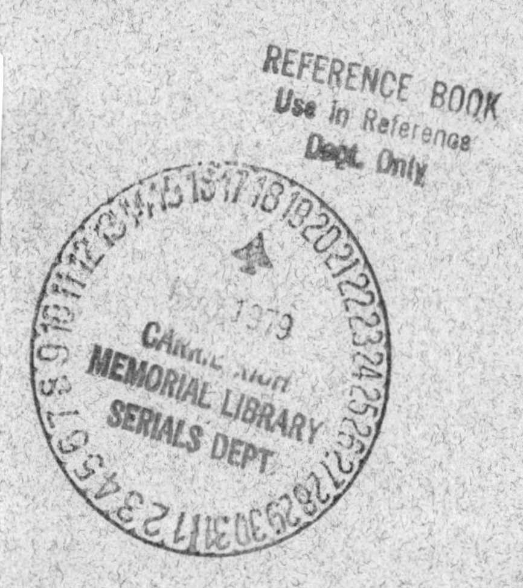

"I find CQ invaluable. It provides the kind of in-depth analysis that is indispensable when you follow Congress. It does not strive for 'color' or 'flare' and consequently does not betray you by playing rhetorical games. Instead it stays with fact and reasoned analysis. I could not imagine anyone who has to stay abreast of public affairs not referring to it regularly."

Director of Public Affairs
Quaker Oats Company

"In this time of so-called 'investigative reporting' by the daily newspapers, it is good to know that there is still a publication in the Nation's Capital that gives honest and thorough treatment to important issues and events."

Chamber of Commerce
of the United States

"Our legal staff has always found CQ to be timely, authoritative and exhaustive of the myriad of events occurring in the Congress. It is attractive and easy to use as well."

General Counsel
National Association of Life Underwriters

From .... Librarians:

"Congressional Quarterly Service is an invaluable tool for the reference librarian. The writing is excellent, complex bills are made understandable. The indexing is fine. Both the staff and our patrons make extensive use of the weekly reports and the yearly almanacs. I would recommend the service for all school and public libraries as well as many specialized libraries."

Reference Librarian
St. Louis Co. Library, MO

"We include Congressional Quarterly Weekly Reports and annual volumes in our curriculum coordinated with the Social Studies Department as one of the basic reference works that is taught to every high school student. I cannot imagine a library not having this important and fundamental reference tool."

Librarian
Darien High School, CT

"Congressional Quarterly Service saves my life (and my fantastic reputation) about once a day! If it weren't for the weekly reports, I would have long since turned in my horn-rimmed glasses!"

Documents Librarian
University of Southern Louisiana

"We find CQ Service one of the most valuable resources in our library."

Librarian
Fullerton Union High School, CA

"Highly recommended for all types of libraries and governmental agencies."

American Reference Books Annual

CONGRESSIONAL QUARTERLY

Almanac

95th CONGRESS

2nd SESSION....1978

VOLUME XXXIV

Congressional Quarterly Inc.

Washington, D.C.

1978 Almanac

Library of Congress No. 47-41081
International Standard Book No. 0-87187-141-6

Congressional Quarterly Inc.

Congressional Quarterly Inc. is an editorial research service and publishing company serving clients in the fields of news, education, business and government. Congressional Quarterly, in its basic publication, the CQ Weekly Report, covers Congress, government and politics. Congressional Quarterly also publishes hardbound reference books and paperback books on public affairs. The service was founded in 1945 by Henrietta and Nelson Poynter.

An affiliated service, Editorial Research Reports, publishes reports each week on a wide range of subjects. Editorial Research Reports also publishes hardbound and paperback books.

Almanac Editor: Mary Cohn
Editorial Coordinator: Sumie Kinoshita
Assistant Editors: Kathryn Waters Gest, John L. Moore, Peg O'Hara, David Tarr, Margaret Thompson, Michael D. Wormser
Editorial Assistants: Imani Crosby, Lynn Krisher
Other Contributors: Judy Aldock, Irwin B. Arieff, Alan Berlow, Christopher Buchanan, Christopher R. Conte, Rhodes Cook, Ann Cooper, Harrison H. Donnelly, Martin Donsky, John Felton, Mark Gruenberg, Charles W. Hucker, Larry Light, Bob Livernash, David M. Maxfield, Ann Pelham, Bob Rankin, Pat Towell, Elizabeth Wehr, Laura B. Weiss, Elder Witt
Indexer: Sharon C. Leuthy; assistants - Lynda McNeil, Diane Huffman, Barbara Risk.
Roll-Call Charts: Amy Millman; Vote Studies: Wayne Walker, Amy Millman
Production: I. D. Fuller (Manager), Maceo Mayo (Assistant Manager)

"By providing a link between the local newspaper and Capitol Hill we hope Congressional Quarterly can help to make public opinion the only effective pressure group in the country. Since many citizens other than editors are also interested in Congress, we hope that they too will find Congressional Quarterly an aid to a better understanding of their government.

"Congressional Quarterly presents the facts in as complete, concise and unbiased form as we know how. The editorial comment on the acts and votes of Congress, we leave to our subscribers." Foreword, Congressional Quarterly, Vol. I, 1945.

Henrietta Poynter, 1901-1968
Nelson Poynter, 1903-1978

CQ

SUMMARY TABLE OF CONTENTS

TABLE OF CONTENTS

Chapter 1—95th Congress, Second Session

Chapter 2—Budget and Appropriations

Chapter 3—Law Enforcement/Judiciary

Chapter 4—Economic Policy

Chapter 5—National Security

Chapter 6—Foreign Policy

Chapter 7—Agriculture

Chapter 8—Transportation/Commerce/Consumers

Chapter 9—Health/Education/Welfare

Chapter 10—Energy/Environment

Chapter 11—Congress and Government

APPENDICES

ERRATA

1976 Almanac p. 5, left galley, paragraph 3: There were 7,268 bills and resolutions (1,488 Senate, 5,780 House) introduced during the session, a marked drop from the 17,015 introduced in the first session of the 94th Congress.

1974 Almanac p. 815, left galley, under Final Action. The bill was cleared by voice vote, not a roll call.

GLOSSARY OF CONGRESSIONAL TERMS

Act—The term for legislation which has passed both houses of Congress and has been signed by the president or passed over his veto, thus becoming law.

Also used technically for a bill that has been passed by one house and engrossed. *(See Engrossed.)*

Adjournment Sine Die—Adjournment without definitely fixing a day for reconvening; literally "adjournment without a day." Usually used to connote the final adjournment of a session of Congress. A session can continue until noon, Jan. 3, of the following year, when by law it automatically terminates.

Adjournment to a Day Certain—Adjournment under a motion or resolution which fixes the next time of meeting. Neither house can adjourn for more than three days without the concurrence of the other. A session of Congress is not ended by adjournment to a day certain.

Amendment—Proposal of a member of Congress to alter the language or stipulations in a bill or act. It is usually printed, debated, and voted upon in the same manner as a bill.

Appeal—A senator's challenge of a ruling or decision made by the presiding officer of the Senate. The senator appeals to members of the chamber to override the decision. If carried by a majority vote, the appeal nullifies the chair's ruling. In the House the decision of the Speaker traditionally has been final, with no appeal to the members to reverse his stand. To appeal a ruling would be considered an attack on the Speaker.

Appropriation Bill—Grants the actual monies approved by authorization bills, but not necessarily to the total permissible under the authorization bill. An appropriation bill originates in the House, and normally is not acted on until its authorization measure is enacted. General appropriations bills are supposed to be enacted by the seventh day after Labor Day before the start of the fiscal year to which they apply, but in recent years this has rarely happened. *(See Continuing Appropriations.)* In addition to general appropriations bills, there are two specialized types. *(See Deficiency and Supplemental.)*

Authorization Bill—Authorizes a program, specifies its general aim and conduct, and unless "open-ended," puts a ceiling on monies that can be used to finance it. Usually enacted before the related appropriation bill is passed. *(See Contract Authorization.)*

Bills—Most legislative proposals before Congress are in the form of bills, and are designated as HR (House of Representatives) or S (Senate) according to the house in which they originate and by a number assigned in the order in which they were introduced, from the beginning of each two-year congressional term. "Public bills" deal with general questions, and become Public Laws if approved by Congress and signed by the president. "Private bills" deal with individual matters such as claims against the government, immigration and naturalization cases, land titles, etc., and become Private Laws if approved and signed.

The introduction of a bill, and its referral to an appropriate committee for action, follows the process given in "How A Bill Becomes Law." *(See also Concurrent Resolution, Joint Resolution, Resolution, in this Glossary.)*

Bills Introduced—In the Senate, any number of senators may join in introducing a single bill. In the House, until 1967 only one member's name could appear on a single bill. Between 1967 and 1978 there was a limit of 24 cosponsors on any one bill. A resolution adopted in 1978 eliminated the ceiling on the number of cosponsors, beginning at the start of the 96th Congress.

Many bills in reality are committee bills and are introduced under the name of the chairman of the committee or subcommittee as a formality. All appropriation bills fall into this category, as do many other bills, particularly those dealing with complicated, technical subjects. A committee frequently holds hearings on a number of related bills, and may agree on one of them or on an entirely new bill. *(See Clean Bill and By Request.)*

Bills Referred—When introduced a bill is referred to the committee which has jurisdiction over the subject with which the bill is concerned. The appropriate reference for bills is spelled out in Senate and House rules. Committee jurisdictions in the House were reorganized in 1974. Bills are referred by the Speaker in the House and the presiding officer in the Senate. Appeals may be made from their decisions.

Budget—The document sent to Congress by the president in January of each year estimating government revenue and expenditures for the ensuing fiscal year and recommending appropriations in detail. The president's budget message forms the basis for congressional hearings and legislation on the year's appropriations.

By Request—A phrase used when a senator or representative introduces a bill at the request of an executive agency or private organization but does not necessarily endorse the legislation.

Calendar—An agenda or list of pending business before committees of either chamber. The House uses five legislative calendars. *(See Consent, Discharge, House, Private and Union Calendar.)*

In the Senate, all legislative matters reported from committee go on a single calendar. They are listed there in order, but may be called up irregularly by the majority leader either by a motion to do so, or by obtaining the unanimous consent of the Senate. Frequently the minority leader is consulted to assure unanimous consent. Only cloture can limit debate on bills thus called up. *(See Call of the Calendar.)*

The Senate also uses one non-legislative calendar, for treaties, etc. *(See Executive Calendar.)*

Calendar Wednesday—In the House on Wednesdays, committees may be called in the order in which they appear in Rule X of the House Manual, for the purpose of bringing up any of their bills from the House or the Union Calendars, except bills which are privileged. General debate is limited to two hours. Bills called up from the Union Calendar are considered in Committee of the Whole. Calendar Wednesday is not observed during the last two weeks of a session, and may be dispensed with at other times — by a two-thirds vote. It usually is dispensed with.

Call of the Calendar—Senate bills which are not brought up for debate by a motion or a unanimous consent agreement are brought before the Senate for action when the calendar listing them in order is "called." Bills considered in this fashion are usually non-controversial, and debate is limited to five minutes for each senator on a bill or on amendments to it.

Chamber—Meeting place for the total membership of either the House or the Senate, as distinguished from the respective committee rooms.

Clean Bill—Frequently after a committee has finished a major revision of a bill, one of the committee members, usually the chairman, will assemble the changes plus what is left of the original bill into a new measure and introduce it as a "clean bill." The new measure, which carries a new number, is then sent to the floor for consideration. This often is a timesaver, as committee-recommended changes do not have to be considered one at a time by the chamber.

Clerk of the House—Chief administrative officer of the House of Representatives with duties corresponding to those of the secretary of the Senate. *(See Secretary of the Senate.)*

Cloture—The process by which a filibuster can be ended in the Senate, other than by unanimous consent. A motion for cloture can apply to any measure before the Senate, including a proposal to change the chamber's rules. It requires 16 senators' signatures for introduction and the votes of three-fifths of the entire Senate membership (60 if there are no vacancies), except that to end a filibuster against a proposal to amend the Standing Rules of the Senate a two-thirds vote of senators present and voting is required. It is put to a roll-call vote one hour after the Senate meets on the second day following introduction of the motion. If voted, cloture limits each senator to one hour of debate.

Committee—A subdivision of the House or Senate which prepares legislation for action by the parent chamber, or makes investigations as directed by the parent chamber. There are several types of committees. *(See Standing, Select or Special.)* Most standing committees are divided into subcommittees, which study legislation, hold hearings, and report their recommendations to the full committee. Only the full committee can report legislation for action by the House or Senate.

Committee of the Whole—The working title of what is formally "The Committee of the Whole House [of Representatives] on the State of the Union." Unlike other committees, it has no fixed membership. It is comprised of any 100 or more House members who participate — on the floor of the chamber — in debating or altering legislation before the body. Such measures, however, must first have passed through the regular committees and be on the calendar.

Technically, the Committee of the Whole considers only bills directly or indirectly appropriating money, authorizing appropriations, or involving taxes or charges on the public. Actually, the Committee of the Whole often considers other types of legislation. Because the Committee of the Whole need number only 100 representatives, a quorum is more readily attained, and business is expedited. Before 1971, members' positions were not individually recorded on votes taken in Committee of the Whole except for automatic roll calls in the absence of a quorum.

When the full House resolves itself into the Committee of the Whole, it supplants the Speaker with a "chairman." The measure is debated or amended, with votes on amendments as needed. When the committee completes its action on the measure, it dissolves itself by "rising." The Speaker returns, and the full House hears the erstwhile chairman of the committee report that group's recommendations.

At this time members may demand a roll-call vote on any amendment *adopted* in the Committee of the Whole. The last vote is on passage of the legislation in question.

Concurrent Resolution—A concurrent resolution, designated H Con Res or S Con Res, must be adopted by both houses but does not require the signature of the president and does not have the force of law. Concurrent resolutions generally are used to make or amend rules applicable to both houses or to express the sentiment of the two houses. A concurrent resolution, for example, is used to fix the time for adjournment of a Congress. It might also be used to convey the congratulations of Congress to another country on the anniversary of its independence.

Conference—A meeting between the representatives of the House and Senate to reconcile differences between the two houses over provisions of a bill. Members of the conference committee are appointed by the Speaker and the president of the Senate and are called "managers" for their respective chambers. A majority of the managers for each house must reach agreement on the provisions of the bill (often a compromise between the versions of the two chambers) before it can be sent up for floor action in the form of a "conference report." There it cannot be amended, and if not approved by both chambers, the bill may go back to conference under certain situations, or a new conference may be convened. Elaborate rules govern the conduct of the conferences. All bills which are passed by the House and Senate in slightly different form need not be sent to conference; either chamber may "concur" in the other's amendments. *(See Custody of the Papers.)*

Congressional Record — The daily, printed account of proceedings in both House and Senate chambers, with debate, statements and the like incorporated in it. Committee activities are not covered, except that their reports to the parent body are noted. Highlights of legislative and committee action are embodied in a Digest section of the *Record,* and members are entitled to have their extraneous remarks printed in an appendix known as "Extension of Remarks." They may edit and revise remarks made on the floor, and frequently do, so that quotations reported by the press are not always found in the *Record.*

Beginning on March 1, 1978, the *Record* incorporated a procedure to distinguish remarks spoken on the floor of the House and Senate from undelivered speeches. At the direction of Congress, all speeches, articles and other materials members inserted in the *Record* without actually reading them on the floor were set off by large black dots. However, a loophole allows a member to avoid the dots if he delivers any portion of the speech in person.

Congressional Terms of Office—Begin on Jan. 3 of the year following a general election and are for two years for representatives and six years for senators.

Consent Calendar—Members of the House may place on this calendar any bill on the Union or House Calendar which is considered to be non-controversial. Bills on the Consent Calendar are normally called on the first and third Mondays of each month. On the first occasion when a bill is called in this manner, consideration may be blocked by the objection of any member. On the second time, if there are three objections, the bill is stricken from the Consent Calendar. If less than three members object, the bill is given immediate consideration.

A bill on the Consent Calndar may be postponed in another way. A member may ask that the measure be passed over "without prejudice." In that case, no objection is recorded against the bill, and its status on the Consent Calendar remains unchanged.

A bill stricken from the Consent Calendar remains on the Union or House Calendar.

Continuing Appropriations—When a fiscal year begins and Congress has not yet enacted all the regular appropriation bills for that year, it passes a joint resolution "continuing appropriations" for government agencies at rates generally based on their previous year's appropriations.

Contract Authorizations—Found in both authorization and appropriation bills, these authorizations are stopgap provisions which permit the federal government to let contracts or obligate itself for future payments from funds not yet appropriated. The assumption is that funds will be available for payment when contracted debts come due.

Correcting Recorded Votes—Rules prohibit members from changing their votes after the result has been announced. But frequently, hours, days, or months after a vote has been taken, a member announces that he was "incorrectly recorded." In the Senate, a request to change one's vote almost always receives unanimous consent. In the House, members are prohibited from changing their votes if tallied by the electronic voting system installed in 1973. If taken by roll call, it is permissible if consent is granted. Errors in the text of the *Record* may be corrected by unanimous consent.

Custody of the Papers—To reconcile differences between the House and Senate versions of a bill, a conference may be arranged. The chamber with "custody of the papers" — the engrossed bill, engrossed amendments, messages of transmittal — is the only body empowered to request the conference. That body then has the advantage of acting last on the conference report when it is submitted.

Deficiency Appropriations—An appropriation to cover the difference between an agency's regular appropriation and the amount deemed necessary for it to operate for the full fiscal year. In recent years deficiency bills have usually been called supplemental appropriations.

Dilatory Motion—A motion, usually made upon a technical point, for the purpose of killing time and preventing action on a bill. The rules outlaw dilatory motions, but enforcement is largely within the discretion of the presiding officer.

Discharge a Committee—Occasionally, attempts are made to relieve a committee from jurisdiction over a measure before it. This is rarely a successful procedure, attempted more often in the House than in the Senate.

In the House, if a committee does not report a bill within 30 days after the bill was referred to it, any member may file a discharge motion. This motion, treated as a petition, needs the signatures of 218 members (a majority of the House). After the required signatures have been obtained, there is a delay of seven days. Then, on the second and fourth Mondays of each month, except during the last six days of a session, any member who has signed the petition may be recognized to move that the committee be discharged. Debate on the motion to discharge is limited to 20 minutes, and if the motion is carried, consideration of the bill becomes a matter of high privilege.

If a resolution to consider a bill *(see Rule)* is held up in the Rules Committee for more than seven legislative days, any member may enter a motion to discharge the committee. The motion is handled like any other discharge petition in the House.

Occasionally, to expedite non-controversial legislative business, a committee is discharged upon unanimous consent of the House, and a petition is not required. *(For Senate procedure, see Discharge Resolution.)*

Discharge Calendar—The House calendar to which motions to discharge committees are referred when they have the necessary 218 signatures and are awaiting action.

Discharge Petition—In the House, a motion to discharge a committee from considering a bill. The motion, or petition, requires signatures of 218 House members.

Discharge Resolution—In the Senate, a special motion that any senator may introduce to relieve a committee from consideration of a bill before it. The resolution can be called up on a motion for approval or disapproval, in the same manner as other matters of Senate business. *(For House procedure, see Discharge a Committee.)*

Division Vote—Same as Standing Vote. *(See below.)*

Enacting Clause—Key phrase in bills saying. "Be it enacted by the Senate and House of Representatives. . . ." A successful motion to strike it from legislation kills the measure.

Engrossed Bill—The final copy of a bill as passed by one chamber, with the text as amended by floor action and certified to by the clerk of the House or the secretary of the Senate.

Enrolled Bill—The final copy of a bill which has been passed in identical form by both chambers. It is certified to by an officer of the house of origin (House clerk or Senate secretary) and then sent on for signatures of the House Speaker, the Senate president, and the U.S. president. An enrolled bill is printed on parchment.

Entitlement Program—A federal program that guarantees a certain level of benefits to persons who meet the requirements set by law. It thus leaves no discretion to Congress as to how much money to appropriate.

Executive Calendar—This is an additional, non-legislative calendar, in the Senate, on which presidential documents such as treaties and nominations are listed.

Executive Document—A document, usually a treaty, sent to the Senate by the president for consideration or approval. These are identical for each session of Congress as Executive A, 95th Congress, 1st Session; Executive B, etc. They are referred to committee in the same manner as other measures. Unlike legislative documents, however, treaties do not die at the end of a Congress, but remain "live" proposals until acted on by the Senate or withdrawn by the president.

Executive Session—Meeting of a Senate or a House committee (or, occasionally, of the entire chamber) which only the group's members are privileged to attend. Frequently witnesses appear at committee meetings in executive session, and other members of Congress may be invited, but the public and press are not allowed to attend.

Expenditures—The actual spending of money as distinguished from the appropriation of it. Expenditures are made by the disbursing officers of the administration; appropriations are made only by Congress. The two are rarely identical in any fiscal year; expenditures may represent money appropriated one, two or more years previously.

Filibuster—A time-delaying tactic used by a minority in an effort to prevent a vote on a bill which probably would pass if brought to a vote. The most common method is to take advantage of the Senate's rules permitting unlimited debate, but other forms of parliamentary maneuvering may be used. The stricter rules in the House make filibusters more difficult, but they are attempted from time to time through various delaying tactics arising from loopholes in House rules.

Fiscal Year—Financial operations of the government are carried out in a 12-month fiscal year, beginning on Oct. 1 and ending on Sept. 30. The fiscal year carries the date of the calendar year in which it ends.

Floor Manager—A member, usually representing sponsors of a bill, who attempts to steer it through debate and amendment to a final vote in the chamber. Floor managers are frequently chairmen or ranking members of the committee that reported the bill. Managers are responsible for apportioning the time granted supporters of the bill for debating it. The minority leader or the ranking minority member of the committee often apportions time for the minority party's participation in the debate.

Frank—A member's facsimile signature on envelopes, used in lieu of stamps, for his official outgoing mail, thus postage-free. Also the privilege of sending mail postage-free.

Germane—Pertaining to the subject matter of the measure at hand. All House amendments must be germane to the bill. The Senate requires that amendments be germane only when they are proposed to general appropriation bills, bills being considered under cloture, or, often, when proceeding under an agreement to limit debate.

Grants-in-Aid—Payments by the federal government which aid the recipient state, local government or individual in administering specified programs, services or activities.

Hearings—Committee sessions for hearing witnesses. At hearings on legislation, witnesses usually include specialists, government officials and spokesmen for persons affected by the bills under study. Hearings related to special investigations bring forth a variety of witnesses. Committees sometimes use their subpoena power to summon reluctant witnesses. The public and press may attend "open" hearings, but are barred from "closed" or "executive" hearings.

The committee announces its hearings, from one day to many weeks in advance, and may invite certain persons to testify. Persons who request time to testify may be turned down by the committee, but most requests are honored.

Both houses have rules against conducting committee hearings in secret, but the House's are much more stringent.

Hold-Harmless Clause—A provision added to legislation to ensure that recipients of federal funds do not receive less in a future year than they did the previous year, if a new formula for allocating such funds would result in a reduction in the amount. To hold a state or city government "harmless" means that neither would be responsible for providing the additional funds or services to make up the difference between the level of benefits previously received and that which would be allowed under the new formula. The federal government would be obliged to provide the additional funds or benefits. This clause has been used most frequently to soften the impact of sudden reductions in federal aid.

Hopper—Box on House clerk's desk where bills are deposited on introduction.

House—The House of Representatives, as distinct from the Senate, although each body is a "house" of Congress.

House Calendar—Listing for action by the House of Representatives of public bills which do not directly or indirectly appropriate money or raise revenue.

Immunity—Constitutional privilege of members of Congress to make verbal statements on the floor and in committee for which they cannot be sued or arrested for slander or libel. Also, freedom from arrest while traveling to or from sessions of Congress or on official business. Members in this status may be arrested only for treason, felonies or a breach of the peace, as defined by congressional manuals.

Joint Committee—A committee composed of a specified number of members of both the House and Senate. Usually a joint committee is investigative in nature, such as the Joint Economic Committee. Others have housekeeping duties such as the joint committees on Printing and on the Library of Congress.

Joint Resolution—A joint resolution, designated H J Res or S J Res, requires the approval of both house and the signature of the president, just as a bill does, and has the force of law if approved. There is no real difference between a bill and a joint resolution. The latter is generally used in dealing with limited matters, such as a single appropriation for a specific purpose.

Joint resolutions also are used to propose amendments to the Constitution. They do not require a presidential signature, but become a part of the Constitution when three-fourths of the states have ratified them.

Journal—The official record of the proceedings of the House and Senate. The Journal records the actions taken in each chamber, but, unlike the *Congressional Record,* it does not include the verbatim report of speeches, debates, etc.

Law—An act of Congress which has been signed by the president, or passed over his veto by Congress; for example, the Civil Rights Act of 1964 (HR 7152) became Public Law 88-352 during the 88th Congress.

Legislative Day—The "day" extending from the time either house meets after an adjournment until the time it next adjourns. Because the House normally adjourns from day to day, legislative days and calendar days usually coincide. But in the Senate, a legislative day may, and frequently does, extend over several calendar days. *(See Recess.)*

Legislative Veto—A procedure permitting either the House or Senate, or both chambers, to block or to modify an administrative action. The specifics of the procedure may vary, but Congress generally provides for a legislative veto by including in a specific piece of legislation a provision that administrative rules or actions taken to implement the legislation are to go into effect at the end of a designated period of time unless blocked by either or both houses. As of 1977, approximately 115 U.S. laws contained legislative veto provisions.

Lobby—A group seeking to influence the passage or defeat of legislation. Originally the term referred to persons frequenting the lobbies or corridors of legislative chambers in order to speak to lawmakers.

The definition of a lobby and the activity of lobbying is a matter of differing interpretation. By some definitions, lobbying is limited to attempts at direct influence by personal interview and persuasion. Under other definitions, lobbying includes attempts at indirect influence, such as persuading members of a group to write or visit their representative or senators, or attempting to create a climate of opinion favorable to a desired legislative action.

The right to attempt to influence legislation is based on the First Amendment to the Constitution, which says Congress shall make no law abridging the right of the people "to petition the government for a redress of grievances."

Majority Leader—Chief strategist and floor spokesman for the party in nominal control in either chamber. He is elected by his party colleagues and is virtually program director for his chamber, since he usually speaks for its majority.

Majority Whip—In effect, the assistant majority leader, in House or Senate. His job is to help marshal majority forces in support of party strategy and legislation.

Manual—The official handbook in each house prescribing its organization, procedures and operations in detail. The Senate manual contains standing rules, orders, laws and resolutions affecting Senate business; the House manual is for operations affecting that chamber. Both volumes contain previous codes under which Congress functioned and from which it continues to derive precedents. Committee powers are outlined. The rules set forth in the manuals may be changed by chamber actions also specified by the manuals.

Marking Up a Bill—Going through a measure, in committee or subcommittee, taking it section by section, revising language, penciling in new phrases, etc. If the bill is extensively revised, the new version may be introduced as a separate bill, with a new number. *(See Clean Bill.)*

Minority Leader—Floor leader for the minority party. *(See Majority Leader.)*

Minority Whip—Performs duties of whip for the minority party. *(See Majority Whip.)*

Morning Hour—The time set aside at the beginning of each legislative day for the consideration of regular routine business. The "hour" is of indefinite duration in the House, where it is rarely used. In the Senate it is the first two hours of a session following an adjournment, as distinguished from a recess. The morning hour can be terminated earlier if the morning business has been completed. The business includes such matters as messages from the president, communications from the heads of departments, messages from the House, the presentation of petitions, reports of standing and select committees, and the introduction of bills and resolutions.

During the first hour of the morning hour in the Senate, no motion to proceed to the consideration of any bill on the calendar is in order except by unanimous consent. During the second hour, motions can be made but must be decided without debate. Senate committees may meet while the Senate is in the morning hour.

Motion—Request by a member for any one of a wide array of parliamentary actions. He "moves" for a certain procedure, or the consideration of a measure or a vote, etc. The precedence of motions, and whether they are debatable, is set forth in the House and Senate manuals.

Nominations—Appointments to office by the executive branch of the government, subject to Senate confirmation. Although most nominations win quick Senate approval, some are controversial and become the topic of hearings and debate. Sometimes senators object to appointees for patronage reasons — for example, when a nomination to a local federal job is made without consulting the senators of the state concerned. Then a senator may use the stock objection that the nominee is "personally obnoxious" to him. Usually other senators join in blocking such an appointment out of courtesy to their colleague.

One Minute Speeches—Addresses by House members at the beginning of a legislative day. The speeches may cover any subject, but are limited strictly to one minute's duration. By unanimous consent, members may also be recognized to address the House for longer periods after completion of all legislative business for the day. Senators, by unanimous consent, are permitted to make speeches of a predetermined length during the Morning Hour.

Override a Veto—If the president disapproves a bill and sends it back to Congress with his objections, Congress may override his veto by a two-thirds vote in each chamber. The Constitution requires a recorded vote. The question put to each house is: "Shall the bill pass, the objections of the president to the contrary notwithstanding?" *(See also Pocket Veto and Veto.)*

Pair—A "gentlemen's agreement" between two lawmakers on opposite sides to withhold their votes on roll calls so their absence from Congress will not affect the outcome of a recorded vote. If passage of the measure requires a two-thirds majority, a pair would require two members favoring the action to one opposed to it.

Two kinds of pairs — special and general — are used; neither is counted in vote totals. The names of lawmakers pairing on a given vote and their stands, if known, are printed in the *Congressional Record*.

The special pair applies to one or a series of roll-call votes on the same subject. On special pairs, lawmakers usually specify how they would have voted.

A general pair in the Senate, now rarely used in the chamber, applies to all votes on which the members pairing are on opposite sides, and it lasts for the length of time pairing senators agree on. It usually does not specify a senator's stand on a given vote.

The general pair in the House differs from the other pairs. No agreement is involved and the pair does not tie up votes. A representative expecting to be absent may notify the House clerk he wishes to make a "general" pair. His name then is paired arbitrarily with that of another member desiring a general pair, and the list is printed in the *Congressional Record.* He may or may not be paired with a member taking the opposite position. General pairs in the House give no indication of how a member would have voted. *(See Record Vote.)*

Petition—A request or plea sent to one or both chambers from an organization or private citizens' group asking support of particular legislation or favorable consideration of a matter not yet receiving congressional attention. They are referred to appropriate committees and are considered or not, according to committee decisions.

Pocket Veto—The act of the president in withholding his approval of a bill after Congress has adjourned — either for the year or for a specified period. However, the U.S. District Court of Appeals for the District of Columbia on Aug. 14, 1974, upheld a congressional challenge to a pocket veto used by former President Nixon during a six-day congressional recess in 1970. The court declared that it was an improper use of the pocket veto power. When Congress is in session, a bill becomes law without the president's signature if he does not act upon it within 10 days, excluding Sundays, from the time he gets it. But if Congress adjourns within that 10-day period, the bill is killed without the president's formal veto.

Point of Order—An objection raised by a member that the chamber is departing from rules governing its conduct of business. The objector cites the rule violated, the chair sustaining his objection if correctly made. Order is restored by the chair's suspending proceedings of the chamber until it conforms to the prescribed "order of business." Members sometimes raise a "point of no order" — when there is noise and disorderly conduct in the chamber.

President of the Senate—Presiding officer of the upper chamber, normally the vice president of the United States. In his absence, a president pro tempore (president for the time being) presides.

President pro tempore—The chief officer of the Senate in the absence of the vice president. He is elected by his fellow senators. The recent practice has been to elect to the office the senator of the majority party with longest continuous service.

Previous Question—In this sense, a "question" is an "issue" before the House for a vote and the issue is "previous" when some other topic has superseded it in the attention of the chamber. A motion for the previous question, when carried, has the effect of cutting off all debate and forcing a vote on the subject originally at hand. If, however, the previous question is moved and carried before there has been any debate on the subject at hand and the subject is debatable, then 40 minutes of debate is allowed before the vote. The previous question is sometimes moved in order to prevent amendments from being introduced and voted on. The motion for the previous question is a debate-limiting device and is not in order in the Senate.

Private Calendar—Private House bills dealing with individual matters such as claims against the government, immigration, land titles, etc., are put on this calendar. When it is before the chamber, two members may block a private bill, which then is recommitted to committee.

Backers of a private bill thus recommitted have another recourse. The measure can be put into an "omnibus claims bill" — several private bills rolled into one. As with any bill, no part of an omnibus claims bill may be deleted without a vote. When a private bill goes back to the floor in this form, it can be defeated only by a majority of those present. The private calendar can be called on the first and third Tuesdays of each month.

Privilege—Privilege relates to the rights of members of Congress and to the relative priority of the motions and actions they may make in their respective chambers. The two are distinct. "Privileged questions" concern legislative business. "Questions of privilege" concern legislators themselves. *(See below.)*

Privileged Questions—The order in which bills, motions and other legislative measures are considered by Congress is governed by strict priorities. A motion to table, for instance, is more privileged than a motion to recommit. Thus, a motion to recommit can be superseded by a motion to table, and a vote would be forced on the latter motion only. A motion to adjourn, however, would take precedence over this one, and is thus considered of the "highest privilege."

Pro Forma Amendment—*(See Strike Out the Last Word.)*

Questions of Privilege—These are matters affecting members of Congress individually or collectively.

Questions affecting the rights, safety, dignity and integrity of proceedings of the House or Senate as a whole are questions of privilege of the House or Senate, as the case may be.

Questions involving individual members are called questions of "personal privilege." A member's rising to a question of personal privilege is given precedence over almost all other proceedings. An annotation in the House rules points out that the privilege of the member rests primarily on the Constitution, which gives him a conditional immunity from arrest and an unconditional freedom to speak in the House.

Quorum—The number of members whose presence is necessary for the transaction of business. In the Senate and House, it is a majority of the membership (when there are no vacancies, this is 51 in the Senate and 218 in the House). A quorum is 100 in the Committee of the Whole House. If a point of order is made that a quorum is not present, the only business in order is either a motion to adjourn or a motion to direct the sergeant-at-arms to request the attendance of absentees.

Readings of Bills—Traditional parliamentary law required bills to be read three times before they were passed. This custom is of little modern significance except in rare instances. Normally the bill is considered to have its first reading when it is introduced and printed, by title, in the *Congressional Record.* Its second reading comes when floor consideration begins. (This is the most likely point at which there is an actual reading of the bill, if there is any.) The third reading (usually by title) takes place when action has been completed on amendments.

Recess—Distinguished from adjournment in that a recess does not end a legislative day and, therefore, does not interfere with unfinished business. The rules in each house set forth certain matters to be taken up and disposed of at the beginning of each legislative day. The House, which operates under much stricter rules than the Senate, usually adjourns from day to day. The Senate often recesses.

Recommit to Committee—A simple motion, made on the floor after a bill has been debated, to return it to the committee which reported it. If approved, recommittal usually is considered a death blow to the bill. In the House a motion to recommit can be made only by a member opposed to the bill, and in recognizing a member to make the motion, the Speaker gives the minority party preference over the majority.

A motion to recommit may include instructions to the committee to report the bill again with specific amendments or by a certain date. Or the instructions may be to make a particular study, with no definite deadline for final action. If the recommittal motion includes instructions, and it is adopted, floor action on the bill continues and the committee does not actually reconsider the legislation.

Reconsider a Vote—A motion to reconsider the vote by which an action was taken has, until it is disposed of, the effect of suspending the action. In the Senate the motion can be made only by a member who voted on the prevailing side of the original question, or by a member who did not vote at all. In the House it can be made only by a member on the prevailing side.

A common practice after close votes in the Senate is a motion to reconsider, followed by a motion to table the motion to reconsider. On this motion to table, senators vote as they voted on the original question, to enable the motion to table to prevail. The matter is then finally closed and further motions to reconsider are not entertained. In the House, as a routine precaution, a motion to reconsider usually is made every time a measure is passed. Such a motion almost always is tabled immediately, thus shutting off the possibility of future reconsideration except by unanimous consent.

Motions to reconsider must be entered in the Senate within the next two days of actual session after the original vote has been taken. In the House they must be entered either on the same day or on the next succeeding day the House is in session.

Recorded Vote—A vote upon which each member's stand is individually made known. In the Senate, this is accomplished through a roll call of the entire membership, to which each senator on the floor must answer "yea," "nay" or, if he does not wish to vote, "present." Since January 1973, the House has used an electronic voting system both for yeas and nays and other recorded votes in the Committee of the Whole. *(See Teller Vote.)*

The Constitution requires yea-and-nay votes on the question of overriding a veto. In other cases, a recorded vote can be obtained by the demand of one-fifth of the members present.

Report—Both a verb and a noun, as a congressional term. A committee which has been examining a bill referred to it by the parent chamber "reports" its findings and recommendations to the chamber when the committee returns the measure. The process is called "reporting" a bill.

A "report" is the document setting forth the committee's explanation of its action. House and Senate reports are numbered separately and are designated S Rept or H Rept. Conference reports are numbered and designated in the same way as regular committee reports.

Most reports favor a bill's passage. Adverse reports are occasionally submitted, but more often, when a committee disapproves a bill, it simply fails to report it at all. Some laws require that committee reports (favorable or adverse) be made. When a committee report is not unanimous, the dissenting committeemen may file a statement of their views, called minority views and referred to as a minority report. Sometimes a bill is reported without recommendation.

Rescission—An item in an appropriation bill rescinding, or canceling, funds previously appropriated but not spent. Also, the repeal of a previous appropriation by the president to cut spending, if approved by Congress under precedures in the Budget and Impoundment Control Act of 1974.

Resolution—A simple resolution, designated H Res or S Res, deals with matters entirely within the prerogatives of one house or the other. It requires neither passage by the other chamber nor approval by the president, and does not have the force of law. Most resolutions deal with the rules of one house. They also are used to express the sentiments of a single house, as condolences to the family of a deceased member or to give "advice" on foreign policy or other executive business. *(Also see Concurrent and Joint Resolutions.)*

Rider—An amendment, usually not germane, which its sponsor hopes to get through more easily by including it in other legislation. Riders become law if the bills embodying them do. Riders providing legislative directives in appropriations bills are outstanding examples, though technically they are banned. The House, unlike the Senate, has a strict germaneness rule; thus riders are usually Senate devices to get legislation enacted quickly or to bypass lengthy House consideration, and, possibly, opposition.

Rule—The term has two specific congressional meanings. A rule may be a standing order governing the conduct of House or Senate business and listed in the chamber's book of rules. The rules deal with duties of officers, order of business, admission to the floor, voting procedures, etc.

In the House, a rule also may be a decision made by its Rules Committee about the handling of a particular bill on the floor. The committee may determine under which standing rule a bill shall be considered, or it may provide a "special rule" in the form of a resolution. If the resolution is adopted by the House, the temporary rule becomes as valid as any standing rule, and lapses only after action has been completed on the measure to which it pertains.

A special rule sets the time limit on general debate. It may also waive points of order against provisions of the bill in question, such as non-germane language, or against specified amendments intended to be proposed to the bill. It may even forbid all amendments or all amendments except, in some cases, those proposed by the legislative committee that handled the bill. In this instance it is known as a "closed" or "gag" rule as opposed to an "open" rule, which puts no limitation on floor action, thus leaving the bill completely open to alteration. *(See Suspend the Rules.)*

Secretary of the Senate—Chief administrative officer of the Senate, responsible for direction of duties of Senate employees, education of pages, administration of oaths, receipt of registration of lobbyists and other activities necessary for the continuing operation of the Senate.

Select or Special Committee—A committee set up for a special purpose and, generally, for a limited time by resolution of either House or Senate. Most special committees are investigative in nature.

Senatorial Courtesy—Sometimes referred to as "the courtesy of the Senate," it is a general practice — with no written rule — applied to consideration of executive nominations. Generally, it means that nominations from a state are not to be confirmed unless they have been approved by the senators of the president's party of that state, with other senators following their lead in the attitude they take toward such nominations.

Sine Die—See Adjournment sine die.

Slip Laws—The first official publication of a bill that has been enacted into law. Each is published separately in unbound single-sheet or pamphlet form. It usually takes two to three days from the date of presidential approval to the time when slip laws become available.

Speaker—The presiding officer of the House of Representatives, elected by its members.

Special Session—A session of Congress after it has adjourned sine die, completing its regular session. Special sessions are convened by the president of the United States under his constitutional powers.

Standing Committees—Committees permanently authorized by House and Senate rules. The standing committees of the House were last reorganized by the committee reorganization act of 1974. The last major reorganization of Senate committees was in the Legislative Reorganization Act of 1946.

Standing Vote—A non-recorded vote used in both the House and Senate. A standing vote, also called a division vote, is taken as follows: Members in favor of a proposal stand and are counted by the presiding officer. Then members opposed stand and are counted. There is no record of how individual members voted. In the House, the presiding officer announces the number for and against. In the Senate, usually only the result is announced.

Statutes-at-Large—A chronological arrangement of the laws enacted in each session of Congress. Though indexed, the laws are not arranged by subject matter nor is there an indication of how they affect previous law. *(See U.S. Code.)*

Strike from the Record—Remarks made on the House floor may offend some member, who moves that the offending words be "taken down" for the Speaker's cognizance, and then expunged from the debate as published in the *Congressional Record.*

Strike Out the Last Word—A move whereby House members are entitled to speak for a fixed time on a measure then being debated by the chamber. A member gains recognition from the chair by moving to strike out the last word of the amendment or section of the bill then under consideration. The motion is pro forma, and customarily requires no vote.

Substitute—A motion, an amendment, or an entire bill introduced in place of pending business. Passage of a substitute measure kills the original measure by supplanting it. A substitute may be amended.

Supplemental Appropriations—Normally, these are passed after the regular (annual) appropriations bills, but before the end of the fiscal year to which they apply. Also referred to as "deficiencies."

Suspend the Rules—Often a time-saving procedure for passing bills in the House. The wording of the motion, which may be made by any member recognized by the Speaker, is: "I move to suspend the rules and pass the bill. . . ." A favorable vote by two-thirds of those present is required for passage. Debate is limited to 40 minutes and no amendments from the floor are permitted. If a two-thirds favorable vote is not attained, the bill may be considered later under regular procedures. The suspension procedure is in order on the first and third Mondays and Tuesdays of each month and usually is reserved for non-controversial bills.

Table a Bill—The motion to "lay on the table" is not debatable in either house, and is usually a method of making a final, adverse disposition of a matter. In the Senate, however, different language is sometimes used. The motion is worded to let a bill "lie on the table," perhaps for subsequent "picking up." This motion is more flexible, merely keeping the bill pending for later action, if desired.

Teller Vote—In the House, members file past tellers and are counted as for or against a measure, but they are not recorded individually. The teller vote is not used in the Senate. In the House, tellers are ordered upon demand of one-fifth of a quorum. This is 44 in the House, 20 in the Committee of the Whole.

The House also has a recorded teller vote procedure, now largely supplanted by the electronic voting procedure, under which the individual votes of members are made public just as they would be on a yea-and-nay vote. This procedure, introduced in 1971, forced members to take a public position on amendments to bills considered in the Committee of the Whole. *(See Recorded Vote.)*

Treaties—Executive proposals — in the form of resolutions of ratification — which must be submitted to the Senate for approval by two-thirds of the senators present. Before they act on such foreign policy matters, senators usually send them to committee for scrutiny. Treaties are read three times and debated in the chamber much as are legislative proposals. After approval by the Senate, they are ratified by the president.

Unanimous Consent—Synonymous with Without Objection. *(See below.)*

Union Calendar—Bills which directly or indirectly appropriate money or raise revenue are placed on this House calendar according to the date reported from committee.

U.S. Code—A consolidation and codification of the general and permanent laws of the United States arranged by subject under 50 titles, the first six dealing with general or political subjects, and the other 44 alphabetically arranged from agriculture to war and national defense. The code is now revised every six years and a supplement is published after each session of Congress.

Veto—Disapproval by the president of a bill or joint resolution, other than one proposing an amendment to the

Constitution. When Congress is in session, the president must veto a bill within 10 days, excluding Sundays, after he has received it; otherwise it becomes law with or without his signature.

When the president vetoes a bill, he returns it to the house of its origin with a message stating his objections. The veto then becomes a question of high privilege. *(See Override a Veto.)*

When Congress has adjourned, the president may pocket veto a bill by failing to sign it. *(See Pocket Veto.)*

Voice Vote—In either the House or Senate, members answer "aye" or "no" in chorus, and the presiding officer decides the result. The term also is used loosely to indicate action by unanimous consent or without objection.

Whip—See Majority Whip.

Without Objection—Used in lieu of a vote on non-controversial motions, amendments or bills, which may be passed in either the House or the Senate if no member voices an objection.

HOW A BILL BECOMES LAW

Note: Parliamentary terms used below are defined in the Glossary.

INTRODUCTION OF BILLS

A House member (including the resident commissioner of Puerto Rico and non-voting delegates of the District of Columbia, Guam and the Virgin Islands) may introduce any one of several types of bills and resolutions by handing it to the clerk of the House or placing it in a box called the hopper. A senator first gains recognition of the presiding officer to announce the introduction of a bill. If objection is offered by any senator the introduction of the bill is postponed until the following day.

As the next step in either the House or Senate, the bill is numbered, referred to the appropriate committee, labeled with the sponsor's name, and sent to the Government Printing Office so that copies can be made for subsequent study and action. Senate bills may be jointly sponsored and carry several senators' names. In the House, until 1967, each bill carried the name of one sponsor only; however, the House April 25, 1967, voted to allow cosponsorship of bills, setting a limit of 25 cosponsors on any one bill. A bill written in the Executive Branch and proposed as an administration measure usually is introduced by the chairman of the congressional committee which has jurisdiction.

Bills—Prefixed with "HR" in the House, "S" in the Senate, followed by a number. Used as the form for most legislation, whether general or special, public or private.

Joint Resolutions—Designated H J Res or S J Res. Subject to the same procedure as bills, with the exception of a joint resolution proposing an amendment to the Constitution. The latter must be approved by two-thirds of both houses and is thereupon sent directly to the administrator of general services for submission to the states for ratification rather than being presented to the president for his approval.

Concurrent Resolutions—Designated H Con Res or S Con Res. Used for matters affecting the operations of both houses. These resolutions do not become law.

Resolutions—Designated H Res or S Res. Used for a matter concerning the operation of either house alone and adopted only by the chamber in which it originates.

COMMITTEE ACTION

A bill is referred to the appropriate committee by a House parliamentarian on the Speaker's order, or by the Senate president. Sponsors may indicate their preferences for referral, although custom and chamber rule generally govern. An exception is the referral of private bills, which are sent to whatever group is designated by their sponsors. Bills are technically considered "read for the first time" when referred to House committees.

When a bill reaches a committee it is placed upon the group's calendar. At that time it comes under the sharpest congressional focus. Its chances for passage are quickly determined — and the great majority of bills fall by the legislative roadside. Failure of a committee to act on a bill is equivalent to killing it; the measure can be withdrawn from the group's purview only by a discharge petition signed by a majority of the House membership on House bills, or by adoption of a special resolution in the Senate. Discharge attempts rarely succeed.

The first committee action taken on a bill usually is a request for comment on it by interested agencies of the government. The committee chairman may assign the bill to a subcommittee for study and hearings, or it may be considered by the full committee. Hearings may be public, closed (executive session), or both. A subcommittee, after considering a bill, reports to the full committee its recommendations for action and any proposed amendments.

The full committee then votes on its recommendation to the House or Senate. This procedure is called "ordering a bill reported." Occasionally a committee may order a bill reported unfavorably; most of the time a report, submitted by the chairman of the committee to the House or Senate, calls for favorable action on the measure since the committee can effectively "kill" a bill by simply failing to take any action.

When a committee sends a bill to the chamber floor, it explains its reasons in a written statement, called a report, which accompanies the bill. Often committee members opposing a measure issue dissenting minority statements which are included in the report.

Usually, the committee proposes amendments to the bill. If they are substantial and the measure is complicated, the committee may order a "clean bill" introduced, which will embody the proposed amendments. The original bill then is put aside and the "clean bill," with a new number, is reported to the floor.

The chamber must approve, alter, or reject the committee amendments before the bill itself can be put to a vote.

Floor Action

After a bill is reported back to the house where it originated, it is placed on the calendar.

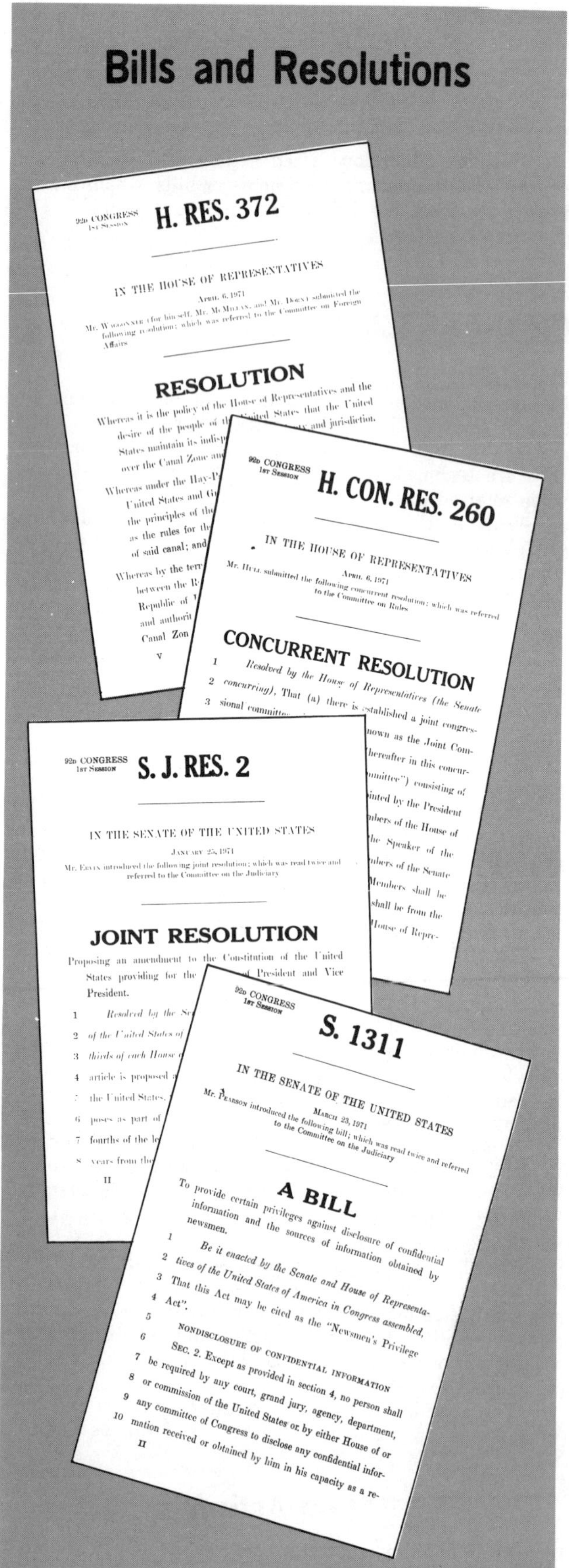

There are five legislative calendars in the House, issued in one cumulative calendar titled Calendars of the United States House of Representatives and History of Legislation. The House calendars are:

The Union Calendar to which are referred bills raising revenues, general appropriation bills and any measures directly or indirectly appropriating money or property. It is the Calendar of the Committee of the Whole House on the State of the Union.

The House Calendar to which are referred bills of a public character not raising revenue or appropriating money or property.

The Consent Calendar to which are referred bills of a non-controversial nature that are passed without debate when the Consent Calendar is called on the first and third Mondays of each month.

The Private Calendar to which are referred bills for relief in the nature of claims against the United States or private immigration bills that are passed without debate when the Private Calendar is called the first and third Tuesdays of each month.

The Discharge Calendar to which are referred motions to discharge committees when the necessary signatures are signed to a discharge petition.

There is only one legislative calendar in the Senate and one "executive calendar" for treaties and nominations submitted to the Senate. When the Senate Calendar is called, each senator is limited to five minutes' debate on each bill.

DEBATE. A bill is brought to debate by varying procedures. If a routine measure, it may await the call of the calendar. If it is urgent or important, it can be taken up in the Senate either by unanimous consent or by a majority vote. The policy committee of the majority party in the Senate schedules the bills that it wants taken up for debate.

In the House, precedence is granted if a special rule is obtained from the Rules Committee. A request for a special rule is usually made by the chairman of the committee that favorably reported the bill, supported by the bill's sponsor and other committee members. The request, considered by the Rules Committee in the same fashion that other committees consider legislative measures, is in the form of a resolution providing for immediate consideration of the bill. The Rules Committee reports the resolution to the House where it is debated and voted upon in the same fashion as regular bills. If the Rules Committee should fail to report a rule requested by a committee, there are several ways to bring the bill to the House floor — under suspension of the rules, on Calendar Wednesday or by a discharge motion.

The resolutions providing special rules are important because they specify how long the bill may be debated and whether it may be amended from the floor. If floor amendments are banned, the bill is considered under a "closed rule," which permits only members of the committee that first reported the measure to the House to alter its language, subject to chamber acceptance.

When a bill is debated under an "open rule," amendments may be offered from the floor. Committee amendments are always taken up first, but may be changed, as may all amendments up to the second degree, i.e., an amendment to an amendment to an amendment is not in order.

Duration of debate in the House depends on whether the bill is under discussion by the House proper or before the House when it is sitting as the Committee of the Whole on the State of the Union. In the former, the amount of time for debate is determined either by special rule or is allocated with an hour for each member if the measure is under consideration without a rule. In the Committee of the Whole the amount of time agreed on for general debate is equally divided between proponents and opponents. At the end of general discussion, the bill is read section by section for amendment. Debate on an amendment is limited to five minutes for each side.

Senate debate is usually unlimited. It can be halted only by unanimous consent by "cloture," which requires a three-fifths majority of the entire Senate except for proposed changes in the Senate rules. The latter requires a two-thirds vote.

The House sits as the Committee of the Whole on the State of the Union when it considers any tax measure or bill dealing with public appropriations. It can also resolve itself into the Committee of the Whole if a member moves to do so and the motion is carried. The Speaker appoints a member to serve as the chairman. The rules of the House permit the Committee of the Whole to meet with any 100 members on the floor, and to amend and act on bills with a quorum of the 100, within the time limitations mentioned previously. When the Committee of the Whole has acted, it "rises," the Speaker returns as the presiding officer of the House and the member appointed chairman of the Committee of the Whole reports the action of the committee and its recommendations (amendments adopted).

VOTES. Voting on bills may occur repeatedly before they are finally approved or rejected. The House votes on the rule for the bill and on various amendments to the bill. Voting on amendments often is a more illuminating test of a bill's support than is the final tally. Sometimes members approve final passage of bills after vigorously supporting amendments which, if adopted, would have scuttled the legislation.

The Senate has three different methods of voting: an untabulated voice vote, a standing vote (called a division) and a recorded roll call to which members answer "yea" or "nay" when their names are called. The House also employs voice and standing votes, but since January 1973 yeas and nays have been recorded by an electronic voting device, eliminating the need for time-consuming roll calls.

Another method of voting, used in the House only, is the teller vote. Traditionally, members filed up the center aisle past counters; only vote totals were announced. Since 1971, one-fifth of a quorum can demand that the votes of individual members be recorded, thereby forcing them to take a public position on amendments to key bills. Electronic voting now is commonly used for this purpose.

After amendments to a bill have been voted upon, a vote may be taken on a motion to recommit the bill to committee. If carried, this vote removes the bill from the chamber's calendar. If the motion is unsuccessful, the bill then is "read for the third time." An actual reading usually is dispensed with. Until 1965, an opponent of a bill could delay this move by objecting and asking for a full reading of an engrossed (certified in final form) copy of the bill. After the "third reading," the vote on final passage is taken.

The final vote may be followed by a motion to reconsider, and this motion itself may be followed by a move to lay the motion on the table. Usually, those voting for the bill's passage vote for the tabling motion, thus safeguarding the final passage action. With that, the bill has been

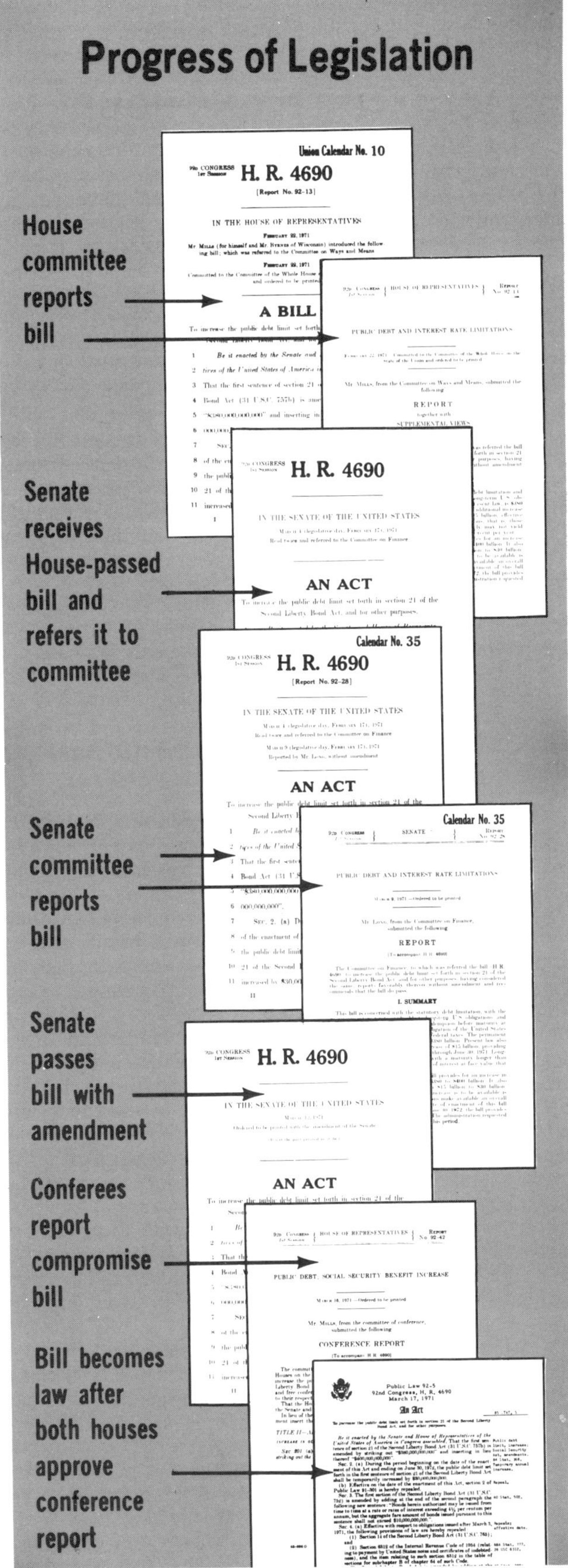

formally passed by the chamber. While a motion to reconsider a Senate vote is pending on a bill, the measure cannot be sent to the House.

ACTION IN SECOND HOUSE

After a bill is passed it is sent to the other chamber. This body may then take one of several steps. It may pass the bill as is — accepting the other chamber's language. It may send the bill to committee for scrutiny or alteration, or reject the entire bill, advising the other house of its actions. Or it may simply ignore the bill submitted while it continues work on its own version of the proposed legislation. Frequently, one chamber may approve a version of a bill that is greatly at variance with the version already passed by the other house, and then substitute its amendments for the language of the other, retaining only the latter's bill designation.

A provision of the Legislative Reorganization Act of 1970 permits a separate House vote on any non-germane amendment added by the Senate to a House-passed bill and requires a majority vote to retain the amendment. Previously the House was forced to act on the bill as a whole; the only way to defeat the non-germane amendment was to reject the entire bill.

Often the second chamber makes only minor changes. If these are readily agreed to by the other house, the bill then is routed to the White House for signing. However, if the opposite chamber basically alters the bill submitted to it, the measure usually is "sent to conference." The chamber that has possession of the "papers" (engrossed bill, engrossed amendments, messages of transmittal) requests a conference and the other chamber must agree to it.

CONFERENCE. A conference undertakes to harmonize conflicting House and Senate versions of a legislative bill. The conference is usually staffed by senior members (conferees), appointed by the presiding officers of the two houses, from the committees that managed the bills. Under this arrangement the conferees of one house have the duty of trying to maintain their chamber's position in the face of amending actions by the conferees (also referred to as "managers") of the other house.

The number of conferees from each chamber may vary, the range usually being from three to nine members in each group, depending upon the length or complexity of the bill involved. There may be five representatives and three senators on the conference committee, or the reverse. But a majority vote controls the action of each group so that a larger representation does not give one chamber a voting advantage over the other chamber's conferees.

Theoretically, conferees are not allowed to write new legislation in reconciling the two versions before them, but this curb sometimes is bypassed. Many bills have been put into acceptable compromise form only after new language was provided by the conferees. The 1970 Reorganization Act attempted to tighten restrictions on conferees by forbidding them to introduce any language on a topic that neither chamber sent to conference or to modify any topic beyond the scope of the different House and Senate versions.

Frequently the ironing out of difficulties takes days or even weeks. Conferences on involved appropriation bills sometimes are particularly drawn out.

As a conference proceeds, conferees reconcile differences between the versions, but generally they grant concessions only insofar as they remain sure that the chamber they represent will accept the compromises. Occasionally, uncertainty over how either house will react, or the positive refusal of a chamber to back down on a disputed amendment, results in an impasse, and the bills die in conference even though each was approved by its sponsoring chamber.

Conferees sometimes go back to their respective chambers for further instructions, when they report certain portions in disagreement. Then the chamber concerned can either "recede and concur" in the amendment of the other house, or "insist on its amendment."

When the conferees have reached agreement, they prepare a conference report embodying their recommendations (compromises). The reports, in document form, must be submitted to each house.

The conference report must be approved by each house. Consequently, approval of the report is approval of the compromise bill. In the order of voting on conference reports, the chamber which asked for a conference yields to the other chamber the opportunity to vote first.

FINAL STEPS. After a bill has been passed by both the House and Senate in identical form, all of the original papers are sent to the enrolling clerk of the chamber in which the bill originated. He then prepares an enrolled bill which is printed on parchment paper. When this bill has been certified as correct by the secretary of the Senate or the clerk of the House, depending on which chamber originated the bill, it is signed first (no matter whether it originated in the Senate or House) by the Speaker of the House and then by the president of the Senate. It is next sent to the White House to await action.

If the president approves the bill he signs it, dates it and usually writes the word "approved" on the document. If he does not sign it within 10 days (Sundays excepted) and Congress is in session, the bill becomes law without his signature.

However, should Congress adjourn before the 10 days expire, and the president has failed to sign the measure, it does not become law. This procedure is called the pocket veto.

A president vetoes a bill by refusing to sign it and before the 10-day period expires, returning it to Congress with a message stating his reasons. The message is sent to the chamber which originated the bill. If no action is taken there on the message, the bill dies. Congress, however, can attempt to override the president's veto and enact the bill, "the objections of the president to the contrary notwithstanding." Overriding of a veto requires a two-thirds vote of those present, who must number a quorum and vote by roll call.

Debate can precede this vote, with motions permitted to lay the message on the table, postpone action on it, or refer it to committee. If the president's veto is overridden by a two-thirds vote in both houses, the bill becomes law. Otherwise it is dead.

When bills are passed finally and signed, or passed over a veto, they are given law numbers in numerical order as they become law. There are two series of numbers, one for public and one for private laws, starting at the number "1" for each two-year term of Congress. They are then identified by law number and by Congress — i.e., Private Law 21, 90th Congress; Public Law 250, 90th Congress (or PL 90-250).

HOW A BILL BECOMES LAW

This graphic shows the most typical way in which proposed legislation is enacted into law. There are more complicated, as well as simpler, routes, and most bills fall by the wayside and never become law. The process is illustrated with two hypothetical bills, House bill No. 1 (HR 1) and Senate bill No. 2 (S 2).

Each bill must be passed by both houses of Congress in identical form before it can become law. The path of HR 1 is traced by a solid line, that of S 2 by a broken line. However, in practice most legislation begins as similar proposals in both houses.

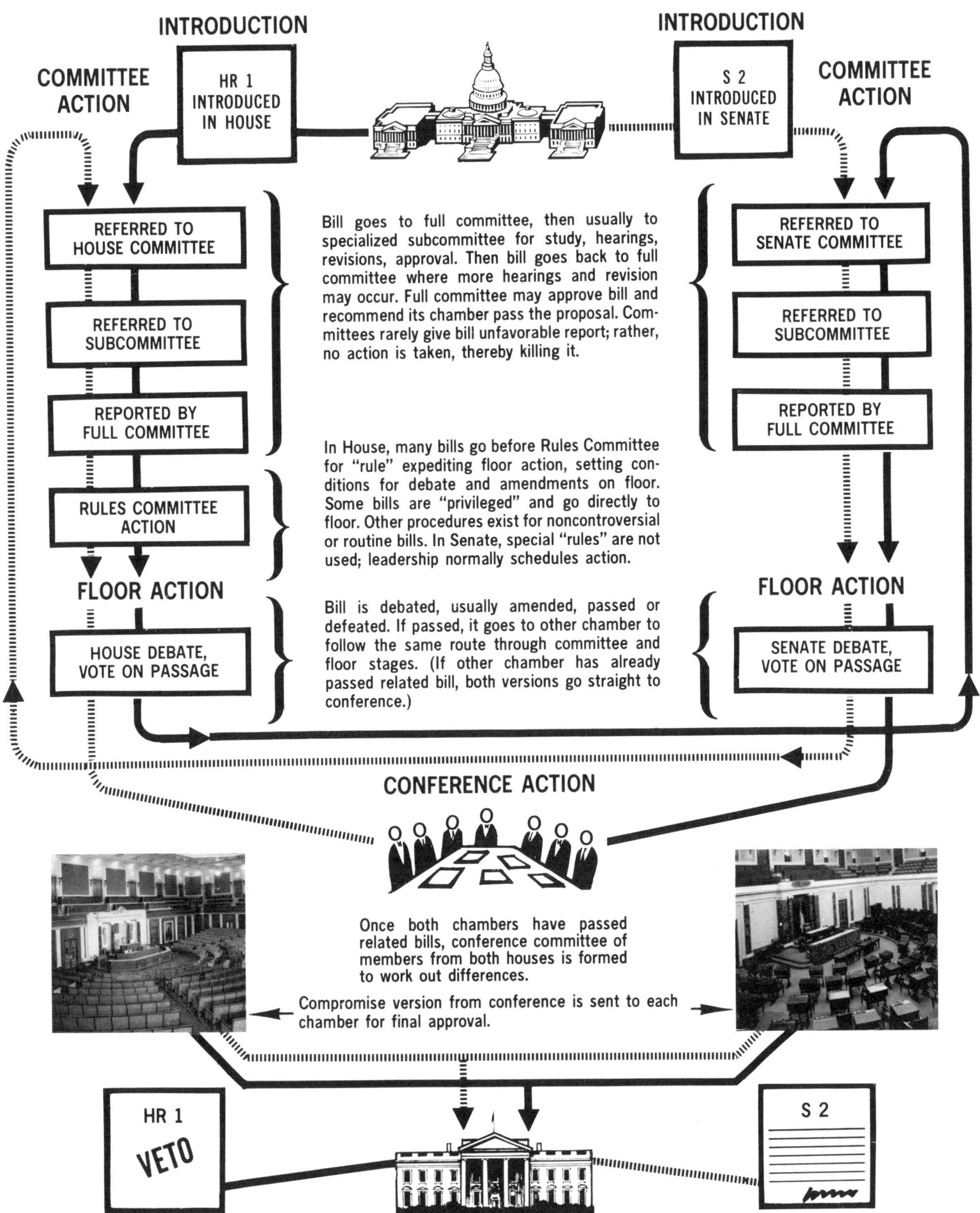

INTRODUCTION
COMMITTEE ACTION
HR 1 INTRODUCED IN HOUSE
INTRODUCTION
S 2 INTRODUCED IN SENATE
COMMITTEE ACTION
REFERRED TO HOUSE COMMITTEE
REFERRED TO SUBCOMMITTEE
REPORTED BY FULL COMMITTEE
RULES COMMITTEE ACTION
REFERRED TO SENATE COMMITTEE
REFERRED TO SUBCOMMITTEE
REPORTED BY FULL COMMITTEE
Bill goes to full committee, then usually to specialized subcommittee for study, hearings, revisions, approval. Then bill goes back to full committee where more hearings and revision may occur. Full committee may approve bill and recommend its chamber pass the proposal. Committees rarely give bill unfavorable report; rather, no action is taken, thereby killing it.
In House, many bills go before Rules Committee for "rule" expediting floor action, setting conditions for debate and amendments on floor. Some bills are "privileged" and go directly to floor. Other procedures exist for noncontroversial or routine bills. In Senate, special "rules" are not used; leadership normally schedules action.
FLOOR ACTION
HOUSE DEBATE, VOTE ON PASSAGE
Bill is debated, usually amended, passed or defeated. If passed, it goes to other chamber to follow the same route through committee and floor stages. (If other chamber has already passed related bill, both versions go straight to conference.)
FLOOR ACTION
SENATE DEBATE, VOTE ON PASSAGE
CONFERENCE ACTION
Once both chambers have passed related bills, conference committee of members from both houses is formed to work out differences.
Compromise version from conference is sent to each chamber for final approval.
HR 1
VETO
S 2

Compromise version approved by both houses is sent to President who can either sign it into law or veto it and return it to Congress. Congress may override veto by a two-thirds majority vote in both houses; bill then becomes law without President's signature.

95TH CONGRESS, SECOND SESSION

CQ

MAJOR LEGISLATION OF 95TH CONGRESS, SECOND SESSION As of adjournment, Oct. 15, 1978

	House	Senate
Democrats	285	62*
Republicans	146	38
Vacancies	4	0

BILL AND BACKGROUND	HOUSE	SENATE	FINAL
National Energy Act. (HR 5146, HR 5037, HR 5289, HR 4018, HR 5263) Enact a range of measures to ensure U.S. energy conservation.	Passed 8/5/77	Program broken into 6 bills; all passed	All signed 11/9/78 PL 95-617-621
Nuclear Licensing. (S 2775, HR 11704) Streamline federal procedures to speed construction of new nuclear plants.	Interior subcommittee markup held 8/15/78	Environment subcommittee hearings began 5/18/78	
Alaska Lands. (HR 39) Decide how many acres of public lands in Alaska will be set aside for permanent federal protection.	Passed 5/19/78	Energy and Natural Resources reported 10/9/78	
Mideast Arms Sales. (S Con Res 86) Disapproval of administration sale of F-16, F-15, F-5E jet fighter planes to Saudi Arabia, Israel, Egypt.		Resolution rejected 5/15/78	No further action required
Financial Disclosure. (S 555) Require public financial disclosure by members of Congress, judges, executive branch officials.	Passed 9/27/78	Passed 6/27/77	Signed 10/26/78 PL 95-521
Lobby Disclosure. (HR 8494, S 2971) Expand registration and information-disclosure requirements covering persons, groups lobbying in Washington.	Passed 4/26/78	Governmental Affairs markup began 5/10/78	
Civil Service Reform. (S 2640) Revise the civil service system to make the federal bureaucracy more efficient.	Passed 9/13/78	Passed 8/24/78	Signed 10/13/78 PL 95-454
Campaign Financing. (S 926) Provide financing of congressional election campaigns from federal tax funds.	Attempt to get floor vote rejected 7/19/78	Killed on Senate floor 8/2/77	
Electoral College Changes. (S J Res 1) Abolish the electoral college and elect the president by direct popular vote.		Judiciary reported 12/6/77	
Labor Law Revision. (HR 8410) Revise the National Labor Relations Act to make union organizing and contract negotiations easier.	Passed 10/6/77	Recommitted to Human Resources 6/22/78	
Humphrey-Hawkins Full Employment. (HR 50) Coordinate government economic policies to reach stated employment goals.	Passed 3/16/78	Passed 10/13/78	Signed 10/27/78 PL 95-523
Airline Deregulation. (S 2493) Encourage airline industry competition by increasing airlines' flexibility to set fares and enter new routes.	Passed 9/21/78	Passed 4/19/78	Signed 10/24/78 PL 95-504
No-Fault Auto Insurance. (S 1381, HR 13048) Establish minimum federal standards for state no-fault auto insurance plans.	Commerce Committee killed 8/1/78	Commerce Committee reported 7/11/78	
Tax Cuts. (HR 13511) Provide individual and business tax cuts to stimulate economic activity.	Passed 8/10/78	Passed 10/10/78	Signed 11/6/78 PL 95-600
New York City Aid. (HR 12426) Provide city up to $1.65 billion in federal loan guarantees, replacing seasonal loan program which expired 6/30/78.	Passed 6/8/78	Passed 6/29/78	Signed 8/8/78 PL 95-339
Welfare Reform. (HR 9030, HR 10950; S 2084, S 2777) Replace existing welfare programs with a consolidated cash and jobs arrangement.	Special subcommittee approved 2/8/78	Finance hearings began 2/7/78; Human Resources hearings began 3/22/78	
Hospital Cost Control. (S 1391, HR 6575) Impose ceiling on inpatient care revenue increases and on capital spending for U.S. hospitals.	Commerce Committee rejected Carter plan 7/18/78	Finance Committee rejected Carter plan 8/3/78	
Panama Canal. (Exec. N, 95th Cong., 1st Sess.) Consent to the ratification of two treaties granting Panama control of the Panama Canal after 1999.	No action required	Treaties approved 3/16/78 and 4/18/78	No further action required

* Includes Harry F. Byrd Jr. (Va.) elected as independent.

The 95th Congress

The 95th Congress that ended a few weeks before the 1978 elections was not an especially unwieldy Congress, but there were new indications of institutional developments that would make both the Senate and House more difficult chambers in which to pass legislation.

In both houses, leaders experienced obstacles to operations that — if not entirely new — at least showed signs of becoming major elements in the legislative process.

Both House and Senate faced delays during the session, and were accused — both by members and outside observers — of becoming unmanageable institutions. The final legislative record didn't prove that Congress was beyond the control of the leadership, but there was little doubt that many new forces were making it a more unwieldy place than it used to be.

New Forces

A considerable amount of the most difficult legislative work that Congress had to do was left for the last six weeks of the session.

Although it is not unusual for delays to appear toward the end of a session, there appeared to be more to the problem in 1978 than the traditional year-end logjam that held up many bills in both chambers. Interviews with more than two dozen members showed that many believed poor legislative relations by President Carter and his White House aides were a factor; but most members thought that Congress itself was an even bigger problem.

Many reasons were cited. Among those mentioned most often were:

Senate Rules. Increased obstructionism in the Senate, where rules make it relatively easy for a handful of members to stall or kill bills. The principal development was new use of the old filibuster technique to keep legislation from coming to a vote.

House Reforms. The substantial reforms in House procedures made during the preceding 10 years, said by many members to have made the chamber more democratic but also more difficult to manage. Power was scattered and new power centers were created.

Assertiveness. Increased congressional assertiveness, which began in the early 1970s when large Democratic majorities in both houses found their plans frequently frustrated by Republican administrations.

Having learned to flex its muscles more, the Democratic Congress was no longer inclined to automatically embrace administration proposals just because they came from a Democratic president.

More Lobbyists. The proliferation of lobbyists — representing everyone from the Chamber of Commerce to the National Electric Sign Association — who had developed sophisticated tactics to fight bills. In addition, the growth of single-issue lobbying organizations put a new type of pressure on members; these groups cared little for a member's overall record, but only whether he or she supported or opposed the organizations' positions.

Lobbying played a prime role in defeat of labor law reform, no-fault auto insurance, hospital cost control and consumer protection agency bills in 1978. It also killed a bill that would have required lobbyists to reveal more about their activities to the public.

Public Mood. A public mood that seldom showed a consensus on major issues because of narrow self-interests. This was a consideration that could change in another Congress, but it reinforced the many other factors that made the 95th Congress a slow-moving one with little apparent overall philosophy guiding it.

Senate Filibuster

A new mood of militancy turned the clubby, custom-bound Senate into a battleground where minorities — often just one or two senators — were increasingly willing to manipulate the rules in order to kill or delay legislation.

95th Congress Leadership

SENATE

President Pro Tempore — James O. Eastland, D-Miss.
Majority Leader — Robert C. Byrd, D-W.Va.
Majority Whip — Alan Cranston, D-Calif.
Democratic Conference Secretary — Daniel K. Inouye, D-Hawaii

Minority Leader — Howard H. Baker Jr., R-Tenn.
Minority Whip — Ted Stevens, R-Alaska
Republican Policy Committee Chairman — John G. Tower, R-Texas
Republican Conference Chairman — Carl T. Curtis, R-Neb.
Republican Conference Secretary — Clifford P. Hansen, R-Wyo.

HOUSE

Speaker — Thomas P. O'Neill Jr., D-Mass.
Majority Leader — Jim Wright, D-Texas
Majority Whip — John Brademas, D-Ind.

Minority Leader — John J. Rhodes, R-Ariz.
Minority Whip — Robert H. Michel, R-Ill.
Republican Conference Chairman — John B. Anderson, R-Ill.
Republican Policy Committee Chairman — Del Clawson, R-Calif.

The most powerful weapon in the arsenal of the militant minority is the filibuster, the last-resort obstructionist technique refined by the late James B. Allen, D-Ala. (1969-78) to thwart the Senate in ways unheard of before the mid-1970s.

Distressed at the number of major House-passed bills held hostage by filibuster threats during the year, some Senate Democrats concluded that changes in Senate rules were necessary in the next Congress. The target of the Democrats would be rules used by Allen in developing his main legacy to the Senate, the post-cloture filibuster-by-amendment.

The post-cloture filibuster "is a violation of every principle I ever learned about fair play," said Dale Bumpers, D-Ark., an advocate of new restrictions on parliamentary delaying tactics. "You don't even have to have a sizable minority" to stage post-cloture delays, he said. The technique was becoming more popular, partly because of the notoriety given to obstructionists, said Bumpers. "The only way you can get press around here, which most members consider tantamount to re-election, is to do something bizarre, be chairman of a committee, or lead a filibuster."

But conservative Republicans, the group most active in delaying Senate action during the Congress, argued that by threatening or conducting filibusters they were simply exercising the minority rights that Senate rules and tradition gave them. Some of the members said their militancy was a response to what they saw as majority efforts to trample on those rights.

"The more threatened we are, the more militant we must become to protect ourselves," said James A. McClure, R-Idaho, chairman of the conservative Republican Steering Committee, which functions as a sort of clearinghouse for Republican objections to bills.

Filibuster Threats

Unlike the House, which limits legislative debates, Senate rules allowed a minority of members to conduct a filibuster (unlimited debate) on any bill unless three-fifths of the full Senate voted to invoke cloture (end debate).

The only thing restricting the number of filibusters was Senate custom, which in recent decades had limited senators to only occasional use of the disruptive tactic. Custom also dictated — prior to Allen's Senate career — that once cloture was invoked, a filibuster was ended.

Public Laws

A total of 410 bills cleared by Congress in 1978 became public laws. Following is a list of the number of public laws enacted since 1965:

Year	Public Laws	Year	Public Laws
1978	410	1971	224
1977	223	1970	505
1976	383	1969	190
1975	205	1968	391
1974	402	1967	249
1973	247	1966	461
1972	483	1965	349

But in a Senate much less inclined to play by the unwritten rules of the past, the filibuster threat was becoming one of the most popular ways to fight legislation. The more militant members who found themselves in a minority — some liberal Democrats as well as the conservative Republicans — made it clear that cloture alone would not stop their filibusters.

Noting the proliferation of filibuster threats in the Senate in 1978, Majority Leader Robert C. Byrd, D-W.Va., said: "It used to be that it was resorted to only infrequently and on the great national issues, mostly civil rights. But anymore, it's just resorted to promiscuously, I think."

Conservative Republican Jesse Helms, N.C., a supporter of some filibuster threats in 1978, dismissed Byrd's protest. "If the shoe were on the other foot, he would be doing exactly what [some] of us have been doing and will probably do to a greater extent in the future," Helms said. "Senator Byrd never fails to use the rules to his advantage, so why the outcry when the minority uses them?"

Actually, there was only one real filibuster in 1978. Because the Senate refused to cut off the six-week talkathon against the labor law reform bill (HR 8410), it never moved into the more controversial post-cloture phase that the bill's opponents were prepared for.

But the long fight over labor law, coupled with lengthy debate on the Panama Canal treaties, took a three-month chunk from the Senate schedule and created a time crunch that made the mere mention of a filibuster as effective as carrying one out.

"One or two members can, when time is running out, resort to obstructionist tactics and endanger any bill that they're opposed to," said Byrd. "And while they're doing that they're also endangering passage of other measures which will be caught in the backlog."

New Independence

Even without the labor law filibuster and the Panama debate, some members believed the Senate would have been troubled by obstructionism. They contended that Senate custom and courtesy, which concentrated power in a few older members and kept younger members from speaking out, had been ignored by newer, more independent senators.

The crop of conservative Republicans elected in the 1970s reflected the new attitude, which rejected the notion that a minority should "surrender quietly and say, 'I give up, they've got the votes,' " said Jake Garn, R-Utah. "As long as extended debate is allowed by the rules, we should use them."

This attitude showed a new "willingness to flout everything," said Fred Wertheimer, vice president of Common Cause.

Waiving Rules. Filibuster threats were not the only delaying tactic that became more popular. Byrd also complained that a new "mind set" in the Senate was causing temporary delays and scheduling problems on even routine, non-controversial bills.

His complaint was prompted by a minor bill setting appropriations for the District of Columbia which was blocked temporarily in August when Republicans refused to waive the rule requiring bills to be on the Senate calendar for three days before being brought to the floor.

Bryd said the rule was routinely waived by Democrats on all but the most controversial bills but had become a "fetish" with Republicans.

Holds on Bills. Another tactic that slowed the Senate was the informal "hold" that any senator could put on a bill. The hold might simply be a request that a bill not be brought up on the floor while the member was out of town. Or it could imply a threat to filibuster.

Even though holds could not officially keep bills off the floor, they became more effective in blocking action in 1978. With the Senate schedule so overburdened, Byrd was reluctant to bring up any bill unless all senators had agreed to a time limit on debate. So a senator with a hold on a bill could block it by simply refusing to go along with a time agreement.

"We've been able to do that [put bills on hold] on several things and get rather large concessions," acknowledged McClure, whose Steering Committee had holds on a number of bills.

Republicans were unmoved by Byrd's contention that such tactics put the Senate in a "straightjacket." Harrison Schmitt, R-N.M., who took the unusual step of asking the Republican leadership to check with him before the three-day rule was waived on any bill, defended use of such rules to "give the minority some ways in which they can exert a small amount of control over the flow of legislation."

Schmitt and others also complained that Byrd, who determined the Senate schedule, was "more interested in the passage of legislation than in the content of legislation." In his rush to pass a long list of bills, they charged, Byrd ignored minority rights and invited retaliation in the form of more delays.

"So long as he wants to use pressure tactics, he's going to have pressure tactics used in retaliation. He's not the headmaster of some school," said McClure.

Senate Cloture Votes, 1977-78

Following is a list of all cloture votes taken by the Senate in the 95th Congress (1977-78). Cloture motions required a majority vote of three-fifths of the Senate (60 members) for adoption, under a rule adopted in 1975; previously cloture could be invoked by a two-thirds majority vote of those senators present and voting. The eight votes in 1978 brought to 140 the total number of cloture votes taken since the adoption of Rule 22 first allowed them in 1917. *(Complete listing of cloture votes from 1919 through 1976, 1977 Almanac p. 813)*

Issue	Date	Vote	Yeas Needed 3/5 Majority
Draft Resisters Pardons	Jan. 24, 1977	53-43	60
Campaign Financing	July 29, 1977	49-45	60
Campaign Financing	Aug. 1, 1977	47-46	60
Campaign Financing	Aug. 2, 1977	52-46	60
Natural Gas Pricing	Sept. 26, 1977	77-17	60
Labor Law Revision	June 7, 1978	42-47	60
Labor Law Revision	June 8, 1978	49-41	60
Labor Law Revision	June 13, 1978	54-43	60
Labor Law Revision	June 14, 1978	58-41	60
Labor Law Revision	June 15, 1978	58-39	60
Labor Law Revision	June 22, 1978	53-45	60
Revenue Act of 1978	Oct. 9, 1978	62-28	60
Energy Taxes	Oct. 14, 1978	71-13	60

Allen Legacy

The tough talk of conservatives and the number of filibuster threats during the session, as well as other delaying tactics used, had their roots in Allen's development of the post-cloture filibuster.

Allen's dilatory post-cloture techniques were known to his mentor, master filibusterer Richard B. Russell, D-Ga. (1933-71), but they were never used until 1976.

Allen had lost a major struggle the year before, when Senate reformers got the cloture requirement reduced from two-thirds of those voting (67 if all members were present) to three-fifths (60) of the Senate. Some thought the change would mark a decline in use of the filibuster.

But Allen continued the solo filibusters that were the major work of his Senate career. When Senate Democratic leaders made new attempts to cut him off in 1976, he broke the unwritten rule that a filibuster ended when cloture was invoked.

The action came on an antitrust enforcement bill opposed by Allen and other conservatives. Allen charged the leadership cut him off before he had actually begun to filibuster, thus violating his minority rights. In retaliation, he called up dozens of amendments, demanded quorum calls and roll-call votes and used other delaying tactics after cloture was invoked. He did not relent until he was offered a compromise. *(1976 Almanac p. 434)*

In 1977, Byrd sought to curb those tactics by making changes in the Senate cloture rule that would have curtailed post-cloture activity. Allen, whose greatest fear was that the leadership might try to further reduce the number of votes needed to invoke cloture, supported Byrd. But Republicans were almost unanimous in opposing any changes that cut back minority tools to delay or block legislation, and eventually Byrd withdrew his proposals. *(1977 Almanac p. 812)*

A few months later, Senate attention again was on the post-cloture filibuster when two liberal Democrats used Allen's techniques to tie up action on the natural gas bill for more than a week. *(1977 Almanac p. 735)*

Ironically, some Republicans who often supported Allen labeled that filibuster "purely obstructionist." But equally repugnant to them and many others were Byrd's tactics in breaking the filibuster. *(1977 Almanac p. 735)*

In the wake of the natural gas debacle, Byrd and Minority Leader Howard H. Baker Jr., R-Tenn., appointed ad hoc committees to come up with proposals for limiting post-cloture filibusters.

Byrd continued to advocate a bipartisan approach to restricting post-cloture tactics, even though the GOP ad hoc committee members refused to meet with the Democrats and the Democrats never met at all.

Some possible proposals for post-cloture rules changes included: reducing the time for roll-call votes, limiting each member to 30 minutes (instead of an hour) of debate after cloture, counting time spent on quorum calls and roll-call votes in the maximum time allotted for post-cloture debate, and making it easier to waive reading of amendments.

An effort to make such changes would raise another issue that always comes up in debate of the cloture rule — whether the Senate can change its rules at the beginning of a new Congress by majority vote without the debate itself

Membership Changes, 95th Congress

Party	Member	Died	Resigned	Successor	Party	Elected	Sworn In
			SENATE				
D	John L. McClellan - Ark.	11/27/77		Kaneaster Hodges Jr.	D		12/12/77
D	Lee Metcalf - Mont.	1/11/78		Paul Hatfield	D		1/23/78
D	Hubert H. Humphrey - Minn.	1/13/78		Muriel Humphrey	D		2/6/78
				David F. Durenberger	R	11/7/78	11/9/78
D	James B. Allen - Ala.	6/1/78		Maryon Allen	D		6/12/78
				Donald W. Stewart	D	11/7/78	11/20/78
			HOUSE				
D	Brock Adams - Wash.		1/24/77	John E. Cunningham	R	5/17/77	5/23/77
D	Bob Bergland - Minn.		1/24/77	Arlan Stangeland	R	2/22/77	3/1/77
D	Andrew Young - Ga.		1/31/77	Wyche Fowler Jr.	D	4/5/77	4/6/77
D	Richard A. Tonry - La.		5/4/77	Robert L. Livingston	R	8/27/77	9/7/77
D	Herman Badillo - N.Y.		12/31/77	Robert Garcia	D	2/14/78	2/21/78
D	Edward I. Koch - N.Y.		12/31/77	S. William Green	R	2/14/78	2/21/78
D	Clifford Allen - Tenn.	6/18/78					
R	William M. Ketchum - Calif.	6/24/78					
D	Ralph H. Metcalfe - Ill.	10/10/78					
D	Goodloe E. Byron - Md.	10/11/78					
D	Leo J. Ryan - Calif.	11/18/78					
R	William A. Steiger - Wis.	12/4/78					

being subject to the cloture rule. The cloture rule required two-thirds of those voting to cut off debate on proposals to make Senate rules changes.

Advocates of cloture rule changes said the Constitution gives the Senate authority at the beginning of each Congress to change its rules — and to cut off any filibusters against the proposed changes — by majority vote.

But opponents said the Senate is a continuing body because only a third of its membership is elected every two years, and therefore the rules carry over from one Congress to another. Thus, they argue, a two-thirds vote is needed to cut off debate on a proposed rules change.

Delays in House

House Reforms

In the House, many members said a series of reforms approved over the previous decade had produced delays and made many chamber operations more difficult.

By breaking the autocratic grip of committee chairmen, the reforms dispersed power and created a more democratic House where junior members had unprecedented opportunities to speak up.

But the House also found that democracy takes up more time. More members demanded consideration of more bills and amendments, sometimes tying up floor action so long that the House began to resemble the Senate during a filibuster.

In addition, democracy enabled many young Democrats to refuse to go along with the party line with far less reprisal from their elders, making it more difficult for party leaders to muster votes.

There were certain efficiencies in the "old system" that governed the House until recent years, said Thomas S. Foley, D-Wash. "But they're not efficiencies I would like to go back to," he hastened to add.

The "old system" was one that concentrated power in the hands of House committee chairmen and party leaders who were always the most senior members. It was "efficient" in the sense that if an administration or anyone else with a bill could persuade a handful of leaders to support it, the legislation usually would pass.

Now, however, "you have to deal with and negotiate with a lot congressmen," said House Budget Committee Chairman Robert N. Giaimo, D-Conn. For instance, instead of just going to the chairman of the Ways and Means Committee to get a tax bill passed, it was necessary to lobby all 37 members of the committee, Giaimo said. Moreover, on the major 1978 tax bill, another half dozen factions with amendments or substitutes had to be negotiated with, he said.

The old autocratic system was broken up gradually, beginning in the late 1960s when the Democratic Caucus was reactivated by reform-minded members. Although seniority was still the key to power, committee chairmen lost much of the control they used to have over colleagues and over the flow of legislation.

One reason was that subcommittees proliferated in the mid-1970s, giving dozens of additional members the chance to head a panel and push out legislation on their own. Moreover, new rules gave subcommittees protection from

Violent Deaths Among Members of Congress Since 1945

Rep. Leo J. Ryan, D-Calif., who was assassinated Nov. 18, was the seventeenth member of Congress to meet a violent death since World War II. Eight were killed in airplane crashes, three in auto accidents and one in an auto-train collision. Two were assassinated and three committed suicide. Of the 17, three were senators: Virgil M. Chapman, D-Ky.; Lester C. Hunt, D-Wyo., and Robert F. Kennedy, D-N.Y.

Five members were campaigning at the time of their deaths: Reps. Clement W. Miller, D-Calif., and Nick Begich, D-Alaska, were campaigning for re-election; Rep. Hale Boggs, D-La., then House majority leader, was campaigning for Begich; Rep. Jerry L. Litton, D-Mo., campaigning for the Missouri Democratic senatorial nomination, was en route to his own headquarters for a victory celebration after the 1976 primary; and Sen. Robert F. Kennedy, D-N.Y., was campaigning for the 1968 Democratic presidential nomination.

Ryan, the only one who died outside the United States, was assassinated while visiting a religious cult in Guyana.

Name	Date of Death	Cause	Place	Age	Years Served
Rep. George J. Bates (R Mass.)	Nov. 1, 1949	Airplane accident	Washington, D.C.	58	1937-49
Rep. Robert L. Coffey (D Pa.)	April 20, 1949	Airplane accident	Albuquerque, N.M.	30	January-April 1949
Sen. Virgil M. Chapman (D Ky.)	March 8, 1951	Auto accident	Bethesda, Md.	55	House 1925-29, 1931-49; Senate 1949-51
Sen. Lester C. Hunt (D Wyo.)	June 19, 1954	Suicide	Washington, D.C.	61	1949-54
Rep. Henderson L. Lanham (D Ga.)	Nov. 10, 1957	Auto-train accident	Rome, Ga.	69	1947-57
Rep. Charles A. Boyle (D Ill.)	Nov. 4, 1959	Auto accident	Chicago	52	1955-59
Rep. Douglas H. Elliott (R Pa.)	June19, 1960	Suicide	Horse Valley, Pa.	49	April-June 1960
Rep. Clement W. Miller (D Calif.)	Oct. 7, 1962	Airplane accident	Eureka, Calif.	45	1959-62
Rep. T. Ashton Thompson (D La.)	July 1, 1965	Auto accident	Gastonia, N.C.	49	1953-65
Sen. Robert F. Kennedy (D N.Y.)	June 6, 1968	Assassination	Los Angeles	42	1965-68
Rep. Hale Boggs (D La.)	Oct. 16, 1972	Airplane accident	Between Anchorage and Juneau, Alaska	58	1941-43, 1947-72
Rep. Nick Begich (D Alaska)	Oct. 16, 1972	Airplane accident	Between Anchorage and Juneau, Alaska	40	1971-72
Rep. George W. Collins (D Ill.)	Dec. 8, 1972	Airplane accident	Chicago, Ill.	47	1970-72
Rep. William O. Mills (R Md.)	May 24, 1973	Suicide	Easton, Md.	48	1971-73
Rep. Jerry L. Pettis (R Calif.)	Feb. 14, 1975	Airplane accident	San Bernardino, Calif.	58	1967-75
Rep. Jerry L. Litton (D Mo.)	Aug. 3, 1976	Airplane accident	Chillicothe, Mo.	39	1973-76
Rep. Leo J. Ryan (D Calif.)	Nov. 18, 1978	Assassination	Port Kaituma, Guyana	53	1973-78

the whims of full committee chairmen. *(1975 Almanac p. 28)*

Accompanying the shift in power was the move to open more House activities to public scrutiny.

In 1973, the House required that all committee and subcommittee bill-drafting sessions and other business meetings be open to the public unless a majority of the committee in open session voted to close the doors to the public. Bill-drafting sessions traditionally had not been open to the public.

In 1970, the House ended non-recorded teller votes by which many key issues were decided. In 1973, the House began use of an electronic voting system that simplified roll-call voting. The change was dramatic. In 1969, the House took 177 roll-call votes; in 1972, 329; in 1973, 541; in 1978, 834. *(CQ Guide to Congress, 2d Edition, pp. 343, 346, 355)*

This opening of committee work sessions and the increase in roll calls enabled constituents and lobbyists to know exactly how each member stood on key issues. But it also created pressure to abandon party loyalty and vote solely on the basis of benefits to a member's district or to special interest groups that support him or her. That made it more difficult for leaders to round up votes, which in turn forced delays in floor action on controversial bills.

The results of those changes were "subtle things" that added up to a considerable impact on the work flow, said House Majority Whip John Brademas, D-Ind. Taken together, the changes increased the obstacles to passage of all bills.

Suspension Calendar

Another trend that developed during the 95th Congress was increased use of the suspension calendar for legislation that many members considered more than routine. The practice had become so common by late in 1978 that it was sharply criticized by members of both parties.

One result was the defeat of a number of bills brought up under suspension; in past years, this seldom occurred.

Suspension Process. The suspension process was supposed to be a time-saving procedure for passing non-controversial House bills.

Under the procedure, regular House rules for debate are suspended, only 40 minutes of debate are allowed and no amendments can be offered unless they are included in the floor manager's motion to suspend the rules. Two-thirds of the members voting are required to pass a bill under suspension.

There are no formal restrictions on what bills a committee chairman can ask the House Speaker to put on the suspension calendar. The unwritten rule is that suspensions are not supposed to be controversial, but it is left up to committee chairmen to define which of their bills are non-controversial.

Increase in Use, Defeats. Congressional Research Service figures showed that extensive use of the procedure in late 1978 was part of a steady growth in use since the 90th Congress, when 167 bills were considered under suspension.

In the 95th Congress, the House considered 449 bills under suspension. Of those, 31 were defeated — a very large number for a procedure intended only for non-controversial matters. By comparison, 25 were defeated in the 94th Congress and only one in the 93rd.

Members said defeat of suspensions, which often surprised even those opposing the bills, increased because of occasional abuse of the system by leaders anxious to ram though bills that otherwise might be subject to sharp debate or amendment.

Also contributing to the number of defeats was a growing unhappiness with the large number of bills considered under suspension.

Growth of the suspension process paralleled a growth in legislation that was being pushed through Congress, partly as a result of the proliferation of subcommittees.

To accommodate all the bills, suspensions — once taken up only every other Monday — were allowed on both Mondays and Tuesdays in 1973. That year, suspensions jumped to 173, more than double the number considered in 1972. In the 95th Congress, suspensions were allowed on Mondays and Tuesdays of every week.

The expansion of days for considering suspensions was creating a legislative Parkinson's Law, according to Rep. William A. Steiger, R-Wis.

"All it did was give committees another excuse to report out another bill," he said.

By September 1978, the suspension procedure had become almost as much a focus of debate as the merits of the bills brought up under this method.

One week, 22 bills were considered under suspension in a two-day period. The following week, 24 bills were taken up under suspension one day and 11 another day.

As the votes continued — one about every five minutes — members grew increasingly unhappy over the procedure. A variety of House members — from liberal Democrats to conservative Republicans — seized the procedure as an argument for voting against bills they opposed.

But probably the most embarrassing suspension vote for Democratic leaders came earlier in the year, in March. The leadership at that time tried to undercut supporters of tuition tax credit legislation by scheduling an education grant bill on the suspension calendar.

The grant bill had been offered by President Carter as an alternative to tuition tax credits, which the president opposed. Fearful that the tax credit supporters might succeed in attaching their bill as an amendment if the grant bill was brought up under regular procedures, Democratic leaders put Carter's bill on the suspension calendar so no amendments could be offered.

Angered by the maneuver, the House didn't even give the grant bill a majority vote. It was soundly defeated, 156-218.

After that, grumbling about the procedure usually focused on large authorization bills brought up under suspension and, as the end of the session neared, the multitude of proposals scheduled under suspension.

Defenses, Criticisms. As the procedure was used more and more in late 1978 to unclog the legislative machinery in the House, members became not at all bashful about admitting they couldn't keep up with the pace when faced with a dozen or more suspension bills in a single day. Attendance during debates on suspension bills usually averaged less than two dozen members, and most members didn't go to the floor at all until roll-call votes actually began.

One Democrat paused on the way to cast his fourth in a rapid-fire series of votes one day, and told a reporter: "I don't know a goddamn thing about the Amateur Sports Act of 1978," referring to the bill he was about to vote on. "So I'll just have to ask someone on the floor. And frankly, I couldn't care less."

"It's too many," said Abner J. Mikva, D-Ill. "On the other hand, at the close of the session what would the alternative be?"

This is the ultimate test of the committee system," said Edward W. Pattison, D-N.Y. "You have to rely on the fact that [suspension bills] are not controversial and that the Republicans and Democrats on the committee are reasonably expert in these things."

But relying so heavily on committees can be dangerous, said Leon E. Panetta, D-Calif. "I frankly had no idea what the impact would be," he said of several tax bills considered in 1978. "Too much of this is done by the seat of our pants."

However, many members still said the process was a valuable parliamentary tool for dealing quickly with relatively minor bills.

What some members — both Democrats and Republicans — did object to was increased use of the suspension calendar for bills they felt should come up under regular rules for full debate and consideration of amendments.

"We're not following the [informal] guidelines" dictating use of the suspension calendar only for non-controversial bills, said Christopher J. Dodd, D-Conn.

"It used to be the suspension calendar was used only for non-controversial items. Now it's for anything they think they can get by," said Robert E. Bauman, R-Md.

James M. Collins, R-Texas, who protested when several large health program authorization bills were brought up under suspension in late 1978, complained that suspension bills are "greased pigs. You turn 'em loose and you can't get hold of them." ▮

The 95th Congress: No Sweeping Changes

With a large majority of Democrats, a Democratic president for the first time in eight years and no more American involvement in Indochina, the 95th Congress was expected by many observers to pass sweeping legislation that would affect the day-to-day lives of many Americans. That, to say the least, did not happen.

The Congress, which adjourned Oct. 15, a Sunday, after a 34-hour weekend session, compiled a respectable legislative record. But legislation that would have led to basic changes in the society — national health insurance, welfare reform, fundamental tax revision and a new urban strategy, to name a few — never got off the ground.

The tax-cut measure that Congress cleared on the last day of the session was significant not because it corrected a tax system that President Carter had called "a disgrace to the human race" but primarily because it was the first tax bill in more than a decade to give most of the relief to taxpayers who were already relatively well off.

Similarly, the energy bill, which also cleared Congress on Oct. 15, did not come near to solving a crisis that Carter had termed "the moral equivalent of war." Although the president hailed its passage, the bill was largely a stopgap measure, the ultimate effect of which was widely disputed.

Carter Victories

However, one of the main themes of the second session of the 95th Congress was that once the president narrowed his priorities and personally entered the fray and coordinated the lobbying he was able to win some important legislative victories. Among them:

- Under intense pressure from the administration, the Senate approved ratification of the Panama Canal treaties, by one vote more than the constitutional two-thirds majority required.
- The president won passage of the compromise natural gas pricing bill, the legislation he eventually called the most critical of the year, despite the opposition of liberals who wanted stiffer price regulations and legislators from oil and gas producing states who wanted no regulations at all.
- On two highly controversial foreign policy matters, the Senate turned down a resolution that would have prevented the president from selling jet fighter planes to Saudi Arabia, Egypt and Israel, and Congress gave Carter the authority to lift the arms embargo against Turkey.
- Carter's veto of a public works appropriations bill, containing funding for popular water projects, was upheld by the House, although the president was opposed by the congressional Democratic leadership. *(Carter vetoes, p. 29)*
- Congress adopted measures restructuring the Civil Service system and lifting many of the federal regulations that had stifled competition in the airline industry. Both laws were expected to have considerable long-term impact.

But there was a price to be paid for those victories. The president's success when he pulled out all the stops led to

Session Summary

The second session of the 95th Congress, which convened at noon, Jan. 19, 1978, adjourned, after an all-night session, on Sunday, Oct. 15. The Senate adjourned at 7:16 p.m. and the House at 6:46 p.m.

The session lasted 270 days. It was the second time in the past three years that a session lasted fewer than 300 days, but only the third time since 1969. The second session was 76 days shorter than the first session of the 95th Congress, but 12 days longer than the second session of the 94th Congress. *(Lengths of sessions, CQ Guide to Congress, Second Edition, chart, p. 338)*

The Senate was in session 159 days and the House 149 during 1978. Both houses took several short breaks during the year.

The all-night session of Saturday, Oct. 14-Sunday, Oct. 15 lasted 30 hours and 46 minutes in the House and 34 hours and 16 minutes in the Senate. The House session was its longest since a 32-hour 17-minute marathon conducted Oct. 8-9, 1968. The Senate's was the first all-night session since Majority Leader Robert C. Byrd, D-W.Va., attempted to break up a filibuster-by-amendment on natural gas deregulation by holding an all-night session on Sept. 27-28, 1977. That session lasted 22 hours and 12 minutes, and was followed (after a 2-hour, 18-minute break) by the regular Sept. 28 session, which lasted 12 hours, 36 minutes. *(All night session, 1977 Almanac p. 736)*

There were 6,927 bills and resolutions (1,617 Senate, 5,310 House) introduced during the session, a decrease from the 7,268 introduced during the second session of the 94th Congress; 15,386 bills and resolutions were introduced during the first session of the 95th Congress.

The president signed into law 410 public bills that were cleared during the second session. He vetoed 17 bills, none of which was overridden.

The Senate took 516 recorded votes and the House, 834. The House total set a new record for the fourth successive year, but the Senate total was substantially below the 635 it cast in 1977. The total of 1,350 votes taken by both houses was one above the previous record, set in 1976. Following are the roll-call vote totals for the past eight years:

Year	House	Senate	Total
1978	834	516	1,350
1977	706	635	1,341
1976	661	688	1,349
1975	612	602	1,214
1974	537	544	1,081
1973	541	594	1,135
1972	329	532	861
1971	320	423	743

criticism from those who thought he had not worked hard enough to achieve passage of other legislation.

Labor leaders, for example, felt that Carter had been lax in his support of a bill that would have changed the labor laws to give unions a stronger hand in collective bargaining. And many blacks criticized the president for not fighting hard enough to obtain passage of a meaningful Humphrey-Hawkins full employment measure.

Moreover, the biggest legislative victories were, in large part, the result of Republican support and were achieved despite prominent Democratic defections. Controversial proposals that did not have much Republican backing — the bill designed to control hospital costs, for example — were defeated.

Assessments

Typically, the post-mortem assessments of the 95th Congress depended on the political views of the assessors.

Sen. Robert C. Byrd, D-W.Va., the majority leader, said that he could not remember a Congress that had dealt with more difficult issues, and he gave the 95th a grade of "A."

The minority leader, Sen. Howard H. Baker Jr., R-Tenn., remarked that "we've got a Democratic president singing a Republican song."

Carter was said by an aide to feel "very proud of this Congress."

Sen. Edward M. Kennedy, D-Mass., said he had never seen a Congress so captive of special interest groups.

Special Interests

Indeed, the one thing that virtually all students of the 95th Congress agreed on was that interest groups, concentrating on one particular issue, were unusually influential.

Business organizations, taking their cue from public affairs activists such as Common Cause and Ralph Nader, organized highly effective grass-roots lobbying campaigns and were able, for example, to block enactment of legislation establishing a consumer protection agency.

The anti-abortion lobby was responsible for enactment of strict language prohibiting the government from paying for most abortions with Medicaid funds or military appropriations.

The women's lobby was surprisingly successful in persuading Congress to extend for 39 months the deadline for ratification of the Equal Rights Amendment.

The health industry took on the administration on the question of mandatory ceilings on hospital rates and prevented one of the president's most significant bills from being enacted.

Not all of the special interests emerged victorious. The pet projects of organized labor — changes in the labor law and repeal of the law against common-situs picketing — were defeated. A measure creating a new Cabinet Department of Education, a favorite of the National Education Association, was rejected despite administration backing.

Consumer activists did not get much of what they wanted from Congress. Nor did the nation's mayors, who sought massive new urban programs, although Congress did provide a new infusion of federal aid to New York City.

Congressional Independence

Congress continued to exercise, even flaunt, its independence from the White House. It was a mood that had taken hold during the Watergate crisis in reaction to the so-called imperial presidency of Richard M. Nixon and had continued through the presidency of Gerald R. Ford.

Carter was resented by some in Congress as an outsider, and he and his legislative staff were viewed by many on Capitol Hill as inept in their dealing with Congress.

From the president's point of view, he was merely eschewing the log-rolling and pork-barrel that had become ingrained in Congress. From the legislators' perspective, Carter was insensitive to political realities.

Nowhere was the conflict more visible than in the two-year fight over federal funding of water projects. In the end, Carter won. But it was only after he had vetoed a popular bill and gone behind the backs of congressional leaders to round up enough votes in the House to prevent the veto from being overridden.

There were some in Congress and the White House who thought that the sustaining of that veto, in the next-to-last week of the session, marked a turning point in the relationship between Congress and the White House. It indicated, they felt, that the pendulum had begun to swing back in the president's favor and that he would be operating from a position of strength for the rest of his term.

Others, however, interpreted the vote differently. They argued that it merely proved that the president — any president, in fact — could win particular battles when he fired his heaviest weapons, but they contended that Carter might have spent so much artillery that he would be weaker in the long run.

Leaders

Rep. Thomas P. O'Neill Jr., D-Mass., and Sen. Byrd, in their first term as Speaker of the House and majority leader of the Senate, were viewed as more forceful leaders than their predecessors and, at the end of the second session, had solidified their positions within the party.

In the Senate, Russell B. Long, D-La., chairman of the Finance Committee, controlled much of the major legislation that passed through the 95th Congress. Occasionally, he was unsuccessful, as in his end-of-Congress effort to obtain a rise in the support price of sugar, but few doubted that he had become the single most influential member of Congress outside the top leaders.

On the other hand, Long's counterpart in the House, Al Ullman, D-Ore., did not have a strong control over the Ways and Means Committee, which was closely divided on many issues that came before it.

Ethics, Investigations

Congress was more concerned with ethics in the 95th Congress than in recent years. Both chambers passed sweeping ethics codes early in 1977 and enacted the rules into law and extended them to other branches of government late in 1978. In the process, both passed strict limits on the amount of outside income members could earn, and the House in 1978 refused by a big margin to repeal the limit.

The legislation also put new restrictions on the "revolving door" between government and private enterprise. In addition, it established procedures for a temporary special prosecutor to investigate allegations of criminal wrongdoing by a president or other high officials of the executive branch.

But in some respects, the 95th Congress was as noteworthy for the laws its members violated as for those they passed. At adjournment time, more than a dozen current or former senators and representatives had been officially accused of criminal or unethical behavior.

Rep. Charles C. Diggs Jr., D-Mich., and former Rep. Richard T. Hanna, D-Calif. (1963-74), were convicted of felonies in 1978. Rep. Daniel J. Flood, D-Pa., and former Reps. Otto E. Passman, D-La. (1947-77), and Frank M. Clark, D-Pa. (1955-74), were under felony indictments when Congress adjourned.

O'Neill and John Brademas, D-Ind., the Democratic whip, among others, were cleared by the House ethics committee of charges stemming from the Korean influence-peddling investigation, but Reps. John J. McFall, D-Calif., Edward R. Roybal, D-Calif., and Charles H. Wilson, D-Calif., were officially reprimanded by the House as a result of the investigation. But the committee had recommended censure of Roybal; the House cut that to a reprimand. Moreover, the debate on the reprimands left observers wondering if the House really took the issue very seriously.

Rep. Joshua Eilberg, D-Pa., was accused by the ethics committee of ethical and criminal violations for allegedly having taken money to represent a Philadelphia hospital before a federal agency, the Community Services Administration.

In the Senate Herman E. Talmadge, D-Ga., Edward W. Brooke, R-Mass., and Birch Bayh, D-Ind., were under investigation for alleged financial misconduct. The investigations were not completed by adjournment.

Legislative Highlights

Foreign Policy, Defense

The 95th Congress was the first since the 87th that did not have to contend with American involvement in Indochina — either actual fighting or the bitter aftereffects. Yet, many of the paramount issues before Congress in 1978 involved foreign affairs and defense policy.

After 38 days of debate, the Senate in April approved ratification of two treaties with Panama, one turning over the Panama Canal to Panama by the year 2000, the second guaranteeing the United States' right to defend the canal after that date.

The next month, on another thorny political issue, the Senate rejected a resolution that would have blocked Carter's plan to sell jet fighters to Saudi Arabia, Egypt and Israel.

Congress also gave Carter controversial victories by lifting the arms embargo against Turkey, rejecting efforts to repeal flatly economic sanctions against Rhodesia and killing the B-1 bomber program.

Carter vetoed a $36.9 billion weapons procurement bill primarily because it called for construction of a costly nuclear-powered aircraft carrier he did not want built. The House sustained the veto, and legislation was then enacted that did not include the proposed carrier.

Congress also adopted a $9.1 billion foreign aid appropriations bill that made no deep cuts in funding and placed no serious restrictions on the use of aid.

Energy, Environment

Congress wrestled with energy policy for two years and, just before adjournment, cleared legislation to raise the price of natural gas gradually until 1985, when price controls were to be lifted altogether, and to provide tax incentives for fuel conservation.

Sen. Ted Stevens, R-Alaska, (left) and Majority Leader Robert C. Byrd, D-W.Va., talk by telephone from Capitol Hill to President Carter at Camp David to inform him that the 95th Congress had adjourned for the year.

Carter claimed success for his energy plan, but it was easy to lose sight of the fact that the broad national energy policy he put forth at the outset of his presidency had largely been abandoned.

Congress refused to go along with the centerpiece of that initial proposal, a tax on domestic crude oil to raise its price to the world level, and declined to approve a tax on business use of oil and gas, as Carter had asked. Moreover, the natural gas pricing legislation that was adopted was a far cry from Carter's plan to expand price controls on natural gas.

In addition to sustaining Carter's veto of the public works appropriations bill containing the water projects Carter did not want funded, Congress voted to extend the life of the Endangered Species Act.

It also created a Department of Energy, imposed strict new controls on strip mining and updated controls on water pollution.

Enforcement of new standards to control toxic auto emissions was delayed, and running disputes over legislation involving nuclear breeder reactors and Alaska lands were put over until the new year.

Taxes, Economic Policy

On the last day of the session, Congress cleared an $18.7 billion tax cut bill that had been written the night before in an all-night meeting of a Senate-House conference committee.

Unlike the tax reduction measures approved by other recent congresses, the 1978 measure was regressive in nature. It provided most of the relief to upper- and middle-income taxpayers (the approximately 50 percent of taxpayers making more than $15,000 a year received 79 percent of the tax relief) and contained little of the language Carter had proposed to eliminate so-called loopholes. Moreover, the bill provided for a reduction of more than $2 billion in capital gains taxes, more than three-quarters of which went to taxpayers making more than $50,000 a year.

Because Congress had voted in 1977 to raise Social Security taxes sharply, the net effect of the tax legislation passed by the 95th Congress was to leave most Americans liable for slightly more taxes than they had been before.

The other major tax measure considered by the 95th Congress — one that would have given parents tax credits to help offset tuition costs — was passed by the House and Senate in different forms but died in the face of a threatened presidential veto.

Congress approved a bill removing many of the federal regulations over airline fares and routes. The bill was intended to reduce air fares by increasing competition, but the Civil Aeronautics Board, perhaps anticipating passage of the legislation, had begun on its own to spur competition before the bill was enacted.

A separate bill that would have provided money to airlines to help them pay for quieter planes died in the adjournment rush.

The Humphrey-Hawkins bill, originally meant to commit the nation to a policy of full employment, was diluted to the point where it was little more than a symbolic statement about Congress' desire to limit unemployment and inflation. It was passed just before adjournment.

A bill that would have raised the domestic price of sugar, opposed by Carter on the ground that it was inflationary, was rejected by the House on the last day of the session.

Another bill that died was one that would have revised the nation's labor law. It was organized labor's highest priority item of the year, but it was killed by a Senate filibuster.

Social Policy

The 95th Congress took few significant steps in the area of social policy.

Liberals and conservatives alike agreed that the nation's welfare system needed to be revamped, but Carter's proposal to do so became caught in a crossfire between those who believed it was too generous and those who thought it too stingy. It was never seriously considered by full committees in the Senate or House.

Similarly, Congress never acted on the major parts of a Carter proposal to redirect urban assistance, although a measure providing long-term financial aid to New York City was adopted.

A bill to limit increases in hospital rates, seen as a necessary prelude to national health insurance, fell victim to lobbying by the health industry. And Carter's blueprint for national health insurance legislation not only met the expected opposition but also was attacked by Sen. Kennedy, the principal congressional advocate of national health insurance.

Congress did pass legislation extending for 39 months the deadline for ratification by the states of the Equal Rights Amendment, which guarantees equality to women, but doubt remained, even as the measure was being passed, that three more states would actually ratify the amendment and make it part of the Constitution.

Probably the most far-reaching social measure that was enacted in 1978 was one that raised the permissible mandatory retirement age for most American workers from 65 to 70.

Elections

Legislation that would have provided for public financing of congressional elections foundered in the House, along with a host of other proposed changes in election laws, even though they had the support of the president and the Democratic congressional leadership.

Agriculture

Agricultural Trade. Legislation designed to stimulate U.S. agricultural exports and thereby help reduce the U.S. trade deficit cleared Congress Oct. 14.

The legislation (S 3447) provided for establishment of up to 25 agricultural trade offices overseas, upgraded the title of U.S. agricultural representatives in at least 10 foreign countries, and authorized the Commodity Credit Corporation (CCC) to provide intermediate-term (three- to 10-year) credit to finance certain agricultural export sales.

The bill also made the People's Republic of China, which many experts considered a potential major new market for U.S. farm exports, eligible for direct CCC short-term credit of up to three years.

Farm Credit, Emergency Farm Legislation. In July, Congress cleared a major overhaul of federal farm lending programs, boosting both the size of loans and interest rates. The bill (HR 11504) also included a new "economic emergency" loan program designed to help established farmers through times when credit was tight.

The new loan program was a direct response to angry lobbying by the militant American Agriculture Movement. Throughout the early months of the year, farmers pressed Congress for relief from economic problems caused by price-depressing surpluses and heavy borrowing.

Also in response to the farmers' pressure, Congress passed a relatively minor revision (HR 6782) of the 1977 omnibus farm law, permitting the administration to raise support levels for wheat, corn and cotton.

Congress cleared that bill after rejecting a controversial "flexible parity" measure that passed the Senate April 10 but foundered in the House. The April 12 House vote on that proposal, which would have sharply raised prices for the three commodities, revealed divided support among farm-state members and opposition from urban members. The Carter administration had objected that flexible parity was very inflationary.

Subsidized Crop Insurance. House and Senate subcommittees held hearings but took no further action on a Carter administration plan to replace the limited federal crop insurance program with a new, subsidized insurance program to cover farmers' losses from drought, floods and other catastrophes. Most existing programs providing grants and cheap loans for disaster losses would be phased out. The administration plan arrived too late for committees to meet the May 15 date for reporting new authorizations. Initial response from both committees was favorable, but insurance companies and the conservative American Farm Bureau were cool to the proposal.

Sugar. Legislation to support domestic sugar producers and authorize U.S. participation in an international sugar pact died in the final hours before adjournment. The House Oct. 15 rejected a conference agreement tailored to administration specifications, though the Senate had accepted it earlier the same day. President Carter had vowed to veto earlier bills as too inflationary.

The House Oct. 6 had passed a bill (HR 13750) mandating import quotas and fees to raise the price of domestic sugar to 15 cents a pound, with automatic increases tied to inflation rates for the five-year life of the program. The Senate passed similar legislation Oct. 13, setting a minimum 16-cent price. Conferees provided a 15-cent base price with supplementary direct payments for 1979 only and 1 percent increases in the "price objective" thereafter. Sugar producers and processors and corn sweetener industry representatives had reluctantly gone along with the lower "price objective" but balked at the direct payment provision, making House passage impossible, according to observers. Members' objections to an unrelated tariff provision also produced some negative votes.

The interim sugar support program enacted in 1977 was due to expire with the 1978 crop year — about July 1979. And the State Department had already begun to seek another deadline extension for ratification of the sugar agreement. But each delay was said to threaten the international pact, which was intended to set minimum world prices for sugar.

Going down with the sugar bill were two unrelated provisions, sought by the administration and added by the Senate as a form of "veto insurance." The first would have extended the president's authority to waive countervailing duties — duties levied on imports to compensate for production subsidies by foreign governments. The second amendment authorized the president to fulfill a longstanding commitment to increase U.S. contributions to an international tin stockpile.

Meat Imports. Congress sent to the president legislation (HR 11545) to protect beef producers from import competion. But Carter pocket vetoed the bill Nov. 10, even though the final, House version was more to the president's liking than a bill (HR 5052) passed by the Senate in May.

The president had objected to a sharp curb, included in the final version, on his authority to lift meat import quotas. Carter and his Republican predecessors had repeatedly used that authority to increase meat supplies, to drive down rising beef prices.

The bill also reversed a statutory formula that pegged the amount of beef and other meats entering the country to domestic production. Consumer groups initially opposed that change, but did not press their case with members. Beef producers, who sought the change, argued that over the long run it would smooth out cyclical price highs and lows in the beef industry. Both sides acknowledged that the issue was more psychological than economic, since the amount of beef imported — about 7 percent of U.S. consumption — was relatively small.

House passage came in the early morning hours of Oct. 13, two days before adjournment. Deciding against trying for a conference to resolve differences, the Senate Oct. 15 passed the House bill by voice vote.

Congress and Government

Civil Service. Congress approved a modified version of President Carter's proposals to revise the civil service system.

Carter's plan, which he called the key to reorganizing the federal government, came in two parts. The first was a reorganization of the Civil Service Commission to split up its conflicting responsibilities as both government personnel manager and board of appeals for employee grievances. The reorganization plan, creating two new agencies to carry out those duties, took effect in August without opposition from Congress.

The second part, opposed by federal employee unions, was a reform bill that passed the House and Senate in differing versions. House and Senate conferees had worked out differences in the two versions, and the final bill (S 2460) was approved the week of Oct. 2.

Carter said his bill would put true merit in the civil service system by abolishing automatic pay raises for many top-level government employees and replacing them with a system of awarding raises or bonuses for good performance. Carter's proposal also would have made it easier for federal managers to get rid of incompetent employees, and it codified the rights of federal employees.

The final bill retained most of the administration's labor rights provisions and Carter's plans to base pay on performance. It also gave managers more freedom to fire incompetents, although it retained more employee protection than the administration had wanted.

S 2640 did not contain new restrictions the administration had wanted in the program that gave veterans preference in hiring for federal jobs. Both House and Senate had rejected most of the restrictions, and it was uncertain whether the administration would propose them again in the 96th Congress.

Ethics in Government. Congress approved legislation (S 555) requiring detailed public financial disclosure by top officials in all three branches of the federal government.

Although the House and Senate had passed bills setting similar disclosure requirements and restricting post-government activity by federal employees, the Senate version included several items not contained in the House bill. The most controversial was a provision for appointment of a temporary special prosecutor in cases of alleged wrongdoing by top government officials. A separate special prosecutor bill (HR 9705) was considered dead in the House, but House conferees accepted the Senate special prosecutor provisions.

Disclosure legislation covering executive branch employees had been proposed by President Carter in 1977. The Senate, as part of what it called Watergate reform legislation, previously had passed a bill covering disclosure by employees in all three government branches.

In the House, where the legislation was stalled for almost a year, attention focused on how it would affect members of Congress. An unrelated issue — a House rule limiting members' outside earned income — was injected into the debate, and other issues in the disclosure bill were virtually ignored by the House. An attempt to repeal the income limit, which was passed in the 1977 House ethics code, was soundly defeated.

Job Discrimination. The Senate Democratic Policy Committee in September killed a resolution (S Res 431) that would have given Senate employees their first formal protection from job discrimination. At a closed-door meeting, the policy committee agreed not to let the resolution come up on the Senate floor in 1978.

Sen. Edward W. Brooke, R-Mass., offered the resolution as an amendment to another bill on the Senate floor just days before the 95th Congress adjourned, but it was withdrawn when it became clear it would be filibustered.

The resolution would have established a new Senate office to try to reach informal agreements settling grievance complaints by Senate employees. Unresolved complaints would have been referred to a six-member Senate Fair Employment Relations Board, and a final appeal could have been made to the Senate Select Committee on Ethics.

The resolution was intended to set up a mechanism for enforcing a new Senate rule, adopted in 1977, forbidding discrimination in hiring and firing on the basis of race, color, religion, sex, national origin, age or physical handicap. The rule was scheduled to take effect in 1979, but supporters said it would be meaningless without an enforcement mechanism.

Ethics Charges. Several members of Congress faced a variety of charges of unethical or illegal behavior during 1978. Some of these charges resulted from the House's investigation of influence peddling by representatives of South Korea.

The other charges grew out of a variety of incidents. They were:

Sen. Edward W. Brooke, R-Mass., was under investigation by the Senate Ethics Committee as a result of allegations that he did not disclose $49,000 in interest-free loans received from a Massachusetts liquor distributor. Senate rules required disclosure of liabilities over $2,500 owed to anyone other than a relative. As a result of the allegations about the loan, Brooke's bitter 1977 divorce trial was reopened and Massachusetts officials launched investigations into other aspects of Brooke's finances.

The special counsel hired by the ethics panel to investigate Brooke resigned Oct. 13, setting off a new controversy. At Brooke's request, the senator appeared before the panel Oct. 24 to deny the charges that either he or his attorneys had hindered the investigation by withholding information. The committee Oct. 25 said there was no evidence to substantiate the charge. Brooke was defeated Nov. 7.

Rep. J. Herbert Burke, R-Fla., pleaded guilty Sept. 26 to charges of being disorderly and resisting arrest in a disturbance at a Florida bar featuring nude dancers.

Burke also pleaded no contest to a related charge of trying to influence a witness to lie about the incident. Burke was fined $150 and required to pay court and investigative costs.

Rep. Charles C. Diggs Jr., D-Mich., was convicted Oct. 7 on charges of taking more than $60,000 in kickbacks from aides on his congressional payroll and putting persons on his payroll who did no official work. Diggs, who was re-elected to a 13th term, said he would appeal the decision.

Rep. Joshua Eilberg, D-Pa., was accused Sept. 13 of illegally accepting more than $100,000 in legal fees to help a Philadelphia hospital obtain a federal grant. Eilberg denied the charge, which was made by the House Committee on Standards of Official Conduct. On Oct. 24, a grand jury issued a one-count conflict-of-interest indictment against Eilberg, who pleaded innocent to the charge Nov. 1. Eilberg was defeated in his bid for re-election.

Rep. Daniel J. Flood, D-Pa., was indicted by a federal grand jury in Los Angeles Sept. 5 on three charges of lying about payoffs allegedly made to him and a former aide. Flood, who was under investigation in other cities for allegedly receiving illegal kickbacks, pleaded innocent to the Los Angeles charges.

A second Flood indictment was announced Oct. 12 in Washington, D.C., where the congressman was charged with 10 counts of bribery and conspiracy.

The indictment alleged Flood and a former aide plotted to "corruptly influence" nine federal government agencies on behalf of businessmen who paid them for help in getting federal grants. Flood was re-elected Nov. 7.

Rep. Frederick Richmond, D-N.Y., pleaded innocent to a charge that he solicited sex for pay. Richmond earlier had acknowledged the morals charge was true. His innocent plea was a technicality designed to make him eligible for a District of Columbia first offender program. Charges against Richmond were dropped after he completed the program.

Sen. Herman E. Talmadge, D-Ga., was under investigation by the Senate Ethics Committee and a federal grand jury on a variety of charges stemming from his financial dealings. During the investigations, Talmadge repaid the Senate $37,125.90 in expenses he had improperly claimed. In addition, Talmadge filed amended personal campaign spending reports for 1973 and 1974 to account for discrepancies between his reports and those filed by his campaign committee.

Other allegations about Talmadge involved a secret campaign account kept by former Talmadge aide Daniel Minchew, who was granted limited immunity to testify before the Senate committee about allegedly illegal deposits made in the account.

Filibusters. Senate Majority Leader Robert C. Byrd, D-W.Va., did not revive his 1977 attempts to limit use of the post-cloture filibuster technique. However, as use of filibuster threats and other delaying techniques increased during 1978, Senate leaders resolved to seek rules changes at the beginning of the 96th Congress. Their efforts were to be aimed at the post-cloture filibuster techniques perfected by the late Sen. James B. Allen, D-Ala. (1969-78), and used or threatened by both conservatives and liberals in fighting legislation.

Congressional Veto. Backers of sweeping legislative veto bills (HR 116, HR 959) that would allow Congress to disapprove any executive branch agency rules and regulations made little headway in 1978. The House Rules Committee finally held hearings on the bills after considerable prodding by chief sponsor Elliott H. Levitas, D-Ga., but the committee said it wanted to study the issue further in the 96th Congress.

Levitas did have more luck pushing the issue on individual bills. A conference report on legislation (HR 3816) authorizing funds for the Federal Trade Commission (FTC) was twice rejected by the House because House and Senate conferees had dropped a House-passed provision allowing congressional veto of FTC actions. The Senate had shown little enthusiasm for most congressional veto proposals.

Sunset Legislation. The Senate passed sunset legislation (S 2) Oct. 11, but the bill died for lack of House action.

S 2, calling for automatic termination of funding for federal programs unless they were specifically renewed by Congress, had been reported by two Senate committees. But chief sponsor Edmund S. Muskie, D-Maine, was unable to bring the bill to the floor because of objections from Majority Leader Robert C. Byrd, D-W. Va., and Majority Whip Alan Cranston, D-Calif.

Muskie finally worked out a compromise with the two leaders, preserving the sunset concept but satisfying their objections that S 2 would create procedural problems for the Senate. However, the compromise was struck less than a month before the Senate was set to adjourn for the year.

Moreover, the House had virtually ignored comparable legislation.

Muskie's only hope for enactment of S 2 was to try to force House acceptance of it by attaching the bill in the Senate to legislation certain to be enacted in the 95th Congress. However, when Muskie offered S 2 as an amendment to the Export-Import Bank extension bill (S 3077), Sen. John Glenn, D-Ohio, also offered an amendment that would have included tax expenditures — such as tax credits or deductions — in the programs subject to sunset review. The Senate committees had dropped tax expenditures from the original Muskie version of S 2.

Glenn's amendment prompted a filibuster by Finance Committee Chairman Russell B. Long, D-La., which continued when the Muskie and Glenn amendments were offered to the tax bill. The Senate voted to invoke cloture on the tax bill Oct. 9, which meant the non-germane sunset amendments could not be considered as riders to S 3077. Muskie later got a Senate vote on sunset. But without a vehicle such as the tax bill, there was no way to force House action before adjournment.

D.C. Voting Representation. A constitutional amendment giving added voting rights and full representation in Congress to District of Columbia residents narrowly squeaked through the Senate Aug. 22 and was sent to the states for ratification.

The Senate adopted the measure (H J Res 554) by a vote of 67-32, one vote more than the required two-thirds majority. The House passed the amendment May 2 by a 289-127 vote, 11 more than the required two-thirds.

Supporters of the amendment were cautiously optimistic about prospects for ratification by 38 state legislatures within seven years, while other observers predicted that opposition in some of the less-populated western and southern states could make final ratification very close. New Jersey was the first to ratify the amendment.

As cleared by Congress H J Res 554 treated the district as a state for purposes of congressional and electoral college representation and for participation in presidential elections and ratification of proposed amendments to the Constitution. It would repeal the 23rd Amendment to the Constitution, which allowed district residents to vote for president and vice president, while limiting district representation in the electoral college to that of the least populous state.

Customs Law Reform. Congress cleared and the president signed a bill (HR 8149) designed to modernize and simplify U.S. customs law.

The bill raised to $300, from $100, the duty-free allowance granted U.S. residents returning from abroad with foreign goods. For goods obtained in U.S. insular possessions such as American Samoa, Guam and the Virgin Islands, the bill increased the allowance to $600, from $200.

Emergency Preparedness Reorganization. President Carter's reorganization of federal emergency preparedness and disaster response programs became effective Sept. 16 after Congress declined to reject the proposal. The House Sept. 14 rejected a resolution to kill the plan. The Senate did not vote on the issue.

The plan created a new Federal Emergency Management Agency and made three transfers into it: the National Fire Prevention and Control Administration, formerly in the Commerce Department; the Federal Insurance Administration, formerly in the Housing and Urban Development Department; and the oversight functions of the Federal Emergency Broadcast System, formerly in the Executive Office of the President. In addition, various functions were to be added to the agency by executive order.

Public Financing, Election Law Changes. A coalition of Republicans and southern Democrats succeeded twice in 1978 in blocking House floor consideration of a proposal to extend public financing to congressional races.

The public financing plan applied only to House general elections and was voluntary. It provided that candidates who participated would be eligible for federal funds on a matching basis.

A bill to establish public financing in Senate general elections fell victim to a filibuster in August 1977, while a similar measure for House general elections was blocked in the Administration Committee two months later.

Uncertain that a public financing bill could pass the House, Democratic congressional leaders in early 1978 promoted an alternative campaign finance bill (HR 11315) that included controversial limits on party and political action committee (PAC) spending.

House leaders contended that they had devised the measure on the assumption there was no majority for public financing and defended HR 11315 as an effective method of curbing excessive campaign spending. They hoped, though, that it might serve as a bargaining chip to gain public financing.

But it brought united Republican opposition and criticism from public financing backers who claimed that it "poisoned the well" for their proposal, which they had intended to add as a floor amendment. By a vote of 198-209, the House March 19 defeated the rule to allow consideration of HR 11315. After the vote the bill was placed on a back burner and not brought up the rest of the session.

Newer House members along with Common Cause and the Democratic Study Group led the second thrust for public financing in July. Bearing the scars of the first battle, the Democratic leadership quietly supported the effort but remained in the background.

Without a majority on the Rules Committee, public financing proponents were forced to try a complex set of parliamentary maneuvers to even bring their proposal to the floor.

They failed, as the House voted 196-213 on July 19 not to allow a public financing amendment to the $8.6 million Federal Election Commission fiscal 1979 authorization bill (HR 11983).

Public financing was the only piece of President Carter's four-part election law package to be actively promoted in Congress in 1978. *(1977 Almanac p. 798)*

The constitutional amendment to abolish the electoral college and elect the president by direct popular vote (S J Res 1) was approved by the Senate Judiciary Committee in September 1977. But the threat of a filibuster prevented floor consideration in 1978.

Legislation to relax the Hatch Act (HR 10) passed the House in June 1977 but lay buried throughout 1978 in the Senate Government Affairs Committee, where Chairman Abraham A. Ribicoff, D-Conn., opposed it. A House effort to attach the measure to President Carter's civil service reform plan failed.

And the centerpiece of the Carter package, election day voter registration (HR 5400, S 1072), had been dormant in Congress since mid-1977. There was no effort to revive it in 1978.

Economic Affairs/Labor

Tax Cuts. In the final hours of the 95th Congress, lawmakers approved an $18.7 billion tax cut to take effect in 1979 (HR 13511).

The reduction was larger than the $16.3 billion cut approved by the House in August, but considerably smaller than the $29.1 billion measure passed by the Senate five days before adjournment.

The overall size of the tax cut was pared back to meet the demands of the Carter administration, which told House-Senate conferees it wanted a cut no more than $1.5 billion above the House bill. A larger reduction, administration officials warned, would create too great a danger of inflation by causing the federal budget to be too large.

While Carter managed to keep the overall size of the tax bill near to the level he wanted, he was less successful in shaping its contents. Almost completely absent from the bill, except for a few tokens, were the various "reforms" the president had proposed to Congress in January.

Indeed, on one major provision Congress took the opposite direction from what Carter proposed. It agreed to a substantial reduction in taxes on capital gains — profits from the sale of land, stock and other assets — by increasing to 60 percent from 50 percent the amount of gains excluded from taxation.

Carter complained that the change benefited the wealthy, but proponents argued that it would encourage new investment and thus cause the economy to grow.

In general, the bill reduced individual income taxes in a manner designed roughly to offset tax increases that would otherwise occur in 1979 as a result of inflation and rising Social Security taxes. However, few taxpayers would have a real net tax cut and some would have an increase.

In addition, it included some structural tax changes — including an increase in the personal exemption to $1,000 from $750 in place of the expiring general tax credit (a change that generally benefits wealthier taxpayers), repeal of the federal tax deduction for state and local gasoline taxes, and a provision that unemployment compensation benefits be taxed when they go to single taxpayers earning more than $20,000 or married couples with incomes above $25,000.

To help the working poor, the bill increased the existing earned income credit to a maximum of $500 from $400. The full credit would be available to people earning between $5,000 and $6,000, and it would phase out at $10,000.

For businesses, the bill included a reduction of corporate income taxes, liberalization of the investment tax credit, a new "targeted" jobs credit for employers who hire the disadvantaged (replacing the expiring general jobs credit), and a variety of miscellaneous provisions. Several sections in the House and Senate bill to liberalize rules governing depreciation of business equipment were dropped in conference in order to reduce the cost of the bill, however.

Social Security Taxes. The ink was barely dry on the paper — a bill approved by Congress in December 1977 to increase Social Security taxes in 1979 and beyond — when lawmakers started having second thoughts.

The 1977 law scheduled a series of Social Security tax hikes in order to restore the retirement system to financial solvency. But efforts to reconsider that action began in January 1978 — a year before its first impact would be felt — when Social Security taxes rose under a previous law. The 1978 hike caused a public outcry, and a number of lawmakers returned to Washington bent on preventing the planned future hikes.

The effort to roll back the 1977 action failed. It was stymied by past precedent, the opposition of President Carter and the congressional leadership, and division among its advocates.

The biggest problem was the principle that the Social Security system should be self-supporting through earmarked payroll taxes. Under that principle, the taxes had to go up to meet projected cost increases. Most efforts to prevent the planned tax increases provided for the use of general revenues instead — an eventuality that some lawmakers warned would result in a loss of fiscal discipline marked finally by deficit financing of Social Security benefits.

The year ended with no action taken, but a commitment by House Ways and Means Chairman Al Ullman, D-Ore., to deal comprehensively with the issue in 1979. In light of the scheduled Social Security tax boost in 1979 — most of which would be offset by income tax cuts approved by Congress — Ullman was likely to be held to that promise.

Budget. Congress began writing its fiscal 1979 budget amidst concerns about high unemployment and a possible economic slowdown. By the time it adopted the budget, inflation and an anti-government spending mood had eclipsed the earlier focus.

In January, President Carter proposed a $500.2 billion budget, coupled with a $24.5 billion tax cut. The deficit, still showing fiscal strains of the 1973-1975 recession, was to be $60.6 billion.

When unemployment dropped more rapidly than expected and inflation surged in early 1978, Congress agreed to scale back the proposed tax cut. That, combined with a downward revision in some spending estimates, enabled lawmakers to adopt a first budget resolution (S Con Res 80) in May calling for a $498.8 billion spending target and a $50.9 billion deficit.

As usual, the resolution won bipartisan support in the Senate, but was opposed by most House Republicans, who favored lower spending and a larger tax cut.

Events following the adoption of the first resolution served to continue the trend toward a smaller deficit. As in the past, federal agencies appeared unable to spend money as rapidly as Congress appropriated it. In addition, approval by California voters in June of a state constitutional amendment slashing property taxes encouraged an anti-spending spirit in Congress. Finally, further concerns about inflation encouraged the belief that a smaller tax cut — and hence a smaller deficit — were advisable.

A change in the prevailing economic and budgetary wisdom was most clearly illustrated by the Senate Budget Committee's shifting attitude toward spending for local public works programs.

The committee had originally supported, with some reservations, proposals to leave room in the first budget resolution for federally financed local public works programs. They were seen as a means to help local governments suffering from recession, and to create jobs.

On the second resolution (H Con Res 683), the committee parted with the House, which had included room for $2 billion of local works spending, and opposed the program entirely. Members argued that the economy didn't justify the program anymore, and that future programs to create jobs should be aimed more directly at the hard-core unemployed.

An impasse over the local public works question prevented a House-Senate conference committee from reaching agreement on the second resolution by the Sept. 15 deadline. The disagreement was skirted several days later, but not before the Senate had gone on record strongly against the program.

The combination of a smaller tax cut, some spending reductions and further downward re-estimates did enable Congress to agree on a $487.5 billion budget carrying a predicted deficit of $38.8 billion — more than $20 billion lower than Carter originally forecast in January.

New York City Aid. Congress agreed in 1978 to provide long-term federal guarantees on up to $1.65 billion in New York City bonds.

In a sharp contrast to the debate that preceded approval in 1975 of a program providing short-term loans to the financially ailing city, the long-term guarantee measure (HR 12426) was approved by substantial margins with almost none of the rancor that marked the earlier action.

The federal loan guarantee agreement was part of a complicated financial plan involving the city and state government, banks and city and state employee pension funds. The pension funds had agreed to provide funds to meet the city's long-term borrowing needs, but only if the loans carried federal guarantees. The banks agreed to make unguaranteed loans on the condition that the pension funds chipped in.

City officials argued that the long-term financing was needed to restore the city to economic self-sufficiency. The short-term loan program, while it enabled the city to stay afloat, was insufficient to cure the city's problems, they said.

Although the final loan guarantee agreement was less than the city had originally sought, and came with some restrictions that city officials opposed, they generally hailed the congressional action and predicted that it would enable New York to get back on its feet.

Public Service Jobs. Congress completed action on legislation extending public service jobs programs that made some cuts from current program levels and benefits.

Authorized under the Comprehensive Employment and Training Act (CETA), the public service jobs had been the target of widespread criticism over alleged corruption and waste. The bills considered by Congress in 1978 extended the public service jobs and job training programs of CETA for four years.

The Senate easily passed its CETA bill (S 2570) Aug. 25. The bill ran into serious trouble in the House, however, and sponsors were able to secure its passage Sept. 22 only by agreeing to a compromise which eliminated an estimated 100,000 public service jobs and held down wages of public service workers. The final version set a goal of 660,000 jobs at current unemployment levels, and limited public service wages to a maximum of $13,200 a year.

Labor Law Revision. A five-week Senate filibuster blocked congressional approval of legislation (HR 8410) revising the National Labor Relations Act. The bill was recommitted to the Human Resources Committee June 22, after six unsuccessful attempts at invoking cloture.

Organized labor's No. 1 legislative priority in the 95th Congress, the bill passed the House easily in 1977. Key provisions expanded the membership of the National Labor Relations Board (NLRB), set deadlines for union representation elections, allowed "equal access" of union organizers to a work place, "debarred" labor law violators from receiving federal contracts, and set back pay awards for newly organized workers whose employer refused to bargain for a contract.

A Sept. 27 attempt to revive the bill, stripped of most of its controversial provisions, went nowhere after opponents made clear that they would oppose any version of the bill in the 95th Congress.

Humphrey-Hawkins Full Employment Bill. Supporters of the Humphrey-Hawkins full employment bill (HR 50) were able to win final congressional approval of their bill in the waning hours of the 95th Congress only by swallowing changes that they had previously considered unacceptable.

The final version that cleared Oct. 15 had been worked out during three days of behind-the-scenes negotiations between Senate sponsors and some of the bill's most outspoken opponents.

The key change made by the Senate compromise was the addition of a national goal of reducing the rate of inflation to 3 percent by 1983 and eliminating it entirely by 1988. Backers of the bill argued that the inflation goal would undermine the measure's primary goal of reduction of the unemployment rate to 4 percent by 1983.

The coalition supporting the bill had had to put heavy pressure on the administration and Senate leaders to get the bill to the floor. A compromise became essential when it became clear that there would not be enough time left in the session to overcome the threatened filibuster against the bill.

Mandatory Retirement. Legislation (HR 5383) protecting most workers from age-based mandatory retirement before age 70 was cleared by Congress early in 1978.

The bill in effect banned mandatory retirement before age 70 by extending coverage under the Age Discrimination Act, which prohibited age-based discrimination in employment against persons between the ages of 40 and 65, to include those between 65 and 70.

The bill removed the existing mandatory retirement age for most federal workers (70), thus allowing those workers to continue on their jobs as long as they were able and willing.

Most of the work on the bill had been completed in 1977; final action was delayed by an extended House-Senate fight over whether to allow corporations and universities to force executives and professors to retire at 65. As cleared, HR 5383 did not contain protections for high-level executives; tenured faculty members were also excluded, but only until 1982.

Energy/Environment

Carter Energy Plan. The determined Democratic leadership of the House, stubbornly wearing down opponents, presented President Carter with a five-part energy package in the early morning hours of Sunday, Oct. 15.

The legislation (HR 5263, HR 5037, HR 5289, HR 5146, HR 4018) contained only remnants of the tough plan originally presented by Carter in April 1977. That program would have raised gasoline taxes, taxed cheaper domestic oil and revamped electricity rate-making. Carter hoped to force Americans to curb their profligate consumption of energy, but Congress refused, preferring generally to encourage conservation, not penalize waste.

However, the president continued to fight for the watered-down plan, calling it his top legislative priority. When it was finally passed, Carter said, "We have declared to ourselves and the world our intent to control our use of energy and thereby to control our own destiny as a nation."

The final 231-168 House vote did not reflect the tense moments that supporters of the plan had suffered in the preceding months.

The energy bill came perhaps closest to defeat Oct. 13, when opponents of the natural gas pricing portion came within one vote of splitting that section away from the more popular parts of the package. Those other sections included government aid for insulating homes and businesses, penalties for gas guzzling cars, reform of utility rate-making and requirements that industries switch from using oil and gas to coal.

But by a 207-206 vote, the House kept the package intact and preserved the strategy of Speaker Thomas P. O'Neill Jr., D-Mass., who wanted to give members just one vote on energy. Standing alone, the gas bill, considered the most important element of the package by supporters, would have been vulnerable to attack by the opposing coalition of conservative Republicans, Democrats from energy-producing states and liberal Democrats worried about higher consumer prices.

But the House vote to keep the five parts together did not clear the way for the energy bill. In the Senate, retiring James Abourezk, D-S.D., Oct. 14 began a filibuster against the only part of the energy package still before the Senate — a conference report on energy taxes. Abourezk, a key opponent of the gas bill, opposed the tax report and instead wanted Congress to pass a Senate version with more generous credits for conservation and solar energy. He vowed to give up his filibuster only if the House passed that Senate bill separately.

But O'Neill refused to allow a House vote on the package until the fifth piece — the tax conference report — was sent over by the Senate. The House had a long wait. Abourezk and a few other senators talked and delayed for about 15 hours — from Saturday morning until 12:30 a.m. Sunday, when they finally gave up. Soon after, the Senate easily passed the conference report on energy taxes, 60-17. Then, after four hours of debate, the House cast its final 231-168 vote about 7:30 a.m.

The stymied tax bill once included the central element of Carter's plan — a tax on domestic crude oil to raise prices to the world level — but it was rejected by the Senate and did not survive the conference. Tax conferees approved tax credits to homeowners and businesses that installed insulation, storm windows, other energy conservation devices and solar, wind or geothermal energy-producing equipment.

While the crude oil tax languished, the Carter administration early in the year focused its attention on the natural gas pricing bill. Conferees were faced with the difficult task of reconciling diametrically opposing views — the House had voted to continue gas pricing controls while the Senate had voted to lift them. A group of conferees meeting behind closed doors finally crafted a compromise, which phased in higher prices until 1985, when controls on newly discovered gas would be lifted. The agreement was designed to end the differences in price between gas sold on the intrastate and interstate markets, which had led to surpluses in producing states where prices weren't regulated, and shortages in consuming states.

With the White House constantly nursing along the fragile agreement, the Senate finally took up the compromise in early September. A move by opponents to send it back to conference, which would have killed it, was defeated Sept. 19, 39-59. The intensive White House lobbying was considered a key factor in that victory and in the 57-42 vote on final passage of the bill Sept. 27.

Endangered Species. A bill aimed at resolving conflicts between endangered species and federal public works projects was cleared by Congress Oct. 15.

The measure (S 2899) established a seven-member Cabinet-level board that could allow construction of dams and other projects, even if they threatened the existence of a species protected by the 1973 law.

Members' desire to soften the law followed a June 5 Supreme Court decision barring operation of the Tennessee Valley Authority's Tellico Dam. The court ruled that the dam would destroy the habitat of an endangered species, a tiny fish called the snail darter.

As passed by Congress, the bill specified that Tellico and the Gray Rocks Dam in Wyoming would receive an early review by the board. A federal court had ruled that the Wyoming project could not be completed because it potentially threatened the whooping and sandhill cranes.

Environmentalists generally did not want to see any change in the law.

To mollify critics of the law, authorization for the endangered species program was for only 18 months, although the Senate version had contained a three-year authorization. The change was intended to permit earlier congressional review of how the law was being administered.

Alaska Lands. Last minute negotiations on legislation to preserve federally owned wilderness in Alaska fell apart in the final hours of the session when Sen. Mike Gravel, D-Alaska, refused to accept a compromise agreement. Conservationists had considered the bill their top priority.

The agreement, crafted in closed meetings Oct. 13 and 14 by key House and Senate leaders and Interior Secretary Cecil D. Andrus, was being readied for the Senate floor when Gravel objected and said he would filibuster the bill. Gravel wanted firm guarantees that pipelines and highways could be built across wilderness to state lands. But the other negotiators refused to go along, noting that access already was provided in House-passed and Senate committee bills.

Restrictions on development of the lands was to expire Dec. 18. Andrus had said the Carter administration would use existing executive authority to continue the restrictions until 1979 when Congress would try again to write a bill.

The House May 19 overwhelmingly passed a bill (HR 39) that classified more than 100 million acres of Alaska into forests, wildlife refuges, parks and other conservation units. The Senate Energy Committee Oct. 5 reported legislation that placed fewer restrictions on use of the federal lands. Conservationists complained that the Senate panel had "mangled" the original administration proposals that were designed to protect wildlife and wilderness from damage by mining, extraction of oil and gas and other development.

Water Policy. President Carter took on the congressional establishment in June when he proposed water policy reforms to tighten control over "pork barrel" federal spending on expensive dams, irrigation channels and other water projects.

When Congress in September passed an appropriations bill (HR 12928) that ignored the reforms, Carter vetoed the bill and won a major victory when the House failed, 223-190, to override it. Supporters of the bill, who included top Democratic leaders, were 53 votes short of the 276 needed to override.

The trigger for the veto was restoration of funding for six projects objectionable to Carter, which he thought had been killed in 1977. In addition, Carter said Congress was starting construction of another 27 projects that, along with the six, would cost taxpayers $1.8 billion over the next several years. He also criticized the bill for mandating the hiring of 2,300 new employees by the two federal construction agencies — the Army Corps of Engineers and the Interior Department's Bureau of Reclamation.

Carter's policy had called for full, up-front funding of new projects, but Congress refused to go along with that proposal, too, which was another reason for the veto.

But Carter and Congress later patched up their differences, at least long enough to agree on a modified replacement for the vetoed measure, which included fiscal 1979 funding for the Department of Energy and the water development agencies. The compromise knocked out funding for the six disputed projects, as well as 10 others added by Congress. Carter said those projects would have cost about $1.6 billion to complete.

Breeder Reactor. Unresolved at the close of the session was the fate of the nuclear-powered breeder reactor at Clinch River, Tenn. The Senate never voted on the authorization bill (S 2692) that would have given the Energy Department the option to kill the demonstration project, which President Carter opposed.

The House had voted in July to continue the project, despite Carter's complaints that the plutonium it produced could be used to make nuclear weapons and that the plant's design was obsolete.

Congress did approve $172 million for the plant in a separate appropriations bill (HR 12928 — HJ Res 1139). But officials said Carter could refuse to spend the money, because Congress had not resolved its dispute over the authorization.

The primary reason the legislation never came up in the Senate was because representatives of oil producing states intended to attach an amendment to it that would end price controls on some domestically produced oil. Democratic leaders wanted to avoid the bitter fight, late in the session.

Tanker Safety. In an effort to curb oil spills, Congress Oct. 3 cleared tougher safety and anti-pollution standards for tankers.

The measure (S 682) had the support of the White House and was similar to an international accord reached in February 1978 by the 62-nation Inter-Governmental Maritime Consultive Organization.

The legislation was prompted by a 1976 accident in which the Liberian tanker *Argo Merchant* ran aground off Massachusetts and dumped 204,000 barrels of petroleum into the ocean. Forecasts that foreign oil imports would continue to grow added impetus to passage.

The bill required tankers and other ships using U.S. ports to carry electronic collision prevention gear, up-to-date charts and at least one English-speaking deck officer. Ships were forbidden to discharge oily water into the sea. Segregated ballasts — one for oil or other cargo, another for water — were made compulsory.

Ships with histories of accidents were barred from U.S. waters. The bill also authorized the government to operate harbor vessel control systems, resembling those for aircraft.

Oil Spill Liability. Congress was unable to reach agreement on legislation to increase the liability of those reponsible for oil spills. The bill (HR 6803) increasing liability also set up a $200 million "superfund" to clean up spills when the source was unknown.

The sticking point was the oil industry's opposition to the Senate version, passed Oct. 5, which extended liability to cover pollution by 271 hazardous chemicals. The fund was to be financed by a tax on transported oil, but the industry protested that it should not have to pay for spills by chemical manufacturers and transporters.

Industry ire was also aroused by another provision that would have allowed states to establish their own funds. The industry said there would be potential for abuse if damaged parties could file claims with different funds.

The industry supported passage of the House-passed version, which limited liability to oil spills alone.

Pesticide Controls. Registration of pesticides was expected to be easier under amendments (S 1678) to pesticide control laws cleared by Congress Sept. 19 and signed by President Carter Sept. 30.

In addition to untangling bureaucratic snarls, the changes gave states additional authority to enforce the pesticides law.

However, the Environmental Protection Agency (EPA) retained authority to oversee their actions. EPA officials also said the bill removed inequities in existing law that gave a marketing edge to longtime pesticide manufacturers and large corporations.

Outer Continental Shelf Leasing. The first overhaul of offshore oil and gas leasing laws in 25 years was cleared by Congress Aug. 22 and signed by President Carter Sept. 18.

The action culminated almost four years of reform efforts, which were bitterly opposed by the oil industry. But the compromise bill (S 9), written by House and Senate conferees during several months of negotiations, was generally supported by most major oil companies, environmentalists and the Carter administration.

The legislation was designed to foster competition for leases on offshore public land and to increase state participation in federal leasing decisions, particularly as offshore activity was expanded from the Gulf Coast to areas in the Atlantic.

Restrictions on drilling and production were tightened to protect the environment.

Seabed Mining. The House July 26 gave a go-ahead signal to U.S. companies ready to take mineral nodules from the floor of the high seas. But Congress was unable to reach agreement on a final bill.

The House vote gave U.S. approval to the mining even though the right to the minerals was in dispute internationally. The ongoing United Nations Law of the Sea Conference had not been able to resolve the question of who could mine the nodules and how the revenues from them could be shared with the world. The legislation (HR 3350) would have applied only until the conference reached agreement on the issue and would have required U.S. miners to get licenses and permits from the government.

Three Senate committees approved similar legislation (S 2053) but wanted to resolve their differences before asking for action by the full Senate. They never reached agreement, so the legislation died.

Coal Slurry Pipelines. An intense lobbying campaign by the nation's railroads led to the stunning House defeat July 19 of a bill (HR 1609) to promote development of coal slurry pipelines.

The vote was 161-246.

Both the Interior and Public Works committees had recommended passage of the bill, but the House, usually responsive to its committees, turned them down.

The pipelines would carry slurry — a mixture of pulverized coal and water — from mines to coal users. Some opponents argued that the pipelines would deplete scarce western water supplies.

But the heaviest opposition came from the railroads, which did not want competitors in the coal-hauling business. Plans in the works called for the pipelines to cross lands owned by the railroads, which had blocked their construction by refusing to grant rights of way. A controversial provision in the bill would have given pipeline developers eminent domain — the power to take private land in the public interest — subject to certain restrictions.

Foreign Policy

Panama Canal. No other single foreign policy issue of 1978 attracted as much attention, aroused as many emotions and consumed as much time and effort of the administration, the Senate and outside lobbying groups as did approval of the Panama Canal treaties. The treaties were the product of negotiations that formally began in 1964 but had in fact gone on intermittently ever since the original pact was signed in 1903. The basic treaty would turn over the U.S.-constructed, owned and operated Panama Canal to Panama by the year 2000. A second treaty — the neutrality treaty — would guarantee the United States and Panama the right to defend the canal after Dec. 31, 1999.

The two treaties were signed by President Carter and Panamanian leader Brig. Gen. Omar Torrijos Herrera on Sept. 7, 1977, but it was not until the spring of 1978 that the Senate consented to their ratification by identical 68-32 votes. The margin was only one vote more than the two-thirds Senate majority needed to consent to ratification of treaties. The neutrality treaty was approved March 16, the transfer treaty on April 18. All told, the Senate debate lasted 38 days, and until the very last, Senate approval of the pacts was in doubt.

Approval of the two treaties was an important foreign policy victory for President Carter, who had staked his administration's ability to conduct foreign policy on their ratification.

A major difficulty in securing approval was adoption of a reservation to the neutrality treaty sponsored by freshman Sen. Dennis DeConcini, D-Ariz., to permit the United States to "use military force in Panama" to reopen the canal if it were closed for any reason. The action immediately provoked an outcry from Panama that threatened to jeopardize the treaties entirely.

However, after weeks of delicate negotiations, the Senate leaderships succeeded in arriving at a compromise. Included in the resolution consenting to ratification of the basic canal treaty was a reservation stating that any action the United States might take to assure that the canal would remain open and secure should not "be interpreted as a right of intervention in the internal affairs of the Republic of Panama."

Jet Sales. Given its first major role in shaping events in the Middle East, the Senate May 15 went along with the Carter administration's controversial plan to sell $4.8 billion worth of jet fighters to Saudia Arabia, Israel and Egypt.

The package contained 60 F-15s for Saudi Arabia — the major issue because of Israel's fears over its security — 50 F-5Es for Egypt, and 15 F-15s and 75 F-16s for Israel.

Under arms sales procedures, House action was not required because the contracts automatically go through in 30 days unless rejected by both chambers.

The Senate's 44-54 decision to turn down a resolution (S Con Res 86) blocking the sales was a victory for the Carter administration but a bitter defeat for Israel and U.S. Jewish organizations strongly opposed to the weapons package.

Sales critics objected to linking Israel's supplies to the Saudi contracts and asserted that the Carter policy would "sap the morale" of the Jewish state. (The administration had said that if the Saudi contracts were rejected, then the other plane sales would be withdrawn.)

Supporters of the sale argued that the United States must be "evenhanded" in its relations with both Israel and the Arab states because of the complex weave of U.S. economic and strategic interests in the Middle East.

Witteveen Facility. Low-income nations plagued by balance-of-payments deficits piled up following the 1973-74 worldwide hike in petroleum prices would get relief under an international program approved by Congress Sept. 28.

The legislation (HR 9214) allowed the United States to participate along with 13 other industrial and oil-exporting nations in a new International Monetary Fund institution — the Witteveen Facility — to assist debt-plagued IMF members.

The United States share of the lending program was pegged at $1.75 billion, with the other donors contributing an additional $8.7 billion.

Countries likely to be assisted were low-income industrial and developing nations: Spain, Portugal, Turkey, Peru, Egypt, Jamaica, Mexico, Zaire, the Philippines and Bolivia.

Loans were to be subject to strict monetary and fiscal conditions the recipients must meet in order to improve their trading positions.

Turkey Arms Ban. Congress sent President Carter a major foreign policy victory Sept. 12 by giving him authority to lift the three-year-old partial arms embargo against Turkey.

Before resuming regular shipments of weapons to Ankara, Carter was required by the fiscal 1979 military aid authorization bill (S 3075) to certify to Congress that Turkey was "acting in good faith" to achieve a "just and peaceful settlement" of Cyprus issues, including the continued removal of Turkish troops from the Mediterranean island. He did this Sept. 26.

Turkey's use of U.S. military equipment in 1974 to invade Cyprus in violation of U.S. laws prompted Congress that year to vote a total arms embargo. It took effect in February 1975 but was modified eight months later to permit sales needed for NATO defenses.

Reversing his own campaign position, Carter argued in 1978 that the partial embargo was too stringent, impeding rather than encouraging any resolution of the basic Cyprus territorial and refugee issues and alienating Turkey from the NATO alliance.

Rhodesia. In the fiscal 1979 military aid authorization bill (S 3075), Congress permitted the president to drop economic sanctions against Rhodesia after Dec. 31, 1978, if he determined that the Salisbury government had: 1) demonstrated a willingness to negotiate in good faith at an all-parties peace conference that included guerrilla factions and 2) a new government had been installed after being chosen in free elections under international supervision.

The Carter administration had opposed the House version of the bill that barred the enforcement of sanctions against Rhodesia after 1978 unless a new government had not been chosen and installed.

The conference decision closely followed the Senate's provision, and was a victory for the Carter administration which had called for an all-parties conference considered essential by the State Department for resolving the Rhodesian civil conflict.

Foreign Aid Appropriations. The foreign aid appropriations bill (HR 12931) survived House and Senate attacks much better than anyone had expected earlier in the year. The final bill was $9.1 billion. This was $1.3 billion less than the administration requested and $2.4 billion above fiscal 1978 appropriations.

Before the House began debate on Carter's $10.4 billion request in early August, the bill was believed to be in such serious trouble that it would be gutted with restrictive limitations on use of aid money and by deep cuts in funding — and possibly defeated entirely.

But intensive lobbying by administration officials and supporters in Congress, and outside groups, including the U.S. Chamber of Commerce, turned the situation around.

In 1977 the House had no reservations about imposing strict conditions on U.S. funds that go to international banks and making substantial across-the-board cuts in funding — decisions the Senate refused to accept and that were dropped in conference. In 1978 the House reversed itself on these issues.

The most dramatic switch came on efforts to tell international lending institutions, such as the World Bank, how they could use U.S. contributions. In 1977 an amendment to bar funds in the bill from being used by the banks for Uganda, Cambodia, Laos and Vietnam was approved overwhelmingly, 295-115. In 1978 the same amendment was rejected 198-203.

Health/Education/Welfare

Health

Hospital Cost Control. The Senate passed compromise hospital cost containment legislation Oct. 12. But Carter administration efforts to bypass House committee and floor action and secure a conference agreement broke down during the last hectic days before adjournment, and the measure (HR 5285) died. Carter had called the legislation critical to his administration's anti-inflation fight.

Neither House committee with jurisdiction had reported the administration bill. Only the Senate Human Resources Committee (in 1977) had approved a bill, which called for immediate national limits on hospital revenues. The Senate Finance Committee instead voted Aug. 3 to report a bill (HR 5285) revising Medicare and Medicaid hospital reimbursement.

The House Ways and Means Subcommittee on Health Feb. 28 had narrowly approved a compromise (HR 6575) that provided the hospital revenue ceilings only if a voluntary industry effort to cut costs failed to meet set goals. That compromise was gutted July 18 by the House Commerce Committee. The standby limits showed up again in the Senate bill, however, along with a Medicare-Medicaid reimbursement provision that was less favorable to hospitals than the original.

The hospital industry and representatives of doctors had fought the revenue limits bitterly, claiming they would damage the quality of patient care. Their lobbying was particularly effective because, for most of the 95th Congress, there was little pressure for the legislation from groups wanting lower hospital costs — the insurance industry, the elderly and organized labor.

National Health Insurance. Worsening economic conditions and the failure of Congress to enact controls on double-digit hospital inflation dampened President Carter's enthusiasm for national health insurance. But, prodded by Sen. Edward M. Kennedy, D-Mass., and organized labor to keep Carter's campaign promise on health, the administration produced a broadly worded set of national health insurance "principles" July 29.

The Carter plan called for universal coverage and comprehensive benefits, but these were to be phased in only as economic factors permitted. Kennedy and his labor allies blasted the plan, saying that it guaranteed that a full health system would never be put in place. Two months later, on Oct. 2, Kennedy released the outline of a labor-drafted proposal that called for universal, comprehensive coverage to begin two years after enactment. The plan also included strict interim controls designed to control health care inflation. Kennedy opened hearings Oct. 9, and planned for congressional action in 1979.

Abortion. Anti-abortion forces in the House broadened their efforts in 1978 to put tighter restrictions on the use of federal funds to pay for abortions — with several notable successes.

Their biggest victory was attaching abortion restrictions to the fiscal 1979 appropriations bill (HR 13635) for the Department of Defense, which in 1977 funded about 26,500 abortions for military personnel and dependents. Congress also prohibited the use of Peace Corps funds to pay for abortions for Peace Corps volunteers. (HR 12931).

Under HR 13635, military abortions would be paid for only when continued pregnancy would endanger the life of the mother or, in the opinion of two doctors, cause severe and long-lasting physical health damage, or in cases of rape or incest, when the offenses are reported promptly to police or a public health agency.

The same conditions were finally attached to the appropriations bill for the Departments of Labor and Health, Education and Welfare (HEW) (HR 12929), which financed abortions for low-income women under Medicaid. The language originally was worked out in 1977 after a five-month struggle to reach a compromise between the House, which wanted to allow abortions only to save the life of the mother, and the Senate, which would have allowed them whenever they were considered "medically necessary."

Sponsors hoped to avoid a similar deadlock on the fiscal 1979 bill by getting both houses to recede from their positions and accept the fiscal 1978 language as a compromise. The House initially refused to go along, voting 216-188 Oct. 12 to stick to its tough stand. But the Senate approved the compromise language and sent the bill back to the House. With adjournment at hand, the House, rather than postpone the battle until 1979 while funding the two departments by a continuing resolution, reversed itself and by a three-vote margin (198-195) Oct. 14 agreed to go along with the wording in the existing law for another year.

The House agreed to accept the compromise language on the first try on the defense bill, approving it by voice vote Oct. 12 only a few hours after rejecting it on the Labor-HEW bill. Some members indicated they trusted defense officials to write strict regulations to enforce the provision, but resented what they regarded as overly permissive HEW regulations allowing abortions to poor women under Medicaid.

House anti-abortion activists successfully delayed action on family planning, health planning and pregnancy disability bills during the year. On the pregnancy disability bill (S 995), after a three-month conference deadlock they were able to retain the substance of a House provision allowing employers to exempt most elective abortions from their health insurance plans. *(Story, below)*

Pregnancy Disability. Legislation prohibiting employment discrimination against pregnant workers cleared Congress on the final day of the session after conferees finally reached a compromise on the abortion issue which had deadlocked them for nearly three months.

The bill (S 995) barred employers from discriminating against women in hiring, promotion or seniority rights simply because they are pregnant. It also required employers to include pregnancy, childbirth and related medical conditions in their health insurance and temporary disability plans. The legislation was intended to overturn the effects of a 1976 Supreme Court ruling that pregnancy did not have to be covered in such plans.

The Senate bill, passed in 1977, included abortions among the pregnancy-related medical conditions employers were required to cover in their medical-disability plans. The House version (HR 6075), passed July 18, allowed employers to exempt elective abortions from such coverage.

House conferees refused to budge from their position and the issue remained unresolved until Oct. 13. Under the compromise finally reached, companies would not be forced to provide medical coverage for abortions, except if the mother's life would be endangered by continued pregnancy or in the case of medical complications. However, they would be required to provide disability and sick leave benefits if a woman had an abortion. The Senate agreed to the conference report by voice vote Oct. 13, the House Oct. 15.

Drug Law Reform. A major administration proposal to revise the way drugs were regulated for safety and effectiveness bogged down in House and Senate health subcommittees, although each held extensive hearings and markup sessions.

Both drug companies and consumer groups objected to features of the complex proposal. Other delaying factors were the unusual number of expiring health reauthorizations and, in the House, lengthy committee deliberations on hospital cost control.

The administration sought to relax certain early testing requirements and make other changes so that promising new drugs could be marketed more quickly. The proposal also called for much fuller disclosure of drug test data and stronger authority to recall new drugs or limit their distribution if post-approval data showed new hazards.

Education

Tuition Tax Credits. Efforts to enact tuition tax credits either as part of a general tax cut or as separate legislation were unsuccessful in the 95th Congress.

Congressional tax leaders dropped a Senate-passed college tuition tax credit amendment to the general tax bill when it became clear that the provision could lead to a veto of the whole bill.

Separate legislation (HR 12050) providing the college tuition credits died when the House and Senate could not agree on tax credits for private elementary and secondary schools.

The fate of HR 12050, which had passed both chambers by substantial margins, was sealed Oct. 12 when the House refused, by a 207-185 vote, to accept a conference report on the bill without the elementary and secondary school credits. Adamant Senate opposition to any pre-college credits killed a last-minute compromise attempt to add only credits for private high-school tuitions to the college credits.

Middle-Income Student Assistance. Although it killed tuition tax credits legislation, Congress did approve new assistance for middle-income families hit by rising college tuition costs.

On the last day of the session Congress cleared the Carter administration's alternative to tuition tax credits (HR 11274), expanding existing federal programs of assistance to college students to include more students from middle-income families.

HR 11274 raised the income cut-off for Basic Educational Opportunity Grants (BEOG) to about $25,000, from $15,000. It also removed the existing income limit for federal interest subsidies on guaranteed student loans.

Action on the bill, which passed the Senate easily in August, had been held up in the House by Rules Committee Chairman James J. Delaney, D-N.Y., a tuition tax credit supporter, who refused to allow a vote on the bill for six months.

Department of Education. Delaying tactics by a small band of House opponents of the proposed new Department of Education succeeded, in the final days of the 95th Congress, in preventing final approval of legislation setting up the new agency.

Opponents, worried that the department would lead to federal control of local education, forced the House leadership to pull the bill (HR 13778) from the schedule by threatening to slow action on other important legislation to a snail's pace.

The Senate had passed its bill (S 991) easily, and even opponents conceded there were enough votes to pass the House bill if it had ever come to a vote.

Under the legislation, the core of the Education Department would have been the Office of Education from the Department of Health, Education and Welfare (HEW). Effective lobbying prevented transfer of the child nutrition, Head Start and Indian education programs into the new department.

Elementary, Secondary School Aid. Congress Oct. 15 finished work on legislation (HR 15) extending and revising the massive Elementary and Secondary Education Act (ESEA) program of federal aid to local schools.

A House-Senate conference committee approved a compromise version of the bill Sept. 27.

The biggest ESEA program provided federal funds to schools educating children from low-income families. A key change made by HR 15 as approved by the conference committee would shift this aid toward wealthy urban states and away from southern rural states; for purposes of determining how much aid to give to each school district, the new formula would count all welfare children as poor, even if their families had incomes over the poverty line.

The measure also allowed some limited growth in the impact aid program. The major recipients of the new assistance would be cities with large numbers of federally subsidized public housing units.

Welfare

Welfare Reform. The Carter administration's proposal for "comprehensive" welfare reform (HR 9030, S 2084) never made it out of the House Ways and Means Committee or Senate Finance Committee in 1978. Lengthy hearings were held and a special Ways and Means subcommittee marked up a bill (HR 10950), but several factors combined to block passage of the legislation: the complexity of the measure, the broad changes contained in it, its $20 billion price tag, and a lack of support from important legislators such as Russell B. Long, D-La., chairman of the Senate Finance Committee.

The passage of California's tax cut initiative, Proposition 13, with its clear message against increased government spending, placed a further damper on the Carter proposal and several other, less sweeping measures introduced in the House and Senate. Administration spokesmen and welfare reform advocates in Congress said they would try again in 1979 to win approval of a comprehensive reform measure.

Housing/Community Development

Urban Policy. Congress gave a lukewarm reception to the package of some 15 bills submitted by the Carter administration as part of the president's urban policy.

None of the four measures singled out by the administration as most important was approved by the 95th Congress. The one piece of legislation considered crucial to fiscally pressed cities — a Senate-passed extension of countercyclical revenue sharing (HR 2852) — was cleared for House floor action on the last day of the session after two weeks of parliamentary maneuvering. But the bill got caught in the rush to adjourn and was never called up.

The administration lost its effort to establish a "soft" public works program designed to provide rehabilitation and maintenance jobs for the hard-core unemployed (S 3186, HR 12993). Sharp opposition from members concerned about the potential inflationary impact of the program left the bills mired in committees in both the Senate and House. Other proposals, including the so-called "centerpiece" of the urban program — a National Development Bank (S 3233, HR 13230) — were put off until 1979.

Most of the smaller spending items in the legislative package — funds for inner-city health clinics, neighborhood volunteer efforts, urban parks and mass transit — were included in authorization measures enacted by Congress for various federal departments.

There were several reasons for the lack of enthusiasm in Congress for the urban package. Many of the major bills were submitted late in the session, thus limiting the amount of time available for hearings and debate. Inflation and the "taxpayers' revolt" suggested by California voters' adoption of the Proposition 13 tax limitation initiative discouraged enactment of measures that called for increased government spending. There were some signs that members of Congress from the "Sun Belt" states of the South and West were increasingly reluctant to approve measures that would provide aid primarily for decaying cities in the "Snow Belt" states of the Northeast and Midwest. Finally, some members who in the past had supported urban aid programs questioned whether new programs were actually needed. Rather, they argued, existing programs should be altered to focus primarily on those cities and communities where help from the federal government was most needed.

Law Enforcement/Judiciary

Judgeships. Legislation creating 117 new federal district court judgeships and 35 new circuit court of appeals judgeships cleared Congress Oct. 7.

The bill (HR 7843) provided President Carter with the largest single block of judicial patronage in the nation's history.

The judgeship bill included a watered-down merit selection provision requiring the president to promulgate "standards and guidelines" for the selection of judges to fill the positions created by the bill. The president was left to decide in issuing those guidelines the future role of the Senate in selecting judges. The Senate traditionally had made the key decisions in the selection process.

The bill as cleared omitted a Senate proposal to split the southern Fifth Circuit Court of Appeals, creating a new 11th Circuit. Instead Congress approved ambiguous language allowing judges in circuits having more than 15 judges to reorganize into administrative units. The kinds of responsibilities those administrative units would have were not defined.

Wiretaps. Congress gave its final approval Oct. 12 to the first major legislative effort to control electronic surveillance conducted in the United States for national security purposes.

The Foreign Intelligence Surveillance Act (S 1566) required intelligence agencies to obtain a judicial warrant for virtually all foreign intelligence surveillance conducted in the United States. The bill provided special protections for U.S. citizens, requiring intelligence agencies to produce evidence that a crime was about to be committed before they could receive a warrant.

The bill, which had its genesis during the Ford administration when widespread disclosures of intelligence agency abuses were made, was a top priority of the Carter administration. The final bill won support from the nation's intelligence agencies as well as the American Civil Liberties Union.

The bill exempted a limited number of National Security Agency surveillances from the warrant requirement. The exact nature of those surveillances was never disclosed.

Magistrates. The House and Senate passed differing versions of a bill (S 1613) to expand the role of magistrates in federal civil and criminal court proceedings in an effort to relieve the caseload burden on judges.

One of several Justice Department "judicial improvement" measures, the bills gave magistrates authority to conduct trials, empanel juries, find facts and enter judgments in certain cases. The House bill required the consent of defendants for criminal trials by magistrates, while the Senate bill provided mandatory magistrate jurisdiction over minor criminal offenses.

Before passing S 1613, the House tacked on a separate, controversial bill (HR 9622) it had passed earlier dealing with litigation between residents of different states. The maneuver was designed to bring the so-called "diversity jurisdiction" bill into a conference with the Senate, which had been unable to consider a similar bill because of one senator's opposition. However, neither the magistrates nor the diversity measure was enacted.

Diversity Jurisdiction. The House passed legislation (HR 9622) abolishing "diversity of citizenship" as a ground for requesting federal court jurisdiction. Abolition or curtailment of diversity jurisdiction was sought by the Justice Department as a means of transferring a small share of federal court cases to state courts.

Diversity jurisdiction provided that citizens from different states who were involved in litigation could have the case tried in a federal court — on the theory that a state court may be biased against the out-of-state litigant.

The Senate Judiciary Committee was blocked by Bill Scott, R-Va., from reporting a bill (S 2094) that would have curtailed diversity use. Scott staged a one-man filibuster against the bill two weeks before the scheduled adjournment of Congress.

The House attached its diversity bill before passing a magistrates bill, assuring Senate conferees on the magistrate bill (S 1613) a chance to consider diversity legislation. Neither of two measures received final congressional approval. *(Magistrates bill, above)*

***Illinois Brick* Overturn.** House and Senate Judiciary committees approved separate bills to overturn a 1977 Supreme Court decision that drastically limited the ability of consumers, businesses and governments to collect damages resulting from antitrust violations.

The bills (HR 11942 and S 1874) allowed individuals or groups to sue for damages resulting from price fixing, monopolies or bid rigging if they purchased the goods from middlemen. The Supreme Court decision in *Illinois Brick v. Illinois* limited collection of damages to direct purchasers only.

A filibuster threat in the Senate prevented the bill from being scheduled. And the House leadership was unwilling to schedule the bill since it saw no chance of Senate approval. The bill died.

Crime Victims Compensation. The House and Senate both passed legislation providing federal funds to states that compensate victims of violent crimes. But the House killed the conference report Oct. 14 on a 184-199 vote. The bill (HR 7010) would have provided grants to states covering a portion of the amount paid to crime victims. Under the House version the maximum award to a victim was $25,000. The Senate bill provided up to $50,000.

Rights of Institutionalized. The House passed legislation (HR 9400) allowing the attorney general to sue state nursing homes, mental institutions, prisons and juvenile facilities where the department found a "pattern or practice" of violations of constitutional rights.

The bill, passed on a 254-69 vote, was aimed at protecting what a sponsor called a "class of uniquely vulnerable persons," such as mental patients who might be totally incapable of asserting their rights.

The Senate Judiciary Committee reported a bill (S 1393) that excluded nursing homes from its coverage and provided fewer protections for prisoners. The Senate did not act on the bill.

Bankruptcy Reform. The first major revision of the nation's bankruptcy laws in nearly 40 years was cleared by Congress Oct. 6.

The bill (HR 8200) was designed to modernize federal bankruptcy law and provide greater protection to consumer debtors as well as to businesses, and to consolidate the laws dealing with business reorganization.

The bill established a bankruptcy court system to relieve federal district courts of the responsibility of handling the large volume of bankruptcy cases filed there.

Criminal Code Revision. The first major revision and consolidation of 200 years of U.S. criminal law was approved overwhelmingly by the Senate Jan. 30.

Passage of the bill (S 1437), which consolidated approximately 3,000 individual statutes, marked the first time a criminal code revision reached the floor of the Senate. Recodification had been debated in the Senate for nearly a decade.

Attorney General Griffin B. Bell called the code the Justice Department's top legislative priority.

Hopes for enactment of the bill in the 95th Congress were dampened as soon as markups began in the House Judiciary Committee. Committee members made it clear they were not interested in the "delicate balance" of compromises that constituted the 682-page Senate bill. Opening the House markup, Criminal Justice Subcommittee Chairman James R. Mann, D-S.C., said the criminal law "should not be subject to trade-offs and compromises in the name of reform."

A week prior to adjournment, the House Judiciary Committee voted not to report a bill but to ask instead for a report setting forth the Mann subcommittee's views on the code revision.

The Senate bill was expected to provide the basis for a debate in the 96th Congress over criminal code reform. One of the major issues it raised concerned the amount of discretion judges should have in meting out sentences.

ERA Deadline Extension. The Senate gave final approval Oct. 6 to a resolution granting states 39 additional months to ratify the Equal Rights Amendment to effective upon Senate passage.

Passage of the resolution (H J Res 638) on a 60-36 vote capped a year-long lobbying effort by backers of the ERA and marked the first time Congress had extended the ratification period for a constitutional amendment since it began setting time limits in 1917.

The extension resolution, approved by the House Aug. 15, did not require the president's signature and became effective upon Senate passage.

When Congress approved ERA in 1972 it set a seven-year time limit on ratification by three-fourths (38) of the states. When Congress granted the extension, 35 state legislatures had ratified ERA. But four states — Idaho, Kentucky, Nebraska and Tennessee — had voted to rescind their ratification. The validity of those actions and constitutional questions surrounding the extension were expected to be decided by the Supreme Court.

Kennedy-King Assassinations Hearings. The House Select Committee on Assassinations concluded its public hearings on the 1963 slaying of President John F. Kennedy Sept. 28 after reviewing a mass of scientific evidence and considering a variety of theories disputing the basic conclusion of the Warren Commission that the crime was solely the work of Lee Harvey Oswald.

Most of the scientific evidence buttressed the Warren Commission finding that Oswald acted alone. The committee appeared to dismantle many of the conspiracy theories about Kennedy's death, but uncovered some new and generally inconclusive evidence linking the slaying with organized crime.

The committee's investigation of the 1968 assassination of Martin Luther King Jr. began Aug. 14 with a week of hearings that included a three-day appearance by James Earl Ray, King's convicted killer. Ray provided little new information to prove his innocence or to implicate others, but speculation about the possibility of a conspiracy in the King case was heightened Sept. 24 when committee member Richardson Preyer, D-N.C., said, "There is evidence which, if it checks out to be credible, would show a conspiracy" in the case.

The King hearings were resumed Nov. 9 and concluded Dec. 1; the committee at year's end concluded that narrowly based conspiracies may have played a role in both assassinations.

Lobbies

Korean Lobbying Probe. The House Committee on Standards of Official Conduct concluded its investigation of South Korean influence-peddling in the House as the session drew to a close.

The investigation, led until Aug. 2 by former Watergate prosecutor Leon A. Jaworski, reported possible criminal wrongdoing by two former House members to the Justice Department and conducted in-house disciplinary proceedings against four incumbents. The two former members, Nick Galifianakis, D-N.C. (1967-73), and John R. Rarick, D-La. (1967-75), were accused of perjury.

A third former member, Richard T. Hanna, D-Calif. (1963-74), entered a bargained guilty plea March 17 to one count of conspiracy to defraud the government in connection with his dealings with Tongsun Park, the Korean rice dealer. Sentenced April 24, Hanna began serving a two-and-a-half year term in federal prison camp May 8.

The committee's strongest recommendation was against Rep. Edward R. Roybal, D-Calif., accused of three counts of failing to report a $1,000 campaign contribution from Park and of lying to the committee. The ethics committee recommended that the House censure Roybal. But on a vote of the full House Oct. 13, Roybal's punishment was reduced to a "reprimand."

That punishment was consistent with the ones the panel recommended for two other House Democrats from California, Charles H. Wilson and John J. McFall. Wilson was accused of lying to the committee about money he took from Park in 1975 as a wedding present; the House approved his reprimand on a 328-41 vote. McFall, accused of failing to report $3,000 in campaign contributions he received from Park, was reprimanded on a voice vote. All three members denied any intentional wrongdoing.

The committee voted 8-0 to take no action against Edward J. Patten, D-N.J. Patten had been accused of violating House rules and New Jersey law by making contributions purported to be his own to a state Democratic organization in 1975 and 1976.

The committee failed to obtain testimony from former Korean ambassador Kim Dong Jo, who was believed to have been a more critical witness than Park. While Jaworski insisted that "the major portion of the facts of Koreagate have been ferreted out and published," he acknowledged that the investigation was incomplete without Kim's testimony.

After resigning as chief counsel, Jaworski criticized current House methods of self-investigation as "ill-conceived." He proposed establishment of independent commissions to investigate charges that involved the Congress or the presidency.

Lobby Reform. Legislation imposing strict new registration requirements on groups that lobby Congress was approved by the House after turning back nearly 20 weakening amendments (HR 8494).

In the Senate, however, the Governmental Affairs Committee failed to resolve differences between supporters of a bill similar to that passed by the House and backed by Common Cause, and supporters of a bill sought by civil liberties groups and business lobbyists.

The Senate's inaction left in doubt the possibility of lobby reform in the 96th Congress. In the 94th Congress each house passed a strong lobby disclosure bill, but differences between them were never resolved. In the 95th Congress both backed off from the more comprehensive measures they had previously approved, as questions about infringement on First Amendment rights took a stronger hold.

The major debates in the 95th Congress focused on whether to require disclosure of grass-roots lobbying efforts such as organized letter-writing campaigns, and disclosure of the names of major organizations contributing to registered lobby groups.

National Security

Defense Spending. Congress generally endorsed President Carter's $126 billion request for Pentagon programs in fiscal 1979. The deletion of the nuclear-powered aircraft carrier, opposed by Carter, cut the Pentagon's principal authorization and appropriations bills by about $1.9 billion. But it was expected that the administration would make up that amount with a special supplemental budget request early in 1979.

Torn between concern about a reported Soviet military buildup and fear of a taxpayers' revolt against government spending, most members felt safest hewing to the middle of the road. Both houses rejected by large margins efforts to raise or lower the defense budget significantly.

The House in May rejected an amendment backed by senior members of the Armed Services Committee to add $2.4 billion to the $127.4 billion recommended by Congress as the defense spending target for fiscal 1979 (S Con Res 80). It also rejected an amendment to transfer $4.8 billion allocated for defense to various domestic programs.

In the Senate, amendments that would have cut $4.6 billion and $1.4 billion respectively from the defense spending target ($129.8 billion) were rejected handily. The Senate also rejected an amendment that would have increased the defense budget by $1.6 billion. By the time Congress considered the Pentagon's annual appropriations bill (HR 13635), California voters had overwhelmingly endorsed Proposition 13, slashing state property taxes. Over the next several weeks, across-the-board cuts of 2-5 percent were made in several department appropriations bills. But the Pentagon remained immune to Proposition 13 fever.

B-1 Bomber. Prodded by White House lobbying of rare intensity, the House in February finally agreed to kill the B-1 bomber program. President Carter had decided to cancel the $23 billion program for production of 244 planes in June 1977, and Congress that year had canceled further funding for the B-1.

But the House refused to remove $462 million previously appropriated to build the first two B-1s. Carter was adamant that the program be terminated, however, and on Feb. 22 the House finally went along, 234-182.

Aircraft Carriers. The effect of congressional action on the defense budget appeared to prod the Navy to accelerate the development of smaller, less-expensive aircraft carriers. These ships would operate vertical takeoff combat planes (called V/STOLs) that would not need the 1,000-foot-long decks of the existing carriers.

The first version of the fiscal 1979 defense authorization bill (HR 10929) incorporated additions to the administration budget that would have given the Navy one more big nuclear-powered carrier while accelerating the development of V/STOL planes and smaller carriers. An effort to kill the big ship had failed on the House floor on a 156-218 vote.

On Aug. 17 President Carter vetoed the bill because of the nuclear carrier. On Sept. 7 an effort to override the veto did not even win a majority of the House, much less the two-thirds required (191-206).

The revised defense bill (HR 14042) acceded to Carter's demand that another carrier not be funded. In most other respects it contained the same programs as those in the vetoed bill, including some of the programs for new types of warships and V/STOL planes. But the final version of the defense appropriations bill dropped the funds that would have gone to convert an existing helicopter carrier to a V/STOL ship.

NATO Readiness. Carter placed heavy emphasis on beefing up the U.S. forces assigned to the defense of Western Europe, and Congress in general supported that policy. But it also stood by the judgments of the congressional committees handling the military construction budget that the European members of NATO were letting the United States bear more than its fair share of the defense burden.

Both the authorization and appropriations bills (HR 12602, HR 12927) for military construction incorporated large cuts in the nearly one-third of a billion dollars requested for combat-related NATO construction. The Armed Services and Appropriations Committees thus hoped to protest the practice of unilaterally appropriating U.S. funds to pay for projects that would benefit the entire alliance, with the intention of seeking reimbursement from the alliance later.

In the future, the committees maintained, they would refuse, except in emergencies, to approve such unilateral financing of NATO projects with U.S. funds.

Strategic Arms Limitation. With negotiations on a new U.S.-Soviet treaty limiting strategic nuclear weapons still incomplete, Congress had no opportunity to act directly on the reported terms of an agreement. But congressional supporters and opponents of the administration approach to SALT spent much time gearing up for an expected fight on the treaty in 1979.

The only SALT-related vote occurred when the Senate in September adopted by voice vote a resolution (S Res 536) directing the president to consult with the Foreign Relations Committee before submitting any important international agreement to Congress in the form of an executive agreement rather than a treaty.

The resolution was prompted by reports the White House might try to evade the two-thirds vote required for approval of a SALT treaty by drawing up a strategic arms limitation pact as an executive agreement. Several days before the resolution was adopted, some of the Senate's strongest supporters of administration SALT policy, including Majority Whip Alan Cranston, D-Calif., publicly warned Carter against trying to circumvent the Senate's treaty procedure.

'Neutron Bomb.' The only congressional effort to halt production of the so-called neutron bomb failed by a large margin. By a 90-306 vote, the House in May rejected an amendment to a bill (S 2693) authorizing the military programs of the Energy Department that would have delayed production of the weapon.

But production still had not commenced when Congress adjourned because the president had decided to defer production for an indeterminate period in hopes of eliciting some restraint by the Soviet Union in its military buildup in Eastern Europe.

In a report, the Senate Armed Services Committee urged the president at least to begin producing the components of the "neutron bomb" so that, if he decided to begin production, the weapon could be deployed quickly.

Korea Troop Withdrawal. Although both the House and Senate Armed Services Committees warned of the risks posed by President Carter's plan, announced in 1977, to withdraw all U.S. ground troops from South Korea, the only votes taken on the issue tended to favor the withdrawal plan.

By a margin of nearly two to one (142-247), the House turned down an amendment to the defense authorization bill (HR 10929) that would have barred a reduction below 26,000 in the number of U.S. troops stationed in South Korea.

The final version of the foreign military aid bill (S 3075) authorized the president to turn over to South Korea the weapons that belonged to the U.S. units there. The estimated value of this military equipment was about $800 million.

Strategic Stockpiles. Several years of work by the two Armed Services Committees to reorganize the national stockpile of strategic raw materials was stalled by pork barrel politics.

Both committees approved legislation (HR 4895) to establish a revolving fund to finance the purchase of new stockpile commodities with the proceeds from disposal of superfluous items. The House had passed the bill in 1977, but the Senate sponsors blocked action on it for fear it would become a vehicle for riders mandating the purchase or sale of particular commodities in order to boost their prices in the open market.

Nuclear Export Controls. With only three dissenting votes, the Senate in February passed a bill setting strict controls on the export of nuclear materials intended for the production of electric power. The bill (HR 8638) aimed at stopping the global spread of nuclear weapons. The House had passed the bill in 1977.

The margin by which the Senate approved the bill concealed strong opposition by the nuclear energy industry and some concern on the part of the White House.

In the first test of the new export licensing procedure, the House in July voted 181-227 not to approve a resolution that would have blocked the export of some reactor fuel to India.

Veterans Pension Reform. Veterans — including all those 65 or older — who were disabled, but not in the course of their military service, were guaranteed a minimum annual income under a bill (HR 10173) reforming the Veterans Administration pension program. Veterans' survivors also received pensions.

Ban on Military Unions. Both the House and Senate passed by large margins legislation (S 274) banning unionization in the armed services. But in the last week of the session, final agreement was stalled over the question of excluding from the ban civilian technicians who were members of the National Guard. The House-passed version had excluded the technicians. On Oct. 14, the Senate accepted the House version, clearing S 274.

Transportation/Commerce /Consumers

Airline Deregulation. It took most of 1977 for legislation (S 2493) to loosen federal regulation of U.S. airlines to get through the Senate Commerce Committee, and 10 weeks for similar legislation to get through the House Public Works Aviation Subcommittee. But both versions were quickly approved once they got to the floor. The Senate approved its bill 83-9 in April and the House passed its version 363-8 in September. A House-Senate conference committee hammered out a compromise bill in short order, and the legislation was given final approval Oct. 15.

The legislation was intended to introduce a measure of free-market competition into the commercial passenger airline industry by limiting the government's authority to regulate air routes and fares.

The Civil Aeronautics Board's authority to regulate the industry would be phased out by 1985 unless Congress acted to extend it. The public was expected to benefit from the substantially lower fares envisioned by the bill's sponsors.

The bill's enactment was in doubt until the final day of the session. Ranking members of the House Public Works Committee had hinted that they would put off final action on the compromise deregulation measure until the Senate completed action on a related bill (S 3279, HR 8729) to provide a subsidy of an estimated $3 billion to $4 billion to the airline companies to help them meet the costs of complying with Federal Aviation Administration (FAA) noise regulations.

The Senate Finance Committee recommended that the Senate delete the subsidy provision from the bill, and the full Senate went along in an effort to get the bill cleared, but the House never acted on the compromise version.

Mass Transit, Highway Programs. Congress completed action on another controversial measure on the last day of the session — legislation (HR 11733) extending the Highway Trust Fund for five years and authorizing federal highway and mass transit aid programs over the next two to four years.

The House-passed version, however, authorized spending of about $61 billion over the next four years, while the Senate-passed bill and the administration sought more modest funding levels. A compromise was reached, authorizing about $51 billion. President Carter had issued a warning that the bill would be vetoed unless conferees came up with a lower funding level.

Waterway User Fees. Final congressional approval of a controversial tax on the fuel used by inland waterway barges was realized after a 38-year effort. Sen. Russell B. Long, D-La., who originally had not favored fees on barges using the inland waterways, made enactment of the tax possible. With the deadline for adjournment only a few weeks away, he had advanced a compromise proposal (HR 8533) combining creation of a waterway trust fund — fed by a barge fuel tax — with an authorization for construction of a new lock and dam on the Mississippi River at Alton, Ill., that was popular in Congress.

Both the House and Senate already had approved legislation to tax barge fuel and authorize the lock and dam's construction. However, each house tacked onto its version of that bill (HR 8309) a string of costly public works water projects that made the bill a likely candidate for a presidential veto. HR 8309 never cleared.

Amtrak, ConRail. Congress passed legislation (S 3040) in 1978 setting up a mechanism for the Transportation Department, with Congress' approval, to trim unprofitable routes from Amtrak's national passenger railroad system in order to cut back Amtrak's growing federal subsidy. However, the legislation as finally approved also barred the department from paring down Amtrak's route system before Oct. 1, 1979.

To bolster the finances of the Consolidated Rail Corp. (ConRail), which early in 1978 said it would need an additional $1.3 billion in order to become self-sufficient by 1982, Congress enacted legislation (S 2788) authorizing an additional $1.2 billion in subsidies for the system over the next five years. The bill was given final congressional approval on Oct. 15.

Merchant Marine Rebating. Legislation to step up the government's effort to combat illegal merchant marine rebating cleared Congress in the final days of the 95th Congress. However, the bill was pocket vetoed by President Carter.

In rebating, steamship companies seek to attract additional business by offering discounts or kickbacks from official rates, a violation of federal law. The legislation (HR 9518) had won House approval in March by a vote of 390-1. The bill became stalled in the Senate, however, when Sen. Russell B. Long, D-La., asked the Commerce Committee to combine the House-passed measure with a bill he had introduced at the request of a New Orleans steamship company. That bill (S 2386) could have had the effect of protecting the New Orleans firm and one other steamship company from competition with outside firms in the lucrative South American shipping trade.

Bowing to pressure from some of his colleagues, Long finally agreed to withdraw his bill from consideration, and the anti-rebating bill passed.

Postal Service. Legislation (HR 7700) to make the U.S. Postal Service more efficient and accountable to the federal government succumbed to postal union and Postal Service management opposition, dying without ever coming to a vote in the Senate.

The legislation would have increased the Postal Service's federal subsidy, reformed its rate-setting procedures and authorized the president to appoint top postal management.

Opposition arose after the Senate Governmental Affairs Committee added an amendment to the bill exempting certain "time-sensitive" mail from the Postal Service's monopoly on first-class service.

The legislation had been passed by the House in April, and approved by the Senate panel in mid-September. However, postal workers fearful of job losses and postal management concerned over potential revenue losses waged a successful campaign to convince the Senate Budget Committee to oppose granting the bill a special waiver from a requirement that bills providing new spending authority be reported to the floor by May 15 of the preceding fiscal year. This had the effect of killing the bill.

Small Business Safety and Health Regulations. A Senate move to exempt certain small businesses from federal occupational health and safety regulations failed when House and Senate conferees dropped the Senate-approved exemption from a bill (HR 11445) extending certain programs of the Small Business Administration.The bill had been passed by the House in April without the exemption provision. The bill, without the exemption, was cleared by Congress, but was subsequently pocket vetoed.

Public Broadcasting. Legislation (HR 12605) reorganizing the nation's public broadcasting system was approved Oct. 14. The measure represented a compromise between the goals set out for the public broadcasting system by President Carter in a 1977 message to Congress and an alternative bill drafted by ranking members of the House and Senate Commerce Communications Subcommittees.

Communications Act Revision. A House subcommittee began hearings during the summer of 1978 on legislation (HR 13015) that would permit marketplace competition to replace much of the existing federal regulation of the communications industry. But after 33 days of testimony, the bill was sent back to the drawing boards for re-introduction in revised form at the beginning of the next Congress.

The schedule set for the bill by its authors, Commerce Communications Subcommittee Chairman Lionel Van Deerlin, D-Calif., and ranking Republican Louis Frey Jr., Fla., called for House passage of the measure in 1979 and Senate passage before the end of the 96th Congress.

Consumer Protection Agency. Congress in 1978 witnessed a gradual shift by liberal and moderate Democrats away from seeking to increase government regulation as a way to protect consumers. Instead, the focus was on trying to eliminate some forms of government regulation in order to make the marketplace more responsive to consumers' interests. The trend was one important reason behind the House's defeat of legislation to establish a federal Office of Consumer Representation.

Despite President Carter's backing, the legislation (HR 6805) was killed Feb. 8 by a vote of 189-227 after having been approved by the House, 208-199, in the 94th Congress, 293-94 in the 93rd Congress and 344-44 in the 92nd. Supporters of the controversial agency surmised the legislation would not be re-introduced in the 96th Congress. The legislation had been before Congress for nine years.

Other Consumer Bills. Congress enacted legislation (HR 2777) in 1978 to establish a National Consumer Cooperative Bank. The administration, which opposed the bill in 1977, reversed itself once the consumer protection agency bill had been defeated and gave its support to the co-op bank.

Other consumer bills sought by Carter did not fare so well, however. Federal no-fault auto insurance legislation (HR 13048), a perennial goal of consumer advocates in Congress, was killed by the House Commerce Committee in August. A bill to authorize the federal government to help underwrite the costs of public interest participation in federal agency proceedings (HR 8798, S 270) died a quiet death in the House and Senate Judiciary Committees.

A bill to streamline Federal Trade Commission proceedings (HR 3816) was killed by the House when the Senate refused to go along with a provision for a congressional veto of commission regulations. Legislation intended to streamline the procedures of the Consumer Product Safety Commission (S 2796) was approved just before adjournment.

Presidential Vetoes, 95th Congress

Following is a list of the 19 public bill vetoes by President Carter during the first and second sessions of the 95th Congress.

Although substantial for a Democratic president with a Congress of his own party, Carter's veto mark was a significant drop from the record of his two immediate predecessors — both Republicans working with a Democratic Congress. Presidents Gerald R. Ford and Richard M. Nixon vetoed 66 and 43 bills, respectively. Unlike Ford or Nixon, Carter did not have any of his vetoes overridden.

In two years in office, Carter already had vetoed more public bills than John F. Kennedy did in three years (nine) and Lyndon B. Johnson did in five years (13). Like Carter, Democrats Kennedy and Johnson had no vetoes overridden by the Democratic Congress.

Thirteen of Carter's 19 vetoes were pocket vetoes, accomplished by his refusal to sign certain bills after Congress adjourned. Two vetoes occurred in the first session of the 95th Congress, and 17 in the second session.

Carter still trailed the all-time veto leaders by a large margin. Franklin D. Roosevelt vetoed 635 bills during his 12 years in office, and Grover Cleveland vetoed 584 during his two separate four-year terms.

In one of only two override attempts during Carter's first two years in office, the House Sept. 7, 1978, sustained his veto of a weapons procurement bill (HR 10929) which authorized funding for a nuclear-powered aircraft carrier that Carter opposed.

In the other override attempt, the House Oct. 5 sustained Carter's veto of a public works appropriation bill which included funding for water projects that Carter wanted to kill. *(For details on all of the vetoed bills, see appropriate Major Congressional Action chapters; for texts of veto messages, see appendix-Presidential Messages.)*

1977

1. S 1811 (Energy Administration Authorization)
   Vetoed: Nov. 5
   No Override Attempt
2. HR 2521 (Rabbit Meat Inspection)
   Vetoed: Nov. 9
   No Override Attempt

1978

3. HR 3161 (Firefighters Workweek)
   Vetoed: June 19
   No Override Attempt
4. HR 10882 (Sikes Act Amendments)
   Vetoed: July 10
   No Override Attempt
5. HR 10929 (Weapons Procurement Authorization)
   Vetoed: Aug. 17
   House sustained Sept. 7, 191-206
6. HR 12928 (Public Works Appropriations)
   Vetoed: Oct. 5
   House sustained Oct. 5, 223-190
7. HR 9370 (Aquaculture Act)
   Pocket vetoed: Oct. 18
8. HR 11445 (Small Business Amendments)
   Pocket vetoed: Oct. 23
9. S 1104 (Legionville Historic Site)
   Pocket vetoed: Nov. 2
10. HR 11092 (Navajo-Hopi Lands)
    Pocket vetoed: Nov. 2
11. HR 11861 (Navy-Maritime Advisory Board Act)
    Pocket vetoed: Nov. 2
12. HR 11580 (Lottery Materials Exports)
    Pocket vetoed: Nov. 4
13. HR 9518 (Ocean Shipping Rebates)
    Pocket vetoed: Nov. 4
14. HR 6536 (D.C. Employees' Pensions)
    Pocket vetoed: Nov. 4
15. S 1503 (Tris Ban)
    Pocket vetoed: Nov. 4
16. HR 13719 (Guam/Virgin Islands Payments)
    Pocket vetoed: Nov. 4
17. S 2416 (Nurse Training Programs)
    Pocket vetoed: Nov. 11
18. HR 11545 (Meat Import Act)
    Pocket vetoed: Nov. 11
19. HR 9937 (Textile Tariffs)
    Pocket vetoed Nov. 11

MEMBERS OF THE 95th CONGRESS, SECOND SESSION....

As of Adjournment, Oct. 15, 1978

Representatives
D 285; R 146
4 Vacancies

A

Abdnor, James (R S.D. - 2)
Addabbo, Joseph P. (D N.Y. - 7)
Akaka, Daniel K. (D Hawaii - 2)
Alexander, Bill (D Ark. - 1)
Ambro, Jerome A. (D N.Y. - 3)
Ammerman, Joseph S. (D Pa. - 23)
Anderson, Glenn M. (D Calif. - 32)
Anderson, John B. (R Ill. - 16)
Andrews, Ike F. (D N.C. - 4)
Andrews, Mark (R N.D. - AL)
Annunzio, Frank (D Ill. - 11)
Applegate, Douglas (D Ohio - 18)
Archer, Bill (R Texas - 7)
Armstrong, William L. (R Colo. - 5)
Ashbrook, John M. (R Ohio - 17)
Ashley, Thomas L. (D Ohio - 9)
Aspin, Les (D Wis. - 1)
AuCoin, Les (D Ore. - 1)

B

Badham, Robert E. (R Calif. - 40)
Bafalis, L.A. (Skip) (R Fla. - 10)
Baldus, Alvin (D Wis. - 3)
Barnard, Doug (D Ga. - 10)
Baucus, Max (D Mont. - 1)
Bauman, Robert E. (R Md. - 1)
Beard, Edward P. (D R.I. - 2)
Beard, Robin L. Jr. (R Tenn. - 6)
Bedell, Berkley (D Iowa - 6)
Beilenson, Anthony C. (Tony) (D Calif. - 23)
Benjamin, Adam Jr. (D Ind. - 1)
Bennett, Charles E. (D Fla. - 3)
Bevill, Tom (D Ala. - 4)
Biaggi, Mario (D N.Y. - 10)
Bingham, Jonathan B. (D N.Y. - 22)
Blanchard, James J. (D Mich. - 18)
Blouin, Michael T. (D Iowa - 2)
Boggs, Lindy (D La. - 2)
Boland, Edward P. (D Mass. - 2)
Bolling, Richard (D Mo. - 5)
Bonior, David E. (D Mich. - 12)
Bonker, Don (D Wash. - 3)
Bowen, David R. (D Miss. - 2)
Brademas, John (D Ind. - 3)
Breaux, John B. (D La. - 7)
Breckinridge, John B. (D Ky. - 6)
Brinkley, Jack (D Ga. - 3)
Brodhead, William M. (D Mich. - 17)
Brooks, Jack (D Texas - 9)
Broomfield, William S. (R Mich. - 19)
Brown, Clarence J. (R Ohio - 7)
Brown, Garry (R Mich. - 3)
Brown, George E. Jr. (D Calif. - 36)
Broyhill, James T. (R N.C. - 10)
Buchanan, John (R Ala. - 6)
Burgener, Clair W. (R Calif. - 43)
Burke, J. Herbert (R Fla. -12)
Burke, James A. (D Mass. - 11)
Burke, Yvonne Brathwaite (D Calif. - 28)
Burleson, Omar (D Texas - 17)
Burlison Bill D. (D Mo. - 10)
Burton, John L. (D Calif. - 5)
Burton, Phillip (D Calif. - 6)
Butler, M. Caldwell (R Va. - 6)

C

Caputo, Bruce F. (R N.Y. - 23)
Carney, Charles J. (D Ohio - 19)
Carr, Bob (D Mich. - 6)
Carter, Tim Lee (R Ky. - 5)
Cavanaugh, John J. (D Neb. - 2)
Cederberg, Elford A. (R Mich. - 10)
Chappell, Bill Jr. (D Fla. - 4)
Chisholm, Shirley (D N.Y. - 12)
Clausen, Don H. (R Calif. - 2)
Clawson, Del (R Calif. - 33)
Clay, William (Bill) (D Mo. - 1)
Cleveland, James C. (R N.H. - 2)
Cochran, Thad (R Miss. - 4)
Cohen, William S. (R Maine - 2)
Coleman, E. Thomas (R Mo. - 6)
Collins, Cardiss (D Ill. - 7)
Collins, James M. (R Texas - 3)
Conable, Barber B. Jr. (R N.Y. - 35)
Conte, Silvio O. (R Mass. - 1)
Conyers, John Jr. (D Mich. - 1)
Corcoran, Tom (R Ill. - 15)
Corman, James C. (D Calif. - 21)
Cornell, Robert J. (D Wis. - 8)
Cornwell, David L. (D Ind. - 8)
Cotter, William R. (D Conn. - 1)
Coughlin, Lawrence (R Pa. - 13)
Crane, Philip M. (R Ill. - 12)
Cunningham, John E. (Jack) (R Wash. - 7)

D

D'Amours, Norman E. (D N.H. - 1)
Daniel, Dan (D Va. - 5)
Daniel, Robert W. Jr. (R Va. - 4)
Danielson, George E. (D Calif. - 30)
Davis, Mendel J. (D S.C. - 1)
de la Garza, E. (Kika) (D Texas - 15)
Delaney, James J. (D N.Y. - 9)
Dellums, Ronald V. (D Calif. - 8)
Dent, John H. (D Pa. - 21)
Derrick, Butler (D S.C. - 3)
Derwinski, Edward J. (R Ill. - 4)
Devine, Samuel L. (R Ohio - 12)
Dickinson, William L. (R Ala. - 2)
Dicks, Norman D. (D Wash. - 6)
Diggs, Charles C. Jr. (D Mich. - 13)
Dingell, John D. (D Mich. - 16)
Dodd, Christopher J. (D Conn. - 2)
Dornan, Robert K. (R Calif. - 27)
Downey, Thomas J. (D N.Y. - 2)
Drinan, Robert F. (D Mass. - 4)
Duncan, John J. (R Tenn. - 2)
Duncan, Robert (D Ore. - 3)

E

Early, Joseph D. (D Mass. - 3)
Eckhardt, Bob (D Texas - 8)
Edgar, Robert W. (D Pa. - 7)
Edwards, Don (D Calif. - 10)
Edwards, Jack (R Ala. - 1)
Edwards, Mickey (R Okla. - 5)
Eilberg, Joshua (D Pa. - 4)
Emery, David F. (R Maine - 1)
English, Glenn (D Okla. - 6)
Erlenborn, John N. (R Ill. - 14)
Ertel, Allen E. (D Pa. - 17)
Evans, Billy Lee (D Ga. - 8)
Evans, David W. (D Ind. - 6)
Evans, Frank E. (D Colo. - 3)
Evans, Thomas B. Jr. (R Del. - AL)

F

Fary, John G. (D Ill. - 5)
Fascell, Dante B. (D Fla. - 15)
Fenwick, Millicent (R N.J. - 5)
Findley, Paul (R Ill. - 20)
Fish, Hamilton Jr. (R N.Y. - 25)
Fisher, Joseph L. (D Va. - 10)
Fithian, Floyd (D Ind. - 2)
Flippo, Ronnie G. (D Ala. - 5)
Flood, Daniel J. (D Pa. - 11)
Florio, James J. (D N.J. - 1)
Flowers, Walter (D Ala. - 7)
Flynt, John J. Jr. (D Ga. - 6)
Foley, Thomas S. (D Wash. - 5)
Ford, Harold E. (D Tenn. - 8)
Ford, William D. (D Mich. - 15)
Forsythe, Edwin B. (R N.J. - 6)
Fountain, L. H. (D N.C. - 2)
Fowler, Wyche Jr. (D Ga. - 5)
Fraser, Donald M. (D Minn. - 5)
Frenzel, Bill (R Minn. - 3)
Frey, Louis Jr. (R Fla. - 9)
Fuqua, Don (D Fla. - 2)

G

Gammage, Bob (D Texas - 22)
Garcia, Robert (D N.Y. - 21)
Gaydos, Joseph M. (D Pa. - 20)
Gephardt, Richard A. (D Mo. - 3)
Giaimo, Robert N. (D Conn. - 3)
Gibbons, Sam (D Fla. - 7)
Gilman, Benjamin A. (R N.Y. - 26)
Ginn, Bo (D Ga. - 1)
Glickman, Dan (D Kan. - 4)
Goldwater, Barry M. Jr. (R Calif. - 20)
Gonzalez, Henry B. (D Texas - 20)
Goodling, Bill (R Pa. - 19)
Gore, Albert Jr. (D Tenn. - 4)
Gradison, Bill (R Ohio - 1)
Grassley, Charles E. (R Iowa - 3)
Green, S. William (R N.Y. - 18)
Gudger, Lamar (D N.C. - 11)
Guyer, Tennyson (R Ohio - 4)

H

Hagedorn, Tom (R Minn. - 2)
Hall, Sam B. Jr. (D Texas - 1)
Hamilton, Lee H. (D Ind. - 9)
Hammerschmidt, John Paul (R Ark. - 3)
Hanley, James M. (D N.Y. - 32)
Hannaford, Mark W. (D Calif. - 34)
Hansen, George (R Idaho - 2)
Harkin, Tom (D Iowa - 5)
Harrington, Michael J. (D Mass. - 6)
Harris, Herbert E. II (D Va. - 8)
Harsha, William H. (R Ohio - 6)
Hawkins, Augustus F. (D Calif. - 29)
Heckler, Margaret M. (R Mass. - 10)
Hefner, W. G. (Bill) (D N.C. - 8)
Heftel, Cecil (Cec) (D Hawaii - 1)
Hightower, Jack (D Texas - 13)
Hillis, Elwood (R Ind. - 5)
Holland, Ken (D S.C. - 5)
Hollenbeck, Harold C. (R N.J. - 9)
Holt, Marjorie S. (R Md. - 4)
Holtzman, Elizabeth (D N.Y. - 16)
Horton, Frank (R N.Y. - 34)
Howard, James J. (D N.J. - 3)
Hubbard, Carroll Jr. (D Ky. - 1)
Huckaby, Jerry (D La. - 5)
Hughes, William J. (D N.J. - 2)
Hyde, Henry J. (R Ill. - 6)

I, J

Ichord, Richard H. (D Mo. - 8)
Ireland, Andy (D Fla. - 8)
Jacobs, Andy Jr. (D Ind. - 11)
Jeffords, James M. (R Vt. - AL)
Jenkins, Ed (D Ga. - 9)
Jenrette, John W. Jr. (D S.C. - 6)
Johnson, Harold T. (D Calif. - 1)
Johnson, James P. (Jim) (R Colo. - 4)
Jones, Ed (D Tenn. - 7)
Jones, James R. (D Okla. - 1)
Jones, Walter B. (D N.C. - 1)
Jordan, Barbara C. (D Texas - 18)

K

Kasten, Robert W. Jr. (R Wis. - 9)
Kastenmeier, Robert W. (D Wis. - 2)
Kazen, Abraham Jr. (D Texas - 23)
Kelly, Richard (R Fla. - 5)
Kemp, Jack F. (R N.Y. - 38)
Keys, Martha (D Kan. - 2)
Kildee, Dale E. (D Mich. - 7)
Kindness, Thomas N. (R Ohio - 8)
Kostmayer, Peter H. (D Pa. - 8)
Krebs, John (D Calif. - 17)
Krueger, Robert (Bob) (D Texas - 21)

L

LaFalce, John J. (D N.Y. - 36)
Lagomarsino, Robert J. (R Calif. - 19)
Latta, Delbert L. (R Ohio - 5)
Leach, Jim (R Iowa - 1)
Lederer, Raymond F. (D Pa. - 3)
LeFante, Joseph A. (D N.J. - 14)
Leggett, Robert L. (D Calif. - 4)
Lehman, William (D Fla. - 13)
Lent, Norman F. (R N.Y. - 4)
Levitas, Elliott H. (D Ga. - 4)
Livingston, Robert L. (Bob) (R La. - 1)
Lloyd, Jim (D Calif. - 35)
Lloyd, Marilyn (D Tenn. - 3)
Long, Clarence D. (D Md. - 2)
Long, Gillis W. (D La. - 8)
Lott, Trent (R Miss. - 5)
Lujan, Manuel Jr. (R N.M. - 1)
Luken, Thomas A. (D Ohio - 2)
Lundine, Stanley N. (D N.Y. - 39)

M

Madigan, Edward R. (R Ill. - 21)
Maguire, Andrew (D N.J. - 7)
Mahon, George (D Texas - 19)
Mann, James R. (D S.C. - 4)
Markey, Edward J. (D Mass. - 7)
Marks, Marc L. (R Pa. - 24)
Marlenee, Ron (R Mont. - 2)
Marriott, Dan (R Utah - 2)
Martin, James G. (R N.C. - 9)
Mathis, Dawson (D Ga. - 2)
Mattox, Jim (D Texas - 5)
Mazzoli, Romano L. (D Ky. - 3)
McClory, Robert (R Ill. - 13)
McCloskey, Paul N. Jr. (R Calif. - 12)
McCormack, Mike (D Wash. - 4)
McDade, Joseph M. (R Pa. - 10)
McDonald, Larry P. (D Ga. - 7)
McEwen, Robert C. (R N.Y. - 30)
McFall, John J. (D Calif. - 14)
McHugh, Matthew F. (D N.Y. - 27)
McKay, Gunn (D Utah - 1)
McKinney, Stewart B. (R Conn. - 4)
Meeds, Lloyd (D Wash. - 2)
Meyner, Helen (D N.J. - 13)
Michel, Robert H. (R Ill. - 18)
Mikulski, Barbara A. (D Md. - 3)
Mikva, Abner J. (D Ill. - 10)
Milford, Dale (D Texas - 24)
Miller, Clarence E. (R Ohio - 10)
Miller, George (D Calif. - 7)
Mineta, Norman Y. (D Calif. - 13)
Minish, Joseph G. (D N.J. - 11)
Mitchell, Donald J. (R N.Y. - 31)
Mitchell, Parren J. (D Md. - 7)
Moakley, Joe (D Mass. - 9)
Moffett, Toby (D Conn. - 6)
Mollohan, Robert H. (D W.Va. - 1)
Montgomery, G. V. (Sonny) (D Miss. - 3)
Moore, W. Henson (R La. - 6)
Moorhead, Carlos J. (R Calif. - 22)
Moorhead, William S. (D Pa. - 14)
Moss, John E. (D Calif. - 3)
Mottl, Ronald M. (D Ohio - 23)
Murphy, Austin J. (D Pa. - 22)
Murphy, John M. (D N.Y. - 17)
Murphy, Morgan F. (D Ill. - 2)
Murtha, John P. (D Pa. - 12)
Myers, Gary A. (R Pa. - 25)
Myers, John T. (R Ind. - 7)
Myers, Michael (Ozzie) (D Pa. - 1)

N

Natcher, William H. (D Ky. - 2)
Neal, Stephen L. (D N.C. - 5)
Nedzi, Lucien N. (D Mich. - 14)
Nichols, Bill (D Ala. - 3)
Nix, Robert N. C. (D Pa. - 2)
Nolan, Richard (D Minn. - 6)
Nowak, Henry J. (D N.Y. - 37)

O

Oakar, Mary Rose (D Ohio - 20)
Oberstar, James L. (D Minn. - 8)
Obey, David R. (D Wis. - 7)
O'Brien, George M. (R Ill. - 17)
O'Neill, Thomas P. Jr. (D Mass. - 8)
Ottinger, Richard L. (D N.Y. - 24)

P

Panetta, Leon E. (D Calif. - 16)
Patten, Edward J. (D N.J. - 15)
Patterson, Jerry M. (D Calif. - 38)
Pattison, Edward W. (D N.Y. - 29)
Pease, Don J. (D Ohio - 13)
Pepper, Claude (D Fla. - 14)

....GOVERNORS, CABINET OFFICERS, SUPREME COURT

Perkins, Carl D. (D Ky. - 7)
Pettis, Shirley N. (R Calif. - 37)
Pickle, J. J. (D Texas - 10)
Pike, Otis G. (D N.Y. - 1)
Poage, W. R. (D Texas - 11)
Pressler, Larry (R S.D. - 1)
Preyer, Richardson (D N.C. - 6)
Price, Melvin (D Ill. - 23)
Pritchard, Joel (R Wash. - 1)
Pursell, Carl D. (R Mich. - 2)

Q

Quayle, Dan (R Ind. - 4)
Quie, Albert H. (R Minn. - 1)
Quillen, James H. (Jimmy) (R Tenn. - 1)

R

Rahall, Nick J. (D W.Va. - 4)
Railsback, Tom (R Ill. - 19)
Rangel, Charles B. (D N.Y. - 19)
Regula, Ralph S. (R Ohio - 16)
Reuss, Henry S. (D Wis. - 5)
Rhodes, John J. (R Ariz. - 1)
Richmond, Frederick (D N.Y. - 14)
Rinaldo, Matthew J. (R N.J. - 12)
Risenhoover, Ted (D Okla. - 2)
Roberts, Ray (D Texas - 4)
Robinson, J. Kenneth (R Va. - 7)
Rodino, Peter W. Jr. (D N.J. - 10)
Roe, Robert A. (D N.J. - 8)
Rogers, Paul G. (D Fla. - 11)
Roncalio, Teno (D Wyo. - AL)
Rooney, Fred B. (D Pa. - 15)
Rose, Charlie (D N.C. - 7)
Rosenthal, Benjamin S. (D N.Y. - 8)
Rostenkowski, Dan (D Ill. - 8)
Rousselot, John H. (R Calif. - 26)
Roybal, Edward R. (D Calif. - 25)
Rudd, Eldon (R Ariz. - 4)
Runnels, Harold (D N.M. - 2)
Ruppe, Philip E. (R Mich. - 11)
Russo, Marty (D Ill. - 3)
Ryan, Leo J. (D Calif. - 11)

S

St Germain, Fernand J. (D R.I. - 1)
Santini, Jim (D Nev. - AL)
Sarasin, Ronald A. (R Conn. - 5)
Satterfield, David E. III (D Va. - 3)
Sawyer, Harold S. (R Mich. - 5)
Scheuer, James H. (D N.Y. - 11)
Schroeder, Patricia (D Colo. - 1)
Schulze, Richard T. (R Pa. - 5)
Sebelius, Keith G. (R Kan. - 1)
Seiberling, John F. (D Ohio - 14)
Sharp, Phil (D Ind. - 10)
Shipley, George E. (D Ill. - 22)
Shuster, Bud (R Pa. - 9)
Sikes, Robert L. F. (D Fla. - 1)
Simon, Paul (D Ill. - 24)
Sisk, B. F. (D Calif. - 15)
Skelton, Ike (D Mo. - 4)
Skubitz, Joe (R Kan. - 5)
Slack, John M. (D W.Va. - 3)
Smith, Neal (D Iowa - 4)
Smith, Virginia (R Neb. - 3)
Snyder, Gene (R Ky. - 4)
Solarz, Stephen J. (D N.Y. - 13)
Spellman, Gladys Noon (D Md. - 5)
Spence, Floyd (R S.C. - 2)
Staggers, Harley O. (D W.Va. - 2)
Stangeland, Arlan (R Minn. - 7)
Stanton, J. William (R Ohio - 11)
Stark, Fortney H. (Pete) (D Calif. - 9)
Steed, Tom (D Okla. - 4)
Steers, Newton I. Jr. (R Md. - 8)
Steiger, William A. (R Wis. - 6)
Stockman, Dave (R Mich. - 4)
Stokes, Louis (D Ohio - 21)
Stratton, Samuel S. (D N.Y. - 28)
Studds, Gerry E. (D Mass. - 12)
Stump, Bob (D Ariz. - 3)
Symms, Steven D. (R Idaho - 1)

T

Taylor, Gene (R Mo. - 7)
Teague, Olin E. (D Texas - 6)
Thompson, Frank Jr. (D N.J. - 4)
Thone, Charles (R Neb. - 1)
Thornton, Ray (D Ark. - 4)
Traxler, Bob (D Mich. - 8)
Treen, David C. (R La. - 3)
Trible, Paul S. Jr. (R Va. - 1)
Tsongas, Paul E. (D Mass. - 5)
Tucker, Jim Guy (D Ark. - 2)

U, V

Udall, Morris K. (D Ariz. - 2)
Ullman, Al (D Ore. - 2)
Van Deerlin, Lionel (D Calif. - 42)
Vander Jagt, Guy (R Mich. - 9)
Vanik, Charles A. (D Ohio - 22)
Vento, Bruce F. (D Minn. - 4)
Volkmer, Harold L. (D Mo. - 9)

W

Waggonner, Joe D. Jr. (D La. - 4)
Walgren, Doug (D Pa. - 18)
Walker, Robert S. (R Pa. - 16)
Walsh, William F. (R N.Y. - 33)
Wampler, William C. (R Va. - 9)
Watkins, Wes (D Okla. - 3)
Waxman, Henry A. (D Calif. - 24)
Weaver, James (D Ore. - 4)
Weiss, Ted (D N.Y. - 20)
Whalen, Charles W. Jr. (R Ohio - 3)
White, Richard C. (D Texas - 16)
Whitehurst, G. William (R Va. - 2)
Whitley, Charlie (D N.C. - 3)
Whitten, Jamie L. (D Miss. - 1)
Wiggins, Charles E. (R Calif. - 39)
Wilson, Bob (R Calif. - 41)
Wilson, Charles (D Texas - 2)
Wilson, Charles H. (D Calif. - 31)
Winn, Larry Jr. (R Kan. - 3)
Wirth, Timothy E. (D Colo. - 2)
Wolff, Lester L. (D N.Y. - 6)
Wright, Jim (D Texas - 12)
Wydler, John W. (R N.Y. - 5)
Wylie, Chalmers P. (R Ohio - 15)

X, Y, Z

Yates, Sidney R. (D Ill. - 9)
Yatron, Gus (D Pa. - 6)
Young, C. W. Bill (R Fla. - 6)
Young, Don (R Alaska - AL)
Young, John (D Texas - 14)
Young, Robert A. (D Mo. - 2)
Zablocki, Clement J. (D Wis. - 4)
Zeferetti, Leo C. (D N.Y. - 15)

Delegates

de Lugo, Ron (D V.I.)
Fauntroy, Walter E. (D D.C.)
Won Pat, Antonio Borja (D Guam)

Resident Commissioner

Corrada, Baltasar (New Prog. - P.R.)

Senators
D 62[1]; R 38

Abourezk, James—D S.D.
Allen, Maryon—D Ala.
Anderson, Wendell R.—D Minn.
Baker, Howard H. Jr.—R Tenn.
Bartlett, Dewey F.—R Okla.
Bayh, Birch—D Ind.
Bellmon, Henry—R Okla.
Bentsen, Lloyd—D Texas
Biden, Joe—D Del.
Brooke, Edward W.—R Mass.
Bumpers, Dale—D Ark.
Burdick, Quentin N.—D N.D.
Byrd, Harry F. Jr.—Ind Va.
Byrd, Robert C.—D W.Va.
Cannon, Howard W.—D Nev.
Case, Clifford P.—R N.J.
Chafee, John H.—R R.I.
Chiles, Lawton—D Fla.
Church, Frank—D Idaho
Clark, Dick—D Iowa
Cranston, Alan—D Calif.
Culver, John C.—D Iowa
Curtis, Carl T.—R Neb.
Danforth, John C.—R Mo.
DeConcini, Dennis—D Ariz.
Dole, Robert—R Kan.
Domenici, Pete V.—R N.M.
Durkin, John A.—D N.H.
Eagleton, Thomas F.—D Mo.
Eastland, James O.—D Miss.
Ford, Wendell H.—D Ky.
Garn, Jake—R Utah
Glenn, John—D Ohio
Goldwater, Barry—R Ariz.
Gravel, Mike—D Alaska
Griffin, Robert P.—R Mich.
Hansen, Clifford P.—R Wyo.
Hart, Gary—D Colo.
Haskell, Floyd K.—D Colo.
Hatch, Orrin G.—R Utah
Hatfield, Mark O.—R Ore.
Hatfield, Paul G.—D Mont.
Hathaway, William D.—D Maine
Hayakawa, S. I.—R Calif.
Heinz, H. John III—R Pa.
Helms, Jesse—R N.C.
Hodges, Kaneaster Jr.—D Ark.
Hollings, Ernest F.—D S.C.
Huddleston, Walter (Dee)—D Ky.
Humphrey, Muriel—D Minn.
Inouye, Daniel K.—D Hawaii
Jackson, Henry M.—D Wash.
Javits, Jacob K.—R N.Y.
Johnston, J. Bennett—D La.
Kennedy, Edward M.—D Mass.
Laxalt, Paul—R Nev.
Leahy, Patrick J.—D Vt.
Long, Russell B.—D La.
Lugar, Richard G.—R Ind.
Magnuson, Warren G.—D Wash.
Mathias, Charles McC. Jr.—R Md.
Matsunaga, Spark M.—D Hawaii
McClure, James A.—R Idaho
McGovern, George—D S.D.
McIntyre, Thomas Jr.—D N.H.
Melcher, John—D Mont.
Metzenbaum, Howard M.—D Ohio
Morgan, Robert—D N.C.
Moynihan, Daniel Patrick—D N.Y.
Muskie, Edmund S.—D Maine
Nelson, Gaylord—D Wis.
Nunn, Sam—D Ga.
Packwood, Bob—R Ore.
Pearson, James B.—R Kan.
Pell, Claiborne—D R.I.
Percy, Charles H.—R Ill.
Proxmire, William—D Wis.
Randolph, Jennings—D W.Va.
Ribicoff, Abraham—D Conn.
Riegle, Donald W. Jr.—D Mich.
Roth, William V. Jr.—R Del.
Sarbanes, Paul S.—D Md.
Sasser, Jim—D Tenn.
Schmitt, Harrison—R N.M.
Schweiker, Richard S.—R Pa.
Scott, Bill—R Va.
Sparkman, John—D Ala.
Stafford, Robert T.—R Vt.
Stennis, John C.—D Miss.
Stevens, Ted—R Alaska
Stevenson, Adlai E. III—D Ill.
Stone, Richard (Dick)—D Fla.
Talmadge, Herman E.—D Ga.
Thurmond, Strom—R S.C.
Tower, John G.—R Texas
Wallop, Malcolm—R Wyo.
Weicker, Lowell P. Jr.—R Conn.
Williams, Harrison A. Jr.—D N.J.
Young, Milton R.—R N.D.
Zorinsky, Edward—D Neb.

Supreme Court Justices

Burger, Warren E.—Minn., Chief Justice
Blackmun, Harry A.—Minn.
Brennan, William J. Jr.—N.J.
Marshall, Thurgood—N.Y.
Powell, Lewis F. Jr.—Va.
Rehnquist, William H.—Ariz.
Stevens, John Paul—Ill.
Stewart, Potter—Ohio
White, Byron R.—Colo.

Cabinet

Adams, Brock—Transportation
Andrus, Cecil D.—Interior
Bell, Griffin B.—Attorney General
Bergland, Bob—Agriculture
Blumenthal, W. Michael—Treasury
Brown, Harold—Defense
Califano, Joseph A. Jr.—HEW
Harris, Patricia Roberts—HUD
Kreps, Juanita M.—Commerce
Marshall, F. Ray—Labor
Schlesinger, James R.—Energy
Vance, Cyrus R.—State

Governors
D 37; R 12; Independent 1

Ala.—George C. Wallace (D)
Alaska—Jay S. Hammond (R)
Ariz.—Bruce Babbitt (D)
Ark.—David Pryor (D)
Calif.—Edmund G. Brown Jr. (D)
Colo.—Richard D. Lamm (D)
Conn.—Ella T. Grasso (D)
Del.—Pierre S. (Pete) du Pont (R)
Fla.—Reubin Askew (D)
Ga.—George Busbee (D)
Hawaii—George Ariyoshi (D)
Idaho—John V. Evans (D)
Ill.—James R. Thompson (R)
Ind.—Otis R. Bowen (R)
Iowa—Robert Ray (R)
Kan.—Robert F. Bennett (R)
Ky.—Julian Carroll (D)
La.—Edwin W. Edwards (D)
Maine—James B. Longley (Ind)
Md.—Blair Lee III (acting) (D)
Mass.—Michael S. Dukakis (D)
Mich.—William G. Milliken (R)
Minn.—Rudy Perpich (D)
Miss.—Cliff Finch (D)
Mo.—Joseph P. Teasdale (D)
Mont.—Thomas L. Judge (D)
Neb.—J. J. Exon (D)
Nev.—Mike O'Callaghan (D)
N.H.—Meldrim Thomson Jr. (R)
N.J.—Brendan T. Byrne (D)
N.M.—Jerry Apodaca (D)
N.Y.—Hugh L. Carey (D)
N.C.—James B. Hunt Jr. (D)
N.D.—Arthur A. Link (D)
Ohio—James A. Rhodes (R)
Okla.—David L. Boren (D)
Ore.—Robert Straub (D)
Pa.—Milton J. Shapp (D)
R.I.—J. Joseph Garrahy (D)
S.C.—James B. Edwards (R)
S.D.—Harvey Wollman (D)
Tenn.—Ray Blanton (D)
Texas—Dolph Briscoe (D)
Utah—Scott M. Matheson (D)
Vt.—Richard A. Snelling (R)
Va.—John Dalton (R)
Wash.—Dixy Lee Ray (D)
W.Va.—John D. (Jay) Rockefeller IV (D)
Wis.—Martin J. Schreiber (D)
Wyo.—Ed Herschler (D)

1 Includes Harry F. Byrd Jr. (Va.) elected as an independent.

MAJOR CONGRESSIONAL ACTION

CQ

Appropriations in 2nd Session, 95th Congress

For fiscal year 1979, in thousands of dollars

Budget Authority (authority to obligate funds) in boldface type

Outlays (funds to be spent in 1979) in italic type

SOURCE: Congressional Budget Office

	Administration Request[1]	House	Senate	Final Action	Page
Agriculture and related agencies (HR 13126—PL 95-448)	**$ 18,090,152** *13,617,017*	**$ 18,014,029** *13,784,054*	**$ 23,365,764** *13,758,424*	**$ 18,288,201** *13,737,996*	145
Defense Department (HR 13635—PL 95-457)	**119,300,283** *105,576,825*	**119,019,278** *105,218,466*	**116,422,972** *104,964,731*	**117,255,621** *105,408,483*	132
District of Columbia (HR 13468—PL 95-373)	**460,090** *429,840*	**277,300** *305,719*	**261,200** *289,619*	**258,200** *286,619*	69
Foreign Aid (HR 12931—PL 95-481)	**10,387,761** *5,568,020*	**7,176,723** *5,395,347*	**9,203,806** *5,443,128*	**9,135,032** *5,445,902*	123
Housing and Urban Development Veterans, NASA (HR 12936—PL 95-392)	**70,557,534** *45,381,049*	**68,208,848** *44,856,515*	**67,656,624** *44,767,409*	**67,911,419** *44,787,745*	78
Interior and related agencies (HR 12932—PL 95-465)	**12,830,967** *9,910,918*	**12,690,544** *9,952,031*	**11,566,413** *9,909,304*	**11,578,692** *9,986,885*	115
Labor, Health, Education and Welfare (HR 12929—PL 95-480)	**74,865,881** *75,133,650*	**57,585,102** *63,258,816*	**56,507,666** *63,404,832*	**57,054,029** *63,423,469*	105
Legislative Branch (HR 12935—PL 95-391)	**1,161,825** *1,184,813*	**922,492** *966,355*	**1,118,244** *1,146,281*	**1,118,244** *1,146,281*	93
Military Construction (HR 12927—PL 95-374)	**4,253,000** *3,212,461*	**3,844,887** *3,189,380*	**3,964,746** *3,170,772*	**3,880,863** *3,154,557*	65
Public Works, Energy Research (HR 12928)[2]	**11,039,449** *9,533,681*	**10,134,801** *9,443,113*	**10,123,345** *9,461,322*	**10,162,252** *9,468,113*	154
State, Justice, Commerce, Judiciary (HR 12934—PL 95-431)	**8,660,076** *10,800,141*	**4,588,718** *7,391,379*	**8,436,480** *10,747,175*	**8,515,354** *10,815,524*	88
Transportation and related agencies (HR 12933—PL 95-335)	**9,268,623** *15,218,013*	**8,847,296** *15,536,342*	**8,568,543** *15,489,729*	**8,747,553** *15,522,889*	61
Treasury, Postal Service and General Government (HR 1930—PL 95-429)	**9,206,161** *9,116,629*	**8,634,300** *8,547,553*	**8,837,206** *8,759,569*	**8,983,261** *8,897,647*	99

1 Includes budget amendments to date.

2 H J Res 1129 (PL 95-482) continuing appropriations for fiscal 1979, was cleared by Congress Oct. 5. However, all bills covered by H J Res 1139 — except public works — were passed before adjournment. H J Res 1139 provided new budget authority of $10,162,251,900 for public works projects in fiscal 1979. H J Res 1139 also provided continuing appropriations for certain labor and health programs whose authorizations were not completed before the regular Labor/HEW appropriations bill passed.

Budget and Appropriations

Congress began writing its fiscal 1979 budget amidst concerns about high unemployment and a possible economic slowdown. By the time it adopted the budget, inflation and an anti-government spending mood had eclipsed the earlier focus.

In January, President Carter proposed a $500.2 billion budget, coupled with a $24.5 billion tax cut. The deficit, still showing fiscal strains of the 1974-1975 recession, would be $60.6 billion. *(Carter budget, p. 49)*

When unemployment dropped more rapidly than expected and inflation surged in early 1978, Congress agreed to scale back the proposed tax cut. That, combined with a downward revision in some spending estimates, enabled lawmakers to adopt a first budget resolution (S Con Res 80) in May calling for a $498.8 billion spending target and a $50.9 billion deficit.

As usual, the resolution won bipartisan support in the Senate, but was opposed by most House Republicans, who favored lower spending and a larger tax cut.

Events following the adoption of the first resolution served to continue the trend toward a smaller deficit. As in the past, federal agencies appeared unable to spend money as rapidly as Congress appropriated it. In addition, approval by California voters in June of a state constitutional amendment slashing property taxes encouraged an anti-spending spirit in Congress. Finally, further concerns about inflation encouraged the belief that a smaller tax cut — and hence a smaller deficit — were advisable.

A change in the prevailing economic and budgetary wisdom was most clearly illustrated by the Senate Budget Committee's shifting attitude toward spending for local public works programs.

The committee had originally supported, with some reservations, proposals to leave room in the first budget resolution for federally financed local public works programs. They were seen as a means to help local governments suffering from recession, and to create jobs.

On the second resolution (H Con Res 683), the committee parted with the House, which had included room for $2 billion of local public works spending, and opposed the program entirely. Members argued that the economy no longer justified the program, and that future programs to create jobs should be aimed more directly at the hard-core unemployed.

An impasse over the local public works question prevented a House-Senate conference committee from reaching agreement on the second resolution by the Sept. 15 deadline. The disagreement was skirted several days later, but not before the Senate had gone on record strongly against the program.

The combination of a smaller tax cut, some spending reductions and further downward re-estimates did enable Congress to agree on a $487.5 billion budget carrying a predicted deficit of $38.8 billion — more than $20 billion lower than Carter originally forecast in January. *(Tax cut, p. 219)*

Fiscal '79 Budget Totals Compared

(in billions of dollars)

	Carter Budget	First Resolution	Administration July Re-estimates	Second Resolution
Budget Authority	$568.2	$568.85	$571.4	$555.65
Outlays	500.2	498.8	496.6	487.5
Revenues	439.6	447.9	448.2	448.7
Deficit	60.6	50.9	48.5	38.8

Fiscal 1979 Budget Targets

Congress completed action May 17 on the first fiscal 1979 budget resolution (S Con Res 80) setting non-binding spending and tax goals for the fiscal year beginning Oct. 1.

The action came after President Carter and Congress agreed to scale back the administration's proposed $24.5 billion tax cut to $19.4 billion and to delay its effective date for three months, to Jan. 1, 1979.

The Senate approved S Con Res 80 by voice vote on May 12, and the House followed suit on a cliff-hanging 201-198 vote May 17. Only two House Republicans — Silvio O. Conte, Mass., and Newton I. Steers Jr., Md. — voted for the resolution. *(Vote 280, p. 80-H)*

By reducing the size of the expected tax cut — its impact during the fiscal year would be to reduce revenues by only $15 billion — lawmakers were able to project a significantly smaller deficit than was forecast in earlier budget proposals by the administration or either branch of Congress.

Provisions

Proposed and final budget targets were as follows *(in billions of dollars)*:

	Budget Authority	Outlays	Revenues	Deficit
Administration				
January budget	$568.2	$500.2	$439.6	$60.6
March 13 re-estimates*	565.6	499.4	439.8	59.6
Senate	566.1	498.9	443.3	55.6
House	569.5	500.9	443.0	57.9
Conference	568.85	498.8	447.9	50.9

* *Figures do not reflect the impact of President Carter's March 27 urban policy proposals or his proposed tax cut revisions announced May 12.*

S Con Res 80 also set non-binding budget authority and outlay targets for the 19 functional areas of the budget.

The resolution targeted $849.1 billion as the appropriate level for the public debt that is subject to statutory limit. An effort to have the debt limit set as part of the budget process had run afoul of constitutional problems. *(Debt limit, p. 283)*

Senate Committee Report

The Senate Budget Committee reported S Con Res 80 (S Rept 95-739) on April 14.

The resolution allowed for total new budget authority of $566.1 billion and outlays of $498.9 billion in the fiscal year beginning Oct. 1. Revenues were targeted at $443.3 billion, with a resulting deficit of $55.6 billion.

The committee reported that its fiscal targets would provide "budgetary stimulus" of $32.5 billion annually — including a net revenue reduction of $25.9 billion and spending increases of $6.6 billion compared to current policy. The revenue figure included extension of tax cuts approved in 1977 that would expire in 1979.

The committee suggested that those policies would maintain a rate of real growth of gross national product (GNP) at about 4.5 percent in 1979, and that unemployment would fall to about 5.7 percent by the end of the year.

The resulting "moderate and steady growth" would add about 4.75 million jobs to the labor force in 1978 and 1979 without adding significantly to the inflation rate, the panel asserted. It predicted a rise in the consumer price index (CPI) of about 5.9 percent during 1978 and 6.0 percent during 1979.

The resolution provided for an increase of $18 billion in budget authority and $6.3 billion in outlays over the spending that would result if Congress merely continued policies with adjustments for inflation and demographic changes affecting entitlement programs.

That spending level was significantly lower than recommended by Senate committees. The targets were $36.5 billion below levels suggested by authorizing committees and $10.1 billion below the Appropriations Committee request.

The revenue figure, which allowed for a $19.4 billion new reduction in taxes during the fiscal year beginning Oct. 1, was $15 billion less than suggested by the Senate Finance Committee.

The committee rejected proposed cuts in Social Security taxes, but it allowed $.5 billion for a tuition tax credit for full-time undergraduate college students.

The committee marked up its version of the budget resolution April 4-12.

The committee followed a slightly different procedure than the House panel. First, it divided each function into a number of "missions," and each mission into a number of "issues."

The House panel worked from "marks" proposed by its chairman, Rep. Robert N. Giaimo, D-Conn.

By deciding on each issue and adding up the resulting totals, the Senate committee derived mission figures. The functional totals then resulted from adding the mission figures.

The Senate panel also considered, in addition to the fiscal 1979 figures, the five-year implications of various decisions. In some cases, senators agreed on 1979 figures but assumed very different policies in the future.

Tuition Tax Credits

Chairman Edmund S. Muskie, D-Maine, led the fight against tuition tax credits.

"I have no doubt this would be inflationary," Muskie said. He argued that implementation of a tax credit to offset college expenses would prompt colleges to increase their tuition. That in turn, he warned, would merely increase pressure on Congress to boost the size of the credit.

Muskie proposed instead adjusting the budget to allow for a modest increase in the maximum grant allowed under the Basic Educational Opportunity Grant (BEOG) program. The increase, which would have cost only $.2 billion in fiscal 1979, was contained in Carter's original budget request. Since then, the president had called for a major expansion of the program to include more middle-income students.

Critics of the tuition tax credit were joined by Ernest F. Hollings, D-S.C., who argued that it would effectively subsidize white students who enroll in private schools to avoid integration.

"You might as well call it a segregation subsidy," Hollings said.

J. Bennett Johnston, D-La., and Dennis DeConcini, D-Ariz., proposed the tuition tax credit previously endorsed by the Senate Finance Committee. *(Tuition credit, p. 248)*

They were persuaded by Henry Bellmon, R-Okla., to modify the budget figures to limit the credit to full-time college undergraduates. The modified proposal was then approved 8-4.

Later, S. I. Hayakawa, R-Calif., tried to amend the proposal to include elementary and secondary school tuition costs. But since such students wouldn't become eligible for tax credits until Aug. 1, 1980, under the Finance Committee proposal, Hayakawa was convinced that the budget resolution need not address the issue at all.

Social Security

Muskie spoke more successfully against a rollback in Social Security taxes. He opposed using general revenues to finance the Social Security system, arguing that the existing payroll tax system gave people "an added sense of security."

He also argued that shifting to general revenue financing would change Social Security into a "welfare program," undermining public support and driving up costs.

Lawton Chiles, D-Fla., pressed for committee endorsement of a plan to provide general revenue financing of the health and disability insurance components of the Social Security system (S 2503, HR 10754). He argued that approach would stimulate the economy and reduce inflation simultaneously.

Hollings may have tipped the balance against a Social Security tax cut, however, when he said general revenue financing would amount to "funding from the general deficit."

"Everyone says balance the budget, balance the budget," Hollings said. "Last year we balanced one [Social Security]. We ought to balance some others."

Chiles' proposal was defeated 6-8.

The committee next defeated, 5-7, a proposal by Pete V. Domenici, R-N.M., to endorse the Roth-Kemp 30 percent across-the-board reduction in income tax rates. The action came after committee staff economist Van Ooms said the tax cut would be inflationary without a matching

$51 billion reduction in spending over the three-year span of the revenue cut.

Debate Specifics

Defense Spending. Hollings and Domenici led a fight against Muskie for higher defense spending. A compromise that followed a series of inconclusive votes finally produced the budget totals: $129.8 billion in budget authority and $116.6 billion in outlays.

Agriculture. The Senate debate also featured an unusual angry confrontation between Muskie and Robert Dole, R-Kan. Muskie, mad at Dole for sidestepping the Budget Committee with a farm bill, sharply criticized the Kansas senator for complaining about Congressional Budget Office (CBO) estimates of the cost of the bill without offering any estimates of his own.

Dole snapped back that "it happened to be an emergency out there in this country," prompting Muskie to "utterly reject" Dole's protestations that he was more concerned about farmers than Muskie.

Jobs, Urban Programs. A number of senators also expressed concerns that — if not in 1979, soon after — jobs programs should be restructured to focus on structural unemployment. The Senate committee didn't quite allow for all of President Carter's urban initiative, cutting in its reckoning $1.8 billion from the $2.4 billion requested for an urban development bank. The Senate panel also disapproved $.2 billion for a demonstration welfare reform project sought by Carter.

Review

After going through all the budget functions, Muskie proposed a "round two" target that would have shaved an additional $4.7 billion in budget authority and $4 billion in outlays.

"I'm really concerned about inflation, and the importance of sending out a message to the country that the Budget Committees are really concerned," he said.

Domenici and Hollings objected, however, to reductions of $1.5 billion in budget authority and $1 billion in outlays for defense in the chairman's proposal.

Muskie warned that there would be a more substantial defense cut proposed on the floor.

"I want to test this committee on the question of whether or not there's a way of saving more money," Muskie said.

"I'm trying to save the defense of the country," replied Hollings. "You're trying to save $4 billion to get the good government award for fighting inflation."

To that, Muskie shot back: "I am as committed to the defense of the country as you are. I just don't believe the defense of the country needs every penny of the $129.8 billion, and you do."

Chiles proposed approving all of the second round cuts except for the defense reduction, although Hollings said that was politically impossible. The South Carolina senator was right — the committee defeated that motion 2-11.

Hollings then moved to table the second Muskie cuts, winning on an 8-7 vote.

The committee then approved the resolution.

Senate Floor Action

The Senate on April 26 approved S Con Res 80, 64-27, setting spending and revenue targets for fiscal 1979 exactly as recommended by the Budget Committee. *(Vote 140, p. 24-S)*

During three days of debate April 24-26, the lawmakers turned down 11 amendments to the committee's proposals, including efforts both to decrease and increase defense spending; to reduce budget targets for programs operated by the Department of Health, Education and Welfare (HEW); to increase the size of the expected tax cut and to reduce federal spending in a variety of other ways.

Noticeably absent from the three-day debate were any challenges to the committee's recommendations opposing general revenue financing of Social Security benefits and endorsing a tuition tax credit for full-time college students. While both recommendations had substantial opposition in the Senate, Budget Committee foes decided for tactical reasons to wait and fight another day.

Muskie himself predicted that the Budget Committee could well face more serious challenges in the future. Past experience, he said, had given rise to the "spectacle of senators who vote for budget resolutions with apparent intention to violate them later.

"Even more discouraging is the apparent cynicism of those who vote against budget resolutions as being too extravagant and then vote for bills which exceed them," he continued.

Muskie defended the committee's actions in a lengthy speech beginning debate on the resolution April 24.

"Notwithstanding these reductions, Mr. President, this budget is not unduly restrictive," he said. "It . . . allows for major new initiatives in fiscal year 1979 in the areas of energy, urban initiatives, the national defense and agriculture."

National Defense. Muskie said the Budget Committee had acknowledged growing concern about "the steady strategic and tactical arms buildup by the Soviet Union," and that it had accordingly voted for real growth in the defense budget. He said it had decided to increase President Carter's defense spending request by $1.4 billion in budget authority because it was concerned about the vulnerability of U.S. intercontinental ballistic missiles (ICBMs) to Soviet attack and because it felt production of the Trident submarine should be accelerated.

Muskie also said the committee endorsed President Carter's pledge to increase the U.S. commitment to the North Atlantic Treaty Organization (NATO).

To hold down costs, Muskie noted that the committee proposed a 5 percent "pay cap" on anticipated federal pay raises in October, and that it expected federal agencies to "absorb" 20 percent of the raise with existing funds.

Human Resources. The chairman said the budget resolution would allow "substantial" funding increases for elementary and secondary education; improvements in provision of health care and nutritional services for low-income pregnant women and young children; improvements in veterans' income security and medical care programs; improvements in health care services and research; and increases in social services grants to the needy.

While acknowledging support for public service employment, Muskie noted that the committee believed the federal government should shift the emphasis of its jobs programs to curing structural unemployment.

Muskie noted further that the committee favored full funding for youth employment initiatives as well as proposals by the president to move workers from Comprehensive Employment and Training Act (CETA) jobs to private sector jobs. He also said the resolution envisioned increases for the work incentive program (WIN). *(CETA, p. 287)*

The chairman said the committee expected welfare reform, including an expansion of the earned income tax credit. But he said the committee would oppose providing fiscal relief to state and local governments in advance of an overall welfare reform plan.

Physical Resources. Muskie said the Budget Committee envisioned continuing major increases for energy supply research and development and for strategic petroleum reserves. He said it also recommended "moderate increases" for natural resources and environment programs, and "major" increases for farm income support programs.

Challenges

Only one of the 11 challenges to the Budget Committee's recommendations came even close to winning approval by the full Senate.

National Defense. George McGovern, D-S.D., and Thomas F. Eagleton, D-Mo., both proposed cutting spending targets for national defense. Later, John G. Tower, R-Texas, recommended an increase.

McGovern, warning that the country was falling into the grip of a "new orthodoxy" concerning defense, proposed reducing national defense spending targets by $4.6 billion in budget authority and $1.5 billion in outlays. That money would be transferred to programs to develop alternate sources of energy, to improve the nation's railroad system, to help regions losing military facilities convert to civilian economies and to provide tuition aid for students.

"We rarely ask the more fundamental questions, whether our defense truly requires real growth in overall expansion of the budget, whether there are less costly alternatives that would buy us just as much in the way of national security, or whether substantial reductions in arms spending can, in fact, enhance our national safety, which I happen to believe," McGovern said.

His amendment was defeated 14-77. A more modest cut in defense proposed by Eagleton — $1.4 billion in budget authority and $.9 billion in outlays — was rejected by a 21-70 vote. *(Votes 130, 131, p. 23-S)*

Eagleton said the cuts could be made without affecting national security at all. He suggested that President Carter had violated a campaign promise to cut defense spending, and he said the Budget Committee had compounded the sin by increasing Carter's recommendations.

Tower argued for an increase in national defense budget authority of $1.6 billion and outlays of $1.2 billion on the grounds that NATO long-term defense planning task forces indicated the need for additional spending to modernize forces in Europe.

He proposed paying for the hike in defense spending by decreasing foreign economic assistance, public assistance and consumer and occupational health and safety programs.

But the amendment ran into trouble when Armed Services Committee Chairman John C. Stennis, D-Miss., praised the Budget Committee recommendation and said there would be time to adjust defense spending totals before the second, and binding, budget resolution in September if necessary.

Tower's amendment was defeated 21-74. *(Vote 138, p. 24-S)*

Human Resources Programs. Harry F. Byrd Jr., Ind-Va., proposed reducing budget authority and outlays in programs run by the Department of Health, Education and Welfare by $5.6 billion.

He said the cut could easily be absorbed since an HEW inspector general's report issued April 3 concluded that the department had misspent between $6.3 billion and $7.4 billion in 1977 due to "waste, mismanagement and fraud."

Muskie argued that the cuts would cause suffering by innocent people since the source of the problems cited in the report couldn't be immediately ferreted out.

The amendment was defeated, 28-48. Later, Byrd returned with a more modest proposal to cut HEW programs by $2.1 billion. It was rejected 38-57. *(Votes 129, 137, pp. 23-S, 24-S)*

Taxes. William V. Roth Jr., R-Del., proposed decreasing the Budget Committee's revenue target by $4.9 billion. That, he said, would approximately accommodate a $25 billion net tax cut beginning on Oct. 1. The Budget Committee had endorsed the concept of a $25 billion cut, but it predicted that the reduction wouldn't take effect until Jan. 1. As a result, the impact in the fiscal year beginning Oct. 1 would be to reduce revenues by only $19.4 billion.

Muskie argued that Roth's proposal would increase the deficit in the coming fiscal year to $60.5 billion — a level he said would be inflationary.

He argued further that the proposal would lead to higher deficits in future years.

The Roth amendment was defeated 22-65. *(Vote 135, p. 23-S)*

Spending Cuts. The Senate considered several amendments to reduce the overall level of spending. William Proxmire, D-Wis., first proposed a $26.1 billion — or roughly 5 percent — cut in budget authority. He described the proposal as an attempt to get Congress to issue "a loud, clear anti-inflation signal" to the country.

Muskie denounced the proposed cut as "arbitrary and indiscriminate." The amendment was defeated 33-57. *(Vote 132, p. 23-S)*

Later, Proxmire proposed a $5 billion cut in budget authority, which Muskie also opposed. In the closest vote on any amendment to the budget resolution, the chairman was upheld, 43-46. *(Vote 134, p. 23-S)*

One other attempt to reduce spending was made by Pete V. Domenici, R-N.M. He suggested a series of cuts totaling $2.2 billion in budget authority and $2.1 billion in outlays. The amendment was defeated, 36-59. *(Vote 136, p. 24-S)*

Also rejected by the Senate were proposals:

- By Carl T. Curtis, R-Neb., to recommit the resolution to the Budget Committee with instructions that the committee prepare a balanced budget, defeated 19-72. *(Vote 133, p. 23-S)*
- By Byrd, Va., to cut $750 million from international affairs spending for international financial institutions, defeated 37-53. *(Vote 139, p. 24-S)*

Unresolved Issues

Two of the most controversial items in the budget resolution — tuition tax credits and the absence of a provision allowing general revenue financing of Social Security benefits — were never directly confronted during Senate action.

Tuition Aid. Critics of the tuition tax credit, setting much of their hopes on a promised presidential veto, were afraid to risk a head-on confrontation in the Senate, where 62 senators had endorsed the concept.

They also were reluctant to press the Senate to endorse the main alternative to tuition tax credits — a proposed expansion of existing student grant and loan programs (S 2539) — because of some questions that had been raised in the Appropriations Committee about technical aspects of the alternative legislation.

In a colloquy on the Senate floor, Claiborne Pell, D-R.I., the prime sponsor of the alternative bill, won a concession from Muskie that the budget resolution didn't absolutely preclude the alternative.

"Whatever happens at the end of the legislative line, whether or not education tax credits or the president's proposal are finally approved by Congress, it seems to me that, in the broad sense, there is room in the budget for some form of college tuition assistance for middle income families," Muskie said.

Appropriations Committee Chairman Warren G. Magnuson, D-Wash., added that his committee wouldn't include money for the alternative program in the regular appropriations bill, but that it might put it in a supplemental. Without committing himself on the issue, he said money for the alternative program shouldn't be included in the budget resolution.

Social Security. The question of Social Security financing wasn't even discussed on the floor. The main Senate sponsor of a general revenue financing proposal, Gaylord Nelson, D-Wis., explained that Finance Committee Chairman Russell B. Long, D-La., had told him that the budget resolution wouldn't preclude the possibility of a general revenue proposal being considered later.

Fiscal Relief. Daniel Patrick Moynihan, D-N.Y., sought assurances from the Budget Committee that its opposition to fiscal relief for state and local governments could be softened before action on the second budget resolution. Moynihan, chairman of the Public Assistance Subcommittee of the Senate Finance Committee, said he hoped Congress could enact a welfare reform plan in 1978, including provisions to relieve state and local governments of part of their welfare cost burdens.

Henry Bellmon, R-Okla., the ranking Republican on the Budget Committee, replied that the committee hadn't envisioned fiscal relief in drawing up the resolution, but he said the Finance Committee could still provide for it by cutting other programs in its jurisdiction.

House Committee Report

The House Budget Committee reported its version of the resolution (H Con Res 559 — H Rept 95-1055) April 14.

As reported, it called for total new budget authority of $568.2 billion and outlays of $501.4 billion. Revenues were targeted at $443.3 billion, and the resulting deficit was $58.1 billion.

However, those figures were revised on the House floor May 3 with adoption of a committee-approved amendment reducing the outlay target by $1.7 billion because of new estimates of the likely cost of agricultural price support programs.

The committee reported that the proposed spending and tax levels would result in real economic growth of 4.4 percent during 1979, with a resulting unemployment rate of 5.8 percent by the end of the year. It predicted 6 percent inflation would continue through the year.

Those economic assumptions were slightly more optimistic than the ones contained in the Senate-approved budget resolution (S Con Res 80) concerning economic growth and unemployment, but a bit more pessimistic concerning inflation.

The House committee agreed to a $7.5 billion cut in Social Security taxes, along with an additional reduction of $10.7 billion in individual taxes, but it rejected the tuition tax credit.

The House panel completed markup of the resolution in three days, April 4-6, approving in large part figures proposed by Chairman Robert N. Giaimo, D-Conn.

Revenues

Noting that his proposal would increase spending over the level proposed by President Carter, and warning about the dangers of renewed inflation, Giaimo argued that the tax cut in the coming year would have to be smaller than recommended by Carter.

The first showdown came on the question of Social Security financing. The committee defeated a Republican bid for a smaller Social Security tax cut than proposed by Giaimo, and it then approved the chairman's $7.5 billion reduction.

While Republicans sought a smaller payroll tax cut, they favored a larger overall reduction in revenues. Barber B. Conable Jr., R-N.Y., proposed a total cut of $38.7 billion — $10 billion more than the chairman recommended.

Conable's proposal included $25 billion in individual and corporate cuts, $3.2 billion in Social Security reductions, $1 billion for a tuition tax credit and $.5 billion in miscellaneous cuts, along with continuation of $9 billion in 1977 tax reductions.

The committee rejected Conable's Social Security proposal, and it later defeated his revenue figures.

Spending

After approving a revenue total, the committee proceeded to consider spending totals for each budget function.

Some committee Republicans, including Ralph S. Regula, R-Ohio, demurred at that approach, arguing that the panel should make at least a tentative vote on overall budget totals before turning to the specifics.

"I don't want to be caught even tentatively voting for a $57 billion deficit," replied Delbert L. Latta, R-Ohio.

Giaimo's specific recommendations were subject to a number of minor amendments, but no serious overall assault. In general, he proposed major spending increases over the president's budget in agriculture, commerce and housing credit, education, employment social service programs, veterans' benefits and transportation.

Major reductions proposed by the chairman from the president's proposals were in defense and interest costs. Both reflected re-estimates of the actual cost of continuing programs, rather than policy differences with the president.

Marjorie S. Holt, R-Md., attempted to substitute for Giaimo's program-by-program approach a plan that she said would allow inflation adjustments in all federal programs, but no new policies. Continuing current services only, she said, would result in budget authority totaling $545 billion and outlays totaling $488 billion — a reduction in the president's budget that would justify his proposed $25 billion tax cut.

The Holt idea was tabled on a 15-8 vote, and when she offered parts of her plan later, they were defeated.

Debate Specifics

Defense Policy. Parren J. Mitchell, R-Md., leader of the Congressional Black Caucus, said he would lead a floor fight to cut defense spending in order to increase human services programs.

Education. Giaimo convinced the committee to include in its reckoning money sufficient to pay for a major extension of student aid and loan programs to middle-income families. The sum allowed would finance the education aid program approved by the Human Resources Committee as an alternative to tuition tax credits.

Jobs Programs. A number of Republicans, led by Conable, were sharply critical of public service employment programs. Conable complained that the programs had become little more than "revenue sharing" for cities, and he warned that many cities were in danger of becoming "wards of the federal government through the back door."

While some proposed cuts in the programs, others — including James D. Mattox, D-Texas — suggested shifting funds away from public service employment programs to training programs. Mattox, whose proposals were defeated, argued that public service jobs too often go to well-trained, well-educated people rather than the "structurally unemployed" who need help.

Despite those complaints, the only major spending change in Giaimo's recommendations that was approved by the committee added $2.5 billion in budget authority and $.3 billion in outlays for "accelerated public works." That proposal, pushed by Majority Leader Jim Wright, D-Texas, was defeated April 5 on an 11-12 vote, but then approved, 15-9, the following day.

Review

When the committee reviewed the end result of its deliberations some members were dissatisfied. A series of proposals were thus made to reduce the spending totals.

The most serious such proposal was offered by Joseph L. Fisher, D-Va. It would have cut controllable budget functions by 2 percent across the board, resulting in a net decrease of $10 billion in outlays and $11.4 billion in budget authority. Fisher proposed using half of the saved money for a tax cut and the other half to reduce the deficit.

Giaimo objected, but he said Fisher's proposal should be kept as ammunition for a floor fight.

"When we go to the floor, we know there are going to be massive pressures to increase this budget," the chairman said, citing especially veterans' programs, agriculture, defense and the tuition tax credit. He suggested holding the Fisher amendment to be used against those who try to increase spending.

Some Republicans argued that the Fisher amendment underscored a flaw in the committee's basic approach.

"Until we're willing to deal with aggregates initially, we're condemned to a meat-axe approach when we're done," said Clair W. Burgener, R-Calif. "Our procedure is wrong. It's merely an adding machine committee."

Robert L. Leggett, D-Calif., agreed. "All we're doing is scorekeeping," he said. "And we're scorekeeping disaster."

The Fisher motion was defeated 11-12, and the committee approved the resolution.

House Floor Action

After five days of contentious debate, the House on May 10 approved, by a four-vote margin, spending and revenue targets for fiscal 1979 that were similar in aggregate totals to the previously approved Senate goals.

As passed by the House, H Con Res 559 called for budget authority totaling $569.5 billion, outlays of $500.9 billion, revenues of $443 billion and a resulting deficit of $57.9 billion. The measure was adopted by a 201-197 vote. *(Vote 255, p. 72-H)*

The House totals were higher than the Senate figures for outlays and budget authority, and slightly lower for revenues. Following passage of H Con Res 559, the House substituted its text for that of the version approved by the Senate April 26 (S Con Res 80).

While the Senate Budget Committee was able to keep its version of the resolution intact during floor action in that chamber, the House committee encountered considerably more resistance from the outset.

Fiscal Policy

The first challenge, led by House Republicans, was aimed at the aggregate targets proposed by the committee. The Republicans criticized the size of the proposed deficit, and they argued that the resolution should sharply reduce spending targets while allowing for a larger tax cut.

Marjorie S. Holt, R-Md., proposed reducing the budget authority target by $21.4 billion to $546.8 billion and outlays by $13.1 billion to $488.3 billion. Revenues, under her amendment, would be reduced by $3.2 billion to $440.1 billion, resulting in a deficit of $48.2 billion, or $9.9 billion below the level contained in the resolution as reported.

Republicans said the Holt amendment was part of a five-year plan to reduce spending and taxes. While criticizing the spending and tax proposals contained in the committee's resolution, their critique went further, embracing the entire approach to budget-writing followed by the committee.

"To the Democrats in Congress, budgeting requires only an adding machine without a subtract button," said Minority Leader John J. Rhodes, R-Ariz. "Nowhere in the Democrat-engineered budget process does a fiscal policy appear. Instead, they first vote *seriatim* on how much they would like to spend in all major governmental programs; they then add up this wish list and take the resulting total and call that the appropriate level of federal spending.

"By working backward like this, the Democrats deny Congress the right to establish a fiscal policy," Rhodes continued. "This year, however, we are refusing to play the game according to their rules."

Holt said her amendment would allow for an 8 percent growth in federal spending — enough to keep programs in pace with inflation without providing real growth. The committee's budget, she said, would increase federal spending by 11 percent.

"I feel we have got to do something to stop high inflation and the rising tax burden on the people," she said.

The amendment was opposed by a number of Democrats who said it would eliminate needed spending programs. It was also criticized by Budget Committee Chairman Robert N. Giaimo, D-Conn., who called it a "good-sounding, wish-type amendment" inconsistent with the spending desires of Congress.

Only one Republican defected from party ranks to vote against the Holt amendment. The nearly-solid Republicans were joined by 58 Democrats in a razor thin 197-203 vote defeating the amendment. *(Vote 230, p. 66-H)*

Taxes. Later, Barber B. Conable Jr., R-N.Y., tried to resurrect the revenue portion of the Holt amendment by proposing an amendment to set revenues at $440.1 billion.

While only $3.2 billion below the revenue total in the committee's proposed resolution, Conable said his figure would allow for a tax cut $10.3 billion larger than the $19.4 billion endorsed by the committee.

Conable explained that his figure was based on an assumption that the annual inflation rate in 1979 would be 7 percent, as opposed to the 6 percent assumed by the committee. As a result, many taxpayers would find themselves pushed higher up the income scale and would thus be forced to pay more taxes, he argued.

Some Democrats criticized the amendment on the grounds that it would increase the federal deficit. Charles A. Vanik, D-Ohio, an advocate in the House Ways and Means Committee of a proposal to allow no new tax reductions in 1979, said that he had "come to believe the Republican assertion that deficits breed inflation."

Republicans Jack F. Kemp, R-N.Y., John H. Rousselot, R-Calif., and Conable all argued that the proposed tax cut probably wouldn't add to the deficit because it would stimulate the economy so much that incomes would rise, pushing tax revenues up with them.

Ironically, the Republicans justified their tax proposals by citing large across-the-board tax cuts proposed by the Democratic administrations of John F. Kennedy and Lyndon B. Johnson.

The 163-239 House vote defeating the Conable proposal was basically party-line, with only 27 Democrats joining the 136 Republicans in support of it, while 236 Democrats and three Republicans opposed it. *(Vote 233, p. 66-H)*

Defense

The House debated for several hours two proposals concerning defense. Parren J. Mitchell, D-Md., sought to reduce defense spending by $4.8 billion in budget authority and $2.8 billion in outlays, and to "transfer" that money to a variety of economic stimulus, jobs and human services programs. His amendment failed 98-313. *(Vote 232, p. 66-H)*

Before that vote, the House turned back a proposal by Samuel S. Stratton, D-N.Y., to increase defense budget authority by $2.4 billion. That would have brought the House in line with the Senate on defense budget authority, while leaving it about $1 billion less in outlays.

The Stratton amendment was soundly defeated, 142-262. *(Vote 231, p. 66-H)*

During the House debate, Stratton and his supporters contrasted the growing Soviet military establishment with moves by President Carter to cancel or slow down several U.S. weapons programs including the B-1 bomber, the M-X missile and various naval vessels.

Stratton said later that Republicans were voting as a bloc against all increases because of the size of the deficit. So the vote really did not reflect opposition to higher spending for defense.

A general assumption that the Navy's shipbuilding program was beset by management problems also contributed to the amendment's defeat, according to some sources. Many members assumed that most of the increase would go to accommodate two nuclear-powered warships costing about $3.2 billion that were added to the president's budget by the Armed Services Committee.

Veterans. Veterans' Affairs Committee Chairman Ray Roberts, D-Texas, managed to increase the Budget Committee's recommendations for veterans' programs by $1.1 billion in budget authority and $844 million in outlays.

Roberts said the increases were needed to accommodate veterans' pension reform (HR 10173), provide cost-of-living benefit increases for disabled veterans and prevent administration plans to eliminate what it considered unneeded beds in veterans' hospitals.

Giaimo vehemently opposed the amendment, arguing that the veterans' affairs budget "is being used for general social welfare purposes rather than chiefly for service-disabled veterans." He said the social welfare purposes could better be achieved through general welfare programs.

After rejecting by a standing vote a proposal by David F. Emery, R-Maine, to pay for the veterans' increase with money from several "welfare" programs, the House approved Roberts' amendment 362-33. *(Vote 234, p. 66-H)*

Tuition Tax Credits

Probably the most embarrassing defeat for Giaimo came when the House approved a motion by Thomas A. Luken, D-Ohio, to reduce revenues by $635 million to allow for a tuition tax credit to offset costs of elementary and secondary schools and college education. Luken said that sum would allow a credit for 25 percent of school costs up to $100 for elementary and secondary school students and $150 for college students.

Giaimo, firmly opposed to tuition tax credits, won Budget Committee support to include in the resolution money for the alternative approach to tuition aid — an increase in spending on traditional student grant and loan programs. He also had included in the committee report several strong statements opposing tuition tax credits.

The committee report prompted credit advocates, who claimed they numbered 262 in the House, to press for an amendment specifically endorsing the concept.

Giaimo sought to prevent that. He argued that the committee's revenue figures would allow for a credit, and that it would be wrong to approve an amendment since it would force a decrease in the revenue aggregate, and thus the deficit.

The chairman conceded that "events" — especially Ways and Means Committee approval of tuition tax credit legislation — had "superseded" the Budget Committee's opposition to the tax credits.

But even that assurance was insufficient to stop tax credit supporters from forcing a vote on the issue. The House first voted 199-173 to favor a tax credit that would include elementary and secondary students as well as college students. It then approved the broad tax credit by a 227-136 vote. *(Votes 240, 241, p. 68-H)*

The Senate had approved the concept of a credit just for college education costs.

Federal Pay, Job Training

The House on May 3:

- Rejected 172-210 an amendment by James A. Mattox, D-Texas, to reduce budget authority and outlays by $255 million so as to allow a pay raise for federal workers of only 5.5 percent. *(Vote 236, p. 68-H)*
- Rejected 123-265 an amendment by Donald M. Fraser, D-Minn., to increase budget authority by $435 million and outlays by $390 million in order to provide for increased job training programs for youths and older Americans. *(Vote 235, p. 68-H)*

Attack on Spending

Voicing concerns that the size of the deficit anticipated in the Budget Committee's proposed resolution would be inflationary, House members voted May 9-10 on a series of amendments to cut spending.

The most serious proposals included one by John M. Ashbrook, R-Ohio, to reduce budget authority and outlays for programs run by the Department of Health, Education and Welfare (HEW) by $3.15 billion; and one by Joseph L. Fisher, D-Va., to reduce budget authority by an additional $8 billion and outlays by $7 billion across the board.

Ashbrook said his proposal was prompted by a recent report that HEW misspent between $6.3 billion and $7.4 billion in 1977 due to "waste, fraud and mismanagement."

A similar attack on HEW spending had been launched in the Senate by Harry F. Byrd Jr., Ind-Va., without success, but Ashbrook won a surprising 198-189 vote supporting his proposal on May 9. Giaimo and the House leadership engineered a second vote that killed the amendment the next day, however, 192-205. *(Votes 246, 254; pp. 70-H, 72-H)*

Fisher, who had nearly won Budget Committee support for an across-the-board spending cut, said his proposal was designed to "send a clear and unmistakable signal through the Congress and the country that we mean to cut outlays and the deficit."

He appeared to have won when the 15-minute voting period expired, but a strenuous 10-minute effort by House Speaker Thomas P. O'Neill Jr., D-Mass., Majority Leader Jim Wright, D-Texas, and Majority Whip John Brademas, D-Ind., managed to produce enough vote changes to convert what had appeared to be a 10- or 12-vote victory margin into a 195-203 defeat for the Fisher proposal. *(Vote 248, p. 70-H)*

Other attempts to reduce spending included amendments:

- By Harold L. Volkmer, D-Mo., to reduce budget authority by $5.4 billion and outlays by $2.8 billion, representing a 2 percent cut in "controllable" budget items. The amendment was defeated on a voice vote.
- By Delbert L. Latta, R-Ohio, for a 5 percent reduction in spending. Latta said the spending cut would save $1.5 billion in interest on the national debt. His amendment was rejected on a voice vote.
- By Robert "Bob" Krueger, D-Texas, to reduce spending by $7 billion, applying the cuts to all budget areas except defense, agriculture and veterans' programs. Krueger had tried the previous day to exempt defense from the proposed Fisher spending cuts. Both of his proposals were rejected on voice votes.
- By Andy Jacobs Jr., R-Ind., calling for a balanced budget and no new tax reduction. Jacobs' amendment would have allowed extension of expiring tax cuts totaling $9 billion through the new fiscal year. It was defeated 45-352. *(Vote 252, p. 72-H)*
- By John H. Rousselot, R-Calif., to balance the budget while allowing for a $30 billion tax cut. It was rejected, 170-226. *(Vote 253, p. 72-H)*

'Sending a Signal'

House members also proposed a number of amendments designed to express their view on a variety of public issues. Those proposals, which eventually were dubbed "cheap shots" by John L. Burton, D-Calif., included:

Panama. George Hansen, R-Idaho, offered an amendment to adjust revenues and spending by the amount they would change if tolls from the Panama Canal were collected by the Treasury. Currently, the tolls were collected and spent by the Panama Canal Co., although the Treasury handled them prior to 1950.

Hansen said his amendment was designed to assert the right of the House to decide on the disposition of the canal. He said the vote was a test of a resolution (H Con Res 347) asserting that no titled U.S. property can be transferred without an act of Congress. *(Panama Canal treaty, p. 379)*

Despite an impassioned speech by Wright asserting that the amendment would "throw a monkeywrench in international machinery," it was approved, 231-170. *(Vote 247, p. 70-H)*

Congressional Salaries. Larry Pressler, D-S.D., proposed to reduce spending by $675,000 — the amount of a 2 percent cut in congressional salaries. His amendment was defeated on a voice vote.

Regulatory Agencies. Garry Brown, R-Mich., sought to cut spending targets by $195.4 million in outlays and $178.2 million in budget authority to reflect reductions in various regulatory agencies, which Brown called "inflationary." The amendment was rejected on a 196-196 tie. *(Vote 249, p. 70-H)*

South Korea. Bruce F. Caputo, R-N.Y., proposed to cut spending by $56 million. Caputo said the cut should be applied to Food for Peace (PL 480) aid to South Korea in order to express congressional disapproval of the fact that the former ambassador, Kim Dong Jo, had refused to cooperate with special investigator Leon Jaworski. The amendment was defeated, 146-254. *(Vote 251, p. 72-H)*

Conference Action

The budget compromise drafted by a Senate-House conference committee May 11, 12 and 15 (S Rept 95-866) won strong bipartisan support in the Senate, even though the revenue figure allowed for a tax cut significantly smaller than recommended by either the Finance or Budget Committees. In part, that reflected a growing consensus that, in view of falling unemployment and accelerating inflation, the economy shouldn't be stimulated as much as many policy makers believed a few months earlier.

"Inflation has increased and unemployment has fallen more than expected," noted Budget Committee Chairmen Sen. Edmund S. Muskie, D-Maine, and Rep. Robert N. Giaimo, D-Conn., in announcing the compromise with the White House on taxes. "Monetary policy has become more restrictive, and interest rates have risen, in response to the fears of higher inflation and weakness of the dollar.

"This reduced deficit will signal Congress' determination to maintain fiscal discipline, reduce inflationary pressures, ease the pressures on capital markets, and maintain the integrity of the American dollar as a reserve asset."

The scaled back tax proposal was immediately hailed by Federal Reserve Board Chairman G. William Miller, who had been calling for just such a shift.

Miller said the decision was "very properly made," and he suggested that it might enable the Federal Reserve Board to ease up on interest rates, which had risen about a half percentage point since Miller took office in March.

"The more discipline we have in fiscal policy, the more pressure we take off monetary policy," Miller said.

House Republican Opposition

The plan didn't draw such a favorable response from House Republicans. House Minority Leader John J. Rhodes, R-Ariz., described the conference committee's budget as "completely inadequate" and "inflationary."

During floor debate May 17, Rhodes and other Republicans complained that the conference committee had reduced the deficit almost entirely by cutting the size of the expected tax cut, rather than by limiting federal spending.

They argued that the smaller tax cut would be inadequate to offset the increase in tax burden resulting from inflation and rising Social Security taxes. Rhodes said inflation would increase taxes $14 billion by pushing taxpayers into higher tax brackets. He said Social Security taxes would rise another $9 billion.

"If you vote for this conference report, you're voting for a tax increase on the American people, and for a $51 billion deficit," Rhodes said.

Defense and Education

The compromise tax proposal cleared the conference committee with relative ease, but the panel was tied up for three days in a debate over spending for defense and a variety of human services programs.

The Senate had proposed a budget authority figure for defense $2.4 billion higher than the House figure. At the same time, the House had set budget authority for education, training, employment and social service programs $2.5 billion higher than the Senate's number.

The two issues became linked during conference committee negotiations in what one budget expert described as an essentially "symbolic and political" exercise.

"There is no way you can fine tune the budgets for those programs the way they [the conferees] did," he said. "They were fighting a symbolic battle over guns versus butter."

After numerous caucuses in which Giaimo tried to gain a consensus among House conferees, the conference agreed to a compromise whereby the Senate reduced its defense figure by $1.1 billion and the House increased its by $1.3 billion; and the Senate increased its social services figure by $1.4 billion in return for a House reduction of $1.1 billion.

That compromise didn't satisfy some House liberals, including conferees Parren J. Mitchell, D-Md., Elizabeth Holtzman, D-N.Y., and David R. Obey, D-Wis. Their opposition to the compromise caused concern that the resolution would be defeated by a coalition of Republicans upset by the smaller tax cut and liberals opposed to the defense increase, but Giaimo managed to hold a slight majority during the final House vote May 17.

Other Tax Compromises

The conferees got past two other potential tax disputes by being deliberately ambiguous. Where the Senate had specifically rejected a Social Security tax rollback and the House had proposed one, the conference committee decided to remain silent on the issue.

On the question of middle class tuition assistance, the conference committee was ambiguous, though not silent. The Senate had endorsed the concept of a tuition tax credit for college students, while the House had included money in the budget for both an expanded student grant and loan program and a tuition tax credit for college and elementary and secondary students.

The conference committee agreed to include half the cost of the grant and loan program ($700 million) and half the cost of the tax credit approved by the House ($300 million).

That, conferees said, would leave room in the budget for whichever approach Congress ultimately approved. Some tax credit advocates weren't happy with the compromise, though. Rep. R. Lawrence Coughlin, R-Pa., called it a "travesty."

The conference agreement also left room in the budget for the following policies:

- A 5.5 percent limitation on federal pay increases for civilian and military personnel, as recommended by President Carter as part of his anti-inflation program.
- Funds sufficient for President Carter's urban initiatives with the exception of $2.4 billion he sought for an urban development bank.
- $1 billion of the House's proposed $2 billion for a new "accelerated public works" program.
- Funds sufficient to accommodate veterans' pension reform, cost-of-living increases and other expansion of veterans' programs.
- $400 million for fiscal relief to states and localities for welfare costs.

Binding Budget Levels

Congress Sept. 23 gave final approval to legislation (H Con Res 683) setting a $487.5 billion spending ceiling for fiscal 1979.

Final action came when the Senate approved the conference version of the resolution by a 47-7 vote. The House had approved the resolution Sept. 21, 225-162. *(Senate vote 393, p. 59-S; House vote 716, p. 204-H)*

The final version of the resolution cut spending more than $11 billion below the level tentatively set in the first resolution in May.

At the same time, it allowed for a tax cut at least $2 billion larger than the $16.3 billion reduction approved by the House in August. The resulting deficit would be $12 billion lower than envisioned in May.

Budget totals, compared to previous figures, were as follows *(in billions of dollars):*

	Budget Authority	Outlays	Revenues	Deficit
First budget resolution	$568.85	$498.8	$447.9	$50.9
Administration July re-estimates	$571.4	$496.6	$448.2	$48.5
House	$561.0	$489.8	$450.0	$39.8
Senate	$557.7	$489.5	$447.2	$42.3
Conference	$555.65	$487.5	$448.7	$38.8

The resolution also called for a public debt limit of $836 billion and set non-binding budget authority and outlay levels for the 19 functional areas of the budget.

House Committee Report

The House Budget Committee reported H Con Res 683 Aug. 8 (H Rept 95-1456).

The committee, armed with the latest projections of the costs of various government programs, approved a spending total for fiscal year 1979 more than $8 billion lower than the target adopted in the May resolution.

The new spending total was included in the committee's proposed second budget resolution, which was approved by the House panel on Aug. 3 by a 15-10 vote.

Budget totals in the committee resolution were: budget authority, $561.5 billion; outlays, $490.5 billion; revenues, $446.8 billion; deficit, $43.7 billion.

Of the projected spending reduction, more than $6 billion reflected downward re-estimates of the costs of various government programs, including defense procurement (down $2.4 billion), Medicare and Medicaid (down $700 million), unemployment compensation (down $700 million) and others.

The second resolution figures approved by the committee did incorporate about $3 billion in spending cuts, already passed by the House, below the first resolution targets. But they also included more than $1 billion in higher spending resulting from House failure to enact some previously expected savings — most notably, hospital cost controls.

The committee's revenue figure would allow a $19.4 billion tax cut beginning Jan. 1. Its impact during the fiscal year which was to begin Oct. 1, would be to reduce revenues by $14 billion.

Before approving the resolution, the Budget Committee rejected several attempts to enact additional spending cuts and a larger tax reduction.

The closest challenge, rejected 12-13, was sponsored by committee Republicans Delbert L. Latta, R-Ohio, Marjorie S. Holt, R-Md., and Barber B. Conable Jr., R-N.Y. It would have set the following budget aggregates: budget authority, $539 billion; outlays, $480 billion; revenues, $445 billion; and deficit, $35 billion.

Conable said that, based on the assumption that inflation would be 8 percent in 1978 and 7.2 percent in 1979, the Republican alternative would allow an annual tax cut of $28 billion with a fiscal year impact of $20 billion. The committee's revenue figure assumed inflation of only 6.9 percent in 1978 and 6.7 percent in 1979.

The committee also rejected, 6-19, a proposal by Joseph L. Fisher, D-Va., to cut spending $5 billion below the committee-approved figures. A proposal by Ralph S. Regula, R-Ohio, to cut $300 billion from countercyclical revenue sharing was rejected, 12-13; and an amendment by Elizabeth Holtzman, D-N.Y., to cut about $410 million from national defense spending was rejected, 10-15.

House Floor Action

The House on Aug. 16 turned back a series of major budget cut proposals — but it approved a relatively modest reduction in spending on public service jobs and fiscal aid to states and cities — as it adopted H Con Res 683, setting binding spending and tax figures for the fiscal year beginning Oct. 1.

By a relatively comfortable 217-178 margin, the lawmakers ended 11 hours of debate by approving the following fiscal 1979 budget aggregates: budget authority, $561 billion; outlays, $489.8 billion; revenues, $450 billion; deficit, $39.8 billion. *(Vote 628, p. 178-H)*

The final figures differed only slightly from the recommendations made Aug. 3 by the Budget Committee.

Only one amendment was approved against the will of the committee. Sponsored by Jim Mattox, D-Texas, it reduced spending totals by $223 billion in budget authority and $673 billion in outlays to reflect House-approved cuts in the Comprehensive Employment and Training Act (CETA), and Senate committee cuts in anti-recession aid to states and cities.

The Mattox amendment was approved, 271-134. *(Vote 623, p. 176-H)*

Budget Committee Chairman Robert N. Giaimo, D-Conn., said the second resolution demonstrated that congressional budget-writers had made "remarkable progress" since the beginning of the year.

The second resolution would limit spending to $9 billion less than the level envisioned by the first resolution. Giaimo estimated that $5.5 billion of the difference reflected lower estimates of the costs of various programs, while about $2.5 billion reflected congressional decisions to reduce expected spending.

"Adoption of this resolution will demonstrate that we can manage the taxpayers' dollars with prudence and discipline, and it will move us solidly along the road toward a balanced budget in the 1980s," Giaimo said.

The Budget Committee chairman predicted that the spending and tax policies established in the resolution would produce modest reductions in unemployment and inflation. He said joblessness would fall to 5.7 percent by the end of 1979, from a projected 5.9 percent at the end of 1978. The inflation rate, he said, would drop to 6.7 percent from 6.9 percent.

Republican Challenge

The Budget Committee recommendation survived by only five votes, 201-206, a Republican challenge led by Marjorie S. Holt, R-Md. Republicans proposed spending almost $10 billion less than the committee figure and leaving room for a larger tax cut as well.

The Republican "alternative" would establish the following budget totals: budget authority, $539 billion; outlays, $480 billion; revenues, $445 billion; and deficit, $35 billion.

Holt said those figures would allow a 7 percent increase in outlays, as opposed to a 10 percent hike envisioned by the committee recommendation. That, she argued, would be enough to maintain current government services even with inflation.

She also argued that the revenue figure would allow for a $28 billion tax cut beginning in 1979, as opposed to the $16.3 billion approved by the House on Aug. 10 and assumed in the committee proposal.

"If the president or Congress want new programs, then it is incumbent on them to find the money by cutting waste and eliminating outdated, ineffective programs," she said.

Democrats scoffed at the claim that a tax cut $12 billion larger than the committee proposal would result in a net loss of only $5 billion more in revenues. The Republicans replied that the Democratic revenue figure was understated because it assumed an unrealistically low level of inflation. In addition, they said, the larger tax cut would encourage economic growth, which would help bring in more revenues.

Giaimo and other Democrats challenged that economic assumption, and they warned that the $10 billion spending cut would force the Appropriations Committees to reconsider various spending bills — a process they warned could keep Congress in session "until Christmas."

Other Amendments

After the Holt proposal was rejected, Delbert L. Latta, R-Ohio, attempted to "compromise" by offering an amendment keeping the Holt budget authority and outlay figures but using the committee's higher revenue total.

That, however, split some Republicans from the party position. Barber B. Conable Jr., R-N.Y., warned that the higher revenue figure might discourage the Senate from increasing the size of the House-passed tax cut, thus thwarting Republican efforts to win a larger tax reduction. The Latta proposal was defeated, 198-204. *(Vote 624, p. 176-H)*

The House also rejected, 155-241, a Democratic effort to reduce spending. Joseph L. Fisher, D-Va., proposed a $5 billion — roughly 1 percent — spending cut. Some attributed the wider margin by which that proposal was defeated to the fact that Fisher, unlike the Republicans, had earmarked where the cuts could be made. *(Vote 625, p. 176-H)*

The only successful attack on the committee proposal came when the House approved the reduction in CETA and countercyclical aid, proposed by Mattox. But the House later rejected, 187-208, a proposal by Elliot H. Levitas, D-Ga., to reduce spending by $753 million by eliminating all money for countercyclical aid. *(Vote 626, p. 178-H)*

Also rejected, 153-235, was a proposal by John H. Rousselot, R-Calif., to reduce outlays to $464.1 billion in an attempt to balance the budget. *(Vote 627, p. 178-H)*

Senate Committee Report

The Senate Budget Committee reported its version of the resolution Aug. 18 (S Con Res 104 — S Rept 95-1124).

As reported, the resolution called for the same budget totals later approved by the Senate: budget authority, $557.7 billion; outlays, $489.5 billion; revenues, $447.2 billion; deficit, $42.3 billion.

The committee said those figures represented a "major" shift in budget policies prompted by changes in the economy. Specifically, the committee noted that inflation had accelerated in recent months, and that unemployment had dropped more than expected.

The committee predicted that gross national product (GNP) would climb 4 percent in 1978 and 3.4 percent in 1979, as compared to the 4.5 percent rates assumed in the first resolution. It said that unemployment would drop to 5.8 percent by the end of 1978, and to 5.6 percent at the end of 1979 — slightly lower than the level foreseen when the first resolution was approved. Inflation, on the other hand, would rise 6.9 percent in 1978 and 6.7 percent in 1979 under the committee's new assumptions — almost a percentage point faster than predicted at the time of the first resolution.

Reductions

The change in economic conditions prompted the committee to press for more spending restraint. Its second budget resolution called for a $9.3 billion reduction in outlays, and an $11.1 billion cut in budget authority below the levels envisioned by the first budget resolution adopted in May.

Of the outlay reduction, $5.1 billion represented technical re-estimates of spending programs, while $4.3 billion reflected actual cuts in planned spending. The committee's total cuts — about 2 percent of the budget — were slightly more substantial than reductions already approved by the House for the second resolution on Aug. 16.

Even with the cuts, spending would grow 9.3 percent over the fiscal year 1978 level. But the committee noted that growth rate would be less than the expected 10.9 percent nominal rate of growth of gross national product (GNP). As a result, the committee said its proposed spending total would result in a decline in the relative size of the federal sector in the overall economy.

The fiscal 1979 figures were part of a Senate committee five-year budget plan under which the federal share of the economy would fall steadily. Spending would rise to $669 billion in fiscal year 1983 under the plan — a rate of growth that would allow the federal share of GNP to drop to 19.9 percent in fiscal year 1983 from 21.7 percent in fiscal year 1979.

The committee's revenue figure assumed the same $19.4 billion annual tax reduction, effective Jan. 1, 1979, that was included in the first budget resolution. In addition, the committee left room in its revenue figures for the continuation of $8.2 billion in tax cuts that would expire at the end of 1978, and $1.2 billion in other "structural" tax law changes — such as a tuition tax credit.

The committee re-estimated the impact of the tax cut, however, concluding that it would only cost the Treasury $14 billion — not $15 billion — during the fiscal year.

The committee reduced its overall spending totals by cutting a number of programs. It hit particularly at some of President Carter's proposed urban initiatives, leaving no room in its budget for the proposed national development bank, enactment of state incentive grants and a "soft public works" initiative. It also allowed no funds for a third-round local public works program.

The committee also suggested that, in light of accelerating inflation and declining unemployment, countercyclical public employment should be phased down, beginning with a reduction of 60,000 in the 725,000 public service jobs during fiscal year 1979.

The committee also assumed a 5.5 percent limit ("cap") on federal employees' pay raises.

Senate Floor Action

The Senate on Sept. 6 easily approved a $489.5 billion fiscal 1979 budget that Budget Committee Chairman Edmund S. Muskie, D-Maine, hailed as "anti-inflationary."

The senators agreed to a Budget Committee recommendation to set a spending ceiling $9.3 billion lower than they had tentatively approved in May. At the same time, they endorsed a floor under revenues for the coming year that would allow a larger tax cut than the $16.3 billion reduction approved by the House in August.

Muskie said the "more restrictive" second budget resolution (S Con Res 104) would result in a deficit considerably smaller than expected earlier in the year. At the same time, he said the revenue figure would allow a tax cut large enough to offset the economically dampening effect of scheduled Social Security tax increases and inflation-induced rises in income taxes, without increasing the overall federal stimulus to the economy.

"This second budget resolution [is] . . . a signal to our citizens and to the private economy that the federal government will lead the way toward reducing inflation without sacrificing jobs," Muskie said.

The final 56-18 vote approving the second resolution, came after the Senate rejected three amendments to cut spending even more than recommended by the Budget Committee. *(Vote 368, p. 55-S)*

Differences between the two chambers and the Carter administration are as follows *(in billions of dollars):*

	Budget Authority	Outlays	Revenues	Deficit
First budget resolution	$568.85	$498.8	$447.7	$50.9
Administration July re-estimates	571.4	496.6	448.2	48.5
House	561.0	489.8	450.0	39.8
Senate	557.7	489.5	447.2	42.3

Before approving the resolution Sept. 6, the Senate substituted the text of S Con Res 104 for that of the House version (H Con Res 683). It also rejected amendments by:

- William Proxmire, D-Wis., to reduce budget authority to $540 billion, 5 percent below the original administration request. The vote was 25-44. *(Vote 365, p. 55-S)*
- William V. Roth Jr., R-Del., to reduce budget authority to $547 billion and outlays to $479.4 billion. Roth's amendment would have exempted from further cuts national defense, agriculture, veterans' benefits, revenue sharing and some other budget areas. The vote was 35-38. *(Vote 366, p. 55-S)*
- Harry F. Byrd Jr., Ind-Va., to reduce budget authority for foreign aid by $2.4 billion. The vote was 32-44. *(Vote 367, p. 55-S)*

Future Spending Restraint

While rejecting those amendments, the Senate gave some indication that it might agree to take further steps to reduce federal spending in 1979. One sign was an amendment offered by Budget Committee member Lawton Chiles, D-Fla., setting a spending and tax plan that would lead to a balanced federal budget in fiscal year 1982. Under Chiles' plan, Congress would commit itself to allow spending increases above levels in his plan only if it would increase taxes to pay for them. By the same token, it would reduce taxes below levels in the plan only if it would reduce spending by a similar amount.

Chiles said the plan should only be violated in times of considerable economic need — he suggested allowing larger deficits than envisioned only during times when unemployment exceeds 6 percent.

The Chiles amendment was ruled not in order because it set spending and tax figures for years beyond fiscal 1979. The budget resolution was limited to that year.

But Muskie said the proposal was worthy of careful consideration. He hinted that it might be an acceptable approach that could be considered as an amendment to the 1974 budget act.

Another indication that the Senate might consider further spending restrictions came when Muskie expressed interest in a proposal by Pete V. Domenici, R-N.M., also a Budget Committee member, to limit federal spending to a certain percentage of gross national product. Domenici raised the possibility of hearings on the idea in 1979.

Conference Impasse

Supporting an unprecedented request from an assertive Senate Budget Committee, the Senate voted 63-21 on Sept. 14 against any new spending for local public works programs. *(Vote 373, p. 56-S)*

The three-to-one vote came in response to a request from Budget Committee Chairman Edmund S. Muskie, D-Maine, that the Senate endorse his panel's strong opposition to House efforts to authorize $2 billion in new public works spending.

Muskie sought the floor vote on public works after the budget conference committee reached an impasse on the issue.

The House had included in its budget resolution $2 billion in budget authority for public works — $1 billion for "Round 3" of conventional public works, and $1 billion for President Carter's proposed labor-intensive "soft" public works.

But the Senate, following the lead of its Budget Committee, included no money for public works in its version of the second budget resolution — even though it had tentatively agreed to include such funds when it adopted the first resolution in May.

Muskie argued that the public works program was no longer justified in light of the decline in unemployment and mounting concerns that federal spending should be cut to reduce the deficit and ease inflation.

The Senate Budget Committee chairman — with strong support from the panel's ranking Republican, Henry Bellmon, R-Okla. — said the new public works spending would be especially inflationary because it would stimulate an already healthy construction sector. Construction employment has been "booming," and shortages had been driving up building materials prices already, Muskie said. The new program would drive wages and prices up further, he argued.

Finally, Muskie warned that the Senate Environment and Public Works Committee, of which he was a member, was in the process of making the public works proposal even worse by easing proposed requirements that it be made more labor intensive (and thus more efficient in creating jobs without driving up materials prices) and that it be focused more than past programs on the hard-core unemployed.

Under President Carter's proposed $1 billion "soft" public works program, 50 percent of the funds would have to go for labor costs, and 50 percent of the people employed would have to be from the ranks of the hard-core unemployed.

But a compromise proposal scheduled to be considered in the Regional and Community Development Subcommittee of the Public Works Committee would drop the labor intensiveness requirement to 40 percent in urban areas and 25 percent in rural areas. The proposal would reduce the percentage of jobs reserved for the hard-core unemployed to 25 percent.

The subcommittee proposal also would extend the program an extra year, during which urban projects would have to be 50 percent labor intensive, and 50 percent of the urban jobs would have to go to the hard-core unemployed. The rural labor intensiveness requirement would rise to 40 percent during the second year, but still only 25 percent of the jobs would have to go to the hard-to-employ. *(Story, p. 311)*

Compromise Efforts

On Sept. 11, the second day of the conference, House Majority Leader Jim Wright, D-Texas, offered to reduce the House public works total to $1.5 billion. Muskie refused to budge.

On Sept. 13, however, Muskie listed among the "elements of possible basis for agreement" the idea of allowing $500 million for public works. He emphasized that all the money would have to go for "soft" public works.

At that, House Budget Committee Chairman Robert N. Giaimo, D-Conn., who was urged to take a tough stand on the matter by House Speaker Thomas P. O'Neill Jr., D-Mass., suggested a compromise figure of $1 billion.

Senate Vote

That was the closest the conferees came to agreeing. On Sept. 14, Muskie went before the Senate seeking approval of a resolution (S Res 562) instructing Senate conferees to insist on no new spending for public works at all.

"The plain fact is that these compromised 'soft public works' proposals would convert the temporary local public works program enacted to deal with the recession into a permanent multi-billion dollar a year fixture in the federal budget," he said.

It was the first time in the four-year history of the congressional budget process that lawmakers had been asked to vote directly on a specific program as part of the budget resolution.

The Muskie proposal was resisted, though somewhat mildly, by Public Works Chairman Jennings Randolph, D-W.Va., whose turf the proposal would most threaten. But any interest he may have had in standing more firmly against Muskie was probably diminished by the fact that the Public Works Committee was sharply divided on the public works issue.

On the 63-21 vote, committee members split 6-6, and two of the three non-voting members were thought likely to oppose further public works spending.

In the wake of the Senate vote, House conferees refused to back down. They noted that the conferees would be discharged if no agreement were reached by midnight on Sept. 19, and at that point new conferees could be appointed. The Senate's instructions to the earlier conferees wouldn't be binding on the new ones, House members argued.

Senate conferees, on the other hand, argued that the Senate vote established that their chamber would reject any public works spending proposal. That meant, they argued, that it would be meaningless to include public works funds in the budget resolution.

Deadlock Ended

The conference report on H Con Res 683 (H Rept 95-1594) was filed Sept. 20.

The conferees cleared the way for final agreement on the budget resolution by sidestepping the public works controversy that had stalled their deliberations since Sept. 14. In effect, they agreed to disagree on the matter, adopting an overall spending figure which each side interpreted differently.

House conferees said the spending total would allow for $700 million in new local public works spending — a figure considerably lower than the $2 billion they said the original House version provided. Senate conferees, on the other hand, said the conference agreement left no room for public works spending at all — a position they took when the resolution first went through the Senate, and one which was reaffirmed by the full Senate on Sept. 14.

Disaster Relief

The face-saving solution to the impasse was resolved with some sleight-of-hand involving spending for federal disaster relief.

In preparing its version of the budget resolution, the Senate Budget Committee had assumed federal disaster assistance programs would cost $1.2 billion (in budget authority) during the fiscal year.

The House Budget Committee had set that figure at $430 million.

The largest single component of those totals was the Small Business Administration's (SBA) disaster loan program, which the Senate predicted would cost $1 billion in budget authority and the House said would cost only $230 million.

During conference committee deliberations on Sept. 11, House Budget Committee Chairman Robert N. Giaimo, D-Conn., conceded that the Senate figure was probably the most "realistic." But he suggested that the conference committee stick with the lower House figure in order to pressure other congressional committees to report legislation reforming the SBA disaster loan program.

Giaimo called the program a "budget buster" — an assessment with which Senate Budget Committee Chairman Edmund S. Muskie, D-Maine, readily agreed.

The Budget Committees had been concerned about the program ever since Congress decided in 1976 to make farmers eligible for it. Previously, farmers had to rely on the Farmers Home Administration for disaster loans. That agency imposed strict requirements on farmers to prove substantial loss of income and to show they could not get credit elsewhere before providing loans. The SBA program did not have such requirements. As a result, a large number of farmers took advantage of the less stringent SBA program.

To make matters worse in the eyes of budget officials, Congress decided in 1977 to lower the interest rates on disaster loans to 3 percent from 6.6 percent.

The two changes, coupled with a drought in 1977, sent costs for the SBA loan program skyrocketing. The SBA originally requested only $20 million to pay for the program in fiscal year 1978. By August, it had revised the figure upward to $2.6 billion.

"In the process of bringing agriculture into the program, they [Congress] dropped all safeguards for the taxpayers," Muskie said on Sept. 11. "Interest rates have been dropped, credit elsewhere tests have been dropped, and there is absolutely no semblance of reform."

While questioning whether Congress would tighten the program in time to affect fiscal 1979 expenditures, Muskie agreed to Giaimo's proposal to use the lower figure in order to exert pressure for reform.

Later, when the conferees reached stalemate on the public works question, that apparently symbolic gesture seemed less important to the Senate Budget Committee chairman.

Public Works Solution

With the Senate conferees bound by the 63-21 Sept. 14 Senate vote instructing them to include no funds for public works (a vote Muskie sought in order to prove there was strong Senate opposition to extending the program), and with the House conferees under pressure from House Speaker Thomas P. O'Neill Jr., D-Mass., to hold out for at least $750 million for public works, Muskie proposed a solution.

The conference, he said, could accept the Senate combined figure for public works and disaster relief. The Senate could interpret that to mean there were no funds for public works and that there was $1.2 billion for disaster relief. The House could interpret to mean that there was $700 million for public works and only $430 million for disaster relief.

That compromise, which was ultimately accepted by the conferees, enabled Muskie to say he had heeded the Senate's instructions to oppose any new funds for public works. In the process, he had forced a test vote in the Senate demonstrating strong opposition to new public works spending.

While the Senate could still enact a new public works program, it would have to do so by eliminating some other program envisioned in the budget resolution.

In the meantime, the compromise enabled Giaimo to report to the House that there was money in the resolution for public works. That would allow the House to pass a new program without incurring Budget Committee opposition.

But if a public works measure were enacted, Giaimo would have to hope that spending on disaster loans met his low expectations, or that some other program fell short enough of anticipated costs to keep the overall spending total within the resolution's ceiling.

Revenues

The public works obstacle thus cleared, the lawmakers quickly resolved their remaining differences.

The $448.7 billion revenue floor they approved was the same figure they had discussed as a possible compromise before their negotiations broke down Sept. 14.

The compromise was up $1.5 billion from the $447.1 billion revenue floor envisioned in the Senate version of the resolution, and it was down $1.3 billion from the $450 billion floor contained in the House version.

The compromise would allow for fiscal year revenue reduction $2 billion greater than the House-approved tax cut. On a calendar year basis, the tax cut could be at least $2 billion greater, and possibly more, depending on the form it would take and how it would be timed.

Middle Income Student Assistance

The conference agreement provided $1 billion to expand middle income student grant and loan programs. That sum included $300 million assumed in both House and Senate resolutions to expand the Supplemental Educational Opportunity Grant (SEOG), college work-study and guaranteed student loan programs. *(Student aid programs, p. 568)*

On top of that, the compromise would leave $700 million to expand the Basic Educational Opportunity Grant (BEOG) program. That was less than the $1.2 billion the House resolution had originally provided, but it kept alive hopes that the expansion could be enacted as an alternative to tuition tax credits.

The Senate resolution had provided no funds to expand the BEOG program because Senate Budget Committee members were afraid it would merely overlap with tuition tax credits, which they said would inevitably be approved by Congress. House conferees argued that eliminating the funds for BEOGs would hurt the chances the program could be enacted instead of tuition tax credits.

The conferees agreed to meet both concerns by including in their report language asserting that it would be "inefficient and duplicative" for Congress to enact both tuition tax credits and the expansion in the grant program. They concluded that Congress should choose between the two.

Jobs Programs

The conference agreement also provided sufficient funds for a larger youth employment program and a larger private sector employment initiatives program, in accordance with House-passed amendments to the Comprehensive Employment and Training Act (CETA) reauthorization. In addition, it provided room in the budget for President Carter's proposed demonstration jobs projects for welfare recipients — a program which the Senate resolution had excluded.

But the agreement, in accordance with both House and Senate resolutions, assumed a reduction in the number of public service jobs. The Senate estimated the reduction to be 60,000 jobs during the fiscal year from a level of 725,000.

Other Issues

The conference agreement also assumed that the total $3 billion in budget authority needed in fiscal 1979 would be provided for the strategic petroleum reserve, but it rejected a House proposal to set that number at $4.1 billion to reflect the full cost of the reserve.

House members had argued that the larger figure was a more accurate way of demonstrating the full cost of the project, even though they agreed that only $3 billion could be spent in fiscal 1979.

On other issues, the conference:

- Provided $300 million for an international grain reserve — down $100 million from the House figure but up from nothing provided in the original Senate resolution.
- Went along with a Senate proposal allowing $200 million more than the $4.9 billion in the House budget for energy conservation and supply programs.
- Split the House-Senate $600 million difference over natural resources and environmental programs — most notably pollution control and abatement efforts — increasing the House budget authority figure to $13.3 billion from $13 billion, and boosting the House outlay figure to $11.5 billion from $11.4 billion. The Senate figures were reduced by a similar amount.
- Assumed that voluntary hospital cost controls would reduce Medicare and Medicaid program costs by $700 million, as compared to the original Senate assumption of $800 million and the original House assumption of $200 million.
- Essentially split their differences on spending for veterans' programs, providing $21.05 billion in budget authority and $20.7 billion in outlays.
- Approved the Senate figures providing for $500 million in budget authority and outlays for fiscal assistance to help state and local governments with their welfare costs.
- Assumed that efforts to limit fraud, waste and abuse in programs run by the Department of Health, Education and Welfare would save $1 billion during the fiscal year.

Carter Asks $500.2 Billion in Spending

President Carter on Jan. 23 provided Congress the final details of his proposed economic strategy by recommending a fiscal year 1979 budget totaling $500.2 billion. Combined with a $24.5 billion net tax reduction, it anticipated a deficit of $60.6 billion.

Characterized by the President as "the administration's first full statement of its priorities, policies and proposals for meeting our national needs," the budget recommended a markedly slowed rate of growth in federal spending, coupled with a middle-of-the-road tax reduction.

It presented no major shift in federal priorities, continuing most programs at levels just sufficient to keep pace with inflation. The few new initiatives had relatively minor fiscal impact during the budget year.

By Carter's analysis—judged to be overly optimistic by some critics—the overall spending and tax proposals would spur solid, but not spectacular economic growth, and thus achieve a modest drop in unemployment. *(Carter economic message, p. 17-E)*

In general, the budget appeared to underscore Carter's philosophy that government should be limited—a view reflected in his proud assertions that he held real spending growth to less than 2 per cent, actually diminishing the relative size of the federal government in the economy.

"In formulating this budget, I have been made acutely aware once more of the overwhelming number of demands upon the budget and the finite nature of our resources," Carter said in the message accompanying the budget. "Public needs are critically important; but private needs are equally valid, and the only resources the government has are those it collects from the taxpayer.... The span of government is not infinite."

Carter estimated that receipts for fiscal year 1979 would amount to $439.6 billion, assuming congressional approval of the proposed tax reductions. The resulting deficit, given $500.2 billion in proposed outlays, was projected to be $60.6 billion.

Besides proposing policies for fiscal 1979, the President's budget contained the most recent estimates for fiscal 1978, which ended Sept. 30. It predicted that outlays would reach $462.2 billion, and that revenues would total $400.4 billion, resulting in a deficit of $61.8 billion.

The revised figures differed from the administration's previous estimates in November 1977, which predicted outlays of $459.8 billion and revenues of $401.4 billion, for a deficit of $58.5 billion.

The newly estimated deficit for fiscal 1978 was very nearly the same as predicted by Congress in September 1977 in its second budget resolution, although it envisioned reaching that bottom line with lower outlays and receipts. Congress set a ceiling on outlays of $458.25 billion and a $397 billion floor on receipts, resulting in a deficit of $61.25 billion.

The $38 billion spending increase proposed by the administration for the new fiscal year represented an 8 per cent rate of growth. That compared to increases of about 15 per cent in fiscal 1978, and 9.9 per cent in 1977, 12.1 per cent in 1976, 20.9 per cent in 1975, 9.1 per cent in 1974 and 6.5 per cent in 1973. In only three years since 1968 had the growth of federal spending been less than 8 per cent.

Most of the increase resulted from continuing current policies through fiscal 1979 with adjustments for inflation and demographic changes. The administration estimated that only $7.8 billion of the spending increase resulted from new spending initiatives. That represented a growth rate of only 1.6 per cent.

The Budget Totals

(In billions of dollars)

	1977 actual	1978 estimate	1979 estimate
Budget receipts	$356.9	$400.4	$439.6
Budget outlays	401.9	462.2	500.2
Deficit (−)	−45.0	−61.8	−60.6
Budget authority	$465.2	$502.9	$568.2

Revised Budget Estimates

In a mid-session review released July 6, the Office of Management and Budget (OMB) issued revised budget estimates for fiscal 1978 and 1979.

The agency reported that federal spending in fiscal 1978 would fall far short of original estimates, resulting in a deficit of about $51 billion rather than the $61.8 billion figure predicted in January.

Moreover, because of President Carter's decision to scale back the size of the tax cut he proposed in January, the fiscal 1979 deficit was estimated at $48.5 billion, not almost $61 billion as previously predicted.

The revised budget totals *(in billions of dollars):*

	Fiscal 1978	Fiscal 1979
Outlays	$452.3	$496.6
Revenues	401.2	448.2
Deficit	51.1	48.5

Administration Priorities

Carter listed several "new priorities" in his budget message, including:

- Energy, with special emphasis on conservation and non-nuclear research development, accelerated acquisition of a strategic petroleum reserve, resolution of problems of nuclear waste management, and research into alternatives to the plutonium-fueled liquid metal fast breeder reactor.
- Human needs, especially a beginning to Carter's welfare reform program, health care for low-income mothers

Budget Terminology

The federal budget is a plan of expected receipts and expenditures, a statement of priorities, an accounting of how funds have been and will be spent and a request for authority to spend public money.

The 1979 budget covered the government's fiscal year beginning Oct. 1, 1978, and ending Sept. 30, 1979.

The federal expenditures reported are most frequently outlays: amounts actually paid out by the government in cash or checks during the year. Examples are funds spent to buy equipment or property, to meet the government's liability under a contract or to pay the salary of an employee. Outlays also include net lending—the difference between disbursements and repayments under government lending programs.

The administration's request to Congress, presented in the form of the budget, is for authority to obligate or lend funds.

Budget authority determines the scope of operations of the government. Congress confers budget authority on a federal agency in general in the form of appropriations.

Appropriations may be for a single year, a specified period of years, or an indefinite number of years, according to the restrictions Congress wishes to place on spending for particular purposes.

Congress also restricts itself in the appropriation process by requiring that an appropriation be preceded by an authorization to appropriate a certain or an indefinite amount of money for a certain purpose over a period of time.

Usually an authorization establishes the scope of a particular program, and Congress appropriates funds within the limits it has previously approved. In the case of authority to enter contract obligations, however, Congress authorizes the administration to make firm commitments for which funds must be appropriated later. Congress also occasionally includes mandatory spending requirements in an authorization, designed to ensure spending at a certain level.

Budget authority often differs from actual outlays. This is because, in practice, funds actually spent or obligated during a year may be drawn partly from the budget authority conferred in the year in question and partly from budget authority conferred in previous years.

and children, major increases in education assistance at all levels, jobs programs (especially for low-income youths), and the start of a program to prevent unwanted adolescent pregnancies.

- National defense, especially an increase in spending for the North Atlantic Treaty Organization (NATO).
- Research and development, earmarked for a 5 per cent real growth in spending.

Carter also suggested that the budget reflected a substantial commitment to urban revitalization, declaring that it attempted "to improve delivery and target existing programs better." He offered no spending total for essentially urban programs, but estimated that they had increased by about $11 billion since 1977.

Carter's promised urban program was not expected until March. James T. McIntyre Jr., director-designate of the Office of Management and Budget, said the new program could be financed partly from a $1.7 billion allowance for contingencies in the budget, but he said the administration might submit to Congress a supplemental budget request.

McIntyre hinted, however, that an urban aid program might require changes in budget authority rather than outlays, suggesting that the administration proposals might emphasize loan guarantees and similar policies rather than direct spending.

The Carter budget proposed an increase in budget authority to $568.1 billion from $502.9 billion. That represented a 13 per cent increase, possibly indicating that the rate of growth in federal spending may speed up again in the future.

Legislative Proposals

The major new legislative proposals in the budget included:

- Expansion of the special supplemental food (WIC) program for women and children, $530 million.
- "A new initiative to provide employment opportunities in the private sector for youth and the disadvantaged," $400 million.
- Expansion of Title I of the Elementary and Secondary Education Act to provide special assistance to disadvantaged areas, $644 million.
- Expanded coverage under the Medicaid program for low-income mothers and children, $381 million; Medicaid cost controls expected to save $399 million.
- Demonstration projects to create 50,000 public sector jobs as part of the 1.4 million jobs eventually envisioned under proposed welfare reform, $200 million.
- A new program to help prevent unwanted teenage pregnancies, $20 million.
- A program to provide federal interest subsidies to local governments that choose to issue taxable bonds, $99 million (proposed budget authority, $7 billion).
- An expanded foster child care program, $64 million.
- A new home ownership assistance program for very low-income families, $6 million.

The Tax Program

One of the administration's top priorities was its detailed proposal for a series of tax reductions totaling $33.9 billion, along with "reforms" that would raise $9.4 billion in revenues. The details were spelled out in the President's tax message Jan. 21. *(Tax message, p. 23-E)*

The proposed reforms, while less ambitious than those promised by Carter during his presidential campaign, were still expected to stir plenty of controversy in Congress.

The administration acknowledged the possibility that lawmakers might approve the reductions without endorsing the full package of reforms, but it insisted that Congress enact a total tax package that would reduce revenues by roughly the same $24.5 billion proposed.

"If we cannot get the reforms, we would be $9 billion short," declared Treasury Secretary W. Michael Blumenthal. "That means we would have to cut back somewhere."

Outlays

The largest increases in the fiscal 1979 budget were proposed in the areas of income security ($12.4 billion, or 8.3

per cent), national defense ($10.1 billion, or 9.4 per cent), health ($5.4 billion, or 12.2 per cent), interest ($5.1 billion, or 11.7 per cent), education ($2.9 billion, or 10.7 per cent), energy ($1.8 billion, or 23 per cent), and international affairs ($944 million, or 14 per cent).

The income security increase included a $9.8 billion, or 10.1 per cent, rise in Social Security.

The most substantial decline in projected outlays was in agriculture, for which the administration projected a $3.6 billion, or 40 per cent, spending decline. That was based on the assumption that "normal weather" during the fiscal year would spare the government the need to make substantial payments to farmers for crop losses. If that assumption were to prove incorrect, expenditures would automatically increase.

Other budget functions that increased less than the overall average, or actually declined, included: community and regional development (down $1 billion, or 10.6 per cent), commerce and housing credit (down $555 million, or 15.8 per cent), general purpose fiscal assistance to states and localities (down $224 million, or 23 per cent), transportation (up $1 billion, or 23 per cent), transportation (up $1 billion, or 6.7 per cent), veterans' benefits and services (up $341 million, or 1.9 per cent), general science, space and technology (up $320 million, or 6.7 per cent), administration of justice (up $192 million, or 4.8 per cent), and natural resources and environment (up $97 million, or 0.8 per cent).

Carter estimated that between 75 and 80 per cent of the budget was "relatively uncontrollable," a situation he predicted would continue for the foreseeable future.

Uncontrollable expenditures included "open-ended programs" and fixed costs, which have risen from 36 per cent of the budget in 1967 to about 57 per cent in the 1979 budget. Carter estimated they will comprise 59 per cent of total spending by 1983.

"Prior year contracts and obligations" accounted for an additional 15 or 20 per cent of the budget considered relatively uncontrollable in the short run.

Current Services Increases

To give a better indication of actual policy changes in the budget, the administration submits each year its "current services estimates." They predict outlays and receipts for the coming year, assuming no change in policies, but only adjustments for inflation in indexed programs and demographic changes.

The current services estimates for fiscal 1979 indicated a spending total of $492.4 billion, and receipts of $463.8 billion, for a deficit of $28.5 billion. Current services budget authority was estimated to be $538.3 billion.

Carter's proposed increase over current services outlays of $7.8 billion represented a growth in the budget resulting from newly proposed policies of only 1.6 per cent. His recommended budget authority total was $29.9 billion, or 5.6 per cent, above the current services estimate.

That meant that new spending accounted for only $7.8 billion of the $32.1 billion addition to the likely 1979 deficit, compared to $24.5 billion in tax cuts. Seen from another perspective, the current services estimates suggested that, for every dollar Carter chose to spend on new policy initiatives, he decided to return $3.14 to the taxpayers in the form of tax reduction.

The current services estimates for 1979 suggested that Carter's top priorities for new policies were energy, defense and education, training, employment and social services programs.

The administration estimated its proposed increases over current services estimates as follows: energy, $2.1 billion; a proposed tax refund for purchasers of fuel efficient cars, $1.3 billion; defense, $1 billion; education, training, employment and social service programs, $1 billion; international affairs, $300 million; transportation, $300 million; an allowance for contingencies, $1.7 billion; and other increases, $1.8 billion.

The administration proposed reducing expenditures below current service estimates by $1.8 billion, including Medicare and Medicaid savings resulting from hospital cost containment, $700 million; Social Security changes, $600 million; and other actions cutting costs, $400 million.

The prospects for the fuel efficiency tax refund were considered very slim in Congress, but the chances of hospital cost containment were slight, too, suggesting that the actual increase over current services estimates might be more on the order of $8.4 billion.

The administration also estimated that, assuming adoption of Carter's proposals for fiscal 1979 and their extension into the future without further policy changes, federal spending would reach $650 billion by 1983.

The Budget Dollar
Where it comes from...

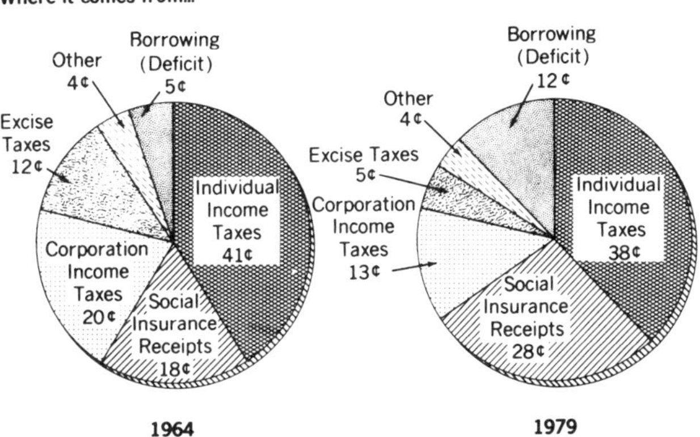

The Budget Dollar
Where it goes...

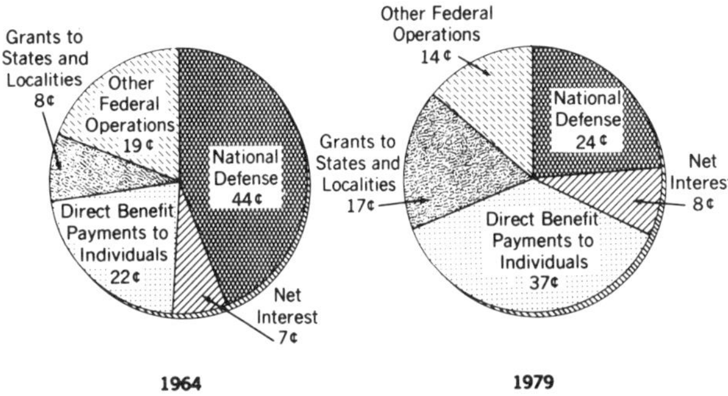

Economic Impact

The administration asserted that its proposed combination of tax reduction and spending increases would stimulate the economy enough to grow at a respectable 4.75 per cent rate in 1979. It predicted that the unemployment rate would drop as a result to about 6.2 per cent by the end of 1978, and to 5.8 per cent by the end of 1979. It suggested

(Continued on p. 54)

Fiscal 1979 Budget by Function: $500.2 Billion in

(in millions of dollars) †

	BUDGET AUTHORITY‡			OUTLAYS		
	1977	1978 est.	1979 est.	1977	1978 est.	1979 est.
NATIONAL DEFENSE						
Military Defense	$108,425	$115,264	$125,567	$ 95,650	$105,300	$115,200
Atomic Energy Defense Activities	2,089	2,512	2,829	1,936	2,308	2,536
Defense-related Activities	−81	38	45	−84	20	45
Deductions#	−*	−2	−2	−*	−2	−2
TOTAL	$110,432	$117,813	$128,439	$ 97,501	$107,626	$117,779
INTERNATIONAL AFFAIRS						
Foreign Economic and Financial Assistance	$ 5,626	$ 6,801	$ 8,335	$ 4,214	$ 5,296	$ 5,407
Military Assistance	676	589	541	494	457	465
Conduct of Foreign Affairs	1,054	1,222	1,240	981	1,115	1,211
Foreign Information and Exchange Activities	400	451	500	386	443	480
International Financial Programs	−744	2,580	3,740	−819	−24	684
Deductions#	−425	−540	−555	−425	−540	−555
TOTAL	$ 6,587	$ 11,102	$ 13,801	$ 4,831	$ 6,747	$ 7,691
GENERAL SCIENCE, SPACE AND TECHNOLOGY						
General Science and Basic Research	$ 1,136	$ 1,267	$ 1,368	$ 1,078	$ 1,190	$ 1,274
Space Flight	2,138	2,198	2,247	2,252	2,192	2,264
Space Science, Applications and Technology	964	1,056	1,210	1,006	1,018	1,150
Supporting Space Activities	340	369	393	343	358	390
Deductions#	−2	−2	−2	−2	−2	−2
TOTAL	$ 4,576	$ 4,889	$ 5,216	$ 4,677	$ 4,757	$ 5,077
ENERGY						
Energy Supply	$ 3,603	$ 3,320	$ 2,869	$ 3,266	$ 4,190	$ 4,113
Energy Conservation	242	842	1,510	143	601	1,402
Emergency Energy Preparedness	445	3,595	4,255	123	2,273	3,284
Energy Information, Policy and Regulation	711	808	1,006	664	799	930
Deductions#	−23	−26	−95	−23	−26	−95
TOTAL	$ 4,978	$ 8,539	$ 9,544	$ 4,172	$ 7,837	$ 9,634
NATURAL RESOURCES AND ENVIRONMENT						
Water Resources	$ 3,664	$ 3,675	$ 3,284	$ 3,241	$ 3,686	$ 3,392
Conservation and Land Management	1,566	2,127	1,755	1,279	2,079	1,579
Recreational Resources	1,236	1,624	1,769	1,014	1,323	1,545
Pollution Control and Abatement	2,691	5,381	5,704	4,279	4,947	5,615
Other Natural Resources	1,087	1,211	1,331	973	1,175	1,268
Deductions#	−786	−1,084	−1,178	−786	−1,084	−1,178
TOTAL	$ 9,457	$ 12,935	$ 12,664	$ 10,000	$ 12,125	$ 12,222
AGRICULTURE						
Farm Income Stabilization	$ 1,351	$ 2,541	$ 5,920	$ 4,485	$ 7,865	$ 4,180
Agricultural Research and Services	1,084	1,223	1,282	1,052	1,244	1,259
Deductions#	−11	−3	−6	−11	−3	−6
TOTAL	$ 2,424	$ 3,761	$ 7,197	$ 5,526	$ 9,106	$ 5,433
COMMERCE AND HOUSING CREDIT						
Mortgage Credit and Thrift Insurance	$ 2,044	$ 2,049	$ 3,206	$ 3,270	$ 467	$ −274
Postal Service	2,266	1,787	1,830	2,267	1,787	1,830
Federal Financing Bank	−143	0	0	−143	0	0
Other Advancement and Regulation of Commerce	1,318	1,548	1,564	1,118	1,272	1,415
Deductions#	−4	−4	−3	−4	−4	−3
TOTAL	$ 5,481	$ 5,381	$ 6,597	$ −31	$ 3,523	$ 2,969
TRANSPORTATION						
Ground Transportation	$ 5,593	$ 9,907	$ 12,803	$ 10,037	$ 11,140	$ 11,990
Air Transportation	3,047	3,328	3,709	2,816	3,269	3,436
Water Transportation	1,683	1,914	2,042	1,749	1,906	1,946
Other Transportation	83	87	86	76	82	93
Deductions#	−42	−86	−66	−42	−86	−66
TOTAL	$ 10,363	$ 15,150	$ 18,573	$ 14,636	$ 16,310	$ 17,399
COMMUNITY AND REGIONAL DEVELOPMENT						
Community Development	$ 3,969	$ 4,706	$ 4,952	$ 3,526	$ 4,049	$ 3,991
Area and Regional Development	8,153	2,106	2,259	2,139	3,976	3,689
Disaster Relief and Insurance	684	1,924	523	634	1,686	1,007
Deductions#	−16	−17	−18	−16	−17	18
TOTAL	$ 12,790	$ 8,719	$ 7,716	$ 6,283	$ 9,694	$ 8,669

Expenditures, $568.2 Billion in Spending Authority

(in millions of dollars)†

	BUDGET AUTHORITY‡			OUTLAYS		
	1977	1978 est.	1979 est.	1977	1978 est.	1979 est.
EDUCATION, TRAINING, EMPLOYMENT AND SOCIAL SERVICES						
Elementary, Secondary and Vocational Education	$ 6,265	$ 6,686	$ 8,443	$ 5,078	$ 5,673	$ 6,484
Higher Education	3,765	4,301	4,588	3,104	3,789	4,289
Research and General Education Aids	1,078	1,238	1,339	927	1,177	1,247
Training and Employment	13,969	4,824	12,287	6,877	10,930	12,787
Other Labor Services	383	451	490	374	440	477
Social Services	4,924	5,335	6,461	4,632	5,468	5,142
Deductions#	−7	−5	−5	−7	−5	−5
TOTAL	$ 30,377	$ 22,829	$ 33,604	$ 20,985	$ 27,471	$ 30,421
HEALTH						
Health Care Services	$ 36,107	$ 41,788	$ 47,987	$ 34,527	$ 39,860	$ 45,097
Health Research	2,654	2,959	3,043	2,543	2,738	2,935
Education and Training of Health Care Work Force	847	868	669	981	836	770
Consumer and Occupational Health and Safety	770	866	917	743	839	887
Deductions#	−10	−12	−12	−10	−12	−12
TOTAL	$ 40,368	$ 46,469	$ 52,604	$ 38,785	$ 44,261	$ 49,677
INCOME SECURITY						
General Retirement and Disability Insurance	$ 84,553	$ 93,013	$105,109	$ 88,642	$ 98,153	$108,396
Federal Employee Retirement and Disability	16,972	18,136	19,654	9,503	10,811	11,995
Unemployment Compensation	16,857	15,360	17,027	15,258	12,360	11,827
Public Assistance and Other Income Supplements	50,184	53,872	49,096	23,601	26,316	27,807
Deductions#	−*	−1	−1	−*	−1	−1
TOTAL	$168,566	$180,381	$190,885	$137,004	$147,640	$160,024
VETERANS BENEFITS AND SERVICES						
Income Security	$ 9,454	$ 10,112	$ 10,535	$ 9,216	$ 9,745	$ 10,275
Education, Training and Rehabilitation	3,984	2,665	2,093	3,710	3,142	2,630
Hospital and Medical Care	5,074	5,657	5,795	4,708	5,436	5,757
Housing	0	0	0	−145	−31	−55
Other Benefits and Services	558	637	653	549	625	652
Deductions#	−1	−3	−3	−1	−3	−3
TOTAL	$ 19,069	$ 19,068	$ 19,074	$ 18,038	$ 18,916	$ 19,257
ADMINISTRATION OF JUSTICE						
Federal Law Enforcement Activities	$ 1,685	$ 1,911	$ 2,015	$ 1,673	$ 1,915	$ 2,011
Federal Litigative and Judicial Activities	863	1,037	1,133	842	976	1,118
Federal Correctional Activities	297	308	353	240	319	373
Criminal Justice Assistance	758	656	651	847	817	717
Deductions#	−2	−8	−8	−2	−8	−8
TOTAL	$ 3,601	$ 3,904	$ 4,144	$ 3,600	$ 4,019	$ 4,211
GENERAL GOVERNMENT						
Legislative Functions	$ 871	$ 908	$ 941	$ 841	$ 900	$ 941
Executive Direction and Management	83	77	81	76	80	80
Central Fiscal Operations	1,963	2,207	2,378	1,930	2,201	2,367
General Property and Records Management	475	279	365	141	366	369
Central Personnel Management	109	119	124	100	120	121
Other General Government	538	644	632	455	632	586
Deductions#	−186	−180	−159	−186	−180	−159
TOTAL	$ 3,851	$ 4,055	$ 4,361	$ 3,357	$ 4,119	$ 4,304
GENERAL PURPOSE FISCAL ASSISTANCE						
General Revenue Sharing	$ 6,658	$ 6,863	$ 6,862	$ 6,762	$ 6,835	$ 6,860
Other General Purpose Fiscal Assistance	2,614	2,829	9,770	2,737	3,026	2,776
TOTAL	$ 9,272	$ 9,691	$ 16,632	$ 9,499	$ 9,860	$ 9,636
INTEREST						
Interest on the Public Debt	$ 41,900	$ 48,600	$ 55,400	$ 41,900	$ 48,600	$ 55,400
Other Interest	−3,807	−4,759	−6,410	−3,808	−4,759	−6,409
TOTAL	$ 38,092	$ 43,841	$ 48,990	$ 38,092	$ 43,841	$ 48,991
CIVILIAN AGENCY PAY RAISES	$ 0	$ 0	$ 1,150	$ 0	$ 0	$ 1,100
CONTINGENCIES	$ 0	$ 0	$ 3,000	$ 0	$ 0	$ 1,700
OFFSETTING RECEIPTS	$−15,053	$−15,619	$−16,021	$−15,053	$−15,619	$−16,021
GRAND TOTAL	$465,231	$502,907	$568,172	$401,902	$462,234	$500,174

† *Figures may not add to totals due to rounding.*
‡ *Primary appropriations.*
# *For offsetting receipts.*
* *Less than $500 thousand.*

SOURCE: Fiscal 1979 Budget

that the tax package alone would add one million jobs that otherwise would not exist in 1979.

Inflation was projected to continue at about the 6 per cent rate, although the administration's new anti-inflation policy was hoped to cut the rate by about one-half of a percentage point each year. *(Economic assumptions, p. 56)*

Those estimates were slightly more optimistic than most. The Congressional Budget Office (CBO) concluded in a study in December 1977 that the combined stimulus would have to be about $2.5 billion higher to achieve the same effect. More recently, Michael Evans, president of the economic forecasting firm Chase Econometrics, estimated that Carter's economic strategy would result in a growth rate of about 4 per cent in 1979. That would be enough to prevent economic deterioration, but not enough to reduce unemployment significantly.

For the years 1980-1983, the administration set an objective of real growth of about 4.75 per cent per year, with unemployment declining to 4.9 per cent by the end of 1981 and to 4 per cent by the end of 1983.

But it also hinted that the 4 per cent goal, contained in the Humphrey-Hawkins full employment bill endorsed by Carter, might be impossible to achieve.

In estimating its "high employment budget"—a measure of government outlays and receipts during periods of high employment—the Carter administration assumed a joblessness rate of 4.9 per cent, rather than the 4 per cent rate traditionally considered full employment.

"These rates are consistent with a 4 per cent rate in 1955, adjusted for changes in the composition of the labor force toward groups that typically experience higher rates of unemployment," the budget document said.

Budget Authority and Outlays by Agency

(in millions of dollars)†

DEPARTMENT OR OTHER UNIT	BUDGET AUTHORITY 1977 actual	BUDGET AUTHORITY 1978 estimate	BUDGET AUTHORITY 1979 estimate	OUTLAYS 1977 actual	OUTLAYS 1978 estimate	OUTLAYS 1979 estimate
Legislative branch	$ 1,043	$ 1,076	$ 1,161	$ 976	$ 1,057	$ 1,175
The Judiciary	430	469	492	392	458	489
Executive Office of the President	78	76	79	73	78	78
Funds appropriated to the President	4,639	8,964	10,974	2,487	4,916	5,089
Agriculture	15,467	17,209	20,026	16,738	22,625	17,727
Commerce	8,204	2,370	2,722	2,606	4,524	4,385
Defense—Military[1]	108,425	115,264	125,567	95,650	105,300	115,200
Defense—Civil	2,495	2,744	2,457	2,280	2,536	2,547
Energy[2]	6,620	10,632	11,642	5,217	8,152	10,087
Health, Education, and Welfare	147,628	162,281	185,007	147,455	164,595	181,265
Housing and Urban Development	33,900	38,143	33,112	5,838	8,411	9,529
Interior	3,708	4,257	4,452	3,194	3,904	4,002
Justice	2,334	2,365	2,457	2,350	2,527	2,533
Labor	31,203	20,676	29,861	22,374	23,742	25,134
State	1,240	1,443	1,465	1,076	1,247	1,355
Transportation	9,298	13,560	17,355	12,514	14,395	15,798
Treasury	49,391	56,571	69,648	49,560	56,688	62,612
Environmental Protection Agency	2,763	5,503	5,627	4,365	5,063	5,679
General Services Administration	304	224	300	−31	289	306
National Aeronautics and Space Administration	3,818	4,063	4,370	3,944	3,982	4,269
Veterans Administration	19,042	19,042	19,048	18,019	18,898	19,238
Other independent agencies	28,253	31,596	32,220	19,878	24,467	24,899
Allowances[3]	—	—	4,150	—	—	2,800
Undistributed offsetting receipts:						
Employer share, employee retirement	−4,548	−5,024	−5,157	−4,548	−5,024	−5,157
Interest received by trust funds	−8,131	−8,595	−9,064	−8,131	−8,595	−9,064
Rents and royalties on the Outer Continental Shelf lands	−2,374	−2,000	−1,800	−2,374	−2,000	−1,800
Total budget authority and outlays	$465,231	$502,907	$568,172	$401,902	$462,234	$500,174

† Figures may not add to totals due to rounding.

1. Includes allowances for civilian and military pay raises for Department of Defense.

2. This agency assumes the energy activities previously performed by the Energy Research and Development Administration, the Federal Energy Administration, and several other agencies.

3. Includes allowances for civilian agency pay raises and contingencies.

SOURCE: Fiscal 1979 Budget

Some economists had argued that a 4 per cent unemployment rate might no longer be the best measure of full employment, but the administration had not endorsed that suggestion. The "high unemployment" estimates in the new Carter budget possibly reflected a shift toward that line of reasoning, however.

Finally, the budget restated Carter's commitment to reduce the size of the federal sector to 21 per cent of gross national product (GNP). The Carter fiscal 1979 budget would bring that percentage down from a 1978 level of 22.6 per cent to 22 per cent.

The budget acknowledged the fading chances of achieving Carter's goal of balancing the budget by 1981, and it stated flatly that that goal might have to be "deferred" if the President decided the economy needed additional stimulus to achieve his economic goals.

The administration stressed that tax reduction would continue to be the favored form of stimulus, in keeping with the President's determination to keep outlays down to 21 per cent of GNP.

Administration Defenses

The President and his top advisers defended the fiscal package from both conservative and liberal attack. Carter called the spending total "restrained," and he pointed with pride to the relatively slow growth rate and the diminished relative size of the budget in the economy. At the same time, he said it included provisions to meet critical national needs.

Treasury Secretary Blumenthal defended the tax portion of the package, saying the reductions were substantial enough to offset the economically chilling impact of scheduled increases in Social Security taxes and inflation, but that the resulting deficit would not set off renewed inflation.

Blumenthal specifically dismissed the "crowding out" theory, which suggests that increased federal borrowing to finance the deficit would create a squeeze in capital markets, increasing interest rates and setting off renewed inflation.

"I suspect there is a persistent tendency to underestimate the depth and resiliency of this country's magnificent financial system," he said.

Budget Director McIntyre reasserted the administration's hopes of balancing the budget by 1981, even though the prospects were conceded to depend on an extraordinarily good performance of the private economy over the next few years.

At the same time, the budget director made clear that, given a choice between a stagnant economy with high unemployment and a balanced budget, the President would "defer" his goal of eliminating the deficit.

BUDGET RECEIPTS BY SOURCE

(In billions of dollars)

Source	1977 actual	1978 estimate	1979 estimate	1980 estimate
Individual income taxes	$156.7	$178.8	$190.1	$223.9
Corporation income taxes	54.9	58.9	62.5	69.1
Social insurance taxes and contributions	108.7	124.1	141.9	160.1
Excise taxes	17.5	20.2	25.5	31.1
Estate and gift taxes	7.3	5.6	6.1	6.5
Customs duties	5.2	5.8	6.4	7.0
Miscellaneous receipts	6.5	6.9	7.2	7.5
Total, budget receipts	$356.9	$400.4	$439.6	$505.4

Federal Outlays-Constant 1979 Dollars

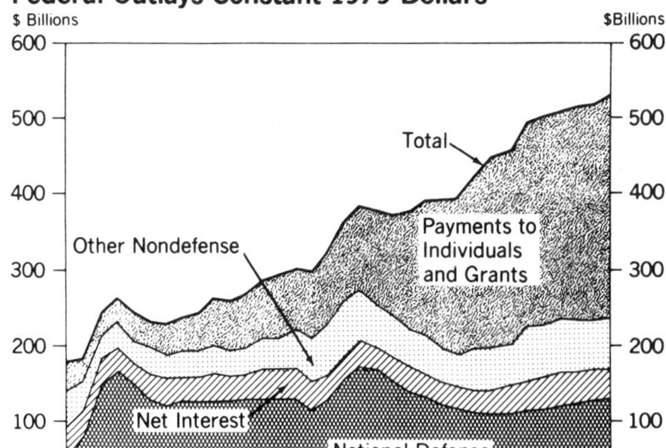

Charles L. Schultze, chairman of Carter's Council of Economic Advisers, described the entire economic package as one "not designed to rescue an economy about to fall into recession," but rather as one to keep a "basically healthy economy" on track.

McIntyre summed up the administration's view of its fiscal plan, calling it "realistic, responsible and responsive to the nation's most critical needs."

Federal Debt and Borrowing

The federal debt was projected to rise in fiscal 1979 by $88 billion, to $873.6 billion, according to the administration budget. The share held by the public was estimated likely to rise from $617.8 billion to $690.8 billion. The rest of the debt was expected to be held by federal agencies or by government trust funds.

Most of the increase in debt was attributed to the federal deficit, although increased federal loan activities also contributed.

The administration estimated that outlays for off-budget agencies—essentially the difference between their new loans and repayments of old ones—would amount to $12.5 billion during the year. Almost all of that sum was attributed to the Federal Financing Bank, which raises money for other federal agencies.

Other off-budget agencies included the Rural Electrification and Telephone Revolving Fund, the Rural Telephone Bank, the Pension Benefit Guaranty Corp., the Exchange Stabilization Fund, the Postal Service Fund and the U.S. Railway Assn.

The administration estimated that new direct loans by on-budget agencies would exceed repayments by $4.3 billion, contributing to the total federal debt.

The administration estimated that total new lending by on-budget agencies would amount to $26.6 billion, and total new lending by off-budget agencies would be $16.8 billion.

In addition, it estimated that the federal government would guarantee or insure net loans totaling $23.2 billion. That sum would not require additional federal outlays, except in cases of default.

Economic Assumptions

(Calendar years: dollar amounts in billions)

Item	Actual 1976	FORECAST 1977	1978	1979	ASSUMPTIONS 1980	1981	1982	1983
Gross national product:								
Current dollars:								
Amount	$1,706	$1,890	$2,099	$2,335	$2,587	$2,858	$3,133	$3,400
Per cent change	11.6	10.8	11.0	11.2	10.8	10.5	9.6	8.5
Constant (1972) dollars:								
Amount	$1,275	$1,337	$1,400	$1,467	$1,537	$1,614	$1,690	$1,761
Per cent change	6.0	4.9	4.7	4.8	4.8	5.0	4.7	4.2
Incomes (current dollars):								
Personal income	$1,383	$1,536	$1,704	$1,892	$2,095	$2,315	$2,538	$2,754
Wages and salaries	892	989	1,099	1,219	1,363	1,521	1,670	1,812
Corporate profits	157	172	192	217	245	274	301	326
Price level (per cent change):								
GNP deflator:								
Year over year	5.3	5.6	6.1	6.2	5.7	5.2	4.7	4.2
Fourth quarter over fourth quarter	4.7	5.9	6.3	6.0	5.5	5.0	4.5	4.0
Consumer Price Index:								
Year over year	5.7	6.5	5.9	6.1	5.7	5.2	4.7	4.2
December over December	4.8	6.9	6.1	6.0	5.5	5.0	4.5	4.0
Unemployment rates (per cent):								
Total:								
Yearly average	7.7	7.0	6.3	5.9	5.4	5.0	4.5	4.1
Fourth quarter	7.9	6.6	6.2	5.8	5.3	4.9	4.4	4.0
Insured[1]	6.4	4.6	4.1	3.6	3.3	2.9	2.6	2.3
Federal pay raise, October (per cent)[2]	4.8	7.0	6.0	6.0	6.0	6.0	5.7	5.4
Interest rate, 91-day Treasury bills (per cent)[3]	5.0	5.2	6.1	6.1	6.1	6.1	5.8	5.3

1. Insured unemployment as a percentage of covered employment.
2. These are the rates used in determining the dollar allowances for additional funds needed to cover pay increases. Agencies will be required to absorb any pay increase in excess of the allowances.
3. Average rate on new issues within period. The forecast assumes continuation of market rates at the time the estimates were made.

SOURCE: Fiscal 1979 Budget

Control Over Lending

The administration of President Ford recommended reforming the government's lending activities by returning the off-budget agencies to the budget. Dismissing the argument that off-budget lending has little fiscal impact since it theoretically requires no net outlays, Ford argued that unifying the separate agencies with the entire budget would lead to greater control.

President Carter made no mention of the Ford proposal, but he agreed that the government needs a "systematic way to consider the resource allocation implied" by the various lending activities and "whether the share of credit transactions being made or guaranteed by the federal government is reasonable."

Specifically, Carter said he would recommend a new set of control procedures, providing that the President and Congress include in their budget processes decisions setting overall ceilings on authority to make direct loans and to guarantee loans, and that annual appropriations acts include limitations on the amounts of direct loans and loan guarantees by individual agencies.

For 1979, Blumenthal estimated that the government would have to borrow about $70 billion, give or take $5 billion, to finance the debt. The rest of the money would be raised from government agencies. That is about the same level of borrowing as in 1978.

Interest on the debt was estimated likely to cost about $48.9 billion.

While that was a substantial sum, the actual size of the federal debt in the economy in 1979 was estimated to be 37.4 per cent of GNP, up from 36 per cent in 1974 but substantially lower than in years before that.

In 1958, for instance, the federal debt comprised 63.3 percent of GNP.

'78 Supplemental: White House Helps Kill B-1

Lobbying of rare intensity by the Carter administration finally killed the B-1 bomber program in February after an eight-month struggle.

Carter had announced his intention to terminate the expensive plane on June 30, 1977, and it had taken until Feb. 22 to get both houses to agree to cancel all funds proposed or previously appropriated for development and production of the aircraft.

Senior Air Force officers and some congressional defense experts had decided that as a matter of practical politics it would have been impossible to reverse President Carter's decision to cancel the B-1 in favor of the new cruise missile. Against that background, the White House and the House Democratic leadership were able to convince enough members that voting against rescinding $462 million that had been appropriated in fiscal 1977 would not save the project, but only further delay the $7.8 billion fiscal 1978 supplemental appropriations bill (HR 9375) to which the rescission was attached.

Politically significant projects funded by the bill included sewage treatment plant construction grants ($4.5 billion), Small Business Administration disaster loans ($1.4 billion) and home heating bill assistance for low-income households ($200 million).

Also provided by the bill was $346.5 million to accelerate development of the cruise missile and to modify existing B-52 bombers to carry them.

House acceptance Feb. 22 of the Senate-sponsored rescission completed action on HR 9375. The Senate Feb. 1 had reaffirmed a position it took in 1977 favoring the plane's cancellation. The conference report on the bill had been cleared Dec. 7. *(Conference report, 1977 Almanac p. 274)*

Breeder Reactor Issue

An important factor in bringing several members around to Carter's position on the B-1 was the Clinch River, Tenn., demonstration fast breeder reactor project.

In November 1977 Carter vetoed the regular fiscal 1978 Energy Research and Development Administration (ERDA) authorization bill in hopes of killing the project. But Clinch River supporters then added to the supplemental $80 million for the project as well as language requiring Carter to use the money to advance the reactor. *(Veto, 1977 Almanac p. 683)*

The White House had been reticent about Clinch River in the weeks before the B-1 votes, refusing to say how Carter would react to such language. However, he invested so much political capital in winning the B-1 rescission that it seemed unlikely he would veto the supplemental to kill Clinch River.

In signing HR 9375, Carter said he would spend the money on the project, as required by the law, but that it would be spent to "complete the system's design...and to terminate the project." But in a letter to Olin E. Teague, D-Texas, chairman of the House Science and Technology Committee, on Dec. 5, 1977, Comptroller General Elmer B. Staats said Carter would be breaking the law if he tried to spend the $80 million to kill the project.

The White House also had under consideration a plan to ask Congress to rescind the money for the reactor. *(See Energy and Environment chapter)*

Administration Lobbying Blitz

Problems in the B-1's early development and its cost—estimated in late 1977 at $101 million a copy — made it an easy target for critics of Pentagon spending.

But the project was supported by Presidents Nixon and Ford, and B-1 opponents were stymied by Congress' traditional reluctance to challenge the White House on major weapons decisions. Eventually, B-1 opponents hit on a tactical ploy that capitalized on this tendency. In 1976 a rider was attached to the annual defense funding bill stipulating that full-scale production of the B-1 would be subject to approval by the winner of the 1976 presidential election.

Carter's opposition to the B-1, announced during the 1976 campaign, appeared to waver once he took office. But by June 30 the former engineer had become convinced the strategic wave of the future was the cruise missile.

Although deeply disappointed, the Air Force quickly accepted his decision. To override Carter would have required the approval of both houses, and the Senate long had been skeptical of the plane.

Gradually, leading congressional defense experts joined the Air Force. By the fall of 1977, Appropriations Committee Chairman George Mahon, D-Texas, was leading the administration's fight in the House. Eventually, he was joined by Jack Edwards, Ala., the senior Republican on the Defense Appropriations Subcommittee. And on the final House vote that carried the day for Carter, the administration was supported by several usually hawkish members of the Armed Services Committee including Chairman Melvin Price, D-Ill., Mendel J. Davis, D-S.C., and Harold Runnels, D-N.M.

Carter had secured congressional cancellation of fiscal 1978 B-1 money by Sept. 8, 1977. But B-1 supporters were able to keep the fiscal 1977 program alive because of members' concern over the possibility that a new strategic arms limitation treaty with Moscow (SALT II) might impose severe limitations on the cruise missile.

The SALT argument and high absenteeism among Democrats beat the rescission move in the House Dec. 6. But Carter was determined to kill the project, and he worked closely with the House Democratic leadership in preparing for a rematch.

At a White House meeting Feb. 17, congressional relations officials from several Cabinet departments were given four or five names from a list of 55 House members thought to be doubtful on the B-1 issue. They were instructed to call the members and press the case for rescinding the B-1 funds in order to free the money in the supplemental. "This is one we really want," a high White House aide told a reporter. "We're willing to spend capital to get it."

The Pentagon's case was pressed by Defense Secretary Harold Brown in phone calls to some members and in a briefing arranged by Mahon for several members the day before the vote. Mahon also circulated a letter from Air Force Chief of Staff Gen. David C. Jones urging the rescission, and, on behalf of Carter, pressed the case against the plane.

Carter phoned several members personally — including Price. And in meetings with some members about other subjects, he brought up the B-1, stressing his determination not to spend the fiscal 1977 money. He also sent a letter to each Democratic member of the Appropriations Committee soliciting support.

Provisions

As signed into law, HR 9375 (PL 95-240) appropriated the following amounts in supplemental fiscal 1978 funds:

	Budget Request	Final Appropriation
Agriculture	$ 4,145,000	$ 102,745,000
Foreign Operations	6,300,000	6,300,000
HUD, Independent Agencies	4,625,000,000	4,638,047,000
Interior, Related Agencies	1,303,792,000	746,813,000
Labor, HEW	110,337,000[1]	350,689,000
Public Works	——	106,450,000
State, Justice, Commerce and the Judiciary	1,408,850,000[2]	1,407,000,000
Treasury, Postal Service and General Government	——	54,000
Transportation	——	18,000,000
Defense	449,000,000	423,800,000
Total	$7,907,424,000	$7,799,898,000

1. Includes $15 million in authority to spend debt receipts.
2. Includes $725 million in Small Business Administration disaster funds requested Oct. 7.
In addition, the bill rescinded $463.4 million appropriated in fiscal 1977 to build two B-1 bombers and the short-range attack missiles they would have carried.

Background

Administration plans to rescind the fiscal 1977 money and thus resolve the B-1 issue for good had fallen victim to the calendar and to lax discipline among Carter's supporters. House Democratic leaders had planned to vote on the rescission in November 1977, when they thought it would be approved. But action on the B-1 was deferred that day when the House first voted to recommit the supplemental bill to the Appropriations Committee because of another controversial provision. When the House finally voted on the B-1 Dec. 6, 78 members did not vote, many of them having already left Washington for the holidays, and several Democrats who usually could be counted on to support the leadership voted against the President's position. The Senate's position favoring the rescission was rejected 166-191.

Senate Democratic leaders had wanted to reaffirm Senate support for the rescission before the December adjournment. A vote was postponed because absenteeism among opponents of the plane made the outcome doubtful.

Maneuvering

In the debate preceding the Dec. 6 House vote, supporters of the B-1 expressed concern over reports coming from Geneva that a protocol to the SALT treaty would, for the first three years, limit to 1,500 miles the range of any air-launched cruise missile deployed. They argued that to reach important targets deep in the Soviet Union, such missiles would have to be carried well within the range of Soviet air defenses; modified B-52s and commercial wide-body jets the administration planned to use for that role would never survive, they argued.

If the fiscal 1977 money were spent to build two B-1s —the fifth and sixth planes—according to this argument, it would keep the contractors in business until late 1979. During that time, resumption of B-1 production would be feasible if a new treaty limited the cruise missile too severely.

On Dec. 19, 1977, Sen. William Proxmire, D-Wis., a leading B-1 foe, asked the Pentagon to comment on the arguments raised in the House debate. In its reply, the Pentagon maintained that B-52s could get close enough to strike Soviet targets with cruise missiles and that the newest model, the B-52H, could penetrate to inland targets at least through 1987. To shoot down the hundreds of cruise missiles that would be set loose in such an attack, it said, would require a revolution in Soviet air defenses.

In any case, according to the Pentagon, rejection of the rescission request would preserve the B-1 production option only for 6-10 months and would require an additional $280-million beyond the fiscal 1977 money already appropriated.

Before Proxmire could use his new arguments, B-1 supporters launched their own attack. Rep. Jack F. Kemp, R-N.Y., who had received a copy of the Proxmire-Pentagon correspondence, drafted arguments countering the Pentagon statements, and Sen. James A. McClure, R-Idaho, inserted the entire mass of material into the *Congressional Record* on Jan. 26, with the B-1 supporters getting the last word.

Kemp said Russia already had in hand the basic equipment necessary to build a cruise missile defense. And he insisted the Pentagon position underrated the ability of a manned bomber using electronic defenses to thwart enemy detection.

Proxmire and John C. Culver, D-Iowa, huddled with Pentagon officials the weekend before the Senate vote to counter Kemp's arguments. Although they conceded that the Russians had some of the pieces of a cruise missile defense system, they said that organizing and extending it over the Soviet Union would take enormous amounts of time and money. And even then, they said, cruise missile development would stay ahead of their defenses as later U.S. models were produced having their own electronic defenses and much greater speed.

On Jan. 31, 1978, the day before the Senate vote, John C. Stennis, D-Miss., Defense Appropriations Subcommittee chairman, circulated to all senators a letter from Air Force Chief of Staff Gen. David C. Jones urging rescission of the B-1 money. While admitting that he still wanted the big bomber, Jones said there was "no realistic probability" that the B-1 would be built. Therefore, he said, the Air Force had other pressing needs for the $742 million it ultimately would cost to build and test the two additional planes.

The Air Force assessment of the political situation — that Carter would prevail in the end, even if Congress kept the B-1 alive a little longer — apparently was persuasive with a number of Democrats sympathetic to the Pentagon, like Stennis, who had long supported B-1 production. After Carter announced his decision on June 30, 1977, Stennis had joined longtime B-1 foes Proxmire and Culver in trying to stop production funding so the money could be put to other defense uses.

Senate Action

A coalition of liberals and conservatives, along with the backing of the Air Force chief of staff, joined forces Feb. 1 to keep the Senate lined up behind President Carter's decision to shelve the B-1 bomber.

By a 58-37 vote, the Senate reaffirmed its position favoring the cancellation of $462 million appropriated in fiscal 1977 for the B-1 bomber program. *(Vote 26, p. 6-S)*

The vote closely paralleled the 59-36 roll call by which the Senate July 18, 1977, had removed all fiscal 1978 B-1 production money ($1.5 billion) from that year's defense appropriations bill. *(1977 Almanac p. 271)*

During five hours of sparsely attended debate, rescission supporters relied heavily on Gen. Jones' argument that the Air Force could not afford to spend $742 million to preserve the B-1 production option for a few more months. And Culver and Proxmire stressed the administration's original justification for canceling the B-1: Over the long-haul, the cruise missile was more likely than the B-1 to baffle Soviet air defenses.

The pro-B-1 side of the debate was dominated by conservative Republicans, including Jake Garn, Utah, John G. Tower, Texas, and Barry Goldwater, Ariz. They cited cancellation of the B-1 as only one of a series of Carter decisions that they said could relinquish strategic superiority to the Soviet Union by slowing modernization of the U.S. nuclear arsenal.

Nearly isolated, ideologically, among B-1 supporters was Majority Whip Alan Cranston, D-Calif., in whose state the B-1 would be manufactured. Cranston denied that he was motivated by constituency pressure, noting that he had voted against many weapons purchases that would have meant jobs for Californians. He insisted the B-1 was needed to hedge against uncertainty over the performance of the cruise missile. And he warned that large-scale deployment of the cruise missile could undercut chances for future strategic arms limitation treaties because limits on these relatively small weapons could not be verified.

The Senate first voted 57-38 in favor of a motion by Stennis killing an attempt by S. I. Hayakawa, R-Calif., to instruct Senate conferees on the appropriations bill to yield to the House position, thus retaining the B-1 money. On the vote, six senators reversed the positions they had taken the previous July; four moved from opposition to support of the B-1 and two from support to opposition, for a net gain of two for continued production of the plane. *(Vote 25, p. 6-S)*

The Senate then voted 58-37 to insist on its position in favor of the rescission and requested a new conference with the House.

House Action

By a surprisingly large margin, 234-182, the House Feb. 22 backed Carter and rescinded the money for the two B-1s. The vote came on a motion by Appropriations Committee Chairman George Mahon, D-Texas, to concur in the Senate's position in favor of the rescission. The House action reversed the December 1977 vote in which the B-1 money was upheld. *(Vote 58, p. 16-H)*

B-1 proponents tried to bolster supporters of the plane against White House and congressional pressure to accept the Senate language quickly in order to clear the $7.9 billion bill. "The agencies could have had this money long weeks ago if the administration had been less engrossed in killing the B-1," said Robert L. F. Sikes, D-Fla. "If we win this fight today for the B-1, we will still get the supplemental."

John Buchanan, R-Ala., an apparent target of the White House lobbying campaign, denounced a phone call to his office by the Environmental Protection Agency's second-ranking congressional liaison official, Larry Snowhite. Snowhite had urged Buchanan to vote for the rescission with the argument that $57 million in sewage treatment money for Alabama was tied up in the supplemental. "Can anyone explain to me the connection between this and the B-1 bomber?" he demanded.

But Carter's supporters, led by Mahon and Joseph P. Addabbo, D-N.Y., noted that the Senate had shown no tendency to give in on its rescission language. And several members rose to recite the litany of pork-barrel projects that would be stalled until the supplemental was cleared.

The substantive discussion of the merits of the rescission retraced the arguments made during the four House B-1 debates in 1977.

Opponents of the rescission insisted the manned bomber could not be supplanted by the cruise missile. The new robot would be helpless against the Soviet Union's dense anti-aircraft defenses, they said, including a new ultra-high-speed missile now under development called the SA-10.

Moreover, the Carter administration already had agreed to limitations on the range of the cruise missile in the arms limitation talks with Moscow, opponents said. These would render the new weapon useless against vital targets deep inside the Soviet Union. Construction of the two planes would keep the contractors in business for a few more months. During that time the Pentagon would retain a realistic option to go ahead with B-1 production if U.S.-Soviet relations took a turn for the worse.

Carter's supporters maintained that in any future attack on the Soviet Union, swarms of the tiny cruise missiles would have a far better chance of slipping through the defenses than would a few hundred B-1s. Noting that no B-1 production money was included in the fiscal 1978 Pentagon budget nor in the fiscal 1979 request, they said that rescission of the fiscal 1977 money was just the logical extension of decisions Congress already had made.

Some members charged that the fight over the bomber had become an institutional test of strength. Robert K. Dornan, R-Calif., in whose district the planes would have been manufactured, argued that completion of the two B-1s would have been no more costly than the cost of their cancellation plus the unemployment payments that would be needed for the 7,000 aerospace workers put out of work by terminating the plane. "What the president is saying here is that he does not want aircraft numbers five and six even if they are free. That is arrogant and absurd."

Armed Services Committee member Davis agreed with the diagnosis, but had a different prescription. "Let us cut out the argument between downtown and the House. Let us let the Air Force get on with the program that they need and let us try to improve them...and not sit here and waste time and money over two planes that will produce nothing."

B-1 Supporters' Strategy

In a last ditch effort to save the planes, Jim Lloyd, D-Calif., moved to table Mahon's motion that the House concur in the Senate's position. But Lloyd was defeated, 172-244. *(Vote 57, p. 16-H)*

Then Dornan demanded that the Mahon motion be split in two. After the House agreed to recede from its own position—the first part of the motion—by a standing vote of 126-110, Dornan moved to amend the second part accepting the Senate position. The Dornan version would have delayed implementation of the rescission until either house of Congress passed a resolution implementing it and, in any case, until 90 days after the Senate had ratified a new strategic arms limitation treaty (SALT II) with the Soviets.

Speaker Thomas P. O'Neill Jr., D-Mass., upheld Mahon's point of order that the Dornan motion was out of order since the SALT negotiations were not germane to the supplemental appropriations bill. The House then adopted the Senate position, 234-182.

Changing from opposition to the Carter position on the Dec. 6 vote to support on the Feb. 22 vote were 31 members, of whom 22 were Democrats: Allen, Tenn.; Andrews, N.C.; Annunzio, Ill.; Bevill, Ala.; Burke, Mass.; Davis, S.C.; Dicks, Wash.; Flood, Pa.; Gammage, Texas; Holland, S.C.; Jenrette, S.C.; Levitas, Ga.; Lloyd, Tenn.; Mann, S.C.; Milford, Texas; Natcher, Ky.; Patten, N.J.; Pepper, Fla.; Price, Ill.; Roybal, Calif.; Runnels, N.M.; and Wright, Texas.

Also switching to support of the rescission were nine Republicans: Conable, N.Y.; Duncan, Tenn.; Quayle, Ind.; Quie, Minn.; Quillen, Tenn.; Ruppe, Mich.; Sawyer, Mich.; Sebelius, Kans.; and Skubitz, Kan.

Switching from support of the rescission to opposition were Democrats Murphy, Pa., and Staggers, W.Va. ▮

Disaster Relief, 1978

With funds for assistance nearly exhausted as a result of severe floods and storms in 1977 and 1978, Congress speedily cleared a joint resolution (H J Res 796) approving a $300 million supplemental appropriation for disaster relief in fiscal 1978.

The House Appropriations Committee reported the measure March 20 (H Rept 95-990). The House approved it March 22 by a 393-4 vote, and the Senate passed it by voice vote March 23. *(House vote 145, p. 42-H)*

President Carter signed the measure into law April 4 (PL 95-255).

The aid program is triggered by the president's declaration of a major disaster or emergency, and is coordinated by the Federal Disaster Assistance Administration (FDAA). *(Background, 1970 Almanac p. 753, 1974 Alma-*

Congress had approved $150 million for fiscal 1978 disaster relief as part of the Housing and Urban Development — Independent Agencies appropriation bill (PL 95-119). *(1977 Almanac p. 279)*

That amount, the House Appropriations Committee said in its report, "was believed sufficient to meet average yearly relief requirements."

But floods in Johnstown, Pa., and Kansas City, plus other natural disasters, cost more than $180 million in fiscal 1978 funds, the report said.

Fiscal Emergency

Severe winter weather conditions in Michigan, Indiana, Ohio, Massachusetts, Rhode Island, Connecticut, California and elsewhere added another $180 million in estimated disaster relief expenses. The FDAA estimated that the total of $450 million appropriated for disaster relief would leave about $43 million for possible disasters during the remainder of fiscal 1978.

During debate in the Senate, Warren G. Magnuson, D-Wash., called the situation a "fiscal emergency." ▮

Disaster Loans, 1978

Congress May 12 cleared and the president May 21 signed into law a bill (H J Res 873 — PL 95-284) appropriating $758 million in supplemental funds for the disaster loan fund of the Small Business Administration (SBA). It was the second such supplemental appropriation in fiscal 1978.

Severe winter weather and the 1977 summer drought drained the SBA's disaster loan fund, prompting President Carter on April 18 to request the additional funding.

The House passed the appropriation bill May 8 by a vote of 346-23. The measure was reported May 2 by the Appropriations Committee (H Rept 95-1105). *(House passage, vote 244, p. 70-H)*

The Senate Appropriations Committee reported the bill May 10 (S Rept 95-801) with two unrelated amendments, one appropriating a $63 million supplement to the Department of Labor's Summer Youth Program and one providing a death gratuity of one year's congressional salary for the widows of three deceased senators. Senate passage of H Res 873 was by voice vote May 11.

The resolution was then returned to the House, which agreed to the Senate amendments May 12, completing congressional action on the bill.

Funding Levels

The resolution provided $750 million to enable SBA to continue providing loans for the repair of physical damage resulting from natural disasters. Final approval of some loan applications had been delayed because of the loan fund's depletion.

The remaining $8 million of the appropriation was earmarked for salaries and expenses of temporary personnel to process and administer the loans.

Congress, in the 1978 Justice, State and Commerce Departments appropriations act (PL 95-86), allocated $115 million for the loan fund. *(1977 Almanac p. 256)*

An additional appropriation of $1.4 billion was included in the 1978 Supplemental Appropriations Act (PL 95-240). *(Weekly Report p. 541)*

The committee report said the most recent SBA supplement was needed to meet the 1978 demand for natural disaster loans expected to total $2.3 billion.

The $758 million supplement and an expected 1978 loan repayment of $255 million brought the disaster loan fund to $2.5 billion for the year. About $210 million of that was for loans to cover catastrophic costs incurred by small business in complying with Occupational Safety and Health Administration (OSHA) and other regulations.

Critics of H J Res 873 argued on the floor that the disaster loan fund was a big spending program that had gotten out of hand because of poor initial budget estimates. They said the fund allowed low-interest loans to disaster victims who could get non-federal financing and who occasionally put loan money in the bank instead of using it for reconstruction.

Neal Smith, D-Iowa, countered that the SBA loans were essential to induce businessmen to seek credit and rebuild in their former locations, thus preventing disaster-stricken communities from being literally wiped out.

Congress previously had cleared a $300 million supplemental HUD appropriation (H J Res 796 — PL 95-255) to cope with floods in Pennsylvania and Missouri and Northeast winter storms. *(Story, this page)* ▮

Transportation Funds

Congress completed action July 20 on the first of 13 regular fiscal 1979 funding bills for federal government departments — an $8.7 billion appropriation for the Transportation Department and related agencies.

The measure (HR 12933 — PL 95-335), contained federal aid for highway, mass transit and other transportation programs, and set a ceiling of $7.95 billion on the amount of money that could be obligated during the year for highway projects funded from the Highway Trust Fund.

The legislation provided $521 million less in budget authority than the amount requested by the administration for fiscal 1979, but the final figure was more than $2.5 billion above the appropriation approved for transportation programs in fiscal 1978.

As approved by House and Senate conferees, the appropriations measure barred the use of fiscal 1979 appropriated funds for implementing or enforcing a June 1977 requirement that passenger vehicles be equipped with air bags. *(Background, 1977 Almanac p. 531)*

Congressional aides and Transportation Department officials, however, said the requirement would not be affected.

They explained that the first deadline for installation of the passive restraint system would not occur until model year 1981, and said the bill specifically permitted the use of appropriated funds for research and development activities related to automobile airbags.

As approved, HR 12933 provided the United States Railway Association with new budget authority $300 million above the president's request. The additional funds were for the purchase of Consolidated Rail Corp. (ConRail) stock to provide a larger federal subsidy for ConRail's fiscal 1979 operations.

HR 12933 was passed by the House June 12 by a vote of 347-25 with an appropriation of $8.8 billion.

The Senate version, approved June 23 on a 55-15 vote, provided new budget authority of $8.6 billion.

The House gave final approval to the conference committee compromise on July 19. The Senate approved it July 20, completing action on the bill.

Final Provisions

As signed into law, HR 12933 made the following appropriations for fiscal 1979:

Agency	Budget Request	Final Appropriation
Transportation Department		
Office of the secretary	$ 45,800,000	$ 44,500,000
Coast Guard	1,505,616,096	1,500,620,096
Federal Aviation Administration	2,518,812,000	2,401,025,000
Federal Highway Administration	145,451,000	251,086,000
National Highway Traffic Safety Administration	84,460,000	83,335,000
Federal Railroad Administration	1,573,170,000	1,462,550,000
Urban Mass Transportation Administration	3,065,000,000	2,361,600,000
Research and special programs	24,420,000	24,760,000
Subtotal	$8,962,729,096	$8,129,476,096
Related Agencies		
National Transportation Safety Board	$ 15,650,000	$ 15,600,000
Civil Aeronautics Board	95,942,000	95,900,000
Interstate Commerce Commission	70,822,000	70,400,000
Panama Canal Zone Government	76,906,000	75,035,000
United States Railway Association	27,200,000	323,000,000
Washington Metropolitan Area Transit Authority	19,374,000	38,142,000
National Transportation Policy Study Commission	0	0
Subtotal	$ 305,894,000	$ 618,077,000
TOTAL	$9,268,623,096	$8,747,553,096

In addition, the bill:

- Prohibited the use of appropriated funds for the implementation or enforcement of any requirement that motor vehicles be equipped with airbags, but permitted the use of such funds for activities related to airbag research and development.
- Limited the amount of money that could be obligated for federal aid to highways from the Highway Trust Fund to $7.95 billion.
- Limited to $593,150,000 the amount of money that could be obligated from the Airport and Airway Trust Fund for airport development grants.
- Directed that a $2 million grant be awarded the Tri-City Airport, in Freeland, Mich.
- Provided $50 million in federal funds for the replacement of the West Seattle bridge in Washington state.

House Committee Action

As reported (H Rept 95-1252) June 1 by the House Appropriations Committee, HR 12933 contained total new budget authority of $8,857,296,096 for fiscal year 1979 operations and programs of the Transportation Department and related agencies.

The committee cut $211,327,000 from the $9,086,623,-096 recommended in the president's budget, but was still $2,630,495,073 over the $6,226,801,023 appropriated for fiscal 1978.

In its report, the committee urged the Transportation Department to purchase American materials and manufactured goods whenever possible.

The committee noted that HR 12933 provided funding for a number of programs for which authorizing legislation was not yet enacted. Appropriations for certain other programs, however, were deferred, including funding for oil pollution liability and compensation, development of multipurpose passenger terminals, intercity subsidies and certain highway projects.

Transportation Department

Office of the Secretary. Because the size of the secretary's office had been trimmed back in a reorganization in 1977, the committee recommended $44.5 million for the office for fiscal 1979, a cut of $1.3 million from the administration's request. Some reductions were made in funding for travel, contractual support and equipment.

No funds were provided for a requested study of auto repair practices. The committee said it felt that regulation of auto repair practices should be left to state and local authorities.

Coast Guard. The committee recommended an appropriation of $1.5 billion, a cut of $8.6 million from the administration's proposed budget. Personnel levels were increased over the president's recommendation because the committee said the additional personnel were needed to adequately carry out the Coast Guard's environmental protection, law enforcement and marine safety programs. Most of the recommended cuts would come out of the Coast Guard's bridge alteration and removal programs.

Federal Aviation Administration. The committee recommended a 1979 appropriation of about $2.4 billion, a reduction of $133 million from the administration proposal. The committee agreed to an increase in the funds for operation of the air traffic control system, but found that cuts could be made in proposed spending for communications services because rate increases anticipated by the administration did not take place.

Federal Highway Administration. The committee recommended that a limit of $8.1 billion be placed on the spending obligations that could be incurred for federal highway aid out of the Highway Trust Fund for the fiscal year. The amount was sharply lower than the $11.1 billion authorization recommended for fiscal 1979 by legislation (HR 11733) approved by the House Public Works Committee, but only slightly less than the $8.5 billion recommended by the Senate Public Works panel.

The committee repeated a warning made annually since 1976 that the transportation secretary should not use the ceiling on obligations to "distort the priorities" established for the federal highway aid programs by Congress.

National Highway Traffic Safety Administration. The committee recommended a cut of $4,250,000 from the administration proposal ($84,460,000) because, it said, the lesser amount was "sufficient" for the agency to carry out its auto safety and fuel programs. Among the recommended cuts were $1 million from a program to develop a consumer automotive rating system and $1.5 million from the agency's automotive fuel economy research program.

The committee recommended a ceiling of $172 million, the amount requested in the administration's budget, for highway safety programs funded from the Highway Trust Fund. According to the committee, $40 million would be for enforcement of the nationwide 55 mph speed limit.

Federal Railroad Administration. The committee recommended full funding of the administration's requests for Northeast rail corridor improvements and for the National Railroad Passenger Corporation (Amtrak).

The $660 million recommended for Amtrak for fiscal 1979 was less than the $768 million authorization (HR 11493) recommended by the House Commerce Committee May 15, but more than the $635 million previously authorized (S 3040) by the Senate.

Though the committee recommended a cut of $500,000 in the agency's appropriation for railroad safety, it directed the agency to conduct an evaluation of existing federal and state railroad safety programs and recommended the addition of 25 new rail safety positions, including 18 track inspectors.

Urban Mass Transportation Administration. The committee recommended total funding for urban mass transit of $3.3 billion, including $2.5 billion in direct appropriations and $850 million in contract authority.

Related Agencies

United States Railway Association. The committee added $300 million to the bill for the purchase of stock of the Consolidated Rail Corp. (ConRail). The 1979 budget did not include any request for stock purchases.

Interstate Commerce Commission. The committee recommended a funding level of $70.4 million for fiscal 1979 for the commission, $422,000 below the administration's request.

The committee also recommended increasing by 30 the number of railroad service agents, to more effectively field complaints concerning what the committee termed ConRail's "uniformly poor" service offered small shippers.

Panama Canal. Despite Senate approval of the Panama Canal treaties, the committee said, the 1979 budget would still provide for continued U.S. operation of the Canal Zone government and the Panama Canal Company. Funding for the new Panama Canal Commission, the committee said, would be considered at a later date.

Civil Aeronautics Board. The committee directed the agency not to use appropriated funds to help underwrite the costs of public interest participation.

House Floor Action

HR 12933, which was approved June 12 by a vote of 347-25, provided the Transportation Department and related agencies with new budget authority of $8,847,296,096 for fiscal year 1979. As passed the bill was $10 million less than the amount recommended by the House Appropriations Committee. *(Vote 379, p. 108-H)*

The $10 million, deleted by voice vote through an amendment offered by Robert E. Bauman, R-Md., had been earmarked for the Federal Highway Administration as the United States' contribution to construction costs of a segment of the Pan American Highway that passed through Panama. Bauman argued that the funds should be deleted because Panama, soon to be the owner of the U.S.-controlled Panama Canal, could afford to pay for the road.

The House issued a warning to the Transportation Department that it might be headed for trouble on its mandate that all new cars be equipped with air bags or other passive restraints by the 1984 model year.

By a vote of 237-143, it approved an amendment by Bud Shuster, R-Pa., prohibiting the department from spending any money during the year to implement or enforce a June 1977 requirement that passenger vehicles be equipped with air bags. *(Vote 377, p. 108-H)*

Though the vote did not scuttle the mandate altogether — because the earliest the air bags would be required on new cars was Sept. 1, 1981 — the program's critics used the vote to warn the department that the mandate might later be reversed.

Though the Senate in October 1977 voted to table, and thus kill, a resolution that would have blocked the department's order, the House never was given the opportunity to vote on the issue. A similar resolution had been rejected by the House Commerce Committee. *(1977 Almanac p. 531)*

After accepting the Shuster amendment, the House rejected, 180-194, an amendment offered by Rep. Bob

Eckhardt, D-Texas, that would have permitted the department to use fiscal 1979 funds for research and development concerning passive restraint systems and to participate in any court action that might result from the department's 1977 passive restraint mandate. *(Vote 378, p. 108-H)*

The House then accepted by voice vote an amendment by Silvio O. Conte, R-Mass., to permit the department to pursue passive restraint research and development but not court action.

Supporters of the air bag requirement argued that the device, if required, would save as many as 9,000 lives annually. Opponents of the mandate argued that air bags were unproven.

In addition to issuing a stern warning to the Transportation Department concerning its air bag requirement, the House also indicated it was paying close attention to the spending habits of the Consolidated Rail Corp. (ConRail). It did so by accepting on voice votes two amendments offered by Toby Moffett, D-Conn., to restrict ConRail's federal funding.

ConRail had come under criticism from some members of Congress for paying "incentive bonuses" to some of its top executives despite the fact that the railroad operated at a loss.

In addition, it was revealed June 9 in press reports that a congressional committee, the Interstate Commerce Commission, the Justice Department and a federal grand jury were investigating a report that ConRail early in 1978 had had 14,000 W-2 income tax forms returned to it by the U.S. Postal Service because the employees to whom the forms had been mailed could not be located.

Though the firm maintained that only about 1,000 of the 14,000 federal income disclosure forms could not be accounted for, the federal investigators apparently were seeking to determine if ConRail had committed fraud by issuing checks to non-existent employees.

The two Moffett amendments barred the use of any funds in the bill for the payment of "incentive bonuses" and prevented ConRail from using any of its fiscal 1979 appropriations until enactment of authorizing legislation.

HOUSE PROVISIONS

As passed by the House, HR 12933 appropriated the following amounts for fiscal 1979:

Agency	Budget Request	House-Passed Appropriation
Transportation Department		
Office of the secretary	$ 45,800,000	$ 44,500,000
Coast Guard	1,505,616,096	1,497,013,096
Federal Aviation Administration	2,518,812,000	2,385,703,000
Federal Highway Administration	145,451,000	221,986,000
National Highway Traffic Safety Administration	84,460,000	80,210,000
Federal Railroad Administration	1,573,170,000	1,534,910,000
Urban Mass Transportation Administration	2,865,000,000	2,461,600,000
Research and special programs	24,420,000	23,100,000
Subtotal	$8,762,729,096	$8,249,022,096
Related agencies		
National Transportation Safety Board	$ 15,650,000	$ 15,600,000
Civil Aeronautics Board	95,942,000	95,900,000
Interstate Commerce Commission	70,822,000	70,400,000
Panama Canal Zone Government	76,906,000	74,000,000
United States Railway Association	27,200,000	323,000,000
Washington Metropolitan Area Transit Authority	19,374,000	19,374,000
National Transportation Policy Study Commission	0	0
Subtotal	$ 305,894,000	$ 598,274,000
TOTAL	$9,068,623,096	$8,847,296,096

Senate Committee Action

HR 12933 was reported (S Rept 95-938) by the Senate Appropriations Committee June 19. As reported, the bill provided total new budget authority for fiscal year 1979 of $8,565,943,096.

The total represented a cut of $702,680,000 from the $9,268,623,096 recommended in the president's fiscal 1979 budget, but the amount was $2,339,142,073 above the sum appropriated for fiscal 1978. *(1977 Almanac p. 237)*

In its report, the committee followed the example of the House Appropriations Committee in urging the federal transportation agencies to "comply with the spirit as well as the strict letter of current 'Buy American' legislation" by purchasing American goods and materials "except in extraordinary circumstances."

Transportation Department

Office of the Secretary. The committee accepted the House-passed appropriation of $44.5 million for the office.

The committee criticized the department for its slow distribution of transportation aid to rural areas in the past, and directed it to do so more promptly in the future.

The committee also scolded the Federal Highway Administration for spending too much money on the 1977 publication of a book entitled "America's Highways." The committee directed the secretary to obtain committee approval before pursuing such projects again.

Coast Guard. An appropriation of $1,509,220,096 — $3.6 million above the administration's request — was recommended by the committee. A major reason for the increase was to improve the Coast Guard's capability to deal with oil spills, the committee explained.

The House-passed appropriation was $8.6 million below the administration request.

Federal Aviation Administration. The Senate committee approved the same appropriation ($2.4 billion) for the agency as that in the House-passed bill. It recommended, however, the hiring of additional environmental review personnel; the House committee had recommended the hiring of additional air traffic control personnel, instead.

The Senate committee recommended deletion of a provision in the House version barring air traffic controllers from using appropriated funds for "familiarization travel" during their leave time. The provision was tacked onto the House bill during June 9 floor debate.

Federal Highway Administration. The committee recommended that a limit of $7.8 billion be placed on spending obligations that could be incurred for federal highway aid out of the Highway Trust Fund for fiscal 1979. The House had agreed to a limit of $8.1 billion, while both House and Senate Public Works committees had recommended higher levels of spending in pending authorization bills.

The committee report directed the transportation secretary to make an estimated $75 million in federal funds available for replacement of the north span of the West Seattle bridge. The report termed the span "deteriorated" and said it had been severely damaged and closed to traffic recently after being hit by a ship.

"Because of the unique and emergency nature of the problem," the report stated, "the committee has relieved the secretary from making the usual findings and other administrative details prior to making funding available for replacement of this bridge. . . ."

The committee also recommended the full $20 million appropriation requested in the president's budget for the Darien Gap Highway. The funds represented the U.S. contribution to construction costs of a segment of the Pan American Highway that passed through Panama.

The House committee had recommended a $10 million appropriation, but the funds were deleted from the bill on the House floor.

National Highway Traffic Safety Administration. The committee recommended restoration of cuts made in the agency's budget by the House. The cuts affected programs to develop a consumer automotive rating system, conduct research in auto fuel economy, and cover expenses of citizen participation in agency proceedings.

Urban Mass Transportation Administration. After shuffling around a number of aid categories, the committee recommended a total of $3.06 billion in funding for urban mass transit aid, including $2.21 billion in direct appropriations and $850 million in contract authority. The committee dropped appropriations of $250 million earmarked in the House-passed legislation for transit operating subsidies not yet authorized by either House or Senate.

Related Agencies

National Transportation Safety Board. The board was directed by the committee to complete a study by March 1, 1979, to determine how the Federal Railroad Administration could more effectively prevent railroad derailments involving hazardous materials.

Civil Aeronautics Board. The committee recommended the same appropriation ($95.9 million) as did the House-passed legislation, but disagreed with the House committee's order that the agency not use appropriated funds to help underwrite the costs of public participation in board proceedings.

Senate Floor Action

HR 12933 was approved June 23 by a vote of 55-15 after the Senate turned back an effort by conservatives to cut mass transit spending by $170 million. *(Vote 172, p. 29-S)*

As passed by the Senate, HR 12933 appropriated $8,568,543,096, an increase of $2.6 million over the committee-approved figure.

The increase, which was contained in an amendment offered by Kansas Sens. Robert Dole, R, and James B. Pearson, R, was to provide for construction of an access road from Lawrence, Kan., to the state's Clinton Reservoir. It was approved by voice vote.

An amendment offered by Richard G. Lugar, R-Ind., to cut $170 million from the appropriation for the Urban Mass Transportation Administration received strong support from Senate conservatives, but was defeated 26-44. *(Vote 171, p. 29-S)*

Conservatives also discussed challenging the $20 million appropriation for the U.S. contribution to construction of the Darien Gap Highway through Panama, but never brought the proposal to a vote.

Instead, the Senate adopted by voice vote an amendment by John Melcher, D-Mont., to require the Transportation Department to take steps to prevent the spread of hoof and mouth disease from Panama to the United States through use of the highway.

SENATE PROVISIONS

As passed by the Senate June 23, HR 12933 appropriated the following amounts for fiscal 1979:

Agency	House-Passed Appropriation	Senate-Passed Appropriation
Transportation Department		
Office of the secretary	$ 44,500,000	$ 44,500,000
Coast Guard	1,497,013,096	1,509,220,096
Federal Aviation Administration	2,385,703,000	2,401,025,000
Federal Highway Administration	221,986,000	257,986,000
National Highway Traffic Safety Administration	80,210,000	86,460,000
Federal Railroad Administration	1,534,910,000	1,413,890,000
Urban Mass Transportation Administration	2,461,600,000	2,211,600,000
Research and special programs	23,100,000	25,420,000
Subtotal	$8,249,022,096	$7,950,101,096
Related Agencies		
National Transportation Safety Board	$ 15,600,000	$ 15,965,000
Civil Aeronautics Board	95,900,000	95,900,000
Interstate Commerce Commission	70,400,000	70,400,000
Panama Canal Zone Government	74,000,000	75,035,000
United States Railway Association	323,000,000	323,000,000
Washington Metropolitan Area Transit Authority	19,374,000	38,142,000
National Transportation Policy Study Commission	0	0
Subtotal	$ 598,274,000	$ 618,442,000
TOTAL	$8,847,296,096	$8,568,543,096

Conference Report

The conference agreement on HR 12933 was reported (H Rept 95-1329) June 29.

Major differences between the two versions were resolved as follows:

Coast Guard. Conferees agreed on $800,000 for the purchase of oil spill pollution prevention equipment. Conferees also directed the Coast Guard to use research and development carryover funds to test an airborne all-weather pollution surveillance system and to improve its pollution cleanup capability.

Federal Aviation Administration. Conferees agreed with the Senate position deleting a House-passed provision that would have barred air traffic controllers from using appropriated funds for "familiarization travel" during their leave time. Conferees said such travel served a useful purpose in educating controllers, but directed the FAA administrator to ensure that the program was not abused.

Federal Highway Administration. A Senate-approved appropriation of $20 million for the Darien Gap Highway, representing the U.S. contribution to construction costs of a segment of the Pan American Highway that passed through Panama, was deleted by conferees. The House had deleted a $10 million appropriation for the highway in earlier floor action.

National Highway Traffic Safety Administration. Conferees provided $125,000 for an experimental program to encourage citizen participation in the agency's rule-making activities. The total appropriated for highway safety approved by conferees was $81,620,000.

Civil Aeronautics Board. Conferees approved expenditures of $150,000 for an experimental program to encourage citizen participation in board proceedings.

Canal Zone Government. Conferees directed that no appropriated funds in the bill be used for capital acquisitions that might be transferred to Panama. For the Canal Zone government, conferees agreed to $1,035,000.

United States Railway Association. Conferees deleted a House-passed provision that would have barred the payment by the Consolidated Rail Corp. (ConRail) of bonuses to its executive personnel.

Airport Grant. The conferees' directive that a $2 million grant be awarded the Tri-City Airport in Freeland, Mich., was not contained in either the House or Senate bills. It first appeared in the conference report. The airport served the Midland, Mich., hometown of Rep. Elford A. Cederberg, ranking Republican member of the House Appropriations Committee.

Military Construction: NATO Projects Cut

The fiscal 1979 military construction appropriations bill (HR 12927 — PL 95-374) cleared Aug. 21 contained only a fraction of the $318 million requested for construction projects in Europe to serve NATO combat missions.

The final version of both that bill and the related construction authorization bill (HR 12602) cut deeply into the request for NATO-related funds. The Appropriations and Armed Services Committees of the Senate and House agreed that such projects should be paid for by the alliance-wide common construction fund, known as the Infrastructure program.

The administration had maintained that other members of the NATO alliance were bearing their fair share of the burden of common defense and that the United States eventually would recoup from the Infrastructure a substantial amount of the funds requested. In the meantime, essential facilities could be constructed.

Congressional action on the appropriations bill left uncertain the status of a $56.9 million storage site for the tanks, trucks and other heavy equipment of an Army division whose personnel could be flown to Europe in a few days in case of an international crisis. The final version of the appropriations bill allowed $20 million less than the request for the so-called POMCUS storage site. Senate-House conferees on the bill said that the difference should be made up by the Infrastructure program. But according to an Army spokesman, construction of the facility could not begin until Congress shifted to the POMCUS site $20 million in funds previously appropriated for other purposes but not yet spent.

In 1978 there were the equivalent of more than five U.S. divisions in Europe and POMCUS equipment for the equivalent of more than two more divisions. In January, Defense Secretary Harold Brown announced a plan to add POMCUS sites for three more divisions so that by 1983 the United States could double — to more than 10 Army divisions — its forces in Europe within two weeks.

The site included in the bill would be the first of the three new facilities.

Provisions

As cleared, HR 12927 appropriated the following amounts for military construction projects in fiscal 1979:

	Budget Request	Final Appropriation
Army	$ 881,900,000	$ 711,509,000
Navy	820,900,000	760,145,000
Air Force	639,100,000	483,264,000
Defense Agencies	176,300,000	194,880,000
Reserve and National Guard	158,900,000	168,900,000
Military Family Housing and Home-owners' Assistance	1,575,900,000	1,562,165,000
Total New Budget Authority	$4,253,000,000	$3,880,863,000

House Committee Action

The House Appropriations Committee reported (H Rept 95-1246) HR 12927 on June 1.

As reported, the bill appropriated $3,964,087,000, a reduction of $408,113,000 in the administration's $4,372,200,-000 request for construction.

NATO Financing

The committee expressed its support for most of the NATO-related projects requested. But it objected to Pentagon plans to pay for them with U.S. funds even though repayment for jointly funded construction projects (the Infrastructure program) subsequently would be sought from the alliance.

Over the years the United States had followed this practice, which the Pentagon calls "pre-financing," for projects totaling $622 million. The Pentagon had argued in each case that the military necessity for the project was too great to await alliance approval.

Military Construction Subcommittee member Ralph S. Regula, R-Ohio, protested to the House June 16 that "the European NATO countries...have benefited greatly from this availability of U.S. funds. This amounts to an interest-free loan."

But Regula went beyond the argument over pre-financing to echo a theme that has been heard in many defense-related congressional hearings: The European allies were sufficiently prosperous to relieve the United States of some of its share of the cost of defending Western Europe.

Tighter Controls

The committee made cuts of $65.9 million to encourage the Defense Department to tighten up on what it saw as slack management of the military construction budget.

Planning and Design Costs. A 6 percent reduction — $12 million — was imposed on the $198.5 million request for design costs. According to the committee, the Pentagon contracted for more design work than subsequently was needed. And despite an overly complex review procedure in effect for such design work, the services still were requesting expensive changes in the completed plans, said the panel.

In order to bring design costs under tighter fiscal management, the committee directed the Pentagon to list them in a separate budget account in future appropriations requests. And it ordered the department to streamline its review procedures for contracted design work.

The panel also ordered the Pentagon to experiment with competitive selection of architectural contractors.

Maintenance of Existing Facilities. By scrimping on maintenance of its existing facilities, the Pentagon was setting the stage for large construction requests in the future as the facilities deteriorated, the committee maintained. "Funds for the maintenance of real property should compete with funds requested for new facilities," the committee said. It suggested that the Pentagon increase its funding of real property maintenance in future years to prolong the life of military facilities.

The only maintenance funds covered by the bill were for military family housing, which the committee increased by $15 million. But it cut overall new construction requests by $10.9 million to emphasize to the Pentagon that it expected the department to step up maintenance programs.

Cost Estimates. Besides the specific program cuts, a reduction of about 1 percent ($43 million) was imposed on the overall amount in the bill. The committee charged that over the previous three years the Pentagon had built up a surplus of more than $300 million because of overestimates of project costs or project cancellations. The committee observed that since the private construction market was not strong currently, the services could expect a continuation of the low bids that had been experienced in recent construction programs. And it said the Army and Navy were allowing too much for unforeseen contingencies in their cost estimates.

Naval Repair Facilities

The committee killed projects totaling $35 million for a Navy plan to develop improved repair facilities at six Navy bases. But it increased by $27 million — to nearly $100 million — the amount appropriated for improvements at Navy shipyards.

The Navy hoped to use the new repair stations to perform some routine maintenance on warships while they remained in the water, allowing them to be in service for longer periods between full-scale overhauls at shipyards.

The committee protested that the proposed repair stations — which eventually would require more than $300 million to construct — would duplicate the work of existing Navy shipyards. The plan would require far more maintenance specialists than the Navy now had, it said. And it would take work away from private shipyards that the Navy had to keep in business in case of emergencies, the panel insisted.

Energy Conservation

Although it noted that the Pentagon had made "significant progress" in developing energy conservation programs, the committee directed the department to improve the efficiency of its equipment for monitoring energy use. And it cautioned the department against cost escalation, after a conservation project was begun, that might make the program no longer economical. The committee implied that the Pentagon might be too enthusiastic about the use of solar power. "Although the concept of solar energy is good, the Defense Department needs to carefully evaluate the benefits of individual systems prior to moving into large capital systems."

Base Realignments

The department would have to give Congress 30 days' notice before it could use any of its funds set aside for minor construction projects for the transfer or relocation of any operation or program from one military base to another. Existing law required prior congressional notification of any base realignments involving significant numbers of civilian Pentagon employees. The committee said it was concerned that Congress' intent to be notified and advised of such major moves might be circumvented if use of minor construction funds became the first step in larger funding requirements in the future.

Continuing its long-term policy of pressing the Pentagon to disperse administrative offices from the Washington, D.C., area, the committee denied $3.5 million requested by the Navy for consolidation at the Washington Navy Yard of various data analysis offices.

House Floor Action

The House passed HR 12927 June 16 by a 278-13 vote. *(Vote 405, p. 116-H)*

As reported May 24, the bill was $408 million less than what the administration wanted. But these cuts enabled the committee to fend off a move by Clarence E. Miller, R-Ohio, that would have cut the overall appropriation by 2 percent, amounting to about $77 million.

But when Miller offered his amendment to the bill, Military Construction Subcommittee Chairman Gunn McKay, D-Utah, and Regula pointed out that the panel already had cut the budget request by almost 10 percent and that any further reduction would undercut U.S. combat readiness.

After the amendment was shouted down by voice vote, Miller asked for a roll call, but no other member then on the floor supported his move; support from 20 members is necessary to force a roll call when the House is considering amendments.

Despite the emphasis on frugality made by some members, others thanked the panel for the funding recommendations it made for certain military installations in their districts. Said Norman D. Dicks, D-Wash.: "I happen to represent a district that has five major defense bases. . . . The [committee] did not give us everything we wanted, but we got most of what we wanted. The committee has been very, very helpful. . . ."

Provisions

As passed by the House June 16, HR 12927 appropriated the following amounts for military construction projects for fiscal 1979:

	Budget Request	House Passed
Army	$ 881,900,000	$ 693,044,000
Navy	820,900,000	729,995,000
Air Force	639,100,000	513,703,000
Defense Agencies	176,300,000	192,680,000
Reserve and National Guard	158,900,000	145,300,000
Military Family Housing and Home-owners' Assistance	1,575,900,000	1,689,365,000[1]
Total New Budget Authority	$4,253,000,000	$3,964,087,000

[1] Includes $119,200,000 for debt reduction.

Senate Committee Action

The Senate Appropriations Committee reported HR 12927 after deleting the entire amount — $318.3 million — requested for NATO-related projects. In its report (S Rept 95-1019) filed July 19, the panel unequivocally endorsed the position previously taken by its House counterpart and by Senate Armed Services. "This adjustment is without prejudice to the projects themselves," the committee insisted. "Rather, the issue here is whether or not the United States should continue to unilaterally finance projects which are of direct benefit to the alliance."

The House committee had made a much less severe reduction, and to demonstrate its commitment to a larger Infrastructure program, it had increased the Infrastructure contribution from $70 million requested to $90 million. The administration planned to add to that new budget authority another $20 million which it expected to recoup from the Infrastructure for NATO-related projects previously funded unilaterally by the United States.

The Senate committee not only did not increase the Infrastructure contribution, it cut it by $5 million to $65 million. A total of $25 million — instead of the planned $20 million — should be recoupable from the alliance "with concerted effort," according to the panel.

Canal Treaty Implementation. The committee said that the Pentagon should be allowed to use existing authority for emergency construction projects needed to implement the Panama Canal treaties, subject to prior approval by the Appropriations Committees of the Senate and House.

The House Appropriations Committee insisted in its report on the bill that any construction related to the treaties should go through the full appropriations process, either as a budget amendment to the fiscal 1979 request or as a supplemental appropriation request.

(Treaty opponents in the House had been waging legislative guerrilla warfare against the pacts by trying to force consideration by the full House of any action that would implement them.)

The Senate panel agreed in principle with the House position that projects of major importance should go through the full legislative process, but insisted that the treaty-related projects were an exception. The administration had testified as early as fall 1977 that it would need to spend $3.5 million during fiscal 1979 to relocate units that would be leaving the Canal Zone. And as a practical matter, a supplemental appropriations bill could not be passed by December when the new facilities would have to be begun.

"It is fairly certain that withholding military construction funds will not stop implementation of the treaty, and it certainly does not absolve the United States from its treaty obligations," the committee said.

Design Costs. The Senate committee agreed with the House panel that the Pentagon could tighten up its management of construction planning and design projects (for which the budget request included nearly $200 million). But it disagreed with some moves taken by the House to enforce greater fiscal discipline.

It restored a $12 million across-the-board cut made by the House in the design and planning programs, saying it doubted that much could be saved. Already, it noted, the fiscal 1979 request for these projects was substantially below the fiscal 1978 request. And most of the projects in the budget were far enough along in their design that the cost estimates were based on relatively firm data.

The Senate committee also rejected a House requirement that the Pentagon experiment with the use of competitive bidding in the award of architectural and engineering contracts. It warned that a heavy price competition might erode the quality of the design work and that the system would be more expensive than it would be worth.

Property Maintenance. The Senate committee also rejected an across-the-board cut of $25.9 million and a partially offsetting increase of $15 million for maintenance of military family housing. There was no evidence for the House contention that the Pentagon had diverted funds away from maintenance of existing buildings in order to build more new ones, the committee said.

As a better way to ensure that maintenance received the proper emphasis, the committee proposed a provision requiring that no less than $635 million of the appropriation be used for property maintenance.

Senate Floor Action

The Senate passed the bill Aug. 3 after rejecting 26-60 an amendment by William V. Roth Jr., R-Del., that would have cut the bill across-the-board by 2 percent. The vote on final passage was 83-4. *(Votes 273, 274, p. 42-S)*

The Senate first had adopted, at the committee's behest, an amendment deleting from the bill items which were not included in the final version of the military construction authorization bill (HR 12602). The amendment also added to the bill the POMCUS storage site ($56.9 million) and some of the NATO-related Air Force projects ($20.1 million). But Construction Appropriations Subcommittee Chairman Walter (Dee) Huddleston, D-Ky., insisted that this was only so the projects could be discussed by the House-Senate conference on the bill.

Cut Rejected. Roth argued that the proposed reduction would put the Pentagon on notice that it must improve its efficiency, just as similar cuts had sent the same message to other federal departments. "It is hard to believe that in this kind of appropriation there is not room for a better job to be done by people in the Department of Defense just as I feel strongly is true of HEW and so forth."

As evidence of the kind of waste he was aiming at, Roth cited the House committee's criticism of the Pentagon's construction planning and design effort.

But Huddleston fought the reduction, pointing out that the House-passed version was some $118 million lower than the committee bill and that the final version no doubt would be a compromise between the two figures. And he argued that, in contrast to other appropriations bills, the military construction bill did not fund the administrative overhead of an agency from which efficiency cuts could be made with little impact on actual projects. Since the Pentagon's administrative apparatus was funded in the separate defense appropriations bill, he maintained, any cuts in the construction bill would impact on actual projects.

Roth retorted that this bill also included administrative overhead — overhead associated with each project. This was the very area in which the House had found so much waste and inefficiency, he said.

Provisions

As passed by the Senate, HR 12927 appropriated the following amounts for military construction projects in fiscal 1979:

	House Passed	Senate Passed
Army	$ 693,044,000	$ 712,053,000
Navy	729,995,000	806,124,000
Air Force	513,703,000	519,984,000
Defense Agencies	192,680,000	173,780,000
Reserve and National Guard	145,300,000	168,900,000
Military Family Housing and Homeowners' Assistance	1,689,365,000[1]	1,703,105,000[1]
Total new budget authority	$3,964,087,000	$4,083,946,000

[1] *Includes $119,200,000 for debt reduction.*

Conference, Final Action

The conference report on HR 12927 (H Rept 95-1495), filed in the House Aug. 15, provided $3.88 billion, nearly $161 million less than the president's request.

The House adopted the conference report Aug. 17 by a vote of 355-24. The Senate adopted it Aug. 21 on an 83-1 vote. *(House vote 632, p. 180-H; Senate vote 333, p. 50-S)*

NATO Projects. The conferees agreed to $36.9 million for the POMCUS site. The remaining $20 million, they said, should be made up from funds paid back by NATO for other projects unilaterally funded by the United States. Alternatively, they said the Pentagon could use the $20 million which they added to the administration's $70 million request for the contribution to the Infrastructure program.

Other major NATO-related projects approved by the conferees included bombproof aircraft shelters ($19.1 million) and additional ammunition dumps ($33 million).

The conferees warned the Pentagon that they would consider unilateral U.S. funding for NATO projects in the future only if other members of the alliance agreed in advance that the project would be repaid on a specific timetable. The Pentagon also would have to convince the Appropriations Committees that the proposed project was militarily urgent as defined by specific criteria.

Panama Canal. On the use of emergency construction authority to build new installations for units which would be leaving the Canal Zone under terms of the Panama Canal treaties, the Senate basically prevailed. Conferees agreed that essential construction which could not await submission of a supplemental appropriations bill would be allowed subject to prior approval by the two Appropriations Committees. But the president would have to certify to those two panels that the construction was essential and could not be delayed pending a supplemental.

Other Items. Projects totaling $10.7 million were approved for two of the proposed four new ship repair stations. These facilities were intended to perform some routine maintenance on warships, allowing them to remain in service for longer periods between full-scale overhauls at shipyards. The House committee was worried that the new stations duplicated existing repair facilities.

For construction of a Space Shuttle base at Vandenberg Air Force Base, Calif., the conferees agreed on $109.9 million. This was the amount requested except for $32.1 million for landing facilities. Conferees said that the landing strip could be deferred until the fiscal 1980 budget and still be ready in time for the first scheduled shuttle flight from Vandenberg.

Both committees had agreed that the California base was needed so heavy military cargos could be launched into polar orbits without sending the launch rocket over heavily populated areas. ▮

D.C. Funds, Fiscal 1978

Congress May 23 completed action on a bill (HR 9005 — PL 95-288) making appropriations for the District of Columbia for fiscal 1978.

As cleared, the bill provided federal funds totaling $396,116,000 — consisting of a federal payment of $276,000,000 made to the city in lieu of property taxes on federally owned and other tax-exempt property, $28,116,000 in lieu of reimbursement for water and sewer services to federal facilities and $92,000,000 in loans to the city for capital outlays.

These funds plus revenues raised by the city were included in the District's budget, which totaled $1,368,623,200. Operating expenses for the city were set at $1,239,449,800 with the remaining $129,173,400 earmarked for capital improvements.

Final action on HR 9005 came when the Senate May 23 adopted the conference report (H Rept 95-1139) on the bill by voice vote. The House had adopted the report by voice vote May 16.

Differing versions of the bill had been passed by the House Sept. 16, 1977, and the Senate Oct. 4, 1977.

However, the House-Senate conference to reconcile the differences was drawn out until May 11, 1978, by a dispute over a proposed convention center in the downtown area. The House bill contained funds for the project; the Senate bill did not. Meanwhile the District government operated at its 1977 funding level under a continuing resolution (H J Res 662) that supplanted the regular appropriations bill. *(1977 Almanac, p. 295)*

A compromise between the House and Senate on HR 9005 provided $27,000,000 to acquire the site for the proposed civic center. However, release of the money was made contingent on the House and Senate Appropriations Subcommittees on the District of Columbia approving a revised and less expensive civic center. Plans originally called for a $110 million complex.

A second prerequisite was proof that anticipated spin-off developments by businesses in the center area will generate enough additional tax revenue to pay off the net annual fixed costs associated with the project.

Convention Center Vote

Before adopting the conference report, the House rejected, 190-199, a motion to table and thus kill the proposed compromise on the convention center. *(Vote 274, p. 78-H)*

The motion was made by Robert E. Bauman, R-Md., who questioned what binding commitments would be required from District businesses to ensure a projected $15 million in new hotels, restaurants and other center-related facilities.

"The question...is whether or not we will require of the D.C. business community...to sign legal documents to assure this additional construction and these various businesses from which revenue is projected?" said Bauman. "This bill contains nearly $400 million in federal taxpayers' money. If...this center costs far more than projected...the city will wind up coming back to Congress asking all Americans to pay the bill. This is the only chance we have to stop this."

Bauman was assured by D.C. Appropriations Subcommittee Chairman William H. Natcher, D-Ky., that the initial $27 million for the center would not be released until participation by the business community had been secured.▮

D.C. Funds, Fiscal 1979

A bill (HR 13468 — PL 95-373) providing $255.2 million in federal funds for the fiscal 1979 District of Columbia budget cleared Congress Aug. 17 with the lowest federal payment since 1975.

The slash in the federal payment to $235 million was the only issue that aroused much criticism in either the House or Senate during debate over the bill, which passed the House July 21 by a vote of 215-32 and passed the Senate Aug. 14 by voice vote. *(Vote 512, p. 146-H)*

The conference report (H Rept 95-1500), filed just two days after Senate passage, passed the House Aug. 17 by a 339-31 margin and passed the Senate the same day by a vote of 76-8. *(Senate passage, vote 326, p. 49-S; House passage, vote 633, p. 180-H)*

As cleared by Congress, the bill set up a District budget of $1,362,317,700, including $1,285,102,700 for operating expenses, an increase of $46 million over the fiscal 1978 appropriation, plus $77,215,000 for the capital improvement program, a reduction of $52.6 million in the city request.

Federal Funds

Included in the District's operating expense budget were federal funds totaling $255.2 million, including a federal payment of $235 million made to the city in lieu of property taxes on federally owned and other tax exempt property, $10.3 million in lieu of reimbursement for water and sewer services to federal facilities, and $9.9 million as the federal share to help retire bonds for the Robert F. Kennedy Stadium.

Not included in the budget but available to the city were an additional $296.9 million in federal grants and $108.6 million in reimbursements, giving the District total resources of $1,767,886,400.

Federal Payment Cut

The $235 million federal payment was $41 million less than the 1978 amount and $82 million below the city's request for fiscal 1979.

Sponsors of the bill said the cut was possible because of the business boom in the District, which had increased revenues from local taxes, and because of a new parking enforcement program that city officials estimated would raise an additional $17.5 million in 1979. The total increase in local revenues was estimated at $42.8 million.

Two members of the Maryland delegation were critical of the federal payment cut. Sen. Charles McC. Mathias Jr., R-Md., said he thought the payment was "too low by perhaps the sum of $26 million," and that a supplemental appropriation might be required.

Rep. Newton I. Steers Jr., R-Md., complained that the cut was punitive because there was no relationship between revenue collected from local residents and revenue lost due to tax-free federal property.

"In other words, the better job the city government does in collecting taxes, the more we 'reward' it by drastically slashing the federal payment," Steers said. "What kind of incentive are we providing the local government to do a good job? Absolutely none."

CETA Fraud and Abuse

The bill imposed limits in public employment hiring under the 1973 Comprehensive Employment and Training Act (CETA). Charges of fraud and abuse in the CETA program, both in Washington and around the country, had led to intense congressional scrutiny of the program. *(Background, p. 287)*

In its report (S Rept 95-1076) filed May 17 the Senate Appropriations Committee said it was "concerned with the abuses to the program that have occurred in the City Council and potentially in other city agencies." It added amendments forbidding the city to supplement a CETA position salary if it resulted in a salary exceeding that for a GS-9 step 1 ($15,090) or if the employee had been employed more than 24 months; or to allow CETA employees to work for an elected official. ▮

Fiscal 1978 2nd Supplemental: $6.8 Billion

Congress completed action Aug. 25 on a bill (HR 13467 — PL 95-355) providing $6.8 billion in fiscal 1978 supplemental appropriations.

The bill was the 10th supplemental appropriations measure for fiscal 1978, but only the second general one. The first major fiscal 1978 supplemental (HR 9375), appropriating $7.8 billion, was cleared in February. *(Story, p. 57)*

The largest single item in the bill, $3.2 billion, went for pay raises for federal employees. Other major items included funds for increased veterans' benefits and mandatory payments to the civil service retirement fund.

Controversy over the bill centered on a $54.9 million appropriation added by the Senate to continue construction of a new Senate office building named after the late Sen. Philip A. Hart, D-Mich. (1959-76). In an unaccustomed break with tradition, the House refused to accept the Senate funding, and the Senate ultimately had to yield on the issue. *(Hart building, box, next page)*

Final Provisions

As cleared by Congress, HR 13467 made the following supplemental appropriations for fiscal 1978:

	Budget Request	Final Appropriation
Agriculture	$ 6,136,000	$ 181,771,000
Foreign operations	38,394,000	24,015,000
Housing, independent agencies	560,777,000	539,553,000
Interior, related agencies	507,547,000	555,628,000
Labor, HEW	487,752,000	394,964,000
Legislative branch	60,027,550	19,157,550
Military construction	73,540,000	8,500,000
Public works	5,350,000	8,700,000
State, Justice, Commerce, Judiciary	665,594,000	649,360,000
Transportation	93,429,000	91,044,000
Treasury, Postal Service, general government	632,220,000	551,600,000
Defense	748,000,000	514,766,000
Increased pay	3,289,680,436	3,214,867,136
Total, Fiscal 1978	$7,168,446,986	$6,753,925,686

House Committee Action

The House Appropriations Committee reported HR 13467 July 13 (H Rept 95-1350). The total fiscal 1978 appropriation was $6.4 billion, $292.1 million less than the administration budget request.

Much of the decrease was due to the lapsed time between the supplemental request and the time that the bill was expected to be cleared. Since the new fiscal year would begin on Oct. 1, the committee reduced funding for many agencies because they would not need all the requested funds in the short time remaining in fiscal 1978.

Pay Raises. The largest single item in the bill (Title II) was $3.2 billion to finance wage and salary increases for federal military and civilian workers required by the October 1977 comparability pay raise. The total was $98.3 million less than the budget request.

Agriculture Department. The committee recommended a total of $183.7 million for agriculture programs, $147.5 million over the administration request.

Much of the increase over the budget went for emergency measures dealing with severe damages caused by drought, forest fires and storms during the preceding year. Unrequested items included $50 million for water storage and waste disposal grants by the Farmers Home Administration, $76 million for the Soil Conservation Service and $20 million for emergency conservation measures of the Agricultural Stabilization and Conservation Service.

Foreign Operations. The committee cut $9.9 million from the budget request for foreign operations, recommending a total of $28.5 million.

Concerned that neighboring oil-rich Arab states were not contributing enough to help Palestinian refugees, the committee cut the request for the U.S. contribution to the United Nations Palestinian relief agency by $1 million, to $8.5 million. The committee approved, however, the full $5 million requested for military credit sales to help Lebanon restore its shattered army.

HUD, Independent Agencies. Most of the $538.6 million for the Department of Housing and Urban Development and independent agencies went for increased veterans' pension, disability and survivors' benefits required by two 1977 laws (PL 95-117, PL 95-204). The committee approved the budget request of $489.6 million for the Veterans Administration (VA) payments.

Interior, Energy. The committee approved a total of $571.2 million for the Interior and Energy departments and related agencies, $63.7 million over the budget request. The bulk of the increase was intended to help the island of Guam recover from a typhoon and build a new hospital.

To help repay firefighting costs of the 1977 fire season, considered one of the worst in history, the committee approved a total of $266.8 million. The funds were to be allocated to the Bureau of Land Management, the Forest Service, the Park Service and the Bureau of Indian Affairs.

The bill included $205 million for surveying and payments to owners of land required for expansion of the Redwood National Park in California. The committee said the appropriation was the first installment of land costs that could run as high as $600 million.

Labor-HEW. Supplemental appropriations of $391.7 million were recommended for the departments of Labor and Health, Education and Welfare (HEW) and related agencies. The total was $96.1 million less than the budget request.

Because most of the increased wages to Comprehensive Employment and Training Act (CETA) workers required by the latest increase in minimum wages had already been absorbed by local governments, the committee turned down the requested $76.5 million for CETA.

The committee approved the $15 million sought by HEW to begin a program of immunization of elderly and chronically ill persons against influenza.

But the committee refused to fund for the first time a 10-year-old program offering federal aid to local schools hit by "pinpoint" natural disasters such as floods, hurricanes

Hart Building: A New 'Palace'?

Spiraling cost estimates for a new Senate office building to be named after the late Sen. Philip A. Hart, D-Mich. (1959-76), made it the subject of increasing controversy during 1978.

The original cost estimate for the building was $47.9 million in 1972, but the Architect of the Capitol in 1978 estimated that the building would cost $122.6 million, and a report released Aug. 14 by the General Accounting Office said the structure would cost much more than that.

To date, the three-acre site for the building next to the Dirksen Senate Office Building had been cleared and excavated, with concrete retaining walls put in the hole dug for the building.

John H. Chafee, R-R.I., and a handful of other senators wanted to see construction stopped there. Chafee introduced an amendment to the legislative appropriations bill (HR 12935) to rescind about $69 million in unspent funds that were appropriated for the building in the early 1970s. About $16 million had been spent on the building as of July 1, but its total price tag was expected to go beyond $122 million. *(p. 93)*

In a statement announcing his amendment, Chafee chided the Senate for wanting to build itself a "palace." He said it was a taxpayer-funded project "designed solely to comfort and coddle the 100 of us."

Much of the criticism was aimed at the "luxury" items in the building. Sen. William Proxmire, D-Wis., gave the Senate in March his "Golden Fleece of the Month" award for the building, which he said "would make a Persian prince green with envy." Among the features criticized by Proxmire were the building's planned rooftop dining room for senators only, a new gymnasium (the Senate already had two gyms) and $1.5 million worth of wood paneling for senators' offices.

However, Chafee's amendment, which drew only seven cosponsors, amounted to little more than a quixotic exercise. Earlier in the year, he introduced a resolution (S J Res 129) to halt construction of the building. The resolution was never taken up by the Senate Rules Committee.

And when Proxmire offered a version of Chafee's amendment during Appropriations Committee markup of HR 12935, it was tabled, 11-5.

During consideration of the fiscal 1978 supplemental appropriations bill (HR 13467), the Senate Aug. 4 voted to allow continued construction of the new building but to include a cost ceiling of $135 million. Then, despite questioning by House opponents as to whether the Senate needed more office space, the Senate added the funds to the House-passed bill Aug. 7, after tabling, 45-29, an effort by Chafee to rescind funds appropriated for the project.

The House adopted the conference report (H Rept 95-1475) Aug. 17 by a narrow margin, but rejected by a 133-245 vote the Senate-passed $54.9 million for the building. On Aug. 25, the Senate bowed to the $54.9 million House cut. *(Vote 630, p. 178-H)*

---

or earthquakes. The administration had sought $26 million for the program. The committee did approve $5 million for rebuilding schools in areas hit by major statewide or regional disasters.

Added to the bill was an unrequested $37.8 million for assistance to states under the Education of the Handicapped Act (PL 94-142). This was in addition to $465 million previously appropriated, and was intended to defray the states' excess costs of educating handicapped children.

The committee criticized the lack of success by HEW in clamping down on defaulters of federally backed college student loans, although it approved the full request for increased costs associated with the program — $224 million. Pointing to a projected $2.4 million decrease in collections on the loans in 1978, compared with 1977, the committee said the department would have to crack down on the defaults, which had been the topic of widespread criticism of the student loan program.

State, Justice, Commerce. The committee-approved total was $256.8 million, $27.8 million less than the administration request.

The $108.8 million for the State Department included the requested $64.1 million for contributions to international organizations and $20.4 million to pay 30 percent of the costs of maintaining the United Nations peacekeeping force in Lebanon.

The committee approved $106 million for programs of the Economic Development Administration, $11 million less than the budget request. The recommendation included $74 million for assistance to firms affected by foreign imports and $21.4 million for economic adjustment assistance to communities.

Treasury, Postal Service. Supplemental outlays for the Treasury Department and general government operations, and payments to the Postal Service, were set at $549.6 million, $82.9 million less than the budget request.

For payments to the Postal Service, the committee recommended $91.7 million, $211,000 below the request. The payments were needed to cover the increased amount that the service gave up by delivering certain types of mail free or at reduced rates after it raised letter rates on May 29, 1978.

Mandatory payments to the civil service retirement fund accounted for $428.8 million, the budget request. Of that amount, $318 million was needed to cover increased pension liabilities caused by the October 1977 pay raise, with the remainder required to cover pension cost increases caused by earlier pay raises.

Defense. The committee approved $600 million for programs of the Defense Department, $148.2 million below the budget request. The department's military and civilian employee pay raises accounted for $2 billion of the $3.2 billion in pay raises in Title II of the bill.

Increases in the consumer price index and in military pay made necessary an additional $169.6 million for retired military pay. The committee turned down an extra $60 million sought by the administration to cover an estimated increase in the number of retirees.

The committee approved the budget request of $58.7 million for two defense communications satellites, after getting department assurances that no further satellites would be needed. The committee had instructed the department in the fiscal 1978 defense appropriations bill to start relying on leased commercial satellites for communications instead of building its own. But the committee agreed to allow two more satellite systems to keep up service until use of the leased satellites could be put into full operation in 1982. *(1977 Almanac p. 265)*

Military Construction. The committee deferred action on a requested $73.5 million for military construction because of the lack of authorizing legislation. The additional funds would be for the increased costs of construction of overseas military facilities and family housing, due to the devaluation of the dollar.

House Floor Action

The House July 20 voted not to commit the federal government to a new program of mass immunizations against influenza.

Still smarting from the sad consequences of the 1976 swine flu vaccinations, the House adopted an amendment to HR 13467 to delete $15 million for new vaccinations in preparation for the 1978-79 flu season.

The administration had sought the funding, which would have gone to immunize elderly and chronically ill persons against three strains of flu expected that winter. But too many members thought it could become a "swine flu II," leading to hundreds of millions of dollars in injuries to persons hurt by the vaccines.

The House also easily adopted another in a series of amendments to appropriations bills offered by Clarence E. Miller, R-Ohio, to cut controllable spending in the bill by 2 percent.

It then passed HR 13467 by a 311-60 vote. The bulk of the $6.3 billion in the bill was required for federal employee pay raises and pension costs. *(Vote 506, p. 144-H)*

Immunization Program

A vigorous lobbying effort by HEW failed to allay doubts that another immunization program could lead to problems like those associated with the 1976 swine flu immunization effort.

The 1976 program was begun because of fears of a new outbreak of the strain of flu that caused the worldwide epidemic of 1918-19. The mass immunization went forward only after Congress agreed to legislation making the federal government responsible for suits for injuries suffered because of the immunizations. *(1976 Almanac p. 548)*

The nation was spared a swine flu outbreak that year — but 120 people died from the immunizations, in particular from a rare paralytic reaction, Guillain-Barre syndrome, associated with the injections. Estimates of government liability because of the program ran up to $1.2 billion. HEW announced in June that it would honor compensation claims without the victim having to prove negligence by anyone.

Unlike the swine flu program, which was intended for virtually the entire population, the new immunization program envisioned by HEW would have concentrated on the estimated 42 million "high-risk" people — the elderly and those with chronic illness.

The proposed program had grown out of the recommendations by a conference of immunization experts in January 1978, which called on the government to undertake a permanent program of flu immunizations for high-risk populations. As developed by the Center for Disease Control, the program would have offered assistance to state and local governments to begin their own immunization programs. The goal for the 1978-79 flu season was to immunize 40 percent of the high-risk population — 17 million — against three flu strains: Russian-A, Texas-A and Hong Kong-B.

John E. Moss, D-Calif., offered the amendment to eliminate the $15 million in the bill for the immunizations, replacing it with an additional $3 million for research and testing of the vaccines by the National Institute of Allergy and Infectious Diseases. The amendment was adopted 268-127. *(Vote 501, p. 144-H)*

Moss argued that the unanswered questions of liability left by the swine flu program, and the unclear evidence that the new plan was necessary, required further study before it was implemented on a mass scale. John D. Dingell, D-Mich., like Moss a strong opponent of the swine flu legislation in 1976, said the new program was sought by "the same good folks who brought you the swine flu program." "Watch out," Dingell said. "They led you astray once."

But Tim Lee Carter, R-Ky., argued that the dangers of runaway costs were slight compared with the threat of thousands of deaths in the event of a serious flu outbreak. "Do the members mean to tell me that for $15 million they are going to risk the lives of 1,200 or more people in this country?" he asked.

Pinpoint Disasters

The House twice turned down amendments to fund, for the first time, a 10-year-old program of federal aid to schools hit by local natural disasters. This "pinpoint" disaster relief, added to the impact aid program by Congress in 1967, was intended to help schools continue operations after being damaged by localized fires, storms or other disasters. But no schools had ever gotten any money from it, because of the lack of appropriations. Some 750 applications from school districts for assistance were pending at the time of House action. *(Background, 1967 Almanac p. 611)*

Albert Gore Jr., D-Tenn., offered an amendment to restore the $26 million for the program that had been deleted by the committee. He said the money was urgently needed to help schools keep teaching children while struggling to rebuild or restore facilities that had experienced calamities.

Responding to a frequent criticism of the pinpoint aid idea, Gore explained that it would not amount to a substitute for insurance for school facilities because the program would only pay the difference between the insured, "book" value of the lost facilities and their actual replacement cost. After examining all the pending applications, he said the committee had been mistaken in saying that most of the requests were for small damages of less than $10,000.

Opponents of the Gore amendment warned that, by funding the pinpoint aid for the first time, the House could be opening the door for spending huge amounts on it in the future. "This program, if it gets launched, will grow and grow and grow," said George Mahon, D-Texas, adding that many local governments were in a better financial position than the federal government to absorb the costs of minor disasters.

The Gore amendment was rejected 166-233. *(Vote 502, p. 144-H)*

After defeat of the Gore amendment, Matthew F. McHugh, D-N.Y., offered an amendment to restore $9.25 million for pinpoint disasters, with the stipulation that no funds be available for claims of less than $200,000. The amendment was immediately thrown out on a point of order, since it set a minimum grant level that was not in the original authorizing legislation.

McHugh then reintroduced his amendment, without the stipulation, but with the clear understanding that the $9.25 million was intended only for schools with claims over $200,000. McHugh said the $9.25 million figure had been obtained by adding up the 42 applications for damages over $200,000, and multiplying by 75 percent, on the assumption that about one-quarter of the claimed damages would be found invalid.

The McHugh amendment was rejected 156-237. *(Vote 503, p. 144-H)*

2 Percent Cut

The Miller amendment reduced controllable spending in the bill by 2 percent, provided that no single program be cut by more than 5 percent. Miller estimated that the amendment would cut $35 million from the $1.75 billion in controllable spending in the bill. The amendment was adopted 256-114. *(Vote 505, p. 144-H)*

Other Amendments

In other action on HR 13467, the House:

- Adopted, by voice vote, an amendment by Jamie L. Whitten, D-Miss., to increase to $80 million, from $76 million, the appropriation for watershed and flood prevention operations of the Soil Conservation Service.
- Adopted, by a 42-13 standing vote, a Robert E. Bauman, R-Md., amendment to prohibit funds in the bill for the U.S. Mission to the United Nations to be used to express the personal opinions of any member of the mission.
- Rejected, on a 75-302 vote, a Philip M. Crane, R-Ill., amendment to delete $275,000 for the U.S. Metric Board. *(Vote 504, p. 144-H)*

Provisions

As passed by the House, HR 13467 made the following supplemental appropriations for fiscal 1978:

	Budget Request	Appropriation
Agriculture	$ 36,136,000	$ 187,706,000
Foreign operations	38,394,000	21,250,000
Housing, independent agencies	559,777,000	538,553,000
Interior, related agencies	507,547,000	571,235,000
Labor, HEW	487,752,000	379,674,000
Legislative branch	8,948,050	9,063,050
Public works	5,350,000	8,700,000
State, Justice, Commerce, Judiciary	284,544,000	256,772,000
Transportation	71,429,000	49,044,000
Treasury, Postal Service, general government	632,470,000	549,600,000
Defense	748,000,000	599,766,000
Increased pay	3,295,539,436	3,197,224,136
Total, Fiscal 1978	$6,675,886,486	$6,368,587,186*

*Subtotals and totals do not include a 2 percent reduction in controllable spending required by the Miller amendment.

Senate Committee Action

The Senate Appropriations Committee reported HR 13467 Aug. 1 (S Rept 95-1061). The committee approved a total of $6.6 billion, $531.9 million less than the budget request, but $303.1 million more than the House-passed amount.

Comparison with individual items in the House-passed bill did not take into account the 2 percent cut in controllable spending ($35.2 million) ordered by the House, since the location of the cuts had to be determined by the executive branch.

Pay Raises. The committee approved the $3.2 billion required to meet the increased wages and salaries of federal workers. The total was $70.8 million less than the latest budget estimate, and $21.6 million more than the House had called for.

Agriculture. For agricultural programs, the committee recommended $151.2 million, $145.1 million more than the budget request and $36.5 million less than the House amount.

Most of the difference from the House level was caused by committee approval of an administration request for a rescission of $30 million from agricultural conservation programs dealing with the effects of the severe 1977 drought. The House had not considered the rescission request. The Senate committee agreed that the increased rainfall of 1978 had removed the need for the extra drought assistance.

The committee went along, however, with the House-approved increases over the budget totaling $150 million. The unrequested funds were $50 million for rural water and waste disposal grants, $80 million for emergency repairs for damages to watershed systems caused by storms and fires, and $20 million for emergency land conservation measures.

Foreign Operations. Supplemental appropriations for foreign operations were set at $22 million, $16.4 million less than the budget request and $790,000 more than the House total.

The committee disagreed with the House decision cutting $1 million from the $9.5 million request for United Nations Palestinian relief programs because the oil-rich Arab nations were not contributing enough to help the refugees. Worried that a cut in support for education efforts would result in increased opportunities for indoctrination of Palestinian youths by radical and terrorist organizations, the committee approved the full request.

Like the House, the committee did not approve the requested $5 million for military credit sales to Lebanon, and $3.6 million for the Peace Corps, because the required authorizing legislation had not been completed.

The committee rejected the requested $200 million to cover the cost of participation in the Supplementary Financing Facility of the International Monetary Fund. The House had not considered the request. The committee said it would consider the estimated $1.8 billion needed for full U.S. participation in the fund once the authorizing legislation was completed. *(p. 424)*

HUD, Independent Agencies. The committee recommended $539.6 million for the Department of Housing and Urban Development, the Veterans Administration and other independent agencies. The total was $21.2 million less than the budget request, and $1 million more than the House wanted.

Committee-approved funding was identical to the budget request and House levels for most items, including the $489.6 million for increased VA pensions. The most important change was that the committee, like the House, rejected $17.6 million of the request for VA assistance to medical schools.

Interior, Energy. Recommending a total of $542.2 million for the Interior and Energy Departments and related agencies, the committee added $34.6 million to the budget request and cut $29.1 million from the House amount.

The committee cut $10 million from the $266.8 million appropriated by the House to help four agencies cope with the 1977 fire season, one of the worst in history. The committee said the reduction should come from Forest Service efforts to prevent forest fires before they happen. Also cut was a $15 million House-passed appropriation for the island of Guam.

The bill included the requested $205 million for land purchases and surveys for the newly created Redwood National Park.

Labor, HEW. The committee granted $281.2 million for the departments of Labor and Health, Education and Welfare. This was $206.5 million less than the request and $98.4 million less than the House amount.

Agreeing with the House that local governments already had absorbed the increased minimum wage costs for Comprehensive Employment and Training Administration (CETA) workers, the committee turned down the request of $76.5 million.

The committee also agreed with the House in turning down the request for $15 million to begin a program of influenza vaccinations for high-risk populations. However, it rejected the $3 million for additional flu vaccine research by the National Institute of Allergy and Infectious Diseases, which the House had adopted in place of the money for mass vaccinations.

Still concerned over the quality of care given to mental patients at St. Elizabeths Hospital in Washington, D.C., the committee turned down the $55.3 million request for construction and renovation. But it said it would consider the money once it received a comprehensive plan for improving all mental health services in the District.

Like the House, the committee refused to fund for the first time a program of federal assistance to schools hit by "pinpoint" disasters. The administration had sought $26 million for it. The committee also went along with the House decision to appropriate an unrequested $37.8 million for assistance to handicapped education programs run by local schools.

Encouraged by the recent efforts by the HEW Bureau of Student Financial Assistance to crack down on ex-students who have not paid back their guaranteed education loans, the committee cut $43.9 million from the $223.9 million request for the Student Loan Fund. The committee hoped that a decline in the rate at which students defaulted on their loans from banks, and increased collections from defaulters, would reduce the amount of money needed for the fund.

Legislative Branch. The committee approved an additional $19.2 million for congressional operations. The original budget estimate was for $60 million.

The $37.5 million sought for the new Senate office building was deferred by the committee, which was awaiting a General Accounting Office report on the full costs of completion. The panel cut $2.3 million from the $10 million requested for the new James Madison Memorial Building of the Library of Congress.

Military Construction. As the House did, the committee deferred action of the $73.5 million military construction request needed to offset the added costs of building family housing overseas caused by the devaluation of the dollar. The appropriation lacked the requisite authorization.

State, Justice, Commerce. The recommended $656.1 million for the State, Justice and Commerce departments, and related agencies, was $399.3 million more than the House total primarily because the committee anticipated a late-coming administration request of $378 million for disaster relief loans from the Small Business Administration (SBA).

The amount of SBA disaster loans had increased sharply since 1976, when Congress declared farmers to be small-business operators, eligible for loans in cases of crop failures caused by drought or other natural disasters. *(Story, p. 60)*

The committee recommended the requested $117 million for public works and trade adjustment assistance by the Economic Development Administration. The panel distributed the $11 million which the House had taken from the community assistance budget, because of lack of authorization, to other programs — largely $8 million for more public works projects.

For renovation of the Marjorie Webster Junior College, in Washington, D.C., to serve as the campus for the National Academy for Fire Prevention and Control, the committee approved $6.2 million. The administration had not sought the funding, but indicated it would not oppose it.

For the estimated 30 percent U.S. share of the costs of stationing 6,000 U.N. troops seeking to maintain peace in Lebanon, the committee approved the budget's $20.4 million. It also accepted the request of $64.1 million for contributions to international organizations.

Transportation. The committee approved $131 million for the Transportation Department, $37.6 million over the request and $82 million more than the House.

The committee allowed the honorable retirement of the Coast Guard icebreaker *Westwind*, which had plowed the frozen waters of the Great Lakes for 35 winters, by appropriating $60 million for its replacement.

The committee added $22 million to the $29.5 million allotted by the House for aid to the Amtrak system, in anticipation of a subsequent request for capital grants to help meet the intercity travel-time goals set by Congress in 1976. The committee disappointed the hopes of intercontinental motorists, by rejecting $20 million requested to hack the Darien Gap Highway through the steamy jungles of Panama.

Treasury, Postal Service. Supplemental appropriations of $551.6 million were set for the Treasury Department, Postal Service and other agencies. The total fell $80.6 million below the budget request mainly because the $70.5 million sought to launch the Federal Preparedness Agency on a massive program of strategic materials stockpiling had not been authorized.

Senate levels stayed close to the House amounts, including the same $91.7 million for the Postal Service and $428.8 million for civil service retirement funds. Also approved was $400,000 so the National Archives could process the Nixon White House tapes.

Defense. Supplemental appropriations for Defense Department programs were set at $514.8 million. The administration wanted $748 million; the House approved $599.8 million.

Committee recommendations stayed close to the House-passed amounts, including the same $48.5 million for increased food costs, $169.6 million for retired pay, $107.9 million for employment of foreign nationals, and $58.7 million for two more Navy communications satellites.

The panel's $130 million appropriation for meeting the increased costs of foreign operations caused by the devaluation of the dollar was $177.3 million less than the budget request, and $85 million less than the House amount. To supplement its total, the committee approved transfer of $100 million from the Secretary of Defense Readiness Fund.

Senate Floor Action

By a substantial margin the Senate voted Aug. 4 to allow continued construction of its new Hart office building.

But, worried by estimates that the structure could end up costing taxpayers more than $200 million, senators agreed to spend no more than $135 million on it.

The actions came on amendments to HR 13467, which the Senate passed by a 69-17 vote Aug. 7. *(Vote 284, p. 44-S)*

Hart Building

John H. Chafee, R-R.I., had for months been the most outspoken opponent of the Hart building. His amendment to rescind $54 million in already-appropriated funds for its construction was tabled by a 45-29 vote. *(Vote 280, p. 43-S)*

Chafee argued that it would be better to write off the $31 million already spent on the project than to sink another $150 million or so into its completion. At the time of the Senate action, contractors had dug the foundation and were erecting the steel framework of the nine-story building.

Supporters of the Chafee amendment denounced the luxury and opulence of the proposed facility. "Never has a building like this been seen. It goes far and away being the most expensive federal building ever constructed," Chafee said. Plans for the building included 16-foot ceilings, a rooftop restaurant, a third Senate gym and a "multimedia center."

Opponents of the Chafee amendment argued that the tremendous growth in the Senate staff had made more working space essential. Having more than tripled in numbers since the 1950s, staffers were so tightly packed in existing offices that they could not do their work effectively, building supporters said.

Chafee responded that the physical limits on staff size set by existing facilities were a good thing. "The only way we are going to cut down on the size of staff is for everybody to be so cram-jammed that they will not be able to add more staff. That is the best thing that could happen to the U.S. Senate," he said.

Noting that the Senate had taken over several nearby buildings in addition to the Russell and Dirksen office buildings, Chafee predicted that Senate staff would grow to fill the Hart building as well.

After rejection of the Chafee amendment, Appropriations Committee Chairman Warren G. Magnuson, D-Wash., offered an amendment to add $54.9 million for the Hart building, which had not been funded in the committee-reported bill. The figure included the originally requested $37.5 million, plus new cost estimates by the General Accounting Office. To make the additional spending more easily acceptable to economy-minded senators, Magnuson included a cost ceiling of $135 million for the entire building and initial furnishings. The amendment was adopted 65-13. *(Vote 282, p. 43-S)*

Flu Vaccines

The Senate by voice vote adopted a Dale Bumpers, D-Ark., amendment to add $8.2 million for the influenza vaccines, after rejecting a Richard S. Schweiker, R-Pa., motion to table the amendment 30-47. *(Vote 281, p. 43-S)*

Bumpers said that, because of delays caused by House rejection of the program, Center for Disease Control officials no longer were hoping to fulfill their original plans of immunizing almost half of the estimated 40 million "high-risk" persons likely to suffer severe illness or death from flu infections. He explained that the money would go only to help states administer immunizations to some 4 million indigent high-risk patients.

Looking back to "one of the biggest medical disasters in recent memory," Schweiker warned that the new program could become a repeat of the swine flu program, which ended up killing 120 people and saving none. To counter the threat of hundreds of millions of dollars in federal liabilities to persons injured by the vaccines, he said, supporters of the program could raise only the chance of a serious flu outbreak. "Why the big hurry? There is no epidemic. Nobody is dying," Schweiker said.

Jacob K. Javits, R-N.Y., strongly objected to what he called the "raiding" of funding for venereal disease control to fund the flu vaccines. Since the flu vaccine program did not have explicit authorization, the Bumpers amendment relied on an unappropriated anti-venereal disease authorization to cover the program.

Other Amendments

By voice vote, the Senate adopted the following amendments Aug. 4:

- Two Magnuson amendments adding $2.9 million for the Rehabilitation Hospital of the Pacific and $8.5 million for an access road to the Trident submarine base in Washington.
- A Patrick J. Leahy, D-Vt., amendment, adding $6 million for rural programs of the Health Services Administration.
- A Schweiker amendment restoring $2.3 million in Peace Corps funds the committee had taken out because of the lack of the requisite authorizing legislation. This was enacted following committee action.

Provisions

As passed by the Senate, HR 13467 made the following supplemental appropriations for fiscal 1978:

	House Appropriation*	Senate Appropriation
Agriculture	$ 187,706,000	$ 151,226,000
Foreign operations	21,250,000	24,305,000
Housing, independent agencies	538,553,000	539,553,000
Interior, related agencies	571,235,000	542,161,000
Labor, HEW	379,674,000	298,325,000
Legislative branch	9,063,050	74,060,550
Military construction	0	8,500,000
Public works	8,700,000	8,700,000
State, Justice, Commerce, Judiciary	256,772,000	656,121,000
Transportation	49,044,000	131,044,000
Treasury, Postal Service general government	549,600,000	551,600,000

	House Appropriation*	Senate Appropriation
Defense	599,766,000	514,766,000
Increased pay	3,197,224,136	3,218,867,136
Less 2 percent of controllable spending	−35,198,000	
Total, Fiscal 1978	$6,333,389,186	$6,719,228,686

* *Individual amounts listed do not reflect a 2 percent reduction in controllable spending required by the House.*

Conference Report

Conferees filed their report on HR 13467 Aug. 10 (H Rept 95-1475).

Conferees agreed on a total of $6.8 billion, which was $359.7 million less than the budget request and $89.6 million more than the Senate-passed amount. The total was $475.4 million more than the House amount, primarily because of $492 million in budget requests that came too late for the House to consider.

Agriculture. The conference report deleted the Senate-approved rescission of $30 million from previously appropriated funds for the Agricultural Conservation Program. The funds, intended to cope with drought and flood conditions arising during 1977, were directed by conferees to be used to meet emergency conditions in 1978.

Foreign Operations. For aid to Palestinian refugee relief programs of the United Nations, conferees approved $9 million, halfway between House and Senate figures. The House had cut the $9.5 million request to $8.5 million because of its belief that Arab governments were not doing enough to help the refugees.

Following enactment of the Peace Corps authorization Aug. 2, conferees restored $2.3 million taken out by the House because of lack of authorization.

Interior, Energy. Conferees approved $35 million for assistance to Guam, compared with the $40 million House and $25 million Senate amounts. The $5 million reduction from the House amount came out of the $10 million originally approved for rebuilding of facilities damaged by a 1976 typhoon.

The Senate-passed total of $194 million for fire-fighting activities of the Forest Service was accepted by conferees, thus cutting $10 million from the House level.

Labor, HEW. Conferees went along with the $8.2 million passed by the Senate for influenza immunization program, which the House had voted to eliminate. Conferees removed the $3 million for flu vaccine research approved by the House as an alternative to the mass immunization program.

Conferees agreed to restore $52.2 million for the Washington, D.C., St. Elizabeths Hospital, which the House had approved but the Senate had removed. They accepted a $6 million Senate appropriation for rural health programs.

The conference committee acknowledged that the Senate committee's decision to cut $43.9 million for expenses of the guaranteed student loan program, on the basis that the rate of student defaults had declined, was too optimistic. The full $223.9 million passed by the House was approved by conferees.

Legislative. In accordance with the long-standing practice that "each body determines its own housekeeping requirements and the other concurs without intervention," conferees accepted the $54.9 million approved by the Senate for its new office building. They also concurred with a Senate amendment adding $7.7 million to complete work on the Madison Memorial Library building.

Commerce. For public works and trade adjustment programs of the Economic Development Administration, conferees included $111.5 million, halfway between the $117 million Senate and $106 million House figures.

Conferees approved the $6.2 million appropriated by the Senate to renovate the Marjorie Webster Junior College campus for use as a national fire service control training academy, but directed that the funds be used instead to purchase a new site for the facility.

Transportation. One of the most difficult issues for the conference committee was resolved when it approved $20 million to begin work on acquiring a new icebreaker for the Great Lakes. The Senate had called for $60 million for full costs of acquisition, but the Coast Guard said it was not ready to purchase a new vessel, so conferees settled on $20 million to get the process under way.

Conferees backed the $51.5 million appropriated by the Senate for the Amtrak system, a figure that was $22 million over the House amount because of a late-coming budget request for additional capital improvements.

Defense. Conferees accepted the Senate plan to cut $100 million from the appropriation covering the increased costs of overseas operations caused by the devaluation of the dollar by transferring $100 million from the Secretary of Defense Readiness Fund.

General Provisions. Having cut $57 million from the total appropriation for items considered by the House, conferees dropped the House-passed provision requiring a 2 percent cut in controllable spending. The House provision would have required the executive branch to decide on the location of the required $35 million spending reduction.

Conferees also accepted a Senate amendment allowing the length of service as an employee of the partisan congressional campaign committees to count for the purposes of determining civil service retirement benefits.

Final House Action

The House Aug. 17 adopted the conference report on HR 13467 by a 198-191 vote. Only personal last-minute lobbying by House leaders saved the report from being recommitted. *(Vote 629, p. 178-H)*

Robert H. Michel, R-Ill., observed that "it was necessary for the Speaker to take the well and turn a number of votes around in order to pass the conference report." Eleven Democrats switched their votes to "yea" from "nay" on the report before the final tally.

After adopting the conference report, the House rejected two of the proposed compromise amendments and returned HR 13467 to the Senate.

Hart Building

The House rejected an old congressional tradition when it voted 133-245 against the conference action in accepting the Senate-passed $54.9 million for its new office building. *(Vote 630, p. 178-H)*

Known as "comity," the principle holds that each chamber must accept the other's decision regarding its own maintenance. Arguing that "this tradition has served the Congress well over the years and I see no reason to break with this tradition at this late date," Appropriations Committee Chairman George Mahon, D-Texas, moved to agree to the funding for the Hart building.

The widespread criticism of the Hart building had focused on its luxury and expense. But House opponents expanded the criticisms to attack the main justification for the building — that the crowded Senate staff needed more room.

Opponents argued that the staff inevitably would grow to fill any new space. Holding down on the available room, they said, would help to put a lid on the rapidly growing congressional staff. "The frills such as the gymnasium and the rooftop restaurant do not bother me as much as the idea of expanding the office people on the Hill," said Steven D. Symms, R-Idaho. "What we need to do is probably to fire half the staff...."

Flu Shots

After agreeing with Health, Education and Welfare Secretary Joseph A. Califano Jr. on safeguards to prevent the proposed mass influenza immunization program from resulting in a repetition of the massive government liabilities caused by the 1976 swine flu program, chief House opponents Dingell and Moss agreed to the $8.2 million approved by the Senate for the program. The House had voted to delete all funding for the flu shots.

Califano made clear that liabilities for damages caused by the shots would be assumed by the states, unlike the swine flu program, for which liabilities were assumed by the federal government.

The House by voice vote agreed to an Albert Gore Jr., D-Tenn., motion to concur in the Senate amount, with an amendment making funds available only until the end of fiscal year 1978.

Campaign Committee Employees

The House refused to accept a Senate amendment to allow former employees of the House and Senate Democratic and Republican Campaign Committees who became federal employees to credit up to 10 years of service with the committees in computing their benefits from the federal retirement system.

To get credit for their years of service, the former campaign committee staffers would have to make a contribution to the federal retirement funds to make up for the fact that they had not made any contributions while working with the committees.

A motion by Adam Benjamin Jr., D-Ind., to accept the Senate amendment was rejected by voice vote.

Final Senate Action

The Senate Aug. 25 yielded to the House rejection of Hart building funds and adopted the conference report by a 61-11 vote, thus clearing the bill. *(Vote 364, p. 54-S)*

Several senators reacted testily to the House cut. Milton R. Young, R-N.D., said he hoped "the action of the House will not create a feud between the two bodies."

Ted Stevens, R-Alaska, said, "If we are going to stop this historic practice of not looking into the expenses of the other body, I think we ought to start by looking at some of the items in the legislative appropriations bill next year."

Charges that the building was overly lavish and that the Senate didn't need the additional space were denied by Appropriations Committee Chairman Warren G. Magnuson, D-Wash.

Magnuson said many senators were suffering from the lack of office space, adding that there "were people sitting on top of one another in my office."

Magnuson released a memorandum designed to correct some of the "distortions and inaccuracies" about the building's costs.

According to the memo:

- Only 15 percent of the building had 16 foot ceiling heights.
- The gymnasium was "in fact a simple basketball court . . . comparable to that which exists on the House side." The gym was described as "austere and simple in its design."
- The Multi-Media Room was "not an overly decorated or opulent room: it is a simple hearing room" for the public, press and electronic media.
- Wood paneling was chosen "not only for the aura of quiet dignity which it exudes, but also because of its cost benefit value."

The memo also said that the building was very energy efficient, and that $18 million of the funds requested had resulted "purely and simply from increases in construction costs resulting from inflation in the economy."

Magnuson said there was about $32 million to continue construction of the Hart building, and that the only effect of the House action would be to increase costs through inflation if completion of the building were delayed.

The Senate also yielded to the House's refusal to accept a Senate amendment that would have allowed former House and Senate campaign committee employees to receive federal pension credits for this service after they became federal employees.

Grain Inspection Costs

President Carter June 26 signed into law a resolution (H J Res 944—PL 95-301) appropriating $6.5 million for fiscal year 1978 for the federal grain inspection program.

The administration had requested the additional funds, which were needed to pay the full cost of the grain inspection program as mandated by the 1977 farm act (PL 95-113).

The 1976 act setting up the federal inspection program (PL 94-582) had provided that the government and users of the service would split inspection fees. But the 1977 act made the government responsible for the full cost of inspection. *(Grain inspection act, 1976 Almanac p. 381; 1977 farm act, 1977 Almanac p. 417)*

"When the 1978 budget was considered, it was assumed that user fees would continue to be collected, so now the Federal Grain Inspection Service is likely to run out of money at approximately 3 p.m. today," Thomas F. Eagleton, D-Mo., told the Senate June 19.

The Senate promptly approved the resolution by voice vote. The House had approved the resolution by voice vote on June 16. It was reported by the House Appropriations Committee May 31 (H Rept 95-1223).

The federal inspection service was created in response to a series of scandals involving private grain inspection firms.

$67.9 Billion HUD Funds Bill Cleared

Congress Sept. 20 cleared the fiscal 1979 appropriations bill for the Department of Housing and Urban Development (HUD), the Veterans Administration (VA) and 16 other federal agencies.

The bill (HR 12936 — PL 95-392) appropriated a total of $67,911,419,000, about $1.6 billion less than sought by the Carter administration. Most of the reductions represented congressional cuts in administration proposals for assisted housing programs.

The total appropriation for fiscal 1979 was also about $7.2 billion below the fiscal 1978 appropriation approved by Congress in 1977. However, about $6 billion of the $7.2 billion represented assisted housing funds appropriated for fiscal 1978 that were not spent and were carried over by HUD to fiscal 1979. *(Fiscal 1978 appropriation, 1977 Almanac p. 279)*

The final bill for fiscal 1979 was about $297 million less than the House version, and about $254.8 million more than the Senate version. The Senate Appropriations Committee initially recommended higher appropriations than the House, but the Senate reduced several spending items during floor debate in order to achieve a 2 percent overall cut in controllable spending.

House and Senate conferees resolved all their differences at one meeting, Sept. 13. The House adopted the conference report by voice vote on Sept. 19. The Senate followed suit Sept. 20.

The major spending items in HR 12936 included $1.3 billion in new contract authority for assisted housing for low and moderate income persons. The new contract authority required total budget authority of $24.3 billion, the actual amount needed to cover the long-term costs of housing contracts made under the various assisted housing programs.

HR 12936 also appropriated $3.75 billion for community development block grants, the major federal urban aid program, and $400 million for urban development action grants, a program begun in 1977 by HUD to stimulate economic revitalization in decaying cities.

The bill also included $18.3 billion for the VA, $5.4 billion for the Environmental Protection Agency (EPA) and $4.3 billion for the National Aeronautics and Space Administration (NASA).

In addition, the bill provided nearly $6.9 billion for revenue sharing and other payments to state and local governments.

Provisions

As cleared by Congress, HR 12936 made the following appropriations for fiscal 1979:

	Budget Request	Final Amount
Department of Housing and Urban Development		
Housing Programs	$28,126,717,000	$26,879,615,000
Community Planning and Development	4,472,000,000	4,453,000,000
Flood Insurance Administration	114,000,000	85,000,000
Housing Counseling	8,000,000	9,000,000
Policy Research and Development	62,000,000	57,500,000
Management and Administration	279,570,000	273,810,000
Total, HUD Department	$33,062,287,000	$31,757,925,000
Federal Disaster Assistance Administration	200,000,000	200,000,000
American Battle Monuments Commission	6,240,000	6,240,000
Consumer Product Safety Commission	41,463,000	40,000,000
Army Cemeterial Expenses	5,200,000	5,100,000
Environmental Protection Agency	5,675,360,000	5,403,946,000
Council on Environmental Quality	3,126,000	3,026,000
Office of Science and Technology Policy	2,621,000	2,476,000
Consumer Information Center	1,186,000	1,146,000
HEW Office of Consumer Affairs	1,737,000	1,700,000
National Aeronautics and Space Administration	4,371,600,000	4,350,200,000
National Commission on Air Quality	4,000,000	2,000,000
National Institute of Building Sciences	—	750,000
National Science Foundation	934,000,000	911,000,000
Selective Service System	9,500,000	7,045,000
State and Local Assistance	6,863,567,000	6,863,174,000
Veterans Administration	18,335,647,000	18,355,691,000
Grand Total	$69,517,534,000	$67,911,419,000

House Committee Action

The House Appropriations Committee reported the bill June 1 (H Rept 95-1255).

The committee recommended $68,208,848,000 in new budget authority for HUD and the 17 independent agencies and offices for fiscal 1979.

The $68 billion was about $6 billion below the amount appropriated for fiscal 1978, and about $1.3 billion below the amount sought by the administration for fiscal 1979.

The committee deferred action on $1,040,000,000 sought by the administration for fiscal aid to "distressed" cities and towns as part of the president's urban program. Legislation to establish the fiscal aid program was pending in the House and Senate. *(Story, p. 313)*

HUD Department

Housing. The committee focused on the question "what mix of subsidized housing programs at what cost" in attempting to decide how much money to recommend for the various categories of federal housing assistance.

On the basis of a study by the General Accounting Office and two studies by the Congressional Research Service, the committee concluded that traditional public housing may be less costly in the long run than the so-called Section 8 program, which provides rent subsidies for low-income persons. The committee did not, however, recommend any major shift of money away from the Section 8 program, although it said it intended to "monitor carefully" the cost and effectiveness of the subsidy program in the coming years.

The committee recommended an additional $1,334,-950,000 in new annual contract authority ($24,650,950,000 in budget authority) for subsidized housing programs, the full amount sought by the administration. The $1.3 billion would support about 400,000 rental units for low-income households in fiscal 1979, although the committee said that estimate did not take into account inflation. Therefore, the committee indicated, the actual number of units would probably be below 400,000.

The committee designated 56,000 of the units for public housing, about 19,000 less than allocated for public housing in fiscal 1978. The remaining 344,000 units would be for subsidized housing under Section 8 with the following distribution: 110,000 units of new construction, 70,000 units of substantial rehabilitation and 164,000 units in existing dwellings.

HUD agreed to finance 380,240 units of Section 8 and public housing in fiscal 1978, according to current estimates.

Of the $1.3 billion in new contract authority, the committee earmarked $37.5 million for public housing modernization, and said it expected HUD to continue to reserve for rural public housing a minimum of 15 percent of the annual contract authority reserved for public housing. But the committee did not impose any further limitations ("set-asides") in allocating housing funds, in line with a request from HUD. The agency had argued that substantial earmarking of housing funds in specific categories impeded management flexibility.

The committee recommended that $4,463,000,000 be provided to meet the costs of subsidized housing contracts made in past years under Section 8, homeownership assistance under Section 235, rental housing assistance under Section 236, low-income public housing, college housing and state housing finance and development agency programs. The funding was $40 million less than the administration request.

For other housing programs, the committee recommended a loan limit of $800 million, the amount sought by the administration, for Section 202 housing for the elderly and handicapped. The $800 million limit should provide about 25,000 additional housing units. The committee also recommended retaining statutes limiting the Section 202 program to qualified non-profit sponsors, providing long-term permanent financing, and requiring that Section 202 loan authority be "on budget" for fiscal 1979, as it was for fiscal 1978.

The committee recommended $723 million for public housing operating subsidies, an increase of $38 million over the fiscal 1978 appropriation, but a decrease of $6 million from the administration's fiscal 1979 request.

The committee also recommended $74 million for a new program of operating subsidies for multi-family housing projects facing default or loss of tenants because of escalating operating costs. Although the committee supported the full request sought by HUD, it expressed concern that the federal agency might be embarking on a new operating subsidy with a substantial "growth potential." The committee prodded HUD to focus on improving the management of the projects, rather than seeking more tax dollars.

Community Development. The committee recommended $3.75 billion for the community development block grant program, the major federal urban aid program. The $3.75 billion was the full amount sought by the administration. The fiscal 1978 appropriation was $3.6 billion.

The committee included language in the bill to limit so-called "non-program" expenditures by any city or town to 20 percent of the annual block grant. The committee cited research by its staff showing that some cities were spending what the committee considered to be exorbitant amounts of money on administrative costs. The committee attributed that partly to a lack of guidance from HUD on what actually constituted "non-program" expenditures. Besides the 20 percent limit, the committee instructed HUD to develop precise definitions for "non-program" and administrative costs.

The committee also recommended $400 million for urban development action grants, the full amount sought by the administration; $50 million for comprehensive planning grants, $7 million below the administration's request; $245 million for Section 312 low-interest rehabilitation housing loans, as sought by the administration; and $20 million for urban homesteading, the amount requested by the administration.

For the federal flood insurance program, the committee recommended $90 million, $24 million below the administration's request. The committee said lower costs for production of flood insurance rate maps allowed the reduction.

The committee also recommended $10 million for housing counseling assistance, $2 million above the administration's request and $5 million above the fiscal 1978 appropriation. The committee said the $2 million increase should be used for counseling programs before potential homeowners make their purchases.

For research and development, the committee recommended $56 million, a cut of $6 million from the administration's request and an increase of $4 million above the fiscal 1978 appropriation. The committee had in the past questioned some of the research projects conducted by HUD. It said in its report that HUD had improved research and development under the Carter administration.

Environmental Protection Agency

Overall, the committee recommended $5,374,446,000 for the Environmental Protection Agency, $300.9 million less than requested by the administration, and about $103.5 million less than the fiscal 1978 appropriation.

Major cuts included:

- $25 million from the budget request for regional planning grants for water pollution control (the so-called Section 208 program). The committee asserted that the Section 208 program had been hindered by poor management and made it clear that no increases in funding would be allowed until the program's direction and management were improved.
- $300 million from funds sought for construction grants for wastewater treatment plants. The committee further

recommended that none of the remaining $4.2 billion should be used for new facilities that would provide "advanced" treatment of wastewater. The committee questioned whether "advanced" treatment plants — the most technically sophisticated systems — had much impact on water quality and public health in relation to the costs involved. The committee denied a request for $4.5 billion in advanced funding for the program for fiscal 1980.

• $8 million from requested funding for research to determine possible future environmental problems. The committee said it was aware of the need for such research, but "extensive management attention" was needed to ensure that the program was not used for research projects that could not be justified elsewhere or had little promise of practical applicability.

National Aeronautics and Space Administration

The committee recommended $4,333,890,000 for the National Aeronautics and Space Administration, $37.7 million less than requested by the administration.

The committee denied $20.5 million requested for development of a new rocket motor to prevent an uncontrolled descent by the Skylab space station. The motor was to be taken to Skylab by the space shuttle, but the committee said the shuttle was unlikely to be ready for a launching before Skylab's probable descent in May-June 1979. The committee said it would reconsider funding for the rocket motor if current efforts to extend Skylab's orbital life appeared likely to succeed.

The committee made it clear that it did not like delays encountered in the shuttle program because of shifting funds from production to development in fiscal 1978. In recommending the establishment of a $30 million contingency fund for the program, the committee said it believed that shuttle development was "in a critical phase and sufficient funds should be made available to protect an eight billion dollar investment in a fourteen billion dollar program."

National Science Foundation

The committee recommended $893,900,000 for the National Science Foundation (NSF), a cut of $40.1 million from the fiscal 1979 request.

In making the recommendation, the committee chided NSF on several counts, reminding the foundation that it was not the only federal agency involved in basic research.

The committee said it had found duplication between research conducted by NSF and research conducted by other federal agencies, and suggested that NSF had "encroached" on the responsibilities of other agencies, particularly in the social sciences.

Veterans Administration

The politically popular Veterans Administration was the only major agency in the bill to receive more money than it had requested for fiscal 1979. The committee recommended $18,460,515,000 for the VA, about $124.9 million above the administration's request.

The major increases recommended by the committee included $32 million for staff positions to enable the VA to keep open about 3,100 beds in its 172-hospital system; nearly $15 million for medical and prosthetic research; and $53 million for 10 major construction projects.

The construction projects were not included in the VA's fiscal 1979 budget request, but were on a list of projects the VA wanted to build in the future.

The committee approved $130 million to build a replacement VA hospital in Portland, Ore. The committee strongly recommended that the hospital be built adjacent to the Emanuel Hospital in Portland, instead of on Marquam Hill, the site favored by the VA. The committee also rejected an attempt by the Carter administration to cancel a proposed new VA hospital for Camden, N.J.

House Floor Action

After rejecting a 2 percent across-the-board funding cut, the House June 19 approved a $68.2 billion appropriation for HUD and 17 other federal agencies.

The House passed HR 12936 by a 332-47 vote, after defeating, 156-222, another in a series of efforts to slash government spending. Those efforts were widely perceived as a reaction to Proposition 13, a property tax roll-back approved by California voters June 6. *(Votes 408, 409, pp. 116-H, 118-H)*

The largest chunk of money in the bill provided just over $32 billion for HUD programs, including $1.3 billion in new contract authority for publicly subsidized housing. That figure represented about $24.6 billion in actual appropriations (budget authority), which reflected the runout costs of long-term housing contracts of up to 40 years.

In fiscal 1979, the new contract authority would provide rent subsidies for an estimated 400,000 housing units, although the actual number of units helped was expected to be less because of inflation.

The second largest item in the bill — $18.5 billion — was appropriated for the Veterans Administration (VA). The VA, whose broad constituency is considered one of the strongest political forces in Washington, was the only major agency whose appropriation was increased by HR 12936 above the request submitted by the Carter administration in January.

The bill also included $5.4 billion for the Environmental Protection Agency (EPA) and $4.3 billion for the National Aeronautics and Space Administration (NASA). Requested funding for EPA was sharply cut.

Floor debate centered primarily on a proposal to cut $133 million from the EPA appropriation and on the proposed across-the-board spending cut.

Across-the-Board Cut

The attempt to cut 2 percent from the total appropriation — about $985 million, according to one estimate — was expected. Clarence E. Miller, R-Ohio, the sponsor of the amendment, had offered it in 1977 during consideration of the fiscal 1978 appropriations bill and again earlier in June on other fiscal 1979 appropriations bills.

Prior to the vote on HR 12936, Miller had been fairly successful on the major bills. His 2 percent cut was tacked on to the Labor-HEW appropriations bill (HR 12929) on June 13, the State-Commerce-Judiciary appropriations bill (HR 12934) on June 14, and the public works appropriations bill (HR 12928) on June 16.

Observers offered several reasons to explain the House refusal to mandate an across-the-board cut in the HUD bill. First, they noted the procedural context. Miller initially lost on a voice vote when he offered his proposal as an amendment to the bill. He then demanded a standing vote, and lost by a 34-53 vote. He then demanded a recorded vote, but was rebuffed. Finally, before passage of HR 12936, Miller moved that it be recommitted to the Appropriations Committee with instructions to reduce appropriations by 2 percent across-the-board, except for programs required by law. That brought a recorded vote, but Miller lost again, 156-222. *(Vote 408, p. 116-H)*

"It's one thing to make the motion on a straight amendment, but trying the cut on a motion to recommit is like really sticking the knife in, and that probably made the vote more of a [political] party matter," said one congressional source.

Edward P. Boland, D-Mass., chairman of the Appropriations HUD Subcommittee, also was credited with skillful handling of the bill on the floor. He had support from Lawrence Coughlin, R-Pa., the ranking Republican on the subcommittee, who opposed the 2 percent cut in a brief floor speech. A week earlier, Coughlin had voted to cut 2 percent from the Labor-HEW bill.

Some members argued that mandating across-the-board cuts actually did nothing but abdicate congressional authority to the executive branch of government. Abraham Kazen Jr., D-Texas, used that argument in opposing the Miller amendment, urging that specific budget cuts, if they were to be made, should be done by Congress "right here on this floor."

But Miller argued that "if we designate each program on the floor we will never have a cut" because members will protect their pet projects.

As it turned out, there was some evidence that members opposed the across-the-board cuts precisely because they wanted to protect their interests.

Coughlin was not the only legislator who voted to cut the Labor-HEW appropriation but opposed the 2 percent cut for HR 12936. Two other members of the HUD Appropriations Subcommittee, Tom Bevill, D-Ala., and C. W. "Bill" Young, R-Fla., also supported the 2 percent Labor-HEW cut but opposed a similar cut for HUD.

In addition, eight members of the Science and Technology Committee who supported the 2 percent Labor-HEW cut opposed the Miller amendment to HR 12936. The Science and Technology Committee handles authorizing legislation for NASA, the National Science Foundation and several other agencies whose appropriations are contained in HR 12936.

Finally, the presence of the Veterans Administration appropriation in the bill may have cooled the budget-cutting ardor.

"The VA is the most sacred cow anywhere," said one Appropriations Committee staff member. The 2 percent cut, he added, would have meant a reduction of about $107 million in VA funds.

A vote analysis showed that 7 members of the Veterans Affairs Committee who supported the 2 percent cut in the Labor-HEW bill switched and rejected it on HR 12936. Those 7 included Ray Roberts, D-Texas, committee chairman; G. V. "Sonny" Montgomery, D-Miss.; and John Paul Hammerschmidt, R-Ark., and Margaret M. Heckler, R-Mass., the first and second ranking Republicans on the committee. No one on the veterans committee who opposed the 2 percent cut in the Labor-HEW bill switched to vote for the cut in the HUD appropriations bill.

Ironically, rejection of the 2 percent cut of HR 12936 came on the same day the sponsor of Proposition 13, Howard Jarvis, was in Washington touring the Capitol and meeting with various members of Congress from both parties. But Proposition 13 was not mentioned by name at all during the more than five hours of debate on HR 12936.

EPA Funding

Garry Brown, R-Mich., proposed the $133 million cut in the EPA appropriations, arguing that such a reduction would reduce the "inflationary impact" of government regulations.

Brown, who as a member of the House Energy Committee had sided with industry in its support of deregulation of natural gas, proposed cuts for EPA's two regulatory areas — abatement and control and enforcement.

Opponents of the cuts argued, however, that trimming $133 million would severely hamper EPA regulatory and enforcement activities in basic areas such as clean water, toxic substances and clean air. The Brown amendment was defeated on a 173-211 vote. *(Vote 407, p. 116-H)*

Other Amendments

The House made only one change in the bill as reported, adopting by voice vote an amendment by Coughlin, to ensure that funds carried over by HUD from fiscal 1978 would not be subject to set asides governing distribution of housing funds.

On other amendments, the House:

- Rejected, by a 13-25 standing vote, an amendment by Young of Florida to add $100 million to the Section 202 housing program for the elderly.
- Rejected two amendments by George E. Brown Jr., D-Calif., that in effect would have shifted $20 million in EPA funds from construction grants to research and development. The first amendment was defeated by a 12-17 standing vote. The second amendment was defeated by voice vote.
- Rejected by voice vote an amendment by Walter B. Jones, D-N.C., to add $200,000 to the appropriation for the Council on Environmental Quality.
- Rejected by voice vote an amendment by Brown of California to add $9 million to the National Science Foundation appropriation for earthquake research.
- Rejected, by a 24-43 standing vote, an amendment by Richard C. White, D-Texas, to add $9,055,000 for the Selective Service System.
- Rejected, by a 27-41 standing vote, an amendment by Elwood Hillis, R-Ind., to add $2,455,000 for the Selective Service System.

Provisions

As passed by the House, HR 12936 made the following appropriations for fiscal 1979:

	Budget Request	House-Passed Appropriations
Department of Housing and Urban Development		
Housing Programs	$28,126,717,000	$27,120,717,000
Community Planning and Development	4,472,000,000	4,465,000,000
Flood Insurance Administration	114,000,000	90,000,000
Housing Counseling	8,000,000	10,000,000
Policy Development and Research	62,000,000	56,000,000

	Budget Request	House-Passed Appropriations
Management and Administration	279,570,000	271,553,000
Total, HUD Department	$33,062,287,000	$32,013,270,000
Federal Disaster Assistance Administration	200,000,000	200,000,000
American Battle Monuments Commission	6,240,000	6,240,000
Consumer Product Safety Commission	41,463,000	40,000,000
Army Cemeterial Expenses	5,200,000	5,100,000
Environmental Protection Agency	5,675,360,000	5,374,446,000
Council on Environmental Quality	3,126,000	2,926,000
Office of Science and Technology Policy	2,621,000	2,476,000
Consumer Information Center	1,186,000	1,166,000
HEW Office of Consumer Affairs	1,737,000	1,700,000
National Aeronautics and Space Administration	4,371,600,000	4,333,890,000
National Commission on Air Quality	4,000,000	2,000,000
National Institute of Building Sciences	—	1,000,000
National Science Foundation	934,000,000	893,900,000
Selective Service System	9,500,000	7,045,000
State and Local Assistance	6,863,567,000	6,863,174,000
Veterans Administration	18,335,647,000	18,460,515,000
Grand Total	$69,517,534,000	$68,208,848,000

Senate Committee Action

The Senate Appropriations Committee reported the bill Aug. 1 (S Rept 95-1060).

The committee recommended $68,464,374,000 in new budget authority for fiscal 1979, $255,526,000 more than the House-passed bill.

The $68.5 billion was $1,053,160 less than the Carter administration budget request for fiscal 1979, and $5,844,-227,000 less than the fiscal 1978 appropriation.

HUD Department

The committee recommended $1,334,950,000 in new contract authority ($24,650,950,000 in budget authority) for subsidized housing programs, the full amount sought by the Carter administration and approved by the House. The committee said the $1.3 billion in new contract authority, along with $6.4 billion in unused budget authority from the 1978 fiscal year, would permit HUD to reserve 396,200 subsidized units for low-income households in 1979, assuming no increase in housing costs over the next 12 months.

The committee designated 56,000 units for public housing, the same designation made by the House. The remaining 340,200 units were designated for the Section 8 rental subsidy program with the following distribution: 108,550 units for new construction, 69,240 units for substantial rehabilitation, and 162,410 units for existing housing.

The committee earmarked $50 million of the $1.3 billion in new contract authority for public housing modernization, $12.5 million above the House-passed bill.

The committee also chided HUD for failing to end "shoppers subsidies" for Section 8 tenants, despite a committee directive to do so and a critical report by the General Accounting Office (GAO). The subsidy program was designed to encourage families to shop for less expensive housing but had not worked out, according to the GAO study.

The committee recommended that $4,460,000,000 be provided to meet the costs of subsidized housing contracts made in past years under Section 8, homeownership assistance under Section 235, rental housing assistance under Section 236, low-income public housing, college housing and state housing finance and development agency contracts. The recommendation was $3 million below the House-passed bill and $43 million less than the administration request.

For other housing programs, the committee recommended a loan limit of $800 million, the amount sought by the administration and passed by the House, for Section 202 housing for the elderly and handicapped. The committee also recommended $729,000,000 for public housing operating subsidies, an increase of $6 million over the House-passed bill; $74 million, the House allowance, for a new program of operating subsidies for multifamily housing projects facing default or loss of tenants because of escalating operating costs, and $20 million for a new program of congregate housing services for elderly and disabled tenants in housing constructed under the Section 202 program.

The administration did not seek and the House bill did not include any funds for congregate services, which provide meals, social services and other needs to help elderly and disabled residents in public housing. But both the Senate and House included authorizations for congregate services in the fiscal 1979 HUD authorization bill (S 3084, HR 12433). *(HUD Authorization story, p. 303)*

The committee recommended a second program not sought by the administration or included in the House-passed bill. The program would provide $4 billion in stand-by authority for emergency purchases of mortgages by the Government National Mortgage Association (GNMA) for use when a depressed housing market threatened to lower housing production, especially in the multifamily area, to what the committee described only as "unacceptable levels."

The funds could be used only when the secretary of HUD found that conditions justified the release of the authority. The committee said the entire $4 billion was to come from "recaptured budget authority" previously provided. Recaptured authority is generated by the sale of mortgages from the GNMA portfolio, cancellations, foreclosures and repayments. Under the program GNMA would be able to purchase HUD-insured and VA-guaranteed as well as conventional mortgages bearing interest rates of 7.5 percent.

Community Development. The committee recommended $3.75 billion for the community development block grant program, the full amount sought by the administration and included in the House-passed bill. The committee also agreed with the House in recommending that administration costs of any grant recipient be held to 20 percent.

The committee recommended $400 million for the urban development action grant program, the amount sought by the administration and approved by the House; $57 million for comprehensive planning grants, the amount sought by the administration but $7 million more than approved by the House; $245 million for Section 312 low-interest rehabilitation loans, the amount sought by the administration and approved by the House; and $20 million for urban homesteading, the amount approved by the House and recommended by the administration.

For the federal flood insurance program, the committee recommended $85 million, $5 million less than the House-approved bill and $29 million less than the administration request.

Environmental Protection Agency

The committee recommended $5,721,971,000 for the Environmental Protection Agency, $347,525,000 more than recommended by the House, and $46,611,000 more than the administration's request.

The committee restored $300 million cut by the House from funds sought for construction grants for wastewater treatment plants. It said the $300 million restoration would enable the administration to continue its 10-year, $45 billion program begun in fiscal 1978 to meet water quality requirements established in the Federal Water Pollution Control Act of 1977.

The committee also recommended restoration of $14 million from a $25 million House cut in the budget request for regional planning grants for water pollution control (the Section 208 program). Furthermore, the committee said that in view of the importance of the Section 208 program, it would "consider any supplemental funding necessary to meet the federal commitment to improve water quality management."

National Aeronautics and Space Administration

For the National Aeronautics and Space Administration the committee recommended $4,358,200,000. That was $13.4 million below the administration request but $24,310,000 above the House recommendation.

In the major departure from the House position, the committee approved a $20.5 million request for development of a new rocket motor to prevent an uncontrolled descent by the Skylab space station. But the committee instructed NASA not to obligate the money until determining that it was feasible to undertake an attempt to reach Skylab in orbit. The committee further instructed NASA, if it decided not to attempt a Skylab reboost or deorbit mission, to submit a rescission proposal to Congress for that portion of the $20.5 million associated solely with such a mission.

The committee also rejected the House position on funds for the second phase of the pad "B" launch complex at Kennedy Space Center, recommending approval of $12.8 million for the project. The committee said a back-up launch pad for the space shuttle should be ready in case any difficulties developed at the prime launch pad.

National Science Foundation

The committee recommended $927 million for the National Science Foundation (NSF), $7 million below the administration request but $33,100,000 above the House allowance. The committee praised NSF for its "excellent initial effort" to publish the results of NSF-sponsored research, and directed the foundation in the future to "take particular care to present this information in terms that are meaningful to laymen" and to present the information in a consistent format including the dates of initiation and termination of each grant together with the cost of the grant to the taxpayer.

Veterans Administration

The committee recommended $18,278,228,000 for the Veterans Administration, $57,419,000 less than the administration request, and $182,287,000 below the amount recommended by the House.

It recommended a cut of $49.3 million in payments for education, training and rehabilitation benefits for veterans and their eligible dependents, saying the reduction would be achieved by prohibiting the use of funds for VA education loans to individuals attending schools where the combined tuition and fees for the academic year were $700 or less.

The committee noted that the program was established by Congress to help students attending "high tuition" institutions, but said a recent report by the General Accounting Office (GAO) found that 72 percent of the loans made since the inception of the program through the end of calendar year 1977 went to veterans attending schools charging low or no tuition.

The GAO found, the committee said, that loans were approved to cover such expenses as installment payments on appliances, home improvements, entertainment and holiday gifts. The committee said it also learned that as of Jan. 31, 1978, 46 percent of all matured loans were in default.

The committee proposed that a House increase of $82,919,000 for medical care be reduced to only $20 million. The committee action in effect rejected about $50 million included by the House for staff increases, and cut $12 million from $32 million designed to enable the VA to keep open about 3,100 beds in its 172-hospital system.

The panel eliminated 11 construction projects not requested by the VA but added by the House. The projects, scattered across the country, totaled about $52 million. However, the committee left a 12th project not requested by the VA but included by the House in the appropriations bill. The project called for $9.8 million for a clinical support building at Mountain Home, Tenn., the home state of Jim Sasser, a Democratic member of the HUD Appropriations Subcommittee that was responsible for the bill.

The committee agreed with one House recommendation instructing the VA to continue plans to build a new VA hospital in Camden, N.J. The Carter administration proposed in January to eliminate the project on the grounds that a new hospital was not needed. A subsequent report by the GAO also concluded the construction of the hospital "is not justified."

But the Carter administration later changed its position after Rep. James J. Florio, D-N.J., whose district includes Camden, threatened to vote against the administration's hospital cost containment bill. In light of that trade, and extensive lobbying by New Jersey's senators, Clifford P. Case, R, and Harrison A. Williams Jr., D, Sen. William Proxmire, D-Wis., chairman of the HUD Appropriations

Subcommittee and an opponent of the Camden project, gave up his effort to block it.

Dealing with another controversial hospital project, the committee directed the VA to build replacement facilities for VA hospitals in both Portland, Ore., and Vancouver, Wash. *(Box, p. 86)*

Although the VA had sought funding for a single replacement facility of 858 beds, to be located in Portland, the committee said the VA should locate high technology services in Portland, with a hospital of at least 600 beds, and provide general medical care services at Vancouver, with a hospital of at least 250 beds. The committee did not, however, make a recommendation on another key aspect of the controversy, the location of the Portland hospital.

Senate Floor Action

On the third try, the Senate Aug. 7 narrowly approved a 2 percent cut in the fiscal 1979 appropriations bill for the Department of Housing and Urban Development (HUD) and 17 other federal agencies.

The cut, which was "targeted" to specific programs in HUD and three other agencies, was adopted after four senators who initially voted against the reduction changed their minds and supported it on reconsideration.

The Senate subsequently passed HR 12936 by an 80-6 vote. *(Vote 293, p. 45-S)*

As passed by the Senate, HR 12936 appropriated $67.7 billion for HUD, the Environmental Protection Agency (EPA), the Veterans Administration (VA), the National Aeronautics and Space Administration (NASA) and various other agencies.

Before the 2 percent cut in total controllable spending under the bill, the Senate measure provided $255.5 million more than the House had approved. But the reduction, which totaled about $810 million, combined with a $2.5 million increase for the Selective Service System, made the Senate version about $552.4 million below the House allowance. The House, which passed HR 12936 June 19, rejected a 2 percent cut during floor debate.

The Senate began consideration of HR 12936 Aug. 4. It finished action Aug. 7, voting on both amendments and the bill itself.

Spending Cuts

Proxmire offered the amendment to cut 2 percent from the proposed fiscal 1979 appropriation. Proxmire argued that the cut was needed in order to hold back government spending and thus help ease inflation and the federal deficit.

"The issue is a very clear-cut one: Are we to make a stand now against ever-increasing federal spending or will we capitulate to the dozens of worthy but costly pressures that drive the budget ever upward?" Proxmire said.

Proxmire "targeted" his cut, however, earmarking reductions in the budgets of specific programs for four agencies included in HR 12936 — HUD, EPA, NASA and the National Science Foundation.

Proxmire offered his amendment as an alternative to an across-the-board, 2 percent cut in controllable spending proposed by William V. Roth Jr., R-Del. Proxmire argued that the Roth proposal would leave it up to the Office of Management and Budget to determine where the actual cuts should be made, thereby allowing the executive branch to ignore or even circumvent actions of the congressional appropriations committees.

Roth indicated during debate that he would accept either his or Proxmire's approach. "Either way helps achieve my objective of slowing down the total cost of government," he declared.

Opponents of proposed cuts argued that the programs funded in HR 12936 that would be hit by the Proxmire amendment provided money for critical needs, especially subsidized housing for the poor.

Initially, the Senate rejected any cut in HR 12936, voting 43-44 against the Proxmire amendment and defeating the Roth amendment by a wider margin, 30-55. *(Votes 288, 289, p. 44-S)*

But then, with parliamentary maneuvering overshadowing the substantive aspects of the debate, the Senate agreed by a 47-41 vote to reconsider its initial rejection of the Proxmire amendment and went on to approve the amendment by a 45-42 vote. Opponents of the 2 percent cut tried some maneuvering themselves, attempting to reconsider the second vote on the Proxmire amendment. But they failed, with the Senate voting 49-39 to table the motion to reconsider. *(Votes 290, 291, 292, pp. 44-S, 45-S)*

Four senators who voted against the Proxmire amendment the first time switched and supported it on the second vote. They were Dennis DeConcini, D-Ariz., Russell B. Long, D-La., Howard M. Metzenbaum, D-Ohio, and Malcolm Wallop, R-Wyo. Floyd K. Haskell, D-Colo., did not vote the first time but supported the amendment the second time. Clifford P. Hansen, R-Wyo., voted for the Proxmire amendment the first time and was paired for it the second time.

There were four other vote switches on the Proxmire amendment. John H. Chafee, R-R.I., and Paul G. Hatfield, D-Mont., supported the Proxmire amendment on the first vote but opposed it on the second. They were joined by Daniel K. Inouye, D-Hawaii, who did not vote the first time. Charles H. Percy, R-Ill., opposed the Proxmire amendment the first time but did not vote the second.

Metzenbaum said through a spokesman later that he voted for the Proxmire amendment in order to be able to make the motion to reconsider the vote. A motion to reconsider can be made only by a senator who voted for the bill or amendment.

Funding Cuts. The Proxmire amendment made the following cuts in HR 12936:

- Reduced additional new contract authority for assisted housing under the Section 8 and public housing programs to $1,310,424,000 from $1,334,950,000 and reduced total budget authority by $510,205,000, to $24,140,745,000 from $24,650,950,000. Proxmire estimated that the new spending as passed by the Senate would enable HUD to fund between 350,000 and 360,000 units of assisted housing.
- Reduced the appropriation for urban development action grants by $20 million, to $380 million from $400 million.
- Reduced the appropriation for Section 312 rehabilitation loans by $15 million, to $230 million from $245 million.
- Reduced the appropriation for EPA water pollution control construction grants by $250 million, to $4.25 billion from $4.5 billion.
- Reduced the appropriation for NASA research and development by $5 million, to $3,290,700,000 from $3,295,-700,000.

• Reduced the appropriation for National Science Foundation research by $10 million, to $836,400,000 from $846,400,000.

Selective Service System

The Senate did agree to one small increase in spending for the Selective Service System, increasing the recommended funding to $9.5 million from $7,045,000.

The $2,455,000 increase came after the Senate rejected a larger increase of $9,955,000 designed to enable the Selective Service System to begin registering 18-year-old men in fiscal 1979.

The debate over Selective Service funding was sparked by Robert Morgan, D-N.C., a member of the Armed Services Committee, one of several senators who used the appropriation bill to voice their concerns about the volunteer Army.

Morgan said the Selective Service System was in a state of deep standby, and did not have any personnel at the state or local level who could register young men in time of emergency.

Morgan ran into some sharp criticism, however, from fellow committee members, including Chairman John C. Stennis, D-Miss.

Stennis said it was inappropriate to mandate registration through an appropriations bill, and that Congress should not act pending completion of a study on manpower mobilization needs by the Department of Defense. Stennis was joined by Sam Nunn, D-Ga., head of the Armed Services Subcommittee on Manpower, who called the amendment "premature."

The Morgan amendment was defeated by a 16-71 vote. But the Senate subsequently adopted by a 46-42 vote an amendment cosponsored by Nunn and Robert Dole, R-Kan., to add $2,455,000 to the appropriation for the Selective Service System. *(Votes 286, 287, p. 44-S)*

The money would enable the system to hire more personnel during fiscal 1979, but would not require registration. The added spending brought the appropriation for the Selective Service System up to the level sought by the Carter administration in its fiscal 1979 budget request.

Veterans Administration

The Senate adopted one other amendment, deleting by voice vote a provision in HR 12936 designed to limit VA educational loans to colleges with high tuition costs. Proxmire accepted the amendment after Alan Cranston, D-Calif., chairman of the Veterans Affairs Committee, said the provision would be attached to veterans legislation. The Senate subsequently attached a provision giving the VA administrator authority to set limits to a veterans housing bill (HR 12028). *(Story, p. 368)*

Provisions

As passed by the Senate, HR 12936 made the following appropriations for fiscal 1979:

	House-Passed Appropriations	Senate-Passed Appropriations
Department of Housing and Urban Development		
Housing Programs	$27,120,717,000	$26,636,512,000
Community Planning and Development	4,465,000,000	4,437,000,000
Flood Insurance Administration	90,000,000	85,000,000
Housing Counseling	10,000,000	8,000,000
Policy Research and Development	56,000,000	59,000,000
Management and Administration	271,553,000	275,851,000
Total, HUD Department	$32,013,270,000	$31,501,363,000
Federal Disaster Assistance Administration	200,000,000	200,000,000
American Battle Monuments Commission	6,240,000	6,240,000
Consumer Product Safety Commission	40,000,000	40,000,000
Army Cemeterial Expenses	5,100,000	5,100,000
Environmental Protection Agency	5,374,446,000	5,471,971,000
Council on Environmental Quality	2,926,000	3,026,000
Office of Science and Technology Policy	2,476,000	2,476,000
Consumer Information Center	1,166,000	1,146,000
HEW Office of Consumer Affairs	1,700,000	1,700,000
National Aeronautics and Space Administration	4,333,890,000	4,353,200,000
National Commission on Air Quality	2,000,000	2,000,000
National Institute of Building Sciences	1,000,000	500,000
National Science Foundation	893,900,000	917,000,000
Selective Service System	7,045,000	9,500,000
State and Local Assistance	6,863,174,000	6,863,174,000
Veterans Administration	18,460,515,000	18,278,228,000
Grand Total	$68,208,848,000	$67,656,624,000

Conference Action

Conferees reached agreement on the differences between the House and Senate versions of the bill and filed a report Sept. 13 (H Rept 95-1569).

HUD Department

Conferees split the difference between the House and Senate-approved figures for annual contract authority for assisted housing programs, settling on new contract authority totaling $1,322,297,000, an amount that would support an estimated 370,000 units of Section 8 and conventional public housing. The conferees directed that none of the reduction from the House-approved amount be taken from the $25.2 million set aside for Indian housing during fiscal 1979.

The new contract authority would require $24,395,848,000 in total budget authority, the actual amount needed to cover the long-term costs of the housing contracts, which usually ran between 30 and 40 years.

The conferees also agreed to earmark $50 million as proposed by the Senate for public housing modernization, instead of $37.5 million proposed by the House. The conferees also approved $727 million for operation of low-income housing projects, $2 million less than proposed by the Senate but $4 million more than proposed by the House.

For subsidized housing contracts made in past years under Section 8 and other assisted housing programs, the conferees approved $4,460,000,000, as proposed by the Senate, instead of $4,463,000,000 as proposed by the House.

The conferees also agreed on $10 million for congregate housing services for the elderly, $10 million less than approved by the Senate. The House bill did not include any money for congregate services. The conferees stated that HUD should use the congregate funds for a "limited pilot program" and should coordinate its efforts with other agencies and organizations that provide similar services. The conferees further said, "The funds are intended for services currently not available rather than to continue programs presently funded from other sources."

The conferees also approved $1 billion in standby authority for emergency purchases of mortgages by the Government National Mortgage Association (GNMA) for use when a depressed housing market threatened to lower housing production. The conferees directed that the funds could not be made available in the absence of a recession in the housing industry. The Senate had sought $4 billion in standby authority, but the House and the Carter administration had not recommended any new standby authority.

The conferees approved $400 million for urban development action grants, as proposed by the House, instead of $380 million as proposed by the Senate. But the conferees accepted the Senate figure for Section 312 rehabilitation loans — $230 million — instead of the figure proposed by the House and Carter administration — $245 million.

For comprehensive planning grants, the conferees approved $53 million, $3 million more than the House figure but $4 million less than the Senate figure. The conferees accepted $85 million as proposed by the Senate for flood insurance, $5 million less than the House figure, and $9 million for housing counseling assistance, $1 million less than the House figure and $1 million more than the Senate figure.

For HUD's research and development program, the conferees split the difference between the House and Senate versions and approved $57.5 million. For HUD management and administration, the conferees approved $524,065,000.

VA Hospital Compromise

Congress moved to resolve a longstanding squabble over the site of a proposed Veterans Administration (VA) hospital in Portland, Ore.

Not surprisingly, the resolution of the controversy involved the acceptance of a compromise designed to please key figures in both the House and Senate.

As a result of the compromise, a new VA hospital was also likely to be built in Vancouver, Wash., about 10 minutes across the river from Portland.

Conferees on HR 12936, the fiscal 1979 appropriations bill for 18 federal agencies, including the VA, accepted the House position on the site of a replacement VA hospital for Portland, and the Senate position on the Vancouver hospital.

Although it did not mandate a site, the House recommended strongly that the VA build a replacement hospital in Portland on a site near the Emanuel Hospital. The VA wanted the new hospital in a section of the city called Marquam Hill, the site of the existing VA hospital.

But congressional investigators said the Emanuel site was better and less costly.

The House recommended $130 million for the new project — the amount needed to build on the Emanuel site and $8.8 million less than needed to build on the Marquam Hill site.

The Senate agreed with the $130 million figure, but did not take a position on the site. However, at the urging of Warren G. Magnuson, D-Wash., chairman of the Senate Appropriations Committee, the Senate also proposed a second replacement hospital for Vancouver, in Magnuson's home state.

The conferees in their report (H Rept 95-1569) said the "evidence appears to support the construction of the replacement hospital at the Emanuel site" in Portland.

Not wanting to dictate what they considered to be an executive branch decision, the conferees did not mandate that the VA build on the Emanuel site. However, adopting the House position, the conferees said no further money would be appropriated above the $130 million if the VA "chooses to disregard the [conferees'] site recommendation."

Further, in a concession to Magnuson, the conferees scaled down the Portland project from 758 to 670 beds and accepted the Senate position that a 180-unit nursing unit be built in Vancouver. The $130 million, the conferees said, should be enough for both projects.

A spokesman for the VA said the agency was studying the conferees' report and had not decided where to build the Portland hospital.

Environmental Protection Agency

Conferees resolved several minor differences between the House and Senate recommendations for appropriations for the Environmental Protection Agency. Conferees also accepted the House recommendation of $4.2 billion for construction grants for wastewater treatment plants. The administration proposed $4.5 billion for fiscal 1979, but the House recommended $4.2 billion.

During its work on HR 12936, the Senate Appropriations Committee restored the $300 million House cut, recommending the full $4.5 billion. But the Senate, during floor action, cut $250 million as part of a selected cut designed to trim 2 per cent from the total appropriation. During conference, the Senate members accepted a further cut of $50 million, accepting the original House recommendation.

National Aeronautics and Space Administration

The conferees resolved a dispute over funding for a new rocket motor to prevent an uncontrolled descent by the Skylab space station. The House had rejected a request by NASA for $20.5 million for the project, but the Senate had approved the request.

The conferees approved the $20.5 million figure, but said NASA should not obligate more than $10 million for continued development of the system without approval of the House and Senate Appropriations Committees. In the absence of committee approval, the conferees said, the remaining $10.5 million would be available only for funding requirements of the space shuttle itself.

The conferees also approved $147,500,000 for construction projects, $1 million less than recommended by the Senate but nearly $13 million more than recommended by the House. The $147.5 million would enable NASA to go ahead with the second phase of the pad "B" launch complex at Kennedy Space Center. The House had cut $12.8 million recommended for the project, but the Senate had restored the cut.

National Science Foundation

The House conferees agreed to accept a Senate provision limiting pay for investigators working under NSF grants to the maximum allowed for a GS-18 government employee ($47,500) unless special approval was given by the NSF director. Proxmire, chairman of the Senate Appropriations Subcommittee responsible for the agencies funded through HR 12936, had complained that some NSF researchers were receiving fairly large salaries for their work. Proxmire called it "academic gold plating."

Selective Service System

Conferees approved $7,045,000 for the Selective Service System, as recommended by the House. The Senate, after rejecting an attempt during floor debate to add $9,955,000 to the fiscal 1979 appropriation, agreed to add $2,455,000. The House, during its consideration of HR 12936, had rejected both increases.

Veterans Administration

The conferees resolved major differences in the VA appropriation by trading back and forth on various programs.

For medical care, the conferees approved $5,334,374,000 — about $28 million less than recommended by the House but $34 million more than recommended by the Senate. The $5.3 billion was about $54.6 million above the fiscal 1979 request submitted by the Carter administration. The conferees said the funding increases should be used in the following manner: $32.3 million for 1,500 additional staff years to keep open existing hospital beds; $18 million for 700 additional staff years to meet anticipated increases in outpatient caseloads above initial projections contained in the fiscal 1979 budget request, and $4.3 million to staff new medical facilities.

The conferees agreed with the Senate that major construction projects were those that cost $1 million or more. The House had agreed to increase the minimum ceiling to $2 million. By accepting the $1 million figure, Congress retained more oversight over VA construction.

The conferees also restored six construction projects added by the House to HR 12936 but removed by the Senate. The projects totaled $34.8 million and included $9.4 million for a 208-bed domiciliary in Bath, N.Y.; $6.3 million for a 120-bed nursing home unit in Livermore, Calif.; $5.2 million for a 120-bed nursing home in Wilkes-Barre, Pa.; $2.7 million for expansion of a clinical laboratory in Cincinnati, Ohio; $4.5 million for a 120-bed nursing home in Temple, Texas, and $6.5 million for an ambulatory care addition in Dallas, Texas. The VA did not recommend the projects in its original submission to Congress, but the projects were then proposed by the House Veterans' Affairs Committee.

Moonrock Study

Scientists in the National Aeronautics and Space Administration (NASA) were able to continue their study of moonrocks through fiscal 1979.

As cleared by Congress, HR 12936 included $1 million for what NASA called "lunar sample analysis."

The House, in its version of HR 12936, recommended $5.7 million for continued study of the assortment of rocks brought back from space visits to the moon.

But the Senate, in its version of the appropriations bill, eliminated the funds, primarily at the urging of Sen. William Proxmire, D-Wis., chairman of the subcommittee that handled the NASA budget.

However, advocates of NASA-funded moonrock study launched a vigorous lobbying effort, and House and Senate conferees agreed to a compromise calling for $1 million for fiscal 1979 for the program.

While the restoration of money made some advocates breathe a little easier, the small amount included in the final bill suggested that NASA would face even more trouble next year in seeking additional money.

Although he had vigorously pushed for elimination of moonrock study money from the NASA budget, Proxmire had said he was not advocating ending all studies. Rather, he had said, research should be conducted through the National Science Foundation.

General Provisions

House managers said they would offer a motion to recede and concur in a Senate amendment designed to prohibit in most cases the use of funds for unsolicited research projects unless recipients share in the cost of the research.

House managers also said they would accept a Senate amendment prohibiting the use of funds appropriated by the bill to pay a consultant at more than the daily equivalent rate paid for a GS-18 employee.

FINAL ACTION

The House adopted the conference report on HR 12936 Sept. 19 by voice vote.

The Senate adopted the conference report by a 75-6 vote Sept. 20, completing congressional action on the bill. *(Vote 377, p. 56-S)*

1978 Urgent Supplemental

Congress July 20 completed action on a fiscal 1978 urgent supplemental appropriations (H J Res 945—PL 95-332) providing $181.7 million for a recently revised program of benefits for coal miners afflicted with black lung disease.

As cleared, the resolution also appropriated $43.5 million for payments to retired railroad workers, $25 million for emergency help to schools affected by desegregation orders, and $3.8 million for administration of the Commerce Department local public works program.

Background

Under legislation (PL 95-239) enacted early in 1978, Congress significantly relaxed miners' eligibility requirements for disability claims as a result of black lung disease. In addition, it created (PL 95-227) the Black Lung Disability Trust Fund, derived from coal excise taxes, to provide disability payments. The more liberal eligibility rules would result in 290,000 more claims in the first year after the law went into effect than were expected under the old law.

Under PL 95-227, the trust fund was to receive a direct appropriation equal to the amount of revenue from the coal tax. *(Black Lung Benefits story, p. 266; 1977 Almanac p. 173)*

House Action

The House Appropriations Committee reported H J Res 945 June 1 (H Rept 95-1236).

As reported, the resolution contained only the $181.7 million for the black lung program. Of that amount, which was $2.2 million less than the budget request, $162.7 million would be used for payment of benefits, with the remaining $19 million going for Labor Department administration of the program.

The House June 9 passed H J Res 945 by a 237-72 vote. *(Vote 373, p. 108-H)*

Senate Action

The Senate Appropriations Committee reported H J Res 945 June 19 (S Rept 95-937).

The committee approved the $181.7 million black lung appropriation, but added $43.5 million for railroad retirement, in order to cover increased benefits payments caused by the effects of a severe winter, the nationwide coal strike, and an increase in the number of workers who were retired by Conrail. The committee also approved $50 million for the Emergency School Aid Act (ESAA), to give more assistance to some 15 large school districts undertaking desegregation plans during the 1978-79 school year.

The Senate June 23 passed H J Res 945 by voice vote. Before passing the resolution, the Senate by voice vote approved an Ernest F. Hollings, D-S.C., amendment to add $3.8 million for the Economic Development Administration, to cope with its increased workload in monitoring the $4 billion local public works program. Also adopted by voice vote was a Dennis DeConcini, D-Ariz., amendment to extend to Aug. 1, 1978, from July 1, the deadline for schools to apply for assistance under ESAA in 1978.

Final Action

Final action came when the House and Senate agreed to a compromise $25 million for ESAA assistance.

The House by voice vote July 19 agreed to the Senate-passed additional funding, with an amendment halving the $50 million for ESAA.

The Senate July 20 then agreed to the House amendment, thus clearing H J Res 945 for the president. ▮

ASCS Supplemental

President Carter July 31 signed into law a resolution (H J Res 1024 — PL 95-330) providing $80.5 million for fiscal 1978 for increased personnel costs of the Agriculture Department service that administered farm price support, commodity reserve and loan programs — the Agricultural Stabilization and Conservation Service (ASCS).

The House Appropriations Committee reported the resolution June 28 (H Rept 95-1326), and the House passed it by a 340-48 vote July 11. *(Vote 457, p. 130-H)* The Senate passed the resolution by voice vote July 24.

H J Res 1024 appropriated $57.1 million for ASCS staff salaries and increased transfer authority to ASCS from the Commodity Credit Corporation by $23.4 million.

Agriculture Appropriations Subcommittee Chairman Jamie L. Whitten, D-Miss., told the House the extra funds were needed because ASCS programs authorized by the 1977 farm act (PL 95-113) had "greatly increased . . . the activities of the county offices" with major administrative responsibilities for them. *(1977 farm act, 1977 Almanac p. 417)* ▮

State, Commerce, Justice

Congress gave final approval Sept. 30 to a bill (HR 12934 — PL 95-431) appropriating $8.5 billion for fiscal 1979 operations of the departments of State, Justice and Commerce, the federal judiciary and related agencies.

The Senate cleared the bill for the president by adopting, 62-7, a conference report (H Rept 95-1565) reconciling differences between the House and Senate versions of the bill. *(Vote 428, p. 63-S)*

The House adopted the conference report Sept. 28 by a 276-61 vote. *(Vote 754, p. 214-H)*

The final appropriation was $144 million less than the Carter administration had requested for the departments and agencies, $78 million above the Senate amount and $3.8 billion above the House amount. The House bill had been slashed prior to passage June 14 on a series of points of order because many of the programs had not yet been authorized.

The final appropriation reflected a Senate floor vote Aug. 3 that lopped $27.7 million from the U.S. contribution to "technical assistance" programs operated by the United Nations.

The conference report included a provision designed to prevent the Federal Trade Commission from promulgating regulations concerning television advertising directed at children. The report also directed the FTC to include foreign producers in any study it made of the structure, conduct and performance of the auto industry. The report noted that fewer than one-third of all 1977 model automobiles sold in the United States were produced in the United States.

The agreement also urged the United States to admit 7,500 Cambodian refugees a year in fiscal 1979 and 1980.

Provisions

As cleared by Congress, HR 12934 appropriated the following amounts for fiscal 1979:

Agency	Budget Request	Final Appropriation
Department of State	$1,262,897,000	$1,234,520,000
Department of Justice	2,471,002,000	2,473,086,000
Department of Commerce	2,422,607,000	2,200,576,000
The Judiciary	495,552,000	489,647,000
Related Agencies:		
Arms Control and Disarmament Agency	16,395,000	16,395,000
Board for International Broadcasting	85,180,000	85,000,000

Agency	Budget Request	Final Appropriation
Commission on Civil Rights	10,752,000	10,752,000
Commission on Security and Cooperation in Europe	521,000	521,000
Equal Employment Opportunity Commission	110,000,000	107,000,000
Federal Communications Commission	68,196,000	70,446,000
Federal Maritime Commission	10,530,000	10,550,000
Federal Trade Commission	66,485,000	64,750,000
Foreign Claims Settlement Commission	1,015,000	—
International Communication Agency	413,327,000	411,009,000
International Trade Commission	13,113,000	12,950,000
Japan-U.S. Friendship Commission	1,500,000	1,500,000
Legal Services Corporation	304,000,000	270,000,000
Marine Mammal Commission	702,000	702,000
National Commission on the International Year of the Child	1,360,000	—
Office of the Special Representative for Trade Negotiations	2,665,000	2,665,000
Commission on Global Hunger and Malnutrition	1,300,000	1,300,000
Renegotiation Board	7,277,000	5,260,000
Securities and Exchange Commission	64,800,000	64,650,000
Small Business Administration	827,100,000	980,500,000
U.S. Metric Board	1,800,000	1,575,000
Total	**$8,660,076,000**	**$8,515,354,000**

House Committee Action

The House Appropriations Committee reported HR 12934 on June 1 (H Rept 95-1253).

The committee-approved bill recommended $8.55 billion for the three departments, the federal judiciary and 18 other agencies, $84 million less than the amount requested by the Carter administration and $1.3 billion less than the fiscal 1978 appropriation. (Fiscal 1978 appropriations were not, however, directly comparable as they included supplemental funding levels not contained in HR 12934.)

The decrease from the administration request was due largely to the committee's decision to fund the Small Business Administration disaster loan program at a lower level because of unexpended balances remaining in the program from fiscal 1978 supplemental appropriations.

The Appropriations Committee request of $8.55 billion was $1.08 billion below the target established by the budget resolution (S Con Res 80) approved May 17. *(p. 35)*

As reported, HR 12934 contained the following major funding provisions:

Department of State. The committee recommendation for the State Department totaled $1,260,291,000, an increase of $108,444,000 over the amount appropriated for fiscal 1978.

The largest item in the amount recommended for State was $833,382,000 for administration of foreign affairs, including salaries and expenses for personnel, expenses for acquisition and operation of buildings abroad, and payments to the Foreign Service retirement and disability fund.

The bill provided $355,392,000 for U.S. contributions to international organizations, including $247,486,783 for the United Nations and related agencies. Travel and other expenses for members of Congress to participate in overseas parliamentary conferences totaled $12,000,000.

Department of Justice. The committee recommendation for the Department of Justice was $2,455,894,000. That amount was $8,408,000 less than the administration request, but $155,275,000 more than the total amount appropriated for fiscal 1978.

The Justice Department appropriation included:

- Antitrust Division, $46,377,000. The figure is $5,369,000 more than the fiscal 1978 appropriation. The increased funding, for salaries and expenses, included money for the division's expenses in litigating cases against International Business Machines and the American Telephone & Telegraph Co. The total figure includes $10,000,000 for grants to states to improve their antitrust capabilities.
- U.S. attorneys and marshals, $196.7 million. A $17.6 million increase over fiscal 1978, the funds would provide 61 additional positions, mostly paralegals, requested for U.S. attorneys.
- Federal Bureau of Investigation, $563,500,000. A $34,046,000 increase over the fiscal 1978 FBI appropriation provided for additional spending of $3,601,000 for domestic security and terrorism investigations. The committee recommendation was $6,750,000 above the level requested by the administration.
- Immigration and Naturalization Service, $294,500,000. The figure represented an increase of $28,050,000 over fiscal 1978, primarily for additional staff created in fiscal 1978 and anticipated in fiscal 1979.
- Drug Enforcement Administration, $192,953,000. An $11,058,000 increase over fiscal 1978 covered pay and related benefits.
- Federal prison system, $356,423,000. A total of $48,097,000 over fiscal 1978 appropriations, primarily to pay employees at new or expanded prisons in New York, Alabama, Oklahoma, Texas, Connecticut, Florida and Kansas.
- Law Enforcement Assistance Administration, $641,488,000. The figure was $3,094,000 below the amount appropriated for fiscal 1978.

Commerce Department. The committee recommended $2,123,152,000 in new budget authority for the Department of Commerce, $299,455,000 less than the administration request but $188,698,000 more than the fiscal 1978 appropriation.

The largest portion of the request, $708,970,000, was earmarked for the National Oceanic and Atmospheric Administration, which is responsible for coastal zone management projects, fisheries, marine and environmental projects, and weather prediction and warning programs. The NOAA request was $79,858,000 below appropriations made available in fiscal 1978.

The fiscal 1979 recommendation for the Economic Development Administration was $513,015,000, an increase of $103,690,000 over the fiscal 1978 appropriation. The amount recommended provided substantial increases in virtually all traditional EDA program areas, including public works projects, business development, planning, technical assistance, research and economic adjustment assistance to communities.

Another large line-item in the Commerce budget was the $481,678,000 appropriated for the Maritime Administration. The amount included $157,000,000 to subsidize domestic construction of ships at prices comparable to those for ships manufactured in foreign shipyards.

Subsidies of $250,000,000 for operating differentials, to allow employment of U.S. seamen, also were included in the bill. The operating differential subsidies were $102,000,000 less than the fiscal 1978 appropriation because of unexpended balances available for the program and because U.S. operators did not make use of subsidies for carriage of grain cargoes to the Soviet Union. U.S. operators spurned the grain cargoes with their subsidies in favor of more lucrative oil cargo contracts.

The Judiciary. The recommendation for the judicial branch was $481,316,600, up $36,998,600 from fiscal 1978. The funds were for operation of the federal courts, including salaries of judges, judicial officers, and employees.

The recommendation included $9,959,600 for the Supreme Court and $443,408,000 for the courts of appeals and district courts. The appeals and district court appropriation was up $32,258,000 from fiscal 1978, in part in anticipation of increases in the number of judges who will sit on the courts.

As reported, HR 12934 included the following appropriations:

Agency	Budget Request	Committee Recommendation
Department of State	$1,262,897,000	$1,260,291,000
Department of Justice	2,464,302,000	2,455,894,000
Department of Commerce	2,422,607,000	2,123,152,000
The Judiciary	486,481,600	481,316,000
Related Agencies:		
Arms Control and Disarmament Agency	16,395,000	16,395,000
Board for International Broadcasting	85,180,000	85,000,000
Commission on Civil Rights	10,752,000	10,752,000
Commission on Security and Cooperation in Europe	350,000	350,000
Equal Employment Opportunity Commission	110,000,000	110,000,000
Federal Communications Commission	67,035,000	68,535,000
Federal Maritime Commission	10,530,000	10,500,000
Federal Trade Commission	66,485,000	63,600,000
Foreign Claims Settlement Commission	1,015,000	—
International Communication Agency	413,327,000	407,709,000
International Trade Commission	13,113,000	12,800,000
Japan-U.S. Friendship Commission	1,500,000	1,500,000
Legal Services Corporation	304,000,000	285,000,000
Marine Mammal Commission	702,000	702,000
Office of the Special Representative for Trade Negotiations	2,665,000	2,665,000
Renegotiation Board	7,277,000	3,000,000
Securities and Exchange Commission	64,800,000	64,650,000
Small Business Administration	827,100,000	1,090,500,000
Total	**$8,638,513,600**	**$8,554,311,600**

House Floor Action

An $8.6 billion appropriation for the Departments of State, Justice, Commerce and 18 related agencies was slashed by more than half June 14 in a House floor debate that called into question the congressional budget process.

Frustrated by the failure of House authorizing committees to approve fiscal 1979 programs by the May 15 Budget Act deadline, managers of HR 12934 sought to dramatize their fear that the authorization process was being turned into a mere formality.

John Slack, D-W.Va., who chairs the Appropriations Subcommittee on State, Justice, Commerce and the Judiciary, made no effort to ward off a series of points of order that excised major portions of his bill.

While a rule waiving points of order had been granted by the Rules Committee, it was not used. As a result, when each unauthorized section of the appropriations bill was called up on the floor, a point of order eliminated it from the bill.

House Rule 21 provides that most appropriations bills cannot be approved until the programs they are intended to fund have been authorized. The points of order were based on that rule.

During the same floor debate, the House continued to respond in its own chaotic fashion to Proposition 13, the property tax roll-back approved by California voters June 6, agreeing on a voice vote to an across-the-board 2 percent cut in the bill. The vote, along with the previously sustained points of order, reduced the $8.6 billion bill to about $3.9 billion.

It was the second time in as many days that the House made an across-the-board cut in an appropriations bill. On June 13, the House voted 220-181 to cut 2 percent from the budgets of the Labor and Health, Education and Welfare Departments. *(Story, p. 78)*

After making the cut, the House approved the State, Justice, Commerce appropriations bill, 359-34.

During floor consideration of HR 12934, the House excised the entire appropriation for the Department of State on a point of order because the authorizing legislation had not been passed.

Major portions of Justice and Commerce Department appropriations were similarly eliminated.

The following amendments were adopted:

- By Carlos J. Moorhead, R-Calif., prohibiting the Legal Services Corporation from using funds for publicity or propaganda designed to support or defeat legislation pending before Congress or any state legislature. Adopted 264-131. *(Vote 391, p. 112-H)*

• By Robin L. Beard Jr., R-Tenn., prohibiting the Commerce Department from using its funds for promoting or conducting trade relations with Cuba. Adopted 241-58. *(Vote 389, p. 112-H)*

• By Clarence E. Miller, R-Ohio, reducing by 2 percent the total appropriation in the bill, except for programs required by law. Adopted by voice vote.

The following amendments were rejected:

• By Mark Andrews, R-N.D., to prohibit the use of funds in the bill to pay Federal Communications Commission salaries for any project that would limit advertising of food products containing ingredients determined to be safe or toys declared safe by government agencies. Rejected on a point of order.

• By John H. Rousselot, R-Calif., to cut $30 million from the Legal Services Corporation budget. Rejected 200-203. *(Vote 390, p. 112-H)*

After completing action on the amendments and points of order, the House approved the bill, 359-34. *(Vote 392, p. 112-H)*

Senate Committee Action

The Senate Appropriations Committee reported HR 12934 on July 28 (S Rept 95-1043).

The committee-approved bill recommended $8.6 billion — $199 million more than the final amount approved by the Senate. The committee recommendation was $1.2 billion less than the fiscal 1978 appropriation. (Fiscal 1978 appropriations were not, however, directly comparable as they included supplemental funding levels not contained in HR 12934.)

Department of State

The committee recommendation for the State Department totaled $1,262,291,000, an increase of $110,444,000 over the amount appropriated for fiscal 1978.

The largest item was $835,382,000 for administration of foreign affairs, including salaries and expenses for personnel, expenses for acquisition and operation of buildings abroad, and payments to the Foreign Service retirement and disability fund.

The bill provided $407,109,000 for U.S. contributions to international organizations.

Department of Justice

The committee recommendation for the Justice Department was $2,484,579,000. The amount was $13,577,000 above the amount requested by the administration, and $183,960,000 above the fiscal 1978 appropriation to date.

Federal Bureau of Investigation, $558,750,000. A $29,296,000 increase over the fiscal 1978 FBI appropriation included additional spending of $2 million above the administration request for domestic security and terrorism investigations. The total committee recommendation was $2 million above the administration request.

Law Enforcement Assistance Administration, $2,-484,579,000. An increase of $16,906,000 over the 1978 appropriation and $20,000,000 above the House allowance, the Senate recommendation was aimed at maintaining LEAA planning grants at current levels and providing funds for the president's urban crime prevention program.

Legal Activities, $383,414,000. The appropriation, $39,569,000 above the 1978 appropriation, provided funding for 241 new positions.

Immigration and Naturalization Service, $299,800,-000. An increase of $33,350,000 over the 1978 appropriation provided for 903 additional positions to handle "intolerable backlogs" in handling of immigration cases.

Federal Prison System, $360,400,000. The appropriation represented a $52,074,000 increase over 1978 funding to date.

Drug Enforcement Administration, $192,953,000. An increase of $11,058,000 over the 1978 appropriation, the amount was identical to that recommended by the House. The increases covered pay and related "non-discretionary increases."

U.S. Attorneys and Marshals, $196,700,000. An increase of $17,625,000 over fiscal 1978 appropriations, the committee report said the funds would provide for 61 additional positions requested by U.S. attorneys, mostly paralegals who "will enable the U.S. attorneys to handle more civil cases, prosecute more white-collar and other criminal cases and improve the quality of appellate work."

Antitrust Division, $46,377,000. An increase of $5,-369,000 over 1978 appropriations is directed at salaries and expenses, including money for the division's expenses in litigating cases against International Business Machines and the American Telephone & Telegraph Co. The appropriation included $10,000,000 for grants to states to improve their antitrust enforcement capabilities.

Commerce Department

The committee recommended $2,417,425,000 in new budget authority for the Department of Commerce, $5,-182,000 less than the administration request, but $482,-971,000 more than the fiscal 1978 appropriation.

The largest item, $738,325,000 for the Economic Development Administration, included $329,000,000 in funding above the 1978 appropriation. The recommendation included $71,466,000 above the administration request to provide for business loans and guarantees.

Funding for the National Oceanic and Atmospheric Administration, which is responsible for coastal zone management projects, fisheries, marine and environmental projects, and weather prediction and warning programs, totaled $737,400,000, a decrease of $51,428,000 from fiscal 1978 and $29,082,000 below the administration request.

Another large line-item in the Commerce budget was the $231,650,000 Maritime Administration appropriation. The appropriation included $157,000,000 to subsidize domestic construction of ships at prices comparable to those for ships manufactured in foreign shipyards.

The Judiciary

The committee recommended $490,675,000 in new budget authority for the judicial branch, up $46,357,000 from the fiscal 1978 appropriation.

The new appropriation included funds to provide an automobile for each of the eight associate justices of the Supreme Court, as well as two additional stenographers for each of the justices.

Senate Floor Action

After rejecting the House approach of a flat 2 percent cut, the Senate Aug. 3 adopted a package of floor amendments that had the same net effect on fiscal 1979 appropriations for the departments of State, Justice and Commerce, the federal judiciary and 20 related agencies.

The Senate pruned HR 12934 to $8.4 billion before passing it on a 62-6 vote. *(Vote 279, p. 43-S)*

The approved amount was $223 million below the $8.7 billion requested by the Carter administration and almost $200 million below the amount recommended by the Senate Appropriations Committee.

The House voted to approve a gutted version of the bill June 14 after points of order resulted in the elimination of numerous items that had not been previously authorized. The deleted items totaled $3.9 billion.

Budget Committee Chairman Edmund S. Muskie, D-Maine, said the bill provided "an excellent example" of how "failure to enact authorizing legislation in a timely way creates problems in the appropriations process...."

During floor consideration of HR 12934, the Senate adopted the following amendments:

- By Jesse Helms, R-N.C., to prohibit the expenditure of funds for certain United Nations "technical assistance" programs, and cutting $27.7 million from the appropriation for such programs.
- By Edward M. Kennedy, D-Mass., to restore $4.27 million to the budget of the Justice Department Criminal Division to provide for positions in the programs on organized crime, fraud, public corruption and narcotics trafficking prosecution. Adopted by voice vote after motion to table rejected, 36-49. *(Vote 275, p. 43-S)*
- By Ernest F. Hollings, D-S.C., reducing funding for several programs in the bill by a total of $26.1 million. Adopted 79-0. *(Vote 277, p. 43-S)*
- By Hollings, to reduce by $150 million appropriations for Economic Development Assistance programs. Adopted 59-19. *(Vote 278, p. 43-S)*

(The Hollings amendments were substitutes for an amendment by William V. Roth Jr., R-Del., to cut each line item in the bill by 2 percent. The Roth amendment, as amended by Hollings, was adopted by voice vote after surviving a 21-60 vote to table and thus kill it.) *(Vote 276, p. 43-S)*

- Howard M. Metzenbaum, D-Ohio, to bar the use of funds to acquire electronic message-switching equipment by the Justice Department.
- By Malcolm Wallop, R-Wyo., to allow expenditure of funds for appointment of special prosecutors by the Justice Department.
- By John Glenn, D-Ohio, to earmark $1 million for anti-arson programs conducted by the Justice Department.
- By Kennedy, appropriating an additional $703,000 for an investigation by the Antitrust Division of the relationship between the Organization of Petroleum Exporting Countries (OPEC) and large oil companies.
- By Kennedy, appropriating an additional $1.4 million for the Federal Justice Research Program and the Office of Management and Finance in the Justice Department.
- By Charles McC. Mathias Jr., R-Md., appropriating an additional $2,591,000 for FBI agent positions.
- By Robert Dole, R-Kan., expressing the sense of the Senate that the attorney general admit into the United States 7,500 additional Cambodian refugees in each of fiscal years 1979 and 1980.

The Senate rejected by voice vote a Dole amendment to prevent funds from being used for the "U.S. interests section" office that the United States opened in Havana as a partial step toward restoration of diplomatic relations with Cuba.

Provisions

As passed by the Senate Aug. 3, HR 12934 made the following appropriations for fiscal 1979:

Agency	House Appropriation*	Senate Appropriation
Department of State	$ 0	$1,234,575,000
Department of Justice	834,441,000	2,484,437,000
Department of Commerce	1,793,034,000	2,262,625,000
The Judiciary	481,316,600	489,675,000
Related Agencies:		
Arms Control and Disarmament Agency	0	16,395,000
Board for International Broadcasting	0	85,000,000
Commission on Civil Rights	0	10,752,000
Commission on Security and Cooperation in Europe	350,000	521,000
Equal Employment Opportunity Commission	110,000,000	107,000,000
Federal Communications Commission	68,535,000	70,446,000
Federal Maritime Commission	10,500,000	10,550,000
Federal Trade Commission	0	65,900,000
International Communication Agency	0	411,009,000
International Trade Commission	0	13,100,000
Japan-U.S. Friendship Commission	1,500,000	1,500,000
Legal Services Corporation	285,000,000	255,000,000
Marine Mammal Commission	702,000	840,000
Office of the Special Representative for Trade Negotiations	2,665,000	2,665,000
Presidential Commission on Hunger	0	1,500,000
Renegotiation Board	3,000,000	6,260,000
Securities and Exchange Commission	0	64,650,000
Small Business Administration	1,090,500,000	840,280,000
U.S. Metric Board	0	1,800,000
Total	**$4,681,543,600**	**$8,436,480,000**

* *Zeroes indicate appropriations deleted on the House floor because authorizing legislation had not yet passed. The total House figure shown does not reflect a 2 percent across-the-board reduction voted by the House.*

Conference Action

The House went to conference with a version of the State-Justice-Commerce appropriation bill that had been gutted during floor debate because of House failure to pass authorizing legislation.

The House bill therefore contained no appropriations for the State Department, the Commission on Civil Rights, the Federal Trade Commission, the Securities and Exchange Commission and numerous other agencies. House conferees relied on the recommendations of the House Appropriations Committee in working out differences with the Senate.

Among the differences resolved by conferees were the following:

International Organizations. Conferees agreed to restore $27,716,000 cut by the Senate from the State Department's budget for contributions to international organizations. The approved amount of $355,392,000 equaled the administration's request.

Antitrust Division. The House agreed to the Senate's recommendation of $46,377,000, instead of $47,080,000, for salaries and expenses of the Justice Department's Antitrust Division.

FBI. Conferees agreed to accept the Senate provision appropriating an additional $2 million above the budget request for FBI domestic security and terrorism investigations. Conferees also agreed to appropriate $2,591,000 above the budget request for FBI bank robbery investigations. The administration wanted to encourage greater state and local responsibility for such investigations.

LEAA. Conferees compromised on funding for the Law Enforcement Assistance Administration and appropriated $646,488,000 instead of the $641,488,000 proposed by the House and the $656,488,000 proposed by the Senate. The amount agreed to included $50,000,000 for planning grants, $7,000,000 for community anti-crime programs, $25,000,000 for law enforcement education and $100,000,000 for juvenile justice and delinquency prevention.

Message Switching. Conferees deleted a Senate proposal to prohibit the use of Justice Department funds for the acquisition of controversial message-switching equipment until approval was given by House and Senate Judiciary Committees.

EDA. Conferees agreed to appropriate $507,525,000 for the Economic Development Administration in the Department of Commerce. The House had proposed $484,325,000 and the Senate $547,775,000. The conference agreement provided $196,000,000 in public works grants and $21,500,000 in business loans and guarantees.

The conference report stated that EDA should not allocate less money to a regional office in fiscal 1979 than that region could expect to receive based on its fiscal 1975-77 percentage share of funds for all EDA programs.

Renegotiation Board. Conferees agreed to appropriate $5,260,000 for funds to terminate activities of the Renegotiation Board. The House had proposed $3,000,000 and the Senate $6,260,000 for termination costs.

Legal Services Corporation. Conferees appropriated $270,000,000 for Legal Services Corporation activities, instead of the $285,000,000 recommended by the House and the $225,000,000 proposed by the Senate.

SBA. Conferees agreed to provide $187,000,000 for operations of the Small Business Administration plus $13,000,000 for disaster loans. The House had recommended $180,000,000 and the Senate $193,000,000.

Final Action

Before adopting the conference report Sept. 28, the House rejected on a non-record vote a motion by Clarence E. Miller, R-Ohio, to recommit the report to the conference with instructions to cut the total appropriation by 2 percent.

After adopting the report, the House Sept. 29 rejected, 143-191, a motion by Neal Smith, D-Iowa, to appropriate $355,392,000 instead of $327,676,000 proposed by the Senate for contributions to international organizations such as the United Nations. *(Vote 755, p. 214-H)*

The House then agreed by voice vote to the Senate figure.

The House also adopted, 231-105, a Senate amendment urging the United States to give special consideration to the plight of Cambodian refugees and urging the Justice Department to admit 7,500 of the refugees in fiscal 1979 and 1980 under its parole authority. *(Vote 756, p. 214-H)*

Senate

The Senate adopted the conference report by a 62-7 vote Sept. 30, clearing the bill for the president. *(Vote 438, p. 63-S)*

Sen. Ernest F. Hollings, D-S.C., said he expected the Carter administration to seek a supplemental appropriation for the $27 million cut from the request for contributions to international organizations.

Legislative Funds: $1.12 Billion

A $1.12 billion fiscal 1979 legislative appropriations bill (HR 12935 — PL 95-391) was approved by Congress Sept. 19. The bill agreed to by House and Senate conferees carried the same price tag as the Senate version.

The annual legislative appropriations bill in recent years had been the vehicle for only one major controversy — funding congressional pay raises. Hoping to avert an election-year floor fight on that issue, House and Senate Appropriations Committees voted to deny a scheduled cost-of-living pay raise to members of Congress and other top federal officials making $47,500 a year or more. Affected would be about 16,000 executive, legislative and judicial branch employees. Federal employees making less than $47,500 would still get the raise, amounting to about 5.5 percent of their current salaries.

A controversial legislative funding issue that surfaced during 1978 and could have tied up the bill instead was taken up Aug. 4 during debate of the fiscal 1978 supplemental appropriations bill (HR 13467). The controversy involved an effort by John H. Chafee, R-R.I., to stop construction of a third Senate office building. The Senate rejected Chafee's proposal and instead voted to put a $135 million ceiling on the total price of the building. However, on Aug. 25, the Senate bowed to an Aug. 17 House cut of $54.9 million for the office building. *(Box, p. 71)*

HR 12935 also became the vehicle for a surprise vote to have House employees — not commercial or public network broadcasters — control television broadcasts of House floor activities. The issue of network versus House control of the broadcasts had been simmering for several months. *(p. 96)*

Provisions

As cleared for the president, HR 12935 appropriated the following amounts for fiscal 1979:

Item	Budget Request	Final Appropriation
Senate	$185,182,000	$185,064,000
House of Representatives	306,049,900	306,016,400
Joint Items	73,773,900	73,727,100

Item	Budget Request	Final Appropriation
Office of Technology Assessment	10,000,000	9,700,000
Congressional Budget Office	11,368,000	11,368,000
Architect of the Capitol	60,613,500	56,506,600
Congressional Research Service	26,379,000	25,553,000
Government Printing Office (congressional printing)	73,961,000	73,961,000
Botanic Garden	1,391,600	1,392,000
Library of Congress	167,006,500	149,093,300
Architect of the Capitol (library buildings and grounds)	2,794,700	2,776,000
Copyright Royalty Tribunal	935,000	805,000
Government Printing Office (other than congressional printing and binding)	34,676,000	34,676,000
General Accounting Office	187,843,000	185,756,000
Cost-Accounting Standards Board	1,850,000	1,850,000
GRAND TOTAL	$1,143,824,100	$1,118,244,400*

* The final bill also provided that of the total budget authority in the act for payments not required by law, 5 percent shall be withheld from obligation and expenditure. (The conference report did not spell out where the withholdings must be made.)

House Committee Action

The House Appropriations Committee May 23 voted to deny top-level government officials — including members of Congress and their highest paid aides — an automatic cost-of-living pay raise scheduled to take effect in October. The amendment was adopted during committee debate on HR 12935.

Republicans had planned to offer the amendment in full committee after a Republican pay raise deferral proposal was defeated in a Legislative Appropriations Subcommittee markup April 25.

But Democrats from the subcommittee subsequently decided to draft their own amendment in an attempt to avert a politically sensitive floor fight on the pay raise. That amendment was offered in full committee by John P. Murtha, D-Pa., who urged passage of it to "speed things up without any demagoguery on the floor."

There was little debate on Murtha's proposal. When Appropriations Committee Chairman George Mahon, D-Texas, quickly called for a vote, Edward J. Patten, D-N.J., complained that he did not know what the committee was voting on. The amendment was approved, 22-8.

The pay raise amendment required a special waiver from the Rules Committee to block parliamentary challenges on the floor. Committee sources expected the amendment to remain intact because, said one aide, "In an election year you're not going to get too many members who will vote themselves a pay raise." In 1977, Congress blocked the annual cost of living raise but agreed to a separate proposal raising members' salaries $12,900 a year. *(1977 Almanac p. 224)*

As approved by the committee, HR 12935 appropriated $922,491,800 for operations of the House and related agencies during fiscal 1979. It did not contain money for operations of the Senate, which is traditionally added by the Senate Appropriations Committee as amendments to the House bill. The budget request for the Senate and its related expenses was $195,130,500.

Following a practice begun in 1977, the committee divided appropriations between two categories — congressional operations, and related agencies that do not provide "primary support" for Congress.

Printing Clerks

Missing from the $922.5 million bill was $33,500 in salaries paid to two House printing clerks. In the past, Democrat David Ramage and Republican Thomas Lankford were paid House funds to print congressional material such as leadership notices.

In addition to their work for the House, both clerks ran private commercial printing businesses in the offices they were given to perform their public jobs. The General Accounting Office reported in 1977 that Ramage and Lankford were each doing at least $1 million a year in private business by printing press releases, bumper stickers and other political material for members of Congress.

The Legislative Appropriations Subcommitte agreed that while the clerks could continue to print material for the House, they would no longer be paid public salaries. The full committee concurred in dropping any appropriations for their salaries.

Republicans William L. Armstrong, Colo., and Lawrence C. Coughlin, Pa., offered several "reform" amendments in the full committee markup, but each was defeated. The two planned to offer the amendments again when the legislative appropriations bill reaches the floor.

The defeated amendments were:

- A Coughlin proposal to cut a total of $6.7 million from the appropriations recommended for members' district office space, constituent communications and consolidated account allowances. Defeated by voice vote.
- An Armstrong amendment to require use of office funds to pay for plants, storage trunks and calendars now provided free to all members. Defeated by voice vote.
- A Coughlin amendment providing General Accounting Office audits of House accounts. Defeated 11-23.

House of Representatives

The committee recommended $306,016,400 to pay for House operations in fiscal 1979. That was an increase of $23,344,300 from the fiscal 1978 appropriation. The committee recommendation included the following:

Members' Compensation. The bill recommended $27,699,300 to pay members' salaries and contributions for retirement, life and health insurance.

Members' Mileage. The allowance for mileage to cover one round trip to the district for each member was continued at the existing level of $210,000 for fiscal 1979. Another $3,494,000 from House contingent expenses (listed below) was recommended to cover the cost of an additional 25 round trips allowed each member.

House Leadership Offices. The committee recommended $2,147,100 for the operations of majority and minority House leaders' offices. In fiscal 1978, the officers were allotted $2,056,600.

House Employees. The clerk, sergeant at arms, doorkeeper and other House employees and officers would receive $26,407,700 for fiscal 1979 operations under the committee's recommendation.

Committee Employees. The committee recommended $24,705,000 for salaries of professional and clerical employees of the 22 House standing committees. That was the same amount appropriated in fiscal 1978.

Committee Studies. The committee recommended $2,895,000 for studies and investigations to be undertaken by its own staff. It also recommended $261,000 for Budget Committee studies.

Law Revision and Legislative Counsels. The law revision counsel office would get $435,000 under the committee recommendation, while the office of legislative counsel would get $1,879,000.

Members' Clerk Hire. The committee recommended $112,648,300 for the salaries of members' personal staff aides. The fiscal 1978 clerk hire appropriation was $107,-192,000.

The committee report noted that the current clerk hire allowance is $273,132 per member, but that some representatives used less than the full amount either by hiring fewer people than permitted or by paying less than the maximum salaries allowed. The report said that if every member used 100 percent of the allowance, the total for clerk hire would be $119,904,948.

House Contingent Expenses. The committee recommended appropriations of $106,729,000 for contingent expenses, with $59,967,000 of that allotted to pay official allowances and expenses of members. The remaining $46,-762,000 was recommended to pay for investigations by standing committees and for operations of special and select committees.

The appropriations for allowances and expenses pay for such office expenses as computer services, mail, equipment, transportation, telephone service and stationery.

Joint Items

The committee recommended appropriations of $73,-727,100 to cover the House share of expenses of committees and services shared with the Senate. That included $2,-353,000 for the Joint Economic Committee, $656,000 for the Joint Committee on Printing, and $2,375,200 for the Joint Committee on Taxation. Other recommendations:

Doctor, Police, Pages. The committee recommended $465,000 to cover costs of the House attending physician, $2,171,000 for Capitol Police operations and $205,800 for the Capitol Page School. The committee also asked the Comptroller General to evaluate education and other services at the Capitol Page School.

Official Mail Costs. The committee recommended $64,944,000 to pay the U.S. Postal Service for the cost of sending franked congressional mail. The committee said that figure was only an estimate of what the fiscal 1979 costs might be.

Capitol Guide Service. The committee recommended $544,000 for permanent and temporary Capitol guides.

OTA, CBO

The committee recommended $9,700,000 for the Office of Technology Assessment.

The committee recommended $11,172,000 for fiscal 1979 Congressional Budget Office operations — $196,000 less than CBO had requested. It also recommended that CBO cut costs by reducing the number of reports it does on its own initiative.

Capitol Architect, CRS

The committee recommended $46,014,000 for the Architect of the Capitol's maintenance of congressional grounds and buildings. That included $21,065,000 for operation of the three House office buildings and two annexes and $13,635,000 for the Capitol power plant.

The committee recommended $25,553,000 for the Congressional Research Service.

Government Printing Office

The committee recommended $73,961,000 to pay for printing and binding of documents for congressional use. That was an increase of $2,287,000 over the fiscal 1978 level. Included in the fiscal 1979 recommendation was $5,090,-400 to print the *Congressional Record*, $9,868,750 to print bills, resolutions and amendments, $4,079,700 to print committee reports, $22,425,000 to print hearings and $2,-225,255 to print House and Senate committee and business calendars. However, those figures covered only the documents that would be used by Congress. Cost of printing copies of the same material for the public or other government officials was included in the GPO "related agency" recommendation listed below.

Related Agencies

The $376,348,300 recommended by the committee for related agencies was divided up as follows:

Botanic Garden. The committee recommended $1,-392,000 for the Botanic Garden in fiscal 1979, an increase of $109,000 from fiscal 1978.

Library of Congress. For all Library of Congress fiscal 1979 expenses, except operation of the Congressional Research Service, the committee recommended $149,093,-300 — $20,139,700 above the previous year. The committee denied most of the Library's request for $3,366,500 for its new James Madison Building. The committee said that because construction delays made it appear the building would not be ready for occupancy until late 1979 or early 1980, it recommended only $268,664 for packing and crating of research materials to move to the building.

Architect of the Capitol. To maintain Library of Congress buildings and grounds, the committee recommended an additional $2,776,000 for the Architect of the Capitol.

Government Printing Office. For expenses of printing material not used by Congress, the committee recommended $34,676,000.

The most costly printed item was copies of the *Congressional Record* sent to executive branch agencies and the public. The committee recommended $9,049,600 for those copies of the Record. The committee also recommended that the public printer increase the subscription price of the Record in order to cover more of the costs.

General Accounting Office. The committee recommended $185,756,000 for the General Accounting Office, an increase of $18,756,000 over its fiscal 1978 appropriations. The recommendation allowed for a net increase of 120 staffers, needed to cope with increased congressional demand for GAO studies, the committee said. It also would cover an increased GAO workload on Department of Defense matters. The committee said about 30 percent of GAO's work involved reports done for Congress. GAO recommendations and suggestions in fiscal 1977 had saved the federal treasury $5,637,059,000, the committee said.

House Floor Action

The House June 14 approved a 5 percent across-the-board slash in funding for Congress' own operations.

The 220-168 vote to cut the fiscal 1979 legislative appropriations bill marked the third time in two days that the House had approved what opponents called "meat ax" amendments to appropriations bills. *(Vote 393, p. 114-H)*

Across-the-board cuts had previously been approved in funding bills for the Labor, Health, Education and Welfare, State, Justice and Commerce Departments.

As passed by the House, 279-90, HR 12935 appropriated $922.5 million (before across-the-board cuts) for the House and related agencies. *(Vote 397, p. 114-H)*

Silvio O. Conte, R-Mass., who opposed a successful across-the-board cut in the Labor-HEW spending bill, offered the 5 percent slash in HR 12935.

"If we really want to be responsive to the taxpayers' revolt expressed in Proposition 13 (a property tax cut measure, in California) we have to look no further than the halls of Congress," he said. Conte suggested his proposal would "show the people that we are willing to do it right here in our own house, which is larded over with fat."

Legislative Appropriations Subcommittee Chairman George E. Shipley, D-Ill., protested that, "We truly have cut this down where we can't stand even a 1 percent cut in this bill." Shipley said Congress "deserves" the money allotted in the bill.

Clarence E. Miller, R-Ohio, sponsor of the across-the-board cut amendments to other appropriations bills, offered a substitute to the Conte amendment that would have called for a 2 percent slash in congressional spending. Miller's substitute was defeated by voice vote. The House then passed Conte's amendment.

The success of Conte's proposal signalled the House mood favored cuts.

One beneficiary of that mood was William L. Armstrong, R-Colo., whose proposal to require use of office funds to pay for plants, storage trunks, calendars and agriculture yearbooks had drawn little interest in previous attempts to pass it. This time, the House adopted Armstrong's proposal, 214-159. That margin included 16 members who switched from "nay" to "aye" after seeing that Armstrong would win. *(Vote 396, p. 114-H)*

The items covered in Armstrong's amendment, now provided to members for free, would still be subsidized by taxpayers. However, Armstrong argued that if members had to pay for them with office funds, they would be less inclined to take them, and spending would be reduced.

After Armstrong's success, Gary A. Myers, R-Pa., offered an amendment to prohibit members from using office funds to pay for flags given to constituents. Flags flown over the Capitol could currently be purchased by members from office funds.

But the House decided it had gone far enough with the calendars and plants. Shipley said it would be too expensive for him to have to use his own money to pay for the flags he gave to Girl Scouts, Cub Scouts and other groups. "What are you going to do when a disabled vet asks for a flag that has flown over the Capitol? Are we going to say we have to have him pay $5?" Myers' amendment was defeated by voice vote.

Broadcast Debate

An unexpected vote on House broadcasts was prompted by an amendment from John B. Anderson, R-Ill., an advocate of network control over House broadcasts.

Anderson, who had pushed for a House vote on the camera control issue, charged that the Democratic leadership was moving close to House purchase of color television cameras without having let the House decide who should run the system. He offered an amendment to prevent House purchase of color cameras, which was defeated, 133-249. *(Vote 394, p. 114-H)*

During discussion of Anderson's amendment, allies of House Speaker Thomas P. O'Neill Jr., D-Mass. — who favored House control of the system — announced they would bring the network versus House issue up for a vote immediately. Their amendment, offered by Adam Benjamin Jr., D-Ind., prohibited anyone but House employees from running the House broadcast system. Currently, House offices could hook up to a closed-circuit system enabling them to watch floor action. But a more sophisticated system was to be installed before the House made any television broadcasts available to commercial broadcasters.

Anderson charged that if the House adopted the Benjamin amendment, "Those who make the news are going to manage the news." He said the issue involved journalistic integrity. "You are saying that the people who are reporting electronically on the proceedings of the House must be employees of this body or they are not qualified, somehow, to operate those cameras," said Anderson.

Majority Leader Jim Wright, D-Texas, said the issue was not journalistic integrity, but "the integrity of the House." Many members feared that if the networks were allowed to bring their cameras in the chamber, they would show members in unflattering poses.

Ronald V. Dellums, D-Calif., openly attacked what he called the "white, male-dominated, chauvinist" media. He charged that journalists frequently ignore statements made by "women, minorities, progressives, thinking people."

Robert K. Dornan, R-Calif., agreed with Dellums' position that the networks should be kept out of the House. But instead of charging indifference to "progressives," conservative Dornan labeled the networks "left of center." Benjamin's amendment was adopted, 235-150. *(Vote 395, p. 114-H)*

Office Account Audits

By voice vote, the House adopted an amendment offered by Lawrence Coughlin, R-Pa., calling for General Accounting Office audits of all House accounts.

Another Coughlin amendment proposed cutting $6.7 million from members' district office space, constituent communications and consolidated account allowances. The amendment was defeated by voice vote.

GOP Offices

Allen E. Ertel, D-Pa., proposed an amendment that would force the National Republican Congressional Committee to move out of House office space by Dec. 1. The Democratic Congressional Campaign Committee, which also had used rent-free House office space, moved out of the federally owned building in November 1977.

Michael T. Blouin, D-Iowa, then offered an amendment to the Ertel proposal that would have required the GOP committee to move out of House space as soon as HR 12935 was enacted. Blouin's proposal touched off a highly partisan, sometimes acrimonious, debate.

The chairman of the GOP committee, Guy Vander Jagt, R-Mich., told the House that new office space was being built for the committee. In the meantime, the committee's attempt to pay rent on the House space it occupied had been turned down by Speaker O'Neill, he said. Vander Jagt called the Blouin proposal a "blatantly partisan proposal which would result in dumping us out in the street in the middle of a campaign at the moment our building is going up." He agreed to accept Ertel's alternative, adding that the committee planned to move into its new building before Ertel's Dec. 1 deadline anyway.

Blouin's proposal was defeated by voice vote. The House then adopted the Ertel amendment by voice vote.

An amendment offered by Robert E. Bauman, R-Md., to prohibit use of funds for legal representation of congressional employees without Congress' approval, was adopted by voice vote.

John L. Burton, D-Calif., offered an amendment to prohibit use of funds in the bill to install pay toilets in the Capitol. Although there were no pay toilets in the Capitol, "the House has been so stupid tonight that I do not know that somebody might not think that it would be improper to have free toilets, paid for at the taxpayers' expense," Burton said. The amendment was defeated by voice vote.

Senate Committee Action

The Senate Appropriations Committee reported HR 12935 (S Rept 95-1024) on July 19.

The bill appropriated $1,118,244,400 for operations of the House, Senate and related agencies. The Senate version was $195,752,600 above the bill passed by the House, but House legislative appropriations bills traditionally do not include funding for Senate operations. Most of the increase recommended by the Senate committee was for Senate operations and the Architect of the Capitol's expenses to maintain Senate offices and grounds.

The Senate bill contained $25,579,700 less than the budget request. The committee report said the reduction from the budget request actually was higher, because the bill included a recommendation that 5 percent of the total bill be cut from payments not required by law. The committee did not state how much the cut would be.

The House had approved a similar across-the-board cut, estimated to be $45 million, in its version of the bill.

Congressional Operations

The bill contained $741,896,100 to pay for congressional operations in fiscal 1979, an increase of $75,518,800 from the fiscal 1978 appropriation. Of the total, $185,064,000 was for Senate operations.

The committee agreed to the $306,016,400 the House had approved for its own operations. Its recommendations for other congressional operations, such as the Capitol Police and the Architect of the Capitol, closely paralleled the House-passed bill.

Committee recommendations for Senate and other congressional expenditures were:

Compensation and Mileage. The committee recommended $6,480,000 to pay for salaries and contributions for retirement, life and health insurance for the senators and the vice president, who serves as the president of the Senate. The recommendation also included funds for members' expenses in traveling between their home states and Congress. Members' travel allowance is 20 cents per mile.

The recommendation was $5,700 more than the 1978 appropriation for compensation and mileage, reflecting an increase in health insurance costs.

Senate Leadership Offices. The bill recommended $25,000 in expense allowances for the offices of the vice president, majority and minority leaders and party whips. The figure was the same as the 1978 appropriation.

Senate Employees. The bill recommended the following amounts for the offices of various Senate employees and officials: vice president, $767,000; president pro tempore, $116,000; majority and minority leaders, $411,000; floor assistants to majority and minority leaders, $103,000; majority and minority whips, $239,000; secretaries of the majority and minority conferences, $132,000; chaplain, $40,000; secretary of the Senate, $4,116,000.

The committee deleted $116,000 requested for the deputy president pro tempore, a post created in 1977 for Sen. Hubert H. Humphrey, D-Minn. (1949-64, 1971-78).

Committee Employees. The bill recommended $10,528,000 for salaries of professional and clerical employees of Senate standing committees. That was $1 million more than the 1978 appropriation.

Conference Committees. For the professional, administrative and clerical staffs of the Democratic and Republican conferences, the committee recommended $750,000. The $62,000 increase over fiscal 1978 appropriations for the conference staffs would provide salary increases, the committee said.

Members' Staff. The committee recommended $70,881,000 to pay salaries of senators' administrative and clerical staff.

Most of the $10 million increase over fiscal 1978 funding was due to including appropriations for legislative staffers — formerly a separate item — in the administrative and clerical allowance, according to the committee.

Sergeant at Arms and Doorkeeper. The committee recommended $19,803,000 for the Senate sergeant at arms and the Senate doorkeeper, an increase of $1,903,000 over fiscal 1978. The committee said $500,000 of the increase was necessary to keep the appropriations at fiscal 1978 levels, which had been boosted by $500,000 in leftover fiscal 1977 funds. Most of the additional increase was to pay for new positions in the Senate computer center.

Included in the sergeant at arms and doorkeeper appropriations was the funding for Capitol Police salaries. The Senate earmarked $8,112,101 to pay for 523 police positions on its payroll. The House sergeant at arms payroll included 629 positions, with a fiscal 1979 appropriation of $9,774,138.

Majority, Minority Secretaries. The committee recommended appropriations totaling $411,000 for the majority and minority secretaries.

Retirement, Insurance. To pay for retirement, life and health insurance contributions and for longevity compensation for certain Senate officers and employees, the committee recommended $7,785,000.

Legislative Counsel. The committee recommended $815,000 for the office of legislative counsel.

Senate Contingent Expenses. The committee recommended $61,662,000 for Senate contingent expenses, which included Democratic and Republican policy committee staff salaries; purchase, lease and maintenance of 20 vehicles for use of Senate officers; document folding; inquires and investigations; postage stamps and stationery.

Joint Items

The committee recommended $2,353,000 for the Joint Economic Committee, $656,000 for the Joint Committee on

Printing and $2,375,200 for the Joint Committee on Taxation. The House had approved the same amounts.

The Senate committee also concurred in these House appropriations: $465,000 for the Capitol's attending physician offices, $205,800 for the Capitol Page School, $544,000 for permanent and temporary Capitol guides, $64,944,000 to pay the U.S. Postal Service for the cost of sending franked congressional mail, and $2,171,000 for general expenses of the Capitol Police and reimbursement to the District of Columbia police department for its 34 officers detailed to the Capitol Police.

OTA, CBO

The committee recommended $9,700,000 for the Office of Technology Assessment, the same as the House-passed appropriation.

The committee restored $196,000 cut by the House from the Congressional Budget Office's (CBO) request. That put the Senate committee's recommendation for CBO operations at $11,368,000. The committee said the restored money was intended to allow CBO to regularly analyze the inflationary impact of major legislative proposals.

Capitol Architect, CRS

The committee recommended $56,506,600 for the Architect of the Capitol's maintenance of congressional office buildings and grounds. That was $10,492,600 above the House appropriation, but the increase reflected maintenance expenses for Senate office buildings and the Senate garage. The House bill did not include any funding for Senate operations.

The committee recommended $25,553,000 for the Congressional Research Service, the same as the House appropriation.

Government Printing Office

The committee concurred in the House appropriation of $73,961,000 for the Government Printing Office to print and bind documents for congressional use.

Related Agencies

The $376,348,300 recommended by the committee for related agencies was divided up as follows:

Botanic Garden. The committee recommended $1,392,000 for operation of the botanic garden and grounds. The figure was the same as the House-approved appropriation.

Library of Congress. For all Library of Congress expenses except operation of the Congressional Research Service, the committee recommended $149,093,300. The House adopted an identical appropriation.

Architect of the Capitol. The committee recommended an additional $2,776,000 for the Architect of the Capitol to pay for maintenance of the Library of Congress and its grounds. The House approved the same amount.

Copyright Royalty Tribunal. The committee recommended $805,000, the same as the House appropriation, for the Copyright Royalty Tribunal.

Government Printing Office. For printing and binding publications used by executive branch agencies and the general public, the committee recommended $34,676,000 in additional Government Printing Office appropriations.

General Accounting Office. The committee recommendation of $185,756,000 for the General Accounting Office was the same as the GAO appropriation approved by the House.

Cost-Accounting Standards Board. The committee recommended $1,850,000 for the Cost-Accounting Standards Board, which set standards for defense contractors and subcontractors.

General Provisions

The committee voted to deny to top federal officials an automatic pay raise scheduled to take effect in October. The House also voted to deny the pay raise.

Following another House move, the committee recommended a 5 percent cut in the bill's total appropriations. The committee's only stipulation was that payments required by law could not be cut.

The committee's 5 percent cut amendment dropped House language requiring that no more than 10 percent could be cut from any one item within the bill. "The deletion of the [10 percent limit] would allow more than 10 percent to be withheld from some appropriations, activities, and projects, a necessity if the intent of the 5 percent reduction is to be accomplished," the committee report said.

Senate Floor Action

Following the lead of the House, the Senate voted Aug. 4 to cut the $1.12 billion fiscal 1979 legislative appropriations bill by 5 percent.

The vote was 72-0 in favor of the $55.9 million cut. The bill, which funds operations of the House, Senate and related agencies, was passed by the Senate, 67-20, Aug. 7. *(Votes 283, 285, p. 44-S)*

Senate debate on the bill, which closely paralleled the House-passed version, was routine.

The House had approved a 5 percent across-the-board cut that would not affect spending mandated by law — such as members' salaries — but would prevent a cut of more than 10 percent in any one item. The Senate Appropriations Committee recommended a similar amendment, but without the 10 percent restriction.

To give their colleagues an election-year opportunity to vote for a spending cut in the congressional budget, the Senate committee requested a recorded floor vote on the 5 percent cut. "While we knew our colleagues would agree with the cut, we would like them to join in the record to show that we are willing to cut our own thing," said Richard S. Schweiker, R-Pa., ranking minority member of the Legislative Appropriations Subcommittee.

After approving the cut, the Senate agreed by voice vote to an amendment clarifying the committee's language, to assure that all appropriations — including those mandated by law — would be considered in computing the size of the 5 percent cut.

The funding levels approved by the Senate were the same as those recommended by the Appropriations Committee.

Conference, Final Action

Conferees quickly resolved minor differences between the House and Senate versions of the bill, and a conference report (H Rept 95-1457) was filed Aug. 9.

Traditionally, the House and Senate each have determined the appropriations needed for their own operations, and the other body has concurred. In funding other congressional operations, the House and Senate versions of HR 12935 differed only on the amount of money for Congressional Budget Office (CBO) operations. The conference committee adopted the Senate version of CBO funding, which was $196,000 more than the House bill. The conferees also agreed to the Senate ceiling of 218 CBO employees instead of the House ceiling of 208.

The conference committee agreed to the Senate language requiring a 5 percent cut in the total bill without affecting items required by law. It dropped the House stipulation that no one item could be cut more than 10 percent.

The conference report also contained some directions for applying the cut. The cut "should be applied by the various agencies, offices and other bodies encompassed by the (bill)," the report said. The clerk of the House and the secretary of the Senate were directed to determine where the cuts would be made in the House and Senate budgets.

The report also directed the librarian of Congress to avoid cuts in several programs and to avoid reducing the library's operating hours "until maximum reductions are made in non-essential library services such as excessive overhead in the librarian's immediate office and the office of the director of the Congressional Research Service."

Final Action

The House adopted the conference report Aug. 17 by a 255-123 vote. The Senate gave its approval by voice vote Sept. 19, completing action on the bill. *(Vote 631, p. 180-H)*

Treasury, Postal Funds

With only a brief debate over pay raise ceilings for federal workers, Congress Oct. 4 cleared and sent to the president the fiscal 1979 appropriations bill for the Treasury, Postal Service, Executive Office of the President and some independent agencies.

The final version of the bill (HR 12930 — PL 95-429) contained nearly $9 billion in new budget authority for fiscal year 1979. That was an increase of nearly $795,567,000 over the fiscal 1978 figure.

Pay Raise Cap. Conferees accepted with minor changes two Senate amendments regarding pay increases for high-level and blue-collar federal employees. The first amendment barred salary increases for federal workers earning $47,500 or more a year. The second placed a cap of 5.5 percent on pay raises for federal blue-collar workers.

Oil Import Fees, Quotas. The only potential stumbling block to final passage — a Senate amendment to bar the president from imposing either fees or quotas on oil imports — was deleted in conference. The conferees cut the provision after receiving assurances from the administration that President Carter would consult with Congress before imposing the fees.

Carter had threatened in 1977 to impose the fees or quotas after House and Senate energy tax conferees failed to reach agreement on a crude oil tax, a measure designed to raise the price of domestically produced oil to the higher price of foreign oil. The fees would have had a similar effect.

However, the Senate by voice vote June 27 voted to block the president from imposing the fees. The vote was on an amendment by Robert Dole, R-Kan. On Sept. 7, the House defeated a motion by Clarence J. Brown, R-Ohio, to instruct House conferees on the Treasury, Postal Service bill to go along with the Senate provision. The House defeated the motion by a 194-201 vote.

Gun Control. An earlier controversy had been resolved when the House voted June 7 to block firearms regulations proposed by the Treasury Department's Bureau of Alcohol, Tobacco and Firearms. Critics charged that the proposed regulations were a first step toward national gun control.

Provisions

As cleared by Congress, HR 12930 appropriated the following amounts for fiscal 1979 *(in thousands of dollars)*:

Agency	Budget Request	Conference Agreement
Treasury Department		
Office of the Secretary	$ 32,381	$ 31,300
Federal Law Enforcement Training Center	15,423	15,000
Bureau of Government Financial Operations	717,687	717,000
Bureau of Alcohol, Tobacco and Firearms	135,522	131,322
U.S. Customs Service	431,350	430,600
Bureau of the Mint	44,274	43,000
Bureau of the Public Debt	183,411	183,000
Internal Revenue Service	2,047,300	2,046,200
U.S. Secret Service	135,899	134,800
Subtotal	$3,743,247	$3,732,222
U.S. Postal Service		
Payment to the Postal Service Fund	1,829,994	1,785,176
Subtotal	$1,829,994	$1,785,176
Executive Office of the President		
President's Compensation	$ 250	$ 250
Office of Administration	7,279	7,279
The White House Office	16,907	16,711
Executive Residence	2,575	2,575
Official Residence of the Vice President	129	129
Special Assistance to the President	1,280	1,280
Council of Economic Advisers	2,042	2,042
Council on Wage and Price Stability	1,753	1,753
Domestic Policy Staff	2,650	2,500
National Security Council	3,432	3,400
Office of Management and Budget	28,353	28,200
Office of Federal Procurement Policy	4,040	3,000
Unanticipated Needs	1,000	1,000
Subtotal	$ 71,690	$ 70,119
Independent Agencies		
Administrative Conference of the United States	$ 1,062	$ 1,062
Advisory Commission on Intergovernmental Relations	1,659	1,659
Advisory Committee on Federal Pay	232	232

Agency	Budget Request	Conference Agreement
Civil Service Commission	$2,853,920	$2,853,605
Committee for Purchase of Products from Blind, Handicapped	441	441
Federal Election Commission	8,224	8,000
General Services Administration	587,577	425,530
U.S. Tax Court	8,715	8,715
Defense Civil Preparedness Agency	96,500	96,500
Subtotal	$3,558,330	$3,395,744
Grand Total	$9,203,261	$8,983,261

HR 12930 also:

- Barred salary increases for federal workers earning $47,500 or more.
- Imposed a ceiling of 5.5 percent on pay increases for blue-collar federal workers.

Background

Gun Control Controversy

On March 21, the Bureau of Alcohol, Tobacco and Firearms issued proposed regulations designed to expand and modernize the bureau's ability to trace guns used to commit crimes. The rules would impose the following restrictions:

- All guns manufactured in the United States would bear a serial number.
- Gun manufacturers, importers and dealers would be required to submit quarterly reports on the sale and disposition of firearms.
- Gun dealers and others involved in firearms transactions would be required to report the theft or loss of any firearms within 24 hours.
- Names and addresses of individual purchasers would not be reported to the bureau.

Supporters of the regulations, including the International Association of Chiefs of Police and the National Council to Control Handguns, argued that they would help to curtail illegal gun trafficking by making it easier to trace guns. They emphasized that individual gun owners would not be required to register under the rules. And they said that the 1968 Gun Control Act gave the agency authority to promulgate the regulations. Also backing the regulations were the National Council for a Responsible Firearms Policy and the National Coalition to Ban Handguns. *(1968 Gun Control Act, 1968 Almanac p. 549)*

Lining up to oppose the regulations were the National Rifle Association (NRA) and the Fire Arms Lobby of America. Contending that the bureau lacked legislative authority to issue the regulations, they accused it of attempting to bypass Congress on the issue of gun control. They blasted the proposed rules as the first step toward national gun control and said the planned tracing system would duplicate efforts of local police and the FBI.

Meanwhile, the House Appropriations Committee voted June 1 to cut the bureau's budget by $4.2 million and to add language to the fiscal 1979 Treasury appropriations bill to block the regulations.

Bureau spokesmen denied that the $4.2 million would be used to fund the tracing program. They said that the program would not be implemented until the second half of fiscal 1979, at the earliest. They added that they would ask Congress for a supplemental appropriation, if the program were put into effect.

Lobbying

The proposed regulations provoked a storm of controversy unmatched in the bureau's history, according to a spokesman for the agency. As of the middle of June, the bureau had received roughly 300,000 letters on the firearms regulations, the majority expressing opposition to the proposed rules. So large was the outpouring of sentiment against the tracing program that the bureau was forced to extend the formal comment period twice — once to May 22 and again to June 30.

The National Rifle Association launched a vigorous campaign to persuade House members to vote in favor of the Appropriations Committee's prohibition against the rules.

"We did our homework in the sense of contacting members," a representative of the NRA said in describing the group's lobbying efforts.

"They were swarming all over us as thick as flies," confirmed one Capitol Hill source, who credited the NRA with a well-oiled and effective lobbying operation.

But a spokesman for the National Council to Control Handguns accused some members of failing to stand up to pressure from the NRA.

"It's a shame these congressmen are intimidated and threatened by the NRA," he said, calling the wrangle over the proposed regulations the "opening skirmish" in a renewed battle over gun control laws.

Some gun control advocates attributed the overwhelming House vote against the firearms regulations to the failure of the administration to develop a comprehensive gun control policy.

"You don't go to Congress with bits and pieces," said David Steinberg of the National Council for a Responsible Firearms Policy.

But Treasury Assistant Secretary Richard J. Davis defended the administration's position. "We just haven't decided what to do on gun control," he said.

House Committee Action

HR 12930 was reported by the House Appropriations Committee June 1 (H Rept 95-1249). The total recommended in the bill was $8,634,300,000. That was $1,155,-992,000 more than the amount appropriated to date for fiscal 1978 and $28,861,000 less than administration requests.

Far larger sums, not included in the bill, were made available under permanent authority to the agencies and activities covered by HR 12930. The permanent budget authority added $82,887,319,000 to the total, an increase of $9,909,872,000 over fiscal 1978. The largest item in this category was interest on the federal debt, expected to reach $55.4 billion in fiscal 1979.

In a general statement, the committee said it had recommended increases over 1978 appropriations primarily to "provide for mandatory and workload increases over which the concerned agencies have very limited control."

"Such additional workload nearly always requires additional personnel, equipment, space and facilities," the report explained.

The committee repeated objections it raised in 1977 to the longtime practice of appropriating funds "by sufferance" for unauthorized activities, such as Executive Office appropriations.

"Where it is considered desirable to continue such items, appropriate legislation should be proposed at an early date," the committee said.

Restrictive Provisions

The committee voted to add two restrictive provisions to the bill. The first prohibited the Bureau of Alcohol, Tobacco and Firearms from carrying out its proposed firearms regulations.

The second barred the Internal Revenue Service (IRS) from issuing rules providing for the taxation of fringe benefits during fiscal 1979. Noting that the House Ways and Means Committee had received a commitment from IRS not to issue such regulations before July 1, 1978, the committee said it wanted to extend the prohibition to give "congressional tax-writing committees the time needed to consider the fringe benefit question." *(Fringe Benefits Tax Ban legislation, p. 270)*

Treasury Department

An appropriation of $3,189,447,000 was recommended for the Treasury Department — $10,800,000 below the budget request.

Bureau of Alcohol, Tobacco and Firearms. In slashing $4.2 million from the budget request of $135,522,000, the committee expressed outrage at the bureau's proposed regulations requiring guns to carry serial numbers.

"The committee has reduced the budget by $4.2 million and directs the bureau not to initiate controversial or sensitive programs without clear legislation and congressional authorization," the report said, tying the budget cut directly to the proposed rules.

In order "to make it abundantly clear to the bureau that it ought not attempt to do by regulation what the Congress has not done by legislation," the committee said it was barring the agency from using any of its funds to put the proposed regulations into effect.

Internal Revenue Service. The committee recommended $2,046,000,000 for the Internal Revenue Service, $1.3 million less than the administration request.

The committee noted that the service had withdrawn its request for a new computer system. "Issues regarding privacy, state of the art of computer technology, cost effectiveness and budget priorities" all were considered in arriving at the decision, the report stated. The committee conceded the need for a new computer, but warned the IRS to protect taxpayers' privacy and ensure cost effectiveness when reviewing alternative systems.

U.S. Secret Service. The committee's recommendation of $135 million was a reduction of $899,000 from the amount requested.

The committee noted that the service had asked for funds to train agents to protect presidential candidates. However, the committee said the Secret Service "ought to be able to provide this training without the increased funding requested."

Postal Service

The committee recommended the full $1,829,994,000 requested for the Postal Service. The largest share of the funds recommended was $920 million in public service costs to reimburse post offices that are not self-sustaining.

Executive Office of the President

In recommending $69,115,000 for the Executive Office, the committee cut $2,575,000 from the administration's request. Personnel reductions and transfers resulting from President Carter's reorganization efforts accounted for much of the funding reduction.

White House Office. The committee allowed 351 positions for the White House staff, the number requested by the administration. The report noted that 485 positions had been allowed in fiscal 1978, but that the president had cut 62 slots and transferred another 72 to the newly created Office of Administration.

Special Assistance to the President. The committee recommended the full $1,280,000 requested for the vice president's executive branch office. The legislative functions of the vice president are funded separately.

Domestic Policy Staff. In recommending $2 million for the Domestic Policy Staff, the committee sharply reduced the administration's budget request of $2,650,000.

The committee acknowledged that the reorganization plan had transferred to the Domestic Policy Staff certain functions of the defunct Office of Drug Abuse Policy and Office of Telecommunications Policy. But it said the $150,000 increase over the 1978 funding level should be adequate to support the five additional positions resulting from the transfer.

Independent Agencies

For the various independent agencies covered by the bill, the committee recommended a total of $3,545,744,000, a reduction of $15,486,000 from the administration request. Some highlights:

Civil Service Commission. The committee took note of the reorganization of the commission proposed under President Carter's civil service reform plan (HR 11280) and requested that it be kept informed of the reorganization's impact on the level of funds appropriated to the agency. The committee cut the administration's request for the commission by $315,000, recommending an appropriation of $120,500,000.

Federal Election Commission. The committee recommended $8 million for the Federal Election Commission (FEC), $244,000 below the administration's budget request.

General Services Administration. The committee recommended $572,830,000 for the General Services Administration (GSA), $12,532,000 less than the administration's request but $192,393,000 more than Congress had appropriated so far for fiscal 1978. (A supplemental request of $71.9 million was still pending for fiscal 1978.)

Most of the increase was for acquisition by the Federal Preparedness Agency of critical materials for the strategic stockpile.

Defense Civil Preparedness Agency. In granting the administration's full budget request of $77 million for the Defense Civil Preparedness Agency, the committee said it was reluctant to "significantly change the president's budget" until the administration "has made specific decisions regarding the direction and emphasis of all aspects of disaster preparedness." The committee also urged the agency to "become more deeply involved" in providing aid during non-military disasters.

House Floor Action

In a defeat for gun control advocates, the House June 7 voted overwhelmingly to block proposed government regulations that opponents charged were the first step toward national gun registration.

The vote came on an amendment offered by Robert McClory, R-Ill. The amendment, rejected 80-314, would have stricken from the bill language prohibiting the Treasury Department's Bureau of Alcohol, Tobacco and Firearms from issuing its proposed regulations and would have restored to the agency $4.2 million cut from its budget by the Appropriations Committee. *(Vote 365, p. 104-H)*

The total appropriation voted by the House for all agencies covered under the bill was $8,634,300,000. The House approved the measure by a vote of 297-98. *(Vote 366, p. 104-H)*

Debate on HR 12930 centered on the controversial firearms regulations.

McClory offered two amendments to reverse the Appropriations Committee's prohibition against the regulations.

The first would have restored the $4.2 million cut from the Firearms Bureau's budget. The amendment also would have stricken language prohibiting the bureau from implementing its proposed gun rules. The amendment was defeated on an 80-314 vote.

A second McClory amendment, which sought only to restore the $4.2 million, was rejected by voice vote.

Charging that Congress had a "hangup" regarding handgun regulations, McClory pleaded with his colleagues to "see these regulations for what they are," rules "directed solely at the subject of law enforcement and the elimination of crime in this country."

Abner J. Mikva, D-Ill., lashed out at the Appropriations Committee for what he called its "punitive" treatment of the Firearms Bureau. He said the committee's action was a signal to the bureau not to issue the gun regulations or "we'll cut your legs off."

However, Delbert L. Latta, R-Ohio, charged that the Firearms Bureau had made "a devious end run around the Congress to get their registration regulations on the books."

"They knew full well they could not get these regulations passed by the Congress . . . or they would have come in here in the first place and requested them," Latta declared.

Before passing HR 12930, the House rejected by voice vote a motion to send the bill back to the Appropriations Committee with instructions to withhold 5 percent of the appropriated funds, except for payments required by law.

Provisions

As passed by the House, HR 12930 appropriated the following amounts for fiscal 1979 *(in thousands of dollars)*:

Agency	Budget Request	House-Passed Appropriations
Treasury Department	$3,200,247	$3,189,447
U.S. Postal Service	1,829,994	1,829,994
Executive Office of the President	71,690	69,115
Independent Agencies	3,561,230	3,545,744
Total, Fiscal 1979	$8,663,161	$8,634,300

HR 12930 also:

- Prohibited the Bureau of Alcohol, Tobacco and Firearms from using funds in the bill to carry out proposed regulations requiring all new firearms to carry a federal serial number and requiring gun dealers and manufacturers to report to the bureau the disposition of all firearms.
- Prohibited the Internal Revenue Service from using funds in the bill to issue regulations providing for the taxation of fringe benefits not already taxed as of July 1, 1978.

Senate Committee Action

The total funding recommended by the Senate Appropriations Committee in its June 19 report on HR 12930 (S Rept 95-939) was $8,984,503,000. This was $350,203,000 more than the House had voted.

Restrictive Provisions. The committee accepted a House-passed provision prohibiting the Bureau of Alcohol, Tobacco and Firearms from carrying out proposed firearms regulations.

It also approved a freeze on salaries for federal employees earning $47,500 or more, and, on a 12-9 vote, an amendment providing a 5.5 percent ceiling on salary increases for blue-collar federal workers. President Carter already had proposed limiting pay boosts for federal white-collar workers to 5.5 percent.

But the committee pointedly rejected House-approved language barring the Internal Revenue Service (IRS) from issuing regulations providing for the taxation of fringe benefits during fiscal 1979. "Legislative responsibility for enactment of our tax laws is vested in the Senate Finance Committee and the House Ways and Means Committee," the report said.

Treasury Department

The committee recommended $3,731,200,000 for the Treasury Department — $541,753,000 above the House allowance. A boost of $543 million in funding for the Bureau of Government Financial Operations accounted for the large increase. The administration requested the funds June 14 to settle 31 states' claims against the Department of Health, Education and Welfare in a dispute over the provision of certain social services. Authorizing legislation was signed into law June 12. *(Social Services Claims bill, p. 582)*

Bureau of Alcohol, Tobacco and Firearms. The committee restored $3,878,000 of the $4.2 million cut by the House from the administration's $135,522,000 request. Expressing its concern over bureau travel expenses and the use of official vehicles for off-duty driving, the committee reduced the administration request by $322,000.

In voting to restore most of the funds cut by the House, the committee said it had received assurances that none of the funds would be used to carry out the controversial gun rules. However, the committee voted to retain language, approved by the House, that would bar the agency from using any of the funds to put the proposed regulations into effect. "It would appear that BATF and the Department of Treasury are attempting to exceed their statutory authority and accomplish by regulation that which Congress had declined to legislate," the committee said.

Postal Service

Anticipating that the increase to 15 cents for first class postage would boost Postal Service revenues by $44,818,-

000, the committee recommended cutting that amount from the House allowance.

Executive Office of the President

An appropriation of $71,309,000 was recommended for the Executive Office — $2,194,000 above the House figure, but $381,000 below the administration's request. Boosts in funding for the Domestic Policy staff, the Office of Management and Budget and the Office of Federal Procurement Policy accounted for the increase over House figures.

White House Office. Noting that 72 personnel slots for the White House staff had been transferred to the new Office of Administration, the committee concurred in the House allowance for the White House staff of 351 positions. The committee also recommended a reduction of $196,000 in the House appropriation for the staff. Lower charges for office space rentals prompted the reduction, the report stated.

Office of Federal Procurement Policy. In approving the full administration request of $4,040,000, the committee restored $1,540,000 denied by the House for the Federal Acquisition Institute, which had previously been funded as part of the Defense Department appropriation. Indicating its endorsement of the institute's program to train procurement personnel, the committee directed it to develop cooperative programs with state and local purchasing officials.

Independent Agencies

The Senate committee recommended $3,396,818,000 for the various independent agencies, $148,926,000 less than the House figure.

Federal Election Commission. Although the Federal Election Commission (FEC) had sought $8,624,000, the administration reduced the request to $8,224,000. The Senate committee backed the administration's request, restoring to the FEC $224,000 cut by the House.

"The House reduction below the president's budget estimate would severely impact on the commission's capability to perform its responsibilities for audit under the Federal Election Campaign Act of 1971," the report stated.

General Services Administration. The committee recommended $426,380,000 for the General Services Administration (GSA), $161,197,000 below the administration request and $146,450,000 below the House allowance.

Most of the reduction in funding came from cuts made in the Federal Preparedness Agency appropriation. The committee cut $174,100,000 from the administration request and House allowance for the agency, explaining that it was denying "without prejudice" a request for funds to buy critical materials for the strategic stockpile. To fund the purchase, authorizing legislation was required, the committee added.

The committee offset the Federal Preparedness Agency reduction with increases over the House allowance for other GSA agencies. The Senate committee cited the "highly publicized fraud investigations underway at the General Services Administration," as its reason for adding $500,000 to the House figure for GSA general management and agency operations.

Senate Floor Action

Jumping on the budget-slashing bandwagon, the Senate June 27 approved a 2 percent across-the-board reduction in fiscal 1979 appropriations for the Treasury Department, Executive Office of the President and certain independent agencies.

The vote to approve the cut came on an amendment to HR 12930 offered by William V. Roth Jr., R-Del. The Postal Service was excluded from the funding cut, but the Senate action was expected to cost the other agencies covered under the bill roughly $144 million.

The Senate also adopted an amendment by Robert Dole, R-Kan., barring the president from using funds in the bill to enforce the imposition of import fees on foreign oil. President Carter had said he might impose such fees if Congress failed to approve his proposed tax on domestic crude oil. The amendment was adopted by voice vote after a motion to table it failed by a 39-49 vote. *(Vote 180, p. 30-S)*

The Senate passed HR 12930 June 27 by voice vote. In addition to the 2 percent funding cut, the Senate also approved amendments cutting $3,878,000 from the budget of the Bureau of Alcohol, Tobacco and Firearms and adding $500,000 to the appropriation for the General Services Administration (GSA).

2 Percent Funding Cut

Asserting that he "was not advocating irresponsible or precipitous elimination of all or any programs contained in the legislation," Roth urged adoption of his amendment to cut funding by 2 percent for each title of the bill except Title II (Postal Service).

But Sen. Lawton Chiles, D-Fla., chairman of the Treasury, Postal Service and General Government Subcommittee, said the bill as reported represented only a 2 percent increase over fiscal 1978 funding levels.

"If there are specific items in this bill that any senator feels are too high, I would like to see those items approached and debated on the merits of those particular items," Chiles argued.

The amendment was adopted by a 55-34 vote. *(Vote 179, p. 30-S)*

Pay Cap

The Senate beat back an attempt by Ted Stevens, R-Alaska, to strike from the bill the provision calling for a 5.5 percent ceiling on wages for blue-collar federal workers. Stevens' amendment was rejected by a vote of 21-69. *(Vote 181, p. 30-S)*

Calling the provision "inequitable," Stevens said it would result in widely varying pay increases for federal blue-collar workers. Federal blue-collar workers within different localities receive wage increases at different times of the year, Stevens explained. If the pay cap were accepted, workers' pay in one locality could be substantially higher than employees' wages in another area, Stevens said.

But Thomas F. Eagleton, D-Mo., who had sponsored the "cap" proposal in the Appropriations Committee, defended the ceiling as an inflation-fighting measure. While Eagleton applauded the president for proposing a 5.5 percent cap on white-collar federal workers' salaries, he said the president's proposal "fosters unjustly preferential treatment" for blue-collar workers, who were not covered under the president's plan.

Other Amendments

In other action on the bill, the Senate:

- Agreed by voice vote to an amendment by James A. McClure, R-Idaho, to delete the committee-approved increase in funding for the Bureau of Alcohol, Tobacco and Firearms. The action was taken to ensure that the bureau did not put into effect proposed firearms regulations, which critics charged were the first step toward national gun control. The House June 7 had agreed to a $4.2 million reduction in the bureau's budget. A motion to table the McClure amendment failed on a 31-61 vote. *(Vote 183, p. 30-S)*
- Adopted by voice vote a Chiles amendment to increase by $500,000 funding for the General Services Administration to allow the agency to hire an additional 25 auditors. Chiles said the amendment was prompted by recent disclosures of widespread fraud and abuse by GSA employees.
- Adopted by voice vote an amendment by Dennis DeConcini, D-Ariz., barring federal agencies from purchasing excessively priced goods and services. The amendment sought to "put teeth" into a May 18 presidential memorandum calling on all agencies to avoid buying such goods, Jim Sasser, D-Tenn., the amendment's cosponsor said.
- Tabled, by an 89-2 vote, an amendment to the McClure amendment, offered by James Abourezk, D-S.D., to prevent payment of any pension or office staff allowance to any former president who has received a presidential pardon for crimes he committed. Abourezk said he hoped the Senate would accept his amendment and then go on to defeat the McClure amendment as amended by it. *(Vote 182, p. 30-S)*

Provisions

As passed by the Senate, HR 12930 appropriated the following amounts for fiscal 1979 *(in thousands of dollars):*

Agency	House-Passed Amount	Senate-Passed Amount
Treasury Department	$3,189,447	$3,727,322
U.S. Postal Service	1,829,994	1,785,176
Executive Office of the President	69,115	71,309
Independent Agencies	3,545,744	3,397,318
Total, Fiscal 1979	$8,634,300	$8,981,125

Energy Victory for Carter

In an energy victory for the Carter administration, the House Sept. 7 narrowly defeated a move to prohibit the president from imposing fees or quotas on oil imports.

The outcome was in doubt until the last several votes were cast, but the 194-201 vote gave the victory to Carter and the House Democratic leadership. *(Vote 643, p. 182-H)*

The vote was on a motion by Clarence J. Brown, R-Ohio, to instruct House conferees on the Treasury appropriations bill (HR 12930) to go along with a Senate provision restricting the president's authority.

Brown argued that import fees, which could be about $5 a barrel, would force consumers to pay millions of extra dollars for oil, and he questioned Carter's assumption that the higher prices would encourage conservation. Brown supported an end to price controls that hold down costs of domestic oil.

House and Senate conferees on the appropriations bill Sept. 29 reconciled their opposing views by agreeing to delete the import fees provision.

Conference Report

The conference report on HR 12930 was filed Sept. 29 (H Rept 95-1673). It recommended total appropriations of $8,983,261,000 for fiscal 1979. That figure included restoration of the 2 percent across-the-board cut in funds proposed in the Senate bill.

Treasury Department

The conferees compromised on $430,600,000 for the Customs Service, cutting the House figure by only $400,000 but adding $4.5 million to the Senate amount. The conferees explained that they "remained convinced" about "the growing menace of airborne smuggling and drug trafficking," and therefore agreed to restore the $4.5 million requested for the acquisition of a high performance interceptor aircraft.

Oil Import Fees. The conferees agreed to delete the Senate provision that would have prohibited the president from imposing fees or quotas on oil imports. The conference report included letters from Treasury Secretary W. Michael Blumenthal and Energy Secretary James R. Schlesinger giving assurances that the administration would consult with Congress before imposing such fees or quotas.

Executive Office of the President

The conferees agreed to the Senate proposal of $16,-711,000 for the White House staff, but compromised on $2,500,000 for the Domestic Policy Staff. That was $150,-000 less than the Senate amount and $500,000 more than the House had approved.

Independent Agencies

Pending the outcome of the authorizing legislation, the conferees approved $39,245,000 as proposed by the Senate instead of $213,345,000 as proposed by the House for the Federal Preparedness Agency. "The sum of $174,100,000 for the procurement, rotation and transportation of strategic and critical materials is denied without prejudice pending completion of the authorization process," the report explained.

General Provisions

The conferees deleted language contained in the House bill that would have prohibited the Internal Revenue Service from issuing rules providing for the taxation of fringe benefits during fiscal 1979. The issue was before a legislative committee, they explained. Legislation prohibiting the IRS from issuing new regulations covering taxation of fringe benefits until 1980 cleared Congress Sept. 19. *(p. 270)*

The conferees reported in technical disagreement modified versions of two Senate amendments. The first barred salary increases for federal workers earning $47,500 or more a year. The second imposed a ceiling of 5.5 percent on pay increases for federal blue-collar workers.

Final Action

House Action. In presenting the conference report on HR 12930, Tom Steed, D-Okla., chairman of the Treasury, Postal Service, General Government Subcommittee, noted that the conference committee bill contained $348,961,000 more than the House figure and $2,136,000 more than the Senate amount. Steed said $543 million appropriated for payments to settle 31 states' claims against the Health, Education and Welfare Department in a dispute over the provision of certain social services accounted for the increase.

After adopting the conference report Oct. 4 by a vote of 247-137, the House went on to consider the federal pay amendments which had been reported in technical disagreement. *(Vote 759, p. 216-H)*

The first amendment, approved by voice vote, made a technical change in the Senate language and barred salary increases for federal workers earning $47,500 or more a year.

The second, approved by a 284-111 vote, placed a 5.5 percent cap on pay raises for federal blue-collar workers. *(Vote 760, p. 216-H)*

A motion to reconsider the votes on the conference report and on the amendments was tabled by a vote of 392-4. *(Vote 761, p. 216-H)*

Senate Action. The Senate approved the conference version the same day by a 70-20 vote. *(Vote 439, p. 65-S)*■

Labor-HEW Funds: Abortion Compromise

Congress avoided another protracted struggle over abortion restrictions by clearing the fiscal 1979 Labor-Health, Education and Welfare (HEW) appropriations bill (HR 12929 — PL 95-480) in the last days of the 1978 session.

Final action came when the House Oct. 14 agreed to an abortion provision that would have remained in effect even if it had not done so. Before it gave in, however, the House once more voted to insist on its tough stand against the use of federal funds for abortions, setting the stage for another campaign by anti-abortion forces in 1979.

The initial House and Senate provisions on abortion had seemed, earlier in the year, to be a prelude to another legislative deadlock like the one that held up Labor-HEW funding for months in 1977. However, in 1978 the Senate did not pass its version of the bill until Sept. 27. With adjournment scheduled for Oct. 14, there was much less time to work in, and both chambers eventually accepted the compromise position that had taken so long to reach the year before. *(1977 action, 1977 Almanac p. 295)*

The House-passed provision had forbidden HEW to pay for abortions for low-income women unless the life of the mother was endangered by continued pregnancy. The Senate provision, by contrast, allowed payment for all "medically necessary" abortions.

The compromise provision eventually adopted in both 1977 and 1978 allowed abortions to save the life of the mother, in cases of rape or incest, when promptly reported to public health or law enforcement officials, or when two doctors found that continued pregnancy would result in severe and long-lasting damage to the mother's physical health.

The key factor in the eventual House approval of the compromise language was its earlier passage of a fiscal 1979 continuing appropriation resolution (H J Res 1139) that contained the same provision. The measure, which provided funds for departments whose regular appropriations had not been completed, would have applied to the Labor and HEW Departments if HR 12929 had not been cleared. *(Story, p. 161)*

Thus the House had a choice between the regular or continuing appropriation — but essentially no choice on which abortion provision would take effect.

Given the lack of alternatives on abortion, HR 12929 eventually won out because it was preferable to the continuing resolution on other funding areas. While the continuing resolution simply extended the fiscal 1978 funding levels into 1979, HR 12929 contained important changes and increases in spending for all Labor-HEW programs.

Looking ahead to 1979, abortion opponents set their goals on the regulations which HEW had written to implement the compromise language. Leading abortion foe Henry J. Hyde, R-Ill., said the "pro-life" forces would be seeking to reduce HEW's 60-day deadline for "prompt" reporting of rape or incest, and to restrict the range of cases of long-lasting physical damage to the mother under which abortions could be performed. While they accepted the principle of "trading a life for a life" implied by the provision allowing abortions to save the mother's life, Hyde said, abortion foes were not willing to accept the idea of "trading a life for a kidney" implicit in a loose definition of long-lasting physical damage.

Total Funding

On money matters, HR 12929 survived its encounter with the budget-cutting mood inspired by California's Proposition 13 relatively intact. The final appropriation sent to the president was $56.1 billion — $1.3 billion under his budget. But most of the difference was a $1 billion reduction, ordered to come out of HEW spending on waste, fraud and abuse, which some critics called a "phony cut." A 2 percent across-the-board cut in spending ordered by the House was dropped in conference, as was another $1 billion cut added on the Senate floor.

The bill did not contain anything for $17.6 billion in budget requests for programs whose authorizations were not completed. Among the important items not considered were public service jobs authorized by the Comprehensive Employment and Training Act, a wide variety of health programs, HEW human development services, ACTION domestic volunteer efforts, and the Community Services Administration.

Final action on HR 12929 did not come in time to avoid delays in spending by the departments, and some anxious moments for their employees. Most of HEW's employees received only half their regular paychecks for the middle of October because the department did not have the money to pay them until HR 12929 became law.

Provisions

As cleared by Congress, HR 12929 made the following appropriations for fiscal 1979 for the Departments of Labor,

Health, Education and Welfare (HEW) and related agencies:

Labor Department

	Budget Request	Final Amount
Employment and Training Administration		
Program administration	$ [90,438,000]	*
Employment and training assistance	[4,852,828,000]	*
Temporary Employment assistance	[5,955,286,000]	*
Community service employment for older Americans	[228,450,000]	*
Federal unemployment benefits	950,000,000	$ 950,000,000
Unemployment grants to the states	21,600,000	21,600,000
Advances to unemployment trust funds	200,000,000	200,000,000
Labor-Management Services Administration	59,954,000	59,754,000
Employment Standards Administration	773,909,000	773,909,000
Occupational Safety and Health Administration	162,730,000	171,224,000
Mine Safety and Health Administration	123,500,000	125,500,000
Bureau of Labor Statistics	94,950,000	94,752,000
Departmental Management	77,947,000	76,317,000
Total, Labor Department	$ 2,464,590,000	$ 2,473,056,000

Department of HEW

Health

	Budget Request	Final Amount
Health Services Administration	$ 678,192,000	$ 712,115,000
Center for Disease Control	153,660,000	162,849,000
National Institutes of Health		
Cancer	858,392,000	917,000,000
Heart, Lung and Blood	432,184,000	485,584,000
Dental Research	57,841,000	61,920,000
Arthritis, Metabolism and Digestive Diseases	249,369,000	287,869,000
Neurological and Communicative Disorders and Stroke	173,610,000	205,000,000
Allergy and Infectious Diseases	159,798,000	183,198,000
General Medical Sciences	185,092,000	231,058,000
Child Health and Human Development	108,855,000	114,305,000
Aging	35,926,000	54,526,000
Eye	82,449,000	100,549,000
Environmental Health Sciences	63,927,000	73,512,000
Research Resources	148,499,000	153,649,000
John E. Fogarty International Center	8,489,000	8,989,000
National Library of Medicine	31,787,000	33,444,000
Office of the Director	19,373,000	19,673,000
Buildings and Facilities	30,950,000	67,950,000
Alcohol, Drug Abuse and Mental Health Administration	815,846,000	816,846,000
Health Resources Administration	384,124,000	507,384,000
Assistant Secretary for Health	52,318,000	51,232,000
Retirement pay	65,083,000	65,083,000
Overseas activities	11,387,000	11,387,000
Health Care Financing Administration	19,481,982,000	19,117,525,000
Subtotal, Health	$ 24,289,133,000	$ 24,442,647,000

Education Division

	Budget Request	Final Amount
Elementary and secondary education	$ 3,353,220,000	$ 3,455,782,000
Impact aid	856,400,000	816,100,000
Emergency school aid	332,700,000	341,350,000
Education for the handicapped	971,825,000	976,637,000
Occupational, vocational and adult education	718,750,000	774,453,000
Student assistance	4,418,243,000	3,922,650,000
Higher education	371,500,000	393,000,000
Library resources	232,837,000	266,475,000
Special projects and training	104,546,000	134,472,000
Guaranteed student loans	750,814,000	739,314,000
Health professions loans	6,500,000	2,500,000
Higher education facilities	2,204,000	2,204,000
Educational activities overseas	2,000,000	0
Salaries and expenses	127,166,000	126,830,000
National Institute of Education	100,000,000	92,300,000
Assistant Secretary for Education	46,257,000	38,483,000
Subtotal, Education	$ 12,394,962,000	$ 12,082,550,000

Welfare

	Budget Request	Final Amount
Social Security Administration		
Payment to Social Security trust funds	$ 760,774,000	$ 760,774,000
Black lung payments	1,016,608,000	1,016,608,000
Supplemental Security Income	5,557,854,000	5,557,854,000
Public assistance	6,823,056,000	6,663,000,000
Refugee assistance	147,500,000	155,300,000
National Commission on Social Security	0	500,000
Special Institutions	178,757,000	178,757,000
Assistant Secretary for Human Development		
Grants to states	2,578,052,000	2,578,052,000
Adoption opportunities	0	5,000,000
Human development services	[3,648,350,000]	
Work incentives	365,271,000	385,000,000
Research overseas	3,490,000	0
Subtotal, Welfare	$17,431,362,000	$17,300,845,000
Departmental management	263,713,000	259,788,000
Waste, fraud and abuse reduction	0	−1,000,000,000
Total, HEW	$54,379,170,000	$53,085,830,000

Related Agencies

	Budget Request	Final Amount
ACTION	[$135,686,000]	*
Community Services Administration	[538,000,000]	*
Corporation for Public Broadcasting	[172,000,000]	*
Federal Mediation and Conciliation Service	22,686,000	22,686,000
Federal Mine Safety and Health Review Commission	4,776,000	4,776,000
National Commission on Libraries and Information Sciences	683,000	648,000
National Labor Relations Board	100,467,000	100,467,000
National Mediation Board	3,969,000	3,969,000
Occupational Safety and Health Review Commission	7,658,000	7,658,000
Railroad Retirement Board	338,000,000	338,000,000
Soldiers' and Airmen's Home	16,939,000	16,939,000
Total, Related Agencies	$ 495,178,000	$ 495,143,000
Grand Total	$57,338,938,000	$56,054,029,000

** Budget request not considered because authorization had not cleared. Figures in brackets not included in total.*

Legislative Provisions

Abortion. Prohibited the use of any funds in the bill to pay for abortions except where the life of the mother would be endangered if the fetus were carried to term; or except for such medical procedures necessary for the victims of rape or incest, when the offenses have been reported promptly to police or a public health service; or except where continued pregnancy would result in severe and long-lasting physical health damage to the mother, when so determined by two physicians.

- Permitted payments for birth control drugs or devices and for operations to terminate tubal pregnancies.

Busing. Prohibited the use of any HEW funds to require, directly or indirectly, the busing of any student beyond the school nearest to his home; included within the scope of the prohibition busing to implement desegregation plans involving pairing, clustering and other methods of restructuring grade levels among schools, with the exception of magnet schools.

OSHA. Prohibited the Occupational Safety and Health Administration (OSHA) from issuing civil fines for first-time health or safety violations of a non-serious nature, unless the establishment involved was cited for 10 or more violations on first inspection.

- Prohibited OSHA from issuing civil penalties for non-serious violations by an employer of 10 or fewer employees if the employer was making a good faith effort to eliminate a hazard found by a consultant.
- Exempted from OSHA regulation all farms with 10 or fewer employees that did not maintain a temporary labor camp.
- Required OSHA to under take a study of alternatives to its regulations limiting occupational exposure to cotton dust.

House Committee Action

The House Appropriations Committee reported HR 12929 June 1 (H Rept 95-1248).

The committee recommended a total of $58 billion for the Labor and HEW departments and related agencies in fiscal 1979. The total did not include $17.6 billion for items requested by the president but not yet authorized by Congress. Nor did the bill contain some $154 billion in automatic annual payments from the unemployment compensation, Social Security, railroad retirement and other trust funds. Another $11.4 billion was provided under permanent appropriations. Taking all spending in the aggregate, the committee estimated that total budget authority for labor, health, education and welfare programs would be $203.5 billion in fiscal 1979, up $23.7 billion from the previous year.

Compared with the budget request for authorized items, $57.3 billion, the committee total was $643 million more than the budget recommendation. The largest increases over the budget levels were a $306 million increase for the National Institutes of Health and a $465 million increase for HEW's education division, which would mostly go for aid to elementary and secondary schools and college students.

As it had done in 1977, before that year's lengthy House-Senate abortion fight began, the committee prohibited the use of funds in the bill to pay for abortions unless the life of the mother was considered to be in danger. Also repeated were previous years' limitations on the use of funds for busing of school children for purposes of desegregation and on activities of Occupational Safety and Health Administration (OSHA) inspectors.

DEPARTMENT OF LABOR

The committee's $2.5 billion recommendation did not include the largest chunk of Labor Department spending, some $10.9 billion for employment and training programs authorized by the Comprehensive Employment and Training Act (CETA). CETA authorization legislation (HR 12452, S 2570) was awaiting floor action in both House and Senate. *(Story, p. 287)*

OSHA. The committee provided $167.5 million for OSHA programs, an increase of $4.7 million over the budget request and $28.4 million over the 1978 level. The increase over the budget request was intended for 86 new compliance and support positions and to guarantee full funding of the remaining 2,800 employees of the agency.

The $21.3 million increase over the 1978 level requested by the administration included $8.4 million for federal payments to state health and safety programs and $5 million for health and safety training for employers and employees.

HR 12929 exempted from OSHA standards farms with fewer than 10 employees, unless the farms maintained temporary labor camps. Inspectors were barred from issuing fines the first time they found a nonserious violation of safety rules, unless they found more than 10 such violations at the same time.

A new limitation prohibited OSHA from restricting work activity because of potential dangers from nearby recreational or hunting activity — a response to an attempt by OSHA to limit logging in areas frequented by hunters.

Other Programs. The committee stayed close to the budget recommendations for the remaining labor programs. It added $10 million to the $996 million total for unemployment insurance services, funding 500 new employees to control fraud and eligibility. Finding that research activities of the department already were adequately funded under specific programs, the committee reduced the requested amount for departmental management by $1.5 million, bringing the total to $76.2 million.

HR 12929 also appropriated $422.3 million from the Black Lung Disability Trust Fund. The fund is financed by a tax on coal mining. The committee estimated that 91,800 persons would be receiving benefits from the fund by the end of fiscal 1979, 86,500 more than were receiving black lung benefits from the Labor Department as of April 1978. Congress earlier in 1978 had substantially loosened the eligibility requirements for benefits. *(Story, p. 266)*

HEALTH, EDUCATION AND WELFARE

The committee approved a total of $55 billion for HEW programs — $641 million more than the budget request and $5.6 billion more than the 1978 level.

Because of a 1977 reorganization of HEW, several programs were transferred to new administrative units. This change made the budgets for these programs difficult to compare with those of earlier years.

Health

Health Services. The committee approved $681.1 million for the Health Services Administration, $2.9 million above the budget request, but $4.5 million below the comparable 1978 level. The largest chunk of health services money, $375.9 million, went to programs aiding the health of mothers and children.

Disease Control. For preventive health programs, including disease control and occupational health, the committee called for $159.1 million, $5.4 million above the budget amount and $20.1 million above the comparable 1978 level. The National Institute for Occupational Safety and Health, funded at $61.9 million, received the bulk of the disease control increase over the budget — $4.9 million.

National Institutes of Health. The many research programs of the National Institutes of Health (NIH) were granted $3 billion, a $305.7 million increase over the budget amount. Most of the increases for the various institutes were earmarked for research grants, in particular projects that were "investigator initiated."

Totals for the institutes that received the largest increases over budget requests included $889.2 million for the National Cancer Institute, $485.6 million for the National Heart, Lung and Blood Institute, $287.9 million for the National Institute of Arthritis, Metabolism and Digestive Disease, $183.2 million for the National Institute of Allergy and Infectious Diseases and $225.1 million for the National Institute of General Medical Sciences. The bill increased the budget request for construction by $37 million, to a total of $68 million, in order to expand the National Institute of Child Health and Human Development.

The committee also added $38 million in research grant funds to the agency's funding, but refused to earmark $4 million of the amount specifically for research on smoking and health, as requested by HEW Secretary Joseph A. Califano Jr.

Mental Health. The committee cut the budget request for alcohol, drug abuse and mental health programs by $10 million, leaving $730 million. Reduced from the budget by $6 million each were research programs relating to mental health and drug abuse. Committee-approved totals for these efforts were $123.4 million and $39.9 million, respectively. Mental health training ($69.3 million) and alcoholism research ($22.2 million) each received $1 million increases over the budget.

Health Resources. Appropriations for the Health Resources Administration were set at $507.4 million, $123 million above the budget and $36.4 million above the 1978 level. The administration had sought a $90 million cut.

All of the increase over the budget was for health resources programs that mostly involve training of health manpower. The largest part of the increase, $59.8 million, was provided for capitation grants to medical, dental and other health training schools. The committee increased several of the programs providing direct assistance to health students, restoring, for example, the $10 million for loans to health professions students that the administration had sought to eliminate.

Health Care Financing. The newly created Health Care Financing Administration, comprising programs previously under the public assistance, Social Security and health services budgets, received funding for Medicare, Medicaid, health quality and cost control activities. The agency received $19.4 billion — $108.5 million less than the budget request.

The committee called for $11.5 billion for mandatory grants to states for Medicaid costs. This was $88 million less than the budget request and was based on the latest Congressional Budget Office estimates of entitlement costs. For payments to health care trust funds for Medicare benefits the committee provided $7.8 billion.

Cut from the budget request was $7 million for review of Medicaid patients by Professional Standards Review Organizations (PSROs). The committee made further cuts in PSRO funding in the budget for administration and management. Finding that the costs of PSROs were skyrocketing, while failing to affect health costs, the committee held the total cost of the PSRO program to the fiscal 1978 level of $139 million, $35 million less than the budget request. Together with reductions in research activities, cuts made by the committee brought the appropriation for administration, management and research to $101.6 million.

Education Division

Elementary and Secondary. The committee added $100 million to the budget request for assistance to schools teaching low-income children, authorized by Title I of the Elementary and Secondary Education Act (ESEA). The recommended total was $3.1 billion, enough to provide an average of $480 for each of the 5.6 million participating disadvantaged children. *(ESEA, p. 557)*

Impact Aid. Pleased that "for a change" it had received a "realistic budget" for assistance to schools educating the children of federal employees, the committee accepted the budget request of $811 million for maintenance and operations, enough to fund the program at the 1978 level. Carter had sought to limit the scope of the impact aid program in proposals for ESEA amendments.

Together with the requested $33 million for impact aid school construction and $12 million for disaster assistance, the total appropriation for assistance to federally affected areas was $856 million.

Emergency School Aid. The committee cut $5.7 million from the requested amount for aid to schools affected by racial desegregation. The total approved was $327 million, $16.8 million more than in 1978.

The biggest cut was a $3 million reduction in spending for "follow the child" programs, which help poor children who are transferred out of regular Title I eligible schools by desegregation orders.

Handicapped Programs. The committee accepted the administration-proposed level of $971.8 million for the education of the handicapped. This was a $349 million increase over the comparable amount in 1978.

For grants to states for handicapped education, the committee approved $804 million, in order to provide 12.5 percent of the average cost of educating each child. The handicapped education authorization called for a 20 percent federal share of costs. Not knowing exactly how many handicapped children there would be next year, the committee adopted the administration funding request.

Vocational Education. The committee added $47.3 million to the budget request for occupational, vocational and adult education, bringing the total to $766 million. The biggest share of the increase, $38 million, was added to vocational programs, in order to prevent the proposed cutback of consumer and homemaker education programs. The total recommendation for vocational programs was $666 million. The committee also added $9.3 million for adult education, bringing the total to $100 million.

Student Assistance. The committee added $257.5 million to the request for assistance for college students, in order to make the funding conform to the proposed middle income student assistance act (HR 11274, S 2539), which would increase assistance and expand eligibility for existing programs. The recommended total for student assistance was $4.7 billion, $1.4 billion more than in 1978.

For basic educational opportunity grants the committee provided $3.4 billion, $233 million more than the budget request. The amount was expected to fully fund the program as expanded by HR 11274, providing grants up to $1,800 per student. For supplemental opportunity grants the committee added $70 million, for a total of $340 million. However, it cut the $600 million budget request for college work-study programs by $80 million.

Figuring on an overall default rate of 11.6 percent, the committee approved $725.8 million to back up private loans to college students — the amount requested by the administration. The loan programs had come under heavy criticism for the large number of students who had defaulted, letting the federal government repay their loans.

Higher Education. As reported, HR 12929 provided $390 million for assistance to higher and continuing education. The total was $20 million over the budget request and $56.5 million over the 1978 amount.

The committee added $25 million to the budget request, for a total of $140 million, for programs aiding disadvantaged students, such as Upward Bound, Talent Search and educational opportunity centers. The committee also restored $18 million for a program aimed at helping universities meet the needs of their communities. The administration had sought to eliminate the program.

The committee deleted the requested $50 million to help colleges and universities remove architectural barriers to the handicapped. However, it said it would consider funding if HEW could come up with estimates of how much it would cost to remove the barriers of all federally assisted institutions, not just those of higher learning.

National Institute of Education. The committee cut $2.5 million from the $100 million request for the National Institute of Education. The reduction was to come out of the amount for research into student achievement and testing, which the committee worried might lead to a national student achievement test.

Libraries. For aid to libraries, the committee approved $258 million, $25.1 million over the budget. The increases were intended to help elementary and secondary schools meet the rising costs of books and to restore a program of grants to college libraries, which the administration had sought to terminate.

Welfare

Income Security. The bill appropriated $14.1 billion for assistance programs of the Social Security Administration, $160 million less than the budget request but $637.5 million more than the comparable amount in 1978.

The committee recommended $6.7 billion for cash assistance programs, primarily Aid to Families with Dependent Children. This was $160 million less than the administration request, a reduction based on the CBO estimate of the amount needed to provide assistance to persons entitled to it.

For supplemental security income, the committee approved the budget request of $5.6 billion. This represented a $185 million actual increase over the 1978 level, enough to provide cost of living increases for the 4.2 million aged, blind or disabled recipients. Payments to the Social Security system to cover benefits for those who had not paid in payroll taxes were set at the budget level of $761 million, $19.6 million above 1978 payments. For the 456,000 miners afflicted with black lung disease, and their dependents, who were the responsibility of the Social Security Administration, the committee approved $1 billion, the budget request.

Human Development. The committee approved the $3 billion budget request for programs under the newly created assistant secretary for human development. The bulk of the funds, $2.6 billion, went for matching grants to state social service programs.

The $3 billion total also included $385 million for the work incentives program (WIN), $19.7 million above the budget. The program helps welfare recipients find jobs.

RELATED AGENCIES

With one small exception, the committee approved the budget requests for eight independent agencies. It approved $100.5 million for the National Labor Relations Board, enough to fund 98 new positions for the agency.

House Floor Action

After chopping an estimated $1.4 billion from spending in the bill, the House passed HR 12929 June 13 on a 338-61 vote after debating it June 7, 8 and 13. *(Vote 386, p. 110-H)*

Haunted by the specter of Proposition 13, the successful California tax-cutting initiative, passed June 6, and determined to force HEW to reduce admitted waste, fraud and abuse in some of its programs, members approved two large, across-the-board cuts in the $58 billion bill reported by the Appropriations Committee. They refused to go along with a Carter administration request to make specific cuts in popular education and health programs, however.

The House also set the stage for another battle with the Senate over the emotional issue of federal funds for abortions. It did so by rejecting the abortion provision of the fiscal 1978 appropriations bill, arrived at after six months of tedious conference negotiations and several dozen roll-call votes on compromise proposals. Instead, the House voted to go back to the more restrictive language of the fiscal 1977 bill, permitting federal funds for abortions only to save the life of the mother.

Spending Cuts

Ironically, House adoption of the broad spending cuts followed the unceremonious scuttling of administration proposals to reduce specific programs. The administration had sought to eliminate increases made by the committee for the National Institutes of Health, elementary and secondary school assistance and college student aid, which together added some $650 million to the budget request.

Administration representatives had importuned committee member David R. Obey, D-Wis., to propose an amendment bringing funding for the programs back to budget levels. But Obey angrily and publicly denounced the attempt, in particular the cutback in college student aid, which would have funded Carter's preferred alternative to tuition tax credits.

Failing with Obey, administration representatives tried to get someone else to offer the cuts. "They were crawling around here like flies," Obey said, "but the good sense of the House prevailed."

Finally, Andy Jacobs Jr., D-Ind., agreed to submit an amendment reducing education and health funds by about $450 million. But, Jacobs said in an interview, administration aides let the proper moment during floor action for offering the amendment slip by without letting him know the time had come. Thus by inaction they missed the chance for the reductions, which Jacobs said would have stood a good chance of approval.

Ken Holland, D-S.C., somewhat reluctantly offered an amendment to cut college student aid by $233 million, but it was rejected by voice vote June 8.

Instead of the specific cuts, the House adopted two Republican amendments, offered by Robert H. Michel, Ill., and Clarence E. Miller, Ohio, which together reduced spending by an estimated $1.4 billion.

Adopted by a 290-87 vote June 8 was a Michel amendment to reduce HEW spending by $1 billion, with all of the reductions to come out of the money going for waste, fraud and other abuses. *(Vote 372, Weekly Report p. 106-H)*

Pointing to an HEW Inspector General's report in April which estimated that between $6.3 billion and $7.4 billion of the department's money was wasted or stolen each year, Michel said the amendment would force HEW bureaucrats to redouble their efforts against abuses.

Opponents of the Michel amendment argued that HEW had already begun thorough efforts to root out waste and abuse. Obey said that, since there was no "line item" in the budget for fraud and abuse, the amendment amounted to an empty political gesture.

Two Percent Cut. The Miller amendment, cutting 2 percent, or about $380 million, from total controllable spending in the bill, was adopted by a 220-181 vote June 13. The amendment limited reduction of any single program to 5 percent. *(Vote 384, p. 110-H)*

Miller said the HEW budget, the third largest budget in the world, was a good place to start heeding the message sent by California voters against government growth. "The vote in California Tuesday on Proposition 13 underscores what the public thinks" about the "explosive cost of government," he said.

But Labor-HEW Appropriations Subcommittee Chairman Daniel J. Flood, D-Pa., observed that, however much they might like across-the-board cuts, most members would shrink from the resulting reductions in popular health and education programs.

According to the subcommittee, controllable spending in HR 12929 amounted to about $19.2 billion. Two percent of that would be $384 million, not the $800 million claimed by Miller on the House floor.

Abortion

In an effort to spare members the "agony" of another lengthy conference deadlock over abortion, Majority Leader Jim Wright, D-Texas, proposed to substitute the 1977 compromise language for the committee provision, which had only allowed federally financed abortions to save the mother's life. Under the rule (H Res 1220), only the Wright amendment and an amendment striking the limitation entirely were in order.

Before the Wright amendment, Louis Stokes, D-Ohio, offered an amendment to remove the abortion provision in the bill, thus allowing unrestricted Medicaid abortions. The Stokes amendment was rejected 122-287 June 13. *(Vote 381, p. 110-H)*

A key point in discussion of the Wright amendment was the effect of the HEW regulations issued to implement the language of the 1977 compromise. Since HEW did not ask states how many abortions they were performing under Medicaid, no one knew for sure what the effect of the 1977 language had been in practice.

Carol Wemer of the National Abortion Rights Action League reported that in some southern states, under the new regulations, abortions had declined to 1 percent of their former number. While not happy with the effects of the new regulations, pro-abortion lobbyists favored the Wright amendment as offering a less restrictive House position in conference bargaining than the committee provision.

But abortion opponents contended that the effect of the regulations went against the anti-abortion positions taken by the House in the past. Henry J. Hyde, R-Ill., said that in the one state from which he had reports, Pennsylvania, the number of abortions had actually increased. "The position of the House was torpedoed and sabotaged by the people who really run the country, the regulators, the bureaucrats," he told the House.

The Wright amendment was rejected 198-212. *(Vote 382, p. 110-H)*

After the vote, Hyde described the defeat of the Wright amendment as a "rejection of HEW regulation," but conceded that the close margin "indicates a disposition to compromise."

"Any compromise will have to be much more tightly drafted" than the 1977 provision, he added. "Where we go from here depends on the stamina of the conferees."

Patricia Schroeder, D-Colo., observed after the vote that some members who voted against the compromise hoped that another long fight with the Senate could be avoided, because Sen. Edward W. Brooke, R-Mass., might be less active than he was in 1977 in leading the Senate fight against restrictions. Brooke was up for re-election in a heavily Catholic state. But he promised June 13 to continue to resist restrictive abortion language.

Other Amendments

In other action on HR 12929, the House:

- Adopted, on a 232-177 vote June 13, a Robert S. Walker, R-Pa., amendment barring use of funds in the bill for implementation of numerical goals or ratios for hiring, promotion or admissions on the basis of race, creed or sex. *(Vote 383, p. 110-H)*
- Adopted, by voice vote, a Mario Biaggi, D-N.Y., amendment prohibiting use of Labor Department funds for any activity that assists illegal aliens.
- Rejected on a 184-216 vote June 13, a Steven Symms, R-Idaho, amendment to reduce funds for the Occupational Safety and Health Administration (OSHA) by $28.4 million. The amendment had previously been adopted on a 201-179 vote June 7 when the House was sitting as the Committee of the Whole. *(Votes 385,367, pp. 110-H, 104-H)*
- Rejected by voice vote June 8 a George M. O'Brien, R-Ill., amendment to add $225 million to help educational institutions remove architectural barriers to the handicapped.
- Rejected, by a 13-20 division vote June 8, an O'Brien amendment to add $7.4 million to the funding for special education projects, in order to make $10 million available for gifted and talented children.

HOUSE PROVISIONS

As passed by the House, HR 12929:

- Appropriated a total of $56.6 billion (estimated) for the Departments of Labor and HEW and related agencies in fiscal 1979.
- Prohibited the use of funds in the bill for abortions unless the mother's life was in danger.
- Prohibited use of funds in the bill to bus children beyond their neighborhood schools in order to achieve racial desegregation, or to force schools to do so.
- Prohibited the use of funds in the bill to enforce quotas, ratios or other numerical requirements related to race, creed, color, national origin or sex in hiring, promotion or admissions procedures.
- Prohibited the Occupational Safety and Health Administration (OSHA) from issuing civil fines for first-time health or safety violations of a non-serious nature unless the establishment involved was cited for 10 or more violations on first inspection.
- Exempted from OSHA regulations all farming operations which employ 10 or fewer persons and do not maintain a temporary labor camp.
- Prohibited OSHA from restricting work in an area because of potential dangers posed by nearby recreational or hunting activities.
- Prohibited the use of funds by the Labor Department for activities that aid illegal aliens.
- Prohibited use of funds for research involving humans without their informed, written consent.

Senate Committee Action

The Senate Appropriations Committee reported HR 12929 Aug. 16 (S Rept 95-1119). It recommended a total of $56.5 billion for Labor and HEW department spending in fiscal 1979. Along with trust funds and permanently appropriated funds, the budget for the two departments and related agencies would be $203.5 billion, $23.7 billion more than the preceding year.

The bill did not include $17.6 billion in budget requests which the committee did not consider because of the lack of authorizing legislation.

The committee's total appropriation was $1.1 billion less than the amount approved by the House June 13, and $868 million less than the budget request. Most of the reduction from the House amount came from a $1.4 billion cut in education funding.

As the House had done through a floor amendment, the committee called for a $1 billion reduction in HEW spending, to come out of departmental waste, fraud and abuse estimated by the HEW inspector general to be between $6.3 and $7.4 billion. However, the Senate bill did not include a 2 percent ($397.2 million) across-the-board cut in controllable spending ordered by the House.

Abortion. The committee adopted restrictions on the use of funds to pay for abortions that were similar to those approved by the full Senate in 1977 — a position that led to a months-long conference deadlock with the House, which wanted stricter curbs. The committee's language permitted paying for abortions for low-income women under the Medicaid program when the mother's life was endangered by continued pregnancy, when a doctor determined that an abortion was "medically necessary," or in cases of rape or incest. The committee made clear that the limitations were not to restrict the providing of intrauterine contraceptive devices or "morning after" birth-control pills.

Busing. The committee bill also repeated language added to the fiscal 1978 Labor-HEW bill banning the use of funds to require the busing of any student beyond the school nearest his or her home. The language included a specific prohibition on implementation of desegregation plans using pairing, clustering, or other restructuring of grade levels among schools.

Student Assistance. The committee cut funding for Basic Educational Opportunity Grants (BEOGs) to college students because it did not want the government to end up paying for both tuition tax credits and increased BEOGs.

As an alternative to the tuition tax credits, the administration had proposed a large increase for BEOGs, asking for $3.1 billion for student grants. The Senate panel reduced this to around the 1978 level, $2.1 billion, which was $1.2 billion less than the House amount. The committee promised to consider an increase for BEOGs, depending on the fate of the tuition credits.

Senate Floor Action

The Senate passed HR 12929 by a 71-13 vote Sept. 27. *(Vote 415, p. 62-S)*

Debate on the controversial abortion and busing provisions in the bill repeated, in much shorter form, the intense arguments that had consumed 10 hours of floor time in 1977. The "warmed-over" nature of the debate contributed to desultory attendance, forcing Appropriations Committee Chairman Warren G. Magnuson, D-Wash., to repeatedly implore his colleagues to come to the floor to offer their amendments, lest he force a quick final vote on the bill in frustration.

Abortion

After running quickly through the arguments for and against Medicaid funding for abortions that had led to a seemingly endless legislative deadlock in 1977, the Senate turned down two amendments to restrict the committee language allowing medically necessary abortions.

Orrin G. Hatch, R-Utah, introduced an amendment to substitute for the committee provision the House-passed provision allowing abortions only to save the life of the mother. The amendment was rejected 30-55 Sept. 27. *(Vote 413, p. 61-S)*

In addition to repeating the substantive arguments on federal abortion funding, supporters and opponents of the Hatch amendment portrayed it in terms of its tactical implications for the conference showdown with the House.

Hatch argued that the Senate had to take a more restrictive position on abortion because the compromise finally reached with the House in 1977 was no longer acceptable to abortion opponents. "Any compromise," Hatch said, "should start, not with the committee language proposed here, but with the language passed into law last year," because of the way HEW had interpreted the 1977 provision allowing abortions when two doctors determined that continued pregnancy would result in long-lasting health damage to the mother. "Last year's language poses almost no obstacle to a Medicaid recipient interested in obtaining an abortion. In short, it is no longer seen as a satisfactory compromise by abortion opponents," he said.

Edward W. Brooke, R-Mass., responded that the Senate had to hold on to the committee language in order to retain at least the 1977 provision in conference. But he opposed immediate adoption of the 1977 compromise, lest it be taken as an admission of weakness before the conference negotiations began. "The House likely would view such an action as not an end to the struggle, but as a sign of weakening of the Senate's determination to protect poor women and as a starting point, a beginning, for extracting further compromises from the Senate," he said.

Using essentially the same argument, Brooke also successfully opposed a Strom Thurmond, R-S.C., amendment to allow abortions to save the life of the mother, or in cases of rape, when reported to law enforcement authorities within 48 hours of the incident, or in cases of incest, as defined by state law. The amendment was defeated 19-66. *(Vote 414, p. 61-S)*

Busing

The Senate voted in favor of broad restrictions on HEW school busing orders by a larger margin than it had in 1977. By a 35-54 vote Sept. 27 it rejected a Brooke amendment deleting committee language prohibiting HEW from ordering busing desegregation plans involving the use of pairing or clustering of schools, or restructuring of grade levels among schools. *(Vote 412, p. 61-S)*

The committee provision, named for Thomas F. Eagleton, D-Mo., and Joe Biden, D-Del., had been added to the Labor-HEW appropriations bill in 1977 because busing opponents felt that HEW was attempting to use the pairing and clustering techniques to get around an earlier congressional restriction, named for Robert C. Byrd, D-W.Va., against busing of children beyond their neighborhood schools.

HEW Secretary Joseph A. Califano Jr., Eagleton explained, had construed the Byrd amendment in the narrowest possible light, deciding that HEW could still order busing in connection with a reorganization of local schools aimed at breaking up patterns of racial segregation. "Mr. Califano put the Congress on notice that he was interpreting the Byrd amendment right out of existence, and the HEW would not feel constrained in its use of busing as an administrative tool to bring about school desegregation," Eagleton said.

To close up this "loophole," the Senate in 1977 approved the Eagleton-Biden provision by a 47-43 vote. *(1977 Almanac p. 307)*

Again opposing the Eagleton-Biden amendment, Brooke argued that it would in fact lead to more, not less, busing. By hampering HEW's efforts to obtain voluntary action against segregation, he said, the amendment would force the issue into the courts, whose authority to order busing was not restricted.

In response, Eagleton cited evidence showing that busing neither helped to end segregation nor improve the education of minority children. Pointing to statistics showing an ever-growing black predominance in major city schools, he argued that busing added to "white flight" from the public schools. He also noted findings by sociologist James S. Coleman, previously a leading academic advocate of busing, that desegregation did not add significantly to minority education achievement.

Affirmative Action

Senate floor managers accepted an amendment offered by S.I. Hayakawa, R-Calif., on behalf of Jesse Helms, R-N.C., to prohibit HEW from requiring the use of racial or sexual quotas in admissions to institutions of higher learning. The amendment, which Helms described as in line with the Supreme Court's Bakke decision against the use of quotas, was adopted by voice vote.

The amendment was a limited version of a House-approved amendment introduced by Robert S. Walker, R-Pa. The Walker amendment banned enforcement of quotas, ratios or other numerical requirements in admissions or hiring; the Helms amendment forbade only quotas in admissions.

OSHA

A complicated parliamentary situation and some vigorous lobbying helped reverse the Senate's position on an Occupational Safety and Health Administration (OSHA) small business exemption from what it had approved in August.

The Senate Aug. 2 approved a Dewey F. Bartlett, R-Okla., amendment to a Small Business Administration (SBA) bill (HR 11445) to prohibit OSHA from making health and safety inspections of most businesses with 10 or fewer employees. *(Story, p. 485)*

The provision was dropped in conference, however, even after Bartlett and Rep. Silvio O. Conte, R-Mass., had proposed a compromise allowing health, but not safety, inspections of small business.

Bartlett revived his compromise proposal as an amendment to HR 12929. Specifically, the amendment prohibited safety inspections of businesses with 10 or fewer employees in industries with occupational injury rates of seven or less per hundred workers, unless a serious injury had already occurred or an employee had filed a complaint with OSHA.

Bartlett argued that the amendment would answer criticisms of his earlier proposals, while still freeing small businesses from the aggravating "nit-picking" regulation with which OSHA was frequently charged. He said it would force OSHA to concentrate on businesses with really serious dangers in the work-place and on the long-term dangers to workers' health.

Opponents of the amendment warned that the classifications used in the Bartlett amendment would lump safe and unsafe businesses together, leaving many workers in dangerous jobs within relatively safe industries unprotected.

The Senate never got a chance to vote directly on the amendment, however. Harrison A. Williams Jr., D-N.J., raised a point of order against the amendment, on the grounds that it was legislation in an appropriations bill. Relying on an obscure Senate rule, Bartlett raised a question of germaneness against his own amendment. The rule holds that a point of order against legislation in an appropriations bill is not valid if the Senate first rules that the amendment is germane to a provision previously passed by the House.

Majority Leader Byrd moved to table the Bartlett question; his motion was agreed to 47-46. *(Vote 409, p. 61-S)*

After the chair sustained the Williams point of order, Bartlett appealed the ruling. Breaking established legislative procedure, Magnuson then moved to table the appeal. According to the Senate parliamentarian's office, no one in living memory had ever tried to table an appeal of a chair ruling. However the tabling motion was approved 50-45. *(Vote 410, p. 61-S)*

In addition to the confused parliamentary developments, on which some senators may have voted on procedural rather than substantive grounds, administration and union forces had lobbied hard against the small business exemption since it passed in August. An OSHA spokesman observed that the adamant opposition of House conferees to the Bartlett SBA amendment may have persuaded some senators to avoid another potentially disruptive issue in conference committee.

Cotton Dust Rules. One restriction the Senate did approve, however, was a delay in implementation of health protections for workers in cotton mills. Approved by a voice vote was an amendment by J. Bennett Johnston, D-La., to put off until May 1, 1979, OSHA rules governing permissible amounts of cotton dust in the cotton industry.

The regulations, which went into effect Sept. 2, reportedly were the topic of an internal dispute within the Carter administration because of fears that the high cost of putting the standards into effect would add to inflation. The standards were intended to protect workers from byssinosis, "brown-lung" disease linked to inhalation of cotton dust.

Impact Aid

Reflecting a changing congressional attitude toward the "impact aid" program of assistance to local schools educating children of federal employees, the Senate Sept. 27 voted 41-52 against an increase in spending for the program. *(Vote 406, p. 60-S)*

Offered by Charles McC. Mathias Jr., R-Md., the rejected amendment would have restored $57.3 million cut by the committee from the budget request. The amendment would have provided a total of $856.4 million of maintenance and operations, construction and disaster assistance to impact area schools, just enough to keep the level of the program even with inflation.

Conceding that the program was in need of further study and possible revision, Mathias maintained that the eve of the next fiscal year was not the time to do it. Senate approval of the cuts, he said, would be a devastating blow to school administrators in small and poor communities. Maryland stood to lose $604,000 under the committee bill.

Opponents of the Mathias amendment argued that Congress had a chance to slow the rapid growth of the program by approving the committee recommendation. Keeping impact aid at the fiscal 1978 spending level would help cut down on the budget deficit and begin to direct the aid to the areas that truly deserve it, they said. Magnuson noted that 38 states would still get more under the committee bill than they had received in fiscal 1978, with only three states facing cuts of more than $100,000.

"Help us to retain this program for those areas of real impact and call a halt to this wild growth that imperils the whole program," Magnuson urged.

Other Amendments

In other action on HR 12929, the Senate approved the following amendments Sept. 25 and 27 by voice vote:

- By Harry F. Byrd Jr., Ind-Va., to increase to $2 billion from $1 billion, the overall reduction of HEW spending, to come out of outlays for waste, fraud and abuse.
- By Robert C. Byrd, D-W.Va., to add $10 million for Health Services Administration aid to victims of black lung disease.
- By Birch Bayh, D-Ind., to increase to $937.5 million, from $925 million, funding for the National Cancer Institute.
- By Magnuson, to add $5 million to the Social Security Administration budget for Indochinese refugees.
- By H. John Heinz III, R-Pa., to add $5 million to the Human Development budget, in order to facilitate opportunities for the adoption of children.
- By Gaylord Nelson, D-Wis., to appropriate $500,000 for the National Commission on Social Security, authorized in 1977 (PL 95-216).
- By Dewey F. Bartlett, R-Okla., to bar the use of any funds in the bill for expenses of the National Commission on the International Year of the Child, 1979.

SENATE PROVISIONS

As passed by the Senate, HR 12929:

- Appropriated $54,507,666,000 for the Departments of Labor and HEW and related agencies in fiscal 1979.
- Barred use of funds in the bill to pay for abortions, unless the life of the mother would be endangered if the fetus were carried to term, or in cases of rape or incest, or when found to be "medically necessary."
- Prohibited the use of HEW funds to require the busing of any student beyond the school nearest his home, including desegregation plans involving the use of pairing, clustering and other methods of restructuring grade levels among schools.
- Prohibited the Occupational Safety and Health Administration (OSHA) from issuing fines for first-time health and safety violations of a non-serious nature, unless the establishment involved was cited for 10 or more serious violations on the first inspection.
- Exempted from OSHA regulations all farms employing 10 or fewer persons.
- Delayed until May 1, 1979, implementation of OSHA rules relating to occupational exposure to cotton dust.

• Prohibited the Department of HEW from requiring the use of racial or sexual quotas in admissions to institutions of higher learning.

Conference Action

By bucking their most divisive issue — abortion — back to the full House and Senate, conferees on HR 12929 were able to report the measure Oct. 6 (H Rept 95-1746).

With adjournment scheduled for Oct. 14, conferees decided to report the differing House and Senate provisions in disagreement, leaving the matter to be settled directly on floor votes.

The final amount approved by conferees was $56.1 billion. This compared with $56.6 billion approved by the House and $54.5 billion approved by the Senate. The total budget request for the two departments and related agencies was $57.3 billion, making the final amount $1.3 billion under the budget. The conferees quietly dropped a much-publicized House provision calling for a 2 percent cut in the spending in the bill, and a $1 billion cut added on the Senate floor.

The conferees accepted spending levels mid-way between House and Senate amounts for almost all programs. The biggest shift made by conferees was the restoration of nearly all the $189 million cut by the Senate from assistance to schools educating children from low-income families, authorized under Title I of the Elementary and Secondary Education Act.

College Student Aid

Conferees agreed on a level of funding for the Basic Educational Opportunity Grants (BEOGs), $2.6 billion, that would allow some middle-income students to benefit from both new direct assistance and tuition tax credits, if they became law. In effect, the conference committee voted to enact the heart of the administration's middle-income student assistance bill (S 2539, HR 11274), at least for fiscal year 1979.

The House had approved $3.4 billion for the BEOG grants, enough to fund expansion of the program to students from families earning between $15,000 and $25,000 a year. But the Senate Appropriations Committee, unwilling to pay for increased grants in addition to the lost revenues caused by the tuition tax credits, provided $2.1 billion for the grants, only enough to hold the program at the existing level.

The administration initially supported the Senate figure, suggesting that any additional funds needed could be provided by a supplemental appropriation if tax credits were not enacted. However, HEW officials later said that the uncertainties caused by the supplemental approach would make it difficult to know how much money to give to students, whose applications for aid in the next school year must be processed early in 1979.

With the fate of the tuition tax credits still very much up in the air, conferees searched for legislative language that would cover all possible outcomes. Lawton Chiles, D-Fla., proposed that the conferees add an amendment to appropriate $2.6 billion for the BEOGs, but prohibit HEW from expanding eligibility to the middle-income group if the tuition credits were enacted. He argued that this approach would prevent "double-dipping" by middle-income students from both the grants and credits, while allowing the BEOG expansion to go forward if there were no credits. *(Tuition credits, p. 248)*

Thomas F. Eagleton, D-Mo., offered a counterproposal to expand the grants even if the credits were enacted. His amendment appropriated the same $2.6 billion, while expanding the BEOG eligibility to the middle-income group. The Eagleton amendment, like the middle-income student assistance bill, allowed BEOGs to families earning up to $25,000 by reducing to 10.5 percent the percentage of its disposable income a family was expected to contribute to a student's education.

Supporters of the Eagleton amendment argued that, given the small size of the tuition credits in 1979, it would be no great loss to let some middle-income families get both credits and BEOGs.

But the $2.6 billion probably will not be enough to pay for grants to millions of new middle-class applicants. So Eagleton included in his amendment a schedule for percentage reductions of individual grants in case there was not enough to go around.

House conferees wanted a higher figure. But Magnuson was adamantly opposed, arguing that anything over $2.6 billion would put the total HEW appropriation over the president's budget. Magnuson also pointed to the estimated $150 million-$300 million in unspent BEOG money that HEW had left over from fiscal 1978, and the possibility of a supplemental appropriation in 1979.

On a 6-4 vote the Senate conferees accepted the Eagleton amendment; House conferees then agreed.

OSHA

Despite a short "filibuster" by Ernest F. Hollings, D-S.C., conferees agreed to drop a Senate provision delaying implementation of Occupational Safety and Health Administration (OSHA) regulations pertaining to dust in the cotton industry.

The Senate had approved an amendment to delay the effect of the OSHA cotton dust rules until May 1, 1979. Although the provision was strongly opposed by organized labor and the Labor Department, sponsors of the bill had accepted the amendment without a roll-call when it became obvious that it would have been approved on a direct vote. The House bill contained no comparable provision.

Working with Hollings, House Appropriations Committee Chairman George Mahon, D-Texas, proposed a compromise amendment to delay the regulations until Jan. 31, 1979, and require a study of other, cheaper ways of protecting workers from cotton dust.

Before House conferees could vote on the proposal, however, William Proxmire, D-Wis., moved that the Senate conferees recede from the amendment. Unwilling to allow a vote on the Proxmire motion, Hollings settled into a prolonged discussion of the issue. He eventually relented, however, and accepted an amendment to remove the delay on implementation of the regulations and require OSHA to submit a study of the issue to Congress by March 1, 1979.

Conferees also dropped a Senate amendment exempting migrant labor camps with 10 or fewer employees from OSHA inspections. The conference report directed OSHA to concentrate its inspections on farms with more than 10 migrant employees.

Educational Quotas

The conference committee deleted two amendments, added on the House and Senate floors, to prohibit quotas in higher education. The conference report contained neither the House provision banning use of HEW funds to enforce racial or sexual quotas or ratios in admissions and hiring, nor a Senate amendment prohibiting quotas in university admissions.

An aide to one senator who supported the anti-quota amendments denounced the conference action as a usurpation of legislative authority, since conferees went directly against actions taken by both houses. Conferees reasoned that the House and Senate amendments, which were to different parts of the bill, were in fact two different amendments, and thus did not have to be retained.

Final Action

The House had threatened to kill HR 12929 when it rejected the compromise abortion provision Oct. 12 after accepting the rest of the conference report by voice vote.

The issue came directly before the House after conferees had decided that they would not be able to settle their differences among themselves. Instead, they simply reported the bill back to both houses with the abortion provisions in disagreement.

Appropriations Committee Chairman George Mahon, D-Texas, moved that the House recede from its own provision and accept the compromise. Telling his colleagues that "the time has come to stop posturing," Majority Leader Jim Wright, D-Texas, urged the House to give up on a position that had no chance of overcoming Senate opposition.

Although he conceded that there were difficulties caused by reliance on the continuing resolution, Robert E. Bauman, R-Md., said any problems caused by the defeat of HR 12929 were small compared with the moral outrage felt by abortion opponents. "The integrity of the Appropriations Committee and the integrity of the process," he said, "is absolutely inconsequential compared with the question of life and death that is before us."

The Mahon motion to recede from the House position was rejected 188-216, a margin that was 14 votes wider than the vote by which the House rejected the compromise language when it first considered HR 12929 in June. *(Vote 790, p. 226-H)*

Although most observers had counted the bill dead for the rest of the year after the House vote, Senate Appropriations Committee Chairman Warren G. Magnuson, D-Wash., refused to give up. He brought the conference report to the Senate floor Oct. 13, where it was approved by voice vote, with the substitution of the compromise abortion language.

The issue then came before the House again Oct. 14. David R. Obey, D-Wis., pointed out that the abortion issue was out of the control of the House, since the continuing resolution had already been passed. The only question remaining, he said, was whether the departments would be funded under a regular appropriations bill, or by "the irregular process of a continuing resolution, which in fact gives departments an excuse to squirrel out from whatever recommendations and admonitions we lay down."

The House then approved Mahon's motion to accept the compromise language by a 198-195 vote, clearing the measure for the president. *(Vote 815, p. 232-H)*

Quotas

In other action on the conference report on HR 12929 Oct. 12, the House narrowly rejected a move to restore anti-quota provisions passed by both House and Senate but dropped by conferees.

The House had passed an amendment prohibiting HEW from enforcing racial or sexual quotas or numerical goals in admissions or hiring by higher education institutions. The Senate had approved language banning university admissions quotas.

Robert S. Walker, R-Pa., sponsor of the House amendment, said he was "shocked and disappointed" by the conference action in opposition to positions taken by both chambers. He moved to recommit the conference report with instructions to House conferees to accept the Senate provision.

The motion was defeated 187-200. *(Vote 787, p. 224-H)*

Interior, Energy Funds

An expanded price break for East Coast refiners of home heating and residual fuel oil — although less than half the break proposed by the Carter administration — was included by Congress in the fiscal 1979 Interior Department appropriations bill.

The $11.6 billion measure (HR 12932 — PL 95-465) also included funding for various Energy Department programs, the Agriculture Department's Forest Service and 10 other commissions and agencies.

In the bill, Congress also acted to protect 20 Colorado River water projects from a court challenge by environmentalists. The legislators' action permitted work to proceed on the projects without a study of what their total impact would be on the Colorado River.

The bill appropriated $1.3 billion less than the administration had requested, largely because $1.2 billion in funding for the Strategic Petroleum Reserve was delayed until fiscal 1980.

Provisions

As cleared by Congress, HR 12932 made the following appropriations for fiscal year 1979:

Agency	Budget Request	Final Amount
Interior Department		
Bureau of Land Management	$488,124,000	$500,937,000
Office of Water Technology and Research	27,154,000	28,357,000
Heritage Conservation and Recreation Service	790,978,000	811,899,000
Fish and Wildlife Service	292,030,000	304,135,000
National Park Service	504,586,000	518,100,000
Geological Survey	583,911,000	640,143,000
Bureau of Mines	168,829,000	147,007,000
Office of Surface Mining Reclamation and Enforcement	114,522,000	115,395,000
Bureau of Indian Affairs	973,481,000	1,034,559,000
Office of Territorial Affairs	156,356,000	179,231,000
Office of the Solicitor	14,895,000	14,585,000
Office of the Secretary	41,607,000	43,200,000
Total, Interior Department	$4,156,473,000	$4,337,548,000
Department of Agriculture		
Forest Service	$1,342,208,000	$1,423,195,000

Agency	Budget Request	Final Amount
Department of Energy		
Fossil energy research and development	$637,451,000	$576,888,000
Fossil energy construction	50,350,000	99,709,000
Energy production, demonstration, distribution	254,692,000	169,181,000
Energy conservation	927,731,000	707,101,000
Economic Regulatory Administration	98,933,000	94,733,000
Strategic Petroleum Reserve	4,250,464,000	3,006,854,000
Energy Information Administration	63,405,000	59,286,000
Total, Energy Department	$6,283,026,000	$4,713,752,000
Department of Health, Education and Welfare		
Indian Health	$542,807,000	$560,789,000
Indian Education	75,735,000	71,735,000
Institute Museum Services	7,752,000	7,852,000
Total, HEW	$626,294,000	$640,376,000
Related Agencies		
Navajo and Hopi Indian Relocation Commission	$ 13,129,000	$ 8,752,000
Smithsonian Institution	130,422,000	129,185,000
National Foundation on Arts and Humanities	295,260,000	294,481,000
Commission of Fine Arts	264,000	263,000
Advisory Council on Historic Preservation	1,553,000	1,178,000
National Capital Planning Commission	1,939,000	1,963,000
Franklin D. Roosevelt Memorial Commission	20,000	20,000
Joint Federal-State Land Use Planning Commission for Alaska	594,000	594,000
Pennsylvania Avenue Development Corp.	27,285,000	27,385,000
Grand Total	$12,878,467,000	$11,578,692,000

House Committee Action

The House Appropriations Committee recommended $12.7 billion in fiscal year 1979 funding. The amount was $174.2 million less than President Carter's request. The bill was reported June 1 (H Rept 95-1251).

The Interior Department was to receive $4.24 billion, a $91.6 million increase over the administration request. But recommended funding for the Energy Department was $5.97 billion, $314.8 million less than the request. The other major item in the bill was $1.38 billion for the Forest Service in the Agriculture Department, which was $38.3 million more than the administration requested.

Department of the Interior

The committee's recommended total of $4,242,184,000 for the Department of Interior was $460.5 million more than fiscal 1978.

Bureau of Land Management. The committee boosted appropriations for the Bureau of Land Management by about $22 million, primarily to improve the management of the 470 million federal onshore acres for which the agency was responsible. Total funding recommended for the bureau was $510.1 million.

Heritage Conservation and Recreation Service. Formerly the Bureau of Outdoor Recreation, this new service was established by the interior secretary in January 1978. The committee recommended $723.7 million for the service, $67.3 million below the requested amount.

A major responsibility of the service was administration of the Land and Water Conservation Fund, about half of which was used for grants to states, with the remainder going for purchase of new national forests, refuges and parks and the improvement of existing conservation areas. The committee recommended $645.8 million for the fund, $79.2 million less than requested. Most of the money cut by the panel had been earmarked to buy parks and other areas not yet authorized by Congress.

Fish and Wildlife Service. The committee increased by $10.97 million the request for the Fish and Wildlife Service, bringing the total recommended to $302.9 million.

National Park Service. The committee emphasized proper maintenance of existing parks and facilities instead of construction of new visitor centers in its recommendation to provide $513.6 million for the park service, an increase of $9.04 million over the request.

The committee criticized the park service's building program. A study by the committee completed in March 1978 "demonstrated that the entire construction planning process was in disarray," the report said. The committee increased funding for advanced planning by $2.7 million, but cut construction funds by $9.6 million.

U.S. Geological Survey. Funding of $635.7 million for the survey was recommended by the committee. The panel added $21.3 million for the survey's investigations and research and $30.5 million for federal exploration for oil and gas in the Naval Petroleum Reserve in Alaska.

Bureau of Mines. The Bureau of Mines, responsible for research on and assessment of minerals, was funded at $132.7 million, $36 million less than requested.

Bureau of Indian Affairs. The committee recommended $1.035 billion for the bureau, $61.9 million more than requested. The increase included $29.8 million more for Indian programs, such as education, housing and community development, and $29.45 million more for construction, primarily of schools.

Department of Energy

In its report, the committee took a number of verbal swipes at the Energy Department.

Instead of bringing order and cohesion to the formerly scattered federal energy programs — the reason the Cabinet-level agency was created in 1977 — the Department of Energy had been disorganized and submitted a poorly drawn budget, the committee charged.

"Lines of responsibility within the organization are unclear," and programs "[are] fragmented," the report said. The department had also been "generally unresponsive" to committee requests for technical information and had been "slow to react administratively," the report said.

The committee also noted that in testimony before the committee, "every responsible official disavowed responsibility for the agency's budget."

Similar criticisms of the Energy Department, its budget preparations and congressional relations were voiced by the House Interstate and Foreign Commerce Committee in its report on the agency's requests for fiscal 1979 budget authorizations.

Jurisdiction over the Energy Department appropriation was split between the Interior and Public Works Subcommittees of the Appropriations Committee. For that reason, funding for the agency was considered by the House in separate pieces of legislation. *(Public Works appropriations, p. 154)*

Among the energy programs included in the bill were fossil energy research, the strategic oil reserve system, energy conservation and internal regulatory agencies, such as the Economic Regulatory Administration.

Fossil Energy Research. The panel reduced by 4 percent the request for fossil energy programs, recommending funding of $614.7 million for the research.

The committee cut $43 million, or roughly 20 percent, from the request for programs aimed at producing liquid and gaseous fuels from coal.

Partially balancing those cuts was a recommended $20 million boost for a program to derive oil from shale and a $10 million hike to increase the rate of gas drawn from existing wells.

Energy Production. The panel urged cuts totaling $51.8 million in a variety of programs designed to increase energy production, including efforts to move new technologies into commercial stages.

Of those cuts, $49 million came from accounts for Naval Petroleum Reserves Nos. 1 and 2. The committee said that in the past three years, the Navy had "been able to reprogram approximately $86 million" from other accounts into these facilities "without adequately explaining to the Congress the need for the increased facility spending."

Energy Conservation. The committee approved $907 million for various energy conservation programs, $2 million more than the department sought.

The committee urged an increase in various residential and commercial conservation programs of $17.3 million. That included an increase of $7.5 million for projects aimed at deriving energy from urban garbage. At the same time, the panel urged cutting the request for industrial conservation by $11.3 million.

The committee also urged cuts of $8.9 million in research and equipment costs for energy saving transportation programs, primarily van pooling.

Strategic Oil Reserve. The panel approved $4.08 billion for the strategic oil reserve system, $165.8 million less than the department sought, even though the committee said it was "appalled that the reserve is at least six months behind schedule in acquiring supplies."

The program was designed to store enough petroleum to cushion the nation in the event of another interruption of imported oil, similar to the 1973-74 Arab oil embargo.

The panel urged cutting $405.2 million from the oil reserve program budget request to cover increased oil costs from the proposed crude oil equalization tax. The tax did not pass.

House Floor Action

The House approved $12.7 billion in fiscal 1979 appropriations June 21 after narrowly rejecting an effort to cut the bill by 2 percent. The vote was 356-50. *(Vote 414, p. 118-H)*

The amount in the bill was $184.2 million less than the amount requested by the Carter administration, but was nearly identical to the recommendation of the Appropriations Committee. It represented an increase of $2.036 billion over fiscal 1978 appropriations.

A potential tie-up in House action on the bill was avoided when Robin L. Beard, Jr., R-Tenn., decided not to offer 682 amendments he had proposed to protest the 1973 Endangered Species Adt. *(Story, Energy chapter)*

Beard withdrew his amendments — one against each domestic and international endangered species — when he won assurances that he would be allowed to seek changes in the law when the House considered the bill (HR 10883) reauthorizing funding for the act.

Two Tennessee Valley Authority (TVA) dams, including the Columbia Dam in Beard's district, had come into conflict with endangered species. The Supreme Court ruled June 15 that TVA's Tellico Dam could not be completed because it would destroy the critical habitat of the endangered snail darter, a small fish.

Two Percent Cut

The House rejected, 198-211, an amendment offered by Rep. Clarence E. Miller, R-Ohio, that would have reduced funding in the bill by 2 percent. *(Vote 413, p. 118-H)*

His name was on a number of attempts on the floor to make across-the-board cuts in appropriations bills.

Sidney R. Yates, D-Ill., chairman of the Appropriations Subcommittee on Interior, defended the bill.

Yates argued that, if the amendment were accepted, the administration, not Congress, would decide which programs to cut. "I think that is a surrender of our responsibility," Yates said. He also said the Appropriations Committee had good reasons for making its recommendations: "We did not do this willy-nilly."

In other action on HR 12932, the House:

- Rejected, 126-282, an amendment by Toby Moffett, D-Conn., to delete the language in the bill prohibiting the Economic Regulatory Administration (ERA) from using any of the funds to pay for public participation in hearings before the ERA. *(Vote 412, p. 118-H)*
- Accepted, by voice vote, an amendment by John D. Dingell, D-Mich., to require that the $4 billion appropriated for fiscal 1979 and 1980 for purchase of oil for the Strategic Petroleum Reserve be spent in fiscal 1979 only.
- Accepted by voice vote an amendment by Carlos J. Moorhead, R-Calif., to cut the appropriations for the energy extension service by $10 million.

Provisions

As passed by the House, HR 12932 appropriated the following amounts:

Agency	Budget Request	House Amount
Department of Interior	$ 4,150,573,000	$ 4,242,184,000
Department of Energy	6,285,216,000	5,960,368,000
Forest Service	1,342,208,000	1,380,526,000
Other Agencies	1,096,760,000	1,107,466,000
Total	$12,874,757,000	$12,690,544,000

Senate Committee Action

The Senate Appropriations Committee wielded its budgetary knife a bit before ordering HR 12932 reported Aug. 2 (S Rept 95-1063).

The panel pared $1.3 billion from Carter's $12.83 billion request. The committee urged total spending of $11,494,763,000. That was almost $1.2 billion less than the House approved for the same programs.

The biggest single cutback was a $1.2 billion reduction in the Energy Department's strategic oil reserve program.

Other heavy cuts were recommended in Interior Department programs to acquire additional recreational lands and to start a natural heritage preservation program, which had not been established by legislation. Reductions also reflected decisions to defer anticipated costs of fire-fighting and various low-priority Interior programs.

Offsetting some of the cutbacks were committee recommendations to boost spending for programs related to renewed leasing of coal tracts, for environmental studies of the Outer Continental Shelf and for a variety of energy research projects.

Interior Department

The panel urged $4.2 billion for the Interior Department, $94.3 million more than the administration requested but $38.9 million less than the House approved. Specific Interior Department subcategories included:

Bureau of Land Management. The panel urged appropriations of $488.7 million for the Bureau of Land Management (BLM) budget, $623,000 more than the administration had sought but $21.4 million less than the House approved.

Most of the difference stemmed from a recommended deferral of advance firefighting expenses totaling $25.2 million. The panel pointed out that apart from that decision, its BLM recommendations involved $24.8 million in program funding boosts.

The panel included two instructions to the agency. First, it noted "with some concern the steady growth of funds devoted to planning, inventory, study and data management activities, often at the expense of resource management." Nearly one-fifth of the agency budget was devoted to paperwork studies, the panel said.

Therefore, the committee told the agency that though studies were important and necessary, the agency's first priority must remain the actual management of resources.

The panel also noted that it was "disturbed over reports of harassment, prosecution and conviction" of people homesteading on Alaskan public lands.

"The few who seek a wilderness experience" there had little or no adverse environmental impact, the report said, "and the committee seriously questions the cost-effectiveness of federal pursuit and harassment. The department should call a halt to this practice immediately."

Heritage Conservation. The committee deleted $5.6 million sought by the administration for a natural heritage preservation program "since the legislative proposals to initiate this program have never materialized. The committee feels a natural heritage program needs to be clearly defined before it can be properly funded."

Land and Water Conservation Fund. Overall, the committee recommended $645.2 million for the fund, $647,000 below the House amount, but $45.2 million more than fiscal 1978.

For federal programs involving land acquisition for the Park Service, the Forest Service, the U.S. Fish and Wildlife Service and related agencies funded through the fund, the committee generally agreed to House-passed reductions of $103.6 million. The only change from the House reductions, the report said, was the restoration of $1 million trimmed by the House from the $7.9 million request for money for the C&O Canal National Historical Park in the Washington, D.C., area.

The panel also urged spending $100 million more than the administration sought to compensate landowners whose property was taken by legislation under the Redwood National Park Expansion Act of 1978 (PL 95-250).

That amount, combined with $205 million pending in a supplemental fiscal 1978 request, would provide the bulk of the $359 million estimated to be needed to cover park expansion costs, the report said. *(Supplemental appropriations bill, p. 70)*

Historic Preservation. The committee recommended spending $100 million for this program, aimed at 2,500 projects. The amount was $55 million more than the administration sought and $40 million more than the House approved.

Of the increase, $5 million was earmarked for maritime projects, such as preservation of historic ships.

Alaska Naval Oil Reserves. The committee urged spending almost $252 million to explore the naval oil reserve in Alaska, $66.5 million above the administration request and $36 million more than the House thought necessary.

The Senate boost, the report explained, equaled the original Navy request. The proposed budget submitted by the administration would have wound down the program and would not have initiated any drilling through fiscal 1980, the report said.

Indian Affairs. The Bureau of Indian Affairs received $755 million in fiscal 1979 under the Senate committee version, $6.2 million less than the administration sought and $36 million less than the House approved.

The committee said investigations launched at its direction by the General Accounting Office (GAO) "largely substantiated the committee's concern that poor program management by the Bureau of Indian Affairs was undercutting Indian services and slowing the implementation of congressional reforms and policies."

The Interior Department and the bureau itself did not dispute those GAO findings, the report said. "The result has been a continuing failure to deliver adequate services to the Indian people despite increased funding," the report said.

Spending for Indian programs had more than quadrupled over the past decade, the report said.

The committee directed the bureau to review its procedures for distributing money to tribes. It charged that Indian schools were "badly managed" and "underutilized" and were characterized by "wide variation in per-pupil funding." It directed the bureau to investigate the Indian education program and report back to the Senate and House Appropriations Committees by Jan. 30, 1979.

Energy Department

The Senate committee voted sharp funding cuts wrapped in scathing language for those Energy Department programs in the bill.

Altogether the panel recommended $4.8 billion for Energy programs, $1.4 billion below the Energy Department request and $1.1 billion less than the House provided. The committee's recommendation held spending for those programs to about 1 percent more than fiscal 1978, the report said.

The largest cut was in the administration's $4.2 billion request for the strategic oil reserve program, designed to cushion the United States against an interruption of oil imports. The committee recommended $3.2 million, about $1.2 million below the administration request and $1 million below the House amount.

"The committee believes the Department of Energy badly overestimated its two year needs for oil purchases," the report said. The request was for fiscal 1979 and 1980. Continued slippage in the program schedule and unanticipated problems in storing the oil "cast doubt on the department's ability to obligate effectively even the $3 billion allowance within the allowed time period," the report said.

The cutback, the committee stressed, was merely a deferral of spending on a program the nation was firmly committed to.

The panel was no less harsh on the Energy Department as a whole. "There is real concern," the report said, ". . . that the new department has serious management and coordination problems that contribute to a lack of a coherent, decisive national energy policy.

". . . As a whole the department's budget justifications were totally inadequate," the report continued.

Similar criticism of the department and its budget was voiced by the House Committees on Commerce and on Appropriations.

The Senate committee's chiding did not stop with the department; Congress also came in for criticism. "Of deep concern to the committee is the fact that most of the department's appropriations recommended in the bill — again this year — are not authorized," the report said.

"This continuing failure of Congress to meet timely spending authorizations and a national energy program must also share the blame for the nation's failure to adopt a vigorous and effective energy policy," the committee said.

That was a reference to the fact that in both chambers in 1978, as in 1977, the measures actually appropriating funds for the Energy Department were passed before the legislation authorizing those funds to be spent. This was contrary to the normal congressional process where authorization bills were intended to set limits for later appropriations.

The authorization bills were held up in 1978 because the leadership in the House and Senate feared policy fights on those bills might endanger chances of passing Carter's energy program. The leadership wanted to push through as much of the Carter program as possible, especially the sensitive natural gas pricing compromise, before allowing an opportunity for divisive policy fights on the authorization bills to arise. Eventually, time ran out and the authorization bills were not passed in 1978.

Fossil Energy. The committee urged spending $589.8 million on fossil energy research programs, $47.7 million less than the administration sought and $25 million less than the House approved.

In that area, the committee recommended a $132 million boost in the administration request for funds to build two solvent refined coal liquefaction plants, which brought the total for them to $152 million.

Also winning generous funding boosts were energy research programs dealing with magnetohydrodynamics and enhanced recovery of oil and natural gas from existing wells.

Conservation. Energy conservation programs won $754 million from the Senate panel, $173.7 million less than the administration wanted and almost $143 million less than the House approved.

The major difference lay in a cutback of $195.6 million for programs aimed at assisting state and local energy conservation programs. The reduction was to compensate for funds appropriated but not spent to carry out portions of Carter's energy program.

Economic Regulatory Administration. The panel cut the administration's request only slightly for this agency, which was responsible for enforcing the complex Energy Department fuel price and allocation programs. The administration asked for $98.9 million; the panel approved $94.7 million.

The panel recommended the deletion of House-passed terms forbidding the agency to provide government funding for intervenors in proceedings before it.

Energy Information Administration. Similarly, the committee cut the administration request for this agency only slightly, from $63.4 million down to $59.3 million.

Senate Floor Action

After resolving a series of serious policy fights the Senate Aug. 9 passed a bill making $11,566,413,000 in appropriations (HR 12932). The vote was 85-5. *(Vote 300, p. 46-S)*

Overall, the Senate version of the Interior spending bill was lean compared to what was sought by the Carter administration and approved by the House.

The president had requested $12.8 billion. The House, which cut Carter's request only slightly, funded expenditures of $12.7 billion.

The Senate Appropriations Committee had recommended total funding of $11.49 billion. But the Senate approved five floor amendments that boosted spending by a total of $71,650,000. Three other amendments, which did not require funding hikes, also were approved.

In some cases, cuts made by the Senate were admittedly inspired by political strategy as much as by perceived needs for reduced spending, according to Walter (Dee) Huddleston, D-Ky., the measure's floor manager.

"I also want to point out to the Senate that there are some decreases that have been made in order to get the attention of our colleagues in the House as we go to conference," Huddleston said. "It is not an unknown tactic. . . ."

Among the major decisions reflected in the legislation was the inclusion of $100 million unsought by the administration to cover costs of expanding the Redwood National Park in Northern California.

Also noteworthy was the decision by the Senate Appropriations Committee to slice more than one-quarter of the $4.2 billion sought by the Carter administration to buy more oil for the strategic petroleum reserve program. The Senate did not try to restore the money the committee had trimmed for that program.

The appropriations bill became the vehicle for several important policy fights. During floor debate, the Senate:

- Rejected a move to slice by 2 percent most of the programs funded in the bill.
- Insisted that work continue on contested construction projects along the Colorado River if an environmental impact statement had been approved for each project.

● Deflected an attempt to legislate on the volatile subject of Alaska land use. A separate Alaska bill failed to reach the Senate floor in 1978.

● Heard several senior leaders berate the Senate for legislating in appropriations bills.

● Compromised on a divisive Energy Department program to subsidize imports of certain refined oil products by East Coast refiners and marketers.

Roth Spending Cut

William V. Roth Jr., R-Del., offered an amendment to cut most of the programs funded in HR 12932 by 2 percent, a response to the so-called "taxpayers' revolt" begun by proposition 13 in California.

Roth termed his 2 percent reduction an "efficiency cut" that would save taxpayers $129 million. ". . . [I]s there anyone in this chamber who can stand up and argue that there is not at least 2 percent administrative slack and fat in every appropriations bill to come before us this year...?" Roth asked.

There were several. Ted Stevens, R-Alaska, led off.

"The increases that the senator from Delaware in this case seeks to eliminate were added in subcommittee in response to specific requests from senators who are on this floor," Stevens said pointedly.

Stevens said if Roth's amendment were adopted, he would urge returning the bill to committee and eliminating "the add-ons requested by any member who votes for the Roth amendment. . . ."

Senate Majority Leader Robert C. Byrd, D-W.Va., who also was chairman of the Appropriations Interior Subcommittee that reported the bill, agreed with Stevens.

Edmund S. Muskie, D-Maine, added that Roth's attempt to cut government spending was the "meat ax approach" that Congress used before its existing budget process was adopted. The old approach "never worked," Muskie said.

Roth lost when the Senate voted 68-25 to table his amendment. *(Vote 296, p. 45-S)*

Oil Pricing

The fight over oil pricing involved a price break for East Coast users of home heating and residual fuel oil, although the amount finally agreed on was less than half that proposed by the Carter administration.

By adopting the compromise, engineered by J. Bennett Johnston, D-La., the Senate was able to avoid a threatened filibuster by northeastern senators who initially feared Johnston would try to block any plan to provide a break on East Coast oil prices.

The action centered on a plan announced June 15 by the Energy Department to increase subsidies to importers of residual fuel oil and home heating oil under the department's complex entitlements program. That program was designed to equalize costs of oil acquisition among the nation's oil refiners. Refiners of domestically produced oil could buy it more cheaply than imported oil. The price of domestic oil was federally controlled. Imported oil prices were dictated by the Organization of Petroleum Exporting Countries (OPEC).

Under the entitlements program, refiners of domestic oil contributed to a federal fund that was disbursed as "entitlements" — or subsidies — to refiners dependent on expensive foreign oil. The fund transferred about $200 million per month among refiners.

Importers of residual fuel oil, a refined product, received a 30 percent entitlement of about 60 cents a barrel. The Energy Department plan would have boosted that to a 100 percent entitlement of about $2 per barrel.

Johnston argued that the Energy Department plan would transfer about $400 million annually to importers of residual fuel oil, most of whom were located on the East Coast, primarily in New England. Of that $400 million, he said, $250 million would be drawn from states not on the East Coast.

Johnston said the plan would lead to higher oil imports and would cause foreign suppliers to raise their prices. Finally, he said, a break for the East Coast would be unfair to other regions. "It was never intended that a $200 million a month slush fund be created to reward the president's friends and punish his enemies," Johnston said.

Defenders of the plan, mostly from the East Coast, said the price break would treat East Coast consumers equitably rather than forcing them to pay more for oil than citizens elsewhere.

To avoid the filibuster, Johnston worked out a compromise with northeastern senators that boosted the existing 30 percent entitlement to 50 percent, but the extra 20 percent would expire July 1, 1979. The administration would have boosted the subsidy to 100 percent. Johnston termed his compromise a "five-sevenths victory and a two-sevenths loss. . . . It is arbitrary, classic compromise."

By a 65-31 vote, the Senate ruled the compromise was germane to the bill. Johnston's amendment then was adopted, 53-40. *(Vote 298, p. 45-S; vote 299, p. 46-S)*

Colorado River

Howard W. Cannon, D-Nev., offered an amendment to allow construction to proceed on water projects already begun in the Colorado River basin if an approved environmental impact statement had been filed on each one.

Cannon said the amendment was a response to a suit by the Environmental Defense Fund that sought an injunction against further construction of projects in the basin until a comprehensive environmental impact statement had been completed assessing the basin-wide consequences of each project.

Cannon said some 20 water projects were under construction in the basin — including such giants as the central Arizona project, the central Utah project and the southern Nevada project — and that each had filed an approved impact statement individually. "The requirement of the law, as it is now understood, has been fully met," Cannon said. The suit would have environmental laws reinterpreted contrary to congressional intent, he said. Court rulings in favor of the petitioners could idle those multi-billion dollar projects for years at high cost.

Stevens agreed, saying he had been one of two original cosponsors of the National Environmental Policy Act of 1969 (PL 91-190), which required environmental impact statements. "We never envisioned . . . these runaway court decisions which would lead to severe personal loss and excessive taxpayer costs . . . .," he said. *(PL 91-190, Congress and the Nation, Vol. III, p. 748)*

Paul Laxalt, R-Nev., said the suit "represents a radical departure in policy. We know there is a fight literally to the death involving the waters of the West. . . . [W]ater in the West is our lifeblood. It is the whole ball game. . . ."

Muskie was the first senator to object to the amendment. "I can only conclude that it is the desire, unstated, to take an action today which would persuade the courts that the Congress has changed its mind and has interpreted the National Environmental Policy Act to mean that a comprehensive impact statement is not required," Muskie said.

"If that is really what the sponsors of this amendment are hanging on to get, I say the place to decide that legislatively is in legislation specifically to that point, fully considered in committee and fully debated on the floor. I am not prepared to surrender it as the price of harmony and regional comity on the floor of the Senate this afternoon," said Muskie, considered by many the leading overseer of environmental legislation in the Senate.

Muskie asserted that the amendment was out of order because it was legislation on an appropriations bill.

Legislating with Appropriations

Muskie's point of order opened a heated debate on the practice of attaching legislative policy issues to appropriations bills.

"I thought we had legislative committees around here to deal with policy," Muskie fumed. "Anyone reading this amendment who could conclude that it is not about as blatant an example of out and out legislation on an appropriations bill, simply cannot read. . . ."

". . . [I]f this trend continues, we need only two committees,... and maybe only the Appropriations Committee, because it is no longer just abortion that comes to us via appropriation bills, it is every conceivable issue," Muskie said, a reference to the perennial controversy over federal payments for abortions that often occurred over the Labor-Health, Education and Welfare appropriations bill. *(1978 version, p. 105)*

The Senate then voted 53-40 to rule the Cannon amendment germane to the appropriations bill. *(Vote 294, p. 45-2)*

After the vote, Frank Church, D-Idaho, and Warren G. Magnuson, D-Wash., joined Muskie in deploring the tendency to legislate through appropriations bills. But that fight was over for the moment, while the Cannon amendment remained unresolved.

". . . [I]n five hours of negotiation today, I offered the sponsors of this amendment everything they asked for except one thing," Muskie said. "I would not concede the right to amend the National Environmental Policy Act with respect to this issue on an appropriation bill. I said the question must be left to the courts, where it is now, or it should be brought to the Senate via the legislative process. . . .

Cannon's amendment then was adopted by a division vote. But Howard M. Metzenbaum, D-Ohio, moved to reconsider. Carl T. Curtis, R-Nev., moved to table, and thus kill, Metzenbaum's motion. Curtis' motion won, 59-33, which settled the issue. *(Vote 295, p. 45-S)*

Alaska Lands

Stevens introduced an amendment designed to block the administration from threatened action to tie up as much as 100 million federal acres in Alaska by administrative order if Congress did not act in 1978 to create park land from that territory.

Secretary of the Interior Cecil D. Andrus had threatened to designate the 100 million acres as national monuments if legislation expanding park land in Alaska did not pass in 1978, which it did not.

Stevens' amendment would have limited the secretary's authority to establish national monuments of more than 5,000 acres. "To create more than 100 million acres of national monuments in a state . . . would be contrary to common sense and would be an absolutely capricious exercise of discretionary authority," Stevens argued.

The amendment threatened to open up the whole debate over Alaska lands. But the discussion was cut short by Henry M. Jackson, D-Wash., chairman of the Energy and Natural Resources Committee, which was attempting to write an Alaska lands bill for action in 1978. Jackson objected to Stevens' amendment, and Stevens withdrew it.

In other action, the Senate adopted by voice vote:

- An amendment by Huddleston, offered on behalf of Sam Nunn, D-Ga., which added $45 million for land acquisition for the Chattahoochee River National Recreation Area in Georgia. Legislation (PL 95-344) authorizing establishment of the park was cleared by Congress Aug. 3 and signed by the president Aug. 15.
- An amendment by Dennis DeConcini, D-Ariz., which added $250,000 for the Bureau of Indian Affairs to maintain the Papago Farms Agricultural Development Project in Arizona.
- An amendment by Wendell H. Ford, D-Ky., which added $20 million for a loan guarantee program to demonstrate alternative fuels.
- Two amendments by Floyd K. Haskell, D-Colo., which added $1.4 million for an oil shale demonstration project and $5 million for research on developing an advanced oil shale recovery technology.
- An amendment by Edward M. Kennedy, D-Mass., transferring to the Community Services Administration from the Energy Department administrative responsibility for about $99.5 million for programs aimed at insulating homes and buildings.

Provisions

As passed by the Senate, HR 12932 appropriated the following amounts:

Agency	Budget Request	Senate Amount
Department of Interior	$ 4,108,973,000	$ 4,248,531,000
Department of Energy	6,283,005,000	4,862,157,000
Other Agencies	2,438,968,000	2,455,725,000
TOTAL	$12,830,946,000	$11,566,413,000

Conference, Final Action

The conference report on the bill was filed Sept. 29 (H Rept 95-1672). The House adopted the report Oct. 5 by a vote of 382-12 and the Senate by a 79-5 margin on Oct. 7. *(House vote 773, p. 220-H; Senate vote 456, p. 67-S)*

INTERIOR DEPARTMENT

The conference committee approved a $4.3 billion budget for the Interior Department, an increase of $89 million more than the Senate version and $95 million more than the House bill.

The biggest single increase approved by the conferees was in the appropriation for the Land and Water Conservation Fund. The $737 million approved was $91 million higher than the House total and $47 million greater than the Senate version.

Colorado River Projects

Conferees went along with the Senate amendment on the Colorado River projects. And the House voted Oct. 2, 206-186, to agree. *(Vote 777, p. 220-H)*

In House floor debate, supporters of the amendment said the comprehensive environmental statement would be an unnecessary hindrance to water projects that had already passed individual environmental impact standards.

House Minority Leader John J. Rhodes, R-Ariz., argued that "the quality of water in the Colorado basin has been studied and studied and studied. I do not know any subject in the country which has received more attention."

And Rep. James P. (Jim) Johnson, R-Colo., said the study demanded by environmentalists "will do nothing more than wind up killing projects. I think that there is a concerted effort that is going on in the country to kill the water development in the Colorado River basin."

Debate on the amendment pitted environmentalist-oriented legislators against each other.

Rep. Paul N. McCloskey Jr., R-Calif., opposed the amendment, even though he said he was not sure that existing law required the comprehensive study sought by the environmental groups.

But Rep. Morris K. Udall, D-Ariz., supported the amendment because one of the contested projects would provide water to his district.

Opponents of the amendment said the basin-wide environmental impact study was needed to determine what the combined effect of the water projects would be on the Colorado River. They noted that a 1976 federal court decision (*Kleppe v. Sierra Club*) said the comprehensive study was required by the National Environmental Policy Act.

Approval of the amendment "would set an ominous precedent for exemptions from the legal requirements" of the environmental policy act, said Rep. James M. Jeffords, R-Vt.

Other major provisions involving the Interior Department were:

- **Alaska Petroleum Reserve.** The bill required speedier exploration than the administration had proposed of the National Petroleum Reserve in northern Alaska. The bill added $30.5 million to the administration request for preparation for oil and gas field drilling in 1980. The bill also added $15 million to the administration request to complete current gas drilling in the Barrow area, but required a study before further drilling could be started.
- **Redwood Park.** The bill provided $100 million to compensate landowners whose property was taken under the Redwood National Park Expansion Act of 1978 (PL 95-250). That amount was in addition to $205 million included in the 1978 second supplemental appropriation (PL 95-355) enacted in August. *(Supplemental appropriation, p. 70)*
- **Lake Tahoe.** The bill appropriated $12.5 million for acquisition of land in the Lake Tahoe area, to slow down development of the area. The states of California and Nevada were to each match half the federal grant, and to agree not to permit additional gambling establishments in the area.
- **Chattahoochee River.** The bill appropriated $30 million for land acquisition for the Chattahoochee River National Recreation Area in Georgia. Legislation (PL 95-344) creating the park was signed by President Carter Aug. 15.
- **Wild Horses.** The bill requested the Bureau of Land Management to review its wild horse and burro program, including possible legislation to allow the bureau to sell the animals to private individuals.
- **Alaska Homesteaders.** The bill took a middle road on the issue of whether the Bureau of Land Management should try to evict homesteaders on Alaska public lands. The Senate Appropriations Committee had criticized the bureau for "harassment, prosecution and conviction" of the homesteaders. The conference report said "individuals using the public lands for a wilderness experience on a temporary basis or for other legitimate uses of public lands should not be subject to harassment and prosecution. The policy of the Bureau of Land Management on the use of public lands should be reasonable as long as indiscriminate unauthorized use is not allowed."
- **Steel Shot.** The bill prohibited the U.S. Fish and Wildlife Service from enforcing a controversial requirement that waterfowl hunters use steel, rather than lead, shot. The requirement could be enforced only in states where it had been approved by state officials.

ENERGY DEPARTMENT

The bill appropriated $4.7 billion for various fossil energy-related agencies in the Energy Department. That represented a $1.6 billion reduction from the administration request.

Major provisions involving the department were:

- **Oil Pricing.** The House adopted the Senate amendment giving East Coast refiners of home heating and residual fuel oil a price break.
- **Strategic Petroleum Reserve.** The bill appropriated $3 billion for the strategic oil reserve program, designed to cushion the United States against an interruption of oil imports, such as the 1973 Arab oil embargo. The administration had requested $4.2 billion for the program, including partial funding for fiscal 1980. But the Senate Appropriations Committee cut the $1.2 billion requested for fiscal 1980 because purchases of oil for the reserve were behind schedule. The committee said the money it cut would be appropriated in fiscal 1980. The conferees agreed with that decision.
- **Energy Conservation.** The conference committee slashed $220 million from the administration request for energy conservation programs. The most drastic cut was in a program of grants to schools and hospitals for energy conservation programs. The administration had proposed a $300.5 million program for fiscal 1979. The Senate Appropriations Committee cut that to $100.1 million — a figure adopted by the conference committee. That appropriation was contingent on enactment of the administration's energy conservation bill (HR 5037) which authorized the program. The Senate adopted the conference report on HR 5037 Oct. 9 and the House adopted the report Oct. 15. *(Provisions, see story, Energy chapter.)*
- **Synthetic Fuel Plants.** The bill appropriated $90 million for construction of two plants that would derive clean synthetic fuels from coal. The administration had proposed building one plant, and the Senate added another $86 million plant. The conference committee compromised with $50 million for one plant and $40 million for another.
- **Public Participation.** The bill prohibited the Economic Regulatory Administration from using any of its funds to pay for public participation in hearings before that agency. The administration regulated oil pricing, allocations and imports.

Foreign Aid Funds Survive 1978 Attacks

Reminded by American labor and industry earlier in 1978 of the commercial benefits to the United States from federal foreign aid programs, Congress Oct. 13 gave final approval to a $9.1 billion appropriations bill (HR 12931 — PL 95-481) for fiscal 1979.

That measure was $1.3 billion less than requested by the administration. But until labor and business lobbyists pointed out to the House during the summer that much of the aid is used to purchase goods and services in the United States, the difference looked as if it would be far greater.

There was even talk that, in the wake of California's tax-cutting Proposition 13, no foreign aid bill could survive in 1978. Critics, including the chairman of the House subcommittee in charge of the funding bill, contended that U.S. contributions to international lending institutions in particular were wasteful and ineffective, often failing to reach the poor.

The final bill was almost $2 billion larger than the House version but most of that was due to a $1.8 billion Senate addition as the U.S. contribution to the International Monetary Fund's new Witteveen Facility. (The money had not been authorized when the House passed HR 12931.) This is an effort by the IMF to help developing nations hit by rapidly rising energy costs. With that amount excluded, the final bill was only about $127 million more than the House version. The final measure was $68 million under the Senate bill. *(IMF loan program, p. 424)*

As in previous years, the Middle East drew the lion's share of the appropriations. Israel was allocated $785 million in economic aid plus $550 million in grants to purchase U.S. military equipment. Egypt drew $750 million in economic aid channeled to the region for promoting long-term peace. Jordan received $93 million and Syria $90 million.

The Syrian funds, however, were momentarily endangered when the House, reacting to that country's intrusion into Lebanon, cut the aid. But the Senate restored the money — and conferees agreed after a long struggle — in order to help win Syria's support for the Camp David peace accords. The Syrian funds weren't earmarked in the bill as they had been before the House cut them out. But the total amount allowed for economic support included $90 million for that purpose. *(Israel-Egypt Camp David Accord, p. 430)*

Provisions

As cleared by Congress, HR 12931 appropriated the following amounts for fiscal 1979:

	Administration Request	Final Appropriation
Title I — Foreign Assistance		
Agriculture/nutrition	$ 673,181,000	$ 605,000,000
Population planning	205,445,000	185,000,000
Health	148,494,000	130,000,000
Education/human resources	109,036,000	97,000,000
Technical aid, energy/other	126,244,000	115,000,000
International organizations	282,150,000	260,000,000
American schools, hospitals	8,000,000	25,000,000
Contingency fund	5,000,000	3,000,000
Disaster assistance	25,000,000	20,000,000
African refugees	——	15,000,000
Sahel development	90,000,000	75,000,000
Narcotics control	40,000,000	38,500,000
Foreign Service fund	24,820,000	24,820,000
Economic support fund	1,875,000,000	1,882,000,000
Peacekeeping operations	29,400,000	27,400,000
AID operations	261,000,000	254,000,000
Israel-U.S. agriculture fund	40,000,000	40,000,000
Inter-American Foundation	7,882,000	10,000,000
Military Assistance	133,500,000	83,375,000
Military training	32,100,000	27,900,000
Title II — Military Credit Sales	674,300,000	654,500,000
Title III — Other Foreign Aid		
Peace Corps	95,135,000	95,000,000
Migration, refugees	90,836,000	111,544,200
U.S. migration, refugee fund	15,000,000	9,500,000
Asian Development Bank	309,643,124	265,000,000
Inter-American Development Bank	914,005,483	763,728,483
International Bank for Reconstruction and Development	665,904,212	163,079,165
International Finance Corp.	40,045,100	40,045,100
International Development Assn.	1,550,000,000	1,258,000,000
African Development Fund	25,000,000	25,000,000
Title IV — Export-Import Bank (limitation on program, expenses)	(5,360,860,000)	(5,360,860,000)
Title V — Witteveen Facility	1,831,640,000	1,831,640,000
Tin Buffer Stock	60,000,000	——
Total	$10,387,760,919	$9,135,031,948

The bill also:

Foreign Assistance — Title I

- Limited economic assistance appropriated for a Yaws immunization program in West Africa to $5 million.
- Provided that development loans to nations whose annual per capita gross national product exceeds $550 but is less than $900 shall be repayable within 25 years and loans to countries over that level shall be repayable in 20 years.
- Prohibited U.S. contributions to the United Nations University in Tokyo.
- Earmarked $3 million for Israeli students studying in U.S.-sponsored centers in Arab countries and Arab students studying in U.S. centers in Israel.
- Earmarked $1 million to control locust plagues in Africa.
- Limited any U.S. contribution to the Sahel development program to 10 percent of all contributions to the program.
- Provided that funds for certain aid programs could not be obligated for others unless the Appropriations Committees were notified 15 days in advance.
- Allocated, in the bill, $785 million in economic support funds for Israel, $750 million for Egypt and $93 million for Jordan. Provided — without earmarking in the bill — $90 million for Syria.
- Allocated $45 million for U.S. aid to southern Africa and provided that not more than $5 million be appropriated for international relief organizations for refugee assistance in Rhodesia.
- Provided that no economic funds be used for a U.S. contribution to the United Nations Relief and Works Agency.
- Provided that not more than $97 million be appropriated for Agency for International Development

Washington expenses and not more than $700,000 for hiring consultants.

- Limited AID personal service contracts to $10 million.
- Established a $210,375,000 ceiling on unobligated and deobligated fiscal 1977 and 1978 funds for military assistance programs. A $30,915,000 ceiling was placed on military training funds.
- Provided a 15 day period for notifying the Appropriations committees of obligations of military aid funds previously deobligated in fiscal 1978.
- Prohibited purchases of new automobiles outside the United States from military aid funds.
- Prohibited the use of funds for the construction of water projects which had not met U.S. construction standards.
- Provided that no more than 15 percent of any appropriation could be obligated or reserved during the last month of availability except for specified programs.
- Allowed fiscal 1978 unobligated balances for international disaster assistance, Middle East special requirements, refugee and migration assistance to carry over to fiscal 1979.
- Barred the use of funds to pay persons serving in the armed forces of recipient nations.
- Prohibited the United States to pay the dues of any other United Nations member.
- Prohibited direct assistance to Uganda, Cambodia, Laos or Vietnam, but exempted payments to graduate students from Uganda studying at U.S. institutions.
- Limited the official residence expenses of the Agency for International Development in fiscal 1979 to $118,000.
- Limited AID entertainment expenses to $13,000.
- Limited AID representation allowances to $96,000.
- Barred funds to any government for aiding its efforts to repress human rights.
- Prohibited use of appropriations for financing the export of nuclear equipment and for training foreign nationals in nuclear fields.
- Prohibited direct U.S. aid to Mozambique or Angola, except to finance the completion of training of Angolan students begun before fiscal 1978.
- Prohibited the transfer of funds between appropriation accounts without the written prior approval of the Appropriations committees.
- Prohibited the use of the Foreign Service Retirement and Disability Fund for paying certain State Department retirees on the basis of their highest one year of service.

Military Credits — Title II

- Allocated $1 billion in military credit sales to Israel, and provided $673,960,000 to finance the fiscal 1979 sales program.

Other Foreign Aid — Title III

- Limited to $320,000 funds available for the United Nations Volunteer Program.
- Barred the use of any Peace Corps funds to pay for abortions.
- Directed the administration to present to Congress in fiscal 1980 a plan to consolidate overseas refugee programs in AID, or an alternative plan if the administration objected to this approach.
- Earmarked $20 million for the resettlement of Soviet and other refugees in the United States on an equitable basis.
- Limited the salaries of the U.S. directors to the international banks to level IV of the executive schedule and alternate directors to level V.
- Stated as the sense of Congress that future U.S. contributions to the international financial institutions should not exceed the following percentages: Asian Development Bank, 16.3 percent; Asian Development Fund, 22.2 percent; African Development Bank, 18 percent; Inter-American Bank, 34.5 percent; Inter-American Bank Fund for Special Operations, 40 percent; International Bank for Reconstruction and Development, 24 percent; International Development Association, 25 percent; International Finance Corporation, 23 percent.

Export-Import Bank — Title IV

- Barred the Export-Import Bank from making loans for the export of nuclear equipment, fuel and services to any nation, other than a nuclear-weapon state, that has detonated a nuclear explosive after the date of enactment.

IMF — Title V

- Limited the salary of the U.S. executive director to the International Monetary Fund to level IV of the executive schedule and the alternate U.S. executive director to level V.

General — Title VI

- Prohibited aid to be used for propaganda purposes within the United States unless authorized by Congress.
- Prevented any appropriations from remaining available for obligation beyond the current fiscal year unless provided in the bill.
- Prohibited aid to any country in default for more than one year on repayment of loans owed the United States.
- Barred use of funds for the Office of Inspector General of Foreign Assistance.
- Prohibited aid to international financial institutions if U.S. representatives cannot obtain loan information.
- Barred use of funds for direct aid or trade with Cuba.
- Prohibited use of funds appropriated for the Export-Import Bank and for direct foreign aid for any government which aids terrorism, unless the president finds the national security requires otherwise.
- Provided that no direct U.S. aid or funds contributed to the Export-Import Bank and the Overseas Private Investment Corporation shall be used for any loan to a nation producing a commodity in surplus on world markets and if harmful to U.S. producers. But the provision would not apply to the Export-Import Bank if its board of directors determined that the benefits to U.S. industry and employment outweigh the injury to U.S. producers of the competing product.
- Directed U.S. executive directors to the international financial institutions to use the voice and vote of the United States to oppose aid by these institutions to other nations for the production of commodities in surplus on world markets or likely to cause injury to U.S. producers.
- Required the president to consult with other nations to develop a standard governing the allocation of development assistance for the production and export of commodities.
- Stated that the president direct the U.S. representatives to the international banks to seek to establish human rights standards to be considered in connection with loan applications.

House Committee Action

Reported by the House Appropriations Committee June 1 (H Rept 95-1250), HR 12931 appropriated $7,352,761,483 in foreign assistance: $3.8 billion in economic aid, $648 million in military credit sales, and $2.8 billion for other foreign aid programs.

Middle East

A major portion of the bill — 32 percent — was earmarked for aid programs to the Middle East where, the committee said, the United States has an interest in the security of Israel, improved relations with the Arab states and a solution to oil supply and price problems. Accordingly, the committee allocated $785 million in security aid for Israel, $750 million for Egypt, $90 million for Syria and $93 million for Jordan — the same amounts requested by the Carter administration and appropriated in 1977.

Human Rights, Arms Sales

Following the lead of the House International Relations Committee, the Appropriations panel chopped $5 million from the administration's $18.1 million military aid request for the Philippines because of alleged human rights violations by the Ferdinand Marcos government. *(Foreign aid authorization, p. 416)*

The committee also cut the administration's $32.1 million request for military education and training programs overseas by 20 percent because of "human rights concerns, as well as the failure to justify many of its military aid programs on national security grounds." The $672.5 million administration request for underwriting military sales credit programs also was cut by 20 percent after Israel, which was allocated $500 million, was exempted. (Each year, Israel is allowed to borrow $1 billion for weapons purchases, but $500 million of this total is forgiven and thus must be appropriated.)

The committee also renewed past criticism of U.S. arms sales to foreign nations. The panel noted that sales had tripled in the last decade with the "vast majority" of them "targeted at the Middle East-Persian Gulf region." As a result, the report argued, "many . . . developing nations are spending huge amounts on their military establishments while their poor live with little prospect of improvement."

The committee also was critical of the increasing sale of sophisticated weapons. "Some countries, such as Iran, have received equipment that is far too advanced in design to be in their inventories," the report said.

Commodities

Justifying its provisions to instruct U.S. officials to vote against loans to countries that compete against U.S. farm commodities, the Appropriations Committee said that it "certainly was not advocating a protectionist stance regarding U.S. trade or assistance to foreign countries." But the committee said it had "difficulty in understanding why we have to provide help in financing foreign producers of competitive commodities. . . ."

Lending Institutions

About one-third of the appropriations were for U.S. contributions to six international lending institutions. The administration had requested $3.5 billion, but the committee reduced this by $876.6 million, to $2.6 billion, still $702.5 million above the fiscal 1978 appropriation level.

The size of the administration's request and the amount of increase over fiscal 1978, however, can be misleading.

The 1979 boost was necessary to fund U.S. pledges to the institutions that have been authorized by Congress but never funded. Had this money been appropriated when originally requested, the fiscal 1979 budget request would have exceeded the 1978 request by $54 million rather than the $835 million required.

The size of the administration's appropriations request also included $1.4 billion (40 percent of the total) for "callable capital" — loan guarantees requiring no budget outlay — that allow the lending institutions to stand behind private loans to developing nations. Should the borrowing nations default — this has never happened — the lending institution then would require member nations to contribute some of its callable funds to pay bondholders.

The remainder of the requested funds, $2.1 billion, was for "paid-in capital" — that is, direct cash transfers to the institutions for assistance to the developing countries.

Committee Recommendations. Of the $2.6 billion total approved by the committee, $966.4 million was for callable capital to six international financial institutions. The balance of the total was for paid-in capital.

Following are the banks for which appropriations were requested, the amount approved by the committee in callable and paid-in capital and the purpose of the institution.

Asian Development Bank. Paid-in: $15 million; callable: $135 million. Established in 1966, the bank's lending activities center on conventional loans to nations in Asia and the Pacific region for agricultural projects. A component — the Asian Development Fund — was created in 1974 to provide loans on concessionary terms; $70.5 million in paid-in capital was provided for this facility by the committee.

Inter-American Development Bank. Paid-in: $27.3 million; callable: $561.4 million. Established in 1959, the bank provides conventional loans to Latin nations for industrial and power projects. Concessionary (low interest) loans are provided by the Fund for Special Operations created in 1965 and allocated $225.3 million in paid-in capital by the Appropriations Committee.

African Development Fund. Paid-in: $25 million. Established in 1973, the fund provides concessionary loans for agricultural and transportation projects in Africa.

International Bank for Reconstruction and Development (World Bank). Paid-in: $30 million; callable: $270 million. Established in 1945, the bank provides conventional loans to developing countries for transportation, power and agricultural projects.

International Development Association (IDA). Paid-in: $1.2 billion. A World Bank affiliate, the IDA was established in 1960 to make loans to the poorest nations on terms they could meet. In 1977, more than 50 percent of its loans were for agricultural projects.

International Finance Corporation. Paid-in: $39 million. The third World Bank affiliate, the corporation was established in 1956 to promote private investment in mining and manufacturing projects in development member countries by lending at conventional rates.

The Difference of a Year

House voting on foreign aid funds in 1978 showed a dramatic turnaround from 1977.

In that year, the House had no reservations about imposing strict conditions on U.S. funds that go to international banks and making substantial across-the-board cuts in funding. But in 1978 the House reversed itself on these issues.

Bank Strings. The most dramatic switch came on efforts to tell international lending institutions, such as the World Bank, how they could use U.S. contributions. In 1977 an amendment by Rep. C. W. Bill Young, R-Fla., to prohibit funds in the bill from being used by the banks in Uganda, Cambodia, Laos or Vietnam was approved overwhelmingly, 295-115. In 1978, the same Young amendment was rejected 198-203.

Eighty-eight members switched their position from support of Young in 1977 to opposition in 1978. Those switches, plus the addition of some members who didn't vote in 1978, were enough to give the administration a major victory. Of the total, 63 members were Democrats and 25 Republicans.

Among the switches were some of the House's senior members including Minority Leader John J. Rhodes, R-Ariz.; George H. Mahon, D-Texas, and Jamie L. Whitten, D-Miss., the number one and two Democrats on the Appropriations Committee; John D. Dingell, D-Mich.; Jack Brooks, D-Texas; William H. Natcher, D-Ky., and Edward P. Boland, D-Mass.

Funding Cuts. The second significant turnaround from 1977 involved across-the-board funding cuts sponsored by Rep. Clarence E. Miller, R-Ohio. In 1977, the House approved a Miller 5-percent general funding cut, 214-168. In 1978, the House refused to go along on a bigger Miller cut — 8 percent — by a 15 vote margin, 184-199.

On this issue, there was a turnaround of 44 members who supported Miller in 1977 and opposed him in 1978: 25 Republicans and 19 Democrats.

Among those Republicans were some senior party members including three on the Appropriations Committee: Elford A. Cederberg, Mich., the ranking member; Robert H. Michel, Ill., the second ranking member and Lawrence Coughlin, Pa. Other prominent Republicans who switched included Majority Leader Rhodes, Barber B. Conable Jr., N.Y., Robert McClory, Ill., Edward J. Derwinski, Ill., John N. Erlenborn, Ill., Tom Railsback, Ill., and Bill Frenzel, Minn.

House Floor Action

The annual foreign aid funding bill escaped from the House much thinner than President Carter wanted but in better overall health than anybody expected.

The House in five days of debate and voting on fiscal 1979 aid appropriations rejected nearly all of the most serious attacks on the bill (HR 12931).

As recently as a month earlier, the bill was believed to be in such serious trouble that it would be gutted with restrictive limitations on use of aid money and deep cuts in funding, and possibly defeated entirely.

Intensive lobbying by administration forces and congressional allies, led by Reps. David Obey, D-Wis., Matthew F. McHugh, D-N.Y., and Silvio O. Conte, R-Mass., aided by outside groups including the U.S. Chamber of Commerce, turned that situation around and gave President Carter a significant foreign policy victory.

As a result, the bill passed by the House 223-167 Aug. 14 appropriated $7.1 billion and contained relatively few restrictions on the use of foreign aid funds that the administration considered unacceptable. *(Vote 617, p. 174-H)*

The total appropriation was $1.3 billion less than the administration request, a cut of about 15 percent. Most of that — nearly $1.1 billion — was cut by the House Appropriations Foreign Operations Subcommittee that drafted the bill.

Floor amendments cut another $176 million from the committee's bill. These came from both general 2 percent cuts and specific dollar reductions including a complete elimination of the $90 million in security assistance budgeted for Syria and almost $25 million for international banks.

But the floor cuts did not touch the $2.6 billion included in the bill for Israel, Egypt and Jordan.

Principal action on HR 12931 occurred the first week in August.

The House put aside the measure Aug. 4 without passing it. The chamber resumed action Aug. 14 and passed it after voting on a number of other amendments.

Funds for Syria

In reaction to recent Syrian attacks on Christian civilians in Lebanon, the House Aug. 2 approved an amendment, 280-103, cutting the full $90 million in security assistance budgeted by the Carter administration for the Middle East nation in 1979. *(Vote 561, p. 160-H)*

The amendment was offered by Edward J. Derwinski, R-Ill., who argued that the funds have given the United States little leverage over the Syrian government's actions, despite earlier State Department reasoning that the country was becoming more moderate and pro-Western.

"And the reason it has not worked," said Derwinski, "is a very simply reason . . . that the Soviet Union pours over $1 billion a year in military hardware into Syria."

The "savage Syrian action" in Lebanon threatens to drag the Middle East closer to all-out war, he said; in attempting to crush the Christians, Syria provoked Israel into a readiness position on the Lebanon border. "Moreover, there is no telling how much damage has been done to the Israeli-Egyptian peace talks."

A substitute offered by Jonathan B. Bingham, D-N.Y., to cut the appropriation by $45 million failed earlier on a 38-78 standing vote. Bingham said that the full amount was "too drastic" a cut that could send the Syrians into the "hands of the Russians."

Bingham pointed to these "positive" signs as reason for maintaining half the aid:

- Syria's movement away from total domination by the Soviet Union.
- Cooperation with the United States in the administration of the U.S. AID program.
- Improvement by the country in the treatment of its Jewish minority.
- Refusal to join Iraq and Libya in their rejection of peace with Israel.

The only other amendment accepted by the House Aug. 2 — on a 70-11 standing vote — was a proposal by John Buchanan, R-Ala., to increase the bill by $10 million for aiding Cypriot refugees.

Rejected were two amendments by C. W. Bill Young, R-Fla., to:

- Cut $49 million for the purchase of rupees to be used in India. Rejected, 194-200. *(Vote 559, p. 160-H)*
- Cut $6.8 million from the bill for the United Nations Development Program. Rejected 189-202. *(Vote 560, p. 160-H)*

Young said the amount represented the U.S. share of funding to countries "like Cuba, like Vietnam, like Uganda. . . ." But opponents argued that the funds were not earmarked for specific countries and that the United States would "punish more than 140 recipient countries" because of U.S. differences with the Marxist states.

Aid Reduction

By a 293-52 vote, the House Aug. 3 cut 2 percent of the $2.8 billion appropriation for Title I bilateral aid programs, except for assistance to Syria, Jordan, Egypt and Israel. The amount would total $45 million. *(Vote 567, p. 162-H)*

The amendment was offered by Tom Harkin, D-Iowa, who said that "there is always a 2 percent waste or 2 percent mismanagement in any of these programs. . . . I think it would be a challenge for the State Department to do as good job with just a little bit less money."

Before approving the Harkin cut, the House by voice vote rejected a substitute offered by Clarence E. Miller, R-Ohio, to cut the bilateral aid program in Title I by 8 percent, except for certain programs. An amendment by Long to exempt certain Title I programs from the original Harkin amendment was defeated by a 14-51 standing vote.

The House approved two other amendments Aug. 3 by voice votes. These were by:

- Bingham, to exempt Uganda graduate students completing their studies in the United States from the prohibition on direct U.S. aid to Uganda.
- James M. Hanley, D-N.Y., to permit the use of U.S. funds for Angolan students who started college in the United States prior to 1978 to finish.

International Banks

By a cliffhanger 198-203 vote, the House Aug. 3 rejected a proposal by C. W. Bill Young, R-Fla., to prohibit any of the funds in the bill for World Bank and other international financial institution loans to Vietnam, Laos, Cambodia and Uganda. *(Vote 566, p. 160-H)*

The issue was a rerun of the battle fought during debate on the fiscal 1978 appropriations bill. But in 1977, Young was successful, winning a 295-115 victory on an identical proposal. *(1977 Almanac p. 286)*

That amendment, which tied up the Senate-House conference on foreign assistance until late in the session, eventually was watered down at the insistence of both President Carter and the Senate, which had refused to accept restrictions on how the international banks used U.S. contributions. A compromise finally was struck when Carter agreed to instruct U.S. officials at the institutions to "oppose and vote against" loans to these countries. At the time, Carter argued that the banks' charters prevented any nation from tying political strings to its assistance. The same arguments were sounded again Aug. 3.

Young pointed out that the bill barred direct U.S. aid for the four countries and that American taxpayers "say in overwhelming numbers there should not be any direct or indirect aid."

The change in sentiment in the House in 1978 was suggested by Young himself during the debate. Members, he said, had heard from the White House, the State, Treasury and Agriculture Departments, church groups, the League of Women Voters, the Chamber of Commerce "and any number of organizations."

Opponents restated their earlier arguments that the Young amendment would play havoc with international lending programs and probably would destroy the banks.

"The Saudis," said Silvio O. Conte, R-Mass., "might use their financial leverage to bar loans to countries that fail to have the 'correct' policy on the Middle East, for example, or others might yield to pressure from the African states to stop loans to countries not endorsing a position like theirs on Southern African questions."

David R. Obey, D-Wis., quoted a letter to House members from eight former treasury secretaries on the issue. "If such restrictive amendments were to be adopted," they said, "they would effectively end U.S. participation in the banks. The charters of these multilateral institutions do not permit the banks to accept funds so conditioned by individual members."

Voting for the Young amendment were 97 Democrats and 101 Republicans; 168 Democrats and 35 Republicans opposed the idea.

A fresh angle was added to the controversy when Tom Harkin, D-Iowa, sent an amendment to the well barring indirect assistance to the governments of Chile, Argentina, Uruguay, South Korea, Nicaragua, Indonesia and the Philippines — all rightist governments long-criticized by human rights activists.

All the governments listed in the Young amendment, said Harkin were communist or socialist, "but the human rights policy of this country should not be ideological; it should be humanitarian." If indirect aid to to be prevented, he added, "let us apply it across the board to both leftwing and rightwing dictatorships."

The House, however, liked this proposal even less than Young's, soundly rejecting it, 41-360. *(Vote 565, p. 160-H)*

Philippines

An attempt by Leo J. Ryan, D-Calif., to cut $5 million from the $13.1 million recommended by the Appropriations Committee for military aid to the Philippines — the administration had requested $18.1 million — was rejected Aug. 3 by a 142-264 vote. *(Vote 563, p. 160-H)*

Ryan insisted that the military aid granted by the United States was not used for protecting the country from external threat but spent by the regime of President Ferdinand E. Marcos, which declared martial law four years ago, "to keep the Filipino people themselves in a state of repression and a state of fear."

Ryan added that the aid level should be reduced to indicate that the United States was "not particularly attracted to the Philippine regime."

Long opposed the amendment, on the basis that the "small military aid program provides a source of leverage" over the Marcos government and that U.S. security is tied to permission by the country for the United States to use major military facilities on its territory.

Other Amendments Rejected

By a 152-236 vote, the House next rejected an amendment by John M. Ashbrook, R-Ohio, to cut $600,000 recommended for military education and training in Afghanistan. Despite the recent switch in the country's leadership to a pro-Soviet, Marxist regime, opponents said it would be a mistake to prejudge it at this time and that flexibility by the United States should be in order until it could be determined whether the country would move into the Soviet orbit. This vote also came Aug. 3. *(Vote 564, p. 160-H)*

An amendment by Harkin to cut $13.5 million from the military training account was rejected by voice vote. Another proposal by Harkin to permit aid to Uganda, Cambodia and Laos if it directly benefited the needy was rejected by 12-33 standing vote. A third amendment by Harkin to ban use of funds for AID entertainment expenses was turned down by a 16-25 standing vote.

The House also rejected by voice vote a plan by Ashbrook to bar indirect U.S. aid to Angola and Mozambique, and an amendment by John B. Anderson, R-Ill., that would have permitted aid to the two countries if it benefited the poor was defeated on a 19-24 standing vote.

International Bank Cuts

The most extensively debated item on Aug. 14 was the attempt by Foreign Operations Subcommittee Chairman Long to cut the committee recommendation for payment to the IDA and IADB by $584,004,483 — about 29 percent of the $2 billion recommended by the Appropriations Committee.

The committee had already cut $420 million — or about 17 percent — from the administration's $2.5 billion request for the two banks.

Long insisted that he was aiming a large funding cut at the banks in order to fend off an across-the-board cut aimed at the entire appropriation. Since mid-June, when California voters had overwhelmingly approved Proposition 13 which slashed state property taxes, the House had approved across-the-board cuts to several appropriations bills. Clarence E. Miller, R-Ohio, who had sponsored many of those cuts, promised not to offer such an amendment to HR 12931 if the Long amendment cutting $548 million from the two banks was approved. Otherwise he would propose an 8 percent reduction.

Obey offered as a substitute for Long's amendment a cut of $24,880,110 for the two banks: $16,280,110 for the Inter-American Development Bank and $8,600,000 for the International Development Association. The amount equaled about 2 percent of the appropriation recommended by the committee for the two institutions.

Obey's substitute was adopted 241-153 and the revised Long amendment was then approved 359-27. *(Votes 609, 610, p. 172-H)*

A professional economist, Long had for years insisted that U.S. bilateral aid and the aid provided by the multilateral banks was misdirected toward prestigious projects benefiting Third World elites but not the great mass of the world's poor. On the House floor, Long buttressed his case by citing an analysis by the Congressional Research Service (CRS) reporting that only about one in eight loans by the IADB was designed to reach directly to the poor. "This may be aiding the poor nations," he said, "but not the poor people."

But Obey and Conte countered that the CRS report also said that the two banks had been directing a rapidly increasing proportion of their funds in recent years to projects designed to directly benefit the poor.

Moreover, they insisted, the amount contained in the bill for the two banks represented an international legal obligation. In the case of the $1.2 billion recommended by the committee for IDA, the contribution had been explicitly authorized by Congress in two parts — $430 million by the 93rd Congress and $800 million by the 95th Congress.

But Long argued that the commitments to the banks were subject to subsequent congressional appropriation.

Costs and Benefits. A second line of debate revolved around the economic advantages — or disadvantages — of U.S. participation in the banks. Long and several other members echoed the line of Bill Nichols, D-Ala., who charged that bank loans were underwriting the development of export-oriented agriculture and industry which was directly competitive with U.S. producers.

Supporters of the banks maintained that the banks' policies barred loans to develop products already in oversupply on the world market. There was no evidence that U.S. exports had been harmed by any bank-funded projects, they added. In fact, participation in the banks was directly profitable, they insisted: for contributions to the banks totaling $4.6 billion since their beginning, the U.S. economy had received payments totaling $10 billion for procurements and salaries.

Aid the Issue? At bottom, for many members, the issue appeared to be one of basic support for, or opposition to, foreign aid. John B. Anderson, R-Ill., cited the U.N.-sponsored goal of .7 percent of a developed nation's gross national product for foreign aid: "Embarrassingly, we have never even come close to achieving this goal. And much of what we classify as foreign aid is in fact military aid — or, if humanitarian or economic aid, is directed for political purposes to developing countries whose income levels do not put them in the ranks of the most deserving."

Conservative Republican Henry J. Hyde, Ill., built his case against the Long amendment on an even higher authority than the U.N.: "The Biblical admonition to give food to the hungry and clothe the naked does not stop when we enter this chamber. . . . An aspect of the greatness of this country is the moral leadership we provide."

But Long-supporter Virginia Smith, R-Neb., saw a different moral imperative: By a huge majority her constituents wanted foreign aid cut. "Well, it is their money, and the judgment of the American people is that we are elected to come here and represent."

Across-the-Board Cuts

The administration's closest call on money cuts came near the end of debate on the bill on Aug. 14.

C. W. Bill Young, R-Fla., offered an amendment to cut by 2 percent all funds in the bill except those directed at Israel and Egypt. Miller then proposed to increase the reduction to 8 percent

The Miller 8-percent proposal was rejected by 15 votes, 184-199. *(Vote 614, p. 174-H)*

The House then approved 289-95 a substitute for the Young amendment offered by Tom Harkin, D-Iowa, which provided for a 2 percent cut only in those portions of the bill that had not already been cut by 2 percent on the House floor. *(Vote 615, p. 174-H)*

The House had approved a cut of $45 million in U.S. bilateral aid programs Aug. 3 by a vote of 293-52. It approved a cut of $12,600,000 in foreign military credit sales Aug. 4 by a vote of 300-29. Both of these cuts amounted to about 2 percent.

Conditions on the Banks

Four amendments dealt with the basic question of whether the United States could bar the multinational banks from using U.S. contributions to "indirectly" aid certain projects deemed inimical to U.S. interests.

In each case, administration supporters maintained that the international institutions could not accept U.S. contributions with those kinds of strings attached. "Do we want to exercise our unhappiness with the few countries we do not like if the cost is to imperil U.S. participation in the international banking structure?" Obey demanded.

But Young and other opponents of the banks argued in each instance that the banks could accept conditional funds and that, in any case, the United States should not simply abdicate its political control over funds channeled through the banks.

Long opposed the amendments, but only reluctantly. He agreed with Young that the banks could accommodate congressional limitations. But the Senate never would accept the provisions, he said, so approval of any limitations merely would prolong the Senate-House conference on the bill until, eventually, the House backed down.

The House adopted two of the limiting amendments on Aug. 14:

- By Young to bar use of any U.S. funds by the IDA to aid Vietnam. Adopted 234-152. *(Vote 611, p. 174-H)*
- By John M. Ashbrook, R-Ohio, to bar use of any U.S. funds to indirectly aid Cuba. Adopted by voice vote.

Two of the limiting amendments were rejected, also on on Aug. 14:

- By Dawson Mathis, D-Ga., to prevent use of any U.S. funds by the banks to establish or expand the production for export of steel, grains, sugar, citrus crops, tobacco, tires or palm oil. The intent of the amendment was to prevent use of U.S. funds to subsidize competitors to U.S. products. (Palm oil is a substitute for soybean oil.) Rejected 143-239. *(Vote 612, p. 174-H)*
- By George Hansen, R-Idaho, to remove from the bill all funds for assistance to Panama. Hansen, a leader of conservative opposition to the Panama Canal treaties, insisted that any aid to Panama should be considered in the context of the legislation to implement the treaties which had not yet been sent to Congress. The House rejected by voice vote a substitute by Harkin that would have removed from the bill all funds for military training or military credit sales for Panama. It rejected the Hansen amendment by 172-202. *(Vote 613, p. 174-H)*

Other Amendments

The House Aug. 14 also rejected an amendment by Mathis that would have limited to one year the $300 million appropriation for the International Bank for Reconstruction and Development.

According to opponents, the appropriation had to be open-ended because some of it was for so-called callable capital — funds pledged by the United States to guarantee private loans to developing nations. None of the banks ever have called any of this guarantee money, but the appropriation was necessary for the pledge to be accepted by the bank. The amendment was rejected by voice vote.

The House also rejected by voice vote an amendment by Ashbrook to reduce funds for the Peace Corps by $1.3 million and to bar Peace Corps operations in the Central African Empire.

Accepted by voice vote was an amendment by Young that directed U.S. governors of each of the six multinational banks to push for the institutions to establish human rights criteria that would be considered in assessing applications for assistance.

An amendment by Young to prevent use of any Peace Corps funds for abortions was adopted by a standing vote of 60-8.

The chair ruled out of order an amendment by Henry A. Waxman, D-Calif., to prevent use of any aid funds for Mexico to destroy marijuana crops with the herbicide paraquat. The prohibition would have been waived if the paraquat were mixed with some other substance that would warn potential users of the marijuana that paraquat had been used on it.

Provisions

As passed by the House, HR 12931 would appropriate:

Program	Budget Request	House-Passed Amount
Foreign Economic Assistance	$4,066,252,000	$3,752,568,000
Foreign Military Sales Credits	672,500,000	635,400,000
Other Foreign Assistance	3,705,568,919	2,788,754,653
Total	$8,444,320,919	$7,176,722,653

Senate Committee Action

The Senate Appropriations Committee reported HR 12931 Sept. 15 (S Rept 95-1194). At that point, the bill totaled $9,202,456,072 — $2.4 billion more than funded in fiscal 1978, $1.2 billion less than requested and $2 billion more than approved by the House Aug. 14.

The increase over the House figure was the result of a $1.8 billion appropriation requested by the president for the U.S. contribution to the International Monetary Fund's new Witteveen Facility.

Middle East

As in previous years, the largest amount in the bill — about one-quarter of total funds — was the U.S. aid program to the Middle East, principally Israel and Egypt. As provided in fiscal 1978, Israel was allocated $785 million in U.S. assistance; Egypt, $750 million and Jordan, $93 million. The committee also approved $90 million for Syria, although the House had deleted this amount during floor action.

The committee stated that it believed the "American support for the economic goals of the Middle Eastern countries does contribute to political stability. American assistance has helped to sustain the policies of moderate leaders; it has encouraged those who have sought to turn confrontation to cooperation."

These funds were contained in a $1.8 billion economic support account, formerly called security supporting assistance.

To strengthen U.S. relations with Turkey following Washington's decision to remove the 1975 embargo on arms sales to that country, the committee provided $50 million, the amount requested.

Arms Sales

To support a $2 billion weapons sales credit program in fiscal 1979, the committee approved a $674 million appropriation. This amount covered $550 million in direct, forgiveable credit to Israel, $17.5 million for Zaire and the remainder for administering the sales program.

Grant military aid continued to decline in fiscal 1979 — the committee approved $84.9 million — as the United States phased out this type of assistance in favor of the military credit program.

A $30.2 million appropriation for military education and training overseas was approved by the committee, $100,000 more than requested, with the comment that the program "serves important national security and foreign policy objectives."

International Banks

In a rambling discussion of the administration's request for $3.5 billion to fund U.S. contributions to six international lending institutions, the committee suggested that the banks must work more actively to meet the basic human needs of the poor overseas. But ambiguously, the panel also said that it was "concerned that the rush to commit the resources of the banks to projects addressing basic human needs may well carry with it more than is intended or desired. . . ."

For the U.S. contribution to the Asian Development Bank, the committee recommended $309.6 million, the same amount requested. The House approved only $220 million. The panel said the bank was the "most cost-conscious and best managed . . . salaries remain relatively modest, its travel costs well-managed. . . ."

The committee approved $763.7 million for the Inter-American Development Bank. The administration had requested $914 million, and the House provided $797.7 million. The panel said it was "concerned over the high U.S. share of the contributions to this institution."

Without comment, the committee recommended only $163 million for the World Bank in contrast to the $665.9 million requested and the $300 million provided by the House.

The World Bank affiliate, the International Development Association (IDA) — it provides loans to the poorest nations on concessional terms — was allocated $1.3 billion by the committee. The administration requested $1.6 billion; the House approved $1.2 billion.

The third World Bank component, the International Finance Corporation, which promotes private investment in developing countries, was granted the full $40,045,000 the administration requested. The House cut the figure to $39 million.

The committee approved $25 million for the African Development Fund, the same amount requested and accepted by the House.

AID Operating Expenses

The committee was extremely critical of the level of AID's operating expenses. "We must conclude that there are still those with AID who do not share the administrator's commitment to minimize operating expenses while maximizing funds for expanding programs of assistance to the poor," the committee stated.

The request of $261 million was reduced to $240 million.

Senate Floor Action

Pressed by its legislative agenda, the Senate Sept. 23 raced through debate on the fiscal 1979 foreign aid appropriations bill before passing the $9.2 billion measure, 39-22. *(Vote 392, p. 59-S)*

The major change in the bill reported by the Appropriations Committee Sept. 15 came on amendments to cut all military aid and economic development assistance to Nicaragua, a total of $8,150,000.

Ruled by President Anastasio Somoza, Nicaragua had been torn by civil strife as large segments of the population opposed continuation of the Somoza family's 40-year control of the government.

Sen. Frank Church, D-Idaho, offering an amendment to withhold $8 million in U.S. economic assistance, urged the United States to disavow the Somoza regime. "The longer we delay," he said, "the greater the chance that the revolution will fall into the hands of the extremists." Church suggested that the United States join with other nations in the region to encourage the formation of a moderate government that "respects human rights and free enterprise."

The Senate also reversed several House amendments approved Aug. 14 that would bar international banks from using U.S. funds for assisting Vietnam and Cuba. But these proposals drew nowhere near the controversy that attended the issue in the House.

The Senate also refused to cut $1.3 billion from the $1.8 billion requested by the administration for the U.S. contribution to the new Witteveen Facility.

Nicaragua, Afghanistan

By voice vote, the Senate agreed to Church's proposal prohibiting the use of funds in the bill for Nicaragua unless the president certified to the Speaker of the House and the chairman of the Foreign Relations Committee that aid "will serve to promote democratic processes in that country."

Church's amendment earlier had been amended by Jacob K. Javits, R-N.Y., to allow assistance if it were for the direct benefit of the Nicaraguan people. And another proposal by Orrin G. Hatch, R-Utah, to include Afghanistan in the aid prohibition also was attached to the Church amendment by voice vote.

The amendment, in effect, cut off $8 million in development assistance budgeted for Nicaragua. Another amendment by Mark O. Hatfield, R-Ore., that cut out $150,000 in military training funds for the Latin government was approved by the Senate on a voice vote earlier.

Africa

By voice vote, the Senate approved an amendment by John Melcher, D-Mont., requiring the State Department to assure that Zambia was taking steps to correct its balance of payments deficit before the $20 million in the bill for economic assistance could be obligated.

An amendment by George McGovern, D-S.D., barring direct U.S. aid to Angola and Mozambique except if the president determined and reported to Congress that such funds would further the "foreign policy interests of the United States" was approved by voice vote.

The purpose of the amendment was to add the exception so it would conform with a provision in the fiscal 1979 security assistance bill, S 3075.

Another Hatch amendment earmarking $5 million for refugee assistance to Rhodesia through international relief organizations was approved on a voice vote.

Cuba, Vietnam

By a 32-31 roll call, the Senate approved a committee amendment that, in effect, deleted House language preventing U.S. funds from being used by the International Development Association for assistance to Vietnam. Opponent Hatch argued that the Senate should go along with the House, but Daniel K. Inouye, D-Hawaii, chairman of the Foreign Operations Subcommittee, countered that this provision would jeopardize the nation's participation in the international banks. *(Vote 390, p. 58-S)*

By a 32-30 vote, the Senate also approved a related committee amendment that dropped the word "indirectly" from a House provision barring U.S. aid to Cuba. Again, the lending procedures of the international banks was at issue. Inouye said the procedures would be in a "shambles" if other countries began attaching conditions to their loans. *(Vote 391, p. 59-S)*

Other Amendments

In rapid succession, the Senate approved these additional amendments:

- By 40-30 roll call, committee amendment deleting House language reducing Title I assistance programs by 2 percent. *(Vote 385, p. 58-S)*

Hatch said the House provision would save the taxpayers money, but Inouye said rather than approving an across-the-board reduction, his subcommittee had considered each account on its own merits.

- By voice vote, Richard S. Schweiker, R-Pa., amendment earmarking $20 million for resettlement of Soviet and other refugees in the United States if not covered by existing refugee programs.
- By 39-20, committee amendment boosting from $220 million, as approved by the House, to $309.6 million the U.S. contribution to the Asian Development Bank. *(Vote 388, p. 58-S)*
- By 41-22, committee amendment increasing from $421.4 million, as approved by the House, to $500 million the U.S. contribution to the International Development Association. *(Vote 389, p. 58-S)*
- By voice vote, Inouye amendment earmarking $3 million for exchange of Israeli and Arab studying in American-sponsored centers in Israel and Arab states.
- By voice vote, Inouye amendment to make available for fiscal 1979 unobligated balances of funds previously appropriated for international disaster assistance, Middle East Special Requirements Fund and U.S. Emergency Refugee and Migration Assistance Fund.
- By voice vote, Schweicker amendment calling for the president to initiate international consultations with member nations of the Organization of Economic Cooperation and Development for reaching agreement on commodities surpluses.
- By voice vote, Edward M. Kennedy, D-Mass., amendment appropriating $1.5 million to assist Cambodian refugees in Vietnam. The only funding addition to the bill made on the floor, the assistance would be channeled through the United Nations High Commissioner for Refugees.

Amendments Rejected

By a 30-37 vote, the Senate Sept. 21 rejected a proposal by Robert Morgan, D-N.C., to delete language in the bill barring the use of any U.S. funds for U.S. contributions to the United Nations University in Tokyo. *(Vote 380, p. 57-S)*

And by a 21-34 vote, an amendment by John Melcher, D-Mont., to cut $20 million from the bill earmarked for helping Zambia improve its balance of payments was also rejected Sept. 21. *(Vote 381, p. 57-S)*

The next day, by a 7-58 vote, the Senate rejected a motion by Hatch to table committee language limiting unobligated and deobligated military aid appropriations for fiscal 1978 and 1979 to $211,875,000. *(Vote 384, p. 58-S)*

By an 18-47 vote, an amendment by Dennis DeConcini, D-Ariz., to reduce to $500 million from $1.8 billion the U.S. contribution to the Witteveen Facility, was rejected.

A letter from Treasury Secretary Michael W. Blumenthal was read on the floor warning that a decision by Congress to eliminate or reduce U.S. participation in the facility, designed to help stabilize the international economy by helping poor countries recover their deficits piled up from oil purchases, could have serious international economic consequences. *(Vote 386, p. 58-S)*

The Senate also turned down, 30-32, a committee amendment that would have deleted House language from the bill barring the use of Peace Corps funds for abortions. *(Vote 387, p. 58-S)*

Provisions

As passed by the Senate, HR 12931 would appropriate:

Program	House-Passed Amount	Senate-Passed Amount
Foreign Economic Assistance	$3,752,568,000	$3,880,531,000
Foreign Military Sales Credit	635,400,000	673,960,000
Other Foreign Assistance	2,788,754,653	2,817,675,072
IMF Facility	———	1,831,640,000
Total	$7,176,722,653	$9,203,806,072

Conference Report

House-Senate conferees filed a report on HR 12931 (H Rept 95-1754) Oct. 10. Approved for fiscal 1979 was a $9,135,031,948 appropriation, including $1,831,640,000 for the new Witteveen Facility. The conference bill was $126,669,295 more than approved by the House, (not including the Witteveen funds on which the House didn't vote because the authorizing legislation had not cleared), but $68,774, 124 less than passed by the Senate. The conference amount was $539,518,948 more than appropriated in fiscal 1978 (not including the Witteveen funds) and $1,252,728,971 below the president's fiscal 1979 request.

Reductions

Before passing HR 12931 Aug. 14, the House accepted amendments to reduce most funds in the bill by 2 percent; excluded were allocations for Israel, Egypt, Jordan and Syria. Conferees, however, deleted these 2 percent cuts, noting that the "House managers considered the effect of this provision in dealing with each of the specific appropriations accounts." Moreover, the final $7.3 billion amount (excluding Witteveen funding) was between the Senate's $7.4 billion recommendation and the House figure of $7.2 billion, the conferees explained.

IDA, Cuba Aid. Conferees dropped two House restrictions: one to bar use of any U.S. funds by the IDA to aid Vietnam and the other to bar use of U.S. funds to indirectly aid Cuba.

Syria Aid

Bowing to President Carter's Middle East peace accomplishments, conferees agreed to accept a Senate amendment providing $90 million in economic support for Syria. The money had been earmarked in the bill by the House Appropriations Committee but was deleted on the House floor in reaction to Syrian attacks on Christian civilians in Lebanon. The Senate restored the funds. Conferees compromised by not earmarking funds for Syria but by increasing the total economic development fund appropriation to allow $90 million for that country.

"The conferees are very much aware of the recent progress made at Camp David," the report said, "and are in agreement that the president should have maximum flexibility in pursuing peace in the Middle East."

Mozambique, Angola

Conferees agreed to a Senate provision allowing the president to directly aid Mozambique and Angola "if he determined and reports to the Congress, that furnishing such assistance would further the foreign policy interests of the United States," but the House refused to accept this decision Oct. 12. *(Below)*

Nicaragua, Afghanistan

Conferees also dropped a Senate provision prohibiting use of any appropriations for direct aid to Nicaragua or Afghanistan unless the aid promoted the "democratic processes" in those countries or helped the poor directly. The conferees did not comment on their action, but the House over the years has been unwilling to restrict aid to Nicaragua despite the dictatorial control of that country by President Anastasio Somoza.

Refugee Aid

Work on the conference bill was reopened Oct. 10 because of a misunderstanding related to U.S. migration and refugee programs. The bill had been approved Sept. 27.

The Senate had called for consolidation of the programs in the Department of State — the initial conference decision — but the conferees later said the programs would be more appropriately placed in AID "since refugee needs are fundamentally humanitarian and development in nature."

The final agreement followed the House view, directing that the administration present a plan in fiscal 1980 for consolidating the programs in AID, but if "this creates difficulties," an alternative plan should be presented, the report said.

The U.S. refugee program, according to the conferees, has operated through three federal agencies and more than a dozen private organizations, becoming an "assemblage of overlapping and frequently competing programs that have resisted reorganizations, central direction and reform at least since 1972. Ongoing programs bear little relationship to need and have perpetuated inexplicable inequities in the types and levels of assistance to which individuals are entitled."

Final Action

House. By a 203-188 vote the House approved the conference report to the bill after first rejecting, 191-201, a motion to recommit it to conference. *(Votes 799, 800, p. 228-H)*

By a 161-204 vote, the House refused to accept the decision of the conference committee to allow the president to waive a ban on aid to Angola and Mozambique if assistance was in U.S. policy interests. *(Vote 801, p. 223-H)*

Robert E. Bauman, R-Md., objected to the move, arguing that the two nations were bases for guerrilla fighters against Rhodesia and Southwest Africa. But Stephen J. Solarz, D-N.Y., replied that the United States needed the cooperation of Angola and Mozambique to bring about majority rule in the two other states and that the conference action simply gave the president flexibility in policy-making.

By a 67-47 standing vote, the House also agreed to accept a Senate amendment barring the use of the Foreign Service Retirement and Disability Fund for paying certain retirees on the basis of their highest year of earning. House conferees had wanted to delete the Senate language *(above)*. House opponents argued the provision was legislation in an appropriations bill.

Senate. By a 60-31 vote, the Senate approved the conference report Oct. 13. *(Vote 486, p. 71-S)*

The Senate subsequently agreed to drop the provision the House refused to accept allowing the president to waive the ban on aid to Angola and Mozambique. This action cleared the bill for the president. ▮

Defense Funds: $117.3 Billion

Just in time to meet the Pentagon's first payroll of fiscal 1979, Congress Oct. 12 cleared for the president a $117.3 billion Defense Department funding bill (HR 13635 — PL 95-457).

The appropriation was about $2 billion below the amount requested by President Carter, but the difference was due to funds deleted from the companion defense authorization bill (S 3486) for a nuclear aircraft carrier that Carter had opposed. The first fiscal 1979 authorization bill for defense was vetoed, and the veto was sustained by the House. *(See p. 321)*

The administration planned to submit a supplemental appropriations request that would reallocate those funds to other programs before submitting its fiscal 1980 budget in January 1979.

Carter Sustained

Together with funds provided in separate bills for military construction, atomic weapons production and annual pay raises, the $117.3 billion in HR 13635 brought the total appropriation for national defense in fiscal 1979 very near the $126 billion requested by Carter.

In addition to holding Congress to his overall recommendation for Pentagon spending, Carter fared well in his most significant disputes with Congress over specific items in the annual appropriations bill. Besides killing the nuclear aircraft carrier, the final version of HR 13635 dropped a key item in a package of shipbuilding projects sponsored by the Senate Armed Services Committee. The intent of the package was to speed the development of smaller, cheaper aircraft carriers using vertical takeoff combat jets.

The final bill also restored almost half of the $350 million the House had cut from the Army's request for ammunition. Carter had strenuously objected to the House action. And the bill allowed about 80 percent of the amount requested to cover anticipated inflation in operating and maintenance costs. The Senate had proposed a far deeper reduction as an incentive to the Pentagon to tighten up its management.

Abortions and Taxes

The double standard many members applied to defense issues was evident in the bill's treatment of two of the most emotionally charged issues of the 95th Congress: abortion and the anti-spending mood symbolized by California's approval in June of a sweeping rollback in property taxes (Proposition 13).

Although the House had approved rigid anti-abortion language, the conference committee on the bill without much fuss subsequently agreed to much less stringent language. This had not been the norm on non-defense legislation to which anti-abortion language had been added.

The Pentagon received even more favored treatment on the spending cut issue. In a year when many appropriations bills for federal departments had been cut across-the-board by 2-5 percent, attempts to cut the defense budget failed as usual. The last such effort of the year, a Senate floor amendment that would have cut the defense bill by 1 percent, lost overwhelmingly, 11-74.

Provisions

As cleared Oct. 12, HR 13635 appropriated $117,255,-721,000 in new budget authority for fiscal 1979. This was about $833 million more than the Senate version contained and about $1.76 billion less than the House-passed bill. (But the House version had included the $2 billion for another carrier.) The following amounts were appropriated:

Program	Administration Request	Final Appropriation
Military Personnel	$27,211,200,000	$27,213,328,000
Military Pensions	10,148,938,000	10,139,838,000
Operations and Maintenance	37,376,200,000	37,336,915,000
Procurement	31,927,600,000	30,238,716,000
(Transfers from prior appropriations)	(0)	(107,000,000)
Research and Development	12,468,000,000	12,156,262,000
(Transfers from prior appropriations)	(0)	(15,000,000)
Special Foreign Currency Program	14,362,000	14,362,000
Working Capital Funds	100,800,000	100,800,000
(Transfer authority)	(750,000,000)	(—)
Related Agencies	53,183,000	55,500,000
Total, New Budget Authority	$119,300,283,000	$117,255,721,000
Total transfers from prior appropriations	0	(122,000,000)
Total funding made available	$119,300,283,000	$117,377,721,000

The bill also:

- Barred the use of Pentagon funds to pay for abortions except when the pregnancy was the result of rape or incest or when the pregnancy risked causing death or "severe and long-lasting physical health damage" to the mother.

House Committee Action

In its report, filed July 27 (H Rept 95-1398), the Appropriations Committee recommended $119,192,571,000 in new appropriations for defense. This amount was $107.7 million less than the administration requested. But the committee also approved use of $160.2 million appropriated in earlier years but not spent.

New Carrier Approved

On a tie vote (26-26), the House Appropriations Committee July 27 rejected a move to delete from the fiscal 1979 defense appropriations bill a $2 billion nuclear-powered aircraft carrier. The ship had been added to the bill by the panel's defense subcommittee by only a one-vote margin (13-12).

The administration wanted no aircraft carrier funds until 1979, when it planned to request a $1.5 billion non-nuclear-powered ship.

By a 28-24 vote, the Appropriations Committee then rejected an amendment that would have substituted the cheaper ship for the nuclear-powered vessel.

The carrier funded by the committee would be the fifth of the fleet to be nuclear-powered.

The panel, however, also increased by $49.6 million (to $221.5 million) funds for development of vertical takeoff combat jets (V/STOLs) that did not depend on the carriers.

A similar approach had been taken earlier in the year by the Senate Armed Services Committee in the related weapons research and procurement bill that eventually was vetoed by the president over the carrier issue.

Carriers and Harriers

The committee majority dismissed out of hand the administration proposal to build a slightly less expensive conventionally powered carrier in fiscal 1980. The additional nuclear-powered ship of the *Nimitz*-class that the Navy wanted would be far superior to the smaller ship, it argued.

The panel also added $412.8 million to buy more combat jets for the carrier fleet than the administration had requested. This brought to $1.76 billion the amount in the bill for 87 carrier planes.

The Navy's plan for V/STOL development placed initial emphasis on a large subsonic plane that would be used for transport and reconnaissance. Not until the mid-1990s at the earliest did they plan to have supersonic V/STOL bombers and fighters.

The Appropriations Committee cut all funds ($31.7 million) requested for the subsonic plane project, which it said the Navy was likely to cancel anyway because of management problems. But it allowed the funds requested for the supersonic V/STOL fighter. An interim V/STOL fighter could be available much sooner from the Marines, it said. This would be an improved version of the British Harrier, a V/STOL light bomber currently used by the Marines. The panel recommended $173 million — more than twice the administration's request — to speed up work on the so-called Harrier "B" that would have a longer range and carry more bombs than the existing version.

According to the committee, this improved Harrier could provide a "logical transition" to the Navy's supersonic fighter of the late 1990s. And the program would foster a climate for more advanced V/STOL research.

For the immediate future, the committee rejected an administration proposal to begin replacing the Marines'

Maritime Power Balance

The House Appropriations Committee's general approach to the U.S.-Soviet naval balance was somewhat less pessimistic than some critics of Carter's Navy budget had been. Comparisons matching a huge Soviet fleet with a much outnumbered U.S. force ignored the fact that "we simply build larger and more capable ships," according to the panel. Many Soviet vessels were small coastal craft or non-combatants.

If the comparison were limited to "major surface combatants," the committee said, the U.S. fleet numbered 198 and the Soviet force 233 (of which 105 were relatively small frigates). And this lineup took no account of the substantial fleets of U.S. allies. The Soviet's allies, on the other hand, had almost no large surface craft, according to the committee.

current Harriers with more A-4M light bombers. New light bombers of some kind were needed to replace the Harriers that had crashed in the four years the Marines had been using the plane. But the Marines and V/STOL supporters maintained that the Harrier's crash record was no worse than that of other combat jets. The committee deleted $113 million for 18 A-4Ms and added $90 million for 15 Harriers.

Making the All-Volunteer Idea Work

Many of the personnel policies scrutinized by the committee were related to the services' efforts to meet their manpower needs in the absence of the draft.

Recruiting. For recruiting expenses and advertising, the panel approved $548 million, $3.5 million less than the budget request. It also cut $4.4 million from the amount requested to pay bonuses that were intended as inducements to enlist in certain essential and hard-to-fill specialties. The committee cited a report by the General Accounting Office (GAO) that said the Army had a personnel surplus in six of the 15 specialties for which it currently was paying such bonuses.

A Pentagon proposal to pay the bonuses in a lump sum when the person enlisted, instead of paying it in annual installments over the duration of the enlistee's tour of duty, was turned down. The installment plan had proven successful, the committee said, and it might be difficult to retrieve lump-sum payments from enlistees who did not complete their service tours.

Training Efficiencies. The panel rejected a proposal to cut from the Navy and Marine recruit training a week currently spent on kitchen duty and other housekeeping chores. This period provided a realistic introduction to the mundane duties that an enlistee inevitably would encounter, according to the committee. And it provided additional time for officers to screen out enlistees who were ill-adapted to a military environment. The committee also ordered the Marines to drop a proposal to cut the time currently spent training recruits in marksmanship and swimming.

As it had done for the last two years, the committee turned down a proposal to merge the basic training programs for Army and Navy helicopter pilots, insisting that the Navy pilots needed special training. But it chided the Air Force for its delay in converting to improved screening methods that would cut down the number of trainees who dropped out of flight school.

Overseas Assistance. The committee approved the $94.7 million requested to begin paying travel and transportation allowances to the families of junior enlisted persons stationed abroad. (The families of senior enlisted men currently received these benefits.)

The existing policy was intended to discourage marriage by junior enlisted men, but with the emergence of the all-volunteer force this no longer was feasible.

But the committee disapproved a $2.8 million request for family financial counselors to assist U.S. personnel stationed in Europe. The committee said the plethora of other Army counselors and the new travel allowances made additional counselors superfluous. The committee also insisted that the Pentagon report on its plans for evacuating overseas U.S. dependents in case of a war.

Fringe Benefits. The committee steered clear of the emotionally charged issue of cutting the cost of traditional fringe benefits for military personnel such as commissaries (supermarkets). It proposed no changes in the current retirement system, but endorsed the April recommendations of a presidential commission and urged the Pentagon not to ignore the study. It approved $10.1 billion for retired pay in fiscal 1979.

The panel cut to $45.4 million (from $55.4 million requested) the funds for tuition assistance to service members pursuing college degrees in their off-duty time. It recommended that priority in receiving such assistance should go to members who were subscribing to the Veterans Educational Assistance Program established in 1976. Under this program, a successor to the education benefits of the "GI Bill," the VA matched on a two-for-one basis the voluntary contribution of a serviceman that would be available for his further education after he left the service.

The committee said this program was an important recruiting incentive for high school graduates. On the other hand, it insisted that a separate program, under which officers pursue advanced degrees while on active duty, should be used only for skills the participants would use in the service. Officers preparing for a second career after leaving the service should use the off-duty, tuition assistance program. Instead, the committee complained, the services were paying over $400 million annually and losing "the talents of high potential individuals who will not be available . . . for one to two years while undergoing training which is, in many instances, of questionable necessity."

For the medical insurance system for military dependents (CHAMPUS), the committee recommended that physicians be reimbursed at a rate of not more than the 80th percentile of the customary charges paid for similar services in the same locality. The legal limit had been the 90th percentile until 1977 (although the Defense Department had limited the payments to the 75th percentile). The fiscal 1978 Defense Department funding bill (PL 95-111) had lowered the figure to the 75th percentile, and that change had become a symbolic target for those in and out of Congress who felt that medical care for servicemen and their dependents was declining.

The committee argued that many more physicians were dropping out of the CHAMPUS program because of poor management than because of the ceiling on reimbursements. But as a sop to those favoring an increase in the payments, it recommended a change to the 80th percentile and urged the Pentagon to tighten up its management of the program.

The Reserves

Several budget additions were proposed by the committee to man and equip the reserves and the National Guard and to improve their combat-readiness. With deep roots in local communities, especially in the South, the reserves always have had strong congressional support. But that support had broadened in the 1970s when, under the "total force" policy, Pentagon planners began assigning important military missions to some reserve units. With the end of the draft, the reserves became the prime source of replacements and reinforcements in case of war.

Recruitment. With the draft gone, all of the reserve components had trouble recruiting enough persons. The committee recommended adding to the budget $4 million for enlistment bonuses and $5 million for re-enlistment bonuses. The House Armed Services Committee had sponsored the re-enlistment program in 1977 and the enlistment bonus in 1978. But the Defense Department had been unenthusiastic about the experiment from the outset. It wanted no new funds to continue the re-enlistment bonuses until it studied the results of the 1977 experiment.

Training. The committee proposed limiting to four the annual number of "make-up" training sessions for which a reservist could be paid. Too many reservists, it said, had poor attendance records at their regular training drills and "made up" the missed sessions by doing administrative chores that had no real training value.

It approved extra meetings of reserve unit leaders to plan the full-unit training sessions. But it insisted that these meetings actually be devoted to planning.

Full-Time Cadres. "Probably the most important factor influencing reserve component readiness is the amount of full-time personnel support available . . . to provide day-to-day management, administration, training and maintenance," said the committee. The Navy Reserve and Marine Corps Reserve relied on active-duty personnel for their full-time cadres. But the National Guard and the Air National Guard relied heavily on a controversial system of "dual-status technicians." Some 67,000 technicians provided the day-to-day administration of reserve units as civilian federal employees. But they also were members of these reserve units and shifted to military status during drill sessions or when the unit was called to active duty.

Critics had argued that the technicians cost much more than active duty personnel of equivalent experience, created an anomaly in the military chain-of-command of the reserve units and offered a foothold for unionization of the military. In 1977 the House Appropriations Committee ordered the Pentagon to phase out the technicians and replace them with active-duty personnel. But in the current report, the panel acknowledged that the proposed switch might be complicated and called, instead, for pilot programs to test several alternative methods of phasing out the technicians.

New Planes. Following the lead of the two Armed Services Committees, the panel recommended adding $257 million to the budget for new aircraft for the reserves: 16 C-130H transports for the Air National Guard ($145 million), seven trainer versions of the A-7D light bomber for the Air National Guard ($96.6 million) and one C-9B transport for the Navy Reserve ($16.1 million).

Civilian Pentagon Employees

The Pentagon employed 340,000 of the 400,000 federal blue-collar laborers — the so-called Wage Board employees. The committee proposed two steps that would curtail future increases in the cost — currently budgeted at $6.5 billion — of employing those workers.

5.5 Percent Pay Cap. One proposal would limit to 5.5 percent any wage increase for Wage Board employees of the Pentagon in fiscal 1979. The Pentagon estimated that without such a provision, the Wage Board formula would require an average wage increase of 9 percent — $170 million more than a 5.5 percent increase would cost.

The president already had authority to impose a ceiling on pay raises for federal white-collar (civil service) employees and on military personnel. President Carter repeatedly announced his intention to hold those groups to a 5.5 percent raise in fiscal 1979.

Wage Board Reform. The more far-reaching committee proposal would completely revamp the existing Wage Board pay system. Theoretically, the current system was intended to ensure that federal blue-collar workers were paid the prevailing rate for their craft in the area in which they were working. But critics, including the House Appropriations Committee, long had argued that the pay computation formula contained various quirks that produced federal pay levels 8 to 12 percent above the locally prevailing rates. This not only fueled inflation and forced private employers to raise their pay scales, according to the committee, but also endangered the jobs of some federal workers. With Wage Board pay rates inflated, according to this argument, it was easier for the Defense Department to justify replacing federal workers with civilian contract employees for certain jobs.

Combat Readiness: Training and Repair

Equipment Overhauls. The committee increased by $170 million the $6 billion requested for major overhauls of planes, engines, tanks and ships. In general, the funds recommended would alleviate the backlog of equipment that was out of service because of needed repairs.

The Army's share — $978 million — would eliminate by the end of fiscal 1979 the backlog of unrepaired tanks and combat vehicles. The Navy would receive nearly $1.6 billion for full-scale overhauls of 71 ships. This amount was for three ships fewer than the Navy requested because the committee concluded that Navy shipyards were not keeping abreast of their scheduled repair deadlines.

The committee acknowledged that the Navy had made progress from the very poor repair record that characterized the fleet in the early 1970s. But it said that serious problems remained, especially in the management of "intermediate" maintenance — jobs too big for a ship's crew, but too small for a major overhaul. The Navy had not worked out a clear division of labor between the shipyards and smaller maintenance facilities that could perform these intermediate jobs, according to the panel.

A $318 million repair ship to carry out intermediate maintenance (called a destroyer tender) was approved. But the committee complained that this was by far the most expensive kind of repair facility to build, and it ordered the Navy to consider using shore bases or repair barges instead of building more tenders.

For overhauls of Navy and Air Force planes and engines, the committee added $182 million to the request. This would avert proposed civilian job cuts at major maintenance depots and would hold the backlog of yet-to-be repaired planes at about the same level as in fiscal 1978.

Operating Tempo. The services maintained that a key to combat readiness was to ensure that ships and planes were operated often enough that crews remained proficient in their jobs. The committee recommended $885.6 million for ship operations, $30 million less than the request. This would force the Navy to cut its tempo of operations by about one day in every three-month period. The Sixth Fleet in the Mediterranean, for instance, would be able to steam about 44 days in each quarter. The committee observed that this would be two or three times the operating tempo of the Soviet Navy and that no cutbacks would be needed at all if the fleet steamed more slowly (to cut fuel consumption) when not in combat exercises.

The committee made only minor cuts in the funds requested for the cost of operating airplanes. But it warned the Pentagon that it expected future budget requests to substitute the use of aircraft simulators for expensive flying hours for some training purposes.

Inflation and Devaluation Protection. The $37.3 billion recommended for operating and maintenance costs included more than $1.45 billion to pay for anticipated inflation (estimated at more than 6 percent except for fuel, which was estimated at more than 10 percent).

This was the second budget in which the Pentagon was allowed to anticipate inflation in its request for operating funds. Before 1978 the services had to cut back scheduled overhauls and operations because of inflation in the 18 months between the preparation of a budget request and the start of the fiscal year.

The committee proposed creation of a new foreign currency stabilization fund to protect the services' overseas operations against fluctuations in the value of the dollar. For fiscal 1978 and 1979, the Pentagon's overseas operations were expected to cost over $1 billion more than planned because of the dollar's drop in value against foreign currency — especially against the German deutschmark and the Japanese yen. Devaluations in the three months beginning in December 1977 alone cost more than $32.2 million.

The Pentagon had been trying to deal with the problem through reprogramming funds appropriated for other purposes or by seeking supplemental appropriations to fund essential overseas operations. But the committee acknowledged that in some cases Congress could not act fast enough to prevent cancellation of training exercises or cutbacks in flying hours for certain units. And the panel said that while the services were quick to seek additional funds when the dollar's value dropped, they were not so quick to turn back funds when the foreign exchange rate moved in their favor.

The committee recommended creating a $500 million fund under the defense secretary's control to hold overseas expenditures on personnel and operations at the real level budgeted by Congress, regardless of foreign currency fluctuations. It would make good any funding shortfall that resulted from dollar devaluation, but it also would absorb any windfalls that might result from any relative increase in the dollar's value. The committee underscored the "anti-windfall" aspect of the new program by commenting that many economists felt the dollar to be undervalued in the world market and likely to rise in value.

The Army and Foreign Aid

The House Appropriations Committee cut $100.4 million for 28 Army helicopters that were to replace equipment left behind for South Korea's use when the U.S. 2nd Infantry Division was withdrawn. In effect, the Army was being required to finance U.S. aid to Seoul, the panel argued, since the equipment would have to be replaced through the Army's share of future defense budgets to the amount of more than $1 billion. The panel "encouraged" the administration to use the regular military assistance program to reimburse the Army for the arms transfer.

The panel also complained that the U.S. Army apparently had a lower priority than foreign governments in receiving newly produced M-60 tanks. In 1977 and 1978 foreign customers either had or were expected to receive their planned allotment of tanks while the Army absorbed production shortfalls that were due to domestic work stoppages and production problems.

Procurement and Research Policy

Duplication Opposed. The committee insisted that it was not opposed to duplicative weapons development programs as such, but it insisted that such programs be kept under tight managerial control by the Pentagon to avoid buying duplicate systems simply because of "artificial roles and mission distinctions and service rivalries."

It singled out as an example the dozen Army and Air Force research programs for missiles or bombs designed to break up massed tank attacks by releasing several small, non-nuclear warheads that would home-in on separate targets. The House Armed Services Committee had recommended consolidating many of the programs under the Pentagon's advanced research agency. But the Appropriations panel left most of the separate programs intact on the assumption that "the necessary attention of all concerned has been obtained."

In the case of an Air Force program to equip its planes for accurate bombing at night and in cloudy weather, the committee approved the $26.5 million requested, but ordered the service to adapt existing Navy equipment. But in other cases, the committee essentially froze spending on projects it deemed duplicative until further study identified one of the contenders as superior. Army and Marine field hospital systems and several positions-locating systems were held up on this basis.

Strategic Warfare

The committee dropped $911.9 million for the eighth Trident missile-launching submarine, which could not be built in fiscal 1979 because of long delays in constructing the first seven of the ships. Concerned over the delay and cost of the new submarines, it urged the Navy to consider putting the new Trident missile into more of the existing Poseidon submarines than the 10 ships currently planned to receive it. The longer range of the Trident missile would allow the submarines to keep their targets within range while sailing through a larger area, thus making it more difficult for Soviet submarine hunters to find them.

The committee also added $3 million for the Navy to study development of a smaller, less expensive missile submarine to succeed the Trident ships.

As in 1977, the committee recommended termination of the decade-long project (Seafarer) to build a large underground radio antenna so that missile submarines could receive orders without revealing their position.

It approved the $41.2 million request for development of a wide-body jet as a launcher for strategic cruise missiles.

Space War. Reported Soviet efforts to develop weapons to destroy space satellites sparked concern over the vulnerability of U.S. satellites used for communications and reconnaissance. Following the lead of the Senate Armed Services Committee, the panel added $15 million (bringing the total to $107.2 million) for two classified projects to defend U.S. satellites.

Tank, Anti-tank Combat

The committee approved the request to begin full-scale production of the new XM-1 tank (368.5 million for 110 tanks in fiscal 1979). But it warned that the Army might not be able to afford its planned production rate of 90 XM-1s a month by the early 1980s. In that period, the committee pointed out, the Army would face huge costs in beginning production of several major weapons. But it said that other NATO members' tank forces would contribute substantially to the military balance with the Soviet Union.

The committee increased by 50 percent — to $147.6 million — funds to modernize existing M-60 tanks with improved gun-aiming equipment. It said the Army should plan to modernize all 4,100 of the M-60s instead of only 1,700 as currently planned.

A total of $25.6 million was recommended for Army and Marine research programs on a tank of the future that would be much smaller and faster than current designs. This included an additional $5 million for the Marine project, as recommended by the Senate Armed Services Committee, so that the vehicle could be in production by 1985.

Chemical Warfare

Following the lead of Senate Armed Services, the panel increased by $4 million — to $24.9 million — research funds for chemical warfare. The Pentagon for years had said it needed some kind of chemical warfare equipment to deter the Soviet's use of their extensive chemical warfare armory. The budget request included $4.9 million for further development of binary munitions — bombs and artillery shells containing two chemicals that, when released, combined to form a lethal gas.

The committee also proposed a provision similar to one requested by the Pentagon that would permit the purchase of foreign-made chemical protective clothes for U.S. troops. In general, clothing was one of the items that had to be purchased from U.S. manufacturers because of so-called Buy-American restrictions.

Submarine, Anti-submarine Warfare

After the Navy had requested $25.2 million to finish development of a towed sonar system for frigates to seek out enemy submarines, it reported that the current design was unworkable. The committee allowed $20.2 million to rig an interim system for the ships and to perfect the new design. Three small listening ships (called T-AGOS, $98 million) designed to track submarines at great distances with a towed sonar system several hundred feet long were deleted by the committee.

The new sonar needed testing before the ships were built, the committee said, adding that it was not convinced the ships would survive in a war.

For continued development of the LAMPS III anti-submarine helicopter, $118.4 million (all but $6.1 million of the request), was approved. But the panel ordered the Navy to simplify the design to control the program's rising cost. And it sought to hold down the costs of submarines designed to hunt enemy subs. Although it approved the $325.6 million requested for another of the fast — and very expensive — 688-class nuclear-powered subs, it ordered the Navy to consider a new type of cheaper submarine — possibly a non-nuclear-powered ship — for the future.

It added $93 million for an experimental ship the size of a destroyer (called an SES) that could move at 80 mph on a bubble of trapped air. The Navy wanted to test the ship as a future submarine hunter, but the administration wanted to cancel the program.

Airlift

Boeing Corp. and McDonnell-Douglas Corp. each had produced prototype cargo jets designed to take off in very short distances, but the administration had canceled the program in the fiscal 1979 budget. The committee added $3 million so that one of the designs could be selected in case the program was restarted in future budgets.

The committee denied the $68.5 million requested to start a program that would pay airlines to modify their wide-body jets so they could rapidly be converted to haul military cargo in case of an emergency. While endorsing the general idea, the committee complained that the cost of the modifications had spiraled to the point where the program might no longer be worthwhile. It told the Pentagon to come back in the fiscal 1980 budget with a cheaper plan.

Communications Programs

The panel approved $4.05 billion for various communications programs, $115.3 million less than the administration request. Of the reduction, $40.5 million was for the Navy's Seafarer submarine communications system and $22.8 million was for communications security equipment. The committee insisted that existing equipment was not being fully used.

Communications Satellites. In 1977 the Pentagon had been forced by the committee to lease its future communications satellites from commercial firms rather than developing its own. The committee was outraged at what it considered the extremely high cost and long development times of the military programs. The committee repeated its insistence that the services move quickly to the leasing approach and it cut $21.7 million requested by the Air Force to begin research on two new communication satellite systems. "There is a robust industrial base to provide leased service [that] would be more cost-effective, more likely to be provided on schedule, and more realistic as to the required number of satellites," said the committee.

Intelligence

A $400 million reduction in the secret amount requested for intelligence programs was recommended by the committee. It said its recommendations differed only in minor respects from the secret recommendations of the House Permanent Select Committee on Intelligence.

It approved an increase to 220 in the Intelligence Community staff used by the Director of Central Intelligence to oversee the several agencies of the intelligence community. The administration had requested an increase to 303. The

The Wild, Blue Simulator

After the increase in oil prices that followed the 1973 Middle East War, the Defense Department set a goal of reducing its total number of flying hours 25 percent by 1981 to conserve fuel. The key to this would be increased use of computer-controlled flight simulators.

The operating costs of military planes ranged from $200 to $4,600 per flight hour. Simulator operations cost from $5 to $180 an hour, and the machines allowed pilots to practice maneuvers that would be extremely hazardous in actual flight. But the Appropriations Committee complained that the flight simulators on which the Pentagon had spent nearly $1.3 billion since 1974 were in use only about half the time and were not being substituted for actual flight operations.

Part of the problem was that the services were not designing training exercises to exploit the advantages of simulators, according to the committee. But part of the problem was that some officers in the military were unenthusiastic about using simulators in lieu of real airplanes. "Pilots take great pride in their ability to fly aircraft in an environment in which the pilot's skill stands between him and disaster. This love and dedication to flying are not satisfied . . . when he is training in the simulator."

The committee ordered the Pentagon to provide a report on simulator use with the fiscal 1980 budget request.

panel warned that the average rank of the existing staff was too high and recommended that more of the members be permanently assigned rather than detailed temporarily from the agencies that the staff was supposed to oversee.

Air Force Tactical Planes

Most of the combat planes requested by the Air Force were approved: 78 F-15 fighters ($1.2 billion), 145 F-16 fighters ($1.3 billion) and 162 A-10 tank-hunters ($839.3 million).

The committee recommended against an Air Force proposal to resume production of U-2 reconnaissance planes ($10.2 million for six planes, the first of a proposed fleet of 25). The new version, called TR-1s, would orbit high on the friendly side of a battle with extremely precise radar and other sensors to give U.S. combat commanders a bird's-eye view of the battle.

But the committee worried that the relatively slow plane could not survive the Soviet array of fighter planes and antiaircraft missiles.

Ammunition

More than $352.9 million was cut from the budget request for new ammunition and Army ammunition production plants. About $63 million of that was for tank ammunition, including training ammunition, that the committee deemed unnecessary since improved ammunition was under development. About $41 million was for new production facilities at three Army ammunition plants. The largest reduction — $22.8 million — was for a metal-working facility at the new Army plant at Bay St. Louis, Miss. The committee argued that ammunition components should be purchased from the private sector, to the extent possible, and that the Army had not adequately explored commercial alternatives to the new facility.

House Floor Action

No fundamental challenges to President Carter's defense policies were posed by the $119 billion fiscal 1979 Defense Department appropriations bill passed by the House Aug. 9.

Although HR 13635 contained a $2 billion nuclear aircraft carrier that the President opposed, Carter had announced he would request a slightly cheaper non-nuclear carrier next year anyway. And the House Appropriations Committee added the carrier only after cutting enough from other projects to keep the total appropriation within Carter's request.

During four days (Aug. 4, 7-9) of debate on the bill, several members complained that the administration was not spending enough on various components of national defense — especially on the Navy. And, as had been the case since 1975, the bill survived all major cuts proposed on the House floor.

Congressional anxiety over the Soviet military build-up, however, did not cancel out the equally strong concern over federal spending. Neither on the House floor nor in the Appropriations Committee was there any move to significantly increase spending in the fiscal 1979 budget above the administration's overall recommendations.

As passed, the bill appropriated $119 billion in new spending authority. This was $281 million less than Carter requested and $173.3 million below the committee-recommended figure. But it also allowed the Pentagon to use $160 million that had been appropriated in previous years but not spent. So the total funding provided by HR 13635 was only $121 million lower than the budget request.

Carrier Opponents Lose

The highlight of House action was the lengthy debate Aug. 7 on an amendment by Sidney R. Yates, D-Ill., to delete the $2.1 billion for the nuclear carrier. The amendment was rejected 156-218. An effort by Bill D. Burlison, D-Mo., to substitute the $1.5 billion conventional carrier that Carter planned to ask for next year was ruled out of order because the fiscal 1979 weapons procurement bill (HR 10929) had explicitly authorized only a nuclear carrier. On May 24 the House had rejected, 139-264, an amendment to the authorization bill that would have replaced the nuclear ship with the conventional one.

Yates and others argued that investing so much money in one ship and its attendant air wing and escort ships would prevent the Navy from buying large numbers of less expensive ships needed to cover potential trouble spots.

Jack Edwards, R-Ala., the senior Republican on the Defense Appropriations Subcommittee, listed various packages of warships that could be bought for the $2.5 million cost of the nuclear carrier. And he insisted there still was time to examine the feasibility of the less expensive carrier favored by the administration.

Appropriations Committee Chairman George Mahon, D-Texas, managing his last Pentagon money bill, maintained that the current fleet of 12 big carriers was enough to handle any enemy other than Russia. And he added that "the carrier will not be a decisive element in a war with the Soviet Union. A war with the Soviet Union would be bang, bang, bang, and what is left would be very little."

But carrier supporters argued that the big ship was an essential instrument of U.S. power. Fewer than 30 overseas airbases remained available to U.S. forces, they pointed out. And many of them were vulnerable to the kinds of political pressure that forced the United States to rely on carriers to support Israel during the 1973 Middle East War. The carrier was a potent political symbol of U.S. global power: "An overwhelmingly dramatic demonstration of the power and the strength and the resolve of this country. It demonstrates as no other thing can do our determination to keep peace in the world," said Bob Wilson, R-Calif.

Opposition by Republicans (23-104) and southern Democrats (16-61) doomed Yates' move. *(Vote 575, p. 164-H)*

Across-the-Board Cuts

The Pentagon proved to be immune to "Proposition 13 fever." By large margins the House rejected several amendments that would have cut portions of the bill by 1 or 2 percent. Similar cuts had been made by the House in several other fiscal 1979 appropriations bills since June when California voters overwhelmingly approved a slash in state property taxes.

The only debate that actually took place on the issue was on an amendment by Harold L. Volkmer, D-Mo., to cut 2 percent from Title I of the bill, which funded military personnel costs. "I believe that the military just as well as HEW or the Treasury Department or anybody else can find 2 percent to reduce . . . if they work hard, and they can still provide a good defense for this country."

Tom Harkin, D-Iowa, argued that there probably was more waste in the military than in other federal agencies because "the tendency is to overlook many inefficiencies and wasteful practices in the name of national security."

Chairman Mahon protested that the Appropriations Committee already had made numerous cuts in the huge bill after months of consideration. "How does it happen that the gentleman from Missouri is so wise, that everybody is wrong but he, and that he feels competent to redraft this $119 billion bill on the House floor in an afternoon?"

Edwards commented that many committee-recommended suggestions to make programs more efficient in the past had been rejected by the House. "If the authorizing committee would face up to some of the things we are talking about . . . perhaps we could cut some money, but that is not in the cards in this bill."

Volkmer's motion was rejected by more than a six-to-one margin (53-327). He later proposed the same reduction in appropriations for operations and maintenance and for procurement. These amendments were rejected by voice vote. *(Vote 573, p. 162-H)*

The House subsequently rejected an amendment by Harkin that would have applied a 2 percent cut to the whole bill (102-252) and a substitute amendment to it by Parren J. Mitchell, D-Md., that would have applied a 1 percent cut (136-222). *(Votes 581-582, p. 164-H)*

Reserve Recruiting Incentives

By 257-121, the House adopted an amendment by G. V. (Sonny) Montgomery, D-Miss., to increase by $15.6 million, to $25 million, funds for enlistment and re-enlistment incentives for the reserves and National Guard forces. *(Vote 572, p. 162-H)*

Montgomery, the Armed Services Committee's leading student of the reserves, said the Pentagon was dragging its feet in implementing the optional enlistment and re-enlistment bonuses and education benefits that Congress had created in 1977. These were intended to reverse the decline in reserve strength that resulted after the draft ended. The Defense Department had spent only half of the $5 million appropriated for these programs in 1977, Montgomery complained, and had requested only $500,000 for them in the fiscal 1979 budget.

Opponents of the amendment conceded that something had to be done about the reserves, but they maintained that more study was needed before Congress could make a major investment in the incentives programs. According to the Pentagon, education incentives had not been noticeably successful in six states that used them to attract National Guard enlistees. And some members of the Appropriations Committee warned that Congress might just wind up funding a bidding match for the same enlistees between the reserves and the active duty forces.

Blue-Collar Pay Reform

The committee's effort to streamline the wage system for federal blue-collar workers was thrown out on a point of order. But an amendment by Richard C. White, D-Texas, to delete the committee's 5.5 percent cap on pay increases for those workers was rejected by a 4-56 standing vote.

These 400,000 so-called Wage Board employees were paid under a system intended to provide the prevailing hourly wage for their craft in the local area. The committee had protested that the Wage Board formula actually led to overpayment of the workers. Since 340,000 of them worked for the Defense Department, the 5.5 percent pay cap alone would save $170 million in the spring 1979 pay raise supplemental appropriations, according to the panel.

White insisted that the pay freeze would be discriminatory since it would not affect the Wage Board employees who worked for other agencies. It would not even have the same effect on all Pentagon workers since workers in different regions received their annual pay raises at different times of the year.

Gladys Noon Spellman, D-Md., protested that her Post Office and Civil Service Subcommittee on Compensation was working on a Wage Board reform bill, but had been sidetracked by President Carter's civil service reform proposal. She agreed that changes were needed, but said the matter was far too complex to be handled by a simple pay cap.

But Mahon and Budget Committee Chairman Robert N. Giaimo, D-Conn., complained that Spellman's panel had taken too long to produce a bill. The pay cap would produce immediate savings while encouraging the subcommittee and Congress to move more quickly on full-scale Wage Board reform, they said.

Contracts and Jobs

The House considered two amendments dealing with the politics of allocating Pentagon contracts. It rejected 165-213 an amendment by James J. Howard, D-N.J., that would have allowed up to 10 percent of the defense budget to be directed to areas of high unemployment even if contract costs were higher in those areas. *(Vote 578, p. 164-H)*

Theoretically, it had been federal policy since February 1952 to target Pentagon contracts to combat high unemployment. But that policy had been eviscerated by the so-called Maybank amendment — added to every defense appropriations bill since 1953 — which forbade agreements involving higher contract costs to target defense procurement orders.

Supporters of the amendment said it would benefit the federal treasury since the resultant economic stimulus would cut welfare costs and increase tax revenues by more than enough to make up for the added procurement costs.

But the amendment was strongly opposed by Mahon, Edwards and others, who insisted the defense budget should not be manipulated for political purposes other than buying the best defense at the lowest cost.

The House also rejected, 72-302, an amendment by Garry Brown, R-Mich., to prevent the Pentagon from buying non-U.S.-made trucks to haul supplies in combat. Reportedly, the Army had been ordered by the Defense Department to look into the feasibility of buying German trucks for use by units stationed in Europe.

The Appropriations Committee had turned down as premature a budget request for $5 million to buy 50 German 10-ton trucks. No studies had yet been made comparing the German trucks with alternative vehicles. But the committee endorsed the basic policy of standardizing the equipment used by NATO forces in Europe. And it raised no objections to a Pentagon decision earlier in the year to buy 10,000 German cars and light trucks in the next seven years for non-combat use.

Brown warned that if his prohibition were not adopted, the Pentagon might present Congress with a *fait accompli* committing the United States to a large purchase of German equipment despite an already unfavorable U.S. balance of trade with West Germany. The United States already had shown its good faith commitment to buying European equipment to further NATO standardization, he insisted, and the alliance would not be harmed if this new purchase were deferred until the U.S. economic situation improved.

But several senior members of the Armed Services Committee and Defense Appropriations Subcommittee warned against interfering with administration plans to further alliance standardization. Mahon observed that the overall balance of trade with all the other NATO members was $3.6 billion in favor of the United States in 1977.

Helicopter Training Consolidation

In a tangled parliamentary situation, the House voted 252-128 to in effect consolidate basic helicopter pilot training under Army control at Ft. Rucker. Navy pilots currently trained at Pensacola, Fla. *(Vote 574, p. 162-H)*

William L. Dickinson, R-Ala., whose district included Ft. Rucker, argued that the consolidation would save the Defense Department an estimated $97 million over the first five years and eliminate 2,000 jobs. He emphasized that only basic training was involved and that the Navy's own training program included less than an hour's flight time over water. The special training over water would be handled in the advance course that the Navy would continue to run, according to Dickinson.

Robert L. F. Sikes, D-Fla., whose district contained the Pensacola base, dismissed the estimated savings as inconsistent with Navy estimates, and he charged that the claimed efficiencies of consolidating the training program were based on untested assumptions of "think-tank civilians." The special demands of navigating over water and landing on ships permeated the entire training program, according to Sikes. And unlike Army helicopter pilots, Navy pilots were given training that would allow them to remain on flying duty throughout their Navy careers.

Medical Care and Abortions

On a point of order, a committee provision was thrown out that would have limited reimbursement by CHAMPUS to not more than the 80th percentile of customary medical charges for comparable services.

By a vote of 226-163, the House adopted an amendment by Robert K. Dornan, R-Calif., that would bar use of funds in the bill to pay for any abortion not required to save the life of the mother. The amendment contained the same limitation that the House earlier had placed on funds appropriated to the Health, Education and Welfare Department. Between Sept. 1, 1976, and Sept. 1, 1977, about 26,500 abortions were performed in military hospitals or paid for by CHAMPUS. *(Vote 584, p. 166-H)*

Other Amendments

The House also rejected amendments:

- By William S. Cohen, R-Maine, to increase by $3.3 million funds for the Navy's supervisor of shipbuilding. Standing vote, 12-26.
- By Robert N. Giaimo, D-Conn., as amended by Margaret M. Heckler, R-Mass. *(identical to separate amendment, below)*, to delete $3 million to continue development of a new diesel engine for use in future combat vehicles; 107-269. *(Vote 576, p. 164-H)*
- By Margaret M. Heckler, R-Mass., to add $1 million for the Army's food research program; 103-277. *(Vote 577, p. 164-H)*

An amendment by Glenn M. Anderson, D-Calif., to require the secretary of the Navy to report on various steps to reduce the health hazard of asbestos used in shipbuilding was ruled out of order.

The House also adopted the following amendments among others:

- By Robert C. McEwen, R-N.Y., to add $2 million for Pentagon assistance at the 1980 Winter Olympic Games. Voice vote.
- By John M. Ashbrook, R-Ohio, to bar the scrapping of certain surplus rifles advertised for sale. Voice vote. The intent of the amendment was to preserve some 290,000 M-1 rifles that the Pentagon had hoped to sell for scrap instead of selling them to private gun clubs affiliated with the Pentagon's civilian marksmanship program. An earlier amendment that would have required the sale of the guns to the clubs was ruled out of order as non-germane.
- By Silvio O. Conte, R-Mass., to drop committee language that would prohibit expansion of the Pentagon's competitive bidding policies for moving the household goods of transferred military personnel, 269-96. *(Vote 580, p. 164-H)*
- The House also approved by voice votes four technical amendments that removed $200.3 million from the bill for items not authorized in the final version of the fiscal 1979 weapons procurement bill (HR 10929). The largest reductions were $90 million for 15 Harrier V/STOL light bombers and $60.6 million for 12 A-7E Navy light bombers.

Provisions

As passed by the House Aug. 9, HR 13635 appropriated the following amounts for Defense Department programs (other than construction) in fiscal 1979:

Program	Administration Request	House-Passed Amount
Military Personnel	$27,211,200,000	$27,191,946,000
Military Pensions	10,148,938,000	10,139,838,000
Operations and Maintenance	37,376,200,000	37,345,105,000
Procurement	31,927,600,000	31,989,164,000
(Transfers from prior appropriations)	(0)	(136,400,000)
Research and Development	12,468,000,000	12,184,608,000
(Transfer from prior appropriations)	(0)	(23,800,000)
Special Foreign Currency Program	14,362,000	13,092,000
Working Capital Funds	100,800,000	100,800,000
(Transfer authority)	(750,000,000)	(750,000,000)
Related Agencies	53,183,000	54,725,000
Total, New Budget Authority	$119,300,283,000	$119,019,278,000
Total transfers from prior appropriations	0	160,200,000
Total funding made available	$119,300,283,000	$119,179,478,000

Senate Committee Action

The Senate Appropriations Committee reported HR 13635 Oct. 2 (S Rept 95-1264). As reported, the bill contained $116,316,635,000 in new budget authority. Significant differences from the House-passed version included the following:

Fringe Benefits

In general, the panel was less sympathetic than its House counterpart to fringe benefits for military members, thus setting the stage for another battle over "erosion of benefits." This was a disputed item in the fiscal 1978 defense funding bill. *(Fiscal 1978 Defense Appropriations story, 1977 Almanac p. 264)*

Critics of the traditional fringe benefits argued that they were intended to compensate for the very low pay of military personnel. But in the last decade, military pay had become roughly comparable with civil service pay rates, so such benefits as subsidies to commissaries no longer were needed, they maintained.

But opponents of this view insisted that the traditional fringe benefits fostered a communal spirit that the military needed because of the extraordinary stresses of military life. And they maintained that service morale was being undermined by the continual whittling away of these traditional benefits in recent years.

The Senate committee cut $113 million from the $338.9 million requested to subsidize commissary operations. This was to be the first stage in a three-year phase-out of the subsidy. The panel also entirely deleted the $79 million requested to transport goods to overseas post exchanges (department stores), insisting that those facilities should charge enough to cover their basic operating expenses. Both of these reductions had been recommended by the panel in previous years, but subsequently restored in conference.

Of more than 10,000 military personnel assigned to various morale and recreation activities, including post exchanges, open messes (restaurants) and publications, the panel ordered that some 1,900 be transferred to more essential military functions. The effect of this policy decision would be to eliminate a partial subsidy for those activities, forcing them to raise their prices or user fees.

The panel cut the $103.1 million requested to give junior enlisted members stationed abroad the same allowance to transport their families as was paid to all other military personnel. The committee, and especially Chairman John C. Stennis, D-Miss., was afraid that the large number of military dependents already in Europe would inhibit the combat effectiveness of U.S. forces in case of an emergency. But senior Army officials had argued strongly that the new benefit was essential to maintain the morale, and increase the re-enlistment rate, of the troops in Europe.

On the other hand, the Senate committee reversed the House decision cutting $10 million from the $55 million requested for a program that would pay 75 percent of the tuition and expenses of servicemen who were going to school in their off-duty hours.

Training

In general, the committee agreed with the House position that some of the administration-proposed cutbacks in the amount of recruit training were too severe. But it disagreed with the House decision adding funds to keep the Marine Corps recruit training period at about 11 weeks (instead of 9 weeks as proposed).

The Senate committee also rejected an administration proposal, supported by the House, to consolidate under Army control all basic helicopter pilot training. The Navy wanted to run its own basic training course.

Reserves

The panel agreed with the House in continuing the enlistment and re-enlistment bonuses that Congress created in fiscal 1978 and 1979 to overcome the declining membership in the reserves.

It added $197 million, which was not requested, for transport planes and training versions of the A-7 light bomber for use by reserve units.

And it rejected a House proposal that the reserves employ reserve members on active duty, instead of civil service technicians, for certain administrative and maintenance services. Reserve units already were burdened with a number of administrative experiments, the committee warned, and one more would just add to the confusion.

On one of the most emotionally charged reserve issues in the budget, the Senate committee agreed in part with the Pentagon's effort — now in its third year — to cut back the Naval Reserve to only those units that would play an important role immediately after any mobilization.

The administration proposed to cut the reserve to 51,500 — from 87,000 — and to phase out an air shuttle service run by the Naval Reserve principally to carry its own members to their training stations.

The House Appropriations Committee had completely rejected the proposed cutback, and added to the budget 1) $74.9 million to keep the reserve at its current strength, 2) $9 million to operate the air shuttle, and 3) $16.1 million for another DC-9 jetliner to beef up the Navy's air transport fleet.

The Senate panel recommended a 74,600-man Naval Reserve — adding only $53.45 million to the budget request — and agreed with the cancellation of the air shuttle, including use of the new DC-9.

Civilian Employees

The committee deleted a House provision that would have prohibited the payment to foreign nationals working at U.S. bases abroad of wages and benefits that were in excess of locally prevailing rates. Foreign labor rates were set by international agreements or contracts that the United States could not unilaterally abrogate, it argued.

Inflation and Devaluation

"A certain amount of inflation in operation and maintenance should be absorbed by [the Pentagon] as a basic, efficacious element of resource management discipline," the committee reasoned. So it cut $618.4 million from the $1.5 billion budgeted to fully cover the cost of inflation on the Pentagon's $36 billion operations and maintenance funds request. The House had allowed the full inflation buffer.

But the Senate committee disagreed with the House position that the Pentagon could save $155 million of the amount budgeted for consumables — everything from paper clips to gasoline — by tighter management practices. It added back all but $24 million of the House cut.

The basic House idea of creating a $500 million revolving fund to protect the Pentagon's budget against devaluation of the dollar was accepted by the Senate panel. But the Senate version differed in some administrative respects.

Procurement Policy

The panel's basic position on Pentagon weapons procurement policy forecast future showdowns with the Pentagon and with the two Armed Services Committees. Senate Appropriations panel members, and especially Lawton Chiles, D-Fla., were determined to force the Pentagon to follow the principles of the Office of Management and Budget's circular A-109 on the purchase of major pieces of hardware.

The basic approach prescribed by A-109 for any government procurement was that the purchasing agency define for industry the job that it wanted done rather than defining the specifications of the hardware it wanted to buy. The assumption was that the agency thus would get the benefit of industry competition not only in producing a specified item for the lowest price but also in coming up with the best concept for solving the problem.

In its report, the committee complained that the Pentagon had begun to develop several important new systems without having defined the problems they were to solve. It told the Pentagon to follow the new procedure in the next budget for several weapons that were important to the military and which the services were reluctant to turn over to industry for their design. These included a system called Assault Breaker that was intended to wipe out large numbers of enemy tanks with multiple, non-nuclear, homing warheads and a long-range mobile ballistic missile.

Strategic Weapons

Both houses had long since given up any hope of being able to fund an additional Trident missile-launching submarine in fiscal 1979 because of snarls in the shipyard where it would be built. But the Senate panel also cut to $55 million the amount appropriated for nuclear power plant components for ships that would be funded in the future. The House had funded nearly five times as much.

The panel deleted all $114 million requested for one of the two anti-ballistic missile (ABM) research projects run by the Army. The canceled program was directed at ABM systems that could be assembled more or less off the shelf from technologies that already had been tested. The committee said that all these approaches were "out of date and unworkable." Left untouched was the $113.5 million requested for another program experimenting in exotic ABM techniques.

Ground Combat Forces

The panel recommended restoration of $55 million for eight cargo helicopters and 12 tank-hunting helicopters that the House committee had deleted on the grounds that they were, in effect, intended as military assistance for South Korea.

House cuts in the Army ammunition budget that the Senate panel restored included $62.7 million for tank ammunition, $50 million for new electronic time fuzes and $46 million for shipping costs. The committee added $20 million to the $64.6 million in the budget for the Army's ammunition plant in Mississippi.

Airlift and Sealift

For a long debated program to modify commercial jetliners so they could haul military cargo in an emergency, the committee approved $7.5 million. And it added to the budget $14 million to complete development of a cargo plane (called AMST) designed to take off and land in relatively short distances. The panel ordered the Navy to design a system for modifying U.S. merchant ships during a crisis so they could haul U.S. troops and their supplies in an amphibious landing.

Combat Aircraft

Small reductions were recommended in the number of Air Force combat planes to be purchased: 120 A-10 tank-hunters (a cut of 42 planes saving $212 million) and 120 F-16 fighters (a cut of 25 planes saving $140 million). No reduction was recommended in the request for 78 F-15 fighters ($1.3 billion).

Warships

The committee approved the funds required for a large package of shipbuilding and research programs that were added to the budget by the Senate Armed Services Committee and included in the final version of the enacted authorization bill (HR 14042). The thrust of the package was to speed the development of smaller, less expensive aircraft carriers carrying vertical takeoff combat planes (V/STOLs).

The committee approved several submarine-hunting projects the House had deleted, including $98 million for three ships (called T-AGOS) designed to locate submarines at a great distance with huge towed sonar sets.

The committee also rejected House reductions in the request for a new sonar for anti-submarine frigates and for an underwater surveillance network.

Other Provisions

The committee recommended against an amendment added on the House floor that would narrowly restrict the use of Pentagon funds for performing abortions in military hospitals or to pay for abortions through CHAMPUS.

It retained a provision added to the defense appropriations bill in 1977 on the Senate floor requiring the Pentagon to report to Congress on the distribution of subcontracts by states. Previously, only prime contracts were reported by states, but a very large part of those sums actually went into the economies of other states.

Senate Floor Action

The Senate approved a $116.4 billion fiscal 1979 Defense Department appropriations bill Oct. 5 after restoring nearly two-thirds of the $349 million cut by the House from the Army's ammunition budget.

In explaining his Aug. 17 veto of the companion weapons authorization bill, President Carter had cited the ammunition budget as one of the vital programs that he said Congress had reduced in order to pay for the $2 billion nuclear aircraft carrier he opposed. *(Veto message, p. 59-E; veto override vote, see National Security chapter)*

But the Senate ignored Carter's objections to cuts it had made in another part of the defense money bill. It insisted on removing $618 million of some $1.5 billion budgeted by the Defense Department to absorb the impact of inflation on the Pentagon's operations and maintenance.

Opponents of the cut had warned that this would force the military to reduce its scheduled training and maintenance activities below the budgeted levels.

HR 13635 was passed by an 86-3 vote. It funded practically all of the military's programs except real property construction. *(Vote 441, p. 65-S)*

As approved, the total amount was about $2.7 billion below the House-passed figure, but the removal of the appropriation for the aircraft carrier accounted for much of the difference.

The Senate took up HR 13635 on Oct. 4, the day after the committee report was filed. Debate that day and the next was dominated by Ernest F. Hollings', D-S.C., challenge to Stennis on the issue of dependents' travel allowances for junior enlisted personnel.

Dependents' Travel Allowance

With his customary flamboyance, Hollings argued the Pentagon's case that extension of the travel allowance to junior ranks was essential for keeping up morale in the era of the volunteer Army.

"We do not want them chasing the mademoiselles, the frauleins, or anybody else. We want them with the families," Hollings said. The problem with the current policy was its inequity, he charged, since there already were 122,500 dependents of service members who had received the travel allowance.

The $95 million Hollings wanted to add to the committee bill would reimburse another 20,000 dependents of junior personnel who had gone to Europe at their own expense and would pay the allowance for another 4,000 dependents who would have the opportunity to go to Europe if they so wished.

Stennis strongly reaffirmed the committee's position: The large number of dependents in Europe was a serious impediment to U.S. combat effectiveness in case of a military emergency on the continent. "Who is going to get to use the highways? That is one thing. Everybody who lives over there will be wanting to move, too. We do not have the cargo [capacity] to bring those people out quickly. Are we going to provide that for that money? What are we going to do about housing? Are we going to build it?" Stennis asked. He wanted to take the issue to conference with the House to work out an interim solution for fiscal 1979 while the Pentagon was put on notice to freeze and, eventually, to cut back the number of dependents abroad, Stennis said.

Eventually, a compromise was struck adding $85 million to the bill, on a voice vote, to pay the allowance for those dependents already overseas. But the Pentagon was warned not to send over any more, pending resolution of the issue in conference.

1 Percent Cut

As was the case on several votes earlier in the year, the Pentagon remained immune to Proposition 13 fever. While fear of a taxpayers' revolt prompted Congress to adopt across-the-board cuts of 2-5 percent in various federal department appropriations bills, an effort to cut 1 percent from HR 13635 was rejected overwhelmingly, 11-74. *(Vote 440, p. 65-S)*

George McGovern, D-S.D., offered the 1 percent cut amendment, arguing that it would "give us a chance to save the dollar from the Germans and the Japanese — and we will count on Senator Stennis' remaining $115 billion to save us from the Russians and the Chinese." Only nine liberal Democrats and two Republicans — Robert P. Griffin, Mich., and Mark O. Hatfield, Ore. — supported the amendment.

Other Amendments

The Senate adopted by voice vote two amendments:

- By Robert Morgan, D-N.C., to appropriate additional funds so as to maintain the size of the Naval Reserve at 87,000, thus reversing the committee's cut in manpower.
- By Mike Gravel, D-Alaska, to appropriate $700,000 for a study of a sea-level canal between the Atlantic and Pacific.

Provisions

As passed by the Senate Oct. 5, HR 13635 appropriated the following amounts for Defense Department programs (other than construction) in fiscal 1979:

Program	House-Passed Amount	Senate-Passed Amount
Military Personnel	$27,191,946,000	$27,201,108,000
Military Pensions	10,139,838,000	10,079,838,000
Operations and Maintenance	37,345,105,000	37,035,492,000
Procurement	31,989,164,000	29,972,377,000
(Transfers from prior appropriations)	(136,400,000)	(70,000,000)
Research and Development	12,184,608,000	11,962,095,000
(Transfer from prior appropriations)	(23,800,000)	(41,000,000)
Special Foreign Currency Program	13,092,000	14,362,000
Working Capital Funds	100,800,000	100,800,000
(Transfer authority)	(750,000,000)	(750,000,000)
Related Agencies	54,725,000	56,200,000
Interoceanic Canal Study Council	——	700,000
Total, New Budget Authority	$119,019,278,000	$116,422,972,000

Total transfers from prior appropriations	160,200,000	111,000,000
Total funding made available	$119,179,478,000	$116,533,972,000

Conference Action

The conference report on HR 13635 (H Rept 95-1764) was filed Oct. 11 after the Senate-House conferees had met for four days, beginning the same afternoon the Senate passed the bill (Oct. 5).

The pressure for quick action was intense. The Senate did not pass the bill until the fifth day of the new fiscal year, and it had not considered a continuing resolution for the Defense Department to provide temporary financing of the Pentagon's operations. Unless the conference report were adopted and the bill signed by the president by the end of the week, it was anticipated that the Defense Department might not be able to meet its first payroll of fiscal 1979.

Throughout the last week of the session, congressional offices were deluged with mail and phone calls from worried Pentagon employees, inquiring about the status of the bill. According to several Capitol Hill aides, some base commanders inadvertently had contributed to the panic by taking precautions such as notifying local lending institutions to prepare for numerous, short-term emergency loan applications.

Although some 520 disagreements between the House and Senate had to be resolved by the conference committee, the task was less hopeless than it appeared. As was customary, the vast majority of the disagreements were dealt with by the Appropriations Committees' staffs. Only those items of special interest to conferees — including items directly affecting their constituents — were discussed at any length by the conferees.

Military Abortions

Conferees agreed to substitute the less stringent abortion limitation language incorporated in the fiscal 1978 Labor/HEW appropriations bill for the more drastic House-approved language. Anti-abortionists had condemned this provision as too loose, and shortly before the House adopted the conference compromise it rejected the same language for the fiscal 1979 Labor/HEW bill. (Just before adjourning, however, Congress agreed to the more liberal 1978 language for the fiscal 1979 Labor/HEW vill as well. *See p. 105)*

But the House anti-abortionists said that they trusted the Pentagon, unlike HEW, to write very stringent regulations governing the application of the legislative language. And they promised not to force a separate House vote on the new abortion language for fear of delaying passage of the defense bill.

The House by a wide margin had voted to add a very rigorous ban on the use of Pentagon funds for non-therapeutic abortions to its version of the defense bill, while the Senate had eliminated all language restricting abortions.

Fringe Benefits

Dependents' Travel Allowances. As recommended by the House, $95 million was approved to pay junior enlisted personnel stationed abroad the same dependents' travel allowance as was paid to all other military members. But to satisfy the intense concern of Sen. Stennis, conferees ordered the Pentagon to report by the end of January 1979 on the extent to which the 122,000 U.S. dependents in Europe inhibited U.S. combat efficiency and endangered the dependents themselves.

Commissaries. A Senate proposal to phase out over three years the nearly $340 million annual subsidy for military commissaries was rejected. And only a small reduction was made in the $79 million requested to ship goods to overseas post exchanges; the Senate had deleted most of the appropriation.

Nearly all the House conferees appeared to be of the opinion that removal of these traditional fringe benefits would undermine military morale. Of the Senate conferees, only Thomas F. Eagleton, D-Mo., who sponsored the commissary subsidy phase-out, strongly supported that position.

Medical Care. In addition to restricting the use of Pentagon funds to pay for abortions, the committee increased the rates at which private physicians would be paid by CHAMPUS in hopes of encouraging greater physician participation in the program.

Training

An administration request to consolidate all basic training for helicopter pilots under Army control was turned down. Although the consolidation had been approved through a House floor amendment, the Senate adamantly supported the Navy's desire to run its own training program at Pensacola, Fla.

Although the House had voted by large margins to approve the consolidation and to instruct its conferees to insist on that position, several of the most active House conferees openly fought consolidation, including Robert L. F. Sikes, D-Fla.).

A proposed reduction in the 11-week basic training period for Marine recruits also was turned down. Noting that the Marine training program took far longer than that of any other service, the administration had proposed a two-week reduction. The Senate agreed to a one-week cut, and Marine headquarters supported that position since it would have released 1,200 Marines for duties other than training. But House conferees were adamant. "They're going to be meaner than anybody else, so it'll take a little longer," quipped Jack Edwards, R-Ala.

Reserves

Both houses had agreed on several additions to the budget request to strengthen the reserves (and thus were part of the final bill), including: 1) additional funds for enlistment and re-enlistment bonuses and education benefits to increase reserve membership; 2) the purchase of new fighter and transport planes for the Air Force Reserve and Air National Guard; and 3) retaining the Naval Reserve at its present strength of 87,000. Since these provisions were in both houses' versions, they were not part of the conference negotiations.

In addition, conferees adopted the House position in favor of maintaining an air shuttle service run by the Naval Reserve to carry its own members to and from their drill units and purchasing a new DC-9 jetliner for the shuttle runs.

Inflation Protection

Of the $1.5 billion requested to cover anticipated inflation in operations and maintenance costs, $188.5 million was to pay the Pentagon's share of the crude oil equalization tax that had been the centerpiece of President Carter's original energy policy. Since the proposed tax had long since been discarded by Congress, both houses deleted that amount from the request.

Of the remaining $1.31 billion, the House cut $43.2 million while the Senate cut $430 million, insisting that this would force the services to run a tight ship financially.

The conference agreement reducing the amount by $260 million, to a total of $1.05 billion, was arrived at indirectly. For those operations and maintenance budget items in disagreement on which the Pentagon had placed the highest priority, conferees adopted the higher of the amounts voted by the House and the Senate. Then the administration's inflation request was reduced by the amount necessary to bring the overall operations and maintenance appropriation within the ceiling available to the conferees.

Foreign Civilian Pay

Over the strong opposition of House conferees and Senate Appropriations Committee Chairman Warren G. Magnuson, D-Wash., a House provision that would have prevented the Pentagon from paying foreign civilian employees at U.S. bases abroad more than they would make at a comparable job in the local economy was dropped.

The State Department had conceded that many foreign employees were overpaid, but warned that unilateral U.S. action would violate existing treaties and labor contracts. The Japanese ambassador to Washington had personally phoned several of the conferees to assure them that the Japanese government was trying to resolve the problem at U.S. bases in Japan.

Magnuson was unimpressed with either plea. "Some days I wonder who the hell [the State Department] represents," he fumed. Nor was he moved by the Japanese ambassador's promises. "They won't deal on anything, they won't help us on the dollar and now they want us to pay more [to Japanese employees at U.S. bases] than our own people," he shouted. "Sometimes I wonder who won the war."

In the end, the House ban was dropped. But conferees ordered the Defense Department to do something to end the overpayment of its foreign national employees.

Helicopters and Foreign Aid

The House had rejected the entire request for cargo helicopters and tank-hunting helicopters that were to be used by U.S. forces in South Korea. Since the equipment would be turned over to South Korea when the U.S. troops were withdrawn under Carter's policy, the Army was, in effect, paying for a foreign aid program, it argued.

The Senate had approved funding for all the helicopters and Senate conferees, especially Magnuson and Richard S. Schweiker, R-Pa., argued strenuously for funding them. They would be built in Philadelphia by the Boeing Corp., headquartered in Seattle.

Reluctantly, the House conferees agreed to a compromise funding the cargo ships. But conferees insisted they be assigned to U.S. forces in Europe and that the Army be reimbursed in a foreign aid appropriations bill for the value of the equipment it would turn over to South Korea once the withdrawal was completed.

Strategic Warfare

Both houses had long since given up on funding another Trident missile-launching submarine in fiscal 1979 since the production snags would make it impossible to begin work on a new ship. But conferees approved $198 million for the nuclear power plant components for Tridents that would be funded in future years. Adm. Hyman G. Rickover, the Navy's nuclear power czar, had warned that if the components were not produced, the production line would have to shut down.

Airlift

As recommended by the Senate, $7.5 million was approved for a long-debated program to design commercial jetliners that could be easily converted to carry military cargo during national emergencies.

New Navy

Conferees dropped the most dramatic component of the Senate Armed Services Committee's Navy V/STOL package. This would have modified an existing helicopter carrier so it could operate V/STOL planes and helicopters as a light aircraft carrier. A new, larger helicopter carrier, to serve as an amphibious attack ship for the Marine Corps, would have been built to replace the converted carrier.

The strongest opposition to the conversion, apparently, came from senior House members who doubted that V/STOL planes ever would match the combat effectiveness of conventional jets.

But important parts of the Senate package were fully funded, including an amount more than double that requested by the administration for development of an improved version of the Harrier V/STOL jet used by the Marines. This improved version could be in service by the mid-1980s. And the conferees approved the $25 million added by the Senate to design a new V/STOL carrier that could be used by the improved plane.

Conferees also approved several Senate-sponsored research projects to develop new types of high-speed ships and to modularize some combat equipment so that it could be quickly installed on warships or on merchant ships in case of war.

Sub Hunting. The conference agreement dropped House cuts made in the budget request for several types of sonar systems designed to locate enemy submarines. And it approved construction of the first two of a new type of picket ship designed to locate submarines at great distances, using large, towed sonar equipment. The House had denied the entire request for three of the ships (called T-AGOS).

Final Action

The House adopted the conference report on HR 13635 by voice vote Oct. 12. A few hours later, the Senate approved it by a vote of 77-3. *(Vote 483, p. 70-S)*

President Carter signed the bill Oct. 13, in time to ensure that Pentagon employees received their paychecks. ▮

Agriculture Appropriations

The Carter administration won a modest victory with the fiscal 1979 agriculture appropriations bill (HR 13125 — PL 95-448), using veto threats to nudge many unwanted policy changes from the final version and to curb over-budget spending proposals.

The final version still appropriated $198 million more than the president had requested, but that was less than half the over-budget additions of the original House version, which had been marked for a veto. (House sponsor Jamie L. Whitten, D-Miss., maintained that the conference agreement actually was $210 million less than the budget request because new borrowing authority shouldn't be included. Whitten had also disputed the administration's claim that the original House bill was $415.8 million over budget.)

Conferees also restored almost all the deep House cuts in expenses for Agriculture Secretary Bob Bergland's office, and they dropped or softened a number of House directives on staffing levels and similar matters. Bergland had said these restrictions would hamstring his administrative efforts.

The final bill also lifted a ban on participation by South Korea in the Food for Peace program. The administration had not taken a position on the prohibition, which had been passed by the House only. The ban was intended to force Korea to send former ambassador Kim Dong Jo to testify before a congressional committee about alleged payoffs to members of Congress.

A major loss for the administration, however, was the refusal of conferees to fund a new program to control non-point source pollution (pesticide runoff from farmland and similar problems). The administration wanted to consolidate existing conservation efforts, administered through three old-line agencies, into a single program which would handle the new pollution control program, among others. A major goal of the reorganization was to redirect funds used for cost-sharing conservation projects, which the administration said were more often used to increase a farmer's yield than to make enduring improvements to farmland. But that initiative, already tangled in an interagency struggle within the Agriculture Department, ran into strong objections in both the Senate and the House. The highly visible and popular cost-sharing programs survived the latest of numerous presidential efforts to end them. Conferees continued to fund the projects, but put a ceiling on the total amount each producer could receive and stressed that the projects should make permanent, conservation-related improvements.

Among other disputed projects that stayed in the final bill were a costly new nutrition laboratory in Boston, small appropriations for urban gardens and wholesale markets, and many plant- and pest-specific research and control programs; all had been deleted by the Senate.

Conferees also decided to permit "super-donuts" — vitamin-fortified pastries — to continue to grace school breakfasts, but only for the current school year. The House had sought to quash an Agriculture Department ban on the breakfast sweets by authorizing local school administrators to decide whether to use them.

The bill appropriated $5.1 billion more than the 1978 appropriation, but spending for Agriculture and related agencies was actually $410 below the prior year's level. The fiscal 1979 total included $5.5 billion in new borrowing authority, which masked the shrinkage. Rural development programs were $81 million below the 1978 appropriation, international food programs down $100 million.

Domestic food programs — food stamps, school lunches, nutritional supplements for infants and pregnant women — were the only area of major growth, with a $217 million increase over fiscal 1978. The food programs are the largest item in the department's budget.

Agriculture programs, including price supports, were down by almost $450 million when the additional borrowing authority was discounted. It was a bill that "demonstrates that no longer should the Senate take for granted full funding of heretofore 'sacred' programs," according to Henry Bellmon, Okla., ranking Republican on the Senate Appropriations Agriculture Subcommittee.

Provisions

As signed into law, HR 13125 made the following appropriations for fiscal 1979:

	Budget Request	Final Appropriation
Agricultural Programs		
Departmental Management	$ 64,680,000	$ 56,103,000
Federal Grain Inspection Service	22,708,000	22,680,000
Agricultural Research Service	331,088,000	379,886,000
Animal and Plant Health Inspection Service	220,213,000	232,141,000
Food Safety and Quality Service[1]	271,475,000	271,104,000
Cooperative State Research Service	158,150,000	174,395,000
Extension Service	262,047,000	275,399,000
National Agricultural Library	7,631,000	7,527,000
Economics, Statistics and Cooperative Service[2]	80,008,000	80,112,000
Agricultural Marketing Service[3]	49,231,000	48,102,000
World Food and Agricultural Outlook and Situation Board[4]	1,009,000	1,009,000
Agricultural Stabilization and Conservation Service	231,056,000	230,767,000
Federal Crop Insurance Corporation	12,000,000	12,000,000
Commodity Credit Corporation	5,500,000,000	5,500,000,000
Subtotal, Agricultural Programs	$ 7,211,296,000	$ 7,291,225,000
Rural Development and Assistance Programs		
Farmers Home Administration	1,178,164,000	1,206,505,000
Rural Electrification Administration	24,833,000	24,805,000
Soil Conservation Service	523,247,000	496,695,000
Agricultural Stabilization and Conservation Service	130,000,000	225,000,000
Subtotal, Rural Development and Assistance Programs	$1,856,244,000	$1,953,005,000
Domestic Food Programs		
Child Nutrition Programs	$1,281,535,000	$1,285,535,000
Special Milk Program	142,000,000	142,000,000
Special Supplemental Food Program (WIC)	555,000,000	569,500,000
Food Stamp Program	5,779,200,000	5,779,200,000
Food Donations Program	12,800,000	12,800,000
Food Program Administration	72,223,000	74,275,000
Subtotal, Domestic Food Programs[5]	$7,842,758,000	$7,863,310,000
International Programs		
Foreign Agricultural Service	$ 51,663,000	$ 53,645,000

	Budget Request	Final Appropriation
International Development Staff	199,000	199,000
Food for Peace (PL 480)	805,900,000	805,900,000
Subtotal, International Programs	$ 857,762,000	$ 859,744,000
Related Agencies		
Food and Drug Administration	$ 306,288,000	$ 305,613,000
Commodity Futures Trading Commission	15,804,000	15,304,000
Subtotal, Related Agencies	$ 322,092,000	$ 320,917,000
Total: Fiscal year 1978 new budget authority	$18,090,152,000	$18,288,201,000
Section 32 Transfers	1,411,575,000	1,411,575,000

1) New service which inspects meat and poultry, formerly a function of the Animal and Plant Health Inspection Service.

2) New service continuing the functions of the former Statistical Reporting, Economic Research and Farm Cooperative services.

3) Includes functions of old Packers and Stockyards Administration.

4) New entity created in 1977 by the secretary of agriculture.

5) The Elderly Feeding Program was transferred to the Department of Health, Education and Welfare.

Loan Authorizations. HR 13125 also provided the following loan authorizations:

- $4,668,232,000 for the rural housing insurance fund. (Budget request: $3,981,132,000)
- $2,074,165,000 for the agricultural credit insurance fund. (Budget request: $1,824,165,000)
- $2,357,276,000 for the rural development insurance fund. (Budget request: $2,257,276,000)
- $1,100,000,000 for the rural electrification and telephone revolving fund. (Budget request: $985,000,000)

Other Provisions. The bill also contained $115 million in funds to liquidate contract authority for the Agricultural Stabilization and Conservation Service.

House Committee Action

The House Appropriations Committee added more than $400 million in new spending to the president's budget, shifted programs around within the Agriculture Department and mandated substantially higher personnel ceilings for certain programs.

Administration cuts in needed research, conservation and rural development "investments" made for a budget that was "seriously out of balance," the committee said in its June 13 report (H Rept 95-1290) on HR 13125.

The president's budget made "no lasting contribution to the nation's economic base," the committee said. By contrast, the committee's bill would safeguard the farm industry — and the economic well-being of the nation, the report said. The report dealt at length with the theme that depressions begin on the farm, and that farm finances in 1978 were as bad as those that led to the 1930s depression.

But the size and distribution of committee amendments for research and conservation prompted one Agriculture Department official to characterize the "investment" as political. "These are highly visible programs back in the district, and there's just a lot of good old-fashioned back-scratching in the bill," he said.

Modest restorations of funds for urban gardens and 4-H clubs and new central-city wholesale markets also reflected political realities — that farm bills are hard to pass unless urban members find in them something of interest.

The types of changes made in the president's budget were longstanding tradition with the House Appropriations Subcommittee on Agriculture, whose chairman, Jamie L. Whitten, D-Miss., is sometimes referred to as "the permanent secretary of agriculture." But in 1978 the extent of subcommittee revisions outstripped that of previous years, prompting an unusual protest visit by Bergland to the House and Senate Appropriations Committees.

Although the administration disagreed, the committee said its many restorations of funds for research, conservation and development projects did not mean any over-budget spending — just a rearrangement of priorities.

The committee recommended a total of $18.014 billion in new budget authority for fiscal 1979, $76 million less than the budget request of $18.09 billion. The bill exceeded the fiscal 1978 appropriation by $5.16 billion, with the big jump caused by a $5.5 billion capitalization for the Commodity Credit Corporation (CCC). Congress in May had raised the limit on CCC borrowing authority to $25 billion, from $14.5 billion. The corporation administers federal price support, commodity loan and disaster payments programs.

The administration claimed that the apparent thrift of the Appropriations Committee was illusory and that in fact the committee had exceeded the president's budget by more than $415.8 million. In a time-honored maneuver, the committee had approximately halved the administration's $9.9 billion request for CCC reimbursement funds and distributed the funds elsewhere.

Typically, the funds are provided later in the year in a supplemental appropriation.

The apparent "savings of $410 million in budget authority ... has no program impact and does not represent a real savings," said Agriculture Secretary Bergland in a letter to Appropriations Committee Chairman George Mahon, D-Texas. Bergland also wrote that the committee changes "would seriously impair my ability and the president's to manage the Department of Agriculture."

In his letter to Mahon, Bergland objected particularly to the subcommittee's changes in conservation projects. Carter had proposed a single, consolidated agricultural conservation program targeted on high priority areas. The committee bill almost doubled the recommended funding level and retained separate administrations. This action subverted the administration's intent to focus on solving pollution-causing soil erosion, rather than on "production-enhancing programs," Bergland said.

Since the Eisenhower era presidents had taken the disputed programs out of the budget, on the theory that the federal government shouldn't invest in improvements that add to the value of a farmer's or rancher's land. Congress has always put them back in.

Agricultural Programs

The committee recommended $6.9 billion for agricultural programs, including departmental management, agricultural research and commodity support and marketing programs. This was $348 million less than the budget request, with much of the savings coming out of administrative budgets for assistant secretary and congressional liaison offices.

Bergland complained that the staff cuts necessitated by the committee action would reduce a policy staff that was already too small. Without adequate staff it would be "impossible to assert any sort of effective policy control over the activities of the department," Bergland said.

Research Grants. While appropriating $15.9 million more than the budget request for the Agricultural Research Service and the Cooperative State Research Service, the committee wiped out a two-year-old competitive grants program that had been intended to "get the best possible technology and get away from automatic handouts to land-grant colleges," as an administration official put it.

The research program had been a battleground for several years, with Congress reluctant to give up the traditional formula (non-competitive) grants to land-grant colleges and agricultural research stations. Members liked them because of their high visibility and because their cost-sharing requirement stretched federal research dollars.

The Carter administration had proposed to double competitive grants through the state research program, to $30 million compared with a fiscal 1978 level of $15 million. That generosity appeared to be at the expense of formula grants, which were cut by $11 million. The committee, finding the administration proposal "unacceptable," dropped competitive grants altogether and restored the formula money, some of which was distributed to a farmers' lexicon of targeted projects, from aquatic weeds through carrots, pickles and onions to wild oats in wheat.

The committee also restored $3.1 million for tobacco production research and $9.4 million for industry-oriented research in processing, storage and distribution efficiency. Big-ticket items included a $21 million human nutrition research center at Tufts University.

Extension Service. The committee added $14.7 million to the budget request, for a direct farmer-to-consumer marketing program, nutrition education and urban gardening and 4-H programs. A $2.5 million addition was to fund demonstrations of solar energy for farm use.

Agricultural Marketing Service. The committee pruned the budget request by $4.7 million for certain administrative expenses, which it said should continue to be covered by non-appropriated (section 32) funds. It added $2 million for an urban wholesale market program that the administration had wanted to kill. The better-sited and more efficient new markets funded by the program meant "higher prices for the farmer and lower prices for the consumer," the committee said.

Farm Income Stabilization. The committee made a $410 million change in the administration request for farm price support programs, loans and disaster assistance. It simply reduced the administration's $990 million estimate of what it would cost to reimburse the CCC for these programs. The remaining $580 million appropriation "will provide ample funds . . . at this time," the committee said.

Rural Development

Farmers Home Administration (FmHA). The committee added $55.7 million to the budget request, for a total of $1.2 billion. It told the Agriculture Department to hire nearly 600 more people to speed up loan processing and otherwise improve agency administration. The department had originally asked for the extra personnel, but lost out when the president's budget was put together.

The committee proposed to cover part of the estimated $7 million needed for these positions with funds subtracted from the office account of the secretary of agriculture. Earlier in the year there had been newspaper reports of long delays in FmHA procedures and failure to inspect property on which money was lent, because of staff shortages. But the personnel ceiling, which showed up in appropriations for several other agencies also, reflected Whitten's preference for "dealing with the old-line administrators he's been dealing with for 20 years," one Agriculture Department official claimed. (The committee also stipulated personnel ceilings for the Soil Conservation Service, the Foreign Agricultural Service and the Agricultural Stabilization and Conservation Service.)

Much of the FmHA increase, about $35 million, was for rural water and waste disposal programs. A $5 million increase was provided for planning grants to rural communities.

Conservation. Recommended increases over the budget request totaled $23.9 million for planning and carrying out watershed and flood prevention projects. That was $57.9 million less than requested in a late-arriving amendment to the budget. The committee added $25.2 million for resource conservation and development work. The committee increased by $90 million the budget request for the Agricultural Conservation Program, which shares with individual farmers and ranchers the costs of projects to enhance soil fertility, control wind and water erosion and conserve water.

The committee added to the budget request $25 million for a cost-sharing water quality program authorized by the 1977 Clean Water Act. It also declared that endangered species whose presence was holding up project work should be removed to "another suitable habitat."

Food Programs

Dominating the bill were food programs, which accounted for $8.8 billion, just under half of all the funds in the bill. For fiscal 1979 the committee recommended $7.95 billion for domestic food programs, including food stamps, nutrition supplements for children, pregnant and nursing women, and school breakfasts and lunches. That was $107 million more than the president had requested. (An additional $1.3 billion was also allotted to these programs from non-appropriated "section 32" funds supplied by import duties, for a total combined spending level of $9.3 billion.)

The committee endorsed the $5.8 billion administration request for food stamps, up $152 million from fiscal 1978, and urged it to move against fraud and abuse in the program.

It added $25 million to the budget request for the "exceptionally successful and beneficial" supplemental nutrition program for women and children (WIC), and it restored an administration cut of $28 million for schools to buy food preparation and storage equipment for the school lunch program.

The committee said local school districts should be able to keep serving breakfasts of "formulated grain-fruit products" — also known as "super donuts" — if they chose to. The vitamin-fortified sweet pastries had been developed at the behest of the Agriculture Department to enable schools without food preparation facilities to offer a breakfast program and to discourage waste. However, responding to consumer complaints that the sugared products encouraged bad eating habits, the department had decided to bar the pastries from federal programs. But the committee said that "nutrition education cannot be taught to children who are hungry."

International Programs

The committee approved the full $805.9 million budget request for the Food for Peace (PL 480) program. It added $2 million to the budget request for development of foreign markets for American-grown commodities. Among farmers' complaints against the Carter administration was that it had failed to stimulate movement of price-depressing surpluses into international markets.

Related Agencies

The committee trimmed $4.5 million from the budget request for administrative expenses of the Food and Drug Administration (FDA) and pruned another $1.5 million from FDA building funds.

It also told the agency not to follow through with its proposed restrictions on using antibiotics in animal feed until it had completed research and hearings on the controversial practice. Concerns that the additives could cause consumer health problems were more theoretical than real, the committee said, adding that the ban could increase the cost of meat to consumers by $1.2 billion a year. The antibiotic additives were used to prevent diseases.

House Floor Action

The House made no changes in the appropriation levels recommended by the committee. It passed the bill 326-59 on June 22. *(Vote 420, p. 120-H)*

Before doing so, it took the unprecedented step of barring South Korea from the Food for Peace program, which provides cheap credit for food purchases by participating nations.

The State Department was dismayed at the precedent set by the House action, which was intended to reverse South Korea's decision to bar a former ambassador from answering questions about alleged payments to congressmen. But President Carter's objections to the bill predated this action, and an Agriculture Department official said the administration "would probably lay low on (the Korea amendment) since it's a congressional matter."

There was little support for the president's budget-cutting position during floor debate. The House turned down a general 2 percent cut, one of the series of across-the-board appropriations reductions promoted by Clarence E. Miller, R-Ohio. Debate focused instead on the Korea food-aid amendment and on an unsuccessful attempt to slice $290 million from the $5.8 billion food stamp program.

Members of the House rarely challenge the appropriations subcommittee's distribution of funds because "Whitten puts in something for everyone," an Agriculture Department official said. More than 300 members contacted his subcommittee about projects in their districts, Whitten said on the floor.

The fact that Whitten was in line for the full committee chairmanship when Mahon retired at the end of the session, and thus could "hand out a lot more than research grants and soil conservation projects," also contributed to the smooth passage of the bill, according to the Agriculture Department official.

Food Stamp Program

The House rejected by a 194-201 vote an amendment by Steven D. Symms, R-Idaho, to reduce the food stamp appropriation by $290 million. *(Vote 417, p. 120-H)*

Symms said the program had been "filled with difficulties, problems, fraud and abuse." Co-sponsor John H. Rousselot, R-Calif., cited a General Accounting Office (GAO) finding that "the federal government is losing over half a billion dollars annually in the food stamp program because of over-issued benefits."

Opponents argued that anti-fraud and other changes in the 1977 agriculture act (PL 95-113) designed to close up loopholes in the program had not yet been given a chance to work. House Agriculture Committee Chairman Thomas S. Foley, D-Wash., also said that the continuing high costs of the program were caused by high food prices. These disguised the fact that "we are consistently lowering the number of people who are receiving food stamps in a very dramatic way from a couple of years ago," Foley said.

2 Percent Cut Rejected

The House rejected, 189-201, an amendment by Clarence E. Miller, R-Ohio, to cut 2 percent from all appropriations except those for the Agricultural Research Service, the Cooperative State Research Service and the Extension Service. *(Vote 419, p. 120-H)*

Miller said excess government spending was "a great crying problem." Whitten responded that since "two-thirds of the items in this bill are mandatory," the reduction would fall harshly on remaining programs.

Aid to South Korea

The House agreed by a 273-125 vote to an amendment by Majority Leader Jim Wright, D-Texas, to prohibit the use of appropriated funds to finance economic assistance to South Korea under the Food for Peace program. *(Vote 418, p. 120-H)*

Wright said Korea food aid amounted to about $56 million and that the refusal of the Korean government to cooperate with House requests regarding the questioning of former ambassador Kim Dong Jo made the cutoff critical. "In defense of the honor of this institution we have no other recourse," Wright said.

Farm state members objected that terminating the program, which was intended to develop foreign markets for American commodities, would harm both U.S. and Korean citizens who had little control over the decisions of the Korean government.

Other Actions

The House agreed by voice vote to an amendment by W. Henson Moore, R-La., to prohibit payments for expenses of parties intervening in regulatory proceedings of the Department of Agriculture, the Food and Drug Administration or the Commodity Futures Trading Commission. Moore said the amendment was aimed at "a creeping invasion of professional litigants" such as consumer advocates whose participation in agency decisions was being solicited by the agencies — at public expense.

HOUSE PROVISIONS

As passed by the House, HR 13125 made the following appropriations for fiscal 1979:

	Budget Request	House-Passed Amount
Agricultural Programs		
Production, Processing and Marketing	$ 1,468,000,000	$ 1,531,000,000
Farm Income Stabilization	5,743,000,000	5,332,000,000

	Budget Request	House-Passed Amount
Rural Development Programs		
Rural Development Assistance	1,203,000,000	1,259,000,000
Conservation	653,000,000	766,000,000
Domestic Food Programs	7,843,000,000	7,950,000,000
International Programs	858,000,000	860,000,000
Related Agencies	322,000,000	316,000,000
Total: Fiscal 1979 new budget authority	$18,090,000,000	$18,014,000,000
Transfers from Section 32	1,412,000,000	1,337,000,000
Direct and insured loan authorizations	8,433,000,000	9,080,000,000

Other Provisions. Prohibited the use of appropriated funds to finance economic assistance to South Korea under the Food for Peace program.

• Prohibited the use of appropriated funds to pay expenses of parties intervening in regulatory proceedings before the Agriculture Department, Food and Drug Administration or Commodity Futures Trading Commission.

Senate Committee Action

The Senate Appropriations Committee reported HR 13125 on Aug. 1 (S Rept 95-1058). In its report, the panel recommended deleting the House-passed proviso on food aid for Korea, stating that an aid cut-off could be counterproductive to U.S. efforts to obtain Korea's cooperation in allowing former ambassador Kim to testify before congressional committees about alleged payoffs to members of Congress.

"Every threat of congressional reprisal to date has been followed by a stiffening of the Korean position," the committee said. "That which a nation might do voluntarily is made the more difficult under threat and when pride and sovereignty are on the line."

Food aid accounted for $8.8 billion of the total $23.4 billion appropriation. The House-passed appropriation totaled $18 billion, including the same $8.8 billion for food aid. But the subtotals differed slightly, with the Senate spending $90.5 million less on domestic food programs and $2.8 million more on international programs.

Other Changes

A late Carter administration request for an additional $5 billion in new borrowing authority for the Commodity Credit Corporation (CCC) accounted for a major part of the big difference between the committee and House bills.

The CCC item masked the fact that the Senate committee proposed $120.8 million less for Agriculture Department programs than did its House counterpart, according to the Senate report. The Senate bill was also $271.9 million more than the budget request (leaving out the CCC item).

Unlike its House counterpart, the Senate panel did not set personnel ceilings for major Agriculture Department agencies. Nor did it follow the House in slashing requested funds for congressional liaison and other administrative functions directly under the secretary of agriculture.

Secretary Bob Bergland had protested these actions, saying that his policy staff would be too small to control the department, and that the personnel ceilings encroached on executive branch powers. The Senate committee suggested that savings could come more appropriately from the congressional liaison offices maintained by the various department agencies. It "reluctantly" declined to set personnel ceilings, but told the department to take care of serious under-staffing problems.

The House committee had extensively revised budget priorities and characterized the changes as needed "investments" in the future of agriculture. The Senate committee modified many of those revisions, funding only those items it judged "highest priority." In a major change, it endorsed full funding of a $990 million CCC reimbursement account that had been about halved by the House. The House had distributed the funds elsewhere and claimed that its bill did not exceed the president's budget.

The Senate committee added $500 million in new loan authority to provide guaranteed loans for moderate-income rural housing. And it restored a $30 million competitive grants program dropped by the House.

It fully funded a $75 million watershed projects request that had been severely trimmed by the House. Other major changes included deletion of a House-passed $15 million appropriation for special targeted research grants, and $105 million for certain conservation projects.

Agricultural Programs

The committee recommended $12.3 billion for agricultural programs, exceeding the House bill by $5.4 billion and the revised budget request by $58 million.

Most of the increase was to cover the extra $5 billion borrowing authority for the Commodity Credit Corporation, which administers price support and disaster programs.

Research Grants. The committee recommended above-budget increases totaling $49 million for research programs of the Agricultural Research Service (ARS) and the Cooperative State Research Service (CSRS). The total appropriation for the two services, including a new, separate buildings and facilities account, was $538 million, about the same as the House appropriation. There were substantial program differences, however.

The Senate panel reversed two major House decisions, restoring a $30 million competitive research program and dropping all but one House-approved increase in special (targeted) CSRS research grants, for a cut of $20.5 million from the House level for these programs.

The year-old competitive program, the committee found, "has great promise and potential for making significant increases in basic agricultural research." On the other hand, the committee said, the special grants were "not of sufficient priority to warrant funding above the budget proposals at this time."

It did, however, retain a $150,000 House increase in research on an insect that attacks soybeans, and added a small $38,000 project in mushroom byproduct utilization. The soybean project was backed by Chairman Thomas F. Eagleton, D-Mo., and the mushroom study was sought by Richard S. Schweiker, R-Pa., according to committee staff.

Senate revisions cut $20.7 million from House-passed increases in research facilities funds, with the biggest casualty a new $21.1 million human nutrition laboratory at Tufts University.

Like the House panel, the Senate committee restored a $3.1 million budget cut in tobacco production research. It also added $2 billion for competitive-grants research in alcohol-based fuels made from farm commodities ("gasohol").

The Senate panel went along with a House restoration of $11.1 million for "formula payments" to support research at agricultural experimental stations and added $4.8 million more to help finance pay raises at the state-federal facilities.

Extension Service. Senate additions for this service were $11.9 million above the budget request of $262 million, and $2.8 million less than the House appropriation, for a recommended total of $273.9 million.

Absent from the Senate version were $10 million worth of House additions for rural development activities, solar farm demonstrations, farm safety programs, urban gardening and other activities that could be "carried on using other funds available to state extension services," in the judgment of the committee.

In their place was a $10 million budget add-on for administrative expenses, including pay raises and retirement benefits for the state-federal services.

Agricultural Marketing Service. The Senate committee rejected a House decision to continue funding $4.7 million of administrative expenses from non-appropriated (section 23) funds opting for a direct appropriation in that amount, as requested by the administration. ("Section 32" funds are provided by the treasury from tariff proceeds.)

It also dropped a $2 million House addition for an urban wholesale market program that the administration had wanted to kill. "City planners and the private sector do not require additional federal research inputs in order to build future wholesale markets," the committee said.

Farm Income Stabilization. The committee approved the full $990.9 million budget request to reimburse the CCC for price support programs, loans and disaster assistance.

The House committee had about halved the request, apparently planning to make up the difference in a later, supplemental appropriation. The Senate committee also boosted CCC borrowing authority to $10.5 billion, the total of the original budget request and a later request by Agriculture Secretary Bergland. The new borrowing authority was $5 billion more than the House appropriation.

In another change, the Senate committee trimmed $10 million from an allotment for expenses of county offices that administer the farm income stabilization programs. Expenses of these offices had jumped $63 million in one year, and the committee had asked the General Accounting Office (GAO) to find out why. If a GAO study showed the money was needed, it could be appropriated later, the committee said.

Rural Development

Farmers Home Administration (FmHA). The committee added $78 million to the budget request, for a total of $1.3 billion for loans and grants to individuals and communities for a broad variety of projects. That was $22.5 million more than the House version.

Most of the above-budget funds, $20 million, were to pay new staff to administer the FmHA programs. The House had told the Agriculture Department to hire nearly 600 more administrators, but the Senate panel said it thought "approximately double that number of new personnel will be needed to meet FmHA workload increases." The agency had been criticized for slow processing and inadequate supervision of its loans, and the administration had been criticized for failing to adequately staff the agency to alleviate these problems.

Like the House, the Senate panel added $35 million to the budget request for water and waste disposal grants and $5 million for rural development planning grants. It also approved up to $500 million in guaranteed loans for housing for above-moderate income families. The administration had requested the increase after submitting the budget, the committee said.

Conservation. The Senate panel dropped 25 new House watershed planning starts, for a savings of $6.9 million. By delaying the new projects, "greater progress can be made on the backlog of 180 projects and $738 million in construction for which planning is already complete," the panel said.

The committee also restored $62.8 million cut by the House from a $75 million budget request for small new watersheds. It also restored the full $57.9 million budget request for watershed and flood prevention operations that had been deleted by the House. In another reversal, the Senate added $10 million to the budget for the Resource Conservation and Development Program, $15 million less than a House add-on.

The program had "accomplished very little that is of national priority," the committee said, adding that the $10 million would be enough to keep it going while the Senate Agrciulture Committee completed a study of all Agriculture Department soil and water conservation programs.

The committee concurred with a $25 million addition by the House to the Agricultural Stabilization and Conservation Service (ASCS) budget for a water-quality (non-point source pollution control) program authorized by the 1977 clean water act. It also added $75 million more than the budget request for the program to the budget of a second agency, the Soil Conservation Service.

The committee cut to $85 million funding for ASCS cost-sharing programs. This was $15 million less than the budget request and $105 million less than the House bill — but enough to continue "enduring practices" that permanently improve the land, the committee said.

Domestic Food Programs

Like the House, the Senate committee endorsed the $5.8 billion administration request for food stamps.

But it deleted an $83 million appropriation for child nutrition programs and said instead that $75 million in over-budget funds should be taken for these programs from non-appropriated section 32 funds. It did not go along with a House-approved directive that local school districts — not the Agrciulture Department — should decide whether they would use "superdonuts" in school breakfasts.

The committee also expressed concern that parents were falsely underreporting their income to make their children eligible for free or inexpensive subsidized school lunches. It earmarked $4 million so state administrations could audit the programs or take other steps to eliminate the problem.

The committee did not go along with a $8 million House add-on for food preparation and storage equipment for the school lunch program, stating that the $20 million budget request was enough "in view of the substantial sums already granted the States for long-lived equipment."

The committee proposed a $14.5 million addition to the budget — compared with a House addition of $25 million — for a supplemental nutrition program for women and children (WIC). "It does not appear that participation rates under the program will grow as rapidly as indicated by the level provided in the House bill," it said.

Related Agencies

The Senate $305.9-million recommendation for the Food and Drug Administration was slightly under the budget and $5.6 million more than the House appropriation. Most of the extra money was for new staff and reflected the fact that the FDA had been given a higher personnel allotment since the House had acted on the bill, according to the committee.

Like the House, the Senate panel trimmed $1.5 million from the budget request for FDA building funds.

The Senate committee also provided $1.5 for a new 19-member national commission that was to report to Congress by December 1979 on potential uses of gasohol.

Senate Floor Action

Disregarding cover-up charges, the Senate refused Aug. 10 to go along with the House in barring South Korea from the Food for Peace program.

Before voting 90-8 to pass the $23 billion agriculture appropriation bill for fiscal 1979, the Senate agreed 71-24 to table — and thus kill — an amendment by Lowell P. Weicker Jr., R-Conn., to keep South Korea out of the food program. *(Votes 308, 304, p. 47-S)*

Opponents of the Weicker amendment argued that the Korean government recently had agreed to secure from Kim answers to written questions, and that more pressure would block further cooperation. But Weicker called "written interrogatories . . . worthless" and told members that if they rejected his amendment, "it adds up to what so far has been called a resounding cover-up."

Weicker said he had quit the ethics panel investigating the payoff allegations because his efforts to get witnesses had been thwarted. His amendment, he said, was an attempt to "bring back into focus what has been to date a shamefully inadequate investigation."

Ethics Committee Chairman Adlai E. Stevenson III, D-Ill., said that Weicker's comments on the uncompleted investigation were "premature."

"If the distinguished senator from Connecticut knew anything about these investigations, he would not make such silly charges," Stevenson said.

Majority Leader Robert C. Byrd, W. Va., backed Stevenson, calling the Weicker amendment "counterproductive." If Weicker "has anything other than innuendos, let him . . . bring it to the Senate floor," Byrd said.

The dispute over aid to Korea was one of several that erupted during floor action Aug. 9 and 10 as floor manager Thomas F. Eagleton, D-Mo., tried to hold off money-adding amendments for what he called "every senator's pet project."

But when the Senate finished, it had added $130.2 million to the committee bill, turned down two efforts to cut funding for food stamps, and refused to follow the House on Korea or in slashing the secretary of agriculture's policy staff.

Railing against "fiscal conservatives" who vote "rather easily for a little $20 million here and a little $100 million there," Eagleton said, "I cannot understand the difference between talking fiscal conservatism and voting for a bloated budget."

Eagleton said his Agriculture Appropriations Subcommittee had received special requests from 85 senators that, if honored, would have added $900 million to the bill. A $400 million over-budget House version already had drawn veto threats, Eagleton warned, urging his colleagues to retain the Senate committee version, which itself was $271 million above the administration's budget request. (The Senate bill also included a $5 billion increase in borrowing authority requested by the administration after its budget submission.)

When the amendments were about completed, the Senate by a 73-24 vote adopted an omnibus thrift amendment that trimmed a total of $126.5 million from 15 different programs. Sponsor Eagleton said that unless the cuts were adopted, a "veto threat is indeed a reality." *(Vote 306, p. 47-S)*

The final version was $3.7 million over the committee bill; for a total of $23,365,764,000 in new budget authority for fiscal 1979. That was $276 million more than the budget request, and more acceptable to the administration than the House version, according to Agriculture Department spokesman James C. Webster.

"We're not particularly happy with an extra $105 million for conservation programs, but administratively it's delightful" compared with the House version, Webster said.

The Senate's biggest addition was $105 million, also approved by the House, for a popular and highly visible cost-sharing conservation program that paid farmers for improvements to their land. Opponents said that the improvements often were either fertilizer applications or irrigation projects that added more to the farmer's income than to the environment.

The Carter administration had tried to limit the program to projects of lasting environmental value only. Sponsor William D. Hathaway, D-Maine, said that about one in four farmers used the provision, and that the funds were important, "particularly in areas where they do not have any subsidy for the crops they grow."

The Senate agreed, by a 55-26 vote. *(Vote 303, p. 47-S)*

Other Amendments

Besides approving the $105 million conservation projects amendment, and rejecting the Weicker amendment, the Senate took these actions:

- Adopted by a 68-23 vote a Melcher, D-Mont., amendment adding $20 million for cost-sharing animal health and disease research programs at veterinary colleges and agriculture experiment programs. Eagleton objected that the bill already provided $42 million for in-house research on animal health and that if states wanted to devote more federal matching funds to this type of research, they could do so. Melcher responded that the states were not using existing veterinary medicine laboratories nor "utilizing all the proper personnel they should have at those laboratories doing veterinary research," even though it was a "cost-effective, money-saving" way of getting the investigations done. *(Vote 301, p. 46-S)*
- Adopted by voice vote a Morgan, D-N.C., amendment adding $200,000 for a National Academy of Science study of recent cotton dust standards issued by the Occupational Safety and Health Administration (OSHA). The OSHA standards were devised to protect textile workers from "brown lung" disease, thought to be caused by breathing in cotton dust. In support of Morgan's amendment, Herman E. Talmadge, D-Ga., donned a protective face mask of the type required by the OSHA standard and announced, "I do not know how good a job it does in keeping out cotton dust. I do know it does a pretty good job of

keeping out air." Talmadge and Morgan argued that the standards were prohibitively expensive for the industry and would price domestic textiles — and jobs — out of the market.

● Adopted by voice vote a Dole, R-Kan., amendment, modified by Eagleton, to add $5 million for grasshopper control measures if a recent infestation in the Midwest continued in the spring of 1979.

● Adopted by voice vote a Chiles, D-Fla., amendment barring implementation of new Agriculture Department standards for thermal insulation in concrete masonry homes. Chiles said that the regulations would make this type of construction "prohibitively" expensive and that the standards were "inappropriate" for warm-weather states.

● Rejected by a 35-51 vote a Stevens, R-Alaska, amendment to delete $1.6 million from the account of the office of the secretary and administration. Stevens said the proposed budget increases for these functions were excessive. Later, after his amendment was rejected, Stevens complained that new Agriculture Department staff had been "shielding the secretary from the policy level officers in his own department," and that there was "an extreme environmentalist cadre" in the department. *(Vote 302, p. 46-S)*

● Rejected by a 38-57 vote, a Lugar, R-Ind., amendment to reduce food stamp spending by $250 million and rejected by a 16-80 vote a Curtis, R-Neb., to cut $2 billion from the food aid program. Both Republicans cited past reports of fraud and abuse in the program and Lugar quoted a General Accounting Office finding that few recipients who should have been required to find work actually had jobs. "To keep talking in terms of cutting off people and bringing about malnutrition and suffering is simply nonsense," Lugar said. *(Votes 305 and 307, p. 47-S)*

Opposing the food stamp cuts were Eagleton and Henry Bellmon, R-Okla., who said that anti-fraud provisions and other restrictions enacted in 1977 had not yet had a chance to work. Eagleton also told the Senate that it was "kidding itself if it believes that it can institute reforms and improvements" in the program by cutting the appropriation. Since it was an entitlement program, all qualified beneficiaries had to be paid and the extra funds would show up in a later, supplemental appropriation, Eagleton said.

Tobacco Research

Claiborne Pell, D-R.I., withdrew an amendment dropping $3.1 million added by the House for tobacco production research. Pell had cited a recent report of a long-term American Medical Association (AMA) study that found cigarette smoking caused "irreversible heart damage and may be responsible" for other health problems including cancer. Opponents from tobacco-producing states including Walter (Dee) Huddleston, D-Ky., objected that the research projects were, in fact, oriented toward eliminating health hazards by improving tobacco strains and similar projects.

Strom Thurmond, R-S.C., added that the research programs were responsible for "today's low tar and nicotine content cigarettes." Pell withdrew his amendment after being assured by Huddleston that "virtually all" the research was health related.

SENATE PROVISIONS

As passed by the Senate Aug. 10, HR 13125 made the following appropriations for fiscal 1979:

	House-Passed Amount	Senate-Passed Amount
Agricultural programs		
Production, processing and marketing	$ 1,531,000,000	$ 1,542,000,000
Farm income stabilization	5,332,000,000	10,733,000,000
Rural development programs		
Rural development assistance	1,259,000,000	1,204,000,000
Conservation	766,000,000	843,000,000
Domestic food programs	7,950,000,000	7,859,000,000
International programs	860,000,000	863,000,000
Related agencies	316,000,000	322,000,000
Total: Fiscal 1979 new budget authority	$18,014,000,000	$23,366,000,000
Transfers from Section 32	1,337,000,000	1,411,000,000
Direct and insured loan authorizations	9,080,000,000	9,960,000,000

Conference Action

Conferees filed their report on HR 13125 Sept. 18 (H Rept 95-1579).

They eliminated House-passed personnel ceilings for all but one of the agencies, the Farmers Home Administration (FmHA). In place of ceilings, conferees adopted "floors" — levels below which department staff could not drop. These floors were at about existing staff levels, and the compromise was viewed as a major victory by the Carter administration.

Conferees also deleted House language prohibiting expense payments for persons intervening in regulatory proceedings before the Agriculture Department, the Food and Drug Administration or the Commodity Futures Trading Commission. But conferees restricted the payments to "intervenors" who lived in the area affected or whose interests were not otherwise represented.

Conferees also resolved these other major differences:

Agricultural Programs

The administration got half its original request — $15 million — for the two-year-old competitive research grants program of the Cooperative State Research Service. The House, irked that the budget funded the program at the expense of cost-shared, targeted contracts and grants for land-grant colleges, had eliminated the new program. Conferees continued it at the 1978 funding level and called for a careful evaluation by the department of individual grants.

A $2.5 million House addition for solar energy research was dropped, a Senate study on the impact of an Occupational Health and Safety Administration (OSHA) standard for cotton dust was funded at half ($100,000) the original level, and a $2 million Senate addition for alcohol fuels research was cut to $500,000. A Senate addition of $20 million for animal health research grants was cut to $5 million.

Conferees restored a $21.1 million House addition for a new human nutrition research facility at Tufts University, and added $1.5 million for operating expenses for a children's nutrition facility at Baylor College of Medicine. The Senate had dropped these projects, which the administration opposed because, while "nutrition research is suddenly very fashionable, people are running off in all directions and it's not at all coordinated," according to a department congressional aide.

These worries were reflected in conference language mandating unusually tight department control over the academic facilities: faculty appointments and research grants were to be reviewed by the Agriculture Department, and directors of both facilities had to be approved by the secretary and were "responsible only to" the department.

Conferees also told the department to set up an independent scientific review board to evaluate research proposals. And the programs were to be closely coordinated with ongoing nutrition research in both the department and at the National Institutes of Health.

Conferees dropped $5 million in contingency funding authority added by the Senate to control midwestern grasshopper infestations that showed up late in the summer. Those insect programs had not "traditionally" covered cropland — only rangeland, conferees noted.

Conferees endorsed a House decision, rejected by the Senate, to continue providing $4.7 million in marketing administrative expenses from non-appropriated Section 32 funds (from import duties).

They did not go along with House treatment of the Commodity Credit Corporation (CCC), the agency that handles farm price support and loan programs. As did the Senate, conferees fully funded a $990 million request to reimburse the CCC for "net realized losses (of) prior years." The House had cut the request to $580 million and distributed the resulting "savings" to other programs.

However, conferees also provided only $5.5 billion in new borrowing authority for the corporation, a little more than half of the $10.5 billion increased authorized in 1978. These adjustments would provide enough working capital for the corporation, conferees said.

Rural Development

Conferees included $7 million more than the budget request for new FmHA personnel, telling the agency to fill 594 new staff positions, all outside Washington. Farmers and farm-state members had complained that chronic FmHA understaffing caused delays in loan applications and inadequate followup.

The final bill also included $500 million for guaranteed loans, added by the Senate at the administration's request, and a House addition of $5 million for rural development planning grants.

Conferees followed the House in deleting a $57.9 million budget request for watershed and flood prevention operations.

They reported in disagreement a provision on the Agricultural Conservation Program — the cost-sharing projects — which got $90,000 of the $105 million additional funds approved by both the Senate and the House. The bill as passed limited to $3,500 the amount a participant could receive, except where a project was carried on jointly among several farms. And it barred funding for projects that were "primarily production-oriented or that have little or no conservation or pollution abatement benefits."

Conferees said they were dropping the non-point source pollution program "since no additional funds or staff were requested for the program." Without additional resources, the new program could detract from existing Soil Conservation Service and agricultural conservation programs, conferees said.

Food Programs

Conferees followed the Senate in adding $65 million in non-appropriated Section 32 funds for child nutrition programs. They also provided $24 million — $4 million over budget — for school food service equipment. The House had added $8 million for this item, but the Senate had dropped the addition because, according to the Appropriations Committee, most schools were adequately equipped. Conferees told the Agriculture Department to track the money carefully, "especially regarding whether the equipment . . . is for new service or replacement."

The new equipment was particularly needed for the anticipated expansion of the school breakfast program, the conferees said. Participation in that program was only 24 percent of the participation level in the school lunch program, their report noted.

Conferees also cut $10.5 million from a $25 million addition by the House for a supplemental nutrition program for women and children (WIC). They made minor adjustments in international food programs and left Korea in the PL 480 program, without comment.

The conferees included $29.3 million for foreign market development as proposed by the House, instead of a lower figure passed by the Senate.

Related Agencies

Like the House, conferees directed the Food and Drug Administration (FDA) to postpone a proposed ban on antibiotics in animal feed. Like the House, they earmarked $250,000 for research on the feed additives, and told FDA not to impose the ban until research results and public hearings on the issue were completed.

A $1.5 million National Alcohol Fuels Commission included in the Senate bill was dropped because it had never been authorized.

FINAL ACTION

The House approved the $18.3 billion conference report Sept. 26 by a 328-31 vote, and the Senate agreed by voice vote the following day. President Carter signed the bill Oct. 11. *(House vote 740, p. 210-H)*

House Sustains Carter Public Works Veto

President Carter secured a major legislative victory Oct. 5, when the House voted to sustain his veto of a public works bill (HR 12928) containing $10.2 billion for water and energy development in fiscal 1979. Subsequently, the administration and Congress reached a compromise on public works funding. It was attached to a resolution (H J Res 1139) providing funds for several agencies for which regular appropriations bills had not been passed. That measure was cleared by Congress Oct. 15 (PL 95-482). *(Story, p. 161)*

The major issue in the debate over HR 12928 was six water projects that had been part of Carter's 1977 "hit list" of 18 projects he wanted killed. They had been removed from the fiscal 1978 appropriations bill in a compromise with Carter. The president contended the 1977 action killed the projects forever; the House and Senate maintained the deletions were for only one year. *(Background, 1977 Almanac p. 650)*

The $20 million in funding for the projects, which would have cost an additional $560 million to complete, was only a small part of the massive appropriations bill.

But the dispute became a symbolic one as Congress and Carter struggled over control of the more than $3 billion spent annually on water development. The "hit list" debate was tied to Carter's efforts to reform overall federal water policy — efforts that had irked many members of Congress. *(Water policy, Energy chapter)*

On June 1, the House Appropriations Committee reported its version of HR 12928, which restored construction or planning money for eight projects deleted in 1977 after Carter said they were environmentally damaging or economically unjustified.

Then, on June 9, Carter asked Congress to fund 36 new projects that met the new criteria included in his water policy. He wanted to signal his support for acceptable water projects and asked for full, up-front funding for the $718 million his new projects starts would cost to complete.

But the full funding was a break from the traditional congressional method of spreading funding over many years. The House June 16 approved legislation that included the 36 new projects, but only provided enough money for one year's work. An effort to delete funding for the eight "hit list" projects failed, and Carter warned he would veto the bill.

The Senate version of HR 12928, passed Aug. 10, contained funds for one year's work on the new water projects Carter requested. But it also included construction money for four water projects and planning money for two other projects that had been on the 1977 "hit list."

House-Senate conferees then worked out a compromise, agreed to by both chambers, that provided construction funding for three of the projects and planning funding for another three. Carter, as he had threatened, vetoed the measure Oct. 5. The House sustained the veto the same day.

Many members saw the House vote as a signal of coming change in the traditional congressional "pork barrel" system of distributing funds for dams, irrigation channels and other water projects. Rep. Silvio O. Conte, R-Mass., described the methods as "little more than back scratching," with members voting without question for their colleagues' projects in return for dams in their district.

But the accord subsequently reached on the bill amounted to only a temporary truce in the continuing struggle between Congress and the president over who would set national water policy. The Senate Appropriations Committee, which gave the first nod to the revised bill Oct. 11, made it clear that the changes, including the deletion of six disputed projects from Carter's 1977 "hit list" would hold only for fiscal 1979.

"By entering this compromise, we are not agreeing to never again consider projects on the hit list," said Sen. J. Bennett Johnston, D-La., chairman of the Appropriations subcommittee that wrote the bill.

Johnston's counterpart in the House, Rep. Tom Bevill, D-Ala., echoed the strains of congressional independence. "We'll give them [the Carter administration] every consideration next year," said Bevill, who had earlier admitted Carter did a "beautiful job" getting votes to sustain the veto. But, Bevill continued, "We will preserve the prerogatives of the Congress."

Bevill and many other members had argued that Congress has the right to decide which projects to fund. Carter wanted the dams, irrigation channels and other projects to meet tough economic and environmental criteria before they were authorized and received federal funds.

Provisions

As cleared by Congress and later vetoed, HR 12928 appropriated the following amounts for fiscal 1979:

Agency	Amended Budget Request	Final
Department of Energy	$ 6,509,027,000	$ 6,085,175,000
Army Corps of Engineers	2,971,165,000	2,636,024,000
Interior's Bureau of Reclamation	735,770,000	579,915,000
Independent Agencies	811,927,000	848,456,000
Water Resources Planning	11,560,000	10,913,900
Total	$11,039,449,000	$10,160,483,900

House Committee Action

The House Appropriations Committee made major changes in the administration's budget request June 1 when it approved fiscal 1979 appropriations for energy research and water and power development (HR 12928—H Rept 95-1247).

Overall, the committee added about $203 million to the administration request for $3.076 billion for dam building and other water resource development activities of the Army Corps of Engineers and the Interior Department's Bureau of Reclamation.

The money added by the committee included the resurrection of the eight deleted water projects as well as more money than the administration sought for other controversial projects on Carter's "hit list" in 1977, such as the Russell Dam, Ga. and S.C., and Applegate Lake, Ore.

In other major increases over the administration request, the committee added $13.3 million for the Tennessee-Tombigbee Waterway, Ala. and Miss.; $5 million for the Red River Waterway, La., and $10 million for the Dry Creek (Warm Springs) Lake and Channel, Calif.

The $203 million also included construction money for 41 new projects that would eventually cost more than $1.3 billion to complete. None had been in the Carter budget.

Carter had wanted to slow down ongoing projects and hold off starting new ones until his long-awaited water policy reforms were in place. But the House panel declined to wait for the policy subsequently announced June 6 and restored the budget and activity to fiscal year 1977 levels.

'Little Game'

Adding new projects to an administration budget is "a little game we play each year," Tom Bevill, D-Ala., chairman of the Public Works Subcommittee, told the committee.

The committee's report listed the projects and the funding recommended for each, but offered an explanation for only a handful of the dozens of increases.

The full Appropriations Committee essentially rubber-stamped the work of Bevill's subcommittee, which spent days in April listening to governors, business people and dozens of members of Congress ask for projects in their districts.

Corps of Engineers

Total funding recommended by the committee for the Corps in fiscal 1979 was $2.654 billion, a $205 million increase over Carter's request and $79 million less than the fiscal 1978 appropriation of $2.734 billion.

In addition to increasing funding levels, the committee recommended that the Corps add personnel and avoid contracting out its work. The panel recommended the addition of 2,150 full-time employees to bring the total number of employees in fiscal 1979 to 30,600.

Funds were recommended for the Corps in these major categories:

- General Investigations (studies): $139.8 million, a $31.7 million increase over Carter's request.
- General Construction: $1.4 billion, a $92 million increase over Carter's request, but $156.6 million less than was appropriated in fiscal 1978.
- Flood Control, Mississippi River and Tributaries: $232.9 million, a $28 million increase over Carter's request.
- Operation and Maintenance: $795.5 million, a $45 million increase over Carter's request.

Bureau of Reclamation

The committee recommended $614.6 million for the Bureau of Reclamation in fiscal 1979, a decrease of $662,000 over Carter's request, and a $63.3 million decrease from fiscal 1978 appropriations.

Funds were recommended for the Bureau in the following major categories:

- General Investigations: $29.9 million, a $7.7 million increase over Carter's request.
- Construction and Rehabilitation: $244 million, a $26 million decrease from Carter's request.
- Upper Colorado River Storage Project: $87.4 million, a $17.1 million increase over Carter's request.
- Colorado River Basin: $74.8 million, a $1 million increase over the president's request.
- Colorado River Basin Salinity Control Projects: $27.3 million, a $15 million decrease in Carter's request that was a carryover of unobligated funds from previous years.
- Operation and Maintenance: $87.9 million, an amount identical to Carter's request.
- Loan Program: $37.7 million, a $14.7 million increase over the president's request.

The committee also recommended $9.7 million for water resources planning by the secretary of the interior. Carter had sought $11.6 million for the Water Resources Council, an interagency council.

Energy

By cutting requested funds for atomic energy defense activities, management and uranium enrichment, the committee was able to increase dramatically the funding for energy research without an overall increase in the Department of Energy budget. The committee cut $298 million from the total request for the department, so the total appropriation recommended was $6.18 billion.

The committee endorsed "an aggressive solar energy development program" by providing $474 million for solar energy, a 37 percent increase over Carter's request. The committee added 20 percent to the request for programs that tap energy from methane gas, hot water springs and other heat below the earth's surface. The program to make usable fuel from biomass, which is agricultural waste and other plant residues, received a funding increase of 96 percent in the committee bill over the president's request.

Another major increase was the addition of $144 million for construction of the Clinch River breeder reactor, subject to House passage of the authorizing legislation. Carter, who wanted to scrap the project, had requested only $13 million to cover final termination costs. *(Authorization bill, Energy chapter)*

The committee refused to increase funding for atomic energy defense construction by 26 percent over fiscal 1978, as Carter had requested. Instead, the committee recommended cutting the request of $533 million to $315 million and criticized the "unsatisfactory situation in management of [Department of Energy] construction activities."

House Floor Action

The House June 16 passed HR 12928 by a vote of 263-59. *(Vote 404, p. 116-H)*

WATER PROJECTS

Challenging the president's veto threat, the House voted 142-234 June 15 against an amendment by Rep. Robert W. Edgar, D-Pa., to prevent spending on the eight projects. *(Vote 400, p. 114-H)*

The Edgar amendment would have prohibited spending for eight projects: Bayou Bodcau, La.; Yatesville Dam, Ky.; Meramec Park Dam, Mo.; Lukfata Dam, Okla.; La Forge Lake, Wis.; Narrows Unit Dam, Colo.; Savory-Pot Hook Dams, Colo., and Fruitland Mesa Dam, Colo.

The administration's effort to cut the eight projects came late and could not match the lobbying for the projects by House members eager to retain congressional control of water project funding.

Majority Leader Jim Wright, D-Texas, Minority Leader John J. Rhodes, R-Ariz., and Public Works Chairman Harold T. Johnson, D-Calif., were among those fighting the Edgar amendment. They worked the floor steadily, sitting beside members and pulling them aside to make their pitch.

One example of the success they were having came from one member who voted with Carter in 1977, but who opposed the president in 1978.

"I have two projects that I want in my district," he said. "They're just small projects we want authorized. Last year I voted for the changes [and with Carter], and I ended up without any water projects." He was told he was more likely to get his projects the next year if he voted for the committee bill.

Other members said they voted with the House Appropriations Committee, which funded the eight projects, because they wanted money for projects in their districts.

But even having the president's support didn't keep members on his side from feeling nervous about rebelling against the system for funding projects.

"It is with a little bit of fear and trembling that I stand before the House today, because I ask to remove eight sacred cows from the House public works appropriations bill," Edgar said. "That simply isn't done."

Like other members, Edgar had been reluctant to lead the fight against the projects. But in a June 8 meeting with

White House officials and environmentalists, he agreed to offer the amendment to delete the eight, Edgar said.

But the administration also wanted to cut funds for new construction starts that did not meet the tougher criteria that were part of Carter's water policy.

Veto Threat

The administration announced June 9 that Carter would veto a bill that included the eight projects and did not comply with his new water policy.

At a June 13 news conference, Carter made the same pledge, saying "We will be working to eliminate the unnecessary spending proposals for water projects in that bill. Unless they are all eliminated, I intend to veto it."

Rep. George Miller, D-Calif., agreed to offer an amendment for the White House to delete new construction funding for more than 20 projects, and add money for 11 new projects proposed by Carter not already in the bill. Carter had proposed 36 new starts. Of those, 25 were already in the bill.

But the morning of the floor vote, Miller decided not to offer the amendment. He said it would have confused the issues and would have been "counterproductive" to passage of the more important Edgar amendment. There was also little support evident for Miller's amendment.

In the meantime, Bevill, floor manager of the bill, had decided to offer an amendment adding $26.5 million for fiscal 1979 for Carter's 11 new projects.

It was accepted by voice vote.

Timing Poor

Bevill and others criticized the administration's timing in announcing the new projects less than a week before the House vote. "This new policy was dropped in our laps at the last minute," Bevill told the House.

His subcommittee, on the other hand, held hearings for 10 weeks and reported out the bill May 3, Bevill said.

"To my knowledge," Bevill said, " nobody from the White House asked to testify before our subcommittee."

"They only respond to stimuli," said one conservationist critical of the administration's tardy efforts against the water projects. "They don't know how to initiate; that's their biggest weakness."

Jacobs Amendment

The House rejected, 108-284, an amendment offered by Andy Jacobs Jr., D-Ind., that would have deleted funding for three projects: Richard B. Russell Dam, Ga. and S.C.; O'Neill Unit, Neb., and the Bonneville Unit of the Central Utah Project, Utah. *(Vote 399, p. 114-H)*

The amendment would have cut $90.8 million from the bill and, Jacobs said, would have saved more than $1 billion required for completion of the projects.

Jacobs said the three projects "raise some of the most serious environmental and ecological questions."

But many members rose to defend the projects in their districts or in neighboring districts. For example, Dan Marriott, R-Utah, said of the Bonneville Unit: "I plead with my colleagues not to turn off the spigot, not to cut our lifeline and not to destroy our vital water supplies."

ENERGY RESEARCH

The House passed intact the part of the bill appropriating funds for energy research. An amendment by Rep. Ted Weiss, D-N.Y., to prohibit funding for the neutron bomb was rejected, 67-259. *(Vote 402, p. 116-H)*

An expected fight over energy research funds was preempted by the rule on the bill, which disallowed any amendment that would make the appropriations contingent on authorizing legislation.

The committee made the restriction to avoid entangling the appropriations bill in a fight among the three committees responsible for the Department of Energy authorization.

The authorization bills (HR 12163, HR 11392) had not yet been taken up by the House. John D. Dingell, D-Mich., had planned an amendment to the appropriations bill that would have made the appropriations subject to authorizing legislation. As it turned out, neither of the authorization bills were passed.

The Commerce Committee, in particular Dingell's Subcommittee on Energy and Power, authorized funds in different amounts and for different purposes than were provided in the appropriations bill. The appropriations bill generally followed the authorizations reported by the Science and Technology Committee, which had been fighting with Commerce and Interior about overlapping jurisdictions.

An already confusing situation would have been compounded by linking the appropriations bill with the authorization bills, the Rules Committee said.

Richard Bolling, D-Mo, a Rules Committee member, recommended that Congress modify the Congressional Budget Act so the appropriations committees would have authorizing legislation available to them earlier in the process. The deadline for reporting authorizing legislation was May 15, which meant that the appropriations committee was often in the middle of its work when it got the authorization bill.

OTHER AMENDMENTS

Final passage came after the House accepted by voice vote an amendment by Clarence E. Miller, R-Ohio, to cut appropriations by 2 percent. The reduction would cut about $206 million from the $10.3 billion committee bill but would not affect payments required by law, Miller said.

The House then refused, 93-228, to make a 3 percent cut in the bill proposed by Silvio O. Conte, R-Mass. Conte said his amendment would have replaced the 2 percent cut with a 3 percent cut. *(Vote 403, p. 116-H)*

Also by voice vote, the House accepted an amendment by John J. Duncan, R-Tenn., to earmark $1,846,000 in the bill for completion of the Tellico Dam in Tennessee. The bill already included the money, and the committee report specified that the funds should be used to complete the dam. But Duncan said he wanted to "make it clear that the Congress intends for this project to be 100 percent complete and used as designed."

The Supreme Court halted construction of the dam June 15 when it ruled that completing it would violate the endangered species law.

PROVISIONS

As passed by the House, HR 12928 appropriated the following amounts. However, the totals do not reflect the 2 percent overall cut in the bill that was adopted on the floor. Miller estimated the cut would reduce the total by $206 million.

Agency	Budget Request	House Amount
Department of Energy	$ 6,481,337,000	$ 6,183,066,000
Army Corps of Engineers	2,448,800,000	2,679,759,000
Interior Department		
Bureau of Reclamation	615,275,000	615,613,000
Water Resources Planning	11,560,000	9,653,900
Independent Offices	811,927,000	853,542,000
Total	$10,368,899,000	$10,341,633,900

Senate Committee Action

Undaunted by threats of a veto, the Senate Public Works Appropriations Subcommittee July 27 funded seven water projects opposed by President Carter and then voted out the $10.2 billion energy and water development bill that contained them.

J. Bennett Johnston, D-La., subcommittee chairman, admitted after the meeting that funding the seven projects could jeopardize the bill because of Carter's veto threats.

Subcommittee Action

The Senate panel also refused Carter's request for full, up-front funding for 26 new projects he proposed June 9. Full funding would force recognition of the enormous long-term construction costs of water projects, according to Carter's reasoning.

The subcommittee funded Carter's requests, but only for one year, the way Congress traditionally funded projects.

Johnston said full funding would "take away congressional prerogatives" that the panel wanted to protect.

Members of Congress preferred annual funding because it gave them a way every year to remind constituents of their work on behalf of a local project.

The seven disputed projects funded by the Senate panel were Bayou Bodcau, La.; Yatesville Dam, Ky.; Meramec Park Dam, Mo.; Lukfata Dam, Okla.; Narrows Unit Dam, Colo.; Savery-Pot Hook Dams, Colo., and Fruitland Mesa Dam, Colo. An eighth disputed project funded by the House, La Farge Lake, Wis., was not funded by the Senate subcommittee because it was deauthorized in an amendment to the waterway user bill passed by the House May 3. *(Waterway bill, p. 513)*

Like the House, the Senate subcommittee provided money to begin construction of many new projects not recommended by the administration. But the senators did not accept all of the 41 new projects approved by the House and substituted instead those they strongly supported.

The senators made other adjustments in the House bill. Among them was an increase of $11 million over the House amount for the Red River Waterway, La., giving the project a total of $56 million in fiscal 1979.

The panel provided a total of $2.68 billion for the Army Corps of Engineers, about $50 million below the House figure. The Bureau of Reclamation, the other major water development agency, received $563 million under the panel's proposal, $53 million less than the House amount.

The panel also approved a resolution that would allow construction of part of the controversial Garrison Diversion Unit, N.D., an irrigation project held up because of Canadian objections to salty discharges into Canadian waters expected from the project.

The resolution would force the administration to spend funds on the part of the project that discharged into U.S. waters. The project was strongly opposed by enviornmentalists who said it would take about 220,000 acres in order to irrigate 250,000 acres.

The resolution was offered by North Dakota Sens. Quentin N. Burdick, D, and Milton R. Young, R, both Senate panel members. They said the project was beneficial.

The panel chose not to vote on a controversial plan to exempt the Bureau of Reclamation from preparing a comprehensive environmental impact statement on several dams planned in the Colorado River Basin. An exemption eventually was included in the Interior appropriations bill (HR 12932).

The Environmental Defense Fund filed a lawsuit to require the study, which the Interior Department later agreed to do.

But a coalition of western representatives and senators did not want the bureau to have to do the impact statement. They argued it was not required and feared it could jeopardize completion of pending Colorado Basin projects.

In addition to funds for water development, the bill contained $6.142 billion for the Department of Energy, and $864 million for the Tennessee Valley Authority and other independent agencies.

Full Committee Action

The Senate Appropriations Committee reported HR 12928 Aug. 7 (H Rept 95-1069) and recommended fiscal 1979 appropriations of $10.12 billion for energy and water resources development. The total was $919.8 million less than requested by the Carter administration.

Major reductions by the committee included a $131 million cut from uranium enrichment programs; $162 million from atomic energy defense activities and more than $500 million from general construction funds for dams and other water development.

Although the House appropriations bill added funds to the administration request for development of solar heating and cooling, photovoltaics and other less conventional energy sources, the Senate bill generally followed the Carter recommendations for energy research and technology development.

For the Clinch River breeder reactor, the Senate bill appropriated $172 million, which would pay for continuing construction of the Tennessee project. The Energy Department authorization bill (S 2692) gave the administration, which opposed the project, authority to complete or terminate construction of the reactor, which cast doubt on whether the money would be spent. However, S 2692 was never cleared by Congress.

In the section on administration of the Energy Department, the committee criticized the department for "great imbalance" in its staffing, with technical programs understaffed while assistant secretaries and other policy management personnel had dozens of new employees.

The panel rejected an across-the-board cut of 2 percent adopted by the House. Johnston said it "doesn't make any sense for ongoing construction work to be deferred."

Senate Floor Action

The Senate Aug. 10 passed its version of HR 12928 by an 89-5 vote. Floor manager Johnston praised it as a "very lean and tight bill that is in the spirit of Proposition 13 [the California tax cut initiative]." *(Vote 309, p. 47-S)*

The Senate bill appropriating $10,123,344,900 was about $916 million less than the administration's budget request. However, $519.3 million of the cut reflected the Senate's refusal to provide full, up-front funding for 26 new water projects as Carter requested.

Presidential press secretary Jody Powell called the bill "budget-busting" and said it was "deceptive" to say the bill was smaller than the administration budget "since it only includes only the first year's funding" for the new water projects.

James T. McIntyre Jr., director of the Office of Management and Budget, criticized the bill for mandating the hiring of 2,300 more federal employes, primarily for the Army Corps of Engineers, and for "excessive funding for breeder reactors."

Included in the bill was construction money for four water projects and planning money for two other projects that were on Carter's 1977 "hit list" and not funded by Congress in 1977.

Few changes were made in the committee bill on the Senate floor, and there were no roll call votes on amendments. Johnston persuaded one senator to cut his amendment from $30 million to $5 million; convinced another not to offer his because the funding had not been authorized and told a third his amendment might guarantee a veto and should be withdrawn.

"I think this would be a very heavy straw that could break the camel's back and surely not only insure but invite and insist on a veto," Johnston told Malcolm Wallop, R-Wyo., who withdrew his amendment.

Wallop wanted to prohibit use of funds in the bill to implement certain provisions of Carter's water policy. Wallop and other western senators were concerned that the policy would end the federal subsidies that provided water at low cost to western users. They were also critical of Carter's plans to require that states and localities pay a larger share of federal water projects.

Other Amendments

In other action, the Senate:

- Accepted an amendment by Frank Church, D-Idaho, to add $5 million for construction of a facility to store spent nuclear fuel. Church reduced the amount from $30 million to $5 million after Johnston said the committee supported a greater emphasis on fuel storage, but felt adequate funds for fiscal 1979 were already provided in the bill.
- Accepted an amendment by Pete V. Domenici, R-N.M., to add $1 million for engineering and design of an electron beam fusion facility in Albuquerque, N.M., and to add $4.2 million for improvements to defense nuclear waste facilities.
- Accepted an Appropriations Committee amendment offered by Johnston to delete the $12 million earmarked for the Meramec Park Lake project in Missouri. In an Aug. 8 referendum on the dam, voters in the state opposed the project two to one.
- Accepted an amendment by Floyd K. Haskell, D-Colo., to add $5 million for final design and initial construction of the Solar Energy Research Institute in Golden, Colo.

Provisions

As passed by the Senate, HR 12928 appropriated the following amounts:

Agency	Amended Budget Request	Senate Amount
Department of Energy	$ 6,509,027,000	$6,059,594,000
Army Corps of Engineers	2,971,165,000	2,633,620,000
Interior Dept. Bureau of Reclamation	735,770,000	566,915,000
Independent Agencies	823,487,000	863,215,900
TOTAL	$11,039,449,000	$10,123,344,900

Conference Report

Conferees filed their report on HR 12928 Aug. 14 (H Rept 95-1490). The conference agreement provided $10,160,483,000 — $878,965,000 below the president's request and $279,389,100 below the amount appropriated in fiscal 1978.

After considerable debate over the eight "hit list" projects contained in the House version, conferees agreed to delete funding for two of the projects: La Farge Lake, Wis., and Meramec Park Lake, Mo. Of the remaining six, conferees proposed funding three of the projects for study purposes only and recommended construction of the other three.

The House agreed to the conference report on Sept. 14, 319-71 *(vote 685, p. 194-H)* and the Senate followed suit on Sept. 27, 86-9. *(Vote 408, p. 61-S)*

On Oct. 5, Carter vetoed the bill, stating that it contained "provisions for excessive, wasteful water projects and ill-advised limitations on efficient program management."

House Override Attempt

Defying its leadership, the House Oct. 5 refused to override President Carter's veto of the bill. The vote to sustain was 223-190. *(Vote 774, p. 220-H)*

The action, with 53 votes to spare, was a stunning victory for Carter, who, assisted by his Cabinet and top aides, blitzed the House with well-organized lobbying.

The promise of a showdown drew more than 200 members to the floor for an hour of debate. They received impassioned speeches for an override by Speaker Thomas P. O'Neill Jr., D-Mass., Majority Leader Jim Wright, D-Texas, and Minority Leader John J. Rhodes, R-Ariz.

Ironically, the president owed his victory to the 62 Republicans who voted with him. They bought his argument that the fiscal 1979 public works appropriations bill was inflationary and would mean spending $1.8 billion over several years on water projects of questionable merit.

Carter said after the vote that it had been a "tough fight" and that he was "gratified by the results." He praised Congress for "its wise and responsible action" in taking a "long step in the battle against inflation."

The margin of victory elated the winners, who had expected a much closer vote.

Frank Moore, chief White House lobbyist, said there were "about 40 undecided" members as late as 11 p.m. the day before the vote, when Carter stopped calling them. He got on the phone again at 8 o'clock the next morning.

According to one southern Democrat who got a call, Carter essentially said he would remember a vote to sustain the veto and promised to return the favor sometime in the future. The Democrat voted with Carter.

On Oct. 4, Carter sent Interior Secretary Cecil D. Andrus, Budget Director James T. McIntyre, chief economic adviser Charles L. Schultze and Army Secretary Clifford L. Alexander to Capitol Hill to defend the veto.

Carter also invited about 30 Republicans to the White House for breakfast on Oct. 5.

The White House efforts got an added boost the morning of the vote, when *The Washington Post* carried a full-page advertisement in which Howard Jarvis labeled the bill the "big spending, big waste, bill of the year." Jarvis, who led the California Proposition 13 movement that cut property taxes, called the legislation an "outrage." Several members were seen carrying the ad in the House chamber.

Compromise Reached

President Carter's veto of the public works bill and the House vote to sustain it, forced legislators back to the drawing boards to try to reach a compromise. The result was an agreement to delete the features in HR 12928 that Carter opposed.

The compromise on the vetoed bill was attached to a resolution (H J Res 1139 — S Rept 95-1317) providing continuing funding for several agencies for which regular appropriations bills had not been passed. *(Story, p. 161)*

The revised energy and public works portion contained about the same amount of money as the original bill. But restrictions were placed on the use of certain funds by the Army Corps of Engineers and the Interior Department's Bureau of Reclamation.

Major elements of the compromise were:

- Deletion of construction funding for the six projects first opposed by Carter in 1977. They would have cost $580 million to complete.
- Deletion of construction funding for 11 new projects that Carter said would have cost about $1 billion to complete. Planning money was retained.
- Deletion of a mandate that 2,300 new employees be hired by the Corps of Engineers and the Bureau of Reclamation.
- A commitment from Congress to hold hearings in 1979 on a policy of full, up-front funding for water projects.
- Funding for the Water Resources Council, which Carter wanted to carry out his new water policy.

Congress, though providing limited funding for Carter's projects, refused to provide full funding. In addition, the legislators added another 26 new projects. Though only limited funding for the new congressional projects was provided in the fiscal 1979 bill, Carter said the projects would eventually cost $1.2 billion to complete and criticized the expense.

In the compromise, construction funding was deleted for one of Carter's projects and 10 of the congressional projects.

Congressional aides said the total cost of completing the new projects that remained in the bill would be $841 million. However, the full price was not contained in the bill, which provided only enough funds for one year of construction or loans.

The Water Resources Council, which Carter wanted to spearhead his water policy reform, was not funded in the original bill, though some money was provided for water resources planning by other agencies. The compromise restored funding for the council and added another $1.7 million for the council to administer the Water Resources Planning Act of 1962.

Final Action

The House passed H J Res 1139 on Sept. 26 by a vote of 349-30. The Senate passed the measure Oct. 15 by voice vote (PL 95-482). *(House vote 739, p. 210-H)*

With a few exceptions, the resolution provided funding identical to that included in HR 12928.

The exceptions were the following:

- No funds could be used for six projects: Bayou Bodcau, La.; Yatesville Lake, Ky.; Narrows Unit, Colo.; Lukfata Lake, Okla.; Fruitland Mesa, Colo., and Savery-Pot Hook, Colo. and Wyo.
- No funds could be used for construction of 10 new projects proposed by Congress and one proposed by Carter. However, spending on pre-construction planning was allowed. The resolution deleted the following new starts proposed by Congress: Animas-La Plata, Colo.; McGee Creek, Okla.; Uintah Unit, Utah; Upalco Unit, Utah; Missouri River Levee System, Units L611-614, Iowa; Kaskaskia Island Drainage and Levee District, Ill.; Cedar River Harbor, Mich.; Burlington Dam, N.D.; Arcadia Lake, Okla., and Big Pine Lake, Texas. Funding was also deleted for a Milan, Ill., project proposed by Carter.
- The provision mandating the hiring of 2,300 new employees by the Army Corps of Engineers and Bureau of Reclamation was deleted.
- Appropriations of $12,681,900 were provided for the Water Resources Council. Congress had provided all but $1,768,000 of that amount but had designated it for water resources planning by the interior secretary instead of by the council.

The report (S Rept 95-1317) accompanying the resolution also said Congress would hold hearings on the administration's request for full, up-front funding of water projects and on other water policy issues.

Provisions

As signed by the president, H J Res 1139 appropriated the following amounts for energy and water development programs:

Agency	Budget Request	Final Amount
Title I—Department of Energy		
Operating expenses:		
Energy research and development		
Solar energy	$ 357,300,000	$ 391,000,000
Geothermal energy	136,700,000	153,200,000
Biomass	36,400,000	41,900,000
Hydroelectric power	28,000,000	28,000,000
Fusion energy	225,000,000	233,000,000
Electric energy systems	38,000,000	38,000,000
Energy storage	55,900,000	55,900,000
Light water reactors	227,350,000	255,350,00C
Liquid metal fast breeder reactor	279,701,000	460,201,000
Other advanced reactors	136,200,000	125,200,000
Space nuclear systems	43,400,000	38,400,000
Environmental research	183,988,000	190,988,000
Basic Energy Sciences	175,600,000	168,100,000
Advanced technology, assessment	16,690,000	5,000,000
Total, energy research	$ 1,940,229,000	$ 2,184,239,000

Agency	Budget Request	Final Amount
Uranium supply, enrichment	81,200,000	65,000,000
General science, research	306,600,000	310,600,000
Atomic energy defense	2,160,083,000	2,137,283,000
Policy, management, support	405,056,000	293,579,000
Carryover from previous years	−11,800,000	−172,270,000
Total, operating expenses	$ 4,881,368,000	$ 4,818,431,000
Plant and capital equipment	1,438,416,000	1,067,971,000
Power marketing	143,573,000	145,473,000
Federal Energy Regulatory Comm.	43,670,000	51,300,000
Special foreign currency program	2,000,000	2,000,000
Total, Department of Energy	$ 6,509,027,000	$ 6,085,175,000
Title II—Army Corps of Engineers	$ 2,971,165,000	$ 2,636,024,000
Title III—Bureau of Reclamation	735,770,000	579,915,000
Title IV—Independent Offices:		
Appalachian Regional Commission	2,220,000	2,220,000
Appalachian regional development	343,700,000	368,700,000
Delaware River Basin Commission	347,000	347,000
Interstate Commission Potomac River	53,000	55,000
Nuclear Regulatory Commission	330,670,000	322,301,000
Susquehanna River Commission	302,000	302,000
Tennessee Valley Authority	134,635,000	154,531,000
Water Resources Council	11,560,000	12,681,900
Total, Independent Offices	$ 823,487,000	$ 861,137,900
Grand Total	$11,039,449,000	$10,162,251,900

Continuing Appropriations

Legislation providing continuing appropriations for a grab bag of programs, including a compromise version of the water projects bill vetoed by President Carter Oct. 5, cleared Congress Oct. 15 in the final hours before adjournment.

The bill (H J Res 1139 — PL 95-482) provided temporary funding at 1978 levels for programs that had not been included in regular appropriations bills for fiscal 1979 because of delays in the passage of authorizing legislation.

Included in this category was about $17 billion in programs administered by the Departments of Labor and Health, Education and Welfare, plus related agencies. The measure provided funding for some of the programs in the Health Services Administration, Center for Disease Control, National Institutes of Health, Health Resources Administration, Office of Education, the Community Services Administration and the Corporation for Public Broadcasting.

Delays in completion of the authorization bill (S 2570) extending the Comprehensive Employment and Training Act (CETA) led to the inclusion of CETA appropriations in H J Res 1139. The bill provided funding at the lower of the current rate or the rate authorized by the House-passed version of S 2570 — about $12 billion. The House had called for a reduction of about 100,000 public service jobs in the program down to a level of 625,000 jobs. *(CETA, p. 287)*

The bill re-enacted the fiscal 1979 water projects bill (HR 12928) vetoed by the president, but threw out funds for six water projects opposed by the administration and provided funding for planning but not for the construction of 11 other projects.

The compromise dropped a provision directing the Corps of Engineers and the Bureau of Reclamation to hire 2,300 new employees, and restored a $12.7 million appropriation to fund the Water Resources Council, an agency the administration said it wanted to help streamline the planning and management of federal water programs. *(Details of compromise, p. 154)*

Passage of the Labor-HEW and Defense Department appropriations bills superseded provisions in the resolution passed by the House Sept. 26 providing continuing appropriations for those agencies. *(Labor-HEW bill, p. 105, defense bill, p. 132)*

Passage of the regular Labor-HEW and Defense appropriations bills also negated abortion language that had been contained in the House-passed version of H J Res 1139.

House Action

The House passed H J Res 1139 Sept. 26, by a vote of 349-30. *(Vote 739, p. 210-H)*

H J Res 1139, reported by the Appropriations Committee Sept. 21 (H Rept 95-1599), provided continuing appropriations for programs funded by the Labor-HEW bill (HR 12929), certain related items not yet authorized, and the defense appropriations bill (HR 13635).

On a voice vote after no debate, the House adopted an amendment making anti-abortion language that applied to Labor-HEW programs applicable to programs covered by the defense appropriations bill.

The defense bill, which passed the House Aug. 9, was slowed in the Senate as a result of President Carter's veto of the weapons procurement authorization bill (HR 10929).

The House passed the Labor-HEW bill June 13 and the Senate approved it Sept. 27.

Senate Action

The Senate adopted by voice vote a number of Appropriations Committee amendments (S Rept 95-1317), including the public works compromise, before passing H J Res 1139 in the early morning hours of Oct. 15.

One of the committee amendments extended from March 31, 1979, to Sept. 30, 1979, the appropriations for the unauthorized portions of the Labor-HEW bill, giving the authorizing committees six additional months to review the programs.

Other amendments adopted by voice vote were introduced by:

- Daniel K. Inouye, D-Hawaii, to repeal a provision of the foreign relations authorization act (PL 95-426) that permitted some foreign service officers to retire based on their highest-paid single year of service.
- Birch Bayh, D-Ind., to remove language from the transportation appropriations bill requiring passage of authorizing legislation before a $300 million appropriation for ConRail operations could be spent.
- Claiborne Pell, D-R.I., to appropriate $3.5 million to implement a settlement over land claims in Rhode Island by the Narragansett Indians.
- Ted Stevens, R-Alaska, to authorize the secretary of commerce to award up to $16 million in grants to the U.S. Olympic Committee to finance construction and maintenance of athletic facilities or for direct operating costs of programs.

Noting that the House had deleted $30 million in authorizations for the Olympic Committee, Stevens told the Senate that "I am quite concerned about the loss of funds from the bill, because I believe the money is essential in making the purposes outlined in the act possible."

He said the money was to be used to restructure the committee "to make it the coordinating body for amateur athletic activity in the country" for reorganizing the 32 amateur sports groups within the Olympic Committee.

The smaller amount he proposed, Stevens said, "meets House concerns for funds being utilized for salaries, studies and other intangibles."

Rejected. An amendment introduced by Lawton Chiles, D-Fla., to cut 68,000 jobs from the anti-recession title of the CETA program in fiscal 1979 was rejected by a vote of 32-44. *(Vote 512, p. 75-S)*

Final Action

The House accepted the Senate amendments by voice vote the same day, clearing the bill for the president. ▮

Across-the-Board Spending Cuts: Few Survived

Following is a list of proposals considered by the House and Senate in 1978 for across-the-board spending cuts in appropriations bills. This list does not include proposals for specific dollar amount cuts in individual programs or agencies, or spending cuts considered in committees.

Agriculture (HR 13125—PL 95-448) — House: 2 percent cut rejected 189-201. Senate: No across-the-board spending cuts considered. Conference: no across-the-board cuts considered.

Defense (HR 13635—PL 95-457) — House: 2 percent cut in military personnel costs rejected 53-327; 2 percent cut to entire bill rejected 102-252; 1 percent cut to entire bill rejected 136-222. Senate: 1 percent cut rejected 11-74. Conference: no across-the-board cuts considered.

Foreign Assistance (HR 12931—PL 95-481) — House: 2 percent cut in bilaterial aid programs (excluding Egypt, Israel, Jordan and Syria) approved 293-52; 2 per cent cut in foreign military credit sales approved 300-29; 8 percent cut rejected 184-199; 2 per cent cut in programs that had not been previously cut approved 289-95. Senate: House-passed 2 percent cut in bilateral programs deleted 40-30. Conference: no across-the-board cuts included.

Foreign Economic Aid (HR 12222—PL 95-424) — House: 5 per cent cut approved 200-172; the amendment cut all programs except food aid and funds for U.S. schools and hospitals abroad. Senate: amendment to give the Appropriations Committees authority to delete 5 per cent approved 57-22. Conference: House-passed 5 percent cut accepted.

HUD-Veterans Administration-Independent Agencies (HR 12936—PL 95-392) — House: 2 percent cut rejected 156-222. Senate: 2 percent cut approved 45-42; the amendment made 2 percent cuts in HUD, Environmental Protection Agency, National Aeronautics and Space Administration and National Science Foundation. Conference: across-the-board cuts converted to specific cuts, resulting in total reduction of approximately 2 percent.

Interior-Energy (HR 12932—PL 95-465) — House: 2 percent cut rejected 198-211. Senate: 2 percent cut tabled 68-25. Conference: No across-the-board cuts.

Labor-HEW (HR 12929—PL 95-480) — House: 2 percent cut approved 220-181. Senate: House cut deleted. Conference: No across-the-board cuts.

Legislative Branch (HR 12935—PL 95-391) — House: 5 percent cut approved 220-168. Senate: 5 percent cut approved 220-181. Senate: House cut deleted. Conference: No across-the-board cuts.

Military Construction (HR 12927—PL 95-374) — House: 2 percent cut rejected by voice vote. Senate: 2 per cent cut rejected 26-60. Conference: no across-the-board cuts.

Public Works (HR 12928) — House: 2 per cent cut adopted by voice vote; 3 percent cut rejected 93-228. Senate: House-passed 2 percent cut rejected in committee. Final: no across-the-board cuts considered in final public works legislation (H J Res 1139—PL-95-482).

State-Justice-Commerce-Judiciary (HR 12934—PL 95-431) — House: 2 percent cut approved by voice vote. Senate: proposed 2 percent cut amended to make specific cuts totaling $176.1 million. Conference: House-passed 2 percent cut rejected by conference committee. House rejected motion to recommit conference report with instructions to reduce total by 2 percent.

Second Supplemental, Fiscal 1978 (HR 13467—PL 95-355) — House: 2 percent cut approved 256-114. Senate: no across-the-board cuts considered. Conference: House-passed 2 per cent cut dropped; $57 million in specific cuts substituted.

Transportation (HR 12933—PL 95-335) — House: no across-the-board cuts considered. Senate: no across-the-board cuts considered. Conference: none.

Treasury-Postal Service-General Government (HR 12930—PL 95-429) — House: 5 percent cut rejected by voice vote. Senate: 2 per cent cut in Treasury Department, Federal Election Commission and General Services Administration budgets approved 55-34; Postal Service not included in cut. Conference: no across-the-board cuts.

Law Enforcement/Judiciary

For the first time since it was created in 1870, Justice Department officials went before congressional authorizing committees in 1978 to justify the agency's programs and expenditures.

The hearing record, including testimony of Attorney General Griffin B. Bell, detailed an ambitious set of legislative goals for the second session of the 95th Congress in the areas of law enforcement and the administration of justice.

A comparison of the department's goals and achievements in 1978 suggests that it was better at identifying problems than either it or Congress was in getting bills approved to solve them. Of 16 top legislative priorities outlined by the department in testimony given in March 1978 before the House Judiciary Committee, only five were enacted by Congress.

Nevertheless, several major pieces of legislation likely to have a long-lasting impact were approved. These included legislation increasing the size of the federal judiciary by more than 30 percent with the addition of 152 new district and circuit court judgeships, and a bill to control the use of wiretaps in the United States for foreign intelligence gathering purposes.

The new judges, to be appointed by President Carter, were likely to shape the character of the federal courts for several decades. The wiretap bill, on the other hand, established an important constitutional precedent in placing limits on executive branch "inherent power" in an attempt to protect the privacy of individual citizens. It was likely to have a considerable impact on legislation that was to be debated in the 96th Congress to further control intelligence agencies.

During 1978, the Congress also cleared a proposed constitutional amendment to give full voting representation in the House and Senate to residents of the District of Columbia, and extended by 39 months the deadline for ratification of the Equal Rights Amendment to the Constitution. *(Congress and Government chapter)*

Left unfinished were the attorney general's top priority, recodification of the entire body of United States criminal law, as well as such other high priorities as legislation to require new registration and reporting requirements for lobbyists, a bill to provide attorneys fees to citizens who prevail in government suits brought against them, and bills dealing with class action lawsuits, antitrust improvements, and illegal aliens.

Many of the bills that failed to become law were approved by either the House or the Senate and were likely to be brought up early in the next Congress. Several of the Justice Department's top priorities — such as a bill to overturn a Supreme Court decision preventing indirect purchasers from suing price-fixers, and a bill to protect the constitutional rights of persons confined in state nursing homes and mental institutions — were killed as a result of filibuster threats in the Senate. Rules changes at the beginning of the 96th Congress were expected to diminish the possibility of the same thing happening to these bills again.

Criminal Code

The bill described by Attorney General Bell as his number one legislative priority in 1978, recodification of the entire body of U.S. criminal law, was the first major piece of legislation to clear the Senate in 1978.

The product of years of negotiations among Senate liberals and conservatives, representatives of conflicting civil liberties and national security interests, the massive bill passed the Senate by a surprisingly wide 72-15 margin. It was the first time in a decade of debate that a recodification bill had reached the floor of either house.

But the underlying assumptions of the Senate-passed bill, that liberals and conservatives had to compromise some of their most strongly held beliefs and that the measure had to be approved or rejected as a package, were resoundingly rejected when the bill was brought up in a House Judiciary subcommittee.

Subcommittee Chairman James R. Mann, D-S.C., summarized the thinking of subcommittee members when he said the criminal law "should not be subject to trade-offs and compromise in the name of reform." Many House committee members also argued that the Senate bill failed to account for the views of certain interested parties, notably defendants.

Wiretapping

Whether it would serve to protect innocent Americans from invasions of privacy by government intelligence agencies was yet to be seen. But the Foreign Intelligence Surveillance Act was clearly one of the most significant accomplishments of the 95th Congress.

A direct outgrowth of congressional hearings documenting widespread abuses by government intelligence agencies, the bill marked the first significant legislative effort to clamp down on invasions of citizens' privacy rights and violations of free speech that reached epidemic proportion in the 1960s.

Requiring a judicial warrant for most foreign intelligence agency electronic surveillance conducted in the United States, the bill was viewed as a major precedent in what promised to be a continuing debate over charters for the FBI, CIA, National Security Agency and other intelligence gathering networks. The Foreign Intelligence Surveillance Act was supported by all the federal intelligence agencies as well as the American Civil Liberties Union.

Administration of Justice

Shortly after taking office in 1977, Bell established a new Office for Improvements in the Administration of Justice which became the fount of numerous legislative proposals in the 95th Congress designed to make the federal court system operate more efficiently.

The most far-reaching achievement in the area was the judgeship bill, creating 117 new district court positions and 35 new spots on the appeals courts.

New judgeships to relieve overloaded court dockets had been called for in many judicial districts for years. But a

Major Justice Department Initiatives in the 95th Congress

Bill	Final Action
Foreign intelligence electronic surveillance controls	enacted
Creation of 152 new federal court judgeships	enacted
Special prosecutor to investigate wrongdoing in the executive branch	enacted
Pregnancy disability rights	enacted
District of Columbia voting representation (constitutional amendment)	cleared for state legislatures
Extension of ratification deadline for Equal Rights Amendment	cleared
Recodification of U.S. criminal laws	passed Senate
Expand jurisdiction of U.S. magistrates	died in House-Senate conference
Mandatory pretrial arbitration	died in committee
Diversity jurisdiction amendments	passed House*
Civil rights of institutionalized persons	passed House*
Lobbying reform	passed House
Federal tort claims amendments	died in committee
Illegal aliens	died in committee
Attorneys fees	died in committee
Class actions	died in committee
Indirect purchaser antitrust suits	died in committee

** Died as result of filibuster threat*

Democratic Congress was never willing to give such an enormous patronage bonanza to a Republican president. So no bill was seriously considered until Democrats had one of their own in the White House.

An amendment to the bill, written in the House, required the president to issue standards and guidelines for merit selection of federal district judges. Carter had been sharply criticized in early 1978 when David W. Marston, a Republican U.S. attorney in Philadelphia, was replaced by a Democrat. Carter had pledged in his campaign to make all appointments of U.S. attorneys and judges on the basis of merit.

Shortly thereafter, Carter issued an executive order establishing merit selection commissions for the appeals courts. But the order did not cover district courts and House liberals and Republicans sought to force Carter into a strong position on merit selection. An executive order issued by the president in November sought to pressure senators to use merit commissions but left the final decision as to whether the patronage system would be put to rest in the hands of senators.

Access to Justice

Other successes in the area of court improvements were less significant than the judgeship bill. Congress gave approval to higher fees for witnesses and jurors to compensate for inflation and provided travel and living expenses that were frequently denied in the past. Congress also provided government paid interpreters to witnesses and parties to lawsuits who did not speak English or had hearing impairments.

But several major court improvement bills did not make it through in 1978. A bill to expand the jurisdiction of magistrates in civil and criminal trials died after the House attached it to a bill opposed by the American Bar Association and Association of Trial Lawyers of America. The more controversial diversity jurisdiction bills would have suspended or severely limited the right of litigants from different states to use federal rather than state courts to decide their disputes.

A bill to encourage use of district court arbitration in civil cases passed the Senate but no hearings were held in the House. The measure, which would have required use of pretrial arbitration on an experimental basis in five to eight districts was viewed as a quicker and less expensive means of resolving court disputes.

Other bills designed to increase access to federal courts, including one to overrule restrictive Supreme Court decisions on standing and another to provide attorneys fees to parties that would otherwise be unrepresented in agency rulemaking, failed to get out of committee. The attorneys fee legislation was subjected to heavy opposition from organized business lobbies.

Finally, a bill that would have given the federal government authority to sue state-run mental hospitals, prisons, and nursing homes where a "pattern or practice" of constitutional rights violations was found was killed by a Senate filibuster threat after winning House approval.

—By Alan Berlow

Senate-Passed Criminal Code Dies in House

The first major revision and consolidation of 200 years of U.S. criminal law was approved overwhelmingly by the Senate Jan. 30, but the measure was not reported by the House Judiciary Committee and did not clear Congress in 1978. In July, the committee's Subcommittee on Criminal Justice had approved a bill that almost completely rejected the recommendations in the Senate-passed Criminal Code Reform Act of 1978.

Senate passage of the 682-page bill, which its principal sponsor, Sen. Edward M. Kennedy, D-Mass., called the "cornerstone of the federal government's law enforcement policy," marked the culmination of 12 years of Senate deliberations. After eight days of debate in January 1978, the Senate passed the measure (S 1437) on a 72-15 vote. *(Vote 21, p. 5-S)*

Past versions of the bill, notably S 1 in the 94th Congress, had been attacked inside Congress and in the liberal press as repressive of basic civil liberties. But in 1978, the first time a criminal code revision reached the Senate floor, the most vocal opposition came from conservative lawmakers seeking tougher criminal laws. Liberal civil libertarians raised few objections.

Major Sentencing Change

The major change from current law provided by S 1437 established fixed, rather than indeterminate, prison terms, virtually eliminating parole and time off for good behavior from the sentencing process.

In addition, the bill established a U.S. Sentencing Commission to set guidelines governing the imposition of sentences by judges. For the first time a sentence could be appealed by a defendant or the government if it fell outside the commission's guidelines.

Other major changes from current law included expansion of civil rights statutes, creation of a trust fund to compensate victims of violent crimes, expanded white collar and organized crime penalties, and reduced penalties for possession of small amounts of marijuana.

Because criminal law enforcement in the United States is primarily a state rather than a federal responsibility, law enforcement would be largely unaffected by the bill. Historically, however, federal statutes have served as a model for state law. And in areas such as the decreased marijuana penalties provided by S 1437 it was expected that the code would have a significant impact on the writing of new state laws.

Spirit of Compromise

The final version of the Senate bill represented a series of compromises between civil libertarians and advocates of tougher criminal laws worked out by Edward Kennedy and Sen. John L. McClellan, D-Ark., a leading advocate of criminal code reform until his death in November 1977. Many of the most controversial provisions of the bill's predecessor, S 1, were dropped as Kennedy and McClellan sought to gain liberal and conservative support.

Although efforts were made during Senate action to resurrect some of the S 1 provisions, such as an expanded death penalty, as well as to drastically revise parts of controversial existing laws, Kennedy was able to convince a majority of senators to support the compromise worked out in the Judiciary Committee. In large measure the bill that passed was the bill reported by the Judiciary Committee in 1977.

Senate Floor Debate

The American Civil Liberties Union (ACLU), which sought numerous changes, called the bill "a dangerous piece of legislation." The ACLU statement attacked the bill for its failure to narrow the conspiracy laws and widening provisions dealing with obstruction of government processes. The latter, the group said, could cover "virtually every strike, picketing activity or mass demonstration at or near a federal facility." The ACLU called on the House to reject a similar bill saying, "The rights of Americans must not be whittled away by Congress."

The ACLU and the Los Angeles based National Committee Against Repressive Legislation (NCARL) provided virtually the only source of public opposition to S 1437 in the Senate. But when the bill came up on the Senate floor the traditional allies of these civil liberties groups were in scant evidence. While Sen. Gary Hart, D-Colo., offered a series of ACLU-supported sentencing amendments and Sen. Alan Cranston, D-Calif., sought to retain the doctrine of strict construction of federal laws, no single liberal led an attack on the bill.

That task was left largely to Sen. James B. Allen, D-Ala., a conservative, who said S 1437 would greatly expand the reach of the federal government in the area of criminal law. Allen raised a series of civil libertarian objections to the bill but also sought tougher criminal laws, particularly in the area of dissemination of pornography.

While Sen. James Abourezk, D-S.D., had considered a number of liberalizing amendments, he dropped his plans to offer them after he succeeded in gaining Senate approval for slightly decreased sentences.

Sen. Jacob K. Javits, R-N.Y., said he decided not to offer a liberal marijuana amendment because "we liberals decided this bill was too important to get hung up" on any single volatile issue.

Virtually the only far-reaching liberal amendment offered was by Sen. Charles McC. Mathias, R-Md., to greatly liberalize the law on dissemination of pornographic materials. And that amendment was tabled overwhelmingly as many senators who normally would have voted for the provision decided it would damage chances of passing the bill. *(Vote 11, p. 4-S)*

Kennedy's Role

Sen. Strom Thurmond, R-S.C., the Republican floor manager of the bill, noted that Kennedy had opposed numerous amendments offered by Democrats in the Judiciary Committee in order to get a bill. Thurmond also asked that "in the interests of achieving a bill that will gain widespread support and acceptance" senators not offer amendments without clearing them with the managers.

Throughout the debate a spirit of compromise worked to dampen opposition to the bill. Where accommodations could be made the managers made them. Where they felt they would endanger the bill, they squelched them.

At one point when Cranston and Allen objected to the bill's failure to state that federal criminal laws were to be construed narrowly, a compromise was reached and the managers inserted the language of strict construction in addition to the language Cranston and Allen had found objectionable, thereby avoiding what threatened to become a protracted floor debate.

In the waning hours of debate Allen insisted on eliminating stiffer penalties for violations of occupational health and safety laws and on reinstating the 1799 Logan Act making it a crime for a private citizen to communicate with a foreign government with the intent of influencing foreign policy. Kennedy accepted the changes. Kennedy had viewed the repeal of the Logan Act as symbolic of the effort to eliminate "archaic" statutes from federal law.

From the outset Kennedy insisted that the major controversies over criminal code reform had been resolved in committee. Passage of the bill was attributable in large measure to his convincing a majority of liberal senators that the bill accomplished significant reforms in "bringing some sense and order out of the chaotic current criminal code" and that, despite ACLU objections, the bill represented a net gain for civil liberties.

But the lack of opposition to the bill on the floor was attributable to several other factors as well. Operating in Kennedy's favor was the fact that few liberals wanted to buck him on a bill to which he had devoted years of effort and for which he had endured frequent criticism from the civil liberties and liberal communities that have been his traditional allies. "The problem in the Senate," according to ACLU Washington Director John Shattuck, was that "no liberals were willing to take on Kennedy in his deal with McClellan.... People were very deferential to Kennedy."

McClellan's endorsement was a factor in gaining conservative support for the bill. And Thurmond took up the standard McClellan left behind. Orrin G. Hatch, R-Utah, who was regarded as a leader on the Republican right, also was seen as an important force in keeping conservatives in line on the bill. Nevertheless, most of the opposition on the passage vote came from the Senate's more conservative members.

Lack of Understanding

In addition to the spirit of compromise in evidence throughout the Senate debate, widespread ignorance of the contents of the bill also contributed to the lack of sophisticated opposition. Throughout the debate, there were rarely more than a handful of senators in attendance on the floor.

Hart said he believed few senators had a thorough understanding of the contents of the bill and acknowledged that that fact frightened him. Sen. Robert Morgan, D-N.C., said he had a "fear of the unknown" in voting for final passage of the bill but hoped the Senate action would contribute to a more enlightened public debate on the measure. Allen said he did not think more than five senators understood what they were voting on.

But while many senators acknowledged that they were relying heavily on the Judiciary Committee recommendation to support the bill (it was approved by the committee 12-2), Allen was openly critical of senators he believed were relying on Kennedy to decide how to vote. "I am just wondering if that is a very good practice that we have here in the Senate, to run by the manager of the bill and ask, 'Well, what about this amendment?' It indicates that senators are not reaching independent judgment on these issues. I wonder if that is the right procedure for us to follow."

Background

The Senate Judiciary Committee approved the Criminal Code Reform Act (S 1437) on Nov. 2, 1977, on a 14-2 vote (S Rept 95-605). The 682-page proposal was reported after three months of markup sessions and approval of approximately 100 substantive amendments. *(1977 Almanac, p. 602)*

Approval of the compromise package was largely the work of Sen. Edward M. Kennedy, D-Mass., and the late Sen. John L. McClellan, D-Ark.

Despite their divergent political philosophies, the two senators collaborated to win committee approval of legislation that had been the subject of Senate debates stretching back a decade. Their collaboration was largely an effort to find a middle ground where law and order conservatives and civil libertarians could find agreement.

The final product represented at least a partial reconciliation of the interests of proponents of expanded federal prosecutorial authority in criminal law and defenders of individual civil liberties. The compromise was reached by dropping a number of the most controversial provisions and at the same time obtaining agreement among committee members that certain provisions that represented no new law but only recodification of existing law would be included without opposition no matter how offensive they might be to certain members of the committee.

S 1437 represented the first comprehensive effort to codify nearly 200 years of U.S. criminal law—approximately 3,000 individual criminal statutes. Lacking any consistent plan or structure, the current criminal code was characterized by the late Sen. McClellan as looking "more like a Tower of Babel than a comprehensible criminal code." In opening the final stage of Senate hearings on the bill, McClellan stated the case against the current code in no uncertain terms: "The plain fact is that the current federal criminal code is a disgrace."

As evidence of the serious disarray of the current criminal law, reform advocates pointed to such items as these:

- Under existing law it was a crime to lie to a ship's captain or to detain a government carrier pigeon.
- Under existing law there were 80 separate theft offenses and 70 separate counterfeiting and forgery offenses, all with their own conflicting definitions and language.
- Existing law included 80 separate terms describing culpable state of mind. These ranged, according to the report on the bill, "From the traditional 'knowingly and willfully,' to the conclusory 'unlawfully,' 'improperly,' and 'feloniously,' to the self-contradictory 'willfully neglects.' " S 1437 delimited only four culpable states of mind.
- Existing law gave judges and parole boards enormous discretion in sentencing. Thus a bank robber could be given a sentence of probation or 25 years in jail. A rapist could get probation or life imprisonment. A bank robber could get 25 years in jail, but a post office robber could get only 10.

In an effort to speed up congressional action on criminal code recodification, Kennedy and McClellan introduced on May 2, 1977, a pared down version of S 1, the controversial criminal code revision proposal that died at the end of the 94th Congress. Many of the most hotly contested provisions of S 1 were eliminated in the new bill, S 1437. The new bill was, in part, the product of negotiations begun during the 94th Congress by Senate Majority Leader Mike Mansfield (D Mont. 1943-77) and was widely viewed as a vast improvement over its predecessor.

Aside from dropping some of the more controversial provisions of S 1, the new criminal code recodification underwent numerous substantive changes in the Senate Judiciary Committee.

The bill was widely regarded as making improvements in rationalizing the definitions of criminal behavior and the concomitant penalties. Supporters of the bill also pointed to new sentencing provisions as a major improvement. These provisions establish nine specific classes of crimes ranging from an "A" felony, punishable by a maximum of life imprisonment, down to an "infraction," punishable by not more than five days in jail. Each specific crime described elsewhere in the proposed code is "graded" to one of the nine classes.

Advocates of the bill believed this classifying process would ensure that maximum punishments for crimes were consistent and accurately reflected society's disapproval of a particular criminal activity, rather than the whim of an individual judge or the idiosyncrasy of a particular piece of legislation.

Another provision to ensure punishment consistency would create a Sentencing Commission to promulgate sentencing guidelines that would direct judges in assigning punishment to a particular criminal. The commission would specify considerations to be weighed by a sentencing judge such as the grade of the crime, the record of the convicted defendant, and any mitigating factors.

Specific reasons would have to be offered by the sentencing judge for any sentence that went outside those guidelines.

Under the bill, federal sentences could for the first time be appealed, with an appellate court reviewing the trial judge's adherence to the guidelines or his reasons for failing to do so.

The bill also reflected increasing public support for "determinate" sentences of predictable duration rather than "indeterminate" sentences typically allowed under existing law. Sentences seldom were certain in length because of parole and "good time" credits given prisoners which could considerably reduce the time actually served. Parole and good time were discouraged under S 1437. Kennedy called the sentencing provisions "the most important reform in the entire bill."

Structure of the Senate Bill

The Senate-passed Criminal Code Reform Act of 1978 restructured the entire body of U.S. criminal law — approximately 3,000 separately enacted pieces of legislation — contained in Title 18 of the U.S. Code.

The bill placed all federal felonies in one integrated code, eliminating many obsolete provisions of current law. Crimes were consolidated so that where current law provided 80 separate theft offenses, the new bill had only one section on theft. And where current law provided 80 separate terms describing culpable states of mind, the new law reduced these to four.

The bill, S 1437, was divided into six titles:

- Title I replaced the existing Title 18 with a new code consisting of a thorough revision of both its substantive and procedural aspects of criminal law. It consisted of five parts.

1. The first part covered general provisions of the criminal law that govern the interpretation and application of the other portions of the code.

The section included general principles of criminal law, definitions of terms used throughout the code, delimitation of federal jurisdiction in prosecuting criminal matters and provisions defining the states of mind that must accompany conduct for it to be criminal.

2. The second part was the main body of the bill listing all federal crimes (except misdemeanors consisting of violations of federal regulatory laws), the jurisdictional provisions allowing federal action on each offense, the maximum penalties for each offense, and defenses that may be offered to prosecution of an offense.

3. The third part described the sentences that may be imposed for each criminal offense and prescription of the manner in which a sentence is to be selected and imposed.

4. The fourth part covered criminal law procedure and administration, which was retained in large part from current law. This part of the bill dealt with such matters as extradition, trial procedure, appellate review, counsel for indigents and release prior to a judicial proceeding.

5. This part covered supplementary civil proceedings that may be conducted in connection with criminal matters. This part of the bill included provisions to compensate victims of violent crimes, authorized forfeiture of property for certain crimes and authorized the use of restraining orders for racketeering offenses.

- Title II set forth amendments to the federal rules of criminal procedure under which the federal court system operates.
- Title III related to agencies that were to implement the new sentencing provisions and the Victim Compensation Board.
- Title IV was a two-page section of the bill dealing with several general provisions including those to continue the existence of the Bureau of Prisons and the Parole Commission.
- Titles V and VI included technical and conforming amendments transferring some sections of the current criminal code to other sections of U.S. law.

Provisions of Senate Bill

Virtually all of the Senate debate on S 1437 focused on Title I and most of that on specific crimes in Part 2. The following analysis of the bill focuses on Title I with particular attention to those sections in which significant changes were made from current law, those that were topics of controversy on the floor or in previous debates, and those that were amended on the Senate floor. The outline follows the numerical ordering of the bill.

Part I. General Provisions, Principles

Chapter 1. General Provisions

This chapter provided for the first time a table of about 100 definitions to be used throughout S 1437, an effort to provide for greater clarity and easier understanding of the law. (Current law provided definitions within each section.)

The chapter also provided that the sections of the bill would be construed in accordance with the "general purposes" of the bill and in "accordance with the rule of strict construction as applied by the federal courts." The committee had sought to eliminate "whatever vestiges remain in the federal system of the artificial canon of 'strict construction,' " which the committee report said had allowed "acquittal of persons who were clearly within the letter and spirit of the law." The strict construction language was replaced in the bill during floor debate.

Chapter 2. Jurisdiction

The underlying basis on which the federal government could enforce laws was set forth. The committee report stated that the bill was written to avoid unnecessary expansion of existing federal jurisdiction and that the bill rested on the "fundamental assumption that the basic responsibility for maintaining the order of our society day-by-day rests with the several states."

Sen. Allen sought to strike a section of the bill stating that the existence of federal jurisdiction is not an element of an offense. *(Vote 19, p. 5-S)*

Allen argued that the issue of jurisdiction should be decided by a jury and not by a judge who might have a personal interest in claiming jurisdiction over a particular offense. The Judiciary Committee concluded, however, that the question of federal jurisdiction should be separated from the elements of an offense because jurisdiction addresses only the question of the government's power to prosecute and not the elements of a crime. The committee view prevailed on the floor but the extent of federal jurisdiction remained one of the underlying philosophical disputes surrounding the bill.

Chapter 3. Culpable States of Mind

This section defined the specific mental states that must accompany the offenses in the code in order for them to be criminal. Current law included 80 separate terms describing culpable states of mind. These ranged, according to the report on the bill, "From the traditional 'knowingly and willfully,' to the conclusory 'unlawfully,' 'improperly,' and 'feloniously,' to the self-contradictory 'willfully neglects.' " S 1437 delimited four culpable states of mind: "intentional," "knowing," "reckless," and "negligent."

Chapter 4. Complicity

This section set forth the circumstances under which a person could be criminally liable for the acts of another individual or of an organization. The section codified the so-called Pinkerton doctrine making a co-conspirator guilty of each specific offense in furthering a criminal conspiracy if the acts were "reasonably foreseeable." Civil libertarians objected that the "reasonably foreseeable" standard was too broad and that each party to an offense should be held to a standard of having "knowingly" aided or abetted its commission. They argued that, as in the Pinkerton case, a defendant could be convicted of a crime committed without his participation or knowledge because each co-conspirator is liable for each offense in furtherance of a conspiracy.

This chapter provided a defense to prosecution if other conspirators had been acquitted because of insufficient evidence.

Chapter 5. Bars and Defenses

This section set forth a general statute of limitations and a bar to prosecution on grounds of immaturity (that the defendant was less than 16 years old). The section left uncodified common law defenses such as insanity, intoxication, unlawful entrapment, and protection of property or persons.

Part II: Offenses

Chapter 10. Offenses of General Applicability

Criminal Attempt. This section made it an offense to "attempt" to commit a federal crime. Currently there was no such specific offense although many individual offenses included attempt provisions. A Judiciary Committee amendment offered by Sen. Joe Biden, D-Del., required that a person's conduct "constitute a substantial step toward" the commission of a crime for him to be guilty of criminal attempt.

Criminal Conspiracy. This section stated that "A person is guilty of an offense if he agrees with one or more persons to engage in conduct, the performance of which would constitute a crime or crimes, and he, or one of such persons in fact, engages in any conduct with intent to effect any objective of the agreement." Civil libertarians raised the same objections to this section as to the "complicity" section cited above, arguing that it broadened federal conspiracy laws.

Criminal Solicitation

This section created a new crime of solicitation, making it an offense to solicit another person to engage in criminal conduct. The section was intended to cover a person who made a serious effort to get another to engage in a crime but was unsuccessful. Under current law a solicitor would not be covered unless he succeeded in having a crime committed. Designed to allow law enforcement officials to intervene in preventing crimes when there was evidence of intent, the section was sharply criticized by civil libertarians who said it could be broadly construed to prosecute discussions of political tactics that might involve commission of an offense even if no crime were actually committed.

Inapplicability to Certain Offenses. This section stated that it is not an offense to attempt to commit, conspire to commit or to solicit the commission of certain offenses, unless they were in fact committed. These included obstructing military recruitment or induction, inciting or aiding mutiny, insubordination or desertion and leading a riot.

Chapter 11. Offenses Involving National Defense

This chapter recodified current law on treason, armed rebellion and insurrection and engaging in paramilitary activity. A new provision was added to the treason section penalizing use of weapons by paramilitary groups that intend to take over a government function by force. The chapter did not recodify, and thereby repealed, the Smith Act, under which it was an offense to advocate the overthrow of the government. While this chapter was the bane of civil libertarians, few changes were made on the Senate floor. Among the controversial provisions were the following:

Sabotage. This section stated it was a crime to damage, tamper with or contaminate any U.S. property used or suited for use in the national defense. Civil libertarians argued that specific types of property that could be "sabotaged" should have been listed in the bill.

Impairing Military Effectiveness. Unlike existing law, the offense of damaging certain property in "reckless disregard" for the consequences was limited to time of war, a national defense emergency and several other situations. Civil libertarians argued that "reckless disregard" could be variously interpreted and that such conduct should be covered by destruction of property statutes or as sabotage if the national defense was involved.

Obstructing Military Recruitment or Induction. This section stated that it was an offense in time of war to interfere with or incite others to interfere with recruitment, conscription or induction. The National Committee Against Repressive Legislation (NCARL) objected that the term "war" could include undeclared wars (such as Vietnam or lesser hostilities) and that the incitement language could cover picketing of induction centers.

Inciting or Aiding Military Insubordination. The section covered mutiny, desertion, refusal of duty and similar offenses found in current law. The ACLU and NCARL both contended the provision should apply only to declared wars.

Espionage and Related Offenses. These sections were largely a recodification of existing law. The Judiciary Committee had originally addressed espionage in S 1 during the 94th Congress, but the revisions resulted in irreconcilable differences between liberals and conservatives. Civil libertarians had hoped to liberalize espionage laws which they argued could be broadly construed to the detriment of First Amendment rights. They cited the indictment of Daniel Ellsberg for leaking the Pentagon papers as evidence of the vagueness of the current statute.

The other offenses included in these sections pertained to disclosure, dissemination and receipt of classified and defense information and failure to register as a foreign agent.

Chapter 12. Offenses Involving International Affairs

The offenses in this chapter were largely a recodification of current law although a new crime was created for conspiring within the United States to assassinate a foreign official.

The Judiciary Committee repealed the Logan Act, a 1799 statute prohibiting private citizens from communicating with a foreign government with the intent of influencing a dispute with the United States. But the Logan Act was reinstated during Senate floor debate at the insistence of Sen. Allen.

The offenses codified in this chapter included attack and conspiracies against a foreign power, recruiting for foreign armed forces and disclosing foreign diplomatic codes or correspondence. The chapter also covered smuggling and unlawful employment of aliens, and fraudulent use of passports and evidence of citizenship.

Chapter 13. Offenses Involving Government Processes

Probably the most controversial chapter of S 1437 was also one of the most expansive. This chapter included six subchapters dealing with obstruction of government functions by fraud and physical interference, obstructions of law enforcement, obstructions of justice, contempt offenses, perjury and false statements and official corruption.

Obstructing a Government Function by Fraud. This section created a new crime for obstructing or impairing a government function through misrepresentation, chicanery, trickery, deceit, craft or other dishonest means. The section included an ACLU-backed committee amendment barring prosecution if the offense was committed solely for the purpose of disseminating information to the public. NCARL objected that the offense was "amorphous" and that as written a person conceivably could be found guilty for giving a postman the wrong directions to a house.

Obstructing a Government Function by Physical Interference. This section created a new crime of impairing by physical obstruction a public servant's performance of a government function. The ACLU objected that the provision could cover virtually any mass demonstration.

Obstruction of Law Enforcement. These sections dealt with such crimes as bail jumping, escape, possession of contraband in prison, flight to avoid prosecution or appearance as a witness, and harboring fugitives. The ACLU and reporters' groups objected to wording which stated that it is an offense to conceal the identity of a person if that hinders law enforcement. These groups argued that concealing the identity of a news source could be covered by this language, raising serious First Amendment issues.

Obstruction of Justice. These sections recodified offenses dealing with bribery of a witness, corrupting, tampering with or retaliating against a witness or informant, tampering with physical evidence, improperly influencing a juror, monitoring jury deliberations and demonstrating to influence a judicial proceeding. The language was considerably more specific than current law which dealt with witness tampering in a broad obstruction of justice statute.

Only one objection to the obstruction of justice provisions was raised on the Senate floor. It related to the section dealing with demonstrations to influence a judicial proceeding. Under this provision it was an offense to attempt to influence such proceedings through picketing, parading or using sound amplifying equipment after being advised that such conduct was an offense. Sen. Allen limited the area in which such an offense could occur to within 100 feet of a building housing a U.S. court. The committee bill had a 200-foot limitation.

Contempt Offenses. Although civil libertarian objections were raised to each of these sections, no modification was made to the committee bill. Civil libertarians argued that judges frequently have abused criminal contempt powers and that the bill would allow continued abuses.

The section stated that it was an offense to misbehave in the presence of a court so as to obstruct justice or to disobey a court order. The committee bill included an ACLU-backed amendment providing a defense to prosecution if the court order was invalid and the defendant sought to obtain judicial review of the order, or if the order was constitutionally invalid and constituted prior restraint on news collection or dissemination.

Civil libertarians also objected to language covering testifying and producing information. They said the section could be used to force reporters to reveal a news source. However, news organizations, which would appear to have the largest stake in this provision, were mostly silent on the issue.

NCARL objected to another section, "Obstructing a Proceeding by Disorderly Conduct," which it said could be used against political dissidents. The provision stated that it was an offense to obstruct or impair an official proceeding by means of "noise that is unreasonable, by means of violent or tumultuous behavior or disturbance, or by similar means."

A section on "Disobeying a Judicial Order" had been opposed by news organizations, but the Judiciary Committee included a defense to prosecution for invalid orders that constituted a prior restraint on collection or dissemination of news, which appeared to satisfy most groups.

Perjury and False Statements. These sections dealt with false statements made under oath and otherwise, in official proceedings and government matters, and the alteration, destruction or concealment of government records. Sen. Dale Bumpers, D-Ark., offered an amendment, accepted on a voice vote, which clarified that perjury, false swearing and false statements had to be done "knowingly."

Civil liberties groups objected to the false statement section which provided that it is an offense to make a false statement to a law enforcement officer or a person assigned noncriminal investigative authority by statute, regulation, rule, etc. The ACLU argued that existing law on making false statements to law enforcement officers was ambiguous and that the section of S 1437 would invite abuses such as a police officer alleging that a person made a false statement.

Sen. Hart offered an amendment to general provisions relating to perjury and false swearing to provide that it was not a defense, in making a false statement in closed sessions of the House or Senate, that it was made to prevent the disclosure of classified information or to protect the national defense. While the amendment appeared to add nothing substantive to current law, it would put witnesses before the House and Senate on notice that they could not claim national security reasons for lying, as was the case with former CIA director Richard Helms. The amendment was adopted on a voice vote.

Official Corruption and Intimidation. These sections dealt with crimes by government officials, including members of Congress. The language made it a crime for public servants to take official actions or use information gained because of their positions for personal gain while public servants or for one year after leaving public service. Previously this offense did not apply to all public servants such as members of Congress.

These sections also stated the offenses of bribery and graft, prohibited trading in public office and made it a crime to retaliate against a public servant.

Chapter 14. Offenses Involving Taxation

This chapter incorporated the federal criminal tax offenses currently in the Internal Revenue Code. The chapter covered internal revenue as well as customs offenses. Largely a recodification, the section on tax evasion allowed criminal prosecution for intent to evade taxes even if no tax actually were due because the individual overlooked deductions he could have claimed.

Chapter 15. Offenses Involving Individual Rights

Civil Rights. Existing civil rights statutes were retained under these sections, but language was added to expand the coverage with respect to sex discrimination. Prosecution of civil rights violations would no longer require evidence of a conspiracy (two or more people) to violate an individual's rights. A single individual or organization could be prosecuted. The requirement that "intent" to violate an individual's rights be shown was eliminated from current law.

Political Rights. The bill provided for the first time a series of statutes covering election fraud—obstruction of elections, registration, political campaigns, etc. Under current law prosecution of such offenses by the federal government had to be done through violations of the civil rights conspiracy statute. The section also included provisions to allow the federal government to prosecute criminal conduct aimed at influencing an election, thus allowing the government to investigate such events as the Watergate burglary. (The federal government had jurisdiction over that offense only because it was committed in the District of Columbia. Had it been committed in one of the states the government might not have been able to pursue the matter.) S 1437 expanded federal jurisdiction to allow prosecution where violations of the crimes in this section occurred in state elections—if the election also involved candidates for federal office.

Privacy. These sections carried forward existing wiretapping statutes and state crimes involving use of eavesdropping devices.

Civil libertarians had sought to place tighter controls on the use of wiretaps against private citizens. But the issue proved too controversial for committee members to resolve.

A section called "Revealing Private Information Submitted for a Government Purpose," made it an offense for a present or former public servant to disclose information in violation of a specific duty imposed on him as a public servant if that information was submitted by a private citizen for a government purpose. The ACLU objected that the provision could be used to insulate documentary evidence of official corruption or wrongdoing from scrutiny by Congress, the press and the public and that it would inhibit "whistle-blowing."

Chapter 16. Offenses Involving the Person

These sections were largely a recodification of current crimes against the person including murder, manslaughter, maiming, kidnaping, aircraft hijacking, battery and sexual assault. The bill made rape and the other sexual offenses apply without regard to the sex of the offender or the victim and included forcible sodomy in the definition of the crime. The statutory rape provision could be committed by females, while consensual acts between peers were eliminated from the offense. The requirement that a rape victim's testimony be corroborated was eliminated and new restrictions were placed on attorneys concerning questioning of victims about past sexual conduct. The spousal exemption for rape was deleted.

A new crime of "reckless endangerment" was created whereby an offense was commited if an individual engaged in conduct which placed or might place another person in danger of death or serious bodily injury.

The code also made "child snatching" a federal crime. The term described the action of a parent who abducts a child from its lawful guardian. Federal kidnaping laws did not cover this crime.

Chapter 17. Offenses Involving Property

This chapter was divided into seven subchapters dealing with property offenses: arson and property destruction; burglary and criminal intrusion, including criminal entry and criminal trespass; robbery, extortion and blackmail; theft and related offenses such as trafficking in stolen property, receiving stolen property, bankruptcy fraud, fraud in a regulated industry, and consumer fraud;

counterfeiting, forgery and related offenses; commercial bribery, labor bribery and sports bribery.

Although largely a recodification of existing law, several significant changes were made by S 1437 under this chapter. The theft section consolidated the 80 separate offenses under current law into a single section.

The extortion section tightened a loophole in current law but also provided an affirmative defense for minor incidents of violence that may occur in the course of picketing in a labor dispute. The ACLU objected, however, that the wording of this section could involve federal law enforcement officials in any labor dispute in which picketing of an employer engaged in interstate commerce "threatened" another person and property damage occurred.

Another section prohibited pyramid schemes for the first time. The section also provided new protections against consumer fraud.

Chapter 18. Offenses Involving Public Order, Safety, Health and Welfare

Among the most controversial chapters in S 1437, chapter 18 included the following seven subchapters: organized crime offenses, including racketeering, washing racketeering proceeds and loansharking; drug offenses; explosives and firearms offenses; riot offenses; gambling, obscenity and prostitution offenses; public health offenses such as distribution of adulterated food and environmental pollution; and miscellaneous offenses, including failing to obey public safety orders.

Organized Crime. A new crime of laundering racketeering proceeds was created to prevent mobsters from investing the proceeds from rackets in legitimate businesses. These sections also tightened up federal loansharking laws and provided tougher penalties for operation of a racketeering syndicate (up to 25 years) than for simple racketeering (12 years).

Drug Offenses. A mandatory minimum sentence of two years for trafficking in an opiate was provided in section 1811, one of only two sections in the code providing mandatory sentences. Possession of less than 150 grams of marijuana was classified as a misdemeanor; possession of less than 30 grams (about one ounce), an infraction under which no imprisonment could be ordered.

The changes in federal marijuana laws, which were not enforced for possession of small amounts, were viewed as a significant precedent for state action by the National Organization for Reform of Marihuana Laws (NORML), a Washington-based lobby.

Explosives and Firearms Offenses. Mandatory sentences of at least two years were provided for commission of violent crimes in which firearms were used.

Riot Offenses. Incitement to riot could no longer be prosecuted unless a riot occurred. A riot was defined to require at least 10 persons rather than three as provided by existing law. The ACLU objected that the riot laws, which were recodified and narrowed somewhat from current law, remained too vague and provided a "convenient tool for discriminatory prosecution and governmental oppression of political adversaries."

Disseminating Obscene Material. The most hotly disputed provision of S 1437 during the Senate floor debate, the section was largely a recodification of existing law under Supreme Court rulings. The Supreme Court ruled that "obscenity" was a matter to be determined by community standards. Conservatives sought to make it easier to prosecute obscenity cases while liberals sought to make it more difficult.

A floor amendment by Sen. Robert Dole, R-Kan., sought to make clear that a jury could use state or local community standards, as opposed to broad national standards in prosecutions of obscenity cases. *(Votes 4, 5, p. 3-S)*

However, subsequent adoption of a committee amendment allowing a defense to prosecution for dissemination of obscene materials if dissemination was legal in the "political subdivision" in which the material was disseminated appeared to make it less likely that an obscenity prosecution would be successful. *(Vote 18, p. 5-S)*

Failing To Obey a Public Safety Order. This section provided a new offense for failure to obey orders by law enforcement officers and certain other public servants. The ACLU objected that the provision could be used to prevent picketing, parading, canvassing or distributing leaflets. A floor amendment narrowed the definition of a public servant to members of the armed forces or militia.

Part III: Sentences

Sen. Kennedy called the sentencing sections "the most important reform in the entire bill." The three chapters of this part along with the chapter on probation, fines and imprisonment provided a major overhaul of the federal sentencing process. This part of the bill attempted to eliminate disparities in sentencing whereby one person could receive a prison sentence for a crime while another who committed the same crime could be paroled.

Many of the changes were opposed by public defender groups. They charged that the bill, written in large measure by Justice Department attorneys, benefited prosecutors at the expense of defendants.

Chapter 20. General Sentencing Provisions

Authorized Sentences. This section, which had no counterpart in current law, stated four basic purposes for sentencing: deterrence, incapacitation, just punishment and rehabilitation.

The section attempted to encourage tailoring the use of probation, fines, imprisonment or a combination of these penalties to the above-stated objectives. The section treated probation as a type of sentence rather than as an alternative to a sentence. Organizations could be sentenced to terms of probation, enjoining them from engaging in specified practices. The section also provided a mechanism for putting an organization out of business if a judge determined that illegal conduct was its usual way of doing business.

Imposition of a Sentence. This section provided guidance to judges in imposing sentences. The section set out the factors a judge must consider in selecting a particular sentence and required the judge to consider the circumstances of the offense and the history and characteristics of the defendant. The section also required the judge to consider the need to avoid unwarranted disparities in sentencing. The section provided a new requirement that the court, at the time of sentencing, state the reasons for imposition of the sentence, and required that if the sentence were outside the range set in the Sentencing Commission's guidelines, a specific reason be stated.

Order of Notice to Victims. Under current law there was no provision requiring that an offender give notice of his conviction to his victims. S 1437 allowed a court to require an individual found guilty of offenses involving fraud or deceptive practices, or an organization found guilty of any offense, to give notice and explanation of the conviction to that segment of the public affected by the conviction or financially interested in it.

The provision was designed to assist citizens affected by these crimes to bring civil suits to recover damages. Courts were empowered to designate the advertising areas and media in which notice was to be given and to approve the form in which notice was given. The section was viewed as providing a major disincentive to corporate crime.

Orders of Restitution. This section expanded current law by permitting a judge to order a convicted defendant who has caused bodily injury or property damage or other loss to pay restitution directly to the victim independent of a condition of probation and in conjunction with any other sentence.

Review of sentences. This provision had no counterpart in current law. It allowed defendants and the government to appeal sentences that fell outside the guidelines established by the Sentencing Commission.

Chapter 21. Probation

Sentence of Probation. Although existing law provided a term of probation of up to five years without regard to the seriousness of the offense, this section provided for differing terms depending on the seriousness of the violation.

Conditions of Probation. This section went beyond current law in requiring that the court provide as a condition of probation that the defendant not commit another crime during probation. This was the only mandatory condition of probation under S 1437. Under current law offenders had to report regularly to probation officers and adhere to other prescribed probation conditions.

Chapter 22. Fines

These sections established the maximum monetary fines that could be imposed for various criminal offenses and specified the criteria to be considered in imposing fines. The sections encouraged greater use of fines, particularly in penalizing white collar crime.

Chapter 23. Imprisonment

Nine classes of offenses were specified with the maximum term of imprisonment for each class. Current law set forth at least 17 levels of confinement ranging from life imprisonment to 30 days. The chapter stated as a general rule that all individual offenders, regardless of the type of offense committed, may be sentenced to a term of imprisonment. The chapter also required that sentences be determinate except in "exceptional" circumstances. Under existing law sentences varied enormously depending on parole conditions and time off accrued for good behavior.

Early parole release under S 1437 was to be made available only in "exceptional" cases. A deterrent to parole violation was provided by a "contingent term of imprisonment" (90 days in a felony case, 30 in a class A misdemeanor) which was applied if a parole condition was violated.

Several important changes in sentencing procedure were made in Title III of S 1437 which established the U.S. Sentencing Commission.

An amendment by Sen. Hart, agreed to on a voice vote Jan. 23, required the commission to consider alternatives to incarceration for first-time offenders convicted of nonviolent crimes. The ACLU had been pushing the Senate to include provisions encouraging alternatives to imprisonment.

A second amendment, offered by Sen. Dole and agreed to on a voice vote, required the commission, in promulgating its guidelines, to assure that persons who commit violent crimes while awaiting trial for another offense would get the maximum penalty or close to it.

Part IV: Administration and Procedure

Chapters 30 through 38 largely consolidated, clarified and codified existing procedural sections of Title 18. The Senate Judiciary Committee did not attempt a comprehensive revision of all the procedural and administrative sections of the code in order to avoid delay in reporting the bill. It recommended that Congress and the Department of Justice begin such a review as soon as the new code was enacted.

The nine chapters that comprised Part IV of the bill were:

- Chapter 30: Investigative and law enforcement authority including that for the Federal Bureau of Investigation, Drug Enforcement Administration, Department of Treasury, Postal Service, Bureau of Prisons, Immigration and Naturalization Service, and Department of Interior.
- Chapter 31: Ancillary investigative authority, including authorization for wiretaps, compulsion of testimony after a claim of self incrimination, protection of witnesses and payment of rewards.
- Chapter 32: Rendition of fugitives and extradition.
- Chapter 33: Jurisdiction of U.S. district courts over offenses occurring within federal jurisdiction, powers of U.S. magistrates to try certain offenses, jurisdiction for arrest warrants and general rules for determination of venue—the place of a trial or a grand jury inquiry.
- Chapter 34: Procedures for appointment of counsel for indigent defendants.
- Chapter 35: Release and confinement pending judicial proceedings, including bail procedures.
- Chapter 36: Disposition of cases involving juveniles and "mental incompetents."
- Chapter 37: Rules for pretrial and trial procedure and rules governing admissibility of evidence and of confessions.
- Chapter 38: Administration of sentences, including probation, fines, imprisonment and early release (corresponding to Part III, sentencing, above).

While largely a recodification of existing laws, these nine chapters included several sections that were noteworthy.

Wiretapping. Several changes in federal wiretap laws were made, including a reduction in the number of investigations of crime in which electronic surveillance may be used, and repeal of the provision claiming "inherent" presidential power to use electronic surveillance. The bill for the first time required a neutral magistrate to find probable cause of a crime before issuing a warrant for electronic surveillance. The wiretap provisions were attacked by civil libertarians who argued that wiretaps were being used without restraint under current law, but no modifications were made on the Senate floor.

Magistrates. The jurisdiction of U.S. magistrates was expanded to cover all misdemeanors and to permit trial of minor offenses carrying six months or less while at the same time eliminating a defendant's right in such cases to elect a trial by jury in a district court.

Pretrial Release. During Senate floor debate on Jan. 25 an amendment by Sen. Dole was adopted on a voice vote expanding the list of violent crimes for which a judge may deny pretrial release. The amendment denied release for serious crimes including murder, rape, armed robbery, and when a hostage is seized to negotiate the release of an accused. A subsequent amendment offered on Jan. 26 by Sen. Sam Nunn, D-Ga., and agreed to on a voice vote further expanded the list of crimes for which pretrial release may be denied to include opiate- and drug-trafficking.

Offenders with Mental Disease or Defect. During Senate debate Jan. 30, Sen. Allen offered an amendment, agreed to on a voice vote, lowering from 45 to 15 days the length of time a person may be subjected to a psychiatric examination for the purpose of determining competency to stand trial. The amendment also allowed a defendant to refuse such an examination if it were requested by the government.

Confessions. This section recodified provisions of the Omnibus Crime Control and Safe Streets Act permitting a confession to be admitted as "voluntary" when *Miranda* warnings—of a suspect's right to remain silent—were not given in certain circumstances. The bill stated that "the presence or absence of any such factors," including *Miranda* warnings, "need not be conclusive as to the voluntariness of the confession." The ACLU argued that this provision seriously undercut the purpose of *Miranda* warnings and removed much of the incentive for police officers to advise suspects of their rights.

House Approach

From the day S 1437 passed the Senate it was clear that agreement with the House depended largely on gaining approval of the basic form and assumptions incorporated in the massive 682-page package.

But from the first day of House markups, it was clear the Judiciary Subcommittee on Criminal Justice did not agree in principle with the Senate. According to Subcommittee Chairman James R. Mann, D-S.C., the Justice Department had provided no evidence of "deficiencies" in current law that needed to be corrected.

According to Mann, "Neither the committee nor anyone with whom the committee has been in communication was able to justify the massive changes in existing laws...."

But there were other areas of fundamental disagreement with the Senate. Mann said, for example, he could not accept what he perceived as the increased federal jurisdiction provided by the Senate bill, one of the major charges leveled against the measure during Senate floor debate.

In addition, Mann and Charles E. Wiggins, R-Calif., said they viewed the Senate's Sentencing Commission as an unnecessarily costly attempt to eliminate disparities in sentencing. Mann characterized the proposal as one that was "never tried or demonstrated" and said he was more concerned with maintaining "individualization of justice" — the ability of judges to make sentencing determinations within a virtually unlimited range of possibilities.

Mann was also critical of what he viewed as the Senate bill's shifting of power from judges to prosecutors, who, he said, would "run the courts" if they were given increased authority to determine sentence ranges.

Wiggins said he believed the advisory guidelines proposed by the House would accomplish the same thing as the Senate guidelines and avoid creation of a new and expensive government bureaucracy.

Shortly before the 95th Congress adjourned, the Judiciary Committee announced that it would not report a criminal code reform bill in 1978. Instead, it asked the Criminal Justice Subcommittee to give its views. Presumably, the report would serve as the basis for any committee action on criminal code reform in the 96th Congress. ■

New Judgeships: A Patronage Plum for Carter

Legislation to create 152 new federal judgeships cleared Congress Oct. 7, after House and Senate conferees rejected a Senate proposal to divide the southern Fifth Circuit into two new appeals courts.

Approval of the new judgeships, the largest number ever created by a single act of Congress, was believed essential to relieve massive backlogs in federal court cases. At the same time, the bill (HR 7843 — PL 95-486) provided President Carter a veritable cornucopia of political patronage.

The Fifth Circuit issue, which had conferees deadlocked for four months, was resolved through adoption of deliberately ambiguous language that would allow circuits having a large number of appeals court judges to experiment administratively with ways of operating the courts more efficiently.

The meaning of the bill's language would not become entirely clear until it was put into practice. What was clear was that the language was designed to let each conferee interpret it to mean what he or she wanted.

While the Fifth Circuit issue dominated the conference, the most significant feature of the bill was that it added 117 new district court judgeship positions and 35 new positions on the circuit courts of appeals to the existing 398 district court judgeships and 97 circuit court judgeships.

The bill provided President Carter with the largest block of judicial patronage in the nation's history. Some Republicans complained that passage of the measure without a merit selection process in place could lead to a wave of partisan political appointments. Although the bill required the president to establish standards and guidelines for the selection of judges on the basis of merit, the president was not required to follow these selection procedures.

Background: 1977 Action

S 11, the "Omnibus Judgeship Bill," was reported by the Senate Judiciary Committee May 3, 1977 (S Rept 95-

117). The 146 judges provided by the committee included 108 new federal district court judgeships.

The Senate passed S 11 May 24, 1977, by voice vote after amending the bill to provide two additional judgeships.

Overriding the plans of its chairman, Peter W. Rodino Jr., D-N.J., to limit the number of new judgeships to 115, the House Judiciary Committee Nov. 30, 1977, ordered reported a bill (HR 7843 — H Rept 95-858) recommending creation of 110 district and 35 circuit judgeships, just three fewer than the Senate approved. House action was held over until 1978. *(Background, 1977 Almanac p. 575)*

1978 House Floor Action

The House passed HR 7843 on Feb. 7, by a vote of 319-80. *(Vote 34, p. 10-H)*

Passage of the bill creating 145 additional federal judgeships came one day after the unofficial release of a report prepared for the Federal Judicial Center, which suggested that many of the new judgeships might not be necessary if current judges were provided improved research and support services to speed handling of cases. The report had not been made available to the Judiciary Committee during its consideration of the bill in 1977. (The Federal Judicial Center is a government research agency for the federal courts. It is connected to the Judicial Conference, the administrative arm of the federal courts, which provided the statistical information used in drafting the House and Senate judgeship bills.)

Debate on final passage of the House judgeships bill found most Democrats and Judiciary Committee members arguing that more federal judges were needed to deal with expanding court caseloads and pointing to Congress' failure to increase judgeships since 1970.

Many Republicans and other opponents of the bill attacked the procedure under which it was brought up, allowing for no amendments and providing a 40-minute limitation on debate. Opponents also criticized the criteria used in determining the need for additional judges and the adequacy of the merit selection provision.

Proponents of the bill led by Judiciary Committee Chairman Rodino, argued that the 145 new judgeships were needed to deal with a 36 percent increase in district court case filings and a 140 percent increase in appeals court filings since 1970. (The federal court system is divided into 11 circuits or appeals courts with 97 judges. The 94 district courts with 398 judges fall within these 11 circuits.)

Proponents said court congestion and delay had eroded the efficiency of U.S. courts. They said that while internal improvements in judicial administration of cases as well as shifting a portion of the caseload to magistrates had increased efficiency, additional judges were still needed.

Criteria Criticized

Opponents of the legislation said the Judiciary Committee relied too heavily on the Judicial Conference in recommending new judges, many of whom might not be necessary.

"I feel we are asked to rubber stamp the requests of the Judicial Conference if we pass the bill as reported by the committee," said Rep. Jack Brooks, D-Texas, a member of the Judiciary Committee. According to Brooks, "in too many areas the courts are not as overburdened as the judges might have us believe. The docket is not as imposing

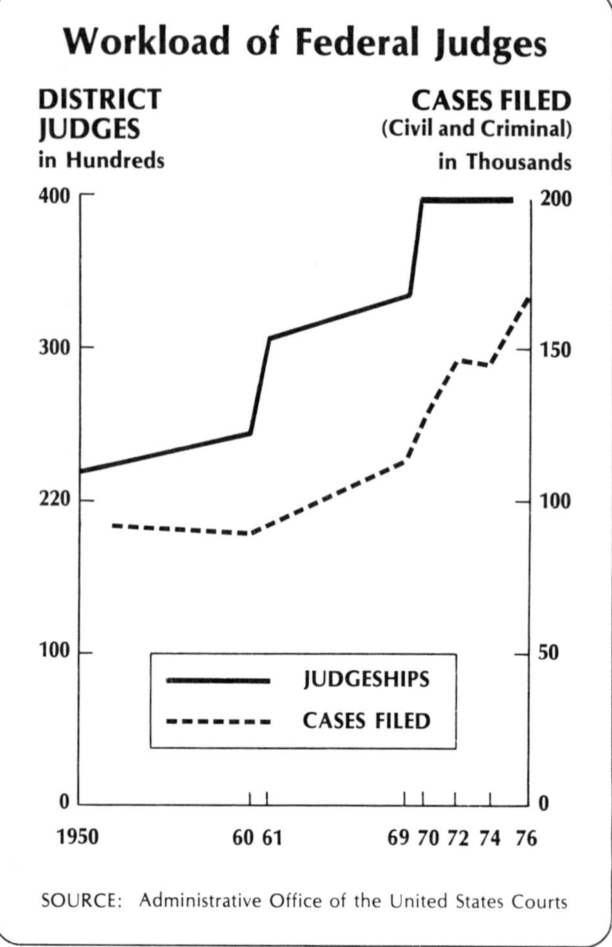

as the statistics they cite may indicate. In too many instances, judges simply need to be more efficient."

The Judicial Conference's methodology was criticized by both Rodino and Rep. Robert McClory, R-Ill., the senior Republican on the committee. McClory said the Judiciary Committee had to rely on "the self-serving statements" of the conference in assessing judgeship needs. He called for an independent agency to assess judgeship needs in the future.

Merit Selection and Marston

Some Republicans questioned the urgency of passing the judgeships bill, noting that the Democratic Congress had avoided creating new federal judgeships when Republicans controlled the White House.

"We somehow were able to struggle along with the same old complement of judges until a Democrat was elected president," said Rep. Bill Frenzel, R-Minn. "Then, and only then, the need for 145 new judges somehow became compelling."

Because President Carter had been accused of failing to keep his campaign pledge to make appointments solely on the basis of merit, the principal point of contention in the House floor debate became a relatively innocuous section of the bill providing for limited application of non-binding merit standards in selecting federal judges.

The bill directed the president to nominate federal district court judges on the basis of merit rather than partisan

Additional District Judgeships

State or Territory	Current Number	Added by Senate Bill	Added by House Bill	Added Under Conference Agreement
Ala.	8	3	4	4
Alaska	2	0	0	0
Ariz.	5	3	2	3
Ark.	4	2	2	2
Calif.	35	7	7	7
Canal Zone	1	0	0	0
Colo.	4	2	2	2
Conn.	4	1	1	1
Del.	3	0	0	0
D.C.	15	0	0	0
Fla.	15	10*	8	9
Ga.	10	6	5	6
Guam	1	0	0	0
Hawaii	2	0	0	0
Idaho	2	0	0	0
Ill.	17	3	4	4
Ind.	7	2	1	2
Iowa	3	1	1	1
Kan.	4	1	1	1
Ky.	6	3*	3*	3*
La.	14	6	5	6
Maine	1	1	1	1
Md.	7	2	2	2
Mass.	6	4	3	4
Mich.	12	5	5	5
Minn.	4	2*	2*	2*
Miss.	5	0	0	0
Mo.	8	3	3	3
Mont.	2	0	0	0
Neb.	3	0	0	0
Nev.	2	1	1	1
N.H.	1	1	1	1
N.J.	9	1	2	2
N.M.	3	1	1	1
N.Y.	41	2	2	2
N.C.	6	3	3	3
N.D.	2	0	0	0
Ohio	13	2	3*	3*
Okla.	6	2	2	2
Ore.	3	2	2	2
Pa.	32	2	2	2
P.R.	3	4	3	4
R.I.	2	0	0	0
S.C.	5	3	3	3
S.D.	2	1	1	1
Tenn.	8	1	1	1
Texas	22	10	9	10
Utah	2	1	1	1
Vt.	2	0	0	0
Va.	8	4	4	4
V.I.	2	0	0	0
Wash.	5	2	2	2
W.Va.	4	2*	2*	2*
Wis.	4	1	2	2
Wyo.	1	0	1	0
Total	398	113	110	117

* Includes one temporary judgeship. The conference report provided that the first vacancy that occurred in each of these judicial districts five years or more after enactment of the bill shall not be filled.

political patronage. But the bill allowed the president to "waive such regulations with respect to any nomination by notifying the Senate of the reasons for such waiver." The provision did not apply to existing judgeship positions already filled or vacancies that might occur among those judgeships.

The provision had been controversial in committee and its adoption was attributable in large measure to support from Republican McClory. While committee Republicans generally supported the provision, they made no effort to insert a tougher merit selection proposal in the bill. But the political climate had changed dramatically since the committee reported its bill in November 1977.

In January President Carter fired David W. Marston, a Philadelphia U.S. attorney who was himself the beneficiary of the political spoils system under President Ford but who had since then won a reputation for prosecuting some of Pennsylvania's top Democrats.

Shortly after it became known that Marston was to be fired, news reports disclosed that the young attorney was investigating two Pennsylvania Democratic congressmen. One of them, Rep. Joshua Eilberg, D-Pa., a senior Judiciary Committee member, had called Carter to ask him to expedite Marston's ouster. Thus when the judgeship bill with its merit selection provision hit the House floor, Republicans had a ready-made forum for their cause celebre. *(Eilberg probe, Congress and Government chapter)*

Rep. Frenzel charged that House Speaker Thomas P. O'Neill Jr., D-Mass., had "gagged and handcuffed" the House in bringing the bill up without allowing amendments. He said the reason was, "so we will not be able to review the Marston scandal, nor to suggest in stronger terms than the timid committee report that we demand merit selection of these judges."

Democrats and some Republicans, including McClory, viewed the merit selection provision quite differently. Rep. John F. Seiberling, D-Ohio, its principal sponsor, said the amendment was "a formal endorsement of Jimmy Carter's campaign promise" that federal judges would be appointed on the basis of merit. Seiberling and others viewed the amendment as "the first effort by the House to remove partisan political patronage" from judicial selection.

McClory argued that "the bill goes as far as the Constitution permits" in limiting the president's authority to make judicial appointments.

Conference Action

Eight Senate and 10 House conferees began meeting on the judgeship bill April 11. They agreed to create 117 new district judgeships and 35 new appeals court positions. To the Senate's satisfaction, conferees also agreed to postpone the effective date for nominations of new judges until Nov. 1, assuring senators up for re-election that they would not have to disclose their choices for the patronage in the middle of their campaigns.

The Senate also prevailed in convincing conferees to accept a watered-down version of the House merit selection provision, which critics charged was likely to have no significant effect on Senate patronage selection of judges.

The most difficult issue to be resolved concerned whether the Fifth Circuit Court of Appeals should be split in two. Resolution of this dispute would determine the fate of the bill and whether President Carter would be handed the largest single block of judicial patronage in the nation's history. It was not until Sept. 20 that conferees reached agreement on this issue.

Judgeships

The House bill contained six district judgeships not included in the Senate bill, while the Senate version contained nine not included in the House bill. Both chambers proposed creating 35 new appeals court judgeships. Had both sides agreed to accept the judges not included in the other side's bill, a total of 154 new judgeships would have been created.

Instead, the conferees accepted 152, rejecting a temporary judge in southern Florida and an additional House-proposed judge for Wyoming.

Merit Selection

A touchier issue proved to be the question of merit selection for district court judges.

The House had voted in February to instruct its conferees to insist on merit selection language sponsored by Seiberling. Seiberling's amendment would have required the president to set forth non-binding "procedures and guidelines" for choosing district court judges on the basis of merit. The language would have allowed the president to waive those criteria simply by notifying the Senate. The motion to instruct conferees to insist on this language was offered by McClory and agreed to by the House Feb. 9, 321-19. *(Vote 46, p. 14-H)*

But Senate conferees resisted even this apparently mild language. They realized, as had the House, that a clear statement in favor of merit selection would make it extremely difficult for the president to avoid setting up merit selection criteria.

Thus the Senate conferees fought to weaken the Seiberling language to preserve the control they have traditionally had over nomination of judges. The conferees agreed to the promulgation of "standards and guidelines" providing, however, that the president could waive them.

Fifth Circuit Issue

Conferees engaged in what one aide described as a "game of chicken" over the Fifth Circuit question, each hoping that as the Congress drew to a close the pressure to approve new judgeships would lead the other side to give in. What had the conferees deadlocked was a debate over administrative efficiency and civil rights.

The Senate bill divided the Fifth, which consists of Florida, Alabama, Georgia, Mississippi, Louisiana and Texas. Under the proposal, favored by Judiciary Chairman James O. Eastland, D-Miss., Louisiana and Texas would form a new 11th Circuit.

Senators argued that since the bill would increase the court from 15 to 26 judges, it would become unwieldy to sit *en banc*. (*En banc* hearings, where all the judges in a circuit hear a case, take place when there are conflicting opinions within the circuit over an issue of major importance.) And senators argued that the large geographical area covered by the circuit already made it difficult to hold *en banc* hearings.

The House bill contained no provision to divide the Fifth. House Judiciary Chairman Peter W. Rodino Jr., D-N.J., prevented inclusion of a Fifth Circuit proposal on the grounds that it was non-germane to a bill to create new judgeships.

But the underlying issue was civil rights, and a majority of House conferees sought to preserve what they viewed as the Fifth Circuit court's balance in favor of strong civil rights decisions. House conferees feared the proposed split would create a Deep South circuit — consisting of Florida, Georgia, Alabama and Mississippi — that would tend not to favor civil rights.

The compromise finally agreed upon evolved out of a series of proposals that had been circulated by both sides. It was locked up Sept. 19 when Attorney General Griffin B. Bell ironed out an agreement acceptable to both Rodino and Eastland.

The compromise, consisting of two parts, stated: 1) "Any court of appeals having more than 15 active judges may constitute itself into administrative units complete with such facilities and staff as may be prescribed by the Administrative Office of U.S. Courts" and 2) "may perform its *en banc* function by such number of members of its *en banc* courts as may be prescribed by rule of the court of appeals."

The proposal would apply not only to the Fifth Circuit, which would have 26 judges under the bill, but to the Ninth Circuit (consisting of 10 western states stretching from Alaska to Arizona), which would have 23 judges.

The key to the proposal was that it allowed large circuits to hold *en banc* hearings with less than the full complement of judges.

Additional Circuit Court Judgeships

Circuit	Existing Judgeships	Added Under Conference Agreement	Total
District of Columbia	9	2	11
First	3	1	4
Second	9	2	11
Third	9	1	10
Fourth	7	3	10
Fifth	15	11	26
Sixth	9	2	11
Seventh	8	1	9
Eighth	8	1	9
Ninth	13	10	23
Tenth	7	1	8
Total	97	35	132

While the proposal would appear to allow the circuits to divide into administrative units that would handle different judicial functions, many observers believed that for the near future any subdivisions within the circuits would be aimed only at dividing up clerical responsibilities.

Several aides said the language simply put in writing authority to make administrative adjustments that already had been implemented in the Ninth Circuit on the initiative of its chief judge.

Other Agreements

Conferees also approved provisions in the final judgeship bill that:

- Modified House language taking notice of the fact that only 1 percent of federal judges were women and 4 percent were blacks, and suggesting that "the president, in selecting individuals for nomination to the federal judgeships created by the act, give due consideration to qualified individuals regardless of race, color, sex, religion or national origin."
- Created 15 high-salaried "supergrade" positions in the Administrative Office of the U.S. Courts.
- Repealed a section of existing law that allowed certain judges to retain their chief judge status beyond the age of 70. The provision was aimed at removing a Utah judge who had since died, making the repeal unnecessary.
- Required persons filling judgeship positions created on a temporary basis to serve at least five years and permitted them to fill the first available vacancy in a permanent judgeship position.
- Made the sections dealing with creation of new judgeships effective upon the promulgation by the president of merit selection standards and guidelines but not before Nov. 1, 1978, and the rest of the bill effective upon enactment.
- Narrowed district court jurisdiction by requiring a $10,000 minimum amount in controversy in certain Interstate Commerce Act freight damage cases.
- Authorized to be appropriated such sums as may be necessary to carry out the provisions of the act. The Congressional Budget Office estimated that a district court judgeship would cost about $250,000 a year after the first year, when the cost would be higher because of start-up expenses. CBO estimated the cost of a circuit court judgeship operation at about $201,000 a year after the first year. Thus, the bill would cost the Treasury approximately $36 million a year.

The conference report on HR 7843 was filed Sept. 28 (H Rept 95-1643).

Final Action

The Senate approved the compromise on the bill Oct. 7 by a 67-15 vote. *(Vote 455, p. 67-S)*

The House had approved the compromise report Oct. 4 by a 292-112 vote. *(Vote 766, p. 216-H)*

Illegal Cigarette Sales

Bootleggers who reap millions of dollars in illegal profits selling cigarettes from states with low taxes may have to switch to another racket or be prepared to fight Uncle Sam under legislation cleared by Congress Oct. 15.

The bill (S 1487 — PL 95-575), aimed at controlling illegal interstate traffic in cigarettes, extended federal antiracketeering laws to cover cigarette bootlegging and provided penalties of up to five years in prison and $100,000 in fines for violations. It provided federal help to states with high cigarette taxes that had suffered major revenue losses through sales of contraband cigarettes brought in from low-tax states.

The final bill — a compromise version of legislation passed earlier by the House and Senate — applied to anyone who knowingly received, possessed, sold or bought the contraband cigarettes, as well as to the actual bootleggers.

Background

Cigarette racketeering is big business. The annual tax loss to states from illegal "buttlegging," as it is known, is conservatively estimated at $400 million. Other estimates place the net — tax free — profits made by illegal dealers at as much as $600 million a year.

A 1977 study by the Advisory Commission on Intergovernmental Relations found that cigarette bootlegging was a serious problem in 14 states in which 50 percent of the nation's population resided. Nearly 70 percent of the states suffer some tax loss from cigarette rackets. In New York City, it has been estimated that one of every two cigarettes sold has been bootlegged.

The origin of the problem and the source of the profits lies in the disparity of tax rates between states. In 1976, the tax on cigarettes in North Carolina was two cents a pack. In New York City it was 23 cents a pack. That $2.10 differential on a carton translates into tens of thousands of dollars in profits on a single truckload of cigarettes run from North Carolina to New York.

Once the cigarettes arrive in New York, or most of the other northeastern states, they may be sold with their North Carolina stamps; if the bootlegger wants to risk a felony charge, counterfeit stamps may be affixed.

The result is huge profits for criminals and hard times for legitimate wholesalers, retailers, drivers and salespeople. One witness cited in the Senate report on the bill estimated that 35 percent of wholesalers and 50 percent of the employees of wholesalers and vendors had been thrown out of business during the 10 year period encompassed by the advisory commission study.

Organized Crime Role

Of the $400 million annual tax loss estimated in the commission study, organized crime operations are believed to reap from $150 to $200 million. Organized crime involvement brings related problems, including truck hijackings of both legitimate and illegitimate cigarette shipments, armed robberies, loan-sharking, corruption of public officials, assaults and murder.

Existing federal law had been aimed primarily at interstate use of the mails to avoid payment of taxes on cigarettes.

According to the Justice Department, the statute employed, known as the Jenkins Act, was designed primarily to assist states in collecting their cigarette taxes and had been ineffective in dealing with the over-the-road bootlegging operations. Violation of the Jenkins Act was a misdemeanor.

Federal anti-racketeering statutes, principally mail fraud, were used against organized crime bootlegging operations, but a Justice Department official said these were inadequate.

Provisions

As cleared, S 1487 contained the following major provisions:

Crimes. The bill:

- Made it unlawful for any person to knowingly ship, transport, receive, possess, sell, distribute or purchase contraband cigarettes.
- Made it unlawful for any person to knowingly make any false statement with respect to the information kept in records concerning transactions of quantities of cigarettes in excess of 60,000.
- Defined "contraband cigarettes" to mean a quantity in excess of 60,000 cigarettes, which bear no evidence of the payment of applicable state cigarette taxes in the state where cigarettes are found, if that state requires such stamps.

Record-keeping. The bill allowed the secretary of the treasury to require persons dealing in 60,000 or more cigarettes to keep records showing:

- The name, address, destination, vehicle license number, driver's license number and signature of the person receiving the cigarettes.
- The name of the purchaser.
- A declaration of the name and address of the recipient's principal in all cases when the recipient was acting as an agent.

H Con Res 755, adopted after passage of the bill, amended the record-keeping section to state that the above information "shall be contained in business records kept in the normal course of business."

The bill further provided that the secretary, with an authorized warrant, could enter premises of persons covered by the bill to inspect records or information kept under the bill's record-keeping provisions as well as to determine actual quantities of cigarettes stored at a premise.

Penalties. The bill:

- Provided fines of up to $100,000 and prison terms of up to five years for knowing violations of the section dealing with illegal transactions of contraband cigarettes.
- Provided fines of up to $5,000 and three years in jail for violation of the record-keeping provisions.
- Allowed for seizure and forfeiture of contraband cigarettes held in violation of the act.

Miscellaneous. The bill provided that nothing in the act affected the jurisdiction of a state to enact and enforce cigarette tax laws.

It authorized to be appropriated "such sums as may be necessary" to carry out the provisions of the act.

Senate Action

The Senate passed its version of the legislation (S 1487) by voice vote Sept. 29, after sponsors agreed to make numerous changes in the bill reported June 28 by the Senate Judiciary Committee (S Rept 95-962) to win the support of southern tobacco-state senators fearful of federal intervention in state tax matters.

The substitute bill contained language stating that the primary responsibility for law enforcement relating to cigarette smuggling still remained with the states. The bill greatly reduced the record-keeping and reporting requirements of the committee bill, which critics said would be burdensome to legitimate tobacco dealers.

The original committee bill was aimed at sales of 30,000 or more cigarettes, the same figure used in the House-passed bill. Senate sponsors agreed to increase the figure to 60,000 in order to emphasize that principal targets of the bill were the larger, organized crime dealers. The modified bill also made trafficking in contraband cigarettes illegal under federal anti-racketeering statutes, as well as under federal criminal statutes.

Edward M. Kennedy, D-Mass., who managed the bill on the Senate floor, said, "Federal law enforcement officials are powerless to do anything about this problem because they have no authority in this area."

Kennedy said organized criminal groups can realize a gross profit of more than $100,000 from sales of a single tractor-trailer of cigarettes.

"One out of every two packs of cigarettes sold in New York City, and one out of every four packs of cigarettes sold in New York State are bootlegged," he said.

House Action

The House Judiciary Committee reported its version of cigarette racketeering legislation Sept 26 (HR 8853 — H Rept 95-1629). It passed the House on a non-record vote Oct. 3 after no debate. HR 8853 was then tabled, and S 1487 was passed as amended to contain the House bill's language.

The major area of disagreement with the Senate was over the reporting and record-keeping requirements, which were considerably more stringent in the House bill.

The House version gave the secretary of the treasury discretion to prescribe the kind and scope of reporting to require of cigarette dealers. The House bill also gave the secretary authority to enter a dealer's premises with a search warrant to inspect records and other documents dealer were required to keep under the bill.

The House bill defined "contraband cigarettes" as 30,000 or more cigarettes not bearing evidence of applicable state cigarette taxes, whereas the Senate version placed the trigger level at 60,000 cigarettes. The House bill provided penalties of up to $10,000 and two years in jail, as compared to the Senate provision of penalties of up to $100,000 and five years in jail.

Conference Action

House and Senate conferees reported a compromise bill Oct. 12, adopting the tougher penalties contained in the Senate bill and detailed record-keeping provisions pushed by House conferees. Reporting requirements contained in both House and Senate bills were eliminated.

A separate concurrent resolution (H Con Res 755) was adopted by both chambers at the request of two tobacco state senators who threatened at the last minute to filibuster the conference report (H Rept 95-1778).

The resolution added a minor clarification to the record-keeping section. It was the last of a series of concessions made to tobacco-state senators to win final approval of the bill.

Record-keeping and reporting requirements included in both House and Senate bills were opposed by senators from tobacco states who saw the bill as an expansion of federal jurisdiction and a potential threat to small-business operators in their states.

While the tobacco lobby could not oppose the bill — since it was aimed largely at sizable illegal operations, including those purported to be controlled by organized crime — its representatives opposed those provisions they thought might inhibit cigarette sales.

The House bill contained broader record-keeping and reporting requirements, authorizing the secretary of the treasury to require records in such form and manner as he prescribed and to require the submission of reports. The House bill specified in considerable detail the kind of information that businesses had to maintain. Conferees agreed to the detailed record-keeping provisions but dropped the reporting requirements entirely.

Conferees also agreed to the Senate definition of "contraband cigarettes," placing the number of cigarettes that would have to be involved before a transaction could become illegal at 60,000 instead of the 30,000 level contained in the House bill. Records had to be maintained only for sales involving more than 60,000 cigarettes. The agreement emphasized that the principal focus of the bill was the large, organized crime operation.

Treasury Study Dropped

Eliminated from the final bill was a Senate-proposed study to be conducted by the Treasury Department that would encourage states to adopt stiffer anti-bootlegging statutes and law enforcement practices. In exchange for dropping the study, which was supported by tobacco-state senators, the conference report re-emphasized that the states were to retain primary responsibility for controlling cigarette bootlegging and that laws in some of the states most directly affected needed to be improved.

Final Action

The Senate approved the conference report Oct. 15, by voice vote, and the House voted 366-0 to accept the report the same day, clearing the bill for the president. *(Vote 821, p. 234-H)*

Congress Approves New Bankruptcy System

The House gave final congressional approval Oct. 6 to the first major revision of the nation's bankruptcy laws in nearly 40 years.

The bill (HR 8200 — PL 95-598) created a new system of bankruptcy judges and was designed to modernize federal bankruptcy law for creditors as well as for consumer and business debtors. It also consolidated laws dealing with business reorganization.

President Carter signed the measure despite objections raised by Attorney General Griffin B. Bell and by Chief Justice Warren E. Burger, who played an unusually active role in shaping the final outcome of the bill.

The compromise version of the bill was put together by Senate and House members and staff without a conference committee.

The House had passed its version of the bill Feb. 1. The Senate did not act until Sept. 7, when it passed a bill (S 2266) that differed from the House bill in several important respects.

After a Sept. 28 meeting of some House and Senate sponsors of the two bills, the House passed on a non-record vote a compromise version of HR 8200. That compromise was never voted on by the Senate as a result of the intervention of the Chief Justice.

The Senate then passed still another compromise Oct. 5 and the House passed it Oct. 6, clearing it for the president. Both votes were voice votes.

Background

The U.S. bankruptcy system dates back to 1898 and underwent its last overhaul in 1938. While bankruptcies declined since the peak of 255,000 in 1976 — the number of bankruptcies had increased substantially since, for example, 1946 when there were only 10,000.

More people are affected by bankruptcy cases each year than by all other civil and criminal litigation combined.

The increase in cases placed enormous stress on the existing system for resolving bankruptcy disputes. That system was run largely by bankruptcy "referees," originally charged with handling the administrative aspects of bankruptcy cases. Over the years, the referees had been given increasing authority over the cases and eventually ended up performing judicial functions, although they officially operated as subordinate officers of the federal district courts.

The House Judiciary Committee had reported HR 8200 Sept. 8, 1977 (H Rept 95-595), but the measure was yanked from the House calendar after its supporters failed to beat back a major amendment that rejected the creation of an independent corps of specialized, life tenure bankruptcy judges and substituted a modification of the existing system. *(1977 Almanac p. 571)*

House Floor Action

The House passed HR 8200 by voice vote on Feb. 1.

The principal debate on HR 8200 was over whether a new body of bankruptcy courts was needed or if the current courts, which are adjuncts to the federal district courts, could be modernized to handle the cases.

An amendment offered by Rep. George E. Danielson, D-Calif., sought to retain the existing court structure, while expanding their jurisdiction, providing that bankruptcy judges be appointed by courts of appeals rather than district courts to enhance the prestige of their judges, and increasing the terms of judges from six to 15 years.

The Danielson amendment, offered as a substitute for HR 8200, had been accepted by the House in 1977, prompting the manager of the bill to withdraw the measure from the floor and hold additional hearings. But the House reversed itself Feb. 1, rejecting the Danielson amendment on a 146-262 vote. *(Vote 21, p. 8-H)*

Major Provisions. As passed by the House, HR 8200 contained the following major provisions:

- Abolished the existing bankruptcy referee system under which bankruptcy courts were subordinate to federal district courts, and established a new bankruptcy court system to become operational Oct. 1, 1983, independent of the federal district courts.

Burger's Lobbying Style Stirs Furor on Hill

Chief Justice Warren E. Burger managed to delay final action on bankruptcy reform in an unusual 11th-hour lobbying effort to have changes made in a compromise version of the bill.

Burger asked Strom Thurmond, R-S.C., to put a "hold" on the bill Sept. 28 to prevent Senate consideration. The request came shortly after the House gave what appeared to be its final seal of approval to the legislation.

The Chief Justice also telephoned Dennis DeConcini, D-Ariz., the principal sponsor of the bill and, according to DeConcini, called the senator "irresponsible" for advocating presidential appointment of bankruptcy judges and making bankruptcy courts adjuncts of appeals courts rather than the lower-ranking district courts.

Burger "not only lobbied, but pressured and attempted to be intimidating," DeConcini said. He said the Chief Justice was "very, very irate and rude."

While Burger succeeded in getting some of the changes he sought, it was less the substance of his concerns than the way he made them known that caused somewhat of a furor on Capitol Hill.

Majority Leader Robert C. Byrd, D-W.Va., said he believed it would be "inappropriate" for the Chief Justice to ask a senator to put a hold on a bill. And DeConcini, while not accusing Burger of any illegality, said he viewed Burger's actions as a violation of the separation-of-powers doctrine.

While lobbying by executive branch officials is commonplace and largely taken for granted, it is unusual to find judicial officials involved in the legislative process.

A Supreme Court spokesman disputed suggestions of impropriety, arguing that Burger spoke to DeConcini and other senators in his capacity as chairman of the Judicial Conference, the policymaking body of the federal judiciary. Burger asked three other senators to stick to the Senate version of the bill and to reject the "compromise" approved by the House.

Burger became actively involved in the bankruptcy debate, which the press had largely ignored until then, just after the House passed the compromise Sept. 28. That vote took the Chief Justice and some senators largely by surprise.

The compromise had been worked out Sept. 26 by a small faction of key senators and congressmen involved in the bankruptcy debate. But other lawmakers, according to aides, hadn't even been informed of the meeting or the compromise before it passed the House. An aide to Thurmond said that "no decision was made to send the bill to the floor" at the meeting. "Because of the hasty [House] action, the Chief Justice asked Senator Thurmond to hold the bill in the Senate until particular provisions compromised against the Chief Justice's views could be resolved."

Burger's specific concerns involved presidential appointment of bankruptcy judges (retained in the final bill), gold-plated retirement benefits for bankruptcy judges (removed), and making the bankruptcy courts adjuncts to the appeals courts (removed).

Burger and the Judicial Conference view bankruptcy judges as a specialized area of practice. The Judicial Conference had resisted changes that would elevate bankruptcy judges to the stature of district or appeals court judges, who are appointed by the president and serve for life.

Burger also objected to having appeals courts review questions of fact rather than the broader questions of law that they currently handle. Had bankruptcy courts been made adjuncts to the appeals courts, as proposed in the original compromise, appeals of bankruptcy court rulings would have gone straight to the appeals courts rather than the district courts.

- Separated judicial from administrative functions in bankruptcy cases, creating U.S. trustees as independent officers under the general supervision of the Justice Department rather than under the bankruptcy judges to handle administrative functions.
- Provided for the mandatory retirement of all sitting bankruptcy judges after the five-year transition period and for appointment of new judges with full constitutional tenure.
- Permitted appeals from bankruptcy courts directly to courts of appeals, skipping district courts.
- Expanded and simplified plans encouraging consumer debtors to repay debts over an extended period rather than to declare bankruptcy.
- Consolidated existing bankruptcy law to encourage business reorganization over liquidation.

Student Loans. On a 54-26 standing vote, the House accepted an amendment prohibiting persons with federally insured student loans from discharging the debts in bankruptcy for five years after the loans become due, except in hardship cases. Supporters argued these bankruptcies increased over 300 percent in four years and would destroy the program. Opponents said defaults, not bankruptcies, threatened the program.

Senate Action

Committee

S 2266 was reported unanimously from the Committee on Judiciary on July 14 (S Rept 95-989). The bill was referred to the Committee on Finance, where tax amendments to the bill were considered, and the measure was reported unanimously from that panel Aug. 10 (S Rept 95-1106).

Floor

Other than agreeing on one substantive amendment and several technical amendments, the Senate approved S 2266 as reported by the Judiciary Committee.

The only significant floor debate came on an amendment by Dewey F. Bartlett, R-Okla., allowing debtors to "reaffirm" and pay off specific debts after being absolved by bankruptcy. The amendment was adopted 51-20. *(Vote 369, p. 55-S)*

Under the amendment, a debtor discharged of an obligation to a creditor by a bankruptcy court could return to the creditor and reaffirm his obligation to pay off a debt if he wished, for example, to reassure continued credit from that particular creditor. The House bill did not allow reaffirmation.

According to Edward M. Kennedy, D-Mass., who successfully opposed the Bartlett amendment in the Judiciary Committee, but was absent for the floor debate, the amendment was "unconscionable" because it went against one of the bill's basic principles — to give a person who has gone through bankruptcy a fresh start.

"The practice of seeking reaffirmation permits unscrupulous and powerful lenders to force persons to reaffirm lawfully discharged debts through job pressure, deceit, and the temptation of an offer of further credit," Kennedy said in a prepared statement.

Bartlett argued that the bankrupt debtor "must have the opportunity to say, if he wishes to say, that he wants to reaffirm certain of these debts." Bartlett's amendment would allow the debtor 30 days to reconsider his decision to reaffirm a debt and to rescind or alter his decision to reaffirm.

Bartlett said the amendment "definitely provides protection for the individual from any kind of abuse or coercion." He said that "the human dignity of the individual" was "at stake" because the "individual who does have large debts does want to put them in order by taking advantage of the bankruptcy laws" but "also wants to shout, loud and clear, that he wishes to reaffirm certain of these debts."

Said Bartlett, "I think it is very important for an individual to have this right."

Kennedy argued that "despite absurd claims to the contrary by some lenders," S 2266 would not deny debtors the right to satisfy their conscience by paying off debts. "There is nothing in the bill to prohibit a debtor from voluntarily making payments if he chooses or feels a moral obligation to do so." But, Kennedy said, "permitting finance companies to condition the extension of further credit on the reaffirmation of debt invites an outrageous evasion of state usury laws."

An aide to one senator credited lobbying by finance companies in favor of the provision for its passage by such a wide margin.

S 2266 established a new system of bankruptcy courts that would operate as adjuncts of federal district courts. (The House bill established a system of courts entirely separate from the district courts.) Under the Senate bill, judges would be appointed for each judicial circuit by the judge of that circuit's court of appeals.

The appointment by the appeals court judges was designed to eliminate the appearance that persisted under existing law that bankruptcy courts were subservient to district courts, and to avoid the apparent conflict in having district court judges rule on appeals from decisions handed down by bankruptcy judges they themselves appointed.

The bill doubled the term of office for bankruptcy judges to 12 years from six in an effort to attract a higher caliber of judges.

S 2266 greatly expanded the jurisdiction of bankruptcy judges to cover all controversies arising out of a bankruptcy case, eliminating situations under existing law where a single bankruptcy case may be litigated in several courts. This comprehensive mandate was designed to reduce the amount of litigation over jurisdictional issues, avoid delays, reduce expenses and generate a more uniform body of bankruptcy case law.

While the House and Senate bills were largely in agreement in expanding the authority of bankruptcy courts, they disagreed over the structure of the courts each created. The Senate bill gave circuit judges authority to appoint bankruptcy judges in the 94 federal judicial districts. The House bill, on the other hand, gave the president authority to appoint the new bankruptcy judges as "Article III" judges, that is, with equal rank and pay with regular federal district judges.

In addition to the major restructuring of the court system for resolving bankruptcy disputes, S 2266 as passed by the Senate contained other provisions that differed from the House bill. Among them were provisions that:

- Modified the system where district judges appointed trustees to look out for the rights of creditors in bankruptcy. Under S 2266 the bankruptcy judge would select a trustee from a panel of prospective trustees selected by the director of the Administrative Office of U.S. Courts. The House bill called for establishing trustees as independent officers under the general supervision of the Justice Department.
- Permitted appeals from bankruptcy courts to the federal district courts. The House bill had appeals going directly to the federal appeals courts.

House-Senate Agreement

Bankruptcy Courts

The principal controversy during the final weeks of debate was whether bankruptcy courts would continue as adjuncts of federal district courts as proposed by the House or of federal appeals courts as proposed by the Senate.

Under the old law bankruptcy cases were handled by "referees," judges appointed by district court judges. The Senate sought to place appointment of the bankruptcy judges to be created by the bill with the appeals courts. Senate sponsors said the appointment of referees by district court judges had led to apparent conflicts when a referee's case was appealed to the judge who appointed the referee — a judge who might be inclined to uphold the views of his appointee.

The compromise retained the bankruptcy courts as adjuncts to the district courts but removed the power of appointment of bankruptcy judges from the district court judges and established a new appeals process.

Bankruptcy Judges

The compromise also included provisions designed to elevate the rank and status of bankruptcy judges, to attract higher caliber judges. Under the final agreement the bill:

- Gave the president power to appoint bankruptcy judges with the advice and consent of the Senate.
- Provided that circuit court counsels could recommend candidates for bankruptcy judgeships to the president, although the president would not be bound to name judges from those recommendations.

• Increased the term of office of bankruptcy judges to 14 years, from six (district and circuit judges serve for life).

• Provided that bankruptcy judgeships be established on a permanent basis by Congress, rather than at the discretion of the U.S. Judicial Conference.

Congress made no specific recommendation on the number of bankruptcy judge positions that were to be created, but it assumed for itself the responsibility of making that determination in the future, a determination previously made by the Judicial Conference.

HR 8200 extended until March 31, 1984, the terms of existing bankruptcy judges. By that time studies were to have been completed and recommendations made by the Judicial Conference on the number of judges deemed necessary. It was expected that from 200 to 250 bankruptcy judgeship positions would be created.

Appeals

HR 8200 as cleared provided for appeals of rulings by bankruptcy judges to the district courts in all cases. However, the bill stipulated that each court of appeals could, by rule, allow an appeal: 1) to a panel of three bankruptcy judges designated by the court of appeals or 2) to a court of appeals if the consent of both parties were obtained.

The compromise recognized that in certain cases it might be inappropriate for a particular district judge to hear a specific appeal, and that in some cases, such as those in rural areas, it might be inconvenient for three bankruptcy judges to review a case, in which instance an appeals court judge could review it.

Jurisdiction

HR 8200 gave bankruptcy judges all the jurisdictional authority that a district court judge would have in handling the same case. Without specifically providing bankruptcy judges the power that life-tenured district court judges have under Article III of the Constitution, bankruptcy judges acquired those powers derivatively, that is, as adjuncts of the district courts.

Practically speaking, this meant that a bankruptcy judge could bring all civil cases pending against a debtor under his aegis for purposes of consolidation. This would help avoid jurisdictional claims such as might arise in a case where a debtor filed for bankruptcy in a bankruptcy court and then found himself the target of a civil suit by a creditor in another court. Under HR 8200 the civil suit would also be brought into the bankruptcy proceeding, so that an effort could be made to deal more equitably with all creditors.

Trustees

HR 8200 largely continued the existing system whereby bankruptcy judges appoint trustees to look out for the rights of creditors. The House bill had sought to completely separate the judicial from the administrative role of bankruptcy judges by giving administrative responsibilities to a new set of trustees under the supervision of the Justice Department.

The compromise bill set up a "pilot" program to test the U.S. trustee plan in 18 of the 94 federal judicial districts. The trustees would be appointed by the attorney general and would serve until 1984, that is, until the end of the transition period when bankruptcy courts would be established on a full-time basis.

Reaffirmation

The Senate bankruptcy bill had included a provision allowing debtors to "reaffirm" debts to creditors, so that the debtor could receive credit from the same source in the future. The amendment would have given a debtor 30 days to reconsider reaffirmation.

The House bill would have banned reaffirmation. Opponents of reaffirmation said it conflicted with the basic purpose of bankruptcy — to give a debtor a fresh start.

The compromise bill prohibited reaffirmation by consumer debtors unless: 1) the debtor consented to reaffirmation and 2) the bankruptcy court found it in the consumer's interest. The debtor would have 30 days in which to reconsider a reaffirmation of a debt. Business debtors would be free to reaffirm debts without the consent of a court.

Other Provisions

HR 8200 also provided:

• That filing fees for most civil cases and bankruptcy cases be increased to $60 from $20. In practical terms the increase was not so drastic since most civil cases carried filing fees of about $50.

• Slightly increased retirement benefits for bankruptcy judges. The benefits were cut back drastically from the version of the bill passed by the House Sept. 28.

• Increased the salaries of bankruptcy judges from $48,500 to $50,000, $5,000 less than the salaries paid district court judges.

• Additional staff for bankruptcy judges, estimated to cost $2 million a year in salaries, and additional personnel for bankruptcy clerk's offices estimated to cost about $3 million a year in salaries.

Final Action

The Senate agreed to the compromise Oct. 5 by voice vote, and the House followed suit the next day. ▮

Justice Dept. Authorization

A $1.69 billion authorization for fiscal 1979 operations of the Justice Department received final congressional approval Oct. 14 (PL 95-624).

The compromise version of the bill (S 3151) eliminated a controversial anti-busing amendment the House had attached, as well as a House provision that would have required the attorney general to issue advisory procedures to help the president in selecting federal district judges on a merit basis.

The Carter administration had requested an authorization of $1.63 billion. The House authorized $1.66 billion and the Senate $1.68 billion.

Legislation appropriating $2.47 billion for the Justice Department in fiscal 1979 already had been signed into law by the president. *(Appropriations, p. 88)*

The appropriation bill (HR 12934) contained funds for the Drug Enforcement Administration and the Law Enforcement Assistance Administration that had been authorized separately from the overall Justice authorization.

Passage of S 3151 marked the first time in the Justice Department's 108-year history that an authorization bill had been passed. The original 1870 act creating the department had been deemed authorization for appropriations until 1976, when Congress voted to require annual authorization, beginning in fiscal 1979. *(1976 Almanac, p. 397)*

Judiciary Committee Chairman Peter W. Rodino Jr., D-N.J., told the House Oct. 14 that "this first exercise of our new responsibility, to be sure, has not been completely smooth — we need, for example, to insure a more rational scheduling process in the future so that the authorizing process will truly precede the appropriations process — but our efforts are nonetheless an important beginning."

Provisions

As cleared, S 3151 authorized the following amounts for fiscal 1979 operations of the Justice Department:

Activity	Administration Request	Final Authorization
General administration	$ 28,996,000	$ 28,996,000
General legal activities	89,884,000	95,481,000
Antitrust Division	46,377,000	47,080,000
U.S. attorneys and marshals	196,736,000	221,736,000
Support of U.S. prisoners	25,100,000	25,100,000
Witness fees and expenses	20,144,000	20,144,000
Community Relations Service	5,353,000	5,353,000
FBI	556,750,000	561,341,000
Immigration and Naturalization Service	298,019,000	320,722,000
Drug Enforcement Administration*	(192,953,000)	(215,000,000)
Federal Prison Systems	362,502,000	362,662,000
Law Enforcement Assistance Administration*	(641,488,000)	(975,000,000)
Total	$1,629,861,000	$1,688,615,000

* Funding for DEA and LEAA was previously authorized under separate legislation; these amounts are not included in the totals shown above.

House Committee Action

In its first review of appropriations authorized for Justice Department activities, the House Judiciary Committee gave the department more money than it asked for. The authorization bill (HR 12005), reported to the House May 12, matched the requested amounts for most programs and increased them in three instances (H Rept 95-1148).

The total authorization of $1.7 billion (plus an estimated $98 million in open-ended authorizations), was approved by the Judiciary Committee April 26 on a 30-2 vote. Opposing the bill were Robert F. Drinan, D-Mass., and Elizabeth Holtzman, D-N.Y.

The bill did not reflect $641 million already authorized for the Law Enforcement Assistance Administration (LEAA) and $193 million for the Drug Enforcement Administration. The department's total authorization for fiscal 1979 including those programs was $2.5 billion.

Since its creation in 1870, the Justice Department never had to go before Congress for authorization of its appropriations. Congress added the requirement to the 1976 LEAA renewal act (PL 94-503), effective fiscal 1979. *(1976 Almanac p. 397)*

FBI Abuses

Alluding to criminal violations by the Justice Department and FBI uncovered in recent years, the committee report stated: "[T]he constitutional trauma of the early decade convinced the committee that a responsible and vigilant oversight by the representative Congress is required if confidence is to be maintained in the institutions of federal government. No component of the federal system is more sensitive to abuse and more fundamental to our liberties than the administration of justice."

In dissenting views accompanying the report, Drinan charged that "in many instances" the Judiciary Committee "rubber stamped" the funding requests made by the Justice Department.

Drinan and Holtzman both objected to funding for FBI domestic and foreign intelligence activities, which they said was not justified by FBI testimony given in a closed committee meeting.

"The FBI assumes and asserts that the numbers and activities of foreign agents operating in the United States are increasing sharply," Drinan said. "No concrete evidence was offered in any of the classified material to document that assumption." Drinan also said the amount of money spent on such FBI programs should not be kept secret.

Merit Selection

In additional views accompanying the committee report, four Judiciary Committee members said they would seek to amend the bill on the House floor to provide for merit selection of federal district court judges.

John F. Seiberling, D-Ohio, Robert McClory, R-Ill., William S. Cohen, R-Maine, and William J. Hughes, D-N.J., said the provision was necessary because a House-Senate conference committee debating a judgeship bill (HR 7843) had rejected a House provision calling for merit selection of district judges. *(Story, p. 173)*

The amendment would require the attorney general to establish procedures to identify individuals who are qualified to be district judges and require the submission of the names of such individuals to the president and the Senate. Under current procedures, individual senators, in effect, select district judges with the consent of the president and the full Senate.

House Floor Action

The House passed HR 12005 Sept. 28 on a vote of 322-21. The bill, which authorized $1.66 billion for Justice Department operations in fiscal 1979, was passed after the House added an amendment prohibiting the department from bringing legal actions that would promote busing of school children. *(Vote 753, p. 214-H)*

Authorizations for two Justice Department components, the Law Enforcement Assistance Administration (administration request $641 million) and the Drug Enforcement Administration ($193 million) had been enacted previously (PL 94-503 and PL 95-137).

The House made no changes in the authorizations recommended by the Judiciary Committee, which exceeded the Carter administration's request by $27.4 million.

The bill as passed contained $1 million more than requested for the Bureau of Prisons, to bring federal facilities into compliance with local fire safety standards, and an increase of $160,000 for the bureau's support for a program providing law school legal assistance for prison inmates.

Other increases included $22.7 million for the Immigration and Naturalization Service and $3.5 million for the FBI's domestic security and terrorism program.

Under the Immigration Service, the bill earmarked $2,052,000 for the Nazi War Crime Litigation Unit. The bill also required the Justice Department to notify the Judiciary committees ahead of time when it planned to reprogram unused funds for new programs or reorganization.

Busing Amendment

The anti-busing ban, sponsored by James M. Collins, R-Texas, was adopted on a 235-158 vote Sept. 26. *(Vote 738, p. 210-H)*

The ban had no effect on school busing plans already in progress or on plans ordered by the courts. It was aimed at plans implemented through actions brought against a community by the Justice Department. Collins argued that busing was too expensive for many school districts, a waste of gasoline and an ineffective and unpopular way of desegregating schools.

Judiciary Committee Chairman Peter W. Rodino Jr., D-N.J., argued in opposition that the amendment interfered with "the exercise of the responsibility of the Department of Justice specifically conferred upon it by the Congress." The Justice Department had been given authority under several statutes to bring suits with respect to school desegregation.

Don Edwards, D-Calif., argued that the amendment unconstitutionally interfered with the executive branch's authority to enforce the law.

Merit Selection

The House adopted on a 206-151 vote an amendment by John F. Seiberling, D-Ohio, requiring the attorney general to promulgate advisory procedures to assist the president in selecting federal district court judges on the basis of merit. *(Vote 752, p. 214-H)*

Seiberling said his amendment, which applied to all judgeship positions that would be filled in fiscal 1979, established for the first time procedures to help identify and evaluate the best qualified potential nominees for federal judgeships. However, the amendment stated that "no nomination or appointment to a United States district court judgeship shall be invalidated on the basis of a failure to comply with this section."

Opposing the amendment, Jack Brooks, D-Texas, argued that a judgeships bill (HR 7843) cleared by a House-Senate conference committee already provided adequate language to assure that judgeships would be filled on the basis of merit.

President Carter pledged during his campaign that he would select judges and U.S. attorneys without consideration of partisan or political influence.

Earlier in the year the president established commissions that were required to select appeals court judges on the basis of merit. But the president was not expected to go as far in issuing guidelines for district courts.

Other Amendments

The House also adopted the following amendments on non-record votes:

- By Henry B. Gonzalez, D-Texas, requiring the FBI to make a written report to a member of Congress on any investigation conducted by the bureau concerning a threat on the member's life.
- By Hamilton Fish Jr., R-N.Y., directing the attorney general to develop special eligibility criteria under the Indochina refugee parole program to enable a larger number of Cambodian refugees to enter the United States.
- By Don Edwards, D-Calif., to permit the FBI to use the proceeds from certain undercover operations to offset costs of similar operations. Edwards said he had in mind situations where the government sets up false fencing operations to apprehend thieves selling stolen goods.
- By Elliott H. Levitas, D-Ga., requiring the attorney general to report to the appropriate congressional committees whenever the Justice Department refrained from enforcing or defending in court any provision of a law that the department determined to be unconstitutional. Levitas argued that his amendment gave Congress an opportunity in legal actions to defend laws it had written. He cited a provision permitting a one-house veto of General Services Administration regulations dealing with the custody of the papers of former President Richard M. Nixon. Levitas said the Justice Department had conceded in a court case that this law was unconstitutional.
- By Seiberling requiring the FBI to classify arson as a major crime, to increase public awareness of the problem and give it greater priority in FBI investigations and prosecutions.
- By Bill Burlison, D-Mo., for the House Permanent Select Committee on Intelligence, on a non-record vote, to make clear that the committee will be apprised of all reprogramming actions affecting those FBI programs that fall within the jurisdiction of the Intelligence Committee, specifically programs having to do with foreign counterintelligence and domestic security and terrorism activities.

Provisions

Fiscal 1979 Justice Department authorizations in HR 12005 and S 3151 were as follows:

Activity	Senate Authorization	House Authorization
General administration	$28,996,000	$28,996,000
General legal activities	98,081,000	89,884,000
Antitrust Division	47,080,000	46,377,000
U S. attorneys and marshals	228,336,000	196,736,000
Witness fees and expenses	20,144,000	20,144,000
Support of U.S. prisoners	25,100,000	25,100,000
Community relations	5,353,000	5,353,000
FBI	564,188,000	560,250,000
Immigration and Naturalization Service	298,019,000	320,722,000
Drug Enforcement Administration*	($215,000,000)	($215,000,000)
Federal Prison System	364,902,000	363,662,000
Law Enforcement Assistance Administration*	($975,000,000)	($975,000,000)
Total	$1,680,199,000	$1,657,224,000

*Funding for DEA and LEAA was previously authorized under separate legislation; these amounts are not included in the totals shown above.

After passing HR 12005, the House tabled it and passed S 3151 with the language of the House bill substituted for that of the Senate bill.

Senate Action

On a nonrecord vote and with no debate, the Senate July 10 approved a $1.7 billion fiscal 1979 authorization for the Department of Justice.

The approved authorization was about $50.3 million above the level requested by the Carter administration and approximately the same as that approved by the House Judiciary Committee May 27.

The authorization bill, S 3151, was reported to the Senate by the Judiciary Committee on May 25 (S Rept 95-911).

The committee report said some of the administration-requested funding levels were not adequate "for the particular agency to meet the need for improved performance of a particular function prescribed by law."

No changes were made in the bill as reported by the committee. The bill provided significant increases in the following areas:

FBI. The FBI received $2 million more than the administration requested for its domestic terrorism activities. While the Office of Management and Budget apparently saw no need for the increase, FBI Director William H. Webster testified in favor of the additional funds.

Also included in the Senate bill was $5.4 million to restore 202 permanent positions for FBI programs to investigate and combat bank robberies.

General Legal Activities. The committee recommended increases for the Civil Rights Division and the Criminal Division totaling $5.6 million. A $2.3 million increase for the Civil Rights Division was provided to handle increased caseloads. A $3.3 million increase for the Criminal Division was provided after the committee asked the Justice Department to reevaluate its original request in light of a rise in criminal activity in certain priority areas.

Antitrust. The committee authorized an additional $703,000 to supplement the Antitrust Division's investigation of multinational oil companies.

U.S. Attorneys and Marshals. The committee estimated that if a bill (S 113), then in a House-Senate conference committee, were passed to increase by 30 percent the number of federal judges, there would be a sizable increase in the demands made on the offices of U.S. attorneys and marshals. The committee provided $30 million above the administration request to beef up those services. An additional $1.6 million was provided the U.S. Marshals Service to add 25 positions to its witness security staff. That program provides protection to persons who agree to testify in high priority organized crime cases. Witnesses and their families may be relocated and given new identities under the program.

As passed by the Senate, S 3151 authorized the following appropriations:

Activity	Administration Request	Senate Authorization
General Administration	$ 28,996,000	$ 28,996,000
General legal activities	89,884,000	98,081,000
Antitrust Division	46,377,000	47,080,000
U.S. attorneys and marshals	196,736,000	228,336,000
Support of U.S. prisoners	25,100,000	25,100,000
Witness fees and expenses	20,144,000	20,144,000
Community Relations Service	5,353,000	5,353,000
FBI	556,750,000	564,188,000
Immigration and Naturalization Service	298,019,000	298,019,000
Drug Enforcement Administration*	($192,953,000)	($215,000,000)
Federal Prison Systems	362,502,000	364,902,000
Law Enforcement Assistance Administration*	($641,488,000)	($975,000,000)
Total	$1,629,861,000	$1,680,199,000

*Funding for DEA and LEAA was previously authorized under separate legislation; these amounts are not included in the totals shown above.

Conference Action

House and Senate conferees reported the conference agreement on S 3151 to the House and Senate on Oct. 12 (H Rept 95-1777).

General Legal Activities. Conferees provided $95 million, an increase over the $90 million in the House bill but less than the $98 million approved by the Senate. The total included an additional $3.3 million for the Criminal Division and an extra $2.3 million for the Civil Rights Division.

Antitrust Division. The House accepted the slightly higher Senate authorization of $47 million. The increase of $703,000 over the president's request was to supplement the division's international oil investigations.

Immigration and Naturalization Service. The Senate receded to the House figure of $321 million, an increase of $22 million over the Senate authorization. Conferees decided that the additional funds were needed to improve efforts to control illegal aliens and to reduce the adjudication and naturalization backlog.

FBI. Conferees provided $561 million, less than the Senate's $564 million proposal but more than the House's $560 million authorization.

U.S. Attorneys and Marshals. Conferees agreed to a total of $222 million, an increase of $25 million over the House figure, to permit supplemental appropriations to cover approximately five months of expenses to handle the increased court activities expected to be generated by a judgeship bill passed by Congress. *(Story, p. 173)*

Federal Prison System. Conferees agreed to $363 million, the House proposal. The figure included $1 million for fire prevention in the Federal Prison System and $160,000 to increase support for legal services for inmates.

Merit Selection. Conferees dropped a House amendment to require the attorney general to promulgate advisory procedures to assist the president in selecting federal district court judges on the basis of merit.

House conferees were persuaded that the amendment was repetitive of language already in the judgeship bill, and that it created a statutory role for the attorney general that may not be envisioned by the president when he issues his "standards and guidelines" for merit selection of judges. Critics of the conferees' agreement said it would perpetuate the patronage system under which senators rather than the president effectively determine who shall be a federal district court judge.

Busing. Conferees dropped a House provision that would have prohibited the Justice Department from bringing legal actions that would promote busing of school children.

'Sting' Operations. Conferees approved language to authorize the FBI to provide funding for its undercover "sting" operations, phony fencing operations set up to apprehend thieves selling stolen goods. The agreement gave the FBI new authority to enter into leasing arrangements and establish bank accounts to support these operations.

McNeil Island Prison. The bill authorized the Bureau of Prisons to submit a plan to ensure the closing of the Washington state prison on or before Jan. 1, 1982. The prison was over 100 years old and seriously overcrowded.

Military Prisons. Conferees gave the Justice Department authority to negotiate with the Department of Defense to develop plans for using military prisons to relieve overcrowding in federal prisons.

Arson. Conferees agreed to a provision requiring the FBI to classify arson as a major crime to help increase public awareness of the problem and give it greater priority in FBI investigations and prosecutions.

Reprogramming of Funds. Conferees adopted a provision to require the Justice Department to inform House and Senate Judiciary committees and other relevant committees of reprogramming of large amounts of funds or of funds that would have a significant effect on program priorities.

Final Action

The Senate adopted the conference report by voice vote Oct. 13. The House adopted the report Oct. 14 by a 271-93 vote, clearing the bill for the president. *(Vote 819, p. 232-H)*

The president signed the bill into law Nov. 9 (PL 95-624).

Jefferson Davis: U.S. Citizen

One of the last vestiges of retribution against the South for the Civil War ended Oct. 17 when President Carter signed a resolution posthumously restoring full rights of citizenship to Confederate president Jefferson Davis.

"It's about time," said Beulah Smith Watts of St. Francisville, La., who at 84 was thought to be the oldest descendant of Davis.

Noting that Gen. Robert E. Lee's citizenship had been restored in 1976, Carter said in signing the document that "it is fitting that Jefferson Davis should no longer be singled out for punishment."

"Our nation needs to clear away the guilts and enmities and recriminations of the past, to finally set at rest the divisions that threatened to destroy our nation and to discredit the great principles on which it was founded. . . ," Carter said.

The resolution (S J Res 16 — PL 95-466) passed the Senate by voice vote April 27, 1977 after the Judiciary Committee reported the measure favorably April 22 (S Rept 95-100).

A companion measure (H J Res 1041) was reported from the House Judiciary Committee Aug. 14 (H Rept 95-1488) and passed the House Sept. 26 by voice vote. It was inserted into the Senate resolution; the Senate agreed to the amended measure Oct. 3, clearing the resolution for the president.

Davis had been specifically excluded from resolutions passed after the Civil War restoring the rights of most Confederate officials.

Controls Tightened on Use of Wiretaps

Congress gave its final approval Oct. 12 to the first major legislative effort to control electronic surveillance conducted in the United States for national security purposes. The House vote was 226-176, clearing the bill for the president (PL 95-511).

The Senate had approved the conference report on the bill, the Foreign Intelligence Surveillance Act, Oct. 9 on a voice vote.

The bill (S 1566) required a warrant for all but one category of foreign intelligence surveillances conducted in the United States and required evidence of criminal activity before a warrant could be issued for surveillance of a U.S. citizen. President Carter signed the bill into law Oct. 25.

Where under existing law only the executive branch handled national security wiretapping and "bugging," S 1566 would involve the judicial and legislative branches as well. The bill sent a message to the White House that Congress no longer recognized executive branch "inherent power" to violate the privacy of Americans in the name of national security.

But where the bill provided a stiff criminal standard for surveillance of Americans, liberals were unsuccessful in attempting to extend these Fourth Amendment protections to foreign visitors to the United States. And despite objections from liberal sponsors of the bill, an exemption from the warrant requirement was included for certain top-secret National Security Agency surveillances, the precise nature and number of which remained a mystery.

S 1566 had its genesis in the Nixon and Ford administrations when congressional committees disclosed widespread intelligence agency abuses of the rights of U.S. citizens. Summarizing the Senate committee's findings, Frank Church, D-Idaho, said: "[T]hrough the uncontrolled or illegal use of intrusive techniques — ranging from simple theft to sophisticated electronic surveillance — the government has collected, and then used improperly, huge amounts of information about the private lives, political beliefs and associations of numerous Americans." S 1566 allowed President Carter to fulfill, at least in part, his campaign promise to stop such activities.

The compromise bill appeared to have won the support of groups representing the frequently divergent interests of national security and civil liberties. All of the nation's intelligence agencies were on record in support of the final version of the bill as was the American Civil Liberties Union.

"From a civil liberties standpoint, the conference bill is — with the exception of the NSA warrant exemption — the best of both [House and Senate] bills," said Jerry Berman, legislative counsel of the ACLU.

The ACLU viewed the criminal standard and warrant requirements as a major precedent for requiring similar safeguards in intelligence agency charters. The charters, which were to be debated in the next Congress, were expected to propose limits to which these agencies can use other investigative techniques such as break-ins, mail openings and reviews of tax returns.

Provisions

As approved by House and Senate conferees, S 1566 amended title 18 of the U.S. Code to authorize applications for a court order approving the use of electronic surveillance to obtain foreign intelligence information. The bill contained the following major provisions:

Targets

S 1566 provided a criminal standard for electronic surveillance of "U.S. persons" *(see definition below)* believed to be engaged in intelligence operations for foreign powers and a non-criminal standard for non-U.S. persons.

The bill allowed court-ordered electronic surveillance if there was "probable cause to believe" the target was a "foreign power" or an "agent of a foreign power." The criminal standard for U.S. persons was less stringent in cases of spying, sabotage and terrorism than the "probable cause" standard provided for other covert activities *(see definition of "agent of a foreign power" below).*

The following major provisions dealing with targets of surveillance:

- Defined a "foreign power" to include:

1) a "foreign government" or "component" of a foreign government [including embassies and consulates], and any "faction of a foreign nation," not substantially composed of U.S. persons;

2) a foreign-based political organization, not substantially composed of U.S. persons;

3) an entity directed and controlled by a foreign government [including businesses], whether it acknowledged that it was so-controlled or not;

4) a group engaged in international terrorism or in preparation of such activities.

- Defined an "agent of a foreign power" to include:

1) a non-U.S. person who acts in the United States as an officer or employee of a foreign power, or as a member of a group engaged in international terrorism or in preparation of such activities;

2) a non-U.S. person who, on behalf of a foreign power, engages in clandestine intelligence activities contrary to the interest of the U.S. when, a) there is evidence to suggest that the person is in the U.S. to engage in such activities or, b) the person "knowingly" "aids," "abets" or "conspires" with someone engaged in such activities;

3) any person, including a U.S. citizen, who knowingly engages in clandestine intelligence gathering activities on behalf of a foreign power that "involve or may involve" a violation of U.S. criminal statutes;

4) any person who "pursuant to the direction of" a foreign intelligence service or network "knowingly" engages in activities that "involve or are about to involve" a violation of U.S. criminal statutes;

5) any person, including a U.S. citizen who knowingly engages in sabotage or international terrorism on behalf of a foreign power;

6) any person who "knowingly aids or abets" any person in the conduct of activities described in sections three, four or five above.

- Defined a "United States person" as:

1) a U.S. citizen;

2) an alien lawfully admitted for permanent residence;

3) an unincorporated association whose membership includes a "substantial number" of U.S. citizens or resident aliens, or a U.S. corporation, except corporations or associations falling within the foreign power definition.

- Provided that no U.S. person may be considered a foreign power or agent of a foreign power solely on the basis of activities protected by the First Amendment to the Constitution.

- Defined "international terrorism" to include activities that:

1) involve violent acts or acts dangerous to human life that would violate federal or state criminal laws if committed in the United States;

2) appear to be intended to: a) "intimidate or coerce a civilian population," b) "influence the policy of a government by intimidation or coercion," or c) affect the conduct of a government by assassination or kidnapping;

3) occur outside the United States or "transcend national boundaries" in terms of the means by which the acts are accomplished, the persons they are intended to coerce or intimidate, or the locale in which their perpetrators operate or seek asylum. (The conference report stated that a criminal standard would apply to U.S. persons engaged in terrorist activities transcending national boundaries.)

Courts

S 1566 provided for federal judicial certification of all electronic surveillance for foreign intelligence purposes in the United States. The role of the judiciary was drastically limited, however, for certain warrantless NSA surveillances. Major court provisions in S 1566 included the following:

- The Chief Justice was to publicly designate seven district court judges from seven of the 11 judicial circuits "who shall constitute a court" to hear applications and grant or deny warrants. Judges were required to provide written statements explaining the denial of any warrant application.
- The Chief Justice was to publicly designate three judges from the district courts to hear appeals by the government from warrants denied. Appeals court judges would also have to state reasons for denying warrants.
- The bill provided that each judge would serve a maximum of seven years, and that judges would serve in Washington, D.C., on a rotating basis with at least two judges serving at any given time.

Warrant Applications

S 1566 sought to prevent indiscriminate use of electronic surveillances through detailed warrant application and authorization procedures requiring executive and judicial branch officials to state in writing the reasons for requesting or granting each warrant.

Applications for warrants under S 1566 required the approval of the attorney general. In most cases applications included the following information, although less complete warrant applications were required for certain categories of foreign powers, primarily those that would not include U.S. persons:

1) the identity of the federal officer requesting the warrant;

2) the identity of the target, if known, or a description of the target;

3) a statement of the reasons the target is believed to be a foreign power or agent of a foreign power and that the premise targeted is used by the foreign power or agent of a foreign power;

4) a statement of proposed minimization procedures;

5) a description of the information sought and the type of communications targeted;

6) a certification by the assistant to the president for national security affairs or an executive branch official or officials designated by the president from among executive officers employed in the area of national security or defense and appointed by the president with the advice and consent of the Senate;

7) a statement by the certifying officer that the information sought is foreign intelligence information, that the surveillance is to obtain that information and that it can't reasonably be obtained by normal investigative techniques;

8) a statement of the method of surveillance and whether physical entry is required;

9) a statement of facts relating to previous warrant applications directed at the same target;

10) a statement of the period of time for which surveillance is requested.

Warrant Approval

In approving orders for electronic surveillance under S 1566 a judge:

- Must determine that the application has all the appropriate authorizations and information required under the warrant application procedures and shall specify that information in the warrant order.
- Must direct that the minimization procedures be followed.
- May, at an applicant's request, direct that a landlord, custodian, or other specified person assist the government in installing electronic surveillance apparatuses or by providing information.
- May approve surveillance for up to 90 days except against certain foreign powers for which a warrant may be issued for up to one year; and may approve extensions for the same periods on the same basis as provided for in the original warrant.

Warrant Exemption

S 1566 provided an exemption from the warrant requirement for certain NSA surveillances directed at "the acquisition of the contents of communications transmitted by means of communications used exclusively between or among foreign powers," and the acquisition of technical intelligence, other than the spoken communications of individuals, from property or premises under the open and exclusive control of a foreign power.

The bill provided that there be "no substantial likelihood that the surveillance will acquire the contents of any communication to which a United States person is a party." It further provided that orders for such surveillances, conducted for periods of up to one year, be certified by the attorney general in writing. The certification would be filed under seal with the seven-judge court and could be opened only in a limited number of circumstances.

Warrantless Surveillance in Emergencies

S 1566 allowed the attorney general to approve emergency surveillance for up to 24 hours without a judge's approval in extraordinary circumstances, provided that:

- A judge was immediately notified that such surveillance was necessary.
- An application was filed within 24 hours.
- Notification of the target of surveillance was allowed if the target was a U.S. citizen and the warrant application was subsequently denied.

Minimization

The use of information obtained through electronic surveillance under S 1566 was limited by provisions designed to protect innocent U.S. citizens who are subjects of surveillance, while at the same time protecting national defense and security interests. Provisions of this section:

- Required federal and state governments intending to disclose evidence obtained by electronic surveillance at a trial, hearing or other proceeding before a court, agency or other government authority, to inform the person affected.
- Allowed a target or other person affected by such surveillance and informed of the government's intention to make the information public, to move to suppress the evidence obtained or derived from such electronic surveillance on the grounds that the information was unlawfully acquired or the surveillance was not made in conformity with an order of authorization or approval.
- Allowed the attorney general to ask a court to block disclosure or suppression of evidence or information obtained through electronic surveillance by filing an affidavit that disclosure or an adversary proceeding would harm national security. Provided that the court review, in private, materials relating to the surveillance to determine if it was lawfully authorized and conducted. Where necessary to make an accurate determination of the legality of the surveillance, allowed the court to disclose to the aggrieved party portions of the surveillance materials.
- Where a court determined that the surveillance was not lawfully conducted, allowed it to suppress the evidence unlawfully obtained, and where the surveillance was legal to deny the motion of the aggrieved person except to the extent that due process required disclosure.
- In circumstances involving the unintentional acquisition of the contents of any radio communication under circumstances where a person has a "reasonable expectation of privacy and a warrant would be required to obtain the information for law enforcement purposes," the contents of the communication shall be destroyed upon recognition unless the attorney general determines the contents indicate a threat of death or serious bodily harm to any person. The provision applied only to communications between individuals within the United States.

Reports and Oversight

S 1566 set forth procedures for reporting to Congress on the application of the act. The bill provided for:

- Semiannual reports by the attorney general to House and Senate intelligence committees concerning all electronic surveillance under the act.
- Reports by the intelligence committees to the full House and Senate on or before one year after the effective date of the act, concerning the implementation of the act. The reports must include an analysis and recommenda-

tions concerning whether the act should be amended, repealed or permitted to continue in effect without amendment.

Penalties

S 1566:

- Provided penalties of up to $10,000 and five years in jail for intentionally engaging in electronic surveillance that failed to conform to the provisions of the act, or for disclosing information obtained by electronic surveillance except as authorized by the statute, knowing or having reason to know that the information was obtained by electronic surveillance.
- Allowed an individual other than a foreign power or agent of a foreign power subjected to an electronic surveillance, or about whom information was obtained through electronic surveillance and publicly disclosed in violation of the act, to sue for damages of $1,000 or $100 a day for each day of the violation, plus punitive damages, plus reasonable attorney's fees and other investigation and litigation costs.

Miscellaneous

The provisions of the bill were to become effective upon enactment, except that electronic surveillance approved by the attorney general was not to be deemed unlawful because the procedures of the act were not followed if the surveillance was terminated or a court order obtained within 90 days following the designation of the first judge.

S 1566 allowed the president, through the attorney general, to authorize electronic surveillance without a court order for up to 15 days following a declaration of war by Congress.

Senate Committee Action

The Senate Intelligence Committee March 14, by a 9-0 vote, approved the Foreign Intelligence Surveillance Act of 1978 (S 1566, S Rept 95-701).

A similar version had been approved by the Senate Judiciary Committee on Nov. 15, 1977 (S Rept 95-604). *(Judiciary bill background, 1977 Almanac p. 596)*

The Intelligence Committee bill required the government to obtain a judicial warrant for electronic surveillance conducted within the United States for foreign intelligence purposes.

Birch Bayh, D-Ind., chairman of the Intelligence Committee, said the criminal activity requirement "was the most difficult and important issue to be worked out" by the committee.

The version of the bill reported by the Senate Judiciary Committee did not include a criminal standard. The sponsor, Edward M. Kennedy, D-Mass., agreed to a non-criminal standard because he thought most Judiciary members would not support a criminal standard unless it had Justice Department backing. The department, which supported a non-criminal standard in the Judiciary Committee, said it could accept the criminal standard in the Intelligence version.

The criminal standard included in the Intelligence Committee bill generally allowed surveillance of a U.S. citizen or resident alien if a court finds probable cause that the person knowingly engages in spying or other "clandestine" activities that "involve or may involve a violation of the criminal statutes of the United States."

Since the criminal standard in S 1566 allowed monitoring conversations of persons who "may" violate the law, it was less stringent than the laws covering domestic criminal wiretaps (such as those used by the FBI against mobsters), which require probable cause that a law has been or is being violated.

Under the Intelligence Committee bill, only persons who are acting as "agents of a foreign power" engaged in "clandestine intelligence activities" were subjected to surveillance. Like the Judiciary bill, the Intelligence Committee bill did not define "clandestine intelligence activities." But in the definition of a foreign agent, the Intelligence bill differentiated two classes of clandestine activities: 1) spying, sabotage and terrorism; and 2) other, more nebulous clandestine activities.

It was the second category that civil libertarians always had feared could allow the greatest abuses. Addressing this concern, the Intelligence bill required that to obtain a warrant to wiretap for activities falling into the second class evidence must be shown that the activities "involve or are about to involve" a violation of the law, rather than that they simply "may involve" a violation of the law.

Safeguards

Conspiracy language that civil libertarians had objected to in the Judiciary Committee bill was clarified to require that an individual know the person he "aids or abets" is engaged in clandestine intelligence activities.

An amendment offered by Sen. Joseph R. Biden, D-Del., provided added safeguards to the conspiracy section to prevent surveillance of U.S. citizens who are engaged solely in exercising their rights of freedom of speech. The amendment provided that "no United States person may be considered an agent of a foreign power solely on the basis of activities protected by the First Amendment to the Constitution."

Both the Judiciary and Intelligence Committee bills provided safeguards for U.S. citizens beyond those provided for aliens. However, foreign visitors to the United States were given increased protection in the Intelligence bill through a tightened definition of a foreign agent.

Under the new language, an alien could be wiretapped if a judge found that: 1) the person is working for a foreign country that engages in clandestine activities contrary to the interests of the United States (the definition assumes that some countries do not engage in such activities) and 2) the circumstances under which the person is in the United States suggest that he or she is likely to be engaging in such activities.

While the Judiciary bill would have lumped many tourists in with spies, the Intelligence bill attempted to make it more difficult to eavesdrop electronically on innocent foreign visitors to the United States.

In another significant change, the Intelligence Committee bill defined as "foreign agents" groups composed substantially of U.S. citizens if they are "directed and controlled by a foreign government." The bill extended to such groups certain protections from surveillance afforded all U.S. citizens. However, the language would appear to allow surveillance of such groups as the Communist Party of the United States, which was ostensibly controlled from Moscow, without evidence that the group was engaging in clandestine activities.

The Senate committee bill created a new court comprised of seven district judges appointed by the chief justice to review applications for electronic surveillance in the United States and to grant or deny orders. The bill allowed the president to authorize the attorney general to approve applications to federal judges for foreign intelligence electronic surveillance.

The bill sought to prevent indiscriminate use of electronic surveillance through detailed warrant application and authorization procedures requiring executive and judicial branch officials to state in writing the reasons for granting each warrant. Under extraordinary circumstances, S 1566 allowed the attorney general to approve emergency surveillance for up to 24 hours without a judge's approval.

The use of information obtained through electronic surveillance under S 1566 was limited by provisions designed to protect innocent U.S. citizens who were subjects of surveillance while at the same time protecting national defense and security interests.

S 1566 set forth procedures for reporting to Congress on the application of the act.

Senate Floor Action

The Senate passed S 1566 April 20, by a 95-1 vote. The lone "nay" vote was cast by Sen. Bill Scott, R-Va. *(Vote 128, p. 23-S)*

The bill was passed with only limited changes from the version reported by the Senate Intelligence Committee.

Seven floor amendments to S 1566 were agreed to by voice votes:

1) An amendment clarifying the intent of the bill that information obtained under the bill's emergency surveillance provisions (allowing surveillance for up to 24 hours without a court order) may be used if the court subsequently approves the surveillance. By Birch Bayh, D-Ind.

2) An amendment acknowledging that congressional committees other than the Senate Intelligence Committee may have a legitimate need for information about surveillance conducted under the bill to carry out their activities. By Bayh.

3) An amendment clarifying the bill's intent that a judge may review intelligence agency compliance with the minimization procedures at any time. By Bayh and James Abourezk, D-S.D.

4) An amendment modifying the language relating to the standard for surveillance of persons engaged in sabotage or terrorism for or on behalf of a foreign power. By Edward M. Kennedy, D-Mass.

The amendment allowed surveillance of persons who knowingly engage in sabotage or terrorism, "or activities in furtherance thereof," for or on behalf of a foreign power. According to Bayh, the term "in furtherance" of sabotage or terrorism would cover acts "supportive of acts of serious violence." Bayh cited as examples the purchase or importation into the U.S. of explosives, planning for assassinations and financing or training for such activities. "The 'in furtherance' provision was also adopted in order to permit electronic surveillance at some point before the danger sought to be prevented — for example, a kidnapping, bombing, or a hijacking — actually occurs," Bayh said.

5) An amendment clarifying the intent of the Judiciary Committee — which had approved the bill in 1978 — that the identity of the target of surveillance *must* be specified in the warrant application if known by the government. By Kennedy.

6) An amendment clarifying the intent of the Judiciary Committee that the "target" of an illegal surveillance may move to supress the contents of any communication acquired by such surveillance in court. By Kennedy.

7) An amendment eliminating the requirement that future amendments to the Foreign Intelligence Surveillance Act proposed by the Senate Select Committee on Intelligence be expedited for consideration in each house. The requirement was considered unnecessary because the bill's criminal standard posed less of a threat to the privacy of U.S. citizens than did an earlier version of the bill which lacked the criminal standard. By Kennedy.

House Committee Action

The House Intelligence Committee June 8 reported legislation requiring warrants for wiretaps in national security cases (HR 7308 — H Rept 95-1283).

On June 30, a House Judiciary subcommittee voted 4-3 to table the bill, thereby preventing consideration by the full Judiciary Committee and avoiding delay in getting the bill to the House floor.

Minority Views

HR 7308 was approved by the House Intelligence Committee on an 8-2 vote. The committee's four Republican members filed dissenting views with the report. The four were Robert McClory of Illinois, Bob Wilson of California, John M. Ashbrook of Ohio and J. Kenneth Robinson of Virginia. "[T]he committee bill represents the very kind of interference with executive authority that frustrates effective foreign policy and national security actions by a responsible chief executive," they said.

The four argued that HR 7308 would: 1) allow judges to interfere with foreign affairs and "political" decisions that should be made by the president, 2) impose warrant requirements that are not required by the Fourth Amendment and 3) threaten national security by making it more difficult to collect intelligence and more difficult to keep intelligence secrets. The four argued that "pressures from administration leaders" prevented intelligence personnel from forcefully opposing HR 7308.

Supporters responded that the restrictions were needed to prevent the kinds of abuses that had been uncovered in recent years; the authorization procedures provided safeguards to prevent a single judge from arbitrarily rejecting a warrant application; intelligence agencies wouldn't support the bills if they were a threat to national security and there would be no delays in getting information because the bill provided for "emergency surveillances" without warrants when the need arises.

Counterproposal

The House Republican Policy Committee came out against HR 7308 July 20, issuing a statement that essentially reiterated the arguments of the four dissenting members of the Intelligence Committee and supported a Republican counterproposal that would be offered on the House floor. The policy committee called the bill "another example of congressional overkill and overreaction in the name of reform of the nation's intelligence community."

House Floor Action

The House passed HR 7308 Sept. 7, by a vote of 246-128. *(Vote 648, p. 184-H)*

Passage came after the House reversed a vote taken Sept. 6 that would have limited the bill's new warrant requirements to surveillance of Americans.

As passed by the House, the bill was similar in its major provisions to the Senate-passed legislation. However, the House bill allowed the government to intercept without a warrant communications it knew were solely between non-U.S. persons.

Debate over HR 7308 pitted members who believed executive orders were adequate to protect individuals from unjustified invasions of privacy against those who argued that more stringent safeguards and greater accountability by those responsible for surveillance were necessary.

Proponents of the bill succeeded in bringing the judicial branch into the warrant process, despite efforts by opponents to retain intelligence gathering largely in the executive branch, with congressional oversight as a safeguard.

Sponsors of HR 7308, led by Morgan F. Murphy, D-Ill., chairman of the Legislation Subcommittee of the House Intelligence Committee, and Robert W. Kastenmeier, D-Wis., chairman of the Judiciary Subcommittee on Courts and Civil Liberties, pursued a floor strategy that called for rejection of any substantive amendments. Sponsors argued that the bill represented a delicate balancing of national security and civil liberties interests and that reaching agreement with the Senate relied on not upsetting the compromise.

McClory Substitute

Opponents saw nothing delicate about the compromise, but rather viewed it as a sellout of national security to civil liberties interests. Robert McClory, R-Ill., who led the opposition, said the measure "goes precisely against the constitutional authority which is reposed in the president."

He said the bill was "a compromise made with regard to our national security intelligence-gathering capability . . . a compromise with the ACLU . . . a compromise made with those who are looking out not for the intelligence-gathering capability but who, in many instances, would like to have this capability eliminated entirely."

McClory, who offered a substitute bill that would have completely gutted HR 7308, pursued an approach of taking the bill apart piece by piece, amendment by amendment.

That strategy, which ultimately proved unsuccessful, largely set the tone for the debate. Since sponsors were arguing that the bill represented the best of all worlds, they offered no amendments of their own and spent the two days of debate defending the bill against attacks by McClory and others.

McClory's substitute bill was not offered until the final hours of debate and was defeated, 128-249. *(Vote 645, p. 184-H)*

The amendment would have eliminated the bill's key warrant requirement, and the requirement that the government produce evidence of criminal activity or intent before snooping on an American. It would have allowed surveillance of U.S. persons if certified by the president, the attorney general and an executive branch official confirmed by the Senate.

McClory argued that his substitute would retain accountability within the executive branch and avoid the risk of national security leaks that would arise from having federal courts hear warrant requests.

The overwhelming vote against the McClory substitute appeared to result largely from what was viewed as its failure to provide any significant new protections to U.S. citizens. McClory temporarily succeeded Sept. 6 in eliminating the warrant requirement for non-U.S. persons on an amendment adopted 178-176. *(Vote 640, p. 182-H)*

But while most House members were less concerned about warrantless taps against foreigners, intensive lobbying by the White House, leadership and intelligence agencies succeeded in convincing a majority in a subsequent vote that warrantless surveillance of foreigners could infringe on the Fourth Amendment rights of U.S. citizens to be secure from illegal searches.

When McClory's amendment eliminating the warrant requirement for foreigners was reconsidered Sept. 7, it was defeated, 176-200. *(Vote 646, p. 184-H)*

Special Court Dropped

The earlier vote on McClory's amendment had, however, resulted in adoption of another significant weakening amendment. Since most foreign intelligence surveillance is directed against foreigners, not U.S. citizens, and since warrants had been eliminated under the first vote on the McClory amendment, Allen E. Ertel, D-Pa., argued there was no need for the "special court" the bill would create to hear government warrant requests.

The House was persuaded by Ertel's logic and voted 224-103 to eliminate the special court provision, leaving the responsibility for hearing warrant requests in the federal district courts. *(Vote 641, p. 182-H)*

Sponsors believed a special court was necessary to assure that intelligence warrant applications would not be scattered in district courts all over the country, increasing the possibility of leaks. It was all but certain the special court provision, which was included in the Senate bill, would be agreed on in conference.

After passing HR 7308, the House tabled it and passed S 1566 with the language of the House bill substituted for that of the Senate bill.

Amendments Adopted

During floor consideration of HR 7308, the House adopted the following amendments:

- By John M. Ashbrook, R-Ohio, expanding the definition of "international terrorism" to include acts dangerous to property. The committee bill included only acts dangerous to human life.
- By Delbert L. Latta, R-Ohio, allowing the president to authorize warrantless electronic surveillance for up to one year during a war declared by Congress.
- By Ertel, allowing the House and Senate Intelligence committees to inform a U.S. person that he or she has been under surveillance, if the committees determine that no foreign intelligence information was obtained and that notification would not harm national security.
- By McClory, requiring that warrant applications be certified by both the assistant to the president for national security affairs and an executive branch official appointed by the president and confirmed by the Senate. The committee bill required only that one or the other certify applications.

• By Ashbrook, deleting the criminal penalties for intentional disclosure of information obtained and for violation of the minimization standards.

• By M. Caldwell Butler, R-Va., making the bill the exclusive "statutory" means by which electronic surveillance may be conducted.

Amendments Rejected

Among amendments or motions rejected:

• By McClory, to return the bill to committee with instructions to report it back with an amendment that would allow warrantless surveillance of official foreign powers. Rejected, 164-207. *(Vote 647, p. 184-H)*

• By McClory to delete the bill's criminal standard, under which the government would have to produce evidence that a crime was to be committed before it could obtain a warrant to conduct surveillance against a U. S. person.

• By Robert F. Drinan, D-Mass., to allow the phone company, landlords and others to refuse to assist in surveillance.

• By Jack F. Kemp, R-N.Y., to require the president to inform the House and Senate Intelligence committees when he has reason to believe an individual with diplomatic immunity is engaging in electronic surveillance in the United States, and to also inform the target of the surveillance and the foreign power if the president determines that to do so would not cause serious damage to national security. Rejected, 154-230. *(Vote 644, p. 184-H)*

After passing HR 7308, the House tabled it and passed S 1566 with the House bill substituted for the Senate version.

Conference Action

Conferees reached a compromise agreement (H Rept 95-1720) on S 1566 Oct. 4 after resolving five major differences between House and Senate versions of the bill. The most significant of these involved NSA surveillances.

NSA Exemption

An exemption for the NSA included in the House bill (HR 7308) confronted Senate conferees with an issue that struck at one of the underlying principles of their proposal — that there should be no warrantless electronic surveillances in the United States. The agreed-on compromise was characterized by one Senate aide as "an immense concession" on the part of the Senate.

Opposing the House provision, Edward M. Kennedy, D-Mass., a principal Senate sponsor of the bill, argued that 1) the exemption would place a "very very special burden" on an attorney general to know when an NSA surveillance would be legal, because it was not clear if an American would be the object of surveillance, and 2) that the exemption could grow into a means of circumventing the purpose of the bill. Kennedy wanted to know at whom exempted surveillances would be directed.

Edward P. Boland, D-Mass., chairman of the House Intelligence Committee, assured conferees that the House did not intend to allow surveillance of lines of communications carrying the conversations of U.S. persons. Morgan F. Murphy, D-Ill., said NSA chief B. R. Inman was concerned primarily with not having to disclose the "means" of surveillance in a warrant application.

And Boland warned that "weakening this provision, we would run into problems taking it [the bill] back to the House" for final approval.

The compromise, which remained far from self-explanatory, provided that the president, through the attorney general, could authorize warrantless surveillance without a court order for up to a year providing that the attorney general certified that the surveillance was directed at: 1) communications "exclusively between or among foreign powers" or 2) the "acquisition of technical intelligence" and not spoken communications emanating from property controlled by a foreign power.

The attorney general was further required to certify that there would be no substantial likelihood that the surveillance would acquire communications to which a U.S. person was a party and would have to report to congressional intelligence committees on NSA compliance with minimization procedures designed to prevent acquisition or dissemination of information falling outside the legal purview of the bill.

While the compromise provided that a certification of an NSA surveillance would be filed with a court, to protect the secret nature of the surveillance the certification would be kept under seal unless: 1) a district court raised a question as to the legality of the surveillance or, 2) the surveillance picked up communications of U.S. persons, in which case the contents could not be used and would have to be destroyed within 24 hours unless a court order were obtained in that period. In processing the court order, a judge could examine the original certification to see if it was legal.

Robert McClory, R-Ill., the leading opponent of the conference agreement, called this compromise "a charade of judicial involvement."

Special Court

The Senate bill contained a provision creating a special court with seven judges designated by the Chief Justice to hear applications for and to grant orders approving electronic surveillance. The bill also provided for a three-judge appeals court to review applications denied by the special court.

The special court had been knocked out of the House bill during floor debate, despite arguments that it was supported by the intelligence agencies.

Instead, the House bill provided that federal district courts throughout the country hear warrant requests. The sponsor of the House provision, Allen E. Ertel, D-Pa., sought to retain it in conference, insisting that the House had overwhelmingly voted not to create a special court.

But the House vote was based largely on the fact that it had previously eliminated the warrant requirement (later restored) for surveillances against foreigners, making the court largely unnecessary.

And Ertel's defense fell apart when he suggested that national security secrets would be safer held in several courts rather than at a single place, a proposition contradicted by each of the intelligence agencies and, conferees suggested, by common sense.

Conferees agreed to a compromise that eliminated the Senate's special court but created a new and distinct court constituted of seven district court judges from seven different judicial circuits appointed by the Chief Justice.

The compromise provided that the seven judges sit in Washington, D.C., on a rotating basis with at least two serving at any one time. Unlike the Senate bill, which would have had the judges handling only warrant applications, the compromise required the judges to handle normal judicial responsibilities as well.

Appeals of warrants denied by the court could be made to a three-judge panel of judges selected by the Chief Justice from the U.S. district courts or courts of appeals.

Foreign Powers

Conferees agreed to drop a provision in the House bill that sponsors of S 1566 said would allow U.S. intelligence agencies to wiretap members of foreign political parties visiting the United States.

An amendment adopted during House floor debate had changed the definition of a "foreign power" to include a "member" of a foreign power. The modified language applied to members of a foreign power engaged in international terrorist activities or in the preparation of such activities and expanded the scope of surveillance of so-called foreign powers to include domestic terrorist groups whose activities transcend national boundaries.

Inherent Power

A House floor amendment, sponsored by M. Caldwell Butler, R-Va., provided that S 1566 would be the exclusive "statutory" means by which electronic surveillance may be conducted for foreign intelligence gathering in the United States.

The single word "statutory" caused considerable concern on the part of sponsors of the bill, who argued that it would undermine a basic purpose of the bill — to circumscribe executive authority to conduct electronic surveillance — and could invite abuses based on claims of "inherent" or non-statutory powers.

McClory defended the inclusion of the word, contending that the president's "inherent constitutional powers" could not be eliminated by legislation.

Opponents of the provision insisted that if the president had "inherent constitutional powers" it was not Congress' responsibility to affirm them. Robert W. Kastenmeier, D-Wis., argued that "there should be no admission of constitutional inherent power. If the president has it, let him assert it."

Kennedy argued that inclusion of the provision would present a "basic stumbling block" to Senate acceptance of the bill. "There is no suggestion [in the Senate debate] that we are making a final and ultimate decision of the range of [executive] authority," Kennedy said. "Let the Supreme Court decide the issue."

Conferees agreed to drop the "statutory" language.

War Powers

Conferees also changed a House provision that would have allowed the president to conduct foreign intelligence surveillance without a court order during wartime for up to one year.

Senate conferees insisted that the wartime exemption was far too lenient and that the president needed authority to act only until Congress could change the law. Conferees agreed to provide warrantless surveillance by the president for up to 15 days.

Final Action

The Senate approved the conference report by voice vote Oct. 9. The House approved the measure Oct. 12, by a vote of 226-176, thus clearing S 1566 for the president. *(Vote 792, p. 226-H)* ▮

Nazi War Criminals

Congress Oct. 13 cleared a bill making it easier for the federal government to deport Nazi war criminals and more difficult for them to enter the United States.

The bill (HR 12509 — PL 95-549) amended the federal immigration and nationality law to exclude from admission into, and to allow deportation from, the United States all aliens who actively persecuted any person on the basis of race, religion, national origin or political opinion under the direction of the Nazi government of Germany.

House Action

The bill was reported to the House by the Committee on Judiciary Aug. 8 on a 20-5 vote (H Rept. 95-1452). The measure passed by the House Sept. 26 by voice vote was narrower in focus than the committee bill, which would have applied to any alien who engaged in persecution on the basis of race, religion, national origin or political opinion.

The bill was tightened through an amendment attached by the floor manager of the bill, Elizabeth Holtzman, D-N.Y., with the support of the subcommittee on immigration. Critics had objected that the term "persecuted" was not defined in the committee bill and could include British soldiers who "persecuted" Catholics in Northern Ireland and white South Africans or Rhodesians who support their governments.

HR 12509 was designed to plug a loophole in the Immigration and Nationality Act that prevented the Immigration Service from taking action to deport suspected Nazi war criminals and to keep out others who wanted to visit the United States. The measure was supported by the departments of Justice and State.

According to Holtzman, "The presence of Nazi war criminals in the United States constitutes the unfinished business of World War II. By taking a forthright stand against allowing these mass murderers a haven in this country, we will not only reaffirm our commitment to human rights but we will be making it clear that persecution in any form is repugnant to democracy and to our way of life."

But what Holtzman and others characterized as "non-controversial" legislation, did not escape criticism from Charles E. Wiggins, R-Calif., on constitutional grounds.

Wiggins "reluctantly" opposed the bill because, he said, it would amount to an ex post facto law and might amount to punishment through legislation.

Because the bill focused solely on Nazi war criminals and because the committee had specific individuals in mind, Wiggins said it might be a bill of attainder, that is, a legislative act that inflicts punishment on named individuals or easily ascertainable members of a group without giving those persons the benefit of a judicial trial.

According to Wiggins, the two Nazis the committee members wanted deported entered the U.S. lawfully and had resided peacefully as citizens or resident aliens.

Holtzman countered that the bill was aimed at a class of individuals, the exact number of whom was not known, and that the Supreme Court had ruled that Congress had the constitutional power to permit deportation of aliens retroactively.

"There is no statute of limitations on murder and there should be no statute of limitations on mass murder," Holtzman concluded.

Senate, Final Action

A similar Senate bill, S 2097, was pending before a Senate Judiciary subcommittee. The panel was discharged, and the Senate Oct. 10 passed HR 12509 by voice vote after adding a second title to the bill that continued for one full year funding for the Indochinese refugee assistance program. The bill, as amended, passed the House under suspension of the rules Oct. 13, clearing the measure for the president.

Antitrust Violations

House and Senate Judiciary Committees in 1978 approved separate bills to overturn a 1977 Supreme Court decision that drastically limited the ability of consumers, businesses and governments to collect damages resulting from antitrust violations.

However, a filibuster threat in the Senate prevented the bill from being scheduled. And the House leadership was unwilling to schedule the bill when it saw no chance of Senate approval. Consequently, the bill died.

The bills (HR 11942 and S 1874) would allow individuals or groups to sue for damages resulting from price fixing, monopolies or bid rigging, even if they were not directly affected by the antitrust violations.

Both committees reported the bills by split votes.

The bills would overturn the high court's ruling in *Illinois Brick v. Illinois*. In that case the state of Illinois and 700 state and local governmental agencies charged that a price-fixing conspiracy by 11 concrete block manufacturers had resulted in $3 million in overcharges.

In a 6-3 decision the Supreme Court ruled that only the first purchaser — and not the state, which made its purchases through a middleman — could recover damages. The limitation of suits to "direct" purchasers shut out "others in the chain of manufacture or distribution" even if they could show they suffered financial losses. *(1977 Almanac p. 4-A)*

According to proponents of the House and Senate bills, the *Illinois Brick* ruling all but nullified the 1976 *parens patriae* act (PL 94-435), under which Congress gave state attorneys general authority to sue on behalf of consumers victimized by price-fixing schemes. *(1976 Almanac p. 431)*

That act was designed to provide a mechanism for dealing with "potato chip conspiracies," where millions of persons may suffer small losses due to an antitrust violation worth millions of dollars to its perpetrators.

"The entire purpose of the *parens patriae* amendments," stated the Senate report (S Rept 95-934), "was to provide an effective remedy for consumers, and consumers rarely deal directly with antitrust violators."

As a result of *Illinois Brick*, proponents of the proposed bills charged, the principal purposes of federal antitrust laws — to provide for enforcement by private parties who have been damaged and to compensate the victims of crime — were seriously undermined.

Direct Purchaser Suits

Opponents of the proposed bills, and a majority of the Supreme Court, argued that the difficulty of proving that overcharges were passed on by a direct purchaser should preclude suits below the level of the direct purchaser. But proponents countered that direct purchasers were unlikely to sue because it would be easier for them to pass the costs on to the consumer.

Proponents said the direct purchaser's interest in maintaining good relations with his source of supplies — on which he is commercially dependent — would act as a powerful disincentive to such suits.

The failure of direct purchasers to protect themselves and their customers against inflated prices resulting from price fixing was illustrated by a case cited in the House report. In that case, out of 2,000 retailers purchasing wheelchairs from a monopoly supplier, not one filed suit, preferring instead to simply pass on the costs.

According to the House report (H Rept 95-1397), "the real victims — the paralyzed and disabled consumers who have no choice but to buy the defendant's products — cannot even be heard in court."

The Senate report on the bill estimated that failure to reverse *Illinois Brick* would cost state governments $500 million from dismissal of pending cases where goods were purchased through middlemen. The House estimated the cost to the federal government at $205 million in four pending cases alone.

'Pass-On' Defense

In giving indirect purchasers a right to sue, the House Judiciary Committee sought to protect defendants from multiple suits.

Committee members reasoned that the number of groups suffering damages could rapidly snowball and a violator could be subject to damages exceeding the triple damages provided in U.S. antitrust law.

According to the House report a defendant "might be liable to a first purchaser for the total overcharge — and in a subsequent suit be held liable as well to indirect purchasers for the portion of the same overcharge probably passed on to them. Such a result (100 percent of the overcharge to the first purchaser, and for example, 60 percent of the overcharge to the indirect purchaser) would unjustly wreak duplicative damages upon defendants."

Ironically, while providing a mechanism for avoiding such duplicative damages, both House and Senate reports noted that there had not been a single case involving multiple recovery of damages during the period prior to the *Illinois Brick* decision, when those damaged directly as well as those damaged indirectly were free to sue.

The protection the committees proposed was a "pass-on defense." Here's how it would work: If defendant A could show that the person bringing the suit, distributor B for example, passed on the overcharges of A's price-fixing conspiracy to retailer C, the defendant would not be liable for damages to B. Nor would A be liable for damages to C if he could show that C passed on the costs to consumers D, E and F and so on.

In providing this defense, the committees partially overturned the Supreme Court's ruling in *Hanover Shoe Inc. v. United Shoe Machinery Corp.* (1968), where the court refused to excuse a defendant who argued that the direct purchaser was not injured because he passed on the overcharges to indirect purchasers.

Those critical of this provision argued that in some instances defendants would play a shell game, avoiding all liability by proving that each particular purchaser in turn passed on the overcharge to someone else.

The Senate bill provided, however, that the defendant who uses this defense show not only that damages were passed on but that they were passed on to someone entitled to recover damages. A House Judiciary aide said HR 11942 would put the defendant in the position of naming persons who could sue him.

According to the Senate report, "The pass-on defense is thus to be allowed only where it does not inhibit the private enforcement of the antitrust laws or create a hiatus in enforcement."

Minority Views

Opponents of the committee bills said they would fail to accomplish their stated goals and would in fact have the reverse effect. Opponents said the bills would: 1) destroy effective antitrust enforcement, 2) deny recovery to the injured and, 3) diminish deterrence of antitrust violations.

The thrust of the minority views was that antitrust laws should be applied fairly and consistently to all damaged parties. Minority views in the House report repeatedly suggested that the signators were looking for stronger antitrust measures than the committee provided.

For example, the minority bemoaned the fact that the bill "reaches only 'purchasers' and 'sellers' " and therefore "excludes creditors, landlords, stockholders, corporate employees, and others even though they were injured."

The minority deplored the bill's exclusion of those purchasers and sellers who are not "in the chain" of manufacture, production or distribution of goods and services. And while the minority opposed inclusion of indirect purchasers in the bill, it complained that the bill unfairly allowed them reduced compensation.

The minority concluded that "if consumers are the ultimate injured party, then neither this bill nor current law provides a generally workable method for putting money back in their pockets."

But what the minority proposed was largely existing law. "The way to help consumers who bear the brunt of illegal overcharges is to prevent the violations from occurring," the House minority view stated. It saw "the true burden of antitrust enforcement" relying on private treble damage actions, specifically actions by direct purchasers.

While proponents of the bill said existing law provided disincentives to such direct purchaser suits, the minority members concluded that HR 11942 itself would discourage such suits in favor of suits and collection of damages by middlemen — including, in some cases, parties that are not injured.

The minority argued that allowing indirect purchasers to sue in addition to direct purchasers would result in a crowded field of claimants and smaller recoveries to the ultimate victors. As a result, they argued, the direct purchasers would be less likely to sue.

Finally, the minority argued, the pass-on defense combined with overturning *Illinois Brick* would result in an "orgy of discovery" as the entire chain of direct and indirect purchasers attempted to establish their injuries. The minority argued that proof of injury beyond the direct purchaser level is difficult and merely complicates the legal process. "It can hardly be denied that the bill would make a process that is already too complex, too slow, and too expensive, insufferable."

Provisions

The Senate Judiciary Committee reported S 1874 the "Antitrust Enforcement Act of 1978," on June 14 (S Rept 95-934). The vote to report the bill was 9-5.

The House Judiciary Committee reported HR 11942, the "Clayton Act Amendments of 1978," on July 26 (H Rept 95-1397). The vote to report that bill was 21-12.

As reported, the bills:

- Reversed the Supreme Court's ruling in *Illinois Brick v. Illinois*, allowing indirect purchasers who proved they suffered damages as a result of violations of federal antitrust law to sue for triple damages as was provided by federal antitrust law since 1890.
- Reversed, in part, the Supreme Court's ruling in *Hanover Shoe v. United Shoe Machinery Corp.*, providing defendants in antitrust actions a pass-on defense exempting them from liability if they could show the company or person bringing the suit passed on the costs of a price-fixing conspiracy.
- Reversed the Supreme Court's ruling, in *Pfizer Inc. v. Government of India*, that a foreign government could sue for triple damages in a U.S. court to recover financial losses resulting from violations of U.S. antitrust laws. (The Senate bill limited recovery by foreign governments to actual damages, while the House bill allowed no recovery by foreign governments.)
- Continued the broad discretion of federal court judges to determine on a case-by-case basis where to cut off a chain of overcharges passed on as the result of a price-fixing conspiracy — that is, determining when an individual claiming damages is too "remote" from the antitrust offense to prove a claim.

Legal Questions

The kinds of questions the courts would have to determine were raised in minority views opposing the bill: "Under the bill, can suit be brought by a retailer who purchased personalized stationery made from price-fixed paper? Is the answer different for the retailer who purchased books? Can suit be brought by a retailer who purchased television sets containing price-fixed picture tubes? Is the answer different for price-fixed printed circuits?"

The House bill would be retroactive to June 9, 1977, the date of the *Illinois Brick* decision. The House drug company amendment would be effective upon enactment. The Senate bill, including its drug company amendment, would be effective upon enactment.

Support and Opposition

Both S 1874 and HR 11942 were highly controversial and were the subject of concerted business lobbying.

The bills were supported by the Carter administration — with reservations — and by all 50 states' attorneys general, represented by the National Association of Attorneys General. Ralph Nader's Congress Watch and a wide range of consumer groups, small business operators and unions also supported the bills.

They were opposed by the Business Roundtable, the U.S. Chamber of Commerce and other big-business groups.

Foremost among Senate opponents of the bill was Orrin G. Hatch, R-Utah, who said he felt the measure was a lawyers' relief bill in disguise. Hatch introduced more than 100 amendments to the bill and threatened to offer up to 300 if the bill came to the Senate floor.

Although the bill never reached the floor of either chamber in 1978, it was likely that Edward M. Kennedy, D-Mass., the principal Senate sponsor, would introduce a more comprehensive bill in the 96th Congress — one that could prove even less satisfactory to the critics of the bills reported in the 95th.

Rape Victim Privacy

Legislation to protect the privacy of rape victims in federal trials received final approval from Congress Oct. 12.

The bill (HR 4727 — PL 95-540) limited the circumstances in which evidence about a rape victim's past sexual conduct would be admissible in a federal rape trial and set strict limits on the introduction of such evidence.

The bill was designed to prevent the routine use of evidence of a victim's prior sexual behavior, evidence that Rep. James R. Mann, D-S.C., said "quite often serves no real purpose and only results in embarrassment to the rape victim and unwarranted public intrusion into her private life."

While rape offenses normally were tried in state courts and more than 30 states already had limited the kinds of questions that can be asked a rape victim, sponsors saw the bill as a model for the remaining states to reform their evidentiary proceedings in rape trials.

Sponsors argued that the lack of limitations on the questioning of rape victims resulted in the failure of many victims to report the crime. Rep. Elizabeth Holtzman, D-N.Y., the principal sponsor of the bill argued that, "Since rape trials become inquisitions into the victim's morality, not trials of the defendant's innocence or guilt, it is not surprising that it is the least reported crime." Holtzman said that as few as one in 10 rapes are reported.

Birch Bayh, D-Ind., who sponsored the bill in the Senate, cited a study in Denver that showed more than 43 percent of reported rapes during the study period were never prosecuted because the victim refused to testify against the defendant.

Legislative History

The Senate approved the bill by voice vote Oct. 12, as passed by the House Oct. 10. There was no opposition in either chamber.

Neither the House nor the Senate held any hearings on the bill in the 95th Congress, although hearings were held on similar legislation in the 94th Congress. Neither the House nor the Senate Judiciary Committee issued a report on the bill. In fact, the Senate Judiciary Committee never even considered it, although similar provisions had been incorporated in the Senate's criminal code reform bill, a measure that passed the Senate Jan. 30 but died in the House. *(Story, p. 165)*

A House Judiciary subcommittee reported the bill, which had 100 House cosponsors, after one of day of markup. It was never officially reported by the full committee, however, because the panel didn't have a quorum the day it was brought up. Thus the bill had to be brought up in the House under suspension of the rules, a procedure normally reserved for non-controversial measures such as the rape bill but requiring a two-thirds majority for passage. Since no one demanded a record vote in the House, however, none was taken.

Provisions

As cleared, HR 4727 created a new federal rule of evidence designed to protect the privacy rights of rape victims. The bill:

- Prohibited the use in evidence of reputation or opinion about the past sexual behavior of the victim in criminal prosecutions for rape or assault with intent to commit rape.
- Restricted the use of direct evidence of past sexual behavior of the victim of a rape or an assault with intent to commit rape to three situations:

1) Where the judge finds after a hearing that admission of the evidence is required under the Constitution.

2) Where the judge finds after a hearing that the past sexual behavior of the victim was with a person other than the accused and that the evidence of that behavior was offered to show that someone other than the accused was the source of semen or injury.

3) Where the judge finds after a hearing that the past sexual behavior of the victim was with the accused and that the evidence of that behavior was offered by the accused solely on the issue of consent.

In the second two cases the evidence could be admitted only if the court found that it was relevant and that its probative value outweighed the danger of unfair prejudice to the victim. In all cases where evidence about the victim's past sexual behavior was admissible, the bill provided that there must first be a private proceeding in the judge's chambers out of the presence of the jury and the general public at which the judge determined the admissibility of the evidence.

Crime Victims Aid

Both chambers passed bills to provide federal funds to states to compensate victims of violent crimes, but the House killed the compromise legislation Oct. 14, on a 184-199 vote. *(Vote 820, p. 232-H)*

The compromise on the bill, the Victims of Crime Act of 1978 (HR 7010), had been worked out by a House-Senate conference committee and reported back to both chambers on Oct. 11 (H Rept 95-1762).

On Oct. 15, the Senate adopted the conference report on a voice vote. The Senate had passed bills to compensate victims of crime in two previous Congresses.

While the House had passed a similar crime victim bill Sept. 30, 1977, on a 192-173 vote, arguments that the cost of the bill had escalated and that a key amendment had been deleted by conferees seemed to prevail when the conference report came up for a final vote.

Charles E. Wiggins, R-Calif., argued that the cost had gone from $90 million to $120 million and that the bill would "become the food stamp program of the Department of Justice . . . the snail darter program that will bring down the Department of Justice." Wiggins said the funding the measure was only the "tip of the iceberg."

Opponents of the bill also objected that an amendment was deleted by conferees that would have set up accounts to benefit victims of federal crimes from book royalties and similar profits accruing to criminals.

Senate Action

The Senate Judiciary Committee June 28 reported its version of a bill (S 551) providing aid to victims of violent crimes (S Rept 95-963).

The bill would provide such states with grants covering 25 percent of the amount they paid to crime victims. The federal grant would not include the state's administrative costs, and would also exclude any amount awarded for pain and suffering, property loss or the part of any award that exceeds $50,000.

The basic provisions of the bill were similar to those in a measure (HR 7010) passed by the House in 1977. *(1977 Almanac p. 570)*

Under the House bill, however, the maximum award to any victim was $25,000, not $50,000.

The House bill also required states to meet several criteria to be eligible for federal reimbursement, while S 551 merely stated that states must "substantially" comply with the criteria.

Both bills would cover 100 percent of compensation paid to victims of crimes subject to federal jurisdiction, including crimes committed on federal property such as a military installation or crimes subject to federal law such as the robbery of a federally insured bank.

Twenty states had programs to compensate victims of violent crimes to cover medical bills, lost wages and other expenses, according to the Judiciary Committee report on S 551.

The report said that the criminal justice system "should be considered to embrace the interests of innocent victims of the criminal, as well as the interests of society as a whole and of the criminal."

It said that the magnitude of the crime problem had put a "severe financial strain" on many states and localities, and that the bill would continue a pattern of federal assistance to the states in many areas of the criminal justice system.

While the bill authorized $40 million in fiscal 1979 with $10 million increments in 1980 and 1981, the report included Congressional Budget Office estimates that the program would cost less than $20 million annually in 1979-81.

The Justice Department told the committee that it endorsed "the basic concept of S 551." However, it suggested that compensation be limited to injuries or death from violent crimes, and that the $50,000 maximum award be lowered to $20,000.

As currently drawn, S 551 "would provide compensation for physical injury or death caused by any criminal act or omission designated by a state," Assistant Attorney General Patricia M. Wald said in a letter to the panel.

"As a result, injuries resulting from criminal negligence, such as reckless driving, might be required to be compensated in whole or in part by the federal government. Also covered might be personal expenses caused by pollution offenses or criminal violations of safety regulations, even though such offenses are not of the nature that have prompted the call for compensation programs."

Provisions

As reported by the Judiciary Committee, S 551:

- Empowered the attorney general to administer the program with the help of a nine-member advisory committee.
- Directed the attorney general to make annual grants to a qualifying state program to cover 25 percent of the compensation for all victims of crimes and 100 percent for crimes subject to exclusive federal jurisdiction such as federal Indian reservations.
- Required a state program to "substantially" meet the following requirements to be eligible for federal reimbursement:

—compensation for personal injuries must be offered to victims of crimes or to surviving dependents if the victim dies as a result of the crime;

—claimants must have the right to a hearing with administrative or judicial review;

—claimants must cooperate with law enforcement officials;

—the financial means of the victim may not be a factor in approving or denying compensation;

—law enforcement officials and agencies must make a reasonable effort to inform crime victims of the program;

—the state must be able to recover from the victim any monies paid to him by the person who committed the crime, up to the amount the state paid to him;

—the state may not require victims seeking compensation to take welfare benefits unless they already were receiving them;

—the program must deny or reduce any claim if the victim contributed to the injury;

—the state must have in effect a law or rule under which the perpetrator of a crime may have to make restitution to the victim or surviving dependent;

—apprehension, prosecution or conviction of the perpetrator cannot be made a condition of an award to the victim or surviving dependents.

- Excluded federal reimbursement for a variety of state expenses, including:

—administrative expenses;

—any amount recovered by the state through legal action against the person who committed the crime or for which the victim has received restitution;

—awards for pain and suffering;

—awards for property loss;

—compensation to any victim in excess of $50,000;

—compensation to any claimant who is entitled to receive compensation from any other source, up to the amount of that compensation;

—awards of less than $100 and for lost earnings based on the loss of less than five work days;

—any awards exceeding $200 a week for lost earnings;

—any award to a claimant who failed to file a claim within one year after the crime, unless the agency found "good cause" for the delay;

—any award to a victim who did not report the crime within 72 hours without "good cause."

- Required the attorney general to report annually to Congress with a statistical description of claims and awards and projected expenditures for the next fiscal year.
- Made the act effective on enactment, with the advisory committee provision to take effect six months later.
- Authorized appropriations of $40 million for fiscal 1979, $50 million for fiscal 1980 and $60 million for fiscal 1981.

Floor Action

The Senate passed the bill Sept. 11 on a voice vote and with no debate. Before passing the bill (HR 7010), the Senate amended it by inserting the text of S 551, which contained language that states must "substantially" comply with criteria to be eligible for federal reimbursement (the House version made compliance mandatory).

Conference Action

The conference report provided that a qualifying state victim compensation program was eligible for a grant of assistance equal to 25 percent of its "cost of paying compensation" to victims of state crimes. It also provided for a grant equal to 100 percent of the "cost of paying compensation" to victims of federal crimes occurring in a state where compensation is paid for similar state crimes (H Rept 95-1762).

Federal payments to the program would not cover state administrative costs.

The maximum federal grant for any victim would be $35,000. The House bill had provided $25,000 and the Senate bill $50,000.

The conference report provided that states could qualify for federal grants if they had a state crime victim compensation program in place that:

- Offered compensation for loss resulting from injury or death caused by a crime.
- Offered judicial or administrative review to an aggrieved claimant.
- Required that claimants cooperate with law enforcement authorities.
- Did not require that a claimant accept welfare benefits unless the claimant was receiving such benefits prior to the crime.
- Denied or reduced a claim if the victim was partially at fault.
- Were able to require that convicted wrongdoers make restitution.
- Did not require, as a condition for an award to a victim, that the wrongdoer be caught, prosecuted or convicted. ▮

Immigration Ceilings

In a move to equalize the treatment of Eastern and Western hemisphere immigrants to the United States, Congress Sept. 20 cleared a bill to establish a single worldwide ceiling to control immigration (PL 95-412).

The measure (HR 12443) combined in the quota — totaling 290,000 — the existing separate ceilings of 170,000 for Eastern Hemisphere immigrants and 120,000 for those from Western Hemisphere countries.

Under the bill, a seven-category preference system would apply equally to all immigrants, without regard to place of origin. A speedup in the timetable for acquiring citizenship, previously available only to refugees from communist and Middle Eastern countries, would be extended to all refugees.

The House Judiciary Committee reported HR 12443 (H Rept 95-1206) on May 18.

The House passed HR 12443 by a 396-20 vote. *(Vote 485, p. 138-H)*

The Senate passed the bill Sept. 20 by voice vote and with no debate, clearing it for the president.

Adoption of a single ceiling represented the third step in a process of immigration reform begun in 1965, when Congress amended the Immigration and Nationality Act of 1952.

The 1965 act eliminated the national origins quota system, which had controlled the flow of immigrants into the United States since the 1920s.

The act endorsed the separate treatment of Eastern and Western hemisphere immigrants. But no country limit or preference system controlled immigration from Western Hemisphere countries. Immigrants from those countries were therefore compelled to seek admission into the United States on a first-come, first-served basis. The result was an eventual backlog of 300,000 applicants for admission.

The situation in Western Hemisphere countries was in sharp contrast to that in the Eastern Hemisphere, where immigrants eligible for admission under one of the family relationship preference categories generally were able to enter the United States immediately.

Legislation in 1976 sought to lessen the disparity in the treatment given immigrants of the two hemispheres. However, because demand under a particular preference system was frequently higher in one hemisphere than in the other, the unequal treatment continued.

Related Actions. Congress Sept. 20 cleared legislation (HR 12508 — PL 95-417) to allow parents of two adopted children to adopt more children under the immigration preference provision of the Immigration and Nationality Act. The bill also liberalized immigration and citizenship requirements for children of parents applying for U.S. naturalization.

Under existing law, additional adopted children had been considered under a non-preference status, along with regular immigration quota applicants, a process that could entail years of waiting.

The House Judiciary Committee reported the bill June 16 (H Rept 95-1301), and the measure passed the House July 18, 413-0. *(Vote 486, p. 138-H)*

The Senate passed HR 12508 Sept. 20 by voice vote and without debate, clearing the bill for the president.

In another action on immigration law, Congress Sept. 28 cleared a bill (PL 95-432) that repealed various unconstitutional, meaningless and unnecessary sections of the Immigration and Nationality Act.

The key provision of the bill (HR 13349) repealed a section requiring a U.S. citizen born outside the United States to one citizen parent and one alien parent to reside in the United States for two years after the age of 14 and before the age of 28. Failure to return could result in a loss of citizenship.

The provision caused hardship to U.S. citizens who lived abroad working for the U.S. government or U.S. corporations.

HR 13349 was reported to the House by the Judiciary Committee Aug. 15 (H Rept 95-1493). The bill was supported by the Justice Department and the Department of State and had no official opposition.

The legislation passed the House Sept. 19 by voice vote and without debate. It passed the Senate Sept. 28. ▮

Judicial Tenure

The running constitutional debate over impeachment returned to Congress Sept. 7, when the Senate passed a bill (S 1423) that would establish an alternative mechanism for removing federal judges from office. However, the House Judiciary Committee held no hearings on the measure, so the bill died at the end of the 95th Congress.

Such a mechanism had been debated for 30 years in the Senate, but S 1423 was the first of its kind to reach the floor of either the House or the Senate.

On a 43-31 vote, the Senate passed the Judicial Tenure Act to establish within the judicial branch a system for investigating and resolving allegations that the condition or conduct of a federal judge requires his or her removal from the bench. *(Vote 371, p. 55-S)*

The bill would create a commission of 12 federal judges to hear complaints against judges and prosecute the most serious ones before a new Court on Judicial Conduct and Disability.

Debate over the bill focused on the constitutionality of the proposed mechanism, an issue that ultimately would have to be decided by the Supreme Court.

Groundwork Laid

While inconclusive, the Senate's constitutional debate laid the groundwork for a more protracted dialogue in the 96th Congress that would hinge on the question of whether federal judges can be removed:

1) only *for* treason, bribery or other high crimes and misdemeanors as provided by Article II of the Constitution, and only *by* Congress to which Article I gave sole impeachment authority or,

2) by other judges based on Article III of the Constitution which states that "Judges, both of Supreme and Inferior Courts, shall hold their offices during good behavior."

Proponents of the Senate-passed bill based their argument for the constitutionality of the proposal on the "good behavior" clause. Opponents argued that impeachment, as provided by Articles I and II, was the only mechanism for removing judges.

Background

Congress historically has been extremely reluctant to use impeachment to remove federal judges from the bench. Impeachment is viewed as a drastic measure as well as being time-consuming. Senate impeachment trials have lasted as long as six weeks, the average trial lasting 16 days.

Only eight federal judges and one Supreme Court justice have been impeached by the House and of those, only four judges were convicted by the Senate and removed from office. The most recent conviction was in 1936.

Because impeachment currently was the only means for removing federal judges, who are life-tenured, and because it had been applied so infrequently, it was widely viewed as an inadequate deterrent to misconduct on the bench — a "mere scarecrow" as Thomas Jefferson put it. And because Congress had not used impeachment in recent cases, such as one involving an allegedly senile chief judge, the Senate Judiciary Committee sought to provide a mechanism less extreme than impeachment.

S 1423 was designed to allow removal of a judge from office in a situation where his or her conduct was deemed inconsistent with constitutional requirements but where Congress would be reluctant to resort to impeachment.

Committee Action

S 1423 was reported to the Senate by the Committee on Judiciary July 24 on a voice vote. Minority views accompanying the committee report (S Rept 95-1035) were submitted by Charles McC. Mathias Jr., R-Md., and Birch Bayh, D-Ind., who led the opposition to the bill on the Senate floor.

Floor Action

Arguments based on the intentions of the Founding Fathers in drafting the Constitution as well as interpretations of the English common law in which the Constitution is rooted, dominated the Senate debate. Pragmatic considerations largely took a back seat to the more esoteric and often highly technical constitutional considerations.

Dennis DeConcini, D-Ariz., who floor-managed the bill for proponents, argued that "we owe constituents an accessible means of protesting judicial conduct that is inconsistent with the behavior required by the Constitution. Conversely, we owe federal judges an alternative to the stigma attached to impeachment proceedings in those cases where aberrant behavior is the innocent product of a poor mental or physical condition."

Sam Nunn, D-Ga., a principal sponsor of the legislation, argued that "congressional inaction on the subject of judicial tenure and discipline has resulted in one of the three branches of government being virtually unaccountable to anyone, even itself."

Opponents, such as Bayh and Mathias, argued that the Judiciary Committee had not heard from enough opponents of the bill. They also objected that the bill would create a mechanism for removing unpopular judges or those who violate social customs.

"The test of a good judge is not whether he can win a popularity contest," Bayh said. He insisted there were "less drastic" alternatives to S 1423, which he said would be constitutional. Bayh suggested "better, more thorough selection methods [for judges], strengthened inter-judicial circuit discipline, and refined pre-impeachment procedures by which impeachment could become an effective mechanism when deemed to be necessary."

Before passing S 1423, the Senate approved a DeConcini motion to table (kill) a Bayh motion that would have recommitted the bill to the Judiciary Committee for further consideration. The tabling motion was agreed to on a 43-33 vote. *(Vote 370, p. 55-S)*

Provisions

As passed by the Senate Sept. 7, S 1423:

- Provided that any individual could file a complaint alleging judicial misconduct or permanent mental or physical disability.
- Established within the judicial branch three components for handling complaints alleging judicial misconduct or permanent mental or physical disability: 1) a committee made up of judges from each circuit or each of the special national courts (Court of Claims, Court of Customs and Patent Appeals, and the Customs Court) to investigate and make recommendations on complaints to, 2) a Judicial Conduct and Disability Commission that may dismiss a case, initiate further investigation and, in cases where it finds conduct inconsistent with the "good behavior" requirement, recommend a formal hearing before, 3) a newly created Court on Judicial Conduct and Disability.
- Provided that the Court on Judicial Conduct could order involuntary retirement, removal, censure or dismissal of a case.
- Provided that either the commission or the judge may seek review of a case by the Supreme Court.
- Authorized the court, in cases involving allegations against Supreme Court justices, to prepare reports to the House recommending that a justice be impeached or censured, or to dismiss the case.

Off-Track Betting

A bill allowing interstate off-track betting (OTB) on horse races, under certain conditions, cleared Congress Oct. 10 (S 1185 — PL 95-515).

The Senate originally passed the bill by voice vote Sept. 26. The House passed an identical bill (HR 14089) also by voice vote Oct. 10, then laid it aside for the Senate measure, thus clearing it for the president.

Though the bill passed easily in both houses, it was not without controversy. Rep. Carlos J. Moorhead, R-Calif., reminded the House that it had overwhelmingly passed a bill in 1976 banning all interstate OTB arrangements. That bill died for lack of time at the end of the 94th Congress. *(1976 Almanac p. 427)*

PRO: 'Peaceful Coexistence'

Supporters of the 1978 bill, in both the House Commerce and Senate Judiciary Committee reports (H Rept 95-1733, S Rept 95-1117) argued that it was necessary for the fiscal health and stability of the racing industry.

"The racing industry expressed concern that unregulated proliferation of interstate OTB could result in diminished employment...and serious damage" to many tracks, especially smaller tracks — and to state revenue from all tracks, the Senate report said.

Supporting the point on the floor, Sen. Warren G. Magnuson, D-Wash., said that Narragansett Race Track in Rhode Island had closed recently, partly because of competition from off-track betting.

"Narragansett just folded up," Magnuson said, "because a fellow could pick up a phone and call New York and make a bet on Aqueduct or Belmont...."

The Senate report noted fears that federal prohibition of interstate OTB would "seriously abridge" state prerogatives in regulating gambling.

At congressional urging, the racing and OTB industries accepted the S 1185 approach of regulating interstate OTB rather than banning it. Supporters claimed this protected both OTB and racing — a $13 billion business, according to Magnuson. The state and local share of OTB receipts in New York and Connecticut — the only OTB states at the time — was $128 million, according to the Senate report.

Supporters of the bill included members from the OTB states of New York and Connecticut, along with others from states that have race tracks.

Sen. Wendell H. Ford, D-Ky., said the bill allowed for "peaceful co-existence" among tracks, states and OTB systems in other states.

CON: 'Encourages Gambling'

Moorhead said that he opposed the bill on ethical grounds. In a dissent to the House committee report, he said that "the whole purpose of the bill is to encourage, aid and abet the fundamental form of gambling which has contributed to the ruin of many families.... The bill...appeals to non-productive, and often immoral, gambling instincts."

During Senate consideration, Adlai E. Stevenson III, D-Ill., objected to allowing race track owners and horse breeders to veto interstate OTB on races in which they are involved. The bill, Stevenson said, tells states that "this [OTB] is no longer a matter of public policy, it is not a matter for the state government to decide.... This, now, is a matter for the industry to decide."

A Stevenson amendment to delete the veto provisions was tabled (killed) Sept. 26, 75-6. *(Vote 405, p. 60-S)*

Despite placating assurances by both committees, about the effects on Nevada bookmakers, Nevada's Democratic Sen. Howard W. Cannon and Rep. Jim Santini opposed the bill. It "substitutes the judgment of the federal government for that of the states in an area — gambling — that...should remain the right and prerogative of the states," Cannon said. Gambling is Nevada's major industry.

Provisions

As cleared, S 1185 prohibited interstate OTB in one state on races in another state except when OTB is approved:

- On a particular race by the sponsoring track, which informs its state's racing commission.
- By the racing commissions of the two states involved.
- By the track after consultations with horse owners and breeders operating there, under a written agreement.
- During a racing season only after consent is obtained from all operating tracks within 60 miles of the OTB office, if the season is fewer than 250 racing days (in order to protect local markets).

The bill also:

- Prohibited (with some exceptions) a state from taking a larger cut of interstate OTB receipts than the state of the affected track takes on a given race.
- Provided for civil suits by states, commissions and tracks against violators.
- Provided for exceptions to the consent rule on days when the track is not running and for 25 "nationally significant" races, such as the Kentucky Derby.

Diplomatic Immunity

Legislation (HR 7819 — PL 95-393) to strip diplomats' staffs and servants of full criminal and civil immunity granted by the United States since 1790 was sent to the president Sept. 18, after the House agreed to the version approved by the Senate Aug. 17.

The House approved the amended bill by a 397-7 vote, clearing it for the president. *(Vote 698, p. 198-H)*

The House passed an earlier version by voice vote July 27, 1977 (H Rept 95-526). The Senate acted Aug. 17, 1978, passing it by voice vote as reported by the Foreign Relations Committee June 26 (S Rept 95-958) and the Judiciary Committee Aug. 11 (S Rept 95-1108).

Besides defining which diplomatic personnel were entitled to immunity from U.S. civil and criminal laws, the bill, at the Senate's suggestion, gave U.S. citizens involved in accidents with diplomats who claimed full immunity to proceed, for the first time, directly against the insurance company holding the diplomat's policy. This provision was expected to ease problems for residents of Washington, D.C., and New York, particularly, who had no recourse for recovering damages when involved in accidents with members of foreign delegations.

HR 7819 also required foreign diplomats to carry liability insurance when operating motor vehicles here.

The law replaced the outmoded 1790 statute defining diplomatic immunity with the Vienna Convention on Diplomatic Relations ratified by the United States in 1972.

Under the Vienna Convention, 4,000 of 6,000 embassy employees in the Washington area would be subject for the first time to civil suits arising from auto accidents, apartment leases, bad checks or other personal contracts.

While the private servants in a diplomat's household were granted full immunity under the 1790 statute, they would lose this protection entirely under the convention and HR 7819. Diplomats themselves as well as their families would continue to enjoy full protection from civil and criminal suits.

Professional staff members would be immune from civil laws, but only when acting in an official capacity, including, for example, driving to a party when required as part of their work. Professional members would continue to receive full criminal immunity.

Families of these staff members would have criminal immunity but no protection from civil suits.

Service staff would be immune from civil and criminal suits — but only in connection with their work. Their families would have no protection.

Combined Magistrates-Diversity Bill Dies

A largely non-controversial bill to expand the role of magistrates in federal court proceedings became caught up in an effort to salvage another House Judiciary Committee bill during the closing days of the 95th Congress.

The gamble failed and both bills ended up dying in a conference committee.

The bills involved were S 1613, the magistrates bill, and HR 9622, which would have abolished "diversity jurisdiction," a legal procedure providing a court forum in disputes between persons who are not from the same state.

While the magistrates bill had passed both the House and Senate with ease, the diversity legislation bill had been the subject of intense debate for at least a decade. A filibuster in the Senate Judiciary Committee had prevented the committee from sending a diversity bill to the floor, but the House had passed HR 9622 by a two-thirds majority.

Diversity Bill

House Committee Action

HR 9622 was approved by the House Judiciary Committee Feb. 22 on a 28-2 vote.

"As a general proposition," the committee report (H Rept 95-893) said, HR 9622 "provides that federal law questions are to be adjudicated in the federal courts, regardless of the amount in controversy; and diversity cases...are to be resolved in the state courts."

The bill also abolished for most cases what is known as the "amount-in-controversy" requirement, which provided that for certain cases to be tried in federal court the amount of a party's claim must be at least $10,000.

The abolition of diversity of citizenship was part of a series of Judiciary Committee efforts to redistribute the responsibilities of federal and state courts and to relieve the caseload before federal district courts.

Sponsors of the diversity bill said it would transfer 30,000 cases from federal to state courts. Figures provided by the Administrative Office of the United States Courts indicated that diversity cases in 1977 accounted for nearly 25 percent of the civil caseload at the trial court level.

About 11 percent of the appeals filed in 1977 were from diversity cases. "[T]he resultant congestion and delay," said the committee report, "makes it clear that some reduction in intake is imperative."

Assigning diversity cases to state courts, advocates of the bill argued, would not impose a serious burden on the latter, since the 32,000 cases pending before 400 federal district judges would be allocated among 6,000 state judges.

Because federal court judges who decide disputes between citizens of different states must rely on state law, it often requires that the judges learn a body of law they are unfamiliar with. Sponsors argued that state court judges would be better qualified to handle these disputes.

While committee members no longer thought interstate rivalries would prejudice the outcome of court cases they did not deny that such prejudices continued to exist against foreigners. As a result the bill allowed parties to disputes between U.S. citizens and aliens or foreign governments to request adjudication by a federal court judge.

At the same time the bill raised from $10,000 to $25,000 the amount-in-controversy required before such cases could go to a federal court.

The amount-in-controversy requirement for disputes between citizens of different states was abolished.

The committee majority members argued that there was no rational basis for requiring such a limitation. "Telling certain citizens, often the poor and oppressed, that although they have had their federal rights infringed, their resultant damages are too insignificant to merit the attention of a federal judge, causes visions of discrimination and unequal treatment," the committee report stated.

Federal court jurisdiction was retained over all civil cases that raised questions of federal law, regardless of the monetary amount involved.

House Floor Action

Opposition to the diversity bill on the House floor Feb. 28 focused on the changes the bill made in existing law, as well as on the procedure under which the bill was brought up.

The bill was considered under a suspension of the rules, normally reserved for non-controversial bills and allowing 40 minutes for debate, no amendments and requiring a two-thirds majority for passage.

Opponents, led by Rep. Dan Glickman, D-Kan., made three substantive arguments against the bill:

- In some urban areas state courts have more onerous backlogs than the federal courts and the bill therefore would add to delays in state court cases, merely shifting the caseload burden.
- The House-passed judgeships bill (HR 7843), creating more than 140 new federal judges, was designed to deal with the caseload problem of federal judges so that the diversity bill was not needed. Supporters countered that the judgeships bill merely temporarily reduced caseloads to a manageable level and that inflation of caseloads would soon dispel those benefits. *(Judgeships bill, p. 173)*

• State courts, unlike federal courts, generally cannot enforce their decisions beyond their jurisdictional boundaries and the diversity bill would raise serious problems concerning venue.

The 266-133 vote to suspend the rules and pass HR 9622 provided the two-thirds majority (266 in this case) needed for approval. *(Vote 72, p. 20-H)*

Senate Committee Deadlock

Through most of 1978, a bill (S 2094) to limit use of diversity jurisdiction remained tied up in the Senate Judiciary Committee on a 2-2 vote.

One of the opponents, Bill Scott, R-Va., filibustered the committee to prevent it from reporting the bill, or the far stronger one passed by the House (HR 9622).

Heavy lobbying by the nation's trial lawyers also helped keep the bill bottled up.

Trial lawyers, many of whom make a living handling "arm and leg" accident and injury cases involving litigation with insurance companies, wanted to preserve their ability to "forum shop" among federal and state courts. The ability to choose the court likely to be more favorable to a client can give an attorney an edge in winning higher settlements for clients and higher fees for themselves.

Despite lobbying against the House bill by the American Trial Lawyers Association (ATLA), the measure passed on a 266-133 vote. But in the Senate ATLA found a more sympathetic audience — the four-man Subcommittee on Improvements in Judicial Machinery.

To kill the bill, the ATLA had to convince only two of the four senators to vote against it. The two, Joe Biden, D-Del., and Malcolm Wallop, R-Wyo., had been lobbied by ATLA, as well as influential local trial attorneys and judges. Supporting the bill were subcommittee Chairman Dennis DeConcini, D-Ariz., and Majority Leader Robert C. Byrd, D-W.Va.

While a bill identical to that passed by the House (S 2389) had been referred to DeConcini's subcommittee, the panel focused most of its attention on a weaker "compromise" (S 2094), which originated at the Justice Department and was sponsored by Judiciary Chairman James O. Eastland, D-Miss.

The Justice proposal would only partially eliminate diversity jurisdiction preventing a plaintiff — in a dispute with a citizen from another state — from bringing suit in a federal court in the plaintiff's home state. The plaintiff still could file suit in the federal court in the defendant's home state or another federal court where venue was granted. And a defendant would retain the right to move a case filed in state court to a federal court.

But while the Justice proposal didn't go nearly so far as the House bill, it failed to win the support of Biden or Wallop and could not be referred to the full Judiciary Committee. Attorney General Griffin B. Bell tried unsuccessfully to persuade Biden to let the bill out of subcommittee. The Justice Department also asked DeConcini to allow the full committee to bypass his subcommittee. But DeConcini said that effort would have to be made by the full committee.

Magistrates Bill

House Committee Action

The House Judiciary Committee reported the Magistrate Act of 1978 (S 1613) to the House July 17 on a 23-7 vote (H Rept 95-1364). The Senate passed its version of the bill in July 1977 (S Rept 95-344).

Congress in 1968 created a new tier of judicial officers known as magistrates to assist federal district judges in a variety of ill-defined areas.

In 1976 Congress expanded the magistrates' jurisdiction and sought to clarify their responsibilities. But it left magistrates' appointment and utilization largely in the hands of the district judges.

In the House, S 1613 was largely the work of the Judiciary Subcommittee on Courts, Civil Liberties and the Administration of Justice, chaired by Robert W. Kastenmeier, D-Wis.

The subcommittee made several changes in the Senate bill to accommodate the interests of committee members and the American Civil Liberties Union. The subcommittee adopted one amendment that allowed only full-time magistrates to handle civil trials (there are about 400 part-time magistrates).

Other amendments clarified the appeal rights of litigants in cases heard by magistrates. A merit selection provision for local magistrate nominating panels also was provided by amendment.

Minority Views. Judiciary Committee opponents of the magistrates bill objected that it would be unconstitutional and would create a "dual system of justice" that would coerce individuals who could not afford to wait for a trial in a district court to consent to trial by magistrate. They said that Article III of the Constitution forbade the delegation of judicial powers to persons who are not life-tenured judges.

According to John F. Seiberling, D-Ohio, "only district court judges — and neither magistrates nor other persons — may dispose of cases, determine controversies, decide matters, issue orders, and pronounce judgments in and for the district courts."

Seiberling further argued that if magistrates were to perform the same jobs as judges they should go through the same appointment process. "The power of federal judges today is awesome," he wrote. "Should we enhance it further by giving to the judges the authority to appoint other judges?"

Supporters of the bill countered that when magistrates try a case, the jurisdiction resides with the district court and is simply being exercised by one of that court's officers. They further argued that both parties must consent to a trial before a magistrate and to the entry of judgment by the magistrate so there is no coercion. Finally, they said, all appeals of a magistrate's decision were to federal Article III courts.

Opponents questioned the freedom of such consent to trial by a magistrate. "It is unlikely that a litigant will hold out for an Article III judge when he or she is poor or denied bail or is suing for badly needed money and is told by an attorney that with a magistrate the trial will be scheduled sooner and conducted more expeditiously," wrote Elizabeth Holtzman, D-N.Y.

Finally, opponents argued that there were better methods of relieving federal court congestion such as the creation of new federal judgeships and the elimination of diversity jurisdiction.

Provisions

As approved by the House Judiciary Committee, S 1613:

- Expanded the jurisdiction of full-time magistrates to: 1) decide civil cases with the consent of the litigants, 2) allow the magistrate to enter a final judgment and 3) permit trial by jury before a magistrate.
- Established a consent procedure to be handled by the clerk of the court so as to prevent litigants from being coerced to accept a trial by magistrate.
- Provided for appeals from a magistrate's decision in a civil trial to the district court and for subsequent review by the appellate court.
- Provided for upgrading of the competence of magistrates through higher standards, such as one requiring that magistrates practice law for at least five years under the highest court of the state or territory.
- Outlined procedures to assure that selection panels choose new magistrates on the basis of merit from a body of applicants broadly representative of the community.
- Required reports to Congress by the Administrative Office of the U.S. Courts on the efficiency and operations of magistrate decisions.
- Expanded magistrate criminal jurisdiction to allow full- and part-time magistrates to try, with the consent of the accused, misdemeanors either with or without a jury.

House Floor Action

In a surprise move, the House added the diversity bill (HR 9622), which it had already passed, as an amendment before passing its version of the magistrates bill (S 1613). The bill passed Oct. 4, 323-49. *(Vote 771, p. 220-H)*

The move to tack on the diversity bill as an amendment was made by Charles E. Wiggins, R-Calif., and adopted by voice vote with no debate.

The House action helped Senate supporters of the diversity legislation to bypass the Judiciary Committee, which had been unable to report its own bill because of Scott's filibuster. Since the Senate already had passed S 1613, the amendment opened up the possibility that the Senate would have a chance to vote on the diversity bill if it cleared the conference committee and reached the Senate floor.

Robert McClory, R-Ill., said the Magistrate Act of 1978 would "do more to streamline our federal courts than any other matter we have considered in this House this year."

The bill was a top priority of the Justice Department, which had been pushing a series of bills to relieve federal court congestion. According to a House Judiciary aide, Attorney General Griffin B. Bell contacted dozens of House members urging them to support the bill.

House debate over S 1613 was minimal and focused on questions of the bill's constitutionality.

In opposing the bill, Robert F. Drinan, D-Mass., took on virtually the entire federal legal establishment, including the American Bar Association and the Judicial Conference. Drinan said the bill was unconstitutional because it elevated magistrates' responsibilities to the level of judges appointed by the president under Article III of the Constitution.

Unlike Article III judges, Drinan argued, the magistrates would not be life-tenured but would serve at the pleasure of district judges. Therefore, he argued, magistrates should not be allowed to dispose of civil cases as are Article III judges.

"Under this bill, the heretofore clear distinction between the functions of magistrates and those of district judges would be lost," Drinan said. "The magistrate would preside over trials in a black robe in the same courtroom used by Article III judges; he would empanel juries, examine witnesses, make evidentiary rulings, find facts and enter judgments...."

"This would debase our balance of powers system, since a legislative or executive act could be nullified by a 'judge' who had not been appointed by the president or approved by the Senate."

In support of the bill, Robert W. Kastenmeier, D-Wis., argued that trial and adjudication of minor offenses including entry of judgment, by magistrates was constitutional because: 1) Magistrates would operate as adjuncts of U.S. district courts and jurisdiction over cases would remain in the district courts and "is simply exercised through the medium of the magistrates"; 2) Both parties would have to consent to trial and entry of final judgment by a magistrate; 3) All appeals of magistrate rulings would be to Article III courts.

Opponents feared the bill would establish a "dual system of justice" that would allow individuals who could not afford to wait for a trial in a district court to be coerced into accepting a trial by magistrate. One of the principal arguments for the bill was that it would allow litigants less formal, more rapid and less expensive means of resolving their disputes.

Besides his diversity amendment, Wiggins offered an amendment to require that both parties agree, when they consent to a trial by magistrate, on whether an appeal will be made with the district court or the appeals court should either side feel the need to appeal. The amendment was designed to prevent forum shopping in the appeals process. It was adopted on a voice vote.

S 1613 as reported by the House Judiciary Committee July 17 provided for civil case appeals only to the district courts.

Differences With Senate. S 1613 as passed by the House differed in several respects from the Senate bill.

The House bill required the consent of defendants for criminal trials by magistrates. The Senate bill provided mandatory magistrate jurisdiction over minor criminal offenses.

The bills also differed in their provisions for "merit selection" of magistrates. The Senate bill provided "procedures" to be set by the Judicial Conference. The House bill specified in considerable detail how magistrate selection panels shall operate in each judicial district. The House bill also specified the criteria to be used for the selection of magistrates by the panels.

Provisions. As passed by the House Oct. 4, S 1613:

- Expanded the jurisdiction of full-time magistrates to: 1) decide civil cases with the consent of the litigants, 2) allow the magistrate to enter a final judgment and 3) permit trial by jury before a magistrate.
- Established a consent procedure to be handled by the clerk of the court to prevent litigants from being coerced to accept a trial by magistrate. The litigants would have to be fully aware of their rights to trial by jury.
- Provided for appeals from a magistrate's decision in a civil trial to a district court or the appeals court and subsequent review by the Supreme Court.
- Provided for upgrading of the competence of magistrates through higher standards, such as one requiring that magistrates practice law for at least five years under the highest court of the state or territory.

- Outlined procedures to assure that selection panels choose new magistrates on the basis of merit from a body of applicants broadly representative of the community.
- Required reports to Congress by the Administrative Office of the U.S. Courts on the efficiency and operations of magistrate decisions.
- Expanded magistrate criminal jurisdiction to allow full- and part-time magistrates to try, with the consent of the accused, misdemeanors either with or without a jury.

(For provisions of HR 9622, added to S 1613 by amendment, see p. 201)

Conference Committee Deadlock

S 1613, as amended by the House to include HR 9622, died in the conference committee.

While House Judiciary members succeeded in bypassing the Senate Judiciary Committee filibuster, they were immediately confronted with a new filibuster threat upon entering the conference committee. Strom Thurmond, R-S.C., and seven other senators already had sent a letter to Majority Leader Robert C. Byrd, D-W.Va., making clear their intention to talk diversity to death if it were brought up on the floor.

Thurmond's new filibuster threat was based on his thoroughgoing opposition to any form of diversity legislation. But in it other senators saw an opportunity for compromise. They hoped the House was bluffing, and that faced with the prospect of losing both bills it would back off.

Thurmond proposed separating the diversity provisions from the magistrates bill and reporting out the latter. But Thurmond's hard line on diversity was met by equal intransigence from House conferees on the magistrates bill.

Robert W. Kastenmeier, D-Wis., the principal sponsor of the House package, made it clear House conferees had no qualms about letting the magistrates bill die. House conferees already had received indications from the Senate side of the table that they were not alone in supporting diversity legislation and were ready to gamble on a Senate filibuster if they could get a bill out of conference. So Thurmond's motion to report only a magistrates bill was rejected. The vote by Senate conferees was 4-4.

The vote against Thurmond signaled House conferees that there was some Senate sentiment against retaining diversity jurisdiction in the bill. But the Senate's position on diversity proved to be more moderate than that of the House.

Rather than abolishing the use of federal courts in diversity cases as the House had proposed, senators suggested a middle-ground position that would curtail diversity jurisdiction to use by defendants only. The proposal, offered by James Abourezk, D-S.D., was identical to a Justice Department compromise that Dennis DeConcini, D-Ariz., had proposed and voted for in his Judiciary subcommittee earlier in the year. If DeConcini, who had voted for Thurmond's motion to strike diversity from the bill, joined the opponents of that proposal on his compromise, it would pass 5-3.

But DeConcini rejected the compromise he previously had embraced and the motion to substitute it for the House provision failed on a 4-4 vote.

That left House conferees with few options. If they couldn't win on the compromise, a vote on full abolition of diversity would be futile.

Arguing that there was no time to resolve the deadlock in the 95th Congress, DeConcini proposed that the conference adjourn. Kastenmeier, hoping that there might still be time to work out a compromise, suggested the conferees recess and try to meet later.

But Kastenmeier changed his mind on the whispered advice of Abourezk and the conference was put out of business.

Abourezk's strategy was grounded in Senate rules, which allow appointment of new conferees if a conference is adjourned, but not if it recesses. It afforded a last-ditch option that was never employed. No new conferees were named.

At that point the game was almost over, but not quite.

Thurmond, fearing the House might again pass a diversity bill and send it over to the Senate as a rider to one of the dozens of bills being rubber-stamped in the final hours of Congress, decided not to take any chances.

He notified the Senate leadership that he was putting a "hold" on every bill that was sent over from the House until the end of the session. Thurmond's move meant that he would be informed before any effort was made to bring up diversity. Any hopes the House had of sneaking the bill through were dashed.

Meanwhile, DeConcini was making one last effort to save the magistrates bill or at least to leave the impression that the House had killed it. He circulated an amendment that would have attached the magistrates bill, which the Senate had approved in July 1977, to an innocuous court siting bill. But his effort was rejected by the Democratic Policy Committee because Judiciary staffers were still trying to work out a compromise diversity-magistrates bill.

Those efforts, which finally fell to pieces the day before adjournment, included an offer to attach a child-snatching bill sponsored by Malcolm Wallop, R-Wyo., to a compromise magistrates-diversity bill. In exchange, Wallop was asked to change his vote to support the diversity substitute he had rejected in conference. Wallop rejected the offer. ▮

Court Boundaries Changed

The Senate agreed Sept. 19 to House amendments to a bill (S 3375) changing the boundaries and locations for federal courts in several states to make them more accessible and eliminate inordinately heavy or light caseloads.

The noncontroversial measure was approved by voice vote, clearing the bill for the president's signature (PL 95-408).

The bill designated new places of holding court in Ashland, Ky., and in Corinth, Miss. It reorganized the geographic boundaries of courts in Louisiana, North Dakota, Florida, Illinois and New York.

The Congressional Budget Office estimated it would cost $200,000 to rent, remodel and provide furnishings for the two new places for holding court.

The Senate Judiciary Committee reported S 3375 Aug. 17 (S Rept 95-1121). It was approved by the Senate Aug. 21 on a voice vote.

The House Judiciary Committee reported virtually identical legislation on Sept. 7 (HR 13331 — H Rept 95-1554). The bill passed the House Sept. 12 on a 362-9 vote. *(Vote 668, p. 190-H)*

After passing HR 13331, the House tabled it and passed S 3375 with the House language substituted for that of the Senate version. ▮

Contracts Disputes Act

The House gave final approval Oct. 14 to a bill designed to speed up the process for resolving disputes between contractors and U.S. government agencies (PL 95-563).

HR 11002, the Contract Disputes Act, established procedures allowing federal agencies to resolve contract disputes through administrative and judicial proceedings.

The Senate passed HR 11002 Oct. 13 and the House approved the amended bill the following day.

The House had approved a slightly different version of the bill Sept. 26 by voice vote and with no debate.

Under existing law prior to enactment of HR 11002, contract disputes were resolved through a system that required a hearing and resolution before an agency board of contract appeals. Only limited access to federal courts was allowed for resolution of such disputes.

The bill authorized each executive agency to settle or adjust any claim or dispute relating to its contracts, except disputes involving penalties or forfeitures that statutes or regulations said must be settled by a specific agency. The bill also provided for contract disputes to be decided by a contracting officer and for the officer's rulings to be appealed to an agency board of contract appeals, U.S. district courts or courts of claims.

A 1972 report by the Commission on Government Procurement stated that existing procedures were unfair to contractors, costly and time consuming. The report made a series of recommendations to Congress, many of which were implemented by HR 11002.

The bill was reported to the House by the Committee on the Judiciary Sept. 8 (H Rept 95-1556) and was reported to the Senate by its Judiciary and Governmental Affairs Committees Aug. 15 (S Rept 95-1118).

Supreme Court Case Review

Responding to an unusual and unanimous request from the justices of the U.S. Supreme Court, the Senate Judiciary Committee recommended that Congress grant the court virtually complete discretion to decide which cases it will review and which cases it will reject. However, there was no floor action on the measure by either chamber in 1978.

The bill (S 3100 — S Rept 95-985) reported by the committee July 13, would eliminate the mandatory jurisdiction of the court to decide certain kinds of cases. That jurisdiction is completely defined by acts of Congress granting a right of appeal in certain cases.

Enactment of S 3100, said the committee, would "be the culmination of a long and historic process converting the appellate jurisdiction of the Supreme Court from one totally obligatory in nature to one that, with a few minor exceptions, will be almost totally discretionary."

Background

The Supreme Court has two kinds of jurisdiction: original and appellate.

Original jurisdiction, the power to hear a case in its initial stage, is spelled out by Article III of the Constitution: It extends to cases affecting ambassadors, public ministers, consuls and to cases to which a state is a party. Congress has no power to affect this jurisdiction.

But Article III made the court's appellate jurisdiction — its jurisdiction over cases coming to it from other courts — completely subject to such "exceptions . . . and regulations" as Congress wished to make. This has been interpreted as giving Congress unlimited power over the court's appellate jurisdiction.

The committee report referred to this power: "To begin with, an 'appeal' to any federal appellate court, including the Supreme Court, is solely a creature of legislative choice. . . . Congress is not compelled by . . . the Constitution . . . to provide aggrieved litigants with any absolute right to take an 'appeal' to the Supreme Court. . . . If Congress wants to make the court's appellate jurisdiction totally discretionary, or totally obligatory in nature, nothing in the Constitution says 'no'."

Until 1891, the court's appellate jurisdiction was completely mandatory. It was obliged to decide all cases which Congress allowed to be appealed to it. Beginning in 1891, with the creation of courts of appeals whose decisions were final in certain types of cases, Congress began to give the court some discretion over which cases it decided and which it rejected. Laws increasing the discretionary jurisdiction — and the court's control over its docket — were passed in 1914 and 1925.

In the 1970s Congress further reduced the mandatory jurisdiction of the court by revising existing laws to eliminate a right of direct appeal to the Supreme Court from district court rulings on certain criminal matters, in civil antitrust cases, in cases involving orders of the Interstate Commerce Commission, and in cases in which the constitutionality of state or federal laws was challenged. *(Congress and the Nation, Vol. IV pp. 587, 590, 616)*

In 1978, cases came to the court by two routes. Most come through the filing of a petition for a writ of *certiorari*, a request for review which the court has complete discretion to grant or deny. Others come by the filing of an appeal, which the court is formally obligated to accept and decide, if it has jurisdiction over the case.

Committee Views

Recommending that Congress eliminate this appeal route — and give all cases an equal chance for review by the court through the grant of *certiorari*, the Senate Judiciary Committee described the continuation of mandatory jurisdiction as "inexcusable and counterproductive."

"It detracts from the court's ability to control its own docket and to effectuate its constitutional mission of resolving only those matters that are of truly national significance," the report stated. Although cases brought under its mandatory jurisdiction accounted for less than 10 percent of all cases brought in the 1976 term, they made up almost half of those argued and decided with full opinion, the report said. It concluded that "a significant number of . . . cases involv[ing] issues of considerable importance are being denied access to the court simply because the court has no time to hear them due to the crush of obligatory appeals."

The committee knew of no opposition to the bill.

Court Views

"To the extent that we are obligated . . . to devote our energies to these less important cases, we cannot devote our time and attention to the more important issues and cases constantly pressing for resolution in an increasing volume," the justices wrote to the committee July 22.

"[A]ny provision for mandatory jurisdiction by definition permits litigants to bring cases to this court as of right and without regard to whether those are of any general public importance or concern," the court's letter said.

To give full review to all mandatory jurisdiction matters in the 1976 term, the justices wrote, would have required doubling the length of the time during which the court heard oral arguments. The alternative, summary disposition of such cases without full argument or written opinions, often resulted in "more confusion than clarity" as to what the court had done, they added. "From this dilemma, we perceive only one escape consistent with past congressional decisions defining the court's mandatory jurisdiction: congressional action eliminating that jurisdiction."

Provisions

As reported, S 3100:

Repealed or deleted sections of federal law which obligate the court to decide cases:

- Where a federal district judge has struck down an Act of Congress in a case in which the United States government, its agencies or employees are involved.
- Where an appeals court has held invalid a state law as conflicting with the Constitution, treaties or federal law.
- Where the highest available court in a state has struck down a federal law or treaty — or upheld a state law against a challenge that it conflicts with the Constitution, federal law or federal treaty.
- Involving the Federal Election Campaign Act, California Indian lands, or construction of the Alaska Pipeline. ▮

Rights of Institutionalized

The House July 28 approved legislation giving the attorney general authority to sue state insitutions that systematically deprive their residents of constitutional rights, but the bill (HR 9400) never reached the Senate floor because of a filibuster threat.

At a cost to the federal government estimated by sponsors at less than $100,000 a year, the bill was designed to protect some of the most helpless segments of society — elderly residents of nursing homes and persons with severe physical or mental handicaps. The major controversy surrounding the legislation was whether it should also apply to prisoners.

The Carter administration and the American Bar Association supported the bill, but it was vigorously opposed by the National Association of Attorneys General, representing top legal officers of the states. A resolution adopted at the NAAG June 1977 convention said the bill would amount to "an unprecedented intervention by an agency of the federal government into the administration of state affairs and the litigation of local concerns."

NAAG argued that:

- The bill was unconstitutional.
- Existing law was adequate to protect residents of state institutions.
- The bill would create unnecessary conflicts between federal and state law enforcement agencies.
- The problems of the institutionalized should be solved through federal-state conciliation rather than by lawsuits.
- The bill provided a judicial remedy where legislative and executive solutions — primarily federal aid to the states — would have a greater impact.

But a statement of findings accompanying the House Judiciary Committee report on HR 9400 concluded: "The dozens of reported cases graphically documenting execrable institutional conditions and practices bely any suggestion that state and local officials are independently capable of protecting their institutionalized residents from unconstitutional abuses. State attorneys general, bound by law to defend the very agencies responsible for maintaining such conditions, are neither willing nor able to serve as advocates for the institutionalized."

Background: Pro and Con

Under existing law, an individual confined to a state institution could sue for violations of constitutional rights under the Civil Rights Act of 1871. This statute, NAAG argued in its 1977 resolution, adequately protected the institutionalized.

But numerous barriers stood in the way of the exercise of the supposed right to sue under that statute.

A sizable number of the persons confined to state institutions are poor and uneducated. And residents of mental institutions and nursing homes often are incapable of identifying or articulating a certifiably illegal abuse or of determining how to assert their rights. Even when these individuals can afford legal representation, they may be reluctant to sue out of fear of retaliation by an institution's staff.

In testimony presented at House hearings in 1977, the National Senior Citizens Law Center said that "many nursing home residents have virtually no human contacts outside the facility, more than half having no close family ties at all. In addition, many nursing home residents must depend on the facilities for assistance in activities of daily life — more than half need help in walking and bathing; nearly half need help in dressing; and more than one in 10 needs help in eating."

Addressing a suggestion by opponents that institutionalized persons be required to exhaust administrative remedies before a federal suit could be brought, Alvin J. Bronstein, director of the National Prison Project of the American Civil Liberties Union testified: "It is unclear to me just how some juveniles (an eight year old) and some mental patients (a person being drugged into near oblivion) would go about 'exhausting their available administrative remedies.' "

But opponents of the legislation, notably NAAG, responded that institutionalized persons had access to a veritable cornucopia of legal services.

In a March 1977 letter to the bill's chief sponsor, Robert W. Kastenmeier, D-Wis., New York Attorney General Louis J. Lefkowitz, one of the most vocal opponents of an earlier version of HR 9400, said the bill was unnecessary because: 1) "The federal constitutional rights of institutionalized persons are well protected now by their representation by various legal groups which are specifically designed to advocate their interests"; 2) Federal and state courts regularly appoint private counsel to represent private litigants; 3) "Numerous clinics and projects attached to law schools, as well as national organizations which represent the interests of institutionalized persons" are available.

Opponents further argued that the agencies funding state institutions (such as the Department of Health, Education and Welfare and the Law Enforcement Assistance

Administration) can cut off funds if a state facility is not complying with federal standards.

Finally, opponents argued that the federal government already could enter lawsuits when invited by a court and as an intervenor.

Legal Resources Disputed

The House committee report on HR 9400 disputed the claims of the attorneys general on the availability of legal resources for the institutionalized. It said: "The resources of the Legal Services [Corporation] and privately funded public interest bars are woefully inadequate to represent the needs of the nation's institutionalized population."

Said Kastenmeier, "The caliber of the public interest bar notwithstanding, it is unacceptable to me to leave enforcement of the constitutional rights of institutionalized citizens entirely in the hands of a small, overworked, underpaid portion of the bar which has voluntarily chosen to make it its business to represent these clients."

Kastenmeier said the federal courts appoint counsel in less than 1 percent of the civil rights petitions filed by the institutionalized.

The Constitution and Federalism

Opponents of HR 9400 based their arguments against Justice Department intervention on the Tenth Amendment to the Constitution, which they said prevents the federal government from interfering in the operation of state institutions.

The amendment states that "the powers not delegated to the United States by the Constitution, nor prohibited by it to the states, are reserved to the states respectively, or to the people."

In a letter to Rep. Kastenmeier in 1977, New York Attorney General Lefkowitz argued: "The running of state prisons, hospitals, juvenile facilities, and similar institutions is peculiarly a matter of local concern to the states. . . . [T]he bill would open the doors of these state facilities to intrusion (or investigation at least) by a federal department which must ascertain 'reasonable cause' and whether corrections have been made. . . ."

Supporters countered that the Constitution takes precedence over state law and policy. Abram Chayes of Harvard Law School argued in House testimony: "The Tenth Amendment is no bar. . . . [N]o power is reserved to the states to confine people in violation of the Constitution of the United States."

Supporters of federal intervention cited Article Six, Section Two of the Constitution (the Constitution as "supreme law of the land") and Article Three, Section Two, ("judicial powers" under the Constitution and laws of the United States extend to "controversies to which the United States shall be a party"). Supporters further argued that the 13th Amendment (slavery and involuntary servitude) and 14th Amendment ("No state shall make or enforce any law which shall abridge the privileges or immunities of citizens of the United States") stipulate that Congress "by appropriate legislation" may authorize the attorney general to bring suit to enforce the provisions of the amendments.

As to the charge that HR 9400 would allow an unprecedented expansion of federal jurisdiction, supporters cited numerous precedents for Justice Department intervention in cases where there is a "pattern or practice" of violations. These included the Civil Rights Acts of 1960 (voting), of 1964 (public accommodations and employment), of 1968 (housing), the Crime Control Act of 1973 and the State and Local Fiscal Assistance Act of 1972 (discrimination in programs receiving federal assistance).

Federal Authority

There currently was no federal statute comparable to the Civil Rights Acts that specifically authorized federal intervention to protect the rights of persons in state institutions.

The Justice Department insisted it had standing to sue where the United States had interests to protect (under the Constitution and 28 USC 517) and that the attorney general has inherent authority to represent such interests in federal courts.

It was not, however, altogether clear what constitutes a "U.S. interest," a question that normally hinges on whether federal funds are involved and whether the institutions receiving federal funds are covered by federal statutes pertaining to the subject being litigated.

Lacking specific authority to initiate suits, Justice had participated in cases involving institutionalized persons at the invitation of a court *(amicus curiae)* or through intervention in ongoing suits. As a result, according to Assistant Attorney General Drew S. Days III, "The ability of the United States to respond to the serious situations existing in many of these state-operated institutions has been dependent upon the selection of litigation by private parties."

In *United States v. Solomon,* a district court stated that the United States may sue in only a few situations without statutory authority — where the victims are the "public at large," where a national emergency exists or where interstate commerce is a factor.

While the Justice Department had never lost a rights of institutionalized case in which it had intervened and that had been decided on its merits, it had a dismal track record on cases it tried to initiate. In the latter the courts supported the states' claims of federalism — the strict separation of federal and state authority — against what they viewed as claims of inherent power from the executive branch.

House Committee Action

Moving to protect what it called a "large and quiescent minority," the House Judiciary Committee approved legislation allowing the federal government to step in when the constitutional rights of institutionalized persons are endangered.

The bill (HR 9400) would authorize the U.S. attorney general to initiate or intervene in lawsuits to safeguard the rights of persons confined to state-operated prisons, mental institutions, nursing homes, juvenile centers and facilities for the chronically ill. Patients in private nursing homes might also be covered under certain conditions.

The committee, which reported the bill by voice vote April 18 (H Rept 95-1058), compiled a chilling hearing record as it prepared the bill.

Hundreds of pages of testimony documented unsanitary and unsafe living conditions, inadequate medical care, cases of torture, beatings, mutilation and deaths in facilities ostensibly designed for the care, protection or improvement of the lives of their residents.

The committee said there is "uniform agreement among those familiar with institutional environments that thousands of individuals continue to be subjected to conditions and practices flagrantly violative of their most basic human rights."

Noting that many of these individuals are poor, inarticulate, mentally impaired or otherwise vulnerable, the committee said that federal intervention on their behalf often is not only justified but essential.

The Justice Department concurred. Assistant Attorney General for Civil Rights Drew S. Days III testified: "The basic constitutional and federal statutory rights of institutionalized persons are being violated on such a systematic and widespread basis to warrant the attention of the federal government."

HR 9400, sponsored by Rep. Robert W. Kastenmeier, D-Wis., would allow the federal government to bring suits against state operated or funded institutions where: 1) the Justice Department finds a "pattern or practice" of violations of the constitutional rights of persons in an institution and; 2) where the attorney general certifies that federal intervention is of "general public importance" and will lead to the vindication of the rights of the institutionalized.

The only committee member to file dissenting views was Allen E. Ertel, D-Pa., who objected to the bill's coverage of prisoners. "State prisoner petitions choke the dockets of federal courts," Ertel wrote. "It is generally agreed that most prisoner complaints are frivolous and ought to be dismissed, no matter how narrowly one defines 'frivolous.' "

House Floor Action

The House passed HR 9400 July 28 by a lopsided 254-69 margin. *(Vote 537, p. 154-H)*

Before passing HR 9400, the House amended the version reported by the Judiciary Committee to provide a lesser degree of federal protection to prisoners than to other institutionalized persons, including those living in nursing homes, juvenile facilities, mental institutions or hospitals for the chronically ill.

Referring to what he called "this class of uniquely vulnerable persons" who would be protected by HR 9400, Kastenmeier said he hoped it would be "virtually impossible to vote against this bill."

But an opponent, Thomas N. Kindness, R-Ohio, objected that there was nothing in the bill to help the states correct the housing, staffing and other problems that he said were the basis for most cases of institutional abuse.

Kindness said that "we ought to be taking the money that will eventually be required to hire lawyers in the Department of Justice and to litigate, and to use it to help the patients and the inmates in these institutions."

When the House began consideration of HR 9400 May 1, it agreed to an amendment by Ertel that deleted prisons and other correctional facilities from the bill. The vote was 227-132. *(Vote 224, p. 64-H)*

During floor debate, Ertel argued that prisoners should not be afforded the protection of the attorney general because they, unlike other groups covered by the bill, generally were aware of their rights and mentally competent to bring legal actions to protect their own rights.

Ertel argued that prisoners had adequate free legal representation and cited statistics he said showed they had made widespread use of the courts.

Opponents of the amendment said conditions in state and local prisons were as bad as or worse than those in any other state institution and that prisoners should not be denied an equal degree of constitutional protection.

Tom Railsback, R-Ill., said the conditions he personally found in inspecting prisons "would have shocked the most callous prosecutor."

Opponents also challenged Ertel on the availability of legal resources for prisoners. Barbara Jordan, D-Texas, said that "despite the demonstrated ability of prisoners to file petitions challenging the constitutionality of their confinement, few, if any, suits securing widespread relief from unconstitutional prison conditions have been brought without the assistance of outside sources, most notably the Justice Department."

Following the vote, Kastenmeier asked to have the bill withdrawn from consideration to give members more time to study the legislation. Kastenmeier said he felt many members did not understand the significance of the vote.

When debate on the bill resumed May 25, the House, with Ertel's support, largely reversed the earlier vote, adopting by a margin of 178 to 109 an amendment by Railsback allowing the government to bring suits on behalf of prisoners if a court determined that conditions in a prison or correctional facility warranted the attention of the attorney general. The recommendation of a court was not required for intervention by the attorney general against any of the other institutions covered by the bill. *(Vote 324, p. 92-H)*

During floor consideration of HR 9400 on May 1, May 25 and July 28, the House also adopted the following amendments on non-record votes:

- By M. Caldwell Butler, R-Va., providing a one-house veto of standards issued by the attorney general to implement a section of the bill establishing grievance procedures for prisoners.
- By Charles E. Wiggins, R-Calif., requiring the attorney general, before intervening in a suit against an institution, to consult with state officials and institutional directors regarding available federal assistance for the correction of deprivations.
- By Wiggins, clarifying the purely advisory role provided inmates and employees of correctional facilities in implementing voluntary grievance systems provided by the bill.
- By Kastenmeier, limiting intervention by the attorney general to cases where conditions cause deprivation of rights and cause "grievous harm." The Kastenmeier amendment was a substitute for a rejected Wiggins amendment that would have limited intervention only to cases where constitutional rights were violated, barring intervention where statutory rights were abused.

Senate Action

The Senate Judiciary Committee approved a bill (S 1393) that differed in several important ways from the House-passed bill.

S 1393, ordered reported July 18 on an 11-6 vote, would not cover nursing homes, and it differed from the House bill in its treatment of prisoners. The Senate committee bill contained no prisoner grievance procedures and it omitted a mechanism, added to the House bill during floor debate, for initiating suits on behalf of prisoners.

Reported July 31 (S Rept 95-1056), the bill had the support of several conservative Republicans on the Judiciary Committee.

However, Robert Morgan, D-N.C., put a "hold" on the bill, refusing to agree to a time limit on debate and threatening to offer numerous gutting amendments if the bill came up. Morgan called the bill "an arrogant grab for power on the part of the attorney general" and viewed it as "a complete usurpation of the rights of states over the management and operations of prisons, jails and nursing homes." ∎

Drug Abuse Programs

Expressing concern over the dismantling of the White House drug abuse office, the Senate Oct. 2 cleared legislation extending for one year federal drug abuse prevention and treatment programs.

The bill (S 2916 — PL 95-461) authorized $229 million in fiscal 1979 for the drug abuse programs, which were administered by the National Institute on Drug Abuse (NIDA). The measure earmarked $45 million for state drug abuse formula grants; $177 million for state project grants and contracts, of which $24 million was authorized for prevention, and $7 million for research into non-addictive drugs for use in the treatment of heroin addiction and for detoxification agents to ease heroin withdrawal.

The measure also required the secretary of health, education and welfare (HEW) to prepare an annual report on the federal drug abuse effort and required state drug abuse agencies applying for grants to include cities, counties and other political subdivisions in their planning process.

Concern over Program

Concern over the impact of the dismantling of the White House Office of Drug Abuse Policy (ODAP) on the federal drug abuse effort prompted the one-year authorization, according to the House Interstate and Foreign Commerce and Senate Human Resource committees. The two committees reported similar bills May 15 (HR 12348 — H Rept 95-1187, S 2916 — S Rept 95-820).

Widely credited with effectively coordinating the federal government's far-flung and frequently warring drug abuse enforcement and treatment agencies, ODAP was also applauded for reducing the availability of heroin to a seven-year low. But President Carter's 1977 reorganization of the executive office led to ODAP's demise. The ODAP staff, reduced to six from 10, was transferred to the White House Domestic Policy Staff. *(1977 Almanac p. 814)*

"We want to take a year to look at the new set-up," said a Senate committee aide, explaining the reason for the transition measure. The aide speculated that the drug programs would undergo a more substantial overhaul in 1979.

Coupled with the resignations in the summer of 1978 of ODAP head Dr. Peter Bourne and NIDA chief Robert L. DuPont, the ODAP dismantling "leaves a big question mark hanging over the whole drug abuse field," according to one drug abuse expert. Bourne resigned after it was reported that he had written a fraudulent prescription for Quaalude, a frequently abused sedative.

"Peter meant a lot to the drug field," commented Peter Goldberg, a policy analyst with the Drug Abuse Council, a private non-profit foundation. The new group "doesn't have Bourne's access to the president," Goldberg said, adding that Bourne had a thorough understanding of the important drug abuse issues.

Legislative History

The Senate approved S 2916 by voice vote May 24. In a time-saving move to avoid a conference, the House Sept. 18 approved by voice vote under suspension of the rules a compromise version of HR 12348 that included four additional Senate-passed provisions. The House then agreed to substitute the provisions of its bill for those of S 2916 and sent the bill back to the Senate, which cleared it Oct. 2. ∎

False Claims Subpoenas

The House cleared a bill Oct. 15 authorizing the issuance of subpoenas of witnesses living anywhere in the United States to appear at trials or hearings resulting from suits under the False Claims Act (PL 95-582).

The bill (HR 12393) amended the act, which allows the United States to bring civil suits in federal district courts to recover double damages and a $2,000 penalty for each false claim made or caused to be made on the United States (H Rept 95-1447).

The bill, which passed the House Sept. 18 by voice vote, allowed the government to subpoena witnesses from anywhere in the country to appear in a false claims action. The Senate passed the bill amended Oct. 13, and the House accepted the Senate amendments Oct. 15. The president signed the bill Nov. 2.

Under existing rules of procedure, courts could issue subpoenas only within their judicial district or up to 100 miles outside the district.

The Justice Department testified that the legislation was necessary because the judicial district where a false claim or fraud scheme occurred often was not the district where the perpetrator resided. Public disclosure of false claims as a result of criminal indictments often prompted the alleged perpetrators to move, forcing the Justice Department to file suit in the person's new district of residence.

In attempting to recover money obtained by fraud against the government, the Justice Department argued that it had been limited in its ability to obtain witnesses because they frequently did not reside within 100 miles of the district where the defendant was charged. ∎

Court Interpreters

The Senate gave final approval Oct. 13 to a bill that was likely to increase the use of court interpreters for defendants in federal criminal and civil actions (PL 95-539).

S 1315 was cleared when the Senate on a non-record vote accepted House amendments. The House passed the bill Oct. 10 on a voice vote (H Rept 95-1687). It had been passed by the Senate Nov. 4, 1977 (S Rept 95-569). The president signed the bill Oct. 28, 1978.

The measure required the Administrative Office of the U.S. Courts to establish a certification process for interpreters used in federal district courts and to maintain on file a list of all certified interpreters.

While existing federal statutes granted discretionary authority to federal courts to appoint interpreters for defendants, these powers were rarely used. As a result, several criminal convictions had been reversed on due process grounds where no interpreter was provided.

The statutory right to appointment of an interpreter would be triggered under the bill when the presiding judicial officer determined that a party or a witness spoke only or primarily a language other than English, or suffered from a hearing impairment.

The federal government would pay the costs of an interpreter's services in all criminal actions initiated by the United States, whether or not the defendant or party was indigent. In civil actions the judge could indicate that all or part of the costs be apportioned among the parties.

The Congressional Budget Office estimated that it would cost $1.4 million in fiscal 1979 and just over $2 million in each of the three subsequent fiscal years.

Juror Fees and Protection

The Senate gave final approval Oct. 13 to a bill that increased the daily fees paid to jurors in federal court proceedings and provided a civil penalty and injunctive relief against an employer who discharged or threatened to discharge an employee because of federal jury service.

The bill (S 2075) originally passed the Senate April 27 (S Rept 95-757). It was approved in amended form by the House Oct. 12 (H Rept 95-1652).

As signed into law Nov. 2, S 2075 (PL 95-572):

- Increased per diem pay for jurors to $30.
- Provided for additional per diem pay to jurors required to attend more than 45 days on juries.
- Replaced statutory subsistence allowances with those to be set by the Administrative Office of the U.S. Courts.
- Increased travel allowances.
- Required private employers in most circumstances to restore a federal juror who had completed service to his previous position or a position of like seniority, status and pay or, if the juror were unable to perform previous duties because of a disability sustained while on jury duty, to a position nearest approximating his previous job.
- Urged state and local governments to grant their employees the same employment rights that were granted private employees under S 2075.

Drug Dependent Offenders

The Senate gave final approval Oct. 13 to legislation (S 3336 — PL 95-537) designed to increase the efficiency of federal programs for rehabilitating drug dependent probationers, parolees and other persons released from prison.

According to the Senate report (S Rept 95-1110) on the bill, the measure would increase the number of supervised "hard" narcotics users, as well as "persons dependent on controlled substances such as barbiturates, amphetamines, hallucinogens, and marijuana" under supervision. The bill transferred the supervisory function from the Bureau of Prisons to the U.S. Probation Service.

The bill passed the Senate on a voice vote Oct. 13, after receiving approval of the House (H Rept 95-1649) Oct. 10 in amended form. The Senate originally passed the bill Aug. 17. The president signed the bill Oct. 27.

S 3336 gave the U.S. Probation Service authority to grant contracts to independent organizations involved in rehabilitation of drug dependent offenders. It required the Probation Service to monitor these contractors to assure that the quantity and quality of services agreed upon were provided.

The program was estimated to cost approximately $3.5 million a year for the first three fiscal years, beginning in fiscal 1980.

Transportation Expenses

The House gave final approval Oct. 10 to a bill authorizing federal judges or magistrates to order travel expenses for indigent defendants charged with criminal offenses.

The bill, S 2411 (PL 95-503), passed the House on a voice vote (H Rept 95-1653). It was similarly approved by the Senate April 27 (S Rept 95-760). The president signed the bill Oct. 24.

The legislation was necessary, sponsors said, because defendants occasionally were unable to afford the costs of transportation to appear in court in a judicial district other than where he or she resided. In some cases this had resulted in defendants being denied release from custody pending trial and had raised questions of whether these individuals were being denied equal protection of the law. The Bail Reform Act of 1966 provided for release from custody pending trial.

The transportation costs were to come out of existing expenses for U.S. marshals.

Witness Fees

Witnesses appearing in federal court and grand jury proceedings or giving depositions were to be compensated at a higher rate than in the past as a result of legislation given final approval by the Senate Oct. 13.

The bill, S 2049, originally passed the Senate April 27 (S Rept 95-756). It passed the House in amended form Oct. 12 on a voice vote (H Rept 95-1651).

The measure increased witness fees, including subsistence and travel allowances, for the first time since 1968. Sponsors said the new levels were necessary to account for inflation and provide the "minimal level of compensation that constitutes a respectable remuneration for witness service today."

As signed into law Oct. 27, S 2049 (PL 95-535):

- Increased the per diem fee for witnesses to $30.
- Replaced the set travel allowance with guidelines directing reimbursement for actual expenses of public transportation and granting allowances for private transportation equal to those granted to federal employees.
- Replaced set subsistence allowances with the subsistence allowance granted federal employees.

Assassinations Hearings

Two years after it was created, the House Select Committee on Assassinations held public hearings related to its investigations into the assassinations of President John F. Kennedy and the Rev. Martin Luther King Jr.

The Kennedy hearings substantially supported the basic conclusion of the Warren Commission that Lee Harvey Oswald fired three shots and that the third killed the president.

But in its summary report released Dec. 31, the committee's last-minute acceptance of an acoustical analysis of the gunfire led it to the startling conclusion that there was a "high probability" that a fourth shot had been fired by a second gunman. The committee said it was "unable to identify the other gunman or the extent of the conspiracy." *(Summary report p. 215)*

Committee investigators also found circumstantial evidence of a conspiracy in the King assassination. While concluding that convicted killer James Earl Ray acted alone, the committee said there was a "likelihood" that Ray had been motivated by a standing offer of $50,000 by a right-wing St. Louis businessman who wanted the civil rights leader slain.

Committee History and Funding

The Assassinations Committee was created in September 1976 when the House voted 280 to 65 to begin a new inquiry into the murders of President John F. Kennedy in 1963 and of civil rights leader Martin Luther King Jr. in 1968. *(1976 Almanac p. 512)*

The new investigations were delayed more than six months, however, after a rift broke out between committee Chairman Henry B. Gonzalez, D-Texas, and chief counsel Richard Sprague, a former assistant district attorney in Philadelphia. *(1977 Almanac p. 591)*

Sprague's intended use of lie detectors and stress evaluators plus a proposed first-year budget of $6.5 million — about six times larger than the House had expected — eroded members' support for the investigation and exacerbated tensions with Gonzalez.

After Gonzalez' attempt in early 1977 to fire Sprague was quashed by the full committee, Gonzalez resigned as chairman March 1.

With House approval for continuing the investigation in doubt, Sprague submitted his resignation March 30. On the same day the House by a 49-vote margin authorized the existence of the committee through the 95th Congress.

The investigation finally began in March 1977 under a new chairman, Louis Stokes, D-Ohio. G. Robert Blakey, a law professor and director of the Cornell Institute on Organized Crime, was appointed chief counsel to the committee June 20.

In 1978, the House continued to muster small majorities in support of the committee's work. H Res 956, which provided $2.5 million for the investigations in 1978, was approved March 13 by a 204-175 vote. *(Vote 110, p. 32-H)*

The 204-175 vote to approve H Res 956 came amid protests that the committee had failed to publicly document what progress, if any, it had made in investigating the assassinations of Kennedy and King.

While committee funding resolutions normally are routinely approved by the House, the assassinations panel had been plagued since its creation by widespread skepticism among House members about the need to further investigate the two murders.

H Res 956, which provided $2.5 million for the assassination investigations during 1978, was approved after the House narrowly rejected an effort to recommit the bill to the Committee on House Administration, which had cut the Assassinations Committee's $2,978,000 request to $2,500,000 (H Rept 95-898).

The recommittal motion, offered by Rep. Robert E. Bauman, R-Md., would have provided $600,000 to continue funding the committee for three months.

Bauman said his amendment would have required the House Administration Committee to provide a summary of the Assassinations Committee's findings to date, an explanation of the direction in which the committee was headed, and a justification for its continued existence. The committee's work had been largely a mystery since Stokes took over as chairman in 1977. Stokes was praised on the House floor for running a "quiet, professional" and leakproof investigation.

The Bauman motion was rejected, 182-198. *(Vote 109, p. 32-H)*

Supporters of continued funding argued that when the committee was reconstituted in 1977 after the resignation of its chief counsel, Sprague, it was extended for the duration of the 95th Congress. They said cutting off funds would not allow the committee to fulfill its original mandate.

Critics of the committee countered that they needed some evidence it was making progress before they would approve the $2.5 million.

Acknowledging that "I cannot produce a smoking gun; I cannot produce a dramatic fact," committee member Stewart B. McKinney, R-Conn., insisted that the committee had developed "a great deal" of new information about the two assassinations. Supporters said the committee would issue a report by the end of the year but that premature disclosures were harmful to the investigation and the reputation of the House.

Support for the often-controversial work of the committee received a boost Sept. 14 when the House voted to give the committee an additional $790,000 to complete its investigations.

The voice vote on H Res 1276 came as the committee was nearing completion of the second week of hearings on the 1963 assassination of President Kennedy in Dallas.

In its report on the funding request (H Rept 95-1555), filed Sept. 7, the Administration Committee said that the Assassinations Committee had been "extremely prudent in the expenditure of funds." The request for an additional $790,000 included $160,000 for scientific projects and $152,000 for expense money. The remaining $478,000 represented a restoration of funds cut from the original request by the Administration Committee.

Hearings on King Slaying

The first week of public hearings on the assassination of Martin Luther King Jr. included a dramatic three-day appearance Aug. 16-18 by James Earl Ray, King's convicted killer, who repeated his claim that he did not shoot the black civil rights leader.

Ray's denials before the House Select Committee on Assassinations appeared to win few converts to his cause and were eroded by the committee's systematic probing into the credibility of his story.

The panel appeared to be developing a theory that Ray, who was appearing in a public forum for the first time since the April 4, 1968, shooting, had trailed King from Los Angeles to Atlanta and finally to Memphis, Tenn., site of the slaying.

The committee produced a change-of-address notice indicating that the mail of Eric S. Galt, a Ray alias, should be forwarded to Atlanta, and two laundry receipts with the Galt name indicating Ray had picked up laundry in that city on April 1. Ray claimed he had left Atlanta several days earlier and had not returned.

As the hearing continued it took on the appearance of the court trial Ray had long requested, with acting Chairman Richardson Preyer, D-N.C., a former judge, presiding and Chairman Louis Stokes, D-Ohio, doing much of the questioning. Ray's lawyer, Mark Lane, frequently voiced objections to the committee procedures.

Appearing under heavy security, Ray said that he did not shoot King, that he had been maneuvered by his former lawyer into pleading guilty, and that he had been framed by a man named "Raoul." But he provided little new information to prove his innocence or to implicate others.

Blames Lawyer

Ray, who recanted his testimony three days after pleading guilty to murder in 1969, told the committee Aug. 16 he had been "maneuvered" by his then-attorney, Percy Foreman, into entering the plea.

He did so, he said, because Foreman had told him that the FBI might harm his family if he didn't, that the judge wanted a guilty plea because "he was afraid blacks might burn down the town" in retaliation for King's death, and because he might receive some of the profits from a book on the shooting by author William Bradford Huie.

Most of Ray's testimony focused on his relationship with Raoul, a mysterious figure who law enforcement officials had never been able to identify and about whom they knew nothing other than Ray's testimony. Ray said he and Raoul had engaged in gun and contraband smuggling in the United States, Canada and Mexico after meeting in a bar in Montreal in July 1967.

"I didn't make no effort to know him well," Ray said of Raoul. "That's a good way to get yourself killed."

Stokes asked Ray to explain the discrepancy between his earlier description to interviewers of Raoul as a 35-year-old blond man and his description to the committee of Raoul as a dark-haired man. Ray said he told the interviewers Raoul was a dark-haired man and that they had published incorrect information.

Ray admitted Aug. 17 that after leaving Los Angeles in mid-March 1968 he had gone to several southern cities including Atlanta, but that he had left Atlanta March 28 for Birmingham and had not returned.

Stokes asked Ray if he wanted to change anything about that statement.

"No," Ray said. "Regardless of how many documents you have up there I didn't return to Atlanta, and if I did, well, I'll just take responsibility for the King case here on TV."

Stokes then introduced the laundry slip indicating Ray was in Atlanta April 1, and said the committee had testimony from witnesses who had seen Ray in Atlanta on that date.

Also during his Aug. 17 testimony, Ray was pressed by Stokes to prove the existence of Raoul.

Ray had only vague answers about possible witnesses to Raoul's existence. "Possibly a barmaid at the Starlight Cafe in Birmingham, possibly a waitress at Jim's Grill in Memphis" had seen Raoul, he said.

Ray's Aug. 18 testimony was delayed when Lane insisted on getting a copy of the handwritten notes Ray had provided Huie. After huddling for 20 minutes, the committee agreed to provide the notes.

Under questioning by Harold S. Sawyer, R-Mich., Ray admitted he had made an unqualified admission of guilt, which led to his 99-year prison sentence. But he still maintained he had been pressured into making the plea by Foreman.

"There's really no big deal about maneuvering a defendant into a guilty plea," Ray said. "All guilty pleas are not made in heaven."

King 'Troubled . . . Nervous'

Earlier in the week, the committee heard from the Rev. Ralph David Abernathy, who was with King when he was killed. Abernathy said the Memphis police and FBI never questioned him about the murder.

During questioning Aug. 14, Abernathy said he had no direct knowledge that King had received a threat to his life, but he cited King's abrupt change in mood to support his belief that King did have some advance warning that his life was in danger.

"He became a different person. He was troubled. He was nervous. He became very jittery," Abernathy told the committee.

Dr. Michael Baden, a criminal pathologist who with two other pathologists was asked by the committee to study medical records in the case, said Aug. 15 it was not possible to determine the precise origin of the shot that killed King.

Ray's Finances Probed

When the committee resumed its hearings on the King slaying in November, it focused on the question of whether Ray had been paid for killing the civil rights leader. In testimony Nov. 15, committee investigators said they had found no evidence to support that allegation.

But a story published in the Nov. 17 *New York Times* said the committee would ultimately conclude that Ray was motivated by a standing $50,000 from from a right-wing St. Louis businessman who wanted the civil rights leader slain.

The *Times* said the offer was made by John H. Sutherland, a patent attorney who was a leader of the racist White Citizen's Council of St. Louis.

Sutherland and businessman John R. Kaufmann — who have since died — were active members of George Wallace's American Independent Party, which in 1968 opened a Wallace campaign office across the street from a tavern operated by Ray's brother John, himself an avid Wallace supporter. The story said the offer was common knowledge in the tavern, which was frequented by men with criminal records as well as Wallace campaign workers, and that Ray probably heard of it by letter or telephone when he was in California in March 1968.

But the story said committee investigators had found no evidence that Ray ever collected the bounty.

The *Times* said sources "familiar with the history of the bounty" contended that the FBI probably learned of its existence in 1967 or 1968, but there was no indication they investigated the matter.

Committee investigator Edward M. Evans told the panel that Ray spent nearly $10,000 from the time of his April 1967 escape from Missouri State Penitentiary until his arrest in London about two months after the April 1968 assassination, but that his income from known sources was little more than $1,000 in that period.

Evans said the July 1967 robbery of $27,000 from a bank in Alton, Ill., was the most likely alternative to Ray's story that he had obtained the money from Raoul.

He said circumstantial evidence suggested that Ray and one or more of his brothers were involved in the robbery.

"The Alton robbery is virtually identical in modus operandi to five other bank robberies in which John Ray was involved, with Jerry Ray participating in at least one of these robberies," Evans said.

The investigators found that Ray spent $250 on clothes and $150 as an advance for an apartment shortly after the robbery.

Foreman Testimony

Percy Foreman, a Houston trial lawyer who defended Ray for a brief period after the shooting, appeared before the committee Nov. 13 and recalled some of Ray's comments during interviews he had with his client.

Foreman said Ray admitted in one interview that his story of Raoul's involvement in the crime was a fabrication.

Foreman denied Ray's charge that he had urged him to plead guilty. He said Ray himself suggested the plea to avoid execution and receive a minimal sentence.

Foreman said he thought Ray's prejudice against blacks was an important motive for the slaying. He said Ray frequently talked about the possibility of a race war between blacks and whites, and that shooting King would make him a hero to the white race.

Witness' Mental Condition

Six witnesses appeared before the committee Nov. 14 to describe the mental condition of Grace Walden Stephens, a 62-year-old woman who on the day of the shooting was staying in the rooming house from where Ray is believed to have shot King. Stephens has said that a man she saw fleeing from the bathroom after the crime was not Ray.

Shortly after the assassination Stephens was committed to a state mental hospital and remained there for 10 years. Mark Lane, Stephens' legal guardian as well as Ray's defense attorney, said Tennessee authorities suppressed her description of the man in the rooming house.

All six witneses, including four doctors, said there was no connection between the King shooting and the decision to commit Stephens.

Police Testimony

During testimony Nov. 9 the committee heard from Alexander Eist, a retired Scotland Yard detective who was assigned to stay continuously with Ray after his arrest in London.

Eist said Ray had "never really told me that he pulled the trigger," but that there wasn't any doubt in his mind "that he was admitting to me that he had done the murder."

During testimony Nov. 10 the committee focused on the lapse in police security in Memphis on the day the crime occurred. The King group's objection to the security arrangements was the main reason the security detail had withdrawn just before the assassination occurred, according to the testimony.

Jerry Ray Appearance

Ray's brother Jerry, appearing before the committee Nov. 30, angrily denounced Blakey's suggestion that he or another Ray brother, John, "or a composite of the two of them" might actually be the mysterious Raoul.

Kennedy Hearings

Opening hearings on the Kennedy assassination in September, the committee heard a great deal of scientific evidence supporting the single-bullet theory — the theory that one bullet struck both Kennedy and John B. Connally — which had often been the target of critics of the Warren Commission report.

During testimony Sept. 8, Vincent P. Guinn, a chemistry professor at the University of California, discussed the results of neutron activation tests he had conducted to determine if samples of bullet lead recovered from the assassination scene had a common origin.

Guinn said his tests showed that fragments of the bullet recovered from Connally's wrist had traces of antimony and silver that matched the bullet found on Connally's stretcher at Parkland Hospital. Also matching were fragments of the bullet that struck Kennedy in the head and the remains of the bullet found in the front seat of the president's limousine.

The committee also heard testimony from ballistics and medical experts disputing the critics' contention that the bullet found on Connally's stretcher could not have struck two men and emerged nearly undamaged.

Dr. Charles Petty, chief medical examiner in Dallas, said the ammunition was "designed to go through people," and that it did not surprise him that it went on into another individual.

Larry Sturdivan, a ballistics expert, said the bullet had struck something before it hit Connally because it was no longer traveling straight. He said the bullet could have been slowed by body muscle before it struck Connally's wrist.

New Acoustics Evidence. In testimony Sept. 11, James Barger, an acoustics expert, testified that a comparison of acoustical tests made in Dallas in August and an accidental police tape recording of the assassination gunfire suggested that the firing of four shots was "a possible conclusion."

Barger said the probability of four shots being fired was "around 50 percent."

Barger conceded that the possibility of error was substantial; committee chairman Louis Stokes, D-Ohio, cautioned against drawing "sensational conclusions from this evidence."

Sept. 12 Testimony. The committee heard from experts on flight trajectories and photographic analysis; all the evidence buttressed the Warren Commission conclusions.

Tom Canning, a specialist in flight trajectories for the National Aeronautics and Space Administration, said his study led to the conclusion that the shots had come from a point near the sixth floor of the Texas School Book Depository building, where Lee Harvey Oswald was believed to have been positioned.

Canning also said he was "confident" that the same bullet that struck Kennedy high in the back was on a trajectory that also would have struck Connally.

A panel of photoanalysts also supported the conclusion that Kennedy and Connally were struck by a single bullet.

Marina Oswald Testimony. Marina Oswald Porter, the widow of Oswald, appeared before the committee Sept. 13 and 14 to describe her impressions of Oswald and the assassination; her testimony added little new substantive evidence.

She said Sept. 13 she was "not qualified" to say whether her husband had killed Kennedy, but that Oswald's attempt to kill Gen. Edwin Walker in April 1963 had led her to believe that he was capable of killing someone.

Under intense questioning Sept. 14, however, she said that in her opinion her husband probably did kill Kennedy.

"Yes, I do believe he did. I believe the man was capable of it," she said.

Asked about Oswald's motives for the slaying, she indicated that mental instability was probably a greater factor than his political beliefs.

Cuban Involvement

In testimony Sept. 18-19, the committee heard evidence about the possibility of Cuban involvement in Kennedy's death.

Evidence presented to the committee Sept. 19 included a tape recording of an April interview by House investigators with Cuban President Fidel Castro, who denied having any involvement in the assassination and described the idea as "insane."

"That would have been the most perfect pretext for the United States to invade our country, which is what I have tried to prevent for all these years, in every possible sense," Castro told the interviewers.

Asked about a statement made to an Associated Press reporter 10 weeks before the Kennedy slaying, in which he warned that plots against him could backfire, Castro said the statement was not given as a threat.

"I did not mean to threaten by that," he said. ". . . I did not mean that we were going to take measures, similar measures, like a retaliation for that."

Castro called "absurd" a report that he knew in advance of an assassination threat against Kennedy. The committee said in a statement that a confidential U.S. government source had told the committee the story might have some substance.

The story also was denied Sept. 18 by two former Cuban consuls in Mexico City and a consulate secretary, who testified regarding a one-week trip Oswald took to Mexico two months before the assassination.

Two of the three witnesses confirmed that it was indeed Oswald who applied for a transit visa to Cuba during a Sept. 27, 1963, visit to the consulate. Committee sources said that handwriting analysis had confirmed that the Oswald who signed the document was the same man captured in Dallas.

The only dissent was from former consul Eusebio Azcue Lopez, who said he thought there were two Oswalds, and that the man who visited the consulate was not the same man who killed Kennedy. The Oswald shown in assassination pictures, Azcue said, seemed younger and heavier than the man who came to the consulate.

Ford Testimony

The committee heard from former President Gerald R. Ford Sept. 21 as part of the examination of the handling of the investigation by the FBI and other federal agencies. Ford, then a House member, served on the Warren Commission.

Ford admitted that the Warren Commission investigation probably would have been broadened had the commission known of CIA plots to kill Castro.

Ford, one of only three surviving members of the commission, said knowledge of the CIA plots "certainly would have required the commission to extend its inquiry into those operations."

"But I don't think they, in and of themselves, would have changed the conclusions," he added.

Ford testified that he didn't understand why the commission had not been told about the CIA plots when one of its members was Allen W. Dulles, a former director of the intelligence agency.

"I had the feeling then that we were getting all the information from the agencies, including the CIA. Obviously, some information, such as on the assassination plots, was not given to us," Ford said. "Why we weren't given it, I frankly don't understand."

Ford added that former CIA Director Richard Helms had given the commission a long memorandum on the possibility of a conspiracy involving Cuba.

Ford acknowledged that for a time he briefed a top FBI official about organizational problems when the Warren Commission was beginning its work. He said there were only two such briefings, and that they stopped when the investigative phase began.

FBI Witnesses

James H. Gale, a retired assistant director of the FBI, told the committee Sept. 20 that Oswald should have been on the FBI's list of subversives, but even if he had it would not have prevented the assassination.

Gale said he was in charge of the investigation that led FBI Director J. Edgar Hoover to discipline 17 FBI employees for not putting Oswald on the list.

James R. Malley, a former FBI inspector who supervised the FBI investigation in Dallas, said the bureau had conducted a thorough investigation of various conspiracy theories before agreeing with the Warren Commission conclusion that Oswald acted alone.

Malley said the possibility of a conspiracy was a constant preoccupation, and that the bureau had looked into the possibility of Cuban involvement and the possible involvement of organized crime in the assassination.

Told by committee investigators that some FBI officials directly involved in organized crime cases had never been asked about the case, Malley insisted that crime syndicate connections had been checked and that other organized-crime agents in the bureau must have been contacted.

Malley said he had never heard Hoover object to the Warren Commission. Hoover reportedly was unhappy with the formation of the commission.

Ruby's Links to Organized Crime

The committee concluded its fourth week of hearings on the Kennedy slaying on Sept. 28, after dismantling several conspiracy theories but opening some potential new leads into others.

While apparently destroying theories that linked the assassination with ultraconservative figures and a man clutching an umbrella near the assassination scene, the hearings explored possibilities that organized crime figures had some connection with the slaying.

Committee investigators found that Jack Ruby had made a large number of "suspicious" telephone calls to alleged crime syndicate figures in the months preceding the assassination, and Cuban exile Jose Aleman testified that

Lottery Export Bill Vetoed

A bill allowing U.S. manufacturers to export lottery materials was pocket-vetoed Nov. 4 by President Carter, with no veto message. The bill had cleared Congress Oct. 13 on voice vote of the Senate.

The House previously passed the bill (HR 11580) by voice vote Oct. 2, after the Judiciary Committee reported it Sept. 27 (H Rept 95-1637). The Senate discharged its Judiciary Committee from consideration of the bill before passage, so there was no report.

The bill permitted the export of tickets and other goods used in lotteries. Restrictions in existing law dealing with interstate commerce in lottery-related goods within the United States were retained. Also left untouched were changes Congress made in federal statutes in 1974 to accommodate state-run lotteries. *(1974 changes, Congress and the Nation Vol. IV, p. 591)*

he had been told by an alleged Mafia chieftain Kennedy "was going to be hit."

But contradicting his earlier statements to committee investigators, Aleman told the committee Sept. 27 that the statement, which he attributed to reputed Florida underworld leader Santo Trafficante, might not have meant that the president was going to be assassinated.

Aleman, who was guarded by federal marshals, said he met Trafficante in the summer of 1963 to talk about business, but that Trafficante instead spent hours talking about the Kennedy administration's investigation of organized crime and Teamsters Union activities.

At one point Aleman said Trafficante told him there was no doubt Kennedy was not going to be re-elected. When Aleman disagreed, Trafficante replied: "You don't understand me. He's going to be hit."

Shifting his earlier interpretation, Aleman said Trafficante meant Kennedy would be "hit" with "a lot of votes for the Republican Party or something like that."

Trafficante appeared before the committee Sept. 28 and was granted immunity from prosecution after using the Fifth Amendment right against self-incrimination and refusing to answer the opening questions.

Trafficante denied having any prior knowledge of the Kennedy assassination or ever telling Aleman that Kennedy would be "hit." He said he did take part in a CIA murder plot against Cuban leader Fidel Castro.

Ruby's possible ties with organized crime were the subject of an extensive committee investigation; Chief Counsel Robert Blakey said the investigation found that Ruby had made a number of telephone calls in the summer and fall of 1963 to associates of Trafficante, Teamsters president James Hoffa, and Mafia chieftains Sam Giancana and Carlos Marcello.

Many of the calls apparently dealt with labor troubles at Ruby's Dallas nightclub, but 13 calls were made to individuals with reputed links to organized crime.

Seven of the calls were to casino gambler Lewis J. McWillie, who Ruby visited in 1959 when he was working in an "organized-crime-controlled casino" in Havana. Ruby also called Irwin S. Weiner, who allegedly "served as a key functionary in the longtime relationship between the Chicago Mafia and various corrupt union officials;" Nofio J. Pecora, allegedly a close associate of Texas syndicate figure Carlos Marcello; Robert G. "Barney" Baker, a Hoffa lieutenant with reputed Mafia connections; and Murray W. "Dusty" Miller, another Teamsters leader the committee said "was associated with numerous underworld figures."

Weiner, Miller and Baker all told the committee that the calls were in connection with Ruby's labor troubles.

McWillie testified that Ruby visited him in Havana for no more than six days in August or September 1959. McWillie told the committee that he knew Trafficante casually, and said he did not know of any contacts between Ruby and Trafficante.

Also appearing before the committee Sept. 26 was Earl Ruby, who testified that his brother always had insisted to him that he acted impulsively and alone when he killed Oswald, and that he had never met him.

Sept. 25 Testimony

During testimony Sept. 25 the committee heard from Louie Steven Witt, who conspiracy theorists argued might have been using his umbrella as a signal when Kennedy was shot.

Witt, who at the time was working in a Dallas life insurance company, said he had brought the umbrella hoping to heckle the president. He said a friend had told him the umbrella was a "sore spot" with the Kennedy family because the president's father, Joseph P. Kennedy, as U.S. ambassador to England had been a supporter of British Prime Minister Neville Chamberlain. Chamberlain's umbrella became a symbol of the appeasement policy with Adolf Hitler.

The committee also heard from photographic experts who testified that photographs did not show Watergate burglars E. Howard Hunt and Frank Sturgess or ultraconservative figure Joseph Milteer at the scene of the assassination.

The possibility that there was more than one Oswald was dismissed by a panel of handwriting experts, who said that all but one of 43 samples of handwriting apparently written by Oswald were written by the same individual.

Joseph P. McNally, a New York City handwriting expert, told the committee that the one exception was a letter dated Nov. 8, 1963, to Texas oil millionaire H. L. Hunt. Conspiracy theorists have said the letter suggests a plot against Kennedy. The original has never been found, but McNally said the photocopy suggested that the Oswald signature could have been forged.

Summary Report

Although agreeing with the basic findings of the Warren Commission — that Lee Harvey Oswald fired three shots from a sixth floor window of the Texas School Book Depository Building in Dallas, Texas on Nov. 22, 1963, and that the third shot killed the president — the committee accepted the findings of acoustical experts that a fourth shot had been fired by a second gunman.

"Scientific acoustical evidence establishes a high probability that two gunmen fired at President John F. Kennedy," the committee said in a summary report released Dec. 31. The report then concluded that the president was "probably assassinated as a result of a conspiracy."

The Role of Counsel

The controversial semi-adversary role played by Mark Lane, James Earl Ray's counsel during his three-day appearance before the House Assassinations Committee Aug. 16-18, was instrumental in leading the committee to propose several recommendations to clarify a counsel's role during a congressional investigation.

The committee proposed that the House examine its rules governing the conduct of counsel in legislative and investigative hearings and consider "delineating guidelines for professional conduct and ethics." It should also consider a change in rules to "provide for a right to appointive counsel in investigative hearings where a witness is unable to provide counsel from private funds."

The commmittee also recommended that the House:

- Consider if Rule 11 of the House should be amended to restrict the current access by all members of the House to classified information in the possession of any committee.
- Examine the adequacy of federal law as it provides for the production of federal and state prisoners before legislative or investigative committees.
- Consider legislation that would authorize the establishment of a legislative counsel to conduct litigation on behalf of committees of the House that was incidental to legislative or investigative activities, and confer jurisdiction for such lawsuits on the U.S. District Court for the District of Columbia.

A financial disclosure bill (S 555) passed in 1978 allowed the Senate to set up such an office. The House showed little interest in the idea.

The acoustical evidence was based on an accidental dictograph belt recording of sounds that were picked up over the open radio transmitter of a police motorcycle.

Acoustical expert James Barger told the committee Sept. 11 that a comparison of acoustical tests made in Dallas in August 1978 with the accidental recording of the gunfire suggested that the probability of four shots being fired was "around 50 percent."

Further acoustical analysis of the recordings was made by New York-based experts Mark Weiss and Ernest Aschkenasy, who testified Dec. 29 that their tests indicated the probability of a fourth shot fired from the area of the grassy knoll to the right of the motorcade was "95 percent or better."

Committee Chairman Louis Stokes, D-Ohio, said the committee had been "very impressed" with the Weiss-Aschkenasy analysis. Stokes denied that the committee had been rushed into a hasty conclusion, noting that the committee staff had anticipated that Barger would draw similar conclusions in his September testimony.

The committee said it was "unable to identify the other gunman or the extent of the conspiracy," but that it found no evidence that either the Soviet or Cuban governments were involved in the assassination.

It firmly ruled out any involvement on the part of the Secret Service, the FBI or the CIA. Richardson Preyer, D-N.C., chairman of the subcommittee investigating Kennedy's death, said there was "not a scintilla of evidence" implicating those agencies.

The committee did not rule out the possibility that individual members of anti-Castro Cuban groups or organized crime might have been involved, but concluded that the groups themselves were not involved.

Although the FBI and the Warren Commission conducted adequate investigations into Oswald's responsibility for the assassination, the committee found that both organizations failed to adequately investigate the possibility of a conspiracy.

By not properly analyzing information it possessed relating to the president's trip to Dallas, the committee found that the Secret Service had been "deficient in the performance ot its duties."

King Findings

The committee concluded that James Earl Ray was responsible for the April 1968 slaying of Martin Luther King Jr. in Memphis, Tennessee.

The report said it was "highly probable" that Ray stalked King for a period immediately preceding the assassination, and that his alibi for the time of the assassination and his story of "Raoul," an alleged accomplice, were "not worthy of belief."

The committee said it believed, "on the basis of the circumstantial evidence available to it," that there was a "likelihood" that Ray assassinated King "as a result of a conspiracy." The committee had developed evidence that Ray was motivated by a standing $50,000 offer from a right-wing St. Louis businessman who wanted the civil rights leader slain. The committee found circumstantial evidence suggesting Ray might have heard of the bounty offer, but no evidence that he ever collected any money.

The committee also developed circumstantial evidence linking Ray's brothers to Ray's criminal activities.

The committee found no evidence that any federal, state or local government agency had been involved in the King assassination, but it did criticize the FBI and the Justice Department for not adequately investigating the possibility of a conspiracy in the case.

Recommendations

The committee made a variety of recommendations for new legislation, including:

- Legislation to make the assassination of a chief of state of any country a federal offense if the offender were an American citizen or could be located in the United States.
- Legislation to codify, revise and reform the federal law of homicide, paying special attention to assassinations.
- Charter legislation for the CIA and the FBI.

The committee also recommended that the Justice Department re-examine its contingency plans for the handling of assassinations, including:

- Insuring that its response took "full advantage of the advances of science and technology, and determining when it should secure independent panels of scientists to review or perform necessary scientific tasks."
- Insuring that the department's "fair trial, free press guidelines, consistent with an alleged offender's right to a fair trial, allow information about the facts and circumstances surrounding an assassination promptly be made public," and negotiating with representatives of the media to obtain through voluntary agreements any photographs or tapes made near the site of the assassination. ▮

Economic Policy

When President Carter sent his fiscal year 1979 budget to Congress, in January 1978, he probably gave the best indication to date of the course of his presidency. A year earlier, the newly elected president had just a few short weeks in which to make his imprint on the federal budget, and while he had proposed significant changes in the program recommended by his predecessor, Gerald R. Ford, he told the nation to wait a year to see a full statement of his budget priorities.

The 1979 budget was thus anticipated more eagerly than most — especially by the various constituencies that had made up the Democratic coalition. Weary after eight years of Republican rule, they had high hopes for a renewal of the Democratic commitment to social programs.

Carter, although he won the presidency without the endorsement of the Democratic establishment, owed much to those groups. But he also had made a campaign commitment to give expression to another sentiment that was sweeping the land — one born of frustration with Vietnam and Watergate — which insisted, in Carter's words, on a more efficient, competent government.

The Economy in 1978

The state of the economy in 1978 gave Carter reasons both for good cheer and for concern. It had recovered doggedly from the worst recession since the 1930s — in the process outstripping the recovery of the other industrialized Western nations. But that performance was clouded by several persistent problems. Despite the strong recovery, unemployment stayed at high levels. Business confidence seemed as yet not fully restored, with the result that new investment was at discouragingly low levels. That gave rise to concerns that the economy would be unable to continue the strong expansion. Inflation appeared to be stuck at a level of 6 percent or higher. Finally, there were indications that the economic recovery was about to run out of steam, even though joblessness was still far above levels traditionally acceptable to Democratic administrations.

Trying to balance the various competing forces represented by his presidency, Carter proposed a budget which he proudly asserted was "lean and tight" but still "compassionate" enough to meet the social needs of the nation. It included a call for a substantial tax cut, which Carter said was necessary to continue the economic recovery and help reduce unemployment. *(Budget, p. 49)*

The promised tax cut and other social program proposals seemed to be in keeping with the traditional Democratic philosophy. The tax cut was consistent with the approach of past Democratic administrations in aiming more relief at lower income groups while at the same time proposing tax "reforms" which would close "loopholes" that benefit the well-to-do.

The budget also included an ambitious proposal to reform the welfare system. Later, under pressure from urban groups, Carter sent Congress a new package designed to help the nation's deteriorating cities to rebuild. He also said he would work to develop other prized liberal programs — including national health insurance.

Taxpayer's Revolt

While some Democrats continued to doubt Carter's liberal credentials, developments through 1978 appeared to suggest that a conservative trend was even stronger than the president had believed.

One of the first indications came from California, where voters June 6 overwhelmingly approved Proposition 13, a state constitutional amendment sharply limiting property taxes. While the meaning of the vote was subject to debate, it appeared to reflect a fairly widespread belief that government spending had grown too rapidly — at least given the results that government was achieving.

The "taxpayer's revolt," as it was dubbed, had a distinctly middle class flavor as it was expressed in Congress. A surprisingly large number of lawmakers denounced Carter's tax proposals on the grounds that they failed to recognize that the time had come to help the "middle class," rather than lower income people. That political view came armed with an economic theory. It asserted that the economy's ills could be traced to a tax system which put too great a burden on "working, productive" people — in the process sapping their initiative to work, save and invest. The result, according to the new theory, was that the economy produced below its capacity — thus causing unemployment — while at the same time suffering inflation because of the resulting shortage of goods and the low labor productivity caused by insufficient business investment.

Whatever the merits of that argument — liberals denounced it as the old "trickle down theory," and its following among economists was relatively small — it proved very persuasive to an inflation-beseiged middle class. The result was that Carter's tax proposal was significantly skewed — most notably by a large cut in capital gains taxes — so that it did relatively more for the well-to-do than any tax bill in recent memory.

In the meantime, the welfare reform proposals floundered, the urban policy was picked apart, and national health insurance was postponed. Growing increasingly concerned about inflation as unemployment dipped and the rise in prices appeared to accelerate — and as an election drew near — Congress chipped away at the budget and scaled back the size of the tax cut. But while strong sentiment to cut spending was expressed in many ways — probably most notably in a series of across-the-board spending cuts added to major appropriations bills on the floor of the House and Senate — most of the congressional reduction in Carter's proposed deficit resulted from scaling back the tax cut and from spending re-estimates based on the inability of various agencies to spend money as rapidly as they had anticipated. *(Spending cuts, p. 162)*

Further Economic Developments

As the year went on, the economy performed in ways not entirely anticipated. Most surprisingly, employment rose much more than expected. That, combined with a new surge of inflation, served to shift the attention of economic policy-makers away from the feared downturn and back to inflation.

Other forces were forcing the administration to take steps to combat inflation. Among them was pressure on the dollar in international money markets. Explanations for the dollar's woes — which caused considerable concern among other Western nations, who feared the increased competitiveness of American products — were varied. Some blamed the United States' tremendous trade deficit, which they said created a glut of dollars abroad. The deficit was caused partly by the nation's continuing heavy dependence on imported oil and partly by the fact that more restrictive fiscal and monetary policies in other nations kept their economies from generating purchasing power for American imports to match the renewed purchases of foreign goods in the revived American economy. The result was that the American hunger for foreign imports far outstripped the market for American products in the other industrialized Western nations. In addition, it was undeniable that American industry had lost some of its competitive superiority relative to the nations of Western Europe and Japan.

But clearly another part of the problem was the relatively high inflation rate in this country, which threatened holders of dollars with a continuing loss of purchasing power.

Carter Inflation Strategy

Early in the year, Carter acknowledged that inflation was a vexsome problem, but his economic policy focused more on the dangers of an economic downturn. The unexpected increase in employment, coupled with a sharp rise in prices, prompted Carter in April to make a stronger commitment to fight inflation. Repeating a promise not to resort to wage-price controls — a bogeyman that frightened the business community, whose confidence Carter was very eager to win both for political and economic reasons — the president renewed a request that business and labor voluntarily keep wage and price increases below the rate for the previous two years. He also acknowledged that government should take the lead in making sacrifices that would help slow inflation, promising further fiscal restraint and citing a number of proposals before Congress that would help bring down prices in specific sectors.

'Guidelines' and the Rescue of the Dollar

By October, Carter's tax reforms were long since moribund. A tax cut was assured, but in its details it bore almost no resemblance to what Carter had proposed. Welfare reform was essentially dead for the year. Parts of the urban program were enacted, but others stood no chance of being approved. Some of the programs Carter had promised as related to his inflation fight — such as an energy program and airline deregulation — had been at least in part achieved. But others — including hospital cost control — were lost. All in all, the record of the 95th Congress gave little cheer to those concerned about inflation.

Pressured by other Western nations, and by domestic political realities as well, Carter strengthened his anti-inflation stance further on Oct. 24 by calling for wage and price "guidelines." He pledged to back up those "voluntary" standards with as much moral suasion and indirect pressure as possible. In addition, he proposed that the next Congress consider linking the tax system to the inflation fight by establishing a system of tax rebates that would go to workers in companies which adhered to the wage guidelines. The rebates would be paid in the event that inflation exceeded the minimum rate to which the government appeared to be resigned for the short run — by then 7 percent.

The new program included a pledge from the Carter administration for even greater budget stringency — a promise that appeared consistent with the spirit of the "taxpayer's revolt," but which raised new questions about how well Carter could hold together the Democratic coalition.

Those doubts were further amplified in the wake of the "Stage II" anti-inflation announcement. Labor expressed strong doubts about the new program, and AFL-CIO President George Meany issued a call for mandatory wage-price controls. But more immediately, the value of the dollar plummeted on international markets after Carter's new inflation address — a sign that foreign currency traders were very skeptical about the new program.

The dollar's new fall prompted the Carter administration to take sudden and fairly drastic action. The decision to intervene on a massive scale in foreign currency trading in order to prop up the dollar, coordinated with Federal Reserve Board action to raise interest rates sharply, sent the dollar rebounding. The immediate crisis, which had threatened seriously to destabilize the international monetary system, force an increase in world oil prices (which are based on the dollar), flood other Western nations with ever-cheaper American imports and set off renewed inflation in the United States, was alleviated.

But the shift in American economic policy evidenced by a more restrictive fiscal and monetary policy gave rise to warnings that the nation could tip into a recession in 1979. The administration denied that was a danger, but there were indications that a recession would be an acceptable price policy-makers would pay to help wring out inflation — provided the downturn was sufficiently mild and short-lived.

The year ended in a state of uncertainty similar to the one in which it began, with businessmen and politicians looking to the administration's fiscal 1980 budget with the same degree of eagerness they had felt about the previous one. All questioned the degree to which the administration would risk recession to hold down the federal deficit — and what domestic priorities it would be willing to sacrifice.

Beyond that were broader questions — questions about whether a relatively mild anti-inflation program could halt the rapid rise of wages and prices, whether Carter could apply the economic brakes and still hold the Democratic coalition that elected him, and — most fundamentally — whether the economy could still afford to complete the liberal agenda with programs such as national health insurance.

—By Christopher R. Conte

Congress Approves $18.7 Billion Tax Cut

Congress gave final approval Oct. 15 to an $18.7 billion tax cut for 1979 which included a substantial reduction in the tax on capital gains.

The bill (HR 13511), one of the last measures to be enacted by the 95th Congress, provided individual income tax reductions that would partially offset Social Security and inflation-induced tax increases for 1979.

In addition, it provided about 4.3 million taxpayers — mostly in the middle and upper income ranges — with generous capital gains tax reductions. It also gave people over age 55 a once-only complete capital gains tax exclusion for up to $100,000 in profits from the sales of personal residences.

For businesses, the bill included a reduction in corporate income tax rates — especially in the $50,000-$100,000 range — and expanded investment tax credits.

President Carter signed HR 13511 without comment Nov. 6 (PL 95-600).

The bill bore little resemblance to the tax program the president had proposed in January. Almost all of his proposed "reforms," except for a few tokens, had been scrapped, and the cuts were skewed much more towards the upper end of the income scale than he had recommended.

But in one respect the administration did assert itself more successfully during the final deliberations that shaped the bill. With Treasury Secretary W. Michael Blumenthal actively participating in the final House-Senate conference, the overall size of the bill was reduced substantially to meet administration budget objectives.

Lawmakers, already committed to the capital gains tax reduction despite liberal complaints that it would mostly benefit the wealthy, found themselves too constrained by those budget limitations to approve other tax cuts large enough completely to offset the expected Social Security and inflation-induced increases in 1979.

The result was that most Americans would have to pay more in taxes in 1979 than they did in 1978, in spite of the new bill. For taxpayers earning less than $40,000, the increases would be modest, but they would grow at income levels higher than that.

The individual tax provisions of the bill marked a sharp departure from the approach of tax laws of the recent past, which were relatively more generous to people at the low end of the income scale, and which generally moved in the direction of limiting the special treatment afforded certain kinds of income such as capital gains.

Indeed, lawmakers, riding the crest of a middle class "taxpayer's revolt," reversed some of the prized liberal "reforms" of the past — cutting back the minimum tax on preferences, and approving a potentially fatal delay of a law that would prevent property from escaping capital gains taxes completely by being held until death.

The "carryover basis" rule, which would have required heirs to pay taxes on the full capital gain on inherited property rather than just that which occurred during their ownership, was a major provision of the Tax Reform Act of 1976. The minimum tax was first adopted in 1969, but it was substantially strengthened by the 1976 act. *(Tax Reform Act, 1976 Almanac p. 41)*

Referring to provisions diluting those two 1976 measures, retiring Sen. Clifford P. Hansen, R-Wyo., concluded Oct. 15: "We've turned around the whole thrust of what tax reform was two years ago."

Liberals sadly agreed. "This bill reverses over 10 years of tax reform efforts," said Robert M. Brandon, director of the Ralph Nader Tax Reform Research Group. "The long effort to eliminate the special treatment of capital gains — the biggest loophole in the tax system for the wealthy — would be dealt a knockout blow unless the president rejects the bill."

Final Provisions

As signed into law, the Revenue Act of 1978 (HR 13511 — PL 95-600) included the following provisions (all were effective Jan. 1, 1979, unless otherwise noted):

INDIVIDUAL TAXES

Rates and Brackets

- Increased the zero bracket amount — the level of income not subject to income tax — to $2,300 from $2,200 for single persons; to $3,400 from $3,200 for married people filing joint returns; and to $1,700 from $1,600 for married people filing separate returns.
- Reduced the number of tax brackets and widened the remaining ones so as to slow the rate at which inflation-induced salary increases would push taxpayers into higher brackets. Rates were reduced in some brackets. For single people, the 25 brackets were replaced with 16 wider ones, ranging from the 14 percent bracket with taxable income between $2,300 and $3,400, to the 70 percent bracket with taxable income above $108,300. For married people, the 15 new brackets ranged from 14 percent on taxable income between $3,400 and $5,500 to 70 percent on taxable income above $215,400.
- Increased the personal exemption to $1,000 from $750, in place of the expiring general tax credit.

Earned Income Credit

- Made the earned income credit permanent, and expanded it to 10 percent of the first $5,000 of income (maximum of $500), to be phased out at a 12.5 percent rate as income rises between $6,000 and $10,000 (previously, the credit was equal to 10 percent of income up to $4,000 and it phased out at a 10 percent rate between $4,000 and $8,000).
- Enabled employees to elect to receive the credit in their paychecks each pay period, instead of when they file tax returns after the end of the year. Employers would reduce their income tax withholding and Social Security tax liabilities by the amount of advance payments made to their employees. Effective July 1, 1979.

Itemized Deductions and Credits

- **Gasoline Taxes.** Repealed the itemized deductions for state and local taxes for motor fuels not used in business or investment activities.

Political Contributions. Repealed the itemized deduction for political contributions, and increased the maximum political contributions credit to $50 for single returns and $100 for joint returns (the credit equaled 50 percent of contributions up to those maximum levels).

Child Care. Provided that payments to grandparents for the care of their grandchildren qualify for the child care tax credit.

Individual Tax Provisions Compared

This table compares the individual tax provisions of the House, Senate and final versions of HR 13511. The total amount of individual cuts for 1979 under the House bill was $10.4 billion. The Senate cuts amounted to $21.1 billion. The final bill provided $12.7 billion in individual reductions.

The three columns on the left show how each version divided the total amount allocated to individual cuts among different income classes. The three columns on the right show the actual average tax reductions each version would provide to each income class. (Expanded income basically includes income minus deductions, but including tax preferences.)

Expanded Income Class *(thousands)*	Percentage Distribution of Tax Cut			Tax Cut as Percent of Existing Law		
	House	Senate	Final	House	Senate	Final
0 to $5	0.5%	2.2%	1.6%	—	74.9%	36.0%
$5 to $10	4.2	14.6	11.6	5.2%	35.3	18.8
$10 to $15	8.0	11.2	7.8	4.8	13.1	6.1
$15 to $20	12.6	14.9	11.6	5.4	12.3	6.4
$20 to $30	27.4	22.6	23.1	6.3	10.1	6.9
$30 to $50	23.2	15.6	20.0	6.1	7.9	6.8
$50 to $100	12.9	9.4	12.3	5.5	7.8	6.8
$100 to $200	4.7	3.9	4.8	3.7	6.0	4.9
$200 and over	6.5	5.6	7.2	4.9	8.2	7.0
Total	100.0%	100.0%	100.0%	5.6%	10.8%	7.2%

Source: Joint Committee on Taxation

Unemployment Compensation

• Provided that unemployment compensation benefits be taxable to the extent they equal one-half the amount by which a taxpayer's adjusted gross income exceeds $20,000 for single people and $25,000 for married people.

Deferred Compensation Plans

• Provided that deferred compensation plans maintained by taxable entities would be governed by regulations in effect prior to an Internal Revenue Service (IRS) proposed regulation issued Feb. 3, 1978. That, in effect, would enable employees of such entities to continue to delay taxes on part of their income by entering into agreements whereby they defer part of their pay until a later date. Effective Feb. 1, 1978.

• Provided that employees of state or local governments or tax-exempt rural electric cooperatives could include the lesser of $7,500 or one-third of their income annually in a tax deferral plan. Plans to which the provision applied were given until 1982 to satisfy the requirements to qualify, but the limitation on amounts that could be deferred was made effective Jan. 1, 1979.

• Prevented employers from claiming deductions for deferred compensation involving independent contractors until the compensation is included in the participants' income. The same principle previously applied to deferred compensation involving employees.

Cafeteria Plans. Provided, in the case of "cafeteria," or "flexible benefit" plans (under which employees may choose from a package of employer-provided fringe benefits), that employer contributions are taxable only to the extent that taxable benefits are selected.

• In the case of "cafeteria" plans that discriminate in favor of highly paid employees, provided that employer contributions are taxable to the extent that the employee could have selected taxable benefits.

• **Profit Sharing.** Clarified rules governing plans under which employees have the choice of receiving cash or having the same amount contributed to a deferred profit-sharing plan. Basically, the bill provided that employer contributions to such plans would not be taxable merely because the employee had a choice to receive cash, provided the plans satisfy normal pension plan rules, do not distribute employer contributions based merely on passage of time or completion of a fixed period of plan participation, and do not include forfeitable employer contributions. Effective Jan. 1, 1980, with transitional rules for plans in existence on Jan. 27, 1974.

Retirement Plans

• Enabled employers who do not maintain retirement plans to make tax deductible contributions to individual retirement accounts (IRAs) maintained by their employees up to the lesser of $7,500 or 15 percent of earned income (compared to the usual limit of 15 percent or $1,500 for IRAs solely financed by employees).

• Permitted employees to supplement employer contributions to IRAs when the contributions are less than the usual limit on deductible IRA contributions — 15 percent or $1,500.

• Exempted employees under collectively bargained pension plans with at least 100 participants from a law limiting benefits to the lesser of 100 percent or $75,000 per year, adjusted for inflation since 1974 ($90,150 for 1978), under certain conditions. The $75,000 limit was reduced to $37,500, adjusted for inflation.

● Permitted distribution of mutual fund stock purchased by a tax-exempt charitable organization or educational institution for an employee after the employee dies, becomes disabled, separates from service, attains age 59.5 or encounters hardship. Previous law prevented distribution before age 65 unless the employee died, or became disabled; and it allowed distribution after separation from service only if the employee had reached age 55.

● Extended to government pension plans the same preferential tax treatment afforded life insurance company income from reserves for annuity contracts sold to non-government pension plans — thus ending a disincentive life insurance companies had in selling the contracts to government plans.

● Made public school teachers and employees of tax-exempt organizations eligible under a law allowing participants in pension, profit-sharing, stock-bonus or annuity plans to convert their shares tax-free into individual retirement accounts or new employer-sponsored plans when they change jobs. Effective Jan. 1, 1977.

Future Spending, Tax Cuts

● Stated, but did not require, that the growth in federal spending should not exceed 1 percent per year, adjusted for inflation, between fiscal year 1979 and fiscal year 1983; that federal outlays as a percentage of gross national product (GNP) should decline to below 21 percent in fiscal 1980, 20.5 percent in fiscal 1981, 20 percent in fiscal 1982 and 19.5 percent in fiscal 1983; and that the federal budget should be balanced in fiscal years 1982 and 1983.

● Stated that if those conditions were met, the tax-writing committees would intend to report legislation providing "significant" tax reductions for individuals to the extent they are justified in light of prevailing and expected economic conditions.

Other Individual Income Tax Provisions

● Extended for one year the tax exclusion for grants under the Uniformed Services Health Professions Scholarship programs. Effective for students entering programs in 1979 to cover amounts received through 1983.

● Extended through 1982 the time during which students could be freed of taxation on canceled student loans by working in certain geographical areas or for certain classes of employers (for instance, a nurse agreeing to work in a rural area).

● Exempted from income through 1983 amounts that employers pay their workers for education.

● Authorized the Internal Revenue Service to contract with private or public non-profit agencies to prepare volunteers to provide tax counseling assistance for the elderly.

● Directed the Treasury Department to study methods by which the process of filing federal income tax returns could be made simpler.

BUSINESS TAXES

Rates

● Reduced corporate income taxes, and established a graduated rate schedule for small corporations, as follows:

Taxable Income	Previous Rate (percent)	New Rate (percent)
0 to $25,000	20	17
$25,000 to $50,000	22	20
$50,000 to $75,000	48	30
$75,000 to $100,000	48	40
Over $100,000	48	46

Investment Tax Credits

● Made permanent the 10 percent investment tax credit.

● Increased to 90 percent from 50 percent the amount of regular tax liability the credit can offset, to be phased in at 10 additional percentage points per year beginning with taxable years which end in 1979.

● **Pollution Control.** Allowed the credit for the full investment, rather than one-half the investment, for pollution control facilities where five-year amortization is elected — provided the facility is not financed with tax-exempt industrial development bonds. Effective for facilities constructed or acquired after Dec. 31, 1978.

● **Building Rehabilitation.** Extended the investment credit to rehabilitation expenditures for business and productive buildings at least 20 years old, excluding residential buildings. Effective Nov. 1, 1979.

● **Chicken Coops, Pigpens, Greenhouses.** Extended the credit to structures used solely for the production of poultry, eggs, livestock or plants. Effective Aug. 15, 1979.

● **Cooperatives.** Extended the credit to cooperatives, effective Nov. 1.

Employer Stock Option Plans

● Extended for three years, through 1983, the law enabling employers to receive an additional 1 percent investment tax credit — above the usual 10 percent— for contributions to employee stock option plans. Employers could claim a further half-percentage point investment tax credit for contributions matched by employees under the extended law.

Targeted Jobs Credit

● In place of the expiring general jobs tax credit, established a "targeted jobs credit" equal to 50 percent of wages up to $6,000 in the first year of employment (maximum of $3,000) and 25 percent in the second year (maximum of $1,500); for employers who hire supplemental security income (SSI) recipients, welfare recipients, handicapped people undergoing vocational rehabilitation, and disadvantaged individuals 18-25, Vietnam veterans under 35, convicts released from custody within the past five years and certain students aged 16-18. Effective 1979-1981 for employees hired after Sept. 26, 1978.

● Included individuals registered under the work incentive, or WIN, program as qualifying under the targeted jobs credit unless they are employed in personal services (such as housework), in which case the credit would be equal to only 35 percent of wages.

Tax Shelters and Partnerships

● Extended to all activities except real estate the "specific at risk rule," whereby taxpayers are prevented from claiming tax deductions for losses larger than their actual economic investment.

• Extended the at risk rules to corporations in which five or fewer individuals own more than 50 percent of the stock (closely held corporations), except for equipment-leasing companies.

• Required the recapture of previously allowed losses when the amount at risk is reduced below zero.

• Imposed a $50 per month penalty on partnerships for failure to file partnership information tax returns.

• Extended to four years from three years the statute of limitations for tax returns involving partnership items.

Industrial Development Bonds

• Increased to $10 million from $5 million the amount of "small issue" industrial development bonds that could be issued tax exempt for acquisition, construction or improvement of land or depreciable property over six years for projects costing no more than that.

• Authorized projects receiving grants under the Urban Development Action Grants (UDAG) program to be financed by up to $10 million in industrial development bonds, even if total capital expenditures were as high as $20 million. Effective Oct. 1, 1979.

• Allowed industrial development bonds used to provide water facilities for industrial, agricultural, commercial and electric utility users to qualify under a law providing for tax exemption for water facilities available to the general public. Effective upon enactment.

• Provided that industrial development bonds used to finance electric generating plants qualify for tax exemption if the energy is sold to a public utility which serves an area no greater than one city and one contiguous area (applied to Power Authority of the State of New York — PASNY — bonds to generate power for New York City and Westchester County). Effective for obligations issued after April 30, 1968.

• Authorized the Tax Court and the U.S. Circuit Court of Appeals for the District of Columbia to issue declaratory judgments with respect to the tax-exempt status of proposed state and local bond issues.

• Authorized certain state and local governments to channel to public charities the profits of certain arbitrage bonds — bonds whose proceeds are invested in other high interest bonds — which were prohibited under a 1976 IRS regulation. Effective upon enactment.

Small Business Corporations

• **Subchapter S.** Increased to 15 from 10 the number of shareholders a small corporation may have to be eligible to elect to be taxed as a partnership under Subchapter S of the tax code.

• Allowed husbands and wives to be counted as one shareholder under Subchapter S.

• Extended the period during which a small corporation may elect to be considered a Subchapter S corporation to the entire previous taxable year and the first 75 days of the current year, rather than a two-month period beginning one month before and ending one month after the beginning of the taxable year.

• **Farms.** Made permanent provisions of a 1977 law (PL 95-30) that exempted two large chicken farms — Hudson Foods of Arkansas and Halifax Foods of Maine — from a provision of the Tax Reform Act (PL 94-455). The provision required farming corporations to use accrual accounting instead of cash accounting and to capitalize preproductive expenses rather than deducting them immediately. *(1977 Almanac p. 101, 1976 Almanac p. 41)*

• Exempted sod farms from the provisions requiring accrual accounting and capitalization of preproductive period expenses.

• Exempted farmers, nurserymen and florists using accrual accounting from a July 18, 1978, IRS ruling that growing crops be inventoried.

• **Miscellaneous.** Required the Treasury Department to conduct a study to determine whether expenditures made in compliance with the Occupational Safety and Health Act (OSHA) or the Mining Safety and Health Act (MSHA) should qualify for the same rapid five-year amortization and special investment tax credit provisions allowed for expenditures made to comply with water pollution laws.

• Provided a three-year extension of the special rule allowing straight-line five-year depreciation for expenditures used to rehabilitate low income rental housing. Effective 1979-1981.

Other Business Tax Provisions

• **Business Entertainment.** Disallowed business deductions for any entertainment facility — such as yachts or hunting lodges — including dues paid to social, athletic or sporting clubs but excluding country club dues.

• **Miscellaneous.** Provided that contributions in aid of construction (other than customer connection fees) received by regulated public gas and electric utilities would be treated as non-taxable contributions to capital by non-shareholders, similar to the treatment afforded public water and sewage facilities. Effective Jan. 31, 1976.

• Ended the tax exemption for amounts received under self-insured accident or health plans if the plans discriminate in favor of officers, shareholders or highly paid employees. Effective Jan. 1, 1980.

• Provided that income or loss from rental of rolling stock to railroads be treated as U.S.-source income, provided the stock is not used outside of the United States for more than 90 days. The provision was designed to prevent the potential loss of lessors' foreign tax credits.

CAPITAL GAINS, PREFERENCES

• **Individual.** Increased to 60 percent from 50 percent the amount of non-corporate capital gains that could be excluded from ordinary taxation. Effective Nov. 1, 1978.

• Repealed the alternative tax for capital gains, whereby taxpayers could elect to pay a tax of 25 percent on the first $50,000 of gain if their rate would otherwise be higher. Effective Nov. 1, 1978.

• **Corporate.** Reduced to 28 percent from 30 percent the tax rate that corporations could elect to pay on capital gains if that rate is less than their regular tax rate.

• **Residences.** Provided that taxpayers 55 years or older could completely exclude from taxation up to $100,000 in gain from the sale of a personal residence once. Effective July 26, 1978.

• Allowed individuals to "roll over" capital gains from home sales (reinvest them in new homes without paying capital gains taxes) more often then the once every 18 months allowed by previous law, if they are required to relocate for work purposes.

• **Study.** Directed the Treasury Department to study the effectiveness of reducing capital gains taxes on stimulating

Individual Income Tax Changes

(1978 Income Levels)

This table shows the impact of HR 13511 as approved by Congress on individual income taxes in 1979, along with the tax increases that would result from inflation and Social Security hikes scheduled to take effect on Jan. 1, 1979, under previous legislation. *(PL 95-216, 1977 Almanac p. 161)*

Single Person

Wage or salary income	Previous law tax	New law tax	Income tax cut[1]	Inflation tax increase[2]	Social security tax increase[3]	Net tax change
$ 5,000	$ 279	$ 250	−$ 29	+$ 35	+$ 4	+$ 10
$ 10,000	1,199	1,177	− 22	+ 47	+ 8	+ 33
$ 15,000	2,126	2,047	− 79	+ 69	+ 12	+ 2
$ 20,000	3,232	3,115	− 117	+ 100	+ 82	+ 65
$ 25,000	4,510	4,364	− 146	+ 153	+ 260	+ 267
$ 30,000	5,950	5,718	− 232	+ 205	+ 260	+ 233
$ 50,000	12,985	12,559	− 426	+ 439	+ 260	+ 273
$100,000	32,235	31,792	− 443	+ 439	+ 260	+ 256

Married Couple, No Dependents

Wage or salary income	Previous law tax	New law tax	Income tax cut[1]	Inflation tax increase[2]	Social security tax increase[3]	Net tax change
$ 5,000	$ 0	$ 0	−$ 0	+$ 0	+$ 4	+$ 4
$ 10,000	761	702	− 59	+ 66	+ 8	+ 15
$ 15,000	1,651	1,625	− 27	+ 62	+ 12	+ 47
$ 20,000	2,555	2,457	− 98	+ 91	+ 82	+ 75
$ 25,000	3,570	3,399	− 171	+ 127	+ 260	+ 216
$ 30,000	4,712	4,477	− 235	+ 188	+ 260	+ 213
$ 50,000	10,610	10,183	− 427	+ 421	+ 260	+ 254
$100,000	29,630	28,878	− 752	+ 621	+ 260	+ 129

Married Couple, Two Dependents

Wage or salary income	Previous law tax	New law tax	Income tax cut[1]	Inflation tax increase[2]	Social security tax increase[3]	Net tax change
$ 5,000	−$ 300	−$ 499	−$ 200	+$ 56	+$ 4	−$ 140
$ 10,000	446	374	− 72	+ 88	+ 8	+ 24
$ 15,000	1,330	1,233	− 97	+ 62	+ 12	− 23
$ 20,000	2,180	2,013	− 167	+ 97	+ 82	+ 12
$ 25,000	3,150	2,901	− 249	+ 124	+ 260	+ 135
$ 30,000	4,232	3,917	− 315	+ 161	+ 260	+ 106
$ 50,000	9,950	9,323	− 627	+ 435	+ 260	+ 68
$100,000	28,880	27,878	− 1,002	+ 673	+ 260	− 69

1. This column represents the tax reduction provided by HR 13511, assuming deductions equal to 23 percent of income. It doesn't include changes in capital gains taxes.

2. This column represents the amount by which taxes would have to be cut in 1979 to offset the tax increase that would occur when inflation pushes taxpayers into higher tax brackets. The numbers assume a 7 percent rate of inflation, and deductions equal to 23 percent of income. They do not include changes in itemized deductions or in capital gains taxation.

3. This column represents the tax increase resulting from a Social Security rate increase to 6.13 percent from 6.05 percent, and an increase in the wage base to $22,900 from $18,900.

Source: Joint Committee on Taxation

investment, increasing the rate of economic growth, increasing employment and raising income tax revenues.

Minimum Tax

• Removed capital gains and excess itemized deductions (deductions other than medical and casualty loss deductions that exceed 60 percent of adjusted gross income) from the list of items subject to the minimum tax of 15 percent on the sum of tax preferences in excess of $10,000.

• Established a new alternative minimum tax, payable only if it exceeds the sum of a taxpayer's regular tax and his minimum tax, levied on taxable income, plus excluded capital gains and excess itemized deductions. After a $20,000 exemption, the tax would equal:

Tax Base Levels	Percent
$0 to $40,000	10
$40,000 to $80,000	20
Over $80,000	25

• Made permanent provisions of a 1977 law (PL 95-30) requiring individuals to include the costs of drilling for oil and gas in their minimum tax base only to the extent that the deductions exceeded their oil and gas income. The provision was designed to protect taxpayers whose main occupation was producing oil and gas from a 1976 law making such "intangible" drilling costs a preference item subject to the minimum tax. *(1977 Almanac p. 101)*

Maximum Tax

• Removed capital gains from the list of preference items which reduce, on a dollar-for-dollar basis, the amount of personal service ("earned") income that is subject to the 50 percent maximum rate. Other, "unearned," income — such as interest and dividends — could be taxed at rates up to 70 percent. The bill removed capital gains from the list of preferences which "poison" the maximum tax under the rule that, for every dollar of tax preference income an individual claims, he loses a dollar of personal service income that falls under the 50 percent maximum.

• For ventures where personal services and capital both contribute to the production of income, removed the existing 30 percent limitation on the amount of income that can be subject to the 50 percent maximum rate on personal service income. That left a "reasonable compensation" test to determine how much income from such ventures can fall under the 50 percent ceiling.

Carryover Basis

• Delayed until 1980 the effective date of provisions of a 1976 law (PL 94-455) establishing that heirs must pay capital gains taxes on the entire gain on inherited property they sell, rather than just the gain that occurred during their ownership. The "carryover basis" provision, originally due to take effect in 1977, would apply to estates of decedents dying after Dec. 31, 1979. *(1976 Almanac p. 41)*

OTHER TAX PROVISIONS

• Provided for the creation of general stock ownership corporations (GSOCs) to be chartered by state governments with stock owned by state residents. The entities would be exempt from corporate taxes, and they would have to distribute 90 percent of their income to owners in the form of taxable dividends. Effective for corporations organized between Jan. 1, 1979, and Jan. 1, 1984 — designed to enable residents of Alaska to acquire an ownership interest in that state's natural resources.

• Nullified an IRS ruling requiring restaurant operators to report employee tips added to checks by charge-account customers, in addition to cash tips reported to management by employees.

• Provided that a surviving spouse who owned a business jointly with his or her decedent can be assumed to have acquired interest in the property for estate tax purposes at an annual rate of 2 percent, for a maximum of 50 percent, provided the spouse can demonstrate that he or she participated actively in the enterprise. The provision was designed to end the "widow's tax" on farms and other businesses.

• Extended to U.S. savings and loan association branches in Puerto Rico a provision by which interest on deposits in U.S. commercial bank branches there is exempt from U.S. taxation. Effective upon enactment.

• Reduced to 2 percent from 4 percent the excise tax on net investment income of domestic private foundations. Effective Oct. 1, 1977.

• Phased out the federal tax on coin-operated gaming devices (slot machines), increasing the credit against the tax for state taxes on the devices to 95 percent from 80 percent beginning July 1, 1978, and repealing the tax after June 30, 1980.

• Directed the Treasury Department to submit to Congress a study on the taxation of foreign owners of U.S. property to determine how to treat income or gain from such property for U.S. tax purposes.

• Extended the amount of time during which legal steps could be taken to qualify certain charitable contributions for special tax treatment — a provision designed to benefit Arkansas College in Arkansas. Effective upon enactment.

• Provided that stock or partnership interests held by the decedent's family are to be treated as being held by a single shareholder or partner for purposes of determining eligibility for provisions allowing extended payment of estate taxes on closely held businesses — a provision designed to benefit the Gallo family, which produces wine in California. Effective upon enactment.

• Excluded from private foundation status (and thus from excise taxes levied on foundations for failure to distribute income) certain long-term care facilities — a provision designed to benefit the Sand Springs Home in Sand Springs, Okla. Effective after Jan. 1, 1970.

• Increased to $5,000 from $1,500 the size of tax deficiencies that could be handled through simple small tax legal procedures.

• Allowed individuals who sold property to cooperative housing corporations and then acquired stock in them to be treated as tenant-stockholders for up to three years — a provision designed to encourage construction of cooperative housing by helping cooperatives during periods of high vacancy to meet the rule that 80 percent of their income be from tenant-stockholders in order for them to qualify for certain tax, interest and business depreciation deductions. Effective for stock acquired after enactment.

• Permitted publishers or distributors of magazines, paperbacks or records to elect to exclude from income amounts attributable to products returned within two months and 15 days (in the case of magazines) and four months and 15 days (in the case of paperbacks and records) after the close of the year in which the sales of the items were made — a provision enabling them to avoid overstating their income in the later year. Effective Oct. 1, 1979.

• Permitted manufacturers to deduct for a taxable year the cost of redeeming discount coupons redeemed within six months of the end of the taxable year — a provision enabling them to avoid overstating their income in the earlier year.

• Prevented the IRS from assessing some very substantial taxes it had been seeking from the Alaska Native Corporations, retroactive to Dec. 18, 1971.

• Made a series of technical corrections to the Tax Reform Act of 1976 (HR 6715). *(HR 6715, 1977 Almanac p. 154)*

• Permitted the Treasury Department to take subordinate liens on farm property which was valued according to its use, rather than fair market value, for estate purposes under the condition that it would be kept in farming for at least 15 years — a provision designed to enable some farms with Treasury liens to obtain loans from banks which require a first lien as a precondition to the loans. Effective Jan. 1, 1977.

• Enabled businesses to carry back product liability losses and apply them against income for 10 years, as opposed to the usual three years for most business losses — a provision designed to help offset the losses by reducing taxes. Effective for losses incurred after Sept. 30, 1979.

• Allowed taxpayers to exclude from income, and hence from taxes, payments received under a variety of agricultural and environmental cost-sharing programs — a provision designed to increase incentives to use the programs. Effective for grants made after Sept. 30, 1979.

• Provided a system whereby taxpayers can, under certain circumstances, receive prompt refunds of overpayments of taxes. Effective upon enactment.

• Eliminated the requirement that married taxpayers claiming the disability income exclusion must file a joint return, thus providing that the exclusion for adjusted gross income over $15,000 could be computed without regard to any income of the other spouse simply by filing a separate return

• Excluded from taxation payments made to Michigan farmers to compensate them for cattle losses resulting from PPB poisoning even if the money was not used to purchase new cattle, so long as the money was used for some farm purpose — a provision nullifying an IRS attempt to tax the payments. Effective Jan. 1, 1975.

• Made technical changes in the laws governing individual retirement accounts.

WELFARE PROVISIONS

• Increased to $2.9 billion from $2.5 billion the ceiling for federal matching funds for social services under Title XX of the Social Security Act, effective for 1979 only.

• Increased the federal matching rate for public assistance programs (aid to the aged, blind and disabled and Aid to Families with Dependent Children) to 75 percent in Puerto Rico, Guam and the Virgin Islands.

• Tripled the maximum annual amount of federal funding for public assistance programs to $72 million for Puerto Rico, $2.4 million for the Virgin Islands and $3.3 million for Guam.

Impact of Capital Gains Cuts

(1978 Income Levels)

This table shows the impact of the capital gains tax reductions approved by Congress as part of HR 13511, excluding the provisions involving taxes on the sale of personal residences. About 4.3 million tax returns would have a tax cut, while 37,000 would have an increase. (Expanded income basically includes income minus deductions, but including tax preferences.)

Expanded Income Class *(thousands)*	Number of Returns *(thousands)*	Average Reduction *(dollars)*	Percentage Distribution of Cut
0 to $5	52	$ 113	.3%
$5 to $10	539	22	.6
$10 to $15	564	45	1.2
$15 to $20	687	73	2.4
$20 to $30	992	112	5.4
$30 to $50	875	275	11.7
$50 to $100	434	1,082	22.6
$100 to $200	118	2,680	14.3
$200 and over	37	25,192	41.4

Source: Joint Committee on Taxation

Carter Proposals

The president's tax program, released Jan. 21, included provisions to reduce personal taxes by $23.5 billion while implementing "reforms" in the personal tax system that would raise $8.4 billion; to reduce business taxes by $8.4 billion while introducing changes to raise $1.1 billion; and to reduce individual and business taxes by an additional $2 billion by eliminating the excise tax on telephone service and reducing the federal unemployment compensation payroll tax.

Carter claimed the net $24.5 billion tax reduction would stimulate the economy to grow at a rate between 4.5 and 5 percent through 1979, as compared to a relatively poor 3.5 percent growth rate without it. He said the reduction would add one million jobs to the national economy, decreasing the unemployment rate to between 5.5 and 6 per cent by the end of 1979. *(Text of message, p. 23-E)*

Carter also said the tax changes were designed to fulfill his promise to make the tax system more progressive. While the reductions would benefit all typical taxpayers with incomes of $100,000 or less, most of the relief—94 percent of it—would go to individuals and families earning less than $30,000 per year, he said.

For a typical family of four earning $15,000 a year, the tax proposals would reduce income taxes by $258, a 19 per cent reduction, Carter said. Families with income less than $15,000 would benefit even more, while families with more income would benefit less.

Tables released by the Treasury Department suggested that a typical four-person family earning $10,000 would have its income tax liability reduced to $134 from $446, a reduction of 70 percent. A four-person family earning $40,000, however, would have income taxes drop to $6,630 from $6,848, a decrease of only 3 percent.

The actual change in taxes paid between 1977 and 1979 under Carter's proposals would differ from those figures, however, because of increases in Social Security taxes already approved by Congress.

The Treasury Department estimated that typical families with one wage earner and four dependents and income less than $20,000 would still experience a net tax reduction, while such families with income above $25,000 would have a net tax increase.

Details of the President's major tax proposals follow:

Tax Reductions

The rates for the individual income tax would be reduced across-the-board by 2 percent, so that they would range from 2 percent for the lowest bracket to 68 percent for the highest bracket, as compared to the existing range of 14 to 70 percent.

Instead of allowing a $750 per person tax exemption and a $35 credit, families would be allowed a $240 credit per person. An exemption is a sum of money removed from a taxpayer's taxable income, while a credit is a sum subtracted from his actual tax liability. Exemptions generally benefit taxpayers in upper income brackets more, because of the high effective tax rates for such brackets.

The tax rate on corporate income above $50,000 would be reduced from 48 per cent to 45 per cent effective Oct. 1, 1978, and to 44 per cent effective Jan. 1, 1980. The rate on corporate income below $25,000 would be reduced from 20 per cent to 18 per cent, and the rate on corporate income between $20,000 and $25,000 would be reduced from 22 per cent to 20 percent.

The existing 10 percent investment tax credit, which was scheduled to drop to 7 per cent in 1981, would be continued permanently at 10 per cent. In addition, it would be liberalized so that it could be used to offset up to 90 per cent of a corporation's tax liability, as compared to the existing 50 per cent ceiling. It also would be extended to investments in industrial and utility structures, in addition to applying to machinery and equipment. Carter also proposed allowing pollution control equipment to qualify for the full 10 percent credit, even if it qualified currently for five-year amortization.

The 4 percent levy on telephone and telegraph service would be repealed Oct. 1, rather than being phased out gradually as provided in existing law. The federal unemployment compensation tax would be reduced to .5 per cent from .7 per cent on Jan. 1, 1979. It was scheduled to drop in the 1980s.

Tax Revision

Carter proposed several changes in itemized deduction provisions in the tax code.

The president specifically recommended eliminating special deductions for general sales taxes, taxes on personal property (except for real estate), gasoline taxes and other miscellaneous taxes.

Carter also proposed eliminating provisions allowing for an itemized deduction of up to $200 for political contributions, while keeping the provision allowing taxpayers to claim a credit of up to $50 against their tax liability for one-half of the amount of a political contribution.

The tax program also proposed combining medical expenses and casualty losses into a single "extraordinary expense" deduction, which would be allowed only when such expenses exceeded 10 per cent of income. A variety of provisions tightening up on the allowance of such expenses were also included in the proposals.

Carter proposed eliminating tax code provisions allowing deductions for purchases of tickets to theater and sporting events, for maintaining yachts, hunting lodges and swimming pools, and for fees paid to social, athletic or sporting clubs.

The president also recommended allowing deductions for only 50 per cent of the currently deductible cost of business meals and beverages.

A related provision would limit deductions for the cost of business-related air travel to the cost of coach, as opposed to first class, fare.

The tax proposals also included a provision that taxpayers would only be allowed to claim deductions for expenses relating to foreign conventions if it could be demonstrated that factors such as purpose and membership made it "reasonable" to hold the convention outside the United States.

The president's tax package included two provisions reducing tax benefits to corporations for overseas activities. First, Carter recommended phasing out over three years provisions allowing U.S. corporations to defer taxes on their export earnings funneled through domestic international sales corporations (or DISCs).

Carter also recommended a three-year phase-out of the provision allowing U.S. corporations to defer taxes on incomes of foreign subsidiaries until the money is repatriated.

The president's proposals included several provisions to crack down on tax shelters used by some upper income taxpayers to limit their tax liabilities. It also had several provisions tightening up on tax preferences for fringe benefits that are applied discriminatorily.

Carter proposed phasing out the existing tax exemption for unemployment compensation benefits for individuals with income above $20,000, and for married couples with income above $25,000.

He also proposed several tax law revisions designed to tighten up on opportunities to avoid taxes by investing in tax-exempt bonds. He said the proposals would not limit the ability of state and local governments to obtain low-cost financing.

Other proposals would cut back on "favored tax status" for financial institutions.

Carter, as expected, backed down from his earlier promises to propose elimination of the special tax treatment on capital gains. But he did propose tightening up on the tax treatment of capital gains for upper-income individuals.

House Committee Action

INITIAL MARKUPS SUSPENDED

Following a tumultuous week in which President Carter's tax proposals were severely battered, the House Ways and Means Committee on April 24 suspended its markup of tax legislation.

A delegation of three House Ways and Means Committee Democrats had gone to the White House April 20 to tell President Carter that his tax "reform" proposals were in serious jeopardy.

The three — Chairman Al Ullman, D-Ore., Dan Rostenkowski, D-Ill., and Joe D. Waggonner Jr., D-La. — were invited by Carter after the committee had rejected several key elements of his tax package. Their message was simple: scale down the proposals or face a substantial defeat. "The committee's actions require a re-evaluation of the whole package," said Ullman after the meeting.

Waggonner, more conservative than the chairman, was more blunt. "He can't win on these reforms," he said. "There is no constituency in the Congress or the country for them."

The meeting at the White House came after a majority on the committee indicated April 17-19 that it intended to tilt Carter's proposed tax cut more toward the middle class.

The coalition, consisting of unified committee Republicans and seven or eight Democrats, scuttled two of the major "reforms" in the president's tax package — his recommendations to end itemized deductions for state and local sales taxes and personal property taxes.

The committee, making its first tentative decisions in a scheduled six-week markup of tax legislation, also sharply scaled down a proposed tightening of medical and casualty deductions. It approved, despite administration opposition, a new tax deduction for charitable contributions.

In one of the few victories it gave the president, the committee did vote to end special tax deductions for state and local gasoline taxes.

In all, the committee's actions pared $6.8 billion from the $10 billion Carter had hoped to raise annually through tax revisions. They also added a new deduction that would decrease revenues by $1.7 billion to $3.6 billion a year.

Still pending before the Ways and Means Committee was a proposal by Charles A. Vanik, D-Ohio, and J. J. Pickle, D-Texas, to scrap Carter's tax cut entirely. They had proposed merely extending tax cuts allowed in 1977. Vanik said April 17 that he had "close to 16 votes" for that proposition on the 37-member Ways and Means Committee.

Sales, Property Tax Deductions

Almost from the outset, it was clear that the Carter "reforms" were in trouble. The panel did approve, 21-16, his recommended elimination of the gasoline tax deduction, for a revenue gain of $1.2 billion annually.

But by back-to-back 18-19 and 17-20 votes, the committee tentatively rejected eliminating the sales tax and personal property tax deductions.

On both votes, the committee's 12 Republicans voted against the reform. They were joined on the sales tax vote by Democrats James A. Burke, Mass.; Omar Burleson, Texas; Waggonner; Otis G. Pike, N.Y.; William R. Cotter, Conn.; Ed Jenkins, Ga., and Pickle.

Those same Democrats were joined by James R. Jones, Okla., in voting with the Republicans against ending the personal property tax deduction.

Barber B. Conable Jr., R-N.Y., explained that some Republicans would support ending the itemized deductions in order to simplify the tax system, but he said they would do so only if the changes wouldn't hurt the middle class.

Figures provided by the administration indicated that 58 percent of the tax increase that would result from ending the sales and personal property tax deductions would fall on people with incomes between $20,000 and $50,000. The figures showed that 82 percent of the increase would fall on people earning between $15,000 and $100,000.

"The proposals have a lot of appeal in terms of simplification and structure, provided we don't stick it in the ear of the middle class," Conable said. "I'll support doing away with them as long as it isn't a redistribution gimmick."

Donald C. Lubick, acting assistant secretary of the treasury for tax policy, said later that President Carter's proposed income tax cuts were designed to neutralize the tax increases that would result from ending the itemized deductions for middle-income taxpayers.

Conable disagreed. The ranking minority member of the committee, Conable said he would insist on more substantial rate cuts for middle-income groups before he would support ending the itemized deductions.

Medical and Casualty Deductions

Carter's proposal to tighten up on medical and casualty deductions won very little support on the committee.

Under existing law, taxpayers could claim deductions for medical expenses that exceeded 3 percent of their adjusted gross income. Drug costs could be included in the medical expense total only to the extent that they exceeded 1 percent of income. Finally, taxpayers could deduct half of the cost of medical insurance premiums, up to $150 a year.

Existing law allowed deductions for casualty losses in excess of $100.

Carter had proposed combining the two deductions into a single "extraordinary expense" deduction, and allowing it only to the extent that the expenses exceed 10 percent of income. That would have raised $2.6 billion in revenues a year.

The committee response was cool. "There is no rational reason why the U.S. government should impose a higher burden on people for medical expenses — especially when we've been so negligent in health care cost control," declared Martha Keys, D-Kan.

Instead of agreeing to Carter's recommendation, the committee endorsed a proposal by Keys and Rostenkowski to tighten up modestly on the deductions. The proposal kept the two types of deductions separate, eliminated the separate partial deductions for medical insurance premiums and the 1 percent floor for medicine and drug deductions, and prohibited deductions for non-prescription medicine and drugs other than insulin. The proposal would increase revenues by only $40 million.

Charitable Contributions

The committee later approved, 20-17, a proposal by Joseph L. Fisher, D-Va., and Conable to allow taxpayers who take the standard deduction to make a special additional deduction from charitable contributions. (The committee later reversed itself and rejected the proposal, 15-22. *p. 230*)

"Charitable giving has decreased as the number of taxpayers taking the standard deduction has increased," Fisher said. He argued that allowing a special charitable contribution deduction would provide an incentive for more charitable giving, and that the increase in such giving would exceed the loss in revenues to the government.

Conable argued further that the new deduction would encourage more charitable giving among lower-income groups. Under existing law, only people who itemized their deductions could claim charitable contributions. Since people who itemized were generally more wealthy, the result was that lower-income people could not benefit as much if they gave to charity, he argued.

"As we have moved to increase standard deductions, we have tended to put charitable policy in the hands of the middle classes," Conable said. "This begins to make charitable contributions look like loopholes."

Officials from the Treasury Department challenged the argument that the special deduction would increase charitable giving. They said that most people in tax brackets that normally used the standard deduction gave only small amounts to charity anyway.

The Fisher-Conable proposal was opposed by a number of committee members who said it would simply complicate the income tax short (1040A) form.

The Treasury Department estimated that the special deduction would decrease federal revenues by about $1.7 billion. Fisher and Conable estimated the loss at $3.6 billion.

Other Decisions

During the first three days of its deliberations, the Ways and Means Committee made several other tentative decisions supporting Carter tax proposals, including:

- Ending the tax deduction for political contributions while keeping the tax credit. It would increase revenues by $3 million annually.

- Extending the "at risk" rule limiting deductibility for tax shelter losses to all activities other than real estate. The rule currently applied only to farming, oil and natural gas exploration and exploitation, motion picture and videotape production and equipment leasing. It denied deductions for losses that exceed an investor's cash outlay plus repayable loans.
- Applying a penalty for failure by limited partnerships to file tax returns.
- Requiring partnerships to provide names and addresses of partners when requested as part of an Internal Revenue Service audit.

The committee tentatively rejected a number of other Carter tax proposals, including:

- Classifying limited partnerships with more than 15 partners as corporations for tax purposes.
- Extending the statute of limitations for partnership tax returns.

Finally, the committee agreed to a modest tightening up of taxation of deferred annuities, although it went nowhere near as far as Carter had proposed.

BILL REPORTED

In an almost total defeat for President Carter, the House Ways and Means Committee July 27 approved a $16 billion tax cut that included a substantial reduction in capital gains taxes.

The committee's 12 Republicans were joined by 13 Democrats on the 25-12 vote endorsing the bill (HR 13511 — H Rept 95-1445) in essentially the "compromise" form proposed by James R. Jones, D-Okla. *(Provisions, box, p. 229)*

One major addition to the Jones proposal, designed in part to mute liberal criticisms of the capital gains reductions, provided homeowners a one-time complete exemption from capital gains taxes on profits up to $100,000 from the sale of personal residences.

In another effort to assuage liberal members, the committee approved a new "alternative minimum tax" to ensure that the new capital gains tax reductions did not make it possible for some very wealthy taxpayers to avoid paying taxes completely.

In addition, an unlikely coalition of committee members approved a provision "indexing" the capital gains tax beginning in 1980, sheltering taxpayers from paying taxes on inflation-induced appreciation of their assets.

The bill bore almost no resemblance to the tax program Carter sent to Congress in January. It excluded almost all of the president's proposed tax "reforms," aimed the benefits of the tax cut primarily toward people in the middle- and upper-income brackets rather than lower down the income scale as suggested by Carter, and included capital gains tax reductions that the president threatened to veto.

"This obviously is not a tax reform bill," said Ways and Means Chairman Al Ullman, D-Ore. "It is an economic tax package. We have voted here a substantial reduction in the deficit. It is very counter-inflationary."

The tax cuts wouldn't take effect until Jan. 1, 1979, so they would only reduce revenues in the fiscal year beginning Oct. 1 by $9.3 billion.

Congress had agreed as part of its first budget resolution to a $15 billion tax cut during the fiscal year. President Carter endorsed that figure.

The Ways and Means Committee had resumed markup sessions July 20, following a three-month hiatus during which the Democratic House leadership and the White House tried unsuccessfully to reach agreement on a tax package.

Ullman drove the committee hard during three days of markup to complete action on the bill, and he described the final version as the "best compromise" possible.

The compromise left the committee's 12 liberal Democrats out in the cold. One of their most outspoken members, Abner J. Mikva, D-Ill., called the bill "outrageous." He threatened to go to the House Democratic Caucus to rally support for a floor fight against the committee action.

Committee Republicans, on the other hand, were quite pleased by the product wrought by them and the 13 more conservative Democrats.

"This reflects the American people's view of tax reform because it is a tax reduction," said the committee's ranking Republican, Barber B. Conable Jr., R-N.Y. "And it helps the middle-class taxpayer in a manner much more substantial than the traditional tax reform bill."

Also pleased was William A. Steiger, R-Wis., who set off the capital gains controversy by proposing a reduction in the maximum possible capital gains rate to 25 percent from 49 percent.

"This is a very significant first step in the reduction of taxes on capital gains," Steiger said. He predicted that the Senate would reduce capital gains taxes even further, paving the way for a "more acceptable" final compromise.

Liberals, who opposed the capital gains tax cut and hoped to skew individual tax reductions toward lower income people, were outgunned throughout the Ways and Means markup.

Their strategy, which was only loosely developed, appeared to include two elements. The first was a substitute amendment prepared by Joseph L. Fisher, D-Va., which would ease capital gains taxes somewhat while leaving almost intact the minimum tax on such gains. The second was the idea of loading the Jones proposal down with so many unattractive amendments that it would eventually sink, leaving the Fisher proposal floating alone.

Instead, the liberals lost most of the amendments they sought, and watched helplessly as the committee approved a number of amendments that undercut the Fisher proposal.

Social Security

The first liberal defeat came on a proposal by Richard A. Gephardt, D-Mo., to provide employers and employees an income tax credit equal to 5 percent of their Social Security taxes during 1979 and 1980. The proposal, which would have cost about $6 billion annually, was designed to offset scheduled increases in Social Security taxes. It was rejected, 11-24, in the first major display of the support for the Jones package. The vote also reflected that rolling back Social Security taxes, a popular issue early in the session, had lost support.

Indexing

The liberals appeared to score a partial victory when some of them helped approve an amendment by Bill Archer, R-Texas, to index the capital gains tax.

Archer's amendment provided that the base value of an asset subject to the capital gains tax would be increased by the same percentage as the rise in the consumer price

Summary of House Bill's Provisions

As reported by the Ways and Means Committee and subsequently passed by the House, HR 13511 provided $10.4 billion in tax cuts to individuals, and $3.8 billion to businesses during 1979. It reduced capital gains taxes by $1.9 billion, of which $1.7 billion was to go to individuals and about $100 million was to go to businesses.

Individual Cuts

About 64.4 million tax returns would receive a tax decrease, averaging $163 per return. The size of the decrease would rise with income, from an average of about $19 for persons with expanded income below $5,000 to an average of $219 in the $20,000-$30,000 income class, to $1,740 in the $100,000-$200,000 class and $9,940 in the over $200,000 income class.

About 2.6 million returns would receive a tax increase averaging $24. The increase, which would fall mostly on single people, would range from $14 in the lowest income class to $1,611 in the highest.

Highlights of the individual tax cuts included:

- A 6 percent widening of income tax brackets designed to prevent taxpayers from being pushed into higher tax brackets as their incomes rise.
- An increase in the zero bracket amount — formerly called the standard deduction — to $2,300 from $2,200 for single persons and to $3,400 from $3,200 for married couples.
- An increase in the personal exemption for each taxpayer and dependent to $1,000 from $750, and elimination of the existing general tax credit. That change accounted for most of the tax increases on single taxpayers.
- Elimination of itemized deductions for state and local motor fuel taxes and political contributions (the existing tax credit for political contributions would be retained).
- A somewhat tightened medical expense deduction.
- A provision that unemployment compensation benefits equal to one half the income in excess of $20,000 for single persons and $25,000 for married persons be taxed.

Corporate Cuts

The bill established a graduated corporate income tax as follows:

- For corporate income up to $25,000, the tax rate would be reduced to 17 percent from 20 percent.
- For income between $25,000 and $50,000, the rate would be reduced to 20 percent from 22 percent.
- For income between $50,000 and $75,000, the rate would be 30 percent.
- For income between $75,000 and $100,000, the rate would be 40 percent.
- For income above $100,000, the rate would be reduced to 46 percent from 48 percent.

Other changes in corporate taxation included:

- An increase in the amount of regular tax liability that could be offset in a single year by investment tax credits to 90 percent from 50 percent, to be phased in at a rate of 10 percent per year.
- Replacement of the existing general jobs tax credit with a targeted jobs credit for employers who hired welfare recipients, supplemental security income (SSI) recipients, unemployed Vietnam veterans and youths who participated in high school or vocational school work-study programs.

Capital Gains Tax Changes

Changes in capital gains taxation included:

- Elimination of the "alternative" 25 percent maximum tax rate on capital gains up to $50,000.
- Elimination of capital gains as preference items subject to the minimum tax and to the "poison" of the maximum tax on earned income. The effect of the two provisions would be to make the maximum possible tax rate on capital gains 35 percent, instead of 49.1 percent.
- Indexation of the basis of capital gains beginning Jan. 1, 1980, so that the amount of gains subject to taxation would be reduced by the amount of the increase in the consumer price index each year.
- Repeal of the capital gains and minimum tax on up to $100,000 in profits on the sale of a principal residence occupied by the owner for at least two years. The provision would be available only once in the life of a taxpayer. It would apply to any sale after July 26, 1978.
- A new "alternative minimum tax" on capital gains that a taxpayer would have to pay if his regular tax liability was less than the new tax. The levy would be equal to 10 percent of the portion of his capital gains exempt from regular taxation, with a $10,000 exemption.

index each year — effectively reducing by the rate of inflation the amount of capital gains subject to taxation. The amendment would take effect in 1980.

While the proposal would have a negligible effect during its first few years, experts estimated that it could eventually cut revenues from the capital gains tax in half. The amendment was approved on a 21-16 vote.

Later, Bill Gradison, R-Ohio, offered an amendment to index the personal income tax, but it was rejected 13-23.

Capital Gains

The biggest blow to the Fisher proposal came when the committee approved on a voice vote an amendment by Sam Gibbons, D-Fla., providing a once-in-a-lifetime complete exemption from capital gains and minimum taxes on profits up to $100,000 from the sale of personal residences.

The Gibbons amendment added about $745 million to the capital gains tax breaks previously included in the Jones bill. But more important, it strengthened the package politically by neutralizing one of the main advantages of Fisher's proposal — namely a proposed capital gains tax break for homeowners.

Referring to the Archer and Gibbons amendments, Jones later said: "I'm not sure I can justify them economically, but politically they strengthen the bill."

The Oklahoma congressman later added one further strengthening amendment to his capital gains proposals. Answering complaints by the administration that the bill would free a small number of millionaires completely from taxes by removing capital gains from the existing minimum tax, he won committee support, 33-3, for a new "alternative minimum tax."

The new tax would be computed quite differently than the existing tax. While the current minimum tax was added on to taxpayers' regular capital gains tax liability, the new tax would only be paid if it exceeded a taxpayer's regular liability.

Conable described it as a "true minimum tax," as opposed to the existing levy, which he called an "add-on tax."

The alternative minimum tax would pick up $120 million in revenues, mostly from very wealthy taxpayers. That compared to $1.2 billion that would be returned, also mostly to wealthy people, through the Jones proposal to remove capital gains from the existing minimum tax.

Fisher Substitute

Fisher tried to outflank Jones' supporters by expanding his original substitute to embrace the proposed Social Security tax credit and other proposals. In its final version, it would have allowed a $23.4 billion tax cut.

Fisher said his proposal would preserve a "meaningful" minimum tax on capital gains, more directly encourage capital investment, focus more relief on middle- and lower-income taxpayers, and provide direct relief for rising Social Security taxes.

Jones complained that the Fisher substitute would add $7.5 billion more to the federal deficit, provide less relief to taxpayers in the "middle" $20,000-$50,000 brackets, and preserve disproportionately high tax rates for married people.

The Fisher proposal was rejected, 13-24.

Other Substitutes

The committee also turned down, 11-24, a substitute by James C. Corman, D-Calif. that would:

- Increase the existing general tax credit to $150 for the first exemption and $110 for all other exemptions, and keep the alternative credit of 2 percent of the first $9,000 of income.
- Retain the existing earned income credit and investment tax credit.
- Reduce corporate tax rates to 18 percent for the first $25,000 of income, 20 percent for income between $25,000 and $50,000 and 46 percent for income above $50,000.
- Include the Gibbons amendment on the capital gains tax exemption for personal residences.
- Provide a targeted jobs credit.

Finally, the committee rejected, 11-26, a proposal by Charles A. Vanik, D-Ohio, and J. J. Pickle, D-Texas, to enact no new tax cut.

Business Entertainment Deductions

While a wide variety of other amendments were considered, the largest number involved a completely unsuccessful attempt by committee liberals to tighten up somewhat on business entertainment deductions.

From the outset, the liberals set their sights much lower than Carter had during his campaign assaults on the "three martini lunch," but even their more modest proposals were consistently rejected.

The most ambitious proposal, by William A. Brodhead, D-Mich., would have limited business entertainment deductions to $44 per person per day. It was rejected, 14-23.

After that, proposals were scaled down progressively until Andy Jacobs Jr., D-Ind., suggested merely disallowing business entertainment deductions for entertaining members of Congress. It was rejected on a voice vote.

In one surprise vote, the committee rejected, 15-22, an amendment by Fisher and Conable to allow taxpayers who take the standard deduction to make a special additional deduction for charitable contributions. The proposal had been tentatively approved by the committee in April.

The Rule

Aware that attempts probably would be made to amend the bill on the House floor, the committee agreed to seek from the Rules Committee a rule allowing floor votes only on complete substitutes to the bill it approved.

Specifically, the Ways and Means panel agreed to allow votes on the Corman, Fisher and Vanik-Pickle substitutes, and also on the Roth-Kemp bill (S 1860, HR 8333) providing a one-third, across-the-board reduction in income tax rates over three years.

Several committee members objected to allowing a floor vote on Roth-Kemp since the bill was never considered in committee, but Ullman said the bill should come to a vote because "it is a political issue in every congressional district." The chairman also expressed confidence that the bill would be defeated on the House floor.

Rules Committee Action

The Rules Committee took up the tax bill Aug. 8-9, in a situation considerably changed since July 27, when the Ways and Means Committee had debated the rule.

A new fight was brewing over Social Security taxes. First, 105 mostly liberal House members petitioned the Rules Committee to allow a floor vote on a proposal by Richard A. Gephardt, D-Mo., to create a new income tax credit equal to 5 percent of Social Security taxes during 1979 and 1980.

The proposal was designed to offset scheduled increases in Social Security taxes. The tax credit would indirectly provide general tax revenues to support the Social Security system, but it would preserve the principle that Social Security benefits should be financed through the payroll tax, proponents argued.

James A. Burke, D-Mass., head of the Social Security Subcommittee of the Ways and Means Committee, opposed the Gephardt plan. He asked for a House vote on either his plan to finance one-third of the Social Security system with general revenues or a more modest proposal to roll back part of the Social Security tax attributable to health insurance — Medicare — and make up the loss with general revenues.

At the same time, Republicans warned that they would try to defeat the rule if the committee refused to allow the House to vote on the Roth-Kemp income tax reduction plan as an amendment to the individual tax portions of the committee bill. A number of Democrats vehemently resisted that proposal, largely because they wanted to avoid the embarrassment of voting against a large tax cut in an election year.

Finally, the committee had been requested by other House members to allow an amendment to the bill adding new solar energy and conservation tax credits previously approved by the House but stalled along with other parts of the president's tax package.

The Social Security issue proved to be the most difficult for the Rules Committee to resolve. In the end, three Democrats — Chairman James J. Delaney, N.Y.; Morgan F. Murphy, Ill.; and John Young, Texas — joined the committee's five Republicans for an 8-7 vote disallowing a vote on the Gephardt proposal. The committee had previously rejected, 6-9, a proposal to allow a vote on the modest Social Security rollback for Medicare.

By another one-vote margin, the committee voted 7-8 against allowing a House vote on the solar energy and conservation tax credit proposal.

In part, committee members were persuaded that allowing the tax credits, which were popular in Congress, to be divorced from the energy package would weaken the chances that the rest of the energy program would be approved.

The Rules Committee concluded by allowing floor votes on Ways and Means Committee amendments, the Vanik-Pickle proposal, and a new Corman-Fisher proposal announced Aug. 4. Republicans eager to force a vote on Roth-Kemp were forced to do so by moving to recommit the bill to the Ways and Means Committee with instructions to amend it by adding the Roth-Kemp individual tax reductions.

House Floor Action

A $16.3 billion tax cut that sharply divided Democrats but won general support from Republicans was approved by the House Aug. 10 after a last-ditch attempt by the Carter administration to amend it fell 32 votes short.

The final 362-49 vote came after an all-day debate in which Republicans derided the administration as "irrelevant" to the decision, and even Democrats who supported the Carter position sought to keep their distance from the president. *(Vote 602, p. 170-H)*

Before approving the bill, the House rejected a final liberal effort to ease the burden of rising Social Security taxes. And, in a vote with strong partisan overtones, it rejected the Republican Roth-Kemp proposal for a 33 percent reduction in income tax rates over three years.

An effort to kill the tax cut entirelv was defeated easily, so HR 13511 was sent to the Senate in exactly the form it emerged from the Ways and Means Committee. That included $10.4 billion in personal tax cuts, $3.8 billion in business tax reductions, and $1.9 billion in capital gains reductions.

The total size of the cut was $4.6 billion less than envisioned by the first budget resolution approved by the House in May. However, it fell about $7 billion short of the amount that would be needed to offset scheduled Social Security tax increases and inflation-induced income tax increases expected in 1979. As a result, many taxpayers would pay more in taxes in 1979 despite the House-passed bill.

Ways and Means Committee Chairman Al Ullman, D-Ore., and James R. Jones, D-Okla., were credited with finding the tax bill compromise despite what some veteran observers described as the greatest Democratic Party divisions on a tax bill in memory.

In the process, Ullman received some criticism from liberal Democrats for failing to develop a package that could better unite their party. But most liberals directed their public complaints about the final bill more toward Carter.

"The president and his advisers were totally naive about the legislative process, and [they] gave the chairman no help," said a bitter Charles A. Vanik, D-Ohio.

Middle Income Relief

The bill approved by the House, in sharp contrast to most tax measures of the recent past, would not increase the progressivity of the income tax. Rather than provide disproportionate relief to lower income people, it would direct most of the benefits of the tax cut to people in the middle and upper income ranges.

Of the $10.4 billion in personal tax reductions, more than 63 percent would go to people earning between $15,000 and $50,000 a year. More than 76 percent of the benefits would go to people earning between $15,000 and $100,000.

The capital gains tax reductions would be even more beneficial to wealthy people. More than 70 percent of the benefits of the special one time capital gains tax exclusion for the sale of a personal residence would go to people earning between $20,000 and $50,000, while only 12.7 percent would go to people earning less than $20,000.

Of the other capital gains tax changes, 60 percent of the benefits would go to people earning more than $200,000, and 96 percent would go to people earning more than $50,000.

Those features of the bill won strong Republican support. Noting that the bill would break with a tradition of "redistributing" income through the tax code, Barber B. Conable Jr., R-N.Y., called the measure "revolutionary."

New Administration Proposal

Treasury Secretary W. Michael Blumenthal, working with disgruntled Ways and Means liberals, made one last, unsuccessful effort to win support for a more progressive tax cut. The new proposal was disclosed by James C. Corman, D-Calif., and Joseph L. Fisher, D-Va., on Aug. 4, more than a week after the Ways and Means Committee completed action on the long-delayed bill.

Corman and Fisher, both of whom had previously prepared detailed complete substitutes for the committee bill, agreed to drop their separate proposals and push instead for two amendments to the bill. The amendments would:

- Increase the general tax credit to the greater of $100 per exemption or 2 percent of the first $9,000 of income, and make some rate reductions. The credit currently was equal to the greater of $35 per exemption or 2 percent of the first $9,000 of income, but it would be eliminated by the committee bill and replaced with an increase in the personal exemption to $1,000 from $750.

The proposal would increase the size of the personal tax reductions by $2.3 billion, to $12.7 billion. Most of the benefits would go to people earning less than $15,000.

- Keep provisions in the committee bill reducing the maximum possible tax rate on capital gains to 35 percent, but replace the committee's "alternative minimum tax" on capital gains with a provision designed to establish a graduated minimum tax.

Specifically, the new capital gains proposal would limit the amount of capital gains excluded from taxation to the amount actually subject to tax.

Under existing law, one-half of total capital gain could be excluded from taxation. But the remaining half could also be sheltered by being offset by ordinary losses. Thus, if a taxpayer could claim losses equal to one-half of his capital gain, he could completely escape taxes on his gain.

The committee bill would allow a minimum tax of 10 percent on the excluded portion of capital gain. That tax would thus equal 5 percent of total gain.

Under the new Corman-Fisher proposal, the special capital gains tax exclusion would be lifted dollar-for-dollar for every dollar of otherwise taxable gain sheltered from taxation. The proposal would provide that the new limitation would never reduce the amount of excluded capital gains below $5,000, however, and it would allow charitable contributions to be deducted from taxable capital gains without triggering the limitation.

The effect of the proposal would be to establish a minimum capital gains tax that could range as high as 17.5 percent. It would increase tax revenues to the government by $300 million over the committee proposal.

Overall, the Corman-Fisher proposal would allow for an $18.1 billion tax cut. Taxpayers earning more than $50,000 would receive less under it than they would under the committee bill, while people earning up to that amount would get more. Most of the added benefits under the proposal would go to people earning less than $15,000.

Administration Role

In a press conference orchestrated to follow the announcement of the new plan Aug. 4, Blumenthal and presidential assistant Stuart E. Eizenstat said the administration "wholeheartedly" supported the "constructive" effort.

Blumenthal said the proposal would provide "much greater relief to low and middle income taxpayers, and would distribute the bill's capital gains relief much more fairly" by avoiding giving huge capital gains windfalls to people who shelter their income.

Blumenthal and Eizenstat refused to call the proposal their own. They said the administration still preferred its own tax package.

Republicans responded to the new proposal with derision. John B. Anderson, R-Ill., called it a "thirteenth hour late-blooming Blumenthal bill." Later, Conable dismissed it as a "latter day attempt to undercut the committee bill."

Jones said that the proposal's sponsors tried to make their bill more attractive than the committee proposal by pumping $2 billion more into the tax cut — even though the committee had decided that a $16.3 billion cut was the largest possible non-inflationary overall tax reduction.

The proposal also ran into some substantive opposition. William A. Steiger, R-Wis., said it would hurt not only people who used tax shelters, but also people with real losses. Finally, Ullman told the House that the administration proposal had been considered in 1969 but rejected because "no one understood it then and no one understands it now."

Rule Vote, Social Security

Liberals were disgruntled with the Rules Committee decision to preclude a vote on Social Security. In a "dear colleague" letter, they called the proposed rule "deplorable" because it gave sponsors of Roth-Kemp "carte blanche" while preventing a vote on the Social Security issue. The letter pointed out that the House Democratic caucus had urged a Social Security tax rollback by a three-to-one margin.

Republicans, on the other hand, were only slightly disturbed with the Rules Committee decision on Roth-Kemp. Delbert L. Latta, R-Ohio, complained that the motion to recommit wouldn't allow a "perfectly clear shot" on Roth-Kemp. Some members, he warned, would be able to claim they voted against the motion not out of opposition to Roth-Kemp but in order to avoid recommitting the bill.

Roth-Kemp co-author Jack F. Kemp, R-N.Y., said he was satisfied with the rule, however. He said the motion to recommit would allow a "clean, clear up or down vote on where all members stand as to lowering the rates on the American people or letting them go up to astronomical proportions in the next 3 to 5 years."

Debate on the rule provided the only chance for floor consideration of the Social Security issue.

Proponents of the Gephardt proposal argued that the amendment, which would add about $6 billion to the tax cut, was necessary to save most taxpayers from a net tax increase in 1979 due to the scheduled rise in Social Security taxes.

Abner J. Mikva, D-Ill., warned that lawmakers would have a hard time explaining in January why people would have more money taken out of their paychecks than before despite the much heralded tax cut.

But Ullman argued that Congress should wait until 1979 to act on Social Security.

"We cannot solve the Social Security problem through an income tax bill," he said. "We have got to solve it in a bill dealing with Social Security itself, and I pledge . . . that we will do that next year."

The liberal effort to amend the proposed rule so as to allow a vote on the Gephardt amendment was blocked on a procedural motion, 284-130. *(Vote 596, p. 170-H)*

Indexing Capital Gains

The House next approved, 249-167, a committee amendment originally offered by Bill Archer, R-Texas, to index the capital gains tax for inflation beginning in 1980. *(Vote 598, p. 170-H)*

Dan Rostenkowski, D-Ill., led the fight against the Archer amendment, under which the base value of an asset subject to the capital gains tax would be increased by the same percentage as the rise in the consumer price index.

Rostenkowski argued that the current preferential tax treatment afforded capital gains already offered protection against inflation, and he said it would be unfair to provide an extra shield — especially when other forms of income, such as wages or interest from savings accounts, received no inflation protection.

Rostenkowski said the proposal would protect "large scale investors" but do nothing for the "average working family." He also warned that it would prove to be very costly in the long-run — experts had estimated that it would eventually reduce revenues from the capital gains tax by 50 percent.

Archer replied that the proposal was the first step in an effort to index the tax system entirely. He argued that taxes on inflated capital gains could result in a net loss in real income for some taxpayers.

Vanik-Pickle

The House next rejected overwhelmingly, 57-356, the Vanik-Pickle proposal to enact no new tax cut. Their alternative to the Ways and Means bill would merely extend earlier tax cuts that were scheduled to expire at the end of 1978. *(Vote 599, p. 170-H)*

Vanik argued that preventing any tax cut would reduce the government's need to borrow in private capital markets, thus easing pressures on interest rates and slowing inflation.

Arguing that deficit financing caused by the large tax cut would lead to inflation, taking away income from taxpayers indirectly even as the tax cut would provide some money to them directly, Vanik claimed that 80 percent of all taxpayers would be better off under his proposal than under the committee bill.

Vanik knew he was fighting a losing battle, however.

"I think it is regrettable that we have to be acting on a tax reduction bill this close to an election," he said. "When we organize the new Congress for those who are here, I hope that a rule will be adopted to provide that no tax cut bill can be considered by the Congress within six months of an election. I want tax laws written by prudent people."

Corman-Fisher

The major tax bill showdown came over the Corman-Fisher proposal.

"Here is the big vote," declared Bill Frenzel, R-Minn. "The Corman amendment will decide whether we will really choose new directions. . . . The Corman amendment redistributes income. The committee bill cuts taxes evenly."

Fisher agreed that distribution of income was at stake in the amendment.

"Very clearly, what we do is provide a little less tax reduction at the very high incomes above $50,000, and apply that . . . to tax reduction in the lower ranges," he said. "But keep this in mind, we do better in tax reduction than the committee bill on incomes all the way up to $50,000.

"Finally, let me point out that behind the Corman-Fisher amendment we now have rallied the support of the administration, the support of the leadership and large numbers of organizations all over the country who speak for small people, ordinary people, average people, whether they are businesses, individuals, families, consumer groups or whatever," Fisher said.

The Corman-Fisher proposal aroused opposition from conservative Democrats who had been instrumental in forming the coalition on the Ways and Means Committee that produced the committee bill.

"This is nothing but a disruptive practice," declared Joe D. Waggonner Jr., D-La., of the proposal.

Directing his fire at the administration, he added: "They will change their mind as they have for months been changing their mind. But we hear it said that the rate cuts are larger. Absolutely they are larger. If you want to increase the deficit, you can make them still larger. If you add the same deficit back to the committee bill, you can have the same rate reduction.

"Make no mistake about it," Waggonner concluded. "If you want larger rate reductions, get ready for a larger deficit."

Even House Speaker Thomas P. O'Neill Jr., D-Mass., in a rare floor speech in support of the amendment, faulted the administration for being slow in developing the alternative.

"The administration has been tardy in bringing tax legislation to this body," O'Neill said. "I truly feel, though, if the amendment . . . had been brought up here five months ago, it would have been the product of the committee by now, and it would have sailed through this Congress."

Even that was inadequate to win the day for the amendment, which was defeated on a 193-225 vote. *(Vote 600, p. 170-H)*

Roth-Kemp

Only the vote on the Roth-Kemp proposal fell along party lines.

As proposed on the motion to recommit the bill to Ways and Means, the Roth-Kemp plan would reduce income tax rates across-the-board by about 33 percent over three years.

During the first year of its implementation, rates would be reduced to a range of 12-63 percent, compared to the existing 14-70 percent range. The rates would be further reduced to a range of 10-56 percent in 1980, and to a range of 8-50 percent in 1981.

The Roth-Kemp tax cut would total $31.9 billion in 1979, rising to $120.7 billion by 1981.

"By recreating the incentive to work, save, invest and take economic risks by reducing the percentage of reward for that economic activity taken by the federal government in the form of taxes, we will have more work, more savings, more investment and more economic risk taking," Kemp argued. "That will expand the total amount of economic activity, expanding the tax base from which federal tax revenues are drawn, providing additional revenues with which to offset federal budget deficits."

Ullman argued that the bill would result in deficits above $100 billion, leading to "disastrous" inflation.

But Conable disputed that claim. He said past tax cuts had been inflationary because they provided most relief to people "who have no choice but to spend them because they are in fact poor people and have no opportunity to do anything else with them."

The Roth-Kemp cuts, on the other hand, would put more money in the hands of the middle class, which Conable said he "hoped desperately" would save more, thus investing and enabling the economy to grow without inflation.

"We have such a tendency to take money away from the middle class and give it to the poor that the result is that we are constantly stimulating consumer demand, and that is why we think of tax cuts instinctively as nothing but inflationary," Conable argued. "Savings instead of consumption, investment rather than indulgence, will make this type of tax cut an economic asset for the country, not an economic liability."

A number of Democrats claimed the Roth-Kemp proposal was a political maneuver not seriously advocated by Republicans. Some responded with stump-like speeches of their own.

Vanik said the measure would require such a drastic reduction in federal spending that people who voted for it should buy a "Kemp-Roth home defense kit. Get a slingshot, a flashlight and a stick, and plan on defending yourself."

Otis G. Pike, D-N.Y., a Democrat who frequently sided with Republicans, returned to his party on the issue.

"Fiscal responsibility has been replaced by political pie in the sky," he said.

On the 177-240 vote defeating the proposal, only three Republicans — Millicent Fenwick, N.J., Paul Findley, Ill., and Charles W. Whalen Jr., Ohio — voted "no." A total of 37 Democrats defected party ranks to vote in favor of the Republican-backed measure. *(Vote 601, p. 170-H)*

Senate Committee Action

The Senate Finance Committee reported its version of HR 13511 Oct. 1 (S Rept 95-1263). The committee approved the bill by a 15-2 vote Sept. 27, following 12 days of markup.

When the markup was completed, the Finance Committee had pumped the House's proposed $16.3 billion in 1979 tax cut to an estimated $22.6 billion. The increase was divided among virtually all taxpayers, through enlarged income tax reductions, more generous cuts for business and — most controversially — a substantial expansion in the House's proposed cut in capital gains taxes.

Before finishing its work on the bill, the Finance Committee disregarded an eleventh-hour warning from Treasury Secretary W. Michael Blumenthal that the bill contained a number of provisions that the administration considered "unacceptable."

But Finance Committee Chairman Russell B. Long, D-La., conceded that some committee decisions would have to be scaled down to avert a veto and to reach an accommodation with the House.

Changes in House Bill

In general, the Finance Committee enlarged House-approved individual income tax cuts — especially for low and middle income taxpayers — in a manner designed to offset expected tax increases that would otherwise occur in 1979 because of the scheduled rise in Social Security taxes and the increase in tax burdens that would result when inflationary wage hikes pushed taxpayers into higher tax brackets.

Under the House bill, some taxpayers would pay more in taxes in real terms in 1979 even after the tax cut. The Finance Committee bill was designed to make sure that as few people as possible faced a net tax increase, but even the income tax reductions it would provide were not considered large enough to result in a real tax cut.

Beyond that, the committee approved the House's proposed reduction in corporate income tax rates, and it added several additional tax cuts for businesses. Most notable among them was a provision allowing businesses more rapid write-offs for new plant and equipment.

The most substantial differences between the House bill and the Senate committee bill concerned capital gains taxes. While the House approved provisions reducing capital gains tax rates for taxpayers in the upper income brackets with large capital gains, the Senate committee's proposed capital gains cuts were both broader and more widely distributed.

At the same time, the Finance Committee bill included a new alternative minimum tax, designed to assure that wealthy taxpayers who sheltered their income did not completely escape taxes.

The Finance Committee bill notably excluded House provisions indexing capital gains taxes for inflation. In fact, the panel rejected repeated efforts by Republicans to add indexing amendments, or at least to provide for additional tax cuts beyond those scheduled for 1979.

The committee also left out of the bill a House provision allowing a once-in-a-lifetime capital gains tax exemption for up to $100,000 in profits from the sale of a personal residence. Instead, it approved a formula providing that all personal home sales would receive more generous capital gains tax treatment than they did under existing law.

Carryover Basis

In addition, the Finance Committee added to its version of the tax bill a controversial provision delaying until 1980 the effective date of one of the most heralded tax "reforms" of the Tax Reform Act of 1976. The delayed provision would require heirs of inherited property to pay capital gains taxes on the entire gain realized on the property — including the gain that occurred before they inherited it.

Prior to 1976, heirs only had to pay taxes on the gain that occurred during the time they owned the property. In tax parlance, they paid according to "stepped up basis." But under that system, gains on property that wasn't sold prior to death escaped taxation.

The reform, called "carryover basis," had been under attack in the Senate, especially from Harry F. Byrd Jr., Ind-Va., since early in the year. Liberals, led by William D. Hathaway, D-Maine, had argued that amendments to resolve admitted administrative problems should be approved before any delay was allowed. They had argued that a delay without the "clean-up" amendments would be tantamount to killing the bill.

Finally, the Finance Committee added a large number of miscellaneous amendments to the tax bill. Some were designed to help relatively small numbers of taxpayers — including some securities firms, sod farmers, restaurateurs, owners of breeding horses and others.

Other amendments were added to the tax bill because it was seen as the only vehicle that could carry them to final passage during the waning days of the 95th Congress. They included a proposal to give $400 million to state and local governments to help defray welfare costs, as well as a number of amendments to improve administration of welfare programs.

The miscellaneous amendments drew fire from Gaylord Nelson, D-Wis., at one point during the markup. "This is welfare, not tax," he said.

To that, Herman E. Talmadge, D-Ga., sponsor of most of the welfare amendments, replied: "But this [bill] is the last train leaving the station."

Responded Nelson: "It's going to wind up with so many flat wheels it won't run."

Dissenters

William V. Roth Jr., R-Del., was one of the two Finance Committee members who refused to endorse the committee bill. He voted against it because he said it helped the rich (with capital gains tax breaks) and the poor (with an expanded earned income credit), but not the middle class.

"I think what we have done here," Roth said of the bill, "is in effect create a new class — the middle class poor."

Roth's efforts to win committee approval of the Roth-Kemp tax cut plan had failed on a succession of near-party-line votes Sept. 18.

The other Finance Committee member who voted against the bill was Nelson. He objected to the capital gains cuts, and he promised to offer a more modest reduction — one he predicted would be acceptable to the administration — as a floor amendment.

Blumenthal Objections

Nelson's proposed amendment — to increase the amount of capital gains excluded from taxation to 60 percent rather than the committee's 70 percent (the figure under existing law was 50 percent) — appeared close to what Blumenthal hinted would be acceptable to the administration in a final appearance before the Finance Committee Sept. 27.

A 60 percent exclusion would reduce the maximum rate on capital gains to 28 percent, Nelson said, as compared to the committee's maximum 21 percent. Blumenthal said that a maximum between 28 percent and 30 percent would be acceptable.

The Treasury secretary also told the committee that indexing would be "unacceptable," and he said the Finance Committee's proposed alternative minimum tax was too weak because it would increase the opportunities for taxpayers to shelter preference income other than capital gains.

While the House bill would remove capital gains as one preference item subject to the existing minimum tax, the Senate bill would completely repeal the existing minimum levy and establish a new alternative minimum tax that would apply to all preference income.

Finally, Blumenthal suggested that the Finance Committee consider a provision to tax capital gains at death. That had long been a goal of tax reformers, and it had been mentioned by liberals such as Edward M. Kennedy, D-Mass., as a fair trade-off for the other proposed capital gains tax reductions. In addition, a capital gains at death provision would effectively sidestep the carryover basis issue by making it a moot question.

Neither the Finance Committee nor Congress appeared to be favorably inclined toward the capital gains at death idea, but Blumenthal tried to convince the lawmakers that the administration would insist on substantial concessions to its proposals.

"The administration wants a tax bill," Blumenthal said. "But the administration does not feel it has to accept any bill just to have a bill."

Budget Squeeze

Blumenthal also warned the Finance Committee that its proposals would cut taxes too far to be consistent with the administration's desire to reduce the federal deficit.

He said the reduction was $1.7 billion deeper in fiscal 1979 than the administration wanted, and that the excess would grow to $5 billion in fiscal 1980 and $6 billion in fiscal 1981.

Several proposals, he said, would have little budget impact in fiscal 1979, while having very substantial effects in subsequent years. The proposed liberalization of depreciation rules for businesses, for instance, would cost only $231 million in fiscal 1979, but the cost would climb to $1.7 billion in 1981.

The capital gains cuts approved by the committee, would cost only about $400 million in fiscal 1979, according to Treasury estimates. But by fiscal 1980, that would climb to $2.6 billion.

Finance Committee members returned repeatedly to the "budget squeeze" problem themselves, although their focus was generally more narrow. They were most concerned to make sure that the proposed tax cut fit what was allowed by the second concurrent budget resolution for fiscal 1979. That was the only year covered by the budget resolution. *(Budget resolution, p. 35)*

The resolution allowed the committee to reduce revenues during the fiscal year to a level $21.9 billion below what would occur with no change in the law. That revenue floor would have to accommodate not only the new tax bill, but $8.2 billion to extend tax cuts due to expire at the end of 1978, and an estimated $2.5 billion in fiscal year impacts from miscellaneous tax bills.

The miscellaneous bills included proposed energy conservation tax credits, tuition tax credits, a reduction in taxes for Americans living abroad, a proposed tax break for airlines to help them reduce aircraft noise, and a wide variety of minor revenue measures.

When the Finance Committee began markup, the total fiscal year cost of the House tax bill combined with the proposed extension of expiring cuts was $18.3 billion. Adding in the cost estimates for the miscellaneous bills, the total came to $20.8 billion, leaving the committee only $1.1 billion to add to the bill. That was not enough even to increase individual income tax cuts enough to offset Social Security and inflation-induced tax increases, let alone allow for the generous capital gains tax cut planned by the committee.

Finance Committee members attacked the budget problem on a variety of fronts. First, they challenged initial Treasury estimates that the capital gains reduction would cost $600 million during the fiscal year. That figure, they said, was "static," failing to take into consideration the fact that a reduction in capital gains rates would induce more rapid sales of capital assets, which in turn would increase total revenues.

Early during the markup, Long produced a thick packet of letters from a number of notable economists. While their opinions about the revenue impact of the capital gains tax cut varied, Long said the general conclusion was that the reduction would cost little. Some even said it would increase revenues.

Prodded by Long, Deputy Assistant Treasury Secretary Emil J. Sunley produced a new administration analysis which suggested that about one-third of the capital gains reduction would be offset by induced capital sales. That would cut the loss in the fiscal year to $400 million.

The Finance Committee chairman wasn't satisfied with that concession, which he called a "split-the-difference" agreement from Treasury. He said he would insist that the capital gains cut would result in no net loss of revenue at all, and he said he might propose an amendment to the tax bill on the Senate floor suggesting that.

"We've got some of these taxes so high they're counter-productive," Long said, arguing that a lower tax rate would produce more revenue. "I personally would not be voting for this kind of cut in capital gains taxes if I didn't believe it would gain revenues."

The committee used a number of other devices to reduce the overall fiscal impact of its proposed tax cut. At Long's suggestion, members agreed to delay the effective date of the new alternative minimum tax until Jan. 1, 1979, even though the capital gains cuts would take effect Nov. 1, 1978. In November and December, taxpayers would still use the existing minimum tax, which would cost the Treasury less in lost revenues.

Similarly, the committee agreed to include its expanded earned income credit in the withholding system beginning only on July 1, 1979 — near the end of the fiscal year. The result was that the $1.8 billion annual tax reduction would only cost the Treasury $200 million during the fiscal year.

In addition, the committee agreed to pare back a proposed extra personal tax exemption for the totally disabled to $500 — half the proposed amount — in order to reduce costs.

By those and other techniques, the Finance Committee was able to produce a tax bill with a fiscal year cost of $12.3 billion. Combined with the extensions, that boosted the total cost to $20.5 billion — still under the $21.9 billion allowed by the budget resolution.

But the committee's tax bill wouldn't leave room for all of the $2.5 billion in miscellaneous tax measures under consideration in Congress. Long acknowledged that, and warned that some proposal must be "squeezed out."

"We've had the pleasure of voting for more tax cuts than we'll be able to enact into law," the chairman said.

Tuition Credit Controversy

In a move that was interpreted by many as indicating lukewarm support for tuition tax credits, Long resisted efforts by Roth to add them to the tax bill.

Roth reasoned that it would be more difficult for President Carter to carry out his threatened veto if they were part of a general tax bill.

Long argued that Carter should have a clear shot at vetoing them. "If the President will sign the [tuitition] tax credit bill, that's it," he said. "But if he sees fit to veto the bill, I'd take the view that if [we] send it back down there on anything else [he'd] veto it too."

The Finance Committee chairman then suggested that rate cuts in the tax bill for middle income families were an alternative to tuition tax credits, saying that the extra benefits would go to the "same class" whether in the form of general rate cuts or tuition tax credits.

Roth resisted linking the two issues, and he vowed to add a tuition tax credit amendment to the bill on the Senate floor. " I don't see how we can say to the middle class we're going to cut their taxes here [in the general tax cut bill] when that money is already committed," he said.

MAJOR PROVISIONS

As reported by the Senate Finance Committee, HR 13511 provided for $15.9 billion in tax cuts to individuals and $4.1 billion to businesses during 1979. In addition, it reduced capital gains taxes for individuals and businesses by between $2.6 billion and $3.6 billion.

Major provisions in the Finance Committee bill follow. All were to be effective Jan. 1, 1979, unless otherwise noted. (**HOUSE** indicates that the provision also was included in the House version of the bill.)

Individual Cuts

Major individual tax provisions:

- For the "working poor," an expansion of the earned income credit to 12 percent of the first $5,000 of earnings (for a maximum of $600). The credit would be reduced $1.20 for every $10 of income above $6,000, phasing out completely at $11,000. Currently the credit was equal to 10 percent of the first $4,000 of income, phasing out at $8,000.

The credit would also be made refundable (so that taxpayers with less tax liability than the credit would receive a refund), and it would be included in the withholding system beginning July 1, 1979. Employers would pay the credit to their employees in regular paychecks, subtracting the amount from their own income or Social Security taxes.

- An increase in the zero bracket amount — formerly called the standard deduction — to $2,300 from $2,200 for single persons and to $3,400 from $3,200 for married couples. **House.**
- An increase in the personal exemption for each taxpayer and dependent to $1,000 from $750, and elimination of the existing general tax credit. **House.**
- Tax rate and bracket revisions. Under the Finance Committee plan, the current 25 brackets would be consolidated into 15 wider brackets for married taxpayers and 16 for single taxpayers.
- An increase in the tax credit for the elderly. Currently the credit was equal to 15 percent of $3,750 for married people over 65, and 15 percent of $2,500 for single people or married people if only one is over 65. The credit was reduced by pension income and by one-half of adjusted gross income in excess of $10,000 for married couples and $7,500 for single people.

The committee increased the base figures to $4,500 from $3,750 for married people, and to $3,000 from $2,500 for single people. It raised the "phase-out" levels to $17,500 from $10,000 for married couples and to $15,000 from $7,500 for singles.

- An increase in the zero bracket amount for single heads of household (single people with dependents) to $3,000 from $2,200. Under existing law, single heads of household had the same zero bracket amount as single people — $2,200 under current law.
- An extra $500 personal exemption for permanently and totally disabled taxpayers or spouses under age 65 who are not receiving benefits as disabled veterans, disabled civil service employees, disabled persons under the Social Security act or other government programs.
- Elimination of itemized deductions for state and local motor fuel taxes. **House.**
- An increase in the tax credit for political contributions to $50 from $25 for single returns, and to $100 from $50 for joint returns. The credit was equal to one-half the amount of a political contribution. The Finance Committee retained the current itemized deduction for political contributions, although members said they would agree to drop the provision, as the House did, provided the House approved the increase in the credit.

Corporate Cuts

Major provisions affecting corporate tax rates included:

- The same "graduated" corporate income tax rate as approved by the House. **House.**

The new rates would be as follows:

Taxable Income	Existing Rate (percent)	New Rate (percent)
0 to $25,000	20	17
$25,000 to $50,000	22	20
$50,000 to $75,000	48	30
$75,000 to $100,000	48	40
Over $100,000	48	46

- An increase in the amount of regular tax liability that can be offset in a single year by investment tax credits to 90 percent from 50 percent, to be phased in at a rate of 10 percent per year. **House.**

The committee rejected, however, a House provision that the credit be extended to expenditures for rehabilitation of industrial structures.

- An increase in the asset depreciation range (ADR) for businesses using the ADR Class Life System to 30 percent from 20 percent. The amendment would allow businesses to establish useful lives for depreciable assets 30 percent longer or shorter than the normal life for such assets. That would make possible quicker (or slower) write-offs.

- A new targeted jobs credit to replace the expiring general jobs credit. The credit would be paid to employers for hiring Vietnam War veterans, persons aged 18-24 from economically disadvantaged families, persons receiving disability benefits under the Supplemental Security Income program (SSI), the handicapped, people receiving general assistance, and people who have been convicted of a felony. The credit would be up to a maximum of $3,000 per employee in the first year of employment, $2,000 in the second year and $1,500 in the third year. The House approved a similar provision, although there were some differences between it and the Senate committee's proposal.
- An increase in the special tax credit for hiring Work Incentive Program (WIN) and welfare recipients to 75 percent on the first $6,000 in wages during the first year of employment, 65 percent in the second year, and 55 percent in the third year. Employers would be allowed a deduction for wages in excess of the amount of the credit.
- A provision making permanent the extra investment tax credit for employers adopting an employee stock ownership plan (ESOP). The ESOP provision, which would otherwise expire at the end of 1978, allowed employers to claim an extra percentage point investment tax credit equal to money they set aside to buy company stock for employees, plus an extra half-percentage point for employer contributions matched by employee contributions. The committee also approved a series of amendments to the law governing ESOPs.

Capital Gains Tax Provisions

Changes recommended by the Finance Committee in capital gains taxes included:

- An increase to 70 percent from 50 percent in the amount of capital gains excluded from taxation, effective Nov. 1, 1978.
- Repeal of the existing minimum tax on tax preferences (which was equal to 10 percent of preference items in excess of $10,000), and implementation of a new alternative minimum tax computed as follows: rates would be applied to taxable income plus all tax preferences, less a $20,000 exemption. The rate would be 10 percent of the first $40,000, 20 percent of the next $40,000, and 25 percent of the excess above $80,000. Taxpayers would pay the greater of the alternative minimum tax or their regular tax liability. The new alternative minimum tax would take effect Jan. 1, 1979.
- A reduction in the corporate capital gains tax rate to 28 percent from 30 percent.
- An amendment delaying until 1980 the effective date of a 1976 law establishing that heirs must pay capital gains taxes on the entire gain on inherited property they sell, rather than on just the gain that occurred during their ownership. The "carryover basis" provision was originally due to take effect in 1977.
- Several provisions liberalizing and extending to all taxpayers the special capital gains tax treatment currently afforded elderly people (over age 65) on the sale of personal residences.

The law currently exempted from capital gains taxes profits from the sale of homes whose price was $35,000 or less. For houses that sold for more than $35,000, the law excluded from capital gains taxes an amount equal to the total gain, multiplied by a fraction, the numerator of which was $35,000 and the denominator of which was the actual sales price.

The committee amendment would increase the $35,000 figure to $50,000, and make it available to all taxpayers regardless of age (provided they owned and used the property as a principal residence for two out of the three years before the sale). It would apply to sales after July 26, 1978.

The amendments wouldn't change the provision completely exempting gains from home sales that were reinvested in a new home within 18 months (the "rollover" provision), or the provision allowing elderly taxpayers to claim special tax treatment on home sale gains not reinvested while using the rollover provision on gains that are reinvested in housing.

- A $20,000 exemption in the existing law providing that the amount of earned income subject to the maximum 50 percent tax rate was reduced by the amount of tax preferences a taxpayer claims (and thus can be subject to ordinary tax rates up to 70 percent). The committee did approve a House provision eliminating capital gains as one of the preference items subject to the "preference poison" law, but it established a Nov. 1, 1978, effective date for the provision, as opposed to the House's Jan. 1, 1979, date.

Welfare Provisions

The committee added to the tax bill several amendments originally contemplated as part of a welfare reform package (HR 7200), which appeared unlikely to win final congressional approval. They included:

- Provision of $400 million in fiscal relief payments for state and local costs incurred under the Aid to Families with Dependent Children (AFDC) program.
- An increase to $2.9 billion from $2.5 billion in the ceiling for federal matching funds for social services under Title XX of the Social Security Act.
- Sections of HR 7200, supported by the Carter administration, to provide incentives for states to develop computerized management information systems for AFDC programs, to provide federal matching funds for child support duties performed by court personnel, to require AFDC recipients to participate in intensive employment search programs, and to penalize AFDC recipients who fail to report earned income to state welfare agencies. *(HR 7200, 1977 Almanac p. 511)*

OTHER PROVISIONS

Other provisions in the Finance Committee bill included:

- An amendment requiring an individual and corporate income tax surcharge to finance any government outlays in excess of $500 billion in fiscal year 1980, $510 billion in 1981, $520 billion in 1982 and $530 billion in 1983, adjusted for increases in the consumer price index in each of those years. The amendment would be suspended in years when unemployment exceeded 7 percent or when war was declared.
- A provision allowing taxpayers to purchase taxable municipal bonds and either exclude the interest from their income, or include the interest and claim a federal tax credit.

Pension Plans

The Finance Committee approved several provisions designed to improve the quality of pension plans.

Currently, employers could provide retirement benefits to employees through qualified pension plans. Such contributions were tax deductible.

Alternatively, workers whose employers did not provide such plans could establish their own Individual Retirement Accounts (IRAs), contributing up to the lesser of 15 percent of compensation or $1,500 annually. Such contributions were deductible.

The Finance Committee agreed to allow employers who did not offer pension plans to contribute to their workers' IRAs up to the lesser of 15 percent of the employee's compensation or $7,500 annually. In addition, if the employer's contributions were less than the usual IRA limit, the employee could make up the difference.

On the other hand, if a worker wished to improve on an employer-provided pension plan, the committee agreed to an amendment allowing him to make deductible contributions to the plan equal to the lesser of $1,000 — if contributions on his behalf were voluntary ($100 if contributions were mandatory) — or 10 percent of his annual pay.

The committee also approved an amendment allowing state and local government employee retirement systems to invest their funds with insurance companies.

Deferred Compensation

The Finance Committee, following the House's lead, approved a number of provisions governing taxation of income which employers and employees agreed to defer. Frequently, deferred compensation plans can help a taxpayer to escape taxes because they enable him to receive his salary at times when his other income is lower, thus putting him in a lower tax bracket.

The deferred compensation amendments were prompted by a regulation proposed by the Internal Revenue Service (IRS) Feb. 3 which would have provided that pay which was deferred at an employee's choice should be taxed as if received when actually earned.

In general, the Finance Committee agreed with a House provision providing that state and local government employees and workers for tax-exempt rural electric cooperatives could defer pay (and thus taxes) up to the lesser of $7,500 or one-third of their annual salaries. The Finance Committee went one step farther than the House, however, and agreed to allow employees of all tax-exempt organizations to take advantage of the rule — an expansion opposed by the Treasury Department.

In addition, the Finance Committee approved a House provision prohibiting employers from claiming deductions for deferred wages of independent contractors until the wages were actually received.

'Cafeteria Plans'

Finally, the Finance Committee agreed to House bill provisions establishing that employee benefits provided under a "cafeteria plan" — a fringe benefit plan giving workers a choice of different benefits — were taxable only to the extent that taxable benefits were elected. The bill also included a provision barring tax exemption for benefits provided under such plans if the plans discriminated in favor of well-paid employees.

Other Employee Benefit Issues

The Finance Committee approved two other amendments affecting taxation of employee benefits.

First, it agreed to an amendment excluding from an employee's taxable income amounts he received from his employer for educational expenses.

Currently, such payments were only deductible if they were directly job-related — a provision which some claimed needlessly discouraged employees from going to school. In addition, the "job-related" provision was said to discriminate against less-skilled workers because executives could claim a broader variety of educational needs to be "job-related."

The Finance Committee amendment included a number of provisions to safeguard against abuses.

In addition, the panel approved an amendment providing that benefits received by corporate officers, shareholders and highly compensated employees under company medical and accident reimbursement plans were taxable to the extent that the benefits exceeded those provided to other employees.

The anti-discrimination amendment resembled one sought by the Carter administration.

Widow's Tax

Another amendment added to the bill by the Finance Committee would eliminate the so-called "widow's tax."

Currently, an estate could be treated as the sole property of one spouse even if held jointly by husband and wife for many years. The result was that when one spouse — usually the husband — died, estate taxes could be quite high.

The committee's amendment would provide that the surviving spouse could be assumed to have acquired interest in the property for estate tax purposes at an annual rate of 2 percent, for a maximum of 50 percent, provided the spouse could demonstrate that he or she participated actively in the enterprise.

Independent Contractors, Tips

The Finance Committee also voted to overrule attempts by the Internal Revenue Service to reclassify some individuals as employees rather than independent contractors. Employers of independent contractors did not pay Social Security taxes or withhold income taxes on behalf of their workers. The IRS had suggested that in some cases that was a ruse, but the Finance Committee amendment would prohibit it from changing its rules.

The committee approved an amendment overturning IRS rulings requiring employers to report employee tips added to a check by charge-account customers.

Other Tax Cuts

The committee added a number of miscellaneous tax reductions which it had approved previously. They included:

- A reduction in the investment income of domestic private foundations to 2 percent from 4 percent.
- A phase-out of the federal tax on coin-operated gaming devices. Currently the federal government allowed an 80 percent credit against the tax for state taxes on the devices. Under the committee amendment, that would be increased to 95 percent for 1979 and 1980, and the tax would be repealed for years after 1980.

• An extension in the moratorium on taxation of student loan cancellations through 1982.

The Tax Reform Act of 1976 declared a moratorium through 1978 on an Internal Revenue Service ruling that if a student loan obligation was forgiven because the recipient served in certain professions in certain parts of the country (for example, if a nurse served in a rural community), the forgiven portion of the loan was taxable.

• A one year extension in the carry-forward period for unused investment tax credits expiring in 1978. The change would benefit a number of airlines.

Industrial Development Bonds

The Finance Committee upheld a tentative decision it had made Sept. 19 to increase the amount of small issue industrial development bonds that could be tax exempt. It would allow tax free issues of $2 million or less for acquisition, construction or improvement of land or depreciable property, or $12 million over six years for projects costing no more than that.

The committee also agreed to allow tax exempt industrial development bonds to provide facilities for furnishing water for any purpose, if operated by a governmental unit which would make water available to the general public. Such facilities would include electric utility, industrial, agricultural or commercial users.

Previous Decisions Upheld

The committee also ratified earlier decisions allowing for establishment of tax-exempt corporations owned by all residents of a state (GSOPs), extending investment tax credits to structures used in food and plant production, making permanent a provision governing the applicability of deductions for intangible drilling expenses for purposes of the minimum tax, and allowing refunding of some tax-exempt industrial development bonds.

It also voted to extend special investment tax credits for railroads to manufacturer-lessors of railroad equipment, to make breeding and draft horses eligible for the usual investment tax credit assumed for livestock, and to provide that payments to electric utilities for capital equipment (such as line extensions) not be considered taxable income (a similar provision currently applied to water and sewerage utilities).

Senate Floor Action

The Senate passed HR 13511 Oct. 10 by an 86-4 vote after a series of floor amendments had swollen the size of the tax cut to $29.1 billion — far beyond the level that President Carter and many congressional fiscal policy leaders said the economy could tolerate. *(Vote 474, p. 69-S)*

The Senate bill, which grew during five days of floor consideration Oct. 5-10, was much larger than the $16.3 billion cut approved by the House or the $22.9 billion reduction recommended by the Finance Committee.

To the particular concern of budget officials, the extra largesse of the Senate was even more accentuated in the years beyond 1979. Floor amendments pushed the annual cost of the bill to at least $55.6 billion by 1983, as compared to $32.2 billion for the House bill and $42.4 billion for the Finance Committee bill.

That "out-year" cost could be even higher — possibly $129.3 billion — should an amendment providing additional tax cuts contingent on spending constraints take effect.

Many senators conceded that the bill as it emerged from the Senate would be inflationary because it would overly stimulate consumer spending and add to the federal deficit. Most agreed that it would have to be pared back in conference to avert a threatened presidential veto. The Carter administration had suggested that even the Finance Committee proposal was too large a tax cut.

Major Changes

In floor action, the Senate substantially increased the amount of tax relief for individuals — expecially those in the middle income ranges — compared to the benefits provided by either the House bill or the Finance Committee proposal.

The average individual tax cut under the Senate bill would be 10.8 percent, compared to 9 percent recommended by the Finance Committee and 5.6 percent under the House bill.

Businesses too would receive a better tax break as a result of Senate amendments — especially one extending for two years the general jobs tax credit, which both the House and Senate Finance Committee had agreed to let expire. Several Senate floor amendments were designed to skew the business tax breaks more to small firms, though.

Only once did the full Senate test the large tax break the Finance Committee proposed giving on capital gains. It overwhelmingly approved the committee's reduction, which was much more generous than the House-approved capital gains provision.

But the Senate significantly altered another provision dealing with capital gains taxes on the sale of personal residences.

The House had approved a once-in-a-lifetime complete capital gains tax exclusion on up to $100,000 in profits from the sale of a personal home. The Finance Committee had proposed a more modest, but reusable break — an exclusion for gains on houses that sell for $50,000 or less, combined with a partial exclusion for more expensive homes.

A Senate floor amendment provided instead a once-only complete exclusion gain on homes that sell for $100,000 or less, combined with a partial exclusion for more expensive ones. But the special break would go only to people who are 55 years of age or older, or who are disabled.

In other floor actions, the Senate overruled the Finance Committee and voted to extend investment tax credits for rehabilitation of commercial and industrial buildings at least 20 years old, and to eliminate provisions allowing taxpayers to claim credits for taxable municipal bonds and providing $400 million in fiscal relief to help state and local governments meet welfare costs.

But the Senate upheld the Finance Committee and rejected the Roth-Kemp across-the-board income tax reductions, and it killed a proposal to index individual income taxes for inflation. It also rejected an effort to force periodic review of tax expenditures — a proposal vehemently resisted by the Finance Committee.

Also during the five days of floor consideration, the Senate turned back proposed tax "reforms" favored by President Carter — including elimination of special tax breaks for domestic international sales corporations (DISCs) and for U.S. corporations operating abroad. Carter's recommendation to limit business entertainment deductions was also soundly rejected.

The Senate did approve by a narrow margin one of Carter's proposed "reforms" — elimination of the deduction for state and local gasoline taxes. Ending the deduction had previously been supported by the House and the Finance Committee.

Finally, the lawmakers added a slew of relatively minor amendments to the tax bill during the five long days of floor consideration. They were dubbed "bearded, one-eyed man with a limp amendments" by William Proxmire, D-Wis., because they were designed to help a relatively small number of taxpayers.

Sunset for Tax Expenditures, Cloture

Floor consideration of the tax bill bogged down during the second and third days of debate, when several senators began efforts to add to the bill various measures which appeared unlikely to have a chance of winning congressional approval unless attached to a "must" bill.

Those moves began when Edmund S. Muskie, D-Maine, proposed attaching as an amendment a "sunset" bill requiring that federal spending programs would terminate automatically once every 10 years unless reauthorized. *(Sunset bill, Congress and Government chapter)*

The controversy mounted when John Glenn, D-Ohio, moved to amend the Muskie proposal with a similar "sunset" provision for "tax expenditures" — deductions, credits, exclusions and other special tax breaks. The Glenn amendment was vehemently opposed by members of the Senate Finance Committee, whose turf would be most threatened by it.

Glenn argued that tax expenditures, which he said totaled $124 billion, should be subject to periodic review. Those arguments were bolstered by Edward M. Kennedy, D-Mass., who said tax expenditures were rising more rapidly than direct expenditures — posing a more serious threat to the budget. He said they should be re-evaluated to assure that they serve sound public policy, are coordinated with direct spending programs, and are the most efficient way to achieve given policies.

But Finance Chairman Russell B. Long, D-La., warned that the Glenn amendment would result, through the elimination of tax expenditures, in massive tax increases. He and other Finance Committee members attacked the use of the word "expenditure" to describe tax breaks, accusing Glenn of assuming, in the words of Lloyd Bentsen, D-Texas, that "all income belongs to the government."

When Glenn said his amendment wouldn't necessarily eliminate any tax expenditures, but would merely require a "systematic review" of them, Carl T. Curtis, R-Neb., accused him of having "child-like faith."

With the sunset debate continuing and other controversial amendments being lined up for consideration later, Long warned that the tax bill was on the verge of being "torpedoed." But the miscellaneous amendments were abruptly cleared away Oct. 9, when the Senate approved, 62-28, a motion by Majority Leader Robert C. Byrd, D-W.Va., invoking cloture. Under cloture, which required the votes of 60 senators, "non-germane" amendments can't be considered. *(Vote 461, p. 67-S)*

Long, who had warned that failure to invoke cloture would destroy hopes for an Oct. 14 adjournment, analyzed the vote with a characteristic homily: "Sunset sounds good, but home sounds a lot better."

Glenn later skirted the cloture problem by offering a scaled down sunset amendment that would be germane. It would apply only to the new tax expenditures recommended by the Finance Committee on the current tax bill — totaling $1.6 billion in 1979 and growing to $18 billion by 1983.

The second Glenn amendment was tabled, on a motion by Long on Oct. 10. The vote was 50-41. *(Vote 471, p. 69-S)*

Budget Problems

Senators readily admitted after the first two days of consideration that budget problems would be the most serious deficiency in the bill.

After defeating by a 38-48 vote on the first day of debate a claim by Budget Committee Chairman Muskie that the Congressional Budget Act (PL 93-344) prohibited enacting tax cuts in fiscal 1979 that would first take effect in fiscal year 1980, Long began supporting Muskie's more general claims that Senate amendments were excessive. *(Vote 444, p. 65-S)*

By voting for future year tax cuts and for amendments with effective dates delayed so as to have minimal effects during the fiscal year covered by the budget resolution (1979), the Senate was able to increase the overall size of the tax cut while staying within the budget for 1979. The result was the substantial increase in the future year cost of the bill.

On the second day of Senate action, Long warned senators that "in their generosity today they have broken the bank." Later, at the conclusion of Senate debate, Muskie said the future year tax cuts went "through the roof."

Still, Muskie won some important budget battles in later days of the debate. On Oct. 9, he made a point of order against an amendment proposed by H. John Heinz III, R-Pa., to establish a $75 refundable tax credit for low income households with one member older than 65 years. The Budget chairman said the amendment would breach the revenue floor established by the budget resolution. The chair upheld Muskie's point of order; and on an appeal of that ruling by Heinz, the chair was sustained, 65-22. *(Vote 460, p. 67-S)*

Later, on Oct. 10, the budget act was used to block an effort to overrule the Finance Committee and keep the existing deduction allowed for state and local gasoline taxes. Muskie said that amendment, offered by Jesse Helms, R-N.C., would also break through the budget revenue floor by cutting $400 million in revenues that the Finance Committee proposal would have gained in repealing the deduction.

Again the chair agreed with Muskie, and was sustained on an appeal, 49-42. *(Vote 472, p. 69-S)*

INDIVIDUAL TAX AMENDMENTS

The major change in the Finance Committee's individual tax proposals came Oct. 6 when Dale Bumpers, D-Ark., and Kennedy won approval, 52-43, of an amendment increasing the recommended $16 billion individual cuts by $4.5 billion. *(Vote 448, p. 66-S)*

Bumpers and Kennedy argued that the Finance Committee bill had provided inadequate protection against inflation to taxpayers earning between $10,000 and $30,000.

Under the Finance Committee bill, they said, people earning between $5,000 and $10,000 would receive cuts sufficient to offset both a scheduled Social Security tax increase and inflation as high as 15.7 percent in 1979. People earning between $50,000 and $100,000 would have a large enough cut to withstand Social Security increases and inflation of 12.1 percent, and people earning more than $200,000 could withstand Social Security increases and inflation as high as 74 percent.

But people in the $10,000 to $30,000 brackets would be able to withstand an inflation rate of only about 8.8 percent on top of their scheduled Social Security tax increases, the senators reported. With the inflation rate currently at about 7 percent and thought to be edging higher, that afforded those people scant protection, they argued.

The Bumpers-Kennedy amendment increased the proposed tax cuts for all income groups, but focused the extra relief on people earning less than $50,000. About 80 percent of the additional relief would go to people in the $10,000-$30,000 range, they said.

Future Year Cuts

Repeatedly the Senate was asked to consider amendments scheduling tax cuts for the future. But it rejected decisively, 36-60, the Republican-inspired Roth-Kemp proposal to phase in across-the-board tax cuts totaling 30 percent over three years, and it also turned thumbs down to a proposal, tabled 53-37, to index the tax system so that taxes would be automatically adjusted to offset tax increases that occur when inflation-induced salary increases push people into higher tax brackets. *(Votes 447, 451, p. 66-S)*

Those proposals fell victim, in part, to the concern that tax increases that were not matched by spending cuts would greatly swell the federal deficit and accelerate inflation.

To meet that criticism, Roth-Kemp supporter Sam Nunn, D-Ga., and a bipartisan group proposed a series of future tax cuts on the condition that spending be reduced as well. Their plan was approved Oct. 9, 65-20. *(Vote 464, p. 68-S)*

The Nunn amendment, also sponsored by Roth-Kemp author William V. Roth Jr., R-Del., Budget Committee member Lawton Chiles, D-Fla., and others, provided for annual tax cuts of about 5 percent for four years beginning in 1980 if certain conditions were met. The conditions included:

- That federal spending increase by no more than 1 percent after inflation each year.
- That the federal government's share of gross national product (GNP) decline to 21.1 percent in 1980, 20.7 percent in 1981, 20.2 percent in 1982, and 19.7 percent in 1983. It was 22.5 percent in 1977.
- That the federal budget be balanced by 1982.

If those conditions were met, under the Nunn amendment, taxes would be cut by about $11.7 billion in 1980, $31.3 billion in 1981, $47.8 billion in 1982 and $73.7 billion in 1983.

Nunn argued that the amendment would help "build a constituency" among the general public to press for spending restraint. His proposal, though seen by some as a device to steal political thunder from Republicans, was quickly embraced by Roth.

But a number of budget experts predicted that the conditions imposed were so unrealistic that the tax cuts would never be triggered. Muskie said the economic assumptions behind the proposal — including its assertion that the federal budget could be balanced by 1982 — would require economic developments "without precedent."

Home Sales

Frank Church, D-Idaho, led the effort, which resulted in a 73-18 vote Oct. 10, to revise the bill's provisions involving capital gains taxes on the sale of personal residences. *(Vote 468, p. 68-S)*

The Finance Committee had amended the House's once-in-a-lifetime complete exclusion for personal home sale profits up to $100,000. Long reasoned that the provision would enable some taxpayers to escape taxes completely on potentially very large income.

But Church said the more modest exclusion proposed by the Finance Committee wouldn't direct the relief where it was needed most — to retiring people ready to sell their homes and move to more modest residences, where they would live off the profits realized in such sales.

By limiting the provision to people disabled or at least age 55, and by allowing it to be used only once, Church was able to increase the size of the exclusion to cover completely homes that sell for $100,000 or less while increasing the total annual cost of the provision by only $27 million — to $322 million from $295 million annually.

Municipal Bond, Tuition Tax Credits

In other actions, the Senate removed from the bill a Finance Committee provision allowing tax credits for people who buy taxable municipal bonds, and it added an amendment incorporating the conference version of a bill (HR 12050) providing tuition tax credits for college expenses.

The Carter administration had sought to end the special tax break provided by tax-free municipal bonds, without at the same time robbing local governments of a valuable revenue source, by proposing to pay direct subsidies to governments that sell taxable bonds. The proposal was met with strong opposition from municipal officials, who feared the direct subsidies would come with strings attached.

John C. Danforth, R-Mo., proposed the taxable bond tax credit idea as a way of ending the tax exemption and preserving the revenue source of local governments without increasing federal control. But he withdrew the amendment on the Senate floor Oct. 7 on the grounds that it had still aroused local opposition.

The tuition tax credit amendment was attached to the bill Oct. 5 by Robert Packwood, R-Ore., in an effort to shelter the measure from a presidential veto, which was considered almost inevitable if the measure went to Carter not linked to a bill with provisions the president wanted. The 67-26 Senate vote on the amendment suggested that Senate support for the proposal might be strong enough to override a veto. *(Vote 449, p. 66-S; tuition credit bill, p. 248)*

BUSINESS TAX AMENDMENTS

Corporate Rates

After a series of votes, the Senate on Oct. 10 agreed, 60-30, to cut the maximum tax rate on corporate income (above $100,000) to 45 percent in 1980 and 44 percent in 1981. *(Vote 467, p. 68-S)*

That cut, which sponsors said would enable businesses to plan in advance, was added to a graduated corporate rate reduction approved previously by the House and supported by the Finance Committee.

It was the third vote the Senate took on corporate rates. Originally, Packwood and Kennedy had proposed a more modest reduction in corporate rates as part of a package deal that included eliminating the provision allowing corporations to defer taxes on export earnings funneled through DISCs.

At the urging of Long on Oct. 6, the Senate split the package in two, approving the corporate rate cut, 48-34, and rejecting the DISC repeal, 28-54. *(Votes 452 and 453, p. 66-S)*

Danforth was defeated on an effort Oct. 10 to cut corporate income taxes further in years beyond 1979. The Senate tabled, 44-37, a proposal to cut corporate rates to 44 percent in 1981 and 1982 on top of the planned 1979 cut. *(Vote 465, p. 68-S)*

But then the Senate adopted, 62-25, an amendment by Gaylord Nelson, D-Wis., replacing a Finance Committee provision allowing businesses to write off business and equipment 30 percent faster than their normal lives (as opposed to the 20 percent faster write-offs allowed under existing law). *(Vote 466, p. 68-S)*

That prompted Danforth to propose for the third time additional corporate rate cuts, on the grounds that the change in depreciation rules would take away one of the major benefits in the bill for large corporations. On that vote he won.

Depreciation

The Nelson amendment substituted for the Finance Committee's increase in write-offs allowed under the Asset Depreciation Range (ADR) system a provision allowing businesses to write off over three years the total cost of the first $25,000 of equipment they purchase each year.

The Nelson amendment would allow the rapid write-offs regardless of the actual life of the equipment, and it wouldn't affect the amount of investment tax credits a firm could claim on the purchase of the equipment. Under existing law, firms could only take the full credit on assets with a full life of seven years or more.

The Nelson proposal was designed to help small businesses, many of which don't use the ADR system because it is quite complex. But Bentsen, the prime sponsor of the ADR liberalization, warned that Nelson's idea would open a new tax loophole. Doctors and lawyers, he warned, would buy business equipment and rent it out, taking advantage of the accelerated depreciation to avoid taxes.

Foreign Earnings

Besides defeating the move to repeal tax breaks for DISCs, the Senate soundly rejected a proposal by Church to phase out the law allowing U.S. corporations to defer taxes on their foreign earnings until the money is brought into the United States. Defeat came Oct. 9 on a 61-17 vote to table the amendment. *(Vote 459, p. 67-S)*

Eliminating DISC and "deferral" were both among the original tax "reform" proposals made by Carter in January.

Kennedy, repeating administration arguments, suggested that DISC had done little to promote exports. Instead, he said, most of the benefits went to very large corporations which would export whether or not the law were in effect.

DISC supporters, including Abraham Ribicoff, D-Conn., countered that anything that might help alleviate the U.S. trade deficit by increasing exports should be maintained. They also suggested that Congress should keep the DISC law to strengthen the administration's hand in negotiating with other countries to reduce trade barriers.

The deferral debate proceeded along similar lines. Church complained that deferral amounted to an "interest-free loan" provided by the government only to businesses that operate abroad. Besides being discriminatory, Kennedy suggested, the provision actually encouraged businesses to keep capital overseas to avoid U.S. taxes — a situation that might decrease the number of jobs that could be created domestically.

Perhaps most damaging to the anti-deferral forces, Packwood cited a Treasury Department report to Carter in September 1977 suggesting that the Departments of State and Commerce recommended keeping deferral on several grounds, including that eliminating it would make it more difficult for U.S. corporations to compete internationally and that it might encourage foreign governments to increase taxes on U.S. firms.

Packwood didn't mention the fact that the President's Council of Economic Advisers termed deferral "unwarranted," and that the Department of Labor recommended removing both DISC and deferral.

Business Entertainment

The Senate, following the House and the Finance Committee, repelled efforts to reduce deductions for business entertainment.

It first rejected Oct. 7, by tabling on a 49-9 vote, an amendment by Kennedy to disallow deductions for 50 percent of the cost of business meals. *(Vote 458, p. 67-S)*

"If there ever was a symbol of the inequity in our tax system, it's the three martini lunch," Kennedy asserted. But other lawmakers, including Bob Dole, R-Kan., and both of Hawaii's senators, argued that reducing the deductions would hurt restaurants and reduce the number of jobs available in the economy.

Kennedy later proposed prohibiting business deductions for the excess cost of first class air fare over coach fare, for sports and theater tickets, and for meals in excess of $25. That was tabled Oct. 10, 70-22. *(Vote 470, p. 69-S)*

One of the few Carter tax "reforms" to survive House and Finance Committee action — the proposed elimination of deductions for state and local motor fuel taxes — was indirectly approved when the Senate voted 49-42 to uphold Muskie's claim that an amendment to restore the deduction would violate the revenue floor in the budget resolution. Helms' effort to restore the deduction might have been more successful if he had offered it earlier, when there was still room in the budget.

"He just came to the window too late, and there wasn't any money left," one Senate staffer observed. *(Vote 472, p. 69-S)*

Other Business Tax Amendments

In other action affecting business taxes, the Senate approved on Oct. 7, 38-31, an amendment extending the investment tax credit to cover expenses incurred in rehabilitating industrial and commercial buildings at least 20 years old. The proposal, sponsored by Howard M. Metzenbaum, D-Ohio, was part of President Carter's program to aid urban areas. *(Vote 457, p. 67-S)*

The proposal was opposed by Long, who argued that government should not encourage rehabilitation of downtown areas in preference to construction in suburban areas nearer to population concentrations.

In earlier action, Oct. 5, the Senate had agreed, 51-42, to continue the existing general jobs tax credit for two more years. On Oct. 10, it liberalized the targeted jobs credit the Finance Committee had approved in place of the general credit by extending it to 16- and 17-year-olds. *(Vote 442, p. 65-S)*

CAPITAL GAINS

Surprisingly, the very large cuts in capital gains taxes recommended by the Finance Committee sailed through the Senate despite the strong opposition of the Carter administration.

That was due in part to the strong support that capital gains tax reductions had gained over months of House debate on the issue, but it was also aided by the almost universal assumption that the Finance Committee provisions would have to be watered down in conference to avoid a veto and to accommodate the House, which was more divided on the issue.

Kennedy led an almost *pro forma* liberal attack Oct. 10 on the committee's proposal. He argued that capital gains tax reductions would be much less efficient than increased investment tax credits, larger corporate rate cuts or accelerated depreciation in encouraging economic growth. Unlike any of those tax changes, large amounts of capital gains tax cuts would be siphoned off into areas not important to economic development — such as real estate — Kennedy said.

He also opposed the committee's cuts as inequitable. Almost half of the $3.2 billion reduction the committee approved would go to taxpayers earning more than $100,000 annually, while only a quarter would go to people earning less than $50,000.

The Massachusetts senator concluded that the arguments that a capital gains cut would be good for the economy were "as gross an example of the trickle down theory as I've seen defended on the floor of the Senate."

His arguments didn't prevail against a series of senators who claimed the cut would restore lost incentives to invest, which in turn would spark the economy to grow.

Kennedy's amendment to keep the existing 50 percent exclusion of capital gains from ordinary taxes, rather than increasing the exclusion to 70 percent as approved by the Finance Committee, was rejected, 10-82. *(Vote 469, p. 68-S)*

A compromise offer somewhere between the Kennedy amendment and the Finance Committee proposal, prepared by Nelson, never came to a vote because a drafting error caused it to be out of order for procedural reasons.

WELFARE PROVISIONS

Danforth, who vigorously opposed efforts by Daniel Patrick Moynihan, D-N.Y., in the Finance Committee to add an amendment providing $400 million in fiscal relief for state and local governments — seen originally as part of a welfare reform plan (HR 7200) — renewed that fight on the Senate floor Oct. 6. His amendment to strike the section was adopted, 52-37. *(Vote 450, p. 66-S)*

But Moynihan did manage to attach another part of the welfare reform bill — including a provision allowing federal payments for parents who adopt children as well as for foster parents — to the tax measure. *(1977 Almanac p. 514)*

OTHER FLOOR AMENDMENTS

In other floor action, the Senate approved amendments:

- Adding to the bill the provisions of another bill (HR 6715) making a series of technical corrections in the Tax Reform Act of 1976. *(HR 6715, 1977 Almanac p. 154)*
- Allowing taxpayers to exclude from income, and hence from taxes, payments received under a variety of agricultural and environmental cost-sharing programs, including the Clean Water Act of 1977, the rural abandoned mines program, the Agricultural Conservation Program (ACP), the Resource Conservation and Development Program, the Water Bank Program, the Emergency Conservation Measures Program, the Small Watershed Program, the Forestry Incentives Program and various state cost-sharing programs. Sponsors John C. Culver, D-Iowa, and Malcolm Wallop, R-Wyo., said the amendment would increase incentives to use the programs.
- Enabling businesses to carry back product liability losses and apply them against income for 10 years, as opposed to the usual three years allowed for most business losses. That would decrease taxes, helping to offset the losses. Sponsored by Culver.
- Requiring that foreigners pay capital gains taxes on the sale of land they owned in the United States. Under some treaties, foreigners could escape such taxes. The amendment would give the administration five years to renegotiate affected treaties before implementing the change. Sponsored by Wallop.
- Allowing teachers and other employees of non-profit organizations to reinvest the assets of their retirement plans in new plans when they changed employers. Sponsored by Moynihan.
- Allowing families to claim the day care tax credit even if the childrens' grandparents did the babysitting. Sponsored by Dole.
- Exempting farm trucks and vehicles used for soil and water conservation from the highway use tax levied against heavy road vehicles to pay for highway maintenance. Sponsored by George McGovern, D-S.D.
- Preventing the Internal Revenue Service (IRS) from assessing some very substantial taxes it had been seeking from the Alaska Native Corporations. Sponsored by Mike Gravel, D-Alaska.
- Extending the amount of time during which legal steps could be taken to qualify certain charitable contributions for special tax treatment. Sponsored by Bumpers to benefit Arkansas College.
- Amending existing law so that certain funds established by the state legislatures of North Carolina and Maryland to guarantee funds in state chartered savings and loan associations could qualify for tax exemption. Sponsored by Robert Morgan, D-N.C.
- Excluding from private foundation status (and thus freeing from certain taxes) long-term care facilities. Sponsored by Dewey F. Bartlett, R-Okla., to benefit the Sand Springs Home in Sand Springs, Okla.
- Increasing to 15 the number of family members who could own stock in a family corporation and still be able to

qualify for inheritance tax deferral rules governing family corporations. Sponsored by Alan Cranston, D-Calif., to benefit the Gallo family, California wine producers.

● Allowing individuals who sold property to cooperative housing corporations and then acquired stock in them to be treated as tenant-stockholders for up to three years. Sponsored by Moynihan, the amendment would help corporations meet the rule that 80 percent of their income be from tenant-stockholders in order for them to qualify for certain tax, interest and business depreciation deductions. Moynihan said the 80 percent rule was difficult to meet when vacancies were high. He argued that his amendment would encourage building of cooperative housing.

● Allowing tax-exempt industrial development bond financing for projects with total costs up to $20 million if they were partially financed by urban development action grants (UDAGs). Sponsored by Birch Bayh, D-Ind., the amendment wouldn't increase the amount of tax-exempt industrial development bonds that could be issued, but would merely allow them to be used to finance larger projects if UDAG grants were involved.

● Providing that the item of preference subject to the minimum tax in the case of low income housing property would be the excess depreciation over double-declining balance depreciation rather than over straight-line depreciation. Sponsored by Jacob K. Javits, R-N.Y.

● Allowing oil producers to claim future tax credits for past taxes paid under a previous law that made retroactive application of the minimum tax to intangible drilling and development costs. Sponsored by Henry Bellmon, R-Okla.

● Excluding from taxation payments made to farmers to compensate them for cattle losses resulting from PPB poisoning, even if the money was not used to purchase new cattle, so long as the money was used for some farm purpose. The IRS wanted to tax the money unless used to replace the dead cattle. Farmers argued they couldn't use the money to buy new cattle because the cattle would be poisoned again. Sponsored by Robert P. Griffin, R-Mich.

● Allowing leased rolling stock used outside of the United States for no more than 90 days to be treated as U.S.-source income (thus preventing the lessors' from losing foreign tax credits). Sponsored by Charles H. Percy, R-Ill.

● Providing that National Research Service awards be treated as scholarships, and hence be tax-exempt. Sponsored by Javits.

● Allowing manufacturers to accrue at the end of the year outstanding discount coupons which were presented for redemption within six months of the end of the year. Sponsored by Spark M. Matsunaga, D-Hawaii, the amendment would save the manufacturers from having to count the coupons as liabilities in the earlier year — thus "overstating" their income in that year.

● Extending similar tax treatment to manufacturers of magazines, paperback books and records. Under existing law, manufacturers had to count as income all shipments of those — even though some would later be returned by distributors. The result was that they overstated their income when the materials were originally distributed. Sponsored by Cranston.

● Allowing New York City to be treated as a single governmental unit, even though it consists of five counties. The amendment would enable planned electric power plants to qualify under a law allowing tax-exempt industrial development bond financing for power facilities built by public power authorities and sold to private utilities in two contiguous governmental jurisdictions. Sponsored by Moynihan.

● Permitting the Treasury Department to take subordinate liens on farm property which was valued according to its use, rather than fair market value, for estate tax purposes. Existing law required the Treasury to take the first lien on such property to assure that it could recapture lost revenue from the lower valuation in the event the land was not kept in farming for 15 years following its inheritance as required. Sponsored by Dick Clark, D-Iowa, who said the first lien requirement prevented some farmers from obtaining credit from banks which required that they hold the first lien as a precondition to making a loan.

● Increasing to $5,000 from $1,500 the size of tax deficiencies that could be handled through the simple small tax legal procedures. Sponsored by Clark.

● Eliminating the requirement that married taxpayers file joint returns to qualify for the income tax exclusion for disability payments. Sponsored by Bumpers.

Conference Action

Final details of the Revenue Act of 1978 (H Rept 95-1800) were worked out in a House-Senate conference committee Oct. 12-15. The work of the conference was determined in large part by the eagerness of lawmakers to avoid a possible presidential veto.

President Carter spelled out his position at an Oct. 12 meeting with the conference's leaders — House Ways and Means Chairman Al Ullman, D-Ore., and Senate Finance Chairman Russell B. Long, D-La.

He then dispatched Blumenthal to the final day of conference deliberations — a marathon session that began at mid-day Oct. 14 and, partly because it was frequently interrupted by the absence of members engaged in other last-minute legislative activities, didn't end until 4 a.m. on Oct. 15.

As recounted by Ullman and Long, Carter made only one firm veto threat during their meeting. They said Carter flatly declared that he would veto any bill that reached his desk containing a provision allowing tuition tax credits.

They also said Carter expressed serious concerns about a Senate-approved amendment, sponsored by Sam Nunn, D-Ga., scheduling across-the-board income tax cuts for four years beginning in 1980 provided that the government meets specified goals to limit the growth of spending.

Finally, they reported that the president was troubled by the overall size of the bill as it emerged from the Senate. Its cost had been only $16.3 billion when passed by the House on Aug. 10, but the Senate had pumped that sum up to $29.1 billion. In addition, the Senate added a number of amendments that would accentuate the cost of the bill in years beyond 1979.

"Revenues are the biggest problem we've got to deal with," concluded Ullman shortly after the meeting with Carter.

Tuition Tax Credits

The threatened presidential veto convinced most conferees that a Senate amendment adding tuition tax credits for college expenses to the bill would have to be dropped.

That became easier when the House and Senate became unable to resolve differences on whether the tax credit should be limited to college-level expenses or whether it should help pay for costs of primary and secondary education too.

After the House voted Oct. 12 to instruct conferees considering separate tuition tax credit legislation to insist on the original House position that elementary and secondary expenses be included, Ullman told the tax conference that he would consider it a "breach of faith" with the House to include a college-only credit on the tax bill.

Long replied that the Senate would refuse to accept a credit that would include elementary and secondary expenses. Pressed to fight for the credit legislation, the Finance chairman replied: "Sign me up for the crusade, but, gentlemen, we're going to have to camp somewhere because we're a long way from Jerusalem."

With House and Senate deadlocked and the presidential veto looming, Long and Ullman both argued that the tuition tax credit amendment would have to be dropped from the bill. Although some conferees were reluctant, that position ultimately prevailed.

Budget Squeeze

Although almost all of the conference deliberations were conducted behind closed doors — with each side caucusing privately and sending its offers to the other side through intermediaries — it was evident that many decisions were reached simply to reduce the overall cost of the package.

Blumenthal told the conferees that the administration's target was a tax cut $1.5 billion larger than the House's $16.3 billion reduction. That required cutting about $11.3 billion from the swollen bill approved by the Senate.

The Treasury secretary made it clear that the administration was concerned as much about the cost of the bill in the years beyond 1979 as it was about the immediate 1979 impact.

The conferees apparently took Blumenthal's advice to heart, as they chopped away numerous costly provisions of the bill. In the end, the $18.7 billion was somewhat larger than the administration's target, but Blumenthal tacitly approved the excess anyway.

The package, surprisingly, fell below the reduction allowed by the second concurrent budget resolution for fiscal 1979. Its fiscal year cost — including extensions of several temporary tax cuts that were due to expire at the end of 1978 — was only about $18.6 billion, below the $21.9 billion fiscal year cut assumed in the budget resolution.

The future year cuts were reduced even more dramatically. The original House bill provided cuts that would total $32.2 billion annually by 1983, and the Senate had increased that figure to $55.6 billion. The bill finally approved in conference would cost $34.1 billion a year in 1983.

Conferees stripped a number of provisions from the bill to reduce its budget impact. Some were removed purely for budgetary reasons, while others fell due to a combination of substantive opposition and budgetary problems.

Future Year Cuts. Among the first provisions to be dropped in conference was a Senate amendment providing corporations with additional corporate income tax reductions in 1980 and 1981.

Earned Income Credit. Conferees also cut costs by scaling back a Senate provision expanding the earned income credit. The credit, which goes to working low income taxpayers with dependents, previously equaled 10 percent of income up to $4,000, and it was phased out gradually up to $8,000.

Carter 'Reforms' Fared Poorly

The Revenue Act of 1978, which Congress sent to President Carter on Oct. 15, contained a few, but not many, of the tax "reforms" that the president had proposed in January.

Most notable among them were provisions eliminating the itemized deduction for state and local gasoline taxes and providing that unemployment compensation benefits be taxed when they go to people with incomes above $20,000.

Both had a shaky time getting through Congress, but they were aided in the final days of the session by the fact that they were revenue-gainers — an advantage in the eyes of many budget-squeezed lawmakers.

Carter's crackdown on business entertainment deductions didn't fare so well. After the House had completely rejected the series of proposals he made in that connection, the Senate had allowed one. It voted to prohibit deductions for the expense of operating and maintaining business entertainment facilities such as yachts and hunting lodges, including dues.

But lobbying in the conference committee helped convince lawmakers to write a last-minute exception to the Senate provision. It allowed deductions to continue to be made for country club dues — a change that cut back the revenue gain to $25 million annually from $100 million.

Also included in the bill was a provision Carter sought extending the "at risk" rule to tax shelters other than real estate. Previous law applied the rule, which limited deductions for tax shelter paper losses to the losses for which a taxpayer had a personal liability, to only some shelters. Carter proposed extending it to all shelters except real estate. The conference went along, with one additional exception — it provided that small equipment leasing firms could still escape the rule.

Finally, the conferees agreed to tighten up slightly on rules governing taxation of partnerships. Partnerships generally are not taxable entities. Instead, their income is taxed as personal income of individual partners. Carter complained that situation made it too easy for some partnerships to hide income from taxation. He proposed classifying some partnerships that qualify for sheltered treatment as corporations for tax purposes.

The conferees didn't go along with that, but they did agree to impose a penalty for partnerships that fail to file partnership information tax returns on time. They also increased the statute of limitations to four years from three years for tax returns involving partnership income — in order to give the IRS more time to audit such returns.

The Senate Finance Committee had proposed increasing the credit to 12 percent of the first $5,000, to be phased out between $6,000 and $11,000.

Conferees cut back the increase to 10 percent of the first $5,000, to be phased out between $6,000 and $10,000. That action cut the cost of the Senate provision to about $1 billion from $1.8 billion.

Indexing. Also dropped from the bill was a House provision to index capital gains taxes for inflation beginning in 1980. While some conferees objected to the provision on the grounds that indexing would set a bad precedent by building automatic inflation adjustments into the tax system, and others objected to indexing taxes on one form of income and not others, cost considerations also weighed heavily in the conference decision. The cost of the provision was expected to rise from negligible levels in 1979 to $2.1 billion annually by 1983.

Business Depreciation. Also victim of the budget squeeze — as well as substantive disagreements — were several provisions liberalizing the rules by which businesses write off new plant and equipment.

Senate conferees first dropped a provision allowing three-year straight line depreciation of the first $25,000 of equipment purchased each year — a change that would have cost $2.4 billion annually by 1983.

Later, the House members agreed to drop from the bill the only remaining major provision on depreciation. It would have allowed more rapid write-offs in the first year after an investment is made.

In dropping those provisions, the conferees in effect rejected recommendations by a number of economic leaders — including Federal Reserve Board Chairman G. William Miller — that liberalizing depreciation would be the best way to encourage industries to invest in new plant and equipment, thus modernizing the nation's industrial capacity.

Acknowledging that, Ullman noted that the conferees had been unable to reach a consensus on the best way to go about liberalizing depreciation.

Deleted Exemptions, Credits and Deductions. The conferees also dropped, essentially for cost reasons, a variety of provisions increasing tax breaks for certain classes of people. Among the eliminated provisions were an extra tax exemption for the handicapped, an increase in the tax credit for the elderly, an extension of the general jobs credit (the conferees did approve a new targeted jobs credit), an increase in the zero bracket amount (tax free income) for single parents, and a provision allowing workers to deduct contributions they make to supplement company-provided pension plans.

Capital Gains

The proposed reduction in capital gains taxes was one provision of the bill not discussed in terms of the budget problem. It was among the earliest major decisions made, and the deliberations focused mostly on ways to devise a reduction that would be substantial, but not so generous as to incur a presidential veto.

The conferees accepted House provisions eliminating the "alternative" 25 percent maximum tax rate on capital gains up to $50,000 (a repeal that would actually increase capital gains taxes for some people in brackets 50 percent and up), and removing capital gains from the list of preference items that are subject to the minimum tax (which is equal to 15 percent of all preference in excess of $10,000).

House and Senate then split their differences on the major issue — an increase in the amount of capital gains excluded from regular taxation to 70 percent from 50 percent. The arithmetic compromise resulted in a 60 percent exclusion.

Finally, the conferees tightened up on a Senate provision involving the minimum tax. Where the House had proposed eliminating capital gains from the items subject to the minimum tax — thus leaving other preference items subject to the minimum levy — the Senate had completely repealed the minimum tax and substituted for it a new "alternative minimum tax" which taxpayers would only pay if it exceeded their regular tax liability.

The administration objected to both the House and Senate provisions, but it was particularly opposed to the Senate approach. Blumenthal complained that the complete repeal of the minimum tax would help some taxpayers escape taxes completely on many kinds of tax preferences in addition to capital gains.

The conference met the objection by keeping the minimum tax for all preference items except excluded capital gains and excess itemized deductions (deductions that total more than 60 percent of adjusted gross income). The lawmakers then agreed to apply the Senate's alternative minimum tax, computed as follows: taxpayers would take the total of their taxable income plus those two preference items, subtract a $20,000 exemption, and apply rates of 10 percent on the first $40,000, 20 percent on the next $40,000, and 25 percent on all income above that. They would then pay their alternative tax total or their regular tax liability, whichever was larger.

Blumenthal said that solution was "much better" than the earlier Senate approach.

It didn't substantially change the beneficiaries of the capital gains reduction, however. Almost 80 percent of the estimated $2.2 billion cut would go to 589,000 taxpayers earning more than $50,000 (out of a total of about 88.5 million taxpayers).

The average capital gains reduction for people in the $5,000-$10,000 range would be $22. But for 37,000 people earning more than $200,000 annually, the average cut would be $25,192.

The conference minimum and maximum tax changes would pick up only $739 million, compared to the $1.3 million derived from the repealed levies.

Homeowners

The final version of the bill marked a similar compromise between the House and Senate approaches to providing special capital gains tax relief to homeowners. It included the more generous House provision exempting $100,000 in gain on the sale of a personal residence from taxation once in a taxpayer's life. But it took a portion of the Senate amendment which limited the special break to people 55 years or older.

That compromise would provide $415 million in tax reductions in 1979, compared to the House provision costing $745 million and the Senate proposal costing $295 million. In addition, it preserved the principle contained in a Senate amendment that the relief should be aimed at elderly people, many of whom would presumably be ready to retire, sell their homes, move to more modest residences and live off retirement income and proceeds of their home sales.

Individual Cuts

Ironically, the conferees left the largest single portion of the bill — income tax cuts for individuals — almost to the end of their deliberations.

By that point, they had designed a package that would allow for the House's $10.4 billion in individual tax cuts (plus $1 billion for the earned income credit expansion) and other provisions boosting the total cost to $17.8 billion.

That was about the total size that Blumenthal said the administration preferred. But pressed by Long, the Treasury secretary said there was room in the budget for an additional $1 billion in cuts above the House reductions.

The Senate Finance Committee had added about $2 billion to the House cuts, and the full Senate had pumped in another $4.5 billion. But Long accepted the $1 billion limitation, and instructed the staff to devise a schedule of rate cuts that would direct the additional $1 billion to the same income groups — those earning between $10,000 and $40,000 — that the Senate agreed had been shortchanged in the House bill.

The result was a new individual tax rate schedule described by one staff member as a "crazy quilt," developed on an "ad hoc basis with no rhyme or reason except that it yields a desired result."

The new schedule reduced the number of rate brackets and widened the remaining ones, as the Senate bill had. It also provided some rate cuts. The overall effect of it was to provide individual income tax reductions that were roughly proportional for all income groups except those below $10,000 (who would qualify for the increased earned income credit). The average reduction was 7.2 percent. For taxpayers earning above $10,000, the cuts ranged between 4.9 percent and 7 percent.

For almost all taxpayers, those reductions were insufficient to offset Social Security tax increases scheduled to take effect in 1979 and the tax increases that were expected to occur when inflation-induced salary increases would push taxpayers into higher tax brackets.

In general, only one earner families of four or more with taxable income of below $19,000 were completely covered by the tax reductions. The net tax increases would be relatively slight for people earning up to $40,000, and they would become larger at higher levels.

Other major provisions involving individual tax cuts had been previously accepted by both House and Senate. They included an increase in the personal exemption to $1,000 from $750 (coupled with elimination of the general tax credit) and an increase in the zero bracket amount (tax free income).

Deferred Compensation, Retirement Plans. The conference agreement included provisions blocking an attempted IRS crack-down on deferred compensation plans. Basically, the bill allowed taxpayers employed by taxable entities to go on deferring taxes on part of their income by entering into agreements with their employers whereby it is withheld and paid at a later date. For people employed by tax-exempt entities, the conferees allowed deferred compensation up to specified limits.

A provision allowing employers who don't maintain pension plans to make deductible contributions to employees' individual retirement accounts survived conference, but one allowing employees to make deductible contributions to employer-provided plans ran afoul of budget considerations and was dropped.

Ullman said taxation of pension plans would be studied further in 1979.

Business Provisions

The major business cuts that were left when the conference completed its action included a reduction in corporate income tax rates and an increase in the amount of regular tax liability that can be offset by the investment tax credit to 90 percent from 50 percent.

One innovation from past business tax policy was the implementation of a "graduated corporate income tax." Whereas corporate income tax was previously taxed at only three rates, the bill established a five-tiered rate schedule which offered special benefits to corporations with income between $50,000 and $100,000.

The administration had opposed the graduated rate schedule, warning that it would encourage some wealthy individuals in those income brackets to escape taxes by incorporating — a change that would qualify them for the lower corporate rates.

But most lawmakers thought of the provision more as being a special help to small businesses — "mom and pop stores," was the catch-phrase. Having lost bids to liberalize depreciation rules and continue the general jobs credit, they insisted on the graduated corporate rate schedule as one provision to help small businesses.

Finally, the business cuts included a special incentive for business to invest in urban areas — a provision allowing investment tax credits for rehabilitation of non-residential business buildings at least 20 years old. That resembled a proposal by Carter.

In addition, businesses were allowed additional relief for product liability losses by being able to claim deductions for such losses against taxes paid as long as 10 years in the past (as opposed to the existing three-year period allowed for most business losses).

Future Year Cuts

Conferees found themselves caught in a political bind between election-minded lawmakers and the president on the issue of future spending and tax policy.

On Oct. 12, the House approved, 268-135, a motion instructing conferees to support the Senate provision scheduling 5 percent across-the-board tax cuts annually between 1980 and 1983 provided spending is held within limits. *(Vote 791, p. 226-H)*

But Blumenthal told the conferees that he would recommend that Carter veto the tax bill if it came to his desk with that provision intact.

"It's not that the president doesn't share the goals of this amendment," Blumenthal said. "[But] we consider this provision unworkable. It would put the government and the budget-making process in a straight-jacket."

The Treasury secretary specifically warned that scheduling tax cuts so far in advance might have the opposite effects from those intended. It might provide tax cuts when the economy was already operating near full capacity — thus causing inflation.

House conferees were divided on the issue. Ullman called the amendment a "political concoction," but Barber B. Conable Jr., R-N.Y., argued strenuously for it.

"We're trying to adopt a fiscal goal," Conable said. "We had better adopt some goals at some point."

Trying to avert a veto, sponsors of the amendment proposed modifying it to provide that the president could cancel the scheduled tax cuts if economic conditions warranted it. Blumenthal refused to accept that too.

Finally, conferees settled on a compromise stating "as a matter of national policy," that the goals of the amendment should be attained. The goals, specifically, were that federal outlays shouldn't increase by more than 1 percent after inflation annually between 1980 and 1983, that outlays should decline as a percentage of gross national product (GNP) to 21 percent in fiscal year 1980, 20.5 percent in 1981, 20 percent in 1982 and 19.5 percent in 1983; and that the federal budget should be balanced in 1982.

If those conditions were met, the compromise said, the tax-writing committees intended to provide "significant tax reductions" if they would be economically justified.

That compromise disappointed advocates. Sen. William V. Roth Jr., R-Del., called it a "pious hope." John C. Danforth, R-Mo., who had sponsored an amendment — also dropped in conference — to require income tax surcharges whenever federal spending rises more than 2 percent after inflation, complained that the conferees had removed all efforts to restrain federal spending.

But, on the other side of the fence, Senate Budget Committee Chairman Edmund S. Muskie, D-Maine, said the spending goals in the compromise appeared to conflict with both the second budget resolution for fiscal 1979 and the Humphrey-Hawkins full employment bill (HR 50) which set a goal of 4 percent unemployment and 3 percent unemployment by 1983. *(Humphrey-Hawkins bill, p. 272)*

Muskie said the goals spelled out in the compromise would keep unemployment at 5.6 percent through 1983.

Miscellaneous Issues

Besides resolving major differences, the conferees had to wade through a slew of minor issues on their way toward an agreement on the tax bill.

Over the long hours of the conference, they removed from the bill provisions exempting farm trucks from the highway use tax, giving businesses extra time to use expiring tax credits (a proposal that would have benefited Texas International Airlines), allowing refunding of certain tax-exempt industrial development bonds (the "E. F. Hutton amendment"), exempting from taxes funds established in Maryland and North Carolina to insure deposits in state-chartered savings and loan associations, and allowing investment tax credits for breeding and draft horses.

More lucky in winning approval were provisions exempting two large chicken farms from a law requiring farms to use accrual accounting; extending investment tax credits to sod farms, pigpens, chicken coops and green houses; exempting from taxes contributions in aid of construction for electric utilities; freeing restaurant-owners from having to report their employees' charge-account tips; phasing out the federal excise tax on slot machines; allowing an Oklahoma long-term care home to escape taxation as a private foundation; removing the excise tax from domestic private foundations; easing requirements for cooperative housing to get special tax treatment; enabling the Power Authority of the State of New York to use tax-exempt industrial development bonds to finance power projects to serve New York City and adjacent Westchester County; liberalizing accounting rules for manufacturers who provide discount coupons and for manufacturers of magazines, books and records; preventing the Internal Revenue Service from limiting the opportunities employers have to escape federal income and Social Security withholding requirements by classifying their employees as independent contractors; allowing employees to escape taxation on payments made by their employers for educational expenses; nullifying tax claims made by the IRS against Alaska Native Corporations; allowing special rapid depreciation of low income rental housing; exempting from taxes government payments to individuals under a variety of environmental and agricultural cost sharing programs; and preventing the IRS from taxing certain payments made to Michigan farmers to compensate them for cattle which were poisoned.

FINAL ACTION

The Senate adopted the conference report on the bill by a 72-3 vote on the morning of Oct. 15, after rejecting, 29-46, a motion to recommit the report with instructions to the Senate conferees to insist on the Nunn amendment. *(Votes 513, 514, p. 75-S)*

Later in the day, the House adopted the conference report by a 337-38 vote, completing action on the bill. *(Vote 832, p. 236-H)*

Tuition Tax Credit Fails Under Veto Threat

Despite overwhelming congressional support at the beginning of 1978 for federal tax breaks for educational expenses, tuition tax credit legislation (HR 12050) died at the end of the 95th Congress.

Both the House and Senate passed bills providing tax credits for college tuition expenses by wide margins, ignoring a threatened veto by President Carter.

But HR 12050 finally foundered on the issue of tax credits for private elementary and secondary schools. Caught between the unwillingness of the House to accept college credits without the private and parochial school tax aid, and a strong Senate majority that was adamantly opposed to any tax breaks below the college level, the bill never made it to the president's desk.

Carter's promise to veto any bill containing tuition credits ended the only other chance for them in 1978, as part of the general tax cut bill. Added by the Senate as an amendment, the college tuition credits were dumped by congressional tax leaders in order to save the rest of the tax reductions. *(Tax cut bill, p. 219)*

Instead of tuition credits, Congress approved the Carter administration's alternative, S 2539, to expand existing federal programs of direct cash assistance to college students to include children of middle class families. Actions on the two competing bills were closely interrelated throughout the year, with the final choice of S 2539 over HR 12050 not settled until the last days of the session. *(Middle Income Student Assistance bill, p. 568)*

Background

Amidst all the debate over tuition tax credits, there was one point that was universally agreed upon — that middle income college students needed help to cope with rapidly rising tuition costs.

Unlike the rich, with adequate resources of their own, and the poor, who could rely on direct federal aid programs, increasing numbers of middle class families were finding themselves unable to meet public and private college costs that had risen more than 35 percent in the preceding five years. "We are rapidly approaching a situation in this country where only the very affluent and the very poor will be able to attend college, and I am convinced that action must be taken to ease the financial plight of middle-income families," said Sen. William V. Roth Jr., R-Del., a leading tuition credit supporter.

An idea that had been proposed in Congress for years, college tuition credits made their strongest previous showing in 1977, when a college credit amendment attached to a Social Security bill had threatened to produce a conference deadlock. *(1977 Almanac p. 161)*

While support for college credits focused on the problems of middle class families, interest in credits for private elementary and secondary schools was directed towards the failing fortunes of the schools themselves. Beset by declining enrollments, many of the largely Catholic-run schools had closed in recent years, leading to fears for the whole system.

But even indirect aid to parochial schools faced a serious obstacle in the constitutional bar against government establishment of religion. The Supreme Court ruled in 1973 that a New York State law providing tax credits for elementary and secondary private schools was unconstitutional.

House Committee Action

The House Ways and Means Committee ordered HR 12050 reported by a 23-14 vote April 11. The committee filed its report on the bill April 17 (H Rept 95-1056).

Before taking the action, which marked the first time it had ever approved tuition tax relief, the committee rejected an attempt to allow credits for elementary and secondary school tuition.

Rejection of the elementary and secondary credits followed a late-starting but intensive lobbying campaign against the credits by a coalition of public education organizations.

As approved by the committee, the bill allowed students or parents of students to reduce their federal income taxes by an amount equal to 25 percent of college tuition expenses, up to a maximum of $100 in 1978. The maximum rose to $150 in 1979 and $250 in 1980. Full-time students and part-timers who took at least half the normal course load for eight months of the year were eligible.

With the inclusion of some 2.5 million half-time students, who were added by the committee, it was estimated that the bill would result in a reduction of tax revenues of about $1 billion by 1981.

Elementary, Secondary Schools

The vigorous lobbying effort by public education groups helped turn around what many considered was the strong position of parochial student aid advocates within the committee. As tuition credit opponent Martha Keys, D-Kan., admitted, "I was scared to death" the committee would approve credits for private elementary and secondary students.

Both the private (largely Catholic) and public school forces were committed to a major effort on parochial student tax credits because both saw it as a "life and death" issue. Catholic educators, faced with a continuing decline in parochial school attendance, argued that a tax break for parents would help to keep their school system from going under completely.

To back up their position, parochial school leaders generated a vast quantity of mail, bringing pressure on committee members from heavily Catholic districts in particular. Three senior Democrats on the committee with large Catholic constituencies, Dan Rostenkowski, Ill., James A. Burke, Mass., and bill sponsor Charles A. Vanik, Ohio, were strong supporters of the credit.

Public school leaders predicted that private school student tax credits could lead to the destruction of the public school system. Constantly growing tax breaks for private education, they said, would lead to a mass flight out of the public schools. "This is a blatant attempt to destroy the public school system," said one opponent.

The public school forces allowed the parochial aid proponents to gain the upper hand at first by their own inaction. As Keys observed, "They let this thing slip up on them," letting their opponents get members' ears without any rebuttal. But once goaded into action, they were able to bring massive pressure to bear on committee members. The lobbying "changed some minds," conceded Bill Frenzel, R-Minn., a leading tuition credit supporter.

The National Coalition to Save Public Education, composed of education and liberal groups, brought some 500 grassroots lobbyists to Washington in the days before the vote. The National Congress of Parents and Teachers brought in its legislative chairmen from states represented by members of the Ways and Means and Rules Committees. The National Education Association had 170 members, all with "their energies focused in one place," according to its president, John E. Ryor.

Vanik Amendment. Parochial student aid was also brought down, ironically, by an attempt by Vanik, its chief sponsor, to make it more acceptable to those who opposed it on constitutional grounds. One of the most important arguments against the aid is that it would violate the constitutional principle against government aid to religion.

To make sure that the elementary and secondary education tax credit would not seem to apply only to religious-oriented schools, Vanik proposed an amendment to make tuition paid to public schools also qualify for a tax credit. The amendment was adopted 19-18 April 10.

But the prospect of appearing to encourage states or localities to start charging tuition in the public schools, by offering a federal tuition subsidy, gave many members second thoughts. Supporters of the amendment pointed out that all but three states had constitutional or statutory prohibitions against public school tuition. But opponents argued that laws and constitutions can be changed, especially if there is the prospect of getting more federal funding to ease the strain on the property tax system.

Upon reconsideration of the amendment, several senior members apparently decided they were unwilling to bring about a possible radical change in American education through the tax code. Ranking minority member Barber B. Conable Jr., R-N.Y., and influential southern member Joe D. Waggonner Jr., D-La., among others, switched sides on the second vote on the Vanik amendment, helping to defeat it by a 12-25 vote.

After defeat of the Vanik amendment, Waggonner moved to delete the elementary and secondary tuition credit, leaving only the college tuition credit. The motion was adopted 20-16: 17 Democrats and three Republicans voted to remove the elementary and secondary credit from the bill, while seven Democrats and nine Republicans voted to leave it.

Opponents of parochial school aid said the disquiet produced when members thought about the consequences of the Vanik amendment was a major factor in the defeat of parochial aid as a whole. "The Vanik amendment did more to knock out elementary and secondary student aid than anything else," said Charles B. Rangel, D-N.Y.

College Credits

By a 20-14 vote the committee adopted a Conable amendment to reduce to 25 from 50 percent the amount of college expenses eligible for a tax credit. The amendment would have reduced the cost of the credit in 1981 to about $780 million if the committee had not later voted to include half-time students.

Conable argued that reducing the credit would save money and help to discourage schools from increasing their tuition to absorb whatever benefits parents got from the credit. But opponents of the amendment argued that it would help high-cost institutions at the expense of community and junior colleges. They noted that the amendment would result in a reduction in benefits for students in schools with tuitions of less than $1,000.

The committee added substantially to the cost of the bill by voting to allow credits for some part-time students. Proposed by Ed Jenkins, D-Ga., the amendment, which committee staff estimated would add over $200 million to the cost of the bill by 1981, was adopted without a recorded vote.

The original version of HR 11776 had allowed a tax credit for those who were full-time students at least four months of the year. Jenkins reasoned that by that standard students who took half a normal course-load for eight months a year should also be eligible. To do otherwise, he said, would discriminate against students who had to work to support themselves.

The committee also adopted, by voice vote, a Frenzel amendment to add laboratory and special course fees to the amounts eligible for a credit.

Tax Deferral

Despite the comfortable 23-14 margin of victory for the college tuition credits, the committee came within an eyelash of dropping the idea entirely and substituting a tax deferral. The tuition credit was saved only by the vote of Ullman, its longtime foe.

Abner J. Mikva, D-Ill., offered a substitute to the whole bill, providing for a deferral of taxes for families with college students. The plan, in effect a loan against taxes, would have allowed taxpayers to put off up to $2,000 a year in tax obligations until the student got out of school, after which the amount owed would gradually have to be repaid.

Mikva argued that the real problem faced by most parents was a temporary cash shortage. The tax deferral scheme would give them more money when they really needed it, he said, without running up enormous costs. While the program would be more expensive at the beginning, estimates were that it would begin to make money in 1988 as parents began to pay their back taxes.

Opponents of the Mikva proposal claimed it would be extremely difficult to keep track of who owed what over an extended period. A Treasury Department representative said the amendment would pose "substantial administrative problems."

Tuition tax credit supporters were surprised by how close the amendment came to victory. The vote was tied 18-18 when it came time for Ullman to vote. He voted against, saying afterwards that the amendment would have caused serious procedural problems in bringing the bill to the floor. Frenzel said the close vote reflected a "strong feeling in the committee against tax credits."

Committee Votes

Following is the 23-14 vote by which the Ways and Means Committee voted to report HR 11776, the tuition tax credit bill. (*indicates proxy vote.)

Yea: Democrats (12) — Ullman, Ore., Burke, Mass., Rostenkowski, Ill., Vanik, Ohio, Gibbons, Fla., Waggonner, La., Cotter, Conn., Jones, Okla.,* Mikva, Ill., Jenkins, Ga., Gephardt, Mo., Lederer, Pa. Republicans (11) — Conable, N.Y.*, Duncan, Tenn., Archer, Texas,* Vander Jagt, Mich., Steiger, Wis.,* Crane, Ill.,* Frenzel, Minn., Martin, N.C., Bafalis, Fla., Schulze, Pa., Gradison, Ohio.

Nay: Democrats (13) — Burleson, Texas, Corman, Calif., Pike, N.Y.,* Pickle, Texas, Rangel, N.Y., Stark, Calif., Jacobs, Ind., Keys, Kan., Fisher, Va.,* Ford, Tenn., Holland, S.C., Brodhead, Mich., Tucker, Ark. Republican (1) — Ketchum, Calif.

* * *

Following is the 20-16 vote by which the committee removed elementary and secondary school tuition from the bill.

Yea: Democrats (17) — Burleson, Corman, Waggonner, Pickle, Rangel, Stark, Pike,* Jones, Jacobs, Mikva, Keys, Fisher, Ford, Holland, Brodhead, Jenkins, Tucker. Republicans (3) — Duncan, Martin, Ketchum.

Nay: Democrats (7) — Burke, Rostenkowski, Vanik, Gibbons,* Cotter, Gephardt, Lederer. Republicans (9) — Conable, Archer, Vander Jagt, Steiger, Crane,* Frenzel, Bafalis,* Schulze, Gradison.

Present: Democrat — Ullman.

Other Action

In other action on amendments, the committee:

- Adopted, by voice vote, an amendment by Bill Archer, R-Texas, to make clear that federal assistance did not justify federal interference in private school operations.
- Rejected, 15-21, an amendment by James G. Martin, R-N.C., to apply the tax credit to only that portion of education expenses that exceeded 5 percent of a family's income.
- Rejected, 12-22, a Fortney H. (Pete) Stark, D-Calif., amendment to make tax credits refundable to persons who paid no income tax.

Rules Committee Action

The House Rules Committee May 10 agreed to allow the House to vote on whether to grant parents of children in private elementary and secondary schools a tax credit for tuition expenses.

By voice vote the committee approved a modified closed rule that permitted an amendment to add elementary and secondary school tuition credits to HR 12050, which granted tax credits for college tuition expenses.

Rules Committee opponents of the elementary and secondary credits made no attempt to block a floor vote on the issue. House Speaker Thomas P. O'Neill Jr., D-Mass., reportedly had wanted the committee to approve a rule barring a vote on the private school credit amendment.

But tax credit foes apparently decided their position would be stronger if they allowed inclusion of the controversial elementary and secondary credits. Said B. F. Sisk, D-Calif., a strong critic of the credits, "By leaving everything in here but the kitchen sink, we've got a better chance to beat it."

Committee members showed a clear awareness of the widespread sentiment among their colleagues for some sort of tuition credits, despite the opposition of President Carter and the House leadership. Claude Pepper, D-Fla., said, "I've never seen a more rapid buildup of support than I have in the last few weeks" for tuition tax relief.

As approved by the committee, the rule allowed votes on three amendments to HR 12050:

- By Vanik, to make tuition at private elementary and secondary schools eligible for a credit.
- By Vanik, to increase to 50 percent from 25 percent the portion of tuition eligible for a credit, up to a maximum of $250 in 1980.
- By Abner J. Mikva, D-Ill., to substitute for tax credits a deferral of taxes equal to college tuition expenses, up to $2,000, to be paid back by the taxpayer within 10 years.

Supporters of the elementary and secondary credits said that, in addition to helping out private schools, the credits would strengthen the public schools. They contended that giving private school parents some tax relief would actually encourage them to vote in favor of public school bond issues, which had been turned down with increasing frequency in recent years.

Opponents said the elementary and secondary credits could be the "death knell" of public education. Shirley Chisholm, D-N.Y., predicted that approval would be the "beginning of the erosion of the common-school system."

Emerging as a "viable alternative" to the tax credits, according to Ways and Means Committee Chairman Al Ullman, D-Ore., was the Mikva tax deferral proposal. Mikva said he hoped the plan could pick up support both from those who thought the modest levels of assistance offered by tax credits were insufficient for hard-pressed parents and from those who opposed the concept of tax credits for tuition. But a tax-deferral supporter on the committee noted that tuition tax credits had become a "buzz-word" on which many members had already committed themselves to their constituents.

Testimony by Joe D. Waggonner Jr., D-La., in favor of allowing a vote on his amendment granting credits for children in profit-making, non-tax-exempt schools revealed a crucial tactical error made by elementary and secondary school credit supporters during Ways and Means Committee markup. Waggonner offered the successful amendment in committee to strike the private school credit. He admitted that he did so in part because of his irritation with its supporters, who had opposed his own amendment. If his amendment had not been rejected, with the help of the private school credit forces, he would not have moved to delete the aid, he said. "They cut off their nose to spite their face," Waggonner observed.

The Rules Committee voted 5-10 not to allow a floor vote on the Waggonner amendment.

House Floor Action

The House June 1 voted to give families federal income tax relief to help pay the costs of private elementary and secondary education as well as college.

But the 237-158 vote in favor of HR 12050 fell short of the two-thirds majority needed to override an expected veto by President Carter. *(Vote 338, p. 96-H)*

Before passing the bill, the House by a narrow 209-194 vote adopted a controversial amendment by Charles A. Vanik, D-Ohio, to make tuition for students in private elementary and secondary schools eligible for the credit. *(Vote 335, p. 96-H)*

As passed by the House, HR 12050 provided a reduction of income taxes equal to 25 percent of tuition expenses for each student in private elementary and secondary schools, and public or private colleges, universities and postsecondary vocational schools. The credit for higher education tuition would be limited to $100 per student in 1978, rising to $250 by 1980. For lower-school tuition credit the limit would be $50, going up to $100 by 1979. The bill would expire after 1980.

The Joint Committee on Taxation estimated that the bill would cost $25 million in lost revenues in fiscal 1978, $635 million in 1979, $1.1 billion in 1980, and $1.2 billion in 1981. About 70 percent of the loss would be due to college credits, 30 percent to the elementary and secondary credit.

The threatened veto by Carter may have helped to generate more votes for the bill. Staff aides observed before the vote that some members intended to vote for the politically popular measure in the firm belief that it would never become law. Paul Simon, D-Ill., said the veto threat meant "you can do two things: You can know the bill's going to be vetoed, and you can tell the folks back home you voted for it."

Lobbying

The intensive lobbying campaign against the private school credits by public school groups, organized as the National Coalition to Save Public Education, was effective, but started a little too late to carry the day. Private and parochial school forces apparently had already gained the upper hand before their opponents even began.

Catholic and other private school groups conducted a strong grass-roots campaign for the credits early in 1978. Public school groups did not mobilize until spring. By then the private school groups had built up such a strong lead that the public educators couldn't quite catch up. William D. Ford, D-Mich., said many members had already committed themselves publicly in favor of the credits before opponents could even present their case effectively.

Nevertheless, the public school lobbying did convert a runaway into a cliffhanger, reducing what some had thought was a 60-vote margin to 15 votes by the time of the vote. Barber B. Conable Jr., R-N.Y., said the close vote was "a tribute to the effective lobbying of the National Education Association," a leading member of the coalition.

The elementary and secondary credits occupied most of the lobbying on the bill. Neither the coalition nor the college and university groups spent much time working against the college credits.

Vanik Amendment

The Vanik amendment offered assistance to the parents of the more than five million private school students, although some parents would not get any assistance because they had no tax liability.

The Joint Taxation Committee estimated that the Vanik amendment would cost $9 million in lost tax revenues in fiscal 1978, $218 million in 1979, $354 million in 1980 and $310 million in 1981.

Supporters of the Vanik amendment argued that private and parochial schools, hit by declining enrollments, needed federal help in the form of tax incentives for parents, in order to keep the tradition of non-public education alive. Parochial school parents, many of whom were from low-income and minority groups, needed some relief from the double burden of public school taxation and private school tuition, they said. Supporters also agreed that the credits could help improve the public schools by preserving needed competition.

Opponents argued that the cost of the amendment and the whole bill, while relatively small to begin with, would inevitably grow over the years into a massive program adding billions to the federal deficit. "This is only the nose of the camel under the flap of the tent, and once this idea gets in, it will grow and grow," said George E. Danielson, D-Calif.

Another key concern about the Vanik amendment was that it would amount to government aid to religion, which is prohibited by the Constitution. Pointing to a 1973 Supreme Court decision declaring a similar New York state law unconstitutional, critics predicted that the measure would be overturned by the courts.

But supporters of the amendment said the House's obligation was to pass legislation, not to try to second-guess the courts. "I do not think our actions ought to be based on any guesses or suppositions about what the court is going to do," Vanik said.

Segregation Issue. Civil rights supporters worried that the Vanik amendment would undermine school integration by subsidizing students in all-white private schools. Parren J. Mitchell, D-Md., said after passage of the bill that "as it is presently written, the bill starts resegregation. A number of these private schools are going to be segregated."

Credits under the bill would be available only to students in schools deemed by the Internal Revenue Service (IRS) to be tax-exempt — a status denied to segregated schools. But critics pointed to a recent study by the Commission on Civil Rights, which found that the IRS granted tax-exempt status to seven segregated schools in Mississippi alone.

Vanik responded with the text of a May 31 letter from IRS Commissioner Jerome Kurtz, who said the IRS was "strongly committed to vigorous enforcement of the racial nondiscrimination requirements." Kurtz conceded, however, that the IRS was unable to monitor every school for segregationist policies.

Democrats voted 107-159 against the Vanik amendment, while Republicans were 102-35 in favor.

Amendments Rejected

By a 142-261 vote the House rejected a second Vanik amendment which would have raised to 50 percent from 25 percent the amount of tuition eligible for a credit. The provision would have added $843 million to the cost of the bill. *(Vote 336, p. 96-H)*

Vanik argued that the amendment was necessary to offer real assistance to students in low-tuition schools. Many parochial schools had tuitions as low as $100 to $200 a year, making the 25 percent credit rather modest assistance, he said.

But the amendment would have had important consequences on college education as well, to the advantage of junior and community colleges. Given the credit maximum, a 50 percent credit would give proportionately much more assistance to students in community colleges, where tuition is measured in hundreds of dollars, than to students in private colleges, where tuition runs into the thousands. Conable, sponsor of the amendment in the Ways and Means Committee to set the credit at 25 percent, argued that the lower percentage would discourage schools from raising their tuition to absorb the benefits meant for families.

The House also rejected, by a 155-239 vote, a substitute amendment for the whole bill, offered by Abner J. Mikva, D-Ill., and William M. Ketchum, R-Calif. The amendment would have established a program of tax deferral for college tuition, allowing parents to put off paying up to $2,000 a year on their income taxes, to be repaid within 10 years. *(Vote 337, p. 96-H)*

Senate Committee Action

Patching together the two most prominent tax credit proposals, the Senate Finance Committee voted 14-1 on Feb. 23 to move the credit proposal to the Senate floor. Substituted for the text of an unrelated House-passed bill (HR 3946 — S Rept 95-642), the Finance Committee measure would:

- Allow a tax credit up to $250 to offset the cost of college and vocational schooling, effective Aug. 1, 1978. That was the essence of a bill (S 311) sponsored by William V. Roth Jr., R-Del.
- Increase the credit to a maximum of $500, and extend it to cover elementary and secondary education costs and also to make graduate and part-time students eligible, effective Aug. 1, 1980. That was the substance of another bill (S 2142) sponsored by Robert W. Packwood, R-Ore., and Daniel Patrick Moynihan, D-N.Y.

Supporters of the tax credits picked up the strongest support yet from Finance Committee Chairman Russell B. Long, D-La. "I am morally committed to support the Roth amendment," he said.

Only Lloyd Bentsen, D-Texas, voted against the tax credit proposal in the Finance Committee. Harry F. Byrd Jr., Ind-Va., voted "present" and Herman E. Talmadge, D-Ga., and Gaylord Nelson, D-Wis., were absent. Bentsen said that while he supported the idea of tuition tax credits, he was concerned about the cost of the proposal endorsed by the committee.

The Joint Committee on Taxation estimated that the combined Roth-Packwood-Moynihan plan would cost $5.3 billion annually by the time it would be fully implemented in fiscal year 1983. The joint committee analysis suggested that 75 percent of the tax credits would go to parents with children in college and vocational schools.

New Proposal

The principal Senate sponsors of tuition tax credit legislation Aug. 3 proposed sharp cutbacks in the amount of tax assistance that their bill would give to students and their parents.

The unveiling of the new tuition credit package followed rejection of the original bill by two Senate committees, and what some observers called a slow erosion in support.

Moynihan, Packwood and Roth announced new amendments that would cut the projected $5.2 billion cost of the original bill (HR 3946) in 1982 to $2.9 billion.

The Senate Finance Committee gave its approval to the compromise by a 12-1 vote the same day, reporting it as HR 12050, the number of the House-passed bill.

In addition to reducing the cost of the credits, the new plan was designed to circumvent the negative recommendations on the bill voted by the Appropriations and Budget Committees Aug. 1 and 2. Sponsors took out the parts of the bill which had resulted in the referral to the two committees.

Key Changes

As reported by the Finance Committee, HR 12050 (S Rept 95-1066) made the following key changes in HR 3946:

- Reduced the maximum credit for elementary and secondary school students to $250, from $500.
- Eliminated eligibility for graduate students and students who took less than half the normal course load.
- Deleted the "refundable" credits, which would result in cash outlays to parents or students whose tax obligations were less than the amount of credit.
- Provided that the credit be reduced by the amount of any other need-based federal educational assistance, such as Basic Educational Opportunity Grants, received by the student.
- Required a Cabinet-level report on the effectiveness of efforts by the Internal Revenue Service to prevent students at racially segregated schools from getting the credit.
- Eliminated eligibility of tuition paid for students at public elementary and secondary schools.
- Delayed to Oct. 1, 1980, from Aug. 1, 1980, the effective date of the elementary and secondary credit and the increase in the college credit to $500 from $250 per student.

Sponsors said they planned to offer the refundability provision on the floor as an amendment.

Appropriations Committee Action. The Finance Committee-reported version of HR 3946 had been referred to the Appropriations Committee because the provision for a "refundable" tax credit for tuition would require a $117 million appropriation in fiscal 1979.

Ernest F. Hollings, D-S.C., moved that the committee report HR 3946 with a negative recommendation. Hollings had been a leader in Senate opposition to credits for elementary and secondary school students. He reportedly had been working to block quick floor consideration of the bill.

The Hollings motion was adopted 13-4. Opposition to the bill reflected a variety of factors, including opposition to the refundable credits and concern over the effect on public schools. "It was obviously not a clear-cut thing," said an aide.

Budget Committee Action. The Budget Committee action against the tuition credits underscored the growing problems facing the bill shown by the Appropriations vote. Robert Dole, R-Kan., observed that "some of us are having second thoughts" about credits for elementary and secondary students. "There's been a lot of erosion of support," he said.

Because the spending in HR 3946 had not all been provided for in the first budget resolution, sponsors of the bill had to get a waiver from the Budget Committee. By a 5-8 vote the committee rejected a Dole motion to report the waiver resolution (S Res 524) favorably. Then by a 9-4 vote the committee reported the resolution unfavorably.

Committee disapproval of the waiver would not have blocked floor consideration of HR 3946, since the Senate could have adopted S Res 524 by majority vote before considering the bill. (The waiver itself was made unnecessary by the new version of the bill reported by the Finance Committee, because it did not contain any spending that required a waiver of the 1979 budget resolution.)

Muskie argued that the committee's responsibility was not to block the bill but to point out its future budgetary implications. Estimating that the bill could cost $14 billion in the next five years, he warned, "once we put this on the books, we'll never get it off. We can't block it, but we sure can raise a big red flag."

Senate Floor Action

After voting 56-41 to delete credits for elementary and secondary school students, the Senate Aug. 15 easily passed HR 12050.

The 65-27 vote for passage of the bill was three votes more than the two-thirds majority required to override a threatened veto by President Carter. *(Vote 319, p. 49-S)*

As passed, HR 12050 allowed an income tax credit — to be subtracted from the amount of federal income taxes owed — equal to half the cost of tuition at colleges or vocational schools. Beginning in the 1978-79 school year, the maximum credit would be $250 per student. The maximum would go up to $500 on Oct. 1, 1980. The bill would expire at the end of 1983.

The Joint Taxation Committee estimated that the bill would result in a revenue loss of $25 million in fiscal year 1978, $578 million in 1979, $947 million in 1980, $1.446 billion in 1981, $1.950 billion in 1982, $1.988 billion in 1983 and $1.711 billion in 1984. The estimates did not take into account the increases in regular student aid provided by S 2539, which would result in a decrease in the amount of credits.

Elementary, Secondary Schools

Most of the attention and lobbying on the bill had centered on the elementary and secondary school credits. The Senate had passed versions of the college tuition credits repeatedly in the past, and there was little organized opposition by interest groups.

But the elementary and secondary credits attracted the opposition of the powerful public education lobby, which worried that federal incentives for private school education would lead to a flight from public schools and cuts in education funding. Lobbyists called defeat of the private school credits a come-from-behind victory, overcoming the once-solid majority support for the provisions of the Packwood-Moynihan bill.

Two southern Democrats, Ernest F. Hollings, S.C., and Kaneaster Hodges, Ark., led the fight against the private and parochial student aid.

The 56-41 vote for the Hollings amendment to remove the private school credits followed the 40-57 rejection of a Moynihan motion to table the amendment. *(Votes 313, 314, p. 48-S)*

Debate on the Hollings amendment focused on three issues: the constitutionality of the parochial school credits, their effects on public education and their budgetary implications.

Hodges observed after the vote that the victory of the Hollings amendment was primarily due to concern that private school aid would weaken the already criticized state of public education, and return the schools to racial segregation. "The critical factor was the effect on elementary and secondary public schools. The more [parochial credit supporters] talked about how poor public education was, the more I thought we needed to strengthen it," he said.

Packwood attributed the success of the Hollings amendment to a "hard core" of 30 to 40 senators who opposed the concept of tuition tax credits, preferring to have all education aid run by the Department of Health, Education and Welfare (HEW). Then there were between six and 12 senators who were most concerned about the constitutionality of the aid, he said, and five or six southerners "convinced that this would be a racist bill." Finally, Packwood charged, there were one or two senators who were "simply anti-Catholic."

Constitutional Question

The constitutionality of the parochial credits posed a formidable obstacle to the Packwood-Moynihan proposal because the Supreme Court had ruled in 1973 (*Committee for Public Education v. Nyquist*) that a related New York state law was unconstitutional. Since most non-public schools were run by the Catholic Church, the court found that tax relief for their tuition would violate the constitutional prohibition against government establishment of religion.

Packwood and Moynihan conceded that there was some question as to the constitutionality of their proposal. But they argued that the court never had ruled on exactly the matter at hand. The only way to find out for sure if their idea was acceptable, they reasoned, was to pass the bill and let the court rule on it.

To strengthen their argument that approval of the parochial credits would not amount to Senate acceptance of their constitutionality, but only set the stage for a clear determination by the court, Packwood and Moynihan offered an amendment to delete from the preamble to the bill a finding that the credits were constitutional. The amendment, which substituted instead a declaration that only the court could settle the question, was adopted 56-42. *(Vote 312, p. 48-S)*

Opponents of the credits argued that the Senate had a responsibility to render its own judgment on constitutionality. "Our job is not to pass the constitutional buck to the Supreme Court simply to get it off our backs," said Thomas F. Eagleton, D-Mo.

Segregation Issue

Central to Hodges' opposition to the private school aid was his concern that it would undermine two decades of efforts to integrate schools in the South. He warned that the bill "will cause resegregation, and give aid and comfort to those who are trying to avoid integrated schools in this nation."

Hodges pointed to the rapid growth in Arkansas and other southern states of private, "white flight" academies set up to avoid integrated public schools. If students of such schools could get federal aid, he said, more whites would depart the public schools, leaving the blacks isolated again.

Supporters of the Hollings amendment also pointed to a recent Johns Hopkins University study which predicted that private school credits would deepen social divisions and encourage segregation. The study, which found that public schools in cities with large black populations had experienced significant "white flight" during the 1960s, warned that the credits could be heavily used by white families in northern as well as southern cities.

Advocates of the private school credits responded that the bill would not allow credits for students in schools found by the Internal Revenue Service to be discriminatory. To strengthen their position, Packwood and Moynihan added to the Aug. 3 version of their bill a requirement that a cabinet-level committee study the effects of the credits on segregation.

Moynihan said the parochial schools that would be the main beneficiaries of the credits had a long record of integration. Many big-city Catholic schools were heavily black, he said, and credits would give aid to black parents who wanted their children to avoid the unruly conditions of many ghetto public schools.

Supporters of the Hollings amendment warned that the effects of the credits on public schools would go beyond the threat of segregation. If the middle class deserted the public schools in favor of private ones, they said, the pressure for adequate funding would decline, leaving the public schools as second-class institutions serving only those who could not afford to get out.

Budget Implications

Budget Committee Chairman Edmund S. Muskie, D-Maine, was the most outspoken critic of the projected costs of the legislation. But he opposed the Hollings amendment, although it cut 40 percent from the revenue loss projected under the committee-reported bill.

Muskie argued that any version of the bill would be a "budget-buster" that would make a balanced budget impossible. Even the scaled-down version of the original Packwood-Moynihan bill. he said, would be like a "Trojan horse," which would "unleash our worst domestic enemies — more deficit spending, more inflation and more unbalanced budgets."

Muskie reasoned, however, that the Hollings amendment would not make what he considered a bad bill any better. The same budgetary arguments, he said, applied to the college credits, which the Hollings amendment would retain, as to the elementary and secondary credits.

"I see no compelling reason to vote against the elementary and secondary part of this very expensive bill which does not apply to the college part as well," Muskie said. Retention of the parochial credits would make the bill easier to defeat entirely, he added.

Income Cap

Howard M. Metzenbaum, D-Ohio, offered an amendment to limit income eligibility for the credit; it was rejected 39-58. *(Vote 315, p. 48-S)*

The amendment would have begun to phase out the credits for families with income over $30,000. Families with incomes over $40,000 would be ineligible for any credits.

Metzenbaum said the amendment would help to hold down revenue losses under the bill, by cutting about $2 billion from its total cost. Calling the $1 billion in the bill that would go to families with incomes over $40,000 "welfare for the rich," he said the bill without an income cap would give the most aid to those who needed it least, while providing little help to low-income families.

Opposing the amendment, William V. Roth Jr., R-Del., said that skyrocketing tuition costs were putting a burden even on upper-middle-income families earning more than the Metzenbaum limit. He pointed to the example of Rep. Michael J. Harrington, D-Mass., who had announced his retirement from Congress because he could not afford to send his children to college on his $57,500 congressional salary.

Refundable Credits

On two votes the Senate refused to waive the rules to allow consideration of an amendment offered by Finance Committee Chairman Russell B. Long, D-La., to provide "refundable" credits, as provided in the bill originally reported by his committee. Refundable credits would give direct cash payments to eligible parents whose tax obligations were less than the amount of the tuition credit.

On a 75-21 vote the Senate sustained a ruling of the chair that the Long amendment was out of order because it required spending for fiscal 1980 prior to adoption of budget targets for that year, a violation of the 1974 budget control act. Then on a 31-62 vote the Senate turned down a Long motion to waive the budget act requirements to allow a direct vote on the amendment. *(Votes 317, 318, p. 48-S)*

Sponsors of the bill had deleted the refundable credits in order to get around the Budget and Appropriations Committees' objections to new spending. But Packwood and Moynihan had made clear that they intended to have the provisions offered as an amendment on the floor.

In offering the amendment, which was submitted in three different forms in order to get around Muskie's budget control objections, Long argued that it would make the bill more equitable while adding only about 10 percent to the costs of the bill. Long said the refundable credit would require about $659 million in appropriations for fiscal 1979-83. After voting to include wealthy citizens by turning down the Metzenbaum amendment, he said, the Senate was obligated to include poor families by allowing a refund for those who otherwise would not benefit.

In addition to his procedural objections to the amendment, Muskie argued that it would not give any help to most poor families. That was because the latest version of the bill had provided that the amount of any federal educational direct grants received by a student would have to be subtracted from the amount of the tax credit. Since most poor students would be eligible for large Basic Educational Opportunity Grants, very few would be able to benefit from the tax credit, even if refundable.

Other Amendments

In other action on HR 12050, the Senate:

- Rejected, on a 21-69 vote, a Goldwater, R-Ariz., amendment to allow a tax credit of up to $150 for residential property taxes paid to support public schools. *(Vote 310, p. 47-S)*
- Adopted, on an 87-0 vote, a Moynihan amendment stating that maintenance of diversity was an important educational goal. *(Vote 311, p. 48-S)*
- Adopted, on an 85-10 vote, a Domenici, R-N.M., amendment providing for increased participation by private school students in programs of categorical education aid. *(Vote 316, p. 48-S)*
- Adopted, by voice vote, a Glenn, D-Ohio, amendment to end the credit after 1983.

Conference Action

A House-Senate conference committee Sept. 28 approved a compromise version of the tuition tax credit bill (HR 12050) that did not include the controversial credits for non-public elementary and secondary school tuitions.

In dropping the elementary and secondary credits and cutting the cost of the bill, conferees on HR 12050 hoped to increase their chances of overcoming a veto. However, in doing so they lost support from many of those who were more interested in the parochial school credits than in the college aid.

On the other hand, the elimination of the parochial credits did not placate the public school lobby, even though the lobby had concentrated most of its fire against those credits, virtually ignoring the college credits for most of the year. Calling the heavy emphasis against the elementary and secondary credits a tactical move, a spokesman for the National Coalition to Save Public Education said the public school forces would oppose the conference report on HR 12050 because it would set a precedent for eventual expansion of the credits to schools below the college level.

Conference committee action on the tuition credits centered around the search for a scaled-down bill that might have some chance of becoming law. Faced with insurmountable Senate opposition to the elementary and secondary school credits, and the Carter veto threat, conferees reduced the cost and scope of the bill in order to pick up the broadest possible support.

The report was filed Oct. 2 in the Senate (S Rept 95-1265), Oct. 3 in the House (H Rept 95-1682).

Both House and Senate conferees began in a difficult situation on the crucial elementary and secondary school credits because members of both delegation majorities were obliged to defend positions they personally opposed. A majority of House conferees opposed the elementary and secondary credits, but had to support the House position in favor, while all but one of the Senate conferees backed the credits — yet they had to go along with the Senate vote against them. As one aide remarked, both sides really wanted to recede to the other's position.

Pilot Program Proposal

Senate sponsors of the bill conceded that a conference report containing a full-blown elementary and secondary credit had little chance of surviving on the Senate floor. But they made one last try at preserving a little piece of the credits, in hopes of expanding it in future years.

Arguing that the margin of defeat in the Senate had been determined by some 10 senators who were most concerned over the questionable constitutionality of the parochial school credits, sponsor Bob Packwood, R-Ore., proposed that the committee try a "pilot program" to test the issue. The idea was to design a limited program that could be the subject of a quick ruling by the Supreme Court, thus opening the way to comprehensive establishment of the credits if the court found them constitutional.

Setting up a program limited enough to win Senate approval but broad enough to obtain a definitive ruling from the court proved rather difficult. More importantly, the idea faced the adamant opposition of Ernest F. Hollings, D-S.C.

Hollings and Kaneaster Hodges Jr., D-Ark., who together had led the successful Senate floor fight against the parochial school tuition credits, had made it clear they would try to talk any conference report containing the credits to death in the Senate. Getting wind of the new proposal, Hollings went over to the conference committee room to tell Finance Committee Chairman Russell B. Long, D-La., he opposed the pilot program; Hollings ended up speaking against the idea to all the conferees. The prospect of a certain filibuster, combined with Long's refusal to actively support the conference report if it contained the test plan, effectively spelled its end with Senate conferees.

Dropping the elementary and secondary credits had its attendant strains among House conferees, however. Reps. Charles A. Vanik, D-Ohio, James A. Burke, D-Mass., and Dan Rostenkowski, D-Ill., were more concerned with preserving the parochial school credits than with the college credits. All three subsequently refused to sign the conference report because it did not contain the elementary and secondary student aid.

House conferees were deadlocked 3-3 on the pilot program, with the proxy on the deciding vote, that of Barber B. Conable Jr., R-N.Y., being held by John J. Duncan, R-Tenn. Instructed by Conable to vote his proxy for any compromise that might improve the chances for enactment of the bill, Duncan cast the decisive vote against the pilot program when it became clear that even the limited proposal would end up killing the bill. The vote ended the chances for any elementary and secondary credit in the conference report.

Provisions

Hoping that a less expensive bill would be harder to veto, conferees generally agreed on provisions that cut the cost of the bill. Senate credit supporters were willing to go along with reductions from their version, on the theory that a "foot in the door" establishing the principle of the credits would lead to expanded benefits in the future.

With practically no objection, Senate conferees agreed to cut their bill's maximum individual tax break in half. The Senate bill had granted a maximum credit of $500 per student, to end on Dec. 31, 1983, while the House bill had allowed no more than $250, ending Dec. 31, 1980.

The conference committee accepted the House version, but extended it one more year, through 1981. As reported, the bill allowed a credit of $100 in calendar year 1978, $150 in 1979, $250 in 1980 and $250 in 1981.

On a key remaining money issue, the rate of the tax credit, conferees reached a compromise that was linked to their decision on the elementary and secondary credits.

The House had backed a 25 percent credit, a position considered more favorable to expensive private colleges, while the Senate had gone with a 50 percent credit, which was thought more advantageous to the less costly public colleges.

Conable had been the most outspoken supporter of the 25 percent credit among House conferees. Recognizing the importance of his proxy vote against the elementary and secondary school pilot program, the three other House conferees who had successfully resisted the test proposal agreed to stick with Conable's position in favor of the lowest possible credit. Resisting Long proposals for a 40 percent or 37.5 percent credit, House conferees finally accepted a 35 percent rate.

Conferees also cut the cost of the bill when they agreed to drop a House provision permitting proportionate allocation of scholarship funds between tuition and living expenses. The House bill had required that any scholarship funds received by a student be subtracted from the amount of tuition costs eligible for a credit, but had allowed some of the scholarship money to be counted as going for living expenses. By requiring that all scholarship funds be subtracted from tuitions, conferees reduced the total expenses eligible for a credit.

The Joint Taxation Committee estimated that HR 12050, as reported by the conference committee, would result in a reduction of federal tax revenues of $330 million in fiscal 1979, $539 million in fiscal 1980, $968 million in fiscal 1981 and $845 million in fiscal 1982.

Conference Report Rejected

HR 12050 was effectively killed Oct. 12, when the House voted to recommit the conference report on the bill with instructions to restore the House-passed elementary and secondary school credits. With no chance of overcoming Senate opposition to the pre-college credits, the 207-185 vote meant the end of the bill, although a perfunctory attempt was made to report a second conference version, containing only credits for college and secondary school tuition. That effort (H Rept 95-1790) was rejected by the Senate by voice vote Oct. 15. *(House vote, Vote 798, p. 228-H)*

The House action stunned credit supporters. "It was a strategy that I would never have expected anyone to take. We weren't fully expecting it to go through," observed one aide.

But opponents felt that the bill had been doomed when the conference committee voted to drop the elementary and secondary credits. "The House never viewed the college credits favorably," remarked Greg Humphrey of the American Federation of Teachers. "We thought that in pulling out the elementary and secondary credits, the whole thing would collapse," he said.

One factor was that elementary and secondary credit supporters figured they would have a better chance of surviving a court test if their credits were coupled with college credits. By diluting the constitutionally questionable parochial credits in the much larger college credits, they hoped they could weaken the argument that parochial credits amounted to government establishment of religion.

In the view of one prominent credit supporter, some members may have been alienated by the heavy pressure against parochial school tuition credits brought by the public education lobby. "They've taken lots of heat — so much heat that they decided to go all the way with the elementary and secondary credits," his aide explained.

Finally, others still hoped that the college credits would survive on the general tax bill. With many Republicans convinced that the president would not follow through on his threat to veto a bill with college credits, there was some sentiment that the credits would become law even if killed as a separate bill. ▮

Social Security Tax Rollback

Despite broad taxpayer discontent, efforts to avert planned Social Security tax increases failed to win congressional approval in 1978.

The payroll tax, which financed the three trust funds that made up the Social Security system, rose in January under a law enacted six years earlier. The resulting public outcry created new doubts in Congress about the wisdom of a series of large tax hikes scheduled to begin in 1979 under legislation approved in December 1977. *(1977 law, 1977 Almanac p. 161)*

Although many members of Congress, including an overwhelming majority of the House Democratic Caucus, favored a tax rollback and changes in financing the Social Security system, opposition from key congressional leaders and the Carter administration succeeded in blocking the effort.

The House Ways and Means Committee May 17 rejected tax rollback legislation, in defiance of a caucus mandate. Subsequent efforts to include a rollback in the general tax cut bill (HR 13511) proved unsuccessful. *(Tax cut bill, p. 219)*

The biggest problem was the principle that the Social Security System should be self-supporting through earmarked payroll taxes. Under that principle, the taxes had to go up to meet projected cost increases. Most efforts to prevent the planned tax increases provided for the use of general revenues instead — an eventuality that some lawmakers warned would result in a loss of fiscal discipline marked finally by deficit financing of Social Security benefits.

Although Congress took no action in 1978, Ways and Means Committee Chairman Al Ullman, D-Ore., pledged to address the issue of Social Security financing in 1979.

Ways and Means Action

Rollback efforts suffered a fatal blow May 17 when the House Ways and Means Committee reversed itself and voted 16-21 against a rollback proposal it had previously approved.

The proposal (HR 12736) would have cut the planned tax hikes and shifted $14.5 billion in general revenues to the system to make up the loss over a two-year period. It had been tentatively approved by the committee May 11 on a 19-18 vote.

Two committee Democrats, including Chairman Ullman, and two Republicans switched from supporting to opposing the proposal, while one Republican reversed his previous opposition and voted in favor of the idea.

Besides Ullman, Ken Holland, D-S.C., Bill Frenzel, R-Minn., and L. A. "Skip" Bafalis, R-Fla., voted against the rollback after supporting it at the May 11 session. John J. Duncan, R-Tenn., who had voted against the proposal at the earlier meeting, supported it on the May 17 vote.

The dramatic reversal was seen by some committee Democrats who had favored the rollback as a direct rebuke to the House Democratic Caucus, which had voted 150-57 April 5 to instruct the Ways and Means Committee to prepare a plan to use general revenues to forestall the scheduled Social Security tax increases.

Although the House had made allowance for a rollback in its version of the first fiscal 1979 budget resolution, the Senate had rejected the proposal. The conference report on the resolution, approved May 17, was silent on the issue. *(Budget resolution, p. 35)*

House Speaker Thomas P. O'Neill Jr., D-Mass., told reporters even before the committee vote that the issue was dead for the year. O'Neill said he doubted there would be further Democratic caucus action, and he reported that President Carter would veto a rollback proposal if it ever cleared Congress.

Later, Senate Majority Leader Robert C. Byrd, D-W.Va., said he would oppose a rollback proposal.

Ullman, who had cast the deciding vote for the rollback on May 11, explained that he had to oppose it as a matter of "conscience" despite his responsibility to the caucus.

He said he was unhappy with the precedent of using general revenues for Social Security.

"In any event, Social Security financing will be the first order of business in the next Congress," Ullman said.

Frenzel and Bafalis said they switched their votes after President Carter reduced the size of his proposed tax cut. They said the smaller overall tax cut wouldn't leave room for both a Social Security tax rollback and a significant reduction in individual and corporate income taxes. ▮

Anthony Dollar Coin

"We've had real birds and buffalo on our coins: surely it's time we had a real live woman."

Concurring in this assessment by Rep. Patricia Schroeder, D-Colo., Congress Sept. 26 cleared a bill (S 3036 — PL 95-447) authorizing the minting of a new dollar coin bearing the likeness of women's suffrage leader Susan B. Anthony (1820-1906). The president signed the bill Oct. 10. It was the first time an American woman had been so honored.

The bill was reported by the Senate Banking Committee Aug. 16 (S Rept 95-1120) and passed the Senate by voice vote Aug. 22. It was reported by the House Banking Committee Sept. 18 (HR 12728 — H Rept 95-1576) and passed the House by a 368-38 vote under suspension of the rules Sept. 26. *(Vote 736, p. 210-H)*

Passage was a victory for both feminists and the Treasury Department. The Treasury proposed the minting of the new coin in the hope that adequate popular acceptance would save an estimated $10 million annually, as well as negate the need for a planned $100 million addition to the Bureau of Engraving and Printing plant. The savings would result from the coin's greater durability — a dollar bill has a life expectancy of about 18 months, the coin, about 15 years.

The new coin was to be larger than the quarter but smaller than the half-dollar.

In hearings held July 17, the Senate Banking Committee heard complaints from bankers and a representative of a retail association, who said the new coin would be costly, requiring redesigned cash registers, currency changers and the money counters. The committee, however, approved the bill unanimously.

The proposal to put Susan B. Anthony on the coin had the support of every major women's organization in the country, ranging from the National Organization for Women to the Daughters of the American Revolution. The Treasury originally had proposed that a mythical figure of "Miss Liberty" adorn the coin.

New York City Aid Extension Cleared

Legislation providing up to $1.65 billion in federal loan guarantees for New York City bonds cleared Congress July 27.

The conference version of the bill (HR 12426 — PL 95-339) was approved by the Senate, 58-35. The bill had been approved by the House July 25 on a 244-157 vote. *(Senate vote 254, p. 40-S; House vote 519, p. 148-H)*

The law authorized, for the first time, federal long-term guarantees (up to 15 years) for city bonds, although guarantees on some short-term bonds were authorized in the first year of the program. Legislation to provide financing for the program cleared Sept. 20 (H J Res 1088 — PL 95-415).

In winning the shift from direct seasonal loans, which had been provided under the previous New York City aid law, the city and the Carter administration scored a major victory.

They had argued that only long-term aid would enable the city to raise needed capital, regain fiscal health and thus restore sufficient investor confidence for it to re-enter public credit markets.

Those markets had closed to the city in 1975, when investors became alarmed at New York's near insolvency — a condition that resulted from recession, the erosion of the city's economic base and serious mismanagement on the part of the city's government.

Congressional approval of the guarantee program reflected a belief that the city had made significant strides in putting its fiscal house in order, that the original seasonal loan program was inadequate to solve the city's long-term problems, and that the guarantee program was preferable to taking the risk of allowing the economic and social disruption that might result from a New York City bankruptcy.

Still, supporters and critics of the measure were quick to assert that the new program would be the last time the federal government would come to the aid of New York City. In addition, arguing that the program caused an unfortunate federal involvement in local affairs, they said the bill would not serve as a precedent for other cities.

Partly to discourage other cities from seeking such help, Congress added to the program a number of conditions. They included requirements for annual audits of city books, a spacing out of the guarantee authority over four years coupled with a provision allowing either branch of Congress to veto guarantees in the second and third years, a provision allowing the guarantees only for bonds purchased by city and state employee pension funds, a requirement that the state of New York and private lending institutions participate in the city's financial plan, and a requirement that the state underwrite at least 5 percent of the guaranteed bonds.

Even with those requirements, city officials hailed the bill, expressing confidence that it would enable New York City to regain its fiscal health.

Final Provisions

In its final form, HR 12426 (PL 95-339):

- Authorized the secretary of the treasury to issue federal loan guarantees totaling up to $1.65 billion for as long as 15 years on New York City bonds.
- Required the secretary to determine, as a precondition to issuing the guarantees, that the city could not obtain enough credit from public credit markets.
- Required the secretary to determine that the city had a financial plan, involving commitments from New York State and private lenders, so that it could avoid bankruptcy if federal guarantees were provided.
- Limited the amount that could be guaranteed during fiscal year 1979 to $750 million. Of that total, guarantees up to $500 million could be extended to long-term city bonds (maturing in one year or more), and guarantees up to $325 million could be extended to seasonal loans (maturing after one year or less) to the city.
- Limited loan guarantees during fiscal year 1980 to $250 million, plus any unused or repaid amount from the sum authorized for fiscal year 1979. Only long-term bonds could be guaranteed during the year.
- Limited loan guarantees during fiscal year 1981 to $325 million, plus any unused or repaid amount from the sum authorized for fiscal years 1979 and 1980. Only long-term bonds could qualify.
- Limited loan guarantees during fiscal year 1982 to $325 million, plus any unused or repaid amount from the sum authorized for fiscal years 1979, 1980 and 1981. Only long-term bonds could qualify.
- Restricted federal loan guarantees only to bonds purchased and held by city and state pension funds.
- Provided that either the House or the Senate could veto proposed guarantees during fiscal 1980 and 1981.
- Terminated the secretary's authority to issue guarantees on June 30, 1982.
- Required the city to pay an annual guarantee fee equal to 0.5 percent of the principal amount of the bonds guaranteed.
- Required the city to balance its operating expenditures and revenues during fiscal years 1979, 1980 and 1981.
- Required the city to have a budget balanced according to generally accepted accounting principles by fiscal 1982.
- Required the city to attempt to sell short-term bonds to the public during fiscal years 1980, 1981 and 1982, and to attempt to sell long-term bonds to the public during fiscal years 1981 and 1982, unless the secretary found such activity against the financial interests of the city.
- Required the city to submit to annual audits of its financial affairs by an independent audit committee.
- Required the city to establish a productivity council to develop ways of making city workers more productive.
- Required New York State to maintain at least its fiscal 1979 level of financial aid to New York City.
- Required the state to maintain an "independent fiscal monitor" to supervise city financial affairs.
- Required the state to establish a special fund equal to 5 percent of the principal and interest of outstanding guaranteed bonds to be used to pay holders of guaranteed bonds in the event of a city default.
- Required the city to use 15 percent of the proceeds from any public sale of unguaranteed bonds after June 30, 1982, to retire guaranteed city bonds.

Background

New York City's financial problems first became a national issue in March 1975, when the city suddenly found itself unable to raise money on the municipal bond market. Subsequent investigation showed, however, that the difficulties began long before that.

Ever since 1960, the city's revenues had been inadequate to meet its rising expenditures. It made up the shortfall through borrowing, and also by using a variety of accounting "gimmicks" that masked the true extent of the city's indebtedness until the problem had grown so large that it could no longer be concealed.

In part, the city's financial weakness resulted from problems familiar to many cities. Its tax base had steadily eroded due to the flight of businesses and affluent taxpayers to the suburbs or other parts of the country, and at the same time the portion of its population most dependent on government services — the aged and disadvantaged — had increased.

In addition, the city provided some of the most extensive public services of any American city. While some have argued that those services were unduly extensive, others have suggested that they were reasonable for a jurisdiction the size of New York.

The fiscal problem was exacerbated by the recession of 1974-1975, during which New York's economy-sensitive income and sales taxes dropped substantially even while the demand for welfare and other social services increased. The result was that the city's annual operating deficit climbed higher and higher.

In 1975, the city had borrowing needs totaling $8 billion, but it was unable to sell any bonds because investor confidence in the city had hit a new low. That raised the danger the city would default on its loans.

The 1975 Solution

Over a period of months in 1975, city, state and federal officials quilted a short-term solution to keep the city solvent.

In June 1975, the state legislature established the Municipal Assistance Corp. (MAC), a state agency authorized to borrow funds to continue essential services in the city. The MAC bonds were to be backed by city-related state tax collections and by state aid payments to the city. Part of the law setting up the new agency required that the city balance its budget in three years — with the exception of about $600 million in expenses that were being funded by the city's capital budget.

In September 1975, another state law was passed requiring the city to develop a three-year financial plan and establishing the Emergency Financial Control Board to supervise the city's financial affairs.

Still later, officials put together a special financing package, which culminated in congressional enactment of the New York City Seasonal Financing Act (PL 94-143), under which the federal government agreed to extend up to $2.3 billion a year in short-term loans to the city. *(1975 Almanac p. 441)*

The act, which caused considerable controversy before winning congressional approval, required the secretary of the treasury to determine that the loans could be repaid during the year they were borrowed before extending them. It also required that the city pay interest on the loans one percentage point higher than the interest rate at which the treasury borrowed money for them.

Other parts of the city's financing package included a virtual freeze on wages for municipal workers; a pledge by city employee pension funds to extend $2.5 billion in loans through June 30, 1978, to meet the city's long-term financing needs; an $800 million annual advance in state aid payments to the city in each fiscal year; and a state law ordering a three-year moratorium on repayment of $2.4 billion in short-term city notes and reducing the interest rate on the notes.

The moratorium was declared unconstitutional in late 1976 by the New York State Court of Appeals, forcing MAC to issue additional bonds to raise money to pay off those loans.

Experience Since 1975

By most accounts, the city had made substantial financial improvements since the 1975 crisis. In testimony before the Senate Committee on Banking, Housing and Urban Affairs on Dec. 14, 1977, Treasury Secretary W. Michael Blumenthal praised the city for taking the following actions to correct its fiscal plight:

- Reducing its work force by more than 60,000 jobs, to a new level of 300,000.
- Negotiating the wage freeze for city workers.
- Eliminating the city's operating deficit.
- Converting $4 billion in short-term notes into long-term MAC bonds.
- Requiring for the first time that students attending city colleges pay tuition. The city also increased its mass transit fares.
- Implementing a $16 million management information and expense control system to improve the city's fiscal controls.

Blumenthal reported that the city had borrowed substantial sums under the seasonal loan program, and that it had repaid each loan with interest on time or ahead of schedule. During the city's fiscal 1976 year (July 1, 1975-June 30, 1976) it borrowed $1.26 billion. In fiscal 1977 it borrowed $2.1 billion, and in fiscal 1978 it borrowed $2 billion, the treasury secretary said.

The seasonal loans had produced a profit to the federal treasury of about $30 million.

Blumenthal told the lawmakers that the Treasury Department increased pressure on the city during the most recent fiscal year to try to find private sources of money rather than rely on the federal loans. That pressure resulted in an attempt by the city in November 1977 to sell between $200 million and $400 million in six-month notes. The effort collapsed, however, when Moody's Investors Service gave the note issue its lowest rating. Moody's agreed that the city was likely to pay off the note issue on time, but it judged the city's financial condition to be "so precarious as not to preclude the possibility of bankruptcy in future years."

The poor rating prompted the issue's underwriters to pull out, leaving New York still shut off from the municipal bond market.

Despite progress, New York City was far from being financially healthy as 1978 began. While the budget was balanced according to state law, considerable sums of expense money were still buried in the capital budget. In addition, the city projected that its revenue shortfall would be $457 million in fiscal 1979, $704 million in fiscal 1980, $903 million in fiscal 1981 and $954 million in fiscal 1982.

Koch's Proposal

On Jan. 20, 20 days after he took office, newly elected New York City Mayor Edward I. Koch unveiled what he called a "candid and realistic" four-year plan to restore the city to financial health.

The mayor proposed reducing the city's workforce by an additional 20,000 jobs over the four years, and he suggested a series of management improvements and purchase reductions to save $174 million in the coming fiscal year.

He said that would leave a $283 million gap to be filled by state and federal aid.

The key element in Koch's strategy included a proposal to continue the seasonal loan program, at decreasing levels, and to begin a new federal and state loan guarantee program.

He proposed that the city be allowed to borrow up to $1.2 billion under the seasonal loan program in fiscal 1979. The borrowing ceiling would drop to $800 million in fiscal 1980, to $400 million in fiscal 1981 and be phased out entirely thereafter.

Under the loan guarantee program, the federal government would guarantee 90 per cent of the value of long-term bonds up to $2.25 billion. The state of New York would guarantee 10 per cent of the value of the bonds, and it would set aside a $225 million contingency fund to back up its guarantee. Koch said the bonds would be sold to New York city and state pension systems.

Senate Opposition

Even before the new proposal was made, strong opposition to any continuation of federal aid to the city had arisen in the Senate.

In a letter to President Carter on Dec. 23, 1977, Senate Banking Committee Chairman William Proxmire, D-Wis., and that committee's ranking minority member, Edward W. Brooke, R-Mass., came out in opposition to extending aid to the city beyond June 1978.

That message was repeated in even stronger terms in a report unanimously endorsed by Proxmire's committee on Feb. 10 (S Rept 95-635).

The report suggested that the city no longer faced the danger of bankruptcy, and it said that continuing federal aid when the immediate crisis was over might encourage other cities to look for federal aid. That, in turn, would "weaken the incentive for fiscal discipline at the local level and erode the foundations of our federal system."

The committee was even more opposed to federal loan guarantees, arguing that they would "greatly increase the federal government's financial exposure, while severely limiting its ability to safeguard its investment through the types of controls that are presently available."

The committee argued in its report that the economic situation in both the city and the nation had improved since 1975. As a result, the city should be in a better position to take care of itself. Even if it was not, the impact of a city bankruptcy would be more "circumscribed" now, because the municipal bond market had stabilized and other cities were in better shape, the report concluded.

House Response

House leaders generally were more supportive of the city than the Senate committee was. Banking Committee Chairman Henry S. Reuss, D-Wis., and the chairman of the committee's Economic Stabilization Subcommittee, William S. Moorhead, D-Pa., said that a preliminary investigation by their staff supported the city's request for more aid.

But, conceding the considerable power of Proxmire on the New York City question in the Senate, they said they would not force House members to face the political difficulties of voting on the controversial issue unless there was a good chance the Senate committee would allow a vote in that chamber.

In the meantime, Moorhead began hearings in his subcommittee to build the case that further aid was needed to prevent a city bankruptcy and to avoid disruption of urban bond markets and possibly the economy in general.

House Hearings

Leadoff witnesses at the hearings on Feb. 21 included Felix G. Rohatyn, chairman of MAC; New York Comptroller Harrison J. Goldin, and Jack Bigel, a municipal union pension consultant.

Rohatyn said the Senate committee plan was "unworkable" because financial institutions and the union pension systems would refuse to buy city bonds without continued federal credit assistance. He said the Senate plan achieved the "appearance of plausibility" by cutting the city's long-term financing requirements by $1.6 billion, but he argued that the city would be unable to re-enter capital markets as long as the lack of that money prevented it from demonstrating "capability to truly balance its budget recurringly."

Goldin and Rohatyn both warned that refusal by the federal government to assist the city could result in bankruptcy. The comptroller noted that the city had met all the "milestones" imposed by the 1975 solution, but he said the city needed long-term help to become truly solvent.

"Without continued federal credit assistance it is not possible to put together a workable financing plan," Rohatyn said. "The risk of bankruptcy in that event is obviously of a very high order. . . . We have proposed a plan which avoids this risk at no cost to the federal government."

The two officials were supported by Bigel, who said that union pension systems could not afford the risk of buying more city bonds unless the bonds were guaranteed by the government. "Our veins are clogged [with city paper]," he said, adding that any pension trustee who agreed to buy city notes without a guarantee "ought to be prepared to go to jail."

The state pension system currently held no city bonds, and its trustee, Arthur Leavitt, said Feb. 22 he would not buy any without an ironclad federal guarantee.

Administration Proposal

The Carter administration on March 2 came out in support of continued federal assistance to New York City, although it proposed less aid than the city had requested.

In testimony before the Economic Stabilization Subcommittee of the House Banking Committee, Treasury Secretary W. Michael Blumenthal asked for standby authority to provide federal loan guarantees for up to $2 billion in city or Municipal Assistance Corp. (MAC) securities for as long as 15 years. The securities would be sold to city and state employee pension funds.

The secretary rejected New York's request for a continuation of the federal seasonal loan program, however.

As a condition to the aid program, Blumenthal said the guarantees would be secured by federal transfer payments to the city and by a New York State special reserve account or pledge of federal transfer payments. He also said he would insist that private lenders buy unguaranteed loans, that the city balance its budget by 1982 and that the state continue to monitor the city's finances.

Estimating the city's four-year capital needs to be $4.5 billion, Blumenthal said refusing federal aid wouldn't be worth the risk of bankruptcy.

"New York City in bankruptcy will prove far more expensive to this nation — both in expense and personal sacrifice — than any modest form of assistance," he said.

House Committee Action

The House Banking Committee on May 3 approved, 32-8, a bill (HR 12426) giving the secretary of the treasury authority to issue guarantees totaling $2 billion for up to 15 years on New York City bonds.

The vote, following favorable action by the committee's Economic Stabilization Subcommittee April 26, was hailed as a good omen by the bill's supporters, who said they had expected a narrower margin.

Subcommittee Chairman William S. Moorhead, D-Pa., said the bill was designed with two principles in mind: first, that a financial failure by the city would have "potentially disastrous national and international effects"; and second, that the city's problems were largely "self-inflicted and that federal aid should thus be "as lean as possible."

During its markup the committee approved a number of amendments, including one to assure that the federal commitment to New York City would be kept at $2 billion. It rejected an attempt by several New York State representatives, led by John J. LaFalce, D, to shield the state from liability in the event the city defaulted on the guaranteed loans. The committee report on the bill was filed May 10 (H Rept 95-1129, Part I).

Major Provisions

As reported by the full House Banking Committee, HR 12426:

- Authorized the secretary of the treasury to issue guarantees totaling $2 billion for as long as 15 years on city bonds. The authority to issue the guarantees would expire on June 30, 1982.
- Imposed as conditions for the guarantees that the city balance its budget, agree to an independent agency monitoring its finances, raise a substantial portion of its long-term borrowing needs from the state and private markets and satisfy the secretary of the treasury that it needed the federal aid.
- Required that the guarantees be secured by federal aid to the city and state, and that the federal government charge a guarantee fee of at least .5 percent per year.

Ways and Means Action

The House Ways and Means Committee also reviewed the bill, adding an amendment to remove the tax exemption from federally guaranteed bonds. The Ways and Means report on the measure was filed May 22 (H Rept 95-1129, Part II).

House Floor Action

The House passed HR 12426 June 8 by an unexpectedly wide margin of 247-155. *(Vote 371, p. 106-H)*

Before passing the guarantee bill, the House rejected, 109-291, a proposal by J. William Stanton, R-Ohio, to extend the seasonal loan program for three years. *(Vote 370, p. 106-H)*

Stanton's motion would have returned the aid bill to the House Banking Committee.

For the most part, the House debate was nontechnical. The most dramatic moments came when Richard Kelly, R-Fla., lashed out at the city for having "the highest welfare benefits and highest wages in the country.

"They have a bunch of politicians who are buying elections," Kelly said. "They have no intention of balancing this budget because, if they do, the whole political house of cards will fall."

The city's case was argued by Majority Leader Jim Wright, D-Texas, who praised New Yorkers for contributing "one dollar out of every ten" for disaster relief and economic development programs in other parts of the country.

"Flood walls in Florida, water projects for the American West, crop supports for the heartland of America — one dollar of every ten that have gone in taxes to support these vital long-term programs has come from the citizens of New York City," Wright said. "New Yorkers are not here asking for a handout; they are only asking for a hand up."

Senate Hearings

The Senate Banking, Housing and Urban Affairs Committee finally began hearings on the issue June 6-7.

The hearings had been long delayed by committee Chairman William Proxmire, D-Wis., an avowed critic of the federal aid proposal. But with the approach of the June 30 deadline — when the current federal loan program for New York City expired — and with progress being made in the city and state governments toward putting together a new solvency arrangement, Proxmire eased his grip on the city aid issue.

The hearings produced some additional encouraging signs for the city. Relaxing his opposition to continued aid a bit, Proxmire said that he would keep an "open mind" on the matter even though he was still "leaning" against it.

Even more important, the chairman said he would allow the committee to vote on the issue, and he predicted that the full Senate would be able to consider it as well.

City and State Developments

The House vote and the beginning of Senate hearings were in part the result of a series of interrelated developments in New York City and the New York State Legislature in Albany.

With Proxmire, Treasury Secretary W. Michael Blumenthal and New York Gov. Hugh L. Carey all applying pressure, the city, its labor unions and the financial community put together several key elements of a new financial plan for preventing a city bankruptcy.

The federal loan guarantees were seen by city officials as the cornerstone of that plan. Under the bill approved by the House, the secretary of the treasury would be authorized to issue guarantees totaling $2 billion (including principal and interest) for up to 15 years on city bonds. The guaranteed bonds would be sold to city and state pension funds.

Other elements of the financial plan included:

- A pledge by banks, savings and loan institutions and insurance companies to buy $1 billion in unguaranteed long-term city bonds. That commitment had been made, subject to several conditions, including congressional approval of the guarantee bill.

• Passage by the New York State Legislature of a bill expanding the borrowing authority of the state-created Municipal Assistance Corp. (MAC) to $8.8 billion from $5.8 billion. MAC had helped raise money for the city since the financial crisis of 1975. The legislature approved the bill May 26.

• Passage by the state legislature of a bill continuing the existence of the Emergency Financial Control Board, which had supervised city financial affairs. The extension, demanded by the financial institutions, Treasury Department and the House-passed bill, was approved by the state legislature along with the MAC expansion.

• Agreement on a contract involving the city and its 200,000-member coalition of municipal labor unions. After the direct intervention of Carey, an agreement was reached June 5.

None of those pieces of the financial plan were put together easily.

New York Mayor Edward I. Koch initially insisted on a labor contract that would cost the city only $610 million. In addition, he demanded that the Emergency Financial Control Board retain the power to veto labor contracts awarded by impasse panels or arbitrators, and he proposed that the panel lose many of its powers over the city's finances after seven years.

City labor unions demanded a larger contract and they strenuously objected to the veto power of the emergency fiscal board over contracts. The financial institutions, on the other hand, threatened to withdraw from the financial arrangement if the legislature weakened the control board.

The final compromises left no one entirely happy. The labor contract — which provided 4 percent pay raises annually for two years — had a price tag of $757 million. The Emergency Financial Control Board lost its veto power over labor contracts, but the new law prevented arbitrators from granting wage increases unless they found that the city could pay for them. The law also authorized the control board to intervene in arbitration to argue against wage settlements it considered beyond the city's ability to pay.

Proxmire Challenge

Proxmire questioned the financing arrangement on several grounds. He said the city could make more substantial spending reductions, called the banks' pledge to buy city bonds "pitifully inadequate," disputed whether city and state pension funds would be so "callous and indifferent" as to refuse to buy city bonds unless they were guaranteed, and — though agreeing that the city wage settlement was "modest" in view of inflation and other labor contracts — suggested that the "cruel" reality was that the city's workers would have to suffer for the city's insolvency.

The Senate Banking Committee chairman also complained that Koch had failed to win a demand that the municipal labor unions "give back" a variety of fringe benefits that had swollen labor costs, and he said that New York State government "hasn't done enough."

Proxmire also raised the possibility that, rather than provide federal loan guarantees, Congress might be wiser merely to continue the existing seasonal loan program.

In support of that suggestion, he cited a letter from former Federal Reserve Board Chairman Arthur F. Burns. Burns warned that the city would face the real danger of going bankrupt without federal aid — a risk he said was too great to take because it would "seriously interrupt" essential services in the city, set off an exodus of people and business from the city that would inflict permanent economic damage, increase interest rates on all municipal bonds, weaken public confidence in the ability of government to handle financial matters, and diminish international confidence in the United States economy.

But Burns called the loan guarantee proposal "a radical departure from the principles of fiscal federalism." He said long-term federal involvement in local affairs could eventually result in city and state governments "withering away," and he warned that the guarantee program might prompt other cities to seek similar aid.

As an alternative, Burns recommended extending the seasonal loan program for three years at diminishing levels each year. Proxmire said the idea was worthy of careful consideration, especially since it would put more pressure on the city to control its finances.

City officials bluntly warned that an extension of the seasonal loan program wouldn't solve their problems.

"Without long-term financing, the city's physical plant — its infrastructure — will continue to deteriorate, economic development will be stifled and the city will stumble from crisis to crisis with no permanent solution in sight," Koch said.

Final Steps

Two months after it completed action on legislation (HR 12426 — PL 95-339) authorizing New York City loan guarantees, Congress approved two final elements of the new financing system:

• H J Res 1088 (PL 95-415), cleared Sept. 20, provided actual appropriations needed for the program.

• HR 12051 (PL 95-497), cleared Oct. 7, permitted New York city and state employee pension funds to retain their tax-exempt status through June 30, 1982, even though they purchased debt obligations issued by or for New York City under terms of the loan guarantee act.

Senate Committee Action

In what its chairman called a "remarkable turnaround," the Senate Banking, Housing and Urban Affairs Committee on June 15 approved legislation to provide up to $1.5 billion in federal loan guarantees for New York City bonds.

The 12-3 vote was a major victory for New York aid supporters, who predicted that final congressional approval and a resulting rescue of the city from bankruptcy were virtually assured.

Their optimism was barely muted by the fact that Banking Committee Chairman William Proxmire, D-Wis., continued to oppose the bill, or by the fact that final congressional action before June 30 was considered unlikely.

City officials expressed some concern about several amendments the Senate panel added to the bill, but they said they could live with them if necessary. The committee reported its amended version of HR 12426 June 23 (S Rept 95-952).

The outcome of the committee vote was uncertain until the day before the markup session that produced the victory for New York City. In February, the entire committee had gone on record declaring that a continuation of federal aid was unnecessary, and as recently as several days before the vote, city supporters were still unable to count a firm majority in support of aid.

The apparent reversal was attributed to several factors, including some last-minute lobbying by President Carter and Vice President Mondale, the decision by several uncommitted senators — most notably Richard G. Lugar, R-Ind. — to support an aid package, and a number of restrictions the committee agreed to place on the aid bill.

Restrictions

Under the bill approved by the committee, the secretary of the treasury would have the authority to guarantee city bonds in the following amounts: $500 million in fiscal year 1979, $500 million in 1980, $250 million in 1981 and $250 million in 1982.

The final installment would be available to the city only if it balanced its budget according to generally accepted accounting principles — something the city was commited to do anyway.

Significant differences between the Senate committee's bill and the legislation previously approved by the House included:

- The $1.5 billion ceiling on the amount of guarantees. City officials and the Carter administration had requested a $2 billion ceiling, excluding interest. The House voted to include interest in the $2 billion figure. Since the Senate committee's bill excluded interest, the actual difference between it and the House bill was about $300 million.
- A provision limiting the guarantees to long-term bonds (those maturing after one year or more). The House bill would allow guarantees on short-term or long-term bonds.
- A limitation on the last $500 million in guarantee authority to 10-year bonds. The House bill would allow 15-year guarantees, while the Senate committee voted to allow guarantees up to 15 years on only the first $1 billion.
- A provision requiring the city to use at least 15 percent of the proceeds from any public bond sales after June 30, 1982, to retire guaranteed bonds.
- A provision allowing either the House or the Senate to veto loan guarantees for New York City in either fiscal years 1980 or 1981.
- A provision requiring the state of New York or an agency of the state to set up a special fund equal to at least 5 percent of the amount of the bonds guaranteed as "co-insurance" to be used to pay guaranteed bond-holders in the event of default.

City Reaction

City officials were generally pleased with the committee action, although some of the amendments caused them some concern. While they planned to use only $1 billion of the guarantee authority, they said they preferred the larger amount provided by the House bill.

They also noted that the shorter life of the last $500 million in guarantees would increase interest costs, and that the possible one-house veto would substantially increase the risks associated with buying guaranteed bonds.

Although he voted against the bill, Proxmire said he would try to expedite floor action on it. (Also voting against the guarantees were John G. Tower, R-Texas, and Jake Garn, R-Utah).

Proxmire noted, however, that the Senate calendar, the refusal of Sen. Harry F. Byrd Jr., Ind.-Va., to agree to limit debate on the issue, and the likely need for a conference committee to iron out differences with the House would probably delay final action until much later than June 30. Proxmire said the delay should cause little concern to city officials, though. "Because of the House vote and the Senate committee action, they should be able to get the funds they need," he said.

Senate Floor Action

The Senate approved a package providing long-term federal loan guarantees up to $1.5 billion for New York City by a 53-27 vote on June 29. *(Vote 197, p. 32-S)*

The lawmakers rejected four amendments before passing HR 12426 exactly as reported by the Senate Banking, Housing and Urban Affairs Committee June 23.

Playing the key role in steering the aid bill through the Senate was Banking, Housing and Urban Affairs Chairman William Proxmire, D-Wis.

Proxmire had been the city's chief antagonist prior to the floor debate, and he voted against the bill. But in recent weeks his stance came to be seen more and more as a "devil's advocate" position designed to force as many concessions as possible from city and state officials and from pension fund, union and bank representatives.

"As I listened to my distinguished chairman," said the Banking Committee's ranking Republican, Edward W. Brooke, Mass., "even though he will vote quietly against the bill, he was so persuasive for the bill that I thought he had persuaded himself that this is a sound bill and that he should support it.

"But I understand my colleague and I understand the message he intends to give."

Amendments Rejected

Proxmire argued against three amendments offered by John G. Tower, R-Texas, to limit New York aid further than recommended by the committee. They would have:

- Terminated any guarantees if the holder of guaranteed bonds — expected to be city pension funds — failed to comply with terms of the city's long-term financing plan. Proxmire said the amendment was well-intended, but he warned that it could defeat the purpose of the bill by prompting pension funds to refuse to buy guaranteed bonds. He said there might be some circumstances — such as a recession — in which a pension fund might legitimately be unable to honor a commitment to lend financial support to the city. The amendment was defeated, 24-63. *(Vote 193, p. 32-S)*
- Required New York State to "coinsure" 10 percent, rather than 5 percent, of the value of guaranteed city bonds. Proxmire warned that proposal, which would increase a special coinsurance fund to $163.2 billion from $81.6 billion, might force the state to decrease its direct aid to the city. The amendment was rejected, 28-61. *(Vote 195, p. 32-S)*
- Reduced the total amount of city bonds that could be guaranteed to $1 billion. Observing that the city, Carter administration and House had all proposed $2 billion in loan guarantees, Proxmire recommended that the Senate stay with the $1.5 billion figure. The amendment was rejected 24-59. *(Vote 196, p. 32-S)*

The Senate also rejected, 28-58, an amendment by Lowell P. Weicker Jr., R-Conn., that would have ordered a federal study to determine what other cities were in financial straits similar to those that forced New York City to seek federal aid. *(Vote 194, p. 32-S)*

Conference Action

The House-Senate conference committee hammered out an agreement on HR 12426 on July 13, after two previous meetings had failed to produce an accord. The conference report was filed July 18 (H Rept 95-1369).

Besides differing on the amount of loans to be guaranteed (the House wanted $2 billion, including principal and interest; the Senate wanted $1.5 billion in principal only), conferees differed over the extent to which Congress should supervise the program.

Congressional Veto

The Senate wanted Congress to play a stronger role. To that end, it proposed an annual ceiling on how much city borrowing could be guaranteed — $500 million in fiscal years 1979 and 1980 each, and $250 million in fiscal years 1981 and 1982 each. It coupled that spacing of the guarantee authority with a provision allowing either branch of Congress to veto guarantees in fiscal years 1981 or 1982.

The Senate also limited the guarantee authority to long-term bonds.

The House, on the other hand, gave the secretary of the treasury discretion in determining when to provide guarantees. It made no provision for congressional veto power.

Senate conferees insisted firmly on the one-house veto. They argued that provision was linked to the proposed spacing of the guarantee authority, since the veto would have no meaning if the guarantees were all provided at the outset.

Seasonal Loans

Senate Banking Committee Chairman William Proxmire, D-Wis., who represented the Senate conferees almost single-handedly through the conference, was firm in his opposition to allowing the guarantees to cover seasonal loans.

Proxmire argued that extending federal guarantees to both seasonal and long-term borrowing would in effect "give the city more" than it got in the expired seasonal financing act. He also argued that private lending institutions in New York City should be called on to make more unguaranteed loans, and he noted that there would be "very little risk" to them in making short-term loans to cover the city's seasonal borrowing needs.

House members, on the other hand, warned that putting too many restrictions on the federal aid could scare away potential investors and defeat the goal of saving the city from bankruptcy.

"We are perilously close to passing a bill that will make sure not only that New York City doesn't make it, but that you and I will have egg on our faces," Rep. Stewart B. McKinney, R-Conn., warned Proxmire.

Trade-Offs

After both sides took initial bargaining postures that conceded little, Rep. William S. Moorhead, D-Pa., the floor manager of the bill in the House, offered a compromise under which the guarantees would be made in two installments, the second one being subject to a one-house veto.

Proxmire said the two installments didn't provide enough clout to Congress, so Moorhead agreed to the Senate four-installment plan, with the one-house veto applying in the second and third years. But Moorhead insisted in turn that some of the guarantee authority be made applicable to seasonal loans during the first two years of the program.

At that, Proxmire softened his strong opposition to seasonal loan guarantees (he said the Senate conferees "caved in" on the issue), agreeing to let the guarantees apply to short-term loans during the first year of the aid program only.

That left only the amount of the guarantee authority in doubt. Because the House and Senate positions were relatively close on that issue (including interest, the total federal liability under the Senate principal-only bill was estimated to be about $1.7 billion, as compared to $2 billion under the House bill), the $1.65 billion principal-only figure was approved fairly easily.

Treasury Department officials estimated that the maximum possible federal liability under the compromise bill would be about $1.9 billion.

Under the final compromise, then, the city was authorized to receive up to $750 million in guarantees during fiscal year 1979. Of that sum, no more than $500 million could be used for long-term loans. The remaining $250 million, plus up to $75 million in unused long-term guarantees, could be used to guarantee seasonal loans.

In the second year, the city could receive up to $250 million in new loan guarantees, plus the unused or repaid guarantees from the first year. No seasonal loans would be allowed, however, and the House or Senate could veto the new guarantees.

In the third year, the city could qualify for an additional $325 million in long-term guarantees. The one-house veto would apply again.

In the fourth year, the city could receive another $325 million in long-term guarantees. There would be no one-house veto, but the city was required to have a budget balanced according to generally accepted accounting principles.

Other Issues

On other points of controversy, the House agreed to Senate provisions:

- Restricting the guarantees to state and city pension funds only. While the city's financial plan envisioned giving the guarantees only to pension fund loans, city officials had hoped to have some "flexibility for unforeseen contingencies."
- Requiring the state to establish a "co-insurance fund" equal to 5 percent of the amount of the bonds guaranteed. The fund would be used to pay guaranteed bondholders in the event of a default.
- Requiring the city to use at least 15 percent of the proceeds of any public bond sales after June 30, 1982, to retire guaranteed bonds. House members originally resisted the proposal on the grounds that it would increase the amount of money the city would have to borrow, making it more difficult to market city bonds.

The Senate conferees yielded to the House on one other major point of controversy. They agreed to drop a provision in the Senate bill that limited the last $500 million in guarantee authority to 10-year bonds. ▮

Mandatory Retirement

Congress March 23 cleared legislation (HR 5383—PL 95-256) to raise the permissible mandatory retirement age for most non-federal workers to 70 from 65, ending a month-long dispute over exemptions for executives and university faculty.

Final action came when the Senate by a 62-10 vote approved the conference report on the bill. *(Vote 78, p. 14-S)*

The House had agreed to the conference report by a 391-6 vote March 21. *(Vote 143, p. 42-H)*

HR 5383 expanded the protections of the 1967 Age Discrimination in Employment Act (PL 90-202), which covered workers between ages 40 and 65, to include those between 65 and 70. This in effect prohibited employers of more than 20 persons from forcing employees to retire before age 70.

The bill eliminated age ceilings for protection of most federal employees, thus barring mandatory retirement of those workers, who previously had to retire at age 70.

HR 5383 also made clear that employees could not be forced off the job for age because of provisions of a seniority or pension system. The Supreme Court had ruled in December 1977 that retirement plans established before 1967 could require mandatory retirement before age 65.

HR 5383 was passed easily by the House Sept. 23 and the Senate Oct. 19, 1977. But differences between the two versions of the bill were difficult to resolve in conference and delayed final action for five months. *(1977 Almanac p. 155)*

Conferees were deeply divided over Senate-passed exemptions for business executives and tenured university faculty. As Sen. Jacob K. Javits, R-N.Y., said, "the fact that we have reached an agreement is itself a wonderful thing, almost a miracle. For a long time it did not appear we would."

After pressure from business and education lobbyists, the Senate had added amendments allowing mandatory retirement between ages 65 and 70 for high-level executives and tenured higher education faculty.

But House members worried that granting exemptions to some groups would open the door to others and end up gutting the bill. The final conference compromise narrowly defined the exempted executives and ended the exemption for faculty in 1982.

Supporters of HR 5383 contended that mandatory retirement at 65 was a cruel anachronism in an era when medical advances allowed many people to remain active and productive into their eighth decade and beyond. Led by House Aging Committee Chairman Claude Pepper, D-Fla., himself a vigorous 77, they argued that the government had a responsibility to protect the rights of older employees who wanted to continue working.

While estimates as to the concrete effects of the bill were sketchy, supporters predicted that it would at least help ease the strain on the Social Security system by allowing some older workers to continue to earn a living on their own. The bill would not affect the ages at which people became eligible for Social Security payments.

Opponents of HR 5383 argued that it would add to the unemployment problems of the young by allowing older workers to hang on to jobs that otherwise would have been open for young people. Sen. Adlai E. Stevenson III, D-Ill., warned that the bill was a step towards a "kind of quasi-civil service set of rules" for private business that would protect inefficiency and hinder efforts to compete with aggressive trading countries such as Japan or West Germany.

Provisions

As signed into law, HR 5383 (PL 95-256) amended the 1967 Age Discrimination in Employment Act to:

- Raise the upper age limit for coverage of non-federal employees to 70 from 65, thereby extending legal protection against mandatory retirement and other age-based employment discrimination, such as in hiring or promotion, effective Jan. 1, 1979.
- Eliminate the upper age limit for coverage of most federal civilian employees.
- Make clear that a provision of the 1967 act was not intended to permit pension or seniority plans to require retirement before the upper age limit.
- Permit until Jan. 1, 1980, mandatory retirement requirements under collective bargaining agreements signed before Sept. 1, 1977.
- Allow forced retirement for employees over age 65 who had been high-level executives for more than two years, if their pensions were at least $27,000 a year.
- Allow, until July 1, 1982, forced retirement of tenured college or university faculty who were between 65 and 70.
- Provide for jury trials of issues of fact in suits brought under the act.
- Retain the statutory age limits for certain federal employees, including Foreign Service and Central Intelligence Agency officers, air traffic controllers, law enforcement personnel and firefighters.
- Require the secretary of labor to report by Jan. 1, 1982, on the effects of raising the age ceiling, and the feasibility of eliminating the upper age limit entirely.

Conference Action

Conferees filed their report March 14 (H Rept 95-950).

Executive and Academic Exemptions

The Senate Human Resources Committee had added amendments to the original Senate bill (S 1784), to exclude from the prohibition on compulsory retirement high-level executives and all tenured educators. Under the amendment those groups still would have been under the other protections of the Age Discrimination Act, but could have been forced to retire between ages 65 and 70.

During floor consideration of the bill the Senate voted to include elementary and secondary school teachers in the protections against mandatory retirement, leaving only the executives and higher education faculty subject to forced retirement before age 70. The House bill did not contain any similar exemptions.

The Senate bill defined as exempted executives "a select group of management" with pensions of more than $20,000 a year, exclusive of Social Security. Critics pointed out that this would be a very broad exemption indeed, since many civil servants and others with long employment would have pension incomes over $20,000.

Supporters of permitting universities to continue to retire tenured professors at 65 argued that education institutions needed to be able to hire young teachers, who would be willing to work for lower salaries. With tenured professors virtually impossible to fire, institutions would be stuck with a group of aging, highly paid instructors if they did not have mandatory retirement.

Conferees retained modified versions of both exemptions. They raised the pension income limit for protection from mandatory retirement to $27,000 from $20,000, and made clear that the exemption applied only to the highest management strata. To protect an employee from being "kicked upstairs" only so he or she could be forced to retire, the compromise limited the exemption to persons who had held their high-level positions for at least two years.

House conferees accepted the exemption for tenured professors, but only until July 1, 1982, in order to give colleges and universities time to prepare for any future problems.

Pension and Seniority Plans

A provision of the 1967 law, intended to encourage hiring of older workers, had allowed employers to limit participation by newly hired older workers in employee pension and insurance plans.

But courts had interpreted the provision to mean that workers could be forced to retire before 65 if that was a provision of their company's pension plan. The 1977 Supreme Court decision *(McMann v. United Airlines)* found that a provision of a benefit plan requiring employees to retire before 65 was lawful if the plan had been established before passage of the 1967 act.

Conferees specifically rejected the court's decision. The final language made clear that retirement or seniority plans could not require workers to retire before age 70. Conferees accepted a Senate-passed exemption, similar to one in the House version, allowing continued mandatory retirement under collective bargaining agreements negotiated before Sept. 1, 1977, until the expiration of the agreement or 1980, whichever came first.

Other Decisions

In other actions, conferees:

- Adopted a House-passed provision abolishing age ceilings for protection of most federal civilian employees, which had not been in the Senate bill.
- Made the effective date of the age limit increase Jan. 1, 1979, as in the Senate bill, instead of 180 days after enactment, as the House had wanted.
- Agreed to a Senate amendment providing for a jury trial in civil cases brought for age discrimination. ∎

Black Lung Benefits

Congress early in 1978 completed action on two measures liberalizing the black lung benefits program and establishing a new financing mechanism to pay for it.

The bills (HR 4544—PL 95-239, HR 5322—PL 95-227), dealing respectively with eligibility and tax provisions, put on a permanent basis a federal program guaranteeing assistance to miners suffering from the debilitating disease.

Repealing a 1981 expiration date on existing black lung legislation, HR 4544 also established more lenient rules for determining who was eligible for the benefits, and provided benefits to most survivors of miners with lengthy work experience. But it did not contain a provision of legislation passed by the House in 1976 that would have presumed that anyone working 30 years in most mines had necessarily contracted the disease, known scientifically as pneumoconiosis. *(1976 Almanac p. 375)*

HR 5322, separated from HR 4544 after a lengthy conference dispute, established a tax of 50 cents a ton on underground-mined coal and 25 cents a ton on surface-mined coal. The tax was to be limited to 2 per cent of the sales price in either case. It was expected to raise about $92 million in the first year.

Conferees had reached agreement on compromise legislation late in the 1977 session, but final action was deferred until 1978. Congress cleared HR 5322 on Jan. 24 and HR 4544 on Feb. 15.

Black lung is caused by chronic inhalation of coal dust. Miners with the disease may suffer a lifetime of difficult breathing, and an early death.

Recognizing the special problems of miners, Congress in 1969 and 1972 approved legislation compensating black lung victims. The federal government undertook to pay workers whose disability claims were filed before 1973, while the coal producers were to pay, through state worker compensation programs, claims filed beginning in 1974. But the government ended up paying those claims as well, since none of the state programs met federal standards. *(Background, Congress and the Nation Vol. III, pp. 707, 725)*

HR 5322 shifted the burden of financing to the coal operators. The new taxes would go into a trust fund to pay claims, filed after 1973, for which no particular operator could be considered responsible. Operators who could be identified as responsible for individual miners' disabilities would pay the total cost of claims through a separate tax-exempt trust.

A top priority of the United Mine Workers, HR 4544 liberalized the rules governing the awarding of benefits, but not as much as the union would have liked. House supporters of the union-backed automatic entitlement provisions granting benefits to all those who had worked for 30 years in the mines (25 years in anthracite coal mines) were forced to drop the idea in the face of substantial opposition. The more lenient "interim" standards used to determine eligibility for benefits, which labor supporters had sought to make permanent, were allowed to stand only until the Labor Department could promulgate permanent standards.

Final Provisions

Eligibility Standards. As signed into law, HR 4544 (PL 95-239):

- Stipulated that continued employment in a mine was not conclusive evidence that a miner was not totally disabled. Miners whose conditions of work had changed, indicating a reduced ability to do mine work, and the survivors of miners who were employed at the time of death, might thus become eligible for benefits.
- Provided that the survivors of miners who had worked more than 25 years in the mines before June 30, 1971, would be eligible for benefits, unless there was conclusive evidence that the miner did not have black lung problems.
- Required the Labor Department to accept as proof of lung impairment X-rays performed by certified radiologists.
- Permitted miners to substantiate their disability claims by means of a complete pulmonary examination.
- Provided that the "interim" eligibility standards developed by the Department of Health, Education and

Welfare (HEW) were to remain in effect until the Labor Department could promulgate permanent standards.

- Required HEW and the Labor Department to undertake reviews of claims previously denied, in light of changes in eligibility requirements made by the bill. HEW would review "Part B" claims, which were filed before 1974, while Labor would handle "Part C" claims, which were filed beginning in 1974.
- Required the Departments of HEW and Labor to undertake broad informational campaigns to inform prospective beneficiaries of changes in the law.
- Authorized establishment of an insurance fund to assist mine operators in meeting their individual obligations to afflicted employees.
- Provided that affidavits as to the prior health of a deceased miner would be sufficient to establish eligibility unless there was medical evidence to the contrary.

Financing. As signed into law, HR 5322 (PL 95-227):

- Established a federal excise tax on coal sales, at the rate of 50 cents a ton on underground-mined coal and 25 cents a ton on surface-mined coal. Limited the amount of tax to 2 per cent of the sale price.
- Established a Black Lung Disability Trust Fund, with an appropriation equal to the revenue from the coal tax, to pay black lung disability claims in cases where no operator could be found to be responsible for the miner's disability.
- Permitted an operator to establish a tax-exempt trust fund to cover its obligations in cases where it was found to be responsible for payment of benefits to afflicted miners.
- Established rules governing the tax-exempt status of the operator trusts and the deductibility of contributions to those trusts.

Legislative History

The House passed HR 4544 Sept. 19, 1977. The Senate passed the bill Sept. 20, after substituting the provisions of its own version of the measure (S 1538). The Senate had completed action on amendments to S 1538 in July, but delayed final passage until the House approved HR 4544.

Conference agreement was held up by a lengthy dispute over the tax provisions. As part of the final compromise reached on the taxation rate, conferees agreed to split the tax provisions from HR 4544 and substitute them for the provisions of an unrelated House-passed bill (HR 5322). This made it clear that the levy was a tax and not an "annual assessment" as provided for by the House. *(1977 action, 1977 Almanac p. 172)*

The Senate passed the amended version of HR 5322, incorporating the tax provisions, on Dec. 15, 1977. The House approved the Senate-passed bill Jan. 24, 1978, clearing the measure for the president.

The conference report on the remaining provisions of HR 4544 was filed Feb. 2 (H Rept 95-864). The Senate approved the conference report by voice vote Feb. 6. The House approved the report Feb. 15 by a 264-113 vote, thus clearing the bill. *(Vote 51, p. 14-H)*

Tax Controversy Resolved

A dispute over the rate of taxation of strip-mined coal delayed completion of conference action for months.

The House had favored a flat assessment on each ton of coal produced. But Senate conferees argued that this would unfairly penalize strip-mined coal, which generally was sold at lower prices than underground-mined coal. Strip-mine operators would thus be subject to a higher tax rate, despite the fact that their workers were somewhat less likely to contract black lung.

The compromise reached by conferees provided for a fixed assessment per ton of coal sold, but at reduced rates for strip mine operators. Underground-mine operators were to be taxed 50 cents a ton for their coal, while strip-mine operators were charged 25 cents. The tax was limited to 2 per cent of the sales price in either case.

Eligibility Compromise

With the tax provisions out of the way, conferees had less trouble reaching final agreement on HR 4544.

Conferees decided that miners seeking benefits should not have to undergo a government X-ray examination to prove disability if they had already been tested by a certified radiologist. The House, responding to complaints of miners that they had to endure repeated X-rays, had voted to require the Labor Department to accept X-rays taken by a miner's physician. The Senate had exempted from government re-examination only miners with more than 25 years experience who had had their X-rays taken by certified radiologists.

Conferees dropped the House-passed requirement that any new disability standards developed by the Labor Department be no more restrictive than the rather lenient "interim" standards developed for use by HEW in judging claims filed before 1974. Conferees accepted the Senate provision allowing the Labor Department to develop its own standards, but stipulated that the "interim" standards were to continue in effect until new ones were promulgated.

The conference version contained a House provision requiring the Labor Department to automatically review in light of the new law the cases of claimants who had filed since 1974 and been turned down. Miners filing before 1974 who had been turned down would be given a chance to refile their claims with HEW. The Senate version had provided only that rejected claimants could refile along with new claimants. ∎

Overseas Private Investment

Congress early in 1978 restored the authority of the Overseas Private Investment Corporation (OPIC) to write new high risk insurance on U.S. business ventures abroad.

The bill (HR 9179—PL 95-268) extended through fiscal 1980 OPIC's operating authority, which had lapsed Dec. 31, 1977.

The House April 11 adopted the conference report on the bill by a vote of 216-185, completing congressional action on the measure. The Senate had adopted the report April 6 by voice vote. *(Vote 175, p. 52-H)*

The bill passed in spite of the opposition of organized labor, which contended that the corporation's activities in providing insurance against the risks of war, expropriation and non-convertibility of currency for U.S. corporations investing in developing countries contributed to a loss of jobs in the United States.

After a companion bill had passed the Senate in 1977 by a 69-12 vote, the House passed HR 9179 Feb. 23, 191-165. *(Senate action, 1977 Almanac p. 390)*

OPIC was created in 1969 to encourage private investment in developing countries. Congress in 1974 extended OPIC's authority through Dec. 31, 1977. *(1974 Almanac p. 519)*

Provisions

As signed into law, HR 9179 (PL 95-268):

- Extended the authority of OPIC through Sept. 30, 1981.
- Repealed a provision of 1974 extension legislation directing OPIC to shift its insurance policies to private insurance companies by Dec. 31, 1980; prohibited OPIC from joint underwriting with private insurers.
- Repealed a 1974 provision directing OPIC to transfer most aid programs to other agencies.
- Directed OPIC to increase its support of U.S. small business by: increasing the proportion of its small business projects to at least 30 percent of all projects; using up to 50 percent of its net income to assist in the development of small business projects; and using its direct loan authority exclusively for small business.
- Encouraged OPIC to give preferential treatment to projects in countries with per capita incomes below $520, and to restrict its activities in countries with per capita incomes above $1,000.
- Prohibited OPIC from assisting any project likely to cause a "significant reduction" in U.S. employment.
- Placed an annual ceiling of $4 million on direct financing of ore or non-fuel mineral projects and $200,000 on surveys for such minerals; explicitly prohibited loans or surveys to finance any project involving the extraction of oil or gas.
- Prohibited OPIC from paying claims to any OPIC-insured investor convicted of bribery of a foreign official in connection with an OPIC-insured project if the bribery was a "preponderant cause" of the loss to the U.S. investor.
- Prohibited OPIC from supporting any project that would result in a "significant expansion of production" of copper before Jan. 1, 1981, or after that date if it would injure the U.S. copper industry.
- Prohibited OPIC from supporting any project to expand production or processing of palm oil, sugar or citrus crops for export.
- Prohibited OPIC from assisting projects in countries that violate human rights, and required the corporation in its annual report to discuss projects in which human rights violations have been considered. Exceptions were permitted if the project was felt to "directly benefit the needy people" in the country or if the activities were found to be in the national security interest of the United States.
- Required OPIC to maintain a profile to measure the economic and social development impact of each project, and to submit annually to Congress a report summarizing the development impact of its activities.

House Action

House passage of HR 9179 came on the second try. The bill had been pulled off the House floor Nov. 3, 1977, when active labor opposition put passage in jeopardy.

Both supporters and opponents of the bill were surprised at the level of opposition that developed during House floor debate Nov. 3. The most ominous development for supporters of the bill was the introduction by Clarence D. Long, D-Md., of an amendment that forced OPIC to provide at least half of its aid to U.S. small businesses.

Jonathan B. Bingham, D-N.Y., chairman of the International Relations Trade Subcommittee and floor manager of the bill, said few small businesses were interested in investing overseas, and that the Long amendment would therefore make the OPIC operation "utterly unworkable."

After the Long amendment was adopted by a 285-111 vote, Bingham withdrew the bill from the floor.

Before bringing HR 9179 before the House again, the International Relations Committee met and informally approved several amendments aimed at reducing opposition to the legislation. The only one that ultimately was offered on the floor required OPIC to give preferential consideration to investment projects in countries with a per capita income of $520 or less and to restrict activities in countries with a per capita income of more than $1,000.

Feb. 23 Floor Action

When the bill was brought to the floor Feb. 23, the amendment giving preferential consideration to projects in countries with per capita income below $520 was routinely adopted by voice vote.

Several amendments were proposed to limit OPIC's activities. Morris K. Udall, D-Ariz., introduced an amendment prohibiting OPIC from providing any insurance or other financial support for any project involving the exploration for or extraction of copper.

That amendment was adopted by voice vote, but the House rejected a broader amendment introduced by Leo J. Ryan, D-Calif., which would have prohibited OPIC from any participation in projects involving aluminum, lead, manganese and zinc as well as copper.

Philip M. Crane, R-Ill., offered an amendment that would have barred the corporation from making any loan or guarantee or insuring the obligations of the National Finance Corp. of Panama without prior House approval.

The amendment, considered a referendum on the Panama Canal issue, was rejected by a 166-199 margin. The House had also rejected a similar amendment in November, 188-215. *(Vote 62, p. 18-H)*

W. Henson Moore, R-La., introduced an amendment prohibiting OPIC from providing any insurance or financial support for any project to establish or expand production or processing of palm oil, sugar or citrus crops for export. That amendment carried by a margin of 191-167. *(Vote 63, p. 18-H)*

Passage

In the final debate before the vote on passage Ryan, one of the staunchest critics of the bill, stressed the jobs issue and particularly the shutdown of tire plants such as the Goodyear Tire & Rubber Co. plant in Akron, Ohio.

"In 1976 OPIC issued a guarantee for a project in Morocco for Goodyear in the amount of $1.8 million," Ryan said. "To do what? To manufacture tires. Now the plant closes over here and a plant opens up over there to do the same thing. The conclusion that I arrive at is that we lost some jobs."

But George E. Danielson, D-Calif., and John F. Seiberling, D-Ohio, rejected Ryan's contention.

Danielson said he planned to vote for the bill because "I have been assured by the Business Roundtable that is not a reason for their closing." Seiberling said that the problem with the Akron plant was not caused by plants in other countries but by competition with modern new plants in other parts of the United States.

The decisive factor in the 191-165 vote for final passage was the better than 2-to-1 support from Republican members. *(Vote 64, p. 18-H)*

Conference Action

Conferees filed their report (H Rept 95-1043) April 5. Major conference agreements:

Small Business

The most sensitive issue concerned an amendment to the House bill introduced by Clarence D. Long, D-Md., which required OPIC to use at least 50 percent of its insurance and financing for U.S. small business.

The conference committee adopted compromise language authorizing OPIC: 1) to give preferential consideration to small business projects; 2) to increase the proportion of projects involving small business to 30 percent of all OPIC projects; 3) to allocate up to 50 percent of its annual net income to assist in the development of projects by small business; and 4) to use its direct loan authority exclusively for small business.

Small business was defined in the reports on the bill as a company below the "Fortune 1000."

Development Guidelines

The conferees adopted broad Senate language requiring the corporation to be guided "by the economic and social development impact" of each project application and to consider their compatibility with other U.S. development programs.

They adopted a House provision requiring OPIC to give preferential consideration to projects in less developed countries with per capita incomes of $520 or less, and to restrict its activities in countries with per capita incomes of $1,000 or more.

The conference report added that it was "understood" that some exceptions, such as projects with "a unique developmental impact," could be approved.

Bribery

The House bill denied payments of claims to OPIC-insured investors convicted of bribery of a foreign official in connection with an OPIC-insured project. The conference committee adopted substitute language under which claims would be denied if bribery was the "preponderant cause" of the loss.

The provision also directed OPIC to adopt regulations to suspend for up to five years an investor's eligibility for OPIC support after an OPIC-related bribery conviction. ▮

Foreign Bank Regulation

Congress gave final approval Aug. 17 to legislation imposing essentially the same regulatory system on foreign banks operating in the United States as domestic banks already had.

The bill (HR 10899 — PL 95-369) cleared Congress when the House accepted a series of Senate amendments adopted in that chamber on Aug. 15 (S Rept 95-1073). The bill initially was passed by the House on April 6 (H Rept 95-910) by a 367-2 vote. *(Vote 164, p. 48-H)*

Similar legislation had been passed by the House in 1976, but the Senate never acted on the earlier measure. *(1976 Almanac p. 88)*

The bill was prompted by the substantial growth in foreign banking operations in the United States. In 1973, there were about 60 foreign banks operating in the country, with assets of about $37 billion. By 1978, 122 foreign banks were operating in the United States, and they had assets of $90 billion.

"Foreign banks in this country are not specialized institutions engaged principally in foreign trade financing on the periphery of our banking system," noted Sen. Thomas J. McIntyre, D-N.H. "They are in the mainstream of our domestic banking system."

While Congress saw a need to bring foreign banking operations under closer control, lawmakers emphasized that the bill was not designed to correct any specific abuses.

"Fortunately, the climate in which this bill has been considered is one of relative calm," McIntyre said. "Foreign banks doing business in the United States have behaved in a responsible manner, and their presence here has been a benefit to the banking industry as a whole. Enactment of a rational framework of federal regulation at this time is appropriate and will serve to avoid future problems while enhancing the competitive environment."

Interstate Banking

The most controversial issue in the bill concerned interstate branching by foreign banks. Under existing law, foreign banks had the privilege of forming branches in other states, even though domestic banks couldn't do so.

While the goal of the bill was to provide equality between foreign and domestic banks, lawmakers decided that prohibiting interstate branching by foreign banks would be inadvisable because it would reduce the flow of foreign capital into the United States by curtailing foreign bank activity. They also noted that a restriction on foreign bank branching would weaken the competitive position for capital of many states relative to a few states — especially New York and California — where most foreign banks currently operated.

To resolve the problem, Congress agreed to allow interstate branching, but to allow interstate branches of foreign banks only to accept deposits related to their international operations. That would continue the international flow of capital while preventing the foreign banks from gaining a competitive advantage in the quest for domestic deposits, bill proponents argued.

Other Issues

On the issue of insurance, the bill spared foreign banks the obligation to insure large "wholesale" deposits, but required them to insure "retail" deposits of individual bank customers.

Concerning regulation of foreign banks, the bill subjected foreign banks to the same regulatory system that domestic banks face, but it provided the Federal Reserve Board with "residual" authority to oversee the operations of foreign banks. That system would enable some centralized supervision of foreign bank operations in the United States.

Finally, the bill provided that the Federal Reserve Board could set reserve requirements for federal and state branches of foreign banks having $1 billion or more in worldwide assets. Arguing that banks with assets that large could significantly affect the flow of money in and out of the country, McIntyre said the provision was necessary to enable the Federal Reserve Board better to control monetary policy.

Major Provisions

As cleared by Congress, HR 10899:

- Allowed the Comptroller of the Currency to waive the requirement that all directors of national banks be U.S. citizens.
- Amended the Edge Act, under which U.S. financial institutions are federally chartered to engage in international financial operations, to ease capitalization requirements so that they could better compete with foreign financial entities.
- Amended the Federal Reserve Act to eliminate provisions that discriminated against foreign-owned banking institutions.
- Allowed foreign banks to establish federally chartered branches or agencies in states that did not prohibit foreign bank operations and where they did not already have state-chartered branches or agencies.
- Allowed foreign banks to establish branches outside of their "home states — provided the branches agreed to accept only foreign source or international banking and finance-related deposits.
- Gave foreign banks the option of applying for deposit insurance, but required insurance by foreign banks accepting deposits of less than $100,000 in states in which deposits of state banks were required to be insured.
- Authorized the Federal Reserve Board to impose reserve requirements on foreign banks.
- Subjected foreign banks to the same system of regulation as domestic banks, but gave the Federal Reserve Board residual authority to examine foreign banks.
- Made future U.S. operations of foreign banks subject to Bank Holding Company Act limitations on their nonbanking activities. *(Banking holding company background, 1970 Almanac p. 874)*
- Ordered a study of the extent to which United States banks operating overseas were subject to discrimination.∎

Fringe Benefits Taxation

Legislation prohibiting the Internal Revenue Service (IRS) from taxing a variety of currently tax-exempt fringe benefits cleared Congress Sept. 19.

The bill (HR 12841 — PL 95-427) barred the Treasury Department from issuing new regulations covering taxation of fringe benefits until 1980. Congressional tax leaders said they intended to study and act on the matter prior to that time.

Other provisions of the bill prevented the IRS from taxing employees on reimbursements they received for expenses in commuting to temporary worksites, and it prevented police officers from being taxed retroactively for cash meal allowances which were ruled to be taxable by the Supreme Court in November 1977.

The temporary ban on taxation of fringe benefits was endorsed by the Treasury Department, which had been trying for several years to include more benefits in the list of taxable items.

The department's last attempt at issuing fringe benefit regulations was withdrawn in December 1976, amid a flurry of objections. The department expected to complete a new study on the matter by the end of 1978 — in time for the planned congressional deliberations in 1979.

Final Provisions

As cleared by Congress, HR 12841:

- Prohibited the Treasury Department from issuing new regulations governing taxation of fringe benefits until 1980.
- Prohibited the department from issuing new regulations regarding tax treatment of expenses incurred in commuting to temporary worksites prior to 1980.
- Legitimized the exclusion of meal allowances from taxable income by police officers between 1970 and 1977, in effect prohibiting retroactive collection of taxes on such income under a Supreme Court ruling of Nov. 29, 1977.
- Allowed police officers to pay taxes on meal allowances retroactively to 1970 if they wished to.
- Provided an income tax exclusion for meals furnished an employee for the convenience of an employer even if the employer imposed a partial charge for the meal.

Background

The IRS interest in taxing fringe benefits derived from Section 61 of the Internal Revenue Code, which defined "gross income" for tax purposes as "all income from whatever source derived." The Supreme Court had ruled that the provision was broad enough to include "any economic or financial benefit."

Some fringe benefits — such as pension or profit-sharing plans and health insurance — were exempted from taxation by act of Congress. Others — including reduced tuition for children of college employees, reduced travel fare for airline, bus and railroad employees, and supper money for employees who worked overtime — had been exempted by IRS regulations.

But a large number of other benefits were currently untaxed because of difficulties involved in valuing them or because of differences of opinion about whether they constituted income.

In 1975, the Treasury Department introduced a discussion draft of proposed regulations to govern taxation of fringe benefits. It proved quite controversial, and was withdrawn in late 1976.

Both the House and Senate had approved legislation barring the IRS from acting until July 1, 1978, but the agency had said it would pursue the matter after that. *(1977 Almanac p. 153)*

In agreeing to the further delay, Ways and Means Chairman Al Ullman, D-Ore., said he would appoint a special task force to study the issue and prepare proposed legislation for action sometime before the ban ended.

That approach was acceptable to the administration. "There should be congressional action," said Donald C. Lubick, acting assistant secretary of the treasury for tax policy. "We're not trying to confound or go against congressional intent." Lubick did argue, however, that Congress should act before too long or the administration would go ahead on its own.

Legislative History

The House Appropriations Committee on May 22 approved an amendment to the Treasury, Postal Service and general government appropriations bill barring taxation of fringe benefits during fiscal 1979, ending Sept. 30, 1979.

That created a jurisdictional dispute with the tax-writing Ways and Means Committee, which on May 25 approved its own bill (HR 12841). The Ways and Means bill was reported (H Rept 95-1232) May 31.

The two committees were prompted to act in large part by an article in the May 8, 1978, issue of *U.S. News & World Report,* which said the IRS was about to start taxing fringe benefits.

The article listed 40 currently untaxed benefits which it said were under scrutiny by the agency. They included price discounts for store clerks, use of company cars by executives, rebates for employees who buy their firms' products, subsidized meals in company cafeterias, lunch and dinner money provided employees in a variety of circumstances, deferred pay for executives who elect to forgo some of their salaries for various tax purposes and others.

The magazine said taxing those benefits would cost "billions" of dollars to taxpayers. Rep. William L. Armstrong, R-Colo., estimated that the average tax burden would increase $240 a year if the IRS got its way.

HR 12841 was passed by the House June 28 on a 386-12 vote. *(Vote 442, p. 126-H)*

The Senate passed the bill by voice vote Aug. 4.

The fringe benefit bill cleared Congress when the House accepted a minor Senate amendment on Sept. 19. The Senate amendment provided that police officers who wished to include meal reimbursements in their taxable income for the purpose of qualifying for larger pensions could do so.

Federal Reserve Problems

Legislation designed to halt the erosion of membership in the Federal Reserve System was set aside by the Senate Banking, Housing and Urban Affairs Committee in late September.

Sen. William Proxmire, D-Wis., the committee chairman, said that he would make passage of such legislation his committee's first priority in the 96th Congress.

The measure (HR 14072) was reported by the House Banking, Finance and Urban Affairs Committee Sept. 19. But House leaders decided not to take the bill to the floor after it became apparent that the Senate would not act in 1978.

Miller Pressure

G. William Miller, chairman of the Federal Reserve Board, pressed hard for enactment of the bill, arguing that it would shore up the Fed's ability to direct monetary policy.

The bill would have required all major federally insured banks to maintain reserves — funds banks must keep on hand or on deposit, without interest, at a Federal Reserve bank — whether or not they belonged to the Federal Reserve, the nation's central banking system.

The bill was also devised to give the Fed more complete information about the nation's money supply.

Proponents of the legislation attributed its demise to the strong opposition of many financial institutions, led by the American Bankers Association.

The association maintained in a statement that "the sweeping changes proposed...haven't been sufficiently analyzed to justify legislative action." It went on to argue that the solution to the problem of the Federal Reserve System's loss of membership was to reduce reserve requirements across the board.

Over the summer, Miller said the Fed might consider paying interest on reserves. He was sharply criticized by the Banking committee chairmen — Proxmire and Rep. Henry S. Reuss, D-Wis. — who contended that the Fed did not have the authority to pay interest on reserves without specific congressional approval.

The bill approved by the House committee was the product of negotiations between the chairmen and Miller.

Background

In testimony before the House committee on July 27, Miller reported that the system had suffered a net loss of 327 member banks over the past eight years. At the end of 1977, there were 5,669 members, out of a total of about 15,000 banks in the country. The decline in membership had reduced the proportion of bank deposits subject to federal reserve requirements to 73 percent from 81 percent in 1970.

Miller warned that the decline in membership would "weaken" the financial system if allowed to continue. Specifically, he warned that the decline would impair the board's ability to implement monetary policy, and the system's ability to adapt to changing policy, by reducing the number of banks that can borrow funds from the Federal Reserve "discount window."

The discount window is one tool the board uses to determine the money supply. By manipulating the interest rate on funds it loans to member banks from the window — the "discount rate" — the board can either encourage or discourage investment. Beyond that, Miller argued, the discount window is an important source of funds for banks, without which the soundness of the system would be less assured.

"The discount window provides individual member banks with a reasonable period of time to make orderly adjustments in their lending and investment policies," Miller said. "The cushion provided by the window facilitates implementation of a restrictive monetary policy in a period of inflationary demands."

Beyond that, Miller argued, the erosion of membership diminished the ability of the board to influence the money supply in another way.

The Federal Reserve Board can implement an expansionary monetary policy by reducing reserve requirements, thus increasing the amount of money in circulation. Conversely, it can slow economic activity by increasing reserve requirements, thus reducing the amount of money in circulation.

Miller conceded that the use of reserve requirements to affect monetary policy had been limited in recent years. He blamed that on the fear that manipulating reserve requirements would accelerate the exodus of banks from the system.

While some economists questioned the usefulness of reserve requirements to influence monetary policy — the board's main tool for implementing monetary policy is its power to buy and sell government bonds in the open market ("open market transactions") — most agreed that universal reserve requirements would at least make it easier to control the money supply.

House Committee Action

The bill was ordered reported by the House Banking, Finance and Urban Affairs Committee by a vote of 22-14 (H Rept 95-1590).

Major Provisions

As approved by the committee, HR 14072 would have:

- Exempted from any reserve requirement the first $50 million held by a bank in checking and savings accounts and the first $50 million held in time deposits (certificates of deposit). Banks whose holdings did not reach that level would not have had to keep any money in reserve.
- Required all banks to maintain reserves on their holdings above $50 million, whether or not they were members of the Federal Reserve. Under existing law, there was no reserve requirement for non-members.
- Limited the range of the reserve requirements. For checking and savings accounts, the Fed could set the range between 6 percent and 8 percent of the holdings above $50 million. For time deposits with initial maturities under 180 days, the range would be 1 to 6 percent. For longer-term time deposits, the range would be 1 to 3 percent. (Under existing law, the ranges were 0 to 16.25 percent on checking accounts, 0 to 3 percent on savings deposits and 0 to 6 percent on all certificates of deposit.)
- Specified that the $50 million exemption figure would grow automatically as overall deposits across the country grew, thus assuring that banks initially exempted from holding reserves would remain exempt unless they grew faster than banks in the aggregate and became large enough relatively to be covered.
- Gave all banks, not just members of the Federal Reserve, access to the system's discount window — meaning that they could borrow money from the Fed.
- Instructed the Fed to develop a system for charging banks for the free services it currently provided, such as check-clearing and pickup and delivery of currency.
- Required all banks, regardless of the size of their deposits or membership in the Federal Reserve System, to provide the Fed with statistical information.

Committee Views

The committee maintained in its report that the measure would improve the Fed's ability to conduct monetary policy, remove the inequities that existed between banks that belonged to the system and those that did not and halt the erosion of membership in the system.

The committee calculated that 95 percent of the nation's banks would be exempt from reserve requirements altogether and that only 240 banks that were not Fed members would have to begin holding reserves.

Committee staff members said that the proportion of total deposits backed by reserves would be reduced from 73 percent to 68 percent.

Minority Views

Several Republicans on the committee filed minority statements. They argued for "an incentive approach to the membership problem rather than a mandated solution." Among the possible incentives, they said, were lowered reserve requirements, the payment of interest on reserves or permission for banks to invest a portion of their required reserves in Treasury securities. ▮

Humphrey-Hawkins Full Employment Bill

Working against the clock, a diverse group of senators produced a last-minute version of the Humphrey-Hawkins full employment bill (HR 50) that was able to gain final congressional approval.

The Senate passed the compromise version of the bill Oct. 13 by a 70-19 vote. The House agreed to the compromise Oct. 15, clearing the measure for the president. *(Senate vote 491, p. 71-S)*

The president signed the bill Oct. 27 (PL 95-523).

The eleventh-hour efforts rescued organized labor's only remaining hope for a major legislative victory in 1978 from what had seemed like certain defeat. Passage was also a victory for the Carter administration, which had worked hard in the dwindling days of the 95th Congress to get the bill to the Senate floor.

Still, the final outcome was a mixed bag for the bill's labor and civil rights supporters, who were forced to accept a measure that, to a considerable extent, was dictated by some of their most vocal legislative opponents — especially Sen. Orrin G. Hatch, R-Utah. By the end, some were calling it the Humphrey-Hawkins-Hatch bill.

As cleared, HR 50 was a far cry from the massive federal jobs and economic planning bill introduced by the late Sen. Hubert H. Humphrey, D-Minn. (1949-1964, 1971-1978), and Rep. Augustus F. Hawkins, D-Calif., during the depths of the mid-1970s recession. *(Background, 1977 Almanac p. 175, 1976 Almanac p. 371)*

The bill that finally reached President Carter's desk was stripped of its original provisions calling for government "last resort" jobs for the unemployed, although it still retained the central goal of reduction of the unemployment rate to 4 percent by 1983.

In addition, the final version contained a new national goal by calling for a reduction of the inflation rate to 3 percent by 1983 and 0 percent by 1988.

Unemployment during 1978 hovered around 6 percent, while inflation as measured by the consumer price index edged toward double-digit levels.

Coretta Scott King, a leader of the Full Employment Action Council, conceded that "we did not get all of the provisions in the bill that we would have liked. But there is no question that this is a major victory and an important first step in the struggle for full employment," she said. "Those who call it symbolic just don't understand how important it is."

Organized labor took a somewhat less sanguine view of the final bill. "It does represent a small symbolic step forward," said Ken Young of the AFL-CIO, "but the Senate weakened it severely."

With the addition of the inflation goal, the legislation was able to pick up support from a majority of Senate Republicans, who voted for it 17-15. Despite his work on the final version, however, Hatch, along with other conservative Republicans, opposed the bill.

Final Provisions

As signed into law, HR 50, the Full Employment and Balanced Growth Act of 1978:

Title I — National Goals and Priorities

● Declared a national policy of promoting full employment, increased real income, balanced growth, a balanced federal budget, growth in productivity, an improved balance of trade and price stability.

● Stated that the purpose of the bill was to better coordinate and integrate federal economic policy through improved management, increased efficiency, attention to long-range problems and a balanced federal budget.

● Stipulated that provisions of the act did not provide authorization for federal controls on wages and prices, production or resource allocation in order to achieve the goals of the act.

● Declared a policy of primary reliance on the private sector, and gave the following order of priority for job creation: regular private sector jobs, private sector jobs with federal assistance, conventional public sector jobs and a last-resort government employment reservoir.

● Encouraged adoption of fiscal policies that would reduce federal spending as a percentage of the gross national product to the lowest possible level consistent with national needs.

● Required the president to include in his economic report to Congress annual numerical goals for the current year (short-term goals) and each of the three succeeding years (medium-term goals) for unemployment, production, real income, productivity and prices.

● Required the president to set the medium-term goals so as to achieve reduction of the unemployment rate to 3 percent among persons aged 20 and over, and 4 percent for persons aged 16 and over, within five years.

● Required further that the medium-term goals be directed towards achieving a 3 percent inflation rate within five years, provided that steps taken to reduce inflation not impede achievement of the unemployment goal. Further required that, after the 3 percent goal had been achieved, succeeding economic reports contain the goal of achieving 0 percent inflation by 1988.

● Allowed the president, beginning with the second economic report after enactment, to propose modifications in the timetables for achieving the unemployment and inflation goals.

● Recommended that the president consider, along with other policies for achieving the goals, development of an agricultural policy aimed at providing full parity for farm prices.

● Required the annual budget of the president to reflect the goals set forth in the economic report.

● Required the Federal Reserve Board to report twice a year on its monetary policies and their relationship to the goals of the act, with the second report each year to include predictions for economic conditions in the next calendar year.

● Required the president to undertake policies to reduce the rate of inflation, including price monitoring, alleviation of product shortages, establishment of commodity stockpiles, increased productivity, increased private sector competition, removal of unnecessary government restrictions and increased exports.

Title II — Structural Economic Policies

● Required the president to propose such structural economic policies as he deemed appropriate to achieve the goals of the act, including consideration of countercyclical employment policies, coordination with state and local governments, assistance to economically depressed regions, youth employment policies and efforts to achieve a high rate of capital formation.

● Permitted the president to establish reservoirs of public employment, if he found that other policies were failing to achieve the full employment goals; stipulated that no new programs were to be put into operation less than two years after enactment.

● Required that any reservoir jobs be set up so as not to draw workers from the private sector, to be useful and in the lower ranges of skill and pay, and to be targeted on individuals and areas with the worst unemployment problems.

Title III — Congressional Review

● Established procedures for congressional review of goals and policies in the economic report and Federal Reserve Board reports.

● Directed the Joint Economic Committee to report to the Senate and House Budget committees by March 15 annually on the short-term and medium-term goals and policies in the economic report, after holding hearings and receiving reports from other committees on their views.

● Gave the congressional Budget committees the option of including in the first congressional budget resolution for the fiscal year recommended economic goals the resolution was designed to achieve.

● Gave Congress the option, if the president declared that the unemployment goals could not be met within five years, of including in the first budget resolution for the fiscal year a congressional determination of when the full employment goal could be reached.

Title IV — General Provisions

● Prohibited discrimination on account of sex, race, age, religion or national origin in any program under the bill.

● Provided that workers in reservoir jobs established under the act be given equal pay for equal work, not less than the federal minimum wage, but stipulated that none of the jobs be of the type covered by the David-Bacon Act's provisions requiring payment of locally prevailing wages on federal construction projects.

House Committee Action

The House Education and Labor Committee Feb. 22 reported HR 50 (H Rept 95-895). The committee had approved the measure by voice vote Feb. 14.

The Rules Committee March 1 proposed a substitute amendment to Title III of the bill, enlarging the Joint Economic Committee's role in congressional review of the economic goals established under the bill. Its report (H Rept 95-895, Part 2) was filed March 3.

LABOR COMMITTEE VIEWS

As approved by the Labor Committee, HR 50 contained only one set of numerical goals, requiring within five years reduction of the unemployment rate to 3 percent of the adult work force (those aged 20 and over) and 4 percent of the overall work force (aged 16 and over). The committee specifically rejected setting numerical goals for other aspects of the economy, such as numbers of jobs, federal spending or income security payments, acknowledging that these would have to be set by Congress and the president as changing conditions warranted.

The committee also rejected direct federal control of the economy in order to achieve the goals of the bill. Throughout the bill it emphasized the importance of the private sector as the source of most new jobs, with massive new public employment to be used only as a last resort.

While it suggested a number of policy options for the president and Congress to consider, the bill did not mandate specific programs to reach the unemployment goal. Its effectiveness for moving the country towards full employment rested on two strategies.

First, the bill would coordinate federal economic efforts towards full employment within a single framework. To coordinate economic strategy, the bill required that the president's annual economic message lay out the goals and policies for attaining full employment in the years ahead. With input from Congress, the Federal Reserve Board and other agencies, this would help to bring balance to overall federal employment efforts, the committee said.

Secondly, the bill would set a national goal that, the committee argued, the president and Congress could ignore or fail to meet at their peril. They would have to do their utmost to meet the target or face the consequences with the voters. The president "will be answerable if it appears that [his policy] results in not moving in accord with the goals and timetable for the reduction of unemployment," the committee predicted.

Inflation Controversy

The Labor Committee rejected the "trade-off" theory of the relationship between unemployment and inflation, which holds that reduced unemployment necessarily brings high inflation. But, recognizing the importance of price stability, the committee included restraint of inflation as a major goal of the bill. To combat inflation the bill proposed a series of strategies, including expansion of production, establishment of commodity stockpiles, increased productivity and tougher antitrust enforcement.

Committee Republicans made the inflationary impact of HR 50 a central point of criticism. They predicted that the expansionary steps needed to reach full employment, together with the wage structure of proposed public service employment under the bill, would lead to severe inflation. "The bill may be committing the nation to 6 percent inflation or worse," the minority views stated, calling the anti-inflation measures in the bill "minimally effective."

To elevate the restraint of inflation to an equal status with the reduction of unemployment, the Republican members proposed that a specific inflation goal be included. An amendment by Ronald A. Sarasin, R-Conn., defeated on a near-party-line vote, would have set an interim goal of the reduction of unemployment to 3 percent within 5 years. The long-term goal would be no inflation at all. The amendment specifically prohibited the president from recommending price controls.

The committee majority responded that a specific inflation goal would move the federal government inevitably into more and more control of wages, prices and the overall economy. "Such a provision in the bill would be a legislated guideline for prices," the report stated. Further, the majority argued, including inflation goals would distract from the primary purpose of the bill, which was to fight unemployment.

Public Service Employment

While its provisions were somewhat more restrictive than in earlier versions of the full employment bill, the Labor Committee text of HR 50 called for establishment of "last resort" public service jobs for the unemployed if all other strategies failed. A key issue concerned whether restrictions on eligibility and pay for those jobs were sufficient to prevent the public service jobs from becoming a magnet drawing workers out of the private sector.

The bill required that all last resort jobs be limited to the lower ends of the pay and skill spectrum. Workers who had left their jobs voluntarily, or who had been unemployed for less than five weeks, would be ineligible. Wages would have to provide "equal pay for equal work," but would not have to meet the prevailing wage in the private sector.

Republicans charged that the "equal pay for equal work" standard, as applied to public service jobs, was nothing less than the prevailing wage in the public sector. Since public sector wage levels set by collective bargaining are often considerably higher than in the private sector, they argued, workers would strongly favor the last resort jobs, draining the for-profit economy of needed employees. The Congressional Budget Office estimated that a prevailing wage standard would require four times as many public service jobs as the minimum wage standard would. "If there is any one area where this bill can produce utterly disastrous effects on the economy, it is in the setting of prevailing wages," the minority said.

Federal Reserve Board

Recognizing that monetary policy could have a crucial impact on unemployment, the Labor Committee required the Federal Reserve Board to report annually to Congress on its intended policies for the coming year. The report would have to outline the relationship between board policy and full employment, with Congress getting a chance to make sure that the policy conformed with full employment strategy. The committee said that this provision would not exceed the historic powers of Congress to supervise the board.

Republicans feared that the provision would lead to politicization of the board. The provision would "put the board on the political chopping block," observed one committee aide. The minority recommended that the sentence in the bill allowing Congress to modify board plans be struck.

RULES COMMITTEE AMENDMENT

The Rules Committee amendment called for the Joint Economic Committee to develop annually a broad statement of Congress' economic goals. By March 15 of each year the committee would report a concurrent resolution setting numerical goals for unemployment, production, productivity and real income. After it was approved by both houses, the concurrent resolution would serve as a guide for future legislation, similar to the outline for spending bills provided by the budget resolution. The Labor Committee bill had provided only for a review by the Joint Economic Committee of the president's Economic Report.

The amendment was proposed by Rules Committee member Richard Bolling, D-Mo., who was also chairman of the Joint Economic Committee. Opponents, notably Senate Budget Committee Chairman Edmund S. Muskie, D-Maine, charged that it would undermine the budget process by setting up a new guideline for action in competition with the budget resolution.

House Floor Action

The House March 16 passed HR 50 after tacking on so many extraneous amendments that critics labeled it a Christmas tree measure.

The vote on final passage, 257-152, came with an ease that belied the difficulties encountered by bill sponsors during four days of floor consideration. Democratic leaders narrowly beat back a series of amendments that sponsors said could have crippled efforts to reach the bill's 4 percent unemployment target. *(Vote 135, p. 40-H)*

Defeated by close margins were amendments to narrow the definition of unemployment and to add provisions calling for a balanced federal budget, reduced income taxes and an inflation rate of 3 percent.

But some additional goals proved irresistible to House members. Since the bill set only a target for unemployment, without authorizing new programs to reach that goal, it was difficult to deny those who wanted to add other goals.

In action March 9, the House added a goal of 100 percent of parity in farm prices. Republican amendments to set inflation and balanced budget targets were defeated March 9 and 16 only after Democrats offered less restrictive substitutes that at least gave members a chance to go on record in favor of price stability and federal economy.

'Christmas Tree' Amendments

Other proposals added to the bill included amendments calling for aid to small business, removal of architectural barriers to the handicapped, use of flexible working hours, balanced regional policies, labor-management cooperation and "appropriate" light-capital technology.

Both supporters and opponents of the bill repeatedly pointed with irritation to the large number of extra goals added. John M. Ashbrook, R-Ohio, observed that "everything but the kitchen sink is going in." Labor Committee member Paul Simon, D-Ill., said during debate that "this bill is moving toward becoming a Christmas tree," overloaded with goals that detracted from the focus on unemployment. Charles E. Wiggins, R-Calif., said that the seedling of the unemployment goal had grown into an "unmanageable Christmas tree," an "unworkable monster," that deserved to be chopped down.

Before passing HR 50, the House killed a move to give the Joint Economic Committee (JEC) broad new responsibility over economic and budget policy.

Symbolic Issue

As passed by the House, HR 50 was a much less comprehensive measure than that proposed some four years earlier by Employment Opportunities Subcommittee Chairman August F. Hawkins, D-Calif. While still committing the nation to a specific five-year unemployment goal, 3 percent for the adult work force (those aged 20 and older) and 4 percent of the overall work force (aged 16 and over), it did not contain earlier proposals for sweeping national economic planning and massive public employment programs.

Nevertheless, the bill retained a strong emotional impact with black and labor groups, who lobbied intensively for it as a symbol of concern for the jobless. House Democratic leaders worked to preserve the bill as a centerpiece of the party program for the November elections. Another factor in support was the desire to create an enduring legislative monument to the late Sen. Hubert H. Humphrey, D-Minn. An emotional welcome was given to Sen. Muriel Humphrey, D-Minn., widow of the bill's cosponsor, when she arrived on the House floor during the vote on passage of the bill.

Opponents of the bill charged that it would be both ineffective in combating unemployment and inflationary. Wiggins, who called the bill "a total waste of time," predicted that "the only Americans hired because of the bill will be those who write the reports" required by it. Republicans favored a substitute establishing a presidential task force on youth unemployment.

Although they lost a substantial number of southern and junior Democrats on key amendments, House Democratic leaders managed to get almost all of their party colleagues to fall into line on the final vote. Democrats voted 233-41 for the bill, while Republicans were 24-111 against.

Passage came as a welcome victory for labor and liberal groups, who had lost a series of key House votes in the past year. One lobbyist for the bill said that six weeks before the vote supporters did not have enough votes to pass the bill.

Inflation Goal

House Democratic leaders March 9 headed off a Republican attempt to add a specific anti-inflation goal by adding their own broad anti-inflation language to the measure.

By a 198-223 vote the House rejected an amendment, sponsored by James M. Jeffords, R-Vt., to set a national goal of a reduction in the inflation rate to 3 percent. *(Vote 100, p. 30-H)*

Instead, the House adopted, on a 277-143 party-line vote, an amendment sponsored by Majority Leader Jim Wright, D-Texas, requiring the president to propose in his annual Economic Report goals for keeping price increases within "reasonable" limits. The amendment was a substitute for the Republican proposal, originally offered by Ronald A. Sarasin, R-Conn. *(Vote 99, p. 30-H)*

Supporters of the 3 percent inflation goal, which paralleled the bill's 4 percent unemployment goal, argued that inflation directly affected many more people than did unemployment. Both problems, they said, had to be dealt with on a coequal basis, with specific goals for each.

To counter these arguments, which appeared to be picking up increasing support in the days before the vote, Wright offered his substitute proposal. It allowed Democrats to show their concern over inflation without committing the bill to a specific target. In addition to requiring the president to set annual inflation goals, the amendment mandated general anti-inflation policies.

Consideration of HR 50 came amid increasing evidence of an improvement in the employment situation and a worsening of inflation. The Bureau of Labor Statistics reported March 10 that unemployment had fallen to 6.1 percent in February, the lowest rate since October 1974.

Minority unemployment, a special concern of bill supporters, dropped to 11.8 percent from 12.7 percent in January. Supporters of the 3 percent inflation goal pointed to another set of economic statistics, released March 9, which showed wholesale prices rising 1.1 percent in February, the biggest inflation increase in three years.

Unemployment Statistics

An amendment offered by Otis G. Pike, D-N.Y., to change the way unemployment statistics were computed, was rejected March 16 by a close margin, 199-204. By excluding certain groups of those currently counted as jobless from unemployment statistics, the amendment could have radically altered the effects of the bill. If implemented, according to opponents, it would have meant that current rates of unemployment would qualify as full employment, thus rendering action under the bill unnecessary. *(Vote 129, p. 38-H)*

The Pike amendment would have excluded strikers and those who had been unemployed for less than four weeks, who had jobs waiting, who were seeking part-time work, or who quit their last jobs. Pike, who opposed the bill as inflationary, said that "there are a few people who are not terribly unhappy being unemployed," and that they should be excluded from unemployment figures. Observing that "we too often use a shotgun when we ought to be using a scalpel," Pike argued that unemployment statistics had to distinguish between those with temporary or voluntary employment problems and the hard-core unemployed.

Hawkins responded that, under the amendment, what was now considered to be 8 percent unemployment would be measured as 4 percent, the full employment goal. "It would mean 8 percent unemployment under current concepts would be the target of the bill under his concepts," Hawkins said.

The Pike amendment came so close to victory that the final outcome was decided by a flurry of last-minute votes and vote switches. Simon observed after the vote that many members who voted for the amendment "didn't understand the full implications of it."

Balanced Budget

By a 205-215 vote, the House March 15 rejected a John M. Ashbrook, R-Ohio, amendment, to give a balanced federal budget a high priority among the goals of the bill. The Ashbrook amendment was an amendment to one offered by Butler Derrick, D-S.C., and Max Baucus, D-Mont., which was in turn a substitute to an earlier Ashbrook amendment. *(Vote 123, p. 36-H)*

The Derrick-Baucus amendment also emphasized the importance of reducing federal deficits. But it provided that balanced budget policies be consistent with full employment policies, thus allowing more flexibility, according to supporters. The Derrick-Baucus amendment was adopted 411-3 after the Ashbrook amendment was rejected. *(Vote 124, p. 36-H)*

Ashbrook said after the vote that the Derrick-Baucus amendment amounted to only "putting in the fine print" a commitment to a balanced budget.

Labor Committee member Ted Weiss, D-N.Y., attributed the close vote on the Ashbrook amendment to the desire of many members to make sure they got on record in favor of a balanced budget. Since some Democrats were not sure they would get a vote on the Derrick-Baucus amendment, he said, they voted for Ashbrook.

GOP Tax Cut Proposal

A Republican amendment calling for the reduction of income taxes as part of employment strategy was offered by Albert H. Quie, R-Minn., and defeated on a 194-216 vote March 15. Originally proposed by Jack F. Kemp, R-N.Y., the amendment set a goal of a permanent reduction in individual federal income taxes by 10 percent a year for three years, accompanied by a 1 percent reduction in corporate taxes annually and an increase in the corporate surtax exemption to $100,000. *(Vote 126, p. 36-H)*

Kemp argued that continuing inflation had caused an increase in tax levels without Congress ever voting on it. As families receive nominally higher incomes along with inflation, they move into higher tax brackets. Thus they end up paying a larger share of their income in taxes even though their real income is not going up, Kemp said. Pointing to the stimulative effect of tax cuts proposed by President Kennedy, he said that the best way to increase employment was to provide increased incentives for saving and investment through tax cuts.

Opponents of the amendment predicted that it could lead to hundreds of billions of dollars of increased federal deficits. Ways and Means Committee Chairman Al Ullman, D-Ore., said that the amendment was "not only bad tax policy, it is extremely bad procedural policy."

Joint Economic Committee Role

The House March 16 voted 259-153 to strike a Rules Committee amendment giving strengthened responsibilities to the Joint Economic Committee in setting congressional full employment policy. *(Vote 132, p. 38-H)*

The Rules Committee had proposed an amendment to Title III of the bill, setting procedures for congressional review of the President's full employment strategy. The amendment required the joint committee to report an annual concurrent resolution detailing congressional goals for employment and economic growth. Action on the concurrent resolution would have been completed before Congress finished work on the first annual budget resolution, which sets guidelines for congressional appropriations.

Although the Rules Committee amendment had the support of Budget Committee Chairman Robert N. Giaimo, D-Conn., it was strongly opposed by other Budget Committee members who feared it would undermine the budget process. A majority of Budget Committee members lined up behind the amendment, offered by Barber B. Conable Jr., R-N.Y., to strike the Rules Committee amendment. The Conable amendment instead allowed the joint committee to offer an amendment on employment and other goals to the budget resolution.

Delbert L. Latta, R-Ohio, called the Rules Committee amendment "a major attack on the jurisdiction of the Budget Committee." Conable argued that the existence of a separate Joint Economic Committee guideline for congressional economic policies would "reduce the Budget Committee to largely an arithmetic function."

Bolling argued that the joint committee resolution would give Congress a chance to "look at all aspects of our society," not just questions of federal spending.

Republican Substitute

The Republican substitute to the bill, offered by Quie, the Labor Committee's ranking minority member, also set a national goal of 4 percent unemployment, but specifically excluded the use of public service employment to reach the goal. It also included goals of a 3 percent inflation rate, 100 percent parity in farm prices, reduction of tax levels, and a balanced federal budget. It was defeated 137-276. *(Vote 134, p. 40-H)*

To combat the most severe unemployment problem, the substitute established a presidential task force on youth employment. The task force was to seek ways of reducing minority youth unemployment to that of non-minority youth, and all youth unemployment to the adult rate.

Other Amendments

In other action on amendments, the House:

- Adopted, on a 264-150 vote March 9, a Quie amendment to establish as a national goal achievement of 100 percent of parity in farm prices. *(Vote 102, p. 30-H)*
- Adopted, on a 239-177 vote March 9, a Jeffords amendment calling for two sets of employment statistics. One set would measure all employment; the second would count workers in public service employment programs as still looking for work, thus giving the public an indication of the extent to which the administration was using temporary jobs programs to meet the high-employment goals. *(Vote 101, p. 30-H)*
- Rejected, on a 114-296 vote, an Ashbrook amendment requiring the president to consider the impact of all federal laws and regulations on the economy. *(Vote 131, p. 38-H)*
- Rejected, on a 196-216 vote, a Robert E. Bauman, R-Md., amendment, to terminate the bill in five years. *(Vote 133, p. 40-H)*
- Rejected, on a 34-65 standing vote, a John H. Rousselot, R-Calif., amendment to require that any last-resort public service jobs under the bill pay wages no more than the minimum wage.

Senate Committee Action

The Senate bill (S 50) was jointly referred to the Human Resources and Banking, Housing and Urban Affairs committees. In contrast to the House committee action, the joint referral produced lengthy delays in reporting the bill, pushing Senate floor action back to the last weeks of the session.

The bill breezed by the Human Resources Committee without encountering any serious obstacles. The committee May 3 ordered S 50 reported by voice vote, without major amendments.

Banking Committee Action

In the Banking Committee, however, the bill faced much stronger opposition. S 50 was reported only after the committee voted June 28 to establish as a national goal the complete elimination of inflation by 1983. The committee ordered the bill reported by voice vote the same day.

Ironically, adoption of the zero inflation goal followed the apparent rejection by the committee of the efforts by its chairman, William Proxmire, D-Wis., to set the more modest goal of 3 percent inflation, as measured by the consumer price index, in 1983. Proxmire had long advocated the 3 percent inflation goal, which the House had rejected in March.

"I couldn't get eight votes for 3 percent," said Proxmire after the committee voted 8-7 to adopt the zero inflation goal. John Sparkman, D-Ala., who held the deciding vote on the otherwise evenly split committee, opposed the 3 percent goal.

But Sparkman was willing to support the zero inflation goal, which had been proposed as an amendment by Harrison Schmitt, R-N.M. The committee had originally rejected the Schmitt amendment by a 10-5 vote June 22.

After modifying his amendment to make clear that efforts to halt inflation should not be allowed to impede achievement of the unemployment goal, Schmitt reintroduced it. He won with the support of Proxmire, Sparkman, and two other Democrats.

Proxmire said he hoped that adoption of the zero inflation goal by the Senate would eventually lead to approval of the 3 percent goal by a conference committee.

Opponents of setting any specific inflation goal predicted that, since the zero goal would be so extraordinarily difficult to attain, it would have less practical effect than the 3 percent goal. Donald W. Riegle Jr., D-Mich., calling the amendment "legislative rhetoric," said that "the zero percent goal renders it meaningless."

Adoption of the inflation goal followed approval of a series of other amendments offered by fiscal conservatives on the committee. Among them were amendments by:

- Robert Morgan, D-N.C., setting a goal of a balanced federal budget; approved by voice vote.
- Proxmire, setting a goal of reduction of the federal budget to 20 percent of the gross national product; adopted 8-4.
- John G. Tower, R-Texas, to allow the president to modify the 1983 4 percent unemployment goal in his first economic report after passage of the bill; approved 8-5.

Supporters of the bill were basically glad to get out of the committee, which they viewed as dominated by unfriendly forces, as well as they did. One lobbyist observed that the recent evidence of popular conservatism also had an impact on the bill. "The political climate has shifted, so we're swimming upstream," he said.

Joint Report

After two months of difficult negotiations, the Senate Human Resources and Banking committees Sept. 6 finally filed their joint report on S 50, the Humphrey-Hawkins full employment bill (S Rept 95-1177).

Labor and civil rights supporters of S 50 viewed the inflation goal in the Banking Committee bill as having disastrous effects on the bill's goal of a reduction of unemployment to 4 percent by 1983. The Human Resources Committee bill, approved May 3, did not contain any specific inflation goal.

Working under new procedures established by the Senate committee reorganization resolution (S Res 4), staffs of the two committees were unable to find an easy way to meld the different versions into one joint report. They settled for reporting the versions as separate substitute amendments for the original bill.

That left unresolved, however, the question of which version the Senate would consider first on the floor.

The Senate parliamentarian's office had already offered an informal opinion that the Banking Committee bill should be considered first. Since the Banking version, by coming after the Human Resources bill, in effect amounted to a substitute amendment to it, a staff member reasoned, then the Banking bill, as any other amendment, would have to be disposed of first.

Pressures

Finally reported by the committees with only about a month remaining in the session, the bill seemed to have only a slim chance of getting to the Senate floor. Faced with a threatened conservative filibuster and an extremely crowded Senate calendar, Majority Leader Robert C. Byrd, D-W.Va., made it clear that he would bring the bill up only if an extended debate could be avoided. "There has to be 60 votes for cloture before they will even think of bringing it up," observed one labor lobbyist.

The labor and civil rights coalition supporting the bill put heavy pressure on the administration and congressional leaders to bring the bill to the floor. At a meeting with Carter Sept. 26, members of the Congressional Black Caucus pushed the administration for a more aggressive effort to bring the bill up for consideration. The meeting resulted in a walk-out by Rep. John Conyers Jr., D-Mich., who had urged Carter to convene a Humphrey-Hawkins summit conference similar to the Middle East summit at Camp David.

Senate Floor Action

Following unsuccessful efforts to attach Humphrey-Hawkins to the tax cut bill (HR 13511), the final compromise was drafted and taken to the Senate floor Oct. 13 as a substitute for the House version of the bill (HR 50). Passage came on a 70-19 vote. *(Vote 491, p. 71-S)*

Compromise Efforts

The shape of the final bill was determined by an *"ad hoc"* committee, composed of the bill's managers and some of its most outspoken opponents, meeting throughout the week of Oct. 9.

Some type of compromise became essential when it became clear that there was not enough time to break a threatened conservative filibuster.

The negotiations opened up sharp strains between the coalition and Senate sponsors, who included Employment Subcommittee Chairman Gaylord Nelson, D-Wis., and Banking Committee Chairman William Proxmire, D-Wis. Nelson insisted that a compromise was the only hope for the bill, even if it meant choking down some objectionable provisions. The labor-civil rights forces, on the other hand, refused to give up without a fight, arguing that they had the strength to avoid provisions on inflation and government spending the *ad hoc* committee wanted to include.

The first version produced by the *ad hoc* committee, presented Oct. 11, was unacceptable to the coalition, even if rejection of it meant the end of the whole bill. Lobbyists continued to press for a cloture vote, scheduled for Oct. 13, and a direct confrontation with their opponents.

But, hours before the cloture vote was to occur, the *ad hoc* committee finally came up with a substantive and procedural package acceptable to all. Based largely on the Banking Committee's report on the bill, the proposal included the inflation goals but left out the spending limits. Along with time agreements on amendments, the idea was to let the Senate work its will on the controversial parts, and then proceed to final passage. It worked.

Inflation Goal

The outcome of the crucial vote on the bill was determined by tactical differences between the labor-civil rights coalition and its senatorial allies.

Although it had campaigned against the setting of a specific inflation target as the chief threat to the bill, the coalition had moved during the weeks before Senate consideration to acquiescence in some form of inflation goal.

Republicans, on the other hand, were absolutely insistent on the inflation amendment. Hatch and others made it clear that they would try to kill the bill if the inflation goals were removed.

The compromise presented by the *ad hoc* committee called for reduction of the inflation rate to 3 percent by 1983 and 0 percent by 1988, with the stipulation that policies aimed at reaching the goals would not override the unemployment goal.

Budget Committee Chairman Edmund S. Muskie, D-Maine, and Muriel Humphrey, D-Minn., offered an amendment to substitute a goal of 3 percent inflation, "at the earliest possible time."

Supporters of the bill were deeply divided on the Muskie-Humphrey amendment. Nelson and Jacob K. Javits, R-N.Y., fearing that its adoption would lead to a fatal filibuster by Hatch, urged their liberal colleagues to vote against the amendment. While the bill had been brought to the floor under a time agreement, there was no limit on the number of amendments — meaning that Hatch could call up the hundreds of amendments he had in his pocket to kill the few remaining hours.

"It is my belief...that there will be no Humphrey-Hawkins bill in this Congress if this amendment succeeds," Javits said.

But the coalition was prepared to call Hatch's dare, arguing that his own party's leadership would not allow a filibuster. "If the Senate had worked its will on the amendment, it would not have permitted Hatch to kill the bill. Politically, the Republicans knew they couldn't permit Hatch to take the responsibility for killing the bill — no way they would have let him do it," said Young of the AFL-CIO.

The coalition came tantalizingly close to victory on the amendment. The vote was tied 41-41 before Dennis DeConcini, D-Ariz., and Thomas F. Eagleton, D-Mo., switched their votes to "nay." Eagleton switched in order to move reconsideration of the vote, in case supporters could round up more votes for the amendment. The final vote was 41-45. *(Vote 489, p. 71-S)*

The Eagleton motion to reconsider the vote was then rejected 39-46. *(Vote 490, p. 71-S)*

Government Spending Limit

If the loss of the inflation goal was unacceptable to Republican supporters of the compromise bill, addition of a specific goal for reducing government spending was unacceptable to the coalition.

Coalition supporters worried that adoption of a spending limitation would preclude new social programs. King said the provision "gave us the greatest trouble," because it could curtail new spending for things like national health insurance.

The compromise package presented to the Senate did not have a spending limit. Proxmire introduced the provision as an amendment, to set a goal of reduction of federal spending as a percentage of the gross national product (GNP) to 21 percent by fiscal 1981 and 20 percent by fiscal 1983.

Noting that Carter had called for reduction of spending to 19 percent of the GNP, Proxmire explained that the current level, over 22 percent, was far in excess of historical levels, which averaged below 20 percent for most of the post-war era.

Muskie responded that the spending limits would tie the hands of the Budget Committees, whose responsibility it was to determine such broad questions as the government's share of the whole economy. Muskie offered an amendment to the Proxmire amendment calling for reduction of the federal share of the economy to the lowest possible level, "consistent with national needs and priorities." The Muskie amendment was adopted by a 56-34 vote. *(Vote 487, p. 71-S)*

Budget Amendment

One verb in the *ad hoc* committee proposal provoked strong opposition from Budget Committee members.

The compromise package provided that, in the event the president decided the 4 percent unemployment goal could not be reached by 1983, the subsequent first congressional budget resolution "shall" contain a new date on which the goal could be met. This in effect meant that the Budget Committees would have to come up with their own ideas of when the goal could be reached, and defend them on the House and Senate floors.

Henry Bellmon, R-Okla., ranking Republican on the Budget Committee, moved to substitute "may" for "shall." Bellmon said the mandatory wording would lead to a "ridiculous" situation in which members had to vote on how soon to get to full employment — a decision, he said, that would inevitably be based on political rather than economic considerations.

Opponents of Bellmon's amendment argued that the mandatory wording was needed in order to make sure Congress got a chance to respond to the president's decision setting back the unemployment goal. But the Senate sided with Bellmon and his amendment was adopted 50-40. *(Vote 488, p. 71-S)*

FINAL ACTION

On Oct. 15, the final day of the session, the House agreed to the Senate amendments by voice vote, completing congressional action on the bill.

Trade Legislation

A bill designed to provide added assistance to workers and firms hurt by import competition was caught in a flurry of last-minute amendments and protectionist sentiment and died in the final hours before adjournment Oct. 15.

The bill, HR 11711, became entangled with two other trade measures, one calling for a ban on any negotiated reduction in textile duties and the other seeking to extend the president's authority to waive countervailing duties designed to offset foreign subsidies on some imports.

The end result was a double defeat for the administration's efforts to complete the final phase of the delicate multilateral trade negotiations in Geneva.

Passage of the ban on textile duty reductions was widely regarded as a largely symbolic expression of congressional frustration over import competition, since it was attached to a minor bill (HR 9937) that the president was not expected to sign. President Carter pocket vetoed the bill Nov. 10. *(Text of Carter statement, p. 67-E)*

The administration's inability to win an extension of the countervailing duty waiver authority was considered a more serious setback, since European governments had pressed for the extension as a gesture of U.S. support in the effort to devise a new code for the treatment of government subsidies. Both European and U.S. spokesmen warned that the lapse of the waiver could imperil the negotiations.

Staff members in both the House and Senate said the defeat of the adjustment assistance bill, to which the countervailing duty waiver was added as an amendment, was largely due to last-minute chaos rather than political conviction.

One of the last measures considered on the final day of the session, the bill became the vehicle for several non-germane family assistance and welfare amendments that members hoped to salvage before adjournment.

"We lost it in the Senate by getting all those family assistance amendments tied to it," said one frustrated supporter of the legislation.

Adjustment Assistance, Duty Waiver

HR 11711 had been reported (H Rept 95-1061) by the House Ways and Means Committee April 18 and passed by the House on a 261-24 vote Sept. 8. *(Vote 654, p. 186-H)*

The Senate Finance Committee reported the bill Oct. 10 (S Rept 95-1313).

HR 11711 attempted to respond to criticisms of the adjustment assistance program, which as originally created provided extra unemployment and retraining benefits to workers and made loans, loan guarantees and special tax deductions available to firms hurt by import competition. *(Background, 1974 Almanac p. 553)*

The measure broadened the coverage of workers and firms, liberalized benefits, accelerated the certification process and delivery of benefits, and provided for industry-wide studies and technical assistance.

Senate Amendments

During Senate floor action Oct. 15, William V. Roth Jr., R-Del., offered an amendment that contained the administration proposal to extend the president's authority to waive countervailing duties on some subsidized imports.

The duties applied to an estimated $607 million in subsidized imports, primarily from Europe, that entered the United States in 1977, resulting in about $47 million in waived duties. The imports were about 1 percent of total imports from Europe to the United States.

The administration proposal, worked out at the last minute with H. John Heinz III, R-Pa., sought to extend the waiver authority to Feb. 15, 1979, if certain conditions were met, with a possible further extension to July 30, 1979.

A similar proposal was also added to the sugar price support bill that the House rejected Oct. 15. *(Sugar bill, p. 462)*

Other provisions of the Roth amendment proposed to limit the duty-free importation of watches with components made in the Soviet Union that enter the United States from insular possessions, primarily the Virgin Islands. In addition, the amendment proposed limited changes in the adjustment assistance provisions of the bill.

Roth's warning that additional amendments would jeopardize final passage of the bill went unheeded as Finance Committee Chairman Russell B. Long, D-La., Jacob K. Javits, R-N.Y., and Birch Bayh, D-Ind., offered the following amendments, all adopted by non-record votes:

● Long, to amend the Social Security Act to provide permanent authority for the federal government to fund child support collection efforts.

● Javits, to permit states to adjust welfare payments when a child eligible under the aid to families with dependent children program was living with an ineligible adult.

● Bayh, to provide Medicare coverage for Pap smear tests for the diagnosis of uterine cancer in women over 55.

The bill was then passed by voice vote and returned to the House.

Final Efforts

The House early Oct. 15 concurred in the Senate amendments, but with further amendments offered by James C. Corman, D-Calif., who was looking for a way to salvage several bills that provided additional funds for foster care, subsidies for adoptions, added protections for children in foster homes, and removed some work disincentives for the disabled.

The final House version also included a substitute for the Senate watch amendment, and deleted the Bayh Pap smear amendment.

By the time the bill returned to the Senate, the House had adjourned. With only a few senators remaining on the floor and facing a take-it-or-leave-it situation on the measure, Majority Leader Robert C. Byrd, D-W.Va., decided against further action. The bill died despite a last-minute call to Byrd from President Carter urging passage of the waiver extension.

Textile Tariff Reduction Ban

Sen. Ernest F. Hollings, D-S.C., — with 46 cosponsors — proposed the ban on negotiated reductions in textile tariffs. He offered the proposal Oct. 12 as an amendment to an unrelated bill passed by the House Sept. 26 (HR 9937) authorizing the General Services Administration to dispose of $24 million worth of Carson City silver dollars. Hollings previously had succeeded in adding the proposal to a bill extending the Export-Import Bank (S 3077), but that measure had sunk under the weight of non-germane amendments. *(Export-Import Bank, p. 397)*

Supporters of the amendment argued that the roughly 2.5 million workers in the industry were particularly vulnerable to import competition, and that an estimated 400,000 jobs had been eliminated by imports over the past decade.

The Senate adopted the amendment and passed HR 9937 by voice vote.

Conference Action

The conference report on the bill (H Rept 95-1806) was broght to the House floor Oct. 15 and adopted by a 198-29 vote. *(Vote 833, p. 236-H)*

Stephen L. Neal, D-N.C., issued a warning to Robert S. Strauss, the president's special trade representative, that Congress was serious about textile imports.

"If he bargains away the jobs and futures of our textile workers, he runs the grave risk of Congress rejecting the entire GATT agreement," Neal said.

The Senate quickly approved the conference report by a 48-13 vote, thus clearing the bill. *(Vote 515, p. 75-S)*

Javits argued that the measure would handcuff U.S. trade negotiators.

"Placing this inhibition upon the negotiators deprives them of a latitude of action which is indispensable to effective consummation of trade agreements and may destroy these Geneva negotiations," Javits warned.

Similar arguments were offered by President Carter in vetoing the bill.

Provisions

As cleared by Congress and vetoed by the president, HR 9937 would have:

● Amended the Trade Act of 1974 to prohibit the reduction or elimination in trade negotiations of duties or import restrictions on certain imported textiles and textile products.

● Authorized the General Services Administration to dispose of $24 million worth of Carson City silver dollars.■

Tax Treaty With Britain

Reversing an earlier vote, the Senate on June 27 approved a new tax treaty with Britain, but not before adding conditions that proponents said were necessary to protect states' rights.

The conditions, contained in a reservation sponsored by Frank Church, D-Idaho, were expected to require renegotiation of the entire treaty.

Approval by an 82-5 vote came only after treaty proponents, including the Carter administration, said they preferred the treaty along with the reservation to no treaty at all. *(Vote 178, p. 30-S)*

On June 23, the Senate had rejected the reservation, 34-44. Advocates of the reservation, arguing that the treaty posed a serious threat to states' taxing authority, were then able to muster enough votes to kill the entire treaty on a 49-32 vote, five votes short of the two-thirds required for approval of a resolution of ratification. *(Votes 169, 170, p. 29-S)*

When the Carter administration let it be known after the June 23 vote that it would prefer the treaty along with the reservation, the Senate agreed to reconsider its action. That paved way for approval of ratification on June 27.

United States Concession

The tax treaty was designed to replace an existing treaty signed by the United States and the United Kingdom on April 16, 1945. It was signed on Dec. 31, 1975, and subsequently ratified by Parliament.

The major concession made by the United States in the treaty would have limited the manner in which states could tax British-owned corporations operating within their borders.

Specifically, the treaty would have prohibited states from using the "unitary" method of accounting in determining the state tax liability of British corporations. Under the unitary method, a state taxes a foreign corporation according to a formula that allocates a certain portion of the corporation's worldwide income to the state according to the state's share of the firm's property, payroll and sales.

The treaty would have forced states to use an "arm's length" accounting method. Under that approach, a state would be required to tax a corporation according to an actual analysis of the firm's income attributable to its activities within the state.

Proponents of the unitary method argued that without that method, it was too easy for corporations to use accounting gimmicks to "hide" income in subsidiaries outside of a state, thus escaping state taxation. They also claimed that the "arm's length" method was too complex, and that states lacked the capability to audit corporate activity in the depth that such a method would require.

Proponents of the "arm's length" method, on the other hand, argued that it was unfair for a state to tax a corporation for income it derived elsewhere. Under the unitary system, they observed, a state could derive taxes on profits earned somewhere else, even if the firm being taxed was actually losing money from its operations within the state.

States' Rights Issue

Church argued that the proposed prohibition on the unitary method amounted to a federal assault on states' rights.

"Whatever tax treaties are good for, they should not be used to usurp for the executive branch of government the power to impose major changes in internal tax policy," he said.

John Sparkman, D-Ala., had previously reported that the proposed U.S.-U.K. tax treaty would serve as a model for treaties to be negotiated with Iceland, Japan, Belgium, Norway and Trinidad. Church argued that those plans made the treaty a dangerous precedent.

The Church reservation to strike the prohibition on unitary accounting was strongly supported by Edward M. Kennedy, D-Mass., who said the treaty "would have the entirely undesirable practical consequence of allowing multinational corporations to lurk in foreign tax havens, hiding behind foreign subsidiaries and corporate shells, sucking income and profits out of the United States, and then thumbing their noses at state tax commissioners in every state."

Only three states — California, Alaska and Oregon — used the unitary method. But Church said his reservation was supported by the governors of Alaska, Oregon and 16 other states, by 26 state tax commissioners, by the AFL-CIO and other organizations.

S. I. Hayakawa, D-Calif., said that he, Alan Cranston, D-Calif., and California Gov. Edmund G. Brown Jr. all supported the treaty, however, on the grounds that it would increase foreign investment in the state by removing a burden that currently discouraged such investment. The benefits to be derived from the increased investment would outweigh the possible disadvantages of losing the right to use the unitary method, he argued.

Jacob K. Javits, R-N.Y., the floor manager of the treaty, cited a letter from Treasury Secretary W. Michael Blumenthal in further support of the ban on the unitary method.

"The inclusion [of the ban] was strongly urged by the British on the ground that the unitary method as applied to United Kingdom corporate groups imposes excessive recordkeeping and reporting burdens and often results in state taxation of income having no connection with the taxing state, thus violating a basic international tax principle," Blumenthal wrote.

"The article will have the salutary effect of limiting a system of taxation which foreign investors often find burdensome, unfair and a disincentive to investment in this country," he said, arguing that the prohibition was "narrowly drawn and a relatively minor concession."

Javits said the entire concession would only cost states $25 million in lost revenue, but he warned that Senate failure to approve it would probably "kill off the whole treaty."

British Concession

That would prove quite costly, Javits said, because the treaty contained some very substantial concessions from the British. Most notable among them was an agreement by the British to extend substantial tax refunds to American investors in British corporations.

The refunds would go to American investors under a provision in the treaty extending to United States citizens the provisions of the British Advance Corporation Tax, or ACT.

Under the British law, shareholders were able to claim a refundable tax credit to offset a tax the British government levies on British corporations according to their dividend payments.

The law was designed to eliminate the "double taxation" of corporate profits — taxation first in the form of the corporate income tax and later in the personal income tax on dividends.

Without the treaty, foreign shareholders of British-owned corporations were unable to claim credits under the British ACT. With the treaty, United States shareholders — most of which are corporations — would qualify for refunds under the British law back to 1973, amounting to about $375 million. In addition, they would receive credits totaling about $85 million annually in the future.

That advantage to American stockholders wasn't enough to convince the Senate to keep the treaty intact, however. Confirming Javits' warning, a British embassy official said after the Senate approved the treaty with the Church reservation that the British government "will have to reconsider its position."

Committee Action

The U.S.-U.K. tax treaty (Exec K, 94th Cong, 2nd Sess) with accompanying protocols was reported by the Senate Foreign Relations Committee April 25, 1978 (Exec Rept 95-18).

The committee estimated that it would result in a revenue loss of $100 million in 1978 and $28 million in 1979, climbing to $45 million in 1983.

Other major provisions besides the prohibition on unitary method accounting for state tax purposes and extension of the provisions of the British ACT to American shareholders in British corporations would:

- Make Britain's "petroleum revenue tax," or PRT, eligible for "foreign tax credit" treatment under U.S. income tax laws. By allowing American corporations to claim a credit against the U.S. taxes for PRT payments, the treaty would provide an incentive for them to drill for oil in the North Sea.

Kennedy argued that the provision was seriously flawed, however, because it would allow American companies to claim the credit for royalties associated with drilling in other countries as well — including Organization of Petroleum Exporting, or OPEC countries — in violation of U.S. energy interests. The Massachusetts senator said he had been assured by the Treasury Department that the treaty would be amended by the two countries so as to prevent U.S. companies from so benefiting from drilling in OPEC countries.

• Provide that highly paid entertainers and athletes would be taxable in the country where they performed regardless of the length of their stay in that country.

Sparkman said the treaty would advance U.S. international economic objectives, which include "the removal of impediments to the free international flow of capital and technology, the prevention of tax evasion, and removal of differential tax rates that discriminate against American investors."

Overseas Income Taxation

After two years of confusion, Congress finally settled on a new system for taxing the income of Americans working abroad.

House and Senate conferees, negotiating during the final day of the 95th Congress, drafted a new system that would generally replace the flat exclusion provided under existing law with a system of extra tax deductions for the "excess" costs of living abroad.

The bill (HR 9251 — PL 95-615) was cleared Oct. 15, when the Senate and House agreed to a conference report (H Rept 95-1798) filed that day.

For the most part, the new arrangement was praised by business lobbyists, who complained that applying U.S. tax rates to Americans living abroad failed to take into account the higher cost of living in many foreign countries.

They said the Tax Reform Act of 1976 (PL 94-455), which sharply reduced the tax break given Americans abroad, imposed tremendous hardships on U.S. citizens working in foreign countries, and made it very difficult for employers to be able to hire Americans. Responding to the complaints, Congress had postponed implementation of the 1976 changes, and they never took effect.

Final Provisions

As signed into law, HR 9251 established rules for the tax treatment of U.S. citizens who are *bona fide* residents of a foreign country or who are present in a foreign country 17 out of 18 months as follows:

• **Excess Foreign Living Cost Deductions.** Allowed a deduction for the excess cost of living over the cost for a person with spendable income of a GS-14, step 1 federal employee (currently $34,442) living in the highest cost metropolitan area in the continental United States (excluding Alaska).

• Allowed a deduction for housing costs in excess of one-sixth of a taxpayer's net earned income.

• Allowed a deduction for the cost of providing dependents the least expensive adequate U.S.-type elementary and secondary education at a school within a reasonable distance of their tax home.

• Allowed a deduction for one round trip annually per year for a taxpayer and his dependents to the location of their last principal residence in the United States or, if there is none, to the nearest port of entry in the continental United States (excluding Alaska).

• **Special Rules.** Provided that taxpayers who maintain a separate household for their dependents in a foreign country because the living conditions at their tax home are adverse, may base the computation of the deductions on the second home rather than the tax home.

• **Hardship Deduction.** Allowed a $5,000 annual hardship deduction for employees working in hardship areas, defined as areas where U.S. government employees would qualify for a 15 percent or higher hardship pay differential.

• **Non-Itemizers.** Provided that the excess foreign cost deductions could be claimed by taxpayers who use the standard deduction.

• **Camps.** Allowed U.S. citizens living in camps — substandard housing provided in enclaves in remote hardship areas close to job sites where alternative housing is not available — to choose between the excess cost deductions or a simple $20,000 exclusion of their income from taxes.

• **Home Sales.** Increased to four years from 18 months the amount of time within which Americans living abroad could reinvest profits from the sale of a personal home in a new home without having to pay capital gains taxes.

• **Effective Dates.** Made the new provisions effective in 1978, but provided that taxpayers could elect to pay taxes in 1978 under either the new system or the old law in effect prior to passage of the Tax Reform Act of 1976. *(PL 94-455, 1976 Almanac p. 41)*

Background

Prior to the 1976 law, U.S. citizens working abroad could exclude up to $20,000 of their earned income from domestic taxes ($25,000 in the case of individuals who had been residents of a foreign country for three years or more). They then paid taxes on amounts above the exclusion as if that were their only income, and they were able to subtract from their tax bills credits equal to the taxes they paid foreign governments.

The 1976 law reduced the exclusion to $15,000 ($20,000 for employees of domestic charitable organizations). It provided further that income above that amount would be taxed at the higher rates that would apply if no income were excluded. In addition, it allowed credits only for foreign taxes paid on income in excess of $15,000.

The law never took effect. It was delayed by Congress because of complaints that it would put an unfair burden on the roughly 140,000 Americans working abroad.

Critics of the new law complained that it failed to take into consideration the higher cost of living in many foreign countries. They also argued that the 1976 law would put American citizens at a competitive disadvantage with overseas citizens of other foreign countries, many of which don't tax the foreign income of their citizens at all.

Because Americans would have to pay higher taxes than citizens of other countries in foreign nations, firms operating abroad would have a strong incentive to hire non-Americans, the critics suggested. That in turn could hurt the U.S. economy, because it would decrease the number of overseas Americans who could convince firms operating abroad to buy American products.

The Treasury Department agreed that the 1976 reform had gone too far, but it insisted that overseas Americans shouldn't have a special tax advantage relative to citizens at home.

Legislative History

As originally passed by the House in 1977, HR 9251 merely delayed until tax year 1978 provisions of the 1976 Tax Reform Act that tightened up on taxation of Americans working abroad. The bill also postponed several other provisions of the 1976 act. *(1977 Almanac p. 153)*

The Senate passed HR 9251 on May 11, 1978, with an amendment worked out in the Senate Finance Committee establishing a new system for taxing overseas Americans. The Senate proposal (S Rept 95-746) was still less generous than the previous law.

Prodded by the Senate action to do more than just delay the 1976 law, the House Ways and Means Committee Aug. 10 reported its own proposal (HR 13488 — H Rept 95-1463), reversing the 1976 clampdown on tax breaks for Americans abroad and replacing it with rules even more liberal than those that predated the 1976 "reform."

The House passed HR 13488 Sept. 25 by a 282-94 vote. *(Vote 733, p. 208-H)*

The House then added its amendment to HR 9251, setting the stage for a conference with the Senate.

Conference Action

The basic difference between the House and Senate versions was that the Senate had eliminated the flat exclusion of foreign income from domestic taxation and replaced it with a system of extra deductions, while the House had kept the exclusion and allowed deductions as well.

Conferees voted to end the exclusion and allow extra deductions for all overseas citizens except those living in camps in hardship areas. Those people would have the choice between the system of deductions and the flat exclusion.

Others would be allowed deductions for the extra cost of living, housing and education, plus one trip home a year. In addition, extra deductions would be allowed for people living in areas recognized by the U.S. government as "hardship" areas. Also included in the bill was a provision allowing overseas Americans more time to roll over the profits from the sale of a personal home into a new home than the law generally provides.

Fiscal Impact

The new arrangement worked out by conferees would be more generous to the roughly 150,000 overseas Americans than the treatment proposed by the Senate, but less generous than the House-approved measure. It would be markedly easier on overseas Americans than the Tax Reform Act of 1976, and only slightly tougher than the law that preceded the 1976 act.

The total cost of the new system in 1978 was estimated to be $411 million, compared to the pre-1976 law costs of $498 million and the 1976 law cost of $180 million.

The original Senate bill would have cut taxes for overseas Americans by $335 million, while the House bill had a price tage of $589 million.

Debt Limit Extensions

Congress twice during 1978 enacted legislation extending the "temporary" ceiling on the public debt, ultimately approving a $798 billion ceiling through March 31, 1979.

Had Congress failed to act, the ceiling would have reverted to its permanent level of $400 billion, leaving the government unable to meet its borrowing needs.

The House rejected Ways and Means Committee efforts to establish the debt limit through the budget control process.

Opponents of the existing system argued that it was a mechanical exercise, since the size of the debt was predetermined by congressional spending decisions.

They also complained that debt ceiling bills had been misused by Congress. They suggested that many members routinely voted against increases in the debt ceiling in order to claim that they opposed deficit spending, even if they voted at other times for the spending bills that caused deficits. *(Previous increase, 1977 Almanac p. 149)*

Other lawmakers argued, however, that the debt ceiling should continue to be considered separately so that members would be forced to go on record as being for or against deficit spending.

Some House members expressed fears that including the debt limit in budget resolutions might heighten difficulties the House already had in approving those resolutions. *(Budget resolutions, p. 35)*

Existing Limit Extended

Congress completed action March 22 on a bill (HR 11518—PL 95-252) extending the temporary public debt limit at its existing level of $752 billion through July 31.

Final action came when the Senate passed the bill by voice vote. The House had approved the measure March 21 by a 233-172 vote. *(Vote 141, p. 42-H)*

The House March 7 had rejected by a 165-248 vote an earlier bill (HR 11180) which would have boosted the ceiling to $824 billion through March 1, 1979, after striking, 277-132, Ways and Means Committee provisions that would have shifted debt limit control to the congressional budget process from that date on. The earlier bill also contained several provisions relating to debt management that were not included in HR 11518. *(Votes 87, 88, p. 26-H)*

In reporting a simple four-month extension March 17 (H Rept 95-984), the House Ways and Means Committee said revised administration outlay estimates indicated that the government would be able to meet its borrowing needs at the existing ceiling through July 31. The administration had requested an increase in the debt ceiling to $871 billion through Sept. 30, 1979.

Budget Link Rejected

The Ways and Means Committee made one further effort to link the debt limit to the budget process.

Immediately following final approval of the first fiscal 1979 budget resolution, the House May 17 considered a Ways and Means Committee proposal (HR 12641 — H Rept 95-1130) to increase the temporary public debt limit to the $849.1 billion target suggested by the budget resolution.

The debt limit, which sets the maximum amount of money the Treasury can borrow to finance government spending, must be set by statute. It thus requires action by House and Senate and the signature of the president.

The budget process, however, is purely a congressional affair, and no presidential involvement is required.

Legal scholars questioned the constitutionality of a procedure whereby the president would be involved in the congressional budget process. To get around that problem, the Ways and Means Committee decided to keep the two procedures separate, but to propose increases in the debt limit immediately following action on the budget resolution.

Many members of Congress had been criticized in the past for approving spending that required an increase in the debt limit and then voting against the increase in the debt limit necessitated by the spending policies.

Barber B. Conable Jr., R-N.Y., said May 17 that such inconsistency might be discouraged by making debt limit votes follow the budget vote. Despite his hope, 57 representatives who voted for the budget resolution that included the debt limit increase voted against the proposed debt limit bill. It was thus defeated, 167-228, with Conable among those voting nay. *(Vote 282, p. 80-H)*

As a result the debt limit remained at the existing level of $752 billion through July 31.

$798 Billion Ceiling Approved

By a 62-31 vote, the Senate Aug. 2 passed and cleared for the president HR 13385 (PL 95-333), raising the public debt limit to $798 billion through March 31, 1979. *(Vote 272, p. 42-S)*

The House had passed the bill July 19 by a 205-202 vote. Only nine Republicans voted for passage of the bill *(Vote 497, p. 142-H)*

The Ways and Means Committee had recommended an $814 billion temporary ceiling, which was roughly what the Treasury Department estimated would be necessary to finance government operations through the first three months of 1979 (H Rept 95-1349).

But the House approved, 363-37, an amendment by Charles A. Vanik, D-Ohio, setting the $798 billion ceiling. *(Vote 496, p. 140-H)*

Vanik's amendment was seen as an attempt to win enough support to get the limit increased. Without any action, the "temporary" limit would expire after July 31, restoring the $400 billion "permanent" limit. With government borrowing needs far in excess of that amount, failure to extend the temporary limit would effectively halt government borrowing. ∎

Filibuster Kills Labor Law 'Reform' Bill

After one of the most intense grass-roots lobbying campaigns in recent history, legislation (HR 8410) revising the nation's labor law was rejected by the Senate.

Six cloture votes were unable to break a five-week conservative filibuster against the bill, which had passed the House easily in October 1977. The measure was recommitted to the Human Resources Committee June 22, and never re-emerged.

The legislation, organized labor's No. 1 legislative priority, would have speeded up the decision-making process of the National Labor Relations Board (NLRB) and made it easier for unions to organize workers and negotiate collective bargaining agreements.

Overbalancing labor's strenuous efforts in support of the bill, business groups threw all of their political power against the measure. In a head-to-head confrontation with the unions' all-out exertions, business forces and their Senate allies were able to stop the bill just short of the 60 cloture votes that would probably have led to eventual passage.

The death of the bill was the most stinging humiliation for the unions in a Congress that was marked by a string of defeats for labor. Labor leaders warned that what they considered to be unfair and inflammatory tactics used against the bill by business could lead to a deterioration of industrial relations and a more militant stance by the unions.

The final fate of HR 8410 was also a defeat for the Carter administration, which worked hard for the legislation after negotiating a new version of it in 1977. But labor's suspicion that the administration had not done all it could have for the bill added to the growing strains between Carter and labor.

Background

If it had become law, HR 8410 would have been the first major revision of the fundamental law governing labor relations since passage of the Landrum-Griffin Act in 1959. *(Congress and the Nation Vol. I, p. 608)*

But while the Landrum-Griffin Act was inspired by allegations of widespread union corruption, the proposed labor law revision was directed largely at what supporters called a clear-cut pattern of denial by a few companies of their employees' right to organize. Pointing to the well-known example of the textile manufacturer J. P. Stevens, advocates of the bill argued that some employers had found it cheaper to defy the law than to allow even the chance of union organization.

Amending the 1935 National Labor Relations Act, which established protections for workers seeking union representation, HR 8410 would have increased the penalties for violations of employee rights and sped up the process of settling unfair labor practice cases.

But opponents of the bill saw another motive in union support for changes in the labor law. Citing figures reflecting a decline in unionization of the work force, and polls showing increased public concern over union power, they argued that organized labor was attempting to use its massive political power to gain an unfair legal advantage in organizing. The bill "makes it mandatory that businesses organize, or they will be clubbed to death," argued its most outspoken Senate opponent, Orrin G. Hatch, R-Utah.

Lobbying

Lobbying on the bill revealed the intense pressure that the combined forces of labor and business were able to bring to bear on Congress in a crucial legislative battle.

Millions of letters and postcards for and against the bill swamped Senate offices. Planeloads of business people, and hundreds of union members, stalked the halls searching for uncommitted votes.

Business groups were particularly effective in bringing out small business representatives to oppose the bill. Unprotected by the corps of labor lawyers maintained by large corporations, small businesses were thought more vulnerable to the legal advantages that HR 8410 would have given to union organizers. Senators were impressed when small business men who seldom lobbied for anything came to Washington to express their concerns. "It's a different type of lobbying," said an aide to an uncommitted senator. "I'm seeing people on this bill that I wouldn't ordinarily see."

Business lobbying was crucial in stopping the momentum that the bill had gained from its easy House passage in 1977. The 257-163 House vote in favor of the bill had seemed to presage quick Senate approval of the bill in 1978. "There didn't seem to be any way to stop it" at the time, said one opponent. *(1977 Almanac, p. 144)*

Senate Committee Action

The Senate Human Resources Committee Jan. 25 approved its version of the bill (S 2467) by a 13-2 vote. Voting against the bill were Hatch and S. I. Hayakawa, R-Calif. The report (S Rept 95-628) was filed Jan. 31.

NLRB Efficiency

Charged with enforcing the protections given to organizing workers by the 1935 National Labor Relations (Wagner) Act, the NLRB had experienced a massive backlog of cases. Half of the complaints filed by workers took over a year to resolve.

As reported, S 2467 added two more members to the five-member board, thus increasing the number of three-member panels that customarily resolve unfair labor practice cases. It would allow the board to summarily affirm—approve without an extended review—decisions of the administrative law judges, who hear testimony and render initial determinations.

Under existing law, the board had no authority to enforce its decisions in unfair labor practice cases. If it awarded back pay to workers, it had to wait to see if the company at fault would comply. If not, the board must ask a federal court to enforce the order, causing extended delays. The bill gave a company losing a board decision 30 days to file an appeal with the court. If it did not, the board could get an order for immediate enforcement.

Opponents of the bill charged that the expansion of the board membership would amount to "packing" it with pro-labor members. They argued that there was no need to radically alter the board's operations, since it already was one of the most efficient agencies in government. "There is no agency in government that is doing a better job today," according to Hatch.

Worker Protections

S 2467 required the board to seek a court order preliminarily reinstating workers who were thought to have been fired because of union organizing activities. It granted workers found to have been discriminatorily fired back pay equal to 150 percent of the wages they would have earned, less the amount earned at other jobs. Existing law provided for straight back pay minus the amount that could have been earned.

The preliminary reinstatement provision would be of immense benefit to unions conducting organizing campaigns. Workers' fear that they would be fired for supporting the union, with only the distant hope of reinstatement, was considered a major obstacle to union organizing. Moreover, the provision would preserve for the union one of its greatest assets during an organizing struggle—the pro-union activists already in the workplace.

'Make Whole' Remedy

Under existing law, a company whose employees had decided to join a union had no obligation to begin serious negotiations with the union over wages, benefits and working conditions. At worst, the company could be forced by the board to open "good faith" negotiations—in the meantime avoiding the wage increases sought by the union.

As reported, S 2467 allowed the board to award to workers whose employer was found to have refused to bargain seriously a back pay remedy based on wage increases won by other workers during the same period. The standard to be used would be the index of collective bargaining wage increases put out by the Bureau of Labor Statistics.

Unions potentially faced a crisis of confidence among their new members if, after winning a representation election, they were unable to quickly produce a new contract. The provision was meant to encourage employers to bargain in "good faith," by presenting them with the prospect of a forced wage increase based on increases received by workers in other industries if they did not.

But the provision raised the specter of government control of collective bargaining, according to opponents. The bill would be a "tremendously bad precedent," observed G. John Tysse, labor relations attorney for the Chamber of Commerce, threatening the principle of free collective bargaining, by allowing the government to "dictate the economic terms of a contract."

Election Time Limits

One of the most controversial provisions of S 2467 set time limits on representation elections. In work units that were plainly appropriate for representation by one union, an election would have to be held between 21 and 30 days after the union filed an election petition, provided half the workers had signed union cards. In cases where there was some question as to what would be the proper bargaining unit, 45 days were granted to hold the election; 75 days were permitted in exceptionally difficult cases.

Behind the struggle over time limits were concrete strategic considerations. In practice, unions tend to file petitions for election when they think they have a solid majority. At the onset of the election period the union is probably near the peak of its strength. For every day that goes by, particularly if the delay is a long one, union support is buffeted by worker discouragement, attrition and employer persuasion.

Victor Kamber, director of the AFL-CIO Task Force on Labor Law Reform, argued that unions "really don't know if [time limits] play into our hands." But opponents contended that "quickie elections" would deny employers adequate time to organize their own campaign against the union. "You can't even get an appointment with a labor lawyer" within the allotted time, Hatch claimed.

Equal Access

One provision generating an emotional response from small business, and causing considerable difficulty within the committee, allowed union organizers access to workers on the job. If, during an organizing campaign, the employer stopped production to lecture the workers on the perils of unionism—the "captive audience" speech—unions would be given a similar opportunity to address employees during working time. If the employer engaged in a "concerted campaign" against the union, but did not halt production, organizers would be allowed to enter non-working areas such as the lunchroom or parking lot.

To allay some of employers' fears about the provision, ranking minority member Jacob K. Javits, R-N.Y., proposed during markup that the provision go into effect only after the union notified the employer in writing that an organizing effort was under way. The amendment was adopted, but the provision remained "anathema" to small business, according to Tysse.

Other Provisions

Other key provisions of S 2467 as reported:

- Barred from federal contracts for three years companies or unions found in willful violation of labor laws.
- Permitted the courts to enjoin strikes not authorized by a certified union. The provision was intended to deal with the "stranger picketing" and "wildcat" strikes endemic in the coal mines of Appalachia.
- Allowed an exemption from union membership or financial support, if required by union security agreements, for members of religious groups with traditional objections to union support.
- Allowed a union not already representing workers within a particular workplace to seek to organize its security guards. Under existing law no union could represent guards if it had any non-guards in its membership.

Senate Floor Action

Senate action on HR 8410, which had been amended to contain provisions of the committee-reported S 2467, stretched over five weeks. In the end, the bill was recommitted to committee June 22, after bill sponsors were unsuccessful on six straight cloture votes.

Open May 16, debate on the bill went on for three weeks before Senate Majority Leader Robert C. Byrd, D-W.Va., tried to invoke cloture. The Democratic leadership elected not to use the "two-track" system, under which part of the Senate's day is allotted to the filibustered bill and part to other bills, in an effort to show its commitment to the labor bill.

Opponents, led by Hatch and Richard G. Lugar, R-Ind., organized themselves into three teams of five to six members to carry on the filibuster. Opponents introduced about 1,000 amendments in order to carry on a "filibuster by amendment" in case cloture was invoked and a regular filibuster was no longer possible.

The first two attempts at invoking cloture fell far short of the required 60 votes. The first vote, June 7, did not even win a plurality of senators, failing 42-47. *(Vote 162, p. 27-S)*

Cloture proponents did better June 8, 49-41, benefiting from three switched votes (Wendell H. Ford, D-Ky., Walter "Dee" Huddleston, D-Ky., and Thomas J. McIntyre, D-N.H.), and several returning absentees. *(Vote 163, p. 27-S)*

Compromise Proposal

After failure of the first two votes, Byrd, with the support of bill sponsors Harrison A. Williams Jr., D-N.J., and Jacob K. Javits, R-N.Y., revealed a compromise proposal, aimed at picking up more support, that focused on four of the most controversial sections of the bill. The compromise would have:

- Limited the "equal access" of union organizers to a company's premises to non-working areas during non-working hours, and exempted businesses with less than 10 employees.
- Extended the deadline for union representation elections to not less than 35 days after an employer was notified of an organizing campaign, and not more than 50 days after an election petition was filed.
- Based the "make whole" remedy, applied against employers not bargaining in good faith, on an employment cost index measuring wage increases given by businesses of all sizes.
- Loosened the "debarment" provision to allow a lifting of the prohibition against government contracts once a company or union was found to have corrected its unfair labor practice.

The proposal also contained a provision, earlier proposed as a separate amendment, to freeze the existing jurisdictional standards of the NLRB, which excluded about three-quarters of all businesses from coverage under the labor law.

In other action June 8, the Senate voted 51-37 to table a motion by Minority Leader Howard H. Baker, R-Tenn., to recommit the bill to committee. *(Vote 164, p. 27-S)*

The next week the Senate took, in quick succession, three cloture votes that were to bring bill supporters to their high-water mark, two votes short of victory.

The cloture motions were rejected:

- 54-43, June 13. *(Vote 165, p. 28-S)*
- 58-41, June 14. *(Vote 166, p. 28-S)*
- 58-39, June 15. *(Vote 167, p. 28-S)*

Four Republicans who had opposed two earlier cloture motions June 7 and 8 switched in favor of cloture during the second round of voting: Charles H. Percy, Ill.; Ted Stevens, Alaska; Robert T. Stafford, Vt. and H. John Heinz III, Pa.

The three cloture votes aimed to limit debate on the Byrd compromise proposal. But the changes did not appear to have been a major factor in the increased support for the cloture motions. Of the four senators who switched to voting for cloture, only one, Heinz, cited the Byrd amendments as an important factor in his changed vote.

On the other hand, filibuster supporters insisted that the Byrd amendments were solely cosmetic in nature. "The garment and shield and sham should be removed from this hypocrisy and nonsense," said Ernest F. Hollings, D-S.C., of the substitute.

Bill Recommitted

At the brink of total defeat, Senate supporters of HR 8410 June 22 beat a strategic retreat.

Following rejection of a sixth cloture attempt by a 53-45 vote, they had the measure recommitted to the Human Resources Committee — a move usually considered tantamount to killing a bill. *(Vote 168, p. 28-S)*

But supporters of the bill vowed that it would live again, recast in a form that could overcome another filibuster like the one that had tied up the Senate since May 16.

Opponents called the recommittal a victory for their filibuster and the intense business lobbying campaign against the bill.

Recommittal of the bill followed last-minute efforts by Byrd to round up the 60 votes needed to invoke cloture. Pressure focused on Edward Zorinsky, D-Neb., and Russell B. Long, D-La., who earlier had voted against ending debate.

Without the recommittal motion, rejection of the sixth cloture vote probably would have doomed the bill, with supporters starting to slip from their 58 vote high-water mark. Minority Leader Howard H. Baker Jr., R-Tenn., said after the June 22 vote that he had commitments from four senators to switch to cloture opposition on later votes.

Discontent with further futile cloture votes was growing in Democratic ranks. Cloture supporter Jim Sasser, D-Tenn., who opposed further cloture attempts after June 23, said that many members were beginning to feel that "the cloture votes are becoming as time-wasting as the filibuster itself." As Thomas F. Eagleton, D-Mo., observed, "If we're stuck at 58 again, then the bill has just about run its course."

The sixth vote originally had been scheduled for June 20, but was delayed for two days — ostensibly because of senators' scheduling conflicts. In the interim Byrd worked out a strategy to keep the bill alive.

Recommittal Strategy

The Byrd move to recommit the bill was agreed to only after tense and complicated parliamentary maneuvering on the Senate floor. Byrd first asked unanimous consent to recommit the bill, thereby eliminating the need for the scheduled cloture vote. Republican opponents responded with agreeable surprise, but Hollings objected.

Byrd, however, had one more card to play — a suggestion by Long that he might vote for cloture if opponents blocked the recommittal motion. Long had obtained agreement for a series of changes in the bill.

With Long's vote, it appeared for a moment that supporters might be able to get cloture after all. But Ted Stevens, R-Alaska, who had voted twice for cloture, quickly announced he would vote against.

With Hollings intent on forcing another cloture vote, and still unable to round up enough votes to win, Byrd switched course and announced that he was going to vote against cloture — an apparent effort to make it impossible to read the final vote total as an accurate measure of Senate sentiment. "Today's cloture vote was meaningless," said an AFL-CIO statement after the 53-45 cloture defeat.

After working out an arrangement with Appropriations Committee Chairman Warren G. Magnuson, D-Wash., who was worried that reappearance of the bill might block essential money bills, Byrd finally secured unanimous consent for his recommittal request. Under the order, HR 8410 was recommitted to the Human Resources Committee, with the understanding that "if and when" it was reported back by the committee, the bill would become the pending business of the Senate, but not before July 15.

Managers of the bill said they would rewrite the measure in committee to make sure they had enough support when they brought it back to the floor, while preserving its central provisions. "We will streamline it, harden it up, make it lean and tough and bring it back," said Javits.

Despite the heavy pro-labor majority on the committee, Baker said that "I really don't expect it to come back." Orrin G. Hatch, R-Utah, said that if it did, "we'd have to go all out against it." Jesse Helms, R-N.C., observed that the time was just too tight for the bill. "Nobody can operate within the time-frame that [Byrd] has now. In my opinion this was a graceful exit for the bill."

Byrd, however, described recommittal as "necessary to keep that bill from being killed." "The issue has not been settled, but it has been temporarily sent back to the committee," he said. "I fully expect the committee to report back a bill . . . and the Senate will take it up."

Final Try

HR 8410 never made it back out of the Human Resources Committee. The bill was stuck in committee for three months while sponsors searched for a package that stood a chance of passage.

Negotiations between labor officials and sponsors revealed two different approaches. Labor favored minimal concessions designed to pick up just two more cloture votes, while Senate sponsors argued that the only hope for the bill was a consensus proposal that would be acceptable to almost all senators. That negotiators were not going to be able to find a satisfactory compromise became clear Aug. 7, when AFL-CIO president George Meany conceded that labor law reform was dead for the 95th Congress.

Feeling that they had an obligation to at least try to bring something back to the Senate before the end of the year, sponsors proposed one last, "bare-bones" version of the bill. Their last-ditch attempt died quietly after opponents made it clear they would resist the bill in any form.

As outlined by Williams Sept. 27, the last version contained almost none of the provisions that had been the focus of criticism during the filibuster. The bill contained so little of what labor wanted that union officials, while supporting it, did not consider it labor law reform.

The final proposed version of HR 8410:

- Dropped provisions of HR 8410 expanding membership of the National Labor Relations Board (NLRB), granting "make whole" remedies, setting timetables for union representation elections, allowing "equal access" to union organizers, and debarring labor law violators from government contracts.
- Granted workers found to have been discharged because of union activities 150 percent of their back pay, minus wages actually earned.
- Allowed the NLRB to seek a preliminary injunction against employers found to have unlawfully refused to bargain for a first contract with a union.
- Set penalties of up to $5,000 a day against willful violators of labor laws.
- Instructed the NLRB to use its rule-making authority to set standards for appropriate bargaining units and schedules for union representation elections.
- Allowed employers to seek federal court injunctions against "wildcat" strikes.
- Allowed international unions to impose trusteeships on union locals to ensure good faith bargaining. ∎

CETA Jobs Act Extended

Despite growing complaints against abuses in public service employment, the 95th Congress approved legislation extending the Comprehensive Employment and Training Act (CETA) relatively intact.

Congress Oct. 15 cleared for the president S 2570, extending the job training and public service employment programs authorized by CETA for four years, through fiscal year 1982. President Carter signed the bill Oct. 27 (PL 95-525).

The final bill authorized, at 1978 unemployment levels, about 660,000 public service jobs, down from the administration's 725,000 job goals for the program in 1978. CETA appropriations were included in a temporary fiscal 1979 funding resolution that permitted spending for about 625,000 jobs. *(Continuing appropriations, p. 161)*

Attention on the bill during much of the year centered on reports of widespread corruption, patronage and waste in public service jobs programs run by local governments.

According to Rep. David R. Obey, D-Wis., CETA had become "the second most unpopular program in the country after welfare."

But the abuses were difficult to deal with legislatively. The decentralized structure of CETA meant that the integrity of the program was largely dependent on the local governments themselves, and their Labor Department overseers.

Initial floor consideration of the House bill (HR 12452) revealed such negative sentiment toward CETA that sponsors were forced to pull it from the schedule for over a month in order to solidify their support.

Despite the lobbying efforts of local government officials, who were the program's strongest organized supporters, the bill eventually passed the House only after sponsors agreed to accept substantial reductions in public service jobs and wages.

The Senate, on the other hand, passed S 2570 easily.

In addition to establishing a revised administrative structure for CETA, S 2570 contained a number of provisions designed to counter frequent criticisms.

To prevent fraud and abuse, the bill increased the authority of the Labor Department to find and root out corruption.

S 2570 also included provisions designed to keep local governments from "substituting" public service jobs for positions they would have normally paid for themselves, thus converting a program aimed at helping the unemployed into another form of revenue sharing. Repeating the existing prohibition against the practice, the bill also limited the length of time individuals could hold public service jobs, and required that half of public service job money be spent on "projects" of limited scope and duration. Both provisions were aimed at ensuring that public service workers did not become, in effect, regular government workers who happened to be paid by the federal government.

In answer to charges that CETA programs failed to "target" efforts on those most in need of assistance, S 2570 limited participation to the economically disadvantaged and unemployed. It placed special emphasis on helping welfare recipients learn skills to get themselves off the public dole.

Final Provisions

As signed into law, S 2570:

Title I — Administration

- **Prime Sponsors.** Designated as "prime sponsors" eligible to receive assistance those local governments, or groups of local governments, with populations of at least 100,000, and those with populations under 100,000 who had previously served efficiently as prime sponsors.
- Required prime sponsors, in order to receive aid under the act, to submit a one-time master plan outlining long-term goals and methods for employment and training programs, and annual plans setting forth what types of services would be provided to which parts of the population during the fiscal year.
- Required state governments, in order to be eligible for funds, to provide coordination and specialized services to prime sponsors.
- Required prime sponsors to set up grievance procedures for hearing complaints from program participants or contractors.
- Gave the secretary of labor authority to revoke prime sponsor funds, all or in part, if the prime sponsor was found to have engaged in discrimination, failed to carry out the objectives of the act, or engaged in substitution of CETA positions for regular jobs; in cases of fraud and abuse, authorized the secretary to withhold funds and require the prime sponsor to carry on programs with its own funds.
- Required prime sponsors and states each to set up planning councils, composed of representatives of interested groups, to help them plan and run their employment and training programs.
- **Authorization Levels.** Provided an open-ended, four-year authorization for Titles I, III, V, and VI of the bill; authorized $2 billion for Title II job training, and $3 billion for Title II public service employment, in fiscal 1979, and open-ended amounts in fiscal 1980-82; authorized $2.25 billion in 1979 and $2.4 billion in 1980 for Title IV, with open-ended amounts in 1981 and 1982 for Title IV Jobs Corps and summer jobs programs; authorized $500 million in 1979 and $525 million in 1980 for Title VII; authorized $350 million in 1979, $400 million in 1980, and an open-ended sum in 1981 and 1982, for Title VIII.
- Limited the appropriation for Title II public service jobs programs, in each of fiscal years 1980-82, to 60 percent of the total amount appropriated for Title II in each year.
- Limited the appropriation for Title III to 20 percent of the annual appropriation for the entire act, excluding amounts for Titles II and VI public service jobs programs.
- **Restrictions.** Limited participation by individuals in any part of CETA to a total of 30 months in any five-year period, excluding participation before Oct. 1, 1978; limited receipt of training allowances to 104 weeks in any five years.
- Required that training be provided for occupations in which there was a reasonable chance of obtaining employment.
- Prohibited substitution of CETA funds to pay for jobs that would have been funded in the absence of the act.
- Limited individual work experience participation to 1,000 hours a year, or 2,000 hours in any five years.
- Prohibited use of funds for contributions to retirement plans for persons enrolled in CETA programs after July 1, 1979, except to the extent that participants had a reasonable chance of benefiting from the plans.
- Required that special consideration in filling public service jobs be given to welfare recipients and Vietnam-era veterans.
- Limited participation by individuals in public service employment to 78 weeks in any five years, except that no more than 26 weeks of service before Oct. 1, 1978, could be counted against the 78-week limit; authorized the secretary to waive the limit in high unemployment areas.
- Set the maximum CETA-paid wage at $10,000 a year, except that the maximum could be increased up to $12,000 in high-wage areas.
- Required that prime sponsors maintain an average public service wage not above $7,200, with increases permitted according to annual changes in area average wages in regular employment.
- Required the secretary to issue regulations against nepotism, conflict of interest, kickbacks, political patronage and other abuses in public service employment.
- Required that workers in CETA-assisted construction projects be paid the locally prevailing wage in accordance with the Davis-Bacon Act.

- Gave the secretary authority to inspect the records of prime sponsors to make sure they were not misusing funds.
- Set up an office of management assistance in the Labor Department to help prime sponsors operate their programs.

Title II — Structural Unemployment

- Combined in a single title all employment and training programs intended to serve the long-term structurally unemployed, including a separate part D authorizing public service employment.
- **Allocation of Funds.** Allocated 85 percent of fiscal 1979 job training and work experience funds to states on the following basis: 50 percent on the basis of each state's proportion of the total amount given to states under the former CETA Title I in fiscal 1978; 37.5 percent in proportion to each state's share of total nationwide unemployment; 12.5 percent according to the share that each state had of the total number of low-income adults in the country.
- Allocated 85 percent of fiscal 1980-82 training funds to prime sponsors according to two formulas. Two-thirds was to be distributed according to the following formula: 50 percent in proportion to each prime sponsor's share of the previous fiscal year allotment, 37.5 percent according to each prime sponsor's share of total unemployment, and 12.5 percent according to each one's share of the total number of low-income adults. One-third was to be distributed to prime sponsors in proportion to the ratio between the number of unemployed living in areas with unemployment rates over 6.5 percent for the preceding year within each one's jurisdiction, and the total number of unemployed living in such areas nationwide.
- Allowed the secretary to make discretionary use of most of the funds not distributed by formula, with instructions to use the money to make sure that prime sponsors got at least 90 percent of their previous year's allocation, and to help cities whose allocations were reduced by changes in techniques for measuring local unemployment.
- **Employment and Training Services.** Authorized employment and training services to the economically disadvantaged including, but not limited to, job search assistance, skill training, on-the-job training, work experience and supportive services.
- Limited eligibility for training programs to persons on or eligible for welfare, or from families with income below 70 percent of the Bureau of Labor Statistics (BLS) lower living standard, who were also unemployed, underemployed or in school.
- Authorized occupational upgrading and retraining programs for employed persons.
- **Transitional Public Service Jobs.** Established a separate section, part D, providing transitional public service employment for the disadvantaged.
- Distributed 85 percent of part D funds according to a formula based equally on each prime sponsor's share of the nationwide total for the following factors: the number of unemployed, the number of unemployed living in areas with unemployment rates over 4.5 percent, the number of unemployed living in areas with unemployment rates over 6.5 percent for the preceding year, and the number of low-income adults.
- Required that part D public service jobs be at the entry level, be combined with training, and lead to regular employment.
- Required that at least 10 percent in fiscal 1979, 15 percent in fiscal 1980, 20 percent in fiscal 1981, and 22 percent in fiscal 1982 of part D funds be spent on training services.
- Limited eligibility for part D jobs to economically disadvantaged persons who had been unemployed for at least 15 weeks or were on welfare.
- Prohibited supplementation of wages paid to part D workers.

Title III — Special Federal Responsibilities

- Authorized the secretary to provide services directly to groups that were a special responsibility of the federal government, including Indians, migrant farmworkers, veterans, the handicapped, older workers, offenders and persons with limited English-speaking ability.
- Made displaced homemakers eligible for special services.
- Authorized research and demonstration projects on employment and training.
- Required establishment of a nationwide system of labor market information, including a computer job bank and new ways to measure local unemployment.
- Authorized a demonstration project to test voucher systems providing funds to employers who hired eligible persons.

Title IV — Youth Programs

- Authorized for two years, through fiscal 1980, a variety of programs designed to test new ways of reducing unemployment among youth, including jobs guarantees for youths in school, community conservation projects and general grants to prime sponsors to run a broad range of youth employment and training programs.
- Extended for four years, through fiscal 1982, the Job Corps program of residential and non-residential centers for jobs training of youths.
- Increased the maximum monthly allowance for Job Corps participants to $60 a month during the first six months of instruction, and $100 a month thereafter.
- Authorized a separate four-year, fiscal 1979-82, program of grants to prime sponsors for the purpose of providing summer jobs to youths.

Title V — National Commission for Employment Policy

- Established a 15-member National Commission for Employment Policy to study and report annually on employment and training goals and policies.

Title VI — Countercyclical Public Service Employment

- Stated the intent of Congress to provide temporary jobs equal in number to 20 percent of the number of unemployed in excess of 4 percent of the work force; if the national unemployment rate was over 7 percent, the goal would be enough jobs for 25 percent of the unemployed in excess of 4 percent of the work force.
- Required the president to report by March 1 of each year the estimated unemployment rate for the year.
- **Allocation of Funds.** Allocated 85 percent of Title VI funds on the following basis: 50 percent to prime sponsors in proportion to each one's share of total unemployment; 25 percent in proportion to each prime sponsor's share of

the number of unemployed living in areas with unemployment rates over 6.5 percent for the preceding year; 25 percent in proportion to each prime sponsor's share of the number of unemployed living in areas with unemployment rates over 4.5 percent.

• Set aside the remaining 15 percent for Indians, discretionary grants by the secretary, and to help cities whose allocations were reduced by changes in techniques for measuring local unemployment.

• **Restrictions.** Required that prime sponsors spend at least 50 percent of their allocations on projects with limited focus and duration, not to exceed 18 months.

• Limited eligibility to persons unemployed for at least 10 of the preceding 12 weeks, who were from families with incomes at or below 100 percent of the BLS lower living standard.

• Limited supplementation of an individual worker's wage to 10 percent of the maximum federally paid wage; limited the total amount that a prime sponsor could add to all its CETA worker's wages to 10 percent of the amount it received under Title VI.

• Required prime sponsors to spend at least 10 percent in fiscal 1979, and 5 percent thereafter, of their Title VI funds on training for participants.

Title VII — Private Sector Initiative

• Established a new, two-year program designed to encourage private sector participation in CETA programs.

• Required prime sponsors, in order to receive assistance under Title VII, to set up private industry councils dominated by business representatives.

• Recommended a wide variety of approaches for providing more private sector jobs to employment and training program participants.

Title VIII — Young Adult Conservation Corps

• Authorized programs, to be administered by the Labor, Agriculture and Interior Departments, to provide work to unemployed youth on conservation projects on public land.

Other Provisions

• Set a penalty of up to two years in jail and a $10,000 fine for persons convicted of fraud and abuse in CETA programs.

• Authorized $10 million in fiscal 1979 for assistance to Labor-Management Committees seeking to improve communication between workers and employers.

Authorizations for Jobs Programs

S 2570 extended CETA programs through fiscal 1982, except for Title IV youth employment demonstrations and the Title VII private sector initiative, which were authorized only for fiscal 1979 and 1980.

Following are the authorization levels for CETA jobs programs in 1979 and 1980. (For fiscal 1981-82, the bill authorized such sums as necessary.)

	1979	1980
Title II		
Job training	$2 billion	open
Public service employment	$3 billion	open[1]
Title III		
Indians, migrant workers, job search aid, veterans, handicapped, projects for middle-aged and older workers	open[2]	open[2]
Title IV		
Youth employment demonstration projects, Job Corps, summer youth jobs	$2.25 billion	$2.4 billion
Title V		
National Commission for Employment Policy	open	open
Title VI		
Countercyclical public service employment	open[3]	open[3]
Title VII		
Private sector initiative	$500 million	$525 million
Title VIII		
Young Adult Conservation Corps	$350 million	$400 million
Labor-management committees	$10 million	open

[1] Limited to no more than 60 percent of the total Title II appropriation.

[2] Limited to no more than 20 percent of the total appropriation for the act minus amounts for Titles II and VI public service employment.

[3] Bill set goal of enough funds to provide Title VI jobs to 20 percent of the number of unemployed in excess of 4 percent of the work force; if the unemployment rate was over 7 percent, the goal would be 25 percent of the number of unemployed over 4 percent of the work force.

Background

CETA developed out of a vast array of job and training programs spawned by Democratic "Great Society" legislation in the 1960s. It featured both centralization of the programs, concentrating overall supervision in the Labor Department, and decentralization, giving control of implementation to local governments.

Studies of Kennedy and Johnson administration manpower programs, which included the 1962 Manpower Development and Training Act (MDTA), the Jobs Corps and Job Opportunities in the Business Sector (JOBS), showed that the programs had a substantial effect on participants' subsequent economic performance, although they had only a limited impact on overall unemployment.

But the programs were difficult to administer, scattered as they were through various government offices. Agencies were forced to make separate contracts with thousands of training centers, making oversight difficult.

The Nixon administration favored an alternative to centrally run manpower programs. In concert with his plans for revenue sharing, President Nixon proposed that manpower funds be given directly to local governments to run their own programs.

1973 Act

Passage of CETA in 1973 was a compromise between Nixon, who wanted to turn administration of manpower programs over to localities, and the Democratic majority in Congress, which wanted public service jobs.

Title I of the act consolidated most of the various manpower programs into a single system of block grants to local governments. Funds were provided by formula to city, county or state "prime sponsors."

Title II established a limited program of public service jobs. It addressed problems of "structural" unemployment by providing jobs for those with long-term employment difficulties. Only persons unemployed for more than a month were allowed to participate. Assistance was provided by formula to areas with unemployment of more than 6.5 percent. *(1973 Almanac p. 346)*

As the recession deepened in the mid-1970s, congressional leaders saw in CETA a vehicle for fighting increasing unemployment. In 1974 Congress added a new Title VI to CETA, authorizing $2.5 billion for public service jobs, allocated on the basis of unemployment rates. But in contrast to the structural emphasis of Title II, Title VI was a "countercyclical" measure attacking unemployment caused by recession. *(1974 Almanac p. 261)*

In 1976 Congress extended and expanded the Title VI public service employment program. In addition to increasing the numbers of positions available, the extension bill contained provisions designed to limit substitution and focus programs on the poor. It required that new positions be used in community projects that could be finished within a year, and be limited to persons unemployed for more than 15 weeks who had low incomes. *(1976 Almanac p. 364; Congress and the Nation Vol. IV, pp. 681-713)*

In 1977 a new CETA Title VIII, designed to aid disadvantaged youth, was added. Title VIII established a Young Adult Conservation Corps and other experimental projects.

Also in 1977, Congress passed a simple one-year extension of CETA, authorizing the program through the end of fiscal 1978. The Carter administration requested a short-term extension in order to gain time to thoroughly study the program and propose substantive changes, as it did in 1978. *(1977 Almanac pp. 116, 119)*

Administration Proposals

President Carter Feb. 22 sent to Congress his proposal for an extension and revision of the CETA system. He emphasized that the plan was aimed at the "structural" employment of minorities and youth, and that its goal was to "make sure that more of our people share in the benefits of growth." *(CETA message, p. 37-E)*

Stressing the need to help those "who have difficulty finding work even when overall economic prospects are good," the president noted that in 1977, "even while unemployment was falling to 4 percent among white males above the age of 20, it was rising — from 35 to 38 percent — among black teenagers."

The Carter administration reauthorization bill called for extension of CETA through Sept. 30, 1982. It would have maintained public service employment at roughly existing levels (725,000 jobs) through fiscal 1979. After that the number of jobs would vary with the unemployment rate. Local areas with high unemployment would have gotten 100,000 jobs regardless of the national unemployment rate. When the national rate exceeded 4.75 percent, another 100,000 jobs would be authorized, with the total rising by 100,000 for every .5 percent increase in unemployment.

To keep local government from substituting CETA workers for traditional positions, the bill called for limiting the time that workers would stay in public service jobs to 18 months. Salaries for participants were to be held below $10,000 a year.

In response to criticisms that CETA had not served those for whom it was intended, the bill limited eligibility to those whose income was below 70 percent of the Bureau of Labor Statistics lower living standard — a limit of about $7,000 for an urban family of four.

To increase the movement of workers from CETA programs to the private sector, the bill established a new program designed to increase linkage with business. Local industry training councils would be set up to plan more on-the-job training and other strategies, particularly those aimed at unemployed youth.

The bill also laid the groundwork for the administration welfare reform plan. It would have funded 50,000 jobs to demonstrate the feasibility of guaranteeing jobs to heads of households in place of welfare.

Committtee Action

SUBCOMMITTEE APPROVAL

House and Senate subcommittees April 26 approved bills extending federal public service job and training programs for four years, through fiscal 1982.

By a 9-4 vote the House Education and Labor Employment Opportunities Subcommittee approved HR 11086, and by a 7-0 vote the Senate Human Resources Employment Subcommittee approved S 2570. The bills were revised versions of legislation requested by President Carter.

CETA reauthorization legislation faced a major obstacle, however, because of continuing congressional concern over substitution of public service jobs for regular local government jobs, and allegations of misuse of funds.

The House Budget Committee April 6 defeated by only a one-vote margin a motion to cut $600 million in outlays for employment and training programs from the first fiscal 1979 budget resolution. While supporting the requested $11.6 billion outlay level for CETA, the Budget Committee said that "it does not endorse the manner in which the programs have functioned," and emphasized "the urgency of correcting these problems in order to warrant continued congressional support for resources being invested in the CETA programs."

House subcommittee members felt limited in their ability to correct substitution problems. Subcommittee Chairman Augustus F. Hawkins, D-Calif., said the panel had "gone as far as we can go" to correct substitution, and that it was up to the administration to crack down.

Both House and Senate bills included some administration proposals designed to prevent fraud involving CETA funds at the local level. The anti-fraud provisions would provide the Labor Department better access to the records of locally run jobs and training programs, and allow it to deal directly with program subcontractors instead of having to go through local government "prime sponsors." The House bill would also establish in the Labor Department an office of audits, investigations and compliance to provide careful auditing of programs.

The Labor Department, meanwhile, had stepped up efforts to use its current authority to uncover fraud in CETA programs. Labor Secretary F. Ray Marshall April 13 announced creation of a permanent special investigations office, charged with correcting abuses in CETA and other department programs. The office, which had been in existence on a temporary basis, was already looking into problems in 11 local jobs programs.

Another CETA controversy involved the formula for distributing funds for "structural" employment and training programs concentrating on the hard-core disadvantaged.

House subcommittee Republicans favored using formulas in existing law, which gave heavy weight to the amount local governments had received in the past for training programs, relative to other areas. Democrats favored a formula that would concentrate money on areas with high unemployment and poverty. The subcommittee ultimately opted for a formula allocating 40 percent of the money on the basis of poverty, 40 percent on local unemployment rates over 6 percent, and 20 percent on national unemployment rates, thus distributing at least some of the funds to all areas.

The Senate subcommittee left it to the full Human Resources Committee to decide on a funding formula.

HOUSE COMMITTEE REPORT

The House Education and Labor Committee reported its CETA bill (HR 12452 — H Rept 95-1124) May 10.

Structural Unemployment

The "permanent core" of CETA as envisioned by the committee was contained in Title II of HR 12452, providing training and jobs for the hard-core unemployed. The bill extended these programs through fiscal 1982; it authorized $4 billion for fiscal 1979.

By establishing a single, separate section providing all services for the long-term unemployed, the committee attempted to clear up the confusion and ambiguity in current practice between structural and countercyclical programs. HR 12452 combined in the new Title II elements of the old CETA Title I, which had authorized job training services for the poor, and old Title II, which authorized part of current public service employment.

Formulas. The formula for allocating money under the new title split urban representatives from a majority of the committee. At the urging of big-city Democrats, the Employment Opportunities Subcommittee had adopted an allocation formula that would have concentrated funds on areas with the worst unemployment problems.

On a 25-10 vote the full committee adopted an amendment by James M. Jeffords, R-Vt., to base the allocation of funds on a combination of formulas in the existing law. Jeffords argued that the current formulas were working well, so there was no need to experiment with new ones. "If it ain't broke, don't fix it," he said.

As reported by the committee, HR 12452 allotted Title II funds on the following basis: 60 percent on the old Title I formula, and 30 percent on the old Title II formula. The remainder was to be available for special programs and cities whose funding was reduced because of recent changes in the way unemployment rates are computed.

Under the old Title I formula, 50 percent of the available money was distributed to prime sponsors on the basis of each one's proportion of the total amount given to all prime sponsors in the preceding year. Each prime sponsor received a share of the next 37.5 percent of the funds that was equal to the ratio between the number of unemployed in its area and the number of unemployed nationwide. The remaining 12.5 percent was distributed according to the share that each prime sponsor had of the total number of poor people in the country.

Under the old Title II, funds were reserved for areas with "substantial" unemployment, defined as an unemployment rate over 6.5 percent for at least three consecutive months in the preceding year. The allotment for a prime sponsor was determined by the ratio between the number of unemployed persons living in areas of substantial unemployment within its jurisdiction, and the total number of unemployed people nationwide who lived in substantial unemployment areas.

Restrictions. The bill contained requirements designed to ensure that Title II met its goal of helping the truly poor obtain regular, permanent employment. Eligibility in the programs was limited to those whose families had incomes below 70 percent of the Bureau of Labor Statistics (BLS) lower living income budget. All programs, including institutional and on-the-job training, work experience and public service employment, were required to have a training component and lead to unsubsidized employment.

HR 12452 contained additional restrictions on public service employment under Title II. Spending on wages for public service employment was limited to half of the total appropriation for Title II. Jobs were to be limited to entry-level positions, and could not be supplemented by local governments out of their own funds. To open public service employment to those who were under-employed as well as unemployed, the bill allowed participation by persons who had worked an average of 20 hours a week or less in the preceding 10 weeks.

Countercyclical Employment

In contrast to the permanent, structural emphasis of Title II, Title VI of HR 12452 authorized a public service employment program providing job aid during periods when the national rate of unemployment exceeded 4 percent. The committee made clear that the countercyclical public service employment would no longer be needed once the goal of national full employment was reached. HR 12452 authorized the program through fiscal 1982.

The bill included a declaration of purpose stating that public service employment under Title VI should provide jobs equal in number to 25 percent of the number of unemployed in excess of 4 percent of the work force. It required the labor secretary to report quarterly to Congress on the funding levels needed to provide that number of jobs. Because the level of public service employment would fluctuate with unemployment, the bill contained no specific authorization for Title VI.

Formula. HR 12452 retained the current formula for allocating the bulk of Title VI funds. Half of the available money was to be distributed to individual prime sponsors on the basis of each one's share of total unemployment. Prime sponsors with unemployment rates over 4.5 percent divided up the next 25 percent of the money, each receiving an amount proportionate to its share of the number of unemployed people in excess of a 4.5 percent unemployment rate nationwide. A prime sponsor's share of the remaining 25 percent was determined by the ratio between the number of jobless living in areas of substantial unemployment within its jurisdiction, and the total number of unemployed living in substantial unemployment areas.

Restrictions. In an effort to curb substitution, HR 12452 required that 50 percent of the public service jobs under Title VI be "projects." A project is a separate undertaking with a clear beginning and end and a physical product — a new bicycle path or a repainted school. Projects are distinct from regular government services, which continue on an ongoing basis.

Three additional restrictions on public service employment also were intended to reduce substitution. Those provisions:

- Limited the amount that prime sponsors could add to their CETA workers' payroll to 10 percent of the amount received from the federal government.
- Permitted prime sponsors to supply additional wages to only 25 percent of their CETA workers in the first year of the bill, 20 percent in the second year and 15 percent thereafter.
- Limited the amount that the local government could add to an individual public service employee's wages to 25 percent of the maximum CETA wage.

Since Title VI was intended to help persons thrown out of work by downturns in the economy, its eligibility standards were somewhat less restrictive than those contained in Title II. Participation in public service employment was limited to persons from families with incomes below 100 percent of the BLS lower living standard, who had been out of work for at least eight weeks.

Improved Administration

Title I of HR 12452 established a revised administrative structure for CETA, combining in one title provisions previously scattered throughout the original law. The committee stated that two prime goals of the provisions were to cut down on needless paperwork for local officials, while at the same time strengthening the authority of Labor Department officials to root out corruption and abuse of funds.

The bill required prime sponsors to submit a comprehensive, one-time "master plan" laying out the general outline and objectives of employment and training programs in the area. Thereafter a prime sponsor would have only to submit annual reports on planned activities for the coming year.

Approval of the plans would be contingent on satisfactory prime sponsor progress towards meeting important national goals, such as serving the right groups, moving CETA participants into unsubsidized jobs, and not wasting money. But the committee specifically rejected the application of rigid national standards to every area. Satisfactory progress towards goals, the committee said, could only be judged in view of local conditions.

To help control local use of funds, HR 12452 established within the Labor Department an independent office of audits, inspection and compliance, similar to the special investigations unit established within the department by Labor Secretary F. Ray Marshall April 13. Along with the new office of management assistance, established by the bill to provide technical assistance to prime sponsors, the audits office would promote efficiency and economy, the committee said.

The bill also contained some administration-requested provisions designed to help the Labor Department take action against fraud. The bill would allow the department to withhold or recover funds from violators, and provide increased access to local records.

The committee set limits on the extent to which CETA funds could be used for payments to state and local government pension funds. Critics of CETA had argued that some governments were using employment and training money to supplement retirement systems of their permanent workers.

The bill allowed pension payments for workers enrolled in CETA before Jan. 1, 1979. After that payments would be allowed only to the extent that CETA workers might actually benefit from the retirement system.

Public Service Jobs Restrictions. Title I of HR 12452 also contained general restrictions on public service employment, applying to both the structural and countercyclical programs. To make sure that CETA workers did not become permanently dependent on the program, the bill limited participation in public service employment to 78 weeks in each three-year period, with some exceptions in cases of unusual hardship. The committee said that this limit, requested by the administration, would also serve to discourage substitution and open CETA programs to more people.

Another provision applicable to all public service employment limited wages to $10,000 a year, except that the limit could be indexed upwards, in accordance with locally high wage standards, to $12,000. In some areas even the lowest-paying available public jobs are over the $10,000 limit. The bill also required that local average wages be set so as to meet a nationwide wage average of $7,800, indexed to consumer price levels beginning in 1980.

Private Sector Initiative

Title VII of HR 12452 established a new, two-year program intended to generate more private sector involvement with CETA. The committee pointed out that while business was the source of four out of five jobs in society, its participation in CETA had been minimal in the past.

The bill authorized $400 million in fiscal 1979 for the new private sector initiative. In order to qualify for funds, prime sponsors would have to set up local Private Industry Councils, dominated by business but including representatives of labor, education and minority groups.

In concert with the councils, prime sponsors could use Title VII funds for a variety of training programs, as long as they allowed for direct participation by businesses. Projects funded under the title might include classroom and on-the-job training, as well as efforts to improve coordination between the employment needs of the private sector and CETA job training.

The committee considered but did not include proposals to authorize funds for "vocational exploration" under Title VII. Under exploration programs for young people currently being tested by the Labor Department, the government paid all the wages of a person who was working full-time for a private employer. This gave young people a chance to check out possible careers, but came close to the concept of wage subsidies strenuously opposed by labor unions.

Special Programs

In addition to providing broad-based employment and training assistance, CETA authorized a number of programs targeting on special groups of the population. HR 12452 extended all but one of these programs, with minor changes, through fiscal 1982. The sole exception, an experimental youth jobs initiative, was extended for only two years.

Title III authorized funds for assistance to groups, such as native Americans and migrant farmworkers, deemed to be the special responsibility of the federal government. The authorization for Title III was limited to 20 percent of the amount authorized by Title II — a limit of $400 million in fiscal 1979.

Newly included in the groups eligible for Title III assistance were displaced homemakers — persons who, after being out of the work force for an extended period, suddenly find themselves in need of work because of divorce or the death of the supporting spouse. Since these people, usually women middle-aged or older, have unusual difficulty in re-entering the work force, the bill authorized special training programs to help them develop skills.

Youth Employment

HR 12452 lumped all but one of the existing special programs for youth employment into a new Title IV of CETA. It extended for two years, through fiscal 1980, experimental youth employment and training projects authorized by the Youth Employment and Demonstration Projects Act of 1977 (PL 95-93). *(1977 Almanac p. 116)*

Also included in Title IV was the Job Corps. The major change made by HR 12452 increased the maximum monthly allowance for Job Corps participants to $100 from $50, their first raise since the beginning of the program in 1964.

The bill authorized $1.9 billion for all Title IV programs in fiscal 1979.

Title VIII of CETA, the Young Adult Conservation Corps, also established in 1977 by PL 95-93, was extended for four years. The corps offered a year-round program of conservation-related work for young adults on public land.

SENATE COMMITTEE REPORT

The Senate Human Resources Committee reported its CETA extension May 15 (H Rept 95-891).

S 2570 was broadly similar to the House version in its revamping of the structure of CETA. Like the House committee, the Human Resources Committee aimed to curb substitution of CETA workers for regular government employees. S 2570 contained a number of administration-proposed provisions designed to increase the authority of the secretary of labor to control prime sponsor abuse of funds.

Following are some of the most important differences between S 2570 and HR 12452 in the key areas of structural and countercyclical unemployment programs.

Structural Unemployment

Like HR 12452, S 2570 consolidated in Title II of CETA a broad range of services for the hard-core, structurally unemployed. However the Human Resources Committee provided the separate training and public service employment parts of Title II with separate formulas for the allocation of funds to local government.

The bill retained from the existing Title I the formula for determining distribution of job training funds. For public service employment under the new Title II the committee adopted an allocation formula that was similar to the formula used for Title VI public service employment, except that money would be more concentrated on areas with especially high unemployment rates.

As reported by the Senate committee, S 2570 would distribute one-third of Title II public service employment funds in proportion to each prime sponsor's share of national unemployment. Another third would be divided among prime sponsors with unemployment rates over 4.5 percent, with each receiving a percentage equal to the ratio between the number of unemployed over 4.5 percent in its area and the total number of unemployed over 4.5 percent nationwide. The remainder of the funds allocated by formula would go to prime sponsors according to the number of unemployed persons living in areas of substantial unemployment within their jursidictions.

Areas of substantial unemployment were defined as having unemployment rates of 6.5 percent or over. A key change made by the committee required that local unemployment rates be set as an average of monthly unemployment rates in the preceding year, rather than as the average of the three months with the highest unemployment rates in the preceding year. This change would shift funds away from areas with seasonal or sharply fluctuating unemployment rates.

S 2570 provided an open-ended authorization for Title II. However, it required that Title II public service employment be appropriated at a level of at least $3 billion a year before any funding could become available for Title VI countercyclical public service employment.

To ensure that CETA beneficiaries not become permanently dependent on the program, or used as part of the regular government work force, the bill limited the length of participation. Total length of service in all aspects of CETA was limited to two and one-half years in any five-year period. Workers in Title II public service employment were permitted to stay on the payroll for only 78 weeks in any five years. A maximum of 1,000 hours in one year, or 2,000 hours in five years, was established for individual use of the work experience aspects of training programs.

The basic eligibility requirement for Title II programs, that participants come from families with incomes below 70 percent of the Bureau of Labor Statistics lower living standard, was the same in the House and Senate bills. S 2570 added an additional requirement that participants in public service employment under Title II be unemployed for 12 weeks before enrollment.

Wages for Title II public service employees were limited to $10,000 a year, although the limit could go up to $12,000 in high wage areas. Local governments were prohibited from adding their own funds to the wages of Title II workers, but those already enrolled could continue to receive such wage supplementation.

Countercyclical Employment

The Senate bill moved even farther away from the administration's proposal to tie the level of Title VI countercyclical public service employment directly to the unemployment rate than did HR 12452. The administration's plan would have set the number of jobs according to the amount that the national unemployment rate exceeded 4.75 percent, while the House bill would have set a goal of providing jobs for one-quarter of the number of unemployed in excess of a 4 percent unemployment rate. S 2570, by contrast, provided a totally open-ended authorization, letting the number of jobs be set each year by the appropriations process.

The Senate committee required that all jobs under Title VI be in "projects" — specific, related tasks that could be finished within a year — in an effort to keep CETA workers from becoming a permanent adjunct of regular local government services. However, local governments would have a chance to extend their projects beyond 12 months if unforeseen events, such as a severe winter storm, delayed completion.

Since Title VI public service jobs were intended only to provide short-term help for the unemployed, the bill limited participation by individuals to one year within any five years. In cases where prime sponsors were having unusual difficulty in finding regular jobs for participants, however, the limit could be extended for up to six months.

Title VI public service wages were also set at a maximum of $10,000 a year, or $12,000 in high-wage areas. But unlike public service employment under Title II, local governments were allowed to add some of their own funds to the wages of Title VI workers. Under S 2570, a local government could add to the total wages of its Title VI workers an amount equal to 10 percent of its Title VI allocation. Supplementation of an individual worker's wage could not be more than 20 percent of that worker's CETA wage. Thus, the most that any public service employee could receive from local and federal governments would be $14,400. However, current CETA workers, some of whom received much more than $14,400, would not be affected by the supplementation limit.

Compared with HR 12452, S 2570 imposed a stricter income eligibility requirement, but lowered the length of time a person had to have been unemployed before becoming eligible for Title VI assistance. Persons from families with incomes below 85 percent of the lower living standard, who had been unemployed for 45 days, were eligible for jobs under S 2570.

Senate Floor Action

The Senate passed S 2570 Aug. 25 by a 66-10 vote after adoption of numerous amendments, including one tightening eligibility requirements for public service jobs and another strengthening the Department of Labor's ability to prevent fraud in various CETA programs. *(Vote 363, p. 54-S)*

As a result of the amendments, and weeks of behind-the-scenes negotiations by key sponsors, S 2570 was passed with little of the criticism and angry debate that marked House floor consideration three weeks earlier and led sponsors to postpone a final vote on the House version (HR 12452) until after the Labor Day recess. *(House action, p. 296)*

The chief sponsors of the measure, Gaylord Nelson, D-Wis., chairman of the Senate Human Resources Subcommittee on Employment, and Jacob K. Javits, R-N.Y., the subcommittee's ranking Republican, acknowledged that CETA had had its share of problems since it was established by Congress in 1973.

But both members argued that CETA had had considerable impact on reducing unemployment and training potential workers and said that with new safeguards written into S 2570 fraud and abuse would be sharply reduced.

Citing amendments added to give the Labor Department more power to crack down on widely publicized abuses of the program, Nelson declared, "This legislation will protect the integrity of CETA funds from fiscal mismanagement at the expense of both the public and those it is intended to assist."

Criticisms

Only two senators offered substantive criticism of CETA during floor debate Aug. 22 and Aug. 25.

Jesse Helms, R-N.C., described CETA as "just another typical example of the futility of throwing tax dollar after tax dollar at a problem."

Helms declared that the "real problem" in the country now was the "big spending policies" of Congress, but he made no attempt to reduce or eliminate funding for what he described as "this massive CETA boondoggle."

Adlai E. Stevenson III, D-Ill., also criticized CETA, arguing that it was a "grossly inefficient means of providing training and jobs for those most in need of both."

Stevenson contended that CETA funds could be better used to reduce the federal deficit and reform the welfare system. Stevenson, who later joined William Proxmire, D-Wis., and eight conservatives in voting against S 2570, did so, he explained, "to protest a well-intentioned but ill-conceived measure which by its costs and waste causes unemployment and inflation."

Otherwise, most senators who spoke generally endorsed the basic aims of CETA while suggesting that weaknesses in the program could be cured.

"I am prepared to argue that CETA — with its basic commitment to decentralized delivery of services to the unemployed — is basically sound in concept," declared Henry Bellmon, R-Okla., in comments later echoed by others.

Fraud and Abuse

During floor debate, the Senate adopted two amendments designed to prevent fraud in CETA programs and provide the Labor Department with enough power to crack down quickly and effectively on violators. Both amendments were adopted with little debate and no opposition.

One amendment, sponsored by Pete V. Domenici, R-N.M., established a monitoring system in the department and extended criminal penalties already in the bill for CETA prime sponsors to contractors and subcontractors. The amendment included a provision establishing a division of monitoring and compliance within the office of the secretary of labor.

The Senate adopted the Domenici amendment by a 91-0 vote after adding a second section to the amendment, proposed by Edward W. Brooke, R-Mass., to establish an office of management assistance to enable the Labor Department to offer management and technical advice to prime sponsors where needed. *(Vote 342, p. 51-S)*

The second amendment, sponsored by Richard S. Schweiker, R-Pa., and adopted by voice vote, was designed to protect against abuses in the public service employment program, especially the problem of "substitution" of regular local government employees with CETA workers and other abuses such as kickbacks, political patronage and nepotism.

The Schweiker amendment gave the secretary of labor the power to suspend funding for a public service employment program accused of questionable use of CETA money until the problem was resolved. It also gave the secretary power to require reimbursement of misspent funds from monies other than those provided by CETA. The House, in its version of the reauthorization measure, adopted a similar provision during floor debate Aug. 9.

The Schweiker amendment was in addition to changes included in the bill by the Senate Human Resources Committee aimed at preventing substitution. The committee provisions expressly prohibited the hiring of a CETA participant when any other person is on layoff from the same or a substantially equivalent position, and required that CETA jobs must be in addition to those that would be funded by a state or municipality. The committee bill also placed time limitations on program participation, limitations on wages and supplementation, and restricted eligibility requirements for public service jobs.

Eligibility Requirements

During floor action the Senate also adopted an amendment, offered by Bellmon and endorsed by the sponsors of the bill, to further tighten eligibility requirements for public service jobs and place greater emphasis on providing jobs for welfare recipients.

Bellmon said his amendment would move the CETA program a "considerable way" in the direction pointed to in a major welfare bill (S 2777) that he and several other senators had sponsored in the Senate.

The Bellmon amendment limited eligibility for Title II public service jobs, which were intended for the structurally unemployed, to persons receiving Aid to Families with Dependent Children (AFDC) or Supplemental Security Income (SSI) benefits, and persons unemployed 15 weeks or more whose family incomes did not exceed 70 percent of the Bureau of Labor Statistics lower living standard. As reported by the committee, S 2570 required 12 weeks minimum unemployment and did not make AFDC and SSI recipients automatically eligible for Title II jobs.

The amendment also revised eligibility requirements for Title VI public service jobs, which were intended to relieve countercyclical employment. The amendment required that persons eligible for the jobs would have to be unemployed for at least 10 of the previous 12 weeks and either have family incomes of less than 85 percent of the Bureau of Labor Statistics lower living standard, or be receiving SSI or AFDC benefits. The committee recommended only 45 days of unemployment and did not make AFDC and SSI recipients automatically eligible.

The Bellmon amendment also eliminated a provision that required Congress to appropriate at least $3 billion for public service jobs for the structurally unemployed under Title II of the bill before any money was appropriated for countercyclical jobs under Title VI. Bellmon said the amendment would leave Congress free to decide the levels and mix of structural and countercyclical public jobs and training programs in each year's appropriations process.

Other Amendments

Altogether, the Senate adopted 34 amendments and rejected one. Many of the amendments made technical changes in S 2570 and were designed to clarify provisions already incorporated in the bill by the committee. Several amendments mandated that specific studies of various employment-related issues be conducted, or specified ways for the Labor Department to reduce paperwork associated with the CETA program, or established certain reporting requirements for the Labor Department.

For example, Robert Dole, R-Kan., won support of one amendment that required prime sponsor planning councils to include representatives of handicapped. Nelson won approval of another amendment that required the department to publish in the *Federal Register* any substantive changes in the method of calculating unemployment at least six months before the new method would take effect.

Sponsors of the bill generally agreed with the amendments, or had no strong opposition, although at least one amendment was accepted with some reluctance.

The amendment, by Helms, prohibited the use of CETA funds to assist or promote union organizing, and prohibited, with some exceptions, compulsory union membership as a condition of enrolling in any institutional training program sponsored by a union unless the program involved individuals employed under a collective bargaining agreement.

Nelson and Javits had little to say about the Helms amendment. "I am not happy with it, but in the interest of facilitating passage of the bill, I interpose no objection," Javits said.

Human Resources Committee sources later said the Helms amendment merely "stated the obvious" and would have no substantive impact.

The Senate rejected one amendment, tabling by a 47-32 vote a proposal by H. John Heinz III, R-Pa., that would have given broad authority to the secretary of labor to establish programs to create employment opportunities in the private sector for CETA workers by making grants to private employers. *(Vote 362, p. 54-S)*

Javits and Nelson said they felt Heinz might have a good idea but no hearings had been held on his proposal. Therefore, they said, more study was needed.

House Floor Action

In sharp contrast to the relatively easy passage of S 2570, House action on HR 12452 was marked by widespread hostility to CETA public service employment.

Sentiment in the House was so strongly aroused by the continuing reports of fraud and abuse in CETA programs that the bill seemed at one point in danger of being killed, or gutted. After being defeated on a series of key votes on Aug. 9, the first time HR 12452 was brought to the floor, sponsors were forced to pull the bill from the schedule for over a month, in order to round up more support.

The bill was finally saved only after sponsors agreed to a series of compromise amendments cutting back the numbers and wages of public service workers.

INITIAL HOUSE ACTION

House debate on HR 12452 Aug. 9 revealed such strongly critical sentiment among House members that leaders pulled the bill off the floor and decided not to bring it up again until after the August recess, lest the legislation be crippled or totally defeated.

House Speaker Thomas P. O'Neill Jr., D-Mass., was apparently determined to complete action on the bill Aug. 9, keeping members in session until 10 p.m. But the House just scratched the surface of the many expected amendments, with the crucial public service employment titles still to be considered.

The late-night session drew a heated reaction from Ronald V. Dellums, D-Calif., who charged that House members were "making a mockery of the legislative process." "We are tearing this legislation apart," he said, ". . .but many of us do not understand what is going on."

Two crucial amendments adopted by the House Aug. 9 lowered the ceiling on wages that could be paid to CETA workers and slashed authorized funding for public service employment.

The cutbacks came despite the strenuous efforts of a CETA task force of House members and intensive lobbying by unions and local government officials, many of whom were heavily dependent on the program. Lobbyists warned that the cutbacks would render the program virtually unworkable, particularly in the expensive urban areas that faced the most severe unemployment problems.

The atmosphere surrounding the bill was so negative that even members who had supported CETA in the past argued that some reductions were necessary to satisfy popular complaints, and to avoid even more stringent congressional restrictions in the future.

Continuing publicity over fraud and abuse in CETA put heavy pressure on members to support some cuts. Robert J. Cornell, D-Wis., observed in an interview that many members felt that "the way to show you're against abuse is to be against the program."

Even more threatening to CETA was criticism directed to more basic questions of how many public service workers to have, and how much to pay them. Conservatives, who had long argued that the job training aspects of CETA should be emphasized at the expense of public employment, were joined by some liberals who feared that the high wages paid to participants were making the program politically indefensible.

Bill manager Augustus F. Hawkins, D-Calif., said Aug. 10 that the bill had been delayed to allow additional lobbying in support of the program by local officials. He said further action on the bill before the recess would result in "individual members taking their feelings out on CETA and responding to their emotions," by approving gutting amendments.

Wage Limits

An amendment offered by David R. Obey, D-Wis., to impose more stringent limits on wages paid to CETA workers was adopted by a vote of 230-175. *(Vote 593, p. 168-H)*

Cosponsored by Budget Committee Chairman Robert N. Giaimo, D-Conn., Ronald A. Sarasin, R-Conn., and others, the Obey amendment limited CETA wages paid by the federal government to $10,000 a year per employee. The committee-approved bill had set the same maximum for most areas, but had allowed wages of up to $12,000 to be paid from CETA funds in high-wage regions.

For the high-wage areas, the Obey amendment did allow local governments to supplement the CETA wages with their own funds, up to a total of an additional 20 percent of wages, or $2,000. The committee bill allowed local governments to add 25 percent of their own money to the federal amount.

In effect, the Obey amendment set a $12,000 limit for high-wage areas and a $10,000 limit for the rest of the country, compared with the $15,000 and $12,500 limits backed by the committee.

The Obey amendment also cut, to $7,000 from $7,800, the required average annual wage of all CETA workers. It allowed the average to be indexed according to the consumer price index.

Obey argued that the amendment was needed to prevent even further cuts in the program by the Appropriations committees. "If the members think we have trouble in passing this bill, I invite them to watch the trouble we are going to have in funding the appropriations down the line," he said, warning that the House Appropriations Committee might approve an amendment to hold all CETA jobs to the minimum wage.

Supporters of the Obey amendment said high wage levels under the CETA program had generated strong public opposition. Obey called CETA "the second most unpopular program in the country after welfare." Robert J. Lagomarsino, R-Calif., said the public "resents the high-paid public payroll jobs that are higher . . . than many jobs in the private sector." "It is much more attractive to be in this program than it is to be in the real world," Sarasin lamented.

Opponents of the Obey amendment predicted that it would make the program very difficult to operate in many areas of the country. That was because CETA workers had to be paid the same amount as regular government employees doing the same job. In some urban areas wages for even the lowest government jobs exceeded the required average wage of the Obey amendment. Thus there would be no easy way to reach the $7,000 average. "In the high-cost areas of this country where we have a large number of poor unemployed, we are in fact going to be killing the CETA program," said Ted Weiss, D-N.Y.

Public Service Jobs Cut

The other key change made by the House Aug. 9 was an amendment that reduced funding for public service jobs. The amendment, offered by James M. Jeffords, R-Vt., was approved 221-181. *(Vote 594, p. 168-H)*

The Jeffords amendment cut about $1 billion from Title VI jobs programs by placing a $3.2 billion cap on the authorization. If unemployment exceeded 6.5 percent, however, the amendment removed the cap.

In place of the $1 billion public service cut, the Jeffords amendment substituted $500 million in extra funding for youth employment and private sector programs: $350 million for Title IV youth programs, $50 million for the Title VIII Young Adult Conservation Corps and $100 million for the administration's new Title VII private sector program. Jeffords said the amendment would still allow for about the same number of jobs, since "you get almost twice as many total jobs in the youth area for the same number of dollars."

Jeffords told his colleagues that CETA priorities needed to be rearranged to meet the greatest need — unemployed young people. Although young people accounted for 50 percent of all unemployment, he said, they were the targets of only 20 percent of CETA funds.

Hawkins said the amendment would end up cutting 100,000 jobs without supplying their replacements for youth. He said the administration had testified that it already had enough money for youth programs and could not effectively use any more.

Pensions

The complex issue of the use of CETA funds for payments to local government pension funds gave members a chance to vote against supplementing local budgets with money intended for job creation. After a complicated series of amendments, the House adopted an amendment by John N. Erlenborn, R-Ill., to ban use of CETA money for payments to retirement plans after 1979. The amendment was adopted 254-148. *(Vote 592, p. 168-H)*

Under existing regulations, CETA funds could be used for contributions to regular government employee pension plans. CETA employees were entitled to the same benefits as other workers doing the same jobs. But very few CETA workers ever stayed on the payroll long enough to qualify for the retirement benefits. Thus CETA payments amounted to a windfall for the pension funds.

The committee bill allowed use of CETA retirement payments for future public service workers only to the extent that they were likely to get the benefits at a later date. Local governments would otherwise have to make the payments themselves.

John Krebs, D-Calif., proposed an amendment to the Erlenborn amendment that was the product of a compromise between bill sponsors, local government officials and public employee unions. Local governments didn't care if CETA funds were used, as long as they didn't have to make the contributions themselves; employee unions didn't worry about who paid, as long as benefits were paid for those likely to draw from the pension funds.

The Krebs amendment eliminated required contributions to retirement programs for CETA workers who were unlikely to benefit from the plans; local government thus would no longer be liable for payments. It allowed federal CETA money to be used if workers were likely to benefit.

But sentiment against use of CETA money for pensions was too strong for the exemption allowed by the Krebs amendment. John M. Ashbrook, R-Ohio, proposed an amendment to the Krebs amendment to strike the exception for those likely to benefit. It was adopted 209-194, after which the Krebs amendment was rejected by voice vote. *(Vote 591, p. 168-H)*

The Erlenborn amendment drew a distinction between payments for immediate benefits, such as health insurance and unemployment compensation, and the retirement plans. It exempted pension plans from the requirement that CETA workers get the same benefits as regular workers, thus absolving local governments from the need to make the payments, and prohibited use of federal funds for the payments beginning Jan. 1, 1980. It allowed payments for the immediate benefits.

Before adopting the Erlenborn amendment, the House rejected a Bill Goodling, R-Pa., amendment to give local governments the option of not paying unemployment insurance for CETA workers. The amendment was rejected 197-211. *(Vote 590, p. 168-H)*

The closest vote of the evening came on an amendment by Andrew Maguire, D-N.J., to tighten the rules for use of CETA funds to pay outside consultants for legal or "associated" services. The amendment, adopted 200-198, allowed such payments if the work performed could not have been done by the local government's employees or the Department of Labor, and the consultant charged a reasonable fee. *(Vote 595, p. 168-H)*

HOUSE PASSAGE

A delicately balanced compromise helped win easy House approval of public service jobs legislation Sept. 22.

In marked contrast with the sharply critical atmosphere prevailing when the House Aug. 9 first took up HR 12452, the bill passed by a solid 284-50 margin. *(Vote 723, p. 206-H)*

The dramatic reversal was largely due to adoption of a substitute bill, worked out by James M. Jeffords, R-Vt., David R. Obey, D-Wis., and Education and Labor Committee Democrats, that cut about 100,000 public service jobs from the committee-reported bill. The compromise included modified versions of restrictive amendments offered by Jeffords and Obey which had been approved by the House Aug. 9.

The compromise helped to alleviate members' concerns about the fraud and abuse frequently charged against the program, without losing the support of the local government officials who were the strongest backers of CETA.

Supporters of the compromise predicted that it would lead to a new focus for CETA. While CETA had been most heavily oriented towards public service jobs since the 1974-75 recession, Jeffords said the bill would reverse that trend, putting more emphasis on job training for the hard-core unemployed.

By agreeing to the compromise, sponsors won a promise from committee Republicans not to offer further major changes on the floor.

While they clearly had the upper hand on the House floor, critics of HR 12452 were worried that any major changes they could win would not survive a conference with the Senate, which had passed a more liberal CETA bill. Jeffords said "a commitment to stand by the bill in conference" had been the most important concession won through the compromise.

Although it approved a string of amendments by voice vote, the House made no major changes in the Jeffords substitute. The only two attempts at altering the shape of the bill significantly were rejected by overwhelming votes.

An amendment offered by Ronnie G. Flippo, D-Ala., would have put back into the bill the estimated 100,000 jobs taken out by the Jeffords substitute, by increasing the numerical jobs goal under Title VI to 25 percent of the number of persons unemployed over 4 percent of the work force. The Jeffords amendment called for jobs for 20 percent of the unemployed over 4 percent of the work force.

Fearful that a return to the committee-approved 25 percent goal would unravel the carefully wrought compromise, Hawkins opposed the amendment. Only Flippo supported his proposal, which was rejected 1-335. *(Vote 721, p. 206-H)*

Despite the sentiment for more emphasis on job training at the expense of public service jobs, which was reflected in the Jeffords substitute, the House also easily turned down a move to cut public service jobs funds in half. Rejected by an 81-252 vote was a motion by John M. Ashbrook, R-Ohio, to recommit HR 12452 with instructions to reduce public service jobs funds to no more than 30 percent of the total appropriations authorized by the bill. *(Vote 722, p. 206-H)*

Ashbrook argued that his amendment would preserve all the money in the bill, while shifting its emphasis to what he called the more efficient job training programs. Noting that public service employment would account for about $9 billion of the $11 billion authorized by the bill for 1979, he said that "Congress should not continue to pour so many dollars into public service employment."

Opposing the Ashbrook motion, Majority Leader Jim Wright, D-Texas, said the Jeffords substitute had gone far enough to correct whatever problems there were in a generally well-run program. "In spite of a few highly publicized irregularities, this program has worked effectively and well in most localities."

Changes Approved

In addition to accepting the Jeffords substitute, sponsors speeded action on the bill by working out modified versions of at least two amendments that could have led to recorded votes. Both amendments were subsequently adopted by voice vote.

Robert Duncan, D-Ore., had planned to offer an amendment to remove the Young Adult Conservation Corps (YACC) from Labor Department jurisdiction, leaving it with the departments of Interior and Agriculture. Instead, Duncan, "in the spirit of compromise," introduced an amendment to increase YACC authorizations by $193 million.

Similarly, Millicent Fenwick, R-N.J., had proposed an amendment to eliminate the National Commission for Employment and Training Policy, an advisory panel established by CETA. "What is the use of a commission if it doesn't act as the ally of the public in relation to Congress?", she asked, arguing that the commission had not helped Congress cope with the problems of CETA. After working with the committee, she settled for an amendment to reduce the membership and term of individual service on the commission, and to allow filing of dissenting views to the commission's report to Congress.

Conference Action

Conferees filed their report on S 2570 Oct. 11 (H Rept 95-1765, S Rept 95-1325).

The final version reported by conferees made a modest overall cut in existing program levels, while shifting the focus of efforts towards job training for the hard-core unemployed.

Restoring about half of the House-passed cuts in public service employment, the conference agreement authorized, at current unemployment levels, about 660,000 jobs. This compared with 600,000 jobs in the House bill, and the administration's 1978 target figure of 725,000 positions.

House critics of the program had agreed to the 600,000 level in return for a commitment from bill manager Augustus E. Hawkins, D-Calif., to stand by the provision in conference. Some opponents of the original House bill had threatened to kill the bill, or fight to reduce its funding, if the final version came back from conference stripped of House cuts in jobs and wages.

Although the conference report allowed some expansion from House levels in the event of high unemployment, it tightened the requirements for assistance to the long-term unemployed. "We lost on slots but got the structure," remarked one staffer. "The bill is a completely different animal."

The conference agreement focused attention on those with the worst employment problems by requiring that assistance go to those who were both unemployed and poor. The bill emphasized giving jobs and training to welfare recipients.

To ensure that help for the disadvantaged went mostly for training designed to cure their long-term problems, and not just for temporary public service jobs with no future, the bill required that all services for the structurally unemployed contain at least some training component. The conference agreement mandated that an increasing amount of the efforts directed towards structural unemployment be concentrated on training.

Prime sponsors, while relieved that the conference agreement did not cut the number of jobs as much as the House bill, worried that the emphasis on training for the structurally unemployed would result in decreased funding for public service employment in the future.

Conferees also approved House-passed transfers of funds from public service employment to youth programs and new efforts to involve the private sector in CETA.

Public Service Jobs

Although much of the discussion on CETA legislation had been directed towards the number of public service jobs to be provided, neither the House nor Senate bills contained specific authorizations for the Title VI countercyclical public service employment section. The Senate bill had been totally open-ended, allowing the number of jobs to be set by the appropriation level each year. The House bill, while also avoiding specific dollar amounts, had called on the Appropriations Committee to provide enough money to fund a number of jobs equal to one-fifth of the number of jobless persons in excess of the 4 percent "full employment" unemployment rate.

Conferees accepted the House goal, with a pressure valve to provide more help when times were bad. In any year in which the president predicted that the unemployment rate for the year would be over 7 percent, the bill called for enough jobs to employ 25 percent of the number of unemployed over 4 percent of the work force.

A factor tending to limit the number of jobs under this arrangement was the requirement that the number of jobs be based on estimates at the beginning of the year of the unemployment rate for the whole year. House Republicans figured that the natural reluctance of any president to predict a distressingly high unemployment rate at the end of the year would tend to hold down the number of jobs.

For wages for Title VI public service job holders, conferees accepted a Senate-passed provision that set a $10,000 general maximum, but allowed increases of up to 20 percent, to $12,000, for workers in high-wage areas. The House bill had enforced the $10,000 limit on CETA-paid wages in all areas.

While they allowed the federal government to pay more than the House bill had permitted, conferees cut down on the amount local governments could add to an individual worker's wage.

Both bills had allowed supplementation of up to 20 percent of the CETA wage; the conference agreement allowed only a 10 percent bonus for individuals in Title VI jobs.

But, under the conference agreement, most wages would be far below the maximum. The final bill required a national public service jobs average wage of $7,200, with individual prime sponsors allowed to have averages no more than 20 percent above the national goal.

The bill limited participation in all public service jobs by individual workers to 18 months within any five-year period.

In an effort to hold down on substitution, the conference agreement required that half of each prime sponsor's Title VI funds be used on projects that could be completed within 18 months. Conferees split the difference between the Senate provision, which had limited projects to 12 months, and the House bill allowing up to two years. However, they dropped the Senate provision mandating that all funds go for limited projects, accepting instead the House provision requiring that all jobs not on projects be in entry level positions.

Conferees adopted the slightly looser House income eligibility criteria for Title VI. The final bill allowed participation by persons from families with incomes up to 100 percent of the Bureau of Labor Statistics lower living standard, compared with the Senate's 85 percent. On the other hand, the conference committee went with the Senate's somewhat looser definition of unemployment as a prerequisite for participation, allowing jobs for persons who had worked up to two weeks in the preceding 12, instead of the House provision requiring joblessness for eight straight weeks.

Structural Unemployment

The key decision made by conferees on Title II programs for the long-term unemployed was the adoption of a Senate provision clearly separating job training and public service employment within the title.

The House bill, while it had required prime sponsors to spend at least half their Title II funds on training, had lumped training and jobs programs together. The Senate had written a separate part D of the title, with its own allocation formula and authorization, devoted to transitional public service employment. No more than 60 percent of Title II funds would be allowed for part D.

Even part D would not be exclusively concerned with public service jobs, however, because of a provision in the conference agreement requiring that gradually increasing amounts, to 22 percent in 1982, of part D funds be spent on training.

The conference agreement also provided separate eligibility criteria for the training and job parts of Title II. To be eligible for training programs, applicants had only to be unemployed, underemployed, or in school, and be from a low-income family. For the public service jobs, participants would have to have been unemployed for 15 weeks or more, and be from a low-income family, or be on welfare.

The limitations on wages and length of service of Title VI public service employees also applied to the Title II jobs. An additional restriction prohibited local governments from supplementing Title II wages with their own funds.

FINAL ACTION

The Senate approved the conference report on S 2570 by voice vote Oct. 13.

The House agreed to the conference report by a 117-28 standing vote Oct. 15, clearing the measure for the president.

Banking Agency Audits

Congress in 1978 approved legislation authorizing the General Accounting Office (GAO) to audit records of federal bank regulatory agencies.

Under the bill (HR 2176 — PL 95-320), the GAO could audit certain transactions of the Federal Reserve Board and member banks, the Federal Deposit Insurance Corporation and the Office of the Comptroller of the Currency.

Sponsors said the legislation was needed to strengthen congressional oversight of the agencies, which had been exempt from audit by the GAO — the investigative arm of Congress — because their funding derived from assessments on banks they regulate.

Congress completed action on the bill June 29 when the House by voice vote approved the version of the bill passed by the Senate May 10. The House had passed a slightly different version of the legislation in 1977. *(House action, 1977 Almanac p. 151)*

Similar attempts to authorize GAO audits of the Federal Reserve System had failed in the last two Congresses. The Federal Reserve had opposed the audits on grounds that they might intrude on sensitive monetary policy matters. HR 2176 exempted monetary policy functions from auditing by GAO. *(1975 Almanac p. 169, 1974 Almanac p. 209, 1973 Almanac p. 278)*

Provisions

As cleared by Congress, HR 2176:

- Directed the comptroller general of GAO to conduct audits of the Federal Reserve Board and its member banks, the Federal Deposit Insurance Corporation and the Office of the Comptroller of the Currency.
- Prohibited the GAO, in auditing the Federal Reserve, to examine international financial transactions; monetary policy matters, including discount window operations, member bank reserves, securities credit, interest on deposits and open market operations; Federal Open Market Committee activities; and all communications among Federal Reserve personnel relating to exempted activities.
- Prohibited the GAO from conducting on-site examinations of banks or bank holding companies without the written consent of the bank regulatory agency concerned.
- Provided safeguards against unwarranted disclosure of confidential and sensitive information.
- Required the comptroller general to report to Congress on the results of the audits.

Banking Regulation

Congress Oct. 15 approved an important package of banking legislation, a large part of which was designed to regulate the activities of bank officials.

The bill (HR 14279 — PL 95-630), which was cleared with little debate in the early morning hours of the last day of the 95th Congress, also contained provisions sought by a variety of competing industry groups.

Many parts of the 260-page composite bill had already been passed by the House, the Senate or both, but it was only after they were tied together into one package overnight that their enactment became possible.

The House approved the measure at 2:30 a.m. by a vote of 341-32. The Senate cleared it by voice vote a few hours later. *(House vote 823, p. 234-H)*

The bill prohibited some of the practices of bank executives that were brought to public attention during the investigation of the financial dealings of Bert Lance, the former director of the Office of Management and Budget. *(1977 Almanac p. 157)*

Other parts of the legislation satisfied various financial industry lobbies and brought their support behind the entire package.

For those interested in curbing abuses by bank executives, the bill provided for tighter controls on insider lending and interlocking directorates among financial institutions and gave expanded authority to bank regulators.

For consumers, the legislation provided safeguards in electronic fund-transfer systems such as computerized bank tellers and limited access by federal authorities to individuals' bank records.

For banks, the legislation eliminated an interest-rate advantage enjoyed by savings and loan associations on so-called transaction accounts, which basically work like checking accounts and were to be offered depositors on Nov. 1.

For savings and loan associations, the measure extended Regulation Q, under which bank regulatory agencies set differential ceilings on interest rates that may be paid on savings deposits, and provided new authority for savings and loans to invest in urban areas.

For mutual savings banks, the bill authorized federal charters.

For New York bankers, the legislation provided authority to offer interest-bearing checking accounts known as negotiable order of withdrawal (NOW) accounts.

The bill also extended the life of the U.S. Export-Import Bank for five years and provided for the public sale of gold medallions.

Provisions

As cleared by Congress, HR 14279:

Title I — Supervisory Authority and Insider Dealings

- Increased the supervisory power of bank regulatory agencies by allowing them, subject to due process safeguards, to:

1) Impose civil penalties on banks or bank officials who violate banking laws.

2) Issue cease-and-desist orders to halt illegal or unsound banking practices.

3) Remove or suspend bank officials who engage in illegal or unsound banking practices.

4) Order banks or savings and loan association holding companies to terminate their ownership of subsidiaries when the ownership is judged to constitute a serious risk to the financial safety of the bank subsidiaries. Nonbank subsidiaries of banks were exempted from the provision, however.

- Required that loans to executive officers or to persons who directly or indirectly or acting in concert with others own, control or have the power to vote more than 10 percent of any class of voting securities of a bank (18 percent in the case of a bank located in a city, town or village with less than 30,000 in population) be subject to the same limits on loans imposed on other borrowers. The prohibition applied to companies controlled by such people and to political or campaign committees which benefit them.
- Prohibited banks from making loans to such "insiders" in excess of $25,000 unless approved in advance by the majority of the board of directors, with the interested party abstaining.
- Required that loans to insiders be made on the same terms available to other borrowers.
- Prohibited overdrafts by bank directors and executive officers.
- Empowered the Federal Deposit Insurance Corp. (FDIC) to make loans to, purchase the assets of or make a contribution to an insured institution in danger of default; and to take similar actions to aid another insured institution to merge with a financially endangered institution.

Title II — Interlocking Directorates

- Prohibited management employees or directors of depository institutions (commercial banks, savings banks, trust companies, savings and loan associations, homestead associations, cooperative banks, industrial banks and credit unions) from serving on any other depository institutions located within either the same Standard Metropolitan Statistical Area (SMSA) or the same city, town or village.
- Prohibited management employees or directors of depository institutions or depository holding companies with total assets exceeding $1 billion from serving on any other depository institution with assets exceeding $500 million.
- Gave individuals who violated the interlocking directorate provisions of the law by dint of previous practice 10 years to comply.

Title III — Foreign Branching

- Permitted the Federal Deposit Insurance Corp. to approve the establishment of foreign branches of state-chartered banks that do not belong to the Federal Reserve System.

Title IV — American Arts Gold Medallions

- Provided for the minting and public sale of one-ounce and half-ounce gold medallions commemorating Americans outstanding in the arts, including Grant Wood, Marian Anderson, Mark Twain, Willa Cather, Louis Armstrong, Frank Lloyd Wright, Robert Frost, Alexander Calder, Helen Hayes and John Steinbeck.

Title V — Credit Union Restructuring

- Established the National Credit Union Administration under the management of a three-member National Credit Union Board. Federal credit unions were required to pay fees to the administration, which was formed to supervise them.

Title VI — Change in Bank Control Act

- Required persons acquiring control of any insured bank to provide notice of the planned acquisition to regulatory officials at least 60 days in advance.
- Authorized bank officials to disapprove a proposed acquisition if they determine it would lessen competition or jeopardize the financial stability of the bank or prejudice the interests of the depositors.

Title VII — Change in Savings and Loan Control Act

- Provided similar requirements for advance notice of acquisition of savings and loan associations, and gave the Federal Home Loan Bank Board authority to disapprove such acquisitions.

Title VIII — Correspondent Accounts

- Prohibited banks which maintain correspondent accounts for other banks from providing preferential loans to executives and major stockholders of the other banks.
- Required insiders to report annually to their boards of directors the loans they have outstanding with correspondent banks.
- Required banks to compile such reports and forward them to regulatory officials.

Title IX — Disclosure

- Required banks to report annually the names of each stockholder who directly or indirectly owns, controls or has the power to vote more than 10 percent of any class of voting securities.

• Required banks to report the amount of all loans to such stockholders, executive officers, and any companies they control or political committees set up for their benefit.

Title X — Federal Financial Institutions Examination Council

• Established a Financial Institutions Examination Council, whose purpose was to prescribe uniform principles and standards for the federal examination of financial institutions by the Office of the Comptroller of the Currency, the Federal Deposit Insurance Corp., the Board of Governors of the Federal Reserve System, the Federal Home Loan Bank Board, and the National Credit Union Administration.

Title XI — Right to Financial Privacy

• Established conditions and procedures whereby government agencies could obtain and share individuals' bank records. In most cases, the law required that individuals receive advance notice that their records were being sought and that they be given a chance to challenge the government's request in court.

• Specified that information obtained under provisions of the title could be used or retained only for the purpose for which it was originally sought.

Title XII — Charters for Thrift Institutions

• Provided state mutual savings banks located in states which authorize the chartering of state mutual savings banks the option of obtaining a federal charter from the Federal Home Loan Bank Board.

Title XIII — NOW Accounts

• Authorized the establishment of NOW accounts (interest-bearing checking accounts) by savings banks in New York State. Previous law authorized such accounts in the six New England states. *(Background, 1977 Almanac p. 152, 1976 Almanac p. 88, 1975 Almanac p. 161)*

Title XIV — Insurance of IRA and Keogh Accounts

• Increased to $100,000 the amount of insurance available for time and savings deposits in insured banks made pursuant to pension or profit-sharing plans.

Title XV — Miscellaneous Provisions

• Extended the prohibition on merchant credit card surcharges for two years.

• Defined "community" for depository institutions serving military personnel.

Title XVI — Interest Rate Control

• Extended for two years, until Dec. 15, 1980, the authority (Regulation Q) of federal regulatory agencies to set the maximum interest rates that banks and savings institutions can pay and eliminated the interest differential between banks and savings institutions in transaction accounts. *(Previous extension, 1977 Almanac p. 152)*

Title XVII — Federal Savings and Loan Investment Authority

• Simplified the investment authority for federal savings and loan associations.

• Gave such associations more authority to invest in urban areas.

• Created a secondary market for rehabilitation loans through the Federal Home Loan Mortgage Corp.

Title XVIII — National Credit Union Central Liquidity Facility

• Created within the National Credit Union Administration a Central Liquidity Facility to loan money to member credit unions facing liquidity problems.

• Authorized any credit union primarily serving natural persons to become a member of the facility by subscribing to its stock in an amount not less than one-half of 1 percent of the credit union's paid-in and unimpaired capital and surplus.

• Authorized the secretary of the Treasury to lend to the facility up to $500 million in the event that it has insufficient funds to meet liquidity needs of credit unions. Interest on the loan would be not greater than one-eighth of a percent above the current annual market yield on oustanding United States obligations.

Title XIX — Export-Import Bank Amendments

• Extended the U.S. Export-Import Bank for five years and increased the Ex-Im Bank's loan guarantee authority to $40 billion from $25 billion. *(Story, p. 397)*

Title XX — Electronic Fund Transfers

• Spelled out the rights and responsibilities of consumers and banks concerning electronic fund transfers, and limited to $50 the liability of a customer for unauthorized funds transfers. *(Story, p. 529)*

Title XXI — Effective Dates

• Made all sections of the act effective 120 days after signing except as follows:

1) Titles IV and XVIII were made effective Oct. 1, 1979.

2) Title XI — cost provisions became effective Oct. 1, 1979. The Securities and Exchange Commission was exempted from the provisions until two years after enactment.

3) Titles XIII, XIV, XV, XVI, XVII and XIX were made effective upon signing.

4) Title XX was made effective upon expiration of 18 months from the date of signing except for two sections — defining consumer liability and prohibiting issuance of a code, card or other means of access to an electronic funds transfer system without a consumer request or application for it — which were made effective 90 days after signing.

Legislative History

Originally, HR 14279 contained merely a one-year extension of Regulation Q. That bill was passed by the House Oct. 11.

When the measure reached the Senate the next day, however, William Proxmire, D-Wis., chairman of the Banking, Housing and Urban Affairs Committee, offered an entirely different version consisting of 15 titles, many of which the Senate had previously passed separately.

Then, when it went back to the House, Fernand J. St Germain, D-R.I., seized the opportunity to attach some sections of the Financial Institutions Regulatory Act (HR

13471), on which his Banking subcommittee had worked for most of the year.

Only provisions of HR 13471 that the House had considered during floor debate Oct. 3-5 were added to HR 14279. The final bill did not include a controversial provision of HR 13471 that would have allowed federally chartered savings and loan associations to issue variable rate mortgages.

Action on HR 13471

HR 13471 (H Rept 95-1383) was approved by a lopsided 34-5 vote by the House Banking, Finance and Urban Affairs Committee on July 18. The 200-page bill contained 20 titles designed to prevent financial excesses by bank insiders, bar interlocking bank directorates, restrict conflicts of interest involving bank regulatory officials, control the sale of financial institutions, and make a variety of other changes in banking laws.

The measure won broad bipartisan support in the House committee — a substantial accomplishment in light of divisions that kept it from winning even subcommittee approval in 1977.

The House committee bill was considerably tougher than a parallel measure (S 71) passed by the Senate in 1977, and it contained a number of provisions not even considered by the Senate. *(Senate bill, 1977 Almanac p. 150)*

Although the House debated HR 13471 on Oct. 3 and went on to vote on a series of amendments Oct. 5, the bill was put aside before action was completed. Sections of HR 13471 upon which the House had acted subsequently were attached to HR 14279. ▮

Housing Authorization

Congress used the fiscal 1979 housing authorization bill to reassert the right of cities and towns to determine, within broad federal guidelines, how to spend some $4 billion annually in community development funds.

Key provisions of the legislation (S 3084 — PL 95-557) aimed to block the Department of Housing and Urban Development (HUD) and its activist Secretary Patricia Roberts Harris from exerting greater influence over the spending of community development funds. The bill also established a process by which congressional committees could review and delay regulations proposed by the department.

The Senate approved the final version of S 3084 by a 77-8 vote Oct. 14. The conferees' decision to remove a Senate amendment blocking a HUD reorganization of its field offices prompted eight senators to oppose the conference report. *(Vote 497, p. 72-S)*

The House cleared the measure for the president Oct. 15, approving the conference report by a 117-6 standing vote.

S 3084 authorized nearly $1.2 billion in new contract authority for fiscal 1979 for an estimated 380,000 housing reservations under the Section 8 rent subsidy and public housing programs.

Reflecting the renewed interest in housing rehabilitation, especially in low and moderate income neighborhoods, the bill expanded the Section 312 low-interest rehabilitation loan program, raising the authorization from $60 million to $245 million for fiscal 1979. President Carter had sought expansion of the loan program as part of his urban policy.

Recognizing that housing rehabilitation was likely to result in the displacement of the poor, S 3084 declared that the federal government, in its administration of housing programs should, where possible, minimize the "involuntary displacement of persons from their homes and neighborhoods."

Two other proposals offered by the president as part of his urban package were also included in the final version of S 3084. The measure authorized $15 million annually for fiscal 1979 and 1980 to finance small neighborhood projects like home weatherization, and established a Livable Cities program to finance art and other cultural projects at the neighborhood level. The Livable Cities program was authorized at $5 million for fiscal 1979 and $10 million for fiscal 1980.

Finally, S 3084 also established a new program, to be administered by the Farmers Home Administration (FmHA), designed to increase home ownership among the rural poor. The program, similar to the Section 8 subsidy program run by HUD, was expected to help as many as 16,000 families during fiscal 1979.

Major Provisions

As signed into law the Housing and Community Development Amendments of 1978 (S 3084 — PL 95-557) contained the following provisions (effective Oct. 1, 1978, unless otherwise noted):

Title I — Community and Neighborhood Development and Conservation

- **Rehabilitation Loans.** Gave priority for low-interest rehabilitation loans (Section 312 of the Housing Act of 1964) to applications from low and moderate income persons who own the property and intend to occupy it after rehabilitation.
- Gave the HUD secretary discretionary authority to charge interest on Section 312 loans above the current 3 percent ceiling when the loans would benefit families with incomes above 80 percent of the median for the area. The higher rates could not exceed the current Treasury borrowing rate.
- Increased the maximum Section 312 loan amount for commercial properties to $100,000 from $50,000.
- Authorized $245 million for the Section 312 loan program for fiscal 1979; allowed up to $60 million to be used during fiscal 1979 for multifamily properties.
- Prohibited future Section 312 loans to be used for improvements that do not meet cost-effective energy conservation standards. This requirement was to take effect 270 days after enactment of S 3084.
- Established guidelines and requirements for Section 312 loans for multifamily properties, in general requiring that the loans be used for housing in low and moderate income neighborhoods.
- Limited Section 312 loans for multifamily housing to properties of less than 100 units, except where the HUD secretary determines that the loan is essential to community development needs and there are no alternative sources of financing.
- **Rehabilitation Loan Insurance.** Gave the HUD secretary authority under Section 203(k) of the National

Housing Act to insure loans made by financial institutions for the rehabilitation of one-to-four family properties used primarily for residential purposes.

● Permitted the Government National Mortgage Association (GNMA) to purchase rehabilitation loans insured under the Section 203(k) program.

● Allowed insurance premium charges up to 1 percent per year for rehabilitation loans insured under Section 203(k).

● **Urban Homesteading.** Authorized $26 million for the urban homesteading program for fiscal 1979.

● Allowed properties owned by the Veterans Administration (VA) to be eligible for the homesteading program.

● **Community Development Block Grants.** Stipulated that estimates of the number of persons expected to reside in a community, for purposes of a housing assistance plan, should cover only individuals who work in the community and live elsewhere, individuals who are likely to work there as a result of projected employment opportunities, or the elderly, regardless of their employment status. Effective upon enactment.

● Further defined the process of determining housing needs to allow housing assistance plans to include estimates based on a community approved state or regional housing allocation plan approved by the secretary. Effective upon enactment.

● Prohibited the HUD secretary from rejecting an application for community development funds because it addresses any one of the three primary purposes of the program to a greater or lesser degree than any other. Effective upon enactment. *(Primary purposes, p. 306)*

● Allowed the HUD secretary to reject a community development block grant application only upon determining that the extent to which a primary purpose is addressed is "plainly inappropriate" to meeting the community development needs and objectives as identified by the community. Effective upon enactment.

● Repealed a prohibition against using community development funds for relocation payments and assistance caused by activities not funded by the block grant.

● **Urban Development Action Grants.** Required communities to submit impact statements analyzing the effect proposed urban development action grants would have on area residents, particularly low and moderate income families and their neighborhoods.

● Required the HUD secretary to take into account the potential impact on low and moderate income families and their neighborhoods in deciding whether to award an action grant.

● Prohibited HUD from excluding small cities and towns from community development programs unless expressly authorized by statute.

Title II — Housing Assistance Programs

● **Troubled Projects.** Authorized up to $74 million in fiscal 1979 in financial aid to Federal Housing Administration (FHA)-insured housing projects facing serious financial trouble; set out criteria to be used by the HUD secretary in determining whether the financial aid should be given to the projects and how the money could be used.

● **Tenant Participation.** Established procedures and guidelines by which tenants of multifamily housing projects can participate in making decisions involving major actions such as rents, improvements in the physical structures and management of the projects.

● **Property Disposition.** Established basic federal policy for management, preservation and disposition of HUD-owned multifamily housing projects; outlined procedures for the HUD secretary to follow in disposing of multifamily housing projects.

● **Elderly, Handicapped Housing.** Required that at least $50 million in Section 202 loans (housing for elderly and handicapped) be set aside for the development of rental housing and related facilities for primarily handicapped persons under the age of 62.

● **Low Income Housing.** Authorized $1,195,043,000 for fiscal 1979 in additional contract authority for the Section 8 rent subsidy program and public housing.

● Earmarked at least $50 million of the new contract authority for modernization of existing public housing projects.

● Allowed Section 8 payments for rental costs faced by mobile home owners who rent the lots on which their mobile homes are located.

● Authorized up to $729 million for operating subsidies for public housing projects.

● **Public Housing Security.** Authorized HUD to begin a demonstration program designed to improve security and alleviate crime in public housing projects and their surrounding neighborhoods.

● Authorized $10 million for fiscal 1979 for various demonstrations; specified that the money should come from the authorization for public housing operating subsidies.

● Authorized the HUD secretary to allow installation of solar units that are economically feasible and cost effective in residential housing assisted through the Section 312, 202 and 8 programs.

Title III — Program Amendments and Extensions

● **FHA Mortgage Insurance.** Extended basic HUD-FHA mortgage insurance and loan programs for one year, through Sept. 30, 1979.

● **Interest Rates.** Extended for one year, through Sept. 30, 1979, the authority of the HUD secretary to set interest rates for FHA-insured mortgage loans at rates above the statutory maximum of 6 percent.

● **Mortgage Purchases.** Extended for one year, to Oct. 1, 1979, the authority of the Government National Mortgage Association (GNMA) to enter into new commitments to buy mortgages under the Emergency Home Purchase Assistance Act of 1974.

● **Comprehensive Planning.** Authorized up to $57 million for fiscal 1979 for comprehensive planning grants.

● **Research.** Authorized up to $62 million for fiscal 1979 for HUD-sponsored research and demonstration projects.

● **New Communities.** Extended to Oct. 1, 1979, the authority of HUD to make special planning assistance grants to private new community developers and state land development agencies.

● **Crime, Riot Insurance.** Extended through Sept. 30, 1980, the authority of HUD to provide new federal crime insurance and riot reinsurance coverage; continued existing reinsurance and direct insurance coverage through Sept. 30, 1983, and extended the deadline for HUD to submit a plan to liquidate and terminate the two programs until Sept. 30, 1981.

● Required that as of Jan. 31, 1979, no risk covered by a statewide FAIR plan be insured at a rate higher than the rates set by the principal state-licensed rating organization for essential property insurance in the voluntary market.

FAIR (fair access to insurance requirements) plans were designed to ensure the availability of property insurance in high-risk areas. *(Background, 1968 Almanac p. 317)*

• **Flood Insurance.** Extended through Sept. 30, 1980, the authority of HUD to enter into flood insurance contracts under the national flood insurance program.

• Extended through Sept. 30, 1980, HUD's authority to provide subsidized flood insurance under the "emergency program" in communities that have adopted minimum flood plain management measures and for which the necessary actuarial rate and flood hazard elevation studies have not yet been completed.

• Authorized up to $114 million for fiscal 1979 for flood insurance studies and surveys.

• Increased the Federal Housing Administration general insurance fund by $165 million for fiscal 1979.

• **Multifamily Mortgage Insurance.** Reduced, from eight to five, the minimum number of family units which must be included in a property covered by a project mortgage insured under Section 207 of the National Housing Act.

• **Day Care for Elderly.** Ended the prohibition against insuring mortgages for day care facilities for the elderly in the Section 232 nursing home and intermediate care mortgage insurance program.

• **Condominium Mortgage Insurance.** Authorized HUD to insure one-family condominium units in non-FHA insured multifamily projects of 12 or more units. To obtain insurance, the project must have been completed at least one year prior to the application for insurance.

• **Neighborhood Commission.** Gave the National Commission on Neighborhoods three additional months to complete its study. *(1977 Almanac p. 122)*

• **Surplus Property.** Lifted restrictions on the transfer of surplus federal land from the General Services Administration to HUD in order to allow the federal housing agency to sell or lease the property for housing for low and moderate income families.

• **GNMA Mortgage Limit.** Increased the maximum original principal obligation of mortgages purchased by the Government National Mortgage Association (GNMA) under its special assistance tandem plan (Section 305 of the National Housing Act) to $55,000 for a one-family residence, $60,000 for a two- or three-family residence, $68,750 for a four-family residence, and, for larger units, $38,000 per dwelling unit ($45,000 in high-cost areas).

• Increased by $500 million the total amount of mortgages GNMA could purchase or commit to purchase after Oct. 1, 1978, under the special assistance program.

• **National Institute of Building Sciences.** Extended the life of the National Institute of Building Sciences through fiscal 1982.

• **Title I Home Loans.** Increased the maximum property improvement loan for multifamily structures to $37,500 from $25,000; increased the loan ceilings within the maximum to $7,500 from $5,000 per unit; increased the maximum repayment period to 15 years and 32 days from 12 years and 32 days.

• **Federal Home Loan Mortgage Corp.** Provided mortgage bankers with direct sales access to the Federal Home Loan Mortgage Corp.; gave the corporation authority to establish various requirements for mortgage bankers to participate in the program. Effective 210 days from enactment, but not before Jan. 31, 1979, or on an earlier date determined by the corporation.

• **Legislative Review.** Established procedures for the House and Senate Banking committees to review regulations proposed by the Department of Housing and Urban Development; allowed the committees, by approval of resolutions or legislation, to delay the effective date of proposed regulations for 90 days.

• **FHA Multifamily Mortgages.** Increased the mortgage limits for non-profit, non-elevator structures insured under Section 221(d)(3) of the National Housing Act (rental or cooperative housing for low and moderate income persons) to $21,563 from $16,860 per family unit without a bedroom; $24,662 from $18,648 for one bedroom; $29,984 from $22,356 for two bedrooms; $38,379 from $28,152 for three bedrooms; and $42,756 from $31,884 for four or more bedrooms.

• Increased limits for non-profit elevator structures under Section 221(d)(3) to $22,692 from $19,680 for a unit without a bedroom; $26,012 from $22,356 for one bedroom; $31,631 from $26,496 for two bedrooms; $40,919 from $33,-120 for three bedrooms; and $44,917 from $38,400 for four or more bedrooms.

• Increased limits for Section 221(d)(4) profit-oriented housing to $19,406 from $18,450 for a unit without any bedrooms; $22,028 from $20,625 for one bedroom; $26,625 from $24,630 for two bedrooms; $33,420 from $29,640 for three bedrooms; and $37,870 from $34,846 for four or more bedrooms.

• **Hospital Refinancing.** Allowed hospitals to refinance existing debts under Section 223(f) of the National Housing Act; established various requirements for refinancing.

Title IV — Congregate Services

• Established a new program designed to provide meals and social services for elderly and handicapped persons living in low-rent housing with group dining facilities. Under the terms of the program HUD would contract with local sponsors to provide the services.

• Authorized $20 million for fiscal 1979, $25 million for fiscal 1980, $35 million for fiscal 1981 and $40 million for fiscal 1982 for the program.

Title V — Rural Housing

• Extended through Sept. 30, 1979, Farmers Home Administration (FmHA) programs for low income repair loans and grants and domestic farm labor housing grants.

• Authorized $48 million for fiscal 1979 for the Section 504 repair loan and grant program.

• Authorized $38 million for fiscal 1979 for Section 516 domestic farm labor housing grants.

• Authorized $5 million for fiscal 1979 for Section 525 counseling assistance, and $5 million for fiscal 1979 for Section 525 technical assistance.

• Authorized an additional $3 million for fiscal 1979 for the Section 523(g) self-help development fund for loans with interest rates below 3 percent.

• Authorized $38 million for fiscal 1979 for Section 514 farm labor housing loans.

• Authorized the agriculture secretary to conduct research, technical studies and demonstrations aimed at stimulating construction and improving architectural design and utility of dwellings and buildings.

• Required the agriculture secretary to study migrant and settled farm worker housing.

• Required the agriculture secretary to develop a notification and appeals procedure for applicants denied FmHA assistance and persons and organizations whose FmHA assistance is substantially reduced or terminated.

• Expand eligibility for Section 521 rural rental assistance to congregate and cooperative housing projects and projects financed by Section 514 loans to public and private not-for-profit sponsors.

• Established a "deep subsidy" program for very low income homeowners who cannot afford FmHA 1 percent interest credit assistance; limited the program to areas found to be unsuitable for rental housing assistance; limited to $440 million the aggregate principal amount of deep homeowner subsidy loans.

• Allowed the agriculture secretary to waive the "credit elsewhere" requirement for farm labor housing loans only in areas where no public or private non-profit sponsor is available and the loan is necessary to provide the housing; established the current Treasury borrowing rate as the interest rate for the loans.

• Required the agriculture secretary to study remote title claims that prevent rural persons from full use of their property; required an interim report on March 1, 1979, and a final report one year after enactment of the act.

Title VI — Neighborhood Reinvestment

• Established the Neighborhood Reinvestment Corp., a public corporation, to promote reinvestment in older urban neighborhoods and continue the work of the Urban Reinvestment Task Force.

• Authorized $12.5 million for fiscal 1979 as the federal government's share in funding the corporation. *(Background, 1977 Almanac p. 154)*

Title VII — Neighborhood Self-Help

• Authorized the HUD secretary to provide grants and other assistance to qualified neighborhood organizations for various housing, economic development and other conservation and revitalization projects in low and moderate income neighborhoods.

• Authorized $15 million for fiscal 1979 and $15 million for fiscal 1980 for the program.

• Established procedures and requirements for funding various projects; required certification by local government that the proposed project is "consistent with and supportive of" the objectives of that local government.

Title VIII — Livable Cities

• Established a Livable Cities program designed to stimulate cultural arts programs in urban communities and neighborhoods.

• Authorized $5 million for fiscal 1979 and $10 million for fiscal 1980 for the program.

• Established procedures and requirements for distributing grants; limited the program to non-profit organizations; required joint administration by HUD and the National Endowment for the Arts; required certification by local governments.

Title IX — Miscellaneous

• **Displacement.** Declared that involuntary displacement of persons from their homes and neighborhoods should be minimized; directed the HUD secretary to study and report to Congress by Jan. 31, 1979, on ways for HUD to minimize involuntary displacement caused by its own housing programs and by both public and privately financed residential and commercial development and housing rehabilitation.

• **Rehabilitation Guidelines.** Directed the HUD secretary to develop guidelines for rehabilitation for voluntary adoption by states and localities; allowed HUD to offer technical assistance to state and local governments in implementing the guidelines.

• **Interstate Land Sales.** Exempted from the Interstate Land Sales Full Disclosure Act fully improved single family lots located within counties and municipalities that have established minimum standards for the development of subdivision lots.

• Excluded U.S. land patents and similar federal grants or reservations from the act's definition of "liens, encumbrances and adverse claims."

• Exempted from the act real estate legally restricted for commercial and industrial purposes.

• Exempted from the act the sale or lease of any improved land on which there is a condominium or on which a condominium is to be built within two years.

• **Paperwork Reduction.** Required HUD and the Veterans Administration (VA) to undertake, where possible, efforts to reduce paperwork, primarily by using uniform forms for various housing programs.

• **Reorganization.** Provided that HUD administrative reorganization plans may take effect only after HUD conducts a cost-benefit study and publishes it in the *Federal Register.*

House Committee Action

The House Banking, Finance and Urban Affairs Committee reported its version of the bill (HR 12433 — H Rept 95-1161) May 15. Much of the debate at both the committee and subcommittee levels focused on the use of community development block grant monies by local governments.

HUD Regulations

The Department of Housing and Urban Development began the debate by proposing in October 1977 that 75 percent of a city's community development funds be used principally to benefit low and moderate income persons. After substantial criticism from House Banking Committee members and interest groups such as the National League of Cities, HUD retreated from the 75 percent proposal and required instead that at least 51 percent of the block grant funds be earmarked for projects benefiting low and middle income persons.

In addition, HUD said it would conduct a "detailed review" of block grant applications in which less than 75 percent of the funds would benefit low and moderate income persons.

HUD Secretary Harris made no apologies for seeking to earmark greater percentages of community development funds for the poor. When she first issued the 75 percent proposal, she declared: "The regulations which we have written . . . send a clear message to our constituents. HUD is targeting its funds more carefully to the needs of the poor."

House Amendment: Primary Purposes

But Rep. Garry Brown, R-Mich., Housing Subcommittee Chairman Thomas L. Ashley, D-Ohio, and other members of the House saw the regulations as circumventing one key tenet of community development block grants —

the right of communities to determine, within some broad categories, how they would spend their funds.

The community development act set out three broad purposes for the use of the money. The act provided that each community, in seeking the grants, must develop a program focused on projects that would: 1) benefit low or moderate income families; 2) aid in the prevention or elimination of slums or blight; or 3) meet any urgent community needs. *(Background, 1974 Almanac p. 345)*

Community development grants had been used for such things as housing rehabilitation, street repairs, parks and playgrounds, community facilities and other neighborhood conservation efforts.

The amendment adopted by the House committee prohibited HUD from disapproving a grant application simply because it gave more or less weight to one of the three spending priorities.

Sponsors of the amendment emphasized that they were in no way opposed to making projects for low and moderate income persons top priority. What they wanted, they said, was to ensure that local communities, and not HUD, made that determination.

"Secretary Harris is saying that she knows what is best. We are saying she doesn't," one committee source said.

Brown and several other Republicans on the committee went a step further in criticizing Harris. In minority views attached to the committee report, the group said that HUD issued a notice to its field offices three days after the community development amendment was adopted by the Housing Subcommittee, directing the offices how to implement the regulations.

"This notice is an affront to the committee and the CDBG program applicants and represents a level of second-guessing by HUD that is plainly inappropriate for the program and plainly inconsistent with the statute," the Republicans charged.

Further, they said, "HUD must learn that the basic constitutional separation of powers provides for Congress, not the executive, to legislate. If HUD desires to redirect the thrust of the CDBG program it should come to Congress and request a change in the law."

House Floor Action

The House passed the bill by a 270-26 vote July 21 after five days of debate. Floor action began June 23, continued June 28-29 and July 20, and was completed July 21. *(Vote 511, p. 146-H)*

Legislative Veto

Controversy centered on whether Congress should have veto power over regulations handed down by the Department of Housing and Urban Development. By a 244-140 vote, the House tacked a "one-house" veto provision on the bill. *(Vote 448, p. 128-H)*

The vote came just eight days after President Carter had sent a message to Congress in which he said he considered the legislative veto unconstitutional and would ignore it. *(Message text, p. 55-E)*

Sponsors initially proposed the amendment as a result of congressional irritation over several regulations proposed and adopted by HUD.

But the presidential message exacerbated feelings in the House, according to several members, and apparently counteracted some White House lobbying against the amendment. A day before the vote, the House leadership counted only 140-150 votes in support of the president.

As it turned out, Carter barely won majority support from his own party, with 137 Democrats voting against the veto amendment, and 118 in favor. Northern Democrats demonstrated the most loyalty, splitting 64-113 against the amendment. But Carter's fellow southern Democrats voted 54-24 in favor of the amendment. Republicans, displaying strong unity, backed the amendment by a 126-3 vote.

As approved by the House, the veto amendment required HUD to submit all housing and community development regulations to Congress, allowing either house 90 days to disapprove them. The amendment provided, however, that regulations would take effect if no committee of either chamber reported a resolution of disapproval within 60 days after the regulations were submitted to Congress. Garry Brown, R-Mich., said the amendment would not apply to setting Federal Housing Administration interest rates.

Arguing for his amendment, Brown contended that HUD was "one of the worst offenders" when it came to trying to undermine legislative intent. He cited the debate over the community development regulations as a "classic example" of HUD overstepping its bounds.

"The executive branch is only supposed to carry out the law, and should not use the regulation writing process to enter the legislative field," Brown declared.

Brown and other Republican supporters of the amendment also sought to gain some political mileage from a comment by House Majority Leader Jim Wright, D-Texas. The day after Carter sent his message to Congress opposing the legislative veto, *The New York Times* quoted Wright as saying the very possibility of a legislative veto "should serve as a brake on the overzealous administrator." Although the Democratic leader voted against the Brown amendment, his words were used as ammunition by amendment supporters.

Housing Subcommittee Chairman Thomas L. Ashley, D-Ohio, floor manager of the bill, led the opposition to the amendment, reminding Brown that HR 12433 already had provisions overturning existing HUD regulations considered by the committee to be improper.

"In my judgment this earlier approach suggested . . . is far more effective than the approach [legislative veto] now suggested," said Ashley, who described the amendment as a "classic case of overkill."

Ashley maintained that requiring HUD to submit regulations to Congress for review raised "very troubling constitutional questions."

Ashley and other opponents of the amendment also said requiring congressional review of regulations would drastically increase paperwork and add "one more element of red tape and delay into the already tedious rulemaking process."

Amendments Accepted

In other action on HR 12433 June 28-29, the House adopted amendments:

- By Charles E. Grassley, R-Iowa, and Wes Watkins, D-Okla., to prohibit HUD from establishing requirements for allocation of community development funds that would limit or exclude access by small communities, unless exclusions or limitations were proscribed by law. Voice vote.

Grassley and Watkins contended that HUD had paid little attention in the past to the community development needs of small cities and towns. Grassley said the amendment was a "starting point" in getting other federal agencies to treat small towns fairly.

• By Brown, Mich., to prohibit HUD from awarding technical assistance grants under the community development program directly to community organizations. The amendment would allow community groups to receive grants only if the money were passed through the local government unit. Voice vote.

• By Ashley, delaying for one year federal housing assistance to uninsured state and low income housing programs. Voice vote.

• By Claude Pepper, D-Fla., to earmark $12 million in Section 202 housing for the elderly for special demonstration projects to develop security measures for elderly public housing. Voice vote.

• By Leon E. Panetta, D-Calif., to establish a special Section 8 demonstration to determine how to get more owners to participate in the rental subsidy program. Voice vote.

• By Bill Green, R-N.Y., to raise the mortgage ceilings for the Section 221 (d) 3 program (mortgage insurance to finance rental or cooperative multifamily housing built by public, non-profit sponsors for low and moderate income households). The amendment would increase the amount of a mortgage which HUD could insure to between $18,450 and $41,494, depending upon the number of units. The new ceilings would be the same as the current mortgage ceilings for Section 221(d) 4 housing, a similar program used by profit-motivated builders. Voice vote.

In action July 20-21 the House adopted amendments:

• By John J. Duncan, R-Tenn., to prevent Social Security cost-of-living increases from being counted as income in calculating rents in federally assisted housing. Duncan argued that Social Security recipients were unable to get any benefit from cost-of-living increases because every time they received an increase their rents were raised. Ashley argued against the amendment, saying the purpose of cost-of-living increases was to cover increased costs of basic needs, like shelter. Recorded vote, 256-38. *(Vote 510, p. 146-H)*

• By James J. Florio, D-N.J., to require the Federal Housing Administration (FHA), the Veterans Administration (VA) and other federal agencies that run housing programs to use the same forms in order to reduce government paperwork and red tape. The amendment also required various housing agencies to form an interagency task force, under the direction of the Office of Management and Budget (OMB), to implement paperwork and regulatory cost recommendations made by the Commission on Federal Paperwork. Voice vote. *(Paperwork commission recommendations, 1977 Almanac p. 748)*

Amendments Rejected

The House rejected the following amendments in voting June 28-29:

• By Robert W. Edgar, D-Pa., to allow community development funds to be used for mass transportation-related projects such as bus shelters. Standing vote, 2-15.

Edgar argued that since community development funds under existing law could be used for streets and parking lots, the funds also should be available for mass transit-related needs. Opponents said funds for bus shelters already were available through the Urban Mass Transit Administration (UMTA) in the Department of Transportation.

• By Tom Hagedorn, R-Minn., to allow non-profit, community organizations to pay below Davis-Bacon Act wage rates for federally assisted neighborhood housing rehabilitation projects. Recorded vote, 173-218. *(Vote 445, p. 126-H)*

Hagedorn argued that the Davis-Bacon Act, because it required paying high, prevailing wages on federally assisted housing, made it difficult for low-income organizations involved in neighborhood rehabilitation to operate. Opponents contended, however, that adoption of the amendment would result in low pay for black and other minority construction workers.

• By Cardiss Collins, D-Ill., to exempt the city of Chicago from a placement formula established under a federal district court decision. The formula prohibited HUD from contracting for new Section 8 construction unless 60 percent of the new units were built in the suburbs and 40 percent were built in the metropolitan area. Voice vote.

• By Millicent Fenwick, R-N.J., to place a ceiling of $100 per month per room for debt service and insurance on the rental subsidy for Section 8 housing. Standing vote, 12-21.

• By Marty Russo, D-Ill., to require all first-time purchasers of FHA-insured mortgages to receive pre-purchase counseling. Recorded vote, 93-285. *(Vote 449, p. 128-H)*

Russo argued that such counseling would cut down the number of loan defaults. But opponents of the amendment, led by Ashley, said that not all persons buying homes needed counseling. They also said HUD was conducting a study to determine how effective counseling actually is and urged Russo to wait until the study was completed.

The House rejected the following amendments July 20-21:

• By James Abdnor, R-S.D., that would have blocked HUD from reorganizing its field offices. Recorded vote, 133-160. *(Vote 508, p. 146-H)*

Abdnor, whose district included Rapid City, where HUD wanted to close an office, contended that the reorganization would not save money as HUD had argued and would make it harder for HUD to deliver services to rural areas.

"The rural areas of this country are getting tired of receiving the short end of the stick from HUD," Abdnor declared.

But Thomas L. Ashley, D-Ohio, chairman of the House Banking Subcommittee on Housing and floor manager of the bill, described the Abdnor amendment as a "flagrant attempt on the part of Congress to interfere with the clear authority of the secretary of HUD to manage and administer the department's field offices."

Ashley said it is a "natural political tendency to go through the accustomed blandishments" when a government reorganizes its offices but said reorganizations "are an effort to conserve money and to derive efficiency in organization and staff. That is why these changes take place."

• By Garry Brown, R-Mich., that would have eliminated a provision in HR 12433 designed to reduce property insurance rates in certain high-risk, urban areas. Recorded vote, 119-185. *(Vote 509, p. 146-H)*

The provision would bring property insurance rates issued under FAIR (Fair Access to Insurance Requirements) plans in line with rates set by principal state-licensed rating organizations for essential property in the voluntary market. Brown argued that the federal government should not interfere with state regulation of the property insurance market. But sponsors of the provision argued that FAIR rates in several states that had FAIR plans were too high for people to afford and amounted to a form of insurance redlining.

Senate Committee Action

The Senate Banking, Housing and Urban Affairs Committee reported S 3084 (S Rept 95-871) May 15. The committee devoted substantial debate to determining proposed spending levels for various assisted housing programs.

Liberals on the committee, led by ranking Republican Edward W. Brooke, Mass., added, on a 9-8 vote, a package increasing authorization levels well above the administration's recommendations for the Section 8 rental housing program, the basic federal housing effort for low-income persons.

The administration had recommended new contract authority for the Section 8 program of $1,195,000,000 for fiscal 1979, enough for about 375,000 units. That recommendation required total budget authority of $24.6 billion to cover the "run out" costs of the program, which often extend as long as 40 years.

But the committee increased the Carter proposal, recommending new contract authority of $1,675,000,000, enough for about 450,000 units. The $1.6 billion in new authority would require total budget authority of about $38.9 billion to cover the run-out costs of the contracts.

The package of spending increases adopted by the committee also included $800 million in operating subsidies for public housing projects, an increase of $71 million above the administration's recommendation.

The committee also voted to establish a new $75 million program of supplementary rent subsidies for very poor tenants already living in federally assisted housing projects in order to reduce their rent to 25 percent of income. The aid would go to residents of about 250,000 units.

Senate Floor Action

The Senate began consideration of S 3084 July 19 and finished July 20, approving it by an 81-3 vote. *(Vote 230, p. 37-S)* Debate focused primarily on three issues — the legislative veto, authorization levels for assisted housing, and the urban development action grant program.

Veto Provision

The legislative veto provision, rejected 29-65, was proposed by Harrison Schmitt, R-N.M., who had carried on a running debate with HUD for nearly a year over a field reorganization planned by the agency. Schmitt was perturbed at HUD's intention to close an office in Albuquerque. *(Vote 228, p. 36-S)*

Schmitt, who during committee markup succeeded in tacking a provision to the bill that in effect would block the reorganization, did not mention his fight during floor debate over the veto provision. Instead, he argued that HUD had repeatedly used regulations to circumvent congressional intent.

"Of all the executive branch departments, I believe the Department of Housing and Urban Development is, unfortunately, one of the worst offenders of this usurpation of legislative power," Schmitt declared.

He asserted that giving either house of Congress the right to veto HUD regulations would make HUD bureaucrats more respectful of carrying out congressional mandates.

"The aim of this amendment is simply to require the department to write regulations which are an accurate representation of congressional intent, and I think the mere existence of legislative veto will insure that that happens. . . ." Schmitt said.

Proxmire and other opponents of the Schmitt amendment countered by saying that Congress should use existing oversight powers to monitor how a federal agency carries out congressional intent. If Congress feels the agency has not acted properly, opponents of the amendment argued, then it should simply pass new legislation.

Immersing itself in continuing review of regulations, argued Wendell H. Ford, D-Ky., "would inject the legislative branch into the day-to-day administrative and regulatory activities of those agencies which we created to administer the laws we wrote."

Spending Battle

The committee's decision to increase the spending levels led Proxmire and three other members to include a statement of additional views with the committee report criticizing the committee's recommendations.

Proxmire wasted little time once floor debate began July 19 in pointing out that he felt "very strongly" that the committee bill went too far in authorizing new spending.

"Inflation is clearly our No. 1 problem today. A higher level of federal spending contributes to that problem," Proxmire said.

But Brooke countered: "Although I recognize our responsibilities to hold down federal spending and sense the 'Proposition 13' fever which has taken hold in both houses of Congress, I strongly believe that housing for low-income families and the elderly is one national priority which should not be lightly disregarded in our rush to slice the federal budget."

The views of Proxmire and Brooke set the tone for a lengthy debate, with liberals like Edward M. Kennedy, D-Mass., and Harrison A. Williams Jr., D-N.J., joining Brooke in arguing for the committee bill.

The effort to trim the spending levels was led by Edmund S. Muskie, D-Maine, chairman of the Senate Budget Committee, and Lawton Chiles, D-Fla., a member of the committee.

Chiles sponsored the $8 billion reduction amendment eventually adopted by the Senate, but he had 10 cosponsors, including Proxmire and three Republican members of the Banking Committee — Henry Bellmon, Okla.; Richard G. Lugar, Ind., and Jake Garn, Utah. The amendment was adopted by a 60-21 vote. *(Vote 223, p. 36-S)*

Muskie and Chiles argued that the amendment would bring the authorization levels in line with the levels recommended by both Carter and Congress in its first budget resolution.

Muskie introduced a letter from Patricia Roberts Harris, the HUD secretary, in which she reiterated the administration's support for the lower spending levels.

"I believe that the budget requests submitted on behalf of this department are sound and fully justified, in light of the balance which must be struck between competing national priorities and the nation's housing needs. I have frequently stated that I shall oppose with equal vigor any efforts to disrupt that balance, either by adding to or reducing the level of funding we have requested. That continues to be my position," Harris said.

The letter, dated July 19, the day of the debate, was requested by Muskie.

Aside from the spending increases for fiscal 1979, Muskie argued that over the next five years the authorization bill would require budget authority of about $45 billion above the 5-year "mission targets" included in the first budget resolution.

In addition to reducing Section 8 spending ceilings to the level sought by the administration, the Chiles amendment reduced the operating subsidies for public housing to $729 million, and eliminated the $75 million new program of supplementary rent subsidies.

Explaining the decision to eliminate the new rent subsidy program, Chiles said it was "purely an income maintenance program."

"Creating a new categorical program of this type would be the opposite of welfare reform," Chiles said. "We believe this is just the sort of narrowly conceived program which the American people are complaining about. It has not been debated, and no one knows what it could ultimately cost."

Robert Morgan, D-N.C., a member of the Banking Committee, nearly succeeded in resolving the fight with a compromise proposal that called for spending levels of about $1.2 billion above the administration and budget resolution levels. Brooke and other backers of the increased funding, sensing a lack of support for their position, voted for the Morgan compromise, but it was rejected by a 42-47 vote. *(Vote 222, p. 36-S)*

Action Grant Change

John G. Tower, R-Texas, offered the amendment to allow cities with "pockets of poverty" to qualify for the $400-million urban development action grant program. The Carter administration opposed the amendment, but a coalition of Sun Belt senators of both parties provided enough votes to approve the change. The Senate defeated a similar amendment in 1977. *(1977 Almanac p. 135)*

Although many cities in Snow Belt states of the Northeast and Midwest could benefit from the amendment, the change would have greater impact in the Sun Belt states of the South and West.

The amendment changed the method of determining eligibility for the grant program. Under existing law, statistical information from an entire city was used to assess whether the city was "distressed" enough to qualify for a grant. The Tower amendment would allow a city to qualify if it had certain areas — defined as census tracts of at least 10,000 persons — that were judged to be "distressed."

The existing formula precluded newer, economically healthy cities from qualifying for the program. Backers of the existing formula said that was the way it should be, because the grant program was designed exclusively for economically distressed cities.

But critics of the formula argued that it did not deal fairly with cities, like Houston or Dallas, that, although healthy economically, still had "pockets of poverty" within their boundaries.

Proxmire, who opposed the Tower amendment, argued that broadening the eligibility standards would restrict HUD's policy of "targeting" action grants to the cities that needed the money most.

Nevertheless, the Tower amendment was adopted by a 47-38 vote. *(Vote 224, p. 36-S)*

In other major action, the Senate agreed by voice vote to add two pieces of Carter's urban package to the authorization bill. The urban proposals were the neighborhood self-help fund and the "livable cities" arts program. Authorization levels for the self-help fund were set at $15 million each for fiscal 1979 and 1980, the same amounts as requested by the administration, and $5 million for fiscal 1979 and $10 million for fiscal 1980 for the arts program. The administration had requested authorizations of $20 million each year for the arts program.

Other Amendments

The Senate also adopted amendments by:

- John A. Durkin, D-N.H., to promote the use of solar energy in federally subsidized housing by requiring HUD to develop solar energy guidelines for owners and local housing officials for the Section 8, 202 and 312 programs. Voice vote.
- William D. Hathaway, D-Maine, to insure that HUD does not discriminate against small cities in its community development programs. Voice vote.
- Howard M. Metzenbaum, D-Ohio, to remove from S 3084 a provision preventing state and local governments from including the value of interest reduction payments or subsidy assistance in assessing the value of multifamily housing projects for property tax purposes. The initial provision was included in S 3084 to counter an expected move in California to include federal assistance payments in the calculation of property tax value. But Metzenbaum said the California effort never materialized. Voice vote.
- Lloyd Bentsen, D-Texas, identical to Rep. Florio's amendment in the House requiring the FHA and VA to use the same forms in order to reduce government paperwork and red tape. Voice vote.
- Chiles, D-Fla., to require the HUD secretary to analyze the amount of paperwork expected to result from new regulations and to publish the results in the *Federal Register*. Roll-call, 93-0. *(Vote 227, p. 36-S)*
- John Sparkman, D-Ala., to exempt the sale of fully improved lots developed in compliance with subdivision regulations of the municipality or county in which the subdivision is located from the filing and disclosure requirements of the Interstate Land Sales Full Disclosure Act. Voice vote.
- Sparkman, D-Ala., to allow FHA-insured mortgage refinancing of hospitals along the same lines as FHA-insured mortgage refinancing for multifamily housing projects. Voice vote.
- Sparkman, D-Ala., to allow HUD in carrying out demonstration projects to study the feasibility of renewing older housing by converting it to cooperatives or condominiums. Voice vote.
- Sparkman, D-Ala., to make Jonathan, Minn., eligible for assistance under HUD's new communities program. Voice vote.
- Javits, R-N.Y. to make state-insured housing projects operated under HUD's Section 236 program also eligible for operating subsidies under the "troubled projects" program. Voice vote.
- Javits, R-N.Y. to increase mortgage limits for rent and cooperative housing built under HUD's Section 221(d)3

program. The amendment would increase the amount of a mortgage which HUD could insure to between $21,900 and $43,158, depending upon the number of units. Voice vote.

- Javits, R-N.Y. to increase from 10 to 20 percent the number of single, non-elderly persons who may occupy public housing and Section 8 housing in a particular project. Voice vote.
- Pete V. Domenici, R-N.M., to allow sponsors of Section 202 housing for the elderly to participate in the congregate services program. Voice vote.
- Robert Morgan, D-N.C., to require the secretary of agriculture to complete a study on problems associated with remote title claims in rural areas by March 1, 1979. Voice vote.
- Dole, R-Kan., to require HUD to conduct a cost benefit analysis of any department reorganizations of field offices before carrying out the reorganization. Voice vote.
- William Proxmire, D-Wis., to continue an existing requirement that the president report to Congress each year on housing construction. Voice vote.

The Senate defeated amendments proposed by:

- Harrison Schmitt, R-N.M., that would have required HUD to conduct an economic impact statement of proposed regulations and publish the statement in the *Federal Register*. Defeated by a roll-call vote of 36-57. *(Vote 226, p. 36-S)*
- Robert P. Griffin, R-Mich., that in effect would have blocked efforts by HUD to prod largely white, middle-class communities into increasing their number of low- and moderate-income residents. Defeated by a roll-call vote of 34-50. *(Vote 229, p. 37-S)*

Conference Report

Conferees reached agreement on the final version of S 3084 and reported it Oct. 12 (H Rept 95-1792).

Community Development

Both the bill and the conference report made it clear that the HUD secretary could not reject community development grant applications simply because they might focus more attention on any one of the three main purposes of the community development program — projects that 1) benefit low or moderate income families, 2) aid in the prevention or elimination of slums or blight, or 3) meet any urgent community needs.

The final language represented a defeat for HUD Secretary Harris, who sought to use the threat of rejecting community development grants (and the loss of money) to prod communities into channeling more money to projects that, in HUD's view, had an immediate benefit for low and moderate income families and neighborhoods.

House conferees argued that they did not oppose making such projects the top priority of the community development program. But they said that decision should be made at the local level, by the community itself.

The final language adopted by the conferees in their report still gave HUD the power to reject community development grant applications, but spelled out the permissible grounds for rejection.

Conferees accepted a House amendment designed to prohibit HUD from using the threat of withholding community development funds to prod communities into increasing housing opportunities for the poor.

Resolving a long-simmering debate over how a community should calculate its housing needs for its community development application, the amendment made it clear that housing assistance plans only need include those persons expected to reside as a result of existing or projected employment opportunities in the community and elderly expected to reside in the community regardless of their employment situation.

That provision was designed to block efforts by HUD to push largely white suburban communities to increase their housing for the poor by using a "fair share" concept based upon the number of low and moderate income persons living in the entire metropolitan area.

House conferees agreed to language in the conference report making it clear that the amendment was not intended to pre-empt a state or judicial requirement that a community undertake a greater share of the responsibility in meeting the housing needs of the poor.

Legislative Veto

House conferees agreed to drop a "legislative veto" provision added during floor action after Senate conferees agreed to a review procedure for HUD regulations.

Under the procedure, both the House and Senate Banking committees were to have an opportunity to review proposed HUD regulations. The procedure also required that a proposed regulation could not take effect for 90 days if either committee reported a resolution of disapproval or actual legislation.

In their report, the conferees indicated that the review procedure was designed for policy matters and "did not include the principle of legislative veto of administrative actions."

That view was reflected elsewhere in the final version of S 3084, as conferees removed a Senate amendment that would have blocked a HUD reorganization of its field offices.

Action Grants

In a victory for the "Snow Belt" states of the Northeast and Midwest, the conferees also rejected another Senate amendment that would have allowed prosperous cities with "pockets of poverty" within their boundaries to qualify for urban development action grants. The amendment was backed primarily by "Sun Belt" senators angry that cities in their states, because of overall economic health, were not eligible for the grants.

S 3084 did require HUD to study the problems of prosperous cities in meeting the needs of distressed areas within their boundaries. ∎

Urban Public Works

Sharing the fate of other major elements of the Carter administration's urban policy package, legislation authorizing a new round of federally supported public works projects did not clear the 95th Congress.

The proposal, which advanced only as far as approval by a House subcommittee, was finally dropped in the face of strong Senate opposition to its possible inflationary impact.

As originally proposed, the public works section of the administration urban package would have authorized $3 billion, over three years, for "soft," labor-intensive public works projects employing large numbers of the low-income unemployed.

The bill was substantially modified by the only congressional panel that did approve it, the House Public Works Subcommittee on Economic Development, which added another $2 billion a year for capital-intensive projects similar to those authorized by Congress in 1976 and 1977. *(Box, below)*

Administration Proposal

The administration proposal (S 3186, HR 12993) called for spending $3 billion — $1 billion each in fiscal 1979, 1980 and 1981 — for so-called "soft" public works projects like renovation and maintenance of public parks, government offices and schools. The program would be "labor-intensive," that is, between 50 and 80 percent of the cost of each project would be spent for labor. Further, about half of the 50,000 jobs the administration said would be created through the program were to be earmarked for low-income, unskilled, unemployed persons.

The "labor-intensive" focus, and the emphasis on hiring unskilled, low-income workers, represented a basic change from the local public works program enacted by Congress in 1976 and expanded in 1977. That program, which pumped $6 billion in federal funds into the economy, was "capital-intensive," focusing on major construction of new projects, and did not require the use of large numbers of unskilled, long-term unemployed workers. *(Urban policy message, p. 45-E)*

House Subcommittee Action

The House Public Works Subcommittee on Economic Development endorsed the "soft" public works program by making it part of a larger public works spending proposal opposed by the president.

Instead of $1 billion sought by the administration for fiscal 1979, the subcommittee approved spending $3 billion, with $2 billion of that to be used to provide a third round of "capital-intensive" local public works projects.

Administration officials opposed continuation of the "capital-intensive" public works program on the grounds that its emphasis on new, major construction was highly inflationary.

But the subcommittee, which was lobbied vigorously by the nation's construction industry, strongly favored a continuation of the current program, and doubted whether the Carter proposal would work. As a result, the subcommittee offered what it considered to be a compromise — a mix of "hard" and "soft" public works programs.

"I think this is working toward a reasonable compromise," said Subcommittee Chairman Robert A. Roe, D-N.J.

Without the additional spending for "hard" public works, Roe said, the administration proposal had little chance of winning congressional approval.

The administration was not happy with the subcommittee compromise.

"The $3 billion is not in accord with the president's program, it is $2 billion over what the president asked," said Robert T. Hall, assistant secretary of commerce for economic development.

The subcommittee drafted its own public works bill (HR 11610) after negotiations with the Carter administration apparently failed to produce a measure acceptable to both sides. Those negotiations included at least two White House meetings involving Carter, Roe and other key members of the Public Works Committee.

The subcommittee met Aug. 15 — two days before the House recessed for Labor Day — to mark up the bill.

The subcommittee proposal called for $2 billion for fiscal 1979 and $2 billion for fiscal 1980 to be spent under the existing local public works program. Under the program, money was distributed to local governments and other public agencies for various capital improvements, such as school buildings, municipal offices, streets and sewers.

The subcommittee also agreed to add another $1 billion for each of the two fiscal years for "soft" public works projects, such as renovation, maintenance and rehabilitation of public buildings, parks and schools. For the "soft" public works program, the subcommittee left intact some key provisions proposed by the administration. At least 50 percent of those employed on the projects would come from the ranks of the hard-core, long-term unemployed. Each project also would require between 50 and 80 percent of the money to be spent on labor costs.

$6 Billion Worth of Projects

Congress enacted the first round of countercyclical public works spending in 1976, providing $2 billion for fiscal 1977 for a variety of quick-starting state and local public works projects across the country.

The program, considered a key element in the Democratic Party's economic recovery plan, was enacted by overriding a veto by President Ford. *(Background, 1976 Almanac p. 68)*

In 1977, Congress provided an additional $4 billion for fiscal 1978 as part of President Carter's economic stimulus package. *(1977 action, 1977 Almanac p. 112)*

The program initially was intended as a countercyclical measure focusing primarily on the building trades and construction industry. Unemployment among construction workers had soared to nearly 20 percent during the 1974-75 recession.

In 1978, in light of the general economic recovery, the Carter administration proposed altering the program to focus on the so-called structurally unemployed. And, reflecting concern about the potential inflationary impact of new construction, the administration proposed an emphasis on less costly, "labor-intensive" projects involving rehabilitation, maintenance and renovation.

Officials in the Department of Commerce estimated that as of July 1978 at least $3 billion of the $6 billion appropriated under rounds one and two had actually been spent, with most of the remainder obligated for other projects. Projects funded under rounds one and two included more than 2,500 water, sewer and utility facilities, more than 2,000 transportation projects (including street and bridge rebuilding), about 650 police, fire and other public safety facilities, and nearly 250 hospital, clinic, nursing home and other health facilities.

The administration had proposed a three-year program of "soft" public works, but Roe said the subcommittee cut the entire public works program back to two years as part of its compromise.

Senate Situation

In the Senate, meanwhile, there was little interest in either "hard" or "soft" public works spending for fiscal 1979.

Quentin N. Burdick, D-N.D., chairman of the Senate Environment and Public Works Subcommittee on Regional and Community Development, ended a markup session Aug. 22 without taking action on the Carter bill (S 3186) because, he told reporters later, he did not have the votes to approve the bill.

"The situation is very iffy at the present time," Burdick said. "Right now we're trying to get the votes."

The Carter administration already had proposed some changes in the program for the first year to provide for a smoother transition from "hard" to "soft" public works.

Amendments submitted to the Senate subcommittee called for reducing the percentage of hard-core, long-term unemployed workers required on each job from 50 percent to 25 percent, and reducing the percentage of money for each project earmarked for labor costs from 50-80 percent to 40 percent. The administration said the initial provisions of the bill would apply in the second and third years.

In addition to lining up the votes needed to approve the bill, Burdick and other supporters of the public works proposal also needed to amend the Senate version of the second fiscal 1979 budget resolution to include funding for local public works. As reported by the Senate Budget Committee Aug. 18, the resolution (S Con Res 104 — S Rept 95-1124) did not allow for any spending for either a third round of the current public works program or "soft" public works during fiscal 1979.

The chairman of the Budget Committee, Sen. Edmund S. Muskie, D-Maine, opposed additional public works spending as unnecessary because of the general economic recovery in the past two years. In a letter to Burdick, Muskie said there was already evidence that strong activity in the construction industry was beginning to fuel inflation, particularly in the cost of lumber and other building materials.

Muskie further argued that the changes proposed by the administration to reduce the "labor-intensity" requirements for the first year of the program would turn the program into a third round of "hard" public works and defeat the purpose of the initial program proposed by the administration.

Budget Defeat

House Democratic leaders gave up on any sort of new public works program for the year after the Senate voted against the idea by a wide margin.

By a 63-21 vote the Senate Sept. 14 went on record as opposing inclusion of new public works spending in the second budget resolution. The $2 billion for public works projects in the House-passed budget resolution had produced a deadlock in conference committee deliberations on the resolution.

Although the budget conference report was ambiguous on the issue, House Speaker Thomas P. O'Neill Jr., D-Mass., yielded in the face of the Senate opposition, "We've agreed that we'd drop that until next year," he said. *(Budget resolution, p. 43)*

Countercyclical Aid Dies; Key Urban Program

Despite intense lobbying by the White House and others, Congress failed to extend an aid program viewed as vital to President Carter's urban policy.

The House leadership decided not to bring up a two-year extension of countercyclical revenue sharing (HR 2852) after opponents threatened to conduct a parliamentary slowdown on the last day of the 95th Congress.

"That was the one sacrificed to get the other things done," said Rep. Richard Bolling, D-Mo.

The lack of House action thus let lapse a program first established in 1976 to provide short-term financial aid to cities and towns as a buffer against the effects of the 1974-75 recession on tax revenues and operating budgets. *(1976 Almanac p. 68; 1977 Almanac p. 110)*

In 1978, despite differences over some key details, the Carter administration and congressional backers both proposed altering the program to channel money primarily to cities with severe, long-term financial problems.

For many cities and counties across the country, the lack of congressional action was expected to force some budget-tightening. The last version of HR 2852 would have pumped about $500 million into local government treasuries in fiscal 1979 and $340 million in fiscal 1980.

"They're going to have to fire some people," declared Tom Cochran, deputy director of the U.S. Conference of Mayors, in assessing the impact on cities.

Some big "Snow Belt" cities in the Northeast and Midwest were hit the hardest. New York City, for example, would have received the largest amount of money under the program — $42.4 million in fiscal 1979 and $43 million in fiscal 1980, according to Treasury Department figures. Chicago would have received the second largest amount, $10.8 million in fiscal 1979 and $11 million in fiscal 1980. Altogether, about 12,000 cities and towns would have received money under the countercyclical measure.

Carter Proposal

Carter urged Congress in his urban policy message March 27 to replace the existing Anti-Recession Fiscal Assistance program, which was to expire Sept. 30, 1978, with a program aimed at cities and towns suffering from long-term economic problems. The existing program, commonly known as countercyclical revenue sharing, was enacted in 1976 and extended in 1977 as a means of providing short-term financial relief to state and local governments suffering from the effects of the 1974-75 recession.

"While the fiscal condition of many state and local governments has improved dramatically over the last three years, many cities and communities are still experiencing severe problems," Carter said in his urban message. "These cities and communities require fiscal assistance

Carter's 1978 Urban Program...

Following is a listing of various bills considered part of the Carter administration's urban program, and how each fared on Capitol Hill in 1978. *(Text, p. 45-E)*

• **Public Works.** A three-year, $3 billion program of labor-intensive public works projects to rehabilitate and renovate public facilities (HR 12993, S 3186). Considered in subcommittees in both the House and Senate, but stiff resistance, particularly in the Senate, led backers to put off consideration until 1978. *(Story, p. 311)*

• **Employer Tax Credits.** Tax credits for employers who hire low-income, unemployed youths. The administration initially proposed that the credit be up to $2,000 per employee for the first year of employment, and up to $1,500 for the second year. Passed, after alteration by tax-writing committees. The final version of the tax bill (HR 13511) included a "targeted jobs credit" of up to $3,000 per employee for the first year of employment, and $1,500 per employee for the second year. *(Tax bill, p. 219)*

• **Development Bank.** A National Development Bank, to be run on an inter-agency basis by a board composed of the secretaries of the Departments of Housing and Urban Development (HUD), Commerce and the Treasury, to guarantee loans totaling $11 billion during fiscal 1979-81 to businesses located in both urban or rural "distressed areas" (HR 13230, S 3233). No action.

• **Investment Tax.** A special tax credit for companies investing in "distressed areas" of 5 percent above the 10 percent investment tax credit allowed on the purchase of new machinery and equipment. The administration also proposed extending the credit to rehabilitation of existing plants and equipment. The tax bill included an expansion of the credit for building rehabilitation, but the 5 percent "differential" was rejected.

• **Fiscal Assistance.** A new aid program for cities with long-term financial problems, to replace the countercyclical revenue sharing program enacted by Congress in 1976 (HR 2852). Passed by Senate, after various changes, including reduction in cost to $500 million for fiscal 1979 from initial $1 billion. Rule granted by House Rules Committee Oct. 14, but never called up for floor action. *(Story, p. 313)*

• **Welfare Reform.** Carter also proposed a change in the fiscal relief portion of the administration's welfare reform bill to allow immediate financial aid to the states. As initially drafted, the reform bill would not provide relief to states until 1981. The administration's welfare reform bill was the subject of lengthy hearings in both the House and Senate, and a special House subcommittee approved a slightly revised version. But no further action was taken. In its final accounting of urban legislation, the administration did not list welfare reform. *(Story, p. 600)*

• **Housing Loans.** An increase of $150 million for fiscal 1979 for low-interest housing rehabilitation loans under the so-called Section 312 program. Congress approved an increase in the authorization of $150 million and in the actual appropriation of $120 million. The authorization was included in the fiscal 1979 housing bill (S 3084). *(Story, p. 303)*

• **Social Services.** An increase of $150 million in the ceiling for Title XX social service grants. Congress approved a larger increase, raising the ceiling to $2.9 billion from $2.5 billion for fiscal 1979 only. The increase was included as part of HR 13511.

• **Volunteers.** A $40 million neighborhood volunteer corps, to be run by ACTION, to create a pool of professionals such as lawyers, architects, planners and others with specialized skills available to help neighborhood renewal programs. Passed by the Senate after the authorization was scaled down, but never considered by the House. Proposal was included in reauthorization legislation for ACTION (HR 11922, S 2617). Measure expected to be considered in 1979. *(ACTION, HEW chapter)*

from the federal government, if they are to avoid severe service cutbacks or tax increases." *(Text, p. 45-E)*

Carter proposed spending $1.04 billion in fiscal 1979 and $1 billion in fiscal 1980.

Changes in Existing Program

Carter proposed several major changes in the current fiscal aid program

State Exclusion. Under the plan, state governments would no longer receive the one-third share of funds they received under the countercyclical program. In proposing that change, the administration argued that the financial condition of state governments had improved to the point where they no longer needed countercyclical dollars.

Dual Formula. The administration proposed altering the eligibility formula in order to "target" funds to the most "distressed" cities.

The countercyclical program went into action when the national unemployment rate rose above 6 percent. In order to receive money, cities had to have unemployment rates above 4.5 percent.

The Carter plan proposed eliminating the 6 percent national "trigger" and leaving the 4.5 percent local unemployment rate as the main eligibility requirement.

In addition, the administration proposed an alternative formula, making it possible for governmental units also to qualify for aid if they had growth rates below the national average during the last five years in two of the following three categories: per capita income, population or employment.

In proposing the alternative formula, the administration argued that unemployment data was not reliable for small towns and rural areas. The second formula, the administration said, was designed to be "sensitive" to "distress" in those areas.

Aid Ceiling. The administration also proposed limiting the amount of money any city could receive under the program. The "cap" would be the amount of money a city

...How It Fared on Capitol Hill

• **Neighborhood Arts.** A "Livable Cities" program to stimulate cultural arts programs in urban communities and neighborhoods. Passed as part of the fiscal 1979 housing bill (S 3084) after authorization scaled down to $5 million for fiscal 1979 from initial proposal of $20 million.

• **Neighborhood Self Help.** A "Neighborhood Self-Help" program authorized at $15 million for fiscal 1979 to provide grants and other assistance to neighborhood organizations for various housing, economic development and other conservation and revitalization programs in low- and moderate-income neighborhoods. Also included in the fiscal 1979 housing bill.

• **Urban Affairs.** An urban parks and recreation program of matching grants to local governments for urban parks and recreation areas. Included in the omnibus parks bill (S 791). Final version authorized $150 million annually for fiscal 1979-82. *(Parks bill, Energy/Environment chapter)*

• **Mass Transit.** An urban mass transit program authorizing $200 million annually for fiscal 1979-83 in aid for urban areas to connect bus and transit lines and to fund economic development projects adjacent to mass transit operations. Included in HR 11733, the main highway bill passed by the 95th Congress. *(Highway bill, p. 536)*

• **Inner-City Health.** Inner-city health spending authorization of $50 million for fiscal 1979 for community health clinics and primary care centers in needy communities. Included in an omnibus health services and centers reauthorization (S 2474). *(Health bill, p. 611)*

• **Education.** Increased federal aid under Title I of the Elementary and Secondary Education Act (ESEA) for cities and other areas with high concentrations of low-income families. Congress approved the administration proposal of a $600 million increase in the Title I authorization, $400 million of which was to be used for aid to cities and other areas with high concentrations of poor families. The administration submitted the ESEA proposal before the urban message, but it subsequently included the spending proposal in its catalogue of urban legislation. *(ESEA extension, p. 557)*

• **Consumer Bank.** A consumer cooperative bank to provide credit, equity and technical assistance to consumer cooperatives. The administration initially opposed formation of the bank when it was first proposed in 1977, but later switched and included it as part of its urban package. Congress approved the proposal (HR 2777) in 1978. *(p. 521)*

• **Crime Prevention.** An increase of $10 million for fiscal 1979 for the Law Enforcement Assistance Administration (LEAA) to develop neighborhood crime prevention programs. Although included in the urban message, the administration later said the proposal would be considered in 1979 as part of its reorganization plan for the LEAA.

• **State Incentive Grants.** A $400 million, two-year program of grants to states to encourage the development of urban revitalization programs at the state level. Hearings on the legislation (S 3209, HR 12893) were held in both the House and Senate, but no action was taken.

• **CETA.** Reauthorization of the Comprehensive Employment and Training Act (CETA). Congress approved reauthorization legislation (S 2570) Oct. 15. Although not a part of the urban message, the administration included the CETA program in its catalogue of urban bills. The measure channeled millions of dollars for public sector jobs into the nation's major urban areas. *(CETA, p. 287)*

• **New York City Loans.** Approval of New York City loan guarantees. The legislation (HR 12426) authorized the secretary of the Treasury to guarantee up to $1.7 billion in loans to New York City for up to 15 years. Although not a part of the urban message, the administration, which backed the measure, also included the New York City legislation in its urban package. *(Story, p. 258)*

received under the existing countercyclical program. Administration officials cited budget restraints and a desire not to increase dependency on the federal government in explaining the need for a ceiling.

House Subcommittee Action

The House Intergovernmental Relations Subcommittee Aug. 2 voted 7-6 to postpone indefinitely consideration of HR 12293, the proposed Supplementary Fiscal Assistance Act. The measure, which would parcel out $1.04 billion in fiscal 1979 and another $1 billion in fiscal 1980 to "distressed" cities, would replace the existing Anti-Recession Fiscal Assistance program.

The vote came after less than 35 minutes of debate and drew angry criticism from supporters of some form of financial help to cities with long-term economic programs.

The Carter proposal, which would distribute millions of dollars to many of the largest cities in the country — cities that had become dependent on current anti-recession funds to fill gaps in the budgets — was in trouble long before the subcommittee met Aug. 2 to mark up the measure.

Back in May, L.H. Fountain, D-N.C., the subcommittee chairman, and several other members, attacked the methods used to decide whether cities were suffering from "distress" and the formula used to parcel out the money. Some members were irked by the fact that some wealthy suburban communities would receive money under the Carter proposal. Moreover, Fountain, a conservative lawmaker with a largely rural constituency, has never been sympathetic to urban fiscal aid.

Finally, while the subcommittee did have some members who supported urban aid, it did not have any members whose districts included big cities in deep fiscal trouble.

Supporters of providing some form of financial assistance realized that, and were prepared to push for an amendment designed to get the bill to the full House Government Operations Committee. Although the committee's chairman, Jack Brooks, D-Texas, had also opposed fiscal assistance, the committee itself was considered more sympathetic than the subcommittee.

Aid backers also turned to House Speaker Thomas P. O'Neill Jr., D-Mass., for some additional help. O'Neill, Frank Horton, R-N.Y., the ranking Republican member of the full committee, and 42 other House members signed a letter urging Fountain to "act in such a way as to permit the full committee to work further on this important issue."

The letter steered clear of endorsing the Carter proposal, focusing instead on the need to continue providing aid to cities that had not shared in the general recovery from the 1974-75 recession.

But the letter apparently had little impact. Before one backer of continued aid, John W. Wydler, R-N.Y., had a chance to offer an amendment, Elliott H. Levitas, D-Ga. moved to postpone consideration of HR 12293 indefinitely. That motion, which was not debatable, effectively cut off any possibility of offering any amendments to the measure.

Wydler and other supporters appealed to Fountain to allow further debate and amendments. "I feel the procedure is just outrageous," snapped Les Aspin, D-Wis., a supporter of the Carter bill.

Aspin reminded Fountain that the subcommittee rarely had followed such a formal procedure, and normally had allowed amendments and substantial debate before voting. Fountain agreed that normally the subcommittee was not so formal, but, he added, "no amount of tinkering can save this piece of legislation."

The subcommittee then approved Levitas' motion by a 7-6 vote. Joining Levitas were Fountain, Don Fuqua, D-Fla.; Glenn English, D-Okla.; John E. Cunningham, R-Wash.; Clarence J. Brown, R-Ohio; and Brooks. Voting against the motion were Aspin, Wydler, Horton and Henry A. Waxman, D-Calif.; John W. Jenrette Jr., D-S.C.; and Michael T. Blouin, D-Iowa.

Aspin later told a reporter that he felt Fountain behaved in an "extremely insulting, and inexcusable manner" by limiting debate and amendments.

Executive Orders

President Carter Aug. 16 signed four executive orders, all designed to put existing federal resources — money, people and programs — to work where possible on behalf of urban areas.

The orders:

- Created an Interagency Coordinating Council to eliminate conflicts between federal agencies in operating urban programs. The council, headed by Jack H. Watson Jr., secretary to the Cabinet and assistant to the president for intergovernmental affairs, had actually been functioning since March.
- Required the General Services Administration, the procuring agency for goods and services, to give priority to suppliers operating in areas of high unemployment.
- Required all federal agencies, including the GSA, to give priority consideration to central city areas in choosing sites for federal offices and facilities.
- Established a process whereby the Office of Management and Budget, in conjunction with various agencies, would analyze proposed new federal programs for their potential impact on urban areas.

Senate Committee Compromise

Following its rejection by the House subcommittee, the countercyclical aid bill was revived, in modified form, by the Senate Finance Committee and substituted for the text of an unrelated House-passed bill.

Prodded by Chairman Russell B. Long, D-La., the committee Aug. 10 adopted a compromise proposal aimed at picking up more support among members of Congress from the Sun Belt states of the South and West, while still retaining the support of the administration and big city mayors.

The Finance Committee compromise (HR 2852) would continue the existing anti-recession fiscal assistance program — commonly known as countercyclical revenue sharing — for two years, through fiscal 1980.

The funding also would remain the same. As long as national unemployment was 6 percent or more, money would be distributed to states and cities that had unemployment rates above 4.5 percent. The program would provide $125 million per quarter plus an additional $30 million for each tenth of a percentage point unemployment exceeded 6 percent. The actual amount of aid would be computed on the basis of a state or city's general revenue sharing allocation and the degree of unemployment above 4.5 percent.

The Senate proposal would make one change in the existing program. Unemployment figures for two quarters, rather than for one, would be used in computing the national unemployment rate. Thus, unemployment would have to fall below 6 percent for two consecutive quarters (six months) for aid to stop. That change was designed to give the program more stability by preventing the aid spigot from shutting off every time the unemployment rate dropped slightly below 6 percent for one or two months at a time.

The Senate compromise contained a second program designed to keep aid flowing to states and cities with higher unemployment rates once the national rate dropped below 6 percent. The second program would keep aid flowing to those states and cities with unemployment rates above 4.5 percent as long as the national rate was between 5 and 6 percent. States would get one-third of the money available under the program, although they could not receive more than they received under the existing program. The alternative program would cost an estimated $650 million in fiscal 1979.

Key Changes

The compromise bill was somewhat different from the measure proposed by the Carter administration. For one thing, the administration sought to remove the "national trigger" from the program, allowing cities and towns to continue receiving aid as long as their unemployment rates exceeded 4.5 percent.

But drafters of the compromise — including Sens. William D. Hathaway and Edmund S. Muskie, both Maine Democrats, and Daniel Patrick Moynihan, D-N.Y. — wanted to preserve the "countercyclical" nature of the program and thus insisted that a national trigger be retained.

Despite initial opposition by the administration, state governments would also continue to receive money under the Senate compromise. The administration bill removed state governments from the aid program on the grounds that for the most part states had budget surpluses and did not need continued aid. The National Governors' Association disputed the administration's contention, and lobbied vigorously to remain in the program.

The compromise also scaled down the size of the program, reducing the Carter administration proposal to spend $1.04 billion for fiscal 1979 and $1 billion for fiscal 1980 to $650 million for each of the two fiscal years.

Dual Formulas

Lloyd Bentsen, D-Texas, raised a critical issue shortly after the Finance Committee began reviewing the proposal drafted by Hathaway and the other senators. Reciting a complaint made by other Sun Belt members during congressional debate on other urban aid programs, Bentsen argued that the Hathaway-Moynihan measure did not give equitable treatment to Sun Belt cities, like Houston, which had "pockets of poverty" within their midsts but did not qualify for aid because their overall tax base was continually expanding and thus in healthy financial shape.

Bentsen cited the 5th ward in Houston, which had several hundred thousand residents, as an example of a "pocket of poverty." That area, he said, was bigger than many Northeastern cities. But because Houston had been able to annex its suburbs, it had a strong tax base, and its unemployment rate was low. That, he said, blocked it from receiving fiscal aid.

Some advocates of countercyclical revenue sharing had argued that cities like Houston did not need the federal aid precisely because they were able to expand their tax bases and thus had additional sources of revenue available. Furthermore, they argued, countercyclical revenue sharing was not supposed to be a "poverty program."

However, philosophy took second place to politics during the committee session. Sponsors of the fiscal aid felt they needed Bentsen's support to get the measure favorably reported, and thus accepted a formula change offered by Long and backed by Bentsen.

Long argued that "no formula is perfect" and said his proposal, because it would result in increased funds for some states, had a better chance of winning congressional approval "for the simple reason that they [the states] would get more money." Adoption of the formula change was necessary, Long said, "if we are going to pass this bill."

The committee eventually agreed to adopt the Long-Bentsen approach, which called for two formulas to be used in determining how much aid each state and its cities would receive. Whichever formula produced the most money for each state and its cities would be used for those jurisdictions.

One formula was the existing one used to allocate countercyclical aid and was based on a state's general revenue sharing allotment and its degree of unemployment. The other formula added by Long and Bentsen would allow allocations for countercyclical aid to be based solely on a state's revenue sharing allotment.

The second formula would increase aid to many Sun Belt states of the South and West, where unemployment was not as great as in Snow Belt states.

Initially, the dual formula would have resulted in a loss of some money for some states, since adjustments would have had to be made when the second formula resulted in a state getting more money than it would have received under the existing counterycyclical formula.

But Long quickly solved that problem. It was "all right with me if we want to add more money" so no state's allocation would be cut back, he said.

The committee agreed, voting 10-5 to raise the authorization from $500 million to $650 million, the amount committee staffers estimated would be needed for each state to receive the maximum amount of money allowed under the dual formulas.

The Long-Bentsen approach drew some criticism. "I think the solution isn't any solution," said John C. Danforth, R-Mo., who argued for a highly targeted approach that channeled aid only to those states and cities with unemployment above 7 percent. Gaylord Nelson, D-Wis., also expressed concern about the second formula.

The committee also accepted one other change pushed by Long to make the bill more acceptable politically. The initial Hathaway-Moynihan draft would have limited aid under the second program to cities and states with unemployment rates above 6 percent. That was changed to 4.5 percent.

The Finance Committee filed its report on HR 2852 Sept. 7 (S Rept 95-1179).

Senate Floor Action

The Senate passed HR 2852 by a 44-8 vote Sept. 23. *(Vote 396, p. 59-S)*

Passage followed rejection, by a 22-30 vote, of an amendment by Lawton Chiles, D-Fla., that would have eliminated the supplementary aid program, thus rendering extension of the program though fiscal 1979-80 virtually meaningless since unemployment was expected to be below 6 percent during fiscal 1979-80. *(Vote 394, p. 59-S)*

The Senate made several significant changes in the bill as reported by the Finance Committee, adopting by voice vote an amendment by John C. Danforth, R-Mo., that reduced the cost of the aid program by about $310 million for fiscal 1979-80 and revised the distribution formula and eligibility requirements in order to funnel aid only to the most financially pressed cities.

Accepting the Danforth amendment, Daniel Patrick Moynihan, D-N.Y., the chief sponsor of HR 2852, declared, "The program will be diminished. I think it is significantly cut back. But it is, if I am not mistaken, consistent with the mood of the Senate today, and in the circumstances I feel the appropriate thing to do is to respond to the mood of the Senate."

Danforth Amendment

The Danforth amendment substantially revised the aid bill as reported by the Finance Committee, altering one key requirement of the existing countercyclical program and rewriting basic elements in the proposed supplementary aid program designed to keep money flowing to "distressed" cities when the countercyclical spigot was turned off.

First, the Danforth amendment raised the eligibility requirement for the existing countercyclical aid program, requiring state and local governments to have unemployment rates above 6 percent in order to receive money. The existing law called for unemployment rates above 4.5 percent.

The Danforth amendment also rewrote the supplementary aid proposal, eliminating state governments, raising the unemployment rate requirement from 4.5 percent to in excess of 6 percent, and eliminating the alternative formula inserted by the Finance Committee. The committee had added the alternative formula as a way of lining up political support from members from less needy districts in the Sun Belt states of the South and West.

By raising the unemployment requirement, and eliminating the alternative formula, the Danforth amendment reduced the estimated cost of the supplementary aid program from $650 million to $340 million, a savings of $310 million.

Under a "hold harmless" provision in the amendment, cities with unemployment rates above 6 percent would not receive reductions in their allocations under either program.

Danforth said his proposal would "bring a little bit of rationality in the countercyclical revenue sharing program by better targeting it to those communities with high rates of unemployment and, therefore, with tax bases which have been eroded."

Lugar Amendment

Besides the Chiles amendment, the Senate also rejected an amendment by Richard G. Lugar, R-Ind., that would have required national unemployment to exceed 7 percent before any aid money would be available under either the countercyclical or supplementary aid program.

Lugar, a former mayor of Indianapolis, argued that the "rationale for spending money comes only if there is in fact national distress and national unemployment that has, in and of itself, triggered this difficulty in cities."

But Moynihan urged rejection of the amendment by citing high unemployment rates in several cities and pointing out that under Lugar's amendment no money would be available to those cities. Moynihan was joined in opposing the amendment by Danforth. The Senate subsequently tabled the amendment by a 40-12 vote. *(Vote 395, p. 59-S)*

Senate Provisions

As passed by the Senate, HR 2852:

Countercyclical Aid

- Extended the countercyclical aid program for two years, through fiscal 1980.
- Authorized $125 million per quarter for the program when the national unemployment rate exceeded 6 percent, with an additional $30 million per quarter for each .1 percent increase in the unemployment rate above 6 percent.
- Limited eligibility for funds under the program to state and local governmental units with unemployment rates above 6 percent.
- Reserved one-third of the money allocated under the program for state governments, and the remaining two-thirds for local governments.
- Calculated the national unemployment rate on the basis of unemployment figures for two consecutive quarters.
- Established a "hold harmless" provision to assure no aid cutbacks for local governments that otherwise would have their allocations decreased because of changes in the method used by the Bureau of Labor Statistics to calculate unemployment.
- Repealed the reporting requirements of the existing law, which required state and local governments to notify the Treasury Department of any changes in taxes imposed or any reductions in services or employees, and further required state governments to report any decreases in state aid to local governments.

Supplementary Fiscal Aid

- Established a second aid program to take effect when the national unemployment rate was between 5 and 6 percent.
- Authorized $85 million per quarter, with a program life of two years, through fiscal 1980.
- Limited eligibility for aid to local governments with unemployment rates above 6 percent.
- Based distribution of funds under the program on the same formula used for countercyclical revenue sharing — degree of unemployment and general revenue sharing allotment.
- Calculated the national unemployment rate in the same manner used to determine the rate under the countercyclical program.

House Action Blocked

Following Senate passage of HR 2852, the House leadership decided to seek a rule from the Rules Committee providing for a straight vote on the issue on the floor.

There, however, proponents of the measure encountered an unexpected obstacle, Rep. James J. Delaney, D-N.Y., the 77-year-old Rules Committee chairman.

Although New York City would be a chief beneficiary of the bill, Delaney initially balked at going along with the leadership.

The Rules Committee finally took up a proposed rule for HR 2852 on the night of Oct. 14. After a lengthy session, the committee voted for a rule, adjourning about 1 a.m. Sunday, Oct. 15.

Conservative Republicans, led by Robert E. Bauman, R-Md., provided the next hurdle. They informed the Democratic leadership that they would begin various stalling tactics if HR 2852 were called up.

An aide to the Speaker said O'Neill refused to take HR 2852 off the schedule for the last day, but agreed not to call it up until after energy and taxes were completed.

By then, however, it was too late. With members leaving the chamber and the Capitol after the vote on the tax bill, it would have been difficult, if not impossible, to obtain a quorum needed to act on the bill.

New Federal Reserve Members

The Senate on March 3 confirmed by voice vote the nomination of Textron Inc. chairman G. William Miller, President Carter's choice as chairman of the Federal Reserve Board. Miller succeeded Arthur F. Burns, whose term as chairman expired Jan. 31. Burns resigned from the Fed March 31.

Nancy H. Teeters was sworn in Sept. 18 as the first woman member of the Federal Reserve Board in the agency's 65-year history.

The former chief economist for the House Budget Committee was nominated in August by President Carter to fill the remainder of former Fed Chairman Burns' 14-year term, which was to expire Jan. 31, 1984.

National Security

At first glance 1978 was a good year for President Carter in defense legislation.

Both the House and the Senate rejected decisively several moves to raise or lower the Defense Department's budget recommendations. And by unexpectedly large margins, Congress supported Carter's position on the year's two major battles over new weapons: the B-1 bomber and a fifth nuclear-powered aircraft carrier, both opposed by the president.

But some other important policy battles were not fought during the year, particularly those on a new strategic arms limitation treaty with the Soviet Union and on Carter's plan to withdraw all U.S. ground forces from South Korea. In each case the president stayed his hand, at least in part for fear of vehement congressional opposition.

Where Carter succeeded, he did so by committing his administration unconditionally to continued growth in Pentagon spending. He based his opposition to the bomber and the carrier on the argument that each would be less effective than other weapons programs: the cruise missile, which was still in the development stage, and smaller, but more numerous, warships.

Congress generally handled defense issues in 1978 the same way they had been handled in the previous four years — the period since the October 1973 Middle East War.

For all the rhetoric about a reassertion of the congressional role in foreign policy decisions, Congress continued to show a strong tendency to defer to the commander-in-chief on the details of military policy.

This presidential flexibility, however, appeared to be contingent on Carter's hewing to a fairly narrow path that depended on a real annual increase in the Defense Department's budget, modernization of Army and Air Force equipment in Western Europe and modernization of the U.S. strategic weapons arsenal.

Modernization Costs

Deferred at least until 1979 was a resolution of the dilemma that would confront both Carter and Congress as the modernization programs move into full swing and begin to cost substantial sums of money. A president who was committed to balancing the federal budget and a Congress elected in the year of a taxpayers' revolt would have to reconcile their fiscal conservatism with new programs that would be extremely costly, even by the Pentagon's standards.

And in the last weeks of 1978, Carter was severely criticized by liberal Democrats, many of whom long had been suspicious that he lacked sympathy with the party's traditional support of domestic welfare programs.

At issue was Carter's reported decision to allow the Pentagon's budget for fiscal 1980 to grow by 3 percent, after taking into account the cost of inflation. Major domestic programs, on the other hand, reportedly were to be severely constrained to keep the total federal budget deficit under $30 billion.

How Much Is Enough?

When the 95th Congress finally went home in mid-October, it became apparent that Congress, during fiscal 1979, would appropriate essentially the amount ($126 billion) the administration requested for national defense for the year.

The largest single money bill in the defense package, the Defense Department appropriations bill, actually was some $2 billion below the amount Carter requested. But this simply was the amount Congress had allocated for the aircraft carrier that Carter finally had killed through his veto of the annual arms procurement bill.

It was considered certain that the administration would submit — and Congress would pass — a supplemental appropriation early in 1979 to reallocate that money to other defense projects.

Through most of the year, Republicans and other conservative groups had bet heavily that Carter would be vulnerable to hard-line attacks on his defense policies. But during 1978 Moscow toned down some of the policies that had vividly conjured up the image of Soviet imperialism on the march, such as its harsh crackdown on Soviet dissidents and its military assistance to Ethiopia in that country's border war with Somalia.

3 Percent Growth Rate

Carter also scored important points in the skirmishing over the size of the defense budget by pledging his administration to a 3 percent annual growth rate. And he presented the budget as giving a strong boost to U.S. forces in NATO.

While hard-line critics charged that both claims were debatable, the administration stood by its position. Desperate to show their eagerness to hold down federal spending without jeopardizing important pork-barrel projects, most members found it comfortable to take Carter's claims at face value.

Carter's position also was buttressed by the fact that many of the weapons with which the hard-liners were most concerned could not have absorbed significant funding increases in any case during fiscal 1979:

- An effort by some members of the Senate Armed Services Committee to increase funds for development of a new intercontinental missile (called M-X) collapsed in May because the Air Force had not yet decided how the new missile would be protected against the large arsenal of increasingly accurate Soviet missiles.
- Several important Army programs — a new tank, two new anti-aircraft missiles, a new armored troop carrier, two new helicopters — all had been delayed at various points in their development cycle during the 1970s. As a result, these weapons had not yet entered production or were just beginning production at a relatively slow pace.
- Long drawn out disputes between the Navy and three of its largest shipbuilders over some $2 billion worth of

contract claims left a general impression — even among some members who could be counted on to support a much larger shipbuilding program — that the Navy just could not absorb more money until it straightened out its management of ship construction programs.

The upshot was that both houses rejected by large margins floor amendments to the first budget resolution that would have increased or decreased the defense spending ceiling from the amounts recommended by the House and Senate Budget committees.

By the time each house acted on the defense appropriations bill, the anti-tax mood in the country, symbolized by California's "Proposition 13," was in full flight. But the few attempts to cut the bill did not present any serious threat. A Senate amendment that would have cut the budget request by a symbolic $1 billion received a mere 11 votes.

The Showdowns: B-1 and the Carrier

Carter beat the supporters of the B-1 and the nuclear carrier by unexpectedly large margins. And in each case the House, in backing the president, reversed at least one previous vote in favor of the new weapons.

But while the White House touted the two victories as clear evidence of Carter's prowess in dealing with Capitol Hill, the circumstances of the two battles suggested some narrow policy bounds within which Carter could exercise such clout.

Alternatives, Not Reductions

In each case, Carter insisted that he was opposing a weapon whose time had passed in order to invest in other projects that would do the same job more effectively. While the immediate effect was to kill a proposed defense expenditure, the promised alternatives would eventually cost about as much as the weapons they were to replace.

The long crusade against the B-1 had laid heavy emphasis on the plane's $100 million-a-copy price tag. But Carter and Defense Secretary Harold Brown based their decision to go with the cruise missile instead of the B-1 on the former's promise of greater effectiveness against Soviet air defenses.

Carter's strategy was even more clear in the White House's efforts to get Congress to sustain his veto of the $2 billion aircraft carrier.

At the insistence of the House Democratic leadership, he stressed that his purpose was not to cut the money from the budget, but rather to spend it on "higher priority" defense projects that would more directly beef up NATO's capability to defend Western Europe. And he unequivocally committed himself to requesting a slightly less expensive, non-nuclear carrier in 1979.

Symbols of Yesterday's War

Despite sophisticated arguments that tried to justify their role in future U.S. strategy, the bomber and the carrier were subjected to heavy criticism as symbols of military obsolescence.

With the end of the Vietnam War, the B-1 had become the surrogate target for critics of Pentagon spending. Capitalizing on the plane's price tag of $100 million-a-copy and its failure to meet some of more extravagant design goals planned for it, critics ridiculed the plane as a plaything for generals. An energetic anti-B-1 lobby bombarded the press and members of Congress with arguments against the plane.

Carrier Veto

Carrier opponents were not as organized as the anti-bomber lobby when Carter vetoed the big ship Aug. 17, but the same themes attracted liberals who were critical of the Pentagon's share of the federal budget and of its presumed influence on U.S. foreign policy: the ship was extremely expensive — $2 billion, without its deckload of planes — and opponents painted images of beribboned admirals swaggering around the quarterdeck to no real purpose.

Other expensive weapons had faced such attacks in the previous decade, but what sealed the doom of the B-1 and the carrier was the skepticism of many members who were not usually inclined to cut Pentagon programs.

House Appropriations Committee Chairman George Mahon, D-Texas, apparently spoke for many members when he said, in opposition to both the bomber and the carrier, that the weapon of the future clearly was the intercontinental missile. Neither the bomber nor the carrier would play more than a marginal role in any conflict with the Soviet Union, according to Mahon.

Skeptical of their value in wartime, horrified by their cost and presented with alternative weapons, which would not have to be paid for in 1978, enough moderates and hard-liners joined the traditional Pentagon critics to kill the two programs.

Brass Hat Support

In the case of the B-1, Carter had the additional advantage of strong support from ranking military leaders, including then-Air Force Chief of Staff Gen. David C. Jones. Jones had fought hard to save the plane, assisted by his colleagues on the Joint Chiefs of Staff. But when Carter decided to cancel the project, Jones decided that it was doomed.

Although the House on several occasions had voted in favor of the B-1, the Senate always had voted decisively against the project.

When House hard-liners tried to keep the program alive in 1978 by spending the money appropriated in 1976 for two of the planes, Jones supported Carter's effort to rescind the earlier appropriation.

The Air Force position was that it preferred to spend the $462 million on other programs that eventually would enter the Air Force arsenal.

The carrier case was different. Admirals campaigned vigorously in support of the nuclear carrier — until Carter vetoed the authorization bill that contained the ship. But many observers felt that the Navy's case was undermined by the long-festering problems with cost-overruns, schedule delays and contract

For 1980

The outrage expressed by liberal members over Carter's plan to increase the Pentagon budget while containing domestic programs was expected to help the president control the size of defense expenditures in fiscal 1980. He would be able to present whatever amount he requested as the middle-of-the-road position between demands for higher and lower Pentagon spending.

Also in 1979, Carter had to seek congressional action on a SALT treaty and, possibly, on his proposed withdrawal of ground troops from Korea. In 1978 he was not really tested on his ability to sell Congress on other than hard-line positions on national security issues.

—By Pat Towell

$35.2 Billion Voted for Defense Procurement

President Carter signed into law Oct. 20 a $35.2 billion fiscal 1979 procurement authorization bill (S 3486 — PL 95-485) for the Department of Defense.

The bill replaced a $37 billion bill (HR 10929) that Carter vetoed because it had authorized almost $2 billion for an additional *Nimitz*-class nuclear aircraft carrier. The veto was easily upheld by the House, providing Carter with a major defense policy victory.

The revised legislation contained identical program authorizations to those in the vetoed bill except for the deletion of $1.93 billion for the aircraft carrier and the addition of $209 million to finance certain settlements between the Navy and two of the largest U.S. shipbuilders.

Vetoed Bill

The first version of the authorization bill incorporated additions to the administration budget that would have given the Navy one more big nuclear-powered carrier while accelerating the development of smaller, less-expensive aircraft carriers and vertical takeoff combat planes (called V/STOLs) that would not require the 1,000-foot-long decks of the existing carriers. An effort to kill the big ship had failed in the House in May on a 139-264 vote.

After the bill was vetoed Aug. 17, House proponents of the ship could not even muster a majority on the vote to override the veto. The vote, taken Sept. 7, was 191-206; to override, a two-thirds majority was necessary.

The fiscal 1978 defense authorization bill had provided almost $36.1 billion for Defense Department programs. *(1977 Almanac p. 332)*

Final Provisions

As cleared for the president, S 3486 authorized the following amounts in fiscal 1979 for Defense Department weapons procurement, research and development:

	Administration Request	Final Action
Procurement		
Aircraft:		
Army	$ 1,017,800,000	$ 972,400,000
Navy and Marine Corps	4,078,800,000	4,381,100,000
Air Force	6,897,700,000	7,028,200,000
Missiles:		
Army	773,200,000	738,100,000
Navy	1,553,600,000	1,583,700,000
Marine Corps	23,100,000	23,100,000
Air Force	1,676,800,000	1,626,500,000
Naval vessels	4,712,400,000[1]	4,470,500,000
Tracked combat vehicles:		
Army	1,532,500,000	1,419,400,000
Marine Corps	21,700,000	24,300,000
Torpedoes	364,100,000	366,800,000
Other weapons:		
Army	104,100,000	109,000,000
Navy	129,800,000	102,000,000
Marine Corps	28,000,000	30,200,000
Air Force	300,000	300,000
Total, procurement	$22,913,900,000	$22,875,600,000
Research, Development, Test and Evaluation		
Army	2,721,400,000	2,661,701,000
Navy and Marine Corps	4,495,912,000	4,504,268,000
Air Force	4,339,100,000	4,164,500,000
Defense agencies	917,000,000	933,400,000
Total, R.D.T. & E.	$12,473,412,000	$12,263,869,000
Civil Defense	96,500,000	96,500,000
GRAND TOTAL	$35,483,812,000	$35,235,969,000

1 Not including a $1.575 billion conventionally powered aircraft carrier later supported by the Carter administration.

Original Bill

House Committee Action

The House Armed Services Committee reported HR 10929 May 6 (H Rept 95-1118) by a vote of 32-4. Authorizations recommended by the panel totaled $37,907,120,000.

The committee made 20 major changes in the administration's weapons procurement requests and more than 150 modifications in proposed weapons research programs. Most of these moves reflected the panel's long-standing criticisms of the Pentagon's priorities.

In its recommendations, the committee:

- Added $2.4 billion to the $35.5 billion requested by Carter for weapons procurement and military research programs, an increase of 6.8 percent.
- Added $3.6 billion for two nuclear-powered warships and for Navy combat planes.
- Added language that would block Carter's plan to withdraw U.S. ground combat troops from South Korea.

But a minority of the committee charged that the panel, by its actions, had "run amok." It hoped to overturn some of the committee's actions by offering the original Carter requests as amendments on the House floor.

The committee had long maintained that the higher cost of nuclear-powered warships was worth the added expense for military reasons. A nuclear ship could run at top speed for great distances without refueling.

The administration had planned to build a $1.25 billion non-nuclear aircraft carrier in fiscal 1980 and to build only non-nuclear Aegis anti-aircraft escort ships for the carriers for the next three years. But the House committee went on record in favor of a nuclear carrier ($2 billion) and a nuclear Aegis ship ($1.1 billion) in fiscal 1979.

The panel also increased the authorization for carrier combat planes: F-14 and F-18 fighters and A-7E light bombers. But it slashed to $15.5 million an $81.8 million request to develop combat jets (V/STOLs) that would not need a big carrier's flight deck to take off and land.

Quick Improvements vs. Future Breakthroughs. Pentagon research had concentrated too heavily on revolutionary new systems that would take a decade to produce. At the same time, it had ignored inexpensive but useful modifications of existing equipment, the committee charged. The panel deleted all $14.5 million requested for a

Major Weapons Authorizations for Fiscal 1979

(in millions of dollars)

	Carter Request		House Passed		Senate Passed		Final Action	
	Number	Amount	Number	Amount	Number	Amount	Number	Amount
Strategic Warfare								
Trident submarine	1	$1,186.7	—	$ 274.8	—	$ 55.0	—	$ 274.8
Trident missiles	86	814.3	86	814.3	86	814.3	86	814.3
M-X missile	—	158.2	—	158.2	—	158.2	—	158.2
Widebody cruise missile carrier	—	41.2	—	—	—	41.2	—	20.6
Civil Defense	—	96.5	—	137.0	—	96.5	—	96.5
Ground Warfare								
XM-1 tank	110	403.1	110	368.5	110	368.5	110	368.5
M-60 tank	480	383.8	480	383.8	240	191.8	410	345.0
M-60 modernization	220	98.4	500	147.6	460	162.1	380	132.4
Infantry fighting vehicle	—	—	—	34.6	—	39.0	—	39.0
M-113 troop carrier	910	74.2	910	74.2	550	44.5	550	44.5
Naval Warfare								
Nuclear aircraft carrier	—	—	1	2,129.6	1	1,930.0	1	1,930.0
Aegis cruiser	—	—	1	1,096.0	—	—	—	369.0
Missile frigate	8	1,533.1	8	1,533.1	8	1,533.1	8	1,533.1
Attack submarine	1	433.0	1	433.0	1	433.0	1	433.0
Surface effect ship	—	—	—	93.0	—	30.0	—	80.0
Tactical airpower								
F-15 fighter	78	1,328.7	78	1,328.7	78	1,328.7	78	1,328.7
F-16 fighter	145	1,375.1	145	1,375.1	145	1,375.1	145	1,375.1
F-14 fighter	24	632.2	36	834.4	28	729.3	36	834.4
F-18 fighter	5	350.5	9	488.5	9	484.5	9	484.5
V/STOL-Related								
A-4M light bomber	18	113.0	—	—	—	—	—	—
Harrier V/STOL light bomber	—	—	15	90.0	—	—	—	—
Advanced Harrier	—	85.6	—	85.6	—	173.0	—	173.0
Other V/STOL research	—	72.4	—	15.5	—	55.5	—	35.5

(Some amounts include funds for spare parts and for advance payments on additional items to be purchased in fiscal 1980.)

SOURCE: House and Senate Armed Services Committee Reports

Navy all-purpose weapons system, called SIRCS, and $3 million for studies of a long-range ocean patrol plane, neither of which would enter service until 1990.

But it added $10 million for alterations to the Army's 500 Chaparral anti-aircraft missile launchers so they could be operated at night or in bad weather. And it added $8.6 million to allow the Navy to begin using a system of data collection that would allow ships to find their targets at much greater ranges. Deciding that 15 years of development and redesigning was enough, it ordered the Army to start producing a new armored infantry carrier. The committee said sarcastically: "For the past 15 years, the United States has had the finest infantry fighting vehicle in the world — on paper."

Budget Problems. The committee had no patience with what it regarded as short-sighted budget cuts that delayed important new weapons or slowed the production of existing models. It increased by at least 50 percent over what the administration wanted the purchase of F-14 and F-18 fighter planes for the Navy. And it restored $93 million sought by the Navy for an experimental surface effect ship (SES) the size of a destroyer that would move at 90 mph on a cushion of trapped air.

But the committee moved to terminate some programs because of their cost. Among these was the Navy's LAMPS III antisubmarine helicopter, which it estimated would cost upwards of $20 million a copy. And it canceled other programs for which it said less expensive alternatives should be used: the EF-111 radar jamming plane and the Army's Scout helicopter.

Duplication Fought. The panel consolidated under the Defense Advanced Research Projects Agency several Army and Air Force research projects using a missile or artillery shell to carry several small warheads, each of which would home in on a target. Strong central management was needed, it said, to reduce costs and eliminate duplication among the projects.

Also given to this agency was control of Navy-sponsored experiments using beams of electrically charged atomic particles as "death ray" weapons. The panel said there were major technical obstacles to be corrected.

Procurement Process Criticized. The committee reiterated its long-standing complaint that it took far too long for new weapons to get from the laboratory into the field.

"Our technology is still one of the great advantages that the United States has relative to the Soviet Union," it said, and, properly exploited, this would allow U.S. forces to offset Soviet numerical superiority. But the potential advantage was being nullified by an unnecessarily prolonged weapon development cycle. The committee noted that it took 19 years for the Army's Patriot anti-aircraft missile to go into service; the Navy's Aegis anti-aircraft system would reach the fleet in its 20th year of development.

By contrast, weapons had been developed in much less time in earlier years. The Polaris submarine-launched missile system took just four years from conception to operation, the committee pointed out.

One reason for the change, in the committee's view, was that weapons development now was overseen by an elaborate system of formal reviews: too many people had a finger in the pie. Many committee members charged the Office of Management and Budget (OMB) with unwarranted intrusion into highly technical military decisions.

And the rigidity of the weapons review process might discourage a common-sense approach to quickly meeting a military need to modify existing equipment. The alternative, the committee warned, was to go through the lengthy and expensive process of developing a new weapon from scratch.

Defense Personnel Policies

The all-volunteer armed services concept generally had been successful so far in getting enough persons for the active forces, the committee said. But there were clouds on the horizon, it warned, and already the reserve forces were in serious trouble.

Selling the Service. All services were coming close to their active duty recruiting goals, although this was in a period when the forces were shrinking. But the cost had been very high — the fiscal 1979 budget request for recruiting was $600 million. And of about 400,000 persons recruited each year, about 160,000 — 40 percent — did not complete their full term of service.

The committee blamed some of this attrition during the first-term of service on a "Madison Avenue approach" to recruiting. Enlistees attracted by such merchandising techniques entered the service without any realistic expectations about military life, and became disenchanted.

"The idea of serving the country through military duty needs to be reinstituted. . . . A recruiting process which does not at all use the concept of patriotism and a citizen's duties and does not realistically present the demands of military life is not acceptable," the committee concluded.

Women in the Service. The recruiting problem was expected to get tougher as the number of men in the 18-21 age group declined over the next 15 years. But the problem could be partially alleviated by plans to increase from 6 percent in fiscal 1977 to 11 percent in fiscal 1983 the proportion of the services made up of women. The committee commented that the military had "benefited substantially" from the increased recruitment of women, but added that it might become necessary to eliminate current restrictions on the use of women in combat.

It suggested that the Air Force might be in a better position than the other services to use more women, since most of its members were not involved in direct combat roles or in jobs requiring great physical strength.

The committee accepted the general intent of an administration proposal to change current law to allow women to serve aboard non-combat Navy ships and, temporarily, on warships that were not expected to face a combat mission. But it amended the proposal to stipulate that such temporary duty would last no longer than six months and that "every reasonable effort" would be made to get the women off the warships if war began.

Training Cuts Rejected. The committee recommended adding about 10,000 men to the 2.06 million active-duty manpower level requested by the administration. Much of the increase was related to the panel's rejection of administration-proposed reductions in the time spent training recruits.

The burden of training recruits would be greater than in the past, the committee argued, because the average intelligence level of recruits had declined, according to standardized test scores. And the proposed cuts would have affected particularly the reserve units, which depended even more heavily on the quality of their formal training since they did not use their military skills on a day-to-day basis.

Reserve Incentives Needed. The committee reiterated its view that various incentives were needed to increase the size of the reserve forces, which were some 30,000 men short of their authorized strength and much smaller than the size recommended by the Pentagon.

The problem had occurred, according to the committee, because at almost the same time as the Pentagon began to rely on reserve units for important military and support missions the draft ended, thus removing an important incentive for persons to enlist in the reserves.

The committee recommended extending for another year authority for the Pentagon to experiment with educational benefits and re-enlistment bonuses as incentives for servicemen to stay in the reserves. And it recommended an additional program of bonuses for first-term enlistments.

As it had for several years, the committee turned down an administration recommendation to cut the Naval Reserve to about 52,000, from its current strength of 87,000.

A Stand-by Draft. Citing the shrinkage of the reserve forces, the committee said the Selective Service System should resume registering and classifying potential draftees so that in an emergency it could deliver personnel to the services quickly. By some estimates, it would take 15 weeks for the draft to gear up from its current "deep-standby" status and deliver the first draftee to a military training base.

Nuclear Warfare

Soviet intercontinental missiles could, within the next 5-10 years, destroy a very large percentage of the present U.S. missile force located in reinforced underground silos, the committee warned. It approved the $158 million requested by the Pentagon to continue development of an improved missile (the M-X). The M-X was intended to nullify the Soviet threat by rolling at random through 15-mile-long tunnels or by being moved from one shelter to another.

But the panel insisted that it was more important to develop a way to protect existing missiles than to develop a new missile. It directed the Pentagon to present by July 1, 1978, a plan to protect U.S. land-based missiles.

The committee cut $912 million requested for the eighth Trident missile-launching submarine because construction of the earlier ones was running far behind schedule. But it allowed $275 million to buy nuclear power plants for the next three Trident ships. And it approved the request for 86 Trident missiles ($890 million), but authorized only $5 million, rather than the $15 million requested, for studies of a longer-range missile.

Continued testing of the B-1 bomber ($105.5 million) was canceled as was a cruise missile carrier adapted from a wide-bodied commercial jetliner ($41.2 million).

Civil Defense. An increase of $40.5 million in the administration's request — to $137 million — was recommended for civil defense programs, much of it for fallout shelters, command posts and communications systems.

Ground Warfare

Both the request and the committee's recommendations for tank warfare were influenced by concern over the huge force of tanks with which Russia could spearhead an invasion of Western Europe.

The requests were approved in full for tank-hunting aircraft: 162 A-10 planes ($885 million), 78 Cobra helicopters ($137 million) and continued development of a new helicopter, the AAH ($117 million).

The first 110 production-line XM-1 tanks ($368.5 million) were approved. And the panel authorized $10.9 million, the amount requested, to begin adapting a German-made gun for use on later models of the tank. But the Investigations Subcommittee charged that the German gun offered no military advantage over the smaller U.S. cannon that was to be used on the first manufactured XM-1s. If the larger gun were installed on the earlier tanks, the total cost could run to $2 billion, the panel said.

Tactical Airpower

The committee approved the requests for 78 F-15 fighters ($1.3 billion), 145 F-16 fighters ($1.4 billion) and three AWACS radar planes ($234 million) to quarterback U.S. planes in an air battle. It also added 16 A-7D light bomber-trainers for the Air National Guard ($141 million).

As favored by the Marines, it dropped 18 A-4 light bombers ($113 million) and substituted 15 Harrier V/STOL light bombers ($90 million). Unlike the Navy, which disliked the Harrier because of its short range, the Marines found the plane, of which they had three squadrons, useful when landing in enemy territory. Bomb-laden Harriers could land in small clearings where they would be available on short notice to provide air support.

Airlift

The first two mid-air refueling tankers, the ATCA, which were modified DC-10 jetliners, were authorized ($143.5 million) by the committee, which also added $9 million to begin putting new, more efficient engines on the existing fleet of KC-135 tankers, which were modified Boeing 707s.

The committee added an authorization for 16 Hercules transport planes for the Air National Guard ($145 million) and $3 million to continue development of a new short-takeoff transport, the AMST, which the administration wanted to cancel.

Naval Warfare

The committee made few changes in the Navy request aside from the issues of nuclear-powered ships and V/STOL.

It approved a request for a nuclear-powered attack submarine ($433 million) and for eight escort frigates ($1.5 billion). Also approved were a destroyer tender ($318 million) and four ships that, although they carry no weapons, were intended to play a major role in blunting a Russian submarine threat.

Three of these ships, called T-AGOS ($98 million), would tow very large underwater listening devices that could detect submarines at great distances. The fourth was a cable laying ship ($191 million) that would be used to maintain the large network of listening devices that were anchored on the floor of the Atlantic and Pacific Oceans to track Russian submarines.

NATO Standardization

The committee recommended reinstating the requirement that the Defense Department be prohibited from purchasing weapons using high-quality steel alloys that were not manufactured in the United States. The requirement had been repealed in 1977 so that the Pentagon could buy some weapons manufactured by European members of the NATO alliance. This decision was intended to promote the standardization of equipment among the allied armed forces. But the committee majority argued that, as a result, U.S. manufacturers were losing the technical edge that had made U.S. weapons superior.

Korean Troop Withdrawal

A committee amendment would prohibit President Carter from removing more than about 6,000 of the 32,000-member 2nd Infantry Division from South Korea until a peace settlement was reached between North and South Korea. Technically, the two Koreas merely had been observing an armistice in the Korean War for the previous 25 years.

The amendment also would bar the removal of any U.S. troops from Korea until Congress enacted legislation to allow the president to turn over to the South Koreans the equipment then used by the U.S. forces there.

House Floor Action

Despite widespread congressional concern about inflation, the House easily blocked moves to overturn the recommendations of its Armed Services Committee before passing HR 10929 May 24 by a 319-67 vote. *(Vote 319, p. 92-H)*

Hoping to capitalize on a wave of anti-spending sentiment that was much in evidence only three weeks earlier in the debate on the first budget resolution, a liberal minority on the committee tried to substitute the administration's original defense requests. President Carter had requested a $35.5 billion bill, but Armed Services subsequently increased it to $37.9 billion.

An overwhelming majority of the House, however, backed the Armed Services Committee and its argument that a wholesale revamping of its work on the floor would be a fundamental attack on the committee system.

The insurgents' strategy also was undercut by the White House, which decided against a head-on collision with the committee.

The substitute containing the administration's weapons authorization levels, offered by Bob Carr, D-Mich., was rejected handily, 115-287. *(Vote 313, p. 90-H)*

The committee's position also was sustained on two important weapons projects: the $2 billion aircraft carrier that the panel added over the president's protests, and a $41 million experimental nuclear cruise missile carrier using wide-body jetliners that was sought by Carter but denied by the committee.

The only victory for Pentagon critics was the deletion from the committee's bill of $8.1 million for an executive jet to be used by the commandant of the Marine Corps. This was the only change made on the floor in the bill's authorization levels.

The committee did not carry the day entirely. The attempt to block Carter's plan to withdraw all U.S. ground troops from South Korea was rejected 142-247. *(Vote 318, p. 90-H)*

This was the first House vote on the withdrawal issue since it became a subject of congressional debate in May 1977. But the vote may have been less an indication of congressional support of the Carter plan than evidence of House deference to the tradition of committee jurisdiction. International Relations Committee Chairman Clement J. Zablocki, D-Wis., argued that the troop withdrawal proposal fell within the province of his panel.

Fiscal Concerns vs. Committee Turf

The strategy of the Pentagon critics was to attack the committee's bill as a fundamentally bad piece of legislation rather than to go after individual weapons systems. The committee had increased the bill $2.4 billion above the Carter request. But the House May 3 had rejected by a very large margin an effort by senior members of the panel to make a much smaller increase in the defense spending ceiling in the first budget resolution (S Con Res 80).

Opening the debate on his amendment, Carr said that during the markup of HR 10929, the committee had added items with a "Christmas-like attitude. . . . We were bending over backward on this secret markup to accommodate the members of the committee and their needs back home."

He maintained that some senior members of the committee who opposed his amendment had warned during the markup that the panel was turning itself into "a Pentagon wish-list . . . a eunuch among congressional committees."

Patricia Schroeder, D-Colo., a committee member, argued that a new bill was needed because the committee had simply disregarded the budget ceilings that would eventually be enforced. "What will happen when this authorization request goes to the Committee on Appropriations is that they will be making the choices if we, the committee, do not manage to keep it within the budget."

But whatever doubts they had expressed during the markup, senior committee members closed ranks against the panel's dissidents. Chairman Melvin Price, D-Ill., circulated a letter to all members describing the move as a threat to the committee structure. If it were effective against Armed Services, he warned, it surely would be used against other panels in the future.

Led by Richard H. Ichord, D-Mo., committee members denounced the Carr move as an attack not only on the panel, but also on Price: "an unmerited and unworthy slur on the great leadership of the gentleman from Illinois," said Samuel S. Stratton, D-N.Y.

Amendments and Arithmetic

The specific approach taken by Carr and his supporters left them vulnerable to charges by Ichord and others that they were trying to mark up the bill in detail on the floor. Because of the small number of members involved in the challenge to the committee bill, and because of disagreements within that group over specific points of defense policy, backers of the move decided against trying to offer their own bill. Instead, they offered Carter's original request minus $912 million for a Trident submarine that everyone agreed was not needed in fiscal 1979.

In order to focus the debate on the committee's performance, instead of on the usual split between defense hawks and doves, they hoped to win the support of Ichord and some other senior committee members who had fought some of the committee additions. The plan was to accept as changes in the Carr substitute amendments by these members that incorporated portions of the committee bill that Carr supporters thought were improvements in Carter's request. By far the most important of these was a $12.5 billion package of research programs that had been handled by Ichord's subcommittee.

But Ichord would not be bought off. Carr's move, he told the House, "borders on the edge of anarchy." By trying, in effect, to mark up the bill on the House floor, Carr would "put the members of the House in a position of voting upon proposition after proposition about which they cannot possibly know enough to cast an intelligent vote."

And to dramatize his position, he pounced eagerly when an arithmetic error was discovered in an amendment by Schroeder to put the committee's research program into the Carr substitute. "By the time the gentlewoman corrects her amendment, by the time we have all the other amendments and the deals that have been made, we are going to be here all week."

Administration Back-pedaling

Whatever chance the Carr move had probably was quashed when the administration May 22 told Price it would accept a $1.5 billion conventionally powered aircraft carrier for fiscal 1979 in lieu of the committee's $2 billion nuclear carrier. This reduced to $850 million the committee's increase over Carter's overall request.

Moreover, the Defense Department had steadfastly refused to support Carr against the committee. "They've got to work with the committee on a daily basis," said one staffer. "They can't fly in the face of the committee, although they can support one or two amendments."

The Carr strategy had received extensive coverage by *The Washington Post,* which, its backers hoped, would rally other liberal Democrats. But only about 50 members were on the floor during debate on the Carr proposal, most of whom were members of the committee.

Before disposing of the Carr substitute, the House rejected, 107-297, Schroeder's amendment that would have incorporated the committee's research program. And it rejected by voice vote another substitute, by Ronald V. Dellums, D-Calif., that would have reduced the bill to $28.4 billion. *(Vote 312, p. 90-H)*

Nuclear Carrier Backed

If Carr's defeat was surprising in light of the budget resolution vote, so was the 139-264 rejection of an amendment by Les Aspin, D-Wis., to replace the committee's nuclear carrier with a conventionally powered ship as agreed to by Carter. *(Vote 315, p. 90-H)*

In March 1977 the House had voted 161-252 against the Armed Services Committee and in favor of Carter's proposal to rescind money appropriated in 1976 as a downpayment for a nuclear carrier. *(1977 Almanac p. 397)*

An Aspin aide insisted that, in contrast to the Carr substitute, this amendment had strong backing from Secretary of Defense Harold Brown.

Aspin did not question the military advantages of the larger nuclear-powered ship. But he maintained that the smaller carrier was adequate for many missions and that the money thus saved could build more ships. "More ships mean that we can be in more places at the same time."

Supporting Aspin, Robert N. Giaimo, D-Conn., observed that there already were four nuclear-powered carriers in the fleet to deal with those missions requiring sustained high speed, the nuclear ship's main advantage. Aspin, on the other hand, argued that the carrier's nuclear power was useful only if its escort ships also were nuclear powered and, he said, there were not enough nuclear escorts for a fifth nuclear carrier.

But the committee denied that the conventional ship would save money if the cost of operating and refueling the ship over its lifetime were taken into account. Even the projected savings in construction costs could not be relied on, they maintained, because a conventional ship had not yet been designed while the nuclear ship funded by the committee would be the fourth of the *Nimitz* class.

Seapower Subcommittee Chairman Charles E. Bennett, D-Fla., argued that the conventional ship was forced on the Navy by administration budgeteers. "But the people who actually have to fight on the scene, and know what they need. . ., say [a nuclear carrier] is not only cost-effective but . . . a better way in which to win a war."

After rejecting the Aspin amendment, the House also voted 106-293 against an amendment by Carr that would have deleted all funds for carriers. *(Vote 316, p. 90-H)*

Cruise Missile Carrier

An attempt to restore funds cut by the committee for the wide-body cruise missile carrier was rejected after a debate that sounded like a bizarre mirror-image of the debate over the B-1 bomber. Thomas J. Downey, D-N.Y., a B-1 opponent, offered an amendment to restore $29.2 million of the $41 million requested. He argued that the new plane should be developed if only as a bargaining chip in the strategic arms limitation (SALT) negotiations with Moscow. This had been the final ploy of the B-1's supporters in their effort to save the plane.

Ichord, who supported the B-1, argued that the wide-body cruise missile carrier was too expensive, at more than $100 million a copy, and that it could never survive Soviet air defenses. These were the primary arguments used by opponents to kill the B-1. Downey's amendment was rejected 145-246. *(Vote 317, p. 90-H)*

Marine Commandant's Jet

The 266-136 vote deleting the funds for an executive jet for the Marine Corps marked the first victory over the Armed Services Committee for House critics of Pentagon spending since 1976. That year, they killed on the floor a $170 million authorization for 12 Navy cargo planes. *(Vote 314, p. 90-H)*

But, as in 1976, the challengers were successful only on a minuscule item that did not involve a major weapons system. And the committee's four senior Democrats had voted against the Marine jet during the markup of the bill.

Schroeder, who offered the amendment, conceded that the plane was not a very big item, but insisted that it was "highly symbolic of the goodies that were handed out" to the services during the committee markup of the bill. She pointed out that no hearings had been held on the 20-seat Gulfstream jet and argued that there was a large pool of executive planes in the Defense Department that the Marine commandant could use.

Supporters of the plane said opponents were taking a cheap shot by labeling the plane an airborne limousine for the commandant. It was intended to be used by several Marine units in Washington, they said, and would replace three old propeller transports that were becoming unsafe to fly. Nearly 100 fewer persons would be needed to maintain the new jet, they said.

Korea Troop Language

The committee's provision requiring that at least 26,000 U.S. combat troops remain in South Korea until both Koreas negotiated a peace treaty was ruled out of order on grounds that it was not germane to the bill. The annual authorization measure set ceilings on the number of active duty troops, but did not specify their location.

But later in the debate, Stratton, whose Investigations Subcommittee had recommended the committee language, offered an amendment stipulating that no funds in the bill could be used to reduce U.S. troops in Korea below 26,000. Since the bill authorized funds only for weapons procurement and research, the legal effect of the amendment was not clear. But supporters of the proposed troop withdrawal were caught off guard and debate on the proposal began before a point of order could be raised against it.

Stratton maintained that during his panel's inspection trip to South Korea in January, "every knowledgeable person to whom our committee spoke . . . agreed that pulling our troops out of Korea would increase the risks of war." His amendment would give Congress an opportunity to express its will on the proposal, he said.

Lester L. Wolff, D-N.Y., chairman of the International Relations Subcommittee on Asia, argued that South Korea was able to fend for itself since it was far more populous and wealthy than North Korea. And the Congressional Budget Office had estimated the annual cost of keeping U.S. forces in Korea at $1.3 billion.

In reply, Stratton said: "It is going to cost a lot more to bring them back to the United States, and . . . it would cost still more if by another miscalculation we were to get into another war in Korea."

Before Stratton's amendment was rejected by nearly a two-to-one margin (142-247), he accepted an amendment by Elliott H. Levitas, D-Ga., allowing the president to remove troops in case of an emergency. *(Vote 318, p. 90-H)*

Canal Zone Bases

By a standing vote of 61-35, the House adopted an amendment by George Hansen, R-Idaho, barring the use of any Pentagon funds to reduce the number of U.S. troops or bases in the Canal Zone unless specifically authorized by law. House conservatives had promised to use such amendments to wage a legislative guerrilla war against implementation of the Panama Canal treaties. In one such move earlier in 1978 treaty opponents added to the first budget resolution (H Con Res 599) language widely interpreted as a slap at the treaties.

Abortion Fight Avoided

An amendment by Bill Goodling, R-Pa., introduced by Gary A. Myers, R-Pa., that would have severely restricted abortions at military facilities was shouted down on a voice vote. Myers' proposal would have subjected abortions funded by Defense Department appropriations to whatever requirements were imposed on abortions paid for by Medicaid funds. After months of wrangling over the fiscal 1978 appropriations bill for the Department of Health, Education and Welfare, Congress had agreed to limit Medicaid coverage to abortions in certain cases of incest and rape and cases in which the mother's life or long-term health otherwise would be endangered. *(1977 Almanac p. 295)*

In a statement released before the debate began, Goodling said that if the same Medicaid limits were not placed on other federally funded programs, the policy would discriminate unfairly against the poor. Between Sept. 1, 1976, and Sept. 1, 1977, according to Goodling, 11,289 abortions were performed in military hospitals and another 15,200 were paid for by CHAMPUS, the Pentagon's hospitalization plan for military dependents.

But the House was able to avoid a recorded vote on the amendment because only 12 members joined Myers in demanding a vote; 20 members were needed when the House debated amendments.

Other Amendments

The House adopted by voice votes four amendments that were accepted in advance by the Armed Services Committee:

- By Elwood Hillis, R-Ind., to allow CHAMPUS to reimburse physicians at a rate of not more than the 90th percentile of customary charges for similar services in the same area. The level had been reduced from the 90th percentile to the 75th percentile by the fiscal 1978 defense appropriation bill on the grounds that Medicare and Medicaid reimbursed physicians at the 75th percentile. Hillis maintained that many physicians charged more than the current CHAMPUS fees and that patients were forced to make up the difference.
- By Lester L. Wolff, D-N.Y., to require an analysis of the productivity of Pentagon employees.
- By David L. Cornwell, D-Ind., to raise from 1 1/4 percent — the percentage under current law — to 2 percent the level by which the secretary of defense would be allowed to exceed the ceiling on civilian Pentagon employment.
- By Ike Skelton, D-Mo., to require a study of the special civil defense needs of areas that would be prime targets for a Soviet nuclear attack because they contained U.S. strategic weapons bases. Whiteman Air Force Base, with 150 Minuteman intercontinental missiles (ICBMs), was located in Skelton's district.

The House also rejected five other amendments:

- By Jim Lloyd, D-Calif., to delete $62.2 million in long-leadtime funds for A-10 attack planes to be requested in 1979. The A-10 was designed with heavy armor so it could fly very low over a battlefield while firing missiles and a cannon at enemy tanks. But Lloyd, a retired Navy pilot, argued that the plane was too vulnerable for the mission. Standing vote, 23-45.
- By Schroeder, to allow the use of military personnel for the 1980 Winter Olympics at Lake Placid, N.Y., only to provide services not available from civilian sources and only if the services were judged by the Pentagon to have some value in training troops. The committee bill gave the secretary of defense authority to assign troops to provide logistic assistance for the games. Voice vote.
- By Myers, to exempt from the bill's ban on the Pentagon's purchases of weapons containing foreign-made specialty metals any arms that were purchased to further standardization within the NATO alliance. Voice vote.
- By Dan Quayle, R-Ind., to eliminate a provision in existing law curtailing the Pentagon's flexibility to replace federal employees with civilian contractors for certain kinds of housekeeping jobs on military bases. Standing vote, 37-61. *(Contracting out issue, 1977 Almanac p. 264)*
- By Dawson Mathis, D-Ga., to authorize increases in the cost-of-living payments to U.S. troops stationed abroad to offset declines in the value of the dollar since Jan. 1, 1977, against the currency of the country in which they were stationed. Army leaders had warned that the rapid decline of the dollar aginst the West German mark was working a considerable hardship on the families of enlisted personnel stationed in Europe. But Military Compensation Subcommittee Chairman Bill Nichols, D-Ala., insisted that the amendment was premature since his panel was in the midst of hearings on the problem. Standing vote, 13-74.

Provisions

As passed by the House May 24, HR 10929 authorized:

	Administration Requests	House-Passed Authorizations
Procurement		
Aircraft:		
Army	$ 1,017,800,000	$ 1,037,400,000
Navy and Marine Corps	4,078,800,000	4,546,780,000
Air Force	6,897,700,000	7,046,400,000
Missiles:		
Army	773,200,000	795,600,000
Navy	1,553,600,000	1,593,700,000
Marine Corps	23,100,000	23,100,000
Air Force	1,676,800,000	1,632,100,000
Naval vessels	4,712,400,000	7,026,100,000
Tracked combat vehicles:		
Army	1,532,500,000	1,518,900,000
Marine Corps	21,700,000	24,300,000
Torpedoes	364,100,000	426,800,000
Other weapons:		
Army	104,100,000	93,100,000
Navy	129,800,000	129,800,000
Marine Corps	28,000,000	30,200,000
Air Force	300,000	300,000
Total, procurement	$22,913,900,000	$25,924,580,000
Research, Development, Test and Evaluation		
Army	2,721,400,000	2,586,215,000
Navy and Marine Corps	4,495,912,000	4,287,009,000
Air Force	4,339,100,000	3,989,400,000
Defense agencies	917,000,000	974,816,000
Total, R.D.T. & E.	$12,473,412,000	$11,837,440,000
Civil Defense	96,500,000	137,000,000
GRAND TOTAL	$35,483,812,000	$37,899,020,000

Senate Committee Action

The Senate Armed Services Committee reported (S Rept 95-826) its version (S 2571) on May 15.

The total authorization recommended was $36,097,534,000, $613.7 million more than Carter requested but $1.8 billion less than the authorization bill (HR 10929) passed May 24 by the House.

Warships accounted for the lion's share of the increase over what the administration sought. Even though cancellation of a Trident missile submarine ($911 million) partly offset the cost of the proposed nuclear aircraft carrier (almost $2 billion), the committee's shipbuilding recommendations added up to a net increase of $890 million.

V/STOL and Politics

The committee went along with a $45 million experiment in the use of V/STOL planes on small aircraft carriers. Specifically, the funds authorized were to convert a Marine landing ship to one that could carry combat helicopters and vertical takeoff planes.

This was the most far-reaching of several recommendations to speed up the Navy's adoption of V/STOL planes, thus allowing the construction of smaller and cheaper aircraft carriers.

But while the committee accepted the conversion proposal, it rejected other initiatives to speed up the transition to V/STOL. In fact, the panel, charging that the Navy was moving too hastily to replace conventional jets with V/STOLs, cut the Pentagon's request for V/STOL research funds.

V/STOL proponents maintained that because of the accuracy of Soviet anti-ship missiles, the Navy could not afford to concentrate all its striking power on its dozen or so big carriers. But if the fleet's firepower was to be spread out across a much larger number of ships, those ships would have to be much cheaper — and thus smaller. V/STOL was the only way to operate combat planes from ships much smaller than the current $2 billion carriers.

But critics of the new technology insisted that only conventional jets could protect the big carriers because of their high speed and sophisticated, long-range weapons. V/STOLs would have neither the speed nor the weapons, they argued, because of the weight and complexity of the special lifting devices that were needed for takeoff.

The Administration and Admirals. The Navy had wanted to build one more nuclear-powered carrier to keep the fleet at a dozen big ships through the end of the century. But it also had embarked on a decade-long development program to produce combat V/STOLs that would replace current jets in the 1990s.

The administration wanted a slightly smaller carrier that would not be nuclear powered. And it cut the request for V/STOL development, expressing doubts that the Navy could produce a plane that would meet its own performance standards.

Hart Naval Package

Gary Hart, D-Colo., the committee's most active member on naval issues and a committed V/STOL supporter, proposed March 22 a complex package of amendments to the administration's requests that would have accelerated the Navy move to V/STOL by:

- Directing the Navy to convert one of its nine helicopter carriers to a V/STOL ship. These vessels carried about 2,000 Marines plus troop helicopters. In 1972 one of them was operated as an experimental V/STOL ship carrying about 14 anti-submarine helicopters and three Harrier V/STOL bombers used by the Marines. Hart proposed a $45 million authorization for the conversion.
- Building a new troop helicopter carrier for the Marines ($770 million) to replace the converted ship.
- Buying 18 Harriers ($108 million) for the converted ship.
- Completing the design of a new class of V/STOL carriers ($25 million).
- More than tripling (to $119 million) funds for development of an advanced version of the Harrier for use by the Marines as a light bomber.
- Developing a new version of the advanced Harrier that would defend the V/STOL ships against air attack ($5.5 million).

Hart reluctantly supported construction of one more big carrier because of the strong congressional support for such a ship. And he dismissed as a poor compromise the administration's proposed conventional carrier. It would be much less capable than a nuclear-powered ship, he said, but still so expensive that large numbers could not be afforded.

But Hart suggested that the committee leave the nuclear carrier out of its version of the weapons bill so that in the Senate-House conference that would write the final version of the bill Senate conferees could agree to take the big ship, backed by the House, for House acceptance of the V/STOL package, on which it had strong reservations.

Committee Compromise

When the Senate committee marked up the authorization bill, Hart's proposal ran up against Tactical Airpower Subcommittee Chairman Howard W. Cannon, D-Nev., who was very skeptical of V/STOL. The resulting compromise allowed the Navy to experiment with V/STOL, using existing equipment, but rejected Hart's basic assumption that modifications of existing V/STOL planes were good enough to arm the fleet.

The committee approved the V/STOL ship conversion, but it also added the nuclear carrier, thus losing a potential bargaining advantage at the subsequent conference negotiations.

And support in the committee for the conversion was less than overwhelming: The conversion program and replacement helicopter ship were approved on a 9-6 vote, and a later move to rescind the conversion failed by only 8-9. Authorization of the replacement ship later was pared back to a $70 million down payment, though the committee insisted it marked a commitment to funding the ship in fiscal 1980. It also approved funds to design a new V/STOL ship.

But Hart's proposals to develop new V/STOL planes fared much worse. The new Harrier bomber for the Marines was approved, but the fighter version for use on V/STOL ships was defeated, 6-12.

Contrary to Hart's contention that the Navy was dragging its feet on V/STOL, the committee charged that the service was moving too fast. It cut to $50 million the Pentagon's $72.4 million request for V/STOL development. "It is the committee's position that considerable additional study and analysis of the whole V/STOL concept should be accomplished before major funding is dedicated to [the new plane]," the panel said in its report.

It directed the Navy to consider new conventional jets in addition to V/STOLs for its next generation of combat planes.

According to several sources, Hart had won support for several of his proposals because committee members were in general agreement that the Navy did not have a clear, coherent vision of its future role. But he had not yet won over the panel on the complex policy underlying his proposals. One staffer surmised that some conservatives had backed Hart simply because his proposals added money to a defense budget that they felt was too small.

Planned Budget Increases

The committee pointed out that the military services were planning spending increases over the next four years that would far outstrip Carter's planned increases in the defense budget. For instance, the Pentagon projected a $12 billion real increase (after inflation) in its fiscal 1980 budget request for weapons, research and pay. But Carter had projected only an $11.3 billion increase, including the cost of inflation.

The Army might face a particularly tight budget crunch because it was either just beginning, or planning to begin within the next few years, the purchase of several expensive new weapons designed to offset the Soviet military buildup in Europe. By 1983 the service planned to have spent more than $22 billion just on new weapons and vehicles, such as helicopters to hunt tanks and carry troops ($7.8 billion), anti-aircraft guns and missiles ($5.9 billion) and the new XM-1 tank ($3.8 billion).

Historically, the committee pointed out, administrations had dealt with the Defense Department's money shortages by cutting back the annual production rate of expensive arms and equipment. But at low production rates, the cost per copy tended to skyrocket.

Strategic Arms and SALT

The panel warned the administration not to slow down any nuclear weapons programs in anticipation of a strategic arms limitation (SALT) treaty with Moscow without first consulting Congress. "Present legislation may not adequately provide for the degree of participation that the committee deems necessary to carry out its responsibilities."

Cruise Missiles. Citing shifting Pentagon explanations of the program to develop air-launched cruise missiles, the committee demanded that the administration set firm timetables and cost estimates for the program. (The missiles were small drone airplanes that could carry a nuclear warhead up to 2,000 miles to within tens of yards of a target. In June 1977 President Carter decided to develop cruise missiles — which could be launched in swarms against the Soviet Union from existing bombers — instead of the B-1 bomber.)

The panel also increased to $81.8 million — an $18.5 million increase — a program to develop a much faster version of the cruise missiles, the ASALM.

By a party line vote of 9-6, the Democratic majority on the committee approved the $41.4 million requested to test the use of wide-body commercial jetliners as cruise missile launchers. Theoretically, each of the big planes could carry up to 70 cruise missiles, launching them from beyond the reach of Soviet air defenses. But critics of the plan insisted the planes would be vulnerable to attack either at their home bases or in the air.

One staffer charged that the administration was moving too fast with a proposal that had not been thought through, simply so Carter could point to the wide-body carrier as his alternative to the B-1. "They don't need the money now [to test the concept], and when they need it they can get it quickly," he said.

But another staffer maintained that the six votes against the test were merely symbolic protests against Carter's cancellation of the B-1. "Revenge is not unknown as a congressional motive," he said.

ICBMs and Space War. Looming large in the committee's thinking was the belief that increasingly accurate Soviet missiles would be able to destroy U.S. land-based missiles (ICBMs) in their underground silos by the mid-1980s. It ordered the Pentagon to report by Sept. 30 on whether it planned to build prototypes of a new, mobile ICBM, the M-X, that could counter this threat. The decision had been delayed pending tests to determine which of several alternative plans for movable missile launchers M-X would use. But SALT hard-liners feared that administration civilian planners were trying to stall the new missile to death.

A Russian attack on U.S. missiles might be coordinated with attacks against the satellites on which U.S. forces depend for early warning. So the committee increased by $15 million — to $107.2 million — the authorization for programs to defend U.S. satellites against attack.

Missile Submarines. Citing construction delays on the seven Trident missile submarines already under contract, the committee delayed authorization of the eighth ship of that class, cutting over $900 million from the bill. And it added $16 million for the Pentagon to begin studies of a smaller, cheaper missile submarine to replace the Trident in the future. *(Trident delays, box, p. 342)*

Critics of the Tridents charged that their size — two football fields long, carrying 24 missiles — made them too expensive and vulnerable to Soviet detection.

The committee insisted that the administration either begin construction of or cancel once and for all a radio transmitter for sending orders to submerged missile submarines. To pick up existing radio signals, submarines had to come very close to the ocean's surface, and the Navy was worried that they could be located by Soviet satellites. But a new radio system, called ELF, could communicate with submarines several hundred feet below the surface using a large, 130-mile-long underground antenna spanning the Michigan-Wisconsin border.

For nearly a decade, three administrations had sought to keep the program alive while deferring a final decision on its construction because of intense local opposition to the plan.

Opponents warned that energy radiating from the antenna could pose a health hazard. But the committee insisted those fears had been put to rest by a National Academy of Sciences-sponsored study. "No technical issues remain to be resolved. . . . This decision is essentially a political one," it said.

Shipbuilding

Beyond the carrier issue, the committee lambasted the Navy for poor management, reflected in slow deliveries and cost overruns, of its shipbuilding program. But the Navy maintained that its legal battles with shipyards involved contracts signed in the early 1970s under procedures no longer in use. The shipyards claimed that those contracts made them bear the cost of construction delays that were caused by Navy-instigated changes in the ship designs.

No lawsuits had arisen out of subsequent contracts, which increased the Navy's liability for any delays. And the first of a new class of missile frigates was commissioned in December 1977 on time and under budget.

But the committee charged that the new contracts would remove only the litigation, not the root cause of the problem: excessive design changes and the consequent delays and cost overruns. The Navy should be much further along in the detailed design of new ships before it sought funding for them, the panel suggested. And it added to the bill a provision establishing a five-member commission to propose improvements in the existing ship contracting system.

Cheaper Ships. The Navy needed more ships than it could afford, according to the committee, partly because it designed ships that were unnecessarily sophisticated for their missions and hence too expensive. It ordered the Navy to consider designing attack submarines that would be cheaper than the current *Los Angeles*-class ships ($433 million a copy). Even non-nuclear-powered subs were to be considered.

Submarine Hunting. Recent developments in underwater detection enabled the Navy to locate Russian submarines as far as 60 miles from a U.S. fleet — too far away to be hit by most anti-submarine weapons. To increase the range of the fleet's anti-submarine punch, the committee directed the Navy to simplify the design of a sub-hunting helicopter (called LAMPS III) that was having cost overruns and development problems. And it added $30 million for development of an experimental destroyer-sized surface effect ship (SES).

Navy, Marine Jets

The committee criticized administration requests to slow down purchases of F-14 and F-18 fighters for the Navy. It added $60 million for four additional F-14s — bringing the total authorization to $584 million for 28 planes. And it recommended that F-14 production continue at the rate of 36 planes a year. It also increased to 9, from the 5 requested, the number of F-18s, which were less expensive than the F-14.

The administration had cut back the planned purchases of both planes because of fiscal constraints. For the same reason the Navy had proposed canceling the F-18 so it could buy more F-14s, which had a long-range missile system that could shoot down Soviet anti-ship missiles.

The committee also rejected the request for 18 A-4 light bombers for the Marines to replace Harrier V/STOL bombers that had crashed. The Marines should rely on an improved version of the Harrier and a bomber version of the F-18, the panel said.

Ground Combat

The Soviet potential for launching a blitzkrieg in Europe using tanks and artillery was a dominant consideration in the panel's actions on ground combat weapons. It approved plans to begin production of the new XM-1 tank. And it recommended that the Army modify more of the current M-60 tanks, including the installation of new gun aiming equipment, to meet the high quality of Soviet tanks.

The Senate panel, agreeding with the House position, directed the Army to begin production of a long-delayed armored vehicle to carry infantry into battle alongside the XM-1 tank. It acknowledged that the new carrier had problems. Critics charged that its high silhouette could give away the hiding place of the tank and that its armor was too thin. But the existing troop carrier had even less armor, and it was too slow to keep up with the new tank. "In our judgment it is time to end this bureaucratic pursuit of the perfect vehicle and to get on with fielding what already has taken us 15 years to develop," said the committee.

To speed up adaptation of a German-designed cannon for the new XM-1 tank, the committee added $37.5 billion.

Airlift. But the committee killed a key element in Pentagon plans to rapidly reinforce U.S. troops in Europe. Called CRAF, the plan would pay airlines a bonus to modify their wide-body passenger jetliners so they could be converted to freight haulers in several hours' time in an emergency. The panel said that conversion of existing jets would be too expensive and that the program should be redirected to pay airlines to order new planes that were designed to be easily converted to carry freight. The $68.5 million program was cut back to $7.5 million.

The committee cut from two to one the number of ATCA mid-air tanker planes (a modified DC-10 jetliner) authorized. The second plane could be deferred until detailed design work was further advanced, it said.

It added funds for eight C-130 transports to replace older planes flown by Air National Guard units. And it added $25 million to complete development of a new V/STOL transport (called AMST) that the administration wanted to cancel.

Korea Troop Withdrawal

Although it expressed deep concern over the military risks of Carter's plan to withdraw U.S. ground troops from South Korea, the panel did not try to block the pullout as had the House Armed Services Committee. But it directed the secretary of defense to give the committee, before any additional troops were pulled out, an analysis of the military and diplomatic effects of the proposed move.

Manpower and the Volunteer Army

The committee basically accepted the manpower ceilings for active duty forces that were requested by the administration, but it cut back proposed reductions that would have resulted from shorter recruit training periods.

All Volunteer Force. "It should be clear that the all volunteer force is a peacetime concept that is not now providing sufficient numbers of reserve personnel and would be hard pressed to provide additional numbers of active recruits should the national security require an expansion of current active force levels," the committee warned.

It charged that some recruiting campaigns placed too little emphasis on patriotism as a motive for joining the service. It directed the Pentagon to study alternatives to current recruiting policies and to report on changes in the current draft law that would shorten the time it would take to re-institute the draft in an emergency.

Reserve Problems. Because the reserve forces played so large a role in military plans once the draft was ended, the committee urged that active duty personnel be assigned to supervise the training of reserve units. And it ordered the Pentagon to submit with the next budget request a plan to reduce the shortage of nearly 300,000 members in the pool of reservists from which the Army planned to replace its casualties during a war. It extended for one year experimental education benefits and re-enlistment bonuses.

Women at Sea. As the House had done, the Senate panel approved provisions that would allow women to be assigned to non-combatant naval ships and, on a temporary basis, to warships not on combat missions. But it insisted that the duration of such assignments be limited.

Senate Floor Action

In two days of debate (July 10-11) on HR 10929, the Senate sent as mixed a set of signals on the Navy's future as had the Armed Services Committee in its version of the bill.

At the same time, it tentatively endorsed the development of smaller, relatively inexpensive aircraft carriers to supplement the current fleet of 12 giant ones. But the Senate also approved construction of one more of the $2 billion, 1,000-foot-long behemoths to replace the World War II-vintage *Midway*, due to be retired in the mid-1980s.

As passed July 11 by an 87-2 vote, the Senate version authorized $36.1 billion for weapons procurement and military research, $615.7 million more than President Carter had requested, but $1.8 billion less than the version passed May 24 by the House. *(Vote 203, p. 33-S)*

Uneasy Truce

Floor action on the bill suggested that the Senate shared its committee's uncertainty about future carrier policy. Evidently willing to explore the new V/STOL approach — at least while the costs were modest — it adopted amendments adding $5.5 million to develop an improved V/STOL fighter and requiring that any future carrier be substantially cheaper than the current large ships. The Senate also rejected an amendment that would have canceled the helicopter carrier conversion proposal.

But the additional $5.5 million authorization was approved by only a five-vote margin (49-44). And the other two floor amendments, which could have tested the extent of Senate support for the new V/STOL approach, were disposed of by voice votes.

In addition to leaving unscathed the authorization for one more big nuclear-powered carrier, V/STOL supporters failed by a three-to-one margin (22-68) to kill the Navy's new F-18 fighter. Hart warned that since the new fighter needed big carriers, their procurement would feed political pressure to build more of the big ships in the future.

NATO, SALT Tensions

Members used the debate to express their concern that the European members of NATO were not paying their fair share of the alliance's defense of Western Europe.

The committee accepted an amendment that would require the president to report to Congress on NATO members' compliance with the alliance policy of increasing defense expenditures by 3 percent annually to offset larger Soviet conventional forces in Eastern Europe.

No amendments were offered bearing on the U.S.-Soviet strategic arms limitation (SALT) talks. But the grim Senate prospect facing the administration's SALT policy was evident in a heated exchange between Henry M. Jackson, D-Wash., a leading critic of Carter's arms control policies, and Thomas J. McIntyre, D-N.H.

Citing published reports of various provisions already drafted on a SALT treaty, Jackson charged that they fit a pattern of administration weakness in dealing with Moscow: "A one-way flow of concessions — from West to East— and an alarming tendency to appease the Russians by accepting their terms on such crucial matters as [SALT]."

McIntyre protested that the treaty could be judged only when all its provisions were viewed in relation to each other. "Why is it," he said, "that people like the distinguished senator from Washington will not allow this treaty to come before us as a finished package, but instead tries to knock it down and defeat it in the eyes of the people before we even have a chance to see it?"

Hart added that a good SALT agreement would improve U.S. ability to face down Soviet probes since it would forestall costly expansions of the strategic force, thus making funds available for improved conventional combat forces.

Soviet Dissidents' Trials. Like other hard-liners, Jackson pointed to Soviet prosecution of dissidents, Anatoly Shcharansky and Aleksandr Ginzburg, as evidence of Moscow's perfidious nature. The trials violated the 1975 Helsinki accords and the 1948 Declaration of Human Rights, he said, "two treaties . . . that the Soviets voluntarily signed. I think that is very relevant to what can be expected of the Soviets in connection with the SALT agreement."

Other Senate hard-liners argued that the SALT talks should be suspended temporarily to show U.S. displeasure at the crackdown of Soviet dissidents. But Senate leaders July 11 produced a less drastic gesture of protest — a resolution deploring the trials and urging the Soviet government to resolve the cases in a "humanitarian" way. *(Protest resolution, p. 369)*

F-18 Fighter

Hart's first attempt to further tilt the bill toward accelerated V/STOL development was through an amendment to delete $983.1 million for continued development of the F-18 fighter and for the first nine production-line F-18s. The amendment would have killed the $14 billion program to produce 800 fighters and light bombers for the Navy and Marine Corps by the late 1980s.

Since the plane could operate only off big carriers, Hart argued, it would be used to justify further construction of the very types of ships the Russians had drawn up plans to sink. "The F-18 plays directly into Soviet hands." The program also would slow development of V/STOLs by absorbing funds that otherwise would be available for the new technology, he insisted.

The F-18 would not even be effective against the Russian missile threat, Hart maintained. It was designed as an extraordinarily agile weapon to attack other planes at short range. Waves of cruise missiles could be stopped only by the F-14 fighter with its long-range missiles and powerful radar, according to Hart. "The F-18s are going to be up there, . . . playing Red Baron, while the carrier is sinking."

Howard W. Cannon, D-Nev., chairman of the committee's Tactical Airpower Subcommittee, led the counterattack in favor of the F-18. Hart's underlying assumption that the Navy could move quickly to V/STOL was wrong, Cannon retorted. Because of their greater complexity, V/STOL planes would weigh from one-third to one-half again as much as conventional planes designed for the same mission, he said. And they would be more costly by nearly the same percentage.

The F-18 was needed to replace some of the Navy's conventional jets, which rapidly were becoming obsolescent, on existing carriers, he said. And they would yield a bonus when the light bomber versions (called A-18s) replaced the existing A-7 bombers. Since the bomber versions would have nearly the same fighter ability as the F-18s, they could be used in either role, greatly enlarging the carrier's air defense force.

Hart's amendment was rejected 22-68. *(Vote 198, p. 33-S)*

Harrier Fighter

Hart was more successful on his second amendment, which added $5.5 million to develop a fighter version of the improved Harrier V/STOL. The basic Harrier was used by the Marine Corps as a light bomber, and the committee had doubled, to $173 million (the Marine's original request), funds for development of an improved version. The improved Harrier would carry more bombs over a greater range. Hart proposed a further modification of the improved Harrier to carry the F-18's radar and air-to-air missiles, and to carry Navy electronic equipment.

Hart insisted that this plane (Harrier B+) would give the Navy a good V/STOL by the mid-1980s to operate off existing helicopter carriers or the new small carriers for which the committee had added design funds to the bill.

Cannon warned that Hart's proposal was another ill-founded effort to push V/STOL design too fast. He said the Navy had estimated that development of the proposed plane would cost $1.4 billion and would slow production of the improved Marine Corps version. And Hart's plane would be inferior to any existing Navy plane, he said.

But Hart prevailed on a 49-44 vote. *(Vote 199, p. 33-S)*

Future of the Carrier

Almost until the final vote, rumors circulated that an effort would be made to delete the big nuclear-powered carrier added by the Armed Services Committee. Officially, the administration still opposed the addition, although it had backed off from its original opposition to building any carrier in fiscal 1979; it now wanted a slightly smaller, non-nuclear-powered ship instead of the nuclear carrier.

But even though the Senate was widely assumed to be dubious about building another big carrier, administration officials did not lobby against it. And Senate skeptics of the big ship decided to swallow one more big carrier, but to make sure that it would be the last.

That position was embodied in an amendment by John C. Culver, D-Iowa, requiring that any future carriers requested by the Pentagon be "substantially smaller and less costly" than either the nuclear ship added by the committee or the smaller conventional ship preferred by the administration.

The president still could request a big ship if he advised Congress that smaller ships were not in the national interest. But in that case, the request would have to be accompanied by an alternate program incorporating smaller ships so that Congress could weigh the matter independently.

The amendment was adopted by voice vote with almost no debate, although Armed Services Chairman John C. Stennis, D-Miss., observed that it would face strong opposition from House Armed Services.

But shortly before the vote on the bill, the entire delicate compromise worked out by the committee was attacked by panel member Robert Morgan, D-N.C., who offered an amendment that would have removed the authorization for conversion of the helicopter carrier to serve as a V/STOL ship.

Until the Navy had a useful V/STOL plane, Morgan argued — and he agreed with Cannon that this might be 20 years off — conversion of the helicopter ship would serve no naval mission and would deprive the Marines of one of its key assault ships. "We are . . . changing the concept of naval warfare," said Morgan. "We are doing it without any kind of testimony having been taken before the committee . . . without the support of the Navy or without the support of any of the other military experts."

Hart, taken by surprise, declared that if the amendment carried, he then would offer an amendment to delete the nuclear carrier from the bill. Hart cited former Chief of Naval Operations Adm. James L. Holloway III, who told Hart he supported the conversion on the condition that 12 big carriers were maintained.

After Stennis and John G. Tower, R-Texas, urged him not to tear up the committee's package, Morgan settled for a voice vote on the amendment, which was rejected.

Ship Research

The Senate also adopted 90-4 a Hart amendment adding $25.2 million for five research projects that would further two other aspects of his plan for a new technology Navy:

- New ship designs that would allow construction of faster ships.
- Modularized combat gear to provide for quick conversion of merchant ships to troop carriers that would transport Marine attack forces. *(Vote 200, p. 33-S)*

NATO: Fair Shares and Readiness

Stennis, floor manager of the bill, expressed the committee's skepticism about whether European members of NATO were pulling their fair share of the load. He welcomed recent pledges by most alliance members to increase their defense spending, but he warned that those commitments would have to be realized.

He insisted that he supported the alliance now as firmly as he had in the early 1970s when he fought widely supported moves in the Senate for large reductions in U.S. troop commitments. But he added: "We are doing far more than was originally intended and far more now, I think, than our rightful share." But he added that he would support the current level of U.S. support for the alliance.

By voice vote the Senate accepted an amendment by Thomas F. Eagleton, D-Mo., requiring the president to report by February 1979 on the current and planned defense expenditures of the other alliance members. It also declared as a matter of policy that future increases in U.S. defense spending should be matched, proportionally, by the other alliance members and required the president to report whether the other members met the alliance goal of a 3 percent annual real increase in defense spending.

Eagleton was supported by Sam Nunn, D-Ga., one of the committee's strongest NATO supporters. Stennis agreed to accept the amendment after Nunn assured him it had been watered down from an earlier version that had called for explicit findings as to which alliance members had increased their budgets by the required percentage.

The same sensitive issue of burden-sharing in NATO surfaced in an amendment by Nunn, adopted by voice

Navy Carrier Studies: A Sea of Paper, an Ocean of Ink

The Navy's next aircraft carrier could float on the ocean of ink that has been used since 1976 in numerous studies of its mission and design.

Persons on nearly every side of the carrier debate have had at least one study providing authoritative support for their views:

Navy Carrier Study (January 1976)

The opening shot in the debate was a Navy study in late 1975 of four nuclear-powered carrier designs. These ranged from a stripped-down version of the current *Nimitz*-class (96,000 tons, carrying 94 planes) to the smallest ship (65,000 tons carrying 53 planes), which could simultaneously launch and land Navy carrier jets.

The study concluded that, for several hypothetical missions, the modified *Nimitz* was superior to the alternatives because: 1) it could carry more planes, launch them faster and carry more fuel and bombs; 2) it could operate planes in rougher seas than could the smaller ships; and 3) building additional copies of the already-designed type would be cheaper per copy than designing and building an entirely new type, unless more than three ships were built.

NSC Study (January 1977)

During 1976 the National Security Council (NSC) considered the effectiveness of fleets of various sizes. The smallest would contain 10 carriers. The study remained classified, but according to a subsequent General Accounting Office (GAO) report the NSC concluded that 12 carriers would be needed to fulfill current U.S. war contingency plans and peacetime commitments. Underlying this decision, apparently, was the assumption that the Navy should continue to station two carriers in the Mediterranean region and two in the western Pacific. For each carrier stationed abroad, the Navy assumed there would be one undergoing overhaul and one training in home waters.

GAO Critique of the NSC Study (December 1977)

The GAO faulted the NSC study for failing to re-examine some basic assumptions that led to the Navy's emphasis on the carrier: 1) it did not consider whether some carrier missions might be performed better or more cheaply by land-based planes, cruise missiles or other large warships; 2) it assumed that carriers were needed to protect the sea lanes between the United States and Europe in case of a Soviet attack on NATO; 3) it assumed that nuclear weapons would not be used in a war at sea. However, the GAO study argued that if nuclear weapons were used, the relatively few large carriers in the U.S. fleet would be vulnerable.

CBO Study (December 1976)

Opponents of building more big carriers fashioned new ammunition out of a CBO study that argued that the Navy should plan either to 1) protect the sea lanes to Europe or 2) attack Soviet forces involved in any land battle in Europe.

According to this study, the first mission revolved on fending off Russian submarines — a task for which the Navy would require neither new carriers nor the expensive Aegis anti-aircraft ships designed to protect carriers near Soviet land bases.

If the Navy were designed for the land-combat role, it would need many more big carriers and Aegis escorts. But the nearer the carriers approached Soviet bases, the greater the proportion of their planes that would be needed for self-defense. Even then, the study argued, the fleet's defenses might be swamped by the sheer number of cruise missiles fired at it.

Sea Plan 2000 (March 1978)

The Navy's rebuttal to the CBO analysis was summed up in a Navy study of what the fleet's role should be in the 1990s. Because ships lasted so long, and the international political situation changed so fast, the United States could not afford to design the Navy to fit specific circumstances. Moreover, direct carrier strikes on Soviet targets were essential to tie down Russian forces. And the fleet would have to operate close to Soviet land bases to reinforce U.S. allies, the study said. This would be feasible because of breakthroughs in defending the fleet against Russian cruise missiles.

A Navy of 10 carriers could do no more than protect the most vital U.S. sea lanes in time of war, it concluded. And it would mean a cutback in the number of carriers stationed abroad in peacetime. The current force of 12 carriers represented the "minimum acceptable risk" to U.S. goals: the ability to protect the sea lanes and launch direct attacks on Soviet forces in time of war. A 14-carrier Navy would provide greater certainty that those missions could be carried out.

Sea-Based Air Platforms (February 1978)

Mandated by a Senate amendment to the fiscal 1978 weapons authorization bill, another Navy study considered the relative merits of various plane-carrying ships ranging in size from the *Nimitz*-class nuclear carrier to destroyers carrying only a small number of helicopters or V/STOL planes.

In five hypothetical situations the study found that for most cases a fleet of *Nimitzes* was more effective than a slightly larger force of smaller, non-nuclear-powered carriers (CVVs), but overall the two forces were "relatively comparable." It also concluded that there were real advantages to smaller ships — which could carry only V/STOL planes — if they were produced in large numbers.

Congressional Research Service (April 1978)

Because the only available V/STOL plane, the Harrier, was militarily inferior to contemporary jets, it would not be worthwhile to build carriers that could not also operate with conventional planes, according to a Library of Congress analysis. But it might be useful to operate Harriers on existing ships that could not handle conventional jets, it concluded.

vote, to release funds appropriated in fiscal 1978 to develop a version of the AWACS radar-warning plane that would be purchased by NATO for joint use. Since the new hardware would not be used on the AWACS version being purchased by the U.S. Air Force, the funds were to be embargoed under the 1978 law until at least one other NATO member signed a contract to purchase the plane.

Nunn assured the Senate that the restriction's intent had been met, since several allied governments were committed to paying for development of the NATO version. But formal contracts had to await parliamentary approval in each country, and the embargoed funds were needed immediately.

Also approved by voice vote was an amendment by Dewey F. Bartlett, R-Okla., to protect U.S. combat equipment stored in Europe against sale to other countries. Large stocks of Army equipment, including tanks, missiles and guns, were stored in Europe to equip reinforcements that would be flown over from the United States in case of a crisis and to replace equipment that would be destroyed during the course of a war. (During the 1973 Middle East war, much of this equipment had been rushed to Israel, and the stockpiles had not yet been fully restored.)

The amendment barred sales of such equipment outside NATO unless the president declared that an international crisis existed. If he approved any sales from the stockpiles during a crisis, he would have to send Congress within 60 days a budget plan for replenishing the stocks.

Personnel Amendments

Naval Reserve. By a 28-64 vote, the Senate rejected an amendment by Robert Dole, R-Kan., that would have increased from 87,000 to 95,900 the size of the Naval Reserve. Dole argued that the higher figure was the number recommended by the most recent Pentagon analysis — made in 1975 — of Naval Reserve requirements. *(Vote 201, p. 33-S)*

But Nunn noted that the committee recommendation — an increase of 35,600 men over the administration's request of 51,400 — would maintain the Naval Reserve at its current strength. Even at that level, he pointed out, the Navy had not found significant assignments for all reserve members. (Beginning in 1976, every budget had recommended cutting the Naval Reserve to about 52,000.) By holding steady at 87,000, Nunn argued, Congress could impress on the administration its insistence that the Naval Reserve be given meaningful assignments.

Retiree Survivors' Benefits. The Senate narrowly rejected (43-46) an amendment by Strom Thurmond, R-S.C., that would have liberalized the existing survivor benefits plan for widows of military retirees that was enacted in 1972. The amendment was identical to HR 3702, which was passed by the House in 1977 by a vote of 391-0. *(Vote 202, p. 33-S)*

Thurmond protested that he had been trying for three years to have hearings held on a similar bill to reverse what the Pentagon conceded were inadvertent inequities in the benefits program.

But Stennis and Budget Committee Chairman Edmund S. Muskie, D-Maine, objected that the proposed changes were far too complex and potentially costly to be approved without exhaustive hearings, which Stennis promised would be held in the near future.

Other Amendments

The Senate approved by voice votes and without debate five additional amendments:

- By Thurmond, to cut $28.7 million from the budget request for modification of Navy anti-submarine torpedoes. The Navy agreed that the reduction was feasible because the original request had overestimated the cost of the program.
- By Barry Goldwater, R-Ariz., to bar use of the $41.2 million authorized for development of a wide-body jet that would be used to launch nuclear cruise missiles until the president submitted to Congress an arms control impact statement on the program.
- By Bartlett, to make the commandant of the Marine Corps a full-fledged member of the Joint Chiefs of Staff. Technically, the Marine Corps was part of the Navy and, under existing law, the commandant sat as a member of the Joint Chiefs only when Marine Corps matters were being discussed. The amendment merely ratified existing practice, Bartlett said, because in recent years commandants had participated in nearly all meetings of the Joint Chiefs.
- By Nunn, to assure that military training was available to, but not compulsory for, women attending the two public and two private colleges that trained their male students in a military curriculum similar to that of the national service academies.
- By Eagleton, to earmark $200,000 of the amount authorized for civil defense for a study of the special civil defense needs of areas that likely would be prime targets for a nuclear attack because they contained U.S. nuclear forces.
- By William V. Roth, Jr., R-Del., to exempt from the Fair Labor Standards Act persons who worked for tips by bagging and carrying out groceries at military commissaries.

Three amendments were withdrawn without a vote.

- By Eagleton, to reform the military retired pay system. After expressing his dismay at the cost of the current military pension system and praising some aspects of the reform proposed by a presidential commission, Eagleton withdrew his amendment in anticipation of President Carter's own reform proposals being sent to Congress early in 1979.
- By Daniel Patrick Moynihan, D-N.Y., to authorize use of military personnel to support the 1979 Winter Olympic Games at Lake Placid, N.Y.
- By Richard S. Schweiker, R-Pa., to restore $78.4 million deleted by the committee for 16 CH-47C cargo helicopters for the Army.

Both Moynihan and Schweiker withdrew their amendments after Armed Services Committee members promised to reconsider the two items, both of which were in the House version of the bill, during the Senate-House conference on HR 10929.

The net effect of floor action was to increase the authorization $2 million over the committee recommendation.

Provisions

As passed by the Senate July 11, HR 10929 authorized the following amounts for weapons procurement, military research and civil defense for fiscal 1979:

	House-Passed Authorizations	Senate-Passed Authorizations
Procurement		
Aircraft:		
Army	$ 1,037,400,000	$ 939,400,000
Navy and Marine Corps	4,546,780,000	4,163,500,000
Air Force	7,046,400,000	6,994,500,000
Missiles:		
Army	795,600,000	669,900,000
Navy	1,593,700,000	1,573,600,000
Marine Corps	23,100,000	23,100,000
Air Force	1,632,100,000	1,626,500,000
Naval vessels	7,026,100,000	5,602,700,000
Tracked combat vehicles:		
Army	1,518,900,000	1,264,000,000
Marine Corps	24,300,000	21,700,000
Torpedoes	426,800,000	335,400,000
Other weapons:		
Army	93,100,000	125,400,000
Navy	129,800,000	74,100,000
Marine Corps	30,200,000	28,000,000
Air Force	300,000	300,000
Total, procurement	$25,924,580,000	$23,442,100,000
Research, Development, Test and Evaluation		
Army	2,586,215,000	2,727,340,000
Navy and Marine Corps	4,287,009,000	4,585,894,000
Air Force	3,989,400,000	4,343,500,000
Defense agencies	974,816,000	904,200,000
Total, R.D.T. & E.	$11,837,440,000	$12,560,934,000
Civil Defense	137,000,000	96,500,000
GRAND TOTAL	$37,899,020,000	$36,099,534,000

Conference Report

The report of the House-Senate conference committee on HR 10929 (H Rept 95-1402) was filed July 31 and was adopted routinely in both houses Aug. 4 by voice votes.

The conference version authorized $36,956,969,000 for weapons procurement, military research and civil defense in fiscal 1979. This amount was $942 million less than had been authorized by the House and $857 million more than had been approved by the Senate. (The breakdown of the authorizations in the bill were identical to those in the revised bill except for the naval vessels category — $6,191,500,000 — which contained the carrier authorization. *See Final Provisions, p. 338)*

The bill exceeded the president's original request by almost $1.5 billion. But the administration had indicated it would accept the authorization of a conventionally powered aircraft carrier, hoping to defuse the congressional attempt to add the more expensive nuclear carrier to the budget.

Not counting the authorization for another carrier, the final version of HR 10929 actually was less than the weapons budget proposed by the president.

Carriers and Costs

For a fifth nuclear powered aircraft carrier, the fourth of the *Nimitz*-class, the bill provided $1.93 billion as recommended by the Senate. An additional $200 million provided by the House to revise the design for protecting ammunition magazines in the proposed carrier was turned down by the conference committee.

Conferees also agreed to Senate-backed additions that would begin design of the new small carrier ($25 million), convert a helicopter carrier to serve as an interim carrier ($45 million) and begin work on a larger helicopter carrier to replace the converted one ($70 million of an estimated total cost of $700 million).

According to one source, the effect of the cut in long-term Navy V/STOL research could be to freeze the plan to have combat planes ready in the 1990s. But Navy witnesses previously had told Congress that major facets of that program likely would be abandoned in any case.

The improved Harrier (called the Harrier B) would carry more bombs and fly greater distances than the version then in service, thus meeting a principal criticism of the plane's usefulness for naval missions. Conferees also agreed to provide $3 million to design a version of the Harrier B that would be especially adapted for service at sea.

Numbers and Costs. The biggest factor in the future of V/STOL may have been the deep concern of many members, including some of the Senate Armed Service Committee's most influential hard-liners, over the high cost of Navy programs.

House conferees watered down several Senate provisions aimed at cutting the cost of future ships, but the final version of the bill:

- Stipulated it to be national policy that future ships were to be "more survivable, less costly and more effective than those currently in the Navy."
- Provided $3 million to design a new missile-launching submarine to replace the current $1.2 billion Trident. The conference report deleted a Senate requirement that the new ship be smaller.
- Incorporated several cuts in Navy research imposed by the Senate to force development of smaller attack submarines for future construction.
- Authorized $369 million for the Aegis anti-aircraft system of a nuclear cruiser, as sought by the House. But only those components that also could be used in a cheaper, non-nuclear Aegis ship would be purchased. Congress had not yet approved the cruiser.

Strategic Warfare

Conferees provided $20.6 million (half the Senate-approved figure) for development of an airplane to carry strategic cruise missiles. The program would be required to consider the feasibility of using military transport planes and the B-1 bomber in addition to commercial jets as potential cruise missile carriers. Proponents of the project hoped that wide-body jets would be able to fire dozens of long-range cruise missiles at Soviet targets from beyond the reach of Russian air defenses.

Opponents, however, dismissed the plan as a feeble substitute for a new penetrating bomber — such as the B-1 — that could get through Soviet defenses to the targets. For further experiments with the four test models of the B-1, conferees allowed $55 million (of $105.5 million requested).

The $48.5 million requested for research on a future cruise missile (ASALM) that would be much faster than the current version was allowed. The Senate had added $18.5 million in hopes of assuring that the new missile would meet its scheduled delivery date of late 1985.

For research on submarine-launched strategic missiles, conferees endorsed the House position. The amount requested for development of the current Trident I was increased by $8.2 million (to $199.97 million) so that a maneuverable warhead to dodge enemy defensive missiles could more easily be added in the future. But the request for studies of a longer range Trident II was cut to $5 million (from $15 million requested). The House committee had complained that the program was too vague.

For the proposed underground radio antenna (Seafarer), the conference agreed to $20 million (of $40.5 million requested). The money could be used only after the president selected a site for the system. Originally planned for Michigan and Wisconsin, the project had been stymied by intense local opposition.

Research on protecting reconnaissance and communications satellites against Soviet attack was increased by $15 million (to $107.2 million). And a project to improve satellite detection of nuclear explosions was increased to $16.1 million (from $9.1 million). A House cut to $3.9 million (from $19.9 million requested) for a new satellite-based missile detection system was upheld, but $4.1 million was allowed, as requested, for coordinating the various attack warning systems.

The $96.5 million requested for civil defense was approved instead of the House recommendation of $137 million.

NATO Buildup

Nuclear Missiles. For various long-range nuclear weapons to be based in Europe, conferees added a total of $11.9 million to the request: $9.9 million for a new version of the 400-mile-range Pershing missile and $2 million for development of a longer range missile. The conferees worried that the Army and Air Force were not coordinating their development projects for medium-range weapons.

They also cut to $20.2 million (from $40.1 million) the request to start purchasing parts for a ground-launched version of the cruise missile that would carry a nuclear warhead. But they added to the budget $30.1 million to start buying parts for a ship-launched version.

Tank, Anti-tank Weapons. For production of a new version of the M-60 tank with improved gun aiming equipment, conferees agreed on $343.6 million for 410 tanks (of $383.8 million requested for 480 tanks). But conferees concluded that only 380 older M-60s could be given the new aiming equipment in fiscal 1979 ($132.4 million).

For armored infantry carriers, conferees agreed to the Senate-passed recommendations: $39 million to begin production of a new infantry fighting vehicle and $44.5 million to continue production of the current troop carrier, which was much less powerfully armed and armored.

A Senate amendment prohibiting sales to non-NATO countries of U.S. equipment stored in Europe was retained. The stocks were intended to equip reinforcements that would be flown to Europe from the United States in a crisis and to replace equipment destroyed during a war.

Alliance Politics. For adaptation of a 120mm German cannon to the Army's new XM-1 tank, conferees agreed to allow $35.6 million. And they rejected a House-passed provision that would have restored the pre-1977 law requiring the Pentagon to buy only American-made products containing the high-quality steel alloys used in weapons. In 1977 the Pentagon had been allowed to waive that limitation so it could buy European weapons for standardizing equipment within NATO.

The conference report language — but not the final version of the bill itself — directed the secretary of defense to submit to Congress by Feb. 1, 1979, the amount spent for defense by each NATO member in fiscal 1978 and 1979.

To produce the first batch of French/German-designed Roland short-range anti-aircraft missiles for the Army, $165 million was allowed. But as a hedge against future problems with Roland, conferees also accepted a House-passed addition of $10 million to develop an improved version of the existing Chaparral short-range missile.

Airlift. For modification of existing commercial jetliners to allow them quickly to be converted to military cargo planes, $28.5 million was approved out of $68.5 million requested. And conferees agreed to add to the budget $15 million to keep alive a project to develop a medium-range short-takeoff transport that the administration tried to kill.

For the first two of a fleet of tanker versions of the DC-10, $143.5 million was approved as requested. And $9 million was added to the request to begin putting new engines on the existing fleet of KC-135 tanker planes.

Recruiting Incentives

Conferees endorsed the Senate committee's requirement that the secretary of defense examine various alternatives to the current all-volunteer military. And they directed the secretary to test an additional alternative: a two-year enlistment (instead of the usual three-year term) for the Army's combat arms and the Navy's engine room jobs. This might attract better qualified enlistees, they said, if it were linked to increased post-service education benefits (which the Pentagon already was authorized to offer).

Conferees also extended for two years the existing system of enlistment and re-enlistment bonuses that the Pentagon paid to attract personnel to key hard-to-fill jobs.

Reserves

Three programs to attract and retain members for reserve and National Guard units were extended for two years: enlistment and re-enlistment bonuses and a system of education benefits.

To modernize the Air National Guard, conferees authorized eight Hercules transport planes ($77.5 million) and 16 trainer versions of the A-7D light bomber ($145.5 million).

Carter Veto

In announcing his vote Aug. 17 of the $36.9 billion weapons procurement bill, President Carter based his decision squarely on the impact of the costly nuclear-powered aircraft carrier added by Congress. *(Veto message, p. 59-E)*

To pay for the $2 billion ship, Congress had cut "into the muscle of our military defense," Carter told a nationally televised press conference Aug. 17. "This is not a question of money. . . . It's a question of how that money is going to be spent."

Carter wanted more of it spent for projects directly related to the U.S. commitment to NATO and for maintaining the combat-readiness of forces already in the field, he said. But many of the congressional changes in the budget to which the president reportedly objected were not contained in HR 10929.

By noon the day after Carter's announcement, neither the White House nor the Defense Department had a list of the specific congressional actions Carter disagreed with, but various sources indicated that he really had two other bills in mind:

• The Senate version of the defense appropriations bill (HR 13635). The Defense Subcommittee reportedly had cut $200 million budgeted for Army ammunition, $437 million for operations and maintenance costs and $200 million for A-10 tank-hunting planes.

• The final version of the military construction appropriations bill (HR 12927), which cut several hundred million dollars requested for NATO-related construction projects in Europe.

According to some sources, the president concluded that he had to show his determination not to fund the carrier so Congress — and especially the Senate Appropriations Committee, which still was marking up the defense bill — would redirect the funds to items on which Carter placed a higher priority. *(Defense appropriations bill, see p. 132)*

Veto Maneuvering

Meanwhile, the administration mounted a public relations campaign which focused almost as much attention on itself as on the veto it was designed to support. Vice President Walter F. Mondale's chief of staff, Richard Moe, headed up a task force that was to meet daily to coordinate administration efforts to sustain the veto.

In a move reminiscent of the administration's massive campaign for public support of the Panama Canal treaties, a group of 250 business and civic leaders from around the country were invited to the White House Aug. 23 to hear the case for the veto. Mondale, Defense Secretary Harold Brown and national security adviser Zbigniew Brzezinski repeated the basic Carter line that NATO and readiness had been slighted to pay for the big ship.

On Aug. 31, a week before the scheduled House vote, the Pentagon announced that Deputy Defense Secretary Charles Duncan would carry the case for the veto to seven television stations scattered across the country.

"Obviously, we are reaching out to the people," said Pentagon spokesman Thomas Ross. He also claimed that a random check of editorial comment showed "overwhelming support" for the veto.

On Aug. 25, the day the Senate went home for its Labor Day recess, its Armed Services Committee mounted its own press campaign against the veto. Quoting from an 18-page analysis prepared by the committee staff, Chairman John C. Stennis, D-Miss., argued that the president's allegations about cuts in NATO and in readiness did not relate to the vetoed bill. In fact, he insisted that the bill went beyond the administration request in these areas by making significant additions.

"The veto message convinces me that the president did not have all the facts before him when he had that message prepared," Stennis concluded.

He conceded that the committee had been anxious not to exceed the budget requested by the president or the spending ceiling set by the congressional budget process; in 1975, he noted ruefully, Armed Services had been forced to rewrite an authorization bill which exceeded the congressional budget ceiling.

But he insisted that the additions and cuts to the administration budget had been made on their individual merits. And he said that the politics of writing the defense bills was so complex that it would have been impossible to coordinate dozens of separate reductions in order to make room for the carrier.

Joining Stennis on the floor, Research and Development Subcommittee Chairman Thomas J. McIntyre, D-N.H. explained the bill's principal changes in the research budget:

• $50 million had been cut from research on the B-1 bomber, which would not be produced.

• $35 million had been cut from eight separate programs (and the remaining money shifted among programs) for development of various weapons that would shoot multiple, highly accurate warheads at several tanks. This new approach had "fallen prey to normal bureaucratic competition," McIntyre said. "Many of the programs were only vaguely defined . . . attempts to get a foot in the door in the competition to be the leader in this new area."

• $50 million had been cut from the Navy's planned research on vertical takeoff jets (but $87.4 million was added to a Marine Corps vertical jet program that would be in service much sooner).

• $116 million had been added for various projects to develop new Navy ships — $36 million of this amount was oriented toward designing cheaper ships in the future, a principal reason cited by Carter for blocking the nuclear carrier.

Later that same day, a Pentagon official reportedly acknowledged to reporters that many of the president's objections related to the appropriations bill and not to the authorization bill. But he insisted that no mistake had been made. "The president vetoed the only bill in front of him because of his opposition to the nuclear carrier," said the official. It was simply a statement of fact, he maintained, that since the $2 billion carrier was being fit into an appropriations bill that was not going to exceed the president's budget request, requested programs of an equivalent value had to be dropped to make room.

Price Letter

On Aug. 31, House Armed Services Chairman Melvin Price, D-Ill., weighed in with a letter to Carter condemning not only the president's arithmetic but also his attitude toward Congress' role in national defense:

"The burden of your message is that Congress does not have a place in defense policymaking except insofar as it is prepared to rubber stamp recommendations of the executive branch," Price wrote. "I reject that philosophy."

He also protested Carter's implication that Congress knowingly had voted for a bill that would weaken national defense just to build the nuclear carrier. And he noted that Carter had not mentioned Navy Secretary W. Graham Claytor's letter to Price in May announcing that the administration would accept the $1.5 billion non-nuclear carrier in 1978 instead of next year as planned.

Earlier Votes

Three times during 1978 the House had voted in favor of the nuclear carrier by relatively large margins, including one such vote only 10 days before Carter acted:

• By 106-293 the House May 24, 1978, swamped an amendment by Bob Carr, D-Mich., which would have deleted the nuclear carrier from the authorization bill. The carrier survived by nearly a 3-to-1 margin, but that might have been deceptive: earlier that day Carr had offered an amendment that would have thrown out the Armed Services Committee's bill and many members were affronted by what they saw as an attack on the committee system. *(Vote 316, p. 90-H)*

Differences Between Vetoed Bill and Budget Request

Programs	Carter Request Number	Carter Request Amount (in millions)	Final Authorization Number	Final Authorization Amount (in millions)	Highlights
Aircraft carrier	—	—	1	$1,930.0	Omitted from request: $1.575 billion non-nuclear carrier administration said it would accept.
Carrier planes	53	$1,557.4	81	1,988.8	Faster production rates for F-14, F-18.
V/STOL development					
Planes		158.0		208.5	Shift to modified Harriers by 1980s instead of new planes. Not counted: bill's cancellation of $113 million of non-V/STOL planes for Marines.
Ships				140.0	
Trident missile submarine	1	911.9	—	—	
Surface effects ship	—	—	—	80.0	
XM-1 tank	110	585.1	110	493.3	Funding readjustments requested by administration and Congress' increase of $27.5 million to adapt German cannon.
M-60 tank (production)	480	383.8	410	345.0	Shift from purchase to modernization gives 90 more tanks for $4.8 million less.
M-60 tank (modernization)	220	98.4	380	132.4	
Infantry fighting vehicle	—	—	—	39.0	Shift to begin production of new type of troop carrier.
M-113 troop carrier	910	74.2	550	44.5	
Multiple anti-tank homing warheads	—	85.5	—	50.5	Funds shifted among eight research projects because of fear of duplication.
Medium-range ballistic missile	—	15.1	—	22.0	Pershing II missile shifted from Army to Air Force.
Air National Guard planes	—	—	24	223.0	Includes attack trainers and Hercules transports.
Strategic warplane research	—	210.0	—	140.9	Includes cuts of 50 percent in research on B-1 bomber ($50.5 million) and cruise missile carrier ($20.6 million).
Strategic attack warning	—	115.3	—	131.3	Increase of $25 million for satellite protection.

(in $ millions)

	Increases Above Carter's Requests	Decreases From Carter's Requests	Net Change From Request
Army			
procurement	$ 97.4	$ 273.7	−$ 176.3
research	54.0	113.7	− 59.7
Navy and Marines			
procurement	2,941.2	1,122.6	+ 1,818.6
research	287.4	279.1	+ 8.3
Air Force			
procurement	253.0	138.2	+ 114.8
research	83.9	258.5	− 174.6
Defense Agencies			
research	47.8	15.0	+ 32.8
Subtotal, procurement)	(3,291.6)	(1,534.5)	(+ 1,757.1)
(Subtotal, research)	(473.1)	(666.3)	(− 193.2)
Total	$3,764.7	$2,200.8	+$1,563.9

•The same day, the House rejected 139-264 an amendment by Les Aspin, D-Wis., that would have substituted a CVV for the nuclear ship in the authorization bill. *Nimitz* supporters fell only four votes short of a two-thirds majority. *(Vote 315, p. 90-H)*

•In a later test, the House Aug. 7 rejected 156-218 an amendment to the defense appropriations bill by Sidney R. Yates, D-Ill., that would have killed the nuclear carrier. Carrier supporters were 32 votes short of a two-thirds majority. An amendment that would have substituted a CVV for the *Nimitz* was ruled out of order. *(Vote 575, p. 164-H)*

Carter Objections

Carter complained that another big carrier would continue the trend toward a smaller number of very expensive Navy ships. But Gary Hart, D-Colo., a leading congressional proponent of moving the Navy toward a larger fleet consisting of cheaper ships, warned that a veto would set back that policy. Inclusion of the big carrier was essential to winning the support of many Senate committee members for the V/STOL acceleration and the concurrence of the House panel, which was even more skeptical of the new approach.

Hart urged the Senate to override the veto, arguing that Carter had ignored the bill's contribution to a new direction for the Navy.

Army Weapons

Although the president maintained that Congress had cut $800 million from the Army weapons budget, the reductions made in the procurement bill totaled only $387.4 million. This was in part offset by additions to the Army budget of $151.4 million.

The cuts included $127.4 million for production overhead costs for the new XM-1 tank contract. But much of this reduction was approved by the administration and did not change the number of tanks authorized.

Other cuts included some management reshuffles prompted by congressional dissatisfaction with the Army's control of various programs. For instance, $15.1 million for programs connected with the Army's 400-mile-range Pershing ballistic missile was cut. Instead, Congress gave the Air Force $20 million to manage the Pershing program. The two Armed Services Committees had been concerned that the long-range missile program was being given too low a priority by the Army and decided that the Air Force was more likely to push it.

Another management-related reduction in Army weapons involved the new A3 model of the current M-60 tank that had more accurate gun-aiming equipment than the earlier M-60 models. Carter had requested $383.3 million to produce 480 new M-60s and $98.4 million to add the new equipment to 220 of the older models already in stock. The Armed Services Committees concluded that by buying fewer new models (410) and modernizing more of the old ones (380), the Army would get 90 more tanks for $4.8 million less.

Air Force Weapons

The net reduction made in Air Force programs in the authorization bill was only $59.8 million, a quarter of the $200 million reduction cited by Carter. But that figure was derived from cuts totaling $396.7 million and additions of $336.9 million.

There were no cuts in Air Force planes and cuts of only $36.7 million in three missile programs. But Carter may have been piqued by the addition of $223 million for 16 trainers and 8 transports for the Air National Guard. And $40 million was cut from a program that was central to Defense Secretary Brown's plan to greatly increase the number of reinforcements that could be flown from the United States to Europe in case of a war. Called CRAF, the program called for modifying civilian passenger jets so they could quickly be converted in an emergency to carry military cargo. Of $68.5 million requested, the bill approved only $7.5 million.

Readiness-Related Programs

Carter's reference to a $500 million congressional cut in programs related to combat-readiness was unclear since the types of programs he mentioned — ship overhauls, training and logistical support — were not contained in the bill to be vetoed.

Overhauls. Major overhauls of ships, combat vehicles, airplanes and airplane engines did not require congressional authorization, but were an important element of the Operations and Maintenance account of the defense appropriations bill. Even if that was what Carter was referring to, his criticism was not relevant to House action on the fiscal 1979 funding bill (HR 13635). Of the $1.6 billion requested in the budget for major ship overhauls, the appropriations bill cut only $41 million. The House Appropriations Committee had argued that the shipyards could not absorb all the scheduled jobs. The bill added $182 million to the administration's request for Navy and Air Force overhauls of planes and aircraft engines. From the Army request of $975 million for major vehicle overhauls, the appropriations bill cut $8.4 million.

Training. Funds for training were not included in the authorization bill, nor were funds authorized for any other personnel costs. But the bill did authorize manpower ceilings, and in that section Congress increased the number of Army and Navy personnel engaged in training by 3,950 above the number requested. The two Armed Services Committees rejected proposed cutbacks in the duration of recruit training for those services.

Logistical Support. The president did not explain what he meant by "logistical support," but according to news reports administration officials said he would like to see up to $500 million of the aircraft carrier funds used instead for spare parts for ships and planes. Spare parts for ships were not separately budgeted in the authorization bill, and the total budget request for airplane spares was only $1.8 billion, from which Congress made almost no changes.

Navy Programs

In addition to the congressionally imposed $1.93 billion for the nuclear carrier, the authorization bill increased Navy procurement funds by $428.4 million for carrier planes. Much of this increase was to increase the production of F-14 and F-18 fighters.

The Armed Services Committees had complained that the slower rate at which the administration planned to buy the aircraft was inefficient and would increase the planes' cost per copy.

Veto Sustained

In a formidable show of Democratic Party unity, the House Sept. 7 voted to sustain Carter's veto of HR 10929.

Although Carter's victory generally had been predicted, the wide margin by which he won came as a surprise. Opponents of the veto, who needed a two-thirds majority of those voting to override, could not even muster a simple majority. The vote to override was 191-206.

Key to the president's decisive win was the administration's success in persuading 41 Democrats to switch their positions on the need to add the $2 billion nuclear-powered aircraft carrier. On Aug. 7, those members had voted to include the carrier. A month later they switched their votes to support the president. *(Vote 642, p. 182-H)*

Although Congress recessed soon after the president vetoed the bill Aug. 17, the Armed Services committees mounted an energetic campaign to override Carter. They criticized his charge in the veto message that they had cut $2 billion from programs to beef up U.S. ground and air forces in NATO in order to fit the carrier into the defense budget. They also argued that Carter had understated the military advantages and overstated the cost of the nuclear carrier compared to a smaller, less expensive oil-fueled carrier the president preferred.

In addition, the House committee in particular maintained that the veto — and Carter's explanation of it — threatened the independent role of Congress in making defense policy.

But in the last several days before the House vote, Defense Secretary Harold Brown and House members who supported the president had insisted that the question was the much narrower one of the nuclear carrier.

After the vote, Majority Whip John Brademas, D-Ind., told reporters that the tone of the president's veto message had not been a major consideration for most members. They understood, he said, that the president was not trying to cut the defense budget but only to spend the money on different priorities than had been recommended by the Armed Services panels. According to Brademas, House Democratic leaders had emphasized to Carter the importance of making this distinction. They also had worked very hard to sustain the veto, he said.

In a House committee meeting the day before the override vote, Chairman Melvin Price, D-Ill., commented that if the veto were sustained the compromise on future small carriers "would have to be abandoned." Only the added money for the advanced Harrier was sure to remain in the new bill since both Armed Services committees strongly supported its development for the Marine Corps.

On Sept. 8, Senate committee member Hart proposed that the new bill include a large, non-nuclear-powered carrier of the same design as the *John F. Kennedy,* which was commissioned about 10 years before.

According to the Navy, a *Kennedy*-class ship, which would be about the same size as the nuclear ship vetoed by Carter, would cost about $1.7 billion if contracted for in fiscal 1979; the smaller carrier favored by Carter was estimated to cost $1.575 billion if contracted in fiscal 1980. But Hart maintained that the smaller ship might well wind up costing more than a *Kennedy* since it had not yet been designed. In the last decade, the Navy had experienced severe cost increases in the first ship of each new design.

While Hart did not believe that any new large carrier was needed militarily, he had argued that one more big ship was essential, as a matter of practical politics, in order to win support in the House — and in the Navy — for a more rapid shift to V/STOL and smaller warships.

Brown Argument

In a nine-page letter to Price Sept. 5, Defense Secretary Brown moved to head off two of the lines of argument that the committees were stressing in their campaign to override the veto. While holding to the Carter line that Congress had cut $2 billion from the total defense budget request in order to pay for the carrier, Brown conceded that only a small part of that amount actually had been cut in the bill that was vetoed. The rest of the cuts, which did not require authorization, were contained in the defense appropriations bill. But he insisted that the reason for those reductions was the carrier, and it was appropriate for Carter to veto the authorization bill as a first step to restoration of the other items whether or not they were in the authorization bill.

Brown emphasized, however, that the veto was based only on the addition of the carrier and that the president was not insisting that Congress undo all of the other changes made in the administration's request. "The president has chosen not to call into question by his veto any of those numerous changes other than the single largest and most disruptive one."

In addition to his elaboration on the figures cited by Carter in the veto message, Brown spent about two and one-half pages trying to head off congressional outrage over the terms in which Carter had characterized the drafting of the original bill.

He assured Price that the administration was not charging the committee or Congress with knowingly voting to weaken national defense in order to fund a pet project. The issue, he said, was the very narrow one of the relative priority of a nuclear carrier compared to other programs which he and Carter believed were more important, given the amount available for defense.

"On reconsideration and reflection it is possible that you may be persuaded that there is merit in the president's judgment in this matter," Brown concluded. "If not, we all will have at least the knowledge of having respected each other's responsibilities and fulfilled our respective constitutional duties."

The jockeying continued in a meeting of the House committee Sept. 6. The majority of panel members drew the issue as a broad challenge to Congress' right to make its own judgment on defense policy. "The president has thrown down the gauntlet as to congressional authority in defense matters," insisted Bob Wilson, R-Calif., the panel's senior Republican.

But supporters of the veto insisted that the issue was simply a judgment call on the carrier: "We certainly aren't [the president's] rubber stamp; nor is he a rubber stamp for us," said Bob Carr, D-Mich. "The issue is simply whether we're going to have a larger number of smaller ships or a smaller number of larger ships."

Another Carter supporter, Patricia Schroeder, D-Colo., lamented the tenor of the veto message, but added, "If we start putting politicians away for heavy rhetoric, then we're all in trouble."

The committee voted 24-6 to urge the House to override the veto in the vote scheduled for the next morning. Voting against the motion were Lucien N. Nedzi, D-Mich.; Jack Brinkley, D-Ga.; Les Aspin, D-Wis.; Ronald V. Dellums, D-Calif.; Schroeder and Carr. The last four members were frequent critics of the Pentagon and of the committee majority.

Another member who usually sided with those four, Thomas J. Downey, D-N.Y., voted with the majority. On two of three votes taken earlier in the year, Downey had supported a nuclear carrier.

Later that morning, House Speaker Thomas P. O'Neill Jr., D-Mass., told reporters he and the rest of the House Democratic leadership remained "foursquare behind the president." Reports circulated that afternoon that pro-administration forces were confident of 175 votes the next day, enough to sustain the veto with a comfortable margin to spare (If all 433 House members had voted on the motion to override, 145 members would have been sufficient to block the motion.)

House Debate

The hour's debate on the motion to override Sept. 7 was even more perfunctory than was usual in the House. Nearly every member of the Armed Services Committee wanted to speak, so time was dribbled out in slices of two and three minutes.

The first indication that the committee had failed to make any headway with its campaign for an override came when Appropriations Committee Chairman George Mahon, D-Texas, and Defense Appropriations Subcommittee members Jack Edwards, R-Ala., and Bill D. Burlison, D-Mo., announced that they would support the veto. They represented the "non-doves" whose skepticism of the big carrier the committee would have had to overcome.

Mahon introduced the only new dimension to the argument, noting that as the House debated, Carter was at Camp David, orchestrating the Israeli-Egyptian summit meeting. "Democrats and Republicans do not wish to destroy the effectiveness of the president of the United States while he sits in the shadow of the summit conference on the Middle East," he cautioned.

Vote Analysis

Many of the 41 Democrats who had backed the nuclear carrier Aug. 7 but supported the president on the veto vote either were members of the party's House leadership or were usually responsive to the leadership. *(Vote 575, p. 164-H)*

Of the 41, 30 had supported the nuclear carrier not only in the Aug. 7 vote, but also in two votes May 27 on amendments to the authorization bill. *(Votes 315, 316, p. 90-H)*

For several in this group, this was the second time they had changed their position on a hotly contested defense issue in order to support Carter. Of the 41, 24 had supported construction of the B-1 bomber in the last House vote taken before Carter announced his intention to cancel the plane. By February, 15 had come around to Carter's position. (Excluding members from California, where the B-1 would have been built, the pattern was even more striking: Of 41 who switched on the carrier, 20 non-Californians originally had supported the B-1, and 14 eventually moved to support Carter's decision to cancel the plane.

Of 19 House Democratic leaders and leadership-appointed whips, 16 supported the veto and only three voted to override.

Republicans had voted in favor of the nuclear carrier and in favor of overriding the veto by nearly identical margins: 104-23 in favor of the carrier; 107-23 in favor of the override.

The voting pattern suggested that a bandwagon effect may have developed on the vote. As members saw that the veto would not be overridden, they decided to go with the winning side. Aspin speculated later that members may have welcomed a chance to vote with the president on this issue in anticipation of having to vote against future vetoes on domestic issues more important to their constituents.

New Defense Bill

Seeking to avoid a prolonged battle over reconstructing the fiscal 1979 weapons procurement authorization bill vetoed by President Carter, the Senate and House Armed Services committees agreed simply to drop the $2 billion aircraft carrier the president opposed.

Senior members of the House committee had warned that if the veto were sustained the bill (HR 10929) would have to be reworked from scratch. In particular, they had said, Senate-sponsored provisions intended to move the Navy more quickly toward the use of small aircraft carriers equipped with V/STOLs would be dropped.

The House panel had accepted these provisions only because the bill contained the money for another big carrier that would carry conventional jet planes.

But time apparently was a major factor deterring members from reopening the dozens of issues that had been thrashed out in the original bill. With the November election less than eight weeks away, Congress was under heavy pressure to adjourn by mid-October to allow members to campaign.

Over in the Senate, Armed Services Chairman Stennis introduced a new bill that was identical in all major respects to the vetoed bill except for deletion of the carrier authorization. "A new start must be made and time is of the essence," he said. "I strongly favor the idea of simply taking the carrier out and passing a new bill without further change."

If a new authorization bill was not passed by Oct. 1 — the start of the new fiscal year — the Defense Department would have to operate under a continuing resolution holding spending for all programs to the levels authorized for fiscal 1978. This would block, for the time being, plans to begin production in fiscal 1979 of the Army's new XM-1 tank and the Navy's F-18 fighter jet. It also would prevent planned increases in the production rate of other new weapons.

After HR 10929 was vetoed, Defense Secretary Harold Brown urged Congress to re-allocate the carrier money among 126 programs — most of which were relatively small — that Congress had cut back either in the procurement bill or in the companion defense appropriations bill. He emphasized to the two committees the importance for U.S. foreign relations of not appearing to cut the defense budget below the $126 billion Carter had requested in January.

The committees agreed that the carrier money should be allocated to other projects. But they told Brown to send up a supplemental appropriations request for that purpose. The cuts originally made in the authorization bill — which totaled about $545 million — had been made after months of careful analysis, they maintained. There was not sufficient time to properly reconsider them before Congress adjourned, they said.

Other than deletion of $1.93 billion for the aircraft carrier, the only authorization change in the new bill was an additional $209 million for the Navy to pay a negotiated set-

Cost Overruns Mount on Navy's Trident

A three-year dispute between the Navy and some of its most important private shipbuilders over construction cost overruns was "the single most influential reason why President Carter chose not to accelerate Navy ship purchases in the 1979 budget," according to a top administration budget official.

But if that was the reason, the president was badly misinformed, said Navy Secretary W. Graham Claytor.

The Navy insisted that the much publicized overruns, delivery delays and lawsuits involved ships contracted for under procedures since abandoned. New contracting procedures were bringing ships off the building ways on time and under budget, it asserted.

But even the Navy conceded that a serious problem remained in building nuclear submarines.

Claims, Costs and Slowdowns

The press had made too much out of the shipbuilding firms' bargaining ploys, according to the Navy. But even if the Navy was right, the attention given them by the media was understandable. The ploys had included claims against the Navy of about $2.7 billion, threats to stop work on warships under construction, and the improbable spectacle of a nuclear cruiser being built under court order.

The Navy and the shipyards agreed that the root of the problem was the contract arrangements used in the late 1960s and early 1970s. Since warships took years to build, the contracts included escalator clauses to protect the builder against inflation. But they also set a ceiling on that protection when ships were not delivered on schedule.

On dozens of ships under construction during this period delays occurred, with each side blaming the other. Under the double-digit inflation prevailing in the early 1970s, the escalator ceiling soon was far exceeded. The contractors petitioned for relief, first with the Pentagon's own contract appeals system and then in the courts.

The Navy maintained that settlements on the pending claims gradually were being worked out and that, in any case, the problem was irrelevant to the ability and willingness of the shipyards to contract for new ships. To prevent a recurrence of the problem, warship contracts in the future offered the builders more protection against inflation. And the proof that the new system worked, the Navy said, was that its new missile frigates were delivered on time and with no cost problems.

Trident Troubles

But the whole cycle of charges, threats and countercharges apparently was just beginning in the Navy's relations with General Dynamics' Electric Boat Division, which was building all of the Trident missile-launching submarines and more than half of the 688-class attack subs.

According to the most recent contractor estimates, the 17 attack subs presently under contract to Electric Boat would be delivered from 2.5 to 3.5 years late. Blaming the delays on the Navy's estimated 35,000 changes in the blueprints for the ships, the contractor filed a $544 million claim and threatened to stop work on the ships in June if the Navy didn't provide more money.

The Navy said the changes were no more numerous than was normal for ship construction and blamed the delay on low productivity by Electric Boat's labor force.

The company and the Navy were in similar disagreement over responsibility for cost overruns of 50 percent and delays of a year and a half on the Trident submarines. The first of these would not be delivered to the Navy until November 1980, according to Electric Boat. And it cost about $1.2 billion instead of the $800 million estimated when the contract was signed in 1974. That did not include the cost of the nuclear power plant or the 24 Trident missiles, which cost about $10 million a copy.

The estimate of the total cost for a fleet of 13 fully equipped Trident ships was about $22 billion.

---

tlement with two major commercial shipyards to end prolonged contract disputes.

Before approving the new version of the defense authorization bill (HR 14042, S 3486), each of the Armed Services committees had voted to kill resolutions that would have blocked the proposed claims settlements.

Shipyard Claims Settlements

The $209 million added to the revised bill was intended to finance settlements of longstanding contract disputes between the Navy and two of its largest ship contractors, General Dynamics Corporation and Litton Industries.

The two shipbuilders' disputes with the Navy involved 1) contracts with Litton to build anti-submarine destroyers and helicopter carriers at its Pascagoula, Miss., yard, and 2) contracts with the Electric Boat Division of General Dynamics to build sub-hunting submarines at its Groton, Conn., facility.

The companies had filed claims against the Navy totaling more than $1.6 billion, arguing that the Navy had been responsible for costly delays in completing several ships and that the contracts, of a type no longer used, did not protect the shipyards against the early 1970s inflation.

The Navy conceded that the two companies were entitled to claims totaling $390 million. But it maintained that much of the loss was due to the companies' poor management of the shipyards and especially to their failure to estimate accurately the time needed to recruit and train work forces large enough to handle the contracts.

Navy Secretary W. Graham Claytor Jr. and Assistant Secretary Edward Hidalgo finally negotiated with the companies a settlement in which the Navy agreed to pay the $390 million, plus $541 million, in return for which the companies would drop any additional claims.

Claytor maintained that the agreement would ensure that both shipyards suffered fixed losses on the contracts and that it dealt out "rough justice" in a tangled situation in which the fault lay both with the Navy and with the contractors. The only alternative, he warned, would be lengthy litigation that would impair the Navy's ability to get new ships built and might, in the end, cost the government more than the settlement being proposed.

The agreement was reached under a law (PL 85-804) that allowed the president to alter the terms of any contract in the interests of national security. But such changes could be blocked by a resolution adopted by either house within 60 days. An earlier effort to resolve the dispute collapsed in 1976 partly because it appeared likely such a resolution might be adopted.

House Committee Action

The House Armed Services Committee reported the revised bill (HR 14042 — H Rept 95-1573) on Sept. 15.

The authorizations as approved by the panel — with the carrier eliminated — totaled $35.2 billion for weapons procurement and military research. The amount was about $250 million below that originally requested by Carter.

On Sept. 12 Brown had sent the House committee the list of items the administration recommended for absorbing the $2 billion that had been authorized for the carrier.

Appearing before the committee the following day, Brown struck the same conciliatory note that distinguished his defense of the veto from the harshly critical tone of Carter's veto message. "[The president] never had the slightest doubt — nor did I — that the original bill reflected the sincere views of the committee as to the way to serve our national defense. Those views were considered with great respect. The veto action was not lightly taken."

But he stressed the political importance of transferring the carrier money to other projects so the defense budget would not have the appearance of having been weakened because of the $2 billion cut. "We must reassure the American public and our allies, and make it clear to the Soviets, that we will not falter in the competition," he said.

Brown's list of items to be restored came under fire from nearly all members of the committee, however, including liberals who had generally sided with Carter on defense issues. Harshest of all was Thomas J. Downey, D-N.Y., who dismissed many of the proposed restorals as "just plain turkeys." And he warned Brown that "in the future, you're going to have a lot of trouble with this committee because it believes it has been politically used [in the veto message]."

Jim Lloyd, D-Calif., complained that the administration's proposals put members in an awkward position since, as a practical matter, they would have to accept the additions without serious analysis or else reject them and face the charge of being "soft" on defense.

Members derided the requested restorals as a "shopping list" of items Congress had cut for lack of merit. Brown now was asking Congress to reverse some of those cuts, which, they said, the Pentagon earlier had conceded were justified, such as 70 tanks the Army said could not have been produced in fiscal 1979 because of production delays. And they pointed out that the list did not include some projects that had been cut back, but which the administration had claimed were of top priority, such as development of a wide-body jet to carry cruise missiles.

But Brown insisted that each of the administration additions was feasible and, taken as a whole, was the best balanced package that could be devised from the set of projects that Congress already had reviewed in considering the vetoed bill.

Brown's underlying assumption seemed to be one he had emphasized in May in testimony to the House Appropriations Committee: Congress simply was not equipped to analyze how the myriad bits and pieces of the defense budget related to each other. Without such analysis, he argued then, Congress might string together a lot of individual programs, each of which was attractive when taken on its merits but which would cost more while providing less defense than an administration-coordinated budget.

And Brown continued to hammer away at the need to get the fiscal 1979 budget back up to the originally requested $126 billion.

Bob Carr, D-Mich., suggested that if Congress simply dropped the carrier money and awaited a supplemental bill observers would understand that there was no intent to cut the defense budget. But Brown retorted: "I would hate, if the Soviets invade Western Europe, to wave signs saying, 'We didn't intend to cut our capabilities.' "

As the hearing progressed, it became evident that committee members wanted Brown to use the carrier money in a supplemental so he could suggest projects other than those that had been proposed in January and so the committee could take time to examine the proposals in detail. Lucien N. Nedzi, D-Mich., urged Brown to single out from his list a few really essential items the committees might accept without much controversy, but Brown declined. The panel then approved HR 14042 36-1.

Senate Committee Action

The Senate Armed Services Committee reported a companion bill (S 3486 — S Rept 95-1197) on Sept. 15.

Like the House bill, S 3486 was virtually identical to the vetoed bill with the exception of the elimination of $1.93 billion for the nuclear carrier.

The only other significant change was the addition of the $209 million for the claims settlement between the Navy and the two shipyards. As reported, the authorizations in the bill totaled $35.2 billion, the same as in the House version.

Before approving the bill, the Senate panel on Sept. 14 also heard from Brown, who was given essentially the same reception as the House committee had given him. Said Stennis: "I don't want to go back over and have to re-chew [the whole bill] ... and have to run the gauntlet of the lobbying." The highest priority, he added, was to pass the bill as quickly as possible.

Thomas J. McIntyre, D-N.H., and Sam Nunn, D-Ga., challenged Brown's support for some of the programs Congress had cut from the vetoed bill, and Brown stuck by the administration list. But his defense of it was more subdued than it was before the House panel, and he seemed resigned to the inevitability of a $35.2 billion bill, followed later by a supplemental authorization bill.

Senate Floor Action

The revised defense measure was approved by the Senate Sept. 26 by an 89-3 vote. *(Vote 402, p. 60-S)*

The Senate made no changes in the committee's recommended authorization levels.

Floor debate on the new version focused primarily on naval issues, with most of the time spent on the shipyard claims. But a potentially more significant development during the debate was a colloquy among key Armed Services Committee members that highlighted a basic conflict between the president and the congressional committees that dealt with defense spending.

Carter had claimed that the nuclear carrier should be killed in order to build cheaper, but more numerous, ships. But the administration had not yet projected any increase in the number of Navy ships to be requested in the next several years. According to some press reports, the number of ships planned by the administration would average only about 13 in each of the next five years.

But substantial majorities of the Armed Services and Appropriations Committees — including influential members who supported Carter's veto of the carrier — agreed with Carter's publicly expressed position that the Navy needed more ships.

A preview of the fiscal 1980 defense budget debate came when Armed Services Committee member John G. Tower, R-Texas, offered an amendment that would have added to the bill an authorization for a large helicopter carrier designed to carry a Marine Corps landing force ($770 million) and two guided-missile armed escort frigates ($320 million).

The procurement bill already contained eight of the frigates, as requested by the administration, and a $70 million down payment on the helicopter carrier. The committee had rejected a slightly different version of Tower's amendment by only two votes, 8-10.

Tower argued that it was essential that Congress act to beef up the Navy since the administration apparently intended to pare away at the annual shipbuilding request. Gary Hart, D-Colo., agreed that Congress had to take the initiative, though he urged Tower to leave the current bill alone to avoid disrupting the Senate's legislative schedule, and promised to work with him on a supplemental authorization bill that would accelerate expansion of the fleet.

Stennis declined to promise Tower quick action on a supplemental, insisting that his panel would have to cooperate with the House committee, the administration and the Navy. But he promised to work hard for early action on it, and he insisted that the supplemental should include "ships only, and not have it tied in with what the Air Force wants, or what the Marines want, or what Navy personnel should be, or what this or that should be."

Stennis even suggested that to expedite a Navy supplemental, the staffs of the two Armed Services panels might work together on a new bill.

Tower then withdrew his amendment.

Proxmire Amendments. By a margin of 5-1, the Senate rejected a Proxmire amendment to S 3486 that would have killed the proposed shipbuilding claims settlement by deleting from the bill the $209 million needed to fully fund the Navy's payment. (The remaining $722 million contained in the settlement had previously been appropriated.) The vote on the amendment was 15-76. *(Vote 399, p. 60-S)*

The Senate then rejected committee-sponsored motions to table, and thus kill, two other Proxmire amendments, and they subsequently were adopted by voice votes. These amendments:

- Required that the comptroller general audit the two shipbuilders' use of the settlement payments to ensure that they were applied only to the Navy contracts and to ensure that they did not give the builders any overall profit on the settled contracts. Motion to table rejected, 39-53. *(Vote 401, p. 60-S)*

- Abolished the Women's Army Corps as a separate part of the Army. Motion to table rejected, 46-46. *(Vote 400, p. 60-S)*

House Floor Action

After two days of debate (Sept 29, Oct. 4), the House passed with amendments the new defense bill by a 367-22 vote. *(Vote 770, p. 218-H)*

The House followed the Senate's example and turned back an attempt to delete the $209 million for the Navy claims settlement.

Downey Amendments. Thwarted by the committee, Downey tried to kill the proposed settlements when the authorization bill came to the House floor Sept. 29. He offered an amendment that would have deleted the $209 million the committee had added. This amount was needed to fully fund the agreed upon Navy payment ($931 million) to the two companies.

The administration had argued that payment above the amount allowed by Navy claims analysts was appropriate to avoid the risk that at the end of a decade's litigation over the claims, the courts might award the companies an even larger sum.

But Downey argued that the Navy analysts had considered the cost and the risk of litigation in arriving at their finding that only $390 million should be paid the companies.

Samuel S. Stratton, D-N.Y., Downey's principal ally on the committee in the fight against the settlements, warned that they would set an expensive precedent for contractors' relations with the Pentagon. "We have said to any big company, 'All you have got to do is put in your claims and the trouble that we have in trying to settle any claims by litigation is so onerous that we will split with you 50-50 on any of your claims.' "

But Seapower Subcommittee Chairman Charles E. Bennett, D-Fla., giving the committee majority's position, said the settlement was the best of several bad alternatives, that it at least would put the mess astern so the firms could get on with building warships. "This is not a bailout, but rather a calculated judgment by the lawyers of the Department of Defense, the Department of the Navy and the Department of Justice that it is in the best dollar interests of the U.S. government," Bennett maintained. "Otherwise, we may have years of litigation and may wind up paying much more."

Downey's amendment was rejected 97-187. *(Vote 758, p. 214-H)*

When the House returned to the authorization bill Oct. 4, Downey proposed to amend the settlement procedure so that future claims costing more than $25 million would require the affirmative support of both houses of Congress. But the amendment was rejected, 111-275. *(Vote 769, p. 218-H)*

Other Amendments. Rejected by voice vote was an amendment by Robert K. Dornan, R-Calif., that would have banned the use of Pentagon funds to pay for abortions. Dornan failed to secure the support of enough members to force a recorded vote on the proposal; 20 members would have been needed to force a vote.

Adopted by voice vote was an amendment by Dan Daniel, D-Va., to exempt from the minimum wage law persons who worked for tips by bagging and carrying out groceries at military commissaries.

Four amendments by Armed Services Chairman Melvin Price, D-Ill., were approved by voice votes. They:

- Extended to Oct. 31, 1978 (from Sept. 30, 1978), the deadline for a Pentagon report to Congress on the plans for preserving U.S. land-based ICBMs despite the increasing accuracy of Soviet missiles.

- Allowed the use for ship design work of $6 million left over from a study of future aircraft carrier types.
- Abolished the Women's Army Corps as a separate unit of the Army.
- Required the General Accounting Office (GAO) to audit the use of funds awarded to the two shipbuilders under the settlement process.

Final Action

In order to get the bill to the president as soon as possible, the Senate Oct. 7 concurred in the House amendments, thus avoiding a time-consuming conference, and cleared the bill. Carter signed S 3486 on Oct. 20 (PL 95-485).

Military Construction

Congress Aug. 17 approved a $144.5 million authorization for NATO projects as part of the $4.1 billion fiscal 1979 military construction bill (HR 12602 — PL 95-356).

The funding was approved despite general agreement that future military construction for NATO should be paid for by the alliance. The Senate had turned down NATO construction funding.

The final version authorized about half of the $288.3 million that had been approved by the House for NATO projects. But $56.9 million was retained for a site to store tanks and other heavy equipment that an extra Army division could use if it had to be flown to Europe quickly during an international crisis.

The total authorization of $4.1 billion was $41.1 million less than had been approved by the House and $129.9 million more than had been passed by the Senate. It was $119.5 million below the president's budget request.

President Carter signed the bill Sept. 8.

Provisions

As cleared for the president, HR 12602 authorized the following amounts for military construction programs for fiscal 1979:

Program	Carter Request	Final Authorization
Army	$ 874,343,000	$ 751,244,000
Navy	769,110,000	790,310,000
Air Force	609,556,000	522,743,000
Defense Agencies	164,900,000	217,610,000
Family Housing	1,695,100,000	1,701,605,000
Reserve Forces	134,800,000	144,800,000
Total	$4,247,809,000	$4,128,312,000

The bill also:

- Required the secretary of defense to transmit the military construction legislative requests to Congress within 10 days from the date the president transmitted the annual federal budget requests.

House Committee Action

As reported May 12 by the Armed Services Committee (H Rept 95-1147), the bill authorized $4,169,444,000 for military construction projects for the fiscal year beginning Oct. 1. The amount was $78.4 million less than the administration had requested.

NATO Buildup

In addition to the equivalent of five and two-thirds Army divisions stationed in West Germany, equipment for almost three additional U.S. divisions was stored there. With the current U.S. air transport fleet, including civilian jetliners that would be requisitioned in an emergency, these reinforcements could be moved to Germany in about two weeks.

But in presenting the fiscal 1979 Pentagon budget to Congress, Defense Secretary Harold Brown had announced plans to add storage facilities for three more divisions in Europe in conjunction with planned improvements in the U.S. air transport fleet. This would allow the United States to double — to about 10 divisions — its ground combat forces in West Germany within a two-week period by 1982.

Tank Storage Bags. The $56.9 million requested for storage of additional military equipment in Europe would permit construction of facilities for one division at three sites west of Dusseldorf near the Dutch border, including $11.5 million for vehicle storage bags. The bags would eliminate the need for 41 warehouses costing upwards of $50 million.

The tank storage bags, which were used by the British Army in Germany for nearly a decade, allowed combat vehicles to be stored with full fuel tanks, thus greatly reducing the time it would take to prepare the tanks and trucks for use. Because of safety considerations, the Army drains the fuel tanks of vehicles stored in warehouses.

Spare Runways. The Pentagon had requested funds to build spare runways at 12 airfields in West Germany and the United Kingdom so that Soviet air attacks could not neutralize all the planes at a base simply by damaging the existing airstrip. According to the plan, alternate runways would be built at each base and the taxiways would be widened so planes could bypass bomb craters.

But the committee denied $40 million requested for the project on grounds that its assumptions were not convincing. Some critics argued that additional runways could too easily be damaged and that it would be more effective to use the money to disperse U.S. planes among more airfields or buy more construction equipment to repair runways damaged by an enemy attack.

Space Shuttle Base

The largest single project recommended by the House committee was $145.6 million for construction of a launching base for the space shuttle at Vandenberg Air Force Base in California.

Construction of the airstrip, in addition to one already planned for Cape Canaveral, Florida, was justified by the Pentagon in terms of its need to put military satellites into a polar orbit around the earth. The shuttle could not be launched into a polar orbit from Florida without passing over densely populated areas. And a large fuel tank that would be jettisoned early in the flight would pass low over Soviet and Chinese territory. Moreover, the shuttle's payload at Cape Canaveral would have to be limited to

22,000 lbs., only two-thirds of the weight that could be carried on a California launch. *(Shuttle authorization, Congress and Government chapter)*

Energy Problems

The bill included $148 million for the fourth annual increment in the Pentagon's energy conservation program. But the committee noted that the program — for which more than $404 million had been authorized in previous years — was justified entirely in terms of predicted energy savings based on engineering analyses. It directed the Pentagon to survey the completed projects to assess the accuracy of those predictions.

And the panel ordered the Pentagon to provide a detailed explanation of the apparent failure of several pilot projects on the use of solar energy at military installations.

House Floor Action

The House passed HR 12602 on May 22 by a vote of 363-18. *(Vote 299, p. 86-H)*

No changes were made by the House in the Armed Services Committee's authorization recommendations.

The House went along with the panel's authorizations for NATO-related projects, and agreed with the committee's denial of funding for a new European headquarters for the Army ($48 million) and for a project to build additional runways at U.S. air bases in Europe ($40 million).

Base Closings Issue

For the first time in three years, the bill did not become the vehicle for congressional opposition to Defense Department proposals to close military bases in the United States. On April 26 the Pentagon announced plans to close or cut back operations at more than 100 bases in 30 states and the District of Columbia. *(Base closings, p. 375)*

Similar efficiency moves in 1976 had drawn intense congressional opposition and resulted in a provision in the fiscal 1978 construction authorization bill requiring prior justification to Congress of any proposed base realignment that affected large numbers of civilian Pentagon employees. *(1977 Almanac p. 343)*

But the House Armed Services Committee, in its report on HR 12602, merely put the Pentagon on notice that it would scrutinize the proposed base changes. And the issue was not raised during the perfunctory floor debate.

Provisions

As passed by the House May 22, HR 12602 authorized the following amounts for military construction in fiscal 1979:

Program	Carter Request	House-Passed Authorization
Army	$ 874,343,000	$ 762,881,000
Navy	769,110,000	811,495,000
Air Force	609,556,000	602,558,000
Defense Agencies	164,900,000	167,610,000
Family Housing	1,695,100,000	1,690,100,000
Reserve Forces	134,800,000	134,800,000
Total	$4,247,809,000	$4,169,444,000

Senate Committee Action

The Senate Armed Services Committee reported its version of the legislation (S 3079 — S Rept 95-847) on May 15.

Demanding that Western Europe pay a larger share of the cost of its own defense, the committee rejected the entire $373 million package of combat-related construction for the NATO alliance requested by the Defense Department.

As reported by the Senate committee, the bill authorized a total of $3,998,432,000 for military construction.

U.S. Funding of NATO

The committee recalled that it had warned the Pentagon in 1977 that it would not support large increases in the construction budget to cover projects that it said should be NATO's responsibility.

It insisted that U.S. forces live with whatever standards the alliance adopted. Rejected, for example, was a request for $1.25 million to allow certain added features for a NATO-funded aircraft hangar.

To signal its support of a construction program paid for on a NATO-wide basis, the panel increased to $150 million, from $90 million requested, the U.S. contribution to the NATO infrastructure program. This is the program through which the alliance members shared the cost of constructing airfields, fuel dumps, war headquarters and other facilities needed by the NATO allies for the joint defense of Europe.

Trident Bases

The committee provided no new authorization for construction of the Trident submarine base at Bangor, Wash. But it re-authorized $16.25 million that had been approved in earlier years, but never funded, for the project. This was $385,000 less than the Navy requested.

For the new Atlantic coast missile submarine base at Kings Bay, Ga., the committee approved the $39.1 million requested.

Energy Programs

Acknowledging that the Defense Department was a leader among federal agencies in energy conservation and in setting ambitious long-term energy goals, the committee nevertheless said this was not enough.

The committee complained that the Pentagon was being too cautious in experimenting with solar and other exotic energy sources for military installations.

In its report, the committee proposed legislation that would allow the Pentagon to underwrite the large initial costs of these non-fossil fuel and non-atomic energy systems. The added expense could be recovered over the life of the facilities, it argued. Such projects might encourage more rapid development of new energy technologies that eventually could reduce U.S. dependence on petroleum, according to the committee.

Solar Energy. The committee added to the bill a requirement that all new military family housing projects and 25 percent of all other construction projects incorporate solar energy systems. As in previous years, the bill included a provision allowing the Pentagon to exceed the congressional authorization for any construction project that incorporated solar energy systems.

Long-term Contracts. Also added to the bill was authority for the Pentagon to enter into contracts of up to 30 years' duration for privately run power plants on military bases. The committee hoped that such long-term contracts would support the development of alternative energy systems — such as geothermal power plants — that might eventually become commercially competitive.

Boiler Fuel Conversions. Several requests for funds to convert power plant boilers from natural gas to fuel oil were not approved by the committee. It argued that this might only delay the shift away from petroleum-based power plants to other energy sources, including coal.

Senate Floor Action

The Senate passed HR 12602 with amendments on July 12 by voice vote.

As passed, the bill authorized $4,000,432,000, $2 million more than the committee authorized, $247 million less than the president requested and $169 million less than the House had agreed to.

The perennial pork-barrel issue of military base closings briefly delayed final Senate action on the bill.

After the bill had been considered, floor manager Gary Hart, D-Colo., delayed a final vote for several hours until he received an answer to a June 23 letter he sent the Pentagon. In the letter, he charged that the Air Force had succumbed to political pressure from the Illinois congressional delegation in deferring the construction of a training center in Colorado. The Illinois delegation had been fighting hard to prevent the closing of a training center in their state.

Bases and Jobs

On April 26 the Pentagon announced it was considering a number of base changes that would reduce payrolls at 81 U.S. bases. Members of Congress predictably expressed their opposition to those moves that would cost their constituents jobs. The Illinois delegation was especially forceful in its opposition to the closing of Chanute Air Force Base, where the payroll of more than 4,000 was the economic backbone of Rantoul, Ill.

On June 15 the Air Force assured Sen. Charles H. Percy, R-Ill., that in its consideration of the Chanute proposal, it would evaluate the advantages of closing, instead, one of four similar training centers, including Lowry Air Force Base in Colorado. Pending a decision, it had deferred construction of a $3.38 million training facility at Lowry.

In his letter, Hart protested that Lowry had not been listed as a candidate for closure April 26. He demanded to know how many other bases were unannounced alternative candidates for closure whose construction was being deferred.

In its July 12 reply, the Pentagon told Hart it always reviewed in detail proposed construction at bases being considered for closing — such as Chanute — and bases that "could reasonably be considered as alternatives" to those prime candidates for closure — such as Lowry.

Hart reported that the Pentagon's reply listed 21 bases that were unannounced alternate candidates for job cuts. And he said he would begin hearings to determine whether any of the $100 million of construction projects authorized at those bases by HR 12602 should be deferred.

Amendments Adopted

Two substantive amendments were adopted by voice vote:

- By John G. Tower, R-Texas, lowering to 300 from 500 the number of civilian jobs that had to be affected before a proposed base reduction activated a full-scale review, as required under existing law.
- By Ted Stevens, R-Alaska, adding $2 million for certain military family housing projects in Alaska.

Provisions

As passed by the Senate, HR 12602 authorized the following amounts for fiscal 1979:

Program	House-Passed Authorization	Senate-Passed Authorization
Army	$ 762,881,000	$ 632,781,000
Navy	811,495,000	753,324,000
Air Force	602,558,000	477,027,000
Defense Agencies	167,610,000	266,900,000
Family Housing	1,690,100,000	1,715,600,000
Reserve Forces	134,800,000	154,800,000
Total	$4,169,444,000	$4,000,432,000

Conference Action

House-Senate conferees filed a conference report (H Rept 95-1448) on the bill Aug. 7. Major differences between the two versions were resolved as follows:

Conferees agreed on an authorization level of $4,128,312,000.

NATO Construction

As in the military construction appropriations bill (HR 12927), the issue was the Pentagon's practice of unilaterally paying for NATO-related construction projects. Maintaining the bureaucratic procedures in the alliance were too time-consuming, the Pentagon for years had requested appropriations to build NATO-related projects, with the intent of later being reimbursed for their cost from the alliance's infrastructure program.

The conferees insisted that except under extraordinary circumstances future NATO-oriented construction should be paid for by the infrastructure fund. But they said that hard and fast application of that rule to the fiscal 1979 budget would have resulted in "unacceptable delay to selected, readiness-related projects."

Conferees agreed to authorize $56.9 million for a site to store tanks and other heavy military equipment that would be needed if an extra Army division had to be flown in from the United States during an international crisis.

In addition to the equipment storage site, the major NATO projects for which the conferees authorized funds included:

- Enlarged Army ammunition storage facilities ($50.8 million).
- Bombproof hangars for Air Force planes based in West Germany ($19.1 million).
- Various communications and command-related projects in Europe ($12.5 million).

The conference committee also approved the entire request ($4.2 million) to improve an airfield in Iceland that was used by Navy anti-submarine patrol planes. The Senate had demanded that Iceland pay 40 percent of the cost since it shared with the Navy the use of the field, but the conferees agreed that it was in the long-term interest of the United States to pay for the project.

Funding Increase. To demonstrate the United States' commitment to an increase in the alliance's construction program, conferees agreed to increase to $120 million from $70 million the U.S. contribution to the infrastructure program. The alliance at the time was negotiating the size of the program for the next five-year plan.

Energy Seed Money

Conferees accepted a Senate provision requiring the use of the most practicable solar power systems in all future military family housing construction and in 25 percent of all future military construction projects. The Senate had hoped that this would create a market for solar energy systems that would encourage expansion of the industry commercially.

The conference committee also agreed to allow long-term contracts (up to 30 years) to encourage the development of power from geothermal sources. The House and Senate Armed Services committees would have to be notified in advance of such contracts.

Final Action

The House adopted the conference report Aug. 16, and the Senate approved it Aug. 17, both by voice votes, completing congressional action.

Arms Control Agency

Congress completed action July 27 on legislation (HR 11832 — PL 95-338) authorizing $18.4 million for fiscal year 1979 for the U.S. Arms Control and Disarmament Agency (ACDA).

As in 1977, the annual authorization for the ACDA became a vehicle for congressional critics of the Carter administration's arms control policies. *(1977 Almanac p. 345)*

In the House report on the bill, a vocal minority of the International Relations Committee had charged that the agency was too eager to recommend risky U.S. concessions in order to conclude arms control agreements with the Soviet Union.

Provisions

As cleared for the president, HR 11832:

- Authorized $18.4 million for ACDA operations in fiscal 1979. (Of the increase, $1 million was to make up for the effects of inflation on the budget estimate of ACDA operating expenses.)

- Directed that future annual ACDA budget requests break down the budget among the agency's bureaus and by the type of expenditure within each bureau.

House Committee Action

The House International Relations Committee approved HR 11832 on April 4 by voice vote. The panel authorized $18.4 million for the agency's activities in fiscal 1979, $2 million more than the administration requested. Of the increase, $1 million was for the operating costs of the U.S. delegation to the Strategic Arms Limitation Talks (SALT) with the Russians. This was necessary, according to the committee's report (H Rept 95-1048) filed April 11, because the dollar had been devalued by 30 percent against the Swiss franc since ACDA's budget request was prepared in late 1977. The result was a substantial increase in the expenses of the U.S. delegation in Geneva.

The other $1 million added by the panel was for the agency's efforts directed at furthering the International Atomic Energy Agency's nuclear safeguards programs. *(Nuclear safeguards legislation, story, p. 350)*

The committee praised the arms control impact statements submitted by the Carter administration as "generally well written, informative and sufficiently analytical to provide new and useful insights into the arms control implications of programs." The committee and the Library of Congress' Congressional Research Service had criticized the impact statements submitted by the Ford administration in 1976 and 1977 as seriously inadequate. *(1977 Almanac p. 345)*

But the committee complained that the value of the statements was diminished by the fact that they reached Congress seven weeks after the president's budget request. It noted that the statements were required by law to accompany the budget proposals.

Supplemental Views

Opponents of the Carter administration's arms control policies restated their position in the committee report. All but one of the panel's 12 Republicans, and two of the committee's Democrats, added supplemental views charging that the ACDA leadership was dangerously biased toward reaching arms control agreements for their own sake.

"ACDA's leadership has lost sight of the fact that arms control is a means to an end, not an end in itself," said 13 of the dissenters. "The persistent refusal of the top ACDA leadership to give consideration to views different from their own single-minded predispositions entails a grave risk that a SALT II agreement will be rejected by the Congress."

They said the SALT negotiations reflected a series of U.S. concessions to Moscow allowing the Russians to field 300 nuclear missiles much larger than any in the U.S. arsenal and exempting from treaty limits the Soviet "Backfire" bomber, which had the capability of hitting U.S. targets under some circumstances.

But a staffer to the committee majority insisted there was no evidence of bias in the agency and said the minority had not even raised the question in the hearings on the bill. The minority views, he said, just reflected "a certain uneasiness as to the direction of U.S.-Soviet relations in general and especially as they relate to SALT."

Verification Dispute. The dissenters said ACDA Director Paul C. Warnke had failed to give the panel an "objective and comprehensive report on the verifiability of arms control proposals" as required by a 1977 law.

On Feb. 23 ACDA sent Congress an analysis of the verification aspects of those portions of a new SALT treaty on which agreement had been reached with the Soviets. These sections were "adequately verifiable," according to an analysis Warnke said had been "prepared and agreed to

Warnke Resignation

Citing personal reasons, Paul C. Warnke announced his resignation Oct. 10 as chief U.S. arms control negotiator.

Warnke returned to his Washington law practice soon after accompanying Secretary of State Cyrus R. Vance to Moscow in late October for another round of talks on a new U.S.-Soviet strategic arms limitation treaty (SALT II).

Warnke's nomination as chief SALT negotiator and as director of the Arms Control and Disarmament Agency (ACDA) was confirmed in March 1977 over the strenuous opposition of Senate foreign policy hard-liners, who charged that he was insufficiently concerned about the growing Soviet military strength. *(Confirmation, 1977 Almanac p. 323)*

Because of the ferocity of the attacks on Warnke personally, observers long had assumed that the burden of selling a SALT treaty to the Senate would be carried by another administration official, such as Defense Secretary Harold Brown.

by the agencies in the executive branch concerned with this issue."

Warnke added: "Although the possibility of some undetected cheating in certain areas exists, such cheating would not alter the strategic balance in view of U.S. programs. Any cheating on a scale large enough to alter the strategic balance would be discovered in time to make an appropriate response."

But the Joint Chiefs of Staff insisted that the report be labeled as an ACDA document since they had not agreed to it. And on March 22 Edward J. Derwinski, R-Ill., wrote Warnke protesting that the report analyzed only the U.S. SALT proposals, that those made by the Soviet Union were ignored. Two days later Warnke sent Congress a verification report on the Soviet proposals. But the analysis still was faulted by Derwinski and others. "It turned out to be a commercial for what's currently going on by Warnke and company . . . rather than a systematic and dispassionate analysis," said a Republican staffer.

House Floor Action

The House April 26 approved HR 11832 by a 332-74 vote. *(Vote 213, p. 62-H)*

Before passing the bill, the House adopted by voice vote an amendment by Paul Simon, D-Ill., authorizing the agency to study the problems of university-based arms control study centers. The House International Relations Committee had warned that they faced a funding crisis.

In a low-keyed debate, several Republicans reiterated the same suspicion of ACDA's political orientation that they had expressed in additional views appended to the committee report.

Research Centers. The arms control centers referred to in the Simon amendment conducted interdisciplinary teaching and research on the international, domestic and technical aspects of arms control problems.

According to a committee staffer, such centers had trained a number of persons currently working on arms control problems in the executive and legislative branches. They were a prime source of independent analysis for both branches of government.

Senate Action

Committee

The Senate Foreign Relations Committee reported an amended version of HR 11832 (S Rept 95-843) on May 15. The Senate version retained the House's authorization level of $18.4 million for the agency's operations and programs for fiscal 1979.

Impact Statements. The committee required that arms control impact statements — including an unclassified version — accompany any budget request for military hardware covered by the statements. The Senate committee complained that the 1978 statements, while very thorough, had not reached the committee until seven weeks after the president's budget request. *(Impact statements, 1977 Almanac p. 345)*

The bill specified that no legislation authorizing or appropriating funds for any program covered by an impact statement could be considered until at least the seventh day after Congress received the impact statement.

When the Senate debated the neutron bomb issue in July 1977, the administration rushed an arms control impact statement to the floor just hours before the showdown vote. *(1977 Almanac p. 381)*

The requirement for impact statements was extended to cover "technology with potential military application" as well as weapons. But the bill also allowed the executive branch to lump together in a single statement groups of programs that were very similar or clearly of minimal importance to arms control.

Study Centers. The Senate committee mandated, as did the House, a study of whether the federal government should assist arms control research centers at certain U.S. universities. Several such research institutes faced serious funding problems because the private foundations that had been providing funds for such programs were cutting back their support.

Budget Reorganization. The committee also amended the bill by directing that future budget requests by the agency break down the budget among the agency's bureaus and by the types of expenditure within each bureau.

Floor Action

The Senate June 8 routinely passed HR 11832 by voice vote without debate or further amendment and returned the bill to the House.

Final Action

On June 16 the House accepted the Senate version except that it deleted the requirement that an arms control impact statement accompany all weapons budget requests.

The Senate July 27 accepted the House change, clearing the bill. ▮

Restrictions Placed on Nuclear Exports

Strict nuclear export controls intended to stop the global spread of nuclear weapons were established by a bill (HR 8638—PL 95-242) signed March 10 by President Carter.

Underlying the nearly three-year-long consideration of the legislation by Congress was concern that the executive branch might be too enthusiastic a promoter of nuclear exports, thus giving inadequate attention to the risks of weapons proliferation.

Particularly worrisome to the bill's supporters was the spread of nuclear fuel processing plants, which produce material that could be used directly in nuclear explosives.

The bill took essentially the approach recommended by President Carter in April 1977. It allowed the export of nuclear material only on condition that it not be used in weapons production either by the original purchaser or by any subsequent purchaser. And it required purchasers to accept safeguards, which would be administered by the International Atomic Energy Agency (IAEA), against clandestine diversion of the material. *(Carter announcement, 1977 Almanac pp. 20-E, 27-E)*

The basic purpose of the various U.S. conditions and IAEA procedures was to ensure that other nations would have "timely warning" of any diversion to weapons of nuclear material from the fuel cycle. This referred to no set period, but rather meant that any diversion would be disclosed long enough in advance of construction of a bomb to give other nations time to try to deter the event.

The timely warning criterion, however, would be short-circuited by certain new types of nuclear power plants and by certain manufacturing processes used in handling fuel for the type of reactor most commonly used. And those technologies also held out the promise of energy independence for those states that depended on fuel imports and thus were vulnerable to political pressure by the supplier nations.

As an incentive for the nuclear fuel consuming states to forgo the apparent advantages of nuclear energy independence, the bill committed the United States to negotiations leading toward creation of an international fuel bank (called INFA) from which nations could purchase nuclear fuel without political preconditions.

Key Provisions

- Directed the president to begin negotiations with other countries to establish an international nuclear fuel bank as a guaranteed fuel source, thus reducing the incentive for countries to build certain kinds of fuel processing plants that would increase the risk of nuclear proliferation.
- Empowered the Nuclear Regulatory Commission to make independent judgments of the proliferation risks involved in licensing nuclear exports.
- Established as the foremost criteria for new detailed agreements by the U.S. government a "timely warning" standard. *(Box, p. 353)*
- Placed non-proliferation conditions on not only the nuclear fuel and equipment exported by the United States but also on any new nuclear material derived from them.
- After 18 months added as another condition for export approval a requirement that the recipient country accept international non-proliferation standards for all its peaceful nuclear facilities, whatever their origin.
- Required that any new agreements for nuclear cooperation mandate a cutoff of U.S. nuclear exports and the recall of material already exported in case of any violation of the non-proliferation conditions.
- Directed the president to try to renegotiate existing nuclear cooperation agreements with other governments in order to incorporate the new non-proliferation standards in the bill.

Legislative History

The House version of HR 8638 was passed Sept. 28, 1977, by a vote of 411-0. The Senate Foreign Relations Committee reported a tougher version Oct. 23 that incorporated commitments by the United States to establish an international nuclear fuel bank and assist other nations' efforts to develop non-nuclear energy sources. Senate floor action was put off until the second session. *(1977 Almanac p. 399)*

Senators sympathetic to the nuclear industry's viewpoint saw no hope of substantially altering the bill. But before passing it Feb. 7 by an 88-3 vote, they were able in collaboration with the administration to amend it to allow somewhat greater flexibility to the executive branch in assessing the proliferation risk of any proposed export. And they won provisions imposing specific timetables on the review process that all export requests would be subject.

The industry supporters had hoped to further modify the bill in a House-Senate conference, but on Feb. 9 the House unexpectedly accepted the Senate version by voice vote, thus completing congressional action.

Background

In the first few years of the atomic age, U.S. policy as embodied in the 1946 Atomic Energy Act forbade exports of nuclear technology for industrial purposes. By 1953 it was evident that nuclear technology was spreading to other industrial nations, and U.S. policy was modified to promote "Atoms for Peace" — intended by the Eisenhower administration to channel the spreading technology into controlled, non-military uses.

But experience gained from the operation of nuclear power generating plants proved usable for less peaceful projects. The Nuclear Non-Proliferation Treaty, put into effect in 1969, was intended to erect a political barrier to weapons proliferation, once the technical obstacles had been eroded. *(1969 Almanac p. 162)*

The single most dramatic event spurring a re-examination of U.S. non-proliferation policy was India's 1974 explosion of a nuclear device. But even before that shock, there was a growing uneasiness about the adequacy of the Non-Proliferation Treaty. A country could amass all the components of a nuclear weapon — leaving itself only hours away from a military capability — without violating the treaty.

By the mid-1970s several other factors appeared to increase the risk that nuclear weapons might spread beyond the six nations that already had exploded nuclear bombs:

- In 1974 India exploded a nuclear device that she insisted was for peaceful purposes. Radioactive material and technology acquired from Canada, France and the United States reportedly was used in the blast.

The shock of that event drew attention to the possibility that a nation could develop nuclear weaponry in a clandestine manner. This would preclude other nations from trying to deter nuclear explosions by diplomatic or other means before the country chose to unveil its new symbol of international status.

India apparently had not diverted any material from a nuclear power plant for its explosion. But U.S. analysts of the nuclear proliferation problem began to concentrate on the vulnerability of the nuclear power plant fuel cycle. At certain points in the process of manufacturing nuclear fuel as an energy source and its subsequent reprocessing, they warned, there was a relatively high risk that weapons-grade material could be siphoned off by the country using the fuel or simply stolen by terrorists. *(Reactor fuel cycle, p. 352)*

- The quadrupling of oil prices in 1973-74 fueled a general insistence by countries that they be self-sufficient in energy.
- Technological developments were imminent both for the commonly used light-water reactor and for the developing breeder reactor that would introduce into the world nuclear economy for the first time large quantities of material (plutonium) that could be converted directly into nuclear explosives without any expensive, complex and time-consuming preparatory steps.
- Global political stability was declining with the emergence of ambitious regional powers resistant to the tutelage of the superpowers.
- Increasingly violent and sophisticated terrorist groups emerged, conceivably capable of exploiting the increased availability of weapons-usable nuclear material.

Fuel Cycles and Foul Play

Nuclear explosives can be constructed out of three elements — plutonium and two isotopes of uranium, U-233 and U-235. None of the isotopes occurs in nature, but all are produced in the course of various nuclear fuel cycles — the industrial operations needed to prepare nuclear raw material for use as reactor fuel and for disposing of it or recycling it after it is used.

The fuel cycles required for different reactor designs present distinctive proliferation risks. The policies announced by the Carter administration and embodied in HR 8638 were intended to prevent diversion of fissionable material for weapons from the fuel cycle most widely in current use — that for the light-water reactors (LWR). The bill also was aimed at discouraging the spread of other fuel cycles that were thought to entail greater proliferation risks than the LWR cycle. The most important of these alternative cycles was that associated with the liquid-metal fast breeder reactor (LMFBR).

National Policy or Terrorist Threat? Any non-proliferation policy must contemplate two kinds of threats. First, a nation not possessing nuclear weapons might decide as a matter of policy to develop them from raw materials used in peaceful nuclear power installations located within its jurisdiction. Such diversion could be either overt or clandestine.

The second threat was that a nation or a terrorist band could seize weapons-usable material by armed force. And this was a threat not only to nuclear exports, but also to U.S. nuclear installations and U.S. nuclear weapons stockpiled overseas.

Light Water Reactor Cycle

'Throwaway' Mode. For the LWR cycle, uranium oxide is recovered from the mined ore and converted to uranium hexafluoride. At an enrichment plant, the concentration of U-235 is increased from the naturally occurring level of .7 percent to about 3 percent.

The enriched fuel then is formed into fuel assemblies that are fed into the power reactor. After several years, the proportion of U-235 in the fuel runs down and it is removed (as spent fuel). But it still contains about .9 percent U-235 and about .5 percent plutonium.

Since the earliest days of nuclear power development, it was assumed that the spent fuel would be reprocessed to tap this energy potential. But if the fuel is not reprocessed — and thus is "thrown away" — certain proliferation risks are reduced because, without the reprocessing plants, the spent fuel is too weak to produce a nuclear bomb.

Theoretically, any country having control over any facility involved in the LWR cycle could divert material for weapons use. The Office of Technology Assessment (OTA) estimated in 1977 that a militarily significant weapon could be constructed from as little as 5 to 10 kilograms of U-233 or pure plutonium, or from 15 to 30 kilograms of uranium enriched to a level of 90 percent U-235. But those materials would be available only if the country possessed uranium enrichment or spent fuel reprocessing plants.

Current International Atomic Energy Agency (IAEA) safeguards probably would preclude covert diversion of spent fuel, according to the OTA. But covert production of weapons-grade uranium would be possible with certain kinds of enrichment plants, given current safeguards.

A terrorist group could obtain weapons material from the throwaway cycle only by stealing the dangerously radioactive spent fuel and carrying out a time-consuming process of chemical separation.

Plutonium Recycling. A national nuclear power facility could recycle the spent fuel from an LWR by chemically separating the plutonium and fissionable uranium, which then could be used again in the fuel cycle. Since plutonium oxide, produced by this step, is directly usable for nuclear explosives, the Carter administration and the sponsors of HR 8638 regarded widespread recycling as entailing very high proliferation risks.

Since the spent fuel is fed through the reprocessing plant in a steady stream, and because of inherent measurement shortcomings of current IAEA safeguards, which are intended to account for all nuclear materials in a nation's fuel cycle, enough plutonium oxide for several weapons a year could be diverted covertly from a reprocessing plant. And if a nation decided to publicly "go nuclear," it would have immediate access to a steady flow of weapons-usable material.

The availability of weapons material in the recycling stage also risked terrorist seizure in the reprocessing plant, the fuel manufacturing plant or in transport between these two facilities.

The Breeder

The liquid-metal fast breeder reactor uses a mixture of plutonium and U-238 oxide for fuel, and this core is surrounded by a blanket of U-238. As a by-product of the core's fission reaction, the blanket is transformed into plu-

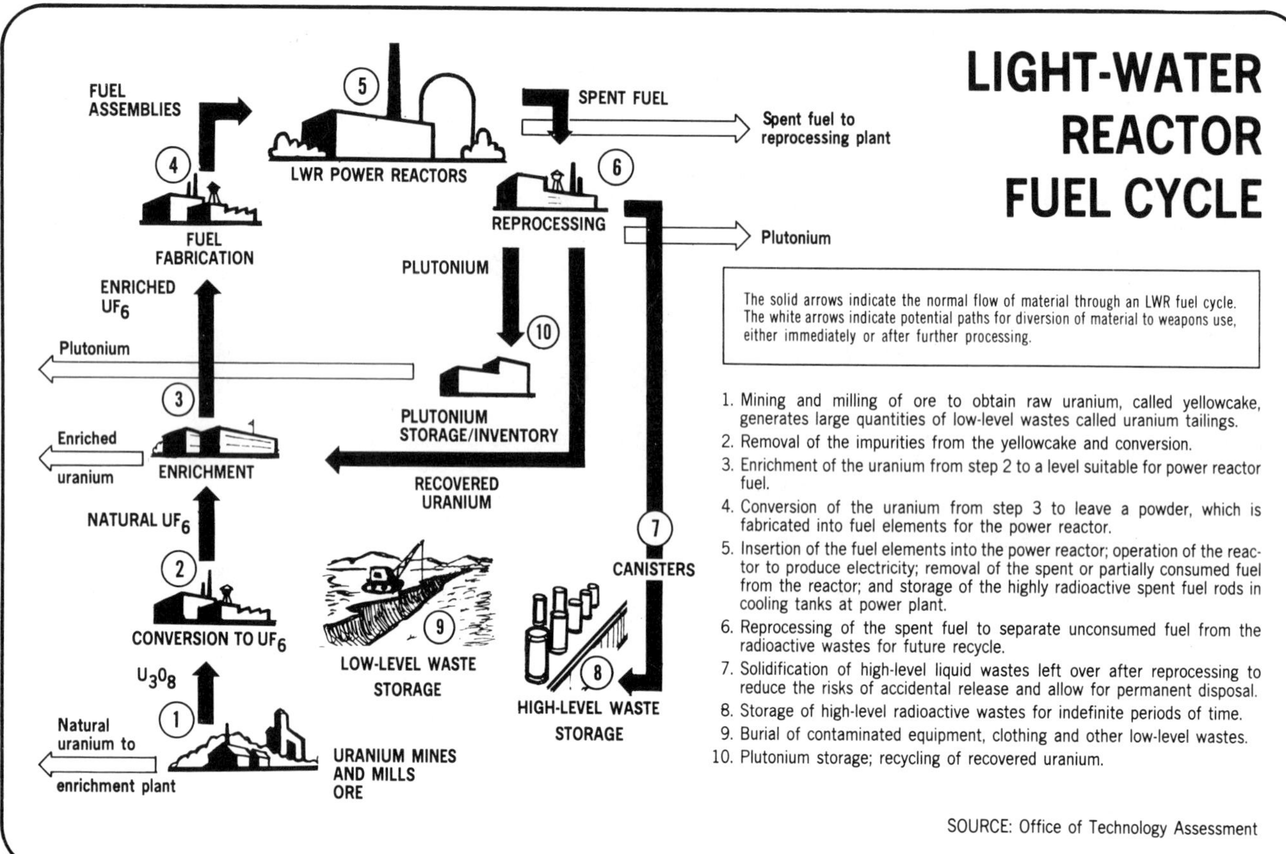
LIGHT-WATER REACTOR FUEL CYCLE
FUEL ASSEMBLIES
LWR POWER REACTORS
SPENT FUEL
Spent fuel to reprocessing plant
REPROCESSING
Plutonium
FUEL FABRICATION
ENRICHED UF6
PLUTONIUM
Plutonium
PLUTONIUM STORAGE/INVENTORY
Enriched uranium
ENRICHMENT
RECOVERED URANIUM
NATURAL UF6
CANISTERS
CONVERSION TO UF6
LOW-LEVEL WASTE STORAGE
U3O8
HIGH-LEVEL WASTE STORAGE
Natural uranium to enrichment plant
URANIUM MINES AND MILLS ORE
The solid arrows indicate the normal flow of material through an LWR fuel cycle. The white arrows indicate potential paths for diversion of material to weapons use, either immediately or after further processing.
1. Mining and milling of ore to obtain raw uranium, called yellowcake, generates large quantities of low-level wastes called uranium tailings.
2. Removal of the impurities from the yellowcake and conversion.
3. Enrichment of the uranium from step 2 to a level suitable for power reactor fuel.
4. Conversion of the uranium from step 3 to leave a powder, which is fabricated into fuel elements for the power reactor.
5. Insertion of the fuel elements into the power reactor; operation of the reactor to produce electricity; removal of the spent or partially consumed fuel from the reactor; and storage of the highly radioactive spent fuel rods in cooling tanks at power plant.
6. Reprocessing of the spent fuel to separate unconsumed fuel from the radioactive wastes for future recycle.
7. Solidification of high-level liquid wastes left over after reprocessing to reduce the risks of accidental release and allow for permanent disposal.
8. Storage of high-level radioactive wastes for indefinite periods of time.
9. Burial of contaminated equipment, clothing and other low-level wastes.
10. Plutonium storage; recycling of recovered uranium.
SOURCE: Office of Technology Assessment

tonium, generating about 15 percent more fuel than is consumed in the core.

This new plutonium is extracted from the blanket in a reprocessing plant and recycled into fuel elements just as in the recycling stage of the LWR cycle. It is vulnerable to diversion or armed seizure at the same points, but there is an important difference. There is more plutonium in circulation in the breeder cycle, and it is in a more concentrated form. Hence, a smaller amount of diverted material is needed to produce an explosive.

Moreover, since the breeder cycle frees a country from any dependence on imported fuel, it would become less vulnerable to the threat of a fuel cutoff as a means of deterring weapons development.

Provisions

As signed into law, HR 8638 contained the following major provisions:

Policy Statement

Contained a sense of Congress declaration that the proliferation of nuclear explosives, or of the ability to manufacture them, was "a grave threat" to U.S. security. Accordingly it was U.S. policy to:

- Pursue international mechanisms to assure fuel supplies for all nations and to improve controls over international transfers of nuclear fuel, equipment and technology in order to prevent the proliferation of nuclear weapons. One aspect of such controls would include the establishment of common international sanctions against violators.
- Affirm the reliability of the United States as a supplier of nuclear reactors and fuel to nations adhering to effective non-proliferation policies.
- Strongly encourage ratification of the 1968 Non-Proliferation Treaty by nations that had not done so.
- Cooperate with other nations in identifying and developing alternative, non-nuclear power sources.

Military Agreements Excluded. Excluded from most of the new procedures established by the bill were agreements between the United States and its allies for cooperative military uses of nuclear material.

Title I — U.S. Reliability as Nuclear Fuel Supplier

The intent of this section of the bill was to assure other nations that the United States would be a reliable supplier of nuclear fuel to nations that pursued anti-proliferation policies. Toward that end, the president was to report to Congress within a year of the bill's enactment on whether expansion of U.S. uranium enrichment plants was necessary to meet both domestic and foreign demands for uranium for peaceful purposes.

International Fuel Bank

The president was urged to begin international negotiations aimed at establishing an international nuclear fuel authority (INFA) that would be authorized to sell nuclear fuel to nations. The agency was prohibited from imposing political conditions except that purchasers had to adhere to a non-proliferation policy. Specifically, the president was directed to ensure that INFA fuel was available only to nations that:

'Timely Warning' Standard

"[T]he standard of timely warning, the basic concept on which the entire international safeguards program rests, is strictly a measure of whether warning of a diversion [of weapons-grade nuclear material] will be received far enough in advance of the time when the recipient could transform the diverted material into an explosive device to permit an adequate diplomatic response. The amount of warning time required will vary (and cannot be defined in terms of a certain number of weeks or months) depending on the type of response which would be needed — i.e., in some cases a bilateral response would be adequate whereas in others a coordinated response by several nations and/or international organizations would be necessary.

". . .Another crucial consideration is the quality of the safeguards in place at the facility. . . . Other factors include whether the nation would have limited access to the material because of multinational control or other barriers, whether the fuel is multinationally owned, and whether the nation has access to any facilities which might be needed to convert the diverted material to a weapons-usable form. . . .

"Other factors which may be taken into account in determining whether there will be a significant risk increase . . . are whether the nation is firmly committed to effective non-proliferation policies and is genuinely willing to accept conditions which would minimize the risk of proliferation; whether the nation has a security agreement or other important foreign policy relationship with the United States; the nature and stability of the recipient's government, its military and security position and the energy resources available to that nation.

"It is important to note that the bill requires that 'foremost' consideration be given to the question of timely warning. . . . There may be circumstances that will suffice and a request may be granted even though timely warning is not present. . . . The committee does wish to emphasize that in the absence of a clear determination that timely warning will indeed be provided, a strong combination of other factors is necessary to compensate for this weakness in safeguards."

SOURCE: Senate Foreign Relations Committee report (S Rept 95-467)

- Accepted International Atomic Energy Agency (IAEA) safeguards on all their nuclear energy activities.
- Did not acquire nuclear explosives.
- Did not establish new uranium enrichment or fuel reprocessing plants. Member nations were required to place any such plants already in existence under international auspices and inspection.

Within six months of the bill's enactment, the president was to submit to Congress proposals for an initial U.S. commitment to the INFA for sale to other nations of an amount of low-enriched uranium sufficient to produce up to 100,000 megawatt/years of power from light-water nuclear reactors. The president also was to report on the desirability of allowing foreign investment in U.S. uranium enrichment plants as an incentive for other countries not to build such plants themselves.

The INFA agreements with other nations were to address the problem of construction of facilities, under international auspices, for handling nuclear fuel and spent fuel. Such agreements were to assure nations placing spent fuel in such international repositories that they would be compensated for the energy content of the spent fuel if the INFA later reprocessed it to extract the energy.

Fuel Cycle Evaluation

The president was directed to invite all nuclear suppliers and consumers to re-evaluate the nuclear fuel cycle for the purpose of finding alternatives to systems using pure plutonium or highly enriched uranium, either of which could be used in the construction of bombs.

Title II — Strengthening International Safeguards

Commitment to IAEA

The bill expressed a "strong commitment" by the United States to the 1968 Non-Proliferation of Nuclear Weapons Treaty and to the IAEA. It pledged U.S. cooperation with other nations to ensure that IAEA had adequate resources. To improve IAEA anti-proliferation safeguards, the United States pledged to work toward:

- Timely detection of possible diversion by any nation of nuclear fuel (or the raw material for such fuel) that could be used to build bombs.
- Timely notification to other nations of the detection.
- Timely response by the international community to any fuel diversion. The bill specifically committed the United States to negotiate with other nations common sanctions that would be applied against any nation that violated its non-proliferation obligations. Also to be negotiated were common procedures to be followed in the event of the theft, loss or sabotage of nuclear materials.

Training Program

The Department of Energy in consultation with the Nuclear Regulatory Commission (NRC) was to establish for the benefit of other nations a training program in non-proliferation safeguards and in physical security measures for nuclear facilities.

Title III — Export Criteria and Organization

Export Criteria

The bill established as criteria for government approval of any nuclear export assurances by the recipient government that it would take specific steps intended to reduce the risk of proliferation of the imported fuel.

In general, these assurances would be required not only for the raw material, fuel or fuel production facilities exported, but also for any such materials or facilities previously exported and any nuclear fuel produced by the recipient country from such materials and facilities.

Before the U.S. government approved the export of nuclear technology that could be used to produce a bomb, the same assurances would be required regarding any nuclear material or equipment that was produced by the recipient nation.

The following conditions were to be applied immediately to any such export request:

- IAEA safeguards must be applied to the export.
- The export must not be used to produce weapons.
- The export must be protected by adequate physical security measures, as defined by the NRC.

- The export must not be transferred to another nation without prior U.S. approval; such approval would be possible only if the potential recipient nation accepted the above conditions.
- In the case of nuclear fuel or raw material, the export must not be reprocessed or enriched without prior U.S. approval.

Beginning 18 months after enactment of the bill, the scope of the above assurances were to be expanded to apply IAEA safeguards to all peaceful nuclear activities and facilities in recipient nations, whatever their source.

This additional requirement could be waived if the president determined that its application would be prejudicial to U.S. non-proliferation goals or to U.S. security, but Congress could override the president's decision by adopting a concurrent resolution of disapproval within 60 days (not counting recesses).

Grounds for Termination. Exports would be barred to any nation that had not previously detonated a nuclear explosive but subsequently:

- Exploded a bomb.
- Violated or withdrew from IAEA safeguards.
- Engaged in activities that could lead to bomb production and failed, in the president's judgment, to stop those activities.

In addition, exports were to be cut off to any nation found by the president to have:

- Materially violated any agreement under which it received nuclear material or equipment.
- Failed to discourage a non-nuclear state from developing a bomb after having encouraged such action.
- Transferred to any non-nuclear weapons state reprocessing equipment, except under terms of an agreement to which the United States was a party.

The president could continue exports in spite of any of these events if he determined that a cutoff would harm U.S. security or non-proliferation objectives. But Congress could override such a presidential judgment by passage of a concurrent resolution within 60 days (not counting recesses).

Export Licensing Procedure

Before the NRC issued a license for any nuclear export, the secretary of state had to rule that the proposed export was not inimical to U.S. security. This judgment was to be reached by a procedure agreed on by the Departments of Defense, Commerce and Energy and by the Arms Control and Disarmament Agency (ACDA) and NRC.

Having received the executive branch judgment, the NRC then could license the export if it found, "based on a reasonable judgment of the assurances provided [by the recipient state] and other information available," that the proposed deal met the criteria established by the bill.

NRC Timetable. The NRC was directed to begin its analysis of an application concurrently with the executive branch agencies. The processing of an application had to be completed within 60 days of receiving the executive branch judgment on the application [the period could be extended another 60 days] unless, within that period, it had begun public hearings or had requested further information from the executive branch. In either contingency, the 60-day period would begin at the end of the public hearings or the receipt of the new information.

Presidential Override. If the NRC evaluation was not completed by the end of the second 60-day period, or if the NRC did not approve the application in light of the applicable criteria, the president could authorize the export by executive order. But Congress could block that approval by adoption of a concurrent resolution within 60 days (excluding recesses).

Criteria Deferral. For license applications for exports made under terms of an existing nuclear cooperation agreement, the requirement in the bill for prior U.S. approval of any reprocessing or third party transfer of any nuclear material of U.S. origin would be waived for the first two years after the bill was enacted. After the two years, the president could continue to waive the provision on a year-to-year basis if he decided that failure to approve exports to any nation would be prejudicial to U.S. security or non-proliferation goals. Congress could override such a presidential decision by joint resolution.

Shortcuts. The NRC was authorized to make a single judgment covering several proposed transactions if they involved the same recipient and were of the same significance for nuclear explosive development. It also was authorized to forgo the full-scale license evaluation if it found there was "no material changed circumstance" between the pending application and the last application approved for an export to the same country. The use of either of these procedures was strictly within the discretion of the NRC.

Nuclear Plant Components. The NRC was authorized to determine, after consultation with the Departments of State, Energy and Commerce and the ACDA, what components of nuclear reactors or fuel handling plants required export licenses because of their special relationship to bomb production.

If a component was not covered by an existing export license dealing with an entire plant and if the executive branch judged the export to be safe, the NRC would approve the export if it were satisfied that:

- IAEA safeguards would be met.
- The components would not be used to produce a bomb.
- The components would not be transferred to a third party without prior U.S. approval.

The Commerce Department, in consultation with the Departments of State, Energy and Defense, the ACDA and NRC, would regulate the export of components that did not require NRC licenses, but which nevertheless could be used in weapons production under certain conditions.

Transfers Without Licensing

In an emergency, the Department of Energy was authorized to export to other countries without a license small quantities of highly radioactive material (less than 500 grams) that were included in laboratory samples, medical devices or monitoring instruments. The department also could transfer to other governments without a license not more than three metric tons of nuclear raw material.

Such transfers could be made by the Energy Department only with the concurrence of the Department of State and after consultation with the ACDA, NRC and the Defense Department.

The same procedure had to be followed for approval of any transfer of technology that could produce nuclear fuel, unless that transfer was authorized by some other agreement made under the terms of the bill.

'Subsequent Arrangements'

The bill established a procedure for approval of "subsequent arrangements" — specific agreements made pursuant to an intergovernmental agreement for nuclear cooperation. These included international arrangements made by the U.S. government involving:

- Contracts for furnishing nuclear fuel and equipment.
- Approvals for transfers to a third party of any fuels, raw material or equipment.
- Arrangements for physical security or for safeguards against diversion of nuclear fuel.
- Storage of spent fuel.

Such subsequent arrangements could be made by the Energy Department only with the concurrence of the State Department and after consultation with ACDA, NRC and the Defense Department. The secretary of state was to have the leading role in any negotiations involving spent fuel storage or third-party transfers. The ACDA director could prepare an unclassified Nuclear Proliferation Assessment Statement for any subsequent arrangement that he viewed as contributing to proliferation.

Arrangements for the reprocessing of spent fuel or for the transfer of more than 500 grams of plutonium could not take effect until they had been referred to the Senate Foreign Relations and House International Relations Committees for 15 days (excluding recesses).

No agreement could be made for reprocessing nuclear fuel in any plant that had not reprocessed it before the bill's enactment, unless the secretary of energy and the secretary of state concluded that the agreement did not increase the risk of proliferation. In making that judgment, "foremost" consideration was to be given to whether the United States would receive "timely warning" of any diversion of the fuel to the manufacture of weapons. The same standard was to be applied to approval of any reprocessing arrangement in plants that had reprocessed fuel prior to the bill's enactment.

The bill established stringent time limits for the various phases of the approval process.

Fuel Storage. Arrangements for spent fuel storage in the United States could be blocked by adoption of a concurrent resolution within 60 days (excluding recesses) of notifying Congress of the proposed agreement. The waiting period for congressional action could be waived by the president for emergency agreements involving small amounts of spent fuel, provided the president notified the congressional committees having jurisdiction.

Title IV — Additional Controls

This section of the bill established new goals for U.S. export policy. It required that any new agreements for nuclear cooperation include conditions to further those goals, and it directed the president to attempt to renegotiate existing cooperation agreements in order to incorporate similar conditions. Essentially, these conditions incorporated in the agreements the same criteria that the NRC was required to use in assessing any individual license application. In general, they were to be applied to all raw materials, nuclear fuel, equipment and technology exported by the United States or derived from U.S. exports.

The new conditions for cooperative agreements were:

- Anti-proliferation safeguards were to be maintained indefinitely, regardless of the duration of other parts of the agreement and whether or not the agreement later was abrogated.

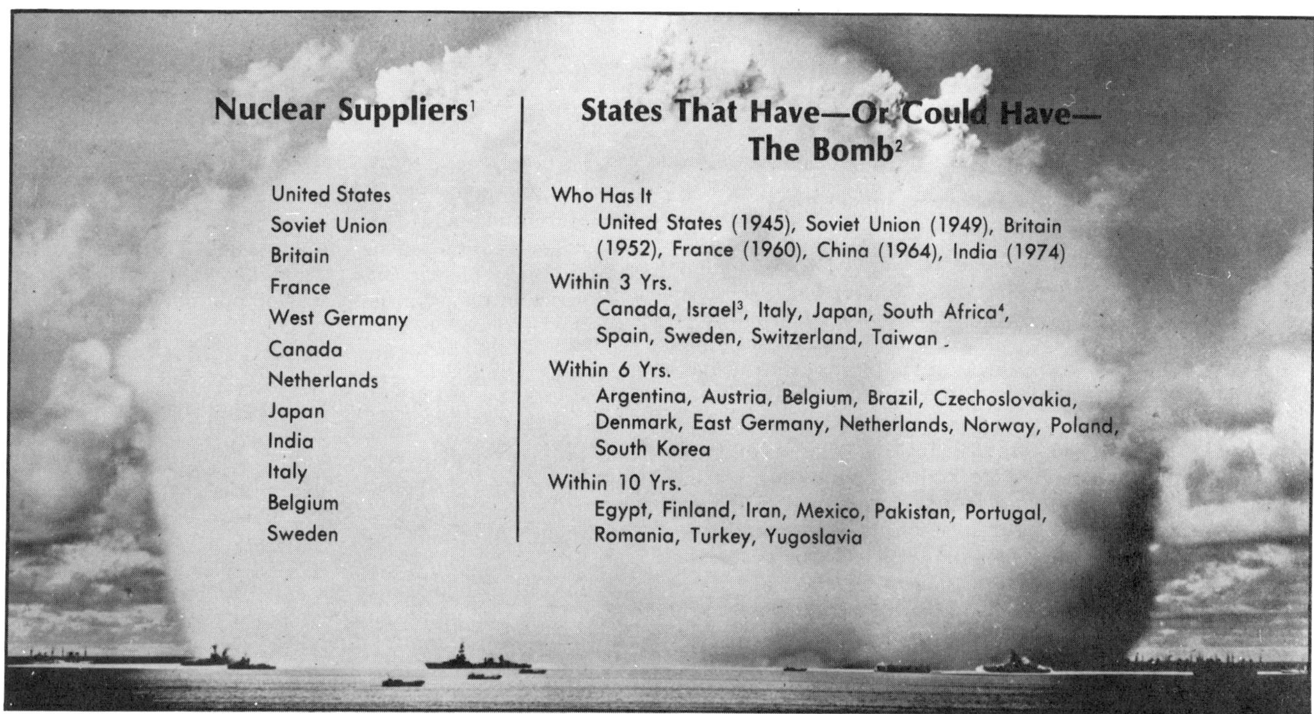

Nuclear Suppliers[1]
United States
Soviet Union
Britain
France
West Germany
Canada
Netherlands
Japan
India
Italy
Belgium
Sweden
States That Have—Or Could Have—The Bomb[2]
Who Has It
United States (1945), Soviet Union (1949), Britain (1952), France (1960), China (1964), India (1974)
Within 3 Yrs.
Canada, Israel[3], Italy, Japan, South Africa[4], Spain, Sweden, Switzerland, Taiwan
Within 6 Yrs.
Argentina, Austria, Belgium, Brazil, Czechoslovakia, Denmark, East Germany, Netherlands, Norway, Poland, South Korea
Within 10 Yrs.
Egypt, Finland, Iran, Mexico, Pakistan, Portugal, Romania, Turkey, Yugoslavia

1. States currently selling nuclear reactors or operating plants to enrich uranium or to reprocess spent reactor fuel. SOURCE: Office of Technology Assessment.

2. This list, prepared by the Energy Research and Development Administration in April 1976, deals only with technical capability. No speculation is implied on the presence or absence of political motivation to develop nuclear weapons. The list contained no mention of West Germany.

3. Most U.S. observers assume that Israel already possesses a modest arsenal of nuclear weapons either already assembled or ready for quick assembly within hours.

4. Preparations for a South African nuclear test reportedly were canceled in August 1977 under strong U.S. diplomatic pressure. Some U.S. observers assume that South Africa retains the technical ability to explode a bomb at any time.

• IAEA safeguards were to be maintained on all nuclear materials, regardless of their origin, in all peaceful nuclear activities in the country.

• Nothing transferred under the agreement was to be used to produce a bomb.

• The United States was given the right to recall any material if the recipient exploded a nuclear bomb or abrogated its acceptance of IAEA safeguards.

• Reprocessing, enrichment or third-party transfer of anything exported under the agreement, and proposed fuel storage sites, had to be approved by the United States.

• Adequate physical security had to be maintained with respect to any nuclear fuel associated with exports under the agreement.

• Any nuclear activity based on technology exported under the agreement was made subject to all the above conditions. But the president could exempt any agreement from this requirement if he thought it necessary for U.S. security or non-proliferation interests.

Approval Procedure. Most proposed agreements were to be negotiated by the secretary of state, with the technical advice and concurrence of the secretary of energy and in consultation with the ACDA director. After consultation with the NRC, proposed agreements had to be submitted to the president by the secretaries of state and energy along with their recommendations and the recommendations of the NRC and the ACDA director. The director also was required to submit an unclassified Nuclear Proliferation Impact Assessment. (Certain classes of agreements were to be submitted to the president by the secretary of energy, others by the secretary of defense.)

If the president approved an agreement, Congress could block it by adoption of a concurrent resolution within 60 days (exclusive of recesses) of receiving the ACDA proliferation impact assessment. For agreements involving relatively small reactors the period for congressional review was 30 days.

International Non-Proliferation

The president was directed to seek international agreement on the following non-proliferation policies:

• No nuclear fuel, equipment or technology would be transferred to any nation that did not agree to 1) abstain from using the exports to make a bomb or from encouraging another nation to do so; 2) accept IAEA safeguards and adequate physical security measures; 3) refuse to transfer the material to any third party that did not accept these conditions.

• Fuel enrichment or reprocessing involving weapons-grade material (and related stockpiling) was to take place only at facilities that were under international auspices and subject to international inspection. Adequate physical security measures would be established for all peaceful nuclear activities, regardless of their origin.

Renegotiation Efforts. The president was directed to try to renegotiate existing nuclear cooperation agreements so as to incorporate the conditions required by the bill. The president, after annual reviews, could recommend changes to Congress, which also could make changes by joint resolution.

The president also was directed to seek safeguards for protecting the international environment from radioactive, chemical or thermal pollution as a result of peaceful nuclear activities.

Title V — Assistance to Developing Countries

The United States was committed to the development of non-nuclear power resources and to aid developing countries to meet their energy needs through such resources.

Specifically, it was directed to establish a program for reducing such countries' dependence on petroleum and developing renewable power sources such as solar energy. The program authorized an exchange of energy scientists and technicians among the United States and the developing countries.

Title VI — Executive Reports

The president was to report annually to Congress on the non-proliferation policy embodied in the act, specifically the progress made in the various negotiations called for by the bill, explanations for the lack of progress on any points, and recommendations for any legislative modifications he thought necessary to achieve the non-proliferation goals set forth in the bill.

The report also was to list any non-nuclear-weapons states that had engaged in any activities that tended to increase nuclear proliferation (including the explosion of a nuclear bomb and refusal to accept IAEA standards).

The president also had to note whether any provisions of the bill proved to be counterproductive and to report on the administrative procedures used to implement them.

Three years after enactment, the comptroller general was directed to report to Congress on the bill's effect on U.S. non-proliferation goals.

Expedited Procedures

An expedited congressional procedure was established to ensure timely congressional action on each of the several presidential submissions required by the bill.

Senate Floor Action

The Senate passed HR 8638 with amendments Feb. 7 by a vote of 88-3. *(Vote 30, p. 7-S)*

Provisions added during the Senate debate included language committing the United States to establish an international nuclear fuel bank and assist developing countries in their efforts to develop non-nuclear sources of energy.

Three days of Senate debate on HR 8638 Feb. 2, 6 and 7 revealed a basic disagreement over the feasibility of containing the spread of weapons-related nuclear technologies. Supporters argued that tighter controls were necessary before additional nations acquired fuel processing plants that produced weapons-usable material.

"While at one time we had a lengthy period in which to take political or diplomatic actions in the event we learned of a diversion from a light water reactor," said John Glenn, D-Ohio, floor manager of the bill, "now in the context of separated plutonium and reprocessing, the time between diversion of material and nuclear weapons has become so compressed that it could be a matter of a very few days or hours of warning."

But opponents maintained that the strategy of limiting access to nuclear technology was foredoomed because the genie already was out of the bottle.

"We live in a nuclear world that has already proliferated," said Minority Leader Howard H. Baker Jr., R-Tenn., "and we must try to keep it from proliferating any more than it has, and try to learn to live with that genie now that he is out of the bottle."

Pete V. Domenici, R-N.M., agreed. "The decision by other countries to build nuclear weapons is a political rather than a technical one. The technology and scientific and technical bases are available to many advanced nations. Only a deliberate political choice separates them from moving ahead. A strategy of non-proliferation based solely on denial of equipment and technology will at most only delay, not prohibit, this possibility."

Carrot or Stick Approach

Not only was the bill's strategy of restricting technology unworkable, according to opponents, but it was applied in a way that would strain the political relationship with other countries through which U.S. influence still could be exerted on behalf of non-proliferation. It was, said James A. McClure, R-Idaho, a leading opponent of the Senate committee version, "an almost no carrot and all stick approach."

The export criteria embodied in the bill were far more stringent than those agreed to Jan. 12, 1978, by a conference of the 12 nuclear supplying nations in London. And the bill's requirements preempted the results of a two-year-long international study of various fuel cycles that had been organized at the suggestion of President Carter.

"...Many of the European countries as well as Japan and others are becoming increasingly offended by the fact that this legislation includes such unilateral and immediate requirements for renegotiation and reconsideration of past agreements," charged McClure.

Faced with U.S. demands that purchasers regarded as unreasonable, said the opponents, customers would merely obtain the same exports from other suppliers who were less fastidious. Brazil's insistence on acquiring a fuel reprocessing plant illustrated the problem, according to Baker. "With or without the United States, Brazil will develop an extensive nuclear program.... Brazil would prefer U.S. technology, [but] only within a framework which eliminates unnecessarily burdensome requirements imposed by the American government," he said.

Supporters insisted the bill offered a big carrot to customers who adhered to firm non-proliferation policies — that of the proposed international nuclear fuel bank (INFA). This would assure customers of a steady supply of nuclear fuel, insulated from the threat of political manipulation, they maintained. They also pointed out that the bill exempted, at least temporarily, several nuclear arrangements between the U.S. and its allies.

The president could approve an export that did not meet the bill's non-proliferation criteria (subject to congressional veto) if he thought the deal essential to national security or to long-term U.S. non-proliferation goals.

But the bill's supporters did place more confidence in the efficacy of mandatory sanctions as the ultimate deterrent against proliferation. Charles H. Percy, R-Ill., who with Glenn helped guide the bill through the Senate, insisted that such a posture by the United States might have prevented India's 1974 nuclear blast. "They were able to do it without any concern that they would have sanctions imposed against them.... We had to thrash around for a couple of years to determine what we would actually do.... But if we had just had a clear-cut policy from the outset that [a nuclear explosion] would be an action so contrary to our policy that we would sever our supply....then I do not think they would have taken the action."

U.S. Reliability as Supplier

McClure and his allies maintained that the export approval procedures would vitiate HR 8638's expressed intent of assuring U.S. reliability as a fuel supplier. They were, he said, "procedurally cumbersome, excessively time-consuming, highly unpredictable" and would provide a field day for anti-nuclear power advocates.

Glenn retorted that the full-scale review process criticized by McClure would operate only in the case of a customer whose nuclear policy was suspect. "In the typical case, however, procedures under the bill will be simpler than under existing law."

By simplifying export procedures and by clarifying export criteria, supporters insisted that the bill would enhance export prospects for the U.S. nuclear industry.

But Glenn and Percy negotiated with McClure a series of amendments designed to impose specific deadlines on the export licensing procedure and bar judicial intervention in certain aspects of that procedure.

Floor Amendments

Nearly all the amendments considered were negotiated by Glenn and Percy and the leading opponents, McClure and Frank Church, D-Idaho. The major changes made in the committee-reported bill were as follows:

Anti-Nuclear Bias? At the insistence of some members who feared the bill could be detrimental to the future expansion of the nuclear power industry, one of the adopted amendments required an analysis by the General Accounting Office (GAO) of the bill's effect on the problem of nuclear proliferation and on the U.S. nuclear industry. The study was to be submitted within three years of the bill's enactment.

To close off one possible line of attack by antinuclear-power activists against nuclear export deals, a statement was incorporated that the bill was officially neutral in the fight within the administration over whether such sales required an environmental impact statement.

NRC Role. The nuclear industry hoped to curb the independent role in export decisions of the Nuclear Regulatory Commission (NRC). Supporters of the industry position charged that in weighing a proposed sale's proliferation risk against its diplomatic and commercial advantages, the NRC would be less likely than the State Department to approve sales.

No industry moves against the NRC's role as spelled out in the bill were brought to an up-or-down vote. Instead, Glenn and Percy replaced them with substitute amendments of their own that made some procedural changes, but preserved intact the basic independence and authority of the NRC in export decisions:

- Authority to define adequate standards of physical security of nuclear facilities at foreign sites remained with the NRC.
- NRC retained the power to determine what exports were relevant to nuclear proliferation and thus required approval under the bill's procedures.
- For certain exports, the president would be allowed to bypass NRC approval if the commission had not made up its mind within 120 days. But the time limit would apply only to the period after the NRC had gathered all necessary information through hearings and inquiries to the State Department. It would be guaranteed access to State Department information on the sale.

Role of Congress. Accepted by a 91-0 vote was an amendment permitting Congress to veto by concurrent resolution any international agreement to store in the United States the spent fuel from foreign nuclear plants. By a narrow margin (47-44) this version, drafted by Glenn, was approved as a substitute for a McClure amendment that would have allowed either house of Congress to veto such an agreement by simple resolution. *(Votes 28, 27, p. 7-S)*

Frequency of Review. By a 56-36 vote, the Senate tabled (killed) an amendment by Domenici that in effect would have required foreign nuclear customers to go through the bill's full-scale review process only once every five years, unless the NRC found that there had been a significant change in circumstances since its previous approval. But Glenn and Percy did accept an amendment allowing the NRC at its discretion to decide that a full-scale review was not necessary for routine exports to regular customers. *(Vote 29, p. 7-S)*

Final Action

The House Feb. 9 on a voice vote accepted the Senate-passed version without change, completing congressional action on the bill.

Submission of the bill to President Carter was delayed for about three weeks while technical and conforming changes (H Con Res 486) were drafted and approved by the House and Senate. This would have been done in the conference committee had the bill been sent there, as McClure and other opponents had expected. ∎

U.S. Intelligence Agencies

Congress completed action Aug. 22 on legislation (HR 12240 — PL 95-370) authorizing funds for the operations of federal intelligence agencies in fiscal 1979.

The amount authorized by the bill was classified.

HR 12240 also authorized $12.7 million for 269 full-time employees of the Director of Central Intelligence's (DCI) staff. The staff assisted the DCI in his budgetary oversight of the various agencies that made up the U.S. intelligence community — the CIA, those agencies run by the Pentagon such as the Defense Intelligence Agency and the National Security Agency and relevant activities of the Departments of State, Treasury and Energy, the FBI and the Drug Envorcement Administration.

The bill incorporated a provision added by the House requiring the attorney general to report to Congress all cases of aliens who were admitted into the United States even though, because of their background, the FBI recommended that they be denied admittance.

Provisions

As cleared for the president, HR 12240:

- Authorized an undisclosed amount for intelligence and intelligence-related activities in fiscal 1979. The amounts authorized for specific programs and the Intelligence Committees' directions to the intelligence community regarding specific programs were listed in a secret annex to the conference report on the bill. This document was available to members of Congress, but not to their staffs.
- Authorized $12.7 million to pay 269 full-time employees of the Intelligence Community Staff of the Director of Central Intelligence.
- Authorized the amount requested ($43.5 million) for the CIA's retirement and disability system.
- Required the attorney general to report to Congress by Oct. 30, 1979, all cases during fiscal 1979 in which the FBI had warned the attorney general that certain aliens who were admitted into the United States by the State Department could have been denied admittance under certain provisions of the U.S. immigration laws. (The controversial provision was drafted out of concern by some Intelligence Committee conservatives that the State Department was routinely admitting into the country potential spies and terrorists over the objections of the FBI. The report was intended to give Congress an indication of the circumstances under which the FBI's warnings were being overridden.)

House Committee Action

The House Permanent Select Committee on Intelligence reported HR 12240 April 20 (H Rept 95-1075, Pt. 1). The Armed Services Committee, which had concurrent jurisdiction over the Defense Department's intelligence-related activities, reported the bill May 9 (H Rept 95-107, Pt. 2)

Because this was the House intelligence panel's first authorization bill, Chairman Edward P. Boland, D-Mass., used the debate to sketch out the committee's procedures and accomplishments.

He noted that the panel's Senate counterpart had received frequent press mention for its investigations of past intelligence failures or abuses. But "this committee," he said, "is, quite frankly, less interested and less oriented toward dragging out past abuses than it is in present operations and legislation."

Created in July 1977, the committee first recruited a professional staff, which numbered 14 compared with a staff of about 25 for the Armed Services Committee. And the Senate Intelligence Committee's staff was much larger than the House's, Boland said. *(1977 Almanac p. 376)*

In late 1977 the three-member Budget Authorization Subcommittee carried out a dry run for HR 12240 by reviewing the fiscal 1978 intelligence community budget. Its review of the fiscal 1979 budget request encompassed 1,800 pages of justification material and another 3,000 pages of testimony. That hearing record, like the annex to the committee report and any other classified material in the committee files, could be requested in writing by any House member.

If the request were approved, the material could be examined either in the committee's offices or elsewhere under supervision of the committee staff.

House Floor Action

Without knowing how much money was being authorized — reported to be upwards of $10 billion — the House June 6 passed HR 12240 by a vote of 323-43. *(Vote 359, p. 102-H)*

Some details of the authorization measure were contained in a supplement to the Intelligence Committee's report on HR 12240 that was available for members to examine in secret. But only eight members checked the classified annex, according to the committee, and — despite heated arguments that the procedure rendered meaningless the House consideration of the bill — only 43 members voted June 6 against the legislation.

Jurisdictional Dispute

Nearly 90 percent of the national intelligence budget was spent by the Pentagon, according to the final report of the 1975-76 Senate Select Intelligence Committee that was chaired by Frank Church, D-Idaho. It said about a third of that amount was managed directly by the armed services and the rest by separate Pentagon agencies including the National Security Agency, which eavesdropped on foreign electronic communications, the Defense Intelligence Agency and the Defense Mapping Agency.

The Pentagon developed, procured and operated most of the complex technical information collectors — including reconnaissance satellites and electronic sensing devices — which provided the raw material for national intelligence. The Church committee commented that these sophisticated information collection tools "have grown capable of serving both the broad interests of the policy-makers and defense planners and the more specific technical interests of the weapons developers and field commanders."

The difference between national intelligence and tactical intelligence, according to the panel, "lies in the eye of the consumer, not in the intelligence-collection activity itself."

Aerial reconnaissance around the fringe of the Soviet Union and counterintelligence operations were two areas managed by the military services that were clearly important for national intelligence, according to the committee.

In the long-drawn-out battle in 1976 to establish a permanent Senate Intelligence Committee, much of the controversy involved the relationship between the new committee and some of the existing committees — principally Armed Services, Foreign Relations and Judiciary — that had jurisdiction over various parts of the national intelligence community.

The Senate finally adopted a resolution (S Res 400) giving the new intelligence panel exclusive jurisdiction over the CIA and joint jurisdiction over the intelligence activities of other agencies. The existing committees could secure sequential referral of legislation covering agencies over which they normally had jurisdiction. "Tactical foreign military intelligence serving no national policy-making function" was explicitly excepted from the intelligence committee's jurisdiction. But that category was not further defined.

An amendment that would have reserved to Armed Services legislative jurisdiction over the Pentagon's intelligence activities was supported on the Senate floor by 11 of Armed Services' 16 members. But the move was rejected 31-63. *(1976 Almanac p. 294)*

The bill authorized funds for all foreign intelligence activities.

The bill also authorized the "intelligence-related activities" of the Defense Department. These were the surveillance and reconnaissance operations of the armed services that were designed to provide intelligence for combat commanders, but which might overlap more general national intelligence operations.

Other provisions of the legislation:

- Approved 241 full-time employees and a budget of $12.4 million for the Intelligence Community Staff. The staff was used by the Director of Central Intelligence to oversee the intelligence community.
- Authorized a payment of $43.5 million to the CIA's retirement and disability fund.
- Required the attorney general in fiscal 1979 to report to the Intelligence and Judiciary Committees of the Senate and House whenever an alien was admitted to the United States whose exclusion had been recommended by the FBI.

Before debating the bill, members agreed to take up the legislation by overwhelmingly adopting the rule (H Res 1205) by a 322-48 vote. *(Vote 357, p. 102-H)*

According to Budget Authorization Subcommittee Chairman Bill D. Burlison, D-Mo., the committee cut President Carter's budget request "substantially, by my definition of substantial." But the bill allowed some real growth over the fiscal 1978 spending level.

James P. (Jim) Johnson, R-Colo., a member of the 1975-76 House select committee that investigated federal intelligence abuses, protested that passage of the bill would grant "a blank check for the expenditure of a lot of money to those who, in the past, have not warranted that kind of trust. . . . I think we are returning to the days when an elite few members of Congress allegedly exercised oversight over the intelligence community. . . ."

The classified annex, Johnson said, was uninformative as to intelligence activities and nearly incomprehensible because of acronyms and technical jargon. "Most members of Congress rather incongruously . . . feel that elected officials are somehow not as patriotic or as trustworthy as non-elected officials," he added.

Committee members insisted that the intelligence community had been candid and forthcoming with the panel, and Burlison noted that the committee staff was available to help members interpret the classified annex.

At least one committee member, John M. Ashbrook, R-Ohio, wondered whether the intelligence agencies were not giving the committee too much information. "I want to know and yet sometimes I think there are areas that it would be better if only the President of the United States and [CIA Director Stansfield] Turner would know what goes on," he said. "The chance of two people leaking is not nearly as much a threat when it comes to vital secrets as [is] sharing these secrets with 13 members of this body."

Several members called for public disclosure of at least the total amount being authorized for intelligence so that the public would have some idea of how the intelligence effort ranked among national priorities. But the committee rejected this idea, Burlison said, because the bare total would be uninformative and would generate pressure to disclose additional details about the budget that could expose delicate intelligence efforts.

But the committee said it annually would review the question of making public at least the total authorization figure.

Intelligence Community Staff. The House approved by voice vote a committee-sponsored amendment increasing by 71 (to 241) the Intelligence Community Staff. This was part of an increase requested by the administration after the committee completed action on the bill. The additional staff would handle new responsibilities assigned the Director of Central Intelligence by an executive order that made him responsible for setting information-collecting priorities for the intelligence community. *(Intelligence reorganization, box this page)*

Aliens Reported. The House rejected, 60-312, an amendment by Ted Weiss, D-N.Y., that would have deleted a requirement that the attorney general report to the House and Senate Intelligence Committees whenever an alien who could legally be excluded under certain provisions of the immigration laws was admitted into the country. *(Vote 358, p. 102-H)*

The Carter administration routinely had been waiving these bars to the distress of the FBI, which claimed that such aliens were a burden on the agency's counterspy operations. The Intelligence Committee maintained that it wanted the reports so it could assess the scope of the situation.

But the House did accept by voice vote another amendment that would limit the reporting requirement to one year and would require the reports to be submitted to the Intelligence and the Judiciary Committees.

Before the bill was passed, Johnson, R-Colo., as a protest offered a motion to recommit the bill to committee. The motion was rejected by voice vote.

Senate Committee Action

Senate consideration of the fiscal 1979 intelligence authorization bill brought to light a continuing jurisdictional tug of war between the Select Committee on Intelligence and the Armed Services Committee over budgetary control of certain Pentagon programs.

At issue was the "gray area" between tactical intelligence — information for combat commanders about enemy forces — and national intelligence — information for top national policy-makers about adversary nations.

The two panels, which shared jurisdiction over the disputed areas, had recommended the same funding levels for fiscal 1979, so there was no showdown fight on the Senate floor. But Armed Services disagreed with the Intelligence Committee's policy recommendation about one classified program.

Intelligence Panel's Report

In its report on the companion bill (S 2939 — S Rept 95-744), filed April 19, the Intelligence Committee argued that the disputed intelligence-related activities category included programs that were clearly important to national policy-makers. These included warning systems that would detect missile and bomber attacks, devices monitoring all nations' space activities and programs that monitor Soviet ballistic missile submarines.

The committee insisted that it had been "scrupulous" in confining its primary interests to national intelligence activities, and it recommended that it continue to share with Armed Services jurisdiction over intelligence-related activities.

Future Costs Hinted. The recommended authorization level in the bill was secret, and the committee did not even report the amount by which its recommendation deviated from the president's request — information that the House Appropriations Committee had reported in each of the previous three years.

But the committee said it had recommended some "major and highly significant new initiatives" that would have a "significant impact" on intelligence costs over the next five years. The new steps, it said, were "absolutely

Intelligence Reorganization

President Carter signed on Jan. 24 Executive Order 12036 reorganizing the intelligence community.

The product of months of negotiations between top-level national security officials, the White House and Congress, the order gave increased authority over intelligence functions to the Director of Central Intelligence.

The order established new restrictions on intelligence activities that threatened the rights of Americans. But it fell short of the goals of civil libertarians aroused by reports of intelligence abuses made public in 1975-76 by the press and congressional committees. The order specifically prohibited only a few of the illegal covert activities of which the intelligence agencies, particularly the Central Intelligence Agency, had been accused in recent years. Assassinations and conducting experiments on unwitting subjects were banned. But the use of American journalists and attempts to overthrow foreign governments were not.

The order placed more emphasis on making government officials responsible for their actions than on spelling out prohibitions as a means of ensuring that intelligence activities did not violate constitutional protections at home or jeopardize U.S. foreign policies.

Under the order, the attorney general was given new authority to guard the rights of American citizens. He was given the responsibility of establishing procedures regulating the use of bugging and other intrusive intelligence-gathering techniques against Americans, both at home and abroad, and the authority to disapprove specific applications of those techniques when he found that they unnecessarily infringed on a person's privacy.

The order centralized in the Director of Central Intelligence authority over the intelligence budget, intelligence "tasking" — assignment of specific responsibilities to particular agencies — and production of intelligence estimates. But the order left with the secretary of defense operational control of the reconnaissance and communications functions that take up the largest portion of the overall intelligence budget.

The order prohibited the use of four intrusive information collection techniques against Americans — electronic surveillance, television monitoring, physical searches, and mail surveillance — unless the president approved the techniques and the attorney general approved its specific application. Physical surveillance of Americans was limited to suspected foreign agents, terrorists, narcotics dealers and current or former intelligence employees thought to jeopardize the secrecy of intelligence methods and sources.

The order prohibited undisclosed participation by intelligence agents in domestic organizations, unless the infiltration was directed against a group composed primarily of foreigners thought to be acting on behalf of another country. It also required disclosure of intelligence agency sponsorship of any contracts entered into with U.S. institutions, except for non-academic institutions where disclosure was thought to undermine the purpose of the contract.

essential" if U.S. intelligence was to meet the needs of national policy-makers.

The intelligence community was in general well managed and responsive to policymakers' needs, the committee concluded. But it ordered the community to study some management techniques that, it said, might improve the community's efficiency. These included coordination of data processing equipment and more explicit analysis of the cost of budget proposals compared to the cost of alternatives and the value of the information to be gained.

Armed Services Report

In its report on S 2939 (S Rept 95-1028), filed July 20, Armed Services protested that the intelligence panel was overreaching its proper role. The Pentagon budget category of "intelligence-related activities" provided "a useful, albeit imperfect, rule of thumb method of defining those tactical programs for which exclusive jurisdiction remained with the Armed Services Committee," according to the panel.

Programs included in that category included funds for research, procurement and operation of military equipment for field commanders, and were primarily "tactical," it maintained. If the intelligence panel left to Armed Services all programs in that category, Armed Services said, it would avoid "innumerable specific disagreements in the future about the nature of each program."

The committee objected specifically to the intelligence panel's comments on one classified intelligence-related program — called TENCAP.

Senate Floor Action

The Senate passed the House bill (HR 12240) by voice vote July 20 after amending it to contain the committee-initiated changes.

Besides authorizing an undisclosed amount for federal intelligence operations, the bill as passed also:

- Approved an addition of 128 employees (for a total of 298 and a budget of $14.6 million for the Intelligence Community Staff.
- Authorized a payment of $43.5 million to the CIA retirement and disability fund.
- Reduced to $3 million (from $4.5 million requested) the amount authorized for contract research.

Conference, Final Action

There were only minor differences between House and Senate versions — dealing with the jurisdictional dispute — and a conference committee filed a report (H Rept 95-1420) on HR 12240 on Aug. 2.

The House approved the conference report Aug. 17 by a vote of 323-30, and the Senate approved it Aug. 22 by voice vote completing congressional action. *(House vote 635, p. 180-H)*

Military Unionization Ban

Essentially all labor union activity in the U.S. military was banned by legislation cleared by Congress on Oct. 15.

The bill (S 274) was sent to the president on the last day of the session when the Senate agreed to minor changes made by the House. The Senate had passed the measure in 1977, and the House acted on it Sept. 26.

The principal change in the House version was a provision exempting from the ban civil service technicians who performed day-to-day administrative and maintenance duties for National Guard units.

The House bill also incorporated several amendments intended to narrow the scope of union activity that would be prohibited, in order to reduce the risk that the bill could be found unconstitutional.

The Defense Department maintained it had taken adequate steps to meet the threat of unionization by issuing regulations in October 1977. These prohibited commanders from negotiating with any military union and barred military members from striking or picketing over the terms of military service. The department had warned that Congress might inadvertently exacerbate the problem by passing a law banning union membership, which might subsequently be declared unconstitutional.

But the House Armed Services Committee, and its Senate counterpart the previous year, were determined to legislate a ban on military unionization. And despite strong skepticism about the bill by a majority of the House Post Office and Civil Service Committee, which also considered the ban, it was called by one opponent a "motherhood" type of bill that few members would question.

Provisions

As signed into law (PL 95-610), S 274 prohibited the establishment of "military labor organizations," which the bill defined as any organization that engaged in or attempted to engage in:

- Negotiations with military or civilian executive branch officials on behalf of members of the armed forces concerning the conditions in the service.
- Efforts to represent individual members of the military before any such official in connection with any grievance or complaint arising out of military service.
- Striking, picketing, marching, demonstrating or in any other way promoting concerted action directed against the U.S. government and intended to induce executive branch officials to change any condition of military service or to recognize the organization as a collective bargaining agent for military members.

The bill also prohibited any serviceman from joining military labor organizations and prohibited anyone from soliciting servicemen to join such organizations and any civilian or military official from dealing with such organizations.

National Guard civil service technicians were exempted from the unionization ban when they were performing their civil service jobs.

The bill affirmed armed forces members' right to join non-labor union organizations, air complaints and grievances, seek information and counseling from any source, be represented by counsel in legal proceedings and petition Congress for redress of grievances.

Background

The issue of military unionization first aroused congressional concern after the nation's largest federal employees' union, the 300,000-member American Federation of Government Employees (AFGE), amended its constitution in September 1976 to permit organization of GIs.

A year later, the union announced that its 1,300 locals had voted overwhelmingly against proceeding with a drive to organize the military. But large majorities of both the House and Senate Armed Services Committees had become alarmed at the prospect of a union organization interfering with the military chain of command, and within two weeks of the union's announcement the Senate passed legislation (S 274) barring union activity in the armed services. *(Senate action, 1977 Almanac p. 388)*

As passed by the Senate, S 274 prohibited any member of the armed forces from joining a labor organization that had as its objectives 1) negotiating through collective bargaining the terms of military service with the federal government; 2) representing servicemen in connection with grievances or complaints, or 3) striking, picketing or engaging in other concerted actions against the government.

The Senate version also barred any government official from engaging in collective bargaining with a military union, and outlawed the use of Pentagon property for union activities.

The bill expressly exempted from coverage fraternal, professional or veterans organizations having none of the forbidden objectives.

House Action

Armed Services Committee

The House Armed Services Committee reported (H Rept 95-894, Part 1) its version of S 274 Feb. 22 after approving the bill 26-0, with two members voting "present."

The only substantive change made in the Senate version by the panel was the exemption of National Guard civil service technicians from the unionization ban insofar as their civil service jobs were concerned. All but a handful of these technicians, however, were required by law to be members of the National Guard units for which they worked, and thus would be prohibited from engaging in union activity in their military role.

Senate committee members had agreed with the argument of senior National Guard commanders that the civilian technicians were performing an essentially military role even when they were working as civil service employees. Allowing unionization of the technicians for part of their jobs, they felt, might lead to unionization of active duty military personnel.

But the House panel decided that a ban on unionization of the technicians in their civilian capacity raised too many constitutional questions and might endanger the entire bill.

The two committee members who voted "present" on the motion to report S 274, Charles H. Wilson, D-Calif., and Patricia Schroeder, D-Colo., joined in filing supplemental views that supported the position of the Defense Department. The bill's outright ban on unionization, even in the absence of any proven threat to military discipline, was hopelessly contrary to the First and Fifth Amendments, they said, despite the committee's efforts to narrow the scope of the bill.

"[S 274] will provide a handy target for legal action by supporters of unionization and, should the [Supreme] Court rule in favor of unions, the Department of Defense would be far more constrained in dealing with the issue than it is currently," they warned. "A legal victory would also undoubtedly prompt even stronger and more organized unionization efforts."

Post Office and Civil Service Committee

The Post Office and Civil Service Committee, to which S 274 was referred concurrently, reported the bill with amendments Aug. 4 (H Rept 95-894, Part 2).

Although it reported the bill favorably, the committee majority's comments were critical, concluding that "S 274 is an overreaction to a potential danger of very restricted proportions. Such a danger, in the unlikely event that it does exist, can be dealt with more effectively by strong, carefully drawn regulations [by the Defense Department]," it said.

But the committee's eight Republicans filed supplemental views that not only endorsed S 274, but urged that the ban be extended to cover the National Guard technicians. They said they would offer an amendment to that effect when the bill reached the House floor.

The only recommendation by the committee that was incorporated in the Armed Services version that was considered by the House was the Post Office panel's narrower definition of "military unions." The panel defined such groups as including any organization "that engages in or attempts to engage in" unionization activities as defined in the bill. Armed Services had defined military unions as any group "that engages in or has as one of its objectives or is substantially likely to engage in" the prohibited activities.

Floor Action

The House considered S 274 under suspension of the rules, a procedure barring floor amendments and requiring a two-thirds vote for passage. This prevented Republicans on the Post Office Committee from offering their amendment to include Civil Service technicians in the unionization ban.

The bill was approved after perfunctory debate by a vote of 395-12. *(Vote 734, p. 208-H)*

Final Action

The Senate Oct. 15 accepted the House changes by voice vote, completing congressional action. ∎

Critical Materials Stockpile

Congress did not complete action in 1978 on legislation (HR 4895) to reorganize the government's stockpile of critical materials.

The Senate Armed Services Committee reported the bill in May with language mandating a three-year reserve of critical raw materials that would be needed for national defense in an emergency. But the legislation was never taken to the floor for a vote.

The Senate bill retained some components of the bill as passed by the House in 1977, including creation of a revolving fund to purchase additional raw materials with the proceeds from sales of surplus materials in the inventory.

Background

The stockpile system was established by the Strategic and Critical Materials Stock Piling Act of 1939 to ensure that the nation would not run short of essential raw materials in case demand increased or imports were cut during wartime or other national emergency.

Some 93 commodities with a total estimated market value of $8.6 billion were stockpiled. Stocks of 41 commodities were in excess of current goals, according to the committee. The estimated market value of this surplus was $4 billion. As of Sept. 30, 1977, surpluses included 14.4 million carats of industrial diamonds (worth an estimated $117.4 million), 139,500,000 troy ounces of fine silver (worth an estimated $632.6 million) and 168,900 long tons of tin (worth an estimated $1.96 billion).

But 53 commodities were stocked at less than the current goals, the panel pointed out, including lead (short 264,000 tons), rubber (short 393,959 long tons) and zinc (short 949,584 short tons).

Some members of Congress had charged recent administrations with juggling the stockpiles for purposes having nothing to do with national security: for example, to manipulate the market price of some stockpiled commodities. In 1975 and 1976 the Ford administration's budget request was artificially reduced several hundred million dollars by counting revenues from sales of stockpiled commodities which, it was generally assumed, Congress likely would not — and did not — approve.

In 1976 the Ford administration announced a new stockpile policy with a goal of accumulating a three-year supply of critical raw materials. As a first step in building up the stockpiles to this level, additional amounts of those commodities that would be needed during the first year of a war in Europe were to be purchased first. In September 1977 the Carter administration reaffirmed that basic policy, but by then the House already had acted to revise the stockpile system.

House Action. Dismayed by executive branch vacillation over stockpile policy, the House Armed Services Committee's Stockpile Subcommittee Chairman, Charles E. Bennett, D-Fla., introduced in 1976 a bill (HR 15081) to establish a revolving fund for stockpile transactions. Since the proceeds of stockpile sales under his bill could be used only for stockpile purchases, he argued, the executive branch would not be tempted to propose stockpile sales for cosmetic budgetary reasons. Neither the House nor the Senate passed the bill during the 94th Congress. *(1976 Almanac p. 323)*

Bennett moved early in the 95th Congress, and on March 31, 1977, the House passed HR 4895, which:

- Established a revolving fund for stockpile transactions.
- Required legislative authorization for appropriations for new stockpile purchases.
- Established a program to acquire strategic materials through barter with foreign countries under existing legislative authority.

Senate Committee Report

The Senate Armed Services Committee reported its version of HR 4895 on May 15 (S Rept 95-846).

The Senate bill also established a revolving stockpile fund. Receipts from the sale of excess commodities were to be used only to purchase other stockpiled commodities until the start of the third fiscal year after the sale was made, at which time any unspent funds would go into the general treasury.

The committee expressed a desire that "stockpile transactions be reasonably balanced for the foreseeable future," so that each year's acquisitions would be paid for by that year's excess sales. With the current surpluses of stockpiled commodities worth more than $4 billion, the panel estimated that major new appropriations would be unnecessary for five to seven years.

Stockpile Consolidation. The bill would have consolidated three separate stockpiles into one National Defense Stockpile and stipulated that it was to be used only for defense needs. HR 4895 authorized the president to identify those commodities that should be stockpiled, and the amounts needed of each. But it specified that the goals should amount to a three-year supply. Only raw materials, not finished products, were to be included, the panel said.

The committee rejected a proposal (S 1810) by James A. McClure, R-Idaho, that would have established a formula linking the stockpile level of any commodity to the amount of U.S. imports of the commodity. Conceding that the formula would protect commodity markets against "indiscriminate" changes in stockpile requirements, the panel concluded nevertheless that the rigid formula would ignore actual wartime requirements for materials and the vulnerability of imports in wartime.

But the committee did limit changes in stockpile goals of a commodity to shifts of more than 10 percent so that commodity markets would not be in constant turmoil over small changes in the Defense Department's stockpile requirements. Changes of less than 10 percent could be made only if justified in advance to Congress.

Procurement Procedures. Additions to the stockpile would have to conform to existing federal procurement regulations. Also, competitive bidding by commodity vendors was to be used as often as possible, and purchases were to be made so as not to "unduly" disrupt commercial commodity markets. U.S. purchasers would have first call on any excess commodities put up for sale.

Existing law required prior legislative authorization of any sales from the stockpile, and the House bill added a requirement for prior authorization of stockpile acquisitions. The Senate committee version also required authorization for both acquisitions and disposals, except in the case of commodities that had a continual turnover because of limited shelf-life.

The authorization for stockpile purchases was to be by lump-sum only so that the commodities markets would not be influenced by prior knowledge of the government's intent to purchase specified amounts of certain commodities. ▮

Veterans' Pension Increase

A 50 percent increase in the maximum pension paid indigent war veterans who were not disabled as a result of their military service was cleared for the president Oct. 15.

In addition to increasing the pensions for eligible veterans and their survivors, the bill (HR 10173 — PL 95-588) created a new formula for allocating the payments. The new system guaranteed veterans a minimum annual income, with the size of their Veterans Administration (VA) pension determined by the difference between that minimum and any income they received from other sources, such as Social Security.

The VA pension program was referred to as the "non-service-connected disability pension" to distinguish it from the "compensation" program for veterans who were disabled in the course of their military service. In general, veterans were eligible for the non-service-connected pension if

Payments for Veterans With No Other Income

	Previous Law	House Version	Senate Version	Conference Version of HR 10173
Veteran Without Dependents	$2,364	$4,000	$3,240	$3,550
Veteran With One Dependent	2,544	5,200	4,284	4,651
Veteran Needing Regular Care	4,344	7,360	6,384	6,781
Surviving Spouse Age 65 or Older	1,824	3,000	2,172	2,379

they served during wartime, had an income below a certain level and were "permanently and totally disabled." But for purposes of the pension program, all veterans 65 and older were considered permanently and totally disabled.

Pension Reform Pressures

The impetus for reforming the non-service-connected pension system came from a belief by the House and Senate Veterans' Affairs committees and the VA that the existing system contained too many inconsistencies in its treatment of veterans. As the two panels and the VA, along with the major veterans organizations, wrangled for five years over the shape of a new pension system, two other ideas took hold that were incorporated in the reform proposal.

- The new system should ensure that eligible veterans were supported above the poverty level.
- It should automatically protect pensioners against increases in the cost of living.

Pressure also was exerted to include in the new system a special increase in the payments to very elderly veterans, especially those of World War I.

In its final form, HR 10173 accommodated, at least in part, all of those goals. But it drew criticism from a newly formed group lobbying for more attention to the problems of Vietnam-era veterans. The Council of Vietnam Veterans warned that the large increases in non-service-connected pensions under the new program would absorb money that should have been focused on those veterans who had been disabled in the course of their military service.

The new program embodied in HR 10173 could turn the fight over VA priorities into a struggle involving billions of dollars if pressure mounted for a parallel increase in the compensation paid to service-disabled veterans.

Historically, the maximum pension for non-service disabled veterans had been substantially lower than the compensation paid to veterans who suffered relatively severe service-connected disabilities. For instance, the maximum non-service-connected pension for a veteran with no dependents under the previous pension law ($2,364) was $900 less than the compensation paid in 1978 to a veteran with a 60 percent service-connected disability, a difference of 38 percent.

Congress enacted a 7.3 percent cost-of-living increase in the compensation payments for service-connected disabilities (HR 11886 — PL 95-479) only days before it cleared the new pension system on Oct. 15. But even with those new rates, the compensation paid a veteran with a 60 percent disability ($3,504) would be $46 less than the maximum pension paid under HR 10173. *(p. 369)*

HR 10173 was passed by the House June 28 and by the Senate with amendments July 31. A House-Senate compromise was reached Oct. 12.

Final Provisions

Minimum Income Level

Both versions of the bill were similar as to the basic design of the new pension system: a minimum income level for pensioners, with eligible persons receiving the difference between that minimum and their income from other sources.

The conference committee set the basic income floor and the various additional allowances at levels between those approved by the Senate and those approved by the House, which generally were higher. For instance, an eligible veteran with no dependents was guaranteed an annual income of $3,550 under the final bill. If he received $2,500 annually in Social Security payments, he would receive a VA pension of $1,050. *(Chart, above)*

Eligibility. As under the previous system, veterans and their widows and surviving dependents were eligible for pensions if the veteran:

- Served at least 90 days in the armed services, including at least one day during wartime.
- Was permanently or totally disabled (for purposes of this law, veterans 65 and older were considered to be permanently and totally disabled).
- Did not have an excessive net worth.

Income Exclusions. The new system dropped most of the existing 18 categories of income excluded from the computation of the veteran's income counted against the minimum income level of the old program. A veteran still would not have to count payments received from public or private relief organizations.

The income of a veteran's spouse had to be counted against the minimum as did the income of a veteran's child, to the extent that the child's income was "reasonably available to" the veteran.

World War I Veterans

The applicable income floor was increased $800 for veterans of World War I or any earlier war. Veterans of these periods had not been eligible for other benefits — tuition assistance and home loans — that were available to veterans of World War II and subsequent conflicts.

The House bill had increased by $804 the income floor for any veteran 80 years of age or older. The Senate bill had provided a 25 percent increase in the income floor of any veteran of World War I or an earlier conflict.

Parents' Indemnity

The conference version instituted a 7.1 percent cost-of-living increase in the dependency and indemnity compensation (DIC) payments to parents of veterans who were killed in service or who died of service-connected disabilities. This provision increased to $3,240 (from $1,824) the DIC payment for a single parent with no other income.

The Senate bill had established a new DIC program that, like the enacted pension program, would have established an income floor for eligible parents. But the Senate version would have limited eligibility to parents who received one-half or more of his or her support from the veteran in the year immediately preceding the veteran's death.

The House version of HR 10173 contained no DIC provision, but the House Sept. 18 had passed a related bill (HR 11887) providing a 6 percent cost-of-living increase in the existing DIC program.

Cost-of-Living Indexing

Both versions of HR 10173 included provisions intended to build into the income floor a cost-of-living escalator linked to the Consumer Price Index of the Bureau of Labor Statistics. The conference version extended the indexing provision to the DIC program as revised by HR 10173.

Social Security Offset

The conference version incorporated a provision approved by both the House and Senate that was intended to ensure that veterans would not suffer a reduction in their pensions because of a cost-of-living increase in their Social Security payments.

Coordination Study

The final bill ordered a study by the General Accounting Office (GAO) describing the coordination between the pension programs of the Veterans Administration and the Social Security System. The report was to describe inconsistencies between the two programs regarding the treatment of needy persons and assess the feasibility of reconciling "unjustifiable" differences.

GI Bill Matching Requirement

Dropped by the conferees was a Senate provision that would have modified a 1977 amendment to the VA education benefits program by making it more advantageous to veterans attending schools in states — mostly in the Northeast — where the fees at public higher education institutions were higher than in other areas.

The 1977 amendment raised to $2,500 the amount eligible veterans could borrow to meet educational expenses. A veteran whose tuition expenses exceeded $700 a year could be forgiven up to two-thirds of the loan if his state of residence paid half of the forgiven amount to the VA. *(1977 Almanac p. 407)*

The Senate provision of HR 10173 would have deleted the state-matching requirement.

Cost

In fiscal 1978 the VA's non-service-connected pension program for veterans and survivors cost about $3.4 billion. The Congressional Budget Office (CBO) estimated that the cost of the program under HR 10173 would increase by $466 million in fiscal 1979 and by $2 billion in fiscal 1983.

But supporters of the bill insisted that this overstated the cost of the new pension plan by assuming that Congress would enact no cost-of-living increases in the existing plan. Assuming that Congress enacted only routine cost-of-living increases in the current law, the increased cost of the new program would be only $258 million in fiscal 1979 and $562 million in fiscal 1983, according to the CBO.

Supporters of the bill argued further that even this calculation overestimated the cost of the new bill since it ignored the fact that many recipients of the new, higher VA pensions no longer would be eligible for other federal welfare payments, including Medicaid. They cited an Office of Management and Budget estimate that the overall effect of HR 10173 would be to save $200 million annually by 1990.

Background

Ever since the Revolutionary War, the United States has paid some form of pension to needy veterans who served in wartime but were not disabled.

As early as 1778 the Continental Congress guaranteed half pay for seven years after the war was over to officers who served for the duration. In 1780 the period was extended to half pay for life. But the pay was awarded whether or not the recipient was needy. The policy was intended to help Gen. George Washington hold together an officer corps around which to build his army.

But the forerunner of the current veterans' pension system was an 1818 law that provided a pension to any veteran of the Revolutionary War who had served for at least nine months and who, "by reason of his reduced circumstances in life, shall be in need of assistance from his country for support." Officers received $20 a month; other veterans, $8. A similar pension was enacted for veterans of all subsequent wars.

According to a study by the Congressional Research Service of the Library of Congress, veterans' pensions through the years generally had become more and more liberal in defining the conditions of eligibility.

Critics of the existing program charged that, in the age of income maintenance and other programs that were available to the entire population, such benefits were not needed.

In 1956 a presidential study commission headed by General of the Army Omar N. Bradley concluded that the "non-service-connected benefits are the lowest priority among veterans programs. . . . Our society has developed more equitable means of meeting most of the same needs, and big strides are being made in closing the remaining gaps. The non-service-connected benefits should be limited . . . and retained only as a reserve line of honorable protection for veterans whose means are shown to be inadequate and who fail to qualify for basic protection under the general Old-Age and Survivors Insurance System [Social Security]."

But veterans' organizations and their congressional supporters adamantly insisted that veterans had a special moral claim on the nation that could not be equated with general welfare programs. "The federal government called these veterans to arms during a time of national crisis," argued House Veterans' Affairs Committee member Chalmers P. Wylie, R-Ohio, during the debate in May on the first budget resolution. "The federal government decided that they should be separated from their families, from their normal occupations, from their communities. The federal government sent many of them off into the unwanted misery of war, and it is the duty of this same federal government to care for them, and their widows and their orphans."

As a practical political matter, Congress in recent decades had never questioned the non-disability pension. "The [Bradley] Commission did not take into account the ability of the pension clientele and its supporting organizations to raise pension levels and insist that VA assistance remain more attractive than the income support programs available to the rest of the population," according to the Congressional Research Service's report.

House Committee Action

The House Veterans' Affairs Committee reported HR 10173 (H Rept 95-1225) on May 31.

Repeal of Current System

The committee recommended repeal of the pension system enacted in 1959 (PL 86-211), which was based on two key variables relating to a veteran's financial status: an income ceiling, above which veterans were ineligible for any pension, and a sliding scale of payments that was determined by the amount of a veteran's outside income. For example, a veteran with no dependents could recieve monthly payments under the existing system ranging from $197 if he had no other income to zero if he had other income of $3,771 or more per year.

The income ceiling and monthly payments were higher if the veteran had dependents and lower for a veteran's widow.

The monthly payments were increased 25 percent for veterans 78 or older. Veterans received an additional $81 a month if they were housebound and an additional $165 a month if they needed constant attention.

Eligibility. Veterans, their widows and surviving dependents were eligible for pensions under the current system if the veteran:

- Served at least 90 days in the armed services including at least one day during wartime.
- Was permanently and totally disabled (for purposes of the law, veterans 65 and older were considered to be permanently and totally disabled).
- Did not have an excessive net worth as determined by the VA.

Income Exclusions. In computing the veteran's income under the current system, all payments from any source were included except for 18 specified exceptions. The most important of these included:

- Donations from public or private relief organizations.
- Other veterans' pensions or compensation.
- All of a wife's earned income.
- 10 percent of all payments from public or private retirement programs (including Social Security).

Pressure for Change

Social Security Increases. Currently, each time Social Security payments were increased, many veterans with pensions moved up the income scale far enough to force their pensions to be reduced. The result was that the pensioner's total income often was reduced by a Social Security increase.

To avoid this, amendments to the current system were proposed that would disregard Social Security increases in computing a pensioner's income. But the House committee insisted that this approach would create a "favored class of pensioners" since increased payments from sources other than Social Security would not be disregarded.

Current Veterans and Survivors Eligible for Payments

	Disability Payments		Non-Disability Pensions	
	Veterans	Survivors	Veterans	Survivors
World War II	1,252,917	114,409	665,537	806,277
World War I	40,679	32,741	260,288	554,431
Korean conflict	238,913	27,686	72,330	237,895
Vietnam era	508,308	96,194	12,438	61,030
Spanish-American War	3	180	367	18,061
Mexican Border Service	4	3	267	620
Indian Wars	0	1	0	56
Civil War	0	8	0	261
Peacetime Service*	213,834	52,208	-	-
TOTAL	2,254,658	323,430	1,011,227	1,678,631

**Eligible only for disability payments.*

SOURCE: Committee reports H Rept 95-1225, H Rept 95-1226 (extracted from VA Report RCS 21-14)

The committee cited VA fears that such a procedure would create an administrative nightmare that "could result in the complete breakdown of the veterans' pension system."

World War I Veterans. Strong sentiment had emerged in recent years for providing special treatment for the 487,000 surviving veterans of World War I. They were the only surviving large group of wartime veterans who did not have access to the education payments and other programs designed to ease the re-entry into civilian life that were given the millions of veterans of World War II and the later conflicts.

Since most World War I veterans and their widows were in their 80s, it was argued that in all likelihood they were the most impoverished segment of the veteran population and the most in need of special assistance.

A bill (HR 9000) with more than 200 cosponsors was introduced during the session that would pay $150 a month (in lieu of all other veterans' pensions) to any World War I veteran or his widow with an income of less than $15,000. But the committee insisted that World War I veterans had received most of the benefits available to veterans of more recent wars. While they had not received readjustment assistance, the panel pointed out that they had received a one-time bonus payment (totaling $3.8 billion) that had not been made to other veterans.

And the panel cited a Congressional Budget Office analysis that concluded that World War I veterans had a higher average income than non-veterans of the same age.

No action was taken on HR 9000 in 1978.

Provisions

As reported by the Veterans' Affairs Committee, HR 10173 established a minimum income level for pensioners and paid eligible persons the difference between that minimum and their income from other sources.

For example, a single veteran below 80 years of age with no dependents would be guaranteed an annual income of $4,000. A veteran receiving $3,000 annually in Social Security benefits would receive a VA pension of $1,000.

The income floor would be $5,200 if the veteran had one dependent and $4,804 if he was 80 or older or was housebound. If he needed constant attention, the floor would increase to $6,160. For the surviving spouse of a veteran, the income floor would be $3,000.

Cost-of-Living Indexing. To protect pensioners against losses of income because of cost-of-living increases in their Social Security payments, the bill would increase pension payments by the same percentage as their Social Security payment increased.

For example, for the veteran under 80 with no dependents who had a Social Security income of $3,000 and a pension of $1,000, a 5 percent cost-of-living increase in the Social Security payment would trigger a corresponding increase to $1,050 in the pension.

Income Exclusions. As under the current pension system, a veteran could be found ineligible for a pension if his net worth was so great that he would be considered self-sufficient. The new system would drop most of the 18 income categories excluded from the computation of the pensioner's income counted against the income floor.

Annual Cost. Currently about 1 million veterans and 1.7 million survivors were receiving non-disability pensions costing about $3 billion a year. The Congressional Budget Office estimated that if HR 10173 were enacted in time to be in effect through nine months of fiscal 1979, it would increase the payments by $853 million. In fiscal 1980, the increased cost would be $1.5 billion.

But the increased income for veterans under the system approved by the committee made them ineligible for payments under the Supplemental Security Income, Medicaid and other federal programs and would save the government about $122 million. Thus the new program would cost $731 million more than the present system for the nine months of fiscal 1979.

House Floor Action

HR 10173 was brought to the floor under suspension of the rules, a procedure that prohibits amendments but requires a two-thirds majority of those voting for passage. The vote was 398-5. *(Vote 441, p. 126-H)*

Glenn M. Anderson, D-Calif., had been urging his colleagues for weeks to vote against HR 10173 under this procedure so that it could be considered anew under regular House rules. Anderson favored adding to the bill a special pension for World War I veterans earning less than $15,000 a year.

But members of the House Veterans' Affairs Committee emphasized that HR 10173 already included higher payments to veterans 80 years old and older. They warned that it would be far too expensive to enact both the new pension system and a special World War I pension.

Several members who had supported the Anderson move indicated they were accepting the committee's bill as a step toward improving the welfare of elderly veterans.

Even without Rep. Anderson's proposal, the House bill added more than half a billion dollars to the $3 billion veterans' pension program.

Senate Committee Action

The Senate Veterans' Affairs Committee reported its version of the pension reform bill (S 2384) July 17 (S Rept 95-1016).

As reported, the Senate bill followed the basic approach of the House bill in designing a new pension system. It set an income floor for eligible veterans; pensioners would be paid the difference between that minimum and their income from other sources.

The guaranteed minimum income for veterans of various degrees of need (number of dependents, amount of medical care required, etc.) was higher in the Senate bill than the payments under the existing pension system, but lower than the income floor set in the House-passed version. As in the House bill, S 2384 contained provisions intended to link the minimum income levels to increases in the cost-of-living and to prevent any veteran from receiving a smaller pension payment because of a cost-of-living increase in his Social Security payments.

The Senate bill had a slightly more restrictive provision than the House measure relating to special treatment to very elderly veterans. It increased by 25 percent the income floor for any veteran of World War I or an earlier conflict, who never had been eligible for the VA education benefits and home loan assistance that had been made available to the veterans of World War II and subsequent conflicts.

The corresponding House provision had increased by $804 the income floor for any veteran 80 or older.

Senate Floor Action

The Senate July 31 by an 85-0 vote passed its version of the pension reform bill as an amendment to the House bill (HR 10173). *(Vote 259, p. 41-S)*

Before passing the bill, the Senate adopted two amendments by voice votes:

- By Jacob K. Javits, R-N.Y., as amended by Alan Cranston, D-Calif., to remove the state matching requirements from the 1977 amendment to the VA's education benefits program. Cranston's modification of the Javits amendment provided that no appropriation resulting from the amendment would be made before the 96th Congress.
- By Henry Bellmon, R-Okla., to require the Office of Management and Budget to study the coordination between the VA and the Social Security System of programs providing benefits to veterans.

Conference, Final Action

A compromise version of HR 10173 was approved by House-Senate conferees just days before the adjournment of Congress *(see final provisions)*. The conference report was filed Oct. 12 (H Rept 95-1768; S Rept 95-1329) and given final approval by the Senate by voice vote the same day and by the House on Oct. 14 by a vote of 387-1. *(Vote 818, p. 232-H)*

The bill was signed into law Nov. 4.

VA Housing Programs

Congress Oct. 2 cleared legislation liberalizing several housing programs run by the Veterans Administration.

The legislation (HR 12028 — PL 95-476) also contained a provision designed to reduce abuses in the VA's education loan program.

Provisions

As cleared by Congress, HR 12028:

- Increased the maximum grant for special housing for severely disabled veterans to $30,000 from $25,000.
- Reduced, to 90 from 181 days, the minimum amount of active duty required of Vietnam-era veterans in order to qualify for VA home loan benefits.
- Gave the VA administrator authority to guarantee loans for home improvements, including energy-related work, at an interest rate higher than the rate set for loans for the purchases of homes.
- Allowed the VA to guarantee loans for the purchase of converted condominiums.
- Increased to $25,000 from $17,500 the maximum loan guaranty for a conventional VA home loan.
- Expanded the VA mobile-home loan program by making it similar to the VA conventional home loan program.
- Authorized the VA administrator to delegate, under certain conditions, responsibility for the inspection of the mobile-home manufacturing process to the secretary of the Department of Housing and Urban Development.
- Gave the VA administrator authority to establish criteria for VA education loans in order to limit eligibility to schools with high tuitions.
- Authorized up to $5 million each fiscal year for fiscal 1979-83 for grants to states for state-owned VA cemeteries.

Legislative History

House Action

The House passed HR 12028 on July 17 by a 373-0 vote under suspension of the rules. *(Vote 476, p. 136-H)*

HR 12028 had been reported (H Rept 95-1332) by the House Veterans' Affairs Committee on June 29. The panel said the bill was necessary in part to keep pace with the impact of inflation on housing costs.

The legislation contained four main provisions. As reported by the committee and passed by the House, HR 12028:

- Increased the maximum grant for special housing for severely disabled veterans to $30,000 from $25,000. The grant, which was limited to 50 percent of the total cost of a house, was designed to help severely disabled veterans wounded in service to obtain housing suited for their special needs. The $25,000 maximum grant was established in the Veterans' Housing Act of 1974 (PL 93-569). According to the committee report, the average cost of special housing was $66,626 during fiscal 1977.
- Reduced, from 181 to 90 days, the minimum amount of active duty required of Vietnam-era veterans in order to qualify for VA home loan benefits. Under existing law, veterans of World War II and the Korean conflict were eligible for VA home benefits after 90 days of active service. But veterans with peacetime service must have served for more than 180 days. The amendment placed Vietnam veterans on the same footing as World War II and Korean veterans. The VA estimated that about 168,000 additional Vietnam-era veterans would be eligible for VA home loan benefits under the provision.
- Increased the maximum VA loan guarantee to $25,000 from $17,000. The VA testified during committee hearings that $25,000 did not afford adequate protection in the eyes of many lenders. According to the VA, increases in average GI loans had reached the point where the VA guarantee covered well below 50 percent of the loan. The $17,500 figure was established in 1974.
- Removed ceilings for mobile home loans guaranteed by the VA. Under current law, a veteran could obtain a VA mobile home loan of up to $12,500 for a single-width home; $20,000 for a single-width home and a suitable lot; $20,000 for a double-width home; and $27,500 for a double-width home and suitable lot.

But there were no maximum loan amounts for conventionally built homes. The VA, in arguing for the changes, said rising costs of production, materials and labor had increased the price of many mobile homes to well beyond the statutory maximums established by law. As a result, the VA said, many veterans were unable to acquire mobile homes without making substantial down payments.

Senate Action

The Senate passed the bill by voice vote with amendments on Aug. 7 after its Veterans' Affairs Committee had approved it July 31 (S Rept 95-1055).

Before passing the measure, the Senate adopted several amendments, including one designed to end abuses of a VA educational loan program. The amendment gave the VA administrator authority to limit eligibility for the loans to veterans attending the most expensive schools.

An investigation by the General Accounting Office (GAO) found considerable abuses of the loan program, with loan money being used to cover such expenses as installment payments on appliances, home improvements, entertainment and holiday gifts.

Initially, the Senate Appropriations Committee had included a provision in the fiscal 1979 appropriations bill for the VA (HR 12936 — PL 95-392) limiting participation in the loan program to individuals attending schools where the combined tuition and fees for the academic year were $700 or more.

But veterans' spokesmen in the Senate, led by Veterans' Committee Chairman Alan Cranston, D-Calif., argued that the provision in HR 12936 was too restrictive, and he worked out a compromise making changes in the VA housing bill.

Final Action

House and Senate members that handled the bill were able to work out differences in the legislation without calling a formal conference. The House then approved the compromise Sept. 28, and the Senate gave its approval Oct. 2, completing congressional action.

Disabled Veterans' Pensions

Congress Oct. 2 cleared for the president a bill (HR 11886 — PL 95-479) providing a 7.3 percent cost-of-living increase in the compensation paid to veterans who were disabled in the course of their military service.

Payments to disabled veterans were based on VA estimates of the extent to which particular types of disability impaired the veteran's ability to support himself. Under HR 11886, the monthly payments ranged from $44 (for a 10 percent disability) to $809 (for a 100 percent disability) for a single veteran with no dependents.

Also increased 7.3 percent were the amounts paid to veterans with dependents. These dependents' allowances were paid to veterans with 30 percent or more disability at a rate proportional to the veteran's degree of disability. The minimum disability for veterans to be eligible for the allowances was 50 percent under the previous law.

HR 11886 also increased by 7.3 percent the payments to survivors of service-disabled veterans. Unlike the payments to veterans, the survivors' payments were based on the rank at which the veteran left the service. HR 11886 increased the payments to widows of privates to $297 per month from $277; payments to a general's widow rose to $760 from $708.

Disability payments totaling about $6 billion were being made to about 2.25 million veterans and 323,000 survivors. The Congressional Budget Office estimated that HR 11886 increased this cost by $324 million in the first year it took effect.

Extension of the additional payments for veterans' dependents with a 40 percent or more disability affected about 147,000 persons at an estimated additional cost of $50 million the first year, according to the CBO.

Legislative History

The House passed HR 11886 on June 28 by a 400-1 vote under suspension of the rules. *(Vote 439, p. 126-H)*

It had been reported by the Veterans' Affairs Committee on May 31 (H Rept 95-1226). In recommending the 6.5 percent cost-of-living increase, the committee said the 5.8 percent increase recommended by the administration was not enough to keep pace with inflation. And it warned that a further increase might be necessary later in the year.

The Senate passed the bill Aug. 7 with minor changes. The companion measure (S 2828) had been reported by the Senate Veterans' Affairs Committee (S Rept 95-1054) on July 31.

The House then made further modifications before approving the Senate amendments Sept. 28, and the Senate agreed to the House changes Oct. 2, clearing the bill for the president.

Other Veterans' Bills

Benefits to a small number of veterans and their survivors would have been liberalized by three bills passed by the House July 25. None of the three was considered by the Senate in 1978.

Disabled Veterans' Survivors

By a vote of 393-9, the House passed HR 11890 providing new benefits for survivors of veterans who had been permanently and totally disabled for at least 10 years before their death. Survivors would receive the same benefits as those applicable where a veteran's death had been related to his military service. *(Vote 518, p. 150-H)*

In its report on the bill (H Rept 95-1230), filed May 31, the Veterans' Affairs Committee estimated that HR 11890 would cost $700,000 in the first year.

Reservists' Retirement Eligibility

By a vote of 390-8, the House passed HR 11823 liberalizing the eligibility for retired pay of military reservists who had completed 20 years of service. *(Vote 514, p. 150-H)*

Under current law, 20-year reservists were not eligible for retirement if they had been in the reserves before V-J Day, but had not served on active duty in either World War II or the Korean War. The bill would make such persons eligible for retirement if they served on active duty during the 1962 Cuban missile crisis or during the Vietnam War.

In its report of the bill (H Rept 95-1076), filed April 20, the House Armed Services Committee estimated that HR 11823 would cost $620,000 in the first year.

Medal of Honor Pension

By a vote of 394-4, the House passed HR 11889 increasing to $200 a month (from $100 under existing law) the additional pension paid to veterans who had been awarded the Congressional Medal of Honor. *(Vote 517, p. 150-H)*

In its report on the bill (H Rept 95-1229), filed May 31, the Veterans' Affairs Committee estimated that HR 11889 would cost about $300,000 in the first year.

Trial of Soviet Dissidents

The trials of Soviet dissidents Anatoly Shcharansky, Viktoras Petkus and Aleksandr Ilyich Ginzburg were condemned by Congress as "deplorable events" that would "inevitably affect the climate of relations" between the Soviet Union and the United States.

A resolution cleared by Congress July 12 (S Con Res 95) stated that the three Russians had supported human

Computer Sale Canceled

President Carter July 18 canceled a major computer sale to the Soviet Union, apparently in retaliation for the 1978 trials of leading Soviet dissidents and two U.S. correspondents working from Moscow. The decision was praised by many members of Congress, who had demanded that Carter impose some economic penalty on Moscow after the conviction of Anatoly Shcharansky.

Carter denied an application by Sperry-Univac to sell a $6.8 million computer to TASS, the Soviet news agency. He also ordered that all oil-production equipment be included in the list of controlled commodities that could be sold to the Soviet bloc only with an export license.

rights principles spelled out in the 1975 Helsinki agreement and for that they were being tried and punished by the Soviet government. "Congress urges the U.S.S.R. Supreme Soviet and its leadership to seek a humanitarian resolution to these cases...," the resolution stated. The measure was approved by the Senate July 11 by voice vote and by the House July 12, 380-10. *(Vote 465, p. 132-H)*

Many in Congress, however, argued that SALT negotiations with the Soviet Union should have been promptly suspended and the U.S. delegates recalled to signal Moscow that the United States would not tolerate the dissidents' trials.

"To go and sit down and debate SALT . . . under these conditions of humiliation . . . makes the U.S. look weak and groveling," said Samuel S. Stratton, D-N.Y.

An attempt in the House by John M. Ashbrook, R-Ohio, to weld a statement onto the resolution calling for termination of the negotiations was ruled out of order during House debate. An attempt to appeal the ruling was tabled, 277-120, a procedural vote that nevertheless reflected which members wanted the House to take stronger action. *(Vote 464, p. 132-H)*

The Carter administration opposed any interruption in the SALT negotiations and refused to cancel Secretary of State Cyrus R. Vance's meeting with Soviet Foreign Minister Andrei A. Gromyko in Geneva as the trials got under way in the Soviet Union.

The department, however, did cancel trips by U.S. environmental and scientific delegations to protest the Soviet trials. But "we will persist in our efforts to negotiate a sound SALT II agreement because it is in our national interest and in the interest of the world to do so," said a July 8 statement issued by Secretary Vance. A major computer deal with the Soviets also was canceled. *(See box, this page.)*

President Carter July 12 condemned the trials as an "attack on every human being who lives in the world who believes in basic human freedom," and Vance conveyed another message from Carter to Soviet leader Leonid I. Brezhnev through Gromyko.

In the middle of the week's developments, U.S. Ambassador to the United Nations Andrew Young drew reprimands from both Congress and the Carter administration for his remarks to a French newspaper that "there were hundreds, perhaps thousands, of political prisoners in the United States."

In Geneva, Young met with Vance, who rebuked the ambassador for his comments. Young then issued a clarifying statement saying that he had never "equated the status of political freedom in the United States with that in the Soviet Union. I know of no instance in the U.S. where persons have received penalties for monitoring our government's position on civil or human rights."

A motion by Rep. Larry P. McDonald, D-Ga., to bring impeachment proceedings against Young was quickly squashed, 293-82, on a tabling motion offered by House Majority Leader Jim Wright, D-Texas. *(Vote 469, p. 134-H)*

Finally, in the Senate July 13, a resolution (S Res 512) was approved, 90-1, expressing support for nominating for the 1978 Nobel Peace Prize individuals monitoring human rights practices in the Soviet Union. The three Russians on trial were members of the investigating team. *(Vote 208, p. 34-S)*

'Neutron Bomb'

Congress approved legislation (HR 11686 — PL 95-509) on Oct. 11 authorizing the production of a new generation of tactical nuclear weapons that would be less vulnerable to terrorist seizure or accidental explosion than the older versions.

The new weapons could be converted rapidly into the so-called neutron bombs if President Carter decided to deploy the weapon.

HR 11686 required Carter to set a deadline for a final decision on whether to carry out the conversion. Once converted, such weapons could discharge massive doses of lethal radiation from a relatively small nuclear blast.

The congressional mandate was incorporated in a $2.97 billion fiscal 1979 authorization bill for military programs of the Department of Energy, which develops and manufactures nuclear weapons and carries out all other nuclear research for the Defense Department. The amount authorized for these weapons was classified, but was reported to be $48.8 million below the fiscal 1979 budget request.

Also authorized by the bill was development of a new Air Force hydrogen bomb designed to survive a plane crash without releasing nuclear contaminants.

Radiation Weapon Controversy

The "neutron bomb" actually was a nuclear warhead for artillery shells and short-range missiles that was designed to produce massive doses of lethal radiation. Its purpose was to deter Soviet tank attacks against Western Europe. The lethal radiation emitted by the warhead would kill tank crews, while the smaller blast would cause less devastation to the surrounding territory than existing U.S. nuclear weapons.

In 1977 the Senate voted by a large margin to approve development of the radiation warheads in the fiscal 1978 nuclear weapons authorization bill, but it added an amendment placing an embargo on the funds for the radiation weapons until 45 days after the president had certified to Congress that production was in the national interest. Congress then could block production of the weapons by concurrent resolution if passed within the 45-day period. *(1977 Almanac p. 381)*

Although President Carter has not yet taken steps to release the funds that were appropriated for fiscal 1978, additional funds for their production were requested in the fiscal 1979 budget.

On April 7, 1978, Carter announced that he would modernize the U.S. stockpile of tactical nuclear weapons, but would defer production of the high-radiation components in hopes that the Soviet Union would show corresponding restraint in its East European arms buildup.

As cleared, final provisions of HR 11686 were the same as those in the Senate-passed version.

Background

The proposed enhanced radiation warheads for the Army's 60-mile-range Lance missile and its 8 inch and 155 mm howitzers were designed to produce an explosion with the force of only a few thousand tons of TNT. But they would produce the same surge of lethal radiation as an older nuclear weapon with 10 times the explosive power. While the heavy blast and fire damage from a neutron weapon would reach out only a few hundred yards, the radiation would be lethal over a radius of more than half a mile.

The new warheads would be especially effective against the concentrated masses of tanks on which Soviet war planning was based. Armored vehicles, although resistant to the heat and blast of "regular" nuclear explosions, would give their crews little protection against neutron radiation.

According to defense planners, the limited nature of the blast and fire damage from neutron warheads made it a better weapon to counter a Soviet armored thrust into West Germany, the likely target of any Soviet attack on NATO.

The existing U.S. tactical nuclear weapons in Europe would be destructive over a much larger radius and could not be used, in many situations, without causing massive damage and high civilian fatalities.

The Army had begun developing a new type of nuclear artillery shell in the early 1970s. But in 1973 Congress canceled the project, in part because of the high projected cost — $904 million for 2,000 8-inch artillery shells.

The Pentagon went back to the drawing board and, in 1974, returned with a new idea for modernizing the arsenal — enhanced radiation warheads, later to become known as neutron bombs. By 1977 the Energy Research and Development Administration (ERDA) — which by law had charge of all nuclear weapons research and production — was ready to begin manufacture of the warheads for the Lance missile and the 8-inch gun. But on June 6, 1977, the project received its first large-scale public notice in a *Washington Post* story headlined, "Killer Bombs Buried in ERDA Budget."

In the ensuing congressional debate, opponents of the radiation weapon warned that because such warheads could be used to defend West Germany without destroying the country, they would make nuclear war more "thinkable" to NATO leaders. Accordingly, there would be pressure to use the weapon in certain circumstances. And once any type of nuclear weapon were used, according to this argument, the conflict would escalate to a global nuclear holocaust.

But proponents of the radiation weapon insisted that precisely because the Russians could more easily envision NATO using the new weapon to repel an attack, they would be deterred from launching the attack.

Export of Uranium to India

The House July 12 rejected a resolution that would have blocked the sale to India of seven tons of uranium for a nuclear power plant. The vote was 181-227. *(Vote 466, p. 132-H)*

The action was the first taken under a law (PL 95-242) signed March 10 by President Carter that was intended to stop the global spread of nuclear weapons. *(p. 350)*

NRC Vote. The Nuclear Regulatory Commission had split 2-2 on whether to approve the sale. (One seat on the commission was vacant.) But President Carter decided to go ahead with the sale in any case. Under the new anti-proliferation law, Congress then had 60 days in which to block the proposed sale by concurrent resolution.

The House International Relations Committee, in a June 21 report (H Rept 95-1314), recommended that the resolution blocking the sale not be approved. But four committee Republicans filed separate views supporting H Con Res 599.

Carrots or Sticks? Supporters of the resolution argued that the sale should be blocked because of India's continued refusal to accept international safeguards on its nuclear facilities.

Since this was the first congressional action taken under the new law, they said, it was necessary to demonstrate the firmness of U.S. resolve to prevent the spread of nuclear weapons.

But supporters of the sale countered that denying India the uranium only would jeopardize negotiations currently under way to secure Indian acceptance of international nuclear safeguards. If the United States did not sell India the fuel, some other nation would.

President Carter had conceded during the 1977 congressional debate that he previously had been unaware of the enhanced radiation weapon program, which was initiated by the Ford administration. But he fought the attempts to kill the program, saying he wanted to retain the option of producing the new weapon. After Congress had acted, however, he said that a decision to produce the weapon would be contingent on a commitment by the NATO allies to allow its deployment on their territory.

Diplomatic Turmoil

Carter's hope that the other NATO members would share responsibility for producing the new weapon ran afoul of domestic politics in several European countries. Several political parties of the non-communist left attacked the new weapon as a peculiarly inhumane device that would accelerate the arms race. Egon Bahr, the general secretary of West German Chancellor Helmut Schmidt's Social Democratic Party, denounced the new weapons as "a symbol of mental perversion."

Schmidt reportedly feared that a public endorsement would jeopardize his governing coalition's 10-vote parliamentary majority. His government insisted that only the United States could decide whether to proceed with production of the radiation warheads.

Exacerbating the situation was an intense Soviet campaign against the weapon. One strategy was to launch a propaganda blitz against it. At the Geneva disarmament

NATO Summit Decisions

An $80 billion plan to beef up the defense of Western Europe included the firmest commitment yet made by NATO members to coordinate the development and production of future weapons.

Approval of the Long-Term Defense Plan was the centerpiece of the NATO summit meeting in Washington May 30-31. The plan, which had been in preparation for more than a year, committed NATO's 13 military members to more than 100 specific projects to modernize their forces, expand their arsenals and tighten the coordination among the combat units of the member nations.

(Of NATO's 15 members, Iceland had no armed forces and France did not formally participate in NATO military planning, in deference to residual Gaullist sentiment in that country. But France was cooperating with alliance military plans and was expected to join in some of the cooperative weapons programs.)

The total cost of the plan would amount to an estimated $60 billion to $80 billion beyond what the NATO members previously had planned to spend on defense. But in a preliminary meeting in May 1977, most of the members had agreed to a 3 percent annual increase (after inflation) in their defense expenditures. A Pentagon spokesman told reporters this would cover most of the increased cost of the long-term plan. He estimated that the United States would wind up paying a little over half the additional cost.

Highlights of the plan included:

Common Weapons Projects. The heads of government of the NATO alliance reportedly selected 15 specific areas in which they would try to cooperate on new weapons development over the next 15 years. These included air-to-air, ship-to-ship and anti-tank missiles and various types of communications.

Reinforcements. The plan endorsed the U.S. project to store heavy equipment for three additional Army divisions in Europe by 1982, "recognizing the need for European allies to provide the necessary support and other facilities." At least two congressional committees had balked at funding storage sites. They insisted such construction was a NATO-wide responsibility. *(See military construction story, p. 345)*

conference, Moscow proposed a treaty banning radiation weapons; and 31 Soviet scientists wrote Carter that his decision on their production would test the sincerity of his campaign promises to slow the arms race.

In addition, Soviet leader Leonid Brezhnev reportedly warned the European NATO governments in strong terms against adding the new weapon to the NATO arsenal.

By March 1978 the Western alliance had moved toward a rough consensus on the issue. Washington would have to make the decision whether to produce the radiation warheads. If Carter decided to go ahead with it, then it would be up to Washington to try to negotiate a cancellation of the decision in return for some commensurate Soviet arms restraint, such as their cancellation of the 2,000-mile-range SS-20 missile or a reduction in Moscow's three-to-one advantage in the number of tanks stationed in central Europe.

Failing any agreement, West Germany then would accept deployment of the warheads on its territory if either Belgium or the Netherlands also endorsed the move. Administration officials pointed out that because of European sensitivity about German military activity, the Bonn government was unwilling to stand alone in calling for a controversial new weapon.

Final approval of the NATO strategy was scheduled for the week of March 20, but was canceled after President Carter became directly involved in the formulation of the U.S. position. Carter apparently wanted a firmer commitment from the NATO allies that the weapons would in fact be deployed if he approved their production.

Congressional Blowup

On April 4 *The New York Times* reported that Carter had decided to cancel the radiation weapon because its deployment would run counter to his goal of nuclear disarmament. According to the story, the decision overrode the advice of Carter's top foreign and defense policy advisers, but was backed by White House political operatives and U.S. Ambassador Andrew Young.

Defense hard-liners reacted swiftly. Many of them linked it to other allegedly unilateral arms decisions by Carter: cancellation of the B-1 bomber, slowing the development of a new intercontinental missile (called M-X) and blocking Navy plans for a new aircraft carrier.

Senate Armed Services Committee member Sam Nunn, D-Ga., who has acquired considerable influence as a NATO expert, warned that cancellation would "place in the minds of the Soviets the image of a timid and hesitant America which lacks the courage to confront the difficult defense choices ahead."

The chairman and several senior members of the House Armed Services Committee wrote Carter a letter protesting the reported decision and urging reconsideration.

Republican Attack

Republicans mounted a concerted attack, beginning with Senate Minority Leader Howard H. Baker Jr., R-Tenn. He told reporters April 4 that a cancellation would be "another in a long line of national defense mistakes," by Carter. "First we gave away the B-1 bomber and now we're going to give away the neutron bomb."

Despite White House insistence that no decision in fact had yet been made, the GOP continued its criticism. Former President Ford, former Secretary of State Henry A. Kissinger, and two of the party's 1980 presidential hopefuls, Sens. Baker and Robert Dole, R-Kan., denounced the reported cancellation at a series of fund-raising dinners April 6.

Also on April 6, Senate Majority Leader Robert C. Byrd, D-W.Va., wrote Carter urging that production proceed in the absence of any Soviet arms restraint in Europe. And he warned the president: "If the United States decides not to proceed with the neutron weapons, and does so without any parallel reduction in Soviet strength, the chances of any SALT agreement being ratified by the Senate are seriously jeopardized."

Rep. Ted Weiss, D-N.Y., and 109 other House members who voted in 1977 to kill the radiation weapon, wrote Carter April 4 to express their support for the cancellation. Just over a quarter of the House had joined Weiss in that 1977 effort.

Carter Decision

Throughout the controversy, the White House insisted that the Times story had been wrong — that no final decision had yet been made. On April 7 Carter announced the decision to delay production, but with an implicit threat to go ahead with it if Moscow showed no matching restraint.

Majority Leader Byrd's immediate reaction was cautious support of the president: "I feel the president is on solid ground if he hopes to use this as an option in disarmament talks and if he can secure similar concessions from the Soviet Union that are verifiable."

But the hard-liners apparently were not mollified by Carter's announcement. "I believe it's a bad mistake that will hurt the NATO alliance, that will interrupt modernization of our tactical nuclear weapons in Europe and, overall, will be harmful to our national security," said Nunn.

House Action

Committee

The House Armed Services Committee May 3 reported (H Rept 95-1108) HR 11686.

The committee recommended an authorization of $2,897,090,000 for the Energy Department's military programs for fiscal 1979. This was $123.2 million less than the administration requested. Of the committee amount, $1.2 billion was to be allocated for weapons development or manufacture.

Other programs covered by the bill included production of nuclear power plants for Navy ships, production of nuclear material for weapons and reactors, and research on inertial confinement fusion (formerly called laser fusion).

The largest change in the administration's proposed weapons programs was the committee's rejection of a plan to modify existing nuclear bombs, at a cost of $32.7 million, instead of producing a new model bomb that was ready for initial production. The new bomb, called the B-77, was designed to be dropped with great precision from a plane flying as low as 100 feet off the ground at supersonic speed. It would have new safety devices to prevent an explosion in case the plane crashed or terrorists stole it. It could be adjusted to produce any of a wide range of explosive yields and it would use much less nuclear material than the bombs it replaced.

Carter intended to incorporate some of these features into the existing B-43 bomb, but the committee said this would cost too much.

A controversial issue that the committee had to deal with was the future of the so-called neutron bomb.

President Carter announced April 7 that he would delay production of the radiation warheads in the hope of eliciting Soviet restraint in its buildup of nuclear and conventional arms. But he said he would modernize the U.S. arsenal of tactical nuclear weapons and reserve the option of adding the high radiation feature later.

The panel authorized Carter to use funds appropriated for other purposes to produce the high-radiation warheads if he 1) certified to Congress that production was in the national interest and 2) secured the approval of both Appropriations Committees.

Floor

The House passed HR 11686 on May 17 by a vote of 348-46. *(Vote 279, p. 80-H)*

During the debate on the bill, the House, by a margin of better than three-to-one turned back an effort to delay a final presidential decision on whether to produce the neutron bomb.

The vote, which came on an amendment by Ted Weiss, D-N.Y., was 90-306. *(Vote 278, p. 80-H)*

By a similar margin, the House in September 1977 had rejected a similar amendment by Weiss to the fiscal 1978 nuclear weapons bill. That proposal would have terminated production of the neutron bomb. These are small nuclear warheads for short-range missiles and artillery shells and were designed to kill enemy tank crews by producing large amounts of lethal radiation from a relatively small explosion. They were widely touted as a counter to the Soviet Union's large tank force. But opponents feared the weapon would foster an impression that tactical nuclear weapons could be used in a limited war. They argued that any such use would escalate into an all-out nuclear war.

After defeating the Weiss amendment, the House also rejected by a standing vote of 12-54 a related amendment by Christopher J. Dodd, D-Conn. This would have extended for another year the provision in the fiscal 1978 bill giving Congress 45 days to veto by concurrent resolution a presidential decision to produce radiation warheads.

Senate Action

Armed Services Committee

The Senate Armed Services Committee reported a companion bill (S 2693 — S Rept 95-961) on June 28 with an authorization of $2,971,484,000 for the national security programs of the Energy Department for fiscal 1979. This was $48.8 million less than the administration requested, but $74.4 million more than the amount approved May 17 by the House.

Besides weapons development and production, the bill authorized funds for research on naval nuclear power plants ($265.6 million) and on inertial confinement fusion power production ($292.2 million).

The committee endorsed the argument that the high radiation weapons would reduce the risk of nuclear war. They were designed to deter Soviet tank attacks against Western Europe. Since their lethal radiation would kill tank crews while causing less damage to surrounding territory, it was argued that Moscow would believe that NATO would be more likely to approve the use of these weapons on allied soil. Therefore, according to this reasoning, there was a better chance that the Soviets would be deterred from launching such an invasion in the first place, and the risk of a U.S.-Soviet confrontation would be reduced.

The panel approved production of a new nuclear warhead for the 70-mile-range Lance missile and the 8-inch howitzer incorporating several improvements over the current versions, but not including the high radiation feature. But Armed Services separately authorized production of the high-radiation features, which could be stockpiled pending a final decision on whether they should be added to the new weapons.

If production of the special components were not authorized until a decision was made, they would not be ready for several years, according to the committee.

Pentagon Report. The committee asked the Pentagon for a report by the end of 1978 that would specify:

- The kinds of arms restraint or other military conditions undertaken by the Soviet Union that would warrant a

U.S. decision to cancel, or delay beyond fiscal 1978, the addition of the high radiation feature to U.S. weapons.

- The prospects for Soviet agreement on such restraints.
- The date by which the United States must decide whether to proceed with the high radiation feature in the absence of a Soviet agreement on specific arms restraints.
- The position of the other NATO allies on the deployment of high radiation warheads on their territory.

Safety Features. Both new warheads — for the Lance and for the artillery shell — would include safety features not on existing U.S. weapons. One was a combination lock that armed the warhead only after the correct six-digit number had been dialed. If the wrong code were dialed more than a few times, the warhead could not be detonated. Another device allowed guards to cripple the warhead if capture were imminent.

The 8-inch artillery shell had additional features to decrease the risk that it could be seized and used by an enemy in wartime. A small rocket motor in the base of the shell reportedly would nearly double the 10-mile range of the existing 8-inch nuclear shell, thus allowing the cannons and shells to be stationed farther from the front line. The new weapon could be readied for use more quickly than the existing shell.

Funds also were authorized for development of a new nuclear shell for the 155 mm howitzer that would contain the same safety improvements as the new 8-inch shell. But the new howitzer shell would not include the high radiation components, as had been planned. Scientists had concluded that the new feature could not be condensed into the small shell.

In additional views, Thomas P. McIntyre, D-N.H., commented that the committee report "perpetuates . . . a disproportionate and distracting controversy about enhanced radiation weapons by focusing exclusively on this one aspect of our modernization of nuclear forces."

He said he supported the high radiation components, but insisted it was "hardly of central importance to the military effectiveness of our [tactical] nuclear forces and may not be as important as the other [safety] improvements."

B-77 Bomb. The new aerial bomb authorized by the bill — the B-77 — would incorporate the six-digit code to prevent unauthorized use. And the high explosive trigger that set off the nuclear explosion would be designed to survive a plane crash without detonating. (No U.S. nuclear weapon ever had exploded in a plane crash, but on at least two occasions a bomb's highly radioactive material was scattered over a wide area when its high explosive trigger detonated in a crash.)

The committee strongly recommended that the new "safe" high explosives be used in all future nuclear weapons. It asked the Defense and Energy Departments to submit a study with next year's budget request reviewing the cost of that policy and the cost of converting all existing weapons to ones using the safer high explosives.

The B-77 was designed to be dropped by a special parachute from planes flying as low as 150 feet. To cut the cost of the new bomb, the committee-approved version would not include a proposed feature permitting a bomber crew to adjust the strength of the nuclear blast according to the size of the target.

Because of the expense of the B-77, the Carter administration had canceled the program, recommending instead that the new safety features be incorporated in a new version of an existing bomb (the B-43). But congressional sources maintained that with the adjustable yield feature removed, the B-77 would be no more expensive than the modified older bomb.

Navy Anti-aircraft Missile. The committee authorized the amount requested (classified) for a nuclear warhead for the Navy's SM-2 anti-aircraft missile.

But it embargoed use of the funds until the administration filed with Congress an arms control impact statement on the weapon.

The SM-2 was a part of the Aegis anti-aircraft system on which the Navy was relying to protect its aircraft carriers against Russian cruise missiles. The existing missile had a non-nuclear warhead.

Pentagon witnesses told the committee the administration was undecided about a nuclear version of the missile both for technical reasons — a nuclear blast might blind the Aegis radar to other approaching missiles — and for political reasons. One political consideration was that when controlled by the high-powered Aegis radar, the nuclear SM-2 might be so good that it would infringe on the 1972 U.S.-Soviet treaty limiting the production of anti-ballistic missile systems.

A second reason for administration hesitation, reportedly, was that the nuclear SM-2 would be designed so that its nuclear warhead could be stored separately aboard ship and inserted into what otherwise would be a conventional, high-explosive warhead. These nuclear components would save space aboard ship. Without the component, Navy ships would have to carry separate missiles that used only nuclear warheads. According to some reports, administration officials feared the new design would greatly complicate negotiations to limit the spread of nuclear weapons since the insertable nuclear warheads were small enough for easy concealment.

Future Testing Needs. The committee requested the secretaries of energy and defense to submit with the fiscal 1980 budget request a report on the reliability of stockpiled U.S. nuclear weapons. The report was to include the judgment of the heads of U.S. nuclear weapons laboratories as to whether continued nuclear tests would be necessary to monitor the reliability of weapons in the stockpile. If the weapons laboratories reported that continued testing was necessary, it could embarrass administration moves to negotiate with the Russians a comprehensive ban on nuclear explosions.

Energy Committee

Portions of the bill dealing with military nuclear programs that might have civilian application were referred jointly to Armed Services and to the Committee on Energy and Natural Resources. The Energy Committee, in the same report filed June 28, recommended reductions of $160 million in the administration's requests for those programs, although most of the cuts involved a bookkeeping change rather than a policy issue.

Inertial Confinement Fusion Research. The panel recommended a $165 million cut in the request for continued research on producing controlled energy from nuclear fusion caused by lasers. At the administration's request, $10 million already in the budget was shuffled among fusion-related projects. Also, $5 million was added to the request for fusion research operations. (Armed Services had proposed a $12.2 million increase.)

Insisting that the high-energy laser (NOVA) research project be funded year-by-year rather than all at once, the committee cut the $187 million request to $10 million.

Floor

The Senate passed the House-numbered bill as amended by S 2693 on Sept. 30 by a 68-1 vote. *(Vote 429, p. 63-S)*

The amounts authorized by the Senate were the same as those that had been recommended by the Senate Armed Services Committee except for those programs with potential civilian applications for which the Energy Committee had recommended different authorization levels. In those cases the Senate bill conformed with the Energy Committee position.

The Senate also adopted Armed Services-sponsored amendments that added several general provisions contained in the House-passed version in hopes of winning speedy House acceptance of S 2693 without having to go to conference on the bill.

Final Action

Congress completed action on HR 11686 Oct. 11 when the House by voice vote agreed to the Senate-passed version of the bill without further modification.

House objections had been anticipated to a Senate provision that barred development of a nuclear anti-aircraft missile for the Navy until the administration sent Congress an arms control impact statement as requested by law. But on Oct. 6 the administration submitted the statement, thus rendering the question moot and making a House-Senate conference to resolve the issue unnecessary.

Related Development

In a related development, President Carter Oct. 18 ordered the Energy Department to begin producing the components that would convert a new generation of tactical nuclear weapons into neutron bombs.

But the components would not be inserted in the warheads for the time being in hopes that the Soviet Union would show some corresponding restraint.

Base Closings Studied

The Pentagon April 26 took the first step toward closing or cutting back operations at some 85 military bases in 30 states and the District of Columbia. The Defense Department estimated the changes could bring annual savings of $337 million and release 14,600 military personnel for other assignments. The plan would cut 8,600 civilian jobs from the Pentagon payroll. In the past, about 85 percent of the civlians affected by such base realignments had either retired or been placed in other federal jobs.

Under procedures mandated by Congress in 1977, the proposed changes had to be analyzed for their effect on the nation's military posture and on the communities that would suffer loss of jobs and population because of the changes. If the secretary of defense then decided to proceed with the base changes, he had to give Congress 60 days to study the move. The required analysis could take six to 10 months for the larger reductions. *(1977 Almanac p. 342)*

Foreign Policy

Negotiation was the key word in American foreign policy during 1978.

Peace talks sponsored by or directly involving the United States were under way in southern Africa, the Middle East, and Latin America. Even Congress and the Carter administration seemed to reach an understanding, through negotiation, on major foreign policy elements. The administration successfully concluded secret negotiations toward the establishment of diplomatic relations with the People's Republic of China, and neared agreement on a pact with the Soviet Union on strategic arms limitation.

But the chances for ultimate success in many crucial negotiations was uncertain as the year drew to a close.

Middle East

For President Carter, the Middle East meant euphoria and frustration in 1978. The euphoria came in September, when in 13 days at Camp David he coaxed and cajoled Egyptian President Anwar Sadat and Israeli Prime Minister Menachem Begin into accepting a "framework for peace" in the Middle East. But then followed three months of agonizing secret negotiations and public declarations by Egypt and Israel that threatened to undo the success of the Camp David accords.

A Dec. 17 deadline for agreement on an Egyptian-Israeli peace treaty passed as each side was accusing the other of reneging on Camp David promises. President Carter appeared to grow impatient as Sadat and Begin became less willing to compromise when the prospects for a peace treaty were so good. He rebuked both sides for squabbling about "little, tiny technicalities."

China

The Camp David meeting was equaled and perhaps surpassed only by the surprise announcement that the United States and the People's Republic of China would assume full diplomatic relations Jan. 1 and end U.S. ties to the nationalist regime on Taiwan.

Although it had long been assumed that the United States eventually would recognize Communist China and break relations with Taiwan, the suddenness of the Dec. 15 announcement startled the world. Particularly surprised were many members of Congress, especially conservatives, who thought Carter had promised to consult with them before severing ties with Taiwan. The president's decision not to involve members of Congress in the decision gave conservative opponents a ready-made issue to fight legislation implementing the new China policy.

Negotiations

United States-sponsored attempts to negotiate peaceful solutions to confrontations around the globe produced mixed results in 1978.

The SALT talks were moving relatively smoothly at the end of the year, in spite of various disagreements on provisions. But serious obstacles had developed in efforts to negotiate a peace in the Middle East and disputes in Nicaragua, Cyprus, Rhodesia and Namibia.

Generally, the American negotiating efforts proved moderately successful only in cases where all parties were predisposed to negotiate. In those cases where one or both parties saw a better chance of success through delay or military action, the negotiating efforts faced long odds.

- **SALT Talks**. The administration was close to completing a strategic arms limitation treaty (SALT) by the end of 1978. But opposition to the treaty was mounting in the United States. Conservative groups argued that the treaty would be a sell-out to the Russians, while a few liberal peace groups claimed the treaty wouldn't do much to end the arms race.
- **Rhodesia**. Along with Great Britian, the United States worked in 1978 to convene a peace conference involving all parties — government and guerrillas alike — in the war in Rhodesia. That attempt seemed close to success in the autumn, but it fell apart when guerrilla attacks escalated and the Rhodesian government expanded its attacks on guerrilla bases in Zambia and Mozambique. By the end of the year most of Rhodesia was under martial law.

Prime Minister Ian Smith established a coalition transition government with three black leaders in March, and said universal elections would be held by the end of the year. But Smith later postponed the elections to April 1979, and announced a new government plan to give whites effective control of the cabinet, further dimming the chances for a peace conference.

As the year ended the Carter administration debated whether to continue the negotiations or to simply withdraw and allow events to run their course, which might have meant an escalation of fighting.

Congress in 1978 again shifted its stand on economic sanctions against Rhodesia, primarily a ban on the importation of Rhodesian chrome. At the request of the Carter administration, Congress in 1977 reimposed a Rhodesian chrome ban that was first implemented in 1968 then lifted in 1971. But in 1978 conservatives moved to again lift the ban by ending all economic sanctions against the country. They didn't win, but Congress did approve language prohibiting the president from enforcing economic sanctions against Rhodesia after 1978 if Rhodesia had agreed to participate in an all-parties peace conference and if a government had been installed by universal, free elections. Because the elections were not held, the sanctions were still in effect at the beginning of 1979.

- **Cyprus**. In August, President Carter convinced Congress to end the arms embargo against Turkey. He argued that the embargo was a major obstacle to persuading Turkey to resume negotiations for a settlement in Cyprus, where traditional rivalries between Turkey and Greece were focused. Three months later the United States proposed a 12-point plan for a federal government in Cyprus with separate Turkish and Greek regions. But that plan met strong objections from both sides, clouding hopes that the ancient dispute could be resolved easily .

• **Nicaragua**. A violent insurrection in September, resulting in the deaths of some 1,500 persons, caused the United States to push for negotiations between President Anastasio Somoza Debayle and his opponents. Long an American-favored dictator, Somoza had lost popular support and the backing of the United States and was kept in power through the efforts of the military. Carter made it clear the United States wanted Somoza to resign.

After balking at U.S. mediation efforts, Somoza in December agreed to release hundreds of political prisoners and to accept a plebiscite on whether he would remain as president. But on Dec. 27 Somoza refused to agree to having the vote supervised by outsiders, which deadlocked negotiations at the end of the year.

• **Namibia**. Along with four other Western powers, the United States attempted in 1978 to persuade South African to accept United Nations-supervised elections in Namibia (South West Africa). The Western plan for elections was accepted by the United Nations and by the guerrilla force challenging South African rule of Namibia.

As part of the effort to persuade South Africa to accept U.N. involvement in Namibian elections, the United States softened its rhetoric against apartheid, and stalled U.N. action on economic sanctions against South Africa.

In December, however, South Africa conducted its own elections in Namibia, which it had controlled since 1920 under a League of Nations mandate. The election was won by a coalition friendly to South Africa.

Human Rights

The Carter administration continued its policy of publicly criticizing nations that violate the human rights of their citizens. But, as in 1977, the administration was itself taken to task for selective application of that policy. Conservatives argued that the United States wasn't paying enough attention to the human rights violations of Communist nations such as the Soviet Union, Vietnam and Cambodia, while liberals challenged the administration policy of near-silence on violations in Uganda, Iran, the Philippines, South Korea and other nations.

Carter himself said little about human rights problems during 1978 until December, when he declared that concern about human rights was the "soul" of U.S. foreign policy. "The effectiveness of our human rights policy is now an established fact," Carter said Dec. 6. "It has contributed to an atmosphere of change — sometimes disturbing — but which has encouraged progress in many ways and in many places."

In his December speech, celebrating the 30th anniversary of the United Nations Declaration of Human Rights, Carter singled out seven nations that "continue to practice repression": Cambodia, Chile, Uganda, South Africa, Nicaragua, Ethiopia and the Soviet Union.

Republican Support for Carter

Republicans supplied the crucial votes for several of President Carter's key foreign policy initiatives in 1978. The Republican aid was most evident — and most needed — in the Senate, where a handful of moderate and liberal Republicans consistently voted to support the Democratic president.

Major issues on which Republicans supplied the decisive votes were:

• Senate ratification of the Panama Canal treaties (16 Republicans supported the president);

• Senate approval of advanced fighter planes to Saudi Arabia (11 Republicans supported the president);

• Lifting the arms sale embargo against Turkey (27 Republican senators supported the president, and 78 Republican House members supported the president);

• Continuation of a moderate policy toward Rhodesia, especially in votes in the Senate (a minimum of 24 Republican senators supported the president on three separate votes).

In spite of their support for the president on specific votes, Republicans tended to paint a gloomy picture of American foreign policy failures resulting from unrestrained Russian blustering.

Senate Republicans in May issued a blistering attack on Carter's foreign policy: "In 15 short months of incoherence, inconsistence and ineptitude, our foreign policy and national security objectives are being challenged around the globe by Soviet arrogance."

American-Soviet Relations

While the United States was busy negotiating disputes around the globe in 1978, the Soviet Union was shoring up old alliances, creating new dependencies and exploiting some of the same conflicts the Americans were trying to resolve. The result was that American-Soviet relations generally were cool, in spite of the importance each side attached to prospects for improved trade and an arms control treaty.

Soviet involvement increased substantially in Vietnam, Ethiopia, Cuba and Afghanistan during 1978. Perhaps most significant, the Soviets were hoping to gain from the turmoil in oil-rich, strategically-important Iran, where American influence was closely tied to the waning power of Shah Mohammed Riza Pahlevi.

Administration officials claimed that the Soviet Union was actually losing ground, especially in Third World countries which needed more economic development support than the Russians could deliver.

For a few weeks in the late autumn a major confrontation appeared possible after the revelation that the Soviet Union had shipped an unstated number of advanced Mig 23 warplanes to Cuba. After a flurry of excitement that threatened a replay of the 1962 Cuban missile crisis, the Carter administration said the planes were not equipped to carry nuclear weapons and were not a direct threat to the United States.

Carter toughened his rhetoric toward the Soviet Union in mid-year, warning the Russians that he was willing to take a hard-line approach if their actions made it necessary.

"The Soviet Union can choose either confrontation or cooperation," the president said June 7. "The United States is adequately prepared to meet either choice."

—By John Felton

Panama Canal Treaties: Major Carter Victory

After a lengthy debate, the Senate in 1978 gave President Carter a major foreign policy victory by consenting to the ratification of two treaties that relinquished American control of the Panama Canal.

The canal victory was the first of several significant foreign policy achievements for Carter during the year. In other actions, Congress:

- Approved sale of sophisticated jet fighter planes to Saudi Arabia over the vigorous objections of the American Jewish community. *(p. 405)*
- Passed a foreign aid appropriations bill with surprisingly modest cuts. *(p. 123)*
- Lifted the partial arms embargo on Turkey. *(p. 416)*
- Rejected proposals to enact tough restrictions on the distribution of American aid abroad, particularly to international financial institutions. *(pp. 403, 123)*
- In addition, Carter was instrumental in persuading Egypt and Israel to agree on a framework for peace in the Middle East. *(p. 430)*

No other single foreign policy issue of 1978 attracted as much attention, aroused as many emotions and consumed as much of the time and effort of the administration, the Senate and outside lobbying groups as did ratification of the Panama Canal treaties. The product of negotiations that formally began in 1964 but had in fact gone on intermittently ever since the original pact was signed in 1903, the basic treaty will turn over the U.S.-constructed, owned and operated Panama Canal to Panama by the year 2000. A second treaty, the neutrality treaty, guaranteed the United States and Panama the right to defend the canal after Dec. 31, 1999.

The two treaties were signed by President Carter and Panamanian leader Brig. Gen. Omar Torrijos Herrera on Sept. 7, 1977, but it was not until the spring of 1978 that the Senate consented to their ratification — and then, only by a razor-thin margin of one vote more than the two-thirds Senate majority needed. All told, the debate had lasted 38 days, and until the very last, Senate ratification of the pacts hung in the balance. *(Text, 1977 Almanac p. 49-E)*

President Carter had staked his administration's ability to conduct foreign policy on their ratification. It was also a victory for the Senate leadership — in particular, Majority Leader Robert C. Byrd (D W.Va.), Majority Whip Alan Cranston (D Calif.) and floor managers Frank Church (D Idaho) and Paul S. Sarbanes (D Md.), as well as for Minority Leader Howard H. Baker Jr. (R Tenn.). One of the major difficulties in securing ratification was adoption of a reservation to the neutrality treaty (the first of the two treaties to be considered, it was ratified March 16 by a vote of 68-32), sponsored by freshman Sen. Dennis DeConcini (D Ariz.), that would permit the United States to "use military force in Panama" to reopen the canal if it were closed for any reason. The action immediately provoked an outcry from Panama that threatened to scuttle the treaties entirely. *(Vote 66, p. 12-S)*

However, after weeks of delicate negotiations, the Senate leadership succeeded in arriving at a compromise. Included in the resolution of ratification to the basic canal treaty (ratified April 18 by the identical 68-32 vote cast on the neutrality treaty) was a resolution stating that any action the United States might take to assure that the canal would remain neutral and secure should not "be interpreted as a right of intervention in the internal affairs of the Republic of Panama." *(Vote 119, p. 21-S)*

Major Treaty Provisions

Panama Canal Treaty

Grants to the United States rights to regulate canal shipping and to manage, operate, maintain, improve, protect and defend the waterway until Dec. 31, 1999, when Panama assumes total responsibility and control of canal activity and property.

States that Panama will participate increasingly in the management, protection and defense of the canal during the life of the treaty.

Establishes a Panama Canal Commission to operate and manage the waterway and to employ a U.S. citizen as its administrator until Jan. 1, 1990, when a Panamanian assumes the position.

Provides that Panamanian laws apply in areas available for use by the United States. But provides that as Panama assumes jurisdiction over the former Canal Zone on the treaty's effective date, a 30-month transition period begins when U.S. criminal and civil laws apply concurrently with Panama's in those areas of U.S. operations.

Prohibits the construction in Panama of any new canal except as the United States and Panama might agree and prohibits the United States from negotiating with other nations for construction of a new route in Latin America except as the two countries agree.

Grants to the United States the right to add a third lane of locks to the existing canal.

Provides that Panama receive 30 cents per net ton in tolls for each vessel passing through the canal during the treaty period.

Requires an annual payment to Panama of $10 million from canal operating revenues and an annual amount up to an additional $10 million if canal revenues exceed expenditures.

Permanent Neutrality Treaty

States that Panama declares the canal shall be permanently neutral and that it shall remain secure and open to peaceful transit by vessels of all nations on terms of equality in times of peace and war.

States that the United States and Panama "agree to maintain the regime of neutrality established by this treaty."

Provides that after the termination of the basic treaty in 1999, only Panama shall operate the canal and maintain military forces, defense sites and military installations within its national territory.

Provides that U.S. and Panamanian vessels of war and auxiliary ships be "entitled to transit the canal expeditiously."

Issues in Debate

At the heart of the debate over the future of the canal — long a symbol of American power and engineering ability — lay basic foreign policy and national security issues. Opponents of the treaty argued that turning the canal over to Panama would, in the words of Sen. Robert P. Griffin (R Mich.) be "a dangerous step, a gamble for the United States and the security of the United States." They argued that such an action would undermine American prestige abroad and represented another in a series of decisions by the Carter administration — among them cancellation of the B-1 bomber, deferment of neutron bomb deployment and withdrawal of U.S. ground forces from South Korea — that, they said, could serve to undermine the U.S. defense posture.

Countered floor manager Church: "A vote against this treaty represents a vain attempt to preserve the past. It represents a futile effort to perpetuate an American colony in Panama against the wishes of the Panamanian people...."

And in televised remarks following ratification of the basic treaty April 18, Carter said, "This is a day of which Americans can feel proud; for now we have reminded the world and ourselves of the things that we stand for as a nation."

Carter went on to say: "These treaties can mark the beginning of a new era in our relations, not only with Panama but with all the rest of the world. They symbolize our determination to deal with the developing nations of the world, the small nations of the world, on the basis of mutual respect and partnership."

As jubilant Panamanians celebrated the final vote, Torrijos appeared on television to declare that the treaties were "the greatest, the most awaited and the most discussed triumph" of his country. Previously, he had warned that Panama would not accept the DeConcini reservation unless there were some modification and had even warned that if the United States attempted to intervene in Panama under the reservation, Panama would destroy the canal.

Implementing the Treaties

The treaties would not go into effect until 1979. Under the terms of a reservation to the basic treaty approved by the Senate April 17, the instruments of ratification could be exchanged by Panama and the United States at any time but they could not become effective earlier than March 31, 1979. The reservation also said the treaties themselves would not take effect until Oct. 1, 1979, unless Congress approved implementing legislation before March 31, 1979.

The House has no constitutional role in ratification of treaties, but sought to get involved nevertheless. Anti-treaty sentiment was thought to be more intense in the House than the Senate.

In mid-year, the House added language to the State Department authorization bill (HR 12598) that prohibited funds authorized by the bill from being used directly or indirectly to effect implementation of the treaties unless authorized by Congress. The Senate bill didn't contain this restriction. However, conferees on the bill specified that funds could be used if authorized either by Congress or the Constitution.

The addition of the Constitution qualification was thought to allow the president under his constitutional treaty-making powers to proceed with implementation of the canal treaties. *(HR 12598 story, p. 411)*

After ratification, there would be a transition period during which Panama would assume some of the Canal Zone functions. Other operations would be maintained by a new U.S. agency. The Panama Canal Commission, composed of five Americans and four Panamanians, that would administer the waterway until the year 2000.

The United States would continue to have primary responsibility for the defense of the canal until expiration of the treaty in 1999, after which date both the United States and Panama would each have the right to defend the canal against threats to its neutrality or to the peaceful transit of ships. In addition, the Senate added a measure to the neutrality treaty that would allow the United States to maintain troops in Panama after 1999 if both countries decided it was necessary.

Background

U.S. government interest in a canal connecting the Atlantic and Pacific Oceans went back at least as far as the early 1830s when President Jackson sent Charles Biddle to explore possible routes across Panama and Nicaragua.

In 1855, a U.S.-owned railroad running across the Panamanian Isthmus was opened. Shippers were quick to use the railroad to transport their passengers and goods across Central America, rather than go round the tip of South America. Pressure to build a canal mounted.

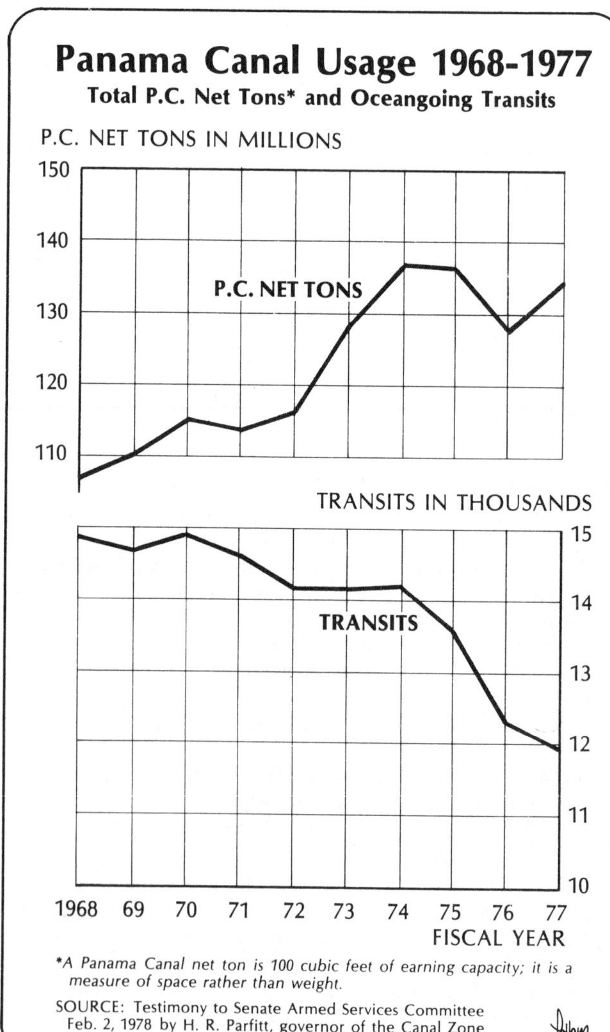

*A Panama Canal net ton is 100 cubic feet of earning capacity; it is a measure of space rather than weight.

SOURCE: Testimony to Senate Armed Services Committee Feb. 2, 1978 by H. R. Parfitt, governor of the Canal Zone

Votes on the Two Treaties

YEAS (68): 52 Democrats; 16 Republicans

Abourezk, S.D.	Humphrey, Minn.
Anderson, Minn.	Inouye, Hawaii
Baker, Tenn.	Jackson, Wash.
Bayh, Ind.	***Javits, N.Y.***
Bellmon, Okla.	Kennedy, Mass.
Bentsen, Texas	Leahy, Vt.
Biden, Del.	Long, La.
Brooke, Mass.	Magnuson, Wash.
Bumpers, Ark.	***Mathias, Md.***
Byrd, Robert C., W.Va.	Matsunaga, Hawaii
Cannon, Nev.	McGovern, S.D.
Case, N.J.	McIntyre, N.H.
Chafee, R.I.	Metzenbaum, Ohio
Chiles, Fla.	Morgan, N.C.
Church, Idaho	Moynihan, N.Y.
Clark, Iowa	Muskie, Maine
Cranston, Calif.	Nelson, Wis.
Culver, Iowa	Nunn, Ga.
Danforth, Mo.	***Packwood, Ore.***
DeConcini, Ariz.	***Pearson, Kan.***
Durkin, N.H.	Pell, R.I.
Eagleton, Mo.	***Percy, Ill.***
Glenn, Ohio	Proxmire, Wis.
Gravel, Alaska	Ribicoff, Conn.
Hart, Colo.	Riegle, Mich.
Haskell, Colo.	Sarbanes, Md.
Hatfield, Mark O., Ore.	Sasser, Tenn.
Hatfield, Paul G., Mont.	Sparkman, Ala.
Hathaway, Maine	***Stafford, Vt.***
Hayakawa, Calif.	Stevenson, Ill.
Heinz, Pa.	Stone, Fla.
Hodges, Ark.	Talmadge, Ga.
Hollings, S.C.	***Weicker, Conn.***
Huddleston, Ky.	Williams, N.J.

NAYS (32): 10 Democrats; 22 Republicans

Allen, Ala.	***Laxalt, Nev.***
Bartlett, Okla.	***Lugar, Ind.***
Burdick, N.D.	***McClure, Idaho***
Byrd, Harry F. Jr., Va.	Melcher, Mont.
Curtis, Neb.	Randolph, W.Va.
Dole, Kan.	***Roth, Del.***
Domenici, N.M.	***Schmitt, N.M.***
Eastland, Miss.	***Schweiker, Pa.***
Ford, Ky.	***Scott, Va.***
Garn, Utah	Stennis, Miss.
Goldwater, Ariz.	***Stevens, Alaska***
Griffin, Mich.	***Thurmond, S.C.***
Hansen, Wyo.	***Tower, Texas***
Hatch, Utah	***Wallop, Wyo.***
Helms, N.C.	***Young, N.D.***
Johnston, La.	Zorinsky, Neb.

Democrats ***Republicans***

With the advent of the Civil War, interest in the canal waned temporarily, to be renewed sporadically over the next 30 years. In 1898, when the battleship *Oregon* took 68 days to sail from San Francisco through the Strait of Magellan to reach the U.S. Atlantic fleet engaged in the Spanish-American War, public demands for construction of a canal became intense.

French interests had already undertaken to build a waterway across the Panamanian Isthmus. A company headed by Suez Canal builder Ferdinand de Lesseps began excavation of a channel, but in 1889 the company went bankrupt. Reorganized in 1894, the new company realized that its only hope to salvage any of its losses was for the United States to decide to build the canal.

The Isthmian Canal Commission set up by President McKinley in 1899 studied the French project. But because the French were asking so much for their property and rights, the commission in 1901 recommended that a passageway through Nicaragua would be cheaper. In the wake of that decision, the French quickly reduced their price—to $40-million—and the commission changed its recommendation and backed the Panama route.

Congress in 1902 approved the Spooner Act agreeing to the French offer if Colombia would agree to deed a strip of land across the Panamanian Isthmus for a canal zone.

Panama had been controlled by Colombia at its southern edge since 1821, when the country had voluntarily joined the Colombian federation. During brief periods Panama enjoyed considerable autonomy, but in 1886 Colombia had reinstated a highly centralized government and treated Panama essentially as a province. This fomented civil strife within Panama and fueled a growing separatist movement there.

In 1903 the Colombia charge d'affaires in Washington, Tomás Herran, negotiated a treaty with U.S. Secretary of State John Hay that conformed to the terms of the Spooner Act. The Senate ratified the treaty in March, but the Colombian government rejected it in August.

Revolt and Treaty

Reluctant to lose the canal and desirous of independence from Colombia in any event, Panamanians staged a successful revolution Nov. 3, 1903. The United States recognized the new government on Nov. 6, and less than two weeks later, on Nov. 18, Hay and the Panamanian minister to the United States, Philippe Jean Bunau-Varilla, signed a treaty giving the United States authority to build the canal.

It was unclear to what extent the United States government aided the Panamanians with their bloodless coup. Indications were that President Theodore Roosevelt at least implicitly approved the revolt—a belief bolstered by the fact that an American warship was sent to Panama during the revolt, anchoring off its north coast near the city of Colon.

Treaty Terms. Ratified by Panama Dec. 2, 1903, and by the U.S. Senate Feb. 23, 1904, the Hay-Bunau-Varilla treaty granted to the United States in perpetuity a 10-mile wide canal zone. Washington also was given all rights, powers and authority over the zone as if it were a U.S. territory. In return, the United States paid Panama $10-million, plus annual fees of $250,000 beginning in 1913.

The treaty was revised in 1936 and 1955, increasing annual U.S. payments to Panama to $1.93-million. Construction of the canal was completed in 1914 at a cost of $387-million.

Dissatisfaction

Immediately after the signing of the treaty, the two countries began to disagree on the question of sovereignty over the canal. The issue reached a head in the early 1960s. In 1959 Panama requested that her flag be flown alongside the American flag in the Canal Zone. Despite strong opposition in Congress, including a House resolution, approved by a vote of 381-12, protesting such action, President Eisenhower allowed the two flags to be flown together at certain sites.

A later order banned the flying of either flag in front of Canal Zone schools. In defiance of that order, U.S. students Jan. 7, 1964, raised the American flag at a high school, touching off a riot that left four Americans and 21 Panamanians dead.

As a result of the riot, Panama broke off diplomatic relations with the United States. They were resumed in April that year, and in December President Johnson announced that the United States would negotiate a new treaty. Johnson and Panamanian President Marco Aurelio Robles announced in June 1967 that three new treaties had been drafted. One of them called for the canal to be administered by a binational commission, but congressional opposition was so strong that the treaties never were submitted for ratification. The following year Panama, which had been taken over by the militarist regime of Gen. Omar Torrijos Herrera, officially rejected the drafts.

New talks were begun in 1970. In September 1973 former Ambassador to South Vietnam Ellsworth Bunker was named chief U.S. negotiator. On Feb. 7, 1974, Secretary of State Henry A. Kissinger and Panamanian Foreign Minister Juan A. Tack signed an agreement of principles as the basis for the formal negotiations.

The eight principles called for an entirely new treaty with a fixed termination date, thus ending the concept of perpetuity; the return to Panama of the territory in which the canal was located; a "just and equitable" share for Panama of the benefits from the canal; a role for Panama in administering the canal during the life of the new treaty and total responsibility for its operation upon termination of the treaty; joint protection and defense of the canal by the two countries; the rights necessary for the United States to regulate the flow of ships through the canal and to operate, maintain and defend it; and provisions for the future enlargement of the waterway.

1976 Campaign Issue

Much of the grass-roots opposition to the 1977 canal treaties already had been generated during the 1976 campaign for the Republican presidential nomination. Seeking a dramatic issue that would help him overcome his early primary losses to President Ford, former California Gov. Ronald Reagan made the return of the waterway the centerpiece of his criticism of Ford's foreign policy.

"We bought it, we paid for it, we built it and we intend to keep it," the former governor said repeatedly. There was no question that Reagan's stance struck a patriotic chord in many Americans across the country.

New Treaty Signed in 1977

President Carter and Panamanian ruler Brig. Gen. Omar Torrijos Herrera signed the two controversial canal treaties on Sept. 7, 1977. Leaders from 26 other Western Hemisphere nations demonstrated their support of the treaties by attending brief signing ceremonies in Washington, D.C., at the Organization of American States.

By a two-to-one margin, Panamanian voters Oct. 23, 1977, approved the treaties that would turn the Panama Canal over to that country by the year 2000.

After the nationwide plebiscite in which two-thirds of the country's 700,000 voters approved the pacts, Gen. Omar Torrijos, the Panamanian leader, said: "I had no doubt it was going to happen this way because I knew our people would not turn their backs on the country when the country demands their presence."

The vote came nine days after President Carter met with Torrijos to clarify key provisions of the treaties that Senate leaders had warned would jeopardize the pacts when they were voted on by the Senate.

There had been concern that Panamanians would react negatively to the treaties after learning that Torrijos had agreed that the United States could "defend the canal against any threat to the regime of neutrality" and that U.S. warships "can go to the head of the line of vessels" waiting to enter the canal.

1977: Congressional Hearings

Building the case for approval of the treaties at the Senate Foreign Relations hearings in the fall of 1977, administration leaders stressed that the pacts would win the United States worldwide respect and "help set the tone" of inter-American relations for years to come.

If the Senate rejected the treaties, Secretary of State Cyrus R. Vance said Sept. 26, the first day of the committee's hearings, "our relations with Panama would be shattered, our standing in Latin America damaged immeasurably, and the security of the canal itself placed in jeopardy." *(Panama Canal issues, p. 379)*

The practical advantage of the treaties for the United States, Vance explained, was that the canal would be open, neutral, secure and efficiently operated without cost to U.S. taxpayers. *(Hearings, 1977 Almanac, p. 403)*

For Panama there would be economic benefits from toll revenues and, most important, full jurisdiction over its own territory, Vance said.

Canal Protection

Both State Department and Pentagon officials bore down on a major contention of treaty critics that if the United States "gives up" the canal, it would not be able to protect the waterway from attack.

The canal's operation could best be maintained, Secretary of Defense Harold Brown said Sept. 27, "by a cooperative effort with a friendly Panama" rather than by an "American garrison amid hostile surroundings."

If Panama and other Latin American countries became hostile to the United States, then protecting the canal against international threats, terrorism and guerrilla actions would become much more difficult, according to the Pentagon chief.

Military authorities have estimated that it would take up to 100,000 men to defend the canal. Even then there was no guarantee against the possibility that someone might sneak in with explosives or lob artillery shells over the heads of American troops and hit the slide-prone sections of the canal.

Witnesses also said the treaties would protect what commercial shipping remained, but added that "the commercial value of the canal" had dwindled. Noting that the passageway could not accommodate supertankers and other large ships and that only about 7 per cent of all U.S. international maritime trade passed through the canal each year, U.S. Ambassador Sol Linowitz said: "It has, to a substantial extent, become economically obsolescent."

Neutrality and Security

The issue of the canal's permanent neutrality and security was woven throughout the week's hearings. Shaped by the Defense Department, the treaty as interpreted by the administration placed the United States under no obligation to consult with or seek approval from other nations before acting to maintain the canal's neutrality.

"We felt strongly," Secretary of Defense Brown told the committee, "that the United States should take whatever action was necessary to maintain neutrality." Added Linowitz: "It is for the United States to make the determination as to how we should respond and how we should defend our rights...."

Earlier, Brown had stated that from a national security standpoint "the use of the canal is more important than ownership." Rather than ownership, the canal's unimpeded use, effective operation and physical security were important to the United States, said Brown. "The treaties provide real security, not paper claims. They offer the firmest and most practical guarantees obtainable that the canal will remain operational, secure and available to the United States."

As he began his testimony, Brown said that the Defense Department "wholeheartedly and fully supports these treaties"—a statement intended to negate suggestions made by the American Legion and other treaty opponents that the Pentagon was going along with the pacts under orders from the president, but that its leaders secretly opposed the agreements.

But Brown and other senior military leaders appearing before the committee noted that they were centrally involved in negotiating the new treaties to ensure that U.S. defense requirements were protected.

Brown called the insinuations of opponents an "insult" to senior military officers and said "such charges do not help the debate any more than would challenging the integrity of the treaties' opponents."

Supporters

The Carter administration had some highly influential backers of the treaties in the persons of former President Ford and former Secretaries of State Henry A. Kissinger and Dean Rusk.

AFL-CIO President George Meany also endorsed the pacts, stating Aug. 29: "I see no reason for us holding on to territory 6,000 miles away just because we built a canal in 1904." The treaties protected the job security, bargaining rights and compensation of about 12,000 union workers in the Canal Zone.

Meany also joined with several other influential statesmen and businessmen to form a Committee of Americans for the Canal Treaties. Members of that committee included former New York Gov. W. Averell Harriman, former Undersecretary of State George Ball, former Ambassador Gen. Maxwell D. Taylor, Mrs. Lyndon B. Johnson, former Senator and Ambassador Henry Cabot Lodge, former Senator and Ambassador John Sherman Cooper, former Senate Minority Leader Hugh Scott, former Sen. Stuart Symington, Du Pont Chairman of the Board Irving Shapiro and Atlantic Richfield Co. Chairman Robert Anderson.

Appearing before the House International Relations Committee Sept. 14, former Secretary of State Kissinger said that the Panama Canal treaties are the "most important and serious" international requests sent to Congress by the Carter administration. "A defeat of the Panama Canal treaties would weaken the President's international authority at the beginning of his term," Kissinger said, and "it would jeopardize our entire Western Hemisphere relationships."

Also appearing at the hearing was former Secretary of State Rusk. Strongly disagreeing with opponents who insisted that the canal's security could better be preserved under the old treaty, Rusk declared: "If, God forbid, it should ever become necessary for a President and a Congress to take strong measures to keep the canal functioning and safe, they would be in a far stronger position to do so under the treaties of 1977." The neutrality pact alone, Rusk said, gives the United States "all that we need to maintain our essential interests...passage and security of the canal itself."

U.S. Cargo Shipped Through Canal

Year	Long Tons* (in millions)	% of All U.S. Ocean-Shipped Cargo
1968	62.5	15.5
1969	67.9	16.1
1970	78.6	16.9
1971	81.8	17.1
1972	70.7	14.9
1973	83.1	14.1
1974	97.0	15.2
1975	91.1	14.4
1976	73.4	11.3

* *Long ton equals 2,240 lbs.*

SOURCE: Panama Canal Company; *Survey of Current Business*

Opposition

Those opposed to the treaties were trying to convince undecided senators that the financial arrangements with Panama were unfair to the United States; that the neutrality treaty was too vague and unclear about U.S. rights; that the canal's security would be jeopardized if the agreements were ratified, and that it was "hypocritical" for the Carter administration to call for other Latin American nations to improve their human rights practices while at the same time agreeing to a treaty with a government headed by the allegedly repressive Torrijos regime.

"From a military viewpoint," American Legion spokesman William J. Rogers told the House International Relations Committee, "a commander never gives away strategic territory which he may have to fight to regain." Dr. John Wasylik, commander of the Veterans of Foreign Wars, said: "What the proposed treaties embody is a slow motion act of strategic self-mutilation."

Former California Gov. Ronald Reagan, the figure the public probably most closely identified with opposition to the treaties, urged that the pacts be rejected because of the possibility that the Soviet Union and Cuba might increase their influence in Panama. "It should never surprise us that whenever the United States withdraws its presence or its strong interest from any areas, the Soviets are ready, willing and often able to exploit the situation. Can we believe that the Panama Canal is any exception?" he said Sept. 9.

The opposition outside the Senate was coordinated by the Emergency Coalition to Save the Panama Canal. An umbrella group inspired by the American Conservative Union, the coalition counted among its members the Conservative Caucus, the American Security Council and the Committee for the Survival of a Free Congress. The coalition periodically held working sessions to develop strategy and to assess which way unannounced senators were leaning.

In addition, both the American Conservative Union and the American Legion conducted letter-writing campaigns against the pacts. *(Lobbying, pp. 388, 389)*

Differing Interpretations

Challenges by two of the Panamanian negotiators to the U.S. interpretation of two key clauses in the treaties dealt an early and severe blow to the pacts' chances for ratification.

Intervention Rights. One of the clauses stated that the United States and Panama "agree to maintain the regime of neutrality established in this treaty"—language U.S. officials said gave the United States intervention powers to keep the canal neutral.

But on Aug. 19, 1977, chief Panamanian negotiator Romulo Escobar Bethancourt said: "[W]e are not giving the United States a right of intervention. What we are giving is an assurance that the canal will be permanently neutral."

And in a conversation with an American embassy official in Panama, reported in a State Department cable made public by Sen. Robert Dole (R Kan.), negotiator Carlos Lopez Guevera said: "Panama cannot agree to the right of the U.S. to intervene."

Priority Passage. Both Panamanian negotiators contradicted the U.S. interpretation of the section in the neutrality treaty that gave American and Panamanian warships the right to "transit the canal expeditiously." Secretary Vance interpreted this clause to mean that "our ships can go to the head of the line."

But Escobar and Lopez both said the United States warships would not be given "preferential rights"—language that was proposed but rejected during the negotiations.

Other Differences. Escobar contended that Panama could close the canal if the waterway was operating at a financial loss. But the United States maintained that other language in the agreements requiring that the "canal shall remain open" repudiated that contention. Escobar also disputed whether the United States would have exclusive rights, as it claimed, to building a new sea-level passageway in another Latin nation. The treaty committed both nations "to study jointly the feasibility" of such a canal.

State Department Response

The State Department sought to clear up some of the misunderstanding over the intervention issue in an Oct. 5 letter to the Senate Foreign Relations Committee. The letter said the explanation of the treaties given to the committee was correct, but added: "The treaty does not give the United States any right to intervene in the internal affairs of Panama, nor has it been our intention to seek out or to exercise such a right."

The letter did not mention the controversy over priority passage for U.S. warships or the other issues raised by Escobar.

Carter-Torrijos Statement

Openly concerned that failure to clarify the conflicting interpretations could scuttle the treaties, Carter met with Torrijos at a hastily called meeting in Washington Oct. 14.

After the meeting, the two leaders issued a statement. On U.S. intervention rights, they said: "The correct interpretation of this principle is that each of the two countries shall, in accordance with their respective constitutional processes, defend the Canal against any threat to the regime of neutrality, and consequently shall have the right to act against any aggression or threat directed against the Canal or against the peaceful transit of vessels through the Canal. This does not mean, nor shall it be interpreted as, a right of intervention of the United States in the internal affairs of Panama."

With regard to passage of warships, the two said they interpreted the treaty to mean that the warships would be assured transit through the canal "as quickly as possible, without any impediment, with expedited treatment, and in case of need or emergency, to go to the head of the line of vessels in order to transit the Canal rapidly."

Statement of Understanding

Following is the text of the statement of understanding agreed to by President Carter and Panamanian leader Brig. Gen. Omar Torrijos Herrera following their White House meeting on Oct. 14, 1977:

Under the Treaty Concerning the Permanent Neutrality and Operation of the Panama Canal (the Neutrality Treaty), Panama and the United States have the responsibility to assure that the Panama Canal will remain open and secure to ships of all nations. The correct interpretation of this principle is that each of the two countries shall, in accordance with their respective constitutional processes, defend the Canal against any threat to the regime of neutrality, and consequently shall have the right to act against any aggression or threat directed against the Canal or against the peaceful transit of vessels through the Canal.

This does not mean, nor shall it be interpreted as a right of intervention of the United States in the internal affairs of Panama. Any United States action will be directed at insuring that the Canal will remain open, secure and accessible, and it shall never be directed against the territorial integrity or political independence of Panama.

The Neutrality Treaty provides that the vessels of war and auxiliary vessels of the United States and Panama will be entitled to transit the Canal expeditiously. This is intended, and it shall so be interpreted, to assure the transit of such vessels through the Canal as quickly as possible, without any impediment, with expedited treatment, and in case of need or emergency, to go to the head of the line of vessels in order to transit the Canal rapidly.

Majority Leader Byrd said the statement improved chances for Senate ratification, but he cautioned that "the great majority" of senators were still uncommitted.

Dole, a key opponent of the treaties, also lauded the statement and said he would offer amendments to incorporate the language of the statement into the neutrality treaty itself.

Amendments and Reservations

Adding amendments was one of three ways the Senate could approve a treaty with qualifications. An amendment to the treaty would change the existing language and terms of the treaty for all parties, thus requiring new negotiations by the two countries.

A reservation was a unilateral recommendation by the United States to modify certain provisions of the treaties, thereby altering U.S. obligations. A reservation modified only the obligations of the nation making the reservation. Adoption of a reservation could open additional negotiations since Panama might file similar reservations.

An understanding was a unilateral statement not intended to modify or limit any of the treaty provisions, but rather to clarify, explain or interpret one or more provisions or to deal with some matter incidental to the operation of the treaty. Such language would not have any legal effect on the treaty.

House Involvement

Hoping to involve the House in the canal controversy on the assumption that the unpopularity of the treaties would influence members to vote against them in an election year, treaty opponents claimed that the House as well as the Senate had to approve any agreement to turn the canal over to the Panamanians. *(House action, p. 412)*

They based this claim on the following reasoning:

- That the United States actually owned the waterway because the Canal Zone was conveyed to the United States in perpetuity by the 1903 treaty.
- That, because the United States owned the property, both the House and the Senate needed to give their consent to the disposal of U.S. land, as required by Article IV, section 3, clause 2, of the Constitution.

This reasoning was disputed by Attorney General Griffin B. Bell at the Foreign Relations Committee's Sept. 29 session. The United States, he said, "is not the sovereign, but it has jurisdiction over the Canal Zone...all the rights, powers and authority which it would possess and exercise if it were sovereign of the Canal Zone."

As to the question of whether proprietary interests of the United States can be disposed of by treaty, or whether authorizing legislation is required (necessitating House concurrence), Bell said a treaty alone would suffice.

House action was required in one area, however. Because of the powers granted the House by the Constitution over fiscal matters, separate legislation was needed for those aspects of the treaties that involved raising revenues or the expenditure of funds.

The implementing legislation was expected to cover 1) the organization and activities of the new Panama Canal Commission, including arrangements for establishing and collecting tolls and payment of funds to Panama; 2) employment and retirement practices of the commission; and 3) adjustments of U.S. courts and law enforcement authorities during the initial 30 months of the treaty.

Key Issues

Some treaty critics said the Oct. 14, 1977, statement by Carter and Torrijos was a "step in the right direction," but they quickly added that even if these interpretations were attached to the treaties as reservations or understandings — a step the Carter administration opposed — there still were other problems with the treaties. Following were the key issues in the debate over the treaties. Most of the arguments were developed during 1977 congressional hearings on the treaties.

Latin Relations

The Carter administration argued that ratification of the treaties "will be the single most positive action" taken by the United States in recent years to advance relations with Latin America. According to the State Department, South and Central American governments have viewed the negotiations "as a litmus test of our intentions toward their countries."

Treaty opponents, however, charged that "perhaps the greatest myth" promoted by the Carter administration and its allies was that Senate rejection would harm U.S. relations with other Latin American countries.

"The support among Latin American nations for these treaties is not nearly as widespread as believed," the American Conservative Union's legislative director, Gary L. Jarmin, told the Senate Foreign Relations Committee Oct. 11. Expressing a view shared by most treaty critics, Jarmin said that privately many Latin leaders were "extremely worried" about the prospect of a Marxist, pro-Cuban government having control of the 51-mile-long waterway.

The conservative organization also contended that Latin American respect for the United States "goes up when we take a tough stance and goes down when we capitulate."

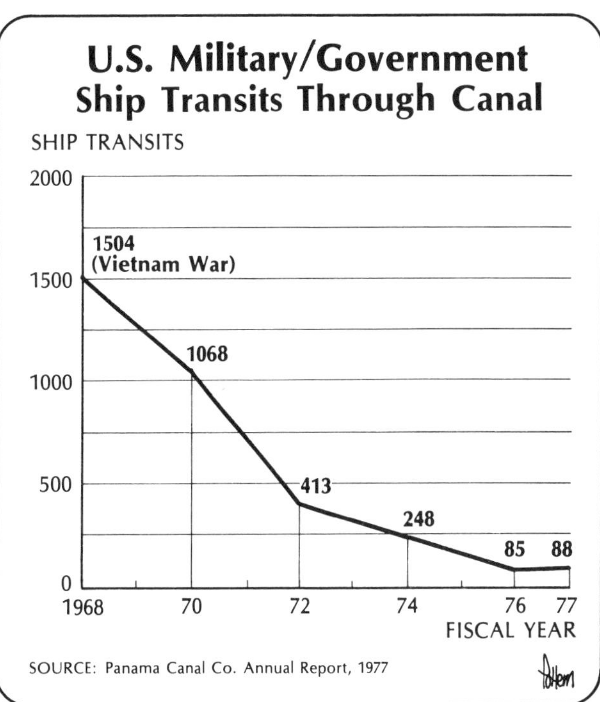

Cuban/Soviet Factor

Disagreeing with the Carter administration's Pentagon brass, former Joint Chiefs of Staff Chairman Thomas H. Moorer warned the Senate Foreign Relations Committee: "Do not be surprised, if this treaty is ratified in its present form, to see a Soviet and/or Cuban presence quickly established in Panama."

Once that happened, Moorer warned, "U.S. security as well as U.S. prosperity would be placed in serious jeopardy" because the Soviets would control the maritime gateway.

But two other former military leaders—Gen. Maxwell D. Taylor and Adm. Elmo R. Zumwalt Jr.—argued that if the United States did not approve the agreements, the Soviets and Cubans would reap political advantages in Latin America. "There will be a lot of cheers in Moscow and Havana," Zumwalt predicted. He noted that "turbulence there is always good news to Moscow—so are American blunders. Let us hope we do not give the Kremlin chiefs the occasion to rejoice, which our rejection of these treaties would undoubtedly afford."

Canal Defense

Treaty backers predicted that the canal would be a frequent target of sabotage and terrorist activity if the treaties were not approved. Taylor maintained that outside terrorists sent in as "hired troublemakers, controlled by Havana or Moscow" would be likely if U.S.-Panamanian relations faltered as a result of the treaties' defeat by the Senate.

Added Sen. Clifford P. Case (R N.J.): "A basic fact which has to be dealt with is the canal's vulnerability.... If we vote to keep the canal 'ours' in the 1903 [treaty] sense, could we end up with a Pyrrhic victory in the form of a useless ditch?"

But since the United States would turn over 10 of its 14 military bases to Panama under the treaties, the waterway would be more vulnerable to attack than it is now, according to Senate opponents. Furthermore, Sen. James B. Allen (D Ala.) said: "Only the naive would doubt that we would very soon see pressure on our forces to withdraw from the four sites retained."

Commercial Value

The Carter administration contended that the commercial value of the canal has diminished considerably as world commerce and shipping patterns changed. Supertankers and other large vessels cannot use the canal, they pointed out. *(Box, this page)*

Not so, argued Sen. Strom Thurmond (R S.C.). He maintained that the canal, "one of a very few vital world waterways," permits rapid two-ocean commerce vital to the nation. In 1975 about 14,000 ships passed through the canal, about 70 per cent of them sailing to or from the United States.

These figures were more important than those cited by the administration, claimed Adm. Moorer, because the United States, for legal and fiscal reasons, has a very small merchant marine, and shipping interests depend on other nations' freighters and tankers to a large degree.

Military Value

Treaty defenders stressed that the nation's aircraft carriers cannot fit through the canal's lock system, but opponents argued that while this is true, about 98 per cent of the Navy's ships can easily transit the canal. Moorer pointed out that the alternative—going around Cape Horn—would add 8,000 miles, 25-30 days and considerable costs to naval operations.

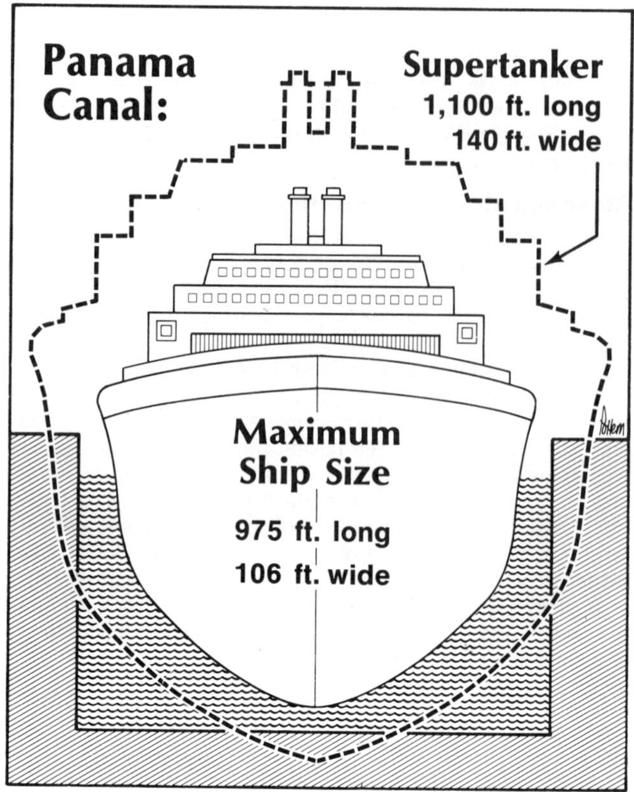

Many modern ships are too big to go through the Panama Canal. The diagram shows the canal's maximum ship size, compared with the dimensions of a typical supertanker.

On a related issue, Thurmond and others said that under the treaty's neutrality provisions unfriendly ships could use the canal, whereas now the United States can deny passage to ships of any adversary during an international crisis or war.

Foreign Relations Committee member Joe Biden (D Del.) dismissed this argument as a "bit of a red herring."

"Why," Biden asked, "would a warship attempt to go into the canal? It would be crazy. To raise that issue is off the mark."

New Canal

Treaty critics also faulted the Carter administration for concluding an agreement that prohibited the construction of a new sea level canal in Central America before the year 2000 unless Panama gave its approval.

But Biden and committee colleague Frank Church (D Idaho) turned this argument around during an exchange with Thurmond. "We're given the exclusive option to build a modern canal in Panama," said Church. "And Panama," added Biden, "can't make an agreement with the Soviet Union."

Payments to Panama

Under the treaties, Panama would receive payments from canal revenues, "which more fairly reflect the fact that it is making available its major national resource—its territory," Secretary Vance told the committee. The treaties, he reminded senators, required no new appropriations, "nor do they add to the burdens of the American taxpayer."

Sen. Robert Dole (R Kan.) called these payments, expected to amount to about $60-million a year until 2000, a "windfall" for the Panamanians, "particularly when we consider the value of real estate and equipment that will be given without charge to the Panamanian government."

Foreign Troops

The basic treaty barred the Soviet Union, Cuba or any other foreign government from stationing its troops in Panama after the year 2000. But the pact made no mention of the years before, a point that worried Thurmond and other critics.

Treaty backers, however, said the key point was that Panama is willing to give up its right to call in Soviet or other foreign troops after the year 2000. "Panama will be the only Latin nation to have signed away those rights," observed Claiborne Pell (D R.I.).

Early 1978: Pressures Mount

As Panama Canal treaty partisans barnstormed the country for public support, the Senate Foreign Relations Committee Jan. 19, 1978, opened a final round of hearings on the two pacts before a markup session Jan. 26.

Majority Leader Robert C. Byrd (D W.Va.) Jan. 13 said he would vote for the treaties "and work for their approval." However, he added that he thought "some form" of language should be added to the treaties clarifying United States' rights to defend the canal and to assure that American military ships could move quickly through the canal in an emergency.

Much of the attention on the canal issue in early 1978 focused on trips: Visits by advocates and critics around the United States to espouse their view, and visits to Panama by a steady stream of senators and representatives.

- Sticking to a six-month-old strategy that based Senate rejection of the agreements on a robust outcry from voters, a coalition of 20 conservative lawmakers left Washington Jan. 16 on a five-day, eight-city campaign to argue that the treaties would harm the nation's security and economic interests.
- On the other side, Secretary of State Vance Jan. 11 flew to Charleston, W.Va., Louisville, Ky., New Orleans and Los Angeles in an escalation of administration lobbying from the lower-ranking State Department speaking tours underway since the pacts were signed in Washington Sept. 7, 1977.
- Six Foreign Relations Committee members returned from Panama the day before the panel's hearings began. That group, which brought to 42 the number of senators who toured the 51-mile waterway, met with Panamanian officials, including General Omar Torrijos, and received political and military briefings from U.S. officials stationed in the country.

Beginning with Majority Leader Byrd's own support announced in mid-January, the pro-treaty forces began to add important new allies to their bipartisan ranks: Minority Leader Howard H. Baker Jr. (Tenn.), then Lloyd Bentsen (D Texas) and next 14 of the Foreign Relations Committee's 15 members, who voted Jan. 30 to send the treaties to the floor. Included in this number were previously uncommitted members Charles H. Percy (R Ill.) and Richard (Dick) Stone (D Fla.).

A Gallup poll released Feb. 1 showed 45 per cent of Americans favoring the treaties, and 42 per cent opposed. This was a substantial change from three months earlier when Gallup found 48 per cent opposed.

Carter Fireside Chat

Prodded by Byrd, who had urged the administration to "use its muscle, its outlets" to win support for the treaties, President Carter gave his first televised "fireside chat" on the issue Feb. 1.

In a series of rhetorical questions, Carter addressed major issues that public opinion polls showed worried Americans most about the new treaties.

- Will the United States have the right to defend the canal? "The answer is yes," Carter said, suggesting that even without the new treaties he would not hesitate to deploy whatever armed forces are necessary to defend the canal.

"But there is a much better option than sending our sons and grandsons to fight in the jungles of Panama. We would serve our interests better by implementing the new treaties, an action that would help to avoid any attack on Panama," Carter said.

- Why should we give away the Panama Canal Zone? As many people say, "We bought it, we paid for it, it's ours."

Here Carter responded that the United States does not own the canal as Ronald Reagan and other treaty opponents have stated. "We have never had sovereignty over it. We have only had the right to use it," Carter stated.

- Are we paying Panama to take the canal? Under the new treaties, Carter explained, payments to Panama will come from tolls paid by ships that use the canal.

Senate Committee Action

To ease the political risk for some senators, the leadership agreed that the Foreign Relations Committee would only make recommendations to the Senate rather than following its usual procedure of attaching amendments, reservations or understandings to resolutions accompanying the treaties to the floor.

The usual procedure would have prevented other members from cosponsoring changes and claiming at home that they had helped improve the agreements. "This procedure allows everyone to have a piece of the action," said Sen. Clifford P. Case (R N.J.), who praised the leadership for a "beautifully coordinated and wisely-planned procedure."

Committee colleague Frank Church (D Idaho) said the bipartisan effort on the treaties "shows how consensus can grow out of the confusion" that settled on the treaties when they were unveiled in September.

New Article

Beginning its "mark-up" Jan. 27, the committee anguished over how to attach to the treaties the Oct. 14 understanding reached by President Carter and Gen. Torrijos that gives both nations the right to defend the canal against any threat to its neutrality and that allows U.S. warships "to go to the head of the line" during emergencies.

Without consulting the Panamanians, the committee

Panama Canal Treaties Spurred Intense Lobby Effort...

In the fall of 1977, as Senate Minority Leader Howard H. Baker Jr. (Tenn.), then uncommitted on the Panama Canal treaties, took his seat at the University of Tennessee/Memphis State football game in Knoxville, even he must have been surprised. Above the stadium a light plane towed a banner calling upon the fans to "Save Our Canal."

Sponsored by the American Conservative Union (ACU), the streamer symbolized the variety of direct and indirect pressures placed on senators in the fight over ratification of the Panama Canal treaties.

Aside from presidential election campaigns and the anti-Vietnam war effort, there had been few political battles in the preceding 30 years to match the national emotion roused by the treaties.

Although the terms of the agreements alone rubbed many raw nerves, those feelings were cultivated and channeled into a massive lobby campaign by a conservative coalition working for the 34 Senate votes needed to reject the pacts.

After the signing of the pacts in September 1977, the opposition fought the treaties with mail campaigns, radio spots, a TV documentary and "truth squads" of Senate and House members sent around the country to apply pressure on those senators still uncommitted. The total cost of these activities, however, could not be determined because many groups were involved, ranging from the American Legion and other veterans groups, to conservative political organizations, to ad hoc committees set up to fight only this issue.

Viewing the position taken by a senator on the issue as a true test of his conservative credentials and hoping the controversy would help expand their own political influence, opponents promised to fight the re-election of any member who supported the agreements.

Treaty Support

Admittedly playing catch-up ball for public opinion on the treaties, private groups aiding the White House in early 1978 began criss-crossing the country for support. They also organized at the grassroots level to show crucial members of the Senate that considerable but untapped support existed for the agreements. At first, the administration and supporters had focused chiefly on Capitol Hill lobbying, leaving the anti-treaty side free to cultivate local opposition.

The State Department reported that by mid-January its officials had participated in 617 "forums" such as TV shows and speaking engagements since September, with another 116 lined up in the next six weeks. But it was not until the first of the year that Secretary of State Cyrus R. Vance took the issue outside Washington. President Carter Feb. 1 gave his "fireside chat" on the merits of the treaties.

"At a minimum our purpose is to get mail to the Senate offices," said a spokesman for the Committee of Americans for the Canal Treaties, Inc., which was established in October by prominent treaty backers. "When a senator—take [John C.] Danforth (R Mo.), for example—gets 12,000 pieces of mail against the treaties, and only 200 for, he can't help but be concerned, although he may be planning to vote for the treaties," the spokesman added. "We're trying to ease that pressure."

Committee for the Treaties, Inc.

Established to mount a "national program of education" about the treaties, the Committee of Americans for the Canal Treaties, Inc. sported a roster of well-known members—former President Ford, Mrs. Lyndon B. Johnson and George Meany, among others enlisted for their opinion-molding abilities. The committee maintained a "loose cooperation" with the White House, although it was "totally independent" of its operations, according to a committee spokesman.

Unlike many of the conservative groups opposing the treaties, the committee planned to disband after the final Senate vote.

Because it had no connection with federal election campaigns, the group could accept contributions from corporations.

Two other activities rounded out the group's efforts: The organization of state committees to drum up local treaty support and a speaker's bureau, whose most active members included former Sen. Hugh Scott (R Pa., 1949-77) and former Ambassador Averell Harriman.

Committee for Ratification

The administration's treaty fight also was aided by the Committee for Ratification of the Panama Canal Treaties. This group was initiated by New Directions, a liberal-leaning foreign policy organization founded in 1976 somewhat on the model of the well known citizens lobby Common Cause. Members of the committee included the AFL-CIO, Democratic National Committee, United Auto Workers, Americans for Democratic Action and the Washington Office on Latin America.

Focused on winning treaty support at the state and local levels, the organization was set up because treaty supporters felt, in the words of one organizer, that "nothing had happened" on lobbying for the agreements after the signing ceremonies in Washington Sept. 7.

The committee's operating budget amounted to only $19,000 for printing costs of a booklet about the treaties and travel expenses of field organizers dispatched by member organizations to rally support for the agreements. States targeted for special attention were Texas, Delaware, Florida, Pennsylvania, Kentucky and Tennessee.

New Directions, itself, however, sent out a 1.1 million mailing to liberal cause backers, such as Common Cause members, asking that they send letters

...As Supporters, Opponents Sought Senate Votes

to senators supporting the treaties. Signed by New Directions chairperson Margaret Mead, the mailing cost $137,500, with $50,000 coming directly from New Directions and the remainder from the Democratic National Committee, United States Steel Workers, Occidental Petroleum and the Communications Workers of America among other organizations.

Like the conservatives battling the treaties, New Directions was not blind to the possibility that the issue could be helpful for its organization building much as the Watergate scandal helped to substantially boost the membership ranks of Common Cause.

Opponents

Opposition to the canal treaties came mainly from conservative organizations and members of Congress, many with political ties to former California Gov. Ronald Reagan, who sparked the canal debate during the 1976 Republican presidential primaries.

Reagan backer Sen. Paul Laxalt (R Nev.), for example, and Rep. Philip M. Crane (R Ill.) were responsible for organizing the "truth squad" of 20 members of Congress who left Washington Jan. 17 on a nationwide, week-long campaign "to focus renewed public interest in the treaties."

The campaign was initially planned in September 1977 at a strategy meeting held at the Virginia home of Richard Viguerie, a publicist for conservative causes. The "truth squad" was financed by $100,000 in individual donations and contributions from eight conservative groups operating under the Committee to Save the Panama Canal. This was a "short-term" organization set up to avoid restrictions placed on member groups under election, lobby and tax laws.

The eight organizations—the most active opponents in the canal fight—were: American Conservative Union, Conservative Caucus, Committee for the Survival of a Free Congress, Citizens for the Republic, American Security Council, Young Republicans, National Conservative Political Action Committee and Council for National Defense.

Besides cooperating on the "truth squad" tour, a number of these conservative organizations plus such others as STOP ERA belonged to the Emergency Coalition to Save the Panama Canal. Organized by the ACU shortly after the treaties were signed, the coalition met in Washington to plan strategy for the Senate battle.

Although conservatives often pooled their efforts and resources, individual organizations continued their own activities. Representative of these groups were the ACU and the Conservative Caucus.

American Conservative Union

The organization sent out at least 1.8 million pieces of mail aimed at raising funds to continue the anti-treaty campaign and to urge recipients to write postcards and letters to Capitol Hill. Mailing lists included the ACU's own in addition to those of the *National Review, Human Events* and other conservative publications.

The organization also sponsored a 30-minute television program shown in 150 cities, anti-treaty newspaper ads that appeared in about 30 cities, a petition drive, and a trip by ACU chairman Crane to Denver in October after President Carter appeared there.

Conservative Caucus

In addition to its work in the anti-treaty umbrella groups, the caucus, which "is organized at the local level" to support conservative causes, sent out 2 million pieces of mail urging letters be sent to Senate and House members. This mailing was handled by Viguerie's company.

The group launched a radio-TV campaign in November 1977, sending to 500 stations messages based on excerpts of Reagan's testimony before a Senate subcommittee in September. The caucus said it hoped to "stem any erosion of anti-surrender sentiment among the general public...."

The White House Lobby

White House marketing of the Panama Canal treaties was aimed largely at the same target pursued by opponents: public opinion.

But there were some differences in approach. Opponents worked directly at grass roots lobbying, while the administration aimed its pitch at opinion-makers. Secondly, the administration had an asset opponents didn't: Invitations to the White House.

Between August 1977 and mid-January 1978, "opinion leaders" from 25 states were invited to high-level White House treaty briefings.

The briefings, some as long as two and a half hours, were conducted variously by the President, his national security adviser Zbigniew Brzezinski, and the Joint Chiefs of Staff Chairman George S. Brown. At each briefing, one of the two treaty negotiators, Ellsworth Bunker or Sol Linowitz, presented the administration viewpoint.

A White House spokesman said the list of those invited was compiled to influence larger segments of public opinion back home. Participants included local elected officials, educators, editorial writers, heads of organizations such as local League of Women Voters, labor leaders and political activists.

In addition to those "opinion leader" briefings, the White House conducted ongoing meetings with editors from around the country. And both the State and Defense Departments sent speakers to reach local groups. Secretary of State Cyrus R. Vance and Secretary of Defense Harold Brown went on speaking tours of their own.

decided that the best way to proceed was to add a new article at the end of the neutrality treaty that would contain the understanding reached in October.

Both the committee and the Carter administration felt it was necessary to avoid giving any appearance that new language had been slipped into the treaties by the United States. But they also hoped to avoid a new Panamanian plebiscite on the treaties, which, they feared, might unravel the agreements and require new rounds of negotiations.

Assistant Secretary of State for Congressional Relations Douglas J. Bennet told the committee that the language "should be put at the end so the Panamanian people know well that's exactly the statement agreed to by Carter and Torrijos before the Oct. 23 plebiscite.

And Jacob K. Javits (R N.Y.) said he was "afraid of splicing the agreement" into existing articles of the neutrality treaty as suggested by Church because "there is some danger they might say, "See, they've changed the treaty.' "

By a 13-1 vote, the committee agreed to add the new article. But that action was short-lived.

Reversal. On Jan. 30, the committee learned from Senate Majority Whip Alan Cranston (Calif.) and others in a 10-member delegation returning from Panama that the approach taken by the committee was unacceptable to Torrijos and could make a new plebiscite mandatory.

Meeting to finish its work Jan. 30 before sending the pacts to the floor, the committee reversed its earlier decision. Instead, it incorporated the Oct. 14 understanding into existing neutrality treaty language. "This is a wise move," said Bennet, changing the administration's earlier position. "A new article might have required a plebiscite, whereas amendments won't."

Case termed the alteration nothing more than a "face saving device" for the Panamanian negotiators that doesn't "really matter" to the United States. Javits called the switch "a change in form, not in substance."

Other Proposals

Before reporting the treaties to the Senate, the Foreign Relations Committee tabled a packet of amendments offered by Sen. Robert Dole (R Kan.) and recommended that four minor understandings be adopted by the Senate.

An amendment he proposed to prevent any country other than Panama or the United States from stationing troops in Panama during the life of the basic treaty was tabled after committee members argued that the amendment was "unnecessary" because of the protection afforded by U.S. troops.

The committee also rejected Dole amendments to remove any language in the treaty giving the United States authority to prevent construction of a new canal in Panama by a third country and barring U.S. negotiations with other Latin countries for a new canal. A State Department spokesman said the United States had wanted the "exclusive right" to build a new canal in Panama. In return, Panama demanded that the United States not negotiate to build a canal in any other country until the year 2000, he said.

Another proposal by Dole to reduce the amount of payments to Panama provided by the basic treaty was tabled after committee members argued that Panama currently was "grossly undercompensated" for use of the canal and that the planned payments were not out of line with funds channeled to Spain and other nations that have security treaties with the United States.

Understandings approved by the committee required that prisoner transfer agreements between the United States and Panama be submitted as a treaty for the Senate's advice and consent; required the inclusion of all reservations, understandings or other statements adopted by the Senate in the "instrument of ratification" itself rather than in separate documents; stated that the United States incurred no financial obligations by the treaties "other than those provided" in the agreement; and stated that the President could discuss new canal routes with other nations but could not conclude an agreement with another nation without Panama's consent.

Debate on Neutrality Pact

The Panama Canal treaties moved onto the Senate floor the first week of February 1978, with the leadership counting 62 members favoring the agreements, 28 opposed and 10 undecided.

On Feb. 22, the Senate took its first vote on the Panama Canal treaties, but the result was considered an inconclusive gauge of senators' positions on the agreements.

The Feb. 22 roll call was 67-30 (67 was exactly the number needed for ratification) in favor of tabling—that is, killing—a move by Sen. James B. Allen (D Ala.) to have the Senate consider the basic Panama Canal treaty before the neutrality pact, the reverse of the order the Senate had been following. Following the vote, the Senate leadership, treaty opponents and uncommitted members all cautioned that the votes cast on this procedural motion were unlikely to fall the same way later. *(Vote 33, p. 7-S)*

It was Allen's position that the Senate should first decide whether the United States should turn the canal over to Panama before debating the neutrality pact. "First things first," asserted Allen. "We should not put the cart before the horse."

But opponents of Allen's move argued that the neutrality pact should be considered before the Panama Canal treaty—it was reported that way by the Foreign Relations Committee—because the United States should know whether it would be able to dispatch troops if needed to keep the canal open before the Senate weighed the merits of transferring the waterway to Panamanian control.

Supporters of ratification, moreover, felt that they would have a better chance to win ratification if the neutrality treaty were debated first. Senate Minority Leader Howard H. Baker Jr. (R Tenn.), in fact said that if the pacts were reversed, "I could not vote for the treaties." Baker said that consideration of the neutrality treaty first "was the logical approach because it would give senators the opportunity to make a judgment on American interests in the canal after the year 2000."

Failing on his motion to reverse the order of the treaties, Allen moved his treaty opposition to a new front Feb. 23, proposing the first of many "killer amendments." Allen's amendment would have allowed the United States to maintain military installations in the U.S. Canal Zone after Dec. 31, 1999, when the waterway was turned over to Panama. But the president would have to certify to Panama before 1999 that the base was essential for defending the canal's neutrality.

Majority Leader Byrd, whose motion to table the Allen proposal was approved by the Senate Feb. 27, 55-34, said that although the plan "looks good on its face and sounds good," it is a "killer amendment." If accepted, Byrd said, the amendment would require new negotiations between the United States and Panama. *(Vote 34, p. 8-S)*

Scott Amendment

The first direct vote on an amendment came Feb. 28 as the Senate turned down, 24-69, a proposal by Bill Scott (R Va.), to prevent the neutrality treaty from taking effect without ratification of the Panama Canal treaty. *(Vote 36, p. 8-S)*

Scott said it was his intention to clarify the "unanswered" question of what was to become of one treaty should the other be rejected by the Senate.

Church argued that existing language in the treaties "makes it abundantly clear" that each treaty must be ratified before the other can take effect.

'Can't Refuse' Amendment

Recasting his first amendment to make it more appealing, Allen Feb. 28 proposed that the United States could maintain military bases in the former Canal Zone area after Dec. 31, 1999, if the United States was at war with a country that might attempt to send its ships through the canal, where they would be allowed passage under neutrality treaty provisions.

Church sensed the amendment's danger: "He is presenting us with an amendment that is exceedingly difficult to reject. It reminds me of that passage from the Godfather, 'I'll make him an offer he can't refuse.' "

Opponents argued that the Allen amendment was unnecessary because the United States could stop enemy ships at either the Pacific or Atlantic approaches to the canal, and if that could not be done, "then we cannot secure the canal anyway."

But Allen insisted that the amendment was necessary to provide for any contingency that might occur at the end of the century and that enemy ships or submarines might be carrying explosives to blow up the canal.

A motion by Church to table the amendment was approved 57-38. *(Vote 37, p. 8-S)*

Allen quickly followed up, proposing a new plan that in time of war the United States could intercept enemy warships sailing for the Panama Canal to prevent them from reaching the neutral waterway.

Opponents, who succeeded in tabling the amendment by a 60-34 vote, pointed out that the U.S. right to intercept enemy vessels on the high seas has nothing to do with the neutrality treaty but is anchored in international practice. *(Vote 38, p. 8-S)*

The Senate rejected three more amendments March 2 as treaty opponents drew their lowest tallies so far.

Treaty opponents drew a larger following when the Senate voted 52-40 March 6 to table an amendment by Allen preventing ships of nations at war with the United States from using the otherwise neutral canal. *(Vote 42, p. 9-S)*

Of the 19 publicly uncommitted senators listed in wire service polls who held the balance in final Senate voting on the treaties, 12 supported Allen's amendment, four voted against the senator and three were absent.

A variation of the tabled Allen amendment was offered by Ted Stevens (R Alaska) but it too was rejected on a 59-34 tabling motion March 8. *(Vote 44, p. 9-S)*

Unable to win a majority on any of the amendments to change language of the neutrality treaty, opponents March 6 unexpectedly agreed to a vote on that pact. The roll call was set for 4 p.m., March 16.

Passage of Neutrality Pact

By one more vote than the 67 needed, the Senate approved the neutrality treaty, 68-32. Following the dramatic roll call—all 100 senators voted at their desks, a rare scene in the chamber—the Senate began debate on the second treaty. *(Vote 66, p. 12-S)*

According to Majority Leader Byrd, treaty proponents had "three or four" votes in reserve that they could have called in if a 67th vote had been needed. One of these, Jennings Randolph (D W.Va.), who faced a tough re-election campaign in 1978, voted "nay" only after it was certain his vote was not required. (Of 26 senators running for re-election, 16 voted for the treaty and 10 against.)

The neutrality treaty vote came on the 22nd day of debate following a frantic last-minute administration lobbying effort. *(Box, p. 392)*

Alterations

The treaty (Exec N, 95th Congress) approved by the Senate—technically, it adopted a resolution of ratification—stated that Panama would keep the canal "secure and open to peaceful transit by vessels of all nations on terms of entire equality...."

But the administration agreed to accept two additions to the treaty. Based on the understanding reached by President Carter and Gen. Torrijos, in October 1977, these alterations gave the United States the right to defend the canal if it were threatened and granted "head of the line" passage privileges for U.S. ships during emergencies. *(Text of understanding, p. 384)*

Besides these changes, the administration accepted two major reservations as the price for winning crucial last minute votes. These reservations, unlike amendments, did not change the text of the treaty. But according to international legal scholars and the State Department, they could carry the same weight, provided Panama accepted the wording.

The administration, however, refused to budge on all amendments proposed by treaty opponents, fearing they would require a new plebiscite in Panama if added.

The two reservations would give the United States the right to work out an agreement with Panama in the future for basing U.S. troops there after Dec. 31, 1999, and also allow the United States to take military action "in Panama" to keep the canal open if it were closed or its operations interrupted. *(Details, below)*

Just before the final vote, the Senate tabled, 67-33, a proposal by Robert P. Griffin (R Mich.) to send the treaty back to the president for renegotiation. Frank Church (D Idaho), floor manager for the treaty, claimed the proposal would lead to war rather than the bargaining table. *(Vote 65, p. 12-S)*

Converts

Throughout the week, uncommitted senators announced which way they would vote on the neutrality treaty, but there were still enough holdouts to keep the outcome in mystery until the last few hours.

A major coup for the pro-treaty side came March 14 when Georgia Democrats Sam Nunn and Herman E.

Carter Sent the Heavy Artillery to Lobby for Treaty

President Carter threw virtually every high official of his administration and the nation's defense and foreign policy establishment into the fray in the final days before the vote on the Panama Canal neutrality treaty March 16, 1978.

The President courted reluctant senators from the White House with a heavy schedule of phone calls and Oval Office visits.

Among those personally lobbying senators were Vice President Walter F. Mondale, Secretary of State Cyrus R. Vance, Secretary of Defense Harold Brown, national security adviser Zbigniew Brzezinski, ambassador Ellsworth Bunker, Deputy Secretary of State Warren M. Christopher, top White House aide Hamilton Jordan and a large team of congressional liaison aides headed by Frank Moore.

The administration was so intent on presenting its arguments personally to wavering senators that any senator could see anyone in the administration upon request, a far cry from past complaints about administration aloofness. At least one senator, at his request, saw all four of the Joint Chiefs of Staff. The top military brass and Brown were consulted by many senators, reflecting concern about the impact of the canal transfer on national security.

But Mondale, as the only Senate veteran in the Carter administration and as the constitutional head of the Senate, was perhaps Carter's most important advocate. An administration lobbyist referred to Mondale as "a living symbol of the administration's concern over this issue," adding that his "personal clout" and his own interest in the canal debate were vital assets.

The late-hour strategy of high-level persuasion reflected a shift in the White House lobbying approach on the treaties.

For months the administration focused on shaping public opinion. The administration invited hundreds of "opinion leaders" to the White House for briefings. Those leaders were expected to help mold public opinion in favor of the treaties.

Administration officials claimed that public opinion had shifted dramatically toward support for the treaties. But some senators, including Edward W. Brooke (R Mass.) complained that the expected groundswell had not occurred.

Nevertheless, it was clear in the final two days of debate the White House did not have the needed 67 votes.

Thus a strategy of personal lobbying and a new flexibility in accepting substantive reservations to the treaties was necessary.

The final flurry of administration efforts to sell the treaties also produced a raft of rumors and press stories that the White House was offering non-treaty-related "deals" to senators. These stories were hotly denied by administration lobbyists. State Department congressional liaison Douglas J. Bennet Jr. stated, "I don't know of a single vote which has been decided by non-germane considerations."

Talmadge declared their support, albeit reluctant, for the agreements.

As reports swirled through Washington that Talmadge had endorsed the pacts in exchange for the administration's support on farm legislation — reports the Agriculture Committee chairman denied — Talmadge said that "had I been President Carter I would not have signed these treaties."

But the Senate now must make the best of this *fait accompli,* Talmadge said, because "we do not want to destroy the bargaining power or diplomatic credibility of the United States" by rejecting the pacts valued by Latin American nations.

Nunn echoed Talmadge's concern about the impact that rejection would have on the president's conduct of foreign policy. "I foresee more potential national security problems if we reject the treaties than if we ratify them," he said.

The administration also drew H. John Heinz III (R Pa.) March 14, who hinged his support on the treaties to passage of the Nunn/Talmadge reservation outlining the right of the United States to station troops in Panama if both governments agreed. *(Details, below)*

On March 15, Finance Committee Chairman Russell B. Long (D La.) joined the administration's side, telling the Senate that although his position probably did "not reflect the view of the majority of voters" of Louisiana, the United States' "moral leadership" overseas would be compromised if the treaties were rejected.

Dennis DeConcini (D Ariz.) also joined the treaty camp after meeting with President Carter March 15 and winning support for his reservation allowing the United States "to use military force in Panama" after the year 2000 to keep the canal open if it were closed for any reason.

Although the reservation would not change the text of the treaty, DeConcini said he had been assured by Carter, the State Department and legal scholars that his proposal "will be binding" on the two nations.

The treaty backers next added Edward W. Brooke (R Mass.) to their ranks, bringing the treaty vote count March 15 to 65, two votes short, according to leadership counts. The administration's 66th vote came the day of the vote when Henry Bellmon (R Okla.) announced his support for the treaty, a judgment he said he arrived at by "instinct and intuition."

Putting the treaty supporters over the top was Paul Hatfield (D Mont.) who succeeded Lee Metcalf (D Mont., 1961-1978), upon Metcalf's death earlier in 1978. Hatfield faced a tough primary campaign from liberal opposition. He hinged his vote on approval of the DeConcini reservation, making a winning vote on that measure critically important to the treaty backers.

The treaty supporters' 68th vote came from Howard W. Cannon (D Nev.) who, Laxalt said, would have voted with the opponents if he had been needed.

Nunn/Talmadge Reservation

Clearing the way for its sponsors to vote for the neutrality treaty, the Senate March 16 approved, 82-16, the Nunn/Talmadge reservation stating that provisions of the pact did not prevent the United States and Panama from working out an agreement for stationing U.S. forces in Panama after 1999.

(Article V of the neutrality treaty stated: "After the termination of the Panama Canal Treaty, only the Republic of Panama shall operate the canal and maintain military forces, defense sites and military installations within its national territory.")

Opponents claimed that the reservation was "meaningless" because it granted the United States no defense role in Panama after 1999, and in any event, there was no language in the neutrality treaty to prevent the two countries from negotiating a base agreement later.

"I cannot understand how anyone would change his vote by having this reservation adopted," scoffed Griffin.

Nunn defended the reservation as a step needed "in terms of the future possibility of base sites, in terms of the overall observation of third countries, and in terms of the future expectations of the Panamanian people." The measure, he added, would "put us in a little better position" if bases are needed in the future.

The Nunn/Talmadge reservation, sponsored by 13 other key senators, was worked out with the administration March 6-10 over a series of lunches at the Capitol after it became clear that the Georgia Democrats and others would not support the treaty without some alteration.

DeConcini Reservation

As the price for winning DeConcini's important vote, President Carter agreed to accept his reservation allowing the United States to use military force in Panama to reopen the canal.

But Panama reportedly was concerned about the reservation, specifically the words "in Panama." On the morning of the final vote, DeConcini told Carter when the president called to discuss the matter that the reservation was the key to his support of the neutrality treaty.

Carter then said the reservation was acceptable, according to DeConcini's account of his conversation with the president.

Before the Senate approved the reservation, 75-23, it rejected a motion to table the proposal, 13-86. An amendment by Allen, providing that DeConcini's reservation would have the same effect as an amendment to the treaty was tabled, 62-36, as a final attempt by treaty opponents to influence the pact's language. *(Votes 64, 62, 63, p. 12-S)*

Other Reservations/Understandings

By a 96-1 roll call, the Senate added another reservation March 15, by Randolph, providing that the two countries negotiate an agreement allowing the American Battle Monuments Commission to administer after 1999 the section of the Corozal Cemetery where U.S. citizens were buried. *(Vote 60, p. 11-S)*

Another reservation was approved by voice vote March 15. Drafted by Long, it called for full consideration of the effects of any toll increase on the trade patterns of the two nations before implementation.

Before the final vote March 16, the Senate took these actions not related to the DeConcini reservation:

- By a 60-37 vote, tabled a reservation proposed by Dewey F. Bartlett (R Okla.) requiring that before the instruments of ratification were exchanged between Panama and the United States, the president determine that Panama had ratified the treaty to comply with its constitution. *(Vote 61, p. 12-S)*
- By voice vote, agreed to H. John Heinz III (R Pa.) reservation requiring that the United States and Panama use revenues of the canal first for maintenance, security and operations.
- By voice vote, agreed to S. I. Hayakawa (R Calif.) reservation stating that either Panama or the United States could "take unilateral action to defend the canal against any threat as determined by the party taking the action."
- By voice vote agreed to an understanding by Church requiring the president to include in the instrument of ratification exchanged with Panama all amendments, reservations, understandings and declarations incorporated by the Senate in the resolution of ratification.
- By voice vote, agreed to an understanding by John H. Chafee (R R.I.) providing that the United States or Panama will determine when there is an emergency or need for its vessels to go to the head of the line at canal entrances.
- By voice vote, agreed to an understanding by Cranston for Brooke that the treaty doesn't obligate the United States to provide economic or military aid to Panama.

Other Amendments

Before approving the first leadership amendment, 84-5, giving the United States and Panama the right to defend the canal against threats to its security, the Senate March 10 tabled two amendments aimed at granting the United States a military role in Panama after 2000. *(Leadership amendment, vote 49, p. 10-S)*

These proposals were by:

- Jessie Helms, R-N.C., giving the United States and Panama the right to take whatever economic, diplomatic or military measures were necessary to defend the canal if it were threatened. Tabled, 58-27. *(Vote 47, p. 10-S)*

DeConcini Reservation

Following is the text of the reservation to the neutrality treaty sponsored by Dennis DeConcini (D Ariz.) and approved by the Senate 75-23 on March 16, 1978:

> ". . .[I]f the canal is closed, or its operations are interfered with, the United States of America and the Republic of Panama shall each independently have the right to take such steps as it deems necessary, in accordance with its constitutional processes, including the use of military force in Panama, to reopen the Canal or restore the operations of the Canal, as the case may be."

Yet the so-called leadership amendment approved by the Senate March 10 giving the United States and Panama the right to "defend the Canal against any threat to the regime of neutrality" contained this proviso:

> "This does not mean, nor shall it be interpreted as a right of intervention of the United States in the internal affairs of Panama. Any United States action will be directed at insuring that the Canal remain open, secure and accessible, and it shall never be directed against the territorial integrity or political independence of Panama."

- Allen, D-Ala., stating that any U.S. action to defend the canal provide that the canal remain open, secure and accessible. Tabled, 53-33. *(Vote 48, p. 10-S)*

The Senate tabled two additional proposals after the vote on the leadership amendment. Those were by:

- Robert Dole, R-Kan., providing that U.S. troops could remain in Panama until Dec. 31, 2009, if the United States and Panama failed to reach an agreement allowing U.S. troops to remain after the year 2000. Tabled, 50-34. *(Vote 50, p. 10-S)*
- Dole, providing that only Panama could maintain troops and military installations in that country "except as Panama and the United States might otherwise agree." Tabled, 45-37. *(Vote 51, p. 10-S)*

By an 85-3 vote, the Senate March 13 approved the second leadership amendment to the neutrality treaty. The addition gave warships of both Panama and the United States the right to go ahead of other ships waiting to transit the canal during emergencies. *(Vote 54, p. 10-S)*

Like the first leadership amendment approved March 10, this language grew out of the "statement of understanding" between Carter and Torrijos.

Three other amendments relating to this language were rejected, however.

Before taking up the resolution of ratification to the neutrality treaty, the Senate March 16 rejected other amendments to the treaty itself.

The first of these was by Allen to allow Panama and the United States to negotiate a later agreement for stationing U.S. troops in Panama after the year 2000. Identical to the language worked out between the White House, Nunn and other senators that was added to the resolution of ratification as a reservation, Allen's proposal was opposed by Majority Leader Byrd.

Any amendment to the treaty automatically opens it to renegotiation, whereas a reservation would not, Byrd said. This was the reason treaty backers had opposed all amendments offered to the neutrality pact. The proposal was tabled, 53-41. *(Vote 56, p. 11-S)*

Other amendments rejected were by:

- Strom Thurmond (R S.C.) authorizing the American Battle Monuments Commission to arrange for the removal of the remains of U.S. citizens from Mount Hope Cemetery, which is located in territory that will pass to Panamanian control upon ratification of the treaties, to the American sector of Corozal Cemetery located in territory that will remain under U.S. control until the year 2000. Tabled, 53-38. *(Vote 57, p. 11-S)*
- Harrison Schmitt (R N.M.) to place the canal under an international management and operating organization composed of Western Hemisphere nations. Tabled, 65-30. *(Vote 58, p. 11-S)*
- Stevens (R Alaska) to make Panama and the United States partners in operating the canal in the future. The amendment was tabled by voice vote.

Compromise Reservation

The language agreed to by Dennis DeConcini (D Ariz.), the Senate leadership and Panama relating to the limitation on U.S. military action in Panama is as follows:

> "Pursuant to its adherence to the principle of non-intervention, any action taken by the United States of America in the exercise of its rights to assure that the Panama Canal shall remain open, neutral, secure and accessible, pursuant to the provisions of this Treaty and the Neutrality Treaty and the resolutions of advice and consent thereto, shall be only for the purpose of assuring that the canal shall remain open, neutral, secure, and accessible, and shall not have as its purpose or be interpreted as a right of intervention in the internal affairs of the Republic of Panama or interference with its political independence or sovereign integrity."

Debate on Basic Treaty

With approval of the neutrality treaty, attention focused on the basic Panama Canal treaty. After defeating a crucial amendment of treaty opponents, the Senate April 5 agreed to hold the final vote on the Panama Canal treaty at 6 p.m. April 18.

Amendments to the pact that turned over the waterway to Panama on Dec. 31, 1999, could be offered by senators until April 13; afterwards debate would begin on the Senate resolution of ratification to which reservations and understandings could be added before the final vote.

Treaty opponents had been counting on at least 45 votes for a key amendment offered by Orrin G. Hatch (R Utah), requiring the House to approve the transfer of U.S. property to Panama before the treaties took effect.

Following the 58-37 vote to table that proposal, Majority Whip Alan Cranston (D Calif.) issued a statement saying that he was "much more confident about final approval of the second treaty." *(Vote 79, p. 15-S)*

But Hatch claimed that the defeat was actually a "victory" because his amendment had won more than the 34 votes needed by opponents to defeat the treaty itself. Treaty backers and some opponents as well discounted this reasoning, pointing out that votes on tabling motions had not been reliable for gauging the final vote on the neutrality treaty.

Hatch had argued that there were "no precedents" for the president to dispose of U.S. property without the House's consent. Opponents argued that the existence of congressional power (Article IV, section 3, clause 2 of the Constitution) to dispose of U.S. property does not preclude a treaty from doing that also.

The framers of the Constitution had been wise, said Strom Thurmond (R S.C.) in requiring both the Senate and House to transfer U.S. property, an assertion dismissed by Majority Leader Robert C. Byrd (D W.Va.). Adoption of the Hatch amendment, he said, "would upset the system of checks and balances of our government because it stands for the proposition that, wherever the Congress may legislate, the president and Senate can not act by treaty."

The Senate April 5 also rejected, 56-36, an amendment by James B. Allen (D Ala.), permitting U.S. citizens employed by the Panama Canal Company to retain their positions until they reached retirement age or resigned. *(Vote 80, p. 15-S)*

Problems Ahead

As the final vote April 18 on the Panama Canal treaty approached, the Senate leadership struggled to find its way over the most troublesome barrier raised thus far to ratification.

In the days following the Senate's approval of the neutrality treaty March 16, little seemed to stand in the way of a second success. But the outlook began to cloud after Panama circulated a letter at the United Nations complaining about the reservation added to the neutrality treaty that gave the United States authority to "use military force in Panama" if the canal were closed for any reason.

This coupled with angry complaints from Panamanian citizens, who found the reservation an anathema to the country's sovereignty, alarmed pro-treaty forces in the Senate who worked to persuade the reservation's sponsor, DeConcini, that some alteration or addition of language to the pending pact was needed to save the treaties. *(Reservation, box, p. 393)*

The problem was complex: to find a way to assure Panama that the reservation did not intend to give the United States the right to intervene in Panama's internal affairs — yet maintain the language that DeConcini had drafted, President Carter agreed to and the Senate approved March 16, 75-23.

How delicate the diplomatic maneuvering was surfaced April 10 when Frank Church (D Idaho), floor manager of the treaties, pleaded with the Senate to "find an appropriate way" to accommodate both Panamanian and U.S. interests over the canal.

DeConcini told the press that he was "optimistic" the dilemma could be resolved. "I am not trying to sink the treaties," he said. "My amendment was never intended to portray the right of the United States to intervene in the internal affairs of that country. My amendment does not use the word 'intervention.' "

What had happened, according to Church, was that Panama was raising objections "to an interpretation of the provision the Senate did not have in mind [intervention] — and in fact disclaimed — in discussing the provision."

Floor Amendments

As the Senate leadership and White House tried to find a way out of the DeConcini obstacle to ratification, debate continued on the floor, with treaty proponents successfully knocking down each new amendment proposed by the opposition. One of these, by Howard W. Cannon (D Nev.), who unexpectedly supported the neutrality treaty March 16, drew 42 votes, the largest total up to that point for an amendment not proposed by the leadership. *(Vote 91, p. 17-S)*

Cannon suggested that the $10-million earmarked in the Panama Canal treaty for police, fire and other public services by Panama be reduced to $5-million.

Cannon told the Senate that the Panama Canal Commission had estimated the annual cost would amount only to about $4.4-million. "Agreeing to a $5-million overpayment will not enhance our relations with Panama," he said.

But Church, who gently countered that this was an amendment on "which reasonable men and women might differ," quoted a $9.9-million figure that the United States now pays for these services. "It seems to me $10-million is not excessive," Church added, considering additional costs for training and start-up services.

An amendment by Robert Dole (R Kan.) offered April 10 was tabled by a 49-40 vote after opponents argued that the proposal to drop one article currently not in favor with either the United States or Panama be offered as a reservation to the resolution of ratification rather than the treaty itself. *(Vote 86, p. 16-S)*

The amendment proposed to remove the article preventing the United States from negotiating with another Latin American nation to build a new canal through its territory and barring Panama as well from contracting with another country to build a new canal across its land.

Passage of Basic Treaty

With the outcome in doubt until the last few hours, the Senate April 18 approved the Panama Canal Treaty by the identical 68-32 vote cast March 16 on the neutrality pact. *(Vote 119, p. 21-S)*

The second and final treaty gave Panama "full responsibility" for running the waterway on Dec. 31, 1999, but until then a joint Panamanian-U.S. commission will oversee the canal's operations. The neutrality treaty agreed to earlier gave the two countries the permanent right to defend the canal and assure that their ships can "go to the head of the line" during emergencies.

But a reservation added to the basic treaty before the final vote stated that any action the United States might take to keep the canal "open, neutral, secure and accessible" did not give the United States the right to intervene in Panama's internal affairs. Panama had insisted upon such a statement after the Senate in March added the DeConcini reservation to the neutrality treaty permitting the United States to "use military force in Panama" to reopen the canal if it were closed for any reason.

Although this issue was the major obstacle facing the treaty leadership during the 38 days of debate that began Feb. 8, the controversy was resolved a day before the final vote. Keeping the Senate, press and public in suspense the last 24 hours were three other senators, who had voted for the neutrality pact, but who later were troubled by the second treaty and other unrelated matters.

"I thought it would be 68-32," one more than the constitutional requirement, said Majority Whip Cranston, "but not until the last hour did it become apparent that we would win. Last night [April 17] I was rather gloomy."

Unlike the March 16 vote, "we had no votes to spare [to call out if needed] this time," said Majority Leader Byrd.

At the White House, President Carter, who had stressed that his ability to conduct the nation's foreign relations would be damaged if the treaties were rejected, told the public: "This is a day of which Americans can always feel proud; for now we have reminded the world and ourselves of the things that we stand for as a nation."

Carter's statement was the positive side of the arguments made by floor manager Church just before the historic roll call. "A vote against this treaty represents a vain attempt to preserve the past," he declared. "It represents a futile effort to perpetuate an American colony in Panama against the wishes of the Panamanian people...."

Yet treaty opponent Robert P. Griffin (R Mich.) insisted to the last that the United States was taking "serious risks" by approving the treaties since, he said, too many issues between the two governments remained unresolved.

Under the terms of a reservation to the treaty approved by the Senate April 17, the instruments of ratification could be exchanged by Panama and the United States at any time, although they would not be "effective earlier than March 31, 1979." And the treaties themselves would not actually take effect until Oct. 1, 1979, unless Congress approved implementing legislation before March 31, 1979.

This legislation, which must be passed by both the House and Senate, and dealt with U.S. employee pensions, the new commission and similar matters, was not expected to be considered until 1979, according to the State Department. And because much of the legislation related to personnel matters of Americans working in the Canal Zone, it was not expected to draw too much controversy.

'A Difficult Decison'

Although the Senate vote was crucial to the White House and the course of U.S. foreign policy, participants in the struggle were crediting the Senate leadership for making the difference between success and defeat. The results, said opponent Paul Laxalt (R Nev.), were achieved "entirely by the effectiveness of the Senate leadership."

Both Majority Leader Byrd and Minority Leader Howard H. Baker Jr. (R Tenn.) "showed tremendous leadership," according to Paul S. Sarbanes (D Md.), one of the treaty's floor managers. When the pro-treaty forces faced the defection by a number of liberal senators outraged by the reservation allowing the United States to use military force in Panama without qualification, it was Byrd and his bipartisan team that worked independently of the White House and State Department to turn this sentiment around. The Carter team monitored the Panamanian positions during this period.

But Sarbanes and others saw those senators who faced election in 1978 as equally critical to the outcome. "Any senator who was up this year was making a difficult decision," he said. When Byrd was asked whether those who voted for the treaties would lose in November, he paused a long while before replying: "People will come around." As it turned out, 16 of the 29 senators running for reelection cast votes for the agreements despite a well orchestrated campaign by conservative organizations aimed at the candidates.

On the final roll call, 22 Republicans and 10 Democrats voted against the treaty; four of the Democrats were from the North, six from the South.

DeConcini Compromise

On the eve of the final vote, the Senate leadership reached its compromise with DeConcini that added the new reservation to the pact assuring Panama that the United States would not intervene in the "internal affairs of Panama" or interfere with "its political independence or sovereign integrity" in the course of keeping the canal open, neutral and secure. *(Box, p. 394)*

The language was approved by a 73-27 vote April 18 after the Senate first rejected a motion to table the compromise, 21-79. *(Votes 114, 116, pp. 20-S, 21-S)*

During the first week of April, Panama's acceptance of the treaties appeared in doubt after the country circulated a letter at the United Nations complaining about the DeConcini reservation. Although President Carter had agreed to the DeConcini reservation as a price for winning the senator's vote on the first treaty, it was not known at the time that Panama found the provision unacceptable. Appearing on "Face the Nation" April 16, Senate Minority Leader Baker said that he was "not advised of the acute concerns that the Panamanians apparently had about the DeConcini amendment until well after the fact.

"As a matter of fact," he added, "the first time I heard about it [Panamanian reaction] was when they posted the letter with member states of the United Nations...."

The problem facing the Senate leadership was to find a way to assure Panama that the reservation did not violate U.S. non-intervention principles while at the same time maintaining DeConcini's wording giving the United States the right to use military force if necessary to reopen the canal if it were closed for any reason. Negotiations with DeConcini were handled by the Senate leadership alone after the Carter administration failed to come up with language that did not alter the thrust of the senator's reservation.

The leadership had worked, Byrd later recounted, "to develop language that would not be directed at the DeConcini reservation but at the same time would enunciate non-intervention principles."

On Sunday, April 16, Byrd and floor managers Church and Sarbanes met with Panamanian Ambassador Gabriel Lewis and Deputy Secretary of State Warren Christopher to present the compromise text. The Senate leaders were informed later in the day that the Panamanian government considered the compromise a "dignified solution to a difficult problem," according to Byrd. The next day, DeConcini agreed to the proposal, telling reporters that he was "very satisfied" with the compromise since it does not "do any violence" to his initial reservation.

The Senate also approved two other DeConcini reservations before the final vote. These were a proposal, accepted by a voice vote, guaranteeing that the United States could act alone in defending the canal during the life of the Panama Canal Treaty, and another reservation, adopted by a 92-6 vote, providing that a maximum annual $10-million payment to Panama from any surplus canal revenues would not accumulate from one year to the next. *(Vote 109, p. 20-S)*

Reaching the agreement with DeConcini and Panama had been the "biggest problem" during debate on the treaties, Byrd said after the vote, but there were other troubles in the last few days, although "lesser in degree." These were to make sure that Howard W. Cannon (D Nev.), James Abourezk (D S.D.) and S. I. Hayakawa (R Calif.) did not carry out threats to vote against the second treaty.

Key Senators

Hayakawa had added to the leadership's troubles by announcing April 14 that he was "reconsidering" his position on the treaties because of the president's recent policy decisions on the neutron bomb, strategic arms limitation talks and other matters that make us "look like a weak nation."

Keeping the Senate in suspense until the final roll call, Hayakawa had met with President Carter, who the senator said promised to consult with him on a regular basis before foreign policy decisions were made. They "made clear to him that the United States was not in retreat," said Cranston.

Abourezk, meanwhile, was upset about an issue unrelated to the treaties: he threatened April 13 to withhold his support for the second pact if the House and Senate energy conferees and the administration continued to meet behind closed doors on energy and natural gas deregulation issues. The last senator to speak before the final vote, Abourezk said that he had "learned" from the White House "that they intend to try to encourage an open democratic process" on the energy negotiations, making it possible for him to vote for the treaty. Later Cranston told reporters that he did not think "any specific promises" had been made to Abourezk, who was planning to retire in 1978.

To win Cannon's vote again this time — he had unexpectedly voted for the neutrality pact — the Senate leaders agreed to support his reservation assuring that interest payments by the Panama Canal Commission on initial U.S. investments in the canal continue for the life of the treaty unless Congress voted otherwise. The proposal, Cannon said, would save the U.S. Treasury about $505-million, according to the General Accounting Office.

Following that reservation's approval by a 90-10 vote, Bill Scott (R Va.) said that it was "disgusting" the leadership was accepting reservations offered April 17-18 "in an effort to placate some of the senators and obtain some votes." *(Vote 118, p. 21-S)*

But Church had argued that the Cannon reservation was acceptable because it gave Congress the final say on whether or not to waive the interest payments.

Other Actions

Besides the reservations resulting from the DeConcini and Cannon negotiations, the Senate approved other additions to the resolution of ratification April 17-18.

A reservation by Russell B. Long (D La.), allowing Panama and the United States to waive their treaty rights giving each the authority to block the other from contracting with third countries for building a new canal was approved April 17, 65-27. Similar language had been proposed by Dole April 10 as an amendment to the treaty itself, but Long said he opposed that approach because it was "objectionable to Panama" and "simply unnecessary" because the treaty allows the two countries to reach new agreements on the matter. *(Vote 99, p. 19-S)*

Floor manager Church accepted the new language as necessary to draw support from Long and others on the final vote. By approving the reservation, "I can not see how the cause could possibly be hindered, but I can plainly see how it could be enhanced," said Church.

By a 90-2 vote, the Senate also approved a reservation by Ernest F. Hollings (D S.C.), providing that the treaty could not obligate the United States to pay Panama any carry over balance in 1999 resulting from the accumulation of annual funds (up to $10-million) available to Panama from toll surpluses not required to cover operating expenses. *(Vote 100, p. 19-S)*

Despite State Department and White House assurances that the United States would not be obligated for an accumulated balance, Hollings said the treaty debate had proven it was best to be "specific now and settle the matter during the ratification process" so there would be no difference of interpretation later.

By an 84-3 vote, the Senate approved a reservation by Edward W. Brooke (R Mass.), providing that the United States and Panama agree to what public services Panama will provide relating to canal operations for which it will receive $10-million annually from the new canal commission. *(Vote 103, p. 19-S)*

By the same vote, another Brooke reservation was accepted, providing that the exchange of instruments of ratification between the two governments not be effective before March 31, 1979, and that the treaties not take effect until Oct. 1, 1979, unless implementing legislation was enacted before March 31, 1979. Brooke said that the "relatively long period of time" between the decision to ratify and the effective date was needed for full consideration of the implementing legislation. The Senate schedule, he said, indicates that the measures could not receive the needed "in-depth attention" in 1978. *(Vote 102, p. 19-S)*

A third reservation offered by Brooke and approved by voice vote stated that the United States was not obligated to provide Panama any foreign assistance because of the treaties.

Among other actions, the Senate agreed to the following understandings by voice vote April 17:

- By John C. Danforth (R Mo.), providing that nothing in the treaty limit U.S. authority through the Panama Canal Commission to incur expenses and make decisions needed for operating and maintaining the canal.
- By Sarbanes providing that any agreement between the two nations relating to prisoner exchanges be concluded in observance of the constitutional process of each country.
- By Sarbanes providing that the president include in the instrument of ratification all amendments, reservations, understandings and declarations incorporated by the Senate in the resolution of ratification.

On the last day of debate, the Senate rejected 10 other proposals offered by treaty opponents. A last attempt by Griffin to send the treaties back to President Carter for renegotiation was turned down, 64-36. To adopt Griffin's proposal, said Church, would not send the treaties back to the negotiating table but rather would produce "deadlock and defiance" between Panama and the United States. ∎

Export-Import Bank

What started out as a non-controversial measure extending the authority of the Export-Import Bank through September 1983 and increasing its loan ceiling to $40 billion from $25 billion almost became the victim of other foreign policy issues and a "Christmas tree" on which a colorful assortment of extraneous legislative ornaments were hung. However, in the end, Congress agreed to a simple extension of the bank's authority by adding the measure to an unrelated bill.

The action came when Congress Oct. 15 cleared HR 14279, a multipurpose financial institutions regulation bill (PL 95-630). *(Financial institutions bill, p. 300)*

The Export-Import Bank extension and related provisions had been contained in House- and Senate-passed bills, but these (HR 12157, S 3077) were abandoned in the final days of the 95th Congress following veto threats by the Carter administration. During Senate debate on S 3077 Sept. 28, a provision barring consideration of cuts in U.S. duties on textiles at international trade negotiations was adopted despite protests from the White House.

However, the textile provisions were added to another bill (HR 9937) that Congress later passed but Carter pocket vetoed. *(Story, p. 279)*

In addition to the textile tariff plan, the Senate-passed measure contained, among other things, authorization for construction of Locks and Dam 26 on the Mississippi River, an extension of the life of the Select Committee on Indian Affairs and an amendment opposing any decision by the president to use the threat of administrative actions to enforce wage and price controls. *(Locks and Dam story, p. 513)*

On the House side, the bill became entangled in controversy over whether to impose trade curbs on South Africa and as well as whether to prohibit the bank from making loans to countries violating human rights.

To salvage the bank extension, House and Senate Banking committee leaders decided to add only non-controversial Ex-Im provisions to HR 14279. This action meant scrapping a number of provisions — besides the textile matter — approved by the Senate Sept. 28. However, language relating to South Africa was retained in the final version of the bill.

Established in 1934, the Export-Import Bank not only makes loans, but provides loan guarantees and insurance to cover overseas political and commercial risks on behalf of American exporters.

Although the bank's commitments are backed by the U.S. government, the bank is self-supporting, extending loans to overseas purchasers on competitive credit terms to encourage them to buy American-made products. It pays dividends of $50 million a year to the Treasury and has never required appropriations from Congress. Because of the United States' two-year string of foreign trade deficits, export promotion as well as a reduction in oil imports was considered essential to reversing this trend.

Provisions

As cleared by Congress, HR 14279:

- Increased to $100 million from $60 million any bank transaction that must be submitted to Congress for review; authorized bank approval after congressional review of 35 calendar days, if either house adjourns for 10 days or more.
- Extended the life of the Export-Import Bank from Dec. 31, 1978, through Sept. 30, 1983, and boosted its loan authority to $40 billion, from $25 billion, in total commitments the bank may have outstanding at any one time, and authorized an increase in the ceiling for loan guarantees and insurance to $25 billion from $20 billion.
- Required the bank to name an officer to encourage exports of non-nuclear energy resources and report annually to Congress on those activities.
- Requested the president to begin international negotiations to end predatory export financing and subsidization practices and to report by Jan. 15, 1979.
- Authorized the bank to provide insurance, guarantees and credit at rates competitive with those provided by export agencies of other governments.
- Stated that the bank shall supplement but not compete with private capital and the programs of the Commodity Credit Corporation to ensure that adequate financing will be available for exporting agricultural products.
- Required the bank to consult with the secretary of agriculture before making a loan, taking into consideration the importance of agricultural commodity exports to the United States and the nation's balance of trade in deciding whether or not to provide assistance.
- Directed the bank to consider whether the aid it provided would have the effect of subsidizing competition with U.S. industries. Required the International Trade Commission to furnish a report assessing the impact of the bank's activities on U.S. industries and employment.
- Authorized the secretary of the treasury to use the Export-Import Bank to counter predatory foreign official financing practices in the United States. If authorized by the Treasury, permitted the bank to provide financing to match that offered by a foreign export program.
- Required the president to report to Congress on international efforts to reach environmental agreements before imposing unilateral environmental review requirements on nuclear exports.
- Prevented the bank from extending credit for any export that would contribute to the South African government's maintaining or enforcing apartheid; for any export to that government unless the president determined that significant progress toward the elimination of apartheid has been made and transmits to Congress a statement describing and explaining that determination; for any export to other purchasers in South Africa unless the secretary of state certified that the purchaser had endorsed and proceeded to adopt the following principles: a) non-segregation of races in all work facilities; b) equal and fair employment for all employees; c) equal pay for equal work for all employees; d) initiation and development of training programs to prepare non-white South Africans for supervisory, technical and clerical jobs; e) increasing the number of whites in management and supervisory positions; f) a willingness to engage in collective bargaining with labor unions; and improving the quality of life for employees.

House Committee Action

In its May 4 report on HR 12157 (H Rept 95-1115), the House Banking Committee said that it was convinced an increase in the bank's financial authority would make U.S. firms more competitive overseas and increase exports significantly. Exporters often are at a disadvantage because Japan, France and other major competing nations offer more liberal government-backed financing, the committee said. For every $1 billion in exports, economists estimate, between 35,000 and 58,000 jobs are created.

But the committee suggested that the bank had been too conservative in its loan policies. By increasing the credit ceiling and encouraging the bank "to become aggressive," Congress can send a signal that U.S. exporters will become "more vigorous and competitive," the committee said.

The American share of the international market has been declining, the committee report said; in 1977, the United States sold 13.2 percent of the world's exports, but that share has declined to 12.7 percent, partly because of the continuing world recession but also a result of the intense competition in international trade.

The committee added a controversial provision, sponsored by Paul E. Tsongas, D-Mass., prohibiting the bank from participating in any transaction in South Africa "until significant progress toward the elimination of apartheid had been determined by the president."

As reported by the committee, HR 12157 also:

- Extended the Export-Import Bank's authority for five years, through September 1983.
- Increased its financial commitment authority to $40 billion, from $25 billion, and authorized a $25 billion ceiling for loan guarantees and insurance.
- Gave the bank permission to approve certain loans after 35 days when Congress was not in session, thus reducing the delay in the existing 25-day legislative period caused by adjournments longer than 10 days.
- Required that all spending authority of the bank be effective for each fiscal year beginning Oct. 1, 1978, to be consistent with current congressional budget procedures.
- Required the Treasury Department, the bank and other relevant government agencies to begin negotiations with the finance ministers of major exporting nations to end predatory export financing programs in foreign markets and the United States.

- Required the bank to give emphasis to aiding new and small businesses in the agricultural export market.

House Floor Action

The House debated HR 12157 June 1 and 2, but delayed finishing because of work on other legislative business. The July 27 passage vote was 314-47. *(Vote 535, p. 152-H)*

A principal issue during floor debate was over aid for companies dealing with South Africa. In the end, the House replaced tough committee-approved language with a milder substitute.

That substitute, sponsored by Thomas B. Evans Jr., R-Del., allowed the bank to make credit available to companies in South Africa if the secretary of state certified that the purchaser had complied with a code of ethics requiring equal and fair employment for all employees and conformed to various other standards.

Tsongas went along with Evans' substitute after headcounts showed that the stronger wording he had sponsored in committee would not survive on the floor.

Evans and others argued that the committee language would result in the loss of jobs for blacks working for American companies in South Africa and that the Export-Import Bank, in any case, was not established to serve U.S. foreign policy interests but rather to promote U.S. trade. "If American companies withdraw from South Africa," Evans said, "severe economic problems will result and South African blacks will be the first to suffer."

Tsongas argued that rejection of the stronger committee language would give the impression overseas that "deep down the Congress feels that economics is more important than the principle of racial equality."

After the Evans amendment was approved by voice vote, the House rejected, 116-219, an amendment by John M. Ashbrook, R-Ohio, to delete the new language. Ashbrook said that he found it "incredible" that Africa would be singled out for trade sanctions while another committee-reported provision exempted the People's Republic of China from a requirement that the president agree before the bank conducts business in a communist country. *(Vote 344, p. 98-H)*

"What we have here is a classic case of liberal doublethink," said Ashbrook.

Later, however, the House dropped the committee-approved China exemption, approving an amendment by Charles A. Vanik, D-Ohio, to delete the language, 179-138. *(Vote 345, p. 98-H)*

During debate July 27, the House adopted two non-controversial amendments on voice votes. They were by:

- Matthew J. Rinaldo, R-N.J., to prohibit the bank from participating in financial transactions with a country aiding international terrorists.
- Clarence D. Long, D-Md., to require the appointment of an officer to the bank's board of directors for advising on exports of goods and services to be used in the development, production and distribution of non-nuclear natural resources.

Before completing work on the bill, however, the House rejected amendments by:

- Long, to prohibit the bank from providing loans to produce any commodity unless the president certified that it was not in surplus in the United States and its importation would not injure U.S. firms and employees producing the same or a competing commodity. Rejected 197-199. *(Vote 531, p. 152-H)*

Debate on the amendment focused mainly on whether Ex-Im Bank credits cost American jobs, particularly in the steel industry. (Long represents a suburban Baltimore district in which Bethlehem Steel Corp. plants and other steel company facilities are located.)

Long argued that jobs in the U.S. steel industry are being lost as a result of "vast imports" of steel from developing nations. He said the Ex-Im Bank shouldn't "subsidize" new plants in these countries. Opponents, led by Stephen L. Neal, D-N.C., replied that developing nations would get steel plants built anyway, with help from other industrialized nations if necessary. As a result, Neal said, "all we do is lose . . . jobs and profits" that construction of steel plants by U.S. firms in those countries would produce.

- Tom Harkin, D-Iowa, to prohibit the bank from making loans to countries which the secretary of state determined grossly violate internationally recognized human rights. Rejected 103-286 *(Vote 532, p. 152-H)*

Harkin had gotten similar language added to House bills in previous years. And in February, the House had accepted a Harkin-offered human rights amendment to International Monetary Fund legislation. *(See p. 424)* But on the Ex-Im bank legislation, the Harkin amendment was opposed by a majority of both parties.

Harkin noted that the bill had a human rights provision aimed at one country — South Africa. He said the legislation should cover other nations, as well.

But opponents argued that existing law applying to the bank already contained language which required that human rights actions by countries "be taken into account" before Ex-Im Bank assistance is made available to companies. Opponents also argued that barring Ex-Im Bank aid wouldn't have any impact on some nations, but would reduce American exports and sacrifice jobs.

Opponents cited a letter from Secretary of State Cyrus R. Vance saying that President Carter opposed the Harkin amendment.

- Garry Brown, R-Mich., to prohibit the bank from extending credit to purchasers of exports if the secretary of state certified they did not endorse fair and equal employment principles. Rejected 90-288. *(Vote 533, p. 152-H)*

- John J. Cavanaugh, D-Neb., to require the bank to submit to Congress an evaluation of the nuclear safety standards in effect in nations to which the bank makes loans for the sale of nuclear reactors. Rejected 106-266. *(Vote 534, p. 152-H)*

Provisions. As passed by the House, HR 12157 contained the provisions of the bill as reported plus the Rinaldo and Long amendments and the human rights amendment directed at South Africa that was approved by the House June 2.

Senate Committee Action

The Senate Banking Committee May 15 reported S 3077 (S Rept 95-844) extending the life of the Export-Import Bank through 1983 and boosting its loan authority to $40 billion total commitments the bank may have outstanding at any time.

Environmental Issue. The committee also took an environmental policy action that kicked up trouble with the

Environment Committee, where the measure, at its request, was referred and reported out July 26 (S Rept 95-1039).

The point of controversy was language that would exempt the bank from National Environmental Policy Act (NEPA) impact statement requirements. But the Environment Committee voted unanimously to delete this section from the bill. "Given the complexity of the issue, it would be inappropriate to legislate further in the absence of a concrete proposal by the administration and without additional hearings," that panel said in its report.

But the Banking Committee took the view that its action "will encourage Congress to accept its responsibility to settle the controversy through legislation."

At issue was the narrow legal question of whether NEPA was intended to have application overseas and the basic question of how to integrate U.S. policy, commercial and environmental interests.

Other Provisions. Besides the bank extension and the environmental exemption, the Banking Committee bill contained these provisions:

- Increased to $100 million from $60 million any bank transaction that must be submitted to Congress for review; authorized bank approval after congressional review of 35 calendar days, if either house adjourns for 10 days or more.
- Required the president to determine and send Congress a list of nations eligible to receive bank-supported exports.
- Required the bank to name an officer to encourage exports of non-nuclear energy resources and report annually to Congress on those activities.
- Requested the president to begin international negotiations to end predatory export financing and subsidization practices.

Senate Floor Action

The bill to extend the life of the bank went to the Senate floor Sept. 29. After three days of debate, numerous amendments had been added that threatened to topple the entire measure.

Textiles. The day the Senate began work on the Export-Import Bank bill, Sept. 29, five amendments were approved, one of them the controversial textile tariff plan.

By voice vote, the Senate approved an Ernest F. Hollings, D-S.C., amendment to prohibit the reduction or elimination of U.S. import duties on textiles and textile products during the current Tokyo round of international trade negotiations. The Senate first voted 21-56 against tabling the amendment. *(Vote 427, p. 63-S)*

After the votes, Adlai E. Stevenson III, D-Ill., the bill's floor manager, announced that he had received a message from the president's special trade representative, Robert Strauss, that he would recommend a veto of the bill containing the provision.

Hollings and other sponsors argued that the textile industry was in terrible shape, running a trade deficit of about $5.2 billion annually. Unemployment, they said, stood at the 331,000 level.

"At the Tokyo round of tariff negotiations we do not want to cut another vein while we are hemorrhaging in this fashion," said Hollings.

Opponents stressed that the trade negotiations should not be required to exempt specific products from global international trade problems. "We would be foolish," said Abraham Ribicoff, D-Conn., "to risk losing all the work and all the possible benefits of an improved international trading system just because one sector wants to be treated differently from any other sector of our economy."

Indian Committee. By voice vote, the Senate Sept. 29 also approved an amendment by James Abourezk, D-S.D., to extend the life of the Select Committee on Indian Affairs for two years, through Jan. 2, 1981. A motion to table was first rejected, 28-55. *(Vote 426, p. 63-S)*

Foreign Service Retirements. On another voice vote, the Senate Sept. 29 accepted a proposal by Daniel K. Inouye, D-Hawaii, repealing a provision in the fiscal 1979 State Department authorization bill (HR 12598) permitting Foreign Service Officers to retire at pension levels based on their highest pay year rather than the traditional three-year average. Inouye said the president might veto the bill if this provision were not altered. *(State Department authorization, p. 411)*

Ex-Im Blacklisting Nations. The Senate Sept. 29 by voice vote accepted an amendment by Stevenson revising committee language relating to nations eligible for bank loans. The Stevenson amendment required the president to maintain a list of those countries ineligible for bank credits, thus establishing "the presumption that all foreign countries are eligible for the bank's credit program unless the national interest requires exclusion." The committee bill required the president to keep a list of eligible nations.

However, this so-called "blacklisting" provision action was reversed on Oct. 2. The Senate that day by a 45-35 roll call approved an amendment by John H. Chafee, R-R.I., simply allowing the president to deny Export-Import credits to countries that harbor terrorists or violate human rights. *(Vote 431, p. 64-S)*

Subsidizing Competition. The Senate Sept. 29 also accepted by voice vote an amendment by Jesse Helms, R-N.C., directing the bank to consider whether the aid it provided would have the effect of subsidizing competition with U.S. industries.

Locks and Dam 26. On Saturday, Sept. 30, the Senate approved by voice vote an amendment by Stevenson to authorize the Army Corps of Engineers to replace Locks and Dam 26, on the Mississippi River at Alton, Ill. The public works project was controversial because it was the sweetener in S 790, the bill to impose fees for barges using inland waterways built with federal funds. *(Waterway user fees, p. 413)*

Predatory Foreign Financing. Another Stevenson amendment relating to the bank was approved by voice vote Sept. 30. It authorized the secretary of the treasury to use the Export-Import Bank to counter predatory foreign official financing practices in the United States.

Wage-Price Controls. H. John Heinz III, R-Pa., also offered an amendment, approved by voice vote, Sept. 30 expressing the sense of the Senate that it oppose any decision by the president to use the threat of administrative actions to enforce wage and price controls.

Nuclear Exports. A second amendment by Heinz Sept. 30 requiring the president to report to Congress on international efforts to reach environmental agreements before imposing unilateral environmental review requirements on nuclear exports was approved by voice vote.

Final Action

When it became clear that the future of the Ex-Im Bank might be imperiled by unrelated issues, the House and Senate Banking committee leaders decided to abandon work on HR 12157 and S 3077 and to add the non-controversial provisions of the bank bill to HR 14209.

Besides dropping the textile measure, they dropped the provision relating to Locks and Dam 26. This issue, however, was resolved in another bill relating to bingo games.

Also dropped was the foreign service retirement amendment, which was tacked onto H J Res 1139, the continuing appropriations bill. *(Story, p. 161)*

And the amendment to extend the life of the Select Committee on Indian Affairs for two years was removed and considered in S Res 405. S Res 405 was passed around 1:30 a.m. Oct. 15 as part of a deal involving an airport noise bill.

A final controversial Senate provision exemption Export-Import Bank projects from National Environmental Policy Act impact statements was put aside.

HR 14279 was approved by the Senate Oct. 12, sent to the House, which added its language relating to bank loans to South Africa Oct. 14, and returned later to the Senate for a final vote. That came in the early hours of Oct. 15 by voice vote, but only after backers — including a House member — persuaded senators not to load up the measure with unrelated amendments that probably would have killed it in the adjournment rush.

The president signed the bill Nov. 10.

Foreign Economic Aid: $1.8 Billion

A $1.8 billion U.S. bilateral aid program for agriculture, health, education and development assistance overseas was approved by Congress Sept. 20 and sent to the White House.

The final bill (HR 12222 — PL 95-424) was routine, although the Senate and House had started work in 1978 to revamp the U.S. foreign aid program. Among the goals had been a plan to restructure the U.S. economic aid program so that it reached the world's poorest nations. Also intended had been a proposal to shift security assistance funds from the annual military aid bill to economic aid legislation because of the non-defense nature of the account, most of which was allocated to Israel and Egypt. *(Military assistance bill, p. 416)*

Most controversial was a proposal to establish a new international development administration to take over economic aid programs run by the State and Treasury departments and the Agency for International Development (AID). *(Box, p. 402)*

But these legislative revisions were put aside in 1978 after the Senate Foreign Relations Committee found its schedule filed by debate over the Panama Canal. The House, however, went ahead with some of these changes, including establishing the new economic aid account. But the conference on the legislation put these revisions aside, recommending they be considered in 1979.

The conference bill totaled $1,795,000,000 — $38.1 million less than authorized by the House, $49.4 million more than approved by the Senate and $43.5 million less than requested.

That total was the amount remaining after a 5 percent across-the-board cut — $93.2 million — was made to the legislation, except provisions for U.S. American schools and hospitals overseas. The House had also excluded agriculture and rural development programs; the Senate approved an across-the-board 5 percent cut.

The bill also included Senate language barring U.S. aid to Vietnam, Cuba and Uganda, but not House provisions prohibiting indirect U.S. aid through international lending institutions or trade with these nations.

Provisions

As signed into law, HR 12222 authorized the following amounts for fiscal 1979:

	Budget Request	Conference Amount
Bilateral Development Aid		
Agriculture/Nutrition	$ 673,200,000	$ 665,200,000
Population Planning	205,400,000	224,800,000
Health	148,500,000	148,500,000
Education/Human Resources	109,000,000	109,000,000
Development Activities/Other	126,200,000	126,200,000
American Schools/Hospitals Abroad	8,000,000	25,000,000
International Organizations	282,200,000	285,500,000
Assembly on Aging	0	1,000,000
Disaster Aid	25,000,000	25,000,000
Locust Control	0	2,000,000
African Refugees	0	15,000,000
Operating Expenses (AID)	261,000,000	261,000,000
Subtotal	$1,838,500,000	$1,888,200,000
Reduction*	0	93,200,000
Total	$1,838,500,000	$1,795,000,000

** 5 percent overall cut as required by the Senate version, except for the exemption for American schools and hospitals abroad as provided in the House bill.*

The bill also:

- Required the president to report to Congress by Feb. 1, 1979, on why food assistance provided under the PL 480 program to the developing nations is not more successful in meeting the needs of those suffering from hunger and malnutrition, along with recommendations to increase the effectiveness of food aid.
- Stated that greater effort must be made in carrying out foreign aid programs to award contracts by competitive selection procedures. Required reports on contracts let in excess of $100,000 between April 1, 1978, and Sept. 30, 1978, without competitive procedures.
- Required a report to be submitted to Congress by Feb. 1 annually on the effectiveness of the U.S. foreign assistance program.
- Prohibited use of funds for aid to Vietnam, Cambodia, Uganda or Cuba.
- Stated that it was desirable to supplement the resources of private and voluntary organizations with public funding for development activities overseas.
- Provided that aid to the least developed countries should be on a grant basis.

Humphrey Aid Plan

Legislation that would place most U.S. foreign aid programs under a new organizational tent close to the White House was introduced Jan. 25 by key members of the Senate Foreign Relations Committee in memory of Sen. Hubert H. Humphrey, D-Minn., who died Jan. 13. But because of its three-month work on the Panama Canal treaties, the committee postponed consideration of the proposals until the 96th Congress.

The bill (S 2420) would establish an International Development Cooperative Administration to take over economic aid programs run by the State and Treasury department and the Agency for International Development (AID).

The new administration's director would report directly to the president, a plan Humphrey had envisioned for raising foreign aid's political profile. The existing AID bureaucracy was a component of the State Department, operating under executive rather than statutory authority.

The Foreign Relations' plan also would transfer the Peace Corps from ACTION, where it was placed by the Nixon administration, to a new institute planned to coordinate volunteer aid programs. The corps, however, would maintain its existing administrative autonomy.

Besides these changes, the new bill would eliminate old sections of the basic 1961 Foreign Assistance Act that had become obsolete and redundant.

The Foreign Relations Committee proposal would remove the bilateral assistance programs from AID ($1.3 billion in outlays budgeted for fiscal 1979), take the contributions ($3.5 billion) channeled by the Treasury Department to the World Bank and other lending institutions for overseas aid and put these programs in the new development administration.

Development and relief aspects of the PL 480 Food for Peace program, which were coordinated by AID, as well as voluntary U.S. contributions to United Nations agencies, also would be folded into the new administration. It would distribute the aid as well as coordinate policy.

The new legislation also proposed the establishment of an international development institute, another component of the new aid administration, that could fund private and public volunteer organizations, including the Peace Corps, which assist Third and Fourth World nations.

The idea here was to set up a "funding window" so that the volunteer groups that need funds quickly for special development projects would not be required to go through normal bureaucratic channels.

The Foreign Relations Committee also recommended that the security assistance program for the Middle East, budgeted at $1.9 billion in new authority for fiscal 1979, be directed to the "greatest possible degree" at basic development problems of the recipients.

These and other countries could be helped by a U.S. aid program that stressed four principal goals, according to the committee bill:

- Alleviation of the "worst physical manifestations of poverty" among the world's poor nations.
- Promotion of conditions that will enable developing nations to achieve "self-sustaining growth with equitable distribution of benefits."
- Encouragement of development programs in which civil and economic rights are respected and enhanced
- Integration of the developing countries into an open and equitable international economic system.

- Established an international disaster assistance fund with authorization for appropriations of "such amounts as may be necessary."
- Required the president to report by Feb. 1, 1979, on steps he has taken to review proposals for an African Development Foundation.
- Required the secretary of state to report to Congress on a proposal to revise the debts owed the United States by a foreign government, at least 30 days before the revision took effect.

House Action

Committee

Reported by the International Relations Committee April 25 by voice vote, HR 12222 (H Rept 95-1087) authorized $3.7 billion for economic aid programs in fiscal 1979. About a third of the assistance was for food, health and education programs ("New Directions") established by Congress in 1973 to assist the world's poorest nations. *(Background, 1977 Almanac p. 360; Congress and the Nation, Vol. IV p. 851)*

Half of the $3.7 billion was earmarked for Israel, Egypt and other Middle East nations which the United States has aided extensively in recent years to encourage peace efforts in the region.

The Middle East funds, however, were included in this legislation for the first time, a shift from their placement in annual military aid bills authorizing U.S. grant aid and weapons credits.

The committee set up a new category for Middle East assistance — an economic support fund — because the aid was channeled into economic development projects, "not military hardware or services." Yet the program stemmed from "political and security considerations related to U.S. foreign policy interests," the committee said.

In other actions, the committee adopted a number of features proposed by Sen. Hubert H. Humphrey, D-Minn. (1949-64, 1971-78), to update the U.S. foreign assistance program, organization and administration. *(Box, above)*

The Humphrey plan called for streamlining existing aid programs to assure that U.S. assistance reached the poorest majorities intended by the 1973 bill.

Most controversial of Humphrey's proposals was the intention to establish a new international development cooperative administration to take over economic aid programs now run by the State and Treasury Departments and the Agency for International Development (AID).

The committee, however, stopped short of approving the reorganization envisioned by Humphrey, adopting instead a provision that "gives a green light" for the president to establish a new development administration, replacing AID, that would coordinate U.S. foreign assistance programs.

The committee said that it had been informed by the executive branch that most of the reorganization proposed by Humphrey could be undertaken by executive orders without additional legislation. The panel wrote that it was advised that the president had decided a new foreign economic aid program should include these features:

- Creation of a new agency that replaces AID and includes "some foreign assistance functions" now performed by other agencies.
- Designation of the administrator of the agency as the principal adviser to the president on development policies and programs. "He will also be the executive branch's chief spokesman to the Congress," the report said.
- Placement of the Peace Corps and the Overseas Private Investment Corporation within the new agency; establishment of a new institute within the agency to support private voluntary organizations and the Peace Corps which assist poor countries, and provision that the agency have "substantial autonomy from the State Department, including having the new agency submit its budget directly to the president."
- Continuation of U.S. Treasury supervision of "U.S. relations with the multilateral development banks while strengthened coordinating mechanisms are tested in the coming year."

It was this last administration decision that differed most substantially with the Humphrey proposal. He had insisted that the Treasury's authority for channeling U.S. aid to the World Bank and other international financial institutions become part of the new agency. Humphrey also had proposed that the new agency be independent of the State Department.

Floor Action

The House May 15 approved a $3.6 billion fiscal 1979 foreign economic aid bill after cutting $153 million from the measure recommended by the International Relations Committee. *(Vote 266, p. 76-H)*

This reduction — a 5 percent, across-the-board cut in all U.S. economic assistance programs in the bill except for food aid and funds for U.S. schools and hospitals abroad — came on an amendment offered by Robert E. Bauman, R-Md. It was approved, 200-172. *(Vote 265, p. 76-H)*

Considering "all the questions about waste and mismanagement" in the aid program, this bill is one that should be cut, Bauman said, insisting that his approach could not be called a "meat axe approach" suggested by the amendment's opponents since food aid programs were exempted from the reduction.

But International Relations Committee Chairman Clement J. Zablocki, D-Wis., pointed out that the bulk of the cut would come from the $1.5 billion economic aid fund in the bill for aiding Israel, Egypt and other nations with important political and security considerations related to U.S. foreign policy interests.

Israel stood to lose $39.3 million if the amendment survived conference committee action. Israel's share of the economic fund, considered in military aid bills until 1978, was set by the committee at $785 million.

The House began work on the bill May 11 approving three amendments. These were by:

- James M. Jeffords, R-Vt., to encourage the use of solar energy technology in Latin American housing guaranty programs. Approved by voice vote.
- Claude Pepper, D-Fla., authorizing $1 million for U.S. contributions to the U.N. World Assembly on Aging. Voice.
- Robert E. Bauman, R-Md., clarifying that none of the funds for international organizations and programs will be used to support "military" activities of the Southwest African Peoples Organization. Voice.

Taking up the bill again May 12, but delaying a final vote until May 15 because of the absence of members, the House approved by voice vote an amendment by John M. Ashbrook, R-Ohio, banning the use of any funds in the bill for direct or indirect aid to Vietnam, Uganda, Cambodia or Cuba. Edward J. Derwinski, R-Ill., sought to soften the amendment by limiting it to direct aid, rather than the "indirect" U.S. funds contributed to the United Nations and other international organizations. His proposal was rejected 148-155. Carter May 11 said he opposed the Ashbrook amendment. *(Vote 263, p. 76-H)*

In other actions, the House approved these amendments by:

- Lester L. Wolff, D-N.Y., prohibiting any funds to be used for aid to the Palestine Liberation Organization. Approved by voice vote.
- John Buchanan, R-Ala., adding $10 million to the bill for aid to Cyprus. Voice vote.
- Bauman, prohibiting economic assistance to Angola, Mozambique, Tanzania or Zambia unless the president determined the aid would further the foreign policy interests of the United States, and he waived the prohibition. Voice.
- Clarence E. Miller, R-Ohio, requiring the president to annually report steps taken to implement a 1974 statute requiring the president, when he determined it was in the national interest, to extend economic and military aid to a country that agrees to exchange raw materials. Voice.
- Robert H. Michel, R-Ill., requiring the secretary of state to include all foreign countries in annual reports on the status of human rights around the world. Voice.
- Tom Hagedorn, R-Minn., requiring the secretary of agriculture to report on the policies of countries receiving U.S. aid funds which are disincentives to agricultural production. Voice.
- David R. Obey, D-Wis., establishing a unified personnel system for all employees of the Agency for International Development. Voice.

Senate Action

Committee

The Senate Foreign Relations Committee reported its bill May 15 (S 3074 — S Rept 95-840). The bill authorized appropriations totaling $1,860,504,000 for fiscal year 1979. The committee bill did not include the $1.8 billion economic support fund contained in the House-passed version.

In its report, the committee noted that only three days of hearings had been held on the bill due to the time consumed by debate on the Panama Canal treaties. Consequently, the report said, "the time spent on the treaties had precluded the careful consideration required for a new initiative in foreign assistance.... The committee plans to give consideration next year to additional changes in foreign assistance policy and the government's machinery for policy implementation."

Floor Action

The Senate passed its version of the House bill (HR 12222) on June 26 by a 49-30 vote. *(Vote 177, p. 30-S)*

Prior to that, the Senate approved by a 57-22 vote a 5 percent cut in the bill. *(Vote 175, p. 29-S)*

Sponsored by Harry F. Byrd Jr., Ind-Va., the cut reduced the total authorization in the bill as approved May 15, by the Senate Foreign Relations Committee by about $93 million.

Unlike a related reduction made by the House, however, the Appropriations Committees under Byrd's proposal would be permitted to decide what foreign assistance programs for food, health, population planning and other activities to cut and by how much.

The House version required a cut of 5 percent in each of the foreign development aid categories, with the exception of food and nutrition programs and aid to overseas American schools.

Byrd said that even with the $93 million reduction, the bill still would authorize $274 million more than was appropriated for foreign aid in fiscal 1978.

"There has to be a halt somewhere," Byrd told the Senate during floor debate. "There has to be some reasonable control over the continued increase in government expenditures.... What the proposal does is restrain the tremendous increase in expenditures being proposed by the . . . committee."

Defending his committee's recommendations, ranking Republican Clifford P. Case, R-N.J., acknowledged that it was the Senate's "duty to listen closely to the cries of alarm by American taxpayers," but senators, he said, "ought to resist the temptation to attack our foreign aid program with a meat axe because it might seem politically expedient in the short run to do so."

In 1977 the Senate on a 28-45 procedural vote in effect refused to endorse a similar 5 percent House reduction in the fiscal 1978 foreign aid appropriations bill. Subsequently, the House position was watered down in conference. *(1977 Almanac p. 293)*

Another controversy that had its roots in the fiscal 1978 bill was embodied in an amendment by Jesse Helms, R-N.C., approved 75-4, prohibiting U.S. aid to nations violating human rights. *(Vote 176, p. 29-S)*

The amendment singled out Vietnam, Cambodia, Uganda and Cuba.

In 1978, the Senate had refused to accept a House provision barring indirect aid — loans made through the World Bank and other international lending institutions — to those nations after bank officials warned that no contributions could be accepted from any country that attached political strings to its donations. *(1977 Almanac p. 286)*

The 1977 controversy was resolved by congressional approval of compromise language requiring U.S. officials at the international banks to oppose any loans to these countries.

The House had revived the issue May 12, 1978, when it approved the Ashbrook amendment barring indirect U.S. aid to the countries mentioned in Helms' amendment.

Helms' amendment had originally contained a phrase barring "direct or indirect" assistance to the four countries. But the phrase was withdrawn after objections to it were voiced by the bill's floor leaders.

In addition to the Byrd and Helms amendments, the Senate approved 12 other proposals, all by voice votes, before passing HR 12222.

All non-controversial, these amendments were offered by:

- Clifford P. Case, R-N.J., to make clear that earmarking of funds ($42.5 million) for the United Nations Relief and Works Agency for Palestine Refugees was for fiscal year 1979.
- Herman E. Talmadge, D-Ga., to require a study by the president of how the U.S. Food for Peace program (PL 480) could be more effectively used to meet the needs of the poor in developing nations.
- Richard S. Schweiker, R-Pa., to instruct U.S. representatives to the United Nations to promote funding of technical assistance for developing countries through the U.N. development program.
- John Sparkman, D-Ala., to establish more precise reporting requirements to congressional authorizing and appropriating committees of Congress for proposed changes in loans and debts to foreign governments where approval of such modifications have not been written into appropriations bills.
- Edward M. Kennedy, D-Mass., to separate the authorizations in the bill for population assistance and health assistance by creating a new section on health and disease prevention.
- Kennedy, to earmark $2 million in the bill for aid to disadvantaged children and orphans in Asia, and making minor changes in the Immigration and Nationality Act relating to adoptions of foreign-born children by U.S. citizens.
- Kennedy, to establish an International Disaster Assistance Fund to allow the United States to provide assistance quickly during an international disaster.
- Case, to authorize $2 million to assist in controlling the locust plague in Africa.
- Dennis DeConcini, D-Ariz., to prohibit use of any funds in the bill for contributions to the United Nations University.
- Helms, to require the Agency for International Development to report on the extent that any foreign loan, grant or credit is likely to have an adverse effect on U.S. employment.
- Case, to require the president to report on steps taken to establish an African Development Foundation.
- Helms, to bar funds in the bill to any nation that allows, permits, supports, or harbors any terrorist groups within its territory.

Conference Report

Senate-House conferees on the economic aid authorization bill filed a report (H Rept 95-1545) Sept. 7 resolving the following major differences:

Conferees adopted a Senate policy statement — the House bill contained no comparable language — supporting an increase in development assistance activities by private and voluntary organizations, "without compromising their private and independent nature," and declaring the desirability of supporting these resources with public funding for development projects.

A House provision authorizing the president to use not less than $1.5 million in development aid for human rights programs was accepted by the conferees.

Conferees also approved a Senate provision providing that aid to the least developed nations should be on a grant basis.

A proposal by the Senate to establish an international disaster assistance fund with authorization of "such funds as may be necessary" was approved by the conferees. The House had authorized $25 million in disaster relief for fiscal 1979.

A House provision authorizing $15 million for aiding African refugees was accepted, though not requested or provided by the Senate.

Conferees agreed to a Senate proposal requesting the president to report by Feb. 1, 1979, on steps he has taken to review proposals for an African Development Foundation.

A 5 percent cut in funds in the bill except for American schools and hospitals abroad was approved. The House had also excluded agriculture and rural development programs; the Senate approved an across-the-board 5 percent cut.

A Senate prohibition on any direct U.S. aid to Vietnam, Cambodia, Uganda or Cuba was accepted by the conferees, but not House language also barring indirect U.S. aid through international banks and loans funds to these countries.

Conferees adopted a Senate provision requiring the secretary of state to send the Foreign Relations Committee, International Relations Committee and Appropriations Committees any proposed agreements that would alter the terms of foreign debts owed the United States at least 30 days before the effective date.

Final Action

The House approved the conference report to the bill Sept. 19 by voice vote, and the Senate accepted the report the following day, also by voice vote, completing congressional action on the measure.

The president signed the bill into law Oct. 6, 1978 (PL 95-424).

Congress Backs Jet Sales to Arabs

Congress in early 1978 backed President Carter's decision to sell $4.8 billion worth of military aircraft to Saudi Arabia, Israel and, for the first time, Egypt.

The proposed sale of America's most sophisticated jet fighter to Saudi Arabia set off a major battle between the large and influential community of Israel's supporters in the United States, and persons — including administration officials — who argued that American policy in the Mideast must be more evenhanded.

In the end the latter group won as Congress refused to block the sale of the planes to any of the three nations. However, the fight principally was over the sale to Saudi Arabia. Few persons in the debate objected to selling Israel more planes, and the aircraft set to go to Egypt was an older type considered a less significant element in the Mideast arms balance.

Carter's victory came May 15 when the Senate voted 44-54 to turn down a resolution of disapproval (S Con Res 86) of the sales. *(Vote 161, p. 27-S)*

This ended the matter because both houses must pass the resolution for it to be effective. As a result, the House never voted on the issue even though opposition to the sales was high in that chamber.

The sales that President Carter proposed to Congress were:

- For Israel, 15 F-15s, sophisticated long-range fighters to add to the 25 previously ordered. The new contract amounted to $480 million. Israel also ordered 150 F-16s, less sophisticated fighter/bombers, but only half were approved for $1.5 billion.
- For Egypt 50 F-5Es, short-range fighter/bombers that were priced at $400 million for the shipment.
- For Saudi Arabia, 60 F-15s costing $2.5 billion.

Carter announced the proposed sales Feb. 14, 1978, but agreed not to give Congress formal notice of the sales until after the Senate disposed of the Panama Canal treaties. *(Story, p. 379)*

Following approval of those treaties, Carter sent the sales contracts to Congress on April 28. Under military sales laws revised in 1976, Congress had 30 days to reject a proposed sale by passing a resolution of disapproval.

In a statement Feb. 14 announcing the sales, Secretary of State Cyrus R. Vance said they were "directly supportive of our overall objectives in the Middle East," that they would help meet each country's security requirements and "will not alter the basic military balance in the region." The sale, Vance added, "will be consistent with the overriding objective of a just and lasting peace."

Although drawing less criticism than the proposed sales to Egypt and Saudi Arabia, the Israeli package was defended by the State Department on the grounds that it would enable Israel to plan for the continued modernization of its air force. "Our commitment to Israel's security has been and remains firm," Vance said.

"Egypt, too, must have reasonable assurance of its ability to defend itself if it is to continue the peace negotiations with confidence," the secretary of state added.

The sale to Cairo marked the first U.S. sale of weapons to that country in two decades. And the sale to Saudi Arabia was the first transfer to that country of the hottest U.S. fighter plane. Equally significant, the proposed sale to Israel was about half the number of planes requested.

The administration's premise was that Saudi Arabia and Egypt had exercised a moderating influence on the Arab side of the Middle East conflict. This was more likely to continue and to affect other Arab states if the United States demonstrated its concern for the security of those countries by providing necessary defense equipment—according to this argument.

Opponents of the sale, prominent among them the American-Israel Public Affairs Committee (AIPAC), argued that U.S. arms sales to the two Arab states simply would feed Arab confidence that they could turn to military measures if Israel resisted their demands. Conversely, the shift in attitude of the United States, long Israel's arsenal against the Russian-supplied Arabs, could only heighten Israel's insecurity and make it less willing to compromise.

Basic policy — not military minutiae — was at issue. But much of the debate also focused on the impact of the sales on the Middle East military balance.

Impact of Sales on Middle East Military Balance...

It is difficult to assess the impact of the sales on the Middle East military balance because the planes are inherently capable of performing a wide variety of combat missions.

How Much? How Far? To use any of the planes as bombers, a country must give up some of the plane's theoretical range. The weight and aerodynamic drag of bombs hung under the plane's wings increases fuel consumption. And the racks from which the bombs are hung could otherwise have been used for extra fuel tanks.

For instance, carrying no bombs, the F-5Es offered to Egypt can fly about 670 miles and return to base. Carrying about 1,000 pounds of bombs, this radius is reduced to 570 miles. Carrying a near-full load of 5,000 pounds the F-5E can reach only about 140 miles.

Even for a given mission, a plane's radius of action can vary. Planners must reduce the range to allow for the fuel-gulping evasive maneuvers necessary in combat. On the other hand, a nation can extend the range of its planes almost indefinitely by mid-air refueling from tanker planes.

In mid-1978 Saudi Arabia had four tankers and Israel reportedly had converted used jetliners into tankers. All three of the planes in the sale package were designed for mid-air refueling, but the necessary plumbing will be omitted from the exported planes.

Optional Equipment. What can be added on to a plane may be as important as what is built into it. And add-ons may be harder for the United States to control.

For instance, as built for the U.S. Air Force, an F-15 can carry only one bomb from each of its three underwing attachments (called "hardpoints"). But the manufacturer has built an adapter (called a "multiple ejection rack") that can carry six bombs from each hardpoint. There is considerable controversy over how easily Israel could duplicate these adapters or whether the Arab states could purchase copies from Soviet or European sources.

F-15

For about $17 million a copy the Saudis and Israelis are being offered what is widely regarded as the world's finest fighter plane. Theoretically able to fly 2,000 mph, the F-15 has climbed seven miles within a minute of take-off.

The plane's radar, which can spot targets more than 50 miles away or flying at tree-top height, guides its four Sparrow missiles which can reach targets 20 miles away. For dogfights at close range, the plane carries a 20 mm cannon and four Sidewinder missiles that home in on a target's heat emissions. A highly accurate computer gunsight projects onto a teleprompter-like screen (called a "heads-up display") so the pilot can read it without taking his eyes off the target.

For a fighter mission (hunting other planes) the F-15's range has been reported as up to 900 miles. But over shorter ranges, the plane could also carry 15,000 pounds of bombs. And the computer gunsight turns out to be an extremely accurate bombsight as well.

The Saudis have insisted that they do not plan to use the plane as a bomber. And the U.S. Air Force has told Congress that the plane would be wasted in that role. The F-16 can carry the same bombload over the same distance at half the pricetag. And while the F-15's radar can map ground targets, the F-16's is more accurate, having been designed for the purpose. Furthermore, in dense, turbulent air close to the ground, the F-15's big wings would bounce the plane around, cancelling some of the gunsight's accuracy.

The plane is designed for quick maintenance. Either engine can be replaced in 20 minutes. The mass of elec-

Background

Four Arab-Israeli wars, along with interim clashes and inter-Arab feuding, have sparked one of the world's most intense arms races. Since the quadrupling of oil prices that began during the 1973 war, Middle Eastern countries have found the means to purchase vast new arsenals of the most modern weapons. Western governments, anxious to pay for the costly oil, have plunged into the Middle East arms market with gusto. None has pursued the sale of weapons in the region with more enthusiasm and success than the United States.

In 1974, the Middle East took 57 percent of all arms exported. And the figure has steadily risen since then.

The Middle East accounts for the bulk of the steep rise in U.S. arms sales. From total sales of less than $1 billion in 1970, sales had jumped nearly ninefold by fiscal 1974, to a total of more than $8 billion. In the past few years sales have hovered around $9- $10 billion. During the years 1973 through 1976 Iran alone purchased $10.9 billion, Saudi Arabia $7.8 billion and Israel $4.4 billion—all from the United States. France and England also have cashed in on the booming arms trade. The Arab countries have also decided to attempt to produce some arms themselves. Money for Egyptian arms purchases and capital investments has been provided largely by Saudi Arabia, Kuwait and smaller Persian Gulf states.

The Egyptians began complaining that the Soviets were dragging their feet in resupplying them with weapons lost during the 1973 war. Then as relations between Egypt and the Kremlin worsened. Egyptian President Anwar Sadat began looking to the West. He had hoped to find the United States willing to supply Egypt with defensive arms, but until 1978, only a few cargo airplanes had been approved. Yet the Egyptian Ambassador to the United States, Ashraf Ghorbal, stated in a May 1977 interview that "If you are going to play ... a very effective role, politically and economically, you must also help militarily."

U.S. Aid to Israel

U.S. military assistance to Israel entered a new phase after the 1973 war. Prior to that time, all U.S. assistance to Israel had been on either a cash sale or credit basis. But because of the magnitude of Israel's needs and the heavy toll the war had taken on the Israeli economy, the United States agreed to provide for the first time outright grants of military aid.

...Could Vary Depending on How Planes Are Used

tronic gear is modularized: If a module fails, it is identified by built-in equipment and the ground crew simply replaces the module — there is no need to diagnose and repair the fault in the module.

F-16

According to Air Force testimony, the F-16, which was designed as a dogfighter, would be about the equal of the F-15 in close combat because of its agility and small size (about half as big as an F-15).

The F-15's chief advantage would be its long-range radar missiles that could destroy the F-16 from beyond the smaller plane's reach. The F-16's radar can search out to 50 miles and can detect very low-flying planes, but it cannot guide radar-controlled missiles (although the necessary additional equipment is available from the radar manufacturer).

The F-16 uses one engine of the type used in the F-15. For a fighter mission, it has a lower top speed (about 1,600 mph) and about the same range as the F-15. But it is half as expensive — about $7 million a copy.

Because the bombing mission was built into the plane's design, it can carry about 10,000 pounds of bombs for a greater range than the F-15. And its radar can pick out smaller ground targets more accurately.

F-5E

Designed expressly for export to U.S. allies, the F-5E combines respectable performance — about 1,000 mph top speed — with low cost and ease of maintenance. Its agility and small size make it a natural dogfighter and it is armed with cannon and Sidewinders. It has a small radar of about 20 miles range and, theoretically, can fly missions out to 650 miles.

Saudi Arabia and Jordan in 1978 had about 150 of the planes.

In recent years, the U.S. Air Force has used squadrons of F-5Es to mimic Russian Mig 21s in training exercises with front-line U.S. planes. Reportedly, the little planes have been surprisingly successful but this could be misleading — the exercises have been conducted under ground rules that stack the deck against the more advanced U.S. planes.

Mirage F-1 and Other Weapons

If the Saudis were denied the F-15 they were likely to buy Mirage F-1s from France. In mid-1978 Egypt, Libya and Morocco already had (or reportedly had ordered) about 130 of these planes which can fly faster than the F-16 and can carry up to 9,000 pounds of bombs.

Opponents of the sales to Egypt and Saudi Arabia cite press reports that France and Egypt have agreed to build an F-1 production line in Egypt. But the State Department has insisted that both governments have denied this.

Arab forces also had in mid-1978 about 130 Mirage III and Mirage V jets that usually carry about 2,000 pounds of bombs. They had about 200 Russian-built Sukhoi 7s that can carry 5,500 pounds of bombs for short distances and about 25 Sukhoi 20s that can carry 11,000 pounds.

The core of Israel's bomb-carrying capacity rested with its U.S.-built planes. These were 200 F-4 Phantoms that carry about 16,000 pounds each and 235 A-4 Skyhawks that carry about 10,000 pounds each. Israel also had about 30 Mirage IIIs and about 100 Israeli-built Kafirs, which are a much improved version of the Mirage III.

President Nixon Oct. 19, 1973, called on Congress to approve his request for $2.2 billion in military aid to Israel in order "to prevent the emergence of a substantial imbalance resulting from a large-scale resupply of Syria and Egypt by the Soviet Union." The U.S. decision to resupply Israel triggered the Arab oil embargo, but this did not deter the United States.

Of Israel's $2.5 billion aid request in 1975, $1.6 billion was to be for military assistance. The State Department held up the request to Congress during the "reassessment" period pending Middle East developments, but requested the aid in September in the wake of the new Sinai accord. Israel received in fiscal 1975 about $1.5 billion in military assistance aid and $740 million in economic assistance. In 1976 Israel received about the same amount of economic assistance but only $1 billion in military credits, half to be forgiven and the other half financed through special loans.

By 1975 Israel's armaments were substantially in excess of what she had when the Yom Kippur war had broken out just two years earlier, from 1,700 to 2,700 tanks and from 308 combat aircraft to 486. Both the Arab and Israeli sides were clearly competing in a massive arms race, one which continued in 1977 and 1978 notwithstanding the constant talk of peace in the area.

This overwhelming U.S. support for Israeli arms assistance was in marked contrast to U.S. policy of less than a decade earlier. The United States, anxious to line up Arab allies in the cold war and to preserve its oil interests in that area, had been reluctant to supply Israel with weapons in the 1950s and early 1960s. *(1977 military aid, 1977 Almanac p. 363)*

The Military Balance

The prevailing assumption in the executive branch in 1978 was that most of Israel's military equipment was superior to most Arab equipment.

What Do They Have? U.S.-built Phantom and Skyhawk jets, which make up the bulk of the Israeli air force, carry many times the bombloads of most Arab planes over greater ranges. The U.S.-built electronic gear that is intended to blind enemy radars is assumed to be a match for the Soviet-built antiaircraft missiles in Arab arsenals.

Moreover, Israel has a substantial domestic arms industry which manufactures locally designed fighter planes, tanks and artillery that are superior to most of what the Arabs can buy from other countries.

Opponents of U.S. sales to the Arabs warned that Israel's qualitative superiority was fading. With their new oil wealth, the Arab states were beginning to buy sophisticated equipment instead of the hand-me-downs with which they once made do. For instance, by summer of 1977 Arab states had in stock or on order about 150 Russian Mig 23s and about 130 French mirage F-1s with much greater bomb loads and range than older Arab planes.

Already facing a substantial numerical inferiority, Israel cannot afford any erosion of its qualitative edge, according to this argument. To stay a jump ahead of modernizing Arab forces over a long haul would impose a crushing burden on the Israeli economy. It might even erode U.S. support for that country if Congress wearied of ever increasing military aid requests.

How Good Are They? The basic judgment of the executive branch agencies was that the Israeli military is far more effective than its Arab opposition on a man-for-man basis. Better training, more combat experience and a more widespread familiarity with modern technology are cited to explain Israeli advantage.

Not only is it assumed that Israeli pilots could outfly their Arab counterparts, but a similar disparity is assumed between the maintenance crews on the two sides. So a much higher proportion of the Israeli planes would be ready to fly if war broke out and they could fly more missions in a day than could the Arab aircraft.

This margin of superiority has been increasing, according to the State Department, because Egypt — by far the largest of Israel's potential foes — has curtailed its training exercises for want of spare parts for its equipment.

But former U.S. intelligence officials challenged this estimate in 1977 in testimony before the Senate Foreign Relations Subcommittee on the Near East and South Asia. The assumption was merely a political rationalization for decisions to pare down Israel's requests for military assistance, according to retired Air Force intelligence chief Maj. Gen. George Keegan.

"The Arabs are training, and they are training well," warned Dr, Joseph Churba, formerly the Air Force's senior Middle East intelligence analyst. "It was proven in the 1973 war that they are quite capable for handling sophisticated military technology if trained well." Churba resigned late in 1976 to protest allegedly anti-Israeli statements by Joint Chiefs of Staff Chairman Gen. George S. Brown.

What's the Bottom Line? "Israel has now, and will retain well into the 1980s, a substantial margin of military superiority — especially air superiority," according to a March 21, 1978, State Department letter to Rep. Gerry E. Studds, D-Mass.

In his May 1977 testimony to the Senate panel, Churba summarized the U.S. intelligence estimate at the time of his resignation late in 1976: "In the worst-case scenario — that is, a war simultaneously breaking out on several fronts — with a Soviet airlift [to the Arabs] and in the absence of an American airlift [to Israel] the Israelis would be able to defeat the combination of Arab armies in a period of one to three weeks, sustaining higher casualties the longer hostilities continue."

But Keegan insisted that this estimate assumed that Israel would continue to perform "miracles on the battlefield" in the face of mounting odds. "One failure in warning, one failure or delay in mobilization, and a number of small failures on strategy and tactics...at the outset of a war can mean the end of the Israeli state," he warned.

Reaction to Proposed Sale

When they were sent to Congress by the president on April 28, the contracts appeared headed for relatively smooth sailing, particularly after administration officials bowed to congressional procedural concerns and backed off earlier insistence that the sales be considered together as a package and that all three deals would be canceled if congressional supporters of Israel blocked the sale to either Arab state.

The main obstacle in the president's delicately constructed $4.8 billion sales plan were contracts for 60 sophisticated F-15 interceptors ordered by Saudi Arabia at $17 million per copy. Considered the world's finest fighter, the aircraft was feared by Israel and its allies in Washington who argued passionately that its sale to Saudi Arabia would alter the Middle East military balance and give the Arab state a dangerous offensive capability.

But the Carter administration defended the sale on the parallel arguments that the plane's primary mission was for defense and that Saudi Arabia needed the 2,000-mph fighter to repel any potential invader, such as Soviet-supplied Iraq. The White House and State Department also noted Saudi Arabia's influence in setting oil prices and regulating supplies.

The day the contracts were sent to the Hill, Vance indicated it would be up to the president to decide whether the sales to Israel and Egypt would go through if the Saudi planes were turned down. Senate Majority Leader Robert C. Byrd, D-W.Va., the following day said the chances for approval of all the sales improved with the administration's decision, as Byrd put it, to "drop the semantic buzz words 'all or nothing package' " insisted on after the contracts were first announced Feb. 14.

But on May 1, 22 of the 37 members of the House International Relations Committee introduced a bluntly-worded resolution disapproving the "proposed package of sales of aircraft" to the three nations. The measure, said one sponsor, Stephen J. Solarz, D-N.Y., "conclusively shows that there are votes to defeat the administration's proposed arms package in the absence of any effort on the part of the administration to reach a compromise."

The position taken by Israeli supporters in opposing the three sales appeared to contradict statements by Israeli Foreign Minister Moshe Dayan and other Jewish leaders who had told U.S. government officials that if the issue came down to the wire, Israel would rather have all the sales go through rather than see Carter reject its order in reaction to adverse congressional action on the Saudi contracts.

Senate Committee Action

The Carter administration's Mideast arms sales plan headed onto the Senate floor May 15, after withstanding a Foreign Relations Committee move May 11 to cancel the contracts.

White House offers to increase the number of sophisticated F-15s for Israel and Pentagon assurances that Saudi Arabia would use its F-15s only for defensive missions were outlined before the Senate committee tied 8-8 on a resolution to disapprove the sales — a victory for President Carter and the Arab states, an upset for the Israeli lobby. *(Details, below)*

Before the vote in the tension-filled committee room, Senate Minority Leader Howard H. Baker Jr., R-Tenn., a panel member, said he had "hoped we could avoid what we are about to do" by negotiation and accommodation with the sales opponents.

Justification

State and Defense Department officials outlined during May 1 Foreign Relations Committee hearings the reasons they believed the Saudi sales were no threat to Israel. But Sen. Frank Church, D-Idaho, holding a McDonnell-Douglas brochure advertising the ordnance available for the F-15, noted that the aircraft has an "immense offensive capability."

"Puffery," replied Secretary of Defense Harold Brown, "is not unknown in the sale of aircraft." The plane's reputation is based on its defensive capabilities, he said. Other Pentagon witnesses argued that it would be "folly" for the Saudis to launch an air strike against Israel, requiring penetration of the "densest air defense in the world."

Brown listed three principal reasons why the F-15 was no military threat to Israel: Saudi Arabia is "well aware of its military limitations" matched against Israel and will not receive its first deliveries until 1981; an attack on Israel would lead to almost certain destruction of the Saudi F-15 force; Saudi Arabia as a nation has never sought confrontation in Middle East conflicts.

But critics of the sale argued that Israel could not take the risk that such a potent weapon will not be used against it, so in case of another regional war, Israel might feel compelled to attack the F-15s at Saudi bases.

Or the Saudis, foreseeing such an Israeli decision, might feel compelled to join an Arab attack, regardless of its own wishes. "There would be pressure on Saudi Arabia to use planes against Israel in war, even if it didn't want to," Dr. Nadav Safran of Harvard University told the Foreign Relations Committee May 4.

In either case, the mere presence of the F-15s in Saudi Arabia could drag the kingdom into war, according to opponents of the sale.

Committee Procedure

Ordinarily the Foreign Relations Committee's vote would have ended the panel's role in the controversy, but to keep control over the issue, members took one additional step May 11 to assure that the Saudi contracts alone were not called up for a vote on the floor.

In order to spare that kind of embarrassing nation-by-nation "popularity contest," as one member put it, the committee voted to report to the floor the resolution (S Con Res 86) of disapproval "without a recommendation."

That action allowed the committee to control the floor debate, and because its resolution was privileged, non-Foreign Relations Committee members were not able to call up other resolutions aimed at specific contracts.

"It's wise now to package these contracts as the administration packaged them," said Church. This move was agreeable to both sides in the controversy and was approved unanimously.

Before voting, committee members anguished over what course the panel and the United States should take on the issue. Despite their divisions, members repeatedly stressed that they could understand how others might come down on the opposite side because the controversy was complicated by so many factors: Middle East peace negotiations, the president's promises to reduce U.S. weapons sales worldwide — a commitment spelled out on May 19, 1977 — and the legitimate defense needs of Saudi Arabia.

Supporters of the three contracts stressed four major themes, including the Soviet presence in Syria, Iraq, Afghanistan and the Horn of Africa. Saudi Arabia "is surrounded by radical states," said Charles H. Percy, R-Ill., who faced re-election in 1978 and was lobbied heavily by Israel's supporters to oppose the sales package.

This side also maintained that the Arab state had given the Carter administration unprecedented assurances on how the aircraft would be used. If the contracts were rejected, the country would turn to France for supplies, and from Israel's standpoint, such a decision would be far worse, they said, because the United States would have no control over how the planes were deployed.

The administration's opponents argued that it was simply the "wrong time" for the sales to be proposed. The Middle East peace negotiations should be allowed a chance, they said, and if that didn't work out, new contracts could be considered at some future time. These senators also complained that Carter had departed from his arms reduction pledges and that the compromise he had offered the committee actually made things "worse" because Israel would receive more F-16s.

In this case, said Richard (Dick) Stone, D-Fla., referring to the entire proposal, "I think less is more."

More Planes for Israel

What Carter offered the committee May 9 was the "firm assurance" that Israel would receive 20 additional F-15s in the 1983-84 period to bring its total to 60, the same number offered the Saudis.

But Jacob K. Javits, R-N.Y., sniffed at this offer, asserting that the administration had "given practically nothing" and the additional planes "would be supplied anyway."

Clifford P. Case, R-N.J., a staunch Israeli backer, noted that the original request from the Jewish state had been for 25 F-15s, a 10-plane reduction Case said he couldn't understand "unless they were telling Israel to be a little more flexible" in Middle East peace talks.

Also presented to the committee was a letter from Secretary of Defense Brown outlining the terms of the Saudi contracts and assurances the planes would be used for "legitimate self-defense" only.

The letters stated that Saudi Arabia had not requested multiple ejection racks, which would allow the fighters "to carry a substantial bomb load" and that the United States would not furnish those items.

But Sen. Stone observed that a draft of the letter circulated on Capitol Hill during the week had said the "Saudis won't purchase" the racks elsewhere. Omission of this in the official letter "raises a question" about how the planes will be used, said Stone.

The Pentagon chief's letter contained these other assurances given by Saudi Arabia: U.S. rights to suspend or cancel deliveries; a ban on basing the planes at Tabuk, 250 miles from Jerusalem, and the requirement that no additional combat aircraft would be added to the Saudi inventory while it received the U.S. F-15s.

Senate Floor Action

In a victory for the Carter administration but a bitter first defeat for Israel and U.S. Jewish organizations, the

Senate May 15 voted 44-54 to turn down a resolution (S Con Res 86) blocking the sales. The vote was preceded by 10 hours of emotional debate on the heavily-lobbied issue. *(Vote 161, p. 27-S)*

Sales critics objected to linking Israel's supplies to the Saudi contracts and asserted that the Carter policy would "sap the morale" of the Jewish state.

Contract supporters argued that the United States now must be "evenhanded" in relations with both Israel and Arab states because of the complex weave of U.S. economic and strategic interests in the Middle East.

"We must have the courage, we must have the guts to face a changing world," said Abraham Ribicoff, D-Conn., referring to Saudi influence on international economic policies and Middle East peace efforts resulting from its oil riches. Ribicoff had been a longtime supporter of Israel.

Although Ribicoff and other administration supporters stressed that their position did not imply any lessening of support for Israel — that "commitment is unshakable," said Muriel Humphrey, D-Minn. — sales opponent Javits told the Senate the vote might not be read that way.

"The Israelis and Americans who feel as I do are likely to read the signal that is going to go out from this chamber quite differently. . . . The vote today may raise doubts now for the first time in 30 years respecting our commitment given the overtone and context of the debate," he said.

Earlier, Javits asserted that Carter's arms sales package was presented by the president "to teach the Israelis a lesson" to be more flexible in peace negotiations.

And other opponents said the sale was an expression of U.S. "nervelessness" in coming to grips with petroleum-based international economics.

Voting Pattern

It was clear throughout the debate that this was one vote many senators had hoped would not occur because of the difficult choice of siding either with Israel or the Arab states. But Senate Majority Leader Byrd said he did not think a floor fight could have been avoided considering the way the sales were packaged.

In one of those odd voting patterns, where liberals oppose liberals, conservatives split with conservatives, it was Republican support that was the key to Carter's victory.

Twenty-eight Democrats opposed the resolution of disapproval, but 33 backed the measure; 26 Republicans made the difference by supporting the sales, while only 11 Republicans voted against them.

On opposite sides were conservatives James B. Allen, D-Ala., and Harry F. Byrd Jr., Ind-Va.; liberals George McGovern, D-S.D., and Frank Church, D-Idaho; Majority Leader Byrd and Democratic Whip Alan Cranston, D-Calif., and Jewish members Javits and Ribicoff.

Lobby Impact

Pressure by the administration began to build May 12, the day after the deadlocked Foreign Relations Committee voted to send the resolution to the floor without a recommendation, when President Carter sent every member of the Senate a letter stating that a rejection of the aircraft for Egypt would be a "breach of trust" with Egyptian President Anwar Sadat who "has turned away from a relationship with the Soviet Union" to work with the United States in the search for peace.

The White House also disclosed that Carter was calling many in the Senate to argue his case. Members of the Cabinet and others in the administration also were reported to have contacted undecided senators before the vote.

On the opposite side, the American Jewish Committee and other pro-Israeli organizations were swamping Senate offices with telegrams, Mailgrams, letters and phone calls as the vote approached, according to aides. Outside the Senate chamber itself, the reception lobby was choked with lobbyists on both sides of the issue.

It was the pressure from Jewish organizations, however, that prompted Sen. Mike Gravel, D-Alaska, and others to state publicly that their votes had become a "litmus test" for future support from Jews, although they had supported Israel on every issue in the past.

"This vote, if it is not done properly, kisses away in the future all kinds of financial support that would inure to a candidate for office," said Gravel. More troublesome, he added, the vote "will cost me some very important personal friendships."

Earlier McGovern warned the U.S. Jewish community's members that if they "press the case for Israel to the point where America loses its capacity to influence the Arab leadership . . . that may set in motion a backlash both in the Middle East and in the United States that can only harm the Israeli cause."

Bob Packwood, R-Ore., defended the lobbying, insisting that Jews have an understandable interest in the homeland of their forefathers as do Poles, Greeks and blacks. "It is with sorrow and disgust, therefore, that I hear the State Department time and again refer to the Jewish lobby or the Israeli lobby in a tone suggestive of a group which puts the interests of another country ahead of the United States."

Administration Criticism

Although voting for the sales package, Senate Minority Leader Howard H. Baker Jr., R-Tenn., said that he was troubled by the way the contracts were linked. To maintain the balance of military forces in the Middle East and to assure Israel of its unique relationship to our interests in the region, Baker called upon Carter to double the number of F-16s to be sent Israel for a total of 150.

(The president May 11 offered to supply Israel 20 additional F-15s in the 1983-84 period to bring its total to 60, the number supplied the Saudis.)

Members of the president's own party as well questioned the way the sales contracts were presented to Congress. Paul S. Sarbanes, D-Md., for example, who had worked alongside Carter throughout the winter on the Panama Canal treaties, said that there "is a question of skill and competence in the art of government" missing on the handling of the aircraft sales.

Arguments for Sale

Administration lobbyists and senators supporting the sales on the floor stressed four major themes to support selling the F-15s to Saudi Arabia: the importance of the moderate Arab states to peace in the Middle East and the need for the United States to maintain balanced relationships in the region; the Soviet presence in the Horn of Africa, Syria and Iraq; the importance of Arab oil to the United States, 20 percent of which comes from the Middle East; and the possibility that Saudi Arabia would turn to France for fighters if the U.S. sale were rejected.

On the latter point, raised by Foreign Relations Committee Chairman John Sparkman, D-Ala., at the outset of the debate, Javits asked: "Do you think they are going to lean on France for their security for the next five years? They are not crazy believe me."

As for the Soviet threat in the region, Frank Church, D-Idaho, said that he remembered when the United States shipped large quantities of weapons to Pakistan because of the U.S. assessment of Soviet threat to that nation. Later, arms were sent to India for the same reason. "In the end, they went to war, using American supplied weapons."

Javits added that if the United States expected Saudi Arabia to defend the area against any Soviet advances, "we had better triple the population in the first place" because Saudi Arabia is an enormous area.

The question of the United States' need for Saudi-supplied petroleum was addressed directly by Ribicoff who said, "People try to avoid it, but let us talk about oil." Noting that the Saudis possess a quarter of the world's oil reserves and have the flexibility to contract or expand production for market stability, Ribicoff said "the fact is that without a stable, predictable supply of oil from Saudi Arabia . . . the West would face the worst depression in the industrial era."

"In essence," countered Daniel Patrick Moynihan, D-N.Y., the aircraft sale is a rationalization of "American nervelessness in the area of international economic policy as well as political and military policy."

State Dept. Authorization

A $2 billion bill authorizing fiscal 1979 funds for State Department programs and related agencies was approved by Congress Sept. 20.

As sent to the president, the $1,969,710,000 bill (HR 12598 — PL 95-426) was $57,470,000 less than the administration's request.

One controversial provision in the Senate's version was eliminated by the conferees. The language had expressed the sense of the Senate that the president consult with the Foreign Relations Committee before deciding whether to submit an international agreement to Congress as a treaty or executive agreement.

That language was the residue of a conflict in the Senate June 29 over a stronger provision allowing the Senate to decide whether pacts with other countries should be submitted as treaties, which need a two-thirds Senate vote, or executive agreements, which don't require congressional action at all. Both the White House and the House opposed this procedure.

The authorization bill, which contains funds for State Department salaries and expenses and U.S. contributions to international organizations and conferences, included a provision stating that the president should review U.S. relations with Cuba and report to Congress by Jan. 20, 1979. The Senate bill had called for an end to U.S. diplomatic and economic relations with Cuba until the country removed its troops from Africa.

Provisions

As cleared by Congress, HR 12598 authorized the following amounts for fiscal 1979:

	Budget Request	Conference Amount
State Department		
Administration	$ 830,143,000	$ 849,118,000
Organizations/Conferences	412,781,000	412,826,000
International Commissions	19,973,000	20,773,000
Migration/Refugee Aid	90,836,000	116,536,000
International-Communications Agency	413,327,000	420,577,000
Board for International Broadcasting	85,180,000	88,180,000
Security and Cooperation in Europe Commission	0	200,000
International Tin Agreement	60,000,000	60,000,000
Hunger/Malnutrition Commission	0	1,500,000
Total	$1,912,240,000	$1,969,710,000

The bill also:

Title I — State Department

- Authorized fiscal 1978 supplemental appropriations of $37,275,000 to pay U.S. arrearages to UNESCO.
- Earmarked $25 million for resettlement in Israel of refugees from the Soviet Union and communist nations in Eastern Europe.
- Earmarked $5 million for assistance for refugees in Africa.
- Established an Assistant Secretary of State for International Narcotics Matters.
- Provided that a U.S. passport may not be restricted for travel in any country other than one with which the United States is at war, where armed hostilities are in progress or where there is a danger to the health or safety of U.S. citizens.
- Stated the sense of Congress that diplomatic or official passports should be issued only to persons in diplomatic jobs or other official positions or who are otherwise eligible for such passports under law.
- Stated that it was the "general policy" of the United States to restrict travel of foreign citizens within the United States only when the government of that country restricted travel by Americans within its borders.

Title II — International Communications Agency

- Provided that the mission of the agency shall be to improve U.S. relations with other countries through educational and cultural activities. (The ICA was created by Reorganization Plan No. 2, approved by Congress in 1977, which consolidated the U.S. Information Agency and the State Department's Educational and Cultural Affairs Bureau. *(1977 Almanac p. 825)*

Title III — Board for International Broadcasting

- Provided that the board could not contribute any funds to Radio Free Europe or Radio Liberty if either permitted a communist nation to use its broadcasting facilities, unless the communist nation permitted the use of its facilities on a comparable basis.

Title IV — Foreign Service Personnel

- Provided that the secretary of state should conduct a review by Jan. 20, 1979, of the personnel needs of the Foreign Service because the United States has expanded diplomatic representation abroad from 80 nations to about 130 since 1960 without a change in staff size.

• Covered, in a number of separate sections, such matters as employment of foreign service family members overseas, payment of special allowances to foreign service employees, counseling persons leaving the service, orientation and language training for family members and rest and recuperation travel benefits.

• Authorized, as part of this effort, a special retirement benefit applicable between Oct. 1, 1978, and Dec. 31, 1979, to encourage certain foreign service personnel to retire. (The conference report noted that the provision would not be a precedent for broadening other government retirement programs. The report said the provision was necessitated by the separate foreign service retirement system and the current lack of senior retirements in the service.)

Title V — Technology and U.S. Diplomacy

• Required the president to report to Congress by Jan. 31, 1980, and each year thereafter, on U.S. agreements involving science and technology, including an analysis of the foreign policy implications and the scientific benefits of these agreements.

Title VI — Policy Provisions

• Required the president to report to Congress by Jan. 20, 1979, on United States' policies and proposals on international communications and information issues.

• Stated the sense of Congress that the president convey to all nations the concern of Congress for the destruction of marine mammals.

• Stated the sense of Congress that the president advise officials of foreign governments which subject foreign news correspondents to harassment and restrictions that the United States considers such mistreatment a potentially damaging factor in overall relations with the United States.

• Stated the sense of Congress that the president continue efforts directed toward achievement of an agreement establishing an international network of nationally held grain reserves.

• Stated that Congress found that "political developments in Spain during the past two years constitute a major step toward the construction of a stable and lasting Spanish democracy," and stated the sense of Congress that the Picasso painting "Guernica" should be returned by the United States to Spain in the near future. (The painting was in the custody of the Museum of Modern Art in New York.)

• Directed the president to report by Jan. 20, 1979, on all discriminatory trade practices affecting foreign relations that have been written into law.

• Stated the sense of Congress that the United States take the initiative in seeking a multilateral agreement governing the use of nuclear-powered satellites, and the administration should report to Congress by Jan. 20, 1979, on actions taken.

• Stated the sense of Congress that the United States should encourage the United Nations to convene a world alternate energy conference in 1981 to consider ways to meet world energy needs through alternate sources.

• Stated the sense of Congress that the president prohibit the export of military, paramilitary and police equipment to Uganda and that the State Department deny visas for military or police training of Ugandan officials until Uganda has demonstrated a proper respect for human rights.

• Required the president to report to Congress by Jan. 20, 1979, on U.S. statutes that discriminate against Americans living abroad.

• Stated as the sense of Congress that the president should negotiate an agreement with Canada aimed at preserving the quality of air above the United States and Canada.

• Stated as the sense of Congress that the president should review U.S. diplomatic and economic relations with Cuba and report to Congress by Jan. 20, 1979, because of the "sharp increase" in Cuban military personnel serving in Africa.

Title VII — Miscellaneous

• Provided that none of the funds authorized by the bill may be used directly or indirectly to effect implementation of the Panama Canal treaties "unless authorized by the Constitution or by act of Congress."

• Prohibited funds from being used for reparations, aid or any other form of payment to Vietnam. Directed the president to continue to seek a final accounting of all Americans missing in action in Vietnam.

• Made permanent the president's authority to regulate the entry of aliens into the United States and to require American citizens to bear valid passports when entering or leaving the country, and repealed criminal penalties for violations of these travel controls. (The president's authority exercised under "emergency" powers had been scheduled to expire on Sept. 15, 1978.)

House Action

The House International Relations Committee reported HR 12598 May 15 (H Rept 95-1160). The bill was passed by the House by a vote of 240-124 on May 31. *(Vote 333, p. 96-H)*

The bill authorized $849.1 million for running the State Department — the largest amount in the legislation — and $412.8 million for U.S. contributions to international organizations and conferences.

Before passing the bill, the House voted on an amendment designed to give it a voice in the Panama Canal treaties. The amendment prohibited the use of any funds in the bill for implementing the Senate-passed treaties without specific approval by Congress. It was passed on a vote of 203-163. *(Vote 332, p. 94-H. Details of House action on Panama Canal, p. 385)*

In other action, the House by a 202-164 vote dropped a committee provision to establish an Institute for International Human Rights — an independent U.S. agency — "to promote universal respect for and observance of human rights." The committee had planned for the institute to sponsor seminars and meetings on human rights, help publish books and other materials suppressed by foreign governments and aid private organizations that support victims of persecution. *(Vote 331, p. 94-H)*

The amendment to drop the section was proposed by Robert E. Bauman, R-Md., who said he feared the organization's independence could "create an awful lot of mischief." The institute's power to give grants to individuals in other countries "sounds much like the activities of the CIA which my liberal friends are so loud in condemning," he said.

By a 237-135 vote, the House struck down a committee provision establishing a commission to study conflict resolution proposals. Committee members wanted the panel to study whether a Center for Conflict Resolution should be established or other methods devised to evaluate how conflicts are started and how they might be resolved. The commission also was expected to study the relationship the center would have to the federal government, its possible size, cost and location. *(Vote 330, p. 94-H)*

John M. Ashbrook, R-Ohio, opposed the plan, arguing that the State Department should be studying these matters anyway. Helen Meyner, D-N.J., said the proposal should be taken seriously because of the rise in international terrorism in recent years.

A third committee provision dropped by the House, by a 16-12 standing vote on an amendment offered by Dan Glickman, D-Kan., would have authorized $100,000 for a study of the possibility for organizing additional parliamentary exchanges between Congress and other nations.

Glickman said, "I do not have any problems with the interparliamentary unions. . . , but we all know that they are a code word to the American people. The code word is 'junket!' " But committee members argued that the funds actually would be spent studying possible reforms and reductions in the number of exchanges.

By voice vote, the House approved an amendment by Ashbrook barring use of any funds in the bill for aid or reparations to Vietnam and requiring the president to continue to obtain a final accounting of all Americans missing in action in Vietnam.

Provisions

As passed by the House, HR 12598 authorized:

(in millions)

Program	Administration Request	House-Passed Amount
Department of State		
Administration	$ 830.1	$ 849.1
International Organizations/ Conferences	412.8	412.8
International Commissions	20.0	20.8
Migration/Refugee Aid	56.3	91.3
International Communications Agency	413.3	417.3
Board for International Broadcasting	85.2	88.2
International Tin Agreement	60.0	60.0
Total	$1,877.7	$1,940.2

The bill also:

- Authorized $47.7 million in supplemental appropriations for fiscal 1978, including $10.5 million for the Board for International Broadcasting and $37.3 million for U.S. arrearages to UNESCO.
- Authorized funds ($60 million) to permit U.S. contributions of tin to the International Tin Buffer Stock.
- Established an assistant secretary of state for International Narcotics matters.

Senate Action

Committee

The Senate Foreign Relations Committee reported the bill May 15 by voice vote (S Rept 95-842).

The committee bill included a controversial provision that would allow the Senate to decide whether pacts with other countries should be submitted as treaties, requiring a two-thirds Senate vote for approval, or executive agreements, which do not. Already sensitive to congressional restrictions on military and economic assistance overseas, the administration opposed the provision. In particular, the administration was bothered because the provision provided that points of order could be raised against implementing legislation to carry out any international agreement if the Senate had approved a resolution stating that the pact should have been submitted as a treaty.

Although the so-called executive agreements have been used by presidents since early in the country's history for carrying out detailed, day-to-day relations with other governments, this practice has increased dramatically since World War II.

"Presidents," said the Foreign Relations Committee, "have too often succeeded in circumventing the requirement of Senate advice and consent by calling treaties 'executive agreements.' "

A motion by Claiborne Pell, D-R.I., to drop the executive agreements provision was rejected on a 7-7 vote.

In additional views, opponents of the provision argued that the language was likely to raise problems in Congress:

- Adding the language to an authorization bill "is not an appropriate way to amend the rules of the Senate."
- The procedure "only invites the House to retaliate" with a resolution of its own allowing a point of order on implementing legislation for any agreement that it feels should be approved by both chambers.
- Retaliatory action by the House, whereby it stakes out specific kinds of agreements in which it wanted to be involved, could result in the Senate actually considering fewer treaties.
- The language added nothing new since the Senate always could act to deny the funding to implement any pact with another country if it felt such an agreement should have been submitted as a treaty.

Floor Action

The Senate passed the $1.9 billion authorization bill June 28, by a vote of 64-17, after agreeing to a compromise on the committee's executive agreements provision. *(Vote 192, p. 31-S)*

When it appeared the committee's executive agreements provision might be entirely deleted during the debate, John Glenn, D-Ohio, offered a compromise, approved by voice vote, merely stating that when a president was considering whether to submit an international pact as a treaty or executive agreement, he "should . . . seek the advice of the Foreign Relations Committee."

A second substitute offered by Clifford P. Case, R-N.J. — a proposal stronger than Glenn's — provided that such agreements submitted without consultation would be subject to points of order when implementing legislation was considered. But it was rejected, 41-48. *(Vote 187, p. 31-S)*

Glenn called his own compromise a "fallback" proposal, requiring that the administration "at least talk to us about what is proposed and whether it will be an executive agreement or treaty."

Another controversial issue debated by the Senate concerned the United States' relations with Cuba.

By a 53-29 vote, it accepted an amendment offered by Dewey F. Bartlett, R-Okla., expressing the sense of Congress that the president should sever diplomatic and economic relations with Cuba until that country removed its military forces from Africa. A George McGovern, D-S.D., motion to table the amendment first was rejected by a 33-55 vote. *(Votes 190, 191, p. 31-S)*

Other Amendments. In addition to the amendments dealing with the executive agreements and Cuba issues, the Senate approved 17 other proposals. All were noncontroversial, and approved by voice votes (unless otherwise specified) and offered by:

- McGovern, adding the words "United States" as a prefix to the new name for the International Communication Agency, authorizing $1.5 million for the Commission on Hunger and Malnutrition and making other minor changes.
- Paul G. Hatfield, D-Mont., requesting the secretary of state to initiate negotiations with Canada on a U.S.-Canadian air pollution control treaty.
- Lowell P. Weicker Jr., R-Conn., calling on the secretary of state to convey to all nations the concern of Congress over the destruction of marine mammals.
- Dennis DeConcini, D-Ariz., establishing the position of Assistant Secretary for International Narcotics Matters in the Department of State.
- Harry F. Byrd Jr., Ind-Va., deleting a section in the bill urging the president to seek a revised U.S. debt settlement agreement with the Soviet Union stemming from debts owed the United States from World War II. Adopted 77-12. *(Vote 189, p. 31-S)* A motion to table the amendment was rejected earlier, 16-74. *(Vote 188, p. 31-S)*
- Glenn, deleting language authorizing six supergrade Civil Service positions (GS 16-18) for the new Board of International Broadcasting.
- Robert Dole, R-Kan., stating the sense of the Senate that the president prohibit the export of military, paramilitary and police equipment to Uganda. *(Uganda trade boycott, p. 428)*
- Dole, expressing the sense of the Senate that Voice of America broadcasts be accurate and objective.
- Dole, as modified by McGovern, barring use of any funds authorized in the bill for establishing diplomatic relations with Angola while military forces of Cuba remain in the African country, unless the president certifies to Congress that the establishment of such relations is in the national interest.
- Harrison Schmitt, R-N.M., prohibiting the use of Radio Free Europe and Radio Liberty facilities by a Communist nation unless that country permits the use of its broadcast facilities by Radio Free Europe/Radio Liberty.
- Daniel Patrick Moynihan, D-N.Y., withholding from the U.S. contribution to the United Nations the U.S. portion of funds that would support the Committee on the Exercise of the Inalienable Rights of the Palestinian People.
- Clifford P. Case, R-N.J., calling for the United States to assist in bringing about an orderly transition to majority rule and protection of minority rights in Rhodesia.
- Pete V. Domenici, R-N.M., stating the sense of Congress that the June arrests of two U.S. journalists by the Soviet Union is in violation of a fundamental freedom of people of all nations and is not consistent with the spirit of detente.
- Byrd, Ind-Va., barring use of any funds authorized by the bill for aid or reparations to Vietnam.
- John Melcher, D-Mont., stating the sense of Congress that the United States enter into negotiations with Canada to develop an agreement governing air quality standards in the two nations.
- McGovern, substituting a "significant increase in" for language in the bill calling for a tripling of the funding of the International Communications Agency for cultural exchange activities.

The Senate rejected on a tabling motion, 48-42, an amendment by Jesse Helms, R-N.C., that would have lifted U.S. economic sanctions against Rhodesia until Sept. 30, 1979. *(Vote 186, p. 31-S)*

Provisions

As passed by the Senate, HR 12598 authorized the following amounts for fiscal 1979:

	Administration Request	Senate-Passed Amount
State Department		
Administration	$ 830,143,000	$ 835,143,000
Organizations/conferences	412,781,000	450,261,000
International commissions	19,973,000	20,773,000
Migration/refugee aid	90,836,000	116,536,000
International Communications Agency		
Salaries/expenses	$ 380,142,000	$ 390,392,000
Technical exchange	13,500,000	13,500,000
Radio facilities	19,685,000	19,685,000
Board for International Broadcasting	85,180,000	88,180,000
Other Programs	—	2,000,000
Total	$1,852,240,000	$1,936,470,000

Conference Report

Senate-House conferees on the State Department authorization bill filed a report (H Rept 95-1535) Sept. 6 resolving the following major differences:

Amounts. Conferees agreed on authorization totals that were $27,030,000 less than the Senate amount and $29,974,000 more than the House total. The final figure was $57,470,000 more than the administration request.

International Communications Agency. A Senate provision changing the name of the new International Communications Agency (ICA) to the United States Agency for Information and Cultural Exchange was opposed by the conferees.

Panama Canal. Conferees modified a House provision, added on the floor, that prohibited funds authorized by the bill from being used directly or indirectly to effect implementation of the Panama Canal treaties unless authorized by Congress. The Senate had no such provision. Conferees kept the provision but added "the Constitution" to the qualification at the end, thus allowing the administration to cite constitutional authority to proceed with the treaties' implementation.

Uganda. Conferees accepted a Senate provision prohibiting export of military and police equipment to Uganda and barring U.S. visas to Uganda officials for training in military and police activities until the Ugandan government demonstrated a respect for human rights.

International Agreements. A provision expressing the sense of the Senate that the president should consult with the Senate Foreign Relations Committee on whether an agreement between the United States and another nation should be submitted to Congress as a treaty or an executive agreement was eliminated by the conferees.

Angola. The Senate had prohibited the use of funds in the bill for establishing diplomatic relations with Angola as long as Cuban forces were in that country, but the conferees dropped this language at the House's insistence.

Cuban Forces. A Senate provision called for termination of U.S. economic and diplomatic relations with Cuba until the nation removed its military forces from Africa. The House bill contained no comparable provision. Conferees drafted language stating that the president should undertake a comprehensive review of U.S. relations with Cuba and report to Congress by Jan. 20, 1979.

Rhodesia. A Senate provision calling for the United States to assist in bringing about an orderly transition to majority rule and protection of minority rights in Rhodesia was put aside by the conferees.

Final Action

The House approved the conference report to the bill Sept. 19, by voice vote. The Senate agreed to the report the following day, by voice vote, clearing the measure for the president.

Anti-Terrorist Bill

Four Senate committees reported a bill to help combat international terrorism by withholding foreign aid and other assistance from uncooperative countries, but the bill did not reach the Senate floor, and the House took no action on similar legislation in 1978.

Reported by the Governmental Affairs Committee May 23 (S Rept 95-908), the Foreign Relations and Commerce, Science and Transportation Committees July 10 (S Rept 95-570) and the Intelligence Committee Aug. 10 (S Rept 95-1079), the legislation (S 2236) required the executive branch to examine its policies and operations for confronting terrorism, whether in the United States or overseas.

A principal provision required the president to submit to Congress every six months a list of countries that give sanctuary to terrorists. When the list is posted, the president then could bar foreign aid, cut off arms sales or turn down export licenses for equipment that might contribute to terrorism.

Except for some executive-legislative branch procedural technicalities, S 2236 was a non-controversial bill that the Governmental Affairs Committee hoped would demonstrate to other nations U.S. readiness to confront the international problem.

The panel counted 1,800 major incidents of terrorism between 1970 and 1977 in which 512 persons were killed by bombings and assassinations, 551 were wounded or injured and 363 kidnapped. At least $146 million in bomb damage was estimated, while "additional cost in terms of human suffering and trauma is incalculable," the committee said. But "perhaps its greatest cost is the profound challenge to the rule of law which it [terrorism] poses."

Need for New Program

The committee said a new U.S. anti-terrorism program was needed because:

- International law has failed to cope with the problem partly because a hero or "freedom fighter" to one nation is a terrorist to another.
- Governments have strongly resisted condemning nations that lend state support to international terrorism and applying sanctions against these states.
- The executive branch had not yet assigned a high priority to combating terrorism.
- International terrorism has posed a threat to the orderly and lawful functioning of governments.
- Civil aviation security programs to protect flights against hijacking, sabotage and other crimes were inadequate. Thirty airline hijackings occurred in 1977 in spite of worldwide security improvements.
- Military operations by commando units raise sensitive political and international law questions. And unless specifically invited, no arm of the U.S. government can take any sort of police action on foreign soil.
- U.S. regulation of explosives has been totally inadequate.

During Foreign Relations Committee markup June 20, the panel accepted a proposal by Jacob K. Javits, R-N.Y., that required the president, in determining which prohibitions shouldn't be applied to a nation on the U.S. terrorism list, to consider a number of factors.

Javits said that under his proposal the president would have to spell out why aid wouldn't be suspended for a country on the list. He argued this would make the president less inclined to grant exceptions.

But State Department liaison Brian Atwood told the committee that Javits' language would send the "wrong message" to other countries because it would focus attention on the reasons that aid prohibitions were not imposed. He said it would be better for the president simply to list the penalties invoked and why they would be imposed.

Frank Church, D-Idaho, argued that the president probably wouldn't bother to list a nation if he later had to tell why he wasn't suspending certain aid provisions.

As a result, the committee amended Javits' proposal to have the president list which prohibitions were "taken" rather than which ones were "suspended."

Major Provisions

As reported by the committees, S 2236:

Definitions. Defined international terrorism as an offense under three existing international conventions and other attempted or threatened unlawful acts that result in death, injury or "forcible deprivation of liberty" or property destruction and which occur in an international context. The bill provided several tests to determine whether there is an international context.

Defined state support of terrorism as furnishing arms, training, direction, financial and other aid to persons or groups with the likelihood that they would be used in acts of international violence or allowing the use of a nation's territory as a sanctuary from extradition or prosecution.

Terrorism Report. The bill required the secretary of state to report to the president and Congress every six months on international incidents of terrorism for examining trends and the effectiveness of U.S. policy.

List of Nations. Required the president to submit to Congress every six months a list of nations supporting acts of terrorism for the purpose of censuring those countries. Libya, Iraq, and Yemen already were on a de facto list submitted in 1977 by the State Department to Sen. Javits.

Allowed the president to remove a nation from the list unless Congress vetoed his action by adoption of a concurrent resolution.

Aid Sanction. Prohibited the United States from providing foreign assistance, authorizing military hardware sales or approving an export license for equipment useable by terrorists for any nation that appeared on the list.

Airport Security. Required the secretary of transportation to periodically assess the effectiveness of security measures at major foreign airports and to display at major U.S. airports a list of international airports with security deficiences.

Exchange Stabilization Funds

Legislation (S 2093 — PL 95-612) supported by the Carter administration to bring Treasury Department expenses for international monetary programs under the budget and appropriations process cleared Congress Oct. 13 when the Senate passed the measure by voice vote (the House had passed it Oct. 11 by voice vote). The bill was reported by the Senate Banking, Housing and Urban Affairs Committee on March 2 (S Rept 95-661) and by the House Banking, Finance and Urban Affairs Committee May 10 (H Rept 95-1126).

This fund was created by a section of the Gold Reserve Act of 1934; profits from gold investments made by the department accrue to the ESF, which often plays a role in international monetary stabilization programs.

Over the years, programs supported by the fund, including short-term credits to Mexico and Great Britain in 1977, have grown steadily, to the $21 million level in fiscal 1976 for salaries and expenses from $117,000 in the 1934-35 period.

Funds for a variety of international activities as well as others the Senate panel termed "only vaguely related" to foreign monetary matters were paid from the Exchange Stabilization Fund (ESF).

Moreover, the committee pointed out, the fund had supported administrative costs not directly related to its purposes. The ESF, for example, paid the salaries of the department's director of the office of regulatory and legislative policy, the director of the office of foreign assets control, and the national intelligence adviser.

S 2093 placed a ceiling of $24 million on the department's fiscal 1979 international monetary expenses and shifted staff paid from ESF funds to regular civil service supergrade positions.

The fund's administrative expenses were audited by the General Accounting Office for the first time in 1974, but at the department's request the bill did not give GAO the authority to audit the fund's "external" activities "for fear [by the department] of jeopardizing confidential relationships with foreign governments," according to the Senate committee.

Military Aid Bill: Turkey Arms Ban Lifted

Congress Sept. 12 sent President Carter a major foreign policy trophy, giving him authority to lift the three-year-old partial arms embargo against Turkey.

Before resuming regular shipments of weapons to that country, Carter was required by House-Senate conferees on S 3075 (PL 95-384), the fiscal 1979 security aid authorization bill, to certify to Congress that Turkey was "acting in good faith" to achieve a "just and peaceful settlement" of Cyprus issues, including the continued removal of Turkish troops from the Mediterranean island.

Turkey's use of U.S. military equipment in 1974 to invade Cyprus in violation of U.S. laws prompted Congress that year to vote a total arms embargo. It took effect in February 1975 but was modified eight months later to permit sales needed for NATO defenses.

Reversing his campaign position, Carter argued in 1978 that even the partial embargo was too stringent, impeding rather than encouraging any resolution of the basic Cyprus territorial and refugee issues and alienating Turkey from the NATO alliance.

The Senate's version of S 3075 would have repealed the embargo outright, but the conferees instead accepted the House version, calling it "de facto repeal" of the 1975 statute.

Stating that it "regrets the lack of progress toward a Cyprus settlement" the conference committee said it intended the "removal of the prohibition be contingent upon a presidential determination and certification to the Congress that resumption of full military cooperation with Turkey is in the national interest of the United States and in the interest of NATO and that the government of Turkey is acting in good faith to achieve a just and peaceful settlement of the Cyprus problem."

The bill also required the president to send Congress every 60 days a report on progress toward reaching a Cyprus solution. And when the administration requested security aid for either Turkey or Greece, the bill required that the president certify it was needed for defensive purposes only.

Rhodesia Issue

A second controversial issue, this relating to Rhodesia, also was resolved by conferees. They permitted the president to drop economic sanctions against Rhodesia after Dec. 31, 1978, if he determined that the Salisbury government had: 1) demonstrated a willingness to negotiate in good faith at an all-parties conference that included guerrilla factions and 2) a new government had been installed after being chosen in free elections under international supervision.

The Carter administration had opposed the House version that barred the enforcement of sanctions against Rhodesia after 1978 unless a new government had not been chosen and installed. The conference decision, which closely followed the Senate's provision, was a victory for the Carter administration, which had called for an all-parties conference considered key by the State Department for resolving the Rhodesian civil conflict.

But the Salisbury government, a coalition of blacks and the white minority led by Ian Smith, had insisted that the black guerrillas fighting alongside Rhodesia's borders lay down their arms and accept its terms for participation in a transition to majority rule. On Sept. 10, Smith declared martial law in parts of Rhodesia and a crackdown on groups representing the black national guerrillas fighting to overthrow his regime.

Provisions

As cleared by Congress, S 3075, which also contained new provisions on human rights, arms sales and transfers of U.S. military equipment to South Korea, authorized $2,817,500,000 in security aid, arms sales credits and military grants for fiscal 1979. This amount was $28.2 million more than requested by the administration, $32.5 million less than recommended by the Senate and $36.8 million less than approved by the House.

The bill authorized the following amounts for fiscal 1979:

	Budget Request	Final Amount
Military Assistance		
Grant Aid	$133,500,000	$133,500,000
Education/Training	32,100,000	31,800,000
Sales Credits	674,300,000	674,300,000
Economic Assistance	1,872,000,000	1,902,000,000
Other		
Narcotics Control	40,000,000	40,000,000
Contingency Fund	5,000,000	5,000,000
Peacekeeping operations	32,400,000	30,900,000
Total	$2,789,300,000	$2,817,500,000

The bill also:

Narcotics Control

● Prohibited U.S. narcotics officials from interrogating or being present during the interrogation of any person arrested in a foreign country without the person's written consent.

● Prohibited the use of foreign aid funds for spraying herbicides on marijuana plants if the herbicides are likely to be harmful to health, unless used with another substance that warned potential users that herbicides had been used.

Human Rights

● Provided that security aid be denied to any nation that violated human rights unless the secretary of state finds that extraordinary circumstances exist which necessitate a continuation of security aid for that country and that it is in the interest of the United States to provide the assistance.

● Barred the export of crime control equipment to a country that engages in a consistent pattern of violation of human rights unless the president certified to the House Speaker and the Senate Foreign Relations Committee chairman that the exports were needed because of extraordinary circumstances. Excluded the NATO countries, Japan, Australia and New Zealand from this provision.

Rhodesian Embargo

● Provided that the United States shall not enforce sanctions against Rhodesia after Dec. 31, 1978, provided that the president determined: 1) that the government of Rhodesia had demonstrated its willingness to negotiate in good faith at an all-parties conference held under international auspices on all relevant issues and 2) that a government has been installed chosen by free elections in which all groups have been allowed to participate freely, with observation by international observers.

Korea Equipment Transfer

● Granted the president authority until Dec. 31, 1982, to transfer defense articles and services to South Korea only in conjunction with the withdrawal of the U.S. 2nd Infantry Division and support forces.

● Stated that it was the sense of Congress that additional withdrawal of U.S. troops from South Korea may seriously risk upsetting the military balance in the region and requires full advance consultation with Congress.

Turkey Arms Embargo

● Provided that the U.S. arms embargo against Turkey no longer have effect if the president determined and certified to Congress that resumption of military cooperation with Turkey was in the interest of the United States and NATO and that Turkey was acting in good faith to achieve a just and peaceful settlement of the Cyprus problem.

● Required that a presidential certification accompany any request for security aid for Greece or Turkey stating that the aid was intended solely for defensive purposes and was not inconsistent with the objectives of a peaceful settlement among all parties to the Cyprus problem.

Military Assistance

Specified that of the $133.5 million authorized for military grant aid, not more than the following amounts could be used for assistance to these nations: Portugal, $27.9 million; Spain, $41 million; Jordan, $45 million; Philippines, $17.1 million; Greece, $35 million. Gave the president authority to increase these amounts by 10 percent.

● Expressed the sense of Congress that the president adhere to a policy of restraint in conventional arms transfers and that not later than Dec. 31, 1979, the president transmit to Congress a detailed report assessing the results and commenting on the implications of multilateral arms sales discussions with other arms suppliers.

● Required that appropriate charges for inventory losses from arms sales be included in the price of defense articles sold to foreign governments.

● Required the transmittal to Congress by Nov. 15 each year of arms sales proposed by the executive branch for the forthcoming fiscal year to countries other than NATO, Japan, Australia and New Zealand.

● Set a military sales ceiling for fiscal 1979 at $2,085,-500,000.

U.S.-China Treaty

● Stated the sense of Congress that any proposed policy changes affecting the mutual defense treaty with the Republic of China be a matter for prior consultation with Congress.

Congressional Travel

● Required the chairman of each congressional committee to report quarterly to the clerk of the House or the secretary of the Senate the amounts spent by committee members and staff from foreign currencies and appropriated funds for foreign travel. (Existing law required only annual reports.)

● Required the clerk of the House and the secretary of the Senate to prepare a consolidated report on a quarterly basis accounting for expenditures by each member and employee or by each group traveling overseas.

• Specified that the reports include amounts and dollar equivalent values of each foreign currency expended and the amounts of dollar expenditures from appropriated funds for travel outside the United States.

• Required reports to be open to public inspection and published in the *Congressional Record* within 10 legislative days after the report is sent to the clerk or secretary by the reporting persons.

Economic Support Fund

• Established an economic support fund to replace the security supporting assistance account in previous military aid bills. Authorized appropriations of $1,902,000,000 for this purpose.

• Earmarked $785 million of the $1.9 billion total for Israel; $750 million for Egypt and $93 million for Jordan. (In their report, conferees also said they intended that $90 million would be provided for Syria.)

• Provided that the total funds earmarked for Israel could be available as a cash transfer if the president ensured that it did not have an adverse impact on U.S. non-military exports to Israel.

• Provided that two-thirds of the assistance to Israel and Egypt be provided on a grant basis.

• Earmarked $65 million of the Egyptian funds for development of private enterprise.

• Stated the sense of Congress that programs which stress regional development or regional scientific and technical cooperation between Israel and its Arab neighbors "can contribute in an important way to the mutual understanding" necessary for Middle East peace. Specified that of the amount authorized for the economic support fund, at least $5 million be available to fund regional programs of this nature.

• Earmarked $60 million for countries of southern Africa. (Conferees said they intended that $10 million of the amount would be used to aid refugees from or in Rhodesia with the funds going through "appropriate international organizations."

• Earmarked $15 million for refugee relief and reconstruction for Cyprus; earmarked $50 million for Turkey.

• Barred aid to Mozambique, Angola, Tanzania or Zambia unless the president reports that assistance would further U.S. foreign policy interests.

Soviet Review

• Stated the sense of Congress that the president in cooperation with Congress should make a full review of U.S. policy toward the Soviet Union.

Senate Committee Action

The Senate Foreign Relations Committee reported S 3075 (S Rept 95-841) May 15 by unanimous vote. The bill authorized $2,886,400,000 in military aid for fiscal 1979.

Turkey

In its report, the Foreign Relations Committee said that "substantial progress" needs to be made in the settlement of the Cyprus dispute before the partial arms embargo imposed by Congress in 1975 on Turkey is lifted.

The committee had voted 8-4 on May 11 to maintain the embargo that allows $175 million in military credits for Turkey in fiscal 1979. The panel also provided $50 million in security aid for Ankara and $140 million in sales credits for Greece.

The committee said that it hoped that "moderate levels of foreign military sales financing for both countries will promote both the prospects for a settlement of the Cyprus dispute and U.S. security interests in the southern European region.

Korea

The committee helped clear the way for President Carter's planned withdrawal of U.S. ground forces from Korea over a five-year period.

The panel provided $800 million in authority to transfer U.S. military equipment to Korea, $275 million for supporting South Korea's military improvement plan plus $90 million to stockpile U.S. ammunition for eventual use by the Koreans.

The proposed troop withdrawal has been controversial. Transfer of U.S. military gear was believed essential for Carter to win support in Congress for the withdrawal.

Human Rights

Noting that Congress had passed legislation providing human rights guidance for all military and economic aid programs overseas, the committee tightened one restriction to specify that no aid could be provided to police or domestic intelligence forces of governments that the executive branch found in consistent violation of rights standards.

John Glenn, D-Ohio, had planned to offer an amendment to reduce the $18.1 million military aid authorization for the Philippines because of alleged rights violations by the government of President Marcos. The report said he did not proceed because of Vice President Walter F. Mondale's trip there when the committee was considering the bill.

Economic Support Fund

The committee created a new $1.9 billion economic support fund to replace the old security assistance program in the military aid legislation. The committee said this decision "reflects more accurately the actual use of these funds: to provide budget support and development aid to countries of political importance to the United States." About 90 percent of the fund was allocated for Middle East nations, with Israel allotted $785 million and Egypt $750 million. The House placed this fund in the economic assistance bill (HR 12222) passed May 15. *(Story, p. 401)*

Arms Sales

Expressing concern that U.S. weapons sales continued to be made at levels similar to past years despite President Carter's May 1977 pledge to lower the level of transactions, the committee drafted 10 arms sales principles intended to serve as guidelines for future sales. The panel said it was its intent to keep the principles non-binding unless it becomes clear that they are not adequately followed by the executive branch. The committee also adopted a provision requiring the White House to send Congress each February an annual arms sale plan for the following fiscal year.

Senate Floor Action

The Senate passed the $2.9 billion military assistance bill (S 3075) on July 26, by a vote of 73-13 *(vote 250, p. 39-S)* after voting to lift the 1974 U.S. arms embargo against Turkey.

The Senate's decision — by voice vote — followed a 57-42 roll call to condition future U.S. shipments to Turkey on that country's progress in withdrawing from Cyprus.

Following the vote, the administration commended the Senate for its "statesmanlike action" and said it hoped that the "House will act in a similar fashion."

In other actions, the Senate approved an amendment that would drop economic sanctions against Rhodesia imposed by the United States if free elections were held under international supervision, cautioned Carter that his Korean troop withdrawal policy may "risk upsetting" the military balance in the region, and requested that any change in U.S. relations with the Republic of China be submitted to the Senate for its views.

Turkey Embargo

When it became clear that the administration's request to repeal the embargo would not carry on its own, Sen. George McGovern, D-S.D., offered compromise language spelling out policies and procedures regarding Turkey, Greece and Cyprus to tack onto the basic provision lifting the embargo. The policy language was brought to the floor by Senate Majority Leader Robert C. Byrd, D-W.Va., and boosted by Lloyd M. Bentsen, D-Texas, and John H. Chafee, R-R.I.

The McGovern language required the president to send to Congress every 60 days a report on progress made toward the conclusion of a negotiated solution of the Cyprus problem.

The provision also provided that when the president requested new funds — military or economic — for any of the three nations, he must certify that U.S. goals for resolving the Mediterranean conflict were being achieved.

The McGovern language also pointedly noted that "the continuing presence of a major Turkish force [on Cyprus] is inconsistent with the legitimate status of Cyprus as a sovereign republic."

The compromise also increased military credits for Greece to $175 million, the same amount allocated Turkey in the military aid bill.

Policy principles outlined in the McGovern compromise stated that U.S. arms transfers to Greek and Turkey would be made "solely for defensive purposes" and "shall not signify a lessening of U.S. commitment to a just solution on Cyprus."

During Senate debate on the remaining embargo language, McGovern hammered at the theme that the main purpose of existing law "is not to curtail Turkey's arms supply but rather to stigmatize that nation for its conduct in Cyprus."

The United States has been pursuing a course, McGovern added, that has produced "very little" in the way of the negotiating success on Cyprus. The repeal would permit Congress to gauge whether Turkey would respond by offering settlement possibilities, and that if the nation was not forthcoming, the embargo could be reimposed by Congress next year, he said.

Chafee pursued the NATO defense theme, contending that the United States is losing "irreplaceable intelligence information from bases in Turkey that have been closed to U.S. forces since 1974.

On the losing side, Paul S. Sarbanes, D-Md., Claiborne Pell, D-R.I., and Thomas F. Eagleton, D-Mo., stressed three themes: repealing the embargo would alienate the Greeks, who have been waiting for Turkey to offer settlement proposals; would remove "any incentive for Turkey to negotiate seriously;" and would communicate to the world that the United States "was not serious" about controlling the use of its weapons.

To the argument that the embargo had not worked, Sarbanes countered that the administration had "undercut" it, never given it a chance. "We have made exceptions to the embargo in terms of arms which have been sent, in the name of realism and pragmatism," he said. "There has been no response [from Turkey]."

The final roll call showed an unusual voting pattern. Democrats voted 30-32. Northern Democrats opposed lifting the embargo, 17-26, while southerners favored the McGovern/Byrd language 13-6. Republicans cast 27 votes for repeal and 10 against the proposal. *(Vote 240, p. 38-S)*

Rhodesian Sanctions

A move by Jesse Helms, R-N.C., to drop U.S. economic sanctions against Rhodesia imposed in 1977 was checked by the Senate July 26 in the second major action on the aid bill. *(Background, 1977 Almanac p. 328)*

On June 28, the Senate had voted 48-42 to table an amendment to the State Department authorization bill to lift the sanctions against Rhodesia, a vote that worried the Senate leadership and the Carter administration. *(Story, p. 401)*

To reduce the support that had developed for Helms' proposal, sanction supporters came up with an alternative, which the Senate accepted. Sponsored by Sens. Clifford P. Case, R-N.J., Jacob K. Javits, R-N.Y. and Daniel P. Moynihan, D-N.Y., the alternative amendment gave President Carter authority to lift the sanctions if two conditions were met by Rhodesia. The president was to determine that:

- Rhodesia had committed itself to negotiate in "good faith" with the guerrilla force known as the Patriotic Front and other parties on all relevant issues, including the terms of future majority rule and protection of minority rights.
- Free elections were held.

The Carter administration, however, objected to the compromise. The administration had backed giving the guerrillas a place in a new Rhodesian government, contending that no government could last without them.

Helms argued that the sanctions should be lifted because a transitional government was in place in Rhodesia and elections were scheduled for Dec. 31. The purpose of the sanctions was to "gradually cripple the economy of Rhodesia to pressure the government of Ian Smith to institute democratic reforms, Helms argued. The principle of democratic majority rule had been established, he said.

But African Affairs Subcommittee Chairman Dick Clark, D-Iowa, strongly protested Helms' proposal: taking that action, he said, could give the white leaders "a false sense of security, thinking that because we lift sanctions, we may, in the last analysis, go further — perhaps, even as many whites hope — come in and militarily defend them." Moreover, Clark said, the amendment would represent a "great setback" for U.S. influence in the Third World.

Javits argued that the alternative approach he backed required the government of Rhodesia to show that it was willing to negotiate with all parties.

The Senate approved the Case-Javits-Moynihan amendment 59-36 after a motion to table the proposal was rejected, 39-57. *(Votes 242, 243, p. 38-S)*

Helms later formally introduced his amendment to drop the sanctions entirely, but this was withdrawn after an amendment by John C. Danforth, R-Mo., to lift the sanctions only between Oct. 1 and Dec. 31, 1978, failed 42-54. *(Vote 244, p. 38-S)*

The Senate action on the Rhodesia issue came on an amendment offered by S.I. Hayakawa, R-Calif., which, after being amended by the Case proposal, was approved 90-6. *(Vote 245, p. 39-S)*

Other Major Provisions

The military aid bill itself authorized $500 million for financing arms sales to Israel, plus an additional $785 million in economic support fund credits for that country. Egypt was allocated $750 million; Jordan, $93 million; and Syria, $90 million.

These funds totalled all but about $600 million of the amount authorized by the measure; the remaining amount was spread among some 50 other nations.

The Senate bill also included a number of provisions to strengthen arms sales procedures enacted by Congress in 1976 to control transfers of U.S. weapons overseas. One required the president to develop an annual arms sales plan for transactions with developing nations.

The bill also created a new $1.9 billion economic support fund to replace the old security assistance program to the military aid legislation.

Korea Amendment

The Senate Foreign Relations Committee had authorized $800 million to cover the cost of transferring U.S. equipment to South Korea as part of the president's five-year troop withdrawal plan, but the Senate July 26 signaled its concern over Carter's basic policy.

By an 81-7 vote, the Senate approved an amendment offered by Charles H. Percy, R-Ill, stating that the scheduled withdrawal of 26,000 troops by 1982 might "seriously risk upsetting the military balance in the region." *(Vote 248, p. 39-S)*

The amendment required the president to consult with Congress, beginning in 1979, on plans for future withdrawals. Language added to the amendment by Sam Nunn, D-Ga., declared that the president should report to Congress on possible effects of any U.S. action on South Korea's ability to deter attacks on North Korea and the reaction anticipated from North Korea.

Reports were requested on South Korean plans to develop an independent nuclear deterrent and the impact of the U.S. pullout on relations with Japan, China and the Soviet Union.

Percy described his amendment as a "strong, strong message" to the president from the Senate and said that the vote margin demonstrated that members representing all political views were "deeply concerned about the program."

In a letter to Senate Majority Leader Robert C. Byrd, D-W.Va., July 20, President Carter objected to Congress placing restraints on his authority to redeploy the troops.

Congressional concern, Carter wrote, "results largely from the incorrect impression that withdrawal will follow a rigid timetable not subject to modification in the light of changing circumstances. This has never been the case."

Nevertheless, the president wrote, "withdrawal based over a four-to-five year period will be sufficiently flexible to accommodate developments" on the Korean peninsula.

Announced in May 1977, the first phase of troop withdrawal schedule, Carter continued, could be deferred until 1979 to give Congress sufficient time to approve the Pentagon's request for transferring U.S. equipment to South Korea.

Other Action: July 25

The Senate approved four other amendments July 25, including one by a 94-0 roll call vote, advising President Carter to consult with the Senate before making any changes in the 24-year-old defense treaty with Taiwan.

The amendment stated that China had "faithfully" carried out its duties and obligations under the treaty. Dole said that before any changes were made in that treaty arising from U.S. policy toward Peking, the Senate should examine the nation's security arrangements in the Pacific region as well as constitutional questions involved in abrogating the 1954 treaty. *(Vote 241, p. 38-S)*

By voice votes, the Senate also approved amendments by:

- Sam Nunn, D-Ga., to require the president to report to Congress on the results of a review required by the 1977 arms control act to distinguish between overseas arms sales that directly contribute to a foreign country's combat capability and those that do not.
- Charles H. Percy, R-Ill., to ban the use of any funds in the bill to spray Mexican marijuana fields with the chemical paraquat if the spraying was likely to cause serious harm to persons who might use the sprayed marijuana.
- By Percy, to include in arms sales contracts to foreign nations appropriate charges for inventory replacement costs associated with sales from Pentagon stocks.

July 26

Besides the action on the Rhodesia sanctions and Korea, the Senate July 26 adopted the following other amendments.

By a 69-25 vote, an amendment offered by Harry F. Byrd Jr., Ind-Va., was approved that sliced $40 million from the $110 million approved by the Foreign Relations Committee for assisting nations in southern Africa (Botswana, Zambia, Lesotho and Swaziland) suffering economically because of racial conflict in that region. The funds were earmarked for aiding African refugees, improving transportation systems, education and job training assistance and economic support. *(Vote 246, p. 39-S)*

Byrd argued that the administration had only requested $70 million and that the additional amount was "unwise" considering that an "already swollen budget" was proposed. African Affairs Subcommittee Chairman Dick Clark, D-Iowa, countered that because of the rapid political change under way in Africa, the aid for fiscal 1979 should be maintained at the same level as appropriated in 1977. "The countries of the region face special problems brought about by the continuing conflict in Rhodesia," Clark said.

Earlier, the Senate by voice vote approved an amendment by Clark earmarking $10 million in the bill for humanitarian assistance to Rhodesian refugees and another $10 million for educational programs in Rhodesia once the U.S. lifted its economic trade sanctions against the country.

In another action relating to Africa, the Senate by voice vote approved a Byrd proposal barring U.S. aid to Mozambique, Angola, Tanzania or Zambia unless the president determined that the assistance would further the foreign policy interests of the United States. The Foreign Relations Committee had not renewed similar language approved by Congress in 1977. *(1977 Almanac p. 363)*

By voice votes the Senate approved the following amendments by:

- Adlai E. Stevenson lll, D-Ill., to provide that the secretary of state be consulted by the secretary of commerce on granting export licenses for shipping equipment overseas that could have military applications for foreign nations. An amendment by Barry Goldwater, R-Ariz., to exclude agricultural commodities from the Stevenson amendment was approved earlier.
- Stevenson, to provide that crime control equipment exported to foreign nations other than NATO countries, Japan, Australia and New Zealand be approved by the Commerce Department with review by the State Department.
- William V. Roth Jr., R-Del., stating that the president should make a "full review" of U.S. policy toward the Soviet Union.
- John Sparkman, D-Ala., to establish procedures to govern the use of appropriated funds and U.S.-owned local currencies for members of Congress and employees traveling overseas on official business. *(Background, 1977 Almanac p. 24-A)*

By an 87-0 roll call, the Senate also approved an amendment by Minority Leader Howard H. Baker Jr., R-Tenn., stating the sense of Congress that the United States should continue to promote direct negotiations between Israel and Egypt. *(Vote 249, p. 39-S)*

"This resolution once more affirms our commitment to the survival of an Israel protected by defensible and recognized borders," Baker said.

The Senate approved a second amendment by Baker deleting a requirement adopted by Congress in 1977 requiring the secretary of state to automatically recommend approval of a U.S. visa application from a member of a communist organization.

Baker said that the amendment, which was approved by Congress "in the afterglow of the [1975] Helsinki Accords," would remind the Soviet Union that "we are willing to hold them to account for their cynical rejection of basic human rights" as indicated by the recent trials of Soviet dissidents.

A motion by McGovern to table the amendment was rejected 42-50. *(Vote 247, p. 39-S)*

House Committee Action

The House International Relations Committee reported its bill, HR 12514 (H Rept 95-1141), May 12 by voice vote. The bill, which did not include economic support assistance, authorized $999.3 million in military aid.

Turkey

Unlike its Senate counterpart, the International Relations Committee, by an 18-17 vote May 3, lifted the partial arms embargo against Turkey.

In its report on the military aid bill, the committee said the four-year-old embargo against Turkey had not worked, U.S. relations with Greece, Turkey and Cyprus had suffered during the period and little progress toward a Cyprus settlement had occurred.

A second reason cited by the committee for lifting the weapons sales ceiling was that it "jeopardized" U.S. national security and protection of the NATO alliance since important intelligence facilities were no longer available in that country. "At a time of a determined buildup in Europe," the committee said, the United States has been unable to shore up its Eastern Mediterranean defenses.

Regarding the Cyprus dispute, the committee said the embargo "has actually impeded negotiations" because "Turkey would not make any meaningful concessions as long as the embargo remained in effect. Meanwhile, its ability to fulfill its NATO responsibilities was deteriorating. In fact, the situation was the worst of both worlds."

But the committee report emphasized that the panel members who voted to lift the embargo expected Turkey to make concessions on the Cyprus territorial issues.

Other Issues

Although they differed on Turkey, the House panel agreed with the Senate Foreign Relations Committee in authorizing the transfer of $800 million in defense equipment to South Korea by 1982 and authorizing $275 million in foreign military sales credits for fiscal 1979.

But the House committee sliced $5 million from the $18.1 million requested for the Philippines because of "the continuing failure by the Philippine government to show significant progress in improving human rights practices as well as its refusal to lift martial law and restore democratic government."

House Floor Action

The House passed the $999 million military assistance bill (HR 12154) on Aug. 2, 255-156. *(Vote 558, p. 158-H)*

By a three-vote margin after an afternoon of emotional debate, the House Aug. 1 gave the Carter administration a major foreign policy victory by permitting the president to drop the U.S. arms embargo against Turkey.

Paving the way for this 208-205 vote to end the arms embargo were at least three factors: an intense, two-month lobbying effort by the White House and the State and Defense Departments; a last-minute compromise amendment drafted by House Majority Leader Jim Wright, D-Texas, on which the vote came; and the willingness of two members to switch their votes when they were desperately needed by the administration. *(Vote 548, p. 156-H)*

Although there were predictions throughout the day that the White House would win by 15-30 votes on the final tally, the repeal forces turned up one vote short — until Butler Derrick, D-S.C., and Richard T. Schulze, R-Pa., changed their votes at the end of the electronic count.

It was the Republican Party, however, that gave Carter his victory. Voting for repeal were 130 Democrats and 78 Republicans; 141 Democrats opposed the president compared to 64 Republicans.

In a statement following the House decision, Carter said the outcome was a "crucial step toward strengthening the vital south flank of NATO" and "will soon make possible the reopening of our military installations in Turkey."

In another major action, the House approved an amendment stating that further withdrawal of ground forces from South Korea may "risk upsetting" the military balance in the Asian region. The House also adopted a proposal prohibiting U.S. economic sanctions against Rhodesia after Dec. 31, 1978, unless the president determined that a government, chosen by free elections, had not been installed.

Turkey Embargo

During the week before the arms vote, the leadership looked for possible compromise routes on the Turkey arms embargo issue. But proposals that continued the embargo or tied its repeal to rigid conditions were opposed by the administration.

The compromise constructed by Majority Leader Wright stated that the embargo could be put aside by the president if he determined and certified to Congress that resumption of full military ties with Turkey was in the "national interest of the United States and in the interest of NATO."

The president also was required to certify to Congress that Turkey was "acting in good faith" to achieve the early return of refugees to their homes, the "continued removal of Turkish military troops from Cyprus, and the early serious resumption of . . . talks" aimed at a settlement of the Cyprus issues.

In a policy statement also contained in the amendment, the administration was required to report to Congress every 60 days on the progress of Cyprus negotiations. In addition, any security assistance requested by the administration was required to be certified by the president as intended only "for defense purposes."

"The embargo has not produced a settlement on Cyprus," said Wright, who had voted for it four years ago. "The southern flank of NATO has been weakened. The relations between Greece and Turkey have deteriorated. The relations of each to NATO have deteriorated."

The amendment, he added, "is not perfect," but it will give all parties a new chance to resolve the Cyprus controversy.

Opponents in the House, led by Majority Whip John Brademas, D-Ind., and Benjamin S. Rosenthal, D-N.Y., argued that repeal would undermine U.S. laws prohibiting the use of U.S. weapons by other nations for unauthorized purposes and would remove any incentive for Turkey to offer settlement proposals. (Turkey now holds about 40 percent of Cyprus territory; the island's population is 80 percent Greek.)

Brademas and other opponents supported an amendment by Dante B. Fascell, D-Fla. — Wright's was a replacement for that — which laid down a number of conditions to be met before the president could lift the embargo. Rejected outright by Carter, these required that:

- Turkey remove its troops from the Cypriot city Famagusta;
- The United Nations run the city and its Greek refugee inhabitants return;
- Talks aimed at a permanent settlement be resumed.

Another proposal by John F. Seiberling, D-Ohio, offered as a substitute to the Fascell proposal, was rejected by voice vote. It was identical to Wright's plan except that either house could veto future weapons sales to Turkey.

Korea Amendment

Following the Senate's lead, the House Aug. 1 approved an amendment relating to President Carter's plan to withdraw U.S. troops from Korea by 1982.

By a 212-189 vote, the House agreed to a proposal by Edward J. Derwinski, R-Ill., stating that it was the sense of Congress that additional withdrawal of U.S. troops from the Asian nation "may seriously risk upsetting the military balance in the region and requires full advance consultation with Congress." *(Vote 549, p. 156-H)*

The language was identical to a provision approved by the Senate July 26.

Derwinski's proposal was a substitute for an amendment by Samuel S. Stratton, D-N.Y., who wanted to limit the president's authority to transfer U.S. equipment to South Korea until Sept. 30, 1979, rather than Dec. 31, 1982, and to cut the value of U.S. military equipment that could be left with the Koreans to $90 million from $800 million. Stratton's amendment — particularly the part involving the $800 million — was intended to prevent Carter from going ahead with the troop withdrawal. Stratton's amendment as revised by the Derwinski language was later adopted 279-117. *(Vote 550, p. 156-H)*

In other actions Aug. 1, the House by voice vote approved an amendment by Lester L. Wolff, D-N.Y., prohibiting the use of international narcotics funds to eradicate marijuana with paraquat unless the herbicide contained another substance warning potential users that paraquat had been used. The House also rejected an amendment by John M. Ashbrook, R-Ohio, prohibiting military training funds to be used in Afghanistan.

Rhodesian Sanctions

In a slap at the Carter administration's policy on Rhodesia, the House Aug. 2, by a comfortable 229-180 vote, approved an amendment designed to remove U.S. economic sanctions against Rhodesia automatically after Dec. 31, 1978. *(Vote 556, p. 158-H)*

Introduced by Richard H. Ichord, D-Mo., as an alternative for a proposal more to the administration's liking, the amendment banned U.S. economic sanctions against Rhodesia "after Dec. 31, 1978, unless the president determined that a government has not been installed, chosen by free elections in which all political groups have been allowed to participate."

Acceptance of the amendment underscored the dissatisfaction in the House with a plan sponsored by the British and American governments calling for a peace conference to be held in which all parties attend, including Patriotic Front guerrillas, to reach a lasting settlement. The State Department believed that a new Rhodesian government, whether popularly chosen or not, could not last without cooperation from the guerrilla forces, and that the U.S. economic sanctions against Rhodesia — imposed by Congress in 1977 — were needed to prod the government of Ian Smith into these talks.

Secretary of State Cyrus R. Vance had addressed this issue on June 21: The U.S.-British plan, which would prompt a "rapid and peaceful transition to majority rule" in Rhodesia, would "bring together" the Patriotic Front with Smith's government, he said. "Neither side can create a new nation, with a decent chance for a peaceful and prosperous future without the participation of the other. And each now rejects the other's claim to predominance during the critical election period."

Vance explained that it was the "hope" of the United States and Britain to "help to bring them together, either to work out power-sharing arrangements among themselves, or to agree on a neutral solution such as the one we have proposed."

The Ichord amendment, however, made no mention of this policy plan, which many criticized as being weighted too heavily on the side of the Patriotic Front, a charge the administration disputed.

The proposal, Ichord stated, "does not require the present government . . . to negotiate with the Communist-backed, admittedly backed by the Soviet Union and Cuba, faction trying to shoot itself into power in Rhodesia."

The Ichord amendment gutted a plan offered by International Relations Committee Chairman Clement J. Zablocki, D-Wis., who suggested an amendment similar to the Case-Javits proposal approved by the Senate July 26. The administration that day quietly had passed the word that it could live with their compromise.

The Zablocki amendment banned U.S. aid sanctions against Rhodesia before Oct. 1, 1979, *if* the president determined that:

- The Rhodesian government had committed itself to "negotiate in good faith" at an all-parties conference held under international auspices on all relevant issues, and
- A government had been installed by free elections in which all groups participated freely with observation by impartial international monitors.

The amendment, of course, was not as absolute as the U.S.-British plan that pinned a new government on talks between Smith's government and the Patriotic Front.

Zablocki said that his amendment would allow U.S. diplomats to continue negotiations to bring about an end to the war in Rhodesia, whereas an amendment by Robert E. Bauman, R-Md. — Zablocki's was a substitute — did not even require elections.

The Bauman amendment, which formed the base for the House debate, barred U.S. economic sanctions before Oct. 1, 1979, *unless* the president determined that the transition government had not committed itself to negotiate in good faith at an all-parties conference and had made no "definite plans" for elections.

The problem with the Bauman language, said Stephen J. Solarz, D-N.Y., is that the sanctions are lifted immediately. ". . .Anybody who knows anything about Ian Smith and how he slips into agreements and then out of agreements," Solarz told the House, "knows that if we lift sanctions now the incentive on the part of the Rhodesian whites to proceed with elections will be significantly diminished, because they will be convinced that they have won the ballgame without having to pay the price in the process."

On top of that, Solarz said, if the sanctions were lifted, the black nations bordering on Rhodesia and the Patriotic Front will accuse the United States of taking sides, and that will mean the loss of whatever opportunity remains to bring all of the parties together for a conference based on the U.S.-British plan.

An amendment by Paul Findley, R-Ill., to the Zablocki substitute was rejected by the House, 176-229, before the vote on the Ichord amendment. Although the Findley amendment, like Bauman's, proposed to lift the boycott immediately — Zablocki's wouldn't have — it allowed the president to reimpose the sanctions if Rhodesia "refused" to participate in an all-parties conference (Bauman said unless Rhodesia had "not committed itself. . .") or "failed to schedule" free elections under international supervision (Bauman said unless Rhodesia has made "no definite plans"). *(Vote 555, p. 158-H)*

Other Actions

By a 147-257 vote, the House also rejected an amendment by Andy Jacobs Jr., D-Ind., prohibiting military aid to South Korea until the House Standards of Official Conduct Committee announced that Kim Dong Jo, former Korean ambassador to the United States, gave testimony regarding the investigation of South Korean influence-buying in Congress. *(Vote 554, p. 158-H)*

Zablocki noted that the House already had voted June 22 to eliminate $56 million in food aid for Korea from the agriculture appropriations bill to encourage that government to cooperate with the House investigation. *(Story, p. 145)*

To cut any military assistance, Zablocki argued, would "run counter to our own national security interests."

By a 166-243 vote, the House also rejected an amendment by Tom Harkin, D-Iowa, prohibiting the delivery of U.S. weapons to Chile sold before the date of enactment of the bill until that government turned over to the United States those Chileans indicted by a federal grand jury Aug. 1 for the 1976 car-bombing deaths of former ambassador Orlando Letelier and an American friend, Ronni K. Moffitt. The House at first had agreed to the amendment by voice vote, but that action was reversed later in the day after the Justice Department, upon hearing of the House action, mounted a quick attack to overturn the vote on the basis that it was inappropriate and premature.

Before the first vote on the Harkin amendment, the House had rejected, 146-260, an amendment by Fortney H. (Pete) Stark, D-Calif., simply banning all weapons shipments to Chile. *(Vote 552, p. 158-H)*

Zablocki argued that the amendments were ill-timed and unnecessary because the United States had "no evidence" that the Chilean government "will not comply with the extradition treaty" bwtween the two nations.

Congress in 1976 halted U.S. military aid to Chile, but some $24 million worth of sales were still in the pipeline, according to Harkin, who said the shipments should be held up until Chile abided by the terms of the treaty.

The House also approved four amendments on voice votes by:

- Wolff, D-N.Y., expressing the sense of Congress that the United States should be responsive to the defense requirements of Israel and should sell that country additional advanced aircraft.
- Wolff, D-N.Y., urging the president to review U.S. policy toward the Soviet Union.
- Dale Milford, D-Texas, requiring the president to report to Congress within 120 days the results of arms sales controls on nonlethal equipment.
- Bauman, requiring quarterly reports by members of Congress on foreign travel and use of foreign currencies.

Conference Report

Senate-House conferees on the security assistance authorization bill filed a report (H Rept 95-1546) Sept. 7 resolving the following major differences.

Turkey Arms Embargo

Conferees rejected the Senate's action requiring repeal of the 1975 embargo on weapons sales to Turkey and followed the House approach. It provided that the embargo would be of no "further force and effect" if the president certified that Turkey was "acting in good faith" to achieve a peaceful settlement of Cyprus issues: the early peaceable return of refugees to their homes and properties, continued removal of Turkish troops from Cyprus and the early serious resumption of talks aimed at a just negotiated settlement.

The conference agreement also required the president to certify that any requests for security assistance for Turkey and Greece be intended solely for defensive purposes, including the fulfillment of NATO responsibilities, and that the aid was not inconsistent with the objectives of a peaceful settlement among all parties.

Rhodesia Embargo

Striking a compromise close to the Senate position, conferees stated that the United States shall not enforce sanctions against Rhodesia after Dec. 31, 1978, provided that the president determined:

- That Rhodesia had demonstrated its willingness to negotiate in good faith at an all-parties conference held under international auspices on all relevant issues; and
- That a government had been installed chosen by free elections in which all political and population groups have been allowed to participate freely, with observation by impartial, internationally recognized observers.

In adopting the compromise, the conferees said it was their intent that the key phrase "has demonstrated its willingness to negotiate in good faith at an all-parties conference" be interpreted to mean that the Rhodesian government has committed itself to attend and participate in such a conference, if held, and that it was not necessary for the conference to convene by Dec. 31, 1978.

The conferees also said that the phrase "all relevant issues" for consideration at an all-parties conference include the terms of majority rule, the protection of minority rights, the Anglo-American peace plan and other matters.

Human Rights

Conferees approved a House provision making it a legal requirement that the United States deny security assistance to governments that engage in a human rights violations on a consistent basis.

Existing law contained more general language stating that it was "the policy of the United States" that aid would be denied these governments. The Senate bill contained no comparable provision.

Conferees also approved a Senate provision requiring exports of crime control equipment to foreign governments to be approved by the Commerce Department and the State Department.

Korea Equipment

Conferees adopted the House provision granting the president authority to transfer defense articles and services to South Korea in conjunction with withdrawal of the U.S. 2nd Infantry Division and support forces, but conferees added the word "only" before "in conjunction . . ." to make certain that the rate and proportion of defense articles transferred correspond to the rate and proportion of troop withdrawals and not any faster.

The Senate provision had authorized the transfer without requiring it to be connected with the U.S. troop withdrawals.

Conferees dropped a House provision placing an $800 million ceiling on the value of defense articles that could be transferred to South Korea in connection with the troop withdrawal. But the conferees said that "under no circumstances" should equipment be transferred that costs more than the replacement value minus a standard depreciation of the defense equipment in possession of the 2nd Division at the time.

Arms Sales

Conferees dropped a Senate provision listing 10 principles to be observed by the executive branch in making arms sales decisions for developing countries.

The conferees said the executive branch should "give consideration" to the principles but that they need not apply in cases "where extraordinary circumstances necessitate a presidential exception or where countries friendly to the United States must depend on advanced weaponry. . . ."

A Senate provision permitting two-thirds of the members of either the International Relations Committee or the Foreign Relations Committee to add 30 days to the existing 30-day congressional review period for arms sales contract was dropped by the conferees. They said the executive branch is expected to cooperate with Congress in acceding to requests for additional time.

Final Action

The Senate approved the conference report Sept. 11 by voice vote. The House adopted the report the following day, 225-126, clearing the measure for the president. *(Vote 670, p. 190-H)*

New IMF Loan Program

Low-income nations plagued by balance-of-payments deficits piled up following the 1973-1974 worldwide hike in petroleum prices were targeted for relief under an international program given final approval by Congress Sept. 28.

Senate and House action on HR 9214 (PL 95-435) allowed the United States to participate along with 13 other industrial and oil-exporting nations in a new International Monetary Fund institution — known as the Witteveen Facility after the IMF's managing director — to assist debt-plagued IMF members.

The United States share of the lending program was pegged at about $1.75 billion, with the other doners contributing an additional $8.7 billion.

The funds would be channeled to IMF member nations that had piled up large balance of payments deficits caused by soaring oil prices following the 1973 Arab petroleum embargo. The loans would be subject to strict monetary and fiscal conditions the recipients must meet in order to improve their trading positions.

Countries targeted for assistance were low-income industrial and developing nations: Spain, Portugal, Turkey, Peru, Egypt, Jamaica, Mexico, Zaire, the Philippines and Bolivia.

Without the new facility, supporters said, a debt-ridden nation would have to impose severe restrictions on imports once its credit was exhausted. This could damage economic growth, reduce living standards and also cause the country's trading partners to suffer.

If the facility was not established quickly, supporters said, the IMF resources might not be adequate to assist countries in managing their payments problems. In that case, indebted nations might be forced to curtail imports, restrict international payments and cut back severely on domestic programs. "The consequences," stated the Senate Banking Committee in its March 13 report (S Rept 95-698) on the measure, "could include political upheaval in countries presently allied with the United States, and the widespread imposition of trade and payments barriers which will reduce U.S. exports and economic growth together with world trade generally."

But conservatives argued that the new fund was simply a new "gimmick" devised by the United States and other oil consumers to avoid dealing with the fundamental problem of international dependence on Arab oil.

President Carter in his State of the Union address had urged Congress to approve U.S. participation in the new loan program.

In addition to authorizing U.S. participation, the bill contained these other major features:

- Clamped a $50,000 lid on the salary paid the U.S. representative to the IMF, currently receiving $83,000.
- Required that the federal budget be balanced beginning in fiscal 1981. The provision, initiated by Sen. Harry F. Byrd Jr., Ind-Va., was a flat requirement. But conferees sought to soften the impact by noting in their report that the provision "may be superseded by the action of future Congresses."
- Banned U.S. trade with Uganda until the president certified to Congress that the country no longer was violating human rights, a policy position initially opposed by the Carter administration.

Provisions

As signed into law, HR 9214:

- **IMF Supplementary Facility.** Authorized the United States to participate in the supplementary financing facility of the International Monetary Fund up to the dollar equivalent of 1,450 million special drawing rights. (The SDR is an international reserve asset whose value is related through a formula to the currencies of 16 IMF member countries. At the 1978 value, the U.S. participation authorized by the bill was put at about $1.75 billion.)
- Required appropriation of the funds necessary for U.S. participation in the IMF facility.
- **Debt.** Required the U.S. executive director of the IMF to seek to assure that no IMF decision on use of the supplementary facility undermines U.S.policy regarding comparability of treatment of public and private creditors in cases of debt rescheduling where official U.S. credits are involved.
- **IMF Salary Levels.** Limited the pay of the U.S. executive director of the IMF to level IV of the government's executive schedule ($50,000 annually in mid-1978) and the pay of the U.S. alternative executive director to level V ($47,500 in mid-1978).
- Directed the U.S. executive director of the IMF to present the IMF's executive board with a "comprehensive set of proposals" to assure that pay of IMF employees does not exceed pay received by persons with similar responsibilities "within national government service or private industry."
- **Human Needs.** Directed the U.S. executive director on the IMF executive board to work for stabilization programs under the supplementary financing facility which, to the maximum feasible extent, promote "productive investment and employment, especially in...activities...designed to meet basic human needs." Required an annual report to Congress on the effect of policies of countries using the new facility on basic human needs.
- Required an annual report from the secretary of the treasury and secretary of state on "the status of internationally recognized human rights" in countries using the new IMF facility.
- **Uganda.** Stated that Congress found that the government of Uganda under General Idi Amin had committed genocide against Ugandans.
- Prohibited any corporation, institution, group or individuals from importing, directly or indirectly, into the United States any article grown, produced or manufactured in Uganda until the president determines that Uganda is no longer committing "a consistent pattern of gross violations of human rights."
- Prohibited the export from the United States to Uganda of any article, material or supply, other than cereal grains and additional food products, until the president determines that Uganda is no longer committing "a consistent pattern of gross violations of human rights."
- **International Terrorism.** Directed the U.S. executive director of the IMF to seek to prevent any assistance by the IMF to any government which allows entry to any person who has committed an act of international terrorism, including aircraft hijacking.
- **Balanced Budget.** Specified that beginning with fiscal 1981, total budget outlays of the federal government "shall not" exceed its receipts.

Background

The International Monetary Fund is a government-supported lending institution established to help member nations correct balance of payments deficits. IMF loans — normally repaid in three to five years with interest — are conditioned on the applying nation adopting fiscal, monetary or exchange rate reforms to improve its trade balance.

IMF funds are drawn from the 132 member nations, but quotas are reviewed and usually increased only about every five years, a process that prevents quick financial response to international trade crises.

Following the surge in oil prices in 1973, a number of developing nations began to pile up huge trade deficits. Commercial banks underwrote large loans to assist these countries, but economists questioned the soundness of lending policies not linked to programs requiring borrowers to improve their trade and economic balances.

The oil-related balance of payments problem in the mid-1970s was compounded by a fall in demand for goods and services in some countries that depressed exports in others.

Some of the exporters did not reduce their own imports equally, choosing instead to borrow to maintain levels of consumption and investment. They continued to face uncertain prospects for their exports because economic recovery outside the United States was sluggish.

To combat these problems, the bill (HR 9214) authorizes the United States to participate in a new $10 billion Supplementary Financing Facility (SSF) within the IMF to aid member countries troubled by oil and trade related deficits.

Fourteen nations, including seven oil exporters, would supply the facility's lending resources. The United States' share, which would require appropriations, was expected to amount to $1.8 billion or 16.7 percent of total subscriptions.

Subscription Shares

(in millions)

		As percent of total
Industrial countries:		
Belgium	$ 182	1.7
Canada	242	2.3
Germany	1,271	12.1
Japan	1,089	10.3
Netherlands	121	1.1
Switzerland	787	7.5
United States	1,755	16.7
Subtotal	$5,447	51.7
Oil exporting countries:		
Iran	$ 829	7.9
Qatar	121	1.1
Saudi Arabia	2,602	24.7
Venezuela	605	5.7
United Arab Emirates	182	1.7
Kuwait	484	4.6
Nigeria	266	2.5
Subtotal	$5,089	48.3
Total	$10,536	100.0

Any member country that met three eligibility criteria would be able to borrow from the new facility:

- The need for balance of payments financing must exceed the amount the country could borrow from existing IMF funds.

- The member's underlying balance of payments problem must require assistance, coupled with adjustment policies, over a period of time longer than the IMF normally grants.

- The member must agree to a detailed economic program to redress its deficits, and the program should be equivalent to the most comprehensive conditions the IMF attaches to its regular credit.

Even with the new financing, commercial funds still would be required, according to the House Banking Committee. Because of the conditions the IMF attached to its loans, private capital was expected to flow more freely to the developing countries, thus supplementing the IMF credit.

In the past, required IMF loan conditions — reducing budget deficits and restraining private credit and money growth, for example — were expected to produce results rapidly, often within one year.

The IMF, the committee said, had been criticized for such a policy that can restore the balance of payments equilibrium only by severely deflationary policies that do not help make a country's economy more competitive in the long run.

In some cases, the Banking Committee said, deflation may be appropriate, while other economies need a longer-term strategy aimed at investment and increased productivity.

By extending programs adopted in conjunction with the new loans to three years, the IMF had taken a step toward adapting its typical stabilization programs to the particular needs of different economies, the committee concluded.

House Action

Committee

The House Banking Committee reported HR 9214 (H Rept 95-853) Jan. 27 by a 27-9 vote. Four amendments also were considered.

By voice vote, the panel approved a proposal that would reduce the salary of the U.S. executive director of the fund from $83,000 to $50,000 and the alternate executive director to $47,000. The committee also approved an amendment requiring the U.S. contribution to the new IMF facility to be reflected in the budget.

By a 17-19 vote, the committee turned down a proposal that would have required the U.S. executive director to the IMF to oppose loans to countries which would contribute to the deprivation of human rights and human needs. Opponents argued that it was not appropriate to attach this language to the bill because the institution is concerned with the balance of payments problems of a country.

By voice vote, the committee also rejected an amendment requiring the U.S. director at the IMF to oppose loans to countries that renegotiate loans with government lending facilities but pay off their loans to private institutions on schedule.

Floor Action

By a comfortable 267-125 vote, the House Feb. 24 approved a $1.8 billion contribution that the United States would put into a new lending facility set up within the IMF. Thirteen other industrial and oil exporting countries would contribute an additional $8.7 billion. *(Vote 61, p. 18-H)*

Before approving HR 9214, the House approved five amendments and rejected an additional two.

At the outset of the four-hour debate Feb. 24, Dawson Mathis, D-Ga., attempted to add language to the bill requiring annual reports on all loans by the IMF, but the amendment was rejected on a 9-27 standing vote.

The leadership then worked out an agreement on an amendment to HR 9214 that made the bill pertain only to the new fund and not to the IMF itself, as inadvertently provided in the committee bill. This was accepted by voice vote. Its effect was to preclude amendments such as Mathis' from being offered. Bill backers didn't want the House to get involved in controversial debate about other aspects of IMF loans.

As part of this floor compromise, the Banking Committee leaders supported an amendment by John H. Rousselot, R-Calif., stating that the U.S. share in the new facility would amount to $1.8 billion, a figure not specified in the committee bill but included in its report.

The House next approved by a 253-141 vote an amendment limiting to $50,000 the salary level of only the U.S. executive to the new facility, rather than the U.S. representative to the IMF itself as provided in the committee bill. The proposal was offered by Banking Trade Subcommittee Chairman Stephen L. Neal, D-N.C., as part of the decision to restrict debate on the bill to the new IMF facility. *(Vote 60, p. 18-H)*

By voice vote, the House also accepted a so-called "big-bank" amendment by John J. Cavanaugh, D-Neb., that required U.S. officials to the new fund to seek to prevent loans by the facility that would be used by a nation to pay off commercial debts while at the same time renegotiating repayment of loans from government sources.

This wording was a substitute for stronger language that would have required U.S. officials to oppose and vote against loans to countries that in the past have renegotiated loans with government institutions but kept obligations to private creditors current.

The idea behind both proposals was to counter what Cavanaugh and others saw as the potential for "bailing out" private banks that had become overextended in international loan markets.

Human Rights Amendment. The House also attached a human rights provision to the bill that Banking Committee Chairman Henry S. Reuss, D-Wis., said was "another in the long history" of rights legislation considered by Congress.

In 1975, Congress declared that U.S. aid could not be channeled to nations that violated human rights standards; in 1977, U.S. officials at the World Bank and other international lending activities were required to "oppose" aid to rights violators. *(Background, 1977 Almanac p. 370)*

Offered by rights architect Tom Harkin, D-Iowa, the new amendment required the U.S. director at the new facility to "oppose" loan transactions that might contribute to human rights abuses. The language had been rejected by the Banking Committee, 17-19, but was approved on the floor by voice vote. The controversy was deflated, according to a committee aide, because the "leadership warned that the bill would not pass the House" without the Harkin amendment.

In previous House skirmishes on rights proposals, liberals and conservatives had teamed up to win acceptance of the language, and it was feared that liberals, failing to win a new rights provision, would join conservatives to oppose HR 9214.

The amendment required the U.S. executive director to the new facility to ensure that monetary and fiscal conditions attached to IMF loans would not contribute to the "deprivation of basic human needs or to the violation of human rights such as torture, cruel or inhumane treatment and degrading punishment." The director would be required to oppose IMF transactions that would contribute to any violations.

Senate Action

The Senate July 31, by a vote of 69-16, approved the bill allowing the United States to participate in a new $10 billion facility within the International Monetary Fund for aiding member countries troubled by oil and trade-related deficits. *(Vote 267, p. 42-S)*

Countries most likely to use the new arrangement, known as the Witteveen Facility, are low-income industrialized nations as well as developing countries with some industry. Portugal, Spain, Turkey, Peru, Egypt, Jamaica, Mexico, Zaire, the Philippines and Bolivia were nations mentioned by the Senate Foreign Relations Committee in its Nov. 15, 1977, report (S Rept 95-603) on the bill.

Uganda

During floor action, the Senate approved a ban on trade with Uganda. Proponents said it was necessary because of that country's violations of human rights. The Senate rejected a non-binding substitute urging the president to consider action against Uganda.

The mandatory trade ban language was offered July 28 by Lowell P. Weicker, R-Conn., and several other senators. Their proposal prohibited imports from Uganda and exports, other than food, to that country until the president certified to Congress that the government of Idi Amin was no longer committing gross violation of human rights.

Weicker complained that President Carter was "unwilling" to cut off trade with Uganda despite reports of torture and slayings by Amin's regime: "So far as I'm concerned, the amendment tells him to do it."

But Frank Church, D-Idaho, opposed Weicker's proposal, offering instead the substitute that simply "urges" Carter to encourage and support international efforts to investigate and respond to conditions in Uganda, including economic restrictions. The amendment was identical to a resolution (H Con Res 612) passed by the House June 12. *(See p. 428)*

Church argued that "virtually every" U.S. coffee company had agreed to voluntarily boycott Ugandan exports following the House vote. An international boycott was now needed, Church insisted. Without it, he said, unilateral action by the United States would be "ineffective" because Ugandan coffee formerly sold to the United States would be absorbed by other coffee-consuming countries.

"A man like Idi Amin," replied Weicker, "does not respond to sense of the Senate resolutions. He only responds when it is clear this nation, and hopefully others, will act."

Church's substitute was tabled 46-30 and the Weicker amendment then approved, 73-1. *(Votes 256, 257, p. 40-S)*

Other Amendments

By a 67-0 vote, the Senate July 28 also approved an amendment by Richard S. Schweiker, R-Pa., requiring that participation by the United States in the Witteveen Facility be subject to the appropriation of funds for that purpose. *(Vote 258, p. 40-S)*

Before passing HR 9214, the Senate July 31 approved five amendments by:

- Robert Dole, R-Kan., to instruct the U.S. director to the Witteveen Facility to oppose any loan to Cambodia or Uganda. The amendment was approved by voice vote after a motion to table was rejected, 30-57. *(Vote 261, p. 41-S)*
- Jesse Helms, R-N.C., to instruct the U.S. director to the Witteveen Facility to oppose any loan to nations assisting terrorists. The amendment was approved by voice vote after a motion to table was rejected, 42-44. *(Vote 263, p. 41-S)*
- Church, to require an annual report to Congress on the observance of human rights, as defined by U.S. law, by each nation drawing funds from the Witteveen Facility. Approved, 57-30. *(Vote 265, p. 41-S)*

The amendment was a substitute for a stringent proposal by James A. McClure, R-Idaho, that defined human rights in terms of "American values," according to Church, rather than internationally recognized standards.

- Harry F. Byrd, Jr., Ind-Va., to require a balanced federal budget beginning in fiscal 1981. Approved, 58-28. *(Vote 266, p. 41-S)*

The Senate also rejected three amendments by:

- James Abourezk, D-S.D., to ensure that the Witteveen Facility did not contribute to the deprivation of human rights of a borrowing country. Tabled, 62-27. *(Vote 260, p. 41-S)*
- Jesse Helms, R-N.C., to restrict average annual salaries of IMF employees to not exceed 5 percent of comparable levels on U.S. Civil Service scales. Rejected, 31-55. *(Vote 262, p. 41-S)*

• Helms, to limit U.S. participation in the facility to a total of five years, through 1983. Tabled, 65-21. *(Vote 264, p. 41-S)*

Conference Report

House-Senate conferees filed a report (H Rept 95-1613) Sept. 22, resolving these differences on HR 9214:

Authorization. Both the Senate and House versions authorized the equivalent of about $1.75 million in special drawing rights for the U.S. contribution to the new facility. The House, however, had not specified when the contributions could be made; therefore, conferees approved the Senate date of Oct. 1.

Salaries. Only minor differences in wording existed between the Senate and House on language limiting the U.S. executive director to the International Monetary Fund to a $50,000 salary, the current amount for a level IV, executive schedule federal employee. The provision reduced the salary from $83,000. The U.S. alternate executive director could receive no more than $47,500 annually.

Conferees also accepted Senate and House language requiring the executive director of the fund to prepare a set of proposals designed to assure that salaries and other compensation paid fund employees were not higher than the pay of other persons in comparable government and private industry positions. The secretary of the treasury was required to report to Congress on these proposals and any salary measures taken by the fund.

Human Needs. Conferees adopted a House provision to encourage Witteveen programs to meet basic human needs "to the maximum extent possible," but they dropped additional House language providing that facility programs "contribute neither to the deprivation of basic human needs nor violation of human rights" and to oppose transactions which would.

Conferees also approved language requiring the Treasury to report to Congress on the effect of Witteveen policies on basic human needs in recipient countries.

Human Rights. Conferees approved a Senate amendment requiring the secretary of the treasury, in consultation with the secretary of state, to report to Congress annually on the status of human rights in nations using the facility.

Debt Rescheduling. Conferees accepted a House provision requiring the International Monetary Fund to seek to assure that no decision on use of the Witteveen facility undermine U.S. policy regarding comparability of treatment of public and private creditors in debt rescheduling where U.S. credits were involved.

Cambodia, Uganda. Conferees dropped Senate language directing the president to instruct the U.S. executive director to the IMF to oppose any aid to Cambodia or Uganda until the president determined and certified to Congress that the country was in compliance with internationally recognized human rights.

Balanced Budget. Conferees accepted a flat requirement added on the Senate floor requiring a balanced federal budget in fiscal 1981. The provision's wording was unambiguous: It stated that outlays "shall not exceed" receipts beginning in fiscal 1981.

On Sept. 14, by a vote of 286-91, the House had instructed its conferees to accept the provision. *(Vote 686, p. 194-H)*

However, conferees sought to soften the impact of the legal language with wording in their explanation of the agreements that said the provision "may be superseded by the actions of future Congresses." In spite of flat wording of the section, conferees said the provision "expresses the feeling" of Congress that the United States should have a balanced budget by 1981.

Terrorism. Conferees adopted Senate language requiring the U.S. director to the IMF "to work in opposition to" — House conferees insisted on this phrase rather than "to oppose" as contained in the Senate provision — any aid to a country that aids international terrorists. The House conferees also had been instructed to accept this Senate amendment.

Uganda Ban. Senate language prohibiting all U.S. exports and imports to Uganda until the president certified to Congress that the African country no longer was violating human rights was accepted by the conferees.

Conferees also approved Senate language directing the president to encourage and support international actions relating to Uganda human rights practices.

There was no comparable House provision, although that chamber June 12 had approved a milder measure (H Con Res 612) that simply "urges" the president to respond to rights violations in Uganda by supporting international economic restrictions and other steps. *(See below)*

Final Action

The Senate approved the conference report on the bill Sept. 25 by voice vote. The House agreed to the report Sept. 28, 238-138, clearing the bill for the president. *(Vote 751, p. 212-H)*

Uganda Trade Boycott

Revolted by reports of torture, murder and other violations of human rights, Congress in 1978 pressed the Carter administration to cut off U.S. trade with the Ugandan government of Idi Amin. Ninety percent of the country's export revenues came from coffee crop sales; and one-third of the crop was shipped to the United States.

The House June 12 approved 377-0 a resolution (H Con Res 612) urging President Carter to clamp an embargo on this trade. *(Vote 375, p. 108-H)*

And on July 28, in action on legislation approving a new International Monetary Fund (IMF) loan program, the Senate passed 73-1 an even stronger measure that imposed a flat trade embargo against Uganda. That proposal prohibited imports from Uganda and exports, other than food, to that country until the president certified to Congress that the government of Idi Amin was no longer committing gross violation of human rights. Conferees on the bill (HR 9214) later accepted the provision. *(IMF loan program, p. 424)*

Meanwhile, major American coffee companies, reacting to the congressional mood, suspended trade with the African country.

But the Carter administration opposed sanctions on trade with Uganda, a position many in Congress found exasperating considering the president's emphasis — and repeated statements — on human rights.

"Our commitment [to human rights] should be measured through actions, and not just moral pronouncements," Don Bonker, D-Wash., disparaging Carter's stance, told the House during debate on the resolution.

Since Amin came to power by a coup in 1971, up to 300,000 Ugandans had been tortured and murdered, according to various accounts. Amnesty International testified before the Senate Foreign Relations Economic Policy Subcommittee June 15 that it was "unable to verify these estimates," but the organization stated the "most serious human rights problem in Uganda is that of killings committed or acquiesced in by government or security officials."

Administration Position

The State Department contended, nevertheless, that an embargo would interfere with U.S. "free trade principles" and would be ineffective, anyway, without support from other purchasing nations. Department officials said that the administration already had taken a number of steps, which was the best way of demonstrating U.S. concern over human rights violations in Uganda. These included:

- No representation by the U.S. government in Uganda.
- A request that U.S. citizens living in Uganda leave the country.
- A ban on U.S. military and economic assistance.
- Instructions requiring U.S. representatives to international lending institutions to oppose and vote against loans to Uganda.
- Termination of U.S. government programs promoting trade and investments in Uganda, although private commercial trade was allowed to continue.
- Restrictions on military-related exports to Uganda, such as helicopters, as well as other exports that could contribute to human rights violations.
- A requirement that Ugandans wishing to visit the United States apply to the State Department for visas. This followed a 1977 disclosure that Ugandan police personnel were in the United States for commercial helicopter training.

The U.S. policy "can be simply stated," Deputy Assistant Secretary of State for African Affairs William C. Harrop told the Senate panel June 26: "It is our policy consciously to distance the United States from human rights violations in Uganda by denying U.S. products and facilities which would directly contribute to continued violations, while actively encouraging more concerted attention to this situation and appropriate actions by the international community as a whole."

Embargo Urged

And yet, key House and Senate members were puzzled by this policy. Foreign Relations Economic Policy Subcommittee Chairman Frank Church, D-Idaho, said at the outset of hearings on the issue in June that he felt "very strongly that this nation cannot sit idly by while genocide is being practiced in Uganda."

After questioning a witness about the administration's "timidity in the face of such bestial action" by Amin's government, Church reported he had once discussed the matter with Carter, who was "worried about U.S. citizens remaining in Uganda and reprisals" that might be brought against them should the United States implement a trade embargo.

Church said that there were fewer than 200 Americans still in the country and that they had been warned by Washington to leave the country. "They've made that choice to stay," Church said.

Another embargo sponsor, House member Don J. Pease, D-Ohio, told the House June 12 that the 100 or so missionaries who had decided to stay "desire that Congress proceed with action on Uganda, despite any possible consequences to them."

Furthermore, the State Department's contention that a U.S. embargo on Ugandan coffee would be ineffective because other nations would refuse to join it at a time of high world prices for the commodity was downplayed by embargo advocates. In the first place, said Rep. Pease, the loss of the U.S. market — one-third of Uganda's exports — would have a "substantial effect" on Amin maintaining his power.

But the Folger Coffee Company, a subsidiary of Proctor & Gamble and one of the companies that had suspended coffee purchases from Uganda, agreed with the State Department that without other nations joining a U.S. boycott, the Ugandan coffee not bought by the United States would be quickly redistributed to other consuming nations.

Another factor contributing to the Carter administration's unwillingness to support an embargo, critics said, was the role of the Congressional Black Caucus, which, like the White House, took no position on the June 12 resolution.

Although individual members of the caucus necessarily voted for the measure when it reached the floor, their support was "lukewarm at best," according to one House source, who added that behind the scenes they were "hoping the issue would go away."

The problem the caucus had with the embargo was that it singled out a black-ruled African government and was not tied to U.S. sanctions against South Africa.

Sen. Mark O. Hatfield, R-Ore., felt that the Uganda situation was "so extraordinary" that it required an embargo. "We're dealing with a madman," Hatfield said. On the other hand, by continuing trade with South Africa and other nations with rights violations, there is "hope that the United States can influence those governments," Hatfield said.

No member of the caucus cosponsored the embargo legislation when it was introduced by Pease and others in 1977. During the House International Relations Committee markup sessions in April that considered mandatory embargo proposals, it was African Subcommittee Chairman Charles C. Diggs, D-Mich., who offered the compromise resolution that simply "urged" the president to ban trade with Uganda.

Peace Corps Authorization

Congress July 25 sent to the president legislation (HR 11877 — PL 95-331) authorizing $112,424,000 in fiscal 1979 for the Peace Corps.

The final authorization level was a roughly even split between the $96.1 million proposed by the House and $125 million recommended by the Senate. The administration requested $95.1 million.

The Senate Foreign Relations Committee said the additional funding was necessary "to cover overseas inflationary cost increases" and to provide the Peace Corps flexibility to upgrade and expand its program.

The compromise figure of $112.4 million was a $29.5 million increase over the $82.9 million Congress authorized and later appropriated for fiscal 1978. *(1977 Almanac p. 376)*

However, the bill also included a $3.7 million supplemental authorization for fiscal 1978, which the administration also requested. The amount was included in the Senate but not the House bill. Conferees said that since House action in April "inflationary and programing factors" had increased pressures on the Peace Corps budget and made the request "fully justified."

In other provisions, the bill as cleared:

- Earmarked $1 million in fiscal 1979 as a U.S. contribution to the United Nations volunteer program.
- Authorized the Peace Corps to provide technical assistance and training to help countries develop their own volunteer service.
- Added a provision urging the Peace Corps to pay particular attention to the integration of women into the national economies of developing countries.
- Extended medical malpractice protection to volunteers involved in providing medical treatment.
- Authorized the assignment of volunteers to work in refugee assistance programs.
- Increased to $20,000 from $10,000 the amount the Peace Corps could pay to settle damage claims.

HR 11877 was reported by the House International Relations Committee April 11 (H Rept 95-1049) and passed by the House April 25 by a 297-102 vote. *(Vote 209, p. 60-H)*

It was reported by the Senate Foreign Relations Committee May 12 (S Rept 95-807) and passed by the Senate June 8 by voice vote.

The conference report (H Rept 95-1333) was adopted by the Senate June 29 by voice vote and by the House July 25 by a 276-120 roll call. *(Vote 520, p. 150-H)*

The president signed the bill Aug. 2, 1978.

Middle East Peace Pact Remained Elusive

Jimmy Carter's most significant foreign policy success during his first two years as president was the Camp David summit meeting, which resulted in a framework for a Middle East peace. Participating in that summit were Israel, Egypt and the United States.

The accords reached at Camp David, the presidential retreat in western Maryland, essentially represented agreements to agree, rather than an actual settlement of the difficult issues dividing the two nations, or the even broader disputes between Israel and all Arab nations.

"This is one of those rare, bright moments of history," Carter declared as the historic accords drafted at Camp David were signed Sept. 17 by Israeli Prime Minister Menachem Begin and Egyptian President Anwar Sadat.

But by the end of 1978, that success was threatened by a renewal of the discord that had made the Middle East a volatile region for thousands of years. As negotiations continued and the euphoria of Camp David dissipated, both Israeli and Egyptian leaders found that agreeing to the specifics of a treaty under political pressures at home was more difficult than agreeing to a "framework" in the seclusion of the presidential retreat in the Maryland mountains.

President Carter repeatedly expressed puzzlement that Israel and Egypt would quibble over what he saw as minor issues. But to both sides, none of the issues were minor. Israeli and Egyption leaders were being asked to resolve long-standing hostilities and to give up positions they considered essential to their national interests.

The negotiations were especially difficult for Israel. In return for a peace treaty, Israel was asked to give up territory that for more than 11 years had served as a buffer against neighboring enemies. Egypt was pressured by other Arab nations not to sign a separate peace treaty with Israel.

Carter's decision to call the Camp David summit was widely seen as a brash gamble that paid off beyond all expectations. The announcement of the summit came in August, just as the president's popularity was at its lowest point and there was increasing speculation that Carter would be a one-term president.

In 13 days of arduous negotiations, Carter, with the aid of Vice President Walter Mondale, convinced Sadat and Begin to accept two agreements that broke new ground. Both Sadat and Begin later said Carter's firmness was the key to the breakthrough.

Two Agreements

There were two agreements at Camp David, one dealing with the Sinai Peninsula and a future peace treaty between Israel and Egypt; and the other a "framework" for settling the future of the West Bank of the Jordan River and the Gaza Strip.

The Sinai agreement contained these major elements:

- Israel would return all the Sinai to Egypt, including three airbases, oil fields and 13 settlements established since the Israeli occupation in 1967. Abandonment of the settlements was left up to the Israeli Knesset, which agreed Sept. 28.
- Israel and Egypt would conclude a peace treaty by Dec. 17. Israel would begin its military withdrawal from Sinai within three to nine months, with final withdrawal to occur within three years. When withdrawal from the Sinai began, Egypt and Israel would "normalize" diplomatic relations. The Dec. 17 deadline was not met.

The West Bank-Gaza strip framework included these elements:

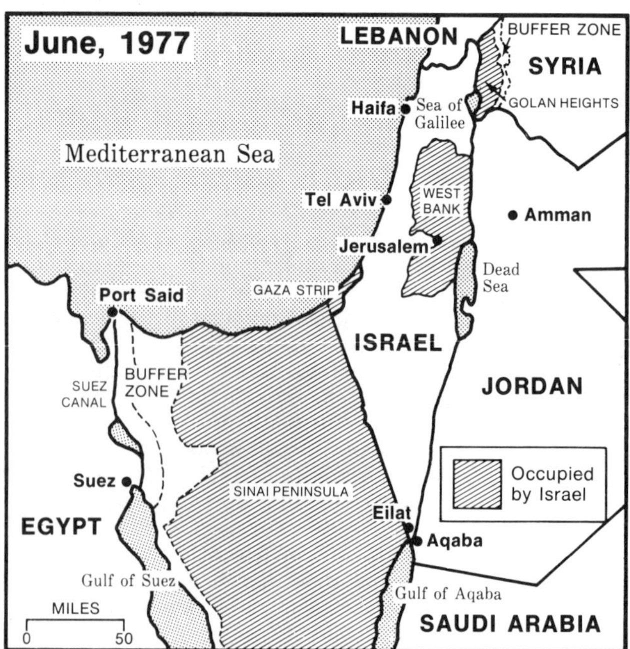

● Negotiations between Egypt, Jordan, Israel and Palestinian representatives would be held over a five-year period to determine the future of the West Bank and the Gaza strip. The Palestinians would have a veto over the final arrangement for those areas. Israel was given a veto over Palestinian representatives if they came from outside the West Bank or Gaza. During the negotiating period, residents of the areas would govern themselves. Most Palestinian leaders in those areas denounced the Camp David accords and said they wouldn't participate in negotiations.

● Israel would maintain troops in the two regions, but the numbers would be sharply reduced and they would be stationed in outposts away from cities.

● The Israeli military government would be withdrawn as soon as an Arab self-governing unit was established to administer the areas and to begin the five-year talks.

Many Issues Untouched

Because they were agreements, not formal treaties, the Camp David accords left untouched several sensitive issues, such as the future of East Jerusalem (occupied by Israel but claimed by Jordan), the eventual date for pull-out of Israeli troops from occupied territory, the eventual legal status of the occupied territory, and the fate of Palestinian refugees scattered throughout the Middle East.

Shortly after the Camp David accords were signed, Secretary of State Cyrus Vance optimistically predicted that a treaty could be signed by Nov. 19. That date was the anniversary of Sadat's historic visit to Jerusalem, when he and Begin pledged that there would be "no more war" between Egypt and Israel.

But it soon became obvious that negotiating the treaty would be a time-consuming process. Predictions of a treaty-signing were pushed back to Dec. 10, the date Sadat and Begin were to receive the Nobel Peace Prize, and then to Dec. 17, the date specified in the Camp David agreement. As the end of the year came, officials stopped predicting when the treaty would be agreed on.

In mid-November Carter expressed frustration that the negotiations had taken so long, and complained that both Israel and Egypt were spending too much time picking over "little, tiny technicalities."

Disagreements

Even before negotiations got underway, disagreements broke out over what had actually been said and agreed on at Camp David; within weeks Egypt and Israel were conducting negotiations through the news media.

While Begin was still in the United States after Camp David, he and Carter were disputing the terms of an agreement on Israeli settlements on the West Bank and Gaza. Begin said Israel could establish new settlements after a three-month moratorium, but Carter said Begin had agreed at Camp David not to establish any new settlements during the five-year negotiating period.

Twice, on Oct. 25 and Nov. 21, the Israeli cabinet approved draft treaties, each time adding reservations that made the drafts unacceptable to Egypt. President Carter had to personally intervene in the talks at two early points to prevent major breakdowns.

Sadat had more freedom than Begin in accepting or rejecting proposals on behalf of his own country, but the Egyptian president was pressured by other Arab nations not to make a separate peace with Israel.

While they were being pressured by the United States to reach agreement, both Sadat and Begin were under intense pressure at home not to make concessions to the other side.

Other Arab nations, including such moderates as Jordan and Saudi Arabia, warned Sadat not to relinquish the rights of Palestinians in the rush toward a peace treaty. And Begin, who led a minority party in a coalition government, was sharply criticized at home for his apparent willingness to abandon Israeli claims to territories occupied in the 1967 war.

On Dec. 10 Secretary Vance started his first effort at shuttle diplomacy in the Middle East to break the deadlock. He got Sadat to agree to a plan to deal with the remaining major problems in side letters to the treaty, rather than in the text of the treaty itself. But when Vance presented that plan in Jerusalem Dec. 13, Begin objected strongly, saying he could not make substantial changes beyond the draft treaty his cabinet had already accepted. Vance returned to Washington with no agreement Dec. 16. American officials publicly rebuked Israel for refusing to accept the latest draft; Israeli officials responded by accusing the United States of taking Egypt's side.

Vance met with the Egyptian and Israeli foreign ministers in Brussels Dec. 24 in an unsuccessful attempt to set up new negotiations.

West Bank and Gaza Strip

Throughout the negotiations, the so-called "Palestinian question" was the key stumbling block.

Egypt wanted Israel to completely abandon all territories occupied in the 1967 war, including the West Bank of the Jordan River and the Gaza strip and the Sinai peninsula.

Begin agreed at Camp David to returning the Sinai to Egypt, and agreed to self-rule by residents of the West Bank and Gaza strip during negotiations on the future of those regions. Palestinians vastly outnumber Israeli settlers in both areas.

Linkage

As negotiations proceeded, the main question became whether, and to what extent, the peace treaty between Egypt and Israel would be linked to the West Bank and Gaza issues. The United States and Egypt insisted that the treaty be linked to the resolution of the occupied territories issue. Israel wanted the treaty, but did not want provisions dealing with the occupied territories.

Sadat continually raised the stakes, first insisting only that the treaty be linked to the future of the occupied territories, then eventually demanding a specific timetable for Palestinian self-rule in those territories. Sadat made those demands largely to soften criticism from fellow Arab leaders, who had accused him of deserting the Palestinians.

At a summit meeting in Baghdad Nov. 2-5, the hard-line Arabs charged Sadat with treason, then offered Egypt $5 billion if Sadat would cut off negotiations with Israel. Sadat refused the offer, making it clear he expected assistance from the United States instead. American officials were distressed that Saudi Arabia and Jordan, two moderate Arab nations, joined in the hard-line attacks on Egypt.

The Israeli cabinet on Nov. 21 finally accepted a vaguely-worded link between the peace treaty and the West Bank-Gaza issues, but flatly rejected any timetable for elections.

Begin contributed to the feud early in the negotiations by announcing plans to expand Israeli settlements on the West Bank. Those plans were bitterly protested by Carter and Sadat, then put on the back burner where they simmered throughout the negotiations.

That issue broke out in the open again Dec. 6 when Israeli sources said the government planned seven new settlements on the West Bank. The government denied that report, and Carter repeated his assertion that the establishment of new settlements would violate the Camp David accords.

As the disagreement over a West Bank-Gaza timetable continued, the United States early in December offered a compromise that would have put the issues in a "side letter" rather than in the treaty itself. Under that compromise, the two sides would have agreed to begin negotiations on the West Bank and Gaza within a month of ratification of the peace treaty. A target date of Dec. 31, 1979, would have been set for elections in those areas.

In the background, the Palestinian Liberation Organization (PLO) rejected all the timetables and self-rule proposals. PLO leader Yassir Arafat said his group was the only true represenative of the one million-plus Palestinians on the West Bank and Gaza, and rejected Sadat's claim that he was negotiating on behalf of the Palestinians and other Arab states.

Just as important as the PLO objection was the refusal of Jordan's King Hussein to participate in the negotiations. The West Bank was administered by Jordan prior to the 1967 war, and the Camp David accords were based on the assumption that Hussein's involvement in the negotiation was crucial.

Egypt's Commitments

A second sticking point developed over Sadat's refusal to accept a section of the U.S.-sponsored draft treaty that pledged Egypt to give the peace treaty precedence over its agreements with other Arab states.

Israel insisted on that section, but Sadat demanded that it be eliminated or watered-down so that his country would not be giving preference to Israel, an enemy, over its fellow Arab countries.

Trade-Off

Vance and Sadat agreed Dec. 13 to a new proposal to settle the issues by forcing each side to make a concession in explanatory letters attached to the treaty.

That compromise would have required Israel to agree to a target date for elections on the West Bank and Gaza strip. Egypt would have accepted the Article Six provision for precedence of the peace treaty, while setting out its position on the issue in a side letter.

But Begin, backed by the Israeli parliament, rejected that proposal as being too favorable to Egypt. At the end of the year Begin said he would be willing to reopen negotiations on the side letters.

American Aid

Implicit in the negotiations was the assumption that the United States would provide substantial aid to both Egypt and Israel once a peace treaty was signed. Although peace in the Middle East generally was seen as being in the long run interest of all parties concerned, the short-term cost would be heavy for both Israel and Egypt.

Beyond short-term aid to help the two countries recover the immediate costs of peace, the Middle East peace initiative clearly would deepen American military and economic commitments for years to come.

Israeli officials estimated that moving its military forces from the Sinai Peninsula to the Negev desert region in southern Israel would cost approximately $3 billion over three years, a huge sum for that nation. To help pay for that move, and for other costs of peace, the Israelis asked the United States for an additional $3.3 billion over three years. At Camp David, Carter committed the United States to building two replacement military bases for Israel in the Negev, at a cost of $300 million to $1 billion.

For his part, Sadat quietly spread the word that he expected the United States to pay a major share of the cost of economic development in Egypt, possibly as much as $10 million to $15 million over five years. The United States had been providing Egypt $1 billion a year.

In December, President Carter said any special aid for Egypt and Israel would have to be legislated separately from the annual foreign aid bill.

Major Points

The frameworks negotiated at Camp David centered on four categories of issues: "the nature of peace," security factors, territorial decisions and the Palestinian role.

Both documents carried commitments for the Arab recognition of Israel as well as the establishment of normal relations between Israel and the Arab nations to advance peace in the Middle East.

The Sinai accord between Israel and Egypt outlined security provisions for the Sinai, including the size and location of Egyptian forces, the introduction of United

Nations troops and new early-warning stations. In the Gaza-West Bank accord, Israel's military presence was defined for the interim period and reduced from the current 11,000 level.

The Sinai accord required Israel to return Sinai territory to Egypt and to withdraw from the airfields on the peninsula, while the West Bank framework called for negotiation of the "final status" of the territories of Gaza and the West Bank and their relationship to neighboring countries.

The fourth issue, that of the Palestinians, was treated in two ways: elected representatives from the West Bank and Gaza would participate in negotiations on the final status of the areas and related talks for a peace treaty between Jordan and Israel. And any final agreement on the two areas would be submitted to representatives of the residents of the areas for their approval.

West Bank Framework

To conclude a Middle East peace treaty, the Camp David negotiators recommended that negotiations over the future of the West Bank and the Gaza follow these steps:

- The governments of Egypt and Israel ("Jordan will be invited") would plan a five-year, transitional "self-governing authority" for the two areas. These negotiations over its powers and responsibilities were expected to take three months. The Arab delegations could include any Palestinians "as mutually agreed" by all the parties.
- As soon as the self-governing authority, called the administrative council, had been "freely elected" by the inhabitants of the West Bank and the Gaza "to provide full autonomy to the inhabitants" of these areas, the present Israeli military government and its civilian administration would be withdrawn.
- Withdrawal of Israeli armed forces to an estimated 6,000 level would then take place and these troops would be stationed in areas away from cities on the West Bank.
- The agreement also would make provision for assuring internal and external security of the areas; a "strong local police force" would be established, and Israeli and Jordanian forces would jointly man control posts at border points.
- Not later than the third year after the transition government took control, negotiations would be held to determine "the final status" of the West Bank and Gaza and its relationship with its neighbors, and to conclude a peace treaty between Israel and Jordan by the end of the transitional period. Two separate but related committees would be convened to handle these talks.

"The general theory for this," said a senior administration official, "is that the negotiation of the final status of Gaza and the West Bank is intertwined with issues which will come up in the negotiation of a final peace treaty. Therefore, they can't be treated in two separate and independent tracts. They have to be treated together."

- The negotiations would be based on all the provisions and principles in United Nations Security Council Resolution 242, which contained the basic formula that Israel would relinquish occupied territories in return for Arab recognition, peace and security.
- The negotiations would resolve, among other matters, the location of boundaries and the nature of the security arrangements and recognize the "legitimate rights of the Palestinian people."

Egypt-Israeli Peace Plan

Compared to the long list of issues purposely ignored or vaguely addressed in the framework relating to the West Bank and Gaza, only one problem divided Israel and Egypt under the accord returning the Sinai to Egypt and establishing "normal relations" between the two countries.

But it was a major one. The question of whether all the Jewish settlements in the Sinai should be dismantled as Sadat insisted nearly wrecked the Camp David talks in the final days, when Begin refused to concede the matter.

The summit impasse was broken when Begin eventually consented to turn the controversy over to the Israeli Knesset for its decision. The Knesset agreed to the dismantling Sept. 28.

"Egypt states that the agreement to remove Israeli settlements from Egyptian territory is a prerequisite to a peace treaty," said a high administration official. "Israel states that the issues of Israeli settlements should be resolved during the peace negotiations."

On other issues that would be incorporated in a peace treaty to be completed within three months of the Sept. 17 framework signing, Israel and Egypt agreed to these points.

- Israel would return all the Sinai to Egypt, including the three air bases it operated on the territory as well as oil fields, and, if the Knesset agreed, the territory occupied by the 13 settlements. If this controversy were not resolved to Sadat's satisfaction, the framework for the peace treaty would be in serious jeopardy.
- All Israeli forces would be withdrawn from the Sinai.
- The airfields abandoned by the Israelis would be used only for civilian purposes in the future, possibly for commercial international flights by all nations.
- The Israeli withdrawal would be accomplished in two steps, with the first major part taking place within three to nine months after the peace treaty was signed. In that period, Israeli forces would withdraw east of a line extending from El Arish on the Mediterranean coast to Ras Muhammed at the tip of the Sinai Peninsula.
- After the interim withdrawal was completed, normal relations would be established between the two countries including full recognition — diplomatic, economic and cultural — termination of economic boycotts and other barriers blocking the movement of people and goods, and protection of citizens of each nation by due process of law.
- The final withdrawal and implementation of the treaty between Israel and Egypt would take place between two and three years from the date of signing of the peace treaty.
- United Nations forces would be stationed in the Sinai west of the Israeli border and Egyptian forces would be limited along the Gulf of Suez and the Suez Canal.
- Israeli ships would be allowed to pass through the canal.

Background: Peace Overture

Paving the way for the Camp David summit and the agreements reached there after 13 days was Sadat's dramatic decision to travel to Jerusalem in November 1977. That trip divided the Arab world more than ever before, but it diminished the psychological debris between Egypt and Israel that had accumulated over a 30-year period and four wars.

Begin indicated he would return sovereignty over the Sinai, a concession no other Israeli government had been willing to make, yet on the question of sovereignty for the

West Bank Begin held firm, vowing never to give up that territory to Arab control.

In December 1977, the two leaders met at Ismailia, Egypt, where Begin presented a 26-point plan for the West Bank, a proposal pinned to local "autonomy" for the Palestinians there during a five-year period. Israeli troops and settlements would remain; the plan contained nothing on the issue of eventual sovereignty for the territory, a critical point for Sadat.

These talks ended in disagreement, and lower-level discussions over the next few months failed to produce any progress.

After another successful meeting in July 1978 at Leeds Castle in England between the United States, Egypt and Israel, Sadat ordered the Israeli military mission out of Egypt, and stated that there would be no further talks until Begin agreed to withdraw from all the territories occupied during the 1967 war.

At this point, President Carter became concerned that the impasse could jeopardize the fragile relations between Israel and Egypt and wreck any chance for peace in the Middle East. He then invited the two leaders to Camp David for informal face-to-face talks aimed at breaking the stalemate. No advance agenda was planned.

Chronology of Camp David

Sept. 5-6. After Begin and Sadat arrived at Camp David — Carter had made the trip the day before — exploratory meetings were held. The president met with Begin alone on Sept. 5, with Sadat the following morning.

Those initial meetings, an administration official said, gave Carter a chance "to set forth at length his views on the unique opportunity the three leaders had to advance the cause of peace, the consequences that we foresaw if there should be no progress, and the key issues, as we understood them and viewed them."

The meetings also gave the president the opportunity to discuss in a preliminary way the objectives of the talks and how they might be structured.

Camp David, the official commented, lent itself ideally to the discussions: It was a chance for easy informality — meetings at different levels, during meals and in cabins with different members of the other delegations.

During the afternoon of Sept. 6, Carter, Sadat and Begin met for the first time at Aspen Lodge. Sadat introduced a new proposal for a comprehensive peace settlement, but the plan, which called for Palestinian sovereignty in the West Bank and the Gaza was tabled at this meeting.

Sept. 7-8. Bilateral talks between the United States and Egypt and the United States and Israel — conducted at various levels — were held "to clarify the proposals that had been put forward" by each delegation. The three leaders were to meet on Sept. 7 for the last time as a group until the summit ended, because, according to one report, it had become clear to Carter that for progress to be made, the two leaders would have to be separated.

Sept. 9-10. By Saturday, Sept. 9, the parties had a clear picture of the major features of the Egyptian and Israeli proposals. "By this time, it became clear that both sides would welcome an effort by the United States to break the deadlock," said a senior administration official.

The Israelis, according to another report, became intransigent over the issue of removing their settlements from the Sinai.

The United States delegation, after receiving directions from Carter, worked during the weekend to produce a draft negotiating text, drawing on the proposals offered by Egypt and Israel but also introducing new language where the positions were far apart, recalled a U.S. official.

It was at this time that separate work began on the Sinai framework separating the differences between Egypt and Israel on Sinai from those involved in the West Bank. The draft texts were discussed separately with the Egyptians and the Israelis by Carter, Mondale, Vance and Zbigniew Brzezinski, Carter's national security adviser.

Sept. 11. On Monday morning, the Israelis gave their reactions to the U.S. text and offered suggestions; the Egyptians went through the same process later in the day.

Revised drafts based on the reactions from each side then were prepared. This shuttle process continued through Sept. 12.

Sept. 13. By Wednesday of the second week, it had become clear to the United States negotiators that there were too many participants in the talks and "that it was necessary to try to reduce the size of the meetings and get down to a small negotiating drafting group," according to a participant.

Carter then asked Sadat and Begin to delegate one person each to meet with him and to meet for trilateral drafting sessions "in an effort to narrow the differences, identify agreed language and draft alternatives for items in disagreement."

On key issues — Sinai settlements, Jerusalem, West Bank settlements and Palestinian rights — the sides remained far apart. "We had to reach a judgment as to what formulations we felt to be fair and reasonable and would protect the vital interests of both sides," said a senior official.

Over an eight hour period, Sept. 13, Israeli and Egyptian officials met with Carter, adjourned for supper and returned for another two-hour session. Bilateral meetings were conducted later and the decisions sent to the drafting team, which worked into the early morning hours.

This process continued on Thursday, Sept. 14, with Carter, Mondale and others reviewing the latest drafts in the morning before planning the next round of talks.

Sept. 15. Without explaining why, Sadat told reporters after the summit ended that he had threatened to walk out of talks on Friday, but was persuaded to remain by Carter.

Also on this day, Mondale persuaded the two parties to set Sunday as the deadline for ending the negotiations and discussed with the two leaders, according to one report, how they all would look to the world if the summit ended in failure.

Sept. 16. Three issues remained — Jerusalem, Sinai settlements and language relating to the West Bank transition period — at the day's outset. During a meeting Saturday night, Begin agreed to take the future of Sinai settlements up with the Knesset and seemed ready to reach agreement on the West Bank Palestinian issue. The decision to exchange letters on Jerusalem came earlier.

Sept. 17. The controversy over Jerusalem surfaced again, but was resolved when the United States agreed to drop the word "occupied" from its draft letter. The final item — the question of Palestinian rights on the West Bank — was resolved about 4:30 or 5 p.m. "I am really not quite sure when it was," said a senior official. "We had all gotten so groggy by that time that we lost track of the time." ∎

Agriculture

Two new elements in farm politics — a militant farmers' organization and farm legislation passed in 1977 — had more success in 1978 than their opponents predicted. As a result, farmers both made more money than the year before and convinced more people that they had some serious financial problems.

Between January and April, the months-old American Agriculture Movement (AAM) came close to forcing a major rewrite of the 1977 farm bill, and it won some unexpected concessions from the Carter administration and Congress. It also was covered extensively in the national media and "was successful in creating a national awareness" of farmers' problems, according to a Library of Congress study.

Meanwhile, the new farm programs that were the target of AAM protests worked well enough in 1978 to raise farm income 29 percent over 1977 levels, according to the Agriculture Department. At year's end, net farm income was expected to total $26 billion, compared with $20 billion in 1977.

Record commodity exports, up 50 percent compared to the 1973-75 period, were a major booster of farm income. Department officials said farmer participation in new set-aside and grain reserve programs, combined with the export sales, had kept farm prices strong enough for efficient producers. However, farmers with unusually high production costs still faced serious financial problems, department officials conceded.

AAM organizers, many from high-risk or low-productivity regions, promised renewed pressures on Washington in 1979 for more aid. But chances for further AAM success seemed dimmed by the improvements in farm income and by the increasingly dominant issue of inflation.

Food prices, a major component in the overall cost-of-living index, rose 10 percent in 1978, compared with a 6.5 percent rate of increase in 1977. Congressional and administration concern with high food costs was a major element in slowing AAM's impressive momentum in the spring. Much of the growth in food spending was caused by spiraling beef prices. Although more than half the retail price of food represents labor, transportation, advertising and other non-commodity costs, soaring cattle prices — up 50 percent from September 1977 — pushed retail prices up rapidly.

Over bitter protests from cattlemen, the president sought to deflate beef prices, first by admitting more cheap, foreign-produced meat into the country and later by vetoing a meat import bill. Even before the meat bill veto, administration lobbyists had wrung from congressional committees less favorable provisions than the cattlemen had wanted. They were similarly successful in winning cuts in sugar legislation, which ultimately failed. These developments suggested that members would be reluctant to risk further food price inflation to meet producer demands.

Farmer Protest. AAM began as a strike organization, but its promised withholding action on commodities never materialized and the movement had its strongest impact as an unorthodox pressure group in Washington, Clinging resolutely to its identity as a "movement", AAM never designated spokesmen, developed detailed positions on agriculture bills, allied itself with established farm lobbies or registered as a lobby.

And AAM as a group did not have any notable impact on the 1978 congressional elections, although members had vowed revenge at the polls on farm-district members who did not support them.

What AAM did do was to dump delegations of angry farmers on congressional and administration offices for about three months. They failed to achieve their major goal of guaranteed 100 percent of parity prices. But before they went home to plant their spring crops, the farmer-lobbyists had:

- Won a moratorium from the administration on Farmers' Home Administration (FmHA) loan foreclosures.
- Won paid land diversion programs for cotton and feed grains and more favorable terms for the new grain reserve program from the administration.
- Prompted creation of a new "economic emergency" loan program under which farmers could refinance debts.
- Won a modest legislative adjustment of the 1977 act.

Farm Income. Near-perfect weather produced record yields in wheat and feed grains during 1978. But where bumper crops a year earlier had produced price-depressing surpluses, many farmers cut overall production in 1978 by idling part of their cropland in the new set-aside program. Strong participation in a new farmer-held reserve program further controlled the flow of commodities to market.

Since September 1977, when Carter signed the farm bill, wheat prices had risen 32 percent and corn prices were up 18 percent. Estimated farm income for 1978 was still well below the 1973 high of $33.3 billion, and farmers' production costs also climbed about 11 percent in 1978. But federal payments to farmers were also up, with an estimated $1.3 billion in deficiency payments due farmers for their 1978 crops. The 1977 figure was $1.2 billion. (Deficiency payments, the difference between market prices and federal "target prices," were available for farmers participating in announced set-aside or land diversion programs.) The combined total of federal payouts to farmers for producer loans, deficiency and land diversion payments and disaster aid came to about $6.2 billion for the year.

Farmers had threatened to stay out of set-aside and reserve programs, and participation in the land program was running behind department expectations. But officials said the rate was "good" for a new program. Farmer use of the reserve program exceeded department projections.

—By Elizabeth Wehr

Pared-Down Emergency Farm Bill Enacted

A persistent lobbying campaign by disgruntled farmers came close to pushing a major agricultural aid bill through Congress in the early months of 1978. But controversy developed over the Senate-passed bill and a subsequent conference version, and the conference report went down to an emphatic defeat in the House.

The result was a scaled-down "emergency farm bill" (HR 6782 — PL 95-279) that mainly left it up to an unenthusiastic Carter administration to increase target prices for crops if it wished. That bill cleared Congress May 4 and was signed into law May 15. The administration indicated it would do little more than raise wheat target prices by about 40 cents a bushel under the new law.

Emergency loan provisions also were added to a farm credit revision bill (HR 11504) in response to the farmers' lobbying pressure. *(Story, p. 446)*

The lobbying effort was spearheaded by the new American Agriculture Movement (AAM), which brought hundreds of farmers to Washington between January and May to lobby personally for aid.

Although the final version of HR 6782 was a disappointment to the AAM, the fact that there was a farm bill at all in 1978 was a surprise to most observers, who had considered it a political impossibility at the beginning of the year.

Provisions

As signed into law May 15, HR 6782 (PL 95-279):

- Authorized the secretary of agriculture to raise the target price for wheat, feed grains or cotton whenever a set-aside (voluntary land diversion program) was established for these crops. The target price increase was to compensate producers for participating in the set-aside; participation costs could include fixed payments on land or equipment which a farmer had to keep up whether or not he planted. Rice would also be covered, under a provision added to the emergency farm credit bill. *(Story, p. 446)*

- Authorized the secretary to raise target prices for other commodities when he increased them for the designated crops. These increases were to be enough to ensure the effective operation of the program — that is, enough to keep farmers from switching their plantings to take advantage of designated crop payments.

- Made three technical changes in the formula for establishing the cotton loan level, and set a minimum loan level of 48 cents a pound. The existing loan level was 44 cents.

- Authorized the secretary to permit farmers to produce crops on set-aside land for the production of gasohol (an experimental fuel combining petroleum and alcohol). In years with no set-aside, the secretary could provide incentive payments to encourage production of gasohol.

- Raised the limit on the Commodity Credit Corporation's borrowing authority to $25 billion, from $14.5 billion, on Oct. 1, 1978.

- Authorized establishment of a federal marketing order for raisins that would permit certain promotional and marketing activities by a grower-producer association.

Background

Financially squeezed between rising production costs and falling market prices, U.S. farmers looked to Congress for help early in 1978. The four-year farm bill enacted in 1977 (PL 95-113) was no help at all, many farmers contended, since inflation-fueled production costs had far outstripped the target prices and loan levels in the bill. Under the price support system begun in 1973, the government paid farmers the difference between what they could get on the market and the so-called target price. *(Financial problems of farmers, 1977 farm bill, 1977 Almanac pp. 415, 417)*

With huge grain surpluses depressing market prices, farm debt at an all-time high and 1977 drought and floods wiping out many farmers' crops, American agriculture was in the worst shape since the Depression, many farmers contended.

Although the AAM's call for a nationwide farm strike in December 1977 was generally ineffective, the organization did focus farmer discontent and spearhead a lobbying campaign that succeeded in generating support in Congress and among the public for more help for farmers.

With tractorcades across the nation, the AAM launched its highly visible lobbying effort in January. Its goal was passage of a "minimum price" law that would prohibit sale of farm commodities at anything less than 100 percent of parity, which AAM defined as production costs plus a reasonable profit.

The new farm movement also sought full control of agricultural policy through a producer board, cessation of agricultural imports until market prices reached 100 percent parity and more timely announcements of marketing and other agricultural information.

What farmers were offered by the Carter administration was encouragement to participate in existing land set-aside and grain reserve programs. Each was intended to raise prices by extracting a substantial volume of existing wheat and grain surpluses from the market. But farmers complained that neither program had adequate incentives, and an Agriculture Department survey at the beginning of 1978 indicated a low participation rate in announced set-aside programs for wheat and feed grains.

The set-aside program was a successor to the earlier "soil bank" programs that paid farmers for not growing on part of their land. But the new version made such payments optional — an option the administration chose not to exercise. Farmers who did not participate in set-asides announced by the Agriculture Department would lose eligibility for target price supports, loans and other benefits.

President Carter Jan. 30 rejected the demand for full parity farm prices as too costly. He insisted that the 1977 farm law would improve the farmers' financial situation if they gave it time to work, and he stated repeatedly that any further increase in farm aid would be vetoed.

Having spent much of 1977 fashioning PL 95-113, Congress was no more anxious than the administration to reopen the question of farm price supports, and Agriculture Committee leaders flatly dismissed the 100 percent of parity demand as having no chance of passage. But the persistent presence of the farmer-lobbyists on Capitol Hill eventually began to pay off.

After briefly disrupting Washington, D.C., traffic Jan. 19 and 20 with tractor-led demonstrations, the striking farmers clogged congressional corridors and offices and "scared the hell out of the Senate," as one aide reported.

House sentiment was mixed, with some urban and suburban members reportedly perplexed by rural styles of speech and dress and by the complexities of farm support systems. Upcoming elections stirred the anxiety of farm district members. The lobby effort spawned numerous meetings at which farmers detailed their bleak financial future and stressed the urgency of congressional action before the 1978 planting season got underway. Members of Congress discussed the political and budget obstacles to further farm aid.

For two months it was impossible to walk around Capitol Hill without being aware of the farmers. They crowded into hearing rooms and nearby hallways, buttonholed individual members, gathered in groups outside congressional office buildings and, as was generally remarked, "just didn't go away."

Eventually, many members grew impatient with the farmers, particularly after several reports of scattered violence and incidents such as the takeover of an Agriculture Department office in Washington in March. However, the AAM was credited by most observers with substantially changing members' perceptions of farmers' financial problems and "creating a climate in which we can do something for farmers," as House Agriculture Committee Chairman Thomas S. Foley, D-Wash., said.

Congress' initial response was more sympathy than substance. The Senate passed a sense-of-the-Senate resolution (S Res 393 — S Rept 95-634) Feb. 9 urging the president to raise loan levels for corn, wheat, soybeans and peanuts and to revive the soil bank program. After an initial spate of non-specific bills calling for 100 percent of parity, numerous substantial bills were introduced that sought to raise existing target price and loan levels (sometimes referred to collectively as "price supports"), tie price supports to cost-of-living increases more directly than in the existing law, limit farm imports (especially beef) and substantially increase farm exports.

As the pressure from angry farmers mounted, both House and Senate Agriculture Committees held marathon hearings in February and March, giving individual farmers, farm lobby organizations, rural bankers and farm-state members of Congress an opportunity to appeal for government action.

Committee Action

Militant farmers, against all predictions, extracted four emergency aid bills from two congressional committees. In just three days — March 13-15 — the House and Senate Agriculture Committees ordered reported:

- A $3 billion, one-year "flexible parity" bill (S 2481) that would guarantee grain and soybean farmers price support payments (target prices) of up to 100 percent of parity, depending on what percentage of their land they agreed to "set aside," or take out of production. The bill also substantially raised loan levels for wheat and corn, and pumped an additional half billion dollars into the Food for Peace (PL 480) program. The bill was sponsored by Robert Dole, Kan., ranking Republican on the Senate Agriculture Committee, and was favored by the militant farmers as an intermediate step toward meeting their financial problems.
- A one-year, $2.1 billion "land diversion" bill (HR 6782) that would pay farmers up to $75 an acre for setting aside up to 31 million acres of wheat, feed grain, cotton and soybean acreage. It was sponsored by Herman E. Talmadge, D-Ga., chairman of the Senate Agriculture Committee.
- Two bills (HR 11504, S 2146) establishing a new $4 billion, two-year "economic emergency" loan program to help established farmers whose regular sources of credit had dried up. The bills also raised individual loan ceilings in existing programs that provided money for mortgage payments (farm ownership loans) and operating expenses.

The House committee moved first, effectively approving the credit revisions March 10 after lengthy markup sessions. *(Story, p. 446)*

The Senate panel approved Talmadge's land diversion bill March 13 and Dole's flexible parity bill two days later (S Repts 95-699, 704).

In an attempt to keep his bill intact and relatively uncontroversial, Talmadge agreed with Dole that the committee would have an opportunity to report each bill separately. Dole's bill had gained substantial support in the Agriculture Committee and elsewhere — at least in part, observers thought — because it contained the AAM catch phrase, 100 percent of parity. If a farmer set aside half his land, under the Dole plan, he would be guaranteed federal price supports at 100 percent of parity, a complex formula designed to give farmers "fair" purchasing power in relation to costs.

Only Kaneaster Hodges Jr., D-Ark., voted against the land diversion measure, saying he had not had enough time to study it.

The only negative vote on the flexible parity measure came from Dick Clark, D-Iowa, who said he feared the impact of higher corn prices on livestock producers. Clark later denounced the bill and said he would not participate in committee "irresponsibility regardless of what the rest. . .do."

Clark questioned the motives of the bill's sponsor, Dole, claiming the measure would "almost certainly destroy the only chance we have to get meaningful help for farm prices this year because there's not any question that this bill will be vetoed. That may well be what Sen. Dole wants, so that he can blame the president for refusing to help farmers." Clark also speculated that "while some senators genuinely support this legislation, I think others are going along with it just to get the issue off their backs."

The committee reported the land diversion legislation as an amendment to a minor House bill (HR 6782) authorizing establishment of a federal marketing order for raisins — that is, permitting certain promotional and marketing activities by a grower-producer association. Because the House had passed the bill in 1977, this maneuver could mean quicker action and less likelihood of substantive amendments.

Strategy Agreement, Breakdown

Talmadge had secured from Majority Leader Robert C. Byrd, D-W.Va., a promise that Panama Canal debate could be interrupted for a day — if Talmadge could secure unanimous consent to limit the time of debate — to bring the land diversion measure to the Senate floor. (Agriculture Committee staff members denied newspaper reports that Talmadge had traded his vote on the Panama Canal treaties for floor time for his bill.)

After the Senate committee, including Talmadge, endorsed the flexible parity bill, Dole expressed confidence that his measure would also be considered then.

Talmadge preferred his measure because in the long run, he said, it would not involve any new spending, since fewer or no deficiency payments — implied by a rising market — would balance out the cost of paying farmers to set aside land. Technically, however, the measure required a waiver of the 1978 budget resolution and action by the Senate Appropriations Committee.

Talmadge managed to get speedy action from the Appropriations Committee, which reported his bill March 17 without recommendation (S Rept 95-705), and the Budget Committee, which approved budget waivers for both the Talmadge and Dole bills (S Repts 95-707, 708).

Talmadge wanted quick action on his bill to speed preliminary cash payments to farmers in time for spring planting — already underway in southern states as his panel acted. The bill provided that half of the land diversion payments — about $2 billion — would be paid to farmers almost immediately. Agriculture Committee staff sources said the Agriculture Department had already begun gearing up to make those payments, and farmers could have a commitment on the amount a week after the president signed the bill, with checks several weeks later.

The strategy was secure through early negotiations between Talmadge, Dole, Byrd and Edmund S. Muskie, D-Maine, chairman of the Senate Budget Committee, on a unanimous consent agreement to limit the time of floor debate. What came out of those negotiations was a plan to spend four hours on each bill and a request that Muskie arrange for budget analyses of each. (Under a unanimous consent request — the format Talmadge was to use to ask the Senate to consider the bills — one objection from a senator could kill the request.)

Accounts of why the agreement fell apart differ somewhat, but the basic elements were that Dole became miffed when he learned that Talmadge planned to allow George McGovern, D-S.D., to add price support hikes to the land diversion bill. This addition was intended to make the bill acceptable to House Agriculture Committee Chairman Thomas S. Foley, D-Wash. A Dole aide said Dole considered the original strategy arrangement void at that point and decided to offer his bill as an amendment to HR 6782 so as not to be left out in a legislative shuffle.

Since Talmadge had attached his bill to the raisin-marketing measure passed by the House in 1977, technically Foley could go directly to the House floor and ask under unanimous consent for a conference.

Senate Floor Action

The Senate responded to militant farmers' pleas for emergency farm aid by passing an unwieldy combination of programs that appeared to join two contradictory strategies for hiking farm income.

By a 67-26 vote March 21 the Senate passed the bill (HR 6782) joining two opposing measures reported a week earlier by the Senate Agriculture Committee and adding a third alternative that had not won the panel's approval. *(Vote 72, p. 13-S)*

To a simple land diversion bill that provided direct payments to farmers who took cropland out of production, the Senate by amendment added hefty boosts in federal target price and loan levels for wheat, corn and cotton. Then it tacked on a flexible parity plan that permitted a farmer to set his own price support by deciding how much land to take out of production. Price supports tended to encourage production, while land diversion was intended to shrink price-depressing surplus production, according to agricultural economists.

Confusion Over Costs

The total cost of the Senate-passed bill was not known because the haste with which it was patched together did not allow time for economic and budgetary analyses by the Congressional Budget Office (CBO), as provided by the 1974 Budget Act (PL 93-344).

Preliminary estimates of the land diversion program alone indicated that its projected payments of $75 an acre for 31 million acres could cost about $2 billion in early outlays. But Talmadge, the measure's sponsor, said that over a four-year period the program would actually save taxpayers money. Improved market prices would lessen the need in the future for price support payments, he said.

Dole disputed a $3 billion price tag put on his flexible parity plan, also asserting that outlays for price supports would be cut by an improved market.

No cost estimates were available for the third element of the bill, the higher target price and loan levels proposed by McGovern.

Nor was there any firm information on how — or whether — these programs would mesh with each other. Dole, who set off an avalanche of amendments with his flexible parity measure, initially claimed that farmers would not be able to "double dip" — take advantage of several programs. But in the course of the debate he said the various elements of the bill were "not mutually contradictory" and that he hoped they could be "married" in conference. Talmadge told reporters after the final vote that he did not see how that legislative marriage could take place. Nothing in the bill as passed prohibited a farmer from collecting several types of benefits — if he could figure out how to do it, according to Senate committee staff sources.

Also lacking during the day-long debate was solid data on how the emergency farm package would affect inflation in general, food prices in particular, commodities exports, and carryover supplies.

An exasperated Muskie warned that the Dole program alone could create severe grain shortages, destabilizing the market and driving up consumer prices. Muskie claimed consumer food prices could rise by as much as $6 billion.

Muskie characterized his colleagues' rush to passage — without economic estimates — as "extremely disturbing," adding, "This is the greatest comedy of errors under the supposed aegis of the budget act that I've ever seen."

Amendments

Talmadge had warned his colleagues against "killer amendments" that would bog down his measure and deprive farmers of early aid. But the disintegration of his strategy showed up as soon as floor consideration began March 21, as amendments spilled out in quick succession.

Dole opened, announcing that he would offer the flexible parity amendment. McGovern followed immediately with the price support hikes, and James B. Allen, D-Ala., proposed raising McGovern's target price for cotton by 10 cents, to 70 cents a pound.

Neither McGovern nor Dole brought up McGovern's proposal, which had been attached by the Agriculture Committee to Dole's bill, to add half a billion dollars to the Food for Peace program. McGovern said he had dropped this provision upon being advised it was "not germane." Privately, committee staff said it had been abandoned because it was "more dollars to hassle about."

At this point, Talmadge, answering a query, acknowledged that he had agreed to take the Dole plan to conference even though he thought it sure to fail. He added that he was ready to accept the Dole plan immediately but the consent agreement required eight hours of debate before a final vote. Other considerations also stood in the way, he said.

With six hours to go before a final vote, the Senate set to work, agreeing to the McGovern amendment by a 58-35 vote, to the Dole amendment by a 55-39 vote, and to nine additional amendments — by voice vote or without objection — directed variously at the three major elements of the bill. *(Votes 69, 71, p. 13-S)*

The Senate also passed by voice vote two resolutions (S Res 415, S Res 418) waiving the limits of the 1978 budget resolution for HR 6782 and S 2481.

It tabled (killed) by a 66-29 vote an amendment by Henry Bellmon, R-Okla., that would have adjusted upwards the graduated scale of acreage set-asides in the flexible parity plan. The effect would be to require farmers to set aside more acres to qualify for each level of payment. *(Vote 70, p. 13-S)*

The only other amendment that failed was a proposal by William D. Hathaway, D-Maine, to establish a 1978 set-aside on potatoes. That proposal was ruled not germane on a point of order raised by Talmadge. The Senate did agree to a Hathaway amendment to prohibit the growing of potatoes on set-aside acreage.

The steady stream of amendments was interrupted periodically by angry outbursts from Muskie, who warned his colleagues against acting with dangerous haste and ignorance.

Muskie, known for his urgent warnings against overspending, seemed unusually exercised because of the extremely short notice he had had on the McGovern and Dole amendments. Muskie said he had not seen the McGovern plan until 10 p.m. the night before, and the Dole plan appeared only 24 hours before that. No one, he added, had asked him to provide estimates on combinations of these elements, and one could simply not add up the costs of the "three-headed monster" of a bill. However, it would surely "add billions to the budget," he said.

Muskie laid out what he viewed as an alarming trend in farm program spending in 1977 — from a Carter budget request of $2.3 billion to a current Budget Committee estimate of $9 billion — not including either the emergency farm bill under consideration or $1.5 billion in a pending special disaster relief appropriation.

In apparent reference to the unremitting AAM pressures, applied in person by great numbers of farmer-lobbyists, Muskie warned, "We're going to vote for this unanalyzed, undigested, inconsistent package for only one reason . . . Don't you suppose other constituencies are watching [and] will learn to do for themselves what the farmers have done?"

Dole responded by attacking CBO projections, which he said were based on the most pessimistic scenarios. McGovern remarked that "two to three billion dollars is just a modest contribution toward the losses farmers are sustaining."

Also speaking against the bill was Bellmon, who warned that "We are about to pass legislation here on which I do not believe the good Lord himself knows what would be the best course of action for any producer."

Howard M. Metzenbaum, D-Ohio, objected to a policy of scarcity in the face of world food problems.

The day after the Senate acted, the President's Council on Wage and Price Stability blasted the Senate bill as passed, claiming that it would add two to five percentage points to the rate of food inflation. In a March 22 statement, the Council said that if the bill were enacted, "it would be one of the most inflationary actions of the federal government in recent years."

Senate Provisions

As passed by the Senate March 21, HR 6782:

Land Diversion Program

- Required the secretary of agriculture to set aside at least 31 million acres of cropland for crop year 1978, in addition to the 15 million acre wheat and feed grain set-asides already announced by the Department of Agriculture. Participation in the additional set-aside was voluntary, but farmers not taking part in the announced program were ineligible for the new one.
- Authorized direct payments to farmers, only for that portion of land they set aside beyond the levels in the previously announced programs. Payments were estimated at about $75 an acre.
- Stipulated the following distribution for the additional set-aside: 15 million acres of wheat, 10 million acres of feed grains, three million acres of cotton, three million acres of soybeans. The Agriculture Department in 1977 had established for the upcoming crop year a 20 percent (11 million acre) set-aside for wheat and a 10 percent (four million acre) set-aside for feed grains. There were no existing set-aside programs for cotton or soybeans.
- Mandated specific market price objectives for the land diversion program, and authorized the secretary to set aside additional land or take certain other steps as needed to bring market prices up to those objectives. The price objectives were: $3.50 a bushel for wheat, $2.50 a bushel for corn, $6 a bushel for soybeans and 60 cents a pound for cotton.
- Waived for the new program the $40,000 upper limit on total payments to an individual farmer authorized by the 1977 farm law.
- Required payments of at least 50 percent of the total due a farmer at the time a program contract was signed.
- Raised the limit on the Commodity Credit Corporation's borrowing authority to $25 billion, from $14.5 billion, effective Oct. 1, 1978.
- Raised existing ceilings on operating loans made by the secretary to $100,000, from $50,000, and on loans guaranteed by the secretary to $200,000; raised existing ceilings on loans for mortgage payments to $200,000 for loans made by the secretary, and to $300,000 for guaranteed loans.
- Authorized the secretary to guarantee commercial loans of up to three years, at commercial rates, on commodities with an established federal loan program. Thus, a farmer could negotiate at a local bank or other lender a federally guaranteed loan, with the dollar amount equaling the federal loan rate times his expected yield. In many cases, commercial lenders put money in farmers' hands more quickly than their federal counterparts. Nothing in the bill required private lenders to make these loans.

- Authorized up to three-year loans on commodities by the Commodity Credit Corporation (CCC). Under existing law, loans by the federal farm lending institution had to be renewed annually.
- Authorized the secretary to set mandatory release prices for commodities held in storage as collateral in the federal loan programs. If the market price on wheat, for example, reached the mandatory release price, the secretary could require a farmer to "release" a portion of his stored wheat — that is, sell it and repay the loan on it.
- Authorized the secretary to "call" (cancel) loans because of market instability caused by short supplies of a given commodity. Canceling the loans would have the effect of releasing more of the commodity to the market, thus stabilizing prices. The secretary could take this action only if the market price equaled or exceeded an established mandatory release price.
- Permitted farmers to use land included in any land diversion program to grow crops devoted to the production of alcohol, for use in "gasohol", an experimental fuel that combined alcohol with petroleum-based fuels, primarily gasoline.
- Prohibited growing of potatoes on any acreage in the land diversion program.

Target Price, Loan Program

- Raised target prices and loan levels for certain commodities, as follows:

Wheat target price to $3.55 a bushel, from $3-$3.05; wheat loan to $2.85 a bushel, from $2.25-$2.35.

Corn target price to $2.50 a bushel, from $2.10; corn loan to $2.25 a bushel, from $2.

Cotton target price to 70 cents a pound, from 52 cents; cotton loan to 50 cents a pound, from 44 cents.

Flexible Parity Program

- Created a sliding scale of target prices for crop year 1978 and linked it with the set-aside program. Participation in the announced set-aside programs was a condition for eligibility and payments would be made only on set-asides in addition to the already established programs.
- Established seven wheat target prices ranging from $3 a bushel for farmers who set aside 20 percent of their cropland to $5.04 a bushel for those who set aside 50 percent of their land. The higher figure represented 100 percent of parity, calculated under the 1910-1914 formula. The existing 1978 target price for wheat was $3 to $3.05.
- Established eight corn target prices, ranging from $2.10 for a 10 percent set-aside to $3.45 for a 50 percent set-aside. The existing target price was $2.10.
- Established a single cotton target price of 70 cents a pound for a 20 percent set-aside. The existing target price was 52 cents.
- Raised commodity loan rates for wheat to $2.85 a bushel, and for corn to $2.40 a bushel, from $2.25.
- Raised the cotton loan rate to 50 cents a pound.
- Revised upward the economic threshold at which grains placed in federal reserves by farmers could be released for the market and eliminated a time factor in calculating that release. The effect would be to strongly discourage farmer participation in the program.
- Permitted grazing and haying on all crop year 1978 set-asides.

Other Provisions

- Authorized establishment of a federal marketing order for raisins — that is, permitting certain promotional and marketing activities by a grower-producer association. This was intended to replace an expiring California marketing order for raisins.
- Required all imported meat to be labeled to show its country of origin.

Conference Action

In a brief March 22 meeting the House Agriculture Committee voted 33-7 to instruct Foley to request a conference on the emergency farm bill. Among the negative votes was John Krebs, D-Calif., author of the original raisin bill that had become the vehicle of the legislation. Krebs said the high cotton target price approved by the Senate would kill cotton exports from his state.

Hours after the committee acted, the House by a 332-63 vote agreed to the conference and the conferees met. The House also rejected 224-167 a motion by W. Henson Moore, R-La., to instruct House conferees to support the Dole flexible parity amendment. *(Vote 149, 150, p. 44-H)*

At the brief conference meeting Talmadge declared himself ready to begin working sessions the next day, March 23, but conferees agreed to postpone further action on the bill until April 3 when a show of hands indicated that members would not be available in sufficient numbers to make up a quorum before then.

Administration Counterattack

Top administration officials warned March 29 that President Carter planned to veto whatever Congress sent him from the grab-bag Senate-passed bill.

In an apparent bid to head off a politically explosive farm aid veto, the administration also came up with its own modest plan to pay farmers to take some cotton and feed grain land out of production, expand domestic grain reserves and buy up surplus wheat for an international emergency food stockpile. *(Details, box, p. 441)*

The new veto threats and the administration proposals, most of which built on existing law and went into place immediately, were laid out at a White House press briefing by Vice President Walter F. Mondale and Agriculture Secretary Bob Bergland.

The eleventh-hour administration scheme was "not intended to derail" the pending Senate bill (HR 6782), Bergland claimed, adding that it represented nothing more than a "timely" response to certain "inequities" in the 1977 farm bill.

Bergland's disclaimer notwithstanding, the Carter administration was known to be deeply worried about budgetary and inflationary implications of either option in the Senate measure.

Bergland said the "massive" land retirement mandated by the bill was particularly disturbing since it would shrink grain supplies to dangerously low levels, leaving consumers, farmers and foreign markets extremely vulnerable to bad weather and the price roller-coaster that poor yields cause. Agriculture Department analyses estimated that the Talmadge scheme would retire a total of 60 million acres, the Dole plan 34 million acres and the Carter program 22 million acres.

Whether the major elements of the Senate bill appeared in tandem or separately, the president would veto

Administration Farm Income Proposals

In the midst of congressional action on emergency farm legislation (HR 6782), the Carter administration March 29 announced a series of actions designed to raise farm income.

Vice President Walter F. Mondale and Agriculture Secretary Bob Bergland said the administration would, effective immediately:

- Create two new paid land diversion programs to retire four million acres of corn land and one million acres of cotton land, in addition to existing wheat and feed grain set-asides already announced for the 1978 crop year. Payments would be figured by a yield-per-acre formula and were comparable to levels provided in the Talmadge land diversion bill, which averaged out nationally to $75 an acre. As under the Talmadge measure, payments could climb well beyond that figure — up to $200 an acre for prime wheat land, for example.
- Lift the existing ceiling on the domestic grain reserve program and waive interest charges after the first year, to encourage producers to hold grain back while market prices strengthened.
- Raise to $4.50 a bushel, from $3.50, the loan rate for soybeans. Loan rates tend to act as a floor for market prices.
- Permit farmers participating in the announced wheat set-aside program to graze livestock on their set-aside land and authorize payments of at least 50 cents a bushel (based on the expected yield on that land if the wheat were harvested).
- Purchase at market prices up to six million tons of wheat for an international emergency food reserve. Existing law authorized purchase of the wheat; the administration asked Congress for new authority to hold the wheat exclusively for world famine aid.

Bergland said the administration would also support legislation to raise wheat target prices moderately — to about $3.50 a bushel from the existing $3-$3.05 level.

The administration's adjustments to existing reserve and set-aside programs, plus some tinkering with price supports, would put an extra $3 billion to $4 billion in farmers' pockets in 1978 if they "take full advantage" of them, Mondale said. Bergland added that most of that income would come from the marketplace, as shrinking supplies drove prices up.

Bergland and Mondale claimed that the administration's "balanced" approach would bail out reasonably efficient farmers — although it would not save "Georgia farmers who grow corn at $8 a bushel" (triple the national average production costs), Bergland noted. Reliance on reserves would also shield consumers from supermarket price shocks, protect sensitive export markets by assuring dependable supplies and permit the United States to aid hungry nations in the event of a world food crisis, the administration spokesmen maintained.

Reaction

Congressional leaders who had spent the last two months listening to angry farmers found the president had proposed too little too late.

Herman E. Talmadge, D-Ga., chairman of the Senate Agriculture Committee, did not offer to withdraw his bill and said he was disappointed with President Carter's meager farm aid plan.

Robert Dole, Kan., the ranking Republican on the committee, had predicted earlier that Carter would mount a "half-hearted effort to delay conference on the bill, with a little sop here and there." He called the president's program a "clear signal" that Carter "doesn't care" about farmers.

An organizer of the militant new American Agriculture Movement (AAM), Bud Bitner, rejected the administration's heavy reliance on reserves to bring prices up. Releasing reserved stocks is a classic maneuver to protect against rock-bottom prices, but it can also be used to damp swings to the upper end of the scale. "Always in the past reserves have been used to depress prices," Bitner claimed, and he pressed AAM demands for a minimum farm price law that would make it illegal to buy or sell commodities at less than 100 percent of parity prices.

---

them, Bergland assured reporters. The "so-called dial-a-parity" (Dole) program carried too great a threat of shortages, he said, while the second (Talmadge) option, even if its acreage levels were brought down to the modest administration goals, would also be axed. By the time it arrived at the White House "it would be unnecessary and it would confuse growers," who would have crops in the ground soon, Bergland said. "If a bill has massive land retirement in it, like the Dole bill, it will be vetoed, whatever its name is," Bergland added.

The Senate proposals "would over the long term do fundamental and irreparable harm to American agriculture and to our economy as a whole," Mondale warned.

Conference Agreement

House and Senate conferees meeting April 3-5 selected the most controversial option, the "flexible parity" program, from the grab-bag bill passed by the Senate.

Conferees dropped the Talmadge land diversion program that would have paid farmers for idling their land. That option had also included the target price and loan hikes proposed by McGovern.

Formal agreement came on the third day of the often confused conference deliberations, which were carried on under the watchful eyes of AAM representatives. Conferees acted without firm estimates of the bill's impact on consumer prices or on the federal budget.

Dole urged his colleagues to go ahead anyway, saying it was probably impossible to calculate the bill's true costs — a claim many economists agreed with. "Everybody who's against the bill is going to dream up the weirdest costs that they can," Dole said. Action was necessary, even though "nobody knows what it will cost consumers and nobody knows if it will help the farmer, although that's what we've been trying to do," he added.

The final version was fashioned from amendments, simplifying Dole's plan, proposed by Reps. Keith G. Sebelius, R-Kan., and W. Henson Moore, R-La.

The conferees repeatedly ignored Foley's attempts to substitute moderate raises in target prices and loans.

Foley urged his alternative because it would extend higher aid levels for the life of the 1977 four-year farm bill. Concerned with raising farmer expectations, Foley warned that there would be "absolute chaos in the countryside" if farm programs reverted to low established levels in 1979 after a brief period of high supports. Conferees informally agreed that revisions in farm programs for 1979-1981 should be attached to two pending farm credit bills (HR 11504, S 2146) reported in mid-March. *(Story, p. 446)*

Howard J. Hjort, chief Agriculture Department economist, warned conferees that adopting a new type of land diversion program would complicate farmers' planting decisions because the department could not sign contracts until it had the law "in hand" — too late for farmers. Department officials had estimated that it would take about 35 working days to write regulations, train program administrators and prepare environmental, inflation, civil rights and other impact statements required by law. That estimate included a waiver of the customary 30-day comment period for regulations.

Rep. Frederick Richmond, D-N.Y., who did not sign the conference report, repeatedly asked how much the plan would cost consumers, and how it could be enacted in time to do farmers any good. Many of his constituents, who were "unfortunately" not taxpayers because of their poverty, could not absorb even $1 to $2 a week in extra food costs, he said.

Votes on Flexible Parity

These votes April 4 shaped the final version of flexible parity:

House conferees by a 9-4 recorded vote agreed to a Moore amendment adding specific target prices for wheat, feed grains and cotton to the three-tier land-diversion plan proposed by Sebelius. Moore's amendment retained Foley's proposed new loan levels.

The House conferees also agreed 7-5 by a show of hands to an amendment by Rep. Dawson Mathis, D-Ga., to raise the corn loan rate to $2.25 a bushel, from Foley's proposed $2.10 figure, and to an E. "Kika" de la Garza, D-Texas, amendment to raise the cotton loan rate to 48 cents a pound, from Foley's proposed 46 cents figure.

By a 9-4 vote, the House conferees accepted the Sebelius flexible parity amendment as amended by Moore and others, in effect replacing the Dole and Talmadge proposals with the revised Sebelius plan.

By a 5-0 show of hands Senate conferees agreed to accept HR 6782 as amended by House conferees. Talmadge did not vote.

Other Conference Action

The following provisions, which had been added on the Senate floor, were eliminated or revised by conferees:

Gasohol. Conferees reworded a Senate-passed provision permitting farmers to plant diverted land with crops to be used for production of the experimental fuel, gasohol.

Tillage, Grazing and Haying. Language clarifying existing authorizations for these practices on diverted lands was dropped after Hjort said it was not needed.

Meat Labeling. Conferees eliminated a provision requiring all imported meat to be labeled to show its country of origin. The provision was opposed by meat packers, who said the extra labeling was expensive and difficult to carry out. It was, however, extremely popular with farmers who were incensed at food imports in general and beef imports in particular.

Loans. Conferees dropped two separate loan program provisions. The first raised existing ceilings on guaranteed and direct loans for operating expenses and mortgage payments. These duplicated provisions in the pending credit bills and should be considered in that context, conferees decided. The second program provided for three-year guaranteed loans at commercial rates based on federal loan rates, and extended to three years federal commodities loans. Conferees dropped it after Hjort said it would make borrowing more expensive for farmers.

Reserve Program. Over Dole's objections, conferees deleted a provision that sharply raised the economic threshold at which grain placed in federal reserves by farmers would be released for the market. Hjort objected that the provision would kill the reserve program by discouraging farmer participation, and that the impact on livestock producers could be harsh. Even without this provision, however, the bill still would discourage farmer participation because the higher loan rates would raise the threshold for release to the market.

Conference Provisions

As agreed to by conferees (H Rept 95-1044), HR 6782:

- Created a voluntary land diversion program for 1978 only, with three levels of participation. The level at which a farmer participated determined his target price. Maximum participation (retiring 50 percent of planted acres) guaranteed a 100 percent of parity target price. (Under a formula established by the 1977 farm law, and unchanged by HR 6782, a 50 percent land diversion requires a farmer to keep one acre out of production for every two that he plants. The effect of this formula is that a 50 percent land diversion in fact idles one-third of a farmer's planted acreage, not one-half. Comparable adjustments apply for the other land diversion levels.) To be eligible, a farmer had to participate in existing land set-aside programs (but not paid land diversion programs).

The levels of participation and their target prices were:

Crop	Diverted Acreage	Target Price
Wheat	20%	$3.50 a bushel
	35%	$4.25
	50%	$5.04
Corn and other feed grains	10%	$2.40
	35%	$3.05
	50%	$3.45
Cotton	0 (not required for lowest-level target price)	60¢ a pound
	35%	72¢
	50%	84¢

- Raised loan rates for the 1978 crop year only, as follows: wheat to $2.55 a bushel, from $2.25-$2.35; feed grains to $2.25 a bushel, from $2; cotton to 48 cents a pound, from 44 cents. The effective date for the new loan rates was Oct. 1, 1978, but payments could be made retroactively to cover commitments to producers on 1978 crops.

- Barred farmers from using the same acreage to qualify for benefits in both existing land diversion programs and in the new voluntary program.
- Authorized the secretary of agriculture to permit farmers to grow crops for gasohol production on set-aside or diverted acreage, and to make incentive payments to producers of gasohol crops when no set-aside or diversion programs were in effect.
- Raised the limit on the Commodity Credit Corporation's borrowing authority to $25 billion, from $14.5 billion, effective Oct. 1, 1978.
- Authorized establishment of a federal marketing order for raisins.

Reaction to Conference Agreement

Conference endorsement of flexible parity surprised both its supporters and opponents. Faced with the possibility that the bill might actually become law, a few Republicans began to back away from it, while Democrats prepared for a difficult House fight that could feature them supporting the Republican bill.

In a "dear colleague" letter April 6, two Illinois Republicans, Paul Findley and Edward R. Madigan, urged a "nay" vote on the bill and Findley told reporters "the farm bill exercise will benefit only President Carter, who will seize upon it to get undue credit as a militant inflation-fighter."

The House Budget Committee April 6 refused to recommend adding enough money to cover the bill to its recommendation on fiscal 1979 farm spending.

Administration. President Carter renewed his veto threat April 11 in an anti-inflation speech to the American Society of Newspaper Editors. He claimed the bill would raise food prices by 3 percent and the overall cost of living by .4 percent, "shatter confidence in the crucial export markets for America's farm products, and cripple American farm families through increased costs."

In an April 6 analysis of the bill the administration said it would take as many as 59 million acres out of production and deficiency payments could range between $3 billion and $9 billion — depending largely on weather. The program would cause shortages — and high prices — in commodities like soybeans that were not included in the program, analysts warned, because farmers would shift to supported crops. The administration also warned that sharp cutbacks in farm production would sabotage ongoing negotiations for international marketing agreements and disrupt local processing, marketing and farm supply industries.

Farm Groups. AAM reaction was evident as conferees completed their work: At a mass meeting in the Capitol rotunda, leaders urged farmers to press members to vote for the measure. The group regarded the bill as a useful stopgap, but still planned to seek a permanent minimum price law that would make it illegal to buy and sell commodities at less than 100 percent of parity.

The American Farm Bureau Federation, a powerful conservative group that has long represented farm interests in Washington, was strongly opposed to the bill, according to spokesman Donald Donnelly. "It's an administrative monstrosity and it will interfere with exports by raising grain prices too high," he said.

But the Farm Bureau found itself pitted against AAM, the National Farmers Union (NFU), which regarded the bill as the best possible legislation this year but "not enough," according to a spokesman, and even some of its own Farm Bureau members. Dole said that state units in Kansas and South Carolina backed his plan.

Consumers. Consumer Federation of America (CFA) director Kathleen F. O'Reilly called the bill "preposterous, because it doesn't speak to the underlying problems that have thrust farmers into the whole boom-bust cycles." Consumers also feared the bill's effect on food prices.

Senate Action

The Senate spent two hours April 10 rehashing themes of earlier debates — farmers' money problems, the real cost of the bill, its political liabilities — before approving the conference report 49-41 *(Vote 85, p. 16-S)*

The narrow eight-vote margin showed that support for the bill had eroded since March 21 when the Senate endorsed the flexible parity concept by a 16-vote majority. And it foreclosed the possibility of a veto override, which required a two-thirds majority in both houses.

Talmadge explained at length why his rejected land diversion plan would have been better, but he urged colleagues to vote for the bill because it was all they had.

Dole said excessive cost estimates by the Congressional Budget Office, based on a "worst case" scenario, had damaged his bill. With moderate — and more realistic — participation and market price figures, the cost would be about $2 billion, not $5.7 billion, he said. Dole suggested that partisan politics were the bill's biggest problem, and he urged colleagues "not to take it out on the American farmer simply because the bill has my name on it."

Dole also reported new Agriculture Department production cost estimates that showed farmers were still not recovering their production costs even though the market had strengthened significantly since last fall. The new figures showed the national average cost of producing wheat at $3.66 to $3.92 a bushel, and corn at $2.54 to $2.71. ("Terminal" wheat and corn prices on April 11, the day after Senate action, were about $3.42 and $2.50 respectively, according to Agriculture Department market analysts. They pointed out that terminal prices were substantially higher — by as much as 50 cents — than what the farmer actually received on the original sale of his crops.)

Budget Committee Chairman Muskie warned that the bill was too costly and that congressional willingness to waive the budget act was seriously eroding the budget process.

Disregarding Muskie's warnings, the Senate voted 49-43 to waive the budget act prohibition on action on fiscal 1979 spending. It then adopted the conference report, 49-41. *(Votes 84, 85, p. 16-S)*

House Action

In a stinging defeat for militant farmer-lobbyists, the House April 12 emphatically rejected the emergency farm bill, sparing President Carter from carrying out his veto threat and apparently dooming chances for a major overhaul of farm policy in 1978.

By a 150-268 vote, with majorities of both Republicans and Democrats voting no, the House voted down the conference agreement on the controversial "flexible parity" bill. *(Vote 176, p. 52-H)*

The magnitude of the defeat left observers gasping. Conventional wisdom was that the vote could go either way, by a narrow margin, because the bill had become deeply embroiled in volatile election-year politics and because divisions within the farm community itself were beginning to show up.

Hours before the final vote House Speaker Thomas P. O'Neill Jr., D-Mass., and Agriculture Committee Chairman Foley had predicted that the bill would pass by a narrow margin. The AAM had counted on 198 sure supporters.

O'Neill had made it clear that he regarded the bill as a disaster, but he let it be known that Democrats could vote whatever way they felt they needed to on the bill. Particularly in western states, members were hurting from farmer animosity toward the Carter administration. No majority whip count was ever taken on the bill.

Floor Debate

The floor debate focused on the substance of the bill, which members had not previously debated, and the certainty of a veto, which the narrow Senate margin showed would stick. Floor managers parceled out one- and three-minute speaking slots, apparently to give as many members as possible a chance to put their views on the public record. More than 40 members, most favoring the bill, spoke.

But the debate showed that the politics of the bill and different regional needs had created deep fissures in each party, and some unusual alliances.

Appropriations Committee Chairman George Mahon, D-Texas, and Minority Leader John J. Rhodes, R-Ariz., both fiscal conservatives, made strong statements supporting the bill, which opponents said would "bust the budget." Mahon, whose state had a strong AAM movement, said the farm crisis was severe and that the admittedly "imperfect" bill was "all we have before us."

Democrat Neal Smith of Iowa urged members to disregard the Democratic president's veto threats and pass the bill, so as to pressure the administration to step up aid for farmers. Another Democrat, Ted Risenhoover, Okla., elicited loud cheers from farmer-packed galleries when he urged the House to "send the bill down to the White House and let AAM work on them."

Majority Leader Jim Wright, D-Texas, apparently acknowledging leadership awareness that many farm-state Democrats needed badly to vote for the bill, said "everybody's on their own." But he said the promised veto and the certainty that override efforts would fail made further action on the bill a "meaningless charade." He asked members to defeat the rule and thereby pressure the Rules Committee into reconsidering its refusal to allow an alternative bill to come to the floor.

(Foley had taken the unusual step of seeking a rule on the conference agreement because he wanted to avoid a point of order on the floor based on the budget law. The committee April 11 granted a rule (H Res 1121) waiving all points of order, but rejected by an 8-7 vote Foley's request that he be allowed to bring a substitute bill to the floor if the House rejected the conference agreement.

Foley had repeatedly asked conferees to accept his less expensive proposal for moderate increases in target prices and loan levels. Opponents claimed that Foley's move in Rules was a last-ditch effort to kill the flexible parity bill by siphoning off votes to an alternative. Foley said many farm-state representatives had pressed him for a bill they could support, and that might escape a veto.)

Republicans speaking against the bill included Silvio O. Conte, from rural western Massachusetts, who called the bill a "boondoggle" and said that "consumers and taxpayers don't have the luxury of being able to take three months off" to lobby Congress.

Paul Findley, R-Ill., representing a state whose American Farm Bureau Federation chapter was often said to call the shots for the national organization, reported that "the majority of farmers in my home state see the enormity for mischief in this bill and they will thank the president for vetoing it." A week earlier Findley warned his colleagues that Carter could capitalize on the veto as an important anti-inflation move. Illinois farmers, working what was often called "the most fertile soil in the world," did not suffer financial problems of the same magnitude as their colleagues further west and in the southeast, where production costs ran higher and drought was bad in 1977.

By voice vote the House adopted the rule on the bill and, an hour later, voted down the conference report 150-268. *(Vote 176, p. 52-H)*

Factors in Defeat

Foley told reporters after the House vote that the controversial substance of the measure and the deep split it created among farmers were probably the decisive factors in its failure. "It is very difficult to pass a bill if there is division within the agriculture community itself," Foley said. Without united farm support, many members from rural districts reportedly shied away from the vote-trading with urban members that was the customary way to get farm legislation approved by the House.

Foley said the veto threat had also weighed heavily against the bill, and a Republican source close to one of the House sponsors, Sebelius, said "it was an anti-inflation vote, pure and simple — for the Republicans anyway."

Democrats and Republicans both reported that lobbying by non-government groups was effective, although minimal when compared with the heavy AAM effort. Republican sources reported well-placed calls against the bill by the Farm Bureau Federation. Church groups, concerned with potential world food shortages, and consumer groups, worried about high food prices, also opposed the measure.

The administration relied heavily on the media, which played up Carter's veto threats and periodic denunciations by the Council on Wage and Price Stability. Democrats said administration lobbyists weren't much in evidence, but Dole told the Senate April 10 that Capitol "halls are filled with lobbyists from the White House trying to shoot down this bill."

Reaction

Bitterly disappointed, AAM farmer-lobbyists massed at the White House where they denounced Carter and promised that members of Congress who had deserted them would feel it in the fall elections.

AAM spokesman Greg Suhler said the bill had fallen victim to "a purely political play on the part of the executive." He also called Congress "derelict in its duty" for failing to press the administration fully to exploit the "flexibility" of the 1977 farm bill; "they [Congress] could have helped us out and prevented all this from happening," he said. He spoke harshly against "lying" members of Congress who had promised AAM to back the measure and then voted against it. But he also attributed defections to "political pressures that we just can't imagine." The group would maintain a volunteer-staffed office in Washington and work in the fall congressional elections, Suhler said. "We're stubborn as mules and agriculture's got some serious problems that still have to be fixed," he added.

Dole, author of the original Senate-passed flexible parity bill, said that "apparently the administration wants American farmers to continue to bear an unfair share of the inflationary burden." The day after the House defeat he introduced a bill (S 2905) to raise wheat target prices to $3.50 from the existing $3-$3.05 level. That was the only farm legislation that Carter had indicated could escape his veto.

Talmadge made no comment. But he was known to feel that the burden was now on the House to come up with some sort of farm bill.

In remarks to reporters after the vote, Foley and House Budget Committee Chairman Robert N. Giaimo, D-Conn., indicated that they still hoped for a modest new farm bill in 1978. Giaimo said the upcoming fiscal 1979 budget resolution would include about $2 billion in uncommitted funds for "new farm initiatives," and he said he would not press budget act strictures about early fiscal 1979 spending decisions because of farmers' special needs during the critical spring planting season. Giaimo had opposed a rule waiving all points of order on the conference agreement because the farm bill violated the budget act.

Foley planned to test the water before deciding on further legislation, but he said he did not want to attach any new proposal to the pending farm credit bill (HR 11504) which had been seen as a vehicle for farm aid. A Foley aide said that was because the administration backed the bill, which included a new $4 billion emergency loan program, and Foley didn't want to jeopardize it.

Second Conference Agreement

House and Senate conferees agreed April 26 to a scaled-down version of the defeated bill.

The agreement, a fine-tuning of grain and cotton price support programs established in 1977, was tailored almost exactly to stringent administration specifications except for a near 10 percent increase in the cotton loan level.

A preliminary $600 million price tag for the bill revealed the very limited use the administration planned to make of the proposed new authority to boost price supports for wheat, feed grains and cotton. The measure's sponsor, Foley, said he doubted that the administration could or would use its new authority to raise commodity prices to "full parity," as suggested by Dole. President Carter's refusal fully to use the authority he already had under the 1977 farm act to aid farmers had been a very sore point among farmers.

Meeting two days after the House requested a second conference, House and Senate conferees agreed without objection to give the president authority to raise target prices for wheat, feed grains and cotton for the next four years — the life of PL 95-113. The president could raise the target prices only when set-aside programs for these commodities were in effect. (The 1977 farm bill gave the president the authority to establish voluntary "set-aside" programs to take cropland out of production. Participating farmers became eligible for federal price supports, while those refusing to participate when a set-aside had been announced lost eligibility for the supports. Under the 1977 law, when market prices fell below the set target prices, farmers were paid the difference.)

Agriculture Department chief economist Hjort told conferees that the change was needed because the 1977 law did not provide enough incentive to attract farmers to the set-aside programs.

Final agreement came after House conferees voted by a 6-4 show of hands for a modified version of Foley's proposal. Voting against the agreement were Republican conferees William C. Wampler, Va.; Sebelius; James P. "Jim" Johnson, Colo., and Moore. Moore had argued that there was "no point" to enacting anything more than a stopgap one-year bill because the administration "is not going to do anything anyway."

Hjort said the president would use the new authority only to raise 1978 wheat target prices — to $3.40 a bushel — since price supports for the other commodities had already been raised by administrative action.

Hjort said several other conference proposals that exceeded administration wishes "worried" him, but he could not say whether they would expose the bill to a veto.

Hjort was particularly concerned with an assortment of technical changes in the complex formula for setting the cotton loan rate. As proposed by David R. Bowen, D-Miss., these changes could raise the rate to about 51 cents a pound in 1979, from 44 cents. A W. R. Poage, D-Texas, amendment to Bowen's amendment stipulated that at no time could the loan rate fall below 48 cents a pound. No cost estimate was available for these cotton loan revisions. House conferees agreed to the Bowen amendment by voice vote.

The second conference on HR 6782 retained three provisions of the original bill, relating to raisin marketing, gasohol and the limit on the Commodity Credit Corporation's borrowing authority. The limit was raised to $25 billion, effective Oct. 1, 1978.

Final Action

The Senate by voice vote May 2 approved the second conference agreement on the bill; the House followed suit May 4 by a 212-182 roll-call vote, clearing the bill for the president. *(Vote 239, p. 68-H)*

Senate approval was abrupt, with neither debate nor recorded vote. In four minutes, with four senators on the floor, the Senate approved the conference agreement without objection, after first approving a budget act waiver (S Res 443). That permitted action on the cotton loan hike for fiscal 1979 before adoption of the first budget resolution for that year.

Before the final vote in the House, Republicans and some California Democrats mounted a last-ditch effort to stop the bill.

The administration had said it would use its new powers only to raise 1978 wheat target prices by a modest 40 cents a bushel.

Despite these assurances, Republicans complained that the bill conferred "unwarranted" and abusable power on the administration. "The secretary of agriculture merrily adjusting prices during an election year is too good a prospect for [Democratic] members to pass up," said John B. Anderson, R-Ill. Other Republicans said the bill could end up costing much more than the one-year, $699 million estimate of the Congressional Budget Office.

The California opponents feared that the higher cotton loan rate would cut into cotton exports from that state. California cotton grown on irrigated land accounted for about one-fifth of the nation's total cotton crop.

Bill Signing

President Carter signed HR 6782 into law May 15. He congratulated Congress for passing the bill so soon after the House defeat of the "unwise and untimely" flexible parity bill.

Carter also announced he would exercise his discretionary authority under the bill to raise wheat price supports to $3.40 a bushel, from $3. This would make wheat producers eligible for some $600 million in additional deficiency payments in 1978, unless the market price rose above $3 a bushel, he said.

Carter criticized the price support increase for cotton in the bill and said he would propose legislation to remove it. He also called on Congress to act on administration proposals to replace disaster assistance programs with an all-risk crop insurance program and to establish an international emergency wheat reserve. ▮

Farm Loan Programs

A major overhaul of federal lending programs for farmers and rural communities, including a new $4 billion "economic emergency" loan program, was enacted in 1978.

The bill (HR 11504) moved relatively smoothly through Congress, carried along with the momentum of a much more controversial emergency farm aid measure. *(Story, p. 436)*

The revision of existing farm loan programs had been in the works since the fall of 1977, but the new emergency loan program was a direct response to three months of lobbying by angry farmers of the militant American Agriculture Movement (AAM). Backed by the Carter administration, it was meant to bail out farmers from a prevailing low-price, no-credit situation that they said had been created by a combination of commodity surpluses, drought losses, spiraling production costs and heavy borrowing. The AAM backed the loan program as a partial, temporary solution to farmers' financial problems.

The House approved the conference agreement on the bill July 19 by a 362-28 vote. The Senate approved it July 20 by voice vote, and President Carter signed it into law Aug. 4 (PL 95-334).

The new "economic emergency" loan program allowed farmers to borrow up to $400,000 for as long as 30 years. Most were expected to use the money to refinance and stretch out repayment of existing debts, but the farmers could also borrow to cover operating expenses, to diversify by starting up new crops, and for other purposes. Farmers could not use borrowed funds to expand the size of their operations by buying or renting more land, however.

Besides creating the new program, HR 11504 raised individual loan ceilings in existing programs administered by the Farmers Home Administration (FmHA). And it upped most loan interest rates, a move intended to stimulate private investors in money markets and private lenders like banks to supply more farm loan money. That change also cut the interest subsidy costs associated with the existing loan programs. Artificially low interest rates were retained only for certain disaster loan programs and for low-income borrowers.

In House debate on the conference agreement, Ed Jones, D-Tenn., said the changes were needed because agriculture, like other sectors of the economy, had experienced "a massive increase in the need for capital and financial credit." Land prices had jumped 132 percent between 1971 and 1977, from an average value of $204 per acre to $474, Jones said. Equipment prices were similarly inflated, and, according to the Department of Agriculture, the index of prices paid by farmers increased 65 percent from January 1972 to January 1978, he added.

Jones, chairman of the House Agriculture subcommittee with credit jurisdiction, said farmers had been saying "for a long time" that they needed expanded credit more than they needed federally subsidized interest.

The Congressional Budget Office estimated that the legislation would prune $4 million from projected FmHA loan program outlays of $252 million in fiscal 1979, with savings of $15 million the following year.

Provisions

As signed into law, HR 11504 amended the 1972 Consolidated Farm and Rural Development Act (PL 92-419) as follows:

- Extended eligibility for all Farmers Home Administration (FmHA) ownership and operating loans to corporations, cooperatives and partnerships owned and run by farmers. These types of loans involved: "direct" loans from federal funds, "insured" loans made by the secretary of agriculture from a revolving loan fund supplied by money from private investors, and federally "guaranteed" loans by private lenders.

Existing Loan Programs

- Raised the limit for individual farm ownership loans to $200,000, from $100,000, for direct and insured loans, and to $300,000 for guaranteed loans.
- Raised the limit for individual farm operating loans to $100,000 from $50,000 for insured loans and to $200,000 for guaranteed loans.
- Raised interest rates on loans as follows: guaranteed ownership and operating loans would be at a rate negotiated between the borrower and lender, although the agriculture secretary could set a ceiling for interest on these loans. For direct and insured loans, the interest would be the "cost of money" to the government (from private investors), with an additional 1 percent added at the discretion of the secretary.
- Authorized the secretary to consolidate or reschedule insured operating loans, including new loans, for up to seven years and to set a new interest rate for the total loan.
- Raised to $500 million, from $300 million, the total amount for grants for water and waste disposal projects in any fiscal year. Authorized grants for up to 75 percent of the cost of an individual project, up from the previous 50 percent level.

New Loan Programs

- Authorized through May 15, 1980, a new "economic emergency loan" program for established farmers, farmer corporations and similar entities with temporary credit problems caused by low farm prices and shortages of lending funds.

• Authorized insured and guaranteed loans for mortgage payments, operating expenses, reorganizing farm operations, refinancing existing debts and similar purposes. Loaned funds could not be used to buy or lease more land. Stipulated that preference for these loans should be given to family farms.

• Raised to 5 percent the interest rate for loans for actual losses caused by natural disasters, thereby eliminating an existing 3 percent rate for portions of these loans. Loans for disaster-associated losses would be made at higher "cost of money" rates.

• Authorized the secretary to make emergency loans on his own finding that an individual's farming, ranching or aquaculture operations had been "substantially affected" by a natural disaster, or to individuals in a presidentially designated major disaster or emergency area. The effect was to make emergency loans more readily available to individual operators struck by an isolated disaster; existing law required an area-wide disaster designation by the secretary or the president for an individual to be eligible for the loans.

• Required Congress to set loan limits for each of the loan programs every three years beginning Oct. 1, 1979. Prohibited the aggregate of outstanding loans in each program from exceeding the limits set by Congress.

• Set a $400,000 ceiling on individual loans under the new emergency program and limited total indebtedness for an individual or farm entity to $650,000 under both new and old loan programs.

• Authorized a 40-year repayment period for economic emergency loans secured by land, and a seven-year repayment period for loans with other types of security, but permitted 20-year non-land loans at the secretary's discretion.

• Provided for a 90 percent FmHA guarantee for the guaranteed loans.

• Retained for these loans the FmHA "no credit elsewhere" test; that is, the applicant was required to show that he had failed to get a loan from private sources.

• Limited the total outstanding amount of these loans to $4 billion at any one time.

• Established a special direct and insured low-interest ownership loan program for loans to beginning or low-income farmers running small farms. Authorized loans at 5 percent, with reduced installment payments during the early years of the loan and larger payments later.

• Authorized loans to farmers for the cost of meeting statutory requirements for abatement and control of waste pollution from agricultural or animal sources.

• Authorized direct, insured or guaranteed loans of up to $1 million per loan for rural communities to acquire and run electrical power transmission facilities. Limited eligibility for the loans to areas that had been receiving power from federal electric power administrations in 1976.

Other Provisions

• Exempted small businesses from a ban on aid to business and industry projects that would shift jobs or business activity from one area to another or cause overproduction.

• Authorized the secretary to permit deferral of loan principal and interest payments for an individual borrower, at the borrower's request. The secretary would determine how long the deferral could last; to be eligible, a borrower must show that he was temporarily unable to make payments due to circumstances beyond his control. Prohibited interest charges for the interest that accrued during the deferral period unless the secretary determined that such secondary interest could be charged.

• Authorized the secretary to hold off foreclosing on loans for individuals in circumstances like those required for a loan deferral.

• Authorized payments from a revolving fund for administrative costs of making loans. The bill also directed the secretary to make sure that only persons "adequately prepared to understand the particular needs and problems of farmers in an area" work in that area.

• Extended through Sept. 30, 1979, the emergency livestock loan program authorized in 1974 (PL 93-357). *(1974 Almanac p. 220)*

• Amended the Beef Research and Promotion Act of 1976 (PL 94-294) to permit majority approval in producer referenda, instead of the two-thirds approval the act required. *(Beef promotion act, 1976 Almanac p. 387)*

• Authorized the secretary to raise the target price for rice in years when a federal set-aside (voluntary land diversion program) was in effect.

• Authorized payments to farmers for projects to control wind, water and other sorts of soil erosion and for emergency water conservation measures.

No new programs were created by this provision. In the first instance, it authorized programs that had been funded by annual appropriations since 1957. In the second case it transferred to the agriculture committees of Congress jurisdiction over certain programs authorized by the Flood Control Act of 1950.

Committee Action

Farm credit revision bills were approved by the House and Senate Agriculture Committees in March, along with several other more controversial farm aid measures — "flexible parity" and land diversion bills favored by the Senate. The administration had taken no position on the latter bills (it later opposed them), but it urged rapid enactment of the credit legislation.

Farmers and their supporters had said early action was critical because the planting season had already begun in the South. Without some notion of what additional help they could expect, farmers could not — and would not — calculate their planting or participate in set-asides, they said.

The House committee moved first, effectively approving the credit revisions March 10 after lengthy markup sessions. The final 39-5 vote to report the bill came March 14 after the committee decided not to honor an administration request to rename the Farmers Home Administration (FmHA), administrator of the loan programs.

Voting against reporting the bill were Republicans Paul Findley, Ill.; Steven D. Symms, Idaho; Edward R. Madigan, Ill.; Margaret M. Heckler, Mass., and Richard Kelly, Fla. Two Democratic committee members were absent: Dawson Mathis, Ga., and Joseph S. Ammerman, Pa.

The report on HR 11504 was issued March 18 (H Rept 95-986).

The Senate bill (S 2146), approved March 15, was reported April 24 (S Rept 95-752).

Both bills established the new "economic emergency" loan program. Individual loans were limited to $400,000 in the House bill, $500,000 in the Senate version. Up to $2 billion was authorized for calendar year 1978 loans with a two-year total ceiling of $4 billion. The House bill would end the program Dec. 31, 1979, the Senate bill May 15, 1980.

The House bill also created a special 3 percent interest loan program to cover mortgage and operating expenses of low-income farmers, including new farmers.

Many of the revisions in existing credit programs made by the two committees were identical. One difference was in the interest rate for emergency loans for farm losses caused by natural disasters. HR 11504 eliminated a special 3 percent interest rate, setting the rate at 5 percent for loans covering actual losses, such as destruction of livestock, and at the prevailing commercial interest rate for loans covering associated losses. S 2146 retained 3 percent rates only for farmers who could not get loans elsewhere; interest on other loans would be "cost of money" plus 1 percent.

Both bills eliminated the existing $225,000 limit on a farmer's total real estate indebtedness. The House bill limited such indebtedness to the value of the farm or other loan security, while the Senate version gave the secretary of agriculture discretion to set annual limitations.

The Senate bill also established new loan authority of up to $1 million per loan for rural communities to acquire and run electrical power plants.

House Floor Action

Twelve days after it shot down the multibillion-dollar emergency farm subsidy bill (HR 6782), the House endorsed the less controversial credit bill. It approved HR 11504 by a 347-23 vote on April 24. *(Vote 205, p. 60-H)*

The major issues debated by the House were whether farmers should be encouraged to go deeper into debt, and whether the FmHA was capable of administering existing and new loan programs.

The lopsided final vote showed that few members agreed with Paul Findley, R-Ill., that the bill should be defeated because it would slow the "very healthy" winnowing out of marginal producers. Findley maintained that instead of handing out more credit, the House should fund payments to help financially "distressed" farmers get "off farm income and not to perpetuate the misery many of them are experiencing in agriculture."

Before the final vote, Republicans led by Edward R. Madigan, Ill., objected to the size of the new emergency loan program because, in their view, it was seriously underfunded. Either the program would fall far short of the expectations it raised or Congress would be asked to shell out far more money than the bill authorized, Madigan warned.

Referring to FmHA projections, Madigan said that if 2 percent of the nation's farmers borrowed $400,000 each, some $5.5 billion in loan funds would be required. And if 50,000 farmers required maximum loans — as FmHA predicted — the program would require $20 billion, Madigan said. (The bill authorized $4 billion for the two-year life of the program.)

In response, Ed Jones, D-Tenn., chairman of the Agriculture subcommittee that had drafted the bill, said few farmers would require the maximum loan amount. Initial FmHA farm ownership loans averaged $50,000, Jones said.

By a 151-215 vote the House rejected a Madigan substitute emergency loan program that provided only smaller, short-term loans to cover operating expenses or installment payments (principal and interest) on existing loans through December 1979. *(Vote 204, p. 60-H)*

Disregarding Findley's warnings that Illinois farmers would "relish" the chance to refinance all their loans, the House agreed by a 32-22 standing vote to eliminate a requirement that only loans incurred after 1973 could be refinanced. Interest rates through the 1960s were so favorable compared with existing rates that farmers were unlikely to refinance many earlier debts, proponents said.

Other Amendments

In other action, the House:

- Agreed by voice vote to a Volkmer, D-Mo., amendment to limit the total indebtedness a farmer could incur under the new emergency loan program and other FmHA programs.

As reported (H Rept 95-986), the bill had permitted an individual to borrow up to $900,000 altogether — $400,000 from the new program and an aggregate of $500,000 from certain other programs with new, higher loan ceilings. While pyramiding the various loans was so difficult that few farmers were likely to do it, that possibility should be eliminated so that more farmers could be served with smaller loans, Volkmer said.

- Adopted by voice vote a Glickman, D-Kan., amendment stipulating that FmHA home ownership mortgages should be offered on terms at least as favorable as those offered by the Department of Housing and Urban Development (HUD) to city-dwellers.

Glickman said inequities between the two programs included the following: a $60,000 HUD mortgage limit, compared with $33,000 under FmHA; 100 percent HUD insurance of eligible loans compared with 90 percent FmHA insurance; an FmHA income ceiling that determined eligibility for the loans, no such restrictions under HUD. Glickman said his proposal, which required FmHA to match HUD terms, was needed to ensure "equal treatment of rural and urban Americans."

Jones and Thomas S. Foley, D-Wash., chairman of the House Agriculture Committee, objected that the change would require an additional $5 billion in loan funds over the next five years while distorting FmHA's mission to help farmers who could not get assistance elsewhere.

- Adopted by voice vote a Bedell, D-Iowa, amendment authorizing the secretary of agriculture to use loan program funds to hire more FmHA employees, and a related amendment by Robert J. Lagomarsino, R-Calif., that FmHA employees be adequately trained to understand local farm needs. Numerous allegations were made about administrative problems with the loan programs, with Iowa members complaining that FmHA was so understaffed that it failed to inspect farm buildings in Iowa on which it had loaned money.

- Adopted by voice vote a Jones, Tenn., amendment that added to the bill authorizations for certain existing soil conservation programs.

Senate Floor Action

The Senate passed S 2146 May 2 by a 92-0 vote. *(Vote 146, p. 25-S)*

The final vote followed a day and a half of desultory debate in a near-empty chamber — a marked contrast to the packed and pressured deliberations on the controversial "flexible parity" farm aid bill (HR 6782).

Low-Cost Disaster Loans

The Senate agreed by voice vote to an amendment by Edmund S. Muskie, D-Maine, to raise to 5 percent, from 3 percent, the interest rate on disaster loans to farmers, effective Oct. 1, 1979. As reported by the Agriculture Committee, the bill continued the existing 3 percent rate indefinitely. The House bill called for a 5 percent rate effective upon enactment.

The amendment was the result of a compromise between Muskie, chairman of the Senate Budget Committee, who thought the low-cost loans too expensive for the government, and James B. Allen, D-Ala., floor manager of the bill.

Muskie said the government should charge borrowers whatever it cost to borrow the money from private investors. He also warned that the cheap loans encouraged excessive borrowing, and he maintained that the FmHA's requirement that a farmer have no other source of credit in order to get a loan was easily eluded. "There is pressure on banking institutions to cooperate with applicants in meeting that test," Muskie said. But Allen, referring to severe financial problems and resulting farmer unrest, responded, "We do not feel that now would be the time to cut back greatly on the low interest rate for disaster loans." He agreed to the higher rate if it were postponed until October 1979.

The Senate agreed by voice vote to eliminate a committee provision that allowed farmers to use the low-cost disaster loans to buy more land. The administration opposed the provision. The House bill also stipulated that the economic emergency loan program could not be used to acquire new land.

Other Amendments

The Senate adopted several other amendments:

- A Bumpers, D-Ark., amendment authorized the secretary of agriculture to raise the target price for rice in years when a set-aside (voluntary land diversion program) had been established. This provision was originally included in the compromise on HR 6782 offered by Rep. Thomas S. Foley, D-Wash., and adopted by conferees as the final version of that bill. Foley had dropped the rice provision when advised it went beyond the scope of the conference. Allen said the administration did not object to adding the provision to the farm credit bill and the Senate adopted it by voice vote.
- An Eagleton, D-Mo., amendment prohibited FmHA from charging interest on the interest of a loan during a period when repayment was deferred to accommodate a borrower's financial problems. FmHA was planning to charge interest during the deferral period, contrary to the intent of the 1977 farm bill (PL 95-113), Eagleton said. Authority to suspend the interest charges was discretionary under that bill. The Senate adopted the mandatory provision by voice vote.
- A Dole, R-Kan., amendment to the Beef Research and Promotion Act (PL 94-294) to permit majority approval of producer referenda, instead of the two-thirds approval the act required. Agreed to by voice vote. *(Beef promotion act, 1976 Almanac p. 387)*
- An Abourezk, D-S.D., amendment to make recognized Indian tribes eligible for FmHA loans for equipment, operating expenses and similar expenditures, agreed to by voice vote. Existing law permitted FmHA loans to tribes only for land acquisition. Abourezk argued that without funds to develop farm operations, the land acquisition loans were not particularly useful to Indians.
- A Clark, D-Iowa, amendment to authorize payments from several revolving funds to beef up FmHA staff was rejected by a 29-62 vote. The House bill included such an authorization. Milton R. Young, R-N.D., objected that the change would improperly short-circuit the appropriations process and would "automatically let any department of government use their own funds for administration purposes." Clark responded that he too disliked the strategy he proposed. But Congress had in the past authorized and appropriated funds for far more staff positions than successive administrations — including Carter's — chose to fill, he said. *(Vote 145, p. 25-S)*

After passing the bill, the Senate moved to substitute the text of S 2146 as amended for the House bill.

Conference Action

Conferees generally followed the House version for the first title of the bill, which revised existing credit programs and added a low-interest loan program for beginning or poor farmers.

The final version of Title II, the new "economic emergency" loan program, represented a compromise between House and Senate bills.

The conference bill also retained miscellaneous House and Senate provisions revising a beef promotion program, reworking authority for certain ongoing farm conservation programs and authorizing higher target prices for rice.

In their July 11 report (H Rept 95-1344), credit bill conferees said they had resolved major House and Senate differences as follows:

- Retained a $400,000 House ceiling on individual loans under the new economic emergency loan program, rejecting a higher Senate ceiling of $500,000. Conferees also agreed to limit total indebtedness of a borrower from the new and existing programs to $650,000. The House bill had required that the amount a producer could borrow under the new program be reduced by his outstanding loans in other Farmers Home Administration (FmHA) programs; the Senate did not limit total indebtedness.
- Retained a new Senate loan program to help rural communities facing electrical power cutbacks because of changes in federal power administrations to operate their own electrical power transmission facilities.
- Dropped a Senate extension of certain 3 percent disaster loans through Oct. 1, 1979.
- Eliminated a House requirement that FmHA home ownership mortgages should be offered on terms at least as favorable as those offered city-dwellers by the Department of Housing and Urban Development (HUD). Conferees said the Agriculture Department had committed itself in June to carrying out administratively what the House had proposed for "above-average income" mortgages. Conferees noted that there was a "serious lack of mortgage credit" for rural families with incomes of up to $20,000.
- Dropped a Senate provision extending to Indian tribes eligibility for FmHA loans for equipment, operating expenses and similar expenditures. Existing law allowed FmHA loans to tribes only for land acquisition.
- Included a Senate exemption for small businesses from a ban on aid that would shift jobs or business activity from one area to another.

Final Action

House

After turning back an effort to stop a change in the ground rules for a producer-run beef promotion program, the House by a 362-28 vote approved the credit bill conference agreement. *(Vote 499, p. 142-H)*

Conferees had retained a Senate provision that permitted a simple majority of beef producers to approve establishment of the program, rather than the two-thirds approval required by the 1976 beef promotion act. A recent referendum had shown that a majority of the producers wanted the program, which they would finance themselves, but the majority was short of the two-thirds required, according to sponsor Sen. Robert Dole, R-Kan.

In a complicated procedural maneuver, Frederick Richmond, D-N.Y., tried unsuccessfully to send the agreement back to conferees with instructions to delete the proposed change. The beef program itself was "strongly opposed by the Consumer Federation of America," Richmond said. The proposed change would result in "an advertising campaign that will add to the retail cost of beef at a time when consumers know, all too well, the effects of the inflationary food price spiral," he said.

Richmond announced his intention but was blocked by a House rule giving the prerogative to recommit to conference to the minority. Steven D. Symms, R-Idaho, who had voted against the credit measure when the House originally passed it, then moved to recommit the conference report, apparently intending to kill it. Without elaboration, Symms told the House that he "opposed" the report. A Symms aide said later that the only thing in the "bankers' bill" that Symms approved of was the beef program.

Richmond moved to end the debate by ordering the previous question, but the resulting 282-105 vote was not a clear indication of members' positions on the beef program, according to Symms' and Richmond's staff. In effect, these sources said, a "no" meant either a vote with Richmond or a vote against the entire package of credit revisions, while a "yea" could mean support for the beef program or a decision not to further delay the bill. *(Vote 498, p. 142-H)*

Following the recorded vote, the House by voice vote rejected Symms' motion to recommit the conference report.

Senate

The Senate by voice vote adopted the conference agreement July 20. In a brief discussion before the vote, Herman E. Talmadge, D-Ga., called the bill the "most significant and far-reaching farm credit legislation" since he had entered the Senate. Talmadge and others then paid tribute to the late Sen. James B. Allen, D-Ala., who had guided the bill through the Senate before his death in June. ▮

Commodity Futures Agency

President Carter Sept. 30 signed into law a bill (S 2391 — PL 95-405) extending the life of the Commodity Futures Trading Commission (CFTC) through fiscal 1982. The agency's authorization was to have expired that day. The Senate had approved the conference report on the bill by voice vote Sept. 28 and the House, also by voice vote, cleared the measure for the president Sept. 29. The Senate originally had approved a six-year extension July 12 and the House passed a three-year bill (HR 10285) July 26.

The unpopular agency that regulates the intricate and risky business of trading futures contracts on commodities won a four-year reauthorization despite congressional animosity and Carter administration efforts to dismember it.

In the end, members decided that many of the young agency's troubles were inevitable growing pains, and that it should continue its difficult task — with more congressional oversight.

The four-year-old commission had been severely and repeatedly criticized as sloppy and ineffective. Most recently a House appropriations subcommittee and the General Accounting Office turned in damaging reports alleging, among other things, that the CFTC had improperly diverted its resources to problems with options sales originating in London. Much of the criticism centered on outspoken CFTC Chairman William T. Bagley, characterized by Sen. Thomas F. Eagleton, D-Mo., as a "windbag" who did not understand the complexities of the futures market. (Bagley resigned his post on Nov. 3 to join a California law firm.)

These controversies showed up in final provisions of the bill. The fixed term of the commission chairman was changed to one served at the pleasure of the president, and trading on most options was suspended until the CFTC could show congressional agriculture committees that it could handle regulation responsibility.

Another change required the CFTC to clear proposed market contracts on financial instruments of the U.S. government or stocks with interested agencies — the Treasury Department, Securities and Exchange Commission (SEC) or the Federal Reserve Board. The administration had proposed transferring regulatory authority for these types of futures contracts to the Treasury and the SEC, and demoting the CFTC to sub-Cabinet status.

The final bill did not include a provision passed by the House and backed by many farmers that would have required public reporting of export sales of commodities within three days. Farmers had complained that market "insiders" had an unfair advantage from advance knowledge of major sales, such as the Russian wheat sales of 1972 and 1977. Conferees, however, decided that that proposal would duplicate an existing program of the Agriculture Department (USDA).

Provisions

As signed into law, S 2391:

- Empowered the president to appoint the CFTC chairman from among the five commissioners, to serve at the president's pleasure.
- Directed the CFTC chairman to follow budget and administrative priorities set by the whole commission when spending commission funds or carrying out its functions.
- Deleted a requirement that the Senate confirm the CFTC executive director.
- Prohibited commissioners and high-ranking CFTC officials from transacting business for others with the commission for one year after leaving office; made the provision effective four months after enactment. The ban covered officials at the GS 16 level and above, and Schedule C appointees — those exempt from civil service by reason of their specialized responsibilities.

• Relaxed a requirement that the CFTC staff a liaison office at the Department of Agriculture (USDA), directing the commission instead to "maintain liaison."

• Required the CFTC to keep the Treasury Department, Federal Reserve Board and Securities and Exchange Commission informed of its activities relating to the responsibilities of the agencies, and to seek agency views on the market and financing implications of futures trading in securities and financial instruments under their jurisdiction. Before the commission could approve an application for a contract market dealing in securities issued or guaranteed by the U.S. government, the application had to be submitted for comment to both the Treasury Department and the Federal Reserve Board. The commission was required to make any agency views on an application part of the public record, and was barred from approving an application for 45 days, or until agency comments were received. Lawsuits based on any aspect of this provision were barred.

• Prohibited commodity options transactions, with two exceptions, until 30 days after the CFTC sent evidence to congressional agriculture committees that it could regulate the transactions; exempted from this ban "trade options" (those between entities that buy or sell the commodity on which the option is based), and certain entities that had been in the business as of May 1, 1978; required any future CFTC regulations on options transactions to set minimum financial and management standards, spelled out in the bill.

• Required a public hearing and a finding that an individual's options transactions were "contrary to the public interest" before the commission could terminate an individual's right to trade options.

• Authorized the commission to bar any options transactions on physical commodities that it finds contrary to the public interest, but only after a public notice and hearing.

• Authorized the commission to permit commingling of customers' segregated funds for different types of transactions, under conditions set by the commission.

• Exempted from mandatory registration and related reporting requirements persons active in "cash market" transactions on agricultural commodities, and non-profit farm groups that advise on cash commodities. (A cash market is one for immediate delivery of and payment for commodities.) These persons were not exempt from other provisions of the Commodity Exchange Act (CEA).

• Required the commission to publish, at least 30 days before adoption, any proposed changes in contract market regulations that it considers of major economic significance; allowed the CFTC up to 60 days after receipt to approve such proposed changes, unless it notifies a market that its proposal violates the commission's statute or regulations. In the latter case, a hearing was required.

• Established CFTC statutory authority to subpoena witnesses and take other actions relating to investigations. (Under existing law, CFTC investigative authority was derived from the Interstate Commerce Act.)

• Required an on-the-record hearing, before cease-and-desist orders or fines were imposed, for a board of trade whose designation as a contract market had been denied, suspended or revoked.

• Empowered states to take civil action against violations of the CEA or regulations based on it. States could seek injunctions or fines. Entitled the CFTC to intervene in any state action brought under this section. Exempted from state actions these entities: contract markets, floor brokers, boards of trade licensed by the commission, and clearing houses. Affirmed that nothing in this section interfered with states' rights to prosecute alleged violations of state anti-fraud statutes.

• Barred the CFTC from disclosing information about traders' business dealings and customers, unless the data had been disclosed in an administrative, judicial or congressional proceeding.

• Eliminated a requirement that the CFTC publish information about traders and their market positions when that data had been supplied to a congressional committee.

• Authorized the CFTC to fingerprint applicants for registration.

• Ended CFTC authority to publish market positions of traders when it is "communicating" with exchange officials or committees about potentially disruptive or harmful market developments.

• Authorized establishment of mandatory-membership professional associations for regulating business practices of members.

• Raised to $15,000, from $5,000, the amount of damages that had to be alleged for arbitration proceedings by a professional association.

• Authorized the commission to delegate registration to professional associations.

• Required each exchange to disclose findings and reasons for any disciplinary action or denial of membership.

• Raised to felony, from misdemeanor status, various fraudulent and deceptive practices, including falsifying registration information.

• Raised to $500,000, from $100,000, the maximum fine for felonies committed by organizations; raised to $100,000, from $10,000, the maximum fine for felonies committed by CFTC staff and agents.

• Authorized appropriations as needed for commission operations for four years, through fiscal 1982.

• Affirmed that reparations proceedings were in order whether the alleged violation was committed by a registered individual or one who had not registered even though required to do so.

• Made a hearing optional, not mandatory, in reparations cases where alleged damages were under $5,000.

• Prohibited leverage transactions on agricultural commodities; required the commission to regulate leverage transactions in gold and silver; authorized it to prohibit or regulate leverage transactions on all other commodities by Oct. 1, 1979; authorized the commission to regulate any leverage transaction as a futures contract if it found that to be appropriate. (But conferees told the CFTC to hold off implementing its decision to treat all gold and silver leverage contracts as futures contracts, until House and Senate committees could hold hearings on the proposal.)

• Authorized the commission to grant use immunity to witnesses appearing before the commission. (Under use immunity, the government grants a witness immunity from prosecution for specific offenses, while at the same time compelling him to testify. The witness is not protected from prosecution relating to the crime on which he testified if the government can obtain evidence independent from the testimony.)

• Required the secretary of agriculture to study and report within one year of enactment on the impact of futures trading on potato marketing.

• Authorized the CFTC to collect "user fees" from entities regulated by the commission, to cover the costs of regulation; barred the commission from implementing any user fee plan until the plan had been approved by both House and Senate Agriculture committees; provided for payment of the fees to the U.S. Treasury, and stipulated that income from the fees would be spent "in accordance with the appropriations process."

Background

Congressional action in 1974 extended the Commodity Exchange Act to cover all commodities that had not been regulated and all other services, rights and interests in contracts for future delivery. (About one-third of the commodities traded in 1973 involved unregulated commodities.) The 1974 act (PL 93-463) created the independent five-member commission in place of a regulatory unit within the Department of Agriculture. It also gave the CFTC the discretion to regulate or ban options trading that was not already illegal, authorized injunctive relief against various violations and empowered the commission to intervene in contract markets to restore orderly trading in emergency situations. Registration requirements were extended to more professionals dealing with the contracts. The 1974 act also included a "sunset" clause allowing the CFTC to expire in 1978 unless it were reauthorized. *(1974 Almanac p. 215)*

Both the General Accounting Office (GAO) and the House Appropriations Subcommittee on Agriculture turned in highly critical reports on the four-year-old agency earlier in 1978. Among other things, the CFTC was said to be ineffective at screening firms and individuals for registration, slow to move against manipulations of the market, slower still at processing reparations claims, and lacking in internal structure. The reports also said the commission had improperly allowed itself to to be sidetracked from its main responsibility by the problems with London options.

The Carter administration recommended transferring CFTC authority over registered securities to the SEC, and giving the Treasury Department the final right to approve or disapprove designation of markets for trading futures contracts on government financial instruments, such as Treasury bonds. The Office of Management and Budget (OMB) proposal also said that the CFTC should be eliminated and that its function should be assigned to a sub-Cabinet agency, comparable to the Environmental Protection Agency. However, the proposal was not received until the final day of Senate Agriculture Committee markup, too late to be considered, according to Chairman Herman E. Talmadge, D-Ga.

Senate Committee Action

In its May 15 report (S Rept 95-850) on S 2391, the Senate Agriculture Committee said the 1974 bill had brought "progress toward encouraging honest and sound dealing. . . . The basic conclusion reached in 1974 that there should be a single regulatory agency responsible for futures trading is as valid now as it was then," it said.

The greatest "substantive" problem since 1974, the committee said, had been with dishonest commodity-related transactions traded "off-exchange" — that is, off the organized, designated contract markets. The CFTC therefore had been forced to divert futures personnel to options-related activities. Thirty of 38 options firms were under investigation and injunctions had been obtained against 60 firms and individuals, the committee said. The states had been effectively prevented from helping crack down on fraudulent options operations by the 1974 law, which pre-empted their commodities futures regulatory authority, the committee said.

Nevertheless, witnesses had told the committee that the young commission had "done a credible job in light of the enormous tasks with which it found itself confronted." Splitting up CFTC regulatory authority among several agencies "would only lead to costly duplication and possible conflict or over-regulation," the committee concluded.

Senate Floor Action

After heaping verbal abuse on the unpopular agency, the Senate decided to give it six more years to shape up.

By an 84-6 vote the Senate July 12 voted to extend the life of the CFTC through fiscal 1984, with no major structural changes. *(Vote 206, p. 34-S)*

Complaints against the commission ranged from sloppy management to failure to fulfill its basic mandate, regulation of the trillion-dollar futures market. Eagleton said he thought the CFTC was "the most messed up federal agency in the government, bar none."

Even the floor manager of the reauthorization bill, Patrick J. Leahy, D-Vt., conceded that the troubled commission was "a strong contender" for the title of "worst" federal agency.

CFTC Chairman William T. Bagley and his four fellow commissioners came in for unusually acid criticism during the Senate debate on S 2391. "Bumblers and sycophants" is the way Orrin G. Hatch, R-Utah, referred to them, and Eagleton claimed that "a lot of the troops on the commission think [Bagley] is a windbag. I happen to think he is, too."

Before passing the reauthorization bill, the Senate rejected an attempt to unseat Bagley and another new, controversial commissioner, David G. Gartner. The vote was on a proposal to dissolve the existing five-member commission and replace it with a newly appointed, three-member unit.

Gartner had come under fire for having accepted, before his appointment, sizable gifts of stock for his children from the president of a Midwest grain company whose business was partially regulated by the CFTC. President Carter and Vice President Mondale had both tried, unsuccessfully, to secure Gartner's resignation when the gifts were publicized after his confirmation. Under existing law, CFTC commissioners could be removed only by impeachment.

But Leahy defended Gartner who, he said, had "bent over backwards" to inform both the White House and the Senate Agriculture Committee of the gifts before his appointment. Leahy urged his colleagues not to "damage . . . a significant piece of legislation just because somebody at the White House screwed up."

While the Senate refused to unseat Gartner and Bagley, the bill as passed reined in the commission's independence somewhat. The fixed, five-year term of the chairman was changed to a position served at the president's pleasure. States were empowered to move against violations of the federal commodities futures statute, and industry associations were authorized to handle reparations proceedings.

The Senate bill also suspended trading in commodity options except for dealers meeting stiff financial and professional standards, and stipulated that the CFTC should not permit options trading to resume unless it could show it had the resources and expertise to regulate it. The risky options market had hatched some notable recent scandals. (An option is, basically, a chance to buy a contract at a future date.)

Also included in the Senate bill was a $1 million-a-year study on the effect of futures trading on the price of farm commodities.

Eagleton launched the attack on the CFTC with an amendment to replace the existing commission with a new one, headed by a single chief. This move would improve the CFTC administratively and had "absolutely and categorically nothing to do with the Gartner controversy," Eagleton maintained. He subsequently withdrew the amendment, saying he had been advised that slashing the commission from five members to one was too drastic.

John Melcher, D-Mont., then proposed to replace the existing commission with a new, three-member Commodities Trading Commission. Melcher said his amendment would extricate both the commission and Gartner from the embarrassment of his continuing as a commissioner.

Opposing Melcher were Leahy, Walter "Dee" Huddleston, D-Ky., and Bob Dole, R-Kan., who said that if the Senate had been mistaken in confirming Gartner, it should not try to undo the mistake at the expense of the commission and the new commissioner. Gartner "came to us with clean hands" and no new charges had turned up since his confirmation, Dole said. Leahy moved to table the Melcher amendment, winning by a 69-23 vote. *(Vote 205, p. 33-S)*

Other Amendments

The Senate took these other actions:

- Agreed by voice vote to a Huddleston amendment re-establishing a maximum fine of $100,000 for felonies under the commodities act. The amendment also specified which sections of the act would carry criminal penalties for violations of CFTC rules and regulations.

The committee bill had raised the maximum criminal penalty to $500,000 and had broadly authorized criminal penalties for violations of the commodities futures statute and of all CFTC regulations and rules based on that statute. Huddleston said the higher criminal fine could exhaust funds that would otherwise be available to pay defrauded customers reparations. And, he said, "the bureaucracy should not have total leeway to create new crimes, particularly felonies, through the issuance of rules, regulations and orders."

- Agreed by voice vote to an Eagleton amendment authorizing "user fees" to be paid to the CFTC by persons whose transactions the commission regulated.
- Agreed by voice vote to a Bellmon, R-Okla., amendment to expand the bill's authorization for state enforcement of the Commodity Exchange Act and CFTC regulations and rules. Bellmon's amendment empowered states to bring civil suits for financial settlements, as well as injunctions, on behalf of residents, if the CFTC were notified of the suit.
- Agreed by voice vote to a Leahy amendment deleting a one-house veto of any CFTC proposal to regulate renewed trading in commodity options.

Leahy said he wanted the veto provision removed "just simply to give us some time to better evaluate" a recent Carter declaration that he would not honor the legislative vetoes. Leahy said the House bill included a similar veto provision, and that he expected the issue to be dealt with in conference.

- Rejected by voice vote an Eagleton amendment to suspend trading in most "leverage" contracts until the CFTC had developed "effective" regulatory methods. These contracts, most commonly used for long-term purchase of precious metals like gold, involve installment payments against future delivery of the commodity.

Leahy said the commission should be allowed to use new discretionary power authorized by the bill to deal with any problems. Huddleston also objected to an outright ban on leverage transactions. Since the scope of this "developing . . . activity . . . in trading" was not yet known, it was unreasonable "to assume that every trade is a fraudulent trade," Huddleston said. He added that anti-fraud laws could also be used to curb abuses.

House Committee Action

Like its Senate counterpart, the House Agriculture Committee rejected an administration proposal to reduce the commission to sub-Cabinet status and parcel out major CFTC responsibilities to the Securities and Exchange Commission (SEC) and the Treasury Department.

Maintaining a "strong, prestigious independent commission" was the best way to ensure a "fair, open" futures market, the committee said in its May 15 report on HR 10285 (H Rept 95-1181).

The committee recommended a three-year reauthorization, because the rapid rate of expansion and change in the industry made early review of the CFTC's mandate "desirable."

House Floor Action

After three sessions (July 21, 25-26) on the complex bill and 14 amendments, the House approved a three-year reauthorization of the CFTC (HR 10285) by a 401-6 vote July 26 and then moved to substitute its text for the Senate-passed measure (S 2391) and request a conference. *(Vote 524, p. 150-H)*

Major issues debated were whether commodities export sales should be quickly publicized to cut the advantage of market "insiders," and whether states should be allowed to pre-empt federal enforcement of key portions of the commodities statute.

The House by a 273-125 vote adopted an amendment by Neal Smith, D-Iowa, requiring reporting within 48 hours of export sales and related information, with public disclosure of the reports on the third day after the sale. *(Vote 523, p. 150-H)*

The amendment was prompted by farmer discontent with the secrecy surrounding massive grain sales to the Soviet Union in 1977 and 1972. In these sales, Smith charged, big grain companies had been able to buy up farmers' stocks at unfair, low prices by masking the "real demand" for the wheat.

The House rejected 141-260 a Baldus, D-Wis., amendment that would allow states to pass and enforce commodities laws if they were identical to key sections of the federal commodities statute. *(Vote 522, p. 150-H)*

Baldus said his amendment was needed to ensure adequate policing of the industry, since the CFTC was not given either "resources (or) manpower to monitor the industry on a nationwide basis." But opponents argued that even though the text of state and federal laws would be identical, interpretations could vary among different state courts, "causing regulatory chaos," according to Steven D. Symms, R-Idaho. Anything other than uniform national enforcement would be a hardship for the industry, opponents said.

The House also:

- Agreed by voice vote to a Glickman, R-Kan., amendment requiring the Securities and Exchange Commission, the General Accounting Office and the CFTC to evaluate the relationship between futures in general and futures on financial instruments like government bonds.
- Agreed by voice vote to a Findley, R-Ill., amendment limiting to nine months a discretionary exemption for certain firms from a general ban on futures trading.
- Rejected by a 6-24 standing vote a Symms amendment to end what Symms called a "double jeopardy" situation. Under existing law, the commission could move in both federal court and administrative proceedings against alleged violations. Opponents of Symms' amendment argued that the authority for dual action should be retained, because the courts could move quickly to enjoin questionable activity while administrative judges with appropriate expertise could deal with the substance of a commodities futures problem.
- Agreed by voice vote to a Foley, D-Wash., amendment deleting a requirement in the committee bill that states could only prosecute certain violations of the commodities statute and regulations under the *parens patriae* doctrine. Foley argued that the "confusing" doctrine, which required a state to demonstrate that a violation had injured its citizens, held up action against criminal violations. With Foley's amendment, states had only to demonstrate that a violation had occurred in order to proceed.
- Agreed by voice vote to a Foley amendment narrowing the bill's conflict-of-interest provision for high-ranking officials by limiting its application to those with confidential or policy-making responsibilities. Foley said the committee's provision, which covered all positions at the GS 16 level or above, would make it hard for the agency to recruit high-caliber lawyers, economists and others with needed expertise.
- Agreed by voice vote to a Panetta, D-Calif., amendment raising to $500,000, from $100,000, the maximum criminal penalty for organizations violating the commodities statute.
- Agreed by voice vote to an AuCoin, D-Ore., amendment requiring a 30-day public notice and comment period before the CFTC approved any contract market rules of "major economic significance."
- Agreed by voice vote to a Richmond, D-N.Y., amendment broadening a provision prohibiting disclosure of confidential, market-sensitive information or the identity of traders and customers until the information had been disclosed in judicial, congressional or administrative proceedings.
- Agreed by voice vote to a Cohen, R-Maine, amendment directing the General Accounting Office (GAO) to study and report within a year on the market impact of futures contracts in Irish potatoes.
- Rejected amendments to disqualify potential commissioners who had received gifts from individuals with interests regulated by the CFTC, and to exempt commodities clearinghouses from direct CFTC regulation.

Conference Action

In most respects the House and Senate bills differed more in detail than in intent. Conferees settled on a four-year reauthorization, compared with the three-year House extension and the six-year extension passed by the Senate. With a few exceptions they simply blended differing features of both bills, retaining most items passed by each house. The report (S Rept 95-1239) was filed Sept. 25.

On the regulation of options, conferees indicated that they did not intend a suspension of trading to become a permanent ban on options transactions. The commission should "expeditiously proceed with plans to implement exchange trading . . . to assure that options will, in fact, be traded on domestic exchanges, to the extent possible with existing commission resources," conferees said.

On the subject of leverage transactions, the conferees expressed surprise at a September CFTC decision to treat leverage contracts in gold and silver as futures contracts, for purposes of regulation. (These contracts, most commonly used for long-term purchase of precious metals, involve installment payments against future delivery of the commodity.) Conferees told the CFTC to hold off final action on the reclassification of the leverage contracts until House and Senate Agriculture committees could hold hearings on the proposed change.

Conferees followed the House in substantially beefing up fines for criminal violations of the commodities statute by organizations. They chose a narrower House conflict-of-interest provision over a Senate version that would have covered many more employees. The Senate bill applied restrictions on post-employment contacts to officials at the GS 15 level and above. The final version imposed restrictions beginning at the GS 16 level.

These provisions were not included by conferees in the final bill:

- A Senate-approved provision designed to protect customer funds from being seized in bankruptcy proceedings against a futures merchant was dropped because the 1978 bankruptcy reform act (HR 8200) included a provision on the treatment of these funds. *(Bankruptcy act, p. 179)*
- Conferees dropped a Senate provision requiring the commission to monitor forward contracts on agricultural commodities for six years and recommend policy changes on the contracts, if needed. Instead, conferees said, Rep. Thomas S. Foley, D-Wash., and Sen. Herman E. Talmadge, D-Ga., chairmen of the House and Senate Agriculture committees, had asked the secretary of agriculture to conduct the study. In a similar decision, conferees retained a House-passed provision mandating a year-long study of the impact of potato futures contracts on the potato market, but assigned responsibility for the study to the Agriculture Department instead of the commission.
- A House-passed requirement that exporters make detailed reports on commodity export sales to the CFTC within 48 hours, with publication of the data the following day, was dropped because the Agriculture Department "already has an export sales reporting program," according to conferees. They noted that the secretary had recently appointed a committee to review the export reporting system and to recommend improvements.
- A Senate provision establishing a national commission to study and report on the impact of futures trading on farm income was deleted, without comment. ∎

U.S. Aquaculture Policy

President Carter Oct. 18 pocket vetoed a bill (HR 9370) that would have provided federal assistance for aquaculture, the controlled cultivation of fish and shellfish. It was his first use of the pocket veto — withholding of the president's signature after congressional adjournment — which automatically kills a bill.

Carter issued a statement saying he was concerned about provisions in the bill giving the industry up to $300 million in loan guarantees and up to $250 million in insurance.

"I am concerned about offering major new government subsidies...unless and until a clear need for them has been established," Carter said. He said the federal government already subsidized fish hatcheries and gave technical assistance to aquaculture interests. *(Message, 64-E)*

As cleared by Congress, the measure (HR 9370) authorized appropriations of $12 million in fiscal 1980 with additions of $10 million in each of the next two years to develop programs and implement a national plan for aquaculture — broadly defined as the raising of plants and animals in a controlled water environment.

The bill was reported by the House Committee on Merchant Marine and Fisheries Oct. 28, 1977 (H Rept 95-778), and passed the House Feb. 15 by a 234-130 vote. *(Vote 52, p. 14-H)*

A similar bill (S 3408) was jointly reported by the Senate Agriculture and Commerce committees Aug. 25 (S Rept 95-1168), and passed the Senate by voice vote Sept. 12. A compromise version of the bill was approved by both chambers Oct. 2, clearing the measure for the president.

Background

Worldwide aquacultural production had roughtly doubled in the past five years and totaled about six million metric tons, about 10 percent of world fisheries production, the committee reports noted.

Countries such as China, Japan and the Soviet Union had been expanding aquacultural production rapidly in recent years. Some countries get up to 40 percent of their fish supply that way — compared to only 3 percent in the United States, the Senate report said. U.S. aquaculture produces salmon, catfish, trout, oysters, mussels, shrimp, clams and other species.

The domestic demand for seafood products may soon outstrip maximum yields by traditional methods, the reports said. U.S. demand — already far ahead of domestic supplies—was expected to increase 80 percent by the year 2000, while most estimates of the maximum global yield of fish were about 50 percent higher than current yields.

The United States imported over 50 percent of its fisheries products in 1976, causing a balance of payments deficit of nearly $2 billion.

Both reports ascribed the slow growth of U.S. aquaculture to a variety of factors, including inadequate funding for aquaculture research; difficulties in obtaining venture capital from the private sector coupled with inadequate federal financial assistance; prohibitively high premium rates for aquaculture insurance, and a lack of leadership, definitive goals and coordination among the federal agencies conducting aquaculture research and development programs. The departments primarily involved have been Agriculture, Commerce and Interior.

Provisions

As cleared by Congress, HR 9370:

- Established a National Aquaculture Council composed of the secretaries of commerce, interior and agriculture; required the council to produce within 18 months a national aquaculture development plan identifying actions the federal government should take to encourage aquaculture production.
- Established an Interagency Aquaculture Coordinating Committee, consisting of the council members plus the directors of six other federal agencies with functions relating to aquaculture, to help improve the exchange of information and coordination among federal agencies.
- Authorized the secretaries of commerce, interior and agriculture to provide matching grants to help implement the national plan and for aquaculture demonstration projects.
- Authorized the secretaries of commerce and agriculture to provide up to $300 million in loan guarantees to cover up to 90 percent of the principal and interest of private loans for the development, operation or refinancing of aquaculture enterprises; also authorized them to issue up to $250 million in direct insurance for stock, property and liability if studies indicated there was a need for such insurance.
- Established a revolving fund in the Treasury Department for carrying out the loan guarantee and insurance programs.
- Authorized appropriations of $12 million in fiscal 1980, $22 million in fiscal 1981, and $32 million in fiscal 1982, with 80 percent of the funds to be divided equally between the Commerce and Agriculture Departments and the remainder going to the Interior Department.

International Wheat Reserve

An administration proposal to establish an international emergency wheat reserve program died at the end of the 95th Congress. Three congressional committees had reported different versions of the plan, but none of the bills came to the House or Senate floor for a vote.

As initially proposed by the administration, the measure would have authorized the secretary of agriculture to buy and hold up to six million metric tons of wheat for emergency food needs in developing countries. The reserves would be released only after domestic requirements and commercial exports had forced curtailment of food aid shipments under the PL 480 (Food for Peace) program.

The major difference between the bill (HR 13835) as reported by the House Agriculture Committee Sept. 12 and the International Relations Committee Sept. 13 (H Rept 95-1564, Parts I and II) was the size of the reserve. The Agriculture Committee set the reserve at three million metric tons, while the International Relations Committee went along with the administration figure of six million tons. The bill died in the Rules Committee.

Instead of reserve stocks, the bill reported by the Senate Agriculture Committee Aug. 24 (S 3460 — S Rept 95-1151) authorized a fund of up to $500 million to purchase grain for humanitarian and disaster assistance.

Committee staff members cited the three conflicting versions of the bill and the crush of last-minute congressional business, plus concerns about the price-depressing effects of a massive reserve, as important factors in the death of the measure.

The administration had hoped to have the bill enacted before the conclusion of ongoing negotiations for a food aid convention as part of a new international wheat agreement. The United States had pledged to provide a minimum of 4.47 million metric tons of grain annually — more than twice its existing obligation — under the new convention.

Agricultural Trade Bill

Congress gave final approval Oct. 14 to a bill designed to boost U.S. agricultural exports by liberalizing credit terms for some export sales and increasing marketing and promotion efforts abroad.

The measure (S 3447 — PL 95-501) allowed the Commodity Credit Corporation (CCC) to extend short-term credit (up to three years) to the People's Republic of China. China had been ineligible under provisions of the 1974 Trade Act.

The legislation reflected a growing feeling that while a surge in U.S. agricultural exports in recent years had little to do with conscious government policy, the government should now move to capitalize on it.

Maintaining a high level of farm sales abroad is critical for two reasons, proponents said:

- U.S. farmers get almost 20 percent of their income from exports.
- Farm exports are one of the biggest positive contributors to the heavily negative — $31.2 billion in 1977 — U.S. balance of trade.

Proponents of the legislation said the United States needed to shed its traditional role as a residual supplier of farm products and be more aggressive if it wanted to maintain its strong position in the face of vigorous sales competition from such countries as Canada and Australia.

They also felt short-term credit for China could help open up a market with great potential for U.S. farm products.

Provisions

As cleared by Congress, S 3447:

- Allowed the Commodity Credit Corporation (CCC) to provide intermediate-term (three- to 10-year) credit for sales that will expand or maintain the importing nation's market for U.S. commodities or improve its capability to purchase and use U.S. commodities.
- Restricted intermediate-term credit to four uses: 1) grain sales to establish reserve stocks as part of an international grain agreement or other stock building plan; 2) sales of breeding livestock such as cattle, sheep or poultry; 3) construction of foreign facilities to improve marketing, storage or distribution of U.S. commodities, or 4) to meet credit competition for export sales.
- Directed the secretary of agriculture to attempt to obtain commitments from purchasers that will prevent resale to other nations of U.S. commodities bought with intermediate-term credit.
- Provided that agreements to sell grain for reserve stocks would not become effective until 30 days after a summary of the agreement had been sent to Congress. The summary was to include a determination by the president that the sale would not injure U.S. commodities producers.
- Exempted intermediate-term credit sales from the provisions of the cargo preference laws.
- Provided CCC short-term credit for private exporters of U.S. commodities who offer deferred payment terms to countries eligible for three-year CCC credit.
- Gave the CCC authority to provide short-term credit to the People's Republic of China.
- Provided that the secretary of agriculture and the secretary of state upgrade the title of U.S. agricultural attaches to agricultural counselor in nations where U.S. competitors assign a diplomat with similar status or where the potential for long-term market development is great.
- Required the appointment of at least 10 counselors within three years after enactment.
- Required the secretary of agriculture, after consultation with the secretary of state, to establish from six to 25 agricultural trade offices abroad.
- Required each trade office to be directed by an agricultural trade officer appointed by the secretary of agriculture.
- Directed that the offices should assist foreign buyers and U.S. trade representatives, coordinate market development activities and establish goals for expanding agricultural markets.
- Upgraded the title of assistant secretary of agriculture for international affairs and commodity programs to under secretary.
- Required the secretary of agriculture to submit an annual report to Congress on U.S. efforts to expand foreign markets for U.S. commodities.
- Required the secretary of agriculture to submit to Congress within six months after enactment a report of the effects on U.S. agriculture of the 1974 Trade Act's provisions limiting nondiscriminatory trade relations with nonmarket economy countries. *(1974 trade act, 1974 Almanac p. 553)*

Background

The crops from about 100 million acres — almost one-third of the U.S. total harvested acreage — have been shipped abroad in recent years. They were worth almost $24 billion in 1977, a substantial segment of the total 1977 gross farm income of $106 billion.

With net farm income slipping from $30 billion in 1973 to slightly more than $20 billion in 1977, the additional income from exports was the difference between a profit and a loss for many farmers.

Farm exports contributed over $10 billion to the plus side of the trade ledger in 1977, and were seen by many in Congress as a major weapon in the effort to reduce the U.S. trade deficit.

Exports also help keep farm prices above federally set target prices and thus reduce or eliminate the federal obligation to pay deficiency payments if prices fall below the target.

The explosive growth in agricultural exports in the 1970s was preceded by a period of relatively modest increases in the '60s, when the total value of farm exports was consistently in the $5 billion to $6 billion range and the net contribution to the trade balance was $1 billion to $2 billion.

Since 1972, when exports climbed to $9.4 billion, shipments abroad had surged, going from $17.7 billion in 1973 to $22 billion in the 1974-75 period and hitting a peak of $23.7 billion in 1977. Estimates for fiscal 1978 indicated farm exports could reach $26 billion.

About four-fifths of the gain in exports came from three commodity groups: grains and feeds such as wheat and corn; oilseeds (soybeans), and animal products (meat, poultry, hides, etc.).

Europe ($10.5 billion) and Japan ($3.8 billion) were the biggest customers for U.S. farm exports in 1977. Other major customers were Eastern Europe, the Soviet Union and the OPEC oil-producing nations. The value of food exports to the OPEC countries had increased almost three times since 1972.

Reasons cited for the surge in agricultural exports included bad weather in China, Russia and Europe that led to crop shortfalls there; greater affluence and consumer and government decisions to upgrade diets, and the decline of the dollar, which made U.S. exports cheaper to buy in many countries.

Senate Committee Action

The healthy state of U.S. agricultural exports was "impressive," the Senate Agriculture Committee said in its Aug. 23 report on S 3447 (S Rept 95-1142), but recent increases appeared to be "more in spite of, rather than the result of, government policy."

There had been some signs in the last year that export gains were being eroded, the committee noted. Farmers and traders were complaining that they were losing sales and facing a reduced market share. "From 1975-76 to 1976-77, for example, wheat exports by Canada, Australia and Argentina increased from 23.2 million tons to 27 million tons — while the U.S. share of the wheat export market decreased from 31.5 million tons to 25.7 million tons," the report said.

In response to this situation, the committee recommended a liberalized export credit program and more aggressive promotion of U.S. farm products.

The intermediate-term credit proposal was intended to help fill the gap between existing short-term CCC credit (six to 36 months) and the Public Law 480 program, which provides 20- to 40-year loans at low interest rates to developing countries.

The objective of the intermediate term program, according to the committee, was to "increase the total world market for grains and other commodities — rather than to compete for shares of the existing market."

The committee said intermediate credit would be appropriate for commodities such as breeding livestock, which usually requires up to 10 years before the initial investment is recouped; building food stocks as part of an international reserve program, and financing projects such as storage and distribution facilities that would increase the capacity to handle farm exports.

The committee also authorized the CCC to provide short-term (less than three years) financing to exporters who must extend deferred payment terms to foreign customers in order to meet sales competition from other countries or to make additional export sales.

It authorized short-term credit financing, including the deferred-payment terms, for commercial sales of commodities to the People's Republic of China.

Providing short-term credit to China would allow the U.S. to offer credit terms comparable to those offered by Canada and Australia, according to the committee report.

The committee made several recommendations aimed at stepping up U.S. efforts at foreign agricultural market development.

Agricultural Counselors. It called for upgrading the title of the senior agriculture representative in at least 16 of the major agricultural missions overseas to "agricultural counselor." Raising the rank of agricultural attaches to counselor would help the U.S. representatives reach key officials in foreign governments, the committee said. Other food-producing nations frequently were represented by an officer with counselor status.

Trade Offices. The committee recommended that the Agriculture Department establish from six to 25 agricultural trade offices overseas.

These offices would stimulate agressive export promotion by consolidating agricultural activities in one office, providing services and facilities for foreign buyers and U.S. trade representatives and increasing the visibility of the U.S. sales effort, the report said.

The United States today "does proportionately less to promote its exports of agricultural commodities than any other major exporting nation," the report said.

Senate Floor Action

The Senate passed S 3447 Sept. 8 by a 65-1 vote. William Proxmire, D-Wis., cast the negative vote. *(Vote 372, p. 55-S)*

The Senate adopted amendments:

- By Kaneaster Hodges Jr., D-Ark., requiring the secretary of agriculture to notify House and Senate agriculture committees 30 days (60 days if Congress is not in session) before the implementation of any agreement for the intermediate-term financing of U.S. grain for foreign reserve stocks.
- By Bob Dole, R-Kan., requiring exports under the PL 480 (Food for Peace) program of at least seven million metric tons annually for the next four fiscal years (1979-1982) unless supplies are not available or there is a lack of need among developing nations. The existing level of PL 480 sales and donations was about five million metric tons a year, Dole said.
- By Robert Morgan, D-N.C., requiring that the 16 agricultural representatives upgraded to the rank of counselor be designated within three years after enactment.

During debate Dick Clark, D-Iowa, said he was "puzzled" and "deeply concerned" about the administration's apparent opposition to the bill.

Clark said he was annoyed about State Department opposition to the sections of the bill requiring trade offices outside of embassies and the upgrading in rank of agricultural officers.

"Frankly, I think this opposition is merely petty bureaucratic wrangling over turf," Clark said. "The State Department fears that USDA may get some authorities under this bill that would reduce the ambassador's ability to control his mission."

Clark said the other administration concern was that the intermediate-term financing provisions might start a trade war with friendly competitors. Other countries were already using intermediate credit, Clark said, and the United States needed to have intermediate credit "to use as a threat in cases where our competitors use it against us."

House Committee Action

The House bill (HR 10584) was jointly referred to the Agriculture Committee, which filed its report July 10 (H Rept 95-1338, Part I), and to the International Relations Committee, which reported its version (Part II) Sept. 14.

As reported by the Agriculture Committee, HR 10584:

- Established an intermediate term credit program similar to S 3447 but without the provisions limiting the use of reserve stocks to emergency relief or requiring a 30-day waiting period before implementation of reserve stock financing.
- Allowed CCC short-term credit for non-market economies for commodities in excess of the average annual amount purchased in the 1975-77 period. The effect of the restriction would be to make China eligible for a large amount of short-term credit and to limit eligibility for the Soviet Union, a heavy purchaser in the 1975-77 period. The Soviet Union was ineligible for commercial credit under the provisions of the Jackson-Vanik amendment to the Trade Act of 1974 (PL 93-618). *(Background, 1974 Almanac p. 553)*
- Created six to 25 agricultural trade offices.
- Upgraded the title of agricultural attache at the more important posts to agricultural counselor.
- Upgraded the position of assistant secretary of agriculture for international affairs and commodity programs to under secretary.

The International Relations Committee limited the number of trade offices to 16, set criteria for their selection and required the concurrence of the secretary of state in establishing them. It permitted intermediate credit for only two purposes: exports of breeding livestock and grains for emergency food reserve stockpiles under international agreements. The broader uses approved by the Agriculture Committee could lead to credit wars, the International Relations panel said.

The committee also reworded the provision allowing short-term credit to non-market countries to exclude the Soviet Union.

House Floor Action

A compromise version of the two committee bills easily passed the House Sept. 25 despite objections that part of the bill constituted an "end run" around existing laws banning trade concessions to communist countries that restrict emigration.

Needing a two-thirds majority to pass under suspension of the rules, the measure (HR 10584) was approved 325-62. *(Vote 725, p. 206-H)*

As passed by the House, the bill would establish up to 16 agricultural trade offices overseas, upgrade the titles of some U.S. agricultural representatives in foreign missions and allow the intermediate-term credit to finance sales of breeding livestock and grain for emergency reserves.

The only controversy over the bill concerned the provision under which the CCC would be allowed to provide short-term credit for nonmarket economy countries for purchases which exceeded the average annual purchases by each country in the 1975-77 period. The major beneficiary of the provision would be the People's Republic of China.

The bill included language that made the Soviet Union ineligible for short-term credit, but did not rule out eligibility for East Germany, Czechoslovakia and Bulgaria.

The provision was criticized by Charles A. Vanik, D-Ohio, as an "end run" around the Jackson-Vanik amendment to the Trade Act of 1974, which banned trade concessions to nonmarket economies unless the president had received assurances from those countries that their policies were leading to free emigration.

Vanik contended that the language of the bill would permit the Soviet Union to receive CCC credits, and said he had "grave reservations" about using China "as a negotiating wedge vis-a-vis the Soviet Union."

There had been no reported cases of emigration from China, Vanik said, while emigration from the Soviet Union had increased 22 percent over 1977. "By providing credits to China, which doesn't even have an emigration system, we are taking a slap at the Soviets," Vanik said. "This action may backfire, causing the Soviets to abandon their growing quiet flow of emigration."

Jonathan B. Bingham, D-N.Y., responded that the original objective of the Jackson-Vanik amendment was to increase the flow of Jewish emigrants from the Soviet Union. U.S. policy had no comparable objective regarding China, he said.

Vanik's criticism of the bill was overshadowed by concerns about record harvests and declining grain prices.

"Given this massive stockpile, the United States must offer the tools to be as competitive as possible in selling U.S. farm products," said Keith G. Sebelius, R-Kan. "Let us sell it, not smell it."

The House bill was endorsed by the administration after language was added by the International Relations Committee strengthening the role of the State Department in the provisions relating to trade offices and agricultural representatives.

Conference, Final Action

Major differences between the House and Senate versions of the bill were resolved when conferees adopted modified versions of the Senate provisions on intermediate credit and short-term credit for China.

The Senate bill limited CCC intermediate credit to four areas: 1) establishment of reserve stocks under an international commodity agreement or stock building plan acceptable to the United States; 2) export sale of breeding animals including cattle, sheep and poultry; 3) construction of foreign facilities to improve handling, marketing, processing, storage or distribution of commodities; and 4) to meet credit competition for export sales.

Conferees chose the Senate restrictions over the narrower House language, which limited intermediate credit to sales of grain under an international grain agreement or for sales of breeding livestock.

Also adopted was the Senate language allowing the CCC to give short-term credit for commercial sales of U.S. commodities to China, rather than the broader House language allowing short-term credit for nonmarket economy countries for purchases exceeding average annual purchases in the 1975-77 period. The House language would have made Eastern European countries such as East Germany and Czechoslovakia eligible for short-term credit.

Conferees adopted the House criteria upgrading the title of agricultural attaches to agricultural counselor in countries where a substantial number of U.S. competitors assign agricultural representatives with a rank similar to counselor, where competition is intense, or where there is long-term potential for market expansion. At least 10 counselors must be appointed within three years; the appointments must be approved by both the secretary of agriculture and the secretary of state.

Conferees also adopted the Senate language calling for the secretary of agriculture to establish up to 25 agricultural trade offices after consulting with the secretary of state. The House bill required the concurrence of the secretary of state and allowed a maximum of 16 offices.

Conferees dropped the Senate provision requiring exports of at least seven million metric tons a year under the PL 480 program.

Final Action. The Senate accepted the conference report (S Rept 95-1315) Oct. 11 by voice vote. The House adopted the report (H Rept 95-1755) Oct. 15 by a 356-4 vote, clearing the measure for the president. *(Vote 827, p. 234-H)*

Foreign Land Ownership

President Carter Oct. 14 signed into law a bill (S 3384 — PL 95-460) requiring all foreign owners of U.S. farm and timberland to report their holdings to the secretary of agriculture.

Media reports of multi-thousand-acre sales and farm anger at rapidly escalating land prices had prompted Congress to pass the first national land ownership reporting system. A June General Accounting Office (GAO) report, one of several studies of the problem, had concluded that there was no effective way to determine how much American farmland was owned or controlled by foreign citizens or corporations.

In all but a few states, the only mandatory reporting of land transactions was at the county level, and owners could easily hide behind corporate identities.

Among the complaints that striking farmers brought to Washington in the spring of 1978 was that rich foreigners looking for investment opportunities were bidding up land prices to exorbitant levels. Many farmers wanted sales to foreign interests prohibited.

S 3384 required detailed reporting of all land transactions involving foreign individuals and corporations. (The law does not apply to permanent resident aliens.) It provided stiff financial penalties for violations of the reporting requirements and required the secretary of agriculture to forward reports on land transactions to states where the deals occurred and to make the ownership reports available in Washington for public inspection. It also provided the secretary with discretionary authority to reach into secondary or tertiary ownership of corporations to determine who really owned or had an interest in U.S. land.

The final version was a House bill (HR 13356), passed Sept. 26 by voice vote by the House, which then substituted its language for a slightly weaker version passed Aug. 11 by the Senate. The original Senate bill had limited the new reporting system to three years and had not included the discretionary authority to pursue the identity of corporate owners.

The Senate Oct. 2 agreed to the House amendment by voice vote, clearing the measure for the president.

Provisions

As signed into law, S 3384:

- Required the secretary of agriculture to complete regulations for reporting of foreign land ownership within 90 days after enactment; made reporting requirements effective when the regulations were completed.
- Required foreign individuals or corporations owning any interest (except a security interest, such as a mortgage) in agricultural land to report that interest and related data to the secretary. Existing holdings were to be reported within 180 days after reporting regulations were complete; future transfers were to be reported within 90 days after the transaction. ("Agricultural land" included acreage used for forestry or timber production.)
- Required the reports to include name, address and citizenship of the owner, location, acreage, price paid and intended use of the land, and other information as required by the secretary. In the case of corporate or other intermediary owners, the reports were to identify the entity's country of origin and principal place of business.
- Required reports from owners who became foreign "persons" (a legal term applying to both individuals and corporations), within 90 days of the change.
- Required reports on foreign-owned land that was converted to agricultural use, within 90 days of the conversion.
- Authorized the secretary to require additional information from any foreign entity (except a government or an individual) with agricultural land interests, such as the name and address of individuals holding any interest in the entity.
- Authorized fines of up to 25 percent of the fair market value of the land involved for failure to report or deliberate false reporting.
- Authorized the secretary to take investigative and other actions as needed to verify the accuracy of reports.
- Required the secretary to analyze the reports, with special attention to the impact of foreign agricultural land interests on family farms and rural communities, and the effectiveness of the reporting system.
- Required the secretary to report his findings periodically to the president and to Congress, with the first report due six months after completion of the reporting regulations.
- Required the secretary to send states, every six months, copies of reports of foreign agricultural land transactions within the states.
- Required the secretary to make reports available for public inspection within 10 days after receipt.

Background

U.S. farmers had complained for years that the rate of foreign investment in U.S. farmland had dramatically increased. They claimed that the devaluation of the dollar had made oil-rich Arabs and affluent West Europeans willing to pay inflated land prices — thereby driving up land prices beyond the reach of American farmers. Real estate brokers reported that in some areas as much as 50 percent of land transactions in 1978 involved foreign investors.

The actual amount of land changing hands may be relatively small; land sales average about 3 percent each year of total farm acreage. But the fact that the supply of land is never going to get any larger, and that the proportion of land under foreign control may be growing fast, worried some administration officials as well as farmers.

Because few states require information on nationality of owners, because actual owners can hide behind corporate identities or other intermediaries, and because land ownership records are scattered through the more than 3,000 countries, nobody has a very good idea how much American land is foreign-owned or controlled. For these same reasons, there was no good way to determine whether the rate of acquisition by foreigners was going up as fast as farmers said it was.

A 1976 law (PL 94-472) set up a Commerce Department office to monitor foreign investment. But that office originally concentrated on business investments and did not deal with real estate.

Senate Action

Without hearings, debate or a printed committee report explaining the bill, the Senate by voice vote Aug. 11 endorsed a mandatory land ownership reporting system for foreign owners or leaseholders — the first such national land registry.

The Senate acted just three days after the Senate Agriculture Committee had reported the bill (S 3384 — S Rept 95-1072). (Days after the Senate action, the committee report still had not been printed, according to committee staff.)

The hasty Senate action disclosed a bit of House-Senate rivalry that staff sources would only discuss "off the record."

Rep. Richard Nolan's, D-Minn., Agriculture Subcommittee on Family Farms had held hearings on a variety of bills dealing with alleged threats to family farms — from corporate and foreign land investments, from housing and other non-farm development, and from other factors.

The bill passed by the Senate was essentially one drafted by Reps. John Krebs, D-Calif., and Charles E. Grassley, R-Iowa. Of the quick Senate action, one House staff member snapped, "They stole our bill."

But sources on the Senate Agriculture Committee said that Chairman Herman E. Talmadge, D-Ga., had long been interested in farmers' complaints about foreign investors. Talmadge had ordered at least six separate studies of the problem that were due to be finished late in 1978. A preliminary General Accounting Office (GAO) report he had requested had showed in June that "foreign investors have acquired 6.3 percent of all farmland in a single county of my state in the past year and a half," Talmadge said in a prepared statement the day the Senate passed the bill.

Talmadge had not planned further action until he had the reports in hand. But when "the House started to move a bill based on the work we've done, there was a little 'don't appropriate our bill' feeling," one Senate Agriculture Committee aide said.

The Carter administration was "nervous" about the bills, according to Agriculture Department spokesman James C. Webster, "because we don't know yet whether foreign ownership is really a problem or not."

House Action

Committee. The House Agriculture Committee reported its bill Sept. 14 (H Rept 95-1570).

Stressing the value of the family-owned farm, it said that increased foreign investment in U.S. farmland appeared to contribute to farmers' economic problems. Recently, "farmland in the United States has had more value as a speculative investment than as a means of production," the committee said, noting that farm land values had more than doubled since 1970. U.S. farmers were being priced out of the market by foreigners willing to pay premium prices, aided by "cheap" U.S. dollars and tax breaks at home, the committee warned.

Media reports indicated "that as much as 40 to 50 percent of the purchases of agricultural land in some areas" were by foreigners, the committee said. But it was hard to assess the extent and impact of the foreign purchases, "primarily because of lack of data."

In a separate statement, John Krebs, D-Calif., one of the bill's co-authors, argued that while much overseas investment was beneficial, that was not the case with investment in farmland, which "creates few new jobs and requires little or no influx of additional capital."

Floor. The House passed HR 13356 Sept. 26 by voice vote, then substituted its language for S 3384.

Most of the debate consisted of statements supporting the measure or clarifying its intent. "We are not intending to take any action here that makes foreign ownership of land impossible or unduly difficult," said Thomas S. Foley, D-Wash., chairman of the House Agriculture Committee. The purpose was merely to provide data, he said.

Dan Glickman, D-Kan., said the land bill paralleled longstanding statutory requirements for disclosure of foreign ownership of U.S. securities.

Final Action

The Senate agreed to the House version of S 3384 Oct. 2, clearing it for the president, who signed it Oct. 14.

At the bill-signing ceremony, the president issued an indirect warning against a next step sought by some farmers — barring or restricting farmland sales to foreign interests.

Without explicitly referring to that proposal, the president cautioned that the new law would not produce "immediate results." Data from the detailed reports would have to be carefully analyzed, the president said, adding that "the policy options that arise from such analysis will have to be considered in the light of overall U.S. trade policies, including our opposition to unnecessary restrictions on international investment flows." ▮

Meat Import Bill Vetoed

Although Congress partially rewrote the bill in response to administration objections that it was too inflationary, President Carter Nov. 11 vetoed legislation (HR 11545) revising the formula for determining how much foreign-produced meat can enter the United States.

The formula changes were useful, Carter said, but the bill was unacceptable because it severely limited the president's authority to suspend meat import quotas, depriving him of "the only anti-inflationary tool available in this area." Carter also objected to a minimum import level set by the bill, which he said would endanger U.S. trade relations abroad. *(Veto message text, p. 68-E)*

The veto came four days after the Nov. 7 congressional elections. Critics charged that the bill's trip from Congress to the White House had been slowed deliberately so that Carter would not have to announce his decision on it before the election and thus anger voters in beef-producing states. Carter's unpopular farm policies already had caused problems for some farm-state Democrats.

The vetoed bill, originally designed to protect U.S. beef producers from import competition, made two major changes in the 1964 meat import act (PL 88-842). It revised the complex formula for calculating meat import quota levels, so that when domestic supplies were scarce and prices high, more imported meat would come onto the U.S. market; imports would shrink when domestic supplies expanded. This "counter-cyclical" factor reversed the effect of the 1964 act. *(1964 act, 1964 Almanac p. 133)*

It also sharply restricted the president's authority to lift the quota. It allowed him to do so in only three instances: a national emergency, a natural disaster that cut domestic supplies severely, or an excessive rise in the farm price of cattle, compared with retail prices. Under the 1964 law, the president had broad discretion to suspend meat import quotas.

Like his Republican predecessors, Carter had angered cattlemen by using that authority June 8 to admit more foreign beef to the country, to counter rising supermarket prices. Cattlemen maintained that the 1978 price rises were part of the normal 10-year cycle of cattle slaughter and herd rebuilding. They argued that the president's decision to admit 200 million more pounds of foreign beef had sharply dropped cattle prices without producing a similar drop in retail prices.

The president's decision to keep the broad quota-waiver authority — by vetoing the bill — ensured price-boosting shortages in the future, cattlemen said. The prospect of future market interventions would discourage producers from rebuilding herds. One official of the Missouri Cattlemen's Association warned that the veto of HR 11545 would trigger "the largest liquidation phase [of cattle] since the depression."

Carter said he was prepared to work with the 96th Congress to pass a countercyclical meat import bill "which will provide the stability and certainty the cattle industry requires, while preserving the president's existing discretionary authority and setting an acceptable minimum access level for imports."

But during House debate on the legislation, key members indicated that they had only accepted an administration version of the countercyclical formula as a tradeoff for the quota waiver authority. Trade laws should be, "insofar as practicable..., self-operative" rather than dependent on presidential discretion, said Charles A. Vanik, D-Ohio, chairman of the Ways and Means Trade Subcommittee.

Background

Cattle producers had long been unhappy with two key provisions of the 1964 meat import act: a "cyclical" import quota formula, and presidential discretion to waive the quota.

The 1964 law required the president to limit the amount of foreign meat brought into the country when imports exceeded a target figure by 10 percent, but allowed suspension of this requirement for economic or national security reasons.

Under the cyclical formula, U.S. production and imports moved up and down together, which meant that just as domestic cattle prices began to rise, more competing foreign meat entered U.S. markets, cattlemen complained. Frequent decisions by Presidents Nixon and Ford to lift the quotas compounded market problems caused by the formula, cattlemen said.

Producers conceded that, in both quality and type, the imports offered little real competition. Most of the foreign meat was low-grade beef used for hamburger, while American herds provided more expensive cuts. Also, imported meat accounted for only 7 percent of U.S. consumption.

But what cattlemen called "psychology" played a major role in the lengthy cattle cycle, they claimed. Producers were reluctant to rebuild herds if they couldn't plan on price rises at predictable points in the cycle, they said.

As beef prices rose in 1978, Carter decided to lift the quota, even though his Council on Wage and Price Stability differed with some Agriculture Department economists on the effectiveness of the action. Beef prices had been climbing dramatically — at an annual rate of 18.1 percent in the last three months of 1977 and 42.4 percent in the first quarter of 1978. These increases pushed up overall food costs which in turn jacked up the Consumer Price Index.

The Council recommended suspension of the quota as one way of fighting inflation. And it said that pending legislation to reverse the quota formula and to severely curb the president's power to lift quotas was "moderately inflationary." The producer-backed proposal would be "disproportionately harmful to lower-income consumers" because they relied more heavily on cheap hamburger prices, the council said.

Agriculture Department economists privately disagreed, maintaining that in fact the bill would keep the price of beef from rising as quickly as it would without legislation. The Consumer Federation of America at first opposed the legislation, echoing arguments of the Wage and Price Council. But that group later backed off, with an explanation that it didn't take positions on trade matters.

Senate Action

The Senate May 5 quietly passed an import bill (HR 5052) that would protect beef producers from import competition. By voice vote and without debate, it endorsed new restrictions on foreign meat imports that were designed to stabilize the cyclical highs and lows of the beef industry.

The bill, reported May 2 by the Senate Finance Committee (S Rept 95-777), was a less restrictive version of an earlier measure introduced by Lloyd Bentsen, D-Texas. It was an amendment in the form of a substitute to a minor tariff bill passed by the House in 1977. (The substance of that bill was enacted as an amendment to another bill.)

Provisions

As passed by the Senate, HR 5052 revised the Meat Import Act of 1964 (PL 88-842) as follows:

- Added a countercyclical factor to the formula for determining when the president must set a quota on unprocessed meat (beef, veal, mutton and goat) imports. The changed formula, based on a ratio between recent beef production and production over a 10-year period, would have the following effect: when domestic supplies were plentiful, less foreign meat could enter the country. When domestic production shrank, more imports could be brought in.

• Extended the quota system to processed beef and veal, with the quota based on average annual imports between 1973 and 1977. The existing requirement that the secretary of agriculture allot a proportion of total imports to each supplying nation was extended to the processed meats.

• Restricted the president's discretion to suspend or increase quotas to two types of situation. The president could suspend or increase quotas during a declared national emergency if national security or domestic shortages required him to do so.

• Provided for even spacing of imports throughout each year, by restricting imports during the first half of each year to no more than 54 percent of the total quota for that year. In years with an expiring quota or without a quota, no more than 54 percent of estimated annual imports could enter the country in the first half of the year.

• Directed the secretary of agriculture to study the regional economic impacts of meat imports and report the results by Dec. 31, 1979.

House Action

Committee. In reporting its bill Aug. 30, (HR 11545 — H Rept 95-1532), the House Ways and Means Committee adopted an administration-approved meat import formula instead of the producer-backed formula endorsed by the Senate in May. The administration formula was designed to respond to market conditions more quickly than the Senate version, and to let more meat into the country.

The committee bill also set an annual minimum for meat imports, but it was less liberal than the administration wanted.

Floor. The House debated HR 11545 Oct. 2, 6 and 12 and passed it Oct. 12, 289-66. *(Vote 802, p. 228-H)*

Before passing its bill, the House took these actions:

• Agreed by voice vote to a Bafalis, R-Fla., amendment requiring the secretary of agriculture to study and report to Congress on the regional economic impact of meat imports. Bafalis suggested that some imports were not nationally distributed, but were stored and later dumped in markets near their point of entry. The Senate bill had included a similar provision.

• Rejected by an 18-43 standing vote a Gibbons, D-Fla., amendment that would restore the president's broad authority to lift import quotas, as in the 1964 act. Gibbons said he had not spoken to the president personally about the restoration, but "I have been assured by people around him that, unless this amendment is adopted, the bill will be vetoed."

Supporting Gibbons amendment were Paul Findley, R-Ill., and Herbert E. Harris II, D-Va., who said the Ways and Means bill would tie the president's hands in international trade talks. Harris warned that the beef limitation would set a precedent for other products, and that the president would "no longer...have trade negotiation authority on any product."

• Rejected by a 131-139 vote a Burleson, D-Texas, amendment to substitute the Senate quota formula for the administration formula included in the House bill. Al Ullman, D-Ore., warned that Agriculture Secretary Bergland had personally approved the House version and that any changes could expose the bill to a veto. *(Vote 786, p. 224-H)*

• Agreed by voice vote to a Smith, R-Neb., amendment eliminating a Dec. 31, 1988, termination date from the bill. The effect of the amendment was to make the changes in the 1964 act permanent.

Smith said the "sunset" limit included in the House (but not the Senate) bill was inappropriate because the program did not involve new federal spending or bureaucracy. Ending the bill at the same time as a cattle cycle ended — as the House bill did — would "undermine" its effect, she said.

• Agreed by voice vote to a Findley amendment authorizing suspension of the quota in the event of a national emergency or natural disaster.

Final Action

Arguing that there was not time for conference action before adjournment, Senate sponsors urged the Senate to accept the House version of the bill. The Senate did so Oct. 15 by voice vote, clearing HR 11545 for the president.

While Bentsen claimed the bill would benefit consumers over the long run as much as it would help cattle producers, Jacob K. Javits, R-N.Y., and Howard Metzenbaum, D-Ohio, disagreed, warning that higher consumer beef prices were sure to result. "I think we have to recognize that this is a cattlemen's bill," Metzenbaum said.

Provisions

As cleared by Congress, HR 11545 would have made these changes in the Meat Import Act of 1964 (PL 88-842), effective Jan. 1, 1979:

• Revised the formula for determining when the president must set a quota on meat (beef, veal, mutton and goat) imports. The new formula was based on the average level of imports for 1968-1977, factored with recent and 10-year domestic production averages, and adjusted with a new countercyclical factor.

• Excluded from the domestic production base of the quota formula all meat produced from imported live cattle that were slaughtered in the United States.

• Authorized the president to lift the quota during a declared national emergency if national security required him to do so, or when natural disaster made domestic supplies "at reasonable prices" inadequate.

• Also allowed the president to increase imports up to 10 percent if the farm price of cattle increased 10 percent faster than the retail meat price in the first two calendar quarters of a year, or to decrease imports up to 10 percent if the opposite situation prevailed.

• Set a 1.2 billion-pound annual minimum level for meat imports, by providing that the quota in any year could not be less than that amount.

• Included in the quota system beef and veal that had been ground or otherwise processed (but not cooked).

• Required the secretary of agriculture to study the regional economic impact of meat imports and to report, with legislative recommendations, to congressional committees by Dec. 31, 1979. ▮

Sugar Legislation Dies

Sugar legislation unexpectedly died in the waning hours of the 95th Congress when the House balked at a conference agreement that had been drafted to Carter administration specifications.

The failure left a pending international sugar agreement (ISA) without ratification, and left domestic producers with an expiring support program.

It also left President Carter without two important powers — renewal of his authority to waiver countervailing duties on imports, which was to expire Jan. 3, 1979, and which Carter said was critical to the success of ongoing international trade talks, and his authority to increase U.S. contributions to an international tin stockpile to fulfill a longstanding treaty commitment.

Both provisions had been tacked onto the sugar bill as "veto insurance" by the Senate, which wanted higher sugar price supports than the president was willing to accept.

In the end, conferees knuckled under to the administration on the price supports, but in doing so made the bill unpalatable to enough House members that they rejected it in the final hours of the session.

The sugar bill had been held hostage during much of the year by Frank Chuch, D-Idaho, chairman of the Senate Foreign Relations subcommittee with jurisdiction over the ISA. Church refused to move on it unless the administration accepted import quotas and fees to raise sugar prices to at least 17 cents a pound with automatic adjustments over five years to allow for inflation, to protect domestic sugar producers from cheap foreign competition. Existing law guaranteed sugar producers at least 13.5 cents a pound through the 1978 crop year.

Consumer groups and the Carter administration fought both the 17-cent price and the automatic adjustment feature (the "escalator"), claiming these would add almost $5 billion to consumer food bills over the five-year period.

Administration aides indicated the president would veto anything above a 15-cents-a-pound price objective with no automatic increases. The administration preferred to supplement the basic price with direct payments from the Treasury to producers if production costs rose in the future. It proposed a price support program, similar to programs for other farm commodities, to raise minimum sugar prices to about 14 cents a pound — a price producers said was too far below their costs of production.

The House passed a bill Oct. 6 (HR 13750) that held the price objective to 15 cents a pound, but included a semiannual inflation adjustment provision unacceptable to Carter.

The Senate passed its version Oct. 13. It cut one cent off the 17-cent price objective recommended by the Finance Committee, leaving it still one cent higher than Carter's minimum, and included the automatic inflation adjustor. It also attached the countervailing duty waiver and tin stockpile authorities.

Struggling to get some kind of a sugar bill enacted before adjournment, conferees bowed to the administration on the 15-cent price objective, added a .75 cent a pound federal direct payment to producers for one year only and emasculated the automatic inflation adjuster.

The Senate went along with the agreement after Finance Committee Chairman Russell B. Long, D-La., insisted it must to avoid a veto. But House members, for a variety of reasons, balked, killing the conference report by a 17-vote margin.

Both the sugar legislation and the unrelated presidential authorities were expected to be reintroduced in the 96th Congress. In addition to Senate ratification of the ISA, both houses would have to authorize stockpiling and financing arrangements prior to U.S. participation.

Background

Americans eat a lot of sugar — about 95 pounds a year per person. But U.S. farmers grow only about half the 11 million tons Americans consume each year. The rest is imported, with most of the imports coming from Third World nations whose economic and political stability often depend on sugar prices.

U.S. sugar production is divided between family-size operations, which tend to be midwestern or western sugar beet farms, and large corporate cane growing and refining companies in the South and Hawaii. The industry's concentration has meant high lump-sum price support payments to corporate sugar producers — as much as $12 million in some instances.

The 1978 battle over sugar policy continued the most recent phase of a struggle begun in 1974 when Congress allowed a 40-year-old sugar price support program to lapse. The demise of that program was credited partly to heavy consumer pressures on Congress and partly to lobby overkill by domestic and foreign producers. *(1974 Almanac p. 225)*

Since 1974 there had been a 7 million ton overall import quota, considered meaningless by producers because imports averaged about 5 million tons annually. Importers, however, had greatly increased their share in the U.S. market since 1974.

1977 Actions

By 1977 Congress felt heavy pressures from American producers for help against the cheap imports. But the Carter administration spent much of the year trying to stave off action until the international sugar negotiations were completed.

In May 1977 Carter rejected as inflationary an International Trade Commission recommendation that an overall quota of 4.3 million tons be imposed on the largest foreign producers — Argentina, Brazil, Cuba, the Dominican Republic and the Philippines. The administration warned that premature action could undermine U.S. negotiations at the sugar talks.

At the same time, Carter set up an interim subsidy program to pay sugar producers up to 2 cents a pound whenever the market price fell below 13.5 cents. That program was later scrapped when a provision to "pass through" part of the payments to farmers was found to be illegal. (Because of the way the industry is set up and because of legislative precedents, government payments go to processors or refiners, who contract with the farmers for a share of the profits once the sugar is sold.)

Late in 1977 Carter bowed to pressures for protection from the cheap import flood set off by anticipation of the new agreement. In November he raised tariffs and fees on imported sugar to bring the price in line with the domestic support level of 13.5 cents.

But his first proclamation failed to distinguish between raw and refined sugar, thus exempting the refined product and leaving it cheaper for industrial users than the domestic versions. Carter closed that gaping loophole with a second proclamation. But the incident created a lot of worries among members of Congress about administration handling of the sugar issue.

Early in 1978 Carter rejected a second trade commission recommendation for import quotas to protect the domestic sugar industry.

The 1977 farm bill started out without a sugar program, but by the time Congress finished with it, it included a price support program added by E. "Kika" de la Garza, D-Texas. The de la Garza amendment, which expired with the 1978 crop year, authorized sugar purchases and loans to support the commodity at not less than 13.5 cents a pound. De la Garza had sought 14 cents, but conferees dropped that level and empowered the secretary of agriculture to end the program if an international agreement was reached guaranteeing the 13.5 cents-a-pound price. The bill also authorized the secretary to set minimum wages for sugar field workers. *(1977 Almanac, p. 417)*

International Sugar Agreement

In October 1977, negotiators for 73 nations agreed to a system of export quotas and stockpiling to stabilize the world market price of sugar at between 11 and 21 cents a pound. With transportation and duties included, this translated to 13.5 cents to 23.5 cents in the United States.

Participating nations would limit their exports and store the sugar until world prices reached 15 cents. The agreement set a "free market" range of 15 to 19 cents — that is, neither quotas nor stockpiling were required when sugar was selling in this range.

The stockpiled sugar would be financed by an international loan fund, supplied with fees on each pound of sugar that moved from one nation to another. Parties to individual sales would determine whether the importer or the exporter paid the fee.

Participating nations also agreed to limit their imports from non-participating nations.

Domestic sugar cane and sugar beet producers, which include multi-million dollar corporations that both grow the commodities and convert them to table sugar, conceded that the pact might bring some order to the international market. But it would not hike prices high enough to cover U.S. production costs and keep them in business, the producers claimed.

Producer groups persuaded strategically placed members of Congress that, in addition to the International Sugar Agreement, they needed backup quotas and fees to limit the flow of foreign sugar into the United States and to keep the domestic industry from being destroyed by underpriced gluts of foreign sugar such as those that plunged world sugar prices as low as 7 cents a pound in the past year. (Agriculture Department figures showed domestic cane and beet production costs averaging around 15 cents a pound; producer associations said 17 or 18 cents was a more realistic figure.)

The sugar pact became a vehicle to try to force the Carter administration to endorse the quota and fee approach. And Carter indicated that if the ISA came to his desk with domestic quotas and fees attached, he would veto the package. Members of Congress involved with the issue did not want to sacrifice the ISA for a domestic program but they were determined to hold out for quotas and fees. Both sides said the pact was sorely needed to relieve chaotic conditions in the world sugar market.

The deadline for ratification of the treaty originally was July 1, 1978, but the Carter administration persuaded participants to delay it — first to Oct. 1, then to Dec. 31, 1978. Since Congress had not approved U.S. participation by the original deadline, a further extension was under discussion as the December deadline approached.

1978 Action

Administration foot-dragging on implementing the 1977 sugar program and on producing a domestic proposal to complement the international pact incensed members of Congress from sugar-producing regions. The delays were widely attributed to two interrelated factors — both disowned by Carter administration officials.

The Carter administration thought the ISA, once it was working, would be enough to protect American farmers without any domestic program, according to some congressional sources. Others suggested that Carter, who had been dogged by charges of campaign indebtedness to Coca-Cola, was trying to pay off with a cheap sugar policy. (Soft drink manufacturers are among the biggest users of sugar.)

Some House members, in Agriculture Committee hearings, suggested the administration wanted to get rid of sugar producers it considered inefficient, and that it cared more about foreign producers than domestic.

The administration countered that its sugar proposal fit with its overall farm policy "to move subsidies from the retail level — where they are paid by consumers in the form of higher prices — to the treasury. The tax system is a fairer way of sharing the cost of farm supports."

The administration did not send its bill to Congress until late May — seven months after the ISA was initialed.

Administration Proposal. The administration's proposal, presented at House and Senate hearings by Agriculture Department chief economist Howard W. Hjort, mandated a sugar target price of 14.05 cents a pound for 1978 or the level authorized by the 1977 farm bill, whichever was higher. After 1978 the target price would be adjusted to reflect average production costs. When the market price fell below the target price, producers would be paid the difference. There was no ceiling on individual payments to producers because of the structure of the industry, Hjort said.

The administration also sought authority to establish import fees and standby authority to impose an overall import quota to bring domestic sugar prices up to a "price objective" of 13.5 cents a pound.

Church-de la Garza Bill. The "sugar stabilization" bills (S 2990, HR 12486) introduced by Church and de la Garza grew out of producer meetings. They mandated a 17 cents a pound price for sugar, to be achieved through import fees and quotas. Both would be adjusted quarterly. The system would come into effect whenever prices fell below 17 cents. (The Congressional Budget Office estimated sugar prices could top 21 cents by 1982 under the bill.)

The bills provided no payments to producers, and no production controls. The program would run for the five-year life of the international agreement. Church claimed that the "1 cent per pound import fee (included in his bill) would add $80 million to the U.S. treasury," so the bill would cost taxpayers nothing. The higher sugar costs would be "borne by sugar purchasers, primarily industrial users." Consumers would be protected by a provision ending the import quotas and fees if the U.S. price rose above the mandated price by 20 percent for 20 days, Church said.

The bills also prohibited sugar imports from non-participating countries and banned sugar imports on which the international fee had not been paid. The president would also be authorized to take other steps necessary for full participation in the International Sugar Agreement.

Lobby Group Interests

The dispute activated powerful lobby groups. The groups tended to keep hands off the international pact but divided sharply on the domestic policy question.

Beet and cane growers backed the quota-and-fee bills introduced by Church and de la Garza. Corn growers also liked the bills because anything that makes cane and beet sugar more expensive creates new customers for their cheaper high-fructose corn syrup. Sugar beet processors had a stake in higher prices, too, since they keep farmers growing beets and thus keep them in business. But some cane refiners opposed the legislation because they rely on cheap imported raw cane sugar to keep their plants going. (Converting beets to table sugar is a one-step process but with cane there is an intermediate "raw" sugar step.)

Organized labor was involved because domestic sugar programs traditionally have included minimum wage provisions for sugar field workers.

Major sugar users — soft drink and candy manufacturers — said publicly that the Church bill was inflationary and privately that "like any other industry, we prefer cheap raw materials." Foreign sugar producers feared that higher cane and beet prices would divert more of the U.S. market to corn sweeteners.

Hearings

Jurisdiction in the House was split between the Agriculture and Ways and Means Committees, a departure from past years when the agriculture panel had exclusive jurisdiction over the matter. The Agriculture Committee began a series of sugar hearings May 23, and the first day's session revealed skepticism among members that the ISA would accomplish its purposes, and hostility to the administration's proposal.

American farmers should not be expected to compete with "dump prices, distressed merchandise prices for sugar that has no home," Rep. Mark Andrews, R-N.D., told the committee.

Much of the House panel's discussion focused on whether the administration's policy was meant to put the "least efficient" producers out of business. If this were true, it would be "outrageous and completely unacceptable at a time when we're trying to become self-sufficient" as a nation, de la Garza told Hjort.

Hjort, struggling to rephrase that formulation, acknowledged that "producers with very high costs and among the least efficient would not be able to produce" under the administration's proposal. An Agriculture Department spokesman said later that such a policy was needed to eliminate the possibility of "huge windfall payments to more efficient producers."

The Ways and Means Trade Subcommittee also held hearings on the sugar legislation.

Senate Lineup

The Senate lineup for the quota and fee approach proposed by Church impressed observers; a third of the Senate signed on as co-sponsors. These included Long, whose Louisiana cane-producers have some of the highest production costs, according to the Agriculture Department, and Spark M. Matsunaga, D-Hawaii, chairman of the Tourism and Sugar Subcommittee. Long's Finance Committee shared jurisdiction with the Foreign Relations panel over the implementing legislation for ISA and the domestic program.

House Committee Action

Agriculture Committee

Congress and the Carter administration moved one step closer to a confrontation over U.S. sugar policy when the House Agriculture Committee Aug. 8 endorsed a bill (HR 13750) that could raise consumer sugar prices by almost one and a half cents a pound. The report was filed Aug. 11 (H Rept 95-1484, Part I).

The two-part bill established a new domestic price-support program for sugar and authorized U.S. participation in the international sugar pact.

Before agreeing by a 37-7 vote to report the bill, the committee had agreed to lower by one cent, to 16 cents a pound, the minimum guaranteed price U.S. sugar producers would get under the bill.

The bill's sponsor, de la Garza, suggested the reduction "as a good faith offer to get this bill moving." But the change was not enough to stave off the threat of a presidential veto, according to Agriculture Department spokesman James C. Webster.

The bill included an automatic "escalator" that would provide for quarterly adjustments in the price guarantee to accommodate inflation — a provision opposed by the administration.

The only other major change the committee made in the de la Garza bill was the addition of a minimum wage provision guaranteeing sugar workers $3 an hour immediately and a 20 cents an hour raise each successive sugar crop year through fiscal 1983, when the legislation was to expire. Other farm workers received $2.65 an hour under the federal minimum wage law.

The committee action on worker wages brought organized labor behind the bill. The Oil, Chemical and Atomic Workers', Longshoreman's and Teamsters' unions all actively supported the bill. The AFL-CIO had agreed to remain neutral, according to an aide to Richard Nolan, D-Minn., sponsor of the wage amendment.

Minimum wage and other worker-protection provisions have long been a feature of sugar legislation and labor had opposed the original version of the bill, which had omitted these features.

Besides guaranteeing worker wages, the Nolan amendment provided an enforcement mechanism like that of the Fair Labor Standards Act. Individual or class-action suits could be brought against employers underpaying their workers, and workers also could opt for a new dispute-resolution mechanism within the Agriculture Department, meant to be speedier and less costly than court action, according to Nolan's aide.

Other provisions of the Nolan amendment required employers to meet state workers compensation requirements, and to refrain from overcharging for goods and services in "company" stores run by producers. Growers who retaliated against workers protesting violations of the wage provision would be subject to fines. The committee agreed to the Nolan amendment by a 33-9 vote.

The Carter administration had little visible support for its alternative, which would mandate a sugar "target" price of 14 cents a pound with upward adjustments after 1978 to reflect average production costs. When the market price fell below the target price, producers would be paid the difference.

Members of the House Agriculture Committee reportedly wouldn't introduce the measure, and it was finally sponsored by Charles A. Vanik, D-Ohio, "by request," a phrase that usually suggests an unenthusiastic sponsor.

Ways and Means Proposal

The Ways and Means Committee Sept. 11 reported a revised version of HR 13750 (H Rept 95-1484, Part II) that it said was "most consistent with our international obligations and obtains the most benefit for producers and consumers."

Like the Agriculture committee version, the bill empowered the president to keep the price of sugar at a stipulated "price objective" — a guaranteed minimum price for producers — with import quotas and fees. But Ways and Means dropped one cent from the price objective and eliminated the escalator feature so that its price of 15 cents would be constant for the five-year life of the program.

If production costs rose above 15 cents a pound, the committee said, the administration was committed to make supplementary direct payments to producers, under authority of the 1949 sugar act. "Your committee's bill does not . . . to repeat, this bill does not contain any direct payments legislation," the committee stressed.

The lower price objective was appropriate, the committee said, because it about matched average sugar production costs. Although some producers spent 16 cents a pound or more, the purpose of the price objective was not to keep them in business. It was simply intended to provide a "floor" for an industry accustomed to "cyclical price swings." It was not intended to "protect the inefficient or to encourage production of a crop in an area which is not competitive," the committee said.

The committee also suggested that the 15-cent price might prove profitable to many producers since, according to administration testimony, that figure "implicitly assumes that everybody just recently bought their land and paid a high interest on it." The implication was that established producers who had bought their land more cheaply would benefit from an extra margin in production costs.

The committee found "the price escalator is where the real cost of the Agriculture Committee bill occurs," adding that it had "nothing to do with the cost of producing sugar." The major flaw of the price escalator was that price hikes for domestic sugar meant equivalent boosts for foreign sugar — about half of all U.S. consumption, the committee said. But those boosts were set by international market developments, not domestic production costs.

Like the Agriculture Committee bill, the Ways and Means version did not put a limit on total payments to individual sugar producers, and it provided for quarterly adjustments to ensure the (lower) price objective. It made no change in the treaty implementation and farm labor provisions of the Agriculture Committee bill.

House Floor Action

The House Oct. 6 passed a compromise sugar bill backed by President Carter — but not before tacking on a controversial automatic price increase provision that the president had vowed to veto.

The final vote on the bill was 186-159. *(Vote 785, p. 222-H)*

The bill (HR 13750) authorized a new domestic sugar support program that assured producers a price of 15 cents a pound, with semi-annual adjustments upward for the next five years. The upward adjustments would be related to increases in costs of production.

The bill mandated import fees and quotas to keep cheaper imported sugar from driving domestic prices below the price objectives. It also authorized U.S. participation in the International Sugar Agreement (ISA) and included minimum wage provisions for sugar workers.

The measure was heavily lobbied. The administration, which originally opposed a quota-and-fee approach, backed the Ways and Means bill as a compromise and urged members to reject the Agriculture Committee version. It was joined by the Consumer Federation of America, which claimed the Agriculture version would add billions to consumer food prices. Industrial sugar users also opposed it, while sugar producers and processors favored it. Several unions representing sugar field and mill workers also worked Capitol Hill in support of minimum wage provisions in both versions of HR 13750.

In a free-wheeling debate, members loudly disputed whether direct payments or the automatic adjuster was more inflationary. Some Republican members, led by Paul Findley, R-Ill., argued that no action in 1978 would be the cheapest alternative.

Findley also warned that a far more expensive sugar program would emerge from a House-Senate conference, and perhaps the White House, because of leverage by Senate Finance Committee Chairman Russell B. Long, D-La. Without naming Long, Findley said, "He has in his hip pocket the energy bill, the tax bill, nobody knows what other goodies. I forecast that the president of the United States, being eager to have [these bills], will hardly be in a position to do other than sign this legislation."

Long had added to his leverage by persuading the Finance panel to tack onto the sugar bill an unrelated tariff measure that the president badly wanted. *(Finance Committee action, below)*

Before passing the bill, the House:

- Agreed by voice vote to the international treaty provisions in the Agriculture Committee bill.
- Agreed by a 194-164 vote to a William A. Steiger, R-Wis., amendment to add the cost-of-production adjuster to the Ways and Means substitute. *(Vote 784, p. 222-H)*
- Agreed by a 67-29 standing vote to a Vanik motion to substitute the Ways and Means domestic sugar program for that of the Agriculture bill.
- Rejected by voice vote a Richard Kelly, R-Fla., amendment to eliminate the minimum wage and other provisions designed to protect sugar workers.
- Agreed by voice vote to a Vanik amendment to extend the existing sugar loan program until "market prices strengthened" as a result of the new quota and fee approach.

Senate Committee Action

The day before the House vote, the Senate Finance Committee reported a similar but more expensive bill (HR 7108 — S Rept 95-1279) that set the guaranteed price ("price objective") at 17 cents a pound, with a more generous automatic adjustment pegged to changes in the cost-of-living index.

The bill's provisions on import quotas and fees, U.S. participation in the ISA and minimum wages for sugar workers were similar or identical to those in the House-passed bill.

What the committee added to the sugar bill was a nine-month extension of the president's authority to waive countervailing duties — duties on imports to compensate for subsidies foreign governments provide for their manufacturers or agricultural producers.

Existing law required the secretary of the treasury to impose the countervailing duties on imports, in addition to regular duties, when a domestic industry complains of a subsidy and the complaint is confirmed. But the 1974 Trade Act (PL 93-618), which directed the president to seek a new international agreement on subsidy practices, authorized waiver of the duties under certain conditions. *(1974 Almanac p. 553)*

The waiver authority was set to expire Jan. 3, 1979. Carter contended the extension was critical to keep the Multilateral Trade Negotiations, which were in their final stages, from collapsing. The waiver itself was controversial.

Senate Floor Action

The Senate passed its version of HR 13750 in the last days of the session — at 12:45 a.m. Oct. 13 — by a 50-22 vote. *(Vote 485, p. 71-S)*

The bill set a 16-cents-a-pound minimum price for domestic sugar producers, to be maintained with import quotas and fees. The price was one cent a pound lower than the Finance Committee had recommended, but one cent higher than the president had said he would accept. Like the House-passed bill, the Senate version also provided for automatic semiannual adjustments of the price objective.

Before passing the bill, the Senate by a 47-25 vote tabled an amendment by Howard M. Metzenbaum, D-Ohio, that would have tailored the bill to administration requirements — a 15-cent price objective and no escalator clause. *(Vote 484, p. 71-S)*

In addition to the extension of the president's authority to waive countervailing duties, added by the Finance Committee, the Senate by voice vote added as further "veto insurance" an amendment by Church authorizing the president to fulfill a longstanding commitment to increase U.S. contributions to an international tin stockpile. The House had passed similar legislation (HR 9486) Sept. 26 by a 308-75 vote. *(Vote 731, p. 208-H)*

Conference Action

In a weary session that began about 5 a.m. Oct. 15, conferees bowed to presidential demands that they drop the automatic inflation adjustment to the base per-pound support price for sugar, and that they adopt a relatively low base or "price objective." Several conferees refused to sign the conference report (H Rept 95-1807).

Conferees finally agreed to the following:

- A base 15-cents-a-pound price objective (guarantee) for fiscal year 1979, with a .75 cent-a-pound direct federal payment for that year only.
- A 15.8-cent price objective for fiscal 1980, and for fiscal 1981-1983, 15.8 cents a pound plus 1 percent of the price objective for the immediately preceding year — an admittedly meaningless "escalator" since it wouldn't begin to keep up with inflation; however, it was a necessary pro forma provision since both House and Senate bills contained escalator clauses.

The agreement also contained provisions on U.S. participation in the ISA, import quotas and fees, minimum wages for sugar farm workers rising from $3 an hour in 1978 to $3.80 in 1982 except in Hawaii and Puerto Rico, other farm labor provisions, extension of the countervailing duty waiver authority until Feb. 15, 1979, and the international tin agreement provisions.

Final Action

Senate. The Senate accepted the conference agreement by voice vote Oct. 15 after voting 36-20 not to recommit it to conference. *(Vote 516, p. 75-S)*

Robert Dole, R-Kan., said the agreement, "dictated by the White House," was totally inadequate. He moved to send it back to conferees with instructions to provide a one-year program with a 15.75-cent market price objective and no direct federal payments to producers. Then Congress could rewrite the program in 1979.

Moving to table Dole's motion, Long agreed that the conference agreement was inadequate for all but the smallest producers, but said there was no chance the administration would agree to any more generous version. He urged the Senate to accept the final bill, "with the firm understanding that we will support a better, permanent bill later on."

House. By a 177-194 vote, the House Oct. 15 rejected the conference report on the sugar bill that the Senate had agreed to a few hours earlier. *(Vote 831, p. 236-H)*

Foley admitted the bill was only a one-year "stopgap." He also noted that many members objected to the direct federal payments to sugar producers which had not been in either bill. But he urged the House to approve the measure as the only thing President Carter would accept.

Opposition came from corn-state representatives who objected that the direct payments to sugar producers were inequitable to corn sweetener producers; sugar-state members who felt the price objective was too low to save small sugar producers from bankruptcy, and from members who said the bill would cost consumers and taxpayers too much. Opposition to the countervailing duty provision by the import-sensitive textile industry also prompted some members to vote against the conference agreement. ▮

Livestock Slaughter

President Carter Oct. 10 signed into law a bill requiring humane procedures for the slaughter of livestock in meatpacking plants.

The measure (S 3092—PL 95-445) expanded existing law, which required humane slaughter only for meat sold to the federal government, to include all livestock slaughtered in federal- and state-inspected plants plus all foreign meat consumed in the United States. The procedure was defined as any method that rendered an animal insensible to pain before it was shackled, hoisted or killed.

The bill was reported by the Senate Agriculture Committee Aug. 1 (S Rept 95-1059) and passed the Senate by voice vote Aug. 7. A companion measure (HR 1464) was reported July 10 by the House Agriculture Committee (H Rept 95-1336) and passed the House by voice vote under suspension of the rules Sept. 19. The language of the House bill was accepted by the Senate Sept. 28, clearing the measure for the president.

Both committees noted that humane slaughter procedures had been adopted by more than 90 percent of all U.S.

meatpacking plants since passage of the Humane Slaughter Act of 1958 (PL 85-765). *(Congress and the Nation Vol. I, p. 707)*

Direct Marketing

A bill authorizing appropriations of $1.5 million in fiscal 1979 to demonstrate methods of direct marketing between farmers and consumers died Sept. 19 after it failed to pass the House under suspension of the rules. The measure (HR 12101 — H Rept 95-1483) would have extended for one year a 1976 law (PL 94-463) designed to find new ways to raise the income of small farmers and lower consumers' food costs. *(1976 Almanac p. 394)*

House Agriculture Committee Chairman Thomas S. Foley, D-Wash., said during floor debate that the additional year was needed so that prototype projects in 23 states and Puerto Rico could be continued through two growing seasons.

Charles E. Grassley, R-Iowa, argued that the bill as originally enacted was intended to be temporary in nature, and that the projects could be better handled by the states.

With a two-thirds majority necessary for passage under suspension of the rules, the bill lost by a vote of 237-163. *(Vote 704, p. 200-H)*

A similar bill (S 2833 — S Rept 95-854) passed by the Senate by voice vote May 24 authorized appropriations of $3 million annually for fiscal 1979 through 1981.

Rural Transportation Study

Concern about the depressed condition of rural railroads led Congress to authorize creation of an advisory task force to study the impact of the decline on the agricultural community. A bill (S 1835 — PL 95-580) directing the secretaries of agriculture and transportation to set up a 16-member task force to study agricultural transportation cleared Congress Oct. 15.

The measure passed the Senate June 8 by voice vote. A companion bill (HR 12917) passed the House by a 352-49 vote Oct. 4 under suspension of the rules. *(Vote 768, p. 218-H)*

The reports filed by the Senate Agriculture Committee May 31 (S Rept 95-923) and the House Agriculture Committee Sept. 21 (H Rept 95-1600) emphasized the poor condition of the nation's rural railroads as a major reason for establishing the task force.

Rail car shortages and rail line abandonments had contributed to a massive shift in agricultural traffic from rail to motor carriers, according to the House report. In some grain-producing areas, the report said, the shift from rail to truck transportation had increased transportation costs to producers by 5 to 7 cents a bushel and required three times more energy to transport the same quantity of grain.

The bill authorized the task force to publish an initial report within six months on the transportation needs of agriculture and impediments to a national rail transportation system that would meet the needs of agriculture. It also required a final report 420 days after enactment that would consider the results of public hearing on the issue.

The task force was to be dissolved 45 days after publication of the final report. Task force members were to be selected by the transportation and agriculture secretaries.

Crop Insurance Proposal

The Carter administration in 1978 proposed to replace disaster aid programs for farmers with a subsidized crop insurance program, but Congress did not act on the plan. The administration planned to reintroduce it in 1979.

The Carter administration said the new program could significantly stabilize farmers' income in future years — without costing taxpayers much more than they were already paying for disaster programs.

The soaring costs and the inequities of handling catastrophes on an ad hoc basis prompted the proposal, which would replace the existing potpourri of limited federal crop insurance, disaster payments and low-cost emergency loans. The Congressional Budget Office put the average annual cost of these programs at some $600 million a year, but the total was expected to be much higher for fiscal 1978 because of heavy disaster losses and record participation in the heavily subsidized loan programs.

The half-billion-dollar subsidized insurance program to cover farmers' crop losses from drought, floods and other natural catastrophes was announced April 26 by Agriculture Secretary Bob Bergland.

Called the Farm Production Protection program, it closely resembled bills introduced in 1977 by Sen. Walter (Dee) Huddleston, D-N.Y., and Rep. Ed Jones, D-Tenn.

The nationwide, all-risk program was intended to end the inequities of the existing system, which Bergland routinely referred to as "a disaster in itself." Now, depending on where farmers live and what they grow, some qualify for help under all or most of the programs, while others are not eligible for any aid.

Under the new plan, any farmer could buy adequate coverage at reasonable prices, Bergland told a May 2 hearing of Huddleston's Agriculture subcommittee on farm prices and marketing.

If Congress acted by July, farmers could buy federal insurance on 18 major crops — about 90 percent of all cropland — by 1980, Bergland said. The existing federal insurance program covered only six crops, on less than 20 percent of the nation's cropland.

Because it would build on an ongoing insurance program using funds now allotted to disaster payments and loan subsidies, the new program would not add much to the federal budget, Bergland said. The first-year cost of the expanded insurance program was estimated at $555 million, compared with $542 million for existing programs. But this expenditure would more than double protection provided farmers against losses — from $7 billion to $15 billion in initial stages, Bergland said. And, "over a 20-year period, this program would pay its own way" as premium payments built up reserves.

Premium prices and levels of coverage for the same crop would vary from region to region and from farmer to farmer. Unlike the existing Federal Crop Insurance Corporation (FCIC) program, which was based on county or regional yields, the new plan would match coverage and premium costs closely to individual performance by farmers. Those in a low-risk area with good production records could buy high levels of coverage for relatively low premiums. Farmers with poorer production records — because of high costs, farming methods or because they worked in disaster-prone regions — would have to pay proportionately more for less coverage.

In the initial phase farmers could insure wheat, cotton, corn, barley, grain sorghum, rice, sugar cane, sunflowers, citrus fruits, dry beans, soybeans, oats, flax, peanuts, tobacco, raisins, sugar beets and rye. The secretary of agriculture would also be authorized to insure timber, livestock and other commodities. These types of coverage would be phased in as actuarial data were developed, Bergland said.

Major responsibility for marketing the new insurance and assessing risk factors and yields would be delegated to county committees that now administer certain other federal farm programs. The local units were best suited to evaluate local conditions, Bergland said. They could write the insurance policies themselves or contract with local private agents to sell them on a commission basis. Funding for the new program would be through the Commodity Credit Corporation.

The direct payment and subsidized loan programs would be effectively ended by a provision barring payments for any commodities covered in the new insurance program. Bergland indicated that some disaster loans, including a new "economic emergency" program enacted in 1978, would continue. *(Loan program, p. 446; existing disaster programs, box, this page)*

Reaction

The proposed insurance program would be voluntary, but many farmers may feel pressured to buy insurance if they have no cheap loan or grant alternatives. The existing assortment of disaster programs was unpopular with farmers, Congress and the administration, but farmers were not expected to welcome the prospect of yet another cost.

The administration claimed that greatly increased levels of protection, the fairness of the new system and the certainty of assistance would be worth the new premium payments. Whether they had sweetened the pot enough to gain farm support was not clear as farm groups got their first look at the plan.

"If farmers have got to pay, the insurance program would have to be about 4,000 percent better than what they've got now," said one spokesman for the militant American Agriculture Movement (AAM).

The conservative American Farm Bureau Federation (AFBF), which runs a sizable insurance program and had urged a larger role for the industry, welcomed the administration initiative but reserved comment on the plan.

The insurance industry had favored a reinsurance scheme, with the government backstopping private all-risk programs. Bergland said he did not expect the industry to embrace the Carter proposal. But he pointed out that private agents could earn sizable commissions, and that the new program could increase "insurance consciousness" in farm areas and stimulate sales of supplementary policies. (Private insurers now cover only crop damage caused by hail.)

Another factor was congressional sentiment for continuing the low-cost emergency loans to farmers. Ending this alternative to insurance was considered to be crucial to the success of the new program, which required broad participation to be financially viable. ▮

Existing Disaster Programs

The major elements of the federal farm relief system are:

- **Disaster Payments.** The wheat, feed grains, cotton and rice disaster payments program, commonly referred to simply as "disaster payments," authorized by the 1973 omnibus farm act (PL 93-86), the 1975 Rice Production Act (PL 94-214) and revised and extended for two years by the Food and Agriculture Act of 1977 (PL 95-113). Under formulas established by law, farmers are partially reimbursed for their losses when natural disasters keep them from planting or reduce their yield.
- **Federal crop insurance,** administered by the Federal Crop Insurance Corporation (FCIC), whose operating expenses are partially paid by congressional appropriation. Because of statutory limitations, FCIC coverage is not sold in about half the nation's counties. Only about 14 percent of eligible acreage is covered.

FCIC is barred by law from operating in actuarially unsound regions—those where the risk of disaster is greatest and thus, those where farmers most need a predictable form of aid. And in areas where it is sold, its relatively low payback rates — averaging 50 per cent of a farmer—s losses — discourage participation.

Another bar to FCIC growth has been financial limits imposed by the program's permanent status as a pilot project. These limits, combined with extraordinary demands, caused FCIC to suspend operations in the 1940s, and in 1977 Congress had to bail it out with two emergency authorizations, doubling (to $200 million) the authorized level for FCIC's capital stock.

- **Emergency loans,** offered at 3 per cent interest by the Farmers Home Administration (FmHA) and the Small Business Administration (SBA). Both pay for similar kinds of losses, but eligibility requirements for SBA loans are less stringent, and since the loans became available in 1977 farmers had flocked to the SBA. FmHA borrowers must prove they cannot borrow money elsewhere and must satisfy "major damage" criteria, but neither requirement applies to SBA loans. Congress in 1976 made farmers eligible for the SBA loans and in 1977 lowered the interest rate for the first $250,000 of a loan to 3 per cent.
- **The dairy indemnity program,** authorized by the 1964 Economic Opportunity Act and amended by PL 95-113, which provides payments to dairy farmers whose milk is removed from market because of contamination by chemicals, toxic substances or nuclear radiation.
- **Emergency drought programs,** authorized in 1977 (PL 95-18), which include a $100 million program to enhance water supplies in federally irrigated areas.
- **Other Programs.** Federal authority also exists for payments to livestock producers whose herds are condemned due to disease, to beekeepers whose swarms are wiped out by pesticides, to transport cattle or hay when disaster strikes, and to finance emergency land repairs to combat erosion or prevent floods.

Transportation/Commerce/Consumers

The Carter administration made some progress in 1978 toward its goal of developing a unified national transportation policy.

However, it found greater success in pushing legislation to let the transportation industries themselves work out their own policies.

But the administration's programs suffered at times from lackadaisical support from its own Transportation Department. Despite Transportation Secretary Brock Adams' congressional background and experience, he was unable to muster sufficient support for a number of administration initiatives and unwilling to go all out for others. And resistance from Congress and transportation interest groups blocked some major Carter goals.

Amidst persistent rumors that he was out of step with the president's program and out of touch with the president himself, Adams was forced to deny in July that he intended to resign from the Cabinet. By the end of the session, however, Adams enjoyed greater success in pushing the Carter proposals.

Deregulation Progress

The administration's most significant achievement was to convince Congress to begin to take the federal government out of the transportation regulation business.

It did this by seeking legislation phasing out federal controls on the commercial passenger airline industry. The airline deregulation legislation, a top Carter priority, was not cleared until the last day of the session.

However, the lengthy and thorough consideration it received in Congress served to allay the fears of its opponents and provided a forum for deregulation advocates to espouse their views. Its approval — and the resultant drop in air fares — was expected to pave the way for other transportation deregulation measures in the next Congress.

Another important legislative accomplishment was enactment of a waterway users fee bill. The payment of fees by users of the nation's inland waterways had been sought unsuccessfully by every administration since Franklin Delano Roosevelt's.

The other major transportation initiative mounted by the administration met with less success. A proposal to restructure the nation's highway and mass transit aid programs fizzled when Congress decided to focus on funding levels rather than on substantive changes.

The Carter administration played mostly a passive role in other transportation areas, seeking either to maintain the status quo or to let Congress set policy with little help from the Executive Branch.

In railroads and trucking, both Congress and the administration put off major policy decisions until 1979 or later. In shipping, Carter opposed most legislative initiatives originating in Congress while waiting for an administration task force to complete a study of the issues and to make recommendations. The task force failed to issue its recommendations before Congress adjourned.

Consumer groups found that heavy Democratic majorities in both houses did little to help along legislation that had enjoyed strong Democratic support in previous Congresses. Instead, moderate Democrats joined with conservative Democrats and Republicans to defeat or delay practically all newly proposed federal consumer programs. One of the few exceptions was passage of legislation creating a federally backed consumer cooperative bank.

After the defeat of a bill to create an agency for consumer affairs — Carter's top consumer priority — the president expanded the powers of his own White House consumer office. But that office was unable to accomplish what advocates of an independent agency had hoped for: a strong, politically unfettered voice for the consumer within the federal government.

Airline Deregulation

Carter's aides had predicted in 1977 that the new president could score an early and easy victory in Congress by supporting airline deregulation legislation because it already had been the subject of extensive congressional hearings during the previous Congress.

Though the victory was to elude him until the last day of the 95th Congress, Carter eventually scored political points through his decision to actively support the legislation.

Even before the deregulation bill was signed, a pioneering Civil Aeronautics Board had demonstrated the legislation's potential by introducing, on a limited basis, a new competitive environment in the commercial airline passenger industry. The board's experiment paved the way for enactment of the legislation by bringing about dramatic reductions in some air fares and increases in service on many routes. Airline company profits soared as ridership skyrocketed.

The success airline deregulation enjoyed was expected to facilitate similar Carter administration efforts involving the trucking and railroad industries.

Despite the airline deregulation measure's success, however, transportation industry deregulation remained a controversial issue in some quarters. Though the airline bill passed both houses by wide margins, for example, it encountered strong resistance in the Senate Commerce and House Public Works Committees. Those same committees were expected to play key roles in the development of trucking and railroad deregulation legislation, as well.

By year's end, a jurisdictional dispute already was brewing between the Senate Antitrust Subcommittee, chaired by Edward M. Kennedy, D-Mass. — a strong supporter of trucking deregulation — and the Senate Commerce Committee, chaired by Howard W. Cannon, D-Nev.

Waterway User Fees

With an assist from a bill dealing with bingo games, and under pressure from the Carter administration, Congress for the first time imposed user fees on the inland waterway barge industry. Legislation imposing the fees had been sought by federal transportation planners for 38 years, but the Carter administration's success in 1978 was due as much to the individual efforts of two key senators as to its own actions.

The Carter administration had asked Congress to require the barge industry to pay a portion of the government's cost of constructing and operating the nation's inland waterway system. But it was the strategy of Sen. Pete V. Domenici, R-N.M., that succeeded in making the fee legislation palatable to the barge industry.

By combining the unpopular fee requirement with approval of a new lock and dam on the Mississippi River at Alton, Ill. — a public works project popular with the barge industry — Domenici managed to steer the fees requirement through both the House and Senate.

That bill stalled, however, when Domenici's colleagues combined it with authorizations for additional water projects totaling several billion dollars, making the combined bill a prime veto candidate.

In a last-ditch effort to get a compromise through Congress, Sen. Russell B. Long, D-La., tacked a new version of the fee and lock and dam combination onto a bill clarifying the tax status of winnings from bingo games sponsored by tax-exempt and political organizations. Using his considerable powers of persuasion, Long pushed the compromise through both houses and on to the White House in only four days.

Highways and Mass Transit

President Carter proposed in January 1978 a modest revamping of the federal government's massive surface transportation aid programs. He also proposed funding levels only slightly above those approved for earlier years.

State and local governments, along with many members of Congress and representatives of transportation interest groups, objected to Carter's funding recommendations. Arguing that more money was needed to meet the nation's highway and mass transit needs, they convinced members of the House Public Works Committee to recommend greatly increased transportation spending.

The ensuing battle between the House and the administration over spending served to obscure the debate over the structural changes the administration had proposed. Though by the session's end Carter had managed to keep transportation spending close to what he considered an acceptable range, many of the structural changes he advocated ended up being lost in the debate over funding.

Though the legislation failed to integrate the highway and mass transit programs, as the administration had proposed, the Transportation Department at year's end proposed combining the Federal Highway and Urban Mass Transportation Administrations into a single Surface Transportation Administration. The merger was expected to substitute a mass transit-highway "partnership" for the competition that prevailed between the two modes of transportation under the existing structure.

Railroads

The nation's railroads remained in poor financial straits in 1978 — a condition that had persisted for over a decade — but the federal government did little to resolve the ailing industry's problems. Instead, both Congress and the administration continued existing programs and put off consideration of railroad policy changes until the next Congress.

Legislation was passed establishing a mechanism for the federal government to weed out unprofitable Amtrak railroad passenger routes in 1979, but leaving the actual choices of what routes to cut to the Transportation Department. The mechanism permitted Congress to veto the department's actions if it disagreed, however.

Congress voted to give the Consolidated Rail Corp. (ConRail) an additional infusion of federal funds to keep it afloat until 1979, when a comprehensive review of the federally subsidized railroad freight company was planned. At year's end, ConRail told Congress it would take substantial deregulation in addition to subsidies to keep it alive.

Commerce and Consumers

Congress' actions in the consumer area in 1978 were mostly negative, from the consumer movement's viewpoint. But Congress did approve legislation creating a national consumer cooperative bank that was expected to provide a boost for the nation's consumer cooperatives. The bank was to be backed by the federal government and was intended to provide loans and technical assistance to consumer cooperatives that had experienced difficulties in obtaining financing.

The Consumer Product Safety Commission, threatened early in the year with extinction by a White House task force, was instead renewed for a three-year period.

For most other consumer bills, however, there were only obituaries. The consumer protection agency, federal no-fault automobile insurance standards, subsidies for public interest group participation in federal agency proceedings, procedural changes for the Federal Trade Commission and legislation to reorganize the U.S. Postal Service all fell victim to a growing conservative trend in Congress during 1978.

In communications, Congress cleared legislation reorganizing the nation's public broadcasting system, accepting many recommendations advanced by the Carter administration. Carter paid little attention to other communications matters, however. Despite the policy vacuum, a House Commerce subcommittee began laying groundwork for a substantial revision of the nation's communications laws in 1979. At year's end, key Senate Commerce Committee members indicated they agreed a revision was in order.

—By Irwin B. Arieff

Carter Dealt Major Defeat on Consumer Bill

The House dealt a major blow to President Carter and the consumer movement Feb. 8 by defeating legislation (HR 6805) to establish an independent Office of Consumer Representation.

The vote was 189-227, and the House's action killed any chance of enacting a consumer agency in the 95th Congress. *(Vote 41, p. 12-H)*

Creation of an agency at the federal level to represent the interests of consumers had been a top priority of the Carter administration.

At the same time, the vote represented a significant victory for the U.S. Chamber of Commerce, the National Association of Manufacturers, the Business Roundtable, and other business-oriented groups. Supporters of the measure blamed the loss on big business' well-financed lobbying effort.

"We regret very much the defeat of the bill," stated White House Press Secretary Jody Powell. "The best efforts of the administration were not able to overcome a well-organized and effective opposition."

"I have been around here for 25 years," remarked House Speaker Thomas P. O'Neill Jr., D-Mass. "I have never seen such extensive lobbying." Both Carter and O'Neill—who had earlier predicted the bill had "a very good chance" of passage—personally lobbied for the legislation. *(Box, this page)*

But U.S. Chamber of Commerce President Richard L. Lesher said the vote indicated the House was reacting to public opposition to a growing federal bureaucracy. The American people, he said, "are weary of too much government in their lives—too much protection, too much of what other people think is good for them."

The House had passed similar legislation in 1971, 1974 and 1975, but on each successive vote the margin of approval was slimmer.

Though the bill's backers had put on an optimistic front before the final vote, many members said later they were aware the consumer agency was doomed even before debate began.

O'Neill said Feb. 9 that the final vote margin had been exactly what was predicted by the House leadership. When asked why he had predicted the bill would win, he replied, "What do you want me to say, that I'm going to lose?"

A White House aide conceded the administration's most optimistic projection had the bill passing by five votes, while the most pessimistic was that the bill would lose by 50 votes. Only 17 Republicans voted for passage.

'We Just Did Our Homework'

By all accounts, lobbying on the bill to create a federal agency to represent consumers was as rigorous as on any issue since the Carter administration took office.

In the 92nd Congress, similar legislation passed the House 344-44. In the 93rd Congress, it passed 293-94 and in the 94th the vote was 208-199.

"Why, all of a sudden, is there this tremendous change," asked House Speaker Thomas P. O'Neill Jr., D-Mass., during debate on the bill, "where people are coming to me and saying, 'I got myself in some difficulty; I made a promise to business along the line that I was going to vote against the legislation.' "

"The corrupting influence of big business campaign contributions, promised or withdrawn, has never been more clear than in the last few days," charged Ralph Nader. "The lesson of today is that we must redouble our efforts so that Congress responds to the needs of consumers rather than the pressure of big business."

The theme of effective business lobbying was echoed by Carter consumer adviser Esther Peterson. "We tried. We tried mighty hard" to pass the consumer agency bill, she said. "We were a little David against a tremendous Goliath, and I guess our little slingshot didn't matter."

But Mary Jo Jacobi, National Association of Manufacturers' director of market regulations and government operations, scoffed at the notion of members of Congress caving in to pressures from big business.

"Contrary to public opinion, we used no strong-arm tactics," she said. "We just did our homework." At the time of the vote on final passage of the legislation, she noted, consumer and White House representatives lined the hallways leading to the House floor. "It was the consumers buttonholing the members on their way in to vote," she said, "and not representatives of business."

Democratic Defections

Comparing the Feb. 8 vote with the one taken in 1975 approving the consumer agency by 208-199, Mark Green, a top aide to consumer advocate Ralph Nader, said HR 6805 lost largely because of defections by moderate Democrats. These same Democrats, Green said, traditionally could be counted on to support consumer bills.

"I'm with you on the merits," Green said many members had told him, "but I can't convince my constituents that this bill is not a move toward big government."

A check by Congressional Quarterly found that 24 members switched their positions on the two votes: 19 who voted for a consumer agency in 1975 voted against it Feb. 8, while five who voted against it in 1975 voted for it this time, for a net increase of 14 members opposed to the agency.

Of these 19, 12 could be classified either as moderate or liberal Democrats.

Members of the 1976 freshman class were opposed to creation of the consumer agency by a margin of 3 to 2. Of the 69 freshmen voting on final passage of HR 6805, 28 supported the agency and 41 opposed it. While 25 of the 28 freshmen voting for the agency were Democrats, the 41 freshmen voting against it were evenly divided along party lines (21 Democrats and 20 Republicans).

The 1974 class gave the agency their support by a margin of 56 to 36.

Carter Consumer Program

Commenting on the fate of Carter's entire consumer program, Carter Press Secretary Jody Powell contended that, "perhaps ironically, the consumer record of this administration may have contributed to the lessening of the pressure for passage of this bill...but the determination of the administration to act to protect the consumer by its appointments and in other ways will remain undiminished and will if anything be intensified."

White House consumer adviser Esther Peterson conceded the push for a consumer agency was dead. "But this is not the end," she added. "This is the end of this bill at this time...but the consumer movement will get stronger. It will not go away."

Peterson denied the bill's defeat was a personal defeat for Carter. "For the President to go down for something he believes in is never a defeat," she said. "It's a terrific political issue. One could really explain to the American people who is making the decisions in Washington."

Did this mean Carter would campaign against the 101 Democrats who voted against the consumer bill? "That's something we have to look at very closely," she said.

Background

The consumer movement had attempted since 1961 to secure passage of legislation establishing an agency at the federal level to represent the interests of consumers. In recent years it had been a top priority, but enactment of such legislation had always eluded pro-consumer agency members.

The Senate approved a bill establishing an Agency for Consumer Protection in 1970. The House approved similar legislation in 1971 and 1974. *(1974 Almanac p. 307)*

Both houses approved a consumer agency bill in 1975, but the House never sent the bill to the White House because President Ford threatened to veto it, and House backers felt they did not have sufficient support for an override. *(1975 Almanac p. 555)*

The bill got a boost in 1977 with the announcement that President Carter strongly supported it. Carter appointed Esther Peterson, who had been consumer adviser to President Johnson, as his special assistant for consumer affairs to lobby for the bill.

Under heavy pressure from the business community to oppose the legislation, and equally heavy pressure from the White House to approve it, the House Government Operations Committee approved a bill (HR 6805) by only a one-vote margin on May 16, 1977. *(1977 Almanac p. 436)*

When the bill became stalled in the House, consumer groups showered potential swing votes with nickels — 5 cents representing the cost per capita of the consumer agency.

A compromise proposal (HR 9718) was unveiled Oct. 13, 1977. The name of the agency was changed to the Office of Consumer Representation (OCR), and the revised legislation proposed a number of sweeteners to enhance its chances for passage.

The House Rules Committee grudgingly voted to send the OCR legislation to the House floor, but Speaker O'Neill pulled the bill from the House calendar Nov. 1 when his vote count indicated the legislation probably would be defeated.

Early in 1978 Carter reiterated his support for a consumer agency, and White House aides pressed the House leadership to again schedule floor action on HR 9718. To drum up support, the White House held a conference Jan. 31-Feb. 1 in Washington, chaired by Vice President Mondale, to lobby 65 national organizations that had not previously participated in the debate over a consumer agency.

"The bill still is a victim" of well-organized opposition from the business community, White House adviser Peterson said on the eve of the House vote. "The vote will be terribly tight—very close," she predicted. "But we are going to go for it."

Floor Action

Though the two-day (Feb. 7-8) debate technically was on HR 6805—the bill reported by the House Government Operations Committee in May 1977 — floor action focused on the watered down substitute (HR 9718) drafted by sponsors to win over additional support for the agency. Before the bill was brought to the floor, the House voted 271-138 to consider it. *(Vote 35, p. 10-H)*

The proposed Office of Consumer Representation was to represent the interests of consumers before federal agencies and courts, encourage and contract for consumer research, studies and tests, suggest consumer legislation to Congress, publish consumer materials, sponsor conferences and investigations concerning consumer matters, and work with state and local governments to promote and protect consumer interests.

The OCR was to participate in agency activities, and seek judicial review of agency decisions, to the same extent as any other private party or person. The office was to act as a clearinghouse for consumer complaints. Twenty consumer offices in other independent and Executive Branch agencies were to be transferred to the OCR, and the Office of Management and Budget (OMB) was required to recommend ways to save at least $10 million by eliminating the various agency consumer offices.

Exempted from the OCR's jurisdiction under the substitute were national security and intelligence functions, the Federal Bureau of Investigation, labor-management disputes and agreements, Department of Agriculture proceedings concerning commodity loans, price supports and purchases and certain other Agriculture Department programs.

Arguments Pro and Con

Debate on the measure followed familiar lines to observers of the consumer agency's tortuous course since it first was approved by the Senate in 1970. *(1970 Almanac p. 607)*

The agency's supporters pointed out that the substitute would have no regulatory powers, but would be able to effectively represent the consumer viewpoint in federal activities. "Business has vast resources to make its views known to federal decision-makers," stated Jack Brooks (D Texas), chairman of the Government Operations Committee and principal sponsor of the bill. "That is fine.... But the consumer interest needs to be heard, too, and at present it rarely is."

The agency, said Toby Moffett, D-Conn., a strong supporter of the legislation, "doesn't have anything to do with regulation or strangling with red tape. We don't want to make a lot of new laws. We want to redirect our efforts to make our old laws work."

Opponents argued that the agency, because it could only represent a consumer viewpoint—and had no regulatory powers — would result only in the addition of another layer of government bureaucracy without much effect on consumer problems. Many of the bill's opponents were quick to point out that the president himself had made an issue of the burgeoning bureaucracy during his campaign.

The American people, said Rep. John B. Anderson, R-Ill., feel that government is "already too big, too intrusive and too bureaucratic."

Others questioned the ability of the office to truly represent consumers. "There is no single consumer interest," remarked John N. Erlenborn, R-Ill. "We ought not to put a single person in the position of determining that interest."

Amendments

Fifteen amendments were offered before the bill was voted down. Four amendments were defeated on recorded votes; 11 were adopted. So many amendments were routinely accepted that some of the bill's opponents charged that this was a conscious strategy of the bill's supporters.

"In an effort to get any legislative vehicle to the other body so that a conference can rewrite the legislation," explained Robert E. Bauman, R-Md., "the leadership embraces any and all amendments, whether they are good, bad or indifferent, so long as they enhance the passage of the bill." The legislation's supporters denied the allegation.

The House defeated, 93-313, an amendment offered by Dan Glickman, D-Kan., to set up independent Offices of Consumer Counsel within each of the existing 23 major federal departments and agencies and a new Justice Department Division of Consumer Protection and Advocacy. *(Vote 36, p. 10-H)*

By a vote of 195-219, the House rejected an amendment by Elliott H. Levitas, D-Ga., requiring that the OCR give the president 30 days' notice before seeking judicial review of a federal agency's action. *(Vote 38, p. 12-H)*

An amendment offered by Dan Quayle, R-Ind., to drop from the OCR bill the exemption for labor disputes and labor agreements was defeated 138-274. Quayle suggested that the labor exemption was included in the legislation because its sponsors felt the bill would not pass otherwise. *(Vote 39, p. 12-H)*

The vote against the Quayle amendment was tacitly interpreted by the bill's sponsors as a vote for the consumer agency, but the margin by which the Quayle amendment was defeated did not accurately indicate the degree of support for the bill on final passage.

Also defeated on a recorded vote was an amendment by Millicent Fenwick, R-N.J., to delete from the OCR bill a provision exempting a number of Agriculture Department programs. The vote was 105-309. *(Vote 40, p. 12-H)*

Included among the amendments adopted were those that barred the OCR from establishing regional offices; required that, when the OCR participated in an agency matter in which there was more than one "substantial" consumer interest, the OCR must represent all of them; barred the agency from participating in any matter concerning firearms; more precisely defined the OCR's right to seek judicial review of agency actions; prohibited the OCR from testing consumer products tested by another agency within the preceding 18 months unless a significant consumer hazard could be demonstrated; and required that, before OCR could be created, the OMB had to certify to Congress that the 20 consumer offices to be transferred to the OCR would result in savings totaling $11 million.▮

FCC Powers - Cable TV

Congress Feb. 6 approved legislation (HR 7442 — PL 95-234) authorizing the Federal Communications Commission (FCC) to regulate the rates charged cable television firms to connect their lines to utility poles and expanding the FCC's authority to levy civil penalties for violations of its rules.

The Senate had passed nearly identical legislation Jan. 31, but the House Feb. 1 objected to two amendments as not germane to the bill and sent the measure back to the Senate.

On Feb. 6 the Senate by voice vote agreed to delete one of the provisions — concerning the types of telephone and related services that could be marketed in Hawaii — but insisted on retaining the other authorizing the FCC to impose penalties on cable TV operators who violated FCC rules. The Senate then returned the bill to the House. The House agreed to the Senate compromise the same day, completing congressional action.

The cable industry attached the cables that carry television signals to its subscribers to an estimated 10 million utility poles, according to testimony received by the Senate and House Communications Subcommittees. The utility companies charged cable firms an average rate of $3.50 per pole per year in 1977, but several major telephone and power companies announced their intention to increase rates dramatically during the year. As of July 1977, there were 27 states in which pole attachment disputes existed, according to cable industry testimony.

At Senate Communications Subcommittee hearings held June 23-24, 1977, cable television industry representatives argued they were totally dependent on telephone and power companies for pole attachments because local governments generally refused to allow cable companies to erect their own poles if another utility already had poles in place.

Cable industry representatives opposed, however, legislation sought by the FCC to expand cable's ability to levy civil fines (referred to as "forfeitures" by the FCC) on violators of its rules. Under existing law, the FCC's authority to levy such fines excluded such classes of communications services as citizens band radios and cable television systems.

Major Provisions

As signed into law, HR 7442 (PL 95-234):

- Authorized the FCC to levy fines of up to $2,000 for each violation of its rules and regulations, in addition to existing FCC penalties, up to a maximum of $20,000 for broadcast station and cable operators and a maximum of $5,000 for all others subject to FCC regulation.
- Required the FCC to observe appropriate due process requirements in assessing fines.
- Barred fines for violations that occurred either one year or longer before the violation was cited by the FCC or prior to the date of issuance of the alleged violator's FCC license, whichever was earlier.
- Authorized the FCC to regulate the rates, terms and conditions for cable television attachments of their lines to utility poles where these attachments were not already regulated by any state authority.
- Required that states certifying to the FCC that they regulated pole attachments also to certify they considered the interests of cable subscribers as well as the interests of utility consumers in their regulatory process.

• Established a formula to guide the FCC in determining just and reasonable rates for the attachment of cable television wires to existing utility poles.

• Required the FCC to issue rules governing the regulation of pole attachments within 180 days of enactment.

• Provided that the legislation take effect within 30 days of enactment.

Legislative Action

The House passed HR 7442 on Oct. 25, 1977 (H Rept 95-721). The House version contained only the provisions authorizing the commission to regulate cable television pole attachments.

The Senate Commerce Committee reported a companion bill (S 1547 — S Rept 95-580) on Nov. 2, 1977. As approved, the bill gave the FCC the authority to regulate the rates, terms and conditions for pole attachments provided a state had not certified to the FCC that it already regulated pole attachments.

The bill required that the FCC issue rules within 180 days of the bill's enactment to carry out the legislation's intent, established a formula to determine whether the regulation was "just and reasonable," and set a five-year limit on the duration of the act's provisions.

The bill extended the FCC's authority to levy civil penalties for repeated or willful violations of its rules to all licensees and operators subject to FCC regulation.

Two amendments were adopted by the Senate before it passed the bill Jan. 31 by voice vote. An amendment offered by Ernest F. Hollings, D-S.C., required states that themselves regulated pole attachments to certify to the FCC that they considered the interests of cable subscribers as well as the interests of utility customers in their regulatory process.

An amendment by Daniel K. Inouye, D-Hawaii, changed Hawaii from an international to a domestic point under FCC rules, to provide domestic common carriers with free entry into the Hawaiian market, thus allowing the island's residents to receive the same types of telephone and related specialized services available in mainland markets. Under existing FCC rules, Hawaii could be served solely by firms called international record carriers, which offered limited services only.

But the House Feb. 1 refused to go along with some of the Senate's additions. It deleted the Senate amendments expanding the FCC's penalty authority and the Inouye amendment relating to Hawaii. Both amendments were rejected as not germane. The House then returned the bill to the Senate.

After the Senate Feb. 6 agreed to delete the Inouye amendment, the House agreed to accept the other provision in dispute, completing congressional action.

Fishermen's Protection Act

Congress Aug. 17 approved legislation (HR 10878 — PL 95-376) extending for three years a voluntary insurance program that reimbursed American fishermen for the loss of their fishing boats through seizure by foreign governments outside U.S. territorial waters.

The program would be expanded under the legislation to include a no-fault insurance system to reimburse American fishermen for damage to their fishing gear and boats.

HR 10878 also strengthened federal protections afforded all endangered and threatened species of wildlife.

Legislative Action

HR 10878 was reported (H Rept 95-1029) by the House Merchant Marine Committee March 31.

As reported, the bill:

• Extended from Oct. 1, 1978, to Oct. 1, 1981, a voluntary insurance program for the reimbursement of losses incurred by U.S. fishermen as a result of the seizure of their fishing boats by foreign governments when a boat was operating in the 200-mile fishery zone of another country.

• Authorized the president to embargo all wildlife products from countries that acted in a manner threatening the continued existence of endangered or threatened species. Under existing law, the president was authorized solely to bar the importation of fish products from a country that conducted fishing operations in a way that diminished the effectiveness of existing international fishery conservation programs.

• Established a Fishing Gear Damage Compensation Fund in the Treasury Department, funded by voluntary contributions from U.S. fishermen, to provide for a no-fault voluntary insurance program to reimburse fishermen for loss of or damage to their fishing gear caused by another vessel, or do to natural causes, occurring within the U.S. 200-mile fishing zone.

HR 10878 was passed by the House April 10 as reported by the Merchant Marine Committee. The vote was 365-14. *(Vote 166, p. 50-H)*

HR 10878 was reported by the Senate Commerce Committee (S Rept 95-816) May 12.

As reported, the bill extended for three years the voluntary insurance program offered American fishermen, but contained no other provisions.

The Senate subsequently passed the bill without further amendment by voice vote May 22 and returned the bill to the House.

Subsequently, the staffs of the House Merchant Marine and Senate Commerce Committees met to work out a compromise. On Aug. 10 the House by voice vote passed a modified version of the bill.

The modification extended the coverage of the Fishing Gear Compensation Fund to damage to fishing vessels as well as to fishing gear, and to damage occurring in U.S.-managed fisheries outside the 200-mile zone.

The modification also provided that the entire cost of the program would be borne by foreign fishing vessels authorized to fish within the U.S. 200-mile zone, except that administrative costs would be borne by American fishing boat owners.

On Aug. 17 the Senate further modified the bill by clarifying that the insurance coverage applied to U.S. crab fishermen operating in the Bering Sea. That same day, the House approved the bill as modified by the Senate, completing congressional action.

U.S. Fish Processing Industry

Legislation giving the U.S. fish processing industry priority over foreign firms in processing fish caught within the United States' 200-mile limit was approved by Congress and signed by the president Aug. 28 (PL 95-354).

The legislation (HR 10732) also authorized fiscal 1979 funding of $30 million for the conservation and management of fish within the 200-mile limit under the Fishery Conservation and Management Act of 1976 (PL 94-265). *(1976 Almanac p. 234)*

The House passed HR 10732 April 10 providing fishery conservation and management authorizations of $40 million for fiscal 1979 and $45 million annually for fiscal 1980 and 1981. *(Vote 168, p. 50-H)*

The legislation had been reported (H Rept 95-1024) March 31 by the House Merchant Marine Committee.

The Senate Commerce Committee, in reporting HR 10732 May 12 (S Rept 95-815), recommended providing an authorization of $30 million for fiscal 1979 only for the fishery programs.

On the Senate floor June 14, however, Warren G. Magnuson, D-Wash., proposed amending the bill by adding to it S 3050, legislation reported (S Rept 95-935) by Senate Commerce that same day.

S 3050 granted the Commerce Department's National Oceanic and Atmospheric Administration authority to deny permit applications from foreign fish processors seeking to buy fish harvested within America's 200-mile limit if a U.S. fish processor also desired to buy the fish. Both the amendment and HR 10732 were approved by voice votes.

The House Merchant Marine Committee subsequently took up legislation similar to S 3050 (HR 13340), reporting it July 7 (H Rept 95-1334).

On July 11, the House passed HR 13340 by voice vote, along with the $30 million authorization provided for fiscal 1979 fishery programs by the Senate-passed version of HR 10732.

A compromise negotiated by the Senate Commerce and House Merchant Marine Committees was agreed to by the Senate Aug. 4 and by the House Aug. 10, clearing the measure.

Transportation Safety Board

A two-year extension of the National Transportation Safety Board was approved by Congress Aug. 14 and signed by the president Sept. 11 (PL 95-363).

The legislation (HR 12106) authorized $16,420,000 for the independent federal agency for fiscal 1979 and $17,650,000 for fiscal 1980.

The board was established by the Independent Safety Board Act of 1974 (PL 93-633) to investigate and help prevent transportation accidents. *(1974 Almanac p. 698)*

The board had requested a two-year funding extension, and the Senate had concurred in passing a companion authorization bill (S 2616) April 27. S 2616 had been reported by the Senate Commerce Committee (S Rept 95-702) April 26.

The House Public Works Committee, however, in its version of the legislation (HR 12106), reported May 15 (H Rept 95-1169, Part I), argued that only a one-year extension should be approved.

The short-term authorization, the committee stated, would pressure the board to act during the next fiscal year to step up its highway safety activities.

The House approved HR 12106 as reported July 10 by a vote of 340-32. *(Vote 455, p. 130-H)*

On Aug. 14, the Senate amended HR 12106 by again approving a two-year extension of the board. On Aug. 17 the House agreed to the Senate version of the bill, completing congressional action.

Fraudulent Mail Solicitation

Legislation to control fraudulent solicitations through the mails was approved by Congress and signed by the president Sept. 9 (PL 95-360).

As approved, S 2543 permitted the Postal Service to order mail containing fraudulent solicitations to be returned to the sender without delivery, and to stop payment on postal money orders made out to the sender of such mail.

The legislation also declared the mailing of fraudulent solicitations to be *prima facie* evidence that the sender was engaged in a fraudulent solicitation scheme.

While the use of the mails for fraudulent solicitations already was barred under existing law, only criminal penalties were provided.

Background

Drafted in response to pleas from the Postal Service that the standard of proof for criminal cases prevented effective enforcement of the law, S 2543 provided civil penalties for violations of the law and made it easier for the Postal Service to prevent future frauds once it learned of attempts to commit them.

Companion legislation (HR 13369) had been approved by the House Post Office Committee (H Rept 95-1401) July 31.

S 2543 was reported (S Rept 95-1077) Aug. 9 by the Senate Governmental Affairs Committee.

The committee said the legislation was needed to prevent fraudulent schemes such as solicitations for advertisements or listings in phony or non-existent directories, for contributions to non-existent charities, or for payment of invoices for goods or services never ordered or never supplied.

Under existing law, such solicitations required that the recipient be informed on the piece of mail that he or she was "under no obligation to make any payments on account of this offer unless you accept this offer," or similar language.

However, according to the committee, such fraudulent schemes continued to proliferate despite the law, especially in the Los Angeles area. Since July 1975, the committee report stated, Postal Service inspectors had investigated more than 500 such schemes and arrested about 60 people.

However, because of the difficulty of bringing criminal cases against violators of the mail fraud statutes, a change in the law was needed to "deny the operators of these schemes the fruits of their labors," the report concluded.

The Senate then passed the bill by voice vote Aug. 14 with a two-year authorization.

The House passed S 2543 by voice vote without amendment on Aug. 17, completing congressional action.

Fiscal 1979 Amtrak Subsidy

Legislation barring National Railroad Passenger Corp. (Amtrak) route cuts before Oct. 1, 1979, was approved by Congress Sept. 23.

The legislation (S 3040 — PL 95-421) also provided Amtrak with a fisacl 1979 federal subsidy of $755 million, including $600 million for operating expenses.

Provisions

As cleared for the president, S 3040:

- Authorized a $600 million federal subsidy for Amtrak fiscal 1979 operating expenses, $130 million for capital acquisitions, and $25 million for payment of guaranteed loans.
- Permitted the Office of Management and Budget to review Amtrak's budget before giving it to Congress.
- Required the transportation secretary to submit to Congress by Dec. 31, 1978, his final recommendations for a basic route structure for Amtrak. The recommendations were to go into effect no earlier than the start of fiscal 1980, but no later than 12 months after being approved by Congress. *(See box, this page.)*

(In their report, House-Senate conferees had instructed the secretary to examine alternative Amtrak fare structures to help it to increase its revenues and thus decrease its dependence on federal subsidies.

(Conferees also asked the secretary, in making his recommendations, to consider the importance of rail passenger service to the tourist industry of the states currently served by Amtrak.)

- Directed the transportation secretary to study the possibility of providing commuter trains with access to "key Northeast corridor terminals" such as New York City's Pennsylvania Station.
- Directed the General Accounting Office to report to Congress by Dec. 31, 1978, on how Amtrak's fare structure affected the intercity bus industry.
- Authorized the Interstate Commerce Commission to hold hearings to determine whether Amtrak's pricing practices were predatory or unfair to competing intercity buses.
- Required Amtrak to make purchases of over $1 million from U.S. sources, unless waived by the transportation secretary. (A "Buy American" provision was contained in both House and Senate bills.)
- Required that Amtrak be operated and managed as a for-profit corporation, even though subsidized.
- Required Amtrak to develop and implement a railroad safety program. (The final bill dropped a provision of the House-passed bill authorizing $250,000 for the program. Instead, conferees asked Amtrak to pay for the program out of its operating funds.)
- Required that firms providing track or facilities to Amtrak be paid solely on the basis of those costs that would not have been incurred had the track or facilities not been provided, except that additional payment was permitted to provide an incentive for good quality track and facilities.
- Authorized the Interstate Commerce Commission to order Amtrak to initiate new services if, after hearings, the commission determined that a petition for new service from a state, regional or local transportation agency was consistent with Amtrak's mandate.
- Gave Amtrak discretionary authority to contract for the provision of state, local or regional commuter rail service.
- Authorized the transportation secretary to develop new and faster trains and related equipment for operations in the Northeast corridor.

Rail Cutback Recommendations

Transportation Secretary Brock Adams announced May 8 that the department had completed preliminary recommendations on a new route structure for Amtrak.

The existing structure, he said, comprised about 27,000 miles, while the department's proposal would trim the system to 18,900 miles.

In 1980, the reduced system would cost taxpayers $547 million in subsidies, Adams said, compared to a subsidy of $665 million projected for the existing system. By 1984, the savings would total $200 million from a projected subsidy of $1 billion for the current system, he said.

Under the proposal, which Adams termed a "political hot potato," rail passenger service would be dropped between Chicago and Florida, Chicago and Mexico, Washington, D.C., and Cincinnati, and Washington, D.C., and the West Virginia-Ohio-Kentucky border.

Two routes would be combined between Chicago and Seattle and between Chicago and Los Angeles-San Francisco.

Maine, New Hampshire, Arkansas, South Dakota, Nebraska, Wyoming, Utah and Nevada would have no service at all under the proposal. Maine, New Hampshire and South Dakota have never had Amtrak service.

Under the plan, no cuts in service could take place before July 1, 1979.

"While this report was being prepared," Adams said in a letter to congressional leaders, "I considered whether federal support of intercity rail passenger service should simply be terminated in light of the large amounts of money we are spending to serve a relatively small segment of the traveling public.

"I have rejected that option, however," Adams said.

Senate Action

COMMITTEE

S 3040 was reported unanimously (S Rept 95-782) by the Senate Commerce Committee on May 4 with a fiscal 1979 authorization of $635 million. Hearings were held on the legislation March 10 and 13.

Bleak Prospects

In its report, the committee provided a bleak view of Amtrak's future financial prospects, and stated that the time had come for Congress to take a hard look at how to cut back the federal government's commitment to national rail passenger service.

"Viewed solely in economic terms," the report said, "Amtrak's rather bleak operating results would suggest little justification for continuing rail passenger service."

The "Amtrak problem," the report continued, "should be faced up to and every effort and sacrifice made by business, labor, government and the passenger public to bring under control and reverse the escalation of these operating deficits."

'Critical Junction'

The government's financial support for rail passenger service had reached a "critical junction," the committee said. Operating deficits had undergone an "intolerable escalation," while Amtrak administrative personnel had increased out of proportion to its needs.

Labor costs, as well, were "uncontrolled and escalating." Though such costs were out of Amtrak's control, this did not justify higher federal subsidies, the committee report stated.

Though Amtrak had claimed increased ridership in recent years, the committee report attributed these increases to the addition of new train service rather than greater load factors on existing trains.

In some cases, the report said, ticket prices were set so low that they were well below Amtrak's actual costs. Passengers attracted by such low fares could not be counted on to continue taking passenger trains when regular fares were in effect. As a result, the report concluded, increased ridership attracted in this manner resulted in greater, rather than lower, subsidies.

Social Benefits Questioned

Finally, the committee report rejected Amtrak's claim that the "social benefits" of rail passenger service — such as energy conservation and lower pollution levels — justified the subsidies. "The realization of these goals," the committee report concluded, "depends on ridership levels not likely to be achieved, at least the way the current system operates."

To deal with the "Amtrak problem," the committee recommended a thorough re-examination of Amtrak's existing routes, services and fares by the Transportation Department, the public and — ultimately — Congress.

Subsidy Level

Of the $635 million authorized by the Senate committee, $510 million was for operating deficits. Amtrak had requested an operating subsidy of $613 million, but the administration had recommended $510 million. In approving the lower figure, the panel required Amtrak to increase fares, adjust service and cut costs in order to finish 1979 within its budget.

FLOOR

The Senate passed S 3040 May 10 by voice vote without making any changes in the authorization levels recommended by the committee.

Russell B. Long, D-La., chairman of the Senate Commerce Surface Transportation Subcommittee, argued on the Senate floor that a comprehensive review of the nation's rail passenger service and its costs to the federal government was needed.

"Amtrak's deficits, which are ultimately paid for by the American taxpayer, have grown unchecked since the corporation commenced operations in 1971," according to Long, "indicating that a fundamental re-evaluation is in order."

The Senate, added Commerce Chairman Howard W. Cannon, D-Nev., "is in a perfect position to effectively reverse the trend of escalating costs associated with Amtrak operations and to help bring about some form of logic and order to the Amtrak system."

During Senate debate on S 3040, one amendment was adopted by voice vote. Offered by Birch Bayh, D-Ind., it would prevent federal funds from being used to purchase steel or rail cars costing over $1 million that were not made "substantially" from American raw materials and manufactured "substantially" in America. Under the amendment, the transportation secretary would be authorized to waive this requirement if it was in the public interest.

Bayh said the amendment was needed to assure that American workers received fair treatment from the government. In some cases, he said, foreign-manufactured goods were sold at less than the cost of production.

Cannon argued the amendment should be rejected because it constituted a "protectionist non-tariff trade barrier" and might encourage other countries to take similar steps against U.S. goods.

Major Provisions

As passed by the Senate, S 3040:

- Authorized for fiscal 1979 for the National Railroad Passenger Corporation (Amtrak) $510 million for operating expenses, $120 million for capital acquisitions and $25 million for payment of guaranteed loans.
- Required the secretary of transportation, after public hearings, to submit to Congress by Dec. 31, 1978, its final recommendations "designating a new basic route system" for rail passenger service. The recommendations were to automatically go into effect 60 calendar days after submission to Congress unless disapproved by either house of Congress. If disapproved, the secretary was to submit revised recommendations.
- Clarified that firms providing facilities and services to Amtrak would be paid solely on the basis of those costs that they would not have incurred had the facilities or services not been provided.
- Authorized the secretary of transportation to develop new and faster trains and related equipment for operations in the Northeast corridor.
- Prohibited grants of more than $1 million for the purchase of steel or rail cars unless they had been manufactured in the United States "substantially" from American raw materials. The secretary of transportation was given authority to waive this prohibition.

House Action

COMMITTEE

HR 11493 was reported by the House Commerce Committee (H Rept 95-1182) May 15 by voice vote.

The committee bill provided a higher subsidy for Amtrak than the administration said was needed for fiscal 1979.

Of the total federal subsidy of $768 million authorized by the committee, $613 million, the full amount requested by the Amtrak board of directors, was for operating costs. The president had requested — and the Senate had approved — an operating subsidy of $510 million.

The administration acknowledged that, with a $510 million operating subsidy, Amtrak would have to increase fares, adjust service and cut costs in order to finish 1979 within its budget.

However, Secretary Adams had informed the committee that, even if Amtrak were to preserve its existing routes and level of service, it would need only $575 million — not the committee-approved $610 million.

Route Cutback

House Commerce Committee action on the Amtrak subsidy bill followed by only one week Adams' May 8 announcement of the Transportation Department's preliminary recommendations on a new route structure.

The department planned to drop over 8,000 miles from Amtrak's 27,000-mile system, including a number of cuts Adams said he expected to be vigorously opposed in Congress.

In any case, the legislation as approved by the committee barred the Transportation Department from modifying existing Amtrak routes before Oct. 1, 1979.

In its report, the committee criticized Adams' preliminary recommendations. The Transportation Department, the report suggested, had not adequately studied all the options open to the federal government for improving Amtrak's financial performance.

Rather than dropping routes, the report suggested Amtrak might do better by improving service, cutting costs, changing labor rules and altering its marketing.

"Although the committee is extremely concerned about the level of Amtrak spending and the failure of Amtrak to develop an effective program of fiscal discipline," the report stated, "the committee feels that full funding of the present system coupled with a prohibition on changes in the present Amtrak route structure are necessary to the integrity of the route re-examination process.

"Public input, careful analysis and calm and dispassionate congressional consideration of the new Amtrak system cannot take place in an atmosphere of emotional clamor over immediate service disruptions," the report concluded.

But in a related development, the General Accounting Office (GAO), Congress' fiscal watchdog, concluded that Amtrak would have to cut back the number of routes it served if it was to avoid continual dependence on federal subsidies. In the first seven years (fiscal 1971-77) of Amtrak's existence, federal grants to the system totaled $2.5 billion.

HR 11493 dealt with the problem by establishing a mechanism for congressional consideration that made it politically difficult for members to support any cutbacks.

Adams had asked that the legislation be written to allow the department's final recommendations on Amtrak's route structure to go into effect automatically 60 days after submission to Congress unless disapproved by either house.

The House Commerce Committee, however, reversed the procedure by providing that the recommended route cuts could go into effect only if approved by both houses.

In supplemental views to the committee report Edward R. Madigan, R-Ill., said: "To require Congress to affirmatively vote to discontinue trains which affect its constituents makes any suggested restructuring of Amtrak a false promise."

Minority Views

In minority views, Reps. Samuel L. Devine, R-Ohio; Clarence J. Brown, R-Ohio; James M. Collins, R-Texas; and Dave Stockman, R-Mich., said HR 11493 should be defeated because "1) Amtrak has failed; 2) Amtrak costs the taxpayers too much; 3) Amtrak provides no public benefits; 4) the freeze in this particular bill guarantees another 18 months of extravagant waste; 5) the bill in effect prohibits even the secretary of transportation from taking off a single Amtrak train, now or in the future."

Referring to a train serving the district of Commerce Chairman Harley O. Staggers, D-W.Va., and threatened with discontinuation, the four members concluded: "It appears that the only way to justify the continuation of a train called the Shenandoah was to freeze every other unprofitable train into the Amtrak system. Only total disregard for the federal tax dollar can justify such crass politicization of Amtrak."

Major Provisions

As reported, HR 11493:

- Authorized a federal subsidy of $768,250,000 for Amtrak for fiscal 1979, including $613 million for operating subsidies, $130 million for capital acquisitions, $25 million for payment of guaranteed loans and $250,000 for development and implementation of a railroad safety program.
- Required the transportation secretary, after public hearings, to submit to Congress by Dec. 31, 1978, his final recommendations for a basic route system for Amtrak. The recommendations were to go into effect only after they were approved by both the House and Senate. The existing Amtrak route structure was to remain unchanged until Oct. 1, 1979, at the earliest.
- Directed the General Accounting Office to study how Amtrak's fare structure affected the intercity bus industry and to report its conclusions to Congress by Dec. 31, 1978.
- Authorized the Interstate Commerce Commission (ICC) to hold hearings to determine whether Amtrak's pricing practices were predatory or unfair to competing motor carriers. The legislation did not alter existing law, however, which exempted Amtrak from rate regulation by the ICC.
- Authorized the transportation secretary to develop new and faster trains and related equipment for its operations in the Northeast.
- Required Amtrak to make purchases costing more than $100,000 from U.S. companies, unless waived by the secretary.
- Authorized the ICC to order Amtrak to initiate new services if, after hearings, the commission determined that a petition for new service from a state, regional or local transportation agency was consistent with Amtrak's mandate. Under existing law, Amtrak was solely responsible for determining which routes it would serve.
- Required that Amtrak be operated and managed as a for-profit corporation, even though subsidized.

FLOOR

The House passed HR 11493 on June 23 by a vote of 204-89. *(Vote 425, p. 122-H)*

Some $13 million was trimmed from the authorization on the floor, leaving a total amount in the bill for Amtrak of $755,250,000.

Members turned back an effort to make a sizable cut in Amtrak's operating subsidy and rejected during the two-day debate (June 21, 23) attempts to curtail routes and delete or weaken a provision requiring that Amtrak "Buy American" materials. *(Box, next page)*

Operating Subsidy

The proposal reducing Amtrak's operating subsidy by $13 million, to $600 million, was approved by voice vote.

Devine had proposed cutting the operating subsidy to $575 million, the amount the administration said would be

Growing 'Buy American' Support

Provisions requiring Amtrak to make major purchases of goods and materials from American companies were contained in both the House and Senate version of the Amtrak legislation.

These "Buy American" provisions reflected a growing concern on the part of many members of Congress that spending public funds on foreign goods and materials hurt American industry and workers and should be further restricted.

At the same time, however, advocates of open and competitive world trade feared the provisions would constitute trade barriers that would invite retaliation from America's trading partners.

Retaliatory closings of foreign markets to U.S. exports, they argued, might end up hurting American business and increasing unemployment more than having no Buy American requirement in the first place.

While such legislation already was on the books — the Buy American Act of 1933 — its critics charged the law was vague and full of loopholes.

Perhaps the most significant loophole exempted from the law's mandate government funds spent by other than federal agencies.

This permitted recipients of federal contracts from agencies such as the Urban Mass Transportation Administration, the Department of Housing and Urban Development and the Environmental Protection Agency to buy goods and materials without regard to their national origin. Also exempted from the requirement were such federally funded firms as Amtrak and the Consolidated Rail Corp. (ConRail).

Attempts to legislate Buy American requirements had met with mixed success.

The Senate Governmental Affairs Subcommittee on Federal Spending Practices held three days of hearings in 1978 on S 2318, a bill to amend the 1933 act, but the legislation was not enacted during the session. The adminstration testified in opposition to the bill. It would have extended the Buy American requirement to state and local government activities funded more than 50 percent by the federal government, and would have attempted to close some of the loopholes in the existing law.

In addition to the Amtrak measure, attempts were made to attach the Buy American requirement to other legislation, including highway bills (HR 11733, S 3073).

sufficient to continue operating passenger trains at the existing level of service.

A cut of that magnitude was strongly opposed, however, by Staggers and Transportation Subcommittee Chairman Fred B. Rooney, D-Pa., who argued that cuts in routes and service would result.

The $13 million cut, proposed by Joe Skubitz, R-Kan., subsequently was agreed to by both Staggers and Rooney as "a good compromise."

While the administration had recommended an operating subsidy of only $510 million — to be accompanied by higher fares, a tighter budget and service cuts — the Amtrak board of directors had requested and the committee had approved $613 million.

'Buy American'

An amendment offered by William A. Steiger, R-Wis., to delete a committee-approved provision requiring Amtrak to buy American goods and materials for purchases of more than $100,000, was defeated by a vote of 93-207.

A subsequent attempt by Stephen L. Neal, D-N.C., to weaken the requirement by giving the Special Trade Representative, rather than the Transportation Secretary, the power to determine when the requirement would harm the "public interest" and thus waive it, also was rejected, by a vote of 121-178.

Defeated by a vote of 119-186 was an amendment by Madigan to provide Amtrak with an automatic mechanism for dropping unprofitable routes.

The amendment would have required Amtrak to drop a route if the federal subsidy for that route rose above $100 per passenger per ride.

Madigan called the amendment "a fair, workable, reasonable standard." He said the standard, if adopted, would require Amtrak to drop existing service from New York to Kansas City, from Chicago to Seattle and from Chicago to San Francisco. Opponents of the amendment argued that Amtrak should be given the opportunity to prove itself before the route cuts were made.

Two minor amendments were accepted. One, offered by Madigan, required Amtrak to submit its budget to OMB rather than directly to Congress.

A second amendment, by Andrew Maguire, D-N.J., directed the transportation secretary to study the possibility of providing New Jersey commuter trains with access to New York City's Pennsylvania Station.

Conference Action

S 3040 was reported (H Rept 95-1478) by the House-Senate conference committee Aug. 11. Overall, the compromise bill was closer to the House recommendations.

Route Cuts. The House-passed bill contained a provision, rejected by the conference committee, that would have made it difficult for the Transportation Department to pare down Amtrak's route structure. Any cutbacks in the rail system recommended by the department would have had to be approved by both houses of Congress. The Senate version — which was accepted by the conferees — permitted cuts to automatically go into effect unless blocked by a vote by either house.

The inclusion of a provision providing a procedure for route cuts was precipitated by Amtrak's decision in November 1977 to drop train service on certain routes unless Congress increased its 1978 subsidy. *(Background, 1977 Almanac p. 556)*

Congress agreed to increase the subsidy, but it also ordered that a study be conducted of Amtrak's route structure, with an eye on dropping the most uneconomic routes.

The conference report was approved by the House Sept. 19 by a 267-127 vote and by the Senate Sept. 23 by voice vote, completing congressional action. *(House vote 705, p. 200-H)*

Related Action

'Southern Crescent' Service

Congress March 21 gave Amtrak its approval to take over operation of the Southern Railway's "Southern

Crescent" passenger train that operated between Washington, D.C., Atlanta and New Orleans.

The train was one of the last long-distance American passenger trains operating outside the Amtrak system. Southern asked the Interstate Commerce Commission (ICC) March 6, 1978, for permission to discontinue the service April 6, citing mounting financial losses.

The congressional action did not require Amtrak to provide the service. Instead, it authorized Amtrak to do so without violating a promise the corporation made to Congress that it wouldn't alter its route structure before completion of a study to determine the recommended level of service Amtrak should maintain for fiscal years 1979 through 1982. *(Background, 1977 Almanac p. 556)*

Congressional assent was given through approval of a resolution (H Con Res 494) unanimously reported (H Rept 95-983) by the House Commerce Committee March 16. There was no Senate committee action. The resolution was approved without amendment on voice votes by the House March 20 and by the Senate March 21, completing congressional action.

Amtrak and Southern Railway already had begun negotiating an agreement by which Amtrak would take over the Southern Crescent service before Congress acted. The Amtrak board of directors March 1 had rejected a draft agreement because of conditions proposed by Southern on track usage and schedule changes.

In a related matter, the ICC voted March 27 to reject Southern's request to discontinue the Southern Crescent passenger service. The commission ordered the company to continue the service while it conducted a study of the situation.

No-Fault Auto Insurance Bill Rejected

For the fourth time since 1971, Congress rejected legislation to set minimum federal standards for state no-fault auto insurance plans.

The 1978 version (HR 13048) was killed Aug. 1 by the House Commerce Committee. A motion to send the measure to the full House was rejected by a 19-22 vote of the committee.

Although companion legislation (S 1381) had been approved by the Senate Commerce, Science and Transportation Committee, the House panel's action ended any chance of enacting the bill in the 95th Congress.

Congressional consideration of HR 13048 was marked by intense lobbying on both sides. It was supported by a number of large insurance companies and a coalition of consumer groups, and opposed by smaller insurance firms and groups representing trial lawyers — who represented auto accident victims and stood to lose business by the curb the legislation would place on court cases.

Though the bill got a boost in 1977 with an endorsement from President Carter — the first president to favor the concept — the administration did not vigorously lobby for the bill, preferring to view the controversial measure's progress from the sidelines. The legislation had been opposed by the Nixon and Ford administrations.

Trial Lawyers Confident

The Aug. 1 vote capped a hurried two-day markup by the House committee.

Lobbyists for the Association of Trial Lawyers had spread word before the vote that they were confident the bill would not be approved, and Commerce members — anxious to get on to other legislation — voted on the motion without debate.

The bill had survived a test vote in the committee July 25, when panel members voted 18-24 to reject a motion to recommit the bill to the Commerce Subcommittee on Consumer Protection.

On the final vote, however, three members who earlier had supported the bill opposed it, two members who had supported the bill July 25 did not vote, and one member not voting July 25 voted no, providing the margin of defeat.

Those switching positions on the Aug. 1 vote were Paul G. Rogers, D-Fla., Jim Santini, D-Nev., and Doug Walgren, D-Pa. Those who voted against recommittal July 25 and did not vote Aug. 1 were John M. Murphy, D-N.Y., and Fred B. Rooney, D-Pa. The member not voting July 25 and voting against the bill Aug. 1 was Joe Skubitz, R-Kan.

Press of Legislation

Though the no-fault legislation was controversial in and of itself, contributing to its defeat were the large number of bills awaiting floor action and the dwindling number of days in which to act on them before Congress hoped to adjourn.

Fourteen senators had written Majority Leader Robert C. Byrd, D-W.Va., July 10 warning him that a time limitation on Senate debate on no-fault legislation (S 1381) would be "very unlikely" and that scheduling the bill on the floor would "lead to a thorough exploration of every question surrounding the no-fault issue."

Though Byrd, through a spokesman, said he had not yet decided whether to proceed with the bill, the letter's message weighed heavily against such a course of action.

Similarly, on the House side Speaker Thomas P. O'Neill Jr., D-Mass., openly discouraged the bill's supporters, stating on at least one occasion that he would not schedule action on the bill this session.

Bob Eckhardt, D-Texas, chairman of the Consumer Protection Subcommittee and a no-fault supporter, said the doubts over whether the bill would be brought to a House or Senate vote made committee approval less likely.

"We were on the very weakest of platforms" in urging panel members to support the bill, he said after the legislation's defeat. "A cautious [member] might have voted 'no' simply because he suspected it would not make it to the floor."

"I don't fault the Speaker," Eckhardt said. "It's his job to set the schedule."

Background

The concept of no-fault automobile insurance gained widespread attention in the United States following the 1965 publication of a book entitled "Basic Protection for the Traffic Victim" by law professors Robert Keeton and Jeffrey O'Connell.

Their argument in favor of substituting a "no-fault" system of compensation for auto accident victims for the existing "fault" system persuaded Massachusetts in 1970 to become the first state to enact a no-fault law.

Committee Vote

Following is a breakdown of the House Commerce Committee's 19-22 vote rejecting the no-fault automobile insurance bill:

Democrats for (18) — Carney, Ohio; Eckhardt, Texas; Florio, N.J.; Gore, Tenn.; Maguire, N.J.; Markey, Mass.; Metcalfe, Ill.; Moffett, Conn.; Moss, Calif.; Ottinger, N.Y.; Preyer, N.C.; Russo, Ill.; Scheuer, N.Y.; Sharp, Ind.; Staggers, W.Va.; Van Deerlin, Calif.; Waxman, Calif.; Wirth, Colo.

Republicans for (1) — Rinaldo, N.J.

Democrats against (9) — Dingell, Mich.; Gammage, Texas; Krueger, Texas; Luken, Ohio; Mikulski, Md.; Rogers, Fla.; Santini, Nev.; Satterfield, Va.; Walgren, Pa.

Republicans against (13) — Brown, Ohio; Broyhill, N.C.; Carter, Ky.; Collins, Texas; Devine, Ohio; Frey, Fla.; Lent, N.Y.; Madigan, Ill.; Marks, Pa.; Moore, La.; Moorhead, Calif.; Skubitz, Kan.; Stockman, Mich.

Not voting (2) — Murphy, D-N.Y.; Rooney, D-Pa.

Under the no-fault plan, auto accident victims were paid by their own insurance companies for medical and rehabilitation expenses, lost wages and funeral costs. At the same time, their right to sue the driver at fault for additional money was limited to the most serious cases.

In return for giving up most of his right to sue a person whose negligence injured him, an auto accident victim was compensated under a no-fault system by increased benefits or lower insurance premiums, or both, from the company that insured him. These extra benefits resulted, no-fault advocates said, from money that went to pay for lawyers' fees and court costs under the fault system as it currently operated. However, no-fault opponents said that the system was not likely to save money for consumers.

State Plans

Since 1971 a total of 16 states had enacted no-fault laws both providing for compensation by the victim's own insurance company and placing restrictions on a victim's right to sue.

The 16 were Colorado, Connecticut, Florida, Georgia, Hawaii, Kansas, Kentucky, Massachusetts, Michigan, Minnesota, Nevada, New Jersey, New York, North Dakota, Pennsylvania and Utah. However, the plans in all of these states except Michigan fell far short of the federal standards being considered in Congress.

An additional eight states had passed laws providing solely for some form of compensation by the victim's own insurance company. These states had not restricted a victim's right to sue, and were not considered "true" no-fault plans by the Transportation Department.

Federal Involvement

In 1971, following publication by the Transportation Department of a $2 million study critical of the auto insurance industry, both the House and Senate held hearings on federal no-fault legislation. The Nixon administration supported the enactment of state no-fault laws rather than federal legislation, however, and a bill was defeated by the Senate in 1972 by a vote of 49-46. *(Congress and the Nation Vol. III, p. 694)*

No-fault legislation again was reported to the Senate floor during the 93rd and 94th Congresses. In 1974, a bill was passed by the Senate but died when the House did not act. In 1976, although the House Consumer Protection Subcommittee — which previously had blocked no-fault — approved a bill, companion legislation was killed by the Senate, 49-45. *(Congress and the Nation Vol. IV, p. 434)*

In 1977, no-fault was revived when the Carter administration became the first administration to endorse the legislation. A Transportation Department report released in July 1977 said that "no-fault automobile insurance works."

In July 1977 congressional testimony, Transportation Secretary Brock Adams said state experience had proved that the no-fault concept worked, but that existing state plans were "quite modest both in terms of benefits and degree of restriction on the right to sue."

He said the administration supported legislation setting minimum federal standards for state no-fault plans that would provide greater benefits while placing greater restrictions on the right to sue than did any existing state plan.

Senate Committee Action

At a Feb. 28 committee session that was to begin markup of the legislation (S 1381), John A. Durkin, D-N.H., announced that, though he supported no-fault, an independent actuarial study of the Michigan experience was needed in order to better predict the bill's impact. Existing studies of Michigan's system, he said, could be biased and inadequate.

Warren G. Magnuson, D-Wash., the bill's principal backer on the committee, opposed Durkin's suggestion, noting that existing studies and the "250,000 pages of congressional testimony" taken so far were sufficient evidence on which to draft the legislation.

However, Commerce Chairman Howard W. Cannon, D-Nev., ranking Republican James B. Pearson, R-Kan., and Wendell H. Ford, D-Ky., said they, too, needed more information before proceeding. They suggested a more comprehensive study encompassing the experiences of a number of states.

Magnuson said he would agree to the study if it could be completed quickly. "If this goes over three weeks," he warned, "you're killing the bill." The meeting adjourned with an agreement that a plan for a study would be drafted for presentation at the committee's next meeting.

Hollings Filibuster

At a March 2 session, however, the study proposal was never permitted to come to a vote. Operating under a Senate rule limiting the meeting to one hour, Ernest F. Hollings, D-S.C., an opponent of no-fault, filibustered against the proposal, and the meeting ended with nothing resolved. "I want us to tread very, very carefully on this before permitting the federal government to enter into a field traditionally left to the states," Hollings said.

On March 7 the committee approved a four-week study that was to consist of an independent actuarial analysis of no-fault plans in effect in Michigan and Colorado and a staff review of existing data from no-fault plans in other states. The study was to be funded by the Transportation Department.

The bill's opponents tried to expand the proposed study in hopes of delaying the bill long enough to kill it for the session, while those backing no-fault legislation opposed the study altogether. The study approved by the committee was seen as a compromise, entailing some delay but still leaving sufficient time for the committee to vote out a bill if it so chose.

Durkin, Riegle Position

Since February the committee's deliberations had been subject to delay after delay while members mapped out strategies, ordered studies and debated a seemingly endless string of amendments.

Many of the amendments, most of an extremely technical nature, were offered by Durkin. Though a cosponsor of the measure, Durkin announced at a May 2 session that he would "find it virtually impossible to vote this bill out" of committee as drafted. The bill, he said, did not adequately protect consumers.

He was joined in faulting the bill's consumer safeguards by Donald W. Riegle Jr., D-Mich., who invited the bill's supporters to work out a compromise with him that would enable him to vote for S 1381.

However, Magnuson and Ted Stevens, R-Alaska, both supporters of the legislation, spurned Riegle's overture, urging him instead to seek to amend the bill on the Senate floor.

'Killer' Amendment

Both Durkin and Riegle said May 2 that much of their opposition was due to the committee's rejection of an amendment offered by Durkin to bar insurance companies from basing different categories of rates on age, sex or geographical distinctions. Only "actuarial experience" could be taken into account in rate-making under his plan.

The amendment's opponents argued it was a "killer" amendment designed to turn no-fault supporters against the legislation. "The amendment seems designed to change the operation and philosophy of the entire insurance industry," Stevens charged. Others argued the amendment simply made no sense.

Durkin and Riegle said the amendment was a necessary "consumer safeguard." The bill as drafted "would provide massive windfall profits for the big insurance companies," Durkin said. He could not explain why many insurance firms opposed the bill. Though consumer groups supporting the bill opposed the Durkin amendment, "consumer groups aren't right all the time," Riegle said.

At the May 9 session, however, both senators said they would not be responsible for killing the bill in committee. Both offered to vote "aye" or "present" in order to avoid this. Both said they would oppose the bill on the floor.

The same day, after spending 10 weeks marking up the bill, the committee voted 9-7 in favor of a motion by Cannon to order S 1381 reported to the Senate.

In the end, only Durkin had to vote "aye" in order to get the bill reported. Riegle, who had passed when his name was first called, then voted "no."

Wendell H. Ford, D-Ky., chairman of the Commerce Consumer Subcommittee, which held hearings on the legislation, offered some insight into why the two senators had decided not to kill the bill in committee.

"I don't believe that I've ever had as much pressure placed on me, and as much work, as on this bill in the four years I've been in the Senate," he said.

The bill's backers, he said, liked to point out the pressure exerted on members by trial lawyers opposed to the legislation. Ignored, but equally as intense, he said, had been the pressure from what he called "lobbying lawyers" — lawyers retained to fight for the bill's passage.

Bill Reported

S 1381 was reported by the Senate Commerce Committee July 11 (S Rept 95-975).

Auto accident insurance reform was needed, according to the committee's report, because the tort liability system in effect in the majority of states was "an unfair and ineffective means for compensating automobile accident victims."

Though 16 states had enacted some form of no-fault insurance, the report said, "most of the plans provide for inadequate benefits or do not sufficiently restrict tort lawsuits, causing increases in insurance costs. Therefore, S 1381 is a necessary and proper exercise of the authority of Congress...."

Minority Views

Three senators submitted minority views to the committee report: Barry Goldwater, R-Ariz., Donald W. Riegle Jr., D-Mich., and Harrison Schmitt, R-N.M.

Goldwater said the committee-approved bill overlooked "six defects" in the legislation: "inconclusiveness, uncertain draftsmanship, cost implications, federalization of insurance, substantial and continuous opposition and discrimination among highway users." The latter "defect" referred to the fact that motorcyclists were not covered by the federal plan.

Riegle said he would seek to amend the bill on the Senate floor to curb large insurance companies' ability to reap "windfall profits" and to provide motorists insured under the no-fault system with additional consumer protections.

Schmitt said the federal government should leave auto insurance regulation to the states.

Major Provisions

As reported, S 1381:

- Declared that Congress found an adequate state no-fault auto insurance system to be a desirable replacement for existing state fault and no-fault systems.
- Set out basic medical, rehabilitation, work loss, death and survivor benefit levels that would constitute an adequate state no-fault system.
- Established limits on the ability of accident victims to seek additional benefits through tort liability lawsuits.
- Required states to require every registered owner of a motor vehicle to purchase no-fault insurance.
- Established basic state consumer protection standards for insurers.
- Preserved the authority of state insurance commissioners to regulate insurers within a particular state.
- Established a state-dominated five-member review panel within the Transportation Department to certify that state plans met the minimum standards established by S 1381 and to recertify the states' compliance with the federal no-fault standards every three years.
- Provided that, if a state did not enact an adequate no-fault plan within four years of enactment of the bill, the review panel would put into effect a system administered by the secretary of transportation that would establish the minimum standards in S 1381 as the standards that would apply to the state's no-fault system.

House Committee Action

The House Commerce Subcommittee on Consumer Protection approved a no-fault measure May 23 by voice vote. Full committee consideration of HR 13048 did not follow, however, until July.

At the urging of the Association of Trial Lawyers of America, House Commerce opponents of the legislation moved July 25 to recommit the bill to the Consumer Protection Subcommittee.

In a vote that surprised even the legislation's supporters, however, the committee rejected the motion to recommit by a vote of 18-24. Recommittal would have killed the bill.

Supporters of the motion, offered by Thomas A. Luken, D-Ohio, either were opposed to the legislation or said it was an untried alternative to the existing fault system of auto insurance.

"What we're talking about is giving it more time for state experimentation," Luken said.

Those opposing recommittal argued that the full committee should assume the responsibility for either rejecting or approving the bill, and not avoid that responsibility by voting to recommit.

To recommit, stated Consumer Protection Subcommittee Chairman Bob Eckhardt, D-Texas, was "to pass the power of the House to a lobbyist."

"The trial lawyers thought they had the votes to recommit," commented a no-fault supporter, who asked not to be named. "They lost it. They counted us as dead, but we're not dead yet. Now our opponents know there's a serious possibility the bill will be reported."

Others involved in the battle over no-fault, however, were not so sure.

Commerce Chairman Harley O. Staggers, D-W.Va., a no-fault supporter, commented during the July 25 session that House Speaker Thomas P. O'Neill Jr., D-Mass., had told him Senate Majority Leader Robert C. Byrd, D-W.Va., would not bring the bill to the Senate floor this session because of the threat of a filibuster.

O'Neill himself had told an insurance industry conference June 21 he would not seek a House vote on no-fault until after the Senate took action.

Staggers' remark prompted Jim Santini, D-Nev., to ask whether continued committee consideration of a bill that apparently was doomed constituted "legislative self-flagellation."

A Byrd spokesman later told Congressional Quarterly "no decision has been made" by the majority leader on a course of action for no-fault.

However, the aide acknowledged Byrd had received a letter sent him July 10 by 14 senators warning that a time agreement on S 1381 would be "very unlikely" and that scheduling the bill on the floor would "lead to a thorough exploration of every question surrounding the no-fault issue."

Though an aide for one of the senators denied the letter constituted a filibuster threat, she admitted the press of legislation awaiting floor action and the relatively few legislative days left before the end of the session indicated that the majority leader "would be crazy to bring the bill to the floor."

Markup by the full Commerce Committee lasted only two brief sessions before members voted 19-22 on Aug. 1 to kill the bill. *(Vote, box p. 483)* ▮

Small Business Bill Vetoed

Legislation to expand many of the federal government's small business assistance programs was pocket vetoed by President Carter. The bill (HR 11445) had been cleared by Congress Oct. 11.

The legislation, Carter said in an Oct. 25 memorandum of disapproval, had some "beneficial features" for small business, but would have strained the federal budget because of its authorizations in excess of the administration's budget projections through fiscal 1982.

HR 11445 would have altered fiscal 1979 authorization levels for a number of Small Business Administration programs already funded by existing law.

The bill also would have authorized SBA funding for fiscal 1980-82; declared it to be a national policy to foster the economic interests of small businesses; continued subsidies on the interest rate paid by the government for SBA natural disaster loans; expanded SBA's small business advocacy role within the federal government, and made it easier for small businesses to raise capital.

During the House-Senate conference committee's deliberations on the final version, administration aides criticized a number of the bill's provisions and threatened a veto if the bill weren't substantially rewritten. Disapproval of the bill did not cause interruptions in federal small business programs because the SBA's 1979 funding already had been authorized by an earlier law, Carter pointed out.

Rep. Neal Smith, D-Iowa, chairman of the House Small Business Committee, said the president's memorandum indicated he had received "bad advice."

House Action

HR 11445 was reported (H Rept 95-1037) by the Small Business Committee April 4. It was approved by the House under suspension of the rules April 10 by a vote of 310-72. A two-thirds vote (255 in this case) was required the pass the bill under suspension. *(Vote 170, p. 50-H)*

Provisions

As passed, the bill provided significantly higher authorization levels for the SBA for fiscal years 1980-1982, but left existing fiscal 1979 authorization levels untouched.

The House-passed bill provided authorizations of $1.365 billion for fiscal 1980, $1.533 billion for 1981 and $1.719 billion for 1982, plus an open-ended authorization for SBA disaster loans for the three-year period.

The House version also increased the interest rate on disaster loans, authorized the financing of loans through the SBA sale of notes to the secretary of the treasury and authorized the president to convene a White House conference on small business.

Senate Action

Committee

HR 11445 was reported (S Rept 95-827) May 15 by the Senate Select Committee on Small Business.

As reported, the bill altered a number of previously enacted fiscal 1979 authorizations for programs administered by the Small Business Administration (SBA) and made numerous minor changes in the SBA's program structure, administration and functions.

The fiscal 1979 authorization provided by the bill was $2,298,500,000, including a $1 billion authorization for the SBA's small business disaster loan program and $5 million for a White House small business conference.

However, because most 1979 SBA programs already had been authorized at higher funding levels, the net effect of HR 11445 was to decrease fiscal 1979 program levels by $267 million.

Under existing law, for example, SBA's disaster loan program was permitted to obligate "such sums as are necessary." The Congressional Budget Office estimated the program would cost approximately $1.4 billion during 1979. Under HR 11445, however, the program was limited to loans totaling $1 billion for the year.

The administration opposed the open-ended authorization provided by existing law, calling it "back door financing" because it enabled the SBA to circumvent the appropriations process.

Other major provisions of HR 11445:

- Increased the federally subsidized interest rate for certain small business disaster loans to 5 percent from 3 percent. Congress first provided for federally subsidized interest rates for SBA and Farmers Home Loan Administration loans in 1977 (PL 95-89). This was done on an emergency basis to help farmers hard hit by severe droughts.
- Authorized the establishment of small business development centers to provide management and technical assistance to small businesses, and to make grants to state, regional and other public and private institutions assisting small business.
- Established a national small business economic program declaring it the policy of the federal government to "foster the economic interests of small businesses."
- Established a White House Council on Small Business and Competition to help the president carry out federal policy on small business, and required the president to report to Congress annually on how the policy was being implemented.
- Strengthened the office and duties of the SBA chief counsel for advocacy.
- Authorized the SBA to license a new type of small business investment company specializing in investment in new and growing businesses, called venture capital small business investment companies.
- Authorized the convening of a White House Conference on Small Business in the fall of 1979. President Carter announced April 6 that he planned to hold such a conference.

In additional views, Dewey F. Bartlett, R-Okla., cited a number of provisions of the bill that troubled him.

HR 11445's repeated references to "small and medium-sized" business, he said, made the legislation ambiguous because "small business" was a concept well understood by the federal government while "medium-sized business" was undefined.

The national policy statement on small business, Bartlett maintained, represented a significant shift from the original Small Business Act of 1953. The 1953 law, he said, stressed the role of small business in preserving free market competition while HR 11445 sought to assist small business solely "in order to assist small business."

Floor

The Senate passed HR 11445 on Aug. 2 by voice vote. Seventeen amendments were adopted, including one by Bartlett to exempt most small businesses with 10 or fewer employees from the requirements of the 1970 Occupational Safety and Health Act (PL 91-596). Only those businesses with a high illness or injury rate would remain subject to federal safety and health standards under Bartlett's amendment. *(Background, box, above)*

The exemption was approved by voice vote after the Senate rejected, 42-51, a tabling motion by Gaylord Nelson, D-Wis. *(Vote 270, p. 42-S)*

OSHA Amendment

Lingering resentment over the Labor Department's record in implementing the 1970 Occupational Safety and Health Act, despite administrative and legislative changes adopted in 1977, was strong enough to win Senate approval of the Bartlett amendment exempting most small businesses from federal job safety and health rules. The amendment was subsequently dropped in a House-Senate conference.

Majority Leader Robert C. Byrd, D-W.Va., said Aug. 5 that the Senate vote was a reaction to the "excesses of the past," when the Occupational Safety and Health Administration (OSHA) engaged in what was widely viewed as overly detailed, nit-picking reporting of minor safety violations.

At the same time, supporters of the amendment portrayed it as merely an endorsement of the policies of OSHA head Eula Bingham, who had attempted to focus the agency's resources on large businesses with potentially the greatest safety problems. OSHA rules currently called for inspectors to devote only 5 percent of their efforts to the types of businesses most likely to be small.

Changes Under Bartlett

Under the Bartlett amendment, most of the 10.5 million workers employed by the 3.9 million businesses with 10 or fewer employees would no longer be covered by OSHA regulations. Only those businesses in industries that the Bureau of Labor Statistics found to average annually more than seven job injuries or illnesses per 100 workers would remain under OSHA supervision.

About 500,000 workers employed by 150,000 small, high-risk businesses still would be covered by OSHA, an aide to Bartlett estimated.

The Bartlett amendment was the latest in a series of attempts in Congress to cut back on the agency's authority. Few ever became law. The most successful vehicle had been the annual Labor-HEW appropriations bills. The fiscal 1978 Labor-HEW bill as enacted contained the following restrictions on OSHA:

- Exempted farms employing 10 or fewer workers from OSHA inspections.
- Prohibited the agency from issuing civil fines for first-instance health and safety violations, unless the inspector found 10 or more such violations.

The fiscal 1979 appropriations bill (HR 12929) contained similar restrictions. *(p. 105; 1977 Almanac p. 295)*

On the 42-51 vote, an overwhelming majority of Republicans (28 of 37) backed the change, while a majority of Democrats (33 of 56) opposed it (ND 30-9; SD 3-14).

An amendment offered by Edmund S. Muskie, D-Maine, and adopted by voice vote, trimmed the authorization levels for SBA programs to the levels recommended by the Senate Appropriations Committee in the fiscal 1979 State, Justice, Commerce appropriations bill (HR 12934).

The amendment trimmed SBA 1979 funding by almost $600 million, from $2,293,500,000 to $1,735,280,000. A $5 million authorization for the White House small business conference was unaffected.

Muskie also offered an amendment to end the federal subsidies on the interest rate paid on SBA disaster loans, bringing the interest rate on such loans up to the federal government's cost of borrowing. The amendment was adopted 54-41. *(Vote 271, p. 42-S)*

The Senate adopted two amendments by Sen. Lowell P. Weicker Jr., R-Conn., trimming the powers of the SBA Office of Advocacy. A number of Bartlett amendments also were accepted, including one to clarify that the federal policy toward small business was to promote free market competition, and another deleting the term "medium-sized business" wherever it appeared in the bill.

Also adopted was an amendment offered by Sen. Nelson to delete from the bill the provision requiring the establishment of a White House Council on Small Business and Competition.

In its place, Nelson proposed a compromise permitting the president, at his discretion, to appoint a special assistant for small business, who would be responsible for most of the functions that would have been assigned to the White House Council. The amendment was approved by voice vote.

Rejected by the Senate on a voice vote was an amendment by Carl T. Curtis, R-Neb., to curb SBA contracts to nonprofit charitable organizations for the federal purchase of wiping cloths.

Curtis argued that organizations such as Goodwill Industries had a competitive edge over for-profit small businesses because they used donated raw materials, while their competitors had to purchase them.

Conference Action

Senate and House conferees filed a conference report on HR 11445 (H Rept 95-1671) on Sept. 29.

OSHA Exemption. The principal disagreement between the two bills concerned the small business exemption from federal occupational safety and health requirements under the 1970 Occupational Safety and Health Act.

Administration officials and representatives of labor unions strongly opposed the Senate-added small business exemption and pressed conferees to drop it.

During its deliberations Sept. 9, the conference committee agreed to a compromise drafted by Nelson. The compromise provided that small businesses, as defined by the bill, having no more than 10 federal health and safety violations of a non-serious nature on first inspection, would not be fined.

The Nelson compromise also exempted virtually all small businesses from certain occupational injury and illness record-keeping requirements and called on the administration to study the effectiveness and accuracy of its statistics and analyses of small business injury and illness patterns.

Authorization Levels. Conferees also agreed to establish authorization levels for SBA programs for fiscal years 1980-82 in the bill. While the House-passed bill had provided authorizations for those years, the Senate-passed bill had merely altered fiscal 1979 authorization levels provided in existing law.

The 1980-82 authorization levels approved by the conferees were higher than those in the House-passed bill.

While the House-passed bill authorized 1980 appropriations of $1.365 billion, for example, the conference version authorized $1.616 billion.

For 1981, the House authorized $1.533 billion, which was increased by the conference committee to $1.607 billion. For 1982, the House authorized $1.719 billion, which conferees increased to $1.943 billion.

Disaster Loans. Conferees dropped a provision of the Senate-passed bill that would have placed a cap of $1 billion on the SBA's authority to obligate fiscal 1979 physical disaster loan funds.

Under the conference committee's bill, the disaster loan program remained free — as under existing law — to obligate "such sums as are necessary."

Conferees dropped provisions of the House-passed bill authorizing the SBA administrator to issue and sell notes to the secretary of the treasury in order to obtain capital for its disaster loan fund, and requiring SBA to submit to Congress all budget requests and legislative testimony or comments at the same time as the information was submitted to the Office of Management and Budget.

The conference report dropped a provision of the Senate-passed bill authorizing the president to name a White House special assistant for small business.

Final Provisions

As approved by House and Senate conferees, HR 11445:

- Authorized appropriations of $1.635 billion for Small Business Administration programs for fiscal 1979, $1.616 billion for 1980, $1.607 billion for 1981 and $1.943 billion for 1982. There was no limit placed on the amount of money the SBA could obligate for physical disaster loans.
- Established an interest rate of 3 percent on the first $55,000 of a homeowner's loans for natural disaster relief made from Oct. 1, 1978, until Oct. 1, 1982. The rate on all other such loans was set at 5 percent on the first $250,000. Interest on loans in excess of those limits was to be paid at the federal government's cost of borrowing, which at the time was 6.58 percent.
- Barred the assessment of fines by the Occupational Safety and Health Administration (OSHA) on businesses with 10 or fewer employees that were found to have 10 or fewer violations on first inspection, provided the violations were not considered serious. If OSHA violations were found on any subsequent inspection, the exemption for such businesses no longer would apply.
- Exempted businesses with 10 or fewer employees from existing OSHA regulations requiring businesses to maintain logs of, and make annual reports on, all their occupational injuries and illnesses, unless the employer was chosen to participate in a statistical survey of occupational injuries and illnesses.
- Authorized the establishment of small business development centers as a pilot program to provide management and technical assistance to small businesses, and to make grants to states and other public and private institutions assisting small business. Authorized grants for the program through fiscal 1982.

• Expanded and defined the duties of the SBA chief counsel for advocacy, strengthening the chief counsel's advocacy role.

• Declared it to be the policy of the federal government to foster the economic interests of small business and to preserve a competitive free enterprise system that would help small businesses develop.

• Required the president to submit annually to Congress a report on "Small Business and Competition," focusing on the economic issues affecting the viability of small businesses.

• Required the Federal Reserve Board, the comptroller of the currency and the Federal Deposit Insurance Corp., in consultation with SBA and the Census Bureau, to report to Congress by Oct. 1, 1979, on the credit needs of small businesses and the extent to which existing financial institutions were meeting those needs.

• Authorized SBA to license a new type of small business investment company specializing in investment in new and growing businesses, called venture capital small business investment companies (SBICs).

• Permitted small business investment companies to place unlimited idle funds in savings and loan institutions; under existing law, such deposits were limited to the amount for which they were insured.

• Authorized the convening of a White House conference on small business, and required that the conference be held no later than June 30, 1980. The bill authorized $5 million for the White House to carry out the conference.

Final Action

The conference compromise was approved by the House Oct. 4 by a vote of 396-10. *(Vote 764, p. 216-H)*

The Senate adopted the report Oct. 11 by voice vote, completing congressional action. ▮

Minority-Owned Businesses

Congress Oct. 10 cleared legislation expanding federal assistance programs for small businesses owned and operated by minorities.

The legislation (HR 11318 — PL 95-507) increased the amount of capital and borrowing power available to minority-owned small businesses through entities known as minority enterprise small business investment companies (MESBICs) and made it easier for such businesses to obtain government contracts.

The legislation also attempted to make existing Small Business Administration (SBA) programs more effective in helping minority-owned businesses to become viable commercial enterprises, and to end abuses in certain of the assistance programs.

Existing programs had not in all cases operated as intended by the drafters of the Small Business and Small Business Investment Acts of 1958 (PL 85-536, PL 85-699), according to the bill's sponsors.

In one program designed to promote the awarding of federal contracts and subcontracts to minority small firms, for example, only 33 of the more than 3,700 firms that participated in the program were found by a General Accounting Office (GAO) study to be solvent and still in business.

The legislation also broadened SBA's surety bond program, expanded SBA's business development program and encouraged federal agencies to let more contracts and subcontracts to minority small businesses.

Final Provisions

As cleared by Congress, HR 11318:

• Increased to 200 percent of its private capital the amount of stock that could be sold to the SBA by a MESBIC licensed before Oct. 13, 1971, or by one licensed after Oct. 13, 1971, but which had a minimum private capital base of $500,000. For MESBICs licensed after Oct. 13, 1971, but with less than $500,000 in private capital, the MESBIC could sell to the SBA stock totaling only 100 percent of its private capital.

• Required that MESBICs formed after Oct. 1, 1979, have a minimum private capital base of $500,000.

• Lowered the interest rate on SBA loans to MESBICs to 3 percent or 3 percent below the government's cost of borrowing — whichever was higher — for the first five years of the loan.

• Broadened SBA's surety bond guarantee program and limited SBA authority to revoke a surety bond guarantee. A guarantee could be revoked only if it were obtained through fraud or misrepresentation or if the total of the guaranteed contract exceeded $1 million.

• Clarified that only small businesses operated and at least 51 percent-owned by socially and economically disadvantaged persons would be eligible for participation in SBA's federal contracting program, in which federal contracts were funneled to small businesses through the SBA. The bill also established criteria for determining whether a group was disadvantaged. Among the socially and economically disadvantaged groups that the legislation specifically identified as being eligible for the program's benefits were blacks and Hispanic and native Americans.

• Established a two-year pilot program requiring one federal agency — to be designated by the president — to make all of its contracts available to the SBA for inclusion in the federal contracting program.

• Established a two-year pilot program authorizing the SBA to waive all federal bonding requirements, under certain conditions, for socially and economically disadvantaged businesses seeking federal contracts.

• Strengthened SBA's existing minority small business development program that provided eligible firms with management and technical assistance, and required that firms benefiting from SBA's federal contracting program participate in the program.

• Revised federal requirements for the submission of subcontracting plans by bidders for federal contracts. For formally advertised contracts, only the low bidder was required to submit a plan for subcontracting part of the work to minority small businesses. For negotiated contracts, the government was required to state in the contract solicitation notice that a minority subcontracting plan would constitute a part of the negotiations.

• Required federal agencies to consult with the SBA in establishing goals for disadvantaged small business participation in federal contracts.

• Established within each agency an "Office of Small and Disadvantaged Business Utilization."

House Action

Committee

The House Small Business Committee reported HR 11318 on March 13 (H Rept 95-949). The bill had been approved by a 27-0 vote.

According to the committee report, minority enterprise small business investment companies had been unable to provide sufficient capital to "disadvantaged" and minority businesses because of statutory limitations placed on the firms and because of insufficient federal funding. In addition, Congress and its budgetary watchdog, the General Accounting Office, found that some non-disadvantaged persons were using minority businesses as "fronts" to seek federal contracts under a program enabling the SBA to negotiate with the government for the purchase of goods from firms owned by the economically or socially disadvantaged.

Major Provisions

As reported by the committee, HR 11318:

- Authorized MESBICs to increase their sales of preferred stock to the SBA by 100 percent above the level authorized under current law.
- Authorized MESBICs to form limited partnerships and to deposit idle funds in any amount in savings and loan associations. Existing law restricted investments in savings and loans, but permitted unlimited investments in conventional banks.
- Authorized the SBA to seek any federal contract for inclusion in its minority business contracting program if the SBA and the responsible federal agency could agree on appropriate conditions. The SBA would be required to certify that it could provide the needed technical assistance to minority businesses seeking such contracts. The SBA could waive federal bonding requirements.
- Required that minorities own at least 51 percent of participating small businesses and control their management and daily business operations.
- Established criteria for determining whether a person or business was "economically and socially disadvantaged."
- Required that federal contractors make efforts to award subcontracts for goods and services to small businesses.

Floor

The House passed HR 11318 by voice vote March 20 under suspension of the rules and sent the bill to the Senate.

Senate Action

Small Business Committee

HR 11318 was reported (S Rept 95-1070) by the Senate Select Committee on Small Business Aug. 8 by voice vote.

As reported, the legislation:

- Lowered the interest rate on SBA loans to MESBICs to a flat 3 percent, from a rate 3 percent below the federal government's cost of borrowing the money.
- Limited to 3 percent the dividend rate paid the SBA for the agency's purchase of MESBIC bonds. Under existing SBA regulations, a MESBIC was required to reimburse the SBA for the difference between the subsidized dividend rate and the then-prevailing free market interest rate at the time the MESBIC redeemed or liquidated its stock.
- Increased the amount of stock a MESBIC could sell to the SBA to two times the MESBIC's paid-in private capital plus any surplus it had.
- Required that newly formed MESBICs have a minimum private capital base of $500,000.
- Established that only small businesses controlled by individuals or groups that were "socially and economically disadvantaged" would be eligible for interest and dividend rate subsidies.
- Broadened SBA's surety bond guarantee program and limited SBA authority to revoke a surety bond guarantee. A guarantee could be revoked only if it were obtained through fraud or misrepresentation or if the total of the guaranteed contract exceeded $1 million.
- Strengthened SBA's existing minority small business development program providing eligible firms with management and technical assistance, and required that firms benefiting from the SBA's federal contracting program participate in the program.
- Required every federal agency to cooperate with the SBA in encouraging the granting of federal contracts to small businesses.
- Established within each agency a small business utilization office.
- Encouraged firms winning federal contracts to formulate plans to subcontract portions of their contracts to minority small businesses.
- Clarified that only small businesses operated and at least 51 percent-owned by socially and economically disadvantaged persons would be eligible for participation in the federal contracting program.

Governmental Affairs Committee

HR 11318 subsequently was referred to the Senate Governmental Affairs Committee, which had requested an opportunity to look at the impact the legislation would have on federal contracting practices.

The committee recommended a number of changes in the bill which, it explained, sought to balance the desire to assist small businesses with good procurement policies.

As amended and reported (S Rept 95-1140) by the panel Aug. 23 by voice vote, HR 11318:

- Required agencies to weigh a firm's plan for minority subcontracting before, rather than after, the firm was awarded a federal contract.
- Prohibited an agency from offering incentives to a firm to improve its minority subcontracting plans after the agency awarded the firm a federal contract.
- Limited SBA's role in the awarding of federal contracts to that of an advisor. "SBA involvement in the actual selection process would be inappropriate and inconsistent with good procurement practices," according to the committee's report.

Floor

HR 11318 was passed by the Senate Sept. 15 by voice vote with two additional substantive amendments.

The sole floor skirmish concerned the requirement that firms competing for federal contracts submit plans for subcontracting part of the work to minority-owned businesses

As drafted by Governmental Affairs, the bill required that practically every bidder for government contracts submit such plans before the contract was awarded.

Sam Nunn, D-Ga., the Small Business Committee's floor manager of the bill, proposed to loosen the requirements under which subcontracting plans would have to be submitted in advance. For advertised contracts, for example, only the low bidder that actually was awarded the contract would be required to submit a plan.

"I believe an unnecessary paperwork and regulatory burden would be created if all offerors had to submit contracting plans," Nunn argued. He said plans would be required to reflect the low bidder's "best efforts" to aid small minority firms.

Despite opposition from several Governmental Affairs Committee members, Nunn's amendment was approved by voice vote.

The Senate, by voice vote, also approved an amendment drafted by Robert P. Griffin, R-Mich., to require the SBA, in subcontracting federal contracts to minority businesses, to consider the price competitiveness of the potential subcontractors.

Conference, Final Action

House-Senate conferees filed a conference report (H Rept 95-1714) on HR 11318 on Oct. 4.

As approved, the legislation represented a combination of the major features of the House-passed and Senate-passed versions of the bill. Both the House- and Senate-passed bills had suggested similar solutions to problems they had found in the existing minority small business programs.

A major dispute in the conference committee concerned the eligibility requirements for the federal contracting program. The House bill provided that black and Hispanic American business groups were assumed to be socially and culturally disadvantaged unless the SBA could prove they were not. Other groups were required to prove they were disadvantaged in order to qualify.

The Senate bill, on the other hand, had proposed uniform criteria to determine a group's eligibility.

Conferees dropped the separate eligibility criterion for black and Hispanic Americans and proposed a compromise set of criteria to determine a group's eligibility.

The House adopted the conference report on Oct. 6 by voice vote, and the Senate approved it Oct. 10, also by voice vote, completing congressional action. The president signed the bill into law Oct. 24.

Intercoastal Shipping Rates

Congress Oct. 3 approved legislation intended to reduce administrative delays in the Federal Maritime Commission's (FMC) regulation of shipping between the United States mainland and such offshore domestic ports as Alaska, Hawaii, Guam, Puerto Rico, the U.S. Virgin Islands, American Samoa and certain other U.S.-owned Pacific islands.

The legislation (HR 6503 — PL 95-475) set deadlines for FMC action on rate changes proposed by steamship companies for such intercoastal shipping, and made it easier for the steamship companies to alter their rates — within specified limits — without prior FMC approval.

FMC Delays

The legislation was needed, according to its backers, to end the delays of from two to four years that it took the FMC to decide rate cases.

HR 6503 was supported by steamship companies serving intercoastal routes, such as Matson Navigation Co. and Sea-Land Service Inc.

The National Industrial Traffic League, a shippers' organization, and representatives of offshore domestic ports opposed the legislation because they feared it made rate increases too easy to put into effect.

The legislation amended the Intercoastal Shipping Act of 1933, which gave the FMC authority to prohibit rates it determined were unlawful.

Under the 1933 law, the commission was permitted to suspend proposed rates for up to 120 days while it judged a rate's lawfulness. However, the 120-day suspension period became inadequate as FMC consideration of such rate cases stretched, in some instances, to four years.

In these situations, a rate went into effect after the 120-day suspension period and remained in effect until the FMC came to a conclusion. If the conclusion was that a rate was unlawful, the commission could order the rate lowered, but it lacked the power to require a refund of shippers' overpayments.

Provisions

As approved by Congress, HR 6503:

- Permitted steamship companies serving intercoastal routes to make general rate increases or decreases of up to 5 percent within a year without prior FMC approval.
- Provided for expedited FMC consideration of the lawfulness of proposed rate changes.
- Required the FMC to complete its determination of whether a rate was lawful within 180 days; if it concluded that a rate was unlawful, it was authorized to suspend the rate and to order the steamship company to refund with interest that portion of the rate it concluded was unlawful.
- Required the FMC to issue guidelines within one year as to what constituted a lawful rate.

Legislative History

HR 6503 was passed by the House May 8 by voice vote under a suspension of the rules, prohibiting amendments. It had been reported (H Rept 95-474) unanimously by the House Merchant Marine Committee on June 30, 1977.

As reported, the legislation had permitted steamship companies to make general rate changes of up to 7 percent within a 12-month period without prior FMC approval. Opposition from Del. Ron de Lugo, D-V.I., however, had convinced the committee to lower the permissible limit to 5 percent in the version of the bill brought to the floor.

The identical measure was reported (S Rept 95-1240) by the Senate Commerce Committee Sept. 26, and passed by the Senate Oct. 3 without amendment, completing action on HR 6503.

U.S. Tuna Industry

Congress May 31 sent to the president legislation (HR 11657) extending the Central, Western, and South Pacific Fisheries Act of 1972. The bill was signed into law (PL 95-295) June 16.

The 1972 act (PL 92-444) authorized $3 million over three years (fiscal 1974-1976) for the development of the tuna fishing industry in the Pacific. No funds, however, were ever appropriated under the act. Instead, the Department of Commerce relied upon funds authorized under a 1954 law providing the department with 30 percent of the duties collected from imported fishery products. These funds were supplemented by matching funds from the tuna industry beginning in 1972.

The tuna fisheries of the central, western, and south Pacific region nonetheless remained an under-utilized source. The tuna yield of the region was estimated at between 800,000 and 1 million tons annually, but in 1976 only 291,000 tons were harvested. It was estimated that the United States alone could harvest as much as 155,000 tons of tuna a year from the Pacific, greatly reducing the U.S. trade deficit in seafood products. In addition, an expanded U.S. tuna industry would provide new jobs for a declining industry.

The House Merchant Marine and Fisheries Committee on April 21 reported (H Rept 95-1079) HR 11657 with an authorization of $27 million over four years (1979-82) to develop fishery resources in the area.

After a brief debate, the House passed HR 11657 May 1 without amendment by a vote of 326-23. *(Vote 220, p. 64-H)*

The Senate Commerce, Science, and Transportation Committee reported the bill (S Rept 95-818) May 12 with amendments.

- The Pacific Tuna Development Foundation, a non-profit corporation headed by representatives from Hawaii, American Samoa, Guam, and the Trust Territory of the Pacific Islands and by representatives of the U.S. tuna industry, was named as an organization the commerce secretary could designate to carry out fishery development projects.
- The commerce secretary was given the authority to begin a cooperative program with member nations in the south Pacific region if the United States became a member of any international south Pacific regional fisheries agency in the future.
- The authorization was increased by $1 million, to $4 million in fiscal 1979, and $5 million annually for each of fiscal 1980-1982 to implement the act. The Senate version authorized a total of $16 million, $11 million less than the House bill.

The Senate passed HR 11657, as reported by the committee, on May 18 by voice vote.

The House May 31 by voice vote concurred in the Senate amendments, completing congressional action.

Additional Funds for ConRail

Acting less than two hours before adjournment Oct. 15, the House approved, and cleared for the president, a bill authorizing an additional $1.2 billion in federal subsidies for the Consolidated Rail Corp. (ConRail) over the next five years. The additional funds had been requested by ConRail in February, and the bill (S 2788) was approved by the Senate in August.

But the crush of legislation in the final days of the session jeopardized final House action. Anticipating that the bill might be caught in the adjournment rush, the House and Senate in the early morning hours of Oct. 15 had approved an additional $300 million in subsidies for ConRail in fiscal 1979 as part of an omnibus resolution temporarily continuing federal programs whose authorizations had not been cleared by Congress.

However, a visit to the Capitol by Transportation Secretary Brock Adams later that morning succeeded in convincing House leaders to bring S 2788 to the floor.

Adams told the House leadership that ConRail might be forced to stop operating in February 1979 without the additional funding. House Commerce Transportation Subcommittee Chairman Fred B. Rooney, D-Pa., speculated that, if the winter were harsh, ConRail might need the additional funds before February.

Major Provisions

As cleared for the president, S 2788 (PL 95-565):

- Authorized the federal government to purchase an additional $1.2 billion in ConRail stock during the period Jan. 1, 1978, through Dec. 31, 1982.
- Ordered ConRail to formulate an employee stock ownership plan, to be funded by transferring up to 15 percent of ConRail stock to the railroad firm's employees.
- Authorized an additional $9 million for reconstruction of the railroad bridge spanning the Hudson River at Poughkeepsie, N.Y.

Background

The Consolidated Rail Corporation (ConRail) chose an unusual method of notifying the federal government to expect requests for additional aid. In its first 21 months of operation, it said in a Dec. 28, 1977, full-page advertisement in several major daily newspapers, ConRail came "very close" to meeting the goals set for it by the government.

However, the advertisement went on, its rolling stock was "in much worse shape than originally reported" and urgently needed replacement and repair. Further, its total traffic was running about 6 per cent lower than forecast.

"Therefore," the advertisement concluded, "additional financing will be necessary."

It was not until Feb. 15, however, that the government was let in on how big the tab would be.

In a proposed five-year plan covering the period Jan. 1, 1978, through Dec. 31, 1982, ConRail revealed that, making generally optimistic assumptions, it would need an additional $1.3 billion from the federal government and $959 million in private financing in order to achieve its goals of improved rail service and financial independence. Some $4.6 billion in grants and loans had previously been given ConRail.

Even then, the railroad warned, "anticipated narrow profit margins" in 1980-82 "will not be sufficient to offset the 1979-80 losses" and will "not provide an adequate rate of return on total capital invested in the railroad."

ConRail began service April 1, 1976, with a mandate to fashion six bankrupt eastern railroads into an efficient and profitable system by 1979. ConRail was designed by the U.S. Railway Association, a quasi-governmental independent agency created by Congress in the 1973 Regional Rail Reorganization Act (PL 93-236). The 1973 act gave ConRail $2.5 billion in federal aid to cover start-up costs, while the 1976 Railroad Revitalization and Regulatory Reform Act (PL 94-210) authorized an additional $2.1 billion through fiscal 1979 in federal loans.

Though ConRail's new projections included $50 million annually for unforeseen problems, the plan was based on a number of "key assumptions" which, if they did not prove true, would make ConRail even more expensive. Some questionable assumptions included eliminating or modifying some railroad union work rules, increasing worker productivity and closing down unprofitable lines.

Transportation Secretary Brock Adams said Feb. 15 he thought no new authorizations would be necessary to continue the system's operations "in a normal fashion into 1979, while permitting capital programs to proceed as planned." For that reason, he said he would recommend that new funding needs be put off until fiscal 1980.

In order to wipe out a projected 1979 budget deficit, Adams was said to be eyeing two programs authorized by the 1976 act to provide aid for railroads outside the ConRail system.

A "Preference Share" program was funded at $1 billion, while a loan guarantee program provided $600 million, for a total of $1.6 billion. According to a U.S. Railway Association spokesman, so far there had been "very little money used" from the two programs.

Five-Year Plan Outlook

Adams said in April he still supported the basic plan and goals established for ConRail in the Railroad Revitalization and Regulatory Reform Act of 1976 (PL 94-210). "The alternatives to ConRail which we faced between 1973 and 1976 [such as nationalization] were not happy ones...[but] should subsequent events show without doubt that ConRail's ultimate need for additional funds is much larger than the $1.3 billion so far identified, then I will be the first to say that we must re-evaluate the premises of the reorganization solution which we adopted in 1976."

At the April 13 hearing of the Senate subcommittee, A. Daniel O'Neal, chairman of the Interstate Commerce Commission, stated that there was a "serious question" whether ConRail could meet its projections as set out in the five-year plan.

"Our preliminary estimate," he said, "is that ConRail will require $1.1 billion to $1.6 billion in funding over and above the $1.3 billion government...funding projected by the plan."

Legislative History

Senate Action

S 2788 was reported by the Senate Commerce Committee (S Rept 95-885) May 15.

At the time the committee began its consideration of the legislation, the administration had not yet determined its policy toward ConRail's request for additional funding, and a bill was drafted by committee staff authorizing the purchase of an additional $600 million in ConRail stock by the U.S. Railway Association, the quasi-governmental agency created to oversee the ConRail system.

In early April, however, Transportation Secretary Brock Adams informed both the House and Senate the administration would support legislation authorizing $1.2 billion of the $1.3 billion ConRail requested.

As reported by the committee, S 2788, in addition to the agreed to $7.2 billion subsidy, ordered ConRail to formulate an employee stock ownership plan, to be funded by transferring up to 15 percent of ConRail stock from the U.S. Railway Association.

ConRail's continuation, the committee stated, was "essential to the nation's economy." But if the railroad was to succeed, the committee warned, "it must quickly make the necessary service improvements that will attract revenue sufficient to support its plant and operation."

Several minor amendments to S 2788 were adopted by the Senate before the bill was passed Aug. 1 by voice vote.

An amendment proposed by Abraham Ribicoff, D-Conn., authorized an additional $9 million for reconstruction of a railroad bridge spanning the Hudson River at Poughkeepsie, N.Y.

The bridge had been damaged by fire in 1974, and the bankrupt Penn Central Railroad failed to rebuild it before transferring its assets to ConRail.

ConRail subsequently refused to rebuild the bridge, calling it uneconomical. Ribicoff charged that the railroad was using the damaged bridge as an excuse for dropping service to the area and added that by repairing the bridge trains running between New York City and New England could save 150 miles. The amendment was approved 48-45. *(Vote 269, p. 42-S)*

House Action

House approval of S 2788 came on the third day the ConRail authorization measure had been debated on the House floor. Approval of the rule providing for the bill's consideration came Oct. 6. General debate was on Oct. 11.

With only minutes remaining in the 95th Congress, the measure's backers explained to their House colleagues that any changes in the bill likely would result in the bill dying in the Senate and ConRail being denied the additional funding.

Nonetheless, two amendments subsequently were offered to the bill on the floor. But neither was approved.

Defeated on a standing vote of 29-58 was an amendment by Toby Moffett, D-Conn., to provide only a $700 million subsidy for ConRail.

Ruled out of order was an amendment by John M. Murphy, D-N.Y., proposing to equalize railroad freight rates within ports. Rep. Barbara A. Mikulski, D-Md., successfully argued that the Murphy amendment was not germane to the ConRail authorization bill.

The House then passed the bill by voice votes without amendment, clearing the bill for the president. ▮

Public Broadcasting

Congress Oct. 15 sent to the president legislation to reorganize the nation's public broadcasting system. The legislation had been proposed by President Carter in October 1977.

The bill (HR 12605) continued multiple-year advance funding for public radio and television, increased the system's accountability to the public and realigned the roles of the major public broadcasting entities.

The bill did not permit public stations to begin editorializing. This had been approved by the House, but subsequently was dropped by House and Senate conferees in drafting the final version of the bill.

As approved, the legislation represented a compromise between the goals set out for the public broadcasting system by President Carter and an alternative drafted in Congress.

Final Provisions

As cleared by Congress, HR 12605 (PL 95-567):

- Authorized $40 million for each of fiscal years 1979-81 for the planning and construction of public telecommunications facilities.

- Transferred administration of the facilities program from the Health, Education and Welfare Department to the Commerce Department.
- Extended eligibility for the planning and construction grants to states, localities and non-profit educational organizations, so long as they were engaged in "public telecommunications" activities.
- Required that at least 75 percent of the grants for facilities be made available to areas not already receiving public broadcast service.
- Required that a "substantial amount" of the facilities grants be available for the expansion of public radio.
- Authorized $1 million annually for fiscal years 1979-81 for nonbroadcast public telecommunications "demonstration" projects, in which public broadcasters were to experiment with new technologies and services.
- Clarified the role of the Corporation for Public Broadcasting (CPB) in the public system. The CPB was the independent, non-profit body created by the Public Broadcasting Act of 1967 to disburse the system's federal funds.
- Authorized for the public system $180 million for fiscal 1981, $200 million for 1982 and $220 million for 1983.
- Required the public system to raise $2 for every $1 in federal funds that it received. Under existing law, the system was required to raise $2.50 for every federal dollar.
- Required the public broadcasting system, in consultation with the General Accounting Office, to institute a uniform system of accounting.

Background

Carter introduced legislation in October 1977 that he said was intended to provide public broadcasting with greater financial stability, insulate it from possible political interference, grant it greater editorial independence and streamline its operations. *(1977 Almanac p. 58-E)*

The bill was greeted with skepticism on Capitol Hill, however. "There are major discrepancies between the rhetoric of the presidential message and the actual provisions of the bill," commented a memo prepared by the staff of the House Communications Subcommittee.

In the months that followed, public broadcasters, congressional aides and White House staffers attempted to work together to revise the Carter bill's provisions.

On April 12, however, House Communications Chairman Lionel Van Deerlin, D-Calif., and Senate Communications Chairman Ernest F. Hollings, D-S.C., introduced their own legislation (HR 12021, S 2883), which differed from the Carter approach in a number of important aspects.

The bill was "designed to build upon the initiative of the president," explained Hollings at the time.

The Hollings-Van Deerlin measure "was drafted hastily," an administration aide later remarked. "They said they wanted to work together with us, but they gave us absolutely no notice they were preparing their own bill," the aide added.

In many ways, the bills are similar, the aide conceded. "Both bills want public broadcasters to have strong equal employment opportunity obligations, to meet in the 'sunshine,' and to have fiscal accountability to the public and to Congress."

The Hollings-Van Deerlin bill, however, dropped administration proposals requiring the Corporation for Public Broadcasting (CPB) to set aside 25 percent of the system's federal funds for a "national programming fund," and allowing certain public broadcasting stations to editorialize and endorse political candidates.

The Hollings-Van Deerlin bill permitted CPB to fund individual programs; the administration proposed to bar CPB from making programming decisions and, instead, wanted it restricted to giving non-specific "block-grants" to production groups, which would in turn be free to determine the specific programs they would produce.

A controversial provision in the Hollings-Van Deerlin legislation not contained in the administration version required free access to the public network's program distribution service by independent producers. Independent programmers had accused public stations of attempting to monopolize the available production money and programming time.

Lawrence Grossman, president of the Public Broadcasting Service, which represented the system's television stations, charged that the provision would open public broadcasting to pornography and other undesirable programs.

Committee Action

Both the House and Senate committees acted quickly in order to complete work on the legislation by the May 15 deadline for authorization bills.

During markup, a number of changes were made in both bills to increase the system's public accountability, give it greater editorial freedom and increase its financial stability. A number of provisions were added that had been proposed earlier by Carter but left out of the Hollings-Van Deerlin bill. *(Demands for greater accountability, box, next page)*

Both bills provided public broadcasting with authorizations for federal funding for three more years — through 1983. The president had requested authorizations through 1985. The legislation followed the president's lead in imposing on the public broadcasting system strong equal employment obligations and requirements that it hold open board meetings and be more fiscally accountable.

Though the president had requested that the legislation permit public stations to editorialize, only the House bill did so. Neither bill, however, set aside 25 percent of the system's federal funds for a "national programming fund" or permitted public stations to endorse political candidates, as Carter also had requested.

The House panel also trimmed back the role the Corporation for Public Broadcasting (CPB) could play in funding individual programs, while the Senate committee's bill did not. The administration had asked that the role of the CPB — the independent, non-profit body created by the Public Broadcasting Act of 1967 to disburse the funds — be cut back in order to better insulate the system from potential political pressure from Congress or the executive.

Both House and Senate committees urged public broadcasting to encourage the production of programming by independent producers. During hearings on the legislation, independents had accused public stations of attempting to monopolize the available production money and programming time.

Senate

S 2883 was reported by the Senate Commerce Committee (S Rept 95-858) May 15 by unanimous voice vote.

In its report, the committee criticized public broadcasting for insufficient employment of minorities and wom-

Tighter Accountability of Public Broadcasting Sought

The public broadcasting legislation imposed tighter public accountability requirements both on individual stations and on the major public broadcasting administrative entities such as the Public Broadcasting Service (PBS), the Corporation for Public Broadcasting (CPB) and National Public Radio (NPR).

The proposed requirements resulted from growing congressional dissatisfaction with existing public broadcasting accountability and a suspicion that federal funds were not being wisely spent.

Many public stations, for example, had no provision for permitting members of the public to attend board meetings, while other federally funded agencies were required to hold their meetings in public under the federal "sunshine" law.

"I don't think the people in public broadcasting understand yet that, when you get public funds, the public comes along with them," commented Rep. Barbara A. Mikulski, D-Md.

As a result of such suspicions and preliminary findings, both House and Senate Communications Subcommittees in late 1977 requested the General Accounting Office (GAO) to 1) review public broadcasting's administrative overhead costs; 2) audit CPB, PBS, NPR and a number of public stations, and 3) review the adequacy of the public system's own auditing procedures.

The GAO findings, though never made public, raised a number of eyebrows on Capitol Hill. Among its conclusions were:

- Of 281 audits of public stations conducted by CPB from fiscal 1975 through fiscal 1977, CPB classified 120 stations as having "serious" discrepancies. The most commonly cited problem was "inadequate accounting for non-federal contributions," while the second most commonly cited problem was "inadequate accounting for grant expenditures." As of Sept. 30, 1977, GAO found that 28 of 175 public television stations and 50 of 191 public radio stations had never been audited by CPB. The existing public broadcasting system was 10 years old in November 1977.
- The CPB "for several years . . . carried forward an excess of assets over liabilities, called 'net assets.' " For 1977, for example, CPB carried forward from 1976 over $8.2 million that was "not budgeted for specific projects." According to GAO, CPB's director of budget "stated that since CPB does not have to return unexpended balances to the Treasury, the department heads have time for thoughtful reflection regarding the spending of federally appropriated funds."
- Federal funds had been disbursed to the CPB on a "lump sum" basis each year. CPT had then invested this money in federal securities in order to earn interest while waiting to spend the money. Thus, "the federal government is paying interest on borrowed money to give CPB its appropriations on a lump-sum basis and paying CPB interest on its investments in federal government securities." GAO estimated that paying CPB on a monthly basis could have saved the federal government $2.9 million during fiscal 1977 in excess borrowing costs and interest payments.
- KCET, the Los Angeles public television station, listed depreciation expenses of $32,000 for the use of fully depreciated equipment and $491,000 "in questionable or unallowable expenditures.... KCET disagreed with the findings."
- WNET, the New York public television station, in 1976 spent $511,000 in direct federal grants for fund-raising appeals and to upgrade the quality of on-air promotional breaks. Asked GAO: "How does the expenditure of [these grants] for auctions and pledge nights relate to educational television and radio programming?"
- Because each federal dollar must be matched by $2.50 in locally raised money, non-federal contributions must be carefully accounted for, GAO stated. Yet a CPB audit of WETA, the Washington, D.C., public station, showed that the station had counted as local contributions $567,000 in advertising spent by the Atlantic Richfield Co. to promote a series of programs it helped underwrite. In each ad, Atlantic Richfield was prominently mentioned as a sponsor of the series, the GAO report noted.
- From 1972 through 1976, CPB spent $91,500 for the services of professional executive search organizations to help it fill six executive positions. In its search for a new president in 1978, CPB had spent $20,600 for an outside consultant and clerical help as of June 1.

en, poor fiscal management, inadequate public accountability, failure to use independent producers, excessive bureaucracy and increased centralization of power in the Public Broadcasting Service (PBS), the public system's television arm.

"Now is the time for public broadcasting to 'get its house in order' so that it can achieve the prominence envisioned for it in 1967," the report stated.

The committee held out increased federal funding in the system's next authorization bill as an incentive for improvement.

As reported, S 2883:

- Authorized $180 million for fiscal 1981 and $200 million annually for 1982 and 1983 for the CPB, to be disbursed by the Treasury on a quarterly basis. The bill also authorized $40 million annually for 1979 through 1981 for the purchase of public telecommunications facilities and equipment for the dissemination of educational and cultural programming by both broadcast and non-broadcast technologies, and $1 million for 1979 for telecommunications demonstration projects. Responsibility for administering facilities grants was transferred from the HEW Department to Commerce.
- Required the system to raise $2.25 in non-federal money for every dollar in federal funds. Under existing law the ratio was $2.50 for every federal dollar.
- Required HEW to enforce equal employment opportunities in public broadcasting. No agency was responsible under existing law.
- Limited CPB overhead costs to 5 percent of total federal funds appropriated.

● Required public broadcasting entities to hold open board meetings in most cases and to make financial reports and audits available to the public.

House

As reported (H Rept 95-1178) by the House Commerce Committee May 15, the companion bill (HR 12605) was similar to the Senate committee's version except that it:

● Authorized $220 million for 1983 for CPB.

● Required the system to raise $2 for every federal dollar.

● Limited public broadcasting executives' salaries to that of a Cabinet officer's.

● Required CPB to spend a "significant portion" of the federal funds on programming, to encourage independent program production, and to use panels of outside experts to review programming proposals "to the maximum extent possible."

● Permitted public stations to editorialize.

Floor Action

House

The House passed HR 12605 July 10 by voice vote.

The legislation was brought to the floor under a suspension of the rules procedure, which generally is reserved for non-controversial bills. Under a suspension, a two-thirds vote is needed for passage and floor amendments are not permitted.

The suspension was successful despite opposition to the Commerce Committee's bill by the Public Broadcasting Service (PBS), the public system's television arm.

PBS's board of directors had adopted a resolution June 28 urging modifications in the legislation. The resolution was adopted despite the urgings of a number of PBS member stations that the reorganization legislation be opposed altogether.

Though other public broadcasting groups supported the legislation, PBS was opposed to provisions requiring public stations to certify their compliance with equal employment opportunity laws; instituting uniform accounting procedures throughout the system; establishing standards for the disbursement of federal funds; requiring stations to make public their board meetings, financial reports and audits; and limiting the salaries of top public broadcasting executives to that of a Cabinet officer's.

During House debate, a number of representatives argued that the measure, because of its controversial nature, should have been brought to the floor under the regular rules and therefore open to amendment.

"Not necessarily on the merits of the legislation, but because it is being brought up under suspension of the rules, I will vote against the legislation," remarked Samuel L. Devine, R-Ohio.

"Anything as important and as widespread and having such an impact on the telecommunications media" should have been brought up under regular procedures, Devine added.

The bill's backers, however, defended both the procedure chosen for the bill's consideration and the bill itself.

"With the acceptance of federal funds, there are always federal requirements and guidelines to ensure proper use of the taxpayer's funds," stated W. Henson Moore, R-La. If public broadcasting opposed controls on the use of federal funds, "then it should no longer seek federal funds."

Despite the opposition expressed to the bill, it carried by a voice vote; a recorded vote was not demanded.

Senate

The Senate passed the bill Sept. 19 by voice vote with amendments.

Attempts to assert additional federal controls on the public broadcasting system's operations were turned back by the Senate.

However, some senators warned they would strongly oppose any attempt to retain in the final version a provision in the House-passed version repealing an existing restriction barring certain public television and radio stations from editorializing.

During Senate action, only minor changes were made in the bill as approved by the Senate Commerce Committee.

Two substantive amendments were adopted, both by voice votes: an amendment by Jacob K. Javits, R-N.Y., to permit individual stations, because of organizational differences, to modify the uniform set of accounting principles mandated by the bill; and an amendment by Harrison Schmitt, R-N.M., requiring the Commerce Department's National Telecommunications and Information Administration to report annually to Congress on its communications activities.

The Senate defeated two amendments that would have increased the degree of federal control over public broadcasting.

An amendment offered by Robert P. Griffin, R-Mich., to fund public broadcasting for only year at a time, was defeated by a vote of 20-63. *(Vote 375, p. 56-S)*

Under the proposed reorganization legislation, public broadcasting funding was authorized for three years. Griffin said his amendment was needed to ensure proper congressional oversight of the system and proper balance in the system's programming.

Also defeated, by a vote of 33-48, was an amendment by James A. McClure, R-Idaho, contained in the House revision that would have limited the salaries of public broadcasting executives to that of a Cabinet-level officer's. *(Vote 376, p. 56-S)*

McClure's initial refusal to agree to a time limitation for debating the public broadcasting legislation had kept Majority Leader Robert C. Byrd, D-W.Va., from scheduling the bill for two and a half months — from late June until mid-September.

Because of several senators' strong opposition to the provision permitting certain public stations to editorialize, it was evident that the Senate would not accept the provision in conference.

"This is a completely inappropriate authority for public broadcasting, and we shall do everything we can to assure that the House position does not prevail on this issue," Schmitt said. "I have a distinct impression that the conferees on the Senate side feel strongly enough on this issue that the House, in fact, will not prevail."

No one contradicted Schmitt's statement.

A number of amendments proposed on the Senate floor subsequently were withdrawn after Hollings, the bill's floor manager, assured senators that their concerns would be addressed next year. Among them were:

● An amendment by Strom Thurmond, R-S.C., that would have prohibited the broadcast of "nudity, obscenity, explicit sexual activity, gross physical violence or morbid torture."

- An amendment by William Proxmire, D-Wis., that would have repealed the fairness doctrine and the equal time rule, under which broadcast stations were required to provide time for the discussion of opposing viewpoints on controversial issues and to give all candidates for a given public office the same opportunity to present their views.
- An amendment by Javits and Alan Cranston, D-Calif., to provide equal employment opportunity in public broadcasting to handicapped persons.
- An amendment by Barry Goldwater, R-Ariz., designed to insulate the public broadcasting system from possible manipulation by the White House.

Conference Action

The conference report (H Rept 95-1774) on HR 12605 was filed Oct. 12.

House and Senate conferees agreed to accept many of the strong public accountability requirements contained in the House-passed bill.

Conferees dropped, however, several of the more controversial aspects of that version. Perhaps the most controversial provision concerned public stations' authority to editorialize. The provision was strongly opposed by several senators during the Senate's debate.

Also deleted from the bill was a House-passed provision that would have required the CPB to judge a public television station's responsiveness to its community, innovativeness, administrative efficiency, reliance on volunteer help and minority employment record in determining its share of federal funds.

In their written report, conferees instructed the public broadcasting system to spend a greater proportion of its funds on programming. The system had come under criticism for administrative waste. Conferees also instructed the system to spend a "substantial amount" of its programming funds on shows by independent program producers.

Conferees warned the system not to become a centralized "fourth network." The growing role in the system's program selection and scheduling assumed by the Public Broadcasting Service, the system's television arm, might harm local stations' ability to serve their local communities, the conference report stated.

Final Action

The conference report was approved routinely by the House Oct. 13 by voice vote and by the Senate Oct. 15 by voice vote. The president signed the bill Nov. 2. ▮

Congress Clears Airline Deregulation Bill

Legislation that eventually would end most federal regulation of the commercial passenger airline industry was cleared by Congress on Oct. 15.

The legislation (S 2493 — PL 95-504) would abolish the Civil Aeronautics Board — the independent agency that regulated the airline companies — by 1985 unless Congress acted to extend it.

A top priority of the Carter administration, the legislation was intended to gradually increase marketplace competition in the passenger airline industry by phasing out federal controls over a seven-year period. Substantially lower fares were expected as a result of the new pro-competition policies.

Carter saw the bill as a key component of his attack on inflation and government red tape. Though the airline measure affected only a very small segment of the nation's economy, it was expected to pave the way toward further administration attempts to cut down on government regulation of business in the next Congress.

'Quick Hit'

Even before Jimmy Carter was sworn in as president in January 1977, his advisers were urging him to declare his support for airline deregulation legislation. Because the issue already had been the subject of extensive hearings in the previous Congress, his aides reasoned, he could score a 'quick hit' — an early legislative victory — by declaring his support for a bill that already was well on its way toward enactment.

Carter's expected easy victory, however, did not materialize. It took most of 1977 for the bill to get out of the Senate Commerce Committee, and 10 weeks for companion legislation to be cleared by the House Public Works Aviation Subcommittee.

But both houses overwhelmingly approved the legislation once the bills got to the floor.

The Senate passed its deregulation bill 83-9 in April. The House bill was passed Sept. 21 by a vote of 363-8.

As cleared for the president, S 2493 instructed the Civil Aeronautics Board (CAB) to stress competition in its regulatory decisions, and ordered it to expedite and simplify its procedures. The bill facilitated the offering of new services and routes by the airline companies, and granted them a measure of flexibility in raising and lowering their fares.

Small communities were given a guarantee that existing levels of air service would be continued for a 10-year period. And airline employees were made eligible for compensation if they lost their jobs, had their wages cut or were forced to relocate due to increased industry competition brought on by enactment of the deregulation legislation.

Carter Goals

As outlined by President Carter in early 1977, the administration sought as essential deregulation ingredients an automatic route entry program, a program to grant unused route authority to air carriers willing to serve those routes, price flexibility and a presumption that competition was in the public interest.

Measured by those standards, Congress gave Carter all he wanted in a deregulation bill. The end product, however, did not reveal the struggles along the way.

Though some airline companies favored deregulation, most strongly opposed it. So did the airline labor unions, which feared deregulation would lead to job losses as the strongest companies drove the smaller ones out of business. And small communities feared that the increased competition would result in service losses as the airlines concentrated on the more lucrative major markets.

In the House, a coalition of Republicans and conservative Democrats kept the deregulation bill boxed up in the Public Works Aviation Subcommittee for weeks while a fight raged over the automatic market entry and unused route authority provisions.

The subcommittee's markup lasted seven weeks while the coalition attempted to weaken or delete the programs and the administration fought to preserve them. The administration finally settled for watered down programs and said it would seek to strengthen them in conference with the Senate. To a great extent, the administration strategy succeeded.

While the House version of the bill was weaker, its supporters had argued that it actually was a stronger deregulation measure because it provided for the abolition of the CAB by 1982 unless Congress acted to extend it.

Supporters of stronger deregulation legislation felt the claim had a hollow ring, however, since it was thought likely that, when the time came, Congress would renew the agency's charter.

As a result, the House-Senate conference version of the bill went far toward making abolition of the CAB more likely. By gradually phasing out the agency's powers over a seven-year period, and establishing precise guidelines for the transfer to other agencies of CAB regulatory functions conferees said should be continued, the bill made it easier to terminate the CAB.

Noise Bill Linkage

At the same time that many airline companies were fighting deregulation, they also were pressuring Congress for legislation to subsidize mandatory airline noise abatement efforts. Key members of the House Public Works Committee responded by insisting on approval of the subsidy as a *quid pro quo* for approval of the deregulation measure.

Noise control legislation originally was proposed by the Ford administration after the Federal Aviation Administration retroactively imposed noise standards on aircraft designed before 1969 and manufactured before 1975.

The airlines were given until 1985 to comply with the standards. As drafted by House Public Works, the noise bill (HR 8729) would have funneled an estimated $3 billion to $4 billion in federal ticket and freight tax funds to the airline companies to help them comply with the 1985 standard.

The linkage between the two bills continued to dog the deregulation bill throughout the session as the noise bill's high price tag made it more and more controversial.

The linkage ended only on the last day of the session, when —to the immense relief of deregulation advocates — the House did not wait for the noise bill to pass before taking up and clearing the deregulation measure. Noise bill opponents then blocked House floor consideration of the noise bill, and that measure died when Congress adjourned. *(Legislative action, p. 504)*

Immediate Effect

"For the first time in decades, we have deregulated a major industry," President Carter said in signing the deregulation legislation Oct. 24. But the new competition in the airline industry was felt even before the new law went into effect.

Under pioneering Chairman Alfred Kahn, the CAB had acted administratively to inject an experimental dose of competition into the commercial passenger airline industry on a limited basis. Under the new competitive policy, both airline ridership and company profits had soared. The airline companies began preparing strategies to capitalize on the new industry environment.

Four days before the deregulation bill was to become law, a line began to form outside the Washington offices of the CAB. Soon, about 30 airline company representatives were standing in the line, patiently waiting for Carter to sign the bill so that they could begin filing for new routes under the liberalized conditions set by PL 95-504.

On Nov. 13 the CAB issued its first decision, awarding 248 new routes to 22 airlines. The routes were those on which fewer than two other companies had been providing a minimum level of service. Of the 22 airlines, six were intrastate carriers receiving their first interstate route awards. State-regulated carriers awarded interstate routes became subject solely to the new law.

At the same time, the CAB permitted nine airlines to retain 52 routes they were authorized to serve, but on which they were not actually operating plane service. Under the new law, the airlines were given 45 days to begin flying on the new routes and 30 days to serve routes they already were authorized to serve. If the companies did not begin service within the designated period of time, the routes were to become eligible for new applicants.

Major Provisions

As signed into law, S 2493:

- Instructed the CAB to 1) place "maximum reliance" on competition in its regulation of interstate airline passenger service, so long as it continued to ensure the safety of air travel; 2) preserve service to small communities and rural areas, and 3) prevent anti-competitive practices.
- Exempted interstate airlines from state regulation of rates and routes.
- Required the CAB and the Transportation Department to recommend to Congress by Jan. 1, 1980, whether the states should be required to share the cost of federal subsidies intended to preserve local air service.
- Required the Transportation Department to report annually to Congress and the CAB on its implementation of airline deregulation under S 2493.
- Required the CAB to report to Congress by May 1, 1979, on whether airlines should be permitted to sell tours to the public and to own and operate travel agencies.
- Set deadlines for many types of CAB actions, and ordered the CAB to simplify and speed up many of its procedures.
- Ordered the CAB to authorize new services that were "consistent with the public convenience and necessity."
- Permitted any carrier with planes carrying 30 or more passengers to provide through-baggage and through-ticketing services.
- Ordered the CAB to grant operating rights to any air carrier seeking to serve a route on which only one other carrier was actually providing service and on which other carriers were authorized to serve, but were not actually providing a specified minimum level of service.
- If two or more airlines were actually providing service on such a route, the CAB was required to determine that granting additional route authority was "consistent with the public convenience and necessity" before permitting additional carriers to serve that route.

An airline not providing the specified minimum level of service on a route could begin providing such service and retain its authority to serve that route. Otherwise, the CAB was required to revoke such unused authority.

• Provided for an automatic market entry program, whereby airlines could begin service on one additional route each year during the period 1979-81 without formal CAB approval. Each carrier also was permitted to protect one of its existing routes each year by designating it as not eligible for automatic market entry by another carrier.

• Required an airline company to give the CAB notice of its intent to suspend or reduce service.

• Authorized the CAB to order an airline to continue to provide "essential air transportation service," and, for a 10-year period, to provide subsidies or seek other willing carriers in order to assure the continuation of essential service.

• Required the CAB to determine, within one year of the legislation's enactment, what it considered to be "essential air transportation" for each point served at the time of enactment. The board was authorized to re-evaluate and adjust, after consultation with local officials, what it considered as constituting essential air service in the future.

• Provided that, after Jan. 1, 1983, the amount of the subsidy paid an airline company based on its carriage of U.S. mail had to take into consideration the company's total revenues. The subsidy program was operated by the CAB.

• Required the CAB to impose rules and requirements on charter airlines that were no more rigid than those it imposed on other classes of air carriers.

• Required commuter aircraft to conform to the safety requirements imposed on larger passenger aircraft "to the maximum feasible extent."

• Exempted from most CAB regulation commuter aircraft weighing less than 18,000 pounds and carrying fewer than 56 passengers. (The Federal Aviation Administration — and not the CAB — was charged with regulating airline safety under existing law.)

• Authorized the CAB to exempt certain classes of service from its regulatory authority as it saw fit.

• Required CAB approval of airline consolidations, mergers, purchases, leases, operating contracts and acquisitions. The burden of proving the anti-competitive effects of such actions was placed on the party challenging an action. Airline company acquisitions by non-airline companies were exempted from the CAB's authority.

• Required the CAB to approve all inter-company agreements affecting air transportation, and ordered the CAB not to approve any agreement reducing competition unless it found that the agreement served a "serious transportation need" or provided "an important public benefit."

• Prohibited the CAB from renewing the airline mutual aid pact unless the benefits it provided an airline company closed down by a labor strike did not exceed more than 60 percent of the company's direct operating expenses incurred during the strike. Pact members also were required to agree to submit issues causing a strike to binding arbitration if the striking employees requested binding arbitration.

• Limited the president's ability to disapprove CAB recommendations concerning international route awards. Under the legislation, the president could disapprove the CAB's recommendation solely on the basis of "foreign relations or national defense considerations."

• Permitted carriers to lower rates 50 percent below or 5 percent above the "standard industry fare" without prior CAB approval. The standard industry fare was defined as the fare in effect on July 1, 1977, subject to semi-annual CAB review. The CAB still was authorized to disallow a fare if it considered it to be predatory.

• Authorized the CAB, the Transportation Department and the Treasury Department to withhold from public disclosure, on request of any individual, information contained in any document or application given the government that might prejudice the U.S. position in any international air negotiations.

• Required the CAB to report to Congress by Jan. 1, 1984, on the implementation of deregulation, and whether the board should be abolished.

• Provided that, unless Congress acted to extend it, the board's authority over domestic routes would end Dec. 31, 1981; that its authority over domestic rates and fares, mergers and acquisitions would expire Jan. 1, 1983, and that the board would be abolished on Jan. 1, 1985. The board's local service subsidy program was to be transferred to the Transportation Department. Its foreign air transportation authority was to be transferred to the Justice and Transportation Departments. Its mail subsidy program was to be transferred to the U.S. Postal Service.

• Made persons employed by an air carrier for at least four years eligible for compensation for a maximum of six years if they lost their jobs, had their wages cut or were forced to relocate due to increased airline industry competition brought on by enactment of the deregulation bill.

• Made commuter and intrastate air carriers eligible for the existing federal loan guarantee program, and extended the program for five years.

Background

Though the Carter administration did not submit its own airline deregulation legislation in 1977, the airline industry became the first target of the White House regulatory reform drive Carter had promised during his campaign for the presidency.

Despite the strong support deregulation received from the White House, however, getting a bill through Congress proved to be an arduous task.

The Senate Commerce Committee held 14 days of hearings in March and April 1977 on two proposed reform bills (S 689, S 292), but the House Public Works and Transportation Aviation Subcommittee gave only sporadic attention to deregulation, concentrating instead on a bill (HR 8729) to reduce aircraft noise.

In June 1977, Senate committee staffers unveiled a compromise deregulation bill they had drafted with the help of key committee members.

After a painful markup spanning 20 sessions, the committee Reported S 2493 on Feb. 6.

Though its critics — primarily representatives of the airline industry and airline labor unions — said the bill would result in service cuts and job losses, United, Southwest, Hughes Airwest, Frontier and other smaller and regional airlines supported a deregulation measure.

At the same time, advocates of a stronger bill, including administration spokesmen, were disappointed at the number of compromises needed to win enough votes to get a bill out of committee. But they generally agreed they could support the measure as reported.

Senate Committee Action

S 2493 was approved by a vote of 11-2 Oct. 27, 1977, and reported Feb. 6 by the Senate Commerce Committee (S Rept. 95-631). Three absent members later cast their votes, making the final tally 13-3.

S 2493 attempted, according to the committee majority, "to provide the domestic air transportation industry with the same competitive incentives which face most other American industries."

In 1898, the report noted, President McKinley awarded a $50,000 federal grant to Samuel P. Langley to achieve the first manned flight by a craft that was heavier than air. Langley earlier had achieved the first unmanned flight. Instead of Langley, however, the first manned flight was made by the Wright brothers, "two unsubsidized mechanical tinkerers," in 1903.

"The lesson of Kitty Hawk" the report concluded, "is that air transportation will be more likely to expand and prosper if the heavy hand of CAB economic regulation is removed from the creative hand of carrier management."

To make the airline industry more competitive, the committee proposed a multifaceted approach, with provisions to require the Civil Aeronautics Board (CAB) to promote industry competition; speed up its decisions; permit air carriers, within limits, to change their fares and serve new routes without CAB approval; provide subsidies to protect "essential" air service to small communities; and create a new class of commuter-type air service practically free of all government regulation. The bill also authorized the secretary of labor to establish a fund to aid airline employees who might become unemployed by the increased industry competition resulting from enactment of the legislation.

The bill, called the Air Transportation Regulatory Reform Act of 1978, was proposed as a series of amendments to the Federal Aviation Act of 1958 (PL 85-726).

Major Provisions

CAB Policy. S 2493 changed the declaration of policy guiding the CAB from one of promoting and protecting the nation's air transportation system to one of: increasing reliance on competition; facilitating entry into the marketplace by new air carriers; preventing anticompetitive and monopolistic industry practices; and maintaining regular air service to small and isolated communities.

Other provisions of the bill were designed to speed up CAB actions; broaden the CAB's authority to prevent potentially anticompetitive agreements, mergers and other actions; and increase the board's discretion to grant exemptions from CAB regulation.

CAB Certification. The legislation enabled the CAB to issue certificates authorizing an air carrier to serve a particular route if the service was "consistent with the public convenience and necessity." Further, the board was instructed that innovative, more efficient, less monopolistic and cheaper service all were "consistent with the public convenience and necessity."

Under current law, the CAB was authorized to certify a particular service only if it was "required" by public convenience and necessity. According to the committee report, the CAB used its discretion under the law "both to prevent any significant entry into the industry by new firms and to frustrate the expansion of existing firms." Between 1950 and 1974, the report stated, the CAB received 79 applications from new firms interested in serving domestic air routes, yet none was granted.

Dormant Authority. The CAB was required under S 2493 to approve within 90 days an application to serve a requested route if 1) only one firm currently was providing regular service on that route, 2) another carrier was authorized to regularly serve the same route, but had not done so for six of the past 12 months, and 3) the carrier's application otherwise met CAB requirements.

The legislation also permitted the CAB to restrict or revoke a carrier's authorization to serve a particular route if the carrier wasn't providing regular service on that route and if another airline applied to serve it.

Under current law, the committee report noted, carriers routinely failed to serve some routes for which they were authorized, but which were served by another airline. These same carriers, however, routinely — and successfully — intervened before the CAB to oppose the authorization of new applicants for those same routes.

Automatic Market Entry. The legislation authorized CAB-certified air carriers, charter airlines, certain Alaskan carriers and major state-regulated (intrastate) airlines to add one additional air route in each of 1979 and 1980, and two additional ones in 1981 and every year thereafter, for a period of 18 months without formal CAB authorization. At the end of the 18-month period, the CAB would be required to permanently authorize service on the additional routes if the carriers had complied with CAB regulations.

Carriers were permitted to choose three routes annually in 1979-81, two routes in 1982 and one in 1983 which would be protected from automatic entry. Federally subsidized carriers were afforded somewhat less protection from automatic entry competition from other carriers, while commuter-type carriers were offered more protection. If the program were found to be causing "substantial public harm," the CAB was authorized to modify the automatic entry program, subject to a veto by either house of Congress.

The automatic entry provision was termed "assuredly modest" by the committee, and was needed, it said, "to provide a meaningful threat of entry to insure that carriers will not fail to provide innovative or lower priced service in those markets in which it is economically feasible."

Charters. The bill preserved the existing limit of 2 per cent of total miles flown on regularly scheduled flights on the maximum number of charter flight miles the major air carriers could fly each year. However, the limit was increased to 5 per cent for smaller carriers and to 10 per cent for regional airlines.

Under a separate provision, carriers certified by the CAB to provide regularly scheduled service were permitted, following a five-year period beginning Jan. 1, 1979, to also be certified as charter airlines and thereby have unlimited charter authority. The legislation instructed the CAB to act to increase the availability of charter flights to the public.

Small Community Service. To ensure that airline deregulation did not result in the loss of service for small communities and isolated areas, the legislation phased out over seven years the current system of airline subsidies based on mail deliveries. This was replaced with a subsidy program designed expressly to preserve "essential air transportation" as determined by the CAB.

Local Air Transportation. The bill provided for CAB certification of a new class of service subject only to the requirement that the aircraft providing the service had no more than 36 seats and that the carrier be "fit, willing and able" to provide the service. The provision permitted commuter-type airlines — currently regulated by the states — to continue to operate in an essentially unregulated manner and still be eligible for the benefits of federal certification such as federal loan guarantees and the ability to write tickets and route baggage using the entire federally certified system.

Fares. The legislation established a zone of "reasonable and just" charges within which a carrier was free to set its fares without prior CAB approval. The zone ranged from 5 per cent above to 35 per cent below the "standard industry fare." This was defined as the fare in effect for a particular service on July 1, 1977, subject to semi-annual CAB adjustment.

Under existing law the CAB had authority to review fares, disallow "unlawful" ones and dictate "lawful" tariffs in their place. The board still could review fares, but was permitted to set only maximum and minimum fare levels in place of fares it disallowed.

Employee Protection. The bill made persons employed by an air carrier for at least four years eligible for compensation for a maximum of three years if they lost their jobs, had their wages cut or were forced to relocate due to increased airline industry competition brought on by enactment of the legislation.

Additional, Minority Views

Five senators filed additional views to the report on S 2493, while three senators expressed dissenting views. Additional views were filed by John C. Danforth (R Mo.), Wendell H. Ford (D Ky.), Robert P. Griffin (R Mich.), Harrison Schmitt (R N.M.) and Edward Zorinsky (D Neb.). Of those with additional views, all voted to favorably report the bill except Zorinsky, who voted "present."

In dissenting views, Sens. Daniel K. Inouye (D Hawaii) and John Melcher (D Mont.) said they voted against S 2493 because of the automatic market entry provisions; Barry Goldwater (R Ariz.) objected to several other provisions as well.

All three senators said the market entry program was likely to cause economic harm to smaller carriers and result in a reduction of service to smaller communities, rather than produce lower air fares through competition.

"The proposed fare flexibility provisions, when added to automatic entry," Inouye said, "would permit the financially stronger carriers to drive the weaker carriers out of the competitive markets. . . . The ultimate result would be monopoly or oligopoly in air transportation simply because there would be no restraint on the growth of the larger carriers."

Senate Floor Action

The Senate passed S 2493 April 19 by a vote of 83-9. *(Vote 127, p. 22-S)*

Senate approval provided a significant victory for the president as well as a rare opportunity for Carter administration officials and senators to credit the vote to close cooperation between the executive and legislative branches. The sole major change made in the Senate further strengthened the deregulation measure.

"This was a fantastic victory for both the Congress and the administration," commented Terrence L. Bracy, Transportation Department assistant secretary for governmental affairs, after the vote.

Sen. Edward M. Kennedy, D-Mass., a key advocate of deregulation who often had been left out of Carter administration strategy decisions in the past, also lauded the "close executive-congressional cooperation on the bill."

During floor debate, senators beat back by large margins a number of attempts to weaken the bill's controversial automatic entry and labor protection provisions.

And the Senate accepted, by a margin of three to one, an amendment to strengthen the deregulation provisions.

"A lot of people were committed to the principles of the bill," stated Howard W. Cannon, D-Nev., chairman of the Senate Commerce Aviation Subcommittee, in noting the wide support for S 2493.

The active lobbying of the airline industry against the bill may actually have worked to the bill's advantage, Cannon suggested. "I think some of the airlines were not as reasonable as they could have been," he said after the vote.

Burden of Proof

The most far reaching amendment accepted on the Senate floor was offered by Kennedy.

Deregulation legislation introduced by Kennedy and Cannon in 1977 provided that an application for a new air transportation service should be presumed by the CAB to be "consistent with the public convenience and necessity" unless an opponent of the application could prove that it wasn't.

But during markup the committee shifted the burden to the applicant. Under S 2493 as approved by the committee, a new application was presumed not to be in the public interest unless the applicant could prove that it was.

The Kennedy amendment proposed reversing the Commerce Committee position and once more shifting the burden of proof to an opponent of the application.

Supporters of the amendment argued that it would provide new applicants with a procedural advantage before the CAB and would provide an additional spur to competition. The opponents argued that it would bring on too much competition, too quickly. The Carter administration supported the amendment.

The amendment passed, 69-23. *(Vote 125, p. 22-S)*

Other amendments adopted on the floor included:

- A Cannon amendment authorizing the secretary of labor to determine the level of compensation given airline employees harmed by airline deregulation.
- A Cannon amendment to enlarge the bill's "zone of reasonable and just" charges within which airlines could alter their fares without prior CAB approval. Under the committee bill, the zone ranged from 5 percent above to 35 percent below the "standard industry fare" as defined in the bill. The Cannon amendment permitted fares to drop as low as 50 percent below the standard industry fare and still remain within the zone. The amendment was needed, Cannon said, because the CAB, under reform advocate Alfred Kahn as chairman, already was approving certain discount fares of up to 50 percent.

Both Cannon amendments were passed by voice vote.

Automatic Entry

George McGovern, D-S.D., who said the bill, if enacted, might result in service losses rather than gains, offered two amendments he said would help preserve the existing services. Both were resoundingly defeated.

One of the amendments would have provided for a more modest program of automatic entry. Cannon argued that the result would have been to "eliminate automatic market entry from the bill and defeat the purpose of this legislation." The administration opposed the amendment, which was defeated 21-72. *(Vote 120, p. 22-S)*

A second amendment would have set minimum standards for "essential air transportation" in the event that an airline canceled an "essential" service and the CAB subsidized a second airline to provide substitute service. Cannon said the bill already authorized the CAB to preserve "essential" services, and argued that the amendment would "tie the CAB's hands." The amendment was tabled by a vote of 80-12. *(Vote 121, p. 22-S)*

A number of other amendments that were defeated would have altered the airline employee protection plan:

- An amendment by Edward Zorinsky, D-Neb., to provide that employees dislocated because of the bill be given hiring priority by other airlines, rather than compensation. Roll call, 43-48. *(Vote 124, p. 22-S)*
- An amendment offered by John C. Danforth, R-Mo., to increase the number of employees protected by the plan. Roll call, 37-54. *(Vote 122, p. 22-S)*
- An amendment by Orrin G. Hatch, R-Utah, to delete the employee protection program from the bill. Roll call, 7-85. *(Vote 123, p. 22-S)*

Another rejected amendment would have permitted the CAB to preempt state regulation of intrastate carriers as soon as they offered interstate service. The amendment was offered by H. John Heinz III, R-Pa. Roll call, 20-72. *(Vote 126, p. 22-S)*

House Committee Action

The House Public Works Committee May 19 reported a companion bill (HR 12611 — H Rept 95-1211) after the measure had been stalled in the Aviation Subcommittee for seven weeks.

The stalemate was created in March when the subcommittee voted to reject legislation it had completed marking up and instead, adopted a substitute bill with few deregulation provisions. The subcommittee was then hurriedly recessed before a vote could be taken to send the substitute bill to the full Public Works Committee.

Aviation Subcommittee

The Aviation Subcommittee's compromise measure, approved by the panel May 9 by voice vote, was somewhat stronger than the substitute tentatively adopted in March, but it still had significantly weaker deregulation provisions than the Senate-passed version.

The compromise retained a modest automatic market entry program under which airlines would be able to serve additional routes, within limits, without prior CAB approval. The controversial provision, considered a key component of deregulation by its supporters, was vigorously opposed by Rep. Elliott H. Levitas, D-Ga., a subcommittee member.

Although Carter announced his support of the subcommittee's action, he said through press secretary Jody Powell that the bill wasn't "as strong as we'd prefer."

Subcommittee Action Delayed. The seven-week stalemate was caused by the subcommittee's approval of a substitute bill, introduced by Levitas, in place of the original deregulation measure backed by the administration. Adopted March 22 by a vote of 13-11, the Levitas proposal lacked almost all deregulation provisions. *(Vote, box this page)*

Vote on Levitas Substitute

Yea (13)	Nay (11)
James Abdnor, R-S.D.	Jerome A. Ambro, D-N.Y.
Thad Cochran, R-Miss.	Glenn M. Anderson, D-Calif.
Billy Lee Evans, D-Ga.	Robert W. Edgar, D-Pa.
Barry M. Goldwater Jr., R-Calif.	Allen E. Ertel, D-Pa.
John Paul Hammerschmidt, R-Ark.	John G. Fary, D-Ill.
William H. Harsha, R-Ohio	Ronnie G. Flippo, D-Ala.
Elliott H. Levitas, D-Ga.	W. G. (Bill) Hefner, D-N.C.
Dale Milford, D-Texas	Harold T. Johnson, D-Calif.
Nick J. Rahall, D-W.Va.	Norman Y. Mineta, D-Calif.
Bud Shuster, R-Pa.	Teno Roncalio, D-Wyo.
Gene Snyder, R-Ky.	Robert A. Young, D-Mo.
Gene Taylor, R-Mo.	
William F. Walsh, R-N.Y.	

The stunned chairman of the panel, Glenn M. Anderson, D-Calif., immediately recessed the subcommittee until April, when he hoped it would be reconsidered and a compromise reached.

"I am keenly disappointed at the action taken" at the March 22 session, Transportation Secretary Brock Adams said in a statement. "Until this last markup session, the subcommittee had come a long way toward adopting the kind of entry and pricing reforms the administration had recommended. . . . None of these provisions would be included under the Levitas amendment."

During the six days of markup — spread over three weeks' time — the subcommittee had before it 68 amendments, 42 of which actually came to a vote.

Because of the complex and technical nature of federal airline regulation and of the legislation itself, the amendments often were extremely difficult for even the sponsors to explain and analyze. If for no other reason, the sheer complexity and magnitude of the task of amending the bill apparently lulled its supporters into a false sense of security.

'Automatic Entry' Reversal. Ironically, the subcommittee had voted 14-9 March 21 to approve a compromise provision, drafted by Rep. Allen E. Ertel, D-Pa., reinstating an automatic market entry program. (The subcommittee on March 8 had voted 15-8 to approve a Levitas amendment dropping the automatic entry language from the bill.)

Those members reversing their March 8 position and voting March 21 to support the Ertel automatic entry provision were Democrats Ertel, Billy Lee Evans, Ga., W. G. (Bill) Hefner, N.C., and Robert A. Young, Mo., and Republicans Bud Shuster, Pa., and Gene Taylor, Mo.

Three of these committee members then switched positions again March 22 and supported the Levitas substitute rejecting automatic entry: Evans, Shuster and Taylor. Nick J. Rahall, D-W.Va., who didn't participate in the earlier votes on automatic entry, also voted for the Levitas substitute, adding to the margin by which the weaker bill was accepted.

Levitas Substitute. The substitute airline bill drafted by Levitas represented a shadow version of the bill as originally drafted.

Those provisions included in the legislation that were dropped from the Levitas substitute included 1) a new CAB policy statement to promote competition; 2) language facilitating CAB route certification; 3) restrictions on the extent to which an airline could be protected by the CAB from competition on routes which the airline was authorized to serve but on which it did not provide regularly scheduled service ("dormant authority"); 4) rate-making flexibility; 5) automatic market entry; 6) a presumption that an application for a new service was "in the public convenience and necessity," and 7) restrictions on industry pooling and antitrust exemptions.

The provisions in the original version that were retained in the Levitas substitute included 1) a continuation of the airline subsidy program for mail service; 2) expedited CAB proceedings; 3) a federal loan guarantee program; 4) consolidation, merger and acquisition guidelines restricting potentially anti-competitive actions; 5) an exemption from most CAB regulation for commuter airlines; 6) a program of federal subsidies for commuter airlines; 7) curbs on the president's authority to receive CAB international route decisions, and 8) an airline employee protection program.

A new provision in the Levitas substitute abolished the CAB as of Dec. 31, 1983. Those functions of the CAB that would have to be continued after the agency's abolition, Levitas said, would be transferred to the Transportation Department, the State Department, the Justice Department and the U.S. Postal Service.

Levitas said the result of the subcommittee's proposed legislation would be "a muddle rather than a free competitive situation." He said he preferred the "full free-entry marketplace approach" that his bill would provide.

Subcommittee Amendments. During markup, the subcommittee accepted a number of amendments to make new market entry and price competition open to a greater number and variety of airline companies:

- An Ertel amendment permitting certification on a first-come, first-served, basis for authority to fly on a route on which dormant authority existed, rather than requiring the CAB to hold a potentially lengthy and expensive hearing to determine which applicant was best qualified.
- Anderson amendments extending to supplemental carriers (charter airlines) eligibility to apply for routes on which dormant authority existed, and suspending airlines' dormant authority if regular service was not begun.
- An amendment by William H. Harsha, R-Ohio, extending to supplemental airlines automatic entry into a limited number of scheduled international routes.
- A Barry M. Goldwater Jr., R-Calif., amendment to ease entry and rates for all-cargo airlines.
- A William H. Harsha, R-Ohio, amendment making supplemental and commuter airlines eligible for federal loan guarantees.

Committee Report

The compromise reached by the subcommittee was adopted by the full committee on May 15 by a 37-5 vote after several minor changes were made in the bill.

"As a general rule," the House Public Works Committee stated in its report (H Rept 95-1211), the policies of the Civil Aeronautics Board (CAB) before 1975 "tended to place restrictions on airline management, which gave it much less competitive freedom than management in other industries."

Since 1975, the report went on, "the board's policies have tended to favor competition and a lessening of regulatory constraints."

The board's new policies "have been accompanied by improved financial results for the industry," the report said, indicating that, "at the least, the industry's experience indicates that lower fares and better service for consumers are not necessarily incompatible with industry profits.

"While the committee has by no means concluded that total deregulation is desirable," the report said, "we are persuaded that it is time for a moderate controlled release of some regulatory fetters."

Major Provisions. As reported by the House Public Works Committee May 19, HR 12611:

- Changed the declaration of policy guiding CAB decisions by directing the board to stress competition, low-fare service, new entries into the airline industry marketplace and prevention of anti-competitive practices.
- Directed the board to approve applications for air transportation service if they were "consistent with the public convenience and necessity."
- Directed the CAB to authorize service within 15 days by the first willing and able carrier applying to serve a route on which unused authority had been granted and which no other or only one other airline actually served. Unused — or "dormant" — authority would occur when an airline was authorized to serve a route yet did not serve it. For routes served by two or more carriers on which unused authority also existed, the CAB would be permitted, within 60 days, to refuse to approve an application for additional service if it concluded the application was inconsistent with the public convenience and necessity.
- Permitted carriers to select one additional market that they wanted to serve during the first year after the legislation's enactment. The CAB would be required to authorize the new service unless it found that it would be likely to seriously harm existing air service, or unless another carrier serving that market notified the board that it wished to be protected from a new entry.

The board was directed to complete a study by June 30, 1980, evaluating the impact of the experimental market entry program and making legislative recommendations to Congress concerning the program's future.

- Authorized the board to regulate intrastate carriers as soon as they began providing interstate service.
- Extended the existing mail subsidy program for 10 years and provided for a new subsidy program to assure continued air service for 10 years to all communities currently served by regularly scheduled carriers.

The CAB was required to recommend to Congress by Jan. 1, 1980, how state and local governments could be made to share the costs of the subsidy programs.

- Permitted air carriers, without prior CAB approval, to raise fares up to 5 percent above the fare in effect for that service one year earlier, or to lower fares by up to 50 percent of the fare in effect one year earlier. If the carrier lowered fares and wasn't satisfied with the result, it also could raise the fare back to its previous level without CAB approval.
- Authorized the CAB to approve "experimental certificates" for innovative services, and to revoke or amend them if the certificate holder failed to provide the proposed service.
- Made commuter airlines eligible for federal subsidies; permitted commuters to enter into joint fare agreements

with regularly scheduled carriers, and increased the size and weight limits for commuter aircraft that would be exempt from many CAB regulations.

- Expedited CAB actions by establishing deadlines for many types of board and administrative decisions and simplifying certain procedures.
- Limited the authority of the president to disapprove CAB decisions in awarding international routes. Under the bill, the president could reverse a CAB decision solely on national defense or foreign policy grounds, not for economic or other reasons.
- Permitted the board to withhold from public disclosure information provided it by air carriers if the information's disclosure would harm the United States' or a U.S. carrier's competitive position on international negotiations.
- Extended the federal loan guarantee program for the purchase of new aircraft for five years.
- Provided for benefits for employees harmed by the legislation's enactment.
- Provided that the CAB be terminated on Dec. 31, 1982, unless Congress acted to renew it.

Additional Views. In additional views, Allen E. Ertel, D-Pa., noted that many of the committee-reported provisions of HR 12611 were weaker than earlier versions of deregulation legislation considered by the committee.

"Given the abundant possibilities for cautious but more substantial airline regulatory reform," Ertel concluded, "the American consumer will be seriously shortchanged if the House does not improve this bill."

Elliott H. Levitas, D-Ga., however, a key architect of the weaker bill, called HR 12611 "a good bill and I urge its approval."

In minority views, Rep. Bob Stump, D-Ariz., said the committee, in reporting the legislation, had "wasted a great deal of time and money on an unnecessary piece of legislation."

"No one has, nor can they, challenge the fact that the nation's airlines provide this country with the finest airline service in the world," he said. "This legislation is not deregulation but reregulation."

House Floor Action

The House passed HR 12611 Sept. 21 by a vote of 363-8. *(Vote 719, p. 204-H)*

During two days of floor debate, ranking Public Works members defended the legislation drafted by their committee as "a delicate balance" between increasing competition and ensuring the commercial viability of the passenger airline industry. Because of that balance, they argued, efforts to strengthen the bill on the floor should be rejected.

Despite their warnings, one additional deregulation provision, offered by Ertel, was approved by an overwhelming margin. Two other efforts by Ertel to revise the bill on the floor were turned back, however.

The successful Ertel amendment reversed the burden of proof for determining that a new service was "consistent with the public convenience and necessity." Under existing law, an application for a new service was considered by the CAB not in the public interest until an applicant could prove it was.

The Ertel amendment provided that an application would be presumed to be in the public interest unless the CAB found evidence that it was not. It was approved, 300-86. *(Vote 717, p. 204-H)*

The amendment was similar to a provision in the Senate bill drafted by Sen. Edward M. Kennedy, D-Mass.

The House rejected by a 7-18 standing vote another Ertel amendment that would have eliminated restrictions on the airlines' ability to begin service on routes on which there was so-called "dormant" — unused — authority.

Under the bill, air carriers could routinely begin to serve routes served by only one other airline without a long CAB proceeding. On routes served by two or more carriers, however, a CAB hearing would be required.

A third Ertel amendment, rejected by a 9-29 standing vote, sought to strike from the bill a provision authorizing subsidy refunds of $433,000 to Frontier Airlines and $1,-042,000 to Mohawk Airlines, which was merged into Allegheny Airlines in 1972.

The payments were intended to reimburse the airlines for incorrect tax loss carryback payments they made in 1964 and 1965 as a result of a change in a CAB tax ruling.

Accepted, 299-78, was an amendment offered by James L. Oberstar, D-Minn., terminating the airlines' mutual aid pact. The pact, sanctioned by the CAB, permitted airlines to earn income during strikes by drawing money from a central fund even though their flight operations were closed down. *(Vote 718, p. 204-H)*

The amendment's supporters argued that the pact rewarded airlines with poor labor relations and was anti-competitive.

Other successful amendments 1) put intrastate airlines on equal footing with CAB-certified carriers in getting federal loan guarantees and being permitted to write tickets and route baggage on connecting lines, and 2) strengthened small communities' protections against service losses.

Legislative Veto Move

Levitas sought to include in the bill language providing Congress with a veto over CAB action — a legislative veto — but was talked out of offering an amendment by Public Works Chairman Harold T. Johnson, D-Calif. Johnson said after the debate that he had told Levitas such a provision would have been unconstitutional. Nevertheless, Johnson voted against the final version of a Federal Trade Commission bill (HR 3816) because it didn't contain a similar legislative veto provision. *(Story, p. 523)*

Noise Control Bill Link

Following House floor action, ranking members of the House Public Works Committee announced at an impromptu press conference that they would wait for word on the Senate's intentions on a related measure — a bill to provide subsidies to airlines and airport operators to reduce aviation noise levels — before deciding on a timetable for a conference with the Senate on the deregulation measure.

The aviation noise bill (S 3279) was pending before the Senate Finance Committee at the time. A companion bill (HR 8729) had been passed by the House Sept. 14.

"I think it's been pretty well understood from the start," commented Public Works Chairman Johnson, "that the House has been working on the noise bill as its first priority, and that the Senate has been working on its deregulation bill.... We hope they stay in tandem."

Would the House still go to conference on the deregulation bill, Johnson was asked, if the Senate rejected the controversial noise measure'

Replied Johnson: "We'll have to cross that bridge when we get to it."

On Sept. 28, however, Public Works Chairman Harold T. Johnson, D-Calif., said he would permit the air deregulation conference to begin work on reconciling the differences between the two versions.

"We'll go slowly" on the deregulation bill while the noise bill wends its way through the Senate, Johnson said. "If any impasse develops, I don't know what we'll do."

Conference Action

The bill was sent to conference Sept. 27, and House-Senate conferees completed their negotiations on the bill before the Senate had considered the airline noise bill. Nevertheless, the conference committee went ahead and reported the deregulation bill (H Rept. 95-1779) on Oct. 12, two days before Congress was scheduled to adjourn.

In conference, House conferees gave in to the Senate's stronger provisions on a number of the key deregulation provisions.

Both the automatic market entry program and the program to ease the granting of new services on routes where there was unused authority had been bitterly fought by the House Public Works Committee, but were strengthened in conference.

One controversial provision of the House bill that was not in the Senate-passed bill was weakened in conference. The House had overwhelmingly adopted on the floor an amendment to end the airlines' mutual aid pact, whereby the major airline companies pooled a portion of their revenues to help each other out during labor strikes.

The mutual aid pact provision approved by conferees permitted the pact to continue, and merely trimmed back its scope largely along lines already agreed to in advance by the pact members.

The future of the pact was one of the most hotly contested issues in the conference committee.

Final Action

The conference version was rushed to the Senate, which had to consider it first, and it was approved on Oct. 14 by an 82-4 vote. *(Vote 501, p. 73-S)*

To the immense relief of deregulation backers, the House did not wait for the noise control bill to pass before taking up and clearing the deregulation bill. By a 356-6 vote, the House Oct. 15 approved the conference report, completing congressional action. *(Vote 826, p. 234-H)* ∎

Airline Noise Control Bill

Congress did not complete action in 1978 on legislation that would have provided commercial airline companies with federal aid to help them pay for quieter planes and engines.

Although the House and Senate had passed differing versions of the bill (HR 8729, S 3279), an attempt in the last days of the session to complete action on a compromise bill that would be acceptable to a majority of both houses foundered.

The main stumbling block was over a provision to provide government subsidies for the airline industry to help them pay for the installation of quieter airplane engines or to retrofit existing engines. Opponents of the provision said the industry was financially able to sustain these costs itself.

Also delaying congressional action on the bill throughout the session was an attempt by the bill's supporters to link it to the airline deregulation measure (S 2493), which they perceived as having much greater support in Congress. But, eventually, growing opposition to the noise control bill convinced the bill's proponents that they did not have sufficient support to block the deregulation measure by holding it hostage to the noise bill. Unlike deregulation, the noise control bill received only lukewarm support from the Carter administration.

Besides the federal subsidy for the airlines, the noise control legislation would have authorized grants to airports to help them reduce their noise levels.

Also in the bill were provisions to increase funding from the Airport and Airway Trust Fund for general airport operations and maintenance.

A controversial provision in the House bill would have imposed a surcharge on airline tickets and freight rates to raise the revenue to pay for part of the cost of engine replacements and retrofitting. The Senate Finance Committee, and the full Senate, subsequently dropped the surcharge provision.

Though the airlines and airport operators argued that HR 8729 was needed to placate communities located near noisy airports and to ensure that financially strapped airlines would be able to meet the federal noise control standards, critics branded the bill a "ripoff" and a "giveaway."

Retroactive Standards

Airline noise control legislation originally was recommended by the Ford administration after the Federal Aviation Administration (FAA) in December 1976 retroactively imposed noise standards on aircraft designed before 1969 and built before Dec. 31, 1974.

The money proposed for airline noise control programs ordinarily would have gone into the Airport and Airways Trust Fund, which is used to pay for airport development and safety programs. The fund, which gets its revenue from the taxes on airline passenger fares and freight charges, had accumulated large surpluses.

Under the legislation, airline companies could use the money diverted from the trust fund for either the retrofitting or replacement of noisy engines, or the replacement of entire aircraft not meeting the 1976 FAA standards.

House Committee Action

Public Works Report

HR 8729 was approved by the House Public Works and Transportation Committee by voice vote Oct. 20, 1977, and reported Dec. 13, 1977 (H Rept 95-836). It:

- Authorized the secretary to award grants totaling $165 million in fiscal 1979 and $250 million in fiscal 1980 to help airport operators prepare noise impact maps and noise compatibility programs and implement the programs. The funds were to come from the Airport and Airway Trust Fund.
- Increased existing authorizations from the trust fund for airport development grants by $560 million for fiscal years 1979 and 1980 (from $585 million to $835 million for fiscal 1979 and from $610 million to $920 million for fiscal

1980), and raised the federal share of such grants from 80 per cent under existing law to 90 per cent for the two years.

- Required the secretary to compile a list of all aircraft not in compliance with federal noise standards as of Jan. 24, 1977, and to determine, for each plane, whether its operator intended to retrofit the plane's engines with sound-absorbing material, replace the engines or replace the aircraft in order to meet the noise control standards.
- Imposed a 2 per cent surcharge on the cost of domestic passenger fares and domestic freight charges, a $2 surcharge on international trips costing less than $100, a $10 surcharge on international trips costing $100 or more and a 5 per cent surcharge on the cost of international freight.

The surcharge was to be deposited by each operator in a separate account, and was to be applied at the rate of 50 per cent of the cost of retrofitting two- and three-engine aircraft; 90 per cent of the cost of retrofitting four-engine planes; 75 per cent of the cost of engine replacement (up to 40 per cent of the cost of replacing the entire aircraft), and either 25 per cent or 40 per cent of the cost of replacement of the entire aircraft, depending on whether the replacement aircraft met noise standards in effect on Jan. 1, 1977, and March 3, 1977, respectively.

- Exempted the funds collected under the surcharge from inclusion in an air carrier's gross income for federal income tax purposes.
- Terminated as of fiscal 1978 the open-ended authorization from the trust fund given the Federal Aviation Administration (FAA) under existing law for air navigation and air traffic control research and development.

In minority views, Rep. Gene Snyder (R Ky.) said the bill was "a bad bill and ought to be defeated." Among the provisions he opposed were those authorizing federal grants for noise maps and noise compatibility planning; federal assistance for the replacement of aircraft which, he said, might already be fully depreciated and "at the end of their useful lives," and exclusion from gross income of surcharge funds. "What a wonderful gimmick," he stated. "Tax free income and the aircraft purchased with the tax free income can be written off against taxable income."

Ways and Means Report

After the noise control bill was approved by Public Works, it had to be considered by the Ways and Means Committee, which has jurisdiction over tax and revenue raising measures.

The bill immediately ran into trouble. Ways and Means split off provisions of HR 8729 dealing with the Airport and Airway Trust Fund and the treatment of the airline ticket surcharge and drafted a separate bill (HR 11986) covering those provisions.

As reported by the Ways and Means Committee April 24 by a 23-11 vote, HR 11986 (H Rept 95-1082) provided a system of taxable credits or refunds — financed by revenues from increased taxes on airline tickets and freight charges — to help airlines defray the costs of replacing or muffling noisy engines or aircraft.

The existing taxes on airline tickets and freight charges were reduced 2 percent by Ways and Means, and a new 2 percent excise tax was levied.

In addition, international passengers would have to pay a tax of $2 on fares less than $100 and $10 on fares of $100 or more, and a 5 percent tax would be imposed on international freight shipments departing the United States.

FAA Role Criticized

The House Government Operatiions Committee issued a number of recommendations on how to improve the federal government's aircraft noise control program, including one recommendation that the president ban the Concorde supersonic transport from landing at United States airports until it could comply with federal noise limits.

In a report entitled "Aircraft Noise and the Concorde" (H Rept 95-879), reported Feb. 9, the committee was especially critical of the role of the Federal Aviation Administration (FAA) in regulating aircraft noise.

Though the FAA was given responsibility for regulation of aircraft noise through 1968 amendments to the Federal Aviation Act (PL 90-411), the Noise Control Act of 1972 (PL 92-574) directed the Environmental Protection Agency (EPA) to advise the FAA on how to regulate aircraft noise.

Following April and June 1977 oversight hearings on the 1972 act by the Government Operations Subcommittee on Environment, Energy and Natural Resources, the committee concluded that 1) the FAA was not doing a good job of regulating airplane noise, 2) the EPA's advice was not being heeded by the FAA, and 3) the Concorde was "noisy, energy inefficient and environmentally unsound."

To remedy these problems, the committee recommended that:

- The president should not permit the Concorde to continue to land at American airports until it could meet U.S. noise standards.
- Congress should consider amending the 1972 Noise Control Act to give EPA primary responsibility for administering the federal noise control program.
- EPA should move more aggressively in developing and policing aircraft noise standards.

Existing charges would be reduced proportionally or suspended.

The taxes would remain in effect for five years, after which the reduced taxes would be restored, or they would be suspended.

An operator of an aircraft not in compliance with the FAA's 1977 noise standards would be eligible to claim a refund or a credit each month against its liability for the new excise taxes.

The operator could claim 90 percent of the cost of retrofitting an aircraft with fewer than four engines; 50 percent of the cost of retrofitting an aircraft with four or more engines; 75 percent of the cost of purchasing a replacement engine, and 25 percent to 40 percent of the cost of purchasing a replacement aircraft, depending on the replacement aircraft's noise characteristics.

Foreign air carriers would be eligible to use the mechanics and revenues of the tax to put them in compliance with the U.S. standards.

In dissenting views on HR 11986, Reps. Charles A. Vanik, D-Ohio, and Fortney H. (Pete) Stark, D-Calif., said the legislation "constitutes the Great Treasury Raid of 1978."

They said the bill should be defeated because it could end up paying the airline industry federal revenues far in

Industry Campaign Contributions

Major airline industry companies and labor unions funneled over half a million dollars into the campaign funds of senators and representatives during 1977 and 1978, according to a Congressional Quarterly study of Federal Election Commission compilations.

Of the $503,704 contributed to congressional campaigns during the two-year period, about 10 percent ($49,110) went to 21 members of the 23-member House Public Works Aviation Subcommittee that helped write the airline noise control legislation.

HR 8729 would funnel an estimated $3 billion to $4 billion in federal user taxes into the coffers of the major airline companies.

Only two Aviation Subcommittee members — William F. Walsh, R-N.Y., and Teno Roncalio, D-Wyo. — accepted no campaign contributions from airline interests; both were retiring at the end of the 95th Congress. Another subcommittee member, Billy Lee Evans, D-Ga., accepted contributions of $2,900, though he was unopposed for re-election in 1978. Top earners on the Aviation Subcommittee included Chairman Glenn M. Anderson, D-Calif., who accepted $6,900 during 1977-78 from major airline industry and labor union political action committees; Norman Y. Mineta, D-Calif., $5,600; Dale Milford, D-Texas, $5,600; Bud Shuster, R-Pa., $3,400, and Gene Snyder, R-Ky., $3,300.

Anderson, Mineta, Milford and Shuster were supporters of the airline noise bill in the Aviation Subcommittee and on the House floor.

Snyder bitterly opposed the noise bill, but worked in the subcommittee to gut or defeat the airline deregulation bill.

The major airline firms studied by Congressional Quarterly included the 10 largest air carriers (according to total annual revenues); an additional six passenger airlines with a significant stake in either the aviation noise or deregulation bills; the two principal airline labor unions; two major air cargo companies and four major manufacturers of commercial aircraft.

A total of $317,650 of the $503,704 in 1977-78 contributions came from the political action committees of the two major airline unions, the Air Line Pilots Association ($122,550) and the Machinists and Aerospace Workers union ($195,100).

Hughes Aircraft Co. contributed $35,764 to House and Senate candidates; Lockheed Aircraft Corp., $30,060; Tiger International Inc., $22,650; Pan American World Airways, $19,840; Western Air Lines Inc., $12,505; McDonnell Douglas Corp., $12,030; United Airlines Inc., $11,750; and Trans World Airlines Inc., $11,650.

All totals were based on Federal Election Commission compilations of political action committee reports and included contributions reported as of September 1978.

excess of what was needed to bring noisy aircraft into compliance with noise standards.

They added that an amendment to make the bill retroactive to Jan. 24, 1977, "would permit a Treasury credit of over $200 million for Eastern Airlines' $778 million purchase of the European Airbus, and a Treasury credit of up to about $350 million to Pan Am for a $480 million purchase of Rolls Royce engines."

Rules Committee Consideration

Before the bill was sent to the floor, the bill's backers sought a "closed rule" — barring floor amendments — to the controversial tax provisions, thus preventing any revisions in the airline subsidy program.

Opponents of the subsidy, led by Charles A. Vanik, D-Ohio, sought an "open rule" from the Rules Committee to permit a floor vote on an amendment to delete the ticket tax provision.

Adoption of the Vanik amendment would have forced some of the airlines to seek fare increases to cover the costs of meeting the federal noise standards.

But rules members Aug. 1 voted down an open rule by a vote of 6-9. In its place, the committee voted to permit amendments only to those portions of the bill aiding airport operators; it recommended a closed rule for the tax provisions aiding the airlines.

Before the vote, lobbying on both sides had been intense. The July 10 issue of *Aviation Daily,* an industry newspaper, reported that airline industry officials had met in Washington in early July to plan how to push the legislation through Congress before the release of second quarter financial reports were expected to show record profits for the airline companies. The airlines' healthy finances, the officials reasoned, could jeopardize support for the bill, according to *Aviation Daily.*

Subsequently, representatives of public interest groups pushing airline deregulation mounted a lobbying campaign to defeat or gut the noise control bill.

"The noise bill is too big a price to pay for the airline deregulation," stated Frances Zwenig, a lobbyist for Congress Watch, in an interview.

"The members of the Rules Committee are being tremendously lobbied by the airlines on the noise bill," Vanik said in an interview. "But their case is not as good as it was a year ago. Their profits are good. I think the deregulation bill can stand on its own."

When HR 8729 was introduced in early 1977, airline revenues had been lagging. But by the summer of 1978 revenues from passenger fares and the airlines' load factors had risen to all-time highs, and the bill's critics wanted the airlines to meet federal noise control standards with their own funds.

House Floor Action

The House passed HR 8729 on Sept. 14 after two days of often heated debate. The final vote was 272-123. *(Vote 684, p. 194-H)*

The bill was brought to the floor Sept. 13. Before the bill was debated, opponents tried to overturn the Rules Committee's "closed rule" recommendation on the subsidy provisions.

The ticket tax provision, Gene Snyder, R-Ky., argued, made the legislation "the most blatant piece of special interest legislation I have seen since I came to Congress in 1963." Appropriations Committee Chairman George Mahon, D-Texas, said the bill "channeled federal funds into private hands" and constituted "back-door spending" because it skirted the congressional authorization and appropriations process.

Its backers, however, defended the bill as a practical solution to the vexing problem of aviation noise.

"I have come to the conclusion that this bill is more good than bad," commented Ways and Means ranking Republican Barber B. Conable Jr., N.Y. He added: "I think this is a classic example of what a mistake it is to build up a great big trust fund for such things as airport safety and not to adjust the tax if a surplus is being created. That surplus becomes a wonderful target for wonderful ideas to spend it in some other area."

But opponents were blocked from attempting to amend the tax section when the House approved a procedural motion designed to end debate on the Rules Committee "closed rule" and proceed to a final vote on adoption of the rule.

Despite a last-minute flurry of vote switches encouraged by opponents of the rule, the procedural motion was approved 199-193, with both parties evenly divided (Republicans — 67-61; Democrats — 132-132). *(Vote 677, p. 192-H)*

With any chance to amend the controversial provisions now blocked, the House went on to adopt the rule on a 236-155 vote. *(Vote 678, p. 192-H)*

The House then approved en bloc the tax portions of the bill as written by the Ways and Means Committee. The vote was 266-133. *(Vote 682, p. 194-H)*

A motion to recommit the bill to the Public Works Committee, offered by Rep. Snyder, subsequently was defeated by a vote of 170-227. *(Vote 683, p. 194-H)*

Amendments

In other action on the bill, the House adopted by voice votes amendments that:

- Made the Environmental Protection Agency an adviser to the Transportation Department on airport noise planning studies; by James J. Florio, D-N.J.
- Authorized an additional $25 million annually from the Airport and Airway Trust Fund for fiscal years 1979 and 1980 for general aviation airport development, with the funds to be divided equally among the 50 states; by Joe Skubitz, R-Kan.
- Extended for two years a demonstration program under which certain states were authorized to administer federal general aviation airport development projects; by William H. Harsha, R-Ohio.
- Made intrastate airlines eligible for federal subsidies for the muffling or replacement of noisy aircraft; by Claude Pepper, D-Fla.

The House rejected, by a vote of 127-246, an amendment by Rep. James J. Florio, D-N.J., to require operators of airports whose noise affected communities in adjacent states to formulate noise control plans. *(Vote 679, p. 194-H)*

Aviation Subcommittee Chairman Glenn M. Anderson, D-Calif., said the amendment ran counter to the voluntary approach to noise control relied on in the bill.

Senate Committee Action

Commerce Committee Report

Companion legislation (S 3279) was considered by the Senate Commerce Committee in 1978 and reported (S Rept 95-976) July 11 by a vote of 7-6.

The Senate Commerce version was similar to the House-passed bill. As approved, S 3279 imposed a noise abatement tax of 2 percent on tickets and freight charges. The Civil Aeronautics Board was empowered to continue, expand or terminate the tax on an annual basis, depending on the financial condition of the airline industry.

Under the House-passed bill, the funds collected by an airline company after the company's planes complied with the noise regulations were to be turned over to the trust fund.

Under the Senate Commerce Committee bill, which incorporated a compromise introduced by Commerce Chairman Howard W. Cannon, D-Nev., an airline was free to use the noise abatement charges for any purpose it wished after its planes were brought into compliance with the regulations.

Transportation Secretary Brock Adams told reporters Sept. 21 the administration supported both the House and the Senate Commerce Committee approaches to the noise problem.

Critics said the administration was pushing the noise legislation solely because the House Public Works Committee had hinted that the bill's enactment was the necessary price it would have to pay to ensure passage of the airline deregulation legislation (S 2493), a top Carter priority.

Provisions. As reported by the Commerce Committee, S 3279:

- Instructed the transportation secretary to devise a method for measuring noise at airports and surrounding areas, and to identify land uses that would be compatible with various levels of noise.
- Established a voluntary noise compatibility planning program, and authorized a total of $150 million from the Airport and Airway Trust Fund for the secretary to make grants to airport operators for planning. The total granted each year was not to exceed $15 million.
- Authorized an additional $35 million annually from the trust fund for fiscal 1979-80 for grants to airport operators to carry out noise compatibility programs, including the purchase of land, noise shielding, restrictions on certain types of aircraft and other controls.
- Created a revolving loan fund of $300 million for the purchase by airport operators of property affected by aircraft noise.
- Required the secretary to prepare a noise control program for National and Dulles Airports in the Washington, D.C., area.
- Barred any person who acquired land near an airport after the date of enactment of the legislation from suing to recover damages from an airport operator for airport noise, unless there was a significant change in the airport's operations after the land was purchased.
- Authorized increases of $100 million in fiscal 1979 and $260 million in fiscal 1980 from the trust fund for commercial and general aviation airport development, operations and maintenance.
- Required the secretary to compile and publish a list of aircraft that did not comply with FAA noise regulations.
- Imposed a 2 percent noise abatement charge on the cost of airline tickets and freight shipments, the funds to be used by airlines to comply with the FAA noise standards. Existing freight and passenger ticket taxes were reduced by 2 percent, to 3 percent from 5 percent, and to 6 percent from 8 percent respectively.

After all of a firm's aircraft complied with FAA noise regulations, "the carrier may expend these funds in any way it chooses," according to the Commerce Committee report.

Indians and Airport Noise: A Deal That Didn't Work

They might have called it the night the Senate Select Committee on Indian Affairs tried to help reduce airport noise.

"It" was the deal cut by James Abourezk, D-S.D., and Howard W. Cannon, D-Nev., in a last-minute attempt by both men to save bills they wanted passed before the 95th Congress adjourned. It didn't quite work.

Abourezk wanted to extend the life of the Indian Affairs Committee, which was set to expire with the 95th Congress. But Cannon was blocking resolutions (S Res 405, S Res 575) to authorize and fund the committee for two years.

Cannon wanted to pass a bill (HR 8729) giving airport operators and airlines aid in reducing the impact of aircraft noise. But Abourezk had made it clear he would filibuster that bill. As the Senate headed into its final session Oct. 14, the standoff between Indian Affairs and airport noise continued.

But Cannon — and the Senate — couldn't afford another last-night filibuster. Abourezk tied up the Senate for 14 hours during its final session, filibustering against the last part of President Carter's energy package. Another talkathon could have turned the last night into a last week. So Cannon agreed to relent on the Indian Committee, in exchange for Abourezk's promise not to block the noise bill.

One More Thing . . .

But Abourezk had one more demand. He wanted Cannon to take out a major provision in the noise bill that could have led to federal aid for airlines in muffling or replacing noisy planes.

Consumer groups had opposed provisions in House and Senate versions of the noise bill designed to subsidize the airlines in meeting a federal noise standard set to take effect in 1985. They argued the subsidy would set a bad precedent of having the federal government aid private enterprise in meeting federal regulations.

Cannon agreed to drop the provision, and the noise bill and the resolutions giving Abourezk's Indian Committee new life were passed in minutes around 1:30 a.m. Oct. 15.

"Not a bad day's work. I saved $3 billion and helped the Indians, too," crowed Abourezk after the deal was struck.

But while Cannon aides admit Abourezk drove a hard bargain, they said the subsidy provision was an easy one for Cannon to give up.

In fact, Cannon originally opposed the House noise bill's subsidies. He later softened that position, supporting a modified version, when House members threatened to hold up Cannon's airline deregulation bill unless he moved forward on noise.

"Cannon had a record of less than overwhelming love for that provision," said Mike Vernetti, Cannon's press aide. And since Cannon felt other sections of the bill — such as new federal grants to help airport operators reduce noise around airports — were still worth saving, he decided to meet Abourezk's second demand.

Abourezk Wins, Airlines Lose

But when the final gavel banged in the 95th Congress, Abourezk, who had chaired the Indian Committee, still came out the winner. Because only Senate passage was required, the two resolutions renewing the Indian Committee became effective as soon as the airport noise-Indian Affairs deal was given its Senate blessing. Cannon, however, still had a full day's wait to see what would happen to the noise bill.

At an early morning caucus Oct. 15, members of the House Public Works Committee decided the Senate noise bill was unacceptable. Cannon aides went home thinking the bill was dead.

But by midafternoon, the House members had put their aides to work in the Speaker's lobby just off the House floor, drafting a new compromise noise bill. They abandoned any subsidy plan for airlines but made changes in other parts of the bill that would make it more palatable to the House.

House Aviation Subcommittee Chairman Glenn M. Anderson, D-Calif., took the compromise to the floor to try to bring it up by unanimous consent. A Cannon aide was posted outside, ready to run the compromise over to the Senate for the final approval necessary there — if Anderson could get it through the House.

Anderson asked unanimous consent but was blocked immediately. The Public Works members went into action, trying to clear away the objection.

Later in the evening, Anderson tried again, and was blocked a second time. He did manage to squeeze in a brief debate on the compromise, but Berkley Bedell, D-Iowa, continued to object.

No House Quorum

The only option left for Anderson was to try to bring the bill up under suspension of the rules. House Speaker Thomas P. O'Neill Jr., D-Mass., would have to be convinced to allow that, and Anderson would then need a two-thirds majority to pass the bill.

But the suspension strategy became moot a few minutes later, when other Public Works Committee members tried to push through a bill authorizing new water resources projects.

The House didn't get a quorum for a roll call vote on the water bill, and the 95th Congress was forced to adjourn, killing the last chance for the airport noise bill.

- Authorized the Civil Aeronautics Board to adjust the levels of the noise abatement charges over a four-year period, beginning one year after the charges were imposed, depending on the airline companies' financial performance. The charge was to be imposed for a maximum of five years.
- Encouraged foreign and domestic air carriers carrying passengers between the United States and other nations to voluntarily comply with FAA noise control standards by permitting them to impose a $3 noise abatement charge on the sale of international passenger tickets, and a 5 percent charge on international freight transport.
- Ordered the FAA to issue a rule by the end of April 1980 to require international aircraft operators to meet FAA noise standards within five years.
- Provided an incentive for the purchase of the newest and quietest airplanes by waiving FAA noise standards for

existing two- and three-engine aircraft if the operator had entered into a binding contract by Jan. 1, 1983, to replace the noisy plane with a new plane.

Finance Committee Amendments

After Senate Commerce completed action on the bill, it went to the Finance Committee, which had jurisdiction over the airline ticket and freight taxes that ordinarily would have gone into the trust fund.

The panel voted Oct. 3 to require the airlines to pay for the muffling or replacement of noisy aircraft from their own revenues, rather than out of funds diverted from the Airport and Airway Trust Fund. In place of the tax, the members recommended merely reducing the existing freight and passenger taxes by 2 percent.

During the markup session, Finance Chairman Russell B. Long, D-La., said he doubted the bill could pass the Senate as originally drafted.

Because of the airlines' strong financial performance, commented Bob Packwood, R-Ore., the airlines should be able to pay for the quieter planes without the subsidy. Packwood called the airline industry one of the nation's "biggest crybabies."

Republicans Carl T. Curtis, Neb., and John C. Danforth, Mo., defended the airline industry, saying its financial condition was not as secure as its detractors implied. If the airlines were forced to raise their rates in order to pay for the needed equipment, they argued, ridership might fall and revenues would then decline.

Finance reported the bill (no written report) Oct. 5.

Senate Floor Action

With only a few days left in the session, the noise bill's backers in the Senate found that floor consideration had been blocked by James Abourezk, D-S.D., who opposed the bill even without the subsidy. A petition for cloture was filed Oct. 12, and a vote had been scheduled for Oct. 14 to end the mini-filibuster. But Abourezk subsequently relented and allowed the bill to come to a vote.

Cannon agreed to delete the subsidy entirely even though he said he favored it. On Oct. 14 he obtained unanimous consent to consider the noise bill, whereupon he offered a substitute for the Senate-passed S 3279.

Besides deleting the subsidy for the airlines, the substitute reduced funding levels to meet objections of the Carter administration and reduced the passenger ticket tax 2 percent, with the savings going to the public.

The Senate then passed the House-numbered bill (HR 8729) without objection as amended by Cannon's substitute and returned the bill to the House. But requests to bring it up for a final vote were blocked and the bill died in the House when Congress adjourned Oct. 15. ▮

Rebating Bill Vetoed

President Carter Nov. 4 pocket-vetoed legislation intended to combat the practice of illegal rebating in ocean shipping.

In rebating, steamship companies seek to gain cargo shipments by offering shippers discounts, or kickbacks, that are below the rates they are required to file with the Federal Maritime Commission, in violation of federal law.

The bill (HR 9518) Carter vetoed would have beefed up the FMC's ability to enforce the anti-rebating laws, increased the penalties for illegal rebating and required foreign flag steamship companies operating in the U.S. trades to obey the U.S. anti-rebating laws.

The legislation also would have prohibited the use of federal criminal statutes to punish violators of the anti-rebating laws. The FMC had argued that the threat of jail sentences hampered the agency's ability to investigate and curb rebating violations.

The legislation had cleared Congress Oct. 13.

Veto Message

In a memorandum of disapproval, Carter said his administration was committed to enforcing the anti-rebating laws, but feared the legislation would upset continuing State Department talks with Japan and several European nations on a wide range of shipping problems, including rebating. *(Veto text, p. 66-E)*

He said he had directed an administration task force on maritime policy to provide him, "by an early date," with recommendations on rebating legislation for the next session of Congress if the talks failed.

The bill had been reported by the House Merchant Marine Committee March 3 and was approved by the full chamber by a 390-1 vote March 22.

The Senate Commerce Committee reported the bill June 28. However, before approving the legislation, the panel agreed to add a provision that was similar to a bill (S 2386) introduced by Sen. Russell B. Long, D-La., in December 1977. Long's measure would have had the effect of protecting two steamship companies from competition with outside firms in the growing South American export-import trade. But before passing the rebating measure Oct. 6, the Senate agreed to an amendment deleting the controversial Long-backed provision.

Major Provisions

As cleared for the president, HR 9518:

- Increased civil penalties for a variety of unfair shipping practices including rebating. The FMC also was permitted to suspend the firm's ability to operate for up to a year.
- Required that steamship firms file periodic written statements with the FMC certifying that it was company policy not to rebate and that the steamship company would cooperate with the FMC in rebating investigations. A firm failing to file the required statement was subject to a $5,000 fine.
- Permitted the FMC, at its discretion, to require similar statements from shippers, brokers and others under FMC jurisdiction.
- Gave the FMC additional investigative powers to expedite rebating proceedings.
- Required the FMC to consult with the secretary of state to determine the impact on U.S. foreign policy of penalizing foreign firms, and permitted the president to prevent the suspension of a steamship firm's ability to operate if required by foreign policy or national security considerations.
- Required the secretary of state to negotiate an agreement with other maritime nations enabling the FMC to obtain information on rebating practices of foreign flag carriers.

• Prohibited use of the federal conspiracy statutes to punish illegal rebating practices committed after Aug. 29, 1972. Conspiracy was prosecuted by the Justice Department, rather than the FMC, and was a criminal, rather than a civil, offense, punishable by a jail sentence. The FMC argued that the threat of jail sentences "chilled" its ability to investigate and curb rebating law violations.

Background

Since rebating schemes are legal in some forms in certain countries and traditionally have been widely practiced in the U.S. ocean trade despite U.S. law, federal policy in the past generally has been to ignore the practice.

One rationale for the government's neglect had been that to strictly police the U.S. fleet—while foreign flag ships remained free to rebate—would harm the U.S. maritime industry's competitive position. Strict enforcement would cause U.S. shipping firms to fold or change their registry to other nations, shippers argued. Should war break out, the argument went, the United States would be at a disadvantage.

Sea-Land Disclosures

Government laxity, however, ended in 1976 with the disclosure to the Securities and Exchange Commission (SEC) that Sea-Land Service, Inc., the world's largest containerized steamship line, had paid out about $19 million in rebates from 1971 to 1975. Sea-Land subsequently settled with the FMC in 1977 and paid fines totaling $4 million.

The FMC, embarrassed by the SEC disclosure, immediately beefed up its enforcement efforts. The agency in 1978 had 27 steamship firms (18 foreign flag and nine U.S. flag carriers) and 215 shippers under investigation.

Both House Merchant Marine Subcommittee Chairman John M. Murphy, D-N.Y., and Senate Commerce Merchant Marine and Tourism Subcommittee Chairman Daniel K. Inouye, D-Hawaii, in 1977 introduced legislation (HR 9518, S 2008) seeking to curb rebating. Both bills, however, also provided a one-year period during which shippers and shipping companies would be immune from "criminal prosecution under the laws of the United States" for disclosing illegal rebating practices.

"The idea was to induce them [violators] to come forward and reveal their violations and settle with the FMC," explained Peter N. Kyros, House subcommittee counsel and former member of the House, D-Maine, 1967-74. "The legislation was introduced for the purpose of being a framework for the formation of policy. As we went through the hearings, the amnesty provision was found to be a matter for which there was little compelling support."

Amnesty Criticized

During five days of hearings held on the House bill in 1977, critics of the amnesty provision pointed out that it could have effects far beyond those intended by its sponsors.

If passed, warned FMC Chairman Richard J. Daschbach in Oct. 20 testimony, the provision "could include immunity from criminal prosecution under laws...administered by the Internal Revenue Service, the Securities and Exchange Commission and the Department of Justice. Thus the penalties from which the rebating carrier or shipper would become exempt by this grant of immunity could be substantial."

Chilling Effect

Adding another twist to the situation, Murphy, Inouye and Ted Stevens, R-Alaska, Nov. 3 wrote Attorney General Griffin B. Bell requesting the Justice Department to delay prosecution of shipping companies accused of paying illegal rebates while Congress considered the rebating legislation.

If grand jury investigations continued while Congress was in the process of acting, the three legislators wrote Bell, these investigations would have "a chilling effect on efforts to secure passage of this legislation."

However, another member, House Merchant Marine Subcommittee ranking Republican Paul N. McCloskey Jr. (Calif.), wrote Bell Nov. 9 that he was opposed to Justice deferring prosecution until Congress had acted. And in subsequent subcommittee hearings, McCloskey pushed for a narrowing of the criminal amnesty provision to make it apply solely to matters under the jurisdiction of the FMC.

On Jan. 25 Bell wrote the four members that prosecutions would continue. "It is our considered judgment that any such suspension of ongoing prosecutive efforts on our part would be without precedent and entirely inappropriate under the circumstances," he wrote.

House Committee Action

The House Merchant Marine Committee March 3 reported HR 9518 by a vote of 28-0 (H Rept 95-922). The bill had been approved by the Merchant Marine Subcommittee Jan. 31.

In its markup session Jan. 31, the subcommittee was presented with an entirely new version of HR 9518, drafted by the majority and minority staffs. The compromise, as adopted by the subcommittee, gave the FMC additional investigative power for rebating proceedings and increased the civil penalties the FMC could levy for violations of the rebating laws.

The legislation enabled the FMC to suspend the tariffs of shippers convicted of rebating, and provided for a fine of up to $50,000 for shippers found to be carrying cargo after a tariff was suspended. The FMC also was authorized to require that shippers file certificates attesting that they did not rebate.

A key section of the compromise rejected HR 9518's original amnesty provision, replacing it with a limited one. Under the compromise, the Justice Department would be barred only from attempting to prosecute a shipper for conspiracy to defraud the FMC by violating the rebating laws. Violations of other laws could be pursued.

In support of the compromise, McCloskey argued that this had been the intent of Congress in 1972 amendments to the Shipping Act of 1916, but that Congress had failed to make this intent clear.

The compromise also set out a proposed policy by which the FMC could apply U.S. rebating laws to foreign flag ships. The FMC would be required to consult with the secretary of state to determine the impact of the possible suspension of tariffs upon foreign policy before penalizing a foreign carrier.

However, subcommittee members said the administration had not yet formulated its policy on foreign flag ships and might request changes in the provision at the full committee level. *(Foreign shipping rates, p. 517)*

McCloskey offered four technical amendments, which were accepted by the subcommittee by voice vote. A fifth amendment, however, was proposed and then withdrawn after Chairman Murphy promised to hold further hearings on the issue by May.

The proposal, McCloskey said, was designed to eliminate "over-tonnaging"—defined as having too many ships for the amount of available cargo. Maritime industry representatives had testified earlier that over-tonnaging was a root cause of rebating, and Chairman Murphy said he agreed with them.

McCloskey's proposal—which has been traditionally opposed by the Justice Department on antitrust grounds—was to permit shippers to form "shippers' councils" to enable them to band together to negotiate with steamship conferences, thus providing a balance to the conferences' antitrust immunity.

House Floor Action

The House March 22 approved the committee version of HR 9518 without amendment by a vote of 390-1. *(Vote 148, p. 44-H)*

The bill was supported on the floor without qualification, except by McCloskey, who said he supported it "with some reservations." McCloskey termed the bill "an experiment," and said Congress — if it approved the legislation — may some day wish to reverse itself on two provisions.

"First," he said, "we give the Federal Maritime Commission broad new powers . . . despite the clear showing . . . that the Federal Maritime Commission . . . has been wholly ineffective in exercising the powers that it has had." If the FMC doesn't improve its enforcement efforts under the new legislation, Congress should consider abolishing it, McCloskey said.

In addition, he pointed out that the legislation would bar criminal penalties for violations of the rebating laws. If rebating continued, McCloskey said, "it may be that stern criminal penalties may be the only way to control this pervasive practice."

Merchant Marine Committee Chairman John M. Murphy, D-N.Y., argued that the legislation "would permit the FMC to carry out its regulatory function to deter rebates in a swift, effective and evenhanded fashion. And, for the first time, foreign-flag ocean carriers would be required to comply with FMC subpoenas and discovery orders or face exclusion from our ocean trades."

Senate Committee Action

The Senate Commerce Committee reported HR 9518 June 28 (S Rept 95-966).

The action came after the panel agreed to add a provision similar to a bill introduced by Sen. Russell B. Long, D-La., in 1977.

Though altered by the committee during markup by the addition of what the committee report termed "certain new safeguards," the provision still could have the effect of protecting two steamship companies from competition with outside firms in the South American shipping trades.

The two companies were Delta Steamship Lines Inc. of New Orleans and Moore-McCormack Lines Inc. of Stamford, Conn.

Long, in a printed statement released in May, said he had introduced the bill "by request of the Delta Steamship Lines, one of my constituents."

Referring to the provision, four Commerce Committee members, Robert P. Griffin, R-Mich., Harrison Schmitt, R-N.M., Adlai E. Stevenson III, D-Ill., and Edward Zorinsky, D-Neb., called it "bad law" and urged its rejection.

In late April, Sen. Long had asked the Commerce Committee to tack onto HR 9518 his bill (S 2386) to expedite FMC approval of pooling agreements by which steamship companies were granted waivers from U.S. antitrust laws in return for consenting to share — or "pool" — the available cargo on a particular route.

As drafted by Long's staff, S 2386 provided that such agreements would go into effect automatically 30 days after being filed with the FMC. Under existing law, the FMC had to rule that an agreement met "a serious transportation need, public benefit or valid regulatory purpose" before it could go into effect or be renewed.

Though the legislation specified that a pooling agreement would be legal only if it permitted all steamship companies to participate in it on an equitable basis, a key provision of the bill required that the agreement would remain in effect during a lengthy review process even if it illegally excluded any company from the pool's sharing arrangements.

According to lawyers familiar with the FMC, the required administrative review process and subsequent court appeals challenging an agreement's legality could take up to four years. During the entire time, a company challenging its exclusion from a pool would continue to be excluded.

Brazilian Connection

Of the shipping markets that could have been affected by the enactment of S 2386, revenues from one trade alone — between Brazil and the United States — totaled about $200 million annually, according to industry estimates.

About 40 percent of the total was shared by two companies, Delta and Moore-McCormack. The two firms, however, were being challenged for a major portion of the trade by the giant U.S. shipping firm, Sea-Land Service Inc. of Edison, N.J. Enactment of S 2386 could have kept Sea-Land out of the Brazil trade for years.

There were a total of 21 pooling agreements approved and on file with the FMC as of early 1978, according to the committee report, 17 of them in the U.S.-Latin American trades.

Of the 17, there were 15 in which either Delta or Moore-McCormack — but not Sea-Land — were parties. Enactment of S 2386 could have affected the renewal of all 15 agreements.

Sen. Long and officials of Delta and Moore-McCormack told Congressional Quarterly in May that they did not intend the legislation to protect the two companies' South American business.

As reported by the Senate Commerce Committee, HR 9518 declared that pooling agreements were "presumptively in the public interest and beneficial to the commerce of the United States." The legislation still provided that such agreements would go into effect automatically 30 days after being filed with the FMC.

However, it also authorized the FMC to suspend the agreement within 30 days of its being filed, for a period of 120 days, if it found that four conditions were met, that:

- It was probable that the agreement ultimately would be found illegal.
- Irreparable injury would result to the party challenging the agreement's legality.

- Suspension of the agreement would not "substantially harm" the parties to the agreement.
- Suspension would not harm trade between the United States and the foreign country affected by the pooling agreement.

In their statement accompanying the committee report, the four senators called the four conditions for suspension "an all but impossible standard of proof." They also said both the 30-day period given the FMC to determine whether or not to suspend an agreement, and the 120-day suspension period would not be adequate for the FMC to reach a conclusion on an agreement's validity.

Rebating — A Chronic Problem

According to the committee report, illegal merchant marine rebating was "a chronic problem which is substantial and serious," and greater efforts to combat rebating were needed because "it threatens the viability of the liner [scheduled] segment of our merchant fleet and is disruptive of our oceanborne trades."

A controversial provision enabling the FMC to obtain information on the rebating practices of foreign flag carriers was retained by the committee, despite a May 12 statement from the governments of Belgium, Denmark, Finland, West Germany, Italy, Japan, the Netherlands, Norway, Sweden and England that they would not agree to permit their citizens to produce documents under U.S.-imposed deadlines. The committee report said the provision was needed to assure that the rebating laws not be applied solely to U.S. carriers.

The provision expediting FMC approval of pooling agreements also was needed to combat rebating, according to the committee report. Because, under pooling agreements, the available cargo was shared equally among all eligible carriers, rebating ceased to be a competitive necessity, the report explained.

In addition, the report said, administrative delays, procedural problems and Justice Department Antitrust Division opposition made FMC approval of pooling agreements "either virtually unobtainable in all too many cases, or the prospects of approval so meager that carriers do not bother applying."

According to FMC records, however, only two agreements were rejected by the FMC after hearings on the previous five years.

As reported by the Senate Commerce Committee, HR 9518 was identical to the House-passed bill, except that it also provided for expedited FMC approval of pooling agreements.

Senate Floor Action

The Senate Oct. 6 passed HR 9518 by voice vote after adopting, also by voice vote, an amendment offered by Merchant Marine Subcommittee Chairman Inouye to delete the controversial Long-sponsored provision.

By mid-September, facing opposition to the measure from Sens. Robert P. Griffin, R-Mich., Edward M. Kennedy, D-Mass., Harrison Schmitt, R-N.M., Adlai E. Stevenson III, D-Ill., and Edward Zorinsky, D-Neb., and under pressure from supporters of the anti-rebating bill to end the controversy, Long agreed to have the provision dropped from HR 9518 on the Senate floor.

"Unfortunately," Long stated on the floor, "some senators felt that the [provision] created a controversy between our shipping laws and our antitrust laws and expressed the view that the [provision] represents an abrupt and sudden change in policy. I happen to disagree, but in view of the lateness of the session, the importance of at least passing HR 9518, and my desire not to engage the Senate in prolonged debate at a time when other bills require action, I . . . approve a modification of the bill on the Senate floor."

In a lengthy statement, Sen. Griffin said the Long-backed provision "would have made bad law and would have been against the public interest. I have worked actively to delete this provision, and I am pleased with the action being taken."

As passed by the Senate, HR 9518 was identical to the House committee- and floor-passed bill.

Final Action. The House on Oct. 13 approved by voice vote an error in the bill's title, clearing the measure for the president.

Rail Public Counsel

A bill (HR 12162) authorizing $2.2 million in fiscal 1979 for the Office of the Rail Public Counsel was rejected by the House Sept. 25. The vote was 188-196. The bill was brought to the floor under suspension of the rules, a procedure requiring a two-thirds vote for passage. *(Vote 727, p. 206-H)*

However, the bill's defeat had little impact on the office's operations. Congress in July approved a fiscal 1979 funding level of $1.85 million for the office in the Transportation Department appropriations measure (HR 12933). *(DOT funds, p. 61)*

A companion bill (S 2789), authorizing $1.6 million for 1979, was passed by the Senate April 27.

The office was created by Congress in 1976 to represent the interests of the public — including communities and consumers of rail services — in proceedings before the Interstate Commerce Commission (ICC).

The office did not begin functioning, however, until President Carter named its first director in late 1977.

At one point, the administration contemplated merging the office into the proposed Office of Consumer Representation. That plan was abandoned, however, after the House defeated the consumer agency bill in February.

Defeat of the rail counsel bill came as a surprise to its backers. James M. Collins, R-Texas, the sole dissenter to the House Commerce Committee's May 15 report (H Rept 95-1174) favoring the bill, argued that the bill should be defeated because the office was "not needed."

Joe Skubitz, R-Kan., backing the legislation, then admitted he had originally opposed creation of a separate office of rail public counsel. What had happened to change Skubitz' mind, John H. Rousselot, R-Calif., asked.

"Nothing," Skubitz replied, "except our colleagues on the floor voted for the thing and provided for the office, so I assume what we ought to be doing is providing funds for the office so that it can operate."

Despite the vote killing the authorization measure, the office still could continue to function in fiscal 1979, ICC officials and congressional staff members explained.

Because the annual funding bill providing the office's appropriation already had been approved by Congress and signed by the president, the office's 1979 funding already was assured, according to a staff aide to the House Transportation Appropriations Subcommittee, even though the funds had not been authorized.

Waterway User Tax Cleared in Final Days

Completing action on a bill whose path through the legislative thicket was as tortuous as any during the session, Congress at session's end cleared legislation imposing a user tax on the nation's inland waterway barge industry.

House backers of the bill (HR 8533) used a shortcut procedure to get the measure through before adjournment. On Friday, Oct. 13, the House brought up and passed the bill under suspension of the rules, which prohibited floor amendments. This ensured that the bill would be passed in the same form as approved by the Senate and thus would not have to go back to the other body and risk being lost in the adjournment rush.

The final vote was 287-123 — just 13 more than the two-thirds majority required for passage under the suspension procedure. *(Vote 805, p. 228-H)*

The Senate had given final approval to HR 8533 on Oct. 10.

HR 8533 had been approved by the House once before. Reported (H Rept 95-1608) by the House Ways and Means Committee Sept. 22 and passed routinely Sept. 25 by voice vote, the original bill merely clarified the tax status of the winnings from bingo games sponsored by tax-exempt and political organizations.

When Sen. Russell B. Long, D-La., conceived of the strategy of drafting a compromise version of the waterway user fee measure that could win congressional approval in the closing days of the session, he chose HR 8533 as the vehicle.

Final Provisions

As approved by Congress, HR 8533 (PL 95-502):

- Authorized $421 million for the Army Corps of Engineers to replace the existing Locks and Dam 26 at Alton, Ill., with a single new dam and 1,200-foot long lock.
- Authorized an additional $4 million for recreational development and replacement of terrestrial wildlife habitats that might be inundated by construction of the new lock and dam.
- Authorized $12 million for the preparation by the Upper Mississippi River Basin Commission of a master plan for the upper Mississippi River system. The plan was to be prepared after public hearings and with the assistance of the Army and Interior Departments. It was to be completed by Jan. 1, 1982.

With the exception of the new lock and dam at Alton, no upper Mississippi River lock, dam or channel was to be built, replaced, expanded or rehabilitated until the plan was approved by Congress.

- Created an Inland Waterways Trust Fund, and provided that the funds in the trust, if authorized and appropriated by Congress, could be spent on construction and rehabilitation projects to aid navigation on the nation's inland and intracoastal waterways.
- Imposed a tax on barge fuel beginning at four cents a gallon on Oct. 1, 1980, rising to six cents on Oct. 1, 1981, to eight cents on Oct. 1, 1983, and remaining at 10 cents after Sept. 30, 1985.
- Specified the inland and intracoastal waterways affected by the legislation.
- Authorized $8 million for a study by the Transportation Departments, in consultation with the Departments of the Treasury, Agriculture, Energy, Justice and the Army, the director of the Office of Management and Budget and the chairman of the Water Resources Council, to recommend to Congress by Sept. 30, 1981, a policy on waterway user taxes and charges.

Background

The waterway user fee proposal began its long journey through the 95th Congress in May 1977 when the Senate Public Works Committee, at the behest of Pete V. Domenici, R-N.M., approved a bill (S 790) to require the government to recover 100 percent of all inland waterway maintenance costs and 50 percent of new waterway construction costs.

To ease the bill's way through Congress, Domenici had suggested — and Public Works had approved — combining the fees with a $421 million authorization for a new lock and dam on the Mississippi River at Alton, Ill. A replacement for the existing Locks and Dam 26 at Alton was a major goal of waterway interests.

The bill was passed by the Senate on June 22, 1977, but in the House it was decided that the measure was a tax, not a fee. Asserting its constitutional prerogative to originate all revenue bills, the House dropped the Senate-passed bill and recommended a different approach.

As drafted jointly by the House Ways and Means and Public Works committees, the new version (HR 8309) imposed a six-cent-a-gallon tax on waterway barge fuel and authorized construction of the new lock and dam at Alton.

Despite a level of cost recovery far below that formulated by Sen. Domenici and passed by the Senate, the House bill was backed by the Carter administration, which said it would work for a higher tax in the Senate.

The House approved that bill on Oct. 13, 1977. *(1977 Almanac p. 542)*

Finance Committee Substitute

Sen. Domenici succeeded in having the House bill placed directly on the Senate calendar to avoid further committee consideration and possible delay. He prepared an amendment to beef up the tax and add user fees to the bill, as well. Transportation Secretary Brock Adams backed up Domenici by warning that President Carter would veto the bill unless it had a "substantial" user fee.

Finance Committee Chairman Russell B. Long, D-La., however, had a different idea in mind. A tireless foe of waterway user fees, Long convinced his Finance Committee to issue a direct challenge to the administration's veto threat by supporting a substitute that delayed the imposition of the barge fuel tax and eliminated the requirement that the waterways recover a portion of their construction costs. In place of a "substantial" fee, Long proposed a 12-cent-a-gallon fuel tax.

In a bitterly fought and heavily lobbied floor fight May 3, Long's proposal won out over Domenici's.

Water Resources Projects

This did not spell the end of the waterway user fee debate, however.

At the same time as it approved the Long-drafted version of the fee bill, the Senate amended it by adding a long list of public works projects in addition to the replacement for Locks and Dam 26. Domenici, the bill's minority floor manager, did not object to the legislation's burgeoning price tag because he reasoned that his Senate colleagues would be more inclined to support the concept of waterway user fees if their states were incidentally to benefit from the additional federal largesse.

By the time the bill was passed by the Senate May 4, the water project authorizations totaled $2.5 billion, including the $421 million for the new lock and dam at Alton.

The House, apparently not wanting to be outdone, decided to compile its own list of favorite water projects before going to conference with the Senate on the bill. The authorizations in the bill swelled to over $2 billion, according to a Congressional Budget Office estimate.

Veto Candidate

The legislation's bloated price tag and the dwindling number of days before the date set for adjourning, however, soon cast a shadow over the bill's chances of enactment.

President Carter's announcement that he would veto the public works appropriations bill (HR 12928) might have been the last straw. "If you dislike the public works appropriations bill," commented a Senate Public Works Committee aide, "you're going to hate HR 8309." *(Public works appropriations, p. 154; water projects legislation, Energy and Environment chapter)*

In early October, Long unveiled a different strategy. He drafted a new compromise, more acceptable to the administration, and tacked it onto a minor House-passed revenue bill (HR 8533). If the Senate passed the package, it could then be returned to the House in time for final approval before Congress adjourned.

Although little time was left, Long's strategy prevailed.

Ironically, the original provision of HR 8533, to which Long tacked on his waterway tax compromise, was deleted. In offering his amendment Oct. 10, Long inadvertently substituted the waterway compromise for the bingo earnings exemption provision instead of just adding it as an amendment to the bill. This procedure wiped out the original intent of the legislation that was returned to the House.

Senate Floor Action

In passing HR 8309 May 4, after three days of debate, the Senate issued a direct challenge to President Carter by approving a waterway user fee scheme that Carter promised to veto. The bill was passed by a 80-13 vote. *(Vote 153, p. 26-S)*

The Senate May 3 rejected, 43-47, the fee proposal drafted by Sens. Pete V. Domenici, R-N.M., and Adlai E. Stevenson III, D-Ill., that had the administration's backing. In its place the Senate adopted the weaker substitute, proposed by Russell B. Long, D-La., by a vote of 88-2. *(Votes 149, 151, p. 25-S)*

Transportation Secretary Brock Adams had written Stevenson just five days earlier that legislation lacking certain provisions of the Stevenson-Domenici proposal "would not be signed." The Long version lacked several of those features Adams said Carter considered key to his acceptance of the bill.

Making Carter's choice more difficult was the fact that the user fee provisions were just part of a massive public works authorization providing almost $2.5 billion for waterway development projects. Most of this amount was added on the Senate floor in 61 amendments, all adopted by voice votes.

Among the authorizations was $421 million for replacement of Locks and Dam 26 on the Mississippi River at Alton, Ill., a project sought eagerly by a number of midwestern and southern senators for over a decade.

"I'm sorry this happened," Adams said in a statement following the Senate's adoption of the Long proposal. "It means there will be no Lock and Dam 26, and there will be no user charge."

In approving the Long alternative on the user charge issue, the Senate voted to impose a fuel tax, as Carter had requested. But it rejected another revenue-raising requirement equally sought by Carter: a fee that would be tied to new waterways construction.

This was the principal difference between the Long and Domenici-Stevenson proposals, and became the key controversy in Senate debate.

Domenici insisted that at least partial recovery of construction costs was a modest price to pay for the extensive federal support already given the inland waterway system. Long, however, argued that the additional fees would harm irreparably the industry as well as the regions it served. He also argued that waterway transportation should be subsidized to a greater extent than other transportation modes because of its greater fuel efficiency.

Also approved as part of the bill was a proposal by Gravel to authorize $8 million to establish a six-member commission to study the feasibility of a sea-level canal in Panama. Gravel was spurned by the Senate, 43-49, in his first attempt to have the commission established. A second effort the next day succeeded, 63-29. *(Votes 148, 152, pp. 25-S, 26-S)*

Another controversy developed over a provision exempting farms relying on federally funded irrigation projects for water in the Kings River, Calif., region from a 160-acre limitation imposed on such farms by a 1902 law.

Malcolm Wallop, R-Wyo., sponsor of the provision, had argued before the Senate Environment and Public Works Committee that the 1944 Flood Control Act — which permitted the Kings River to be dammed — should not be governed by the acreage limitation placed in the 1902 Reclamation Act. The Supreme Court in February 1977 had upheld a lower court decision that ruled otherwise.

Alan Cranston, D-Calif., who offered an amendment to remove the exemption, argued that the provision unjustifiably benefited a single area. In California alone, he noted, farmers in nine other areas may have to sell acreage to meet the limitation.

Cranston suggested that Congress pursue a more general and cautious approach to the 160-acre limitation problem. His amendment carried 52-37. *(Vote 147, p. 25-S)*

Major Provisions

As passed by the Senate May 4, HR 8309:

- Imposed a tax on fuel used by inland waterway barges. The tax was to go into effect either on Jan. 1, 1982, or at the time construction began on replacement of Locks and Dam 26 at Alton, Ill., whichever occurred first. The tax was to begin at 4 cents a gallon, rising to 12 cents a gallon over a 10-year period. The tax was to be devoted to waterway maintenance and operation.

- Authorized $421 million for replacement of Locks and Dam 26 at Alton, Ill.
- Authorized $20 million for establishment of an Upper Mississippi River System Council to prepare a comprehensive plan for management of the upper Mississippi River waterway system to be sent to Congress by July 1, 1982.
- Authorized construction — or additional federal funds — for approximately 100 waterway development, flood control and other waterway-related projects. New authorizations in the bill totaled over $2 billion in addition to the funds for replacement of Locks and Dam 26 at Alton. (The latter was the only public works project that was included in the House-passed version.)
- Established an international commission for further study of the feasibility of a sea-level canal in Panama.

House Action

Because of Carter's threat to veto the Senate-passed version of HR 8309, House leaders cautiously approached their decision on how to proceed with the legislation.

Because the Senate passed bill provided for both waterway user fees and water resources authorizations, while the House-passed bill provided solely for the barge fees, the House decided it had to consider the water resources section separately before the bill could go to conference.

At first, House Public Works Committee leaders simply ordered committee staff members to study the 100-odd waterway projects in the Senate-passed bill and make recommendations to the committee on the merits of each of them. "A lot of these projects [in the Senate bill] really came out of left field," a committee aide remarked.

On June 8 Ray Roberts, D-Texas, introduced HR 13059, the Water Resource Development Act of 1978. This legislation authorized certain water projects contained in the Senate-passed waterway bill as well as a number of new ones. The bill was reported Aug. 9 (H Rept 95-1462). About one-third of the projects were in both the House committee bill and the Senate measure.

Compromise Reached

A new controversy was injected into the waterway fees measure on Sept. 30, when Sen. Adlai E. Stevenson III, D-Ill., offered an amendment authorizing the replacement of Locks and Dam 26 — but omitting waterway fees — to an unrelated Export-Import Bank bill (S 3077). Stevenson offered the amendment during a Saturday session when only a few senators were present. The amendment was adopted on a voice vote. *(Export-Import Bank, p. 397)*

Following Stevenson's successful move Sept. 30, an angry Sen. Domenici let the Senate know he would filibuster the Export-Import Bank bill or the conference report on the bill in order to prevent congressional approval of the lock and dam authorization without the fees.

At that point, Senate Finance Committee Chairman Long offered a second compromise proposal.

He wanted to tack a new version of the fees-plus-lock-and-dam bill onto a "minor revenue bill" that had already passed the House and take it to conference and get the House to accept it.

The Long compromise, which was agreeable to Stevenson and Domenici as well as to Transportation Secretary Brock Adams, had begun to take form in August. It was circulated to interested parties for their comment in September, but disappeared by the end of the month.

Long said Oct. 2 that waterway users had opposed the compromise but that he was willing to push the legislation despite their opposition. Also opposed to the compromise had been environmental groups and the railroads.

The waterway users opposed the bill because they felt it was too strong, while the railroads and environmentalists opposed it because they felt it was not strong enough.

In the end, Long's strategy proved successful and the compromise acceptable.

Final Action

Senate. HR 8533 was passed by the Senate Oct. 10 by voice vote after having been amended by Long's substitute funding a new Locks and Dam 26 and creating the Inland Waterways Trust Fund and the barge tax.

Long, speaking on behalf of the bill, called the legislation "about as complete a compromise as we could work out."

Sens. John C. Danforth, R-Mo., Adlai E. Stevenson III, D-Ill., Thomas F. Eagleton, D-Mo., and Harrison Schmitt, R-N.M., all noted that, in the Long-drafted bill, the imposition of barge fees, starting in 1980, was not tied to the beginning of construction of the new lock and dam — as in the version approved by the Senate May 4. They said the Senate should reconsider the fee issue if construction of the lock and dam were unduly delayed.

The project had been tied up in the courts by the railroads and environmentalists since the Army Corps of Engineers first proposed replacing the existing facility in 1968.

Domenici was absent Oct. 10. However, he commented in a printed statement that the compromise should be approved even though it was only "a start" toward creating what he called "a better balance in national transportation policy."

Only William Proxmire, D-Wis., spoke against passage of the compromise. He said that construction of a new Locks and Dam 26 was too high a price for the taxpayers to pay for "so small" a user fee.

"We may be hoping to buy improved transportation on the Mississippi," Proxmire stated, "but we are selling the taxpayers down the river."

House. The House completed action on the bill Oct. 13 by passing the Long compromise under suspension of the rules by a 287-123 vote. *(Vote 805, p. 228-H)*

No member spoke in opposition to the lock and dam authorization, but some criticism of the user tax was voiced, both by those who opposed it and those who maintained it was inadequate. Some House members agreed with their Senate colleagues that Congress should delay the user tax if construction of a new lock and dam at Alton was not begun by 1980.

Bingo Provision. The sponsor of the original bingo provision, Rep. William M. Brodhead, D-Mich., after discovering that it had been omitted from the bill, succeeded in getting it restored.

A concurrent resolution (H Con Res 754) was drafted making corrections in the enrollment of the bill. This had the effect of adding his provision as a new title. After the House passed it, it was rushed to the Senate, which accepted it by unanimous consent, thus approving the bingo addition. ▮

Commerce Act Streamlined

Legislation to streamline the language of the Interstate Commerce Act and related laws was signed by the president Oct. 17.

The bill (HR 10965 — PL 95-473) placed in one new section of the United States Code all federal laws dealing with the regulation of interstate commerce. It made "absolutely no substantive change in existing law," according to House Law Revision Counsel Edward F. Willet Jr.

The legislation was drafted by Willett in response to a requirement of PL 93-554, a law that created the Office of the Law Revision Counsel as an independent and nonpartisan office in the House of Representatives. It directed the office to codify each of the 30 titles of the United States Code that had not yet been brought up to date and re-enacted.

The codification of the interstate commerce laws, dealing with federal regulation of the railroads, water carriers, motor carriers, pipelines and freight forwarders, was the first part of an attempt to codify all federal laws dealing with transportation. The entire transportation section was expected to be ready for congressional consideration during the 96th Congress, Willett said.

HR 10965 was reported (H Rept 95-1395) by the House Judiciary Committee on July 26. It was approved by the House Sept. 19 by voice vote without amendment.

The Senate passed the bill Sept. 25 in identical form except for correction of typographical errors. The House approved the bill as corrected by the Senate on Sept. 26, clearing the measure.

Coast Guard Authorization

Congress completed action on legislation (HR 11465 — PL 95-308) authorizing $1,419,463,000 for the Coast Guard for fiscal 1979.

Final approval came June 14 when the House, by voice vote, concurred in the Senate-passed authorization.

The House had passed companion legislation April 17, but the bill subsequently was amended by the Senate Commerce Committee and by the Senate May 19.

As cleared for the president, HR 11465 authorized $969,906,000 for the Coast Guard's fiscal 1979 operating expenses; $379,954,000 for 1979 acquisition, construction and improvement of facilities and equipment; $34,603,000 for 1979 alteration or removal of bridges; $25 million for 1979 research and development, testing and evaluation; $10 million annually for 1979 and 1980 for federal aid to state boating safety programs, plus a supplemental authorization of $5,479,000 for fiscal 1978 operating expenses.

House Action

Committee

HR 11465 was reported (H Rept 95-1030) by the House Merchant Marine and Fisheries Committee March 31 by a unanimous voice vote.

As reported, the legislation authorized appropriations of $1,397,743,000 for the Coast Guard for fiscal year 1979. The total was $119,132,000 above the administration request of $1,278,611,000 for the year.

In its report, the committee said it was "gravely concerned" that the administration's recommended budget and manpower levels were inadequate for the Coast Guard to perform its duties.

Especially in the areas of marine safety and marine environmental protection, the report concluded, "the complement of Coast Guard personnel is stretched beyond reasonable limits in attempting to execute the Coast Guard missions."

HR 11465 as reported by the committee authorized $958,186,000 for Coast Guard operating expenses for fiscal 1979, $13.4 million over the administration's request; $379,954,000 for acquisition, construction and improvement of facilities and equipment for aiding navigation, $100.7 million above the administration's request; $34,-603,000 for the alteration or removal of bridges that obstructed navigation, the total recommended by the administration; and $25 million for research and development, testing and evaluation, $5 million more than the administration's request.

Among the specific items accounting for the differences between the administration's recommendations and the committee-approved sums were: $60 million for a replacement icebreaker for the Great Lakes, $30 million for an additional medium-endurance cutter and $5 million for research and development related to the Coast Guard's ability to clean up oil spills on the high seas.

The legislation also established a fiscal year 1979 personnel ceiling of 39,331, an increase of 911 over the administration's request of 38,420.

Floor

HR 11465 was passed by the House April 17 under suspension of the rules, prohibiting floor amendments. The vote was 357-13. *(Vote 188, p. 56-H)*

Senate Action

Committee

As reported by the Senate Commerce Committee May 12 (S Rept 95-817), HR 11465 was identical to the House-passed bill except for the following major additions:

- Authorized $10 million annually for fiscal 1979 and 1980 for federal aid to state boating safety programs. The administration had requested $3 million for fiscal 1979 and nothing for fiscal 1980, proposing to phase out the program at that time.
- Extended an exemption from certain federal safety standards for fishing tender and cannery tender vessels operating out of Alaska, Oregon and Washington, and exempted from Coast Guard inspection until Jan. 1, 1983, fish processing barges operating out of Alaska, Oregon and Washington.
- Required the Coast Guard to evaluate the adequacy of existing procedures for cleaning up oil spills on the Columbia River.

The committee report said the study was needed to prepare for a possible major increase in oil transportation on the river due to the 1977 opening of the Trans-Alaskan oil pipeline.

Floor

The Senate passed HR 11465 by voice vote May 19 with one amendment.

The amendment, approved by voice vote, was sponsored by Sen. Warren G. Magnuson, D-Wash. It increased the authorization level for the Coast Guard for fiscal 1978 from $887,521,000 to $892,900,000, and increased the authorization for the Coast Guard's fiscal 1979 operating expenses from $958,186,000 to $969,906,000.

Magnuson said the additional authorizations were needed to assure that supplemental funds requested by the administration — to increase certain Coast Guard law enforcement activities — did not surpass existing authorization levels.

The increases were earmarked primarily for better enforcement of fisheries laws — particularly the 200-mile fishing zone — and increased efforts against drug smuggling.

Final Action

The House June 14 by voice vote agreed to the Senate-passed version of the bill and the Senate authorization levels, thus clearing the measure for the president. ▮

Maritime Authorization

Legislation (S 2553 — PL 95-298) authorizing $496,792,000 in fiscal 1979 appropriations for the Commerce Department's Maritime Administration was cleared by Congress June 12 and signed into law June 26.

The Senate passed its version of the legislation on April 24, and the House approved a slightly higher funding level for the Maritime Administration in companion legislation (HR 10729), passed May 23.

On June 12 the Senate accepted the House-passed version, clearing the measure.

Legislative History

Senate Action

S 2553 was reported by the Senate Commerce Committee (S Rept 95-741) April 19. As reported, the bill authorized appropriations of $494,778,000 for Maritime Administration programs for fiscal 1979. The administration had requested $494,628,000.

Of the total funding authorized, the bill provided $157 million for ship construction; $262.8 million for construction subsidies based on the cost of U.S. labor as compared to foreign labor and on a ship's national defense capabilities; $17.4 million for research and development; $22,483,000 for maritime education and training expenses; and $34,845,000 for the national defense reserve fleet.

The bill also raised the ceiling on the government's ship construction loan guarantee program from $7 billion to $10 billion.

S 2553 was passed by the Senate April 24 by voice vote, with no debate and without amendment.

House Action

As reported (H Rept 95-1155) by the House Merchant Marine Committee May 15, HR 10729 authorized appropriations of $496,792,000, including $157 million for ship construction; $262.8 million for construction subsidies; $17.5 million for research and development; $24,647,000 for maritime education and training; and $34,845,000 for the national defense reserve fleet.

The bill also raised the ceiling on the government's ship construction loan guarantee program to $10 billion.

In additional views filed with the report, Paul N. McCloskey Jr., R-Calif., called for a revision in the basic laws governing the U.S. shipping trade. He encouraged the administration to develop policy recommendations, but added that, in the meantime, he would offer a series of amendments to the bill on the House floor designed to begin the revision process.

In debate on the legislation May 22 and 23, the House accepted several technical amendments to the bill, but turned back every McCloskey amendment. The bill was then passed by a vote of 326-82. *(Vote 310, p. 88-H)*

During floor consideration, floor manager John M. Murphy, D-N.Y., said the American merchant fleet was "in a deplorable state," and argued that the federal maritime programs and subsidies were "vital to keeping afloat as much of the fleet as we presently have."

No member spoke out in opposition to the authorization bill's passage, but McCloskey unsuccessfully offered a series of amendments to curb or cut back the subsidy and loan guarantee programs, to curb or cut back the wage subsidy programs, and to alter certain maritime labor union practices, privileges and subsidies. *(Vote 300, p. 86-H; votes 307, 308, 309, p. 88-H)*

One amendment offered by McCloskey would have barred the use of federal money for the construction of liquefied natural gas (LNG) carriers.

The bill authorized subsidies of $102 million for the construction of two LNG carriers for fiscal 1979. McCloskey noted, though construction of two LNG carriers was authorized for fiscal 1978, that construction was delayed while the administration reviewed the LNG carrier program. The amendment was rejected by a voice vote.

Final Action. The Senate accepted the House-passed version of the bill June 12, clearing it for the president. ▮

Foreign Shipping Rates

Legislation to combat Soviet merchant fleet undercutting of the prices charged by U.S. firms for shipping goods between the United States and other countries was signed into law Oct. 18.

The legislation (HR 9998 — PL 95-483) authorized the Federal Maritime Commission to prevent vessels owned or controlled by a foreign government from setting predatory rates for the carrying of goods in the U.S. foreign shipping trade.

The FMC prohibition of such rates could be overturned by the president for national defense or foreign policy consideration, under the new law.

Provisions

As cleared by Congress Oct. 3, HR 9998:

- Authorized the Federal Maritime Commission to disapprove any rate charged by a "controlled carrier" for up to 180 days if the rate were found, after appropriate notice and hearings, to be below a level determined by the commission to be "just and reasonable."

(Under existing law, disapproving a shipping firm's rates had the effect of suspending the firm's ability to carry cargo between the United States and other nations.)

- Defined "controlled carrier" as any firm that carried cargo in the United States foreign trade and was owned or controlled by a foreign government.

(According to the House committee report on the bill, the shipping firms of 40 nations could be considered "controlled carriers" under the bill's definition, but "only the Soviet Union has thus far utilized its controlled carriers to significantly penetrate United States liner trades.")

- Set out criteria to guide the commission in determining whether a rate was "just and reasonable."
- Authorized the commission to require that a controlled carrier justify the basis for a given rate in order to permit the commission to judge whether the rate was "just and reasonable."
- Permitted the president to block a commission's order to disapprove a rate for national defense or foreign policy reasons.

Background

The FMC, an independent regulatory agency, regulated the ocean shipping industry. Under existing law, shipping firms engaged in the U.S. trade were required to notify the FMC of the rates they charged for each service they offered. They were prevented from setting prices that the commission determined to be harmful to the national interest.

But the existing regulations had been unable to contain the growing number of Soviet ships entering the U.S. trade and attracting business by offering shippers prices well below those offered by competing lines.

Growing Soviet Penetration

In 1971 Soviet penetration of the U.S. export-import trade — routes served by ships carrying goods between the United States and other nations — was only 0.3 percent, but by 1977 that figure had grown to 3.4 percent, according to FMC figures.

During that period, the number of U.S. trade routes served by Soviet ships grew from one to "at least 16," FMC studies also reported.

The Soviet merchant marine achieved that rate of growth by offering shippers rates from 10 to 50 percent below the rates offered by its competitors.

Because the Soviet ships were owned and operated by the Soviet government, they were not constrained to turn a profit on their services.

Instead, according to the U.S. maritime industry, some members of Congress and representatives of the U.S. armed services, the Soviet Union operated its fleet of merchant marine ships in order to earn foreign currency, to employ Soviet citizens, to furnish military support in case of war and to provide a worldwide network of intelligence collection.

The Soviets' resultant pricing system "makes competition untenable," according to House Merchant Marine Committee Chairman John M. Murphy, D-N.Y.

According to a 1978 Navy Department report, "Understanding Soviet Naval Developments," the Soviet Union's merchant marine "can compete economically in international markets and provide many other services in support of state policy, while maintaining the ability to respond rapidly to provide extensive military support. Thus, the merchant fleet provides the USSR with a growing capability for the worldwide projection of political, military and economic influence."

Soviet Response

The Soviet Union, on the other hand, argued that its shipping policies were no different than any other nation's.

Writing in the July 1978 issue of *New Times*, a Soviet weekly, USSR Merchant Marine Minister Timofei Guzhenko said the Western view of Soviet merchant marine operations was made up of "groundless and ill-intentioned insinuations."

Soviet shipping constituted "only a fraction of the world merchant fleet," he said, "and the increase in its tonnage accounts for a little more than 1.5 percent of the total increment in world tonnage."

"Notwithstanding the attempts of certain quarters to block the activity of the Soviet merchant marine in international shipping," Guzhenko said, "our sea transport will continue to develop in accordance with the needs of the USSR national economy."

Legislation Sought

Many shippers in the United States favored the lower rates offered by the Soviet fleet and did not object to the growing Soviet maritime presence.

But the U.S. shipping industry, composed of shipbuilders, shipping lines and maritime labor, suggested in 1975 that Congress enact legislation to curb the Soviet pricing practices.

After hearings were held on several proposed bills during the 94th Congress, the FMC in July 1976 succeeded in negotiating with the USSR the Leningrad Agreement, in which the Soviets agreed not to charge rates lower than those offered by other carriers.

In May 1977, however, the FMC notified the House Merchant Marine Committee that the Leningrad Agreement had not been complied with by the Soviet Union.

Legislative Action

House

HR 9998 was reported (H Rept 95-1381) by the House Merchant Marine Committee July 19 by voice vote.

"The committee has concluded," the report stated, "that the rate-cutting activities of controlled carriers in the U.S.-liner trades demand a swift and just resolution."

The purpose of the legislation, the report said, was "to preserve legitimate competition among all common carriers engaged in the foreign commerce of the United States, ensure the survival of the American merchant marine, provide a means to monitor and check, if necessary, the future penetration of state-owned carriers into U.S. trade, and thus maintain and promote our international trade."

During its consideration of the bill, the committee rejected an amendment proposed by the administration to "avoid the possibility of curtailing legitimate cost-justified competition."

The amendment would have permitted a controlled carrier's rate to stand so long as it was either at least 85 percent of the rate posted for the same service by an existing shipping conference or the same or higher than the posted rate of any independent carrier.

The committee, in rejecting the amendment, argued that it would permit a controlled carrier to offer, in effect, a 15 percent across-the-board discount below other carriers' rates. This would nullify the desired effect of the bill, it was argued, which was to prevent controlled carriers from undercutting without justification the rates set by U.S. firms.

Other amendments suggested by the administration were adopted, including the provision permitting the president to disapprove a commission action for reasons of national defense or foreign policy.

HR 9998 was brought to the House floor under suspension of the rules, which barred amendments and required a two-thirds vote for passage. During the brief debate, no member spoke against the bill, and it was passed overwhelmingly by a 329-6 vote. *(Vote 541, p. 154-H)*

Senate, Final Action

The Senate Commerce Committee Sept. 29 reported the House-passed bill without amendment (S Rept 95-1260).

The bill then was passed by the Senate Oct. 3 in identical form by voice vote, clearing the measure for the president.

Freight Rail Lines Aid

The president Nov. 8 signed legislation broadening federal assistance for freight rail operations that served local communities.

Under the bill (S 2981 — PL 95-607), the Local Rail Service Assistance Act of 1978, branch rail lines carrying less than 3 million gross tons of freight per mile annually qualified for assistance.

S 2981 was designed primarily to assist financially hard-pressed freight lines that provided the only economically feasible transport service to a community. Federal assistance under the bill included both loans and grants.

The legislation amended an existing program of rail aid that was mandated by the Department of Transportation (DOT) Act. The DOT Act, which established the Transportation Department in 1966, had set guidelines for allocating assistance to the nation's light density rail lines.

This formula, as amended by S 2981, gave first priority to areas that would be most affected by the abandonment of uneconomic light density lines that were still in use. Two-thirds of the federal assistance was earmarked for these lines; the balance was set aside for the restoration of previously abandoned lines.

The new formula was to take effect in fiscal 1980; until then, the existing railroad aid programs, authorized by the 1976 Railroad Revitalization and Regulatory Reform Act, were to remain in effect. By concentrating on attempting to keep existing financially-strapped branch lines afloat, the bill reversed the emphasis in the DOT Act on resurrecting abandoned lines.

Although the rail assistance act redirected previously authorized funding for rail aid programs, no additional funding was authorized by S 2981.

The light density branch lines that qualified for federal aid under S 2981 were based on guidelines established by the Interstate Commerce Commission.

Final Provisions

As signed by the president, S 2981 (PL 95-607):

- Redirected previously authorized funds for rail assistance programs allocated by the 1966 Department of Transportation Act by concentrating more money on rail lines that needed the infusion of funds to continue operating. (The authorization for fiscal 1979 under the 1966 act was $67 million.) No state would receive less than 1 percent of the appropriation for any fiscal year in which federal rail assistance was authorized.
- Earmarked two-thirds of all authorized funds for deteriorating, but still operating, lines, with the remaining third used to restore abandoned lines.
- Made rail branch lines that carried less than 3 million gross tons of freight per year eligible for aid.
- Established a fixed 80-20 federal-state cost-sharing ratio for rail assistance for financing improvements to operating branch lines. Abandoned lines that were reopened were eligible for federal assistance for three years, with the share of federal operating subsidies for these lines set at 80 percent the first year and 70 percent the remaining two years.
- Permitted each state to expend not more than $100,000 or 5 percent of its allocation each fiscal year, whichever was higher, to meet the costs of establishing and/or maintaining its light density freight rail program.
- Amended the Interstate Commerce Act to reinstate, until July 1, 1980, restrictions on the ICC's authority to suspend a railroad's rate increases or decreases. (The "rate flexibility" provision, which expired Feb. 5, 1978, permitted railroads to raise and lower rates by up to 7 percent.)
- Empowered the ICC to order a railroad to install "safe and adequate" facilities and equipment. The agency could only exercise this power after examining and holding hearings on the condition of a railroad's facilities.
- Required the Federal Railroad Administration (FRA) to immediately consider the Chicago, Milwaukee and St. Paul Railroad's need for emergency assistance. The bill did not authorize any funds for this assistance, but merely ordered the FRA to review the railroad's condition.

Background

S 2981 reversed the emphasis in existing law on resurrecting abandoned lines and providing them long-term operating subsidies. While federal aid was channeled into these lines in an attempt to get them operating again, financially-strapped lines still in operation were deprived of an infusion of funds that might save them from being abandoned also.

The 1973 Regional Rail Reorganization Act, which became effective in 1974, authorized rail assistance for 6,000 miles of branch lines in the Northeastern states that were excluded from the Consolidated Rail System, established the same year. *(1973 Almanac p. 465)*

The rail assistance program in the 1973 act expired in April 1978. The Northeastern states' railroads were incorporated into a national program under the 1976 Railroad Revitalization and Regulatory Reform Act. A total of $360 million was authorized under this act through June 30, 1981. Rail lines that the ICC determined no longer met "public convenience and necessity," or those cited for abandonment by the final system plan set up in the 1973 act, received funds under the 1976 act.

Approximately 12,000 miles of light density branch lines nationwide were eligible for rail assistance before enactment of S 2981. This expanded to an estimated 93,833 miles of track eligible for federal aid under the revised allocation formula in S 2981.

Legislative History

Senate Committee Action

S 2981 was reported (S Rept 95-1159) by the Senate Commerce, Science and Transportation Committee on Aug. 25 by voice vote. As reported, the Senate bill differed from its House counterpart, HR 11979, in its eligibility criteria and allocation formula.

The Senate committee's bill emphasized federal aid to restore operating lines rather than channel funds in order to revitalize abandoned rail lines. S 2981 made branch lines that carried 3 million gross tons of freight per mile annually eligible for this aid, as opposed to a 5 million cut-off limit in the companion House bill.

House Committee Action

HR 11979 was reported (H Rept 95-1482) by the House Interstate and Foreign Commerce Committee on Aug. 11.

Panel member Tim Lee Carter, R-Ky., proposed to repeal a 1976 amendment to the Interstate Commerce Act that he said gave preference to large rail shippers over small ones. Carter said his amendment "would have provided meaningful assistance to thousands of small shippers who need railroad cars," but could not get them. But the full committee rejected the amendment.

Eight members of the Transportation Subcommittee, which considered the bill, filed a dissenting view with the committee report. They criticized the full committee for excluding a provision on freight rates for recyclable materials. They noted that the ICC had asked the full committee to give it "another chance to remove all railroad freight rates for the transportation of recyclable materials" that were pegged as unreasonable or discriminatory.

The House committee's bill was the same as the Senate committee's version except that it:

- Provided $100,000 each fiscal year to states for rail planning assistance. The balance of available federal funds would be used to assist in resurrecting abandoned lines.
- Made lines that carried 5 million gross tons or less per mile per year eligible for federal assistance.
- Empowered states to determine the criteria for branch rail line eligibility for financial assistance.

Senate Floor Action

S 2981 was passed Sept. 23 by voice vote after the Senate approved three amendments, as follows:

- By Wendell H. Ford, D-Ky., as a substitute for committee language establishing criteria empowering the ICC to require a railroad to provide "safe and adequate service." Under the floor amendment, the ICC had to make certain specific findings before it could exercise this power.
- By Howard W. Cannon, D-Nev., directing Conrail to expand its commuter service only if it were subsidized by the state or a local authority making the request for expansion.
- By John Melcher, D-Mont., to require the Federal Railroad Administration to consider the Milwaukee, Chicago and St. Paul Railroad's need for emergency financial assistance.

House Floor Action

With congressional adjournment nearing, floor manager Fred B. Rooney, D-Pa., delayed House debate on the bill in hopes of informally working out a compromise that, according to Rooney, "would be acceptable to all parties," including the Senate and the administration. Rooney offered the substitute to eliminate the need of a conference.

The compromise included the Senate's provision on eligibility of branch rail lines for assistance and the Senate's formula for awarding this assistance. The House agreed to limit eligibility for aid to those lines hauling no more than 3 million gross tons (rather than 5 million).

HR 11979 was passed by voice vote Oct. 13 under suspension of the rules. The Senate-numbered bill, as amended by the language of Rooney's compromise in HR 11979, then was passed and returned to the Senate.

Final Action

In the Senate, Melcher on Oct. 15 tried to tack on an amendment to allow two neighboring states to apply for a discontinued Amtrak route. Under the amendment, Amtrak would continue to operate the route, with the costs subsidized by the states. But Melcher subsequently agreed to withdraw the amendment.

The Senate then concurred in the House compromise language by voice vote, thus clearing the bill. ▮

Tris Ban Reimbursement

Legislation ordering the federal government to reimburse companies for their losses incurred as a result of a 1977 ban on the sale of Tris-treated children's sleepwear was pocket-vetoed by President Carter Nov. 4.

The legislation (S 1503), Carter said in a memorandum of disapproval, "would establish an unprecedented and unwise use of taxpayers' funds to indemnify private companies for losses incurred as a result of compliance with a federal standard."

If not vetoed, Carter said, the bill could have placed the government in the position of having to pay industry "each time new information arises which shows that a product used to meet regulatory standards is hazardous. This would be wrong."

'Hazardous Substance'

The proposal to reimburse companies grew out of a 1971 federal regulation requiring children's sleepwear to be made flame resistant. A second federal standard, for larger sizes of sleepwear, went into effect in 1974.

Manufacturers commonly relied on the flame-retardant chemical Tris to meet the federal standards. In 1977, however, the Consumer Product Safety Commission (CPSC) banned Tris as a "hazardous substance." Under the CPSC ruling, manufacturers were required to repurchase all unsold or unwashed children's garments made from Tris-treated fabric.

Carter noted that, though the CPSC did not ban Tris until 1977, information concerning Tris' carcinogenic properties became available as early as 1974. "Some firms stopped using Tris after this test information became available, but other firms did not," Carter said.

"If this bill became law the potential would exist for compensation of firms who marketed the Tris-treated material after they knew, or should have known, that such products constituted a hazard to the health of children," Carter said.

The Congressional Budget Office (CBO) estimated the legislation would force the government to pay out approximately $51 million to clothing manufacturers over a three-year period.

Though some Tris-treated garments subsequently were exported to foreign countries that had not banned the sale of such garments, many of the garments resulted in a total loss for the manufacturers.

SBA Assistance

At the same time that he vetoed the reimbursement legislation, President Carter wrote Small Business Administration (SBA) head Vernon Weaver instructing him to assist eligible firms harmed by the 1977 Tris ban "to the fullest extent possible under existing loan programs," to enable those firms to remain in business and to preserve their employees' livelihoods.

Legislative History

The legislation was sought by clothing manufacturers and by members of Congress dismayed with the manner in which the federal government first ordered manufacturers to fireproof their garments and then banned the most commonly available fireproofing treatment.

The bill was opposed by Ralph Nader's Congress Watch, a consumer group, which argued that the manufacturers were as much to blame for the losses as the government.

The government had not ordered manufacturers specifically to use Tris, the group argued, but merely ordered them to fireproof their garments. Tris was used because of its high consumer acceptability, according to clothing manufacturers.

S 1503, giving the U.S. Court of Claims jurisdiction to determine the losses incurred as a result of the 1977 ban on Tris was reported (S Rept 95-584) by the Senate Judiciary Committee Nov. 2, 1977, and was passed by the Senate Jan. 20, 1978, by voice vote.

An amended version of the bill was reported (H Rept 95-1747) by the House Judiciary Committee Oct. 10 — just five days before Congress adjourned.

In a strong dissent to the majority's views, the Judiciary Committee's Robert F. Drinan, D-Mass., said the legislation was a bad precedent and would reduce a manufacturer's incentive to produce safe products.

Nonetheless, the bill was passed by the House Oct. 12 under suspension of the rules by a vote of 304-90. *(Vote 797, p. 226-H)*

The House version of the bill subsequently was approved by the Senate Oct. 13, clearing the bill for the president. Senate approval was by voice vote. ▮

Consumer Co-op Bank

Legislation to encourage the development of consumer cooperatives was cleared by Congress and sent to the president Aug. 9.

The legislation (HR 2777) established a national consumer cooperative bank and a technical assistance program to make loans to co-ops and help them develop.

The House narrowly passed its version of the co-op bill in July 1977.

The Senate passed a more modest version on July 13, 1978, by a 60-33 vote.

A compromise bill was approved by the Senate July 27 on a voice vote, and by the House Aug. 9 by a vote of 236-164, completing action on the measure.

While the administration's initial opposition to the bill during 1977 had harmed its chances in the House, President Carter's subsequent endorsement of the legislation in early 1978 gave a boost to the bill in the Senate. Given much credit for the administration's turnabout — and for the comfortable margin of victory in the Senate — was vigorous lobbying by White House consumer adviser Esther Peterson.

Major Provisions

As approved by Congress, HR 2777 (PL 95-351):

- Stated that Congress concluded that cooperatives had been hampered in their development and that a national consumer cooperative bank was therefore needed.
- Created a National Consumer Cooperative Bank, to be located in the District of Columbia, to make loans, commitments for credit, loan guarantees and other financial services available to non-profit consumer cooperatives.
- Provided that the bank's 13-member board of directors initially be appointed by the president, but that the board eventually was to become self-perpetuating as it became increasingly self-sufficient, except that one director, representing the interests of small business, would continue to be appointed by the president.
- Authorized $300 million in federal funds to purchase stock in the bank to provide seed money during the bank's first five years, and required the bank, beginning in 1990, to retire federally owned stock on a regular basis until the bank became financially self-sufficient, at which time all stock would be owned by the bank's member cooperatives.
- Provided the bank with borrowing authority of 10 times its paid-in capital plus other earnings.
- Encouraged the bank to provide loans to co-ops having low-income members or benefiting low-income persons.
- Established, within the bank, an Office of Self-Help Development and Technical Assistance, and authorized $75 million over the office's first three years to promote and assist the development and operation of consumer co-ops.
- Authorized $4 million for fiscal 1979 and additional sums "as necessary" for 1980 and 1981 for administrative costs of the bank and for the technical assistance program.

Background

The National Consumer Cooperative Bank Act was passed by the House in similar form in July 1977 by a vote of 199-198. Before approving the bill, the House had rejected a substitute measure — supported by the Carter administration — that would have provided for a two-year study of cooperatives, their role in the economy and existing sources of aid for cooperatives. *(1977 Almanac p. 441)*

Throughout House consideration, the administration had opposed the legislation. "Although the administration sympathizes with the objectives of consumer cooperatives," Bert Lance, then director of the Office of Management and Budget, wrote June 29, 1977, "we have concluded that adequate justification does not exist for the establishment of a new federal bank and the expenditure of billions of dollars of federal funds for the purchase of capital stock and debt to finance consumer cooperatives."

Following a review of the administration's position in late 1977, however, and at the urging of Carter consumer adviser Esther Peterson, the administration reversed its position on the legislation. The White House, Treasury Assistant Secretary Roger C. Altman announced in January, "now has a better appreciation for the needs of consumer cooperatives than we did" in 1977.

The administration switch pleased Sen. Thomas J. McIntyre, D-N.H., chairman of the Banking Subcommittee on Financial Institutions and a supporter of the legislation. "I am personally most gratified by your testimony here," McIntyre told Altman. "I am certain we can forge a very responsible bill of which both the Congress and the President can be duly proud."

Senate Committee Action

As reported (S Rept 95-795) by the Senate Banking Committee May 10, HR 2777 was pared down substantially from the House-passed version, with most of the changes following the administration's recommendations.

The House-passed measure created a National Consumer Cooperative Bank; authorized the creation of from four to 12 regional banks; established an Office of Consumer Cooperatives in the ACTION agency to provide technical assistance to cooperatives and to administer a self-help development fund; provided the bank with borrowing authority of 10 times its paid-in capital plus other earnings; and authorized a total of $500 million for the bank and $250 million for the self-help development and technical assistance programs over five years.

Committee Amendments. As amended by the Senate Banking Committee, HR 2777:

- Replaced the bank's authority to create regional banks with authority to create regional offices.
- Placed responsibility for the self-help development and technical assistance programs with the bank, rather than with ACTION.
- Established loan targets and safeguards to promote aid to low-income areas, discourage excessive loans to housing cooperatives, and prevent granting an unfair competitive advantage to cooperatives that might compete with small businesses.
- Provided the bank with borrowing authority of five times its paid-in capital plus other earnings.
- Authorized $300 million for the bank over five years and $75 million for the self-help development and technical assistance programs.

Committee Views. In its report, the committee concluded that cooperatives could play a valuable role in helping consumers fight rising prices, and that the development of cooperatives had been "greatly hampered by the general unavailability of conventional credit and lack of technical assistance."

In response to critics of the bill, who said during Senate hearings that the legislation would aid cooperatives to the detriment of small businesses, the committee stated:

"The proposed National Consumer Cooperative Bank is not a hand-out, give-away or a subsidy program. Only sound loans which have a reasonable expectation of being repaid are to be made. Interest rates charged borrowers will be at competitive rates."

"To assure that no unfair competitive advantage is granted to cooperative borrowers," the report continued, "the bill requires that loans be made on a sound business basis. These loans will be successful only if there is an economic need and if the purposes of the loan are not already being met on a competitive basis."

In additional views on HR 2777, four senators said they opposed the legislation as drafted by the committee.

The four, all of whom voted against reporting the bill, were William Proxmire, D-Wis., John G. Tower, R-Texas, Jake Garn, R-Utah, and Richard G. Lugar, R-Ind. (The fifth senator who voted against reporting the legislation was Harrison Schmitt, R-N.M.)

"Rather than a lack of bank credit," the four stated, "we believe a lack of technical assistance is the major factor behind the slow growth of consumer cooperatives." They also said the legislation could harm small businesses.

For these reasons they said they would propose an amendment similar to the substitute bill that had been supported by the Carter administration in 1977. The amendment, they said, would provide for a two-year study of cooperatives' technical and financial needs and a two-year pilot lending program.

Senate Floor Action

The Senate passed HR 2777 July 13 by a 60-33 vote after rejecting four amendments offered by Garn, Lugar, Proxmire and Tower. *(Vote 212, p. 34-S)*

The Senate rejected all of them by similar margins. It then passed the bill as reported.

The legislation's supporters said an additional lending institution was needed to help consumer cooperatives because existing financial institutions did not adequately serve cooperatives. They argued that the weakening amendments would jeopardize the bank's ability to become self-sufficient.

"This bill will be particularly helpful in making it possible for low-income consumers in deteriorating rural and urban areas to solve many of their own problems," stated Thomas J. McIntyre, D-N.H., the bill's floor manager. "However, the need for a source of credit is general among all types of consumer cooperatives because most traditional commercial lenders do not understand the structure of cooperatives or the importance of the commitment of their members."

Opponents argued that the federal aid granted cooperatives by the legislation would unfairly give them a competitive edge over existing small businesses, and would harm existing lending institutions. They also argued that there was no proven need for the bank and expressed the fear that the bank's loans would end up going to wealthy suburban cooperatives rather than to poor urban ones, in order to ensure the bank's success.

"There is no proof, there is no adequate evidence, that this bank is really needed," Tower said during the debate, and Lugar said that to guarantee the bank's financial stability was contradictory to its purpose, which was to "help poor people."

Defeated by the Senate were amendments to:

- Substitute a two-year pilot lending program and a study of the need for a cooperative bank for the committee-backed bill. By Tower, rejected 35-59. *(Vote 207, p. 34-S)*

- Require the bank to determine, for each loan, that the loan would not harm existing small businesses and that the area was not already served by existing lending firms. By Lugar, rejected 35-57. *(Vote 209, p. 34-S)*
- Bar the bank from making any loan unless the borrower had been turned down by two other lenders. By Lugar, rejected 35-58. *(Vote 210, p. 34-S)*
- Require the bank to make 50 percent of its loans to cooperatives having low-income members. By Lugar, rejected 36-56 *(Vote 211, p. 34-S)*

Conference Action

HR 2777 was reported (H Rept 95-1399) by a House-Senate conference committee July 28.

As approved by the committee, the legislation was closer to the Senate-passed bill than to the House-passed version. Most of the changes made by the Senate had been recommended by the administration.

The House conferees agreed to support the Senate position on the amount of seed money the federal government would provide the bank, on the composition and selection of the bank's board of directors, on making no provision for regional banks, on the authorization for administrative costs, on the structure and funding of the technical assistance program, and on encouraging loans to low-income groups.

Senate conferees agreed to the House position permitting the bank to borrow up to 10 times its paid-in capital plus other earnings; the Senate bill had limited the bank's borrowing authority to five times its paid-in capital plus other earnings.

Final Action

The Senate approved the conference report by voice vote July 27, and the House followed suit Aug. 9 by a vote of 236-164, clearing the bill for the president. *(Vote 586, p. 166-H)* ▮

Consumer Participation Bill

Legislation (S 270, HR 8798) to authorize the federal government to help underwrite the costs of public participation in agency proceedings died a quiet death in the 95th Congress.

The legislation had been declared by the White House to be a top consumer priority following the House defeat Feb. 8 of legislation to establish a federal Office of Consumer Representation. *(Story, p. 473)*

But the bill never gathered sufficient support to win approval by either the House or Senate Judiciary Committees.

The bill's supporters said the White House had never vigorously pushed for enactment, but they conceded that a stronger administration commitment probably would have made little difference.

"We probably didn't have the votes to have the bill reported by either committee," one public interest group lobbyist stated.

Legislative History

The Senate Judiciary Committee on a tie vote of 8-8, Aug. 4, 1977, failed to report S 270.

In the House, HR 8798, the companion bill, was approved by the Judiciary Committee's Subcommittee on Administrative Law and Governmental Relations on July 27, 1977. It was the second time the subcommittee approved the bill in 1977, the full Judiciary Committee having sent it back to the subcommittee May 12 of that year for a number of minor changes after the panel had already considered it.

The bill as drafted authorized $10 million annually for a three-year experiment to encourage private individuals and groups to participate in federal agency proceedings.

Agencies would be permitted to award attorneys' fees, fees and costs of experts and "other cost of participation" to those who 1) represented an important interest or point of view that would not otherwise be fairly represented, 2) themselves had little economic interest in the outcome of the proceedings in comparison to the costs of participation, and 3) did not otherwise have sufficient resources to participate in the proceeding.

Public Interest Coalition

The legislation was supported by a coalition of groups, including the Consumer Federation of America, Congress Watch, the Council for Public Interest Law, Consumers Union, the J.C. Penney Co., Common Cause, the National Association for the Advancement of Colored People, the National Council of Senior Citizens, Environmental Action and the Sierra Club. It was opposed by the National Association of Manufacturers, the Grocery Manufacturers of America, and number of utilities and nuclear power firms and the Pacific Legal Foundation. ▮

FTC Reorganization

Controversy over the congressional veto issue led to the defeat of legislation authorizing funding for the Federal Trade Commission (FTC) for fiscal years 1978-81.

The legislation (HR 3816), which would have streamlined the agency's proceedings and strengthened its power to issue and enforce orders and subpoenas, was killed when the House Sept. 28 voted for the second time in 1978 to reject a conference compromise on the bill.

Both times, opponents argued that the conference report should be rejected because House and Senate conferees had refused to include in the bill a provision providing for a congressional veto of FTC actions. The veto was needed, they argued, to keep a congressional rein on the FTC's "unelected bureaucrats."

Supporters called the second conference report a fair compromise.

Both conference reports had been routinely approved by the Senate, which was opposed to the congressional veto.

The vote rejecting the second conference report was 175-214. *(Vote 750, p. 212-H)*

The House's action did not jeopardize the agency's existence. The final version of the fiscal 1979 State, Justice, Commerce and Judiciary appropriations bill (HR 12934 — PL 95-431) contained $64,750,000 for the commission. *(State, Justice appropriations, p. 88)*

Major Provisions

As approved by a House and Senate conference committee, but subsequently rejected by the House, HR 3816:

- Required the president to appoint persons qualified by training, education or experience to serve as FTC commissioners, and to ensure that the commission was "well balanced, with a broad representation of various talents, backgrounds, occupations and experience appropriate to the functions of the commission."

- Prohibited former commissioners and high-level staff members from communicating with agency commissioners or employees concerning official agency business — and from participating in agency proceedings — for a period of one year after they left the agency. The prohibition did not apply to personal matters, nor to former employees representing the United States, as would occur if the person had gone to work for a different federal agency.
- Provided the FTC with an additional 25 high-level staff positions.
- Barred executive branch political clearance of any commission employee except the general counsel.
- Exempted savings and loan institutions from FTC jurisdiction over unfair methods of competition and unfair or deceptive acts and practices, and from the commission's authority to conduct investigations, compile information and require the filing of reports.
- Increased the penalties for ignoring FTC orders and subpoenas, modified the deadlines for compliance with such orders and subpoenas and prohibited court challenges to orders or subpoenas before the agency had announced it intended to enforce them.
- Permitted the FTC to initiate suits to enforce its subpoenas or orders in any judicial district in which the commission's inquiry was being carried on.
- Required the FTC to respond within 20 days to citizen petitions for FTC actions.
- Provided that a commission rule would not go into effect if a joint resolution of disapproval were passed by Congress and signed by the president. If the president vetoed the resolution, Congress would have an opportunity to override the veto. Expedited procedures were established for House consideration of joint resolutions of disapproval. The commission was to submit to Congress a paperwork and "judicial impact" analysis of each rule it issued.
- Authorized appropriations for the FTC of $65 million for fiscal 1978, $70 million for 1979, $75 million for 1980 and $80 million for 1981.

Background

Both the House and Senate had passed differing versions of HR 3816 in 1977. The bill was designed to strengthen the consumer protection and enforcement powers of the FTC. Both bills streamlined legal procedures so that the agency could more easily pursue broad actions against suspect business practices. The legislation also greatly increased FTC fines for failure to comply with certain fair trade practices.

But in a setback for consumers, the House Oct. 13, 1977, deleted a controversial provision that permitted class action suits based on FTC rulings. The deleted provision would have allowed individuals and groups harmed by violations of FTC trade regulations to sue for damages. Court decisions in 1974 and 1975 had effectively barred such suits by prohibiting third-party intervention in commission rulings and by requiring individual notice to each member of a class action suit.

The Senate-passed version contained a provision, rejected by the House, to require simultaneous submission to Congress and the executive branch of agency budget and legislative recommendations.

Among the other differences that had to be resolved by House-Senate conferees were:

- The House-passed provision for a congressional veto of FTC rules and regulations.
- A provision in the Senate bill directing the FTC to seek appointment of a receiver for businesses accused of cheating customers, or similar relief, to prevent "siphoning away" of assets before a final determination of wrongdoing could be made. The House deleted this provision during floor action.
- A Senate ban on White House political clearance of "supergrade" appointees to the FTC and the Consumer Product Safety Commission. The House had struck a similar provision that was applicable to the FTC. *(Background, 1977 Almanac, p. 552)*

First Conference Action

House and Senate conferees filed the first conference report (H Rept 95-892) on HR 3816 on Feb. 22.

House conferees accepted the Senate position on two of the most controversial provisions.

The conference agreement authorized the FTC to go to court to prevent firms accused of engaging in unfair or deceptive practices from wasting their assets in trying to avoid reimbursing wronged consumers.

Business interests — and the House — had opposed the provision, arguing that FTC staff members might use this authority to scare small businesses into signing consent orders rather than mounting serious legal defenses of their business practices.

The compromise contained no provision for a congressional veto, as contained in the House-passed version.

House members angry with the size and growing power of the federal bureaucracy had argued that Congress' ability to nullify FTC actions was the sole way to assure that the agency remained accountable to the public. Under the House provision, an FTC regulation could be overturned by approval by Congress of a concurrent resolution. (A concurrent resolution, which cannot become a law, does not require the president's signature to take effect.)

It was largely this widespread dissatisfaction with "big government" and an "unchecked" federal bureaucracy that led the House to reject the conference report Feb. 28. Backers of the legislation said the 146-255 vote came as a complete surprise. The report had been routinely approved by the Senate by voice vote on Feb. 22. *(House vote 73, p. 22-H)*

During the House floor debate on the report, members repeatedly characterized the FTC as an agency run by unelected "bureaucratic dictators." They urged the House to reject the conference report and insist that conferees reinstate the veto provision in order to keep a tighter rein on the agency's activities.

Consumer Defeats

The vote was the second blow to consumer legislation in the span of a single month. The House Feb. 8 defeated (189-227) legislation backed by President Carter to establish a federal Office of Consumer Representation (OCR). *(OCR, p. 473)*

At the same time, the vote was another victory for representatives of small business, the National Association of Manufacturers and the Grocery Manufacturers of America, which had worked to defeat both bills.

Dissatisfaction with the continuing growth of the federal bureaucracy also was frequently cited in the debate that preceded the vote killing the consumer agency bill. A check by Congressional Quarterly found that 199 of the 255 members voting to reject the conference report on the FTC Act amendments also had voted against establishing the consumer agency. Of the 199, 84 were Democrats and 115 were Republicans.

"The message is that the government is getting too big, that the FTC is one of the worst agencies in the federal government, and that we've got to rein it in," explained James P. Carty, the National Association of Manufacturers' regulatory reform and consumer affairs director. He acknowledged that the association used the names of consumer agency opponents as a "target list" for lobbying against passage of the FTC conference report.

But Elliott H. Levitas, D-Ga., a leader of the floor fight against the conference report, denied the vote was anti-consumer. "Many members told me after the vote that this was clearly on the single issue of the congressional veto," Levitas said in an interview. "This is an important issue." He added that, in his opinion, lobbying on the bill had not been heavy. "I didn't hear from a single lobbyist on this bill one way or the other," he said.

Levitas also had opposed the consumer agency bill.

Second Conference Report

After the House defeated the conference report on Feb. 28 and requested a second conference to rewrite the disputed provisions, Senate Commerce Committee Chairman Howard W. Cannon, D-Nev., and Consumer Subcommittee Chairman Wendell H. Ford, D-Ky., at first decided not to respond to the House request. A congressional veto, the senators reasoned, might be worse than having no bill at all.

As the summer months passed, however, Cannon and Ford agreed to meet with House conferees in an attempt to craft a new compromise.

Second Conference

In a mid-August meeting, Senate conferees rejected outright the House's insistence on the congressional veto provision.

Rep. Bob Eckhardt, D-Texas, the bill's floor manager, then suggested language providing for congressional cancellation of FTC rules through House and Senate adoption of a joint resolution of disapproval. Under this plan, the president would have the power to veto the resolution, but Congress still could override the veto.

To expedite consideration of resolutions of disapproval, Eckhardt proposed setting deadlines and establishing special procedures and rules for Senate and House committee and floor action on such resolutions.

In exchange for considerably weakening the congressional veto provision, Eckhardt proposed a concession to House conferees: dropping from the bill the provision authorizing the FTC to try to prevent firms from wasting their assets in order to avoid having to reimburse aggrieved consumers.

Senate Leadership Objections. Before agreeing to the Eckhardt proposal, Ford told House conferees the expedited procedures provision would have to be approved by the Senate leadership.

Both Majority Leader Robert C. Byrd, D-W.Va., and Minority Leader Howard H. Baker Jr., R-Tenn., subsequently rejected the plan, stating that the expedited procedures were unnecessary and conflicted with existing Senate rules.

In a final compromise effort, Eckhardt proposed that the expedited procedures apply solely to House consideration of resolutions of disapproval.

This plan was agreed to by all Senate conferees and all but three House conferees (Robert (Bob) Krueger, D-Texas; James T. Broyhill, R-N.C.; and Samuel L. Devine, R-Ohio). The second conference report was filed (H Rept 95-1557) Sept. 8. Again the Senate routinely approved the report on Sept. 11.

Rules Committee Action

One more stumbling block remained before the second conference report was able to go to the House floor.

Though HR 3816 as originally approved by the House in October 1977 contained the congressional veto language, it did not provide for expedited House consideration of concurrent resolutions of disapproval.

Reps. Broyhill and Levitas notified Eckhardt that, if the bill were brought to the House floor, they would raise a point of order against its consideration. Because the conference report contained language providing for expedited consideration of resolutions of disapproval, the conference version, they stated, exceeded the scope of both the Senate- and House-passed bills, a violation of House rules.

In order to avoid a point of order being raised, Eckhardt had to ask the Rules Committee to grant a waiver of the rules. At a Sept. 14 session, Rules heard Eckhardt's request for a waiver, but took no action.

In a subsequent meeting, held on the morning of Sept. 19, several Rules members said they opposed the waiver. Rules Chairman James J. Delaney, D-N.Y., said such a move required careful deliberation. He suggested the bill be left to die at the end of the session.

After the morning Rules session, but before the afternoon vote, however, Delaney and others on the panel changed their minds.

Voting largely along party lines, Rules approved, 8-5, a resolution giving Eckhardt his waiver of House rules and sending the bill to the floor. Only one Democrat, Christopher J. Dodd, Conn., voted against the resolution, and only one Republican, John B. Anderson, Ill., voted for it.

House Floor Action

The bill died when the House Sept. 28 voted 175-214 to reject the second compromise version. *(Vote 750, p. 212-H)*

The vote to reject the second report was closer than the 146-225 vote by which the House had rejected the first version. Fifty-one members participating in both votes switched from opposition to the bill in February to support on Sept. 28, while only 13 switched from support for the bill in February to opposition in September. ▮

Product Safety Agency

Acting on the final day of the session, Congress approved an extension (S 2796) of the Consumer Product Safety Commission (CPSC) for three years. The bill was signed into law (PL 95-631) Nov. 10.

A White House task force earlier had recommended a shorter extension for the CPSC, with an eye to abolishing or reorganizing the controversial agency during the 96th Congress.

However, President Carter personally decided to reject the task force's recommendation. Siding with White House consumer adviser Esther Peterson and Senate Commerce Consumer Subcommittee Chairman Wendell H. Ford, D-Ky., Carter decided instead to seek a three-year extension, but with minor changes in the agency's procedures.

A bill similar to that recommended by Carter won Senate approval Aug. 4.

However, a companion bill (HR 12442) became stalled in the House over a controversial provision governing the export of unsafe consumer products.

The controversy arose in connection with the export of fabric and clothing treated with Tris, a chemical used for years as a fire retardant in children's sleepwear before being found to be a carcinogen. *(Tris ban, p. 520)*

The CPSC had decided in October 1977 that it lacked authority to ban the export of Tris-treated clothes. In May 1978, however, with two new members, the commission reversed itself and voted that it did have such authority.

The House Commerce Committee, attempting to clarify the commission's powers, during its markup of HR 12442 approved an amendment requiring the CPSC to notify foreign governments of a risk to safety or health posed by the export of materials found — or proposed to be designated — unsafe for American citizens.

Eight of the committee's members, however, unhappy with the amendment, blocked floor consideration of the bill until a compromise could be worked out.

They argued that to require the commission to notify foreign governments of a product's export even before the product had formally been designated unsafe amounted to depriving the exporter of his constitutional guarantee of due process under the law.

House Commerce Consumer Protection Subcommittee Chairman Bob Eckhardt, D-Texas, subsequently drafted a compromise bill acceptable to the eight dissenting Commerce Committee members.

The new version, introduced on the House floor Oct. 15 as a substitute bill, dropped the notification requirement for the export of products only proposed to be designated unsafe.

It added a provision proposed by Stephen L. Neal, D-N.C., permitting the CPSC to suspend development of its own mandatory safety standards in order to permit an industry to develop its safety program. It also incorporated a number of the procedural changes provided in the Senate-passed bill.

The compromise bill was passed by the House Oct. 15 by voice vote. The House changes then were routinely approved by the Senate later that day, also by voice vote, completing congressional action.

Major Provisions

As cleared for the president, S 2796:

- Authorized $55 million for the CPSC for fiscal 1979, $60 million for 1980 and $65 million for 1981.
- Required manufacturers to give the CPSC advance notice of the export of any product, substance or fabric not in compliance with an existing safety standard, and required the CPSC to notify the appropriate foreign governments of the hazard associated with the exported product.
- Established a Toxological Advisory Board to provide the CPSC with technical assistance on first-aid instructions contained in labels on toxic household products.
- Provided that the chairman of the CPSC was to serve at the pleasure of the president. Under existing law, the chairman retained his post throughout his term.
- Permitted the commission, under certain circumstances, to develop its own mandatory safety standards. Under existing law, standards were developed largely independent of the agency by outside experts.
- Authorized the CPSC to make existing voluntary product safety standards mandatory, and to delay imposition of a mandatory standard in order to permit an industry to develop its own voluntary standard.
- Required the CPSC to study all its existing rules and make recommendations to Congress within 18 months of the legislation's enactment on how to simplify and modernize them.

Background

Established in May 1973, the Consumer Product Safety Commission was the first independent regulatory agency created since the New Deal.

In the Consumer Product Safety Act (PL 92-573), however, Congress did not merely dust off and press back into service the New Deal approach of creating new agencies to correct each alleged abuse of the free enterprise system. Instead, Congress attempted an innovative approach keyed to the regulatory problems of the 1970s.

The new law, according to an October 1976 study by the House Commerce Subcommittee on Oversight and Investigations, "represented in many respects the most advanced congressional thinking on the techniques of federal regulation. The act incorporated a number of concepts of regulatory reform. Indeed, many current proposals for regulatory reform appear to be its progeny."

Yet since its inception the CPSC had been subjected to an unrelenting stream of criticism from consumers, business interests and Congress itself. The criticism peaked Feb. 8 when the commission chairman, S. John Byington, announced his resignation, effective June 30, to "depoliticize" congressional hearings on extending the agency's authorization.

"I believe it is essential in the weeks ahead," Byington wrote President Carter in his letter of resignation, "that we focus our attention on [the agency's] goals and achievements, our present priorities and activities as well as future options for CPSC—rather than on me personally. The public stands to gain little by the latter, but a great deal by the former."

Byington had been asked to resign Jan. 13 by Sen. Wendell H. Ford, D-Ky., following release of a Civil Service Commission report alleging 30 cases of CPSC abuse of the government's personnel rules. The alleged violations occurred, the report stated, "against a backdrop of management unconcern for and, in some instances, outright contempt for principles of merit."

(Susan B. King, whose nomination as a commission member had been confirmed by the Senate Feb. 28, was appointed by President Carter to replace Byington as chairman on June 29.)

Under Byington, the already-troubled agency drew a steady stream of critical government evaluations:

- On July 26, 1976, the General Accounting Office criticized the CPSC for inefficient management, poor use of available resources and poor enforcement of its laws.
- A September 1976 report prepared by an internal management task force concluded that "while some

progress has been made in implementing the Consumer Product Safety Act and related legislative mandates, the CPSC remains far short of reaching levels of performance reasonably expected of an institution of its size, funding and technical expertise."

- An October 1976 report by the House Commerce Oversight and Investigations Subcommittee found that the agency "has fumbled over arranging its priorities, run into complex problems in seeking to maximize public participation and delayed launching an effective enforcement program."
- A December 1977 GAO study criticized the slowness of its procedures in using the "offeror" process to issue mandatory safety standards. The report noted that since it had been created, the agency had issued only three standards: for swimming pool slides, architectural glass and matchbook covers. Though by law an offeror was to take only 330 days to develop a proposed standard, the average for the three standards was 834 days.
- A 1977 Civil Service Commission personnel survey found that, of those responding, only 43 per cent of CPSC's employees felt their agency was doing a good job. The commission called the CPSC employees' responses to this and other questions "significantly unfavorable" compared to all other federal agencies surveyed.

Senate Committee Action

S 2796 was reported by the Senate Commerce Committee May 15 (S Rept 95-889).

As reported, the legislation authorized $55 million for the CPSC for fiscal 1979, $60 million for 1980 and $65 million for 1981.

The agency should be extended for three years, according to the committee report, "because the commission must have a sufficient opportunity to engage in realistic long-term planning and the setting of priorities, as well as sufficient time to further improve the commission's past performance and to address and correct the shortcomings that have been noted during the commission's brief existence."

Acting on White House's suggestions, the panel added language to the authorization legislation to:

- Provide that the agency chairman serve at the pleasure of the president. Under existing law, the chairman retained his post throughout his term.
- Authorize the CPSC to participate directly in the development of mandatory safety standards in certain narrow circumstances. Under existing law, standards were developed largely independent of the agency by outside "offerors."
- Authorize the CPSC to make existing voluntary product safety standards mandatory, without going through the "offeror" process.

Senate Floor Action

The Senate passed S 2796 Aug. 4 by voice vote. During the debate, no member spoke in opposition to an extension of the agency.

Three amendments were adopted by voice votes with little discussion.

Two of them, agreed to in advance by the Commerce Committee, further defined the procedure the CPSC was to follow when it chose to develop a mandatory safety standard.

Under existing law, the commission was obliged to contract with an outside group in developing safety standards, but the committee had recommended that the commission be permitted to develop standards on its own in certain circumstances.

The first two amendments, offered by Ford, required the commission to consult with interested industry and consumer groups before beginning to develop a safety standard, and deleted a provision that would have required the commission to offer to subsidize such groups' participation in the development process.

A third amendment, offered by Harrison Schmitt, R-N.M., required the CPSC to study all its existing rules and to make recommendations to Congress within 18 months of the legislation's enactment on how to simplify and modernize them.

House Committee Action

HR 12442 was reported (H Rept 95-1164) by the House Commerce Committee on May 15 by voice vote.

As reported, HR 12442 followed the Senate's lead in extending the agency for three years.

HR 12442 provided the agency with the same funding levels for 1979 through 1981 as did S 2796. Both bills also permitted the commission independently to develop consumer product safety standards under certain conditions and to adopt the existing voluntary safety standards as proposed mandatory standards.

The House committee's bill, however, omitted a provision contained in the Senate version providing that the agency chairman serve at the pleasure of the president.

The House bill went beyond S 2796 by requiring the commission to notify foreign governments of a risk to health or safety posed by the export of consumer products, fabrics and related materials found — or proposed to be designated — unsafe for American citizens.

Before approving this provision, the Commerce Committee rejected a stronger version that would have given the CPSC the authority to prohibit the export of such goods.

Henry A. Waxman, D-Calif., had sought to give the commission that authority.

Waxman, in his request, had attempted to clarify the commission's authority, but the question remained unanswered. Although the committee majority maintained that the bill left untouched the commission's May 1978 decision that it had the necessary authority, eight congressmen, in separate views, maintained the authority was lacking.

James T. Broyhill, R-N.C., James M. Collins, R-Texas, Samuel L. Devine, R-Ohio, Robert (Bob) Krueger, D-Texas, Norman F. Lent, R-N.Y., Richardson Preyer, D-N.C., Paul G. Rogers, D-Fla., and Dave Stockman, R-Mich., in separate views, took strong issue with the entire provision requiring the commission to notify foreign governments of potential hazards posed by the export of certain products.

They said they were especially concerned that the requirement would apply even to products only proposed to be banned or otherwise regulated. This could deprive an exporter of the constitutional guarantee of due process under the law, they argued.

House Floor, Final Action

After a compromise had been drafted that was acceptable to the eight dissenting Commerce Committee members, a substitute bill was introduced on the House floor Oct. 15. It was accepted that day by voice votes in both chambers, completing congressional action.

Truth in Lending Changes

Legislation to streamline federal disclosure requirements for credit transactions was approved by the Senate in 1978, but the House failed to act on the measure.

The legislation (S 2802) would have amended the Truth in Lending Act of 1968 (PL 90-321) by making required disclosures of the actual cost of goods purchased on credit more understandable to consumers, less difficult for creditors to observe and easier for federal agencies to supervise. *(1968 law, 1968 Almanac p. 205)*

According to the Senate committee report on the bill, disclosure requirements were "too lengthy and difficult to understand. Creditors, on the other hand, had encountered increasing difficulty in keeping current with a steady stream of administrative interpretations and amendments, as well as highly technical judicial decisions.... In addition . . . the level of administrative enforcement by the federal bank agencies [has been found to be] seriously inadequate."

Though the committee report said the legislation was sought equally by consumer and creditor representatives, a number of consumer groups testified in opposition to the legislation during Senate hearings held in July 1977.

Consumer representatives testified in favor of provisions of the proposed legislation requiring the Federal Reserve Board to issue model credit transaction forms and requiring creditors to use simple English and a streamlined format to highlight important credit information.

However, "this can hardly be considered a consumer bill," commented Ellen Broadman, an attorney with Consumers Union. "We should not be gutting the existing law's disclosure requirements until we show that the information disclosed is not useful to consumers."

She said consumer representatives also opposed provisions narrowing creditors' civil liability in cases of private legal action under the Truth in Lending Act.

Senate Action

The bill was unanimously approved by the Senate Banking Committee on March 23 (S Rept 95-720), and the bill was passed by the Senate May 10 by voice vote.

As passed by the Senate, the major provisions of S 2802 were identical to the version reported by the Banking Committee.

During Senate debate on S 2802, Donald W. Riegle Jr., D-Mich., chairman of the Banking Subcommittee on Consumer Affairs, said the legislation was needed because "the typical disclosure statement given to consumers is far too lengthy and difficult to understand. Creditors have had a difficult time keeping up with a steady stream of administrative rulings. And many lenders who have tried to comply with the act in good faith have nonetheless, due to the act's complexities, found themselves in violation and subject to litigation."

Jake Garn, R-Utah, the sole senator to speak in opposition to the bill, said he feared it would increase creditors' paperwork burden without commensurate creditor and consumer benefits.

The sole amendment to be offered on the floor concerned a provision in the bill authorizing the appropriate federal agencies to order a creditor to refund the difference between the stated and actual cost of credit if the creditor understated the finance charge. The amendment was adopted by voice vote.

The amendment, offered by Richard G. Lugar, R-Ind., left to the agency's discretion the ordering of refunds of sums less than $1. For larger sums, if finance charges were regularly or willfully understated, restitution would be mandatory.

The amendment also left to the enforcing agency's discretion the determination of whether such payments should be repaid with interest. The committee report had stated it was the committee's "belief" that interest should be included in any "restitution formula."

Although the bill was subsequently referred to the House Banking, Finance and Urban Affairs Committee, that panel took no action on the legislation in 1978.

Provisions

As reported (S Rept 95-720) by the Senate Banking Committee March 23, and passed by the full Senate May 10, S 2802:

- Simplified the format and language of disclosures required to be given consumers concerning credit transactions. Other required disclosures were modified or dropped.
- Required the Federal Reserve Board to issue model forms for common credit transactions.
- Designated Oct. 1 of each year as the effective date for administrative amendments and interpretations of regulations, so that creditors would need to correct their forms only once a year.
- Limited the civil liability of creditors who committed unwitting or "technical" violations of the disclosure requirements. Under the proposed legislation, civil liability would be limited solely to violations of the basic disclosure requirements. Lesser failures to disclose information would no longer be liable for private legal action.
- Gave the federal agencies having jurisdiction additional enforcement powers including the authority — retroactive to 1974 — to order a creditor to refund the difference between the stated and actual cost of credit if the creditor understated the finance charge. (Consumer groups sought retroactivity to 1969.)
- Authorized the Federal Reserve Board to study the feasibility and value of publishing consumer credit guides in a few selected markets. The guides would compare the annual percentage rates charged by all creditors in that market.
- Exempted agricultural credit and credit for the purchase of mobile homes costing more than $25,000 from the Truth in Lending Act's requirements.
- Eased existing restrictions on advertising credit rates "in the hope of enhancing creditor competition."
- Required creditors to make "good faith" efforts to refund credit balances to consumers when the balance remained in a consumer's account for more than six months. Under existing law, creditors were required to refund the balance solely on request.

Electronic Banking Services

Congress did not complete action in the 95th Congress on legislation (HR 13007, S 3156) that, for the first time, would have established federal regulation of money transfers through electronic transfers.

Although the legislation was given overwhelming approval by the House in July, it was never acted upon by the Senate.

Many of the provisions in the legislation were, however, subsequently incorporated in an omnibus banking bill (HR 14279 — PL 95-630) by the Senate, and they were retained in the final version of that bill. *(Provisions incorporated in HR 14279, see p. 530; story, see Economic Policy chapter, p. 300)*

Consumer Protections

The electronic funds transfer (EFT) legislation would have established consumer rights and safeguards for users of electronic banking systems, whereby bills were paid and deposits and withdrawals made by means of electronic banking terminals, pay-by-telephone systems, pre-arranged direct deposit and automatic payment of funds and point-of-sale fund transfers. *(Background, 1977 Almanac p. 446)*

The bill limited to $50 a consumer's liability for unauthorized transfers through theft or fraud and spelled out other rights as well as the liabilities afforded both consumers and banking institutions that used EFT systems.

Though the sponsors of the legislation argued that federal regulation of EFT systems was needed to assure their acceptance by consumers, banking industry representatives maintained that federal restraints on so new a technology might cripple its development.

Seven states — Wisconsin, Iowa, Colorado, Minnesota, Montana, New Mexico and Kansas — already had enacted laws regulating EFT. Federal regulation was recommended in the October 1977 report to Congress by the National Commission on Electronic Fund Transfers.

"Electronic banking is rapidly growing and spreading across the country," stated Frank Annunzio, D-Ill., chairman of the House Banking Consumer Affairs Subcommittee, during a brief House debate on HR 13007.

Yet most consumers, he said, "are not aware of the great risks they run in using EFT services today. Some consumers have, to their great misfortune, found out these risks the hard way — after their money was stolen and the financial institution refused to recredit their account."

The recent advent of electronic banking brought new convenience to consumers and permitted banks to expand the types of services they could offer their customers. Twenty-four-hour-a-day banking via electronic terminals, for example, made unforeseen purchases and last-minute plans easier to carry out.

At the same time, the loss of a customer's 24-hour banking card and accompanying secret identification number could lead to substantial financial losses through the card's unauthorized use.

The unsolicited distribution by mail of such cards by some banks enhanced the odds that at least some cards would go astray and be misused.

House Committee Action

The House Banking Committee reported HR 13007 June 21 by a 37-0 vote (H Rept 95-1315).

In its report, the committee stated the legislation was needed because "this new payment mechanism lacks established rules, responsibilities and rights."

"Most crucial" among these rights, the report noted, were the determination of who should be liable for unauthorized funds transfers and whether or not firms should be permitted to distribute electronic fund transfer cards — similar to credit cards — on an unsolicited basis.

Because the federal government had not yet decided these questions, the report said, "consumers are being made to bear the cost of unauthorized transfers. Unsolicited distribution is permitted."

Though critics labeled federal legislation "premature," there was "clear evidence of need" for federal action, the report said. "Every day there are more and more cases reported in which consumers have lost thousands of dollars in transactions involving EFT services."

The legislation, the report stated, "will protect consumers and be pivotal in making EFT acceptable to consumers. Both financial institutions and consumers have much to gain from this legislation."

Major Provisions

As reported by the House committee, HR 13007:

- Required financial institutions to disclose to consumers the terms and conditions of electronic fund transfers.
- Required institutions to confirm each fund transfer to consumers either at the time of the transfer or by subsequent notice.
- Required institutions to furnish each account holder with periodic statements of transactions, service charges and bank balances.
- Required institutions to provide a mechanism for correcting errors and to inform account holders of the mechanism.
- Limited the financial liability of institutions to reimburse an account holder for losses due to the account holder's own negligence or fraud. In cases in which the losses weren't due to the account holder's negligence or fraud, the institution was held liable for all losses above $50.

The committee said it considered the $50 liability limit for account holders the key to consumer acceptance of EFT systems.

- Placed the burden of proof on the institution to show that a transfer was an authorized one when an account holder claimed it was unauthorized.
- Barred the issuance of EFT cards or other means of access to a consumer's account unless it was in response to a request from the consumer.
- Barred merchants from setting a higher price on goods or services paid for by check than would be charged if paid for by EFT.
- Provided that violators of the law regulating EFT systems would be civilly liable for damages caused by any violations, and facilitated the filing of class action suits against violators.
- Provided that "willful and knowing" violators of the law would be held criminally liable.

Minority Views

In dissenting views, Reps. John H. Rousselot, R-Calif., George Hansen, R-Idaho, and Charles E. Grassley, R-Iowa, argued that the legislation would require excessive paperwork, impose operational burdens on financial institutions, and provide opportunities for "bounty-hunter" lawyers to profit by suing financial institutions to seek civil damages for technical violations of the law.

House Floor Action

The House passed HR 13007 Aug. 11, by a 314-2 vote. *(Vote 607, p. 172-H)*

Though a number of minor amendments were adopted on the House floor, no one spoke against the legislation.

Even those members of the Banking Committee who earlier had filed a strongly worded broad-brush dissent to the committee report on the bill voted for HR 13007.

All the amendments were adopted on voice votes and with the approval of the bill's floor managers. The amendments were largely technical in nature.

An amendment offered by John H. Rousselot, R-Calif., clarified that, though the legislation barred merchants offering EFT services from imposing a surcharge on the purchase of goods by check, it did not bar merchants from offering discounts for payment by EFT, check or cash.

"If it is cheaper to transact business through EFT, we should ensure that merchants and financial institutions have the opportunity to pass these savings on to the customer," Rousselot said. "Moreover, merchants should have the option of offering a discount to encourage EFT use as a marketing tool, regardless of cost."

Senate Committee Action

S 3156, the companion Senate EFT bill, was reported (S Rept 95-915) by the Senate Banking Committee May 26 by a vote of 8-2.

The committee said it "believes that this new generation of financial services offers the public significant new choices in personal banking and has the potential to be of great benefit to consumers."

Because of the unanswered questions concerning rights and liabilities, however, "the committee believes the Congress should enact an 'EFT Bill of Rights' for consumers which addresses these issues."

As reported by the Senate panel, S 3156 was quite similar to HR 13007. Among the principal differences between the two bills, S 3156:

- Did not attempt to set a standard for determining whether unauthorized transfers were due to an account holder's negligence. Instead, the committee recommended solely limiting a consumer's liability to a maximum of $50.
- Provided a more limited liability for financial institutions subject to civil suits filed as a result of violations of the law, and omitted House provisions facilitating class action suits against violators.
- Provided that a consumer's obligation to transfer funds was "suspended" when a system malfunction prevented completion of an electronic transaction. The provision was designed to assure that a system breakdown would not result in a consumer being declared in default due to late payment on a mortgage or insurance policy, for example.

In additional views, Sens. Harrison Schmitt, R-N.M., John G. Tower, R-Texas, Robert Morgan, D-N.C., Jake Garn, R-Utah, and Richard G. Lugar, R-Ind., argued that the federal regulation imposed by the legislation would be "burdensome" and would harm — rather than help — EFT's development. They suggested that EFT regulation be left to the states until more abuses of the existing system of regulation became documented.

Provisions in Banking Bill

As incorporated in the omnibus banking bill (HR 12479), the EFT provisions:

- Required financial institutions to disclose to consumers the terms and conditions of electronic fund transfers.
- Required institutions to confirm each fund transfer to consumers either at the time of the transfer or by subsequent notice.
- Required institutions to furnish each account holder with periodic statements of transactions, service charges and bank balances.
- Required institutions to provide a mechanism for correcting errors and to inform account holders of the mechanism.
- Limited the financial liability of institutions to reimburse an account holder for losses due to the account holder's own negligence or fraud. In cases in which the losses weren't due to the account holder's negligence or fraud, the institution was held liable for all losses above $50.
- Placed the burden of proof on the institution to show that a transfer was an authorized one when an account holder claimed it was unauthorized.
- Barred the issuance of validated EFT cards or other means of access to a consumer's account unless it was in response to a request from the consumer.
- Provided that violators of the law regulating EFT systems be civilly liable for damages caused by any violations, and facilitated the filing of class action suits against violators.
- Provided that "willful and knowing" violators of the law be held criminally liable.
- Provided that a consumer's obligation to transfer funds was "suspended" when a system malfunction prevented completion of an electronic transaction. ▮

Postal Reform Bill Dies

Opposition from the three major postal workers unions on the U.S. Postal Service killed for the session legislation intended to make the Postal Service more efficient and accountable to Congress and the executive branch.

The legislation, which was passed by the House in April, was pronounced dead after the Senate Budget Committee in September voted to deny the bill (HR 7700) a waiver from the provisions of the Budget Act of 1974.

That act required legislation providing new spending authority to be reported to the floor by May 15 of the preceding fiscal year. HR 7700, as amended by the Senate Governmental Affairs Committee, was not reported until Sept. 13.

Under the act, before legislation reported after May 15 could be brought to the floor, the Senate was required to approve a resolution waiving the Budget Act requirement. But the Budget Committee voted 5-9 Sept. 26 against allowing the waiver.

At issue was a proposed increase in the Postal Service's public service subsidy, but with a four-year freeze on the cost of first-class mail. Estimates of postal revenues that would be lost annually through a first-class rate freeze ranged from $35 million, the figure advanced by proponents of a freeze, to between $1 and $2 billion annually, the amount cited by the Postal Service.

Another controversial provision, opposed by postal union and management groups, would have exempted from the Postal Service's monopoly on first-class mail certain "time-sensitive" letters — such as business communications and financial information.

A third issue concerned the future of the Postal Service's parcel post delivery system and the question of whether that service could be subsidized with income from first-class mail in order to remain competitive with private delivery services.

Background

According to its sponsors, the main purposes of the Postal Service reorganization legislation were to make mail service more efficient and to reinstate a measure of congressional and executive branch control over its operations. HR 7700 was to accomplish this by making the postmaster general a presidential appointee, increasing the federal subsidy for mail services and altering the criteria for determining postal rates. Reversing a mandate of the 1970 Postal Reorganization Act (PL 91-375), the bill dropped a requirement that the Postal Service operate on a profitable basis.

That requirement was intended to insulate postal operations from federal government interference and politics and to free taxpayers from the burden of ever-rising federal subsidies.

The 1970 law established an independent postal corporation, the U.S. Postal Service, whose board of governors and postal rate commission — rather than the president and Congress — chose the postmaster general, set the rates, and oversaw its operations. To help get the new Postal Service on its feet, federal subsidies were authorized for a period stretching until 1984. *(1970 Almanac p. 341)*

1977 Action

HR 7700, the omnibus postal reorganization bill, was reported by the House Post Office and Civil Service Committee on Nov. 3, 1977. It stressed the need for better mail service rather than a balanced budget and largely abandoned the effort to attain an unsubsidized, profitable mail service envisioned by Congress in the 1970 act. The committee's bill also made the postmaster general a presidential appointee, gave Congress veto power over postal rate increases and nearly tripled the federal subsidy for postal services.

President Carter had criticized the Postal Service during his 1976 election campaign, but there was little in the House committee bill favored by the administration. In testimony delivered in September 1977, Office of Management and Budget official W. Bowman Cutter said the White House was especially opposed to increasing the federal subsidy for the Postal Service.

The bill also bore little resemblance to proposals made by a congressionally created Postal Service Commission in April 1977.

The commission recommended cutting mail delivery to five days a week, continuing the appointment of the postmaster general by the Postal Service board of governors and giving the Postal Rate Commission, not Congress, the final authority for setting rates.

The commission's proposals were immediately criticized by House Postal Operations and Services Subcommittee Chairman James M. Hanley, D-N.Y.., who said he was disappointed by the report's focus on service cuts rather than on improvements.

Carter Delay

In January 1978 Carter asked House Speaker Thomas P. O'Neill Jr., D-Mass., to delay further action on the measure. The bill should be held up, Carter explained, at least until after upcoming labor union negotiations were concluded. A three-year contract involving the 600,000 unionized employees of the Postal Service was to expire July 25.

The legislation's chief backers, Hanley and Postal Personnel and Modernization Subcommittee Chairman Charles H. Wilson, D-Calif., dashed off an angry letter to Carter accusing him of trying to scuttle the bill.

"Unfortunately," the two chairmen wrote Carter, "the truth is that throughout the consideration of this proposal...there has been a serious lack of continuing communication between the administration and the developers of the legislation. Perhaps this is understandable in view of the inexperience of some of the new, young administration staff people who have been responsible for liaison on this issue. Frankly, however, as experienced legislators, we must say that this situation has been unprecedented, even during Republican administrations."

The letter reportedly ruffled feathers at the White House. But an aide to the Post Office and Civil Service Committee said: "We may have a little cooling off now. Everyone's a bit angry. But as soon as tempers have cooled ... I imagine there will be some serious negotiating on the bill."

Negotiations

That prediction was borne out. Having previously requested O'Neill to delay floor consideration of HR 7700, the White House agreed to let the bill come to a vote after Hanley and Wilson agreed to a number of changes sought by the administration and said they would introduce a substitute version of the legislation incorporating those changes when the bill came to the House floor.

The changes agreed to, Hanley told the Rules Committee March 14, made "significant modifications in HR 7700 as reported, but maintains its basic thrust. That thrust is to give both the president and Congress a greater voice in the establishment of postal policy, eliminate the ill-fated 'break-even' policy and provide authorization for adequate public service funding, ensure a postal rate

Among the modifications approved by Hanley and Wilson were:

- Elimination of a provision authorizing a congressional veto of postage rates set by the Postal Rate Commission.
- Elimination of a provision providing for a public service subsidy of 15 percent of the postal budget for fiscal years 1979-1980. Instead, it was decided to increase the existing annual subsidy by $800 million, to $1.7 billion from $920 million, for fiscal 1979 through 1981.
- Retention of the postal board of governors. The existing law was to be modified to let the president appoint the board chairman, who would be authorized to hire an independent auditing staff to check up on the postmaster general's performance.

• Agreement on allowing the president to appoint the postmaster general for a fixed four-year term, to run concurrently with the president's.

Administration Reservations

Despite the changes, presidential assistant Stuart E. Eizenstat wrote Post Office Committee Chairman Robert N. C. Nix, D-Pa., March 14 that "we continue to have a number of serious reservations and objections to the bill. The president has indicated that he will not commit himself to signing postal legislation until he has had an opportunity to review it in its final form."

However, in a follow-up letter the next day, Eizenstat wrote: "Although the administration cannot support HR 7700 on the floor, we will not oppose it at that time.... We hope to be able to resolve any problems we now have with the proposed postal legislation during the balance of the legislative process."

To the legislation's opponents, the Eizenstat letters were evidence that the bill was not needed. "Deep down in my heart, I hate to see the president's own party inflict this kind of monstrosity upon him," John H. Rousselot, R-Calif., told the House when the measure came to the floor March 20.

"There is no question . . . that this legislation provides for assistance increases in an already crowded deficit and budget, to say the least," remarked Budget Committee Chairman Robert N. Giaimo, D-Conn. "What disturbs me about this bill, quite frankly, is that neither the Postal Corporation nor the president of the United States seem to favor it. I do not know why we are forcing that upon them, that being the case."

Hanley and Wilson defended the bill. "The principal reason [for his opposition] is that the president still does not understand this legislation," Wilson explained. "He has been so distant."

"The mail to our offices and meetings back home indicates that Americans of all kinds are more fed up with mail delivery and the Postal Service now than ever before," Hanley said. "This, let it be said, is a fact of political life that no responsible elected official can or should ignore in a democracy."

HR 7700's backers had the White House's approval to go ahead with the bill, but the fact that the administration still opposed a number of its provisions considerably weakened the sponsors' arguments. Instead of completing floor debate in one session, as planned, the House took four days (March 20-21, April 5-6) to complete action.

House Floor Action

Passage of the legislation April 6 was by a lopsided margin of 384-11, but the vote did not reflect the controversies surrounding a number of amendments proposed during four days of debate. *(Vote 163, p. 48-H)*

Key changes made in the bill on the floor included a proposal by Tom Corcoran, R-Ill., to set the Postal Service's federal subsidy at whatever level — above the existing $920 million annually — that the Postal Service said it would need to cover its public service costs, and language by Paul Simon, D-Ill., to prevent the Postal Service from subsidizing the cost of parcel post deliveries with revenues from either the Treasury or other classes of mail.

The Corcoran amendment was in direct opposition to President Carter's insistence that federal subsidies to the Postal Service be kept as low as possible. On the other hand, another Corcoran amendment accepted by the House abolished the postal board of governors, in effect leaving the president ultimately responsible for the preparation of the

Reprieve for Parcel Post Delivery Rates?

During House action April 5 on the Postal Service reorganization legislation (HR 7700), an amendment was approved by almost a three-to-one margin to clarify congressional intent that the Postal Service's parcel post deliveries were to "pay their own way."

Simon Amendment

Subsidies for "idea mail" such as first-, second-and third-class mail, explained Paul Simon, D-Ill., the sponsor of the amendment, were desirable. But Congress didn't intend, he said, that the Postal Service use its federal subsidy to keep parcel post rates below cost — thus helping it compete with private parcel delivery firms such as United Parcel Service.

Simon's amendment, adopted by a vote of 292-112, instructed the Postal Service to set its rates so as to recover all costs of its parcel deliveries.

Simon, then, was "a little surprised," he later admitted, to discover that the House the next day had routinely approved a seemingly unrelated amendment that nullified his "clarification" language.

"At the very last moment," explained the next issue of the newsletter of the National Association of Letter Carriers, Postal Personnel Subcommittee Chairman Charles H. Wilson, D-Calif., "managed to have adopted, by voice vote, a little understood amendment that has the practical effect of wiping out the Simon amendment. Thus we are protected against the Simon attack on our parcel post business, and we are grateful to Congressman Wilson for his skill and alertness...."

The amendment, Wilson explained on the House floor April 6, "would simply provide the postmaster general with some contracting authority, so that when the volume of mail of a particular mailer or groups of mailers justify [a contract for the transportation and delivery of mail], it could be undertaken."

Flexibility for Postmaster General

"Don't be confused by Wilson's floor speech," a Postal Personnel Subcommittee aide explained later. "The amendment provides that, regardless of any other provision of the act, if the postmaster general feels a rate is too high, he can lower the rate," including that for parcel post.

"The situation is extremely complex," the committee aide explained. "The problem with the Simon amendment was that it tried to legislate a complicated issue from the floor. Simon said he wanted to keep the status quo [concerning the competitive situation between the Postal Service and private delivery firms]. We feel the Wilson amendment will preserve the status quo."

postal budget through his authority, granted by the bill, to hire and fire the postmaster general.

The Simon amendment's backers said it was necessary to protect such private parcel delivery systems as United Parcel Service from unfair Postal Service competition. Its opponents argued that the amendment would cause the rates for both the Postal Service's and private system deliveries of packages to increase 65 percent.

Because a number of provisions in the Hanley-Wilson substitute went further than Carter wished in increasing the subsidy and government control over the Postal Service's operations, the debate often cast conservative Republicans such as Edward J. Derwinski, R-Ill., and Rousselot in the role of defending a Democratic president from his own party.

"Don't saddle the president with the burden of managing the Postal Service," argued Derwinski in opposing the Corcoran amendment to abolish the postal board of governors — an amendment Carter opposed. But the amendment was passed by voice vote.

In other floor action, the House:

- Adopted, 292-112, the Simon amendment to require the Postal Service to recover all direct and indirect costs in setting rates for parcel post. *(Vote 159, p. 48-H)*

A less comprehensive substitute, offered by Clifford Allen, D-Tenn., with the backing of the Post Office Committee, was rejected 147-257. Rather than forbidding parcel post subsidization altogether, the Allen amendment would have permitted subsidization so long as the Postal Service's parcel post rates didn't undercut or discriminate against the rates set by private delivery firms. *(Vote 158, p. 46-H)*

- Adopted, 203-189, an amendment by Corcoran to require the Postal Service to spell out in detail how it spent its federal subsidy the preceding fiscal year and how it proposed to use its subsidy for the upcoming year. (The federal subsidy, under existing law, was limited to helping underwrite the costs of certain "public services.") The amendment prohibited Congress from approving an appropriation for the Postal Service unless such information was supplied. It also provided for an open-ended authorization, but not less than the existing $920 million subsidy. *(Vote 162, p. 48-H)*

- Adopted by voice votes amendments by Jerry Huckaby, D-La., to delete the requirement that the Postal Service spend 1 percent of its annual budget on research and development, leaving this determination to the postmaster general; by Wilson, to give the postmaster general limited authority to contract for the transportation of mail instead of relying exclusively on rates set by the Interstate Commerce Commission *(See box, p. 532);* and by Trent Lott, R-Miss., to exempt from the Postal Service's monopoly on first class mail timely material that was delivered by courier.

- Rejected a number of amendments by Patricia Schroeder, D-Colo., that attempted to prevent the Postal Service from using revenues from first class mail to subsidize other classes; an amendment by Henry B. Gonzales, D-Texas, to bring back the "penny postcard"; an amendment by Rousselot to end the Postal Service's monopoly on first class mail, and an amendment by John M. Ashbrook, R-Ohio, to reinstitute a congressional veto over postal rates.

Provisions

As passed by the House, HR 7700:

- Established criteria for the setting of postal rates, including a 60 percent ceiling on the amount of direct costs attributed to a particular class of mail in calculating the rate for that class. The remaining direct and indirect costs could be allocated among the different classes based on commercial and social judgments made by the postal rate commission. The rate for parcel post was required to recover all of its direct and indirect costs. Uniform rates were mandated for the news content of second class and controlled circulation publications, regardless of the distance the publication was sent. A discount was provided for the first 250,000 copies of newspapers and magazines that didn't qualify for existing pre-sort discounts.
- Provided for presidential appointment of the postmaster general, subject to Senate confirmation, and abolished the postal board of governors.
- Set ceilings on the salaries of top postal officials.
- Authorized a congressional veto of proposed nationwide changes in the level of service provided by the Postal Service. The provision was identical to a separate piece of legislation (HR 9146) passed by the House March 13, 1978. *(See related development below)*
- Required the Postal Service to detail by function, on an annual basis, how it would spend its federal subsidy, and annually to authorize a subsidy equal to what the Postal Service said it would need to perform those functions. The $920 million annual authorization through fiscal 1984 provided under existing law was set as the minimum level of the subsidy. A continuation of six-day-per-week mail delivery and the retention of money-losing small post offices were included in the types of service to be subsidized. The legislation required the Postal Service to hold a public hearing before closing a post office.
- Permitted the Postal Service to represent itself in litigation related to postal rates and classification.
- Required the Postal Service to contract with available U.S. steamships for international mail transportation by sea.
- Revised existing law concerning the rates for books and other educational materials to clarify which were eligible for preferred rates.

Senate Committee Action

HR 7700 was reported (S Rept 95-1191) by the Senate Governmental Affairs Committee Sept. 13 by a vote of 9-0. The reported bill was an amended version of legislation (S 3229) introduced June 20 by Sen. John Glenn, D-Ohio, chairman of the Senate Governmental Affairs Subcommittee on Federal Services. The Glenn draft won cautious endorsement from the administration.

Unlike the House-passed version, the Senate committee bill retained the existing 15-cent first-class mail rate through fiscal 1982, maintained the Postal Service's federal subsidy at its existing level through 1982 and authorized the president to appoint the chairman of the postal board of governors.

The panel's bill also revised the Postal Rate Commission's rate-setting criteria and required the Postal Service to improve its bookkeeping procedures.

The House version did not freeze the price of first-class postage. It fixed the Postal Service's annual subsidy at whatever the postmaster general said was needed to serve the public effectively. It abolished the postal board of governors and authorized the president to appoint the postmaster general. As did the Senate bill, it revised the postal rate commission's rate-setting criteria.

Parcel Post Future

Perhaps the most significant controversy faced by the committee in considering the bill concerned the future of the Postal Service's parcel post delivery service.

Because the Postal Service was required to serve both urban and rural areas, while private competitors such as the United Parcel Service were able to confine their services to heavily populated — and thus more profitable — areas, the Postal Service in the early 1970s found its parcel post costs rising more quickly than revenues.

In order to remain competitive with the private delivery services, the Postal Service began to subsidize parcel post with income from its first-class service.

In a December 1976 decision, however, the U.S. Court of Appeals for the District of Columbia ruled that the Postal Rate Commission must, to the extent reasonably possible, base its rate for each service on that service's actual costs. It based its decision on the language of the 1970 Postal Reorganization Act (PL 91-375).

HR 7700 as drafted by the House Post Office Committee had proposed reversing the Appeals Court decision by placing a cap of 60 percent on the amount of direct costs the Postal Service could recover in establishing a rate for a particular service.

The Postal Service had been recovering about 65 percent of the costs of parcel post service. The Appeals Court decision would have required the Postal Service to collect about 75 percent of the service's costs from its parcel post rates.

The provision had been sought by postal workers fearful that higher parcel post rates would steer more business to the private delivery services, eventually driving the Postal Service's parcel service out of business.

The House had adopted an amendment by Paul Simon, D-Ill., to require the Postal Service to recover all direct and indirect costs in setting rates for parcel post. That amendment was backed by the International Brotherhood of Teamsters, whose members that were employed by United Parcel Service stood to gain from the parcel post service's demise.

The situation was further confused by adoption of an amendment by Charles H. Wilson, D-Calif., to "clarify" the amendment's intent. That amendment, in fact, was found to have reversed the intent of the Simon amendment. *(Box, p. 532)*

Senate Compromise

When the Senate committee marked up the bill, John C. Danforth, R-Mo., proposed an amendment having the same effect as the Simon amendment.

Glenn argued against it. "I do not believe that it was the intent of Congress [in the 1970 law] to force cost allocations that would put a particular service out of business," he said. "I would not like to see the Postal Service go out of the parcel delivery business until we have the data to make that decision and have that judgment."

As an interim solution, the committee fixed the ceiling on costs to be recovered for each service at 65 percent, the existing level, until after fiscal 1982, and it asked the General Accounting Office to propose a permanent solution.

The compromise was offered by committee Chairman Abraham Ribicoff, D-Conn., and accepted by voice vote.

Major Provisions

As reported by the Senate committee, HR 7700:

- Extended the existing public service authorization of $920 million annually through fiscal 1982.
- Froze the existing 15-cent rate charged for first class mail through fiscal 1982.
- Established new ratemaking criteria and set a 65 percent ceiling on the amount of direct costs the Postal Service could recover in setting the rate for a given service. The bill also required the Postal Rate Commission to develop an improved method of allocating costs in calculating rates, and increased the commission's independence from the Postal Service.
- Provided that the president could designate the chairman of the postal board of governors. Under existing law, all governors were appointed by the president, subject to Senate confirmation, but the chairman was chosen by fellow board members. The board's duties were outlined "in order to provide improved definition for the role of the board in the overall management structure of the Postal Service," according to the committee report.
- Provided a discount for the first 250,000 copies of newspapers and magazines that didn't qualify for existing pre-sort discounts.
- Permitted "qualified" political committees to benefit from third class bulk mail discount rates. Labor unions and the national political parties were able to benefit from these lower rates under existing law.
- Provided a discount for the mailing of children's classroom reading publications that contained no paid ads.
- Required the Postal Service to submit annually to Congress detailed information on its budget and operations.
- Exempted from the Postal Service's monopoly on first-class mail the delivery by private firms of certain "time-sensitive" letters.
- Authorized the Postal Service to levy civil penalties of up to the cost of the unpaid postage on mail users who failed to affix the proper postage to their mail.

Budget Committee Action

In its Sept. 26 report (S Rept 95-1244) denying the bill a waiver from the provisions of the 1974 Budget Act, the Budget Committee said it was concerned about the proposed subsidy increase, combined with the four-year freeze on the cost of first-class mail, as well as the provision exempting from the Postal Service's monopoly on first-class mail certain "time sensitive" letters.

The latter provision, sponsored by Thomas F. Eagleton, D-Mo., had been adopted as an amendment to the bill Aug. 16 by the Governmental Affairs Committee.

At the committee markup, Eagleton termed the proposed amendment's impact on the Postal Service "relatively inconsequential." Glenn did not oppose the Eagleton amendment.

After the amendment was approved, however, Postmaster General William F. Bolger wrote Budget Committee Chairman Edmund S. Muskie, D-Maine, that the bill would harm the Postal Service's financial well-being.

Representatives of the American Postal Workers Union, the National Association of Letter Carriers and the Mailhandlers Union also lobbied the Budget Committee's members, arguing that the amendment would result in postal worker unemployment.

"We cannot stress enough the importance of defeating this postal reform bill, along with its damaging amendments," the letter carriers union told its members in late September. The bill's enactment, the union said, "would mean a drastic loss of mail volume to private delivery systems — resulting in a loss of jobs for letter carriers."

After the Budget Committee action, the unions wrote Senate Majority Leader Robert C. Byrd, D-W.Va., urging that he not schedule the bill for floor action.

By the beginning of October, the postal workers' efforts had paid off. The bill never came to the Senate floor.

Related Development

A mechanism for congressional disapproval of changes in the level of postal services proposed by the Postal Service was approved by the House, but was not acted on by the Senate in 1978.

By a vote of 371-6, the House March 13 passed a bill (HR 9146) to permit either house of Congress to veto proposed changes by adopting a resolution of disapproval within 60 calendar days from the date it was announced by the Postal Service. *(Vote 107, p. 32-H)*

The bill was unanimously reported by the House Post Office and Civil Service Committee Nov. 2, 1977 (H Rept 95-796, Part I).

The legislation was introduced in September 1977 by Post Office Committee Chairman Robert N. C. Nix, D-Pa., in response to a plan announced in May by then-Postmaster General Benjamin F. Bailar to cut back mail deliveries from six days per week to five.

Bailar's plan was cut short by strong congressional opposition. Congressional backers of HR 9146 said the bill would establish a formal procedure for congressional review of such plans.

Bailar resigned from the Postal Service, announcing Feb. 16 he would become executive vice president of United States Gypsum Co. The Postal Board of Governors March 1 named Deputy Postmaster General William F. Bolger to succeed Bailar. ▮

Consumer/Business Disputes

Legislation to provide federal assistance to the states to help them establish and promote procedures for resolving minor consumer disputes was killed by the House Oct. 12.

The bill (S 957) had been passed by the Senate June 29, but died when the House, by a vote of 224-166, failed to get the two-thirds vote (260) needed to pass the bill under the suspension of the rules procedure. *(House vote 796, p. 226-H)*

The legislation's backers said the bill was needed to provide fair and inexpensive mechanisms for the resolution of minor disputes between consumers and businesses.

Because of the costs and delays involved in seeking redress in the regular court system, minor disputes often remained unresolved because of practical considerations, they said.

Further, lawyers and judges said they supported the legislation because providing separate forums for the resolution of these minor disputes would permit the regular court system to concentrate on more significant cases.

"All Americans should have access to forums which provide just settlements of even the most minor disputes," Wendell H. Ford, D-Ky., chairman of the Senate Commerce Consumer Subcommittee, said on the Senate floor June 29. "There is a need to assure access to justice for all citizens, both through more effective courts as well as through nonjudicial settlement procedures."

Opponents of the bill argued that the $95 million authorized over five years for the encouragement of such mechanisms was too high a price to pay. They also argued that the bill should not have been brought up under a suspension of the rules, a procedure that barred floor amendments.

A similar bill died at the end of the 94th Congress. That version had been passed by the Senate, but the House took no action on it.

S 957 had the support of the American Bar Association, Chamber of Commerce, Conference of Mayors and other local government, civic and consumer groups.

Senate, House Action

S 957 was reported (S Rept 95-210) by the Senate Commerce Committee May 16, 1977. It was the third time the committee had reported such legislation, which it called the "Consumer Controversies Resolution Act." *(Earlier action, 1977 Almanac p. 443)*

As reported, S 957:

- Established within the Federal Trade Commission (FTC) an office to award grants to states for the development, establishment, improvement or support of state consumer/business dispute programs and to encourage and help develop innovative concepts and approaches to the resolution of consumer controversies.
- Authorized $15 million for fiscal 1978 and $25 million for fiscal 1979 for grants to the states and for the FTC's administrative costs.

Following Commerce Committee approval, S 957 was referred to the Senate Judiciary Committee at Judiciary's request. Some members of Judiciary had expressed concern over the extent of the regulatory powers granted the FTC by the bill and whether the legislation infringed on states' rights by giving the federal government jurisdiction over state courts.

Commerce gave Judiciary only 60 days to study the bill and make its recommendations, but the time period expired and was extended twice at the request of Sen. Edward M. Kennedy, D-Mass.

Finally, on Sept. 21, 1977, Judiciary decided to take no action on the bill and approved it for floor action. Instead of formal committee action, Kennedy decided to propose a substitute bill, which he introduced in November 1977.

Consumer Subcommittee Chairman Ford, however, disagreed with some aspects of Kennedy's bill, and the two senators' staffs began to negotiate a compromise. In late June, a new substitute bill was agreed upon and introduced with both Ford and Kennedy as cosponsors.

As drafted by Ford and Kennedy, the substitute bill more precisely defined the types of state mechanisms that would be eligible for federal funds; transferred the program from the FTC to the Justice Department; authorized $3 million annually for fiscal years 1978 through 1982 for administration and $15 million annually for fiscal years 1978 through 1982 for program grants.

The Senate passed the legislation as amended by Ford and Kennedy June 29 by voice vote.

The House Commerce Committee reported S 957 (H Rept 95-1654) Sept. 28, with further amendments, but the bill died in the House Oct. 12 when the motion to suspend the rules and pass S 957 failed to get the necessary two-thirds majority vote.

Investor Protection Act

Amendments to the Securities Investor Protection Act of 1970 (PL 91-598) were cleared by Congress May 10.

The legislation (HR 8331 — PL 95-283) provided additional protections for individual investors in the event of the bankruptcy of their broker or dealer. It streamlined and expedited broker-dealer liquidation proceedings, and provided customers with additional safeguards against financial losses by brokerage houses. Insurance coverage was increased.

Legislative History

HR 8331 was reported by the House Commerce Committee (H Rept 95-746) Oct. 26, 1977, and was passed by the House Nov. 1 by voice vote.

Similar legislation was reported by the Senate Banking Committee (S Rept 95-763) April 25 and passed by the Senate April 26 by voice vote.

The House May 2 reconsidered HR 8331, adopting several provisions of the Senate-passed bill but rejecting two others. Although the House asked for a conference, the Senate May 4 agreed to the House charges with further amendments, whereupon the House added still another change May 9. On May 10 the Senate agreed to the final House-passed version, completing congressional action. *(1970 act, 1970 Almanac p. 865)*

Carter Signs $54 Billion Highway Bill

President Carter signed into law Nov. 6 legislation (HR 11733 — PL 95-599) providing nearly $54 billion in federal aid for highways and mass transit over the next four years.

In approving the measure, Carter ended nearly a year-long battle over the future direction of the massive federal surface transportation aid programs with only a partial victory.

Carter had sought to keep highway and transit aid spending down, warning that his number one priority of reducing inflation would be jeopardized otherwise. Instead — though the administration succeeded in substantially lowering the sums of money sought by the House Public Works Committee — it ended up with a bill totaling nearly $7 billion more than it asked for.

Carter also had proposed to streamline and integrate federal transportation policies in order to make them more responsive to the needs of state and local governments and align them with other important administration goals such as energy conservation and pollution control.

Although the administration achieved some reforms, it fell short of its goals.

As cleared by Congress, the bill went only part way in 1) keeping mass transit and highway projects from competing with each other for federal dollars, 2) eliminating many of the restrictions on state and local government use of surface transportation aid dollars, and 3) requiring that energy conservation, land use planning and pollution control be considered in the planning of mass transit and highway projects.

HR 11733 was passed by the House Sept. 28 and by the Senate Oct. 3. A conference compromise on the bill was approved by both the House and Senate by voice votes on Oct. 15, completing congressional action.

Highlights

The bill funded virtually all federal-aid highway, highway safety and mass transit programs for four years, fiscal 1979 through 1982. Authorizations for construction of the Interstate Highway System were lowered from the levels provided in existing law for the years fiscal 1980-83.

The Highway Trust Fund and the taxes that fed it were extended for five years, fiscal 1979 through 1984. To facilitate long-term planning, HR 11733 also provided a fifth year of funding (from general revenues) for a mass transit aid program aimed at subsidizing the largest projects.

The legislation consolidated some narrow aid programs to provide more flexible mass transit and highway safety funding, and made some progress toward Carter's goal of combining the planning process for both highway and mass transit projects. Many of the individual transit and highway aid programs were restructured.

A number of changes were made in the way the cost of a highway or mass transit project was allocated between the federal government and state and local authorities.

The administration had proposed equalizing — and in many cases decreasing — the federal share of most kinds of projects. This was intended to stretch the limited number of federal dollars available and to enable local officials to design transportation systems on their merits rather than on the amount of federal money a particular project design might bring in.

But as approved, the federal share of many types of projects was increased, limiting the reach of the federal money authorized. And the bill equalized the federal and local shares of certain programs only within broad categories of transportation aid, retaining the disparities between the different categories.

For example, the federal share of the cost of most non-Interstate highway programs was set at 75 percent, which was an increase in many cases from 70 percent. For most mass transit capital projects, the federal share was set at 80 percent.

For mass transit projects substituted by local authorities for interstate highway segments, the federal share was set at 85 percent, while the Interstate segments remained 90 percent federally funded.

Highway Program Shift

In the legislation, Congress began to shift the emphasis of its highway programs from building new roads to maintaining existing ones.

As originally conceived, federal Highway Trust Fund revenues were to be used solely to put a nationwide highway system into place. Maintenance was to be a state responsibility.

But as the states' maintenance efforts dwindled in the face of budgetary shortages, Washington was forced to assume more and more responsibility for maintenance of federally built highways in order to preserve its investment in the system.

Interstate highway resurfacing, restoration and rehabilitation was made a permanent federal program, and its funding was increased. A fixed proportion of the federal funds authorized for the primary and secondary route systems also was earmarked for roadway maintenance.

An existing bridge replacement program was expanded to cover bridge repair projects, and the funding for the program was greatly increased.

The legislation also set a final deadline for completion of the Interstate Highway System, enlarged the Appalachian highway system, began new programs to subsidize intercity bus service and bikeways, encouraged state enforcement of federal truck weight limit laws and the 55-mile-per-hour national speed limit, and required that most major purchases of surface transportation equipment and supplies be manufactured in the United States substantially from American materials.

Funding Level Controversy

The biggest battle between Congress and the Carter administration over the bill concerned the levels of funding for the transportation programs.

The Carter administration sought an authorization of about $47 billion over the four-year period. Under its proposal, spending from the Highway Trust Fund was to be held to about $7 billion to $8 billion annually, approximately the amount that was paid into the fund each year in taxes.

Though the Senate fashioned a bill quite similar to the White House model, the House refused to go along.

As drafted by its Public Works Committee, HR 11733 originally authorized $66.5 billion in federal funds over the four-year period, including an annual drain from the Highway Trust Fund of over $11 billion.

Though Office of Management and Budget Director James T. McIntyre on Sept. 20 labeled the bill "currently the biggest threat to the budget pending in Congress," the House agreed to cut only $5.6 billion from the total approved by Public Works.

An effort to cut the bill further — mounted by House Budget Committee Chairman Robert N. Giaimo, D-Conn., and supported by the administration — was rejected by a lopsided vote.

Carter Ultimatum. After House and Senate leaders had appointed conferees to negotiate a final version of the bill, President Carter invited them to the White House Oct. 10 and announced that he considered an authorization of $52.4 billion for four years to be an "acceptable" figure. But anything more than that, he told the conferees, would be "unacceptable." Though the word "veto" never was mentioned, "he was very firm and the conferees knew what he meant," according to one participant.

Comparison of Transportation Funding

(in millions of dollars)

	Carter Administration Recommendations[1]	HR 11733 as cleared by Congress
FISCAL 1979:		
Highway Programs		
Interstate highways	$ 3,675	$ 3,550
Primary roads	1,500	1,550
Bridge replacement	450	900
Other highway aid	2,107	2,781
Highways, subtotal	$ 7,732	$ 8,781
Highway Safety Programs	$ 225	$ 309
Mass Transit Programs		
Discretionary grants	1,218	1,375
Formula grants	1,356	1,515
Other mass transit	842[2]	960[2]
Mass transit, subtotal	$ 3,416	$ 3,850
Total	$11,373	$12,940

1. Some categories have been restructured to match the legislation as cleared by Congress.
2. Assumes expenditures of $675 million for mass transit projects funded with money originally intended for the construction of segments of the Interstate Highway System reclassified as non-essential.

While the House conferees expressed a willingness to yield during their meeting with the president, they mounted a vigorous defense of the House bill during the subsequent conference committee negotiations.

When the final version of the bill emerged from the conference committee Oct. 14 — the day before the end of the 95th Congress — it was evident that the House had indeed yielded on the bill's total funding level, which fell from the $60.9 billion approved by the House to $51 billion.

House Compromise?

However, some of the decrease was illusory and some was expected to be erased by the next Congress.

The $51 billion total, for example, did not include an estimated $2.8 billion — not specifically authorized in the bill — that was expected to be spent on mass transit projects substituted for Interstate highway segments deemed "non-essential." This brought the bill's total to $53.8 billion.

In addition, the conference committee achieved many reductions simply by shaving a disproportionate amount off the authorization for the fourth year for several of the largest programs in the bill. Fiscal 1982 authorizations were more than $1 billion less than fiscal 1981's.

For example, the bill authorized from $1.55 billion in 1979 to $1.8 billion in 1981 for primary system highways. For 1982, however, only $1.5 billion was authorized. For secondary system routes, the authorization fell to $400 million for 1982, from $500 million in 1979 and $600 million in 1981.

House Public Works Surface Transportation Subcommittee Chairman James J. Howard, D-N.J., explained on the House floor Oct. 14 that the lower 1982 authorizations were "the result of what I hope will prove a passing [administration] obsession with large numbers, coupled with an astonishing ignorance of the true capability of the trust fund. . . ."

Taxes That Feed the Highway Trust Fund

	Taxes Levied Under Previous Law	Taxes as of Oct. 1, 1979[1] Postponed to Oct. 1, 1984, Under HR 11733
Retailers: Diesel and special motor fuels	4 cents per gallon	1½ cents per gallon
Manufacturers		
Gasoline	4 cents per gallon	1½ cents per gallon
Lubricating oil	6 cents per gallon	6 cents per gallon
Trucks, buses, trailers	10 percent of manufacturer's price	5 percent of manufacturer's price
Truck and bus parts	8 percent of manufacturer's price	5 percent of manufacturer's price
Tires for highway use	10 cents per pound	5 cents per pound
Tubes	10 cents per pound	9 cents per pound
Tread rubber	5 cents per pound	None
Other: Use tax on highway vehicles in excess of 26,000 pounds gross weight	Annual tax of $3 per 1,000 pounds	None

1. On Oct. 1, 1979, without enactment of legislation to extend the Highway Trust Fund, the tax money would go into the general fund.

"We sympathize with their position," he continued, "and in an attempt to accommodate their concerns we focused the final cuts that were necessary to reach agreement in the fourth year of the bill. In a further spirit of compromise, we may well be back before the expiration of this bill to give our program needs some updated attention. . . . We will be back."

"One must be suspicious of the House conferees' intent in proposing this accommodation," Senate Budget Committee Chairman Edmund S. Muskie, D-Maine, said on the Senate floor only minutes later. "The Senate will want to watch with interest and should be prepared to oppose any increase for fiscal 1982 authorizations which are not fully justified by firm evidence of new program needs not currently foreseen," he warned.

Carter Approval

After the conferees completed drafting the final version of the bill, and both the House and Senate had approved the conference report Oct. 15, only Carter's signature remained to make the bill law.

According to *The Washington Post,* a nervous Frank Moore and Jody Powell, Carter's congressional liaison and press secretary respectively, asked Surface Transportation Subcommittee Chairman Howard late on the 14th how he would vote on the president's energy package the next day.

Howard, in turn, asked the two whether Carter would sign HR 11733 despite the fact that it went over Carter's $52.4 billion ceiling.

Moore and Powell replied that they could not speak for the president, whereupon Howard informed them that he would vote "no" on the energy package and take three other New Jersey Democrats with him.

Soon afterward, according to the Post, Carter told House Speaker Thomas P. O'Neill Jr., D-Mass., that he would sign the transportation bill. Howard voted "aye" on the energy package.

Transbus Delay

Another important controversy dealt with in the context of the highway bill concerned the future of the transbus, a new type of urban transit bus intended to be more accessible to the elderly and handicapped.

The bus had been developed by the Transportation Department in response to a mandate from Congress that federally funded transportation projects be accessible to the elderly and handicapped. The department spent more than $27 million developing it.

Transportation Secretary Brock Adams had ruled in May 1977 that all transit buses purchased with federal funds after Sept. 30, 1979, would be required to meet the transbus specifications. During its consideration of the highway and mass transit funding legislation, however, the House Public Works Committee approved a provision — sought by the General Motors Corp. — calling on Adams to reevaluate the transbus program. General Motors officials explained that they were unwilling to retool their bus manufacturing facilities at that time in order to meet the transbus specifications.

The uncertainty created by the request to re-evaluate the program forced a consortium of three cities — Los Angeles, Miami and Philadelphia — to drop plans to buy more than 500 transbuses in advance of the Transportation Department deadline.

However, the provision was dropped after the Transportation Department succeeded in negotiating a compromise with General Motors, a coalition of 13 organizations representing the elderly and handicapped, and key members of the House Public Works Committee. The compromise enabled the department to go ahead with its transbus plans, but delayed the bus' debut for a number of years.

Provisions

As cleared by Congress, HR 11733 contained the following major provisions:

Title I—Federal Aid Highways

Interstate Highway System. The bill lowered the funding levels provided in existing law for Interstate Highway System construction, as follows:

Authorized $3.25 billion for fiscal 1980, $3.5 billion for each of fiscal years 1981 and 1982, and $3.2 billion for fiscal

1983. Under existing law, $3.625 billion annually was authorized for Interstate highway construction during the four-year period. Existing authorizations of $3.625 billion annually for fiscal years 1984-90 remained unchanged.

HR 11733 encouraged completion of the Interstate system by requiring that the states, by Sept. 30, 1983, either submit an environmental impact statement for every segment of Interstate highway already proposed or withdraw the segments from the system. Segments — or the substitute projects that replaced them — were required to be either under construction or under contract to be constructed by Sept. 30, 1986.

With minor exceptions, no new segments were permitted to be added to the Interstate system after the legislation's enactment. Interstate funds not obligated by a state after two years were to be reallocated by the transportation secretary to states with ready-to-go Interstate projects.

Interstate resurfacing, restoration and rehabilitation was made a permanent program and authorized at $175 million annually for fiscal 1979-80 and $275 million annually for fiscal 1981-82.

Mass transit projects substituted for segments of the Interstate Highway System designated as "non-essential" were made eligible for 85 percent federal funding. Interstate segments remaining in the system continued to be eligible for 90 percent federal funding.

Other Federal-Aid Highways. Primary system authorizations were set at $1.55 billion for fiscal 1979, $1.7 billion for 1980, $1.8 billion for 1981 and $1.5 billion for 1982. For 1978, $1.35 billion had been authorized under existing law.

A priority primary route program was established by setting aside $125 million of each year's authorization for obligation at the transportation secretary's discretion to projects of unusually high cost or unusually long construction time. The Transportation Department was instructed by the conference report to consider a portion of U.S. Route 19, in Florida, for inclusion in the priority primary program.

For the secondary federal-aid highway system, the bill authorized $500 million for 1979, $550 million for 1980, $600 million for 1981 and $400 million for 1982.

The states were required to spend at least 20 percent of both primary and secondary highway system funds for resurfacing, restoration and rehabilitation. The federal share for most non-Interstate highway programs was increased to 75 percent from 70 percent under existing law.

Authorizations for a number of other minor categorical programs were continued.

The legislation also:

- Imposed a ceiling of $8.5 billion for fiscal 1979 federal-aid highway and highway safety obligations.
- Authorized a study of ways to speed up highway traffic slowed at rail crossings by extensive rail transportation of coal.
- Added 125 miles to the Appalachian highway system.
- Consolidated existing carpool and vanpool demonstration programs and made them permanent programs. A total of $15 million was authorized for the programs for fiscal years 1979-81.
- Authorized $20 million annually — $10 million from the Highway Trust Fund and $10 million from general funds — for fiscal years 1979-82 for bikeways construction.
- Authorized demonstration projects permitting vending machines in rest areas adjacent to Interstates.
- Authorized the payment to the state of New Hampshire of 90 percent of the savings resulting from building a parkway in the Franconia Notch, N.H., area instead of an interstate link. The funds were to be used to improve alternative routes around Franconia.
- Authorized a total of $50 million during fiscal years 1979-81 for construction of a bypass highway around Prairie Creek Redwood State Park in California.
- Directed the Transportation Department to study the feasibility of an additional bridge across the Columbia River between Vancouver, Wash., and Portland, Ore.
- Ordered the transportation secretary to carry out an express bus transportation demonstration project in the Sherman, Texas-Denison, Texas, area.
- Authorized $200,000 from the Highway Trust Fund for use by the state of Minnesota in preparing an environmental impact statement on the construction of the Scott County-Hennepin County Highway 18 bridge near Bloomington, Minn.
- Authorized $30 million over two years for design and construction of a traffic flow management demonstration project on the Long Island Expressway in New York state.
- Required the Transportation Department, in cooperation with other interested federal agencies, to recommend to Congress legislative changes that could reconcile apparent conflicts in existing clean air and transportation laws.
- Required the transportation secretary to report to Congress by July 1, 1979, on the desirability of designating highways in Alaska and Puerto Rico for inclusion in the national Interstate Highway System.
- Established a 19-member National Alcohol Fuels Commission to investigate the potential of alcohol fuels.

The commission was required to report its findings and recommendations to Congress by Feb. 1, 1979.

Bridge Replacement and Rehabilitation. The legislation authorized $900 million for fiscal 1979, $1.1 billion for 1980, $1.3 billion for 1981 and $900 million for 1982 for highway bridge replacement and rehabilitation.

The federal share of the cost of bridge replacement or rehabilitation was increased to 80 percent, from 75 percent under existing law. From 15 percent to 35 percent of the total amount allocated to each state was to be used to replace or rehabilitate bridges not on federal-aid highways.

Of the amount authorized for fiscal 1979, $54 million was to be set aside for two demonstration projects designed to test the feasibility of reducing the time between the filing of a request for approval of a bridge replacement project and completion of the project. The U.S. Grant bridge near Portsmouth, Ohio, was allocated $30 million, and the bridge across the Ohio River at Huntington, W.Va., was allocated the remaining $24 million.

Highway Beautification Act. The legislation required that compensation be paid by the states for the removal of any roadside sign located adjacent to federal-aid highways and not in compliance with federal law, no matter what the reason for the sign's removal.

The legislation also permitted the installation adjacent to federal-aid highways of flashing lights to display public service information or advertising of goods and services available on the property on which a sign was located.

Title II—Highway Safety

The legislation authorized from the Highway Trust Fund $175 million annually for fiscal 1981-82 for highway safety programs carried out by the National Highway Traffic Safety Administration (NHTSA).

Highway safety programs conducted by the Federal Highway Administration (FHA) were authorized from the trust fund at $25 million annually for the four-year period.

For highway safety research and development activities, $10 million annually was authorized for the FHA and $50 million annually for the NHTSA, for the four years.

For NHTSA enforcement of the 55-mile-per-hour national speed limit, $55 million was authorized for fiscal 1979 and $67.5 million for each of fiscal years 1980-82.

For pavement marking, $65 million was authorized from the trust fund for each of fiscal 1979-81. For elimination of road hazards, $125 million was authorized for fiscal 1979, $150 million annually for fiscal 1980-81 and $200 million for fiscal 1982. The increased authorization for fiscal 1982 hazard elimination was provided because of the termination of pavement marking as a separate categorical grant program, beginning that year.

For school bus driver training, the bill authorized $2.5 million annually for fiscal years 1979-82. For grants to states developing innovative approaches to highway safety — a new program — $5 million was authorized from the trust fund for fiscal 1980, $10 million for 1981 and $15 million for 1982. A total of $20 million was authorized from the trust fund for the collection of national accident data and $16 million from the trust fund for promotion of a national highway safety campaign.

Two existing rail-highway crossing categorical grant programs were consolidated and provided with an annual authorization of $190 million for the four-year period covered by the bill.

In other provisions, the bill:

- Required states to certify that they were enforcing the 55-mile-per-hour speed limit, and directed the transportation secretary to reduce a state's apportionment of highway funds by up to 5 percent for fiscal 1980-82 and by up to 10 percent for 1983 and thereafter if a state did not meet minimum federal compliance standards in enforcing the national speed limit. Incentive grants of up to 10 percent of a state's annual apportionment of highway safety funds were also available to states that further stepped up their enforcement efforts.

- Encouraged state safety programs that promoted the use of seat belts.

- Directed the transportation secretary to make a full study of the impact of a provision of the 1976 Highway Safety Act amendments (PL 94-346) that had barred the secretary from mandating that states enact laws requiring motorcycle riders to wear safety helmets.

- Directed the transportation secretary to make a one-year study of the effect on the states of a mandatory national driver registry system.

- Directed the transportation secretary to report to Congress by Dec. 31, 1979, on national efforts to detect and prevent marijuana use by operators of motor vehicles.

- Barred the use of federal highway safety funds for the retrofitting of most federal- and state-owned motor vehicles with airbags.

Title III—Mass Transit

HR 11733 authorized a total of $15.6 billion for mass transit aid over five years: $3.17 billion for fiscal 1979, $3.27 billion for 1980, $3.47 billion for 1981, $3.67 billion for 1982, plus an additional $1.58 billion for fiscal 1983 to extend the discretionary grant program, in which funds for major transit projects were distributed at the discretion of the transportation secretary, into a five-year program.

Discretionary Grants. Of the total authorization, $7.48 billion was for a reorganized discretionary grant program. By year, the program was authorized at $1.375 billion for fiscal 1979, $1.41 billion for 1980, $1.515 billion for 1981, $1.6 billion for 1982 and $1.58 billion for 1983. An existing $2 billion in discretionary grant contract authority, remaining from earlier authorizations, was repealed, to be replaced by the new authorizations.

The discretionary grant program was restructured to permit the secretary to focus it on those mass transit projects involving major investments of federal funds.

The legislation required that at least $350 million of the total funds in the program be spent on the reconstruction and improvement of existing public transit systems. Up to $200 million annually was earmarked for urban development projects involving transit facilities, and $45 million was earmarked for projects along the Northeast rail corridor.

A set proportion of the total funds was earmarked for planning and technical studies and for the development of innovative approaches to transit services.

Formula Grants. The bill retained $850 million in previously approved contract authority for fiscal 1979 and $775 million for fiscal 1980 that remained from earlier authorizations for the formula grant program, in which transit funds were allocated to states and urban areas according to a fixed formula.

Total authorizations for the formula grant program were $1.515 billion for fiscal 1979, $1.58 billion for 1980, $1.665 billion for 1981 and $1.765 billion for 1982. Included in this total were authorizations for the basic formula grant program, a second grant program directed at the nation's largest cities (known as a second tier program), the bus capital grant program and a commuter rail and fixed guideway grant program.

Separately authorized second tier, capital and commuter rail-fixed guideway grant programs were created by the bill. A $250 million annual authorization was earmarked for the nation's largest cities. The capital program was created to fund routine bus purchases and construction of bus-related facilities.

New formulas for the allocation of these program funds were established by the bill, but a formula for capital grants was provided solely for the first two years of the four-year program. Congress was expected to legislate a new formula for the program before fiscal 1981.

The legislation required transit systems receiving federal funds to hold public hearings before increasing fares or making substantial changes in their level of service.

The legislation also:

- Authorized $10 million annually for grants to universities and colleges to establish transportation research centers.

- Permitted mass transit systems crossing state lines to petition for exemption from Interstate Commerce Commission regulation of a system's services and fares.

Highways Have Dominated U.S. Transportation Policy

Federal support for highway construction programs has dominated U.S. transportation policy since passage of the Highway Act of 1956. That law (PL 84-627) channeled highway user taxes — principally on gasoline — into the Highway Trust Fund to pay the federal share of the programs.

Two key projects were financed from the trust fund. The first was the Interstate Highway System authorized by Congress in 1956 and originally intended to be completed by 1972. Under this program the federal government provided 90 percent of construction funds and the states the remaining 10 percent.

The total cost of the interstate system was set at $41 billion in 1956. By 1972, the estimated cost of the system had risen to $76.3 billion, with a completion date of 1980. By 1978 the expected cost had risen to about $100 billion. Legislation approved in 1976 extended the completion date to 1990 for the 42,500-mile system.

The second program financed from the Highway Trust Fund was construction of federal-aid primary, secondary and urban roads, which were funded on a 70-30 matching basis with the states.

An Explosion of Cars

The dramatic growth of the interstate highway system was accompanied by a parallel explosion in the number of cars, which increased from an estimated 25.8 million in 1945 to about 80 million in 1967 while the number of bus and subway riders declined from 23 billion to 7.7 billion in the same period.

By the early 1970s the consequences of this growth in urban areas — traffic congestion and disruption of neighborhoods from highway construction — had created an increasingly vocal coalition of urban interests pleading for a "balanced" transportation system with more emphasis on mass transit.

In the early 1970s the transportation debate focused on the Highway Trust Fund, which had often accumulated a surplus in revenues as a result of its lucrative user taxes.

The first successful effort to permit use of trust fund money for purposes other than highway building occurred in 1973 when Congress cleared a bill (PL 93-87) to help finance mass transit projects.

The Senate voted 49-44 to allow this. But the House rejected similar language, 190-215. *(1973 Almanac p. 435)*

After a two-and-a-half month deadlock, conferees pushed through a compromise. In fiscal 1974 cities could buy buses or build subways with funds from general revenues; total federal spending was to be offset by a reduction of the same amount in the $780 million urban share from the Highway Trust Fund. In fiscal 1975 cities were permitted to use this same method in spending up to $600 million for mass transit purposes and to tap the trust fund directly for up to $200 million for buses only.

For fiscal 1976, cities became eligible to use as much of the $800 million urban share of the trust fund as they desired for either buses or rail transit.

The 1976 extension of the highway program (PL 94-280) further liberalized the trust fund by allowing states to reject completion of non-essential segments of the Interstate system and use the funds intended for those segments for mass transit projects. *(Background, Congress and the Nation Vol. I, p. 524; Vol. II p. 228; Vol. III pp. 149, 171; Vol. IV pp. 508, 550)*

HR 11733 (PL 95-599) made no additional mass transit inroads into the Highway Trust Fund.

- Created a new formula grant program for non-urbanized areas.
- Required the transportation secretary to recommend to Congress, within one year, its proposals for establishment of a basic "no-frills," low-cost mass transit system.
- Authorized $25 million for a high-speed "jetfoil" over-the-water demonstration transit project for the New York City region.
- Required the transportation secretary to recommend to Congress by Jan. 1, 1980, a formula that would consider the severity of an area's air pollution problems in determining its share of federal mass transit funds.
- Authorized $40 million annually for four years for the purchase, construction or improvement of intercity bus terminals, and an additional $30 million annually for subsidies for the initiation, improvement or continuation of intercity bus service.

Title IV—'Buy American'

The transportation secretary was barred from using funds authorized by the bill to purchase any articles, materials or supplies costing more than $500,000 that were not from the United States.

Title V—Highway Trust Fund

The Highway Trust Fund was extended for five years, from Sept. 30, 1979, through Sept. 30, 1984. All existing taxes feeding the trust fund were continued at their existing levels, except that a system of refunds and tax credits was established for taxicab fuel purchased during 1979-80 in areas where ride-sharing was permitted.

The legislation authorized a four-year study by the Transportation Department of the costs of the federal-aid highway system and the share of the costs paid into the Highway Trust Fund by each class of highway user. A final report on the study was to be submitted to Congress by Jan. 15, 1982.

The treasury secretary was to recommend to Congress by April 15, 1982, improvements in the structure of the highway excise tax system.

Background

President Carter disappointed mass transit backers in 1977 when he left mass transit out of his proposed energy conservation program and decided not to seek new money for mass transit programs before fiscal 1980. When Transportation Secretary Adams proposed that part of Carter's proposed standby gasoline tax (later rejected) go to mass transit, and supported the idea in testimony before the House Ways and Means Committee, the White House pointed out that the idea was Adams' alone.

Concerned that additional mass transit money would be needed for fiscal years 1978 and 1979, Sen. Harrison A. Williams Jr. (D N.J.) pushed through the Senate June 23, 1977, a bill (S 208) to increase mass transit authorizations over a five-year period. *(1977 Background, see 1977 Almanac p. 529)*

The House Public Works and Transportation Subcommittee on Surface Transportation, chaired by Rep. James J. Howard (D N.J.), began hearings in 1977 on its own proposal (HR 8648), which combined mass transit and highway funding.

In the House, mass transit and highway programs were considered by a single committee; in the Senate, mass transit authorizations were under the jurisdiction of Sen. Williams' Banking, Housing and Urban Affairs Subcommittee on Housing and Urban Affairs, while highway authorizations were considered by the Environment and Public Works Subcommittee on Transportation, chaired by Lloyd Bentsen (D Texas).

Howard sought to raise the gasoline tax to supply the higher funding provided in the House bill. But when he proposed an amendment to the energy bill in August 1977 seeking a 5 cent increase in the gasoline tax (2.5 cents for highways and 2.5 cents for a separate mass transit fund), the proposal was soundly defeated by the House. Several members stated during the floor debate that this was a transportation matter, not an energy matter, and therefore should be dealt with separately.

The Howard subcommittee continued its hearings on HR 8648 in September and October 1977, and Secretary Adams asked that markup of the bill be held off until the administration could formulate its own proposals.

In testimony before the subcommittee, Adams said the Transportation Department plan would be based on six factors: the decreasing supply of energy resources; a need to streamline the regulatory process; a desire for a cleaner, safer and quieter environment; the urban crisis; unemployment; and the President's commitment to a balanced budget by fiscal 1981.

Administration Recommendations

The administration's bill was formally submitted to Congress on Jan. 26. As drafted, the legislation was intended to streamline and integrate federal mass transit and highway policies, make them more adaptable to state and local needs and align them with other domestic goals sought by the administration such as a balanced budget, energy conservation and pollution control.

One of the first things Brock Adams did after becoming Transportation Secretary in 1977 was to establish a task force to review existing federal highway and mass transit programs and recommend how to improve them.

What the task force found, Adams said later, was "a crazy quilt" of aid programs.

"We have different recipients for our highway and transit programs," he explained. "Assistance for transportation planning is fragmented. Federal-local matching ratios are a hodge-podge of numbers. . . . In short, many of our programs are outdated, inflexible and arbitrary."

Adams recommended to President Carter that a number of highway and mass transit programs be consolidated and made more flexible for state and local government use by abolishing a number of the rigid grant categories defined by existing law.

He recommended that the government adopt a uniform federal-state matching grant formula for most types of transportation projects in order to encourage local authorities to design programs based on their merits rather than on the amount of federal money a particular plan would bring in. Adams proposed that federal, state and local authorities formulate transportation projects that considered land use plans, energy usage and social, economic and environmental needs.

Carter's goal of a balanced budget by fiscal 1981 kept spending levels low in the legislation he subsequently introduced. But by and large, the rest of Adams' proposals were embraced in the Carter bill.

Carter's legislation (HR 10578) proposed to use the same federal matching grants formula for all but one of the various mass transit and highway programs. Under current law, Washington's contribution ranged from $90 for every $10 in local money to $70 for every $30, depending upon the program. The administration recommended spending $80 in federal funds for every $20 in local funds for all programs except the Interstate Highway System, where the ratio remained at $90-$10.

The administration also proposed consolidating planning programs for both highways and mass transit, and asked the Transportation Department to prepare a reorganization plan merging the Urban Mass Transportation Administration (UMTA), the Federal Highway Administration (FHWA) and other related agencies into a single surface transportation agency within the Department of Transportation. The proposed reorganization was to be submitted to Congress by Sept. 30, 1979.

OMB Cutbacks

Some of the funding levels proposed by the administration represented cutbacks from Transportation Department recommendations. In some copies of the administration's draft proposals, the original dollar figures had been crossed off and lower amounts inserted, but the totals had been left unchanged. When one congressional aide requested a clarification, a DOT official merely added up the figures that had been penciled in and supplied the new total as the correct one.

Transportation Secretary Adams sought approval from the Office of Management and Budget (OMB) of $3.9 billion for mass transit for fiscal 1979, but this was trimmed to $3.2 billion. Among the OMB cuts was $450 million intended for urban revitalization, a program developed by the Transportation Department to be part of a new urban policy package. But the White House delayed announcement of the program until March, and any additional funding for transportation under the new program had to be submitted to Congress later in the year as part of a supplemental appropriations request.

Environmentalists and others who had hoped to convince the administration to open up the Highway Trust Fund were disappointed by the Carter bill. The administration had considered the idea of establishing a separate mass transit fund financed by a hike in the gasoline tax or a crude oil equalization tax.

A Nov. 11, 1977, Transportation Department memo explaining the administration's proposals noted that, because the department was "firmly committed" to making transportation users supply the needed revenues "wherever possible and practical," a separate "mass transit fund" should be established. One major drawback to coordinating mass transit and highway needs, the memo went on, "has been the fear of 'busting the trust fund' and shortchanging legitimate highway needs in order to emphasize mass transit. This barrier will be somewhat lowered by a direct source of transit funding."

When Carter's proposals reached Congress, however, the separate mass transit fund was not included. Instead, the administration chose to expand the existing mass transit urban formula grant program, funded from general revenues and subject to the regular congressional appropriations process. The administration had never considered a phase out of the Highway Trust Fund or transferring significantly more of its revenue to mass transit.

Mass Transit Projects

The existing mass transit discretionary grant program was changed under the administration bill from a broad program capable of funding all mass transit capital projects at the discretion of the Transportation Secretary to a narrow program covering only major ones. The administration wanted the program extended for five years (through fiscal 1983) "in order to provide for advance planning," according to the department.

The urban mass transit formula grant program, which apportioned federal funds to states and urban areas with populations as low as 50,000 according to a fixed formula, was expanded to compensate for the restrictions placed on the discretionary grant program. Under the administration bill, the grant program became the sole source of funds for routine bus and subway and trolley car replacement and for modernization of rail and bus facilities and equipment.

The bill set a stricter limit on federal underwriting of mass transit operating expenses than that contained in existing law, but the new limitation was expected to affect only a handful of transit systems in small urban areas. Another provision permitted up to 50 per cent of the funds allocated to a given area to be used for urban highway projects instead of mass transit.

The administration attempted to encourage urban revitalization by permitting the funding of economic development projects adjacent to transportation projects.

The apportioning of mass transit funds was to be based on a new and more complex five-part formula based on population, density, "bus seat miles" and the age of the existing bus fleet, rail miles and commuter train miles. At the time the draft bill was completed, the Transportation Department had not yet determined what would be the impact of the new formula.

The administration's proposed urban highway program was to complement the mass transit formula grant program, with both serving the transportation needs of urban areas with populations over 50,000. Under existing law, the federal-aid urban highway program served areas with populations as small as 5,000; the administration bill transferred transportation programs for urban areas with populations of from 5,000 to 50,000 to a new rural and small urban program.

The highway portion of Carter's program permitted funds to be allocated directly to urban areas with populations of 1 million or more—bypassing state governments—while funds for smaller urban areas were to continue to be distributed to the states. A portion of the funds could be used on roads that weren't previously part of the federal-aid primary road system, on small urban and rural program projects and on mass transit capital projects. The proposal also facilitated grants for carpooling and vanpooling by consolidating and expanding existing programs contained in three different laws.

Highway Policy Redirection

The administration bill attempted to redirect the federal highway program from one of continuing construction of new roads to that of maintaining existing ones. A permanent fund was proposed for Interstate highway resurfacing, restoration and rehabilitation projects.

Completion of the Interstate system was encouraged by requiring that construction of all segments be under contract for construction by Sept. 30, 1986, and that, after Sept. 30, 1982, the secretary of transportation could not approve an Interstate segment unless the environmental review process for that project had been completed.

The Highway Trust Fund and the taxes that fed it were extended until Sept. 30, 1983, but the administration's proposed authorization from the fund for the Interstate system was cut by $125 million annually — to $3.5 billion a year through 1990.

The legislation committed $1.9 billion over four years for rehabilitation and replacement of highway bridges. Under existing law, the government could finance only the replacement of damaged bridges. A May 1977 Transportation Department study identified 40,000 bridges on the federal-aid highway system alone that needed replacement or rehabilitation, at an estimated cost of $12 billion. The administration proposal was well above current funding levels.

Rep. Howard's bill authorized $2 billion for the rehabilitation program.

The administration measure encouraged the transfer of funds for segments of the Interstate system deemed nonessential to other highway or mass transit projects by changing the formula by which funds were allocated to the states. It reasoned that this would spur completion of essential segments. The bill also made the substituted projects eligible for federal funding at the Interstates' 90-10 federal-state matching ratio. Under current law, funds transferred from the Interstate program were matched at a 70-30 ratio for other highway projects and at 80-20 for mass transit projects.

The administration also proposed to consolidate eight separate highway grant programs into a single federal-aid primary system; three existing rural and small urban area programs into a unified small urban and rural transportation aid program; and six different highway safety programs into a single grant program giving greater flexibility to state and local governments.

House Committee Action

Subcommittee Consideration

The task of considering the Carter administration's proposals fell to the House Public Works Committee's Surface Transportation Subcommittee.

At the time the administration submitted its legislation, the House Surface Transportation Subcommittee already had held 18 days of hearings on the Howard bill (HR 8648).

Because its work on highway and transit legislation was so far advanced, the subcommittee scheduled only one additional day of hearings, on Feb. 1, 1978, for the administration to present its recommendations. Following the hearings, the subcommittee staff began drafting a new bill (HR 11733) to use as a vehicle for subcommittee markup.

Discussing the subcommittee's new version March 22, Chairman Howard called it "undoubtedly the most significant piece of transportation legislation ever to come before [the House]. . . . I am proud of this bill and look forward to bringing it to the floor."

Transportation Department officials, however, greeted the bill with alarm.

Although it did not mandate an increase in the gasoline tax, as Howard earlier had suggested would be necessary to obtain new revenue, the legislation called for $11.1 billion in fiscal 1979 spending for highway and highway safety programs, compared to $10.5 billion in the earlier version and $7.7 billion proposed by the administration.

For mass transit, the subcommittee bill contained $4.4 billion for 1979, compared to $4.2 billion in HR 8648 and $3.2 billion in the administration's bill.

The subcommittee also increased by 14 the number of categories of federal highway and transit grants. The panel thus ignored administration suggestions that most categories be consolidated into more flexible programs. Different matching formulas for different types of projects were retained, rejecting the administration's recommendation that a uniform formula be substituted.

Other provisions of the subcommittee draft bill would have the effect of encouraging completion of the entire Interstate Highway System, no matter how costly or controversial the remaining unbuilt segments might be. The administration, on the other hand, had sought to encourage areas with unbuilt segments to either complete them or transfer the funds to other transportation projects.

Single Project Authorizations. Among the provisions in the subcommittee bill that benefited the districts of individual members of Congress were:

- An authorization of $50 million for a "demonstration project" establishing "jetfoil transportation" (a type of high-speed boat) between Long Branch, N.J., Sandy Hook State Park, N.J., and New York City, "for the purpose of determining the feasibility of utilizing this technology in providing certain public mass transportation service." Though no hearings were held on the jetfoil project, Howard and committee aides traveled to Hong Kong to see an operating jetfoil transit system, a committee aide explained.
- Language authorizing the Transportation Department to fund a "demonstration project" for construction of "a bypass highway from a point south of Prairie Creek Redwood State Park through the drainage of May Creek and Boyes Creek to extend along the eastern boundary of Prairie Creek Redwood State Park within Humboldt County, Calif., for the purpose of determining the extent such bypass highway will divert motor vehicle traffic around such park so as to best serve the needs of the traveling public while preserving the natural beauty of the park."

The bill authorized $50 million for construction of the bypass. The bypass would be located in the district of subcommittee member Don H. Clausen, R-Calif. It was not the subject of hearings, but rather grew out of a 1976 study, a committee aide explained.

- A feasibility study of an additional bridge across the Columbia River between Vancouver, Wash., and Portland, Ore. No cost was given for the study, and no hearings were held on the proposal. The bridge would serve the congressional district of Mike McCormack, D-Wash., a subcommittee member.
- A directive that a rural public transit "demonstration project" be carried out "in and in the vicinity of the Sherman, Texas-Denison, Texas, area." No cost was given in the bill. The project would be in the congressional district of subcommittee member Ray Roberts, D-Texas, who requested that the provision be put in the bill, according to a committee aide. No hearings were held on the proposed project.
- A requirement that the transportation secretary include a 13.2-mile segment of California Route 17 in the Interstate Highway System. The highway, in the congressional district of George Miller, D-Calif., has a particularly high accident rate, and the provision would make that segment eligible for rebuilding with 90 percent federal funding. No hearings were held on the provision. No cost estimate for the segment was given in the bill.
- A clause permitting the federal government to reimburse the West Virginia and Ohio state governments for the cost of constructing a toll bridge across the Ohio River at Huntington, W.Va. The bridge, which would be located in the district of Nick J. Rahall, D-W.Va., a subcommittee member, was not discussed in hearings, but Rahall and Chairman Howard visited the bridge site in early 1978, according to a committee aide. No statement of cost was given in the bill.
- Authorization for the state of New Hampshire to downgrade a planned Franconia Notch Interstate Highway segment to the status of a parkway, and to use the leftover federal funds for other New Hampshire roads. Construction of the Interstate segment had been opposed by environmental groups.

The parkway, which would be located in the district of subcommittee member James C. Cleveland, R-N.H., was discussed in 1973 hearings, according to a committee aide. No statement of cost was contained in the bill.

Transbus Delay Sought. The profusion of public works provisions in the House subcommittee bill caused Senate aides drafting companion legislation to label the House measure "pure pork."

Moreover, two other provisions of the bill were included to help a single corporation. Neither provision was in the earlier subcommittee version or mentioned in 1977 or 1978 hearings.

The provisions were drafted to favor the letting of Transportation Department contracts to GM for the purchase of buses.

The provisions, pushed by GM Transportation Affairs Director Roland Ouellette, involved a May 1977 Transportation Department regulation requiring all federally funded buses purchased after Sept. 30, 1979, to be of a type that would be more accessible to the elderly and handicapped.

The Transportation Department, which developed the specifications for the special bus, called it the "transbus." The department completed the specifications for the new bus in March.

The federal government was expected to spend an estimated $480 million annually for transbuses.

A key provision sought by GM and included in the subcommittee bill would have required the secretary of transportation to re-evaluate the transbus program and report his recommendations to Congress by Jan. 1, 1979.

The uncertainty created by the request to re-evaluate the transbus program forced a consortium of three cities — Los Angeles, Miami and Philadelphia — to drop plans to buy more than 500 transbuses in advance of the Transportation Department deadline.

The uncertainty also caused one potential transbus manufacturer — AM General Corp. — to shut down most of its transit bus manufacturing operation, and another — Grumman Flexible Corp. — to notify the Transportation Department that it was no longer willing to bid for transbus construction contracts.

The only other American firm that manufactured urban transit buses was the GMC Division of General Motors.

Trust Fund Spending. The Surface Transportation Subcommittee's markup of HR 11733 made few changes in the legislation as drafted by the subcommittee staff. The bill was then approved by the full Public Works Committee in similar form.

Following its approval by Public Works, the bill was expected to breeze through the Ways and Means Committee — which had jurisdiction over the taxes that feed the Highway Trust Fund — on its way to the House floor. Ways and Means traditionally had acquiesced in Public Works' recommendations.

Ways and Means, however, did not react in the traditional manner.

A draft study by the Congressional Budget Office had concluded in April that Public Works was attempting to finance a four-year highway program with six years' receipts from the Highway Trust Fund, "apparently avoiding the need for an immediate increase in highway taxes."

Faced with proposed trust fund spending levels of about $11 billion to $12 billion annually, and estimated trust fund receipts of only about $7 billion to $8 billion annually, Ways and Means members Sam Gibbons, D-Fla., and Barber B. Conable Jr., R-N.Y., delayed committee action by proposing an amendment requiring that trust fund spending be linked to anticipated revenues.

In mid-July, Surface Transportation Subcommittee Chairman James J. Howard, D-N.J., offered to propose an amendment on the House floor to trim the bill by about $1.4 billion annually.

He proposed to cut $300 million from the Interstate program, $150 million from primary route aid, $50 million from secondary highways, $500 million from bridge replacement and rehabilitation and about $400 million from mass transit programs.

Gibbons and Conable said the Howard compromise was inadequate and promised to press for more cuts, as well as for only a three- or four-year extension of the trust fund's life, instead of the six-year extension sought by Public Works.

On Aug. 1, however, Ways and Means rejected attempts to tie highway spending to anticipated trust fund revenues, and agreed to a five-year extension.

Public Works Report

The House Public Works Committee reported HR 11733 (H Rept 95-1485) on Aug. 11.

As reported, HR 11733 consisted of five titles: federal-aid highway construction; highway safety; mass transit operating assistance and construction; miscellaneous legislative provisions; and the extension of the Highway Trust Fund.

The four-year authorization bill, the committee report stated, "is the longest authorization period ever established for a total highway and safety program. It is the largest program ever established in highways and mass transit."

Title I — Federal-Aid Highways

Interstate Highway System. To hasten completion of the full Interstate system, the committee recommended increasing annual Interstate authorizations to $4 billion for fiscal years 1980-1989 and $2.33 billion for the system's expected completion in fiscal 1990. Under existing law, the annual Interstate authorization for fiscal years 1980-90 was $3.625 billion.

Early completion of the Interstate system was encouraged by requiring that all environmental impact statements for unfinished segments be completed by Sept. 30, 1984, and that construction be begun on rights-of-way acquired on all segments by Sept. 30, 1986.

Interstate resurfacing, restoration and rehabilitation was authorized at $175 million annually for fiscal 1980-81 and $275 million for fiscal 1982-83.

Other Federal-Aid Highways. The authorization for primary system construction aid was increased to $2.1 billion annually from the fiscal 1978 level of $1.35 billion. The secondary system authorization was increased from the $400 million approved for 1978 to $650 million annually over the four-year period covered by the bill. The urban system authorization remained at $800 million annually, as in 1978. Most other minor highway program levels remained the same.

A total of $125 million annually in primary aid funds was made available, at the secretary's discretion, for unusually expensive projects. Each state was required to reserve at least 36 percent of its primary aid funds for resurfacing, restoration and rehabilitation.

The federal share of most non-Interstate aid highway projects was increased to 80 percent, from 70 percent under existing law.

"Energy impacted" public roads — such as roads subjected to increased coal hauling traffic — were made eligible for rehabilitation under a newly created program; $50 million annually was authorized for the program. An additional $50 million annually was authorized to separate railroads from highway crossings when extensive rail transportation of coal threatened to excessively slow highway traffic. The federal share for both programs was set at 80 percent.

Highway Beautification Act. A number of changes were proposed in the Highway Beautification Act of 1965 (PL 89-285). Localities were barred from removing billboards and roadside signs without federal compensation; the secretary was required to approve requests for exemptions from the 1965 act for illegal signs that, if removed, would pose an economic "hardship" for their owner; and electronic signs featuring flashing, moving or intermittent lights were permitted to be installed in many areas where they had been barred under a number of federal-state agreements.

Bridge Replacement and Rehabilitation. Authorizations totaling $2 billion annually were provided for bridge replacement and rehabilitation. The 1978 authorization was $180 million, and, under existing law, only bridge replacement was eligible for federal funding. The federal share for the bridge program was increased to 90 percent from 75 percent under existing law.

Other Highway Provisions. In other provisions, HR 11733:

- Authorized $25 million annually for bicycle facility construction.
- Authorized the transportation secretary to reimburse West Virginia for the federal share of the cost of construction of a toll bridge across the Ohio River at Huntington, W.Va., after which the bridge was to become a toll-free bridge.
- Authorized demonstration projects permitting vending machines and the selling of lottery tickets in rest areas adjacent to Interstates.
- Authorized $50 million for construction of a bypass highway around Prairie Creek Redwood State Park in California.
- Authorized $30 million for design and construction of a traffic flow management demonstration project on the Long Island Expressway in New York state.
- Required the Transportation Department to study and report to Congress by Jan. 1, 1979, whether Alaska and Puerto Rico should be allocated routes to be made part of the national Interstate system.
- Required the department to recommend to Congress legislative changes that could reconcile apparent conflicts in existing clean air and transportation laws.
- Directed the department to study the feasibility of an additional bridge across the Columbia River between Vancouver, Wash., and Portland, Ore.
- Ordered the secretary to carry out a demonstration rural highway public transit demonstration project in the Sherman, Texas-Denison, Texas, area.
- Authorized the payment to the state of New Hampshire of 90 percent of the savings resulting from building a parkway in the Franconia Notch, N.H., area instead of an Interstate. The funds were to be used to improve alternative routes around Franconia.
- Ordered the secretary to fund the construction of access roads to Lake Raystown in Huntingdon County, Pa.
- Ordered the secretary to fund a railroad-highway crossing demonstration project in Hammond, Ind.
- Imposed a ceiling of $10.9 billion on fiscal 1979 federal-aid obligations, and ordered the secretary to obligate funds equally to all programs until the ceiling was reached, without establishing priorities or withholding funding from any particular programs.

Title II — Highway Safety

HR 11733 authorized from the Highway Trust Fund $200 million annually for highway safety programs carried out by the National Highway Traffic Safety Administration (NHTSA); $25 million annually for highway safety programs conducted by the Federal Highway Administration (FHA); $50 million annually for NHTSA, and $10 million annually for FHA, for highway safety research and development activities; $7.5 million annually for schoolbus driver training; $100 million annually for NHTSA enforcement of the 55-mile-per-hour national speed limit, and $5 million for fiscal 1980, $10 million for 1981 and $15 million in 1982 for grants to states developing innovative approaches to highway safety.

The bill also authorized $150 million annually from the trust fund and $100 million annually from general funds for rail-highway crossing improvements; $10 million annually from the trust fund for the collection of national accident data; and a total of $16 million for promotion of a national highway safety campaign.

In other provisions, the bill:

- Required states to certify that they were enforcing the 55-mile-per-hour speed limit, and directed the transportation secretary to reduce a state's apportionment of highway funds by up to 5 percent in fiscal 1980-82 and by up to 10 percent in fiscal 1983 and thereafter, if a state did not meet minimum federal compliance standards in enforcing the 55-mile-per-hour limit.
- Directed the secretary to make a full study of the impact of a provision of the 1976 Highway Safety Act amendments (PL 94-346) barring the secretary from mandating that states enact laws requiring motorcycle riders to wear safety helmets.

The 1976 law reversed a 1966 NHTSA standard requiring motorcycle riders to wear helmets and a 1975 Transportation Department decision to withhold federal funds from states without helmet laws. *(1976 Highway Safety Act, 1976 Almanac p. 669)*

Following enactment of the 1976 law, the committee report explained, a number of states repealed existing helmet laws and the number of motorcycle accident fatalities subsequently rose to record levels. This, the report explained, "was certainly not anticipated when the 1976 act was passed."

Title III — Mass Transit

HR 11733 authorized a total of $4.6 billion annually for fiscal years 1979-82 and provided $4.5 billion annually for fiscal years 1983-88 for mass transit programs.

Of the total authorization, $1.86 billion annually was for the existing discretionary grant program, whereby funds were distributed at the discretion of the transportation secretary. A set proportion of the total grant program was earmarked for planning, rehabilitation and modernization of existing transit systems, purchase of rail rolling stock, construction or extension of "fixed guideway" systems, and other capital projects.

An existing $2 billion in discretionary grant contract authority, remaining from earlier authorizations, was repealed, to be replaced by the new authorizations.

The bill retained $850 million of existing contract authority for fiscal 1979 and $775 million for fiscal 1980 remaining in the formula grant program, by which funds were allocated to states and urban areas according to a fixed formula.

Added to existing authorizations was $125 million for fiscal 1980 and $900 million for each of fiscal years 1981 and 1982. An additional $250 million annually for fiscal years 1979-82 was to be allocated according to a second formula favoring the largest urban areas.

An additional $400 million annually for four years was earmarked for urban transit bus replacement.

The bill also:

- Permitted the secretary to consider a bus's "life cycle costs" in awarding contracts, and directed the secretary to review a Transportation Department requirement that all buses purchased with federal funds after Sept. 30, 1979, be of a type more accessible to the elderly and handicapped.

The provisions, included in the bill at the behest of the General Motors Corp., concerned the specifications for a new type of bus, called the "transbus," developed by the Transportation Department in response to a congressional mandate.

- Authorized $100 million annually for fiscal 1979-82 for commuter rail passenger service aid.

- Authorized $125 million annually for four years for rural public transit aid.
- Authorized $50 million annually for the construction, acquisition or improvement of intercity bus terminals, and an additional $50 million annually for grants for other transportation terminal projects.
- Authorized $50 million annually for four years for the initiation, improvement or continuation of intercity bus service.
- Placed a ceiling of $675 million annually on mass transit projects to be funded from the Treasury as substitute projects for non-essential segments of the Interstate Highway System.
- Authorized $30 million for a high-speed "jetfoil" over-the-water demonstration transit project between Long Branch, N.J., and New York City.

Title IV — Miscellaneous Provisions

Buy American. The bill barred the purchase of materials with funds authorized by the legislation unless the materials were produced or manufactured in the United States.

Truck Brake Anti-locking Standard. The bill barred for two years the use of authorized funds to enforce a controversial truck brake anti-locking standard promulgated by the NHTSA in 1975. The so-called "121 standard" was issued before the brake had been fully tested, and was declared invalid and ordered removed by a U.S. appeals court in April 1978.

The NHTSA decided to appeal the ruling to the Supreme Court, and Rep. Dan Marriott, R-Utah, asked the committee to include a moratorium on the standard's enforcement in the surface transportation legislation.

Opponents of the system contended that it was excessively expensive and that malfunctions may have been responsible for as many as 18 deaths.

Congressional Veto. The bill gave Congress veto power over proposed Transportation Department rules and regulations.

Disapproval was to occur if both houses adopted a resolution of disapproval within 90 days, or if either house adopted a resolution of disapproval within 60 days and the other house did not then, within 30 days, disapprove the resolution of disapproval. Unchallenged rules could go into effect after 60 days.

Title V — Highway Trust Fund

This title extended the Highway Trust Fund financing mechanisms for five years, from Sept. 30, 1979, through Sept. 30, 1984.

All existing taxes feeding the fund were continued at their existing level, except that an exemption was granted fuel used by taxicabs in areas where cabs were not prevented by government or company regulation from implementing a shared-ride program. The exemption did not apply to gas-guzzling cabs of 1978 or later model year.

A four-year study by the Transportation Department of the costs of the federal-aid highway system and the share of the costs assumed by each class of highway user also was authorized. The administration proposed a three-year study, but the American Trucking Associations argued that three years was not a sufficient period of time. The four-year period approved by the committee meant that the study would be submitted to Congress by Jan. 15, 1982, an election year.

A second study, to be completed by the Treasury Department by April 15, 1982, was to recommend improvements in the structure of the highway excise tax structure.

Minority Views

In minority views, Rep. Gary A. Myers, R-Pa., scored the committee for "overindulging itself in committing future highway funds that are not now available from the Highway Trust Fund."

In separate views, Ways and Means members Gibbons, Conable, Charles A. Vanik, D-Ohio, Otis G. Pike, D-N.Y., Fortney H. "Pete" Stark, D-Calif., William A. Steiger, R-Wis., Bill Frenzel, R-Minn., and Bill Gradison, R-Ohio, criticized fellow Ways and Means members for approving "deficit financing ... at the expense of the taxpayer."

Senate Committee Action

While the House Public Works and Ways and Means Committees had fashioned a single bill to deal with the federal highway and the mass transit programs, four different Senate committees dealt with the same programs in separate bills.

Highway authorizations were considered by Senate Public Works, highway safety by Senate Commerce, mass transit funding by the Banking Committee and the Highway Trust Fund extension by Finance.

Public Works Committee

The Federal Aid Highway Act of 1978 (S 3073) was reported (S Rept 95-833) May 15 by the Senate Environment and Public Works Committee by a vote of 14-0.

The bill as reported proposed a number of changes in the structure and direction of federal aid highway programs. It also provided authorizations totaling $8.5 billion from the Highway Trust Fund for these programs for fiscal years 1979-80 and provided authorizations for the Interstate Highway System for fiscal years 1980-81.

According to the committee report, S 3073 "provides for more expeditious completion of the Interstate system and sets the stage for increased emphasis on rehabilitation and preservation of the existing highway network, including a new impetus for bridge...rehabilitation."

As reported, S 3073 adopted a number of recommendations put forward last winter by the Carter administration concerning funding levels, program consolidations and changes in program goals.

Highway authorization levels were kept in line with expected revenues from the trust fund, the committee stressed. To permit authorizations to "clearly exceed revenues over a comparable time period" could lead in the future to "drastically reduced" program levels or tax increases decided "in a crisis context." Either outcome would weaken the trust fund concept, the report concluded.

The statement was an apparent reference to HR 11733, which, as reported by the House Public Works Committee, authorized trust fund expenditures of about $11 billion annually for 1979-82, to be financed from trust fund receipts estimated at from $7 billion to $8 billion annually.

Following Public Works approval of HR 11733, an alarmed Carter administration endorsed an amendment to the bill to limit spending from the trust fund to amounts equal to revenue projections for a given year.

Interstate Highway System. As reported, S 3073 authorized $3.5 billion annually for the Interstate Highway System for fiscal years 1980-81 and provided a number of incentives for accelerating completion of the system or dropping nonessential segments. The annual authorization for fiscal 1979 was $3.25 billion.

The bill required that Interstate projects be either under construction, under contract for construction or completed by Sept. 30, 1986. It also changed funding allocation formulas to encourage completion of "essential gaps" in the system, increase the funds available to states able to construct segments faster than existing procedures permitted, and make Interstate substitute projects eligible for the same 90 percent federal funding level as the Interstate segments themselves.

Rehabilitation. The bill established a resurfacing, restoring and rehabilitation ("3R") fund for Interstate routes of $175 million annually for fiscal years 1979-80, and increased authorizations for bridge replacement and rehabilitation from the $180 million already authorized for fiscal 1978 to $450 million annually for 1979-80.

Highway Authorizations. S 3073 authorized annually from the trust fund $1.5 billion for the federal-aid primary road system, $675 million for the secondary road system, $700 million for urban highways and $285 million for the highway safety improvement program.

The bill authorized an additional $485 million annually for fiscal years 1979 and 1980 for road aid projects requiring appropriations.

Authorizations for a number of other minor categorical grant programs were continued. One new categorical grant program created by the bill authorized $20 million annually for two years for the construction of bikeways.

Grant Program Consolidations. Among categorical grant programs consolidated into larger grant programs under the bill were two vanpool and carpool demonstration programs; three highway safety construction programs, and two rail-highway crossing categories.

Other Major Provisions. As reported, S 3073 also:

- Permitted states to transfer up to 50 percent of their primary, secondary and urban highway funds to other transportation projects.
- Established as a national policy a requirement that transportation planners consider environmental, energy conservation, social, cultural and land-use factors in establishing policy.
- Provided urban areas with a mechanism for replacing metropolitan planning organizations designated for them by state governors.
- Required the use of domestic products and materials — other than petroleum products — in federally funded highway projects costing more than $1 million. The requirement could be waived by the transportation secretary.
- Directed the transportation secretary to study how different classes of highway users contributed to the costs of highway construction and maintenance and to evaluate the equitability of the distribution of highway taxes among all classes of users. The secretary was required to report his findings to Congress by January 1982.
- Directed the transportation secretary to study the need for federal truck size and weight limits, and to report his recommendations to Congress by January 1981.
- Provided that states not adequately enforcing the national 55 mile per hour speed limit be penalized by having a portion of their federal highway aid funds withheld.

Senate Banking Committee

As reported (S Rept 95-857) by the Senate Banking Committee May 15, the Federal Public Transportation Act of 1978 (S 2441) closely paralleled the Carter administration's recommendations sent the committee in January. The bill was approved unanimously.

"The committee fully supports the president's stated objectives for a coordinated and rational national transportation policy," the committee stated in its report. "Of the challenges the United States faces on many fronts, the harsh realities of our energy extravagance and inefficiency are among the most serious. . . . But one essential ingredient in the total solution will be greater dependence and ever increasing reliance on public transportation to provide the mobility our population demands."

The major problem the committee found with the administration's proposals, the report explained, was "the inadequacy of the funding levels." Although mass transit authorizations for fiscal 1978 — not counting transfers from the Interstate account to fund substitute mass transit projects — totaled $2.4 billion, and the Carter administration recommended $2.6 billion for fiscal 1979, S 2441 as approved by the committee authorized $3.4 billion for fiscal 1979 federal mass transit aid.

The committee also altered the administration's recommendations on restructuring existing formula and discretionary grant programs, and rejected altogether a recommendation to create a combined mass transit-highway aid program for small urban and rural areas.

The committee also adopted by a vote of 8-7 a controversial amendment offered by Edward W. Brooke, R-Mass., to authorize an additional $891 million over four years to subsidize up to 50 percent of a transit system's operating deficits, so long as the total federal operating subsidy did not exceed one-third of total operating costs. The provision would result in a marked increase in operating subsidies for Boston, New York and San Francisco.

Secretary Brock Adams, in a May 1 letter to the committee, said the administration opposed the amendment.

Major Provisions

S 2441 as reported:

- Authorized in federal aid to urban mass transportation $3.4 billion for fiscal 1979, $3.7 billion for 1980, $3.8 billion for 1981 and $3.9 billion for 1982.
- Narrowed the existing discretionary grant program to permit the transportation secretary to make loans and grants at his discretion, primarily for the construction of major new transit systems and extension of existing ones.

Included under the discretionary program were grants for construction costs of such systems; acquisition of equipment, facilities and real estate; the funding of new technology demonstration projects; grants or loans for urban development projects related to transportation, and for improvements in urban transportation facilities.

- Broadened the existing grant program in urban areas where federal transit aid was apportioned according to a fixed formula. The program continued to be the major source for funds to purchase equipment for public transit systems and to subsidize such systems' operating deficits, but was expanded to cover the costs of routine bus replacement, the modernization of bus facilities and equipment, the special transportation needs of the elderly and handicapped and commuter rail operating subsidies.

The formula by which the funds were allocated was altered to consider an area's population and population density, the age of its bus fleet, the number of miles the system served annually, and the size and capacity of existing mass transit services in the area. The formula also was altered to favor the largest urban areas.

- Created a new program within the Urban Mass Transportation Administration (UMTA) to provide capital and operating subsidies for the mass transit needs of small urban and rural areas.
- Directed the transportation secretary to discourage the purchase of transit materials and equipment from countries that offered those goods for sale at less than the cost of production or otherwise erected nontariff trade barriers.
- Provided a mechanism for urban areas to reject metropolitan planning organizations designated for them by state governors.

Commerce Committee

S 2541 was one of two Senate bills providing funding for highway and motor vehicle safety programs, which were administered primarily by NHTSA, an agency of the Transportation Department.

The bill, reported (S Rept 95-870) May 15 by the Senate Commerce Committee, authorized funds for NHTSA activities under the Highway Safety Act of 1966 (PL 89-564).

(The other NHTSA authorization bill (S 2604) concerned programs provided under the National Traffic and Motor Vehicle Safety Act of 1966 (PL 89-563) and the Motor Vehicle Information and Cost Savings Act of 1972 (PL 92-513).)

S 2541 comprised only Title II of HR 11733, the omnibus highway-mass-transit-highway safety legislation reported by the House Public Works Committee Aug. 11.

Under the 1966 Highway Safety Act, NHTSA was authorized to award incentive grants and to develop mandatory safety standards to help states and localities develop their own safety programs for motor vehicles, drivers and highways.

In 1976 Congress asked the Transportation Department to evaluate the standards issued under the 1966 law and recommend improvements both in that law and in the existing standards.

Carter Recommendations

In March 1977 the Transportation Department convened a highway safety conference to help it formulate its recommendations. Legislative revisions were proposed by the department in early 1978 as part of the Carter administration's Highway and Public Transportation Act of 1978.

The administration bill proposed retaining mandatory safety standards and data collection requirements only for certain highway safety goals, and substituting federal guidelines for others. Areas for which mandatory standards were recommended were those in which national uniformity was considered essential.

Substituting guidelines for federal standards in all other areas would give the states greater flexibility in adapting their highway programs to local conditions, the administration argued.

The administration bill also recommended consolidating the existing categorical grant programs into a single highway safety grant program, and providing for a federal share of $80 for every $100 of a project's cost.

Under existing law, the federal share was $70 of every $100.

In marking up the legislation, the Commerce Committee accepted some of the administration recommendations.

Provisions

As reported by the Commerce panel, S 2541:

- Authorized from the Highway Trust Fund $175 million for each of fiscal years 1979 and 1980, and $200 million for each of fiscal years 1981 and 1982, to carry out highway safety programs.
- Authorized $50 million annually from the Highway Trust Fund for fiscal years 1979 through 1982 for NHTSA highway safety research and development.
- Authorized from the Highway Trust Fund $5 million for fiscal 1980, $10 million for fiscal 1981 and $15 million for fiscal 1982 for grants to states developing "innovative" approaches to highway safety. Under existing law, the grants were awarded as "incentives" to reduce highway fatalities.
- Continued the formula under existing law providing that the federal share of highway safety program funding be $70 of every $100 spent; the other $30 was provided by local funding.
- Provided a formula for apportioning the federal highway safety funds to the states according to their population and miles of public roads.
- Required that mandatory safety and data collection standards be retained concerning the licensing of drivers, rules of the road, traffic records, highway design, construction and maintenance, traffic control devices, vehicle titling and registration and theft prevention. Existing highway safety standards in such areas as traffic safety education, motorcycle and pedestrian safety, emergency medical services, traffic adjudication systems, vehicle inspection and maintenance, pupil transportation and identification of locations with high accident rates were converted into guidelines.
- Required states to certify that they were enforcing the 55-mile-per-hour nationwide speed limit and directed the transportation secretary to reduce a state's apportionment of funds by up to 5 percent in fiscal years 1981 through 1983, and by up to 10 percent in fiscal 1984, if a state did not meet minimum federal compliance standards in enforcing the 55-mile-per-hour limit.
- Identified the increased use of safety belts and improved enforcement of the 55-mile-per-hour limit as high priority safety programs, and permitted the transportation secretary to apportion to the states up to 25 percent of their total funds for such high priority programs.

Finance Committee

The Finance Committee considered and approved the trust fund provisions on Oct. 3, but did not issue a written report on their portion (S 2440) of the overall authorization. S 2440 extended the taxes which fed the Highway Trust Fund.

House Floor Action

Ignoring administration pleas for major reductions in spending levels, the House Sept. 28 gave overwhelming approval to a $60.9 billion, four-year highway and mass transit funding bill.

The vote approving HR 11733 was 367-28. *(Vote 749, p. 212-H)*

The legislation was the first combined highway and mass transit bill ever to be fashioned by a single congressional committee, the House Public Works Committee.

The House action represented a victory for Public Works and a setback for President Carter and House Budget Committee Chairman Robert N. Giaimo, D-Conn., both of whom had urged the House to make significant cuts in the highway and mass transit funding levels.

During five days of debate on the bill beginning Sept. 15, the House adopted only one amendment that reduced the legislation's authorization levels.

That amendment, offered by Public Works Surface Transportation Subcommittee Chairman James J. Howard, D-N.J., cut $5.6 billion from the $66.5 billion approved by Public Works. The Howard amendment had been agreed to in advance by senior Public Works members. The panel wanted to avoid a showdown with Ways and Means Committee members over authorizing expenditures from the Highway Trust Fund in excess of the fund's anticipated revenues.

Administration officials and Giaimo, however, felt that the Howard amendment was not enough.

'Biggest Threat to the Budget'

In a Sept. 20 briefing, Office of Management and Budget Director James T. McIntyre told reporters the bill "is currently the biggest threat to the budget pending in Congress." He and Transportation Secretary Brock Adams warned that if further cuts were not made in the bill the president would veto it.

They supported an amendment sponsored by Giaimo to cut spending from the Highway Trust Fund to the level of the fund's anticipated receipts. The amendment, rejected by the House Sept. 21, would have cut annual trust fund spending from the more than $11 billion proposed in HR 11733 to about $8.3 billion.

A similar amendment to the related S 3073 had been adopted by a vote of 86-0 by the Senate.

The bill would be acceptable to the president, Adams said, "if we can get between the Giaimo amendment and the Senate bill" in conference.

The vote rejecting the Giaimo amendment, however, was lopsided — 111-238. Voting against it were 143 Democrats and 95 Republicans. Only 93 Democrats and 18 Republicans supported Giaimo. *(Vote 720, p. 206-H)*

Other Amendments

In the five days the House debated the bill, 43 amendments were considered, of which 30 were adopted.

Beautification Act Changes. The House rejected, 76-199, an amendment by Peter H. Kostmayer, D-Pa., to delete from the bill three provisions the Transportation Department contended would gut the 1965 Highway Beautification Act. *(Vote 724, p. 206-H)*

The provisions prohibited localities from removing billboards and roadside signs near federal-aid highways unless their owners were paid federal compensation; required the transportation secretary to approve requests for exemptions from the 1965 act for illegal signs that would pose an economic "hardship" for their owner if removed; and permitted electronic signs featuring flashing, moving or intermittent lights in areas where they had been previously barred under various federal-state agreements.

Howard, opposing the Kostmayer amendment, argued that the provisions were intended "to strengthen and fully effectuate the Beautification Act's purposes." Kostmayer argued that the bill made "a very basic and fundamental change" in existing law.

Highway Safety Changes. Two successful amendments weakened federal highway safety efforts.

- An amendment by William H. Harsha, R-Ohio, eased compliance deadlines and lessened required state efforts to enforce the nationwide 55 mile per hour speed limit. The amendment, however, provided incentives for states to step up enforcement by authorizing additional federal highway safety funds.
- An amendment by Bud Shuster, R-Pa., prohibited the use of federal highway safety to purchase airbags for vehicles owned by state and federal governments.

James C. Cleveland, R-N.H., succeeded in winning adoption of an amendment to encourage the use of safety belts by requiring states to use a certain proportion of their federal highway safety funds for safety belt programs.

Transbus, Weight Limits. An amendment by Mario Biaggi, D-N.Y., deleted the provision calling for a reevaluation of the Transportation Department's Transbus specifications. The effect of the amendment, accepted by voice vote, was to permit the department's program to fashion a bus more accessible to handicapped and elderly persons to go forward.

The amendment had been agreed to in advance by the bill's floor managers.

Sam Gibbons, D-Fla., who as chairman of the Ways and Means Oversight Subcommittee had been critical of lax state enforcement of truck size and weight limitations on federal-aid highways, offered an amendment designed to facilitate enforcement of those limitations.

The amendment required the states to certify annually to the federal government that they were enforcing the limitations, and permitted the transportation secretary to reduce by 10 percent the amount of federal highway aid destined for states not enforcing the limitation. The existing penalty of a 100 percent reduction in state funds was not workable, Gibbons stated. It was adopted by voice vote.

The House, by a vote of 12-380, reversed an earlier vote that had approved an amendment by Barry M. Goldwater Jr., R-Calif., to bar the Federal Aviation Administration from having access to the files of the National Driver Registry. *(Vote 748, p. 212-H)*

Senate Floor Action

In sharp contrast with the House, the Senate backed budgetary restraint over national highway spending in its consideration of the legislation.

During Senate debate, the bill's floor manager urged colleagues to resist approving substantial additional spending in order to preserve the integrity of the Highway Trust Fund.

"The basic question," argued Lloyd Bentsen, D-Texas, chairman of the Senate Public Works Transportation Subcommittee, "is not how much the program needs, but the measure of resources available to sustain it. We must weigh needs against available trust fund revenues and do the best we can with the funds we have."

The House, Sen. Bentsen observed during Senate debate, "has been less reticent" about living within the confines of the trust fund.

"They are going to take an expensive and inflationary bill to conference and we shall have to negotiate them down from that figure if the integrity of the trust fund is to be preserved."

Four-Part Package

The Senate completed action on the highway and highway safety portions of the bill on Aug. 18 and 21 respectively. Work on the mass transit and Highway Trust Fund portions was considered and passed Sept. 28 and Oct. 3 respectively.

Finally, after action on all four titles of the Senate bill had been completed, it was given the House-passed bill number (HR 11733), approved and sent to conference.

Future of Trust Fund

At the same time as the Senate toed the line on fiscal integrity, it strongly supported preservation of the Highway Trust Fund, despite a significant change in its direction.

The Senate voted 10-75 Aug. 21 to reject an amendment offered by Sens. Edward M. Kennedy, D-Mass., and Lowell P. Weicker Jr., R-Conn., to terminate the trust fund. *(Vote 336, p. 51-S)*

Kennedy and Weicker had offered similar amendments since 1971. All were defeated, but the lopsided defeat this time was the Senate's most decisive endorsement of continuing the fund.

The endorsement came as key members of Congress and administration officials admitted that the fund's original purpose had been largely fulfilled, and urged a major change in its direction — the first since the fund was created in 1956.

The change was to shift the goal of the federal highway aid program from financing new construction to maintaining existing roadways.

As originally conceived, federal trust fund revenues were to be used solely to put a federal highway system in place. Maintenance was a state responsibility.

When the states failed to hold up their end of the bargain, however, federal policymakers agreed to take up the slack.

"It makes little sense to spend over a hundred billion dollars for a highway network and then permit it to crumble for lack of maintenance," Sen. Bentsen said Aug. 18. "We have no choice but to protect this enormous investment, and maintenance is the key to protection."

"You will see more and more of this as the Interstate System completes," Transportation Secretary Brock Adams told reporters in January. He announced at that time that the Carter administration supported retaining the trust fund at its existing level despite a declining need for additional highway construction.

Spending Hikes Rejected

Senators showed their willingness to keep highway spending lean in a number of ways.

Only two amendments accepted on the floor added funds to the spending totals approved by the Commerce and Public Works Committees.

An amendment offered by John C. Culver, D-Iowa, and adopted by voice vote, authorized an additional $75 million annually for bridge replacement and rehabilitation. The amendment raised from $450 million annually to $525 million the amount of federal money to be spent to keep highway bridges safe.

"The number of unsafe bridges in this country is simply appalling," Culver argued in support of his amendment. No one spoke against the increase.

An amendment offered by Edward Zorinsky, D-Neb., adopted by voice vote, authorized an additional $350,000 for a study of the impact of coal trains on communities located next to rail lines on which the hauling of coal had recently increased.

At the request of Public Works Chairman Jennings Randolph, D-W.Va., an amendment offered by Adlai E. Stevenson, D-Ill., to authorize an additional $125 million annually for high-cost federal highway projects, was withdrawn from consideration.

The additional funds already had been approved as a part of HR 11733 as reported by House Public Works, and Randolph said he would consider the provision favorably in conference with the House.

Also withdrawn under pressure from the bill's floor managers was an amendment by Sens. Dewey F. Bartlett and Henry Bellmon, both R-Okla., to authorize $640,100 for Arkansas' share of a bridge on Interstate Highway 40 over the Arkansas River.

The Senate rejected, by a vote of 8-45, an amendment offered by Charles McC. Mathias Jr., R-Md., to authorize the federal government to make to the state of Maryland an advance payment of 100 percent of the costs for construction of a new tunnel under Baltimore Harbor as part of Interstate Highway 95, even if the sum advanced exceeded the total federal share allocated for the project. *(Vote 327, p. 50-S)*

Also rejected, by a vote of 37-51, was an amendment by Walter (Dee) Huddleston, D-Ky. to authorize an additional $100 million for rehabilitation of roads damaged by coal hauling. *(Vote 334, p. 50-S)*

The Senate then went on to approve by a vote of 86-0 an amendment by Robert Morgan, D-N.C., to declare it to be national policy that highway spending increases "should be consistent with the rate of growth of revenues from existing sources, the ability of states responsibly to obligate increased federal funds, and a sound overall federal fiscal policy." *(Vote 335, p. 51-S)*

Though Morgan said the amendment would "require" that trust fund expenditures not exceed revenues, his colleagues portrayed it as a symbolic gesture to the House of the Senate's concern over the fiscal integrity of the fund.

Killing the Trust Fund

The 10-75 vote rejecting the Kennedy-Weicker amendment to terminate the Highway Trust Fund altogether reflected the substantial support that existed in the Senate to maintain the existing federal aid highway program. *(Vote 336, p. 51-S)*

The vote also showed the declining strength of trust fund opponents. The 10 votes for the amendment was the smallest number to support Kennedy and Weicker since the two began offering this proposal in 1971.

Voting for the amendment were Sens. Edward W. Brooke, R-Mass., John H. Chafee, R-R.I., Alan Cranston, D-Calif., Jacob K. Javits, R-N.Y., Kennedy, Mathias, Claiborne Pell, D-R.I., Charles H. Percy, R-Ill., William Proxmire, D-Wis., and Weicker.

"We have a job to do, an important job," Bentsen argued in opposing the Kennedy-Weicker amendment. "We must complete the Interstate System as rapidly as possible and we must maintain what we have built. Take away the trust fund and you will inhibit — perhaps cripple — our ability to do the job."

In floor action Sept. 28 on the mass transit provisions (S 2441), senators executed an intricate series of maneuvers that reduced mass transit spending levels in the bill by $1.891 billion for the fiscal 1978-82 period and then added to the bill a fifth year (fiscal 1983) authorization of $1.58 billion.

As finally approved by the Senate, the bill authorized about $14.5 billion for urban mass transit aid over the five-year period. The total did not include an additonal $2.8 billion over four years in Interstate Highway System funding that was expected to be transferred to mass transit projects built as substitutes to proposed Interstate segments that subsequently were dropped.

As approved by the Banking Committee, the bill had authorized $14.8 billion for urban mass transit programs over four years.

The floor maneuvers had been worked out in advance through negotiations between the bill's floor managers and Transportation Secretary Brock Adams.

The agreement, Adams wrote floor manager Harrison A. Williams Jr., D-N.J., in a Sept. 26 letter "reaffirming the position of the administration," would result in authorizations representing "the upper limit on the funding levels that are acceptable during the time frame covered by S 2441."

"It is my strong desire," Adams wrote, "that this point be emphasized when the House and Senate conferees meet to resolve the differences on future highway and transit funding." On voice votes, the Senate approved an amendment by Robert Morgan, D-N.C., to reduce by $1 billion the level of authorizations over the four-year period covered by the bill, and a Williams amendment authorizing $1.58 billion for the mass transit discretionary grant program for fiscal 1983.

The Senate subsequently deleted from the bill, 74-15, a provision authorizing a federal subsidy of up to 50 percent of an urban transit system's operating costs, so long as the total federal operating subsidy did not exceed one-third of the system's total operating costs. Budget Committee Chairman Edmund S. Muskie, D-Maine, offered the amendment to delete the subsidy. *(Vote 416, p. 62-S)*

"The cuts proposed on the floor [by Morgan and Muskie] would have crippled the construction and improvement programs underway in many cities across the country," Williams said in a printed statement after the measure was passed.

"That is why it was so necessary to add the fifth year authorization to make sure funds were on hand to keep these projects on schedule."

Mass Transit Subsidy

The provision deleted by the Muskie amendment had been added to the bill in the Banking Committee through an amendment, adopted 8-7, offered by Edward W. Brooke, R-Mass.

The provision was "strenuously" opposed by the administration, according to Adams' Sept. 26 letter. The administration said the provision would have cost the federal government an estimated $891 million over four years, and would have resulted in a marked increase in operating subsidies for only a few cities, including Boston, New York and San Francisco.

Brooke was not a party to the agreement between Secretary Adams and the bill's floor managers. He defended the subsidy provision, arguing that many smaller cities' transit systems already received the equivalent of a 50 percent subsidy on their operating costs through the formula grant program. Under the program, federal funds were allocated to transit systems on the basis of a fixed formula. He termed the subsidy a matter of "equity."

Other Amendments

A number of minor amendments to the highway portion of the bill were adopted by the Senate on voice votes. Among the more significant changes were amendments:

- To permit the transportation secretary to reallocate a state's unused urban highway funds to other states — by Thomas F. Eagleton, D-Mo.;
- To require the Transportation Department to study the potential for reducing urban blight adjacent to federal highways located in central business districts — by Warren G. Magnuson, D-Wash.;
- To relieve states of the need to reimburse the trust fund for funds spent on Interstate highway construction or acquisition of rights-of-way if an Interstate segment subsequently was withdrawn from the system and the land put to another public conservation or recreational use — by Javits.

In floor action Sept. 28, the Senate approved an additional 13 amendments to the mass transit portion of the surface transportation legislation, all on voice votes. None of these amendments increased the authorization levels in the bill.

Among the significant changes made by the amendments were the following:

- Permitted mass transit systems crossing state lines to be exempted from Interstate Commerce Commission regulation of joint fare agreements between the different areas served; by Walter (Dee) Huddleston, D-Ky.
- Provided a single uniform planning system for all urban mass transit grant programs; by Williams.
- Permitted the use of funds earmarked for a single transit mode to be used for development of comprehensive mass transit programs relying on a combination of modes to meet an area's particular transit needs; by Williams.
- Required the transportation secretary to submit to Congress within one year of the legislation's enactment recommendations for a formula that would consider the severity of an area's air pollution problems in determining its share of federal mass transit funds; by Floyd K. Haskell, D-Colo.
- Made more flexible federal requirements that state and local governments pay their share of the costs of operating and maintaining mass transit systems; by Alan Cranston, D-Calif., and Patrick J. Leahy, D-Vt.
- Permitted the Transportation Department to make "incentive" grants from a fund earmarked for the encouragement of technical innovation of transit systems that had been operated, in the transportation secretary's opinion, in a "particularly meritorious" manner; by Edward M. Kennedy, D-Mass.

Two of the amendments that were adopted by the Senate affected programs unrelated to urban mass transportation.

An amendment by Wendell H. Ford, D-Ky., relieved automobile tire retreaders from record-keeping requirements imposed on them by the National Traffic and Motor Vehicle Safety Act of 1966.

Ford said the records were needed solely to recall a retreaded tire and noted that only eight of 66 million retreaded tires manufactured since the reporting requirement was imposed had actually been recalled.

With the Transportation Department's concurrence, the Senate already had passed legislation (S 2604 — S Rept 95-861) May 22 relieving the retreaders of the record-keeping requirement. However, that bill — providing authorizations for certain activities of the National Highway Traffic Safety Administration — was never considered by the House during the session.

The Senate also routinely approved an amendment by John Melcher, D-Mont., requiring the National Railroad Passenger Corp. (Amtrak) to notify the governor and legislature of each state in which it intended to drop train routes, and permitting states to enter into agreements with Amtrak to subsidize the continuation of routes Amtrak announced it intended to discontinue.

Trust Fund Extension

By voice vote, the Senate Oct. 3 adopted as a new title of the surface transportation aid bill a series of provisions extending the Highway Trust Fund for five years.

As approved by the Senate, the provisions were almost identical to the corresponding title of the House-passed bill.

The Senate was obliged to wait until early October to complete action on the bill because the House did not complete its version of the trust fund extension until Sept. 28. Under the Constitution, the House is required to originate all revenue measures.

As approved by the Senate, the final title extended all existing taxes that fed the trust fund; provided for a four-year study by the Transportation Department of the costs of the federal-aid highway system and the share of the costs assumed by each class of highway user, and asked the Treasury Department to recommend by April 15, 1982, improvements in the structure of the highway excise tax structure.

Dropped from the Senate bill was a provision of the House-passed version that granted an exemption from the fuel tax for taxicabs in areas where cabs were permitted to implement shared-ride programs.

The trust fund provisions were approved by the Senate without change.

Conference Instructions

In naming Senate conferees Oct. 3 to the House-Senate conference committee, Lloyd Bentsen, D-Texas, carefully defined which titles of the bill each Senate committee's conferees would be permitted to work on.

In areas where the interests of two committees overlapped, Bentsen stated, a majority of the conferees from each committee would be required to agree before a proposed compromise provision would be considered approved.

Conference Report

HR 11733 was reported (H Rept 95-1797) by a House-Senate conference committee on Oct. 14.

In its overall funding level the bill more closely resembled the Senate-passed legislation, but in its broad policies and specific programs it bore a closer resemblance to the House-passed measure.

Retained in the compromise version were most of the narrow categorical programs that had been provided by the House bill. Also retained from that bill were the wide differences in matching shares from program to program, the separate planning requirements for highway and mass transit projects, the major increases in spending for the bridge rehabilitation program, a subsidy program for intercity buses and a wide array of provisions specifying individual projects to be funded.

Some of the more controversial provisions of the House-passed bill were dropped in conference, while others were merely shifted from one section to another or combined with other programs.

House Provisions Dropped

Dropped were a $200 million authorization for rehabilitation of "energy-impacted" public roads — roads subjected to increased coal hauling traffic — and another $200 million program for improvement of rail-highway crossings in areas where traffic had been slowed by long coal-hauling trains.

Also dropped were a congressional veto over proposed Transportation Department rules and regulations; a ceiling of $675 million annually on mass transit projects to be funded by the Treasury as substitutes for non-essential segments of the Interstate Highway System, and a two-year moratorium on Transportation Department enforcement of a controversial truck brake anti-locking standard promulgated by the NHTSA in 1975.

On April 17, 1978, the U.S. Court of Appeals overturned much of the truck brake standard. After the Supreme Court declined to review the lower court decision, the Transportation Department announced it would not enforce several provisions of the standard. Conferees said they expected the entire issue to be reviewed during the 96th Congress.

Conferees dropped one provision of the House-passed bill that would have jeopardized the goals of the Highway Beautification Act of 1965. The provision had required the transportation secretary to approve all requests for "economic hardship" exemptions from the 1965 law's requirement that illegal billboards be torn down.

Nonetheless, Sen. Robert T. Stafford, R-Vt., said Oct. 14 that other Beautification Act modifications that had been accepted by the conferees had so weakened the original legislation that "I think it is time to admit the ... act is a failure and to seek its repeal."

Finally, a provision establishing a National Alcohol Fuels Commission that was contained in neither the House nor the Senate version of the legislation, was inserted in the bill during the conference at the request of Sen. Birch Bay, D-Ind., and subsequently accepted by both houses.

Final Action

Both the Senate and the House completed action on the bill on the final day of the session — Oct. 15 — by adopting the conference report by voice votes, sending the bill to the president. ▮

'Pothole' Repair Bill Dies

An "emergency" measure that would have granted federal aid to the states for repair of potholes caused by the harsh winter weather of 1977-78 died in the 95th Congress. The Senate on Oct. 15 had tacked on a water projects authorization measure before passing the legislation (HR 10979) by voice vote, but the bill died in the House several hours later when Congress adjourned. *(Water projects legislation, Energy and Environment chapter)*

Acting with uncharacteristic speed, the House had approved the highway repair bill Feb. 21. Introduced Feb. 14, the House Public Works Committee reported the bill (H Rept 95-889) Feb. 20. The bill was taken up under suspension of the rules procedure — prohibiting floor amendments — and was passed by the House the next day by a 274-137 vote. *(Vote 53, p. 16-H)*

The legislation would have authorized $250 million from the Highway Trust Fund to be allocated to the states to reimburse 100 percent of the cost of repairing weather-related damage to highways and urban mass transit railbeds. The legislation specified that the funds were to be spent "in addition to, and not in substitution for," repairs normally undertaken by the states themselves. Each state, the District of Columbia, Puerto Rico and Guam were eligible for the funds, and no state was to receive less than one-half of 1 percent or more than 7 percent of the total funds available. ▮

Home Insulation Safety

Compromise legislation (S 2401) establishing an interim safety standard for cellulose home insulation was passed by both the House and Senate June 29, clearing the measure for the president. The bill was signed into law July 11 (PL 95-319).

The measure set mandatory safety standards for flammability and corrosion of cellulose insulation. It was drafted because of congressional dissatisfaction with the pace of the Consumer Product Safety Commission's (CPSC) response to the danger of home fires caused by cellulose insulation.

Major Provisions

As cleared by Congress, S 2401:

- Established an interim product safety standard for cellulose home insulation similar to the standard already put into effect by the General Services Administration (GSA) for federal purchases of insulation. The standard was to go into effect 60 days after the legislation's enactment.
- Provided the CPSC with mechanisms for enforcing the standard; for making technical changes in the standard before it went into effect; for incorporating future GSA changes in its insulation standard into the interim CPSC standard, and for promulgating a final standard on an expedited basis.
- Limited judicial review of both the interim and final standards.
- Required the CPSC to report periodically to Congress on its enforcement efforts, and required other federal agencies to report violations of the standard to the CPSC.

Background

As the price of heating oil and electricity rose dramatically in the mid-1970s, the demand for home insulation materials skyrocketed. President Carter, in his 1977 energy message to Congress, set a goal of insulating 90 percent of American homes by 1985 in order to conserve energy.

Cellulose insulation products made up an estimated 40 to 50 percent of the market for insulation of existing homes. According to CPSC, "heightened risks of injury [from cellulose home insulation] stem from the current high demand for home insulation, inexperienced new manufacturers who may use poor facilities, inadequate or improper chemical treatment of products to achieve flame retardancy, and incorrect installation by consumers or professionals who place insulation near recessed lighting fixtures, chimney flues, or other heat sources."

The CPSC was first asked to develop mandatory insulation standards in an October 1976 petition filed by the Denver, Colo., district attorney's consumer office.

When, by January 1978, the CPSC still had not acted on the petition, Wendell H. Ford, D-Ky., chairman of the Senate Commerce Consumer Subcommittee, introduced legislation to establish an interim standard.

On Feb. 9 the CPSC called for proposals for mandatory safety standards.

Legislative History

The Senate took up and passed S 2401 on Jan. 23 by voice vote without amendment. There was no committee report.

A related bill (HR 11998) was reported (H Rept 95-1116) by the House Commerce Committee on May 4. Committee action followed the April 26 release of a report by the committee's Oversight and Investigations Subcommittee (Subcommittee Rept 95-52) that stated that the CPSC had been "derelict in failing to set safety standards for various types of insulation."

The committee decided to legislate interim standards, according to the committee report, because "experience has shown that [the CPSC's rulemaking] process can take a substantial period of time...."

The House then passed the Senate-numbered bill, as amended by HR 11998 in committee, by voice vote.

A conference committee was convened to resolve differences between the two versions, and a report was filed (H Rept 95-1322) June 28.

Both the House and the Senate by voice votes approved the conference report June 29, completing congressional action. ▮

Health/Education/Welfare

A mood of budgetary austerity dominated consideration of health, education and welfare programs in 1978, both inside and outside of Congress.

The tax-cutting, anti-spending desires of the voters, symbolized by California's Proposition 13, had a great effect on social programs, which are often associated in the public mind with the worst of government waste and inefficiency.

The November election defeats of several liberal Democratic senators and the election of a Congress seen as somewhat to the right of the 95th foretold an even more conservative outlook on social spending in the future.

Rapid inflation added to the problems of the social service system, putting new strains on the local and private financing of health, education and welfare efforts, while discouraging increased federal assistance.

Carter administration hopes for major changes in health insurance and welfare systems were frustrated by the new conservative spirit. Congress was clearly reluctant to approve new programs with the potential to add billions of dollars to federal spending.

Social programs were also being curtailed on the local level. School operations in California and Ohio were cut back following voter rejection of taxes. And some states appeared to be moving toward "deliberalization" of welfare eligibility and benefits.

Health

The cost question clearly dominated debate on health programs. U.S. medical costs were growing about twice as fast as the overall rate of inflation, and spending for health services in 1978 averaged out to more than $800 per man, woman and child. In six years the nation's aggregate medical bill had nearly doubled, in 15 years it had quadrupled, and since 1950 it had increased more than eleven-fold, according to the Congressional Research Service.

The economics of national health insurance, pledged by President Carter in his 1976 campaign, caused a deep rift between Carter and Sen. Edward M. Kennedy, D-Mass. Carter favored a step-by-step approach, with benefits or coverage of groups phased in only if the economy permitted. Kennedy blasted this scheme, and launched extensive hearings on a labor-drafted health plan. He argued that the only way to eliminate the costly inequities and duplications of the existing "non-system" was to create at one time — and soon — an all-inclusive federal health system. *(Story, p. 630)*

Congress' Mixed Record. Congress had a mixed record on saving health dollars in 1978. On the one hand, the Proposition 13 vote and general uneasiness about inflation prompted some cost-cutting votes on popular health programs. But when the proposed savings appeared to be at the expense of the powerful health care industry, thrift went out the window.

About 85 percent of federal health programs were up for renewal in 1978, and long-time observers were surprised at Congress' repeated pruning of authorizations well below levels recommended by health subcommittees. Often the cuts were recommended by the subcommittee chairmen after unusual floor defeats on health bills, to forestall further challenges.

While economizing on existing health programs, however, Congress balked at regulating hospital income, the one step the Carter administration said would significantly slow the ominous acceleration of health care spending.

One of the most significant factors in 1978 health policy debates appeared to be members' heightened sensitivity to the highly emotional issue of access to health care — much of it due to a 1977 fracas over proposed federal health planning guidelines intended to eliminate underused hospital beds and facilities. The guidelines had set off an avalanche of protests, mostly from rural and small-town constituents who feared they would force shutdowns of health resources in areas that already suffered from medical service shortages. Congress called on the Department of Health, Education and Welfare (HEW) to accommodate rural needs, and the 1978 final version included exemptions for small hospitals and clarified that the guidelines were advisory, not mandatory. *(1977 Almanac p. 523)*

The 1977 experience brought the access issue strongly, and unpleasantly, to the attention of members, including many who usually paid little attention to health matters. The reported similarity of many of the protest letters suggested to some that the hospital industry had orchestrated the outcry. If so, it got good mileage out of its effort, for not only were the guidelines softened but the "rationing of health care" argument shaped many members' objections to the cost containment bill as well as a reauthorization of the planning system itself. *(Stories, pp. 616, 619)*

Other Cost-Control Developments. As Congress struggled with health legislation, the Carter administration moved ahead on several other fronts to deal with health cost problems. Anti-trust lawyers at the Federal Trade Commission (FTC) were scrutinizing the health care industry for evidence of anti-competitive patterns, such as restrictions on advertising by physicians, fee-setting and accreditation, and constraints on consumer information and state health regulation. In November, an FTC administrative law judge found that American Medical Association bans on physician advertising restricted competitive pricing for services, causing "substantial injury to the public." Opponents of the FTC anti-trust activities warned against such blunt interventions in medical economics.

On the theory that preventing illness was less expensive than treating it, a special HEW task force began surveying existing programs to prevent disease and promote health, and developing new initiatives. Only about 4 percent of federal health dollars were being spent on such activities. Creation of the task force came just as Congress was writing into several health bills modest new disease-prevention and health promotion programs. A third development was creation of a new disease-prevention and environmental health coalition that hoped to marshal efforts and resources of more than 100 lobby groups against business opposition to environmental and occupational health regulation.

Abortion Issue. The growing militance of the anti-abortion movement was apparent across the country. Members of Congress who opposed the use of any federal funds for abortion succeeded in attaching anti-abortion amendments to more bills than ever before. Anti-abortion forces played key roles in some 1978 congressional races, and vowed to continue their fight against those on their "hit list" for 1980. And at the urging of "pro-life" lobbyists, the legislatures of 13 states had petitioned Congress to call a constitutional convention to ban abortion in the United States; 34 were needed to require the convention call.

Education

Education was also a target of the taxpayers' revolt. At a time when total education spending represented almost 8 percent of the gross national product, a larger share than that consumed by defense, voters were becoming increasingly reluctant to approve new local taxes to pay for schools. In Ohio, for example, almost 60 percent of school bond issues were rejected by voters in June elections. In California, school officials announced service cutbacks and looked to more state aid to make up for shortages caused by Proposition 13's limit on local property taxes.

The schools' financial problems were compounded by militant demands by teachers for higher pay. The National Education Association counted more than 75 teachers' strikes in September, double the number in 1977.

Public concern over education continued to focus on the issue of discipline in the schools. According to the National Center for Education Statistics, more than twice as many persons polled cited discipline problems as the major problem facing education, as pointed to the next most frequently mentioned subject, school integration.

Another problem that attracted new efforts by state governments was the growing evidence that many students were graduating from the public education system without having acquired the basic skills needed to function adequately in society. The National Assessment of Education Progress estimated that 13 percent of 17-year-old high school students were functionally illiterate.

In response to this, 36 states had instituted some sort of minimal competency testing since 1975. But educators strongly resisted suggestions from some members of Congress that national competency standards be instituted.

In his Feb. 28 education message to Congress, President Carter called for a large increase in education funding to cope with these and other problems. Overall, he called for $12.9 billion for the education division of HEW, a 24 percent increase over fiscal 1978 and a total increase of 46 percent and $4 billion in the last two fiscal years. For elementary and secondary education, he proposed a 15 percent jump, for a total of $6.9 billion — the largest increase since enactment of the Elementary and Secondary Education Act (ESEA) of 1965. He also proposed new programs to improve basic skills and educational quality.

Desegregation. Another key educational issue, the use of affirmative action programs to correct past discrimination against minorities, was the topic of a historic Supreme Court decision in 1978. *(Regents of the University of California v. Bakke, story, p. 8-A)*

Supporters of affirmative action reacted with cautious optimism to the court's finding that such programs were constitutional, arguing that the decision vindicated the consideration of race in university admissions. But opponents of the use of quotas in admissions also found much to be pleased by in the decision.

The use of busing to eliminate racial segregation in public schools continued in 1978 without much of the intense strife that surrounded it in the early 1970s. But polls showed that a large majority of Americans opposed the tactic. In Los Angeles, a busing plan went into effect without violence but with a boycott by thousands of white students, fueling charges by busing opponents that such plans added to "white flight" from big city schools.

Private Schools. The 1978 congressional debate over tuition tax credits for private elementary and secondary schools followed a decade-long decline in enrollments among the largest private education sector, parochial schools run by the Roman Catholic church. But there were some indications that the trend was slowing or reversing. Catholic educators said the increase in big-city parochial school enrollments was due to the desire of many parents to take their children out of the chaotic conditions prevailing in some public schools.

At the end of 1978, private school forces were mobilizing to fight a tentative decision by the Internal Revenue Service to review the tax-exempt status of private schools with low minority enrollments that had been formed at the time local public schools were being desegregated. The regulation was intended to enforce prohibitions against tax exemptions for segregated schools, but was strongly opposed by conservatives who claimed the ruling would declare schools guilty of segregation unless they could prove themselves innocent.

Welfare

The Carter administration began 1978 with high hopes of succeeding with a presidential campaign promise to overhaul the nation's welfare system. But within months it reluctantly had placed its comprehensive welfare reform measure on the back burner, where it remained for the rest of the year.

After the administration gave up its effort, several members of Congress offered less sweeping "reform" plans. Although the proposals generated some committee hearings, none made it to the floor of either the House or Senate. At the end of the year, officials in the White House and HEW and social welfare activists were debating whether to offer another, scaled-down welfare reform plan in 1979. *(Story, p. 600)*

While voices from all sides of the political spectrum agreed that there were serious problems with the existing system, there was little consensus on the details of welfare reform, and this stymied efforts by both Democrats and Republicans to achieve legislative action. Some observers also suggested that the liberal coalition that had regularly lined up broad support for social welfare programs in the mid-1960s had lost considerable clout on Capitol Hill and was unable to muster the political leverage necessary to generate majority votes on behalf of key issues. ▮

Massive Aid to Education Programs Extended

President Carter Nov. 1 signed into law legislation (HR 15 — PL 95-561) extending the massive Elementary and Secondary Education Act (ESEA) programs of assistance to schools for five years, through fiscal 1983.

The final version of the bill, which cleared Congress Oct. 15, made no changes in the fundamental concept behind the heart of ESEA, the Title I program of compensatory education assistance to schools educating children from low-income backgrounds.

Proposals to change the focus of Title I from low-income children to all children with problems in educational achievement never got far. However, limited consideration of educational achievement in allocating compensatory funds to individual schools was allowed by the bill.

The major change made by HR 15 in compensatory education was a revision of the formula allocating funds to states that was expected to benefit northern and urban states at the expense of southern and rural areas. By fully counting all welfare children as poor, even if their families had incomes above the poverty level, the new formula would give an especially large bonus to New York, Michigan and California.

The bill also allowed limited use of a 1975 poverty survey that found increased numbers of poor in the North and decreased numbers in the South, compared with the 1970 census; use of the survey would thus send more money to northern states. Pointing to one state, Alabama, which was found to have had more than a one-third decline in poverty since 1970, critics said the survey was clearly biased against uncovering the true extent of poverty in rural areas.

As had occurred many times in the past, presidential proposals to cut back the impact aid program of assistance to schools educating children of federal employees were rejected. However, the final version of the bill did include a provision that was expected to lead to reduced funding for those parts of impact aid which the administration had wanted to cut or eliminate.

Most of the many other ESEA programs were extended without major changes. The bill retained the concept of categorical grants for specific educational efforts, such as for libraries, bilingual instruction and adult education, instead of single block grants to states or localities.

Included was an administration proposal to establish a new program to help states develop their own standards of minimum academic competency for students. Because of declining performance by high school graduates, many states had begun to implement programs to make sure that students did not graduate without essential academic abilities — programs which the bill sought to encourage. However, sponsors made clear that the new help was not to lead to a national system of minimum education standards.

Another administration proposal in the bill established new assistance for teaching of the basic skills of reading, writing and mathematics.

In response to repeated complaints from educators groaning under the heavy paperwork burdens imposed by ESEA, the bill cut down on the number of required applications and set up a coordinating body to oversee all federal education paperwork demands.

Both House and Senate bills passed easily. The House passed HR 15 by a 350-20 vote July 13. The Senate passed its version (S 1753) by an 86-7 vote Aug. 24.

The last major revision of ESEA programs was in 1974. The programs were given a one-year extension in 1977. *(1974 Almanac p. 441; 1977 Almanac p. 480)*

Provisions

As cleared by Congress, HR 15:

- Extended the Elementary and Secondary Education Act for five years, through fiscal 1983. (Busing provisions — Title II of the 1974 act — and other provisions not changed by HR 15 remained in effect.)

Title I — Compensatory Education

- **Basic Grants.** Provided that the basic grants to school districts educating economically disadvantaged children be determined by multiplying the number of eligible low-income children by 40 percent of the average per pupil expenditure in the state, except that the average could be no less than 80 percent nor more than 120 percent of the national average per pupil expenditure.
- Provided that one-half of any amount appropriated for the program in excess of the fiscal 1979 amount be distributed to states according to the number of children in each state from families with incomes below 50 percent of the national median income, as determined by the 1975 Survey of Income and Education (SIE) conducted by the Bureau of the Census.
- Directed the commissioner of education to use the most recent data, or conduct a new survey, in any state which the SIE found to have experienced a greater than 25 percent decline in the number of poor children compared with the 1970 census.
- Raised to 100 percent, from the two-thirds in existing law, the number of children in each state from families receiving Aid to Families with Dependent Children (AFDC) in excess of the poverty level to be counted in the formula for allocating funds, beginning in fiscal 1980.
- **Special Incentive Grants.** Authorized, beginning in fiscal 1980, a new program of incentive grants that would give school districts in states with eligible compensatory education programs $1 in extra Title I funds for every $2 spent by the state on its own program; limited the total amount given to school districts in a state to 10 percent of the regular Title I funds received by schools in that state.
- **Concentration Program.** Authorized a new concentration program, funded at $400 million in fiscal 1979, to distribute additional Title I funds to schools in counties that had more than 5,000 poor children aged 5-17, or poor children making up more than 20 percent of enrollment.
- Guaranteed every state at least one-quarter of 1 percent of the total funding of the concentration program.
- **Program Requirements.** Required school districts to rank schools according to the number of poor children served, for the purpose of distributing Title I funds. However, schools with few poor children but many children with low educational achievement could be ranked before schools with more poor children but fewer low achievers, with the approval of the district parental advisory committee and the state.
- Outlined the steps that local education agencies had to take to receive funds, including establishment of paren-

tal advisory boards, maintenance of adequate records, establishment of a complaint resolution procedure, and maintenance of efforts in excess of what would have been done without the assistance.

• Required equal expenditures for Title I-eligible children attending private schools.

• Allowed schools whose enrollments were more than 75 percent Title I-eligible children to operate compensatory programs for the entire student body.

• **Special State Programs.** Authorized assistance to state programs educating children of migrant workers, handicapped, neglected and delinquent children, providing 40 percent of the state average per pupil expenditure for each child, within the limits of 80 percent and 120 percent of the national average per pupil expenditure.

• **Other Provisions.** Outlined the duties of state educational agencies under the title, including review of local applications, technical assistance, monitoring and audits of local programs.

• Gave the commissioner authority to withhold funds to school districts for violations of regulations under the act.

• Established a 15-member National Advisory Council on the Education of Disadvantaged Children.

Title II — Basic Skills

• Authorized a new program of grants to states and school districts for improvement of instruction in the basic skills of reading, mathematics and oral and written communication.

• Authorized the first $20 million of annual appropriations for Title II for a program of direct federal grants. Any excess would go to state-run programs, allocated according to student populations.

• Extended an inexpensive book distribution program, funded at $9 million in fiscal 1979, $10 million in 1980, $11 million in 1981, and $12 million in 1982 and 1983. The program provides 75 percent of the cost of the books, with the remainder provided by non-profit and local government agencies.

Title III — Special Projects

• Authorized a program of grants to education agencies for a variety of special education projects, including innovative teaching techniques, energy conservation curriculum development and personnel training.

• Provided separate five-year annual authorizations for the following education programs: metric ($20 million), arts ($20 million), youth employment ($7.5 million), law ($15 million), environment ($5 million in fiscal 1979, $7 million in 1980, $9 million in 1981, $11 million in 1982 and $13 million in 1983), health ($10 million) and criminal offenders ($5 million).

• Reserved portions of discretionary grant funding for the following education programs: pre-school partnership, consumer and population.

• Established a new biomedical enrichment program, funded annually at $40 million, to provide science instruction to minority students at the secondary school level.

• Established an Office of Environmental Education in the Office of Education.

Title IV — Consolidated Programs

• Extended consolidated programs providing assistance to states, based on student populations, for educational improvement and resources.

• Authorized assistance to private schools for secular materials, services and equipment on an equal basis, for each child, to that provided to public schools.

• Authorized grants for library and instructional materials.

• Authorized grants, distributed on a competitive basis, for assistance to schools in developing innovative ways of improving education; required that half of any increases in funding over the fiscal 1979 level go for compensatory education innovation.

• Established a new program providing assistance to schools for guidance, counseling and testing programs, with an annual authorization of $50 million.

Title V — State Leadership

• Outlined the duties of state and local education agencies participating in programs under the act; authorized funds to help states carry out their responsibilities.

• Established a 15-member National Council on Quality in Education; authorized similar state advisory councils.

Title VI — Emergency School Aid

• Extended the program of assistance to school districts experiencing the effects of racial desegregation; authorized $245 million for the program in fiscal 1980 and the three succeeding years.

• Decreased to $155 million from $185 million a year the funds to be distributed to states on the basis of a formula tied to minority populations, thus increasing the amount to be distributed at the discretion of program administrators.

• Authorized $7.25 million in fiscal 1980 for "follow the child" services assisting children transferred out of Title I schools by desegregation plans.

• Made eligible for assistance those school districts that were undertaking voluntary or court-ordered desegregation plans, or were planning to do so.

• Reserved at least $20 million a year for assistance to magnet schools.

Title VII — Bilingual Education

• Authorized $200 million in fiscal 1979, $250 million in 1980, $300 million in 1981, $350 million in 1982 and $400 million in 1983 for grants to schools undertaking bilingual education programs.

• Made eligible for bilingual services students who had difficulty in speaking, reading, writing or understanding English to the extent that they were denied an opportunity to learn successfully in classrooms where English was the language of instruction.

• Allowed participation by English-speaking children in bilingual programs, up to 40 percent of bilingual classes.

• Allowed the commissioner of education to terminate assistance to school districts after five years of participation, unless it was shown that the district had been operating the program successfully, did not have the resources to pay for it on its own, and continued to have significant numbers, or had experienced recent influxes, of bilingual children.

• Required that teachers in bilingual programs, to the extent possible, be proficient in both English and the second language.

Title VIII — Community Schools

• Authorized grants to states, school districts and other public agencies for the purpose of encouraging use of school facilities to provide educational, recreational, health and other services to the surrounding community.

● Provided for a decreasing federal share of financial support for the community programs.

● Prohibited federally funded community programs from duplicating services already offered by other government agencies, unless the commissioner determined that the schools and the other agencies were collaborating.

Title IX — Additional Programs

● Authorized assistance to states and local schools for development of programs meeting the special needs of gifted and talented children; authorized $25 million in fiscal 1979, $30 million in 1980, $35 million in 1981, $40 million in 1982 and $50 million in 1983 for gifted and talented education assistance, with 75 percent to be distributed to states according to student populations, provided that appropriations were at least $15 million, and the remainder available for discretionary grants.

● Established a new program of assistance to states to develop and implement minimum standards of education proficiency.

● Authorized $80 million annually, beginning in fiscal 1980, for programs encouraging equity for women in education, and helping schools meet the requirements of Title IX (sex discrimination) of the Education Amendments of 1972. *(1972 Almanac p. 390)*

● Established a new demonstration program, funded at $15 million in fiscal 1979, for assistance to 15 school districts seeking to reduce crime in their schools.

● Authorized $15 million annually for ethnic heritage programs.

Title X — Impact Aid

● Increased flexibility in impact aid funding by requiring that only 65 percent of the entitlements in the second tier be fully funded, thus removing restrictions on where Congress, though the appropriations process, chose to put any additional funding.

● Guaranteed local schools at least 90 percent of the impact aid funding they received in the previous year.

● Repealed the existing limitations on payments for children in federally assisted public housing.

● Repealed the "absorption" provision of the 1974 ESEA amendments that required schools to assume the costs of educating federally dependent children up to 3 percent of their enrollment.

● Reduced to 20 percent, from 25 percent, the percentage of enrollment made up by students whose parents both lived and worked on federal property a school district had to have in order to qualify for extra payments as a "heavily impacted" district.

● Directed the president to appoint a 10-member commission to review the impact aid program and recommend changes by Dec. 1, 1979.

Title XI — Indian Education

● Increased payments for school districts educating Indian children who lived on reservations to 125 percent of the impact aid payments for children of federal employees who lived on federal property.

● Required that school districts receiving payments for Indian children set up procedures for increased participation by Indian parents in their children's education.

● Required promulgation of minimum academic standards for the education of Indian children, and criteria for Indian boarding schools.

● Placed primary authority for Indian education with the Office of Indian Education Programs of the Bureau of Indian Affairs.

● Removed Indian education personnel from coverage under Civil Service regulations.

Title XII — Administration

● Authorized $4 million a year to help states develop plans to equalize education spending among school districts within a state.

● Required establishment of a 15-member advisory panel on school finance in the Department of Health, Education and Welfare.

● Called for establishment of procedures designed to reduce the amount of paperwork required from schools receiving federal assistance, including three-year rather than annual applications.

● Required states and local education agencies to submit single applications outlining procedures for compliance with the requirements of the act.

● Established procedures for enforcement of regulations, including withholding of funds.

● Required establishment of a Federal Education Data Acquisition Council to review and coordinate data collection activities.

● Created an Office of Non-Public Education within the Office of Education.

● Directed the National Institute of Education to conduct a National Assessment of Educational Progress, to report at least every five years on student performance; authorized $10.5 million a year through fiscal 1983 to conduct the assessment.

● Provided that no student can be required to submit to psychiatric or psychological examination, testing or treatment in which the primary purpose is to reveal information on personal matters ranging from political affiliation and income to sex behavior and illegal acts.

Title XIII — Other Education Programs

● Authorized $210 million in fiscal 1979, $230 million in 1980, $250 million in 1981, $270 million in 1982 and $290 million in 1983 for adult education programs.

● Extended assistance to the education of Indochinese refugee children through fiscal 1981.

● Authorized grants for adult education programs for immigrants.

Title XIV — Defense Department Schools

● Provided statutory authority for the schools of overseas military dependents run by the Defense Department; required an advisory committee for each school, an Advisory Council on Dependents' Education, and a study of the dependent school system.

Title XV — Miscellaneous Provisions

● Established a National Commission on the International Year of the Child, as proclaimed by the United Nations for 1979.

● Established a commission to study proposals to create a National Academy of Peace and Conflict Resolution.

Background

Since the last revision of ESEA in 1974, there had been considerable discussion about the effectiveness of Title I programs and the method used to distribute the funds.

In 1974, after a bruising regional fight, Congress cut the amount of Title I money available to certain northeastern and midwestern states by reducing payments for children from families who received Aid to Families with Dependent Children (AFDC) in excess of the poverty level. A few states, notably New York, Michigan, California, Illinois and Pennsylvania, made big enough welfare payments to bring a large number of families over the official definition of poverty. The 1974 change reduced to two-thirds from 100 percent the number of AFDC children over the poverty level who were counted in determining a state's allocation. *(1974 Almanac p. 441)*

Title I was expected to serve about 5.6 million children in fiscal 1979, out of about nine million eligible. The fiscal 1978 appropriation was $2.7 billion. The Carter administration sought a $644 million increase for fiscal 1979. Fourteen thousand school districts are served. The average grant per student is about $400. Two-thirds of the students served are in grades 1-6.

Many of the questions about the program were answered by a National Institute of Education study mandated by the 1974 amendments. NIE determined that the program apparently works. First-graders studied made average gains of 12 months in reading and 11 months in mathematics in the seven-month period between their testing in the fall and the spring. Third-graders gained eight months in reading and 12 months in math.

Another study, completed in 1976 for the U.S. Office of Education, also found that Title I programs were retarding or preventing the relative decline in achievement among disadvantaged children that they said would almost certainly occur in the absence of such programs.

Distribution of Funds

NIE also looked at how Title I funds were distributed.

Researchers determined that two-thirds of the money went to major cities and rural areas and about one-quarter went to suburban areas.

But the actual amounts those areas received per child varied considerably. Suburban areas got 11 per cent more and central cities 15 per cent more than did non-metropolitan areas. The nation's largest cities received 18 per cent more per child than did rural areas.

The variation was caused by the formula factor that weighted allocations based on average state expenditures, so that per-pupil Title I expenditures were higher in predominantly urban and suburban states than in predominantly rural ones, the report said. South Carolina and Georgia, for example, received $163 per eligible child in 1977 compared to $244 per child in New York and $228 per child in Pennsylvania.

The differences showed up sharply when regional aspects of distribution were noted. The South, which had 45 per cent of the eligible children, received almost 40 per cent of the total allocation. But more than half of the states in the South received the minimum $163 per eligible child because of the low level of current expenditure per pupil, compared to the $200 per eligible child received by almost all northeastern states. *(Regional distribution of funds, box, this page)*

Regional Distribution Of Title I Funds

(Fiscal 1977)

Region	Eligible Children *(millions)*	Per Cent	Funds *(millions)*	Per Cent
Northeast	1.62	18.8	$378.9	22.9
North-Central	1.80	21.0	367.4	22.2
South	3.90	45.5	660.5	39.9
West	1.26	14.7	246.7	14.9

SOURCE: National Institute of Education

The NIE study also determined that if AFDC-eligible children were not included in the formula that distribution of funds would have been considerably different. Those eligible under the AFDC portion of the formula were unevenly distributed around the country. About 75 per cent of them lived in five states—New York, Michigan, California, Illinois and Pennsylvania. Those states contained only about a quarter of the children counted because they were from poverty families. Inclusion of the AFDC children had the effect of raising the allocations to the nation's largest cities by $36 million.

Overall, inclusion of the AFDC children resulted in a 20 per cent gain in allocations ($29.4 million) for the large northeastern cities, a 12 per cent gain ($13 million) for north-central cities, a 3 per cent gain ($1.9 million) for western cities. Large southern cities lost $8.1 million, or 7.1 per cent of what their allocations would have been without the AFDC counts, the study found.

Other Programs

Of the many other programs covered by ESEA, two that had come under particular scrutiny were the impact aid and bilingual education programs.

Impact Aid. Like every president since Truman, Carter wanted to cut the impact aid program, which was designed to compensate school districts for the effects of non-taxable federal property. One-fourth of the nation's school districts received the aid, for 2.5 million federally connected children. The money — $770 million in fiscal 1978 — goes into nearly every congressional district. It was the only type of federal aid to local schools not earmarked for particular programs, and so was very popular with local school officials. However, critics said much of the aid went to well-off school districts that simply spent less of their own money on education as a result.

Bilingual Education. Since establishment of the federal bilingual education program in 1967, there had been constant debates about its purpose and effectiveness.

It originally was designed to fund demonstration projects to help non-English-speaking children gain language skills so they could enter English-speaking classrooms. In fiscal 1978, the $135 million appropriated was expected to support 565 demonstration projects in 67 different languages serving approximately 255,000 of the estimated 3.6 million children eligible. The money also was expected to provide in-service training for about 38,000 teachers.

Many of the questions about the program dealt with whether it should continue to move children as quickly as possible into regular classrooms or whether it should be a more permanent program stressing bicultural education. The bicultural approach had its strongest supporters in the Hispanic community where in some areas bilingual classes had attracted wide community interest.

A study of the bilingual program for the Office of Education found that 75 percent of the 5,300 students enrolled in Title VII classrooms examined in the study were of Hispanic origin. But less than one-third were of limited English-speaking ability. All of those studied were in grades two through six.

About 85 percent of the directors of the projects surveyed indicated that Spanish-dominant students remained in the bilingual project even after they were able to function in school in English. Only 5 percent of the project directors indicated that a student was transferred to an English-only classroom once he learned English well enough to function.

Administration Proposals

The administration did not propose any changes in the basic Title I funding formula, but it did ask for extra aid for districts with large concentrations of poor children. President Carter requested $400 million in fiscal 1979 for the program, which would aid 3,500 school districts which had either 5,000 or more poor children or in which 20 percent or more of the enrollment was poor. In his education message to Congress Feb. 28, Carter also called for:

- An incentive matching grant program to encourage states to establish their own compensatory education programs.
- Changes in the Emergency School Aid Act (ESAA) to target desegregation assistance funds where they were most needed. *(ESAA, 1972 Almanac p. 385)*
- Reform of the impact aid program, including elimination of payments for children whose parents work on federal property outside the county in which the school district is located; a two-year cap on payments to children living in public housing, followed by a phase-out of those payments; an "absorption" provision that would reduce funding for lightly impacted districts by eliminating payments where children of federal employees amounted to less than 3 percent of a district's enrollment, and a gradually declining hold-harmless provision so that no district would receive less than 75 percent of its previous year's payments over the next three years.
- New emphases on basic skills and educational quality.
- Changes in the bilingual education program.
- Equitable treatment of private school pupils. *(Text of education message, p. 40-E)*

House Committee Action

The House Education and Labor Committee reported HR 15 May 11 (H Rept 95-1137).

Expressing satisfaction with the general course of the compensatory education services authorized by Title I of ESEA, the committee opted for a "fine tuning" instead of a major overhaul. The most important changes made by the committee shifted the distribution of compensatory funds away from southern and rural states to the advantage of wealthier, more urbanized states, generally in the Northeast and Midwest.

Earlier in 1978, staff aides and education lobbyists had noted a widespread reluctance to tamper with the formula for fear of reopening old wounds left by the 1974 fight. But members from northeastern and midwestern states, sensing a "prime regional issue," as one aide put it, organized themselves to regain some of the ground lost in 1974. Led by William D. Ford, D-Mich., and James M. Jeffords, R-Vt., they won two important changes in committee. Supporters of the changes were aided by the heavy preponderance of "Snow Belt" representatives on the committee.

AFDC Change. As reported by the committee, HR 15 restored to full count the number of children from AFDC families over the poverty level, beginning with fiscal year 1980. Using the 1979 allocation total, the Library of Congress' Congressional Research Service (CRS) estimated that this change would bring especially large proportional increases to five states: Hawaii (9 percent), Michigan (8 percent), New York (5 percent), Connecticut (4 percent) and Wisconsin (3 percent). On the other hand, every southern state stood to lose because of the change. The biggest loser would be Texas, which would receive a cut of about $3.8 million.

Supporters of the change said it would have a temporary impact at most. Since the official poverty level had been going up with consumer prices, the number of AFDC children counted as poor was expected to go down, unless states continued to increase their AFDC payment levels. This development should gradually work to reduce the effect of the AFDC change.

The amendment to fully count AFDC children, offered by Ford, was originally defeated on a 17-17 vote of the committee. After agreeing to reconsider the amendment, the committee adopted it by an 18-17 vote.

Second Change. The second important change made by the committee would distribute Title I appropriations in excess of the 1979 amount on the basis of a 1975 survey of poverty instead of on the 1970 census and would change the definition of poverty. The amendment, also offered by Ford, was adopted on a 21-14 vote.

Supporters of the change argued that the census had become outdated for determining 1978 poverty. But the 1975 Survey of Income and Education (SIE), conducted by the Census Bureau, found such large changes in the distribution of poverty compared with the census that critics contended it was based on unfair sampling techniques. The survey seriously undercounted rural poverty, they charged, causing sharp reductions in the number of poor found in the southern states, where poverty is more prevalent in rural areas than in the cities.

To determine the number of poor people in each state using SIE data, the bill defined poverty as an income of less than one-half of the national median income for a family of four. This expanded the number of "poor" children, making some 12 million eligible, compared to about 8 million under the existing Orshansky poverty index.

Using an estimate of the amount of 1980 appropriations in excess of the 1979 level, the CRS found that use of the new survey would generally result in a relative decrease in funds for southern states. The states suffering the largest cuts would be Alabama (35 percent), Mississippi (24 percent) and Louisiana (23 percent). No state would receive an absolute decrease, since the SIE formula would apply only to funding in excess of the 1979 level.

Two small states, Nevada and Vermont, would get the biggest increases — 105 and 68 percent, respectively, while

Alaska and the District of Columbia would suffer the largest relative declines — 41 and 31 percent.

To cushion the effect of this change, the committee adopted an amendment allowing the states in which the SIE found more than a 25 percent decline in the number of poor children to have their allocation based on a new state survey or the best other data available.

Under the change in the AFDC formula, 37 states would lose money, while 13 states and the District of Columbia would gain. Under the 1976 poverty survey, 28 states would receive relative increases in funding, while 22 states and the District would have relative declines.

Private School Students. Noting that less than 4 percent of private school students living in Title I districts received compensatory education services even though they were eligible under existing law, the committee required that equal expenditures be made on them.

Quie Proposal. A proposal to base the Title I funds allocation on the educational rather than economic disadvantages of children, which had been expected to spark controversy, was not brought up in committee. Sponsored by ranking minority member Albert H. Quie, R-Minn., the plan would have concentrated funds on children who did poorly on standardized tests.

Recognizing that "the opposition was too strong," Quie decided not to offer the proposal. The bill did contain, however, a provision allowing school boards to concentrate funds on schools with special problems of educational deprivation.

Concentration Funds

HR 15 authorized an additional $400 million in Title I money for school districts with high concentrations of low-income students. Recognizing the special problems of big-city schools in poverty areas, the committee adopted the Carter administration's proposal to provide increased assistance to school districts that had more than 5,000 poor children, or had poor children making up more than 20 percent of enrollment.

Together with the other changes in the Title I formula, the "concentration" program would provide generous increases for school systems in the nation's largest cities. Among the 28 cities that belong to the Council of Great City Schools, the council estimated, the biggest winner would be New York City, which would get $24.3 million more in 1981 than it would have under the existing formula. Increases to other large cities were: Chicago, $10 million; Los Angeles, $6.5 million; Detroit, $6.5 million; Philadelphia, $5.1 million.

State Incentives

Another new program authorized by HR 15 would provide incentives for states to establish and fund their own compensatory education programs. The bill authorized a program of matching grants that would give states $1 in extra Title I funds for every $2 they spent on their own compensatory programs. In order to qualify for the incentives, state programs would have to spend at least half of their money in areas with high concentrations of low-income students. Grants to states would be limited to 10 percent of each one's Title I allocation.

Impact Aid

The committee rejected administration proposals to cut back on the impact aid program for areas educating children of federal employees. Instead, the committee, saying payments were already inadequate, expanded eligibility for the program and increased benefits for certain groups of children.

The bill repealed a provision of the 1974 ESEA law which eliminated from the payment formula the number of children in an area whose federal employee parents worked in another state. It also restored full payments for children whose parents worked for the federal government in a county other than the one in which they lived. CRS estimated the changes would cost the government an additional $32 million in 1979.

HR 15 provided increased assistance to areas for educating military dependents and the handicapped. It increased the amount available to areas with large numbers of military dependents who did not live on federal installations, at an estimated cost of $18 million in the first year. For handicapped children of military personnel and Indians, the bill guaranteed payment of the full excess cost of special education, at an estimated cost of $35 million.

Finding that "school districts are already not being paid adequately by the federal government for these children," the committee decided to repeal the existing "absorption" provision, which required that school districts on their own assume the cost of educating the number of federal dependents who constitute 3 percent of total enrollment. The Department of Health, Education and Welfare (HEW) estimated the provision would cost $42 million in 1979.

HR 15 removed restrictions on impact aid payments for some 660,000 children who live in public housing. The committee reported that in some cities the payments made up for only a small fraction of the amount of taxes lost because of public housing. The provision would add an estimated $110 million to the cost of the program in 1979, according to CRS. In addition, the bill deleted the existing restriction limiting the use of public housing impact aid funds to compensatory education, thus allowing the money to be used for general operating purposes.

Indian Education

Rejecting the concept of "doing things for Indians," the committee called for allowing more participation by native Americans in the educational process.

Title XI of HR 15 outlined the procedures that local school districts would have to set up to make sure that Indians who lived on nearby reservations had a voice in how and what their children were taught. To reward school districts that offered more opportunities for participation by Indian parents, the bill added an extra 25 percent to the payment for each child who lived on a reservation.

On the grounds that non-educators should not be in immediate control of schools, the committee consolidated authority over schools run directly by the Bureau of Indian Affairs into the bureau's Office of Indian Education Programs. HR 15 required the bureau to establish national standards for Indian education programs, dormitory schools and school construction and to work out a formula for allocating funds on the basis of student costs.

Bilingual Programs

Title VII of ESEA authorized funds for demonstration and training projects designed to assist students for whom English is a second language to function in school. HR 15 authorized extension of these "bilingual" programs for five years.

The committee made clear that federal assistance to local bilingual education programs should be considered temporary start-up funds, not a permanent subsidy for operations at the local level. It found that individual districts were continuing to receive bilingual funds year after year, without assuming responsibility for the programs on their own. To ensure that local bilingual programs not become permanently dependent on federal funding, the bill included an administration-proposed five-year limit on the time that a district could receive the assistance.

The bill clarified the definition of students who were eligible for bilingual services. Recognizing that the existing definition of eligible students as those with "limited English-speaking ability" was incomplete for students who also needed to read and write effectively in English, the committee changed the definition to take in children with "limited English-language skills."

HR 15 also tightened up on the widespread practice of allowing children who are fluent in English to participate in bilingual classes. However, the committee recognized the value of mixing some English-speaking students into bilingual classes in order to help those with limited English abilities to learn faster.

The bill provided that special "pull-out" classes devoted solely to English instruction would be open only to students with limited English ability. But other projects funded by the bilingual program as part of regular classroom instruction could be open to English speakers in proportion to their enrollment in the school as a whole.

Proficiency Standards

Title VIII of HR 15 established a new program of assistance to states to encourage development of minimum standards of educational proficiency. The committee noted that a number of states, concerned with evidence of declining educational competence of public school graduates, had already begun their own systems of testing and offering remedial instruction for students who did not meet minimal standards of competence.

The bill authorized grants to states to assist in developing and implementing proficiency standards. The committee took pains to make clear, however, that the bill in no way called for establishment of national proficiency standards, arguing that such standards were best left to states. *(Background, 1977 Almanac p. 524)*

Emergency School Aid

Title XI of HR 15 extended the Emergency School Aid Act (ESAA), which was enacted in 1972 to provide assistance to school districts that were undergoing desegregation or that had high concentrations of minority students. The bulk of funds are distributed to states on the basis of minority population. *(1972 Almanac p. 385)*

The committee found that the formula tying funds to state's minority populations limited the ability of program administrators to respond quickly to local problems. In some states with few segregation problems, money was available for which there were no applicants; in others, the massive desegregation problems of big-city schools monopolized the entire amount for the state.

To provide more flexibility in fund distribution, the bill lowered to $155 million from $185 million the amount of funding which had to be distributed to states on the basis of the formula. It also strengthened the authority of federal program administrators to redistribute unused money to areas that really needed it.

The bill authorized $7.25 million a year for "follow-the-child" services. These would be available to assist disadvantaged students who, because of a desegregation plan, had been transferred out of a Title I school into a school not eligible for Title I assistance. The money would go to provide compensatory services to the newly transferred students, who otherwise would not be eligible for help.

However, the committee made clear that other funds under ESAA were not intended primarily to provide compensatory services. A recent study showed that over two-thirds of ESAA funds go to instruction in basic skills. HR 15 placed first priority for funding on programs to cope directly with the problems of desegregation, such as training teachers to handle racial incidents.

Consolidated Program

The 1974 ESEA extension consolidated various programs of categorical assistance to schools in a single Title IV. Part B of the consolidated title provided assistance for school libraries, instructional materials and guidance counseling services. Part C funded programs of educational innovation, seeking new ways of teaching basic skills, environmental and career education and other subjects.

The committee found that the consolidation of the programs was succeeding in attaining its goal of reduction of paperwork and administrative requirements. HR 15 extended Title IV programs for five years, and increased the authorization for Part C programs to $450 million from $350 million.

Recognizing that the "people-oriented" guidance programs of Part B did not fit in too well with the "things-oriented" library programs, the committee created a new Part D devoted to guidance, counseling and testing services. The first-year authorization for the new section was $80 million.

To ensure that the Part C innovative projects included efforts directed towards the central focus of ESEA, compensatory education, the bill required that half of the increased authorization for the program fund new ways to provide compensatory education. HR 15 also contained a five-year limit on the length of time local districts could receive innovative program funds, in order to encourage them to begin to sponsor more such efforts on their own.

Miscellaneous Programs

Title VI of HR 15 authorized a grab-bag of special programs directed toward selected educational subjects and types of children.

The committee found that the right-to-read program had reached only a small fraction of the adults and children whose poor reading ability was holding back their functioning in society. Right-to-read programs offer special funding to state and local education agencies, conduct demonstration projects, and distribute low-cost books to students to encourage them to read more.

Concluding that the states had been most effective in operating right-to-read programs, the committee transferred the bulk of administrative duties from the Office of Education to state education agencies. HR 15 also added mathematics to the topics of instruction under the program. The bill authorized $147 million for the reading and math programs in fiscal 1979.

The committee established as separate sections three projects formerly under the Special Projects Act. Set up with separate authorizations were experimental programs relating to gifted children, women's educational equity and community education. Remaining under the special projects authority were programs encouraging metric, career, consumer and arts education. Population education was included as another part of the special projects section.

For programs directed at talented and gifted children, HR 15 provided a separate authorization of $10 million in 1979, rising to $25 million in fiscal 1982 and 1983. For women's educational equity, including national demonstration projects and services to local schools attempting to correct problems of sex discrimination, the bill authorized $80 million in each of fiscal years 1980-83. For community education programs, which attempt to make use of school facilities to help offer educational, recreational and cultural services to the community, the bill authorized $68 million in fiscal 1979. It required state and local governments to gradually increase their matching payments to the federal community education grants.

HR 15 also established a new program to help minority high school students prepare for medical school. The committee found that disadvantaged students were often behind in the race for medical school admissions before they got to college, because of inadequate preparation in the basic sciences. The bill would authorize $40 million for grants to colleges and universities to operate courses in remedial science instruction for disadvantaged high school students.

Administration

The committee called for stepped-up study of ways to equalize educational spending within states. Finding that recent efforts by states to equalize spending among school districts were at best only slowing down a trend toward greater disparities, the committee authorized $4 million a year to assist states in developing equalization plans and required a study by the National Institute of Education of what else the federal government could do to help.

Other provisions of Title XIII of HR 15 addressed what many educators considered to be the overly burdensome paperwork requirements of ESEA. Recognizing that people resent having to provide the government with the same information more than once, even when the data was required by different agencies, the committee designated the National Center for Education Statistics as the coordinator of information needs of the various education agencies. Other suggestions by the committee for reducing the resentment over paperwork included allowing more time to fill out forms, avoiding requests for unnecessary data, giving feedback to educators on the results of studies and balancing the information needs of a program with its overall importance.

House Floor Action

A series of regional and fiscal compromises helped guide the ESEA five-year extension (HR 15) through the House, where it passed by a vote of 350-20. *(Vote 472, p. 134-H)*

Before passing the bill, the House voted to cut up to $215 million from the committee-approved version of the impact aid program, bowing to the possibility of a veto and a changing attitude toward the long-popular program of aid to schools in areas affected by federal installations. The administration had wanted an even larger reduction.

Some regional vote-trading helped to block an attempt to shift funding for compensatory education aid in favor of southern and rural states, although many more states would have benefited from the change. The Education and Labor Committee had altered distribution of funds in favor of a few northern and urban states.

As passed by the House, HR 15 authorized more than $10 billion a year for a wide variety of aid programs for elementary and secondary schools. In general the bill avoided major changes in the 13-year-old education act.

Impact Aid

After prolonged negotiations, Education and Labor Committee Chairman Carl D. Perkins, D-Ky., offered an amendment designed to placate administration opposition to the impact aid provisions in the committee bill, without cutting too much from a program that benefits schools in almost every congressional district. At full funding of the program, the Perkins amendment would cut $215 million from impact aid provisions approved by the committee.

The administration had sought impact aid cuts which would have reduced spending for the program by over $300 million by 1982. The committee not only rejected these proposals, but restored some cuts made by the 1974 ESEA extension.

The Perkins amendment did not reduce the program below existing levels, but only cut some of the increases made by the committee. The amendment deleted provisions in the committee bill allowing payments for children whose federal employee parents worked in another state from the one in which they lived (the out-of-state B category), increasing payments for children whose parents worked for the federal government in another county (out-of-county B's), and guaranteeing full payment of the excess costs of educating handicapped children of military personnel and Indians.

Part A payments go for children whose parents live and work on federal property, while Part B goes for those who either work or live on such installations.

Perkins said the amendment was necessary "in order to make sure the bill is not vetoed by the administration." Budget Committee Chairman Robert N. Giaimo, D-Conn., supported the amendment, saying that the committee-approved provisions were "potential budget-breakers."

But Herbert E. Harris II, D-Va., who, along with other Washington, D.C.-area representatives, stood to lose most from the elimination of aid to out-of-state B's, said that the program should not be cut because of its relatively unrestricted, unbureaucratic nature.

"It is the one education program that does not immerse itself in all sorts of red tape," but "gets money down to . . . the kids," Harris said.

The Perkins amendment was adopted by voice vote.

The House rejected, however, a further cut in the program proposed by Robert H. Michel, R-Ill. The Michel amendment would have restored existing law regarding payments for children living in subsidized public housing. The committee bill had eliminated restrictions on payments for public housing children, at an estimated cost of $110 million.

Opponents of the Michel amendment said it would endanger the delicate compromise put forward in the Perkins amendment. It was rejected by voice vote.

Title I Formula

The House July 12 rejected, on a 175-212 vote, a Mickey Edwards, R-Okla., amendment to restore to the bill existing language regarding Title I payments for children whose families received Aid to Families with Dependent Children (AFDC) payments in amounts above the official poverty line. *(Vote 468, p. 134-H)*

Under existing law, only two-thirds of such children in each state were counted for the purpose of determining state allocations under Title I. The committee had voted to restore full counting of all AFDC children.

Calling the committee change "patently unfair," Edwards argued that it would benefit a few states that made high welfare payments, at the expense of 37 states. He pointed out that three states, New York, Michigan and California, would get about three-quarters of the $24.6 million that would be redistributed under the committee version. "This bill as it now stands is largely another aid to New York bill," he said.

Opponents of the Edwards amendment argued that tampering with the Title I formula would undermine the careful regional compromises worked out in committee and on the floor. "We have a real well-rounded package here that we cannot unravel a thread at a time," said Michael T. Blouin, D-Iowa.

Albert H. Quie, R-Minn., observed after the vote that, by agreeing to support an earlier Blouin amendment, bill sponsors had picked up votes against the Edwards amendment from members whose states would have benefited from it. The Blouin amendment provided substantial increases in funding to small and rural states under a new concentration funds program created by the bill.

Concentration Funds

The Blouin amendment, passed by voice vote July 12, guaranteed small states at least one-quarter of 1 percent of the $400 million authorized for the new program distributing extra funds to schools with especially high concentrations of poor children.

Blouin said the amendment was "an eminently fair way to give equity to the states that were disadvantaged by the other parts of the [Title I] formula." He said the administration and most education organizations supported it. The larger states would give up about 1.5 percent of their concentration funds so that each small state could receive at least $1 million, Blouin said. Shirley Chisholm, D-N.Y., said the shift would result in a "disproportionate, fantastic rise in educational funds to the small states." Vermont, for example, would go from $5,000 to $1 million, and Wyoming from $2,000 to the minimum $1 million grant, Simon said.

The House rejected by voice vote, however, a move to further dilute the concentration program so that it would be available to almost every school district in the country.

The committee bill made school districts in counties with more than 5,000 poor children, or where poor children made up more than 20 percent of enrollment, eligible for the concentration program. John M. Ashbrook, R-Ohio, proposed an amendment that would have made counties eligible if the proportion of poor students equaled the average percentage of poor children in the 50 counties with the largest enrollments — a standard of about 2 percent poor enrollment.

Ashbrook argued that the 5,000-student or 20 percent criteria discriminated against small rural areas, even if they had pockets of poverty. He pointed out that large school districts, by sheer numbers, could qualify, even if their percentage of poor children was very low, while very poor rural areas could not.

Opponents of the amendment argued that it would undermine the whole purpose of the new program, which was to concentrate funds on the special problems of dense poverty areas. According to Perkins, the administration had said it would not seek funds for the program if the Ashbrook admendment was adopted, since it would change the focus of the program.

State Incentives

The House also rejected an amendment to provide more widespread participation in a new program offering matching grants for state compensatory education programs. Defeated by a 150-240 vote was a Quie amendment to allow school districts to apply for matching grants for their own compensatory programs, if there was no statewide program. *(Vote 467, p. 134-H)*

Quie explained that the amendment would allow participation by schools where state funds were distributed but not specifically earmarked for compensatory education. If a local agency had its own program, he said, then it too should be eligible for matching grants.

Frank Thompson Jr., D-N.J., from a state that already had a strong compensatory program, argued that the amendment would negate the intent of specifically encouraging state programs. He predicted that the amendment, by allowing local option, could lead to "a nightmare of overlapping and incompatible procedures."

Community Schools

The House voted to prohibit federally funded community education programs, which involve using school facilities for non-school activities, from duplicating services already offered by other government agencies, unless the U.S. commissioner of education determined that the school and the other agency were collaborating.

Marjorie S. Holt, R-Md., had offered an amendment to prohibit duplication of services by schools unless the other government agency approved. Fearing that this would amount to a veto power over community school programs, Dale E. Kildee, D-Mich., offered a substitute amendment to allow duplication if the commissioner determined that collaboration existed between school and agency. The Kildee amendment was adopted 197-195. *(Vote 470, p. 134-H)*

Holt portrayed the difference between the two amendments as a question of federal versus local control — a view that probably led to the extreme closeness of the vote. "It's a philosophical difference. Does the local government make the decision or do we do everything at the federal level?" she asked.

Ashbrook Substitute

By a 79-290 vote the House rejected an Ashbrook substitute for the whole bill that would have radically revised the nature of federal elementary and secondary education aid programs. *(Vote 471, p. 134-H)*

The Ashbrook amendment would have substituted for the various categorical programs a single block grant to states, based on school enrollments. The same total amount of money would have been distributed, but in a single payment to each state, to use for education as it saw fit. The impact aid program alone would have retained its separate authorization.

Senate Committee Action

The Senate Human Resources Committee approved its bill (S 1753) May 15 (S Rept 95-856).

Title I Formula

An agreement between Chairman Harrison A. Williams Jr., D-N.J., ranking minority member Jacob K. Javits, R-N.Y., and Education Subcommittee Chairman Claiborne Pell, D-R.I., settled within the committee the contentious issue of the formula for Title I funds.

Like the House committee, the Senate panel included the change in the count of welfare children. It agreed to count all children aged 5-17 from AFDC families over the poverty level, reversing the change made by the 1974 law which had shifted aid away from the northern, urban states to southern and rural states. However, the Senate version did not provide for use of the 1975 Survey of Income and Education to count poverty.

The change would result in a "short-run gain for a few states," according to Education Subcommittee counsel Jean Frohlicher. But additional benefits in the long run presumably would decline, since the number of AFDC families over the poverty level would decline as the poverty level itself increased with inflation.

Other elements of the agreement reached by the Senate committee expanded the proposed concentration program, which would provide extra money to areas where poor children numbered more than 5,000 or made up 20 percent of enrollment. The committee broadened the base of the program by allowing whole counties, rather than individual school districts, to qualify for the 5,000-student or 20 percent enrollment standard, thus including many rural districts with more than one school district.

The committee also set aside $400 million for the concentration program, and guaranteed small states at least one-quarter of 1 percent of the entire concentration funding.

Impact Aid

The Senate committee voted down proposals by Pell to make modest cuts in the impact aid program.

Pell offered an amendment, supported by the administration, to eliminate payments for children of federal employees who work outside the county of residence. Noting that the change would save some $45 million a year, supporters argued that there was no need to give federal funds to counties that were not being directly affected by a parent's federal employment. The amendment was rejected 5-9.

The committee also rejected, by a 7-8 vote, a Pell motion to delete payments in the Education Subcommittee's version of the bill for children of employees of post office service centers on federally owned land. Javits, chief spokesman for the new payments, said only a small number of facilities for regional processing of mail are located on federal land.

Private School Aid

The Senate committee rejected a proposal to provide new, unrestricted assistance to private schools. Pell described the proposal as an alternative to legislation granting tuition tax credits to parents of students in private elementary and secondary schools. Telling his colleagues they needed to show that they really did care about private education, Pell offered a new title to the bill to increase assistance to non-public schools for textbooks, health testing and other pupil-related services, and to provide all-purpose loans to private schools for maintenance and operation.

While the specific, pupil-related grants to private schools had clear precedent, Pell conceded that the constitutionality of general purpose loans to private schools had never been tested in the courts. Javits voiced strong doubts that the loan program would withstand the constitutional prohibition on aid to religion, because churches operate a large percentage of the nation's private elementary and secondary schools. Pell agreed to remove the loan program, leaving only the restricted grants.

Bilingual Education

Responding to criticisms by New York City teachers and others that Hispanic and other minority children were staying in federally funded bilingual classes long after they had gained command of English, the Human Resources Committee tightened the definition of students who were eligible for the program.

Concerns about the bilingual program were reinforced May 8 by the release of an Office of Education study which found that less than one-third of students in bilingual programs had serious problems with speaking English. The study also found that in 85 percent of the bilingual projects students were kept in the special classes even after they had the ability to function in school in English.

The Education Subcommittee had made students eligible for the programs if they were reading and speaking below their grade level. Arguing that such a standard would make half the students eligible for special classes, Javits convinced the committee to allow students to stay in only long enough to have had a sufficient opportunity to master English.

Senate Floor Action

After rejecting a federal aid program for parochial schools and an amendment to limit school busing, the Senate Aug. 24 passed a bill authorizing about $55 billion for elementary and secondary education over the next five years. The vote was 86-7. *(Vote 358, p. 53-S)*

During two days of debate, the senators adopted 44 amendments to the bill (S 1753 — S Rept 95-856), including some major changes in the impact aid program. But they defeated attempts to make even more drastic cuts in impact aid and to delete a new program designed to improve basic skills, such as reading and writing. Opponents of the basic skills program argued that it impinged on local control of schools. The amendment to delete the program was rejected on a 30-62 vote. *(Vote 356, p. 53-S)*

No Senate floor amendments were offered involving the Title I formula.

School Busing

The debate over busing involved an attempt by Delaware Sens. William V. Roth Jr., R, and Joe Biden, D, to attach to the bill the text of S 1651, which was reported by the Senate Judiciary Committee in 1977.

S 1651 was the first bill ever reported by a congressional committee that sought to restrict the courts' authority to order busing as a remedy in desegregation cases. All previous congressional action had sought to limit the authority of HEW to order busing. *(1977 Almanac p. 510)*

The amendment would have barred any court from ordering busing without first determining that a "discriminatory purpose in education was a principal motivating factor" for the violation the busing was designed to correct.

It would have prevented the courts from ordering more extensive busing than "reasonably necessary" to restore the racial composition of "particular schools" to what it would have been had there been no discrimination.

The amendment would have affected any busing order that was not final or which had not taken effect by June 27, 1977. When the bill was considered by the Judiciary Committee in 1977 opponents predicted that 60 school districts would be affected. Among them was Wilmington, Del.

Roth said the amendment was intended to "establish guidelines that are consistent with the United States Constitution regarding the circumstances under which courts" could order busing. He argued that most people opposed busing, that it did not improve educational quality or better race relations and that it caused white flight from public schools.

Opponents of the amendment charged that it was unconstitutional and that it was an unfair encroachment by the legislative branch on the power of the judiciary. They also said the bill would interfere with the school desegregation process, which was working throughout the country.

Pell, floor manager of the bill, opposed the amendment, saying it would prevent courts from ordering busing to correct discrimination caused by housing patterns.

S 1651 as reported by the Judiciary Committee was never brought to the floor because of a threatened filibuster. The same threat was made during debate on the amendment Aug. 23.

Edward W. Brooke, R-Mass., described the measure as "the most pernicious amendment" ever introduced on the subject and said he had drafted 95 amendments to it.

Pell eventually moved to table the Roth amendment, which killed it. The tabling motion narrowly passed, 49-47, after a plea from Majority Leader Robert C. Byrd, D-W.Va., who said he favored the substance of the amendment, but urged members to table it because of the Senate's tight schedule. *(Vote 348, p. 52-S)*

Biden told reporters later that the closeness of the vote signaled a "death knell" for the pro-busing position in the Senate. "This is not a harebrained amendment," he said.

Parochial Aid

The Senate bill included a provision, not in the House version, authorizing $500 million a year in fiscal 1979-83 for grants to private schools.

The grants could be used for secular textbooks, standardized tests, speech, hearing and psychological diagnostic services, guidance and counseling, secular instructional materials and equipment and transportation. In addition, the bill created an Office of Non-Public Education in the Office of Education.

Asserting that the section was a clear unconstitutional entanglement of church and state, Sen. Ernest F. Hollings, D-S.C., moved to strike it from the bill. His amendment was approved, 60-30. *(Vote 352, p. 53-S)*

Hollings said that 90 percent of the schools that would get the grants were parochial and that the $2.5 billion total cost of the program would be better spent on public schools. He also asserted that it was "at least as unconstitutional" as tuition tax credits for non-public elementary and secondary school students, which the Senate had defeated Aug. 15. *(Tuition tax credit, p. 248)*

Pell, defending the committee bill, said the panel had attempted to word the provision in a manner consistent with what it believed were the tests of constitutionality — that the programs have a secular purpose, that their principal effect be that they neither advance nor inhibit religion and that they not foster an excessive government entanglement with religion.

He noted that 9 percent of the nation's children are educated in non-public schools.

Impact Aid

The Senate adopted changes in the impact aid program, which is designed to compensate school districts for the effects of non-taxable federal property.

The biggest assault on the program came from Sen. Thomas F. Eagleton, D-Mo., who offered an amendment to knock out all aid for "B" children, those whose parents live or work on federal property. He said it would save $374 million a year. The amendment was defeated 20-66. *(Vote 354, p. 53-S)*

But some less sweeping changes were more successful.

The Senate adopted an amendment by Warren G. Magnuson, D-Wash., deleting a provision from the bill increasing mandatory payments for children living in public housing projects by $120 million. The amendment would give the Appropriations Committee, which Magnuson chaired, discretion in making the payments.

The amendment was adopted, 62-22, but not before producing some angry words from members from urban areas. *(Vote 353, p. 53-S)*

Describing his remarks as "brutally frank," Javits asserted that the committee bill increased aid for public housing students so that big cities "could get in on all this dough. . . .

"Now if we are knocked out we are being discriminated against and [it will be] necessary for us to go after the whole impact aid program. I promise, we will. The big cities of the country . . . will wake up and they will join me. They will knock it all out," Javits said.

Also adopted, 57-35, was an amendment by Henry Bellmon, R-Okla., which wiped out the tier system for making impact aid payments. The system was created in 1974. The effect of the amendment would be to give the Appropriations Committee discretion in determining how to fund the program. *(Vote 357, p. 53-S)*

Conference Action

Conferees filed their report on HR 15 Oct. 10 (H Rept 95-1753).

Impact Aid

The conference committee compromise on the impact aid program centered around a Senate-passed amendment eliminating the "tier" system of funding.

Existing law provided three funding tiers. In the first tier, all categories of impact aid got 25 percent of their entitlement. In the second, however, the different categories were to receive varying percentages of the remainder of their entitlements. Districts with large numbers of military dependents were to get all they were due, for example, while districts with "B" children whose parents worked on federal property in another county were to receive only 28 percent of what they were due.

To make the funding distinctions stick in the appropriations process, the law required that the second tier be fully funded, or not at all. Anything left over could go to the third tier.

The appropriations committees complained that the provision tied their hands by preventing decisions as to the varying importance of the parts of impact aid.

In order to increase flexibility in the appropriations process, the Senate deleted the tier system, thus turning over all levels of funding to annual budget determinations. The House bill retained the tier system.

The conference compromise retained the tier structure but allowed more funds to be directed according to appropriations decisions. The final version accomplished this by requiring a minimum of 65 percent of existing entitlements in the second tier, beginning in fiscal 1980.

The effect of this provision was to preserve in the second tier the existing ratio of mandatory payments for different categories. But once the reduced required amounts were provided, the appropriations process could proceed to allocate additional funds according to annual determinations.

To make sure school districts were not faced with sudden drops in funding because of appropriations decisions, the compromise included a 90 percent hold-harmless provision guaranteeing recipients most of what they got the year before.

The big winners under the compromise could be cities with large numbers of children in federally subsidized public housing. Under existing law, there had been no payments for public housing in the second tier. The House bill removed this restriction, while the Senate bill did not.

The conference version contained the House provision, thus counting public housing children like all other impact aid children.

The final bill did not contain administration proposals to eliminate payments for B children whose parents worked outside the county or state in which they lived. But by reducing mandatory payments for the Bs in the second tier, the bill allowed the appropriations process to cut funding for the program, whose popularity in Congress had been slipping.

Title I Formula

Conferees compromised on proposed revisions of the Title I compensatory education formula by delaying their implementation and limiting their scope.

Both the House and Senate bills removed a restriction in existing law that, for the purpose of computing Title I allocations, limited the count of welfare children whose families were over the poverty income level to two-thirds of their number. But the House bill did not put the change into effect until fiscal 1980, while the Senate had approved it for 1979.

The conference agreement put the full counting provision into effect immediately for the new concentration program of extra assistance to districts with high proportions of poor children. However, for the bulk of Title I funds, the change was not to go into effect until 1980.

Another House-passed formula change, which, like the change in welfare counting, was expected to result in a shift of Title I funds to northern and urban states, had required use of poverty data from a 1975 income survey for allocating future funds appropriated in excess of the fiscal 1979 level. The Senate bill contained no similar provision.

Conferees agreed to accept use of the new survey for half of the appropriations in excess of the 1979 level.

Conferees approved, with restrictions, a House-passed provision taking tentative steps in the direction of allocating Title I funds on the basis of educational achievement, rather than income levels. In response to pressure for use of achievement data in the Title I formula, the House had accepted a limited provision allowing school districts to rank schools with severe educational deprivation over those with more poverty but better progress in learning by students.

The Senate conferees accepted the provision, which was not included in their bill, with an amendment allowing use of achievement data only if approved by parents and the state.

Bilingual Education

For bilingual programs, conferees modified a House provision barring most schools from receiving bilingual project aid for more than five years. The final agreement prohibited termination of the aid if the school was operating the program well, could not afford to do it on its own, and continued to have bilingual students, or had experienced a recent influx of non-English speakers.

The conference committee accepted a Senate provision limiting participation by English speakers in bilingual programs to 40 percent of any bilingual class. The House bill had provided a somewhat looser restriction allowing English-speaking participation in bilingual classes proportionate to the enrollment of the whole school.

Conferees produced a new definition of who was eligible for bilingual instruction. Some teachers had complained that children were being kept in bilingual classes long after learning English. The final bill allowed participation by children who had sufficient difficulty in speaking, writing or understanding English that they could not learn successfully in classrooms where instruction was in English.

Final Action

The Senate approved the conference report on HR 15 by voice vote Oct. 12. The House agreed by a 349-18 vote Oct. 15, clearing the measure for the president. *(Vote 828, p. 236-H)*

College Student Assistance

President Carter Nov. 1 signed legislation (S 2539 — PL 95-566) providing new financial assistance to help middle-class college students cope with rapidly rising tuition costs.

Final congressional approval of the bill, which came Oct. 15, the last day of the session, marked the successful conclusion of a year-long campaign by the administration and public education forces to enact an expansion of existing federal student aid programs in place of the proposed tuition tax credits legislation (HR 12050). HR 12050 died at the end of the 95th Congress. *(Story, p. 248)*

Standing all year as an alternative to the tuition tax credits, the legislation, known as the Middle Income Student Assistance Act, was proposed by the administration in response to the widespread support for the credits, which Carter strongly opposed. The student assistance bill was held up for most of the year by tuition credit supporters, who feared that its enactment would mean the sure death of the credits.

Both the Carter proposal and the tuition credits were attempts to cope with what was widely recognized as a serious problem: the growing burden on middle-income families caused by rapidly increasing educational costs. The costs of higher education went up 77 percent between 1966 and 1976. But middle-income families remained ineligible for federal programs helping students from low-income backgrounds. "Increasingly, middle-income families, not just lower-income families, are being stretched to their financial limits by these new and growing costs of a college or university education." Carter said when he announced his plan Feb. 8.

In signing the final bill into law Nov. 1, along with the Elementary and Secondary Education Act Amendments, Carter called it "an historic expansion of federal assistance to education . . . similar to the GI Bill as a landmark in the federal commitment" to aid college students.

Provisions

As cleared by Congress, S 2539:

- Reduced to 10.5 percent the amount of its discretionary income a family was expected to contribute to a student's college education for the purpose of determining awards under the Basic Educational Opportunity Grants (BEOG) program. The provision effectively expanded eligibility for the grants to include students from families with incomes between $15,000 and $25,000.
- Removed the existing $25,000 income limit for participation in the federally subsidized portion of the guaranteed student loan program, thus allowing all students borrowing under the program to have the interest on their loans paid by the federal government while they were in school.
- Established a schedule for reductions of individual BEOG awards, in the event that not enough funds were appropriated to provide full grants to all those who were eligible, that would preserve the full awards for students from low-income families and make the biggest percentage reductions in the grants for students from the higher-income group.
- Increased the required minimum annual funding for Supplemental Educational Opportunity Grants to $370 million, and for the college work-study program to $500 million.
- Required that the assets of independent students be treated, for the purposes of determining BEOG awards, in the same fashion as the assets of families with dependent students.
- Allowed funds obtained from guaranteed student loans to be fully counted as part of the expected family contribution used to determine the amount of a BEOG award.

Carter Proposal

The Carter college student aid proposal was divided into three parts:

- Basic Educational Opportunity Grants. The plan requested $3.1 billion for fiscal year 1979, up from $2.1 billion in 1978, to provide assistance to a total of 5.3 million students. Students from families earning between $16,000 and $25,000 would become eligible for grants of $250 each.

The maximum grants available to low-income students would rise to $1,800 from $1,600. The average grant for lower-middle-income families earning $8,000 to $16,000 would go up to $1,050 from $850.

- College Work-Study. A $165 million increase over the $435 million appropriated in 1978 was requested. The work-study program, which pays for 80 per cent of a student's part-time job, would be expanded to include more than one million students. Over a third of the students would come from families earning over $16,000.

- Guaranteed Student Loans. To guarantee student loans and help pay interest costs, Carter requested $867 million for fiscal 1979, up from $540 million in 1978. The income limit for eligibility in the program would go up to $45,000 annually, from $30,000. *(Text of Carter message, p. 40-E)*

Senate Committee Action

The Senate Human Resources Education Subcommittee approved its version of the middle income student assistance bill (S 2539) Feb. 22.

The bill, sponsored by Claiborne Pell, D-R.I., was similar, but not identical, to the proposal by the Carter administration. In essence, it would expand the Basic Educational Opportunity Grant program so that more middle-income families could qualify for aid. The existing income cutoff point was about $15,000 for a family of four. The bill approved by the subcommittee would increase that ceiling to about $25,000.

The Carter proposal would guarantee a $250 grant to all eligible families with income up to $25,000. The subcommittee bill would provide aid on a sliding scale, so that families would receive aid according to their need. A typical family of four earning $25,000 would qualify for a grant of about $250 under the bill.

The subcommittee also approved an expansion of the college work-study program to at least $600 million, as proposed by Carter; and it agreed to eliminate the income eligibility limit under the guaranteed student loan program. Carter had proposed increasing the limit to $45,000 from $30,000.

The full Human Resources Committee then approved S 2539 Feb. 24.

Before taking that action, the committee approved an amendment, offered by Thomas F. Eagleton, D-Mo., to increase spending for the Supplemental Education Opportunity Grant program, which provides money to colleges for student financial aid, by $100 million. The amendment reduced the sum in the bill for work-study by the same amount.

While most committee members agreed with Pell, several, including Richard S. Schweiker, R-Pa., and S. I. Hayakawa, R-Calif., emphasized that they would prefer the tax credit approach. Schweiker complained that the Pell bill was being sent out of committee "as a club against the other bill."

The committee report was filed Feb. 28 (S Rept 95-643).

Senate Floor Action

By a 68-28 vote, virtually the same margin by which it had approved the tax credits (HR 12050) the day before, the Senate Aug. 16 passed S 2539, which would expand existing federal student aid programs. The bill was passed without amendment. *(Vote 320, p. 49-S)*

The major change in aid programs made by S 2539 would effectively expand eligibility for Basic Education Opportunity Grants (BEOG) to include students from families with incomes between $15,000 and $25,000 a year, making an estimated 1.5 million more students eligible. Grants would range between about $1,000 per student at a $15,000 income level to $300 at a $24,000 income.

The bill also expanded the default-ridden guaranteed student loan program (GSL) by allowing students regardless of income to receive federal interest subsidies on their bank loans while they were in college. Banks have been reluctant to make unsubsidized loans, since it is much more expensive to bill students individually for periodic interest payments than it is to send one bill to the government to cover all its subsidized loans.

Provisions

As passed by the Senate, S 2539:

- Reduced to 10.5 percent from 20 percent of discretionary income the expected family contribution used to compute the amount of BEOG grants.
- Increased required minimum funding to $500 million from $237.4 million for college work-study programs, and to $370 million in fiscal 1979 and $450 million in 1980, from $130.1 million, for supplemental educational opportunity grants.
- Repealed the existing $25,000 income eligibility limit for subsidized GSL loans.

House Committee Action

By a 32-3 vote the House Education and Labor Committee March 8 approved its version of the middle income student assistance bill (HR 11274), authorizing an additional $1.2 billion in federal student assistance spending.

HR 11274 would increase federal assistance to middle-class students by altering the formula that determines how much their families are expected to contribute to their education. Unlike the Carter plan, it would provide more money to families at the lower end of the middle-income spectrum than to those at the high end. The Carter plan would give a flat $250 to all students from families earning between $16,000 and $25,000.

Under existing law, families were expected to contribute 20 percent of their "discretionary income" — regular income minus taxes, a living allowance and unusual expenses — toward their children's education. If discretionary income was over $5,000, families had to contribute 30 percent of the excess. The family contribution is substracted from education costs to determine the award under the Basic Educational Opportunity Grant program (BEOG).

HR 11274 would reduce the family contribution to 10.5 percent of all discretionary income. If Congress failed to appropriate enough money to fully fund the program at 10.5 percent, the rate would go up to 12 percent.

At 10.5 percent, families with one child at a $3,600-a-year college could get a grant if its income was below $26,100. At the 12 percent rate, the income limit would be about $23,500. The Senate bill (S 2539) provided for a flat 10.5 percent rate.

The bill would remove income eligibility requirements for guaranteed student loans. Carter had requested an increase in the income eligibility limit to $40,000 from $25,000. This would make all but about 2 percent of families eligible, so the committee decided to go ahead and remove the limit altogether, thereby saving the costs of the income reporting requirements.

The committee defeated by an 11-20 vote an Erlenborn amendment to provide for continued collection of income information, not to determine eligibility, but for the purpose of analyzing the program.

The committee report was filed March 14 (H Rept 95-951).

Administration Move Thwarted

The Carter administration and the Democratic leadership in the House were thwarted March 20 when they tried to advance an expanded college student aid program and prevent a vote on tuition tax credits.

They had sought to promote the educational grant bill (HR 11274) while simultaneously blocking a vote on tax credits by bringing the bill up for action under suspension of the rules. That procedure prohibits amendments, although it also requires a two-thirds vote for passage.

The House was evidently angered by the maneuver, voting 156-218 against considering the educational grant program under those conditions. *(Vote 136, p. 40-H)*

The strategy used by the tax credit foes, far from strengthening their cause, may have produced the opposite effect. Shortly after the showdown on the House floor, Ways and Means Committee Chairman Al Ullman, D-Ore., announced that his committee would mark up a tuition tax credit bill April 10-11. Ullman previously had stalled action on tuition tax credits, but the House vote was so strong it appeared to have forced him to act on the matter.

On the other hand, Rep. William D. Ford, D-Mich., suggested that the vote would be in the long-run interest of tax credit foes. He said a number of powerful lobby groups representing public school interests were alarmed at the depth of the support demonstrated for the tax credit approach to aid to education. He predicted those groups would now launch a serious effort to defeat the tuition tax credit concept.

Sequence of Events

The next episode in the grants-versus-tax credits controversy began March 16, when the House Rules Committee began hearings on the grant bill.

Bill Frenzel, R-Minn., asked the Rules Committee to allow him to propose on the House floor an amendment providing tuition tax credits of up to $500.

A spokesman for Frenzel said he sought Rules Committee clearance for his amendment only after he became convinced that Ullman would not allow action on tuition tax credits in the Ways and Means Committee.

The Rules Committee did not complete its deliberations on the bill March 16, so it scheduled a further hearing for March 21.

William D. Ford, D-Mich., chairman of the Postsecondary Education Subcommittee and sponsor of the grant bill, said he became convinced during the March 16 hearing that the Rules Committee would allow the House to consider a tax credit amendment to his bill.

The idea of skirting the Rules Committee and scuttling Frenzel's amendment was planned at a White House meeting March 17. The *Washington Star* quoted presidential domestic policy adviser Stuart E. Eizenstat following the meeting as saying, "The political hardball season has begun."

The White House strategy proved to be more of a wild pitch. In a "Dear Colleague" letter March 20, Frenzel, Albert H. Quie, R-Minn., and Lawrence Coughlin, R-Pa., denounced the move as "a brazen plot by our leaders to squelch tuition tax credits."

They noted that over 250 members of the House were cosponsors of tuition tax credit legislation, and complained that the suspension of the rules procedure would preclude them from considering any tax credit amendments. They suggested that the House should refuse to second the motion to suspend the rules, thus blocking the maneuver without actually voting on the grant bill.

House Floor Action

After its consideration under suspension of the rules was rejected by the House, HR 11274 sat idle for some five months. Despite pressure from Ford, Rules Committee Chairman James J. Delaney, D-N.Y., a tuition tax credit supporter, refused to schedule further action on a rule for the bill.

After receiving pressure from the White House, the Rules Committee finally granted a rule on Oct. 5.

For all the difficulties it experienced in getting to the floor, HR 11274 sailed through Oct. 14 by voice vote and without major amendment.

Sponsors had cleared the way for quick final action by the Senate by altering the committee-reported bill to conform more closely to the Senate-passed bill (S 2539), in the process dropping several significant provisions. Floor manager Ford said provisions changing the guaranteed loan and state student incentive grant program would be considered during reauthorization of the Higher Education Act in 1979.

Other than the 342-38 vote on adoption of the rule (H Res 1425), the only recorded vote during consideration of the bill was on an amendment offered by John N. Erlenborn, R-Ill., to prohibit the government from paying interest on guaranteed student loans (GSL) going to students from families earning over $40,000 a year. *(Vote on rule, Vote 816, p. 232-H)*

In its original proposal to Congress, the administration had suggested that the income limit for eligibility for interest subsidies on GSLs while a student was in school be increased to $45,000 from $25,000. The House Education and Labor Committee, noting that the limit would exclude only a few students, while still involving a lot of paperwork on income reporting, decided to abolish the income eligibility limit altogether.

Critics of abolishing the income limit feared that it would lead to a reduction of loans going to low-income students. This was because, in general, banks didn't like to make unsubsidized GSLs, since it was a lot more bother to collect interest from students than from the government. If all students were eligible for subsidies, critics reasoned, then banks would rush to make loans to wealthier students, who had better connections and were more likely to repay. Since most banks have limited amounts available for GSLs, this would tend to reduce loans going to low-income applicants.

The Erlenborn amendment was rejected 86-301. *(Vote 817, p. 232-H)*

After passing HR 11274, the House substituted its provisions for S 2539.

Final Action

The Senate agreed to the House-passed version of S 2539 by voice vote Oct. 15, clearing the measure for the president.

Department of Education

President Carter wanted it, numerous education-related interest groups supported it, House and Senate committees approved it and the Senate passed it — but a bill to create a new Department of Education in the Cabinet was stymied on the House floor by a small band of the proposed department's foes.

Opponents were primarily concerned that creation of the department would result in federal domination of traditionally independent local schools. The American Federation of Teachers and the AFL-CIO also opposed the bill.

At first, it appeared that the bill would easily clear Congress despite some bitter struggles within the bureaucracy, interest groups and members of Congress over exactly what would be in the new department. In particular, the controversy focused on the proposed transfers of Indian education, science education programs, the Head Start preschool program and the school lunch (child nutrition) program out of their existing bureaucratic homes into the new department. As a result of vigorous lobbying, both House and Senate bills omitted the transfer of the Head Start, school lunch and Indian education programs.

Originally slated for House floor action late the week of Oct. 2, the bill (HR 13778) was pulled from the schedule Oct. 4 after it became clear that opponents were prepared to slow House proceedings to a snail's pace to prevent it from coming up.

"The straw that broke the camel's back," as one aide put it, was a demand by Robert S. Walker, R-Pa., that the House clerk read out loud the entire conference report on a bill on the schedule before HR 13778. Faced with that type of dilatory tactic, House leaders decided to shelve the bill so they could get action on other important legislation before the scheduled Oct. 14 adjournment date.

If the bill had come up, opponents had introduced nearly 100 amendments to it. While some of the amendments dealt with serious issues, such as the transfer of Defense Department schools to the Education Department, aides admitted that many others were intended solely to waste time.

Background

Unlike many other countries, for whom a centralized educational system was a vital component of nation-building, the United States traditionally avoided a strong federal role in education. It was not until 1867 that a federal education agency, called the Department of Education but not represented in the Cabinet, was established.

The first Department of Education was quickly downgraded to the status of a bureau of the Interior Department. For the next 70 years it limped along as a small, record-keeping office, collecting information on the modest federal education efforts. Proposals for a separate department surfaced periodically, but got nowhere. In 1939 the renamed Office of Education was transferred to the Federal Security Agency, which became the Department of Health, Education and Welfare (HEW) in 1953.

With the tremendous expansion of federal education programs in the postwar period, arguments for a separate department grew more attractive. During the 1960s, several studies of government organization recommended establishment of a separate department, as well as related reorganization proposals.

One alternate plan, still occasionally put forward, would model HEW along the lines of the Defense Department. Sub-Cabinet secretaries of health, education and social services would be established, each with independent bureaucratic structures, but serving under the HEW secretary. Another model called for establishment of a Department of Human Resources, including HEW and a vast array of programs from other departments. This plan was backed by President Nixon.

In 1972 Congress established an Education Division, headed by an assistant secretary for education, within HEW. It included the existing Office of Education. *(1972 Almanac p. 387)*

One of the main arguments for a separate education department was the confusing and contradictory structure of the existing federal educational administration. In 1978, the hundreds of different federal educational programs were located in more than 40 different agencies. As Sen. Abraham Ribicoff, D-Conn., chief sponsor of S 991, observed, "Today federal education efforts are really scattershot; there's no focus or coordination."

Lumping all these programs in one department, however, proved to be very difficult politically. For every program going into the department, some other department would have to lose power and money. Agencies and interest groups were willing to fight to resist giving up long established relationships for an uncertain future in the Education Department.

The strongest supporters of the new department were involved in elementary and secondary education. The National Education Association (NEA) and organizations of local education agencies used their substantial political muscle to round up broad backing for the idea in Congress. These groups felt they would get a more sympathetic hearing from an education department than they had from HEW.

Other groups were not so keen on the idea precisely because they feared the department would be too close to that constituency. Higher education organizations were basically neutral on the question. The American Federation of Teachers (AFT), arch-rival of the NEA for the allegiance of the nation's teachers, opposed creation of a separate department.

The bill was also opposed by a coalition of labor and civil rights groups, who feared their influence would be reduced in a department dominated by professional educators.

HEW Secretary Joseph A. Califano Jr. long opposed the new department, a position commonly thought to be based at least in part on reluctance to divide up his and future HEW secretaries' massive bureaucratic power.

As a presidential candidate, Carter came out in favor of the department in 1976, and won the first presidential endorsement of the NEA in its history. On April 14, 1978, the administration called for including in the department almost exactly what Ribicoff and other Senate backers wanted.

The Ribicoff bill put the following major agencies into the new department: HEW's Education Division, Head Start program and education-related activities of the Office for Civil Rights; the Defense Department's armed forces dependent schools; Bureau of Indian Affairs schools, now under the Interior Department; the Agriculture Department's school lunch program and graduate school; college housing loans, now in the Department of Housing and Urban Development; the National Science Foundation's Education Directorate, and the National Foundation on the Arts and the Humanities.

The Carter plan would have put everything proposed by S 991 in the department, except for the arts and humanities foundation.

As outlined by Office of Management and Budget Director James T. McIntyre Jr., the Education Department would have a budget of $17.5 billion — nearly $14 billion of it from existing HEW programs — and would employ 23,325 workers.

A majority of the Senate signed up as cosponsors of various bills to create a new department. House bills creating a department had 120 cosponsors.

Transfer Fights

The shape of the new department was almost as important to many educators as the fact of its existence.

"Some transfers are hard to accomplish politically," said Senate Governmental Affairs Committee staffer Bob Heffernan. Indeed, a few programs with at least a theoretical place in the new department were out of the question because of political opposition. Transfer of job training programs from the Labor Department, for example, was unacceptable to organized labor, while veterans' groups were strongly against the suggested transfer of the G.I. Bill and other veterans' educational programs from the Veterans Administration.

National Science Foundation. Particularly troubling to the higher education community was the proposed transfer of the education functions of the National Science Foundation (NSF) to the Education Department. NSF's Education Directorate funds science education research, grants fellowships to graduate students and provides additional training to science teachers. Its budget in fiscal 1978 was $74 million, about 10 percent of the total NSF budget.

University educators and scientists feared that putting the directorate in a new department would undermine existing relationships and reduce the status of science education.

Arts and Humanities Foundation. A similar concern was expressed over inclusion of the National Foundation on the Arts and Humanities in the new department. Although it held out the possibility of a future transfer, the administration decided not to recommend an immediate shift — its major difference with S 991.

The foundation is composed of separate Endowments for the Arts and for the Humanities, which make grants to individuals and institutions working in those fields.

School Lunch. School nutritionists worried about the prospect of having programs like school lunch administered outside the Agriculture Department. Having had to struggle to gain full status within Agriculture, they were wary of what might happen to them in the Education Department. They felt they could not always count on educators to fully appreciate the value of their programs, according to Faith Gravenmier of the American School Food Service Association. A new department might result in a loss of funding, she said, since "school nutrition funds might be lumped in with all other federal education funds, and in the inevitable listing of priorities" end up worse off.

All 18 members of the Senate Agriculture Committee April 19 announced their opposition to the transfer.

Defense, Indian Schools. The Education Department would come closest to actually running schools if it received school programs from the Defense Department and Bureau of Indian Affairs (BIA). The Defense Department operates 260 schools outside the United States for dependents of military personnel. The BIA runs schools on Indian reservations with some 50,000 students. Altogether, these two programs would account for some 16,500 of the new department's 23,325 employees.

Opponents of these transfers argued as a matter of principle that the department should not get involved in directly running schools. Rufus E. Miles, author of an influential report supporting a separate education department, pointed out that there would be negative effects regardless of how successful the department was in operating schools.

Head Start. Some civil rights groups opposed the transfer of the Head Start program from HEW's Office of Child Development to the Education Department. Head Start officers preschool help to children age 3 to 6 who come from disadvantaged backgrounds. It also runs programs to teach parenting skills and nutritional information.

Head Start programs have a heavy community and parent involvement. Parents sit on local Head Start boards and help develop curricula. Community groups worried that their influence would be submerged within a department dominated by professional educators. Budget Director McIntyre promised unspecified safeguards to make sure that Head Start within the Education Department would still retain "maximum involvement of families and the community."

Committee Action

The Senate Governmental Affairs Committee reported S 991 Aug. 9 (S Rept 95-1078). The House Government Operations Committee reported HR 13778 Aug. 25 (H Rept 95-1531). The Senate bill was approved unanimously, the House bill by a 27-15 vote.

Both bills established a Cabinet-level federal Department of Education, but the Senate version would transfer to it more programs than the House bill would.

Department Organization

The bills established essentially similar structures for the new department.

S 991 established seven offices within the department that would be headed by assistant secretaries: the offices of elementary and secondary education; postsecondary education; occupational, adult and community education; special education and rehabilitative services; child nutrition; Indian education, and educational research and development. The bill also set up an office of education for overseas dependent children, headed by an administrator.

HR 13778 set up corresponding offices, but did not include those for occupational and Indian education and child nutrition.

Both committees called for a strong role for the Office for Civil Rights within the department. Each bill contained provisions designed to maintain the independence and authority of the director of the office, including the right to report directly to Congress without the approval of the education secretary. Civil rights groups had worried that transfer of education-related functions of the HEW civil rights office would weaken efforts against discrimination.

Both bills also provided for an inspector general and general counsel for the department.

The committees split, however, on establishment of two coordinating committees in the department. The House committee deleted a provision, contained in S 991, establishing on a permanent basis the Federal Interagency Committee on Education, composed of representatives of other federal agencies with remaining education responsibilities.

But, despite the fears of some members that it would become a "national school board," the House committee approved the Intergovernmental Advisory Council on Education, with some changes from the Senate committee's version. While S 991 called for a 22-member council, with no more than 11 members from one political party, the House bill provided for 20 members, with no partisan restrictions. The council would be composed of state and local government officials, educators and members of the public.

The House report made clear that the council should not be dominated by education lobbyists, as some opponents feared that it would.

Administration

In general, the House bill contained more restrictions on the activities and authority of the department than the Senate version.

HR 13778 contained a specific prohibition against federal control of education. The Senate bill, as amended in committee by William V. Roth Jr., R-Del., stated that the new department was not intended to interfere with the traditional local decision-making process in education.

The House bill placed a limit of 113 on the number of "supergrade" (GS-16, 17 and 18) civil service employees of the department, a restriction not included in the Senate bill. The House bill allowed an increase of 43 supergrade positions from the existing payroll; S 991 allowed the department 50 more positions.

The Senate bill gave the education secretary authority to reorganize the structure of the department, provided that offices or agencies explicitly established by law were not altered or abolished. However, the Senate committee added a list of existing offices, including the National Institute of Education, which the secretary could consolidate or abolish after consultation with Congress. The House committee gave the secretary authority to reorganize any organizational entities not established by the bill, but specifically denied authority to set up new offices.

A similar restriction was contained in the House provisions giving the secretary authority to reorganize regional and field offices of the department. While the Senate bill gave the secretary a free hand to rearrange the local offices, the House committee removed the authority to establish new field offices.

Both committees agreed on removing a provision in the administration proposal allowing the secretary to rearrange or add to the many educational advisory committees. Acting on a recommendation from the Senate Human Resources Committee, the Governmental Affairs Committee, like the House panel, deleted the provision. This left alteration of the advisory bodies still subject to the General Education Provisions Act, which allows Congress to disapprove such proposals.

The House committee added two amendments limiting the secretary's rule-making authority. As reported, HR 13778 made the issuing of rules and regulations subject to the General Education Provisions Act, ensuring that department regulations would be subject to all the many and varied congressional veto procedures provided by the act. The bill also required that all rules and regulations be accompanied by estimates of their economic impact.

Program Transfers

Indian Education. The House committee did not transfer Indian education programs operated by the Bureau of Indian Affairs (BIA) to the new department. The Senate committee did, rejecting 4-7 an amendment by Ted Stevens, R-Alaska, to leave them in the BIA.

The amendment had the support of major Indian organizations, including the National Congress of American Indians (NCAI) and the National Tribal Chairmen's Association.

Indian opposition to the transfer of their education programs seemed to contradict a long history of mistrust towards the BIA. As Ribicoff observed, "If there's one agency the Indians don't like, its the BIA."

But Stevens argued that recent changes in Indian policy had made Indians feel that they would do better staying with the BIA. "Suddenly they feel that they're getting control over this program. They're doing better in education, and the reason is that they're controlling it," he said.

Since passage of the Indian Self-Determination Act of 1974, tribes had begun to operate schools by themselves, under contract with the BIA. While Indians continued to have serious criticisms of the BIA, "we don't want it dismantled. We don't want to be fragmented," said Georgianna Tiger of the NCAI.

Stevens also argued that, while the transfer might be appropriate in the long run, the decision to move the programs had been taken without sufficient consultation with Indians themselves. Indian organizations said administration support for the move contradicted a Carter campaign promise not to take any actions toward Indians without checking with tribal representatives.

Because of the controversies that led to their exclusion from the House bill, S 991 contained limitations and protections on the transfer of the Indian education programs. The bill allowed a three-year period for transition to the new department, in order to give time for extensive consultations with native American organizations. The committee called for appointment of a person of Indian heritage as assistant secretary for Indian education, and suggested establishment of an all-Indian advisory council on education. It emphasized that the transfer should not impinge on the historic trust responsibilities of the federal government to the tribes.

Child Nutrition Programs. The House committee did not transfer the $3 billion child nutrition programs run by the Agriculture Department to the new education department, but the Senate committee did — barely.

The provisions of S 991 transferring child nutrition were a limited version of the original Carter proposal. In order to get enough votes in the committee to defeat an attempt to delete the nutrition programs entirely, offered by Charles H. Percy, R-Ill., supporters had to agree to let the commodity purchase aspect of the programs remain within the Agriculture Department. Even then, Percy's amendment failed to carry in committee only by an 8-8 tie vote.

As was the case with the Head Start program, child nutrition groups, fearing that their programs would suffer from neglect under professional educators, were able to mount intense pressure against the move. A coalition of agricultural producer and nutrition groups strongly opposed the transfer, as did the Senate Agriculture Committee.

Head Start. The Senate committee avoided a potentially contentious floor struggle when Ribicoff agreed during markup July 11 to remove Head Start from the bill, thus leaving it within HEW. The House committee bill did not include transfer of the program.

Science Programs. The Senate committee bill included transfer of the science education part of the National Science Foundation to the proposed new department, but the House committee agreed to an amendment that deleted the transfer.

Additional Views

Separate views attached to the Senate report focused on the remaining controversial transfers to the Education Department. Percy, Muriel Buck Humphrey, D-Minn., and John C. Danforth, R-Mo., opposed the nutrition transfer, arguing that it "would not solve any problems; it would create new ones." Ted Stevens, R-Alaska, argued against the Indian transfer, saying it would undermine the administration's commitment to include Indian leaders in making decisions affecting their people. Roth and Danforth added that the purpose of the department should be to simplify federal regulations and reduce paperwork requirements on local schools, not to expand federal control.

Dissenting views in the House report concentrated on attacking the idea of the department as leading to more federal control. In separate statements, five Democrats and eight Republicans repeated their opposition to the entire bill. Leo J. Ryan, D-Calif., a former teacher and school superintendent, called the bill "the worst bill I have seen in my six years in the House...a massive shift in the emphasis by the federal government from supporting (local and state) efforts to establishing and implementing a national policy in the education of our children."

Paul N. McCloskey, R-Calif., promised to offer an amendment to require the department to be smaller and spend less than the combined agencies it would replace.

In addition, nine Republicans and two Democrats opposed transfer of Department of Defense overseas dependent schools to the Education Department.

Senate Floor Action

The Senate easily passed its Education Department bill (S 991) by a 72-11 vote Sept. 28. *(Vote 422, p. 62-S)*

Debate, running intermittently over three days, touched on both the fears of opponents that the department would lead to federal control of education and the effects of transfers of various educational programs out of their existing bureaucratic homes and into the new department. *(Programs transferred, box, next page)*

Programs Transferred

Major programs to be transferred to the Department of Education by S 991 (as passed) and HR 13778 (as reported):

Program	Agency	Fiscal 1978 Staff	Fiscal 1978 Budget (in millions)
Education Division	HEW	3,600	$10,500
Inspector General (relating to education)	"	117	3.5
Office for Civil Rights (relating to education)	"	1,102	33.3
Special Institutions	"	1	44.8
Telecommunications Demonstration	"	12	31**
Health Professions Student Loans	"	21	20
Nursing Loans and Scholarship Programs	"	24	31.5
Rehabilitative Services Administration	"	342	976.3
Office for Handicapped Individuals	"	14	.69
Advisory Council on Education Statistics	"	1.5	††
Institute of Museum Services	"	15	28
Graduate School*	Agriculture	—	†
Overseas, Dependent Schools	Defense	10,000	350
Law Enforcement Education Loans	Justice	9	30
Selected Science Education Programs*	National Science Foundation	40	56
College Housing Construction Program	Housing and Urban Development	3	111**

† Not subject to federal appropriations or civil service.
** Fiscal 1979 request.
†† Under $1 million ($29,000)

SOURCE: Senate Governmental Affairs Committee

But, unlike their allies in the House, opponents made no concerted effort to prevent a vote on final passage.

Much of the controversy over the bill had been defused after Ribicoff bowed to overwhelming opposition to the transfer of two programs to the department. Effective mobilization of the constituencies of the Head Start and child nutrition programs, which President Carter had wanted to include in the department, made deletion of the programs from S 991 inevitable.

The Head Start transfer had been dropped by the Governmental Affairs Committee before the bill was reported. The child nutrition transfer, which had survived in committee only by a tie vote, was clearly doomed after Percy collected a majority of the Senate as cosponsors for his amendment to leave the programs with the Agriculture Department.

The Percy amendment, introduced by Stevens, was adopted by voice vote Sept. 20, without resistance from Ribicoff.

Other Votes on Transfers

Ribicoff did oppose, unsuccessfully, removal of the most controversial remaining transfer, that of Indian education programs from the Bureau of Indian Affairs (BIA). A Stevens amendment to delete the transfer was adopted 47-39. *(Vote 419, p. 62-S)*

Most major Indian education groups had opposed the transfer, fearing that it would lead to a breakup of the BIA and erosion of the federal trust responsibilities to the tribes. Stevens argued that the most important reason to oppose the move was simply that the people affected didn't want it. "The whole spirit of self-determination will be violated if Congress does not listen to [Indian organizations] as they represent their people in telling us they do not support this move," Stevens said.

Ribicoff responded that BIA education efforts were "a mess." Joined on the issue by James Abourezk, D-S.D., chairman of the Select Committee on Indian Affairs, Ribicoff argued that the concerns of Indian organizations did not outweigh the sad history of BIA education, as shown by the low achievement scores and high dropout rates of Indian students. Abourezk claimed Indian organizations had been manipulated into opposition by BIA officials afraid of losing their bureaucratic turf.

Senators from western states, representing most Indians, voted 17-6 in favor of the Stevens amendment. Two westerners who opposed the amendment, Pete V. Domenici, R-N.M., and John Melcher, D-Mont., had earlier introduced an amendment, approved by voice vote Sept. 19, to protect trust and self-determination rights in the transfer.

Two other attempts to prevent transfer of education programs were unsuccessful, however. Proceeding from a general opposition to the bill as another step toward a federal takeover of local education, Harrison Schmitt, R-N.M., offered amendments to prevent transfer of Defense Department overseas dependent schools and science education programs of the National Science Foundation (NSF).

Schmitt argued that the dependent schools were an integral part of overseas peacetime military operations, and as such best left with the Defense Department. Opponents of the move feared in addition that the schools would become "test tubes" for experiments in educational innovation by department officials.

Unlike the child nutrition transfer, the dependent school move was supported by important members of the committee that would lose its jurisdiction over the program. Armed Services Committee members Henry M. Jackson, D-Wash., and Sam Nunn, D-Ga., supported the transfer, arguing along with Ribicoff that it would help bring an up-to-date education to military dependents and correct some of the serious problems experienced in the department's European schools.

The Schmitt amendment on defense schools was tabled by a 65-23 vote. *(Vote 418, p. 62-S)*

As approved by the committee, S 991 transferred about three-fourths of NSF science education funding to the new department. Programs for teacher training and development of elementary, secondary and undergraduate curricula would be moved; graduate research training would remain with the foundation.

Opposing the transfer, Schmitt stressed that the scientific community and most of higher education was against it. Scientists and universities were worried that their concerns, amply represented in the relatively small NSF, would be swamped in a new department dominated by elementary and secondary education interests.

The Schmitt science amendment was tabled by a 62-23 vote. *(Vote 420, p. 62-S)*

Other Amendments

In other action on S 991, the Senate:

- Approved by voice vote Sept. 20 a William V. Roth Jr., R-Del., amendment to require Congress to set an annual ceiling on the number of departmental personnel.
- Approved by voice vote Sept. 20 a Humphrey amendment to rename the Department of Health, Education and Welfare as the Department of Health and Human Services.
- Tabled by a 70-14 vote Sept. 28 an S. I. Hayakawa, R-Calif., amendment to substitute for the bill establishing the Education Department a bill requiring the National Institute of Education to study the need for a separate department. *(Vote 421, p. 62-S)*

Federal Aid to HMOs

Legislation that would convert federal aid for health maintenance organizations (HMOs) from an experimental, demonstration project basis to more substantial, continuing support cleared Congress on the last day of the session.

A three-year, $164 million reauthorization (S 2534 — PL 95-559) for federal grants and loans for the prepaid group medical practices was cleared for the president Oct. 14 by voice vote by the Senate. The House had approved the conference agreement Oct. 13 by a 309-33 vote. *(Vote 812, p. 230-H)*

The final bill was considerably less ambitious than either the five-year extension originally sought by the Carter administration or the five-year, $415 million bill reported by the Senate Human Resources Committee. The measure was scaled down by both the Senate and the House.

The administration had proposed new financial incentives to encourage enrollment of Medicare and Medicaid beneficiaries in the health plans. And it wanted to exempt HMOs from certain restrictions of the federal health planning process.

It did not win these changes, but even the shorter reauthorization was considered a substantial reaffirmation of federal involvement in HMOs. In one important change, the bill added new financial support for HMO outpatient facilities, key to the plans' emphasis on reducing costly hospitalizations. The total amount of support for various stages of development and operation was raised, and certain requirements for staff and services offered were relaxed for the early, financially difficult years when an HMO builds membership.

The administration had enthusiastically promoted the money-saving potential of the prepaid plans, which provide comprehensive health services to members for fixed fees. Because the health care groups must live with an annual budget, dictated by members' fees, there is a strong incentive to avert costly acute illness when possible, to cut back on excessive tests or other procedures and to stress preventive care, health screening and other innovations. For these reasons, and because the HMOs offer competition to the conventional fee-for-service type of health care, the administration wanted a major expansion of the federal support program.

But before either House or Senate committees reported the reauthorization legislation, the existing federal HMO program came under fire for slipshod management practices which included endorsing multimillion-dollar HMO loans without a fixed loan policy. And charges resurfaced that certain HMOs were defrauding their members and the federal government, or were so poorly managed that they would fail and default on federal loans. These charges, outlined in reports by the General Accounting Office (GAO) and the Senate Governmental Affairs Subcommittee on Investigations, figured prominently in debate on the HMO reauthorization. The doubts created by the reports, plus growing congressional resistance to expensive health programs, resulted in the more modest three-year reauthorization.

The proposed incentives to promote Medicare-Medicaid enrollments in HMOs never emerged from committee, in large part because some of the most memorable HMO abuses involved Medicaid HMO enrollments authorized by California in 1972. An administration proposal to exempt HMO ambulatory (outpatient) care facilities from federal planning review — thus putting them on an equal footing with outpatient services started by other entities like fee-for-service group practices — died with the health planning reauthorization (HR 11488). A Health, Education and Welfare (HEW) official in the HMO program said the administration would ask Congress again in 1979 for the Medicare-Medicaid and planning law revisions. *(Health planning bill, p. 616)*

In response to the criticisms of HMOs and the federal support program, the final bill included detailed HMO financial reporting requirements, with criminal penalties for false reporting. It also ordered the GAO to evaluate HEW efforts to improve its management of the program.

Provisions

As cleared for the president, S 2534:

- Authorized a three-year total of $164 million for grants, contracts and loans for health maintenance organizations — $31 million for fiscal 1979, $65 million for fiscal 1980 and $68 million for fiscal 1981.
- Increased to $2 million, from $1 million, the maximum amount an entity could receive for initial HMO development grants, contracts or loan guarantees, beginning Sept. 30, 1979; made grants available for up to three years.
- Permitted established HMOs to receive initial development funds for significant expansions of services or membership.
- Increased to $4 million, from $2.5 million, the total amount an HMO could receive in initial operating loans and loan guarantees; raised to $2 million, from $1 million, the maximum amount an HMO could receive under this section in any given year. In fiscal 1979 an HMO could borrow up to the higher levels only if the HEW secretary determined that the extra funds were needed to preserve the fiscal soundness of the HMO.
- Authorized the secretary to take possession of property or take any other steps needed to keep an HMO from defaulting on a federal operating loan or guaranteed loan.

- Authorized the secretary to provide loans and loan guarantees up to $2.5 million for constructing and equipping HMO ambulatory care (outpatient) facilities. The loan guarantees were only for private non-profit HMOs providing new ambulatory care to medically underserved populations. (The ambulatory care funds were not included in the aggregate limits for development and operating funds, and an HMO proposing several separate ambulatory care facilities could borrow up to the limit for each facility.)
- Established a new HMO management internship program, providing stipends for individuals and support funds for HMOs or other training entities.
- Required the secretary to provide HMO technical assistance grants, for both start-up and operating phases.
- Required certain employers, with the consent of an employee, to provide payroll deductions for HMO payments. This provision applied to employers who were required by existing law to provide workers with an HMO option and who provided conventional health insurance coverage either through payroll deductions or through full payment of premiums for workers.
- Required HMOs periodically to submit financial reports to HEW, identifying owners and describing transactions with "parties-in-interest" (persons with an interest in both the HMO and an entity providing goods or services to the HMO); required the reports to include evidence that the HMO was "fiscally sound," and to cover any organizations related to an HMO by common ownership or control.
- Required HMOs to disclose the financial reports to members upon request.
- Required the secretary to review the reported parties-in-interest transactions for adverse impact on the financial status of HMOs, if he thought a review was needed; required him to report annually to Congress on the review program.
- Authorized disqualification of HMOs that failed to file the financial statements.
- Provided criminal penalties of up to $25,000 in fines and up to five years' imprisonment for intentional falsification of the financial reports.
- Limited HMO enrollment practices for Medicaid beneficiaries to methods approved by the secretary.
- Authorized HMOs to enroll student members at special rates based on health risks of students as a group rather than at community rates.
- Specified that HMOs must have administrative and management capabilities "satisfactory" to the secretary.
- Exempted public HMOs from a requirement that the HMO policy-making body must be one-third HMO members, with representation from medically underserved populations in its service area; required instead that they establish advisory boards with comparable membership; authorized the advisory boards to make policy decisions if the public HMO delegated that power to them.
- Removed an existing limit on HMO contracts for services with non-physician providers (hospitals, home health agencies, clinical laboratories, optometrists, dentists and others); retained an existing limit on HMO contracting with doctors not working full-time for the HMO; allowed HMOs to use medical groups not meeting statutory requirements for amount of total practice devoted to HMO patients, for up to 48 months after qualification.
- Authorized HMOs to collect workmen's compensation or private health insurance payments for services to an HMO member who was eligible for these benefits.
- Required HMOs to reimburse members for health services that were provided by another entity only when the care was provided on an emergency basis.
- Limited to "good faith" efforts HMO responsibility for health care during natural disasters, wars or other uncontrollable events. Labor disputes were not included in this exemption.
- Permitted HMOs to refuse to cover unusual or infrequently provided services such as sex-change surgery.
- Required the General Accounting Office to evaluate HEW's management of HMO grant and loan programs, and to report its findings to Congress by May 1, 1979.
- Extended statutory conflict-of-interest prohibitions for federal employees (18 USC 207, 208) to state and local government employees handling substantial Medicaid expenditures. The prohibitions included former government employees and their associates in the private sector.
- Exempted new HMO outpatient facilities and services from federal health planning system reviews, but only for purposes of Medicare-Medicaid reimbursement. (Existing law required certificate of need approval for such facilities before including an appropriate proportion of their cost in overall payments for Medicare and Medicaid services.)

Background

In 1971, President Nixon proposed an ambitious program of federally assisted HMOs. Among other things, Nixon advocated development by the end of fiscal 1976 of 1,700 HMOs, to enroll 40 million people. His ultimate goal was enrolling 90 percent of the population — "if they (so) desire" — in the prepaid health plans, according to a 1971 HEW report.

By the 1972 election, however, Nixon had backed off from his original broad endorsement, reportedly at the insistence of the American Medical Association (AMA) and his personal physician. The AMA had long regarded any other payment system than fee-for-service to be unethical.

Another early advocate of an extensive HMO system was Edward M. Kennedy (D Mass.), who won Senate approval in 1972 of his wide-ranging, $5.1 billion HMO bill. By the time an HMO bill won final approval in 1973, however, it had shrunk to a $375 million "experimental" program that effectively limited the number of federally assisted HMOs over a five-year period to about 100.

The 1973 law (PL 93-322) required HMOs to offer enrolled members basic health services for a set fee and to provide supplemental services to enrollees contracting for them at an additional cost per service. Federal grants and loans were provided to generate and support new HMOs until they became qualified and financially viable. *(1973 law, 1973 Almanac p. 499)*

In 1976 Congress loosened the stringent HMO eligibility and benefits standards mandated by the 1973 act, following complaints from HMOs and organized labor that meeting them could push HMO costs so high that their premiums would not be competitive with those of regular health insurance plans. *(1976 Almanac p. 544)*

As of February 1978, 168 HMOs were functioning, serving about six million people. Of these, only 52 plans, serving about four million people, had met federal standards, according to HEW. The Carter goal was to have 172 federally qualified HMOs in operation by 1982.

1978 Action

The Carter administration moved on several fronts in 1978 to foster HMO growth. Major elements of the Carter initiative included:

- A modest legislative proposal to boost financial support for HMOs and eliminate various barriers to HMO enrollment of Medicare and Medicaid patients. The president's fiscal 1979 budget upped funding for the federal HMO program by about 16 percent, to $30 million.
- A drive to enlist big business support for HMOs.
- Actions by the Federal Trade Commission (FTC) to curb discrimination by insurers or local practitioners against HMOs and combat other practices that might restrain their growth.
- Internal improvements in the administration of the federal HMO program.

The Senate Human Resources Subcommittee on Health and Scientific Research began hearings March 3 on S 2534, a bill that reflected much of the president's program, except for Medicare and Medicaid amendments. Its principal sponsor was Richard S. Schweiker, R-Pa., author of the 1976 HMO bill, with Kennedy listed as cosponsor.

The bill was the product of a collective effort involving the Washington Business Group, the AFL-CIO, aides to Schweiker and Kennedy, health policy staff at HEW, and the Consensus Group, a coalition that sprouted several years ago to lobby for HMOs and helped shape the 1976 HMO amendments. Consensus Group members included HMO trade associations (the Group Health Association of America, the American Association of Foundations for Medical Care) and the insurance industry.

Thus, most of the interested parties — with the major exception of the AMA — had a hand in crafting the Schweiker bill. For the most part their reaction to the finished product was favorable.

Senate Committee Action

In its May 15 report on S 2534 (S Rept 95-837), the Committee on Human Resources proposed a $415 million authorization for the federal HMO program through fiscal 1983. Ceilings on initial grants for starting HMOs were raised, as were ceilings on operating loans for plans that had "qualified" (met federal standards).

The committee said the HMO program had proved itself, but that it had been "systematically undercut by previous HEW leadership." HMO enrollment had increased only 5.2 percent in the past year, the committee said. "It is clear that HMOs will not be able to achieve their true potential without expanded and more efficient federal efforts," the committee asserted.

It proposed these major changes in existing law:

Construction Loans. Construction loans and loan guarantees were authorized. According to the committee, an important cost-saving feature of HMOs was their emphasis on out-patient care instead of hospitalization. But HMOs had trouble raising money for creating these facilities from private sources "because they often lack the equity base and the financial history to attract capital."

Service Exemptions. Existing law made providing basic and supplemental health services "without limitations as to time or cost" a requirement for federal qualification. But this requirement has "restricted HMO development" because it produced "extremely narrow qualification rulings," the committee said. For that reason the committee authorized qualification of HMOs whose "contracts with members contain certain exclusions relatively common in the insurance industry," such as exemptions from coverage during natural disasters or insurrections. Under this amendment an HMO also would not be liable for health conditions of an enrollee who was covered by a workmens' compensation statute, or for certain infrequent or unusual procedures such as transsexual surgery.

Payroll Deduction. Existing requirements that employers offer HMO coverage as an alternative to traditional health insurance in certain circumstances had been undermined when employers refused to deduct HMO fees from employees' paychecks, according to the committee. If employers were required to offer HMO coverage and if they had the capability to make the deductions, they had to do so if workers wished it, the committee said.

Financial Disclosure. The committee decided against an outright ban on certain types of transactions, such as those between non-profit and for-profit entities with overlapping directorships. Despite much study, the committee was unable to single out types of transactions that were so consistently abused as to warrant such treatment, it said. The committee concluded that it would be more useful to require "careful screening of potential conflicts of interest for their adverse effect." It expanded financial reporting requirements and required HEW to review the reports to locate abuses.

Health Planning. The existing planning process established by a 1974 law had worked against HMO development, the committee found. "Because [HMOs] compete with the fee-for-service system, [they] are frequently given unobjective appraisals" in required certification procedures by physician- or hospital-dominated planning agencies, the report said. The committee proposed special review criteria for HMO applications to build inpatient facilities, plus other changes.

Senate Floor Action

By a 71-1 vote the Senate July 21 passed a $185 million reauthorization for HMO loans and grants for three years, through fiscal 1981. The bill (S 2534) also included a five-year authorization for a new HMO management training program. *(Vote 231, p. 37-S)*

Before passing the bill, the Senate sliced two years and $330 million from the committee version and beefed up anti-fraud provisions by adding criminal penalties.

Neither the Senate bill nor a House version (HR 13655) included Carter administration proposals to encourage HMOs to enroll the poor and elderly beneficiaries of the two federal health plans, Medicaid and Medicare. These were withdrawn before they could be formally considered by the House and Senate committees.

The thrust of the Senate amendments and the fate of the Medicare-Medicaid initiative revealed congressional resistance to the all-out development of HMOs sought by the administration.

In part, congressional coolness was attributed to members' touchiness about spending bills in the wake of the anti-tax Proposition 13 vote in California. Schweiker decided after that vote to reduce spending levels and the length of the authorization when the HMO bill came to the floor, according to his aide, David Main.

But the critical factor in the go-slow attitude of members appeared to be renewed charges of fraud in certain HMOs and of inept management of the federal program by the Department of HEW.

Two reports extremely critical of HMOs appeared in the late spring. One, by the General Accounting Office (GAO), focused on defects in the administration of the federal program and fiscal problems of the health plans. The second, issued in April by the Senate Governmental Affairs Subcommittee on Investigations, chaired by Sam Nunn, D-Ga., detailed numerous abuses in the California Medi-Cal program. The report said some HMOs had conducted high-pressure and misleading enrollment drives among the poor residents in ghettos and barrios. Contracted services were not provided patients, while some HMO operators improperly diverted government funds paid for the Medicaid enrollees into their own for-profit companies.

Amendments

The Senate took these actions on the HMO bill:

Planning Act. Agreed by voice vote to a Kennedy-Schweiker amendment deleting proposed revisions in the health planning act (PL 93-641) relating to HMOs.

The proposed revisions had provoked opposition from some members who said they unfairly favored HMOs, or interfered with doctors' rights to purchase equipment or states' rights to tailor certificate-of-need laws to local conditions. Kennedy said the proposed changes were "more germane to the consideration" of a proposed extension (S 2410) of the planning law.

Nunn Amendment. Agreed by voice vote to a package of changes proposed by Nunn, as follows:

- Shortened the HMO reauthorization to three years, from five.
- Reduced funding for the program to $185 million, from $415 million. Besides dropping the last two years' worth of funding altogether, Nunn's amendment trimmed back spending for the remaining three years (fiscal 1979-81) from the $210 million proposed by the committee.
- Delayed until fiscal 1980 committee-proposed increases in individual HMO grants to $2 million.
- Delayed until fiscal 1980 a proposed increase to $5 million, from $2.5 million, for HMO operating loans. The amendment provided an exception which would allow the secretary of HEW to authorize the higher level in fiscal 1979 if he determined that an HMO needed the extra funds for survival.
- Added criminal penalties for willful falsification of financial disclosure reports to HEW. The committee bill had authorized disqualification for HMOs submitting false or inadequate information.
- Prohibited door-to-door enrollment of HMO members. The prepaid plans could still canvass door-to-door for new members, but could not complete membership procedures in the home.
- Directed the GAO to evaluate HEW's administration of the HMO program and report to Congress by May 1, 1979.

Kennedy backed Nunn's proposals to cut funding and toughen anti-fraud provisions.

House Committee Action

The 1978 reauthorization changed the federal commitment to HMOs from the relatively limited role of funding demonstration projects to one of providing "support for HMO development on a continuing basis," the House Commerce Committee said in its Aug. 11 report (H Rept 95-1479) on HR 13655.

Although development of the prepaid plans was "not without risk," their potential for health care savings and other benefits justified continuing federal aid, the committee found. It also said it was "encouraged" by administration efforts to improve HEW management of the HMO program.

Compared with the fee-for-service sector, HMOs saved 10 to 40 percent of health care costs, with much of the savings coming from "eliminating the overuse of inpatient hospital services," according to the committee. HMOs also could deliver "high quality" health care "in innovative modes," such as increased use of non-physician medical professionals and health screening programs. Many HMOs also had "impressive" peer review and quality control programs, the committee said.

As reported, the House committee bill authorized $63 million each year for 1980 and 1981. (A fiscal 1979 authorization was included in HR 12460.) Like the Senate bill, HR 13655 raised loan ceilings — only to accommodate inflation, according to the committee report — and loosened certain service requirements for the prepaid plans. These relaxations were intended to make the HMOs more competitive in price with conventional health insurance plans, and to postpone (or revise) some staffing requirements until an HMO had enough members to pay for full staff.

The House bill also followed the Senate measure in authorizing new support for construction and equipping ambulatory care facilities, and it established a new management training program and a mandatory financial reporting program.

The House bill (but not the Senate) authorized special rates for students to encourage their enrollment in HMOs. Because students had relatively fewer illnesses, private insurers covered them more cheaply and so students tended not to join the more expensive HMOs, the committee found. They should be encouraged to do so "so they will be more likely to consider the HMO option in the future," the committee said. The committee stressed, however, that HMOs serving only students could not be federally qualified. Existing law required broadly representative HMO membership for qualification.

The House bill (but not the Senate) authorized the secretary of HEW to waive for existing Blue Cross-Blue Shield HMOs a requirement that one-third of the HMO policy-making board be members of the health plan. The committee said that in order to be federally qualified, these plans would still have to meet all other organizational and operational requirements. It further ruled out any federal assistance for these plans. The committee instructed HEW to watch carefully for anti-competitive behavior or other negative market factors when deciding on the waivers. The committee said the waiver was appropriate, to protect the substantial private investment in the plans.

Dissenting Views. In dissenting views, five committee members objected to the waiver as "an unwarranted suspension of the already limited public accountability of these organizations." The waiver appeared "inconsistent with the intent of the HMO legislation," since hospital administrators controlled Blue Cross and physicians controlled Blue Shield, the dissenters claimed.

House Floor Action

The House passed the committee version of HR 13655 by a 327-60 vote Sept. 25, adding a $25 million authorization for fiscal 1979 from HR 12460 and then substituting its text for the Senate-passed bill (S 2534). *(Vote 728, p. 208-H)*

Proponents stressed the money-saving potential of the prepaid health plans and said HEW was moving satisfactorily to clean up program problems.

The only major objections came from Commerce Committee Republican James M. Collins, Texas, who had made a practice of attacking health reauthorizations he considered too expensive on the House floor.

Collins' major complaints were that HEW couldn't handle the money it was now receiving, much less new funds, and that "right now HMOs are now a success." He cited a GAO report on the shaky financial prospects of a group of federally supported HMOs and said the government "should not be exposed to additional financial risk."

Conference Action

The biggest difference between House and Senate bills was in overall authorization levels. Conferees in their Oct. 13 report (H Rept 95-1784) leaned toward the less generous House bill, with a three-year total that was $21 million less than the Senate approved and $13 million more than the House figure. (The conference report listed the Senate-passed total as $170 million for three years, but the bill passed by the Senate had also included a separate $15 million authorization for a new training program, for a $185 million total.)

In most of the major policy changes, the differences were relatively minor. In most cases conferees traded off the differences without making major changes.

Conferees dropped two House provisions that permitted HMOs to receive funds authorized for migrant and community health centers and that waived required participation by HMO members in policy-making boards for Blue Cross-Blue Shield HMOs. (Another bill cleared by Congress, S 2474, authorized grants to the health centers for converting to a prepaid basis.)

Conferees retained two House provisions that were not in the Senate bill. The first extended federal conflict-of-interest prohibitions to state and local Medicaid administrators, and the second permitted special rates for student HMO members. ▮

Domestic Violence

The Senate passed legislation establishing a new federal grant program to help fight what had been described as a national epidemic of family violence, but a similar bill died in the House.

The Senate bill (S 2759) was passed by voice vote Aug. 1. It authorized up to $30 million a year in fiscal 1979-83 for grants to states and other agencies for "spouse abuse" shelters and other community activities designed to prevent family violence and treat victims.

The House defeated similar legislation (HR 12299) May 23. The bill was brought up under suspension of the rules, which requires a two-thirds vote for passage. It was defeated 201-205, and was not brought up again under regular procedures. *(Vote 302, p. 86-H)*

The House measure, in the drafting stages for more than a year, authorized up to $125 million during fiscal 1979-83, primarily for the community shelters. It was reported May 10 by the House Education and Labor Committee (H Rept 95-1127).

The sponsors were stunned by defeat of the bill. They viewed spouse abuse as a major social ill, with millions of persons, mostly women but also some men, beaten each year by their spouses, and felt the magnitude of the problem was recognized by other legislators. No opposition had surfaced during subcommittee hearings and sponsors did not think the modest amounts of federal spending authorized by the bill — $15 million for fiscal 1979 — would create any outcry.

Even some opponents were surprised at the vote. John M. Ashbrook, R-Ohio, one of two members to criticize the bill during floor debate, initially doubted that more than a couple of dozen legislators would vote against the bill. But the rhetoric of Ashbrook and M. Caldwell Butler, R-Va., who also argued against the bill, apparently had some impact.

Among reasons members cited for voting against the bill were: the feeling that the federal government should not intrude in what should be a state or local matter; unwillingness to add to federal spending or to the programs of the Department of Health, Education and Welfare (HEW); the feeling that spouse abuse programs could be run through the Law Enforcement Assistance Administration with only minor changes in existing law, and resentment over the large number of bills brought up under suspension, which bars members from proposing amendments.

Senate Bill

The Senate bill was reported by the Human Resources Committee May 15 (S Rept 95-824) and adopted without amendment Aug. 1.

Floor manager Alan Cranston, D-Calif., urged its passage, saying the federal government should take the lead in dealing with a social problem that he said has had tremendous costs for both the victims and American society in general.

After the bill was passed by a voice vote, Harry F. Byrd Jr., Ind-Va., asked to be recorded as voting "no," and launched into a criticism of the measure. "I think the citizens of the United States — the hard-working taxpayers, as well as the retired persons on fixed incomes — need protection from the devastating ravages of inflation far more than they need any new multimillion-dollar programs at HEW," Byrd asserted.

As passed by the Senate, S 2759:

- Authorized up to $30 million a year in fiscal 1979-83 for domestic violence programs.
- Established a National Center on Domestic Violence in the Department of Health, Education and Welfare (HEW) to administer the grant programs and act as an information clearinghouse for domestic violence programs.
- Authorized regional centers on domestic violence.
- Provided for research into the causes of domestic violence.
- Established an Interagency Coordinating Council to coordinate federal domestic violence programs and promote the use of volunteers serving under the Domestic Volunteers Service Act of 1973 in such programs. ▮

Kidney Dialysis Program

President Carter June 13 signed into law legislation (HR 8423 — PL 95-292) to encourage persons with end stage renal disease (kidney failure) to conduct their own dialysis treatments at home or in special self-care facilities with professional assistance, or to choose kidney transplants. Both were said by proponents to be less expensive and more healthful alternatives to costly hospital-based dialysis.

Under existing law, home dialysis patients had to bear a substantially greater portion of the treatment costs than those entering hospitals for the life-sustaining treatments.

The measure, a compromise between House- and Senate-passed measures, emphasized priorities of regional planning groups and individual physicians and patients in selecting appropriate treatment. Provisions endorsed by the House in 1977 for a strong federal role involving national goals and sanctions for enforcing those goals were watered down. Health committee sources credited these changes partly to fallout from a controversy that erupted in the fall of 1977 over national health planning goals.

Soaring Medicare spending for hospital-based dialysis, coupled with a dramatic decline in less costly home care, prompted congressional action. Since 1972, when Congress created the Medicare renal disease program, the number of patients dialyzing at home had dropped to 10 percent from 40 percent, largely because of the financial incentives introduced for hospital treatment, according to proponents. The annual bill for the program was $1 billion and had been projected to reach $6 billion by 1992 — for a relatively small patient population (estimated to reach 75,000).

Provisions

As signed into law, HR 8423:

- Waived the three-month waiting period for Medicare coverage of dialysis costs for patients who enroll in a self-dialysis training program.
- Authorized Medicare reimbursement for all supplies used in home care and for periodic monitoring and maintenance visits at home by trained dialysis personnel.
- Also authorized reimbursement to facilities that set up and maintained self-dialysis units for patients interested in self-care but unable to perform it at home.
- Authorized Medicare to reimburse dialysis facilities for the "reasonable cost" of buying and installing and maintaining dialysis machines in patients' homes.
- Broadened Medicare coverage for patients undergoing kidney transplant operations. The new coverage included up to three months of hospitalization while awaiting a kidney transplant and coverage for 36 months after surgery, compared to 12 months under existing law. If the transplant failed, hospital coverage would resume immediately.
- Stipulated that Medicare coverage included kidney donors as well as recipients.
- To increase cost-effectiveness, directed the secretary of Health, Education and Welfare (HEW) to implement new reimbursement methods, such as setting rates prospectively, establishing target rates and classifying comparable facilities. Facilities that improved management and thereby cut costs would keep part of these savings.
- Directed the secretary to establish a network of renal disease peer review organizations that would set goals for identifying patients for self-care or transplants and oversee dialysis facilities; required patient membership in the organizations.
- Authorized the secretary to prohibit, by regulation, conflicts of interest in the membership of the individual review organizations making up the national network.
- Authorized the secretary to promulgate national guidelines, for advisory purposes only, for renal disease treatment.
- Directed the regional peer review organizations to identify facilities and providers "not cooperating" with the established goals, and assist them in developing plans to facilitate cooperation.
- Authorized the secretary to suspend or end approval ("certification") for reimbursement to uncooperative facilities until the department found "reasonable efforts" toward cooperation with the goals. These decisions would be partially based on annual reports on performance of providers submitted by the network review organizations.
- Authorized the secretary to base decisions to certify new or expanded facilities partly on the network's goals and performance.
- Stated that Congress intended that the maximum number of patients for whom home dialysis or kidney transplant was "medically, socially and psychologically" acceptable use those treatments.
- Authorized pilot projects in the purchase of new or used dialysis machines for home use by patients, and experiments to reduce program costs and encourage donation of kidneys and other organs.

Legislative History

House Action

The House passed HR 8423 Sept. 12, 1977. The bill stated a national goal, that a majority of new renal disease patients use self-dialysis or receive a kidney transplant. It also directed the regional units of the network to set goals for identifying patients for self-care or transplants, and to review regional facilities' success in meeting those goals. Under the House bill a regional agency could report facilities that consistently failed to meet these goals to the secretary of Health, Education and Welfare (HEW), who could withhold a facility's certification. Areas with low self-dialysis rates could lose federal certification for additional facilities or beds. *(1977 Almanac p. 517)*

Senate Action

With no discussion and without objection the Senate April 10 passed HR 8423 by voice vote.

The Senate-passed bill, which was reported by the Finance Committee March 22 (S Rept 95-714), was in most respects identical to the version the House approved in 1977. But several changes made by the Finance Committee were disturbing to members of the House Ways and Means Committee, who requested a conference.

The House members were concerned with Senate deletion of provisions for a national dialysis policy and related language that spelled out responsibilities of a national "network" of peer review agencies.

The Senate bill retained the review network but limited its functions to advice and review. According to a Finance Committee aide, this change and elimination of the national goal reflected backlash against unpopular 1977 HEW hospital use guidelines. Doctors' objections that a national goal would distort decisions on the best treatment for individual patients were also a factor. *(Hospital guidelines controversy, 1977 Almanac p. 523)*

The deleted goal was itself a watered-down remnant of the original bill, which had set specific percentages of patients that should perform self-dialysis — by set deadlines. That provision grew from allegations of profiteering and conflict of interest on the part of physicians involved with dialysis facilities.

House members also found "too sweeping" Senate language barring persons with financial interests in dialysis facilities from membership in the review network units, according to a Ways and Means aide.

Final Action

The final compromise, introduced by Dan Rostenkowski, D-Ill., chairman of the House Ways and Means Health Subcommittee, followed Senate action in deleting the numerical national goal. Instead, each entity in a national network of dialysis peer review organizations would establish goals for its own region. National goals could be articulated by federal guidelines, but these would only be advisory. However, HEW could end or suspend Medicare reimbursement of facilities that did not cooperate with regional goals established by the peer review organizations.

The House approved the compromise language May 1 without objection, and the Senate followed suit May 24 by voice vote, clearing the bill.

Child Pornography

President Carter Feb. 6 signed into law legislation (S 1585—PL 95-225) making it a federal crime to use children for prostitution or the production of pornographic materials.

The bill, cleared Jan. 24 by a 401-0 House vote, also banned the sale and distribution of obscene materials depicting children in sexually explicit conduct if the materials were mailed or transported in interstate commerce. *(Vote 9, p. 4-H)*

The Senate had approved the conference report on S 1585 Nov. 4, 1977. *(1977 Almanac p. 521)*

Congress acted in response to evidence that the sexual exploitation of children for profit had become a multimillion-dollar-a-year business in the United States.

John Conyers Jr., D-Mich., chairman of the House Judiciary Subcommittee on Crime, which drew up the bill, praised Congress for approving legislation "which is both constitutional and protects the rights of children."

Conyers was the leader of the House conferees who insisted on adding the word "obscene" to the section of the bill penalizing sellers and distributors of child pornography.

The original House bill did not cover distributors, but the House instructed its conferees to accept the Senate-passed "Roth amendment," which did. Conyers and others, including Justice Department attorneys, had feared the bill would be declared unconstitutional on First Amendment grounds unless it specified that pornographic materials must be obscene if sellers and distributors were to be prosecuted under the act.

Several House members, including Dale E. Kildee, D-Mich., House sponsor of the Roth amendment language, said that although they felt insertion of the word "obscene" watered down the bill somewhat, the measure still would provide significant new protection for children.

John M. Ashbrook, R-Ohio, said passage of the bill put the attorney general "on notice that the Congress expects some special treatment, some special prosecution of those who would profiteer from child abuse, child pornography and the sexual exploitation of minors."

Conyers said that although the bill did not set a stricter standard of obscenity for materials using children, as some members had suggested, "we are confident that juries will find materials with children in them obscene under present standards."

Provisions. As cleared by Congress, S 1585:

- Made it a federal crime to cause any child under 16 to engage in sexually explicit conduct for the purpose of producing materials that are mailed or transported in interstate commerce, or if the person knows or has reason to know that the materials are intended to be so used. A parent or guardian who knowingly permitted a minor to engage in such behavior would also be guilty.

- Prohibited the sale or distribution of any obscene materials that depict children engaging in sexually explicit conduct if such materials have been mailed or transported in interstate commerce.

- Provided penalties of up to 10 years in prison and $10,000 fines for first offenders; minimum penalties of 2 years in prison and maximum penalties of 15 years and $15,000 fines for repeat offenders.

- Prohibited the interstate transportation of males as well as females under 18 for the purpose of engaging in prostitution or other sexually explicit conduct for commercial purposes; provided penalties of up to $10,000 and 10 years in prison for violation of this section.

Social Services Claims

President Carter June 12 signed into law a bill clearing the way for settlement of a longstanding dispute over social services claims between 28 states and the Department of Health, Education and Welfare (HEW).

The measure (HR 11370 — PL 95-291) provided $543 million for HEW to distribute to the states to settle the claims. It was passed by the House May 23 by a 377-25 vote and by the Senate May 25 by voice vote. *(Vote 306, p. 88-H)*

The dispute began in 1972 when HEW refused to pay about $1.6 billion to 19 states and sought reimbursement of about $830 million from 22 states, including 13 of the first group of 19.

HEW had changed the criteria for states to qualify for federal aid for a variety of social service programs, including day care, welfare and drug abuse programs, and then used the new criteria to disallow new claims and seek reimbursement of payments already made to states.

On taking office, HEW Secretary Joseph A. Califano Jr. initiated a negotiated settlement in order to dispose of the claims without tying up federal lawyers in years of court actions.

Under the terms of the settlement, the states accepted the $543 million instead of $1.6 billion and HEW agreed to drop its efforts to recover the $830 million.

Older Americans Act

Congress Oct. 6 cleared legislation extending through fiscal 1981 the Older Americans Act, the basic federal government effort on behalf of the nation's 35 million elderly citizens.

The legislation (HR 12255 — PL 95-478) consolidated the administrative structure of programs for the aging, substantially increased authorizations for various social services, health and nutrition programs, and continued the push for improved legal protections for older Americans, especially those confined to nursing and rest homes. It established a separate authorization for home-delivered meals for the elderly, in addition to group feeding programs already in the bill.

For fiscal 1979-81, HR 12255 authorized $4 billion for social services, nutrition programs, multipurpose centers, community jobs and volunteer programs for persons 60 or more years old.

Claude Pepper, D-Fla., the 78-year-old chairman of the House Select Committee on Aging, described HR 12255 as a "renewed commitment" by Congress to "improve the lives of older people and to assure them a decent place in our society."

The program had grown tremendously in the 13 years since it was enacted. When the act was passed in 1965 (PL 89-73), the authorization was only $17.5 million. For fiscal 1976-78, Congress authorized $1.7 billion. The act was last extended in 1975. *(1975 Almanac p. 680; 1965 Almanac p. 356)*

The House had passed HR 12255 on May 15, the Senate on July 24.

Provisions

As cleared by Congress, HR 12255:

Older Americans. Extended the Older Americans Act of 1965 for three years, through fiscal 1981.

- Consolidated administration of social services, multipurpose centers and nutrition programs.
- Authorized $730 million for fiscal 1979, $835 million for fiscal 1980 and $1 billion for fiscal 1981 for programs under the act. *(Authorizations, box, this page)*
- Gave the Commissioner on Aging in the Department of Health, Education and Welfare (HEW) the authority to review and comment on all federal policies affecting the elderly; required him to advise, consult and cooperate with heads of other federal agencies that run programs involving the elderly; required them to consult with him before establishing programs that substantially involve the elderly.
- Prohibited full-time officers or employees of the federal government from serving on the Federal Council on Aging; eliminated the requirement that the secretary of HEW and the Commissioner on Aging serve as ex officio members of the council; authorized the council to have its own independent staff, appointed by the chairman; required it to conduct a study examining the purposes and effectiveness of programs authorized by the Older Americans Act.
- Required the National Information and Resource Clearinghouse for the Aging to collect information on transportation services for the elderly provided by federal, state and local public agencies.
- Required the Commissioner on Aging to prepare a study on the need for a separate legal services program under the Older Americans Act.
- Allowed grant and contract recipients to enter into agreements with profit-making organizations, provided the organizations demonstrated "clear superiority" over public agencies in regard to the services they offered.
- Expanded the purposes of the Older Americans Act to include providing "a continuum of care" for the "vulnerable" elderly; added health screening and pre-retirement and second career counseling as eligible services to be offered under the social services section of the act.
- Eliminated separate authorizations for multipurpose centers, legal services and ombudsman programs, merging them under authorizations for social services.
- Required states to reserve $20,000, or 1 percent of their social services allotments, whichever is greater, to establish and operate long-term care ombudsman programs.
- Required state agencies on aging to establish procedures to assure the confidentiality of files maintained by ombudsman programs.
- Prohibited associations of long-term care facilities from being designated to administer ombudsman programs.
- Retained the existing funding formula, which based a state's share of federal funds under the act on the relative proportion of persons aged 60 or over; increased the amount earmarked for rural areas in each state by 5 percent; added a waiver provision for those states which showed that there were insufficient numbers of rural elderly to warrant the 5 percent increase or that they were already meeting the needs of the rural elderly.
- Allowed the Commissioner on Aging to contract with public or private agencies within a state to run social services programs if the state failed to qualify for funds.
- Established a 3-year planning cycle for area agencies.
- Required that 50 percent of each area agency's social services allotment be spent on programs associated with access, in-home services and legal services.
- Required area agencies to designate where feasible a "focal point" for service delivery in order to improve coordination of services.
- Required that area plans give preference to elderly persons with the greatest economic or social needs; required area agencies to "make assurances" that they will conduct outreach activities, with special emphasis on the rural elderly.
- Allowed area agencies to enter into agreements with other agencies administering programs under the

Authorizations

As cleared by Congress, HR 12255 authorized a total of $4.042 billion for fiscal 1979-81 for programs for older Americans, as follows *(in millions of dollars)*:

	1979	1980	1981
Social services	$ 300	$ 360	$ 480
Congregate meals	350	375	400
Home-delivered meals	80	100	120
Subtotal, Older Americans Act programs	$ 730	$ 835	$1,000
Community service employment for the elderly	350	400	450
Volunteer programs for the elderly	80	92.5	105
Total	$1,160	$1,327.5	$1,555

Rehabilitation and Social Security Acts to develop and implement coordinated transportation services.

• Required that 25 percent of the non-federal share for the delivery of social services be met from state or local public sources.

• Allowed the Commissioner on Aging to reimburse states for funds provided for disaster relief, providing up to 5 percent of a state's social services allotment; required the commissioner to set aside 5 percent of funds appropriated for model projects for disaster relief payments.

• Authorized a minimum level of assistance per meal of 30 cents in fiscal 1979-81.

• Required the Commissioner on Aging to develop and implement a national manpower policy, in cooperation with other federal agencies.

• Required the Commissioner on Aging to conduct several studies, including one exploring the possibility of transferring all federal transportation programs to a single administrative unit and a second on the differences in costs, service delivery and access between rural and urban areas for the elderly.

• Authorized grants to organizations and agencies to develop "comprehensive, coordinated systems of community long-term care" for the elderly.

• Reserved $5 million of authorizations for model projects for special demonstration projects on legal services for the elderly, and up to 15 percent of model project appropriations to develop projects of "national significance."

• Authorized the secretary of HEW to establish model projects designed to relieve elderly Americans of the "burdens of high utility service and home heating costs."

• Authorized insurance under the National Housing Act of mortgages for construction of multipurpose centers.

Community Service Employment. Extended the community service employment program for the elderly for three years, through fiscal 1981; authorized $350 million for fiscal 1979, $400 million for fiscal 1980 and $450 million for fiscal 1981.

• Authorized the secretary of labor, after consulting with the administrator of the Environmental Protection Agency (EPA) and the secretary of energy, to create part-time jobs for the elderly involving environmental improvement and energy conservation.

• Authorized the secretary to develop innovative job opportunities for the elderly through work sharing and other experimental programs, involving prime sponsors in the Comprehensive Employment and Training Act (CETA) program, labor organizations, business and industry.

• Authorized the secretary of labor on his own or by request to review intrastate distribution of community service employment funds.

• Authorized the secretary of labor to enter into agreements to assure transition of public service jobs to the private sector.

• Raised the income eligibility criteria from the poverty index to 125 percent of the poverty index.

Indian Tribes. Authorized the Commissioner on Aging to make grants to Indian tribes for social services, legal services, nutrition programs and ombudsman programs for Indians 60 years or older.

Volunteer Programs. Extended volunteer programs for the elderly under the Domestic Volunteer Service Act of 1973 for three years, through fiscal 1981.

• Authorized $25 million for fiscal 1979, $30 million for fiscal 1980 and $35 million for fiscal 1981 for the Retired Senior Volunteer Program (RSVP), and $55 million for fiscal 1979, $62.5 million for fiscal 1980 and $70 million for fiscal 1981 for the foster grandparent/senior companion program.

• Raised the foster grandparent/senior companion stipend to $2 per hour, conditioned upon enough money being appropriated to maintain the existing level of participation in the program.

• Extended eligibility for participation in foster grandparent/senior companion programs to elderly persons with incomes up to 125 percent of the poverty level; gave special consideration for participation to elderly with incomes at or below the poverty level.

White House Conference on Aging. Authorized a White House Conference on Aging in 1981.

Racial and Ethnic Study. Required the U.S. Commission on Civil Rights to conduct a study of discrimination based on race or ethnic background in any federal program which affects older persons.

Age Discrimination. Allowed persons who claimed to be harmed by alleged violations of the Age Discrimination Act of 1975 to file civil suits; required that all administrative remedies be exhausted first.

House Committee Action

The House Education and Labor Committee reported HR 12255 on May 13 (H Rept 95-1150). The bill authorized a total of $789 million in fiscal 1979, $911 million in fiscal 1980 and $1.08 billion in fiscal 1981 for Older Americans Act programs.

The committee recommended changes in the administration of the social services and nutrition programs at both the federal and local levels.

In an effort to enhance the political clout of the elderly within the federal bureaucracy, the committee proposed to have the Commissioner on Aging report directly to the secretary of HEW rather than to an assistant secretary, as under existing law. That would help make the commissioner a more "effective and visible advocate" for the elderly, the committee said.

The committee also recommended that the Federal Council on Aging, an advisory body, have its own staff because of the "unwillingness of the Department of HEW to provide the necessary staff and resources." It also recommended removing the HEW secretary and the commissioner of aging from the council in order to make it a more independent advocate for the elderly.

At the local level, the committee recommended establishing one administrative structure to run the social services, multipurpose center and nutrition programs. Under the existing program, about 40 percent of the nutrition programs were run independently of the social service projects and multipurpose centers, which were administered by area agencies on aging. The area agencies usually covered one or several counties within a state.

To ensure adequate funding for all three programs, the committee recommended that separate authorizations for each grant program be continued, but it said placing nutrition programs under the administration of area agencies would "eliminate duplicative and overlapping functions" in such areas as outreach, advocacy, planning and staff training.

The committee cited data compiled by the Administration on Aging, which showed that in 1977 about 2.8 million elderly participated in the nutrition program. "That means that only about one out of three of the estimated 8 million older persons eligible for the program are being served," the committee said.

Nutrition program directors, fearful of losing their independence and control over their operations, lobbied against the consolidation, but the committee sided with the area agencies.

"It is . . . the committee's hope that consolidation will increase the visibility, political strength and significance of area agencies on aging in the community. . .," it said.

By authorizing the volunteer programs for the elderly run by ACTION for only one year instead of three, the committee said it "put ACTION on notice that its handling of these programs will be closely watched by Congress during the next year."

The Carter administration had proposed a fund cut in the Retired Senior Volunteer Program (RSVP) which would have meant the dropping of 30,000 volunteers, an action the committee called "unreasonable, unwarranted and insensitive." After protests from members of Congress and senior citizens, the fund cut was restored.

House Floor Action

The House passed the three-year extension of the Older Americans Act on May 15. The politically popular measure (HR 12255) sailed through by a 361-6 vote under suspension of the rules. *(Vote 270, p. 78-H)*

The bill authorized $4.2 billion in spending during fiscal 1979-81, a sharp increase over the $1.7 billion authorized by Congress for fiscal 1976-78. The bill also consolidated the administration of programs under the act, and extended for one year several volunteer programs for the elderly run by ACTION under the Domestic Volunteer Service Act.

Senate Committee Action

The Senate Human Resources Committee reported the bill May 15 (S 2850 — S Rept 95-855). The committee focused attention on what it described as the "fragmentation" of the federal approach to assisting senior citizens by citing the proliferation of programs in seven areas: employment, health care, housing, income maintenance, social services, training and research and transportation.

The committee said there were nine employment programs in one executive department and two independent agencies; seven health care programs in two departments and one independent agency; 10 housing programs in two executive departments; six income maintenance programs in two departments and three agencies; 11 social services programs in two departments and two agencies; six training and research programs in one department, and four transportation programs in one department.

Therefore, the committee said, it sought to avoid further fragmentation in developing the 1978 amendments to the Older Americans Act, and proposed consolidation of existing service titles under the act. Further, it said it limited the extension of the act to two years since the Carter administration had pledged "major policy decisions" in the field of aging in 1979.

In proposing the consolidation of service programs, the committee took an approach somewhat similar to that taken by the House committee. Both the Senate and House bills placed control of the social services, health and nutrition programs in the hands of area agencies on aging, which usually cover one or several counties within a state.

The House, however, retained separate authorizations for each of the programs established by the act. The Senate bill abolished the separate authorizations, except in the case of nutrition programs.

The Senate committee report said the separate authorization was retained to assure that "funds appropriated for nutrition will be reserved for that purpose." However, it declared that "nutrition services are not to operate in isolation from other social services within the community."

The committee also sought to prod area agencies into providing more in-depth services by requiring that at least 50 percent of each area agency's allotment be targeted for programs involving so-called "access services" (transportation, outreach, and information and referral), in-home services (homemaker-home health aides, visiting/telephone reassurance and chore-maintenance) and legal services.

The committee said that despite 1975 amendments to the Older Americans Act designed to establish priority programs, it was "concerned that few services are provided in-depth in local communities." Rather, the committee said, "there appears to be a scatter-gun attempt to provide a wide array of services, none of which adequately serves the needs of the elderly in the community."

Senate Floor Action

The Senate passed S 2850 by an 85-2 vote on July 24. *(Vote 239, p. 38-S)*

The two-year extension of the act authorized expenditures of $1.2 billion in fiscal 1979 and nearly $1.4 billion in fiscal 1980.

Home-Delivered Meals

Floor debate focused primarily on an amendment offered by Edward M. Kennedy, D-Mass., to provide separate authorizations for home-delivered meals with spending ceilings of $100 million for fiscal 1979 and $120 million for fiscal 1980.

The Kennedy amendment was adopted by a 59-29 vote after the Senate rejected, by a 30-60 vote, a motion by Thomas F. Eagleton, D-Mo., to table the Kennedy amendment. *(Votes 234, 235, p. 37-S)*

Eagleton was chairman of the Human Resources Subcommittee on Aging, which is responsible for the Older Americans Act. Kennedy was the second-ranking Democrat on the subcommittee. While both men vigorously advocated passage of S 2850, they disagreed vehemently on the need for a separate authorization for home-delivered meals.

Kennedy argued that under the existing structure the two basic nutrition programs — congregate meals and home-delivered meals — were forced to compete with each other. He claimed his amendment would provide for 215,000 home-delivered meals daily in fiscal 1979 and 258,000 meals daily in fiscal 1980. In 1978, he said, only about 72,000 home-delivered meals were served daily.

He further argued that his amendment would not reduce support for the congregate meals, under which meals for the elderly are served daily at group settings such as churches, schools and senior citizen centers. In 1978, about 480,000 persons received meals daily under that program. The proposed authorizations for the nutrition program — $375 million in fiscal 1979 and $425 million in fiscal 1980 —

would provide for 800,000 meals daily in 1979 and 900,000 meals in 1980.

Kennedy acknowledged that "we are going to hear complaints" that the amendment exceeded the budget targets, but he said that unless a separate authorization was established, "we are effectively putting the needy elderly people and the shut-ins in conflict with each other to try and get the scarce resources."

Eagleton argued that the Kennedy amendment increased the authorizations for the nutrition program far more than necessary, pointing out that the authorizations already in the bill represented a 50 percent increase from existing spending levels.

Eagleton hinted that the Kennedy amendment might result in a presidential veto. He read excerpts from a letter from HEW Secretary Joseph A. Califano Jr., stating the administration's opposition to the Kennedy amendment on budgetary grounds.

Eagleton moved to table the amendment, but Kennedy had the votes. Kennedy did accept one change in the amendment, allowing a provision by William D. Hathaway, D-Maine, to give states the authority to use funds allocated under the basic nutrition program for home-delivered meals, if the separate allocation for home-delivered meals did not provide enough money to meet the demand.

Other Amendments

The Senate adopted 16 other amendments to S 2850, most of which involved technical changes designed to clarify various administrative provisions in the legislation.

Besides the Kennedy amendment, an amendment offered by Pete V. Domenici, R-N.M., generated some debate, although it was eventually adopted by voice vote.

The Domenici amendment altered the funding formula so largely rural states would receive proportionally more money for social services, health and nutrition programs.

Domenici said he proposed the amendment because, "it costs more to deliver the services to those who live in small communities in the rural parts of our respective states than it does in big cities."

Critics disagreed. "It is a very expensive proposition to live in a city, not just New York City, or Providence, or St. Louis or Kansas City, cities of even more modest size," said Eagleton. "To say there is to be built in an inherent bias, a tilt, in formula in favor of rural America to the detriment of urban America, I think is to belie the fact of where the great social needs of this country exist today," he added.

But Domenici had lined up enough votes. That was evident when the Senate rejected a compromise offered by Jacob K. Javits, R-N.Y., that would have left the formula intact but given the HEW secretary discretion to use up to $5 million to offset excessive costs in rural areas. The Javits compromise was rejected by a 22-70 vote. *(Vote 238, p. 38-S)*

At that point, Eagleton and other opponents of the Domenici amendment realized that they had lost and did not bother to seek a roll call on the amendment, allowing it to be adopted on a voice vote.

Under existing law, Older Americans funds were distributed on the basis of the number of elderly Americans 60 years old or above in each state. The Domenici amendment would add a second factor in determining the fund distribution. After the number of elderly Americans had been calculated for each state, one-half of the number of elderly living in rural areas would be added to the total elderly population. Funds would then be proportioned to the states.

However, no state would lose money, as the Domenici amendment included a "hold harmless" provision that would ensure that each state receives no less than it did during fiscal 1978. In effect, the new formula would apply to new monies allocated in the coming years.

Conference Action

Conferees filed their report on HR 12255 (H Rept 95-1618) on Sept. 22.

Conferees had little difficulty resolving differences in the two versions of the legislation, trading off on most provisions, usually accepting whichever side was more favorable to the elderly.

Senate conferees accepted a three-year authorization for the act, as favored by the House. The Senate version had contained a two-year authorization.

House conferees agreed to eliminate separate authorizations for multipurpose centers, legal services and ombudsman programs, accepting a Senate provision merging them with authorizations for social services.

In establishing the home-delivered meals program, the conferees said they expected the administration to "follow carefully" the development of the program and "discourage its use unless necessary" because of such factors as illness, an incapacitating disability or extreme transportation problems.

The conferees required that each meals project provide at least one "hot, or other appropriate" meal per day. The phrase "other appropriate" was included to allow flexibility in cases where climatic conditions may make the serving of a hot meal undesirable. Despite the flexibility, however, the conferees made it clear the emphasis should be on hot meals.

Elderly Volunteer Programs

Senate conferees agreed to include in HR 12255 amendments to the various programs for elderly Americans authorized in the Domestic Volunteer Service Act of 1973. The House had included these amendments in HR 12255, but the Senate amendments initially were included in S 2617, a separate authorization measure for the entire volunteer services act. Congress failed to complete action on S 2617. *(Story, p. 635)*

The House had called for a one-year extension of the programs in order to put ACTION, the agency that administers them, "on notice that its handling of these programs will be closely watched by Congress during the next year."

ACTION had proposed earlier in 1978 a substantial reduction in the volunteer programs for the elderly in order to concentrate more on various community organizing activities. However, objections from key congressmen resulted in a restoration of the proposed cuts.

In conference, the House agreed to go along with the Senate and endorse a three-year authorization for the elderly volunteer programs. However, the conference agreement noted that House and Senate committees intended to conduct "regular oversight" on all facets of ACTION's administration of the programs, with "special scrutiny" of ACTION's budget requests in fiscal 1980 and future years. The oversight would be conducted to "assess the extent of the

ACTION agency's commitment" to the elderly volunteer programs, and to determine whether administration of the programs should be transferred to the Administration on Aging, the conferees said.

Final Action

The House approved the conference report on HR 12255 on Oct. 4 by a 399-3 vote. The Senate followed suit Oct. 6 by voice vote. *(House vote 762, p. 216-H)*

New Head Start Formula

Ending a politically sensitive dispute with "Snow Belt-Sun Belt" overtones, Congress established a new formula for distributing federal funds for Head Start programs across the country. The new formula was designed to equalize, over time, the distribution of Head Start funds to all states, ending the emphasis on about 25 states, mostly in the South.

The formula was contained in legislation (HR 7577—PL 95-568) extending the Economic Opportunity Act of 1964 for three years, through fiscal 1981, and making other, less significant changes in Head Start and other poverty programs established under the act.

Congress cleared HR 7577 Oct. 15 after House and Senate conferees ended a month-long deadlock and worked out an agreement on the Head Start formula, the most important aspect of the legislation.

Except for the Head Start formula, HR 7577 made no major changes and established no new programs. Rather, the legislation concentrated on improving the administration of programs run by the Community Services Administration (CSA) and the Department of Health, Education and Welfare (HEW).

The legislation might make it possible for local community action agencies to receive more federal money in the future. HR 7577 increased the federal share of funding for the grass-roots agencies to 80 percent, from 60 percent, and reduced the share of funding required from local communities to 20 percent, from 40 percent.

But additional federal funds would be available only if Congress increased the appropriation for the community action programs. If the appropriation was not increased, local agencies would wind up with less funds because, while the actual amount of federal money they would receive would remain the same, their local shares would be reduced.

Because HR 7577 cleared Congress so late, the Appropriations Committees did not have time to consider the fiscal 1979 budget request for any of the programs authorized under HR 7577. That would be done as part of the fiscal 1979 supplemental budget.

Under the new Head Start formula most states would receive increased allocations for fiscal 1979, although that assumed eventual approval by Congress of the $680 million requested by the administration for Head Start for fiscal 1979. The new formula guaranteed that no state would receive less than it did during fiscal 1978.

With some exceptions the new formula would parcel out Head Start money on the basis of a poverty index that took into account a state's share of low-income children 5 years old and younger, and the number of recipients in each state's Aid to Families with Dependent Children (AFDC) program. *(State allocations, box, this page)*

As approved by Congress, the new formula would distribute at least 78 percent of the total Head Start appropriation to states on the basis of the poverty index. The remaining funds would be set aside for various uses, including "hold harmless" payments to make sure that all states received at least what they did during fiscal 1978, and special supplemental payments to provide small increases to several states that were slightly "over-funded" in the past.

The new formula was largely the result of private negotiations involving congressional staff and key members of the conference committee — Carl D. Perkins, D-Ky., chairman of the House Education and Labor Committee, and Gaylord Nelson, D-Wis., chairman of the Senate Human Resources Subcommittee on Employment and Poverty.

Reflecting a position initially taken by Nelson and others whose states were "under-funded" in the past, the new formula was designed to ensure that all states eventually will receive funds solely on the basis of the poverty index. The formula also took into account a concern voiced by Perkins and others whose states were "over-funded" and would lose money if allocations were based solely on the index. The new formula guaranteed that no "over-funded" state would receive less than it did during fiscal 1978. It also allowed for slight increases for states that had been moderately "over-funded" in the past, such as Kentucky.

The guarantee was based primarily on the assumption that Congress would provide yearly increases in the appropriation for Head Start.

Provisions

As cleared by Congress, HR 7577:

- Extended the Economic Opportunity Act of 1964 for three years, through fiscal 1981.

Head Start Funds

Based on a proposed appropriation of $680 million for fiscal 1979, most states would receive increases in Head Start funds ranging from 6 to 11 percent under the new formula.

Six states considerably "over-funded" in the past would not receive any increases.

Receiving increases of 10.97 percent would be Arizona, California, Connecticut, Georgia, Illinois, Maryland, Massachusetts, Michigan, Nevada, New Jersey, New York, North Dakota, Ohio, Oregon, Pennsylvania, Puerto Rico, Rhode Island, South Dakota, Texas, Utah, Virginia, Washington and Wisconsin.

The following would receive increases of 6 percent: Alabama, Arkansas, Delaware, District of Columbia, Hawaii, Idaho, Iowa, Kansas, Kentucky, Louisiana, Minnesota, Missouri, Montana, Nebraska, New Hampshire, New Mexico, North Carolina, South Carolina, Tennessee and Vermont.

Florida would receive an increase of 6.47 percent, Indiana, 8.86 percent, and Maine, 8.21 per cent.

The six states that would not receive any increases under the formula are Alaska, Colorado, Mississippi, Oklahoma, West Virginia and Wyoming.

- Authorized $5 million for fiscal 1979, $6 million for fiscal 1980 and $8 million for fiscal 1981 for research and demonstration programs.
- Removed the prohibition against establishing a community action agency (CAA) in a county or multicounty unit with a total population under 50,000. This should make it easier to establish community action agencies in rural areas.
- Required a minimum of 15 persons to serve on the board of a local CAA in order to ensure a minimum level of participation by the local community.
- Allowed public and private non-profit agencies to operate summer youth recreation programs in areas where community action agencies do not exist or are unable to run the programs.
- Established an experimental employment and training program for low-income persons who are unemployed or underemployed, with special emphasis on youth.
- Set the federal share of financial assistance to community action agencies at 80 percent, and the local share at 20 percent.
- Placed a ceiling of $18,000 per year on employee salaries, but allowed exceptions in cases where there is a need for specialized or professional skills or where prevailing local salaries are considerably higher than $18,000.
- Authorized $3 million for fiscal 1979, $5 million for fiscal 1980 and $7 million for fiscal 1981 for special poverty programs in rural areas.
- Authorized $3 million for fiscal 1979, $5 million for fiscal 1980 and $8 million for fiscal 1981 for national programs for migrant and other seasonal farm workers.
- Established a formula for distributing federal funds for Head Start programs across the country; based the formula primarily on a state's relative share of children ages 0-5 living with families with incomes below the poverty level and a state's relative share of AFDC (Aid to Families with Dependent Children) recipients.
- Required the secretary of HEW to distribute at least 78 percent of the Head Start appropriation on the basis of the formula.
- Required the HEW secretary to reserve 20 percent of remaining Head Start funds for programs for Indians, migrants and handicapped youngsters, for "hold harmless" payments to ensure that no state receives less than it did in fiscal 1978, for training and technical assistance activities, and for other purposes to be determined by the secretary.
- Reserved the remaining 2 percent of funds for Head Start programs in the trust territories and special supplemental payments for states.
- Required the HEW secretary to operate Head Start programs in accordance with Head Start performance standards; prohibited any lowering of standards.
- Expanded eligibility for the Follow Through program to children who participated in other federally assisted pre-school programs besides Head Start.
- Specified the types of services that Follow Through programs are to provide. They include educational, health, nutritional, social and other comprehensive services.
- Authorized $70 million for fiscal 1979, $85 million for fiscal 1980 and $100 million for fiscal 1981 for the Follow Through program.
- Established public reporting requirements for research, demonstration and pilot projects conducted under the Follow Through program.
- Reduced the size of the National Advisory Council on Economic Opportunity from 21 to 15 members; required that at least one-third of the council membership be poor persons, one-third representatives of the poor, and one-third representatives of the general public.
- Extended the life of the council for three years, through fiscal 1981; prohibited the council from making expenditures that exceed $225,000 for fiscal 1979, $250,000 for fiscal 1980 and $275,000 for fiscal 1981.
- Required the director of the Community Services Administration (CSA) to consult with community action agencies and state economic opportunity offices in developing a five-year national poverty action plan.
- Authorized $70 million for fiscal 1979, $85 million for fiscal 1980 and $105 million for fiscal 1981 for community economic development programs.
- Authorized the president to establish a National Advisory Community Investment Board.
- Defined the type of programs that may be conducted by Community Development Corporations to include community business and commercial development, community physical development, training and public service employment, and social service programs that support and complement community business and commercial development programs; defined social service programs to include recreation services.
- Allowed cooperatives to be eligible for grants under community economic development programs; added community development credit unions to the list of projects that may be conducted with development loans.
- Authorized $4 million for fiscal 1979, $7 million for fiscal 1980 and $10 million for fiscal 1981 for evaluation of poverty programs.

Background

Distribution of Head Start funds had been an issue for several years. During the first 10 years of the program, until 1975, funds were allocated to individual programs solely at the discretion of the agency running Head Start — first the Office of Economic Opportunity and, since 1969, HEW.

The original intent was to channel the funds to states with high concentrations of poor people. As a result, congressional researchers found, a handful of states, mostly in the Southeast, received the great bulk of Head Start money in the early years of the program.

Mississippi, which by many measurements of social and economic health was considered the poorest state, benefited the most. According to congressional researchers, about 70 percent of Mississippi youngsters eligible for Head Start were enrolled in the program. Nationally, only 16 percent of those eligible were enrolled.

Not all southern states received disproportionately large allocations of funds, however. Congressional aides who studied Head Start funding said Georgia, for example, had been under-funded in relation to its poverty population, while several non-southern states, Wyoming and Alaska, had received substantially larger shares of funds than their number of poor people would indicate.

In 1974, Congress adopted a formula, effective in 1975, that was designed to distribute Head Start funds more equitably to the states. The formula was based on the number of pre-school children from low-income families and the number of welfare recipients in each state. The formula also included a "hold harmless" clause to ensure that no state would receive less money than it did in 1975. *(1974 Almanac p. 495)*

Application of the formula, however, had proved difficult. HEW and the two committees with jurisdiction over Head Start — House Education and Labor and Senate Human Resources — disagreed over how cost-of-living increases mandated by the Appropriations Committees for fiscal 1976, 1977 and 1978 should be calculated with respect to the "hold harmless" clause. The Congressional Research Service (CRS) and the General Accounting Office both were called in to study proposed HEW allocations of Head Start funds; both concluded that HEW did not follow the statutory formula in its allocations for fiscal 1978.

As a result, the CRS said, 24 states received less Head Start funding than they were eligible for based on their poverty population; the rest received more, with one state receiving nearly five times its fair share.

Consequently, both committees attempted again in 1978 to devise a more equitable funding formula.

CAA Funding

The change in the federal-local funding ratio for local community action agencies was sought by both the CSA and directors of the local programs. They argued that the 40 percent local contribution, which could be met either with cash or with "in-kind" contributions such as office furniture or supplies, was difficult to meet. The CSA said other poverty programs required only 20 percent local matching and cited other federal programs that required none.

The House committee noted in its report, "Every community action agency executive director who testified before the Subcommittee on Economic Opportunity expressed fear for the financial stability of their agencies under the existing financial assistance formula."

The committee also cited the ninth annual report of the National Advisory Council on Economic Opportunity, which urged the return to 80 percent federal funding because local communities "have been unable or unwilling to provide the funds necessary to compensate for the reduction in federal funding."

The Economic Opportunity Act of 1964 provided for a 90 percent federal share for community action programs. The share was decreased to 80 percent in 1967 after antipoverty programs had become more acceptable to communities. The formula was altered again in 1974, with the federal share reduced to 70 percent for fiscal 1976 and 60 percent for fiscal 1977. A slightly higher federal contribution was allowed for community action agencies in small towns and rural areas, with a $300,000 budget established as the maximum an agency could have and still receive a higher federal share. CSA was also given the authority to issue waivers to those agencies unable to raise the 40 percent local share.

House Committee Action

The House Education and Labor Committee wrote a formula it said would correct some of the inequities without reducing the funding for any existing Head Start program. It reported HR 7577 (H Rept 95-1151) on May 15.

The House formula would first set aside 13 percent of Head Start funds for programs in the territories and for discretionary use by the secretary of HEW. Second, each state would receive an amount equal to the amount it received in the previous fiscal year. This was in effect a floating "hold harmless" provision.

Third, most states would receive a 6 percent increase for cost-of-living. Eligibility for the cost-of-living increase would be determined by comparing the amount each state would be eligible to receive (of the Head Start funds not included in the 13 percent set aside for territories and discretionary use) on the basis of its number of welfare recipients and low-income children, to the amount the state actually was receiving. Those states that would receive less than 200 percent of the amount they were entitled to under the poverty formula would receive cost-of-living increases.

The formula was designed to provide new money for Head Start programs in all states except those that had been substantially "over-funded" during the last decade. According to data prepared by the committee, three states — Mississippi, Wyoming and Alaska — would not qualify for the 6 percent cost-of-living increase.

Finally, whatever funds were left would be distributed on the basis of the poverty formula: 50 percent based on the number of public assistance recipients in each state and 50 percent on the number of children aged 0-5 from low-income families.

According to committee statistics, all the states except Mississippi, Wyoming and Alaska would get total increases during fiscal 1979 of between 8 and 9 percent, based on an appropriation of $595 million.

"The new formula recognizes the history of the program and, unlike the current formula, provides for a distribution which will not seriously damage the programs of one state in order to benefit another," the committee said.

Committee sources said it made no sense, politically or otherwise, to reduce funds for a program that had turned out to be so successful and popular over the years.

House Floor Action

The House passed HR 7577 July 26 by a 346-38 vote after rejecting 158-224 an amendment by Bill Goodling, R-Pa., to restore the 60-40 federal-local funding match for community action agencies. *(Votes 529, 528, pp. 152-H, 150-H)*

Goodling conceded that increasing the federal share to 80 percent could result in more money if Congress were inclined to increase the appropriation. But, Goodling said, funding for community action agencies remained the same between 1972 and 1977, and was adjusted upward only slightly in fiscal 1978 to reflect the higher cost of living.

"Knowing the mood of the Congress at the present time and realizing the mood throughout the country, I cannot imagine that the Committee on Appropriations is going to be so generous as to come up with a 20 percent increase to offset what they (community action agencies) are going to lose on the local effort if we go to 80-20," Goodling said.

Proponents of the return to the 80 percent federal share, led by Perkins, argued that the 40 percent local contribution placed a hardship on community action agencies. "A return to 80-20 would allow local agency administrators to devote primary attention to program development and operation," rather than worrying about funding, Perkins said.

The existing 60-40 formula was "totally unrealistic in light of present economic conditions," Perkins said, particularly hurting rural areas with minimal tax resources and little private business.

Perkins acknowledged that if the total federal appropriation remained the same it "might be true" that the agencies would wind up with lower budgets.

But he said he hoped local communities would continue to provide contributions above the 20 percent requirement, and that the appropriations committees would increase the funding.

The House also approved by voice vote an amendment by Jerry Huckaby, D-La., that would make it easier to establish community action agencies in rural areas. Existing law prohibited their establishment in a county or multicounty unit with a total population under 50,000.

Huckaby's amendment removed the population barrier but still required a proposed agency to meet other eligibility criteria set by CSA, including the requirement that at least 20 percent of the area's families must be below the poverty level.

Senate Committee Action

The Senate Human Resources Committee reported its bill (S 2090) on May 15 (S Rept 95-892).

The committee took an approach to the formula problem that differed from the House. It did not use the special cost-of-living factor or a hold harmless clause.

The committee said its method of distributing Head Start funds was designed "with the premise that all states would receive 100 percent of what they are eligible for based on their poverty populations."

Further, the committee said, "The formula reflects the intent that over time all states should eventually receive only formula funds; the need for a hold-harmless will disappear as the distribution of allocations among the various states is equalized by application of the formula."

The Senate formula would first set aside up to 2 percent for Head Start programs in the territories and up to 20 percent for the discretionary use of the HEW secretary. Of the remaining 78 percent of the funds, 50 percent would be distributed to the states on the basis of the relative number of low income children ages 0-5 in each state, and 50 percent on the basis of the relative number of public assistance recipients in each state.

The Senate committee said a cost-of-living factor was unnecessary because as appropriations were increased to reflect, in part, cost-of-living increases, the increases would be passed on automatically through the formula.

The Senate committee report did not contain a breakdown of how much each state would receive in fiscal 1978 if the formula were used, or how many states would receive increases or decreases in their Head Start funds. But committee aides and others who studied the Senate formula said some states could face reductions in their allocations in the next two years. Among them, according to one source, was Kentucky, home of Democrat Carl D. Perkins, chairman of the House Education and Labor Committee.

The Senate formula set a base allocation for all Head Start programs; no state could receive less than it did in fiscal 1975, exclusive of the cost-of-living increase granted then. In adopting the floor, the committee said it believed this level of funding would prevent "massive disruption" of any program.

The committee also sought to soften the blow of any potential reduced funding by allowing the HEW secretary to use his discretionary fund for hold harmless payments, to be phased out over a 10-year period.

The Senate formula would guarantee that each state would receive a percentage of its fiscal 1978 funding level until appropriations were increased to the point where total funding was based on the poverty formula. It would allow discretionary funds to be used in fiscal 1979 to maintain each state at a level of funding equivalent to its fiscal 1978 funding level. In each year after fiscal 1979, the hold harmless payment would be reduced by 10 percent. So, in fiscal 1980, for example, a state would be able to receive a hold harmless payment to enable it to maintain its funding level at 90 percent of its fiscal 1978 funding. In fiscal 1981, the hold harmless payment would be enough to enable it to maintain funding at 80 percent of fiscal 1978.

"As appropriations increase, each state will be eligible for increases from the funds distributed according to relative poverty populations. This will reduce dependency on hold harmless payments, and in fact, all states will gradually convert to total funding based on their relative share of the poor," the committee said.

Senate aides conceded that the formula was complicated, but they argued that it was necessary to truly equalize Head Start funding among the states. The House formula, they argued, would not solve the problem. "In the House, no state would lose, but it doesn't solve the problem," said one committee staff aide. "Our formula would hold some states back and allow others to catch up, until the funding is equal."

Senate Floor Action

The Senate approved S 2090 Aug. 1 by voice vote. At the time of the vote only the measure's two chief sponsors, Gaylord Nelson, D-Wis., and Jacob K. Javits, R-N.Y., were on the floor.

The Senate adopted several amendments by voice vote, including one by Richard S. Schweiker, R-Pa., that would prohibit basing eligibility for emergency fuel bill payments solely on delinquency in paying bills, and an amendment by Nelson similar to the Huckaby amendment adopted by the House.

The Senate also adopted a Nelson amendment that:

- Established specific authorization levels for research and demonstration projects of $5 million for fiscal 1979, $6 million for 1980 and $8 million for 1981.
- Established authorization ceilings for the rural loan program of $3 million for fiscal 1979, $5 million for 1980 and $7 million for 1981.
- Established authorization ceilings for technical assistance grants for programs for migrant and seasonal farm workers of $3 million for fiscal 1979, $5 million for 1980 and $8 million for 1981.
- Reduced the authorization for the Follow Through program to $70 million for fiscal 1979, $85 million for 1980 and $100 million for 1981, from the $90 million, $110 million and $130 million recommended by the committee. (The House version of the bill authorized $70 million, $80 million and $90 million for those fiscal years, plus $100 million for fiscal 1982 and $110 million for 1983. It also expanded the program.)
- Reduced the authorization for the community economic development program for fiscal 1979 to $70 million from $80 million, and established authorization ceilings of $85 million for fiscal 1980 and $105 million for 1981 instead of the open-ended funding recommended by the committee. (The House bill authorized $50 million in fiscal 1979 and such sums as were necessary for 1980-81.)

- Established authorization levels for evaluation programs conducted by the CSA of anti-poverty programs at $4 million for fiscal 1979, $7 million for 1980 and $10 million for 1981.
- Set the maximum annual compensation for community action employees at $18,000.

Nelson said his amendment was offered in response to concerns expressed by James A. McClure, R-Idaho, about the authorization levels and the open-ended authorizations in the bill.

Mike Gravel, D-Alaska, also offered an amendment requiring that the official poverty level be adjusted upward by a specified percentage formula in any area where the cost of living was 25 percent above the urban U.S. average. He contended that the existing 25 percent adjustment for his state "woefully understates the cost-of-living problem" there. After some discussion, he withdrew his amendment on being assured that the Human Resources Committee would study the problem.

Conference, Final Action

House and Senate conferees reached agreement on the final version of HR 7577 and reported it Oct. 11 (H Rept 95-1766).

Most of the differences in the House and Senate versions of the measure were worked out by committee staff and required only perfunctory ratification by the conferees. Only two issues required extensive negotiations between the conferees — the Head Start formula and the makeup and proposed extension of the National Advisory Council on Economic Opportunity.

The House conferees, spurred primarily by Goodling, ranking minority member of the House Economic Opportunity Subcommittee, pushed to limit the extension of the council for one year and drastically cut its funding.

Goodling argued that the council was a waste of money and only duplicated the activities of the CSA. But Senate conferees, more sympathetic to the council, rejected the House position, arguing instead for some less sweeping changes designed to make the council more effective. The House conferees eventually gave in, although strict limitations were placed on funding for the council. Goodling, who was not satisfied with the compromise, declined to sign the final conference report.

Congress cleared HR 7577 for the president on the last day of the 95th session.

Both chambers approved the conference report by voice vote, with little debate.

Congress Clears $5 Billion Handicapped Aid

Congress Oct. 15 cleared and sent to the president legislation expanding federal government programs for the handicapped.

The legislation (HR 12467 — PL 95-602) substantially increased authorizations for existing programs and established several new ones, including a pilot jobs program patterned after the highly successful community employment program for the elderly. Total authorizations in the bill were more than $5 billion over a four-year period.

The legislation also established a National Institute for Handicapped Research, and strengthened efforts to provide legal protection and equal opportunities for the estimated 20 million-35 million handicapped persons in the country.

It changed the formula for state grants for vocational rehabilitation so that in the future more funds would go to the more populous states, and it broadened the definition of "developmentally disabled" persons to be served by the legislation to include an estimated 300,000 to 400,000 additional persons.

HR 12467 extended two existing laws. It extended the Rehabilitation Act of 1973 for four years, through fiscal 1982, and authorized $4.9 billion for programs under that act. It also reauthorized the Developmental Disabilities Services and Facilities Construction Act for three years, approving expenditures of $341 million in fiscal 1979-81 for those programs. *(Rehabilitation Act background, 1976 Almanac p. 619; Developmental Disabilities Act background, 1975 Almanac p. 599)*

The House had passed the rehabilitation measure May 16 by a 382-12 vote under suspension of the rules. It passed the Developmental Disabilities Act extension (HR 12326) Sept. 19, also under suspension, 397-3.

The Senate passed a combined measure (S 2600) by an 81-1 vote Sept. 21 after reaching a compromise with the Carter administration over authorization levels. A veto had been threatened if the bill was not scaled down from the five-year, $8 billion authorization approved by the Senate Human Resources Committee.

Provisions

As cleared by Congress, HR 12467 extended the Rehabilitation Act of 1973 for four years, through fiscal 1982, and the Developmental Disabilities Services and Facilities Construction Act for three years, through fiscal 1981. HR 12467:

Rehabilitation Act Amendments

- Authorized for basic state grants $808 million for fiscal 1979; tied authorizations for fiscal 1980-82 to the Consumer Price Index, setting maximum ceilings of $880 million for fiscal 1980, $945 million for fiscal 1981 and $972 million for fiscal 1982.
- Authorized $244 million for fiscal 1979, $365 million for fiscal 1980, $465 million for fiscal 1981 and $310 million for fiscal 1982 for other programs under the act. *(Authorizations, box, p. 593)*
- Allowed state agencies to contract with profit-making organizations for on-the-job training and related services for the handicapped if they find the organizations are better qualified to provide such services than non-profit agencies and organizations.
- Required state agencies to establish sufficient information and referral programs for handicapped persons.
- Established procedures by which a handicapped person or his parent or guardian can review and appeal decisions concerning the person's written individualized rehabilitation program.

● Authorized direct grants to Indian tribes for vocational rehabilitation programs, with the federal government to pay 90 percent of the costs.

● Altered the funding formula for basic state grants to provide that of the money appropriated in excess of the fiscal 1978 level, 50 percent shall be allocated to the states on the basis of the present formula without squaring the state per capita income factor. All other funds will be allocated under the existing formula.

● Lifted the limitation on the number of client assistance projects that may be established; required client assistance projects to help handicapped persons pursue legal, administrative or other appropriate remedies to ensure protection of their rights under the act.

● Increased to five years from three years the total period of time in which a project may receive funds for innovation and expansion programs.

● Raised the minimum state allotment from the current one-fourth of 1 percent of the total appropriation or $2 million, whichever is greater, to one-third of 1 percent of the total appropriation, or $3 million, whichever is greater. This would increase funding for small states.

Research. Established a National Institute of Handicapped Research within the Department of Health, Education and Welfare (HEW); specified that the director be appointed by the president and confirmed by the Senate.

● Required the director to develop within 18 months a long-range plan on research activities affecting handicapped persons.

● Gave the institute responsibility for establishing and supporting research and training centers and for conducting research and demonstration projects, including model projects in preschool activities for handicapped children and in employment training activities, programs for handicapped youngsters, the elderly handicapped and the deaf.

● Established a research fellowship program for the institute.

● Authorized a research program to develop and demonstrate innovative methods to attract and retain professionals in the handicapped field to serve in rural areas.

● Established an Interagency Committee on Handicapped Research to promote cooperation among federal departments and agencies conducting rehabilitation research programs.

● Authorized the secretary of HEW to conduct research and demonstration projects concerned with the interrelated needs of handicapped individuals, elderly, children, youths, adults and families.

Special Projects, Centers. Authorized demonstration projects to improve rehabilitation services for the deaf and blind regardless of age or vocational potential.

● Allowed special project grants to be used for renovation and construction of facilities, where appropriate.

● Authorized grants to state and public non-profit agencies and organizations for paying part or all of the cost of starting recreation programs for the handicapped.

● Authorized the establishment of "comprehensive rehabilitation centers" to provide a broad range of services to the handicapped, including information and referral, counseling, job placement, health, educational, social and recreational services.

● Provided federal mortgage insurance and 2 percent interest subsidies for construction of rehabilitation facilities by non-profit private organizations; set a $100 million ceiling on the total amount of loan guarantees that can be outstanding at any one time.

● Authorized grants to states or local agencies to pay up to 90 percent of the cost of rehabilitation services for handicapped migrant farm workers or members of their families.

● Authorized training of personnel specializing in job development and job placement for handicapped individuals, personnel in the fields of medical, social and psychological rehabilitation, and interpreters for the deaf.

National Council. Established a 15-member National Council on the Handicapped within HEW, to advise and make recommendations on programs for the handicapped. Members would be appointed by the president and confirmed by the Senate; at least five must be handicapped or parents or guardians of handicapped persons.

Architectural, Transportation Barriers. Provided for the appointment of 11 public members to the Architectural and Transportation Barriers Compliance Board, including eight who are handicapped; also designated as members of the board the heads (or their designees) of the departments of HEW, Transportation, Housing and Urban Development, Labor, Interior, Defense and Justice, the General Services Administration, Veterans Administration and U.S. Postal Service.

● Required the board, in cooperation with other federal agencies, to develop and enforce standards for overcoming barriers to the handicapped and ensure that any waiver or modification of a standard is based upon findings of fact and is not arbitrary and capricious.

● Included communications barriers as within the scope of the board's authority.

● Required the board to submit to the president and Congress within 12 months a report on the money needed by each state to provide handicapped persons access to all programs and activities receiving federal assistance.

● Authorized technical assistance to public or private groups to help in complying with the act or with accessibility standards.

● Authorized grants to state vocational rehabilitation agencies to study the costs of removing architectural barriers.

Discrimination Against Handicapped. Provided that the non-discrimination provisions of the Rehabilitation Act of 1973 (Sections 504, 501b) apply to any program or activity conducted by any executive agency.

● Provided that remedies, procedures and rights under the Civil Rights Act of 1964 apply to complaints filed under the non-discrimination sections of the Rehabilitation Act of 1973.

● Allowed the awarding of "reasonable attorney's fees" as part of the costs of bringing suit to enforce the non-discrimination statutes.

● Allowed courts, in fashioning an equitable remedy for handicapped persons who allege employment discrimination, to take into consideration the cost of workplace accommodations needed, the availability of alternatives or other appropriate relief.

● Established an Interagency Coordinating Council to develop consistent policies among federal agencies responsible for enforcing the non-discrimination sections of the 1973 act.

● Clarified that only those alcoholics or drug abusers who cannot perform the duties of the job in question or who present a danger to property or the safety of others are not covered by the employment protections (Sections 503 and 504) of the 1973 act.

Employment Programs. Established a pilot community service employment program, to be administered by the Department of Labor, to provide full and part-time community service jobs for the handicapped.

- Required that jobs pay at least the minimum wage and do not result in the displacement of previously employed workers.
- Allowed the secretary of labor to contract with public or private non-profit organizations, including governmental units, to operate specific jobs projects; specified that the federal government would pay up to 90 percent of the costs of the projects.
- Required that projects funded by the secretary shall offer appropriate placement services to handicapped employees to assist them in obtaining unsubsidized employment when the project ends.
- Established a second jobs program designed to provide on-the-job training to handicapped persons; authorized the commissioner of the Rehabilitation Services Administration to run the program through contracts with private industry; authorized the federal government to pay up to 80 percent of the costs of the program.
- Required employers to pay handicapped workers the applicable minimum wage and provide benefits comparable to those received by other employees.
- Authorized the commissioner to make grants to handicapped persons to enable them to operate commercial or other enterprises and to develop or market their services and products.

Comprehensive Services for Independent Living. Established a new funding category to improve services for severely handicapped persons with little potential for gainful employment, including grants to states to provide "independent living services" like counseling, psychological and related services, housing, transportation, attendant care, physical rehabilitation, therapeutic treatment, recreational activities, interpreter services and other needs to severely handicapped persons. The programs would be run by state vocational rehabilitation agencies.

- Authorized the establishment of special centers for independent living for the severely handicapped, including older blind persons.
- Authorized grants to states for advocacy and legal protection programs for the severely handicapped.

Developmental Disabilities

- Broadened the definition of developmentally disabled by changing from a "categorical" definition based on specific, clinically diagnosed mental or physical impairments to a "functional" definition based on an individual's inability or limited ability to perform certain roles and tasks expected within a social environment; defined a developmental disability as a severe, chronic disability which is attributable to a mental or physical impairment or combination thereof, is manifested before age 22, is likely to continue indefinitely, results in substantial functional limitations in certain specified areas, and reflects the need for lifelong, individually planned services.
- Required the secretary of HEW to make a special report to Congress on the impact of the new definition by Jan. 15, 1981.
- Established four priority areas for services to the developmentally disabled: case management, child development, alternative community living arrangements, and non-vocational social developmental services.
- Required state planning councils on the developmentally disabled to jointly develop the state plan with the state agency that runs the programs.
- Required that at least half the membership of state planning councils be persons with developmental disabilities, or their parents or guardians.
- Abolished the National Advisory Council on Services and Facilities for the Developmentally Disabled in order to avoid duplication and overlap with the National Council on the Handicapped.
- Provided that the establishment of protection and advocacy programs should not be interpreted to override existing federal bans on lobbying with federal funds.
- Authorized the secretary of HEW to fund special projects designed to attract and retain professionals to serve in rural areas.

House Action

The House Education and Labor Committee reported HR 12467 May 13 (H Rept 95-1149).

The bill passed the House May 16 by a 382-12 vote under suspension of the rules. *(Vote 273, p. 78-H)*

There was only minimal debate on the measure. A couple of members questioned the wisdom of voting on a major authorization measure under suspension, but their

Authorizations

As cleared by Congress, HR 12467 authorized the following amounts for programs under the Rehabilitation Act of 1973 *(in millions of dollars):*

	1979	1980	1981	1982
Vocational Rehabilitation				
Basic state grants*	$ 808	$ 880	$ 945	$ 972
Innovation and expansion	45	50	55	60
Research and Training				
Research	50	75	90	100
Training	34	40	45	50
Community Service Employment	35	50	75	100
Comprehensive Services and independent living	80	150	200	**
Totals	$1,052	$1,245	$1,410	$1,282

Authorizations for basic state grants for fiscal 1980-82 will be based on the Consumer Price Index, but cannot go above $880 million for fiscal 1980, $945 million for fiscal 1981 and $972 million for fiscal 1982.

***Such sums as necessary. HR 12467 also authorized such sums as necessary for the National Institute of Handicapped Research, Indian tribes, special projects, National Council on the Handicapped, Architectural and Transportation Barriers Compliance Board, Projects with Industry, and Business Opportunities for Handicapped Individuals.*

HR 12467 also contained the following authorizations for programs under the Developmental Disabilities Services and Facilities Construction Act *(in millions of dollars):*

	1979	1980	1981
State grants	$55	$ 65	$ 75
University affiliated facilities	12	14	16
Protection and advocacy	9	12	15
Special projects	20	22	26
Totals	$96	$113	$132

comments were largely ignored. For the most part, those who spoke praised the legislation and stated their commitment to helping the handicapped.

"There is landmark legislation providing the necessary commitment which will permit greater independence for millions of disabled and handicapped citizens of this nation," declared Mario Biaggi, D-N.Y., a cosponsor of the bill.

On Sept. 19, the House passed the Developmental Disabilities Act extension (HR 12326), also under suspension, 397-3. *(Vote 700, p. 198-H)*

Senate Action

Committee. The Senate Human Resources Committee reported S 2600 May 15 (S Rept 95-890). It recommended a five-year extension of the programs with authorizations totaling more than $8 billion.

Veto Threat. HEW Secretary Joseph A. Califano Jr. said July 20 that unless the Senate committee bill was substantially changed, he would recommend that President Carter veto it. He cited the "adverse budgetary impact" as well as "serious administrative difficulties" in the bill. The committee had added some new programs to those proposed by the administration and authorized far more funding for some others than HEW wanted.

In the weeks after Califano's letter, administration officials and negotiators for the Human Resources Subcommittee on the Handicapped worked out authorization levels acceptable to both sides.

Floor Action

Faced with the threat of a veto, the Senate Sept. 20 scaled back proposed authorization levels for federal programs for the handicapped for the next three fiscal years.

It agreed by voice vote to cut nearly half a billion dollars from committee-approved authorizations for fiscal 1979-81 for programs under the Rehabilitation Act and the Developmental Disabilities Act. It also agreed to limit the authorizations to three years instead of five.

It then passed the authorization measure (S 2600) Sept. 21 by an 81-1 vote. There was little debate on the floor; the authorization cuts had been worked out in negotiating sessions beforehand. *(Vote 379, p. 57-S)*

Even after the Senate adopted the authorization levels agreed to by the administration and subcommittee, James A. McClure, R-Idaho, succeeded in cutting further the proposed spending ceilings for protection and advocacy programs.

McClure argued that the proposed authorizations were well above what the Carter administration had requested, and he questioned whether sharp increases in legal advocacy programs for handicapped persons could be used efficiently.

The administration and subcommittee had agreed to reduce ceilings for advocacy programs from $101 million for fiscal 1979-81 to $80 million for the three fiscal years. But an amendment offered by McClure and adopted by voice vote after some quick floor negotiations reduced the total authorizations for advocacy programs to $51.5 million for 1979-81.

Despite the reductions, which were spread among all programs except basic state grants, the authorization levels approved by the Senate were about $245 million above the levels recommended by the administration for fiscal 1979, according to committee staff.

Besides reducing the authorization levels, the Senate acquiesced to a second administration demand that the extension authority be limited to three years instead of five as proposed by the committee. The administration was joined in calling for a scale-back from five to three years by the Senate Budget Committee. The committee, while approving a budget waiver for the bill, expressed concern over "long-term commitments involving increasing expenditures in entitlement programs" and said "such programs should be reviewed more frequently in light of changing needs and conditions."

Most of the debate on S 2600 centered on an effort by senators from the most populated states to alter the distribution formula for state vocational rehabilitation grants, the major program under the Rehabilitation Act.

Led by Jacob K. Javits, R-N.Y., and Harrison A. Williams Jr., D-N.J., they succeeded in changing the formula during markup by the Human Resources Committee, which Williams chaired. But they failed during floor action, accepting instead a compromise that retained the existing formula.

The new formula proposed by Javits and Williams would have parceled out basic grants to states on the basis of population. Under existing law, the distribution formula was based on population and per capita income.

Hoping to ease potential criticism from smaller states, Javits and Williams proposed that the new formula apply only to new money appropriated during fiscal 1979 above the appropriation for fiscal 1978.

But senators from smaller, rural states, especially in the South and West, did not buy that proposal, and succeeded during floor debate in removing the formula change proposed by the committee. Although Williams and Javits, ranking Republican on the committee, endorsed the new formula, the chairman of the Subcommittee on the Handicapped, Jennings Randolph, D-W.Va., did not. He played a key role in marshaling support to reverse the committee recommendation.

Javits and Williams argued that the existing formula had served a critical role when it was first established in 1954. The basic philosophy behind it, Williams said, was to help low-income states that needed proportionately more money to start up their programs.

But the two argued that income gaps among states had closed considerably in the last decade, thereby making the existing formula outmoded and weighted against big states like New York, New Jersey and California.

Opponents of the formula change argued that it would severely limit the amount of new funding their states would receive in the coming years. "It will be a mortal blow to my state," said Dale Bumpers, D-Ark., who led the floor fight against the new formula.

Aside from the financial impact, Bumpers disputed contentions that per capita income was not a relevant measure of state need.

Randolph noted that the subcommittee favored retention of the existing formula. He had no objection to increased funding for the larger states, he said, but it should not be done at the expense of "handicapped who happen to live in the lower-income states."

Bumpers initially proposed a floor amendment to remove the new formula from the bill. Javits sought to alter the Bumpers amendment, but then accepted another compromise which retained the existing formula for the distribution of all vocational funds appropriated for the basic state grant program.

However, the compromise, adopted by voice vote, gave the secretary of HEW authority to make special appropriations to needy states if money were available. Javits and others said they hoped that would enable New York and other states to receive extra funds during fiscal 1979.

Other Amendments

Other amendments adopted by the Senate, all by voice votes, included:

- By Randolph, defining preschool children eligible for special model programs for severely handicapped as those children up to age 5, instead of 3, as proposed by the committee.
- By Robert P. Griffin, R-Mich., allowing governors to determine which state agency would be responsible for operating comprehensive services programs for the severely disabled. The committee bill gave state vocational rehabilitation agencies the authority.
- By Randolph, establishing a National Institute of Handicapped Research.
- By Howard W. Cannon, D-Nev., exempting alcoholics and drug abusers from employment protections of the Rehabilitation Act of 1973 (Sections 503, 504) in cases where the health condition could prevent the person from performing the essential functions of the job in question.
- By McClure, to ensure that establishment of protection and advocacy programs would not be interpreted to override provisions making it a federal offense to lobby with federal funds.

Conference Action

Conferees reached agreement on the final version of the measure and filed their report (H Rept 95-1780) Oct. 13. They had little difficulty resolving differences in the two versions of the measure, generally compromising on most provisions. The House, for example, had approved a five-year extension of the Rehabilitation Act, while the Senate had approved a three-year extension. The conferees resolved the difference by approving a four-year extension.

The conference committee also resolved a dispute over the funding formula for basic state vocational rehabilitation grants by accepting a slight change in the mathematical equation used to determine state allocations.

The change was not expected to have much immediate impact, since it will only affect 50 percent of any additional appropriations made in the future above fiscal 1978 funding levels. But in the long run, the altered formula will channel greater percentages of money to higher per capita income states like New York, New Jersey and California. Advocates of the formula change had argued that the existing formula was weighted against the most populous states. Opponents accepted the change because it would have little immediate impact and would not reduce allocations for other states.

Conferees also took care in their report to outline in detail their views on the definition of a developmental disability. The new definition would cover everyone covered under the existing definition, they stressed, but would also include as many as 400,000 other persons. The new definition, pushed primarily by the Senate, sought to move away from a definition of developmental disabilities based on "categorical" impairments to a definition with a "functional" base. The House bill had listed specific conditions, including mental retardation, cerebral palsy, epilepsy, autism and dyslexia.

Final Action

Final action on the measure came Oct. 15 when the House approved the conference report by a 365-2 vote shortly after the Senate had approved it by voice vote. *(House vote 829, p. 236-H)* ▮

Nurse Training Aid Vetoed

On the final day of the session, Congress cleared legislation (S 2416) extending federal support for nurse training programs for two more years at existing spending levels, but President Carter pocket-vetoed the measure Nov. 11.

The veto drew an angry blast from nursing leaders who suggested that the "discriminatory" pocket veto was motivated by sexism in the White House. "We cannot help but wonder if [the veto] had anything to do with the fact that nursing is predominately a woman's profession," said Barbara Nichols, president of the American Nurses' Association.

Carter said he would not sign the nurse training bill (S 2416) because its spending levels were "excessive," particularly since two decades of federal aid to nursing schools had all but ended nursing shortages. Other forms of federal aid were available to nursing students, Carter pointed out, adding that "future federal assistance should be limited to geographic and specialty areas that need nurses most." *(Veto text, p. 68-E)*

Carter had asked Congress to end most nurse training aid, except for $20 million worth of special projects and nurse practitioner training funds. But Congress had continued a broad range of grants — at more than $200 million a year — through 1980.

Because a continuing resolution continued the nursing education programs at existing funding levels through fiscal 1979, the veto would not abruptly terminate nursing education programs.

However, three largely black health professions schools (Meharry Medical College, Tuskegee School of Veterinary Medicine and Xavier School of Pharmacy) were also affected by the veto because the bill had doubled the authorization for financial distress grants, which they needed badly. Congressional sources predicted that that increase would be added to other health legislation early in 1979; they also suggested that Carter would have no more success in killing the nursing programs than President Ford had. Ford's 1975 veto of a similar reauthorization was overridden, because "it's hard for members to vote against the nurses. There are a lot of them in every district, they're effective, and they always hit members with the 'discrimination against women' argument," as one congressional aide explained. *(1975 action, 1975 Almanac p. 591)*

Nurses argued that national health insurance would greatly increase the nation's need for nurses. Congressional supporters of the bill also said that the overall numbers of trained nurses made the supply appear to be more generous than it actually was. Of about 1.3 million nurses, 500,000 were not practicing full time, and maldistribution compounded the problem. Nurses were still in short supply in many rural and inner-city areas, and there were not enough specially trained nurses to fill teaching, administrative and research positions, proponents of the bill said.

Although there was some confusion as to the final total authorized by Congress, the nurse training bill sent to the White House far exceeded the president's budget request. In his fiscal 1979 budget the president had sought to end per-student ("capitation") grants to schools for all health professions, including nursing, and to cut back other nurse training aid programs to a $20 million total. The fiscal 1979 total for the bill that cleared Congress was, according to the Congressional Budget Office (CBO), $272.2 million. The bill also authorized $275.1 million for fiscal 1980, according to CBO.

In his Oct. 13 presentation of the conference report to the House, Commerce Committee Chairman Paul G. Rogers, D-Fla., used lower figures of $208 million and $209 million for the two years. The House committee did not consider two types of expenditures, for loan repayment and scholarship grants to nursing schools, to be "line items," and it excluded spending for these programs from its totals. However, CBO maintained that, in the case of the scholarship funds, there was a two-year, entitlement-type formula written into the Public Health Service act and continued by the bill, so it included dollar figures for these items in its version of the authorization. The Senate Human Resources Committee also used the higher CBO figures.

A new $5 million authorization for clinical training of nurse anesthetists was the only major change the bill made in existing programs. The House committee, which proposed the new program, said it would save money because annual salaries of nurse anesthetists averaged about a third of fees charged by physician-anesthesiologists for similar services.

The bill also made minor changes in other health professions programs.

Committee Action

In its May 15 report on the bill (S Rept 95-859), the Senate Human Resources Committee said hospitals were complaining of acute nursing shortages, particularly in inner city and rural areas, where medical services of any sort were often scarce. Chicago hospitals, for example, were unable to fill 2,000 nursing positions.

The committee also argued that abrupt cuts in federal support would cripple nursing education and that future health policies could create additional demands for nurses. The president's decision was "premature and unsubstantiated," the committee said, promising a full review of national nursing needs once several studies were finished.

The House Commerce Committee argued similarly in its May 15 report (HR 12303 — H Rept 95-1189). New priorities such as national health insurance and prepaid group practices (health maintenance organizations) could affect both the number and the type of nurses needed, the committee suggested. Also, nurses with advanced training to fill administrative and teaching positions were still in short supply, the committee said.

Floor Action

The Senate passed S 2416 June 7 by voice vote, and the House passed HR 12303 Sept. 19 by a 393-12 vote. *(Vote 701, p. 198-H)*

The Senate bill authorized a total of $542.3 million through 1980 for grants, loans and loan interest subsidies for construction, capitation aid, student loans and scholarships and various types of advanced and specialized training programs.

The House bill authorized $553.5 million for the same period. The more expensive House version included a new $5 million program to train nurse anesthetists and a $6 million increase in the fiscal 1979 authorization for the National Health Service Corps. That program was designed to bring medical services to communities needing them badly.

Both bills extended through fiscal 1983 authorizations as needed for nursing student loans and scholarships. This provision was meant to ensure that students beginning their training with federal assistance before fiscal 1981 could complete their educations.

The bills also ended a $5 million distress grants program for financially troubled schools. These funds were transferred to special projects, where there was a great demand for extra funds, according to the committees.

Conference, Final Action

Conferees retained most features of the similar House and Senate bills, including the nurse anesthetist program passed by the House. The only major change was deletion of a House-passed $6 million increase in the fiscal 1979 authorization for the National Health Service Corps. In their Oct. 13 report (H Rept 95-1785), conferees did not explain why they had refused to boost that authorization.

The conferees retained a House authorization for "yet another study" on national nursing needs even though both the Department of Health, Education and Welfare (HEW) and the nursing profession were already working on the issue. Given the "longstanding — and thus far unresolved — controversy" between the department and the profession on "the need for federal support of nursing education programs," an "independent" study was needed, the conferees said.

Conferees said they were raising the levels of individual and aggregate loans for health professions students (medicine, osteopathy or dentistry) for two reasons: to keep pace with rising tuition costs and to offset an undesirable concentration of National Health Service Corps (NHSC) awards at the most costly medical schools. "The Congress . . . never intended the NHSC scholarship program to be a vehicle for the subsidization of expensive medical schools," conferees noted.

Final Action. The House endorsed the conference agreement by voice vote Oct. 13, the Senate Oct. 15, clearing it for the president.

Provisions

As cleared by Congress and vetoed by the president, S 2416 would have:

Nursing Education. Extended authorizations for two years, through fiscal 1980, for these nurse training programs: grants, loans and loan interest subsidies for construction, capitation aid, student loans and scholarships and various types of advanced and specialized training programs; also extended authorizations, as needed, for nursing student loans and scholarships for fiscal 1981-1983 to ensure that students beginning their training with federal aid before fiscal 1981 could complete their educations. The new authorization included a $5 million increase for special projects grants.

- Deleted authority for financial distress grants.

• Established a new program of traineeships for professional nurses in training to become nurse anesthetists; authorized $2 million for fiscal 1979 and $3 million for fiscal 1980 for this program.

• Eliminated a general loan forgiveness authority but authorized the secretary of health, education and welfare to forgive up to 85 percent of a nursing education loan for persons working in medically underserved areas.

• Directed the secretary to contract for a study of national nursing needs, including future needs if a national health insurance program were enacted; required submission of the report, including legislative recommendations, by Oct. 1, 1979.

Other Health Professions Programs. Raised to $15,000 a year, from $10,000, the amount a medical, dental or osteopathic student could borrow under the federally guaranteed loan program; raised to $60,000 from $50,000, the total indebtedness permitted each student.

• Authorized the secretary to extend beyond three years the service obligation of a National Health Service Corps scholarship recipient, to permit completion of an internship or other advanced clinical training.

• Raised to $10 million a year, from $5 million, the authorization for financial distress grants to health professions schools (medicine, osteopathy, pharmacy) under the Health Professions Educational Assistance Act (PL 94-484) for fiscal years 1978-80.

• Provided a temporary relaxation of new eligibility requirements for public health traineeships, to allow students mistakenly admitted in 1978 to programs under old standards to complete their education.

• Revised a requirement for participation of health professions schools in the area health education center program, deleting a requirement that each participating school conduct a training course for nurse practitioners or physician's assistants; instead, permitted participating schools to omit such programs if another participating school in its area offered the training. ▮

Pregnancy Disability, Rights

In a sweeping expansion of working women's rights, the 95th Congress passed legislation (S 995 — PL 95-555) to ban employment discrimination on the basis of pregnancy and require disability and health insurance plans to cover pregnant workers.

After a three-month stalemate, House and Senate conferees in October agreed to modify anti-abortion language that had threatened to scuttle the bill. The Senate approved the conference report by voice vote Oct. 13, the House Oct. 15, clearing it for the president.

As cleared, S 995 amended Title VII of the 1964 Civil Rights Act to prohibit discrimination against pregnant women in any area of employment, including hiring, promotion, seniority rights and job security. It also required employers who offered health insurance and temporary disability plans to provide coverage to women for pregnancy, childbirth and related medical conditions. The bill was intended to reverse the 1976 Supreme Court decision, *General Electric v. Gilbert,* which held that employers were not required to include pregnancy in their disability pay plans. *(Background, 1977 Almanac p. 486)*

Both supporters and opponents of the new law characterized it as a dramatic broadening of working women's job rights and benefits. A spokesman for the U.S. Chamber of Commerce also criticized it as "excessively costly." Labor and women's rights organizations had sought the legislation.

The stage for a renewed congressional battle over abortion was set in March when the House Education and Labor Committee reported its version of the pregnancy disability bill (HR 6075) containing an anti-abortion amendment. The House approved the bill July 18.

The Senate had passed a similar bill by a 75-11 vote in 1977, but it had tabled by a 44-41 vote a floor amendment that would have exempted elective abortions from coverage in medical benefit and disability pay programs. *(Senate bill, 1977 Almanac p. 486; 1977 abortion fight, 1977 Almanac p. 295)*

The last-minute compromise came after Senate conferees agreed to accept a modified version of the House-passed anti-abortion language that was quite similar to the original House provision.

Provisions

As cleared by Congress, S 995:

• Amended Title VII of the Civil Rights Act of 1964 to make discrimination on the basis of pregnancy, childbirth or related medical conditions illegal in all matters of employment, including hiring, promotion and seniority rights as well as receipt of benefits under fringe benefit programs.

• Provided that employers could exempt elective abortions from health insurance programs except if the life of the mother were endangered if the fetus were carried to term, or in the case of medical complications resulting from abortion; required employers to provide disability and sick leave benefits to women receiving abortions; permitted employers to provide health and all other benefits for abortions if they wished.

• Provided that the bill take effect immediately upon enactment except for the provision relating to fringe benefit or insurance programs, which would take effect 180 days after enactment.

• Prohibited employers from reducing the level of their benefit packages to come into compliance with the measure until one year after the date of enactment or until the expiration of any collective bargaining agreements in force at the time of enactment.

• Provided that where the costs of medical-disability plans were shared by employers and employees, increased costs due to compliance with the bill could be apportioned in the same proportion already established.

House Committee Action

The House Education and Labor Committee reported HR 6075 on March 13 (H Rept 95-948). The bill was similar to the version passed by the Senate in 1977.

However, the House committee added a provision to exempt elective abortions from medical benefits or disability pay programs. Medical complications resulting from abortion would be covered, and the bill would not prevent employers from providing benefits for abortion if they wished.

The House anti-abortion amendment was offered by Edward P. Beard, D-R.I., who said employers should not be forced to pay benefits for a procedure they did not believe in. The amendment was rejected on a 3-5 vote by the Subcommittee on Employment Opportunities Feb. 2, but the full Education and Labor Committee reversed that position March 2, voting 19-12 to exempt abortion from medical and disability coverage unless it was required to save the life of the mother. The committee then voted 25-6 to report the bill.

The committee said the bill was needed to "clearly establish that the prohibition against sex discrimination in Title VII of the Civil Rights Act of 1964 includes a prohibition against employment-related discrimination on the basis of pregnancy, childbirth or related medical conditions." It did not require employers to treat pregnant workers in any special way, or set up health or disability plans if they did not already have them, the committee pointed out; it simply provided that pregnant women were entitled to the same benefits as other workers.

The committee cited a Labor Department estimate that the bill would raise the costs of disability insurance nationwide by about $191 million, or 20 cents a week per worker, assuming an average disability period of 7 and one-half weeks and an average benefit payment of $80 a week. The AFL-CIO had estimated the cost at $130 million, while the Health Insurance Association of America estimated it at $571 million. It had no reliable estimates for health insurance cost increases, the committee said.

Like the Senate bill, the House committee bill gave employers 180 days to comply with the fringe benefit requirements, and prohibited them from reducing benefits as a means of coming into compliance with the measure for at least a year, or until the expiration of any collective bargaining agreements in force at the time of enactment. It also provided that where employees and employers shared the cost of health and disability insurance plans, any cost increases could be shared proportionately.

Minority Views

The House committee's adoption of an anti-abortion provision was denounced in minority views by Ted Weiss, D-N.Y., a sponsor of the original bill.

Weiss said the provision constituted a new form of discrimination against women employees and would put the burden of the battle over abortion on employers and labor unions. He said no employers had asked for the abortion exemption, and that not one of the states that require pregnancy disability coverage had such an exemption in its law. (About half the states have such laws.)

"The only group which actively came forward to promote the anti-abortion provision was the United States Catholic Conference, the conference of bishops, and never at a public hearing," Weiss said. "In fact, there is not a single word of testimony on the record supporting the anti-abortion amendment in this bill."

Weiss noted that some anti-abortion groups had supported the bill without the amendment, feeling that such a provision was unnecessary, that the bill was by nature "pro-life" because its provision of benefits and job security would encourage pregnant workers to carry their babies to term rather than electing to have abortions.

"If this legislation, which can be considered nothing but 'pro-life,' must be amended by those who oppose abortion, no bill which comes before the House . . . can be insured of freedom from such an amendment," he said.

House Floor Action

In a vote that sharply divided women's rights activists, the House July 18 passed HR 6075 by a vote of 376-43 under suspension of the rules, a procedure intended for non-controversial legislation. Bills taken up under suspension require a two-thirds vote for passage, and floor amendments are prohibited. After passing HR 6075, the House agreed to substitute its provisions for those of S 995. *(Vote 490, p. 140-H)*

By the time the bill reached the House floor, it enjoyed broad backing from the administration and a coalition of labor, civil rights, "pro-life" and women's rights groups. Business conducted only a low-key lobbying campaign against what some termed "the motherhood bill." But controversy continued to swirl around the bill's anti-abortion amendment and the use of the suspension calendar to stave off a divisive floor fight over that issue.

The decision to consider the bill under suspension drew fire from some feminists, who labeled it "inappropriate" in view of the controversial nature of the anti-abortion provision. Complaining bitterly that the suspension procedure allowed members to duck the prickly abortion issue, representatives of the National Organization for Women (NOW), the National Abortion Rights Action League (NARAL) and the Religious Coalition on Abortion Rights said consideration of HR 6075 under suspension could set a precedent for future abortion votes.

Lining up in support of the strategy were the American Civil Liberties Union (ACLU) and the National Women's Political Caucus (NWPC). They argued that a bitter floor fight over the abortion language would have threatened the bill's passage. Attempts to knock out the anti-abortion provision would be more effective during the House-Senate conference on the measure, they insisted.

Support and Opposition

Supporters of pregnancy disability pay argued that discrimination based on pregnancy was at the root of women's employment problems because employers' views on pregnancy had relegated many women to marginal, low-wage positions.

Opponents of the bill, including the U.S. Chamber of Commerce and the National Association of Manufacturers, countered that pregnancy is a voluntary condition that should not be regarded as an illness. They also expressed concern over the high cost of the legislation, citing estimates of $571 million a year for disability payments and $1 billion for health and medical expenses.

But the key opposition to the bill came from within the ranks of the women's movement, particularly from "pro-choice" groups, which oppose restrictions on abortion. Although the National Abortion Rights Action League and the Religious Coalition on Abortion Rights both stopped short of actively lobbying against the bill, they did not mute their dissatisfaction with the suspension move.

The decision to place HR 6075 on the suspension calendar was prompted by the fear that the bill would remain lodged in the Rules Committee, according to sources. Even if the bill were reported, backers feared a protracted floor fight over the abortion provision would have severely damaged the bill's chances for passage.

Insisting that suspension was used "not to stifle debate but to speed up the process toward enactment," Ronald A. Sarasin, R-Conn., said that a motion to strike the abortion language would not have been "in the best interests of the vast majority of working women."

"The cold fact is that whatever procedure we utilize, this House is not going to approve a bill without the abortion provision in it," Sarasin said.

But, arguing against the bill, Weiss said the measure substituted "a new form of discrimination for the one it seeks to eliminate." Weiss insisted that the measure would give the employer sole discretion concerning coverage for abortions in employee benefit packages.

Beard said collective bargaining agreements would provide employees with a voice in the decision over whether to include abortions in benefit plans. But "most employees are not represented by unions," Weiss countered, adding that the bill put "the burden on unions and employers to be subjected to pressure on pro- and anti-abortion matters."

The 43 members who voted against the bill included some who objected to the anti-abortion language and some who sided with business' contention that maternity pay was a matter for labor-management negotiations and not for the federal government.

Conference Action

Conferees met several times in July and August, but the House conferees refused to budge from their strong anti-abortion position. By a 9-4 vote Aug. 1 they rejected a Senate compromise offer that would have required abortion coverage in health and disability plans but exempted religious organizations, such as schools, from the requirement.

Conferees did not meet again until the last week of the session.

With Harrison A. Williams Jr., D-N.J., Human Resources Committee chairman, taking the lead, Senate conferees Oct. 12 offered to broaden the so-called conscience clause language to include sole proprietors with religious or moral objections to abortion. But the House participants once again spurned the Senate's attempt at compromise, voting 9-4 to back the Beard language.

With the aid of Rep. Augustus F. Hawkins, D-Calif., Senate and House conferees crafted the final compromise language late the night of Oct. 12, according to a House aide. Perkins then cleared the language with House anti-abortion members, who promised not to block the measure when it reached the House floor, the aide said.

The compromise abortion language which finally emerged stuck close to the original House provision. The conference language allowed employers to exempt elective abortions from medical coverage, except if the life of the mother were threatened, or in the case of medical complications resulting from abortion. But in a minor weakening of the original House provision, employers were required to provide disability and sick leave benefits to women recovering from an abortion.

A Senate aide conceded that the final language did not deviate far from the original House provision. But Senate conferees were willing to swallow the abortion pill in order to see the pregnancy disability measure enacted, he explained.

Women's rights and "pro-choice" groups lauded the bill as an important women's rights milestone. But they registered indignation over the compromise abortion language.

"We were disappointed that the abortion language couldn't be struck or narrowed," said John Shattuck, director of the American Civil Liberties Union's legislative office. However, Shattuck said he did not view the provision as one of the "more serious blows" to the pro-choice movement.

Other pro-choice groups strongly disputed that assessment, expressing outrage at the conference language. ∎

Child Abuse, Adoption Act

President Carter April 24 signed into law (HR 6693 — PL 95-266) legislation broadening the federal government's role in treating and preventing child abuse and neglect.

The legislation could result in slightly higher federal spending for child abuse programs. It would enable the federal government to begin a modest attack on a related, growing national problem — sexual abuse of children.

HR 6693 also expanded the federal government's role in promoting the adoption of foster children. Among other things, it instructed the Department of Health, Education and Welfare (HEW) to develop model adoption codes for use by the states and to establish a national adoption information exchange system to match children with foster parents.

The bill extended for four years, through fiscal 1981, the Child Abuse Prevention and Treatment Act of 1973 (PL 93-247). The act began the federal government's involvement in fighting child abuse, primarily through special demonstration programs and research activities. *(1973 Almanac p. 513)*

The House and Senate had passed different versions of HR 6693 in 1977. *(1977 Almanac p. 518)*

Sponsors of the measure, led by Alan Cranston, D-Calif., chairman of the Senate Human Resources Subcommittee on Child and Human Development, and John Brademas, D-Ind., chairman of the House Education and Labor Select Education Subcommittee, worked out their differences and submitted a compromise agreement to the House April 10 and the Senate April 12. Both chambers accepted the agreement by voice vote.

Initially, the Senate version of the bill contained provisions allowing grants to states for adoption subsidies. Those provisions were later removed from the bill and attached to HR 7200. *(Child pornography, story, p. 582; 1977 Almanac p. 511)*

The House-passed bill included criminal penalties for persons convicted of sexually exploiting youngsters, but those provisions were dropped after the president signed into law in February another bill establishing such penalties. *(1977 Almanac p. 520)*

Provisions

As cleared by Congress, HR 6693:

Child Abuse

- Extended the Child Abuse Prevention and Treatment Act for four years, through fiscal 1981.

- Set authorization levels for child abuse programs at $25 million for fiscal 1978, $27.5 million for fiscal 1979, and $30 million each for fiscal 1980 and 1981.
- Permitted funding of ongoing child abuse treatment and prevention programs as well as demonstration projects. Under existing law, funding was restricted to research, demonstration projects and grants to the states. The new authorization would enable successful demonstration programs to be converted into continuing operations.
- Increased the percentage of money earmarked to states from the 5-20 percent range set in 1973 to a minimum of 25 percent for fiscal 1978 and 1979 and a minimum of 30 percent for fiscal 1980 and 1981.
- Directed the secretary of HEW to establish research priorities for the child abuse effort and to make all necessary resources available to the National Center on Child Abuse and Neglect.
- Directed the national center to "disseminate" as well as "compile, analyze, and publish" its research findings and training materials and develop a plan for coordinating activities of all agencies and organizations that deal with child abuse.
- Allowed public participation in the formulation of policy by placing three public members on the Advisory Board on Child Abuse and Neglect.

Sexual Abuse. Broadened the definition of child abuse to include "sexual exploitation."

- Established a new spending category for treatment and counseling programs designed specifically to deal with sexual abuse of youngsters. Authorization levels were set at $3 million for fiscal 1978, $3.5 million for fiscal 1979, and $4 million each year for fiscal 1980 and 1981. At least three treatment centers were required.
- Defined "sexual abuse" as the obscene or pornographic photographing, filming or depiction of children for commercial purposes; rape, molestation, incest, prostitution or other forms of sexual exploitation under circumstances which harmed or threatened the child's health or welfare.

Adoption

- Required the secretary of HEW to centralize all departmental activities involving adoption and foster care, to set up a national system for collecting and analyzing adoption and foster care data from the states, and to conduct an education and training program on adoption and adoption assistance programs.
- Required the secretary to establish a national adoption information exchange system coordinated with similar state and regional systems to match waiting children with adoptive parents.
- Set authorization levels of $5 million a year for fiscal years 1978-1981 to run the adoption programs.
- Required the secretary of HEW to set up a panel of 11 to 17 experts in the area of adoption to review conditions and practices in the field and to develop a model adoption code.
- Required HEW to conduct a study of so-called "black-market" adoptions. ▮

Welfare Reform Stalled

Legislation proposing a comprehensive reform of the welfare system remained stalled in House and Senate committees at the end of the 95th Congress. Besides the Carter administration proposal (HR 9030, S 2084), several other, more modest reform bills were introduced — but they never reached the floor of either chamber.

Interest groups representing the nation's governors, state legislators, county officials and mayors lobbied aggressively for Carter's legislative package, which was introduced in 1977. The proposal was approved, with some slight changes, in February 1978, by the House Welfare Reform Subcommittee, which had been specially created to consider Carter's plan.

When none of the panel's parent committees — Ways and Means, Education and Labor and Agriculture — took action on the bill (HR 10950), the administration and congressional advocates of welfare reform began to negotiate. In early June, administration and House leaders reached agreement on the broad outlines of a welfare reform bill substantially scaled down from the president's proposal.

But later that month, while staff aides were still attempting to work out actual draft legislation, House Speaker Thomas P. O'Neill Jr., D-Mass., pronounced the legislation dead for the 95th Congress. O'Neill said June 22 that the Senate leadership had informed him it was too late in the session for a major welfare reform bill to reach the Senate floor. Others said that, in the aftermath of the so-called "tax revolt" which led to approval of Proposition 13 in California, Congress was not interested in major new federal expenditures for welfare.

Several other bills were introduced after that, producing a few flickers of revived interest but no further action.

About 32 million persons were to receive benefits under Carter's proposed system, which would roll together the existing Aid to Families with Dependent Children (AFDC), Supplemental Security Income (SSI) and food stamp programs and replace them with a flat cash grant. About 30 million persons received aid under the existing programs. *(Carter proposal, existing welfare system, background, 1977 Almanac p. 471)*

The administration's plan had two tiers. The upper one was for those not expected to work or for whom no job was available—the aged, blind and disabled, single parents with children under 7, single parents with children between 7 and 13 if a job and day care were not available and two-parent families with children if one parent was incapacitated. The lower tier was for those expected to work—two-parent families with children, single parents with their youngest child over 13, and single persons and childless couples unable to find full-time work.

The crux of the jobs program would be creation of up to 1.4 million jobs and training slots, 300,000 of them part-time, and placement of numerous participants in private sector jobs. The new jobs were intended to provide work for all low-income families with children, not just persons receiving welfare under the existing system. The Labor Department estimated that about 57 per cent of those participating in the jobs program would be the so-called working poor—persons receiving only food stamps or no income supplement at all under the existing system.

As Carter outlined his plan, it would cost $30.7 billion in 1978 dollars. But later estimates put the cost at $31.1 billion. The administration calculated that $28.3 billion of that amount would come from existing programs or savings and $2.8 billion would be additional cost. However, not included in the total was $3 billion in expanded earned income tax credits for middle-income persons who would not receive income supplements.

House Action

To expedite consideration of President Carter's welfare reform package, House Speaker Thomas P. O'Neill Jr., D-Mass., created a special subcommittee to handle the legislation. The subcommittee, chaired by James C. Corman, D-Calif., held hearings in the fall of 1977 and then went to work marking up a bill.

Ullman Plan

While the subcommittee was plugging away at writing a welfare bill based on the president's plan, House Ways and Means Chairman Al Ullman, D-Ore., Feb. 2 unveiled his own reform program (HR 10711), which he said was affordable and achievable in the 95th Congress. Ullman asserted that President Carter's welfare plan had no chance of passing in 1978.

Unlike the Carter program, which scrapped existing welfare programs in favor of a single cash payment, Ullman retained and revised those programs. The president proposed creating 1.4 million public service jobs for recipients unable to find work in the private sector. Ullman's proposal expanded the existing Work Incentive (WIN) program to provide about 500,000 public jobs, but he said his program did more than Carter's to encourage private sector employment.

"We don't have the money or the experience to open up a million new public jobs," Ullman said. "You don't solve the welfare problem with public jobs. You have to put them in private jobs. That is our main thrust."

If preliminary estimates were correct, the Ullman plan would cost considerably less than the administration program, primarily because of the difference in the public jobs to be produced and because states would receive less fiscal relief.

According to estimates by the Joint Committee on Taxation and the Ways and Means Committee staff, Ullman's program would cost between $7.5 billion and $9 billion more than existing programs. The Congressional Budget Office (CBO) put the additional cost to the federal government of the administration bill at $17.36 billion. Both estimates were for fiscal 1982.

Comparison with Carter Plan. Ullman's plan had a few characteristics in common with the Carter program. It established national eligibility standards for recipients, set national minimum benefit levels, made intact families eligible for assistance, made private sector jobs more attractive than those in the public sector, simplified administration, cut fraud and abuse and provided some fiscal relief to states.

But it differed in many more respects. Ullman's plan retained food stamps, SSI for the aged, blind and disabled and AFDC. It provided a national minimum benefit — to be paid in cash and food stamps — but that benefit varied among states to reflect differences in median family income. Cash benefits would not vary by family size although food stamp benefits would. Some of the benefits paid to recipients with relatively high annual incomes would be recouped through the tax system.

Ullman's plan also phased out cash assistance at a lower level than under the Carter plan. But expansion of the earned income tax credit would make up the difference if the recipient were in a private job. "They're getting the same amount of money but from an employer through the earned income tax credit instead of from the government," a staff member said. "It reduces stigma and saves going to the welfare office."

Ullman Plan Rejected. Less than a week after its unveiling, the Ullman plan went down to defeat at the hands of the Welfare Reform Subcommittee. By a 13-16 vote, the subcommittee rejected Ullman's proposal, and then went on to report its own bill.

Subcommittee Bill

A bill incorporating nearly all of the major points in President Carter's program was ordered reported Feb. 8, 1978, by the special House subcommittee. But there were few indications that the administration's success in pushing and preserving its program would continue. One immediate sign of trouble was the narrow margin — 13-16 — by which the subcommittee had turned down the Ullman proposal.

After turning down Ullman's substitute, the subcommittee voted 26-3 to report its own bill (HR 10950). All of the panel's nine Republicans voted in favor of the Ullman proposal, as did four Democrats. All but one of the six votes against reporting the subcommittee bill came from Republicans.

Before casting his opposing vote, Thomas S. Foley, D-Wash., chairman of the House Agriculture Committee, asserted that the subcommittee bill "cannot pass the Congress or the House in anything like its present form."

Several Republicans who voted in favor of the subcommittee bill indicated they were doing so in order to keep the welfare reform process moving, but said they had reservations about parts of the measure.

In urging defeat of the Ullman proposal, Corman noted that the major difference in the costs of the two plans was in the amount of money earmarked for jobs and for fiscal relief to the states.

"The higher expenditures in the subcommittee bill are justified on both counts," Corman said. "There is no way to get state relief without spending more money.... It costs more for people to work than merely to give them a welfare check. You're way ahead when you put people to work. It gives them dignity, self worth, and their work is of value to the community."

The subcommittee bill then went back to the panel's three parent committees — Ways and Means, Education and Labor and Agriculture.

Search for Compromise

Welfare reform went on the back burner after the House subcommittee agreed on its version of the bill. When the issue resurfaced in April, it had a different focus. No longer were people concentrating on the "comprehensive" welfare measure proposed by Carter.

Instead, key legislators, their aides and officials in the Department of Health, Education and Welfare (HEW) had begun studying four different welfare measures, including the Carter proposal, looking for similarities and possible areas of compromise.

Besides the administration bill (HR 9030, S 2084), the other measures getting scrutiny included HR 10950 — the Carter plan as amended by the subcommittee; HR 10711, the Ullman plan and S 2777, sponsored by a bipartisan group of senators led by Howard H. Baker Jr., R-Tenn., the Senate minority leader; Abraham Ribicoff, D-Conn., a former HEW secretary; Henry Bellmon, R-Okla., and John C. Danforth, R-Mo.

Baker-Bellmon Proposal

The Baker-Bellmon welfare measure took what its sponsors called an "incremental" approach to welfare reform, proposing limited changes in existing welfare programs without altering the basic structure of the overall system. It was introduced in March 1978.

Some major players in the welfare debate, including Daniel Patrick Moynihan, D-N.Y., chairman of the Senate Finance Subcommittee on Public Assistance and chief sponsor of the Carter bill in the Senate, viewed the introduction of the Baker-Bellmon bill, regardless of its chances of passage, as an important step toward generating support for welfare reform in the 95th Congress. He called it a "very important option" to be considered if the Carter bill did not move.

One administration official who had lobbied for the Carter bill was more succinct. Welfare reform, he said, "was pretty much dead in the water" before Baker and the other senators introduced their bill.

Status of Carter Proposal

The Baker-Bellmon bill came at a time when high-ranking officials in the HEW bureaucracy and in the White House were just about ready to throw in the towel on welfare reform for the 95th Congress. Many on Capitol Hill agreed that there was little prospect for passage of the Carter proposal.

The Carter proposal, as amended by the Corman subcommittee, would increase existing welfare costs by about $20.22 billion, according to Congressional Budget Office estimates. The administration disputed that estimate, but the different cost figures only increased uncertainty over the Carter measure.

The cost of the administration proposal generated substantial opposition. Even in a non-election year, one congressional aide said, a program with such a large price tag would be received skeptically.

Secondly, while administration officials argued that fundamental changes were necessary, they conceded that Congress was not likely to accept them all at one time. "Congress likes to do things in bits and pieces," one official asserted.

Thirdly, key committee chairmen, like Ullman, Foley and Russell B. Long, D-La., of the Senate Finance Committee, expressed opposition to major sections of the Carter plan. For example, Foley opposed "cashing out" food stamps and merging the program with other welfare benefits into one single cash payment. His committee had jurisdiction over the food stamp section of the bill, and few thought its members would buck him.

Long, whose committee shared jurisdiction over the measure in the Senate, repeatedly stated his opposition to providing cash benefits to single individuals and childless couples. "It's my judgment that you don't need any more people on welfare," Long declared.

Move Toward Compromise

Thus, administration officials conceded, "political realities" dictated that some compromises had to be made if a welfare reform measure was to be enacted in the 95th Congress.

HEW Secretary Joseph A. Califano Jr. signaled the administration's readiness to talk during little-noticed testimony March 23 before the Senate Human Resources Committee. Califano pointed to the Ullman and Baker-Bellmon bills, noted several similarities with the Carter plan, and declared, "In short, the introduction of the Ullman and Baker-Bellmon-Ribicoff proposals reflects an emerging consensus for significant reform upon which to build."

If the areas cited by Califano did provide the basis for a possible compromise welfare bill, it meant that Carter was giving up, at least for the time being, two major elements of his plan: the merging of various existing welfare programs into one single cash grant, and extending cash benefits to single individuals and childless couples.

Those were considered two of the most controversial portions of the Carter plan, and generated the most opposition. Extension of benefits to single individuals and childless couples was widely viewed as a major step toward a guaranteed minimum income, a step many in Congress did not want to take.

Compromise Agreement

The Carter administration and House leaders reached agreement in June on the broad outlines of a welfare reform bill substantially scaled down from the president's original proposal. The fundamentals of a compromise bill were worked out at a June 7 meeting in the offices of Ways and Means Chairman Ullman.

The compromise bill was expected to cost $9 billion to $12 billion more than existing welfare programs. It reportedly retained the existing system of cash payments and food stamps, provided between $1.5 billion and $2.5 billion in fiscal relief for states, expanded the earned income tax credit, streamlined administration of the welfare system, provided for between 600,000 and 700,000 public service jobs, set a minimum national benefit standard for AFDC of about $4,200 for a family of four (65 percent of the official poverty level) and required states to provide AFDC benefits for so-called "intact" families where the husband lived at home.

But while staff aides were at work on draft legislation, O'Neill announced to a meeting of House Democratic whips June 22 that the Senate leadership had informed him that it was too late in the session for a major welfare bill to make it to the Senate floor.

Others said the Senate really wasn't in the mood to debate major increases in federal spending for welfare in light of Proposition 13.

Soundings by O'Neill and others in the House, including Corman, found a similar lack of interest.

The assessment by congressional leaders ended efforts to fashion a compromise welfare bill. Although negotiators had made some progress, cost was still a big problem when the discussions came to an end. The Corman bill had a price tag of $20.22 billion. Ullman had said Congress would not support anything costing more than $5 billion to $6 billion. Negotiators had come up with a bill costing about $14 billion, well above what Ullman was willing to support.

Cranston-Moynihan-Long Bill

Only a week after O'Neill pronounced welfare reform dead another drive was under way to steer a welfare bill through the 95th Congress.

At a press conference June 28, Alan Cranston, D-Calif., and Daniel Patrick Moynihan, D-N.Y., proposed what they called a "no frills" welfare plan which would cost $5 billion when fully effective in fiscal 1981. The initial cost for fiscal 1979 was estimated at $1 billion to $2 billion.

The "no-frills" bill (S 3470), which was also sponsored by Long, was introduced in August.

The proposal had three key sections: expanded tax credits for the working poor, tax credits for employers who hire welfare recipients, and fiscal relief for states and localities.

The fiscal relief was expected to be the most politically attractive aspect of the proposal. Increased federal funding of welfare would ease the financial burden on states and localities and could be cited by Congress as an example of how concerned its members were over state and local tax burdens.

"The infusion of additional federal funds that we are proposing will, in effect, cut in half the size of the welfare bill for states, cities and counties across the nation," Cranston said.

Many observers believed the passage of Proposition 13 in California, Cranston's home state, made fiscal relief — and the welfare measure itself — even more appealing. Cranston cited the property tax rollback approved by California voters as one of the reasons for developing the new welfare proposal.

The enormous financial impact the Cranston-Moynihan plan would have on California and New York — the two together would receive about one-third of the fiscal relief — led some cynics to see the measure primarily as a financial bail-out for the two states. But other observers pointed out that California and New York rightly deserved the money, since they had the highest welfare rolls.

Beyond that, however, the Cranston-Moynihan plan created some political problems for a host of people and interest groups that supported broader changes in the welfare system, including liberals like Corman and Rep. Charles B. Rangel, D-N.Y., the nation's governors and other state and local elected officials, and the Carter administration.

All saw the measure as too limited, focusing only on fiscal relief and tax incentives without making any structural changes in the welfare system itself.

Ways and Means Bill

Corman and Rangel had an alternative to the fiscal relief portion of the Cranston-Moynihan plan. The two House members were pushing HR 13335, which would provide $400 million in temporary fiscal relief to states for fiscal 1979 only.

Corman and Rangel saw the measure as a way to provide fiscal relief to states on a temporary basis until broader welfare changes were enacted by Congress.

HR 13335 was reported by the Ways and Means Committee July 18 (H Rept 95-1373), but never came to the House floor. (A last-minute effort by Moynihan to add such a provision to the tax bill in the Senate also failed, so no fiscal relief was enacted.)

Kennedy Bill

On Sept. 14, two days after complaints about the "no-frills" Cranston-Moynihan measure were voiced before the Senate Finance Subcommittee on Public Assistance, Sen. Edward M. Kennedy, D-Mass., introduced his version of welfare reform legislation (S 3498).

The Kennedy bill, which had an estimated total cost of $7.1 billion for fiscal 1979, would establish a minimum national benefit level of 65 percent of the poverty level, mandate coverage to "intact" families, establish a new set of "rights and responsibilities" for welfare recipients, provide fiscal relief for states and localities through increased federal payments for AFDC, establish incentives and penalties designed to improve administration and cut down errors, and expand the earned income tax credit for the working poor.

Kennedy acknowledged that little time remained in the current session to consider his bill. But he said he introduced his proposal so the Senate would have an opportunity to debate it if it decided to take up welfare before adjournment.

If not, Kennedy indicated, he would work in 1979 with the Carter administration and others interested in welfare reform to develop an acceptable bill. ▮

Cancer Research, Ethics

President Carter Nov. 9 signed into law a bill mandating an intensive study of the ethics of genetic counseling and other difficult health issues, and adding a major new direction to federal cancer research.

The House by voice vote Oct. 15 cleared the multi-part, $4 billion reauthorization (S 2450 — PL 95-622) that re-established a national commission to study medical ethics problems and provided two-year extensions for disease research and control programs of the National Cancer Institute and the National Heart, Lung and Blood Institute. Half of the reauthorization, $2.1 billion, was for cancer programs.

The bill also continued for two years various types of federal aid to community mental health centers, and continued assistance programs for medical libraries. The Senate had passed the bill by voice vote Oct. 14.

The ethics of genetic counseling was one of several topics the ethics commission was directed to study. Its predecessor had focused on protection of human participants in medical research but the new commission had a broader charge, reflecting current concerns with such issues as a uniform definition of death ("brain death," for example, as compared with the traditional standard based on cessation of heartbeat and other "vital signs").

The reauthorization of the cancer programs reflected a judgment that what started out as President Nixon's "blitzkrieg" war on cancer had lengthened into a classic war of attrition, with no victory in sight. The 1971 National Cancer Act had conferred special status on the cancer institute and reflected a view that massive infusions of money into targeted research could produce an early cure, in much the same way that stepped-up federal spending had put men on the moon. *(1971 act, Congress and the Nation Vol. III, p. 566)*

By 1978, however, there was strong statistical evidence that personal habits such as smoking and environmental factors such as pollution played a major role in the incidence of cancer. And many scientists viewed cancer as a highly complex group of diseases, with multiple causes, rather than as a single entity.

The 1978 reauthorization cleared by Congress included new statutory authority for the secretary of health, education and welfare (HEW) to test substances for carcinogenicity (cancer-causing properties) and other harmful effects, and ordered research on low-level ionizing radiation, implicated in cancer.

The bill also mandated annual publication of a list of substances known or suspected to be carcinogenic. The list would have no legal force — that is, presence of a substance on it would not be grounds for another agency with regulatory reponsibility to move against that substance. Still, the proposal had attracted considerable opposition from conservative members and chemical industry representatives, who argued that data on carcinogenicity was still too imprecise to justify the damage that would be done to a product by inclusion on the list.

The reauthorization also added new stress on disease-prevention measures, including new information programs for medical practitioners and for the public, to be conducted by the cancer and heart-lung-blood institutes. Funding authorization levels were not dramatically raised for either institute.

There were few changes for the mental health centers, other than a relaxation of service requirements for the start-up period of a center. Some centers had found that providing the mandated range of services from the first day of operation was too costly.

Most of the policy changes, except for the ethics commission, originated in the House Commerce Committee. The Senate Human Resources Committee had decided on a simple one-year extension for the mental health centers and the health institutes, anticipating a full-scale review of the centers and all the National Institutes of Health in 1979.

The final version of the legislation was a compromise worked out by committee staff and members without a formal conference when it appeared that time was about to run out for the 95th Congress. It combined elements of several earlier bills.

The only piece of the final bill that the House had passed was a three-year mental health centers reauthorization, approved Sept. 19 as part of a health centers bill (HR 12460). The House had not acted on a bill (HR 12347) reported in May by the Commerce Committee that extended the health institutes for three years and made policy changes stressing disease prevention and environmental and behavioral factors in the diseases. There had been no House legislation reported comparable to the ethics commission bill (S 2579) that passed the Senate June 26. The Senate had added the provisions of S 2579 to a simple one-year extension (S 2450) for the two institutes and the mental health centers, which also was approved June 26.

Authorizations

As cleared by Congress, S 2450 authorized the following amounts for fiscal 1979-81 *(in millions of dollars):*

	1979	1980	1981
Mental health centers			
Planning	$ 1.5	$ 1	—
Initial operations	34.5	35	—
Consultation, education	20	3	—
Conversion	30	25	—
Financial distress	25	—	—
Rape prevention	8	9	—
State mental health programs	5	20	$ 25
Medical libraries	15	16.5	18.5
Cancer Institute			
Control programs	90.5	103	—
Research, other programs	924.5	927	—
Heart, Lung and Blood Institute			
Prevention, control programs	40	45	—
Research, other programs	470	515	—
National Research Service Awards	197.5	210	222.5
Ethics Commission[1]	5	5	5
Totals	$1,866.5	$1,914.5	$271

[1] S 2450 also authorized $5 million for this program in fiscal 1982.

Provisions

As cleared by Congress, S 2450:

Community Mental Health Centers. Authorized through fiscal 1980 support for grants to mental health centers for costs of planning, initial operations, consultation and education programs and conversion of facilities; extended financial distress grants through fiscal 1979 only; authorized state mental health program support through fiscal 1981, and rape prevention programs through fiscal 1980. *(Authorizations, box, this page)*

- Raised to five, from three, the number of financial distress grants a center may receive, and broadened eligibility standards for the grants.
- Relaxed existing minimum service requirements for initial operations grants, to permit centers to begin operations with six basic services, if the secretary of health, education and welfare (HEW) approved a plan for adding other mandated services within three years. The six services that had to be provided initially were inpatient, outpatient, emergency, screening and referral, followup and consultation and education. The basic services had to be provided for all age groups.
- Permitted centers to share certain services (inpatient, emergency, transitional or "halfway house" services), if the services were accessible to patients in both centers' service areas and if the secretary approved the arrangement.
- Deleted a requirement that centers operated by hospitals or public entities be governed by a separate board; allowed them instead to establish advisory boards.
- Earmarked appropriations for state-level monitoring of the mental health centers.
- Authorized centers to keep up to 5 percent of excess grant funds from other sources, if they spent the money to improve services.

Biomedical Reseach. Extended federal assistance programs for medical libraries through fiscal 1981.

- Extended National Heart, Lung and Blood Institute and National Cancer Institute programs through fiscal 1980.
- Required both institutes to step up their efforts to provide information both to doctors and other health professionals and to the general public; directed the Heart-Lung-Blood Institute to include disease-related information on nutrition and environmental pollutants.
- Added non-voting, ex officio members from these federal agencies to the National Cancer Advisory Board:

National Institute for Occupational Safety and Health.
National Institute of Environmental Health Sciences.
Department of Labor.
Food and Drug Administration.
Environmental Protection Agency.
Consumer Product Safety Commission.

• Amended membership requirements for the board to include experts in environmental carcinogenesis and treatment of cancer.

• Required the cancer institute to expand and intensify its research on preventing cancer caused by occupational or environmental exposure to carcinogens.

Research Service Awards, Other Provisions. Extended the National Research Service Award program through 1981; extended to five years, from three, the maximum period an individual could receive the awards; authorized cost-of-living adjustments in the stipends; relaxed some service pay-back requirements.

• Authorized the secretary to provide research substances or organisms in certain circumstances. This provision was intended to improve research by ensuring uniform materials for comparable experiments, by providing very rare or costly substances, or by assisting laboratories that couldn't afford a given substance.

• Directed the secretary to conduct research and testing of substances for their capacity to cause cancer (carcinogenicity), severe birth defects (teratogenicity), significant and basic changes in genetic material (mutagenicity) or other harmful biological effects.

• Required the secretary to establish a research program on the biological effects of low-level ionizing radiation, and to review federal research programs on the topic.

• Directed the secretary to support research and information programs on human nutrition.

• Required the secretary to publish an annual report on carcinogens, including a list of all substances known or thought likely to be carcinogenic, evaluations of existing regulatory efforts to control specific substances, surveys of federal agency testing and research results.

• Authorized the director of the National Institutes of Health to hire up to 200 consultants.

• Broadened the scope of alcohol abuse programs to include, when appropriate, the impact of alcoholism on families of alcoholics.

Ethics Commission. Established an 11-member President's Commission for the Study of Ethical Problems in Medicine and Biomedical and Behavioral Research, with representatives from biomedical and behavioral research, medicine, humanities, social sciences and other natural sciences. Full-time federal employees were barred from membership.

• Required these agencies to maintain liaison with the commission: the Departments of Defense and HEW, Central Intelligence Agency, Office of Science and Technology Policy, Veterans Administration and National Science Foundation.

• Directed the commission to report every two years on human research policies and their implementation in all federal agencies.

• Directed the commission to conduct special studies on the impact of income and place of residence on the availability of health services and on the ethical and legal implications of these subjects:

Informed consent in medical contracts.

The desirability of a uniform legal definition of death.

Genetic counseling and information programs.

Confidentiality of patient records in research, and access of patients to such records.

• Required publication of commission recommendations on programs or policies of a federal agency, with opportunity for public comment; required the agency to either adopt the recommendation or, within six months, publish its reasons for deciding not to do so.

• Barred the commission from disclosing trade secret information or medical records that were protected by the Freedom of Information Act.

• Authorized $5 million a year for commission operations through fiscal 1982; authorized commission activities through the first quarter of fiscal 1983 if the extra time was needed to complete its work.

House Committee Action

HR 12347

The House Interstate and Foreign Commerce Committee reported HR 12347 (H Rept 95-1192) May 15. It recommended three-year extensions of the cancer and heart-lung-blood programs, and directed both institutes to give special attention to environmental and behavioral factors in their research, control and information programs. The committee also proposed returning the two institutes to comparable status with the other National Institutes of Health, deleting provisions for presidential appointment of their chiefs and direct reporting to the president.

In other changes, the committee told the cancer institute to draw up a list each year of all known and suspected carcinogens, and to review data on human exposure to the substances and the success of related regulations. The committee also directed both institutes to step up efforts to move their research discoveries out of the laboratory and into general use, through continuing education programs for doctors and other professionals and through increased public information activities.

HR 12460

The Commerce Committee also recommended a three-year extension and made substantive changes in the mental health centers program. It reported HR 12460 on May 15 (H Rept 95-1186). The bill also included reauthorizations for migrant and community health centers, the federal health maintenance organization (HMO) program and rape prevention. *(HMO program, story, p. 576; migrant, community health centers, p. 611)*

House Floor Action on HR 12460

The three-year, $1.9 billion reauthorization bill (HR 12460) passed the House Sept. 19 by a 302-102 vote under suspension of the rules. *(Vote 702, p. 198-H)*

Over Republican objections to funding increases, the House agreed to raise federal spending in fiscal 1979 by almost 50 percent for federal programs delivering mental health services and for centers providing health care to migrant farm workers and medically underserved rural and urban communities.

By fiscal 1981, spending for the federal health programs would exceed the fiscal 1978 authorization by 78 percent and the fiscal 1978 appropriation by 98.3 percent, according to dissenting Republicans on the House Commerce Committee.

Committee Republicans James T. Broyhill, N.C., and James M. Collins, Texas, also objected during floor debate to what Broyhill called "huge increases in authorizations." Both were prevented from offering cost-cutting amendments by the suspension procedure.

Floor manager Paul G. Rogers, D-Fla., defended the higher authorization levels, arguing that the outpatient health programs actually saved federal health dollars by "substituting for more expensive inpatient services."

Besides extending the health centers programs, the bill provided one-year extensions for a special rural health program and for start-up support for prepaid group medical practices (health maintenance organizations). It continued for three years the federal rape prevention program, and relaxed certain statutory standards for community mental health centers. Most of these programs were previously authorized in 1977 by an omnibus one-year extension (PL 95-83) of health programs. *(1977 Almanac p. 453)*

Senate Action

The Senate June 26 by voice vote passed a simple one-year extension (S 2450) of community mental health centers, the National Cancer Institute and the National Heart, Lung and Blood Institute. The authorizations in the bill totaled $2.2 billion.

The programs should have a "thorough, thoughtful review" in the next Congress before they were continued for a longer time, sponsor Edward M. Kennedy, D-Mass., told his colleagues. One reason for postponing revisions of the mental health program was the late-arriving recommendations of a presidential commission, which could not be incorporated into the committee bill by the May 15 budget deadline, according to the Senate Human Resources Committee.

Before passing S 2450, the Senate agreed to two amendments — by Kennedy, to add the research subject commission to the bill, and by Orrin G. Hatch, R-Utah, to add an emphasis on treatment for families of alcoholics to the mental health programs. The Senate Human Resources Committee had reported S 2450 May 15 (S Rept 95-838).

Senate Action on S 2579

By a 68-10 vote the Senate June 26 approved a four-year, $24 million authorization (S 2579) for a President's Commission for the Protection of Human Subjects of Biomedical and Behavioral Research. *(Vote 173, p. 29-S)*

The bill re-established and upgraded the status of an existing national commission, requiring presidential appointment of commissioners and Senate confirmation of the chairman. That panel, which was due to expire in October, reviews and makes recommendations on research policy and practice for projects funded by the Department of Health, Education and Welfare (HEW). The new panel would look at all agencies whose biomedical or behavioral research involved human subjects.

Included for the first time would be classified projects of the Defense Department and the Central Intelligence Agency.

The commission would also study other ethical-legal questions relating to health, such as the desirability of a uniform legal definition of death, which varied from state to state.

Reports of serious research abuses had prompted Congress in 1974 to establish a two-year advisory commission to suggest regulations for biomedical and behavioral research involving humans. Among the abuses brought out at hearings were experimental use of drugs on uninformed subjects, without proper medical follow-up, and a multi-decade study that withheld medical treatment from syphilis patients. Legislation authorizing the commission was extended for one year in 1976 and for another six months in 1977 (PL 94-573, PL 95-203). *(Background, 1974 Almanac p. 379; 1976 Almanac p. 566)*

Commending the existing commission, the Senate Human Resources Committee said in its May 15 report (S Rept 95-852) that its activities should be extended to all biomedical and behavioral research funded by the federal government.

Much of the floor debate turned on the question of whether a non-elected entity should be making what opponent Jesse Helms, R-N.C., called "life and death decisions." A leading foe of abortion, Helms invoked the specter of euthanasia and suggested that the commission — or at least certain influential segments of the medical profession — were insensitive to a basic human right to life. He sought unsuccessfully to eliminate provisions instructing the commission to conduct special studies on genetic counseling and on definitions of death.

The Senate agreed by voice vote to a Helms amendment stipulating that the genetic counseling study shall "evidence concern for the essential equality of all human beings, born and unborn." It also adopted by voice vote a second Helms amendment requiring commission membership to be balanced to represent various viewpoints. And it agreed by voice vote to a Richard S. Schweiker, R-Pa., amendment stressing that commission findings were entirely separate from either Congress or the executive branch, and that its recommendations "cannot be binding on any department or agency."

After passing the bill the Senate agreed to add it as an amendment to S 2450, a bill extending funding for community mental health centers and biomedical research. This move was intended to ensure a House vote on extending the commission, as there was no comparable measure pending in the House.

House-Senate Compromise

As a middle ground between the one-year Senate extensions and the three-year House reauthorizations, the compromise proposal provided two-year extensions for the mental health centers and the two institutes. It also included a four-year authorization for the ethics commission, and made a few minor changes in the Senate bill. It cut $1 million a year from the $6 million authorization level proposed by the Senate, and added to the commission's charge a study on health services availability.

The compromise also included most of the policy changes recommended by the House Commerce Committee for the two institutes and for the mental health programs. However, there were these differences between earlier versions and the final bill:

- Authority for "supplemental" grants, to support mental health centers operations past the eighth year, was deleted. However, because many centers would be completing their eighth year in 1978, the compromise included a $25 million House recommendation for financial distress grants in fiscal 1979.
- A Senate authorization of $2.5 million for mental health center construction was not included in the compromise.
- House provisions intended to integrate the mental health center system with the federal health planning

system were deleted from the final version because they duplicated language in a proposed extension (HR 11488) of the planning law. However, Congress adjourned without completing action on the planning reauthorization, and that program was simply extended without change by a continuing resolution (H J Res 1139) *(Health Planning bill, p. 616)*

Health Care Research

Congress Oct. 15 cleared a three-year, $378-million reauthorization (S 2466 — PL 95-623) for federal health statistics and health care research programs.

The bill provided statutory authority for a newly created health technology evaluation center at the Department of Health, Education and Welfare (HEW). It also authorized both the center and a related new national advisory body to advise the secretary of HEW on whether and to what extent Medicare and Medicaid should pay for new health technologies applied to their beneficiaries.

Health economists had partially blamed spiraling health care costs on wasteful duplication and inappropriate use of such expensive equipment as the half-million-dollar computerized X-ray machine known as the CAT scanner. The medical and economic worth of certain specialized treatment units, such as hospital coronary care units, and certain surgical procedures had also been questioned. Paradoxically, there had also been some complaints that information about new medical developments was difficult for many practitioners to come by. The new center was authorized to address both of these problems through direct research and projects carried out under federal grants and contracts.

The increasing prominence of cost issues in health care also showed up in new authority for studies on environmentally-related diseases and health conditions. The bill required the secretary to report periodically to Congress on a broad, ongoing study of the present and future costs of environment-related diseases and disabilities. A second new study was to evaluate the desirability and privacy problems with setting up a new federal program to study health effects of exposure to hazardous substances, locate victims of exposure and assist with medical follow-up.

The environmental-cost study was to use conventional fiscal yardsticks of cost such as medical care expenses and lessened productivity, and it was also to put dollar values on such intangibles as social and emotional impact of the health problems. Proponents said such a wide-ranging study was needed to find out whether new pollution controls and similar protections were in fact more costly to the nation — as some business opponents maintained — than doing without and paying for the resulting health problems.

The bill had been substantially reduced from earlier proposals, after opponents objected to higher spending levels and increased bureaucracy. The Senate June 26 rejected a committee bill authorizing a three-year total of $440 million and elevating the three centers to the status of National Institutes of Health. A $318 million version was approved by the Senate Aug. 9; it kept the existing status of the centers. House approval of similar but more expensive legislation (HR 12584), with a three-year total of $429 million, came Sept. 25.

The House approved the conference report on the bill by voice vote Oct. 13, the Senate Oct. 15.

Provisions

As cleared for the president, S 2466:

- Authorized a three-year (through fiscal 1981) total of $378 million, as follows: for the National Center for Health Services Research, $120 million; for the National Center for Health Statistics, $185 million; for the National Center for Health Care Technology, $73 million.
- Directed the secretary to add certain priorities to health statistics and health services research, including health care costs and cost increases, and effectiveness and impact of health care technology.
- Required the secretary to support manpower training programs in health care research, statistics and technology evaluation.
- **Health Statistics.** Authorized the Center for Health Statistics to provide, at cost, statistical analyses and studies for public and non-profit private entities.
- Strengthened the existing local-state-federal Cooperative Health Statistics System by requiring coordinated participation by federal agencies, authorizing grants to state and local health agencies for costs of data collection, and authorizing guidelines for uniform data-collection.
- Authorized the center to aid health planning agencies in interpreting and using health statistics.
- Directed the secretary to standardize health data and information collection under HEW statutory authority.
- **Health Care Technology.** Established a National Center for Health Care Technology.
- Authorized the center to support evaluations of health care technology for safety, effectiveness and cost effectiveness, social, ethical and economic impact; also, factors affecting use of technologies and methods of disseminating information about them.
- Authorized the center to make recommendations on health care technology with respect to all HEW statutory responsibilities, including reimbursement policy (such as Medicare and Medicaid payments for health services).
- Authorized the secretary to support existing or new facilities to conduct health care technology studies, with a goal of at least three such centers in operation by Sept. 1, 1981; stipulated that the centers were to be within established academic or research institutions and specified staff and other requirements.
- Required both peer group review and review by the new National Council on Health Care Technology for grants exceeding $35,000.
- Established a National Council on Health Care Technology to advise the secretary and the center director on health care technologies, to develop "exemplary standards, norms, and criteria" for the use of particular technologies and to review certain research projects and grants.
- **Studies, Other Provisions.** Directed the secretary to conduct an ongoing study of existing and future health costs of pollution and other environmental conditions (including those of the workplace). The study was to be conducted by the National Academy of Sciences, with a first report to congressional health committees within 18 months of enactment and subsequent reports every two years thereafter.
- Directed the secretary to submit to Congress, by Jan. 1, 1981, a plan for standardizing collection of statistical

and epidemiological data on effects of environment on health.

- Directed the secretary to establish, within two years of enactment, guidelines for collection and processing of information relating to workplace and other environmental conditions and public health; required protection from disclosure for medical records and trade secrets; required review of the guidelines every three years and, if needed, revision.
- Directed the secretary to study the desirability of a federal system to locate individuals exposed to hazardous substances, study the health outcomes of such exposures and assist exposed individuals in securing medical care, if needed.
- Directed the secretary to study the impact on use of health services of the March 1978 United Mine Workers collective bargaining agreement that required copayment for health services; required the study results to be reported within 30 months of enactment; earmarked $1 million (health services authorizations) for the study.

Senate Action

Committee. The Senate Human Resources Committee reported S 2466 May 15 (S Rept 95-839). The bill approximately doubled existing spending levels for health care research, authorizing $440 million through fiscal 1981. It extended existing health statistics and health services research centers at greatly increased funding levels and upgraded them in status to National Institutes of Health. The centers were first authorized in 1974, and extended for one year in 1977. *(1974 Almanac, p. 420; 1977 Almanac, p. 453)*

The bill also created a new national institute to evaluate medical technology.

Floor. Persuaded by arguments against an expensive new bureaucracy, the Senate rejected the bill June 28 by a 30-48 vote. *(Vote 174, p. 29-S)*

Opponent Robert Dole, R-Kan., said that was too much money for a plan that promised "no meaningful improvement" in the "mediocre" performance of existing research facilities (the National Center for Health Services Research and the National Center for Health Statistics). The scheme represented the "beginning of a vast bureaucratic entity," Dole claimed. He also warned that "overregulation in development of medical technology could have a disastrous impact" on medical practice in general.

Sponsor Edward M. Kennedy, D-Mass., said that the important work of the health statistics and health services research units had "never been sufficiently appreciated" within the federal government. These types of research also had suffered from "intense bureaucratic rivalries," leading in some cases to duplicate efforts and in others to wasteful withholding of information, a situation "bordering on administrative chaos," Kennedy said. (At least two other HEW entities, the Health Care Financing Administration and the Center for Disease Control, do major statistical and epidemiological studies.)

While the bill did not envision the centralization of all existing health care research efforts into one "superagency," Kennedy said, upgrading the status of the research units would give "focus, strength and vitality" to their work.

The day after Senate action on the bill William D. Hathaway, D-Maine, moved to reconsider the vote. That action left the way open for another vote on the measure.

Second Vote. The Senate reversed itself Aug. 9 and passed, by a 74-19 vote, a scaled-down version of S 2466. *(Vote 297, p. 45-S)*

The bill provided a three-year, $318 million reauthorization for two national research centers that deal with health care delivery and health statistics. The bill also formally authorized the already existing health technology office in HEW and a new national advisory council that would develop standards for use of significant new medical procedures.

The Senate bill directed the new medical technology office to coordinate, fund and set priorities for research. The 18-member advisory council was to advise the HEW secretary on the optimum use of new technologies and distribute its findings throughout the nation's health care community.

Kennedy offered the scaled-down version of S 2466 as a floor amendment, which the Senate accepted by voice vote.

As passed by the Senate, S 2466 authorized spending through fiscal year 1981 at about 30 percent above existing levels for the National Center for Health Statistics ($140.4 million) and the National Center for Health Services Research ($107.6 million). For the new Office of Health Technology and the national advisory board it provided a three-year total of $70 million.

House Action

Committee. The House Commerce Committee reported its version of health care research legislation May 15 (HR 12584 — H Rept 95-1190).

The House bill provided a simple extension of the health statistics and services units in their existing status and provided for special research emphasis on environment-related diseases and conditions. HR 12584 also provided for a new health technology study unit under the assistant secretary for health of HEW.

The committee's concern for health costs was evident throughout the report. On the one hand, the committee suggested, any apparent savings from watering down statutory controls on pollutants could be gobbled up by increased costs of treating environment-related diseases and conditions. It directed the secretary of HEW to study and report periodically to Congress on the cost of environment-related health conditions, and directed the health statistics center to prepare guidelines for creating a national data base on environmental conditions and public health.

The committee bill authorized $113 million for fiscal 1979 for stepped-up statistical work, health services research and technology assessment. That figure compared with a fiscal 1978 authorization of $62.2 million and a fiscal 1979 budget request of $74 million for statistics and health services research. The bill's three-year total was $429 million. The need for adequate information on which to base health policy decisions justified the jump in spending, the committee said.

In separate views, committee Republicans Samuel L. Devine, Ohio, James M. Collins, Texas, and Dave Stockman, Mich., said the bill was too expensive and that it could lead to federal control over the use of health care technology.

Floor. Before passing HR 12584 by a 306-77 vote under suspension of the rules Sept. 25, the House briefly debated whether it was more inflationary to pay for the various studies and other programs it authorized, or to continue without the additional information. Attention focused on the work of the newly established health technology office and on the study of the costs of environment-related health conditions. *(Vote 729, p. 208-H)*

Collins said the bill was far too expensive, and that the nation did not need another new federal agency, "least of all in HEW." He said the House committee bill "builds up to a 138 percent increase" by fiscal 1981 over current spending levels. He called the environmental study a "wild goose chase," observed that "money does not cure everything," and noted that "people are going to die from one thing and another" regardless of federal studies.

Sponsor Paul G. Rogers, D-Fla., and other proponents argued that a better data base on environmental and technology issues could end by saving the nation money.

Andrew Maguire, D-N.J., a junior member of the House Commerce Health Subcommittee that had drafted the bill, justified the technology office by noting that "medical technology added $8 to $12 million to the nation's hospital bill" in a decade (1966-76).

Conference Action

Conferees leaned toward the more generous House bill in setting three-year authorization levels, which were $51 million less than the House-approved total and $70 million more than the lean Senate version. They blended provisions from the similar House and Senate bills, adopting, with few exceptions, about everything each body had passed. The final report on S 2466 (H Rept 95-1783) was filed Oct. 13.

Conferees retained a House provision explicitly authorizing the new technology center to make policy recommendations to the secretary, including advice on Medicare and Medicaid payment policy. Conferees also stressed the dual function of the technology center, saying it should both "stimulate scrutiny" of health care technology and "encourage the the rapid dissemination" of technologies of proven value. Also included in the final version was House authorization for a study of the issues involved in setting up a broad federal system to deal with the health effects of exposure to hazardous substances.

From the Senate bill, conferees kept an authorization for a special study of a recent United Mine Workers collective bargaining agreement that required union members to share costs of medical benefits.

Absent from the final version was a House-approved requirement for a report on health care technology activities. Conferees also dropped a Senate provision authorizing the assistant secretary for health to develop policy and make decisions on patent rights for inventions developed with HEW funds. Instead, conferees cited "dissatisfaction with the pace" with which these decisions now are made, and told the department to review its policy. Delays in the patent rights decisions "deprive taxpayers of the potential benefits of research and development financed with federal monies," conferees said. ∎

Family Planning, SIDS

Withstanding a final assault by anti-abortion House members, Congress Oct. 15 cleared legislation authorizing funds for three years for family planning and sudden infant death syndrome programs.

The bill (S 2522 — PL 95-613) authorized $1.07 billion for family planning services and $12.5 million for sudden infant death syndrome (SIDS) programs in fiscal 1979-1981.

The authorizations were brought to the House floor as part of an omnibus health services bill, HR 12370. After beating back a series of anti-abortion amendments by Robert K. Dornan, R-Calif., the House approved HR 12370 Oct. 13 by a vote of 343-27. It then agreed by voice vote to substitute the family planning and SIDS provisions for the text of the Senate-passed family planning-SIDS bill, S 2522.

The Senate approved the House amendments by voice vote Oct. 15, clearing the bill for the president.

As originally passed by the Senate June 7, S 2522 had authorized $2.6 billion for fiscal 1979-83 for the family planning programs, $1.6 million more than the House version.

Chagrined at the lack of opportunity to offer amendments, House anti-abortion members had helped defeat HR 12370 when it first came up under suspension of the rules Sept. 25, a procedure that bars floor amendments.

Provisions

As cleared for the president, S 2522:

Family Planning. Authorized $200 million in fiscal 1979, $230 million in fiscal 1980 and $264.5 million in fiscal 1981 for family planning services, including natural family planning services, services for infertile couples and family planning services for teenagers.

- Authorized $3.1 million in fiscal 1979, $3.6 million in fiscal 1980 and $4.1 million in fiscal 1981 for programs to train family planning personnel.
- Authorized $105 million in fiscal 1979, $120.8 million in fiscal 1980 and $138.9 million in fiscal 1981 for family planning and population research programs, including biomedical research projects and programs to develop new contraceptive devices.
- Authorized $700,000 in fiscal 1979, $805,000 in fiscal 1980 and $926,000 in fiscal 1981 for programs to develop and make available family planning information, including educational materials, to all persons desiring such materials.
- Required that family planning pamphlets and other information materials be suitable for the group or community to which they are to be made available, taking into account educational and cultural background and community standards; required review and approval of such materials by an advisory committee broadly representative of the community or group.

Sudden Infant Death Syndrome. Authorized $3.5 million in fiscal 1979, $4 million in fiscal 1980 and $5 million in fiscal 1981 for programs to provide information on the causes of Sudden Infant Death Syndrome (SIDS) and to provide counseling to families affected by SIDS.

Background

Family Planning

Until the 1960s, family planning services generally were available only through private physicians and clinics. In 1967, however, Congress passed the Child Health Act as part of the Social Security Amendments of 1967 (PL 90-248). It required states to make family planning services available to Aid to Families with Dependent Children (AFDC) recipients and provided special project grants for the services. *(1967 Almanac p. 892)*

In 1970 Congress passed the Family Planning Services and Population Research Act (PL 91-572) which established an office of Population Affairs in the Department of Health, Education and Welfare (HEW), and added a Title X to the Public Health Service Act which authorized funds for family planning services, training, information and education programs, and population research. The act stipulated that all family planning services must be provided only on a voluntary basis, and it contained a prohibition against using Title X funds for abortions; however, funds are provided to clinics that provide abortion counseling and referrals. *(1970 act, 1970 Almanac p. 570)*

Nearly 4,300 of the nation's 5,000 family planning clinics receive some Title X funds.

Teen-age Pregnancy. Of the roughly 21 million young people in the United States between the ages of 15 and 19, some 11 million were thought to have had sexual intercourse, according to the Senate Human Resources Committee. In addition, 20 percent of the eight million 13- and 14-year-olds were believed to be sexually active. Approximately one million teen-agers became pregnant annually, and almost 600,000 gave birth.

These pregnancies were frequently unwanted. A higher incidence of low birthweight infants, a higher percentage of pregnancy and childbirth complications and higher rates of school dropout, unemployment and welfare dependency were some of the problems that plagued teen-age mothers.

The rate of elective abortions among teen-agers was also high. In 1976, one-third of the estimated 1,100,000 abortions performed in the United States involved teen-agers.

Sudden Infant Death Syndrome

An estimated 6,000-7,000 infants succumbed each year to Sudden Infant Death Syndrome. These children died suddenly, unexpectedly and quietly in their cribs, during what had been considered normal sleep. SIDS, or "crib death," was the leading cause of death of infants one to 12 months old, according to the Human Resources Committee.

In 1974, Congress passed the Sudden Infant Death Syndrome Act (PL 93-270), which provided funds for research on the causes and prevention of SIDS. *(1974 Almanac p. 433)*

Although researchers had not been able to uncover a specific cause for SIDS, recent studies had shown that the syndrome resulted from a number of developmental, environmental and biological factors, rather than from a single mechanism, as previously believed.

Senate Action

Committee

The Senate Human Resources Committee reported S 2522 (S Rept 95-822) on May 15. It authorized for fiscal 1979-83 a total of $2.635 billion — $2.586 billion for family planning and population research programs and $49 million for Sudden Infant Death Syndrome programs.

The committee lumped together under one title family planning and Sudden Infant Death Syndrome program authorizations. SIDS programs were formerly grouped with genetic disorders. But research calling into question the genetic basis of the disorder and emphasizing the importance of pre-natal care in its prevention prompted its inclusion under the same title as family planning programs, the committee explained.

Teen-age Pregnancy. Blasting the administration's budget proposal for services to pregnant adolescents as inadequate, the committee earmarked a total of $544 million for family planning services to teen-agers. The administration had set aside $18 million for expanded services to teen-agers; $8 million of that amount would have come from existing services to adult women.

The committee's higher authorization was "warranted in view of the high rates of unwanted pregnancies among adolescents," it said, adding that the funds would be used to support counseling, information and education programs targeted at teen-agers.

The committee expressed concern over the high rate of abortions among teen-agers. "Undoubtedly, many of these abortions could have been avoided with greater availability of effective family planning methods," the report stated.

The committee also added a provision directing family planning agencies to encourage minors, "whenever feasible," to seek parental consent before furnishing them with contraceptives or other family planning services.

Abortion. In addition to continuing the existing ban on use of funds in the bill to provide abortions, the committee added a "conscience clause" that prohibited HEW from requiring individuals employed by family planning groups to provide abortion counseling or referrals, if such activity was contrary to their religious or moral convictions. HEW was also prohibited from terminating funding to a project that refused to offer abortion counseling and referrals.

Other Programs. The committee added a new authorization of $49.5 million for services to infertile couples.

In recommending an authorization of $750 million for family planning and population research projects, the committee expressed concern over the high cost of contraceptive research and development. To spur commercial development of new contraceptive devices, the committee recommended providing private firms with exclusive contraceptive marketing and development rights.

Information and educational materials on so-called natural family planning methods should also be developed, the report stated.

The committee recommended strengthening and clarifying the duties of the deputy assistant secretary of HEW for population affairs and placing him or her in charge of the Office of Population Affairs.

"The committee believes that the responsibilities given the [deputy assistant secretary] are of sufficient importance and size to warrant the full-time attention of the occupant of that position," the report stated, expressing concern over the fact that he had been assigned duties outside of the areas of family planning and population research.

Sudden Infant Death Syndrome. Noting that the existing SIDS program suffered from a "certain amount of fragmentation of personnel," the committee directed HEW to establish a separate administrative unit with adequate staff to carry out the program.

Pointing out that the "post mortem examination is vital in alleviating the guilt feelings of most SIDS parents," the committee recommended a study of death investigation laws and systems throughout the United States. It also stressed the importance of additional research into the impact of crib death on surviving family members.

Floor Action

The Senate passed the bill by voice vote without debate on June 7.

House Action

The House Interstate and Foreign Commerce Committee reported HR 12370 (H Rept 95-1191) May 15. It recommended $1.07 billion for fiscal 1979-81 for family planning and population research programs. Although no funds were set aside specifically for adolescent pregnancy prevention, the committee said it was "committed" to addressing the needs of teen-agers.

Funding for family planning services was boosted by nearly 50 percent, from a fiscal 1978 authorization of $208 million to a fiscal 1979 level of $309 million.

First Floor Vote

By a tie vote of 193-193, the House Sept. 25 rejected HR 12370 under suspension of the rules. *(Vote 730, p. 208-H)*

Sponsor Paul G. Rogers, D-Fla., blamed the setback to the health services bill partly on members' resistance to suspension votes on major bills — "It was a lot of money to do under suspension" — and partly to lobbying by abortion foes. "I think the right-to-lifers were busy on this one," Rogers said. The target for the lobbying was the family planning program, which opponents said was improperly promoting abortion. Nearly half the funds in the bill went for family planning.

Rogers urged members to reject arguments that the bill was too expensive, or that the family planning programs encouraged abortion. "A vote for this bill is a vote against abortion. [Family planning] is the only national program which will actually prevent the condition which could lead to a request for abortion," Rogers said. A ban in existing law on using the funds to pay for abortions was being observed, Rogers said, adding that "there is no evidence that a single abortion has been performed with [these] funds."

Robert K. Dornan, R-Calif., objected that the statutory ban on funding for abortions was being circumvented by federally funded groups that referred clients to abortion services. Family planning grants were supporting "Planned Parenthood and other groups which promote abortion and controversial publications, films, etcetera, which undermine generally accepted standards and values about sex and sexual conduct," Dornan said.

Dornan said he wanted to amend the bill to bar funding to any entity which "directly or indirectly provides abortion services . . . counseling . . . or referral services." He also sought authorization for grants to "single service organizations that provide only natural family planning as a means of child spacing."

Existing law required family planning organizations to offer comprehensive services. Dornan claimed that HEW withheld grants from groups that did not deal with abortion as a method of spacing births.

House Passage

The House by a 343-27 vote passed the health services bill (HR 12370) Oct. 13, after agreeing to amendments by Rogers and Tim Lee Carter, R-Ky., to cut $388 million from the committee bill. The funding cuts were adopted by voice vote without discussion. *(Vote 811, p. 230-H)*

Before approving the bill, the House by voice vote adopted an amendment by Carter requiring review and approval of family planning pamphlets and other education materials by local advisory committees to ensure that they would not outrage community sensibilities. It rejected another amendment requiring parental notification before providing contraceptives to children under 16.

The House also rejected a series of anti-abortion amendments, directed at the family-planning program, proposed by Dornan. Most were rejected by voice or standing votes, but there was a 137-232 recorded vote against recommitting the bill to committee with instructions to add a ban on using family planning funds directly or indirectly for abortions, abortion counseling or abortion referrals. *(Vote 810, p. 230-H)*

Dornan urged recommittal on grounds that the bill's "expensive programs" were "beyond the spirit of what Congress or the nation really wants." Rogers said the ban proposed by Dornan would be "devastating" to efforts to reach teen-agers likely to become or already pregnant.

To avoid yet another assault on the family planning program by pro-life members, House sponsors of the bill decided to separate the controversial provisions from the rest of HR 12370. The decision was prompted by assurances that the Senate would accept House authorization levels for the family planning programs without a conference, thus eliminating the risk that anti-abortion House members would attack HR 12370 once again when the bill returned to the House for a final vote, according to a House source.

After passing HR 12370, the House by voice vote agreed to subtract the family planning and sudden infant death syndrome provisions from that bill, adding them instead to the text of the Senate family-planning bill, S 2522. It then agreed to substitute the rest of HR 12370, plus the health services title of HR 12460, for the text of the Senate-passed health services-centers bill, S 2474. *(Story, below)*

Health Services, Centers

The 95th Congress in its last hours cleared omnibus health legislation (S 2474 — PL 95-626) extending support for health facilities serving doctor-short areas and for programs targeted on specific health problems such as hypertension.

The $2.9 billion authorization also included new initiatives to head off unwanted teen-age pregnancies through increased counseling and other services, and to promote better health through preventive programs like water fluoridation. The various programs were authorized for one, two or three years.

Final action came during the round-the-clock Oct. 14-15 session, when conferees quickly endorsed compromises worked out by staff and both houses cleared the conference report for the president. The House approved it by a 110-27 standing vote, the Senate by voice vote.

The only objection to the conference report came when Robert E. Bauman, R-Md., urged members to recommit (kill) the bill because conferees had removed a requirement that parents of young adolescents be notified if their children used the family planning or pregnancy prevention services. That issue, plus efforts by abortion foes to bar funding for abortion counseling or referrals, had helped defeat a major component of the bill in the House when it was first brought up under suspension of the rules.

A second major objection to the reauthorizations — money — had surfaced and been dealt with earlier. House and Senate sponsors Paul G. Rogers, D-Fla., and Edward M. Kennedy, D-Mass., both cut funds on the floor from committee-recommended totals. Conferees did some additional fiscal trimming, cutting back on proposed spending levels for the teen-age pregnancy prevention program and new hospital-based primary care services.

The Health Services and Centers Act cleared for the president had a complicated legislative history. The Senate had stitched together a health services reauthorization (S 2474), a disease prevention-health promotion package (S 3116) plus a teen-age pregnancy bill (S 2910) in floor action Sept. 29. The House had passed its health centers bill (HR 12460) Sept. 19, rejected the health services bill (HR 12370) under suspension Sept. 25, and finally passed a cheaper version of HR 12370 late Oct. 13. *(HR 12460, p. 603; HR 12370, p. 609)*

Absent from the final omnibus bill were a community mental health centers reauthorization that had passed the House as part of HR 12460, and reauthorizations for family planning and sudden infant death syndrome programs that had been part of HR 12370. The mental health centers were reauthorized along with biomedical research programs in S 2450, and the other two programs were transferred to S 2522 and cleared separately. *(S 2450, p. 603; S 2522, p. 609)*

Provisions

As cleared for the president, S 2474 authorized a total of $2.9 billion for one-, two- and three-year extensions and new authorizations for a variety of public health programs. *(Authorizations, box, p. 613)*

It also made these revisions:

Migrant and Community Health Centers

- Authorized centers to fund improvements to private property, with the permission of the owner, to eliminate the source of an environmental health hazard, if no other funds were available; authorized the secretary of Health, Education and Welfare (HEW) to earmark appropriated funds for this purpose.
- Made pharmaceutical services a primary (required) rather than a supplemental service.
- Authorized centers to keep a portion of payments for services from third-party payors and to spend that money for administrative or physical improvements; required the HEW secretary to approve construction projects if they required more than half of these funds.
- Authorized the secretary to make grants for conversion to a prepaid basis for providing services for some or all of the population a center served.
- Waived partially a requirement that public agencies sponsoring health centers delegate decision-making to a separate governing board, but retained a requirement that the public agency allow the board to decide on services to be offered, hours of service, director of the center and budget; limited appropriations for public agencies using the waiver.

For Migrant Health Centers Only: Redefined a "high impact area" as one with 4,000 migratory and seasonal agricultural workers in residence (instead of 6,000), and required the secretary to rank programs by need and distribute funds according to that ranking.

- Made aged or disabled former migrant workers and members of their families eligible for services.
- Required applicants for migrant health center funding to set priorities on certain environmental and supplemental health services and required the secretary to fund those priorities, if the center as a whole were funded, or explain why he did not.
- Repealed authority for grants to pay for converting existing facilities into migrant health centers.

For Community Health Centers Only: Required the centers to develop referral relationships with one or more hospitals.

- Barred the secretary from requiring a center to provide a full range of services in rural areas where such services "are not practical."
- Required the secretary to provide grant recipients with lists of federal and non-federal resources to improve the environment and nutritional status of individuals in the center's service area.
- Required the secretary to equalize urban-rural distribution of the centers when approving grants for the centers.

Technical Assistance

- Authorized grants for technical assistance to state government and private entities to assist community, migrant or other health centers with planning, developing and operating functions; limited grants to $3 million a year for an individual center for three years, with a per-grant limit of $500,000.
- Established a primary health care advisory committee to review applications and required a report to Congress by March 1, 1981, on the effectiveness of entities providing assistance under the grants.

Primary Care

- Established new authority for grants to public and private non-profit community hospitals for planning, developing and operating primary care centers in medically underserved areas.
- Required the new primary care centers to be administered separately from the hospital sponsoring them, to deliver primary health care services and appropriate supplemental services, and to be staffed by at least three primary care physicians (except that one nurse practitioner or one physician assistant could substitute for one doctor in physician-short areas).
- Required primary care grants to be awarded so as to assure equitable urban-rural distribution.
- Limited planning and development grants to $150,000 per project.
- Required the General Accounting Office to submit by March 1, 1981, a comparative study of the hospital-based primary care centers and community health centers.
- Established new authority for grants and contracts to public and private entities to either demonstrate new methods of delivering primary health and dental services or to conduct research on delivery of services; required the projects to serve medically underserved areas, and barred funds for projects eligible for other types of federal support; provided separate authorizations for urban and rural projects, with rural projects receiving more than four times the amount of urban projects. This provision provided statuto-

ry authority for continuing research and demonstration projects, funded with appropriations since 1975, known as Health in Underserved Rural Areas (HURA) Programs.

• Required reports from the secretary of HEW on these topics: health care needs of immigrants and individual American Indian and Alaska native tribes, by June 30, 1979; the National Health Service Corps, by Feb. 1, 1979; continuing education programs for health personnel in medically underserved areas, by Jan. 1, 1980.

Health Services

• Continued formula grants to states for comprehensive public health services through fiscal 1979; converted this support to health incentive grants of at least $1 per capita, depending on state contributions, for fiscal 1980.

• Continued formula grants to states for hypertension programs (screening, detection, diagnosis, prevention, referral for treatment) through fiscal 1979; converted this support to project grants for fiscal 1980 and 1981.

• Authorized grants to state and local governments for community and school-based fluoridation projects, for fiscal 1980 and 1981.

• Authorized, for fiscal 1979 only, funds for immunizing high-risk individuals against influenza; prohibited spending any appropriated funds for this purpose unless the secretary submitted by June 30, 1979, a complete report on health and legal liability problems of immunization programs, including the 1976 swine flu program.

• Required the secretary to study the long-term effects on child development of lead in the blood.

• Required the secretary to provide cost-sharing grants for fiscal 1980-82 for state preventive health services; required states to provide detailed plans for dealing with the cause of at least one of the five leading causes of death within the state.

• Required the secretary to conduct five demonstration programs to test, in rural and urban areas, methods for delivering comprehensive disease prevention services to specific populations; authorized funds for fiscal 1979-81.

• Required the secretary to establish research and community- and school-based programs to identify causes of childhood smoking and alcohol consumption and to discourage these behaviors; authorized the programs for fiscal 1980-81.

• Required the secretary to report within two years of enactment on health risks of smoking, including risks of common cigarette additives.

• Required the secretary to submit by Dec. 1, 1980, and every third year thereafter a national health statistics profile on disease prevention.

• Assigned to an existing HEW health information office new authority to make grants for state physical fitness councils, for model projects to improve physical fitness, for research on sports injuries, and for a national conference in 1979 on teaching and fitness.

• Created a new national panel for promotion of child health; directed the panel to set child health goals, develop a national child health plan and report legislative and other recommendations within 18 months of enactment.

• Limited the eligibility of an emergency medical service for federal support to five grants, replacing a five-year limitation on that support.

• Authorized for fiscal 1979-81 support for community-based health and other services targeted on unwanted adolescent pregnancies, and for a study of the problem.

Authorizations

As cleared by Congress, S 2474 authorized the following amounts for health services and centers in fiscal 1979-81 *(in millions of dollars):*

	1979	1980	1981
Comprehensive health services,			
formula grants	$103	—	—
incentive grants	—	$150	$170
Hypertension programs	20	24.5	29
Home health services			
Demonstration	11	12	13
Training	1.5	2	2.5
Lead-based paint poisoning prevention	14	14	15
Immunization (children)	51	39.5	45
Rodent control	14.5	15.5	17
Other disease control	1	1	1
Venereal disease control	45	51.5	59
Genetic disease programs	17.5	21.5	26
Hemophilia programs	4	5	6
Blood separation centers	2.5	3	3.5
Child health panel	1	—	—
Community health centers			
Planning	6.3	7.5	9
Operation	341.7	397.5	463
Technical assistance	3	3	3
Migrant health centers			
Planning	2.2	2.5	2.9
Operation	40.8	46	52.1
National Health Service Corps	7	—	—
Primary care			
Hospital-based centers	5	25	30
Research, demonstration			
Rural	18	20	22
Urban	4	4.5	5
Preventive health services, formula grants	—	20	60*
Fluoridation	—	5	5
Comprehensive prevention demonstrations	6	8	8
Childhood, adolescent smoking and alcohol			
Research	—	5	5
Prevention programs	—	10	10
Physical fitness			
Promotion	—	6	6
Sports medicine research	—	1.5	1.5
Adolescent pregnancy			
Prevention, health care services	50	65.5	75
Study	.5	—	—
Total	$770.5	$966.5	$1,144.5

* S 2474 also authorized $75 million for this program in fiscal 1982.

• Continued for fiscal 1979-81 federal support for the following categorical health programs: childhood immunization, rodent and other disease control, venereal disease control, genetic disease screening and counseling, and hemophilia programs (including blood separation centers).

Senate Committee Action

Health Services, Primary Care (S 2474)

Uneven distribution of doctors and medical treatment sources was still a national problem, despite "the presence of ample medical...manpower and facilities," the Human Resources Committee said in its May 15 report on S 2474 (S Rept 95-860). "Large groups and geographic areas" were still without health care, while "expensive and duplicative treatment facilities and medical specialists" clustered in certain areas, the committee found.

To help fill in the gaps, the committee authorized two new grants programs, one for primary care facilities run by hospitals and a second for demonstration programs. It also extended through fiscal 1983 the community and migrant health centers programs, which provided comprehensive medical services to medically underserved populations.

Certain categorical health programs were also extended, with little change, as follows: through fiscal 1979 — comprehensive public health and disease control grants, lead-based paint poisoning prevention, hypertension screening and control activities; through fiscal 1981 — hemophilia, home health and genetic disease programs.

The committee bill also established a new national commission that was to evaluate ongoing federal efforts to correct medical maldistribution and recommend improvements within 18 months. The related problem of health manpower would be dealt with in 1979 in a general review of federal support for health professions training.

To encourage the three types of centers to increase their support from third-party payors (federal and private health insurers), the committee authorized the centers to use such "earned income" for a variety of improvements. This income would not reduce federal support for a center. To encourage the centers to convert to prepaid financing, the bill authorized special grants. The secretary was to ensure, by regulation, that the new emphasis on earned income did not cause abuses such as discrimination against patients without third-party coverage or service cuts. And patients would be guaranteed the right to continue paying on a fee-for-service basis, the committee said.

Disease Prevention, Health Promotion (S 3116)

The success of hypertension screening and control activities and the other categorical programs, plus dramatic results of several recent experimental projects, justified new spending and new authority for disease prevention programs, the committee said in its Sept. 15 report on S 3116 (S Rept 95-1196). But these types of projects now received "less than 3 percent of total health spending," the committee noted.

The committee authorized new programs to promote physical fitness, combat childhood smoking, fund fluoridation of water supplies and contribute to preventive health programs targeted for specific population groups.

The committee also provided fiscal 1980-81 reauthorizations for certain categorical public health programs, including hypertension screening and control, childhood immunization, rat control and lead-based paint poisoning. (Fiscal 1979 extensions for these programs were included in S 2474.)

These new programs were proposed by the committee:

Preventive health services at both state and local levels, authorized through fiscal 1982. States would be eligible for formula grants, ranging from 25 cents to 50 cents per capita depending on state funding levels, for preventive health projects. The committee stressed that the new federal funds should not be used to treat existing disease conditions.

States were required to develop plans to reduce mortality rates for at least one of the five leading causes of death within the state. The secretary of health, education and welfare (HEW) could cut post-planning-phase funds if states failed to implement their plans effectively. The committee stressed that in program evaluations, results — "changes in health status" — would be far more important than "tracing how states spend each federal dollar."

In addition to the state-level cost-sharing program, the committee authorized five community-based demonstration programs in rural and urban areas to evaluate delivery methods for "comprehensive preventive health services to defined populations."

Smoking. The number of teenage girls that smoke and the quantity of cigarettes they smoked had both risen dramatically since the 1960s, the committee found, adding that "childhood and teenage smoking is highly predictive of adult smoking." It provided new funds for research and demonstration projects on behavioral and health aspects of smoking, and projects to discourage childhood smoking.

The stiff anti-smoking program of the disease-prevention bill originally proposed by Kennedy had required expanded health-hazard labeling for cigarettes, non-smoking areas in all federal buildings and interstate carriers (trains, airplanes, buses), and a graduated tax on cigarettes, with the highest tax for cigarettes with the most tar and nicotine. It did not move out of the Commerce Committee "because Wendell H. Ford, D-Ky., chairs the subcommittee with jurisdiction," according to a Human Resources staff source. Ford often defends the interests of his tobacco-growing constituents.

Fluoridation. Every dollar spent on water fluoridation saves an estimated $35 in dental treatment costs, according to the committee. The committee authorized funds for project grants to communities for either treatment of the community water supply or more limited programs in schools. The new program was "entirely voluntary," it said.

Fitness. Citing lower incidence of illness, reduced sick-leave and other benefits for participants in organized fitness programs, the committee devised a plan to encourage participation and support research in physical fitness and sports medicine. The major components of the $15-million, three-year program were a new office of physical fitness and sports medicine in the Department of HEW; grants to state fitness councils and to public and private entities for model projects on improving fitness; research funds, and a national conference on the topic in 1980.

Additional Views. Two Republican committee members, Orrin G. Hatch, Utah, and S. I. Hayakawa, Calif., did not challenge the basic value of preventive health programs. But both said the committee bill was too expensive, particularly the new physical fitness program which Hatch labeled "wildly luxurious."

In a third separate view, Donald W. Riegle Jr., D-Mich., said that improved nutritional and safety labeling of food was an important part of any preventive health program, and he urged action on the issue in the next Congress. Riegle had sponsored a food labeling bill which was largely incorporated into Kennedy's original preventive health measure but was dropped from the final committee version. The Senate Commerce Committee, which shared jurisdiction over the issue, had indicated it would not report a bill unless the House produced a food-labeling measure, according to a Riegle aide. The Senate had enacted labeling bills in 1971, 1974 and 1976. The Human Resources panel took testimony on food labeling but did not consider the legislative proposal in 1978.

Teenage Pregnancy Prevention (S 2910)

The Human Resources Committee reported S 2910 Sept. 21 (S Rept 95-1206) after making several key changes in a proposed administration bill.

As reported, S 2910 authorized $210 million in fiscal 1979-81 for health and social service programs for pregnant teenagers, particularly those under 17 years of age.

The original administration bill, which authorized $60 million in fiscal 1979, gave equal emphasis to prevention of teenage pregnancy and to programs for pregnant girls and their families. It did not specify a target population.

The committee recommended providing grants to public and private non-profit agencies that agreed to offer a specific list of core services, including pregnancy testing, maternity counseling and referral, and nutritional information and counseling. The administration bill required agencies to include some, but not all, of a suggested list of services.

The commiteee deleted a provision in the administration bill that required an agency receiving funds to earmark up to 50 percent of those funds for the creation of new programs for pregnant teenagers. The bulk of the grant money was to be used to coordinate existing services.

Calling the arbitrary ceiling "unrealistic, unwarranted and ill-advised," the committee contended that the major problem facing many communities was not lack of coordination but the lack of services themselves.

The administration bill included no language dealing with the controversial abortion question. As reported, S 2910 prohibited the use of funds authorized under the program for abortions. It also required grant recipients to inform pregnant teenagers of the availability of abortion counseling. And, although grant recipients would not be required to provide the counseling themselves, they would be required to refer girls to facilities that did provide such counseling.

Senate Floor Action

The Senate stitched the three bills together on the floor and passed them as S 2474 Sept. 29 by a vote of 82-4. *(Vote 425, p. 63-S)*

As he had on three other health bills earlier, Kennedy led off debate with a money-cutting substitute for the main bill (S 2474) under consideration. The Senate agreed to the funding cuts without objection.

As reported by the Human Resources Committee, S 2474 had authorized a total of $3.3 billion for up to five years for some — but not all — of the health services (categorical) programs and for the health care centers. Kennedy's substitute dropped the last two years of funding, eliminated a new $5 million study on maldistribution of health resources and cropped proposed authorization levels. The amendment cut the committee-approved spending levels for fiscal 1979 by 19 percent, for fiscal 1980 by 14 percent and for fiscal 1981 by 13 percent, Kennedy said.

Kennedy noted that he had been "working closely with the Senate Budget Committee to assure most effective allocation of scarce health care dollars." That panel had been one source of Senate hostility to high health spending in 1978.

After the funding cuts on S 2474 were adopted, Kennedy proposed, and the Senate agreed by voice vote, to add S 3116 as an amendment. It was, Kennedy said, the "first major piece of legislation targeted toward disease prevention and health promotion." And the American Medical Association backed the bill, Kennedy reported, noting that "the AMA and I have had our disagreements in the past. . . ."

Before agreeing to add on S 3116,the Senate agreed by voice vote to several minor amendments and rejected an effort by William Proxmire, D-Wis., to eliminate the physical fitness title of the bill. The amendments reintroduced a financial need factor into the formula for determining funding levels for states and authorized a special HEW study on the health care needs of Alaska natives and Indians.

Proxmire, who was known in Washington for jogging the five miles between his home and Capitol Hill, said the title was too expensive and too bureaucratic. "Now we are beginning to move in the direction of the Peoples' Republic of China, with some kind of program where everybody will do calisthenics on order."

Kennedy replied that the proposed program, which included funds for media presentations, research on sports injuries and a new coordinating office within HEW, was "extremely modest" and would supplement — but not duplicate — existing efforts.

The Senate retained the fitness title, agreeing 47-39 to a Pell, D-R.I., motion to table Proxmire's amendment. Pell had originated the fitness proposals. *(Vote 423, p. 63-S)*

The only extended debate was on the abortion issue. Richard S. Schweiker, R-Pa., ranking minority member of the Human Resources Subcommittee on Health, defended the committee language on counseling for the teenage clients of the pregnancy services. "Under the bill it is presumed that the individual seeking services wishes to carry the fetus to normal delivery unless the individual indicates a desire for abortion counseling," he said.

But Robert T. Stafford, R-Vt., disputed that interpretation. He said the bill's presumption was that the pregnant teenager was undecided about how to deal with the pregnancy. Jacob K. Javits, R-N.Y., supported Stafford's claim, arguing that providing federal support only for teenagers planning to carry their babies to term was "unconstitutional and wrong, morally and legally." The Senate rejected Stafford's amendment, agreeing 66-19 to a Kennedy motion to table. *(Vote 424, p. 63-S)*

The Senate agreed by voice vote to amendments:

- By Helms, R-N.C., to require notification of parents or guardians when a federally funded adolescent pregnancy center provided contraceptives to children under 16.
- By Wallop, R-Wyo., to provide for a $500,000, one-year study on existing federal efforts to curb the rising rate of teenage pregnancies. Wallop had objected to the adolescent pregnancy prevention initiative on the grounds that similar existing federal efforts had never been proven successful.
- By Dole, R-Kan., to limit the amount of earned income a migrant, community or primary health center could invest in converting to a prepaid reimbursement system. (Such payment systems, the basis for health maintenance

organizations, require reserve funds, similar to those of private insurers, to cover extraordinary patient expenses not fully covered by premiums.)

House Action

The House passed its health centers bill (HR 12460 — H Rept 95-1186) on Sept. 19 by a 302-102 vote. *(Vote 702, p. 198-H; story, p. 603)*

It rejected its health services bill (HR 12370) by a 193-193 tie vote under suspension Sept. 25, but passed a cheaper version Oct. 13 by a 343-27 vote. *(Votes 730, 811, pp. 208-H, 230-H; story, p. 609)*

Before passing HR 12370, the House cut $388 million from the $2.7 billion version reported by the Commerce Committee May 15 (H Rept 95-1191). The committee had justified the bill's spending levels by stressing the money-saving potential of preventive health measures.

The House bill did not contain anything comparable to the Senate-passed programs on water fluoridation, smoking or physical fitness. Nor had the House passed legislation comparable to the primary care provisions of S 2474.

Another difference was that the House bill provided a one-year authorization for a program to inoculate high-risk individuals. The Senate bill explicitly banned using any of the funds in the bill for influenza immunization.

Conference Action

In their Oct. 15 report (H Rept 95-1799), conferees resolved major differences between House and Senate bills as follows:

- Adopted a less restrictive House provision authorizing community and migrant health centers to keep payments for services from third party payors. The Senate version had directed the secretary of Health, Education and Welfare (HEW) to allow centers to keep the funds only if they were spent to expand or improve the center or used as a reserve fund for putting the center on a prepaid-fee basis. The final version said only that the extra funds should be reported to the secretary, and could be used for service improvements. Conferees also stated that centers should be allowed to keep at least half the money and that approval by the secretary was required if more than half that money was used for construction.
- Retained a House provision for new technical assistance grants for community, migrant and other primary health care providers.
- Retained a Senate provision for new grants for hospital-based primary care centers in medically underserved areas. They also kept a related new authorization program for primary care research and demonstration projects. For the hospital-based centers, conferees cut to $150,000, from $500,000, the per-project limit on planning and development grants, and halved the three-year authorization for the program, to $60 million, from $120 million. For the demonstration projects, conferees retained the $60 million, three-year authorization for rural projects, but cut support for urban projects to $13.5 million, from $16.5 million.
- Followed the House and Senate in providing for a one-year continuation of formula grants for comprehensive public health services, and converting them to cost-sharing "incentive" grants thereafter. But they cut to two years, from three, the authorization for the incentive grants.
- Included a Senate-passed program to promote fluoridation of community water supplies and school-based fluoridation programs.
- Followed the House in authorizing influenza immunization funds for fiscal 1979. But they barred any spending for the program unless HEW fulfilled, by June 30, 1979, a long-overdue commitment to report on the 1976 swine flu program. The Senate bill had prohibited spending for flu immunizations because a report required by the 1976 swine flu act (PL 94-380) had never been filed. Conferees expressed particular concern over the absence of recommendations for dealing with serious legal problems created by the 1976 program. In that program the federal government had assumed legal responsibility for adverse health effects of the flu vaccine, and numerous claims were still outstanding. *(1976 Almanac p. 548)*
- Kept, without change, two new preventive health grant programs passed by the Senate. One provided matching funds for state preventive health programs; the second authorized a limited number of demonstration projects for delivering preventive health services to targeted populations.
- Retained new Senate authorizations for programs to promote physical fitness and discourage childhood smoking. However, the conferees did not establish a separate HEW fitness office, and they expanded the anti-smoking initiative to cover child and adolescent consumption of alcohol. Conferees also kept a House authorization for a new national panel on child health.
- Kept a Senate provision authorizing new services to prevent and deal with unwanted adolescent pregnancies. They dropped a requirement in the Senate bill that parents of persons under 16 using the services be notified, and they cut authorizations to a three-year total of $190 million, from $210 million.

Health Planning Bill Dies

A three-year extension of the controversial system for allocating health resources such as hospital beds and expensive diagnostic machines went down to a surprise defeat under suspension of the rules in the House Sept. 18.

The health planning measure (HR 11488) later was granted a rule, but never made it back to the floor in the crush of last-minute legislation. Instead, the programs in the bill received a simple one-year extension under an omnibus continuing resolution (H J Res 1139) passed at the end of the session. *(Story, p. 161)*

The Senate July 27 had approved a three-year extension of the health planning system (S 2410) that included a stiff limit on doctors' buying very expensive diagnostic and treatment equipment.

The House defeat was blamed on a volatile mix of rumor, irritation with the planning system and annoyance over the short-cut procedure used to bring the $1.49 billion reauthorization bill to the floor.

In an unusual sequence the House produced — and then lost — the two-thirds majority needed to pass the bill under the suspension procedure. Sponsor Paul G. Rogers, D-Fla., had already left the floor thinking the bill had passed, when 29 members changed their "yea" votes to "nay," thereby defeating the measure on a 261-141 vote. Under suspension, 268 votes were needed to pass the bill. *(Vote 699, p. 198-H)*

The bill reauthorized the nation's controversial health planning system, which was established in 1974. The 1974 act was given a one-year extension in 1977 to give the Carter administration time to review the program and recommend changes. *(1974 Almanac p. 405; 1977 Almanac p. 451, 453)*

Committee Action

Although some members wanted to require the elimination of costly surplus hospital beds and services, the House Interstate and Foreign Commerce and Senate Human Resources Committees decided that 1978 was not the year to force that emotional issue. Both committees reported bills May 15 (H Rept 95-1185, S Rept 95-845).

Both bills instead provided payments to hospitals that chose voluntarily to shut down underused facilities or convert them to other uses. Both bills also made many minor changes in the complex, multi-level planning system — amounting to "a tune-up, not an overhaul," according to one committee aide.

A storm of protest had erupted when the Department of Health, Education and Welfare issued guidelines in 1977 that appeared to mandate hospital closings, particularly in rural areas. *(1977 Almanac, p. 523)*

What the 1977 dispute told members of the health panels was that "people want state and local control" of decisions about health care delivery, said Commerce Committee aide Robert Crane. The reported similarity of many letters suggested a second lesson — that the health care industry had lost none of its ability to mount a powerful lobbying effort on Capitol Hill.

The committees responded by increasing the role of governors and local elected officials in state and regional planning processes and instructing the secretary of HEW to make sure the planning panels were "broadly representative" of community interests. Many of the planning agencies had been accused of catering to the local medical establishment and ignoring the health needs of the poor and minority groups.

The House and Senate committees recommended revisions in these features of the 1974 planning law:

Certificate of Need. The Senate bill required certificates of need for new equipment valued at $150,000 or more, regardless of where it was located. This change, requested by the administration, was needed to stem proliferation of duplicative services, according to the committee report. A Harvard University study had shown that of 839 CAT scanners, 46 located in hospitals were privately owned and at least 112 were in doctors' offices. The scanners cost up to $500,000 each.

The House bill required certification for similarly expensive equipment if it were going to be used on inpatients. All planned equipment purchases of that size were to be reported to state agencies so they could determine if use would be confined to inpatients. Nothing in the House bill kept a hospital from "discharging a patient for an hour, carting him across the street for a test, and readmitting him," an HEW official said.

Both bills required certificate of need decisions to be consistent with state health plans. The House bill also required certification for home health services. These were proliferating in areas with large elderly populations, according to the House report.

Unneeded Services. The Senate bill authorized $600 million over three years for a new program to retire debts, terminate personnel and cover other costs of hospitals closing underused inpatient services, merging them with other facilities or converting them to alternate uses such as outpatient clinics or long-term nursing care.

Depending on whether whole hospitals or individual services shut down, elimination of the nation's 100,000 surplus hospital beds could save between $2 billion and $4 billion each year, the Senate report predicted. "Scattered" closings would reduce savings.

The House bill provided a much smaller, $12 million demonstration grant program. The impact of decertification on hospital employees and physician privileges and other questions should be explored, the committee said.

Access to Planning Process. The Senate bill required governors' "concurrence" with state health plans, while the House version made governors' approval mandatory.

Both bills broadened conflict of interest provisions to bar HSA members from participating in decisions affecting institutions where they or relatives worked, sat on the board of directors or had other substantial interests. The Senate bill went further, barring HSA members from deciding matters affecting institutions in competition with those in which they had an interest.

To end reported self-perpetuation of HSA governing boards, the Senate bill prohibited the boards from naming new members. The House bill required that at least half the board members be appointed by another method. Both committees urged appointment of members representing varied community interests. But both declined to set quotas for minority, poverty and other population groups that claimed they were underrepresented in the planning process. Instead, they instructed the secretary to enforce an existing requirement that the boards be "broadly representational."

Other changes were intended to facilitate consumer participation and to encourage representation of sparsely populated rural areas.

Guidelines. Both committee reports emphasized that the national guidelines were to be "benchmarks," to be weighed with local and regional needs. The House committee said HSA plans did not have to conform to national guidelines.

Authorizations. The Senate bill authorized almost a billion dollars more than the House version, $2.48 billion through fiscal 1981 compared to $1.49 billion for the same period in the House bill. The difference reflected the Senate's much larger program for eliminating excess beds, its decision to retain the state allotment program and almost uniformly more generous funding for various programs.

The House bill, however, devoted $110 million more to the project grants program. Part of that was for the existing program to eliminate safety hazards and bring hospitals up to state accreditation standards, and part was for a new program to develop outpatient clinics in medically underserved areas.

Senate Floor Action

The Senate passed S 2410 by voice vote July 27 after narrowly rejecting an effort to gut a provision that limited doctors' buying very expensive medical equipment.

"It was the first time in 10 years the AMA [American Medical Association] lost in Congress," said one aide to the bill's author, Edward M. Kennedy, D-Mass.

What the Senate agreed to do was to require anyone buying medical equipment worth more than $150,000 to get a type of state approval known as a "certificate of need" for the purchase. That meant the buyer had to demonstrate that patients needed the equipment and that it did not duplicate existing resources. The AMA objected bitterly to the provision.

Existing law required certification only for hospital-owned machines. Proponents of the Senate measure claimed that doctor groups were sabotaging the law by buying the machinery after hospitals had been turned down. They said equipment duplication pushed medical costs up.

Authorizations in the bill as passed were $915 million below those reported by the Human Resources Committee, which had recommended a total of $2.5 billion through fiscal 1981 for the planning program. Kennedy himself suggested the funding cuts, which left a total three-year authorization of $1.6 billion. That was similar to a pending House bill which authorized $1.49 billion.

Kennedy said data received since markup had convinced him that the cuts were appropriate. But although he spoke in terms of excess health facilities and administrative problems of the Department of HEW, the cuts, along with other versions in his amendment, seemed equally dictated by political data. Kennedy had twice run into Senate hostility to expensive health legislation and, reportedly, agreed to the cost-cutting changes when they were proposed by Robert Dole, R-Kan., and others.

The chairman of the Senate Budget Committee, Edmund S. Muskie, D-Maine, had planned a floor amendment to slash a state allotments program that provided funding for health facilities construction. Kennedy's amendment eliminated that program and halved a proposed $600,000 authorization for a new program to encourage hospitals to eliminate or convert to other uses unneeded hospital beds. The amendment was adopted by voice vote.

AMA Amendment

Anticipating what he called a "gutting" AMA amendment on the equipment provision, Kennedy opened debate with a strong attack on it.

Efforts by local planning units to control the explosion of expensive equipment had been subverted by physician groups which often set up shop with the desired machines near the hospital, Kennedy said. The target of his amendment was the half-billion-dollar computerized X-ray machine known as a CAT scanner.

"It is self-evident that planning cannot work if the same piece of expensive medical equipment will or will not be subject to certificate-of-need laws on the basis of who happens to purchase it," Kennedy said.

The complicated "AMA amendment" was proposed by Walter "Dee" Huddleston, D-Ky. The basic thrust of Huddleston's amendment was to give the states discretion to extend certificates of need to health care providers other than hospitals.

It was, Huddleston said, "simply ... a 'states' rights' amendment."

Orrin G. Hatch, R-Utah, said that the proposed extension into the "private office setting" was a " 'first step' to a regulatory foothold over all individual practitioners of medicine, eventually bringing them under the complete umbrella of government control."

In response, Kennedy cited examples of physician purchases of CAT scanners to circumvent negative decisions by planning agencies.

"We cannot bow to the power of the American Medical Association to gut any kind of effective cost containment," Kennedy said.

"While the AMA is promoting this self-serving amendment, which would place physicians in a special class, they are the only major health care group that supports the amendment," he added.

About half of hospital cost inflation was traceable to "technology and equipment," Kennedy said.

Supporting Kennedy, Richard S. Schweiker, R-Pa., cited an estimate that within two years "we will be paying a billion dollars a year for CAT scanners." He also defended the proposed revisions of HMOs as needed correctives of the 1974 health planning act.

Schweiker moved to divide the Huddleston amendment into two parts for votes. As each part came up, Kennedy moved to table. The Senate agreed by a 57-40 vote to table part one, relating to separate treatment for HMOs by state certificate-of-need statutes. By a 50-45 vote it also agreed to table part two, which would have eliminated mandatory state certificate-of-need coverage of non-institutional equipment. The Senate also agreed 47-45 to a Kennedy motion to table a Javits, R-N.Y., motion to reconsider. *(Votes 251-253, p. 40-S)*

House Floor Action

The House Sept. 18 defeated HR 11488 under suspension of the rules. The defeat was blamed on a combination of factors, including annoyance with the health planning system and a late-blooming rumor that the bill would "overregulate" doctors' offices (although the House provision on purchase of major medical equipment was less stringent than the Senate provision).

Other highly charged health issues, including scarcity of medical resources, genetic counseling and abortion, were invoked by one member, Robert K. Dornan, R-Calif. Dornan, a leading opponent of abortion, had urged during floor debate that health planning agencies be required to conform their health plans to the medical ethics embodied in the Hippocratic oath, or explain why they did not do so.

Dornan cited his constituents' concerns about the "huge moral vacuum under which (health) policy decisions are being made."

Dornan had also wanted to amend the bill to remove new protections from lawsuits for planners, and reverse the consumer-majority requirement for planning boards. This would mean requiring a majority of doctors and other health providers on the boards.

Dornan was also very concerned with recommendations of certain planning agencies, according to an aide, including approval of facilities providing abortions, alleged limits on the amount of time hospital staffs could spend with critically ill patients, and fetal screening of certain population groups for genetic defects associated with those groups.

Members apparently were more than usually receptive to objections because of mounting irritation with what some considered abuse of the suspension calendar. ∎

Medicare-Medicaid Benefits

The House Sept. 18 passed legislation (HR 13097, HR 13817) to make home health care — nursing, physical therapy and similar services — more available to the elderly beneficiaries of Medicare.

However, the Senate's Medicare-Medicaid revisions were in legislation (HR 5285) that included hospital cost control provisions, it died at the end of the session, so the benefit changes were not enacted. *(HR 5285, below)*

The Carter administration opposed new health benefits for budgetary reasons.

With only two dissenting votes the House agreed to unlimited home health visits for beneficiaries, dropping an existing curb on the number of visits that would be reimbursed. It also dropped a prior-hospitalization eligibility requirement, eliminated a $60 deductible and adopted other changes designed to make more home care available to more of the aged ill.

The home health revisions were part of a collection of minor benefit and administrative changes in Medicare and Medicaid that were approved under suspension of the rules.

Benefits revisions for Medicare were included in HR 13097, which passed by a 398-2 vote. *(Vote 695, p. 198-H)*

Changes affecting peer review, nursing care beds in acute-care hospitals and auditing procedures for both federal programs were included in a second bill (HR 13817) which passed 359-40. *(Vote 696, p. 198-H)*

Proponents of fuller home health benefits argued that expanding in-home care could save money by keeping beneficiaries out of more expensive nursing homes and hospitals. But some health economists minimized potential savings, warning that expanded home-care services would do little more than supplemental institutional care, as is now the case.

The benefits bill (HR 10397) would have added $95 million to a $29 billion Medicare budget in fiscal 1979. The annual cost of the new benefits, which also included direct payments to non-M.D. health professionals and several demonstration projects, would rise to $223 million in fiscal 1983, when the authorization would expire. Savings from administrative changes included in HR 13817 would have amounted to $20.5 million in fiscal 1979, dropping to $15.3 million in fiscal 1983.

These estimates were included in the Aug. 31 reports of the House Ways and Means Committee on HR 13097 (H Rept 95-1533) and HR 13817 (H Rept 95-1534).

Dan Rostenkowski, D-Ill., chairman of the Ways and Means Health Subcommittee, said in debate that budget limitations precluded many other improvements in benefits sought by the elderly. Lobbyists for the aged and their congressional advocates, including Claude Pepper, D-Fla., and Toby Moffett, D-Conn., argued that gaps in the federal program left many heavy medical expenses uncovered. Preliminary HEW figures for fiscal 1977 showed that the nation's 25 million elderly — or their insurance companies — spent an estimated $2 billion-plus on outpatient prescription drugs, another $2 billion on uncovered hospitalization expenses (deductibles, co-insurance) and $300 million on eyeglasses, hearing aids and similar medical applicances. ▮

Hospital Cost Control Legislation Dies

Hospital cost control legislation, which had been pronounced dead for the year repeatedly during 1978, was resurrected and passed by the Senate Oct. 12. But it never made it to the House floor, and the measure was buried at the end of the 95th Congress.

The bill passed unexpectedly by the Senate in the waning days of the session was a watered-down version of the legislation the administration had sought as a crucial element of its fight on inflation. President Carter also had said such legislation was a necessary prerequisite for any system of national health insurance.

The president's proposal had been gutted by the House Interstate and Foreign Commerce Committee in July and rejected by the Senate Finance Committee in August, so the fact that it re-emerged in any form came as a surprise to almost everyone.

Carter himself said in a speech Sept. 20 that he had given up any hope for passage of the legislation, blaming the "selfish concerns" of the hospital and medical lobby for its failure. But administration officials pushed the fight anyway, apparently to get what political mileage they could from the issue, and the surprise Senate victory was the result.

The Senate-passed bill (HR 5285) was a compromise sponsored by Gaylord Nelson, D-Wis. It would have left cost-cutting to hospitals on a voluntary basis as long as they met set goals, but mandated strict revenue controls if hospitals failed to reduce the rate at which their spending grew to about 12 percent a year by the end of 1979 and keep it at that level through 1983. It allowed a number of exemptions. The bill also would have converted Medicare and Medicaid to a prospective payment system for hospitals.

The administration originally had proposed a mandatory 9 percent cap on increases in hospital spending in the first year and less in subsequent years, with no voluntary phase, and a national limit on capital expenditures by hospitals. Its proposal was strenuously opposed by the hospital industry and the U.S. medical establishment.

The administration said it would reintroduce cost control legislation in the 96th Congress. At year's end it reportedly was considering tying it to a proposal to provide federal coverage for catastrophic health costs, in order to gain support for the measure.

Background

President Carter early in his administration singled out hospital costs as the first target in a drive to put the brakes on skyrocketing health care costs — costs that were rising, and fueling inflation, at a much faster rate than other basic costs of living.

Hospital costs had been rising at the rate of 15 percent a year or $1 million a day — 2½ times faster than the Consumer Price Index, according to the Department of Health, Education and Welfare (HEW). Health care costs not only hurt individual citizens and their insurers, but an increasing portion of the federal budget was being taken up by costs of Medicare, Medicaid and other federal programs. *(Background, 1977 Almanac p. 499)*

Carter sent his legislative proposals (HR 6575, S 1391) to Congress in April 1977. He called for quick approval so that the program could go into effect Oct. 1, the start of the 1978 fiscal year.

1977 Committee Action

However, only one of the four committees with jurisdiction over the proposal approved it in 1977. The Senate Human Resources Committee approved a revised version of S 1391 drafted by Edward M. Kennedy's, D-Mass., Health Subcommittee. The House Interstate and Foreign Commerce Subcommittee on Health, chaired by Paul G. Rogers, D-Fla., also approved a clean bill (HR 9717) in late 1977. *(1977 Almanac p. 506)*

Both revised versions took a less drastic approach to hospital operating costs than the original. Both retained a wage "pass-through" provision sought by labor, but only the Senate version made it mandatory — and it included a "loophole" big enough to have earned it labor's enmity. That was a provision that exempted from the federal law those states with their own cost control agencies. The Rogers bill exempted fewer states than the Kennedy bill.

In other changes, the Rogers bill added financial incentives to encourage hospital cost-cutting, while the Kennedy bill placed a moratorium on new capital investment by hospitals.

A third panel, the Senate Finance Subcommittee on Health, did not hold hearings on the administration plan until late in the year, focusing its efforts instead on a rate-setting measure (S 1470) for Medicare-Medicaid reimbursements that was crafted by its chairman, Herman E. Talmadge, D Ga.

The fourth committee with jurisdiction, Rep. Dan Rostenkowski's D-Ill., Ways and Means Subcommittee on Health, split 7-6 on a number of preliminary votes. As 1977 drew to a close, Rostenkowski failed repeatedly to field a quorum to complete work on the bill.

In part the delay was caused by the press of other House business, notably the massive energy and Social Security bills. Progress also was hampered by factors common to all the health committees—lack of enthusiasm for the bill and annoyance at the administration's alleged lobbying deficiencies.

Substantively complex, the bill was difficult to sell. A further liability was the calibre of its opponents—the well-financed hospital industry and medical establishment. Most "supporters" were lukewarm and, in the case of organized labor, decidedly frosty. Labor fought the bill until the committee agreed to a provision protecting hospital worker wages.

Labor wanted soaring health costs controlled, but feared that any hospital savings would come disproportionately from workers' salaries. Their fears were not softened by statements from several members that wages, in fact, did offer a good opportunity for savings.

One of the bill's biggest problems was the almost total absence of supporting groups. The insurance industry and elderly groups were said to favor the bill. But they did not aggressively pursue committee members and staff until late in the game. The bill's benefits were difficult to dramatize because most Americans did not directly pay their own hospital bills.

The legislation also suffered from implications that cost controls meant service cutbacks — a theme well orchestrated by the hospitals. Most members of Congress would rather give more than less health care to their constituents.

Finally, as one lobbyist for the elderly complained, "The administration didn't do the basic educational job for members of Congress and staff." And Kennedy publicly chastised Carter for not building a public constituency for the bill.

On Nov. 1 Rostenkowski challenged the hospital industry to come up with a plan to police its own costs voluntarily.

1978 Action

Attention was refocused on the hospital cost bill early in 1978 by its prominent place in the fiscal 1979 health budget, and by a Feb. 1 announcement by Rostenkowski that he would like to give hospitals a 12-month reprieve, to see if they could cut their costs voluntarily.

In its budget presentation in January, the administration strongly urged enactment of hospital cost control legislation, which it said would cut the national health bill by $2 billion — including $730 million in Medicare and Medicaid payments — in fiscal 1979. Without cost constraints, the administration warned, the federal bill for Medicare and Medicaid would leap to $70 billion from $42 billion — a 60 per cent increase — between 1979 and 1983.

Hospitals' 'Voluntary Effort'

On Jan. 30 the industry announced creation of a national steering committee and a network of state "medical and hospital committees." The major goal of the "Voluntary Effort," as the program was called, was to reduce the growth rate of hospital expenditures by 2 per cent the first year and by an additional 2 per cent the second year. The program's focus on hospital spending differed from the Carter targeting of hospital income. The Voluntary Effort was organized by the American Hospital Association, the Federation of American Hospitals and the American Medical Association.

Besides pruning hospital expenditures, the voluntary program set goals of "no net increases" in hospital beds and "restraint in new hospital capital investment." Implementation was left to the state committees, which were advised to provide technical assistance and use public disclosure and a certification procedure.

It was this program that Rostenkowski proposed to let run for a year. But, he told a Washington meeting of the American Hospital Association Feb. 1, "since nothing stimulates volunteers more quickly than the genuine fear of a draft," he would also push for mandatory "fallback federal controls...to assist you" if the voluntary effort failed.

The administration response to Rostenkowski's move was flat rejection. Speaking on behalf of the President, HEW Secretary Joseph A. Califano Jr. said Feb. 2 that past performance of the hospitals showed the plan "couldn't work." Although hospitals had promised to hold the line on costs in 1974 when they sought relief from national wage and price controls, "costs have been rolling along" at double the national rate of inflation since then, he said.

The delay proposed by Rostenkowski would "cost the American people $7.5 billion, and the taxpayers almost $3 billion," Califano warned.

Ways and Means staff member John J. Salmon said that giving the hospitals "a chance — to fail or make a go of it" seemed the only way to break up the logjam. "The votes [for the administration proposal] just weren't there in the committee," Salmon said.

Rostenkowski Bill

Concessions to the hospital industry and a lobby fight that pitted the White House against organized labor Feb.28 dislodged a compromise version of President Carter's plan for controlling hospital costs from the House Ways and Means Subcommittee on Health.

After chewing over the unpopular proposal for nearly a year, the panel voted 7-6 to send to the full committee a substitute bill drafted by Rostenkowski. The outcome was uncertain until the final roll call as unhappy hospital and labor lobbyists sought to tilt the closely divided panel against the compromise.

The committee gave hospitals about a year to trim their spending voluntarily before a mandatory federal limit on revenue increases was imposed. The goal for the voluntary phase was to cut the annual growth rate of hospital spending from the current 16 percent level to 12 percent within two years, with a constant rate thereafter. The mandatory phase, to be activated if the voluntary program failed, permitted 9 percent growth in the first year, although adjustments could bring that figure to 12 percent. By 1983 the permissible rate of increase under the mandatory program would drop to 10 percent.

While neither the administration nor the hospital industry "warmly embraced" his bill, Rostenkowski said, it might serve as the basis for a compromise. Administration and congressional health sources privately conceded that Rostenkowski's move had bettered the bill's chances politically.

Even so, Rostenkowski's compromise won no ardent converts in his subcommittee during markup sessions at the end of February. Distaste for the measure reached across party lines. Ranking Democrat James C. Corman, Calif., said he still preferred immediate, mandatory controls, while fellow Democrats William R. Cotter, Conn., and Otis G. Pike, N.Y., said that the Department of Health, Education and Welfare (HEW) was probably incapable of running the program.

Republican members, led by Bill Gradison, R-Ohio, objected strenuously to a special adjustment for wage hikes for blue-collar hospital workers. Wages plus benefits accounted for about 50 percent of hospital budgets, Gradison said, adding that hospital administrators could more easily prune these costs than those for programs originating in Congress.

The exemption was unfair, Gradison said, and he proposed similar "pass-throughs" for food, energy, Social Security and unemployment compensation payments, pensions, depreciation, interest and malpractice insurance. Republicans also warned that limiting hospital revenues without controlling the rising costs of goods and services they bought was unworkable, unfair and damaging to health care.

Nevertheless, the committee rejected — by a tie vote — a congressional veto proposal and three other weakening amendments that went to the heart of the mandatory program. It did agree to limit the duration of the mandatory program to four years after it was "triggered" into effect. It added Gradison's pass-throughs for energy and malpractice costs, and it cut back a heavy tax penalty for noncompliance during the mandatory phase. It also relaxed certain aspects of the voluntary portion of the program, meeting some of the industry's objections to that feature.

Neither the hospital industry nor organized labor found the Rostenkowski bill acceptable in either its original or amended form. The Carter administration indicated its endorsement by not objecting strenuously in markup sessions but HEW officials said they still hoped for immediate mandatory controls.

Absent from the Rostenkowski bill was an administration proposal, retained by the Rogers bill, to place an annual national limit of $2.5 billion on capital expenditures by hospitals. Also deleted were financial incentives added by the Commerce subcommittee to encourage hospital cost-cutting and to promote elimination of unneeded hospital beds. Rostenkowski dropped these features for jurisdictional reasons and "because his subcommittee wouldn't pass them," according to a Ways and Means aide.

Compromise Efforts

Compromise efforts got underway after Rostenkowski's panel reported out his bill.

In April, Carter health officials, who had spent a year stonewalling objections by labor that their bill would depress hospital worker wages, offered concessions to labor leaders — a Kennedy-style wage pass-through in the federal program and in state agencies created after enactment of the bill.

And the four key subcommittee chairmen, who had differed sharply on how best to control costs, agreed to agree, apparently to avoid a floor fight on the highly technical and heavily lobbied issue.

Kennedy and Rogers, who had backed the mandatory controls in the administration bill, appeared by April to have agreed to go along with Rostenkowski and Talmadge on legislation allowing hospitals a chance to police their own costs voluntarily first, with mandatory controls only if they failed to meet set goals. Talmadge in February had flatly rejected the notion of a uniform revenue cap for all hospitals, and indicated he found the idea of a voluntary effort with standby controls attractive.

The strategy of cost control proponents was to try to bring Rostenkowski's bill, as revised by Rogers, through the full Commerce Committee before taking it to Ways and Means. It was thought that a favorable vote in Commerce would give the measure some momentum in Ways and Means, which was considered less sympathetic to cost-control legislation.

In addition to providing for standby federal controls on hospital revenues if the voluntary program failed to meet specified goals, Rogers' bill imposed a $3 billion national ceiling on capital expenditures by hospitals for expansion, major equipment purchases and similar outlays, and added financial incentives for good performance.

The continued opposition of both the hospital industry and labor slowed progress on the bill. Labor reportedly felt that administration concessions on the wage pass-through met its objections for the mandatory controls phase, but not for the voluntary phase. The Commerce Committee pulled the measure from its markup schedule in May after concerted administration lobbying failed to win enough votes for the compromise.

Commerce Committee Action

The House Commerce Committee finally began marking up the bill in early June, and continued until mid-July, when it voted to scrap the hard-fought, much-amended proposal.

A motion by Bob Gammage, D-Texas, to recommit to subcommittee — in effect, kill the bill — was rejected by a 16-24 vote June 7, but members continued to offer numerous amendments to water down the bill, and a gutting substitute by Jim Santini, D-Nev., failed June 13 by only a two-vote margin, 20-22. That vote was considered a truer index of narrowly divided committee sentiment, since many proxies had been cast on the recommittal motion.

Wage Pass-Through. The committee agreed 15-13 to a wage pass-through amendment by Bob Eckhardt, D-Texas. To protect hospital workers' wages, wage costs would be excluded from calculations on whether the voluntary phase goals had been met. In the mandatory phase unions could request wage pass-throughs and state cost-control programs would have to provide protection for blue-collar hospital wages comparable to those offered by the federal program.

The Eckhardt amendment prompted members to offer a string of pass-throughs — for the costs of utility bills, malpractice insurance, food and petroleum-based products. The first two were narrowly defeated — 19-20 and 19-21. The third and fourth were declared out of order for procedural reasons, but their sponsor, Timothy E. Wirth, D-Colo., said he hoped the "mischief that was just raised here reflects the nonsense of adding pass-throughs."

Stockman Amendment

On June 21, the committee by a one-vote margin, 20-21, adopted an amendment that cut deeply into the bill's projected savings in hospital costs.

The amendment, offered by Dave Stockman, R-Mich., went to the heart of a basic but largely unarticulated assumption of the administration's controversial hospital bill: controlling rising hospital costs involves holding down increases in hospital admissions. Many health economists blamed double-digit inflation in hospital bills partly on efforts by some hospitals to fill their beds, with more concern for cash flow than medical needs of the patients.

What Stockman's complicated amendment did was to remove the financial disincentive in the original bill for a hospital increasing its patient load after the base year. Or, as its opponents explained it, the amendment created a strong incentive for hospitals to push admissions upward. Stockman's amendment also lessened the benefits to a hospital decreasing its patient load.

Stockman's amendment was so complicated that the day it was adopted opponents were unable to say just how much it damaged their bill. Even the following day, damage reports varied. Rogers said it would cut the savings from $30 billion over the next five years to $24 billion, still "a heck of a savings." CBO estimated that even if the amended formula did not create a growth in hospital admissions, five-year savings would be down to $16.5 billion. HEW estimates showed that if hospital admissions went up by 3.5 percent annually, there would be no savings.

The deciding vote for the crippling Stockman amendment was cast by Tim Lee Carter, R-Ky., ranking minority member of the Commerce Health Subcommittee, who until then had been voting with Rogers and the administration on the bill.

Rumors of administration vote-buying — with water projects, delayed military base-closings and lesser plums such as primary-time visits to congressional districts by prominent administration officials — "turned me off," Carter told the committee June 21.

What particularly irked him was a well-publicized claim by James J. Florio, D-N.J., that he had agreed to keep voting for the bill in return for an administration go-ahead on a new $75 million Veterans Administration hospital in his Camden district.

Having first voted "nay," Carter changed his vote to "yea" when it appeared that the amendment might lose.

Other Amendments. The committee adopted amendments permitting an adjustment in the mandatory phase revenue limit for hospitals with a sudden growth in Medicare patients; fixing 1977 as the base year for the program; barring Medicare and Medicaid reimbursement for hospital capital expenditures found to be unneeded; exempting small rural hospitals from the cost control program, and loosening restrictions on small hospitals using beds on a "swing" basis (alternating between acute and long-term care).

By a 20-21 vote it rejected an attempt by James T. Broyhill, R-N.C., to add a one-house veto provision, and by a 12-27 vote turned down an amendment that would clamp down on physician charges to elderly patients covered by Medicare. The amendment, proposed by Toby Moffett, D-Conn., was designed to require doctors to accept Medicare benefits — about 80 percent of "customary and usual" fees — as full payment for in-hospital charges.

It also rejected by a 20-21 vote an amendment by David E. Satterfield III, D-Va., to eliminate the capital expenditure ceiling.

In other committee action, Richardson Preyer, D-N.C., proposed and then withdrew an amendment intended to soften the impact of the crippling Stockman amendment. The Stockman amendment eliminated features of the bill intended to discourage greatly increased hospital admissions. Committee aides said Preyer failed to "come close" to getting enough votes for his amendment.

Bill Gutted

After six weeks of markup, the committee by a 22-21 vote July 18 voted to scrap its bill and replace it with a Republican substitute offered by Broyhill. *(Committee vote, box, p. 623)*

It was a stunning loss for the president, and most observers figured it probably meant the bill was dead for the year.

The result of the committee's decision was that the bill (HR 6575) simply endorsed the hospital industry's voluntary efforts to cut back their costs by 2 percent a year. The Broyhill substitute dropped mandatory federal regulation of hospital revenues altogether.

"This amendment is so extreme that it's just a gutting of the bill," said Rogers.

After adopting the Broyhill amendment the committee voted 15-21 to report the bill, with Rogers reluctantly voting "aye" and Chairman Harley O. Staggers, D-W.Va., voting "no."

Many members were clearly uncertain as to whether it was worse to report the bill or kill it in committee, and did not answer on the first roll-call for reporting the bill. Sixteen committee members did not vote on reporting the bill.

Rogers said he "did not approve" of the final version but that he hoped repairs could be made in the Ways and Means Committee or on the House floor.

The Broyhill amendment adopted by the committee was a four-part measure joining provisions drafted by Santini, Rogers, Stockman and Carter.

The central provision duplicated the earlier Santini amendment, dropping the mandatory cost control program altogether.

A second provision developed by Carter authorized grants to states for up to 80 percent of the expenses of state hospital cost containment programs.

A Stockman section revised the Carter administration's proposed ceiling on hospital capital expenditures. The original Carter plan included a $2.5 billion national ceiling on major hospital spending each year. Stockman boosted the ceiling to $4 billion and reworded the provision to exempt many types of hospital improvements from the limit. Stockman aides said the changes were intended to give local health planning agencies more leeway in allotting health care resources. Rogers said the changes would send the industry off on a "bed-building spree."

The Commerce Committee bill also provided for financial incentives to encourage hospitals to merge, close or convert to other uses underused acute-care beds. Rogers had convinced his Health Subcommittee to add this feature to the administration's basic proposal in 1977.

Committee Vote

Following is the vote by which the House Interstate and Commerce Committee adopted the Broyhill substitute to HR 6575, the hospital cost containment bill:

Yes (22): Democrats Dingell, Mich.; Rooney, Pa.; Satterfield, Va.; Krueger, Texas; Sharp, Ind.; Santini, Nev.; Russo, Ill.; Luken, Ohio, and Gammage, Texas; Republicans Devine, Ohio; Broyhill, N.C.; Carter, Ky., Brown, Ohio; Skubitz, Kan.; Collins, Texas; Frey, Fla.; Lent, N.Y.; Madigan, Ill.; Moorhead, Calif.; Moore, La.; Stockman, Mich., and Marks, Pa.

No (21): Democrats Staggers, W.Va.; Moss, Calif.; Rogers, Fla.; Van Deerlin, Calif.; Murphy, N.Y.; Eckhardt, Texas; Preyer, N.C.; Carney, Ohio; Metcalfe, Ill.; Scheuer, N.Y.; Ottinger N.Y.; Waxman, Calif.; Wirth, Colo.; Florio, N.J.; Moffett, Conn.; Maguire, N.J.; Markey, Mass.; Walgren, Pa.; Gore, Tenn., and Mikulski, Md.; Republican Rinaldo, N.J.

Senate Committee Action

The Senate Finance Committee Aug. 3, by a 7-11 vote, rejected an administration-backed hospital cost control measure and approved a more limited version (S 1470) sponsored by Talmadge, that applied only to hospital bills paid by Medicare and Medicaid. The committee added the provisions to a minor, House-passed tariff bill (HR 5285) and reported the measure Aug. 11 (S Rept 95-1111).

Talmadge had begun to move June 20 on his own bill after standing back for more than a year while the other three committees struggled with the administration's hospital cost control proposal.

After the president's plan was shot down in the House Commerce Committee July 18, the administration tried to make Talmadge's bill the vehicle for its hospital cost control effort. President Carter himself reportedly telephoned senators on behalf of the compromise administration amendment, sponsored by Nelson, while heavy lobbying pressure against it was brought to bear by the hospital and medical associations.

The administration and the Kennedy-Nelson forces continued to fight for the compromise after its rejection by the Finance Committee, and it was an amended version of the Nelson amendment that finally passed the Senate Oct. 12, only to die at the end of the session for lack of House action.

Talmadge Bill

The Talmadge bill aimed at replacing the traditional fee-for-service system of paying hospitals with a pre-set, fixed-fee system—but only for bills paid by Medicare and Medicaid. The fee-for-service system was criticized by health economists on grounds that it provided powerful financial incentives for more hospitalizations and more treatments and tests.

Talmadge proposed to gradually phase in a "prospective" reimbursement system, with different rates for different types of hospitals. Under the bill, Medicare and Medicaid would reimburse a hospital for routine "bed and board" costs at the average rate for its type, with bonus payments for hospitals with below-average costs. Hospitals whose charges exceeded the average by up to 15 percent would be fully reimbursed, but charges above that level would not be reimbursed.

In a major change from earlier versions of the proposal, similar controls for "ancillary" costs — drugs, X-rays, laboratory tests and other variable expenses — would not be adopted unless Congress enacted legislation requiring them. A staff draft had provided that a fixed-rate payment system for those costs would be implemented in the future by a national commission unless the secretary of HEW objected.

The administration had two major objections to Talmadge's bill: that it was limited to the two federal programs instead of covering all sources of hospital income, and that it didn't begin to save enough money.

Although the bill forbade hospitals to shift uncovered costs for Medicare and Medicaid patients to other payors, the administration warned that hospitals would do just that, avoiding any meaningful efforts to economize.

And the bill would save "only about $500 million over the next five years, or 100 times less than [the original administration plan] and 60 times less" than the latest compromise, according to Nelson.

The administration was also unhappy that the bill as reported omitted two important cost-saving features of earlier versions: a limit on payments to hospital-based physicians (anesthesiologists, radiologists, pathologists), and automatic phase-in of reimbursement limits for costly "ancillary" services like lab tests and drugs.

Unless the Senate accepted the Nelson amendment on the floor, HEW officials said, they would recommend to the president that he veto the bill.

Talmadge's bill had the qualified support of two leading opponents of the Carter plan, the Federation of American Hospitals and the American Hospital Association.

It was bitterly opposed by organized labor because, of all the alternatives pending, it was the least favorable to blue-collar hospital workers.

Provisions. In addition to establishing the prospective reimbursement system for hospital bills of Medicaid and Medicare patients, HR 5285, as reported:

● Authorized establishment, by Jan. 1, 1979, of an 11-member Health Facilities Costs Commission. Directed the commission to monitor the new routine-cost reimbursement system, study extension of the system to ancillary services and other health care providers like nursing homes and home health services, and recommend any proposed changes to Congress.

● Authorized reimbursement on a cost basis for extra expenses incurred by a hospital in closing down excess acute-care services or converting them to other uses such as long-term nursing care. Payments could be used to retire debts or pay interest on them and for severance pay for employees.

● Required approval by a state health planning agency of capital expenditures exceeding $150,000 as a condition for Medicare and Medicaid reimbursement for those expenses and for operating costs associated with those expenditures. Existing law gave the secretary of HEW discretion to deny reimbursement for capital expenditures exceeding $100,000 which had not been approved.

● Provided special benefits for physicians agreeing to accept "assignment" for all their Medicare patients — that is, agreeing to accept Medicare benefits as full payment for charges to Medicare patients. Physicians agreeing to the voluntary program would receive an "administrative cost-saving allowance" of $1 per patient visit, and would use simplified claim forms. Claims from participating doctors would be given priority handling.

● Authorized Medicare reimbursement for office overhead, routine laboratory work and other expenses associated with surgery performed in physicians' offices or in outpatient surgical facilities that were not part of a hospital. Existing law authorized reimbursement for the physician's fee only when an operation was performed outside a hospital.

● Raised the existing limit on the fee a doctor starting a new practice in a medically underserved area could charge Medicare; also permitted established doctors in these areas to charge the higher fee.

● Placed a ceiling on future increases in calculating a region's "prevailing fee," the basis for Medicare reimbursements for doctors. Doctors would not be reimbursed for charges that were more than one-third above the statewide median charge for a given service.

● Barred the HEW secretary and state agencies from releasing the names of doctors participating in Medicare and Medicaid, or the amounts of payments to them.

● Required states to deny Medicaid benefits for up to a year to persons who disposed of "significant" assets — by giving them away or selling them below market value — in order to become eligible for Medicaid benefits.

● Made numerous changes in the administration of the Medicare and Medicaid programs.

Nelson Amendment

The Nelson amendment included several concessions to opponents. Like the compromise worked out earlier in the year by Rostenkowski, Nelson's plan endorsed the industry's voluntary effort to control hospital costs. It provided for stand-by mandatory controls on hospital revenues from all payors if the voluntary goals to cut hospital revenue increases to about 12 percent annually were not met.

There was a broad "pass-through" exemption to protect blue-collar hospital worker wages. And under mandatory revenue limits each hospital would have its own limit based on its expenses. The industry had objected that Carter's original across-the-board 9 percent revenue limit for all hospitals was a "meat-ax" approach that could force hospitals with unusual costs out of business.

The amendment applied the fixed-rate payment system to all hospital charges — those paid by private insurers and individuals as well as by Medicare and Medicaid. The system was similar to that in the Talmadge bill, but its version of incentives and penalties was less favorable to hospitals than Talmadge's.

Under the Nelson amendment, the hospitals' voluntary cost control effort and the new reimbursement system would run at the same time. Mandatory controls would go into effect if the voluntary effort failed to meet its goals, and they would apply to all revenues, not just routine costs. In addition to financial penalties (reduced reimbursement) for hospitals failing to comply, there would be tax penalties for both hospitals and other payors (insurance companies) for overcharges or overpayments.

A similar reimbursement system for ancillary costs would be developed by July 1981. Until then the voluntary effort would apply.

Several exemptions were added to the Nelson amendment to build support for it. The compromise:

● Exempted wage hikes for nonsupervisory hospital employees from calculations in both the voluntary and mandatory phases of the program, including state cost containment programs.

● Exempted from mandatory controls hospitals with annual admissions of less than 4,000.

● Exempted from mandatory controls hospitals in states with cost control programs that either met the voluntary goals or were at least as comprehensive and effective as the federal (mandatory) program.

Senate Floor Action

The Senate Oct. 12 handed President Carter a surprise victory on hospital cost containment — a victory built on hardball lobbying, compromise, parliamentary ambush and a pervasive belief that a "yea" on the controversial bill was "safe" because the House couldn't pass it before adjournment.

By a 42-47 vote the Senate refused to table, and then adopted by voice vote, the Nelson amendment. *(Vote 480, p. 70-S)*

After agreeing to a number of amendments that, among other things, placed stringent limits on payments to hospital-based physicians (anesthesiologists, radiologists, pathologists), the Senate then passed HR 5285 by a 64-22 vote. *(Vote 482, p. 70-S)*

Earlier it had tabled by a 69-18 vote the tougher, original administration cost containment bill as reported in 1977 by the Human Resources Committee. *(Vote 479, p. 70-S)*

Factors in Victory

Inflation was the dominant theme of Senate debate and after the vote, sponsors credited their success to new congressional awareness of "the rising concern of Americans about rampant inflation in the health care industry," as Kennedy put it.

But there were also these other factors, weighing against the administration's earlier reputation for failing to build lobby support or to compromise on the hospital issue:

Strenuous lobbying. According to Health, Education and Welfare (HEW) sources, these groups were pushing the compromise: organized labor, private insurance trade associations, and many groups that depend on federal "categorical" (targeted) health funds — state and local governments, nurses, speech and hearing, epilepsy, community and mental health groups, plus Kaiser Permanente, the massive West Coast health maintenance organization and other representatives of HMOs. Many of these groups had been told by HEW Undersecretary Hale Champion that federal dollars sucked into Medicaid and Medicare for their massive hospital expenditures would not be available for the categorical health programs.

Surprise. An Oct. 9 cloture vote banning non-germane amendments to the tax bill killed Kennedy's plan to tack hospital cost controls onto that high-priority bill, apparently dooming the hospital measure for the year. But calling on old promises for a floor vote on the issue from Senate Majority Leader Robert C. Byrd, D-W.Va., and Finance Health Subcommittee Chairman Herman E. Talmadge, Kennedy engineered a dramatic confrontation that forced the floor action.

The method was to load cost containment onto a controversial sugar bill (HR 13570) which, in turn, had been tacked onto a welfare measure (HR 7200) by Finance Committee Chairman Russell B. Long, D-La. When the smoke cleared, Long's sugar bill had been temporarily bumped from the agenda and the welfare bill was out of sight.

Senators who often defended AMA interests argued sharply against the bill during debate but did not attempt to slow it down with procedural delays, apparently lulled by the common belief that the administration did not have enough votes for passage. Kennedy fostered that belief, ostentatiously telling AMA officials at an Oct. 10 hearing, "We haven't got the votes" for the compromise. Yet days before that, Kennedy had told HEW lobbyists that the votes for the compromise were there.

Compromise. The Senate bill authorized standby revenue caps on the nation's hospitals if they failed as a group to meet the cost-reduction goal. Unlike the original administration plan, which imposed an across-the-board 9 percent cap on all hospitals (with no voluntary phase), the Senate bill provided that each hospital would have its own tailor-made income ceiling, derived from a mix of expenses and inflation adjusters. Blue-collar wages would be "passed through" in all phases — not counted in determining compliance. Labor had actively fought cost containment until it won this administration concession during the summer.

The Senate compromise also exempted numerous hospitals from the mandatory controls, a feature that brought an unknown but significant number of senators on board.

Nelson's amendment exempted from mandatory controls hospitals with annual admissions under 4,000, hospitals in states that met the voluntary goals or that had their own mandatory rate control programs, and individual hospitals that met the voluntary goal even if the state where they were located failed to do so.

One hospital lobbyist snapped that 7,000 hospitals would seek the exemption — about the total number of hospitals in the nation.

The relatively weaker impact of Nelson's bill was pointed up by estimated five-year savings in health care spending — $23 billion for the Nelson compromise, compared with $33 billion for the Carter proposal.

Final Action

In the end, no further action occurred after the Senate vote and the compromise died — but not without massive input from industry and administration lobbyists.

"We ran out of time. There wasn't enough time to let members know that the Senate bill met a lot of the objections that people had had before," said Richard D. Warden, HEW assistant secretary for legislation. The Senate bill provided numerous types of exemptions from mandatory hospital revenue limits, and opponents claimed the administration was buying senators' votes with the exemptions.

By noon the day after the Senate vote the industry lobbyists were camped out in the Capitol, shuttling between the Speaker's rooms, the reception room just off the House floor, the Ways and Means committee room, the tax bill conference and members' offices.

Attention focused on the Ways and Means panel because it had not reported a hospital cost bill. Rostenkowski sought committee authorization to ask the House to go into conference without floor consideration of the Senate bill. But hours before adjournment Oct. 15 Rostenkowski let it be known that — as he had always maintained — the votes were not there for cost containment in the Ways and Means panel.

Among other things, Rostenkowski ran into a major legislative overload problem that magnified whatever problems members may have had with the hospital bill. The Democratic leadership and many of Rostenkowski's Ways and Means colleagues were already up to their teeth in tax, energy and sugar conference negotiations. It was not a good time to load on one more bill, especially one as complex and unpopular as hospital cost containment.

Dying with the cost containment bill was a major Medicare-Medicaid reimbursement reform (HR 5285) that had been incorporated in the compromise, and two minor House Medicare-Medicaid bills (HR 13097, HR 13817) that could have been tacked on to the compromise in conference. *(Story, p. 619)*

Child Nutrition Programs

Although he cited reservations about the final bill, President Carter Nov. 10 signed into law legislation (S 3085 — PL 95-627) extending child nutrition programs for four years, through fiscal 1982.

Carter said he hoped the 96th Congress would make the changes necessary to satisfy his concerns, including a reduction in the spending entitlement for fiscal 1980 for the supplemental feeding program for women, infants and children (WIC). He said he signed the measure because "key members of the House and Senate committees [that oversee the program] have assured me that they will promptly enact a reduction of at least $50 million in the 1980 entitlement."

A spending level of $800 million for fiscal 1980, plus the conversion of the program from an authorization to an entitlement for fiscal 1979 and 1980, had drawn a veto recommendation from the Office of Management and Budget (OMB), reportedly on grounds that the provisions were highly inflationary. However, other agencies, including the Departments of Agriculture and Health, Education and Welfare, the Community Services Administration, WIC backers and various anti-poverty activist groups, lobbied the White House on behalf of the measure.

As originally reported by House and Senate committees, the legislation would have made WIC an entitlement program for all four years of the authorization. The program had been plagued since its establishment by uncertain funding. However, the Senate Appropriations Committee objected to creating another entitlement program, and the Senate agreed to cut the entitlement provision to two years; the House went along with that compromise.

Although the spending levels and entitlement provision were "significant problems," Carter said, the bill contained other changes in the nutrition programs advocated or backed by the administration. Those changes included provisions designed to reduce administrative expenditures for the school feeding programs and expand the child care food program.

Congress had refused to go along with several other administration proposals, including making the school breakfast program mandatory in schools with large numbers of poor children, eliminating children aged 3 to 5 from the WIC program, and ending the special milk program.

In extending both WIC and the child care food program, S 3085 made few major changes in existing law; principally it aimed to better target the food aid and to provide incentives for program expansion.

Provisions

As signed into law, S 3085 amended the National School Lunch Act and the Child Nutrition Act of 1966 as follows:

Child Care Food Program

- Made the child care food program permanent and authorized such funds as necessary to carry out the program.
- Established eligibility requirements for participation in the program.
- Simplified payment rates for participating institutions, except family and group day care homes, as follows: in institutions where at least two-thirds of the children enrolled are eligible for free or reduced-price school meals, the state will receive reimbursement for all meals at the reimbursement rate for free school meals; in institutions where between one-third and two-thirds of the chldren enrolled are eligible for free or reduced-priced school meals, the state will receive reimbursement for all meals at the rate for reduced price meals; in institutions where less than one-third of the children enrolled are eligible for free and reduced-price school meals, states will be reimbursed at the rate for paid school meals.
- Provided that reimbursement rates be adjusted semiannually on the basis of the "food away from home" component of the Consumer Price Index (CPI).
- Established a separate rate schedule for family and group day care homes. They would receive a payment for food and labor costs and payments for administrative costs up to limits prescribed by the secretary of agriculture, without a requirement for documentation of those costs.
- Required that institutions sponsoring family and group day care homes, rather than the individual homes, must satisfy the requirements regarding tax-exempt status; allowed reimbursement for administrative expenses to institutions that sponsor family and group day care homes; allowed such a home to function as its own sponsoring organization.
- Required the secretary of agriculture to conduct studies on the administrative costs for institutions participating in the program, on food service operations and on licensing problems faced by institutions and family and group day care homes; authorized up to $2 million for the studies.
- Increased to $6 million from $3 million the amount available for food service equipment assistance for child care institutions participating in the program.
- Allowed direct reimbursement by states to food equipment suppliers under certain conditions.

Special Supplemental Food Program (WIC)

- Extended the special supplemental food program for women, infants and children (WIC) for four years, through fiscal 1982.
- Established an entitlement of $550 million for fiscal 1979 and $800 million for fiscal 1980; authorized up to $900 million for fiscal 1981 and $950 million for fiscal 1982.
- Established as law the existing eligibility requirements contained in Department of Agriculture regulations, with the addition of an income limit. Limited program participation to pregnant, postpartum and breastfeeding women, infants and children up to age 5 who are determined to be at nutritional risk and whose incomes are below the standard for reduced-price lunches under the National School Lunch Act (195 percent of the poverty level).
- Defined nutritional risk, basing it on specific medical and nutritional causes; expanded the definition to include conditions that predispose persons to inadequate nutritional patterns and nutritionally related medical conditions, including alcoholism and drug addiction.
- Allowed simultaneous operation of the commodity supplemental food program and the WIC program in the same area; required the secretary of agriculture to issue regulations to prevent receipt of benefits under both programs.
- Expanded authority for nutrition education in the WIC program through a series of new requirements.
- Required the secretary to establish procedures to facilitate program participation of migrants as they move from state to state.

School Lunch, Milk Programs

- Reduced the federal reimbursement rate to states for reduced-price lunches by 10 cents, making the reimbursement rate 20 cents below the free lunch rate, with one exception: where all schools in a state charge less than 20 cents for a reduced-price lunch, the reimbursement rate for reduced-price lunches would be set at a level where the average reimbursement per lunch, plus the charge paid by the student, would equal the free lunch reimbursement.
- Allowed schools to provide free milk to children who are eligible for free lunches.
- Changed the reimbursement rate for milk in the special milk program from the "food away from home" series of the Consumer Price Index to the Producer Price Index for fresh processed milk.
- Based the annual adjustment in the commodity donation rate for the school lunch program on changes in

the Price Index for Food Used in Schools and Institutions, rather than changes in the CPI's "food away from home" series.

- Eliminated the requirement that schools serving both lunches and breakfasts account for each program separately.
- Increased the authorization for equipment funds to $75 million from $40 million for the school breakfast program.
- Provided increased assistance of 10 cents more per free breakfast for schools if they have high percentages of poor youngsters.
- Prohibited the secretary of agriculture from limiting or prohibiting the use during the 1978-79 school year of formulated grain-fruit products currently used in the school breakfast program; allowed the secretary to issue final regulations banning the use of the products 60 days after notifying appropriate congressional committees.

Other Amendments

- Increased funding for state administrative expenses for the child nutrition programs by raising the administrative cost limit to 1½ percent of the funds spent nationwide during the second previous fiscal year on school food programs.
- Raised the minimum state allocation for administrative costs to $100,000 from $75,000.
- Provided an increase of $750,000 in state administrative expense funds for operating the summer food program.
- Established one uniform set of poverty guidelines for all Agriculture Department food programs, with the national income limit for free school meals set at 125 percent of the poverty guidelines.
- Required the secretary of agriculture to conduct a study of the cost and feasibility of requiring schools to offer a choice of menus, in an effort to reduce plate waste.
- Established criminal penalties of up to $10,000 in fines and five years in prison for fraud and embezzlement in connection with the child nutrition programs.
- Authorized 14 pilot projects in providing lunches free to all children in a school, regardless of income.
- Authorized the secretary to purchase seafood commodities for donation in the school lunch program.

Senate Committee Action

The Senate Committee on Agriculture, Nutrition and Forestry reported S 3085 May 15 (S Rept 95-884). The committee recommended extension of child nutrition programs, incorporating in the bill improvements designed to reach more of the nutritionally "needy," distribute funds more equitably and strengthen nutrition education requirements.

Bill sponsor George McGovern, D-S.D., noted that "one way to reduce the nation's medical bill, that is now approaching some $200 billion, is by sound preventive health measures to keep ourselves from becoming ill in the first place. . . . These programs are designed . . . to head off much greater costs that would otherwise result later on in life."

WIC Program

The committee authorized $3.2 billion for WIC for fiscal 1979-82.

Carol Tucker Foreman, assistant secretary of agriculture for food and consumer services, had testified at an April 12 hearing that the WIC program was "one of the most effective and successful health and nutrition programs operated by the federal government." She cited studies showing WIC had significantly reduced anemia among participants, improved weight and height and led to a substantial increase in health clinic visits by children and pregnant women. That increase led to wider nutrition education and increased immunizations, she said.

Two major changes were made in the WIC program, tightening eligibility standards and attempting to assure funding at specified levels.

Eligibility. The committee considered two factors, income and age. The existing program allowed participation by all children in an area served by a WIC program who met local income guidelines and were found to be in "nutritional need" of supplemental food. Under these requirements, children of middle- and upper-income families were sometimes eligible for benefits. The committee decided to limit participation to persons whose household incomes did not exceed 195 percent of the federally established poverty level. Opponents of the income standard said the provision would eliminate many needy people from the program, but an Agriculture Department spokesperson said most state and local agencies already used such a standard.

Neither the House nor Senate bill contained a change in WIC, sought by the administration, to lower the age of eligible children to three years from five. The administration had argued for concentrating the limited resources available on children in the most crucial periods of development.

The "nutritional risk" requirement for recipients was redefined. The committee deleted specific examples, but included patterns which might lead to inadequate nutrition, such as alcohol or drug addiction.

Funding. The committee suggested two measures to eliminate uncertainty about WIC program funding. One would require allocations to each state or local agency applying to conduct or expand WIC programs, using a formula devised by the agriculture secretary. The committee set aside 20 percent of total funds for administration. Previously, administrative funds were designated as up to 20 percent of funds generated by program participation. Under this system, administrators did not know how much they would have available each year until food vouchers were redeemed. As a result, they tended to shy away from expansion.

Secondly, the committee recommended that WIC be entitled over the four-year authorization period. Entitlement would guarantee funding each year at levels set in the legislation. It would allow WIC to bypass annual review by the Appropriations Committee, which recommends funding for each program up to the level authorized by law. This move, like the setting aside of administrative funds, was designed to reduce agencies' uncertainty over how much they would receive each year.

McGovern called it "perhaps the most controversial provision of the bill." He said "entitlement is crucial, in the short run at least, to provide for program growth." McGovern cited the "unusual history of the . . . program, which includes a continuous series of impoundments, lawsuits and court orders to spend funds that remain in effect through September 1978. . . ."

The Appropriations Committee, charged with enforcing provisions of the Congressional Budget Act, was opposed to the guarantee of funding. But it finally agreed to report a compromise provision to entitle WIC funding for 1979 and 1980, and authorize appropriations for 1981 and 1982.

The Agriculture Committee also moved to strengthen nutrition education. While existing law called for it, S 3085 strengthened that law by requiring nutrition education standards, training, learning materials, regular evaluation by state agencies and one-fifth of funds set aside for nutrition education.

Child Care Food Program

With an eye to expanding the child care food program, the committee relaxed eligibility standards for participating institutions.

Previously, institutions had to go through a time-consuming licensing process, which discouraged many small, family or group day care homes from applying.

The committee provided that if licensing were inaccessible, child care centers could be funded by showing either that they had received government food program funds in the past and properly used them, or that they met certain approval standards to be established by the secretaries of HEW and agriculture.

Robert Dole, R-Kan., said the new flexibility in licensing would allow more centers and homes to sponsor programs. He claimed it would not reduce safeguards, since "all participating institutions are still expected to meet appropriate local health and safety standards."

The committee also revised reimbursement schemes, establishing one payment rate for all child care centers. Each center would be funded on the basis of whether two-thirds or more, one- to two-thirds, or one-third or less of children in the center were eligible for free or reduced-price meals under the National School Lunch Act. Family and group day care homes were authorized to receive flat payment rates.

The child care food program was recommended for permanent authorization, eliminating the need for Congress to vote on the life of the program after some future expiration date.

School Breakfast Program

The committee did not endorse the administration-supported expansion of the school breakfast program, but included incentives for greater participation.

One provision keyed reimbursement rates to the percentage of needy people served by each school's food program. If a school population included at least 50 percent children considered "especially needy," that school would be eligible to receive reimbursement as if all the children were needy.

The bill also allowed participating schools to do joint administration and record-keeping for lunch and breakfast programs, eliminating more difficult separate accounting for the two programs.

The committee increased to $75 million from $40 million the authorization for assistance to schools buying or replacing food service equipment.

Bob Greenstein of the Agriculture Department said the administration was "disappointed" in the failure to require expansion of school breakfasts. But he said the administration had "strongly supported" proposals for expansion incentives that were voted in.

Other Programs

S 3805 set the federal reimbursement rate for schools offering reduced-price lunches at 20 cents less than the amount provided to schools for free lunches served. Under existing law, schools got 10 cents less for each cheap meal than for a free meal. But most schools have charged 20 cents for the reduced-price lunches, picking up an "extra dime" in the process.

Under the special milk program, children judged to be at severe "nutritional risk" were given extra milk. The committee approved use of the wholesale price index for fluid milk instead of the food-away-from-home index.

The committee also amended a 1977 law to place more administrative responsibility on states for the summer food program.

Senate Floor Action

The Senate passed S 3085 July 21 by a 68-0 vote. *(Vote 232, p. 37-S)*

The way was cleared for quick action on the measure by a compromise between the Agriculture and Appropriations Committees over whether to create a new "uncontrollable spending" entitlement program.

The Senate compromise allowed guaranteed, entitled funding for the program for two years, after which spending would be subject to regular appropriations.

The Appropriations amendment, brought up by Lawton Chiles, D-Fla., eliminated WIC funding entitlement for fiscal years 1981 and 1982, but allowed it during 1979 and 1980. The compromise amendment also reduced WIC funding in fiscal 1979 from $600 million to $550 million.

McGovern called the amendment "reasonable" and urged its passage, but not before saying he felt the Agriculture Committee proposal for four-year entitlement was more appropriate for the WIC program, which should be viewed as a "special case" because of its historical difficulty in obtaining authorized funds.

The percentage of food service equipment assistance funds that were "reserved" for schools without meal service facilities was reduced to 40 percent from 50 percent by an amendment by John Melcher, D-Mont. The percentage reserved still represented an increase over the existing 33 1/3 percent. Melcher said the amendment would allow greater flexibility in states' distribution of funds to institutions, retaining the incentive for schools to initiate breakfast programs while removing "potential harm resulting from decreasing the unreserved" funds.

The full Senate joined the committee in refusing to mandate schools' participation in the school breakfast program. Patrick Leahy, D-Vt., proposed mandatory elections in school districts which had not yet implemented breakfasts. If a majority of parents voted for the breakfast program (at least 50 votes) a school would be required to implement it the next year. McGovern, shying away from the mandate, which was opposed by the American Food Service Association, asked that the amendment be withdrawn in lieu of hearings on the subject early in 1979. Leahy consented.

The Senate also adopted amendments:

- By Edward M. Kennedy, D-Mass., to encourage the use of fish in the programs, hopefully as a vehicle to promote consumption of less popular but edible fish types.

- By Robert Morgan, D-N.C., to authorize pilot projects in up to 14 school districts to study the feasibility of free school lunches for all children.
- By Robert Dole, R-Kan., to require the agriculture secretary to periodically review foods used in the programs, to assure quality and perhaps avoid "super donuts" — nutritious confection-type breakfast items opposed by many people who feel children will learn improper eating habits consuming them for breakfast.

A proposal by Orrin G. Hatch, R-Utah, to exclude from the WIC program women who have had abortions but might fit into the "postpartum" (after-childbirth) category, was withdrawn after McGovern clarified that these women already were ineligible.

House Committee Action

The House Education and Labor Committee reported HR 12511 May 15 (H Rept 95-1153). The bill extended the WIC program through fiscal 1982, setting higher authorization levels the first two years than the Senate did. The committee recommended $650 million for fiscal 1979, $850 million for fiscal 1980, $900 million in 1981 and $950 million in 1982.

The committee recommended entitled funds for WIC for fiscal 1979-82. But the House Appropriations Committee July 27 approved a clarifying amendment to deny entitlement, saying the WIC program was by definition subject to the regular appropriations process. The House Appropriations report (Part II of H Rept 95-1153) said the entitlement would contribute to spending in excess of the current budget resolution.

Differences

House provisions for the child care food program differed from the Senate only in that licensing would be slightly stricter.

The school breakfast program was changed to mandate breakfasts in "needy" schools — those where 50 percent or more of lunches were served free or at reduced rates. The percentage required to mandate breakfasts dropped to 45 percent in 1980-81 and 40 percent in later years. Schools with less than 125 students were exempted from the requirement.

The committee also recommended that schools be considered in compliance even if they did not implement the program in one or two "needy" schools, if they opted to use an alternative school serving just as many or more needy children.

The committee determined that all schools required to offer breakfasts under state law could receive higher reimbursement rates.

House Floor, Final Action

Like dozens of other bills passed by the 95th Congress, the fate of the bill remained uncertain until the final days of the session. HR 12511 was still pending on the House calendar when the session entered its final days.

Fearing that the bill would die — major differences existed between the Senate and House versions — key legislators on both sides began private negotiations as the last weekend session began. Early Oct. 15, they reached agreement, and quickly steered the final bill through the House and Senate. Sponsors in the House took S 3085 as passed July 21 by the Senate, substituted the compromise language, won House approval by a voice vote, and returned it to the Senate, which also approved it by voice vote.

The compromise focused on three issues:

Entitlement Issue. House sponsors agreed to drop their effort to make the WIC program an entitlement for all four fiscal years, accepting the Senate plan, which called for entitlements for fiscal 1979 and 1980 and authorizations for fiscal 1981 and 1982.

Mandatory Breakfast Program. House negotiators also backed off from their desire to require school districts with high concentrations of low-income students to participate in the school breakfast program. Supporters of the provision cited the "significant impact" the breakfast program has had on the nutritional health of youngsters but said not enough school districts were taking advantage of it. Therefore, they argued, the program should be made mandatory in districts with many children who otherwise would go without breakfast each day.

But others questioned the wisdom of mandating the breakfast program when the school lunch program was not required. The Senate bill, although it did not mandate participation, contained various provisions designed to increase the number of schools involved in the breakfast program. Negotiators subsequently accepted the Senate provisions, which increased funding for schools buying or replacing food service equipment, allowed participating schools to do joint administration and record-keeping for lunch and breakfast programs, and keyed reimbursement rates to the percentage of needy youngsters served by each school's food program.

'Super Donuts.' Finally, House and Senate negotiators resolved differences over an amendment added during Senate floor debate designed to ban the use of the fortified grain-fruit products in the school breakfast program. The Dole amendment, which was backed by various activist groups, directed the secretary of agriculture to review the use of alternative foods in the child nutrition programs, with an eye toward banning the products.

Opponents of the alternative foods felt such a provision would give the Department of Agriculture the right to ban the foods by issuing regulations. But, just to make sure, the amendment contained wording which prohibited the use of alternative foods that were designed to substitute for more than one food component in the daily basic meal requirement. The fortified foods made by various manufacturers were designed to substitute for two or more components in the basic meal requirement. Such products as Huzzah!, Morning Break and Super Donut contained servings of both fruit and grain. Acceptance of the amendment probably would have resulted in the end of those and other alternative foods, since, according to several analysts, manufacturers would lose the economic benefit gained in combining two requirements in one food product.

The push for the Dole amendment reflected longstanding controversy over the alternative foods. Many felt that serving such items as Super Donuts, which were viewed as "junk" foods by nutrition advocates, while attempting to teach good eating habits, was hypocritical.

But the House bill did not contain a provision similar to the Dole amendment. In the final negotiations, members accepted wording which would still allow the Department of Agriculture to review the alternative foods. However, the agency could not issue any regulations banning the foods until after the current school year.

National Health Insurance

President Carter in 1978 found himself between a rock and a very hard place on the issue of national health insurance.

Prodded by labor and Sen. Edward M. Kennedy, D-Mass., to make good on his 1976 campaign promise of a "comprehensive national health insurance system with universal and mandatory coverage," Carter did issue a statement of general principles on July 29 and directed Health, Education and Welfare (HEW) Secretary Joseph A. Califano Jr. to draft a health plan to be submitted to Congress in 1979. But he said that to hold down federal spending, the program would have to be phased in gradually.

Labor leaders criticized the president's plan as too little, too slow, and in October Kennedy launched a series of nationwide hearings on his own comprehensive, labor-backed Health Care for All Americans Act. Labor had hoped to make health insurance a campaign issue in the 1978 congressional elections, but it was overshadowed by concerns about inflation and federal budget-cutting. Some observers also suggested that Kennedy was pushing the issue for his own political gain.

While the administration still insisted the federal government could not afford a major new health program in the immediate future, at year's end it was exploring the possibility of linking its hospital cost containment proposal to a limited federal program of coverage for catastrophic health costs. Carter had insisted hospital cost control was a necessary prerequisite to national health insurance, but Congress had failed to enact his plan in 1978. *(Story, p. 619)*

Administration Proposal

In his directive to Califano, Carter said any national health plan should assure that all Americans have comprehensive health care coverage and quality health care, with freedom to choose their doctors, hospitals and health delivery systems. It should include "aggressive" cost containment measures and not be inflationary. The plan should be phased in as the economy permits, be financed by multiple sources and include a "significant" role for the private insurance industry, with "appropriate" government regulation, Carter said.

The plan should be designed so that additional public and private expenditures for improved health benefits and coverage would be substantially offset by savings from greater efficiency in the health care system, and should involve no additional federal spending until fiscal 1983, the president said.

It also should provide resources and develop payment methods to promote such major reforms in delivering health care services as substantially increasing the availability of ambulatory and preventive services, attracting personnel to underserved rural and urban areas, and encouraging the use of prepaid health plans. It also should assure consumer representation throughout its operation, he said.

Reaction. If members of Congress were pleased with the 10 broadly drafted "principles," few said so.

The announcement came when few members wanted to go on record supporting such a potentially costly initiative. On the other hand, labor leaders and Kennedy blasted the president for not going far enough. Kennedy called a press conference to reject the principles and denounce what he called Carter's "failure of leadership" on the health issue. AFL-CIO President George Meany and other labor leaders also expressed disappointment with Carter's plan.

Kennedy-Labor Plan

Two months after breaking with Carter on the economics of national health care, Kennedy and his allies in organized labor launched their new drive for national health insurance, insisting that the nation can no longer afford to do without it.

Although the "Health Care for All Americans Act of 1979" would be costly to put in place, "once cost containment takes effect, the nation will pay less for health care under national health insurance" than if nothing were done, according to Kennedy.

After rejecting Carter's July proposals, the labor coalition Committee for National Health Insurance (CNHI) had quickly drafted the plan Kennedy released Oct. 2.

The labor plan would place a new federal Public Authority (PA) in charge of a mixed system that would combine heavily regulated private insurance with expanded federal health programs for the poor, disabled and elderly. The PA would "contract" with state agencies to implement the program, but the division of state-federal responsibilities was not spelled out.

A package of basic health benefits would be mandated for all Americans, with employers paying most of the cost for their employees and dependents, and the federal government picking up the tab for the unemployed and the elderly. Fixed, annual budgets — with fee schedules for doctors and budgets for hospitals — would be set after annual negotiations among the PA state units, insurers, doctors, hospitals and other health providers.

Kennedy's timetable was enactment in 1979, with most benefits in place two years later and a complete program by 1985. During the two-year interim period, strict revenue limits on doctors and hospitals would be imposed, to get health care spending under control.

The benefits would be delivered through existing providers — hospitals, health maintenance organizations, federally subsidized primary health care centers, plus newly developed providers that could get federal subsidies.

Premiums for the private insurance would be related to wages rather than to the health history of the insured group, as is now the case. Insurers would have to open enrollment, disregarding medical histories of individuals. They would be allowed to pool funds, through several national consortia, to provide back-up insurance to cover high-risk beneficiaries.

Without national health insurance, the nation would spend an estimated $361.6 billion on health care in 1985; with the plan, the nation's health bill would be $31 billion less according to CNHI estimates.

Reaction. Hearings Oct. 9 and 10 before Kennedy's Human Resources Subcommittee on Health featured almost ritual exchanges between Kennedy and witnesses, who had gone over the basic issues many times in the past. Kennedy introduced his first national health insurance proposal, an "all-federal" program, in 1971.

The American Medical Association (AMA) viewed the new features of Kennedy's plan — private insurance participation and private sources of funding — as "beneficial," according to Dr. James H. Sammons, AMA executive director. But even with these concessions, the labor-Kennedy plan meant "rationed" medical care, wasteful bureaucratic expenses and destruction of the high quality of care now available to Americans, he said.

Spokesmen for labor and senior citizens groups praised the plan.

Kennedy also held hearings in New York, Chicago, West Virginia and Detroit, where families detailed the financial woes that resulted from severe or lengthy illnesses.

Clinical Lab Regulation

For the third time in three years, Congress failed to complete action on legislation to strengthen and broaden regulation of laboratories that do medical tests.

Two House committees reported a clinical laboratories bill (HR 10909) similar to one (S 705) that the Senate had passed in 1977. The House briefly debated the bill Oct. 2, but when the end-of-session crunch came, there were six health reauthorizations to clear in three days, and a cluster of amendments to the labs bill. House leaders refused to shove the labs bill onto their overcrowded schedule and Congress adjourned without a House vote. *(Senate action, 1977 Almanac p. 493)*

That sequence was almost an exact rerun of 1976, when the Senate easily endorsed a slightly stronger measure and a majority of the House approved it. The bill died, however, because House sponsors failed to muster the two-thirds majority needed for passage under suspension of the rules, and time ran out before they could schedule a second vote. *(1976 Almanac p. 557)*

Although the lab bill's chronic problems suggested blocking efforts by organized opposition, proponents said that was not the case, and cited numerous exceptions and delays that had been written into successive versions of the bill to soften its immediate impact. Instead, health observers credited the House failure to vote to such factors as the legislative overload of other health bills, late-surfacing amendments from a few conservative opponents of regulation, and absence of an active sponsor in the House. "It was nobody's pet bill in the House, although [Senate sponsor] Jacob K. Javits, R-N.Y., pushed it as far as he could. When the House leadership saw all those amendments, they got gun-shy and wouldn't schedule it," said Dennis W. Weissman of the American Society for Medical Technology. Weissman said the group would press again in 1979 for passage.

Like S 705, the House bill required the secretary of health, education and welfare (HEW) to set national standards for quality control, record-keeping, employee proficiency and other aspects of laboratory operations. It also required licensing of all labs by HEW, but authorized the secretary to delegate this function to states with equivalent programs.

Like the Senate bill, the House bill included a "whistle-blower" provision to protect employees who reported violations of the act. It authorized warrantless inspections of the labs — as did S 705 — but softened the impact of this provision by requiring prior written notices to labs before inspections. The Senate bill had required one unannounced inspection per lab, per year.

The House bill was reported by the Interstate and Foreign Commerce Committee March 24 and by Ways and Means July 12 (H Rept 95-1004, Parts I-III).

Drug Law Reform

The Carter administration asked Congress to make major changes in the way drugs were regulated for safety and effectiveness, but the proposal went no further in 1978 than extensive hearings and some revision by health subcommittee staffs. The legislation was expected to be reintroduced in 1979.

Under the plan announced March 16 by Joseph A. Califano Jr., secretary of Health, Education and Welfare (HEW), consumers could buy new drugs much earlier after they were developed than was the case, and they would have far more information about the effectiveness and health risks of all drugs. Manufacturers would be relieved of many costly and time-consuming pre-marketing test responsibilities. And the Food and Drug Administration (FDA), which regulated drugs, would gain new powers to remove hazardous drugs from the market, penalize manufacturers that violated the law and in some cases approve new drugs before testing was completed.

The administration bill weakened existing restrictions on drug exports and on protection of human subjects in the earliest stages of drug experimentation. And it contained language that would effectively wipe out state laws legalizing the controversial drug laetrile, promoted as a cancer cure.

If enacted, the bill would be the first major revision of drug regulation law since 1962 and the third since the first drug law was passed some 70 years ago. Califano said that with 1.5 billion prescriptions being written each year for some 60,000 prescription drugs, the time had come to replace the "horse-and-buggy law with a jet-age law." *(Background, Congress and the Nation Vol. I, p. 1159; Vol. II, p. 705)*

Drug manufacturers had pushed for revision, arguing that time-consuming and expensive pre-market testing requirements severely cut their incentives for developing new drugs. Developing a new drug could cost as much as $20 million under existing restrictions, Califano said. Consumer health groups had also sought legislation to make information on drug hazards more widely available and to counter the spiraling costs of drugs. The administration bill did not address the question of drug costs directly, although it contained provisions designed to stimulate competition within the industry and to inform consumers of comparative prices of prescription drugs.

The administration proposal followed on the heels of at least 10 years of effort by members of Congress to amend the drug law, Califano noted. Appearing with Califano — and on the bill's sponsor list — were Sens. Edward M. Kennedy, D-Mass., and Jacob K. Javits, R-N.Y., and Rep. Paul G. Rogers, D-Fla., key health committee members.

Also preceding the proposal were three months of constrenuous lobbying and redrafting by FDA and HEW, representing an effort "to create a fabric of consensus to carry the message," as FDA Commissioner Donald Kennedy put it. After releasing a hefty first draft last fall, the FDA conducted public hearings with representatives from the industry, consumer health and medical groups, labor unions and associations of the elderly. The last two groups share a concern with how drug costs eat up health plan benefits.

However, there still were numerous areas of disagreement among interest groups and among members of Congress over provisions of the bill — indicating a long and difficult course to enactment.

Details of Proposal

The heart of the administration proposal was a new approval procedure based on a "monograph" — published descriptive standard for each generic drug. Because the new system would make substantial changes in data requirements and disclosure of safety and efficacy test results, it was the subject of concerted lobbying by drug manufacturers, who feared loss of trade secrets, and by consumer health advocates, who warned of dangerous omissions or falsifications.

The generic (non-brand name) standard would be issued as the final step for marketing approval. Individual manufacturers would be licensed to produce their brand-name versions under restrictions set out in the monograph. The existing system granted multiple approvals for similar drugs on a brand-name basis. The first manufacturer to seek approval for a new drug entity would be protected by a five-year ban on any other manufacturer using that data to support its own application. After the five-year period, other manufacturers could make the drug without duplicating the originators' tests.

Breakthrough drugs could be conditionally released before monograph acceptance for medically compelling reasons.

The monograph would constitute the final approval for marketing, but it could be amended or revoked at any time by the Secretary of HEW to reflect new data on the drug.

The new system would make no changes in the existing sequence of pre-approval animal and clinical testing. But less information would be required on early test stages than is now the case, while substantially more would be required, and disclosed, in the end stages.

Manufacturers' data on drug safety and effectiveness was kept confidential until final approval and then released only in limited form. This confidentiality had functioned as a sort of "second patent" since the FDA usually required competitors seeking approval of similar products to go through at least some scientific investigation.

The administration bill required only submission of a "scientific summary" with the initial application, and publication of safety and effectiveness data two to three months before the public hearing. (Other "trade secret" data, including manufacturing processes, would be submitted to advisory committees but was not subject to disclosure.)

The Health Research Group strongly disapproved this provision because it did not require disclosure of raw data. Without this material, the accuracy of the data summaries could not be determined, a spokesman said. The question of how much data should be publicly available and at what stage in the approval process was viewed as one of the most difficult problems in the bill.

Other major provisions of the administration bill:

- Loosened existing drug export law to permit sales of unapproved drugs to a foreign country on its request, unless the HEW secretary determined that the drug would create a public health problem. Existing law prohibited export of drugs not approved for the U.S. market.
- Made "unreasonable and substantial risk of illness or injury" the standard for immediate recall of a drug, rather than "imminent hazard," and set deadlines for the various phases of the longer approval procedure.
- Authorized the secretary to require drug companies to monitor and report adverse effects of their drugs for at least five years after monograph approval.
- Authorized the secretary to require post-approval tests of drugs.
- Permitted very limited tests of new drugs on human subjects in a preliminary test period without proof that the proposed tests will yield scientifically valid and reliable data, as was required. Because most new drugs are discarded in this early stage, because it would save time and money, and because it could be done "without appreciable increase in the risk" to test subjects, HEW said, it was a desirable method of speeding new drugs to consumers.
- Required patient information inserts in most prescription drugs, spelling out side effects and other information provided only to doctors. The FDA could waive this requirement and might do so for drugs used as placebos and in certain other instances, an FDA official said.
- Placed new restrictions on drug advertising, including penalties for false promotional statements. The secretary was authorized to require corrective advertising.
- Prohibited drug companies from giving doctors free samples or gifts worth more than $5.
- Declared invalid, for purposes of drug regulation, the distinction between "intrastate" and "interstate" commerce. This provision would wipe out state laws legalizing laetrile, and was intended to prevent similar problems in the future, an HEW lawyer said.
- Raised criminal penalties to $25,000 for an individual and $50,000 for a company, from $10,000. (These fines could be aggregated for multiple offenses.)
- Established civil penalties for violations of the drug law — $10,000 for an individual, $25,000 for a company.
- Authorized expert witness fees and other methods of encouraging public participation in the approval process.
- Established a national center for pharmacological research.

Certain elements of the proposal resembled components of bills proposed in the past by Rogers, Kennedy and Javits, but some provisions prominent in previous bills were conspicuously absent, including proposals to:

- Make the FDA an independent agency, outside HEW, with Senate confirmation of the FDA commissioner. Sen. Kennedy said he would offer such an amendment to the administration bill.
- Create a national board to evaluate test data of drug companies. Sen. Gaylord Nelson, D-Wis., had proposed that this testing be carried out by the government, at the expense of the manufacturers.
- Strengthen controls on drug testing in human subjects.

The pressures for legal laetrile had generated another type of bill in Congress, a "medical freedom of choice" measure introduced by Rep. Steven D. Symms, R-Idaho. That bill simply eliminated the efficacy requirement. A later version also provided for a one-house veto of a drug regulation decision which had adverse economic effects, and streamlined some approval procedures. ▮

Child Health Program

Concern that legislation broadening health care coverage for poor children would mark the first step toward liberalization of cash welfare programs helped kill the measure in the last hectic days of the 95th Congress.

The legislation, called the Child Health Assessment Program (CHAP), would have replaced Medicaid's widely criticized Early and Periodic Screening, Diagnosis and Treatment Program (EPSDT). The program would have raised the average federal payment to the states to carry out the screening program and would have made more poor children eligible for Medicaid by expanding coverage in all states to children living in needy two-parent households. CHAP would have added another 1.7 million to 2.5 million children to the Medicaid rolls. *(Background, 1977 Almanac p. 494)*

The legislation, proposed by President Carter in 1977 (HR 6076), drew strong bipartisan and interest group support. However, neither the House nor the Senate version was ever brought to the floor for a vote.

"It was everyone's second priority," said a spokeswoman for the Children's Defense Fund, who along with the American Medical Association and a host of other health groups lobbied vigorously in support of CHAP.

But concerns about the program's cost and about the provision that liberalized Medicaid eligibility by allowing poor children from intact families to receive aid also helped scuttle the legislation.

In the Senate, a last-minute push by the bill's sponsor, Abraham Ribicoff, D-Conn., sparked a hasty Finance Committee markup of Ribicoff's bill (S 1392). The panel then attached CHAP provisions to a minor House-passed Medicaid bill (HR 9434) and approved the measure Oct. 10.

But Carl T. Curtis, R-Neb., engaged in some deft parliamentary maneuvering that ensured the measure would never reach the floor. Under the Senate's so-called three day rule, floor consideration of a bill is prohibited until three weekdays following members' receipt of a copy of the committee report. The rule may be waived under unanimous consent, but Curtis let it be known that he would object to such an attempt.

The Finance Committee filed its report (S Rept 95-1310) late Oct. 12. Since the bill could not have been taken up until Oct. 17 under the three day rule, the measure died with Congress' Oct. 15 adjournment.

The House briefly debated its CHAP bill (HR 13611 — H Rept 95-1310) Oct. 11. However, the measure was never brought up for a vote because of its poor chances for Senate action, according to a House source.

Social Services Funds

Congress in 1978 raised the ceiling for social services funds under Title XX of the Social Security Act to help meet the rising costs of the entitlement programs. The increase, for fiscal 1979 only, was enacted as part of the omnibus tax bill that cleared Congress Oct. 15 (HR 13511 — PL 95-600).

The ceiling was raised to $2.9 billion from $2.5 billion. The $2.5 billion ceiling had been in effect since 1972.

The House had passed legislation (HR 12973) July 25 to raise the ceiling to $2.9 billion in fiscal 1979, $3.15 billion in fiscal 1980 and $3.45 billion in 1981.

HR 12973 also extended or amended provisions affecting several Title XX programs, including day care, and authorized the use of Title XX funds for emergency shelter for abused adults. These provisions died with the end of the 95th Congress.

The House passed the bill by a 346-54 vote under suspension of the rules. *(Vote 516, p. 148-H)*

President Carter had proposed an increase of $150 million in Title XX spending for each year during fiscal 1979-82 as part of his urban program, but the House Ways and Means Subcommittee on Public Assistance raised the ceiling. The Ways and Means Committee reported the bill June 21 (H Rept 95-1312).

The Senate Finance Committee reported HR 12973 Oct. 9 (S Rept 95-1306).

DNA Regulation

Congress in 1978 shelved efforts to enact legislation to regulate a controversial form of genetic research — recombinant DNA or "gene-splicing."

Two House committees reported a weakened version (HR 11192) of legislation considered in 1977, but no floor action was taken. *(1977 action, background, 1977 Almanac p. 492)*

For the second time in a year, Sen. Edward M. Kennedy, D-Mass., once a strong advocate of stiff regulation, withdrew his bill (an amended version of S 1217 as reported in 1977) to extend federal regulation to academic and commercial research involving the substance, deoxyribonucleic acid.

Instead, Kennedy suggested the Carter administration use existing authority under the Public Health Service Act to extend federal safety standards for DNA research to all laboratories. The administration had contended it needed specific authority from Congress to do so, but in December it announced new regulations anyway.

Environmental groups and some scientists had pushed for federal regulation of all DNA experimentation on grounds that it could pose safety hazards to the public. Existing rules covered only research that received federal funds.

Some DNA researchers themselves earlier had expressed the same fears, but by 1978 a strong lobby of academic and commercial DNA researchers, professional organizations and university officials argued that these fears had proved groundless and that no federal regulation was needed.

Although the bills were modified in 1978 to satisfy most of the universities' objections to the 1977 versions, many scientists still opposed any legislation as an infringement on academic freedom. Others supported a relatively weak federal law, since that appeared to be the only way to preempt (override) stiffer state or local statutes. Harvard University, one of several universities favoring federal preemption of local DNA laws, was subject to a landmark local DNA ordinance in Cambridge, Mass., and similar proposals were pending in several other states.

Kennedy's proposal to skip new legislation and use the Public Health Act instead had the tacit support of some environmental groups, since that act apparently would permit state and local DNA regulations to continue in force, and at the local level environmentalists might have more influence.

Environmentalists generally conceded that academic DNA projects had not turned out to be dangerous, but they feared hazards could still result from large-scale industrial application of the new technology. DNA experiments were expected to result in new drugs, agricultural products and industrial chemicals. Some environmentalists suggested that money was a factor in some researchers' opposition to federal controls, since they stood to gain from commercial application of their research.

The 1978 measures extended the NIH safety standards for recombinant DNA research to all public and private laboratories for two years only. The 1977 bills had set no time limit on the regulation.

The new bills also directed the secretary of HEW to regulate the research, but provided no blueprint. Local biohazard or biosafety review committees, mandatory in 1977, were made optional, and there was no explicit requirement for public-interest representation on a national advisory board. These changes, plus a pre-emption clause in the House bill, elicited a strongly worded dissent from six members of the House Commerce Committee.

House Committee Action

The House Interstate and Foreign Commerce Committee reported HR 11192 March 24 and the Science and Technology Committee followed suit April 21 (H Rept 95-1005, Parts I and II). The Commerce Committee voted 17-6 to report the bill, the science panel 24-4.

Both committees said the bill was intended to protect the health of the public and the environment, because the "best informed scientists" still thought some protection was needed. Since DNA research also was "of exceptional value to science," a second purpose was to "prevent the imposition of unnecessarily restrictive state and local requirements," the report said.

Dissenting Views. The six dissenting members of the Commerce committee warned that local review committees — even if they were set up under the non-mandatory provisions of the bill — would be nothing more than peer review groups, "with corporations or educational institutions conducting DNA research . . . policing themselves. . . . We totally reject the view that the people are incapable or unworthy . . . and that only a regulatory or research elite can make reasoned decisions on the complex regulatory issues of the day," they asserted.

Other trouble spots, in the view of the dissenters, included:

- Inadequate standards for selecting personnel to enforce the act.
- Overly broad authority for the secretary to exempt "low-risk" DNA projects, as well as those designed to assess the dangers of DNA research in general. The absence of clear standards and of opportunities for public review, such as hearings, were both considered objectionable.
- Omission of explicit health and legal safeguards for laboratory workers.

Objection was also registered by Mike McCormack, D-Wash., of the Science committee, whose background in nuclear energy research had earned him some standing as a House expert on scientific matters. McCormack said the bill "set a dangerous precedent" when no need had been demonstrated for federal regulation, and that "freedom of inquiry is as indispensable as freedom of speech." He also said researchers "really intent" on violating the safety guidelines could easily do so.

Provisions

As reported by the two House committees, HR 11192:

- Extended NIH safety guidelines for conditions of recombinant DNA research (physical facilities and organic materials used) and types of experiments permitted to all public and private investigators, for two years.
- Authorized the secretary of Health, Education and Welfare (HEW) to revise the guidelines.
- Authorized the secretary to exempt recombinant DNA activities that did not constitute "a significant risk to health or the environment."
- Required investigators or institutions involved in any recombinant DNA activity to report both ongoing and planned DNA work to the secretary.
- Authorized these penalties for violation of the guidelines and reporting requirements: civil fines of up to $5,000 a day for each violation; suspension or cancellation of federal research funding for the project; injunctions against continued violations, and seizure and destruction of materials involved in violations.
- Authorized inspectors appointed by the secretary to inspect DNA facilities, without warrants, "during normal business hours;" barred persons involved in a research project or having a direct financial interest in it from serving as that project's inspector.
- Authorized the secretary to allow a state or local law to supersede the federal law only if that law were at least as stringent as the federal statute and if it were shown to be necessary to protect health or environment.
- Authorized the secretary to support research on health and environmental risks of recombinant DNA activities, and permitted the secretary to exempt those research projects from the guidelines.
- Stipulated that the secretary's authority to regulate DNA activities did not supplant workplace inspection and other authority established by the 1970 Occupational Safety and Health Act (PL 91-596).
- Established a study commission, appointed by the secretary, to study and report on federal policy for activities "involving the genetic modification of organisms and viruses."
- Directed the secretary to provide for protection against improper disclosure of trade secrets or similar proprietary information.

New DNA Regulations

HEW Secretary Joseph A. Califano Jr. Dec. 17 announced new regulations that would relax federal safety rules for DNA research and provide for more input by non-scientists into decisions on what experiments should be done.

He also said he was asking the Food and Drug Administration and the Environmental Protection Agency to use existing authority to regulate commercial DNA experiments.

The new regulations exempted about one-third of the experiments from federal "containment" requirements and authorized the secretary to permit, on a case-by-case basis, hazardous experiments that had been banned. The regulations, effective Jan. 1, 1979, also increased the number of non-scientists serving on local review committees and a national advisory board.

Congressional staff who worked on the DNA bills said the relaxation of the safety rules and the public participation provisions were acceptable, but that bills to cover private industry were still likely in 1979. It was not clear from Califano's announcement that industrial projects could be effectively regulated without new legislation, they said.

ACTION Authorization

Congress failed to complete action on legislation extending various domestic volunteer programs run by ACTION, including the major effort, VISTA.

The Senate passed a reauthorization measure (S 2617) July 21, but the House never took up its version (HR 11922). As a result, Congress will be required to consider extension legislation again in 1979. ACTION programs were funded until then under a continuing resolution (H J Res 1139). *(Story, p. 161)*

Besides extending VISTA and other volunteer programs, the bills contained authority for a $40 million neighborhood volunteer program proposed by President Carter as part of his urban policy. *(Urban policy, p. 314)*

Inclusion of the neighborhood program in the House measure was the principal reason the measure was never taken up on the floor. Republican members of the Education and Labor Committee had sharply criticized the proposal as ill-considered, lacking in direction and too expensive. They promised a lengthy floor fight if the bill was called up.

The measure was on the House calendar for the last weekend of the 95th session but the leadership, anxious to avoid delays in the push for adjournment, did not call it up for debate.

Committee Action

The Senate Human Resources Committee approved the neighborhood program with little difficulty, but the White House had to do some last-minute arm-twisting to get it through the House Education and Labor Committee.

Both committees reported their bills May 15 (H Rept 95-1152, S Rept 95-823).

The Senate bill extended ACTION and its programs for three years, with an authorization of $643.2 million. The House bill authorized spending of $210.4 million over two years.

Although the neighborhood program was considered a relatively minor part of President Carter's urban package, the White House lobbied vigorously for it when it ran into trouble in the House Subcommittee on Economic Opportunity.

The program would have provided grants to cities and towns to hire volunteer coordinators, who in turn would recruit lawyers, accountants, architects and other professionals to do volunteer work for neighborhood organizations. It also would have provided grants up to $15,000 for small neighborhood revitalization projects such as converting abandoned lots into basketball courts or small parks.

The subcommittee originally approved the program despite a lack of hearings; doubts about the budget request, which allotted 25 percent of the $40 billion total for administrative costs, and antipathy, particularly among Republican members, to ACTION and its director, Sam Brown, former anti-war activist and liberal politician.

(ACTION also had come under sharp criticism in Congress because it proposed no funding increases in fiscal 1979 for two volunteer programs for the elderly and a 25 percent cut for a third program. That set off a howl of protest in Congress, where the popular programs had substantial support. ACTION later backed off from its budget proposals, but many members of Congress remained hostile to the agency.)

Subcommittee Chairman Ike F. Andrews, D-N.C., later announced he would move to delete the neighborhood program in full committee markup on grounds that ACTION had not had adequate time to plan a major urban initiative, and that the program was potentially inflationary and excessively costly. However, after vigorous White House lobbying, Andrews agreed not to offer the amendment.

The Office of Management and Budget, seeking to ease Andrews' concern about the inflationary impact, rushed off a letter arguing that the volunteer effort generated by the paid coordinators would more than offset the effects of the increased spending.

The administration also accepted a provision limiting administrative costs to 13 percent.

Andrews said the White House prodded him into supporting the program by appealing to party unity and stressing loyalty to the president and his urban program.

A defeat for the first bill in the urban package to come before a committee would represent a "severe blow" to the impetus behind the entire urban program, he was told.

Although Andrews agreed to go along with the program, he said he still questioned the need for federal spending to stimulate local volunteer programs.

Neither the House nor the Senate committee recommended fundamental changes in the ACTION agency or any of its programs, although the Senate panel approved significant increases in authorization levels for senior citizen volunteer programs (Retired Senior Volunteer Program, Foster Grandparent and Senior Companion programs). The House bill did not include these programs, since the House had already passed legislation extending them for one year. *(Story, p. 583)*

Both bills included higher pay for VISTA volunteers, raising the monthly stipend to $75 from $50.

The Senate committee made several changes designed to ensure that ACTION focused attention on rural areas as well as urban areas. S 2617 also gave ACTION authority to operate volunteer programs for victims of "spouse abuse."

The House committee recommended changes designed to strengthen the National Voluntary Service Advisory Council, which has been inactive since 1975.

In another step to improve public accountability, the House bill also required the council and the director of ACTION to submit their annual reports to Congress as well as the president.

Senate Floor Action

The Senate passed S 2617 by voice vote July 21 after adopting amendments reducing funding levels and placing tight restrictions on the proposed neighborhood volunteer program.

One restriction would require ACTION to notify Congress in advance of virtually every planned expenditure of money for the program. The Senate also required ACTION to increase spending on volunteer programs for the elderly before any money could be spent on the new urban program.

The amendment, which also was approved by voice vote without opposition, was worked out during negotiations involving Alan Cranston, D-Calif., the bill's floor manager; Jacob K. Javits, R-N.Y., ranking Republican on the Human Resources Committee; Gaylord Nelson, D-Wis., and Pete V. Domenici, R-N.M., both of whom had raised questions about the program.

The amendment:

- Reduced the committee-approved $40 million annual authorization for the urban volunteer program in fiscal 1979-81 to $25 million in fiscal 1979, $27.5 million in fiscal 1980 and $30 million in fiscal 1981.
- Eliminated a provision from the volunteer program that would have allowed ACTION to establish 10 "regional resource centers."
- Provided for coordination between ACTION and the Community Services Administration, and gave priority to existing, local community action agencies in the selection of organizations to serve as "lead agencies" in operating the volunteer program.
- Required ACTION to submit to the appropriate committees of Congress a program plan describing the proposed "nature, scope and geographic distribution" of each program, grant and contract awarded under the volunteer program and regulations and guidelines issued to run the program. The information would have to be submitted to Congress at least 60 days before a grant or contract was awarded or a guideline took effect.
- Required the agency to increase spending for the Older American volunteer programs by $10 million before any new funds could be used for the urban program, and required that the first $8.1 million spent for the urban volunteer program be used for several specified priority activities that primarily would benefit older Americans.

The amendment also included a provision sought by Robert Dole, R-Kan., to ensure that persons who took VISTA or other volunteer jobs, all of which carry low stipends, could not obtain public assistance, unless they were receiving it before joining the volunteer program. ▮

Environmental Education

The House Feb. 21 by voice vote under suspension of the rules approved a five-year extension of the Environmental Education Act of 1970 (PL 91-516). The bill (HR 10570) authorized expenditures totaling $45 million through fiscal 1983, allowed multiple-year funding of environmental education projects and abolished the Advisory Council on Environmental Education, which the Education and Labor Committee said had not been "very active, visible or effective" (H Rept 95-885).

The 1970 act was last extended in 1974. *(1970 act, 1970 Almanac p. 512; 1974 action, 1974 Almanac p. 834)*

The Senate Human Resources Committee did not act on the bill, but the five-year authorization was added to HR 15, the Elementary and Secondary Education Act extension, which was signed into law Nov. 1 (PL 95-561). *(Story, p. 557)* ▮

Alcohol, Drug Abuse

Congress July 24 cleared a three-year extension of the Alcohol and Drug Abuse Education Act (HR 10569 — PL 95-336), authorizing appropriations of $10-million in fiscal 1979, $14 million in fiscal 1980 and $18 million in fiscal 1981.

The program provides grants to schools and community groups for demonstration programs and trains school teams to deal with local drug and alcohol problems. Enacted in 1970 (PL 91-527) as a result of widespread concern over the growing problem of drug and alcohol abuse among young people, the law was extended in 1974 (PL 93-422). *(1970 Almanac p. 586)*

The House Education and Labor Committee, which reported HR 10569 (H Rept 95-884) Feb. 16, said the need to prevent abuse remained a high national priority, and urged the administration and the congressional appropriations committees to increase funding for the programs, which the committee said were highly effective. The fiscal 1978 appropriation for the program was only $2 million of an authorized $34 million.

The House passed a five-year $67.6 million extension of the act Feb. 21 by a 409-0 vote under suspension of the rules. *(Vote 55, p. 16-H)*

The Senate passed a three-year, $42 million reauthorization (S 2915 — S Rept 95-819) May 23 by voice vote after adding a non-germane amendment — a hold-harmless clause to ensure that colleges participating in the veterans' cost-of-instruction program would not lose eligibility as a result of declining enrollments of veterans. The amendment extended a provision of the Education Amendments of 1976 (PL 94-482). The House had included a similar provision in HR 11274, the Middle Income Student Assistance Act, but due to an oversight the Senate failed to do so.

The House accepted the Senate version of the bill by voice vote July 24, clearing it for the president. ▮

Doctor Recruitment Aid

Congress cleared legislation Oct. 13 designed to help government agencies recruit and retain physicians by providing bonus payments of up to $10,000 a year.

The measure (S 990) was intended to alleviate the difficulties experienced by many agencies in hiring physicians at normal government pay scales or for assignment in geographically unpopular locations.

The bill passed the Senate by voice vote May 25 after being reported May 15 by the Governmental Affairs Committee (S Rept 95-864). The House passed the bill by voice vote under suspension of the rules Oct. 3, and the Senate Oct. 13 accepted the bill as amended by the House, clearing the measure for the president.

As cleared by Congress, S 990 (PL 95-603):

- Allowed an agency to offer a bonus payment to government physicians of up to $7,000 annually if the physician had worked for the government for less than two years, or up to $10,000 if the physician had worked more than two years.
- Restricted the bonus payments to positions where the agency could prove there was a recruitment and retention problem.
- Provided that no service agreements could be arranged after Sept. 30, 1979, and that none could extend beyond Sept. 30, 1981.
- Provided that physicians who failed to complete at least one year of service under the agreement must refund the bonus.

The legislation did not apply to physicians in the Defense Department or Veterans Administration, who became eligible for bonus payments of up to $13,500 under legislation cleared in 1974 and 1975. *(Defense physicians, 1974 Almanac p. 642; VA physicians, 1975 Almanac p. 415)* ▮

Energy and Environment

President Carter managed to get an energy bill through Congress in 1978, but the measure promised to have little effect on the way Americans produced and consumed increasing quantities of energy.

Its major purpose was to decrease oil imports by encouraging Americans to conserve oil and gas, to switch to other fuels such as coal when possible and to produce more oil and gas from domestic reservoirs.

On signing the bill, Carter remarked, "We have acquitted ourselves well as a nation while the world watched. We have shown the will and courage to face this complex problem."

But, while the legislation may have faced the energy problem, it stopped far short of solving it. Energy consumption in the United States continued to grow in 1978. It increased 2 percent over 1977 consumption and was expected to go up again in 1979.

About half of that energy was provided by oil and about 45 percent of that was imported. Only new supplies from Alaska's North Slope, in its first full year of production, kept imports below 1977 levels.

Concern increased in 1978 about the effect the high level of imports was having on the decline of the dollar on foreign money markets, the $34 billion trade deficit and continued inflation. The decision by the Organization of Petroleum Exporting Countries (OPEC) to increase prices by 14.49 percent in 1979 promised to exacerbate the situation.

Though perceived as a great political victory for the administration, the bill was drastically rewritten as it moved slowly through Congress.

Most painful to reach was the compromise on natural gas pricing policy, an incredibly complex scheme that by 1985 would end federal controls on the sale of newly discovered natural gas. The administration and its supporters struggled for months to overcome opposition from what one congressman called a "weird" coalition of legislators favoring continued controls and those preferring to lift controls.

But the administration failed to jar out of the Senate Finance Committee what was clearly the most important part of the original bill — a new policy to bring domestic oil prices up to world levels. Carter wanted to rebate the additional cost to consumers through a crude oil equalization tax, but Finance Chairman Russell B. Long, D-La., wanted the oil industry to get the extra revenues. His opposition, which stalled the bill in his committee, was enough to kill the measure even though the House passed it.

Other Energy Legislation

The attention paid the energy bill left Congress little time for other energy-related measures. For example, the fiscal 1979 authorization for the Department of Energy was not passed because of the threat of lengthy haggling over amendments, which congressional leaders feared would distract from work on the energy bill.

Other energy highlights of 1978 were:

- The first overhaul of offshore oil and gas leasing laws in 25 years. The new act, four years in the making, was expected to end uncertainty that had slowed development of frontier areas on the federally owned Outer Continental Shelf off the Atlantic coast.
- Defeat of efforts to spur construction of special pipelines to carry coal slurry — pulverized coal mixed with water. The railroad industry, joined by westerners concerned about depletion of scarce water supplies, got the credit for defeating the administration-backed bill.
- The first full year of operation of the Department of Energy, during which it spent more than $10 billion.
- Continued difficulties for the nuclear industry. Public concern about safe disposal of radioactive nuclear waste was one of the central problems plaguing the industry, but government in 1978 provided only studies of the waste, not solutions. Congress did not complete action on a bill supported by the industry that would have shortened the time it takes to get a nuclear plant licensed by the government.
- Writing of regulations to implement the strip mining law of 1977, which required coal miners to restore strip-mined land. But the regulations were criticized by industry and even by some within the Carter administration, who considered them inflationary.
- No resolution of the long-running dispute between Carter and Congress over the plutonium-powered nuclear breeder reactor at Clinch River, Tenn. Carter continued his attempts to terminate the project, which he said was obsolete and over-priced.

Environmental Issues

Carter drew high praise from environmentalists for his record in 1978 on conservation and pollution control. Though noting some shortcomings, such as inadeqate funding of toxic substances control and "a contradictory and confusing nuclear policy," the leaders of major U.S. conservation organizations, in a year's end news conference, endorsed Carter's actions.

Among the highlights they cited were the president's veto of several water projects, protection of Alaska's wilderness and a "policy of unprecedented openness" that included meeting with environmentalists on numerous occasions.

Alaska Lands

The dominant event in 1978 that dealt with the environment was President Carter's sweeping move to restrict use of 56 million acres of federally owned wilderness in Alaska.

The action, based on authority from a 1906 law, earned Carter the highest praise from conservationists, who called him the "greatest conservation president of all time." The president created 17 new national monuments.

Congress earlier had a chance to win similar praise by passing legislation to protect some of the federal land in Alaska in parks, wildlife refuges and other conservation units. But, despite an overwhelming vote by the House, months of work by committees and last minute negotiations, no legislation was given final approval.

The protections from mining, oil and gas drilling, logging and other harmful uses that were provided by Carter were permanent. However, Carter and Interior Secretary Cecil D. Andrus said the administration wanted the next Congress to pass legislation similar to what Carter supported in 1978.

Though it failed to act on Alaska lands, Congress did pass other sweeping legislation, which was considered to be the largest parks bill in history.

The measure authorized expenditure of $1.2 billion for more than 100 parks and projects in 44 states. Because it brought new federal money for parks to so many districts, the bill earned the label of "park barrel," in recognition of its similarity to "pork barrel" funding of hospitals, dams and other federal projects in a member's district.

Pollution Control

The dramatic move to protect Alaska's wilderness was in sharp contrast to the continuing, tedious implementation by federal agencies of laws designed to clean up the nation's water and air.

Clean air laws, for example, were amended in 1977, and regulations to carry out those revisions were written in 1978. States, cities and industry were starting to respond as the year ended. Clean water laws were also updated in 1977, and the court challenges to the regulations began in 1978.

Pollution control was increasingly focused on toxic substances and how they affected health. The danger of poisonous chemicals was vividly illustrated by the evacuation during the summer of 239 homes at Love Canal in Niagara Falls, N.Y., because they had been contaminated by chemical dumps.

But federal agencies writing regulations continued to face sharp disagreements about whether small amounts of toxic chemicals caused health risks, particularly risk of cancer. Often cleaning up the last bit of a poison was the most expensive part of pollution control.

Administration officials concerned about inflation had urged those writing regulations to pay more attention to the costs of health and environmental controls. Carter officials warned of the inflationary impact of regulations and adopted some of the same arguments used in the past by industries and by cities faced with cleaning up municipal water supplies.

To monitor inter-agency squabbles about balancing inflation and government regulations, Carter set up a Regulatory Analysis Review Group, headed by Environmental Protection Agency Administrator Douglas Costle.

Water Policy

When Carter and Congress fought in 1977 over several water projects he wanted to kill, the president promised to send Congress in 1978 a proposal for a new national water policy. The promised proposals went to Congress in June, but not in time to affect committee decisions about funding of dams and other projects for fiscal 1979.

Because of the timing and Carter's failure to propose legislation to carry out the policy, there was no debate in 1978 on general, overall questions of water policy. That was expected in 1979 when the legislation was to go to Capitol Hill.

Instead, Carter and Congress repeated the 1977 scenario and tangled over funding of several specific projects that Carter considered economically and environmentally unsound.

But rather than giving in to the powerful supporters of the projects, Carter carried out his threat to veto the public works appropriations bill that contained funding for six projects he thought were killed in a 1977 compromise. Even though Democratic leaders of the House wanted to override the veto, they fell 53 votes short of the two-thirds needed.

—By Ann Pelham

Energy Bill: The End of an Odyssey

The determined Democratic leadership of the House, stubbornly wearing down opponents in the wee hours of the morning, presented President Carter with a five-part energy package on Sunday, Oct. 15.

The vote was held up by a 15-hour filibuster by Senate opponents. But at 7:30 a.m. sleepy House members cast the final vote on the five-part package and cleared it for the president. The vote was 231-168.

The legislation passed by Congress contained only remnants of the tough plan originally presented by Carter in April 1977, that would have raised gasoline taxes, increased the price of domestic crude oil through taxes and revamped electric rate-making. Carter wanted to force Americans to curb their profligate energy consumption, which required the United States to import about 8 million barrels of oil per day. That figure represented about 45 percent of the current consumption rate of 18.2 million barrels per day. *(Carter plan, 1977 Almanac p. 708)*

But Congress, worried about the political repercussions of higher prices and buffeted by intense lobbying from industry and other interest groups, chipped away at Carter's plan. The gasoline tax, for example, was dropped early, and the Senate defeated the key element — a tax on domestic crude oil to raise prices to world levels.

Generally, the legislators chose to encourage conservation rather than penalize waste.

The decision-making spawned some of the bitterest fights in years, with members allied or divided by region, by party, by ideology. An example of the depth of the split was the 207-206 House vote Oct. 13 by which members chose to keep the controversial natural gas pricing bill in a package with the four other more popular parts of the bill. *(Vote 806, p. 230-H)*

Although the plan had been watered down, Carter and Energy Secretary James R. Schlesinger continued to fight for it, learning new ways to persuade politicians in the process. When the bill was finally passed, 18 months after it was proposed, Carter said, "We have declared to ourselves and the world our intent to control our use of energy and thereby to control our own destiny as a nation."

Import Savings

Just exactly what effect the energy bill would have was the subject of some dispute. A primary goal of Carter's original plan was to cut oil imports, which the White House projected would be between 11.5 million and 16 million barrels per day by 1985, without new legislation. The original goal was to use a combination of conservation, increased production and substitution of coal for oil and gas to keep 1985 imports at 4.5 million barrels less than projected.

But Congress rewrote the original proposal. The tax section, for example, which accounted for 43 percent of the savings projected by the White House, was substantially changed by Congress. Though Carter wanted to force industry to switch from oil and gas to coal, Congress provided only encouragement, but no punishment if industries chose not to comply. Carter also wanted stiff penalties for gas guzzling cars, but Congress, while keeping the penalties, weakened them.

As those and other provisions were dropped or softened, the natural gas pricing section became the most controversial part of the bill. Carter had wanted to continue regulation, extending federal price controls to gas sold within producing states. The House agreed with Carter, but the Senate voted for deregulation of prices. The protracted conference between the two houses threatened the future of the entire energy package. But the administration and a few congressional negotiators finally came up with an agreement that doubled the price of newly discovered gas by 1985, when controls would be lifted.

The natural gas bill originally had not been counted on by Carter to contribute to savings of imported oil. But Department of Energy figures released after final passage predicted savings of from 1 million to 1.4 million barrels of oil per day from the natural gas provisions.

Total savings in imported oil from the legislation were estimated by the administration to range from 2.39 to 2.95 million barrels of oil per day by 1985.

THE PACKAGE

Highlights of the bill included:

Natural Gas (HR 5289 — PL 95-621). Prices of newly discovered natural gas were allowed to rise about 10 percent a year until 1985, when the price controls would be lifted. Special pricing categories were set up to make industrial users pay the brunt of the higher prices until the cost reached a certain level, when residential users were to assume more of the burden. Some price controls were extended for the first time to gas produced and sold within the same state.

Installation of new decorative outdoor gas lights was forbidden, and existing lights were to be shut off in three years.

Carter originally had proposed that price controls be extended to the gas sold within producing states with the general philosophy that gas, an ideal residential fuel, be saved for that purpose by switching industrial and utility users to other fuels.

Coal Conversion (HR 5146 — PL 95-620). New industrial and utility plants were required to be built to use coal or a fuel other than oil or gas. Existing utility plants using oil or gas were to switch to other fuels by 1990, and the energy secretary could order some industries, on a case-by-case basis, to switch fuels. But the energy secretary could also exempt utilities and companies from the requirements if certain conditions, such as an inadequate supply of coal, existed.

Originally, Carter had proposed a stiff tax on industrial use of oil and gas that would have given gas users a clear economic incentive to convert to coal, but that tax was dropped by Congress.

Utility Rates (HR 4018 — PL 95-617). State utility commissions and other regulatory agencies were required to consider the use of energy-saving methods, such as pricing electricity lower in off-peak hours to avoid heavy loads in the middle of the day and discontinuing discounts for large volume users. The energy secretary was authorized to intervene in the regulatory proceedings to argue for energy-saving measures.

Carter had wanted state agencies to be required to follow certain federal guidelines in rate-making in order to

ENERGY BOXSCORE

A chart detailing House and Senate action on key parts of President Carter's energy program follows.

The dates given for approval of the various pieces reflect final floor votes. The dates for rejection of programs are the days on which floor votes on the questions were taken or when committee reports were issued that did not contain those Carter proposals.

Carter Energy Proposal	House Action	Senate Action	Conference	Final Action
Tax credits for home insulation (HR 5263)	Approved August 5, 1977	Approved Oct. 31, 1977	Maximum $300 credit approved and conference report filed Oct. 12, 1978	Senate and House passed conference report Oct. 15, 1978
Boost in gasoline tax *(1977 Almanac p. 708)*	Rejected Aug. 4, 1977	Rejected by Finance Committee Oct. 21, 1977		
Tax on "gas guzzling" cars (HR 5263)	Approved Aug. 5, 1977	Rejected; ban on their production approved instead Sept. 13, 1977, as part of HR 5037	Approved and conference report filed Oct. 12, 1978	Senate and House passed conference report Oct. 15, 1978
Rebate of "gas guzzler" tax to buyers of gas saving cars *(1977 Almanac p. 708)*	Rejected by Ways and Means Committee June 9, 1977	Not considered		
Mandatory energy efficiency standards for home appliances (HR 5037)	Approved Aug. 5, 1977	Approved Sept. 13, 1977	Approved Oct. 31, 1977; conference report filed Oct. 10, 1978	Senate passed conference report Oct. 9, 1978; House passed conference report Oct. 15, 1978
Extention of natural gas price controls, with higher price ceiling (HR 5289)	Approved Aug. 5, 1977	Rejected; approved ending federal price controls for new gas Oct. 4, 1977	Agreement to end federal price controls on new natural gas by 1985, reached May 24, 1978; conference report filed Aug. 18	Senate passed conference report Sept. 27, 1978; House passed conference report Oct. 15, 1978
Tax on crude oil (HR 5263) *(1977 Almanac p. 708)*	Approved Aug. 5, 1977	Rejected by Finance Committee Oct. 21, 1977	Killed by conference	
Tax on utility and industrial use of oil and natural gas (HR 5263) *(1977 Almanac p. 708)*	Approved, weaker than Carter plan Aug. 5, 1977	Approved, but weaker than House or Carter plan Oct. 31, 1977	Killed by conference	
Authority to force utility, industrial conversion from oil, gas to coal (HR 5146)	Approved Aug. 5, 1977	Approved, but weaker than House version Sept. 8, 1977	Compromise reached Nov. 11, 1977; conference report filed July 14, 1978	Senate passed conference report July 18, 1978; House passed conference report Oct. 15, 1978
Reform of electric utility rates (HR 4018)	Approved Aug. 5, 1977	Rejected by Finance Committee Sept. 19, 1977	Compromise reached Dec. 1, 1977; conference report filed Oct. 6, 1978	Senate passed conference report Oct. 9, 1978; House passed conference report Oct. 15, 1978

save energy. But Congress, arguing that the states should continue to oversee the utilities, refused to make it mandatory to follow the guidelines.

Conservation (HR 5037 — PL 95-619). Utilities were required to give customers information about energy conservation devices such as insulation and storm windows. Though the utility could not sell the devices or install them, the utility could arrange for the installation and allow customers to pay for the improvements through utility bills. Direct loans from utilities to consumers of up to $300 were allowed.

Over the next three years, schools and hospitals were to receive $900 million to install energy-saving equipment. Grants and government-backed loans would be available to low-income families for home conservation investments. Mandatory efficiency standards were authorized for 13 major home appliances, including refrigerators, furnaces and water heaters, with the standards to take effect in the mid-1980s.

Carter's original proposal had called for a more aggressive role for utilities and mandatory conservation standards for new residential and commercial buildings. But, generally, this was the least controversial of the five parts and came through Congress relatively intact.

Taxes (HR 5263 — PL 95-618). Homeowners and businesses would get tax credits for installing energy-saving devices in their buildings. Homeowners were eligible for a credit of 15 percent on the first $2,000 spent on insulation or other devices, for a maximum of $300. Investment in solar, wind or geothermal energy equipment made the homeowner eligible for a tax credit of up to 30 percent on the first $2,000 and 20 percent on the next $8,000, for a total maximum credit of $2,200.

A 10 percent investment credit was made available to businesses that installed specified types of energy conservation equipment. The bill also provided tax incentives for companies that produced synthetic fuels from coal or other resources.

Cars that used fuel inefficiently, known as gas guzzlers, were to be taxed to discourage manufacture and purchase. Starting with 1980 models, new cars getting less than 15 miles per gallon (mpg) would be taxed $200. The tax and mileage standards would increase every year so that by 1986, cars getting less than 12.5 mpg would be taxed $3,850.

Taxes on 1986 models would apply to all cars getting less than 22.5 mpg.

The administration had wanted the gas guzzler tax to start on 1978 models averaging less than 18 miles per gallon, with the first year penalty ranging from $52 to $449. And by 1986, Carter wanted to be taxing heavily any car that got less than 27.5 miles per gallon.

Central to Carter's original energy proposal were taxes on industrial use of oil and gas, a wellhead tax on domestically produced crude oil to bring the price to world levels and authority to add a tax of five cents per gallon of gasoline each year through 1989 if gasoline consumption exceeded target levels. All of those proposals were dropped by Congress, which emphasized tax credits instead.

Major Provisions

NATURAL GAS PRICING

As cleared by Congress, HR 5289:

Title I — Wellhead Pricing

Price Controls. Established a scaled ceiling price for "new" gas starting at $1.75 per million British thermal units (MMBtu's) as of April 20, 1977 — the date Carter proposed his energy program.

- Provided that the initial price would rise monthly to cover inflation as measured by the gross national product (GNP), plus .2 percent, plus another 3.5 percent, until April 1981; and plus 4 percent thereafter, instead of 3.5 percent.
- Defined new natural gas found onshore to include gas from 1) new wells at least 2.5 miles from a "marker" well — one producing commercial quantities of gas between Jan. 1, 1970, and April 20, 1977; 2) a new well with a bottom depth 1,000 feet below the nearest and deepest well bottom within 2.5 miles; 3) a newly drilled onshore reservoir.
- Defined "new" offshore gas to include gas from new leases or from new reservoirs in old leases.
- Excluded from the "new" category 1) gas located "behind the pipe" — in an untapped reservoir adjacent to a well being drilled; 2) gas "withheld" from production; 3) gas from Alaska's Prudhoe Bay.
- Provided that new wells in old onshore reservoirs would draw a new ceiling price of $1.75 per MMBtu and would increase at a rate equal to inflation. Some of this gas would be deregulated by 1985.
- Provided that all other interstate gas would draw a ceiling price of $1.45 per MMBtu as of April 20, 1977, and that price would rise by the GNP inflation rate.
- Provided that gas sold under existing intrastate contracts would draw a new price equal to the contract price or the new gas ceiling price, whichever was lower.
- Directed that gas sold under an interstate contract that expired — a "rollover" contract — was eligible to draw the higher price between the applicable "just and reasonable" standard under existing law (the Natural Gas Act — PL 75-690), or $.54 per MMBtu.
- Provided that gas sales under expiring intrastate contracts would get the contract price or $1 per MMBtu, whichever was higher.
- Provided that all gas sold under rollover contracts would draw price increases equal to inflation.
- Specified that certain categories of "high cost" gas would be deregulated about one year after enactment.
- Included in that category gas 1) from wells deeper than 15,000 feet; 2) from geopressurized brine; 3) from coal seams; 4) from Devonian shale; and 5) produced under conditions determined by the Federal Energy Regulatory Commission (FERC) to pose unusual risks or costs.
- Provided that gas produced from "stripper" wells — those producing on average not more than 60 thousand cubic feet (Mcf) per day — would draw an initial ceiling price of $2.09 per MMBtu, which would rise according to a special monthly inflation formula.
- Specified that state severance taxes were not to be considered part of any ceiling prices set by the act.

Decontrol. Eliminated federal price controls as of Jan. 1, 1985, on 1) new natural gas; 2) deep new onshore wells; and 3) existing intrastate contracts over $1 per MMBtu as of Dec. 31, 1984.

- Provided that either the president or Congress could reimpose controls for one 18-month period.
- Specified that the authority to reimpose price controls existed only from July 1, 1985, until June 30, 1987.
- Provided that either the House or Senate could veto the president's decision to reimpose controls, but that both houses would have to act together to reimpose controls.

Title II — Incremental Pricing

- Required FERC to develop within 12 months of enactment an incremental pricing rule for industrial boiler fuel facilities. The rule would define which low priority gas consumers would bear the increased costs of gas disproportionately to ease the impact on high priority gas users.
- Directed FERC to develop a second incremental pricing rule within 18 months of enactment that would broaden the application to more low priority users.
- Specified that the second incremental pricing rule would be subject to veto by either house of Congress.

Energy Bill Imported Oil Savings

(Thousands of barrels of oil equivalent per day)

Legislation	Projected Savings by 1985
Conservation (HR 5037)	
Building improvements/appliance standards	410
Automobile, truck fuel efficiency standards*	265
Utility rate reform (HR 4018)	0 to 160
Natural gas pricing** (HR 5289)	1,000 to 1,400
Coal conversion (HR 5146)	300
Energy taxes (HR 5263)	
Residential credits for conservation	225
Crude oil tax (rejected by Congress)	0
Gasoline taxes (rejected by Congress)	0
Gas guzzler tax	80
Business credits for conservation	110
Total	*****2,390 to 2,950**

*Assumed that penalties set in the Energy and Policy Conservation Act for makers of gas guzzling cars would be raised to the maximum level of $10 for each tenth of a mile a car exceeded the national fleetwide average fuel consumption rate. By 1985 that standard would be 27.5 miles per gallon.

**The range depended on the degree to which increased use of natural gas displaced use of oil. Domestic natural gas, for example, could displace imported liquified natural gas, instead of oil.

***The administration projected that, without the legislation, oil imports in 1985 would range from 11.5 million to 16 million barrels of oil per day.

SOURCE: Department of Energy

• Directed that any costs that could be passed along to low priority users under the incremental pricing rules be placed in a special account. Incrementally priced users would have to pay the higher gas costs until their gas expenses equalled the cost of substitute fuels.

• Required FERC to determine what the competitive cost of substitute fuels would be, on a regional basis.

• Directed that once an incrementally priced industrial facility reached the price level for gas equal to that of an alternative fuel, the pass-through of higher gas costs to that facility would be limited to the amount necessary to keep it at the alternative fuel price.

• Required distributors to pass through the higher gas costs to incrementally priced industrial facilities instead of rolling the extra charges into all consumer rates.

• Exempted from incremental pricing 1) certain small industrial boiler fuel facilities; 2) specific agricultural uses; 3) residences; 4) small commercial uses; 5) schools; 6) hospitals and other institutions, and 7) electric utilities.

• Empowered FERC to provide other exemptions subject to congressional review.

• Provided that existing gas imports would be exempted from incremental pricing.

• Required distributors to roll Alaska's Prudhoe Bay gas into general consumer rates. (Conferees gave this subsidy to Alaskan gas development, the report explained, "because they believed that private financing of the pipeline [to be built to move the Alaskan gas] would not be available otherwise.")

Title III — Emergency Authority

• Authorized the president to declare natural gas emergencies.

• Authorized the president to authorize any interstate pipeline or local gas distributor to make emergency purchases of gas under short term contracts.

• Authorized the president in emergencies to allocate supplies to meet high priority needs.

• Provided that gas could not be allocated until the emergency sales option had been exhausted.

• Barred the president from taking gas from one class of users in one state to give to the same class of users in another state.

• Required compensation for allocated gas.

• Authorized FERC to allow interstate pipelines to move gas for intrastate pipelines or distributors, and vice versa.

Title IV — Curtailment

• Specified that in the event of gas curtailment, the last uses to be curtailed would be residences, small commercial uses, schools, hospitals and like institutions, and other uses when the energy secretary determined that curtailment to them would endanger life, health or property maintenance.

• Specified that certain agricultural uses would have priority after the uses spelled out above.

• Specified certain industrial processes or feedstock uses would hold the next curtailment priority.

Title V — Administration

• Provided FERC with general rule making authority.

• Authorized the state or federal agency with regulatory jurisdiction over gas production to determine the category for which a given well qualified.

• Authorized FERC to review agency decisions.

• Provided both civil and criminal penalties for violations of the act.

• Gave the energy secretary power to intervene in state proceedings concerning gas production.

• Provided judicial review authority modeled on that under the existing Natural Gas Act.

Title VI — Coordination with Existing Law

• Reserved to states the right to mandate lower price ceilings than provided by the act.

COAL CONVERSION

As cleared by Congress, HR 5146 had seven titles:

Title I — Goals, Definitions

The first title set forth the act's purpose and defined key terms.

Among its purposes was to cut oil imports and stimulate use of coal and other plentiful substitute fuels to save dwindling supplies of oil and gas. One key definition specified that regulatory orders in the measure applied to existing utility plants or major fuel burning installations only if they burned fuel at rates of at least 100 British thermal units (Btu's) per hour or more. A British thermal unit is the amount of heat required to raise the temperature of one pound of water by one degree Fahrenheit at or near 39.2 degrees Fahrenheit.

New utility power plants or major fuel burning facilities were defined as those on which construction began or which were acquired after April 20, 1977, the date Carter proposed his energy program. New plants were subject to different terms than existing ones in some sections of the proposed law.

Title II — New Facilities

Title II flatly barred new electric power plants and new major fuel burning installations from burning oil or natural gas as their primary energy source. It also directed that all new power plants be built with the capability to burn coal or another alternate fuel instead of oil or gas.

The title also gave the energy secretary power to issue rules prohibiting broad categories of new major fuel burning installations from burning oil or gas in uses other than boilers. The secretary further was empowered to prohibit on a case-by-case basis the burning of oil or gas for uses other than boilers in new major fuel burning installations.

Temporary Exemptions. Temporary exemptions of up to five years could be granted for use of gas or oil. The burden of proving worthiness for an exemption would be on the applicant. Temporary exemptions could be won if:

- The applicant demonstrated that coal or other substitute fuels would be inadequate or unreliable.
- The plant site were physically incapable of adjusting to use of alternate fuels.
- Environmental constraints required the continued use of oil or gas.
- The applicant could show he would be in compliance with the act at the end of the exemption period by using synthetic fuels.
- The secretary determined the exemption would be in the public interest.

Permanent Exemptions. Permanent exemptions could be granted if it were shown that:

- Coal or other alternative fuels would not be available throughout the useful life of the facility.
- The use of coal or other fuels would preclude the obtaining of capital.
- State or local laws precluded compliance, except those laws passed solely to allow the plant to escape the act.
- The facilities were to use cogeneration technology.
- Gas or oil were to be used in mixture with coal or other fuel substitutes.
- Gas or oil were required for emergency operation, with the secretary to define what constituted an emergency.
- A permanent exemption were necessary to assure reliable service.
- A new power plant were to be used as a "peakload" facility, i.e., used only when customer demand on the power system was at defined "peak" levels.

Permanent exemptions also could be won for new plants:

- To be used as "intermediate" load facilities for use of oil only, subject to specific conditions.
- For which the use of coal or other fuels would not be feasible technically due to special needs to ensure product quality.
- That required gas- or oil-fired units to cover their operations during specially scheduled equipment outages.

Condition on Exemptions. Section 213 of Title II required that before granting any temporary or permanent exemptions — except in the case of fuel mixture and peakload exemptions — the secretary had to find that use of a mixture of oil and coal or other fuels was not economically or technically feasible.

Title III — Existing Facilities

Existing electric power plants were prohibited from burning natural gas after Jan. 1, 1990, except under rigidly defined circumstances. Power plants that did not use gas as a primary fuel during 1977 were prohibited from converting to its use.

Existing electric power plants that burned gas were prohibited from consuming more of it than they burned on average between 1974 and 1976.

Existing electric power plants awaiting judgment on petitions for continued use of gas, which were filed prior to Jan. 1, 1990, could continue to use gas pending the outcome of their petitions.

The energy secretary was empowered to order oil or gas burning power plants or existing major plant facilities, which by design were capable of burning coal or other fuels, to cease burning oil or gas. But the burden of proof that the plants could burn substitute fuels would be on the government.

Exemptions. A full range of temporary and permanent exemptions, like those available for new power plants and industrial facilities, were available subject to conditions similar to those for existing plants.

In addition, temporary exemptions to prohibitions on oil or gas use were available to existing plants if the secretary were convinced the plant would later comply by use of innovative technologies, or if the plant were due to be retired within certain time restrictions.

Similarly, permanent exemptions were available under the same kinds of conditions as for new plants and if the plant were to use liquid natural gas and the appropriate federal or state environmental agency certified that coal use there would violate environmental laws.

Also, before any exemptions could be granted for existing plants, the secretary would have to be satisfied that fuel mixtures could not be used.

Title IV — Other Prohibitions, Authorities

The energy secretary was empowered to prohibit the use of natural gas in new or existing boilers used for space heating if the boiler consumed as much as 300,000 cubic feet of gas per day and could run on oil.

Decorative Lighting. The measure prohibited new outdoor decorative lights fueled by natural gas and empowered the secretary to prohibit gas pipeline and distribution companies from delivering gas to residential, commercial or industrial customers for such purposes. Existing residential and municipal outdoor gas lights had to comply by Jan. 1, 1982.

The gas lamp ban could be exempted for lights on memorials or in areas of historical significance upon petition to the secretary from appropriate federal, state, or local government agencies or historic associations.

Civil penalties for violations of the gas lamp ban would be assessed against the local gas distribution company up to $500 per lamp, and up to $500 per day to a maximum $5,000 for industrial violators.

Emergency Powers. The president was authorized to allocate coal, to order any plant to cease burning oil or gas and to suspend the terms of the law in time of severe energy supply emergencies, as defined in existing law or as he declared. Presidential orders under such emergency powers would be for the extent of the emergency or 90 days, whichever was less.

Title V — System Compliance Option

This title was designed to ease the transition from oil and gas dependence for utility systems, such as those in southwestern states, that were almost entirely dependent upon natural gas to fuel their plants.

Under Title V, such utilities would have the option of submitting compliance plans by Jan. 1, 1980, identifying their gas-dependent plants and outlining how they planned to comply with the mandatory phase-out of natural gas boiler fuel consumption by 1990. The plan would have to include commitment not to build new baseload capacity electric power plants that used oil or gas as their primary fuels. The utility also would have to pledge, in lieu of all other exemptions under the act, to phase all gas-fired power plants into only peak or intermediate load use by Jan. 1, 1995, and into peakload use only by the end of 1999. The secretary could extend the 1999 date five years under criteria for peakload or emergency exemptions.

Title VI — Financial Assistance

Title VI provided that when a governor declared an area of his state to be impacted because of development of coal or uranium, the federal government could provide cash grants to ease the impact, subject to conditions.

The governor would have to demonstrate to the energy secretary's satisfaction that:

- The development had increased employment directly over the past year by 8 percent or was projected to do so by at least that much annually for the next three years.
- The increase would require substantial public facilities such as schools and roads.
- State and local governments could not handle the financial burden.

Once an area was designated an energy impacted area, the secretary of agriculture could give 100 percent planning grants to affected states or localities to help plan how to cope with the development's impact. Land for public facilities or housing also could be acquired with such funds.

The legislation authorized $60 million for fiscal 1979 and $120 million for fiscal 1980 to cover program costs.

Pollution Control Loans. Section 602 authorized loans for existing power plants to finance the cost of installing pollution control devices required to burn coal under the act. The measure authorized $400 million for such purposes in both fiscal 1979 and 1980.

Title VII — Administration

Title VII dealt with promulgation of rules under the act, provided judicial review rights and listed enforcement provisions and penalties for violations. Penalties ranged up to one year in prison and a $50,000 fine for each criminal violation and up to $25,000 for each civil violation.

The act authorized $1.9 million for the program in fiscal 1978.

Title VIII — Miscellaneous Provisions

Title VIII combined a series of miscellaneous provisions. Among them was an authorization for $100 million for rehabilitation of branch line railroads to enable them to better carry coal. The money would go to the Railroad Rehabilitation and Improvement Fund.

UTILITY RATES

As cleared by Congress, HR 4018:

- Required that, within three years of enactment, each state utility commission or non-regulated electric company consider, with appropriate public hearings, implementation of the following federal standards for rate making on a utility-by-utility basis:

1) Setting of rates to reflect the actual cost of providing electric service to each class of consumers.

2) Prohibition of the use of "declining block rates" under which the cost of electricity decreased as consumption increased, unless the block rates reflected actual costs.

3) Use of "time-of-day" rates that reflected the cost of providing power at peak hours, when all power plants and back-up facilities were in use, versus the cost of power at off hours.

4) Use of "seasonal" rates when different seasons of the year affected the costs of providing electricity.

5) Use of "interruptible" rates when the cost of providing power was less when service could be interrupted.

6) Offering of other "load management techniques" to consumers when they would be practicable, cost effective, reliable and provide useful management advantages to the utility.

- Provided that if the state commissions did not comply voluntarily, the Department of Energy or any affected rate payer could request the commission to consider those standards. If intervention was denied, the department could seek an order for compliance from a federal court.
- Required each commission, within two years of enactment and to the extent deemed appropriate by each commission, to: 1) prohibit or restrict master metering, 2) adopt procedures to review automatic adjustment clauses, 3) adopt procedures to prohibit rate discrimination against solar, wind or other small power systems, 4) adopt procedures to provide consumer information, 5) prohibit charging rate payers for advertising and 6) adopt procedures to protect rate payers from abrupt termination of service.
- Required each state utility commission, within one year of enactment and annually thereafter, to report to the Department of Energy on its progress in considering and putting those standards into effect.
- Required the Department of Energy, within 18 months of enactment and annually thereafter, to report to the president and Congress its analysis of those commission reports and recommendations for further federal laws.
- Provided that if a consumer "substantially contributed" at "significant financial hardship" to a proceeding in which he prevailed, then the utility would have to compensate the consumer for reasonable costs incurred in the intervention.
- Provided that state commission actions on the standards would be subject to review in state courts only, not federal courts, except as existing federal law guaranteed the right to appeal to the U.S. Supreme Court.
- Authorized grants of $58 million each in fiscal 1979 and 1980 for states to use in implementing the rate reforms, with most funds to be spent on additional personnel.
- Authorized the Federal Energy Regulatory Commission (FERC) to order utilities to interconnect their facilities and to exchange energy supplies, subject to tests of reasonableness and judicial review.
- Authorized FERC to order a utility to "wheel" power from one supplier to another, subject to tests of reasonableness.
- Required FERC to review for up to one year the potential advantages of utility pooling of resources and to report to the president and Congress on its findings.

- Provided for disclosure of interlocking relationships between the top officials of public utilities and the top officials of banks, energy companies and related industries.
- Established an Office of Public Participation within FERC.
- Required that the energy secretary study and report on gas utility rate procedures within 18 months of enactment.
- Authorized the federal government to provide loans for up to 90 percent of the cost of feasibility studies for small hydroelectric projects on existing dams.
- Authorized government loans of up to 75 percent of the costs of such projects, subject to certain conditions.
- Required the interior secretary to expedite his review of and recommendations on crude oil transportation systems.
- Authorized the president, in emergency situations, to prohibit power plants from burning natural gas to generate electricity when the plant had the capability to burn petroleum products.

CONSERVATION

As cleared by Congress, HR 5037:

- Required that gas and electric utilities inform their customers of available energy-saving measures and offer to inspect homes to point out other energy saving steps.
- Required utilities to offer to arrange for financing and installation of home energy conservation improvements, such as insulation and storm windows, and allowed utilities to make direct loans of up to $300 for such improvements unless prohibited from doing so by state law.
- Allowed customer costs for insulation and other home energy conservation measures to be paid through utility bills, regardless of who installed them.
- Authorized the Department of Energy to spend up to $200 million in each of fiscal years 1979 and 1980 for weatherization grants to low-income families, with grants limited to $800 for the costs of materials for each home, except in certain cases. To qualify, a family's income could not exceed 125 percent of the national poverty level.
- Authorized the Government National Mortgage Association (GNMA) to purchase $3 billion in loans from commercial lenders to provide subsidized low interest loans for energy conservation improvements to families whose income was below the median income for their area.
- Authorized GNMA to purchase an additional $2 billion in loans, provided the energy secretary decided the purchase was necessary, to provide loans at market rates for energy conservation improvements by households with incomes above the poverty level.
- Authorized GNMA to purchase up to $100 million in loans to provide loans at market rates to homeowners for purchase and installation of solar energy systems.
- Authorized $295 million in fiscal 1979 and $400 million in fiscal 1980 for grants to schools and hospitals for energy conservation improvements. The grants would be distributed according to population, with consideration also given to such factors as area climate and costs of fuel. No single state could receive more than 10 percent, and each would receive at least 0.5 percent, of the total appropriated.
- Doubled the maximum penalty assessed an automaker whose fleet had an average fuel efficiency below the national standard set in the Energy Policy and Conservation Act of 1975 (PL 94-163). The penalties could be raised as high as $10, up from $5, per car for each tenth of a mile in excess of the average.
- Provided that the penalty could be increased if the transportation secretary found the increased fine would result in substantial energy savings in future auto production and would not increase unemployment, hurt competition or increase automobile imports.
- Required the Energy Department to set mandatory energy efficiency standards for 13 major home appliances, with the effective date not later than the mid-1980s. Appliances covered were refrigerators, furnaces, room and central air conditioners, water heaters, freezers, dishwashers, clothes washers and dryers, home space heaters, television sets, kitchen ranges and ovens, humidifiers and dehumidifiers.
- Authorized spending $100 million through fiscal year 1980 for demonstrations in federal buildings of solar heating and cooling technology.
- Authorized spending $98 million through fiscal year 1981 to acquire and operate photovoltaic solar electric systems to provide energy needs of federal agencies.

TAXES

As cleared by Congress, HR 5263:

Title I — Residential Credits

Insulation. Provided a nonrefundable income tax credit of 15 percent of the first $2,000 (maximum $300) spent by homeowners to install insulation and other specified energy-conserving improvements at their principal residence.

- Provided the credit would be available for expenditures made between April 20, 1977, and before Jan. 1, 1986.
- Provided that credits would carry over for two years, through Jan. 1, 1988, if the credit exceeded the amount of tax the homeowner owed.
- Specified that credits for expenditures made in 1977 would be claimed, along with 1978 credits, on 1978 tax returns and that the carryover would apply only to taxes owed in 1978.
- Provided that the credit would be available for expenditures made for insulation, furnace replacement burners for cutting fuel consumption, flue opening modifications, furnace ignition systems to replace gas pilot lights, storm or thermal windows or doors, automatic energy-saving setback thermostats, caulking or weather stripping, meters displaying the cost of energy usage or other items specified in regulations by the energy secretary.

Solar. Provided a nonrefundable credit of 30 percent of the first $2,000 and 20 percent of the next $8,000 — for a total maximum of $2,200 — for homeowners who installed solar, wind or geothermal energy equipment in their principal residences.

- Provided the credit would be available for expenditures made between April 20, 1977, and Dec. 31, 1985.
- Provided a credit carryover if the credit exceeded the amount of taxes owed by the homeowner and specified that the carryover would apply through taxable years ending before Jan. 1, 1988.
- Specified that credits for expenditures made in 1977 would be claimed, along with 1978 credits, on 1978 tax returns and that the carryover would apply only against taxes owed in 1978.

• Specified that the credit would apply to "passive" as well as "active" solar systems. "Passive" refers to building design while "active" means the use of mechanical devices, such as fans.

Title II — Transportation

Gas Guzzler Tax. Imposed a "gas guzzler tax" on the sale by the manufacturer of passenger cars — beginning with model year 1980 — that used fuel inefficiently, with certain exceptions for ambulances, police cars and other emergency vehicles.

• Set the taxes as follows:

1) For model year 1980, taxes ranged from $550 for cars that got less than 13 miles per gallon (mpg) to $200 for cars that got at least 14 mpg but less than 15 mpg.

2) For model year 1981, taxes ranged from $650 for cars that got less than 13 mpg to $200 for cars that got at least 16 mpg but less than 17 mpg.

3) For model year 1982, taxes ranged from $1,200 for cars that got less than 12.5 mpg to $200 for cars that got at least 17.5 mpg but less than 18.5 mpg.

4) For model year 1983, taxes ranged from $1,550 for cars that got less than 13 mpg to $350 for cars that got at least 18 mpg but less than 19 mpg.

5) For model year 1984, taxes ranged from $2,150 for cars that got less than 12.5 mpg to $450 for cars that got at least 18.5 mpg but less than 19.5 mpg.

6) For model year 1985, taxes ranged from $2,650 for cars that got less than 13 mpg to $500 for cars that got at least 20 mpg but less than 21 mpg.

7) For model year 1986, taxes ranged from $3,850 for cars that got less than 12.5 mpg to $500 for cars that got at least 21.5 mpg but less than 22.5 mpg.

Gasohol. Exempted from the federal excise tax on motor fuel, gasohol sold after Dec. 31, 1978, and before Oct. 1, 1984, if the gasohol was at least 10 percent alcohol. The exemption would apply only if the alcohol was made from products — such as grain or solid waste — other than petroleum, natural gas or coal. Gasohol is a blend of gasoline and alcohol.

• Directed the Treasury secretary to expedite applications for permits to distill ethanol for use in the production of gasohol. Directed the energy secretary to make annual reports to Congress on the use of alcohol in fuels from 1980 through 1984.

Excise Taxes. Repealed as of Dec. 31, 1978, the 2-cent-a-gallon reduction of the excise taxes on gasoline and special motor fuels and the refund of the 6-cent-a-gallon tax on lubricating oil for gasoline, special fuels and lubricating oil used for nonbusiness, non-highway purposes (such as lawnmowers and snowmobiles) and for motorboats.

• Specified that there would be no change in the exemptions for commercial fishing vessels.

Buses. Repealed the 10 percent manufacturers excise tax imposed on the sale of buses over 10,000 pounds, which were sold on or after April 20, 1977.

• Repealed the 8 percent manufacturers excise tax on the sale of bus parts and accessories.

• Removed the excise taxes on highway tires, inner tubes, tread rubber, gasoline, other motor fuels and lubricating oil for private intercity, local and school bus operations.

Commuter Vehicles. Provided a full 10 percent investment tax credit for "commuter highway vehicles" used in van pooling if the vehicles could carry at least nine adults, were used at least 80 percent of the time for van pooling for transporting employees to and from work and were acquired after the date of enactment and placed in service before Jan. 1, 1986.

Title III — Business Credits

Alternate Energy Property. Provided a special 10 percent investment credit for businesses that installed specified equipment, limited to 100 percent of tax liability, but provided that the credit rate was 5 percent for property financed with tax exempt industrial development bonds.

• Provided that the credit would be available for property acquired and placed in service after Sept. 30, 1978 and before Jan. 2, 1983.

• Defined equipment eligible for the credit as equipment for producing synthetic fuel, geothermal energy and solar and wind energy if installed in connection with a new building. Hydroelectric and nuclear equipment and structures did not qualify; nor did "passive" solar equipment.

• Excluded from eligibility for the credit persons trading with educational, religious, charitable and scientific organizations, electric utility cooperatives, state and local governments and public utility property.

• Provided that the credits, except those for solar and wind energy equipment, were not refundable.

Specially Defined Energy Property. Provided a special 10 percent investment credit, which could be applied against 100 percent of tax liability, for eligible property placed in service after Sept. 30, 1978, and before Jan. 1, 1983.

• Included as eligible property recuperators, heat wheels, regenerators, heat exchangers, waste heat boilers, heat pipes, automatic energy control systems and other items specified by the energy secretary that reduced the amount of heat wasted or energy consumed in existing industrial processes.

Energy Property Tax Credit. Provided the special 10 percent tax credit, which could be applied against 100 percent of tax liability, for eligible property acquired or placed in service after Sept. 30, 1978, and before Jan. 1, 1983.

• Included as eligible property specified recycling equipment, shale oil equipment and equipment to produce natural gas from geopressured brine.

Denial of Credit. Provided that portable air conditioners, portable space heaters and boilers fueled by oil or gas and other specified equipment would not be eligible for the credit if it were placed in service after Sept. 30, 1978.

Depreciation. Provided special treatment for depreciation of a natural gas or oil fueled boiler replaced before it was no longer useful.

Geothermal. Provided a percentage depletion allowance for gas produced from geopressured brine of 22 percent for production in 1978-1980, 20 percent for 1981, 18 percent for 1982, 16 percent for 1983 and 15 percent for all years thereafter.

• Specified that geothermal provisions would take effect on Oct. 1, 1978, and would apply to taxable years ending on or after Oct. 1, 1978.

Geopressured Natural Gas Depletion. Provided that natural gas produced from geopressured brine would be eligible for special treatment under the Natural Gas Policy Act of 1978.

• Provided that the 10 percent depletion for natural gas produced from geopressured brine would be allowed only for wells drilled after Sept. 30, 1978 and before Jan. 1, 1984. Wells drilled within that period would continue to be entitled to percentage depletion for their entire producing lives. But wells drilled before and after those dates would be treated as natural gas wells as under existing law.

- Provided that the section would take effect Oct. 1, 1978, and would apply to taxable years ending on or after Oct. 1, 1978.
- **Drilling Costs.** Allowed a deduction of intangible drilling costs for geothermal wells, which would be separate from that from oil and gas wells. The provision did not affect wells producing natural gas from geopressured brine.

Title IV — Miscellaneous Provisions

- Exempted the sale of lubricating oil from the 6-cent per gallon manufacturers excise tax if the oil were sold for use in a mixture with previously used or waste lubricating oil that had been cleaned, renovated or rerefined.
- Specified that for the exemption to apply, the blend of old and new oil had to consist of 25 percent or more of waste or rerefined oil. All of the new oil in a mixture would be exempt from the tax if the blend contained 55 percent or less new oil. If the mixture contained more than 55 percent new oil, the excise tax exemption would apply only to the portion of the new oil that did not exceed 55 percent of the mixture.

THE PROCESS

The fate of the energy package, particularly the natural gas pricing and tax portions, remained in doubt until the last day of the session, Oct. 15.

All five pieces began the year in a conference committee and remained there for many months. Three parts of the bill — coal conversion, utility rate reform and conservation — had been generally agreed upon by conferees in late 1977, but not formally approved.

But further action on those relatively non-controversial sections of the bill was delayed by long-running disputes over natural gas pricing and energy taxes. The majority of the natural gas conferees refused to finish up the other sections until they had resolved the gas controversy. In the tax conference, Sen. Russell Long, D-La., chairman of the Finance Committee, led senators in their refusal to meet on taxes until an agreement had been reached on natural gas.

For most of the year, it looked as through the gas pricing section would fail, that compromise was impossible. Nearly every time conferees appeared close to agreement, some new difficulty seemed to present itself. The opposition was a powerful coalition of consumer advocates who felt prices would go up too fast and industry sympathizers who asserted that price controls would not be lifted fast enough. The deadlock on natural gas threatened the entire energy package.

The Strategies

The Senate chose to handle the energy bill as it had in 1977, when it chopped the Carter bill into five measures and voted on each separately. It did the same with the conference reports; each was voted on as it emerged from the conference committee.

In the House, however, Speaker Thomas P. O'Neill, Jr. D-Mass., insisted on keeping the package together and permitting only one up or down vote on energy. That way, he reasoned, members could not approve the popular parts of the package without facing the more politically difficult questions of gas pricing and taxes.

O'Neill had employed a similar strategy in 1977 when the energy package went through the House the first time as one bill (HR 8444). He wanted to treat the conference reports the same way, postponing House action until all the reports had been passed by the Senate. Then the House would be permitted one final vote on the whole package.

But O'Neill's strategy came very close to failing. On Oct. 13, opponents of the natural gas pricing portion came within one vote of splitting that section away from the more popular parts of the package.

But even that crucial House vote did not clear the way for the energy bill. The next day in the Senate, retiring James Abourezk, D-S.D., began a filibuster against the only part of the energy package still before the Senate — the conference report on energy taxes. Abourezk, a key opponent of the gas bill, opposed the tax report and instead wanted Congress to pass a Senate version (HR 112) with more generous credits for conservation and solar energy. He vowed to give up his filibuster only if the House passed that Senate bill separately.

But O'Neill refused to allow a House vote on the package until the fifth piece — the tax conference report — was sent over by the Senate. The House had a long wait. Abourezk and a few other senators talked and delayed for about 15 hours — from Saturday morning until 12:30 a.m. Sunday, when they finally gave up. Soon after, the Senate easily passed the conference report and sent it to the House. There, four hours later, at 7:30 a.m. Oct. 15, the House approved the whole package.

Natural Gas

The first meeting of the year for the gas conferees was delayed by the death of Sen. Lee Metcalf, D-Mont., who died in his sleep Jan. 11. All 18 members of the Senate Energy Committee were conferees and had split 9-9 on price deregulation. Metcalf had supported Carter on continuing federal price controls on natural gas sales.

Supporters of Carter's plan needed a sympathetic senator appointed to maintain that balance. But senators wanting to end price controls threatened a floor fight if Sen. Henry M. Jackson, D-Wash., chairman of the Energy Committee, tried to arrange the appointment of a pro-regulation senator to Metcalf's conference seat. Eventually, two senators were elected to the Energy Committee, but not to the conference committee.

On Feb. 23, the 17 Senate conferees resumed daily sessions behind closed doors.

Tentative Senate Compromise

Several weeks later, on March 7, nine Senate conferees announced they had formed a shaky coalition behind a compromise plan to end federal price controls on new natural gas by 1985. The coalition was so shaky that the three Republicans who were part of the nine-member majority — Pete V. Domenici, N.M.; James A. McClure, Idaho, and Mark O. Hatfield, Ore. — said they would back out if House conferees tried to alter the agreement significantly.

Initial reaction from leading House conferees was cautious. They praised the Senate for hard work and good faith and pledged to analyze the compromise in a spirit of reconciliation.

But John D. Dingell, D-Mich., who had led the fight against gas dergulation since coming to the House in 1955,

Gas Price Hike Upheld

The Supreme Court declined Feb. 27 to overturn a controversial 1976 Federal Power Commission (FPC) ruling that almost tripled natural gas prices.

Without dissent, the justices left standing a lower court decision upholding the FPC rate hike. Associate Justices Potter Stewart and Lewis F. Powell Jr. did not participate in the case.

A coalition of consumers and municipal gas systems, led by the American Public Gas Association, charged that the FPC decision had been based on inadequate evidence and that it would have a "devastating" impact on consumers.

The FPC approved the rate boost July 27, 1976, after a two-month study. The higher price levels were designed to cover gas producers' costs plus a 15 percent return on investment. *(Background, 1976 Almanac p. 171)*

Under the FPC's ruling, newly discovered gas sold in interstate commerce after Jan. 1, 1975, could draw prices of up to $1.42 per thousand cubic feet (mcf), up from the old rate of $.52 per mcf.

The ruling also allowed that ceiling price to rise by one penny per quarter, starting Oct. 1, 1976, as an inflation adjustment. Through that mechanism, the current ceiling price for new natural gas sold in interstate commerce was $1.48 per mcf, and was to rise one cent April 1.

The FPC ruling also set a new price ceiling of $1.01 per thousand cubic feet for gas produced in 1973-74.

said he found major portions of the compromise " quite troublesome." And, he said, if Senate Republican coalition members intended the compromise as a "take-it-or-leave-it" proposition, "I would be compelled to leave it."

Of the nine Senators who backed the compromise, four had been committed to backing Carter's plan to continue regulation, while five had favored deregulation.

Carter had proposed boosting the price ceiling for new natural gas from $1.48 per thousand cubic feet (mcf) to $1.75 per mcf, with the new price to rise as oil prices rose. Carter's plan also called for providing that gas produced and used in the same state would be subject to price controls and allocations for the first time.

The Carter supporters in the coalition were Jackson, Dale Bumpers, D-Ark., Frank Church, D-Idaho, and Spark M. Matsunaga, D-Hawaii. The five former deregulation supporters in the coalition were the three Republicans plus Democrats Wendell H. Ford, Ky., and J. Bennett Johnston, La.

The Terms

Under key terms of the compromise "tentative agreement in principle":

- Price controls for new natural gas would expire Jan. 1, 1985.
- The president or Congress could reimpose controls for a two-year period any time after June 30, 1985, if prices went too high.
- In the period before 1985, new gas prices would start at $1.75 per mcf and would rise annually at a rate equal to the rise in the consumer price index plus 3.5 percent through April 20, 1981; and plus 4 percent from then through 1984.
- New onshore gas was defined as gas from new wells at least 2.5 miles from the surface location of an old well or at least 1,000 feet deeper than any well within 2.5 miles. Also qualifying as new gas would be gas from reservoirs which had not been in commercial production before April 20, 1977. New offshore gas was defined as gas from a lease commissioned since April 20, 1977, or from a reservoir discovered since July 27, 1976.
- State severance taxes would not be included in terms specifying first sale prices.
- The president, after declaring a natural gas emergency, would have authority to allocate natural gas from low priority users to others for up to 120 days.
- Certain "high cost gas" would be freed from price regulation immediately after passage of the bill. That category would include gas produced from Devonian shale, geopressurized brine, new wells drilled to depths below 15,-000 feet and occluded gas from coal seams.
- Gas from low-yield "stripper" wells producing up to 60 mcf per day would qualify for first sale prices of $2.09 per mcf, with annual price escalation rates the same as for new gas.
- Within 18 months of enactment, the Federal Energy Regulatory Commission would be required to issue a rule providing that major fuel burning installations would bear the increased costs for new high-priced gas until their fuel costs equalled the reasonable cost of other substitute fuels, such as oil.

March 22 Conference

On March 22, the House and Senate conferees held their first public session in three months. The results were inconclusive.

Senate conferees voted 10-7 to offer formally to the House their compromise plan to deregulate new natural gas by 1985.

House conferees did not vote directly on the Senate compromise. Instead, they voted 13-12 to accept it with an amendment. The amendment was their own substitute compromise.

Superficially, the House version was built on the same concepts as the sensitive Senate compromise. But close analysis revealed it would make extensive and fundamental changes in it.

Standing Room Only

The two-hour conference session took place before a standing room only crowd in an atmosphere of growing disorder, frustration, confusion and bad temper.

After the House conferees voted for their substitute, the Senate conferees mirrored their tactic. They voted 10-7 to accept the House version with an amendment. The amendment was the original Senate compromise that they had endorsed just an hour before.

"This is like the Mad Hatter's tea party," one veteran Capitol Hill reporter commented in an aside.

One Senate conferee asked Energy Chairman Jackson where that left the issue. Jackson said it left it where it was after the House conferees' vote, but admitted he was not sure what that meant.

"You can see why I have urged strongly that we engage in quiet diplomacy," Jackson said. "I think these public get-togethers before we get our ducks in a row create nothing but trouble."

Carter Statements on Gas Deregulation

President Carter startled many observers at a March 9 press conference by endorsing a phased-in end to government regulation of natural gas prices.

The surprise came because for almost a year Carter had fought hard to continue government price controls over natural gas. In that time, some of the harshest rhetoric he had employed as president was issued to denounce the oil and gas companies for trying to end such federal gas price regulation.

From the record, it was clearly true that Carter as a candidate for president called for phased-in deregulation. It was also true that in his April 20, 1977, speech on energy to a joint session of Congress that he pledged to "work carefully toward deregulation."

But his National Energy Plan clearly called for continuing federal price controls on natural gas. The controlled prices would be higher and the control system would be different under Carter's plan. But the point was that gas would not be deregulated.

Most important, when it appeared that either house of Congress was about to vote to deregulate new natural gas, Carter strongly and publicly denounced the moves. At those times he seemed to argue that the oil and gas lobby was pushing for total deregulation of all natural gas, both newly discovered and that already flowing from old wells. But that was not the case.

The gas deregulation legislation which threatened Carter's program in the House in July and which triumphed in the Senate in October 1977, aimed only at deregulating new natural gas — although "new" gas was liberally defined. In arguing against those deregulation measures, Carter incorrectly implied they would end regulation over all gas. A representative compilation of Carter's statements on natural gas deregulation follows:

June 16, 1976

Presentation to the Democratic Platform Committee: "For natural gas, we should deregulate the price of only that natural gas not currently under existing contract (less than 5 percent) for a period of five years. At the end of the period of time, we should evaluate this program to see if it increases production and keeps gas-related products at prices the American people can afford."

Oct. 19, 1976

Letter to Texas Gov. Dolph Briscoe, D: "First, I will work with the Congress, as the Ford administration has been unable to do, to deregulate new natural gas."

April 20, 1977

Energy speech to joint session of Congress: "I want to work with the Congress to give gas producers an adequate incentive for exploration, working carefully toward deregulation of newly discovered natural gas as market conditions permit. I propose now that the price limit for all new gas sold anywhere in the country be set at the price of the equivalent energy value of domestic crude oil, beginning in 1978. This proposal will apply both to new gas and to expiring intrastate contracts. It would not affect existing contracts."

April 22, 1977

News conference: **Q:** "Mr. President, do you foresee a recommendation to eventually take the cap off of gas; that is, as long as there is a cap on it, it would seem to be regulated? . . .

A: "I think that would still have to remain for future analysis. I believe that . . . setting the natural gas price at its equivalent in oil is an adequate level of deregulation. Others, of course, want complete deregulation of oil and gas.

"I don't think it's possible for us to do that in the immediate future. I think the adverse impact on consumers and on our economy would just be too severe. . . ."

Sept. 24, 1977

Campaign speech at Norfolk, Va.: "I put forward to the Congress a comprehensive energy package. Part of it calls for deregulation, over a period of time, of natural gas. . . . But the gas companies — very powerful in Washington as you well know — want to deregulate immediately and add tremendous costs to the American public, not only for new gas to be discovered in the future but for gas that already has been discovered and that will be coming to you in any case. . . .

"I hate to veto a bill that a Democratic Congress passes, but you can depend upon it: I'll protect your interests when the bill crosses my desk."

Sept. 26, 1977

White House remarks: "The Congress has been lobbied continuously by the oil and gas industry to deregulate the price of new natural gas. . . . There comes a time when we must ask how much is enough. . . . It's time for the public interest to prevail over special interest lobbyists."

Sept. 29, 1977

Press conference: "I do not support complete deregulation of natural gas prices which would provide windfall profits without increasing supply. Deregulation would cost consumers an extra $70 billion by 1985 but would increase supplies very little, if any."

Oct. 13, 1977

News conference: Carter denounced "potential war profiteering in the impending energy crisis. This could develop with the passing months as the biggest ripoff in history." . . .[T]he oil companies apparently want it all. . . . If we deregulate natural gas prices, then the price will go to 15 times more than natural gas prices were before the oil embargo."

Oct. 28, 1977

Question and answer session with visiting newspaper executives: "As I said in my campaign and also as I said to the Congress when I made my energy speech last April, we are working toward deregulation of natural gas."

Nov. 4, 1977

Question and answer session: "I don't believe that I've changed my position. I don't interpret it that way. My position was that I would work with Congress, as had President Ford, for deregulation of natural gas. . . . The difference is in the rapidity with which natural gas is deregulated. . . .

March 9, 1978

News conference: **Q:** "Mr. President, are you willing to accept energy legislation that in a few years would lead to the deregulation of natural gas?"

A: "Yes, I am. This was a campaign statement and commitment of mine — that I thought natural gas should be deregulated. In my speech to the Congress last April, I repeated this hope and I think a long phased-in deregulation process without any shock to our national economy would be acceptable."

The conference then adjourned for Easter recess with no new meeting date set.

The session had revealed several things.

Fragile Coalition. First, the fragile Senate coalition behind the compromise had been badly shaken by the extent of the changes called for by the House compromise.

Clear evidence of this came after the session broke up. Thomas L. Ashley, D-Ohio, Speaker O'Neill's personal coordinator on the energy conference approached an angry Sen. Domenici in an apparent peacemaking effort.

Domenici had made it clear that his support for the Senate compromise was tenuous and that he would back out if the House insisted on tampering much with its terms.

Domenici seethed as he talked to Ashley. "You prepared a whole new deal," he said, referring to the House plan. That was not his understanding of what had been tacitly agreed upon, he said. The Senate coalition had been assured that if it could strike a bargain, the House and the Carter administration would go along with little resistance. Instead, Domenici fumed, the House offering included at least "12 major changes."

Second, it also was apparent from vote splits on both sides that the coalitions behind the compromise plans were thin and insecure.

Conservative Republicans joined with consumer-oriented Democrats to oppose each compromise, although the alliances were formed for different reasons. The Republicans thought the plans achieved deregulation too slowly and insufficiently; the liberals thought even phased deregulation would rob consumers while handing undeserved windfall profits to the oil and gas industry.

Splitting the Bill. A third potentially significant development was that extensive support appeared to be growing among both House and Senate conferees to split the Carter energy program into separate bills. If progress toward agreement on natural gas pricing were to bog down again, as it had so often in the past, several leading conferees said, they would break loose the three non-controversial portions of the program already resolved in conference and pass them without resolving natural gas pricing and major energy taxes.

House-Senate Differences

Ironically, the compromise proposals put forward by House and Senate conferees showed the two sides were closer than ever before.

A majority of House conferees formally went on record for the first time in favor of phasing out federal price controls over new natural gas.

Controls would end Dec. 31, 1984, under the Senate plan and six months later under the House plan.

The House version would accept the Senate price structure in the interim, with one major change. The Senate plan would set new gas prices at $1.75 per thousand cubic feet (mcf) as of April 20, 1977, with annual boosts equal to the rate of inflation as measured by the Consumer Price Index plus 3.5 percent through April 20, 1981, and plus 4 percent thereafter.

The House version would tie the inflation adjustor to changes in the gross national product, which was more stable.

The most important changes called for by the House were in defining what gas would be "new" and hence would qualify for high prices and eventual deregulation. The Senate compromise terms were extremely broad, so that almost any newly drilled well — even into existing reservoirs currently producing — could draw the high prices. The House version would redraft several technical sections to cut back severely the amount of gas eligible for high prices.

In other major conflicts, the House plan would require a system of "incremental pricing" whereby industrial gas consumers would bear the burden of paying for new high priced gas disproportionately at first, while smaller gas consumers would indefinitely draw lower priced gas from wells still under controls. The Senate version required only that such pricing plans be drafted and submitted to Congress for separate approval.

The House version also would substantially redraw terms empowering the President to allocate gas supplies and a section allowing either the President or Congress to reimpose price controls.

The Votes

Voting with the majority in the Senate conferees' 10-7 split to endorse their compromise plan were Republicans Domenici, Hatfield and McClure, and Democrats Johnston, Ford, Jackson, Church, Bumpers, Matsunaga and Floyd K. Haskell, Colo. Haskell's vote came by proxy and was a surprise. Facing a hard re-election fight, he delivered a message through Jackson that his vote March 22 did not mean he would support the plan later.

Opposing the Senate compromise were three Democrats — John A. Durkin, N.H.; James Abourezk, S.D., and Howard M. Metzenbaum, Ohio. They were joined by four Republicans — Clifford P. Hansen, Wyo.; Dewey F. Bartlett, Okla.; Paul Laxalt, Nev., and Lowell P. Weicker Jr., Conn.

Opposing the House compromise were Joe D. Waggonner Jr., D-La., an oil-state conservative, three consumer-state liberals — Toby Moffett, D-Conn., Charles A. Vanik, D-Ohio, and Charles B. Rangel, D-N.Y. — and all eight Republican House conferees: John B. Anderson, Ill.; Clarence J. Brown, Ohio; Frank Horton, N.Y.; John W. Wydler, N.Y.; Garry Brown, Mich.; William A. Steiger, Wis.; James M. Collins, Texas, and Bill Archer, Texas.

Carter Intervenes

Faced with a standstill on gas, President Carter intervened personally in the dispute April 11 by calling key conferees together for a series of White House meetings.

On April 12 Carter met separately with a group of House Republican conferees in an effort to soothe their anger at being shut out of the closed-door sessions that key conferees had been holding in the Capitol.

After the April 12 meeting, Clarence Brown of Ohio reported that Carter said "he would support, in effect, anything that came out of the conference."

All sides reported that Carter's intervention renewed their dedication to resolve their differences. But after three days of White House meetings, serious differences continued to divide the conferees.

One published report indicated that Senate conferees listed eight specific areas of disagreement as the April 13 meeting began and that the House side then added four more.

Protest Vote. Meanwhile, the House overwhelmingly went on record April 13 to protest the practice of key conferees meeting privately in informal meetings instead of in public as both chambers' rules required.

Toby Moffett, a key conference leader on behalf of those favoring continued federal controls on gas prices, forced a floor vote on the question. To finesse the parliamentary confusion of the issue, Moffett's motion had to be phrased as a formal instruction to close the conference. Moffett hoped it would be strongly voted down as a signal to conference leaders that the House wanted the meetings open. The House agreed with him, voting down the motion 6-371. *(Vote 184, p. 54-H)*

The April 21 Agreement

A major breakthrough in the gas debate came one year and one day after President Carter presented Congress with his omnibus energy program. On April 21 a small group of leading House and Senate conferees ended four months of stalemate by agreeing to end federal regulation of prices for new natural gas beginning Jan. 1, 1985.

But the agreement had been reached by fewer than a dozen of the 43 conferees involved.

Marathon Session

Most of the final agreement was reached during a marathon 13-hour session stretching until 3:30 a.m. April 21. With Energy Secretary Schlesinger pushing the small group each step of the way, the leading House and Senate conferees settled all but two technical points, according to key participants.

They reconvened for another tense two and a half hours April 21 at 11 a.m. in plush but cramped quarters in an obscure third floor room of the Capitol.

J. Bennett Johnston, D-La., created a deadline by insisting he had to catch a plane at 1:30 p.m.

As the Senate delegation and the House members caucused in different rooms about 100 paces apart, Schlesinger periodically emerged in shirtsleeves to shuttle messages back and forth. Each venture into the hall by any participant brought a crush of questions from about 100 reporters and technicians milling about outside.

In the end, Johnston left without agreeing.

But at 1:25 p.m. a burst of applause from inside the caucus room signaled the impasse had been broken.

"We have been able to merge our differences for the first time in 30 years [on the issue]," announced Henry Jackson.

And John Dingell, who had doggedly insisted on terms to protect consumers from too steeply rising gas bills, pledged: "I'm going back and I'm going to try to sell this proposal to my colleagues."

PROVISIONS

Following are the main points of the agreement reached April 21 by leading House and Senate conferees, according to a summary prepared by the Senate Energy Committee. The agreement:

Price Controls

- Imposed price controls on all categories of natural gas, both interstate and intrastate, effective between enactment of the legislation and Jan. 1, 1985.
- Mandated an end to federal price regulation, effective Jan. 1, 1985, of new natural gas, of most gas currently sold in intrastate commerce and of natural gas from new wells deeper than 5,000 feet located in old reservoirs.
- Specified that gas freed from price controls would remain free from those controls at least between Jan. 1, 1985, and July 1, 1985.
- Provided that either Congress or the president, subject to veto by both houses of Congress, could reimpose price controls at any time between July 1, 1985, and July 1, 1987.
- Provided that the level of reimposition would be set by statute and would vary by type of gas.
- Provided that reimposed controls last 18 months.
- Specified that authority to reimpose controls could be used only once.

New Gas Definitions

- Defined new onshore gas as gas from new wells 2.5 miles beyond an existing well or 1,000 feet deeper than an existing well, or gas from new wells into reservoirs that had not produced in commercial quantities before April 20, 1977.
- Excluded from the new gas definition gas which producers intentionally had withheld from the market.
- Defined new gas from the outer continental shelf as gas from leases issued after April 20, 1977.
- Defined as "special development incentive gas" gas from new wells in an old reservoir within 2.5 miles of an old well, provided the new well met spacing requirements.
- Provided that special development incentive price gas from wells shallower than 5,000 feet would be freed from federal price regulation on July 1, 1987, unless price controls had been reimposed. If controls had been reimposed, that gas would be freed from regulation at the end of the reimposition period.

Interim Price Scale

- Provided that in the interim period between enactment of the legislation and Jan. 1, 1985, new natural gas ceiling prices would increase at a level equal to inflation as measured by the Gross National Product (GNP) deflator plus 0.2 percent, plus 3.5 percent as an incentive to gas producers, through April 20, 1981. The 3.5 percent producer incentive would rise to 4 percent on April 20, 1981, effective to Dec. 31, 1984.
- Specified that the starting price for that interim pricing scale would be $1.75 per million British thermal units (MMBtu's) as of April 20, 1977, (which staff estimated equalled about $1.93 as of April 21, 1978).
- Provided that in the interim period prior to Jan. 1, 1985, gas qualifying as special incentive price gas would draw price increases equal to inflation as measured by the GNP deflator plus 0.2 percent. The base price would be $1.75 per MMBtu as of April 20, 1977, (an estimated $1.86 as of April 21, 1978).
- Provided that special development incentive price gas from wells shallower than 5,000 feet would draw prices from a scale splitting the difference between its old price increase rate and the new price increase standard.
- Specified that prices for old gas not under contract or under federal regulation would be allowed to increase at a rate equal to the inflation rate. The starting price was estimated to be $1.45 per MMBtu as of April 20, 1977, or $1.54 as of one year later.
- Provided that outer continental shelf gas from reservoirs discovered after July 27, 1976, in old leases would draw new gas prices, but would not be deregulated.

Rollover Contracts

●Provided that as contracts for interstate gas sales expired or "rolled over," the new ceiling price for that gas would be 54 cents per MMBtu if the original contract price were below that level. If higher, the new ceiling price would be limited to the old contract price.

●Provided that as contracts for intrastate gas expired, the new ceiling price for that gas would be $1 per MMBtu if the contract price were below that amount and would be limited to the contract price if higher.

●Provided that for intrastate gas contracts existing at the time of enactment of the legislation, price escalator clauses would apply until the contract price equalled the new gas price.

Allocation Powers

●Provided that in times of natural gas supply emergencies, the president would have powers to allocate gas supplies after voluntary emergency sales were exhausted.

●Limited the president's emergency allocation powers to a set of ordered priorities. First, he must allocate gas from boilers capable of being fired by coal, including those fed by either interstate or intrastate gas. Second, he could allocate gas used by other low priority users served by interstate pipelines only. Third, he could allocate gas owned by low priority end users.

Regulatory Powers

●Provided the Federal Energy Regulatory Commission (FERC) with authority to specify duration of gas contracts and specified that outer continental shelf contracts would be for a minimum of 15 years.

●Provided FERC with authority to provide a right of first refusal on interstate contracts.

●Empowered FERC to issue rules and regulations under the legislation.

High Cost Gas

●Provided that upon the effective date of the first FERC incremental pricing rule, gas from Devonian shale, methane gas from coal seams, gas from new wells drilled below 15,000 feet deep and gas derived from geopressurized brine would be deregulated immediately.

●Authorized FERC to establish price incentives to encourage investment in development of other kinds of high cost gas.

●Specified that the authority given FERC was to be exercised prior to the drilling of wells and that the authority was not to be "cost based;" i.e., limited to covering the costs of production.

Stripper Wells

●Provided that stripper wells were wells producing gas not associated with oil at a maximum efficient production rate of 60 thousand cubic feet (mcf) per day or less.

●Set a ceiling price of $2.09 per mcf for gas from stripper wells, with the price ceiling to rise at the same rate as for new gas.

●Specified that gas from stripper wells was not to be deregulated.

●Directed FERC to provide a rule allowing wells that qualified as stripper wells to increase production if the producer used recognized production enhancement techniques.

Incremental Pricing

●Directed FERC to devise within 12 months of enactment a rule mandating that industrial consumers of gas as boiler fuel should bear the disproportionate burden of paying higher costs for the higher-priced gas flowing under the act.

●Specified that schools, hospitals and other similar institutions and agricultural users would be exempt from this "incremental pricing" provision.

●Specified that those eligible industrial boiler fuel users would have to pay the increased costs of gas disproportionately until their gas costs reached the costs of buying substitute fuel; i.e., the cost of No. 2 fuel oil as determined regionally. No. 2 fuel oil was the grade of oil used in home heating.

●Directed FERC to develop a second incremental pricing rule within 18 months of enactment which would apply incremental pricing terms to other low priority gas consumers.

●Specified that the second incremental pricing rule would be subject to a one house veto by Congress.

●Specified that incremental pricing rules would apply only to users served by interstate pipelines.

●Specified that incremental pricing would apply to that portion of an interstate pipeline's cost of certain supply categories that exceeded $1.48 per MMBtu, adjusted for inflation.

●Spelled out those categories as new natural gas, rollover contract gas previously fed solely into the intrastate system and special development incentive price gas.

●Provided that incremental pricing also would be applied to deregulated high cost supplies if the price of those supplies exceeded the price of imported No. 2 fuel oil plus 30 percent.

●Provided that imports of liquid natural gas would be incrementally priced, but also provided that approved projects could qualify for a "grandfather" clause.

●Specified that liquid natural gas import projects pending before the Department of Energy and those determined by FERC to involve binding contractual and financial commitments would be priced under the existing Natural Gas Act.

●Provided that natural gas imports that exceeded the new natural gas ceiling price and were in excess of existing contract volumes also would be priced incrementally.

Squabbling Continues

By April 24, the optimism generated by the April 21 agreement was waning. On the 24th, conferees cancelled a public meeting scheduled for the 26th when it became apparent that a majority of the 25 House conferees would not support the compromise.

President Carter and House leaders, anxious for agreement, spent the week of the 24th trying to round up the last few votes needed. Reportedly, the pressure concentrated on two House conferees — Henry S. Reuss, D-Wis., and James C. Corman, D-Calif. — who voted for the March 22 compromise offer.

Both told reporters they believed the April 21 compromise was overly generous to the oil and gas industry. Reuss also said that he feared the gas compromise would pave the way for adoption of Carter's proposed crude oil equalization tax, which Reuss opposed.

Corman, conversely, insisted he would oppose the April 21 compromise at least until conferees on energy taxes

Carter on Natural Gas Compromise

Following is the White House transcript of President Carter's remarks at a news briefing Aug. 18 on the natural gas compromise. Energy Secretary James R. Schlesinger also took part in the briefing.

THE PRESIDENT: Good morning, everybody.

Last night the House and Senate conferees on the energy legislation reached agreement on one of the most difficult aspects of the entire energy package, and that is natural gas, ending a 30-year debate on this question.

Now the conference report will go to the House and Senate for further action.

This is a major step forward under the most difficult of circumstances and I and everyone in our country owe the House and Senate conferees a debt of gratitude for their assistance and tenacity and their willingness to accommodate their own deeply felt personal and sectional interests in the best interests of our country.

The legislation, when passed, will give us a new national market, making available new supplies of natural gas, which will be at a lower price than competitive foreign oil.

The bill is specially designed to protect home owners and small business leaders, small businesses.

It is also designed to give industry adequate supplies of natural gas at a good and competitive price. The bill encourages additional American production of natural gas, gives better prices in the future, and more sure prices in the future for those producers, at the same time protecting the interests of consumers.

We have been especially careful in natural gas legislation and the other elements of the overall energy package to protect the interests of the poor, the underprivileged and those who don't have the flexibility to accommodate changing prices.

The next step will be for the Senate to make a decision about the conference committee report.

My hope and expectation is that the individual Members of the Senate will show the same deep interest, a willingness to be flexible, a willingness to accommodate the needs of our Nation, as have the conferees themselves.

There is no doubt that this legislation, when passed, will protect the security interests of our country. It will protect the energy interests of our country. It will help us to assure continued prosperity and jobs for the American people, it will help us to control inflation, it will also help us to have a more stable economy and to protect the integrity of the dollar overseas.

All these benefits that will come from this legislation when and if it is passed, I am sure, will be an inspiration to the Members of the House and Senate to act expeditiously and positively on this very difficult and challenging but very important legislation.

Jim, are you prepared to answer questions?

SECRETARY SCHLESINGER: Yes, sir.

THE PRESIDENT: Secretary Schlesinger, who has done a superb job in bring together opinions and working very continuously with legislation that is perhaps as complex as any that has ever faced the Congress, will now answer questions that you might have.

QUESTION: Did you have to make any promises to [Reps. Charles B.] Rangel [D-N.Y.] and [James C.] Corman [D-Calif.] that we should know about to get them to sign?

THE PRESIDENT: That you need to know about?

QUESTION: That we should know about. (Laughter) Did you have to promise them something?

THE PRESIDENT: No. The only thing they were interested in was that I would repeat for the Congress and for the American public my interests along with theirs to protect the interests of the poor and the underprivileged, not only in this particular legislation, but in other aspects.

QUESTION: But no deals?

THE PRESIDENT: No.

reached an agreement that included a strong crude oil tax and a strong tax on utility and industrial use of oil and gas as Carter proposed and as the House approved in 1977. The energy tax conferees had not met since Dec. 7, 1977. *(Oil taxes, background, 1977 Almanac p. 708)*

THE MAY 4 SESSION

House and Senate conferees next met in public May 4, but spent most of the session quarreling about closed meetings.

No vote was taken on the April 21 compromise, apparently because House leaders lacked firm commitments for approval from a majority of their conferees. But conference Chairman Harley O. Staggers, D-W.Va., announced that a vote on the plan would be taken May 9.

The compromise pricing proposal, the result of an "intensive and emotional struggle," is the "best hope we have for resolution of this issue," Staggers said.

Senate Energy Chairman Jackson asserted that the compromise proposal was "neither left nor right ideologically, but clearly in the center."

Costs of Proposal

According to estimates by the House Commerce Energy Subcommittee, the compromise proposal was expected to provide by 1985 about $23 billion more in revenues to natural gas producers than the House-passed bill, which kept more controls on gas prices.

Compared to existing regulations, the compromise would give producers an extra $9 billion, the staff study said. The Senate-passed bill would have increased revenues to producers by $46 billion or more by 1985 over existing regulations, committee staff said.

Differences Flare Up

The inconclusive, raucous public meeting of the conferees came two days after the tenuous agreement among leading conferees threatened to come apart.

The problem was that the conferees disagreed about what they had agreed upon.

On May 2, House conferees met in closed session on one side of the Capitol with Energy Secretary Schlesinger while, on the other side of the building, Senate staff — and, from time to time, senators — waited for a scheduled 2 p.m. meeting of the two sides to begin.

Eventually, the two sides met together and, by 10 p.m. that night, had again worked out their differences.

Delays in Vote

Opponents of the compromise proposal, already upset because it had been worked out in closed session by a select group of conferees, also fussed at the May 4 meeting about not being able to vote on the compromise.

But Jackson, a leader of the small group that worked it out, asserted that, "we'd be charged with railroading" if the vote were held before members had a chance to read the document detailing the compromise.

But Jackson also noted, "The name of the game happens to be votes."

Sens. Weicker, Metzenbaum and other conferees tried to sidetrack the compromise proposal by raising points of order about the closed sessions and about new provisions in the compromise that were not in the Senate bill.

But Staggers and Jackson insisted that the group of conferees had not acted officially as conferees, but as individual members.

"The truth is," Jackson said, "we meet in members' offices all the time. . . . This was just the longest, most protracted discussion, meeting, 'getting together thing,' probably in congressional history, but that doesn't change the substance [that it was informal]."

DEADLOCK REMAINS

The May 9 date set by Staggers for a vote on gas came and went as House conferees continued their search for a majority.

Attention was focused on one man — Joe D. Waggonner, D-La., — thought by supporters to be the key to getting a majority of the 25 conferees. They could count as supporters 12 of the 13 votes they needed.

Waggonner, from a gas producing state where gas prices were not federally controlled, was concerned because the compromise would extend limited federal controls to the intrastate sale of gas.

Another representative from a gas producing state, Charles Wilson, D-Texas, also had problems with the provision on intrastate gas. But Wilson had won new language to benefit producers that would keep the government from holding prices down to the generally low levels set in contracts signed before the 1973 Arab oil embargo.

Waggonner and Wilson also eventually worked out a compromise with Bob Eckhardt, D-Texas, that after 1985 would raise the price ceiling for certain existing intrastate contracts under which the price per thousand cubic feet was more than $1.

On May 9, the seriousness of the stalemate prompted Speaker O'Neill to say for the first time that he was considering splitting up the five-part package. Such a move would dim substantially chances for passage of the crude oil equalization tax, an unpopular piece of the package, which Carter had described as its centerpiece.

Whatever O'Neill's announcement meant for the future of the tax, it apparently won Reuss' vote for the gas compromise. Reuss opposed the tax.

Two More Meetings

House conferees on natural gas held two more uneventful meetings on May 9 and 10. A third meeting scheduled for May 11 was cancelled when supporters of the compromise again didn't have the votes for a majority.

The conferees spent most of their time listening to staff explain the compromise and asking questions of each other about the proposal.

At one point, Toby Moffett, who opposed deregulation and the compromise, tried to end the proceedings. "I move we dispense with this explanation," he said. "It's not serving any useful purpose [as evidenced] both by the [poor] attendance and by the fact that we have already heard this explanation."

But, one by one, supporters of the compromise spoke up. "I would hate to be deprived of this edification," said Richard Bolling, D-Mo.

"I yet find several areas of this very complicated question of what constitutes new natural gas" that are confusing said Eckhardt. "I still need an explanation of it."

Moffett's frustration was evident. Because supporters of the compromise weren't sure they had enough votes, "there is a great penchant for discussion, dialogue, reflection. It's rather obvious what's going on here," Moffett said.

His motion was ruled out of order by Staggers, chairman of the conference and a supporter of the compromise.

MAY 24: DEADLOCK BROKEN

The deadlock was finally broken May 24 when House and Senate conferees voted to accept a proposal for deregulation that even supporters said they did not like.

The final vote was far from dramatic as weary conferees cast their ballots, but the action represented the most significant move toward deregulation of natural gas since Congress had begun fighting over the issue 30 years before.

On May 23, House conferees who opposed the deregulation plan had tried unsuccessfully to derail the compromise with amendments. But in late afternoon, the final vote, as predicted, was 13-12.

The next day, Senate conferees also spent hours defeating crippling amendments and, about 6 p.m., finally approved the plan, 10-7.

President Carter praised the conferees' "historic agreement" and predicted it would cost consumers "no more than they would pay if today's inadequate regulatory system were to be maintained."

He predicted that new supplies of natural gas would move from intrastate markets, where prices were higher, into interstate markets, where prices were low but shortages had occurred.

Conference Action

At the meeting of House conferees May 23, Toby Moffett led the opposition to the compromise.

The proposal "lines [the] pockets" of the gas industry "without getting much in return for the public," Moffett said. The push to "get a bill" had led House conferees to go "against the will of the House" and agree to a proposal "crafted and agreed to in an atmosphere . . . of political hysteria," said Moffett, who did not participate in the closed-door sessions that led to the agreement.

His concern about the benefits of deregulation to producers was shared by Staggers, conference chairman, who took the industry to task at the meeting of the full conference May 24.

The bill is "generous to you," said Staggers, addressing the gas industry in general. He warned he would consider it "treason against the interests of America if you withhold gas from the marketplace in the future." Monopolistic actions or price fixing would bring "corrective legislation that would be unwelcome to you," Staggers said.

A leader of the Senate opposition to the agreement was James Abourezk, D-S.D., who called the deregulation a "rip-off" and "rape of the American consumer." The sole beneficiary of the proposal will be the "titans of the oil and gas industry, whose lust for profits has been unmatched in the annals of American business," he said.

FLOOR ACTION DELAYED

In the weeks after May 23, staff worked to translate the delicate gas agreement into legislative language and to write the report to go with the bill.

The task proved difficult. Conferees saw the final terms for the first time July 31. Some members who earlier had agreed to the compromise balked at signing the report, contending that the final language was not what they thought they had agreed upon. The disagreements held up floor action.

By mid-August the situation looked bleak for the bill's supporters. Three of the 13 House conferees who had agreed to the May 24 compromise — Reuss, Waggonner and Wilson — were refusing to sign. Of the 10 senators who had okayed the compromise, four were withholding support. They were Johnston and Repubicans McClure, Hatfield and Domenici.

Basically, the defectors said the formal legislative language was not what they had agreed to in principle. But shifting political winds may have been just as reponsible for their change of heart.

Reuss, for instance, had been reluctant to go along with the agreement initially because he said it rewarded the gas industry at the expense of consumers. One of the reasons he yielded to heavy pressure to support the agreement was his announced concern that President Carter have evidence for world leaders that the United States was dealing with its energy problems.

Reuss' support came before Carter's attendance at a mid-July economic summit meeting in West Germany. The legislator's later refusal to sign the report came after the summit.

Industry's Objections

Wilson, Waggonner and the four Senate conferees pulling back were gas industry partisans who preferred immediate deregulation of new natural gas to the complex, phased system proposed under the agreement.

They argued that the compromise language meant prices would rise more slowly between 1978 and 1985 than they thought the May agreement had provided. They also objected to terms giving the president powers to allocate gas in intrastate markets. And other technical terms were different from those agreed on in May, they said.

But other pressures were at work, too. The two Louisianans, for instance — Sen. Johnston and Rep. Waggonner — reassessed their support for the gas compromise in part because of a case pending before the Federal Energy Regulatory Commission (FERC).

The case involved the United Gas Pipeline Co. of Shreveport, La., one of the nation's largest natural gas pipeline companies. A tentative FERC ruling blocked the company's plan to give preference to Louisiana gas customers when gas supplies were short, as they had been repeatedly in periods of high demand.

Johnston and Waggonner made personal pitches to the commission to overturn the preliminary judgment. Waggonner publicly linked the case to his vote on the gas compromise, and Johnston made a telephone call to commission Chairman Charles Curtis stressing how important the case was to him.

Their interest stemmed from fears that the combination of the commission ruling and the deregulation compromise could leave Louisiana with severe gas shortages. The compromise would extend federal controls for the first time to gas sold in states where it was produced, like Louisiana. And it would free such gas for distribution to other states.

Meanwhile, the compromise also was drawing even heavier fire from a diverse range of interest groups. Among them were the U.S. Chamber of Commerce, the Independent Petroleum Association of America, the AFL-CIO, the Consumer Federation of America and the Americans for Democratic Action.

Cats and Dogs?

For those curious about how the Senate-House conferees on President Carter's energy bill continued to drone on without resolution, the events of June 7 may prove instructive.

What started out as debate on national energy policy quickly degenerated into a quixotic discussion of dog and cat food.

Although the basic principles of a natural gas pricing agreement had finally been agreed to May 24 after six months of hard, secret bargaining, several highly technical questions remained.

On June 7, conferees were presented with a staff-drawn definition of "essential agricultural user," which would have protected the use of gas in the production of, among other things, animal feed.

Sen. Howard M. Metzenbaum, D-Ohio, objected. He said dog and cat food production should not supercede the national interest in energy policy.

Staff explained the provision was intended for beef cattle farmers and other essential agricultural purposes, not dog and cat food production.

Metzenbaum insisted the staff language be amended to exclude dog and cat food.

Debate ensued.

Sen. John A. Durkin, D-N.H., wondered if Metzenbaum's dog and cat amendment shouldn't be altered to exempt food for Alaskan dogs, because they are essential to sled transportation.

Senatorial tongues were planted firmly against cheeks.

Sen. Clifford P. Hansen, R-Wyo., contributed the thought that sheep dogs, too, were important, and their food should be excluded.

Conference Chairman Rep. Harley O. Staggers, D-W.Va., told Metzenbaum he could not go along with the amendment because there were too many voting dog and cat owners in his district.

The audience howled.

Sen. Wendell H. Ford, D-Ky., wanted hunting dogs differentiated from Metzenbaum's dogs.

At length — roughly 30 minutes of much more of the same — Senate conferees adopted Ford's amendment to Metzenbaum's amendment by a show of hands, then quickly voted down Metzenbaum's amendment, as amended.

New Gas Ceiling Price Projections

	Status Quo Intra-state	Status Quo Inter-state	House Bill	Senate Bill	Conference Agreement
1978	$1.82	$1.50	$1.87	$2.84	$1.99
1979	1.93	1.59	2.04	3.79	2.21
1980	2.04	1.69	2.24	4.73	2.42
1981	2.17	1.79	2.44	4.64	2.65
1982	2.30	1.89	2.65	4.58	2.91
1983	2.44	2.01	2.87	4.53	3.19
1984	2.58	2.13	3.11	4.50	3.50
1985	2.74	2.26	3.36	4.48	3.86

Price per million Btu's, as of midyear each year. Projection assumes 6 percent annual inflation..

SOURCE: Conference Committee

Energy Department 1985 Natural Gas Retail Price Projections

(in million Btu's, 1978 dollars)

	Current Law	House Bill	Senate Bill	Conference Agreement
Residential	$3.22	$2.92	$2.97 to $3.62	$3.31
Commercial	3.02	3.46	3.70 to 3.19	3.25
Raw Material	2.38	2.77	2.98 to 2.67	2.55
Industrial	2.35	2.81	3.02 to 2.69	2.59

SOURCE: Department of Energy/Energy Information Administration

AUG. 17 AGREEMENT

The months of haggling seemed to be nearing an end on Aug. 18 when a majority of House and Senate conferees signed the conference report (S Rept 95-1126) and seemingly cleared the way for floor action on the embattled agreement.

In the House, James Corman and Charles Rangel did an unexpected about-face and signed the conference report after a personal appeal from Carter in a late-night White House session. Their decision came on the eve of a three-week House recess.

Corman and Rangel were needed to replace Waggonner and Reuss, the two House conferees who had given their verbal endorsement to the agreement in May, but then refused to sign the final report. They were the 11th and 12th House conferees to sign. The 13th signature, providing a majority, came from Charles Wilson.

Asked how he had persuaded the two reluctant House conferees, Carter told an Aug. 18 press conference that the two liberal Democrats had wanted reassurance that the gas agreement would protect "the poor, the underprivileged" from higher gas prices. Carter denied that any deals had been made to get the two signatures.

Also at the White House meeting were Domenici and McClure, but they said that factors other than presidential persuasion caused them to sign the report Aug. 17. They provided the needed majority of Senate conferees.

Heading for the Floor

As the beleaguered gas bill headed for the Senate floor, it seemed subject to attack from all sides.

Opponents, led by Sen. Abourezk, were threatening to filibuster the measure. But its chances of approval on a straight up or down vote did not look good either.

Recommittal Sought

On Aug. 23, a coalition of 18 senators representing both ends of the political spectrum announced they would not support the agreement. The group, including opponents and proponents of gas price deregulation, said the compromise would "lead to a situation worse than under the status quo."

The senators, representing both producing and consuming states, said they would move to send the conference report back to committee when the agreement reached the floor. By that time floor action had been postponed until after the Labor Day recess.

The senators said their motion also would require the conferees to finish action on the utility rate reform and conservation portions of the energy plan, which they asserted had been "held hostage to the gas bill."

The coalition of 11 Democrats and seven Republicans was glued together with opposing interests. Some of the senators opposed the gas provisions because they believed consumers would be badly hurt by higher prices. Others opposed the agreement because it did not decontrol the price of gas fast enough to suit the gas industry and encourage production.

All of the Republicans in the group supported deregulation when the Senate voted on the question Sept. 22, 1977. All but one of the Democrats voted against deregulation. *(Vote 389, 1977 Almanac p. 58-S)*

Democrats in the coalition were Metzenbaum, Abourezk, Durkin, Edward M. Kennedy, Mass.; William Proxmire, Wis.; George S. McGovern, S.D.; Birch Bayh, Ind.; Gaylord Nelson, Wis.; Donald W. Riegle Jr., Mich.; Muriel Humphrey, Minn., and Wendell R. Anderson, Minn. Muriel Humphrey had not been a member of the Senate when the deregulation vote was taken.

Republicans supporting the coalition were Hansen, Weicker, Dewey F. Bartlett, Okla.; John G. Tower, Texas; Henry Bellmon, Okla.; Richard G. Lugar, Ind., and Jake Garn, Utah.

In a "Dear Colleague" letter circulated Aug. 24, they asserted that the restrictions the compromise imposed on the intrastate market would reduce producer incentive and that it would mean higher prices for consumers without assuring additional supply.

Breeder Deal

Also complicating approval of the conference agreement was McClure's announcement Aug. 23 that the president had softened his opposition to breeder reactors in return for McClure's signature on the conference report. *(Breeder background, energy authorization bill, p. 684)*

But by the next day there were signs that the agreement with McClure might have backfired. Senate Republican leader Howard H. Baker Jr., Tenn., said Aug. 24 that he would not try to stop the filibuster against the compromise. Baker feared the agreement with McClure could shift funding away from the Clinch River breeder reactor in his state to some other breeder project. Baker's announcement was significant, because without his help, supporters would have trouble getting enough votes for cloture.

Also waivering because of the concessions to McClure were two signers of the conference report — Republican Mark Hatfield and Democrat Dale Bumpers. Both opposed the Clinch River project and had fought hard in the Energy Committee for the administration position against it. Bumpers told Congressional Quarterly it was "unbelievable" that Carter would promise to spend $1.5 billion on a type of reactor Carter opposed.

McClure Compromise

Just what Carter and McClure had agreed on was the subject of some dispute.

According to Michael D. Hathaway, legislative assistant to McClure, the agreement postponed the decision to terminate or construct the breeder reactor at Clinch River, Tenn., until March, 1981. In the meantime, work would continue on design of Clinch River, and components for the project would continue to be purchased. At the same time, government researchers would try to come up with another, more modern type of breeder reactor that would not use plutonium or, if plutonium were the fuel, would be designed to prevent its diversion to nuclear weapons. One of the reasons Carter had opposed the Clinch River project was his fear that the plutonium would be used to make nuclear bombs.

Then, according to Hathaway, one of four options would be chosen in 1981: construction of Clinch River; cancellation of Clinch River and construction of the more modern breeder; construction of both projects or construction of neither.

COMPROMISE'S PROS AND CONS

As the date neared for a floor vote on the gas bill, it became clear that nobody really liked the compromise.

Even supporters had little enthusiasm for the complicated bill. Carter Perkins, a vice president of Shell Oil Co., said, "It's not a good bill, but if that's all we can get, it's better than the status quo."

Congressional authors of the compromise were just as lukewarm about the product. "It's the best we can hope for," Jackson said often.

Energy Secretary Schlesinger was somewhat more enthusiastic. "On balance, this bill is good for producers, it is good for consumers and, above all, it is good for the nation itself," he said.

Opponents were vociferous in their criticism. 'It's a mess, a disaster," said Talbott Smith, an associate manager of the U.S. Chamber of Commerce.

Only heavy lobbying by the Carter administration, which touted the agreement as the key to meaningful energy legislation for the 95th Congress, gave the conference report a chance of approval. And at that point, the chances of passage did not look good. *(Lobbying, box, next page)*

Uncertainties Spur Debate

Voting on the natural gas bill posed an "interesting Catch-22 situation" for senators, Dale Bumpers, told his colleagues in a Senate floor speech Sept. 12.

"It does not make any difference how you vote," Bumpers said. "You are going to get it. Gas prices are going to go up if we defeat the bill, and they are going to go up if we pass the bill. You just book that."

Except for those higher prices, little else related to the gas compromise could be booked with certainty, either by supporters or opponents. But the difficulties of predicting the future did not stop either side from trying.

Depending on whom one believed, the bill would either increase gas production, or slow it down; aid the dollar, or harm it; curb inflation, or fan it; encourage industry to use more gas, or prompt switches to oil; be easier to administer than existing law, or spawn a regulatory nightmare.

The crystal ball was even cloudier after Jan. 1, 1985, when price controls would expire. The predictions on the charts and diagrams did not extend beyond that date.

The Administration Line

The most elaborate arguments for the gas compromise were expounded by the Carter administration.

As lobbying for the bill intensified, administration officials emphasized the link between the gas bill and the ailing dollar.

"Unless Congress acts soon on a natural gas bill," President Carter wrote in an Aug. 31 letter to senators, "the world will remain convinced of our unwillingness to face the energy problem, with continuing uncertainties and pressures on the dollar in foreign exchange markets."

Energy Secretary Schlesinger repeatedly stressed the international aspects of the legislation. "It is a very important symbol, internationally, of America's ability to face up to its energy problems," he said in late August.

Two basic aspects of this international argument stood out: the psychological impact U.S. action on energy would have on the image of the United States abroad and the actual impact the predicted decrease in oil imports associated with the bill would have on the trade deficit.

At an economic summit in Bonn in July, Carter promised Chancellor Helmut Schmidt of West Germany, Prime Minister Takeo Fukuda of Japan and others that the United States would have in place, by the end of 1978, a plan to cut imports by 2.5 million barrels of oil per day by 1985. Left vague was how the reduction would be accomplished, but administration officials believed passage of the gas bill would be a step in that direction.

The picture of the United States taking direct action on energy was supposed to shore up the dollar in international money markets, which in turn would slow domestic inflation, according to the administration. "At present, every 1 percent decline in the dollar's value against the currencies of the countries from whom we import adds .1 percent to the consumer price index," Carter told senators in the letter.

But the validity of these claims of a psychological boost to the dollar were challenged by opponents of the compromise. "We might as well pass a blank sheet of paper and just write 'energy bill' across the top of the sheet of paper and hope to fool somebody," said Russell B. Long, D-La., chairman of the Senate Finance Committee and one of the bill's powerful opponents. "What good will it do us to pass such a bill in the hope of fooling some foreigner?"

But the brunt of the opponents' criticisms were against the second part of the administration's argument: that passage of the bill would cut oil imports.

White House Lobbyists Employ the Hard Sell . . .

On the afternoon of Aug. 28, two dozen executives from major paper, textile and glass companies crowded into the Roosevelt Room in the White House to hear the hard sell for the natural gas pricing bill.

Some of the executives were dead set against the bill. Others were ambivalent. Not one could be counted on as a solid supporter.

First, according to the notes taken by one man who was there, Energy Secretary James R. Schlesinger, using multi-colored charts and new figures on gas production developed by his department, described the substance of the legislation (HR 5289).

Next, G. William Miller, the ostensibly independent chairman of the Federal Reserve Board, argued that passage of the compromise bill — any bill, really — was essential to the stabilization of the value of the dollar against foreign currencies.

Finally, an hour or so into the meeting, the Carter administration's super salesman took the floor. It was a "time for candor," Robert S. Strauss, the president's all purpose adviser, told the businessmen, and he was not about to pretend that the compromise bill was first-rate legislation. But, he went on, "it no longer makes a difference whether the bill is a C-minus or an A-plus. Certainly, it is better than a zero, and it must pass."

Then, in the same folksy style he used to raise money for George McGovern in 1972 and to win votes for Jimmy Carter in 1976, in the same Texas drawl with which he spoke to Japanese negotiators on trade policy and labor leaders on inflation, Strauss made his pitch.

"This is close enough," he asserted, "so a half-dozen bankers I had in this morning and the people in this room could pass or defeat the bill."

At least some of the executives must have been impressed. Those from the glass and paper companies remained opposed to the bill, but their opposition seemed somewhat muted after the session at the White House. Some of those from the textile industry switched to active support for the administration's position.

That meeting was one of a dozen held in the White House with key industrial consumers of natural gas in the three weeks before the bill was brought up on the Senate floor Sept. 11.

There were similar sessions, for instance, with representatives of the insurance, steel, automobile, construction and aerospace industries. A group of bankers had lunch with President Carter in the family dining room. One hundred thirty of the most ardent industrial opponents of the bill were called to the East Room on Sept. 6.

The meetings were the cornerstone of the White House effort to win passage of the natural gas bill, the focus of the most extensive administration lobbying on a piece of domestic legislation since Carter took office.

By all accounts, the lobbying was effective. In late August, only a handful of important businessmen could be counted on to support the legislation. On Sept. 11, the Department of Energy supplied all senators with a list of 55 major industrial and financial corporations and 20 trade associations that were backing the bill.

Administration Strategy

The administration's basic problem was that the bill that came out of conference committee was the product of so many compromises that it had a wealth of natural opponents and no strong supporters. Therefore, according to administration officials, the strategy, designed primarily by Schlesinger, Strauss and Vice President Walter F. Mondale, was to mount a campaign to neutralize the opposition, while pleading for support on the grounds of national prestige and loyalty to the president.

The day-to-day tactics were planned by a group of ranking aides from the White House and the Department of Energy, who met every weekday morning from mid-August on in the White House office of Frank B. Moore, assistant to the president for congressional liaison.

The regulars at the 8:30 a.m. meetings were Hamilton Jordan, the president's chief political adviser; Anne Wexler, special assistant for political matters; Stuart E. Eizenstat, head of the domestic policy staff; Gerald Rafshoon, the president's media adviser; three top officials from the Department of Energy; one of Strauss's assistants, and two of Mondale's aides, William C. Smith and Gail L. Harrison. Danny C. Tate, the White House's chief Senate lobbyist, usually presided over the meetings and William H. Cable, the lobbyist assigned to the House, normally attended.

Participants at the meetings said that most of the time was spent deciding which senators should be approached by Strauss, which by Schlesinger, which by Mondale and which by the president himself.

Many uncommitted senators reported receiving repeated calls from each of them. "It's been Carter, Schlesinger, Strauss, Mondale and then they start all over again," said an aide to Sen. Patrick J. Leahy, D-Vt.

Sen. John C. Culver, D-Iowa, visited Alaska over Labor Day weekend and reportedly received a call from Carter on the natural gas issue at 5 a.m. Alaska time.

All told, a White House spokesman said, the president telephoned 26 senators that weekend. The following weekend, during breaks in the Middle East summit talks, he called several more from Camp David.

Once the bill hit the Senate floor, Mondale began to spend most of his time in the Capitol, buttonholing senators on the floor and calling them into his private office just off the Senate chamber. Mondale was given much of the credit for swinging Sen. Edmund S. Muskie, D-

The Department of Energy estimated that the gas bill would cut oil imports by 1.4 million barrels per day by 1985. This was based on the assumption that an additional 2 trillion cubic feet (tcf) of gas annually would be available in the lower 48 states, plus additional supplies from Alaska of about another .8 tcf annually. Roughly translated, each 1 tcf of gas would provide energy equivalent to that from about 500,000 barrels of oil per day, thus leading to the prediction of savings of 1.4 million barrels of imported oil per day.

Though it appeared straightforward, the equation was based on a long string of assumptions, each of which was at-

. . . To Win Senate Support for Natural Gas Bill

Maine, the influential chairman of the Budget Committee, to the administration's point of view.

"They don't talk about the merits of the bill," one senator said. "They tell you that the president needs a bill to pass to save face politically and that the country needs it for international prestige."

But, most of all, the administration's strategy was to seek support from special interest groups that could, in turn, put pressure on senators to back the bill. Wexler was in charge of finding out from senators the interest groups that were leaning most heavily on them, and it was representatives from those groups who were invited to the White House.

Entire industries were split. Some important oil companies, like the Atlantic-Richfield Corp., agreed to support the bill, and others, like Exxon, were persuaded to remain neutral. Some oil companies, like Amoco, continued to oppose the bill.

The steel industry and the automobile manufacturers were also divided, and many important financial institutions, including the Manufacturers Hanover Trust Co. and the Bank of America, came out for the president. The farm lobby was also split, with the American Farm Bureau Federation, for instance, opposing the bill, and the National Grange supporting it.

The divide-and-conquer tactics showed results. A ranking congressional staff member noted, for example, that Sen. Robert P. Griffin, R-Mich., could not support the bill as long as all the major automobile makers were in opposition, but once the Chrysler Corp. announced its support, Griffin, too, felt free to do so.

Opposition Strategy

Opponents of the bill were an unusual coalition of senators and interest groups. Some of them believed that the compromise bill would not lift price regulations on natural gas fast enough while others felt it would allow gas prices to rise too fast.

For example, Sen. Russell B. Long, D-La., one of the most ardent supporters of deregulation of gas prices, met regularly to plot strategy with Sens. James Abourezk, D-S.D., and Howard M. Metzenbaum, D-Ohio, who led a filibuster in 1977 against deregulation legislation. *(1977 Almanac p. 735)*

Other senators who worked to round up votes against the bill included Edward M. Kennedy, D-Mass.; Howard H. Baker Jr., R-Tenn., the minority leader; John Tower, R-Texas, and Clifford P. Hansen, R-Wyo.

The interest groups working against the bill were equally unlikely bedfellows. Amoco officials, for instance, were working hand-in-glove with James Flug, director of Energy Action, an organization devoted to representing consumer interests against those of the oil companies. Lobbyists for the Chamber of Commerce of the United States consulted regularly on tactics with representatives of the AFL-CIO and the United Auto Workers. George Meany, president of the AFL-CIO, and Douglas A. Fraser, president of the UAW, wrote all senators urging defeat of the bill, primarily on the ground that it would be too costly to consumers.

For the most part, those against the bill concentrated on maintaining their strength against administration forays. Republicans were urged not to extricate the president from his political dilemma, and efforts were made to persuade Democrats that the compromise measure was such bad legislation that they could not afford blind loyalty to the administration.

Trade-off Controversy

Throughout the late summer, reports surfaced that the administration had made improper political trade-offs to win the votes of crucial senators. All the reports were denied by administration officials.

On Aug. 23, Sen. James A. McClure, R-Idaho, said he had agreed to support the bill and left the impression that he had done so in exchange for administration support for a $417 million energy research project in his state. Carter denied any deal. *(Details, Clinch River breeder reactor, p. 684)*

On Sept. 2, *The Detroit News* reported that Sen. Paul Hatfield, D-Mont., had been offered a federal judgeship if he would vote for the natural gas bill. Hatfield and Jody Powell, the White House press secretary, said there was no truth to the report.

On Sept. 7, *The Washington Post* reported that the administration had promised tax relief, protection against imports and other aid to steel and textile manufacturers in order to obtain their support for the bill. The next day, the Post printed a letter from Strauss in which he called the allegation "so far from the truth as to do disservice not only to me but to the nation."

Rep. Clarence J. Brown, R-Ohio, ranking Republican on the House Subcommittee on Energy and Power, took note of alleged "threats, promises and warnings" in a letter he sent to more than 100 corporate officials. He urged the businessmen "not to be cajoled into silence or coerced into support by misinformation, threats of retaliation or untoward offers of reward."

Brown then charged in his letter that Schlesinger had warned industrial users of natural gas that they would lose their right to make emergency gas purchases from the intrastate market, which had to be approved by the independent Federal Energy Regulatory Commission, if the bill were defeated. Schlesinger said that he had not made such a threat.

tacked by the bill's opponents. The disputes spilled over into such predictions as how much domestic gas would be produced; what types of wells would provide it, which would determine price; what the average gas price would be; what the price of other fuels, such as oil and coal, would be.

Current Situation

Earlier legislation and court rulings going back to 1938 had created two separate markets for natural gas in the United States. Gas produced and sold within the same state was not federally regulated and was known as intrastate gas. Gas sold across state lines was federally regulated, by the Federal Energy Regulatory Commission, and was known as interstate gas.

Because producers had been able to get higher prices in the intrastate market, where the price was not regulated, they tended to sell the gas there. About 40 percent of domestic gas was sold on the intrastate market. This had led to plentiful and even surplus supplies in producing states such as Louisiana, and shortages in states such as North Carolina, which bought on the interstate market.

Both those favoring price regulation and those opposing it recognized the problem caused by a dual market. But the two sides favored different solutions.

One proposed solution had been to extend federal controls to the intrastate market, thus removing the advantage of selling within producing states. But producers resisted this concept, preferring a different solution. They favored removal of price controls from the interstate market so those buyers could compete equally for gas supplies with intrastate users.

The Carter administration initially took the first approach and proposed in the 1977 energy plan to extend federal controls to intrastate markets. The ceiling price would have been raised to equal the cost of domestic crude oil, estimated at $1.75 per thousand cubic feet (Mcf).

The House basically agreed with Carter. But the Senate took the opposite approach and voted to lift price controls from the interstate market within five years.

The conference agreement combined the two solutions.

Production and Supply

The art of predicting what supplies would be available if the bill were passed was so uncertain that analysts came up with no less than six estimates of 1985 supplies. They ranged from the Independent Gas Producers Committee's prediction of 5 trillion additional cubic feet annually, to the Energy Department's 2 tcf, to the more conservative Congressional Budget Office's estimate of .7 to .8 tcf in additional supplies.

The new gas from Alaska, which the administration estimated at 800 billion cubic feet annually, was counted in the total new gas from the bill because of price subsidies the bill provided for Alaska gas. The higher priced Alaska gas would be rolled into the price of all gas, forcing all users to share the cost burden.

The administration assumed that the intrastate market could provide an additional .7 to 1 tcf annually, without additional discoveries. In other words, the administration thought that much gas was being held back from the interstate market because the price was not high enough. As evidence, they noted the price of intrastate gas had dropped from an average of $1.85 per Mcf in early 1977 to $1.75 per Mcf in early 1978.

Another assumption by the Department of Energy and the administration was that the higher prices would spark new drilling and production, particularly of gas found below 15,000 feet. The price of gas from these deep reservoirs and other expensive, hard-to-reach areas would be deregulated by the bill within one year of enactment.

But opponents who preferred deregulation objected to these assumptions, arguing that:

- The amount of surplus gas in the intrastate market was vastly overestimated.
- Producers would be discouraged from drilling, not encouraged to drill by the new laws, because the price through 1985 was not high enough, and complying with federal regulations would be costly. Besides, producers would not know when they started drilling what category of gas the government would decide their new wells fell into. That determined the price. The bill set up 17 categories of new gas.
- The ceiling price meant that interstate buyers would be limited in their ability to outbid intrastate buyers.

Consumer and labor groups that opposed the bill also questioned claims that it would increase supplies. Instead of encouraging use of gas, they said the jump in price of 250 percent by 1985 would cause users to switch from gas to oil. This would increase oil imports, not curb them, they argued.

Price

Consumer groups opposing the bill were sharply critical of the effect the higher gas prices would have on low-income families. The Carter administration believed that higher prices were an effective way to increase production and encourage conservation.

But groups such as the Consumer Federation of America disagreed. "Experience since 1970 demonstrates that even 100 percent price increases have failed to yield increased production," according to the federation. "For billions of dollars more, we get less."

The administration and congressional proponents of the gas compromise said they had cushioned residential users from higher prices by a provision called "incremental pricing." The highest price gas would be newly discovered gas, and certain industrial users, such as those using gas as boiler fuel, would bear this higher cost initially.

But consumers pointed out that residential users would still be paying higher prices for gas than would industry.

But administration charts also showed that the estimated cost of domestic gas would still be less in 1985 than the estimated cost of oil, liquified natural gas (LNG) and other substitutes. What would happen after 1985 was an open question.

The administration also pointed out that interstate gas users were paying for high-priced LNG and other substitutes because not enough domestic gas was available. With the additional domestic gas they said would be produced and brought onto the market, those higher priced fuels could be replaced with domestic gas.

All in all, the price, as Bumpers predicted, would certainly go up. The transfer of money from consumers to producers was expected to be about $29 billion more over the next six years than under existing law, according to the Department of Energy. Other predictions ranged from $9 billion to $50 billion.

Outlook for 1985

One of the things that worried opponents of the compromise the most was what might happen in 1985, when price controls in the bill were scheduled to expire.

Opponents favoring no regulation worried that Congress and the president might continue controls beyond 1985. The bill gave them authority to reinstitute controls for one 18-month period six months after they were lifted.

Senate Floor Action

Senate floor debate on the gas bill finally began Sept. 11. Supporters of the measure averted the threatened filibuster by agreeing not to vote until Sept. 19 on the motion to send the bill back to conference committee. Opponents thought the extra time could win more votes for the recommittal motion.

But heavy White House lobbying turned the extra days of debate into an advantage for the bill's supporters.

Metzenbaum Amendment

The recommittal motion sponsored by Metzenbaum was to instruct conferees to strike all provisions relating to gas pricing, except the section allowing some higher prices across-the-board to reflect the extra cost of Alaska gas. The measure would still contain authorization for the president to allocate gas in an emergency.

Though Metzenbaum and others argued recommittal would lead to an acceptable bill, Majority Leader Robert C. Byrd, D-W.Va., and Energy Chairman Jackson insisted it would kill any chance for major energy legislation in the 95th Congress or for some time to come.

"This motion . . . would sabotage the efforts of 17 months in this Congress, the best chance we have had in more than three decades of finding a solution to our natural gas pricing problem," Byrd told the Senate.

Besides, Jackson noted, House conferees had told him that even if the bill were recommitted, they would not meet again to consider it.

As the debate droned on, speeches were made and repeated. Arguments, already hashed over during original House and Senate passage of the pricing bills and the 10 months of conference meetings, were presented again. Only a handful of senators were on the floor during most of the speechmaking and, from time to time, the number shrunk to as few as two or three.

At one point, during confusion about whose turn it was to speak, Abourezk remarked lightly, "At this point, I don't know anybody who wants to talk . . . I could make [a speech] to fill the dead air time, but I'll need to repeat it tomorrow."

During the frequent lulls in debate, conference reports on other issues and minor bills were slipped into the schedule and routinely approved.

On Sept. 19, about half an hour before the scheduled 3 p.m. vote, the Senate turned away from debate on a Department of Education and back to natural gas.

Abourezk, arguing for recommittal, called the compromise "monstrosity legislation." Kennedy, sitting beside Abourezk, rose to add his voice against the compromise, also labeling it an "absolute monstrosity. Something better can be developed" in another conference, Kennedy said.

Metzenbaum also urged recommital of "a bill . . . that everyone has agreed is not a good bill . . . The only argument that has been made for it is that it is the only bill in town."

But those favoring the compromise — and opposing recommittal — were heading into the showdown with two new supporters picked up that morning — Majority Whip Alan Cranston, D-Calif., and Sen. Maryon Allen, D-Ala., The momentum, and the vote counts, were on their side as Vice President Walter F. Mondale, in the chair, directed the clerk to call the roll. The motion to recommit failed, 39-59. *(Vote 374, p. 56-S)*

Forty-four Democrats voted against the recommittal motion, along with 15 Republicans. Those voting to recommit included 21 Republicans and 18 Democrats.

THE LAST DAY

In the days between the Sept. 19 recommittal vote and Sept. 27, the date set for the final vote on the conference report, debate on gas droned on intermittently. But generally the Senate shifted to other business, putting the gas bill aside and waiting for the scheduled vote.

"I think it sort of begs the questions to imply that this subject needs more debate," Hansen told the Senate. "If there ever were any subject that has been debated, it has to be the natural gas bill."

On Sept. 26, led by Robert Dole, R-Kansas, opponents made a second try at sending the measure back to conference. Like the first recommittal vote, the motion was to instruct the conferees to approve presidential authority to allocate gas in emergencies and to delete all pricing provisions except those relating to Alaska gas. Dole also added a clause giving priority to agricultural users.

The Senate rejected the motion, 36-55. *(Vote 404, p. 60-S)*

The Final Vote

On Sept. 27, about half an hour before the scheduled 1 p.m. vote on the conference report, the Senate turned once again to debate on natural gas pricing.

Metzenbaum recited a litany of complaints against the bill and warned the Senate this would not be the final vote on gas pricing. "No senator should yield to the temptation to believe that after today, the natural gas issue will be a thing of the past," Metzenbaum said. "It will not be, not by any means. It is an issue that will come back time and again to this body."

But Charles H. Percy, R-Ill., repeated the argument that the pending gas bill was the best possible. "It is this compromise or nothing for several years," he said.

Abourezk, who like Metzenbaum preferred price controls, told the Senate somewhat bitterly, "This has been one of the most frustrating fights I've ever been involved in." All of the senators he had talked to and told, "It's a lousy bill," had not disagreed with him, said Abourezk, who was retiring from the Senate. "Instead of arguing with me, each and every one said, 'I know, but I'm going to vote for it anyway.' "

Those who really preferred regulation but supported the compromise anyway were labeled "born again regulators" by Abourezk. Drawing smiles from Jackson and others on the floor, Abourezk said they should realize "it ain't going to help them one single bit when they have to face their constituency that is going to pay the price of this lousy, stinking natural gas bill."

When Hansen got his chance to speak, he apparently wanted to resolve some legal technicalities and asked Jackson a lengthy question that was sprinkled with editorial comments about the bill, such as how it would "swindle" the American people. Jackson, who had grinned during Hansen's speech, told him, "I enjoyed the question." Jackson started answering Hansen, but Hansen's allotted time ran out. Both men sat down without another word.

Byrd, who was a key factor in lining up votes behind the bill, called it a "legislative milestone" and "the most complex and divisive issue the Senate has faced in this 21-month session."

Jackson, speaking as the first call to vote went out, said the measure would "give us a better law" and help reduce oil imports.

The vote began, with Vice President Mondale in the chair.

There were no real surprises as the senators generally repeated the votes they had cast on the two recommittal motions.

Schlesinger walked into the visitors' gallery above the Senate floor, his pipe in his mouth. A Senate guard scurried over to tell him no smoking was allowed.

The final tally was 57-42. *(Vote 407, p. 61-S)*

The vote brought to a head a months-long ordeal for Jackson, who once told the Senate he had given "the best of my life for the last more than 12 months on the energy program — and 90 percent of that on the gas bill, working into the midnight oil."

After the vote, Jackson turned to shake hands with his two top aides, Betsy Moler and Mike Harvey, who had sat beside him in the chamber during the lengthy debate and worked many extra hours on the legislation. Then he reached across the aisle to Hansen. Metzenbaum came up to join them, grabbing elbows, shaking hands. Then Jackson moved along, greeting Abourezk with a big handshake. All were smiling.

In Mondale's office, just off the floor, the victory call was placed to Carter. Later, the president praised the Senate leaders for pursuing "one of the most difficult pieces of legislation that the Congress has ever faced in the history of our country. . . .

"I think it proves to our nation and to the rest of the world that we in this government, particularly the Congress, can courageously deal with an issue and one that tests our national will and our ability."

The Last Lap

Even before the final Senate vote, Speaker O'Neill was marshaling his forces in the House to push the energy package through.

The Speaker appointed a 40-member task force to shepherd the measure, and named Rep. Phil Sharp, a 36-year-old Democrat from Indiana, to head the lobbying effort. The job of the task force was to provide rapid, accurate information about the energy bill.

Opponents of the gas bill in the House, as in the Senate, were an unlikely coalition of conservatives favoring an end to controls on gas prices and liberals supporting tight regulation.

For example, Minority Leader John J. Rhodes, R-Ariz., was working against the bill with the man who narrowly lost the 1977 race for majority leader, Phillip Burton, D-Calif. Clarence Brown of Ohio continued the alliance he formed on the conference committee with Connecticut Democrat Toby Moffett, even though Republican Brown wanted controls lifted and Moffett wanted regulation to continue.

THE FINAL HOURS

The last lap for the energy bill began the morning of Thursday, Oct. 12, when the Senate took up the conference report on energy taxes. Quick approval was expected so the tax report and the four other bills cleared by the Senate could be put before the House Rules Committees. Approval from Rules, which was meeting that morning on the other side of the Capitol, was needed before a final House floor vote.

But Abourezk had other ideas. Senate action on the tax bill gave Abourezk one last shot at the natural gas pricing bill. As long as the Senate vote was delayed, House leaders would have an incomplete version of the package they wanted to put before the House. That meant delays in the House vote on natural gas pricing, which might help opponents.

When someone made the routine request that the reading of the bill be dispensed with, Abourezk shouted, "I object." What followed was a one hour and 15 minute recitation by the clerk. Abourezk's efforts forced Majority Leader Byrd, anxious to vote on other bills, to withdraw the bill from the floor. Byrd also filed a cloture petition to limit debate, which was to be voted on Saturday. The Senate then went on to other business.

But over in the House Rules Committee room, that was a minor irritant compared to the major problem looming before those seeking a single vote on the five-part energy package. Opponents of the gas bill were pushing Rules to reject the packaged bill, believing they had a better chance to defeat the gas bill with a separate vote.

But after an all day session, neither side had won. A motion to keep the package intact and a motion to allow it to be split both failed on a 8-8 tie.

But the next day, Oct. 13, the panel voted 9-5 to approve the rule permitting only one vote.

B.F. Sisk, D-Calif., one of three Rules Committee Democrats who voted with Republicans against the rule Oct. 12, was lobbied heavily by the House Democratic leadership and the Carter administration. He voted for the rule Oct. 13.

Two other Democrats, Shirley Chisholm, D-N.Y., and Gillis W. Long, D-La., who voted against the rule on Oct. 12, softened their position Oct. 13 and voted "present."

Later, Clarence Brown blamed Sisk's reversal on "probably the most pressurized arm twisting we have seen since President Carter took office."

Rule Floor Vote

Later in the afternoon of the 13th, in a dramatic 207-206 vote, the House agreed to consider the five parts as one package. *(Vote 806, p. 230-H)*

The victory for the president came only after several members voted late or switched their votes. When Millicent Fenwick, R-N.J., went to the well of the House to change her vote, the tally was 207-206. But Fenwick picked up an orange card, changing her vote to "present." That tied the vote, 206-206.

Then Thomas B. Evans Jr., R-Del., voted "aye," and Speaker O'Neill banged his gavel. The single vote on the energy package was agreed to.

The vote actually was on a procedural motion, which opponents of the gas bill hoped to defeat. That would have given them a chance to try to force a separate vote on gas. The motion to actually adopt the rule providing for the single energy vote was passed by voice vote.

Clarence Brown, an ardent opponent of the gas bill, placed great significance on the vote on the rule.

"The National Energy Act passed the House [Oct. 13] by one vote," Brown said on the floor Oct. 15. "Technically, of course, the final passage vote will occur today, but I am politically correct because I am enough of a realist to know that a majority of my colleagues will find it impossible to vote against 'an energy bill,' regardless of how ill-conceived and counterproductive the bill may be."

The Filibuster

But as the House cleared one obstacle to final passage, another skirmish was developing. A group of House members — Reps. Christopher J. Dodd, D-Conn., James M. Jeffords, R-Vt., Richard L. Ottinger, D-N.Y., and others — preferred a tax credit bill (HR 112) already passed by the Senate to the one reported by the energy tax conferees. HR 112 had no credits for business and provided bigger credits for homeowners. Dodd and company wanted the House to approve that bill and drop the conference version. *(Energy taxes, below)*

They found an ally in Abourezk. As long as he delayed the Senate vote on the tax conference report, the House could not vote on a five-part package. The House group hoped the House leadership would get impatient, agree to take up HR 112 and then vote on a four-part energy package.

Abourezk began his filibuster in mid-morning Oct. 14 — after the Senate voted 71-13 for cloture. He and a few other senators continued to tie up the proceedings by demanding quorum calls and using other stalling tactics. *(Vote 493, p. 72-S)*

By late afternoon, Dodd was shuttling back and forth, carrying the message to Speaker O'Neill that Abourezk would end the filibuster as soon as O'Neill agreed to take up HR 112. But the Speaker, who had worked for months to keep the package together, wouldn't give in.

But neither would Abourezk. As evening wore on, House members clustered near the Senate floor to watch.

Majority Leader Byrd, becoming increasingly irritated, begged for an end to the filibuster. House leaders had assured him, Byrd said, his voice rising, "that in no event will they allow the House to be blackmailed into calling up HR 112 and acting on it. That bill is down the drain, dead — d-e-a-d."

O'Neill "gave me his word," Byrd said. "And the majority leader [Jim Wright, D-Texas] gave me his word."

A couple of hours later, about 12:30 a.m. Oct. 15, Abourezk finally wound down.

Calling the energy bill "extremely bad, noxious legislation," Abourezk said, "Whom it pleases I am not certain, but I know it will not please the people we are supposed to represent."

The 46-year-old senator apologized for inconveniencing his colleagues, but insisted, "I do not regret having made this effort."

Byrd thanked Abourezk "for myself and on behalf of the Senate."

The energy tax conference report was then passed, 60-17. *(Vote 511, p. 74-S)*

House Floor Debate

The House finally began to debate the energy bill about 2:45 a.m. Thomas Ashley, chairman of the Ad Hoc Energy Committee, led off. Only about two dozen members were on the floor. Most of them were sleeping elsewhere, having heard the arguments on the energy bill many times before.

"Millions of words have been exchanged. Millions of words have been printed.... Now is the time to declare," Ashley said, aware there was little left to say. "We have an energy bill which can be translated into a comprehensive national energy policy," he said. Later, he called it "an initial foundation for a national energy policy." "This is the best thing we could come up with," said Staggers.

Opponents were harsh in their criticism of the natural gas section. The gas bill, charged John Anderson, became "merely a convenient vehicle for the president to prove his supposed new dynamism, macho and legislative competence....

"The bill is, indeed, a marvel of tangled regulations and bureaucracy at its worse."

Brown of Ohio accused the White House of unfair lobbying tactics. "In mid-August, the smart money was betting that Congress would vote down the natural gas legislation. But that was before the White House invited the chief executive officers of major U.S. corporations to Washington for a little straight talk about the realities of doing business in a federally regulated environment," he said. Brown charged that business leaders were "threatened, promised and cajoled into passive opposition, silence or grudging support of this legislation."

The arguments continued through the scheduled four hours of debate.

When the time for a vote came, the leadership asked for a quorum call first, giving the scattered members an extra 15 minutes to get to the floor. Finally, about 7:30 a.m., with Energy Secretary James R. Schlesinger looking on from the gallery, the House voted 231-168 for the five-part energy bill. *(Vote 824, p. 234-H)*

Energy Taxes

Progress on energy taxes was even slower than on the gas bill.

Tax conferees held no meetings between Dec. 7, 1977, and July 13, 1978, primarily because Russell Long, chairman of the Senate Finance Committee, insisted that the gas pricing controversy be resolved before the tax issues were settled. After that, the conferees did not meet again until Sept. 29.

Largely responsible for the tax hangup was the crude oil equalization tax, which Carter had dubbed the centerpiece of his program. The tax would raise the controlled price of American-produced oil to world levels over three years. Designed to stimulate energy conservation, the tax would drive up prices of all petroleum-related goods. Economists had estimated that it would boost gasoline prices by about seven cents a gallon.

Under Carter's proposal, revenue from the tax would be rebated to the public, though Long and other legislators argued that the money should be applied toward more energy production instead.

'Dead Horse'

Chances for passage of the tax had never looked very good and looked bleaker and bleaker as the year wore on.

In March, Long announced that the crude oil tax could not pass the Senate in 1978 "under any imaginable set of circumstances."

". . .[T]he White House is beating a dead horse when they are talking about that crude oil equalization tax," Long said. He said outraged public reaction to the stiff increases in Social Security taxes passed by Congress in 1977 made passage of the oil tax impossible in an election year.

Energy Chairman Jackson was not quite so negative at that stage when asked if he agreed with Long's assessment of the situation. "Clearly, the only honest answer I can give is that taxes at this stage of the election year are very difficult," Jackson said.

At the same time, Toby Moffett, generally a strong supporter of the president's tax program, was quoted as saying the crude oil tax was " dead as a door nail."

PREPARATION FOR THE SUMMIT

Despite the gloomy predictions from Capitol Hill about the crude oil tax's fate, the administration was reluctant to give it up.

The president was scheduled to go Bonn, West Germany, July 16 and 17 for an economic summit conference with other western leaders. He would have liked nothing better than to arrive with positive news on the oil tax.

Aware that leaders of other western nations were insisting that the president take action to cut heavy U.S. oil imports, congressional leaders tried to arrange things so Carter could at least claim to be making progress.

The July 12 remarks by French President Valery Giscard D'Estaing in the Paris newspaper *Le Monde* appeared typical of the attitude of western leaders.

"At the present time," Giscard said, "an important reduction in [U.S.] oil imports is the precondition for an improvement in the world economy . . . In my view, this is the most important single source of upheaval in the worldwide network of trade and payments."

Hoping to put on a good front for the summit, Senate and House energy tax conferees met July 13. The meeting was intended at least in part to show a skeptical world that Carter's plan was not dead.

But the session produced few signs of life for the taxes. No decisions were made, and there was no significant debate. Several conferees suggested the main Carter energy taxes were dead, especially in light of the nation's burgeoning "taxpayer's revolt."

INSULATION, SOLAR CREDITS

As the crude oil tax languished and debate on the gas bill droned on, proponents of the less controversial pieces of the energy tax bill grew increasingly concerned.

Included in the measure were tax credits for homeowners and businesses that installed solar energy collectors, insulation and other energy-saving devices. Proponents of those credits argued that they were being "held hostage" to the crude oil tax and that the impasse had disillusioned and created hardships for homeowners who had made improvements on the assumption that they would be eligible for the credits.

In an effort to liberate the solar credits, a group of senators, led by Gary Hart, D-Colo., moved in August to tack them onto a minor tax bill (HR 112). On Aug. 23, by voice vote, the Senate agreed.

In addition to creating hardships for homeowners, Hart argued, Congress' inaction had had a "devastating effect"on the solar industry. Business had dropped since the announcement of Carter's energy plan in April, 1977, because consumers were waiting for Congress to act before investing in expensive solar equipment.

He estimated that the amendment would cost $978 million a year.

Gravel's Maneuvers

Debate on the bill was prolonged because of an attempt by Mike Gravel, D-Alaska, to attach tax breaks for producers of energy to Hart's amendment.

The provisions in Gravel's amendment had been passed by the Senate in 1977 as part of the energy tax bill, as had the provisions Hart proposed. And they were stalled in conference along with the insulation and tax credits.

HR 112, the tax bill being used as the vehicle for the solar and insulation credits, had been reported from the Finance Subcommittee Gravel chaired. That bill, which passed the House Feb. 28 under suspension of the rules, reduced from 4 percent to 2 percent the excise tax on investment income of private foundations.

Hart moved to table Gravel's amendment. The motion was agreed to 53-43. *(Vote 350, p. 52-S)*

Gravel then reintroduced his amendment after adding to it provisions giving credits for gasohol production and small hydropower projects. That amendment was defeated, 42-54. *(Vote 351, p. 53-S)*

The Hart amendment and the bill then were passed by voice vote.

Provisions

The Hart amendment provided tax credits for installation in principal residences of conservation or solar or renewable source energy equipment.

A tax credit would be subtracted from the amount due the government after a tax had been computed. The credits would be applicable to equipment installed between April 20, 1977, the date of the president's energy message, and Dec. 31, 1985. Credits could not be refunded but could be carried forward for two years if they were not used in the year earned.

For solar and other renewable source energy equipment, the amendment allowed a maximum credit of $2,200. For up to $2,000 in expenses, a homeowner could take a 30 percent credit ($600 maximum), plus a 20 percent credit on expenses between $2,000 and $10,000 ($1,600 maximum).

Qualifying for the credit would be equipment for:

- Solar heating, cooling and hot water heating, including passive solar (building design);
- Wind energy for non-business residential purposes;
- Geothermal.

For residential energy-conserving improvements, a maximum $400 credit would be allowed. For up to $2,000 in expenses, a homeowner could take a 20 percent credit.

Improvements qualifying for the residential energy conservation credit were:

- Insulation;
- Replacement boilers or furnaces;
- Boilers or furnaces replaced to reduce fuel consumption;
- Devices to modify flue openings to increase efficiency;
- Electrical or mechanical furnace ignition systems to replace pilots;
- Storm or thermal windows or doors;
- Automatic energy-saving setback thermostats;
- Caulking or weatherstripping of doors or windows;
- Heat pumps to replace electric resistance heating systems;
- Meters that displayed the cost of energy use;
- Replacement fluorescent lighting systems;
- Evaporative cooling devices;
- Space heating devices, other than fireplaces, designed to burn wood or peat.

CONFERENCE ACTION

It was not until after the Sept. 27 Senate vote on gas that conferees again turned their attention to energy taxes. By then the crude oil tax was considered officially dead.

On Sept. 29, the conference met but reached no agreement.

Insulation, Solar Credits

After two long days of meetings Oct. 3 and 4, the conferees agreed on a tax credit for homeowners who insulated their houses and for homes and businesses that installed solar heating devices. The maximum credit agreed on was $300.

This was $100 less than approved earlier by both House and Senate and by the Senate as part of HR 112. However, the amount was not in dispute among the conferees who on their own decided to cut back in order to reduce the cost of the bill to the government. Critics of the credit had argued that homeowners should not receive a tax break for doing something they probably would do anyway.

The credit would be equal to 15 percent of the first $2,000 spent by homeowners on insulation, storm windows, caulking, weatherstripping and other specified energy-saving measures. It would be available for improvements made between April 20, 1977, and 1985.

Homeowners who installed solar, wind or geothermal energy equipment would be eligible for a maximum credit of $2,200, also retroactive to April 20, 1977. For up to $2,000 in expenses, a homeowner could take a 30 percent credit, plus a 20 percent credit on expenses between $2,000 and $10,000.

Credits for improvements made in 1977 would be claimed on 1978 tax returns.

Conferees also agreed on a non-refundable 10 percent credit for businesses effective Oct. 1, 1978.

The credit would be available for boilers, burners for combustors other than boilers, geothermal power equipment, not including turbines or generators, equipment for producing synthetic gas, pollution control equipment required by regulation, solar or wind energy equipment and equipment for heat recovery, recycling, shale oil production and geopressurized methane production.

The conferees adjourned at 10 p.m. Oct. 4 after the House conferees adopted, 18-6, a package of provisions that eliminated an industrial use tax on oil and retained a gas guzzler tax that would begin with 1980 model cars that used excessive amounts of fuel.

On Oct. 12, the conferees finally completed their work and reported the bill (H Rept 95-1773). They agreed to drop the proposed tax on industrial use of oil and natural gas, but retained the gas guzzler tax.

FINAL ACTION

Senate floor action on the energy tax bill began Oct. 12, but was quickly cut short by Abourezk's filibuster attempt. Majority Leader Byrd pulled the bill from the floor, filed a cloture petition to be voted on Saturday, Oct. 14, and the Senate went on to other business. *(Details, p. 663)*

Cloture was voted early Saturday, but that did not stop Abourezk, who continued his stall into the early hours of Oct. 15 by spreading out his allotted debate time and using delaying tactics, such as quorum calls. When he finally quit, the tax bill was passed easily and was sent to the House for consideration with the rest of the energy package.

Conservation

Although generally noncontroversial, the energy conservation bill also ran into some snags. It was bogged down along with the other portions in the arguments over the gas bill. And it also had a controversial provision, approved by the Senate in 1977, that banned production of gas guzzling cars.

House and Senate conferees were in agreement that production of big cars that wasted gas should be discouraged, but they had considerable difficulty trying to decide how to do it.

The Senate wanted to ban by 1980 production of cars getting less than 16 miles to the gallon. But the House preferred President Carter's proposal to levy a tax on gas guzzlers.

The tax was conditionally approved in late 1977 by the energy tax conferees. Final agreement depended on a decision by the non-tax conferees not to endorse the Senate ban.

At a June 21 meeting of non-tax conferees, Senate members were reluctant to give up the ban when prospects were bleak at that point for congressional approval of the gas guzzler tax.

"The tax conferees have been sitting on this since last December," Energy Chairman Jackson lamented. "That tells me something. There's no real determination to do anything about the tax portion."

But House conferees, led by Thomas Ashley, argued that the Senate ban would not save gas and would penalize smaller automobile manufacturers. 'I am concerned about the major auto employer in my district," said Ashley, referring to an American Motors Co. plant in Toledo.

The impasse was fueled by the lack of firm information on how much gas either the tax or the ban would save. A Department of Energy study was inconclusive, the conferees complained.

When Sen. Howard Metzenbaum tried to use the department study to discredit the claim that the tax would save gas, John Durkin reminded Metzenbaum, "Yes, but it also says your [ban] would have zero [savings]."

In addition to the ban, the Senate wanted to change existing law to double penalties for automakers with cars that did not meet specific mileage standards.

The impasse continued until July 25, when Metzenbaum announced that he would give up his fight for the Senate terms banning production of gas guzzlers.

But that still left the question of tougher penalties.

CONFERENCE ACTION

The conferees met again on Sept. 28 and, after a full day of haggling, reached accord on tougher penalties for auto makers who produced fleets of gas guzzling cars.

The Senate conferees agreed to drop their ban on production of cars that did not meet minimum fuel consumption standards in return for an agreement by House conferees to increase penalties under an existing gas-mileage law if certain conditions were met.

The existing law, the Energy Policy and Conservation Act of 1975 (PL 94-163), penalized auto makers if their fleets had an average fuel consumption rate that exceeded the national standard. The existing standard was an average of 18 miles per gallon. It was to increase to 27.5 miles per gallon in 1985. *(1975 Almanac p. 220)*

The Senate wanted to double the penalty for not meeting the standard to force compliance. For each tenth of a mile in excess of the average, an automaker would be charged $10, up from $5, per car. But the House insisted on, and won, a provision making higher penalties dependent on certain findings. They also authorized a range of penalties, from $5 up to $10.

Michigan Democrat John Dingell resisted the tougher penalties, worried they would lead to layoffs in his district. Energy Chairman Jackson at one point whispered to a colleague, "John's like a stone wall."

As the arguing began, Dingell insisted that the increased penalties be contingent on findings by the secretary of transportation that they definitely would lead to energy savings and would not harm the economy.

"The moral equivalent of war, and we just lost it," Metzenbaum said quietly after one of Dingell's aides recited a long list of procedures necessary to meet the requirement. The reference was to Carter's description of the energy crisis.

The difficulty of showing absolutely that the penalties would result in energy savings and would not harm the economy would "drag out the hearings, literally for years, and that's not achieving the objective, which is energy savings," Metzenbaum said.

Metzenbaum then tried to define more loosely what the secretary would have to prove. He suggested the secretary need show only that the penalties would "be likely to lead to" energy savings. Others offered other phrases.

The Auction

The dickering over a few words caused Rep. Paul D. Rogers, D-Fla., to lose patience.

"What about $7.50?" Rogers asked. suggesting that conferees simply raise the $5 penalty without requiring formal findings by the secretary.

"I'll take that," Metzenbaum replied from the other end of the table.

"$7.50," announced Rogers.

"This is not an auction," grumbled Dingell.

"$7.50 is not bad," Rogers implored Dingell. "Why not, John?"

"I'll make the same offer I did with the $7.50," said Dingell, insisting on the requirement that the secretary make a substantial finding.

Just then there was a vote on the House floor. But agreement seemed imminent, and Rep. Bob Eckhardt, missing the vote, tried another phrase.

"What about 'will result in or tend to compel' substantial energy conservation?" he asked.

"Let's take 'tend to compel,' " said Rogers, looking at Dingell. "That's all right."

"That's your judgment, not mine," said Dingell.

"I'll take 'tend to compel,' " offered Metzenbaum.

"Let me just put a little paragraph on the end," said Dingell, still not willing to give in.

The impatience in the room seemed to swell. Dingell made his last stand: "My signature is not only needed on this report, but my support is needed on the gas bill."

The thinly veiled threat rankled Jackson. "In my 38 years here, I have never said my vote on one thing would affect my vote on another unrelated issue," he told Dingell.

Dingell didn't apologize.

House members returned from voting. The talk returned to words.

"Significantly encourage," suggested Rogers.

Rep. Joe Waggonner strolled back in from voting, calling out like an auctioneer, "Going up to $7.50, $8, give me $8 and a half, $9." The conferees laughed, still able to see the humor in their situation.

" How about 'affect'?" someone asked.

"Will result in or affect," said Dingell, agreeing.

"Howard?" asked Jackson.

"That's not bad," Metzenbaum replied.

A little more haggling and a phrase seemed finally to fly: "Result in or substantially further."

"Sold," said Staggers, banging his gavel.

As the meeting adjourned, someone pointed to the master draft that had the final language and said, "You better get a Xerox of that."

FINAL ACTION

Although differences over the conservation bill had been resolved by the conference, its report (S Rept 95-1294) was not filed immediately. Conferees who opposed the gas bill withheld their signatures from the report, aware that a delay in final Senate action could foul up House plans to cast a single vote on the package.

The conferees eventually relented and the report was filed Oct. 6. The Senate then adopted the conference report Oct. 9, with an 86-3 vote, sending it on to the House for consideration with the rest of the package. *(Senate vote 463, p. 68-S)*

Coal Conversion

The first piece of Carter's energy program to emerge from the conference committee was the coal conversion measure, which was reported July 13. It was a watered-down version of the president's proposed regulatory scheme to force utilities and major industries to burn coal or other fuels instead of oil and natural gas. Multiple grounds for exemptions had been included by the conferees, weakening Carter's original proposals. In addition, the tax penalties for using oil and gas, designed to accompany the coal conversion scheme, were voted down by tax conferees.

Carter supporters, like Senate Energy Chairman Jackson, argued the measure would result in savings of slightly more than one million barrels of oil per day by 1985.

But Carter critics, like ranking Energy Committee Republican Hansen, claimed the bill would save no more than 250,000 barrels of oil per day by 1985.

Harsher critics, like Dewey Bartlett, insisted that the bill was unnecessary because, where possible, industry was switching to coal already because it made better economic sense than using oil or gas. Bartlett also asserted that the measure actually would increase U.S. dependence on foreign oil, because it directed some facilities to stop burning gas by 1990, and the only other fuel some of them could burn would be oil.

Senate and House conferees reached final ageement on basic compromise principles for the coal conversion bill on Nov. 11, 1977. But the hangup over natural gas pricing threw the entire package into a freeze until June.

The conference report (S Rept 95-988) on the coal conversion bill was drafted in a rush, and it was not until July 13 that a majority of conferees from each chamber signed it. Even then, the final language of the bill and report never was discussed in an open meeting, a fact that outraged House Republican conferees, all of whom refused to sign it.

The bill went to the Senate floor July 14. The Democratic leadership hoped to get quick Senate passage before Carter's economic summit conference July 16 in West Germany. The hope was to allay foreign fears that the United States was doing nothing to curb its massive oil imports, which had been blamed for a number of worldwide economic problems.

But Harrison Schmitt — one of six senators, all Republicans, who voted against the bill — forced a delay in the vote until July 19 by insisting upon time to ask extensive questions. Majority Leader Byrd called Carter in Bonn late July 14 to assure him the measure would pass the coming week.

The conference report was finally adopted July 18 by a lopsided 92-6 vote. *(Vote 215, p. 35-S)*

Utility Rate Reform

There was little debate in 1978 over the utility rate reform section of the energy plan because conferees had resolved most of the questions in 1977. All that remained was for staff to put the agreement into legislative language and to draft the conference report.

In November and December, 1977, House conferees on the bill gave in to Senate demands that the states retain the power to force electric utilities to reform the way they billed customers.

President Carter had proposed, and the House had passed, a series of minimal federal reforms revising utility billing practices, which the states would have been required to carry out. The reforms were designed to spread customer demand for electricity more evenly, avoiding the existing pattern of "peak" demand periods. It was hoped the change would result in energy savings and reduce the need for utility expansion.

But the Senate had argued that the proposed reforms were experimental and needed further tests of experience before they could be mandated. The Senate had also insisted that regulation of utility rates was properly a state function, not a federal one.

Although the conference agreement was softer than the House bill, its backers asserted that it was much stronger than the original Senate version. And it would guarantee, they said, that each state utility commission consider thoroughly a wide variety of innovative rate reforms.

It guaranteed that the Department of Energy could intervene before a state regulatory commission hearing on a proposed utility rate increase and made the case for rate reforms.

And it provided that, whenever consumer advocates succeeded in winning adoption of their proposed reforms, utilities would have to pick up the consumer group's expenses for making the case.

The conferees also reached the following agreements:

Wheeling. The Federal Energy Regulatory Commission (FERC) could order a utility to "wheel" power from one supplier to another, subject to tests of reasonableness.

Pooling. FERC had to review for up to one year the potential advantages of utility pooling of resources and report to the president and Congress on its findings.

Interconnection. FERC would be empowered to order utilities to interconnect their facilities and to exchange energy supplies, subject to tests of reasonableness and judicial review.

Lifeline Rates. A Senate provision was abandoned that required utilities to offer elderly persons 62 and over enough electricity to cover heating, lighting, cooking, refrigeration and other essential needs at rates no higher than that utility's lowest rate.

Final Action

Once the legislative language and the conference report were drafted, the utility rate bill ran into snags similar to those facing the conservation measure. Some conferees who opposed the natural gas pricing bill withheld their signatures from the utility rate measure, hoping to delay plans for a House vote on the whole package and possibly defeat the gas bill.

They eventually signed, however, and the report (S Rept 95-1292) was filed Oct. 6. It was passed by the Senate Oct. 9 with a 76-13 vote and then sent to the House for consideration with the rest of the energy bill. *(Senate vote 462, p. 68-S)*

Oil Reserves Plan Rejected

By voice vote, the Senate April 17 unilaterally rejected a Department of Energy plan to double the nation's strategic oil reserve capacity to one billion barrels and to limit possible sites for storage of 20 million of those barrels earmarked for use by New England.

Rejection of the plan represented less of a defeat for the Carter administration than might be assumed.

Opponents made clear they supported expansion of the strategic oil reserve, designed to stockpile oil for use in emergencies, such as interruption in foreign imports similar to the Arab embargo of 1973-74. Their opposition centered on the narrower issue of where to put New England's share of the stockpile.

Under the 1975 Energy Policy and Conservation Act (PL 94-163), major changes in government fuel price or allocation programs had to be submitted to Congress. Unless either house passed a resolution of disapproval within 15 days of submission, the plans — termed "energy actions" — took effect. The strategic oil reserve expansion plan, designated "Energy Action DOE Number One," was submitted to Congress April 4 and would have taken effect April 20. *(1975 law, 1975 Almanac p. 220)*

On April 7 Sen. Edward M. Kennedy, D-Mass., filed a resolution of disapproval (S Res 429) cosponsored by all of the New England senators. They objected to terms of the plan requiring that storage sites for New England's reserves cost no more than the program's primary storage sites along the Gulf of Mexico, primarily in Louisiana.

New England is heavily dependent on imported oil and oil products. Its senators hoped to store the emergency stockpiles closer to home. They argued that the terms mandating a cost limit would, in effect, leave no alternative but to store the New England oil in Louisiana.

The Senate Energy Committee voted 16-0 April 11 to back Kennedy's resolution disapproving the plan. In its report (S Rept 95-738), the panel suggested that the administration submit a second plan limited to expanding the strategic oil program capacity and omitting restrictions on New England's reserve sites.

Continental Shelf Leasing Bill Cleared

The first overhaul of offshore oil and gas leasing laws in 25 years was signed by President Carter Sept. 18 (S 9 — PL 95-372).

The long-sought changes were given final approval by the House Aug. 17, on a 338-18 vote, and by the Senate Aug. 22, on an 82-7 vote. *(House vote 634, p. 180-H; Senate vote 347, p. 52-S)*

The bill was designed to foster competition for leases and increase state participation in federal leasing decisions. Restrictions on drilling and production were tightened to protect the environment.

Congress had been struggling for almost four years to reach agreement on the controversial legislation, which had been bitterly opposed by the oil industry. However, the latest compromise was generally accepted by most major oil companies, environmentalists and the Carter administration.

The congressional action came within days of the first commercial discovery of oil and gas deposits off the Atlantic coast. Texaco Inc. announced Aug. 14 it had struck gas about 100 miles from Atlantic City, N.J.

It was this coming expansion of offshore drilling to the Atlantic from the Gulf of Mexico that prompted the push for reform of the Outer Continental Shelf Lands Act of 1953.

The East Coast states, protective of their healthy resort and fishing industries, sought, and won in the new law, more control over potentially harmful offshore activities.

Enactment of the new rules governing Outer Continental Shelf (OCS) exploration was expected to spur development on the Atlantic shelf, which was an extension of the continent that stretches up to 200 miles from shore. *(Map, next page)*

In particular, leasing of tracts off the coast of New England, in an area known as Georges Bank, was likely to go forward. The state of Massachusetts and a conservation group had held up scheduled 1978 leasing with successful court suits, arguing that the new law should be in place before additional drilling was allowed.

The U.S. Geological Survey had estimated that potential recoverable resources of from 10 to 49 billion barrels of crude oil and from 42 to 81 trillion cubic feet of natural gas were located on the OCS of the United States.

OCS lands began three miles from the shoreline, where state jurisdiction ended. The federally held lands had been under the jurisdiction of the Department of Interior. However, some authority for offshore energy development was transferred by the new law to the year-old Department of Energy. The energy secretary was to write many of the rules the interior secretary would have to follow in administering the law.

Background

The Senate originally passed S 9 in July 1977 by a 60-18 vote. A weaker OCS bill (HR 1614) was reported in the House, but the Rules Committee blocked floor action on the legislation during the 1977 session. *(1977 Almanac p. 662)*

In 1976, a dissatisfied House recommitted the conference report on an earlier OCS bill by a 198-194 vote. *(1976 Almanac p. 113)*

Final Provisions

As cleared by Congress, S 9 amended and modified the Outer Continental Shelf Lands Act of 1953 (PL 83-212).

Exploration and Development

Title I called for more aggressive management of the Outer Continental Shelf, submission of plans by lessees for active exploration and development of OCS tracts and more involvement of coastal states in OCS activities.

New provisions were added to the 1953 law to:

- Require the appropriate Cabinet secretary to develop a comprehensive five-year program for OCS leasing that was to consist of a schedule of proposed sales indicating the size, timing and location of activities. Considerations in developing the program were to include the relative environmental sensitivity and marine productivity of different areas and the return of a "fair market value" for the public lands leased.
- Direct the secretary to solicit recommendations regarding the leasing program from the governors of affected states and from interested federal agencies. If the recommendations were rejected, the secretary was to explain the reasons for doing so.
- Require an environmental study of each general area proposed for leasing.
- Provide for a study, review and, if necessary, revision of safety regulations to ensure safe operations on the Outer Continental Shelf.
- Provide that the interior secretary and the secretary responsible for the U.S. Coast Guard enforce the regulations, along with any other "applicable federal officials."
- Permit "any person having an interest which is or may be adversely affected" to file a suit against any person, including a government agency, for alleged violation of the act or of a lease, or against the secretary for alleged failure to perform a non-discretionary act or duty.
- Set civil penalties of up to $10,000 per day for failure to comply with the act; set criminal penalties of up to $100,000 (per day for some violations) and 10 years in prison or both for deliberate violation of the act or regulations issued under it.
- Require submission of a development and production plan for all future leases and all existing leases where no oil or gas had yet been discovered, except for leases in the Gulf of Mexico.
- Provide that the interior secretary review and approve or disapprove the plan. If a plan were not submitted or complied with, the secretary could cancel the lease.
- Provide that the plan set forth a description of the specific work to be performed; a description of all facilities and operations located on the OCS; the environmental safeguards to be implemented; all safety standards to be met; an expected rate of development and production and a time schedule for performance and any other relevant information required by the secretary.
- Required a lessee to give the secretary access to all data and information relating to OCS activities.
- Provide that the secretary share the information, except for proprietary information, with the affected states.

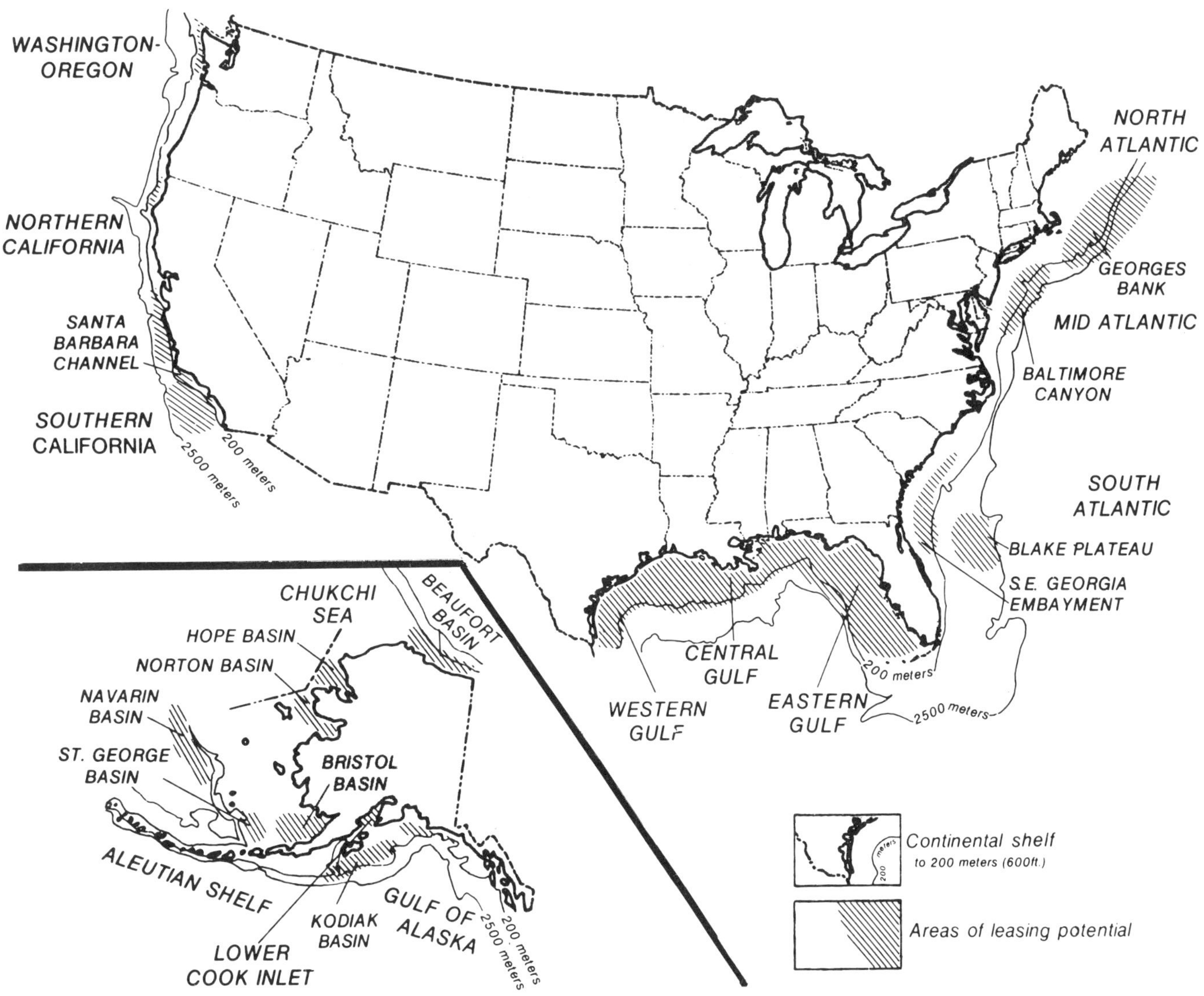

Existing provisions were amended to:

- Transfer to the energy secretary functions of the interior secretary relating to:

(1) Fostering of competition for federal leases including, but not limited to, prohibition on bidding for development rights by certain types of joint ventures.

(2) Implementation of alternative bidding systems authorized for the award of federal leases.

(3) Establishment of diligence requirements for operations conducted on federal leases including, but not limited to, procedures relating to the granting or ordering by the interior secretary of suspension of operations or production as they related to such requirements.

(4) Setting rates of production for federal leases.

(5) Specifying procedures, terms and conditions for acquisition and disposition of federal royalty interests taken in kind.

(The interior secretary retained responsibility for conducting lease sales, for monitoring the effect of exploration and development on the environment and for generally enforcing the OCS law. The interior secretary also retained authority to suspend or cancel a lease.)

- Establish a liaison committee of top Energy and Interior officials to coordinate administration of the act.
- Provide that a lease be suspended or canceled, after suspension, if there was threat of harm or damage to life (including fish or other aquatic life), to property, to any mineral deposits, to the national security or to the marine, coastal or human environments.
- Provide that a lease be suspended or canceled if the lessee failed to comply with the terms of the lease or act.
- Provide new bidding procedures to be used in addition to cash bonus bids with a royalty of at least 12.5 percent, including variable royalty, variable net profit, fixed net profit and work commitment bidding procedures. The secretary was authorized to use other, unspecified systems if, after 30 days, neither house of Congress had passed a resolution disapproving the alternative system.
- Mandate that new bidding systems be used in at least 20 percent and not more than 60 percent of the tracts offered for leasing in all OCS areas during each of the next five years.
- Allow leases, currently set for five-year terms, to have a term of 10 years where the secretary found the longer pe-

riod to be necessary in areas with "unusually deep water or other unusually adverse conditions."

- Require that lessees offer for purchase at least 20 percent of OCS-recovered crude oil or natural gas to small refiners.
- Permit the attorney general, in consultation with the Federal Trade Commission, to conduct a review of lease sales and make recommendations as to whether the sales indicated a situation inconsistent with antitrust laws. If the secretary rejected the attorney general's recommendations, the secretary would have to notify the lessee and the attorney general of the reasons for his decision.
- Retain language in the 1953 law which provided that: "Any agency of the United States and any person authorized by the secretary may conduct geological and geophysical explorations in the Outer Continental Shelf, which do not interfere with or endanger actual operations under any lease maintained or granted pursuant to this act, and which are not unduly harmful to aquatic life in such area."
- Require that a lessee submit to the secretary a plan for exploring a leased OCS tract that included a schedule of anticipated exploration activities; a description of equipment to be used; the general location of each well to be drilled and other information deemed pertinent by the secretary.

Offshore Oil Pollution Fund

To deal with spills from offshore production and transportation of oil, a new Title III was added to:

- Establish an Offshore Oil Pollution Compensation Fund of up to $200 million, funded by a three-cent per barrel fee on oil produced on the OCS.
- Provide that owners and operators of offshore facilities and vessels have unlimited liability for cleanup of oil spills and a liability for damages of up to $35 million for offshore facilities and of $300 per gross ton, up to $25,000, for vessels.
- Authorized the president to clean up an oil spill, using money from the fund, if the owner or operator responsible would not clean up or had not been identified.
- Provide that damaged parties can make claims to the fund and be paid by the fund, with the fund subsequently acquiring the claimant's rights to sue the spiller.

Fisherman's Contingency Fund

To aid commercial fishermen whose livelihood was jeopardized because of OCS activity, primarily damage to equipment, Title IV was added to:

- Establish a Fishermen's Contingency Fund of up to $1 million, with area accounts established therein of up to $100,000.
- Require each lessee to pay into the fund up to $5,000 per calendar year per lease, permit, easement or right of way.

Amendments to the Coastal Zone Management Act

Contained in Title V were amendments to the Coastal Zone Management Act of 1976 (PL 94-370) to:

- Modify the formula used to distribute OCS formula grants to base allocation of funds on new acreage leased adjacent to a coastal state (50 percent); oil and gas produced adjacent to a coastal state (25 percent); and oil and gas first landed in the coastal state (25 percent).
- Ensure that no state eligible under the existing formula would receive less than 2 percent of the total appropriation. States not eligible under the formula, but which were in the region of affected coastal states, would be entitled to receive 2 percent of the total if the secretary of commerce determined that the state was affected by OCS activity and could use the money as required by the coastal zone act.
- Provide that no state could receive more than 37.5 percent of the total.
- Authorize appropriation of $130 million annually for the OCS formula grants.
- Authorize appropriations of $5 million annually to help states carry out their responsibilities under the OCS act.

House Floor Action

After accepting a hodgepodge of amendments that calmed many critics, the House Feb. 2 voted 291-91 to approve HR 1614. *(Vote 29, p. 10-H)*

The House Rules Committee, which had prevented the bill from reaching the House floor in fall 1977, voted 8-6 on Jan. 23 to clear the bill for floor action.

HR 1614, as passed, would increase environmental controls, provide for more state participation in federal leasing of offshore tracts, share federal revenues from lease sales with coastal states and broaden competition for leases by changing bidding procedures.

Even though the House had defeated 187-211 an industry-backed substitute on Jan. 26, adoption of the various amendments during the four days of floor debate gained the support of key opponents for final passage. *(Vote 11, p. 4-H)*

The House-passed bill was "the Breaux substitute by another name," said Rep. John B. Breaux, D-La., who had originally pushed an industry version of the legislation. "I'm very pleased," he said of the final bill.

A turning point in the House floor debate came on Jan. 31 when the chief sponsors accepted changes in the two provisions that had sparked most criticisms.

First, OCS Committee Chairman John M. Murphy, D-N.Y., and committee members did not challenge an amendment by Rep. David C. Treen, R-La., to strike the bill's separation of leases for exploration from leases for production, a procedure known as dual leasing.

Industry officials had charged that this provision, sought by the administration to open up the leasing process, would reduce incentives and cause delays in production. Treen also criticized the partnership of the federal government and private companies during the exploration stage that was called for in the bill.

After Treen's amendment was accepted by voice vote, Rep. Gerry E. Studds, D-Mass., a key supporter of the committee version of HR 1614, proposed an amendment to weaken government authority to conduct pre-lease drilling in order to discover a tract's potential. His move was an effort to defuse criticism by opponents. *(Box, next page)*

"My amendment removes the only remaining language in the bill which has been construed by some as authorizing federal exploratory drilling," Studds told the House, which accepted his amendment 328-77. *(Vote 16, p. 6-H)*

Though his amendment was modified by Treen, the effect was to return to 1953 language, which authorized the government to permit or contract for pre-lease exploration. The Studds amendment clarified that the government could not do the exploration itself, an authority implied in the 1953 act.

OCS Bill: Effective Lobbying on Both Sides

The red capital letters in the full-page newspaper advertisement were two inches high: "If dependence on foreign oil is what you want, HR 1614 will get it for you."

The National Ocean Industries Association (NOIA) wanted to be sure the House knew that NOIA's 345 members opposed pending Outer Continental Shelf (OCS) legislation, even if it cost them more than $11,000.

"Propaganda," bill supporter Rep. Gerry E. Studds, D-Mass., called the various ads. "Red herrings," he labeled their claims that the bill would lead to an imaginary outfit dubbed FOGCO, a federally operated oil and gas company.

To a House aide trying to garner support for the very complicated bill, the ads were one more headache. "You've got full-page ads, with screaming headlines, saying 'We're industry, we know this bill is going to be an unmitigated disaster,' " said the aide. "It's got to have an effect. How do you counter that sort of rhetoric?"

The members of the House Ad Hoc Select Committee on the Outer Continental Shelf eventually countered it by agreeing to take out offending sections on dual leasing and federal exploratory drilling. This defensive effort by the bill's supporters was evidence that their opponents were having some effect.

"It was a full-court press," said James Flug of Energy Action, a consumer and environmental organization, when asked about the oil and gas industry efforts against the committee bill.

Letter Writing Campaign. In addition to dramatic, full-page newspaper ads, individual companies and associations that represented them used some fairly sophisticated techniques to generate interest in the bill in districts far removed from the coast.

For example, Exxon Corporation, which refused to support even a watered down substitute proposal endorsed by most companies, sent letters to each of its stockholders explaining its opposition to HR 1614 and suggesting that letters be written to Congress. Many responded.

NOIA, with a membership that included producing companies, diving contractors, caterers, makers of drilling rigs and other support services for OCS activity, tried to capitalize on its diversity with the same sort of "grass roots" lobbying.

"This bill is so complicated," said Charlie Matthews, NOIA president. "The average member of Congress...who's not associated with the coast, not associated with this issue, well, he has so many demands, he can't know the details. I have tried to get my [member] companies to write and say, 'I'm in Oshkosh and I manufacture widgets that they use in Houston on drilling rigs. I oppose this bill.' "

Matthews also coordinated the placement of ads in a Washington newspaper by other groups, such as the Association of Diving Contractors, which also belonged to NOIA. The divers wanted to keep the Occupational Safety and Health Administration from getting jurisdiction over OCS activity, and they succeeded.

United Business Community. When the South Carolina banking community started calling Rep. John W. Jenrette Jr., D-S.C. about HR 1614, he was a little confused about why they should be interested.

"I started asking questions about dual leasing and revenue sharing, and the guy finally had to admit he was returning a favor for a fellow in Texas," said Jenrette, who voted against the position of the banking community and oil and gas interests.

"They're trying to work some trades" with votes on other bills, such as labor law, said another southern Democrat who had been contacted by local members of a national business community that was apparently united against the OCS bill.

Various segments of the energy industry had already been working together on the energy legislation before Congress. "There's a real need to be together," said Talbott Smith, associate manager of the resources and environment division of the Chamber of Commerce.

Breaux as Lobbyist. The old coalition of Republicans and southern Democrats, boosted by the solidarity of the Louisiana and Texas delegations, was operating on the OCS issue.

One of the reasons the coalition hung together on most votes was Rep. John B. Breaux, D-La. "When the issue is this complex, many members take their cues from the neighboring delegation," explained one committee aide.

"Breaux has been very effective," admitted a Carter administration lobbyist.

Administration Efforts. With the rash of votes on amendments and substitutes, both sides could claim some victories, and the administration was credited with the initial defeat of the weaker Breaux substitute, as well as with getting the bill through the reluctant Rules Committee.

"They made the difference," said a House aide, and Breaux agreed.

In 1976, when the conference report on similar OCS legislation was recommitted in the waning days of the 94th Congress, the Ford administration had been working hard against passage. *(1976 Almanac p. 113)*

The Carter administration came through quickly with separate letters from Energy Secretary James R. Schlesinger and Interior Secretary Cecil D. Andrus renewing their endorsement of the committee bill after Republicans on the House floor raised the specter of a divided administration.

Deputy Under Secretary of Interior Barbara Heller, who formerly lobbied for the Environmental Policy Center on the same issue, spent hours nursing the legislation through the House. Liaison staff from Interior and Energy, operating out of a room near the House chamber, kept a close watch on the progress.

The major criticism of the administration effort was the arrival on the Hill just before Rules action of some 50 primarily technical amendments that the adminstration wanted in the bill. Members of the Rules Committee who sought to delay floor action seized on the amendments as another reason for postponing debate.

Studds later explained his action. "You can go down in flames like we did two years ago, or you can try to get a bill that has some very good things in it," he said.

Alternative Bidding Systems

In addition to criticizing dual leasing and federal drilling, the industry and its supporters in the House had focused their attention on the bill's proposed changes in bidding procedures for OCS leases.

"We have finally got to the hub of why the major oil companies are opposed to HR 1614," Rep. William J. Hughes, D-N.J., told the House when it took up bidding changes. "It is because we are tampering with the bonus bid system. It is as simple as that. All the other is window dressing."

Under the bidding system currently used most of the time, an up-front, cash-bonus payment was required before a lease was granted. Critics said this system favored major oil companies and kept out smaller companies that could compete if the lease were based on royalties from future production instead of the early cash payment.

The committee bill had mandated the use of such alternative bidding systems at least half the time, while Breaux had sought to mandate continued use of the bonus system at least half the time.

The House eventually agreed to an amendment by Rep. David F. Emery, R-Maine, that would require use of alternatives in at least 20 per cent and up to half the sales. The amendment was a substitute for an amendment by Treen that would have simply eliminated the 50 per cent bidding requirement.

Though the 219-188 vote appeared to be a defeat for the administration and the committee, Rep. George Miller, D-Calif., a leader in the debate, had another idea. "We have the acceptance, with a Republican author, of a mandate on alternative bidding systems," Miller said later. "We never had that before." *(Vote 19, p. 6-H)*

The House had previously rejected, 196-207, a substitute proposed by Rep. Clarence J. Brown, R-Ohio, to apply alternative bidding systems to at least 10 percent and no more than 30 percent of the lease sales. *(Vote 18, p. 6-H)*

The House later strengthened its support of alternative bidding by accepting a Miller amendment that would allow the secretary of interior to decide on which tracts to use alternative systems. The amendment killed language in the committee bill that had required that the tracts be selected randomly. Under the Miller change, a secretary such as Andrus who wanted to increase the impact of alternative bidding could apply the new systems to the choice tracts. The amendment was adopted 225-174. *(Vote 23, p. 8-H)*

Revenue Sharing

Sympathetic to the problems that coastal states would face in handling OCS-related activity, the committee bill authorized grants of $125 million annually through fiscal 1984 to those states.

But the level of funding wasn't high enough for Hughes. "Tax revenues always lag behind" the impacts, he said.

Hughes broke with the committee and offered an amendment to share with the states 20 per cent of the federal revenues from OCS leasing, up to $200 million annually. The House accepted his amendment Feb. 2, 278-120. *(Vote 27, p. 8-H)*

The revenue sharing in Hughes' proposal was similar to the defeated Breaux substitute, but Hughes, like the committee bill, channeled the money through the Coastal Energy Impact Fund that was established by the Coastal Zone Management Amendments of 1976 (PL 94-370). The impact fund would direct the money toward needy areas and keep some strings on how it was used by the states, Hughes said.

Hughes also changed the formula for distributing the money. Instead of basing it half on the area leased and half on the oil and gas landed in a state, as the committee did, Hughes based the allocation half on leasing, 25 per cent on the amount of oil and gas produced offshore and 25 per cent on the amount landed onshore.

The Carter administration said the Hughes proposal was too expensive and objected to the concept of revenue sharing. However, even though the proposal called for earmarking 20 per cent of the revenues, the normal appropriations process would still have to provide the money to the states.

During the roll-call vote on the Hughes amendment, representatives huddled around the table from which Murphy was operating as floor manager for the bill. He had a copy of a Commerce Department estimate of how each state would benefit from the different formulas.

Because Hughes increased the maximum annual funding to $200 million, every coastal state was shown with an increase under his proposal. However, the percentage of the total each state would receive changed less than a percentage point.

The state with the largest share of the funds would be Louisiana, which would receive about 30 per cent.

Other Amendments Accepted

The House also adopted amendments that:

- Retained the authority in existing law to make new regulations apply to existing OCS activity from the date of the regulations. The amendment offered by Rep. John D. Dingell, D-Mich., Feb. 1 was strongly supported by the administration and was accepted by voice vote. Dingell removed new restrictions in the committee bill that allowed the application of regulations to existing leases only "where there is a finding of serious or irreparable harm or damage."
- Deleted the provision expanding the authority of the Occupational Health and Safety Administration (OSHA) to OCS activities. Rep. Hamilton Fish Jr., R-N.Y., argued that the Coast Guard, not OSHA, had necessary expertise.

"We have enough problems without bringing OSHA into the picture," said Breaux. The amendment, opposed by labor, was accepted by a standing vote, 58-23, Feb. 1.

- Clarified language in the committee bill establishing a Fishermen's Gear Compensation Fund and increased the maximum payment from the fund for a single incident from $10,000 to $75,000. The fund would be financed by annual fees of $5,000 from each offshore leasing company. The amendment, offered by Studds, was accepted by voice vote Feb. 1.
- Authorized $5 million in annual grants to states for 80 per cent grants for costs associated with their increased role in federal decisions on offshore leasing. The amendment, offered by Murphy Feb. 2, was accepted by voice vote.
- Changed the position of a lease holder seeking compensation from the federal government for a lease cancellation. The amendment, proposed Jan. 31 by Rep. Charles E. Wiggins, R-Calif., deleted the compensation formula in

the committee bill which would have subtracted revenues that a lessee received from the losses for which he could be compensated. It substituted language stating that cancellation would not foreclose claims for compensation required by the Constitution. The amendment was accepted, 208-194. *(Vote 17, p. 6-H)*

Amendments Rejected

The House rejected amendments that would have:

- Deleted the bill's requirement that offshore operators hire American citizens unless an insufficient number were qualified and available to work. The amendment, proposed by Charles W. Whalen Jr., R-Ohio, was rejected Feb. 2 118-280. *(Vote 25, p. 8-H)*
- Required that all offshore drilling rigs, platforms and other equipment be built and registered in the United States. The Murphy amendment, known as "Buy America," was rejected Feb. 2, 201-208. *(Vote 26, p. 8-H)*
- Deleted the requirement that coastal states receiving funds for OCS impacts must have a federally approved coastal zone management plan. Offered by Treen Feb. 2, it was rejected 159-230. *(Vote 28, p. 8-H)*
- Modified several provisions through a substitute for the entire bill. The substitute, offered by Fish and rejected 143-229 Jan. 26 after the vote on the Breaux substitute, would have deleted dual leasing, struck provisions expanding OSHA authority to offshore activities, and applied alternative bidding systems to 10 to 30 per cent of lease sales. *(Vote 12, p. 4-H)*

Conference Action

House and Senate conferees haggled off and on for months, starting in March and ending in July, before finally filing their conference report (S Rept 95-1091) Aug. 10.

Though the basic outlines of the two bills were similar, there were some substantive and numerous technical differences that had to be worked out. Many of the same conferees had met on OCS legislation in 1976, but the House recommitted that conference report late in the 94th Congress. *(Recommittal, 1976 Almanac p. 113)*

Federal Exploration

The most controversial provision — one that had doomed the bill in the past — was a Senate mandate that the federal government determine what oil and gas was deposited offshore before leasing the public land.

The House had refused to require federal exploration, but did retain language in the 1953 act authorizing the interior secretary to conduct "geological and geophysical explorations."

The compromise worked out by the conferees retained the exact 1953 language, dropping a House modification. Although Interior Secretary Cecil D. Andrus claimed the language gave him authority to conduct explorations, any use of the authority was almost certain to be challenged in court. The conferees did not interpret the law in their report, and the resulting ambiguity was a major reason the compromise was acceptable to some House conferees.

Bidding Procedures

Both the House and Senate modified bidding procedures in hopes of encouraging smaller, independent companies to bid on OCS leases. Critics of the current system said big, wealthy oil companies were favored by the existing requirement that bidders pay large sums in advance in order to get a lease.

Alternative bidding systems would allow a leaseholder to pay the government royalties as the oil or gas was produced from the tract, instead of paying the up-front, "cash bonus."

The House wanted such alternative systems to be used in at least 20 percent and not more than 50 percent of all lease sales during each of the next five years. The Senate wanted to mandate that alternative procedures be used in at least 50 percent of the leases offered in previously undeveloped areas.

The compromise required that alternative bidding systems be used in at least 20 percent and not more than 60 percent of the tracts offered for leasing in all OCS areas during each of the next five years.

The conferees dropped a Senate provision, added on the floor by Sen. J. Bennett Johnston, D-La., that would have required the secretary to select randomly the areas for which alternative bidding procedures would be used. Without a requirement for random selection, a secretary who favored alternative bidding could pick out the choicest tracts for alternative procedures.

The conferees also dropped a Senate provision that called for use of a dual leasing system off the coast of Alaska. Dual leasing was a new system that provided separate leases for exploration and then for development, thus giving the secretary more information before leasing for development.

Other Issues

Among other compromises, the conferees also:

- Modified a House requirement that OCS activities comply with national air quality standards. The conferees agreed that air pollution from OCS activities should be regulated when it "significantly affects the air quality of a state." The conferees said they did not intend that the air mass above the OCS meet the standards, but that it be controlled to prevent harmful effects on the air above an adjacent shoreline.
- Modified a House provision that allowed local governments, as well as states, to submit recommendations to the secretary. Local governments could still make proposals, but their comments would have to be forwarded to the secretary by the governor of the state.
- Dropped a House provision that earmarked 20 percent of federal OCS revenues for the Coastal Energy Impact Fund, a revolving fund that had given loans and bond guarantees to states providing services and facilities to support coastal energy activity. The conference report contained a standard authorization of $130 million annually for the fund, which would also provide OCS formula grants.

Final Action

House Action

The House gave final approval to the conference report on Aug. 17. The vote was 338-18. *(Vote 634, p. 18-H)*

Senate Action

The Senate adopted the conference report on Aug. 22, 82-7, clearing it for the president. *(Vote 347, p. 52-S)* ▮

Coal Slurry Bill Killed by Heavy Lobbying

An intense lobbying campaign by the nation's railroads led to the stunning defeat July 19 of a bill to promote development of coal slurry pipelines. The measure was rejected 161-246. *(Vote 492, p. 140-H)*

HR 1609 was debated on the House floor July 17 and 18 and votes on amendments began July 19.

Proponents — led by Bob Eckhardt, D-Texas, the measure's sponsor, and Morris K. Udall, D-Ariz., chairman of the Interior Committee — argued the bill was necessary to provide another means of moving the increased loads of needed coal and would benefit consumers by providing competition to the railroads. Bringing coal to gas- and oil-producing states like Texas, would free those fuels for other uses elsewhere. Lastly, they argued the pipelines were less harmful to the environment than the trains used by railroads.

Opponents of the measure — led by Fred B. Rooney, D-Pa., chairman of the Commerce Subcommittee on Surface Transportation, and Joe Skubitz, R-Kan., ranking minority member of the Interior Committee and of Rooney's subcommittee — argued it would deprive railroads of vitally needed future income, would drain scarce western water and would give an unwarranted grant of federal power to private developers.

In defeating the bill, the House took the unusual step of turning its back on the judgment of two House committees — Interior and Public Works — that had urged passage of the measure.

Coal slurry pipelines would pump a mixture of pulverized coal and water from mines to coal users like utilities. Five major pipelines had been on the drawing boards for years, but they would cross lands owned by railroads. The railroads, anxious to block competition in the lucrative coal hauling business, had thwarted pipeline development by refusing to grant rights of way.

HR 1609 would have given the Department of the Interior authority to grant pipeline developers federal powers of eminent domain — the power to take private lands in the public interest — subject to certain restrictions.

Railroad Opposition

The railroad industry, led by the Association of American Railroads and rail-affiliated unions, spearheaded opposition to the bill. As the measure neared a floor vote, the group called in members from all over the country to press their regional congressmen to defeat it.

The railroads were aided by some farmers and landowners concerned about the impact of slurry pipelines on their property and by some environmentalists and western state House members fearful that the pipelines would deplete scarce western water supplies.

But only one environmental group, the Environmental Policy Center, ever testified against the bill. And western state members voted for the measure by a nearly two-to-one margin.

Although the Carter administration had announced in January that it would back HR 1609, with amendments, it ultimately took no position on the bill as reported.

The Senate Energy Subcommittee on Public Lands and Resources, chaired by Dale Bumpers, D-Ark., completed three days of hearings June 19 on two coal slurry pipeline measures (S 707, S 3046) but took no further action.

Background

A similar bill was rushed through the Senate in 1974, but never got out of committee in the House. Further hearings stalled action in 1975. In 1976, the Office of Technology Assessment (OTA), a congressional research agency, began a comprehensive study of coal slurry pipeline issues, and the controversy largely lay dormant while Congress awaited the report, which was issued Jan. 19. *(Background, 1976 Almanac p. 110; 1975 Almanac p. 836)*

OTA Study

The 190-page OTA report, released 18 months after the congressional agency's board decided to analyze the slurry pipeline controversy, concluded that both pipelines and railroads had some advantages and some disadvantages as methods for hauling coal.

In major conclusions, the OTA report said that:

- In some circumstances, slurry pipelines could haul coal more cheaply than railroads, but each case varied.
- There was enough western water for such pipelines to be viable, but such use could deprive future needs.
- Given eminent domain powers, pipelines would enjoy significant regulatory advantages over railroads.
- Without federal or state eminent domain powers, pipelines would have a hard time competing, but that the pipeline industry could develop without federally given powers of eminent domain.
- Growth of a slurry pipeline industry would cut future railroad profits.
- Coal development would not be significantly boosted nationally by the use of slurry pipelines.
- Both posed differing threats to the environment.

Interior Committee Action

In two House Interior Committee markup sessions on HR 1609 Feb. 8 and 14, the panel adopted a series of amendments aimed at making the measure more palatable to defenders of railroads and states' water rights.

On Feb. 8, the panel approved by voice vote an amendment requiring the interior secretary to make specific findings on the extent to which a pipeline project would impair the financial integrity of railroads. Also by voice vote, the committee approved an amendment to require the secretary to solicit recommendations from the Department of Transportation and the Interstate Commerce Commission (ICC) on how a pipeline would affect other modes of transportation.

Debate was more emotional on states' water rights.

"One of the rationales used by opponents of this bill has been to raise the fear that we were going to come in and seize somebody's water," noted Udall, who backed the measure. Udall stressed that he wanted to make sure the bill in no way infringed on states' water rights. Eckhardt agreed.

Teno Roncalio, D-Wyo., who opposed the bill, led successful attempts to amend it. On Feb. 8 he offered an amendment, approved by voice vote, which spelled out that nothing in the measure should be construed as "affecting in any way existing law" governing states' rights to control their own water allocation.

On Feb. 14, Roncalio proposed an amendment to prohibit licensing of a western pipeline unless at least half the water to be used in it were surface water. The amendment also said the federal government would be barred from licensing a pipeline before all necessary state permits were issued. When several states shared jurisdiction over a water source, permits from each would be required.

Udall and Eckhardt argued that for federal legislation to require each project to have a certain percentage of ground and surface water was itself an infringement on states' water rights.

Roncalio's amendment was rejected, first on a 9-9 show of hands, then on a roll call, 19-20.

A third Roncalio amendment was adopted, however, 27-16, which would impede pipeline licensing. Under the amendment, a western pipeline could not be licensed unless the U.S. Geological Survey first conducted a comprehensive study of the project. For a license to be issued the study would have to conclude that use of water as planned would not cause a significant adverse impact on the area's water table. The amendment also provided that no federal license could be granted unless all necessary state permits had already been issued.

BILL APPROVED

HR 1609 was ordered reported by the House Interior Committee Feb. 22 on a 30-13 vote.

The surprisingly lopsided committee vote was a defeat for a coalition of railroads, environmentalists and rail-dependent unions which had opposed the measure vigorously. Credit for the victory was shared by a variety of business groups, utilities, construction trade unions and the coal industry.

Whether the Carter administration could claim victory was difficult to say. It supported the bill to complement its energy program. But it conditioned its support upon the adoption of several major changes in the legislation. Yet the administration never submitted formal amendments to the Interior Committee embodying the changes it testified it wanted.

Further complicating the assessment was the fact that when the panel's ranking Republican, Joe Skubitz, R-Kan., offered an omnibus amendment virtually identical to what the Carter administration had said it wanted, the committee rejected the proposal overwhelmingly.

The critical changes in HR 1609 came on amendments adopted in the markup sessions Feb. 8 and 14.

Eckhardt credited those amendments with easing many members' fears, leading to the surprising one-sided victory.

Markup continued Feb. 21 and 22. Skubitz offered his amendment reflecting the Carter administration position that the Departments of Transportation, Energy and Interior each should have veto power over issuance of eminent domain licenses for slurry pipelines. It was rejected 9-29. A second Skubitz amendment to give the Interstate Commerce Commission sole authority over slurry pipelines was ruled non-germane.

Also ruled out of order was a substitute bill (HR 10014) by Philip E. Ruppe, R-Mich., which would have given the Department of Energy power to regulate any kind of coal carrier along certain designated "energy priority routes"—a fundamental change in existing regulatory law.

Voting not to report HR 1609 out of the Interior Committee were: Robert E. Bauman, R-Md., Goodloe E. Byron, D-Md., James J. Florio, D-N.J., Ron Marlenee, R-Mont., Austin J. Murphy, D-Pa., Nick J. Rahall, D-W.Va., Teno Roncalio, D-Wyo., Eldon Rudd, R-Ariz., Jim Santini, D-Nev., Joe Skubitz, R-Kan., Steven D. Symms, R-Idaho, Bruce F. Vento, D-Minn., and James Weaver, D-Ore.

REPORT FILED

The House Interior Committee report on HR 1609 (H Rept 95-924, Part I) was filed March 3.

The report said railroads would carry most of the increased coal loads required in the future, but in some instances coal slurry pipelines would be preferable transport modes for economic and environmental reasons. The legislation was necessary, the report said, to enable development of the pipeline option where desirable.

To illustrate that pipelines could be superior economically, the report cited a 1977 Interstate Commerce Commission decision known as the Houston case. The commission authorized a rate of $15.60 per ton for coal hauled by train from Montana to a point near Houston, Texas. "This transportation cost is over 200 percent of the price of coal," the report said. "The delivered cost of coal will exceed the cost of natural gas."

The committee noted that the high transportation costs worked against President Carter's energy program, which sought to turn utilities and industries away from use of scarce fuels like natural gas and oil when other more plentiful fuels like coal could be used.

"Moreover, while the Public Utility Commission in Texas has led the nation's coal conversion program by refusing to certify any new natural gas generating units in recent years, the chairman of the commission has recently stated that 'two and threefold transportation cost increases could well force us to seriously reconsider our position on conversion,' " the report said.

The committee also defended pipelines on environmental grounds. Conceding that they required large amounts of water, the report argued that other forms of coal utilization, such as electricity generation at the mouth of a mine or coal gasification, required even more water.

Also, the report said, use of pipelines where feasible "can minimize the detrimental environmental and social impacts associated with large-scale transportation of coal by railroads...."

The main roadblock retarding pipeline development, the report said, had been the refusal of railroads to allow pipeline projects to cross their rights of way. Pipeline developers had fought the obstruction in court but, the report noted, "it may take years" for court resolution.

The report also said pipeline projects could not rely on winning state grants of eminent domain because authority granted might vary from state to state and might be unavailable where needed.

Federal legislation was necessary to save time and money, the report concluded. It also observed that federal eminent domain legislation would enable Congress to regulate pipelines built under the measure.

Water Rights

The report was careful to spell out how the committee bill protected state water rights, a reflection of the intense debate on that subject when the panel marked up the bill.

Referring to Roncalio's amendment, the report stressed that the legislation was not meant "to set federal water policy" and was in no way meant "to be construed as altering the traditional state role in allocating its water resources."

The amendment "makes exceedingly clear that the grant of a federal certificate of eminent domain authority cannot be read to imply preemption of state control over water allocation or use," the report said.

Railroad Impact

The legislation also raised concern over the impact pipelines might have on competing modes of transportation, primarily railroads. "The committee recognizes that railroad revitalization is an important national goal, but sees no reason to deny consumers the benefits of healthy competition in the coal transportation market," the report said.

The bill as reported provided that before granting eminent domain to a pipeline project, the secretary of the interior would have to consider recommendations from the secretary of transportation and the Interstate Commerce Commission about whether the pipeline would impair the financial integrity of a competing transport mode.

Additional Views

Five western Republicans filed a supplemental statement to the report alleging that, contrary to the committee's intent, adoption of the Roncalio amendment opened the door to federal intrusion on state water rights.

By requiring the U.S. Geological Survey to study areas under consideration for pipeline construction to assure there would be "no significant adverse impact" on the water table, the five wrote, the amendment would introduce the Interior Department into interstate allocation of water for the first time. " 'Significant adverse impact' is an elusive term, subject to varying interpretations, a term which would permit certain subjective decisions by the secretary," they said. Signing the statement were Manuel Lujan Jr., N.M., Robert J. Lagomarsino, Calif., Eldon Rudd, Ariz., Don H. Clausen, Calif., and Keith G. Sebelius, Kan.

"Nothing is more absurd than the total misconstruing of the water amendments offered by me to HR 1609," Roncalio responded in a separate statement in the report.

His amendment would limit only the granting of federal eminent domain authority, making it contingent upon a finding that there was adequate ground water, he said. "Nothing in my amendment in any way limits a state's right to control its own ground water resources," Roncalio insisted.

In a separate "minority views" section, ranking Republican Skubitz, asserted that the bill was not necessary, encouraged wasteful use of water, fragmented transportation policy, provided a special interest windfall, would lead to unfair depreciation of farm land, would benefit a few states at the expense of others and would promote a technology that would "seriously weaken the national railroad system."

Provisions

As reported by the Interior Committee, HR 1609:

- Authorized the secretary of the interior, or appropriate federal agency heads, to grant rights of way through federal lands for coal slurry pipelines.
- Authorized pipeline developers holding certificates of convenience issued by the interior secretary to acquire needed rights of way through eminent domain when negotiation failed.
- Prohibited the power of eminent domain from being exercised to acquire lands owned by the United States, any state or lands held in trust for Indian tribes.
- Stated that nothing in the act should be construed to mean that eminent domain powers could be used to acquire or develop water.
- Specified that the power of eminent domain could be wielded only by a holder of a certificate of public convenience issued by the secretary of the interior.
- Authorized the secretary to issue such certificates if the specific project were found to be in the national interest and were capable of serving as a common coal carrier.
- Directed that the secretary analyze the project before issuing the certificate and that he make certain findings and consider the extent to which the project would: 1) meet national coal needs, 2) need power of eminent domain to avoid delay, 3) disrupt the environment more than alternate choices, 4) affect the water table of the area, 5) be likely to financially hurt other competing modes of transport, 6) be likely to result in lower rates for coal transport, 7) be likely to result in environmental damage at the end of the pipeline due to disposal of water.
- Directed the secretary to consider recommendations from the transportation secretary and the Interstate Commerce Commission when considering possible financial impacts of pipeline projects on railroads.
- Specified that any pipeline built under the act must be a common carrier.
- Prohibited any pipeline company certified under the act from shipping any coal through the line which it owned, which it mined or over which it had any control.
- Provided special exceptions to that prohibition for pipelines that pumped coal received from several mines if it were destined for many users, and for pipelines designed as feeder lines if they served as common carriers and if the secretary decided the exception was in the public interest.
- Prohibited certification of any pipeline controlled by a person who used or would use the coal transported by it.
- Provided that any pipeline receiving certification must guarantee that rights of way could be obtained across the pipeline's territory by other carriers.
- Specified that as a condition of granting a certificate, the secretary must insist that a pipeline right of way be subject to additional uses compatible with the pipeline's operation.
- Provided that pipelines proposed west of the 100th meridian west longitude (which runs north-south through the Great Plains states) would not be granted certificates unless the U.S. Geological Survey had performed a comprehensive study of the affected area showing that use of ground water in the line would not cause significant adverse effects on the water table.
- Specified that regardless of the findings of the study, no certificate could be granted unless the applicant first had obtained all necessary permits or authorizations required by states having jurisdiction for use of any water.
- Required that prior to issuance of any certificate, at least one public, formal hearing be held in the District of Columbia under the provisions of the Administrative Procedures Act.
- Required the interior secretary to request recommendations from the secretary of transportation and the Inter-

state Commerce Commission regarding the likely impact the proposed project would have on competing modes of transportation.

- Required the assurance of the attorney general and the Federal Trade Commission that certification of a proposed pipeline would not violate antitrust laws.
- Guaranteed to states that conditions they placed upon use of water by pipelines would be binding under the legislation, provided the conditions were legal under state law.
- Specified that nothing in the legislation would be construed as preempting any law governing water use.
- Required that all pipelines covered by the legislation be buried to the maximum extent practicable.
- Required also that to the maximum extent practicable pipeline rights of way be replanted.
- Prohibited any pipeline from pumping slurry unless certified under the act or unless agreement was reached with the interior secretary guaranteeing that other carriers could obtain rights of way across the pipeline's lines.
- Provided that pipelines in operation as of Jan. 1, 1978, were not covered by the act.

Public Works Committee

The House Committee on Public Works and Transportation, which shared original jurisdiction with the Interior Committee, voted 23-20 May 16 to report the bill. The report (H Rept 95-924, Part 2) was filed May 25.

Changes in Bill

Public Works made only four significant changes, otherwise accepting the bill as reported from Interior.

First, the panel broadened the role played in the eminent domain licensing process by the Department of Transportation and by the Interstate Commerce Commission. The report stressed that as amended HR 1609 would ensure that the commission would have full regulatory authority over rates charged by slurry pipelines licensed under the act. "Lack of such control might place the railroads at a regulatory disadvantage," the report said.

The panel also loosened Interior's controls on ownership of licensed pipelines. The Interior Committee language was aimed at promoting competition in the fuel and fuel transport industry. Public Works said Interior's definition of pipeline ownership control was too strict and might limit investment in slurry pipelines. The two committees reached agreement on a compromise definition.

Third, Public Works required that the U.S. Geological Survey study the likely water table impact of a slurry pipeline project anywhere in the United States, not just in the West, as the Interior version provided.

And fourth, Public Works added language requiring congressional approval of rules or regulations put forward under the act by the interior secretary.

Separate Views

In separate views filed with the Public Works report, David E. Bonior, D-Mich., said approval of the legislation was premature until more studies could be made. He voiced concern that it might lead to damage of the environment and jeopardize railroads.

In a separate section of minority views, five committee members charged that the bill had been considered too hastily. They also said the bill was unnecessary to move coal, would damage the railroads financially, would not ensure lower energy costs to consumers and would promote unwise use of water. They also asserted that a transportation agency, not the Interior Department, should be the licensing agency. And, they said, portions of the bill unfairly restricted coal owners. Lastly, they said, waste water from slurry pipelines could present unknown environmental threats. The lengthy dissent was signed by Republicans William H. Harsha, Ohio, Bud Shuster, Pa., Arlan Stangeland, Minn., James C. Cleveland, N.H., and Democrat Robert W. Edgar, Pa.

Commerce Committee Action

Amid charges of foul play and deception, the House Interstate and Foreign Commerce Committee voted 19-9 July 11 to urge the House to kill HR 1609.

Rep. Bob Eckhardt, D-Texas, sponsor of the measure and a Commerce Committee member, hotly accused opponents of the legislation of trying to trick him into being absent from the meeting so they could more easily turn the vote against his bill.

Rooney Subcommittee Report

The committee had before it a report from the Subcommittee on Transportation and Commerce, chaired by Rooney, Commerce's leading opponent of HR 1609.

The subcommittee held two hearings on coal slurry pipelines in early February. Three substitutes to HR 1609 were put forward by panel members but were abandoned by the subcommittee in late June. Instead, the panel drafted the report, which attacked HR 1609.

The report (committee print 95-96) argued at length that:

- The bill provided unprecedented, extraordinary and unfair federal powers of eminent domain to private carriers.
- Sufficient rail capacity to haul coal already existed.
- Pipelines were expensive and could burden consumers.
- Railroads would be denied a chance to compete with pipelines because the lines would be committed to long-term supply contracts up to 30 years.
- The railroad industry would be hurt because it needed the increased capital that future coal traffic would bring.
- As many as 16,000 railroad jobs could be lost if slurry pipelines were fully deployed.
- Slurry pipelines used too much water and HR 1609 failed to provide adequate protection of state water allocation rights.
- Water discharged at the end of slurry lines could damage the environment.

"The committee believes that the question of coal slurry pipelines is primarily a transportation issue because of its impact on the established transportation system," the report declared. "While the financial success of private companies is not the responsibility of Congress, the continued viability and indeed, revitalization of the national railroad system has been identified as a matter of important public interest," the report said.

"The loss of coal traffic could deal a serious blow to the hopes of survival of marginal railroads. . . . In short, the industry's capital requirements far outstrip its current financial ability," the report said.

Federal promotion of coal slurry pipelines as HR 1609 provided would amount to federal subsidy for a special interest at the expense of genuine "common carrier" transport systems, like railroads, which should weigh heavier in the national interest, the report argued.

Shouting Match

At the July 11 Commerce meeting, Eckhardt arrived late but got there just before the vote. He charged that he would have arrived on time had he not been deceived by Rooney. Rooney denied the charge.

Commerce Chairman Harley O. Staggers, D-W.Va., refused to recognize the loudly protesting Eckhardt until after the vote.

When Eckhardt was recognized, he insisted that the vote had been out of order because the Commerce Committee did not have jurisdiction over HR 1609.

Staggers rejected Eckhardt's point of order, citing a March 20 letter from House Speaker Thomas P. O'Neill Jr., D-Mass. In the letter, O'Neill denied Commerce jurisdiction over the bill but said that since the measure might affect railroads — customarily under Commerce jurisdiction — the bill would be withheld from floor consideration temporarily to "allow your committee to . . . develop a position on the legislation."

Eckhardt charged that on the day before the Commerce vote, Rooney had assured him he was dropping his effort to get Commerce to oppose the bill. Thus assured, Eckhardt said, he decided to skip the meeting and have a medical examination.

Eckhardt said he rushed out in the middle of his physical exam when informed that Commerce intended to act on the measure.

"This member was deceived. . . ." Eckhardt shouted. If members can't count on each other's words, "we make of this committee a jungle, a sort of Jim Bowie duel (in which) you turn two people with knives loose in a darkened room and let 'em go at each other," he said.

"I never assured you of anything," Rooney replied. He told Eckhardt he should have sent the committee a note from his doctor and then it certainly would not have taken up HR 1609 in his absence.

The day after the Commerce vote — perhaps reflecting how close both sides expected the floor vote might be — House Majority Leader Jim Wright, D-Texas, and Interior Committee Chairman Morris K. Udall, D-Ariz., held a hastily called press conference to re-emphasize their support for the bill.

Both termed it a major energy bill because it would help plants and utilities to burn coal instead of oil and natural gas, consistent with President Carter's energy policy. Both also termed it a pro-consumer bill because it would provide competition to railroad transport, which they said could lead to lower prices. Both also asserted that the measure would not infringe on states' water rights.

House Floor Action

The House defeated HR 1609 July 19 by a 161-246 vote. *(Vote 492, p. 140-H)*

Of 75 voting House members from 13 western states, including Alaska and Hawaii, 47 voted for passage compared to 28 against.

A Congressional Quarterly vote breakdown showed that 45 Republicans voted for passage compared to 90 against; 116 Democrats voted for the bill and 156 against. Southern Democrats split almost evenly — 43 for passage and 41 against. But Northern Democrats voted heavily for the railroads, with 73 backing the measure compared to 115 voting against it.

Defeat of HR 1609 killed the legislation for the 95th Congress. However, Robert B. McNeil, spokesman for the Slurry Transport Association, the pro-pipeline lobby group, said it would press the fight again in 1979. The group included contractors, utilities and pipeline suppliers.

McNeil noted that proponents had convinced a majority of two House committees that the bill was needed and had won about 40 percent support on the House floor. With that much success, he said, "You just don't walk away and forget it."

Asked what the pipeline backers could do next time to win, McNeil said, "You have to translate this some way into how it can affect every congressional district . . . I think not only we have that problem, I think the president has that problem," he added, referring to President Carter's frequent inability to pass energy legislation.

The administration supported the principle of developing slurry pipelines, but insisted the bureaucratic procedures for issuing grants of eminent domain should differ from those set out in HR 1609. Consequently, the administration had no position on the bill and did not lobby for its passage.

The administration proposal, McNeil said, "was an unworkable, cumbersome kind of thing. I think they're going to have to rethink that." ▮

Redwood Park Expansion

Legislation (HR 3813—PL 95-250) that nearly doubled the size of northern California's Redwood National Park by providing for federal acquisition of 48,000 acres of privately owned timberland was cleared by Congress March 21.

Created by Congress in 1968, the park originally was 55,000 acres. The first, second, third and sixth tallest trees in the world were within it, towering with other ancients over a narrow strip of park land along Redwood Creek. *(Background, 1977 Almanac p. 678)*

Backers of the park expansion argued that nearby logging operations had caused soil erosion and silt build-up throughout the Redwood Creek watershed, threatening the existence of some of the world's tallest and oldest trees. Opponents countered that the trees were not in danger but that the park's expansion would threaten the area's economy and up to 2,000 jobs.

The legislation expanded the park by 48,000 acres upon enactment. It also gave the secretary of the interior standby authority to acquire up to 30,000 additional acres from adjacent lands in a designated "park protection zone" if necessary to protect the trees.

Provisions

As signed into law, HR 3813:

- Provided that 48,000 acres be annexed and added to the Redwood National Park immediately upon enactment.
- Provided that an additional border area of 30,000 acres designated as a "park protection zone" would be subject to acquisition by the secretary of the interior upon his finding that failure to acquire all or part of that territory would endanger the park.

- Vested jurisdiction over claims for compensation arising from the bill under federal district courts for the district where the land was located.
- Authorized $33 million, effective Oct. 1, 1978, for a forest rehabilitation program in the park area.
- Declared all timber felled after Oct. 15, 1977, within the existing park or area to be acquired to be federal property.
- Directed the secretaries of interior, agriculture, commerce and labor to undertake federal actions to assist the local economy in the park's region. Timber and mill workers affected negatively by the legislation were to be given hiring preference for relevant programs through Sept. 30, 1983.
- Directed the secretary of the interior to continue to make appropriate payments to affected local governments to offset their loss in property taxes.
- Authorized expenditure of funds from the general treasury to compensate private landowners dispossessed because of the park expansion.
- Guaranteed financial compensation through Sept. 30, 1984, to workers laid off or fired as a direct result of the park expansion.

Senate Action

The Senate approved its version of the bill (S 1976) Jan. 31 on a 74-20 vote. *(Vote 24, p. 6-S)*

Senate backers of the park expansion bill, led by its sponsor Alan Cranston, the Senate majority whip and California's senior senator, argued that nearby logging operations had exacerbated soil erosion and silt build-up throughout Redwood Creek watershed, threatening the existence of the trees.

"Redwoods, Mr. President, are not just a California resource but a national heritage," Cranston told the Senate. "Preserving them is not just a California problem, but a national challenge."

Opponents of the park's expansion, led by S. I. Hayakawa, a Republican and California's junior senator, argued that private property rights, tax dollars, the local economy and up to 2,000 jobs were endangered rather than trees.

The question of how many jobs would be lost as a result of park expansion was a key issue during debate. The measure's defenders disputed the 2,000 job loss estimate asserted by Hayakawa. Sen. James Abourezk, D-S.D., floor manager of the bill by virtue of his chairmanship of the Energy Subcommittee on Parks and Recreation, said a survey of affected timber companies conducted by his subcommittee indicated that at most 921 jobs would be lost, and perhaps as few as 260. And much of that negative impact could be offset by special terms in the legislation, such as authorization for $33 million to pay for a "labor intensive" forest rehabilitation program in the area, he said.

Two features of the Redwood Park expansion bill were unusual. First, there was no cost ceiling for land acquisition. This was necessary because the measure called for the immediate "legislative taking" of the 48,000 acres.

That provision was an unusual example of the legislative branch employing the government's inherent power of eminent domain, usually exercised by the executive within dollar limits set by the legislature. The backers of the provision argued that because massive tree cutting was imminent in the area to be acquired there was no time for bargaining over acquisition costs.

The Senate Committee on Energy and Natural Resources estimated the total cost of acquiring the 48,000 acres at not more than $359 million. But actual costs were to be determined through court proceedings.

The second unusual feature of S 1976 was its provision for standby authority to the secretary of the interior to acquire some or all of an additional 30,000 acres if land practices in that "park protection zone" threatened the park's trees. That authorization was estimated to require not more than $60 million.

Amendments. Hayakawa offered four amendments, three of which were rejected. His most drastic proposal would have deleted from the bill the provision for acquiring up to 30,000 extra acres for the "park protection zone."

Hayakawa argued that the extra acreage was not only unnecessary to the park but also that, under the standby authority, owners of the land would be afraid to make use of their acreage for fear of provoking the Interior Department into seizing it. His amendment was rejected, 28-65, after Clifford P. Hansen, Wyo., the Energy Committee's ranking Republican, assured that the extra land would be acquired only if a clear threat to the park could be documented. *(Vote 23, p. 6-S)*

A second Hayakawa amendment sought to delete two parcels totaling 8,300 acres that were not in the same watershed as the rest of the acquisition. The amendment was rejected by a standing vote.

Another Hayakawa amendment, to keep determination of compensation costs to landowners within the jurisdiction of the U.S. Court of Claims instead of transferring that authority to federal district court was rejected 36-57. *(Vote 22, p. 6-S)*

Hayakawa's only victory was on his amendment to require the secretary of agriculture to study timber harvest in the nearby Six Rivers National Forest to see if the timber yield could be increased, thereby providing more jobs to the area. Cranston and Abourezk supported the amendment, which was accepted by voice vote.

Also agreed to by voice vote was an amendment by Ted Stevens, R-Alaska, to require that funds to cover compensation costs be taken from the general treasury rather than from the Land and Water Conservation Fund. Stevens argued that costs for added park acquisition could drain the fund and rob other necessary projects.

House Action

House approval of the measure came Feb. 9 on a 328-60 vote. *(Vote 43, p. 12-H)*

House passage was easier than expected. The bill's sponsor, Rep. Phillip Burton, D-Calif., drafted a compromise version modeled on the Senate bill after the Senate approved its measure, and park expansion opponents found the Burton compromise less distasteful than the original House bill.

The key change was Burton's dropping of terms allowing federal regulation over timber practices on lands near the park. Instead, he substituted the Senate-passed provision of a 30,000-acre park protection zone.

House debate was relatively short and low key, providing tacit testimony that Burton's compromise was destined from the outset to win. Debate often took a religious tone.

"What kind of a country is it if we can't protect these tall trees that were here at the time of the birth of Christ?" argued Morris K. Udall, D-Ariz., chairman of the House Committee on Interior and Insular Affairs.

"I first visited the redwoods—heavens, it must've been 35 years ago," recalled Burton. "...It is a cathedral-like experience. An awesome and moving and—I don't want to be blasphemous—but it's almost a religious-like experience," Burton said.

From the other side of the ecclesiastical spectrum, Rep. Steven D. Symms, R-Idaho, argued, "When the good Lord gave us these resources, he gave them to us with the idea we should use them and replenish them."

The attack on the bill was led by Don H. Clausen, R-Calif., whose district included the entire park. Clausen said the people who lived there did not want the park expanded and the trees were in no danger.

The key vote came on a Clausen motion to recommit the bill to the Interior Committee with instructions to strike the park protection zone and to cut back the park expansion from 48,000 to 14,000 acres.

Clausen's recommittal motion was rejected, 116-274. *(Vote 42, p. 12-H)* The measure, changed by the Committee of the Whole to embody Burton's substitute, then passed the House, 328-60.

Conference, Final Action

Conferees did not alter basic terms of the legislation that were common to both Senate and House bills. They provided that the California park would be expanded by 48,000 acres immediately upon enactment by federal "taking" of privately owned timberland.

Both bills also provided that the secretary of the interior would have standby authority to acquire up to 30,000 additional acres from adjacent lands in a designated "park protection zone."

In settling relatively minor disparities between the House and Senate bills, conferees agreed to:

- Senate terms specifying that money to cover private landowners' claims would be appropriated by Congress instead of being drawn from the Land and Water Conservation Fund as provided under the House bill.
- Senate terms authorizing $33 million to rehabilitate forests in the park area, rather than the $12 million provided in the House bill.
- Senate terms giving jurisdiction over landowners' claims against the government to the federal district court for the area in which the land was located, rather than in the U.S. Court of Claims as in the House bill.

House Action

The House approved the conference report on HR 3813 (H Rept 95-931) March 14 on a 317-60 vote. *(Vote 120, p. 36-H)*

There was little debate. Once controversial, the measure had drawn little opposition since the Burton compromise was worked out prior to initial House passage.

Senate Action

The Senate voted 63-26 March 21, clearing the bill for the president's signature. *(Vote 73, p. 13-S)*

Senate debate centered on language accepted by conferees providing that timber workers and others who lost their jobs due to the park expansion would be guaranteen equivalent salaries for six years if unable to find suitable substitute work.

Clifford P. Hansen, R-Wyo., ranking minority member of the Senate Committee on Energy and Natural Resources which reported the bill, led the fight against the conference report because of that provision.

Hansen said the original Senate bill, which he had backed, provided adequate job compensation coverage for workers. The income guarantee provisions added by conferees, he said, created a dangerous precedent.

The measure's floor manager, James Abourezk, D-S.D., chairman of the Energy Subcommittee on Parks and Recreation, argued that the government reimbursed people when it took their property and it ought to do the same when it took their jobs. ▮

Land Management Bureau

Criticizing administration funding requests, the Senate cleared and sent to the president Aug. 8 legislation authorizing $2.1 billion for the Bureau of Land Management (BLM) in fiscal 1979-82.

The bill (HR 10787 — PL 95-352) authorized $479.7 million for the bureau's operations in fiscal 1979. That amount was $119.8 million more than the administration budget request, but only $19.7 million higher than the amount the BLM itself had sought. The hefty funding boost over the president's budget request was prompted in large part by a desire to spur rehabilitation of the nation's deteriorating rangelands.

The bill also increased the interest rate that states paid on federal loans to help them cope with the impact of mining. And it authorized $10 million beginning in fiscal 1980 for funds to buy private lands needed to assemble acreage for the King Range National Conservation Area in California.

Provisions

As cleared, HR 10787:

- Authorized $2.1 billion for the Bureau of Land Management (BLM) in fiscal 1979-82. *(Authorizations, box, next page)*
- Increased the interest rate that states paid on federal loans to help them cope with the impact of mineral development to roughly 4.5 to 5.5 percent, or the rate paid on state-issued tax-exempt bonds, from 3 percent.
- Authorized $10 million beginning in fiscal 1980 for funds to buy private land needed to assemble acreage for the King Range National Conservation Area.

Background

For years, the BLM, the largest federal land management agency, operated under the jurisdiction of thousands of outmoded public land laws. But in 1976, Congress passed the Federal Land Policy and Management Act (PL 94-579), which set for the first time in a single statute the BLM's authority to manage its land. The act also required authorizations for BLM operations every four years. *(Background, 1976 Almanac p. 182)*

In recent years, BLM had come under fire for the management of its rangelands. The 1975 BLM Range Condition

Authorizations

As cleared for the president, HR 10787 authorized the following amounts for the Bureau of Land Management for fiscal 1979-82* *(in millions of dollars):*

	1979	1980	1981	1982
Lands & resources management	$312.1	$329.3	$361.3	$393.3
Land acquisition, construction, maintenance	22.6	22	25	27
Payments to states in lieu of taxes	105	108	111	114
Mineral impact loans to states	40	50	57	65
Total	$479.7	$509.3	$554.3	$599.3

**The bill also authorized such sums as were necessary for increases in salaries, employee benefits and other non-discretionary costs, and $10 million beginning in fiscal 1980 for acquisition of land for the King Range National Conservation Area in California.*

Report painted an alarming picture of the condition of BLM rangelands, indicating that only 2 percent were in excellent condition.

House Action

Committee. The House Interior and Insular Affairs Committee, which reported HR 10787 May 10 (H Rept 95-1121), authorized a total of $2.2 billion in fiscal 1979-82 for the BLM.

Stating that it was "in general agreement" with the BLM's funding requests, the committee blasted the administration for submitting a proposed budget that "falls dramatically short of the levels requested by BLM for the fiscal year 1979 portion of their four-year authorization."

The committee also criticized the president's fiscal 1979 requests to improve BLM rangelands and recommended a boost of $7.5 million in fiscal 1979 over the president's figures.

Floor. The House approved HR 10787 July 11 by voice vote under suspension of the rules, a procedure that requires a two-thirds vote for passage and does not permit floor amendments.

Teno Roncalio, D-Wyo., explained a committee amendment, added to the bill after it was reported, to raise the interest rate on federal loans designed to help states provide services to cope with the impact of mineral mining. The amendment raised the rate to roughly 4.5 to 5.5 percent, or the interest charged on state, local government and other tax-exempt bonds, from the existing 3 percent level. Roncalio said the Interior Department had refused to launch the program because of the existing low rate. The program was passed in 1976, but had never been put into effect.

Senate Action

Committee. The Senate Energy and Natural Resources Committee reported S 2234 May 9 (S Rept 95-789). The committee authorized $2.1 billion in fiscal 1979-82 for BLM operations.

Echoing the House Interior Committee's views, the Senate committee chastised the administration for making inadequate budget requests for the agency. And, like the House committee, the Senate panel opted for the most part to go along with the Interior Department's funding recommendations for fiscal 1979-82.

The committee also expressed concern over the condition of BLM rangelands and recommended an increase in fiscal 1979 for range management of $9,928,000 over the president's proposal of $31,357,000.

Floor. The Senate approved S 2234 by voice vote July 27, after a brief debate on two amendments by Dale Bumpers, D-Ark., and one by Clifford P. Hansen, R-Wyo. All the amendments were adopted by voice vote.

The first Bumpers amendment was nearly identical to the House-passed amendment increasing the interest rate on state mineral mining impact loans, except for a provision basing the interest rate on state tax-exempt bonds only.

The second Bumpers amendment added $19.9 million in fiscal 1979 to authorizations for lands and resources management and $1.7 million in fiscal 1979 to the land acquisition, construction and maintenance authorization.

The final amendment, by Hansen, increased to $10 million, beginning in fiscal 1981, the authorization for funds for land acquisitions for the 52,500-acre King Range National Conservation Area.

The Senate then substituted the provisions of S 2234 for those of HR 10787 and approved the measure by voice vote.

Final Action

The House approved the Senate version of HR 10787 by voice vote Aug. 2, adding an amendment that changed to fiscal 1980 the date on which funds would begin to be authorized for King Range.

The Senate then approved the House version as amended Aug. 8, clearing the bill for the president. ▮

Environmental Research

Support for the role of the Environmental Protection Agency (EPA) in pollution control research was given a boost Oct. 4 when Congress cleared a bill (HR 11302) authorizing $400,564,000 in fiscal 1979 EPA research and development funds.

The final authorization was a nearly even split between the $374.8 million authorized by the Senate May 26 and the $432.9 million authorized by the House April 27.

The final amount was more than $75 million over the administration request.

Provisions

As signed into law, HR 11302 (PL 95-477) authorized the following (in millions):

Program	Budget Request	Final Amount
Energy*	$114.8	$129.8
Air Quality	52.7	59.7
Water Quality	48.4	53.4
Drinking Water	16.2	20.2
Solid Waste	11.6	11.9

Program	Budget Request	Final Amount
Noise	——	4.0
Pesticides	12.0	12.0
Radiation	.9	2.5
Interdisciplinary	34.8	36.3
Toxic Substances	10.5	12.8
Subtotal **	301.7	342.5
Program Management	23.1	23.1
Special Programs	——	35.0
Total	$324.8	$400.6

**Conferees split the energy authorization into $100.3 million for air and $29.5 million for water.*
***Totals may not add due to rounding.*

House Committee Action

The Science and Technology Committee filed its report (H Rept 95-985) March 17. It authorized $431,338,000 for fiscal 1979. The administration asked for $324,128,000.

The largest addition to the president's request was for energy-related programs. The committee added $23.6 million to the $114.8 million sought by the administration.

The additions included $14.8 million for studies of potential health and ecological effects of burning coal and synthetic fuels and $7.5 million to study controlling pollution from fuel processing techniques.

The committee authorization in the energy area did not include $14 million in programs that the president had indicated earlier that he intended to switch to the Department of Energy.

The committee added $19.1 million to EPA air pollution research programs. Of that, $10.5 million would be used to study the effects of pollutants on health, the relationship between adverse health effects and air quality and the effects of geography and seasons on air quality.

The remainder, $8.6 million, was added to the administration's request for research aimed at controlling industrial emissions. The committee said it was "impatient" with the "low level" of resources being devoted to this area. EPA "does not seem to give sufficient assistance to developing the means, control technology, to meet the standards the agency itself promulgates," the report said.

The committee specifically asked EPA to develop control technologies for toxic hydrocarbon emissions from textile plants, for emissions from printing plants and for hydrocarbon emissions from petrochemical plants.

An additional $11.3 million was added to the $48.4 million administration request for water quality programs. Included in the increase was $3 million for pollution control studies in the Great Lakes, $3 million for studies of "nonpoint" sources of pollution such as agricultural runoff and $1 million for studies of the effects of waste disposal into the oceans.

In EPA's drinking water research program, the committee added $4 million for ground water research.

The committee also added a number of special authorizations for programs not included in the president's budget request. The largest among them was $25 million for grants to demonstrate technologies that would turn wastewater into safe drinking water.

House Floor Action

The House April 27 approved HR 11302 authorizing $432,908,000 in fiscal 1979.

The 367-33 vote indicated approval for the additions to the bill made by the Science and Technology Committee, which added $107.2 million to the administration's request. *(Vote 218, p. 62-H)*

The measure incorporated authorizations which in previous years had been included in three different bills.

During debate, George E. Brown Jr., D-Calif., chairman of Science and Technology's Environment and the Atmosphere Subcommittee, said that during markup subcommittee members added funds to the administration request in certain areas to indicate what type of research they believed should have the highest priority.

". . .[T]he quality of the regulatory work done by [EPA] can only be as good as the quality of the supporting research which goes into establishing solutions to the pollution problems they are addressing. . .," Brown said.

He asserted that the Office of Management and Budget had approved a 12 percent increase over fiscal 1978 for the regulatory phase of the EPA program but only a 1 percent increase for research and development.

"A significant fraction of EPA's problems in the past have been caused by a lack of credible information," Brown said. "Although credible information is exactly what should be generated by the EPA research program, such information has not always been forthcoming."

Two amendments were adopted by voice vote.

One of them, by Elizabeth Holtzman, D-N.Y., raised the funding level for microwave radiation research to $2.5 million from $930,000.

Holtzman said she was "deeply concerned about our lack of scientific information about the hazards of microwave radiation." She cited a General Accounting Office study which found that there was no official health standard on acceptable levels of microwave exposure, that existing research was inadequate to formulate standards and that preliminary results of an EPA research program had shown that "low level exposure to microwaves has had serious health effects."

The other amendment, offered by Brown, required EPA to establish guidelines for the quality of water resulting from waste water demonstration projects.

Provisions

As passed by the House, HR 11302 authorized the following (in millions):

Program	Budget Request	House Authorization
Air Quality	$ 52.7	$ 71.8
Water Quality	48.4	59.6
Drinking Water	16.2	20.2
Solid Waste	10.9	11.9
Pesticides	12.0	10.0
Radiation	.9	2.5
Interdisciplinary	34.8	38.3
Toxic Substances	10.5	12.2
Energy	114.8	138.4
Subtotal*	301.1	364.9
Program Management	23.1	23.1
Special Programs	—	45.0
Total	$324.1	$432.9

**Totals may not add due to rounding.*

Senate Committee Action

The Environment and Public Works Committee filed its report (S Rept 95-877) May 15.

Among the committee additions to the bill was $4 million for research on noise control and the health effects of noise pollution. Neither the administration nor the House had included noise control research in the bill.

The committee noted that "a very modest but suggestive body of evidence has developed in recent years on the relationship of excessive noise levels to diseases related to physiological stress and sleep disturbance," but that research in this field "is almost non-existent."

Funding Changes

The committee raised the administration request for air quality programs by $6 million — $1 million for research on the effects of air pollution on plants and $5 million for research on the effect of air pollution on the stratosphere. The Senate authorization in that area was $13.1 million below the House figure.

In water quality programs, the Senate raised the administration request by $2 million for studies of water quality in the Great Lakes and $1 million for evaluating the relationship of water quality and soil erosion.

Other additions to the administration request included $1 million for microwave radiation studies, $1 million for research to develop alternatives to certain toxic industrial chemicals and $1 million for studies of energy production from municipal wastes.

The committee added language to the bill prohibiting the transfer of $14 million in energy-related pollution control research funds from EPA to the Department of Energy. The transfer had been proposed by the president. The report said it was "unsound public policy to separate pollution control technology from pollution control regulation."

In all, the House total was $22.6 million more than the Senate in the energy area.

Several special authorizations included in the House bill were also added to the Senate bill in generally the same amounts. However, the Senate authorized $15 million, compared to $25 million in the House bill, for grants to demonstrate technologies that would turn waste water into safe drinking water.

Senate Floor Action

Legislation authorizing $374,811,000 in fiscal 1979 was passed by the Senate May 26 by voice vote without debate.

The bill (HR 11302) included $16 million more for EPA programs and $34 million more for special programs than the administration request.

The House April 27 authorized appropriations of $432,908,000 for the agency. That was $58.1 million more than the Senate bill and $108.1 million more than the administration request. Carter originally had sought $324,128,000, but the request later was revised upward by $638,000 for solid waste programs, which brought the total request to $324,766,000.

The committee authorized $3 million for grants to citizens groups concerned about long-term environmental trends, an authorization that was not in the House bill.

Also established was a committee to coordinate research on ocean pollution.

Provisions

As passed by the Senate, HR 11302 authorized the following (in millions):

Program	House Authorization	Senate Authorization
Air Quality	$ 71.8	$ 58.7
Water Quality	59.6	51.4
Drinking Water	20.2	16.2
Solid Waste	11.9	11.6
Pesticides	10.0	12.0
Radiation	2.5	1.9
Interdisciplinary	38.3	34.8
Toxic Substances	12.2	11.5
Noise	—	4.0
Energy	138.4	115.8
Subtotal*	364.9	317.8
Program Management	23.1	23.1
Special Programs	45.0	34.0
Total	$432.9	$374.8

* *Totals may not add due to rounding.*

Conference Action

The conference report (H Rept 95-1593) was filed Sept. 20.

Conferees resolved a major difference between the bills by accepting a Senate amendment barring the switch of $14 million in pollution control research from EPA to the Energy Department and $14 million in health effects research from Energy to EPA.

"It is unsound public policy to separate pollution control technology from pollution control regulation," the conference report said. "Regulations should be based on sufficient research and adequately demonstrated techniques, so that the agency can make informed and dependable decisions as to pollution control regulations."

Conferees authorized $100.3 million for energy-related air quality programs, which was $15 million more than the EPA request, $14 million more than the Senate bill and $8.6 billion less than the House bill. The increase was intended for energy-related emission control technology and health effects research.

In the health and ecological effects program, conferees accepted the Senate level of $37.4 million, $6 million more than the administration request. The additional funding was earmarked for long-term research on the relationship between adverse health effects and air quality.

Conferees agreed to raise the administration request for water quality programs by $5.1 million, including $3 million for research to develop methods of controlling industrial pollution. Conferees accepted the Senate figure of $15 million, rather than the $25 million authorized in the House bill, for grants to demonstrate technologies to increase the availability of drinking water through the reuse of waste water.

Final Action

The Senate adopted the conference report by voice vote Sept. 26. The House adopted the conference report by voice vote Sept. 26. The House approved it Oct. 4, 387-15, clearing it for the president. *(Vote 763, p. 216-H)* ▮

Energy Authorization Bills Fail to Clear

Legislation to authorize programs for the Department of Energy for fiscal 1979 failed to clear in 1978, leaving in limbo the future of the controversial breeder reactor at Clinch River, Tenn.

Three authorization bills (S 2692, HR 12163, HR 11392) were reported by committees. Two of them, S 2692 and HR 11392, never reached a floor vote. The third measure, HR 12163, was passed by the House July 17 but was not taken up by the Senate.

The legislation languished when the Democratic leadership in both houses refused to bring it up for fear it would become the vehicle for several controversial attempts to remove or modify price controls on oil.

The leaders wanted to avoid a major floor fight on energy until after Congress had completed action on President Carter's energy package. But the energy bill did not clear until the final day of the session, which did not leave enough time before adjournment for action on the Energy Department authorization. *(Energy bill, p. 639)*

Clinch River Reactor

Because Congress failed to act, spending for the Clinch River reactor project — which was opposed by the administration — continued at the rate of about $15 million a month.

Without a new bill providing authority to modify or terminate the plutonium breeder, the Energy Department had to continue to operate under existing authority, which required construction. The $172 million appropriated for the project in fiscal 1979 in the public works appropriations bill (HR 12928 — H J Res 1139) had to be spent on new parts, engineering, design and other scheduled work on the $2.56 billion reactor. *(Public works appropriation, p. 154)*

Carter wanted the project killed because he said it was too expensive, its design was obsolete and it would lead to the spread of nuclear weapons. The reactor would produce plutonium, a nuclear fuel that could be used to make bombs.

Throughout the year, the administration attempted to work out some sort of compromise that would end the project.

But in July, the House voted twice to refuse to allow the administration to terminate the breeder. The two votes were on amendments to HR 12163.

But the Senate Energy Committee, in its bill (S 2692) reported July 5, gave Carter authority to end the Clinch River project. The committee bill required the administration to develop another breeder reactor demonstration project instead.

McClure Compromise

Still another alternative was presented in August when Carter — trying to round up votes for his beleaguered energy package — reached an agreement involving Clinch River with Sen. James A. McClure, R-Idaho.

Unlike the 1978 Senate committee bill, the McClure compromise did not require a commitment from Carter to construct another breeder, according to Michael D. Hathaway, legislative assistant to McClure.

The agreement would postpone the decision to terminate or construct Clinch River until March, 1981. In the meantime, work would continue on design of Clinch River, and components for the project would continue to be purchased. At the same time, government researchers would try to come up with another, more modern type of breeder reactor that would not use plutonium or, if plutonium were the fuel, would be designed to prevent its diversion to nuclear weapons.

Then, according to Hathaway, one of four options would be chosen in 1981: construction of Clinch River; cancellation of Clinch River and construction of the more modern breeder; construction of both projects or construction of neither.

The agreement also reportedly included support by the administration for a $417 million energy research project in Idaho that Carter previously had opposed.

The agreement was never put to a Senate vote because the bill did not come to the floor.

BACKGROUND

For decades, energy planners had looked to "breeder" reactors as the future source of electric power. Conventional nuclear power reactors used only one to two percent of the potential energy in the scarce uranium they used as fuel, according to a study by the General Accounting Office (GAO). "Breeder" reactors, however, would extract more than 60 percent of the potential energy in uranium and would "breed" more fuel than they consumed.

But breeder reactors also produce plutonium, a byproduct of nuclear fission that does not occur in nature. Breeder reactors would run on a fuel blend of uranium and plutonium and would produce a great deal more plutonium than conventional reactors, providing an endless supply of breeder fuel.

Plutonium, however, can be used to make nuclear bombs. It also is highly poisonous and can cause cancer if inhaled or exposed to an open wound. It remains radioactive for thousands of years and thus presents storage problems once it is spent as fuel.

Since 1970, American development of a commercially viable breeder reactor technology was keyed to a project to build a trial demonstration plant at Clinch River near Oak Ridge, Tenn.

The Clinch River reactor was designed to have a 380 megawatt capacity at a cost of about $2.5 billion.

Original plans called for site preparation to begin by October 1977 and construction to start one year later, with plant operation to begin in mid-1984. *(Background, 1977 Almanac p. 692)*

President Carter on April 7, 1977, announced plans to turn away from use of plutonium as a nuclear fuel because of the dangers of nuclear weapons proliferation.

As part of that policy, he later asked Congress to cut funding for the Clinch River project from $150 million to $33 million in fiscal 1978, enough to cover termination costs.

Congress refused to go along. The House insisted on providing the full $150 million while the Senate authorized $80 million to sustain the project through fiscal 1978. Conferees agreed on $80 million, accompanied by language asserting the will of Congress that the project continue.

Casting his first veto, Carter killed the authorization bill (S 1811) Nov. 5. *(1977 background, 1977 Almanac p. 692)*

Carter's Clinch River Stand

Although President Carter remained firmly opposed to construction of the Clinch River nuclear breeder reactor, the reasons for his stand reportedly changed.

That was the consensus of eight nuclear and five utility industry leaders who discussed the project with Carter for about an hour at the White House June 14.

"I found it very interesting that President Carter stated that concern over [nuclear] proliferation — his original reason for canceling Clinch River — is no longer his basis for opposing the project," wrote Kenneth A. Roe, chairman and president of Burns and Roe, Inc., a nuclear consulting engineering firm, in a June 26 letter to House Science Committee Chairman Olin E. Teague, D-Texas. ". . .The president made it clear that his opposition to the project is now on the basis of timing and budgetary reasons," Roe wrote.

Similar observations were included in several other letters to Teague from industry executives present at the meeting. Teague inserted the letters in the July 14 *Congressional Record.*

A White House spokesman disagreed with the interpretation of the leaders and denied that the president's remarks at the meeting indicated a change in position. "All the factors [timing, cost and weapons proliferation] have been important from the beginning and still continue to be," the spokesman said. She suggested that Carter may have emphasized the timing and budget questions because of the nature of the audience.

Carter first turned against the Clinch River breeder project on April 7, 1977, when he announced a campaign to steer the United States away from use of plutonium. Plutonium is a uranium by-product that would fuel the breeder planned for Clinch River and also would be produced by it. Plutonium also can be used to make nuclear bombs.

By late April, Carter was demanding that Congress cancel the Clinch River breeder project because of the plutonium threat to world peace. *(1977 Almanac, p. 692)*

By Nov. 5, 1977, when Carter vetoed an authorization bill (S 1811) because it included funds for the Clinch River project, his opposition was based primarily on grounds that the project was too expensive and would be technologically obsolete, and only secondarily on fears of nuclear proliferation. *(1977 Almanac, veto text p. 63-E)*

1978 Action

The Clinch River project remained alive, however, because Congress also included the $80 million in a fiscal 1978 supplemental appropriations bill (HR 9375).

The $7.3 million bill included funds for several projects which Carter could not afford to sacrifice. He signed it on March 7 but said he would spend the $80 million to kill the Clinch River breeder.

But Comptroller General Elmer B. Staats ruled March 10 that if the president did that he would be breaking the law. In a letter hand-delivered to the White House, he said funds for the project were authorized to be spent only on its construction, not its termination. Administration officials ordering funds spent to kill the project would be held personally liable for the money, he said.

But there was one way the president could legally end the project. Staats explained it in a March 6 letter to Sens. Henry M. Jackson, D-Wash., and Clifford P. Hansen, R-Wyo., chairman and ranking minority member respectively of the Senate Energy Committee.

The original contract between the government and private utilities to build the project allowed any party to begin contract termination under specific conditions. One eligible criterion was if any necessary government license were delayed six months or more, Staats noted. He pointed out that the Clinch River schedule already had slipped 18 months and said that delay would qualify as grounds for the government to kill the contract.

But if Carter pursued that strategy, some observers noted, the issue probably would end up in the courts and take so long to resolve that the project would effectively be killed anyway.

Administration Compromise Offer

In his fiscal 1979 budget request Jan. 23, President Carter asked for only $13 million for the Clinch River project to cover final termination costs.

But in late February the House Science Subcommittee on Nuclear Energy voted 17-6 to boost the authorization level another $159 million to continue the project.

To avoid further fighting, the administration led the effort to compromise. In a March 17 letter to Science Committee Chairman Olin E. Teague, D-Texas, Energy Secretary James R. Schlesinger explained his proposal to "redirect the nation's breeder program...(which) would in our view strengthen the breeder...program."

Under the compromise, the Clinch River plant would be shelved. In its place the Department of Energy would undertake a 30-month study of alternate breeder technologies feasible for a plant two to three times as big as the one planned. The compromise made no firm commitment to actually build any breeder reactor; however, it did not rule out construction later.

The Clinch River project would be stopped short of construction work upon completion of systems design and component testing, Schlesinger said. The overall government breeder research program then would focus on study of "a larger, advanced fission facility" which administration spokesmen said would have a capacity of up to 900 megawatts.

The study would examine alternate fuel options aimed at minimizing plutonium availability, Schlesinger said. The administration proposed spending $33 million in fiscal 1979. Also, he added, 90 percent of the design crew working on Clinch River — 850 professional employees — would be kept together as a team and transferred to the new project.

SCIENCE COMMITTEE FIGHT

An amendment to the energy authorization bill generally embodying the compromise was offered to the Nuclear Energy Subcommittee by its chairman, Walter Flowers, D-Ala. Flowers' amendment, however, called for spending $48 million in fiscal 1979 and specified that the study end by March 31, 1981. The amendment also had Teague's backing.

The compromise drew heavy fire April 4 at a Nuclear Subcommittee hearing. The plan, without any commitment to build a breeder, was "totally unacceptable" said B. B. Parker, president of Duke Power Co., on behalf of the Edison Electric Institute, the trade association of private electric utilities.

Breeder reactors remained the nation's best future hope for electricity, Parker said, and the Clinch River project "is an essential step in providing this option."

Echoing Parker's views were spokesmen from the American Public Power Association, the National Rural Electric Cooperative Association, Westinghouse Corp., General Electric Co., Stone & Webster Engineering Corp., Rockwell International Corp., and other industrial suppliers of nuclear equipment.

Also opposing the compromise was James M. Cubie of New Directions, the only environmental action group testifying. Cubie said Carter's 1977 veto underscored his determination to kill Clinch River, which Cubie said meant the project was dead. He also cited Staats' opinion that Carter legally could cancel the contract unilaterally, voiding the necessity of a compromise.

The compromise, Cubie said, could be negotiated in the Senate into a strong pro-breeder position, and even as drafted in the House it represented a "commitment to move forward with commercial demonstration of the breeder reactor," which Cubie said he opposed.

April 11 Action. Recalling that Carter vetoed a 1977 bill (S 1811) in an effort to kill the project, Flowers argued before the committee April 11 that it was futile for Congress to try to force a president to build something he was determined to scrap.

"It's obvious to me that we are at an impasse with the administration," he said. "This is designed to get us off of square one. . . . It's designed to give the administration maximum flexibility." Flowers said the compromise left open the option to build a breeder reactor later.

Mike McCormack, D-Wash., assailed the compromise. "The effect is to kill the Clinch River breeder reactor project and to substitute for it a vague study, to be completed in 1981 — after the next presidential election," he said. "The result would be that this nation would lose another five to seven years in breeder development.

"We are already desperately late in committing ourselves to a breeder project," McCormack said.

Ranking Republican John W. Wydler, N.Y., said Carter's stance indicated his "apparent determination that the United States be a second rate nuclear power." Wydler said the Soviet Union would have three breeder reactors operating by the end of the 1980s and that most European nations were committed to the same goal.

George E. Brown Jr., D-Calif., spoke for a coalition of about 10 Science Committee members opposed to the project. The compromise was "completely unnecessary" Brown said, because Carter could kill the project unilaterally if he chose. But in the interest of avoiding prolonged confrontation with the White House, he said, he would support the compromise.

Brown and six others sharing his views met with Carter April 10. Reportedly, Carter assured them he would not make a commitment to build any breeder reactor in 1978 and that he would step up funding for research on non-nuclear energy alternatives such as solar and geothermal power.

Gary A. Myers, R-Pa., moved to table, and thus kill, the compromise amendment. His motion won, 20-18. Four "yea" votes and three "nay" votes were cast by proxy, however, and Chairman Teague insisted that the House parliamentarian declare whether the proxy votes were legal before he would certify the vote. The panel adjourned until April 12, pending the parliamentarian's ruling.

April 12 Action. The next day Teague announced that the House parliamentarian had ruled the proxies were valid, and the Flowers compromise was tabled.

Flowers then offered another amendment modeled on his earlier one, but giving the administration more flexibility to act, he said. Opponents, however, said it would do more than his first amendment to ensure the death of the Clinch River project.

Marilyn Lloyd, D-Tenn., in whose district the project would be built, then offered an amendment authorizing $35 million for a study like the one called for under the administration-backed compromise. But the amendment left untouched a separate authorization providing $172.5 million to continue work on the Clinch River project. The compromise would have eliminated that. The amendment eventually passed, 25-14.

House Action

Action on the Energy authorization bills was held up by a months-long turf fight among three House committees for jurisdiction over the Energy Department budget.

The squabble pitted the Science Committee against the combined team of Commerce and Interior. The origins of the dispute lay in the formation of the Energy Department in 1977. The new Cabinet-level department was created by combining many independent federal agencies and sub-units of other departments. *(Energy Department, 1977 Almanac p. 609)*

Dispersed, they fell naturally under the jurisdictions of several House committees. Energy Research and Development Administration (ERDA) programs, for example, were under the control of the House Science and Technology Committee. Similarly, energy regulatory programs were administered by the Federal Energy Administration (FEA), and House oversight of that agency was the duty of the Commerce Committee. Interior's jurisdictional claims stemmed from its oversight responsibilities for environmental programs. The departmental fiscal 1979 budget request was the first one presented since the department was created.

The dispute raised many important questions.

The most immediate ones were what to do about two competing versions of the department's fiscal 1979 authorization, which in some cases contained conflicting policy initiatives and funding levels for the same programs.

One measure (HR 12163) was primarily the product of the Science Committee and ostensibly confined itself only to authorizations for research and development programs. As reported by the Science Committee, that bill authorized $5.87 billion for civilian energy research programs. But both Commerce and Interior won referral of certain sections of that bill to their panels and adopted many amendments to it.

In addition, Commerce and Interior jointly produced their own version of a fiscal 1979 authorization bill (HR 11392). That measure dealt primarily with departmental regulatory and administrative programs, and authorized a total of $7.121 billion as reported by Commerce, with $2.6 billion the figure approved by Interior for the programs in that bill over which it claimed jurisdiction. The Science Committee voted 32-2 June 6 to report that version to the House with the recommendation that it "not pass."

Also at stake was whether Science or Commerce and Interior would increase their respective roles overseeing the Energy Department. If any panel were to gain power at the expense of the others, there could be far-reaching implications for congressional relations with the Energy Department. The Science Committee typically backed high-cost, high technology solutions to policy problems. An example was its stand on Clinch River.

Commerce, on the other hand, had established a history of strict and at times hostile oversight over energy programs and officials subject to its jurisdiction. Generally considered more sympathetic to consumer and environmental activists than Science, an increased oversight role by either Commerce or Interior at Science's expense likely would influence energy policy formation.

Legislative History

On Feb. 16, Energy Secretary Schlesinger submitted a bill proposing fiscal 1979 authorizations for the Energy Department. That measure (HR 11137) was introduced by request by Science Chairman Teague.

But the day before Teague had introduced HR 10969, the fiscal 1979 authorization for department programs that the Science Committee believed fell under its jurisdiction.

On March 8, Commerce Chairman Harley O. Staggers, D-W.Va., and Interior Chairman Morris K. Udall, D-Ariz., introduced HR 11392, covering fiscal 1979 authorizations for the department programs they believed fell under the jurisdiction of their committees. Some items overlapped and conflicted with the Science bill.

On April 18, the Science Committee by voice vote ordered its version reported as a "clean bill", which was filed April 20 as HR 12163 (H Rept 95-1078, Part 1). Two days later, Speaker Thomas P. O'Neill Jr., D-Mass., ordered HR 12163 referred to Interior and Commerce as a result of a March 10 Staggers and Udall request. After amending it, Interior ordered the bill reported by voice vote May 15 (H Rept 95-1078, Part 2). Commerce ordered it reported May 15 by voice vote and filed its report May 19 (H Rept 95-1078, Part 3)

The Commerce and Interior amendments to HR 12163 were the same as their decisions in their own version of the authorization bill, HR 11392. Interior ordered that bill reported by voice vote May 15 and filed its report (H Rept 95-1166, Part 1). Commerce ordered the bill reported May 15 by a 25-16 vote and filed its report (H Rept 95-1166, Part 2) May 19.

Speaker O'Neill insisted that the Science Committee mark up the Commerce/Interior bill, and on June 6, without discussion of the specific provisions in the measure, the panel voted 32-2 to report HR 11392 to the House with the recommendation that it not pass.

Committee Action

THE COMMERCE VERSION

Though they introduced HR 11392 together, the Commerce and Interior Committee sections of the legislation were separate.

Commerce claimed more territory than Interior. Total authorizations for Energy Department programs claimed by Commerce reached $7.65 billion. Of that amount, $4.1 billion was for development of the strategic petroleum reserve system.

For the most part, Commerce recommendations were to cover administrative costs in the various Energy Department divisions, such as the Federal Energy Regulatory Commission or the Energy Information Administration.

The Commerce Committee report (H Rept 95-1166 Part 2) noted that total funds authorized by the panel were $553.7 million less than the Energy Department requested for those programs.

The major changes imposed by Commerce stemmed from its concern not to duplicate decisions made by the conferees on Carter's omnibus energy legislation.

The Commerce report noted that the department's fiscal 1979 authorization requests included about $593 million for programs already included in the energy bill. The Commerce Committee deleted all such funds from HR 11392.

Entitlements

One of the most controversial sections involved an Energy Department plan, announced in May, to administratively boost subsidies paid to East Coast oil refiners by refiners elsewhere in the nation.

The program, known as the "entitlements" program, was designed to balance out American refiners' oil acquisition costs in the face of rising world oil prices. The entitlements program was generally conceded to be one of the most complicated regulatory schemes ever devised by the federal government.

Under the program, refiners dependent on expensive imports for most of their oil supplies were paid cash subsidies by other refiners whose primary supplies came from domestic oil fields. Domestic oil was much cheaper.

The Energy Department proposed boosting the rate of "entitlements," or subsidies, paid by refiners of domestic oil to those, located mainly on the East Coast, whose supplies were primarily foreign.

The Senate Energy Committee voted 17-1 in May to oppose the program, which would cost $500 million a year. But on May 11 the House Commerce Committee rejected, 24-16, an attempt by W. Henson Moore, R-La., to stop the subsidy plan.

Republicans charged the plan was bait to pick up votes for Carter's stalled energy program.

On May 15, Commerce voted again on Moore's amendment. That time the count was 22-20 to uphold the administration plan.

The Commerce report expressed "deep concern" over the department's entitlements program providing subsidies to importers of refined oil products, which were different from imports of crude oil. The committee pledged to hold hearings on the entitlements program.

Uranium Enrichment

Commerce included a separate Title V in HR 11392, which rejected the department's request to boost fees it charged for enriching uranium, a process that turned it into fuel for nuclear reactors.

The department reasoned that though its current fees covered government costs, they were below what private enterprise would charge, and therefore, by providing the service, the government was subsidizing nuclear power.

The Commerce Committee called for a study.

House Supports Coal Liquefaction Plant

In one of the few decisions actually made on the Energy authorization bill, the House voted July 14 to spend $75 million for construction of a plant that would make liquid fuel from coal.

The vote was noteworthy because it provided a preview of congressional reaction to Energy Department plans to increase spending dramatically for facilities that made liquid fuel and gas from coal, shale and other sources.

In previous votes in 1975 and 1976 the House had refused to back loan guarantees for private companies wanting to develop synthetic fuels commercially. Fiscal conservatives and liberals favoring other types of energy had joined in opposing the guarantees.

The 165-132 vote provided funds as part of HR 12163 for initial construction costs of the plant to be built by Gulf Oil Corp. in West Virginia. It was to use a process called SRC-II (solvent refined coal). *(Vote 475, p. 136-H)*

The plant was expected to cost more than $600 million, of which about 80 percent would be federally funded.

The liquid product would cost twice as much as oil, with even higher prices as the plant geared up. In addition to paying most construction costs, the government would subsidize the market price.

Without government aid, Gulf would not build the project because the expensive fuel would not be marketable. "Our stockholders would go bananas and with good reason" if Gulf acted alone, said Dan Denning, a Gulf official based in Washington.

But the government wanted to increase energy supplies, and the plant eventually could produce daily an amount of fuel equivalent to 100,000 barrels of oil for use in existing, oil-using facilities. Every day, the process would turn about 30,000 tons of dirty, high-sulfur Appalachian coal into a less polluting, more usable product.

Energy Department officials argued that the Gulf project and others like it were needed because the government had a responsibility to prepare for predicted higher oil prices and possible future shortages on the world market. Synthetic fuels had become known as an "insurance policy" against the energy crunch expected in the 1980s.

"We believe strongly that we need these options in place in the early to mid-1980s," said Robert R. Hanfling, executive assistant to Deputy Energy Secretary John F. O'Leary.

But opponents argued that the federal government should not get into the business of commercializing new technologies.

One opponent, Dave Stockman, R-Mich., charged that "this is a deal in which the taxpayers take all the risk and Gulf gets any benefits."

Funding such projects without waiting to review the entire range of possibilities for synthetic fuels meant the creation of a "gigantic pork barrel," Stockman said.

Decisions would be based "not on rational economics, but merely on the basis of the tugging and hustling politically for the projects within the authorizing and appropriating committees," Stockman said.

Politics' Role

Politics did give the Gulf project a boost in the House Commerce Committee, where it was first considered, although the project eventually ended up attached to the Science Committee version, HR 12163. Rep. Walter Flowers, D-Ala., offered the floor amendment to HR 12163 authorizing the plant when it appeared that the Commerce version, HR 11392, was in trouble.

Congressional sources said the plant would be built near Morgantown, W.Va., in the district represented by Commerce Chairman Harley O. Staggers, D. "Gulf is not stupid," said one source.

One committee member said only the "sheer power of the chairman" had kept the project in the Commerce Committee's energy authorization bill.

A move by Stockman on May 15 to delete the authorization failed 17-23 in committee.

Another Commerce member, describing Staggers' lobbying for the project, said it was a classic example of "reaching in and trying to grab something for your district just because you sit with a gavel in your hand."

Staggers, asked about his role in the panel's decision, said he "didn't do any arm twisting" to get votes. He called the proposal "good for the country" and also noted the project did not originate with him.

The idea came from Gulf and the department.

Using federal grants, Gulf had been working since the 1960s on a technology to derive liquid, solid or gaseous synthetic fuels from coal. Satisfied with its progress on coal liquefaction, Gulf proposed to the Energy Department that a commercialization plant be built near the coal fields in West Virginia. The government owned the domestic patent; Gulf, the foreign rights.

The Commerce panel was considering the commercialization project because it was expected to be part of the Energy Department's pending "Phase II" supplement to the 1977 national energy plan.

Nuclear Fuel Storage

The Commerce Committee added $3 million to the department budget to pay for a study of and to select sites for the temporary storage of spent fuel from nuclear power plants, including foreign ones.

The same section also directed the Energy Secretary to construct spent nuclear fuel storage facilities at one or more sites away from reactors, but provided no funds for that purpose.

The section mandated that a report on the study's progress be issued within three months of the legislation's enactment. It further required the department to prepare a detailed report for Congress on the facility to be located away from reactors.

Dissents, Other Views

Richard L. Ottinger, D-N.Y., filed a separate statement with the Commerce report stating his "deep concern" over the provision committing the government to build at least one "away-from-reactor" storage facility.

The provision permitted the department, rather than utilities which produced the spent fuel, to pay for the facility's entire cost, Ottinger said. The provision was "topsy turvy," he charged, because it made the commitment before the mandated studies were completed.

Building spent nuclear fuel storage facilities away from reactors "involves a tremendous risk to health and safety," Ottinger said, because the material was so lethal. By the year 2000 the thousands of rail and truck trips needed annually to haul all the spent fuel would present grave dangers, he said.

Ottinger inserted a May 16 letter from the Council on Environmental Quality opposing the provision because it restricted the application of environmental laws to nuclear fuel storage facilities.

In a separate response, John E. Moss, D-Calif., and Bob Gammage, D-Texas, sponsors of the spent nuclear fuel provision, said the environmental law would not be unreasonably restricted.

The Gulf Project. In another statement, Dave Stockman, R-Mich., Timothy E. Wirth, D-Colo., Moore, and Robert (Bob) Krueger, D-Texas, denounced Section 704, which authorized $75 million toward development of a plant to produce synthetic fuel from coal.

The four charged the section was a disguised attempt to benefit Gulf Oil Corp.'s planned facility for Morgantown, W.Va. Commerce Chairman Harley O. Staggers, D-W.Va., whose district would house the plant denied there was any deal. *(Synthetic fuel project, box p. 688)*

Department Challenged. In a final section of minority views, eight Commerce Republicans denounced the Energy Department as disorganized and confused, deplored increased funding for regulatory programs and blamed federal oil price regulation for driving up oil imports and thus injuring consumers the regulations were designed to protect.

THE INTERIOR VERSION

The Interior Committee claimed jurisdiction over those Energy Department programs inherited from the Interior Department, such as several regional power administrations, as well as over various programs with direct environmental policy impacts such as spent nuclear fuel.

For those programs under Interior's jurisdiction, the Energy Department requested fiscal authorizations of $2.6 billion. The committee approved total authorizations of $2.64 billion, or $39.9 million more than requested.

Nuclear Fuel

The Interior report (HR 11392 — H Rept 95-1166, Part 1), paid particular attention to the issue of managing spent nuclear fuel. The committee said states probably should have veto power over federal decisions to store nuclear wastes within their boundaries.

The committee announced its full support for programs to expand a spent nuclear fuel storage facility in New Mexico and to construct temporary nuclear fuel storage facilities at sites removed from reactors.

Uranium

Like Commerce, Interior deleted an Energy Department request to boost its fee schedule for enriching uranium. Instead, the panel directed the department to perform a study of uranium enrichment costs.

Interior also recommended more than quadrupling spending to clean up piles of radioactive tailings from abandoned uranium mills. Uranium ore is refined at mills; tailings are radioactive residue from the milling process.

The department had sought $3.5 million for that purpose, but the committee added another $15 million. The tailings were concentrated at 22 sites in eight western states. Three were in Utah, one in Salt Lake City. Dan Marriott, R, of Salt Lake City, was the prime mover behind the funding boost. *(Tailing cleanup legislation, p. 750)*

THE SCIENCE VERSION

As reported by the Science Committee, $2.83 billion — 51 percent of the Energy Department's fiscal 1979 civilian budget — went toward nuclear energy programs (HR 12163 — H Rept 95-1078, Part 1). The authorization was $239.6 million more than the department requested. The largest single addition was for the nuclear project that sparked the most controvery — the Clinch River nuclear breeder reactor.

Clinch River Reactor

Referring to its April 12 vote to defy Carter and continue funding for Clinch River, the report said that "by this action, it is the intention of the committee that notwithstanding the present or future structure, pace, timing and objectives of the overall [breeder] program, the [Clinch River project] shall be pursued so as to maintain the viability of all project arrangements and objectives....

"...[T]he committee remains convinced that authorization of Clinch River as a demonstration plant project is not, and never was intended to be, a commitment to the introduction of commercial breeder reactors," the report said.

Minority Views — A bipartisan group of 14 members led by Flowers, filed a statement with the committee report opposing the panel's decision to continue development of the Clinch River project.

The 14 members argued that because the Carter administration had committed itself firmly to killing the project, it was necessary to reach a compromise. The members said they favored the ill-fated administration-backed compromise offered in committee by Flowers.

In a separate statement, 11 Republican committee members defended the panel's decision to continue full funding for Clinch River, saying "We cannot expect other developed nations to take us seriously in matters of nuclear technology or safeguards" unless the plant is built.

Other Breeder Programs

Clinch River had the highest profile, but it was not the only nuclear breeder program recommended for funding in the bill.

The Clinch River breeder would be a single demonstration model of the type known as the "liquid metal fast breeder reactor." Total Clinch River funding as reported by the Science Committee was $172.5 million in fiscal 1979. But total funding for all research on liquid metal fast breeder technology was $500.3 million, more than twice that much, and $220.6 million more than the administration sought.

In addition, the bill provided $45.9 million for water cooled reactor research, $34.5 million for gas cooled thermal reactor research and another $24.5 million for research on gas-cooled fast breeders.

An additional $25.2 million was designated for capital equipment costs for the liquid metal fast breeder program and another $7.1 million for similar expenses in other breeder programs.

For other nuclear fission reactor programs, the committee recommended $267 million, or $10.7 million less than the administration sought. The cut was urged in a program aimed at determining how much raw uranium and thorium, both nuclear fuels, was held by the United States.

Fusion. The panel urged boosting research on magnetic fusion, an alternative nuclear process for producing electricity, by $15.9 million above the departmental request, to a total of $241 million.

Nuclear Wastes. The Science Committee recommended adding $3 million to the Energy Department's request for $152.1 million to develop storage sites for nuclear wastes. The addition was earmarked to cover increased research on the feasibility of firing nuclear wastes into space.

Solar

Solar energy advocates, disappointed with the recommended cutback in funding for solar energy research in President Carter's initial fiscal 1979 budget, could draw cheer from the Science Committee's actions.

In his January budget, Carter asked for $341.5 million for all Energy Department solar programs. On May 16, in his belated Phase Two energy program, the president urged transfers of roughly $100 million from other Energy Department accounts to boost solar programs, a direct response to the growing popularity of the alternative energy source.

But before Carter's response — which came too late for consideration by committees trying to complete markup of money bills by May 15 — the Science Committee had already voted to boost Energy Department solar authorizations by $134.7 million, for a total recommended level of $476.2 million.

Most of the increase went to programs aimed at turning sunlight into electricity. Of the total $476.2 million solar budget, solar electric research took the lion's share, $349 million.

The panel urged spending $125 million for development of solar photovoltaic cells, which convert sunlight to electricity directly on contact. That was $49.2 million more than was sought in the administration's January budget. The program was authorized $76.5 million in fiscal 1978.

The program was aimed at refining the already proven photovoltaic technology to make the units cost competitive with other energy systems. They could be used on a small scale, such as in individual homes or factories, or could be harnessed to power full-scale utility power plants, the report noted.

"[The Energy Department] believes that the following cost goals can be realized: the reduction of solar cell costs from the 1977 level of $11 per peak watt to $2 by 1982, to 50 cents by 1986 and to the 10 cent to 30 cent range by 1985," the report said. "Achievement of the $11 per peak watt level in 1977 instead of the planned goal of $14 put the program about one year ahead of schedule," the committee observed.

"Work done by industry, universities and others indicates that very rapid growth in the photovoltaic market may occur when the cost reaches $1-$2 per peak watt," it added.

Wind. Also falling under the bill's solar electric program division were efforts at producing power by harnessing the wind — air movement caused by the sun's heat.

The committee noted that research efforts in the past two years had concentrated on small wind systems designed for limited applications, such as one house or one factory. The earliest market for small wind systems was believed to be in rural areas, the report said. It noted that three sizes of wind systems were being developed for that market capable of producing one, eight or 40 kilowatts of electric power.

The panel boosted the administration's wind energy request by $20 million, to $59.3 million. Half the hike went to step up research on small-scale wind turbine systems and the other $10 million was split between two programs aimed at using wind to power electric plants producing 2.5 to 3 megawatts of power, or up to 3,000 kilowatts.

Ocean Energy Conversion. The panel also boosted the administration's request for money for research on converting oceanic temperature differences into electricity. The program was increased by $28.9 million over the administration request to $62.1 million. The program was authorized at $36 million in fiscal 1978; the administration had recommended cutting it to $33.2 million.

Other Solar. The remainder of the Energy Department's solar research efforts concentrated on adapting solar power to directly heat and cool buildings and to be used in industrial and agricultural processes.

In January, the administration sought to reduce funding for those programs and requested $81.1 million for them in fiscal 1979. That was below the estimated fiscal 1978 program obligations of $106.3 million. The Energy Department request for fiscal 1979 initially was $97.6 million, but the Office of Management and Budget sliced that cutback further, to $81.1 million, which became the official administration request.

The Science Committee recommended boosting that by $36.5 million, to a total authorization of $117.6 million.

Biomass

The Science Committee almost doubled the administration's request for $26.9 million for research on squeezing energy from biomass — organic material consisting of plant or animal wastes or agricultural products raised specifically for energy conversion. The panel added $25.7 million, for a fiscal 1979 total of $52.6 million. Included in the increase was $10 million earmarked to speed construction of a direct combustion wood burning plant near Lincoln, Maine, and $5 million for research on converting plant wastes to methanol, a form of alcohol designed to supplement gasoline as automobile fuel.

Geothermal

The committee added $16 million to the administration's request for funds to research how to convert the earth's innate heat into electricity or applied heat, for a new total of $145.7 million. Geothermal programs were authorized about $107 million in fiscal 1978.

Hydroelectric

The Science Committee voted to almost double the fiscal 1979 authorization for small-scale hydroelectric power sites.

The administration sought $8 million, and the panel added $7 million more for a $15 million total authorization, the same as fiscal 1978, although only $8 million was appropriated for that year.

The committee noted that Federal Energy Regulatory Commission (FERC) figures showed that as of Jan. 1, 1976, there were 105,000 megawatts of undeveloped electric capacity available at large hydroelectric sites around the nation. Another 200,000 megawatts of unused capacity were potentially available at smaller sites, the report said. That represents "a significant energy resource," that can be harnessed by the year 2000, the panel concluded.

The extra money authorized by the committee was earmarked for a program aimed at speeding conversion of existing small dams to electricity generators, the report said. Eligible dams would be those up to 70 feet high or with water storage capacities of up to 22,000 acre feet.

Conservation

A program aimed at encouraging municipalities to develop systems to convert sewage sludge and other organic waste into fuel highlighted a variety of energy conservation programs that received generous funding boosts from the Science Committee.

"Energy conservation" included a wide variety of efforts aimed at developing machines, buildings and transportation systems that increased energy use efficiency.

The Energy Department request for such programs was $356.6 million, compared to $284 million in fiscal 1978. But the Science Committee urged an additional $93.8 million for those programs, for a total of $450.4 million.

The municipal waste development program was created by the 1978 Energy Department authorization bill (PL 95-238). But the administration's fiscal 1979 budget request did not include funding for the program because the request was sent to Congress before the bill creating the program was signed into law Feb. 25.

The Science Committee also recommended a $21 million hike for a program aimed at developing more efficient automobile engines capable of running on exotic fuels. The increase would go to a program devoted to development of an engine that would have at least 30 percent better fuel efficiency than conventional auto engines and would still meet the most stringent exhaust emission standards, according to the committee. The program also was aimed at producing engines capable of running on any liquid or gaseous fuel. The budget boost was designed to speed development to attain a demonstration stage within five years.

Another $25 million boost from the panel was earmarked for development of a fuel cell demonstration project. Fuel cells produce electricity directly from fuel without combustion and are nearly pollution free.

The project was expected to cost the government $250 million over seven years, with equal or greater contributions from the fuel cell industry and participating electric utilities, according to the report.

Coal

The Science Committee substantially reworked the Energy Department budget request for coal programs.

Coal research and development operations programs were reduced by a total of $28.8 million. Plant and capital equipment authorizations sought by the administration were sliced by $151 million.

Research programs aimed at producing liquid fuels from coal were cut by $20.7 million to $84.1 million. The report explained that members believed in liquefaction research but made the cut to weed out "unnecessary second generation projects" to provide better focus on more promising technologies.

A major decrease in that category was the panel's decision to end funding for the so-called "Cresap Test Facility," which cut the departmental request by $13.5 million. The committee explained its action by citing "enormous cost overruns" at the test center and terming its value "minimum."

Coal gasification projects were cut by $23.9 million below departmental requests to a total of $98.5 million. The reduction was not as severe as it appeared, the report said, because the panel decisions were based on a secondary "minimum budget" presented by the Energy Department that listed only $78 million for those programs.

A related but separate budget category involved an Energy Department request for $191 million for design and construction of a synthetic pipeline gas demonstration plant. The plant would be capable of converting up to 3,800 tons of coal daily into 58 million standard cubic feet of gas per day.

Two competing designs were under study, one by the Continental Oil Co. and the other by the Illinois Coal Gasification Group.

The Science Committee authorized only $40 million for the project, the portion of the $191 million sought by the department for fiscal 1979. The report explained that congressional control over the project would be retained more easily if authorizations were approved annually.

High Physics

Similar reasoning lay behind the committee's seemingly drastic cut of $172.5 million for a technically complex physics program known as an intersecting storage accelerator and code named "ISABELLE." The project was designed to enable nuclear physicists to conduct previously impossible atomic experiments.

The Science Committee recommended authorizations of $92 million for the project for fiscal 1979. Total estimated cost of the undertaking was $275 million.

Oil and Gas

The Science Committee boosted research funding for oil and natural gas projects by $37 million, raising the total program cost to $111.5 million for fiscal 1979. The fiscal 1978 authorization was $79.6 million.

Of the increase, $16 million was for perfecting techniques for recovering more oil from wells after initial recovery efforts ended. Enhanced oil recovery research was budgeted for $46 million by the Energy Department and raised to $62 million by the panel.

Another $20 million of the recommended increase was earmarked for accelerating department programs aimed at obtaining natural gas supplies from geopressurized acquifers along the Gulf Coast, from Western gas-bearing sands and from Devonian shales in the Eastern states.

Environment

The Science Committee voted to boost authorizations for the Energy Department's environmental research programs by $28.2 million, to a total of $312.7 million, or about $6 million more than fiscal 1978.

Included in the hike were recommended spending increases of $6.7 million for research on the health and ecological effects of coal combustion, $6 million for research on the safety and control of liquid natural gas and $1.5 million for research on the effects of electric fields near high voltage overhead transmission wires.

Commerce, Interior Amendments

Both the Commerce and Interior Committees were referred several sections of HR 12163. Amendments to that bill proposed by Commerce (H Rept 95-1078, Part 3) and by Interior (H Rept 95-1078, Part 2) reflected their decisions on programs included in their own version of the authorization bill (HR 11392).

Floor Action

On July 17, the House voted 325-67 to pass HR 12163, which authorized $4.5 billion in fiscal 1979 funds for civilian research and development programs in the Department of Energy. The measure also contained full funding for the Clinch River breeder reactor. *(Vote 481, p. 138-H)*

Clinch River

The arguments on Clinch River echoed those of past years.

Debate centered around the administration "compromise" amendment, offered by Flowers. It was the same proposal he had submitted earlier to the Science Committee.

The amendment authorized $55 million and directed the secretary of energy to finish only the design work on the Clinch River project. The Energy Department would be required to study advanced breeder reactor concepts and recommend to Congress by March 31, 1981, how to proceed toward development. But the amendment contained no commitment to ever build anything.

Proponents of the compromise, including Science Committee Chairman Teague, argued that Carter was determined to kill Clinch River, that the president held enough votes to make a veto stick, and, therefore, that the project was as good as dead.

"The amendment is the very best that Congress is going to come out with in dealing with the administration," Flowers said. ". . .That is why I recommend it."

Proponents also argued that at the end of the three-year study the administration would likely decide to build a demonstration breeder reactor two to three times larger than the one planned for Clinch River, so the breeder development program would come out ahead.

Teague said Carter had personally assured him that he favored development of breeder reactors, but not the one at Clinch River. And Don Fuqua, D-Fla., ranking Science Democrat, noted that the bill provided $375 million for breeder research apart from Clinch River, which the administration supported.

But Clinch River defenders could not be convinced.

Citing unanimous support for the project from the nuclear power and utility industries, they argued the project was essential for development of nuclear-generated electricity in the United States. The nation would fall hopelessly behind Western Europe and Japan in developing nuclear technology if it were scrapped, the defenders asserted.

Clinch River defenders were led by Marilyn Lloyd, D-Tenn., in whose district the project was located; Mike McCormack, D-Wash., chairman of the Science Subcommittee on Advanced Energy Technologies, and John W. Wydler, R-N.Y., Science's ranking minority member.

"I suggest that we would be in a much stronger position in the conference committee, where we can actually deal with the president, if we reject the Flowers amendment," McCormack argued.

"Then, we are in the position to tell the president that we can force him to veto it if that is what he intends to do, and tell the American people that he intends to kill the breeder program.

"Let him be the executioner, not us," McCormack said.

On Friday, July 14, the House rejected the Flowers amendment, 142-187. *(Vote 474, p. 136-H)*

The decision to put the question to a vote on a Friday when many members were certain to be absent and home campaigning was considered peculiar. A close vote was expected, although with Teague and Flowers pulling for the compromise, it appeared that the administration had a good chance of winning.

The evening before the vote the House leadership was officially undecided on what legislation to bring to the floor the next day. Nevertheless, on Friday, despite high absenteeism, the closely fought issue was allowed to come to a vote.

The administration lost by 45 votes. There were 103 absentees. Ninety-six Democrats voted against the amendment and 68 Democrats failed to vote.

However, administration sympathizers tried again Monday, July 17. Hamilton Fish, R-N.Y., moved to recommit the bill to the Science Committee with instructions that the panel add the Flowers amendment language.

"[I]f we are to have a bill then this compromise is an essential part of it," Fish said, observing the high absentee rate for the first vote. "I happen to have several things that I want very dearly in this measure and I would hate to see it vetoed," Fish explained.

Debate was short and repetitious, and the House rejected Fish's motion, 157-238. *(Vote 480, p. 136-H)*

Coal Plant

Flowers was more successful in pushing an amendment to add $75 million to cover initial construction costs for a plant to make liquid fuel from coal using a process called SRC-II (solvent refined coal). Only Gulf Oil Corp. was ready to demonstrate the process in a commercial-sized plant. *(Details, p. 688)*

Flowers argued that the nation's need for new energy supplies was so pressing that the time was at hand for Congress to authorize public funding to demonstrate the process. His amendment was adopted 165-132. *(Vote 475, p. 136-H)*

Gary A. Myers, R-Pa., offered a substitute amendment that would have authorized only $60 million for studies and initial design activity for several competing coal liquefaction technologies. He said that his amendment, unlike Flowers', would allow the administration a choice on what technology to pursue. Myers' substitute was rejected by voice vote.

Richard L. Ottinger, D-N.Y., argued that both amendments were improper because the plants to be built would be so big they should be considered commercial-stage undertakings instead of research-level projects. Commercialization projects more properly fell under the jurisdiction of the Commerce Committee, he argued, and he noted that the Commerce version of the Energy Department authorization bill (HR 11392) included funds for such a plant.

John D. Dingell, D-Mich., chairman of the Commerce Energy and Power Subcommittee, said the Commerce version ensured congressional oversight of the plant's construction, which Flowers' amendment did not. The Commerce bill, Dingell said, restricted spending to engineering and design and barred expenditures for land acquisition or construction. The Commerce bill also specified that eligible projects had to be selected by competitive bids, which Flowers' amendment did not.

The strongest criticism of Flowers' amendment, however, came from Dave Stockman, R-Mich. Stockman argued that fuels produced by the SRC-II process would cost at least $20 to $30 per barrel, or 50 percent higher than current world oil prices. Therefore, production of such fuels could not be justified economically, he said, which was why private enterprise was holding back on them.

"...I think an executive from Gulf Oil Corp., the major beneficiary of this proposed project, had the last word about a month ago when he said that if the Gulf Oil Corp. was investing its own money and funds in this project, the stockholders would go bananas," Stockman said.

Stockman also made public two contradictory letters he received the same day from the Office of Management and Budget (OMB) regarding the authorization in the Commerce bill for the coal plant. In the first letter, the administration said it opposed the plant. But in the second it said it favored the provision with minor alteration. OMB estimated the plant would cost a total of $600 million through fiscal 1983.

Jurisdictional Dispute

The Ottinger-Flowers exchange on Flowers' coal plant amendment illustrated the rivalry between Science and Commerce that had delayed the Energy Department authorization bills from reaching the floor.

On June 23, the two committees announced in the *Congressional Record* that they had compromised jurisdictional differences. They then outlined proposed substitute versions of HR 12163, the Science Committee bill, and HR 11392, the Commerce and Interior version.

The substitute bills eliminated authorizations that were duplicated or overlapped in the original committee bills, which resulted in some changes in program totals. However, the changes reflected shifts of program accounts from one bill to the other, rather than new spending levels.

As a result of the compromise, HR 12163 as passed by the House July 17 authorized a total of $4.5 billion for research and development programs, $1.3 billion less than the amount originally reported by the Science Committee.

Oil Pricing Controversy

The second authorization bill, HR 11392, had been expected to come to the floor shortly after approval of HR 12163. But it was yanked from the schedule, and eventually died, because of a controversial amendment that would have decontrolled the price of about half the oil produced in the United States.

Majority Leader Jim Wright, D-Texas, said he intended to offer the amendment to HR 11392, which would have provided $6.2 billion in fiscal 1979 authorizations for non-research civilian Energy Department programs.

But the House Democratic leadership held up consideration of the bill when informed by Henry M. Jackson, D-Wash., chairman of the Senate Energy Committee, that if Wright's amendment passed the House, several Senate conferees would retract their approval of the natural gas pricing compromise. Those members objected to the amendment, they said, because together the oil and gas proposals would give exorbitant profits to the oil and gas industry. At that point, the gas pricing compromise was threatening to fall apart at any moment, and leaders in both houses did not want to risk alienating any of the compromise's supporters.

The Proposal

Wright's proposal would have broadened the definition of "stripper" oil wells, defined as those that produced less than 10 barrels of oil per day. Under existing law, oil from those wells sold at unregulated prices and drew the world price of about $14 per 42-gallon barrel.

Wright's amendment would have expanded the definition to include some wells producing up to 35 barrels of oil per day. Most of the 75,000 wells that Wright estimated would be added to the "stripper" category under his amendment produced oil that sold at a controlled price of about $5.50 per barrel.

Under Wright's proposals, wells eligible to draw unregulated prices would be those:

- Up to 2,000 feet deep that produced no more than 20 barrels per day.
- Up to 4,000 feet deep that produced no more than 25 barrels per day.
- Up to 6,000 feet deep that produced no more than 30 barrels per day.
- 8,000 feet or deeper that produced no more than 35 barrels per day.

Wright termed such wells "marginal" and argued that wells cost more money the deeper they go. Deep wells that produced little oil did not pay their owners to keep them in production, he said.

Wright said his amendment was intended to keep in production up to 75,000 wells that might otherwise be shut down, which would lock in production of 1.5 billion barrels of oil that could be drawn by 1985.

John D. Dingell, D-Mich., chairman of the House Commerce Energy and Power Subcommittee, told the Rules Committee Wright's amendment would result in little increased oil production, would apply to about half the oil produced in the nation and would cost consumers about $300 million a year.

Wright told reporters later that Energy Secretary James R. Schlesinger had promised to achieve much of what Wright sought via administrative rules, but Wright said Schlesinger had failed to honor such pledges in the past.

Senate Action

The controversy over oil pricing also held up action on the Senate version of the Energy authorization bill (S 2692). Senators from oil-producing states were expected to press to end federal price controls on some domestically produced oil.

As a result, the leadership did not bring the bill to the floor, because they feared such an amendment would turn votes away from the delicate compromise on natural gas pricing that was the joint leadership's primary energy priority.

The two issues were closely related because both the gas compromise and any oil plan would raise the prices consumers paid for oil and natural gas while handing oil and gas producers billions in new profits. On the other hand, proponents of both proposals said they would increase energy supplies.

Committee Action

S 2692 was introduced March 8 at the administration's request by Energy Committee Chairman Jackson. Nineteen days of hearings were held by the panel and its subcommittees before markup began May 3 for 15 sessions. On June 20, the committee voted 15-0 to report the bill. The 307-page report (S Rept 95-967) was filed July 5.

As reported, S 2692 authorized $10.3 billion in fiscal 1979 for civilian programs in the Department of Energy, $420.7 million more than the administration sought.

The committee noted that $646.8 million in authorizations under S 2692 duplicated decisions approved by conferees on various portions of Carter's energy program. The report explained that the duplications were intended to continue existing programs that might otherwise be cancelled if the Carter energy program were not enacted.

Budget Act Concerns

The committee gave a verbal slap to the Carter administration for its budget presentation. Similar displeasure was voiced in the House by the Interstate and Foreign Commerce Committee.

The Senate committee said it was "disturbed" by administration spokesmen who said the president's proposed budget "has consciously underfunded various programs in the expectation of submitting major 'supplemental' appropriations requests later in fiscal year 1979.

". . .In the judgment of the committee the congressional process of annual authorizations cannot be effective or rational if major policy decisions which will impact on the current and next fiscal years are habitually withheld by the administration until initial budget decisions have been completed by the Congress," the committee report said.

In 1977, the report continued, late submissions by the administration of major energy policy proposals had forced the committee to obtain budget waivers, which upset the Budget Committee. Despite that inconvenience, however, the Energy Department again waited until May 15 — the Congressional Budget Act deadline for reporting authorization bills — to submit requests for energy authorizations totaling $130 million.

"The adverse effects upon the budgetary process of such a delayed request is self-evident," the report said.

Clinch River

Unlike the House, which had insisted that work continue on the Clinch River reactor, the Senate committee would have allowed Carter to cancel the project. Had the bill reached the floor, a major fight was expected.

The committee voted to allow Carter the option of full finding for Clinch River — $172.4 million — or for the first time allow him legal authority to terminate the Clinch River contract. If Carter chose to kill Clinch River, the committee bill committed the government to later design and build a new breeder reactor demonstration project. The final conceptual design plan for the new project would be required to be in Congress' hands by March 31, 1981.

Diehards on both sides of the debate were expected to press their cases for all or nothing resolution of the conflict, but committee sources said they were confident the panel's compromise would survive the Senate floor.

Research and Development

The administration sought a total of $2.67 billion in new budget authority for fiscal 1979 Energy Department research and development programs. The committee boosted that by $700 million to a new total of $3.37 billion.

Coal. The committee urged $826.3 million for research dealing with coal, $208.1 million more than Carter sought.

Most of the recommended increase went toward two plants aimed at deriving clean fuels from coal. The panel approved a $132 million hike in construction funds and an $11 million boost in operating expenses for the two plants.

Both plants would use the "solvent refined coal" process to produce the fuels. One plant, that would produce a liquid fuel, was authorized for the first time and would get $93 million, most of the funding boost. The other, previously authorized, would produce a solid fuel and was recommended for a funding hike of $46 million.

The committee also boosted administration requests for coal gasification projects by $35.5 million.

Peat. One innovation tucked into the bill by the Energy Committee was $4.5 million not requested by the administration for research on deriving gaseous fuels from peat.

"Peat is a very large resource, possibly as large as all of our oil and gas resources combined," the report said. Located primarily in Michigan, Wisconsin and Minnesota, peat often was referred to as "young coal," the report said, and was considered a better material for gasification.

MHD. The panel recommended a $38 million increase above the administration's $72.3 million request for work on developing an electricity generation system employing magnetohydrodynamics (MHD). MHD "is based on direct conversion of heat to electricity by passing a high temperature, high velocity electrically conducting gas through a magnetic field. The principle is similar to a conventional turbine generator system," the report said. It noted that a joint study by the National Science Foundation, the National Aeronautics and Space Administration and the former Energy Research and Development Administration, which became part of the Energy Department, had found MHD to be the most promising technology for advanced electric power conversion.

Oil. The Energy Committee voted to boost by $14 million the administration's request for $46 million in new budget authority for research on how to extract more oil from conventional wells.

"Two-thirds of the oil discovered to date remains in the reservoirs and cannot be recovered with current practices and economics," the report said. It noted that 88 billion barrels of oil potentially could be pulled from conventional domestic wells if advanced extraction techniques — known as enhanced oil recovery — were perfected. Energy Department plans called for increasing oil production by 910,000 barrels per day by 1985 above the level that industry efforts alone would produce, the report said.

Gas. Similarly, the administration's request of $21.3 million for enhanced natural gas recovery research was boosted by $17.5 million. The increase was allocated as follows: $6 million for research on eastern gas shales, $6 million for western gas sands, $4 million for methane from coal and $1.5 million for deriving gas from geopressurized aquifers.

Solar. The panel recommended a major boost for solar research programs. It added $78.3 million to the Carter request of $309.2 million for a new total of $387.5 million.

Of the increase, almost all went toward efforts to translate sunlight and its effects — like ocean heat and wind — into electricity. The largest solar category boost was a $31 million hike for research on photovoltaic systems, which would convert sunlight directly into electricity on contact. The administration had sought $75.8 million for photovoltaic research, which was $400,000 less than in fiscal 1978.

The committee also voted to boost funding by $20 million for deriving electricity from the wind using windmills. The objective was to make wind power economically competitive with conventional technologies, the report said. The administration's request for wind energy research was $34.2 million.

Another $15 million of the recommended hike in solar program spending was designated to boost research on converting ocean heat into electricity. The administration had sought $32.5 million for that effort, $2.8 million below the fiscal 1978 level. In addition, the committee added $10 million for construction of physical test facilities known as the OTEC-1 module.

Geothermal. The administration requested $129.7 million for research on geothermal power — tapping the earth's innate heat — a $23 million boost over fiscal 1978. But the committee added another $18.5 million.

Fusion. The committee recommended a $24.2 million increase above the administration request for research on a variety of highly technical nuclear physics approaches to produce electricity. The increase brought the total for those programs to $358.4 million.

Nuclear Fuel. The committee urged an $82.5 million increase for programs dealing with storage and disposal of nuclear wastes. The total authorization for those programs was $329.9 million.

The committee added $30 million for storage of spent nuclear fuel. The administration had sought $3 million. The ten-fold increase was to cover initial costs for a 5,000 metric ton spent fuel repository.

Such a repository would be needed by 1983, the report said, to ensure orderly continued operation of the nation's nuclear power plants, which otherwise would run out of spent fuel storage space.

The committee required that the governor of the state chosen to house the repository be informed in writing by the energy secretary. The governor could veto placement of the repository there unless it already was the site of ongoing nuclear activity, the committee said.

Expressly exempted from the veto clause was the Barnwell, S.C., site of a dormant nuclear fuel reprocessing facility. The bill would not allow the South Carolina governor to veto use of that site.

The committee also added $18.5 million above the administration request to continue the work of a technical team at Barnwell. The panel specified that those funds were intended solely for research and development and could not be used to reprocess spent nuclear fuel there.

The Barnwell site had been the target of a massive anti-nuclear protest demonstration in April 1978.

For research on how to reuse spent fuels and better safeguard nuclear fuel processes, the administration sought $48.8 million in operating expenses. In fiscal 1978 appropriations, those programs received $92.4 million. "Due to the severe decrease" evident, the committee report said, the panel decided to add $46.5 million to research programs in that category.

Other Nuclear. The committee recommended a major boost in research on gas-cooled thermal nuclear reactors, reactors cooled by gas, not water like conventional nuclear power plants. There were three types of gas-cooled reactors: high temperature, very high temperature and gas-cooled fast reactors. The high temperature reactor could use a more flexible range of enriched uranium than conventional nuclear power plants, and produced less plutonium, the report said.

The administration sought $28.5 million for gas-cooled thermal reactors, less than the previous year's appropriation. The committee urged an increase of $20 million.

But the panel cut the administration proposal for gas-cooled fast reactors by $6 million. The administration had sought $30.5 million for that program, up from $14.7 million in fiscal 1978. The new total urged by the committee was $24.5 million.

Lastly, the committee recommended a significant increase in funding for research to improve the performance of conventional light water nuclear power reactors, which provided about 10 percent of the nation's electricity. The administration sought $23.9 million for such research; the panel boosted that by $10 million.

Hydroelectric. The committee almost doubled the $8 million request for funds to assist public and private sector development of low-head hydroelectric facilities at small dam sites. The panel added $7 million, for a total of $15 million.

The only limitation was that the dams built with the money not generate more than 15 megawatts capacity. By contrast, most nuclear power plants generated about 1,000 megawatts.

Biomass. The committee urged almost doubling research spending on obtaining fuels from biomass — forest, farm and animal wastes or plants grown as energy sources.

The administration sought $26.9 million for the program, $6.15 million more than fiscal 1978. The committee urged boosting the request by $21 million.

Other Programs

In addition to research and development programs, the committee bill covered the full range of Energy Department civilian activities.

Coal Loans. The committee added $6.5 million for the Coal Loan Guarantee program created under the 1975 Energy Policy and Conservation Act. The program was intended to stimulate coal production by allowing the department to guarantee loans to small coal producers who otherwise would be unable to obtain financing.

The committee said at least 350 coal producers would be eligible for the loans. The Energy Department request for $6.87 million for the program in a supplemental appropriation in late fiscal 1978 was blocked by the Office of Management and Budget (OMB), the report noted. The panel approved $6.87 million for it in the fiscal 1979 authorization bill, although there was no administration request in 1978.

Loan Guarantees. In a related area, the committee added $20 million to cover loan guarantees for construction and start-up costs of demonstration facilities for production of alternate fuels from coal, oil shale, biomass and other resources.

FERC. The Federal Energy Regulatory Commission (FERC) inherited most of the duties of the defunct Federal Power Commission (FPC), including regulation of interstate electric and gas sales. The FPC also had a long backlog of cases that the new agency inherited when the Energy Department was created.

FERC studies indicated that the commission's workload would increase by 12.1 percent during fiscal 1978, the report said. FERC and the department wanted more staff and money for fiscal 1979 to handle the increased load and to cut back the backlog, but OMB slashed the departmental request. As sent to Congress, the administration request for FERC called for 1,391 staff positions — 12 fewer than in fiscal 1978 — and $43.6 million in fiscal 1979 authorizations — $9.5 million more than the previous year but $7.2 million less than the department wanted.

The committee boosted the FERC authorization to $57.2 million, including funds for an additional 323 employees that FERC said it needed.

ERA. The Economic Regulatory Administration (ERA) within the Energy Department was responsible for enforcing the mass of regulatory programs concerning oil prices and allocation. The committee approved $69.8 million for the agency's operations, $9.8 million more than the administration sought.

The committee specified that it wanted the regulatory agency to lean hard on the 34 major oil refiners in the United States and ease up on small refiners in conducting audits to see if the refiners complied with price and allocation laws.

On Dec. 4, 1977, the ERA formed an Office of Special Counsel to determine through audits whether the nation's major refiners had made illegal overcharges for oil sales between May 1973 and December 1976. Estimates showed that up to $5 billion in overcharges may have occurred.

The administration had called for $23.8 million for that special investigation office. The office asked Congress for an additional $13.8 million. The committee approved both requests.

But the Senate panel cut $3.5 million from the administration request for funds to cover expenses for monitoring the compliance of small refiners, importers and oil sellers with fuel price and allocation laws.

"The president's request for these compliance activities represents a 22 percent increase over the fiscal 1978 estimate," the committee observed.

"The committee finds difficulty in reconciling this proposed increase with the department's contention that a phase out is under way of compliance and enforcement efforts directed against small firms. . . .

"The committee understands that open audits under this activity contain potential settlements of approximately $400 million. However, the committee also understands that potential recoveries from major refiners have been estimated to be in excess of $5 billion," the report said.

Therefore, the committee said, investigative efforts aimed at compliance should concentrate on the refiners "where the largest gains are to be made."

Entitlements

Section 604 of S 2692 barred the Energy Department from carrying out its announced plan to boost subsidies to importers of residual oil.

Under the existing "entitlements" program, refiners dependent on expensive foreign fuels had their fuel acquisition costs subsidized by payments from refiners who bought cheaper, federally price controlled domestic oil. The committee said the entitlements fund transferred about $200 million among domestic firms each month.

Under existing law, importers of residual oil, a finished oil product, were paid 30 percent entitlement benefits, which amounted to about a 60 cent per barrel subsidy. Residual oil was used primarily for boiler fuel by utilities, hospitals and other large institutions.

The system worked to the benefit of foreign refineries, especially those in the Caribbean, who were subsidized by the system. They also were aided by another policy, which required domestic refiners selling more than 5,000 barrels per day of residual oil in the East Coast market to forfeit about $1 per barrel in entitlements payments for each barrel over 5,000.

Together, the report argued, those two fuel policies kept imports of foreign residual oil high and "stifled" attempts to expand domestic refinery capacity to serve the East Coast.

In recent months, the report noted, the Energy Department had announced plans to increase the subsidy on imports of residual oil from the existing 30 percent level to a full 100 percent entitlement benefit.

'Reverse Entitlements'

At the same time, the department planned to remove the "reverse entitlements" penalty assessed against domestic suppliers of residual oil to the East Coast.

"An increase in the subsidy to a full 100 percent would transfer at least an additional $500 million annually from domestic consumers of petroleum products to imports of residual fuel oil," the report said. The benefits of the extra $500 million would be shared among foreign refiners, East Coast marketers and consumers of the imported oil, at the expense of the rest of the country, the report said.

The committee language blocking the change in the entitlement program was designed, the report said, "to reassert a measure of congressional control over the administration of the benefits of the entitlements fund."

A break for East Coast refiners later was approved as part of the Interior appropriations bill (HR 12932). *(Interior appropriations, p. 115)*

Pesticides Marketing Bill

Legislation designed to end the bureaucratic snarls tying up registration and marketing of pesticides was cleared by Congress Sept. 19.

The Senate Sept. 18 passed by voice vote the conference report (S Rept 95-1188) on S 1678 — PL 95-396, which extended through fiscal 1979 and amended the Federal Insecticide, Fungicide and Rodenticide Act (PL 94-140). The House passed the measure Sept. 19, also by voice vote, clearing it for the president.

The legislation left intact the basic philosophy that the public should be protected from harmful poisons.

But the revisions were directed at making it easier for farmers to find effective pesticides on the market. The new procedures authorized by the bill allowed the Environmental Protection Agency (EPA) to simplify registration of pesticides.

EPA had been drowning in data about the 35,000 pesticides on the market. Under the modified law, the agency was able to register pesticides according to their chemical composition instead of by their product name, a change known as "generic" registration that allowed EPA to focus its efforts on about 1,400 basic substances.

EPA would also get help from states, which were given new authority to enforce controls on pesticides once state governments met standards designed to maintain minimum, nationwide controls on the substances.

The changes were prompted by two main factors: EPA's failure to meet deadlines, set in a 1972 law, for assessing the safety of pesticides and farmers' complaints that the law was hindering food production by fouling up the pesticides market.

EPA officials also said the bill removed inequities in existing law that had given a marketing edge to longtime pesticide manufacturers and large corporations.

The measure also gave the public access to information about the effect of a pesticide on human health and the environment.

In addition to the reforms, the bill extended the Federal Insecticide, Fungicide and Rodenticide Act of 1975 (PL 95-140) through fiscal 1979 and authorized $54.5 million in fiscal 1978 and $70 million in fiscal 1979 to carry it out.

Both the House and Senate passed pesticide bills in 1977. The conference on the two versions took several months to reach a compromise. *(1977 Almanac p. 680)*

Conference Action

The large chemical companies that developed most pesticides preferred the House bill. It gave them a longer period to have "exclusive use" of the health and safety data they developed to support their products. The House bill also gave more power to the states, which in most cases were sympathetic to farmers and thus to the pesticides industry.

Environmentalists, on the other hand, supported the Senate bill, which did not allow exclusive use of safety data and gave less authority to the states.

Both sides claimed some victories from the conference.

Two major differences confronted the conferees when they started meeting in April—how much authority states would have for registering pesticides and how long a company could have exclusive use of the safety data it developed on a pesticide.

State Registration. The House bill expanded the power of states to register pesticides for intrastate use and removed EPA's right to review a state's decisions.

In conference, EPA and the Senate fought to retain EPA oversight of state actions so the public — nationwide — would be assured of a minimum level of protection from dangerous chemicals. The conferees agreed to retain existing EPA authority to veto a state registration, but did give the states a larger role in the registration process.

Exclusive Use. The new, 1972 requirements for safety data had the effect, in many cases, of extending the period during which a company that patented a pesticide had exclusive use of the product. Normally, after a patent expired, other companies could market the pesticide. The corporations that developed a pesticide claimed that the newly developed safety data were trade secrets and went to court to protect that claim.

In the meantime, other companies, as well as the public, were unable to see or use the data, and smaller companies that could not afford to duplicate the expensive tests were shut out of a large sector of the marketplace.

Both the House and Senate bills attempted to solve the problem by limiting the number of years of exclusive use and, after that, requiring companies to share the data for a fee. Both gave the public access to the data.

The House provided that a company could have five years of exclusive use of the data, and that during the next five years other companies could use the data to register identical products if they paid for the information. That protection also applied to any data submitted after the initial registration to justify registration of additional uses of the pesticide or to comply with new EPA requests.

EPA and Senate conferees complained that the House bill allowed a few companies to control the safety data for years and thus monopolize the market. Exclusive use would also hinder "generic" registration, they said. The Senate bill allowed no period of exclusive use and required that the developer of the information be compensated for use of the data for seven years after it was submitted to EPA.

The compromise worked out by the conferees gave those who developed new chemicals in the future 10 years of exclusive use of the safety data and an additional five years of compensation from others who used the data. The period of exclusive use coincided with the time during which a patent protected the product; as a result, the pesticides law did not give any extra edge to the large companies that developed new products.

For extra health and safety data on products already on the market, a company could not claim exclusive use, but would be compensated by other companies using the data for 15 years after the data were submitted. ▮

Water Resources Council

Legislation (S 2701 — PL 95-404) authorizing a one-year extension of the Water Resources Council was cleared by Congress Sept. 18. Funding for the council was provided in a continuing appropriations bill (H J Res 1139) that cleared Congress Oct. 15. *(Story, p. 161)*

The House passed the conference report (H Rept 95-1494) on the bill Sept. 15, 304-22. The Senate passed the report by voice vote Sept. 18, clearing it for the president. *(Vote 691, p. 196-H)*

Continuation of the council was imperiled July 11 when the House passed a bill (HR 11655) abolishing it and transferring its duties to the Department of the Interior.

The 13-year-old council was made up of department and agency heads who monitored national and regional water supplies, coordinated federal, state, regional and river basin water programs and administered a grant program to states for water resources planning.

Under President Carter's proposed water policy, the council was to review all new water projects. *(Water policy, p. 759; message text, p. 50-E)*

The council was established in 1965 to assess the national water situation. It was to oversee establishment of several river basin commissions that would study water needs and resources in their regions and suggest plans for developing sources of water. The council also was to recommend legislative solutions where necessary. Six river basin commissions operated in all but two areas of the country.

The Senate supported the administration and authorized continuation of the council in fiscal 1979 when it passed S 2701 May 25 by voice vote.

House conferees agreed to support the Senate provision extending the council one year, but reduced its administrative budget by $660,000 from $3,328,000 to $2,668,000.

Provisions

As cleared by Congress, S 2701:

- Authorized $2,886,000 in fiscal 1979 for administration of river basin commissions.
- Authorized $2,668,000 for the Water Resources Council.
- Authorized $3,179,900 for special studies and regional plans, including $828,900 for a study of the Columbia River Estuary; $459,000 for a Great Lakes water and energy study; $308,000 for a New England Port and Harbor Study; $135,000 for a Hudson River Basin Study and $150,000 for a study of flood plain management in the Connecticut River Basin.
- Authorized $3 million in fiscal 1979 for planning grants to states.

House Action

The House Committee on Interior and Insular Affairs reported HR 11655 May 15 (H Rept 95-1158). The original bill, introduced at the administration's request, called for continuation of the council while the administration studied water policy and reorganization proposals.

"The valuable work of the council is continuing with increased interest from all concerned with water and related land," Interior Secretary Cecil D. Andrus, council chairman, said in a letter urging the council's continuation. "Its programs to assess the water problems of this nation . . . will continue to assist greatly the water resource management programs of both federal and state governments."

However, the committee amended the bill to abolish the council as of Sept. 30, 1978.

Impetus for the amendment, offered by Nick J. Rahall, D-W.Va., came from the Appropriations Subcommittee on Public Works, which was responsible for funding the council's activities.

In an April 18 letter to Rahall, Tom Bevill, D-Ala., chairman of the appropriations subcommittee, and John T. Myers, R-Ind., its ranking minority member, urged that the council be disbanded.

"We feel that there is no need to extend the Water Resources Council," they wrote, adding that elimination of the council would go along with Carter's avowed intention to eliminate unnecessary bureaucracy. Transferring administration of the council's duties to the Interior Department would save $1,320,000, they said.

An amendment similar to Rahall's was offered by Manuel Lujan Jr., R-N.M., when the Interior Subcommittee on Water and Power Resources marked up the bill April 20, but it failed. Rahall's amendment was adopted by the full Interior Committee April 26, 20-13.

The House passed HR 11655 July 11 under suspension of rules, a procedure that does not permit amendments and requires a two-thirds vote for passage.

During floor debate, Lujan asserted that the Interior Committee had had "the patience of Job with this council over the past 10 years and that this action [to abolish it] is long overdue."

He charged that the council "was more interested in building and maintaining its own little bureaucratic empire than it was in completing the work it was given to do."

Dan Beard, deputy assistant secretary for land and water in the Interior Department said later that the administration was "most disappointed" in the vote.

Senate Action

The Senate Committee on Environment and Public Works reported S 2701 May 15 (S Rept 95-835). The committee said the council's authorization should continue through fiscal 1979 and recommended $14.1 million.

The Senate passed S 2701 by voice vote May 25.

Final Action

The conference report on the bill passed the House Sept. 15, 304-22 and the Senate by voice vote Sept. 18. ▮

Nuclear Licensing Reform

The Carter administration's nuclear licensing reform plan, designed to aid the ailing nuclear industry by speeding plant licensing, failed to clear Congress in 1978.

The last hope for even limited action by the 95th Congress was in a House Energy panel chaired by Morris K. Udall, D-Ariz. But Udall abandoned his plan for an "informal" markup Aug. 14 when he ran into resistance from members of his Interior Subcommittee on Energy.

Neither the House Commerce Committee, which shared jurisdiction, nor the Senate Environment Committee reported a licensing reform bill in 1978.

"We should give guidance [to the Carter administration] before we fold our tents for the year," Udall told the panel. The Department of Energy proposed a reform bill (HR 11704) in March that was attacked both by industry and environmentalists.

But James Weaver, D-Ore., who opposed the administration bill, said it would be "going into the snake pit for no purpose" to hold a markup where there was no hope of further action.

Bob Carr, D-Mich., agreed with Weaver. He complained that the administration had devised changes to end delays in nuclear licensing without first pinpointing what caused the delays.

Jonathan B. Bingham, D-N.Y., argued that a markup would be useful because the panel could "crystallize" its thinking and "be further along when we come back next year."

When a motion by Carr to end the markup appeared about to fail, Carr noted the absence of a quorum. The eight members present were one shy of the required number.

At that point, after a brief attempt to find another member, Udall gave up trying to meet on licensing reform in 1978.

Background

After 11 months of bureaucratic infighting, the Carter administration March 17 unveiled its proposal to streamline the licensing of nuclear power plants.

"We believe at the present time that the nuclear option is barely alive," Energy Secretary James R. Schlesinger told a news conference. The proposed bill, a department release said, "is intended to assure that nuclear power will remain a viable option."

Schlesinger said the proposed legislation would cut from 10 to 12 years to about 6.5 years the period between the decision to build a nuclear power plant and the time it was licensed to operate.

But because it would take several years before the proposal could be implemented, he said, "It will be a decade approximately before we begin to see the effects of these new procedures."

President Carter had called for streamlining the licensing process April 20, 1977, in his energy policy speech to Congress. The Energy Department had prepared a draft bill by August, but objections to it from other agencies and environmental and public interest groups led to months of internal administration debate and redrafting.

In the end, however, it appeared Schlesinger had won the bureaucratic war; the bill as submitted was strikingly similar to what his department had proposed originally. *(Background, 1977 Almanac p. 708)*

The proposed legislation was introduced into both chambers of Congress March 21 (S 2775, HR 11704).

Reaction

Initial reactions served warning that the proposal faced a rocky road.

The Atomic Industrial Forum, the nuclear industry's trade association, welcomed the bill but said it "needs substantial improvement."

Environmentalists and public interest groups said the bill gave short shrift to environmental concerns, unfairly restricted public access to the licensing process, ignored the real reasons behind nuclear power's development problems, failed to remedy existing problems associated with nuclear plants, such as where to store nuclear wastes, and proposed ineffective reforms which existing law already provided.

"It's a badly conceived, badly drafted and badly motivated piece of legislation," said Anthony Z. Roisman, a lawyer with the Natural Resources Defense Council. "[The bill] represents the final corruption of the president's moral and political courage on the nuclear issue. . . . The president has chosen to pay the price of losing his environmental constituency in exchange for a legislative proposal that will not win him a new constituency. This is curious politics for an election year."

Proposed Provisions

As introduced, the bill:

- Authorized the Nuclear Regulatory Commission (NRC) to approve sites for nuclear plants prior to the filing of a construction permit. The site approval would be valid for 10 years and could be renewed for 10 year periods.
- Authorized the NRC to approve standard nuclear reactor designs prior to the filing of a construction permit and independent of where the plant would be located. The approval would be valid for five years and renewable for periods of three years.
- Authorized the NRC to grant construction permits and operating licenses jointly, avoiding the existing system providing opportunities for two sets of hearings.
- Required states rather than the NRC to determine whether applicants needed the extra power that a proposed plant would provide.
- Allowed states, or voluntary regional groups of states, to assume some or all responsibility for assuring that proposed nuclear power plants met environmental impact standards set forth under the National Environmental Policy Act of 1969, a duty of the NRC under existing law.
- Specified that when states chose to administer environmental assessments, their findings would not be subject to challenge by the NRC or by a federal court review of NRC action.
- Reserved to NRC all authority to assess radiological health and safety questions.
- Permitted the NRC to issue interim operating licenses, valid for up to one year, before the completion of a hearing if there were an urgent public need or emergency and all matters concerning health and safety were resolved first.
- Cut back public hearings by mandating that if an opportunity once existed in any hearing for discussion of an issue, that issue could not be raised at later hearings unless significant new information had surfaced in the interim.
- Required the NRC to hold a formal hearing before granting a site permit, approving a standard design or issuing a joint construction/operation license.
- Required NRC to hold courtroom-style hearings for all health and safety issues, but required less formal legislative-style hearings for environmental challenges.
- Provided government funding for a five-year pilot program to cover costs of citizen intervenors. ▮

Seabed Mining

Companies eager to take minerals from the sea floor got a go-ahead signal July 26 from the House, which passed a bill (HR 3350) governing industrial mining on the ocean floor. However, the legislation died in the Senate because of objections from Sen. James Abourezk, D-S.D.

Abourezk, who retired at the end of the 95th Congress, blocked a "unanimous consent" agreement to limit debate on the bill (S 2053). As a result, the leadership refused to call it up. Abourezk opposed unilateral U.S. legislation on seabed mining prior to international agreement on rules to govern the mining.

As passed by the House, the bill would require that those mining the seabed have government licenses or permits and that they abide by government regulations designed to protect the environment. U.S. companies would have to pay taxes on mining profits even though the minerals would come from international waters.

The companies would have to turn some of their profits over to an international fund that eventually would be shared with other countries for mining operations.

The legislation would apply only until the adoption of an international treaty worked out by the ongoing United Nations Law of the Sea Conference.

Under U.S. interpretation of international law, the minerals were available to anyone under the concept of "freedom of the high seas." But U.S. mining companies had been unwilling to proceed because of changes in international law contemplated by the conference. They wanted the legislation as an indication of U.S. support of high seas freedoms. They said a firm U.S. policy would allow them to obtain from lenders the millions of dollars needed to buy mining vessels.

The mineral nodules, strewn on the ocean floor, contain manganese, copper, cobalt and nickel. Other resources, including oil and gas, lay beneath the seabed, but the technology for extracting them was still being developed. A seabed mining bill was expected to set precedents for development and distribution of the other high seas resources.

Four House committees — Merchant Marine, Interior, International Relations and Ways and Means — worked on the bill and developed a compromise proposal.

A Merchant Marine requirement that the government guarantee the mining companies' investment in the event of an unfavorable treaty was dropped when the other committees would not accept it.

Background and Controversies

The nodules sought by seabed miners were located in the high seas, far beyond any nation's territorial claims. Traditional high seas law said the nodules belonged to whoever got to them first.

But this old sea law, a favorite of pirates, was being rewritten by officials from more than 150 nations who were meeting as the Law of the Sea (LOS) Conference. Guiding the long-running conference on ocean law was a 1970 United Nations resolution, agreed to by the United States, that held the seabed resources to be the "common heritage of all mankind."

But participants in the conference disagreed on the application of this philosophy.

Developing countries said it entitled them to financial and technical assistance for seabed mining from industrialized countries. Some even claimed the right to control access to the seabed. Many of these developing countries were chief world suppliers of maganese, copper, cobalt and nickel, the minerals in seabed nodules. They wanted to protect themselves from competition from the seabed.

To the United States and other industrialized countries, the "common heritage" philosophy did not mean that the developing countries, with the majority of the votes in the conference, should control access to the seabed. The dispute over seabed mining threatened resolution of other issues facing the conference, which many U.S. officials considered more important or at least as important as seabed mining. These issues were outlined to a House committee by LOS Ambassador Elliot Richardson, who said an LOS treaty should:

- Provide a framework of law to accommodate competing ocean uses.
- Preserve high seas freedoms, including navigation and similar uses in the 200-mile economic zone.
- Maintain maximum freedom of scientific research.
- Provide a framework for protecting the marine environment.
- Establish a comprehensive dispute settlement mechanism.
- Establish an international regime for mining the deep seabeds which assured nondiscriminatory access under reasonable conditions for U.S. miners.

The desire for a treaty that spoke to all of these concerns had prompted continued U.S. participation in the LOS conference.

But U.S. mining companies interested in mining the nodules had grown impatient with the slow progress at the conference, which was first convened in 1958. The miners wanted domestic legislation that endorsed their efforts to mine the seabed.

Kennecott Copper, U.S. Steel and Lockheed were eager to begin scooping up nodules with giant vacuum cleaners and other special equipment they had been testing. But they said the shadow of the LOS negotiations kept them from getting the necessary financial backing for the multi-million dollar operations. They wanted legislation to provide guarantees for their investments in case the United States signed an LOS treaty that jeopardized their operations by giving control of the high seas to countries unsympathetic to private enterprise.

At first, the Carter administration opposed any seabed mining legislation, fearful it would hinder the LOS negotiations. But, after a frustrating session in the summer of 1977, the administration reassessed its position and decided to support a form of seabed mining legislation. Perhaps, the officials reasoned, it would spur conference negotitions.

According to Richardson, any bill supported by the administration had to:

- Not provide investment guarantees.
- Be interim until a treaty was signed.
- Share financial benefits with the international community.
- Concentrate on exploration, providing only a broad framework for the exploitation stage of mining.
- Designate no specific sites for mining.
- Not require that processing plants be located in the United States.
- Provide for environmental protection and sound resource management.

House Committee Action

The most divisive issue confronting congressional committees considering the legislation (HR 3350) — and one on which compromise was difficult — was the question of providing federal investment guarantees to U.S. mining companies. The House Merchant Marine Committee supported the guarantees, while the House Interior and International Relations Committees opposed them.

In addition, the Merchant Marine Committee, which oversees the Commerce Department, gave jurisdiction over seabed mining to that department, while the Interior Committee, which has jurisdiction over the Interior Department, placed jurisdiction there.

Following negotiations among the committees' staffs, an agreement was reached to drop the investment guarantees. Supporters of the guarantees realized the provision was not likely to pass the House and, if approved, would draw a veto from Carter. Then a new dispute arose over whether to create an international revenue sharing fund to pay for future seabed mining ventures.

The concept of shared revenues was a cornerstone of the U.S. approach to setting up new rules on how the world should share the resources of the seabed and the high seas. However, no specific administration recommendation on how a revenue sharing fund should operate domestically had been put forward.

None of the three committees set up a revenue sharing fund in the versions of HR 3350 that they reported, though all called for future, separate legislation establishing such a fund. An International Relations amendment would have blocked permits for mining until a fund had been set up.

This link between the fund and the permits was pushed by the administration, but was not acceptable to the Merchant Marine Committee. The committee did not want the miners, already facing uncertainties of the Law of the Sea conference, to have to wait for Congress to act again to set up a fund before being able to mine.

At one point, the negotiators were close to agreement on including a specific revenue sharing proposal in HR 3350. But the Treasury Department insisted that tax treatment of revenues from seabed mining, already put off for future legislation, be tied to revenue sharing, either in this bill or a future bill.

The problem with including taxes and revenue sharing in HR 3350 from the beginning of action was that the Ways and Means Committee would also have jurisdiction, adding a fourth committee to an already complicated situation. Because of the desire to give Richardson a bill for the LOS conference, the committees had tried to avoid a time-consuming referral to Ways and Means.

In addition, the committees wanted a specific proposal for revenue sharing from the administration, which was unable to clear up internal differences on the issue during several months of congressional action.

The State Department opposed the Treasury requirement that no permit for mining be issued until Congress had passed legislation governing the tax treatment of seabed mining — and the Carter administration subsequently agreed not to offer the Treasury proposal.

Merchant Marine Bill

As reported by the Merchant Marine Committee Aug. 9, 1977, HR 3350 established interim regulation of seabed mining until an international ocean treaty could be negotiated. The bill disclaimed U.S. sovereignty over any area of the seabed.

It also required that:

- Miners have a license from the Commerce Department to explore the seabed and a permit to recover minerals.
- Applicants be financially responsible and technologically capable and that their activities not interfere with other countries' exercise of high seas freedoms, conflict with any international obligation of the United States or pose an unreasonable threat to the quality of the environment.
- Facilities to process seabed nodules be located in the United States.
- Ships used in seabed mining activities be documented under laws of the United States.
- A programmatic environmental impact statement be filed on seabed mining in a generally defined ocean area and that environmental impact statements then be filed on each permit or license granted.
- Any eligible licensee or permittee be entitled to payments from the federal government covering 90 percent of non-recoverable losses, or up to $350 million per mining site, caused by U.S. agreement to an international treaty. A U.S. district court would decide the amount of compensation.
- Only licensees or permittees who chose to contribute to the Ocean Mining Fund would be eligible for the investment guarantees. Their annual contribution, to be set by the secretary of commerce, could not be less than ¼ percent nor more than ¾ percent of the investment made by the licensee or permittee in seabed mining in the preceding year.
- The secretary of commerce, within 180 days of passage of HR 3350, submit legislative recommendations to Congress on establishing a special seabed fund. The fund would be shared with the international community if a treaty were signed that required such contributions from seabed miners.

Interior

Amendments to HR 3350 reported by the Interior Committee on Nov. 7, 1977, required that:

- It be U.S. policy to seek protection in an international treaty for U.S. licensees and permittees to continue their operations on the seabed.
- The secretary of interior administer seabed mining laws.
- Applications for licenses or permits be submitted to the attorney general and the Federal Trade Commission for antitrust review and recommendations.
- Licensees or permittees use the best available technology economically achievable to protect the environment.
- Licensees or permittees be required to allow federal officials aboard any vessel used in mining-related operations.
- The investment guarantees section be deleted.
- Licensees or permittees monitor the environmental effects of their operations and furnish information gathered to the secretary if requested.

International Relations

Amendments to HR 3350 reported by the International Relations Committee Feb. 16, 1978, required that:

- Conservation of natural resources and protection of life and property at sea be added to the purposes of the bill.
- It be U.S. policy to seek protection in an international treaty for U.S. licensees and permittees to continue their operations on the seabed.
- The disclaimer of sovereignty be strengthened by also disclaiming "exclusive control" over any area of the seabed.
- Licenses or permits be allowed to be issued even after an international agreement was in force if they were consistent with it.
- Ships documented under laws of reciprocating states be allowed to be used in seabed mining operations.
- The executive agency have flexibility to approve location of processing plants in order to weigh the desire to create U.S. jobs against the multinational nature of the mining and other U.S. foreign policy considerations.
- The investment guarantees section be deleted.
- An international revenue sharing fund be authorized, with details to be worked out by the executive agency.

Contributions to the fund from seabed miners would go to international seabed mining ventures if a treaty were signed that called for such ventures.

- No licenses or permits be issued until legislation governing tax treatment of mining and the revenue sharing fund took effect.

Ways and Means

The House Ways and Means Committee April 27 approved a proposal to require that companies mining the deep seabed contribute to a trust fund for international development of the seabed.

Including the trust fund in the bill (HR 3350) made the measure acceptable to many internationally-oriented House members who had opposed it, and cleared the way for House action.

Ways and Means was the fourth House committee to act on the legislation to regulate seabed mining.

Companies harvesting mineral nodules from the ocean floor would have to pay an excise tax of .75 percent of their annual revenues into the "international revenue sharing fund" approved by Ways and Means.

The Carter administration and the three other committees that reported out the measure — Merchant Marine, Interior and International Relations — all supported the concept of such a fund. However, approval was needed from Ways and Means because it had jurisdiction over all tax matters.

House Floor Action

The House passed HR 3350 July 26, by a vote of 312-80. *(Vote 527, p. 150-H)*

The four panels that reported the bill had been unable to agree on whether the Interior or Commerce Departments should administer the seabed mining program and left the issue to the full House to decide.

John B. Breaux, D-La., chairman of Merchant Marine's Oceanography Subcommittee, led the fight to place administration with the Commerce Department's National Oceanic and Atmospheric Administration (NOAA). NOAA had studied the environmental effects of ocean mining and handled ocean-related matters. Breaux's panel had jurisdiction over NOAA.

Interior Chairman Morris K. Udall, D-Ariz., argued that the Interior Department, which was responsible for onshore mining and development of oil and gas on the outer continental shelf, should logically oversee seabed mining. His committee had jurisdiction over Interior.

Edward J. Derwinski, R-Ill., summed up the situation when he called the dispute a "little civil war between departments of our government."

The vote was very close, and the lighted scoreboard in the House chamber showed the score tied several times. Finally, as the last 25 or so votes were cast, Commerce pulled ahead and won the race 214-184. *(Vote 525, p. 150-H)*

In another close vote, the House rejected, 199-202, an amendment by Paul N. McCloskey Jr., R-Calif., to require companies to define the area they intended to mine in a "work plan" to be submitted to the government when they applied for a license or permit. Under the amendment, a license or permit still was required, but it would not specify the area to be mined, other than describing it as the area defined in the "work plan." *(Vote 526, p. 150-H)*

McCloskey argued that not specifying the site in the official government license would remove "any inference that in enacting this bill the U.S. government is claiming jurisdiction over any area of the seabed beyond the 200-mile limit of the United States."

McCloskey said the "words may be seen by some to be cosmetic," but he argued that the language was important.

Breaux, opposing the amendment, said the bill already denied any claim of U.S. jurisdiction. He pointed out that the "work plans" would not be public documents, so that information about what areas were mined would not be readily available. Under the committee bill, licenses and permits would specify the area to be mined and would be published in the *Federal Register,* Breaux said.

Bingham, chairman of the International Relations Economic Policy and Trade Subcommittee, said he supported the amendment, but advised the House not to "overestimate the importance" of the amendment because it was only "a difference in terminology."

Access by U.S. Miners

The Merchant Marine Committee bill had contained a "grandfather" clause stating that U.S. policy would be to seek a treaty that would allow U.S. miners continued access to the seabed. However, the committee language was weakened by a floor amendment offered by Millicent Fenwick, R-N.J., much to the dismay of Breaux.

Breaux argued that the changes would represent a shift in U.S. policy at the Law of the Sea conference.

Fenwick's amendment, adopted on a non-record vote, said any international agreement should "allow" U.S. miners to continue operating, that operations should be able to continue in a "similar" way and that the treaty should not "unreasonably" impair investments. The Merchant Marine language, which was in the bill when it reached the floor, said any international agreement should "recognize the rights" of miners to continue operating that operations should be able to continue in "substantially the same way" and that the treaty should not "materially" impair investments.

In other action, the House adopted amendments by:

- John M. Murphy, D-N.Y., to require that ships used for mining and processing be registered under the U.S. flag.
- Murphy to require that at least one ship used to carry the minerals to shore for processing be registered under the U.S. flag.
- James M. Jeffords, R-Vt., to strengthen the bill's requirement that NOAA cooperate with the Environmental Protection Agency in monitoring the environmental impacts of the mining.
- George Miller, D-Calif., to make regulations issued under the law apply retroactively to mining operations under way at the time of issue.

The House rejected an amendment by Fortney H. (Pete) Stark, D-Calif., to require that 10 percent of mining profits go to the fund that would be shared internationally. The bill required that only .75 percent of the revenues be earmarked for the fund.

House Provisions

As passed by the House, HR 3350:

Title I — Regulation

- Stated that in regulating the mining activities of U.S. citizens on the high seas, the United States was not asserting sovereignty over or ownership of any area of the deep seabed.

- Provided that the act was interim, pending U.S. approval of an international agreement to govern mining of the seabed.
- Required any U.S. miner to get from the Commerce Department a license to explore the seabed and a permit for commercial recovery of the minerals.
- Required that the mining vessel, the processing vessel and at least one carrier used to transport minerals to shore be documented under the laws of the United States.
- Required the commerce secretary, before issuing a license, to determine that applicants were financially responsible and had the technical expertise to mine.
- Required the secretary to determine, before issuing a license, that planned mining activities would not 1) interfere with the operations of other countries exercising freedoms of the high seas; 2) conflict with international obligations of the United States; 3) provide an unreasonable threat to the quality of the environment. If circumstances changed so that mining activities began to affect adversely those conditions, the commerce secretary could modify restrictions in the permit or license.
- Provided that terms of permits and licenses could not be modified by the secretary if the national interest in obtaining the hard mineral sources outweighed the potential injury to the quality of the environment intended to be remedied by the modifications.
- Required the secretary, in modifying the terms, to consider whether the modification would cause significant economic loss to the miner that would outweigh the injury to the environment that the modification was supposed to correct.
- Authorized the secretary to suspend a license or permit to avoid conflict with an international obligation.
- Required that a 90-day period be provided before issuance of a permit or license for an anti-trust review of the application by the attorney general and the Federal Trade Commission.
- Authorized the secretary to override a recommendation by the attorney general or the Federal Trade Commission to deny an application if he notified the agencies first of his decision.
- Required the secretary to give written notice of his intent to deny, suspend or revoke a license or permit and allow an applicant, permittee or licensee up to 180 days to correct a deficiency if the extra time was requested by the miner within 30 days after the notice from the secretary.
- Required the secretary to prepare a programmatic environmental impact statement that would generally assess the effect of ocean mining on the environment.
- Required preparation of an environmental impact statement under the National Environmental Policy Act of 1969 before approval of any license or permit.
- Required the license or permit to specify the area of the seabed to be mined.
- Required the secretary to set performance requirements.
- Required that records of miners be accessible to the government for audits and other purposes and to the public, except for information protected by trade secrets laws.
- Provided that federal officials would be allowed on board mining vessels.
- Authorized the president to designate a country as a reciprocating state if it had an interim legal framework for exploration and commercial recovery of minerals and recognized U.S. licenses and permits. In return, the United States would honor the mining operations of reciprocating states.

Title II — Transition to Treaty

- Stated it was the intent of Congress that an international agreement signed by the United States provide nondiscriminatory access to the seabed for U.S. citizens; allow U.S. citizens who already had mining operations underway to "continue their operations under similar terms, conditions and restrictions" as those imposed by U.S. regulation and "not unreasonably impair the value of investments" already made.

Title III — Penalties

- Authorized the secretary to assess civil penalties of up to $50,000 for each violation of regulations issued under the law.
- Authorized the secretary to assess criminal penalties of up to $250,000 a day against anyone who willfully and knowingly violated the seabed regulations.
- Authorized appropriation of such sums as necessary to carry out the act.

Title IV — Tax

- Imposed a tax of 3.75 percent of the "imputed" value of minerals removed from the deep seabed. The imputed value was equal to 20 percent of the fair market value of the minerals. The tax would be equivalent to .75 percent of the fair market value.
- Provided that the tax revenues would be held for 10 years in the Deep Seabed Revenue Sharing Trust Fund, which would be used to make any contributions required by an international deep seabed treaty. If a treaty were not in effect after 10 years, Congress would decide how to use the money in the fund.

Senate Committee Action

The Senate Energy and Natural Resources Committee approved seabed mining legislation (S 2053) May 2. The bill was approved by the Senate Commerce, Science and Transportation Committee Aug. 10 and by the Foreign Relations Committee Sept. 11.

The differences in the committees' bills were to be resolved on the Senate floor. Progress was complicated by the overlapping jurisdiction of the various committees.

The measures approved by the Commerce and Foreign Relations committees differed in several important respects from the one adopted earlier by the Energy Committee and from the bill that was passed by the House. (Commerce, Energy report: S Rept 95-1125; Foreign Relations report: S Rept 95-1180)

U.S. Ships. The Commerce and Foreign Relations committees added a controversial provision that would require all ships licensed for the recovery or processing of seabed minerals to be built in the United States. Furthermore, licensed companies would have to use at least one U.S. flag vessel to transport their recovered minerals to shore. The ships involved would be guaranteed construction and operating subsidies from the federal government.

The provision was necessary, the Commerce Committee said in its section of the report it filed jointly with the Energy Committee, "to ensure that the advanced technology will remain available to the nation and will not be freely exported to the site of cheapest construction" and to "enable the United States to enforce the environmental provisions of S 2053 and federal construction and safety requirements."

In addition, the committee said, the provision would stimulate the maritime industry and create thousands of jobs in shipyards and at sea. The maritime unions lobbied heavily for the provision.

The Congressional Budget Office estimated that the construction subsidies would cost the Treasury nearly $200 million from fiscal 1980 through 1983.

Sen. Robert P. Griffin, R-Mich., who voted against the bill in both the Commerce and Foreign Relations committees, attacked the ship-building provision as "an appalling power play" by maritime interests. The provision was also opposed by the Carter administration. A similar provision was contained in the House bill.

Investment Guarantee. The Commerce and Foreign Relations committees rejected a provision approved by the Energy Committee that would guarantee the investment of U.S. mining companies against an unfavorable Law of the Sea treaty. The Carter administration strenuously opposed the insurance system, which was not part of the House bill.

Domestic Production. The Senate Energy and Commerce committees adopted language requiring that all ore mined by U.S. companies be processed in the United States. That provision was rejected by the House and by the Senate Foreign Relations Committee.

Lead Agency. The Commerce Committee's bill would place the direction of the seabed mining program in the National Oceanic and Atmospheric Administration, a part of the Commerce Department and an agency over which the committee had jurisdiction. That was also the position taken by the House. The bills approved by the Energy and Foreign Relations committees would put the Interior Department, over which the Energy Committee had jurisdiction, in charge of the mining program.

Toxic Substances Control

What began as a noncontroversial authorization for toxic substances control was defeated by the House June 12 as members protested government spending and federal controls on business.

Rep. James M. Collins, R-Texas, led the fight against the Environmental Protection Agency (EPA) authorization, arguing that "America has too many duplicated, money spending, paperwork agencies."

The failure of the bill (HR 12441 — H Rept 95-1163) was a surprise to supporters, who had sought its passage under suspension of the rules. This procedure requires approval by two-thirds of the voting members instead of a simple majority, and does not permit any amendments. The vote was 190-188, 62 votes shy of two-thirds. *(Vote 376, p. 108-H)*

"They weren't voting on reasonableness or rationality; it was just emotion," said one agency official. "It was Proposition 13 all over."

The June 6 approval by Californians of Proposition 13 forced drastic reductions in property taxes. Observers speculated that it sparked some votes against the bill by members eager to be on the record against federal spending.

Toby Moffett, D-Conn., brought up the California vote when he spoke for the bill and against Collins: "I might say to my friend from Texas that he cannot be accused of jumping on the Proposition 13 bandwagon; his credentials in that area were well established long before that vote."

Moffett went on to say, "We might agree that there is too much government. There is also too much cancer, too many birth defects." Moffett said the control of toxic subtances was an area where "no one else [but government] is going to do the job."

The bill would have increased the authorization for implementation of the Toxic Substances Control Act of 1976 (PL 94-468) from $16 million to $50 million for fiscal 1979. The funding would allow EPA to start enforcing the act, which is designed to evaluate the safety of chemicals before they enter the marketplace. *(Background, 1977 Almanac p. 676)*

But Collins complained that the act would be a costly burden for chemical companies, particularly small firms. Collins also criticized the bureaucracy spawned by environmental controls.

Omnibus Parks Bill

The largest parks bill in history, authorizing $1.2 billion for more than 100 parks and preservation projects in 44 states, was passed in the closing days of the 95th Congress.

The legislation (S 791 — PL 95-625) was shepherded through by Rep. Phillip Burton, D-Calif., chairman of the Interior Subcommittee on Parks. In an effort to accommodate senators and to speed passage of the measure, Burton had the House pass three versions of the bill.

His efforts paid off when the Senate Oct. 12 accepted by voice vote a modified version of one of the House bills and returned it to the House. The bill, the National Parks and Recreation Act of 1978, was cleared by the House Oct. 13, also by voice vote.

Major elements of the bill included:

- Expansion by 16,200 acres of **Sequoia National Park, Calif.,** to include an area known as Mineral King Valley. Formerly managed by the U.S. Forest Service, the site had been sought by the Walt Disney Corp. for a ski resort, a use not usually allowed in a park.
- Designation of 37 miles of the **Middle Delaware River** as a wild and scenic river, a classification that prohibited construction across the river of the controversial Tocks Island Dam.
- Authorization of $125 million through fiscal 1983 to acquire undeveloped areas in the **Santa Monica Mountains** in Los Angeles and Ventura counties in California for a national recreation area.
- Authorization of an **urban parks** program providing $150 million annually in fiscal 1979-1982 for grants to rehabilitate recreational facilities, including basketball and tennis courts.

'Park Barrel'

Because the bill encompassed so many projects in so many states, members referred to it as the "park barrel" bill, a play on the name given to legislation called "pork barrel" that spreads federal dollars to dozens of congressional districts.

The number of projects in the bill prompted some bantering among senators during floor debate. "Is there any state other than Kansas that did not end up with a park?" asked Sen. Robert Dole, R-Kan.

"Did we leave you out, Bob?" asked Sen. James Abourezk, D-S.D., chairman of the Energy Subcommittee on Parks and floor manager of the bill.

"I have two more years in my term," noted Dole, as the laughter continued in the chamber.

Sen. Clfford P. Hansen, R-Wyo., also on the parks subcommittee, offered Dole a little sympathy. "It is my understanding that six states — five others — did not make it."

"I appreciate that," replied Dole. "We will have a meeting later."

Major Provisions

As cleared by Congress, S 791 authorized development and expansion of dozens of existing parks and established several new national parks, seashores, trails and wild and scenic rivers.

Major expansions were authorized for:

- Sequoia National Park, Calif.: addition of 16,200 acres known as Mineral King Valley.
- Cuyahoga Valley National Park, Ohio: addition of 2,670 acres.
- Delaware Water Gap National Recreation Area, Del. and Pa.: addition of acreage held by the Army Corps of Engineers for Tocks Island Dam.
- Golden Gate National Recreation Area, Calif.: addition of 4,000 acres.
- Point Reyes National Seashore, Calif.: addition of 2,000 acres.
- Chesapeake and Ohio Canal National Historical Park, Washington, D.C., Md., W.Va.: addition of 600 acres.

Nearly 2 million wilderness acres were established in 8 existing park areas. The additions exceeded the total acreage of all U.S. park land previously designated as wilderness:

- Buffalo National River, Ark.: 10,529 acres.
- Carlsbad Caverns National Park, N.M.: 33,125 acres.
- Everglades National Park, Fla.: 1,296,500 acres.
- Guadalupe Mountains National Park, Texas: 46,850 acres.
- Gulf Islands National Seashore, Fla. and Miss.: 1,800 acres.
- Hawaii Volcanoes National Park, Hawaii: 123,100 acres.
- Organ Pipe Cactus National Monument, Ariz.: 312,600 acres.
- Theodore Roosevelt National Memorial Park, N.D.: 29,920 acres.

The bill authorized creation of 11 new parks, seashores, historic sites and recreation areas:

- Edgar Allen Poe National Historic Site, Pa.
- St. Paul's Church, N.Y.
- Kaloko-Honokohau National Historic Park, Hawaii.
- Palo Alto Battlefield National Historic Site, Texas.
- Santa Monica Mountains National Recreation Area, Calif.
- Ebey's Landing National Historical Park, Wash.
- Friendship Hill National Historic Site, Pa.
- Thomas Stone National Historic Site, Md.
- Maggie L. Walker National Historic Site, Va.
- New River Gorge National River, W.Va.
- Jean Lafitte National Historical Park, La.

The bill established the following new trails:

- The Oregon Trail running from Independence, Mo., to Portland, Ore.
- The Mormon Pioneer Trail running from Nauvoo, Ill., to Salt Lake City.
- The Continental Divide National Scenic Trail running from the Montana-Canada border to the New Mexico-Mexico border.
- The Lewis and Clark Trail running from Wood River, Ill., to Columbia River, Ore.
- The Iditarod Trail running from Seward, Alaska, to Nome, Alaska.

The bill authorized $150 million annually in fiscal 1979-1982 for grants to cover up to 70 percent of the cost of the rehabilitation of recreation facilities in urban areas.

Segments of the following rivers were added to the National Wild and Scenic Rivers system:

- Pere Marquette River, Mich.
- Rio Grande, Texas.
- Skagit River and tributaries, Wash.
- Upper Delaware River, N.Y., Pa.
- Middle Delaware River in Delaware Water Gap National Recreation Area, N.Y., Pa. and N.J.
- North Fork of American River, Calif.
- Missouri River, Neb., S.D.
- St. Joe River, Idaho.

House Action on First Bill

The first bill (HR 12536) was reported by the House Interior Committee May 15 (H Rept 95-1165) and passed by the House July 12 on a vote of 341-61. *(Vote 463, p. 132-H)*

Debate on the measure extended over several days. Most of it involved attempts by members to remove rivers and wilderness areas in their states from the bill because their inclusion would preclude development.

However, the biggest change in the bill reported from the Interior Committee was acceptance of a package of 70 amendments that cut $220 million in authorizations from the measure. The changes, which chipped a little away from many different proposals, were worked out with the Carter administration, which had been concerned about the high price tag on the bill. They were offered by Phillip Burton, D-Calif., floor manager of the bill, and were adopted by voice vote.

Tocks Island

A major floor fight was over Tocks Island. Debate centered on the addition of 37 miles of the Middle Delaware River within the Delaware Gap National Recreation Area to the national wild and scenic rivers system — a designation that prohibits construction of any dams on a free-flowing river.

Frank Thompson Jr., D-N.J., failed in his effort to delete the designation of the Middle Delaware and thus save the dam. His amendment was defeated 110-275. *(Vote 456, p. 130-H)*

Thompson said the dam had been promised in the 1950s to southern New Jersey for water supply and flood protection. He complained that the parks bill provided a backdoor deauthorization even though four studies of alternatives ordered by Congress were incomplete.

Those opposing the Thompson amendment were led by Peter H. Kostmayer, D-Pa., who argued that the historic and scenic river should not be destroyed for a dam with questionable benefits.

Even the Army Corps of Engineers, "the ultimate dam-builders," opposed the project, said Kostmayer, who had distributed small vials of Delaware River water to each member of the House.

Helen Meyner, D-N.J., whose district bordered the designated segment of the Middle Delaware, joined Kostmayer in opposing the dam. "We must not consign our heritage to the bottom of a putrid lake," she told the House.

Upper Mississippi

Another fight involved designation of the Upper Mississippi in Minnesota as a wild and scenic river.

Members adopted an amendment by James L. Oberstar, D-Minn., which put off designation of the river as wild and scenic for at least a year while a master plan was prepared detailing what areas would be involved. It was adopted 205-192. *(Vote 461, p. 132-H)*

Debate on both sides of the amendment was conducted almost entirely by members of the Minnesota delegation.

Oberstar and other opponents of the designation argued that existing studies of the Upper Mississippi did not delineate where development would take place and what properties would be acquired if the river were designated wild and scenic.

"What we have here," Oberstar said, "[is] a rubber-stamped proposition sent over by the administration, a proposition approved by the committee and sent to the House floor. We do not know what the boundaries of the corridor are or the extent of acquisition."

"People in Minnesota are upset about this," he continued. "They do not know whether they want a wild and scenic river on the Mississippi or not, because they do not know what it means. They do not know what it entails."

Opponents of the amendment were led by Bruce F. Vento, D-Minn. Vento argued that hearings in and studies of the area that would be affected by the designation provided adequate information.

"There is nothing to be gained and much to be lost by the adoption of the study provision or deletion amendments," Vento said. "A delay in designation can only mean increased federal costs, harmful development of the riverbank and a repudiation of the wild and scenic rivers designation process which Congress establish to resolve conflicts."

Proponents also noted that President Carter, in his 1977 environmental message, had recommended wild and scenic designation for the Upper Mississippi and that it also was supported by Vice President Walter F. Mondale of Minnesota. However, opponents asserted that the designation was opposed by Minnesota's senior senator, Wendell R. Anderson, D. *(Environmental message, 1977 Almanac p. 30-E)*

Other Action

Among other amendments adopted by the House were those by:

- William C. Wampler, R-Va., to delete from the bill the designation of about 12,700 acres as wilderness in the Cumberland Gap National Historical Park, Ky., Tenn. and Va. The change was adopted by voice vote.
- Max Baucus, D-Mont., to delete from the bill the designation of 927,550 acres as wilderness in Glacier National Park, Mont. The amendment was adopted 216-181. *(Vote 459, p. 132-H)*
- Richard C. White, D-Texas, to reduce the area the bill designated as wilderness in the Guadalupe Mountains National Park from 58,000 acres to 46,850 acres. The amendment was adopted by voice vote.
- Jerry M. Patterson, D-Calif., providing for a study of the Irvine Coast-Laguna, Calif., for inclusion in the national park system, that reduced the acreage to be studied from 20,000 to 17,000 and reduced the amount authorized for the study from $250,000 to $50,000. It was adopted by a 37-16 division vote.
- Among the amendments rejected was one by Steven D. Symms, R-Idaho, to change the boundary of the Hells Canyon National Recreation Area, Idaho, to exclude the Blue Jacket mining area. It was rejected 147-249. *(Vote 460, p. 132-H)*

Second Bill Cleared

After the House passed its first parks bill (HR 12536) July 12, there was little action on the measure in the Senate Energy Committee, which was bogged down first with the natural gas bill (HR 5289) and then with Alaska lands legislation (HR 39). As the scheduled adjournment neared, Burton realized that the only way to get a bill cleared was to avoid a time-consuming conference.

On Oct. 4, Burton won House passage of a new version of the bill, which he attached to a minor Senate parks bill (S 791) dealing with the Sawtooth National Recreation Area in Idaho.

Burton needed to attach the provisions to a Senate bill so that the measure would be immediately available for floor action and would not be referred to the Senate Energy Committee, which had already considered S 791.

The most controversial provisions of the original House bill, HR 12536, were left out of S 791 in an attempt to ensure Senate passage. Because of Senate rules, objections from one or two senators could have blocked passage in the busy closing days.

Two such projects were the Manassas National Battlefield Park in Prince William County, Va., and Crater Lake National Park in Oregon.

Sen. William L. Scott, R-Va., killed the proposed 1,800 acre expansion of the Manassas Park near Washington, D.C. Real estate developers had taken over much of the surrounding area, and park planners had wanted to expand the Civil War battlefield memorial to protect it from suburban sprawl. But the Prince William County Board of Supervisors objected to the park expansion, partly because it would have eroded the county tax base. Scott successfully fought to delete the project before the Senate took up the revised parks bill.

Sen. Mark O. Hatfield, R-Ore., deleted another proposal which designated 127,500 acres of the Crater Lake National Park in Oregon as a wilderness area. Although that proposal would not have expanded the park, it would have restricted recreational uses, and thus ran into opposition from local authorities.

Several of the remaining controversial projects, described as "cats and dogs" by one House aide, were included in a separate bill (S 491) passed by the House Oct. 4, but never taken up in the Senate.

Among the controversial provisions put in S 491 were designation of San Antonio Missions in Texas as a national historic park. The project was opposed by some senators and administration officials because of possible conflicts between church and state that might result from continued church operations inside the facility and Department of Interior management on the outside. However, that park eventually was created in another bill (S 1829).

Another controversial provision would have changed the name of the Indiana Dunes National Lakeshore to Paul H. Douglas Indiana Dunes in honor of the late Democratic senator from Illinois (1949-67). Douglas was instrumental in establishing the park, but Indiana's senators, Democrat Birch Bayh and Republican Richard G. Lugar, opposed the name change and any bill that included it.

But there were still some complaints in the Senate. Burton spent a lot of time on the Senate floor, trying to work out individual problems, and Senate and House staff met to resolve the differences. Eventually, the Senate came up with a package of about 27 amendments to S 791, many of them minor, and Sen. James Abourezk, D-S.D., prepared to offer the changes on the Senate floor.

Among the major changes included in the 27 amendments were the following:

- Deletion of a House provision that would have reimbursed the Walt Disney Corp. for losses incurred by the addition of Mineral King Valley to the national park system. In addition, the Senate wanted language clearly stating that downhill skiing would be incompatible with management of the area as a park.
- Modification of a House provision that would have allowed government condemnation of homes within the Fire Island National Seashore in New York if a home were 50 percent destroyed by a hurricane or other disaster and were located on the dunes or in a community 50 percent destroyed by the natural catastrophe. The Senate wanted language to allow government condemnation and purchase only of property in a special Dunes District on the beach and then only if the property owner started building after the date S 791 was enacted.
- Deletion of the North Country National Scenic Trail running from New York to North Dakota because of questions from senators and because, according to Senate aides, no hearing was held on the trail. Also to be deleted was government authority to buy lands on or along any trail, though areas could still be designated as trails.

Still Another Version

But before Abourezk could attach the amendments to S 791, Burton, afraid time would run out on the bill, added them to yet another measure. On Oct. 11, he attached the text of S 791 plus the 27 amendments to another bill, HR 6900, which the House readily passed.

As it turned out, the Senate Oct. 12 had time to take up the second version, S 791. HR 6900 died.

In addition to adding the package of 27 amendments, the Senate adopted an amendment offered by Sen. Charles McC. Mathias Jr., R-Md., to expand the boundaries of the Hampton National Historic Site near Towson, Md.

Rejected were amendments offered by Sen. Mike Gravel, D-Alaska, to delete the designation of the Middle Delaware River and thus avoid obstructing the Tocks Island Dam, and by Sen. S. I. Hayakawa, R-Calif., to delete the addition of Mineral King Valley to the Sequoia National Park.

S 791 then went back to the House, which approved it by voice vote Oct. 13.

Pennsylvania Avenue Development

In the flurry of bill-passing, the legislators left out of S 791 the authorization for the Pennsylvania Avenue Development Corporation, the overseer of improvements to the avenue between the White House and Capitol Hill. The authorization had been included in the first House parks bill, HR 12536. The House Sept. 29 then resurrected and passed another bill (S 2566) containing the corporation's authorization and sent it to the Senate.

But the Senate Oct. 12 added several items to the bill, including the deauthorization of the Cross Florida Barge Canal, a controversial project supported by some House members. Rather than have the development corporation tangled up with that and other controversies, the House added the authorization for the corporation to still another Senate bill (S 1829).

That bill also included authorization for the San Antonio Missions National Historical Park in Texas, which was included in the original House-passed parks bill, but not in the final version.

The House and then the Senate approved S 1829 (PL 95-629) on the final day of the session. S 2566 died.

A provision creating the War in the Pacific National Historical Park in Guam was pulled from the original House-passed parks bill and added to S 2821, which cleared Congress Aug. 4 (PL 95-348). ▮

Endangered Species Curbs

Congress Oct. 15 cleared legislation allowing exemptions under the Endangered Species Act so that future conflicts with public works projects — such as the one that pitted a tiny fish against a Tennessee dam — could be avoided.

As signed into law, the bill (S 2899 — PL 95-632) set up a Cabinet-level board to consider permitting construction of federal projects, even though they might kill off species protected by the 1973 law (PL 93-205). *(Endangered Species Act background, 1973 Almanac p. 670)*

The drive in Congress to make the law more flexible was sparked by a June 15 Supreme Court decision barring operation of the Tennessee Valley Authority's (TVA) Tellico Dam, which already had been built. The court, in a 6-3 decision, ruled that opening the floodgates of the $119 million dam would destroy the critical habitat of a three-inch fish called the snail darter.

Rearguard Tactics

The sentiment to soften the law was so strong in Congress that members allied with environmentalists early on gave up fighting the concept of exemptions. Instead, members such as Rep. John D. Dingell, D-Mich., concentrated their efforts on keeping modifications of the law to a minimum.

At one point, Rep. Robin L. Beard Jr., R-Tenn., a critic of the law, threatened to introduce 682 amendments to the bill, lifting protection for many species, if his views did not prevail. In the past, Beard had sought fruitlessly to get an exemption to the law for TVA's Columbia Dam in his district.

Environmentalists scored one of their few victories when the conference committee rejected a House provision granting automatic exemptions for both Tellico and the Gray Rocks Dam in Wyoming. A U.S. District Court had ruled that the Wyoming project could not be completed because it threatened an area along the migratory patterns of the whooping and sandhill cranes.

Meeting on the final day of the session, the conferees settled on mandating an early review of the Tellico and Gray Rocks projects by the Cabinet-level board.

Generally, however, the law's critics had their way. For instance, the conferees retained a House provision limiting funding authorization for administration of the act to 18 months. The Senate version authorized funding for three years.

Critics wanted the shorter authorization period so they could hold oversight hearings sooner on how the changed law was being implemented. Also, many members were influenced by word that a General Accounting Office study, due out February 1979, would criticize the administration of the existing law.

Conference and final action on S 2899 came quickly because the authorization for the Office of Endangered Species had expired Sept. 30. A wide variety of federally funded projects — such as airport expansion, highway construction and dam building — were forced to halt because they could not complete a legally required consultation with the office.

The review board created by S 2899 consisted of seven persons. Its rulings were to be based on recommendations made by a lower-level, three-member panel.

The bill first was passed by the Senate July 19 by a huge 94-3 margin. The original Senate bill provided only for a Cabinet-level board.

Provisions

As approved by Congress, S 2899 (PL 95-632):

- Set up a seven-member Endangered Species Committee to determine whether a project should be exempted. At least five votes would be needed to grant an exemption. The board would be composed of the secretaries of agriculture, the army and the interior; the chairman of the Council of Economic Advisers; the administrators of the Environmental Protection Agency and the National Oceanic and Atmospheric Administration; and a presidential appointee from the affected state, as recommended by its governor.
- Established a lower-level, three-member board to hear cases and make recommendations to the Cabinet-level group. This panel would be made up of one member appointed by the interior secretary; one from the affected state, as suggested by its governor and appointed by the president; and an administrative law judge selected by the Civil Service Commission.
- Required that a project meet three tests to receive an exemption. It would have to demonstrate that 1) there was no "reasonable and prudent alternative," 2) its benefits to the public outweighed the continued existence of a species and 3) it was of national or regional significance.
- Mandated that the Cabinet-level board establish methods to save a species if it were doomed by the approval of a project. Breeding a species in captivity or transplanting it to another locale would be two such ways.
- Required that the interior secretary review the endangered species list every five years to see if some species might be dropped and some added.
- Required public hearings by the Interior Department for designation of endangered species' critical habitats. The hearing had to occur in the same area where the proposed site designation was located.
- Restricted the authority to apply for an exemption to governors, the federal agency concerned and the holder of a federal permit or license to build and operate a project.
- Allowed any person to appeal the review board's decision in court.

Background

The snail darter's victory over the dam in a June 15 Supreme Court decision was, to many in Congress, a stupefying absurdity — a signal that the law, passed amid great fanfare five years earlier, had gone too far.

In its decision, the court ruled 6-3 that the Tellico could not operate, even though it was virtually complete, because shutting its floodgates would wipe out the endangered snail darter. The fish's critical habitat — the special biological surroundings it needed to survive — would be obliterated by closing the dam and the 1973 law forbade any federal project from harming an endangered species.

Other than the $119 million Tennessee dam, only one project had been stopped by the law, the $50 million Gray Rocks Dam in Wyoming. Two other dams under construction, the Columbia in Tennessee and the New Malones Lake in California, were headed for a conflict with the act.

After the Supreme Court ruling, editorial cartoonists and television comedians had a lot of fun over the issue, while Rep. Helen Meyner, D-N.J. expressed her concern for such imaginary endangered birds as the "Ruffled Spouse" and the "Double-breasted Seersucker."

In the view of many, it was bizarre that a federal law that protected such storied creatures as the grizzly bear and the bald eagle should be extended by the Interior Department — whose Endangered Species Office designated which species were to be protected — to cover obscure, seemingly insignificant little things like mollusks, beetles and snapdragon plants. Brushed aside was the environmentalists' argument that even the smallest elements in the earth's ecological system are vital.

"It might have been different if the bald eagle or the California Condor were involved," lamented Toby Cooper, program director of the Defenders of Wildlife. "That's how you got this smear campaign going against the Endangered Species Act."

Although clashes between projects and species had been few in the five years of the law's operation — just four court decisions had been rendered — many in Congress perceived that federal protection of wildlife was running amok.

"There is not a district in this country that will be immune from the kind of problem we are facing unless the law is changed," warned Rep. John Buchanan, R-Ala.

As complaints flooded in from developers and state and local officials about the application of the law, members came under increasing pressure to change it, if not abolish it altogether. Typical was the request that an exasperated Rep. Tom Bevill, D-Ala., once reportedly made to Interior Secretary Cecil D. Andrus "to get the snail darter off my back."

"According to the law, the Defense Department's first priority was protecting endangered species and its second priority was national defense," said David R. Olson, a House Appropriations Public Works Subcommittee aide.

Following the court's Tellico ruling, even a number of members considered pro-wildlife began wondering whether the law needed to be reined in. Interior Committee Chairman Morris K. Udall, normally a friend of the environmentalists, remarked on the floor that conflicts between obscure species and projects "get the whole act into trouble, into disrepute."

In testimony before the Senate Environment Committee in April, Donald C. Simpson of the Pacific Legal Foundation, a pro-development group, illustrated the ludicrous level which many believed the act had reached.

Noting the White House's longstanding rodent problem, Simpson said, "After 20 years of interbreeding in an isolated location such as [the executive mansion], it is possible that unique subspecies or lower taxa have developed for which the White House is a critical habitat. Should not the extermination of these unique mice be enjoined?"

The act's defenders argued that the Endangered Species Office was not as arbitrary as the critics pictured it.

"The law worked well," said Keith M. Schreiner, associate director of the Fish and Wildlife Service and overseer of the office. "We implemented hundreds of programs, put out full regulations and saved lots of endangered species."

In addition to placing a species under the federal mantle — maximum penalties for harming or capturing a protected creature was a year in jail and $20,000 fine — Schreiner noted that the office also tried to increase the lifeform's population. "Our goal is to get it off the list," said Schreiner.

According to Schreiner, the listing process was well organized, divided into at least 10 steps. The aim was to make a designation, in the parlance of the office, "sue-proof."

Some environmentalists said the office had moved too slowly. "It's dragged its heels on a number of occasions," said the Defenders of Wildlife's Cooper.

In the United States, there were 177 animals and 15 plants listed as endangered, as of September 1978. Threatened species — a category for lifeforms that were slightly less imperiled — numbered 37 animals and two plants.

Of the almost 6,000 consultations between the office and builders to see if a project met the law, only four had reached court, up through September 1978.

Often, Schreiner said, compromises were worked out before an issue got to court. He cited the case of the Furbish lousewort, an obscure Maine snapdragon that stood in the way of the $533 million Dickey-Lincoln hydroelectric project. The office arranged to transplant the two-foot lousewort elsewhere, letting the dam go forward. (The project had another problem, though. It was opposed by the Carter administration.) *(1977 Almanac p. 650)*

Senate Action

The Senate Environment and Public Works Subcommittee on Resource Protection approved S 2899 May 2 on a voice vote. A bipartisan group of subcommittee members had developed the proposal for a special seven-member federal board that could exempt projects from the endangered species law if the board members decided the benefits of the project "clearly outweigh[ed]" the value of the threatened species.

The bill was reported by the full committee May 15 (S Rept 95-874). The Senate passed the bill July 19, on a 94-3 vote. *(Vote 221, p. 36-S)*

Passage of the measure followed the 22-76 defeat July 18 of a key, weakening amendment sponsored by John C. Stennis, D-Miss. *(Vote 216, p. 35-S)*

Stennis, a longtime advocate of federal dams and waterways, wanted to exempt from the law any project for which funds had been appropriated or contracts let before the law was enacted or on which construction was 50 percent completed.

His amendment also would have left resolution of any conflicts between species and projects up to the federal agency building the project.

Giving construction agencies that responsibility is "a bit like putting the fox in charge of the henhouse," complained John H. Chafee, R-R.I.

Efforts to strengthen the bill were no more successful than moves to weaken it.

Gaylord Nelson, D-Wis., who planned to offer an amendment to retain the existing 1973 law, chose not to when it was obvious the amendment would get few votes.

Another Nelson amendment, which would have limited exemptions to projects well under way, also failed, 25-70. *(Vote 219, p. 35-S)*

John C. Culver, D-Iowa, led what was often an emotional floor debate. "It does on the surface seem stupid to save something like a snail darter, some crazy bat, some crayfish, something called a Furbish lousewort," Culver told the Senate, referring to other species that threatened the future of certain projects.

But, he continued, "it is also true, in my judgment, that we have the ethical and moral responsibility to pass on to future generations, in as pristine a state as possible, what we in turn have inherited."

The loss of species has accelerated rapidly since prehistoric times, when one species was extinguished every 10,000 years, Culver said. Around the year 1600, the rate increased to one every 1,000 years, Culver said, until "today, from one to 20 species are extinguished from our global environment every single year."

"The cause of our accelerated pace of natural extinction is man," Culver said.

People *vs.* Fish

But Stennis and others argued that the law was still too tightly written even with the committee's changes. "This law as it is now is crippling," Stennis said.

Bill Scott, R-Va., tried several times to limit application of the law to certain species. "People are more important than fish," Scott told the Senate.

One Scott amendment would have limited the definition of threatened species to those that were "of substantial benefit to mankind." The proposal was defeated July 18, 2-87. *(Vote 218, p. 35-S)*

The Senate did accept an amendment by H. John Heinz III, R-Pa., that would make it more difficult to exempt a project. Heinz's change required that the members of the board themselves — not substitutes — cast the actual votes on whether to exempt a project. Five of the seven members would have to vote for an exemption. In all but the final votes on a case, the board members could be represented by an assistant, but only one whose post was high enough to require Senate confirmation.

Members of the board would be the secretaries of the interior, agriculture and the Army; the chairman of the Council on Environmental Quality, the administrators of the National Oceanic and Atmospheric Administration and the Environmental Protection Agency and the governor of the state in which the project was located.

Members also adopted a Nelson amendment reducing from $2.5 million to $750,000 the annual authorization for the board. Another Nelson amendment, which also was adopted, required preparation of an environmental impact statement on the threatened species or its critical habitat before the board could grant an exemption.

Most conservation groups preferred that existing language in the law be retained. They, along with Nelson, argued that hundreds of conflicts between species and projects had been worked out. The Tellico Dam, Nelson contended, was the exception, not the rule, and should never have been started in the first place.

House Alternatives

Meanwhile, opponents of the Endangered Species Act were making other attempts to get around the law.

Rep. Beard opened the way for House changes when he tried to tie his criticism of the endangered species law to the fiscal 1979 Interior appropriations bill (HR 12932).

Beard proposed 682 amendments, each one prohibiting use of funds in the bill for protection of federally listed endangered species. He also included species found only in foreign countries. Consideration of the amendments would have taken hours, perhaps days.

But, at the last minute, Beard agreed to drop the amendments when he was assured that he could amend the Endangered Species Act itself, his original purpose.

Beard had been one of the most vocal House opponents of the act. But his efforts to exempt a dam in his district — TVA's Columbia Dam — from the law had gotten nowhere in the Merchant Marine Committee.

Instead, the committee, which had written the law in the first place, wanted to take a measured look at how it was working before considering amendment or exemptions.

Committee Action. To meet the deadlines of the Congressional Budget Act, the Merchant Marine Committee March 31 reported HR 10883, which extended funding for the law (H Rept 95-1026). The committee made no change in Section 7, which protected species from federal actions.

The provisions of that bill were later included in HR 14104, which was reported unanimously by the Merchant Marine Committee Sept. 25 (H Rept 95-1625). That measure, providing for a six-member review panel, was slightly different from the Senate bill (S 2899).

House Floor Action

Bargaining was intense over the make-up of the board, with both sides pushing for inclusion of officials they felt would be more sympathetic to their views.

But tempers flared when the bill reached the House floor, especially after amendments were approved giving exemptions to the two dams.

At one point, Andy Jacobs Jr., D-Ind., shook his fist at Dingell, whom he accused of using "abusive language," and declared, "Somebody around here is about to become an endangered species if he comes up to me that way again without a pistol."

The House Oct. 14 passed HR 14104 on a 384-12 roll-call vote and substituted its text for that of S 2899 so the conference committee would be working with one bill. *(Vote 814, p. 232-H)*

The House approved amendments:

- Reducing extensions of funding authorization for the Office of Endangered Species, in the Department of the Interior, from three years to 18 months. Beard insisted on the change, threatening to tie up the House indefinitely if he did not get it. Funding for the office was $23 million in fiscal 1979 and $12.5 million for the period from Oct. 1, 1979, to March 31, 1980. The Department of Commerce, which also administered the act, was given $2.5 million for fiscal 1979 and $12.5 million for the following six months.
- Stipulating that the Gray Rocks Dam and Reservoir, known as the Missouri Basin Power Project, satisfied the requirements of the act and did not need to go before the review board. The standing vote was 29-14.
- Exempting the Tellico Dam and Reservoir Project from the provisions of the act. The amendment's sponsor, John J. Duncan, R-Tenn., whose district contained the dam, argued that the project no longer threatened the snail darter. A large number of the fish had been transplanted to another river, he said. The vote was 231-157. *(Vote 813, p. 230-H)*
- Striking language from the House bill that directed courts to give preference over other matters to appeals of endangered species rulings by the review board.
- Requiring the secretary of the interior to consider the economic impact of designating an area the critical habitat of a species.
- Exempting military activities related to preparedness from the provisions of the act. This allowed maneuvers, equipment testing and other training to go forward despite the presence of an endangered species. Other military-related activities, however, such as the building of an officers' club, would continue to be subject to the law.
- Permitting appeals of board decisions to begin in the circuit court of appeals, rather than in the U.S. district court, where calendars were more clogged and the chances of delay greater.

Conference Action

The major change made in conference was to alter the composition of the Cabinet-level board, tilting it slightly more toward the pro-development side. The chairman of the Council on Environmental Quality, included in both House and Senate bills, was replaced by the chairman of the Council of Economic Advisers (CEA).

Early review for the Tellico and Gray Rocks projects was substituted for automatic exemption using the argument that special consideration for the two dams in the bill would undermine the integrity of the act.

Other major House amendments were accepted by the conference committee.

Both houses swiftly approved the conference report (H Rept 95-1804) by voice votes Oct. 15. ▮

Sikes Act Amendments

In response to President Carter's veto of legislation authorizing funds for certain fish, wildlife and recreation programs, the Senate Sept. 25 cleared and sent to the president a new bill that significantly reduced funding for those programs.

The new measure (HR 13745 — PL 95-420) replaced an earlier bill (HR 10882), known as the Sikes Act amendments, vetoed by Carter July 10. The president said the authorization levels in HR 10882 were too high, and he objected to a provision requiring agencies to justify funding requests that were below levels authorized in the measure. No funds had ever been requested for Sikes Act activities.

As cleared, HR 13745 was similar to the vetoed bill, but did not contain the funding justification provision.

The new bill authorized $79.5 million in fiscal 1979-81, $93.5 million less than the vetoed measure. HR 13745 authorized $9 million for the Interior Department — $4.5 million less than in HR 10882 — and $4.5 million for the Defense Department — the same as HR 10882 — to develop with states fish, wildlife and recreation programs in military lands over the three years.

HR 13745 also authorized $30 million — $10 million less than HR 10882 — for the Interior Department to work with states to develop fish and wildlife projects on Bureau of Land Management, Energy Department and National Aeronautics and Space Administration lands. An additional $36 million — $79 million less than HR 10882 — was recommended for Forest Service and other Agriculture Department fish and wildlife programs.

Background

The Sikes Act, passed in 1960, directed the Defense Department to develop jointly, with the Interior Department and the states, a fish and wildlife conservation program for military lands. Military bases cover 25.4 million acres. *(Background, Congress and the Nation, Vol. I, p. 1067)*

The act was amended in 1968 to authorize the Defense Department to develop a public outdoor recreation program. And in 1974, Congress added a provision directing the Interior and Agriculture Departments to develop cooperative programs with the states for fish and wildlife programs on certain agency lands. The Interior Department also was placed in charge of fish and wildlife resources on NASA lands and on some lands that eventually became part of the Energy Department.

Action on Vetoed Bill

House Action. The House Merchant Marine and Fisheries Committee reported HR 10882 (H Rept 95-1025) March 31. It authorized $23.5 million a year in fiscal 1979-81.

The committee recommended $4.5 million for Defense Department fish, wildlife and public recreation programs and $6 million for Interior Department technical assistance for the three years. It also authorized $60 million for Agriculture and Interior Department fish and wildlife programs in fiscal 1979-81.

Noting that the Agriculture Department had supported Sikes Act activities with funds drawn from other programs, the committee assured the department that it could "consider its authorization under the Sikes Act as supplemental to its other authorizations for wildlife conservation activities."

The House passed the bill April 10 under suspension of the rules, a procedure that permits no amendments and requires a two-thirds vote for approval. The vote was 377-8. *(Vote 167, p. 50-H)*

Senate Action. The Senate Environment and Public Works Committee reported a companion bill (S 2987—S Rept 95-873) May 15. The committee recommended authorizations of $51 million in fiscal 1979 and $61 million in fiscal 1980. The two-year total was $112 million, compared to a $70.5 million total for three years in the House bill.

The committee authorized $9 million in funds for Interior Department technical assistance to military bases, $3 million above the House amount. Authorizations for Interior Department fish and wildlife development programs were $10 million for fiscal 1979 and $15 million for fiscal 1980. Part of those funds were for Energy Department and NASA projects. The committee also recommended $35 million for fiscal 1979 and $40 million for fiscal 1980 for the Department of Agriculture, compared to $10 million each year in the House bill.

Calling the use of funds from other sources for Sikes Act programs "unsatisfactory," the committee added a requirement that agencies justify budget requests falling below authorized amounts.

The Senate passed S 2987 by voice vote May 25. The next day the provisions of S 2987 were substituted for those in HR 10882 and the House bill was approved as amended.

Final Action. On June 12, the House approved the Senate version of HR 10882, but amended it to extend the authorization through fiscal 1981. The Senate approved the House amendments June 26 by voice vote.

In his veto message July 10, Carter said he objected to a provision in the bill requiring agencies to justify funding requests that fell below the bill's authorization levels. No funds had ever been requested for the Sikes Act, although agencies had drawn funds from other programs to support some of the Sikes Act's activities.

Carter also blasted Congress for more than doubling the act's authorization from the fiscal 1978 level, an increase he said was unnecessary. The president pointed out that Sikes Act funds would supplement money already made available under other, more general land management programs.

Senate and House sources and representatives of various environmental groups charged that the Office of Management and Budget (OMB) "arm twisted" the president into vetoing the measure. The sources said OMB was reportedly unhappy with the amounts authorized in the bill and with the budget justification clause. An OMB spokesman declined to comment.

But insisting that the authorization level was "realistic," Ken Hampton of the National Wildlife Federation also endorsed the budget justification language as a necessary tool to prod the administration into requesting money for Sikes Act programs.

Action on HR 13745

Responding to Carter's veto, the House Merchant Marine and Fisheries Committee Aug. 18 reported HR 13745 (H Rept 95-1519). It was passed by the House Sept. 19 by voice vote. The Senate Environment and Public Works Committee attached the new Sikes Act authorization to HR 2329, a bill to improve the administration of

Interior and Commerce department fish and wildlife programs (S Rept 95-1175). But the new authorization was deleted from that bill on the floor Sept. 25. The Senate then approved HR 13745 by voice vote, clearing it for the president.

Nongame Wildlife Bill

A fierce lobbying campaign by the Carter administration, business and labor effectively killed for the 95th Congress legislation that some of its opponents called the "son of endangered species."

The legislation would have provided federal funds to help states protect nongame animals. Much of the opposition centered around a provision that would have allowed states to take land for wildlife habitat, which would preclude any commercial development on it.

The federal endangered species law prohibited construction of federal public works projects if they would harm endangered species. *(Endangered species act, p. 707)*

No existing federal law supported the conservation of nongame fish and wildlife — those species, such as songbirds and chipmunks, that are not hunted or trapped.

Two existing laws provided for the conservation of game species. And states also supported game conservation through the sale of hunting and fishing licenses.

The Senate version of the bill (S 1140), passed May 24 with little opposition, provided federal matching grants to states to help them develop and carry out specific nongame projects, such as songbird viewing areas or long-range nongame conservation plans. The plans could include acquisition of land for fish and wildlife habitat.

The House bill (HR 10255) was scheduled to be taken up in June under suspension of the rules, a procedure that requires a two-thirds vote for passage and that does not allow floor amendments. But the administration, business and labor groups lobbied hard to push the bill off the suspension calendar, and it eventually became stalled in the Rules Committee. Under the House version, the federal government would reimburse the states for preparation of state game and nongame long-range plans, as well as for the development of specific nongame projects.

The Opposition

Office of Management and Budget (OMB) opposition to the need for a specific nongame conservation program and to the program's cost were at the root of administration dissatisfaction with the bill, according to a White House staffer.

In his 1977 environmental message, President Carter endorsed a federal program to improve protection for nongame wildlife. But an administration spokeswoman said, "It's one thing to express some concern and another to start a whole new program." *(Environment message, 1977 Almanac p. 30-E)*

"A full-blown program is skipping a step," she said, adding that the administration would have favored a more limited bill to provide funding for nongame planning only.

The U.S. Chamber of Commerce, the International Brotherhood of Teamsters, the International Union of Operating Engineers and the United Brotherhood of Carpenters and Joiners of America spearheaded the lobbying campaign to kill the bill, according to House Merchant Marine and Fisheries Committee aides.

The organizations' opposition was keyed to the provision allowing states to acquire land for wildlife habitat, which would take land away from development. They also objected to a provision that directed federal agencies, to the greatest extent possible, to conduct their activities in a way that was least environmentally damaging.

A House committee aide disputed the critics' contention that the bill would stop development. With the bill's provision for long-range planning, the states would have been able to assist developers in choosing sites that were least environmentally damaging, he said.

Background

The U.S. Fish and Wildlife Service estimated that about 83 percent of the approximately 3,700 vertebrate species of fish and wildlife (birds, mammals, fish, reptiles and amphibians) inhabiting the United States were in the "nongame" category — not hunted for food, fur or sport.

In recent years, the population of nongame fish and wildlife had declined, generally because of the loss of wetlands, open space and other wildlife habitat to water pollution, agriculture and other uses. The game population, however, had remained relatively stable, largely as a result of two laws — the 1937 Pittman-Robertson Wildlife Restoration Act (PL 75-415) and the 1950 Dingell-Johnson Sport Fish Restoration Act (PL 81-681), which funded the conservation of game species. Both acts provided federal matching funds to states, with the federal government providing 75 cents for every 25 cents put up by a state.

Forty-five states had some kind of nongame conservation program. However, the total investment in nongame efforts was small because states had to either divert money from the two federal programs or appropriate separate state funds for nongame conservation.

Senate Action

The Senate Environment and Public Works Committee reported S 1140 May 15 (S Rept 95-872).

As passed May 24 by voice vote, S 1140:

- Authorized $20 million in fiscal 1979, $30 million in fiscal 1980 and $40 million in fiscal 1981 for grants to states to develop nongame fish and wildlife long-range conservation plans or to carry out individual nongame conservation projects.
- Defined "nongame" as those vertebrates — mammals, birds, reptiles, amphibians and fish — that were not hunted, trapped, fished or otherwise consumed, as well as game animals that inhabited urban or suburban areas.
- Allowed states to add invertebrates to the nongame category.
- Set the federal share of project costs at 90 percent in fiscal 1979-80; thereafter, the federal share decreased to 75 percent. Projects undertaken jointly by two or more states would receive a 90 percent federal share.
- Provided that beginning in fiscal 1982 none of a state's share could be funded from the sale of hunting, fishing and trapping licenses. In fiscal 1981, up to 5 percent of a state's share could be funded from these sources. In fiscal 1979 and 1980, there was no such restriction.

House Action

The House Merchant Marine and Fisheries Committee reported HR 10255 on April 4 (H Rept 95-1036). It differed in several ways from the Senate-passed measure. The committee recommended providing grants to the states to develop long-range game and nongame conservation plans. For up to 10 years after the date of enactment, the federal government would reimburse the states for up to 90 percent of the costs of developing and revising statewide plans and for developing specific nongame conservation projects. After that, up to 75 percent of those costs would be eligible for reimbursement.

The committee recommended that federal agencies, to the greatest extent possible, conduct their activities in accordance with the state's conservation plan. The committee recommended an authorization of $10 million annually in fiscal 1979-81 for the development of the comprehensive plans and a total of an additional $90 million in fiscal 1979-81 for carrying out nongame projects.

Tanker Safety

Legislation designed to curb oil spills and impose stricter safety standards on tankers was cleared by Congress Oct. 3.

The measure (S 682—PL 95-474), aimed at reducing the chances of spills, was prompted by several tanker accidents. The *Argo Merchant,* for example, a Liberian vessel, ran aground off Massachusetts in 1976, dumping 204,000 barrels of petroleum into the sea.

Tanker traffic was expected to increase in U.S. ports because of the surging demand for foreign oil. In 1978, about 35 tankers arrived in American harbors each day, carrying eight million barrels of crude oil.

The bill mandated better control of ship traffic and required tankers to install electronic gear to prevent accidents.

It also sought to decrease the discharge of oil during routine tanker operations. About 85 percent of the ocean's oil pollution came from the discharge of oily water used to clean tanks.

A program similar to that contained in the bill was proposed by President Carter in March 1977. The measure's provisions generally followed an international accord reached in February 1978, by the 62-nation Inter-Governmental Maritime Consultive Organization. *(Carter message, 1977 Almanac p. 14-E)*

Background

The bill first was approved by the Senate on a voice vote May 26, 1977. Several of its requirements were stiffer than those eventually set by the international conference, notably a provision mandating double bottoms for new ships as of Jan. 1, 1980. *(1977 Almanac p. 668)*

The House Merchant Marine Committee reported its own version (HR 13311) July 21 (H Rept 95-1384). Reacting to concerns that the Senate-approved bill might jeopardize the international accords, the committee left out the double hull requirement.

A second difference between the House and Senate versions was that the Senate required that more ships be retrofitted with separate ballasts — one for carrying oil or other cargo, another for water — and separate crude oil washing systems. The washing systems were designed to curb pollution by ending the release of oily water into the sea.

Major Provisions

As cleared by Congress, S 682:

Manning. Authorized the transportation secretary to require a federally licensed pilot on each vessel operating in U.S. waters when state law did not so require.

Investigations. Expanded federal authority to investigate accidents at sea.

Entry restrictions. Barred any vessel carrying oil or another hazardous material from operating in U.S. waters or transferring cargo in any U.S. port if the vessel 1) had a history of accidents, 2) failed to comply with U.S. laws and regulations, 3) did not meet U.S. manning requirements, or 4) did not have at least one licensed deck officer who could clearly understand English.

- Provided that all of those requirements would become effective immediately on enactment, except the manning requirements, which would become effective 18 months after enactment.
- Gave the cabinet official in charge of the Coast Guard (in peacetime, the secretary of transportation; in wartime, the secretary of the Navy) the authority to issue different regulations for domestic sea trade than those imposed by the multi-nation agreement.

Traffic control. Authorized the government to operate harbor vessel traffic control systems, resembling those for aircraft.

Minimum standards. Required new crude oil tankers of 20,000 deadweight tons (dwt) or more to install a cargo tank protection system, segregated ballast tanks and a crude oil washing system; required new tankers of 20,000 dwt or more not carrying crude oil to have a cargo tank protection system.

- Required existing crude oil tankers of 40,000 dwt or more to install segregated ballasts or a crude oil washing system, generally by June 1, 1981.
- Required installation by Jan. 1, 1986, of segregated ballasts or crude oil washing systems in tankers between 20,000 and 40,000 dwt if they were at least 15 years old.
- Required existing crude oil tankers of 20,000 dwt or more to install inert gas systems by June 1, 1983, in most cases.
- Required existing vessels of 40,000 dwt or more to install segregated ballasts by June 1, 1981, or to operate with clean ballast tanks.
- Required existing tankers of 20,000 dwt to 40,000 dwt, which were at least 15 years old, to install segregated ballasts by Jan. 1, 1985.
- Required tankers of 40,000 dwt or more or existing tankers of 20,000 dwt to 40,000 dwt fitted with high capacity tank washing machines to install an inert gas system by June 1, 1983; required vessels of 70,000 dwt or more to comply by June 1, 1981.
- Required all "self-propelled" vessels of 10,000 gross tons or more — a definition that excluded most barges — to have a dual radar system, a computerized relative motion analyzer to warn of impending collisions, an electronic position-fixing device, adequate communications equipment, a sonic depth finder, a gyrocompass and up-to-date charts.
- Required that equipment be installed by June 1, 1979, except for the relative motion analyzer which had to be installed by July 1, 1982.
- Required that all tankers serving drilling rigs on the U.S. outer continental shelf have segregated ballasts by June 1, 1980.

Inspections. Set up an annual inspection requirement for vessels using U.S. ports.

Lightering. Put controls on lightering, the practice of transferring oil offshore from deepdraft supertankers to tankers able to negotiate shallow U.S. harbors. If a ship had ignored U.S. lightering regulations, it could not unload oil in a U.S. port.

Dumping. Prohibited any ship from docking in a U.S. port if it had dumped wash water at sea.

Penalties. Authorized the secretary to assess civil penalties of up to $25,000 for each violation, or in the case of a continuing violation, $25,000 a day.

- Set criminal penalties of up to $50,000 or a prison term of up to five years or both; if the criminal offense involved use of a dangerous weapon or constituted a common law battery, the penalty was a fine of up to $100,000, a prison term of up to 10 years, or both.

House Action

The Merchant Marine Committee reported the bill July 21 (H Rept 95-1384, Part I).

One of the measure's major goals was to increase federal control over the operations of tankers to help avoid collisions and to keep wayward tankers from running aground.

The bill authorized the government to operate vessel traffic control systems, similar to air traffic control. An operating center in each port would oversee ship movement in and out of the harbor and along navigable waterways. Controllers could require that ships follow certain routes at certain speeds and could monitor their progress.

Such systems already were in operation in Puget Sound, San Francisco Bay, Houston-Galveston Ship Channel and the Berwick Bay Bridge area in Louisiana. Systems were planned for New York and New Orleans harbors.

Some authority to require that foreign ships comply with U.S. rules was in existing law, but the committee bill clarified and expanded that authority. Ships not in compliance could be kept out of port or forced to anchor outside a harbor.

The bill also provided that a federally licensed pilot could take over the helm of a foreign ship to steer it into a U.S. port if the country where the ship was registered did not have piloting standards. All U.S.-flag ships would have to be operated by a licensed pilot.

Authority for the Coast Guard to investigate tanker accidents also was clarified by the bill.

The House easily passed the bill Sept. 12, 366-6. After the House passed its bill, it substituted the House-passed language for the Senate version of S 682. *(Vote 664, p. 190-H)*

Final Action

Because there was little time left in the session, the bill did not go to a conference committee. Instead it went directly back to the Senate. On Sept. 30 the Senate accepted the House changes by voice vote and inserted its own minor alterations. The Senate amendments broadened federal authority over tankers serving offshore oil drilling platforms and allowed the government to impose tighter standards on domestic shipping than were called for in the international protocol. House language permitting the accords to be exceeded was deleted. On Oct. 3 the House concurred in the Senate additions by voice vote. ▮

Oil Spill Liability

Legislation that would have increased the liability of those responsible for oil spills died during the final days of the 95th Congress because of a disagreement over whether hazardous chemical spills should be covered by the bill.

The measure (HR 6803) also established a $200 million "superfund" to pay for spill cleanup when the source was unknown. The fund would have been financed through a tax on transported oil.

The oil industry opposed the bill for a number of reasons. One sticking point was a provision in the Senate version (S 2083—S Rept 95-1152), extending liability to spills of 271 chemicals deemed dangerous by the Environmental Protection Agency. The oil industry argued that it should not have to pay for spills by chemical transporters and manufacturers.

Industry also disliked a provision in the Senate bill allowing states to set up their own funds. The industry contended it would create a potential for abuse, because damaged parties could file claims with different funds.

The chemical liability and state fund provisions were inserted in the Senate version of the bill by Edmund S. Muskie, D-Maine.

Muskie said a study was needed of how much chemical firms should be assessed for spill damages. If a chemical liability fund were set up, he said, chemical companies should be reimbursed with interest for payments they had made into the oil "superfund." Muskie also argued that states should continue to be permitted to write their own standards.

Wending Through Congress

S 2083 passed the Senate by voice vote Oct. 5 and its language was substituted for HR 6803, which the House had approved Sept. 12, 1977, 332-59. The House-passed bill limited liability to oil spills alone. *(House Action, 1977 Almanac p. 670)*

Muskie was eager to keep the bill out of a conference committee, where the industry stood a greater chance of removing the two disputed provisions. House and Senate staff sought to hammer out a compromise, but were unable to agree on chemical liability and separate state funds.

The House Oct. 12 amended HR 6803 to remove the provisions added by the Senate with which it disagreed.

Muskie, however, was adamant about inclusion of chemical liability and state funds. He prevented the House-amended bill from coming up on the Senate floor and resolved to try again in the next session, according to sources.

The bill would have consolidated existing federal oil spill funds and hiked the liabilities imposed under them. The measure was spurred by the large volume of oil spills, which resulted from increased U.S. importation of petroleum.

Under the Federal Clean Water Act of 1977 (PL 95-217), the liability of ships for oil spills was $150 per gross ton or $250,000, whichever was greater. Other laws governed deepwater ports and loading Alaska oil onto tankers. *(Clean Water Act background, 1977 Almanac p. 697)*

According to the Coast Guard, from 1972 through 1976, there were an average of 12,291 spills a year. The origins of 2,588 of them were unknown.

Provisions

Both versions of HR 6803:

- Established an oil spill liability fund with a $200 million ceiling to pay for damages in which the spiller could not be identified. It was to be financed through a tax of 3 cents per barrel on oil received by refineries.
- Made owners and operators of vessels, storage facilities and offshore drilling rigs liable for damages to parties injured by spills into navigable waters unless a spill was caused by an act of war, a natural phenomenon or negligence by the federal government.
- Limited the liability of an offshore drilling facility to $50 million.
- Limited liability of a deepwater port to $50 million.
- Required owners or operators of vessels over 300 tons using U.S. waters, including foreign ships, to carry insurance or other financial guarantees that they could meet the liabilities set by the bill.

The chief differences were that the Senate:

- Sought to preserve the power of states to impose additional requirements or liabilities regarding spills. Thirty-two states already had enacted such laws.
- Extended liability to 271 hazardous chemicals as listed by the Environmental Protection Agency.
- Set the liability for ships at a minimum of $300,000 or $300 per gross ton, whichever was higher. No ceiling was established.

The House version:

- Stipulated that no one could be required to contribute to any fund other than the one set up by the bill.
- Allowed a state to maintain its own standards and permitted a damaged party to sue in state courts. But judgments could be paid only from the federal fund.
- Rejected placing liabilities on chemicals. Instead, a civil penalty of up to $50,000 would be assessed for all but cases of willful negligence and misconduct, in which the spiller could be fined a maximum of $250,000.
- Set the liability level for a ship at $300,000 or $300 per gross ton, whichever was higher, but unlike the Senate bill, established a maximum of $50 million. ▮

Ocean Pollution Research

Citing the need to study the long-range impact of chemical pollutants on marine life, Congress April 24 cleared legislation establishing a federal ocean pollution research program.

The bill (S 1617 — PL 95-273) established a five-year ocean pollution research plan administered by the National Oceanic and Atmospheric Administration (NOAA), and authorized $5 million for it in fiscal 1979.

Major Provisions

As cleared by Congress, S 1617:

- Required the development of a five-year plan to coordinate all federal ocean pollution research, development and monitoring efforts.
- Required that the plan be submitted to Congress and the president on or before Feb. 15, 1979, and that it be revised every two years.
- Required NOAA to administer the plan in consultation with the director of the Office of Science and Technology Policy and with other appropriate federal agencies, such as the Environmental Protection Agency (EPA).
- Required that the plan establish cost-effective research priorities, contain a list of existing federal ocean pollution research programs and recommend changes in federal ocean pollution research policy.
- Required the establishment within NOAA of an ocean pollution research program.
- Authorized $5 million for fiscal 1979.

Background

Ever since the 1967 *Torrey Canyon* tanker oil spill off the southwest coast of England, researchers had attempted to assess the long-term impact of oil and other chemical pollutants on the marine environment.

Eight federal departments, nine independent agencies and 37 sub-agencies administered existing ocean pollution research programs. But critics charged that the federal program was haphazard, with little to show in the way of solid research results.

Senate Action

Spurred by the criticism, the Senate Commerce, Science and Transportation Committee included an ocean research pollution plan in the 1977 Tanker Safety and Vessel Act (S 682). The plan was struck during floor debate on the measure in May 1977. *(1977 Almanac, p. 669)*

Sen. Warren G. Magnuson, D-Wash., then introduced the plan as a separate bill. It was referred to the Environment and Public Works Committee, which discharged it July 26 without a report.

As discharged, S 1617 designated NOAA as the lead federal agency for developing a one-year research and development plan. The bill authorized $5 million for fiscal 1978 and $6 million for fiscal 1979.

The Senate passed S 1617 by voice vote Aug. 3. The only substantive change was a Magnuson amendment increasing the plan from one to three years.

House Action

The House Science and Technology and the Merchant Marine and Fisheries Committees shared jurisdiction over the bill. The Science Committee filed Part I of the report (H Rept 95-626) Sept. 26, while the Merchant Marine Committee filed Part II on Oct. 17.

The Science Committee lamented "the nearly total lack of any efforts to determine long-term fates and effects of various pollutants in the marine environment."

The committee increased the plan's duration to five years and authorized $10 million for it for fiscal 1979.

The Merchant Marine Committee urged a strict, cost-effective approach to deciding research priorities. It provided for a three-year plan and cut the authorization level to $5 million for fiscal 1979.

The House approved S 1617 Feb. 28 by voice vote under suspension of the rules. Under a compromise forged by the two House committees and offered as an amendment by Rep. George E. Brown Jr., D-Calif., a five-year, $5 million program was authorized.

Final Action

The Senate April 24 agreed by voice vote to the House changes. ▮

Oceans, Atmosphere Committee

Legislation (HR 10823 — PL 95-304) authorizing fiscal 1979 appropriations for the National Advisory Committee on Oceans and Atmosphere (NACOA) was cleared by Congress June 14.

The advisory committee was created in 1971 (PL 92-125) to advise Congress and the executive branch on the development and implementation of a national policy on oceans and coastal zone management.

The House Merchant Marine Committee reported the legislation March 30 (H Rept 95-1013).

As reported, HR 10823 authorized $572,000 for the advisory committee for fiscal 1979, and extended by one year the terms of committee members appointed by the president in January 1978.

The bill passed the House without amendment April 17 by voice vote.

The Senate Commerce Committee reported the bill (S Rept 95-862) May 15 with a technical amendment. The legislation passed the Senate as reported on June 5 by voice vote.

The House approved the Senate bill June 14.

Marine Mammal Protection

The House June 28 cleared and sent to the president legislation authorizing $47.1 million in fiscal 1979-81 for the Marine Mammal Protection Act.

The measure (HR 10730 — PL 95-316) authorized $14.8 million for fiscal 1979, $15.6 million for fiscal 1980 and $16.8 million for fiscal 1981. The bill also included funding for matching grants to state marine mammal protection programs for a variety of marine mammal research projects.

The act, passed in 1972, set a permanent moratorium on most killing of ocean mammals and on the importation of marine mammal products. The ban applied to seals, sea lions, whales, porpoises, dolphins, sea otters, polar bears, manatees and walruses. The act also provided for a three-member commission to conduct research and to monitor the activities of the Commerce and Interior Departments under the act. *(Background, 1977 Almanac p. 673)*

The House Merchant Marine and Fisheries Committee, which reported the bill (H Rept 95-1028) March 31, provided a total authorization of $13.7 million in fiscal 1979, $14.8 million in fiscal 1980 and $16.6 million in fiscal 1981.

The committee chided the Commerce Department for what it termed "inadequate" funding of outside research projects, and designated $6.1 million for research grants. Included were funds for research on the east coast whale population, bottlenose dolphins and dall porpoises.

The House approved HR 10730 April 10 without amendment, 380-5. *(Vote 165, p. 50-H)*

The Senate Commerce, Science and Transportation Committee reported the bill (S Rept 95-888) May 15. The committee recommended an additional $2 million for research and monitoring of the bowhead whale. Noting the controversy surrounding Alaska natives' subsistence hunting of the species, the committee suggested that "incomplete data on population levels of the bowhead whale" was partly responsible for the furor.

The Senate approved the bill June 7 by voice vote.

Provisions

As cleared by Congress, HR 10730 authorized:

	1979	1980	1981
Interior Department	$ 2,350,000	$ 2,660,000	$ 3,376,000
Commerce Department	11,425,000	11,925,000	12,425,000
Marine Mammal Commission	1,000,000	1,000,000	1,000,000
Total	$14,775,000	$ 15,585,000	$16,801,000

Public Grazing Land Laws

The first overhaul in 44 years of the nation's range management laws was cleared by Congress Oct. 11.

The bill (HR 10587 — PL 95-514) established a new grazing fee system for ranchers whose livestock fed on the 260 million acres of federal rangeland. The bill also included a compromise provision establishing methods to reduce overpopulations of wild horses and burros.

The Bureau of Land Managment (BLM), the agency responsible for overseeing federal ranges, had estimated that 80 percent of the land was in poor shape, partially as a result of large numbers of roaming burros and horses. The bill authorized $365 million in fiscal 1980-99 for maintenance and improvement of the land.

The bill set up a new grazing fee system that reduced charges to ranchers in periods of low beef prices and raised them when beef prices went up. The formula was expected to bring in additional revenue, although cattle producers were happy about its flexibility, which would help them when beef prices plummeted.

The White House had expressed reservations about the new fee schedule, which was the first set by legislation. The administration felt that it would mean a continued subsidy to ranchers using federal lands. The 1978 monthly fee for public land was $1.51 per animal, compared to $7.06 for private land.

Provisions

As cleared by Congress, HR 10587:

- Required the secretaries of agriculture and the interior to draw up and periodically update an inventory of range conditions.
- Authorized $365 million for range improvements — $15 million annually in fiscal 1980-1986 and no less than $20 million per year for fiscal 1987-1999.
- Stipulated that at least 80 percent of the $365 million go to actual improvement projects and limited to 15 percent the amount to be spent for hiring and training additional personnel.
- Required that the secretary of the interior prepare an environmental assessment record on any project before spending money on it. If the secretary decided that a project would have a harmful ecological effect, he could order an environmental impact statement performed.
- Adopted a formula for setting grazing fees that was tied to beef prices and forage values (the cost of hay and other feed). In years when beef prices were depressed, the fees would be lowered — and vice versa in good years. The

annual increase or decrease in fees was limited to not more than plus or minus 25 percent of the previous year's fee. This plan was to run on a seven-year trial basis, through fiscal 1985.

- Provided that least $10 million per year from fees, or 50 percent of the total collected, whichever was greater, would go into the range betterment fund. Under existing law, half the revenues had to go into the fund, but no minimum amount was set.
- Underscored the congressional intent that most grazing leases should be for 10 years, unless the interior secretary agreed to shorter terms in individual cases.
- Authorized grazing district advisory boards for national lands in 16 western states.
- Exempted from the act all national grasslands, which had been set aside to guard against future dust bowls. They had their own separate fee schedules.
- Directed the interior and agriculture secretaries to experiment with incentive programs offering lower fees for permit holders whose stewardship would improve range conditions. A report to Congress on their findings was due no later than Dec. 31, 1985.
- Allowed excess wild horses and burros to be destroyed in a humane manner by federal or state game officials, provided the destruction was done selectively. Old, sick and lame animals were to be killed first.
- Limited adoption to four animals per individual, unless the interior secretary ruled that a person was capable of caring for more than that. Ownership of the animals was to be transferred after one year to the person who adopted them.
- Mandated the interior secretary to keep an inventory of free-roaming horses and burros and to perform a study, with the help of the National Academy of Sciences, on procedures to determine excess animals. The results were to be delivered to Congress no later than Jan. 1, 1983.

Background

Before 1934, public lands in the West not set aside as national forests or parks were used freely by livestock owners for grazing their animals. Homesteaders and miners could stake claims on the arid land, with the idea that their interest would help settle the West.

But in 1934 Congress decided to stop giving away the federal lands and to keep what was left in better shape. The Taylor Grazing Act retained the lands for federal use and gave the government authority to charge for their use. The fees and other federal funds were to pay for revegetation, reforestation and water conservation measures.

But the fees were low, and additional available federal funds were inadequate to prevent further deterioration of the range. Conservationists also criticized BLM for allowing overgrazing and for not promoting other uses of the "multiple use" land, such as for wildlife habitat.

The Forest Service also allowed grazing on its land and was authorized in 1905 to charge a "reasonable fee."

Ranchers vs. the Government

From the start, the fees were resisted by the ranching industry, which alleged that the government did not have authority to charge fees. But over the years various court challenges failed.

The fees charged were always low and did not cover government costs of maintaining the land. Several studies of the fees were conducted and, in 1966, an interdepartmental survey recommended raising the fee from 33 cents to $1.23 per animal unit month (AUM) — the charge for one cow to graze for one month.

Then, in 1968, the secretaries of agriculture and the interior instituted a new fee formula and schedule, using the 1966 charge as a base figure and making annual adjustments to reflect changes in private grazing land fees. The new formula — designed to bring the government fair market value for its land — was to be phased in over 10 years.

But four moratoriums on the scheduled increases — three by the executive branch and one by Congress in 1976 — kept the fee low. The 1976 charge of $1.51 per AUM remained in effect in 1978. The commercial rate for private land for 1978 was $7.06 per AUM, while the fair market value for federal land, adjusted for differences in quality between private and federal land, was $2.38 per AUM.

After completing another study, this one required by the Federal Land Policy and Management Act of 1976 (PL 94-579), the secretaries of the interior and agriculture said on October 21, 1977, that they would speed up implementation of the 1968 formula so fees charged would represent fair market value, probably by 1980 or 1981. The increases would be held to not more than 25 percent annually until the fair market value was reached; then annual increases could not exceed 11 percent. The secretaries rejected market conditions as a factor in setting grazing fees.

Under the secretaries' formula, fees for 1978 would be raised from $1.51 to $1.89 per AUM. In 1979, the fee would increase to $2.28 per AUM.

Congress, reacting to protests by the ranching industry, resisted the new formula. A one-year moratorium on a fee increase (HR 9757 — PL 95-321) was cleared by Congress June 29.

House Committee Action

Earlier in 1978, the House Interior Subcommittee on Indian Affairs and Public Lands, after making a study of grazing fees, recommended that Congress legislate, for the first time, a formula for setting grazing fees. The full Interior Committee approved the bill by voice vote April 26.

As approved by the panel, the new grazing fee formula, to be carried out on a seven-year trial basis, would consider as a factor the difference between the cost of beef production and the market value of beef. In other words, the fee would reflect current beef prices; if prices were low, the fee would be low.

The committee, in its report (H Rept 95-1122), noted that the formula proposed by the secretaries would cause a hardship on the ranching industry. The higher fees, the report stated, "when considered along with the rapidly escalating costs for other aspects of livestock production, would place an increasing, and perhaps crippling, burden on the many livestock operations which are heavily dependent on the use of public grazing lands."

However, the Carter administration, in the report of the two secretaries, noted that, for about 72 percent of the ranchers, the average fee increase per year per rancher under their proposal would be only $60.

House Floor Action

The House passed HR 10587 June 29 by voice vote.

The easy passage of the bill — despite the controversial grazing fee formula — could be attributed in part to the pending retirement of floor manager and Interior subcommittee chairman Teno Roncalio, D-Wyo.

"This may very well be my swan song as one of the lawmakers of this House," Wyoming's lone representative told the House.

Interior Chairman Morris K. Udall, D-Ariz., who said he doubted the new grazing formula would achieve the ideal of fair market value, nevertheless praised the bill and Roncalio. Other members joined in the praise.

Floor debate had been expected on provisions of the bill making changes in the laws protecting the wild horse and burro herds that roam on grazing lands. The bill required that herds be culled of excess animals if adoption programs failed to reduce their numbers.

Rep. Newton I. Steers Jr., R-Md., had planned an amendment to strike the changes. Steers and some animal protection groups worried that the bill would make it mandatory, not discretionary, to kill excess animals.

But major environmental groups, such as the National Audubon Society and the Sierra Club, generally supported the bill's provisions on horses and burros. They were concerned that the increasing numbers of horses and burros were destroying the habitat of native wildlife.

Opposition from these groups and the committee meant probable failure for Steers' amendment. According to an aide, Steers decided not to offer the amendment because of fears that its defeat would be interpreted as a signal that Congress was no longer concerned about protecting the wild horses and burros.

Provisions

As passed by the House, HR 10587:

- Required an inventory of range conditions.
- Authorized an additional $360 million for range improvement through fiscal 1998 — $15 million annually in fiscal 1979 through 1986 and $20 million per year after that.
- Directed that minor range improvements, such as soil erosion projects, cattle guards, attempts to revegetate with native plants and some fencing, need not be accompanied by environmental impact statements.
- Established a formula for setting the fee for grazing on public land that considered the base price set in 1966, the annual forage value index, the price of beef production and the market price for beef.
- Guaranteed that at least $10 million annually would go into the range improvement fund instead of half the revenues from fees, as in existing law.
- Directed the secretaries of the interior and agriculture to experiment with programs that reward with lower fees permit holders whose stewardship improved range conditions.
- Reiterated the congressional intent that most leases and permits for grazing be for 10 years.
- Directed the secretaries to maintain a "current and scientific" inventory of the number of wild, free-roaming horses and burros on federal land.
- Required that the secretaries make annual determinations of whether overpopulation of wild horses and burros existed; if there was overpopulation, mandated consideration of sterilization or natural controls (such as disease and parasites) for reducing the population. If those methods did not work, directed the secretaries to remove excess animals by first culling from the herd old, sick or lame animals and killing them in a humane fashion. If overpopulation was still a problem, directed that the animals be rounded up for adoption. If there were still excess animals, the secretaries were directed to destroy additional animals.
- Instructed the secretaries to conduct the adoption program in a more humane way and to contract with animal protective groups to conduct inspections and report on the treatment of adopted animals.

Senate Action

The Senate Energy and Natural Resources Committee reported HR 10587 Sept. 23 (S Rept 95-1237), and the Senate passed the bill Sept. 30, 59-7. *(Vote 430, p. 63-S)*

The chief difference between the two versions was the Senate's rejection of a House-approved provision permitting BLM to kill excess burros and wild horses if demand from people wanting to adopt them was low.

The change, made by the Senate Natural Resources Committee, was at the behest of animal protection groups.

Howard W. Cannon, D-Nev., said he hoped the House language would be put back in conference. "The states are free to manage the numbers of deer, antelope and big horn sheep which inhabit the same territory," he said. "The wild horse, however, is presently in a special status."

Widespread slaughter of the free-roaming animals for use in dog food prompted Congress to extend them federal protection under the Wild Horse and Burro Act of 1971 (PL 92-159). *(Congress and the Nation, Vol. III p. 789)*

Conference Action

House and Senate conferees filed their report on HR 10587 Oct. 6 (H Rept 95-1737).

The major difference between the House and Senate versions involved how to handle reduction of the horse and burro herds. The House had voted June 29 to permit the BLM to kill excess animals if demand from people willing to adopt them was low. But on Sept. 30, the Senate knocked out that provision at the urging of animal protection groups, such as the Humane Society of the United States.

The conference agreement, reached Oct. 6, made some concessions to the animal protection groups, but to their dismay, still called for killing excess animals as a last resort. The conference committee required that the interior secretary maintain an inventory of the free-roaming animals and set up criteria to determine excesses. If sufficient adoptions could not be arranged, sick, lame and old animals would be killed first.

Under an existing 1971 law (PL 92-159), the animals were protected to curb their widespread slaughter for use in pet food. According to the protection groups, a loophole in the law allowed unlimited adoptions, which they said some pet food suppliers exploited by "adopting" large numbers of animals and then sending them to the butcher's block.

The conferees on HR 10587 agreed to close that loophole by restricting adoptions to four animals per person, unless the interior secretary determined that an individual could humanely care for more.

Final Action

The conference report on the measure was approved in the House Oct. 10 by voice vote. The Senate adopted it Oct. 11, also by voice vote. ∎

Private Rangeland Bills

A trio of bills aimed at improving management and output of the nation's private forests and rangelands was cleared for the president June 16.

The bills (HR 11777 — PL 95-313, HR 11778 — PL 95-307 and HR 11779 — PL 95-306) authorized the agriculture secretary to provide technical assistance and education programs designed to increase timber yield and conserve such renewable forest resources as fish, game, water, wildlife habitats, forage and recreation areas.

HR 11777 combined into one statute nine forest improvement programs, including disease and insect control, rural fire protection and urban forestry, and it provided for cost-sharing programs with state forestry agencies.

HR 11778 consolidated and expanded the Forest Service's authority to conduct forest and rangeland renewable resource research.

HR 11779 strengthened the Agriculture Department's forestry extension program by authorizing $15 million annually for 10 years to establish forest renewable resource courses in land-grant and other colleges and universities.

Background

In 1970, about 69 percent of the nation's area, 1.6 billion acres, was classified as forest and rangeland by the U.S. Forest Service. Of that, a 500 million acre area roughly equal in size to the states of Alaska, Texas, Arkansas and Virginia combined was commercial timberland.

Private individuals and corporations owned 59 percent of the commercial timberland; the forest industry, 14 percent; the federal government, 21 percent, and state and local governments, 6 percent, according to the Senate Agriculture Committee.

But according to forestry experts, the portion held by private, non-industrial owners had been yielding only about half its capacity.

After enactment in 1976 of the National Forest Management Act (PL 94-588), Sen. Herman Talmadge, D-Ga. asked the Forest Service to draft a bill to use forest management, research and Agriculture Department extension programs to increase benefits from private forest lands. *(Background, 1976 Almanac p. 192)*

House Action. The House divided the Forest Service draft bill into three parts, the Cooperative Forestry Assistance Act (HR 11777), the Forest and Rangeland Renewable Resources Act (HR 11778) and the Renewable Resources Extension Act (HR 11779).

The committee unanimously reported the bills May 15 (H Repts 95-1183, 95-1179, 95-1184).

The House May 22 passed all three bills under suspension of the rules. HR 11777 was approved 373-2; HR 11778, 373-3, and HR 11779, 377-7. *(Votes 292, 293, 294, p. 84-H)*

Senate Action. In the Senate, the Agriculture, Nutrition and Forestry Committee considered three companions to the House measures (S 3033, S 3034 and S 3035) and ordered them reported May 10 (S Repts 95-879, 95-880, 95-881).

The Senate June 7 agreed to the committee's technical amendments to the bills, substituted the language of the Senate bills for that of the House measures and then passed the bills by voice vote.

Final Action. The House June 16 agreed to the Senate's technical amendments by voice vote, clearing the bills for the president.

Provisions

As signed into law July 1, HR 11777 (PL 95-313):

- Authorized a rural forestry assistance program to aid state foresters in developing improved tree seeds, planting trees and seeds for reforestation, advising landowners in management and forestry practices.
- Authorized a cost-sharing incentives program for small landowners to encourage development and protection of non-industrial private forest lands.
- Authorized the agriculture secretary to provide technical assistance to local governments to encourage urban forestry programs.
- Increased the maximum acreage landowners could hold to participate in cost-sharing incentive programs to up to 1,000 acres generally and up to 5,000 acres in special cases from 500 acres.
- Expanded the forestry insect and disease control program to include protection of wood products, stored wood and wood in use.
- Established a rural fire disaster fund for states with rural fire emergencies.
- Authorized such sums as needed to carry out programs under the act.

As signed into law June 30, HR 11778 (PL 95-307):

- Authorized the agriculture secretary to conduct forest and rangeland renewable resources research.
- Directed the secretary to analyze and survey the status of renewable resources in the nation's forests and rangelands.
- Authorized the agriculture secretary to award competitive grants to federal, state and local agencies and private agencies and institutions for renewable resources research.
- Expanded the secretary's authority to accept and use donations of money and property for research and established a U.S. Treasury fund for deposit of research donations.
- Authorized such sums as needed to carry out programs under the act.

As signed into law, HR 11779 (PL 95-306):

- Required the agriculture secretary to provide renewable resource education programs in cooperation with land-grant colleges and colleges and universities eligible for aid under the McIntire-Stennis Act of 1962 (PL 87-788).
- Required development of a state renewable resources extension program by state extension service heads and administrators of colleges and universities eligible for the new education programs.
- Required the secretary to prepare a series of five-year plans beginning in 1980 for the guidance of state renewable resources extension programs.
- Authorized appropriations of up to $15 million annually for 10 years beginning in fiscal 1979.

Timber Bids

Congress in 1978 repealed a 1976 law mandating sealed bids for national forest timber sales. The action came Feb. 6 when the House cleared a Senate-passed bill (S 1360 — PL 95-233) by voice vote.

The 1976 law, the National Forest Management Act (PL 94-588), required sealed bids unless the Secretary of Agriculture determined otherwise. Added in conference, the provision grew out of allegations that the traditional western practice of oral bids led to collusion. Once the law was enacted representatives from western states objected that it was endangering their timber industry. The industry was dependent on national forest timber, the argument ran, and consecutive oral bidding was necessary to give local lumber mills a fair chance to outbid timber interests from outside the area. Under sealed bidding, timber purchasers are allowed only a single bid. *(1976 Almanac p. 192)*

As originally reported to the Senate, on July 6, 1977, by the Energy and National Resources Committee (S Rept 95-333), S 1360 repealed the sealed bid requirement and directed the secretary to monitor sales to prevent collusion. The Agriculture and Justice Departments opposed the bill.

The Senate passed S 1360 Sept. 14, 1977, by voice vote after amending it to allow the Agriculture Secretary to choose whatever bidding method he deemed necessary. The amendment provided that when the secretary permitted oral bidding he should first require sealed bids. Only prospective buyers whose sealed bids equaled or exceeded the appraised value of the timber would be allowed to participate in subsequent oral bidding that would then begin with the highest sealed bid.

As reported June 9, 1977, by the Agriculture Committee, the companion House bill (HR 6362 — H Rept 95-402) simply repealed the sealed bidding requirement in the 1976 law and established an advisory committee on timber sales. When it came to the House floor Agriculture Committee Chairman Thomas S. Foley, D-Wash., proposed a substitute to bring it in line with the Senate bill. The substitute was adopted, 295-78, after rejection 136-239, of a further substitute by John Krebs, D-Calif., that would have restored the language of the 1976 law. *(Votes 32, 33, p. 10-H)*

New Wilderness Areas

The National Wilderness Preservation System was expanded by 1.3 million acres spread through 17 areas in 10 western states under a bill (HR 3454 — PL 95-237) cleared by Congress Feb. 9.

The Senate had endorsed the conference report (H Rept 95-861, S Rept 95-626) Feb. 8, 83-5. The House cleared it the next day on a 333-44 vote. *(House vote 44, p. 12-H; Senate vote 31, p. 7-S).*

The bill had been reported by the House Interior and Insular Affairs Committee July 27, 1977 (H Rept 95-540) and by the Senate Energy and Natural Resources Committee Oct. 11, 1977 (S Rept 95-490).

The conference bill was the product of many compromises. The House bill initially passed Sept. 12, 1977, would have included 1.17 million acres in 16 national forests in nine western states. The Senate bill passed Oct. 20 called for the addition to the system of 1.25 million acres in 14 national forests in eight western states.

Under the final version, new wilderness areas or additions to existing ones were distributed as follows: four in Oregon, three in California, three in New Mexico and one each in Arizona, Colorado, Utah, Montana, Wyoming, Idaho and one overlapping the Oregon-Washington border.

Seven of the wilderness areas were identical in both the original House and Senate bills. Of the areas that had no counterparts, one House-approved area was deleted by conferees. Three House-approved areas were approved, as were two Senate-approved areas. Conferees deleted a 55,210 acre addition to the Galiuro Wilderness in Arizona which had been included in the House bill but not the Senate.

In each of three areas where both houses had approved new areas but had varied widely in assigning acreage totals, the Senate-approved total was much closer to the conferees' final decision.

An area receiving special attention was the new 180,000 acre Wenaha-Tucannon Wilderness overlapping the Oregon-Washington border. Conferees laid out extensive controls over logging activities in the border areas, noting that the region contained many valuable timber stands, but observing "these lands are important habitat for Rocky Mountain Elk as well."

Gospel-Hump. A major addition to the wilderness system was creation of a new area in north-central Idaho, known as the Gospel-Hump area, provided originally only in the Senate bill. The Senate bill established a 206,000 acre wilderness with an additional 92,000 acres of contiguous land to be managed under a multi-use resource development plan, and another 45,000 acres designated as "development areas."

The conference bill adopted the Senate version, with one change. Terms allowing snowmobile travel along one wilderness trail were deleted after it was decided that the precedent might lead to their intrusion elsewhere.

A major portion of the bill was devoted to outlining creation of a management plan for the Gospel-Hump area. The secretary of the interior was directed to appoint a seven member committee to oversee drafting of the plan, which was to be carried out within four years of enactment.

Refuge Revenue Sharing Act

Legislation to boost payments to counties that lost tax revenues because federal fish and wildlife refuge areas were located within them was cleared by Congress Sept. 29 and signed into law Oct. 17.

The bill (HR 8394 — PL 95-469) revised existing formulas that compensated counties for lands the U.S. Fish and Wildlife Service took from the tax rolls for use as wildlife refuges.

Counties had complained that existing payment schemes did not adequately compensate them for the loss of tax revenues. And, because of the low payments, counties did not want refuges on their lands.

The bill's formulas were patterned after payment schemes contained in the 1976 Payment in Lieu of Taxes Act (PL 94-565). Under that act, which excluded fish and wildlife refuge lands, the federal government made annual tax loss compensation payments to counties that contained National Park Service, Forest Service and certain other federal lands. *(1976 Almanac p. 190)*

HR 8394, known as the Refuge Revenue Sharing Act, established two payment formulas: one for refuge lands purchased from private owners and one for public domain lands — lands owned by the federal government that were turned into wildlife refuges.

Under existing law, counties received for purchased lands the greater of three-quarters of one percent of the adjusted original cost of the land or 25 percent of the net proceeds from the sale of certain refuge products, such as timber or gravel. HR 8394 added a third payment option — 75 cents per acre, based on the land's existing fair market value rather than its original cost.

For public domain lands, HR 8394 maintained the existing scheme, under which counties received 25 percent of the net proceeds from product sales distributed according to a formula in the Payment in Lieu of Taxes Act.

The bill also authorized open-ended appropriations to make up the difference between product revenues and the amount the counties were authorized to receive.

The Congressional Budget Office (CBO) estimated that for fiscal 1979 wildlife refuge areas would generate between $5.5 million and $8.1 million from various products' revenues but that the federal government would be required to pay to the counties between $9.5 million and $10.1 million. The CBO estimated that the federal government would pay out an additional $3.3 million to $5.3 million to make up the difference between product revenues and the amount of payments.

In addition, the bill revised an existing restriction that required counties to spend their refuge revenue sharing funds on public schools and roads only. And it required the counties to give a portion of the funds to other local government units that lost tax revenues because of the location of refuge areas within their jurisdiction.

Legislative History. The House Merchant Marine and Fisheries Committee reported HR 8394 May 15 (H Rept 95-1197). In addition to revising the payment formulas, the committee recommended adding oil and natural gas to the list of products whose sale revenues could be distributed to the counties.

The House approved HR 8394 June 6, 340-28, under suspension of the rules. *(Vote 354, p. 100-H)*

The Senate Environment and Public Works Committee reported HR 8394 (S Rept 95-1174) Aug. 31 and deleted the House provision regarding oil and gas revenues.

The Senate passed HR 8394 by voice vote Sept. 25 with an amendment. The House agreed to the Senate amendments Sept. 29, by voice vote, clearing the bill for the president.

Water Resources Research

A bill (S 2704 — PL 95-467) consolidating water resources research was cleared by the House Oct. 2 and sent to the president.

The measure, which authorized $36.5 million in fiscal 1979 and $57.4 million in fiscal 1980, provided federal grants to state water institutes for research and boosted funding for research on salt water conversion.

The bill also provided a single legal authority for the operations of the Interior Department's Office of Water Research and Technology. *(Background, 1964 Almanac p. 507; 1971 Almanac p. 794)*

The bill emphasized "technology transfer" — the translation of research findings into designs, construction, testing and demonstration to develop efficient methods for supplying and using water as a product.

Provisions

As cleared by Congress, S 2704:

- Provided $8.1 million in fiscal 1979 and $9.45 million in fiscal 1980 for matching research grants to state water institutes; authorized $150,000 for each institute in fiscal 1979 and $175,000 in fiscal 1980. The grants would be provided on a 2 for 1 federal-state cost sharing basis.
- Directed the secretary of the interior with the assistance of the institutes to develop a five-year water resources research program indicating goals, priorities and funding requirements.
- Authorized $750,000 in fiscal 1979 and $1.35 million in fiscal 1980 for a program of competitive 2 for 1 grants in technology transfer designed to encourage the institutes to develop new initiatives to disseminate information to other organizations.
- Authorized competitive matching grants of up to $6 million in fiscal 1979 and $8.5 million in fiscal 1980 for additional special research by the institutes.
- Authorized additional competitive matching grants of up to $5.2 million in fiscal 1979 and $8 million in fiscal 1980 to support research by educational institutions, private firms and foundations, government agencies or any interested individual.
- Authorized $1 million in fiscal 1980 for the secretary to support programs demonstrating the technical and economic viability of systems or techniques that improve water or the water-related environment.
- Authorized $12 million in fiscal 1979 and $14 million in fiscal 1980 for research on the conversion of salt water or other impure water.
- Authorized $10 million in fiscal 1980 for the construction of a salt water conversion demonstration plant. (Earlier legislation — the Water Research and Conservation Act of 1977 (PL 95-84) — had authorized four such demonstration projects and provided funding of $40 million.)
- Authorized $4,464,000 in fiscal 1979 and $5.1 million in fiscal 1980 in additional funding to carry out the act.
- Authorized the secretary to maintain a national information center on water research.
- Required establishment of a center for cataloging scientific research on water, including all federal projects in progress or scheduled.

Background

During the past 26 years, Congress had provided piecemeal funding in varying amounts for water research. Money was focused on educational institutions, and authorizations were extended as legislators saw fit when laws expired. In an attempt to begin national coordination of such research, the Ford administration created the Office of Water Research and Technology from two Interior Department divisions. Ford's fiscal 1977 budget called for a combined program of research on water resources and saline conversion, removing salt from water. But Congress refused to endorse the merger, funding saline conversion only, and leaving the research office without a legislative mandate.

Senate Action

The Senate Committee on Environment and Public Works reported S 2704 on May 15 (S Rept 95-836).

The committee set authorizations at $36.5 million for fiscal year 1979, and $38.7 million for fiscal year 1980. The administration asked for $27.1 million for fiscal 1979 but did not specify a fiscal 1980 sum.

The only major change from the administration request was in Title II, which provided support for development of saline conversion techniques. The committee authorized an additional $10 million for construction of demonstration plants. But it turned down an administration request that 50 percent of the cost of the plants be borne by state and local government sponsors. Because of the importance of developing conversion techniques, and the expenses already faced by local sponsors in complying with the law, the committee reasoned that cost-sharing was "inappropriate."

The Senate passed S 2704 May 25 by voice vote without debate.

House Action

The Committee on Interior and Insular Affairs reported HR 11226 May 15 (H Rept 95-1156). The committee recommended $36.5 million for fiscal 1979, the same amount in the Senate-passed bill. But for fiscal 1980 it recommended $72.9 million, $34.2 million more than the Senate amount.

The panel deleted language to require that state institutes receive and review all grant and contract applications for academic research in their areas.

The committee also called for a requirement, not in the Senate bill, that all rules and regulations formulated in connection with the bill be sent to Congress for 45 days before becoming effective.

The House passed HR 11226 July 11 by voice vote under suspension of the rules and then substituted its language for that of the Senate bill.

Final Action

The Senate approved the House amendments Sept. 25 and made further changes. The House then approved the Senate amendments Oct. 2, clearing the measure.

Noise Control Programs

Legislation directing the Environmental Protection Agency (EPA) to encourage state and local noise control programs and to conduct a research and technical assistance program on noise was cleared by Congress Oct. 13.

The bill (S 3083 — PL 95-609) originally was passed by the Senate by voice vote July 19. The House passed its version (HR 12647) Oct. 10 by voice vote under suspension of the rules, and then substituted its language for that of S 3083. The Senate accepted the House changes Oct. 13, thus clearing the measure.

The House-passed measure differed from the Senate bill in two ways. It reduced the authorization from two years to one year, fiscal 1979, and mandated a joint study by EPA and the Transportation Department of how the noise from airports in one state affected communities located in adjoining states.

Both bills included penalties of up to $10,000 a day for manufacturers whose products violated federal noise standards.

Provisions

As cleared by Congress, S 3083:

- Directed EPA to develop and distribute information and educational materials about the health effects of noise and effective noise control methods.
- Directed EPA to conduct and finance research on such topics as the psychological and physiological effects of noise, noise control technology, equipment for noise control programs, the economic impact of noise and the use of economic incentives (including emission taxes) on noise control.

(The EPA research and development authorization (HR 11302) included $4 million for noise control research. *EPA authorization, p. 681)*

- Required EPA to administer a program of grants to states, local governments and authorized regional planning agencies to identify noise problems, develop noise control programs and evaluate techniques for controlling noise.
- Directed EPA to buy monitoring and other equipment for loan to states and localities.
- Directed EPA to identify trends in noise exposure and to determine the effectiveness of noise control programs.
- Established regional technical assistance centers to assist state and local noise control programs.
- Directed EPA to provide technical assistance to state and local governments, including preparation of model state and local legislation for noise control.
- Required the Federal Aviation Administration (FAA) to respond to EPA's proposed regulation on aircraft noise within 90 days after an FAA hearing and required the FAA to provide an explanation if it rejected an EPA recommendation.
- Mandated a joint EPA/Transportation Department study of how noise from airports affected communities located in adjoining states.
- Provided civil penalties of up to $10,000 per day for manufacturers who distributed new products in violation of EPA noise emission standards.
- Authorized appropriations of $15 million in fiscal 1979.

Legislative History

The Noise Control Act of 1972 (PL 92-574), reauthorized by the legislation, required the EPA administrator to set maximum noise levels that could be tolerated without adversely affecting health, and authorized the EPA to establish noise emission standards for commercial products like motors or air conditioners, to study the effects of noise on humans and to develop improved noise control methods. *(Background, 1976 Almanac p. 210)*

The House and Senate committees that handled the 1978 measure noted that the federal noise research budget had plummeted from about $55 million in fiscal 1973 to roughly $30 million in fiscal 1977.

The Senate Environment and Public Works Committee, which filed its report on S 3083 May 15 (S Rept 95-875), concluded that EPA's noise control program "has been ineffective as a regulatory program to reduce noise" and "enjoys little of EPA's resources or attention."

The committee said the EPA had been "totally frustrated" in its recommendations to the Federal Aviation Administration (FAA) on the control of aircraft noise. EPA officials told the committee they had been "ineffective in influencing the FAA's decisions despite 11 regulatory proposals made to the FAA."

HR 12647, reported by the Interstate and Foreign Commerce Committee May 15 (H Rept 95-1171), included an amendment requiring owners of major airports and the local government with jurisdiction over area land use to file a satisfactory noise abatement plan with the EPA and the Transportation Department. *(Airport noise, p. 504)*

Reclamation Dam Repair

A bill giving the secretary of the interior authority to order repairs on unsafe Bureau of Reclamation dams was cleared by Congress Oct. 14 after the House amended the measure to ensure that water users would bear the cost of repairs for normal wear and tear.

The measure (S 2820—PL 95-578) was cleared for the president after the Senate agreed to accept the language of the bill (HR 11153) passed by the House the same day. The Senate had passed its own version July 28 by a vote of 77-1. *(Vote 255, p. 40-S).*

As originally proposed by the administration, the bill authorized the interior secretary to repair 13 older Reclamation dams and to fix others as they were identified. Most of the repair costs would have been borne by the water users.

But the versions reported by the Senate Energy and Natural Resources Committee (S Rept 95-810) and by the House Interior Committee (H Rept 95-1125) provided that the federal government would pay for all repairs and authorized $100 million for them.

During floor action, the House accepted by voice vote an amendment by Lloyd Meeds, D-Wash., that retained the $100 million authorization but spelled out that the federal money could only be used for modifications to bring the dams up to the latest "state-of-the-art" engineering standards for dam safety. The cost of repairs needed because of normal deterioration would be borne by the water users.

Major Provisions

As cleared by Congress, S 2820:

- Permanently authorized the interior secretary to perform structural modifications to ensure the safety of Bureau of Reclamation dams.
- Limited the authorization to ensure that modifications would be for dam safety purposes only and would not provide additional storage capacity or user benefits.
- Provided that repair costs resulting from normal deterioration would be borne by the users, while the cost of modifications needed because of changes in engineering criteria for dam safety would be paid by the federal government.
- Authorized appropriations of $100 million for fiscal 1979 and ensuing years.
- Provided that no funds for actual construction could be authorized until 60 days after a report on the project had been submitted to Congress by the interior secretary.

Other Legislation

Two other bills promoting dam safety were passed by the Senate June 9 by voice vote, but died because no action was taken on them in the House.

The broadest proposal, S 2437, attempted to provide an incentive to states to undertake dam safety programs without relinquishing the federal role in states that had no program.

The other bill, S 2444, sought to expedite dam inspections by the Army Corps of Engineers by giving corps engineers right of entry to all dam sites and access to permanent records.

Climate Research

A program designed to centralize planning and improve coordination among the widely scattered federal agencies working on climate research was signed by President Carter Sept. 17.

The bill (HR 6669 — PL 95-367) directed the president to establish a national climate program and define the roles of the 12 federal agencies concerned with climate. It established a National Climate Program Office in the Department of Commerce to coordinate the program, and authorized $60 million for it in fiscal 1979 and $75 million in fiscal 1980.

After House passage Sept. 9, 1977, by a 282-60 vote, the Senate approved the legislation April 24 by voice vote. The conference report (H Rept 95-1489) was filed Aug. 14 and agreed to by the Senate Aug. 17 and by the House Sept. 6, both by voice vote.

Background

Both the House and Senate reports on the bill emphasized that existing scientific capacity to forecast climate was limited despite the substantial impact of climate on the U.S. economy.

The Senate report (S Rept 95-740) was filed April 18 by the Commerce Committee. The House report (H Rept 95-206) had been filed May 6, 1977, by the Science and Technology Committee.

The legislation was needed, according to the Senate report, to respond to three major needs; better federal planning and management, more research on basic climatic phenomena and more effective use of climate-related information.

"Each agency tends to develop its own climate-related activities without regard for what other agencies are doing; coordination has been haphazard," the Senate report said. "No national program or plan exists which specifies objectives, priorities, agency responsibilities and appropriate funding, and no agency has been designated as the lead agency responsible for developing and implementing a national climate program."

The report called the existing $52 million annual budget for federal climate research "inadequate," and recommended a broad program in basic and applied research with special emphasis on forecasting.

The report also recommended increased involvement of state and local governments and the private sector in receiving and using climate information.

Provisions

As cleared by Congress, HR 6669:

- Directed the president to establish a national climate program and to submit to Congress six months after enactment a preliminary five-year plan stating goals and priorities and defining the roles of the various federal agencies in the program. A final plan was required one year after enactment.
- Directed that the program include: 1) assessment of the effect of climate on the environment; 2) basic and applied research; 3) methods for improving long-range climate forecasts; 4) global data collection; 5) systems for the management and dissemination of climatological data; 6) measures for increasing international cooperation in climate research; 7) mechanisms for intergovernmental

climate-related studies and services; and 8) experimental climate forecast centers.

- Directed that the program encourage cooperation with and participation by other domestic and international organizations and agencies involved in climate-related programs.
- Directed the secretary of commerce to establish an advisory committee of users and producers of climate data to advise the secretary and Congress and to establish interagency groups to encourage coordinated management of the program by all federal agencies.
- Authorized the secretary to establish federal/state cooperative activities in climate studies and services.
- Authorized the secretary to provide matching grants to states with approved state climate programs. The grants could be made available to universities, state agencies or private organizations.
- Directed that the intergovernmental program include 1) studies of climatic effects on agricultural production, water resources and energy needs; 2) atmospheric data collection and monitoring on a statewide or regional basis; 3) advice to state and local agencies on climate-related issues; 4) information to users within a state regarding climate and its effects; and 5) information to the secretary regarding state needs for information and services.
- Required the secretary to submit an annual report on the program to the president and Congress.
- Authorized general appropriations to the secretary of $50 million in fiscal 1979 and $65 million in fiscal 1980, plus $10 million each in fiscal 1979-80 for intergovernmental program grants. ▮

Drought Aid Extension

Congress Jan. 31 cleared legislation extending the deadline for completion of water reclamation, irrigation and other emergency drought projects authorized in 1977.

By voice vote the House Jan. 30 and the Senate Jan. 31 approved a bill (HR 10532 — H Rept 95-854 — PL 95-226) that gave the Secretary of the Interior discretionary authority to extend certain construction projects past a Jan. 31 cut-off date set by PL 95-18, a drought-aid bill.

It was the second time an extension for the projects had been granted at the request of the administration. More time was needed because bad weather and shortages of supplies had held up completion of at least 66 drought-related projects, according to Interior Secretary Cecil D. Andrus. No new spending or new projects were authorized by the measure, which simply permitted work to continue on projects contracted before Sept. 30, 1977. *(PL 95-18, earlier extension, 1977 Almanac p. 678)* ▮

Carter Acts to Preserve Alaskan Wilderness

Earning a reputation as a conservationist president, Jimmy Carter acted in 1978 to protect from commercial development millions of acres of pristine Alaskan wilderness.

Carter's action came at the end of a year in which Congress haggled over but was unable to agree on legislation (HR 39) to set aside even bigger chunks of the nation's largest state. The legislation failed in the closing hours of the session when Sen. Mike Gravel, D-Alaska, blocked efforts at compromise by key House and Senate leaders.

Action on the Alaska issue by the 95th Congress had been considered crucial because existing restrictions on use of 80 million acres of Alaska expired Dec. 17. Under the 1971 Alaska Native Claims Settlement Act (PL 92-203) Congress had until that date to decide which of the federal government's vast holdings in the state should be classified as "national interest" lands and receive special protection as national parks, wildlife refuges, wild and scenic rivers or national forests. *(Explanation of laws, next page)*

Proponents of preservation of vast wilderness areas argued that Alaska was the United States' last frontier. The president had called an Alaska bill his highest conservation priority.

When Congress failed to act, Carter made his move. Using authority provided in the Antiquities Act of 1906, he acted Dec. 1 to create 17 new national monuments, which prevented mining, logging and other commercial development on 56 million acres — an area the size of Minnesota. The move more than doubled the size of the national park system.

The "risk of immediate damage to magnificent areas," Carter said, made it "imperative to protect all the lands and preserve for Congress an unhampered opportunity to act next year."

Both Carter and Interior Secretary Cecil D. Andrus said the monuments were created to preserve the fragile scenery until Congress could try again in 1979 to pass an Alaska lands bill.

House Action

The Alaska Lands Subcommittee of the House Interior Committee began markup of an Alaska bill early in the year. The full committee ordered HR 39 reported March 21 by a 32-13 vote. The report (H Rept 95-1045, Part I) was filed April 7.

In subcommittee markup, conservationists retained the advantage on the most divisive aspect of the legislation — the number of acres to be designated as wilderness. Some public land classifications, like national forests, allowed development such as oil and gas exploration and mining. But such uses were not permitted by the wilderness designation. *(Land uses, boxes, pp. 729, 731)*

Arctic Wildlife Refuge

One example of the conflict between development and preservation was the fight over designation of wilderness in the 1.2 million acre Arctic National Wildlife Refuge in northeastern Alaska. The area, thought to be rich in oil, also was the calving ground for Alaska's healthiest caribou herd, a key stopping point for millions of migrating birds and a home for some 31 species of wildlife. The administration and the Interior subcommittee had supported wilderness designation for the area.

The Administration's Tools

A number of existing laws gave the administration authority to restrict use of federal land in Alaska. They were:

Alaska Native Claims Settlement Act of 1971 (PL 92-203). This law gave Alaska natives the right to select 44 million acres of the 226 million federally owned acres in Alaska. The law also set aside 80 million acres of federal land for consideration as national parks and refuges. Included in the 80 million acres were some lands that the state wanted as part of the 104 million acres it was granted when it became a state in 1959. It had not finished choosing its land when the 1971 law was passed.

The law provided that once the federal parks and refuges were selected, under Section 17 d(2), then the state, or d(1) lands, could be chosen. If the d(2) designation expired, then all federal land in Alaska not already in parks or refuges would be set aside to allow the state to select from it. Use of this d(1) land also was restricted, but some mining and mineral exploration was allowed. Land not selected for either category would continue to be managed by the Bureau of Land Management (BLM).

Federal Land Policy and Management Act (PL 94-579). Known as the BLM "organic act," this law set out general policy for management of the more than 470 million acres of federal land in the agency's jurisdiction.

The law required the interior secretary to study all roadless areas of 5,000 acres or more to determine whether they should be protected as wilderness, a designation that generally prohibited development.

The Interior Department said the secretary could use the law to earmark for wilderness study millions of federally owned acres in Alaska. Most of the federal land in Alaska was managed by BLM.

According to the law, the land under wilderness study would have to be managed in a way that would not destroy existing wilderness features. Congress eventually would decide what land was actually designated as wilderness, but in the intervening years of study millions of acres could be closed to development and held in limbo, a situation many Alaska leaders wanted to avoid.

Antiquities Act of 1906. This law gave the president authority to use executive orders to create national monuments, in which use of the land was restricted in the same way as it was in national parks. It required an act of Congress to remove the monument designation.

Fish and Wildlife Act of 1956 (PL 84-1024). This act gave the interior secretary authority to take any steps needed to conserve and develop fisheries and wildlife resources, including the establishment of refuges for fish and wildlife.

During full committee markup, John F. Seiberling, D-Ohio, chairman of the Alaska Lands Subcommittee, fought efforts to open the refuge to private oil and gas development. Seiberling proposed an amendment, accepted 21 to 19, which allowed the federal government to use seismic testing and exploratory drilling to try to determine oil and gas potential in the refuge. In five years, a report would be made to Congress on the potential reserves; Congress would then decide whether to allow private development.

Interior Committee Action

As reported by the Interior Committee, HR 39 classified 95 million acres of federally owned lands in Alaska into parks, preserves, wildlife refuges and forests. The committee called the bill the "most significant conservation measure ever laid before the House."

Of the 95 million acres, 50 million were designated as wilderness. Another 24 million acres in existing conservation units also were classified as wilderness.

"Nowhere else in our country, after four centuries of settlement and development, will we ever again have this opportunity to capture and save the living wildness of such great expanses," the committee said.

The committee report also noted that the bill was a compromise.

"It will not 'lock-up' the mineral and energy resources of this land, but will provide for their discovery and development in the national interest and subject to the control of Congress," the report said.

The committee also pointed out that the lands HR 39 would place in conservation units were already federal lands. "It [the bill] will not take land from anybody else nor will it require appropriations of funds for acquisition, since this land already belongs to the nation," according to the report.

Boundaries were drawn so that, whenever possible, potential oil and gas deposits and minerals veins would be left outside of protected areas, according to the committee. About 70 percent of the hard rock mineral deposits in Alaska would be excluded from protected areas, along with about 95 percent of the potential oil and gas deposits.

To accommodate sport hunting and fishing, as well as mineral development, the committee carved preserves out of proposed parks. The preserves would be open to hunting and fishing and eligible for a special minerals access process; parks would be closed to those uses.

Special Access

The special minerals process in the bill allowed access to mineral deposits, including oil and gas, in preserves and refuges if it were in the national interest.

Oil and gas leasing had been allowed in refuges, but not in preserves. Both types of conservation units had been closed to hard rock mining.

The committee developed this mechanism for loosening controls on use of the land because members felt that shutting all of the protected acres to mining would be too restrictive, the report said. With the special process, 51 million of those acres could be opened to mining and oil or gas development. Some 14 million acres, or about 20 percent of the state, would still be closed to those uses.

The new process would require approval by the interior secretary and Congress of any application for such development. Instead of allowing miners to stake claims on hard rock deposits, as under existing law, HR 39 would set up a leasing program.

Wilderness Designation

In still another compromise, the committee substantially reduced wilderness designations from the 146

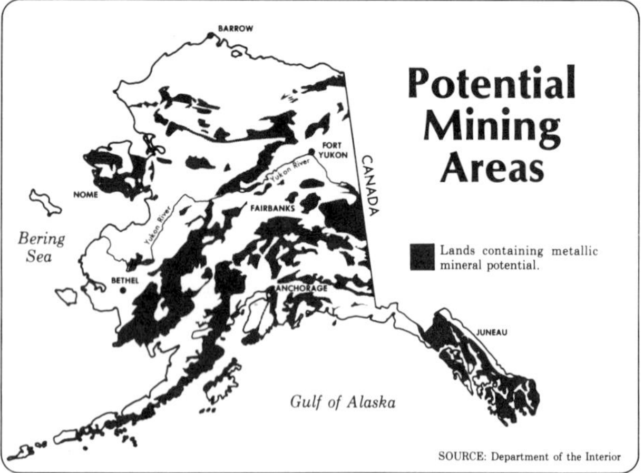

million acres proposed in the original HR 39 to 74 million acres. The administration proposed 46 million acres as wilderness.

The committee said it used the wilderness designation to provide extra protection in refuges and preserves that it wanted closed to the minerals process. The administration did not propose a plan for access to minerals and opposed the committee's proposal. Administration officials said their plan to designate lands as parks or refuges would have provided adequate protection. *(Administration plan, 1977 Almanac p. 672)*

The committee protected more acreage than the administration requested but with fewer restrictions on its use.

Because of concerns about access to holdings within protected areas and to state and native lands nearby, the committee also set up a procedure for cutting transportation and utility corridors through protected areas. As in the minerals process, an application for a road, pipeline or other corridor across a conservation unit would have to be approved by the secretary and then by joint resolution of Congress.

The committee also guaranteed that those native and non-native Alaskans using the public lands for subsistence could continue to do so even if the lands were placed in wilderness or restrictive conservation units. A compromise worked out on this potentially explosive issue would require that the state be responsible for the subsistence program, with federal oversight.

Merchant Marine Committee Action

The Merchant Marine Committee, which had jurisdiction only over the wildlife refuges in the bill, reported its version May 4 (H Rept 95-1045, Part II).

Merchant Marine added acreage to several refuges designated by the Interior Committee and created new refuges in the Copper River delta in southern Alaska and at the National Petroleum Reserve in northwest Alaska.

But the committee reduced the 28 million acres designated as wilderness by Interior to about 20 million acres.

In a move supported by conservationists, the committee deleted the Interior provision calling for the special government study and exploration of the oil and gas potential of the Arctic Wildlife Refuge. Robert L. Leggett, D-Calif., whose Merchant Marine Fish and Wildlife Subcommittee handled the bill, argued that any exploration would harm the caribou and other wildlife there. He said he agreed with President Carter that any oil and gas there should be the last to be developed by the United States.

Rep. Don Young, R, Alaska's only representative in the House, had been pushing to have more areas open to development. While he lost on the Arctic Wildlife Refuge, he was more successful in deleting a 600,000 acre section from the Yukon Flats Refuge in central Alaska so it could be developed by the state.

The administration and conservationists contended that the area was the "heart" of the 10 million acre refuge and that the recreational development, mining, agriculture and other uses planned by the state would severely harm the rest of the refuge, which was of international significance because of its wildlife.

In other action, the Merchant Marine Committee:

- Deleted Interior's special provision allowing mining in refuges if approved by Congress.
- Set up cooperative state-federal management of the Bristol Bay drainage in southwest Alaska, which included three wildlife refuges and patches of state and federal lands.
- Loosened restrictions on aquaculture development, primarily fish hatcheries, in two wilderness areas.

Rules Committee Action

Floor action on HR 39 was delayed until mid-May because of a dispute in the House Rules Committee.

Opponents of the measure were attempting to block or delay action on the bill.

Rep. Lloyd Meeds, D-Wash., one of the opponents, argued that "it would be unwarranted to make House members vote on a very tough labor versus conservation issue when there is absolutely no chance, at this time, of it going to the Senate floor." Meeds had sponsored an amendment to the bill in the Interior Committee that would have cut wilderness acreage in half. It was defeated 20-24.

Some labor groups, including the Building Trades Department of the AFL-CIO, opposed the bill because of fears that wilderness and park designations would cost labor jobs in timber, mining and oil and gas development. But other labor groups, such as the United Auto Workers, supported the bill.

The chances for Senate floor action were considered shaky at that time because the Senate Energy Committee, which had jurisdiction, had not taken it up because members were tied up in the natural gas pricing debate. In addition, Alaska's senators had threatened to filibuster the bill.

Corporate Lawyer, River Pilot Vied Over Alaska Lands

Throughout the debate on the Alaska lands bill, John F. Seiberling, D-Ohio, and Don Young, R-Alaska, were on opposite sides of the fight.

Young's style was direct, sometimes boisterous. Seiberling was more subtle, but no less determined or capable of a wry comment when he was displeased.

The corporate lawyer from Akron and the former river boat pilot from Fort Yukon were leaders throughout House skirmishes over the bill.

Seiberling

Traveling down the rushing Charley River in 1975, John Seiberling had his first exposure to the "absolutely fantastic" beauty of Alaska.

After that he became an expert on the state. Show him a photograph of an Alaskan mountain peak, and Seiberling probably could name it.

In 1978, Seiberling, 59, chairman of the House Interior Committee's Alaska Lands Subcommittee, often traded float trips for hearing rooms.

The once stubborn conservationist grew adept at swapping votes and soothing ruffled feathers as he steered the massive bill through the panel.

Much of it was tedious work. Don Young jokingly called Seiberling "iron pants" because he could sit for 12 to 14 hours a day at public hearings on the bill.

Interior's hearing room, decorated with Seiberling's color photographs of Alaska, was always jammed with conservationists, oil and gas lobbyists, Interior Department officials and others following the bill. The tension, the pressure from different sides, was obvious.

"I never saw such lobbying in my whole life," Seiberling said in an interview.

Seiberling earned a reputation as a fair chairman.

Even Young was generous in his praise of Seiberling's work. "He has been more than fair in his treatment of me," said Young.

As he worked out compromises, Seiberling found himself opposed from time to time by the committee's most ardent conservationists, a role he had assumed on some other issues. But this time was different. Seiberling said: "I was the chairman. I had responsibilities."

A Conservationist Grandfather

Though patient with opponents of the Alaska bill, Seiberling disliked their motives. The idea of preserving Alaska's wilderness for future generations of Americans "puts to shame those money-grubbers looking only at their immediate profit," he said.

His philosophy of conservation was similar to his grandfather's. The elder Seiberling, owner of a tire manufacturing company, once gave land for a park near Akron. Asked later if he regretted not holding on to the increasingly valuable land, the grandfather pointed to the people using the park and replied, "Those are my dividends."

Young

Don Young fought particularly hard to keep part of Yukon flats in northeast Alaska out of the federal park system.

It was no wonder. For years that area was Young's home as he piloted a river boat on the Yukon River and checked fur traps in the flats and nearby mountains.

Young, the frontiersman, did not even have running water in his Fort Yukon home. "I was the original streaker," he cracked, describing runs to the outhouse in below zero temperatures.

Like Seiberling, Young, 44, had little time for the outdoors in 1978 because of his fight over Alaska lands.

Bill Unnecessary

"The bill's not needed," said Young, who preferred that the Bureau of Land Management (BLM) continue to oversee the bulk of the 230 million federally owned acres in Alaska. BLM allowed grazing, mining, oil drilling and other development.

Putting 100 million of those acres into protected parks, refuges and other systems would just mean than "50 or 100 years from now, when the crunch comes down here [for minerals and energy]. . .they'll rip us up like you've never seen," said Young.

The "they" Young referred to was the federal government. It would, he said, open the protected areas to miners and drillers "without any concern for the environment or what the consequences would be for the state."

Young wanted to postone the classification of the land into conservation systems to provide more time to learn about minerals and other resources.

"Let private industry do it on a time schedule basis," said Young of the studies and the development.

Though conservationists said Young was short-sighted because the development could ruin the wilderness forever, Young used the same argument against them. "They're living for today, not thinking of tomorrow," he complained. In the Alaska bill reported by the Interior Committee there was no planning for that future energy crunch, he said.

Alaska still was recovering from another time the federal government needed some of its resources, Young said. "We're still picking up the barrels and garbage the government left" in the National Petroleum Reserve when it searched for oil in the 1940s, he said.

May 9 Compromise

The measure got a boost May 9 when leaders of the Interior and Merchant Marine committees endorsed a "consensus" they had developed as a means of simplifying House action on the bill.

However, the consensus (HR 12625) also provided further ammunition for Rules Committee members who were critical of the Alaska measure for restricting development of the state's resources, including oil, gas and mineral development.

Meeds and Rep. B.F. Sisk, D-Calif., for example, charged that neither committee had actually voted on the consensus and that no report was filed on it. Meeds also charged that the consensus would "put everything in Alaska out of bounds for mineral entry," something that neither committee had done.

Supporters reiterated their contention that the measure left most of the state's resources open to development.

Rep. Morris K. Udall, D-Ariz., chairman of the Interior Committee, said the intent of the consensus was to keep Rules from having to referee the two committee's disputes and to simplify House consideration of the bill.

But Meeds protested. "You are asking, in effect, to replace the work of both committees with this document," he said.

And Trent Lott, R-Miss., noted that it was "unusual to force a bill through that is opposed by the two senators and the representative [of the only state affected]."

Finally, after two days of hearings, the Rules Committee voted 11-5 May 16 to send the Alaska bill to the full House. The rule granted was broadly drawn to allow various substitute bills to be introduced on the floor, including the consensus and the Meeds proposal.

THE 'CONSENSUS'

The most significant difference between the consensus bill and the Interior and Merchant Marine versions was that the consensus tightened restrictions on hard rock mining on conservation lands.

The consensus dropped the special access provision in Title IX of the Interior bill, which allowed Congress to open any federal land in Alaska — except parks and wilderness — to mining. Park preserves and wildlife refuges, usually not open to mining, would have been eligible in Interior's version.

Dropping the special access to minerals provision meant that all conservation lands, except forests, would be closed to mining. As a result, the consensus actually was more restrictive than either the Interior or Merchant Marine versions.

Though Merchant Marine had deleted Interior's Title IX, Merchant Marine interpreted existing wildlife refuge law as saying that the interior secretary could open refuges to hard rock mining if it were compatible with the wildlife.

Under the consensus version, the secretary could allow oil and gas leasing when compatible with wildlife, but not hard rock mining. The change essentially followed existing law.

The consensus also generally embodied what the Carter administration had sought in its proposed Alaska legislation.

Administration officials had proposed applying existing laws to refuges and parks, which they said would provide a balance of protection and access. The administration had opposed the Interior plan which, in effect, exposed more areas to mining through the Title IX access process, but then closed still other areas to mining by designating them as wilderness.

"This [consensus] approach," said Seiberling, in a statement prepared for delivery on the floor May 9, "recognizes that the boundaries of the [preserved areas] were carefully drawn to exclude the great majority of lands containing some potential for the occurrence of metallic minerals and oil and gas."

The American Mining Congress, already opposed to the bill, found the consensus version even less acceptable.

Keith Knoblock, a spokesman for the group, called the new proposal "a step backwards." Both companies and the government would "never be able to get in there, not even to look," for mineral deposits, he said.

Wildlife Refuges

Generally, the consensus included Merchant Marine's designations of wildlife refuges, which added about 3.1 million acres to the refuges that were created or expanded by Interior. The compromise expanded the existing refuge system in Alaska by about 55 million acres.

Of the two new refuges proposed by Merchant Marine, the consensus included one — a 1.2-million-acre refuge in the Copper River delta that would be carved from existing national forest. The second proposed new refuge — the 22.5-million-acre National Petroleum Reserve on the North Slope — was not included in the agreement.

Merchant Marine's designation of wilderness acreage in refuges also was included in the consensus. Merchant Marine had voted to protect about 20 million acres — about 8.5 million fewer than Interior — as wilderness.

Other Changes

The compromise also included the modifications Merchant Marine had made to the Interior bill regarding the subsistence use of conservation lands by natives.

The consensus did not include a Merchant Marine proposal for a cooperative federal and state management plan for the Bristol Bay region in the southwestern part of the state just north of the Alaska Peninsula.

Floor Action

The House resoundingly endorsed the consensus bill May 19 on a 277-31 vote. *(Vote 290, p. 84-H)*.

Don Young, who generally spoke for state officials, failed in his effort to open more of the proposed park land to private and state development.

The measure, which put about 100 million acres of federal Alaska land into national parks, refuges and wilderness, had powerful backers — two House committees, the House leadership and the Carter administration.

Lobbying by those for and against the bill was fierce. Mining, timber and oil and gas interests opposed it, while conservationists ran a well-organized grass roots campaign in its favor. But after the first test votes, it was clear the conservationists, waiting outside the chamber and sporting buttons showing a caribou, were winning.

The only victory for industry came May 19 when the House voted in favor of an amendment by Jim Santini, D-Nev., calling for a study by the interior secretary of mineral deposits in Alaska. The amendment directed that the study, with recommendations for development, be presented to Congress by Oct. 1, 1981. The amendment was adopted 157-150. *(Vote 288, p. 84-H)*

But that victory for industry was muted because mining companies and other developers had sought an overall reduction in the acreage to be protected as wilderness. On May 18, the House had refused, 119-240, to adopt an amendment by Meeds that would have cut the wilderness acreage in half. *(Vote 286, p. 82-H)*

Another key vote came May 18 on a proposal by Young to give the state about five million acres of the proposed park land. But the House also rejected that move by a heavy margin, 141-251. *(Vote 285, p. 82-H)*

By a vote of 67-242, the House May 19 refused to accept a Young motion seeking passage of a substitute proposal by Meeds. The Meeds substitute included a reduction in wilderness acreage, the removal of the land Young wanted for the state from the proposed park land and other changes designed to make the bill more acceptable to development-oriented interests. *(Vote 289, p. 84-H)*

THE DEBATE

Debate on the measure, called the most important conservation bill of the century, was colorful, though marked in its early stages by hassles over procedure.

Supporters talked about the beauty of the Alaskan wilderness and its wildlife.

"It is the kind of experience that the pioneer and the discoverers of America must have had when they came upon this vast, unspoiled, pristine land, teeming with magnificent wildlife," said Seiberling.

"I am confident," said Udall, "that Alaska lands legislation can be enacted into law this year so that you and I, and your children and grandchildren, and my children and grandchildren, will be able to know that a part of our great natural heritage located in the state of Alaska will be protected and preserved for the enjoyment and edification of all people for all time."

Opponents were just as forceful.

"A turkey is a turkey is a turkey," Young said of the bill. The proposed park lands "are also areas that have their uses," he said. "Those uses must be for this nation, for recreational purposes, for oil and gas, for all the 31 minerals which we import today."

Robert E. Bauman, R-Md., who opposed the bill, called it "a cheap shot" for members not from Alaska. "If you want to go with the environmentalists, if you want to throw one their way, if you want to vote for federal action that you would never permit to be done in your state, go ahead, vote for it," Bauman said. "Or you can try to face the issue fairly and squarely."

From time to time, supporters and opponents of the bill brought maps and charts into the well of the House chamber to illustrate their points. Members often opened on their desk tops the maps of Alaska that had been folded into the backs of the committee reports on the bill.

In the Speaker's Lobby, a hallway and sitting room adjacent to the front of the chamber, several dozen color photographs of Alaska taken by Seiberling were on display.

Wilderness Amendment

The two-to-one defeat of the Meeds proposal to halve the wilderness area was a surprisingly solid victory for conservationists. Meeds had tried to portray his approach

Types of Conservation Units

Following is a listing and description of the different types of conservation units Congress considered for Alaska.

In its bill (HR 39),the Senate Energy Committee classifed 97.13 million acres of federal land into seven types of units and designated as wilderness 37.2 million acres in new and old conservation units.

The House put 122.3 million acres into conservation units, including 22.5 million acres already withdrawn as the National Petroleum Reserve. It also created 66 million acres of wilderness in new and old units.

National Parks and Monuments. Managed by the National Park Service, these areas are set aside to protect outstanding scenic and other natural values. Camping, fishing, hiking and other activities normally are allowed. But mining, oil and gas development, logging, trapping and hunting usually are not.

National Park Preserves. These units also are managed by the park service and are treated as parks except that the taking of fish and wildlife for subsistence purposes and for sport, including guided hunting, is allowed under appropriate state and federal regulations.

National Recreation Areas. The interior secretary manages these areas for public recreational use, including hunting, fishing and camping. In addition, the secretary can permit development of minerals and other resources under controls that protect fish and wildlife and other natural resources in the area.

National Wildlife Refuges. The primary purpose of a refuge is the preservation and enhancement of fish and wildlife and their habitat. Recreation activities, including hunting and fishing, are usually allowed if compatible with that purpose. The interior secretary can also allow oil and gas exploration if compatible with the wildlife.

National Forests. Forests are managed by the U.S. Forest Service, which is part of the Department of Agriculture. Multiple uses — logging, grazing, trapping, mining, oil and gas development and hunting — are allowed. The forest service also replants trees to maintain the yield.

National Conservation Areas. These areas are managed by the Bureau of Land Management (BLM) as multiple use lands, but with special consideration given to protection of wildlife and other resource values. BLM is directed to develop a land use plan for national conservation areas that identifies fragile areas that are not suited to development or where certain activity should be restricted.

Wild and Scenic River. This designation protects flowing rivers and a corridor of land along the banks from dams and other water resource development projects.

Wilderness, a designation that overlays a park, refuge or other system, is a management approach that restricts commercial development, such as road building, mining or construction of resort facilities. But an activity like hunting can continue in a wilderness if it is already allowed in that system; i.e., hunting could continue in a forest also managed as wilderness.

as a compromise that protected some land but also accommodated development.

The wilderness designation is "the mischievous part of this bill" that "prevents growth and development for Alaskans," Meeds told the House. The minerals and other resources the bill would cut off from development are also needed by the rest of the country, he said.

But Udall told his colleagues, "Wilderness is what this bill is all about." The bill reflects a balance between protection and development, he said, urging defeat of the Meeds amendment.

"We are going to give the caribou a chance to survive, or we are going to let them go the way of the buffalo in the lower 48. We have compromised; we have recompromised; we have compromised again," Udall said, referring to cuts made by committees in the acreage to be protected.

Meeds proposed that there be 33 million acres of wilderness, primarily in parks, instead of the 66 million acres sought by the Interior and Merchant Marine Committees, which had jurisdiction over the bill.

His amendment would have removed the wilderness protection from the Arctic Wildlife Refuge, which would have allowed oil and gas development in the fragile tundra.

Meeds said the refuge areas proposed for wilderness by the committees had not been studied enough and noted that procedures in the Wilderness Act of 1964 (PL 88-577) had not been followed.

He also said the wilderness area proposed for the national forests would cause job losses in southeast Alaska.

But Seiberling disputed both charges. Saying the areas had not been studied "is just failing to look at the facts as they are," Seiberling said, pointing to the thick reports from the Interior Department and the 17 volumes of committee hearings that were stacked before him on a table.

The threat of job losses in southeast Alaska had been remedied in committee, he said, because the wilderness acreage had been reduced.

Young, endorsing the Meeds proposal, contended that the delay in designating wilderness would not be harmful. "Nothing precludes us from making it wilderness at a later date," after study by government and private industry of possible oil and mineral deposits.

But Seiberling disagreed. "If we put land in wilderness, or a national park, or a refuge, that is not an irreversible decision," he said, because Congress could later change its mind. "But if we cut all the timber, the wilderness is gone, and if we dig out all the minerals, they're gone, and the true lock-up has taken place."

Federal land that was not put into national parks, refuges or forests would remain under the control of the Bureau of Land Management, which permitted development.

State Land Amendment

The state of Alaska wanted about five million acres of the proposed park land for recreation, residential development and industry. Young, offering an amendment to delete the acreage from HR 39, argued that his state deserved the land because it still did not have title to all of the 104 million acres the federal government gave the new state in 1958.

"I am sorry to say that statehood did not terminate our status as a colony," Young said. "We are still ruled largely by Washington...." Later he added, "One thing we must remember is that the state of Alaska feels as if this Congress has broken its word. And believe me, I honestly believe the legislation before us, without this amendment, does exactly that."

But Seiberling, Udall and others disputed Young's claims of state's rights and said he had already won many boundary changes and lands for his state. Seiberling said the Alaska Lands Subcommittee adopted 85 of 89 amendments offered by Young.

But Teno Roncalio, D-Wyo., appeared ready to compromise with Young. "If I vote for these 14 amendments, which include up to five million acres, will the gentleman accept the rest of this bill and vote for it?," he asked Young.

"Let us put it this way," Young replied. "I would not support the bill, but I would not actively oppose it either."

Rules Action

In broadly drawing its rule to allow substitute bills to be introduced, the Rules Committee inadvertently created a loophole that also allowed nongermane amendments to be offered.

John M. Ashbrook, R-Ohio, saw the mistake as an opportunity to defeat the bill and said he would offer a gun control substitute. Supporters of the bill also were worried about other nongermane substitutes.

If a substitute is accepted, it displaces the original bill.

But the bill's supporters worked out a parliamentary solution to the dilemma. After the Meeds substitute was offered on the floor, Udall offered another substitute. That meant that, under the rules, a third substitute would not be in order.

The Udall substitute, then, was the one that the House spent two days amending. Once it was accepted, the Meeds substitute and the original bill were displaced.

The Udall substitute was identical to the consensus bill, but included Interior's "unlock" provision that allowed mining in nonwilderness areas if Congress and the interior secretary believed it would be in the national interest.

Other Amendments

During floor action May 18, the House accepted by voice vote amendments by:

- Leggett to create the North Slope wildlife refuge from the approximately 22.5 million acres known as the National Petroleum Reserve.
- Peter H. Kostmayer, D-Pa., to make the entire Cape Krusenstern area into a park, removing the designation of "preserve" from 350,000 acres in the northern portion.

By voice vote May 19, the House accepted amendments by:

- Leggett to adjust the boundaries of three proposed national wildlife refuges to permit the state of Alaska to select the areas as part of its statehood entitlement of 104 million acres. The deletions were 65,000 acres from the Togiak refuge; 95,000 acres from the Innoko refuge along the Yukon River and 70,000 acres from the Selawik refuge on the Baldwin Peninsula.
- Ralph S. Regula, R-Ohio, to retain the name Mount McKinley Mountain for the peak within the Denali National Park, which was the new name the bill gave to the expanded Mount McKinley Park.
- Kostmayer to add about 47,000 acres to the Kobuk Valley National Park, bringing total park acreage to about 1.72 million acres.
- Seiberling to clarify that HR 39 would not affect the right-of-way for the route of the Alaska natural gas pipeline

Conservation Unit Activities

	Oil and Gas Development	Mining	Logging	Hunting
Parks	no	no	no	no
Preserves	no	no	no	yes
Refuges	yes*	no	no**	yes***
Forests	yes	yes	yes	yes

** The interior secretary may allow oil and gas development in a refuge but only if it is compatible with enhancement of wildlife and its habitat.*

*** Logging is not allowed unless connected with a wildlife management practice, such as removing certain trees to provide a cover more beneficial to wildlife.*

**** Hunting is usually allowed under conditions that differ from refuge to refuge. There are refuges where hunting is not allowed.*

that was approved in the Alaska Natural Gas Transportation Act of 1976 (PL 94-586). The right-of-way was through the Tetlin wildlife refuge created in the bill.

PROVISIONS

As passed by the House, HR 39:

Title I: Policy Statement

The title set out five congressional policies to guide implementation of the legislation. The bill provided that:

- Designated public lands in Alaska should be set aside immediately upon enactment as part of federal conservation systems in order to preserve wildlife, free-flowing rivers and other resources.
- Administrators of conserved lands should consider intangible values, such as scenic beauty, equally with values that could be quantified, such as oil and gas deposits.
- The public should have access to the lands "consistent with the purposes" for which they were conserved.
- Persons dependent on the land for subsistence should be allowed to continue that lifestyle.
- The Interior Department and other agencies implementing the act should consider the desire of the state and native corporations to maintain a viable economy and provide employment for the citizens of Alaska.

Title II: National Parks

The three existing national parks in Alaska were expanded and 10 new parks were created, increasing the state's total park acreage from 7.5 million acres to 50.2 million acres.

Certain areas of the parks — about 16 million acres — were designated preserves. Activities not allowed in parks, such as sport hunting and fishing, would be allowed in the preserves.

The new parks and preserves established by the bill were:

- **Aniakchak,** a 510,000-acre area on the Alaska peninsula highlighted by its 30 square mile caldera, the collapsed cone of a large volcano. About one-third of the area was designated as preserve.
- **Bering Land Bridge,** a 2.5 million-acre preserve. Part of the area once was linked to Asia by a 1,000-mile-wide land bridge. Valuable geologic deposits there provide information about ice ages in the Pleistocene period and about Siberian hunters who crossed the bridge to Alaska more than 25,000 years ago. The area is also the nesting ground for birds that migrate to six continents.
- **Cape Krusenstern,** an unusual series of 114 beach ridges along the cape, each an ancient shoreline. They show where succeeding generations of Eskimos lived over a 4,500-year period. The ridges and other evidence of Eskimo culture make the 540,000-acre area north of the Arctic Circle significant as an archaeological site.
- **Gates of the Arctic,** an 8.1-million-acre area of rugged peaks and deep canyons in the central portion of the Brooks mountain range in north central Alaska. The Interior Department had called the site "America's ultimate wilderness." Like many of the other new parks, it is prime habitat for bear, Dall sheep and wolf and is a primary migration route for the once-great Arctic caribou herd. About 60,000 acres were designated as preserve
- **Kenai Fjords,** a unique interface of ice fields and rain forest, which supports a diverse population of marine mammals and sea birds. The 420,000-acre park is a two and a half hour drive from Anchorage, the state's largest city, which is in south central Alaska.
- **Kobuk Valley,** home of the Kobuk River which meanders across this 1.7-million-acre park in northwest Alaska, 35 miles above the Arctic Circle. The area has a variety of habitats, including arctic wetlands, open tundra and 25 square miles of sand dunes, remnants of prehistoric dunes that once covered more than 300 square miles.
- **Lake Clark,** a 3.5-million-acre area called the "Switzerland of Alaska." Known for its vegetation and wildlife, the area straddles the Alaska and Aleutian mountain ranges in the southern part of the state. Glacier-created lakes border the park to the west and to the south is the 50-mile-long Lake Clark. About 1 million acres were designated as preserve.
- **Noatak,** the largest Alaskan river basin unaffected by man's activities. The Noatak River flows through the middle of the 6.1-million-acre preserve. Bordered by the Gates of the Arctic to the east and Kobuk Valley to the south, the area has perhaps the most diverse array of flora in the northern hemisphere and a rich diversity of birds and mammals.
- **Wrangells-St. Elias,** a 12-million-acre area in south central Alaska that encompasses most of the Wrangells, St. Elias and Chugach mountain ranges. Ten of the highest peaks in North America are located within it. Some of the world's largest and most active glaciers are found in the park, which is rich with wildlife. About 3.4 million acres were designated as preserve.
- **Yukon-Charley,** a 1.7-million-acre area on the Canadian border in central Alaska. The preserve would protect the upper Yukon River, a diverse area with a rich history as a trade route, and the Charley River basin, a generally undisturbed area that includes one of Alaska's best white water rivers. The area has fossil deposits estimated to be 700 million years old.

The bill added acreage to the following areas:

- **Denali,** a 1.9-million-acre park established by Congress in 1917 as Mount McKinley Park. The park, in southern Alaska, would be expanded by 3.4 million acres to protect the highest peak in North America, the spectacular glaciers nearby and moose, caribou and grizzly bear habitats. An additional 400,000 acres were designated as preserve.
- **Glacier Bay,** one of the most extensive wilderness sand beaches on the Pacific coast. Established as a monument in 1925, it would be expanded by 540,000 acres into a

2.8-million-acre park. The area, in the northern part of the Alaska panhandle, includes the Alsek River valley and rapidly flucuating glacial ice.

• **Katmai,** a 2.8-million-acre area in southern Alaska established as a monument by President Woodrow Wilson in 1918 after a 1912 volcanic eruption. HR 39 expanded it by 1.1 million acres of park and 210,000 acres of preserve. The new area includes an ecosystem large enough to protect a healthy population of giant Alaskan brown bear and other wide-ranging mammals, such as moose and caribou. The watersheds protected within Katmai provide the pristine waters needed to produce salmon.

Title III: National Wildlife Refuges

HR 39 established 12 new wildlife refuges with a total of 49.7 million acres and added 27.1 million acres to five existing wildlife refuges.

In a refuge, the needs of the wildlife receive priority over other uses, such as hunting or oil development. In a number of cases, however, recreational use of refuges, including hunting, had been found compatible with the maintenance of the wildlife habitat.

Under existing law, the secretary of interior determined whether mining or oil and gas development was compatible.

Many activities usually allowed in refuges would be prohibited in areas within them designated as wilderness. None of the wilderness areas within refuges would be eligible for mineral development.

The new wildlife refuge areas created by the bill were:

• **Alaska Maritime,** 500,000 acres encompassing a variety of islands, capes and other federally-owned coastal areas stretching from Cape Lisburne in northeast Alaska to Forrester Island in southeast Alaska. The refuge would protect millions of seabirds and other marine wildlife.

• **Alaska Peninsula,** a patchwork of 1.6 million acres of federal land designed to protect a variety of wildlife, including caribou, sea otters, falcons and salmon.

• **Becharof,** a 1-million-acre refuge on the upper Alaska Peninsula, including a unique brown bear habitat and protection for other wildlife.

• **Copper River,** a 1.2-million-acre area in the southeastern part of the state, north of the Gulf of Alaska. The main feature of the refuge is the marshland and tributaries in the Copper River Delta, an important breeding ground for ducks, migratory birds, salmon and other wildlife. Part of the area was formerly in the Chugach National Forest.

• **Innoko,** a 2.7-million-acre area in western Alaska including a unique transition area between tundra and forest which provides a nesting area for more than 380,000 ducks and 65,000 geese that migrate south across the continental United States in the fall.

• **Kanuti,** a 1.5-million-acre area in central Alaska near the Arctic Circle that would protect moose, caribou and bears and provide a nesting area for thousands of migratory birds.

• **Koyukuk,** a 3.7-million-acre area north of the Yukon River in central Alaska, which includes a nesting area for tens of thousands of ducks and geese and which supports populations of moose, beaver, mink and caribou.

• **North Slope,** a 22.5-million-acre area in the northwestern tip of Alaska that was the existing National Petroleum Reserve. It is rich with wildlife and home of the Western Arctic caribou, a once healthy herd of 250,000 animals that, between 1972 and 1978, dropped to about 75,000 animals. Designation of the area as a refuge would not affect the continued exploration for oil and gas there being carried out by the government under the Naval Petroleum Reserves Production Act of 1976. Wildlife resources there were placed under the management of the U.S. Fish and Wildlife Service, which was expected to encourage drilling only during the winter months, when the fragile tundra was frozen.

• **Nowitna,** a 1.5-million-acre area along the Yukon River in central Alaska that includes wetlands habitat for more than 250,000 waterfowl that migrate south through the lower 48 states.

• **Selawik,** a 3.3-million-acre area in northwest Alaska where three river deltas converge. It provides habitat for tens of thousands of migratory waterfowl as well as other birds and wildlife.

• **Tetlin,** a 776,000-acre area in east-central Alaska which serves as a nesting area for thousands of waterfowl annually. Thousands more birds from Canada and the continental United States use the refuge during periods of drought in those areas.

• **Yukon Flats,** a 9.4-million-acre area in northeast Alaska straddling the Arctic Circle. The area, Alaska's largest interior valley, includes lowlands around the Yukon River, the fifth largest river in North America. The area's 40,000 shallow lakes make it an outstanding waterfowl production area.

The bill expanded the following national wildlife refuges:

• **Arctic,** an 8.9-million-acre refuge in the northeast corner of Alaska that was established in 1960. Another 9.9 million acres would be added. The area includes tundra, coniferous forest, glaciated valleys, snow-covered peaks and habitat that is particularly fragile, such as tundra desert, which receives less than six inches of precipitation each year.

• **Kodiak,** an existing 100,000-acre refuge that would be expanded by adding much of Kodiak Island, an island in the Gulf of Alaska noted for the 2,000 brown bears that roam it, and Afognak Island, formerly part of the Chugach National Forest.

• **Togiak,** the new name for the expanded Cape Newenham Refuge. The addition of 3.1 million acres would increase the size to 4.1 million acres. The area, in southwest Alaska near Bristol Bay, supports a variety of wildlife, including more than 32 species of land mammals.

• **Yukon Delta,** a 15.5-million-acre refuge created by adding 13.9 million acres to existing Clarence Rhode and Hazen Bay National Wildlife Refuges. Along the Bering Sea in western Alaska, the area harbors more than 170 species of birds. Each fall 50,000 swans, 700,000 geese and 2.3 million ducks leave the area to migrate south.

• **Kenai,** a 1.7-million-acre area — across the inlet from Anchorage — established by President Franklin D. Roosevelt in 1941. Another 250,000 acres would be added to round out habitats for Kenai moose, Dall sheep, trumpeter swans and other wildlife and to protect spawning areas that support one-third of the Cook Inlet area's multimillion dollar salmon fishery.

• The area six miles seaward of coastal refuges would be managed by the Seaward Area Management Planning Committee, consisting of two state officials and one each from the U.S. Fish and Wildlife Service and the Commerce Department's National Oceanic and Atmospheric Administration. The committee was charged with protecting the marine ecosystem and insuring that activities such as offshore development of oil were carried out in a manner compatible with preservation of the marine resources.

- Another cooperative planning group of state and federal officials was established to study the tracts of state and federal lands in the Bristol Bay region on the Alaska peninsula. Within three years after enactment, the interior secretary, along with the governor and other state officials if they chose to participate, were to develop a management plan for Bristol Bay to be submitted to Congress and to the state legislature for approval.

Title IV: National Forests

No new national forests were created by HR 39, though the two existing forests, both on the Alaska panhandle in the far southeast part of the state, were expanded.

Three areas — Kates Needle, Juneau Icefield and Barbazon Range — added 1.5 million acres to the Tongass National Forest.

Nellie Juan and College Fjord, two land areas totaling 1.3 million acres, were added to Chugach National Forest.

Title V: National Wild and Scenic Rivers

Segments of a total of 22 rivers in Alaska were protected by the National Wild and Scenic Rivers System. Seven of the protected rivers were outside the boundaries of other conservation systems; 12 were totally within protected preserves or refuges and 3 rivers straddled protected and unprotected areas.

The protected rivers not totally within other conservation units were: Birch Creek, Fortymile, Gulkana, Alagnak, Killik, Noatak, Nowitna, Unalakleet and Yukon (Ramparts section).

Title VI: Wilderness

To retain the vast areas of wilderness in Alaska that were unaltered by man's activities, HR 39 added another layer of protection to 66 million acres of proposed and existing parks, refuges and forests. Those areas were added to the National Wilderness Preservation System established by the Wilderness Act of 1964 (PL 88-577).

But the bill specified that certain activities, prohibited in some wilderness in the lower 48 states, would be allowed in Alaska wilderness areas. Hunting and fishing would be permitted in most cases in national forests, preserves and wildlife refuges, but not in parks.

Mechanized equipment, such as airplanes, snowmobiles and other vehicles, were allowed in Alaska wilderness where the use already had been established. Cabins could remain in use.

The secretaries of the interior or agriculture also could allow fisheries management in wilderness areas, but fish hatcheries were allowed only on four sites already identified and only with certain restrictions.

In the national parks, 12 wilderness areas were established for a total of 41.6 million acres. Because mining, hunting and timber cutting already were prohibited in parks, the wilderness designation added little extra protection. The designation was, in essence, a direction to the National Park Service that visitor facilities and other recreation-oriented development not be allowed in those wilderness areas.

New wilderness acres established by the bill in national parks and preserves were:

- 290,000 ares in the Aniakchak National Monument.
- 700,000 acres in the Bering Land Bridge National Preserve.
- 5.4 million acres in Denali (formerly Mt. McKinley) National Park and Preserve.
- 8.1 million acres in the Gates of the Arctic National Park.
- 2.8 million acres in Glacier Bay National Park.
- 3.6 million acres in Katmai National Park.
- 340,000 acres in Kenai Fjords National Park.
- 1.1 million acres in the Kobuk Valley National Park.
- 2.6 million acres in the Lake Clark National Park and Preserve.
- 6.1 million acres in the Noatak National Preserve.
- 9.6 million acres in the Wrangell-St. Elias National Park and Preserve.
- 1 million acres in the Yukon-Charley National Preserve.

The wilderness areas in 14 existing and proposed national wildlife refuges totaled 20 million acres. They were:

- 2.9 million acres in the Alaska Maritime Wildlife Refuge, including the Aleutian Islands, Unimak and Semidi Wilderness areas.
- 13.1 million acres in the Arctic National Wildlife Refuge, known as the Arctic Wilderness.
- 400,000 acres in the southern and eastern parts of the Becharof refuge.
- 1.2 million acres in the Innoko refuge.
- 300,000 acres in the Izembek refuge.
- 300,000 acres in the Kanuti refuge.
- 1.4 million acres in the Kenai refuge, including areas known as Canoe Lakes, Chickaloon, Andy Simons and Mystery Creek.

In the two national forests, a total of 3.9 million acres were classified as wilderness, including 1.5 million acres in the Chugach and 2.4 million acres in the Tongass. Timber cutting was allowed in those sections.

Title VII: Subsistence

Alaska natives and non-natives were guaranteed the opportunity to continue subsistence uses of public lands. The state of Alaska would be responsible for developing a program to monitor hunting and fishing.

The interior secretary was to comment on and monitor the state plan, as were local and regional councils. If the state did not implement any plan or did not make changes suggested by the secretary — and the natural stability and productivity of the fish and wildlife were threatened — the secretary could close the lands to subsistence hunting.

The federal government would reimburse the state for up to 50 per cent of the costs of the program, or up to $5 million annually.

Title VIII: Land Transfers to Natives and State

The transfer of federal lands to natives and the state was expedited under procedures set out in this title. The simplified and speedier process updated the Alaska Native Claims Settlement Act (PL 92-203) and the Alaska Statehood Act (PL 85-508).

An Alaska Native Land Bank was established to assist native corporations in preserving undeveloped land. The federal government was authorized to pay litigation costs for the native corporations for three years after enactment.

Title IX: Transportation and Utility Systems

The procedure for permitting a highway, pipeline or other right-of-way across a conservation unit was clarified by this section.

Applicants would have to submit a proposal to the interior secretary. The secretary would make a recommendation after considering whether the transportation corridor would be in the public interest and compatible with the conservation unit and whether there were "economically feasible and prudent alternatives."

The secretary's recommendation, whether favorable or unfavorable, would go to Congress, which would have to pass a joint resolution of support within 120 days in order for the application to be approved.

Title X: Coordination

An 11-member Alaska Advisory Coordinating Council was established to conduct studies of Alaska and advise the interior secretary for a 10-year period. Federal agencies were to contribute 65 per cent of its operating costs with state agencies contributing the remainder. Federal, state and native representatives would sit on the council.

Title XI: Administrative Provisions

The interior secretary was authorized to:

- Construct visitor facilities.
- Acquire lands within conservation units, but without using federal powers of eminent domain.
- Issue regulations on customary travel across conservation units.
- Establish a program to hire qualified local residents without regard to certain civil service regulations.
- Prepare management plans for park and wildlife units and submit them to Congress within five years of enactment.
- Close all areas of the national parks in Alaska to taking of fish and wildlife, except for authorized subsistence uses in all areas and to authorize sport hunting and fishing in preserve areas.
- Exempt from the restrictions, for 20 years or life, existing licensed hunting guides who would otherwise suffer hardship when the parks were closed to hunting. Guides could continue to operate within Katmai, Gates of the Arctic and Wrangells-St. Elias.
- Exempt from the restrictions, for 20 years or life, licensed commercial trappers in Cape Krusenstern, Kobuk Valley and Denali.

Title XII: Miscellaneous

This title authorized several miscellaneous studies and exemptions.

Title XIII: Minerals Assessment

The interior secretary was authorized to continue assessment of mineral, oil and gas deposits in the public lands in Alaska. The government could contract with private companies for research, such as core drilling. The activity would be regulated so that it would not cause lasting environmental damage and would be compatible with the purposes for which the units were established, such as wildlife protection.

In addition, the president was directed to develop a procedure for evaluating applications from individuals or companies wanting to explore for or extract minerals, oil and gas on public lands. The president was to report to Congress by October 1, 1981, his recommendation for this procedure, as well as any public information on what deposits were thought to be located in Alaska.

Senate Action

Throughout the year, there were predictions, which eventually came true, that the Senate would not pass an Alaska lands bill in 1978.

The state's two senators — Ted Stevens, R, and Mike Gravel, D — indicated early in the year that they would filibuster any Alaska bill they found unacceptable.

Their feelings prompted Senate Majority Leader Robert C. Byrd, D-W.Va., at a May 6 news conference, to proclaim that "prospects are not good" for Senate action on an Alaska lands bill.

"That bill will be filibustered," he said. "I will not support cloture on a matter that affects one state when the senators from that state are vigorously opposed. I wouldn't want a bill that affected only West Virginia crammed down my throat."

Energy Committee Action

The Senate Energy Committee was late getting started on the Alaska bill because members were tied up throughout the year in the debate over President Carter's energy bill. *(p. 639)*

However, markup eventually began June 22.

Stevens attempted to work with the panel and sat in on the sessions. He was allowed to offer amendments but could not vote because he was not a member of the committee. He said he was attempting to work out a compromise, but vowed to fight any bill that restricted development of vast areas of Alaska.

Gravel, on the other hand, made no pretense of trying to compromise and said that even if the Senate passed an acceptable bill, it would be butchered by House conferees.

During the week of July 10, Gravel forced the Senate panel to meet early in the morning, with poor attendance the result. He did so by objecting to the committee's usually routine "unanimous consent" request for permission to meet while the Senate was in session. But on July 13, Byrd, with the help of Minority Leader Howard H. Baker Jr., R-Tenn., invoked an obscure parliamentary rule that allowed the two leaders to bypass the "unanimous consent" requirement and permit a committee to meet.

Gravel tried to fight the leaders by staging a one man filibuster the night of July 13. But after almost four hours, he gave up.

His tactic apparently riled Byrd, who had been sympathetic to the Alaska senators but wanted the Senate to conduct its business without interruption.

"If the senator wants to conduct himself in that way, he is perfectly free to do so," said Byrd when Gravel threatened to continue his filibuster for days. "What I am saying is he is losing points if he does."

Stevens also urged Gravel to reconsider and reminded him of the Senate tradition of not passing legislation opposed by both senators in the affected state. "The Senate is more likely to abide by the tradition of the Senate if we, in turn, abide by the tradition of the Senate," Stevens told Gravel on the floor.

Alaska's Senators Shared a Goal, Not Much Else

Across the hall from the committee room where hours were spent shaping Alaska lands legislation was the office of that state's Democratic senator. But Mike Gravel did not use the proximity to lobby his colleagues on the bill. Instead, he tried to kill it.

Meanwhile, inside the same Energy Committee hearing room, Alaska's other senator was on the dais for every tedious markup, trying to get an Alaska lands bill his state would find "livable."

Not even a member of the committee, Republican Ted Stevens was working, as usual, within the system.

The tactics of the two senators were as different as their personalities. They admitted they really didn't get along. But they shared a goal: stopping those who wanted to preserve as wilderness millions of federal acres in Alaska.

"We are not going to live under the yoke of the great white father and have to go get a permit from one of his minions to live," Stevens told reporters, complaining about the powers of the secretary of the interior.

Gravel had charged on the Senate floor that a "radical environmental group" within the government was gaining control of "stragetically located" land in Alaska and would thus be able to "thwart any and all economic development in the balance of Alaska."

Gravel the Maverick

Gravel preferred his own "guerilla tactics" to what he described as Stevens' "walk down a primrose path." The cooperative nature of his colleague galled Gravel, who wanted to postpone action on the bill until 1979.

Slick, smooth-talking Gravel never worried about ruffling senatorial feathers with his unconventional remarks and tactics. He perturbed many senators in June 1971, for example, when he held a late-night session of his Buildings and Grounds Subcommittee just so he could read into the record the secret Pentagon Papers.

That he was breaking unwritten Senate rules did not bother Gravel any more than the fact that he had been elected as a "hawk" and was acting like a "dove."

However, despite some setbacks, Gravel's tactics at times were successful. One congressional source described Gravel as a "high roller — he takes an extreme position and then he somehow pulls it off."

An example of a Gravel success was Congress' 1973 decision to exempt the Alaska Pipeline from requirements for an environmental impact statement.

One of Gravel's opponents on Alaska, Sen. John A. Durkin, D-N.H., who represented conservationists on the Senate Energy Committee, described Gravel as "another wild card in the deck."

Two New Alaskans

Both Gravel and Stevens were adults when they made Alaska their home.

Gravel did a stint in the Army and then finished college at Columbia University, working part-time as a cab driver to earn tuition money. When he graduated, at age 28, he headed for Alaska, driving someone else's car and eating peanut butter sandwiches along the way.

In contrast, Stevens' route to Alaska was as a young member of the Republican establishment. A Harvard Law School graduate, Stevens worked for a Washington, D.C., law firm until, at 30, he was named U.S. attorney for the 4th district in Alaska, a position he held for three years.

While Gravel was selling real estate in Alaska and becoming friendly with the wealthy men who eventually would finance his political campaigns, Stevens was back in Washington working, ironically, for the Interior Department, which later became his nemesis.

Starting in 1956, he worked as the department's legislative counsel and then became solicitor in 1960, the last year of President Eisenhower's second term. In 1961, he opened a law practice in Alaska.

Both men served in the Alaska legislature in the 1960s. Gravel tried unsuccessfully for the U.S. House in 1966. He won his Senate seat in 1968 after relying heavily on television advertising.

Stevens, a less flamboyant compaigner, lost a Senate race in 1962, was appointed to a vacant seat in 1968 and then won the 1972 election. He was reelected handily in 1978.

Stevens the Traditionalist

Stevens's orderly life style matched his reputation as a patient, even-handed builder of compromises. The moderate senator apparently had the respect of his colleagues, for he was rewarded with the post of minority whip at the start of the 95th Congress. But Stevens was not so even-tempered that he never showed a burst of temper or a flash of cunning.

Stevens had been blunt in his criticism of conservationists lobbying for Alaska wilderness, although in keeping with his "nice guy" image, he did meet with the lobbyists. "Wilderness is not for the people who live there [in Alaska]," Stevens said. "It's for visitors who are very wealthy." He considered conservationists part of that "healthy and wealthy elite."

Stevens agreed that some additional federal land in Alaska — that of "national significance" — should be set aside as parks. But, in the House bill, he argued, the lines that restricted use had been drawn with too broad a brush, around more acres than should be protected.

Stevens wanted to protect the "basic core areas" and permit access to the lands. He opposed establishment of any wilderness in Alaska.

But the boyish senator conceded he would have to be flexible. "Pragmatically, I know we'll not get a bill without some wilderness," he said.

Stevens' Position

Originally Stevens, like Gravel, had planned to use every available tactic to stop Senate passage of the bill. But he later decided he would be more successful if he also tried to change the bill in committee, with the filibuster on the floor a possibility should the Energy Committee vote out an unacceptable bill.

Two factors apparently influenced Stevens: politics in Alaska and what would happen if no Alaska bill were passed.

The two Republican candidates for the Alaska gubernatorial nomination had taken different positions on the Alaska bill. Stevens, unwilling to pick a favorite, had been caught in the middle.

Candidate Walter J. Hickel, a former governor and interior secretary, agreed with Gravel that the bill should be killed by Senate inaction. But the incumbent, Jay S. Hammond, wanted the Senate to modify the House bill. Hammond narrowly won in the Aug. 22 primary and went on to win reelection.

The other reason for Stevens' more determined efforts at compromise was the realization that the Carter administration had the authority under existing law to continue to prohibit development on federal land in Alaska even if Congress did not pass a bill in 1978.

As a result, simply killing the bill would not accomplish what Stevens and other state leaders wanted — removal of the existing hold on development, not an indefinite extension of it. The state wanted the land issues settled so it could plan development and select the rest of the lands the federal government had granted Alaska when it became a state.

COMMITTEE DECISIONS

In a major test vote, the committee July 25 endorsed a plan to allow limited federal exploration for oil and gas beneath the Arctic Wildlife Refuge.

Arctic Wildlife Refuge

The tough decision — whether to drill for oil and risk disruption of wildlife — was essentially put off for six years while the interior secretary studied the potentially oil-rich area on Alaska's North Slope. Congress, after reviewing the secretary's recommendation and study, would then vote on whether to drill.

The panel's decision differed from the House bill, which designated the 8-million-acre area as wilderness, a classification that prohibited oil and gas exploration.

The Senate panel July 24 rejected, 7-12, a proposal by John A. Durkin, D-N.H., to designate the area as wilderness.

Also rejected, 9-10, was a proposal to limit the study area to 1.8 million acres and designate the rest of the refuge as wilderness.

On July 27, the committee decided to require that the government study the mineral potential of all federal lands in Alaska. But it barred core drilling, a study technique, in national parks and monuments.

Conservationists Disappointed

Markup of the Alaska bill plodded on through the fall with Stevens continuing to press for concessions to the state.

A number of the committee's decisions were disturbing to conservationists who considered the measure the conservation "vote of the century."

Chuck Clusen of the Sierra Club, who headed the Alaska Coalition, said in early September that conservationists were "very disappointed" in what the Energy Committee had done.

In addition, Udall and Seiberling also had problems with a number of the committee's decisions. "There are a dozen things in there [the Senate bill] now that make it unacceptable," Udall said.

THE FINAL PRODUCT

Conservationists and the House leaders were no happier with the final version of the bill reported Oct. 9 (S Rept 95-1300). The vote to report was 18-1. Dewey F. Bartlett, R-Okla, was the lone dissenter.

Like the House measure, the committee bill, also called HR 39, classified about 100 million federal acres as parks, forests and refuges. But conservationists accused the Senate panel of mangling the original proposal and said the committee bill did little to restrict development of fragile wilderness.

Udall and other House leaders also said they would not accept the Senate bill without some changes, and began meeting with Senate leaders in an attempt at compromise.

Scars of Markup

The committee held more than 40 markup sessions, and the final bill bore the scars of the weeks and weeks of compromising.

Stevens argued tenaciously against anything that resembled the House-passed bill. Conservatinists were represented by Durkin, who fought against Stevens. Jackson, often distracted by the natural gas issue and others, usually took a position somewhere between Stevens and Durkin.

Attendance at the markup sessions was seldom very good, with Jackson, Durkin and Stevens joined by other senators from time to time. Generally, the committee informally accepted or rejected a proposal without taking a formal vote.

The same lobbyists — for mineral, timber, oil and gas interests and conservation organizations — who had followed the months of House markup spent hours in the Senate committee hearing room, waiting for meetings to begin and watching the very slow progress.

At first, Jackson had hoped to finish in July, then in August. Then he finally stopped making predictions.

Stevens, aware that his chances of getting a bill to his liking increased as the session waned, did little to speed the action.

Stevens' Objections

Stevens, who had called the committee's early decisions on the bill "livable," also was no fan of the final product, which he termed "unacceptable." Last minute actions by the panel had made the bill "totally unlivable as far as my state is concerned," he asserted.

HR 39. Stevens also was unhappy that the committee had chosen to call its bill HR 39. That was the number of the measure originally introduced for conservationists and retained as the number of the rewritten House-passed bill that Stevens had been fighting.

"I'd hoped you would report a Senate bill," Stevens complained to Jackson. "HR 39 is anathema. No one at home will understand you've made any changes at all."

The use of HR 39 also fueled Stevens' anger at other committee actions Oct. 4.

A Borax Corp. claim for a molybdenum deposit in the Misty Fjords area of southeast Alaska was included in a park preserve, instead of in a forest as Stevens had wanted. Although the law allowed the mining of existing, valid mining claims within preserves, Stevens was worried the Park Service would place such tight restrictions on the mining operation that it would be uneconomical. In forests, there were fewer restrictions on such development. Molybdenum is used to make steel.

"You're changing the rules in the middle of the game," charged Stevens. The Borax claim was seen by many Alaskans as symbolic of the mineral potential there that might not be developed because of federal restrictions on development of resources on federal lands.

"I have no desire to cut off" development of the deposit, said Jackson. "It's just a matter of maintaining standards." Pollution from the mine could harm wildlife and the important fishing industry nearby, committee aides said. The committee agreed with Jackson on a 12-4 vote.

Stevens also objected to a decision to place in wilderness — the most restrictive land classification — a section of the Wrangell-St. Elias National Park that had been classified as a preserve. No hunting, except for traditional subsistence hunting, would be allowed in the wilderness.

Conservationist Concerns

Although the Senate panel voted to classify about 100 million acres into conservation areas, conservationists said that figure was misleading and that many Senate classifications provided little protection for natural values.

The Senate panel, for example, placed about 12 million acres in "conservation areas" run by the Bureau of Land Management (BLM). Grazing, timber cutting, mineral development and extraction of oil and gas were allowed but BLM would have to study the conservation potential of the lands before any of those activities could begin. Conservationists said the designation provided almost no protection.

The committee's biggest cuts were in the acreage designated by the House for wildlife refuges — areas managed for the enhancement and protection of wildlife, with no mining permitted and with restrictions on other development. The House had created 56 million acres of wildlife refuges from existing federal lands; the Senate bill called for about 35 million acres, leaving the other acreage in categories such as BLM conservation areas and national forests where there was less restriction on use and development.

Wilderness, the most restrictive land classifiction, was considered by conservationists as the key to preserving Alaska. The Senate designated about 30 million acres as wilderness, compared to 65.5 million acres in the House bill.

Most representatives of industry said they generally saw the Senate bill as preferable to the House version.

PROVISIONS

As reported by the Senate Energy Committee, HR 39 provided the following:

Title I: Purposes, Definitions

The title stated that congressional intent in the act was to:

- Preserve unrivaled scenic and geological values associated with natural landscapes.
- Provide for the maintenance of sound populations of and habitat for wildlife species, including those dependent on vast, relatively undeveloped areas.
- Preserve in their natural state extensive unaltered arctic tundra, boreal forest and coastal rain forest ecosystems.
- Protect resources related to subsistence needs.
- Protect and preserve historic and archeological sites, rivers and lands and to preserve wilderness resources and related recreational opportunities including but not limited to hiking, canoeing, fishing and sport hunting.
- Maintain opportunities for scientific research on undisturbed ecosystems.

Title II: National Parks

Three existing national parks in Alaska were expanded by the bill and eleven new parks were created, expanding park acreage in the state from 7.5 million acres to 51.8 million acres.

Certain sections of the new areas were designated as preserves and national recreation areas, classifications in which additional uses were allowed, such as hunting. *(Classifications and uses allowed in each, p. 729)*

The new parks, preserves and national recreation areas established by the bill were:

- Aniakchak, a 138,000 acre monument and a 376,000 acre preserve on the Alaska Peninsula.
- Bering Land Bridge, a 2.5 million acre preserve on the northern Seward Peninsula.
- Cape Krusenstern, a 560,000 acre preserve north of the Arctic Circle.
- Gates of the Arctic, an area in the central portion of the Brooks Mountain Range consisting of two parks totalling 4.8 million acres, with one centered on the Alatna River-Arrigetch Peaks Area and the other on the Gates of the Arctic; a park preserve of 2.1 million acres between the two parks and two national recreation areas, totalling 1 million acres.
- Kenai Fjords, a 567,000 acre park on the southern coast of the Kenai Peninsula.
- Kobuk Valley, a park preserve of 1.5 million acres, with a monument of 190,000 acres around the unique Kobuk Sand Dunes.
- Lake Clark, a 2.4 million acre park around Lake Clark in south central Alaska, with 1.2 million acres designated as preserve.
- Misty Fjords, a 1.53 million acre preserve in the Coast Mountains in southeast Alaska in the Tongass National Forest.
- Noatak, a 5.4 million acre preserve and a 386,000 acre national recreation area in the Noatak River drainage in the western Brooks Range.
- Wrangell-St. Elias, a 12 million acre mountainous area in south central Alaska, including an 8.5 million acre park, a 2.5 million acre preserve and a 1.2 million acre national recreation area.
- Yukon-Charley, a 1.7 million acre preserve along the upper Yukon River near the border with Canada.

The bill added acreage to the following existing units:

- McKinley, an existing 1.9 million acre park that would be expanded to include another 2.6 million acres of park land and 1.2 million acres of preserve.
- Glacier Bay, an existing monument along the Pacific coast that would be expanded by 523,000 monument acres and 57,000 preserve acres into a 2.8 million acre monument.
- Katmai, an existing 2.7 million acre monument in southern Alaska that would be expanded by adding 936,000 acres of park and 409,000 acres of preserve.

Title III: National Wildlife Refuges

The bill proposed establishment of eight new wildlife refuges, totalling 18.77 million acres, and expanded three existing wildlife refuges by 18 million acres.

The new areas were:

- Alaska Maritime Wildlife Refuge, 460,000 acres encompassing a variety of islands, capes and other federally owned areas stretching from Cape Lisburne in northeast Alaska to Forrester Island in southeast Alaska.
- Becharof, 990,000 acres on the upper Alaska Peninsula.
- Innoko-Kaiyuh, two separate units totalling 3.85 million acres along the east bank of the Yukon River below Galena.
- Kanuti, 1.4 million acres in central Alaska.
- Koyukuk, 3.5 million acres north of the Yukon River in central Alaska.
- Selawik, 2.1 million acres in northwest Alaska.
- Tetlin, 765,000 acres in east-central Alaska.
- Yukon Flats, an area in northeast Alaska straddling the Arctic Circle that included 5.7 million acres in refuge, with adjacent areas designated as a new forest, the Porcupine National Forest, and a national conservation area, the Steese National Conservation Area, to be managed by the Bureau of Land Management.

The bill expanded the following national wildlife refuges:

- Arctic, an existing 8.9 million acre refuge in the northeast corner of Alaska that was expanded by 5.7 million acres.
- Clarence Rhodes, an existing refuge in the Yukon and Kuskowin River deltas that was expanded by 11.1 million acres.
- Kenai, a 1.73 million acre moose range across the inlet from Anchorage that was expanded by 240,000 acres.
- Kodiac, a 50,000 acre island in the Gulf of Alaska.

Title IV: National Conservation Areas

Though still managed by the Bureau of Land Management (BLM) as multiple-use federal lands, with logging, mining and grazing allowed, national conservation areas receive special management consideration to protect recognized scenic, recreational and historic values.

The Interior secretary may regulate the mining and other activities to protect the natural resources of a conservation area.

The bill established four national conservation areas and a national recreation area to be managed by BLM:

- Baird Mountains, 2.2 million acres in northwest Alaska bordered by the Noatak Preserve, the Kobuk Valley Monument and Preserve and the Selawik Wildlife Refuge. Caribou migrate through the area, which has hard rock mineral potential.
- Chandalar, 808,000 acres in the upper Chandalar drainage in the eastern Brooks range, adjacent to the Arctic Wildlife Refuge.
- Nowitna, 3.1 million acres in the Nowitna River watershed in central Alaska.
- Steese, 1.2 million acres in the Birch and Preacher Creek drainages adjacent to the Yukon Flats Wildlife Refuge.
- White Mountains, a 1 million acre national recreation area in the White Mountains east of Fairbanks.

Title V: National Forests

A new 5.5 million acre national forest, the Porcupine National Forest, was created in northeastern Alaska along the Porcupine River and near the Arctic Wildlife Refuge and the Yukon Flats Wildlife Refuge.

The bill also added about 3 million acres to the Chugach and the Tongass National Forests, the two already existing forests in Alaska:

- Three areas — Nellie Juan, College Fjord and Copper River — totalling 1.6 million acres, were added to Chugach. The Copper River section was to be managed as if it were a wildlife refuge, with protection of fish and wildlife and their habitat as the primary purpose.
- Three areas — Kates Needle, Juneau Icefield and Brabazon Range — were also added to Tongass, the largest national forest. The addition increased its size by 1.5 million acres.

Title VI: National Wild and Scenic Rivers

Segments of 24 rivers in Alaska were added to the National Wild and Scenic Rivers System. The rivers protected in the system had to be left in their natural state, which prohibited construction of dams or discharge of pollutants into the rivers.

Rivers located within parks that were added to the system were Alatna, Aniakchak, Charley, Chilikadrotna, John, Kobuk, Mulchatna, Noatak, North Fork of Koyukuk, Salmon, Tinayguk, Tlikakila and part of Alagnak.

Rivers located within refuges that were added to the system were Andreafsky, Ivishak, Selawik, Sheenjek and Wind.

Rivers located outside conservation units that were added to the system were Beaver Creek, Birch Creek, Delta, Fortymile, Gulkana, Unalakleet and part of Alagnak.

Title VII: Wilderness

New wilderness areas established in national parks and preserves were:

- 1.9 million acres in the existing Mount McKinley National Park.
- 4.8 million acres in the Gates of the Arctic National Park.
- 2.8 million acres in the expanded Glacier Bay National Park.
- 3.4 million acres in Katmai National Park.
- 190,000 acres in the Kobuk Valley Preserve and Monument.
- 2.5 million acres in Lake Clark National Park and Preserve.
- 5.4 million acres in Noatak National Preserve.
- 8.7 million acres in Wrangell-St. Elias National Park and Preserve.

New wilderness areas established in wildlife refuges were:

- 1.3 million acres in the Aleutian Islands unit of the Alaska Maritime National Wildlife Refuge.
- 300,000 acres in the existing Izembek National Wildlife Refuge.
- 1.3 million acres in Kenai National Wildlife Refuge.
- 250,000 acres in the Semidi National Wildlife Refuge.
- 910,000 acres in the Unimak National Wildlife Refuge.

New wilderness areas totalling 2.88 million acres were established in the Tongass National Forest. The bill required study of the wilderness potential of 2 million acres in the Chugach National Forest.

In order to avoid a possible reduction in timber production because of prohibitions on logging in wilderness, the committee set as a goal the maintenance of timber production in the Tongass at 520 million board feet annually, which was the average level between 1970 and 1977.

As part of efforts to increase harvests and reach that goal, the bill authorized a program of intensive forest management, to be funded at $10 million a year, with another $5 million available for loans to timber purchasers for buying equipment and implementing technologies that would reduce waste of tree stumps and other wood products.

However, because of the "generally unsettled timber supply picture in the Tongass," described in the committee report, the senators also wanted to provide a backup source of timber to insure that the production goal would be met. Instead of designating an additional 1.76 million acres of wilderness in the Tongass, the area was placed in a special management category closed to mining and logging.

Anytime within 10 years after the designation, the Interior secretary could recommend to Congress that timber sales be allowed in the special management area. The House and Senate, by concurrent resolution, would have to approve the waiver of the prohibition on logging within 60 calendar days of continuous session of Congress after the proposal was submitted.

Title VIII: Subsistence

Alaska natives and non-natives dependent on the wildlife and other resources of the public lands for food, clothing and other life-supporting uses were guaranteed the opportunity to continue those "non-wasteful subsistence uses." The state of Alaska would continue to carry out traditional state responsibilities for management of fish and wildlife and would be required to develop a plan for overseeing subsistence use of the lands. The interior secretary was to comment on and monitor the state plan, as were the five regional and several local advisory councils the secretary was directed to establish.

The federal government was authorized to reimburse the state for up to 50 percent of the costs of the subsistence management program, or up to $5 million annually.

Title IX: Land Transfers to Natives and State

The transfers of federal lands to natives and the state were expedited under procedures set out in this title, which updated the Alaska Native Claims Settlement Act (ANCSA) (PL 92-203) and the Alaska Statehood Act (PL 85-508). *(PL 92-203, Congress and the Nation, Vol. III, p. 783)*

Delays in transfer of land to village corporations had been caused in part by a backlog of applications by natives for allotments available to them under 1956 amendments to the 1906 Alaska Native Allotment Act. Though ANCSA repealed the allotment law, applications received through Dec. 18, 1971, were still honored. However, those claims were still not resolved in 1978 and had delayed delineation of the boundaries of native villages and other procedures so that only 5 million of the 44 million acres given to natives under ANCSA had been conveyed.

Passage of HR 39 would "summarily approve allotments in all cases where no countervailing interest requires full adjudication," the committee report said. Once the allotments were resolved, land transfers to natives under ANCSA would be expedited.

The bill also set up an Alaska Native Land Bank to help native corporations preserve undeveloped land.

For the state, the bill included several provisions proposed by the state that expedited conveyance of the remainder of the 104 million acres given to the state when statehood was granted. The bill also provided for immediate, legislative conveyance of most of the acreage not in dispute.

The bill also extended the existing 20-year moratorium on taxing of undeveloped lands conveyed to natives by requiring that the 20-year moratorium begin at the date of conveyance of each tract of land.

Title X: Federal North Slope Lands Study

This title directed the interior secretary to study all federal lands on the North Slope in north central Alaska. The study, to be completed in eight years, was to examine energy, wilderness and wildlife values and to make recommendations on best use of the land.

Within six months of enactment, the secretary was to present Congress a plan for exploration for oil and gas in the Arctic Wildlife Refuge, which was in the North Slope area. The plan could include geological activities, such as seismic surveys, but no core drilling was authorized on the refuge. Within six years of enactment, the secretary was to report to Congress any proposals for test core drilling.

But before any oil or gas in the refuge could be developed, Congress would have to authorize it.

The bill also required the interior secretary to establish an oil and gas leasing program on all other federal conservation lands in Alaska where such activity was allowed. The program would include all national recreation areas, Bureau of Land Management conservation areas, national forests and river protection zones surrounding wild and scenic rivers.

The secretary also was to conduct an assessment of the mineral potential of all public lands in Alaska and to report to Congress by Oct. 1, 1981.

Title XI: Transportation and Utility Systems

This title established procedures so permanent transportation facilities, such as pipelines, highways or power lines, could cross conservation units where existing law generally prohibited such facilities.

Approval of the facilities would depend on findings by the:

- Transportation secretary that there was no economically feasible or prudent alternative route and mode of access.
- Interior secretary (or the agriculture secretary in the case of forest wilderness) that the right of way would be compatible with the purposes for which the conservation unit was established.

If the officials did not agree, the route proposal would go to the president for a decision.

The bill required that Congress give its approval for routes through national parks.

The bill also:

- Guaranteed access for traditional activities, such as subsistence or sport hunting, fishing, berry picking and travel between villages.
- Continued use of transportation such as float and ski planes, snowmachines, motorboats and dogsleds.
- Guaranteed access for economic and other purposes to state, private or native holdings within conservation units.

Title XII: Federal-State Cooperation

This title established a 12-member Alaska Land Use Council to recommend uses for federal or state lands, negotiate land exchanges and identify specific opportunities for cooperation among the state, federal government and natives.

Members would include heads of the principal federal and state agencies in Alaska dealing with land and resource management. In addition, there would be two co-chairmen: the governor of Alaska and a federal official appointed by the president and confirmed by the Senate.

Title XIII: Administrative Provisions

This title:

- Required the interior secretary to submit, within five years, management plans for the new conservation units to the appropriate congressional committees.
- Authorized the interior secretary to acquire lands within conservation units, but limited his authority to acquire improved property.
- Authorized the interior secretary to acquire significant archeological and paleontological sites, up to a total of 7,500 acres, that were closely associated with nearby conservation units and could be managed as part of those units.
- Authorized the interior secretary to plan for a visitors' center at a site of up to 1,000 acres adjacent to the Alaska Highway and to plan similar centers in Anchorage and Fairbanks.
- Authorized the agriculture secretary to plan for a similar visitor center in Juneau, Ketchikan or Sitka.
- Authorized the interior secretary to establish a program to hire qualified local residents without regard to civil service regulations.
- Authorized the interior secretary to study the possibility of a Denali Scenic Highway between Mount McKinley Park and McCarthy.
- Authorized fishing and hunting for sport and subsistence purposes in national preserves in Alaska.

Title XIV: Amendments to Settlement Act

This title dealt with native land settlement. It included a resolution of tax interpretations by the Internal Revenue Service that had been unfavorable to natives and authorized land exchanges among the federal government, the state and natives.

Title XV: Mineral Assessment

This title authorized the president to recommend to Congress that mineral development be permitted on specific lands in Alaska usually closed to mining if there was an urgent need for such development that outweighed other resource values of the lands.

Scramble for Compromise

As Congress went into its final hours, there were frenzied last minute negotiations to pass an Alaska bill. But the negotiations fell apart when Gravel refused to accept a compromise agreement.

Gravel also objected to an extension of the existing protections. His filibuster threats kept the Senate from voting.

The compromise, worked out by House and Senate negotiators and Andrus, would have put 96 million acres into conservation units and designated 50 million acres in new and existing units as wilderness.

Gravel's Objections

Gravel's plans to block passage of the bill, with a filibuster and other tactics, had always threatened the measure. But in an Oct. 12 letter to Stevens and Byrd, Gravel appeared to have changed his mind. He said he would not block the bill.

The Citizens for the Management of Alaska Lands, the Alaska Lands Steering Council and other Alaska politicians had convinced him, he said, that "we should attempt compromise for a bill this year."

Until that point, House and Senate leaders had made feeble attempts to reach a compromise they could attach to the Senate Energy Committee's Alaska bill on the Senate floor. If the plan succeeded, the House was to approve the agreement and send it, without a conference, to the president.

Gravel's announcement that he was dropping his filibuster plans hit the negotiators like a shot of adrenalin. Chances of passing a bill increased.

Andrus cut short a western trip. Key House and Senate leaders holed up with him in a room under the front eaves of the Capitol. The band of committee aides, Interior officials, lobbyists and others who had followed the legislation for more than a year and a half camped outside the closed meeting.

For awhile, hopes were high. On Oct. 13 the hangers-on started a pool on what time an agreement would or would not be reached. Stevens plunked down his dollar and bet on 10:50 a.m., Oct. 14, as the time a bill would be agreed on.

After a day and a half of meeting, the negotiators were close to what would have been a remarkable compromise. Then Gravel issued an ultimatum. He demanded that the bill guarantee that specific rights of way be designated for pipelines, railroads, highways or other types of transportation across federal conservation areas to state-owned lands.

Udall and Seiberling had already agreed to many changes that weakened the House-passed bill. But Gravel's request, which would have laid out certain routes opposed by nearby native villages, was too radical for them to accept. The House bill and the Senate committee bill guaranteed access to state lands, but authorized the interior secretary to restrict the type of access and put conditions on its use in order to protect the conservation unit.

But Gravel insisted that his demand for seven transportation corridors be met. Later, in an interview, he charged that, without the corridors, the bill would effectively "take" the 105 million acres of state-owned lands because there would be no access to the land's resources.

"They can't have it all," Gravel said. "We have to have a place to live, too. . . . They would have fixed it so we would not have a viable economic existence."

The negotiators discussed Gravel's "bottom line," but soon after, about 11 a.m., the meeting broke up. Stevens declared to those outside, "It's all over. No bill."

Stevens, who had worked for months to get a bill acceptable to Alaskans, did not curb his anger at Gravel in an encounter on the Senate floor about 5:30 a.m., Oct. 15.

"You've got yourself a big battle now, buddy," Stevens shouted at Gravel, charging there would be delays in the transfer of federal land to the state without a bill. "You carry that burden," Stevens said, pointing his finger at Gravel.

Durkin, who spoke for conservationists on the Senate panel, wanted to place the blame for the bill's demise. "The compromise foundered on two words," he said, "and those two words are 'Mike Gravel'."

Administration Moves

After the compromise failed, the administration went to work.

On Oct. 25, the Interior Department released an environmental impact statement on the various methods it could use to protect the land. And Interior Secretary Andrus reiterated the administration's intention to use authority already provided by law to protect federally owned wilderness until Congress passed legislation establishing conservation units.

Stevens and the Alaskans were unhappy with the situation for a variety of reasons.

Lamenting the fact that no bill was passed, Stevens noted that land conveyances to the state and natives of more than 100 million acres still owed them since statehood would continue to be delayed.

As for the classification of land into conservation units and other issues, Stevens said, "I really don't see how we're going to do much better next year. I realize Alaskans believe [the compromise worked out at the end of the session] is too much, but we're trying to practice the art of the possible."

Stevens and others also worried that their task would be even more difficult in the 96th Congress if the administration had created millions of acres of monuments. It requires an act of Congress to remove land from the monument category.

"The burden would be on us to downgrade the areas, to convince our colleagues to change the map," Stevens said.

Alaska's Lawsuit

On Oct. 30, the state of Alaska filed suit in federal district court in Anchorage to stop the administration from setting aside land. The suit challenged the legality of the Antiquities Act of 1906, which gave the president authority to create national monuments, similar to national parks.

The suit also questioned the adequacy of the environmental impact statement and asked whether the period the government provided for public comment on it would give Alaskans, especially those in remote villages, enough time to respond. Comments were due Nov. 22.

The lawsuit sought a permanent injunction against creation of monuments. The state charged there was no basis for use of the Antiquities Act or of the 1976 Federal Land Policy and Management Act (PL 94-579). The latter permitted the secretary to earmark millions of acres for study as wilderness. Congress eventually would decide what land was actually designated as wilderness, but in the intervening years of study millions of acres could be closed to development and held in limbo.

The state's appeal for additional time to comment on the impact statement was denied Nov. 24 by U.S. District Judge James von der Heydt in Anchorage. The judge also refused to grant a temporary restraining order against any federal actions to restrict use of the federal Alaska lands.

Andrus Acts

On Nov. 16, Andrus used authority in the land policy and management act to withdraw from development about

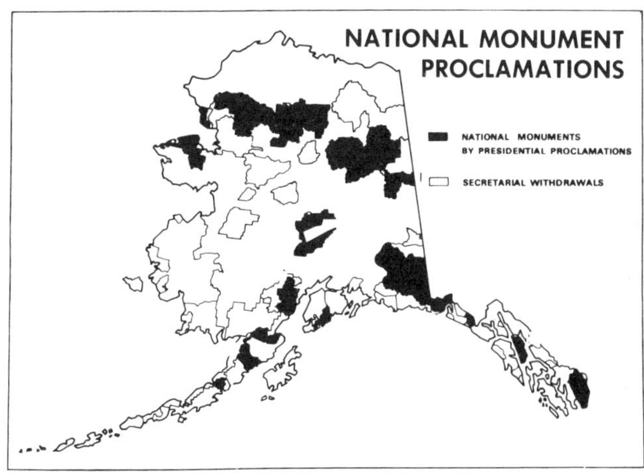

110 million acres of federal land. The next day Carter rejected a proposed compromise worked out between the state and federal officials. It would have held up the state's lawsuit for a year in return for a promise from Carter not to establish monuments.

When Andrus moved to restrict use of the 110 million acres, he was blasted by Stevens. "I'm astounded," he said, "at the artibitrary and capricious actions," which he asserted put an end to further "good faith" negotiations between federal and state officials on the state's lawsuit.

Andrus said his actions were "aimed at protecting the integrity of Alaska lands. . .because it assures that there will be no questionable mining claims or other complications regarding this land until final decisions are made."

Andrus was particularly concerned about mineral claims that could be made under an 1872 mining law. Such claims, officials said, could damage the fragile wilderness and complicate land ownership. The law, written when prospectors rode donkeys and carried pick axes, allowed a company that discovered minerals on public land open to mining to file a claim for ownership of the minerals and the site.

The section of the land policy and management act cited by Andrus, Section 204(e), allowed restrictions on development when the interior secretary, the Senate Energy Committee or the House Interior Committee determined existence of an "emergency situation" that threatened the natural state of the land.

The day before Andrus acted, he got a letter from House Interior Chairman Udall in which Udall urged Andrus to take "extraordinary measures" to protect the land because of the current "emergency situation."

Carter Uses 1906 Law

On Dec. 1, Carter made sweeping use of the Antiquities Act of 1906 to add another layer of protection to 56 million acres already withdrawn by Andrus. The president created 17 new national monuments, which more than doubled the size of the national park system.

A spokesman for conservationists in the Alaska Coalition said Carter had "exceeded the efforts" of Theodore Roosevelt and become "the greatest conservation president of all time." Not since Roosevelt put 65 million acres in forest reserves had a president acted to protect so large a chunk of federal land.

Because only an act of Congress could undo the permanent protected status of the monuments Carter designated,

Alaska officials accused the administration of pre-empting the legislators.

Alaska Gov. Hammond said Carter had "made unilaterally what should have been a congressional decision providing for public and state participation." Hammond said Carter's "extremely restrictive" actions had confirmed the state's "worst fears."

However, Andrus said the land would not have been adequately protected between Dec. 17 — the date the protections ran out — and the time Congress could act. "If we had adequate protection, I would not have put the president and myself through this exercise," Andrus told reporters. "We simply could not afford to gamble."

The Antiquities Act, which authorized the monuments, was "by far the strongest authority we have available," Andrus said. The administration created the monuments believing it was "in the best interests of the American people not to make light of these threats of litigation," Andrus added.

The bulk of the 56 million acres set aside as national monuments was included in the House and Senate bills as part of the national park system.

Carter could have made monuments of all of the 110 million acres being considered by legislators for parks, wildlife refuges and other conservation systems. But Andrus recommended designating only the 56 million acres because that action could be most readily defended under the 1906 law, he said.

In addition to creation of monuments, the administration also was moving to use authority in the 1976 land management law to establish wildlife refuges in Alaska.

Stevens was less than pleased with the administration's action. At a Dec. 14 news conference, he blasted Carter, accusing him of responding to "the desires of the absolute extremist environmentalists.

He also said Carter's move "destroyed the basis of the compromise reached in the 95th [Congress but not passed at the end of the year].

The Monuments

Thirteen of the monuments created by Carter were to be managed by the Natinal Park Service. They were:

- Aniakchak; 350,000 acres.
- Bering Land Bridge; 2.6 million acres.
- Cape Krusenstern; 560,000 acres.
- Denali, an enlargement of Mt. McKinley Park; 3.9 million acres.
- Gates of the Arctic; 8.2 million acres.
- Glacier Bay; an enlargement of an existing monument by 550,000 acres.
- Katmai; an enlargement of an existing monument by 1.4 million acres.
- Kenai Fjords; 570,000 acres.
- Kobuk Valley; 1.7 million acres.
- Lake Clark; 2.5 million acres.
- Noatak; 5.8 million acres.
- Wrangell-St. Elias; 11 million acres.
- Yukon-Charley; 1.7 million acres.

Two monuments were to be managed by the Fish and Wildlife Service, which would allow sport hunting. Those monuments were Yukon Flats, 10.6 million acres, and Becharof, 1.2 million acres.

Two monuments would be managed by the Forest Service. Those were Admiralty Island, 1.1 million acres, and Misty Fjords, 2.2 million acres. ▮

Boundary Waters Area

Congress Oct. 15 cleared a compromise bill (HR 12250) that allowed limited motorboat use to continue in the popular Boundary Waters Canoe Area in northern Minnesota.

The acrimonious dispute over whether users of canoes or motorboats should have top priority in the area had split the state, and politicians ranked the issue with abortion in terms of voter interest.

Canoeists had long opposed the special exemption for the Boundary Waters wilderness that allowed the use of motorboats on the 1,000 lakes that lace the one million acre area. They argued that the motors spoiled the pristine setting. But restrictions on use of the boats were resisted by local motorboat users and resort owners dependent on guests who used the boats to fish.

The dispute eventually spilled over into Congress.

Provisions

As signed into law, HR 12250 — PL 95-495:

- Allowed continued use of motorboats on 23 of the 124 major lakes, which meant no change in 52 percent of existing motor boat use.
- Allowed continued use of motorboats until the year 2000 on seven additional lakes.
- Allowed continued use of motorboats on a permanent basis on the major portions of the five largest lakes: Basswood, Trout, Saganga, Seagul and Lac La Croix.
- Designated 1.077 million acres of wilderness within the Boundary Waters Canoe Area.
- Required that the wilderness be managed in accordance with the Wilderness Act of 1964 and the Eastern Wilderness Act of 1975, with the exceptions for Boundary Waters in the 1964 act repealed.
- Prohibited the use of snowmobiles except along two portages that allowed winter access to Canada from the United States.

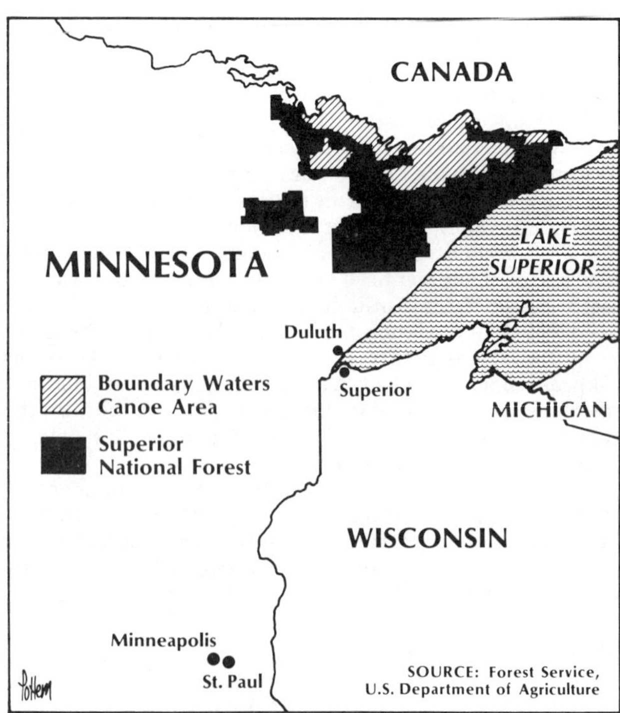

- Allowed owners of resorts to require purchase of their property by the federal government until Sept. 30, 1983. The price would be equal to the fair market value as of July 1, 1978.
- Required the secretary of agriculture to terminate timber contracts within Boundary Waters within one year of enactment.
- Authorized $8 million each year in fiscal 1979-83 for more intensive forest management of nearby national, state and private lands.
- Provided that no mining be allowed in the Boundary Waters wilderness unless the president declared a national emergency and Congress passed legislation opening the area to mining.

Background

Boundary Waters, the largest wilderness area east of the Rocky Mountains, is located in Superior National Forest near the Canadian border. It is laced with 1,000 lakes that give visitors water routes deep into virgin forest. The same routes were once used by Indian fur traders.

Canoeists said the sight and sound of motorboats skittering across the lakes disrupted the experience of being in a wilderness. They, cross country skiers and other users wanted to restrict the use of motorboats and snowmobiles in the area.

For years, though, fishermen had used motorized boats to find good fishing spots and to trawl for trout and bass. They stayed in about 60 lodges located along the lakes. Lodge owners and small shop owners said they would lose their business if motorboat use were restricted.

Minnesota Politics

Many city dwellers in Minneapolis-St. Paul and other southern cities sided with the canoeists. Blue-collar workers in Duluth and miners scattered across northern Minnesota generally appeared to favor the motorboaters, polls showed.

The split made picking a winning position difficult for Minnesota politicians seeking statewide office.

There had been continued conflict over Boundary Waters since the early 1900s, but the debate intensified in 1964 when the area was designated a wilderness by the National Wilderness Preservation Act (PL 88-577). The law contained an exemption for Boundary Waters that allowed logging, mining and motorboating there, uses normally prohibited in wilderness areas.

For many years, a big obstacle to removing the exemption was the argument that logging jobs would be lost if timber cutting were banned.

But the logging conflict was resolved in April when Rep. James L. Oberstar, D-Minn., whose district included Boundary Waters, agreed that timber cutting in the area should be stopped. He was convinced by state and federal officials that additional timber to fulfill existing contracts and to meet future needs was available in the adjacent Superior National Forest and on nearby state lands.

Use of motorboats, then, remained the only conflict between Oberstar, who sought to maintain the exemption for Boundary Waters, and supporters of legislation to remove it. No mining had ever occurred in the area so that activity was never an issue.

House Action

COMMITTEE ACTION

On April 26, the Interior Committee, by voice vote, ordered reported a proposal on Boundary Waters worked out by its Subcommittee on Parks (H Rept 95-1117).

The subcommittee had spent months trying to reconcile the opposing views of Oberstar and Donald M. Fraser, D-Minn., who wanted the area protected as full-fledged wilderness. Fraser represented the Minneapolis area and was running for the Senate seat formerly held by the late Sen. Hubert H. Humphrey. Fraser was defeated in the primary.

Though neither Fraser nor Oberstar sat on the Interior Committee, one Minnesota Democrat, Bruce F. Vento of St. Paul, did. He, with subcommittee chairman Phillip Burton, D-Calif., moderated the dispute, working toward a compromise that protected the resort owners, but also phased out use of motorboats.

However, Oberstar said he was still not satisfied with the compromise and said he wanted fewer restrictions on motorboat use.

The committee bill removed the exceptions made for Boundary Waters in the 1964 Wilderness Act.

Logging would be phased out after one year. The committee directed the agriculture secretary to provide timer from Superior National Forest and other nearby national forests to fulfill existing contracts and meet future needs. The state of Minnesota also agreed to try to provide substitute timber.

The bill also authorized $8 million annually for fiscal 1979-83 for additional tree planting and other more intensive management on national, state and private land in Minnesota.

Use of motorboats generally would be prohibited, except on a few peripheral lakes where boats of less than 10 horsepower could still operate. One interior route could be used for five years after enactment.

Resort owners suffering hardships from the bill's restrictions on motorboat use could require federal purchase of their property.

FLOOR ACTION

Because both sides agreed to end logging and prohibit mining in the national wilderness, the only remaining conflict when the bill reached the floor was over use of motorboats and snowmobiles in the wilderness.

And on June 5, the House voted 213-141 to reduce motorboat use in Boundary Waters. *(Vote 350, p. 100-H)*

The Debate

"What we are down to in this Boundary Waters Canoe Area bill today is, who will use the area?" Oberstar told the House. "It is the people question. Who is going to use the area, those from thousands of miles or hundreds of miles away, or those who live in the area, whose lives and livelihoods are dependent upon the small businesses, the small outfitter[s], the small resorts — the people who live there year-round?"

But Oberstar's plea for giving local users priority was countered by Vento, Fraser and Burton, floor manager of the bill.

The heavy demand for access to Boundary Waters from all users, including canoeists, motorboaters, loggers and others, meant the "threat to this wilderness is very real and increasing at a dramatic rate," said Vento. "Unless these demands are faced through the legislative process, we will lose one of the largest wilderness areas through overuse and abuse."

A compromise worked out by Vento, Fraser and Richard Nolan, D-Minn., balanced national and local concerns and allowed 41 percent of existing motorized use to continue until 1984, and 36 percent to continue until 2010, Vento said. After that, he said, 24 percent of existing motorized use would be permitted.

Vento Substitute

The compromise, the agreement ultimately adopted, made the following changes in the committee bill:

- Eliminated the National Recreation Area of 220,000 acres that would have linked the two sections of Boundary Waters.
- Established a Mining Protection Area along road corridors and other areas that had been part of the proposed National Recreation Area.
- Continued, except for July and August, motorboat use on Newton Lake and the lower portion of Basswood Lake (Jackfish and Pipestone Bays) until the year 2000 and on Big Trout Lake and Lake Saganaga until 2010.
- Increased to 25 the allowable horsepower on six peripheral lakes. The change meant many lodge and resort owners — and their guests — could continue use of existing motors, which was not restricted under existing law.

Senate Action

The House bill was opposed by Minnesota's two Democratic senators, Wendell R. Anderson and Muriel Humphrey. Senate procedures allowed them to block action in that chamber.

But a compromise worked out by two Minnesota groups was eventually accepted by the Senate Energy Committee, which reported a bill Oct. 4 (S Rept 95-1274). Sens. Anderson and Humphrey accepted that compromise, as did national conservation groups including the National Audubon Society and Friends of the Earth. The Senate passed the bill Oct. 9 by voice vote.

Conference and Final Action

In conference, the House agreed to the Senate provisions. The conference report (H Rept 95-1790, S Rept 95-1327) was filed Oct. 12. The House and Senate both adopted the conference report on the last day of the session. The House vote was 248-111. *(Vote 825, p. 234-H)*

Major amendments to the House bill provided:

- Continued use of motorboats on 23 of the 124 major lakes, which meant no change in 52 percent of existing motorboat use. The House bill had kept open 11 of those 124 lakes, leaving 25 percent of existing use unaffected.
- Continued use of motorboats until 2000 on seven additional lakes. The House had allowed motorboat use through 2010 on five additional lakes.
- Continued use of motorboats on a permanent basis on the major portions of the five largest lakes: Basswood, Trout, Saganga, Seagull and Lac La Croix. The House did not provide continued motorboat use on a permanent basis on any of the five largest lakes. ∎

Solar Satellite Research

The drive by the nation's aerospace industry to increase federal support for construction in space of giant solar power satellites received a boost June 22, when the House passed legislation authorizing research funds. However, the measure never got to the Senate floor.

By the one-sided vote of 267-96, the House approved a bill (HR 12505) providing $25 million in fiscal 1979 funds for stepped-up research on the satellites' feasibility. The bill called for studies "leading to a solar power satellite ... and the placing of a demonstration satellite unit or units into orbit...." *(Vote 421, p. 120-H)*

Backers of the idea — including such firms as Grumman Aerospace Corp., Boeing Aerospace Corp., Lockheed Missile and Space Co., McDonnell Douglas Corp., and others — said the satellites could be the answer to projected future energy supply shortages.

Opponents said the satellites would cost too much, would be environmentally dangerous and were designed mainly to provide a federal bail-out for the moribund aerospace industry.

The satellites would weigh up to 20,000 tons, would stretch as much as 10 square miles and would have to be built in space. They would operate from a fixed orbital position 22,000 miles above Earth. The sunlight they collected would be converted to microwaves, which would be beamed to Earth-based antennae, turned into electricity and fed into conventional utility power grids.

After House passage of HR 12505, sponsored by Ronnie G. Flippo, D-Ala., the measure went to the Senate where it was referred to the Energy Subcommittee on Research and Development. The panel took no action on the bill.

In a related development, the Senate June 28 authorized $500,000 for the National Science Foundation (NSF) to study the feasibility of solar satellites. The provision was included in the fiscal 1979 NSF authorization bill (HR 11400). *(Story, Congress and Government chapter)*

House Committee Action

HR 12505 was ordered reported May 9 by the House Science and Technology Committee on a 30-1 vote. Richard L. Ottinger, D-N.Y., was the lone dissenter.

The panel's report (H Rept 95-1120) said the solar satellite technology was feasible and that economic studies projected it would be cost competitive with other power generation methods in the future. Aside from producing electricity, the report said, other possible benefits of such satellites included expansion of high technology industries, more jobs and possible U.S. export of energy and technology.

The report said the legislation would require the Department of Energy and the National Aeronautics and Space Administration (NASA) to prepare a comprehensive plan on how to develop the technology.

"The operation of the solar power satellites could produce environmental effects, several of which involve a large degree of uncertainty and will require much more understanding before their effects can be reliably quantified," the report said.

The committee estimated that continuation of the government research program would require $245 million through fiscal 1983 in addition to the $25 million authorized for fiscal 1979.

The report included position statements from the Department of Energy and NASA saying the legislation was not necessary and would prematurely push the existing research program.

Ottinger filed a dissent with the report detailing his views that the project would be expensive and dangerous.

Among Ottinger's charges were that microwave technology presented a broad range of possible threats to health and safety, that cost projections varied widely and that the bill explicitly committed the government to commercial demonstration of a solar satellite. He also said the satellites would have possible military applications and that the materials required to build them would increase American dependence on foreign minerals.

House Floor Action

Proponents of the measure gave repeated assurances on the House floor June 22 that HR 12505 did not commit the nation to construction of any satellite. They said it would only accelerate the research effort from "merely paper studies toward hardware verification," in the words of Mike McCormack, D-Wash.

Ottinger led the opposition. He persuaded the bill's proponents to strike language mandating a study of nuclear satellites. The motion to strike was agreed to by voice vote.

SBA Solar Loan Program

Legislation creating a $75 million loan program for small businesses involved in the solar energy, renewable energy and energy conservation fields was cleared by Congress June 19.

The bill (HR 11713 — PL 95-315) authorized $30 million in fiscal 1979 for the Small Business Administration (SBA) to make direct loans to eligible businesses. It also authorized $6.75 million in fiscal 1979 so SBA could insure $45 million in guaranteed bank loans for such companies.

The bill made loans available for plant start up, construction, conversion or expansion for firms producing solar, renewable source or energy conservation equipment. Engineering, architectural and consulting firms in those fields also were eligible.

Sponsors of the bill said it was needed to provide startup capital for untested new energy businesses that had had difficulty obtaining financing from commercial sources or through regular SBA loan programs.

Provisions

As cleared by Congress, HR 11713:

- Authorized direct and guaranteed loans to small businesses to finance plant construction, conversion, expansion (including land acquisition) or start up or to buy or acquire equipment, facilities, machinery, supplies or materials to enable those businesses to design, engineer, manufacture, distribute, market, install or service solar, renewable source or energy conservation equipment.
- Defined eligible solar energy equipment as active or passive solar thermal energy equipment or photovoltaic cells.
- Defined eligible energy conservation equipment as that on the conservation measures list of the Department of Energy or that determined to be eligible by the SBA administrator.
- Defined eligible renewable energy equipment as that involved in the production of hydroelectric power; wind energy; energy from wood, grain, biological waste or other biomass or energy from industrial waste or cogeneration.
- Provided that the loans could go to engineering, architectural or consulting firms in the solar, renewable source or energy conservation fields.
- Limited guaranteed loans to $500,000 and direct loans to $350,000.
- Prohibited loans from being used primarily for research and development.
- Limited SBA's participation in the guaranteed loan program to 90 percent of the loan.
- Required applicants to apply for non-federal credit first.
- Limited loan repayment time to 15 years.
- Set interest rates at the same level as general SBA loans, bank rates for guaranteed loans and the prevailing government interest rate plus one-quarter percent for direct loans.
- Provided that applicants for special energy loans did not have to have so sound a financial status as applicants for general loans.
- Required that in determining who should get a loan SBA consider the quality of the product or service, the applicant's technical qualifications, sales projections and financial status of the business.
- Authorized the SBA to conduct seminars to inform the public of the availability of the new loans.
- Authorized SBA grants to groups for training seminars in solar and renewable source energy equipment and energy conservation measures.
- Authorized $36.75 million for fiscal 1979 to provide $30 million in direct loans and $45 million in guaranteed loans. (Of that amount, $6.75 million was authorized to cover losses in the guaranteed loan program).

House Action

The House Small Business Committee reported HR 11713 April 19 (H Rept 95-1071).

The committee said that small businesses had been unable to compete with large corporations in gas, oil, coal and nuclear energy. As a result they had concentrated their limited capital on developing new technologies, such as solar energy, energy from renewable sources and energy conservation devices, the report said.

In 1978, about 860 small firms were involved in manufacturing, servicing or distributing solar energy and energy conservation equipment, the committee estimated. But, the report noted, large corporations were producing a growing share of the nation's solar collectors. At the same time, small businesses had found it increasingly difficult to borrow capital for entering into or expanding in the field.

"Small business persons admit that private capital is available from very large corporations, especially major oil companies," said the committee report. "Invariably, however, a precondition to . . . such capital is the surrender of controlling interest in the small business concern."

The committee also quoted a report from the Department of Energy which determined that firms in the solar energy field had received "no effective assistance from SBA." The administration granted only three energy-related loans between October 1977 and March 1978, the committee said.

SBA, based on its own estimation of the state of the solar energy art, had "apparently determined that (loan) applicants did not demonstrate the required assurances of ability to repay loans," according to the committee.

"The committee is aware that loans made to businesses involved in these new and emerging energy fields may be associated with somewhat higher than normal risks," the report said. "Nevertheless, it intends, by the express language of this bill to signal clearly to SBA the committee's determination that (these) . . . loans . . . should be made."

Dissenting views were filed by M. Caldwell Butler, R-Va., and John J. LaFalce, D-N.Y. They said it was "unwise for Congress to single out one part of one industry and tell the SBA to throw out its well established standards in this instance."

The House passed the bill May 2, 375-17, under suspension of the rules, which meant no amendments were permitted. *(Vote 225, p. 64-H)*

Bedell argued that big business' interest in small business' energy developments had too often led to the acquisition of small companies by larger ones.

"We should reverse this trend," Bedell said. "Otherwise, we will have yet another segment of the energy market controlled by a handful of large companies."

But Butler, who opposed the bill, said the measure would substitute Congress' judgment for the SBA's in making loans and would set a dangerous precedent of "adopting whatever loan program happens to be in style, regardless of its validity."

Senate Action

The Senate Small Business Committee substituted its language for that of House-passed HR 11713 and reported the measure May 15 (S Rept 95-828).

The bill made loans available for plant start up, construction, conversion or expansion for firms producing solar, renewable resource or conservation energy equipment. It also added engineering, architectural and consulting firms in the energy field to the eligibility list.

The committee said the loan program was needed to provide capital for untested, new energy businesses that had had difficulty obtaining financing from commercial sources or through regular SBA loan plans.

It also expanded the definition of conservation equipment eligible for funding and, to provide flexibility for new developments in the field, left it to the SBA administrator to determine what new equipment could be come eligible.

The Senate passed HR 11713 May 24 by voice vote and without debate.

Final Action

When the bill was returned to the House June 16, members amended it further and prohibited loans from being used primarily for research and development. The House also stipulated that the $36.75 million authorized in the bill was for fiscal 1979.

The bill was then returned to the Senate, which cleared it by voice vote June 19.

'Sun Day' Resolution

A resolution (H J Res 715 — PL 95-253) proclaiming May 3 as "Sun Day" to celebrate the promise of solar energy was cleared by the Senate March 14 on a voice vote. The House passed the measure March 6 by a 348-7 margin. *(Vote 84, p. 24-H)*

Sun Day was modeled after Earth Day in 1970, which highlighted the growing environmental movement.

House members voting against Sun Day were Robert E. Badham, R-Calif.; Gunn McKay, D-Utah; Gary A. Myers, R-Pa.; David R. Obey, D-Wis.; Otis G. Pike, D-N.Y.; Samuel S. Stratton, D-N.Y.; and David C. Treen, R-La.

Solar Energy Cell Program

An aggressive 10-year federal program for developing solar photovoltaic cells as a commercially competitive technology cleared Congress in the final days of the session. The cells convert sunlight directly into electricity.

As cleared by Congress, the bill (HR 12874 — PL 95-590) authorized $125 million in fiscal 1979 funds for research and development by the Department of Energy on solar photovoltaic technologies. The bill also established a statutory framework for the conduct of the Solar Photovoltaic Research, Development and Demonstration programs.

Legislative History

HR 12874 was ordered reported unanimously by the House Committee on Science and Technology. The report (H Rept 95-1285) was filed June 9.

In the report, the panel said solar photovoltaic cells were first developed in the early 1950's and were used extensively in the U.S. space program to provide electric power for spacecraft. But the high cost of the cells limited their widespread use on Earth.

"In order for the systems to compete with conventional energy systems and achieve broad commercial applications photovoltaic system costs will have to be reduced by a factor of 10-20 over the next 10 years," the report said.

The committee estimated that the program would require a total of $1.57 billion through fiscal 1987.

Under the bill, public and private entities could apply to the Energy Department for up to 75 per cent of the costs of purchasing and installing photovoltaic systems.

Administration Position

Mike McCormack, D-Wash., floor manager of the bill, said the Carter administration had taken no position on the measure. In its fiscal 1979 budget, the administration called for $76 million for solar photovoltaic research.

In mid-May the administration revised its request upward by adding $30 million to the $76 million, but that was less than the Science Committee had urged.

HR 12874 passed the House easily without opposition June 28 under suspension of the rules, a procedure that requires the approval of two-thirds of voting members and does not permit amendments. The vote was 385-14. *(Vote 444, p. 126-H)*

There was one preliminary vote when Barry M. Goldwater Jr., R-Calif., demanded a second on the motion to pass the bill. The second was ordered 376-5. That vote was not related to the substance of the bill. *(Vote 438, p. 126-H)*

In the Senate, the Committee on Energy and Natural Resources Sept. 21 voted 17-0 to recommend passage of a similar bill. The bill passed the Senate Oct. 10 by voice vote, and the House agreed to the Senate version Oct. 13, clearing the measure for the president.

Coal Leasing Amendments

Congress Oct. 13 cleared a bill (S 3189 — PL 95-554) authorizing the interior secretary to exchange some leased federal coal lands in Utah and Wyoming for other lands where mining would have a less damaging effect on the environment.

But Congress put off a decision on the issue of giving the interior secretary general authority to swap federal coal leases in order to preserve environmentally valuable land.

The Senate version, passed by voice vote Sept. 20, gave the secretary authority to exchange or purchase leases to help resolve cases where there could be undesirable social or environmental damage from mining.

The bill was reported Aug. 25 by the Energy Committee (S Rept 95-1169). The measure was prompted by industry complaints about cumbersome requirements of the Federal Coal Leasing Amendments Act of 1975 (PL 94-377). *(1976 Almanac, p. 108; 1977 Almanac, p. 617)*

The House Interior Committee had debated giving the interior secretary broad authority to swap leases, but finally settled on a case-by-case approach (HR 13553). It voted to give the secretary authority to exchange the leases held by three companies, because they conflicted with a highway route in Wyoming and with potential wilderness areas in Utah. The measure was reported Sept. 27 (H Rept 95-1635).

HR 13553 was passed by voice vote under suspension of the rules Oct. 3. The House then substituted the language of its bill for S 3189, and the Senate accepted the amended version by voice vote Oct. 13, thus clearing it for the president.

Provisions

As cleared by Congress, S 3189:

- Allowed the interior secretary to exchange specific federal coal leases in Utah and Wyoming for land of equal value. The leases were held by Utah Power and Light Co., Texaco Inc., and Wyodak Resources Development Corp.
- Authorized the secretary to sell, at fair market value, coal that had to be removed to exercise a federally granted right of way.
- Authorized the secretary to modify an existing lease with the addition of up to 160 acres of lands that cornered the lease without requiring that the entire lease, not just the new lands, become subject to the provisions of the 1975 Coal Leasing Amendments, which placed a mandatory 12.5 percent royalty on all surface-mined coal. *(Coal Leasing Amendments, 1976 Almanac p. 108)*
- Repealed a provision in existing law prohibiting women miners in underground mines on federal lands.
- Directed the secretary to study the public value of the Lake DeSmet reservoir and its surrounding lands in Johnson County, Wyo.
- Authorized the secretary to exchange federal coal lands for the Lake DeSmet area if he determined the area should be obtained and preserved.

Oil Shale Development

A bill requiring the government to test three methods of squeezing oil from shale rock was passed by the Senate June 27. The measure (S 419) required the Department of Energy to contract with private firms to run up to three federally-owned plants to do the testing. The House took no action on the bill, which passed the Senate 61-23. *(Vote 185, p. 31-S)*

Sponsored by Floyd Haskell, D-Colo., the measure authorized $1.4 million in fiscal 1979 funds. Of that, $1 million covered general start-up and administrative costs and the remaining $400,000 was for a program of special planning grants to state and local governments that suffered because of the bill.

In addition, the legislation authorized $40 million in loan guarantees in fiscal 1979-80 to cover state and local planning and development projects necessitated by the bill's passage.

The Senate Energy Committee estimated that if the plants actually were funded, they would cost from $275 million to $400 million to build and would have annual operating costs of $30 million to $40 million. Revenues from the oil produced would go to the federal treasury.

The only floor opposition to the measure was led by Clifford P. Hansen, R-Wyo., ranking minority member of the Senate Energy Committee. Hansen opposed having the federal government assume full financial responsibility for the projects. He proposed an amendment to require industrial participants to assume part of the financial risks or provide alternative incentives to oil shale production. It was rejected 34-51. *(Vote 184, p. 30-S)*

Committee Action

The Senate Energy Committee voted 12-5 April 26 to report out S 419; all five opponents were Republicans. The report (S 95-802) was filed May 10.

"It is the judgment of the committee that the nation cannot afford to await, as has been the case for 20 years, the demonstration of the commercial viability of oil shale technologies by private industry and should begin now to test these technologies at public expense," the report said.

Oil shale, a sedimentary rock containing organic material called kerogen, can be converted to a liquid and recovered as oil. There are potentially up to two trillion barrels of shale oil in the United States, most of it within a 17,000 square mile area in western Colorado, eastern Utah and southwestern Wyoming, the report said. By comparison, there are only 657 billion barrels of oil in worldwide petroleum reserves. Almost 80 percent of the nation's oil shale is on publicly-owned lands, the report said.

There are various processes for deriving oil from shale. Most involve fracturing the rock and heating it to about 900 degrees Fahrenheit. This can be done either by mining the ore, cracking it and then processing it in above-ground plants or by any of several processes achieved below ground, known as "in-situ."

Although there have been attempts dating back to the 1860's to produce oil from shale, none has been commercially successful. Given the nation's pressing need to produce more fuel, the committee said, the government should step in to stimulate development of a workable process.

The report included written statements from the Department of the Interior and the Office of Management and Budget opposing the legislation as unnecessary and as likely to duplicate an Interior program begun in 1973. Under that program, choice federal shale-rich lands were leased for oil shale development. No oil had yet been produced as a result of the program.

Minority Views. In minority views filed with the report, Sens. Hansen and Dewey F. Bartlett, R-Okla., opposed the legislation as "wholly unnecessary and unjustified." It would cost too much and would not prove the commercial viability of any project because the government would swallow all economic risks, they said.

Provisions

As passed by the Senate, S 419:

- Directed the secretary of energy to determine the commercial viability of three technologies for oil shale production.
- Directed the secretary to invite proposals for the design, construction and operation of oil shale demonstration projects.
- Directed the secretary to select the three most attractive project proposals submitted, but allowed him discretion to select fewer if there were not three worthy candidates.
- Provided that if three projects were selected, at least one had to employ an above ground process and at least one had to operate as an "in situ," or below ground, process.
- Specified that all three projects had to be located at a single site if feasible, but allowed the secretary discretion to choose multiple sites.
- Directed the secretary to give priority to lands of the Naval oil shale reserves.
- Directed the secretary to consult with the secretary of the interior before designating any public lands for oil shale development.
- Required the energy secretary to consult with the governor of any involved state and with any affected political subdivision before selecting any project.
- Provided that at least one public hearing be held in the area most affected by commercial development of oil shale before completion of the official evaluation of the project's feasibility.
- Gave the United States title to any invention conceived by participants in the projects.
- Allowed the secretary to license any invention arising from work under the act.
- Created a panel to advise the secretary on impacts of the act on local and state governments and the environment.
- Specified that the panel consist of 10 members including a representative each from the Council on Environmental Quality (CEQ), the Interior Department, the Environmental Protection Agency, the state affected, plus three elected representatives from local governments to be appointed by the area's regional governmental council and three representatives from citizen environmental groups to be appointed by the CEQ chairman.
- Directed that oil produced from the projects be used, stored or sold by the secretary, with revenues paid into the federal treasury.
- Authorized the secretary to issue up to $20 million in loan guarantees in both fiscal 1979 and fiscal 1980 to provide financial backing for community planning and development projects required by the act and to waive repayment.
- Authorized the secretary to make up to $200,000 in fiscal 1979 in grants to state or local governments for such purposes.
- Created a special "Oil Shale Commercialization Test Special Fund" to handle the loan and grant monies.
- Authorized an additional $200,000 to cover administrative costs arising from establishment of the fund.
- Specified that nothing in the act modified or superseded any state laws governing water control rights.
- Authorized $1 million in fiscal 1979 for the act. ▮

'Dealer Day in Court' Bill

The House June 6 cleared and sent to the president legislation to protect gas station owners from the arbitrary cancellation of their franchises. Final action came when the House approved Senate amendments to the bill (HR 130 — PL 95-297) by voice vote.

The measure also required refiners to determine gasoline octane ratings and post them on the pump.

A third section required the Energy Department to study the extent to which producers, refiners and other motor fuel suppliers subsidized retail and wholesale sales with profits from other operations.

The first two titles of the bill were basically uncontroversial. They were similar to HR 130 as passed by the House April 5, 1977. *(1977 Almanac, p. 746)*

The first title was designed to protect gasoline station franchise holders from arbitrary or discriminatory lease cancellation. Under the measure, franchise agreements could not be terminated or left to expire without renewal unless specific standards of reasonableness were satisfied, as spelled out in the bills. Contested franchise cancellations would be heard in federal court.

Title II required refiners to determine their gasoline octane ratings and to display the ratings at gasoline station pumps. It also required the Federal Trade Commission (FTC) to draft rules mandating motor vehicle manufacturers to display proper octane requirements on each new vehicle. Violations would be enforceable by the FTC.

But the Senate Energy Committee added a third title, which sparked controversy. It prohibited gas stations from being subsidized with funds or services derived from other operations performed by their parent companies.

"...[F]ranchise termination or nonrenewal of a franchise relationship are not the only means at the disposal of a refiner or distributor supplier to exert pressure on a retailer or a distributor," the committee report explained. "The control of supply and the pricing of that supply provide powerful instruments for influencing profitability and, in many cases, the survival of a retail operation.

"Any refiner or distributor supplier who also operates his own outlets at the retail or wholesale level can, by subsidizing those outlets, place a sharp limit on the prices any independent competitor can afford to charge. ... This flexibility can be used to eliminate independent buyers ...," the report said.

Provisions

As cleared by Congress, HR 130:

Title I: Franchise Protection

- Prohibited a franchisor from arbitrarily cancelling or failing to renew a franchise agreement with a gasoline distributor or retailer.
- Provided that the franchisor could terminate an agreement if he met certain standards of reasonableness defined under the law; among these standards were a franchisor's decision to cease selling gasoline in a geographic area or failure of a gas station owner to maintain a clean facility.
- Required a franchisor to provide at least 90 days advance notification of termination or non-renewal of a franchise; less than 90 days notice was permitted if reasonableness could be shown.
- Required a franchisor to provide at least 180 days advance notification if the termination was based upon a

decision to discontinue selling gasoline in a geographic area; required the franchisor to notify the governors of affected states.

- Provided a retailer or distributor with the right to file a civil suit in federal court; placed upon the franchisor the burden of proving compliance with Title I.

Title II: Octane Disclosure

- Required refiners to test gasoline to determine the octane rating; required suppliers and distributors to certify the rating.
- Required retailers to post octane ratings at the point of sale.
- Directed the FTC to issue rules requiring auto manufacturers to display octane requirements on new cars.

Title III: Motor Fuel Subsidies

- Required the Energy Department to conduct a study to determine the extent to which producers, refiners and other suppliers of motor fuel subsidize company-owned gasoline stations with funds or services derived from other operations performed by their parent companies.
- Required that the study include an examination of how subsidization is predatory and presents a threat to competition.
- Required the Secretary of Energy to report to Congress the results of the study and to make legislative recommendations within 18 months after the date of enactment.
- Provided authority to the president to take interim steps to prevent predatory pricing policies, subject to approval by Congress.

Senate Committee Action

The Senate Energy Committee voted 11-7 March 22 to report two identical bills (HR 130, S 743) to prevent unfair gas station franchise cancellation. The reports (HR 130 — S Rept 95-731, S 743 — S Rept 95-732) were filed April 10 and April 11 respectively.

An Energy Committee spokesman said the unusual step of filing separate reports on two identical bills was taken at the request of John A. Durkin, D-N.H., a panel member who sponsored S 743. Durkin wanted to have a Senate numbered bill on the floor to provide more tactical flexibility during debate and in conference, the spokesman said.

Eight committee members filed dissents to passage of Title III. They argued it would have an anti-competitive effect despite its intent, that there was insufficient evidence that it was needed, that the Justice Department and the Federal Trade Commission opposed it and that the remedy was unworkable.

Signing those dissents, separately in some cases and in joint filings in others, were Dale Bumpers, D-Ark., J. Bennett Johnston, D-La., Mark O. Hatfield, R-Ore., James A. McClure, R-Idaho, Dewey F. Bartlett, R-Okla., Paul Laxalt, R-Nev., Clifford P. Hansen, R-Wyo., and Wendell H. Ford, D-Ky.

Unlike the other seven, Ford voted to report the bill because, he said in his statement, he thought Titles I and II were necessary and hoped Title III could be "worked out on the floor."

Hansen alone noted objections to Title I as well, "because in my judgment, it constitutes unwarranted and unfair intrusion into the contractual relationships between sellers and buyers of motor gasoline."

Senate Floor Action

The Senate passed HR 130 May 9 on a 95-0 vote, after accepting a last-minute compromise amendment by Dale Bumpers, D-Ark., that provided for an Energy Department study of how oil refiners subsidize the sale of gasoline to stations. *(Vote 159, p. 27-S)*

The Bumpers amendment replaced the controversial Title III section of the measure reported by the Senate Energy Committee that prohibited refineries from subsidizing sales to gasoline stations they owned with funds or services derived from other operations of their company.

The National Congress of Petroleum Retailers, representing station owners, and the National Oil Jobbers Council, representing wholesalers, both favored outlawing subsidies from refiners. But while the jobbers supported the committee version of Title III, the retailers withheld their support from the controversial title in hopes of aiding passage of the rest of the bill.

Attempts to modify Title III dominated the debate on HR 130, which began May 5 and resumed May 9.

Bumper's amendment required the Energy Department to conduct a study of the extent to which producers, refiners and other motor fuel suppliers subsidize retail and wholesale sales with profits from other operations. The department also was required to make legislative recommendations to Congress within 18 months after the date of enactment. The amendment gave the president authority to develop interim methods for maintaining competition in gasoline sales. The amendment was adopted by voice vote.

Sen. Pete V. Domenici, R-N.M., author of Title III as reported by the Energy Committee, said the study called for in the amendment was like "prescribing aspirin for a severed jugular." But he conceded that the original Title III lacked sufficient votes for passage.

Sen. Edward M. Kennedy, D-Mass., then offered an amendment to make the findings of the Energy Department study available to the Federal Trade Commission (FTC) and the Justice Department.

The Energy Department should share its information with the agencies "that have the primary responsibility for protecting the little guy, the corner gas station," Kennedy argued in support of his proposal.

But the amendment was denounced by Bumpers, who warned that "the Secretary of Energy would not get into the front door," if the oil companies thought the Justice Department or the FTC would get the information.

Kennedy chided Bumpers for believing that "those nice, benevolent oil companies" would "give us all the information we want."

But Bumpers shot back that the Kennedy proposal provided no more clout for extracting information from the oil companies than his own amendment.

Members voted 55-38 to table the Kennedy amendment. *(Vote 158, p. 27-S)*

Final Action. The House accepted the Senate amendments to HR 130 by voice vote on June 6, clearing the bill for the president.

Strip Mining

Legislation authorizing $100 million in fiscal 1979-80 to carry out the 1977 strip mining control law (PL 95-87) was cleared by the Senate July 28 and sent to the president. *(Background, 1977 Almanac p. 617)*

The bill (S 2463) increased the amounts originally provided under the Surface Mining Control and Reclamation Act for federal enforcement and state inspection programs and for aid to operators of small mines who were required to conduct various hydrologic and geologic tests.

The bill authorized $25 million each in fiscal 1979 and 1980 for state enforcement and federal inspection programs. Another $25 million in each of those years was authorized for the testing program. Under existing law, authorizations were pegged at a total of $30 million annually for the three programs.

The Senate Energy and Natural Resources Committee, which reported S 2463 May 9 (S Rept 95-788), recommended $25 million annually for fiscal 1979-80 for the enforcement and test programs. An additional $15 million was authorized for the test program for each of the next 13 fiscal years.

The Senate approved S 2463 by voice vote May 16.

The House Interior and Insular Affairs Committee reported its version of the bill (HR 11827—H Rept 95-1143) May 12. The committee limited the authorization for the enforcement programs to $25 million for fiscal 1979, but provided such sums as necessary in fiscal 1980.

The House and Senate committee staffs worked out a compromise substitute bill. The bill retained the Senate-approved authorization of $25 million annually for fiscal 1979-80 for the enforcement programs, but eliminated the Senate's provision for 13-years of authorizations after fiscal 1980 for the small mine operators program.

The House approved the substitute version of HR 11827 July 11 by a 323-74 vote under suspension of the rules, a procedure that requires a two-thirds vote for passage and does not permit amendments. *(Vote 458, p. 130-H)*

The House then substituted the provisions of HR 11827 for those of S 2463 and returned the bill to the Senate, which passed it July 28 (PL 95-343).

Uranium Mill Waste Control

A program to clean up some 25 million tons of potentially hazardous uranium wastes was cleared by Congress Oct. 15.

The bill (HR 13650 — PL 95-604) mandating the cleanup also provided for stricter controls on future handling and disposal of wastes from the processing of uranium.

A substitute version of the bili was passed by the Senate Oct. 13. The House amended that substitute Oct. 14, and the Senate then accepted the final House version.

The major dispute between the two houses was resolved when the Senate agreed to accept House language calling for the federal government to pay 90 percent of the cleanup cost, with the remaining 10 percent to be paid by states where the wastes were located. The Senate had previously insisted that the federal government pay 100 percent of the cleanup costs.

Under existing law, no federal agency had explicit authority to regulate or dispose of wastes at abandoned uranium mills.

Under existing law, the NRC licensed and regulated 11 operating mines and mills. States regulated 14 operating mines and mills. But once the operations closed down, the NRC no longer had jurisdiction over the uranium wastes.

The Environmental Protection Agency (EPA) had some jurisdiction over the tailings. But Sen. Pete V. Domenici, R-N.M., told the Senate that EPA would not be able to issue regulations governing the wastes for several years, possibly not before 1984.

Scientists and environmentalists had become concerned about the possible health hazards from the wastes — called "tailings."

Over the years about 25 million tons of the radioactive tailings were generated by 24 mills. The mills originally were operated under federal contracts for the production of uranium for nuclear weapons. The tailings had been considered harmless, and often were used in building construction.

Several members of Congress from western states pushed legislation to clean up the sites where the wastes had been dumped and to store the wastes so they would no longer present public health dangers.

Processing mills and waste dumping sites were located in Colorado, Arizona, Idaho, New Mexico, Oregon, Pennsylvania, Texas, Utah and Wyoming.

Sharing Cleanup Costs

Estimates of the cost of cleaning up the uranium wastes at 24 sites ranged as high as $200 million, depending on how much work was needed at each site.

The Carter administration had proposed, in S 3078, that the federal government pay 75 percent of the cleanup costs, with the remaining 25 percent to be paid by states where the wastes were located. That proposal met strong resistance from western governors, who argued that the federal government should pay the entire cost because the uranium was milled for federal use.

In the House, a plan was adopted providing for a flat 90-10 split between the federal and state governments.

When the House bill reached the Senate Oct. 13, the 90-10 split also was adopted, although the Senate Energy Committee, which had jurisdiction over the bill, had originally proposed that the federal government pay 100 percent of the costs.

The Senate also went along with a House provision which said that money for the cleanup would have to be provided each year in the Energy Department authorization bill. The fiscal 1979 authorization (HR 11392) was not passed by the 95th Congress.

No money was appropriated to start the cleanup in fiscal 1979, but a House Interior Committee aide said actual cleanup work could not begin for at least a year.

Future Regulations

Title II of HR 13650 required the NRC and the Environmental Protection Agency (EPA) to develop standards for disposal of uranium wastes in the future.

The bill also provided that the uranium wastes would become the property of the state or federal government. The disposal sites would be turned over to the state or federal government unless the NRC determined that government takeover was unnecessary.

The Senate had attached the provision for future uranium waste regulations to the fiscal 1979 NRC authorization. But that provision was no longer necessary once Congress enacted HR 13650, and it was dropped. *(NRC authorization, p. 752)*

Provisions

As cleared by Congress, HR 13650:

- Gave the Nuclear Regulatory Commission, in cooperation with the Environmental Protection Agency, authority to develop standards for the safe disposal of wastes from uranium processing mills.
- Directed the Energy Department to enter into agreements to clean up 22 abandoned disposal sites with states where the uranium wastes were located.
- Provided that the federal government would pay 90 percent of the cleanup costs, with the remaining 10 percent paid by the states, but specified that the federal government would pay 100 percent of the cleanup costs at two sites located on Indian lands.
- Gave states the right to "participate fully" in the selection and implementation of procedures to clean up the wastes.
- Required that the uranium wastes be turned over to the federal government or to the states where they were located.
- Required that waste disposal sites be turned over to the state or federal government, unless the NRC determined that such a turnover was unnecessary.
- Directed the NRC to conduct a study to determine if it had the authority to compel the owners of two active processing mills in New Mexico to clean up abandoned uranium wastes on their property. If the NRC determined that it did not have that authority, the commission could enter into an agreement with the state of New Mexico for a government-run cleanup program.
- Directed the attorney general to conduct a study to determine if the private companies owning uranium waste disposal sites could be held liable for damages caused by the wastes. Any damages collected from the companies would be used to help pay the cleanup costs.

House, Senate Committee Action

The Senate Energy and Natural Resources Committee ordered reported its uranium wastes cleanup bill (S 3078) Oct. 3 (S Rept 95-1266). On Sept. 26, the House Commerce Committee ordered reported the House bill (HR 13650), which had been stalled for more than a month. The House Interior Committee, which shared jurisdiction on the issue with Commerce, had reported its version of HR 13650 Aug. 11 (H Rept 95-1480).

The major difference among the three cleanup bills concerned how much of the cost was to be shouldered by the federal government.

The Carter administration originally called for the federal government to pay 75 percent of the cost, with the remaining 25 percent paid by states where abandoned mills were located.

The House Interior Committee raised the federal share to 90 percent, but said that no state would be required to pay more than one-fourth of 1 percent of its general revenues. If the state's 10 percent share exceeded that level, the federal government would make up the difference. Colorado, Utah and Pennsylvania were the only states that would be affected by the ceiling.

The House Commerce Committee went along with the 90 percent federal share, but refused to back the provision for higher shares in Colorado, Utah and Pennsylvania. Rep. Clarence J. Brown, R-Ohio, said the 10 percent state share "is not unreasonable."

Rep. John D. Dingell, D-Mich., argued that increasing the federal share "could conceivably serve as a pattern for future legislation of this type. It would be extremely dangerous and a bad precedent."

The Senate Energy Committee was more receptive to the pleadings of the governors of those states. The panel adopted an amendment by Sen. Pete V. Domenici, R-N.M., requiring the federal government to pay 100 percent of the cleanup costs.

"Why shouldn't the federal government pay for the whole thing?" Domenici asked fellow committee members. "This was the federal government's responsibility in the first place." Four of the mill sites were in New Mexico.

In its version, the House Interior Committee authorized $180 million for fiscal 1979. That was in addition to the $3 million for cleanup included in the Department of Energy authorization bill (HR 11329). *(Energy Department authorization, p. 684)*

The Commerce Committee bill provided for the cleanup funds to come out of the annual Energy Department authorization, but did not specify an amount.

The Senate Energy bill authorized $3 million for fiscal 1979, with the stipulation that future funds be authorized each year.

All three versions:

- Required federal ownership of uranium mill sites, although the Senate bill allowed states to take over sites after they were cleaned up.
- Required the federal government to pay 100 percent of the cleanup costs for wastes sites on Indian lands.
- Gave states the authority to concur in the type of cleanup activity and the location of disposal sites for tailings.

The Senate Energy and House Commerce bills directed the attorney general to study whether private corporations owning uranium waste sites could be held liable for environmental damage. The attorney general could then file suit to recover damages, which would be used to help pay the cleanup costs.

Floor Action

The House passed HR 13650 Oct. 3 under suspension of the rules on a standing vote of 13-0.

Under the House bill, the federal government would pay 90 percent of the cleanup and storage costs of potentially hazardous uranium wastes, with the remaining 10 percent to be paid by states where the waste dumps were located.

The House bill directed the Nuclear Regulatory Commission (NRC) to clean up 22 abandoned uranium disposal sites. The bill also directed the NRC to study the disposal sites at two active uranium mills in New Mexico to determine what should be done about the wastes there.

In addition, the bill required the attorney general to determine if the private companies that milled the uranium, under contract to the federal government, could legally be required to pay part or all of the cleanup cost.

The House-passed bill also:

- Provided for federal ownership of uranium waste disposal sites.
- Required the federal government to pay 100 percent of the cleanup costs for wastes sites on Indian lands.
- Gave states authority to concur in the type of cleanup activity and the location of disposal sites for tailings.

The Senate Sept. 18 had passed a measure calling for future regulation as part of the 1979 authorization bill (S 2584) for the NRC, but that provision was later dropped in conference, when HR 13650 was cleared.

Following negotiations among House and Senate committee members, the Senate Oct. 13 by voice vote passed an amended version of HR 13650. In addition to directing studies by the secretary of energy, the Environmental Protection Agency and the attorney general, the bill reduced the states' share of the cost of the cleanup program to 10 percent from 25 percent.

Final Action. The House accepted the Senate amendments Oct. 14 by voice vote, with primarily technical amendments, and the Senate agreed to the bill the same day, clearing the measure for the president. ▮

Energy Research

The Senate Feb. 8 by voice vote sent President Carter a new version of the energy research bill (S 1811) he vetoed Nov. 5, 1977. The new bill (S 1340 — PL 95-238) was identical to the earlier measure except that it dropped the two provisions opposed by the president: authorization of $80 million to continue work on the Clinch River breeder reactor and language revising uranium pricing arrangements. It had been passed by the House by voice vote Dec. 7, 1977. *(1977 Almanac p. 683; breeder reactor, p. 154)*

S 1340 provided $6,081,400,000 for energy research programs in fiscal 1978. During brief debate, senators stressed that passage of the authorization without Clinch River funds should not be construed as deauthorization of the project. Funding for the project in fiscal 1978 was contained in a supplemental appropriations bill (HR 9375). ▮

Nuclear Agency Funds

Congress Oct. 15 cleared and sent to the president a bill authorizing $333 million for the Nuclear Regulatory Commission in fiscal 1979. That amount was $900,000 more than the House had voted and $3.4 million less than the Senate approved.

The bill (S 2584 — PL 95-601) directed the NRC to undertake major studies on the adequacy of safeguards at nuclear power plants and of the role to be played by states in the storage of nuclear wastes.

The Senate passed its version Sept. 18. The House adopted its bill (HR 12355) Oct. 4.

The energy and public works appropriations bill (HR 12928 — H J Res 1139) appropriated $322.3 million for the NRC in fiscal 1979. *(H J Res 1139, p. 154)*

Provisions

As cleared by Congress, S 2584:

- Authorized $333,007,000 for NRC operations in fiscal 1979, an increase of $35.3 million over fiscal 1978.
- Earmarked $1.152 million for studies of unresolved nuclear safety issues and to reduce a backlog of license applications.
- Earmarked $1 million for studies and evaluations of alternative fuel cycles.
- Required the NRC to prepare a report on ways in which states might participate in the siting, licensing and development of nuclear waste storage and disposal facilities.
- Earmarked $650,000 to develop a plan for a long-range study of the health effects of low-level radiation.
- Required the NRC to prepare an annual report on the adequacy of safeguards at facilities licensed and regulated by the commission.
- Tightened NRC internal operations by including new prohibitions on conflicts of interest involving contracts and requiring more careful commission scrutiny of its contracts.

Senate Committee Action

In the Senate, the Committee on Environment and Public Works urged funding boosts totaling $5.725 million above the administration request (S 2584 — S Rept 95-848).

The committee also urged shifts totaling $8.1 million within the administration's request.

Nuclear Waste Program. The biggest change was the committee's decision to substantially increase funding and staffing for nuclear waste management programs. The administration sought $8.125 million in that area, and a total of 41 employees. The committee recommended adding $4.45 million and 15 people.

The report noted that although the Energy Department had taken the lead in trying to find a permanent solution to the nuclear waste problem, the NRC held prime responsibility to protect public health and safety by licensing and regulating nuclear waste disposal facilities.

The report said that since the commission budget request had been submitted to Congress, the administration had stepped up its efforts to solve the nuclear waste problem. As a result, the report said, the commission had asked for an extra $4 million in fiscal 1979 beyond the original request.

State Grant Program. In a related move, the committee authorized $500,000 to cover grants to any state designated to house a long-term nuclear waste storage or disposal facility. The grants, to be awarded by the commission, were designed to allow affected states to independently review storage proposals. The administration had not sought funding for such a program.

Senate Floor Action

The Senate Sept. 18 by voice vote passed the bill making fiscal 1979 authorizations of $336.4 million for the Nuclear Regulatory Commission. Passage came after adoption of a floor amendment that provided for future NRC regulation of uranium wastes and mandated a study of which federal agencies should have jurisdiction over radioactive wastes of all kinds.

Calling for expanded NRC authority, Sen. Gary Hart, D-Colo., said the uranium wastes "are just as radioactive as the original uranium ore from which they came. In fact, if tailings are not properly controlled, they can be more dangerous than radioactive wastes generated by power plants and nuclear weapons programs."

Hart and Pete V. Domenici, R-N.M., sponsored the amendment giving NRC additional authority over uranium wastes. Hart was chairman of the Nuclear Regulation Subcommittee of the Environment and Public Works Committee.

As passed by the Senate, the amendment required the NRC and the EPA to develop standards for the storage of uranium mill tailings. After three years, the NRC would license and regulate all uranium tailing disposal sites, including previously abandoned sites. States would be allowed to maintain jurisdiction over mill sites if their standards were as rigid as the federal standards.

The amendment did not directly address the issue of immediately cleaning up uranium mill sites that were already abandoned.

Nuclear Waste Disposal

The Senate amendment also required a study by March 1978 of the costs and benefits of expanding NRC regulations of all nuclear wastes, including those from nuclear power plants. The study would help Congress develop legislation in 1979.

Hart told the Senate that waste disposal "has received a low priority from both Congress and the federal agencies in the past." A committee staff member said part of the reason was that it is unclear which agencies should have jurisdiction over the various aspects of nuclear waste disposal and management.

The Senate Environment Committee recommended a 55 percent boost in the administration's budget request for nuclear waste disposal and management programs. The administration had sought $8.125 million and 41 employees for the licensing and regulation of waste disposal facilities. Citing "a strong need for increased federal efforts" in the area, the committee added $4.45 million and 15 people.

Citizen Participation

Sponsors of the authorization bill avoided a potentially sticky floor fight over the issue of paying for citizen participation in NRC proceedings.

Sen. Patrick J. Leahy, D-Vt., proposed an amendment adding $500,000 to the NRC budget in fiscal 1979, and $3 million in fiscal 1980, for an "Office of Nuclear Energy Public Counsel." The counsel would represent communities and citizen groups before the NRC. But Leahy withdrew the amendment when Hart promised his subcommittee would hold hearings on the matter in 1979.

The House Commerce Committee included $2 million for a public counsel in its NRC authorizations bill (HR 12355). *(See below)*

Sen. Dale Bumpers, D-Ark., offered, then withdrew, two amendments to cut what he called "exorbitant" authorizations for studies.

One amendment would have sliced $300,000 from a $500,000 program of grants to states for studies of proposed nuclear waste disposal sites.

But after Hart defended the study, Bumpers withdrew the amendment, saying: "I am not going to ask for a roll call vote. If I did, based on normal mentality around here, people would think I needed a saliva test, asking for a roll call over $300,000."

Bumpers also withdrew an amendment eliminating a $500,000 program of grants to states for studies of proposed nuclear waste disposal sites.

Provisions

As passed by the Senate, S 2584:

- Authorized $336.4 million for NRC activities in fiscal year 1979, an increase of $38.7 million over fiscal 1978.
- Included in that amount $14 million in new and expanded NRC programs, including nuclear waste disposal and management, nuclear reactor safety research and advanced reactor research.
- Gave the NRC authority to license and regulate, after three years, inactive uranium mining sites.
- Directed the NRC to study nuclear waste disposal regulations, including the question of which agencies should have jurisdiction over disposal sites.
- Directed the NRC and the EPA to prepare a plan for a long-range study of the health effects of low-level radiation.
- Required the NRC to review its process for selecting and training members of the Atomic Safety and Licensing Board.

House Committee Action

Commerce Bill

In its May 15 report, the House Interstate and Foreign Commerce Committee recommended additions totaling $3.43 million to the commission request (H Rept 95-1089, Part 2).

Of that, $2 million went for a program to pay the expenses of citizens who participated in proceedings before the NRC. Another $1.5 million went to the Office of Nuclear Reactor Regulation to beef up staff and programs for resolving safety issues and reducing the backlog of license applications. And the remaining $285,000 went for a program to insure the safety of nuclear exports.

As reported by the Commerce Committee, the $2 million would be used by the commission to establish a five-year program to help pay costs of eligible citizen intervenors.

"The purpose of this program is to enhance the quality of commission decisions and actions by helping fund public participation and representation in commission proceedings," the committee said. Because issues covered by the commission are so complex and technical, the report observed, consultant and legal fees necessary for effective participation sometimes run from $25,000 to $100,000 per issue. "This expense is a severe impediment to full participation," the report said.

Under the program, the commission would determine whether citizen participants qualified for aid. The committee said that to be eligible, a citizen participant had to present a view or interest that no other participant had presented adequately, and that the citizen's contribution to the proceeding had to be substantial.

Eligibility also would be determined in part by the public participant's resources. "This does not mean that the participant must be destitute or be without the capacity to obtain additional resources," the report said. "The operating criterion is the sufficiency of the participant's funds which are available to allow effective participation."

Seven Commerce Republicans, led by ranking minority member Samuel L. Devine, Ohio, said in separate views that the provision was "premature, unnecessary and will only lead to further delays in the nuclear power plant licensing process, a regulatory process which everyone conceded is already too long."

The seven noted that the administration had included similar citizen intervenor funding provisions in its proposal to speed up nuclear power plant licensing (S 2775, HR 11704). *(Nuclear licensing bill, p. 698)*

". . . [W]e feel that if this concept is to be explored, it should be considered as part of this comprehensive reform package where full hearings can be held," they wrote. They pledged a floor fight to strike the terms from the NRC bill.

Interior Bill

The House Interior and Insular Affairs Committee reported its version of HR 12355 April 26 (H Rept 95-1089). The committee bill did not authorize funds for citizen intervenors, but in additional views filed with the committee report, seven Democrats, including panel chairman Morris K. Udall, D-Ariz., called for such a program and announced they would support the idea on the floor.

As reported by the Interior Committee, HR 12355 authorized $330.95 million in fiscal 1979 for the NRC, $285,000 more than the administration's $330.67 million request.

All of the increase went to boost funding for safeguarding exports of nuclear materials. The change was proposed by Clement J. Zablocki, D-Wis., chairman of the International Relations Committee.

In its report, the committee also urged the commission to assign a higher priority to development of gas cooled reactors as an alternative to the current generation of "light water" fission nuclear reactors. The panel also directed the commission to prepare an annual report on safeguard programs in the domestic nuclear power industry.

In other comments, the committee called for consolidation of commission offices in a central location in downtown Washington, D.C. Currently, the NRC was scattered in 12 locations, the report said.

House Floor Action

The House Oct. 4 approved the fiscal 1979 authorization for the Nuclear Regulatory Commission without having to deal with the controversial issue of providing federal money for citizen participation in NRC proceedings. The bill was passed by voice vote under suspension of the rules.

A House Commerce Committee amendment providing $2 million for citizen participation was withdrawn before the NRC authorization bill (HR 12355) came to the House floor.

House Republicans had promised to fight the citizen participation funding, and a protracted floor dispute on the issue could have tied up the entire NRC authorization bill.

The House bill authorized $332.1 million during fiscal 1979 for the NRC, an increase of $1.4 million over the NRC request.

Most of the difference — $1.2 million — came from a Commerce Committee amendment that authorized the commission to hire 35 additional employees to speed up the processing of nuclear power plant applications.

The citizen participation provision produced a strong reaction from Republicans who generally opposed federal funding for citizens' groups that intervened in regulatory actions.

Rep. Clarence J. Brown, R-Ohio, said it would be "a dangerous thing for the government to use tax revenues to finance one particular point of view before a regulatory commission."

One strong supporter of the citizen participation funding, Rep. Morris K. Udall, D-Ariz., said he would try in 1979 to get that provision added to Carter administration proposals to streamline the nuclear power plant licensing process. Those proposals were introduced earlier in 1978 but died in the 95th Congress.

In floor debate on the NRC bill, Udall said citizens who intervene in NRC cases should be reimbursed for their expenses because they "make important contributions to the regulatory process."

As passed by the House, HR 12355 also:

- Required the NRC executive director to prepare an annual report on the status of safeguard programs in the domestic nuclear power industry. The first report would be due Feb. 1, 1979.
- Specified that $6.3 million in commission authorizations be used to accelerate review and research of gas cooled reactors as an alternative to the current generation of "light water" fission nuclear reactors.

Conference, Final Action

Conferees filed their report on the bill Oct. 14 (S Rept 95-1796).

The conferees eliminated a provision that would have authorized the commission to regulate hazardous wastes from uranium processing mills. The provision had been attached by the Senate. But Oct. 14 Congress cleared HR 13650, which gave the commission the authority to regulate those wastes and which mandated a federal-state cleanup program. *(Uranium wastes, p. 750)*

Conferees adopted a Senate provision requiring the NRC to conduct a study by March 1979 of the costs and benefits of expanding NRC regulations to all nuclear wastes, including those from nuclear power plants. The study would help Congress develop legislation in 1979.

The House adopted the conference report Oct. 14 and the Senate followed suit Oct. 15. ∎

Energy Boom Town Aid

Federal aid to energy boom towns died in the 95th Congress because of a disagreement in the Senate over whether to give grants as well as loans to affected communities.

A bill (S 1493), sponsored by Sen. Gary Hart, D-Colo., was aimed at helping communities whose services were overburdened by a sudden population explosion brought on by energy development, such as the opening of a coal field.

As reported by the Senate Environment Committee June 27, the bill provided $750 million in loans and grants to municipalities and Indian tribes over five years, with $150 million available annually. Each year, $15 million would go for grants; $15 million for emergency loans, loan guarantees or grants; and the remaining $120 million for a revolving loan fund run by state governments.

But the bill ran into trouble when it was referred to the Senate Governmental Affairs Committee. There, Energy Subcommittee Chairman John Glenn, D-Ohio, was skeptical about the need for grants. He reasoned that boom towns would develop local tax bases large enough to repay loans easily.

Advocates of grants replied that some communities would never realize sufficient tax revenue to build the hospitals, sewers and other facilities necessary to accommodate the increased population.

Glenn's subcommittee voted to knock out loans. But after negotiation with supporters of the Hart version, Glenn softened his position. At his behest, the full Governmental Affairs Committee Sept. 28 agreed to allow grants on a case-by-case basis if the secretary of commerce determined that there was "no practical alternative."

But backers of the Hart version were not satisfied with this either. They argued that the "no practical alternative" phrase did not adequately spell out the criteria.

"Some states prohibit going into debt," said a Hart staffer. "Does this mean that they have to try to change their constitutions to qualify?"

The staffs of the two committees tried to work out a compromise in the hectic closing days of the session, but failed.

A plan in the House to seek passage of a companion bill (HR 13559), which resembled the Hart version, also failed.

Observers said inland energy impact legislation likely would be enacted in 1979, when there would be time to fashion a compromise in the dispute over grants. ▮

Chattahoochee River

Acquisition of 6,300 acres for national parkland along Georgia's Chattahoochee River was authorized by Congress Aug. 3.

The bill (HR 8336 — PL 95-344) earmarked $73 million to purchase riverfront tracts near Atlanta.

The House passed the bill Feb. 14, by a 273-79 vote. *(Vote 49, p. 14-H)* It had been reported by the Interior and Insular Affairs Committee Sept. 8, 1977 (H Rept 95-598).

The Senate Energy and Natural Resources Committee reported the bill May 12 (S Rept 95-812), and it passed the Senate, amended, July 21. The House agreed to the Senate bill, with an amendment, July 31, and the Senate agreed to the House amendment Aug. 3, clearing the measure for the president. ▮

Liquefied Energy Gases

A bill to provide tougher federal regulation of the land transport and storage of highly explosive liquefied natural and petroleum gases passed the House in 1978, but the Senate took no action on the proposals.

The bill (HR 11622) was approved by the House Sept. 12 by voice vote and was substituted for the text of S 1895, a minor Senate-passed bill. There was no Senate companion to HR 11622, however, and the Senate declined to consider any of the House provisions on such topics as safety requirements for liquefied natural gas (LNG) storage facilities and reporting requirements for gas pipeline operators. Thus the bill died at adjournment.

Background

Liquefied petroleum gas (LPG) accidents in Spain and Mexico claimed about 200 lives, plus increasing publicity about the dangers of LNG had focused attention on the potential hazards of the fuels.

A report by the General Accounting Office (GAO), released July 31, detailed some of the dangers.

LNG. LNG is natural gas that has been reduced to −261 degrees Fahrenheit and the compressed 1/600th of its volume to make it easier to store and transport. The United States imported LNG from Algeria. Surplus domestic natural gas also was turned into LNG during slack periods so it could be stored for later use. Tank trucks sometimes carried LNG from storage facilities to terminals where it was distributed for home heating or industrial use. When the gas was needed, the LNG was regasified and fed through existing pipelines.

In 1978, LNG provided less than 1 percent of the nation's energy, but the Department of Energy predicted that by 1985 21 percent of the gas consumed in the United States would be imported.

There were two facilities receiving LNG ships from abroad — one at Everett, Mass., in the district of Edward J. Markey, D-Mass., cosponsor of the legislation, and the other at Cove Point, Md.

A typical tanker carried up to 125,000 cubic meters of LNG, and larger, 33-million-gallon ships were expected to be in service soon. There also were 121 "peak shaving" facilities — used to liquefy and store gas during slack periods — with a combined storage capacity of 2 million cubic meters. Nearly all of them were located in or near highly populated areas, according to the House Commerce Committee.

The committee estimated that if Energy Department estimates were true, three large LNG tankers would be entering U.S. waters on an average day and three to five new LNG storage facilities would have to be built. HR 11622 did not deal with LNG shipping.

LNG is heavier than air at -261 F, but becomes lighter than air when it warms to -160 F. "As it warms," the committee said, "LNG vaporizes and expands its volume significantly — eventually reaching 600 times its liquid volume — and moves with the prevailing winds. The drifting gas cloud that results could be ignited by any spark — even one as small as that caused by an auto horn."

The committee estimated that an accident involving release of 125,000 cubic meters of LNG from a typical tanker could produce a flaming cloud 20 miles long and five miles wide.

An LNG accident in Cleveland in 1944, caused when a storage tank gave way, killed 128 persons, injured 300 and caused $7 million in property damage.

A spokesman for the American Gas Association asserted that the structural problems that caused the 1944 accident had been corrected and that all plans for future LNG import facilities called for them to be located in remote areas. "The safety record speaks for itself," he said.

He said LNG facilities were reviewed by the Department of Energy. "We feel [the bill] is duplicative of regulations and authority already in current law," he said.

LPG. LPG is the name given to a whole category of fuels, including propane and butane, used for home heating, crop drying and other purposes. LPG normally was shipped by truck, rail or barge to one of the nation's 8,000 storage facilities where it was redistributed to consumers. LPG is heavier than air. If it were released, it would form a highly flammable cloud clinging to the ground and sinking into sewers and subway tunnels.

The committee said that 9,000 gallons of LNG or LPG, the amount carried by the average truck, could fill 110 miles of a 6-ft. sewer or 15 miles of a 16-ft. subway tunnel, "turning them into subterranean bombs of enormous destructive potential."

Some LPG explosions erupt "with enormous power creating a fireball and mushroom cloud which resembles that associated with nuclear explosions," the committee said. "The force of the explosion can propel a ruptured tank like a rocket, trailing liquid flame hundreds of feet."

The committee said the fact that LPG storage facilities often included more than one tank increased the danger.

In testimony before Congress, Francis H. McAdams, a member of the National Transportation Safety Board, reported that although LPG was involved in only 9.7 percent of all reported liquid gas pipeline accidents in the previous nine years, it caused 65.5 percent of the reported deaths, 48 percent of the injuries and 30.5 percent of the property damage.

The committee said that there were 225,000 miles of pipe used to transport LPG.

Natural Gas. The Commerce Committee also addressed the hazards of natural gas, which was distributed to 44.6 million residential customers and accounted for more than 40 percent of domestic industrial energy consumption.

The committee said that about 750,000 natural gas leaks were reported each year. In 1976, 1,500 of those resulted in accidents that caused 63 deaths and 366 serious injuries.

Of the 1.4 million miles of natural gas lines in service, about 90 percent were built after 1971, the year the natural gas Pipeline Safety Act of 1968 (PL 90-481) went into effect. As a result, most lines were not covered by federal safety regulations, the committee said. *(Background, Congress and the Nation, Vol. II, p. 813)*

Information about pipelines built before 1971 was sketchy, but experts had speculated that some were built in the late 1840s, the report said, noting that one company was using pipe that it bought second-hand and installed 116 years before.

"Thus, the very pipeline which, due to age and less sophisticated technology at the time of installation, may be expected to present the greatest hazard, has not been subject to safety standards, and will not be required to be subject to such standards until an accident occurs," the report said.

The Gas Association spokesman said complying with the reporting requirements would be very expensive and that the cost would be passed on to consumers. He also questioned the value of the required data.

He said a committee provision requiring utilities to report all leaks they knew about or should have known about was ambiguous. "If they were known, they would have been reported," he said.

GAO Report

In a 6½ pound report, "Liquefied Energy Gases Safety," submitted to Congress July 31, the GAO warned that a major spill of liquefied energy gas (LEG) in a densely populated area, caused by accident, natural forces or sabotage, could be catastrophic. The report made a number of recommendations for improving the safe storage and transport of LEG.

The GAO said its findings were based on visits to 37 import, storage, shipyard, transportation and design facilities in the United States and Japan.

The President of the American Gas Association, George H. Lawrence, called the report "misleading" and said it "fails to present an objective picture."

"The facts show that LNG can be transported and stored safely and the potential hazards can be and have been anticipated in the design of LNG facilities and ships."

Storage

GAO investigators recommended that new large LEG storage facilities be located in remote areas because of the possibility of tank failure and that only those LEG storage facilities in remote areas be expanded in size or use.

The GAO recommended that storage tanks be in the ground, with the highest level of fluid below ground level, a procedure used in Japan, and that storage tanks be built and operated to standards similar to those applied to nuclear plants.

Congress, the report said, should enact legislation requiring armed guards at LEG facilities to prevent sabotage and extending federal authority to cover large LEG storage facilities not covered by federal regulation.

The GAO recommended that transportation of LEG through densely populated areas be banned unless delivery was impossible otherwise. Special care should be taken to keep trucks away from hazards such as overpasses, high-speed traffic and roadside abutments that might cause accidents, investigators said.

The report concluded that existing liability and compensation systems in the event of an accident did not provide enough incentives for safety.

The GAO recommended that Congress pass legislation that would require corporations transporting, storing or using large amounts of flammable materials to carry the maximum liability insurance available and that the corporations contribute to a federal hazardous materials compensation fund.

The legislation also should give the attorney general authority, on behalf of injured parties, to sue companies or persons responsible for incidents, and should allow injured parties to sue all companies in the corporate chain for all damages beyond those covered by insurance and the fund, the report said. In addition, the liability limits for owners and charterers of ships and barges carrying hazardous materials should be raised, investigators recommended.

The report also recommended establishment of an Energy Health and Safety Regulatory Agency, which would include the Nuclear Regulatory Commission; the pipeline safety aspects of fuel transportation on land, now handled by the Transportation Department; safety aspects of importing energy, now handled by the Energy Department, plus all of the safety responsibilities formerly carried out by the Federal Power Commission.

Congress also should consider including in the agency the safety regulation of LEG carried by truck and train, investigators said.

The agency should be completely independent of the Energy Department, or it could be included within the department if there were strong statutory provisions ensuring its independence, the report said.

House Committee Action

The committee reported HR 11622 May 15 (H Rept 95-1167), and authorized $13.5 million for the bill in fiscal 1979.

The committee noted that the 1968 act gave the Transportation Department responsibility for setting standards for the safe design, construction, operation and maintenance of liquid and gas pipelines and related facilities. But the committee accused the department of failing to "forcefully and effectively" carry out the law.

The department's Office of Pipeline Safety Operation, designated to carry out the program, had not had a permanent director for seven of the previous 10 years.

"Lacking effective leadership," the report said, "the office has tended to follow the path of least resistance, adopting industry 'consensus' standards, delaying entry into controversial areas, and generally avoiding facing up to the hard issues of public safety by adopting the most conservative interpretation of its authorities and responsibility."

The committee chided the department for failing to adopt standards for the siting, design, operation and maintenance of LNG facilities.

To deal with the problem, the committee bill stipulated that no one could serve as acting director of the office for more than 180 days. If a permanent director were not appointed by then, the secretary of transportation had to personally administer the office. The panel said it would exercise "vigorous oversight" to assure the provision was met.

Setting Standards

To deal with the LNG standards question, the bill required the transportation secretary to approve construction of all new LNG facilities, but did not give the secretary authority to select the sites.

Six months after passage of the bill, the secretary would have to establish standards for the location, construction, operation and maintenance of new LNG facilities. Within nine months of enactment, minimum standards regarding the operation of existing LNG facilities would have to be established.

The bill spelled out criteria the secretary was to use in setting standards. In developing operating standards, for example, he was directed to consider, among other things, security measures to prevent sabotage, a problem of some concern to the panel.

In testimony before a Commerce subcommittee, Monte Canfield Jr., director of GAO's Energy and Minerals Division, asserted that security measures and physical barriers at LNG and LPG facilities "are generally not adequate to deter even an untrained amateur saboteur.... [S]torage tanks are vulnerable to sabotage efforts within the known capabilities of terrorist groups."

Under existing law, violations of LPG regulations were dealt with in the criminal code, which had made prosecution difficult because criminal negligence had to be proved, congressional aides said.

The committee bill made the transportation and storage of LPG subject to the same sections in the civil code as natural gas, which, the aides said, would make prosecution easier.

The committee said the change was recommended by GAO and the National Transportation Safety Board, and "corrects a deficiency in the law which has allowed this highly volatile product to be regulated as other, much less dangerous, petroleum products."

Natural Gas

On natural gas, the committee did away with the grandfather clause, which exempted many pipelines from the 1968 act.

HR 11622 authorized the transportation secretary to order pipeline operators to remove hazards in lines.

The bill also required all operators to provide information on line safety, such as location, age, type, the material transported and geological conditions. The secretary was authorized to exempt some operators from reporting if the requirements imposed undue administrative and financial hardships or if the costs exceeded the safety benefits.

Noting that half of all pipeline accidents were the result of construction activity, the committee required that operators file a detailed description of their lines with the local or state agencies that approved construction.

Leaks. The bill also required operators to report all pipeline leaks they knew about or should have known about.

"The committee adopted this requirement after hearing evidence that operators frequently have reason to believe that leaks are occurring or are likely to occur in certain parts of their facilities, but take no action until the existence of the leak is actively brought to their attention. . .," the report said. "The committee intends this requirement to serve as an inducement to such operators to aggressively seek out and correct leaks."

According to Energy Department figures supplied by the committee, 216 billion cubic feet of gas were lost each year through leaks, at an annual cost of $430 million.

The statistical information on leaks would be compiled to enable the secretary to order corrective action before an accident by knowing what type of pipe was the most accident prone, the report said.

Liability

Because the damages associated with an LNG explosion could be so great, the committee required the secretary to determine whether companies had adequate insurance. The secretary could then order LNG facility operators to maintain an adequate degree of financial responsibility.

The committee said it adopted the provision "out of concern that the public be protected against catastrophic losses, but at the same time the committee does not intend to impose impossible financial burdens upon persons engaged in the production, storage and transportation of LNG."

Minority, Dissenting Views

In minority views filed with the report, five Republican members objected to the reporting requirements on LPG and natural gas pipelines. The provision would require utilities to report and gather "a massive amount of essentially useless information at great expense to the consumer," they said.

Floor Action

The House passed HR 11622 Sept. 12 by voice vote. The bill had been slated to reach the floor July 26, but it was pulled off the schedule because its sponsors — John D. Dingell, D-Mich., chairman of the Commerce Subcommittee on Energy and Power, and Markey — objected to the Rules Committee's action on the bill.

The Rules Committee voted July 25 to bar a conference on HR 11622 and the minor Senate-passed bill (S 1895), but reversed itself Aug. 10 and approved a rule allowing the House to substitute the provisions of HR 11622 for those of S 1895, a routine reauthorization for the Department of Transportation's Office of Pipeline Safety. The House made the substitution after passing HR 11622.

As passed by the House, HR 11622 authorized the secretary of transportation to require natural gas pipeline operators to remove hazards in their lines and to provide information on line safety, such as location, age, type of material transported and geological conditions. The bill also required operators to report all pipeline leaks they knew about or should have known about.

Under the bill, the transportation secretary was authorized to approve construction of all new LNG facilities. However, the secretary was not given the authority to select sites. The secretary was also directed to establish standards for the location, construction operation and maintenance of new LNG facilities within six months after the date of enactment. The bill authorized $13.5 million in fiscal 1979 to carry out the program.

Supporters argued that the tougher safety regulations were needed to prevent catastrophic explosions and fires that could result from ignition of LNG or LPG truck or storage tank leaks.

They also argued that the poor condition of a large percentage of natural gas pipelines made the bill's pipeline leak reporting requirement necessary.

Opponents of the legislation countered that the natural gas industry has maintained an exemplary safety record. They argued that pipeline leaks were easy to spot and that the bill would force gas companies to pass on the cost of what they called the bill's onerous reporting requirements to consumers.

The House passed HR 11622 by voice vote after adopting an amendment by Robert W. Edgar, D-Pa. It required the transportation secretary to conduct a study to determine whether LPG storage and transportation facilities should be covered by the act. The amendment required the secretary to report to Congress within one year of enactment.

Provisions

As passed by the House, HR 11622:

Title I — Fuel Transportation

- Required the secretary of transportation, upon determining that a pipeline was hazardous, to require the operator to remove the hazard.
- Spelled out the criteria the secretary was to use in determining whether a pipeline was hazardous.
- Required the secretary to issue regulations requiring pipeline operators to prepare general descriptions of their facilities, including the physical characteristics of the facility and the materials transported.
- Required operators to submit a detailed description of the location of their pipelines to state and local authorities who approved construction activities; in lieu of submitting a description, authorized operators to participate in a system whereby they would be notified of construction activity in the area of their lines.
- Required the secretary to exempt operators from the reporting requirements if he found the financial or administration burdens of the requirements would not justify the benefit or if complying would significantly increase consumer rates, provided the exemption did not endanger public health or safety.
- Within three years of enactment, required the secretary to set up a data processing system containing the information on pipeline location, reported leaks, accidents and incidents.

Reporting Leaks. Required pipeline operators to report all leaks, specifying their location, injury or property damage that resulted and corrective action taken. (Existing Department of Transportation regulations required that most of this information be provided.)

- Required the secretary to provide an exemption to the reporting requirements if the financial or administrative burdens of reporting did not justify the results.

LPG Transport. Placed the transportation by pipeline of liquefied petroleum gas (LPG) in interstate or foreign commerce under the jurisdiction of the act.

- Permitted the secretary to regulate any LPG storage facility with a capacity of 30,000 gallons or more or if used in conjunction with other facilities with a combined capacity of 30,000 gallons or more.
- Directed the secretary, within three months of enactment, to adopt interim minimum federal safety standards for pipeline facilities to bring them under the act.

Other Facilities. Authorized the secretary to regulate facilities or equipment other than pipelines used to transport gas on land.

Inspectors. Required that federal standards include minimum training and education requirements for pipeline inspectors.

- Beginning Dec. 31, 1981, barred the secretary from funding state programs unless the state demonstrated that it would use federal funds to train and educate employees.
- Required the secretary to determine the minimum number of pipeline safety inspectors needed by a state.

Authorization. Authorized $11.5 million in fiscal 1979 to carry out Title I. Of that, $4.5 million was designated as the federal share of the state certification program; $1 million for data processing, and $6 million for other sections.

Title II — Siting, Safety of LNG Facilities

- Defined a liquefied natural gas (LNG) facility as a storage tank, pipeline or other structure for transportation, storage, use or conversion of LNG in interstate or foreign commerce, but specified that the definition did not include structures or equipment on navigable waters.

Safety, Siting Standards. Required the secretary, within 180 days of enactment, to establish minimum standards for the location, design and construction and operation of any new LNG facility.

- Within 270 days of enactment, required the secretary to establish minimum standards for the operation of any existing LNG facility.
- Specified that no new LNG facility could be built or an existing facility expanded until the secretary determined that the construction, operation and maintenance of that facility would meet the standards.
- Barred the secretary from approving construction of an LNG facility unless the applicant submitted a contingency plan detailing the steps to be taken in case of an LNG accident or supply interruption.
- Provided that the standards would not apply to construction of facilities if the application for approval had been filed before March 1, 1978; and specified that those would be considered existing facilities.
- Provided that only operations standards would apply to existing facilities; but if the capacity of an existing facility were to be expanded, the construction standards would apply to the expansion.
- Provided that all new facilities would be subject to all of the standards.
- Required the secretary, in determining minimum standards for new stationary facilities, to consider 1) how they would be used; 2) alternative locations; 3) existing and projected population, demographic characteristics and land uses of alternative locations; 4) physical aspects of each

location; 5) medical, legal and fire prevention capabilities of the location, and 6) costs of construction, operation and maintenance and the desirability of remote location.

- Required the secretary, in developing standards for the design and construction of any new LNG facility, to consider 1) thermal resistance and other characteristics of materials to be used in construction, 2) design factors, such as insulating concrete and vapor containment barriers, 3) characteristics of the LNG to be stored or converted, such as whether the gas was in a liquid or solid state, 4) public safety factors of one design compared to alternative designs and 5) directed that special attention be paid design elements intended to prevent and contain LNG spills.
- Required the secretary, in developing standards for the operation of any LNG facility, to consider 1) the condition, features, type of equipment and structure used in the facility, 2) fire prevention and containment equipment of the facility, 3) security measures to be used to prevent sabotage, 4) training techniques in regard to the equipment, 5) operation and security measures and 6) other factors pertaining to the safe handling of LNG.
- Specified that any standard would become effective 30 days after the date issued unless the secretary determined that an earlier or later date was necessary to better assure compliance.
- Permitted state agencies to adopt additional or more stringent standards for intrastate LNG facilities provided those standards were compatible with the federal minimum standards; but provided that no state could adopt or continue standards for interstate LNG facilities after the new federal standards became effective.

Financial Responsibility. Required the secretary, within nine months of enactment, to study the risks associated with LNG production, transmission and storage and the methods of assuring financial responsibility for those engaged in such activities, and to report to Congress with recommendations for legislative and administrative action.

- Authorized the secretary, if he felt that the operator of an LNG facility did not have adequate insurance or financial responsibility, to notify the operator, who would be allowed a hearing to show cause why an order should not be issued.
- Authorized the secretary, after the hearing, to order the person to maintain the required amount of financial responsibility.
- Provided that a person subject to such an order could seek judicial review in the U.S. Court of Appeals within 60 days after the order was issued.

Enforcement Provisions. Imposed a civil penalty of up to $50,000 for persons violating the standards and financial responsibility requirements.

- Imposed a criminal penalty of up to $50,000 or up to five years in prison or both for violation of the standards and financial responsibility requirements.

Authorizations. Authorized $2 million for fiscal 1979 for the standards and financial responsibility sections.

Title III — Miscellaneous

- Set a fine of up to $15,000 or a prison term of up to 15-years for any person who injured, destroyed or tried to injure or destory a pipeline facility used in the interstate transmission of gas, petroleum or liquefied gas.
- Provided that no one could serve as acting director of the Office of Pipeline Safety Operations or as acting director of the Materials Transportation Bureau of the Transportation Department for more than 180 days.
- Required the secretary to personally carry out the functions of the position if a director of the office or bureau were not appointed within 180 days after a vacancy occurred. ▮

Carter Water Policy, Projects Proposed

A national water policy designed to tighten executive branch control over federal spending for expensive dams and other water projects was announced by President Carter in 1978. But legislation spelling out the policy — expected to be the real test of how successful the president would be in persuading Congress to change the way it funded projects — had not been sent to Capitol Hill by year's end.

However, there were some preliminary skirmishes between Carter and Congress over water policy.

On Oct. 5, the president successfully vetoed the fiscal 1979 public works appropriations bill (HR 12928) because it contained funding for a number of projects that did not meet the environmental and economic criteria in his water policy. *(Public works appropriations, p. 154)*

The House sustained the veto and a compromise was eventually reached that was acceptable to the president.

But the victory was not total. In addition to proposing the water policy, the White House had also recommended that Congress fund three dozen new projects at a total cost of $718 million. The White House wanted Congress to provide the full cost of completing the projects in the bill. But Congress refused and appropriated only enough for one year, which was the traditional method of funding.

The Carter Proposals

Carter made his water policy announcement June 6. It drew limited praise from environmentalists, who had hoped for more changes, and from western governors, who preferred business-as-usual.

The administration proposal placed new emphasis on water conservation as a national goal and called for more state participation in the planning and funding of water projects.

Future authorizations for projects were to meet tougher criteria for enhancing conservation, providing national economic benefits and protecting the environment, according to the policy.

A new review panel was to provide for the first time an independent, uniform analysis of all federal water projects that would be available to budget makers and to the public.

However, Carter did not seek legislation to raise the interest rate used to compute benefits and costs of projects despite complaints from critics that the rate was artificially low and skewed analysis in favor of construction.

The Carter proposal also had no effect on the existing federal obligation to irrigate huge tracts of arid western land, usually at low cost to farmers. About 80 percent of all

Highlights of the Carter Plan

Here are the main points in President Carter's water policy, which was announced June 6. Carter said the administration would:

- Add water conservation as a specific component of the national economic and environmental objectives of water projects.
- Require consideration of a non-structural solution to a water resources problem whenever a dam or other structure was planned.
- Require throughout the government uniform procedures for analysis of benefits and costs. A manual would be developed by the Water Resources Council within 12 months.
- Establish a staff within the Water Resources Council to conduct independent reviews of the preconstruction plans for projects to ensure they were consistent with the government-wide standards and policy.
- Give priority to projects for annual funding or authorization if: 1) the benefit-cost ratio were high, 2) there were no adverse environmental consequences, 3) benefits were widely distributed, 4) water conservation was stressed and nonstructural solutions had been considered, 5) there was evidence of active public support, including support from state and local officials, 6) the state government was sharing more of the costs than required under the existing system, 7) there were no significant international or inter-governmental problems, 8) more federal and state costs were recovered from sale of water or power provided by the project, 9) the project complied with relevant environmental statutes and 10) funding for fish and wildlife damages was provided to the state at the same time the project was constructed and in sufficient amounts.

Cost Sharing

- Require, with appropriate legislation, that states share in the costs of construction of federal water projects authorized in the future. The state share would be 10 percent for projects that provided water supply, hydroelectric power or other saleable resources, and five percent for projects, such as flood control, where nothing saleable was provided. For projects authorized, but not yet built, a state contribution would mean "expedited executive branch consideration and priority for project funding." Soil Conservation Service projects would be exempt from the cost-sharing requirements.
- Equalize cost-sharing for structural and nonstructural flood control alternatives. The federal government would pay 80 percent of nonstructural solutions even though states usually supply land and easements, a large part of the costs of a non-structural project. Without this equal treatment, states would choose a structural alternative over a non-structural alternative because it would require a lesser contribution from the state.
- Direct all federal agencies and departments that administer programs that affect water supply or consumption to encourage conservation.
- Require that new and renegotiated contracts for irrigation or other water from the Bureau of Reclamation be for five years, not 40 years as had been the practice, and that operation and maintenance costs be recovered in the new contracts. More attention would also be paid to who qualified for subsidy or having debts forgiven under the "ability to pay" clause in existing law.
- Allow, with appropriate legislation, states the option of charging more than cost for federally supplied municipal and industrial water.
- Increase, with appropriate legislation, from $3 million to $25 million the grants available each year to states for water planning on a 50-50 matching basis.
- Authorize, with appropriate legislation, $25 million in annual grants to states for technical assistance in water conservation programs. States would match the funds on a 50-50 basis.
- Establish a task force of federal, state and local officials to continue to address water-related problems.
- Require federal agencies to work promptly to inventory and quantify federal reserved and Indian water rights.
- Direct agencies to request funds for mitigation of environmental damage at the same time construction and other funding is requested.
- Accelerate implementation of Executive Order No. 11988, which required agencies to protect flood plains and discourage flood plain development.
- Direct the secretaries of army, commerce, interior and housing and urban development to reduce flood damages by acquiring flood-prone land when it would be consistent with primary program purposes.
- Direct the agriculture secretary to improve watershed programs of the Soil Conservation Service by working with the Fish and Wildlife Service, encouraging land treatment of soil erosion instead of structural solutions and conducting periodic post-project monitoring.

water consumed in the United States was used for irrigation in the West.

Little incentive was provided in the policy for better management of groundwater supplies by western states, a concern of federal officials. Depletion of groundwater reservoirs, along with wasteful irrigation practices, were seen by conservationists as highly inconsistent with the growing demand for the West's limited water supply.

But western governors, upset at possible federal infringement on traditional state water rights, talked Carter out of anything other than promises of more federal cooperation and assistance in state water management.

The mild tone of the policy also reflected the administration's desire not to prompt a response anything like the uproar from the West and Congress that greeted the president's previous major water project proposal — a 1977 "hit list" of 30 water projects that he wanted killed. *(Background, 1977 Almanac p. 650)*

Carter eventually reached a compromise with Congress in 1977 that stopped or phased out construction of 10 projects that had been on his original list. He also promised that the administration would study water problems and offer a new national policy before he tried to stop any additional projects.

To cool the West's reaction to the "hit list" and to the pending water policy, Carter in early 1978 sent Vice President Walter F. Mondale and Interior Secretary Cecil D. Andrus on a goodwill trip to the West, during which they promised that any new water policy would not infringe on the rights of states to manage and control their own water.

State Participation

The major legislative proposal in the policy was for states to share the costs of projects they wanted built. By providing up to 10 percent of construction costs, a state could buy a voice in the decision about which projects would be built first and in which order.

Andrus said the cost-sharing "would for the first time put the governors in the decision making process." Under the existing system, Congress generally made the decisions. Having states pay was expected to weed out controversial or less desirable projects from the federal budget.

For projects authorized after enactment of cost-sharing legislation, states would have to put up 5 percent of the cost of flood control projects and 10 percent of irrigation and hydroelectric projects. But no state would have to pay more than one quarter of 1 percent of its general revenues for any one project.

For already authorized projects, a contribution from a state would give a project priority in the administration's budget over other projects with no state funding.

The administration had considered requiring states to pay 25 to 50 percent of project costs, but pressure from the western governors and others led officials to scratch all but limited cost-sharing.

Benefit-Cost Analysis

Under existing law, the only projects built were those for which costs did not exceed national economic and environmental benefits.

The benefit-cost analysis of a project by the federal construction agencies was sent to Congress as justification for construction of a project.

Those seeking reforms in water policy had criticized the way the agencies calculated benefits and costs. In his message to Congress describing the water policy, Carter said that "in some cases, benefits have been improperly recognized, 'double-counted' or included when inconsistent with federal policy or sound economic rationale."

One of Carter's options for reform, which he did not choose, was to ask Congress to raise the discount and interest rates used to compute costs and benefits. The rate, just under 7 percent at the time, had fallen behind inflation and, because it was lower than the actual cost of money, weighted any benefit-cost analysis in favor of construction projects. The formula for the rate could increase up to .25 percent a year.

But Congress had been expected to resist any effort to change the discount rate. In his message to Congress, Carter said the existing formula for computing the discount rate was "reasonable."

But Carter did mandate that those seeking solutions to water problems consider conservation as a benefit. He also instructed that planners give non-structural solutions, such as buying a flood plain for recreation, equal consideration with structural alternatives, such as dams.

Details of how to carry out the directive were to be spelled out in executive orders and in a manual for government-wide benefit-cost analysis that the federal Water Resources Council was directed to issue within one year.

Conservation

The manual was to be one way the administration would define conservation.

The western states wanted to be sure that dams built to store water were considered to be conservation measures. Democratic Gov. Scott Matheson of Utah, chairman of the water committee of the National Governors' Association, said he wanted the administration to appreciate the "different kinds of problems faced by different parts of the country."

Generally, westerners thought water conservation meant using dams to store runoff during rainy seasons so the water was available in dry seasons. Easterners, plagued by century-old leaky water pipes, thought water conservation meant replacing or rehabilitating their water systems. Both groups wanted federal recognition of and aid for their versions of "conservation."

As part of the push for conservation, the policy called for authorization of $25 million for grants to states for water conservation programs. Another $25 million was to go to states for water planning. The grants were to be "seed money" for states and cities to begin coming up with ways to conserve water.

As another way to encourage conservation, the policy made proper conservation measures a condition for getting federal grants for sewage treatment, additional water supplies from federal projects and other federal aid.

Review Council

Having an analysis of water projects by the independent review panel was intended to improve executive oversight of the usually independent-minded construction agencies — the Army Corps of Engineers, the Interior Department's Bureau of Reclamation, the Agriculture Department's Soil Conservation Service and the Tennessee Valley Authority.

All of the agencies had different ways of computing benefits and costs and brought different biases to their analysis. The manual of new procedures was designed to

President Carter Backed 36 New Water Projects. . .

Following is a list of the 26 construction starts and the 10 planning starts for water projects that President Carter recommended Congress fund in 1978. The descriptions include funding actions — if any — taken on the projects by the House Appropriations Committee prior to Carter's announcement. In all except two cases, the San Juan harbor and Chicagoland projects, the descriptions include the expected total cost to the federal government of the projects.

Army Corps of Engineers

Planning Starts

Ardsley, N.Y. A flood control program in Westchester County. The project would provide channel improvement, levees, walls and other improvements along the Saw Mill River. The corps estimated that planning and building would cost the federal government $1.9 million. Benefit cost ratio was 1.02 to 1. The committee included $100,000 for the project.

Bassett Creek, Minn. Designed to provide flood control along Bassett Creek, a tributary of the Mississippi in the Minneapolis area, the project would require $9.2 million in federal funds to complete. Plans called for improvements to divert flood waters to golf courses, parks and other open spaces to protect homes, businesses and industries. Benefit-cost ratio was 1.4 to 1.

Chaska, Minn. The project, which would cost the federal government $11.8 million, would improve levees, create new pumping stations and create a flood bypass channel away from residential and commercial areas of Chaska, located on the Minnesota River in the south central portion of the state. Benefit-cost ratio was 1.08 to 1.

Chicagoland Underflow Plan, Ill. This project would provide tunnels, retention reservoirs, upgraded sewers and improved sewage treatment to handle storm water, which had caused sewer backup and flooding in Chicago and 52 adjacent communities. Advanced engineering and design costs were estimated at $7.7 million with no estimate given for construction costs. The committee included $1 million for the project. Benefit-cost ratio was 1.4 to 1.

Goleta and Vicinity, Calif. The project, which would cost the federal government $28.7 million to complete, would provide flood protection for the Goleta Valley area in Santa Barbara County. The project would involve channel improvements for a growing urban area subject to frequent severe flooding. Benefit-cost ratio was 1.3 to 1.

Kahoma Stream, Hawaii. This flood control project on the island of Maui would cost the government $4.3 million to complete. Improvements in the stream channel and construction of a levee and debris basin would provide protection for about 415 homes and numerous businesses. Benefit-cost ratio was 1.2 to 1.

Placer Creek, Idaho. The project, which would cost the federal government about $3.5 million to complete, would provide for construction of a reinforced concrete channel to protect about 55 acres of developed urban property in Wallace, in northern Idaho. Benefit-cost ratio was 1.04 to 1. The committee included $50,000.

Ponce Harbor, Puerto Rico. The $4.3 million project would improve navigation in Ponce Harbor, an open bay about midway on the south coast of Puerto Rico. The project would provide deeper water for ships carrying such cargo as lumber, chemicals and fresh fish. Benefit-cost ratio was 12 to 1. The committee included $100,000 for the project.

San Juan Harbor, Puerto Rico. Deepening and widening channels in the harbor, which handled 80 percent of all cargo entering or leaving Puerto Rico, was the main aim of this project. The proposal called for funding only the advanced engineering and design phase, which would cost $340,000. No estimate was given for construction costs. Benefit-cost ratio was 1.6 to 1.

Willapa River at Raymond, Wash. The project plan provided for construction of a levee system to protect the central business and residential district of Raymond, Wash., in the southwestern part of the state. Benefit-cost ratio was 1.3 to 1. The committee included $100,000 for the $1.8 million project.

Construction Starts

Barbers Point Harbor, Hawaii. The project would provide Oahu Island with its second deep draft harbor. In addition to alleviating congestion at Honolulu Harbor — about 16 miles away on the island's southwest coast — the project also would serve the Barber Point industrial complex. The federal cost was estimated at $46.6 million. The benefit-cost ratio at the time the project was authorized was 2.1 to 1. The committee provided $5 million.

Big South Fork National River and Recreation Area, Ky. and Tenn. The project would establish a national recreation area along the Big South Fork River and its tributaries in northeastern Tennessee and southeastern Kentucky. The $140 million estimated federal cost would pay for limited clearing of areas for primitive campgrounds, access roads and historical sites. Lodges and other facilities would be provided in adjacent areas.

Blue River Channel, Mo. This project would modify the channel along the Blue River in Kansas City for flood control. Cost to the federal government would be $114 million. Benefit-cost ratio was 1.6 to 1. The committee included $500,000 for the project.

Hartwell Lake (fifth unit), Ga. and S.C. Located on the Savannah River in Georgia and South Carolina, the project would consist of adding a fifth 66,000 kilowatt unit to the four existing generating units completed in 1962. Cost to the federal government was estimated at $18.4 million. Benefit-cost ratio was 2.2 to 1.

Honolulu Harbor, Hawaii. The project, which would cost the federal government $7.7 million, would deepen the channels in Honolulu Harbor, Hawaii's primary port, to improve navigation. Benefit-cost ratio at the time it was authorized was 12.2 to 1, although it was considerably lower, 5.7 to 1, using the current discount rate. The committee included $2 million for the project.

Hoonah Harbor, Alaska. The project would provide protection for the harbor situated on the northeast shore of Chichagof Island in southeast Alaska. It was designed to increase efficiency and reduce boat damage and maintenance costs in the overcrowded harbor. Federal costs

. . .House Committee Voted Funding for 25

were estimated at $5.5 million. The benefit-cost ratio was 4.5 to 1. The committee included $2 million.

Los Angeles-Long Beach Harbor, Calif. The project, which would cost the federal government $19.1 million, would provide dredging of a portion of Los Angeles Harbor adjacent to the city of Long Beach. Existing depths were inadequate to handle larger container and scrap metal vessels, the corps said. Benefit-cost ratio was 7.6 to 1. The committee included $5 million.

Lower Snake River Fish and Wildlife Compensation Plan, Idaho, Ore. and Wash. The $78.2 million plan would compensate for the losses in fish and wildlife that resulted from construction of four lower dams on the Snake River. The project provided for acquisition of more than 25,000 acres for easements, wildlife habitat and fish hatcheries. Benefit-cost ratio was 1.4 to 1. The committee included $5.2 million.

Metlakatla Harbor, Alaska. This $7 million project would increase the size and capacity of the harbor, located on Annette Island in southeastern Alaska. The small size of the existing harbor caused damage to vessels and docks, the corps said. Benefit-cost ratio was 1.2 to 1.

Milan, Ill. The project would involve construction of levees and improved drainage facilities to provide flood protection to the villages of Milan and Big Island. It would cost the federal government $11.2 million. Benefit-cost ratio was 3 to 1 at the time the project was authorized but was 1.6 to 1 under the current discount rate. The committee included $250,000.

North Nashua River, Mass. The project would provide flood protection to Fitchburg, Mass., the center of industry and commerce in central Massachusetts. Federal cost was estimated at $2.3 million. Benefit-cost ratio was 4.2 to 1 at the time the project was authorized and was 2.6 to 1 at current discount rates. The committee included $1.35 million for the project.

Point Place, Toledo, Ohio. The project, which would cost the federal government $6.3 million, would provide for construction of a seawall, a levee, pumping stations and storm drainage facilities for Point Place, a section of Toledo subject to flooding by Lake Erie. Benefit-cost ratio was 1.2 to 1.

Port Everglades Harbor, Fla. Deepening of the ocean entrance channel of Port Everglades Harbor for improved navigation was the primary purpose of this project, which would cost the federal government about $28.6 million. The port is located on the southeast coast of Florida. Benefit-cost ratio was 1.5 to 1. The committee included $2 million for the project.

Prairie du Chien, Wis. Flood control was the primary purpose of the project, which would cost the federal government about $4 million. The plan provided for flood proofing and land use controls plus evacuation and relocation of some residences and businesses. Benefit-cost ratio was 1.09 to 1. The committee included $500,000.

St. Lucie Inlet, Fla. Intended to stem beach erosion and to aid navigation, the project would cost the federal government about $5 million. Benefit-cost ratio was 1.5 to 1. The committee included $1.5 million for the project.

Two Harbors, Minn. The project would provide for dredging in the Two Harbors area on Lake Superior, 26 miles north of Duluth, to improve commercial navigation. The project would cost the federal government $260,000. Benefit-cost ratio was 6 to 1.

Winona, Minn. Flood protection for Winona, a community of 26,500 in southeastern Minnesota would be provided by the construction of levees and floodwalls. Cost to the federal government would be about $26 million. Benefit cost ratio was 2.1 to 1. The committee included $2 million for the project.

Bureau of Reclamation

Construction Starts

Oroville-Tonasket Unit, Chief Joseph Dam Project, Wash. This $55.3 million irrigation project would provide water for nearly 10,000 acres of apple orchards in north central Washington. Benefit-cost ratio was 1.9 to 1 at the time the project was first proposed and 1.5 to 1 using the current discount rate. The committee included $700,000.

Glen-Colusa Irrigation District, Calif. A $17 million federal loan would be required so the water district along the Sacramento River could reconstruct a 70-year-old pumping plant and rehabilitate its main canal. The committee included $4.75 million for the project.

Hidalgo and Willacy Counties, Dist. 1, Tex. An $11 million federal loan would be used to expand and rehabilitate the existing irrigation and drainage system in the lower Rio Grande Valley. The committee included $200,000 for the project.

Overland Ditch and Reservoir Co., Colo. The project called for construction of a new earthfill dam on Grand Mesa in western Colorado, which would require a $1.7 million federal loan. The new dam would replace an existing unstable one. The committee included $386,000.

Hidalgo County Water Improvement Dist. 2, Texas. The project would require a $16.1 million federal loan to replace a 70-year-old pumping plant that the bureau said was in dangerous condition. The committee included $1 million for the project.

Pleasant Valley County Water District, Calif. This irrigation project in Ventura County would require a $4.7 million federal loan. Private wells would be acquired and new ones drilled to conserve water and electrical energy lost in excess pumping. The committee included the entire cost of the project.

Rainbow Municipal Water District, Calif. This southern California irrigation project called for construction of a number of new reservoirs, pumping plants and pipelines. It would require a $9.9 million federal loan. The committee included $2.1 million for the project.

South Weber Water Improvement District, Utah. This irrigation project would enable the water district, located along the Wasatch Mountains, to rehabilitate and improve existing water delivery systems. The committee included the entire $1.72 million cost of the project.

West Bench Irrigation District, Mont. The project would convert the existing gravity irrigation system to sprinklers in a 5,660 acre area near Dillon. The change would allow conservation of water and electrical energy. A $3.1 million federal loan would be required.

make all agency analyses uniform. The new policy also would provide a check for the agencies' work, which would be reviewed by staff working under the Water Resources Council.

The review process was to apply to future authorizations and to already authorized projects not already under construction. The project review would be sent to the Cabinet secretary responsible for the construction agency. Then the secretary would send the report — along with the department report on the project and a budget request, if warranted — to the Office of Management and Budget (OMB), which would make final budget recommendations.

Carter's New Projects

On June 9, three days after the announcement of his water policy, Carter asked Congress to fund 36 new projects that would cost the federal government $718 million to complete. It was the first time in four years the White House had recommended new water project construction.

The $718 million represented the total construction costs for almost all of the projects. Carter sought fiscal 1979 outlays of $68.2 million, but asked for fiscal 1979 budget authority for the whole package.

Eliot R. Cutler, associate director of OMB for natural resources, energy and science, who announced the new projects at a news conference, noted that the administration's decision to seek lump sum funding for all of the projects was a "sharp departure from past practice."

"We are clearly flying in the face of congressional custom," Cutler said. "We are doing it on purpose."

Traditionally, Congress' annual appropriations for water projects covered only the amount that would be spent in that fiscal year.

"We propose that Congress . . . recognize up front what the total cost of projects will be, not indulge in artificial means of financing [water projects] — purchasing enormous mortgages that the American public cannot afford in the long run."

Cutler urged Congress to use the full-funding procedure in subsequent years "so that the full magnitude of the funding commitments involved in these projects will be very clear to the Congress and the people." Similar procedures were used to fund long-term defense and housing programs. He asserted that all of the new starts met Carter's criteria for water projects.

In determining which projects to fund, the administration put a priority on those that would produce hydroelectric power, Cutler said. However, only one project, Hartwell Lake in Georgia and South Carolina, was designed for that purpose. Other purposes emphasized were flood control to protect existing development in flood prone areas, navigation improvements to aid commerce and rural and agricultural improvement, he said.

No New Dams

No new dams were among the Carter starts. Most of the projects called for construction of levees, improvements in existing irrigation systems and harbor dredging to accommodate larger ships.

Among the new projects recommended by Carter were 17 construction starts for the Army Corps of Engineers, nine for the Bureau of Reclamation and 25 for the Soil Conservation Service. Ten new corps planning starts also were included.

Of the corps projects, 14 were designed for flood control, nine for navigation, one for hydropower, one for recreation, one to preserve fish and wildlife and one to stop beach erosion.

The Conservation Service projects, which would require $75 million to complete, would be selected during the year, Butler said. They would be built in small watersheds.

The corps projects would require $522.4 million of the $718 million total. About $120.5 million would go for Bureau of Reclamation projects, all of which were designed to improve irrigation.

Water Project Authorizations

While the administration was preparing its water policy and recommendations for new starts, the Senate had been at work creating its own list of water projects.

In early May, the Senate tacked about $2 billion in federal funding for about 100 waterway development, flood control and other waterway-related projects onto a controversial waterway user fee bill (HR 8309). Supporters of the bill, which imposed a tax on waterway users, favored addition of the projects because they thought they would garner additional support for the tax. *(Waterway user fee bill, p. 513)*

The Senate first agreed to adopt as a unit a $767 million package of authorizations and miscellaneous public works provisions passed by the Senate in June 1977 as part of an earlier version (S 790) of the user fee bill. That died when the House subsequently considered HR 8309, which it passed in October 1977. *(1977 Almanac p. 542)*

The Senate then went on to approve an additional 61 amendments — all by voice votes — authorizing another $1.7 billion for numerous public works projects.

A number of the authorizations approved by the Senate were so-called "phase one" projects — those that were still in the design and engineering stage at the Army Corps of Engineers.

Under a 1974 law (PL 93-251), Congress provided that water projects first had to be approved by Congress for design and study. They would later be approved for construction if found to be feasible by the Corps. *(Background, Congress and the Nation Vol. IV, p. 296)*

However, in anticipation of the administration's new water policy, OMB had been holding back many projects that had gone through phase one and been submitted to it for clearance before being sent to Congress.

House Action

When the Senate version of HR 8309 reached the House, the leadership there was faced with a problem. The House version had included only the barge fees, not the water projects. As a result, the House decided it had to consider the water resources section of the bill separately before the legislation could be sent to conference.

On June 8, Ray D. Roberts, D-Texas, chairman of the Public Works Subcommittee on Water Resources, introduced HR 13059, which authorized certain water projects contained in the Senate-passed waterway bill and a number of new ones.

Committee Bill

On Aug. 9, the Public Works Committee reported HR 13059 (H Rept 95-1462), which included a plethora of water

The Last Bill to Die in the 95th — and How It Happened

The last bill to be killed by the 95th Congress seemed like one of the unlikeliest candidates for an obituary.

Death came about 6:30 p.m. Oct. 15. Official cause was lack of a quorum in the House, which also forced the House to adjourn *sine die.*

Many assumed that tired members, aware that adjournment was near, simply went home. Indeed, those who wanted to see the bill die admit that luck and last-night confusion was on their side. But the fatal House blow to HR 10979, a water resources bill, was not nearly as accidental as it appeared.

Popular Projects

With $1.4 billion for 158 new projects scattered liberally through 46 states, the water resources authorization bill was the kind of legislation that had lots of friends in Congress.

Despite the "pork barrel" taint that water projects had acquired in the 95th Congress, earlier versions of the authorization bill had passed easily in both houses. All that remained was final approval of a compromise worked out informally by House and Senate conferees.

However, some diehard opposition to the projects remained in both House and Senate — as Mike Gravel, D-Alaska, discovered when he tried to bring up the conference agreement in the Senate about 5 a.m. Oct. 15.

Gravel tried to attach the water projects to an innocuous bill (HR 13514) naming a federal building in Shreveport after retiring Rep. Joe D. Waggonner Jr., D-La. But James Abourezk, D-S.D., and John A. Durkin, D-N.H., spotting an unidentified, thick stack of papers on Gravel's desk, leaped to their feet, ready to object.

In the confusing final hours of a congressional session, it is not unusual for a member to slip through one bill that could create controversy as a "rider" on another bill that is so innocuous no one pays attention to it.

Durkin had been watching for Gravel to make just such a move with legislation gutting executive branch authority to protect federal lands in Alaska.

Abourezk, the self-appointed liberal watchdog of the evening, had been watching for anyone to make just such a move on anything.

Both pounced when Gravel barely had the name of the Waggonner bill out of his mouth.

Gravel quickly explained that the sheaf of papers on his desk was the water resources bill, pointing out that both New Hampshire and South Dakota would get projects under the proposal.

But Abourezk objected to Gravel's unanimous consent request to bring up the bill.

'Just Being Ornery'

'He was just being ornery," an Abourezk aide said later, adding that Abourezk did not oppose any of the projects in the bill.

Abourezk's orneriness saved the day — temporarily — for Patrick J. Leahy, D-Vt., who had put a hold (a request that the majority leader not allow it to come up) on the bill. Leahy wasn't on the floor when Gravel made his move, but by the time he raced to the chamber Abourezk had everything under control.

Gravel later tried a second time to get unanimous consent to bring up the water projects. Leahy objected.

It looked like the projects were dead when the Senate began a recess at 12:30 p.m. Gravel told his aides working on the water bill to go home.

However, Leahy talked to Gravel and Majority Leader Robert C. Byrd, D-W.Va., asking them again to observe the senatorial courtesy of honoring his hold, just in case the Senate went back into a legislative session before final adjournment.

But about two hours later, Byrd called the Senate into session again to let Gravel bring up a reduced version of the water resources bill. By that time, Leahy had left town. So had Minority Leader Howard H. Baker Jr., R-Tenn., who also had a hold on the bill. Abourezk had decided against continuing his objection, leaving only William Proxmire, D-Wis., to fight the projects. But Proxmire earlier had withdrawn a hold he had on the bill, so he put up only a token fight.

Then, with Byrd's blessing, the water resources language was inserted in HR 10979, a bill authorizing pothole repairs. The pothole language was dropped completely, and the new water resources bill was passed and sent to the House.

Disappearing Representatives

That sent environmentalists, who opposed the water projects, scurrying to find their friends in the House. Because the bill had to be brought up there by unanimous consent or under suspension of the rules, which requires a two-thirds majority for passage, the environmentalists asked friendly members to be on the lookout for a unanimous consent request.

When Allen E. Ertel, D-Pa., made the request, Robert W. Edgar, D-Pa., and other opponents were ready with loud objections.

Ertel's next move was to try to pass the bill under suspension. Edgar demanded a roll call vote, knowing the House was dangerously close to not having a quorum. Members had begun to leave for home after passage of the tax cut bill, and the previous roll call had drawn only 11 more votes than were necessary for a quorum.

Just to be sure a quorum didn't show, "We urged members not to be there so we could sink this piece of legislation," said Brent Blackwelder of the Environmental Policy Center. Some members agreed to the environmentalists' request, although Blackwelder and others said they didn't know how many. Edgar was one who withheld his vote, casting it only when it became obvious a quorum wouldn't show.

The final 129-31 tally (five members voted present) was more than 50 short of a quorum. The House was forced to adjourn, ending any chance to revive the water projects bill or other legislation before the session ended. *(Vote 834, p. 236-H)*

Noting the better than 4-to-1 margin in favor of the bill, Blackwelder acknowledged, "We wouldn't have been able to win in the House" if a quorum had shown up for the vote.

projects incompatible with Carter's policies. The plan was for the House to pass HR 13059 and then to go to conference with it and HR 8309.

As approved by the Public Works Committee, HR 13059 included funds for 120 projects in 33 states and one territory. The committee estimated the cost at $1.29 billion, although the Congressional Budget Office put the price at $2.1 billion. Twenty-eight new construction projects were authorized. Eleven "Phase I" planning projects also were authorized. Most of the other funding was for alterations to projects already in the works.

The committee did not estimate the total cost of completing the projects, which environmentalists charged could run as high as $3.5 billion. In addition, many authorizations were for only part of a project so the authorized amount did not reflect the full commitment of funds necessary for completion.

The largest projects authorized by the committee were:

- Expanding Gulfport Harbor, Miss., at a total cost of $44.9 million — $26.5 million for dredging and $18.4 million for equipment. Opponents charged the bulk of the benefits for deepening the harbor would go to E.I. duPont deNemours and Co., which had a plant nearby.
- Building three electrical generators for the already constructed Libby dam project on the Kootenai River in Montana. Total cost would be $38 million. The generators would have a capacity of 76.4 megawatts.
- Constructing the Parker Lake Dam on Muddy Boggy Creek in Oklahoma. The project would supply power to the surrounding area and prevent flooding. It would cost $21.7 million.

President Carter's water policy fared poorly in the bill. The committee broke even its own less restrictive rules to accommodate certain projects.

In several cases it waived federal requirements that localities share costs of a project. And it declared benefit-cost ratios to be favorable for some projects even if costs exceeded benefits or if no benefit-cost study had been done.

FLOOR ACTION

HR 13059 went to the House floor Oct. 4 and passed on a 303-73 vote. It then went to a conference committee with the Senate. *(Vote 772, p. 220-H)*

The House Democratic leadership originally had planned to couple HR 13059 with HR 8309, the Senate bill that included water projects, waterway user fees and authorization for construction of a new Lock and Dam 26 on the Mississippi River near St. Louis.

However, Russell B. Long, D-La., chairman of the Senate Finance Committee, indicated that he would seek to attach the user fees and the Lock and Dam 26 authorization to a minor revenue bill and let the water projects stand on their own.

In the House debate, Rep. David E. Bonior, D-Mich., complained that 37 of the project authorizations had not received clearance from the Corps of Engineers as required.

COMPROMISE BLOCKED

The compromise water project authorization, which had been separated from the waterway user fees, did not come to the floor again until the last day of the session.

That day, Oct. 15, the Senate tacked the staff-negotiated compromise on the projects onto HR 10979, a highway repair bill. The Senate then passed the measure by voice vote.

But the bill died in the House several hours later when — in the last roll call of the session — a quorum failed to show up to vote on it. The vote was 129-31, more than 50 short of the number needed. *(Vote 834, p. 236-H)*

Environmentalists had opposed the projects as "pork barrel" legislation, and when the time came for the House vote, they urged members to stay off the floor. *(Details of bill's death, p. 765)*

The compromise version that eventually died incorporated virtually all major projects in the earlier House and Senate versions. The compromise was aimed at avoiding sending the bill to a time-consuming conference committee.

The compromise sought to mollify the measure's critics, including the administration, who opposed 37 projects because they had not been cleared by the Army Corps of Engineers. The compromise stipulated that those projects had to receive clearance before detailed planning or construction could begin.

Provisions

Among the projects authorized by HR 10979, as passed by the Senate, were:

- Libby reregulating dam power units, Mont.; $43 million.
- Gulfport Harbor, Miss., channel deepening; $31.1 million.
- Ft. Randall Dam-Lake Francis Case Project, S.D., a pumped storage hydro-electric facility; partial authorization of $30 million.
- Kaw Lake, Okla., water treatment and pipeline project, to supply water to town of Stillwater; $27 million to be repaid to federal government.
- Caesar Creek, Ohio, water supply project; $33 million to be repaid over 50 years.
- Sacramento River, Calif., flood protection; $25 million.
- Willow Creek, Ore., modification of existing flood protection project; $24 million.
- Parker Lake, Muddy Boggy Creek, Okla., dam project for water supply in central part of state; $28.4 million to be repaid.
- Tug Fork, W.Va., flood protection and dredging on the Big Sandy River; $100 million.
- Cleveland Harbor, Ohio, modification of existing widening and deepening program; $30.4 million.
- McNary Lock and Dam, Ore., powerhouse on the Columbia River; $75 million for initial authorization of the $548 million project.
- Jefferson City, Mo., flood control; $32.3 million.

Congress and Government

Concerned about the federal government's tarnished public image, Congress took actions in 1978 aimed at boosting public opinion about ethics and efficiency in all three branches of government.

The two biggest steps taken toward that goal were enactment of laws reforming the federal civil service system and requiring detailed public disclosure of financial holdings by members of Congress and top officials in the executive and judicial branches.

But in trying to deal with ethics problems involving some individual members, Congress may have done its image more harm than good.

A series of embarrassing accusations of criminal or unethical behavior involving members plagued both the House and Senate in 1978. Three House members were indicted on felony charges during the year, and one of them later was convicted. Four members were charged with ethical violations by the House Committee on Standards of Official Conduct, and the Senate Ethics Committee investigated two of its members for alleged unethical behavior.

The full Senate was not called upon in 1978 to act in either ethics case investigated by its committee or in a separate probe of South Korean influence-peddling. But the House conducted a bitter, divisive debate after its ethics panel recommended punishment for three members charged with wrongdoing in the South Korean scandal.

The committee recommended that the House reprimand California Democrats Charles H. Wilson and John J. McFall and censure Edward R. Roybal, D-Calif. However, after a debate featuring criticism of the committee's procedures and its differing recommendations for punishment, the House rejected a resolution to censure Roybal and instead voted reprimands — the lightest possible punishment — for all three Californians.

Looking beyond its internal problems, Congress heeded election-year constituent complaints about the federal bureaucracy by passing two bills aimed at making the federal government more efficient and reducing waste in federal programs. One was the civil service reform bill, which was heavily promoted by the administration. The other was a measure setting up inspector general offices in 12 federal agencies. The new inspectors general, appointed by the president, were given subpoena and investigatory powers to fight waste and fraud in government programs.

A Senate subcommittee also held hearings on a scandal involving massive fraud and abuse in the General Services Administration, but no other congressional action was taken on the issue.

The subcommittee, investigating newspaper reports that had exposed the scandal, found abuses involving false claims for benefits and services, collusion among contractors and bribery of officials. Investigators said the abuses could be traced to lack of competitive bidding and irregular auditing procedures within GSA, as well as the traditional practice of filling GSA jobs by political patronage.

Constitutional Amendments

Two constitutional amendments were debated at great length during 1978.

One of them, giving full representation in Congress to the District of Columbia, was approved after opponents in the Senate abandoned their effort to kill it by filibuster. The amendment still had to be ratified by 38 state legislatures before it could take effect.

Also debated was a resolution giving the states 39 more months to ratify the Equal Rights Amendment (ERA). Congress approved ERA in 1972 and gave the states seven years to ratify it. However, only 35 of the 38 states needed for ratification had passed the amendment by the end of 1978. The new deadline set by the resolution was June 30, 1982.

Government Operations

Several legislative proposals that would have made fundamental changes in federal government operations were not acted on in 1978 but were expected to be revived in the 96th Congress. They included:

- **Sunset.** Sunset legislation, which would require automatic termination of funds for most federal spending programs if they were not specifically reauthorized after a comprehensive congressional review every 10 years. A sunset bill passed the Senate shortly before Congress adjourned for the year, but the House did not act on it.
- **Lobby Disclosure.** A lobby reform bill, calling for more detailed disclosure of lobbying activities by interest groups. The House passed a lobby disclosure bill but the Senate Governmental Affairs Committee never resolved a philosophical split among its members to produce a bill.
- **Campaign Financing.** Legislation to provide public financing for congressional races. House Republicans and southern Democrats twice blocked floor consideration of a public financing bill during 1978.
- **Congressional Veto.** Bills to give Congress a veto over regulations written by executive branch agencies. Broad legislative veto proposals, which traditionally have been rejected by the Senate, made no headway in the House during 1978. However, the House did include a legislative veto provision in a bill authorizing funds for the Federal Trade Commission. The bill eventually died because of House insistence that the legislative veto remain in it.
- **Appropriation Bill Riders.** Limitations on legislative riders offered as amendments to appropriations bills. Although many members of the House and Senate agreed that there should be restrictions on adding legislative amendments to appropriations bills, there was no consensus on what the restrictions should be. Neither body acted on proposals to limit legislative riders.
- **Senate Job Bias.** A resolution to give Senate employees protection from job discrimination. A filibuster threat prompted sponsors to withdraw the bill, which would have

set up a mechanism for enforcing a new Senate anti-discrimination rule. The rule, scheduled to take effect in 1979, marked the first official protection for Senate employees from discrimination in hiring and firing.

The death of the resolution meant the Senate Ethics Committee had sole authority to enforce the rule when it took effect. But supporters of the resolution said its enforcement mechanism would have given Senate workers more protection than they were likely to get from the committee.

The House did not have any formal anti-discrimination rule.

- **Congressional Terms.** Resolutions limiting the number of terms members of Congress can serve. Although the Senate held hearings on several proposals, neither body showed much interest in term limitation bills. Similar proposals have been introduced — with no success — since the first Congress convened in 1789.

Televised Debate

Plans to begin televising House floor debates in 1978 were set back when the House Rules Committee decided it needed to come up with a more sophisticated broadcast system than the House originally had planned. The committee said a test system operated in 1977 produced poor pictures and sound, and House broadcasts were put off until the 96th Congress.

During 1978, television networks continued their battle to bring their own cameras into the House chamber. But the House leadership resisted network arguments and assured members that the cameras recording debate would be operated by House employees. The networks would be allowed to pick up a "feed" from the House-run broadcasts, the leadership said.

In the Senate, National Public Radio was permitted to broadcast floor debate of the Panama Canal treaties — the first time such broadcasts had been allowed. But there were no plans to broadcast other debates or to begin television broadcasts from the Senate.

Civil Service Reform

President Carter in March made civil service reform his top domestic legislative priority when he unveiled proposals to change the system. He said his plan would help fulfill his campaign promise to reorganize the federal bureaucracy and make it more responsive to the public.

Carter's plan — the most comprehensive reform of the system since the civil service was set up in 1883 — called for reorganizing the Civil Service Commission into two new agencies.

In addition, Carter proposed legislation that he said would put true merit in the civil service system by basing pay and job security on performance. Those and numerous other changes in the civil service were approved after months of intense administration lobbying, giving Carter one of the biggest legislative victories in his first two years as president.

Financial Disclosure

Although the ethics bill covered all three branches of the federal government, nearly all of the debate focused on how it would affect Congress.

The disclosure bill was the final piece of ethics legislation in a series of reform measures considered by the House and Senate in 1977 and 1978. A small but highly vocal group of House members managed to tie up the bill for months by threatening to use it as a vehicle for undoing a major reform in one of the earlier bills — the limit imposed on members' outside earned income.

House Democratic leaders considered passage of the financial disclosure bill essential as a *quid pro quo* for a House vote in 1977 raising congressional salaries. But they also wanted to keep intact the outside earned income limit.

The leaders put off House action until fall, when election-conscious members were unlikely to vote against the new ethics bill or for repeal of the previous ethics reform. The ploy worked well: An effort to repeal the limit was soundly defeated and the bill passed with no trouble.

—By Ann Cooper

Public Financing, Campaign Spending Bills

Support from some of the biggest names in Washington — including President Carter and House Speaker Thomas P. O'Neill Jr., D-Mass. — was not sufficient to move legislation calling for public financing of congressional elections in 1978.

Although Congress voted public financing for presidential races in 1974, efforts to extend the concept to congressional campaigns remained stalled on dead center.

Public financing seems to be one of those "good government" issues that draw widespread praise as an abstract concept but fewer votes as a concrete piece of legislation. "Support for public financing has always been very tentative," observed Rep. Edward W. Pattison, D-N.Y. "People make statements for it who are not really in favor of it."

A bill to establish public financing in Senate general elections fell victim to a filibuster in August 1977. A similar measure for House general elections was blocked in the Administration Committee in October of that year. And House backers failed in two parliamentary maneuvers in 1978 to attach a public financing proposal to campaign finance bills. *(Background, 1977 Almanac p. 798)*

One of those bills, HR 11315, contained another controversial feature that would lower limits on contributions and expenditures by parties and multicandidate political action committees (PACs). The bill was reported March 16 by the House Administration Committee over the strong criticism of Republicans who had expected a bill similar to the 1977 Senate-passed version (S 926), which made basically non-controversial changes in the Federal Election Campaign Act (last amended in 1976) concerning campaign reporting and disclosure requirements.

After the measure was reported by the committee, a coalition of Republicans and disgruntled Democrats combined to defeat the rule to allow consideration of the leadership-backed measure.

The 198-209 March 21 vote to defeat the rule on HR 11315 had two practical effects. First, it blocked consideration of the bill's provision to lower the limits on spending by parties and political action committees. Second, it killed any hopes of adding to the bill an amendment allowing public financing of House general election campaigns. *(Vote 142, p. 42-H)*

In a second attempt to secure a public financing measure, supporters of the concept then turned to a generally non-controversial Federal Election Commission authorization bill (HR 11983) as a vehicle for the public financing amendment. The House July 19 refused to approve a parliamentary maneuver that would have allowed floor consideration of the amendment. By a 213-196 vote on a procedural motion (H Res 1172), the House blocked consideration of public financing as an amendment to HR 11983. *(Vote 493, p. 140-H)*

Proponents of public financing had made no effort to win a favorable rule in the House Rules Committee, where they lacked majority support. Instead, they developed a complex alternative strategy, which hinged on defeating the rule for HR 11983 on the floor and then winning approval of a substitute that would have permitted their amendment.

The vote on H Res 1172 was billed as a clear indication of the strength of public financing forces in the House. "A vote on this rule," House Administration Committee Chairman Frank Thompson Jr., D-N.J., told his colleagues, "is tantamount to your position on public financing."

Committee Action on PACs Bill

Resisting Republican efforts to gut the bill, Democrats on the House Administration Committee March 16 reported the controversial campaign finance legislation (HR 11315 — H Rept 95-982) that would lower limits on contributions and expenditures by parties and multicandidate political action committees (PACs).

The vote to report the bill was 16-9, with South Carolina's Mendel J. Davis the only Democrat to join the Republicans in opposition.

Angry Republicans, viewing the lower limits as a direct threat to their ability to challenge entrenched Democratic incumbents, were particularly upset with the limits on party spending, which would reduce from $30,000 to $10,000 the amount national, congressional and state party committees combined could contribute directly to a federal candidate in an election year. The bill also would lower from $20,000 to $5,000 the total amount the same party committees could spend on behalf of a federal candidate in a general election for services such as polling and staff assistance. Transfers between party committees, allowed by existing law, would be prohibited if it was made as a contribution or expenditure for a candidate. National and congressional committees, which currently operated under separate contribution limits, would be combined under one limit.

An analysis of party contributions to House candidates in 1976 and a compilation of party finances for most of 1977 by the Federal Election Commission (FEC) show how seriously the Republicans could be crippled by the changes.

In 1976, 39 percent of the Republican House candidates received more than $10,000 from party committees. Only 11 percent of the Democratic candidates, in contrast, received at least $10,000 from party sources.

In 1977, while affiliated Democratic committees raised $8 million through most of the year, Republican committees raised more than three times as much, $24.3 million. The cash-on-hand disparity was even greater, with Republican committees enjoying a nearly 10-1 advantage over their Democratic counterparts, $8.2 million to $867,000. *(Chart, next page)*

Republicans were caught off-guard when the controversial bill was unveiled by the committee March 4. They had expected a bill similar to the 1977 Senate-passed version (S 926), which made basically non-controversial changes in the Federal Election Campaign Act.

The White House was kept apprised during drafting of the House bill, but the controversial section on party and PAC limits was devised solely by Democrats on the committee and its majority staff.

While Republicans were initially surprised by the contents of HR 11315, they reacted quickly with a barrage of criticism. Party leaders like House Minority Leader John J. Rhodes, R-Ariz., and Republican National Committee Chairman Bill Brock denounced the bill as a blatant Democratic power grab and a reaction to Republican fund-raising successes that threatened the survival of the party.

No abuse had been shown under the existing law, they claimed, charging that the Democrats were trying to change the rules in the middle of the election.

"It's incredibly piggy," concluded Rep. Bill Frenzel, R-Minn. "It's a punitive, anti-Republican bill."

Democratic proponents of the legislation contended that the low limits provided a needed curb to increasing expenditures by the parties and special interests in House and Senate races. "The presidency can no longer be bought, but House and Senate seats can," said committee Chairman Thompson.

Democrats cited the proliferation of PACs — up from 608 at the end of 1974 to 1,261 in October 1977 — and increases in PAC and party spending the last two years as evidence that concentrated amounts of big money in House races was increasing.

They noted that interest group spending rose from $12.5 million in congressional races in 1974 to $22.6 million in 1976, according to Common Cause, and that an FEC survey covering most of 1977 found that $23.6 million had already been collected by PACs. *(Chart, below)*

Party spending also was getting out of hand, proponents of HR 11315 said, arguing that the 1977 special elections were little more than auctions. According to FEC figures, Republican Party committees contributed more than $400,000 to House candidates in 1977, compared to $27,000 by Democratic committees. Republican candidates won three of four special elections, all seats previously held by Democrats.

Committee staffers added that the existing limits for parties and PACs never were intended to be applied without public financing. As it is, one committee staff member remarked, "The law is one big loophole."

The charge that the Democrats were trying to change the rules in midstream concerned some party members, but not Thompson, who claimed: "We're never in the middle of a game. We have two-year terms and we're constantly running."

Political Action Committee Receipts, 1977

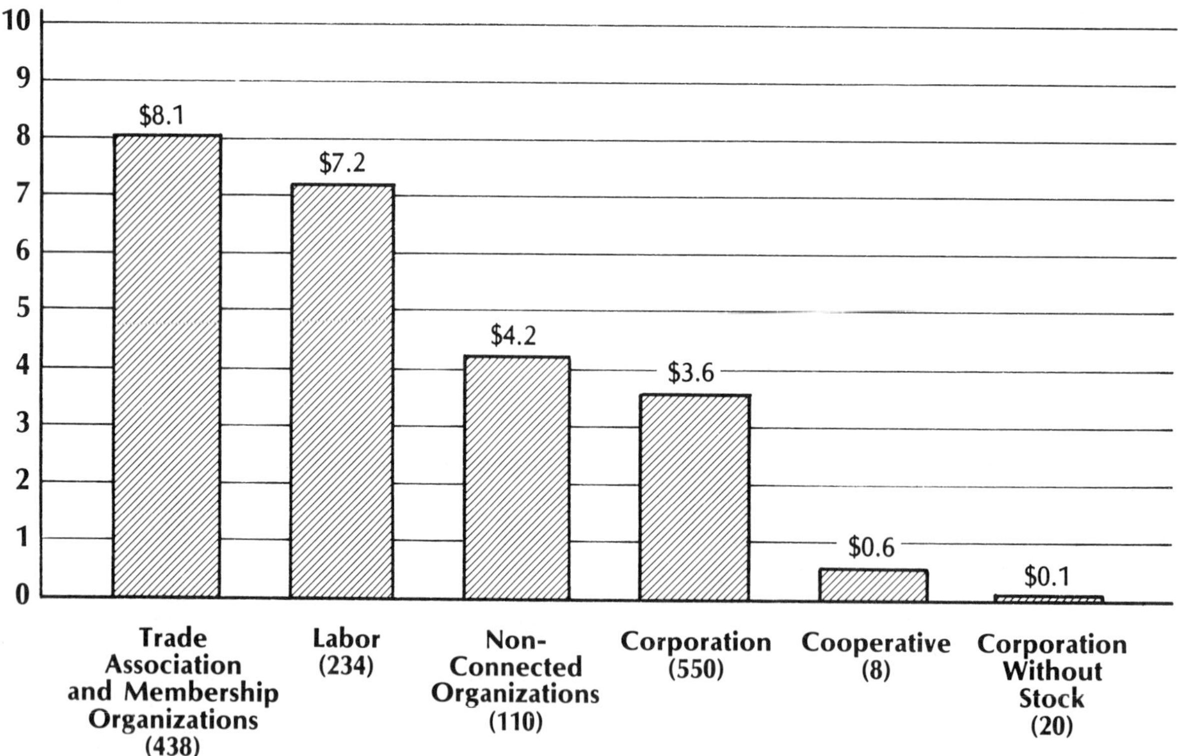

NOTE: Receipts are adjusted to subtract transfers of funds between affiliated committees. Figures are as of Sept. 30, 1977, for committees filing quarterly reports and Nov. 30, 1977, for committees filing monthly reports. In parentheses are the number of PACs in each category.

SOURCE: Federal Election Commission

Still there was the feeling among some Democratic members of the committee that the drive for such a controversial campaign measure in the midst of an election year might recoil against the Democrats. "The timing is terrible," Rep. Edward W. Pattison, D-N.Y., told Congressional Quarterly. "My opponent will accuse me of taking money away from him."

Indeed, Republicans gained an unusual ally when Common Cause announced it opposed the bill. Common Cause feared that the Democrats' proposal would polarize the House on the campaign finance issue, dimming the chances for winning needed Republican votes for a public financing provision they sought to be added to the bill on the House floor. "It's over-partisan," remarked Common Cause Vice President Fred Wertheimer. "They played into the hands of the opponents of public financing."

Democratic Dominance

Throughout the sessions, it was obvious that Democrats controlled the committee. Although Republicans offered an even 100 amendments during the five-day markup, they were unable to make any substantive changes in the bill.

The dominance of the Democrats was evident on the first vote, a motion by Charles E. Wiggins, R-Calif., to delay markup until several days of hearings had been held. His motion was defeated on a straight party-line vote, 8-16. Other Republican-backed amendments lost by a similar margin, with the key amendment to restore the existing party and PAC limits to the bill losing by a vote of 9-13. Mendel Davis was the only Democrat to bolt and join the Republicans.

Although the Republicans fought hard to restore the party contribution and expenditure limits, they spent comparatively little time defending the proposed cuts in PAC contributions from $10,000 to $5,000 per candidate in an election year. In part it was probably due to a realization that the reduction would apply to both labor unions and corporate PACs, although traditional "non-partisan" labor efforts such as voter registration and get-out-the-vote drives were still permissible. Also, it was becoming apparent to Republicans that incumbents, primarily Democrats, were the main beneficiaries of PAC contributions.

This was underlined by an FEC survey of PAC spending in 1977 that showed that only one category of multicandidate committees, the non-connected PACs, had given a majority of its contributions to Republican candidates. Non-connected PACs include political committees such as Ronald Reagan's Citizens for the Republic. Other categories, including corporate PACs, had given a majority of contributions to Democratic candidates. *(Chart, p. 772)*

In addition to halving the amount PACs could contribute to candidates, the committee voted for stricter requirements governing the creation of PACs. To qualify as a multicandidate committee with the $2,500 per election contribution limit ($5,000 total in an election year), HR 11315 called for a PAC to have at least 50 contributors and make contributions of at least $500 to five or more candidates within a two-year period. Existing law required only that contributions be made to five candidates without a threshold figure. Democrats claimed the stricter requirements would curb the creation of bogus PACs designed to aid only one candidate.

While attention focused on the controversial contribution and expenditure limits, most of HR 11315 dealt with simplifying candidate and committee reporting requirements and increasing the permissible activity of political parties.

The bill would permit state and local party committees to pay the costs of certain campaign materials — such as buttons, bumper stickers and posters — without counting them as a contribution or expenditure; would allow a state party committee to spend either $20,000 or two cents multiplied times the state's voting age population, whichever is greater, on behalf of the party's presidential candidate; and would entitle party committees to the same postage rates as qualified non-profit organizations.

Except for the section revising party and PAC contribution and expenditure limits, HR 11315 was similar to S 926, which passed the Senate Aug. 3, 1977, by a vote of 88-1.

House Action on Public Financing

The direct focus of House floor action on HR 11315 was not on the spending limits provisions, but rather, on the attempt to add the public financing amendment to the bill. That attempt was blocked on March 21, when the House voted 198-209 to defeat a rule that would have allowed consideration of the amendment. *(Vote 142, p. 42-H)*

The vote was a defeat for the Democratic House leadership, which had actively promoted the bill; Common Cause, which had made public financing its top legislative priority; and the Carter administration, which, although staying on the sidelines in the House struggle, had included public financing as part of its package of election law revisions.

Assessing Blame

In assessing blame for the defeat, public financing proponents and the Democratic leadership pointed fingers at each other.

Common Cause officials claimed that in reporting a bill that cut back party contributions to federal candidates from $30,000 to $10,000 and PAC contributions from $10,000 to $5,000, the House Administration Committee had created a highly partisan, polarized atmosphere. It was impossible to win Republican support for public financing, they claimed, when the bill contained a provision that Republicans viewed as a thinly veiled effort to neutralize their fund-raising advantage.

"The whole partisan squabble undercut us," claimed Michael Cole, the legislative director for Common Cause.

Public-financing supporter Abner J. Mikva, D-Ill., tended to agree with the Common Cause assessment, charging that HR 11315 had emerged from committee as a "dirty, sullied-up vehicle" for public financing. "A majority of the Democrats were talking with each other," he said of the controversial provisions, "but ignored the minority of Democrats and the Republicans."

Another supporter, Barber B. Conable Jr., R-N.Y., reportedly had lined up about 25 Republicans to vote for the public financing amendment, but Conable himself objected to the "partisan" environment in which the bill was being considered and joined other Republicans in opposing the rule.

House Speaker Thomas P. O'Neill Jr., D-Mass., Majority Whip John Brademas, D-Ind., and House Administration Chairman Frank Thompson Jr., D-N.J., all countered criticism by claiming the defeat was a rejection of public financing, which was viewed by most Republicans as an incumbents' protection measure and by many Democrats as a boon for challengers.

Most newspaper editorials around the country were lambasting the bill as a blatant Democratic power grab. Even Thompson's hometown paper, the *Trenton Times,* editorially condemned it as a "legislative 'dirty trick.' "

In an effort to defuse some of the controversy, Thompson on March 18 offered to restore party spending to its existing level. "I hope that my amendment," he wrote, "will now close the sideshow and allow us to get back to the serious work of voting on an election reform law that includes partial public financing. . . ."

But for Republicans the Thompson offer was not enough, since it did not restore the provision allowing transfers of funds between different party committees.

And in any case most Republicans were in no mood to accept the bill in any form. "The way the initial bill was dropped on us," said Bill Frenzel, R-Minn., "we were past trusting."

House Republicans caucused before the vote, discussed the situation, and agreed to oppose the rule.

Debate

In the floor debate which preceded the vote, Republicans focused their criticism on the "extraordinary and irresponsible" process in which the bill was developed, citing the spending provisions as anti-Republican and attacking Democratic "steamroller" tactics that had brought the bill to the floor less than three weeks after it was unveiled. "This is a bill that never should have been born," concluded Rhodes.

Two Democrats also spoke against the rule, B. F. Sisk of California and Mendel J. Davis of South Carolina. Davis, the only Democrat on the committee to vote against reporting HR 11315, charged that the bill was an indictment of the Democratic Party. "It says," he told the House, "that our party has not done its job in fulfilling its obligation to raise money."

Democratic backers of HR 11315 argued that the issue of public financing was worthy of House consideration and that the bill would be brought up under an open rule, permitting Republicans to offer any amendments they wanted. Besides, there were needed, non-controversial reforms in the bill, they added, such as a reduction in the number of campaign financial reports a candidate had to file, an elimination of random audits of candidates and improved enforcement mechanisms within the Federal Election Commission. ". . .Ninety percent of this bill is not controversial," explained Thompson.

But by an 11-vote margin, the rule to consider the bill was defeated. Republicans voted as a unanimous bloc against it, 0-140, and were joined by a majority of southern Democrats, 35-49.

Northern Democrats overwhelmingly favored the rule, 163-20, but there were some notable defections among veteran northeastern Democrats that included Rules Committee Chairman James J. Delaney of New York; John H. Dent, Joseph M. Gaydos and Robert N. C. Nix, all of Pennsylvania, and Robert H. Mollohan of West Virginia.

Younger Democrats produced a heavy majority in favor of the rule, with members elected since 1974 backing consideration by a 94-18 margin. Only three non-southern members in the large Democratic classes of 1974 and 1976 voted against the rule.

The problem, Frenzel assessed, was not so much the contents of the bill or the ineptitude of the leadership (al-

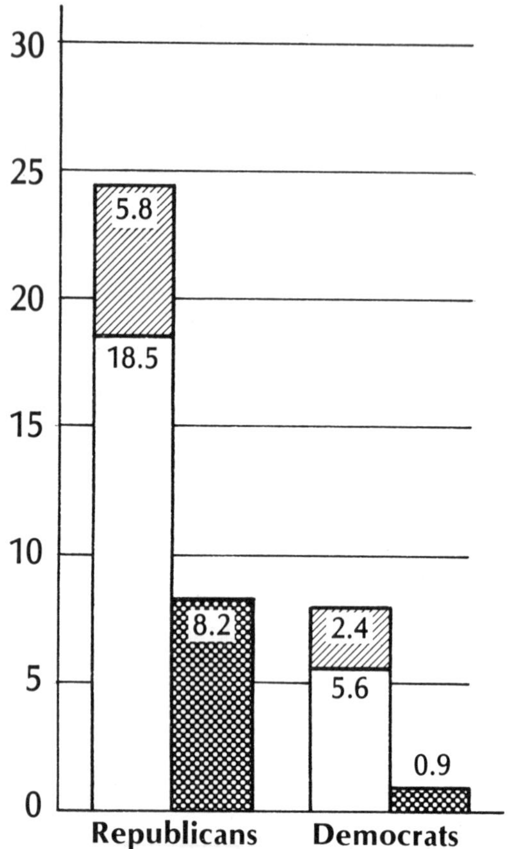

NOTE: Receipts are adjusted to subtract transfers of funds between affiliated committees. Cash-on-hand figures do not include any debts and obligations reported as owed by the committees. Figures are as of Sept. 30, 1977, for committees filing quarterly reports and Nov. 30, 1977, for committees filing monthly reports.

SOURCE: Federal Election Commission

though they were both factors), but a changing mood in Congress against programs designed to make sweeping reforms in the system. "Congress no longer has a lot of confidence in programs to cure the world's ills," he observed. "We may have seen the last gasp of public financing for federal elections."

House Action on HR 11983

Stymied in March when a majority in the House blocked consideration of HR 11315, public financing proponents switched tactics. In a "Dear Colleague" letter sent out to House members May 11, four leaders in the public financing fight indicated they would try to amend the rule governing the generally non-controversial Federal Election Commission authorization bill (HR 11983) to make the public financing amendment in order. As approved by the Rules Committee May 9, such an amendment to HR 11983 would not be in order.

Again, public financing supporters were rebuffed, when the House July 19 voted to accept the rule governing consideration of HR 11983 that made their amendment out of order. *(Vote 493, p. 140-H)*

A diverse House coalition that included a majority of Republicans and southern Democrats, as well as a significant number of veteran northern, big-city Democrats, managed to block the proposal.

On the unsuccessful vote July 19 to allow House consideration of the public financing proposal, Democrats in the class of 1974 voted nearly unanimously (54-4) in support. Only Robert Duncan of Oregon, Joseph D. Early of Massachusetts, John P. Murtha of Pennsylvania and Leo C. Zeferetti of New York voted against public financing.

A large majority of the non-southern members of the class of 1976 also voted for consideration, but by a narrower margin (25-9).

In contrast, an overwhelming majority of Republicans (106 of the 136 who voted) and southern Democrats (62 of 84) voted against considering the public financing proposal.

Vigorous White House backing could have made a difference. But after making public financing of congressional races part of a four-piece election law package in 1977, the White House remained well in the background. "It's one of more than several examples that can be cited," claimed Republican cosponsor John B. Anderson of Illinois, "where they've paid lip-service to an idea but have not mounted a high-powered campaign behind it."

Common Cause Vice President Fred Wertheimer agreed, adding that the White House had said it would lobby for the measure but had ended up doing nothing. "They wound up ducking," he said.

Two major changes were made in the proposal after the March setback: The effective date was pushed back from 1978 to 1980, and the candidate spending limits were raised from $125,000 plus $25,000 for additional fund-raising costs to $150,000 plus $30,000 for fund raising.

The rest of the proposal remained the same. It applied only to House general elections and was voluntary. Candidates would have 10 days after their nomination to decide whether or not to accept public financing.

Those who did would first have to raise $10,000 on their own in contributions of $100 or less, with 80 percent of the total in contributions from residents of their own state. Funds would then be matched up to the spending ceiling.

Candidates accepting public financing would also have to agree not to spend more than $25,000 out of their own pockets. In 1976 there were 68 House candidates who loaned or directly contributed more than $25,000 to their own campaigns, including 10 candidates who gave at least $100,000. Freshman Rep. Cecil Heftel, D-Hawaii, paced the list with $507,000 in personal loans.

The public financing plan called for removal of the spending ceiling where a candidate who did not accept public money spent in excess of $25,000 in personal funds or raised or spent in excess of $75,000. In such cases, candidates who signed up for public financing could receive up to $50,000 more in federal money.

In spite of the setbacks, public financing was the only piece of the Carter election package visible in Congress in 1978. Election day voter registration, the widely heralded keystone of the package, was heavily criticized in 1977 for its fraud potential. It had not been heard from since November 1977, when Ohio voters overwhelmingly rejected an election day registration law nearly identical to the Carter plan.

Legislation to relax the Hatch Act to permit increased political activity by federal employees won House approval in 1977, but was stymied in the Senate Governmental Affairs Committee, where Chairman Abraham Ribicoff, D-Conn., continued to oppose the legislation and few actively supported it in 1978.

The constitutional amendment to abolish the electoral college and elect the president by direct popular vote was approved by the Senate Judiciary Committee in September 1970. Although the amendment enjoys bipartisan support, the threat of a filibuster delayed consideration.

Proponents of public financing promised to renew the fight in 1979. They hoped that with 60 to 80 new members and an increasing public awareness of the impact of special interest spending on congressional races, their chances would be improved. "It's an idea that is far from dead," said Anderson.

Yet it was also far from adoption. There has been no public clamor for congressional public financing, and while the proposal drew some vocal support in Congress as a "good government" issue, resistance remained formidable.▮

ERA Deadline Extended

The Senate gave final approval Oct. 6 to a resolution granting states 39 additional months to ratify the Equal Rights Amendment to the Constitution.

Passage of the resolution (H J Res 638) on a 60-36 vote capped a year-long lobbying effort by backers of the ERA and marked the first time Congress had extended the ratification period for a constitutional amendment since it began setting time limits in 1917. *(Vote 446, p. 66-S)*

Supporters of the extension knew victory was at hand two days before the final vote, when the Senate rejected a key amendment that would have allowed states that already ratified ERA to rescind their actions during the extension period. The rescission amendment, sponsored by Jake Garn, R-Utah, was rejected 54-44. *(Vote 435, p. 64-S)*

ERA forces indicated that Birch Bayh, D-Ind., principal Senate sponsor of the extension, would have withdrawn it from consideration had the Garn amendment been adopted. Bayh said the Garn proposal "would have effectively killed any chance for final ratification" of ERA. The

The Proposed Amendment

"Section 1. Equality of rights under the law shall not be denied or abridged by the United States or by any State on account of sex.

"Section 2. The Congress shall have the power to enforce, by appropriate legislation, the provisions of this article.

"Section 3. The amendment shall take effect two years after the date of ratification."

—Proposed by Congress March 22, 1972 (H J Res 208)

period for ratification had been set to expire March 22, 1979. The new deadline was June 30, 1982.

The extension resolution, approved by the House Aug. 15, took effect upon Senate passage. Although his approval was not required, President Carter signed the measure Oct. 20.

Court Tests Expected

The Constitution did not specify a time limit for the ratification process. When Congress approved ERA in 1972 it set a seven-year time limit on ratification by three-fourths (38) of the states. To date, 35 state legislatures had ratified ERA. But four states — Idaho, Kentucky, Nebraska and Tennessee — had voted to rescind their ratification. The validity of those actions and constitutional questions surrounding the extension would almost certainly have to be decided by the Supreme Court. *(Background, 1977 Almanac p. 601; constitutional debate, 1977 Weekly Report p. 2493)*

Phyllis Schlafly, national chairwoman of Stop ERA, insisted that regardless of the Senate action, ERA would expire March 22, 1979, if it did not receive the approval of 38 states. Predicting that the 15 states that had rejected ERA would stick to their positions, Schlafly said lawsuits challenging the extension would be filed by states that had ratified, states that had not and states that had rescinded their action. Those suits were likely to be based on the fact that the extension was approved by a simple majority vote in Congress, rather than a two-thirds vote.

The Senate Oct. 3 affirmed the House view that the extension amendment required only a simple majority. It rejected, 33-57, an amendment by Bill Scott, R-Va., that would have required a two-thirds vote. *(Vote 433, p. 64-S)*

In a closing statement on the Senate floor just before the final vote, Bayh said, "It has been clear in every court decision and in every action of the U.S. Congress that the Congress has the authority to determine what is a reasonable time for ratification of a constitutional amendment. . . .

"We are asking the Senate to join the House in declaring that 10 years is a reasonable time for the ERA. This is no ordinary constitutional amendment. We are dealing with the rights of over half the people in the country."

Amendments Rejected

Backers of the extension feared that any change in the resolution passed by the House would kill its chances of approval because only a few days remained in the session. They and White House lobbyists therefore adopted a "no amendment" policy to avoid a conference with the House. Their efforts proved a complete success.

During Senate debate Oct. 3 and 4, the following amendments were rejected, besides the Garn rescission and Scott two-thirds amendments:

- By Adlai E. Stevenson III, D-Ill., as a substitute for the Garn resolution, to provide that the Congress express no opinion with respect to the effect of the action of any state legislature in rescinding its ratification of the proposed ERA. Rejected 4-92. *(Vote 434, p. 64-S)*
- By Scott, to permit a state legislature to rescind its ratification of ERA after March 22, 1979. Rejected 39-55. *(Vote 436, p. 64-S)*
- By Scott, proposing a substitute amendment to the Constitution to provide that equality of rights not be denied on account of sex. Rejected 14-79. *(Vote 437, p. 64-S)*
- By Scott, establishing Jan. 1, 1980, as the deadline for ratification of ERA. Rejected 10-84. *(Vote 438, p. 64-S)*
- By Scott, to permit a state legislature to rescind a ratification of ERA and to recognize any rescission of such ratification made before the date the ERA extension resolution became law. Rejected 26-64. *(Vote 432, p. 64-S)*

House Hearings

A House Judiciary subcommittee completed hearings May 19 on H J Res 638.

In its three final days of hearings, the Subcommittee on Civil and Constitutional Rights heard testimony from Phyllis Schlafly, an arch opponent of ERA, who argued that stretching out the seven-year deadline would be viewed by the public as tampering with the Constitution.

Eleanor Smeal, president of the National Organization of Women, which was behind the idea of an extension, countered that if Congress failed to extend the cutoff date it would be "setting back the clock of progress for the advancement of the rights of women in this society."

Supporters of the extension argued that the seven-year cutoff was arbitrary and that more time was needed for the measure to be understood by the public.

House Committee Action

Proponents of the Equal Rights Amendment to the Constitution scored a major victory July 18 when the House Judiciary Committee voted to extend the date for ratification by the state until June 30, 1982 (H Rept 95-1405).

By a 19-15 vote, the committee approved H J Res 638 after agreeing to a key amendment reducing the proposed ratification extension from seven years to three years, three months and eight days. That amendment, sponsored by Don Edwards, D-Calif., and adopted 17-16, was a compromise to win votes for the extension.

Edwards, the resolution's principal sponsor along with Elizabeth Holtzman, D-N.Y., said H J Res 638 might encounter some difficulty in the House Rules Committee but that House Speaker Thomas P. O'Neill Jr., D-Mass., had promised to help get it to the floor. Passage by the House "will be a cinch," Edwards said.

The key committee vote came on the Edwards' amendment to reduce the extension period. Edwards, who earlier said he had the votes to win a seven year extension, said he had to shorten the period to win support of four committee members. But Edwards' compromise almost fell apart.

Narrow Margin

Shortly before the committee was to vote on the amendment, Harold S. Sawyer, R-Mich., considered the swing vote on the committee, said he was unaware of any compromise and would vote against the amendment. Chairman Peter W. Rodino Jr., D-N.J., then called a 15 minute recess during which Sawyer was lobbied for his vote. But Sawyer refused and voted against the Edwards amendment. He later voted to report the resolution.

Absent for the vote was Jim Santini, D-Nev., an opponent of the extension. In his absence, the amendment carried 17-16. Santini told Congressional Quarterly he missed the vote because one of his pet projects, the coal slurry pipeline, was being debated on the House floor. There were no votes on that bill during the committee's debate over ERA. Santini also said he had instructed that his proxy be cast in favor of the compromise because a three year extension was preferable to seven, even though he preferred no extension. *(Coal slurry story, p. 674)*

Edwards later acknowledged that, "We didn't have the votes counted right."

Rescission

Having lost on the extension compromise, opponents turned their attention to an amendment by Tom Railsback, R-Ill., to allow states to rescind earlier ERA ratification. It was rejected 13-21.

While most constitutional scholars who testified in the House said that ratification of a constitutional amendment was irrevocable, some said it might be required if an extension for ratification were allowed. Four state legislatures — Idaho, Kentucky, Nebraska and Tennessee — had voted to rescind. Supporters of rescission such as Railsback said it would be "fundamentally unfair" to allow extension but not rescission.

Opponents argued that rescission was not provided by the Constitution and would encourage states to be less careful in considering future amendments.

Two-thirds Approval

In another constitutional debate, the committee decided against requiring a two-thirds — rather than a simple majority — vote by the House and Senate for an extension.

Harold L. Volkmer, D-Mo., who wanted to write a two-thirds requirement into the resolution, was blocked on a committee procedural vote, 23-8. That vote came on an Edwards' amendment to take up H J Res 638 as approved by his Subcommittee on Civil and Constitutional Rights. Had Edwards lost, Volkmer could have proposed considering the bill with a stipulation that it needed a two-thirds House majority for approval.

Proponents of a simple majority vote argued that the mode of ratification and the time limitation required no more even though an amendment to the Constitution itself required a two-thirds vote. Volkmer argued that it was unlikely the original ERA would have gotten a two-thirds vote by the House and Senate had there been a ratification period of more than seven years. He said that the extension was part of the process of amending the Constitution and therefore required a two-thirds vote.

The committee later rejected an amendment by M. Caldwell Butler, R-Va., to send the bill back to the subcommittee for consideration of whether a two-thirds vote was necessary. The amendment was defeated 15-19.

Key ERA Votes

These were the three key votes on the ERA ratification extension:

- The Edwards amendment reduced from seven years to three years, three months and eight days the period of extension for ratification. It was agreed to 17-16.
- The Railsback amendment sought to allow states that had already ratified the ERA to rescind their ratifications during the period of extension. The amendment was defeated 13-21.
- Approval of H J Res 638 extending the period of time for states to ratify the ERA. The vote was 19-15.

	Edwards Amendment	Railsback Amendment	Approval
Peter W. Rodino, Jr., D-N.J.	Yes	No	Yes
Jack Brooks, D-Tex.	No	Yes	No
Robert W. Kastenmeier, D-Wis.	Yes	No	Yes
Don Edwards, D-Calif.	Yes	No	Yes
John Conyers, Jr., D-Mich.	Yes	No	Yes
Joshua Eilberg, D-Pa.	Yes	No	Yes
Walter Flowers, D-Ala.	No	No	No
James R. Mann, D-S.C.	No	Yes	No
John F. Seiberling, D-Ohio	Yes	No	Yes
George E. Danielson, D-Calif.	Yes	No	Yes
Robert F. Drinan, D-Mass.	Yes	No	Yes
Barbara C. Jordan, D-Texas	Yes	No	Yes
Elizabeth Holtzman, D-N.Y.	Yes	No	Yes
Romano L. Mazzoli, D-Ky.	No	No	No
William J. Hughes, D-N.J.	Yes	No	Yes
Sam B. Hall, Jr., D-Tex.	No	No	No
Lamar Gudger, D-N.C.	Yes	Yes	Yes
Harold L. Volkmer, D-Mo.	No	No	Yes
Herbert E. Harris II, D-Va.	Yes	No	Yes
Jim Santini, D-Nev.	—	Yes	No
Allen E. Ertel, D-Pa.	Yes	Yes	Yes
Billy Lee Evans, D-Ga.	No	Yes	No
Anthony C. Beilenson, D-Calif.	Yes	No	Yes
Robert McClory, R-Ill.	No	No	No
Tom Railsback, R-Ill.	No	Yes	No
Charles E. Wiggins, R-Calif.	No	Yes	No
Hamilton Fish, Jr., R-N.Y.	Yes	No	Yes
M. Caldwell Butler, R-Va.	No	Yes	No
William S. Cohen, R-Maine	Yes	No	Yes
Carlos J. Moorhead, R-Calif.	No	Yes	No
John M. Ashbrook, R-Ohio	No	Yes	No
Henry J. Hyde, R-Ill.	No	Yes	No
Thomas N. Kindness, R-Ohio	No	Yes	No
Harold S. Sawyer, R-Mich.	No	No	Yes

House Floor Action

The House voted Aug. 15 to give states an additional 39 months to ratify the amendment, moving the ratification deadline back to June 30, 1982.

The House approved the extension, H J Res 638 (H Rept 95-1405), on a 233-189 vote after rejecting a key amendment sponsored by Railsback that would have allowed states to take back their approval of ERA during the extension period. *(Extension passage, vote 621, p. 176-H)*

Sponsors threatened to pull the extension resolution from the floor if the House approved Railsback's amendment. It was rejected, 196-227. *(Vote 620, p. 176-H)*

Before the vote on the Railsback amendment, extension proponents won an important procedural victory when the House agreed to consider the resolution under a rule (H Res 1295) allowing passage by a simple majority, rather than the two-thirds vote required for constitutional amendments. The rule was adopted by voice vote, after a motion to end debate was agreed to, 243-171. *(Vote 618, p. 176-H)*

Later in the debate, the House tabled — and thus killed — a resolution (H Res 1315) to require a two-thirds approval vote. The tabling motion by Edwards was agreed to 230-183. *(Vote 619, p. 176-H)*

Rescission Amendment

The major debate over H J Res 638 came on the Railsback amendment. Railsback argued that it would be unfair to the 35 states that have voted ratification to extend the deadline without at the same time giving states an opportunity to change their minds about ERA.

Four state legislatures that once voted to approve the ERA — Idaho, Kentucky, Nebraska and Tennessee — later voted to rescind. But the courts had never ruled on the legality of rescission and the question was unlikely to be resolved before 38 states had ratified the ERA. Railsback said his amendment would not sanction rescissions voted before the extension period began.

Edwards, sponsor of the ERA extension, countered that "the constitutionally established process in effect for 200 years would be sorely damaged" if Railsback's amendment were adopted.

"The message would go out that Congress says ratification is conditional," Edwards said, "that states would not have to take ratification seriously because they could rescind next year. It would make every state a battleground during every session . . . for every constitutional amendment in the future."

Margin of Approval

The other major debate concerned the margin of approval necessary for passage of an extension of the ERA.

Charles E. Wiggins, R-Calif., said it was his opinion that "approval of this pending resolution by two-thirds of the House is constitutionally required if the resolution is to have any effect at all after January 3, 1979."

Wiggins argued that the resolution was not a law because it would not be submitted to the president, that it was not a treaty, and that it could not be a constitutional amendment unless it were approved by a two-thirds House majority. Without the "super majority," Wiggins said, the bill would be "merely an opinion which will lack any force of law."

Supporters countered that the question of how much time would be allowed for ratification of a constitutional amendment was a matter of "detail," separate from the issue of the amendment itself, and that there was nothing sacred about the seven-year time limitation included in the ERA when it was passed in 1972.

They said the length of time for ratification depended only on whether the amendment remained an issue that was contemporaneous with the needs of the society for which it was intended at the time of passage.

Said John B. Anderson, R-Ill., "I do not happen to think that a 10-year ratification period in any way strains the 'contemporaneous' approval standard as set forth by the Supreme Court in *Dillon [v.] Gloss*. In that decision, the court held the Congress could set a time limit on ratification, provided it was reasonable. . . ."

Opponents concentrated on constitutional and legal arguments while at the same time insisting that they supported the purposes of the ERA. Supporters, on the other hand, made frequent appeals to members not to forget the purpose of ERA and the symbolic import of failing to allow more time for the ratification.

"The negative symbol, if we vote against this today, will be heard around the world," said Millicent Fenwick, R-N.J. "What does this say to the people of the developing countries and to the women in those countries? It says that even this country, the United States of America, does not really want to admit that women are equal citizens here." Fenwick attacked opponents saying they "pretend to be concerned with matters that are strictly legal, but they are not. They are finding ways to avoid a step toward this new freedom. . . . They are evasions of a simple but important question."

While ERA supporters were pleased at the House action, they were even more pleased by the subsequent passage in the Senate, where a filibuster had been threatened.

As the House began debating extending the time for ratification of the ERA, an Associated Press-NBC poll showed that more than half the American people opposed a seven-year extension of the deadline, although a majority of the public continued to support the ERA. ■

Science Authorization

By voice vote Sept. 29, the Senate cleared a bill (HR 11400 — PL 95-434) authorizing $934.4 million for fiscal 1979 activities of the National Science Foundation (NSF). The measure exceeded President Carter's budget request by $400,000.

In his budget, Carter requested a $77.6 million authorization for science education, instead of the $82 million NSF wanted. The House restored the funding to the $82 million level.

The Senate raised the education figure to $87.7 million on June 28, on recommendation of its Human Resources Committee.

In an agreement worked out with the Senate, the House later split the difference, leaving an $84.8 million education authorization in the bill — $7.2 million more than Carter requested.

Of the $7.2 million hike, $2 million would be spread among other programs authorized by the bill, to increase science education opportunities for women; $1.3 million of the increase would pay for additional graduate science fellowships for minority schools.

The House-Senate agreement urged the NSF to submit a two-year authorization in 1979 for fiscal 1980 and 1981.

To keep the bill from greatly exceeding Carter's budget request, the agreement called for authorizations for six budget categories at levels below what Carter sought. Senate floor manager Edward M. Kennedy, D-Mass., said that the overall $934.4 million figure still represented "3.4 percent real growth in the foundation's research and science education programs."

Provisions

As cleared for the president, HR 11400 authorized the following totals for NSF programs *(in millions)*:

Program	Budget Request	Final Authorization
Mathematical and physical sciences and engineering	$268.3	$265.7
Astronautical, atmospheric, earth and ocean sciences	227.3	224.7
Biological, behavioral and social sciences	158.0	157.0
U.S. Antarctic Program	50.7	51.2
Science education	77.6	84.8
Applied science and research applications	67.0	69.7
Scientific, technological and international affairs	24.3	23.5
Program development and management	54.8	53.3
Special foreign currency program	6.0	4.5
Total	$934.0	$934.4

House Committee Action

The House Science and Technology Committee reported the bill March 20 (H Rept 95-993).

"The committee believes that the level of support . . . requested by the president is proper," the report said. "The committee believes that the nation's scientific community could use larger amounts effectively but concurs with the president's judgment that the nation cannot afford a larger investment at this time."

The committee also applauded Carter's plan to increase funding for basic research by 11 percent across all federal agencies. But the NSF authorization in that area was $751 million, a slightly below average 10 percent hike.

The committee came up with the overall $400,000 increase in the administration request by cutting $3.2 million from each of two research programs — the mathematical, physical sciences and engineering program and an ocean drilling program — while adding $2.4 million for Antarctic research and $4.4 million for science education.

The five other NSF program authorizations were unchanged from the president's request.

The committee said it was distressed by Carter's decision to cut NSF's original $82 million request for science education to $77.6 million.

Deploring the "downward trend" in funding for science education, the committee restored the difference, increasing funding in that area by 10.8 percent.

The committee also designated $2 million for establishment of a program to research the needs of the handicapped, recommended that future NSF authorizations be for two years, and endorsed NSF's fiscal 1978 program allocating $4.5 million for joint university-industry research projects.

'Big vs. Little' Science

Charging that the NSF had yielded to pressure to fund what it called "big science" projects, the committee barred further major expenditures for such programs until a set of priorities and a system for balancing support between big and little projects had been set up.

The committee defined "big science" projects as those that involve many scientists, equipment "too expensive to lie idle" and which are likely to produce a breakthrough. "Little science" projects were defined as those that can be done by one or a few scientists and do not involve expensive equipment.

The committee suggested that Congress consider requiring NSF to request a specific authorization for each new big science project.

Deep Sea Drilling

The bulk of the $3.2 million cut by the committee for the deep sea drilling project would have gone for studies to determine if special systems needed to drill at extreme depths could be built and for drilling site surveys. The administration sought $4.2 million for the program.

Drilling to 30,000 feet would be conducted at continental margins — points at which land masses meet — and in deep trenches, at three times the depths previously explored. Taking core samples from those areas would provide data on the location of gas and oil deposits, volcanic activity and potential earthquakes, a committee aide said.

The committee limited spending for the project to $1 million in fiscal 1979 to be used to study conversion of the ship *Glomar Explorer* or other drilling alternatives.

The *Explorer,* then in storage in California, formerly was used for salvaging sunken ships and was once used by the CIA to raise portions of a Russian nuclear submarine. The federal funds would be used to study methods of converting the *Explorer* so it could extract core samples from the ocean floor.

In dissenting views, Eldon Rudd, R-Ariz., asserted that the impact of inflation on academic salaries had not justified the steady increase in the NSF budget since 1969.

He also said that NSF grants were weighted toward large states with prestige institutions and that federal audits had shown grant funds were poorly supervised.

House Floor Action

After a traditional wrangle over exotic research projects, the House April 18 approved HR 11400 by a 364-37 vote. *(Vote 194, p. 56-H)*

The bill provided $400,000 more than the $934 million sought by President Carter and represented an 8 percent increase over the previous year. The amount approved by the House plus $6.9 million appropriated in fiscal 1978 and carried over would give the agency a program level of $941.3 million in fiscal 1979.

No changes were made in the committee approved authorization level. Debate focused on increased funding for conversion of the *Glomar Explorer* and a proposed $6 million reduction of funding for research projects.

Ocean Drilling

An amendment to restore the $3.2 million cut by the committee from the ocean drilling program was offered by John B. Breaux, D-La., chairman of the Merchant Marine Oceanography Subcommittee.

Breaux said testimony before his subcommittee indicated that cutting the administration's request to study conversion of the *Glomar Explorer* could add $25 million to $30 million to the anticipated $450 million long range cost of the deep sea drilling project because it would delay it for a year.

Tom Harkin, D-Iowa, argued that NSF had not justified the additional expense of the Glomar study and that the foundation had not yet decided to go ahead with the drilling project.

The amendment was defeated 111-291. *(Vote 192, p. 56-H)*

Questionable Research?

John M. Ashbrook, R-Ohio, sought to cut $6 million from the $158 million the bill authorized for biological, behavioral and social sciences, an area Ashbrook tagged as the source of "many questionable grants."

One example he noted was a $63,200 study of the hormones of homosexual seagulls off the California coast.

"Many NSF grants are little more than intellectual welfare to support research we don't need, the results of which are often wrapped up in academic double-talk," said Ashbrook.

But opponents argued that important scientific breakthroughs often come from basic research "where you don't know if you are going to find anything."

Harkin cited several "silly grants" with serious results, including one on dog urine that led to information on the functioning of human kidneys and another on red hair that provided data on inheritance of sickle-cell anemia.

"They (grant recipients) need to study not what we as politicians think they should study, but what their training and curiosity leads them to study," said James G. Martin, R-N.C.

The amendment was defeated, 174-229. *(Vote 193, p. 56-H)*

Provisions

As passed by the House, HR 11400 authorized the following *(in millions):*

Program	Budget Request	House Authorization
Mathematical and physical sciences, engineering	$268.3	$265.1
Astronomical, atmospheric, earth and ocean sciences	227.3	224.1
Biological, behavioral and social sciences	158.0	158.0
U.S. Antarctic program	50.7	53.1
Science education	77.6	82.0
Applied science and research applications	67.0	67.0
Scientific, technological and international affairs	24.3	24.3
Program development and management	54.8	54.8
Special foreign currency program	6.0	6.0
Total	$934.0	$934.4

Senate Committee Action

The Senate Human Resources Committee May 15 reported S 2549, providing an NSF authorization of $957.1 million in fiscal 1979 and $1.08 billion in fiscal 1980 (S Rept 95-851).

Before voting, 14 to 1, to report the bill, the committee adopted a Health Subcommittee amendment that added to the administration's $934 million request $12.1 million for science education programs and $10.5 million for applied science and research applications.

Kennedy had expressed concern during subcommittee hearings that science education had comprised an increasingly smaller portion of the NSF budget in the 1970s.

Included in the committee-approved amendment was a provision authorizing NSF to spend up to $500,000 to study the feasibility of transmitting solar energy to Earth through satellites made of material from the moon or near-Earth asteroids.

In minority views to the committee report, Orrin G. Hatch, R-Utah, objected that the bill authorized $16.2 million more than the 1979 program level of $940.9 requested by NSF. Hatch also charged that the 7 percent annual inflation in academic salaries assumed by the bill was unrealistic, that NSF research projects often returned little for the investment involved and that they were poorly monitored. He objected to a two-year authorization until the monitoring process could be tightened.

Senate Floor Action

The Senate June 28 battled back an amendment limiting international scientific cooperation and approved a $934.4 million fiscal 1979 NSF authorization.

The Senate-approved authorization plus $6.9 million appropriated in fiscal 1978 and carried over would give the agency a program level of $941.3 million in fiscal 1979.

HR 11400 was passed by voice vote after the Senate agreed to a budget-cutting floor amendment worked out by Kennedy and a coalition of conservative senators.

The compromise was fashioned in the wake of Senate cuts in appropriations for several major departments and with the warning that taxpayers would not stand for excessive spending on exotic-sounding research grants.

The amendment limited S 2549 to a one-year authorization and slashed $22.2 million from the $957.1 million authorization recommended by the Human Resources Committee, leaving the 1979 NSF budget at the same $934.4 million level approved by the House April 18. But within the overall amount the House and Senate versions differed considerably.

The amendment cut $16.2 million from administration requests for seven NSF programs, including five basic research programs. At the same time, it added $16.6 million to the science education and applied science and research application programs. The result was a $400,000 net increase in the authorization requested by the administration.

Education programs increased by the substitute included those focusing on minorities, women and the handicapped; providing scientific and technical support for citizens' groups; providing funds to examine the ethical implications of science and technology and assisting high school and college students in getting experience in scientific research projects.

The $10.2 million cut in basic research programs set the fiscal 1979 authorization for basic research throughout NSF at $744.8 million. That provided an 8.3 percent increase over the $688 million NSF expected to spend on basic research in 1978. Carter had set a goal of 11 percent increase in basic research funding and 5 percent real growth in research across all federal agencies.

The amendment retained programs authorizing $2 million to research the needs of the handicapped, setting aside 15 percent of applied science funds for small businesses and authorizing $4.5 million for cooperative grants for academic and industrial researchers.

"The taxpayers have begun a revolt which may grow to rival the Boston Tea Party," Hatch said in supporting the amendment.

It "...serves as evidence that this Congress will begin to make good its promises to the people...to hold down spending.... Special projects which may temporarily suffer due to such belt tightening will in the long run exhibit the health and strength characteristic of a sound economy."

Dole Amendment

Robert Dole, R-Kan., introduced an amendment to prohibit NSF funds from being used for any international scientific activity in a country that denied participation on the basis of scientists' racial, ethical, religious or political views.

Opponents argued that the NSF director, who would be responsible for restricting funds in such cases, would have no accurate way of knowing when participation had been denied in a foreign country; that much of the most valuable scientific data had resulted from international exchange and that the scientists being cut off from contact with the United States otherwise could be valuable agents in enlightening countries that suppress human rights.

"I am naturally disappointed that some agencies of government and a large segment of the organized scientific community apparently do not support this amendment," Dole said.

"But I seek support now for human rights from a much larger constituency, the American public."

Kennedy said that the Dole amendment "is the worst way to further our human rights objectives." He said it would affect not only the Soviet Union but 17 other nations in all parts of the world.

Dole withdrew the amendment.

The Senate then substituted the language of S 2549, as amended, for that of the House-approved bill and passed HR 11400 by voice vote.

Provisions

As passed by the Senate, HR 11400 authorized the following *(in millions):*

Program	Budget Request	House Authorization	Senate Authorization
Mathematical and physical sciences and engineering	$268.3	$265.1	$266.3
Astronomical, atmospheric, earth and ocean sciences	227.3	224.1	225.3
Biological, behavioral, and social sciences	158.0	158.0	156.0
U.S. Antarctic program	50.7	53.1	48.5
Science education	77.6	82.0	87.7
Applied science and research applications	67.0	67.0	73.5
Scientific, technological and international affairs	24.3	24.3	22.3
Program development and management	54.8	54.8	51.8
Special foreign currency program	6.0	6.0	3.0
Total	$934.0	$934.4	$934.4

Final Action

The House and Senate informally agreed to split the difference in the bill's authorization for science education. The House approved the compromise Sept. 19 and the Senate agreed Sept. 29, clearing the measure for the president. ▮

NASA Authorization

Legislation (HR 11401 — PL 95-401) authorizing $4,401,600,000 in fiscal 1979 for the National Aeronautics and Space Administration (NASA) was cleared by Congress Sept. 19 after House and Senate conferees agreed to add $30 million to the amount requested by the Carter administration.

The compromise represented a nearly even split between the $4,388,600,000 authorized by the Senate May 18 and the substantially larger $4,415,300,000 authorized by the House April 25. The administration requested $4,371,-600,000.

The bill included $4 million to initiate production of a fifth space shuttle orbiter, the plane designed to carry payloads to and from low Earth orbit.

Cost-conscious administration officials favored a four-orbiter fleet, but the unified position of the House and Senate was in favor of five orbiters. Under current projections, an increase of $53 million would be required in fiscal 1980 for a five-orbiter fleet, though delays in the development of the orbiter engine could change funding requirements considerably.

Provisions

As cleared by Congress, HR 11401 authorized the following *(in millions):*

Program	Budget Request	Final Amount
Research and Development		
Space Shuttle	$1,439.30	$1,443.30
Space flight operations	311.90	315.90
Launch vehicles	76.50	74.00
Physics and astronomy	285.50	285.50
Lunar and planetary exploration	187.10	187.10
Life sciences	40.60	42.60
Space applications	274.30	280.30
Technology utilization	9.10	12.10
Space research and technology	108.30	111.30
Aeronautical research and technology	264.10	275.10
Energy technology applications	3.00	5.00
Tracking and data acquisition	305.40	305.40
Subtotal	$3,305.10	$3,337.60
Construction of Facilities	152.50	150.00
Research and Program Management	914.00	914.00
Total	$4,371.60	$4,401.60

House Committee Action

Criticizing the Carter administration for its "apparent lack of interest" in planning for the future of the space program, the House Science and Technology Committee March 15 reported HR 11401.

The report (H Rept 95-973) appeared to be another round in a game of fiscal merry-go-round that began when NASA submitted an authorization request of $4.48 billion to the White House. The Office of Management and Budget (OMB) sliced $108 million off the NASA request, and the House committee restored many of the OMB cuts. It recommended an authorization of $4,415,300,000.

The administration requested $4,371,600,000 for NASA, an increase of $323 million over the fiscal 1978 authorization.

The largest additions in the committee report were $26.7 million for aeronautical research and technology, dropped by OMB and restored by the committee, and $14 million added for space applications programs.

The applications money included $4 million to initiate the development of STEREOSAT, a remote sensing satellite that would provide geological data to facilitate mineral exploration.

Potentially the biggest disagreement concerned the administration decision to maintain four orbiters in its space shuttle program rather than five. The committee added $4 million to the $1.44 billion space shuttle program to maintain the option to purchase a fifth orbiter without incurring an estimated $220 million in additional costs. Total cost of the orbiter — an airplane-sized reusable space craft — was estimated at $600 million.

The committee said it favored the five-orbiter fleet "to provide flexibility for exploitation of the orbiter capabilities and to provide a backup for any unforeseen loss of a vehicle." It added that significant savings could be realized if production of the fifth orbiter was initiated in fiscal 1979.

The administration's preference for a four-orbiter fleet was based primarily on cost, but had also been affected by NASA's decision not to modify for actual space flight the vehicle dropped from a Boeing 747 for approach and landing tests. That orbiter could be redesigned for space flight at an estimated cost of $50-60 million.

Aeronautical Research

The committee was most active in changing the aeronautical research and technology program, which it criticized for being top-heavy with short-term programs.

To help correct this "imbalance," it cut $12 million from programs designed to improve the performance retention characteristics of engine components and apply advanced aerodynamic technologies to subsonic transport aircraft. It added $8 million to the "very promising" variable cycle engine components program and $4 million to the supersonic cruise research program.

The variable cycle engine program, the committee said, would evaluate advanced technology components "which offer significant performance benefits combined with reduced noise and pollution characteristics."

The committee fully restored the $26.7 million dropped by OMB for the flight test phase of the composite primary aircraft structures program, which was designed to develop and test new, lightweight material for aircraft structures.

Citing the potential for fuel savings with the lighter materials, the committee called the OMB reduction "short-sighted."

Space Applications

The committee continued to be enthusiastic about NASA's space applications program, adding $14 million for earth resources detection and monitoring after OMB had reduced the request by $20.7 million.

In adding $4 million for the development of STEREOSAT, the committee insisted that NASA implement cost-sharing with the industrial users of the data. Another $10 million was included for demonstration programs, increases in support for technology transfer to states, advanced crop prediction and advanced data analysis.

The committee also expressed concern that NASA did not request funds to initiate a follow-on to SEASAT, which was concerned with the detection, monitoring and forecasting of ocean conditions (and which stopped transmitting data Oct. 10). It urged the agency to propose the program for the next authorization.

Energy Research. Responding to the "continuing energy crisis," the committee called solar satellite power "one of the potentially most promising sources of energy." It added $6 million in two programs to increase work in power conversion and microwave energy technology, to develop solar energy cells appropriate for space, and to increase work on the problems involved in transmitting the energy from space to earth.

Space Flight Operations. The committee made a $10 million general reduction in development, test and mission operations and a $7 million increase in advanced programs. It cited a further need to define systems for future space shuttle missions in the 1980s as the reason for the increase.

Launch Vehicles. The administration request for expendable launch vehicles was reduced by $5 million to $71.5 million, with the explanation that there were "opportunities for reducing NASA costs during the phaseout" of the program.

Technology Utilization. The committee added $5.5 million to the $9.1 million requested by the administration for technology utilization programs, with most of the increase for work on transferring NASA technology to bioengineering applications.

House Floor Action

HR 11401 sailed through the House April 25 by a vote of 345-54. *(Vote 207, p. 60-H)*

The only opposition to the bill was from Ted Weiss, D-N.Y., who offered an amendment to delete $27.9 million in research and development funds for an advanced supersonic transport aircraft (AST/SST).

Weiss had offered a similar amendment in 1977 during debate over the fiscal 1978 NASA authorization. The bill cleared by Congress incorporated a substitute to the Weiss amendment which permitted a feasibility study of the plane but stipulated that design or development of a prototype aircraft would require a separate authorization.

Weiss argued that the program should be dropped because NASA was working toward the development of a prototype rather than engaging in pure research. Congress killed the SST program in 1971 after complaints about the environmental hazards of the airplane. *(1971 Almanac p. 130)*

Supporters argued that the proposed NASA program was strictly research-oriented and was designed to solve some of the environmental and economic problems of supersonic flight.

After a quorum call Weiss' request for a vote on the amendment was rejected.

By voice vote the House accepted an amendment introduced by Gary A. Myers, R-Pa., requiring the NASA administrator to report to Congress on the implementation of the administration policy on conflicts of interest, standards of conduct and financial disclosure.

Provisions

As passed by the House, HR 11401 authorized the following *(in millions):*

Program	Budget Request	House Authorization
Research and Development		
Space Shuttle	$1,439.30	$1,443.30
Space flight operations	311.90	308.90
Launch vehicles	76.50	71.50
Physics and astronomy	285.50	285.50
Lunar and planetary exploration	187.10	187.10
Life sciences	40.60	40.60
Space applications	274.30	288.30
Technology utilization	9.10	14.60
Space research and technology	108.30	111.30
Aeronautical research and technology	264.10	292.30
Energy technology applications	3.00	6.00
Tracking and data acquisition	305.40	304.40
Subtotal	$3,305.10	$3,353.80
Construction of Facilities	152.50	147.50
Research and Program Management	914.00	914.00
Total	$4,371.60	$4,415.30

Senate Committee Action

The Commerce, Science and Transportation Committee reported HR 11401 on May 10 (S Rept 95-799).

Fifth Orbiter

The committee agreed with the House action adding $4 million to the bill to initiate production of a fifth space shuttle orbiter.

The report called the acquisition of a five-orbiter fleet a "prudent and sensible decision and one necessary to meet civilian and defense needs in the most economical way."

The report estimated that four orbiters would be $2 billion to $2.5 billion more expensive to operate over their 10-year life than a five-orbiter fleet.

The main reason a smaller fleet costs more, the report said, was that a second system — expendable launch vehicles — would have to be used as a backup system by the Department of Defense and others for a much longer period into the 1980s.

Exploiting the Shuttle

A total of $10 million was added to two programs to exploit the capabilities of the space shuttle:

- The committee restored $7 million requested by NASA but dropped by the Office of Management and Budget (OMB) for advanced programs in the space flight operations program. The money was to be used for systems studies of the space shuttle, and included $2 million for preliminary design of a 25 kilowatt power module to provide additional electrical power for experiments.
- The committee also added $3 million for shuttle studies in the space research and technology program.

Two other additions were made by the committee: 1) $2 million in the life sciences program for studies of the human response to long-duration space flight, and 2) $1 million for further studies in the energy technology applications program.

Disagreements with the House

The major disagreements between the House and the Senate committee were in the aeronautical research and space applications programs.

The committee did not go along with a House decision to add $26.7 million for an accelerated effort to make aircraft more energy efficient by developing lighter and stronger bodies of combined materials such as fiber and epoxy. The committee cited NASA testimony that the problem of "free-floating" graphite fibers used in these composite structures was "under study, and that the extent of the program was unknown."

The Senate also disagreed with the House decision to add $12 million to supersonic aircraft research with an offsetting reduction in the aircraft energy efficiency program.

Also rejected was a House addition of $14 million to the space applications program, including $4 million for development of the STEREOSAT satellite.

The committee rejected House cuts of $10 million in space flight operations, and $5 million in the expendable launch vehicles program.

Senate Floor Action

Congressional support for a fifth orbiter for the space shuttle program solidified May 18 when the Senate went along with House action inserting funds for the additional vehicle into HR 11401.

The Senate bill authorized appropriations of $4.39 billion; this was $17 million more than the Carter administration request but $26.7 million less than the amount approved by the House.

The Senate passed HR 11401 by voice vote after perfunctory debate. No amendments were introduced.

Provisions

As passed by the Senate, HR 11401 authorized the following *(in millions)*:

Program	House Authorization	Senate Authorization
Research and Development		
Space Shuttle	$1,443.30	$1,443.30
Space flight operations	308.90	318.90
Launch vehicles	71.50	76.50
Physics and astronomy	285.50	285.50
Lunar and planetary exploration	187.10	187.10
Life sciences	40.60	42.60
Space applications	288.30	274.30
Technology utilization	14.60	9.10
Space research and technology	111.30	111.30

Program	House Authorization	Senate Authorization
Aeronautical research and technology	$ 292.30	$ 264.10
Energy technology applications	6.00	4.00
Tracking and data acquisition	304.40	305.40
Subtotal	$3,353.80	$3,322.10
Construction of Facilities	147.50	152.50
Research and Program Management	914.00	914.00
Total	$4,415.30	$4,388.60

Conference, Final Action

The biggest disagreements between the House and Senate were in the space flight operations, aeronautical research and space applications programs.

In the space flight operations program, conferees agreed to retain $7 million added by the Senate for advanced programs and to cut $3 million from development, test and mission operations, for a net gain of $4 million. The House had made a net reduction of $3 million in the space flight program.

In aeronautical research the Senate had rejected the House decision to add $12 million to supersonic aircraft research and $26.7 million for research with combined materials, such as fiber and epoxy, to make aircraft bodies lighter and stronger.

Conferees agreed as a substitute to add $11 million to the NASA request for work on supersonic aircraft technology, aerial applications and composite materials.

The Senate also had disagreed with the House addition of $14 million in the space applications program, including $4 million to initiate production of STEREOSAT. Conferees instead added $6 million to the NASA request, including $1 million for STEREOSAT.

The Senate adopted the conference report (H Rept 95-1509) by voice vote Aug. 17. The House adopted it Sept. 19 by a vote of 321-54, clearing the bill for the president. *(Vote 708, p. 200-H)*

Senate Inaction Kills Lobby Reform Bill

Legislation imposing strict new registration and reporting requirements on groups that lobby Congress passed the House in April 1978 but never came to the Senate floor because the Governmental Affairs Committee could not agree on the kind of bill to report.

The House-passed bill was designed to replace the 32-year-old Federal Regulation of Lobbying Act.

The 1946 law was directed at individuals and organizations whose "principal purpose" was to influence the defeat or passage of legislation. It required such lobbyists to register and file reports with the Secretary of the Senate and the Clerk of the House.

But the law was largely unenforceable. Only four cases were prosecuted under it. And a 1954 Supreme Court decision upholding the constitutionality of the law severely limited its application.

The bill reported by the Judiciary Committee, HR 8494, was considerably less stringent than legislation passed by the House during the 94th Congress by a vote of 291-74. That bill and a Senate-passed lobbying bill never went to conference and died at the end of the session. *(1976 Almanac p. 477)*

Throughout the years of debate over lobbying reform, the major difficulty had been to fashion a bill that would ensure disclosure of essential information by major lobbying organizations while assuring that the requirements did not discourage groups from making their views known to public officials.

As approved by the Judiciary Committee, HR 8494 seemed to have accomplished the delicate balancing of constitutional rights with the need for information that all parties to the legislation agreed was essential.

The bill required annual registration and quarterly reporting with the comptroller general by major paid lobbying groups that make oral or written lobbying communications on legislative matters with representatives, senators and about 100,000 top level executive branch officials.

Individual communications were exempted as were communications with a House member by organizations located in a member's district or with a senator by organizations located in the senator's state. And the committee had set a threshold high enough to satisfy most groups that small lobby organizations would not be covered.

As a result, when the bill came out of the Judiciary Committee it had the support of a diverse group of lobbying interests, including Common Cause and Ralph Nader's Congress Watch, the ACLU and various environmental and church groups, as well as major business organizations.

But that support crumbled after action on the House floor, where amendments were adopted that greatly expanded the scope of the bill.

The U.S. Chamber of Commerce and other business groups that had once advocated the bill, or at least said they could live with it, opposed the bill, as did the American Civil Liberties Union. Aligned against them were the White House and AFL-CIO as well as Common Cause and Ralph Nader's Congress Watch, which had criticized what they viewed as major loopholes in the bill as reported by the Judiciary Committee.

The two alliances were split over a pair of amendments adopted by the House:

- An amendment requiring lobby organizations to report expenditures for grass-roots lobbying activities, such as computerized mass mailings designed to bring constituent pressure on congressmen.

- An amendment requiring lobbying organizations to disclose the names of major groups contributing $3,000 or more to their operations. Both amendments were supported by Common Cause and Congress Watch and opposed by business and civil libertarians.

These two issues consumed most of the debate in House and Senate committees and on the House floor. In the end, supporters and opponents of the two amendments could not resolve their differences, making it uncertain whether a lobby reform bill could clear in the 96th Congress.

House Committee Action

The House Judiciary Committee reported the lobby disclosure bill on March 24 (H Rept 95-1003), after having approved it by voice vote Feb. 23.

The major debate in the Judiciary Committee was over the "threshold" for determining which organizations should be covered by the lobbying law. Debate focused on the amount of expenditures and the number and kinds of communications that should trigger registration.

The committee finally agreed on a formula that would require registration by: 1) any organization which spends $2,500 in any quarterly reporting period ($10,000 a year) to lobby or to draft lobbying communications, or 2) any organization that spends $2,500 a quarter for lobbying and employs one or more persons who lobby 13 or more days per quarter or two or more persons who lobby seven or more days per quarter.

The final threshold appeared to satisfy most groups, except for paid professional lobbyists who are hired by an organization to lobby for a limited amount of time on a particular issue. These lobbyists feared they would lose business as a result of the amendment, which they argued set up a double standard that will intimidate organizations not to use the services of professional lobbyists as a way to avoid the registration requirement.

In another controversial action, the committee accepted an amendment offered by Don Edwards, D-Calif., that eliminated a provision in the bill requiring disclosure of major solicitations to generate grass-roots letter-writing campaigns.

The exclusion of this and several other hotly disputed provisions made the committee bill more controversial for what it did not include than for what it did.

Two Judiciary Committee members, Republicans Charles E. Wiggins of California and Henry J. Hyde of Illinois, filed dissenting views to the report. They said the bill addressed unproved abuses, that it violated the right of privacy and that it placed excessive burdens on the right of citizens to petition the government.

House Floor Action

The House passed HR 8494 April 26, by a vote of 259-140, after three days of debate and after turning back nearly 20 efforts to weaken the bill. Two major amendments that significantly expanded the bill's disclosure requirements were adopted. *(Vote 216, p. 62-H)*

Immediately upon passage of the Public Disclosure of Lobbying Act, the White House issued a statement from President Carter praising the vote and urging prompt Senate action. "This bill will enable the American people to understand and see more clearly how the legislative process is being affected by organizations that engage in significant lobbying activities," said Carter, who had pledged during his presidential campaign to push for lobby reform.

Common Cause also hailed the House action. Legislative director Mike Cole said the bill "strikes a proper balance between individual citizens' right to petition their government and the public's right to know what organizations are doing to pressure Congress."

But the two amendments that expanded the bill's coverage to require disclosure of 1) grass-roots lobbying efforts and 2) the names of major organizations contributing to lobby groups led major business, civil liberties, church and environmental groups to charge that the bill interfered with privacy and with citizens' rights to petition public officials.

The American Civil Liberties Union said the bill set up "unprecedented surveillance of political activities" by the government.

At the beginning of House debate, HR 8494 generated only marginal opposition, and the House overwhelmingly adopted the rule (H Res 1139) under which it was considered. *(Vote 195, p. 58-H)*

But as the floor debate progressed, conflicts became clear in arguments over virtually every major section of the bill.

"We have labored carefully to try to bring about an adequate disclosure of lobbying activities without at any time treading on the constitutionally protected rights of the people to petition their government for redress of grievances," said floor manager George E. Danielson, D-Calif., at the outset of debate.

The bill's principal opponent, Charles E. Wiggins, R-Calif., acknowledged that he was going to "tilt at windmills" and try to have the bill sent back to committee. Rejecting Wiggins' constitutional arguments, the House overwhelmingly defeated an attempt to kill the bill.

But by the second day of floor debate, the House had adopted two highly controversial amendments that led to sharply defined alliances for and against the bill:

- The first, sponsored by Walter Flowers, D-Ala., required lobby organizations to report expenditures for grass-roots lobbying activities, such as computerized mass mailings designed to bring constituent pressure on congressmen. The amendment was adopted, 245-161. *(Vote 197, p. 58-H)*
- The second, sponsored by Tom Railsback, R-Ill., required any lobbying organization that spent more than 1 percent of its total budget on lobbying to report the names of organizations from which it received more than $3,000 a year in dues or contributions. It was approved 251-135. *(Vote 201, p. 58-H)*

Contributors. Railsback's amendment was offered only after an amendment to require disclosure of the names of major individual contributors was rejected. The follow-up amendment requiring lobbies to disclose only the names of contributor organizations appeared to mollify most of those who argued that disclosing individuals' names might discourage people from contributing to unpopular causes and would seriously erode free speech.

Railsback said the amendment covering organizations was essential because, "Without disclosures of major contributors . . . it would be difficult to know that the Calorie Control Council is an organization which receives its principal financial backing from soft drink manufacturers opposing the saccharin ban; or that the Electric Consumers Resource Council is financed by the big electric industry; or that the Natural Gas Supply Committee is supported by the major oil companies."

Railsback said the lack of a contributor disclosure provision "invites the establishment of front organizations that mask the real source of lobbying activities." Opponents objected that organizations were no different from individuals and that their right to privacy would be abridged by the amendment.

Grass-Roots Lobbying. Flowers' grass-roots lobbying amendment was clearly the most controversial matter to come up on the floor. Opponents objected that the amendment would place a massive record-keeping burden on members, employees or affiliates of lobbying organizations.

Rep. Don Edwards, D-Calif., said that if Sears Roebuck qualified as a lobbying organization and met the threshold for reporting in a given quarter, and if a local Sears outlet encouraged its employees to write congressmen on some issue beneficial to the parent company, local Sears offices all over the country would have to keep records for the national office so that all lobbying communications by employees would be reported.

Supporters of the amendment insisted that it did not apply to any organization that did not already meet the threshold for reporting and therefore hit only large lobby organizations. They said the amendment was necessary because grass-roots lobbying is becoming more popular.

Exemptions. Two efforts were made to broaden the bill's exemptions for groups of individuals. Both were unsuccessful.

An amendment by Thomas N. Kindness, R-Ohio, would have expanded the geographical exemption from the bill's registration requirement to anyone living or working in a congressman's district or a county or standard metropolitan statistical area, all or part of which is in a member's district.

The Kindness amendment was defeated, 195-212. *(Vote 196, p. 58-H)*

A second effort to expand the exemptions in the bill was offered by Rep. Jim Santini, D-Nev. Santini's amendment sought to exempt organizations of state or local elected or appointed officials who lobby in Washington. Such organizations as the National Governors' Association would have been exempted under Santini's proposal, which was rejected on a division vote, 28-33.

Disclosure Threshold. Two efforts were made to change the bill's threshold for determining which organizations must register and file reports. One would have greatly expanded the coverage of the bill while the other would have narrowed it. Both were rejected by voice votes.

Other Changes. Before passing the bill, the House made several other changes.

A Railsback amendment aimed at Ralph Nader proved to be a crowd pleaser and was adopted on a standing vote, 33-22. It required a reporting organization to identify its chief executive officer, whether paid or unpaid, and the issues on which he lobbied.

"The failure to cover Ralph Nader, and others like him," said Rep. Robert McClory, R-Ill., "has become the most notorious 'loophole' in HR 8494." There was little opposition to the amendment, which Nader lobbyist Andrew Feinstein characterized as "the first step towards licensing the exercise of First Amendment rights."

The amendment also required reporting organizations to identify the persons who lobbied on the 15 issues on which the organization expended its greatest efforts.

The House also adopted:

- An amendment by Wiggins to extend to 30 days, from 15, the time for organizations engaging in lobbying activities to register.
- An amendment by Harold L. Volkmer, D-Mo., to require the comptroller general to refer all apparent violations of the act to the attorney general.
- An amendment by Thomas N. Kindness, R-Ohio, stating that communications dealing only with the status, existence or subject of an issue are exempted. Adopted 207-188. *(Vote 215, p. 62-H)*
- An amendment by Gary Myers, R-Pa., that required reporting organizations to report lobbying activities carried out by their retainees on the House or Senate floor, or in any of the adjoining rooms. Myers said the amendment would "relieve current members of Congress of whatever they want to attach to the often very embarrassing situation of having former members who have access to the floor discussing issues which they ought not to be discussing on this floor." House rules prohibit former members from lobbying on the House floor.
- A Wiggins amendment that required a reporting organization to disclose the expenditure for a dinner or similar event held for a federal officer or employee only if the cost exceeded $500.

Weakening Amendments Defeated

Numerous efforts to weaken HR 8494 were defeated. Among those rejected were:

- A Kindness amendment that sought to broaden the geographic exemption to exclude from the bill's coverage communications made to a member by an organization having its principal place of business in the member's state rather than just in his or her congressional district. Rejected on a standing vote, 13-17.
- An amendment by Jim Santini, D-Nev., that sought to exempt organizations of state or local elected or appointed officials. Rejected on a standing vote, 28-33. A second Santini amendment, which sought to direct the General Accounting Office to study lobbying activities of organizations of state and county elected officials and to delay until January 1980 their coverage under the bill, was rejected, 197-211. *(Vote 214, p. 62-H)*
- A Kindness amendment that sought to cover "volunteers" used by an organization to lobby.
- An amendment by John F. Seiberling, D-Ohio, that would have raised the bill's threshold so as to cover only organizations that spent $5,000 a quarter on lobbying rather than $2,500 and would have covered only organizations with paid officers or employees. Rejected on a standing vote, 15-22.
- A Kindness amendment that would have included expenditures for travel to and from Washington for the purpose of lobbying in the computation of lobbying expenditures.
- A Kindness amendment that sought to delete the requirement that reporting organizations disclose salaries paid to lobbying organizations or individuals. Rejected on a standing vote, 6-23.
- A Kindness amendment that sought to limit coverage of the bill to only oral lobbying communications.
- A Kindness amendment that sought to reduce civil and criminal fines to $5,000, from $10,000, and to reduce the limit on imprisonment for violations to one year, from two. Rejected on a standing vote, 6-16.
- Two Kindness amendments that sought to strike the bill's requirements that the comptroller general establish cross-indexing and coding systems and compilations and summaries of information reported under the bill.
- A Kindness amendment that sought to delay the effective date of the act from Oct. 1, 1978, to Oct. 1, 1979.
- An amendment by Larry Pressler, R-S.D., to apply the bill's registration and reporting requirements to the lobbying activities of the White House legislative liaison operations and federal departments and agencies. Rejected, 44-350. *(Vote 200, p. 58-H)*

House Provisions

As passed by the House April 26, HR 8494 contained the following major provisions:

Who Can Be Lobbied?

Lobbying activities covered by HR 8494 were limited to those communications made to a "federal officer or employee." The definition included a member of the House or Senate, a delegate or resident commissioner, an officer or employee of Congress, the comptroller general and certain high-level employees of the General Accounting Office, as well as officers of the executive branch from the Cabinet level down to assistant secretaries (executive schedule levels I through V).

What Is a Lobbying Organization?

The bill provided a twofold test for determining which organizations had to register and report on their lobbying activities on legislative matters. Organizations that qualified under either test were required to register. The "applicability" section of the bill:

- Required registration and reporting by any organization that spends more than $2,500 in any quarterly filing period to retain an individual or another organization to make "lobby communications" or "for the express purpose of drafting such communications."
- Required registration and reporting by an organization that spends $2,500 a quarter on oral or written lobbying communications and

1) employs one individual who spends all or part of 13 days in any quarter lobbying or,

2) employs at least two individuals who spend all or part of seven days a quarter lobbying (the $2,500 threshold in this provision was an aggregate expenditure test, so that an organization spending $1,000 for one lobbying communication and $1,600 for 12 others would meet the threshold).

"Organizations" were defined as groups of individuals, corporations, foundations, associations, labor organizations, societies, joint stock companies, some organizations of state or local elected officials that engage in lobbying (such as national associations of state or local elected or appointed officials, including the National Governors' Association and the U.S. Conference of Mayors), "foreign agents" covered by the Foreign Agents Registration Act, and colleges and universities, including certain state colleges and universities. Corporations owned or controlled by the United States government were exempted from the definition.

"Affiliate" organizations were defined to include any organization formally associated by agreement or ownership with another organization, so that one organization maintains actual control or has the right of potential control over all or part of the activities of the other. Included in this definition are:

- Certain units of religious denominations or conventions or associations of churches.
- State and local units of national membership organizations.
- Organizations that are members of national trade associations, business leagues and labor organizations or federations that otherwise qualify under the definition.

What Is Lobbying?

The section defining "lobbying communications" included:

- An oral or written communication directed to any member or employee of the House or Senate to influence the content or disposition of a bill, resolution, treaty, nomination, hearing, report or investigation.
- Oral or written communications to certain officers or employees of the executive branch, the comptroller or deputy comptroller general and certain officers or employees of the General Accounting Office, concerning bills, resolutions, treaties and other measures that have been transmitted to or introduced in the House or Senate.

Exempt Communications. The following were excluded from the definition of "lobbying communications."

- Communications to a federal officer or employee that do not concern the above legislative matters but have to do with other government matters such as regulations, executive orders, contracts and so forth.
- Communications made at the request of a federal officer or employee, such as testimony before a committee or information submitted for inclusion in a public hearing or record.
- Non-paid communications made through a speech or address, through a newspaper, book, periodical or magazine published for distribution to the general public, through a radio or television transmission, or through a regular publication of an organization published in substantial part for purposes unrelated to influencing legislation.
- Any communication by an individual for redress of grievances or to express a personal opinion.
- Communications on any subject directly affecting an organization to a senator or his staff — if the organization's principal place of business is located in the state represented by that senator.
- Communications with a member of the House or his staff — if the organization's principal place of business is located in a county within which all or part of a member's congressional district is located.
- Communications with representatives, senators or their staffs that deal only with the "existence or status" of any issue, or which seek only to determine the "subject matter of an issue."
- An individual who is a member or an officer, director or employee of an organization should not be presumed to be speaking on behalf of his organization in every instance but is entitled to express his views as an individual so that such expression is not necessarily a lobbying communication. (According to the committee report on HR 8494, "the general test would be whether the communication is made for the organization pursuant to the employee's general or specific responsibilities as an employee.")

Registration and Record-Keeping

HR 8494 required that lobbying organizations register annually and that they keep certain records of their lobbying activities. The bill required:

- Registration with the comptroller general no later than 30 days after engaging in lobbying activities (such registration is effective until Jan. 15 of the following year).
- Reregistration by Jan. 30 of the following year if the quarterly filing threshold is met.
- Identification of the organization, including its name and address, principal place of business, the general nature

of its business and the names of the organization's executive officers and directors (even if they were not paid).

- Identification of employees or retained individuals who qualify as lobbyists.
- Notification of the comptroller general if an organization terminates lobbying activities.
- Retention by the organization or retained lobbyist of "such records as are necessary" to file registrations and reports required under the act. (The bill prohibited the comptroller from requiring records beyond those normally maintained by the organization.)
- Preservation of such records for at least five years after the close of the quarterly filing period they cover.

Reports

Lobbying organizations were required to file quarterly reports with the comptroller within 30 days of the end of the quarter. Lobbying organizations that did not meet a threshold had to file a statement to that effect. Those meeting a threshold were required to report:

- An identification of the organization filing (similar to that provided under the registration provision).
- Total expenditures made by the organization or a retainee for lobbying communications during the period (including costs for mailing, printing, advertising, telephones, consultant fees, gifts or other expenditures made to or for the benefit of a federal officer or employee).
- An itemized listing of each expenditure of $35 or more made to or for the benefit of any federal officer or employee (including members of Congress) and the name of the recipient.
- Expenditures for receptions, dinners or other similar events held for a federal officer or employee if the cost to the reporting organization exceeded $500.
- The name and address of organizations contributing $3,000 or more during the calendar year to a lobbying group and the amount given if the contribution was spent in whole or in part for lobbying and the lobbying group spends at least 1 percent of its budget on lobbying activities.
- A description of the issues on which the organization expends a significant amount of lobbying effort, and the name of any retainee or employee as well as the chief executive officer of the lobby group, whether paid or unpaid, who engaged in lobbying on one of those issues on behalf of the organization.
- The name of any lobbyist retained by an organization and the name of any employee who meets the lobbying threshold, the amount of money spent to employ the employee or retained lobbyist, and that portion of expenditures made in connection with lobbying by such individuals.
- A statement that lobbying communications were made on the floor of the House of Representatives or Senate or in adjoining rooms if such communications were made by an employee or retainee of a reporting organization.
- Disclosure of each known "direct business relationship" between the reporting organization and a federal officer or employee the organization sought to influence in the quarterly reporting period.
- Lobbying activities (such as those listed above) engaged in by an affiliate organization meeting a threshold if such activities are not reported by the affiliate itself.
- Disclosure of each known "direct business relationship" between the reporting organization and a federal officer or employee the organization sought to influence in the quarterly reporting period. Under the provision, designed to prevent conflicts of interest, "direct business relationship" meant a relationship between the organization and any federal officer or employee in which:

1) the federal officer or employee was a partner in such organization or,

2) the federal officer or employee was an employee of the lobbying organization or a member of its board of directors or similar governing body or,

3) the organization and the federal officer or employee held a legal or beneficial interest in excess of $1,000 in the same business or joint venture (excluding stock holdings in publicly traded corporations, insurance policies and leases made in the ordinary course of business that are provided on terms that would be available to the general public).

Grass-Roots Lobbying. The reports section of the bill also required disclosure of grass-roots lobbying solicitations — requests an organization makes to other individuals or organizations to lobby on an issue. Organizations would report solicitations made through advertisements if such solicitations reached or could be reasonably expected to reach 500 or more persons, 100 or more employees of an organization, 25 or more officers or directors or 12 or more affiliates. Reports on grass-roots lobbying required disclosure of:

- The issue with which the solicitation was concerned.
- The means employed to make the solicitation and an indication of whether the recipients were in turn asked to solicit others.
- An identification of any persons retained to make the solicitation.
- The approximate number of persons solicited, if the solicitation is made through the mails or by telegram.
- An identification of the publication or radio or television station where the solicitation appeared and the total amount expended on such advertisements if the amount expended exceeded $5,000.

"Solicitation" under this provision included communications directly urging, requesting, or requiring another person to advocate a specific position on a particular issue and seeking to influence a member of Congress, but did not include communications between registered lobbying organizations.

Public Records

Public record-keeping provisions in the bill required that the comptroller general:

- Establish filing and indexing systems to make the registrations and reports publicly accessible.
- Make copies of registrations available by five days after the date a registration is filed.
- Compile and summarize the information contained in registrations and reports in each quarterly filing period and make that information available to the public within 60 days after the close of such period.
- Submit an annual report to the president and Congress detailing the comptroller's activities.
- Refer all apparent violations of the act to the attorney general.

Enforcement

The attorney general was given responsibility for enforcing the lobby disclosure act. The bill provided that:

- Alleged violators be notified of possible violations, except when it might interfere with enforcement of the act.
- The attorney general use "informal methods of conference and conciliation" as the first line of enforcement.
- If informal methods fail the attorney general may institute a civil action in the judicial district in which the organization is based or transacts business.
- The attorney general may institute criminal proceedings if a violation of the law is found.
- In civil actions brought under the act, a court may award attorneys' fees and expenses to the prevailing party (other than the government) if the court determines the action was brought "without foundation, vexatiously, frivolously, or in bad faith."
- Organizations or individuals knowingly violating the registration, record-keeping or reporting sections of the law or rules or regulations are subject to civil penalties of not more than $10,000 for each violation.
- Individuals or organizations willfully and knowingly making false statements or failing to provide information required under those sections may be fined up to $10,000 or imprisoned for up to two years or both for each violation.
- Any individual who sells or uses information retained under the public record-keeping sections for soliciting contributions or business may be fined up to $10,000.

Other Provisions

HR 8494 also contained these provisions:

- Authorizations of $1.6 million for each of the first three fiscal years in which the act was to be in effect.
- The act's registration, record-keeping, reporting and enforcement provisions were to take effect on the first day of the first calendar quarter following promulgation of rules for registration, reporting and record-keeping; the bill otherwise was to be effective Oct. 1, 1978.
- The Federal Regulation of Lobbying Act of 1946 was repealed.
- Rules or regulations under the registration, record-keeping and reporting sections were to take effect 90 days after they were submitted to Congress, unless either House adopted a resolution disapproving the rules or regulations by majority vote.
- The act exempted those practices covered by the Federal Election Campaign Act of 1971. (This technical language was included to distinguish lobbying law from the law governing political parties and elections.)

Senate Committee Action

The Senate Governmental Affairs Committee began marking up its lobby bill (S 2971) on May 10 and 11, but the bill was shelved in late July as key senators were unable to reach agreement on how to get a bill to the floor.

The bill as introduced by the committee's chairman, Abraham Ribicoff, D-Conn., was considered far more rigorous than the House-passed bill.

Besides requiring more groups to file reports, Ribicoff's original bill contained more comprehensive grass-roots lobbying and contributor disclosure provisions than the House-passed bill, and more extensive coverage of lobbying of executive branch officials.

Ribicoff's original bill contained a complicated two-tiered threshold, which allowed lighter reporting responsibilities for groups engaging in less substantial lobbying. The threshold test was based on the amount of time and money an organization spent on lobbying and the frequency of contacts.

An amendment adopted on a voice vote changed the threshold to cover groups that: 1) spent $1,750 (rather than the $1,250 in the original bill) in a quarter to retain an outside lobbyist, or, 2) paid one employee to make two oral lobby communications a day on each of 10 days in a quarter, or paid two employees to make oral communications on each of five days a quarter (for a total of 20 communications).

The original threshold in S 2971 was considered more far-reaching than the House bill in terms of the number of groups that would be covered. The House bill required registration and reporting by groups that: 1) spent $2,500 a quarter for a retained lobbyist, or, 2) spent $2,500 a quarter for lobbying by one or more employees on a specified number of days.

But the final Senate committee proposal was in some ways more lenient than the House-passed threshold. It applied only to oral communications, where the House threshold included written lobbying communications. And the Senate amendment specifically exempted small groups that lobby on six or fewer consecutive working days a year and non-Washington based groups that are "locally oriented" and have a total annual budget of less than $75,000.

Unlike the House bill, the Senate threshold could also be triggered by indirect or grass-roots lobbying, such as mass mail solicitations encouraging citizens to contact their congressmen on an issue. This provision would, for example, require a small church lobby group that spent $5,000 in a quarter on a newspaper ad concerning abortion to register and file a report.

This threshold was widely opposed by business and public advocacy groups.

Charles McC. Mathias Jr., R-Md., and Edmund S. Muskie, D-Maine, had the votes to win committee approval for five or six major amendments they planned to propose. The amendments would have eliminated requirements for disclosure of grass-roots lobbying efforts and the names of major contributors to lobby groups, exempted organizations of state or local elected officials from the reporting requirements and eliminated the bill's criminal sanctions.

Ribicoff said he would not manage his bill on the Senate floor if it were "emasculated" by the Mathias-Muskie amendments. "I couldn't manage a bill I didn't believe in," he said. "I would prefer someone else manage it so I could offer strengthening amendments on the floor."

But Muskie wasn't interested in managing such a bill and Ribicoff couldn't find anyone who was.

Consequently, despite vigorous lobbying by the White House and Common Cause, no compromise was reached in committee, and the bill never got to the Senate floor. ▮

Customs Law Revision

House adoption Sept. 19 of the conference report on the bill (HR 8149) to modernize and simplify U.S. customs law culminated nearly a year of legislative activity on the bill and cleared it for the president (PL 95-410).

The House had passed the bill Oct. 17, 1977, by a 386-11 vote. *(1977 Almanac p. 817)*

The legislation was the first major revision of customs procedures in more than two decades. In that time the value of U.S. imports increased five times, entries increased from 1.1 million in 1956 to 3.4 million in 1976, and the number of travelers processed doubled from 130 million to 266 million.

Senate Committee Action

In its report (S Rept 95-778) filed May 2, the Senate Finance Committee said the bill had three major objectives: 1) to develop more efficient procedures for handling the paperwork and financial aspects of import transactions, 2) to relate the amount of a penalty for false statements to the degree of guilt of the offender, and 3) to expedite the processing of goods and individuals.

In a key change from the House bill, the committee increased the duty-free allowance granted returning U.S. residents on foreign goods and goods obtained in U.S. insular possessions such as American Samoa, Guam and the Virgin Islands.

The House bill increased the duty-free allowance for travelers returning from foreign countries from $100 to $250, while the Senate bill raised the allowance to $500.

For travelers returning from insular possessions the House bill raised the allowance from $200 to $500; the Senate bill increased the allowance to $1,000.

The Senate bill also allowed U.S. residents arriving from insular possessions to apply the $1,000 exemption to articles they bought there and then shipped home. The House bill had no similar provision.

Senate Floor Action

The Senate passed HR 8149 by voice vote June 7.

The Senate accepted an amendment to the bill allowing existing law related to penalties for false filing to remain in force if the violations were the subject of an ongoing investigation by the Customs Service.

The amendment, introduced by Carl T. Curtis, R-Neb., was designed to allow the Customs Service to impose stiff penalties if its investigation of abuses in the importation of Japanese television sets found violations of current law.

Speaking in favor of the amendment, Robert Morgan, D-N.C., said the abuses were part of a "broader conspiracy" that had "virtually decimated our domestic television industry."

Provisions

As passed by the Senate, major provisions of HR 8149:

- Modified entry procedures to allow the release of goods when an entry document was filed. All documents would have to be filed within 10 days after filing the entry document, and estimated duties would have to be deposited within 30 days. (Under existing law full documentation and payment of the duty were required before release.)
- Authorized Customs to send importers a monthly statement for all goods arriving in the billing period.
- Imposed record-keeping requirements on importers and strengthened Customs' authority to inspect importer's books and records.
- Modified existing law regarding penalties for false statements from a fixed penalty regardless of the nature of the violation to different penalties for violations involving fraud, gross negligence and negligence. Allowed judicial review for unresolved issues.
- Imposed a flat 10 percent duty on non-commercial imports for personal use up to a value of $600 above the personal exemption. A flat 5 percent rate would apply to goods from insular possessions.
- Retained the existing provision under which merchandise held for one year without payment of duties was considered unclaimed and was sold by the government. The House bill reduced the time period to six months, but Customs officials, upon reconsideration, supported retention of the one-year period.
- Placed a one-year limit on the time allowed Customs to make a final assessment of duties on an item. (Existing law permitted duties to be assessed many years after the entry of goods.)
- Included provisions similar to the House bill allowing entry of merchandise with copied trademarks for non-commercial personal use, but added an amendment providing for notification of the trademark owner, forfeiture to the government of all such goods and delivery to a government agency or charitable institution. (Under existing law Customs was permitted to sell such goods after forfeiture, putting them back into competition with legitimate trademark goods.)
- Prohibited duty-free entry for any individual including an officer of the federal government or a member of Congress.
- Required an annual authorization for the Customs Service beginning with fiscal year 1980.

Conference Action

The House adopted the conference report (H Rept 95-1517) on the bill Sept. 19 by a 360-1 vote. *(Vote 709, p. 200-H)*

The Senate had adopted the report Aug. 25 by voice vote.

A key difference between the House and Senate bills was the amount of the duty-free allowance granted U.S. residents returning from abroad with foreign goods. The House bill had raised the existing $100 allowance to $250, while the Senate bill had raised it to $500. Conferees agreed to raise the allowance to $300.

For goods obtained in U.S. insular possessions such as American Samoa, Guam and the Virgin Islands, the House bill had raised the $200 allowance to $500 and the Senate bill had increased it to $1,000; conferees agreed on increasing the allowance to $600.

The duty-free exemption would apply to articles being shipped home only if the articles were purchased and shipped from the insular possessions.

The House agreed to a Senate amendment allowing existing law relating to penalties for false filing to remain in force, if the violation occurred before the date of enactment of HR 8149 and was the subject of an investigation by the Customs Service.

Japanese TV Sets

The amendment would allow the Customs Service to impose stiff penalties if it found violations in its current investigation into the importation of Japanese television receivers.

The House also accepted a Senate amendment concerning commercial goods carrying copied trademarks seized by the Customs Service. The amendment provided for notification of the trademark owner, forfeiture to the government of all such goods and their delivery to a government agency or charitable institution.

Final Provisions

As cleared by Congress, HR 8149:

- Modified entry procedures to allow the release of goods when an entry document was filed. All documents would have to be filed within 10 days after filing the entry document, and estimated duties would have to be deposited within 30 days. (Under existing law full documentation and payment of the duty were required before release.)
- Authorized Customs to send importers a monthly statement for all goods arriving in the billing period.
- Required importers to keep records pertaining to imports for up to five years and strengthened the authority of Customs to inspect importers' records. Provision was made for issuing summonses to record-keepers. (Existing law had no such record-keeping requirement.)
- Modified existing law regarding penalties for false statements from a fixed penalty regardless of the nature of the violation to different penalties for violations involving fraud, gross negligence and negligence. Allowed judicial review for unresolved issues. (Existing law required mandatory penalties, including forfeiture of merchandise for violations occurring as a result of simple negligence, and did not provide full and effective judicial review.)
- Exempted from the new penalty provisions any alleged anti-dumping violation involving Japanese television receivers if the alleged violation occurred before the date of enactment or was being investigated by the Customs Service before the date of enactment of the bill.
- Required all customshouse brokers to file a report with the Treasury Department by Feb. 1, 1979, and every third year thereafter. The report would state whether the broker was actively engaged in business and give the name and address of the business.
- Increased the personal duty exemption for returning U.S. citizens from $100 to $300 on foreign goods and from $200 to $600 on goods obtained in U.S. insular possessions. The duty free allowance of one liter of liquor per adult was extended to cover non-residents as well as residents.
- Authorized a flat 10 percent duty on non-commercial imports for personal use up to a value of $600 above the personal exemption. A flat 5 percent rate would apply to goods from insular possessions.
- Retained the existing provision under which merchandise held for one year without payment of duties was considered unclaimed and could be sold by the government. The House bill had reduced the time period to six months, but Customs officials, upon reconsideration, supported retention of the one-year period.
- Placed a one-year limit on the time allowed Customs to make a final assessment of duties on an item. (Existing law permitted duties to be assessed many years after entry.)
- Allowed entry of merchandise with copied trademarks for non-commercial personal use; amended provisions regarding commercial imports with copied trademarks to include notification of the trademark owner, forfeiture to the government of all such goods and delivery to a government agency or charitable institution. (Under existing law Customs was permitted to sell such goods after forfeiture, putting them back into competition with legitimate trademark goods.)
- Prohibited duty-free entry for any individual including an officer of the federal government or a member of Congress.
- Required an annual authorization for the Customs Service beginning with fiscal year 1980.

Civil Rights Commission

Congress gave final approval Sept. 28 to legislation (S 3067 — PL 95-444) extending the life of the Civil Rights Commission for five years and expanding the agency's jurisdiction to cover discrimination based on age or handicap.

The bill added age and handicap to the commission's jurisdiction, which already covered discrimination based on race, color, religion, national origin and sex.

The commission, established under the Civil Rights Act of 1957, originally was authorized to study discrimination based on race, color, religion, or national origin. In 1972, discrimination on the basis of sex was added to the commission's jurisdiction.

The agency had no enforcement powers, but could submit reports, findings and recommendations to the president and Congress.

Senate Action

The Senate passed S 3067 on June 27 by voice vote, with no report and no debate. The bill as introduced called for a five-year extension of the commission, but this was amended on the floor to a three-year extension.

Rather than a specified amount, the bill authorized "such sums as are necessary" for the commission's operations, which were expanded to cover age and handicap discrimination.

House Action

HR 12432, a bill to extend the commission, was reported to the House on a voice vote of the Judiciary Committee on May 12 (H Rept 95-1140).

The committee recommended approval of the commission's request to have age and handicap discrimination added to its scope of authority.

In minority views, Republican members of the committee criticized the bill's funding level, which they said will have doubled by 1980. The minority said the commission's costs were "escalating at an exorbitant rate" and that its work was duplicative of that performed by other federal agencies.

The House passed HR 12432 by voice vote Sept. 6 extending the life of the Civil Rights Commission for five years.

Two amendments were adopted during floor debate July 28 and Sept. 6. One by M. Caldwell Butler, R-Va., prohibited the commission from lobbying before state or federal legislative bodies and a second, sponsored by David C. Treen, R-La., and Tom Hagedorn, R-Minn., barred the commission from studying or recommending any action on abortion.

Lobbying. Opponents of the Butler amendment, among them bill sponsor Don Edwards, D-Calif., argued that there was little evidence that the commission had engaged in lobbying.

Edwards argued that the amendment could "gut" the commission's most important function — its authority to make findings and recommendations. Without this authority, "the commission's courageous voice will be mute," he said. Butler assured supporters of the bill that that was not his intention. His amendment, acted on July 28, was adopted 159-125. *(Vote 540, p. 154-H)*

Abortion. Treen said his anti-abortion amendment, approved Sept. 6 by a 234-131 vote, was necessary because abortion "is not a civil rights matter." *(Vote 638, p. 182-H)*

"...No one denies that, unfortunately, minorities are disproportionately represented among the poor. But that analysis surely does not authorize the commission to appraise every law . . . that may impact poor persons," Treen said.

Opponents said the commission should at least be allowed to study the effect of federally funded abortions on the poor to determine if the laws provide or deny equal protection.

Amendments Rejected. The House on July 28 defeated an effort by Butler to delete the provisions authorizing the commission to study age and handicap discrimination. His amendment was rejected 87-224. *(Vote 539, p. 154-H)*

Also rejected, by voice vote Sept. 6, was an amendment by Paul N. McCloskey Jr., R-Calif., to limit the extension to three years, as in the Senate bill.

After passing HR 12432, the House substituted it for S 3067 and passed the Senate bill.

Provisions. As passed by the House, S 3067 authorized $12.8 million for fiscal 1979 and $14 million for fiscal 1980, an increase of $5.2 million over the commission's request for the two-year period, to cover expenses associated with its new responsibilities concerning age and handicap discrimination.

Conference, Final Action

The conference report was filed (H Rept 95-1626) Sept. 25. Approval came on non-record votes. First the House and then the Senate adopted the report Sept. 28.

Abortion Studies. Despite its expanded jurisdiction, the commission was slated to operate under at least one significant new restraint. Conferees agreed to retain a House provision barring the commission from studying or recommending any action on abortion.

Sponsors of the extension argued that the commission had operated within its jurisdiction in researching and reporting a study on the "Constitutional Aspects of the Right to Limit Childbearing," the only study of abortion in the commission's 21-year existence.

But House conferees argued that because of the 234-131 House vote in favor of the anti-abortion amendment, it was unlikely the conference report would be adopted were the provision deleted.

Lobbying. Conferees also agreed to a House provision that prohibited the commission from lobbying Congress or state and local governing bodies. The import of this provision remained unclear because the conference report suggested: "The managers agree that the commission is not now nor has it ever been authorized to lobby and is (*sic*) confident that appropriate administrative and or criminal remedies are available to prevent such abuses."

Other Provisions. Conferees agreed to adopt the House bill's five-year extension, rather than the Senate's three-year extension as part of a compromise retaining the Senate's open-ended authorization proposal. Senate language provided "such sums as are necessary" to carry out the commission's functions for one year. The House version had called for authorizations of fixed amounts for fiscal 1979 and 1980, totalling $26.7 million.

Conferees also agreed to require at least one advisory committee in each state, and to allow the commission to create additional voluntary committees where necessary.∎

'Flexitime' Bill Cleared

The Senate passed and cleared for the president Sept. 15 a bill authorizing a three-year experiment in flexible and compressed work schedules for federal agencies and their employees (PL 95-390).

HR 7814 required the Civil Service Commission to establish a voluntary program in selected executive agencies and military departments to test the effect of flexible hours on employees and their families, the efficiency of government operations, mass transit and energy consumption and federal government employment opportunities.

"Flexitime" would require employees to be present during core hours, for example 11 a.m. to 6 p.m., but would let them choose quitting and starting times before and after core time.

Compressed time requiring 80 hours of work spread over fewer than 10 work days in a two-week period would permit experiments with four-day work weeks.

For such experiments, the bill suspended regulations requiring premium pay for work after 6 p.m. or in excess of eight hours a day or 40 hours a week.

HR 7814 was also an amendment to HR 11280, the Civil Service Reform bill passed by the House Sept. 13. Rep. Stephen J. Solarz, D-N.Y., sponsor of the flexitime bill, succeeded in attaching it to HR 11280 through a voice vote. Solarz said HR 7814 was stalled in the Senate and was unlikely to pass in 1978 unless it was attached to another bill. *(Civil Service reform, p. 818)*

A House Post Office and Civil Service subcommittee staff member said that the Solarz amendment was withdrawn by House conferees Sept. 18. But Solarz's office said he had "a commitment from the leadership of the House conferees" to retain the amendment until the president signed HR 7814. President Carter signed the bill into law Sept. 29.

Provisions

As approved by Congress, major provisions of HR 7814:

- Required the Civil Service Commission to establish an experimental program involving a sufficient range and number of executive branch positions to evaluate flexible schedule effectiveness.
- Suspended regular overtime provisions of federal law for the experiment and provided for special computation of overtime and premium pay.
- Limited the experiment to three years from the effective date of Oct. 1, 1978, or 180 days after enactment, whichever was later.
- Allowed agencies not selected for the experiment to opt for flexible schedule programs.
- Allowed agencies to request exemption from the experiment and to request termination of a disruptive flexible schedule.
- Allowed agency heads to restrict employees' choice of arrival and departure times, exclude certain employees or groups of employees from the experiment and restrict the use of flexible hours.
- Allowed employees to request exemption from a program that created personal hardships.
- Required that employee participation be voluntary and approved by employee organizations or by a majority of workers in a unit without an organization.

- Prohibited coercion of employees in choosing whether to participate, what hours to work and whether to choose compensatory time or payment for overtime hours worked.
- Allowed employees to work overtime rather than taking leave to compensate for absences for religious observances.

House Committee Action

The Post Office and Civil Service Committee Jan. 25 voted 23-1 to report HR 7814 (H Rept 95-912). The committee noted the success of private sector flexible hour programs involving between 1.5 million and 2.2 million workers and the results of similar federal programs that have included 90 government units and about 164,000 workers.

Those results warranted the three-year experiment to see if flexitime would work government-wide, said the report.

"The evidence presented at hearings of the Subcommittee on Employee Ethics and Utilization on the Federal flexible work hours programs indicated that thus far, they have produced a range of positive benefits and the problems that arise are not unresolvable," the committee report said. Any difficulties, it said, resulted from poor planning.

Rep. Edward J. Derwinski, R-Ill., representing administration views, filed a dissenting opinion against the bill's requirement that all executive agencies have a flexitime program.

House Floor Action

The House May 25 approved HR 7814, 288-57. It had failed March 13 to receive two-thirds approval needed for passage under suspension of the rules. *(Passage, vote 332, p. 92-H; failed suspension, vote 105, p. 32-H)*

Bill proponents argued that flexible hour experiments resulted in improved employee morale and productivity, decreased tardiness and sick leave, energy savings from employee travel at non-peak traffic periods and opportunities for those with restricted hours to enter the work force.

Opponents said the flexible schedules would aggravate the public image of government employees as specially privileged and would encourage moonlighting. They objected to a provision they said would allow employee unions to negotiate hours under the experiment.

The House adopted by voice vote a compromise amendment by Solarz and Derwinski giving agencies not selected by the Civil Service Commission for the experiment a choice of whether to have a flexitime program. A second Solarz amendment adopted by voice vote allowed employees to work overtime rather than taking leave to compensate for time off for religious observances.

"Flexitime is one of those ideas which benefits virtually everyone and harms practically no one," Solarz said.

An amendment by Richard C. White, D-Texas, to strike a requirement that flexitime hours accord with any union contracts was defeated, 9-20, by a non-record division vote.

White said he didn't want to give employee unions the statutory right to negotiate flexitime hours. Opponents of the amendment said the unions were granted that right in a 1962 executive order by President John F. Kennedy and that a statutory precedent was set in the 1970 Postal Reorganization Act (PL 91)375). *(Postal Reorganization, 1970 Almanac p. 341)*

Senate Action

The Senate Human Resources Committee Aug. 23 voted unanimously to report a companion bill, S 517 (S Rept 95-1143). The bill was reported 10-1 out of the Governmental Affairs Committee July 24. Ted Stevens, R-Alaska, the lone objector, "wanted to make sure employees could vote before the system was implicated," an aide to the Governmental Affairs Committee said. She added that Stevens voted for HR 7814 on the floor.

S 517 would have delayed implementation of the flexitime experiment until six months after it had been signed into law, as opposed to the three-month period provided in HR 7814.

S 517 was indefinitely postponed after its House counterpart was passed. The Senate passed HR 7814 without amendment by voice vote. ▮

Part-Time Careers Bill

A bill easing requirements for hiring part-time federal workers — but not until fiscal 1981 — was signed into law by President Carter Oct. 10.

The bill (HR 10126 — PL 95-437) made it easier for federal agencies to hire workers for up to 32 hours a week. Previous law set the federal workweek at 40 hours, divided into eight-hour days. A related measure signed into law allowed "flexitime" working-hour experiments as well. *(Flexitime bill, above)*

The bill "will help us tap the energies and talents of people who, for various reasons, are unable to work full time," Carter said. "Along with the recently enacted 'flexitime' bill, this legislation will provide more flexible — and more productive — working arrangements for federal employees."

As reported by the House Post Office and Civil Service Committee (H Rept 95-932), HR 10126 allowed federal agencies to designate vacant posts that were best filled by part-time arrangements.

The bill prohibited any agency chief from abolishing an occupied full-time post to convert it to part-time status. It also barred agencies from requiring employees to switch to part-time work or lose their jobs. Positions covered by labor union contracts with the government, where the contract fixed the workweek, were not covered. Also exempt were positions of grade GS-16 and above — the Senior Executive Service posts of Carter's civil service reform bill.

The Congressional Budget Office estimated that the bill would add 3,000 part-time employees a year for four years beginning in fiscal year 1979. The CBO estimated the additional cost at $23,678,600 for fiscal years 1979-82.

The House passed HR 10126 by a 294-84 vote on March 13. *(Vote 106, p. 32-H)*

Before passing the measure by voice vote Aug. 25 the Senate delayed its implementation until Oct. 1, 1979. A similar bill, S 518 (S Rept 95-1116) was postponed indefinitely. Before clearing HR 10126 for the president Sept. 26, the Senate agreed to a House amendment further delaying its effects until Oct. 1, 1980.

The Senate report on the bill said that "the enactment of part-time legislation would authorize the federal government to undertake some very significant initiatives to enhance its position as a model employer...." ▮

Vetoed Firefighters' Bill

A vetoed bill (HR 3161) shortening the workweek of federal firefighters went back to the Post Office and Civil Service Committee June 28 by a 279-109 House vote. *(Referral, vote 433, p. 124-H)*

The referral vote came after Herbert E. Harris II, D-Va., conceded that proponents of the bill did not have the votes to override President Carter's veto. "As the Post Office and Civil Service Committee develops Civil Service reform legislation, I will offer the bill as an amendment to that bill," Harris said. He was the bill's sponsor.

In a debate over the referral motion, Harris told Robert E. Bauman, R-Md., "this is a better strategy than a premature vote on a veto override that my colleague well knows has little chance of passage."

Bauman had pressed for an up-or-down veto override vote. "The real reason for this referral," he said, "is to avoid embarrassment for those members who would now switch their votes away from federal firefighters in deference to the president, who vetoed a good bill that is badly needed."

HR 3161 would cut the basic workweek for 11,500 federal firefighters to 56 hours, from 72. Pay also would be reduced, but by 9.5 percent. Carter claimed that reducing the workweek by a larger amount in effect gave the firefighters a 15 percent hourly pay increase.

Edward J. Derwinski, R-Ill., who led the original fight against the bill on the House floor, again praised what he called Carter's "spunky" veto. He said it was consistent with Carter's "hard-hitting campaign to control bureaucratic sprawl...."

HR 3161 fell victim to the third veto of President Carter's administration on June 19.

It was Carter's first of 1978. In 1977, he vetoed the initial version of the fiscal 1978 Energy Department authorization bill, as well as a measure to establish a federal inspection program for rabbit meat. *(1977 Almanac pp. 63-E, 64-E)*

Carter said the bill extends "unwarranted advantages" to the firefighters and "offends the ideals of fairness that should guide this administration."

"I am not prepared to accept its preferential approach," he added. *(Veto message, p. 55-E)*

Carter said HR 3161 "would reduce the firefighters' workweek without reducing the premium pay which was designed for a longer standby schedule.

"In effect it would raise firefighters' total hourly pay by more than 15 percent . . . without overtime pay, the increase is almost 30 percent."

Carter said such a raise would not be justified, particularly in light of his recommendation of a 5.5 percent pay raise cap for all federal workers, as part of his anti-inflation campaign.

Carter also contended HR 3161 would require the Defense Department alone to hire 4,600 more firefighters, at an annual cost of $46.7 million, in order to maintain present protection of facilities.

House Committee Action

As reported Feb. 28 by the Post Office and Civil Service Committee (H Rept 95-911), HR 3161 would reduce the workweek of the 11,559 civilian federal firefighters to 56 hours from 72. Average pay for the firefighters, including overtime, would decline by about 9.5 percent. The average salary for a firefighter — $15,407 a year under existing law — would go to $13,938 under the bill.

The Congressional Budget Office (CBO) estimated that in order to fully staff the firefighting squadrons after the hours were cut, 2,200 new firefighters would have to be hired. CBO estimated the net cost of that (after salary cuts for current firefighters) at $24.3 million in fiscal 1979.

Administration officials objected to what they termed a pay hike for current firefighters.

In a letter to Post Office Committee Chairman Robert N. C. Nix, D-Pa., Civil Service Commission Chairman Alan Campbell charged the bill would make the firefighters "a favored class of employees." He added that reducing the workweek by 16 hours without a similar reduction in premium pay (for hazardous and/or constant standby duty) "provides an additional increase . . . for these employees of approximately 30 percent."

Under existing law, federal firefighters worked a 72 hour week. The week was split into three 24-hour segments plus rest periods. Each segment included eight hours of active duty followed by 16 hours of standby duty during which a firefighter could be called on at any time.

Of the 11,559 firefighters affected by the bill, approximately 10,500 worked for the Defense Department according to the committee report. Their duties there included preventing and fighting munitions dump fires, chemical fires and aircraft fuel and radioactive waste fires. Also affected by the bill would be U.S. Forest Service firefighters in the Agriculture Department.

Four Republican committee members, in a minority report to the bill, quoted Navy Department testimony about firefighters' duties in a different context. "Time spent [on] actual fire calls averages about two hours per week. . . . Most assignments consist of only light work, for example, training or manning alarm rooms."

House Floor Action

In the face of presidential opposition, the House passed HR 3161 April 12 by a 241-129 vote. *(Vote 178, p. 52-H)*

The House defeated a similar bill Aug. 4, 1976, by a 204-184 margin. *(Vote 458, 1976 Almanac p. 128-H)*

Proponents of HR 3161, led by Patricia Schroeder, D-Colo., chairman of the House Post Office Employee Ethics and Utilization Subcommittee that considered the bill, claimed the firefighters "work 33 percent more hours each week than municipal firefighters, but receive only 12.5 to 23 percent more pay." Schroeder said federal firefighters spent more time on fire prevention than their municipal counterparts and had to be ready to fight unusual fires, such as in nuclear power plants and military aircraft.

Opponents, led by Derwinski, repeated administration arguments and cited President Carter's proposed 5.5 percent lid on federal employee pay raises.

"I find myself this afternoon once again in the interesting position of administration spokesman urging rejection of this special interest legislation," Derwinski said. "I have been looking in vain to the other side of the aisle for a member of the president's party to present the White House viewpoint. There are dozens of special interest bills like this stacked up in [committee]," he charged. "If we let this one roll, it is 'Katy, bar the door,' [and] they all come rolling out."

Senate, Final Action

The Senate passed HR 3161 by voice vote June 5, after the Governmental Affairs Committee reported it on May 15 (S Rept 95-867). Executive branch opposition was reiterated in hearings before the committee's Civil Service and General Services Subcommittee. Civil Service Commission representatives told the panel that the bill would "establish federal firefighters as a favored class of employees" through changes in overtime and standby payment provisions.

After agreeing by unanimous consent to a Senate technical amendment, the House June 7 cleared the bill.■

D.C. Representation

A proposed constitutional amendment giving full representation in Congress to District of Columbia residents cleared a crucial hurdle Aug. 22 when the Senate passed it and sent it to the states for ratification.

"Any thread could have broken, up until the last moment," said one jubilant lobbyist after H J Res 554 had passed 67-32, one vote more than the required two-thirds majority. The House had approved the resolution March 2, 289-127.

District Delegate Walter E. Fauntroy, D, called the victory a "masterpiece of strategy and timing," while floor manager Edward M. Kennedy, D-Mass., cited the bipartisan support for the resolution.

"Strong bipartisan support was able to raise what is a fundamental issue of justice and equality," Kennedy said, "that people who have fought in our wars and have a population greater than that of seven other states ought to have voting representation in the Congress of the United States."

Other supporters were quick to mention that the amendment still required ratification by 38 state legislatures.

"We can't afford the luxury of savoring the victory too long," said Ruth Hinerfeld, president of the League of Women Voters.

Jason Boe, president of the National Conference of State Legislatures, said he expected ratification to be "very close." He said the state legislatures' voting pattern could follow that in the Senate vote, where strong opposition came from some of the less-populated western and southern states.

Final Provisions

As cleared by Congress, H J Res 554:

- Treated the District as a state for purposes of congressional and electoral college representation and for participation in presidential elections and ratification of proposed amendments to the Constitution.
- Repealed the 23rd Amendment to the Constitution. The amendment allowed District residents to vote for president and vice president, while limiting District representation in the electoral college to that of the least populous state.
- Required ratification by 38 states within seven years after passage.
- Provided that implementation of the amendment would be legislated by Congress at a later date.

Background

The victory was a milestone in the protracted struggle for voting rights in the District.

Twenty-three times since 1800 congressional representation for the District had been sought, mainly on the grounds that taxation of District residents without representation in Congress was undemocratic.

In 1970 Congress cleared legislation (PL 91-405) giving the District one non-voting delegate to the House. Once before, during an 1871-75 experiment in a territorial form of government, the city had had a non-voting delegate. *(1970 action, 1970 Almanac, p. 312)*

The 1961 ratification of the 23rd Amendment enabled District residents to vote for president and vice president but restricted D.C. representation in the electoral college to the number of electors granted the least populous state. The District had a 1970 census population of 756,510, larger than that of 10 states. The least populous had three electors.

A council, mayor and increased self-governance were granted the District by 1973 home rule legislation (PL 93-198). But, under Article I of the Constitution, Congress retained power to legislate for the District and to veto its local laws. *(District of Columbia home rule, 1973 Almanac p. 734)*

Proposals for congressional representation were reported in 1967, 1972 and 1976. But only the 1976 proposal reached the House floor, where a 229-181 vote fell 45 short of the two-thirds majority needed for approval. *(Background on proposals for representation, 1972 Almanac, p. 654, 1976 Almanac p. 507)*

House Committee Action

The House Judiciary Committee Feb. 16 reported H J Res 554 (H Rept 95-886) by a vote of 27 to 6.

As reported, H J Res 554 provided that:

- The District of Columbia be treated as though it were a state for purposes of representation in Congress and the electoral college and be allowed to participate in the ratification process of proposed constitutional amendments.
- The people of the District would exercise the rights and powers conferred by the resolution, but Congress would retain its power to establish the mechanisms by which they did so.
- The 23rd Amendment to the Constitution would be repealed.
- The proposed constitutional amendment would not take effect unless ratified by the legislatures of three-fourths of the states within seven years from the date of its submission.

The provision requiring ratification within seven years was added to the resolution in committee by voice vote. It was proposed by M. Caldwell Butler, R-Va., and was intended to ensure that the deadline could not be extended by a simple majority vote of Congress. The Justice Department had said in the case of the Equal Rights Amendment that Congress could extend the deadline for ratification by a simple majority vote because the time limit was contained in the resolving clause rather than in the body of that amendment. *(ERA, p. 773)*

Committee Views. Saying the original disenfranchisement of the District appeared to be more a result of circumstances than of design, the committee said "no reasonable basis exists" for its continuation.

Nevertheless, the committee said it felt the District "should not be transformed into a state." It said the proposed amendment would not give the District a state's powers, constitute a foundation for statehood or change the constitutional powers and responsibility of Congress to legislate with respect to the District.

The committee said it expected that if the amendment were ratified, the size of the House and Senate would be increased temporarily to accommodate the new District members, so that no other states would have their representation reduced. Congress would have to decide whether to permanently increase the membership or reapportion the existing seats after the 1980 census.

Five Judiciary Committee members filed dissenting views saying they had sympathy for the problem but felt H J Res 554 — creating a "pseudo-state" — was the wrong solution. They urged establishment of a commission to draw new boundaries for the federal enclave that would exclude most of the District's residential areas.

Butler filed separate views calling for a voting House representative only. He said the Senate and state legislatures would never agree to add two entirely urban-oriented members to the Senate.

House Floor Action

The House passed H J Res 554 March 2 by a 289-127 vote, 11 votes more than the required two-thirds majority. *(Vote 78, p. 22-H)*

The vote marked the first time a proposal for full congressional representation of the District had passed either chamber. The resolution proposed by Don Edwards, D-Calif., also was the first to grant full electoral college representation and ratification rights to the District.

The House agreed by voice vote to the committee amendment placing the ratification deadline in the body of the resolution.

It defeated, by a 7-11 standing vote, a substitute amendment by Butler that would have retained the 23rd Amendment and granted the District representation only in the House.

Butler said H J Res 554 "went too far" in making the District look like a state without giving it a state's responsibilities. He said his proposal offered a "kite that will fly" and that the House was the logical place to start, since the House is representative of the people while the Senate is representative of the states.

'No More and No Less'

Supporters of H J Res 554 argued that, especially in view of U.S. pressure for human rights elsewhere in the world, it was morally wrong to deny District residents the same representation in Congress as other U.S. citizens.

"We want no more and no less than that to which all Americans are entitled and to do that we must be represented in both the House and the Senate," Del. Walter E. Fauntroy, D-D.C., told the House. "Nothing more is needed; nothing less will satisfy the dictates of conscience."

Proponents argued that the Senate and the states should be allowed to decide on the amendment and that the people of the District should have a voice in special kinds of decision making, where one chamber has exclusive or dominant jurisdiction.

"The question before us is not whether this proposed amendment will be acceptable to the other body and ratified by the state legislatures.... The question is rather whether the House of Representatives will act responsibly today to accord...to District residents their constitutional right and privilege," said Robert McClory, R-Ill.

A motion by Charles E. Wiggins, R-Calif., to recommit the resolution to the Judiciary Committee with instructions that it consider a resolution to return populated areas of the District to Maryland was rejected by voice vote.

Before approving the proposed amendment, the House split by similar margins on adoption of the rule (H Res 1048) providing for floor consideration of H J Res 554, and on two votes March 1 and 2 to consider the Edwards resolution in Committee of the Whole. *(Votes 75-77, p. 22-H)*

Senate Action

The Senate Aug. 22 passed H J Res 554, 67-32, one vote more than the required two-thirds majority. *(Vote 346, p. 52-S)*

On April 24, the resolution had been placed directly on the Senate calendar without having been referred to the Judiciary Committee.

Kennedy's opening speech Aug. 16 summarized most of the arguments in favor of the amendment:

- It was a question of "fundamental rights and human justice" that District citizens "should have a voice in the decisions of the Senate and the House."
- The population of the District was larger than that of several other states.
- Residents of the District paid $1.4 billion in federal taxes in fiscal 1977, an amount greater than the taxes paid by 11 states.
- District residents fought and died in Vietnam and other wars.
- A study by the Library of Congress had found that Brazil and the United States were the only two among 115 nations in the world with elected legislatures to deny representation for citizens of their capital cities.

Opposition to the amendment focused on three issues:

- Lacking rural areas and natural resources, the District did not fit the traditional notion of a "state."
- The amendment was a violation of Article V of the Constitution, which declared that "no state, without its consent, shall be deprived of its equal suffrage in the Senate." Opponents argued that admission of the District would dilute the votes of current states in the Senate without their consent.
- A more suitable solution would be to link the District to Maryland, either by ceding the District's territory back to Maryland (full retrocession) or by allowing District citizens to vote in Maryland elections (partial retrocession).

Changes Blocked

Opponents failed on the first day of debate, Aug. 16, to prevent the measure from being taken up on two procedural motions, agreed to 64-28 and 71-22. *(Votes 322, 323, p. 49-S)*

An agreement to limit debate was reached the following day after opponents were defeated 68-22 and 52-33 on motions to table (kill) two proposed amendments. As part of the agreement, under which a vote on the amendment was scheduled for Aug. 22, Majority Leader Robert C. Byrd, D-W.Va., withdrew a cloture petition he had filed to cut off debate.

When debate resumed Aug. 21, supporters fought off five more amendments, and then defeated an additional seven amendments.

Opponents, led by Bill Scott, R-Va., James A. McClure, R-Idaho, and Orrin G. Hatch, R-Utah, introduced without success one weakening amendment after another; many proposed some form of retrocession.

The final effort to squelch the resolution involved a point of order made by Hatch that the proposed amendment was in violation of Article V, states' rights to equal suffrage.

Byrd countered that "it was too late in history to argue that granting representation in Congress to the District of Columbia would deprive any state of its equal suffrage in the Senate."

A motion to table the Hatch point of order was agreed to, 65-32. *(Vote 344, p. 52-S)*

The resolution was put to a vote after the final proposed change was tabled.

Amendments Killed

In all, supporters managed to kill 14 weakening amendments by tabling them.

The rejected amendments were offered by:

- Carl T. Curtis, R-Neb., to require a balanced federal budget; tabled 68-22. *(Vote 324, p. 49-S)*
- Melcher, to provide representation for the District in the House as though it were a state and in the Senate as though it were a part of Maryland; tabled 52-33. *(Vote 325, p. 49-S)*
- Scott, to give states the power to decide on the abortion issue; tabled 48-19. *(Vote 328, p. 50-S)*
- McClure, to prohibit states from rescinding ratification of the amendment; tabled 67-5. *(Vote 329, p. 50-S)*
- McClure, to grant to District residents the authority to implement the provisions of the amendment; tabled 50-28. *(Vote 330, p. 50-S)*
- McClure, to return the District to Maryland; defeated 47-35. *(Vote 331, p. 50-S)*
- McClure, to grant statehood to the district; tabled 67-17. *(Vote 332, p. 50-S)*
- McClure, to treat the District as part of Maryland for purposes of representation in the Senate; tabled 46-36. *(Vote 337, p. 51-S)*
- McClure, to grant similar representation to cities with populations larger than the District; tabled 79-6. *(Vote 338, p. 51-S)*
- Scott, to treat the District as a state for purposes of representation in the House, but not in the Senate; tabled 60-28. *(Vote 339, p. 51-S)*
- Scott, to provide a method for filling vacancies in the District congressional delegation; tabled 69-22. *(Vote 340, p. 51-S)*
- Scott, to assure District residents the right to implement provisions relating to representation in Congress; tabled 76-16. *(Vote 341, p. 51-S)*
- Dewey F. Bartlett, R-Okla., to prohibit the establishment of any new congressional committee having jurisdiction over District legislative matters; tabled 63-31. *(Vote 343, p. 52-S)*
- Melcher, to provide for direct representation in the House for the District but representation in the Senate as though it were part of Maryland; tabled 60-37. *(Vote 345, p. 52-S)*

Amateur Sports Revamping

A major reorganization of the nation's amateur sports structure won the approval of Congress Oct. 15 — minus a $30 million authorization that later was pared down to $16 million and attached to another bill.

Although the bill was designed to end 50 years of squabbling among amateur sports organizations, there were indications that the next Congress would see a new fight over federal funds for one of the organizations, the U.S. Olympic Committee.

The House passed the bill (S 2727) by voice vote Oct. 13 after adopting on a non-record vote an amendment by Harold L. Volkmer, D-Mo., that dropped the $30 million authorization. The Senate passed S 2727 as amended by voice vote Oct. 15, clearing it for the president (PL 95-606).

But later that same day, Ted Stevens, R-Alaska, one of the prime Senate supporters of S 2727, successfully attached a $16 million authorization of fiscal 1980 funds for sports medicine and training programs to a resolution (H J Res 1139) continuing appropriations for agencies whose fiscal 1979 appropriations had not yet cleared.

The Senate and the House both agreed to Stevens' move by voice vote, clearing the continuing resolution for the president. *(Continuing resolution story, p. 161)*

According to a spokesman for S 2727 supporter Rep. Robert W. Kastenmeier, D-Wis., approval of the $16 million authorization meant that the whole fight over whether the Olympic Committee should receive a federal grant would be renewed during consideration of the 1980 budget.

Congressional budget rules forbid any new authorizing legislation for the fiscal year beginning Oct. 1 from being reported after May 15 of the previous calendar year. Thus the Olympic money should have been reported before May 15, 1978. A similar delay prevented the $16 million from being included in the 1979 budget.

The fight over the $30 million for the Olympic Committee had helped defeat House passage of S 2727 on Sept. 26. With a two-thirds majority needed for passage under suspension of the rules, the 244-158 vote by the House was 24 votes short. *(Vote 737, p. 210-H)*

Background

A January 1977 report from the President's Commission on Olympic Sports, established by President Ford in 1975, was the preliminary basis for S 2727. Among its findings were:

- A longstanding conflict between the National Collegiate Athetic Association (NCAA) and the Amateur Athletic Union (AAU) sometimes prevented the best American athletes from competing internationally, including in the Olympics.
- "There is no truly effective system for [coordinating] amateur athletics in this country."
- Conflicts among a "weak" USOC, the NCAA, the AAU and separate national governing bodies (NGBs) in other sports, hindered amateur grass-roots competition, facilities and development, and contributed to the other problems.

The panel recommended a structure similar to that contained in S 2727, but added that the USOC should be superseded as the main governing amateur sports body by a new authority having the same powers S 2727 granted to the USOC.

Senate Action

The NCAA and AAU both vigorously objected to the bill during Senate Commerce Committee hearings (S Rept 95-770) in October 1977. Both organizations disliked proposals that an athletes' "bill of rights" be written into the law. NCAA executive director Walter Byers said that schools and colleges should be able to veto an athlete's competing in non-school sports contests.

Sen. Ted Stevens, R-Alaska, prime Senate sponsor of the bill, successfully sought changes in the USOC constitution guaranteeing some athletes' rights. Backing up those changes would be the bill's arbitration provisions.

Both the NCAA and the AAU later supported the bill. The NCAA grudgingly gave its support after the USOC changed its voting rules so that the AAU could not dominate the NCAA within the Olympic body.

The Senate passed S 2727 (S Rept 95-770) by voice vote May 8.

House Action

The Judiciary Committee on a 24-7 vote Sept. 21 ordered reported an amended version of the Senate bill. It was reported Sept. 25 (H Rept 95-1627), but the printed report was not available until after the Sept. 26 floor vote.

The Sept. 26 House vote defeating the measure came under a suspension of the rules, requiring a two-thirds majority for passage and permitting no amendments. The lack of opportunity to amend the bill was a key to its defeat. Members particularly objected to the $30 million grant, arguing that they should have been able to amend or delete that provision. Members also complained that the Judiciary Committee report on the bill, which contained opposing views, was not available to them when the bill was called up.

Opponents of the $30 million grant charged that $18 million would go for an "amateur sports bureaucracy." They pointed to a USOC budget summary admitting that that amount of money would go for administrative costs.

John F. Seiberling, D-Ohio, questioned whether the grant was a one-time-only affair, as proponents claimed. "I view it as a foot in the door," he said. "We know how hard it is to shut off federal dollars once they start flowing."

Seiberling and Thomas N. Kindness, R-Ohio, argued that members should have an opportunity to separately vote on the grant. Kindness said that Judiciary's Administrative Law Subcommittee had unanimously deleted the money, and Seiberling said that the 18-13 Sept. 21 Judiciary Committee vote to restore the funds indicated that it was too controversial for consideration by suspending the rules.

Supporters of the bill included Jack F. Kemp, R-N.Y., and several other House members who were once-active athletes. Ralph Metcalfe, D-Ill., a former Olympic sprinter, said, "It would be travesty if we let slip from our grasp the opportunity to end over 50 years of quarreling" between the NCAA and the AAU.

"Their squabbles have only served to penalize our amateur athletes. I was a victim of their disputes. I have seen other victims of their disputes."

Noting that Kemp and other Republican fiscal conservatives were "suddenly embracing the opportunity to spend $30 million," Seiberling said that "they also seem to be in favor of federal regulation into what has up to now been the quintessence of private initiative — amateur athletics."

Romano L. Mazzoli, D-Ky., said the bill injected too much federal authority into resolving the feud. "I do not think Congress should be sucked into combat between the AAU and the NCAA," he said.

Final Action, Provisions

The bill was brought up again on the House floor Oct. 13 under a rule allowing amendments during the floor debate.

Supporters of the authorization claimed the money was a one-time-only grant to help reorganize the committee and end the wrangling among amateur athletic groups that had hampered past U.S. efforts in the Olympics.

Opponents pointed to an admission by Olympic Committee officials that $18 million of the original $30 million request would go for administrative costs. The committee claimed the money was a key part of the bill.

Both Sen. Stevens and Rep. Robert H. Michel, R-Ill., who argued for passage of the funds in the continuing resolution, pointed to safeguards in both S 2727 and H J Res 1139 on spending the money contained in H J Res 1139. The safeguards were adopted in both houses by voice vote before passage of S 2727 and included in the provisions of the resolution.

Under S 2727 as cleared, the Olympic Committee must report yearly to congressional committees on all grants made to it. Included in its report would be full disclosure of "how the funds are and will be spent." Stevens and Michel said the safeguards would prevent the money from being spent on what opponents termed "an amateur sports bureaucracy."

The opponents, however, were still uneasy. Seiberling, who opposed both authorizations, said after the smaller one passed that the $16 million "would extend the long arm of the government into amateur athletics and into the taxpayer's pocket to pay for it."

Also adopted on the floor were several Judiciary Committee amendments to S 2727, later agreed to by the Senate. In addition to Michel's "full disclosure" amendment, they:

- Eliminated a Senate-passed provision authorizing the committee to accept transfers of surplus government property. According to a Judiciary Committee aide, the Olympic Committee "had its eye on an abandoned military base in Colorado." The provision was dropped after Government Operations Committee Chairman Jack Brooks, D-Texas, said his panel would consider the request.
- Keyed spending of any authorized funds, though not included in S 2727, to "purposes outlined in Sec. 104 of the Olympic Charter," but said the secretary of commerce "may" — not "shall" — disburse the money.

The Senate passed the amended version of S 2727 by voice vote Oct. 15.

White House Staff

A legislative cloud that hovered over most of the White House staff since 1939 was finally dissipated by the 95th Congress in the last days of the 1978 session.

By voice vote Oct. 14, the House cleared a conference report (H Rept 95-1639) on a bill (HR 11003) authorizing salary levels for, and setting limits on the number of, top White House staffers. President Carter signed the bill into law Nov. 2 (PL 95-570).

The Senate previously passed the conference report on Oct. 7, also by voice vote.

The bill authorized levels and numbers of top presidential, vice presidential, Domestic Council and Office of Administration staffers. The old federal law had allowed the president 14 staff members, compared with an actual White House staff of more than 300. Though Congress annually had approved appropriations for the larger staff, the money had been challenged on the floor several times for its lack of authorization. Opponents often claimed that under Article I, Section 8 of the Constitution, appropriating the money for an unauthorized staff was illegal.

Under HR 11003, specific limits were set on the number of persons hired at the salary levels of GS-18 and above. Unlimited hiring at lower salary levels was authorized, although yearly appropriations were required to pay for the staff.

The bill allowed the continued use of detailees and outside consultants, but this and other White House staffing practices would for the first time have to be reported by the president to Congress.

Explicit authorization also was given for staffs and support services for the vice president and the spouses of the president and vice president.

The bill was lauded by its sponsors as a needed and rational way of ending the confused, topsy-grown White House staffing procedures. Supporters also noted that the reporting provisions allowed Congress some oversight ability for White House staffing for the first time.

Opponents responded that the bill's staffing provisions were too lavish, noting that the number of high-level staffers authorized would be nearly double the current actual number. Opponents also criticized the reporting requirements as inadequate. Republican members twitted a number of Democrats for having about-faced on the authorizing legislation, since it was proposed under Republican presidents but never enacted.

House Action

Committee. The House Post Office and Civil Service Committee reported HR 11003 (H Rept 95-979) on March 16 by unanimous voice vote.

The committee said that the legislation was needed because the lack of specific authorization subjected White House appropriations to points of order when they were being considered on the House floor. In 1977 conferees warned that future appropriations would not be approved unless they were authorized. *(1977 Almanac p. 243)*

Floor. The Carter administration and the Democratic House leadership suffered a temporary setback April 4, when the bill first went to the House floor. It was brought up under a suspension of the rules, usually reserved for non-controversial measures, and failed to obtain the necessary two-thirds margin of approval. The 207-188 vote fell 57 votes short of the needed 264 votes in favor. *(Vote 156, p. 46-H)*

Bill Cable, top White House liaison with the House, said after the April 4 vote that the administration had been surprised by the outcome. He said he believed the bill's intent had been misunderstood, as indicated by floor debate. While members attacked the bill as an expansion of the White House staff, Cable stated that no such expansion was planned.

During floor debate on April 4, sponsors argued that HR 11003 was needed to clarify the presidential authority to hire and maintain a full-sized staff at the White House. Legally, sponsors pointed out, the White House staff should only number 14. In fact, the core White House staff stood at 351, with the full executive office of the president numbering more than 1,500.

Patricia Schroeder, D-Colo., chairperson of the Post Office and Civil Service Employee Ethics Subcommittee, said that the White House staff had been built up over the last 40 years by "all sorts of different ways of phonying up the records" of who actually works for the president at the White House.

The principal means of "phonying" the size of the White House staff had been the use of consultants and detailees — employees of an executive branch agency, typically a Cabinet department, who actually worked in the White House but were paid by their home agency and showed up on its budget.

Herbert E. Harris II, D-Va., argued that the bill allowed Congress for the first time to maintain genuine oversight of the size and deployment of the White House staff.

Opponents argued that the reporting requirements in the bill were inadequate, particularly with regard to the reporting of the use of detailees, and that the bill authorized too many high-level, large-salary positions. It provided for 50 executive level employees, those paid from $52,500 to $57,000 a year. If all those slots were filled, it would double the number of executive level White House employees.

On the bill's second time up for consideration, the House April 13 voted 265-134 to pass HR 11003. *(Vote 183, p. 54-H)*

During April 13 floor action, an amendment offered by Benjamin A. Gilman, R-N.Y., was adopted by voice vote. Its principal effect was to tighten the reporting requirements affecting detailees in the White House for less than six months.

An amendment to the Gilman amendment, offered by J. J. Pickle, D-Texas, also was adopted by voice vote. It required the annual reports to include the names of each employee of the White House, the amount paid to each and a brief job description and general title.

A second Gilman amendment intended to shorten the permanent authorization to four years was rejected, 171-232. The amendment would have required the next president to resubmit a staff authorization request within one year of assuming office. *(Vote 181, p. 54-H)*

Also rejected, 85-320, was an amendment offered by Steven D. Symms, R-Idaho, that would have barred the use of any authorized staff funds for lobbying state legislatures on proposed constitutional amendments. Symms noted his opposition to the activities of former Carter aide Mark Siegel in organizing state lobbying efforts on behalf of the Equal Rights Amendment. *(Vote 182, p. 54-H)*

Earlier, the House voted 395-1 to adopt the rule, H Res 1128, under which HR 11003 was considered. *(Vote 179, p. 54-H)*

Senate Action

Committee. The Senate Governmental Affairs Committee reported HR 11003 (S Rept 95-868) on May 15.

The only change it made in the House-passed bill involved reporting requirements. It dropped the House requirement that the president report individually on every employee. Instead, it required reporting of the number of and amount paid to employees in specific pay categories and of the number of and amount paid to experts, consultants and federal employees loaned from other departments.

Floor. The Senate passed the bill by voice vote July 14.

The only differences between the House and Senate versions of the legislation were in the length of the authorization — the House made it permanent while the Senate limited it to five years — and in provisions setting out what information the president had to provide to Congress.

As passed by the Senate, HR 11003 authorized the president to hire up to 25 employees for Exective Level II positions (up to $57,500 per year), 25 for Executive Level III up to $52,500, 50 above the GS-16 level (up to $47,500) and an unlimited number below GS 16. If all of those positions were filled, it would nearly double the number of employees in the top three salary levels who, as of July 1, 1978, numbered 59.

The bill also authorized staff and support services for the vice president, the spouses of the president and vice president, the domestic policy staff and the Office of Administration. The president was given an open-ended authorization for his official expenses including entertainment, staff travel and White House maintenance. But those expenses had to be verified by the comptroller general.

Senate opponents charged that the bill authorized excessive staff and spending levels, especially in light of Carter's campaign promises to cut White House staff and his appeals to the public to fight inflation through smaller wage increases.

Proponents argued that the bill's reporting requirements would prevent the president from abusing his hiring power or hiding staff size through the use of detailees and consultants. They added that the congressional oversight provided for in the bill would check excessive spending.

The decision to limit the authorization to five years came on an amendment by William V. Roth, R-Del., which was adopted by voice vote. The amendment barred spending under the bill after Sept. 30, 1983.

Earlier, the Senate voted 16-56 against an amendment by Jesse Helms, R-N.C. to limit funds for the president's offical expenses to $20,019,700 in fiscal 1979. Helms said the figure represented a 7 percent increase for inflation over the $18,710,000 budgeted for those expenses in fiscal 1978. *(Vote 213, p. 35-S)*

Conference, Final Action

As agreed upon by conferees and accepted by the Senate Oct. 7 and the House Oct. 14 by voice votes, the president under HR 11003 could hire up to 100 top-level ($47,500 or higher annual salary) staffers, plus however many employees he needed below that level. The vice president could hire 11 top-level employees, plus however many he needed below that level.

The spouses of both top officials also were authorized to use the staff to "assist in the discharge of the duties and responsibilities" of holding the two offices.

The effect of the measure was to legalize the White House staff, the staff of the Executive Office of the President and the vice presidential staff. The measure also raised the White House travel authorization to $100,000 from $40,000, and continued the authorization of $1 million for the president's "unanticipated needs." However, the president was required to report on how the contingency money was spent within 60 days after the beginning of the new fiscal year.

The measure also authorized the hiring of temporary outside consultants and the detailing of other executive branch agency employees to the White House, but with some restrictions. Such "borrowing" of other agency employees had been a favorite method of expanding the White House staff over the years.

Conferees retained a Senate amendment keeping confidential the names, occupations and salaries of every specific White House employee. However, they supported a House provision making HR 11003 the permanent White House staff authorization bill. A Senate "sunset" provision would have terminated the staff authorization at the end of fiscal 1983.

The bill authorized "such sums as may be necessary" for White House maintenance, presidential and vice presidential entertaining and subsistence expenses for government employees who travel abroad on official business connected with either presidential or vice presidential travel. ▮

Federal Information Centers

By voice vote Oct. 5, the Senate agreed to House amendments to a bill (S 3259) authorizing $7 million for expansion of federal information centers in 1980, clearing the measure for the president (PL 95-491).

The bill also officially authorized the federal information center network, which had been in existence — and receiving about $4 million in appropriations — since the first experimental center was established in 1966.

Also given official statutory authorization by S 3259 were the federal telecommunications fund and some automatic data processing equipment. The House added the two other authorizations to the Senate-passed bill during debate Sept. 25 (H Rept 95-1530).

By voice vote, the House passed its version of the bill (HR 13688) adding the three authorizations to the Federal Property Act of 1949. It then substituted HR 13688's provisions for those of the Senate bill by voice vote.

During Senate consideration of S 3259 on Sept. 12, before passage by voice vote (S Rept 95-1129), the committee report noted that the centers' "principal beneficiaries were poor people least informed and knowledgeable about the government."

House Government Operations Committee Chairman Jack Brooks, D-Texas, said that "there are now centers in 38 major cities . . . but about half of our citizens still do not have this service available."

Rep. Frank Horton, R-N.Y., added, "this bill makes it possible for every citizen to pick up the phone, dial a number and find out in one call exactly where to get the information" sought about federal programs and procedures. ▮

Inspectors General Bill

With the specter of fraud and corruption in the General Services Administration (GSA) looming in the background, the House Sept. 27 passed a bill establishing inspector general offices in 12 federal agencies (PL 95-452).

The House cleared HR 8588 for the president by unanimous consent, after agreeing to Senate amendments. The

Senate passed HR 8588 by voice vote Sept. 22, after hearings in June and July before the Governmental Affairs Committee (S Rept 95-1071). The House originally passed the bill by a 388-6 vote on April 18. *(Vote 189, p. 56-H)*

Each presidentially appointed inspector general would be subject to Senate confirmation and would have full subpoena and investigatory powers to move against waste and fraud in government programs, according to sponsor Rep. L.H. Fountain, D-N.C.

The affected agencies were: departments of Agriculture, Commerce, Housing and Urban Development, Interior, Labor, and Transportation; the Community Services Administration, Environmental Protection Agency, GSA, National Aeronautics and Space Administration, Small Business Administration and the Veterans Administration.

The position was modeled after one established by law in the departments of Health, Education and Welfare (PL 94-905) and Energy (PL 95-91, section 208).

HEW Secretary Joseph A. Califano Jr. told the House Government Operations Committee July 27, 1977, that "the inspector general concept was one of the most important ideas in years for strengthening the management of complex government programs." (H Rept 95-584). HEW Inspector General Thomas Morris had recently disclosed fraud and waste in Medicare and Medicaid programs.

A Sept. 18 General Accounting Office study said that up to $25 billion annually could be lost to crime and fraud within the government.

Several provisions of the bill attempted to insulate the inspectors general from political pressure: When a president removes an inspector general, he must tell the Congress why he does so. The inspectors general must be nonpartisan nominees chosen for ability in accounting, auditing, law and investigations, among other aspects. And the inspector general's reports to Congress may not be changed by agency heads before submission.

The bill also provided that an inspector general may conceal the identities of lower-level "whistleblowers" — federal employees who report fraud or mismanagement.

The Senate added the Defense Department to the bill, without requiring a separate inspector general. The legislation ordered the defense secretary to make twice-yearly reports, drawn from service audit agency records, to Congress. It authorized the secretary to designate an inspector general, subject to confirmation, within the department. ▮

Presidential Papers

Congress followed up a 1974 law designed to prevent the destruction of former President Nixon's tapes and papers by clearing Oct. 15 broader legislation making most of the papers of outgoing presidents public property (PL 95-591).

After being favorably reported by the House Government Operations Committee Aug. 14 by a vote of 33-2 (H Rept 95-1487), the bill (HR 13500) was passed by the House by voice vote under suspension of the rules Oct. 10.

The Senate passed the measure by voice vote Oct. 13 after adding an amendment, which the House accepted Oct. 15, clearing the measure for the president.

Background

Presidential papers traditionally had been considered the property of a president when he left office, but the issue came to a head in the aftermath of the Watergate scandal in 1974.

President Nixon reached an agreement with Arthur Sampson, then general services administrator, that would have given Nixon ownership and control of his tapes and papers and allowed him after five years to destroy any tape.

Congress overruled the agreement when it passed legislation (S 4016 — PL 93-526) directing Sampson to keep possession of Nixon's papers and tapes and requiring explicit congressional authorization for destruction of those materials. *(Background, 1974 Almanac p. 654)*

Provisions

While the 1974 act applied only to the Nixon materials, HR 13500 established the public ownership of all future presidential records beginning with the 1981 presidential term.

Under the bill most presidential records become public property at the end of a president's tenure in office.

The president could retain personal records, including diaries and journals, materials relating to private political matters, or materials connected with the president's election or the election of any other officials.

The president also would retain the right to restrict access to certain materials for up to 12 years if the documents fell within one of several categories, including national defense or foreign policy, trade secrets, confidential advice between the president and his advisers, personnel files or files relating to presidential appointments.

As cleared by Congress, HR 13500:

- Defined presidential records to include all documents created by the president or his staff that related to the official duties of the president; documents dealing with political activities would only be included if they related to the president's official duties.
- Defined personal records to include documents of a personal nature that were unrelated to the president's official duties, such as diaries, journals, or other personal notes; political materials that were unrelated to the president's official duties; and materials connected with the president's own election or with the election of any other official that had no bearing on the president's official duties.
- Declared that the federal government owned all presidential records and that the records were to be managed by the archivist.
- Allowed the president to dispose of documents considered to have no value. The president must, however, notify Congress 60 days before the disposal date, and he must also notify and get an opinion from the archivist, who retains the right to advise Congress that the records are of special interest.
- Provided that the archivist would assume control of the documents upon the conclusion of the president's last term, and that all records would be placed in a facility operated by the archivist.
- Authorized the archivist to dispose of documents considered to have insufficient value to warrant preservation.
- Allowed the president to restrict for up to 12 years access to records if: 1) they were authorized to be kept secret in the interest of national defense or foreign policy; 2) they related to presidential appointments; 3) they were specifically exempted from disclosure by law; 4) they contained trade secrets and commercial or financial information obtained from an individual on a confidential basis; 5) they were confidential communications requesting or sub-

mitting advice between the president and his advisers; and 6) they were personnel or medical files that would constitute an invasion of personal privacy.

- Allowed persons denied access to restricted records to file an appeal with the archivist, who would make a determination within 30 days after consultation with the former president.
- Allowed all records to be made available: 1) to respond to a court order or subpoena dealing with a civil or criminal proceeding; 2) to an incumbent president if they were needed for the conduct of current business and were not otherwise available; 3) to Congress if they were needed for the conduct of its business and were not otherwise available; and 4) to the former president or his representative.
- Provided similar treatment for vice-presidential records.

The amendment added by the Senate directed the archivist to make all unrestricted presidential papers available to the public and declared that the exemption in the Freedom of Information Act for intra- and interagency memorandums and letters should not apply to unrestricted presidential papers.

Overseas Voting Rights

An "apple pie and motherhood" bill designed to encourage more people to vote was given final approval in the closing hours of the 95th Congress with a multimillion-dollar subsidy for Democratic and Republican campaign committees tacked on.

The bill (S 703) prevented states from using the fact that an American living overseas voted in a state or federal election as evidence of residency for tax purposes. Sponsors said many Americans living abroad don't vote out of fear of having to pay additional taxes.

Attached to the voting rights bill as cleared was a provision the Congressional Budget Office (CBO) estimated would cost taxpayers $2.5 million in 1979 and $4.7 million in 1980 in subsidized mail rates for Democratic and Republican national and state campaign committees.

The Senate had passed the bill May 9, 1977 (S Rept 95-121). The House Administration Committee reported S 703 Sept. 13 (H Rept 95-1568) and the House passed the measure Sept. 19 by a vote of 327-78, after adding the mail subsidy. *(Vote 703, p. 200-H)*

The Senate accepted the House amendment Oct. 13 by voice vote, clearing the bill for the president (PL 95-593).

In remarks entered in the *Congressional Record,* Claiborne Pell, D-R.I., urged the Senate to accept the provision because it "will provide a measure of relief to the financially burdened political process."

In addition to the mail subsidy, S 703 contained these major provisions:

- Required the states to provide for absentee registration and voting in federal elections by members of the armed forces and the merchant marine and their dependents.
- Required the secretary of defense to design a standardized postcard to serve as a simultaneous application for both registration and absentee ballot.
- Extended coverage of the bill to include U.S. citizens who possess acceptable forms of identification other than current passports or State Department identification.
- Provided that certain qualified political committees might utilize the third-class postal rate applicable to a non-profit organization. (This provision was not included in the Senate version of the bill.)

The bill applied only to federal elections, leaving states free to tax Americans living abroad who voted in state or local elections.

Only for 'Qualified Committees'

The subsidy provision entitled certain "qualified political committees" to use low-cost mail rates that were available to other non-profit organizations. Those "qualified" committees would include any "national committee" or "state committee" as defined by the federal election law, but not non-party or "candidate" committees such as the "Jones for Congress Committee."

Theoretically, the provision could provide subsidies to minor parties such as the Libertarian and U.S. Labor parties. But for practical purposes, the principal beneficiaries of the subsidy provision would be the Democratic and Republican Party committees.

The bill specifically stated that the term "qualified political committee" included "the Republican and Democratic Senatorial Campaign Committees, the Democratic National Congressional Committee, and the National Republican Congressional Committee."

Support for the bill was, as one advocate described it, "a bipartisan effort." No one opposed the provision on either the House or Senate floor.

Mary Maginniss, a CBO analyst, said her cost projections were based exclusively on costs resulting from use of the subsidy by Republican and Democratic campaign committees. She said CBO assumed costs from other party committees would be "negligible."

"In most states only the Republican and Democratic parties would be included," she said.

David L. Shurtz, who worked on the bill for Charles E. Wiggins, R-Calif., said, "It's obvious the Democratic and Republican campaign committees were the authors of this thing. . . . They were looking for a nice convenient non-controversial bill" to attach the provision to. (Wiggins supported the provision, but opposed the bill.)

The non-profit mail rates sought by the Republican and Democratic campaign committees provided that letters may be sent for 2.7 cents a letter, rather than at the 8.4 cents-a-letter rate then paid by the committee using third-class bulk mail.

Guayule Rubber Research

Congress Oct. 15 cleared legislation authorizing $30 million over a four-year period for research and development to encourage commercial production of natural rubber from guayule, a desert shrub common in the Southwest.

The bill (S 1816 — PL 95-592) was given final approval after the House and Senate agreed on a compromise version that split administrative jurisdiction evenly between the Commerce and Agriculture Departments.

As reported by the Senate Environment and Public Works Committee May 15 (S Rept 95-829) and passed by the Senate by voice vote May 26, the bill gave exclusive jurisdiction to the Commerce Department and authorized appropriations of $30 million over four years.

The House passed its version (HR 12559) by voice vote under suspension of the rules Sept. 19. It authorized $55 million over four years and gave jurisdiction to the Agriculture Department. The bill had been reported by the Science and Technology Committee Aug. 17 (H Rept 95-1512).

The compromise was approved by the Senate by voice vote Oct. 7. The House approved it Oct. 13 with an amendment exempting a group of farmers in Virginia, Tennessee and North Carolina from penalties for mistakenly growing a type of tobacco subject to quota restraints. The Senate accepted the amended bill by voice vote Oct. 15, clearing the measure.

The bill marked a second attempt by the federal government to promote commercial production of the plant. A similar project started during World War II ended in 1946 when cheaper rubber from Southeast Asia returned to the world market after the area was freed from Japanese control.

Supporters argued that with the price of natural rubber at 50 cents a pound and expected to go higher, guayule could be produced at a competitive price. They also said guayule production would decrease U.S. dependence on foreign sources of supply, help the nation's balance of trade and provide some economic stimulus to areas of chronic unemployment in the Southwest such as Indian reservations.

Provisions

As cleared by Congress, S 1816:

- Established a joint commission on guayule research and commercialization consisting of three members from the Agriculture Department, three from Commerce, one from the Interior Department's Bureau of Indian Affairs and one from the National Science Foundation.
- Authorized the commission to establish goals and broad policy and to make recommendations to the secretaries of agriculture and commerce on grants and contracts.
- Authorized the secretary of agriculture to conduct research and development to promote effective and economical methods for large-scale cultivation of guayule, including seed collection and stockpiling, breeding and selection programs to improve latex yields, and experimental plantings of guayule in arid and semiarid regions of the United States.
- Authorized the secretary of commerce to test and demonstrate the economic feasibility of the manufacture and commercialization of natural rubber from guayule, including research on extraction and processing techniques, analysis of usable byproducts, improving manufacturing technologies and evaluating the marketability of rubber derived from guayule.
- Authorized the secretaries, after consultation with the secretary of state, to cooperate with the Mexican government in guayule research and development.
- Authorized appropriations of $30 million over four years beginning in fiscal 1980.

Carter Reorganization Plans

President Carter submitted four reorganization plans to Congress in 1978. All went into effect, after Congress handily rejected resolutions of disapproval.

Under legislation passed in 1977 (PL 95-17), the president was given authority to reorganize the executive branch — authority that Carter during his presidential campaign had said would be a top priority for his administration. As cleared by Congress, the legislation allowed the president to submit reorganization plans to Congress. A legislative veto provision in the bill stipulated that a reorganization plan would take effect unless disapproved by either the House or Senate within 60 days after submission. Two reorganization plans took effect in 1977. *(Background, 1977 Almanac p. 749)*

The four plans which took effect in 1978 were:

- A consolidation of most fair employment enforcement programs into the Equal Employment Opportunity Commission. The House approved the plan April 25 by defeating a resolution of disapproval, 39-356.
- A reorganization of the Civil Service Commission, which was part of the president's proposal to revamp the civil service system. The House rejected the resolution of disapproval Aug. 9, 19-381. *(Civil Service reform, p. 818)*
- A merger of federal emergency preparedness and disaster response programs into a new agency. The House rejected the disapproval resolution Sept. 14, 40-327.
- A reorganization of the administration of the Employee Retirement Income Security Act, transferring most of the administrative functions to the Treasury Department from the Labor Department. Both chambers rejected resolutions of disapproval by voice votes.

Fair Employment Programs

President Carter's proposal to consolidate most fair employment enforcement programs into the Equal Employment Opportunity Commission (EEOC) went into effect May 6 after Congress passed up its chance to block the plan within 60 days. *(Carter message, p. 38-E)*

"The plan will improve enforcement of equal employment opportunities and reduce the burden of equal employment enforcement on business by consolidating the agencies involved," Carter said as Reorganization Plan No. 1 of 1978 took effect.

Some 18 government entities had been enforcing employment discrimination statutes.

Carter submitted the plan Feb. 23 under a law that allowed presidential reorganization plans to take effect automatically if neither house voted to disapprove them within 60 days. The House approved the plan April 25 by defeating a resolution of disapproval (H Res 1049) 39-356. *(Vote 210, p. 60-H)*

The House Government Operations Committee filed its report on the plan April 19 (H Rept 95-1069).

The committee concluded that the plan would be "beneficial to those whose rights are being protected," and would "reduce the impact on the business community that has resulted from the proliferation of governmental units administering related programs."

The committee added that the laws to be administered by the EEOC "contain widely varying standards and procedures" and that "duplications and inconsistencies must be addressed by legislation."

As approved by the House, the plan:

- Shifted to EEOC from the Civil Service Commission functions relating to equal employment opportunity for federal government employees and federal employment of the handicapped.
- Shifted to EEOC from the Labor Department functions relating to wage discrimination between men and women under the Equal Pay Act (PL 88-38) and employment discrimination against the aged under the Age Discrimination in Employment Act. (PL 90-202).

• Abolished the Equal Employment Opportunity Coordinating Council on July 1, 1978 and transferred its duties to the EEOC.

The Senate Governmental Affairs Committee unanimously endorsed the plan April 20 by reporting a similar disapproval resolution (S Res 404) with the recommendation that it not pass (S Rept 95-750). The Senate failed to act on the resolution before the May 5 deadline.

Approval was conditioned, however, on Carter's promise to the Governmental Affairs Committee that he would delay implementation of a federal employment provision until 1979, provided the 95th Congress passed the administration's proposed civil service reform bill (HR 11280).

The disputed provision gave EEOC power in discrimination cases to overrule the Merit Systems Protection Board (MSPB) proposed in the civil service bill as an independent agency to rule on federal employees' merit system violations and discrimination complaints.

The committee feared the mixed jurisdiction might result in forum shopping by aggrieved employees, conflicting decisions from the two agencies, inefficiency and delay in the complaint process, and the precedent of an executive agency overruling an independent, regulatory one.

Disaster Units Merger

President Carter's reorganization of federal emergency preparedness and disaster response programs went into effect Sept. 16, two days after the House rejected a resolution (H Res 1242) to disapprove the reorganization plan, Carter's third of 1978. The vote was 40-327 against the measure. *(Vote 687, p. 196-H)*

The Senate did not vote on the plan. The Senate Governmental Operations Committee supported it by voting unanimously Aug. 17 to report a disapproval resolution (S Res 489) unfavorably (S Rept 95-1141).

Carter submitted the plan to Congress June 19. *(Text of president's message, p. 53-E)*

"For the first time, key emergency management and assistance functions would be unified and made directly accountable to the president and Congress," Carter said.

Goal: Reduce Inefficiency

The purpose of the plan was to merge federal preparedness, mitigation and response plans into one agency to deal with man-made and natural disasters and protection of the population in case of nuclear attack.

The plan also would ensure that existing emergency resources — such as warning, communication and evacuation facilities — would be used for civil defense purposes in case of attack as well as for disaster-related emergencies. It would provide a better basis for evaluating the cost effectiveness of disaster and relief spending.

An administration study begun in August 1977 found that federal statutes and executive orders for dealing with emergencies were outdated, causing jurisdictional disputes, inefficient delivery of services and uncertainty in federal agencies about emergency preparedness policy.

The study also found that the federal government lacked a clear understanding of the relationship between attack and peacetime preparedness activities and of its role in assisting states in disaster relief and recovery.

"The present situation has severely hampered federal support of state and local emergency organizations and resources which bear the primary responsibility for preserving life and property in times of calamity," Carter said.

To deal with these problems, the reorganization plan and a series of executive orders:

• Combined five existing agencies into the Federal Emergency Management Agency.

• Transferred six other emergency preparedness functions to the new agency.

• Created an Emergency Management Committee to advise the president on meeting civil emergencies.

• Gave responsibility for overseeing civil defense programs in the new agency to the secretary of defense and the National Security Council.

Consolidated into the new agency were: the Defense Civil Preparedness Agency (DCPA) of the Department of Defense; the Federal Disaster Assistance Administration (FDAA) and the Federal Insurance Administration (FIA), both of the Department of Housing and Urban Development; the Federal Preparedness Agency (FPA) of the General Services Administration; and the National Fire Prevention and Control Administration of the Commerce Department.

The functions of the DCPA, FDAA and FPA were transferred to the new agency by executive order after the reorganization plan went into effect and those three agencies were abolished. The fire prevention and flood insurance programs remained intact within the new agency.

Similarly transferred were the functions of the community weather emergency preparedness programs of the National Weather Service and the earthquake hazard reduction program, the dam safety coordination program and the federal emergency broadcast system, all carried out by the White House Office of Science and Technology.

The new agency also would be responsible for federal response to terrorist acts.

Office of Management and Budget Director James T. McIntyre Jr. said the reorganization plan would cut disaster spending, estimated at $600 million in fiscal 1979, by $10 million to $15 million a year and would eliminate about 300 of the 2,300 positions involved in disaster preparedness and response functions.

The administration anticipated no cut in expenditures by the programs transferred to the new agency.

Committee Action

The House Government Operations Committee reported H Res 1242 Aug. 21 (H Rept 95-1523) with a 29-4 vote in favor of a recommendation that it not pass.

Though it expressed concern that Carter would implement much of the plan through executive order not requiring congressional approval, the committee supported the proposal.

The report said the proposed new agency would have two major advantages: It would make a single agency accountable to the president and Congress for all federal emergency preparedness and response activities, and it would provide a single point of contact for state and local governments.

Provisions

The reorganization plan created a new Federal Emergency Management Agency and made three transfers into it:

• The National Fire Prevention and Control Administration, formerly in the Department of Commerce.

- The Federal Insurance Administration, formerly in the Department of Housing and Urban Development (HUD).
- The oversight responsibility for the Federal Emergency Broadcast System, formerly in the Executive Office of the President.

The report said the president by executive order was to transfer into the new agency the functions of the Defense Civil Preparedness Agency in the Department of Defense, the Federal Disaster Assistance Administration in HUD, and the Federal Preparedness Agency in the General Services Administration.

Also added to the agency by executive order were oversight of the earthquake hazards reduction program; coordination of federal activities to promote dam safety; responsibility for aiding communities develop readiness plans for weather-related emergencies; coordination of natural and nuclear disaster warning systems; and coordination of planning to reduce the consequences of major terrorist incidents.

The Congressional Budget Office estimated that the reorganization would save between $10 billion and $15 billion annually through increased efficiency and reduced duplication of effort.

Pension Regulation

By voice votes near the end of the session, both houses of Congress rejected separate resolutions disapproving President Carter's fourth reorganization plan.

The plan, as submitted by Carter, reorganized the administration of the Employee Retirement Income Security Act (ERISA) by transferring most of the administrative functions to the Treasury Department from the Labor Department. *(Text of plan, p. 59-E)*

By voice vote Oct. 12, the House rejected disapproval resolution H Res 1308. Government Operations Committee Chairman Jack Brooks, D-Texas, noted that minor differences between the panel and the White House had been compromised in advance. One difference changed the date for a submission of a report to Congress by the president on ERISA administration from April 30, 1980, to Jan. 31, 1980. The committee reported the measure (H Rept 95-1658) Sept. 29 with a recommendation that it not pass.

By voice vote the next day, the Senate rejected a similar resolution of disapproval (S Res 537). The resolution had been reported by the Governmental Affairs Committee on Sept. 28. The panel recommended by an 11-0 vote that S Res 537 be rejected. ▮

Congress Ends 'Koreagate' Lobbying Probe

A year and a half after they began their investigations, ethics committees in the House and Senate wound up their probes into alleged South Korean influence-peddling on Capitol Hill without recommending any severe disciplinary action against colleagues linked to the scandal.

The investigation by the House Committee on Standards of Official Conduct drew to a close Friday, Oct. 13, in a bang of hyperbole, a whimper of opprobrium and a mass of uncertainties about the future of the House ethics process.

The investigation, which began some 18 months earlier with reports that as many as 115 members of Congress had taken illegal gifts from South Korean agents, ended with the House voting its mildest form of punishment, a "reprimand," for three California Democrats: John J. McFall, Edward R. Roybal and Charles H. Wilson. *(Background, 1977 Almanac p. 820)*

Similarly, the Senate Ethics Committee, concluding its 17-month Korean investigation, issued a report Oct. 16 that recommended no disciplinary action against any incumbent or former senator.

A third committee investigating U.S.-Korean relations concluded that the South Korean government sought to bribe U.S. officials, buy influence among journalists and professors, extort money from American companies and rig military procurement contracts to win support for what the panel called the "authoritarian" government of President Park Chung Hee. In its final report, released Nov. 1, the House International Relations Subcommittee on International Organizations said that South Korean government's illegal activities went beyond its legal and extra-legal lobbying efforts. The 450-page report, which outlined the history of U.S.-Korean relations, indicated that the South Koreans frequently pursued policies antithetical to U.S. interests. The most notable of these incidents involved South Korean efforts to develop nuclear weapons, a project the subcommittee said was abandoned by 1975.

House Investigation

Completing its "Koreagate" investigation Oct. 13, the House Committee on Standards of Official Conduct issued reports (H Repts 95-1741, 1742, 1743) charging McFall, Roybal and Wilson with official misconduct involving cash contributions from Korean rice dealer Tongsun Park and statements made to the House standards committee concerning those payments.

In the closing arguments on the House floor, heard by fewer than a third of the members, questions about the ability and willingness of the House to discipline its members were raised anew. The Standards Committee was criticized both for being too harsh in its findings and, in the end, for its inability to make the toughest of its charges stick.

Presented with reports on the committee's findings only hours before being asked to vote on them, few members evidenced any reluctance to uphold the committee's suggested reprimands of McFall and Wilson (H Res 1415 and H Res 1414). But confronted with the choice of voting to uphold the panel's recommended "censure" of Roybal (H Res 1416), who was of Hispanic descent, and suggestions that such a vote would be perceived as racist, a majority of the House backed off from the tougher recommendation.

The House rejected the resolution to censure Roybal 219-170 and then adopted a reprimand on a voice vote. Wilson's reprimand was voted 329-41 and McFall's was approved on a voice vote. *(Votes 807 and 808, p. 230-H)*

Censure is the harshest form of punishment the House can mete out short of expulsion, a course of action ethics Chairman John J. Flynt Jr., D-Ga., said was considered in committee for Roybal but rejected.

Background

The House Standards Committee Korea investigation, begun in January 1977, was renewed in early 1978, when Tongsun Park returned to Washington to answer questions about his role in South Korean influence-buying on Capitol Hill.

For months the Justice Department and subsequently the Standards Committee under Special Counsel Leon Jaworski had negotiated with the Seoul government to gain Park's testimony. On Dec. 30, 1977, the Justice Department announced an agreement with the South Korean government to obtain Park's testimony in exchange for a grant of immunity from prosecution. (Park was indicted on 36 charges, including bribery, conspiracy, mail fraud, making illegal political contributions and failing to register as a foreign agent. He pleaded innocent to all charges.) The agreement, which stipulated that Park testify only in Justice Department cases, was immediately denounced by Jaworski and Standards Committee Chairman Flynt.

Flynt labeled the deal a "facade" that would allow Park to refuse to testify on Capitol Hill. "Congress will not sit idly by and accept this insult," he said.

On Jan. 4 Flynt issued a statement saying that the committee would subpoena Park to appear before his panel immediately upon the South Korean's return to the United States. It was the first of a series of pressure tactics used by Flynt and Jaworski that led to an announcement Jan. 31 of agreement with South Korea for Park's testimony.

Flynt's Jan. 4 threat to subpoena Park was followed up two days later by an announcement from Jaworski that "we have requested that the South Korean government make Mr. Park available for testimony in proceedings of the committee at such time as the committee may schedule them." In making that announcement Jaworski separated the House investigation from the Justice Department probe, making it clear the House was ready to go its own way to obtain Park's testimony.

On Jan. 20 Jaworski asked the House for a resolution calling on the South Korean government to give unlimited cooperation to the committee's investigation. Three days later, on Jan. 23, a resolution was introduced in the House insisting that the South Korean government make Park, former Ambassador Kim Dong Jo and other officials available for questioning before the Standards Committee. The resolution, backed by Speaker Thomas P. O'Neill Jr., D-Mass., and Republican Minority Leader John J. Rhodes of Arizona, warned that the U.S. alliance with South Korea and American military and economic aid would be jeopardized if the Koreans continued to resist congressional requests for information.

On Jan. 31, Ambassador Yong Shik Kim presented his government's agreement on Park's "voluntary" testimony to O'Neill and the Speaker indicated that a vote on the House resolution had been shelved — at least temporarily.

Park began testifying before the Standards Committee Feb. 28. But even before he returned to the United States, his credibility had been called into question. In 17 days of Justice Department interrogation in Seoul in January, he had denied that he was an agent of the South Korean Central Intelligence Agency, a statement that ran counter to a substantial body of evidence developed by House committees.

By the end of his first week of testimony before the House Standards Committee, Park's credibility was even weaker. Members in attendance described his responses to questions as "incomplete" and "evasive." Several members said they did not believe his answers.

Former Rep. Hanna Pleads Guilty

Former Rep. Richard T. Hanna, D-Calif. (1963-74), pleaded guilty March 17 to one count of conspiracy to defraud the government.

Hanna's action averted his going to trial on a 40-count indictment. The trial had been set to begin March 20.

Hanna admitted that he had agreed to use his office to help South Korean rice dealer Tongsun Park and that he had received $200,000 for his efforts between 1969 and 1975.

Sentenced April 24, Hanna began serving a 2½ year term at a federal prison camp May 8.

Park House Testimony, Passman Indictment

Park completed his public testimony before the House Standards Committee April 4, denying to the end that he was a Korean government agent.

Park also denied that he had conspired with former Rep. Otto E. Passman, D-La. (1947-77), to buy influence for South Korea.

Passman was indicted March 31 by a federal grand jury in the District of Columbia on charges of bribery and conspiracy to defraud the United States in connection with rice sales to the South Korean government. The indictment named Passman as the recipient of $213,000 in illegal payments from Park. An April 28 indictment accused him of failing to report $143,000 on his income taxes and of evading taxes of $77,000. Park was named as an unindicted co-conspirator. Passman, who was chairman of the House Appropriations subcommittee that dealt with rice and other Food for Peace commodity sales as well as foreign aid, had denied any illegal or improper conduct in the Korean influence-buying scandal. (Passman was defeated in a primary re-election bid in 1976.)

During his testimony, Park said that most of his payments went to three former House members — Passman, who Park testified received cash and gifts of between $367,000 and $407,000; former Rep. Richard T. Hanna, D-Calif., who allegedly received $262,000; and former Rep. Cornelius Gallagher, D-N.J., who Park said got $211,000.

Hanna pleaded guilty March 17 to one charge of conspiracy to defraud the government. *(Box, above)*

Park said he paid the three men because they helped him retain his lucrative job as the exclusive agent for U.S. rice sales to Korea. Park received $9 million in commissions from that job between 1970 and 1975.

O'Neill Disputes Report

Park denied to the Standards Committee that he reported his payments to U.S. congressmen back to South

Korean officials. He said he did not know how four purported reports got into his house.

One of the reports said that House Speaker Thomas P. O'Neill Jr., D-Mass., during a 1974 trip to Korea, asked Park to make contributions to House members and their wives. O'Neill branded the report "self-serving and a total fabrication," and denied that he had ever done anything more for Park than get him tickets to the 1969 World Series.

Park testified that he had no idea who wrote the report, but that it was false.

On July 13, the Standards Committee issued a report clearing O'Neill and stating that the only thing the Speaker did of "questionable propriety" was to accept two parties in his honor paid for by Park.

The lengthy report said the committee found nothing to warrant action against other House members whose names had figured in Park-related allegations. Besides O'Neill, they were Reps. E. "Kika" de la Garza, D-Texas, Thomas S. Foley, D-Wash., John M. Murphy, D-N.Y., Frank Thompson Jr., D-N.J., Melvin Price, D-Ill., Morris K. Udall, D-Ariz., Edward P. Boland, D-Mass., John B. Breaux, D-La., and Majority Whip John Brademas, D-Ind.

Focus Shifts to Kim

Once the agreement to obtain Park's testimony had been settled, the brunt of the Standards Committee's pressure on South Korea shifted to obtaining an agreement on the testimony of former Ambassador Kim Dong Jo.

"Kim Dong Jo is immeasurably more important to us than Tongsun Park," Jaworski said Jan. 16. "This whole thing was run right out of the Korean embassy ... and the Korean government might as well stop kidding itself. We're not going to rest until we've got everything."

Several witnesses had told investigators that Kim or his wife delivered envelopes containing $100 bills to congressional offices. Kim reportedly had more contacts among senators than Tongsun Park.

On Feb. 5 Jaworski called on President Carter to order the State Department to help the committee obtain the testimony of Kim. Three days later, on Feb. 8, Secretary of State Cyrus R. Vance responded. Addressing a House International Relations subcommittee, Vance said that U.S. aid to South Korea should be based on military needs and not used as leverage to get testimony on alleged influence buying. It was the kind of encouragement Seoul was looking for. *(Aid cutoff threat, box, next page)*

The administration position remained the same. Justice Department officials apparently never tried to question Kim or other Korean diplomats because they believed them to be protected by diplomatic immunity, which South Korea had invoked.

The problem was simple: There are more American diplomats who have been accused of making political payoffs abroad than foreign diplomats accused of making payoffs here. Graham Martin, former ambassador to Italy, was reported to have made $9 million in payoffs to Italian politicians in 1972.

Despite the pressure, congressional committees were unsuccessful in their efforts to obtain Kim's testimony.

Jaworski Withdraws from Probe

Leon Jaworski withdrew from active participation as special counsel to the House Korea lobbying investigation Aug. 2, raising in his departing comments the very questions that underlined the inquiry from its inception.

Jaworski criticized the House's ability to investigate its own members, questioned the commitment of the chairman of the investigating committee, and took several shots at the Justice Department for its part in the Korean influence peddling inquiry.

At the same time, Jaworski appeared to have little difficulty giving his own investigative efforts a gold star in a report to the House leadership and the members of the Standards Committee.

"It is my opinion that everything that could be done was done," Jaworski said, dismissing as "extreme demagoguery" suggestions that the House could have threatened South Korea with a cutoff of military aid to obtain the testimony of former ambassador Kim Dong Jo.

Jaworski, who said he would be available to the committee for consultation, said the investigation had successfully exposed South Korean influence efforts and possible misconduct by congressmen.

"[T]he major portion of the facts of Koreagate have been ferreted out and published," he said. "They cannot be ignored by public officials tempted in the future to yield to greed. They cannot be ignored by officials who have been careless in dealing with persons whose backgrounds and intentions are not clearly known. And they cannot be ignored by foreign governments."

Standards Committee Hearings

Public hearings by the Standards Committee on the charges against Roybal, McFall, Wilson and Patten began Sept. 14.

During the first day of hearings, Roybal confirmed testimony by Tongsun Park that he gave Roybal a $1,000 cash contribution, which the committee alleged Roybal failed to report. Roybal said his failure to report the contribution was "a mistake of judgment."

The Standards Committee had accused Roybal of violating House rules in failing to report the campaign contribution and of converting the cash to his own use. It also had accused Roybal of testifying falsely in statements to the committee that he never received the money and, later, that he received the money but gave it to his re-election campaign.

Park told the committee under oath that he gave Roybal $1,000 in cash after then-Rep. Passman told him he had "two dear friends" who needed campaign contributions. Park said Passman later arranged for him to meet Roybal in Passman's office, where he gave Roybal the money.

Roybal confirmed Park's recollection of the events, but said he did not catch Park's name when he received the money and never asked Passman who the man was who gave him $1,000. Roybal testified that he previously told committee investigators he never met Park and never received money from him "because I didn't know that the man was Tongsun Park."

He said he had previously denied receiving money from a Korean national because "I didn't know that Tongsun Park was a Korean national. It could have been a Korean who was a citizen of the United States."

In addition to Roybal, statements of alleged violations were released in July by the committee against McFall, Wilson and Patten. None of the four congressmen named by the committee faced federal charges.

Korean Aid Cutoff Threat Fails

On May 24, the House International Relations Committee unanimously approved a resolution (H Res 1194) warning South Korea that the House would consider cutting off economic aid if former Ambassador Kim Dong Jo did not cooperate in its investigation of alleged bribery attempts.

Leon Jaworski, special counsel to the House Korean investigation, had asked for a resolution threatening an aid cutoff in order to obtain Kim's testimony.

Jaworski announced May 10 that the South Korean government had refused to make Kim available for questioning. Later that day, in action on a bill setting budget targets, the House voted 146-254 against cutting off aid to South Korea. *(Vote 251, p. 72-H)*

The resolution approved by the International Relations Committee was a watered-down version of the one Jaworski had requested. That resolution would have required the House to cut off non-military aid unless South Korea made Kim available for sworn testimony.

Members of the committee and the State Department expressed concern that the stronger resolution would establish a bad precedent, inviting other countries to ignore diplomatic immunity and coerce testimony from diplomats.

The State Department said the Carter administration could not support the resolution because of its "overt pressure."

The State Department suggested Jaworski accept an offer from Seoul to allow Kim to be questioned by House Speaker Thomas P. O'Neill Jr., D-Mass., by telephone. Jaworski responded that the offer would make "a mockery of Congress."

"It is my opinion," Jaworski said, "that the people of this nation will not accept legal niceties as an explanation for the failure of Congress to complete its investigation of corruption in its own chambers."

The House approved the non-binding resolution by a vote of 321-46 on May 31. *(Vote 326, p. 94-H)*

In action on another bill — agriculture appropriations (HR 13125) — the House June 22 voted 273-125 to cut $56 million in economic aid to Korea. The vote came on an amendment by Majority Leader Jim Wright, D-Texas, to delete the Korea funds from the Food for Peace program. *(Vote 418, p. 120-H)*

Wright said the House had "no other alternative" than to approve the amendment if it was to preserve its honor. "A cloud of suspicion has hung over the House; that cloud must be dispelled," he said.

Kim resigned his post as foreign affairs assistant to South Korean President Park Chung Hee the day after the House vote. Kim said he was "indignant at the coercive American action" but quit because he was "sorry for causing trouble" for his country.

Wright told the House that since its 321-46 vote May 31 in favor of a resolution threatening an aid cutoff, the Republic of Korea had refused to make any concessions in making Kim available for interrogation.

Jaworski wrote House Speaker O'Neill that he had offered to accept written responses from Kim rather than sworn statements.

House Minority Leader John J. Rhodes, R-Ariz., who supported the resolution, charged that Jaworski "has given away the ballgame.... It seems to me that the counsel has already given away the possibility of obtaining meaningful testimony from Kim Dong Jo."

Rhodes and other members said an unsworn statement would be ineffectual and unacceptable to them. "I would rather have nothing from Kim Dong Jo than to have a statement not under oath," Rhodes said.

Members who opposed the Wright amendment said it was a "hollow gesture" that stood little chance of evoking Kim's testimony and that even if it worked charges against members could not be brought unless Kim testified under oath in U.S. court proceedings.

Rep. Neal Smith, D-Iowa, said the Wright amendment was the "weakest possible tool" that could be used to gain Kim's testimony and that it would hurt U.S. farmers because a glut of agricultural commodities on the world market would lead Korea to buy products from non-U.S. firms.

On Aug. 10, the Senate refused to go along with the House's action. Before voting to pass HR 13125, the Senate agreed 71-24 to table — and thus kill — an amendment by Lowell P. Weicker Jr., R-Conn., to keep South Korea out of the food program. *(Vote 304, p. 47-S)*

Opponents of the Weicker amendment argued that the Korean government had agreed to secure from Kim answers to written questions, and that more pressure would block further cooperation. But Weicker called "written interrogatories ... worthless" and told members that if they rejected his amendment, "it adds up to what so far has been called a resounding cover-up."

Weicker said he had quit the Senate ethics panel investigating the payoff allegations because his efforts to get witnesses had been thwarted. His amendment, he said, was an attempt to "bring back into focus what has been to date a shamefully inadequate investigation."

Ethics Committee Chairman Stevenson said that Weicker's comments on the uncompleted investigation were "premature."

"If the distinguished senator from Connecticut knew anything about these investigations, he would not make such silly charges," Stevenson said.

Majority Leader Robert C. Byrd, W.Va., backed Stevenson, calling the Weicker amendment "counterproductive." If Weicker "has anything other than innuendos, let him ... bring it to the Senate floor," Byrd said.

House and Senate conferees upheld the Senate position on lifting the ban. *(Agriculture funds, p. 145)*

McFall. The ethics committee lodged three charges against McFall: 1) that he received a $3,000 "contribution" from Park in October 1974 and failed to report it as required by federal law; 2) that he converted Park's 1974 contribution to his personal use and failed to keep his campaign funds separate from his personal funds, in violation of Rule 6 of the House Code of Official Conduct and; 3) that he received cash contributions and gifts from Park "under circumstances which might be construed by reasonable persons as influencing the performance of his government duties, in violation of Rule 5 of the Code of Ethics of Government Service."

McFall responded in writing, seeking a dismissal of the charges. He said that each count failed to "state facts constituting a violation of the Code of Official Conduct or any other applicable law, rule, regulation, or standard of conduct."

In his 19-page response, McFall conceded that he received $3,000 from Park in 1974, that he never returned it and never reported it. But he said he was not required to report it because he never unconditionally "accepted" the contribution and because he never "received" it as a contribution. The ethics committee staff response to McFall's explanation said that "the argument is completely without merit."

McFall also argued that his purpose in receiving the contribution, rather than Park's purpose in giving it, determined whether he had to report it.

The staff recommendation stated: "The statute unambiguously requires reporting of gifts *'made'* 'for the purpose' of influencing an election. Moreover, it is shocking to suggest that a candidate could unilaterally decide to use for some purpose of his own, money which was given to him solely to help elect him to office."

Wilson. The ethics committee alleged that Wilson deliberately withheld information when he answered a questionnaire from the committee concerning contributions from Park.

Wilson told the committee in July 1977 that he received no money from Park. But in a letter dated Feb. 7, 1978, he informed the committee that he and his wife had received wedding gifts from Park including $600 in U.S. currency. A staff memorandum on the case stated that "it is plainly unethical for a congressman to lie to a committee of Congress even if he later admits that he lied."

Patten. The ethics committee charged Patten with violating a New Jersey law by identifying as his own contributions from Park that Patten passed on to a county political organization. Patten denied the charge in a written response asking that the charges be dismissed. A staff response to Patten's motion said, "The respondent's papers ignore all the evidence except that which the respondent views as supportive of his position."

Final Arguments, Committee Action

On Sept. 27, the House Standards Committee voted to recommend that the House censure Roybal on three counts of failing to report a $1,000 campaign contribution from Park and lying to the committee.

The committee also recommended that the House "reprimand" Wilson for lying to the committee about money he took from Park in 1975 as a wedding present.

The 9-0 vote to recommend censure of Roybal was the strongest action the committee had ever taken against a member of the House. Censure required that the accused congressman stand before the House to hear the charges against him. The recommended reprimand of Wilson, which came on an 8-1 vote, is a weaker form of punishment than censure. Wilson would not have to be present when the House read its findings against him.

In final arguments before the ethics committee, committee counsel John Nields said, "Congressman Roybal has lied to this committee, lied to this institution repeatedly, and his latest version of the facts is also untrue."

Roybal's attorney, Richard Hibey, said Roybal received the cash but did not intentionally lie about it and that his earlier conflicting statements to the committee were the result of a faulty memory. "What you have before you is not a liar but an honest man who has made an honest mistake, an error in judgment, and is not the perjurer he is being painted by the staff."

In his testimony, Wilson said he forgot about the envelope of cash Park had given him at his wedding in South Korea in 1975. He said that when he responded to the committee's questionnaire, he thought the panel was looking for gifts intended to influence his congressional work, not gifts given "as a courtesy at the time of a wedding." Wilson said in a statement following the committee action: "I'm deeply disappointed that the committee was unwilling to accept the fact, which I swear is absolutely true, that I had completely forgotten about the wedding present when I responded to the questionnaire."

In earlier action, the committee heard final arguments in its cases against McFall and Patten.

McFall said his efforts on behalf of Park were aimed only at assuring that California rice would be sold to South Korea. McFall said he did not "see any connection" between his gifts from Park and his efforts to sell the rice.

McFall said he wrote two letters on behalf of Park to South Korean President Park Chung Hee and that with Park's permission he put cash contributions intended for his campaign into his office account instead of reporting them as campaign contributions. He said he did not put them into his campaign account because he misunderstood federal law and believed he could not accept a campaign contribution from a foreign national in 1972 and 1974.

But under cross examination by Nields, McFall acknowledged that he had taken a contribution in 1972 from a Chinese national. He also said that only cash contributions went into the office account. Asked why, he said, "I don't know," but denied that it was an effort to prevent the contributions from being traced. McFall also acknowledged that after the House adopted a July 1974 rule requiring members to report the name of contributors to office accounts, he never put another cash contribution into the account.

In an emotional table-pounding defense before the committee Sept. 26, Patten denied ever receiving "a penny" from Tongsun Park.

"I have never in my life been accused of unethical or illegal conduct, let alone engaged in such activities," the 73-year-old New Jersey Democrat told the committee.

On Oct. 4, the Standards Committee voted to recommend that the full House reprimand McFall for failure to report a $3,000 campaign contribution he received in cash from Park. However, the committee rejected the two other, more serious, charges against McFall.

On the same day, the committee found Patten not guilty of the charges against him.

House Floor Action

In floor action Oct. 13, the House accepted the committee's recommendation of a reprimand for McFall and Wilson, but killed 219-170 the resolution to censure Roybal, reducing his punishment to a reprimand. Wilson's reprimand was voted 329-41 and McFall's was approved on a voice vote. *(Votes 807, 808, p. 230-H)*

Throughout the Standards Committee hearings and the floor debate, none of the three congressmen acknowledged any illegality or wrongdoing.

On the House floor, Roybal contested the recommended punishment. Both McFall and Wilson said they accepted the committee's judgment. And the ensuing debate said as much about their culpability or innocence as about how members perceive their own ethical responsibilities and the House system of ethics.

The debate was viewed by Flynt as the conclusion of the House mandate to determine whether members accepted anything of value from the government of South Korea.

But it was also a debate, as Walter Flowers, D-Ala., defined it, on "whether we are going to continue to operate with a Committee on Standards of Official Conduct...."

The strength of the House ethics system was called into question from the beginning, on the resolution to reprimand Wilson. Wilson accepted the reprimand but insisted he was "innocent," had "very little to apologize for," and that the reprimand was "harsh," "cruel," "unjust and unfair."

He said he chose not to contest it because it would teach that "we in the House of Representatives are prepared to accept ethical standards for ourselves which are higher than those imposed upon any other citizen."

But he also said he believed the judgment "essentially exonerates me of serious wrongdoing," and that the committee had merely recommended that he be "chided" for a "careless mistake."

System Criticized

If Wilson's remarks could be construed as a defense of the system, his defenders' remarks could not.

"The entire thing to me stinks to high heaven," said Ronald V. Dellums, D-Calif. "I challenge not the personalities who serve here but the process itself, the structure of the institution." Dellums said the committee held no "judicial proceedings" and that it was not representative of Congress.

William "Bill" Clay, D-Mo., called the proceedings an "inquisition to suppress the heresy" of three "relatively inconspicuous" members "marched into this coliseum to face the lions and cheering mobs while bloodthirsty scribes sit perched high in the press gallery awaiting the carnage."

But by the time the House got around to the most serious charge — the censuring of Roybal — the lions' den had turned into a den of pussycats and the credibility of the ethics process had been challenged.

But defenders of the system also contributed to pointing up its weaknesses. While critics said it was harsh and arbitrary, others such as Flowers, said it deliberately had delivered a "light stroke" to the miscreants because the House could not conduct full judicial proceedings. "We are not looking for anybody's blood, "Flowers said. "We are trying to present a fair, moderate, middle-of-the-road case which we think represents a reasonable approach by reasonable people on the committee...."

While critics blasted the lack of "evidence" and the failure of the committee to issue reports in time for members to read them, other members openly acknowledged that they were voting purely on the basis of the committee's recommendations.

John W. Nields Jr., chief counsel to the committee, said the reduction of Roybal's punishment to a reprimand "arose out of the hostility expressed towards the committee by members on the floor."

"It looked as though the ethics committee had no taste for bringing this kind of report to the floor...," Nields said. "It will be painful for the next ethics committee to bring a similar thing to the floor unless there are indications the House will view such actions favorably."

Related House Probe

In tandem with the House Standards Committee, the House International Relations Subcommittee on International Organizations had been investigating the lobbying scandal since early 1977.

Unlike the ethics panel, however, its main concern was the impact on U.S.-Korean relations, not the wrongdoing of individuals.

At a hearing March 15, the subcommittee released documents backing up previous reports that President Park Chung Hee personally directed the Korean lobbying campaign.

Chairman Donald M. Fraser, D-Minn., said the summaries of U.S. intelligence reports showed that President Park was involved in discussions at his Blue House executive mansion that resulted in the lobbying effort.

Fraser stopped short of giving any indication that the South Korean president knew of or approved the disbursing of money to members of Congress. Nor did he disclose how the intelligence agencies were able to obtain reports on discussions within the Blue House.

William Porter, who was U.S. ambassador to Korea at the time, testified that he was skeptical about the authenticity of the report, although he conceded he had no evidence it was inaccurate.

"They knew how to keep secrets from us," Porter said. "I would not bet on that, necessarily, as a useful report on what went on at those meetings."

The Washington Post had reported in October 1976 that President Park had initiated the Korean lobbying effort and that U.S. intelligence reports "apparently" included tape recordings of the conversations obtained through electronic eavesdropping.

Korea Election Gifts

Sanitized summaries of U.S. Central Intelligence Agency documents released by the International Organizations Subcommittee March 22 revealed evidence that high-level officials in the Nixon administration were aware of illegal South Korean government influence-buying activities on Capitol Hill but did nothing to stop it.

The summaries stated that Korean President Park "was directly involved in directing the contribution of several hundred thousand dollars to the Democratic Party" in 1968.

A Nov. 24, 1971, memo from then-FBI Director J. Edgar Hoover said the Korean presidential mansion was directly involved in the contribution to the Democrats.

The intelligence summaries were based on secret National Security Agency (NSA) interceptions of cable traffic between the South Korean government and its embassy in Washington. The information was transmitted to the FBI and, according to the memoranda, to Attorney General John N. Mitchell and Henry A. Kissinger, national security adviser to President Nixon.

Mitchell Testimony

In testimony before the subcommittee, Mitchell, who was on medical furlough from prison where he was serving sentences for Watergate crimes, said he remembered receiving only one of three memos about Korean lobbying from Hoover. Mitchell said he never saw the memo alleging contributions to the Democrats and that he was sure he would have remembered it because of "the reference to hundreds of thousands of dollars to an election I had just gotten through managing on the other side."

A spokesman for Kissinger said the former national security adviser had "no recollection" of seeing any of the memos.

News reports said the subcommittee had also received reports that the Republican Party got a smaller contribution from the Korean government in 1968. The amount was reported to be in "six figures."

The memoranda released by the subcommittee included severe limitations placed by the FBI on the use of information obtained from the secret wire interceptions "to preclude any investigation whatsoever," even though "criminal activities are strongly indicated."

Michael Hershman, deputy staff director of the subcommittee, said the NSA did not request the restrictions when it passed the top secret cables on to the FBI.

William McDonnell, the FBI agent who drafted the memos for Hoover, said the bureau did not initiate criminal investigations because an intelligence officer said doing so might compromise the "sensitive source" of the charges.

The credibility of the reported South Korean government contribution to the Democrats was called into question by Rep. Edward J. Derwinski of Illinois, the ranking Republican on the subcommittee, who suggested that some of the intercepted messages were deliberate distortions by KCIA agents in Washington to impress their bosses in Seoul.

The intelligence summaries also stated that the Korean government was spending "large sums" to "develop control over" American and Korean journalists, that two congressional staff aides were connected with the KCIA, that Tongsun Park had made payments to a member of Congress and was acting under KCIA direction, and that a second congressman had sought contributions from Tongsun Park.

Allegations that Park was "under Korean Central Intelligence Agency direction" weren't passed on to the FBI Washington field office by the FBI headquarters. At the time the field office was conducting an investigation of Park at the State Department's request to determine if Park was acting illegally at the behest of the South Korean government. The field office found no grounds on which to act against Park.

An "eyes only" memo to Mitchell and Kissinger dated Feb. 3, 1972, reported that a congressman who had sought contributions from President Park Chung Hee said that Tongsun Park should be made Korea's chief U.S. lobbyist.

The top officer on the Korean desk at the State Department between 1970 and 1974 provided additional testimony concerning Park's relation to the South Korean government. Donald Ranard testified that he believed Park was under the control of the Korean CIA. Ranard said he believed Park "had an integral role, a very important role" in the Korean government's effort to win influence illegally among U.S. officials. Park had testified that he never worked for the Korean government.

The subcommittee released a summary of intelligence messages from Seoul warning U.S. officials that Park was "receiving assistance from the KCIA . . . and was under the KCIA's control, but was not an 'agent' as such." The summary appeared to support Park's assertion that he contributed $750,000 to some 30 congressmen as a businessman and not to buy influence for Seoul.

Hancho Kim Trial

Former Korean CIA agent Sang Keun Kim, the government's key witness in the perjury and conspiracy trial of Maryland businessman Hancho Kim, said he was unsure the defendant gave any money to members of Congress. S. K. Kim testified March 22 that about $44,000 of the money he gave to Hancho Kim came from a $100,000 check provided the KCIA agent by Tongsun Park.

S. K. Kim defected to the United States in November 1976. He said he feared he would be imprisoned if he returned to South Korea. At the time he was the second-ranking KCIA agent attached to the Korean embassy in Washington.

S. K. Kim testified that although he delivered $600,000 in cash from the KCIA to Hancho Kim, Hancho Kim never told him if any money had been paid to members of Congress. Hancho Kim had denied receiving any money from S. K. Kim. S. K. Kim said Hancho Kim told him he had gotten congressmen to speak on behalf of South Korea in Congress.

Asked if he believed payments were made to congressmen, S. K. Kim replied: "I had no confidence that he [Hancho Kim] gave the money. . . . He spent money entertaining congressmen in a festive way, but there was no accounting of how it was spent. I was too low-ranking a guy to question Kim."

S. K. Kim underwent three days of questioning that ended March 23.

Hancho Kim was charged with conspiracy to defraud the United States by plotting to interfere with the workings of Congress and of making false statements to a federal grand jury. He allegedly conspired to pass $600,000 to members of Congress on behalf of the Korean government.

Hancho Kim became the first person to stand trial in connection with the Korean influence-buying case. His trial began March 15.

Rep. Tennyson Guyer, R-Ohio, became the first sitting congressman to testify publicly in any of the Korean investigations when he appeared March 28 at the trial of Hancho Kim. Guyer said he had done political favors for Kim but that they were no different from favors he did regularly for constituents. He said he received no money from Hancho Kim.

Guyer said he inserted three statements based on information from Kim into the *Congressional Record.* He said he shared Kim's concerns for the security of South Korea. Guyer also said he tried unsuccessfully to get Kim an appointment with President Ford.

On May 19, Hancho Kim was sentenced to six months in jail for conspiring to corrupt members of Congress in return for favors for Korea and of lying to a grand jury about receiving $600,000 for the plot. Kim was ordered to serve three years on each of two counts, but U.S. Disrict Court Judge Thomas A. Flannery said the sentences would be suspended after Kim served six months. Kim was convicted April 8 for conspiring to defraud the United States. Kim's conviction was the second growing out of the Korean scandal. The first person convicted was former Rep. Hanna.

Rev. Moon Connection

A former Korean military intelligence officer who was a top aide to Rev. Sun Myung Moon said March 22 that he received $3,000 in $100 bills from the Korean CIA.

Bo Hi Pak, interpreter for the Korean evangelist, said he received the money from Sang Keun Kim, the former

KCIA agent. But he insisted he took the cash only as a favor to Yang Doo Won, a high-ranking KCIA official in Seoul, and that he passed it on to a Unification Church member from Japan as reimbursement for expenses incurred on an anticommunist speaking tour of Korea.

Pak had no explanation for why the KCIA rather than another Korean agency handled the "reimbursement."

House International Relations subcommittee staffers were quoted as saying they did not find Pak's explanation convincing.

Pak's testimony before the Subcommittee on International Organizations March 22 was the first indicating that Moon's church had received money from the KCIA.

In that session Pak attacked news reports based on Central Intelligence Agency documents released by the subcommittee which said the Unification Church was founded by a director of the Korean CIA in 1961. He said the Church was founded in 1954 and challenged the CIA to swear to its evidence before the subcommittee.

A CIA report dated Feb. 26, 1963, based on statements from an undisclosed source, said "Kim Chong Pil organized the Unification Church while he was director of the ROK [Republic of Korea] Central Intelligence Agency, and has been using the Church, which has a membership of 27,000, as a political tool."

The reports reinforced the subcommittee's principal hypothesis, that senior officials of the Nixon administration were aware of the South Korean lobbying effort but failed to act on evidence they had obtained.

Chairman Fraser contended that "initiative for action pursuant to the intelligence reports was sporadic, half-hearted and inconclusive, with the result that Korean activities, which were both improper and illegal, continued to expand and gain momentum for some five years."

Final Report

In its final report, released Nov. 1, the International Organizations Subcommittee traced the origins of the South Korean lobbying campaign to fears in the early 1970s that U.S. support was waning. The report indicated that high-level U.S. government officials allowed the Korean lobbying effort to continue without interference because of an "attitude of permissiveness" that placed a premium on keeping Korean troops engaged in the Vietnam War.

The same attitude, the report said, sought to "maintain credibility for the U.S. position in Korea as an unyielding commitment to resist the threat of Communist aggression."

The committee's case study of a foreign government's influence-buying efforts also detailed the often illegal operations of organizations controlled by South Korean evangelist Sun Myung Moon. The report produced new evidence showing what it called "the Moon organization's" involvement in the production and sale of armaments.

Origins of Lobbying Effort

The investigation of Korean-American relations, headed by Donald M. Fraser, D-Minn., found that the initial objectives were to ensure congressional approval of a $1.5 billion military aid package between 1971 and 1975 for South Korea and to prevent further withdrawal of U.S. troops.

From 1972 onward, the committee said, the Koreans had another objective: "to convince Americans that Park's authoritarian government was justified" for reasons of national security and economic development.

The committee said the lobbying effort, directed from South Korea, began in 1970 and involved South Koreans operating either out of motives of patriotism or profit. In Washington, Tongsun Park's George Town Club, established with Korean CIA (KCIA) assistance, became a lobbying center for the Korean government.

KCIA operations in the United States included: 1) recruitment of American businessmen, congressmen and academics to advocate South Korea's policies, 2) visits to Korea by influential Americans, 3) use of commissions from U.S.-financed rice sales for KCIA activities, 4) infiltration of the Korean community in the United States to counter criticism of the Park government, 5) obtaining classified U.S. government information by cultivating U.S. officials.

Executive Branch Awareness

The Fraser committee concluded that by 1971 "appropriate agencies of the executive branch" were sufficiently aware of "questionable" Korean government activities to "warrant taking action toward halting the activities and preventing recurrences."

Instead, the report stated, "the activities were allowed to continue until a major scandal erupted five years later."

The committee said that by late 1971:

- The State Department and U.S. embassy in Seoul regarded Tongsun Park as an unregistered South Korean agent, presumed to be connected with the KCIA, who was offering gifts of cash to congressmen.
- The State Department believed Radio of Free Asia, sponsors of which included prominent Americans, was controlled by the KCIA.
- The State Department had indications that Kim Kwang, an aide to then-Rep. Cornelius E. Gallagher, D-N.J. 1959-73, was a KCIA agent.
- State Department officials suspected that Suzi Park Thomson, an aide to then-Speaker Carl Albert, D-Okla. 1947-77, was working for the KCIA.
- The FBI had information that "convinced its own officials" that "criminal activities [by Korean agents] are strongly indicated," that a KCIA agent working as a congressman's aide had made a "payoff" to the congressman, that Park had made payments to congressmen using money received in rice deals and that a congressman had sought campaign contributions from President Park and recommended that Tongsun Park be put in charge of Korean lobbying in the United States and of Korean rice purchases.

The Fraser committee concluded that "no effective action was taken to deal with any of these reported activities." The report suggested that the Justice Department and FBI whitewashed an investigation of Radio of Free Asia. And the report concluded that despite information strongly indicating that Tongsun Park worked for the KCIA, the Department of Agriculture was told Park had no connection with the government of South Korea when it queried the "appropriate" agencies in connection with Park's becoming a rice agent.

The report also indicated that former Secretary of State Henry A. Kissinger knew of allegations of payoffs to Rep. Gallagher four years before the Justice Department began a full-scale investigation during the Ford administration. Kissinger, the report stated, brought evidence of bribery to Ford's attention in 1975 when it indicated involvement of several congressmen.

Gallagher, formerly chairman of a House Asian affairs subcommittee, served 17 months in jail after pleading guilty to a tax charge.

Armaments

While the Rev. Sun Myung Moon was best-known for his "Unification Church," the Fraser report indicated that Moon's involvement with the South Korean government extended to the arms business. In 1977, the report stated, a Moon-controlled business in Korea approached Colt Industries in Korea to get permission to export M-16 rifles being manufactured in Korea. The report said the Moon organization was "apparently acting on behalf of the Korean government."

The M-16 incident was cited as evidence of South Korea's repeated requests that the United States allow it to become an arms exporter. The committee recommended that a task force of federal agencies investigate whether Moon's effort to export M-16s violated the U.S. Arms Export Control act and other possible violations of tax, banking, currency and foreign agent laws by Moon and his followers.

A spokesman for the Unification Church condemned the report as "prejudiced and biased." A Korean embassy spokesman denied any ties between his government and the Moon organization.

Other Findings

Among the committee's other findings were the following:

- That the Moon organization provided at least $1.2 million to capitalize the Diplomat National Bank in Washington in apparent violation of federal banking laws, and that Tongsun Park purchased $250,000 of stock in the bank in apparent violation of securities law.
- At least $8.5 million of American corporate funds were diverted to the ruling party in South Korea in connection with the 1971 elections.
- The Korean government negated the competitive bidding practices of the U.S. government by keeping contracts for U.S. military procurement artificially high, at a cost of millions of dollars to the U.S. Treasury.
- In 1970, a Korean government official attempted to bribe an official of the Voice of America, the U.S. propaganda network, apparently for the purpose of limiting unfavorable news about the Korean government.

In minority views to the report, Reps. Edward J. Derwinski, R-Ill., and Bill Goodling, R-Pa., said that they did not endorse all the findings. However, they said that they supported the section on the Moon organization and agreed that it "may have violated U.S. laws" and should be investigated thoroughly.

Senate Investigation

The Senate Ethics Committee concluded its 17-month Korean investigation with an Oct. 16 report (S Rept 95-1314) that recommended no disciplinary action against any incumbent or former senator.

At the same time the committee referred to the Justice Department evidence of possible law violations involving Birch Bayh, D-Ind., former Sen. Jack Miller, R-Iowa (1961-73), and aides to Bayh, Miller and Sen. Hubert H. Humphrey, D-Minn. (1949-64, 1971-78).

The possible illegalities involved perjury in all cases and acceptance of a campaign contribution on federal property, as well as failure to report a campaign contribution in the Bayh case.

The committee also released a somewhat ambiguous finding that Bayh was in "neglect of his duties" as a senator in failing to tell the committee in his written statements about an offer of a sizable campaign contribution from Tongsun Park, who the committee said was a South Korean government agent.

Bayh denied that he intended to mislead the committee.

"Neglect of duty" apparently was an unprecedented finding that carried no disciplinary penalty and required no vote or other action by the full Senate.

Finally, the committee report cleared numerous current and former senators of wrongdoing in the "Koreagate" affair. Most of those findings had been disclosed in the committee's interim report released in June.

Interim Report

In its first report on its secret inquiry into Korean influence peddling in the Senate, the committee revealed that shortly before his death in November 1977, Sen. John L. McClellan, D-Ark., acknowledged accepting an illegal $1,000 campaign donation from Tongsun Park. The report, issued in June, indicated that McClellan had violated the law and that there was conflicting testimony on the activities of Bayh, Miller and Humphrey.

McClellan Case

Ethics Committee Counsel Victor Kramer said that in October 1977 McClellan, the chairman of the Senate Appropriations Committee, asked to speak with him. McClellan related that he had received a $1,000 cash contribution from Park a few days prior to the November 1972 general election.

McClellan said he did not recall what he did with the funds, but they were not listed in publicly filed campaign reports as was required by the 1971 federal election law. McClellan said he never discussed any legislative matter with Park.

Park testified that his gift to McClellan was "close to $2,000 or even more" but that a portion of the money was sent back "with the explanation that the senator wanted to keep only $1,000."

The Senate report produced no hard evidence of impropriety on the part of Sen. John G. Tower, R-Texas. A member of the Ethics Committee, Tower had disqualified himself from participating in the inquiry because his name had been associated with Park. Tower acknowledged receiving gifts of jewelry from Park, but said they were worth less than $25. Committee counsel Kramer said the committee had not had the jewelry appraised.

The committee report also noted previously reported contributions from Park to Harry F. Byrd Jr., Ind.-Va., Spark M. Matsunaga, D-Hawaii, and former Sens. Stuart Symington, D-Mo., and Joseph M. Montoya, D-N.M.

The Bayh Case

The central questions in the Bayh case turned on two issues: 1) conflicting statements Bayh gave the committee concerning a campaign contribution offered to him by Tongsun Park and, 2) the events surrounding a meeting that took place in an office in the Capitol on Oct. 8, 1974.

The first issue provided the basis for the committee's Oct. 16 finding that Bayh was in "neglect of his duties." The second was the basis of the committee's referral to the Justice Department.

'Neglect of Duty'

In a questionnaire sent all 100 sitting senators and 56 living former senators who served in the Senate from 1967, the Ethics Committee asked in several different ways whether senators ever had received or been offered anything of value in excess of $35 by Tongsun Park.

In his response to the committee in October 1977, Bayh answered that he had never accepted anything of value from Park, and twice said he had not been offered anything of value from Park or someone he "now suspected" was a representative of the South Korean government.

In addition, Bayh stated in a July 1977 letter to committee Chairman Adlai E. Stevenson III, D-Ill.: "At no time, did he [Park] offer me any money, honorary degrees, trips to Korea, or any of the other numerous items we've all read about in the newspapers."

But in his testimony before the committee in April 1978 Bayh acknowledged that Park offered him a sizable contribution at a meeting in October 1974. Bayh said he refused to accept the contribution: "I had reflected on it; had come to the conclusion that that was not the kind of thing I wanted any part of. . . . I did not feel that it was the thing to do so far as my campaign was concerned to take money from someone who was not an American."

(Park testified that he had no recollection of Bayh's commenting on the propriety of accepting contributions from foreigners and that Bayh accepted the money.)

Bayh acknowledged that there were "rather pointed inconsistencies" between his July 1977 letter and his sworn testimony concerning offers from Park. He termed the contradictions "a mistake."

Bayh said he did not recall Park's offer until some time after his July letter and after Park had testified that he gave Bayh's administrative aide Jason Berman $1,500 to $1,800 for the Bayh campaign. Bayh said he remembered the offer in trying to figure out "why or how it was possible" for Park to make such a statement.

Bayh also testified that in answering the question about offers of money, "what was going through my mind was the sizable dollar figures that had been related, the offer of bribes and payoffs had been the thread of all the notoriety, as opposed to the kinds of offers that were purely legal on their face. . . . I testified here that he did offer a campaign contribution to me, [but it was] not illegal."

The committee report noted that Bayh had acknowledged in his July letter and his later testimony that Park's contributions and gifts to members of Congress had made front-page news for a long time prior to July 1977 and that both the Justice Department and congressional committees had launched investigations.

The committee concluded: "This publicity should have jogged the memory of any senator, especially any senator who was a close social friend of Mr. Park [as Bayh was], so that he would recall an offer of a contribution made directly to the senator by Mr. Park. Thus there appears to be no reasonable justification for Senator Bayh's misleading statements to this committee that Mr. Park had not offered him any 'money' or 'anything of value in excess of $35.' "

The committee also found, however, that, "in view of significant conflicts in the evidence, there is insufficient proof to establish that Senator Birch Bayh, his family, staff or campaign committees accepted a campaign contribution from Tongsun Park." And the committee said there was no evidence Bayh took any official action at the suggestion or request of Park.

Criminal Evidence

The second and more serious aspect of the Bayh case concerned conflicting testimony about where a contribution the "Hoosiers for Birch Bayh" committee received and reported was made, and whether it was received by Bayh or his aide Berman.

The committee concluded that "there is substantial credible evidence that Senator Birch Bayh, or his aide Jason Berman, received a $1,000 campaign contribution from Edward Merrigan on Oct. 8, 1974, in the Capitol of the United States of America." (The report said Merrigan was a friend of Park's.)

Receipt of a campaign contribution on federal property is a crime carrying penalties of up to $5,000 and three years in jail. There are apparently few precedents for the statute having been enforced. Bayh denied that he received the contribution at the Oct. 8 meeting.

The committee's evidence against Bayh and Berman included the following:

- Merrigan's testimony that he "made a $1,000 contribution to Senator Bayh sitting at his desk," at a meeting Oct. 8, 1974, at which Park and Berman were also in attendance. Merrigan said he "didn't give it [the $1,000] to anyone else but Senator Bayh, I am convinced. I wasn't there to give it to anyone else."
- Park's testimony that Merrigan "actually pulled out his checkbook, out from his suit pocket. And I was somewhat bewildered that he took the checkbook out right then and there and wrote out the check." Park said he recalled that the check was for $1,000 and believed it was given to Berman but was unsure on the latter point. Park said, however, he believed the contribution was made *before* Bayh arrived at the meeting.
- Merrigan's check was dated Oct. 8, 1974.
- Bayh's campaign schedules and calendars showed that he and Berman were in Washington on only one day in October 1974 — the eighth.
- A letter dated Oct. 14, 1974, found in a box marked "Jay Berman," which was sent out over Bayh's name thanking Merrigan for coming by the Senate and making a $1,000 contribution, and stating that Berman would stay in touch with Merrigan and Park.
- A list of contributions compiled in Indiana on Oct. 9, 1974, listing Merrigan's $1,000 contribution.
- A record of deposit of the Merrigan check in an Indianapolis bank on Oct. 9, 1974. The committee report stated: "It is extremely unlikely that the check could have been mailed to the Washington, D.C., office after the 5 o'clock meeting held on October 8, 1974, and have been received in the Indiana office on October 9, 1974. Instead, the evidence confirms the testimony of Mr. Merrigan and Mr. Park that the check was given to Senator Bayh or Mr. Berman at the meeting on October 8, 1974, and indicates that the check was carried back on a return flight to Indiana."

Bayh acknowledged that Merrigan made a $1,000 contribution in October 1974 but testified: "I don't think the Merrigan contribution was even discussed in any way, shape or form at that meeting. In fact, in my mind, I don't know what he was doing there."

In his first appearance before the Ethics Committee, Bayh said he had a "very strong recollection" of the October meeting and that during it Park offered him a contribution. But in his second appearance Bayh testified that his "memory is not as sharp as I wish it were" and that he was no longer sure that Park's offer had been made at the meeting.

Bayh said it was "conceivable" he met Park before the meeting or some time earlier in the year, but that he was "absolutely positive" he rejected Park's offer of campaign assistance.

While Berman first testified that Merrigan "did not say that he was going to make a contribution" at the meeting and did not do so, he later said it was "entirely likely" the meeting occurred on Oct. 8, 1974, and "entirely possible" Merrigan offered a contribution at the meeting.

Bayh said he was not "dead certain" the meeting occurred the eighth, that he had "no recollection whatsoever of the theatrics of [Merrigan] whipping out the checkbook and then giving it to me" and that Merrigan "did not give me a campaign contribution in person." He testified he was certain the contribution was not made in his presence.

Assuming the conclusions of the committee were correct as to the time and place of the Merrigan contribution, the Justice Department still had to determine *who* received the contribution — Bayh or Berman. Without greater certainty on that point, prosecution appeared unlikely. If the recipient issue were resolved, the Justice Department would likely have an additional crime to deal with — perjury.

Perjury

While the committee report did not specifically state which testimony might be perjurous in the Bayh case, page references in a footnote to the report suggested several possibilities. These involved conflicting testimony on the Merrigan contribution, conflicting testimony on receipt of a Park contribution, and conflicts between Bayh's responses to the committee questionnaire and his oral testimony. If it could be established that Park gave a contribution to Bayh or Berman, an additional crime, failure to report the contribution, would have been committed.

Bayh and the committee also disagreed over whether his statement that he and his wife had been the guests of honor at a dinner hosted by Park and costing $3,800 was thorough enough. The disagreement appeared unlikely to provide a basis for a serious legal challenge.

The committee referred all evidence of potentially perjurous statements in the Bayh case to the Justice Department. It also referred similar evidence in the Miller and Humphrey cases.

Humphrey and Miller

The Ethics Committee concluded that Park made a contribution of at least $5,000 in cash in April or early May 1972 to the Humphrey presidential campaign and that it was not reported as required by the federal election law.

It found, however, that there was no evidence Humphrey was ever aware of the contribution. The committee concluded that Humphrey's deputy campaign manager, John Morrison, "personally accepted the contribution from Mr. Park under circumstances that were difficult to forget and that it is highly unlikely that Mr. Morrison does not remember meeting Mr. Park and receiving the contribution."

Morrison testified that he did not believe he ever met Park, could not recall a contribution of $5,000 in cash made to the Washington office and that he did not know of any contributions by Park to the 1972 Humphrey campaign. "I am not saying that it didn't take place," Morrison testified, "but I do not believe that it did."

The committee also reported that Park made a contribution of $3,000 in cash to the Miller senatorial campaign but that there was insufficient evidence to determine who initially received the contribution. "The evidence demonstrates that Senator Jack Miller or some member of his staff, other than Stanley Browne, must have known about Tongsun Park's contribution in 1972; the evidence is not sufficient to establish which of these people had such knowledge." Browne was Miller's administrative assistant.

The committee further reported that "much of the testimony of Stanley Browne is not accurate; however, the evidence is not sufficient to establish that Mr. Browne testified falsely when he said that he returned Tongsun Park's contribution." ▮

Franking Bill Dies

A bill that would have written into law significant changes in congressional use of the frank for mail died in the Senate during the rush to adjournment.

The bill (HR 7792) would have placed into law the restrictions on franking privileges adopted by the House and Senate ethics code in 1977. *(1977 Almanac, pp. 770, 778)*

Those restrictions were put into effect by the ethics codes, and were not affected by the failure of HR 7792 to pass. The House had passed HR 7792 by voice vote July 12, 1977.

The Senate Governmental Affairs Committee had amended the bill to make it easier for senators to send bulk mail to constituents. The amendment might have enabled some senators to substantially increase the amount of mail sent out under the frank.

The bill was reported by the committee Sept. 15 (S Rept 95-1195), but was held up at the request of Sen. Adlai E. Stevenson III, D-Ill., chairman of the Senate Ethics Committee. An aide said Stevenson wanted the committee to hold hearings on the bill, but was unable to call the hearings because of the press of other committee business.

In the closing days of Congress the bill also was threatened by a series of proposed amendments which would have loosened some of the restrictions on franked mail. A Governmental Affairs Committee aide said the amendments were not acceptable to the committee.

The franking privilege allows members of Congress to send letters and packages under a reproduction of their signature (where a stamp usually goes) without being charged for postage. In 1976, members sent 421.4 million pieces of franked mail, at a cost to the taxpayer of $51.8 million.

Simplified Mailing

Under postal regulations in effect since 1964, House members are allowed to send franked mail to "postal patrons," thus avoiding the need to supply a name and address for each piece of mail. House members also have been able to send mail by third class, which costs about half as much as first class.

But senators have been severely restricted because of the 1964 regulations that resulted from four years of bickering between the House and Senate.

Senators are allowed to send franked mail only first class, addressed to specific names at specific addresses. Mail with wrong names or addresses is either forwarded or returned to Senate offices.

As a result, most senators have been forced to keep massive mailing lists on the Senate computer. The lists must be updated continuously, because about one in five Americans moves each year.

In a letter to the committee, Sen. Bob Packwood, R-Ore., said "it is impossible for a Senate office to maintain a current statewide mail list when changes of address are occurring so quickly that even the Postal Service has difficulty keeping pace."

In 1977, the Governmental Affairs Committee considered, but rejected, giving senators the same "postal patron" privilege that House members have. The committee's views came in a report on the franking system in October 1977 (S Rept 95-566) as directed by the Senate ethics code.

Instead, the committee suggested that senators be given the same bulk mailing privileges that are available to the general public. That would enable senators to send mail marked "occupant," but they would still have to supply specific street addresses or box numbers. ▮

House Bill Cosponsorship

The House passed a resolution (H Res 86, H Rept 95-1612) Oct. 10 eliminating the ceiling on the number of cosponsors who can sign on to a bill.

The resolution was scheduled to take effect Jan. 3, 1979. After that date, all members who wanted to cosponsor a bill could be added to the original bill introduced in the House. Previously, a member's bill could be cosponsored by only 24 other members. When there were more than 24 cosponsors, an identical bill had to be printed under a different number.

Supporters of the resolution, which passed by voice vote, said it could save about $177,000 a year in printing costs. The clerk of the House based the savings on an estimate that 3,500 fewer bills would have to be printed if there was no limit on cosponsorship.

The resolution was reported by the House Rules Committee Sept. 22. It would allow cosponsors to remove their names from a bill by unanimous consent up until the day the bill was reported from committee, and it would allow reprinting of a bill with a list of new cosponsors if 20 or more members had been added since the last printing.

Senate Administrator

The Senate Rules Committee April 26 rejected the idea of hiring an administrator to take over operation of Senate support services.

Instead, the three officers who oversee most of those services were told by Rules Chairman Claiborne Pell, D-R.I., to streamline their fragmented administrative structure.

Pell's instructions killed a proposal (S Res 166) to establish a Senate administrator who would pay bills, buy supplies and run custodial and other services now scattered under the jurisdiction of the Architect of the Capitol, the Senate Sergeant at Arms, the Secretary of the Senate and the Rules Committee.

Streamlining Functions

After the three officers agreed to meet informally with members of Rules to discuss streamlining their functions, Pell said S Res 166 would be "set aside."

The resolution, introduced by John C. Culver, D-Iowa, and 30 cosponsors, would have implemented a recommendation made by the Commission on the Operation of the Senate in December 1976. *(Background, 1977 Almanac p. 790)*

The commission said that day-to-day internal Senate operations were hampered by an antiquated administrative structure.

Many inefficiencies stemmed from overlapping jurisdictions giving two or more Senate officers authority to perform the same duty, such as buying or moving furniture, the commission said. A centralized administrative office could increase efficiency and make the Senate operate in a more business-like fashion, according to the commission.

Culver's proposal got a hostile reception from former Rules Chairman Howard W. Cannon, D-Nev., at a 1977 hearing. Cannon said the commission's recommendations contained errors and overlooked some changes that had been made in Senate administration.

Officers Testify

Pell, who took over the committee in 1978, scheduled the April 26 meeting to hear from witnesses who did not get to testify before Cannon. They included the three officers who would lose authority to the proposed administrator. Architect George M. White, Secretary J. S. Kimmitt and Sergeant at Arms Frank "Nordy" Hoffmann each made it clear in testimony that they opposed the idea of an administrator.

Instead, they embraced Pell's suggestion to maintain the structural status quo while adopting new jurisdictional guidelines that would leave just one officer in charge of each support service.

By offering the alternative, Pell avoided taking a position on the resolution. His plan gave the officers a way to meet some of the commission's criticisms without relinquishing most of their duties. ▮

Smithsonian Authorizations

President Carter signed into law Oct. 5 a bill allowing the Smithsonian Institution to acquire Washington's Museum of African Art.

The measure (S 2507 — PL 95-414) passed the Senate by voice vote May 16 after being reported by the Rules Committee May 9 (S Rept 95-793). A companion bill (HR 10792) was passed by the House Sept. 18 by a vote of 350-54. *(Vote 697, p. 198-H)*

The Senate agreed to accept the language of the House bill Sept. 22, clearing the measure for the president.

Rep. Lindy Boggs, D-La., said the museum, worth $10 million, would be deeded to the Smithsonian. The $1 million authorized for appropriations for museum operations in fiscal 1979 would be partly offset by revenues of about $375,000, she said.

The act established a 15-member museum commission to be appointed by the Smithsonian's regents; at least 10 members of the museum's current board of trustees must be appointed to the commission. Commission members will serve for three years.

Related Action

Congress Oct. 14 cleared legislation (S 1029 — PL 95-569) authorizing $21.5 million for construction of a support facility to house and preserve part of the Smithsonian Institution's burgeoning collection.

The planned new facility contained about 239,000 square feet of space, most of it for storage of collections of the Museum of Natural History, and was to be built on a 21.5 acre tract at the Suitland Federal Center in Silver Hill, Md.

The bill was reported by the Senate Rules and Administration Committee May 4 (S Rept 95-783) and passed the Senate May 9. It passed the House under suspension of the rules Sept. 25 after being reported Sept. 12 (H Rept 95-1559) by the Public Works and Transportation Committee. ❚

R.I. Indian Claims

A settlement between the Narragansett Indians and the state of Rhode Island over land claims in the town of Charlestown was approved by Congress and signed by the president in September.

The bill (HR 12860 — PL 95-395) provided that the state would transfer about 900 acres of its lands and the U.S. government would purchase and transfer about 1,000 acres of private lands to a state-chartered, Indian-controlled corporation to administer the land settlement.

The settlement arose out of lawsuits filed by the Narragansett Indians that were similar to suits pending in Maine and other eastern states.

The suits have contended that lands lost by the Indians since 1790 were taken in violation of the Indian Non-Intercourse Act of 1790, which provided that all land transactions between tribes and white settlers required approval by the federal government. The claims generally have been upheld in the courts.

The Narragansett tribe filed suit in 1975 against the state of Rhode Island and a number of private landowners; the Indians were seeking about 3,200 acres of public and private lands in Charlestown.

The suits were consolidated into a single action and on Feb. 28, 1978, a settlement was reached between the Indians and representatives of the town and state.

The agreement provided that all the 900 acres of public settlement lands and 75 percent of the 1,000 acres of private settlement lands would be permanently held for conservation purposes.

HR 12860 authorized appropriations of $3.5 million to carry out the settlement and authorized payments of up to $175,000 for options to buy the private lands.

The bill was reported Aug. 8 by the Committee on Interior and Insular Affairs (H Rept 95-1453), and passed by the House under suspension of the rules Sept. 12 by a 249-122 vote. *(Vote 663, p. 190-H)*

The Senate passed HR 12860 Sept. 15 by voice vote after the Indian Affairs Committee had reported a companion bill (S 3153) July 11 (S Rept 95-972).

Congress cleared a $3.5 million appropriation to implement the settlement shortly before adjournment Oct. 15. The money was contained in the continuing appropriations bill (H J Res 1139). *(Continuing resolution, p. 161)*❚

Access to Agency Records

A bill loosening restrictions on access to federal government papers was signed into law by President Carter Oct. 5.

The new bill (S 1265 — PL 95-416) allowed the National Archives to accept other agencies' records after 30 years, rather than after 50 years. It also barred the placement of curbs on access to the records once they were transferred, except in certain circumstances.

Rep. Richardson Preyer, D-N.C., who guided the bill through House floor debate and voice vote passage Sept. 25, said that under the new law the General Services Administrator and the Archivist of the United States must agree to agency-proposed access curbs in order for the curbs to take effect.

If such curbs were agreed upon, they would last for 30 years after transfer of the documents, rather than 50 years. Under previous law, the 50-year curbs could be unilaterally imposed by the chief of the agency sending the documents to the archives.

The effect of the change was to put a 60-year maximum time limit on inaccessibility of documents, rather than a 100-year time limit.

Preyer noted that the National Archives had requested that the legislation be passed in hearings before his House Government Operations Information and Individual Rights Subcommittee (H Rept 95-1522).

The Senate passed the bill April 3, also by voice vote (S Rept 95-710).

Under other provisions of S 1265:

- The administrator may remove all restrictions on access to records of defunct agencies having no successor agencies.
- The administrator, the archivist and the agency chief may "for reasons . . . in relevant statutory law" bar access to "specific bodies" of records for longer than 30 years.
- A 1952 agreement between the Census Bureau director and the archivist, barring access to individual census information for 72 years after it was gathered, shall remain in force. Changes in the release of individual census data shall be made only after both the census director and the archivist agree to them, and after the proposed changes are published in the *Federal Register*. ❚

D.C. Pensions Bill Vetoed

Criticizing what he called "abuses" of disability pensions, President Carter Nov. 4 pocket-vetoed a bill (HR 6536) changing the pension rules for many Washington, D.C., public employees. The bill had cleared Congress Oct. 13.

Carter said he agreed with the main purpose of the bill, which was to put pension plans of D.C. police, firefighters, teachers and judges on a sound financial footing. But he said "a large part" of the plans' financial problems "derives from abuses of the disability retirement statutes which were permitted to flourish by those responsible for their effective administration."

Carter also objected to providing $1.63 billion in federal funds to the pension plans over the next 25 years. He said HR 6536 "overstates the degree of federal responsibility" for the indebtedness of the plans. *(Veto text, p. 66-E)*

Proponents of the bill were disappointed by Carter's move. An aide to Thomas F. Eagleton, D-Mo., who had guided the bill to Senate passage, said a similar measure to solve the funding problem would be introduced in 1979. Eagleton had warned Congress that it would have to be responsible for the costs of pension plans it had imposed upon the D.C. government since 1916, for which it had not provided adequate funding.

Carter added he would support an Office of Management and Budget (OMB) proposal to contribute $462 million to the pension funds over the next 25 years. The OMB views were rejected during House committee consideration of HR 6536 in 1977.

Carter also objected to awarding disability pensions for non-service injuries aggravated by active duty to D.C. employees already on the payroll. The bill retained such awards — which had come under fire following the award of such full-pay pensions for non-service-but-aggravated-by-it injuries to a former police chief and a former fire chief in early 1978 — but banned them for future employees.

Legislative History

The House cleared HR 6536 by voice vote Oct. 13. The Senate had agreed to the conference report (S Rept 95-1293; H Rept 95-1713) by voice vote Oct. 6. The House originally passed the bill Sept. 26, 1977, by a 348-21 vote (H Rept 95-335), while the Senate agreed to the original version of HR 6536 by voice vote Aug. 24, 1978 (S Rept 95-1025). *(1977 House vote, Vote 541, 1977 Almanac p. 158-H)*

As cleared by Congress, HR 6536: authorized $1.63 billion in federal payments to the pension funds from fiscal 1979 through fiscal 2003 to cover the unfunded liability; barred future award of service-connected disability pensions for non-service injuries aggravated by active duty; required that disability pensions for future uniformed officers be equal to the percentage of disability (rather than the existing all-or-nothing system of disability awards, which would continue for current officers); reduced federal payments to the funds if disability pensions for current officers were greater than 102 percent of what they would be under the new, tighter rules; and established an 11 person board to manage the police, fire, teachers' and judges' pension funds under provisions laid down by the Employee Retirement Income and Security Act. ∎

Indian Preference Laws

The House June 26 defeated a Senate-passed bill that would have allowed non-Indian employees of two federal Indian agencies to retire earlier and with greater benefits than other Civil Service workers.

S 666 was designed to aid non-Indian employees adversely affected by laws giving Indians preference in the agencies' hiring, promotions and other employment practices. The bill failed, 118-204, to receive the two-thirds approval needed for passage under suspension of the rules. *(Vote 429, p. 122-H)*

The measure would have permitted non-Indian employees of the Bureau of Indian Affairs (BIA) and the Indian Health Service (IHS) to retire after 25 years of federal service or at age 50 with 20 years of service. Early retirement would have been available only until the end of 1985 and only to those employed continuously by either agency since June 17, 1974.

Such retirees would have received annuities based on 2.5 percent of their first 20 years' salary and 2 percent of additional years' pay. Those annuities were substantially greater than the amounts allotted other Civil Service employees, who generally must work until at least age 55 for full benefits or be penalized for early retirement.

The bill was reported by the Senate Governmental Affairs Committee Jan. 24 (H Rept 95-615). The Senate passed the measure by voice vote Jan. 30.

The House Post Office and Civil Service Committee reported the bill June 13 (H Rept 95-1288) with the agreement of the Committee on Interior and Insular Affairs, which shared jurisdiction but issued no report.

Court Upheld Law

Supporters said during House debate that the bill was needed because Indian preference laws and a series of court decisions beginning in 1974 had required the agencies to give preference to Indians in hiring, promotions, transfers and employee cutbacks.

Acting on a case that raised some of the same issues involved in the historic *Bakke* case four years later, the Supreme Court in 1974 upheld the Indian preference law by an 8-0 decision. The court said in *Morton v. Manconi* that the law did not call for racial preference but was an employment criterion intended to further the cause of Indian self-government and to make the Bureau of Indian Affairs more responsive to its constituent groups.

In its June 28 decision in *Bakke*, the Supreme Court outlawed using racial quotas in college admissions, but it said race could be taken into consideration in choosing applicants. *(Bakke decision, p. 8-A)*

The preference laws, proponents of S 666 said, had stymied the careers of non-Indians, resulting in low morale and inefficiency. They argued that the early retirement plan would aid the 3,000 non-Indians involved and open more agency positions to Indians as others retired.

Indian Takeover Feared

Opponents painted the bill as a move to give further preference to Indians and raised the specter of an Indian takeover of the agencies as non-Indians retired. At the same time, they pointed out that the measure was unfair to all other Civil Service employees, including Indians and non-Indians not retiring early, since none of them would get the special benefits.

They argued the cost of the bill — $142.9 million in added Civil Service retirement fund appropriations over 30 years — was unjustifiable. The Civil Service Commission had agreed during September hearings that the cost would be excessive.

Opponents also argued that the bill misused the retirement system as a solution to personnel problems that should be handled administratively.

President Ford gave the same reason for vetoing a nearly identical bill (HR 5465) on Sept. 24, 1976. *(1976 Almanac p. 24-A)*

Observers said the Indian preference tag hung on the bill, together with a general reluctance to increase benefits for any Civil Service workers, was instrumental in bringing about the 118-204 roll call vote that defeated the bill. Committee staff said no effort would be made to bring the bill up under a new rule.

— PL 95-608) was passed in response to complaints that state agencies were taking children from poor, uneducated Indian parents who did not know their rights. It required approval of tribal courts for adoptions of Indian children, court-appointed counsel for indigent parents or guardians in the proceedings, and other safeguards. It also authorized $26 million in fiscal 1979 for programs to keep Indian families together, including counseling, day care, homemaker and child recreation services.

Indian Legislation

Sensing an anti-Indian "backlash" in Congress, 2,800 American Indians from throughout the country journeyed to Washington, D.C., in July to speak up for Indian interests and lobby against passage of 11 bills that would have restricted their hunting, fishing and land-claim rights.

The bills went nowhere in the 95th Congress, but tribal leaders feared "anti-Indian" legislation would return in the next session, perhaps to a better reception.

Indians attributed the backlash to increasing Indian assertiveness, and particularly to tribal land claims. Indians had been pressing their case in the courts and in Congress for compensation or the return of lands they say were illegally taken from them by the federal government over the past 200 years. Some of the lands contain valuable energy resources; some estimates say 25 to 40 percent of U.S. uranium, almost one-third of western coal and at least 5 percent of the nation's oil and natural gas reserves were on land already controlled by Indian tribes, and Indians were asserting their rights to other lands containing timber and water resources.

Land Claim Bills. Congress cleared legislation settling one large land claim, and planned hearings on another in 1979. The conflict resolved was in Rhode Island, where the Narragansett tribe sought 3,200 acres in state and private lands. Under the settlement approved by Congress, the Indians were to receive 900 acres of state land and $3.5 million from the federal government for individual grants of up to $75,000 to buy private property. *(Story, p. 815)*

The 96th Congress would have to decide whether to approve an out-of-court settlement between the state of Maine and the Penobscot and Passamaquoddy tribes, which had claimed more than half the land in the state. Under that settlement, the tribes would get $37 million in federal funds to purchase 100,000 acres of timberland from large paper companies.

Other Legislation. Other legislation enacted by the 95th Congress that affected Indians:

- Permitted tribes to administer food stamp programs on reservations. *(PL 95-113, 1977 Almanac p. 461)*
- Made tribes eligible for community development grants from the secretary of housing and urban development. *(PL 95-128, 1977 Almanac p. 126)*
- Authorized $80 million in fiscal 1979-81 to provide $4,000 grants to full-time students in tribally controlled community colleges. The legislation (S 1215 — PL 95-471) was aimed at improving education at the 20 Indian community colleges, 18 of which were not accredited. Proponents said such institutions were necessary because many Indians were ill prepared, either scholastically or culturally, to attend colleges far from their reservations.
- Provided safeguards for Indian families in cases of involuntary adoption. The Indian Child Welfare Act (S 1214

Trade Commission Funds

Legislation (HR 11005 — PL 95-430) authorizing appropriations of $12,963,000 in fiscal 1979 for the operations of the International Trade Commission (ITC) cleared Congress Sept. 28.

The ITC, which determined whether or not increased imports were injuring an industry under the provisions of the Trade Act of 1974 (PL 93-618), requested $13,113,000.

The House version of the bill (H Rept 95-1060), passed May 15, authorized $12,813,000.

The Senate version (S Rept 95-914), passed June 28, contained the higher figure requested by the ITC.

House and Senate sponsors agreed to split the difference between the two bills without a formal conference. The House approved the compromise Sept. 19 and the Senate agreed Sept. 28, thus clearing the measure for the president.

U.S. Fire Administration

The Senate by voice vote Sept. 22 approved a one-year extension of funds for the United States Fire Administration (USFA), clearing the bill for the president.

The measure (HR 11291 — PL 95-422) also changed the name of the agency, formerly the National Fire Prevention and Control Administration, and moved it from the Commerce Department to the newly created Federal Emergency Management Agency, as called for in President Carter's reorganization of federal emergency agencies. *(Reorganization plan, p. 801)*

The bill, which authorized $24,352,000 for the USFA in fiscal 1979, and $5.6 million for the Center for Fire Research, passed the House May 15 by a 360-11 vote. *(Vote 268, p. 76-H)*

The Senate passed its version of the bill (S 1794 — S Rept 95-798) on June 13 by voice vote.

At House and Senate Appropriations committees' request, the revised final bill authorized possible sale of the former Marjorie Webster Junior College in Washington, D.C., which had been considered as the location for a proposed National Fire Academy.

Office of Management and Budget officials told the panel that the cost of converting the site for the academy had doubled. The Science and Technology Committee had recommended (H Rept 95-992) that $6,043,000 of the USFA authorization be used to renovate the college academy site. If the college site were sold, the proceeds would be applied toward the acquisition and preparation of a new academy site.

Congress Approves Civil Service Reforms

Congress gave the green light to President Carter's plan for reorganizing the Civil Service Commission by clearing a bill (S 2640 — PL 95-454) that was a modified version of his blueprint for reforming the civil service system. Carter signed the bill Oct. 13.

Carter's plan, sent to Congress in March, was reworked extensively by both the House and Senate. But the compromise bill approved by House and Senate conferees still contained all but one of the basic changes the president had proposed for injecting merit into civil service pay systems and giving federal managers more flexibility to fire incompetent employees. The final bill was the most extensive revamping of the federal employment system since the civil service system was established in 1883.

The Senate quickly approved the conference agreement by voice vote Oct. 4. The House passed it, 365-8, Oct. 6, clearing the bill for the president.

The bill contained Carter's plan for a Senior Executive Service (SES) of top federal employees, a merit pay system for middle-level management, increased management flexibility in firing incompetent employees and statutory labor rights for federal employees. It did not contain Carter's proposals for curtailing veterans' preference in federal hiring. *(See box, p. 825)*

The bill was in danger several times in the seven months the House and Senate spent working on it. The administration and congressional backers fought off filibuster threats, vehement opposition from federal employee unions and other perils that seemed to pop up every time it appeared the bill had clear sailing.

What It Does

Major provisions in the final versions of the House and Senate bills were similar, but differed in some respects from the administration's original bill. S 2640 contained these major features:

• **New Agencies.** The functions of a new Office of Personnel Management (OPM) and Merit Systems Protection Board (MSPB), authorized by Carter's Reorganization Plan No. 2, were defined.

The two new agencies will replace the existing Civil Service Commission, with OPM taking over personnel management functions and MSPB becoming the new board of appeals for employee grievances.

• **Merit System, Banned Practices.** Merit system principles and prohibited personnel practices were defined. The bill also spelled out procedures for investigating and punishing prohibited personnel practices, including reprisals against employees who blow the whistle on government wrongdoing.

• **Incompetent Workers.** Federal managers were given slightly more flexibility in firing incompetent employees. However, the final bill did not give management nearly as much leeway as Carter had requested in firings based either on incompetency or misconduct. The appeals process spelled out for adverse actions — such as a firing or suspension — retained substantial protections for employees who challenge agency actions.

• **New Senior Corps.** A new Senior Executive Service (SES) was authorized. As finally agreed to by the conferees, SES would consist of about 8,000 top federal managers and policy-makers. Carter had proposed an elite corps of about 9,200 top employees, but Congress exempted several intelligence agencies from the SES.

Employees in the new service would be eligible for substantial cash bonuses. They would have less tenure than civil service employees, and they could be transferred more easily within an agency or between agencies.

• **Merit Pay.** Merit pay was established for federal employees at civil service levels GS-13 through GS-15. Although employees at those levels were still entitled to some of the automatic comparability raise given to all civil servants each year, other raises would be based on detailed evaluation of individual performance. In addition, those in the merit pay system were entitled to some cash bonuses not available to other civil service employees.

• **Labor Practices.** A Federal Relations Authority — comparable to the National Labor Relations Board for private sector employees — was established to hear complaints about unfair labor practices in federal employment.

• **Employee Limit.** A ceiling on the total number of federal employees was established for fiscal 1979-81. However, the final bill gave the president slightly more flexibility in exceeding the ceiling than the House, which drafted the original, administration-opposed, ceiling.

• **Unions.** The rights of federal employees to join labor unions and bargain collectively on certain personnel practices and policies was established in law. Previously, those rights were granted only by executive order, subject to change by the president with no congressional review.

The bill did not give federal employees the right to strike to negotiate for pay or fringe benefits or to require agency shops where employees would have to pay union dues regardless of whether they belonged to the union representing their unit. Federal employee unions had wanted those more sweeping rights, but all were opposed by the administration and rejected by Congress.

Although the unions attacked the reform bill as far too management-oriented, it still gave them something they had sought for years — statutory protection of federal employee rights to organize and bargain collectively.

The only major Carter proposal rejected by Congress was curtailment of veterans' preference in federal hiring.

Final Provisions

As approved by House and Senate, S 2640:

Title 1 — Merit System Principles

Merit Principles

• Applied the bill's merit system principles, as defined below, to all executive branch departments and agencies, the administrative office of the U.S. courts and the Government Printing Office (GPO).

• Required hiring and promoting of federal employees solely on ability, knowledge and skills.

• Required fair and open competition for federal jobs.

• Barred federal employment discrimination on the basis of political affiliation, race, color, religion, national origin, sex, marital status, age or handicapped condition.

Action on Reorganization Plan

On a 19-381 vote, the House Aug. 9 killed a resolution (H Res 1201 — H Rept 95-1396) that would have blocked the president's civil service reorganization plan (Reorganization Plan No. 2). Under the Reorganization Act passed by Congress in 1977 (PL 95-17), the president can submit plans to Congress for reorganizing federal agencies. The plans take effect unless disapproved by the House or Senate within 60 days. *(Vote 587, p. 166-H)*

The Senate did not vote on a resolution (S Res 464 — S Rept 95-1049) that would have blocked the civil service reorganization, so the plan became effective Aug. 11.

The reorganization plan calls for dividing up the CSC's conflicting duties of being chief government personnel manager and the appeals board for employee complaints. A new Office of Personnel Management (OPM) will take on CSC management responsibilities, such as conducting civil service examinations, training, and administration of pay and benefits.

Employee complaints will go to a new bipartisan Merit Systems Protection Board (MSPB). A third office, the Federal Labor Relations Authority (FLRA), will be headed by a bipartisan panel that will hear complaints about unfair labor practices. CSC Chairman Alan K. Campbell said the changeover to the new agencies would be completed by Jan. 1, 1979.

The House resolution to block the plan was killed after a short debate. The only member to speak against the plan was Newton I. Steers Jr., R-Md., who said it would "politicize the machinery of government."

The Government Operations Committee had unanimously endorsed the plan July 19.

- Required that federal pay rates be determined with consideration of national and local rates paid by private enterprise.
- Required employees to avoid conflicts of interest.
- Provided that employees be retained on the basis of their work performance.
- Protected employees from arbitrary action, personal favoritism and partisan political coercion.
- Prohibited use of official authority to coerce political activity by federal employees.
- Protected government whistleblowers from reprisals for certain disclosures of government wrongdoing.
- Authorized the president to issue personnel management rules, regulations and directives to carry out the merit system principles.

Prohibited Personnel Practices

- Excluded government corporations, the FBI, the Central Intelligence Agency (CIA), the Defense Intelligence Agency (DIA), the National Security Agency (NSA) and the General Accounting Office (GAO) from having action taken against them for the prohibited personnel practices listed below.
- Authorized the president to exempt other intelligence units from the prohibited practices provisions.
- Prohibited discrimination against federal employees as defined by sections of the Civil Rights Act of 1964, the Age Discrimination in Employment Act of 1967, the Fair Labor Standards Act of 1938, the Rehabilitation Act of 1973 and laws prohibiting discrimination on the basis of marital status or political affiliation.
- Prohibited reprisals against federal employees who refused to engage in political activity, and barred any coercion to force political activity by a federal employee.
- Prohibited influencing a person to withdraw from competition for a job in order to aid another's job chances.
- Prohibited giving an employee or applicant unauthorized preference in order to improve or injure the prospects of an individual.
- Prohibited nepotism in appointments or promotions.
- Prohibited reprisals against an employee who disclosed to the public or to other federal officials a violation of a law, rule or regulation; mismanagement; gross waste of funds; abuse of authority; or substantial and specific danger to public health or safety.
- Provided that in order to be protected, the employee's disclosure could not have violated certain statutes or an executive order dealing with classified material.
- Prohibited reprisals against an employee or job applicant who exercised a legitimate appeal right.

FBI

- Required the Attorney General to establish special procedures for protecting whistleblowers in the FBI from reprisals.

GAO Review

- Authorized the GAO to conduct audits and reviews of agency compliance with civil service laws and regulations.

Title II — Appraisal, Adverse Actions

Office of Personnel Management

- Made the OPM an independent body within the executive branch.
- Provided that OPM would be headed by a director and a deputy director appointed by the president and confirmed by the Senate.
- Gave the OPM director a four-year term, subject to removal by the president.
- Authorized the director to appoint up to five associate directors, who would be in the SES.
- Authorized the OPM director to administer and enforce civil service statutes.
- Authorized the OPM director to delegate any of his or her personnel management functions — except conducting most competitive examinations — to the heads of executive branch agencies, or to other agencies employing people in competitive service.

Merit Systems Protection Board

- Made the MSPB a three-member, bipartisan body appointed by the president and confirmed by the Senate.
- Provided that the MSPB members would serve seven-year, nonrenewable terms, and could be removed by the president only for inefficiency, neglect of duty or malfeasance in office.
- Required Senate confirmation of the president's choice for chairman of MSPB.

● Authorized the president to appoint an MSPB special counsel, with Senate approval, for a five-year term.

● Authorized the president to remove the special counsel only for inefficiency, neglect of duty or malfeasance in office.

● Authorized the MSPB to hear and adjudicate appeals from employees or applicants for federal jobs, and to enforce its orders.

● Authorized MSPB to review OPM rules and regulations, and to veto rules that constituted prohibited personnel practices.

● Authorized MSPB, its special counsel or any administrative law judge appointed by the board to issue subpoenas.

● Authorized the special counsel to receive and investigate allegations of prohibited personnel practices.

● Required the special counsel to notify an employee when an investigation of the employee's complaint has been terminated.

● Authorized the special counsel to initiate — without receiving specific complaints — investigations of prohibited personnel practices.

● Prohibited the special counsel from disclosing the identity of an employee who filed a complaint, unless disclosure was necessary to carry out the investigation.

● Provided that the special counsel may require an agency to investigate and file a written report on a whistleblower's allegations of agency wrongdoing if the special counsel found substantial likelihood that the allegations were true.

● Required that an agency's report on an investigation of a whistleblower's allegations must be sent to Congress, the president and the special counsel, and it must be reviewed by the special counsel.

● Authorized the special counsel to recommend to the MSPB corrective action to be taken if he or she determined there are reasonable grounds to believe a prohibited personnel practice has occurred.

● Required the special counsel to report to the attorney general and the head of the agency involved if he or she found cause to believe a criminal law had been violated.

● Required the special counsel to report noncriminal violations to the head of an agency and to require an agency to report on what was done with the special counsel's recommendations.

● Required the special counsel to maintain a public list of noncriminal matters referred to agency heads, along with the agency actions taken.

● Authorized the special counsel to investigate political activity prohibited by the Hatch Act.

● Authorized the special counsel to bring a disciplinary action against an employee who committed a prohibited personnel practice, or who knowingly and willfully refused or failed to comply with an MSPB order.

● Provided that any recommendation for disciplinary action against a top presidential appointee should be dealt with by the president rather than the MSPB.

● Authorized the special counsel to seek corrective action of a pattern of prohibited personnel practice by an agency or individual, such as hiring or promotion practices which violate merit system principles.

● Provided that any employee against whom a complaint has been filed with the MSPB was entitled to an opportunity to respond orally and in writing, to be represented by an attorney, to have a hearing before the board, an administrative law judge or other board employee, to have a transcript kept of the hearing and to have a written decision and reasons supporting it from the board.

● Authorized the board to order the following disciplinary actions: removal, reduction in grade, debarment from federal employment for not more than five years, suspension, reprimand or a civil fine of up to $1,000.

● Provided that there would be no administrative appeal of a board decision.

● Provided that a federal employee served with a disciplinary order by the board could appeal the action to the U.S. Court of Appeals.

● Authorized any MSPB member to stay a personnel action for up to 15 days if the special counsel had reasonable grounds to believe the action was a prohibited personnel practice.

● Authorized any member of the board to extend the stay for an additional 30 days at the request of the special counsel.

● Authorized MSPB to extend a stay indefinitely if it agrees with the special counsel's determination after hearing oral or written comment from the special counsel and the agency involved.

Performance Evaluation

● Provided that all executive branch agencies and departments, the administrative office of the U.S. courts and the GPO would be required to develop performance appraisal systems and to abide by procedures spelled out for firing or demoting employees.

● Exempted government corporations, the GAO, the CIA, the DIA, the NSA and other intelligence units designated by the president from the performance evaluation requirements.

● Replaced the practice of annually evaluating each federal employee's work as satisfactory, unsatisfactory or outstanding with a more complex performance appraisal system.

● Authorized agencies to develop their own performance appraisals, based on general guidelines set by OPM.

Incompetence

● Required an agency to give an employee at least 30 days advance notice in writing that he or she was to be fired or demoted because of unacceptable performance.

● Required the agency to include information about why the employee's performance was unacceptable.

● Guaranteed the employee the right to an attorney and to reply orally and in writing to the agency notice.

● Required the agency to make a final decision, in writing, on whether to fire, demote or retain an employee within 30 days after the expiration of the notice period.

● Required that a firing or demotion for incompetence must be based on examples of unacceptable performance during the previous one-year period.

● Provided that after an agency gave an employee notice of unacceptable performance, if the employee's performance improved and continued to be acceptable for one year, any record of the unacceptable performance must be removed from the employee's official records.

Misconduct

● Defined the rights of employees who are notified of a suspension of 14 days or less for misconduct or some other cause besides unacceptable performance.

● Provided that employees who are fired, furloughed without pay, suspended for more than 14 days, or reduced in grade or pay for misconduct or other reasons (besides unacceptable performance) must receive a 30-day advance written notice of the proposed action.

● Guaranteed those employees the right to have an attorney and to answer the notice in writing and orally.

● Required the agency to put its final decision and reasons for the decision in writing.

● Authorized the agency, at its own discretion, to hold a pretermination hearing for an employee who had been notified of an adverse action for any reason other than unacceptable performance.

● Defined the rights of administrative law judges who are notified of an agency's planned action against them.

Appeals

● Gave employees of covered agencies the right to appeal an adverse action for unacceptable performance, misconduct, or other cause, to the MSPB.

● Provided that a competitive service employee who is eligible for veterans' preference could appeal to the MSPB a firing or demotion by an agency otherwise exempt from the bill's appeals procedures.

● Required MSPB to grant all appellants a hearing and the right to be represented by an attorney.

● Authorized the board to refer any case appealed to it to an administrative law judge or other board employee, except that any case involving a firing must be heard by the board, an experienced appeals officer or an administrative law judge.

● Provided that in order for MSPB to uphold the agency's decision in an adverse action case, the agency must show an action based on unacceptable performance was supported by substantial evidence.

● Provided that to uphold an action involving misconduct or any other charge besides unacceptable performance, the agency must be supported by a preponderance of the evidence.

● Provided that an agency's decision in an adverse action case would not be upheld if the employee could show the decision involved procedural error which substantially impaired the employee's rights, involved discrimination or involved a prohibited personnel practice or otherwise violated the law.

● Provided that the decision on the appeal was final, unless a party to the appeal or the OPM director petitioned the board for review within 30 days after announcement of the decision, or unless the board decided to reopen the case.

● Required an agency to pay reasonable attorneys' fees for an employee if the employee won on appeal to the MSPB and the board determined that payment was warranted in the interest of justice or if the decision was based on a finding of discrimination.

● Required the board to announce a deadline for taking action on each appeal filed with it.

● Gave both the MSPB and the EEOC jurisdiction over discrimination complaints filed by federal employees, but provided that if the two agencies disagreed on a final decision, it shall be referred to a special panel composed of one member of MSPB, one member of the EEOC and one person appointed by the president and confirmed by the Senate.

● Gave employees or federal job applicants the right to appeal board decisions to the courts.

● Allowed OPM to appeal certain board decisions to the courts.

Title III — Staffing

Miscellaneous

● Authorized agencies to accept unpaid student volunteers, as long as they did not displace federal employees.

● Authorized hiring of reading assistants and interpreters for blind or deaf federal employees.

Veterans' Preference

● Eliminated preference in federal hiring for non-disabled retired military officials at or above the field grade rank of major.

● Permitted non-competitive appointment of veterans with at least a 30 percent service-related disability to certain federal jobs.

● Required an agency to notify a veteran with at least a 30 percent disability if the agency decided he or she was not eligible for an appointment because of physical disability, and allowed the veteran to ask OPM to review the agency's decision.

● Required an agency to notify a veteran with a disability of 30 percent or more if he or she was passed over on a federal hiring list in order to hire a non-veteran, and gave the veteran an opportunity to ask OPM to review the decision.

● Gave veterans with a service-related disability of at least 30 percent more protection from federal job layoffs than other veterans.

Double Dippers

● Prohibited retired military officers who are appointed to federal jobs from receiving retired pay and a federal salary totaling more than the rate paid to Executive Schedule level V employees.

● Provided that the ceiling would apply only to those who became eligible for retirement and took federal jobs after the effective date of the bill.

Job Notification

● Required OPM to notify the U.S. Employment Service of all job openings in the competitive service.

Minority Recruitment

● Required the OPM to develop a minority recruitment program for federal agencies.

Employment Limitation

● Limited the total number of full and part-time civilian employees in the executive branch (excluding the Postal Service and the Postal Rate Commission) to the number employed on Sept 30, 1977.

● Made the ceiling effective from Sept. 30, 1979, to Jan. 31, 1981.

● Authorized the president to employ more people than the limit allowed if he determined it was in the national interest, but barred the number of additional employees from exceeding the percentage increase in the U.S. population from Sept. 30, 1978.

Title IV — Senior Executive Service

• Established a Senior Executive Service (SES) of executive managers whose compensation, retention and tenure was contingent on individual performance.

• Defined SES positions as those executive branch jobs currently classified above GS-15 of the general schedule and below Level III of the executive schedule held by managers, supervisors and policy-makers who are not appointed by the president and confirmed by the Senate.

• Exempted from the SES government corporations, Foreign Service employees, the GAO, the FBI, the CIA, the DIA, the NSA, positions in the Drug Enforcement Administration (DEA) which are excluded from the competitive service, administrative law judges and other executive branch units designated by the president whose principal function was intelligence.

• Gave the president authority to exempt other agencies from SES.

• Authorized the OPM to determine every two years the number of SES employees for each agency, based on agency requests.

• Provided that the number of career SES employees never could be less than the number of SES-level positions that were reserved for career employees prior to enactment of the bill.

• Limited the number of non-career appointees in the SES to no more than 10 percent of the total number of SES employees in all agencies.

• Required that not more than 30 percent of all SES positions could be filled by persons who have less than five continuous years experience in the civil service just prior to their appointment to SES.

• Required each agency to set up a program for recruiting career employees for the SES.

• Required OPM to set criteria for judging candidates for career SES positions, based on performance and other qualities.

• Required OPM to establish one or more qualifications review boards to certify executive qualifications of candidates for initial appointment to career jobs.

• Provided that more than half the members of the qualifications review boards must be career civil servants, and that all board members must be chosen on a non-partisan basis.

• Required each agency to appoint executive resources boards of persons inside the agency who would review qualifications of certified candidates and make hiring recommendations to the agency.

• Established a one-year probation period for career SES appointees.

• Permitted agencies to choose their own non-career SES appointees, based on the general qualification guidelines for career appointees.

• Provided that SES career appointees may, after 15 days' notice from the agency, be reassigned to any other SES position in the same agency or may be transferred to an SES position in another agency.

• Provided for reassignment of noncareer appointees.

• Provided that career appointees could not be involuntarily reassigned within 120 days after appointment of a new agency head or a new immediate supervisor.

• Provided that career appointees with at least seven years of service could be granted a sabbatical leave up to 11 months if the employee agreed to return to civil service for at least two years after the sabbatical.

• Provided that career appointees could be removed from SES any time during their one-year probation.

• Provided that an SES employee notified that he or she was to be removed from the service for less than fully successful managerial performance was entitled to an informal public hearing before an official designated by the MSPB.

• Provided that career SES employees, who had been appointed from the civil service and were removed from SES during probation, could be moved back to a civil service job, as long as they had not been dismissed from SES for misconduct, neglect of duty, malfeasance or — after probation — for less than fully successful performance.

• Established criteria for performance appraisals.

• Required each agency to set up, in accordance with OPM regulations, performance review boards for annual evaluations of SES employees to be used in determining performance for incentive bonuses as well as removal of unsatisfactory employees.

• Authorized the president, based on OPM and agency recommendations, to name no more than 5 percent of SES employees each year as meritorious executives and to give each of those executives incentive bonuses of $10,000.

• Authorized the president to name no more than 1 percent of SES employees per year as distinguished executives, and to give them bonuses of $20,000.

• Authorized agencies, based on the recommendations of their performance review boards, to give SES career employees performance awards of not more than 20 percent of each executive's base pay.

• Limited the performance awards to no more than 50 percent of an agency's SES employees in a year.

• Limited the total compensation an SES employee could receive in one year from salary, awards and performance pay to no more than the annual salary of employees at Level I of the Executive Schedule.

• Gave SES employees the right to appeal disciplinary actions to the MSPB.

• Allowed an employee removed from SES for less than fully successful performance to retire early if he or she had completed 25 years of government service, or was 50 years old and had completed 20 years of service.

• Gave top-level employees in the civil service at the time of enactment of the bill the option of not joining SES.

• Provided that SES will become fully operational in all covered federal departments and agencies nine months after enactment of the bill but gave Congress the option of terminating it after five years.

• Provided that in order to terminate SES, Congress would have to pass a concurrent resolution within 60 days after the five-year period expired.

Title V — Merit Pay

Merit Pay

• Directed the OPM to establish a merit pay system, based on performance appraisals, for managers and supervisors in grades GS-13 through GS-15 by Oct. 1, 1981.

• Provided that employees in the merit pay system would get only half of the annual pay comparability adjustment computed for civil service employees, unless OPM authorized a larger comparability payment.

Cash Awards

• Authorized agencies and the president to pay cash awards of not more than $10,000 to employees in the merit pay system for actions contributing to the efficiency, economy or other improvement of government operations, for substantially reducing paperwork or for special actions taken in the public interest.

● Authorized an agency, with the approval of OPM, to pay cash awards of up to $25,000 to employees in the merit pay system for highly exceptional and unusually outstanding performance.

Title VI — Research, Demonstration, Other Programs

● Exempted from research and demonstration programs government corporations, the GAO, some DEA employees, the FBI, the CIA, the DIA, the NSA and other executive agencies designated by the president that have intelligence as their principle function.

● Authorized OPM to conduct research and development projects for improved federal personnel management.

● Required OPM to give advance notice of any demonstration project to Congress and to employees likely to be affected by the project.

● Limited demonstration projects to no more than 5,000 employees and no longer than five years, with certain exceptions.

● Prohibited OPM from conducting more than 10 demonstration projects at a time.

Title VII — Labor-Management Relations

● Gave federal employees the right to join labor unions and bargain collectively on certain employment conditions.

● Exempted the GAO, FBI, CIA, NSA, Tennessee Valley Authority, Federal Labor Relations Authority (FLRA) and the Federal Service Impasses Panel from the labor-management provisions.

● Established the FLRA as a bipartisan, three-member independent agency.

● Provided that FLRA members would be appointed by the president with the approval of the Senate for five-year terms and could be removed by the president only after notice and hearing and only for misconduct, inefficiency, neglect of duty or malfeasance in office.

● Authorized the president to designate one member as chairman of the FLRA.

● Provided that the president would appoint a general counsel, to be confirmed by the Senate, to the FLRA for a five-year term.

● Provided that the general counsel could be removed by the president at any time.

● Authorized the general counsel to investigate and prosecute unfair labor practices.

● Authorized the FLRA to supervise union elections, hold hearings on and resolve complaints about unfair labor practices and resolve other labor rights issues.

● Authorized the FLRA to order an agency or a labor group to stop an unfair labor practice or to take any remedial action judged appropriate by the authority.

● Prohibited negotiations between agencies and federal employee labor unions on matters reserved as management rights, which included agency mission, budget, organization and internal security practices; hiring, assigning, directing, laying off and retaining employees in the agency; suspending, discharging, reducing in grade or pay or taking other disciplinary action against employees; work assignments; contracting out and carrying out agency mission during emergencies.

● Provided that agencies and labor groups could negotiate numbers, types and grades of employees or positions assigned to any organizational subdivision, work project or tour of duty; technology, methods and means of performing work; procedures management must observe in exercising its rights and arrangements for employees adversely affected by exercise of management rights.

● Required agencies to give exclusive recognition to a labor organization chosen by a majority of the employees in a unit who cast votes in a secret ballot election, if the organization met certain other requirements.

● Required the FLRA to investigate all petitions challenging a union's representation and to supervise union elections.

● Spelled out procedures for elections.

● Required agencies to give national consultation rights to labor organizations meeting certain requirements, and required them to inform those organizations of any proposed substantive changes in employment conditions and to permit the organizations to present views and recommendations on the proposed changes.

● Required a union with exclusive recognition rights to represent the interests of all employees in the unit it represents, regardless of whether they belonged to the union.

● Gave a union with exclusive representation rights authority to be represented at certain meetings between employees and management concerning grievances, personnel policy or practices, general conditions of employment or disciplinary action.

● Required agencies and unions to negotiate in good faith, and defined other union and agency duties.

● Required an agency — at no cost to a union with exclusive recognition rights — to deduct union dues from the paycheck of a union employee who gives written authority for dues withholding.

● Defined unfair labor practices for agencies and unions.

● Provided that a labor union could challenge an agency's compelling need for any rule or regulation dealing with its employees, and provided that the FLRA would make a determination on the agency's challenge.

● Required agencies to inform unions with exclusive representation rights to consult with those unions on government-wide rules or regulations that would make a substantial change in employment conditions.

● Authorized the FLRA general counsel to investigate charges of unfair labor practices against unions or agencies.

● Authorized the FLRA to hear and adjudicate cases involving unfair labor practice complaints.

● Authorized the FLRA to order a halt to an unfair labor practice, to require a union and an agency to renegotiate a collective bargaining agreement or to require reinstatement of an employee with back pay, if the authority found a preponderance of the evidence supported the charges of unfair labor practices brought against either an agency or a union.

● Established the Federal Service Impasses Panel within the FLRA to consider disputes when third party mediation between an agency and a union has reached an impasse.

● Provided that the panel would have at least seven members appointed by the president to five-year terms.

● Established standards of conduct for labor organizations.

● Required that any collective bargaining agreement between an agency and a union must provide procedures for grievance settlements.

● Defined procedures for negotiation of grievances and gave employees the option of using statutory procedures or negotiated grievance procedures to resolve discrimination complaints.

● Provided judicial review of some FLRA final orders.

● Limited the amount of official time employees could use for labor union activities.

● Authorized all FLRA members, the general counsel, the Federal Service Impasses Panel or any employee designated by the FLRA to subpoena witnesses.

● Applied the Back Pay Act of 1966 to federal employees in certain situations.

Title VIII — Grade and Pay Retention

● Incorporated provisions of a bill (HR 9279 — H Rept 95-994, parts 1 and 2) to provide retention of grade and pay for employees adversely affected by job reclassification when an agency's work force is reduced, but limited to two years the period in which employees reduced in grade because of reclassification or layoffs could retain their previous higher grade.

Title IX — Miscellaneous

● Provided that the bill would take effect 90 days after its enactment, with exceptions spelled out for some sections.

Administration Proposal

During the election campaign and after taking office, Carter strongly urged governmental reorganization. In his 1978 State of the Union address he called civil service reform "absolutely vital" to "a government that is efficient, open and truly worthy of our people's understanding and respect."

In a March 2 message spelling out his proposals, Carter said the civil service system "has become a bureaucratic maze which neglects merit, tolerates poor performance, permits abuse of legitimate employee rights and mires every personnel action in red tape, delay and confusion. Civil service reform will be the centerpiece of government reorganization during my term in office."

In that March message, Carter sent Congress a draft of his proposed reorganization of the Civil Service Commission, along with legislation making fundamental changes in civil service policies. *(Message, p. 43-E)*

The president's package of civil service changes had been developed from a study by a team of 110 civil servants and business and academic representatives. The Personnel Management Project's year-long study resulted in a two-part administration proposal.

The ideas in the administration plan were not new, and many were variations of changes sought by previous presidents. However, Carter's package and the importance he placed on its passage — in his March 2 speech, he said the proposals "will be the centerpiece of government reorganization during my term in office — marked the first major effort by a president to change the merit system established in the Pendleton Civil Service Act of 1883. That act ended the era of the spoils system and replaced it with a merit system for choosing government workers. The act set up a bipartisan Civil Service Commission (CSC) to help federal agencies fill jobs by open, competitive examination.

The reorganization plan was formally submitted to Congress May 23. It would take effect Aug. 11 unless the House or Senate voted to block it. On Aug. 9, the House killed a resolution that would block the plan. The Senate did not vote on a similar resolution, so the plan became effective Aug. 11. *(See box p. 819)*

The administration reform bill was introduced in the House and Senate March 3 (HR 11280, S 2640). A separate labor-management relations section was submitted by the administration May 10.

Reorganization Plan

Responding to widespread criticism about the CSC's conflicting roles as federal personnel manager and protector of employee rights, the administration proposed splitting the agency in two.

Responsibility for personnel management, such as examinations, training and administration of pay and benefits, would be given to a new Office of Personnel Management (OPM). The office would be run by a presidentially-appointed director and deputy director.

The CSC's function of adjudicating employee complaints would be the responsibility of a new Merit Systems Protection Board (MSPB), which would hear most appeals and complaints from federal employees or applicants for federal jobs. The three-member board would be bipartisan, and members could be removed only for cause. The board members would be named by the president with Senate confirmation.

A special counsel for the board, appointed by the president, would prosecute political abuses and merit system violations and would investigate charges of reprisal actions against employees who disclose unlawful activity.

A third office set up by the reorganization plan would be the Federal Labor Relations Authority (FLRA), a bipartisan panel that would handle complaints about unfair labor practices. The FLRA would be an independent agency and would take over functions that were assigned to the Federal Labor Relations Council and the Labor Department.

Reform Bill

Whistleblower Protection. The administration bill would protect from reprisal those persons who blow the whistle on their bosses or other federal employees for violating laws or regulations. The MSPB special counsel would handle whistleblowers' complaints about reprisals.

Employee Appeal Rights. Appeal rights for veterans in federal jobs are spelled out by law. However, the right to appeal "adverse actions" (such as firing for unsatisfactory performance or reducing an employee's grade or pay) taken against other federal employees is granted only by executive order. The administration proposal would put appeal rights for all federal employees into statute.

However, in order to streamline appeals of adverse actions and make it easier for managers to get rid of incompetent employees, the administration proposal would reduce from three to two the number of administrative appeals available to an employee.

Under existing law, an employee could appeal an adverse action to the CSC with a guarantee of a hearing. Two subsequent appeals within the CSC were possible.

The administration bill would give MSPB authority to hear appeals, but the board would grant a hearing only in cases where an employee disputed the facts on which an agency based its decision. Under the proposal, an agency's decision would be upheld unless the employee could show the MSPB that the decision involved discrimination, was arbitrary and capricious or was not supported by substantial evidence.

Veterans' Preference. The administration proposal would leave intact lifetime veterans' preference for disabled veterans, including disabled military retirees. Other veterans would be entitled to preference in hiring for 10 years after leaving the service.

Preference in federal hiring had been given to veterans by automatically adding points — 10 for disabled veterans and five for those with no disability — to their civil service exam scores. The scores were a major factor used in ranking applicants competing for federal jobs.

Under the administration plan, veterans' preference would be eliminated for top-level retired military officers. Those below the rank of major or lieutenant commander who retired after at least 20 years in the service would be eligible for preference for three years after retirement.

Veterans who have federal jobs would be protected from layoffs during their first three years of employment, **instead of the lifetime protection they had in existing law. After the three years, they would be given an extra five years in seniority as protection against layoffs.**

Veterans' preference could not be used by those seeking Senior Executive Service positions that would be established under the administration plan.

The proposal would change the "rule of three," which requires agencies to select employees from the top three candidates on civil service lists, to a "rule of seven," allowing selection from among the top seven applicants.

The proposal would expand the number of noncompetitive federal jobs available to Vietnam-era and disabled veterans.

Senior Executive Service. The administration plan would set up a Senior Executive Service (SES), consisting of about 9,200 managers from GS-16 through Level III of the executive schedule. Employees in those top-level positions at the time of enactment of the bill would be given a choice of going into SES or staying in the existing system.

New appointees to the service would serve a one-year probationary period. All SES employees would be evaluated in an annual performance review. Those judged inadequate by their superiors could be transferred back to GS-15, and they would have no right to appeal the decision. Top management would have the right to tranfer SES employees from one agency to another.

SES employees would not get automatic pay raises for longevity, but those who ranked high in performance reviews would be eligible for bonuses. At least 90 percent of the SES employees would have to be career officials.

Merit Pay. Another 72,500 managers and supervisors at grades GS-13 through GS-15 also would no longer receive automatic pay increases awarded only for longevity. Under the administration plan, the OPM would develop a merit pay system for those employees, allowing agencies to award raises on the basis of performance.

Labor-Management Relations. The administration proposal would put into law the executive order first issued in 1962 that gave collective bargaining rights to federal employees. Collective bargaining would be limited to personnel policies and practices and working conditions.

The proposal would not permit agency shops, where employees must pay union dues even if they are not members of the union representing their colleagues. It also would not allow federal employees to strike, and it would not permit bargaining on wages. Collective bargaining would be allowed on grievance procedures.

Reactions

Release of the reorganization plan and the reform bill brought responses from a variety of interest groups.

Most endorsements were qualified, and some groups commented on only one aspect of the proposals. For instance, most veterans' groups denounced the proposed changes in veterans' preference, while several women's groups endorsed the proposed preference changes without commenting on other aspects of the bill.

The most intense opposition came from veterans' groups and from labor unions representing federal employees.

Labor had the longest laundry list of complaints about the administration proposals. Most of the unions warned the plan would curtail employee rights and lead to a return of the spoils system.

Some specific labor complaints:

- The unions endorsed the plan to split up CSC's management and employee protection functions, as well as establishment of the independent FLRA to supervise union elections and handle unfair labor complaints. But most criticized the plan of having a single presidentially appointed director, who would appoint OPM's associate directors. The plan "lays the groundwork for a massive politicization of the federal work force," charged Vincent L. Connery, national president of the National Treasury Employees Union (NTEU). Connery's organization is the third largest federal employee union, representing over 100,000 workers.

A major exception to union criticism of the reorganization plan was the AFL-CIO and its affiliate, the American Federation of Government Employees, representing 58 percent of all federal workers, excluding Postal Service employees. AFL-CIO legislative representative Kenneth Meiklejohn endorsed the reorganization plan and praised the proposed FLRA.

- Unions criticized the administration's "streamlined" appeals proposal, saying it would curtail employees' due process rights. They argued that an employee who is fired, suspended or downgraded in rank or pay should be guaranteed a hearing. In addition, instead of requiring the employee to show agency error, discrimination or lack of substantial evidence in order to overturn an adverse action, "Government should have the burden of proving its reasons for the action taken against the employee," said John L. White, director of legislation for the National Alliance of Postal and Federal Employees.

- Formation of a Senior Executive Service would contribute to politicization of the civil service, some union spokesmen said. They argued that without the civil service's job protections, SES employees would serve at the whim of the president's top political appointees.

- Unions rejected the administration's labor-management relations proposals because they would not expand the scope of collective bargaining to include items

Vets Job Preference Rule Hurts Women, Minorities . . .

Even Alan K. Campbell, the college professor President Carter chose to run the Civil Service Commission (CSC), acknowledged that civil service reform was an arcane issue that did not exactly capture the public's imagination.

But while most of the administration's 128-page civil service revision bill produced more public yawns than public interest, one portion was destined to create the sort of storm that usually clouds debate on such emotional issues as abortion, amnesty or gun control.

The issue was veterans' preference, the program that helps boost veterans into federal jobs and protects them from layoffs once they get on the federal payroll.

While no one argues that veterans should not get some hiring advantages in exchange for their military service, the administration proposal limited the lifetime preferences able-bodied veterans enjoyed. Federal managers responsible for affirmative action hiring complain that preference puts veterans — usually white males — at the top of the civil service hiring lists, pushing equally qualified non-veteran women and minority applicants out of the running for federal jobs.

The administration also argued that the lifetime preference enjoyed by older veterans is a disadvantage to the 8.5 million Vietnam-era veterans who must compete against them for federal jobs.

'A Lot of Voters'

However, with almost every one of the nation's powerful veterans' groups lined up to oppose any change in the veterans' preference program, administration supporters acknowledged they faced a difficult job in attempting to cut back veterans' advantages in federal hiring.

For the veterans' groups, preserving lifetime veterans' preference will be a "test of strength," said American Legion Lobbyist Phil Riggin. "We are labeling this as a testing ground of our ability to persuade Congress to do what we want them to do," Riggin said. The American Legion, the largest veterans' group, has 2.6 million members. "That's a lot of voters," Riggin pointed out.

Partly because of their large numbers, veterans' groups enjoy a high rate of success in lobbying Congress for veterans' benefits such as pensions and education aid. For instance, when the House in 1978 approved three bills to increase old age and disability pensions for veterans, one of the bills drew only 16 negative votes, another was opposed by five members and only one member opposed the third.

Congressional supporters of the administration bill warned that the intense lobbying expected on the veterans' preference issue would overshadow the rest of the bill when it reached the full House and Senate.

Veterans' Reward

The concept of rewarding U.S. veterans after service to their country is an old one, dating to the Revolutionary War. Congress in 1944 approved the Veterans' Preference Act, extending hiring advantages to persons who suffered no injury in order to compensate them for "career interruption." Retired military personnel, who draw government pensions, also are eligible for veterans' preference.

But there is considerable disagreement about the intent of the 1944 act. Donald H. Schwab, of the Veterans of Foreign Wars, told the Senate Governmental Affairs Committee: "Veterans' preference was never intended to be merely a readjustment benefit, but a lifetime reward."

Veterans' supporters in Congress agreed, arguing that to reduce the preference would break a contract implied in the 1944 act. "Are we going to recognize the obligation incurred by this government . . . or are we going to say it's over, we're going to change the ground rules?" said James M. Hanley, D-N.Y., to the applause of dozens of Disabled American Veterans crowded into a June 28 House Post Office and Civil Service Committee markup session.

But Patricia Schroeder, D-Colo., who successfully fought Hanley's effort in committee to keep veterans' preference unchanged, argued that the 1944 act was designed to help veterans re-establish their careers, not to give veterans hiring preference the rest of their lives.

World War II veteran Morris K. Udall, D-Ariz., the major supporter of the administration bill on the House committee, agreed.

"I served 30 years ago," said Udall. "I wasn't injured. Most of the time I was punching a typewriter or being an administrative officer. The United States gave me an education, a law degree, helped me buy my first house, enabled me to get a loan to buy the building I had my law office in. Why should the non-disabled like myself have some preference 30 years after I was in service?"

What It Does

Under the 1944 act, veterans who were not disabled in the service automatically have five points added to their scores on the civil service examinations that determine eligibility for federal jobs. Disabled veterans and their spouses, the mothers of veterans who died in military service and surviving spouses of veterans (as long as they are not remarried) received 10 points. Disabled veterans also are put at the top of lists for those eligible for federal jobs.

The preference points are reusable if a veteran gets one federal job and later decides to compete for another one. A veteran at the top of a Civil Service Commission list of persons competing for a job cannot be passed over by an agency without getting permission from the commission.

Veterans also get preference in keeping their jobs if an agency must lay off workers. Some jobs — such as guards, custodians and elevator operators — are reserved solely for veterans eligible for preference.

Veterans' preference does not apply to persons who entered peacetime service after Oct. 14, 1976, and who leave without a disability. But because of the lifetime preference rule, about 28 million veterans still enjoyed the hiring advantages, according to the CSC. Only about 150,000 persons are hired from the civil service lists each year.

... Congress Modified But Did Not End the System

Problem for Women, Minorities

Those advantages translate into disadvantages for women, minorities and younger veterans who compete for federal jobs, the administration argued.

Thus, the government's obligation to reward veterans conflicts with its obligation — mandated in 1972 amendments to the Civil Rights Act — to provide equal employment opportunity to all job applicants.

The biggest problem comes in trying to recruit and hire women and minorities for upper level jobs, according to the administration. For instance, while women held 77.3 percent of all jobs at levels GS-1 through GS-4 in 1976, they held only 2.8 percent of the better-paid, more prestigious jobs at levels GS-16 through GS-18, according to CSC figures. Minorities held about 5 percent of the higher level jobs.

Campbell said the percentages at higher levels were not likely to increase much for awhile, even if veterans' preference was changed, because the top positions are usually filed by promotion from lower levels. Women and minorities are only slightly better represented at the next steps down from GS-16, Campbell said. In grades GS-13 through GS-15, about 5.7 percent of the jobs are held by minorities and about 5 percent by women.

CSC officials said they could not estimate how many jobs might be opened up to women and minorities if veterans' preference is curtailed. But they said a 1977 General Accounting Office (GAO) study showed veterans' preference had been a formidable barrier to hiring women and minorities.

Among examples GAO cited were:

- A woman who scored a near-perfect 99 on a civil service examination for accountant/auditor positions in San Francisco would have ranked 12th on the list of those qualified for jobs if no veterans' preference points were allotted. However, when veterans' preference was figured in, the woman — a non-veteran — dropped to 111th on the civil service hiring list that agencies must use in selecting competitive service employees.
- A Dallas woman got a perfect score on the nationwide air traffic control specialist examination. That would have put her in seventh place before figuring in veterans' preference. Instead, she ranked 147th. The top 83 persons on the list were male veterans. GAO found that if veterans' preference points had been excluded in making the list, 16 of the top 83 would have been women.
- All of the top 81 persons listed as eligible for correctional officers jobs in Atlanta had scores boosted by preference points. In 82nd place was a woman who had no preference. If all veterans' preference points were eliminated, that woman would have been first on the list.

GAO singled out preference for retired military officers — who accounted for about 5 percent of the total federal work force — as an important barrier to women. "Veterans' preference for retired military personnel is, in our opinion, contrary to the idea of compensating veterans for time lost in their careers," the agency said.

Despite the GAO figures showing how extra points for veterans can push women's civil service examination scores far down hiring lists, veterans' groups contend preference does not discriminate against women and minorities.

"Laws or regulatory provision do not discriminate, it is people who discriminate in their implementation of such laws and regulations," said Norman B. Hartnett of the Disabled American Veterans, in a statement prepared for the Senate committee.

Outlook

The original administration proposal called for limiting the preference for those veterans who were not disabled to the 10 years after they left the service. It would have protected them from layoffs from a federal job for three years. Disabled veterans would have maintained lifetime preference.

After criticism that the plan would hurt Vietnam-era veterans who served in the 1960's, the administration agreed to a compromise allowing use of preference for 15 years after leaving the service. However, a veteran could only use the preference to get one federal job. He or she would then be protected from layoffs for eight years.

The Senate committee rejected the compromise.

But in a surprise vote, the House Post Office and Civil Service Committee adopted it. Although the administration had predicted success before the House committee vote, the comfortable 16-9 margin was a surprise. Committee sources and lobbyists supporting the compromise said the argument that it would help Vietnam-era veterans seemed to persuade some members to vote for it.

But the House committee vote may have served to make veterans' groups all the more determined in fighting the issue when it came to the floor. Although they had succeeded in backing other legislation to increase their own benefits, veterans' groups were unhappy with administration and congressional action on other issues, such as the Panama Canal treaties and the pardon of draft evaders.

Fighting against the veterans' groups, and for the administration proposal, was a coalition composed of Common Cause, the Chamber of Commerce, the Business Roundtable, Congress Watch, the National Urban League and one liberal veterans' group, the American Veterans Committee, which had about 25,000 members. Several women's groups also lobbied for the change.

Edward J. Derwinski, R-Ill., one of the House committee members who voted against changing veterans' preference, said he had warned the administration against tackling such a highly emotional issue. Although Derwinski supported most of the rest of the administration bill, he predicted the fight over veterans' preference could endanger the whole package.

"In an election year, when the veterans get stirred up the Congress is going to react to it," he said.

Derwinski's prediction proved to be an accurate one. In a major defeat for the administration, both chambers voted to drop most provisions eliminating veterans' preference. The only provision they maintained was one that excluded from veterans' preference non-disabled military retirees who left the service at the rank of major or above after 20 years of service.

such as wages, and because they would not allow agency shops.

Some organizations representing public managers, such as the American Society for Personnel Administration and the National Academy of Public Administration, endorsed the bill. The Business Roundtable announced its support, singling out the SES proposal for particular praise.

Other endorsements came from 16 former Republican and Democratic Cabinet officials, who praised the shift to incentive pay for top federal managers. "Tying financial rewards to standards of organizational and individual performance provides a critically needed tool to make government work well," the Cabinet officials wrote to House and Senate members.

The Chamber of Commerce praised most of the proposals but opposed formation of the independent FLRA and objected to some of the administration's labor-management proposals.

Chamber Vice President Jack Carlson said his organization would oppose any parts of the bill "encouraging expansion and power of public unions" because, "We think that any proposed legislation ought to be neutral on either encouraging or discouraging civil servants to join a union."

The administration's whistleblower protections were criticized by public interest groups and the government's best-known whistleblower, A. Ernest Fitzgerald. Fitzgerald, who revealed Air Force cost overruns of $2 billion in building the C-5A transport plane, said some aspects of the administration plan actually would provide whistleblowers with less protection than they currently had against reprisals by their superiors.

Consumer activist Ralph Nader called the proposal a "minuscule" change.

Critics of the administration whistleblower protections said they should be expanded to protect those who reveal waste and mismanagement in government that doesn't necessarily constitute violations of law or regulation.

Controversies

One of the most controversial aspects of Carter's reform proposals was curtailment of the preference veterans received in federal hiring. The American Legion and other veterans' groups, who felt their federal benefits programs had been unjustly criticized, quickly announced their opposition to the proposed changes. Their intense lobbying campaign was successful: both the House and Senate adopted amendments to the bill that dropped almost all of the suggested changes in veterans' preference. The final version of the bill excluded from veterans' preference non-disabled military retirees who left the service at the rank of major or above after 20 years of service, but left intact preference for all other veterans.

Another potential roadblock to the administration's plan involved the issue of labor rights. At one point, it was thought that the labor controversy would kill the bill. Labor groups opposed to the plan charged that it would reduce job security and make the federal government's 2.8 million workers responsive to the whims of the president and his top political appointees.

But public administrators, including Cabinet officials who served in previous administrations, said the president's plan would give the government's top managers new incentives to perform well, while making it easier for them to get rid of incompetent employees.

After arduous behind-the-scenes negotiations in both chambers, the final compromise version of the legislation gave labor groups several changes they had sought. It put labor rights into statute, protecting them from being changed by the whims of a president. It established the Federal Labor Relations Authority (FLRA), giving federal employees their own equivalent of the National Labor Relations Board that deals with private sector labor disputes. It also required agencies to automatically withhold union dues — without charge to the unions — from union members' paychecks, and it allowed employees to seek union arbitration of grievances.

Throughout the lengthy congressional debate on the civil service reform bill there lurked the possibility that the measure could become a "Christmas tree" if members agreed to tack on controversial amendments to what many considered a veto-proof bill. One such "ornament" was a measure (HR 3161) vetoed in June by Carter that would reduce the workweek of federal firefighters. That measure was tacked onto the bill by the House Post Office and Civil Service Committee, but was later defeated on the House floor on a point of order.

One of the largest "ornaments" the House committee tacked onto the bill was the text of the Hatch Act revision bill (HR 10) loosening restrictions on political activity by federal employees. Although the administration supported the Hatch Act revisions, it opposed adding them to the civil service bill. House and Senate Republicans also opposed adding the revisions to the civil service reform bill. As with the firefighters bill, the Hatch Act addition was dropped on a point of order on the House floor.

Senate Committee Action

The Senate Governmental Affairs Committee held 12 days of hearings, with testimony from 86 witnesses, on the reorganization plan and the reform bill.

The committee then met in six markup sessions on S 2640, where it rejected the proposed changes in veterans' preference but kept most of the other administration proposals largely intact. The bill was approved by the committee, 11-2, June 29. It was reported July 10 (S Rept 95-969).

In justifying the need for changes in the civil service, the committee report said, "The public is ill served by the existing civil service system. When programs fail or are damaged by mismanagement and incompetence, both the taxpayer and the program beneficiary suffer."

The committee said that procedures set up to judge applicants and employees on their merit, and to protect employees from arbitrary management decisions, also had functioned to protect incompetent employees.

"Moreover, the system's rigid procedures — providing almost automatic pay increases for all employees — makes it as difficult to reward the outstanding public servant as it is to remove an incompetent employee," the report said.

Major amendments considered by the committee included:

Veterans' Preference. By a 7-9 vote, the panel rejected a compromise plan to curtail veterans' preference.

The compromise, backed by the administration, would have allowed able-bodied veterans to use preference to get one federal job in the 15 years after they left the military service. Disabled veterans would retain lifetime preference. The compromise also would have protected veterans in federal jobs from layoffs for eight years, instead of the three-year protection originally proposed by the administration.

Even committee members who were sympathetic to the compromise admitted it created problems for passage of the entire package of civil service changes. Jacob K. Javits, R-N.Y., who voted for the compromise, said veterans' preference would dominate floor debate and could kill the whole bill.

In rejecting the compromise, the committee agreed to leave the existing veterans' preference program intact, giving all veterans who served prior to October 1976 a lifetime boost into federal jobs.

After the compromise was defeated, the committee adopted, 13-1, a proposal by Javits to set up a task force of members from Governmental Affairs and the Senate Veterans Affairs Committee to study possible changes in veterans' preference. The task force was to report to the Senate by 1979.

Whistleblower. An amendment offered by Muriel Humphrey, D-Minn., and adopted by the committee expanded the whistleblower protections in the administration proposal. Humphrey's amendment expanded the definition of reprisals that whistleblowers would be protected from, as well as the definition of protected whistleblower activities.

Firing Burden of Proof. The panel agreed to make agencies prove their case for firing an employee, if the employee appealed the firing to the MSPB. The administration proposal would not have required agencies to make an initial showing that their evidence supported firing an employee, and it would have upheld the agency's action unless the employee could prove agency error, discrimination or arbitrary action. This change resulted from an amendment sponsored by Charles H. Percy, R-Ill.

Senate Floor Action

By an overwhelming 87-1 vote, the Senate approved S 2640 on Aug. 24. *(Vote 361, p. 54-S)*

Senate floor managers Abraham Ribicoff, D-Conn., and Percy, set the stage for passage of S 2640 by letting their colleagues chip away at the administration proposal without tearing out any big chunks.

Percy and Ribicoff, backed by the administration in most cases, accepted 15 amendments to the bill. But although some of the accepted amendments included proposals the administration previously had opposed, none made major changes in the thrust of the bill.

In fact, the tedious, seven-hour debate seldom addressed basic issues in the bill — such as creation of a Senior Executive Service (SES) or establishment of labor rights — and instead focused on details of how those basic ideas would be implemented. The debate was studded with quorum calls designed to stall while senators worked out details on the numerous amendments.

A major factor encouraging accommodation of amendments was the lack of a time agreement on debate. Ribicoff and Percy aides had spent weeks working out an agreement with Charles McC. Mathias, R-Md., and Ted Stevens, R-Alaska, who opposed the bill in the Governmental Affairs Committee. But that effort was thwarted by Jake Garn, R-Utah, who, in retaliation for Carter's veto of a defense bill (HR 10929), said Aug. 17 he would block any effort to limit debate. *(Defense authorization, p. 321)*

With no agreement to limit debate, the bill could easily have been filibustered or delayed in the closing weeks of the 95th Congress. Thus, when Orrin G. Hatch, R-Utah, presented the floor managers with what Percy called "a rather bulky package of amendments" the day of the debate, Percy and Ribicoff aides and Civil Service Commission Chairman Alan K. Campbell met with Hatch to try to work out compromises acceptable to both sides.

The administration also decided against trying to restore its controversial proposals to reduce veterans federal hiring preference. That move prevented divisive debate.

Instead of fighting for its own preference proposals, which were rejected by the Senate Governmental Affairs Committee, the administration accepted an amendment by Alan Cranston, D-Calif., to abolish veterans' preference for able-bodied military retirees who left the service at the rank of major or above after 20 years of service. Cranston's non-controversial change was adopted by voice vote.

Compromise

The negotiations involving aides to Ribicoff, Percy, Mathias and Stevens produced an amendment cosponsored by the four senators that made several changes in S 2640. The amendment, which was accepted by the administration, was adopted by voice vote.

Mathias and Stevens had stressed objections to three parts of the bill: Giving responsibility for federal management policy to an Office of Personnel Management (OPM) headed by a presidential appointee; allowing agencies to conduct competitive examinations for federal jobs; and establishing the SES without — in the opinion of the two Republicans — adequate protection against its politicization.

The compromise agreed to by the four senators did not fully accept the positions of Mathias and Stevens. But it moved enough in their direction to satisfy both Republicans, who presented no obstacle during floor debate.

The compromise they accepted did not contain their recommendation that a three-member, bipartisan board should head the OPM. But it did give the Merit Systems Protection Board (MSPB), an independent agency set up to consider federal employee grievances, authority to veto any OPM rule or regulation that MSPB found violated merit system principles or constituted a prohibited personnel practice. OPM would still be headed by a single presidential appointee.

The compromise amendment restricted the instances where an agency could give a competitive examination, leaving much of the examination authority with OPM. It also ordered that jobs that were career positions at the time of enactment of the bill could not be converted to politically appointed jobs when they became part of SES, except under certain circumstances.

Mathias said the amendment would mean about 5,100 of the 9,200 jobs expected to be converted from civil service to SES positions would have to be certified as career jobs by the OPM director. S 2640 already specified that not more than 10 percent of SES jobs could be non-career positions. But Mathias and Stevens had argued that unless specific positions were made career jobs, an administration could juggle the designations of career and political jobs in a way to make nearly all SES positions political.

Double Dippers

On a voice vote, the Senate adopted an amendment by H. John Heinz III, R-Pa., to prevent retired military officers appointed to federal jobs from getting a federal salary and retired military pay totaling more than Executive Schedule V salaries — $47,500 in 1978.

Heinz' amendment, like the House committee amendment it was patterned after *(see below)*, would affect only those who retired after the effective date of the bill. Before it was adopted, the Senate rejected, 32-58, a motion by John Glenn, D-Ohio, to table it. *(Vote 360, p. 54-S)*

Glenn and Barry Goldwater, R-Ariz., who both draw military pensions in addition to their congressional salaries, said it was hypocritical to consider retired military double dippers without looking at former members of Congress who drew federal salaries in addition to their congressional retirement pay.

"I am getting a little sick and tired of hearing the man in uniform kicked around," said Goldwater.

Labor Interests

A group of three amendments introduced by Hatch — after negotiations with the administration and Percy and Ribicoff staffers — was adopted by voice vote.

However, Hatch made several changes in the language of his amendments when several senators raised questions about protection of labor interests. Hatch's amendments, as modified by others, would require secret ballot elections on union representation. They would revoke the recognition rights of a union that willfully or intentionally did not prevent a strike by federal employees. They also guaranteed free speech rights for both opponents and proponents of union representation, as long as they were not coercive or threatened reprisals.

Summary of Floor Changes

Before passing S 2640 Aug. 24, the Senate made the following changes in provisions of the bill as reported by the Governmental Affairs Committee:

- Excluded from veterans preference non-disabled military retirees who left the service at the rank of major or above after 20 years of service.
- Provided for appointment of veterans with a service-related disability of 30 percent or more to certain non-competitive jobs.
- Required that a veteran passed over on a federal hiring list must be notified of the agency's reasons for the decision and given 15 days to appeal it to the Office of Personnel Management (OPM).
- Gave disabled veterans more protection from federal job layoffs than non-disabled veterans.
- Authorized hiring of reading assistants and interpreters for blind or deaf federal employees.
- Authorized the Merit Systems Protection Board (MSPB) to review OPM rules that violated merit system principles or constituted a prohibited personnel practice.
- Authorized the MSPB special counsel to order an agency investigation of a whistleblower's allegations if the special counsel believed the allegations were likely to be valid.
- Exempted the Foreign Service from certain provisions in the bill.
- Prevented retired military officers appointed to federal jobs from getting a federal salary and retired military pay totaling more than Executive Schedule V salaries.
- Required secret ballot elections on union representation.
- Required that exclusive recognition of a union would be revoked if the union willfully and intentionally failed to take action to prevent a strike, work stoppage or slowdown.
- Provided for judicial review of Federal Labor Relations Authority decisions on unfair labor practice charges.

House Committee Action

In the House, the administration's reorganization plan was referred to the Government Operations Committee, while the reform bill (HR 11280) was sent to the Post Office and Civil Service Committee. The committee reported the bill July 31 (H Rept 95-1403).

When the committee finished lengthy hearings on the bill in May, Democrats on the panel caucused several times to draft their own civil service bill that would serve as the vehicle for markups.

The caucuses led to a committee print that strongly reflected the desire of unions to give federal employees more protections and collective bargaining rights. But although the committee print was the result of Democratic negotiating, Democrats on the panel disagreed on many portions of it.

Evidence of the Democratic discord was in abundance at the opening markup meeting June 21.

The pattern of offering numerous amendments to each title of the bill — including many from Democrats — was set. Democrats split on most votes. Committee Republicans were frequently united in backing administration positions on amendments, giving beleaguered ranking majority member, Morris K. Udall, D-Ariz., the votes he needed to hold together the administration package. In a sign of its unhappiness with the administration, the committee agreed by only a one-vote margin to let administration officials comment on amendments as they came up.

Major Actions

Whistleblower. The first major change approved by the committee was an amendment offered by Colorado's Rep. Patricia Schroeder, D, to expand whistleblower protections.

Schroeder's amendment was similar to the Humphrey amendment approved by the Senate committee. However, before adopting the Schroeder amendment, the Post Office Committee added to it the language the Senate committee had dropped, requiring agencies to investigate and report on whistleblowers' charges. *(Senate action, above)*

Job Hearing, Firing. The committee divided on two major labor-backed amendments, siding with labor on one and with the administration on the other.

The first labor amendment, sponsored by Stephen J. Solarz, D-N.Y., would have guaranteed a hearing to employees notified of an adverse action against them. The hearing would take place before the employee was actually suspended, fired or reduced in rank or pay.

Some federal agencies had granted employees a "pretermination" hearing. But the administration opposed a government-wide guarantee of such hearings, arguing that it was contrary to HR 11280's purpose of streamlining the civil service.

Although the committee had previously voted overwhelmingly in favor of a bill (HR 6225) guaranteeing federal employees a pretermination hearing, it reversed itself and rejected the Solarz amendment, 10-15.

On the question of firing employees for incompetence or misconduct, the committee supported labor's position in favor of requiring an agency to show that the action was based on a "preponderance" of the evidence. The committee adopted that standard and rejected a less stringent evidence test that had been proposed by Udall.

Veterans' Preference. In action on June 28, the committee voted in favor of a compromise proposal, backed by the administration, to modify the existing veterans' preference rule. The compromise adopted was the one rejected by the Senate Governmental Affairs Committee *(see above).*

Under that compromise, able-bodied veterans could use the preference resulting from military service to help get one federal job in the 15 years after he or she left the service. Disabled veterans would retain lifetime preference. The compromise also protected veterans in federal jobs from layoffs for eight years, instead of three years as the administration originally proposed.

Playing to a hearing room filled with Disabled American Veterans and DAV auxiliary members, James M. Hanley, D-N.Y., charged that the administration changes would put "the integrity of the federal government into jeopardy." Hanley proposed an amendment that would keep veterans preference unchanged.

Rejecting the argument that the preference law amounted to an unchangeable contract between the government and veterans, Udall said: "No principle ought to be so sacred that you can't go back and question it."

Udall supported the compromise which was introduced by Schroeder and backed by the administration. Compromise supporters argued it would focus preference on those who needed employment help the most: Vietnam-era veterans. Schroeder's amendment passed, 16-9.

Other major amendments adopted included:

"Rule of Three." A Solarz proposal to drop the administration's plan of allowing employers to hire from among the top seven candidates for a job. By a voice vote, the panel agreed to keep intact the "rule of three," requiring agencies to pick employees from among the top three applicants for a job.

Protecting Pay Levels. An amendment by Committee Chairman Robert N. C. Nix, D-Pa., to add his bill (HR 9279) on downgrading of federal employees to the reform bill. Nix's bill would protect the pay of federal employees whose jobs are downgraded in a grade reclassification or agency reorganization.

Hatch Act Bill. Support for Carter's civil service reform proposals had been strong among committee Republicans, who often joined a minority of the Democrats to beat back amendments opposed by the administration. But that unusual coalition crumbled July 13 when the committee agreed to add the labor-supported Hatch Act revision bill (HR 10) as a new title.

The Hatch Act bill, which would have loosened restrictions on the political activity of federal employees, was passed by the House in 1977 but was stalled in a Senate committee. Although Republicans seldom acknowledged it publicly, many privately said they feared the federal work force was heavily Democratic and that Hatch Act changes would benefit that party much more than the GOP. *(1977 Almanac p. 808)*

SES Experiment. A substitute for the administration SES proposal, introduced by Gladys Noon Spellman, D-Md., July 13, would make SES a two year experiment in three federal agencies named by the president.

Echoing the arguments of labor groups that opposed SES, Spellman said the administration proposal would let presidents load their top management jobs with political friends. At hearings she held in several federal agencies, Spellman said she found, "This SES was the one thing that struck terror in the hearts of civil servants."

Others agreed with her that the SES idea needed a trial run before Congress voted to make it permanent.

But ranking Republican Edward Derwinski, Ill., opposed Spellman's amendments, saying "This is no time to turn reform into a test tube baby."

Udall, the administration's strongest supporter on the committee, said SES was intended to develop a corps of well-qualified managers who — aided by other parts of the bill making it easier to fire incompetent employees — could improve government efficiency. "My overriding priority is to shake up this government and give managers the ability to manage," he said.

Spellman's amendment might have been defeated if the committee had acted on it the same day. But instead, the committee moved on to reconsideration of the Hatch Act bill, which it had defeated earlier.

When the vote was taken on the Spellman amendment four days later, Derwinski had led the Republicans away from the administration position to create pressure for dropping the Hatch Act changes. Spellman's amendment was adopted, 13-8. Udall changed his vote at the last minute — making the tally 14-7 — so he could ask for reconsideration of the amendment later. However, he did not exercise that option.

Scope of Bargaining. A version of the bill drafted by committee Democrats would have expanded the scope of union bargaining on behalf of federal employees to nine areas excluded by the administration proposal.

William (Bill) Clay, D-Mo., one of the leading backers of the Democratic proposal, said it represented major concessions on the part of labor and its supporters. Labor had agreed to drop pay and benefits from the list of bargainable items it wanted, while concessions the administration said it had made "have been so insignificant as to render them virtually meaningless," Clay said.

At the committee's final markup July 19, Cecil (Cec) Heftel, D-Hawaii, offered the administration's more limited proposal for bargaining rights, which was defeated, 8-16.

The committee then adopted, 14-10, a Udall substitute to permit bargaining on six of the nine items Clay sought to include in the bill. Udall's compromise drew support from some members who feared the more far-reaching Clay proposal would not survive on the House floor. "I'd rather have six of the nine than none at all," said Solarz, who voted with Udall.

Udall's amendment would give federal employee unions the right to bargain on government regulations dealing with job classification, promotion standards, numbers and types of employees assigned to jobs, travel expenses, layoff standards and the amount of paid time employees can spend serving as union negotiators.

Agency Shop. Udall successfully pushed another "compromise" amendment on the agency shop issue that was a clear defeat for the pro-labor forces.

Unions argued that because they were required to represent equally all employees in a unit — including those who don't join the union — they should be able to collect dues from all of them. But the administration opposed forcing non-union members to pay dues.

An administration proposal barring agency shops was defeated, 9-16. Then Udall's proposal, which also would not allow agency shops, was adopted, 15-10. The only change Udall made was to require agencies to withhold, without charge to the unions, dues from union members' paychecks. In existing law, unions must bargain with agencies to get dues withholding.

On the agency shop issue, Udall picked up votes of members who said they supported the labor unions' position but did not think it would prevail on the House floor.

Firefighters Bill. Herbert E. Harris II, D-Va., offered the amendment tacking on the firefighters work week bill (HR 3161). Carter had vetoed the bill June 19.

Udall, protesting the "Christmas tree" practice of loading down the bill with controversial, unrelated legislation, said approval would be "a slap in the face of the president." But Solarz defended the tactic of adding a vetoed bill to another bill the president wanted very badly as "a time-honored legislative strategy."

Harris' amendment was defeated on an initial vote, but it was adopted, 14-10, on reconsideration.

Reconsidering SES. When the committee had dealt with a last-minute flurry of amendments, Udall moved to report the bill as marked up, minus Spellman's SES amendment. Udall's move would have restored the administration SES proposals to the bill but left all other sections as the committee had written them.

A Republican move to table the whole bill was defeated, 7-14. But Udall's motion was also defeated, 12-13.

Administration officials had expected that the Spellman amendment could be reversed by Udall's tactic. However, most Republicans on the committee were still angry about the Hatch Act amendment. Only Derwinski and two other Republicans supported Udall.

The committee's final 18-7 vote ordered the bill reported as the committee had written it, including the Spellman amendment.

House Floor Action

Supporters of the administration's civil service reform bill survived a political endurance test and the opposition of federal employee unions to win overwhelming House approval of the president's proposals Sept. 13. The vote to approve HR 11280 was 385-10. *(Vote 676, p. 192-H)*

The bill had been tentatively listed for House action in early August. But despite administration urging for quick action, House Democratic leaders at one point decided to put off the bill until after the late August recess.

However, at the urging of Udall, House Speaker Thomas P. O'Neill Jr., D-Mass., announced Aug. 10 that the bill would be taken up the next day. Udall said he had told House leaders he hoped the bill could be completed in one day, but he acknowledged that would be a difficult task.

The quick scheduling of the bill incensed some Post Office Committee members, who had little more than 24 hours' notice that the bill would be on the floor. William (Bill) Clay, D-Mo., quickly began preparing dozens of amendments to delay final action on the bill.

Clay and others indicated the unexpected scheduling of the bill may have been influenced by the absence of top Washington officials of the American Federation of Government Employees (AFGE). The officials were in Chicago for the union's annual convention, where rank-and-file members voted Aug. 7 to withdraw their support from Carter's civil service proposals.

In addition to withdrawing support from Carter's civil service proposals, AFGE — the largest representative of federal employees — also voted to censure Carter and accused him of lying about federal pay raises.

The AFGE action was in retaliation for Carter's support of a 5.5 percent ceiling on a federal pay raise scheduled for October.

Debate on the bill was abandoned when Clay made it clear he would not stop his procedural delaying tactics, which were designed to protect parts of the bill supported by federal labor groups.

The House resumed consideration of HR 11280 on Sept. 7. On Sept. 6, Udall and Carter officials had sought an agreement with Clay, who opposed changes the administration wanted in the committee bill's labor relations provisions. Clay's other major concern was the Hatch Act revisions, which had been added to the bill by the Post Office and Civil Service Committee despite administration opposition.

Clay said he was willing to drop the Hatch Act provisions and go along with some labor relations changes if he got a letter from the president strongly urging Senate action on the Hatch Act bill in 1978.

But when a White House aide read him the letter the administration had prepared Sept. 6, Clay rejected it as too weak and vowed to block the bill any way he could. "I really don't care to talk to [the administration] any more about compromise," Clay said just before launching his Sept. 7 attack against the bill.

During the Sept. 7 debate, the only progress made by supporters of the bill came when Lloyd Meeds, D-Wash., raised a point of order against two titles of the bill — the one containing the Hatch Act provisions and another containing provisions of a bill Carter vetoed (HR 3161) reducing the workweek of federal firefighters that was tacked on to HR 11280 by the Post Office Committee.

Meeds' point of order was sustained, eliminating both titles from the bill.

Although that administration-backed parliamentary maneuver angered Clay, four days later he announced he would drop his delaying tactics because he had received a new letter from Carter stating the president's intention to tell Senate leaders of his "concern" that HR 10 had not been acted on. "Hopefully consideration and action will be taken without undue delay — prior to adjournment," Carter wrote to Clay.

Once Clay was mollified, Udall tried to move ahead with the bill and finish it Sept. 11.

But when debate began, floor managers Udall and Derwinski were bombarded with amendments. Although most were defeated, the debate droned on until members began booing and hissing to drown out some members trying to explain their amendments.

It was nearly midnight before Udall decided to postpone final action on the bill. When the bill came up again Sept. 13, another barrage of amendments drew out debate for almost five hours before the bill was passed.

Veterans' Preference

Most of the numerous amendments taken up during the last two days of debate were defeated. Those that were adopted by the House made few major changes in the bill, and some were accepted by the administration and Udall.

The only major administration defeat on an amendment came Sept. 11 when the House voted to drop almost all proposed changes in veterans' preference.

Although the committee version of veterans' preference represented compromises from the original administration proposal, the administration agreed to back a further compromise when the bill reached the floor.

That proposal, offered by David E. Bonior, D-Mich., would have changed the committee bill to allow veterans who served in combat in Vietnam to use veterans' preference to get one federal job within 15 years after leaving the service or before 1986, whichever came later.

Bonior said his amendment would give 1.5 million Vietnam veterans a longer period to use their preference than they would have had under the committee bill. Under his amendment, Bonior said, about 20 million older veterans would no longer be eligible for preference. That would give Vietnam veterans, women and minorities a chance to move up on federal hiring lists, he said.

However, James M. Hanley, D-N.Y., who offered a successful amendment striking nearly all proposed changes in veterans' preference, disputed Bonior's claim.

Hanley argued that since Vietnam veterans would have less than lifetime preference under Bonior's amendment, they would be better off under the present system.

In addition, said Hanley, it would be unjust for the federal government to change the 34-year-old preference system for millions of veterans who had been given lifetime preference. "The issue at stake here this afternoon is the integrity of the federal government," he said.

Skubitz offered an amendment to Bonior's proposal, which would have made Korean War combat veterans eligible for preference until 1986. Skubitz' amendment was defeated by voice vote.

The House then defeated the Bonior amendment, 149-222. However, Hanley's victory was padded by several vote switches and votes cast after it became apparent Bonior had lost. The tally before the switches and late votes was 160-202. *(Vote 657, p. 188-H)*

The House adopted Hanley's amendment, which was similar to one approved by the Senate in August. It abolished veterans' preference for able-bodied military retirees who left the service at the rank of major or above after 20 years of service. It preserved lifetime preference for all other veterans. The vote was 281-88. *(Vote 658, p. 188-H)*

Labor Relations

When the House took up the bill again to consider another 13 amendments Sept. 13, it rather painlessly resolved an issue that had been under negotiation between the administration and Post Office Committee members for months.

By a 381-0 vote, the House agreed to a complicated compromise that, for the first time, would put into law provisions governing federal labor-management relations. *(Vote 673, p. 192-H)*

The compromise gave federal labor unions more rights than the administration had originally proposed, but it fell far short of many of labor's demands.

During the Sept. 13 debate, James M. Collins, R-Texas, offered an amendment that would have erased the additional rights agreed to by the committee and substituted the language of the executive order. Udall offered a substitute to the Collins amendment, which also would have reduced the scope of bargaining but would have retained several other committee provisions that strengthened labor rights.

Udall's substitute had been worked out with the administration and labor supporters on the Post Office Committee. Even though the Collins amendment was closer to the original administration proposal, the administration backed Udall's compromise. Administration officials said they realized that unless they gave in on some labor rights issues they would lose the support of Clay and other labor backers.

Before voting on the Collins and Udall proposals, several amendments by John N. Erlenborn, R-Ill., were adopted to the Udall substitute, further chipping away at labor rights. The House then approved the Udall substitute by voice vote and unanimously adopted the Collins amendment as modified by Udall.

Other Amendments

FBI Exemption. By voice vote, the House agreed to changes worked out by Collins and Udall to exempt the FBI from some of the bill's provisions. The Udall-Collins amendments exempted the FBI from SES and from research and demonstration projects authorized by the bill. They also would set up a separate mechanism for hearing complaints from whistleblowers within the FBI, and the attorney general would be required to issue regulations for protection of whistleblowers.

Review of Personnel Regulations. An amendment by Joseph L. Fisher, D-Va., would authorize the MSPB to review OPM rules and regulations and to veto any OPM regulations that constituted a prohibited personnel practice. The Fisher amendment, accepted by the administration and adopted on a voice vote, was similar to an amendment adopted by the Senate.

Employment Ceiling. By a 251-96 vote, the House adopted an amendment by Jim Leach, R-Iowa, setting a ceiling on the number of full- and part-time employees the executive branch could employ. Excluding Postal Service employees, the executive branch could not have more than 2,119,000 employees — the total federal workforce in January 1977. Leach's amendment would expire Jan. 20, 1981, the day Carter's current term expired. *(Vote 659, p. 188-H)*

Flexitime Bill. The House adopted an amendment by Solarz, tacking on a House-passed bill (HR 7814) to establish an experimental flexible time program for federal employees. Solarz said the bill was stalled in the Senate and was unlikely to pass in 1978 unless it was attached to another bill. HR 7814 passed the House May 25. A companion bill (S 517) was reported in the Senate Aug. 23. *(See p. 790)*

Labor Rights. An Erlenborn amendment to delete the labor-management provisions of the bill was rejected Sept. 11 by a 125-217 vote. *(Vote 661, p. 188-H)*

Two days later the House by voice votes accepted several Erlenborn amendments on labor rights. These amendments did the following: allowed the president to fire the FLRA general counsel only for cause; required an election be held before a union is given formal recognition; required that a union participating in or backing a strike by federal employees would lose its recognition; and deleted provisions requiring a union recognition election even when there are unresolved issues such as who is eligible to vote.

Pretermination Hearing. A Hanley amendment to guarantee a federal employee a hearing within 90 days after being notified of an adverse action was rejected, 15-23.

Income Limit. John M. Ashbrook, R-Ohio, proposed an amendment that would have limited the outside income of federal employees at level GS-13 or above to 15 percent of their federal salaries. Ashbrook's amendment was defeated, 134-254. *(Vote 674, p. 192-H)*

Summary of Floor Changes

Before passing HR 11280, the House made the following changes in provisions of the bill as reported by the Post Office and Civil Service Committee.

- Exempted the FBI from SES provisions, research and demonstration projects and whistleblower provisions.
- Required the attorney general to issue rules and regulations providing whistleblower protection for FBI employees and applicants for FBI jobs.
- Required the General Accounting Office to make annual reports to the president and Congress on the activities of OPM and MSPB.
- Prohibited OPM from delegating to agencies its authority to conduct competitive examinations, except in certain instances.
- Authorized MSPB to review OPM rules and regulations, and to veto rules that constituted prohibited personnel practices.
- Authorized MSPB, its special counsel or any administrative law judge appointed by the board to issue subpoenas, but did not extend the authorization to other MSPB employees.
- Defined a pattern of recurring discourtesy in dealing with the public as unacceptable performance subject to discipline.
- Excluded from veterans preference non-disabled military retirees who left the service at the rank of major or above after 20 years of service, but left intact preference for all other veterans.
- Prohibited federal employment one year after enactment of the bill from being higher than the January 1977 level, with the ceiling to remain in effect through the president's current term of office.
- Authorized hiring of reading assistants and interpreters for blind or deaf federal employees.
- Required that at least half of the members of qualifications review boards set up by OPM be career civil service employees.
- Authorized an experimental flexitime program for federal employees.
- Reserved as management rights (not subject to bargaining) authority over hiring, firing, promoting, demoting, determining staffing needs, agency mission, budget, organization, number of employees, internal security, contracting out, work assignments and work direction.
- Required that exclusive recognition of a union would be revoked if the union supported a strike by federal employees.

Conference Action

The conference report on S 2640 was filed in the Senate Oct. 4 (S Rept 95-1272) and in the House on Oct. 5 (H Rept 95-1717).

Udall had predicted quick conference action after the House passed the bill Sept. 13.

But when Udall called the conference to order the following week, it was clear the process wouldn't be as painless as he had hoped. House and Senate members restated their positions at the opening meetings with little indication of where they were willing to compromise.

"I'm disappointed at the pace the conference is going," Udall said Sept. 25, several meetings into the conference.

As if in response, the conferees finally began haggling in earnest, methodically moving through a stack of 25 major differences that House and Senate committee staffers had compiled in an "A" memo. Dozens of less controversial differences, outlined in "B" and "C" memos, for the most part were worked out behind the scenes by staff.

Among the compromises reached on "A" memo differences were:

- The conferees agreed to make the SES a government-wide program immediately, in all but a few executive branch agencies. However, after five years Congress could terminate the SES by passing a concurrent resolution. The congressional veto would have to be passed in the 60 days following the five year period.

The Senate had voted to make SES a permanent, government-wide program immediately.

The House had approved SES as a phased-in experiment beginning in three federal departments or agencies. After the first two years, SES would have become government-wide if Congress did not veto it.

Although the conference report retained the House provision for a congressional veto, "The way it's set up the momentum would be against that concurrent resolution passing," said a Senate aide.

- The conference report retained the existing requirement that an agency must have a preponderance of evidence to uphold the firing of an employee for misconduct. But they agreed to give federal managers more flexibility in firing incompetent employees by requiring only that they have substantial evidence to back up the action. The "preponderance" and "substantial" evidence tests are legal requirements an agency must meet if an employee appeals his or her firing.

The House had wanted to keep the tougher "preponderance" test for proving the agency's case in all firings. The Senate had set less stringent tests for firings in cases of misconduct or incompetency.

- The conferees agreed that if a discrimination complaint from a federal employee can't be settled under the administrative procedures set up in the bill, a final decision will be made by a three-member panel composed of one person from the Equal Employment Opportunity Commission (EEOC), one from the Merit Systems Protection Board (MSPB) set up in Carter's civil service reorganization plan and one independent person.

The House, reflecting the position of civil rights groups, had left final decisions on discrimination complaints up to EEOC. The Senate had given MSPB final administrative authority, but the U.S. Court of Appeals would have made a final determination if EEOC disagreed with MSPB's decision.

- The middle level federal managers in the new merit pay system will get only half of the annual comparability pay raise given to civil service employees, under the conference compromise. The comparability raise, computed on the basis of salaries in the private sector, is automatically given to civil service employees.

The House had voted to give employees in the merit pay system a full comparability raise every year, in addition to their new merit increases. The Senate wanted to give the president's chief personnel manager the discretion to withhold all or part of the comparability raise for merit pay employees.

- In the complex sections of S 2640 spelling out labor rights, the conferees agreed to most of the House provisions expanding those rights slightly beyond the labor rights spelled out by existing executive order.

The conference compromise gave federal employee unions more latitude than the Senate had provided in negotiating with federal agencies. It also retained a House provision requiring agencies to automatically withhold union members' dues, at no expense to the union. In addition, it modified a House provision to allow employees to have a union representative at meetings on disciplinary actions.

Stevens Threat

With the end in sight Oct. 3, Udall kept dangling his gavel, ready to end the conference. Three times, he pronounced the meeting over. And three times he was interrupted by members who wanted just one last crack at changing the bill.

In the last of those interruptions, Sen. Ted Stevens, R-Alaska, threatened to kill the bill if the conferees did not change a minor provision to assure some military reserve officers that they could get high-paying civil service jobs and still draw full military retirement pay.

Both the House and Senate had voted to restrict those "double dippers" by preventing retired military officers from drawing a federal salary and retirement benefits totaling more than Executive Schedule V salaries — $47,500 in 1978. Some retirees collected as much as $80,000 a year from their benefits and federal salaries.

The House would have exempted from the ceiling anyone drawing both retirements pay and a federal salary at the time of the bill's enactment. The Senate would have gone further by exempting military reservists eligible for, but not yet drawing retirement pay, from the ceiling.

"I don't think this is equitable," shouted Stevens, who acknowledged he did not know how many people would be affected. "If I have to defeat this conference report on this basis, I'll try it," he threatened.

Udall said he hoped Stevens wouldn't "shoot down" the bill just because the senator thought it would shortchange "a couple of hundred reservists, who really aren't on food stamps or welfare." But then Udall recommended that the House give in to Stevens.

Humphrey, Dirksen Memorials

The House voted April 18 to authorize $7.5 million for memorials honoring two former Senate leaders.

As cleared for the president on a 267-127 vote, the bill (S 2452 — PL 95-270) authorized $5 million for the Hubert H. Humphrey Institute of Public Affairs at the University of Minnesota and $2.5 million for development of the Everett McKinley Dirksen Congressional Leadership Research Center in Pekin, Ill. *(Vote 190, p. 56-H)*

The legislation originated in the House as a memorial to Humphrey, D-Minn., who died in January. House approval came Feb. 21 on a 356-53 vote. *(Vote 56, p. 16-H)*

But Senate Republicans tacked on money for a memorial to Dirksen, R-Ill., before the bill passed March 22 by voice vote.

The Senate version picked up opposition from both Democrats and Republicans when the bill was returned to the House, although there was little debate before the vote.

Principal House supporters of the Humphrey memorial went along with the Dirksen addition, pointing out that Congress had honored several congressional leaders with similar memorials.

But Rep. Robert E. Bauman, R-Md., who opposed the legislation both times it came before the House, denounced the Senate's Dirksen amendment as "a classic example of political back scratching." Bauman argued that taxpayers should not be financing memorials to former congressmen. "Where is this going to end? The possibilities are almost endless in which the taxpayers will be asked to fund projects for every deceased statesman," he said.

With Stevens pacified, Udall finally got to bang his gavel, ending the conference.

Final Action

The Senate agreed to the conference report by voice vote Oct. 4. The House followed suit on Oct. 6, by a vote of 365-8. *(Vote 783, p. 222-H)*

Carter Signs Government-Wide Ethics Bill

Detailed financial disclosure by top federal officials and new restrictions on post-government activity by former federal officials were mandated by the government ethics bill (S 555 — PL 95-521) signed into law by President Carter, Oct. 26.

Carter said the bill "responds to problems that developed in the highest levels of government in the 1970s."

The final bill codified the public financial disclosure requirements passed as new ethics codes in the House and Senate in 1977. It also required public disclosure by top executive and judicial branch employees. The bill provided administrative procedures to assure compliance with the disclosure requirements, but civil penalties could be imposed for knowing and willful violations.

Restrictions were tightened on the "revolving door" that allows government employees to move freely to private jobs lobbying their former agencies. Penalties for violation of the post-government restrictions ranged from administrative actions to criminal fines or jail sentences.

In addition, the bill established an Office of Government Ethics to monitor financial disclosure and conflicts of interest in the executive branch.

Major Provisions of Financial Disclosure Bill

- Wrote into law the financial disclosure provisions of the Senate and House ethics codes adopted by both chambers in 1977. Those codes were enforceable only by internal penalties such as a reprimand; writing the codes into law allowed violations to be enforced with fines. However, the final bill provided only civil penalties; criminal penalties were dropped.
- Applied the same disclosure requirements to the president, vice president, top-level executive branch officials, Supreme Court justices, federal judges and other top employees of the judicial branch.
- Also applied the disclosure requirements to candidates for federal office with the reports for 1978 due by Nov. 1, just a week before the general elections. However, 1978 candidates were exempted from any penalties for failure to comply with the disclosure requirements.

  The provision was directed principally at House candidates. Both incumbent senators and representatives disclosed financial data in the spring under the congressional ethics codes. The Senate code sought to apply the requirement to challengers also, even though the ethics code was not binding on anyone outside the Senate. Nevertheless, Senate challengers in general complied. Under S 555, disclosures made under the ethics code met the requirements.
- Required disclosure of earned income, by source, type and amount, unearned income by categories of value (such as $5,000-$15,000 and $15,000-$50,000) and honoraria totaling $100 or more in a year. In addition, certain information about gifts had to be disclosed.
- Also required disclosure by category of value of information about property holdings, debts and interests in trades or businesses.
- Required disclosure of certain information about finances of a spouse and dependent children.
- Provided civil but not criminal penalties for disclosure violations. Maximum penalties would be $5,000.
- Required that the public have access to the information disclosed.
- Required the reports to be filed by May 15 of each year with the first reports under the law due in 1979 for calendar 1978.
- Established an Office of Government Ethics in the Office of Personnel Management, which was created in 1978 by President Carter's reorganization proposal splitting the Civil Service Commission in two. The new ethics office would develop rules and regulations on government conflicts of interest and other ethical problems, and monitor and investigate compliance with federal ethics laws.
- Placed new restrictions on business activities of federal workers who leave the government. In general, the bill expanded existing law to further restrict the freedom of a former government employee to represent private firms in matters before the government in which the employee was in some way involved while on the federal payroll. These provisions were to take effect in mid-1979.
- Established a mechanism for court appointment of a special prosecutor to investigate criminal allegations against high-level government officials, including the president, vice-president and Cabinet-level officers. Only the attorney general could ask the court to name a special prosecutor; no other mechanism was provided. The special prosecutor mechanism would go out of existence in five years.

The bill also set up a mechanism for appointment of a temporary special prosecutor to investigate criminal wrongdoing by the president, vice president and other top executive branch officials.

The final version also permitted the Senate to set up an Office of Senate Legal Counsel to represent members, officers, committees or the Senate as a whole in litigation.

Two-Year Gestation

Both chambers passed their ethics codes, covering members of Congress, at the beginning of the 95th Congress. But action on bills to require disclosure by other federal officials lagged. *(1977 Almanac p. 763)*

The requirements of the ethics codes were enforceable only through congressional procedures such as disciplinary actions against a member. Stiffer penalties through the legal system, such as civil or criminal charges, weren't possible without more legislation.

The final bill passed by Congress covered the executive and judicial branches and provided civil fines but no criminal penalties.

The Senate passed its version of S 555 in mid-1977. However, companion legislation languished in the House until late in the year when it was reported by several different committees, all of which had some jurisdictional responsibility. *(1977 Almanac p. 578)*

In 1978, the jurisdictional problem had to be resolved in order to make the bill manageable on the floor. This was accomplished eventually when the four committees involved agreed to back one compromise bill on the floor. However, the bill had languished for several months before the compromise was struck.

Penalties, Income Limit Issues

One key issue that contributed to delay was a provision in early versions of the bill imposing criminal penalties on persons who violated the disclosure requirements. Opponents said that a criminal charge, even if later disproved, could ruin a politician's career. Criminal penalties were dropped from the compromise.

A second issue involved a provision in the ethics codes limiting outside earned income of members to 15 percent of their salaries — $8,625 at the salary level in effect in 1978. That limit, which was to go into effect in 1979, had drawn criticism from a small but vocal group in Congress.

House opponents of the limit mounted a campaign to get a vote on repealing it when the House took up the financial disclosure legislation. The fear that they might win contributed to the Democratic leadership's reluctance to bring the bill to the floor.

However, the ceiling opponents lost, and lost big. The House in September rejected by a 97-290 vote a proposal to repeal the earned income limit. Members who backed the repeal claimed that they were hurt by the vote's proximity to the November elections. Some said members had told them privately they did not like the income limit but could not vote against it just before the elections.

After the income issue was settled, the House went on to pass its version of the disclosure legislation (HR 1) with little controversy. That occurred Sept. 27 by a 368-30 vote.

Conferees reached agreement surprisingly quickly. The conference report on the bill (S 555 — H Rept 95-1756) was adopted by the Senate Oct. 7 by voice vote and by the House Oct. 12 by a 370-23 roll call. Before that final vote, the House defeated a motion by Charles E. Wiggins, R-Calif., to reject the section setting up a mechanism for appointment of a temporary special prosecutor. The vote on Wiggins' proposal was 49-344. *(Votes 793, 794, p. 226-H)*

Provisions

As signed into law, S 555:

Title I — Legislative Branch Disclosure

- Required all members, their principal assistants, congressional officers and employees paid at the GS-16 salary level or higher, and any candidate for congressional office to file annual public financial disclosure reports.
- Required all reports, except those from congressional candidates, to be filed by May 15 each year with the clerk of the House or the secretary of the Senate.
- Required candidates for congressional office in 1978 to file reports by Nov. 1, 1978, but exempted 1978 candidates from any penalties for failure to comply with the disclosure requirements.
- Required candidates in future elections to file reports within 30 days of becoming a candidate or by May 15, whichever was later.
- Required new officers and employees who are principal assistants or are paid at the GS-16 salary level or above to file reports, beginning Jan. 1, 1979, within 30 days after assuming their positions if they had not previously held legislative branch positions covered by the bill.
- Required all members, officers and employees covered by the legislative branch disclosure requirements to report the source, type and amount of earned income from any source (other than their U.S. government salaries) and the source, date and amount of honoraria received during the preceding calendar year and aggregating $100 or more in value.
- Required members, officers and employees to report the source and type of unearned income received from dividends, interest, rent and capital gains received during the preceding calendar year and aggregating $100 or more in value.
- Required candidates and new officers or employees to file the same information about income for the year of filing and the preceding calendar year.
- Required reporting of each item of unearned income in one of the following categories: Not more than $1,000, greater than $1,000 but not more than $2,500, greater than $2,500 but not more than $5,000, greater than $5,000 but not more than $15,000, greater than $15,000 but not more than $50,000, greater than $50,000 but not more than $100,000, or greater than $100,000.
- Required all persons covered except candidates and new officers and employees to disclose the source and a brief description of any gifts of transportation, lodging, food or entertainment aggregating $250 or more in value received from any source other than a relative during the preceding calendar year.
- Exempted gifts of food, lodging or entertainment received as personal hospitality from the reporting requirements.
- Required all persons covered except candidates and new officers and employees to disclose the source, a brief description and estimated value of all gifts (other than transportation, lodging, food or entertainment) aggregating $100 or more in value received from a source other than a relative during the preceding calendar year.
- Exempted gifts with a fair market value of $35 or less.
- Required all persons covered except candidates and new officers and employees to disclose the source and a brief description of reimbursements from a single source aggregating $250 or more in the preceding calendar year.
- Required all persons covered to disclose the identity and category of value of any interest in property held in a trade or business, or for investment or production of income, with a fair market value over $1,000 at the close of the preceding calendar year.
- Excluded from disclosure personal liabilities owed by relatives to the reporting individual or any deposit of $5,000 or less in a personal savings account.
- Required all persons covered to disclose the identity and category of value of the total liabilities owed to any creditor (other than a relative) exceeding $10,000 at any time during the preceding calendar year. This did not include a mortgage on the individual's personal residence or loans for cars, household furniture or appliances.
- Exempted reporting outstanding liabilities on revolving charge accounts unless the liability was more than $10,000 at the close of the preceding calendar year.
- Required all persons covered except candidates and new officers and employees to include a brief description, the date and category of value of real property (other than personal residence) or stocks, bonds or other securities purchased, sold or exchanged in the preceding calendar year if the amount involved exceeded $1,000.
- Exempted from reporting requirements any transaction solely between the reporting individual and his or her spouse or dependent children.
- Required all persons covered to report any positions held during the current calendar year with businesses, nonprofit organizations, labor groups or other institutions, except for religious, social, fraternal or political groups.
- Required all persons covered except candidates and new officers and employees to report terms of agreement about any future employment planned by the reporting individual.
- Provided that in reporting property holdings, liabilities and purchase, sale or exchange of real property or securities, individuals should list each item in one of the following categories: Not more than $5,000, greater than $5,000 but not more than $15,000, greater than $15,000 but not more than $50,000, greater than $50,000 but not more than $100,000, greater than $100,000 but not more than $250,000, or greater than $250,000.
- Permitted reporting of real property values as the price on the date purchased or the assessed value for tax purposes, as long as the method used for determining the assessed value was described in the report.
- Required reporting individuals to list the following information about a spouse's finances: source of any earned income over $1,000; source and type of unearned income

received from dividends, interest, rent and capital gains received during the preceding calendar year and aggregating $100 or more in value; source and brief description or estimated value of any gift or reimbursement which is not received totally independent of the spouse's relationship to the reporting individual; and certain assets, liabilities and transactions of the spouse (unless the reporting individual certified that he or she had no control over them and would not receive any economic benefit from those interests).

- Required reporting individuals to list unearned income of dependent children, and to list their assets, liabilities and transactions unless the individual certified that he or she had no control over them and did not receive any economic benefit from them.
- Exempted from reporting requirements a spouse permanently separated from the reporting individual.
- Required that an individual with holdings in a qualified blind trust report the category of the amount of income received by the individual, the individual's spouse or dependent children, but did not require reporting of the holdings or source of income.
- Defined the requirements of a qualified blind trust, and gave House and Senate ethics committees authority to determine whether a blind trust qualified under the law.
- Authorized the attorney general to bring civil charges against a reporting individual or the trustee of his or her qualified blind trust for negligent or knowing and willful disclosure or receipt of information specifically required to be kept confidential about a qualified blind trust.
- Required the clerk of the House and secretary of the Senate to make reports available to the public within 15 days after they are filed.
- Provided that reports be available to the public for five years, after which they were to be destroyed.
- Barred use of the reports for any unlawful purposes, commercial use (other than in news reporting), solicitation of money or determination of an individual's credit rating.
- Provided civil penalties of up to $5,000 for persons who make illegal use of the reported information.
- Provided that designated committees in the House and Senate should review all reports to see if they were properly and completely filed.
- Required the committees to notify any reporting individual who did not file an accurate report and give the individual an opportunity to correct it.
- Provided that an individual who complied with recommendations of the committees shall not be subject to any sanctions provided in the bill.
- Provided for civil penalties of up to $5,000 against any persons who knowingly and willfully filed a false report or failed to file a report.
- Required the General Accounting Office (GAO) to monitor compliance with the legislative branch disclosure requirements.

Title II — Executive Branch Disclosure

- Required the president, vice president, candidates for those offices, executive branch employees paid at level GS-16 or above, military officers paid at grade O-7 or above and certain other executive branch employees to file annual public financial disclosure reports.
- Required persons nominated by the president to posts requiring Senate approval to file financial disclosure reports within five days after their nominations were sent to the Senate.
- Required candidates for president or vice president to file reports within 30 days of becoming a candidate or by May 15, whichever was later.
- Required new officers and employees who are in positions covered by the bill to file reports within 30 days after assuming their positions if they had not previously held executive branch positions covered by the bill.
- Required all others subject to executive branch disclosure to file reports by May 15 of each year.
- Required all executive branch employees (except new officers and employees) covered by the disclosure law to report the source, type and amount of earned income from any source (other than their U.S. government salaries) and the source, date and amount of honoraria received during the preceding calendar year and aggregating $100 or more in value.
- Required disclosure of the source and type of unearned income from dividends, rent, interest and capital gains received during the preceding calendar year exceeding $100.
- Required reporting of each item of unearned income in one of the following categories: Not more than $1,000, greater than $1,000 but not more than $2,500, greater than $2,500 but not more than $5,000, greater than $5,000 but not more than $15,000, greater than $15,000 but not more than $50,000, greater than $50,000 but not more than $100,000, or greater than $100,000.
- Required disclosure of the source and a brief description of any gifts of transportation, lodging, food or entertainment aggregating $250 or more in value received from any source other than a relative during the preceding calendar year.
- Exempted gifts of food, lodging or entertainment received as personal hospitality from the reporting requirements.
- Required disclosure of the source, a brief description and estimated value of all gifts (other than transportation, lodging, food or entertainment) aggregating $100 or more in value received from a source other than a relative during the preceding calendar year.
- Exempted gifts with a fair market value of $35 or less.
- Required disclosure of the source and a brief description of reimbursements from any source aggregating $250 or more in the preceding calendar year.
- Required disclosure of the identity and category of value of any interest in property held in a trade or business, or for investment or production of income, with a fair market value over $1,000 at the close of the preceding calendar year, excluding a personal savings account of $5,000 or less.
- Required disclosure of the identity and category of value of the total liabilities owed to any creditor (other than a relative) exceeding $10,000 at any time during the preceding calendar year.
- Excluded from disclosure mortgages on a personal residence or loans for cars, furniture or appliances.
- Required reporting of revolving charge account liabilities only if they exceeded $10,000 at the close of the preceding calendar year.
- Required a brief description, the date and category of value of real property (other than personal residence) or stocks, bonds or other securities purchased, sold or exchanged in the preceding calendar year if the amount involved exceeded $1,000.
- Exempted from reporting requirements any transaction solely between the reporting individual and his or her spouse or dependent children.

• Required disclosure of any position held during the current calendar year with businesses, non-profit organizations, labor organizations or other institutions except religious, social, fraternal, charitable or political groups.

• Required non-elected executive branch officials covered by the title to report the source of any income (other than from the U.S. government) over $5,000 received in the two calendar years prior to the year in which the report was filed and to include a brief description of the work done for that income.

• Required reporting of the terms of agreement about any future employment planned by the reporting individuals.

• Provided that in reporting property holdings, liabilities and purchase, sale or exchange of real property or securities, individuals should list each item in one of the following categories: not more than $5,000, greater than $5,000 but not more than $15,000, greater than $15,000 but not more than $50,000, greater than $100,000 but not more than $250,000, or greater than $250,000.

• Required candidates, nominees and new officers and employees to report the same information required of other executive branch employees, except for gifts, reimbursements, and purchase, sale or exchange of real property or securities. Required those persons to report income for the year of filing and the preceding calendar year.

• Permitted reporting of real property values as the price on the date purchased or the assessed value for tax purposes, as long as the method used for determining the assessed value was described in the report.

• Required reporting individuals to list the following information about a spouse's finances: source of any earned income over $1,000; source and type of unearned income received from dividends, interest, rent and capital gains received during the preceding calendar year and aggregating $100 or more in value; source and brief description or estimated value of any gift or reimbursement which is not received totally independent of the spouse's relationship to the reporting individual; and certain assets, liabilities and transactions of the spouse (unless the reporting individual certified that he or she had no control over them and would not receive any economic benefit from those interests).

• Required reporting individuals to list unearned income of dependent children, and to list their assets, liabilities and transactions unless the individual certified that he or she had no control over them and did not receive any economic benefit from them.

• Exempted from reporting requirements any financial disclosure by a spouse permanently separated from the reporting individual.

• Required that an individual with holdings in a qualified blind trust report the category of the amount of income received by the individual, the individual's spouse or dependent children, but did not require reporting of the holdings or source of income in the trust.

• Defined the requirements of a qualified blind trust and gave the Office of Government Ethics authority to determine whether a blind trust qualified under the law.

• Authorized the attorney general to bring civil charges against a reporting individual or the trustee of his or her qualified blind trust for negligent or knowing and willful disclosure or receipt of information specifically required to be kept confidential about the qualified blind trust.

• Exempted campaign receipts or expenditures from the disclosure requirements.

• Required the president and vice president to file reports with the Office of Government Ethics, candidates to file with the Federal Election Commission and other employees to file with their agencies.

• Required military officers to file with the secretary of their branch of service.

• Provided civil penalties of up to $5,000 for anyone who knowingly and willfully falsified a report or failed to file a report.

• Authorized the president to exempt the reports of undercover intelligence agents from public disclosure.

• Authorized the president to allow intelligence agents to file false disclosure reports to cover their identities.

• Barred use of the reports for any unlawful purpose, for any commercial use (other than in news reporting), for determining a person's credit rating or for soliciting money.

• Provided civil penalties of up to $5,000 for unlawful use of the reports.

• Required reports to be available to the public for six years, after which they were to be destroyed.

• Required agencies that received reports to review them within 60 days and to give reporting individuals an opportunity to correct any errors.

• Excluded the president, vice president and candidates for those offices from the administrative procedures set out for making corrections of violations.

• Authorized the president to require any executive branch employees not covered by the bill to file confidential financial disclosure reports.

• Gave the comptroller general access to executive branch disclosure reports in carrying out GAO statutory responsibilities.

• Required filing of the first executive branch disclosure reports May 15, 1979, to cover the preceding calendar year.

Title III — Judicial Branch Disclosure

• Required financial disclosure reports to be filed by Supreme Court justices, federal judges and judicial branch employees who are authorized to perform adjudicatory functions or who are paid the equivalent of a GS-16 salary or above.

• Required presidential nominees for judgeships to file disclosure reports when their nominations were sent to the Senate.

• Required judicial branch personnel to disclose the same information required in the executive branch disclosure provisions, but did not include the requirement of reporting sources of income over $5,000 during the previous two years and gave authority to approve a qualified blind trust to the Judicial Ethics Committee.

• Authorized the attorney general to bring civil charges against a reporting individual or the trustee of his or her qualified blind trust for negligent or knowing and willful disclosure or receipt of information specifically required to be kept confidential about the qualified blind trust.

• Exempted campaign receipts or expenditures from the disclosure requirements.

• Required judicial branch employees to file the annual reports with a Judicial Ethics Committee to be established by the Judicial Conference of the United States.

• Authorized the committee to monitor and investigate compliance with the disclosure requirements.

• Provided civil penalties of up to $5,000 for knowingly and willfully filing a false report or failing to file a report.

● Required the committee to make the disclosure reports available to the public for six years, after which they would be destroyed.

● Prohibited use of the reports for any unlawful purpose or any commercial use other than news reporting.

● Prohibited use of the reports for establishing a person's credit rating or soliciting money.

● Provided civil penalties of up to $5,000 for unlawful use of the reports.

● Authorized the committee to require confidential disclosure reports from judicial branch employees not covered by the bill.

● Required the first judicial branch reports to be filed May 15, 1979, covering the previous calendar year.

Title IV — Office of Government Ethics

● Established an Office of Government Ethics, to be headed by a director appointed by the president with approval of the Senate, in the Office of Personnel Management.

● Authorized the director to develop rules and regulations pertaining to conflicts of interest and ethics in the executive branch, to monitor and investigate compliance with the executive branch financial disclosure requirements, to review reports for possible violations of conflict of interest laws and regulations, to issue advisory opinions, to order corrective actions and to consult with agency ethics counselors.

● Authorized appropriations of $2 million for each of five fiscal years, beginning with fiscal 1979, for the Office of Government Ethics.

Title V — Post Employment Conflict of Interest

● Barred former executive branch, independent agency or District of Columbia employees from representing anyone before their former agencies in connection with any proceeding, investigation or other matter that the former employees personally and substantially participated in while working for the government.

● Barred former government employees from appearing before a federal agency for two years on matters that were under their official responsibility before leaving the government.

● Barred former officials above GS-16 who had significant decision-making or supervisory authority and top-ranking military officers from representing anyone formally or informally on any matter pending before their former agency for one year after leaving government.

● Authorized the director of the Office of Government Ethics to apply the one-year ban to other former officials not covered by the bill's definition.

● Set maximum penalties for violation of the permanent, one- and two-year bans at $10,000 and two years in prison.

● Provided that former employees could provide information to their former agencies about an area in which they had special knowledge, as long as they received no compensation other than that normally paid to witnesses.

● Provided that in lieu of criminal penalties against a former employee who violated any of the bans on contact, a department or agency head could take disciplinary action against him or her, including barring any business communication between the former employee and the agency for five years.

● Exempted from the conflict of interest provisions persons who left government prior to July 1, 1979.

● Made the provisions effective July 1, 1979.

Title VI — Special Prosecutor

● Required the attorney general to conduct an investigation when he or she received information that any federal criminal law (other than a violation constituting a petty offense) had been violated by the president, vice president, Cabinet-level officials, senior White House aides, top Justice Department officials, the director or deputy director of the Central Intelligence Agency, the Internal Revenue Service commissioner, any persons who held the above positions during the incumbency of the president or during the term of the previous president (if that president was from the same political party), a national campaign manager or the chairman of a national campaign committee.

● Required the attorney general to complete a preliminary investigation of allegations within 90 days.

● Required the attorney general to report to a special court unit on whether the allegations appeared substantiated by the investigation.

● Required the attorney general to apply to the special court unit for appointment of a special prosecutor, if the attorney general determined that the allegations warranted further investigation.

● Specified that if the attorney general finds that the matter is so unsubstantiated that no further investigation or prosecution is warranted he or she would notify the court of this and the court would have no power to appoint a special prosecutor.

● Required the attorney general to apply to the court for appointment of a special prosecutor if the Justice Department had been unable to determine within 90 days whether the allegations were substantiated or not.

● Required the attorney general to repeat the investigation and report procedures if additional specific information was obtained after the initial 90-day investigation.

● Specified that a majority of the members of either political party on the Judiciary committees of either house of Congress may request in writing that the attorney general apply for appointment of a special prosecutor. Required the attorney general to respond to the request within 30 days, indicating what action was taken and, if no application was made for appointment, the reasons why.

● Set up a special three-judge unit in the U.S. Court of Appeals for the District of Columbia Circuit as the body with authority to receive and act on the attorney general's applications.

● Authorized the court unit to appoint a special prosecutor and define the prosecutor's jurisdiction after receiving an application from the attorney general.

● Gave the special prosecutor power to perform all investigative and prosecutorial functions and powers of the Justice Department and its officials.

● Authorized the special prosecutor to hire employees as needed.

● Required the special prosecutor to report periodically to Congress and to advise the House of any information that might constitute grounds for an impeachment.

● Prohibited removal of the special prosecutor from office, except by impeachment and conviction, or by personal action of the attorney general for extraordinary impropriety, physical disability, mental incapacity or any other condition that substantially impairs the prosecutor's performance.

- Required the attorney general to give a report stating reasons for removal of a special prosecutor to the court unit and to the House and Senate Judiciary committees.
- Allowed a special prosecutor removed from office by the attorney general to seek court review of the action.
- Provided for termination of a special prosecutor's office when the special prosecutor notified the attorney general that his or her investigation was completed, or if the court unit determined that the special prosecutor's investigations were over.
- Required the special prosecutor to give the court unit a final report describing disposition of all cases and reasons for not prosecuting any matter within the prosecutor's jurisdiction.
- Prohibited the Justice Department from investigating any matters under the special prosecutor's jurisdiction.
- Set a termination date for the special prosecutor mechanism five years after enactment of the bill.
- Authorized the Chief Justice of the United States to assign three judges to serve on the special court unit for two-year terms.
- Required the attorney general to write rules ordering Justice Department officials not to participate in any investigation or prosecution if their participation could result in a personal, financial or political conflict of interest, or the appearance of conflict.
- Provided that violation of the conflict of interest rule should result in removal from office.

Title VII — Senate Legal Counsel

- Established an office of Senate Legal Counsel, to be headed by a chief counsel and a deputy counsel appointed by the president pro tempore of the Senate.
- Required that the counsel and deputy counsel be lawyers.
- Provided that the Office of Senate Legal Counsel was accountable to a joint Senate leadership group consisting of the president pro tempore, the majority and minority leaders and the chairmen and ranking minority members of the Senate Judiciary and Rules committees.
- Required a two-thirds vote of the members of the joint leadership group, or adoption of a privileged resolution by the Senate, to order the counsel to defend the Senate or any member, officer or unit of the Senate in any civil action or proceeding involving a subpoena.
- Required adoption of a privileged resolution by the Senate before the counsel could bring a civil action to enforce a subpoena.
- Defined other duties and powers of the Office of Senate Legal Counsel.
- Provided that in any action or proceeding where the Senate legal counsel was representing the Senate or a Senate member or unit, the attorney general would have no authority to represent the Senate except at Senate request.

House Action

The House late in the session passed its version of the financial disclosure legislation. But for a long time there was considerable doubt that a bill would ever emerge from that chamber.

The matter was complicated because several different bills had been reported by different committees. This created a difficult jurisdictional and parliamentary problem.

But more important was the politics. House sentiment against ethics reform proposals was running high when 1978 began. In particular, many members disliked the limit on outside earned income that was imposed in the 1977 House ethics code.

As a result, a few outspoken opponents of the limit organized a campaign to repeal the ethics code provision. They found a receptive audience in the House Rules Committee which in the spring voted to allow a House floor vote on repeal.

From then on the House leadership — which was strongly committed to retaining the limit — maneuvered, delayed, and rounded up votes until it was clear that the ethics bill would pass and the income limit repealer would be defeated. In addition, there were numerous other conflicts over the disclosure and other sections of the bills, all of which took time to iron out.

But by fall this all had been accomplished and the ethics bill sailed through the House largely intact after the repealer effort went down to a huge defeat.

Background

Financial disclosure bills were reported by four House committees in 1977. A bill (HR 11941) from the Select Ethics Committee, chaired by Richardson Preyer, D-N.C., codified financial disclosure rules for members of Congress and extended disclosure requirements to candidates for Congress. The House Judiciary Committee wrote a bill (HR 1) setting disclosure requirements for executive and judicial branch officials. A third bill (HR 6954) dealing only with executive branch disclosure was approved by the Armed Services and Post Office and Civil Service committees.

In addition, the House Judiciary Committee in 1978 reported a separate bill (HR 9705) calling for a temporary special prosecutor for certain criminal investigations of top executive branch officials. But because some members planned floor amendments to expand that bill to cover investigations of Congress, HR 9705 was never brought up for floor action.

Major Provisions: HR 11941, HR 1

Legislative Branch Disclosure. HR 11941, the Select Committee on Ethics' bill covering disclosure in the legislative branch, would require detailed financial reports to be filed every May 15 by members of Congress, elected officers of the House and Senate, candidates for federal office, and employees of members, officers or committees who are paid at least as much as a GS-16 civil service employee. (HR 11941 was a revised version of a bill — HR 7401 — reported by the ethics committee in 1977, H Rept 95-574.)

If a member had no employee compensated at that level, he or she would have to designate at least one principal employee to file a detailed financial disclosure report.

The reports, which would be made available for public inspection by the Clerk of the House and the Secretary of the Senate, would list income, gifts, reimbursements, personal liabilities, securities, business or investment property, and interest income. Exceptions would be made in some categories, and income and holdings below certain levels would not have to be reported.

Less detailed reports, which would also be made public, would be required from spouses and dependents. Spouses would have to report the source — but not the amount — of earned income, as well as certain gifts and reimbursements. Both spouses and dependents would have to report certain assets and liabilities.

Penalties for filing a false report or failing to file at all would be a maximum fine of $5,000 for a civil violation. Maximum criminal penalties, for knowing and willful falsification or failure to file, would be a $10,000 fine and a year in jail.

Executive, Judicial Disclosure. The Judiciary Committee bill (HR 1) covered financial disclosure by executive and judicial branch employees.

It would require annual reports to be filed by the president, vice president, candidates for those two offices, federal judges, officials and employees of the executive and judicial branches who are compensated at the GS-16 level or above, other employees in confidential or policy-making positions, and presidential nominees whose appointments must be confirmed by the Senate.

Judicial and executive branch employees would be required to report (with some exceptions) gifts and reimbursements, outside earned income, personal property for business or investment, liabilities, interest in — or purchase or sale of — real property, and positions held with businesses or other groups (except religious, social, fraternal or charitable groups). Spouses and dependents would be required to file less detailed reports.

The president, vice president and their top employees would file reports with the Office of Government Ethics. Candidates for president or vice president would file with the Federal Elections Commission. Other executive branch employees would file with their agencies, while judicial branch employees would file with the Judicial Conference of the United States.

Penalties for false reports or failure to file would be the same as those for the legislative branch contained in HR 11941.

Government Ethics Office. An Office of Government Ethics would be established to audit the reports and monitor the reporting program.

Conflicts of Interest. Existing conflict of interest laws would be broadened. HR 1 would extend to two years the existing one year prohibition on a former top official's contact with an agency on matters that had been under his or her general supervision.

It would also establish a broader ban — effective for one year — on formal or informal contact on any other matters with the agency for which the official formerly worked. *(Details on provisions, 1977 Almanac p. 584)*

Special Prosecutor Bill

Six years after the events known as Watergate began, a House committee approved a bill calling for a temporary special prosecutor for certain criminal investigations of top executive branch officials.

The House Judiciary Committee approved the bill (HR 9705) by a 24-6 vote (all six negative votes were from Republican members) and ordered it reported May 16. The committee reported the bill June 19 (H Rept 95-1307).

The proposal — approved twice before by the Senate — would set up a mechanism for choosing a temporary special prosecutor to handle investigations of criminal allegations involving the president, vice president and other top executive branch officials. Its supporters said it would eliminate the potential conflict of interest in having the attorney general — a political appointee — investigating the president who appointed him or other top executive branch officials who could put pressure on the Justice Department.

As reported by the House Judiciary Committee, the bill would not apply the special prosecutor mechanism to investigations involving members of Congress.

The committee in May rejected, 7-26, an amendment calling for a temporary special prosecutor in some investigations involving members of Congress — including the Korean influence-peddling allegations. *(Korea story, p. 803)*

The special prosecutor legislation was one of several post-Watergate reforms that have been proposed in recent Congresses. It was part of a Senate Watergate reform bill (S 555) passed in 1977 that also included requirements for financial disclosure by top federal officials.

Supporters of the special prosecutor legislation said it would eliminate the potential conflict of interest facing an attorney general who must deal with allegations of crimes committed by the president who appointed him or other top-level executive branch officials who are in a position to put pressure on the Justice Department.

In such circumstances, the bill would authorize the attorney general to request appointment of a temporary special prosecutor by a panel of judges. It would allow removal of the special prosecutor only by the attorney general, and only under circumstances spelled out in the bill.

The amendment to apply the special prosecutor mechanism to investigations of some members of Congress was offered by Elizabeth Holtzman, D-N.Y.

Holtzman's proposal called for a temporary special prosecutor in the ongoing 1978 Justice Department Korean investigation, in criminal probes involving members of the majority and minority leadership in the House and Senate, and for allegations of crimes involving three or more members. A House Judiciary subcommittee earlier defeated similar language.

Holtzman argued that her amendment would avoid any appearance that an investigation of a member of Congress was influenced by political considerations.

It was the Korean special prosecutor provision that backers of HR 9705 feared could jeopardize the bill's chances for consideration in 1978. Although the amendment was soundly defeated when Holtzman offered it during Judiciary Committee markup, some of the bill's supporters said it would be difficult for many members to vote against it on the floor during an election year. A vote against a Korean special prosecutor might be construed as a vote against a full investigation of the scandal, they said.

Outside backers of the special prosecutor bill, such as Common Cause and the American Bar Association, opposed adding Congress to the bill. They argued that the conflict of interest inherent when the Justice Department investigates fellow executive branch officials is not a problem in Justice probes of members of Congress. They also argued that the Justice Department had been adequately investigating the Korean scandal.

The House Judiciary Committee report said that although the drive for special prosecutor legislation stemmed from the Watergate scandal, "the need did not originate with Watergate." It cited the scandal that led to the resignation of former President Eisenhower's aide Sherman Adams as an example of a high level conflict of interest case that called for handling by a special prosecutor.

Five Republicans filed dissenting views, arguing that during Watergate "the government proved itself so conspicuously effective that we cannot accept" that HR 9705 is needed to reassure the public of executive branch integrity.

The Republicans said the attorney general and the president already have the power to appoint a special prosecutor. "If an attorney general cannot be trusted to enforce the law against the executive, the remedy is impeachment and not the cloning of an additional attorney general to do the job of the first," they said.

Signing the dissenting views were: Charles E. Wiggins, Calif.; Robert McClory, Ill.; M. Caldwell Butler, Va.; Carlos J. Moorhead, Calif.; and Thomas N. Kindness, Ohio.

Senate Action. President Carter in his 1977 government ethics package endorsed special prosecutor legislation.

The Senate in passing its ethics bill (S 555) included a special prosecutor provision. In addition, the Senate approved a floor amendment by Donald W. Riegle, D-Mich., and H. John Heinz III, R-Pa., calling for a special prosecutor on the Korean scandal in Congress.

In a Sept. 30 letter to Sen. Abraham Ribicoff, D-Conn., chairman of the Governmental Affairs Committee, President Carter said the administration strongly opposed the amendment.

Earlier, the White House in a letter to the House Criminal Justice Subcommittee at the time the panel was marking up the special prosecutor bill said the administration felt the mechanism should be limited "to cases of great magnitude where potential conflicts of interest for the attorney general are real and intense. Normally, allegations about any but the highest executive officials, or about members of Congress do not fall in this class."

Summary of Delays

Although all of the ethics bills were ready for House consideration by spring, various specific controversies and lingering resentment in the House over ethics proposals delayed floor action until fall, shortly before the election.

Following is a summary of the delays, which are explained in more detail in the following pages.

After a stormy two-day session, the Rules Committee in April agreed to send the ethics bills — except for the special prosecutor bill which was not yet reported — to the House floor. Rules also agreed to allow non-germane amendments to be offered, giving the House a chance to reconsider the outside earned income limit.

Faced with a complicated parliamentary situation and antagonism toward any new ethics reforms, House leaders pulled the disclosure bills from the floor calendar in late April.

Three months later, chairmen of the subcommittees that drafted different versions of executive branch disclosure requirements agreed to unite behind a substitute version.

On Aug. 1, the three chairmen were joined by Preyer in introducing a bill (HR 13676) that combined the ethics committee's bill on congressional disclosure requirements with the substitute on executive branch disclosure. The new bill also contained the judicial branch disclosure requirements from HR 1, as well as HR 1's version of an Office of Government Ethics.

The legislative branch disclosure requirements of HR 13676 differed in several respects from HR 11941. The new version exempted from disclosure some items required in the earlier bill, including alimony, child support and real property that was not held for investment or production of income.

Executive branch disclosure sections of HR 13676 did not contain the Post Office Committee bill's provisions of partial confidentiality for reports filed by career civil service employees or Armed Services' provision of confidentiality for the reports of career military officers.

However, on Aug. 3 the Rules Committee again balked as members rehashed old arguments raised against the bill.

But less than two weeks later, on Aug. 15, the committee voted to send HR 1 to the floor and provided parliamentary means to merge key parts of the other ethics measures.

A little more than a month later, on Sept. 27, the House passed HR 1 by a huge margin, 368-30, after soundly defeating an attempt to repeal the House outside earned income limit.

Details of House Action

First Rules Delay

After a stormy two-day session, the House Rules Committee April 12 agreed, 13-2, to send to the floor three bills (HR 1, HR 6954, HR 11941) requiring financial disclosure by government officials. But the panel also agreed, 9-6, to allow a non-germane amendment to be offered giving the House a chance to reconsider the outside earned income limit approved in 1977 as part of the House ethics code.

As a result of the latter vote, House leaders pulled the financial disclosure legislation from the calendar. It had been scheduled for floor action April 12.

Several Rules members who voted in favor of reconsidering the limit had outside income that could be curtailed if the rule took effect. They included James H. (Jimmy) Quillen, R-Tenn., who led the fight to allow the amendment; Shirley Chisholm, D-N.Y.; Morgan F. Murphy, D-Ill.; and Claude Pepper, D-Fla.

The ethics code approved in 1977 said that, beginning in 1979, members could not earn outside income totaling more than 15 percent of their public salaries. At the 1978 congressional pay level, the limit would be $8,625. The code did not limit unearned income, such as stock dividends. *(1977 Almanac p. 767)*

During the 1977 debate, the House overwhelmingly defeated a move to strike the income limit.

David R. Obey, D-Wis., a chief architect of the ethics code, fumed that Quillen's attempt to strike the limit "is a last gasp of a few guys who want to be able to unravel what we did last year." He added: "It's outrageous. It stinks. It smells. It's stupid."

The open rule granted by the committee would have sent HR 1, covering executive and judicial branch disclosure, to the floor as the original bill. HR 11941, covering members and candidates for Congress, would have been incorporated as a title of HR 1 and HR 6954, dealing only with executive branch disclosure, would have been offered as a substitute for sections of HR 1.

Rules Debate. Several Rules Committee members used the two-day debate as a forum to repeatedly denounce the income limit and the proposed codification of congressional financial disclosure requirements, which were also part of the 1977 ethics code. Among the most outspoken critics were Quillen, Murphy, B. F. Sisk, D-Calif., and Rules Chairman James J. Delaney, D-N.Y.

Opponents of the income limit and disclosure said the House had gone too far in trying to reform itself.

Delaney predicted that if the reporting requirement were enacted, "You're going to make every member of Congress resign." Delaney spoke at length about his own stock holdings, which he claimed would take so much time to report that complying with the law would amount to "a full-time job. I wouldn't be able to do anything else."

Other members painted images of congressmen being indicted by "runaway U.S. attorneys" for failure to report their financial assets exactly right. Murphy said a district attorney using his office as a political springboard could ruin an innocent congressman's career just by indicting him under the disclosure requirements. Although the pending bill would require proof that a congressman willfully and knowingly made a false statement on a financial disclosure statement, Murphy said, "It's not the trial we're concerned about. It's the indictment. It ruins you."

Murphy warned that, "We're just opening ourselves to pressures from an executive branch that disagrees with our political philosophies."

Preyer, testifying before the committee on HR 11941, countered that, "We're already in that situation." The ethics code required members to file a financial report under House rules. HR 11941 would make the rule federal law. But Preyer said even if it didn't pass members would be subject to felony charges under existing law if they filed a false report with the federal government.

Opponents of the income limit argued that unless it was repealed, only rich people or those afraid to try another job would continue to run for Congress. "This bill is a massive invasion of the privacy of people. Many people will think it's not worth it to continue to run for public office," predicted Chisholm.

Floor Action Postponed

At a meeting April 24, Democratic leaders and key committee members decided to pull the financial disclosure bill (HR 1) off the calendar for the second time. Floor debate had been scheduled to begin the next day.

The decision came after a series of leadership meetings with several groups of House Democrats. The leadership found plenty of rank-and-file resistance on specific issues, as well as on the general idea of passing a new ethics bill. A number of Democrats told their leaders the House had gone far enough in setting ethical standards, and one more bill amounted to overkill.

In addition, about 100 amendments had been introduced, thus assuring a complicated debate that could have stretched on for days.

House leaders also feared a lengthy battle over modification of a key part of the 1977 House ethics code that barred members — beginning in 1979 — from earning more than $8,625 in any year beyond their congressional salaries of $57,500.

The biggest change proposed in HR 1 would be detailed financial disclosure requirements for candidates for federal office and top executive and judicial branch officials. But virtually all objections raised by House members concerned financial disclosure for themselves, which was already mandated by the 1977 ethics code. The first reports required under that code were due April 30.

Preyer, chairman of the Select Ethics Committee, and other backers of the bill said Democratic whip counts showed the anti-reform backlash was not strong enough to defeat the bill. Preyer said some of the opposition developed as members began filling out their disclosure reports to meet the April 30 deadline. "I think that probably didn't improve the emotional atmosphere," he said.

But the procedural confusion and the threat to the outside earned income limit were considered major problems that the bill's backers hoped to alleviate before scheduling it for floor action again.

Whip counts on an amendment to kill the income limit showed the vote outcome was uncertain because many members said they were undecided on the issue. House leaders, who had labored hard for the earned income rule in 1977, did not want to take a chance on having it repealed.

Bill Agreement Reached

The chairmen of House subcommittees in mid-summer settled many of their differences on financial disclosure bills. It was thought this would clear the way for floor action by the middle of August, but new problems arose in the Rules Committee. As a result, a House vote was delayed until late September.

The bills already had been pulled from the House schedule in the spring when parliamentary problems and anti-reform backlash threatened the measures.

Among the problems prompting House leaders to withdraw the bills in April was the fact that HR 1, written by the House Judiciary Committee, differed from an executive branch disclosure bill (HR 6954) drafted by the Armed Services and Post Office and Civil Service Committees. Armed Services and Post Office had planned to oppose sections of HR 1 dealing with executive branch disclosure and to offer HR 6954 as a substitute. The disagreement among committees promised to cause parliamentary confusion and lengthy debate.

To reduce the confusion, floor managers of HR 1 and HR 6954 — George E. Danielson, D-Calif., of Judiciary, Patricia Schroeder, D-Colo., of Post Office, and Samuel S. Stratton, D-N.Y., of Armed Services — agreed in late July to seek a procedural compromise. As a result, they planned to offer a substitute for HR 1's executive branch disclosure provisions.

The substitute contained some compromises but did not resolve some disagreements among the committees. For instance, the substitute did not give disclosure reports filed by military officers any of the confidentiality that Armed Services had voted for in HR 6954.

However, those working on the executive branch disclosure substitute said it would greatly simplify floor consideration of the bills. Schroeder said it would eliminate a major fight among the committees involved, and it would reduce the time needed for general debate. "It won't be nearly as complex," she said.

Second Rules Delay

House leadership efforts to schedule floor action on financial disclosure legislation were thwarted by the House Rules Committee Aug. 3.

The chairmen of four panels that wrote legislation to require financial disclosure by top federal officials told Rules they had settled many of their differences that had led to postponement of floor action last spring.

But Rules, which never got around to hearing from two of the chairmen Aug. 3, instead rehashed old arguments raised against the bill (HR 13676) and postponed further consideration of it until Aug. 10. HR 13676 was a clean bill that combined financial disclosure provisions of various other bills.

Several Rules members were openly hostile to the bill and welcomed the comments of Charles E. Wiggins, R-Calif. Rules Chairman James J. Delaney, D-N.Y., allowed Wiggins to testify against the bill before giving two sponsors an opportunity to testify on its behalf.

Also discussed at length by Rules was the outside earned income limit that the House imposed on its members in an ethics code approved in 1977.

However, sponsors of the disclosure legislation expressed optimism that their bill would be approved by Rules. Bolstering their position was their request for a rule that would allow a floor vote on an amendment to delete the outside earned income limit.

The rule requested by the financial disclosure sponsors would not allow other non-germane amendments, as Rules had agreed to do last spring.

Backers of HR 13676 conceded that Rules members appeared very sympathetic toward Wiggins' arguments against the bill. Wiggins warned that the financial disclosure reports, which were already required under House and Senate rules, would be used by political opponents to damage the careers of members of Congress.

Rules Committee Approval

For the second time in 1978, the House Rules Committee voted to send to the floor a bill (HR 1) requiring detailed financial disclosure by top federal officials.

The committee also agreed Aug. 15 to let the House vote on repeal of the outside earned income limit it approved in the 1977 House ethics code.

The Rules Committee action provided a new plan for House debate, which simplified a messy parliamentary situation that had helped keep the bill from the floor for months. For instance, in April the Rules panel voted to allow an unrestricted number of amendments to the income limit during debate on HR 1. House leaders feared that would lead to a complicated and protracted fight.

Under the new rule approved by the committee, only one amendment on the income limit was allowed. That amendment, which would completely eliminate the outside income limit, had to be permitted specifically by the Rules Committee because it was not germane to the disclosure bill.

The Rules Committee's quick, quiet consideration of HR 1 on Aug. 15 was in sharp contrast to its lengthy, heated debate on the bill in the spring.

At the Aug. 3 meeting, HR 1 opponent Wiggins, warned that the bill's criminal penalties for false reporting could ruin the political careers of House members who made accidental errors.

Although the bill's backers protested that Wiggins' charges were unfounded, they finally agreed to drop all criminal penalties from the bill.

That change was reflected in a new bill (HR 13850) presented to the Rules Committee Aug. 15. The chief sponsors of HR 13850 — who also were the floor managers for HR 1 — were to offer the new bill as a substitute for HR 1 when it reached the floor. HR 13850 was based on an earlier compromise (HR 13676) reached by the four floor managers.

Despite concessions by backers of disclosure legislation, there was a final attempt to delay the bill in Rules Aug. 15. By a 5-5 vote, the committee defeated a motion by Morgan F. Murphy, D-Ill., to put off a final vote. Several members voted present.

Murphy said later he wanted more time to work out a compromise amendment on the income limit issue. Murphy's amendment would have raised the outside earned income ceiling to $15,000 a year, with additional increases allowed for inflation.

Murphy, a lawyer whose practice would be sharply curbed by the new income limit, had been a major opponent of the ceiling. He and James H. (Jimmy) Quillen, R-Tenn., who was sponsoring the amendment to strike the income limit, said there was growing sympathy in the House for a repeal of the earned income ceiling.

House Floor Action

After months of delay, the House passed a government ethics bill Sept. 27 requiring detailed public financial disclosure by top officials in all three branches of the federal government. The bill (HR 1) also would put new restrictions on post-government activity by federal employees, aimed at reducing conflicts of interest. In addition, it would set up a new Office of Government Ethics to police executive branch integrity.

Before approving the bill, 368-30, the House adopted an amendment easing the conflict-of-interest restrictions on some contacts between former employees and the agencies they worked for. *(Vote 746, p. 212-H)*

But most of the compromise version of HR 1 created by four House committees remained intact. After passing HR 1, the House inserted its text in a similar disclosure bill (S 555) passed by the Senate in 1977.

The House bill's provisions requiring executive branch disclosure and restricting contact by former employees were similar to proposals made by President Carter.

But both the Senate and House bills expanded on Carter's proposals by also requiring federal judges and members and top level employees of Congress to make public disclosure of their income, assets, liabilities, gifts and reimbursements. Provisions covering disclosure in Congress would codify the detailed disclosures required by ethics codes passed by the House and Senate in 1977.

During debate on HR 1 Sept. 20, an attempt to repeal a House rule limiting members' outside earned income was soundly defeated.

Although the House spent another full day debating the bill Sept. 27, most of the emotion was gone after the income limit issue was settled. The bill's managers defeated most of the two dozen amendments offered Sept. 27.

The major change adopted by the House came in the provisions designed to reduce use of the "revolving door" by officials who leave government posts to take jobs with organizations or companies their agencies regulated.

As passed, HR 1 would permanently prohibit former government officials from representing private interests on matters in which they were "personally and substantially" involved while in government service. It would prohibit them from involvement in matters that were under their formal responsibility for two years after leaving the government. And it would — with certain exceptions added on the House floor — prohibit top level officials who leave the government from contacting their former agencies for one year on any matter pending before the agency.

Outside Income Limit: Can It Be Evaded?

For the second time in the 95th Congress, the House in late 1978 voted on one of the most ticklish internal issues it had faced in recent years: limiting the outside income of members.

As in 1977, House members in 1978 voted overwhelmingly in favor of the income ceiling. In 1977, the vote was 79-344; in 1978 it was 97-290. *(1977 Almanac p. 767)*

The votes reflected in part the reluctance of many members to support a proposal that the public might interpret as strictly self-interest — particularly when representatives already were earning $57,500 a year.

Both the Senate and House limited the outside earned income of members, starting in 1979, to the equivalent of 15 percent of congressional salaries. At the existing level, that would be $8,625. The limits were part of the ethics codes of both chambers. The House votes came on efforts to remove the limits from the code.

Effectiveness Questioned

The one-sided House votes did not end debate over the effectiveness of the limit, however. Several House members with substantial outside earned income argued that they would get around the limit by incorporating their businesses and taking the income in dividends rather than salaries.

But the drafters of the ethics code, and staff members of the House Select Ethics Committee, argued that members will not be able to avoid the limit.

Ethics Committee member Rep. Lee H. Hamilton, D-Ind., who helped draft the ethics code, said the limit "will be difficult to get around" because the rule is "clear-cut." But Hamilton refused to rule out the possibility that some members will be able to avoid the limit.

Disputes over whether income is earned or unearned will be settled "on a factual basis" by the Committee on Standards of Official Conduct, Hamilton said.

Ethics Code Definition

The ethics code defines outside earned income as "wages, salaries, professional fees, honorariums and other amounts (other than copyright royalties) received or to be received as compensation for personal services actually rendered."

In other words, income that is earned as a result of performing a service is subject to the limit.

But there is a major exception: "In the case of a member engaged in a trade or business in which the member or his family holds a controlling interest and in which both personal services and capital are income-producing factors, any amount received by such members [is exempt from the limit] so long as the personal services actually rendered by the member in the trade or business do not generate a significant amount of income."

That section was inserted to protect members from having to give up family farms and other small businesses. Opponents have questioned the phrase "significant amount of income," saying it is vague and subject to varying interpretations.

Two Views of Issue

At least three members said they planned to use that exemption in order to get around the income limit:

- Rep. Claude Pepper, D-Fla., an attorney who reported $26,285 in legal fees during the fourth quarter of 1977, said he would incorporate his law firm and start drawing dividends.
- Rep. Gene Snyder, R-Ky., said he planned to incorporate his real estate and law firms. He reported earning $58,431 from his real estate business and $4,362 in legal fees in 1977.
- Rep. Bud Shuster, R-Pa. said his income was already protected under his tire store-real estate business of BTI Investments Inc. He reported fourth quarter 1977 income of $42,406 from that firm.

"As a general rule, a person who owns a business can take his income in dividends," Shuster said. "This limit doesn't apply to anybody like me who owns a small, family-type business." Shuster said he was a minority stockholder, but held no position in his business. "I don't spend much time at all" on the business, he said.

But Rep. Hamilton and other supporters of the ethics code argued that members would not be able to get around the income limit just by changing the name of a company or by calling their income dividends rather than salaries.

"The source of income, I don't think, is the pertinent point," Hamilton said. "The question is whether personal services were rendered" to the company by the member.

The only income that is exempt from the limit, Hamilton and others said, is "return on equity" such as profits, dividends, rent or royalties.

They contended the income is earned if the member renders any services on behalf of the firm, such as meeting with law clients or showing property to a prospective purchaser of real estate.

Hamilton conceded that "it is possible for a member to have return on equity" from a law firm, and thus escape the limit. "But this applies to a very few members, because most members who are lawyers . . . it is clear that they are giving services" to the law firm.

If the character of a member's income is in doubt, Hamilton said, "we're going to have to get the facts. There will have to be a factual determination made by the ethics committee."

Obey Commission Opinion

The Commission on Administrative Review (the Obey Commission) which drafted the ethics code, foresaw the possibility that some members would try to evade the income limit.

In its report (H Rept 95-73) to the House in February 1977, the commission warned that "care should be taken to prevent members from circumventing [the limit] by incorporating themselves into a family business and then withdrawing what in reality are fees for personal services in the form of dividends or profits."

But the commission did not specifically recommend what should be done to prevent such a practice.

Income Limit Retained

An attempt to repeal the limit on members' outside earned income was resoundingly rejected by the House Sept. 20.

By a three-to-one margin, the House voted to keep intact its Rule 47 restricting the outside earnings of members to no more than 15 percent of their congressional salaries. The rule becomes effective in 1979.

The emotional, lengthy debate on the income limit was dominated by opponents of the ceiling. "They feel very deeply," acknowledged ethics bill sponsor George E. Danielson, D-Calif., who had to postpone the financial disclosure legislation partly because debate on the income limit stretched late into the evening.

But despite their emotional appeals to the House, opponents of the income limit fared little better than they had in a 1977 vote on the same issue. The Sept. 20 vote was 97-290 to kill a repeal amendment; a similar amendment was defeated in 1977, 79-344. *(Vote 714, p. 202-H)*

The limit was approved overwhelmingly in 1977 in the House's new ethics code. It was considered a *quid pro quo* for House acceptance of a 1977 salary increase boosting members' pay to $57,500 a year, a 29 percent increase. House leaders fought hard for the limit.

James H. (Jimmy) Quillen, R-Tenn., sponsor of the repeal amendment, and others who supported repeal said there was growing resentment against the income limit in the House.

However, the lopsided margin against Quillen's amendment showed there had not been substantial change since the 1977 vote.

Quillen's amendment did draw the support of 37 members who had voted in favor of the income limit in 1977. Among them were six members who were to leave Congress at the end of 1978.

But another 13 members who had opposed the limit in 1977 voted to keep it in 1978. In addition, nine opponents of the income limit in 1977 did not vote on the Quillen amendment.

Quillen supporters said they were hurt by the vote's proximity to the November elections. Some claimed members had told them privately they did not like the income limit but could not vote against it just before the election.

During debate, Quillen called the income limit "irrational" because it restricted what members could earn from personal services but did not put a lid on their unearned income such as stock dividends or rent. The rule implied that earned income "is tainted but the other is pure," said Quillen.

Several opponents argued that the income limit would discourage many people from running for Congress.

"We are going to be left with the very wealthy," said Henry J. Hyde, R-Ill. "Or we are going to be left with social activists who leap from college, from working with Ralph Nader, and then into Congress."

But David R. Obey, D-Wis., chief architect of the 1977 ethics code, said the income limit would not change the nature of Congress because relatively few of the current members actually would be affected by the income limit. "Ninety percent of the members of this House have already severed their past relationships with their previous businesses," he said.

Obey added that the income limit was necessary to show the public that members gave their congressional jobs "undivided attention."

Ronald V. Dellums, D-Calif., whose income from honoraria would probably be curtailed by the income limit, made a highly personal appeal that won applause from conservative Republicans who rarely agreed with his liberal views.

"Some of the old codgers here that have put their children through college and paid off the mortgage, you do not care," said Dellums. Instead of restricting the income of members who still had families to raise, "Why not specifically deal with how members of Congress are bought, and deal with that question," he said.

Income limit supporter Newton I. Steers Jr., R-Md., said that even with the ceiling members could have an income of $66,000 a year — including their congressional salary. "Maybe our constituents are entitled to somebody who can more closely approximate their needs and not somebody who is able to earn vast sums which put us out of touch with reality," said Steers.

Other Action Sept. 20. Other amendments considered before the House postponed HR 1 included:

Candidate Disclosure. A proposal by Charles E. Wiggins, R-Calif., to exempt congressional candidates from the financial disclosure requirements. Rejected, 34-365. *(Vote 712, p. 202-H)*

Amount, Source Disclosure. An amendment by Gary Myers, R-Pa., to require candidates for federal office to disclose only the source — not the amount — of their income. Rejected, 39-353. *(Vote 713, p. 202-H)*

Conflicts of Interest. An amendment by Carlos J. Moorhead, R-Calif., to strike provisions from the bill that would prohibit former government employees from having any business contacts with their former agencies for one year after leaving the agency. Rejected, 112-259. *(Vote 715, 202-H)*

Other Action Sept. 27. Among amendments considered Sept. 27 were:

- A proposal by Bill Frenzel, R-Minn., to restrict the outside earned income of about 750 executive branch presidential appointees. Those employees could not earn outside income totaling more than 15 percent of their government salaries. Frenzel's amendment, adopted by voice vote, was a substitute for an amendment by John M. Ashbrook, R-Ohio, that would have applied the income limit to about 14,000 employees.
- A proposal by Patricia Schroeder, D-Colo., to create a corps of 75 ethics counselors in the Office of Government Ethics. In its version of disclosure legislation, the House Post Office and Civil Service Committee had included the ethics counselors to supervise reporting by civilian employees. The compromise considered by the House gave the supervising job to employees within each executive branch agency, although the Office of Government Ethics would have authority to monitor and investigate compliance. Schroeder's amendment was defeated, 4-22.
- A proposal by Henry J. Hyde, R-Ill., to set up a mechanism for appointment of a temporary special prosecutor to investigate certain allegations of wrongdoing by top government officials. Hyde's amendment was similar to a bill (HR 9705) reported by the House Judiciary Committee in June. However, Hyde's amendment would have applied the special prosecutor mechanism to members of Congress, who were not included in the committee bill. The amendment was ruled out of order.

Provisions

As passed by the House, HR 1:

Title I — Legislative Branch Disclosure

• Required all members and congressional officers, their principal assistants, all congressional employees paid at the GS-16 salary level or higher, and any candidate for congressional office to file annual public financial disclosure reports.

• Required all reports, except those from congressional candidates, to be filed by May 15 each year with the clerk of the House or the secretary of the Senate.

• Provided that candidates for congressional office and others required to file reports did not have to disclose gifts and reimbursements received when they were not subject to the disclosure requirements.

• Required candidates for congressional office to file reports by Nov. 1, 1978, or within 15 days after becoming a candidate, whichever occurred later.

• Required all persons covered by the disclosure law to report the source, type and amount of income from any source (other than their U.S. government salaries) received during the preceding calendar year and aggregating $100 or more in value.

• Required disclosure of the source and a brief description of any gifts of transportation, lodging, food or entertainment aggregating $250 or more in value received from any source other than a relative during the preceding calendar year.

• Exempted gifts of food, lodging or entertainment received as personal hospitality from the reporting requirements.

• Required disclosure of the source, a brief description and estimated value of all gifts (other than transportation, lodging, food or entertainment) aggregating $100 or more in value received from a source other than a relative during the preceding calendar year.

• Exempted gifts with a fair market value of $35 or less.

• Required disclosure of the source and a brief description of reimbursements from a single source aggregating $250 or more in the preceding calendar year.

• Required disclosure of the identity and category of value of any interest in property held in a trade or business, or for investment or production of income, with a fair market value over $1,000 at the close of the preceding calendar year.

• Excluded from disclosure personal liabilities owed to relatives or any deposit of $5,000 or less in a personal savings account.

• Required disclosure of the identity and category of value of the total liabilities owed to any creditor (other than a relative) exceeding $5,000 at the close of the preceding calendar year. This did not include a mortgage on the individual's personal residence or loans for cars, household furniture or applicances.

• Required a brief description, the date and category of value of real property (other than personal residence) or stocks, bonds or other securities purchased, sold or exchanged in the preceding calendar year if the amount involved exceeded $1,000.

• Exempted from reporting requirements any transaction solely between the reporting individual and his or her spouse or dependent children.

• Required reporting terms of agreement about any future employment planned by the reporting individual.

• Provided that in reporting property holdings, liabilities and purchase, sale or exchange of real property or securities, individuals should list each item in one of the following categories: Not more than $5,000, greater than $5,000 but not more than $15,000, greater than $15,000 but not more than $50,000, greater than $50,000 but not more than $100,000, or greater than $100,000.

• Exempted campaign receipts or expenditures from the disclosure requirements.

• Required reporting individuals to list the following information about a spouse's finances: source of any earned income over $1,000, source and brief description or estimated value of any gift or reimbursement which is not received totally independent of the spouse's relationship to the reporting individual and certain assets, liabilities and transactions of the spouse (unless the reporting individual certified that he or she had no control over them and would not receive any economic benefit from those interests).

• Required reporting individuals to list assets, liabilities and transactions of dependent children unless the individual certified that he or she had no control over them and did not receive any economic benefit from them.

• Required that an individual with holdings in a blind trust must disclose the total holdings and income from the trust.

• Required the clerk of the House and secretary of the Senate to make reports available to the public within 15 days after they are filed.

• Provided that reports be available to the public for five years, after which they shall be destroyed.

• Barred use of the reports for any unlawful purpose, or commercial use (other than in news reporting).

• Barred use of the reports for determining an individual's credit rating or for soliciting money.

• Provided civil penalties of up to $5,000 for persons who make illegal use of the reported information.

• Provided that the House Standards of Official Conduct Committee and the Senate Select Committee on Ethics should review all reports to see if they were properly and completely filed.

• Required the committees to notify any reporting individual who did not file an accurate report and give the individual an opportunity to correct it.

• Provided that an individual who complied with recommendations of the committees shall not be subject to any sanctions provided in the bill.

• Provided for civil penalties of up to $5,000 against any person who knowingly and willfully filed a false report or failed to file a report.

Title II — Executive Branch Disclosure

Part A — Filing Requirements

• Required the president, vice president, candidates for those offices, executive branch employees paid at level GS-16 or above, military officers paid at grade O-7 or above and certain other executive branch employees to file annual public financial disclosure reports.

• Required persons nominated by the president to posts requiring Senate approval to file financial disclosure reports when their nominations were sent to the Senate.

• Required all executive branch employees covered by the disclosure law to report the source, type and amount of income from any source (other than their U.S. government salaries) received during the preceding calendar year and aggregating $100 or more in value.

- Required disclosure of the source and a brief description of any gifts of transportation, lodging, food or entertainment aggregating $250 or more in value received from any source other than a relative during the preceding calendar year.
- Exempted gifts of food, lodging or entertainment received as personal hospitality from the reporting requirements.
- Required disclosure of the source, a brief description and estimated value of all gifts (other than transportation, lodging, food or entertainment) aggregating $100 or more in value received from a source other than a relative during the preceding calendar year.
- Exempted gifts with a fair market value of $35 or less.
- Required disclosure of the source and a brief description of reimbursements from any source aggregating $250 or more in the preceding calendar year.
- Required disclosure of the identity and category of value of any interest in property held in a trade or business, or for investment or production of income, with a fair market value over $1,000 at the close of the preceding calendar year.
- Required disclosure of the identity and category of value of the total liabilities owed to any creditor (other than a relative) exceeding $5,000 at the close of the preceding calendar year.
- Excluded from disclosure mortgages on a personal residence or loans for cars, furniture or appliances.
- Required a brief description, the date and category of value of real property (other than personal residence) or stocks, bonds or other securities purchased, sold or exchanged in the preceding calendar year if the amount involved exceeded $1,000.
- Exempted from reporting requirements any transaction solely between the reporting individual and his or her spouse or dependent children.
- Required disclosure of any positions held with businesses, nonprofit organizations, labor organizations or other institutions except religious, social, fraternal, charitable or political groups.
- Required reporting of the terms of agreement about any future employment planned by the reporting individuals.
- Provided that in reporting property holdings, liabilities and purchase, sale or exchange of real property or securities, individuals should list each item in one of the following categories: up to $5,000, from $5,000 to $15,000, from $15,000 to $50,000, from $50,000 to $100,000 or greater than $100,000.
- Required reporting individuals to list the following information about a spouse's finances: source of any earned income over $1,000, source and brief description or estimated value of any gift or reimbursement which is not received totally independent of the spouse's relationship to the reporting individual and certain assets, liabilities and transactions of the spouse (unless the reporting individual certified that he or she had no control over them and would not receive any economic benefit from those interests).
- Required reporting individuals to list assets, liabilities and transactions of dependent children unless the individual certified that he or she had no control over them and did not receive any economic benefit from them.
- Required disclosure of certain information about blind trusts.
- Exempted campaign receipts or expenditures from the disclosure requirements.
- Required the president and vice president to file reports with the Office of Government Ethics, candidates to file with the Federal Elections Commission and other employees to file with their agencies.
- Required military officers to file with the secretary of their branch of service.
- Provided civil penalties of up to $5,000 for anyone who knowingly and willfully falsified a report or failed to file a report.
- Required each agency and others authorized to make them available to the public for five years.
- Authorized the president to exempt the reports of undercover intelligence agents from public disclosure.
- Authorized the president to allow intelligence agents to file false disclosure reports to cover their indentities.
- Barred use of the reports for any unlawful purpose, for any commercial use (other than in news reporting), for determining a person's credit rating or for soliciting money.
- Provided civil penalties of up to $5,000 for unlawful use of the reports.
- Required agencies that received reports to review them within 60 days and to give reporting individuals an opportunity to correct any errors.
- Authorized the president to require any executive branch employees not covered by the bill to file confidential financial disclosure reports.
- Required filing of the first executive branch disclosure reports May 15, 1979, to cover the preceding calendar year.

Part B — Office of Government Ethics

- Established an Office of Government Ethics in the Civil Service Commission, to be headed by a presidentially appointed director subject to Senate approval.
- Authorized the office to monitor and investigate executive branch compliance with the financial disclosure requirements, to order corrective action by employees or agencies, and to oversee federal conflict of interest laws.

Part C — Conflict of Interest

- Barred former executive branch, independent agency or District of Columbia employees from representing anyone before their former agencies in connection with any proceeding, investigation or other matter that the former employees personally and substantially participated in while working for the government. Maximum penalties for violation of this ban were $5,000 and one year in prison.
- Barred former government employees from appearing before a federal agency for two years on matters that were under their official responsibility before leaving the government.
- Barred former officials above GS-16 and top-ranking military officers from representing anyone formally or informally on any matter pending before their former agency for one year after leaving government.
- Set maximum penalties for violation of the one- and two-year bans at $10,000 and two years in prison.
- Exempted from the one-year ban former government employees who were licensed or certified by a professional organization that met certain conditions.
- Provided that former employees could provide scientific or technological information to the federal government, notwithstanding the prohibitions on contact, under certain conditions.
- Exempted from the conflict of interest provisions persons who left government prior to July 1, 1979.

- Limited the outside earned income of non-judicial, full-time presidential appointees to no more than 15 percent of their government salaries.

Title III — Judicial Branch Disclosure

- Required federal judges and their employees who are paid the equivalent of a GS-16 salary or above to file annual financial disclosure reports.
- Required presidential nominees for judgeships to file disclosure reports when their nominations were sent to the Senate.
- Required judicial branch officials to disclose the same information required in the executive branch disclosure provisions.
- Required judicial branch employees to file the annual reports with a Judicial Ethics Committee to be established by the Judicial Conference of the United States.
- Authorized the committee to monitor and investigate compliance with the disclosure requirements.
- Provided civil penalties of up to $5,000 for knowingly and willfully filing a false report or failing to file a report.
- Required the committee to make the disclosure reports available to the public for five years.
- Prohibited use of the reports for any unlawful purpose or any commercial use other than news reporting.
- Prohibited use of the reports for establishing a person's credit rating or soliciting money.
- Provided civil penalties of up to $5,000 for unlawful use of the reports.
- Authorized the committee to require confidential disclosure reports from judicial branch employees not covered by the bill.
- Required the first judicial branch reports to be filed May 15, 1979, covering the previous calendar year.

Conference Action

Conferees on the bill reached agreement quickly.

In major decisions, conferees approved a mechanism for choosing a temporary special prosecutor to investigate alleged criminal wrongdoing by the president and other top executive branch officials. The special prosecutor provisions, contained in the Senate version of S 555, were not in the House bill.

Separate special prosecutor legislation (HR 9705) was reported from the House Judiciary Committee in June. But because some members planned floor amendments to expand that bill to cover investigations of Congress, HR 9705 was considered dead.

The conferees dropped provisions to set up a permanent Office of Government Crimes, which had been in the Senate bill. A congressional legal counsel, also called for in the Senate bill, was dropped. However, the conferees agreed to allow the Senate to hire its own legal counsel to defend the Senate in litigation.

A House provision making some exceptions to the bill's revolving door restrictions was dropped by the conferees. However, the bill's one-year restriction on contact between top-level officials who leave government and their former agencies was narrowed to include only high officials who had significant decision-making or supervisory authority.

Final Action. The conference report was adopted by the Senate by voice vote Oct. 7 and by the House Oct. 12, 370-23. *(Vote 794, p. 226-H)*

Sunset Legislation

"Sunset" legislation that would require automatic termination of funds for most federal spending programs if they were not specifically reauthorized after a comprehensive review every 18 years passed the Senate 87-1, Oct. 11. *(Vote 475, p. 69-S)*

But despite the widespread popularity of the sunset review concept, similar bills in the House never emerged from committee. Only an extraordinary parliamentary coup could have gotten the Senate bill (S 2) through the House in the closing hours of the 95th Congress, and chief sponsor Edmund S. Muskie, D-Maine, acknowledged the changes for such a coup were almost nil.

However, for Muskie, just getting a Senate floor vote in the 95th Congress had become a matter of principle.

Before the Oct. 11 vote Muskie had predicted that his latest of several versions of S 2, cosponsored by a majority of the Senate, would pass easily — if he could just bring it up for a vote.

But for three years, he said, various versions of the bill had been delayed by "one damn thing after another."

Background

The sunset concept, popular with many younger members of Congress and supported by President Carter, drew its most significant opposition from some committee chairmen who felt it would erode their authority, give them a heavy new workload and perhaps cause inadvertent termination of some worthwhile programs.

When Muskie — who chaired the Senate Budget Committee — tried to get a sunset bill to the Senate floor in the 94th Congress, he met strong opposition from the Rules and Finance Committees. The bill was withdrawn from the Senate schedule late in the second session. *(1976 Almanac p. 505)*

Muskie attracted 59 cosponsors — about half Democratic, half Republican — when he reintroduced the idea as S 2 in 1977. The Governmental Affairs Committee approved the bill in June, 1977, after exempting tax expenditures — such as tax credits or deductions — from the sunset review process.

S 2 then went to the Rules Committee, where it was bogged down for nearly a year.

Although he had cosponsored Muskie's original bill, former Rules Committee Chairman Howard W. Cannon, D-Nev., made no secret of his dislike for S 2's automatic termination provision.

Muskie tried, but failed, to get Cannon to set a deadline for Rules action on the bill. Instead, Cannon held one day of hearings in September 1977 on S 2 and a proposal (S 1244) from Joe Biden, D-Del. Then he handed the sunset issue to a group of Senate staffers for a study. The staff group included representatives of Muskie, Biden and Senate committees.

1978 Compromise

That group did not report back to Rules until April 19, 1978, when it recommended a plan requiring increased congressional oversight — minus the key sunset termination provision.

By that time, Cannon had moved on to the chairmanship of the Senate Commerce Committee and Rules was taken over by another S 2 cosponsor, Claiborne Pell, D-R.I.

At an April hearing, Pell asked for another review of sunset proposals. This time, the General Accounting Office (GAO) got the study assignment. GAO came up with its own recommendations for a sunset bill, which were presented to Rules June 8.

Rather than choosing one of the alternatives given to the committee, Pell asked GAO to meet with representatives of Muskie and Biden to try to work out a compromise. Left out of the compromise negotiations was the staff group Cannon had assigned to study sunset.

The negotiating group quickly came up with a compromise, which the Rules Committee marked up June 21.

Automatic Termination Dispute

The compromise retained the termination provision, requiring most federal programs to face extinction unless they were reauthorized every 10 years.

At the markup session, Cannon complained that the staff group he had assigned to study sunset had been left out of the final negotiations.

He blasted the bill as a "weekend compromise" and warned that automatic termination was "going to be a very dangerous proposition." With the threat of termination, "no program could have any hope of continuity," Cannon said.

Pell, who avoided a verbal match with Cannon, read a letter of support for S 2 written by President Carter. Pell said the compromise maintained the "general thrust" of Muskie's original S 2 and marked "one last try" to get a sunset bill through the committee.

Cannon offered the staff draft as a substitute for the compromise version of S 2, but it was defeated, 5-2. Harrison A. Williams, D-N.J., who chaired the Senate Human Resources Committee, joined Cannon in supporting the oversight proposal without automatic termination.

The committee then voted 6-1 for the compromise version of Muskie's bill, with only Cannon dissenting.

A Muskie aide said the Rules Committee version of S 2 still contained "the guts of the bill" because it retained automatic termination and set in law the schedule for review and reauthorization of federal programs.

The aide said the Rules bill was likely to be the language considered on the floor if S 2 were scheduled this year. And he predicted the Rules bill would draw the support of Governmental Affairs Committee members, who approved a different version in 1977.

Reauthorization Cycle Length

A major difference in the two versions of S 2 was in the length set for the reauthorization cycle. Governmental Affairs would have required most federal programs to come up for review, and possible termination, every six years. Rules required review and reauthorization every 10 years. Rules also expanded the number of programs, such as civil rights, that would be protected from the automatic termination provision. Those programs still would be subject to the bill's comprehensive review procedures.

The Rules Committee version included review of regulatory agencies, which had been omitted by the Governmental Affairs Committee. Governmental Affairs assumed that regulatory agency review would be dealt with in a separate bill (S 600). But S 600 did not move out of subcommittee in 1978.

Senate Rules Committee Action

The Senate Rules and Administration Committee reported S 2 (S Rept 95-981) July 13.

Citing California's recent vote in favor of cutting property taxes, the report said, "It is clear that taxpayers expect more rigorous, critical, and systematic evaluation of government spending programs." Current review of federal programs by congressional committees "is neither systematic, comprehensive, nor uniform," the committee said.

The key to forcing systematic, comprehensive review, the report argued, was the sunset bill's "requirement that government programs expire unless periodically reauthorized by the legislature."

Additional Views

Cannon filed additional views objecting to the bill's provision for automatic termination of programs that were not specifically renewed by Congress. "I fear that 'automatic termination' could mean 'inadvertent termination,' " Cannon wrote.

In his additional views, Williams urged the Senate to try the sunset system as a two-year experiment. He said the demands on congressional committees that would be created by sunset review could cause a "catastrophic" backlog of legislation.

Republicans Mark O. Hatfield, Ore., and Robert P. Griffin, Mich., joined Dick Clark, D-Iowa, in objecting to the bill's exemption of tax expenditures from the sunset review process. The trio called tax expenditures — which include tax credits, deductions, deferrals and exemptions — "the functional equivalent of direct spending programs."

Major Provisions

As reported by the Senate Rules and Administration Committee, S 2:

- Established a 10-year reauthorization cycle for most federal programs with reauthorization deadline dates for general areas (such as social services, energy supply or defense related activities) set in the bill. (Tax expenditures were not included.)
- Required termination of funding for any program subject to sunset review that was not specifically reauthorized before its expiration date.
- Limited the authorization of any program to no more than 10 years.
- Exempted from the funding termination requirement retirement and disability programs, Medicare, civil rights programs, some veterans programs, and interest on the national debt.
- Prohibited Congress from considering a bill to reauthorize a program during a year when the program was scheduled for sunset review until the authorizing committee had completed its report on the review and evaluation.
- Required the General Accounting Office (GAO) and the Congressional Budget Office to prepare an inventory of federal programs, subject to congressional review.
- Required GAO to issue a revised inventory after consultation with Congress, and to revise the inventory after each session of Congress.
- Provided that related programs dealing with a certain area of legislative policy should be considered and reauthorized in broad program categories.
- Required that sunset reviews of programs at a minimum must set objectives for programs and assess whether

they have been met, identify programs with conflicting or overlapping objectives, assess alternatives to the programs and study their regulatory, privacy and paperwork impacts.

- Required committees conducting sunset review and evaluation to report on their review and recommendations to the House or Senate no later than May 15 of the year in which the program was scheduled for review.
- Established an 18-member, independent Citizens' Commission on the Organization and Operation of Government to conduct a nonpartisan study of the organization and operation of all executive branch offices.
- Required the commission to report its findings and recommendations by July 1, 1983.

Senate Floor Action

Once the bill left Rules in July, Muskie began working on the Senate leadership to schedule it. But Majority Leader Robert C. Byrd, D-W.Va., Majority Whip Alan Cranston, D-Calif., and other influential senators wanted Muskie to make some changes. The leaders were concerned that procedures established by the committee bill would make some federal spending programs highly vulnerable to presidential vetoes or filibusters.

To calm those fears — and get his bill scheduled — Muskie devised a procedural safety valve that would allow Congress to vote for continued funding of a program one year past its sunset date if the program's reauthorization bill ran up against a veto or a filibuster.

With the safety valve in place, Byrd and Cranston signed on as cosponsors of the new S 2 introduced by Muskie Sept. 26.

But the delay caused by having to compromise with the leadership put Muskie in the same position he was in two years earlier. Competition to bring bills to the floor in the last two weeks of the session was fierce, and sunset was hardly a priority since the House had never acted on it.

So Muskie presented the compromise as an amendment, hoping to attach it to a bill — such as the tax cut measure — that was certain to be enacted before adjournment.

Muskie's first choice of a vehicle for sunset was the Export-Import Bank authorization bill (S 3077), which several other senators had already spotted as a potential "Christmas tree" to carry unrelated bills that would not be brought up on their own. But S 3077 was pulled off the Senate floor when it was loaded down with one too many ornaments. *(Ex-Im Bank authorization, p. 397)*

Muskie and others then turned to the tax bill. Once the sunset amendment was introduced, however, John Glenn, D-Ohio, introduced an amendment that would have added tax expenditures to the sunset process.

Muskie supported the amendment, even though it torpedoed his chances of attaching sunset as a rider to unrelated bills moving through the 95th Congress in its closing days.

The Glenn amendment was opposed by Finance Committee Chairman Russell B. Long, D-La., who thwarted Muskie's attempt to add sunset to the tax cut bill (HR 13511) by filibustering against Glenn's proposal.

Foiled in the attempt to get a vote on sunset as a "rider" amendment, Muskie renewed his push to bring the bill up by itself in the last four days before the Oct. 14 adjournment target. On Oct. 11, Muskie found his opportunity.

The Senate, waiting for an ad hoc committee to reach a compromise so it could consider the Humphrey-Hawkins bill (HR 50), found itself with little to do in the afternoon. Glenn agreed to drop his tax amendment, clearing away the final roadblock so Muskie could bring up sunset for a symbolic vote. The bill passed, 87-1. ▮

Ethics and Crimes

Congress' image with the public suffered further during the 95th Congress as a number of present and former members were officially accused of criminal or unethical behavior.

One House member — Rep. Charles C. Diggs, D-Mich. — was convicted on felony charges involving illegal diversion of employees' salaries to his personal use. Two others — Reps. Joshua Eilberg, D-Pa., and Daniel J. Flood, D-Pa. — were awaiting trial on separate felony indictments as the year ended. Eilberg also was charged with improper conduct by a House ethics committee, but these proceedings ended when he was defeated for re-election.

In addition, three representatives were accused of unethical conduct following an investigation of alleged South Korean influence-peddling in Congress. All were reprimanded by the House. The three were Reps. John J. McFall, Edward R. Roybal and Charles H. Wilson, all Democrats of California. In the Senate, a similar investigation produced evidence that one senator — Birch Bayh, D-Ind. — may have been touched by the Korean scandal. *(Story, p. 803)*

Also in the Senate, two members — Edward W. Brooke, R-Mass., and Herman E. Talmadge, D-Ga. — were under investigation for conduct allegedly in violation of Senate rules.

Of these sitting members of Congress facing the most serious charges, two were defeated for re-election: Eilberg and Brooke. Others were returned to office, some — such as Diggs — by lopsided margins. (A few other members had less serious conflicts with the law. *Box, next page)*

Rep. Charles C. Diggs Jr.

Rep. Charles C. Diggs Jr., D-Mich., was sentenced Nov. 20 to a maximum of three years in prison for illegally diverting more than $60,000 of his congressional employees' salaries to his personal use. Diggs was convicted on Oct. 7. He won re-election to a 13th term in the House Nov. 7.

Diggs was indicted March 23 on 35 charges of mail fraud (the mails allegedly were used in the salary kickback scheme) and making false statements to the government.

Specifically, Diggs was accused of taking kickbacks from three of his congressional employees and putting three other persons on his congressional payroll who did no work for Congress. The three congressional staffers allegedly were given raises by Diggs with the stipulation that they use the extra money to help pay the congressman's debts.

The three persons who allegedly drew federal pay for no work were employees of Diggs' funeral home business in Detroit. The indictment alleged that Diggs used federal money to pay them for working in his private business.

Diggs was traveling in Africa when the indictment was announced. His office released a statement saying he was innocent and criticizing the timing of the indictment, which came just days before Diggs was to meet President Carter in Nigeria.

House Members Jailed or Charged

The conviction of Rep. Charles C. Diggs Jr., D-Mich., on felony charges was the most serious action against a member of Congress in 1977-78 but it was only one of a number of criminal or ethical problems faced by representatives and senators.

In addition, a number of former members had their troubles with the law during the period.

Following is a list of present or former members who faced criminal charges or were in prison during the period of the 95th Congress.

Former Rep. Hugh J. Addonizio, D-N.J. (1949-62), served five years in federal prison for conspiring to extort $235,000 from contractors doing business with the city of Newark, N.J., while he was mayor. He was released from prison on a court order in April 1977.

Rep. J. Herbert Burke, R-Fla., was indicted in July 1978 on charges stemming from an incident at a nude go-go bar in Dania, Fla. He was charged with intoxication, resisting arrest without violence and trying to influence a witness to lie about the incident. He pleaded guilty and was fined $150. Burke was defeated for re-election in November.

Former Rep. Frank Clark, D-Pa. (1955-74), was charged in Pittsburgh in September with 13 counts of mail fraud, perjury and income tax evasion.

Rep. Charles C. Diggs Jr., D-Mich., was convicted Oct. 7 of illegally diverting more than $60,000 of his congressional employees' salaries to his personal use. He was sentenced Nov. 20 to three years in prison, but he said he would appeal the conviction. He was re-elected to his 13th term in November with 80 percent of the vote.

Rep. Joshua Eilberg, D-Pa., was indicted Oct. 24 by a federal grand jury for illegally receiving compensation after helping a Philadelphia hospital to get a $14.5 million federal grant. Eilberg was defeated for re-election in November.

Rep. Daniel J. Flood, D-Pa., was indicted on 13 criminal charges of lying about payoffs allegedly made to him and a former aide, of bribery and of conspiracy. The charges all grew out of claims that Flood improperly used his influence as a member of Congress to benefit private interests, in return for bribes. He was scheduled for trial in January 1979.

Former Rep. Edward A. Garmatz, D-Md. (1947-73), escaped bribery conspiracy charges in January when the Justice Department acknowledged that a key witness had lied to a grand jury and forged documents. Garmatz was indicted in September 1977 on charges of accepting up to $15,000 from shipping companies in return for help on legislation that benefited them. Charges were dropped. *(1977 Almanac p. 63-A)*

Former Rep. Richard T. Hanna, D-Calif. (1963-74), was serving a 2-year term at a federal prison camp. He pleaded guilty in March 1978 to conspiracy to defraud the government in connection with dealings with South Korean businessman Tongsun Park. Hanna entered prison May 8.

Former Rep. James F. Hastings, R-N.Y. (1969-76), was paroled from federal prison in Florida June 5, 1978, after serving 14 months of a 20-month to five-year term. He was convicted in December 1976 on 28 felony counts of taking payroll kickbacks from congressional employees. *(1977 Almanac p. 64-A)*

Former Rep. Henry Helstoski, D-N.J. (1965-77), still faced federal bribery charge as the year ended. He was indicted in 1976 of accepting cash bribes to introduce bills to allow illegal aliens to remain in the United States. But a decision on the charges was put off when Helstoski challenged the indictment as unconstitutional under the Speech or Debate Clause which provides that "for any Speech or Debate in either House" a member "shall not be questioned in any other Place." An appeals court upheld the indictment, reasoning that the truth or falsity of the bribery charges could be proved without reference to legislative acts. But the court also held that the clause did prevent the prosecution from introducing into evidence private bills sponsored by Helstoski and correspondence and conversations about them. The Supreme Court in late 1978 agreed to review that ruling.

Former Rep. Andrew J. Hinshaw, R-Calif. (1973-77), was released in June 1978 from a California prison after serving seven months of a one-to-14 year term. He was convicted in December 1976 of soliciting and accepting bribes while he was Orange County tax assessor. *(1977 Almanac p. 64-A)*

Former Rep. Otto E. Passman, D-La. (1947-77), pleaded not guilty in June 1978 to charges of accepting $213,000 in illegal payments from South Korean businessman Tongsun Park. Passman also had been charged with failing to report $143,000 on his income taxes and of evading taxes of $77,000.

Rep. Frederick Richmond, R-N.Y., pleaded innocent to a charge that he solicited sex for pay. Richmond earlier had acknowledged the morals charge was true. His innocent plea was a technicality designed to make him eligible for a District of Columbia first offender program. Charges against Richmond were dropped May 3 after he completed the program.

Former Rep. Richard A. Tonry, D-La. (1976-77), was discharged from federal prison Feb. 10, 1978, after serving six months on four misdemeanor charges of violating the federal election law. He resigned from the House in May 1977, just before a House committee would have recommended that he be unseated because of fraud in an election he won. *(1977 Almanac p. 62-A)*

However, Diggs reportedly had known for some time that the indictment was expected. The Justice Department had been investigating the allegations for almost a year.

Diggs, who had been married three times and had six children, was known to have substantial debts. His financial problems, which had plagued him for years, were apparently related to his alimony and child support obligations.

Six of the charges in the 35-count indictment brought against Diggs were dropped before his 10-day trial began.

Diggs' trial opened Sept. 26 in the U.S. District Court in Washington D.C. Prosecutor John Kotelly charged at the opening of the trial that Diggs "devised personally the scheme to defraud the United States." But Diggs' attorney David Povich said that one of the congressman's aides allegedly involved in making the kickbacks had given Diggs the money voluntarily.

Key witness for the government was Jean G. Stultz, Diggs' former congressional office manager. Stultz testifed that Diggs raised her salary in order to use the money to pay his personal bills. She said she feared she would lose her job if she didn't cooperate.

Government prosecutors said Diggs got kickbacks from Stultz and two other employees, Felix Matlock and Ofield Dukes. Matlock, who continued to work in Diggs' Detroit district office, said he went along with letting Diggs raise his salary to pay bills because he "didn't want to make any waves."

The prosecution also charged that Diggs put Geralee Richmond — who continued to work for the congressman — and George Johnson on his congressional payroll to conduct his personal business and pay off personal debts.

Diggs contended during the trial that Stultz and other employees had paid his bills, but had done so voluntarily out of their salaries.

Five black leaders, including UN ambassador Andrew Young and Coretta Scott King, testified as character witnesses for Diggs. However, they said they did not have personal knowledge of the congressman's finances.

Rep. Daniel J. Flood

Rep. Daniel J. Flood, D-Pa., a senior member of Congress and chairman of a powerful Appropriations subcommittee, was indicted on 13 criminal charges in 1978. His trial was set to begin Jan. 15, 1979, in Washington, D.C. Flood was re-elected to the House in the November elections.

In addition, the House Standards of Official Conduct Committee announced Feb. 8 that it was informally investigating Flood, but no formal move against the Pennsylvania representative was made by the committee in 1978.

Sept. 5 Charges

The indictment charges came from a federal grand jury in Los Angeles Sept. 5 on three charges of lying about payoffs allegedly made to him and a former aide.

Flood was charged with lying to a grand jury in June 1977 when he denied receiving $5,000 from William Fred Peters, a former trade school operator, and when he denied taking $1,000 from former Washington lobbyist Deryl Fleming, who once represented Peters' school.

The third charge alleged that Flood lied in October 1977 when he testified at the trial of a former aide that he did not know Peters had given the aide $5,000 in 1972. The aide, Stephen Elko, was convicted in 1977 of accepting bribes from Peters and Fleming.

Each charge against Flood was punishable by five years in prison and a $10,000 fine.

Flood denied the grand jury's charges and said they were "made by desperate men under pressure."

Oct. 12 Charges

Flood was indicted Oct. 12 on 10 additional counts: nine of bribery and one of conspiracy. These indictments came from a federal grand jury in Washington D.C. They alleged that Flood and Elko schemed to "corruptly influence" federal agencies on behalf of businesses, in exchange for bribes.

The indictment alleged that Flood received payments — ranging from $5,000 to $27,000 — from several individuals in exchange for the congressman's help in getting them grants or other forms of federal aid or approval. One of the bribery counts also alleged Flood was promised $100,000 for another favor for a Pennsylvania home builder.

Trial. Charges in both indictments were set for trial in Washington under an agreement between attorneys for Flood and federal prosecutors.

Investigations

Flood had been under investigation in a number of cities during the year including Los Angeles, Washington, New York and Philadelphia. The wide-ranging Justice Department probes of Flood were known to have drawn on testimony from Elko, who began cooperating with federal investigators after his conviction.

Each investigation was looking into allegations that Flood, in exchange for money, was using his congressional influence to help businessmen, constituents and others to get contracts or other favorable treatments from the federal government.

Flood, a 74-year-old, 15-term congressman, was chairman of the Appropriations subcommittee that controlled federal labor, health, education and welfare spending.

Elko, who was Flood's administrative assistant until he resigned under pressure in 1976, reportedly told federal investigators that Flood received more than $100,000 in exchange for using his official influence as a congressman.

Elko reportedly gave investigators information in an investigation of Flood and Rep. Joshua Eilberg, D-Pa., in connection with federal financing of a Philadelphia hospital. *(Eilberg, p. 855)*

In addition, investigators quizzed Elko about allegations that a New York rabbi paid bribes for favors from Flood. Rabbi Lieb Pinter pleaded guilty May 8, 1978, to charges that he bribed Flood. Flood was not charged at the time, and he denied he had been bribed. But the Oct. 12 indictment included charges that Pinter paid $6,500 for Flood's help in getting grants from the Labor Department and the Community Services Administration.

Federal bribery statutes forbid public officials from accepting anything of value in exchange for officials acts.

Prior to the indictments, the most damaging allegations reported about Flood were contained in statements given to federal investigators by former aide Elko and lobbyist Fleming.

Elko alleged in an affidavit that Flood received more than $100,000 in exchange for official favors. Fleming told investigators that he handed Flood $1,000 in 1972, shortly after a letter bearing Flood's signature was sent to the U.S. commissioner of education to help the business that Fleming represented.

Fleming in 1977 was given immunity from prosecution by the Justice Department in exchange for his testimony concerning alleged organized crime influence in Congress and federal agencies. The immunity agreement was disclosed in October at Elko's trial.

Marston Issue

Flood's name also came up during the year in a controversy over President Carter's firing of a U.S. attorney in Philadelphia — David W. Marston. The controversy arose when it was reported that Flood's Pennsylvania colleague, Rep. Joshua Eilberg, had asked Carter in November 1977 to get rid of Marston, who was located in Philadelphia.

Just prior to Eilberg's call to the president, Marston's office opened an investigation of the financing of a Philadelphia hospital — the Hahnemann Medical College and Hospital of Philadelphia — that obtained $14.5 million in federal funds. Flood, who pushed the appropriations for the hospital grant through Congress, and Eilberg, whose law firm represented the hospital, were part of the inquiry.

Eilberg denied knowing about the investigation at the time he called Carter. Eilberg said his call was politically motivated: He wanted Marston, a Republican appointee, replaced by a Democrat. Carter eventually fired Marston.

Stories About Flood

Besides newspaper reports based on statements by Elko and Fleming, there had been numerous media reports about other favors Flood had done over the years.

The alleged favors ranged from helping a firm in his district get about $60 million in defense contracts to persistently pressuring the Agency for International Development to set up a $10 million livestock development project in the Bahamas. Those incidents did not contain allegations that Flood had taken money in exchange for his influence, and they were not included in the indictments.

But other stories did involve matters that later on were to be part of the grand jury indictments. Typical is the matter of the West Coast schools.

West Coast Schools Case. Justice Department investigations of Flood's political favors primarily had their roots in the federal government's successful prosecution of Elko on charges that he accepted bribes in exchange for helping private vocational schools get federal aid. In July 1974, Justice began investigating Automation Institute of Los Angeles, a firm that owned six vocational schools in California. But Justice did not get very far, because the company's president and the records of his West Coast Schools disappeared after the schools had folded in May 1973.

About a year after Justice said it began inquiring about the school, the Senate Permanent Subcommittee on Investigations opened a probe of the federally insured student loan program, where the federal government guarantees loans made by private firms to students.

Committee investigators tracked down William Fred Peters, president of West Coast Schools, whose real name was Freddy LaVerne Braneff. Hearings by the Senate panel focused on Peters and other school officials and irregularities in their handling of student loans.

Peters and others associated with the schools later were convicted of bribery, fraud and tax evasion in connection with student loans at the school.

Among the information turned up by the subcommittee was a disclosure that even though five of Peters' schools were not fully accredited — which was necessary to receive federal aid such as the student loan program — they got several temporary waivers from HEW.

The temporary eligibility was authorized by former Education Commissioner Sidney P. Marland Jr. after presistent pressure from Flood's office to get the schools accredited. The schools never met federal requirements for accreditation, but Marland's authority to grant temporary eligibility allowed them to continue receiving student loan money until they folded.

HEW officials acknowledged that the pressure from Flood's office was what kept the schools in the loan program. One letter bearing Flood's signature, but apparently drafted by Elko, told Marland the failure to accredit the schools was "a shocking case of misfeasance, nonfeasance and possibly malfeasance, which is simply beyond my understanding."

The Washington Star reported Feb. 17, 1978, that Peters told federal investigators he paid a total of $50,000 in 1972 and 1973 to Elko and Fleming and that he thought most of the money had been passed on to Flood, even though he personally had not paid Flood, and didn't know how much of the cash reached the congressman.

In 1977, Elko and a business associate, Patricia Brislin, were indicted on charges that they received $25,000 in bribes from Peters and Fleming, a former lobbyist who also was a longtime Elko friend and represented Peters' schools.

The indictment charged that Elko and Brislin received the money in exchange for Elko's use of Flood's power as Labor-HEW Appropriations Subcommittee chairman. Peters and Fleming were named as unindicted co-conspirators in Elko's indictment. Flood, who later testified he knew nothing of any money paid in exchange for the letters, was not named.

Elko and Brislin were found guilty on the bribery charges in the fall of 1977 after a trial in U.S. District Court in Los Angeles. Flood's testimony at that trial led to one of the charges in the Sept. 5 indictment — that he lied when he said he did not know Peters gave Elko $5,000 in 1972. Elko and Brislin were subsequently ordered to testify before federal grand juries on other matters, in exchange for immunity from prosecutions that might result from that testimony. Their testimony was instrumental in developing other charges in the two indictments against Flood.

Rep. Joshua Eilberg

Rep. Joshua Eilberg, D-Pa., in the fall faced charges from a federal grand jury and a House committee stemming from his alleged involvement in a Philadelphia hospital controversy.

Grand Jury Charge

On Oct. 24, a Philadelphia grand jury charged Eilberg with illegally receiving compensation after helping a Philadelphia hospital to get a $14.5 million federal grant.

The grand jury issued a one-count conflict-of-interest indictment against Eilberg, along with 19 other charges made against the former president of the hospital and two men connected with the company that monitored the hospital's construction. The conflict of interest charge against Eilberg carried maximum penalties of $10,000 and two years in prison.

Eilberg issued a statement saying he was innocent of the charge and blasting the timing of the indictment, which came just two weeks before the Nov. 7 election in which he was seeking his seventh House term. He was defeated in that bid.

The indictment charged that Eilberg received compensation from Hahnemann Medical College and Hospital in Philadelphia through law firms for help Eilberg and fellow Pennsylvania Democrat Daniel J. Flood gave the hospital in getting the grant.

Flood was not charged in the indictment, but was indicted in the fall in other cases on 13 counts of bribery, perjury and conspiracy to influence federal officials in exchange for bribes. *(Details, above)*

The indictment did not specify what compensation was received between April 1975 and December 1977. Hahnemann got the $14.5 million federal grant to build an addition from the Community Services Administration (CSA) despite the agency's conclusion that "serious question exists as to the feasibility of this project." An appropriation to fund the grant had been pushed through Congress by Flood prior to CSA's decision to make the grant. Eilberg's Philadelphia law firm was hired — on the recommendation of a Flood aide — to help arrange the hospital's financing to build the addition.

Eilberg pleaded innocent Nov. 1 to the charge. After entering his plea in a Philadelphia court, Eilberg told reporters that the charges against him were "really bookkeeping irregularities." He said the timing of the indictment was "a deliberate attempt to influence the voters in my congressional district on the eve of the election."

House Ethics Committee

On Sept. 13, the House Committee on Standards of Official Conduct brought its own charges against Eilberg in connection with the hospital grant. However, the committee's proceedings against him ended with his election defeat because the panel would no longer have jurisdiction to pursue charges.

The committee formally charged Eilberg with three counts of receiving improper payments from Philadelphia law firms with which he had been associated. The most specific count alleged that he received more than $100,000 from three law firms "under circumstances which might be construed by reasonable persons as influencing the performance of his government duties." Eilberg received that money from March 1975 through 1977, the committee said.

The committee charged that Eilberg violated federal law which prohibits members of Congress from receiving outside compensation for matters relating to the federal government. The committee also said Eilberg violated the House ethics code by conducting himself "in a manner that did not reflect creditably on the United States House of Representatives."

The committee voted 7-0 to make the charges.

Sen. Herman E. Talmadge

Sen. Herman E. Talmadge, D-Ga., one of the Senate's senior members, faced a number of charges in 1978 growing out of personal and political finances.

By the end of the year, Talmadge's finances were under investigation by a federal grand jury and by the Senate Ethics Committee. In December, the committee set in motion a trial-like process to determine what, if any, action should be taken on alleged wrongdoing by Talmadge. The committee said there was "substantial credible evidence" of possible improprieties by Talmadge. *(Details, below)*

Senate Funds

Among the issues being investigated were charges that a former aide to Talmadge falsely obtained Senate funds and passed them on to the senator and his family.

Former Talmadge administrative assistant Daniel Minchew told *The Washington Star* in August that he had withdrawn Senate expense money, totaling almost $13,000, in Talmadge's name during 1973 and 1974. Minchew said he acted on Talmadge's instructions. He said the money went to the senator and his family.

The Star reported that a knowledgeable source who had reviewed Talmadge's financial records said the vouchers filed by Minchew were false. Talmadge said he never received any of the $13,000 and denied that Minchew acted on his orders. The grand jury and the Ethics Committee, both of which were looking into the matter, subpoenaed records from the Riggs National Bank in Washington D.C. where Minchew deposited the money.

Senate Expenses Repayment

In another development, Talmadge repaid the Senate $37,125.90 in improperly claimed expenses.

The repayment included about $24,000 he had received as reimbursements for official expenses that had never been incurred. It also included more than $11,000 that Talmadge had claimed for expenses that are not reimbursable under Senate rules.

Talmadge said the improper expense claims involved "errors in judgment" by his staff aides. The amount of improper claims was determined by a private auditing firm that Talmadge hired to review his records after the Star questioned some of his claimed expenses.

The check Talmadge sent to Senate Secretary J. Stanley Kimmitt Aug. 18 did not include the $13,000 that Minchew allegedly collected in false claims. Those funds "were procured without my knowledge or consent...," Talmadge wrote to Kimmitt.

Cash Gifts

On May 21, the Star reported that Talmadge received thousands of dollars in gifts from friends and supporters during 31 years as a public official.

Talmadge said the gifts, which he never reported as income, were in amounts of $5 to $20. In addition, he said meals, lodging and most of his clothes were given to him free of charge, enabling Talmadge to live on only about $25 a week in "pocket money."

The revelations about the cash gifts were prompted by the information — brought out in court proceedings involving a divorce settlement between Talmadge and his wife Betty — that Talmadge had written only one check for "cash" between 1970 and 1976. Talmadge's most recent Senate financial disclosure report, as well as information gathered in the divorce proceedings, had showed that his net worth was more than $1 million.

Subsequent news stories reported that Talmadge had received thousands of dollars in unreported income from an annual birthday dinner held in his honor.

Funds from his birthday dinners, which had been held annually for three decades, were treated as gifts and not reported as income. *The Washington Post* reported that guests at the dinner, who paid $25 each to attend, often did not know Talmadge.

By treating the birthday money and other small cash payments as gifts to help him pay for "day-to-day incidental expenses," Talmadge avoided reporting them as income. Talmadge said the "pocket money" gifts were not campaign contributions and therefore did not have to be reported for income tax purposes.

Talmadge in July announced he would continue to accept cash from constituents but wouldn't keep the money for personal use. Future gifts would be given to a "worthy" cause.

Campaign Funds

News stories following the May 21 Star report also revealed that Talmadge had not reported spending about $27,000 in personal funds on his 1974 campaign.

Talmadge aides claimed that failure to report the money on sworn reports filed with the Senate was an oversight and would be corrected by filing amended reports.

Talmadge had spent his own money for travel, constituent meals and other campaign expenses, according to aides. Although he did not report those expenditures, he was subsequently reimbursed for them by his political campaign committee.

In mid-summer, Talmadge did file amended personal campaign spending reports covering his 1973 and 1974 reelection expenditure.

The amended statements filed in July accounted for $26,912 that Talmadge later said he spent on the campaign. That sum was the amount his political campaign committee had given him in 1974.

Secret Campaign Account

The Star reported Aug. 26 that a secret campaign account was kept in Talmadge's name at the Riggs National Bank. The Star said the account allegedly was used to deposit the $13,000 in expense claims made by Minchew, as well as some unreported campaign contributions. According to the Star, about $26,000 in campaign contributions was put in the fund.

Talmadge said he did not authorize the account and did not know about it until the bank records were subpoenaed. In late November, he told reporters the secret bank account was "simply a case of embezzlement by a former administrative assistant."

But an attorney for Minchew, who was authorized to use the account, said Minchew's actions as Talmadge's administrative assistant were all taken with the senator's knowledge or consent.

Georgia Land Sale

Newspaper reports in July said that Talmadge made more than $600,000 from the sale of land that he purchased after getting inside information that an interstate highway interchange would be built on it. Talmadge bought the land in 1967 as part of an investment group, Terminal Facilities Inc., after being told by a Georgia friend, W.W. Stribling, that an interchange would be built on it. Talmadge sold the land in 1972.

Although the transaction did not appear to violate law, Talmadge's ex-wife Betty contended that profit from the sale belonged to her. She said the original land investment, which Talmadge made in her name, had been a gift to her from the senator.

The Georgia Supreme Court in June, noting that Talmadge never paid gift taxes, agreed with Talmadge that it was not a gift and the profits belonged to him.

Senate Ethics Committee Action

Two days after the initial Washington Star story on May 21, the Senate Ethics Committee announced it would consider whether it should launch a formal investigation of Talmadge. Talmadge subsequently wrote to Chairman Adlai E. Stevenson III, D-Ill., asking that the panel "expeditiously determine whether this practice violates any law, regulation, procedure or provision of the Senate rules and ethics code."

While the Ethics Committee staff had been put to work on a preliminary inquiry, Stevenson said it was possible that acceptance of the cash gifts did not violate Senate rules.

The Senate ethics code passed in 1977 forbade members from accepting gifts of over $100 in aggregate value during a year from any individual or group having a direct interest in legislation before Congress. It also required members, beginning in 1979, to report cash gifts aggregating $100 or more from one source, as well as gifts of transportation, lodging, food or entertainment aggregating $250 or more from one source during a year. The numerous sources of Talmadge's gifts were not known, nor was it known whether any of the gifts exceeded the ethics code limit.

When asked in testimony at his divorce proceedings where he got his "pocket money," Talmadge said: "I don't know." He was only slightly more specific with the Star, telling a reporter the gifts came from friends and supporters. "They come up and say they know I have a lot of expenses back in Washington and they want to help me," he told the Star.

Committee's Formal Action. It was not until late in the year that the committee decided to move to formal proceedings in the case. By a 4-1 vote Dec. 18, the committee decided to proceed into formal adjudicatory hearings.

The last ethics trial of a senator was in 1967 when then-Sen. Thomas Dodd, D-Conn., was censured after the Senate Select Committee on Standards and Conduct said he had used money raised at political affairs to pay personal bills.

Five Charges. In accordance with Senate and committee rules, Ethics Chairman Stevenson and Vice-Chairman Harrison Schmitt, R-N.M., sent the Georgia Democrat a letter specifying the charges that would be taken up at the hearing and a summary of supporting evidence.

The letter, later made public, indicated that the five charges to be considered by the committee were:

- Talmadge converted campaign contributions to personal use.
- Talmadge submitted false expense vouchers to the Senate for reimbursement of expenses that were never incurred.
- False reports of campaign receipts and expenditures were filed with the Senate secretary.
- Taxes on gifts of stock to Talmadge's ex-wife Betty were not reported.
- Gifts and property owned were not reported, as required, to the Senate.

One allegation, however, was not included in the committee's charges. Stevenson said that the panel could not find enough evidence to pursue charges that Talmadge had "committed any impropriety or violated any Senate rules" during various real estate transactions in Georgia.

Ribicoff Dissent. The charges leveled by the committee were adopted from findings reported by special counsel Carl Eardley. The only dissenting vote against approving Eardley's recommendations was that of Sen. Abraham Ribicoff, D-Conn. Sen. John Tower, R-Texas, who was not present at the Dec. 18 meeting, indicated that he would have voted for the expanded probe.

Ribicoff said in a statement after the Dec. 18 meeting that he had voted against the trial hearings because he felt that would conflict with a current grand jury inquiry.

However, Stevenson in a post-hearing press briefing, said there were no apparent conflicts between the Ethics

Committee investigation and any grand jury proceedings against Talmadge.

Sen. Edward W. Brooke

Sen. Edward W. Brooke, R-Mass., was under investigation by the Senate Ethics Committee during 1978 as a result of allegations that he did not disclose $49,000 in interest-free loans received from a Massachusetts liquor distributor.

The investigation and the publicity given to Brooke's finances were damaging to his effort to win re-election to the Senate, and were thought by many political observers to be instrumental in his election defeat on Nov. 7. Despite the defeat, the Senate Ethics Committee still was expected to issue a final report with its findings from the investigation.

Senate rules required disclosure of liabilities over $2,500 owed to anyone other than a relative. As a result of the allegations about the loan, Brooke's bitter 1977 divorce trial was reopened and Massachusetts officials launched investigations into other aspects of Brooke's finances.

Documents Controversy

The investigation of Brooke's finances was clouded by a new controversy in October, when the special counsel hired by the Ethics Committee charged that some of Brooke's financial documents had been withheld.

In late October, the Ethics Committee — at Brooke's request — held two days of hearings to give Brooke an opportunity to present his view of the controversy. The committee on Oct. 25 said it had no evidence that Brooke was personally responsible for withholding or altering documents sought by the panel.

Newspaper Reports

Brooke's troubles began when *The Boston Globe* noted discrepancies between the senator's financial disclosure report, filed in May, and sworn testimony he gave a year earlier in divorce proceedings in Massachusetts. Brooke and his wife Remigia had been granted a divorce in December 1977, but it was not to take effect until June 15, 1978.

In his court statement, Brooke said he had received $49,000 in interest-free loans over a 10-year period from A. Raymond Tye, a Massachusetts liquor distributor. But the money he had said he owed Tye was not listed in the financial disclosure report Brooke filed with the Senate.

Under rules adopted in 1977, personal liabilities over $2,500 — except those owed to relatives — must be reported in Senate disclosure forms filed annually.

The Globe May 26 reported that Brooke initially told the paper he still owed Tye the $49,000. However, Brooke later told the paper that he had only received $2,000 in loans from Tye. The other $47,000, he said, was money from an insurance settlement he administered on behalf of his mother-in-law, who died in 1977.

Mother-in-Law Link

In a press conference May 27, Brooke admitted he had made "a misstatement" in the court deposition. But he left unclear whether the $47,000 — which was part of a settlement his mother-in-law received after she was severely injured in a car accident — was a loan.

Senate financial disclosure rules did not require reporting of loans from relatives. But at a June 8 press conference Ethics Committee Chairman Adlai E. Stevenson III, D-Ill., said, "I believe that at the time [Brooke got the money] if it was a loan from a relative it was required to be disclosed."

Brooke later indicated he had used some of the $47,000 for his personal expenses, but intended to pay it back. One possible purpose of Brooke's "misstatement" was to make his debts appear larger and thus reduce his liability in the divorce. However, in a court hearing June 7 to review the divorce settlement, Brooke said he "made up the story" because "I did not want [his mother-in-law's] funds made public.... I did not want to bring out the family matter."

At the May 27 press conference, Brooke accused his family — specifically his daughter, Remi — of giving details of the divorce proceedings to reporters in order to hurt him politically. Before stories about his false statement on the loans appeared, Brooke was thought to be headed for a comfortable re-election in 1978.

Ethics Committee Action

The committee's Oct. 25 statement came after two days of hearings requested by Brooke to rebut charges that his attorneys had delayed the four-month-old investigation of alleged financial wrongdoing.

The charges came from Richard J. Wertheimer, who resigned Oct. 12 as special counsel for the Brooke investigation. In a letter to the committee, he claimed that representatives of Brooke altered documents and tried to "delay and frustrate" the probe. When Stevenson made Wertheimer's letter public, Brooke responded in an emotional Senate floor speech by demanding a hearing before the committee on the former special counsel's charges.

The request was granted, and on Oct. 24 Brooke made a statement before the committee denying that either he or his attorneys had hindered the investigation or altered documents.

The committee also allowed Wertheimer to present a lengthy statement detailing the charges made in his resignation letter. Brooke objected when Wertheimer's statement was distributed to reporters at the hearing, saying: "I just can't believe this is happening in this country, much less this committee."

However, Stevenson resisted Brooke's objections, and Wertheimer told the committee that he had found at least six alterations in Brooke's financial records. He also renewed his charges that Brooke's attorneys had withheld documents sought in the investigation.

Brooke Rebuttal

The committee resumed the hearing Oct. 25, giving Brooke an opportunity to rebut Wertheimer's statement. Again, Brooke denied Wertheimer's charges, emphasizing an earlier statement he and his attorneys had made that only one document was altered to correct a clerical error. And again, Wertheimer repeated his charges that Brooke's attorneys had withheld documents.

The committee statement issued after the hearings was supported by Stevenson and the other three panel members who attended the sessions. Brooke expressed satisfaction with the statement that there was no evidence he personally hindered the probe.

But the committee's statement only went to the charge that Brooke had withheld or altered documents. The statement did not address a charge by Wertheimer that representatives of Brooke had hindered the probe. ▮

Senate Job Bias Plan

After helping outlaw job discrimination and assuring minimum work conditions for most Americans, the Senate in the 95th Congress moved cautiously toward labor protection for its own workers.

But the effort produced only a provision in Senate rules making job discrimination illegal. No enforcement mechanism was provided. Attempts in 1978 to create that mechanism died under assaults by many senators.

A resolution (S Res 431) with enforcement procedures was approved by the Governmental Affairs Committee, but never came to a vote. The resolution was approved in the spring, but remained in limbo until September when the Democratic Policy Committee told sponsors that it would not be brought up for action. An end-of-the-session effort by backers to force a floor vote by attaching the resolution to another bill died under a filibuster.

Supporters said there was considerable behind-the-scenes opposition to the proposal. Much of it seemed grounded in the refusal of many senators to accept any limits on their power to hire and fire employees.

S Res 431 would have provided a mechanism to enforce Rule 50, which was part of the Senate ethics code adopted in 1977. The code said that members could not discriminate in employment on the basis of race, color, religion, sex, national origin, age or physical handicap.

However, the non-discrimination rule was to take effect Jan. 3, 1979, in any event. This meant that any job bias claims arising from it would have to be handled by the Senate Ethics Committee. Several senators said they doubted many of their colleagues realized this. They said opponents of S Res 431 seemed to believe that there wouldn't be any job bias rule in effect if the resolution were killed.

House

As part of the Senate code, the non-discrimination rule did not apply to House employees, who were not covered by any formal grievance procedure. About a quarter of the members of the House set up a voluntary grievance system that covered only employees working for those members.

Members who joined signed a pledge that they would not discriminate in employment on the basis of race, color, religion, sex, national origin, age, parental or marital status or handicap.

Most of those who signed up were from the reform-minded classes elected in 1974 and 1976. Few House leaders took the anti-discrimination pledge. Among the Republican hierarchy, only John B. Anderson, R-Ill., signed. The Democrats' top officers unanimously shunned it.

Backers of the system acknowledged that it was hampered severely by its lack of enforcement authority and the fact that it did not cover every member of the House.

Senate Proposal

Congress has exempted itself from the major civil rights laws passed to protect virtually all workers in private employment, leaving Capitol Hill employees with no legal recourse for discrimination complaints.

A few former congressional employees have gone to court with employment complaints, but their charges that members of Congress violated their constitutional due process rights have met with only limited success.

If S Res 431 had been approved, it would have been the first time that either house of Congress formally agreed to give its employees some protection against discrimination.

The resolution would have established a Senate Fair Employment Relations Office to collect information for an annual report on employment practices in Senate offices. The office also would try to conciliate informal discrimination complaints filed by Senate employees or individuals who applied for Senate jobs.

If the office were unable to help the employer and employee reach a settlement, the employee could file a formal complaint with a six-member Senate Fair Employment Relations Board. The board, composed of Senate-selected private citizens, would judge whether discrimination had occurred. It could recommend remedies such as promotion, reinstatement to a job or a monetary settlement. If either party were unsatisfied with the board's decision, he or she could file an appeal with the Senate Ethics Committee.

As a practical matter, a complaint would stop there. A Senate employee could go to court, but a court challenge could not be based on the Senate's anti-discrimination rule because it had no legal force. It was only part of the Senate rules.

Committee Action

The Governmental Affairs Committee reported S Res 431 (S Rept 95-729) on April 7. The resolution was referred to the Human Resources Committee. But that committee didn't really want it. On May 9, it passed the issue to the Senate. The panel said it declined to take a position on the resolution because it did not believe it had jurisdiction over "internal operations of the Senate." The action put the resolution on the Senate calendar.

But in late September, the proposal was killed in the Democratic Policy Committee. At a Sept. 20 closed-door meeting, the committee rejected the efforts of Sen. John Glenn, D-Ohio, to get a floor vote.

PROVISIONS

As reported by the Governmental Affairs Committee, S Res 431:

Senate Fair Employment Relations Board, Office

- Established a Senate Fair Employment Relations Board, composed of three members chosen by the majority leader and three chosen by the minority leader.
- Required that the members of the board be selected from private life and have a demonstrated commitment to fair employment relations.
- Barred former members, employees or officers of Congress from serving on the panel for at least three years after leaving Congress.
- Provided travel expenses and pay for members of the board when they are conducting the board's business, to be paid from the Senate contingent fund.
- Required the board to meet at least four times a year.
- Ordered the board to set policies and guidelines for carrying out the Senate's anti-discrimination rule.
- Directed the board to supervise the operations of the Senate Fair Employment Relations Office and to appoint its director.
- Gave the board authority to hear and make decisions on complaints alleging violations of the anti-discrimination

Congress Outside Many Laws

Among major laws that do not apply to Congress — or give members a special status — are:

Civil Rights Act of 1964, and amendments to it contained in the Equal Employment Opportunity Act of 1972. Both laws established anti-discrimination protections for employees, as well as an enforcement mechanism allowing them to seek redress.

National Labor Relations Act. Under this law, employers were required to recognize and bargain with unions, and employees were protected from unfair labor practices.

Fair Labor Standards Act. Minimum wage, overtime compensation and child labor standards were dealt with in this law.

Equal Pay Act. Women were guaranteed the same pay men received for comparable work after this law, amending the Fair Labor Standards Act, was approved in 1963.

Age Discrimination in Employment Act. This law protects employees between 40 and 65 from discrimination based on their age.

Occupational Safety and Health Act. Employers must maintain certain health and safety standards for the protection of their employees under this law.

Freedom of Information Act. Congress forced the executive branch to open its files to the public, but kept its own documents under wraps.

Privacy Act. Congress also ordered the executive branch to keep a tighter lid on information it keeps on individuals, except to let those people see their own files for correction or amendment.

State and Local Income Taxes. It took two tries, but in 1977 Congress finally got a law on the books that saves members from paying state and local income taxes in Maryland, Virginia and the District of Columbia, where they reside during congressional sessions. The law primarily affected about 125 members living in Maryland, because Virginia and the District of Columbia had already freed members residing in their jurisdictions from local taxes.

Conflicts of Interest. Federal law currently prohibits executive branch employees from participating in government dealings with companies in which they have a financial interest. There is no such prohibition on Congress, and in fact many members have financial interests in areas — such as banking, law and agriculture — handled by the committee on which they serve.

However, both houses of Congress in 1977 passed stringent ethics codes that require detailed public disclosure of these financial interests.

---

rule, and to appoint hearing examiners to hear formal complaints.

- Established a Senate Fair Employment Relations Office to be headed by a director who could only be removed by a majority vote of the board.
- Authorized the director to implement the board's policies on anti-discrimination.

Complaints and Violations

- Allowed any Senate employee or person applying for a Senate job to seek advice about employment rights from counselors in the Fair Employment Relations Office within 60 days after an alleged discriminatory act.
- Authorized the director to waive the 60-day deadline.
- Allowed Senate employees or persons applying for Senate jobs to file an informal complaint with the director within 20 days after seeking counseling at the Fair Employment Relations Office.
- Required the director to give a copy of the complaint to the senator or Senate employee named by the complainant.
- Ordered the director to investigate the alleged violations and report findings and conclusions to the board, the complainant and the respondent within 45 days.
- Authorized the director to informally try to arbitrate an agreement between the complainant and the respondent in cases where the director believed a discriminatory act had taken place.

Formal Complaints and Hearings

- Allowed the complainant to file a formal complaint, made under oath, with the board if the director was unable to help the parties reach an informal settlement.
- Allowed a complainant to ask the board to review an opinion by the director that no discriminatory act had occurred.
- Provided that the complainant could file a formal complaint if the board disagreed with the director's opinion and found reason to believe a violation had occurred.
- Ordered a hearing by a board-appointed hearing examiner on each formal complaint.
- Ordered the hearing examiner to give the board a report with findings and recommendations after a hearing.
- Ordered the board to issue a decision within 60 days after the filing of a formal complaint.
- Authorized the board to order remedial actions — such as employment, re-employment, promotion, a salary raise or a monetary settlement — when it found the anti-discrimination rule had been violated.

Appeals to Select Committee on Ethics

- Allowed either the complainant or the respondent to appeal a decision by the board to the Select Committee on Ethics within 30 days.
- Ordered the Ethics Committee to issue a decision on the appeal within 60 days after it was filed.
- Authorized the Ethics Committee to order remedial action if it found a violation of the rule.

Records

- Provided that all records kept on a case remain confidential and available for inspection only by the complainant, the respondent, the board, the fair employment office and the Ethics Committee.
- Required that decisions and orders from the board or the Ethics Committee be made public. ∎

SPECIAL REPORTS

CQ

The Court's Year: Centrist, Shifting Alliances

Questions of government power and official accountability dominated the issues decided by the Supreme Court during its 1977-78 session.

These decisions came from a court on which there was no dominant philosophical majority to consistently guide the justices' actions. Taken as a whole, the decisions reflected a "centrist" court with shifting alliances among the justices.

The many divided votes on cases indicated that the court's middle-of-the-road position was less the result of choice than of coincidence and compromise.

By its decisions, the court affected many of the powers and rights of states, the immunity of government officials, government regulation and the ever-recurring search and seizure questions.

Highlights

Public discussion of the court's activities, however, focused on a single case. In October the court heard argued the case of Allan Bakke, the white engineer who charged that "reverse discrimination" had blocked his effort to get into medical school. Not until June 28 did the court announce its decision, in favor of Bakke and in support of affirmative action programs as well. The *Bakke* case illustrated, as much as any, the absence of a clear philosophical trend to the court's actions.

The court's ruling in favor of affirmative action in the *Bakke* case led a list of more than a dozen major rulings that found favor with liberal observers. Among them were its decisions reducing the immunity of cities and executive branch officials to lawsuits brought by persons wronged by official action. In addition, the court backed the continued existence of an endangered fish, the snail darter, against the arguments of the Tennessee Valley Authority.

The court struck down still more death penalty laws, upheld a federal judge's order directing reform of state prisons, expanded the rights of consumers faced with termination of their utility service and gave defendants in criminal cases a new opportunity to challenge the way evidence against them was obtained.

Conservative groups were cheered as well, by the court's striking down racial quota systems, widening state tax powers, finding part of the controversial Occupational Safety and Health Act unconstitutional, and rejecting challenges to the growth of the nuclear power industry.

Furthermore, the court took a conservative stance to uphold the power of the Federal Communications Commission to restrict the broadcasting of certain programs to hours when fewer children were listening, to back the power of police to search newspapers offices and the authority of a sheriff to keep newsmen out of his prisons at all times except when the general public might enter too.

Five 'Swingers'

As in the 1976 term, the two ends of the philosophical spectrum were each held by two justices.

On the conservative end were Chief Justice Warren E. Burger and Justice William H. Rehnquist; on the liberal side were Justices William J. Brennan Jr. and Thurgood Marshall.

In between — and swinging with varying degrees of regularity between the two groups were Justices Byron R. White, Potter Stewart, Harry A. Blackmun, Lewis F. Powell Jr. and John Paul Stevens. Powell and Stevens, in particular, played key roles in a number of decisions.

Since Justices Powell and Rehnquist became the third and fourth members of the court named by President Nixon (in the middle of the 1971 term), they — with Chief Justice Burger and Justice Blackmun — have often been described as the "Nixon bloc" of justices. Whatever validity the phrase had in earlier court terms, it clearly lost with the October 1977 session.

A statistical analysis of the court's votes by *The New York Times*, published July 4, revealed that the foursome — who voted together on as many as three of every four, or at least on two of every three, cases in previous terms — agreed on only one of every three in the 1977 term. The *Bakke* vote clearly revealed this divergence. Burger and Rehnquist voted together, joined in part by Powell. Blackmun voted with the "liberal" majority in the case, also joined in part by Powell.

The decisions came from a court on which there was no dominant philosophical majority to consistently guide the justices' actions. Taken as a whole, the decisions reflected a "centrist" court with shifting alliances among the justices.

State Powers

Governors and mayors found their powers and responsibilities taking on new shape under the pressure of more than two dozen of the court's decisions during the term.

State officials were the first to feel the impact of the *Bakke* ruling. The court ordered admissions officers at the University of California at Davis Medical School to admit Allan Bakke — and to cease their use of a quota for minority applicants.

The Taxing Power

Amid the national debate over state taxes, spurred by California's adoption of Proposition 13, the Supreme Court with little fanfare moved to enlarge state power to tax the interstate businesses operating within their boundaries.

For decades, the court had severely restricted state power to tax these companies, viewing such taxes as unconstitutional burdens on the flow of interstate and foreign commerce.

But in 1976, the court overruled a century-old ban on state taxation of imported goods still in the warehouse. And in 1977, it discarded its rule against state taxes on the "privilege" of doing business in the state.

Under the old rationale which viewed most state taxes of this sort as unconstitutional, the court twice — in 1937 and 1947 — had struck down Washington state taxes on stevedoring activity, the loading and unloading of ships. But in 1978 the court, citing its 1977 decision on "privilege" taxes, overruled the two earlier decisions against the state and upheld the stevedoring tax.

Explaining the decision, Justice Blackmun wrote that the court now recognized that "a state has a significant interest in exacting from interstate commerce its fair share of the cost of state government. . . . All tax burdens do not impermissibly impede interstate commerce. The . . . [constitutional] balance tips against the tax only when it unfairly burdens commerce by exacting more than its share from the interstate activity."

The court also backed the right of states to work together — in a MultiState Tax Compact — to coordinate their taxing of interstate corporations. A number of affected corporations, led by United States Steel, challenged the compact as unconstitutional, because Congress had not formally approved it. The court rejected that challenge, holding that only compacts which enhance state power vis-a-vis federal power must be explicitly approved by Congress.

Supreme Court Building

Most states base the taxes they assess against interstate corporations on three factors — the company's payroll in the state, its property in the state and its sales (or other measure of the amount of business done) in the state.

Iowa, however, uses only the single factor of sales within the state. Upholding this formula as permissible, Justice Stevens reaffirmed the court's belief "that the states have wide latitude in the selection of apportionment formulas and that a formula-produced assessment will only be disturbed when the taxpayer has proved by 'clear and cogent evidence' that the income attributed to the state is in fact 'out of all appropriate proportion to the business transacted . . . in that state'. . . ."

Oil, Water and Garbage

State regulation came under scrutiny from the justices in some half dozen cases, of which the states won four.

The justices backed Maryland's law barring major integrated oil companies from operating service stations in that state, but they struck down — as infringing on federal prerogatives — Washington state's ban on supertankers in Puget Sound. The court backed the right of states to control the use and allocation of the water within their boundaries — even against claims by federal reclamation projects and national forests.

Implicitly supporting similar laws in all 50 states and more than 500 cities, the court upheld New York City's landmark preservation law — against a challenge from Penn Central Co., the owner of Grand Central Station. The company challenged the law as an unconstitutional "taking" of private property, after the city rejected their plans to build a skyscraper on top of the terminal. The court rejected that challenge, finding the law a proper exercise of the state's "police" power to protect the public welfare.

But New Jersey lost its effort to halt the flow of out-of-state garbage into its dumps and landfills. Ruling that even garbage fell under the protection of the Constitution's commerce clause, the court ruled that New Jersey violated the basic purpose of that clause when it attempted "to isolate itself from a problem common to many by erecting a barrier against the movement of interstate trade" with this ban.

Alaska saw its "Alaska Hire" law struck down by the court which found it unconstitutional for a state to require employers — even those engaged in exploiting a state's natural resources — to give preference to state residents in hiring. The court said that violated the Constitution's directive that citizens of one state be granted all the "privileges and immunities" of citizens by any other state. The right to work is clearly such a privilege, the court held. But the court upheld New York's right to require that all its state troopers be citizens and Montana's right to charge non-residents much higher hunting license fees than charged to Montanans who wished to hunt the state's elk.

The Right to Light

In a major enlargement of consumer rights, the court declared that "utility service is a necessity of modern life," of which the state cannot deprive someone without due process of law. This extension of 14th Amendment protection to utility service provided by muncipally-owned utilities was expected to require revision in the complaint and termination procedures of those agencies. The court held

The Perils of the Zig-Zag Course

The lack of a dominant philosophical majority created problems for those who looked to the Supreme Court for guidance in making policy and drafting laws.

The issue of capital punishment — and the court's decisions on that question over the six years from 1972 to 1978 — illustrated the zig-zag pattern of the current court. The only change in membership during that time was the replacement of Justice William O. Douglas in 1975 by Justice John Paul Stevens.

In 1972 the court found existing death penalty laws too vague in setting the standards which judges and juries could use in deciding whom to sentence to death. Thus those laws were invalidated because the court found that the broad discretion they allowed in sentencing resulted in great unfairness in the imposition of the death penalty.

Four years later, the court reviewed the new capital punishment laws adopted by states to replace those struck down in 1972. Upholding those which set out clear guidelines for sentencing, the court struck down others which made death the mandatory sentence for first-degree murder. The Constitution, held the majority, required consideration of the individual crime and the individual defendant before the sentence of death could be imposed fairly. Mandatory sentences for first-degree murder precluded such individual consideration and were unconstitutional.

In 1978, the court struck down Ohio's death penalty law because it limited too strictly the mitigating factors that a judge could consider in deciding whether or not to impose a death sentence. In writing the majority opinion, Chief Justice Burger conceded that "the signals from this Court [on capital punishment] have not . . . always been easy to decipher. . . ." *(Lockett v. Ohio, Bell v. Ohio)*

Two other justices were not quite so euphemistic. "The Court has now completed its about-face" since its 1972 ruling on capital punishment, wrote Justice White. He criticized the court for retreating to a position allowing the imposition of the death penalty by a judge "as an exercise of his unguided discretion after being presented with all circumstances which the defendant might believe to be conceivably related to the appropriateness of the penalty for the individual offender."

"The court has gone from pillar to post," wrote Justice Rehnquist, "with the result that the sort of reasonable predictability upon which legislatures, trial courts, and appellate courts must of necessity rely has been all but completely sacrificed."

He warned that the court was "totally unleashing" sentencing discretion. "I am frank to say," he added, "that I am uncertain whether today's opinion represents the seminal case in the exposition by this Court of the Eighth and Fourteenth Amendments as they apply to capital punishment, or whether instead it represents the third false start in this direction within the past six years."

that customers must be given a full opportunity to resolve billing disputes before their service is terminated.

Politics and Corporations

Recognizing for the first time the protected right of corporations to participate in political discussion, the court struck down a Massachusetts law that restricted corporate spending on issues to be resolved through a referendum.

Speaking for the five-man majority, Justice Powell wrote that speech itself was what the amendment protected, regardless of its source: "If the speakers here were not corporations, no one would suggest that the state could silence their proposed speech. It is the type of speech indispensable to decisionmaking in a democracy, and this is no less true because the speech comes from a corporation rather than an individual. The inherent worth of the speech in terms of its capacity for informing the public does not depend upon the identity of its source. . . ."

The dissenting justices warned that the court's ruling could result in corporate domination of political debate, drowning out the also-protected political speech of individuals.

Official Immunity

City, state and federal officials all lost some measure of the immunity from damage suits they had claimed in previous years when faced with charges that they had violated federal law or constitutional rights in the course of their official duties.

Cities were dealt a double blow by the court.

In March the court refused, 5-4, to extend to cities the immunity which states enjoy from antitrust suits. Such immunity would protect municipal agencies only if the challenged action was taken at express direction of the state, wrote Justice Brennan for the majority. In dissent Justice Stewart warned that such damage suits could impose "staggering costs" on city treasuries, bankrupting cities who lost cases.

But an even more unsettling ruling came two months later. Early in June the court reversed a 1961 decision and held that cities and city agencies were not exempt from civil rights damage suits.

"Local governing bodies," wrote Justice Brennan, "can be sued directly . . . [under federal law] for monetary, declaratory, or injunctive relief, where, as here, the action that is challenged to be unconstitutional implements or executes a policy statement, ordinance, regulation, or decision officially adopted and promulgated by that body's officers . . . [or the alleged injury is] visited pursuant to governmental 'custom' even though such a custom has not received formal approval through the body's official decision-making channels. . . ."

State Immunity

More than a decade of litigation protesting conditions in Arkansas' prisons produced a Supreme Court ruling in

Freedom of the Press

"The First Amendment does not 'belong' to any definable category of persons or entities: it belongs to all who exercise its freedoms," wrote Chief Justice Burger in April.

The court's decisions during the 1977-78 term studiously avoided giving any impression that the freedom-of-the-press guarantee granted special privileges to the news media beyond that available to individual citizens who sought to communicate their ideas. Burger said he saw "no difference between those who seek to disseminate ideas by way of a newspaper and those who give lectures or speeches and seek to enlarge the audience by publication and wide dissemination."

In the case of *The Stanford Daily*, the court rejected the argument that the First Amendment, combined with the Fourth Amendment rights of persons not suspected of any crime, justified requiring prosecutors and police to use subpoenas rather than search warrants to obtain information from newsmen and newspapers. The vote was 5-3.

Media Limits

Subsequently, the court rejected the claims of television newsmen for greater access to state prisons than that generally afforded to the public. This time the vote was 4-3. Chief Justice Burger said the Constitution doesn't mandate "a right of access to government information or source of information. . . . Like all other components of our society, media representatives are subject to limits."

Writing separately, Justice Stewart showed his disagreement with Burger's press views. Referring obliquely to earlier Burger comments on "special" First Amendment rights, Stewart said: "That the First Amendment speaks separately of freedom of speech and freedom of the press is no constitutional accident, but an acknowledgement of the critical role played by the press in American society."

FCC Powers

First Amendment claims by the press also met defeat in two Federal Communications Commission cases. In one, the court held that the FCC did not violate rights of newspaper owners by forbidding them, in the future, to acquire a broadcast outlet in the same town as their newspaper. In the second, the court held that the FCC did not violate any First Amendment freedoms of radio broadcasters by telling them that they could not air certain offensive programs during hours when children were certain to be part of their audience.

The record of free press cases was not entirely one of losses for the press. The court unanimously ruled that Virginia violated the First Amendment by fining a newspaper for publishing a true and accurate account of confidential state judicial review proceedings concerning discipline of a state judge. Chief Justice Burger wrote the opinion — omitting any mention of freedom of the press, however, and focusing instead on the First Amendment's protection for free discussion of governmental affairs.

late June 1978 that narrowed the freedom of a state to disregard federal court orders with impunity.

Frustrated by state disregard of his suggestions that improvements should be made in state prison conditions, a federal judge in Arkansas finally ruled that some of the conditions in the prison were so bad as to be unconstitutionally cruel punishment, directed the state to make specific changes in the prison regimen and to pay the attorneys' fees for the persons bringing the suits against the state. The state challenged this action on a number of points, asserting that the judge was infringing state sovereignty and immunity.

The Supreme Court — with only Justice Rehnquist dissenting — backed all points of the judge's order. Given the state's "bad faith" response to the earlier directives from the judge, the fee award was quite proper, wrote Justice Stevens. "Federal courts," he pointed out, "are not reduced to issuing injunctions to state officials and hoping for compliance."

State judges, however, won Supreme Court affirmance of their immunity from damage suits. A woman sterilized without her consent, after a state judge approved her mother's petition for sterilization, sued her mother, the doctor and the judge for damages. The court, divided 5-3, held the judge immune from such charges.

It is "a general principle of the highest importance to the proper administration of justice that a judicial officer, in exercising the authority vested in him, [should] be free to act upon his own convictions, without apprehension of personal consequences to himself," wrote Justice White for the court. In dissent, Justice Stewart argued that the majority was allowing judges "like . . . loose cannon, to inflict indiscriminate damage."

Federal Officials

By indirection, the court also allowed a new loophole to open in the heretofore solid immunity that members of Congress and their aides had enjoyed from damage suits arising from actions related to their legislative duties.

Lower courts rejected the request of Sen. John L. McClellan, D-Ark. (1942-1978), and several of his aides that a damage suit against them be dismissed because of their congressional immunity. The damage suit was brought by persons who argued that McClellan and his aides had violated their constitutional rights by seizing some of their papers.

After hearing the congressional defendants' appeal asking the justices to rule that immunity did protect them from such a suit, the court dismissed the case. The justices said that it made a mistake when it decided to review it. That action allowed the lower court rulings to stand and the damage suit to proceed to trial.

Earl Butz, Richard Nixon's controversial secretary of agriculture, was in the news again late in June, as the Supreme Court ruled that neither he nor any other high-ranking federal executive official was absolutely immune from a damage suit filed by an injured citizen.

Federal officials had no more immunity in most situations than state officials, wrote Justice White for the court, which divided 5-4 on the issue. Federal officials were protected by a qualified immunity for any official actions which they could show to have been reasonable at the time they were taken and to have been taken in good faith, the court held. But an absolute immunity could not be asserted by most federal officials to suits alleging that they had injured someone by acting unconstitutionally.

"It is not unfair to hold liable the official who knows or should know he is acting outside the law" wrote White, and "insisting on an awareness of clearly established constitutional limits will not unduly interfere with the exercise of official judgment."

Government Regulation

In eight major cases involving government regulation, the court upheld agency action five times, and overturned agency arguments in three other instances.

The court upheld the Federal Communications Commission's order decreeing an eventual end to joint ownership of a town's newspaper and broadcast outlets. It also upheld an FCC order admonishing a radio station for broadcasting indecent material at 2 o'clock in the afternoon.

The power of the ICC to substitute its own rate structure for that of the owners of the Alaska Pipeline was backed by the court, as was the authority of the Nuclear Regulatory Commission to make decisions concerning the expansion of the nuclear power industry.

The court held that Congress acted unconstitutionally when it authorized inspectors for the Occupational Safety and Health Administration (OSHA) to inspect, without search warrants, business premises for violations of health and safety standards.

But the court upheld congressional approval of a statutory limit on the liability of the nuclear power industry in the event of a nuclear accident.

The court applied the letter of the Securities Exchange Act to hold that the Securities Exchange Commission (SEC) had been acting illegally when it suspended trading in stocks under investigation not only for a single 10-day period, as the law provides, but for consecutive 10-day periods running into months and even years. The SEC thus lost use of one of its major tools for dealing with suspected stock fraud and manipulation.

Divided 5-4, the court opened the door to more challenges to Environmental Protection Agency (EPA) decisions concerning emissions standards. The justices ruled that a company, charged with violating EPA rules concerning demolition of buildings, had a right to challenge those rules.

Searches . . . and Searches

Media protest over the court's ruling allowing police to search newspaper offices obscured the fact that defendants won three out of four major search-and-seizure cases decided during the term.

In the first case, which arose out of an arson investigation, the court in May required fire officials, returning to investigate the origin of a fire after the flames were extinguished, to obtain the consent of the owner of the damaged premises — or a search warrant — in order for the search to be constitutionally proper. The court acknowledged, however, that "the fire truck need not stop at the courthouse in rushing to the flames."

In June, the court flatly rejected Arizona's argument for a "murder scene" exception to the general rule that police searches be authorized in advance by warrants. "The mere fact that law enforcement may be made more efficient can never by itself justify disregard of the Fourth Amendment" protection of citizens against unreasonable search and seizure, wrote Justice Stewart for the court.

The following week, the court for the first time gave defendants an opportunity to challenge evidence against them by arguing that it was obtained as a result of a search warrant based on lies.

If a defendant could make a substantial showing that police used false statements in order to convince a magistrate that they had probable cause to search a place, then he should be granted a full hearing at which to present his evidence of that charge, held the court. And if he could establish his charge, the evidence against him should perhaps be excluded from use at trial. "The requirement that a warrant not issue 'but upon probable cause supported by Oath or affirmation,' " wrote Justice Blackmun, "would be reduced to a nullity if a police officer was able to use deliberately falsified allegations to demonstrate probable cause. . . ."

In 1971, county police, armed with a warrant, searched the offices of the Stanford University campus newspaper, seeking evidence of the identity of persons who had injured policemen in the course of a demonstration at which a newspaper reporter and photographer were present. Subsequently, the paper, backed by most of the nation's media associations, charged that the search had violated its Fourth and First Amendment rights.

> *"Under existing law, valid warrants may issue to search* any *property, whether or not occupied by a third party, at which there is probable cause to believe that the fruits, instrumentalities, or evidence of a crime will be found."*
>
> —Justice Byron R. White

The newspaper argued that a subpoena — rather than a search warrant — was the constitutionally proper way for law enforcement officials to seek evidence in the possession of a third party not suspected of any involvement in a crime, particularly if that third party were a newspaper.

The Supreme Court rejected that argument — as to third parties and as to newspapers. The First Amendment aspect of the ruling drew the most attention, but the Fourth Amendment — "innocent third party" — issue was likely to have a broader impact. Divided 5-3, the court held that nothing in the Fourth Amendment required that search warrants only be issued for searches of places occupied or owned by persons suspected of crime. "Under existing law," wrote Justice White, "valid warrants may issue to search *any* property, whether or not occupied by a third party, at which there is probable cause to believe that the fruits, instrumentalities, or evidence of a crime will be found."

In dissent, Justice Stevens warned that the consequences of allowing police searches of the homes and offices of innocent third persons were "extremely serious. . . . The only conceivable justification for an unannounced search of an innocent citizen is the fear that, if notice were given he would conceal or destroy the object of the search."

MAJOR DECISIONS

CRIMINAL LAW

Searches and Seizures

United States v. Ceccolini, decided by a vote of 6-2, March 21, 1978. Rehnquist wrote the opinion; Blackmun did not participate; Brennan and Marshall dissented.

The exclusionary rule against the use of illegally obtained evidence does not prevent the voluntary testimony of a witness in a perjury case concerning evidence she saw discovered years earlier in an inadvertent, but illegal, search.

Michigan v. Tyler, decided by votes of 7-1 and 6-2, May 31, 1978. Stewart wrote the opinion; Brennan did not participate; Rehnquist, White and Marshall dissented in part.

The Fourth Amendment guarantee against unreasonable search and seizure does not require fire officials to obtain a search warrant to search the location of a suspicious fire during the fire or immediately after the flames are extinguished. But that guarantee does require that subsequent searches of the site be authorized by a warrant; if they are not, any evidence then obtained is not usable in court.

Zurcher v. The Stanford Daily, decided by a vote of 5-3, May 31, 1978. White wrote the opinion; Brennan did not participate; Stewart, Marshall and Stevens dissented.

The Fourth Amendment does not preclude or limit the use of search warrants for searches of places owned or occupied by innocent third parties not suspected of any crime. "Under existing law, valid warrants may be issued to search *any* property...at which there is probable cause to believe that fruits, instrumentalities, or evidence of a crime will be found...."

The First Amendment guarantee of freedom of the press does not require that information concerning a crime which is suspected to be in the possession of a newspaper be sought by a subpoena rather than a search warrant.

Mincey v. Arizona, decided by votes of 9-0 and 8-1, June 21, 1978. Stewart wrote the opinion; Rehnquist dissented in part.

There is no "murder scene" exception to the warrant requirement of the Fourth Amendment. In general, it remains the rule that warrantless searches "are *per se* unreasonable under the Fourth Amendment — subject only to a few specifically established and well-delineated exceptions." Evidence obtained in a warrantless four-day search of the apartment where a murder had been committed was not admissible in court.

Interrogation of a wounded and hospitalized suspect by police, disregarding his calls for an attorney, produced involuntary statements which may not be used in any way against him because they have been obtained in violation of his constitutional rights.

Franks v. Delaware, decided by a vote of 7-2, June 26, 1978. Blackmun wrote the opinion; Rehnquist and Burger dissented.

When a defendant makes a substantial showing to defend his charge that police used false statements to obtain a search warrant — used to obtain evidence against him — the Fourth Amendment requires that he be given a pre-trial hearing to examine that charge. If his charge is proved at the hearing — and the remaining information upon which the warrant was based is insufficient to justify its issuance — the evidence obtained by the search is inadmissible.

Wiretapping

United States v. New York Telephone Company, decided by votes of 9-0, 6-3 and 5-4, Dec. 7, 1977. White wrote the opinion; Stewart, Stevens, Brennan and Marshall dissented in part.

Pen registers, devices which intercept only numbers dialed from a particular telephone, not the conversations conducted on the instrument, are not governed by Title III, the wiretapping section of the 1968 Crime Control and Safe Streets Act. A federal court has the inherent power to authorize installation of such devices, and to order a third party — the telephone company in this case — to provide technical assistance to government agents in installing the pen registers.

Scott v. United States, decided by a vote of 7-2, May 15, 1978. Rehnquist wrote the opinion; Brennan and Marshall dissented.

Apparent disregard, by federal agents, of the requirement of Title III of the Omnibus Crime Control and Safe Streets Act of 1968 that electronic surveillance be conducted in such a way as to minimize the interception of irrelevant conversations is not sufficient reason to exclude evidence obtained by a wiretap from use in court.

Double Jeopardy

Arizona v. Washington, decided by a 6-3 vote, Feb. 21, 1978. Stevens wrote the opinion; White, Marshall and Brennan dissented.

The Constitution's protection against double jeopardy does not protect from retrial a defendant whose previous trial was declared a mistrial due to misconduct by his defense counsel — despite the fact that the trial judge did not make any specific finding of the reason for the mistrial declaration.

United States v. Wheeler, decided by an 8-0 vote, March 22, 1978. Stewart wrote the opinion; Brennan did not participate.

The Fifth Amendment guarantee against double jeopardy does not bar prosecutions by separate sovereigns of the same person for the same action. An Indian defendant convicted in tribal court of certain crimes may be tried again by federal authorities for those same actions.

Burks v. United States, Greene v. Massey, decided by votes of 8-0, June 14, 1978. Burger wrote the opinion; Blackmun did not participate.

The Fifth Amendment double jeopardy clause forbids a second trial of a person whose first conviction has been overturned because of insufficient evidence. The clause does not forbid a retrial of a person whose first conviction is overturned because of trial error.

Crist v. Bretz, decided by a 6-3 vote, June 14, 1978. Stewart wrote the opinion; Burger, Powell and Rehnquist dissented.

State courts must use the same rules as federal courts to determine when jeopardy "attaches" during a trial — that is, when a defendant is actually placed in jeopardy within the meaning of the Fifth Amendment. Thus state courts must rule, as federal courts do, that jeopardy attaches once a jury is sworn in.

Sanabria v. United States, decided by a 7-2 vote, June 14, 1978. Marshall wrote the opinion; Blackmun and Rehnquist dissented.

Once a person is acquitted of a crime — even if the acquittal results from an error — the double jeopardy clause bars his retrial for that action. "[T]here is no exception permitting retrial once the defendant has been acquitted, no matter how 'egregiously erroneous' " the acquittal.

United States v. Scott, decided by a 5-4 vote, June 14, 1978. Rehnquist wrote the opinion; Brennan, White, Marshall and Stevens dissented.

A judge's decision, upon a defendant's motion, to dismiss charges in mid-trial, due to factors unrelated to guilt or innocence, does not preclude government appeal of that ruling and a retrial of that defendant if the government's appeal is successful. *United States v. Jenkins* (1975) allowing the government to appeal such rulings only so long as the success of the appeal would not result in a new trial is overruled.

Self-Incrimination

Lakeside v. Oregon, decided by a 6-2 vote, March 22, 1978. Stewart wrote the opinion; Brennan did not participate; Stevens and Marshall dissented.

The Fifth Amendment protection against self-incrimination does not forbid a state trial judge to instruct a jury, over defense objection, that they should not draw any adverse inference from the fact that a defendant did not testify in his own defense. *Griffin v. California* (1965) forbade adverse comment, not all comment, on a defendant's silence.

Right to Counsel

Moore v. Illinois, decided by an 8-0 vote, Dec. 12, 1977. Powell wrote the opinion; Stevens did not participate.

The right of an alleged rapist to have the aid of an attorney was violated by his being confronted with his alleged victim at a preliminary hearing in the absence of his lawyer — and by use of her identification of him at his trial.

Holloway v. Arkansas, decided by a 6-3 vote, April 3, 1978. Burger wrote the opinion; Powell, Blackmun and Rehnquist dissented.

The effective aid of legal counsel was denied to three defendants charged with and tried together for the same offense growing out of the same occurrence when the trial judge, over their objection, appointed the same public defender to represent all three of them. Joint representation is not *per se* a denial of the right to counsel but in this case it resulted in a conflict of interest that prevented effective representation of all three defendants.

Fair Trial

Ballew v. Georgia, decided by a 9-0 vote, March 21, 1978. Blackmun announced the court's decision, but no one opinion had the support of a majority of the court. White, Powell and Brennan wrote separate opinions.

In order to fulfill the constitutional guarantee of trial by jury, state juries must be composed of at least six members.

United States v. MacDonald, decided by an 8-0 vote, May 1, 1978. Blackmun wrote the opinion; Brennan did not participate.

A defendant may not — before his trial — appeal a federal court order refusing to dismiss the charges against him on the basis of his assertion that he has been denied his right to a speedy trial.

Capital Punishment

Lockett v. Ohio, Bell v. Ohio, decided by a vote of 7-1, July 3, 1978. Burger wrote the opinion; Brennan did not participate; Rehnquist dissented.

Ohio's death penalty law — which precluded consideration of age, minor role in crime, lack of intent to cause death and other mitigating factors by sentencing authority in murder case — is unconstitutional. "In all but the rarest kind of capital case," the Constitution's ban on cruel and unusual punishment and its guarantees of equal protection and due process require that the sentencing judge or jury be allowed to consider, as a mitigating factor, "any aspect of a defendant's character or record and any of the circumstances of the offense...."

Due Process

Bordenkircher v. Hayes, decided by a 5-4 vote, Jan. 18, 1978. Stewart wrote the opinion; Blackmun, Brennan, Marshall and Powell dissented.

Due process is not violated by a prosecutor's use — in the plea bargaining process — of a threat to bring an additional indictment against a defendant if the defendant did not accept the prosecutor's offer of a bargain. "[I]n the 'give-and-take' of plea bargaining, there is no...element of punishment or retaliation so long as the accused is free to accept or reject the prosecution's offer.... [T]he course of conduct engaged in by the prosecutor in this case, which no more than openly presented the defendant with the unpleasant alternatives of forgoing trial or facing charges on which he was plainly subject to prosecution, did not violate the due process clause of the 14th Amendment."

United States v. Grayson, decided by a 6-3 vote, June 26, 1978. Burger wrote the opinion; Stewart, Brennan and Marshall dissented.

In determining the sentence to be imposed upon a convicted defendant, the trial judge may properly take into account his belief that the defendant lied during the trial, and increase his sentence accordingly.

CIVIL RIGHTS

Jobs

Christiansburg Garment Company v. Equal Employment Opportunity Commission, decided by a vote of 8-0, Jan. 23, 1978. Stewart wrote the opinion; Blackmun did not participate.

A federal district court has the discretion to award attorneys' fees to an employer who successfully defends himself against a charge of illegal job discrimination under Title VII of the 1964 Civil Rights Act, if the court finds that the charge was "frivolous, unreasonable or without foundation, even though not brought in subjective bad faith." The claim of a prevailing defendant to attorneys' fees in a Title VII case is not as strong as that of a prevailing plaintiff — and in this particular case, no such award is justified.

Furnco Construction Company v. Waters, decided by votes of 9-0 and 7-2, June 29, 1978. Rehnquist wrote the opinion; Marshall and Brennan dissented in part.

To rebut charges of job discrimination in violation of Title VII of the 1964 Civil Rights Act, an employer must show that he has legitimate reasons, not illegal ones, like race, for his challenged hiring, firing or promotion decisions. As support for his defense, an employer may introduce statistics showing that he employs a substantial number of minority workers in certain jobs. However, statistics showing "a racially balanced work force cannot immunize an employer from liability for specific acts of discrimination."

Reverse Discrimination

Regents of University of California v. Bakke, decided by votes of 5-4 and 5-4, June 28, 1978. Powell announced the judgment of the court; Stevens and Brennan filed separate opinions; Stevens was joined by Burger, Rehnquist, and Stewart; Brennan was joined by Marshall, White and Blackmun.

A special admissions program for a state medical school under which a set number of places were set aside for minority group members — and white applicants were denied the opportunity to compete for those seats — clearly violated Title VI of the 1964 Civil Rights Act which forbids the exclusion of anyone, because of race, from participation in a federally funded program.

Admissions programs which consider race as one of a complex of factors involved in the decision to admit or reject an applicant are not unconstitutional in and of themselves. "Government may take race into account when it acts not to demean or insult any racial group, but to remedy disadvantages cast on minorities by past racial prejudice, at least when appropriate findings have been made by judicial, legislative, or administrative bodies with competence to act in this area."

Sex Discrimination

Nashville Gas Company v. Satty, decided by a vote of 9-0, Dec. 6, 1977. Rehnquist wrote the opinion.

The sex discrimination ban in Title VII of the 1964 Civil Rights Act forbids employers to divest women workers of their accumulated seniority when they take maternity leave, but allows them to refuse sick pay to those workers when their absence is due to pregnancy and childbirth.

Quilloin v. Walcott, decided by a 9-0 vote, Jan. 10, 1978. Marshall wrote the opinion.

State law making consent of natural mother sufficient for adoption of illegitimate child does not deny father of illegitimate child equal protection or due process.

City of Los Angeles v. Manhart, decided by votes of 6-2 and 7-1, April 25, 1978. Stevens wrote the opinion; Brennan did not participate; Burger and Rehnquist and Marshall dissented in part.

Under the Civil Rights Act of 1964, the fact that the average woman outlives the average man does not justify an employer's requiring women to pay more into pension funds than men workers earning the same pay. The 1964 Act requires that employers' decisions focus on the individual, not the generalization. "Individual risks, like individual performance, may not be predicted by resort to classifications proscribed by Title VII....[W]hen insurance risks are grouped, the better risks always subsidize the poorer risks...."

Santa Clara Pueblo v. Martinez, decided by a 7-1 vote, May 15, 1978. Marshall wrote the opinion; Blackmun did not participate; White dissented.

The Indian Civil Rights Act does not give federal courts jurisdiction over sex discrimination suits challenging tribal rules for determining membership in pueblo.

Age Discrimination

United Air Lines Inc. v. McMann, decided by a 7-2 vote, Dec. 12, 1977. Burger wrote the opinion; Brennan and Marshall dissented.

A *bona fide* retirement plan adopted in 1941 and requiring retirement at age 60 cannot be considered a subterfuge to evade the provisions of the Age Discrimination in Employment Act, enacted in 1967.

Lorillard v. Pons, decided by an 8-0 vote, Feb. 22, 1978. Marshall wrote the opinion; Blackmun did not participate.

The Age Discrimination in Employment Act allows a jury trial upon demand of a person seeking reinstatement, lost wages and money damages for loss of job in violation of the act.

INDIVIDUAL RIGHTS

Aliens

Foley v. Connelie, decided by a 6-3 vote, March 22, 1978. Burger wrote the opinion; Marshall, Brennan and Stevens dissented.

States may constitutionally require that state policemen be citizens; policemen fall within the category of persons who participate in the formulation or implementation of public policy for whom a citizenship requirement may be appropriate. "[W]e extended to aliens the right to education and public welfare, along with the ability to earn a livelihood and engage in licensed professions, the right to govern [however] is reserved to citizens."

Citizens

Hicklin v. Orbeck, decided by a vote of 9-0, June 22, 1978. Brennan wrote the opinion.

"Alaska Hire" law that required employers in jobs related to the development of the state's oil and gas resources to give a hiring preference to state residents violates the Constitution's requirement that "citizens of each state...be entitled to all privileges and immunities of citizens in the several states."

Consumers

Memphis Light, Gas & Water Division v. Craft, decided by a vote of 6-3, May 1, 1978. Powell wrote the opinion; Stevens, Burger and Rehnquist dissented.

"[U]tility service is a necessity of modern life" and a state may not deprive someone of that service without due process of law. Municipally owned utility is required by the 14th Amendment to give customers full opportunity to resolve billing disputes before service is terminated to the customer.

Students

Board of Curators of University of Missouri v. Horowitz, decided by votes of 9-0 and 6-3. Rehnquist wrote the opinion; Blackmun, Marshall and Brennan dissented in part.

The constitutional guarantee of due process does not restrict the right of school officials to dismiss a student from school for poor academic performance. Due process does not require, in these circumstances, that the student be given a hearing at which he or she may contest the reasons for his or her dismissal.

Carey v. Piphus, decided by a vote of 8-0. Powell wrote the opinion; Blackmun did not participate.

Students suspended for disciplinary reasons — without notice and a hearing as required in that circumstance by due process — may be awarded no more than nominal damages against school officials unless they are able to demonstrate that they suffered actual injury from the suspension.

ELECTION LAW

Voting Rights

United States v. Board of Commissioners of Sheffield, Ala., decided by a vote of 6-3, March 6, 1978. Brennan wrote the opinion; Stevens, Burger and Rehnquist dissented.

The requirement imposed by the Voting Rights Act of 1965 upon all affected areas that changes in voting procedures be cleared with the attorney general before being implemented extends "to all entities having power over any aspect of the electoral process within designated jurisdictions."

FIRST AMENDMENT

Freedom of Press

Landmark Communications Inc. v. Virginia, decided by a vote of 7-0, May 1, 1978. Burger wrote the opinion; Brennan and Powell did not participate.

The First Amendment prohibits a state from penalizing a newspaper for printing a truthful and accurate report of state commission proceedings — required by law to remain confidential — concerning the possible disciplining of a sitting state judge. "Whatever differences may exist about interpretations of the First Amendment, there is practically universal agreement that a major purpose of that amendment was to protect the free discussion of government affairs."

Federal Communications Commission (FCC) v. National Citizens Committee for Broadcasting (NCCB), Channel Two Television Co. v. NCCB, National Association of Broadcasters v. FCC, American Newspaper Publishers Association v. NCCB, Illinois Broadcasting Company v. NCCB, The Post Company v. NCCB, decided by a vote of 8-0, June 12, 1978. Marshall wrote the opinion; Brennan did not participate.

The Federal Communications Commission did not exceed its authority — nor did it infringe upon First Amendment rights — by ordering a halt to future formations of jointly owned newspaper/broadcasting station combinations in the same community, and by requiring divestiture of such combinations when they involved joint ownership of the only newspaper and only broadcast outlet in a community — unless continued existence of that monopoly was shown to be in the public interest.

Houchins v. KQED Inc., decided by a vote of 4-3, June 26, 1978. Burger wrote the opinion; Marshall and Blackmun did not take part in the case; Stevens, Brennan and Powell dissented.

A federal district court erred in ordering a sheriff to grant news media greater access to county jail facility than granted to public at large. "Neither the First Amendment nor Fourteenth Amendment mandates a right of access to government information or sources of information within the government's control."

Freedom of Speech

First National Bank of Boston v. Bellotti, decided by a vote of 5-4, April 26, 1978. Powell wrote the opinion; White, Brennan, Marshall and Rehnquist dissented.

State law banning corporate expenditures relative to referendum issue which does not materially affect corporation's business impermissibly abridges political speech protected by the First Amendment. "If the speakers here were not corporations, no one would suggest that the state could silence their proposed speech. It is the type of speech indispensable to decisionmaking in a democracy, and this is no less true because the speech comes from a corporation rather than an individual."

Federal Communications Commission v. Pacifica Foundation, decided by a vote of 5-4, July 3, 1978. Stevens wrote the opinion; Brennan, Marshall, Stewart and White dissented.

The Federal Communications Commission violates neither the First Amendment guarantee of free speech nor the Federal Communications Act by regulating the time of broadcasts of material which is offensive and indecent, yet not obscene.

Freedom of Speech and Association

Ohralik v. Ohio State Bar Association, decided by a vote of 8-0, May 30, 1978. Powell wrote the opinion; Brennan did not participate.

The First Amendment protection of free speech is not violated by the action of a state bar to discipline an attorney for soliciting clients in person, for pecuniary gain, under circumstances which pose dangers of fraud, undue influence, intimidation and other "vexatious conduct" — all of which the state has a right to prevent.

In re Primus, decided by a 7-1 vote, May 30, 1978. Powell wrote the opinion; Brennan did not participate; Rehnquist dissented.

"[C]ollective activity undertaken to obtain meaningful access to the courts is a fundamental right within the protection of the First Amendment." That right was violated by state bar action publicly reprimanding an attorney affiliated with the American Civil Liberties Union for soliciting clients. The reprimand was a result of her letters, to women who had been sterilized as a condition of receiving welfare, which informed the women that the ACLU would provide free legal representation if they wished to sue the doctors who had performed the operation.

Church and State

McDaniel v. Paty, decided by a vote of 8-0, April 19, 1978. Burger wrote the opinion; Blackmun did not participate.

The First Amendment right to free exercise of religion is violated by state constitutional provision declaring ministers and priests ineligible to serve in state legislature.

Obscenity

Pinkus v. United States, decided by a vote of 8-1, May 23, 1978. Burger wrote the opinion; Powell dissented.

Trial court, in federal obscenity prosecution, erred in instructing jurors in case that children should be included in their definition of the "community" as they attempted to define the community standards against which material should be judged obscene.

BUSINESS LAW

Antitrust

Pfizer Inc. v. The Government of India, decided by a 5-3 vote, Jan. 11, 1978. Stewart wrote the opinion; Blackmun did not participate; Burger, Rehnquist and Powell dissented.

Foreign governments are "persons" entitled to sue American corporations for treble damages for antitrust violations under the Clayton Act.

National Society of Professional Engineers v. United States, decided by a vote of 8-0, April 25, 1978. Stevens wrote the opinion; Brennan did not participate.

The ban on competitive bidding — included in the code of ethics of professional engineers — constitutes price-fixing and is illegal under the provisions of the Sherman Antitrust Act.

National Broiler Marketing Association v. United States, decided by a vote of 7-2, June 12, 1978. Blackmun wrote the opinion; White and Stewart dissented.

The Capper-Volstead Act, which provides an exemption for farm cooperatives from the federal antitrust laws, does not cover a cooperative organization which includes even one member who does not produce a product — who, in this case, does not breed, hatch or grow chickens.

St. Paul Fire & Marine Insurance Company v. Barry, decided by a vote of 7-2, June 29, 1978. Powell wrote the opinion; Stewart and Rehnquist dissented.

Consumers and policyholders may sue insurance companies for violating federal antitrust law by banding together to boycott, coerce or intimidate individual consumers and/or policyholders. These individuals may bring such suits under an exemption in the McCarran-Ferguson Act, which protects insurance companies from federal regulation.

United States v. U.S. Gypsum Company, decided by votes of 7-1 and 6-2, June 29, 1978. Burger wrote the opinion; Blackmun did not participate; Rehnquist and Stevens dissented in part.

Trial error requires reversal of price-fixing convictions of four wallboard manufacturers. However, companies may not use as a complete defense to charges of price-fixing the argument that their exchange of price information among themselves was simply an effort to comply with the Robinson-Patman Act, which forbids price discrimination among customers.

Taxation

Department of Revenue of State of Washington v. Association of Washington Stevedoring Companies, decided by a vote of 8-0, April 26, 1978. Blackmun wrote the opinion; Brennan did not participate.

Neither the commerce clause — authorizing federal regulation of interstate and foreign commerce — nor the import-export clause — banning state taxes on imports or exports — is violated by Washington State's general business and occupation tax on stevedoring activity. Earlier rulings — *Puget Sound Stevedoring Company v. State Tax Commission* (1937) and *Joseph v. Carter & Weekes Co.* (1947) — invalidating such a tax as in violation of the commerce clause are overturned. Such a tax does not unfairly burden interstate commerce nor does it exact from the enterprise anything more than compensation for the services it is provided by the state.

Moorman Manufacturing Company v. Bair, decided by a vote of 6-3, June 15, 1978. Stevens wrote the opinion; Brennan, Blackmun and Powell dissented.

A state formula, based upon a single factor, sales, for computing the portion of an interstate business' net income which is attributable to business within the taxing state is not unconstitutional. "States have wide latitude in the selection of apportionment formulas and...a formula-produced assessment will only be disturbed when the taxpayer has proved by 'clear and cogent evidence' that the income attributed to the State is in fact 'out of all appropriate proportion to the business transacted...in that State'...."

Zenith Radio Corporation v. United States, decided by a vote of 9-0, June 21, 1978. Marshall wrote the opinion.

The non-excessive remission, by Japan, of an excise tax on electronic products exported from that country is not a bounty or grant triggering the requirement of U.S. tariff law that the United States impose a countervailing duty to equal the remitted Japanese taxes.

State Powers

United States Steel Corporation v. Multistate Tax Commission, decided by a vote of 7-2, Feb. 21, 1978. Powell wrote the opinion; White and Blackmun dissented.

The Multistate Tax Compact is not unconstitutional — although it has not received the formal approval of Congress. The Constitution's requirement of congressional consent for interstate compacts traditionally has been applied only to agreements which result in the formation of a combination tending to enhance state power at the expense of federal supremacy. The tax compact is not such a combination.

Exxon Corporation v. Maryland, Shell Oil Company v. Maryland, Continental Oil Company v. Maryland, Gulf Oil Corporation v. Maryland, Ashland Oil Inc. v. Maryland, decided by a vote of 7-1, June 14, 1978. Stevens wrote the opinion; Powell did not participate; Blackmun dissented.

Maryland did not act unconstitutionally when it banned the operation of service stations within the state by companies which produced or refined petroleum products. Neither the due process nor the commerce clauses of the Constitution are infringed by that ban.

Allied Structural Steel Company v. Spannaus, decided by a vote of 5-3, June 28, 1978. Stewart wrote the opinion; Blackmun did not participate; Brennan, Marshall and White dissented.

The Constitution's ban on state action impairing the obligation of contracts is violated by a state pension benefits protection law which increased the pension liability of some companies beyond that voluntarily undertaken in existing pension agreements.

Securities Law

Securities and Exchange Commission v. Sloan, decided by a 9-0 vote, May 15, 1978. Rehnquist wrote the opinion.

The Securities and Exchange Commission does not have the authority under the 1934 Securities Exchange Act to suspend trading in a security, summarily, for consecutive 10-day periods amounting to months or even years. The 1934 act permits such suspensions for one 10-day period only.

Occupational Safety

Marshall v. Barlow's Inc., decided by a vote of 5-3, May 23, 1978. White wrote the opinion; Brennan did not participate; Stevens, Blackmun and Rehnquist dissented.

The provision of the Occupational Safety and Health Act of 1970 — which allows warrantless inspections of businesses covered by the Act's requirements — violates the Fourth Amendment's guarantee against unreasonable search and seizure. "The Warrant Clause of the Fourth Amendment protects commercial buildings as well as private homes." When a businessman objects to such a search of his premises, the Occupational Safety and Health Administration inspector may obtain a search warrant simply by showing that "reasonable legislative or administrative standards for conducting an...inspection are satisfied with respect" to the establishment he seeks to search.

LABOR LAW

Sears, Roebuck & Company v. San Diego District County Council of Carpenters, decided by a vote of 6-3, May 15, 1978. Stevens wrote the opinion; Brennan, Stewart and Marshall dissented.

State courts have jurisdiction to rule on an employer's request that the court order workers to stop picketing on private property in violation of state trespass laws. State jurisdiction is not defeated or pre-empted by the fact that the picketing activity itself might be protected by federal labor law.

American Broadcasting Companies Inc. v. Writers Guild of America, West, Inc., Association of Motion Picture and Television Producers Inc. v. Writers Guild, National Labor Relations Board v. Writers Guild, decided by a vote of 5-4, June 21, 1978. White wrote the opinion; Stewart, Brennan, Marshall and Stevens dissented.

Unions engage in an unfair labor practice when they discipline members who hold supervisory jobs and who cross picket lines during a strike in order to continue doing those jobs.

Eastex Inc. v. National Labor Relations Board, decided by a vote of 7-2, June 22, 1978. Powell wrote the opinion; Rehnquist and Burger dissented.

Federal labor law protects the right of union members to distribute a union newsletter in non-working areas of a plant during non-working hours, even though the contents of the newsletter do not relate solely to the relationship between management and its employees.

Beth Israel Hospital v. National Labor Relations Board, decided by a vote of 9-0, June 22, 1978. Brennan wrote the opinion.

Freedom of communication is a major element of an employee's right to organize and bargain collectively. Without any evidence of harm resulting from distribution of union literature in hospital eating places used primarily by employees, a hospital may not ban such distribution in those places.

ENERGY AND ENVIRONMENT

Adamo Wrecking Company v. United States, decided by a vote of 5-4, Jan. 10, 1978. Rehnquist wrote the opinion; Stewart, Brennan, Blackmun and Stevens dissented.

A federal jury before whom a person is prosecuted under the Clean Air Act for violating an emission standard may determine whether or not the regulation violated is in fact an emission standard within the meaning of the Act. In the case at hand, the emission standard was not such a standard at all, but instead was a work practice regulation, and so the conviction for violating it was overturned.

Ray v. Atlantic Richfield Company, decided by votes of 7-2 and 6-3, March 6, 1978. White wrote the opinion; Marshall, Brennan, Rehnquist, Stevens and Powell dissented in part.

Federal Ports and Waterways Safety Act of 1972 asserted federal authority over questions of the size of tankers permitted to enter U.S. waters and over safety design requirements for tankers. Therefore, a state's ban on supertankers in its coastal waters must fall, as must its safety design requirements for tankers. States may require that ships engaged in foreign trade carry a state-licensed pilot while in state waters, and that tankers have a tug escort while in certain state waters.

Vermont Yankee Nuclear Power Corporation v. Natural Resources Defense Council, Consumers Power Company v. Aeschliman, decided by a vote of 7-0, April 3, 1978. Rehnquist wrote the opinion; Powell and Blackmun did not participate.

Federal courts have only a limited role to play in reviewing decisions of the Nuclear Regulatory Commission (NRC) concerning the expansion of the nation's nuclear power capability. In the absence of constitutional constraints or compelling circumstances, courts should leave agencies like the NRC free to determine their own rules of procedure and methods of inquiry.

The court overturned two rulings of a federal court of appeals which had required the NRC to reconsider two decisions concerning licensing of new power plants.

Tennessee Valley Authority v. Hill, decided by a 6-3 vote, June 15, 1978. Burger wrote the opinion; Powell, Blackmun and Rehnquist dissented.

The Endangered Species Act — reflecting the intent of Congress to halt and reverse the trend toward species extinction — demands that the Tennessee Valley Authority not put into operation a new dam, when completion of the dam would destroy the habitat of an endangered species of fish.

Philadelphia v. New Jersey, decided by a vote of 7-2, June 23, 1978. Stewart wrote the opinion; Rehnquist and Burger dissented.

A state violates the commerce clause, designed to ensure the free flow of interstate commerce, when it prohibits the disposal, within its territory, of waste originating outside the state. "All objects of interstate trade merit commerce clause protection; none is excluded by definition at the outset."

Duke Power Company v. Carolina Environmental Study Group, Nuclear Regulatory Commission v. Carolina Environmental Study Group, decided by a vote of 9-0, June 26, 1978. Burger wrote the opinion.

Congress did not act unconstitutionally when it enacted a $560-million ceiling on the liability of the nuclear power industry for damages resulting from an accident at a nuclear power plant. That limitation does not deprive citizens of life, liberty or property without due process of law or take private property without just compensation.

The decision to impose such a limit and the limit adopted were neither arbitrary nor irrational and thus were well within the power of Congress.

Penn Central Transportation Company v. City of New York, decided by a vote of 6-3, June 26, 1978. Brennan wrote the opinion; Rehnquist, Burger and Stevens dissented.

New York City's landmark preservation law as applied to restrict the use of a particular historic landmark is not an unconstitutional government "taking" of property without just compensation to the owners. Such laws do not authorize a taking of property any more than zoning laws; both are proper exercise of the state "police" power to safeguard and promote the general welfare.

California v. United States, decided by a vote of 6-3, July 3, 1978. Rehnquist wrote the opinion; White, Brennan and Marshall dissented.

Federal appropriation, purchase or condemnation of water rights for reclamation projects must be conducted in keeping with the requirements of the relevant state law. Once waters have passed through a dam or other reclamation project their distribution to individuals is controlled by state law.

GOVERNMENTAL IMMUNITY

Stump v. Sparkman, decided by a vote of 5-3, March 28, 1978. White wrote the opinion; Brennan did not participate; Stewart, Marshall and Powell dissented.

A state judge who approved a mother's petition to have her teen-aged daughter sterilized, without the daughter's being informed or giving her consent, is protected by judicial immunity from a civil rights damage suit by the daughter protesting this violation of her rights. "A judge will not be deprived of immunity because the action he took was in error, was done maliciously, or was in excess of his authority; rather, he will be subject to liability only when he has acted in the absence of all jurisdiction."

City of Lafayette, Louisiana v. Louisiana Power & Light Co., decided by a vote of 5-4, March 29, 1978. Brennan wrote the opinion; Stewart, White, Rehnquist and Blackmun dissented.

Cities are not, simply by virtue of their municipal status, exempt from federal antitrust suits. *Parker v. Brown* (1943) exempting states from such suits covers cities only when their challenged actions are taken at the express direction of state policy.

Monell v. Department of Social Services of the City of New York, decided by a vote of 7-2, June 6, 1978. Brennan wrote the opinion; Rehnquist and Burger dissented.

City officials, municipalities, and municipal agencies are not exempt from civil rights damage suits brought under the Civil Rights Act of 1871; *Monroe v. Pape* (1961), insofar as it held that cities and their agents and agencies were exempt from such suits, is overruled as wrongly decided.

"Congress did not intend municipalities to be held liable unless action pursuant to official municipal policy of some nature caused a constitutional tort.... [A] local government may not be sued for an injury inflicted solely by its employees or agents. Instead, it is when execution of a government policy or custom...inflicts the injury that the government as an entity is responsible...."

Butz v. Economou, decided by a 5-4 vote, June 29, 1978. White wrote the opinion; Rehnquist, Burger, Stewart and Stevens dissented.

Federal government officials do not have absolute immunity from damage suits based on their performance of official duties. Federal officials, even when acting to carry out congressional directives, are subject to the restraints of the Constitution. "Federal officials will not be liable for mere mistakes in judgment whether the mistake is one of fact or one of law. But we see no substantial basis for holding...that executive officers generally may with impunity discharge their duties in a way that is known to them to violate the United States Constitution or in a manner that they should know transgresses a clearly established constitutional rule."

FEDERAL COURT POWERS

Hutto v. Finney, decided by an 8-1 vote, June 23, 1978. Stevens wrote the opinion; Rehnquist dissented.

After extended litigation and lack of cooperation from state officials in response to previous suggestions and directives from the federal court, a federal district judge acted within his power when he set a limit for the state's use of certain types of punishment in its prisons — finding indefinite use of one punishment to be unconstitutional — and when he ordered that the attorneys' fees for the prevailing plaintiffs bringing the case protesting prison conditions be paid from state agency funds.

MISCELLANEOUS

Nixon v. Warner Communications Inc., decided by a 7-2 vote, April 18, 1978. Powell wrote the opinion; Marshall and Stevens dissented.

Neither the Constitution nor common law requires release from custody of the court of the "White House tapes" used as evidence at the trial of former White House aides for their part in the Watergate cover-up. The claim of broadcasters and recording companies to a right to access to the tapes, to inspect and copy them for commercial purposes, is rejected. Congress has created a procedure for processing and releasing all materials of historical interest from the Nixon administration to the public, including the recordings at issue in this case.

National Labor Relations Board v. Robbins Tire and Rubber Company, decided by a 9-0 vote, June 15, 1978. Marshall wrote the opinion.

The Freedom of Information Act does not allow an employer charged with an unfair labor practice to find out the evidence assembled against him by the National Labor Relations Board. Exempt from disclosure under that law are the statements of witnesses whom the board would call to testify on the charge. These statements are exempt as investigatory records compiled for law enforcement purposes — disclosure of which would interfere with enforcement proceedings. ▮

Nominations and Confirmations

Senate Rejects Few Carter Appointments

Except for his efforts to fill vacancies on the Federal Election Commission (FEC), President Carter had little trouble getting his major nominees for federal office confirmed by the Senate in 1978.

Of 3,054 civilian nominations Carter sent to the Senate, 3,010 were confirmed. Four nominations were withdrawn and 40, mostly to relatively minor positions, failed to win confirmation. *(List of major 1978 confirmations, p. 17-A)*

FEC Fight

Two of the failed nominees, and one of the withdrawals, concerned the FEC — continuing Carter's problems with FEC nominees that began during his first year in office.

In 1977, Carter had named former congressional aides Samuel D. Zagoria and John W. McGarry to the bipartisan election agency, but political problems prevented the Senate from confirming either man. *(1977 CQ Almanac p. 48-A)*

Zagoria, Friedersdorf. Carter resubmitted the Zagoria and McGarry nominations in early 1978, but the uproar continued. Concerning the Zagoria nomination, Republican congressional leaders Rep. John J. Rhodes of Arizona and Sen. Howard H. Baker Jr. of Tennessee reiterated that Carter broke his pledge that he would follow their recommendations in filling an open GOP seat on the FEC. Zagoria, a former aide to Sen. Clifford P. Case, R-N.J., had not been recommended by Baker or Rhodes. Carter eventually withdrew Zagoria's name on Aug. 15. (Zagoria won confirmation later for a slot on the Consumer Product Safety Commission.)

To fill the GOP slot, Carter on Oct. 10 nominated former White House legislative liaison Max L. Friedersdorf, who had been recommended by GOP congressional leaders. The Senate Rules Committee did not act on Friedersdorf's nomination before the 95th Congress adjourned.

McGarry. The Rules Committee approved McGarry's nomination by a 7-2 vote on Aug. 25, even though committee hearings had exposed discrepancies between the financial disclosure statements McGarry filed with the clerk of the House and his income tax returns.

McGarry, then special counsel for the House Administration Committee, also drew GOP fire for his close ties to House Speaker Thomas P. O'Neill Jr., D-Mass. A filibuster threat by the GOP leadership prevented the Senate from considering the McGarry nomination in the final days of the session.

Carter renewed the controversy by naming McGarry to a recess appointment to the FEC Oct. 25. Neil O. Staebler, a Democrat McGarry was supposed to replace, angrily said he would challenge the recess appontment in court. Staebler, whose term expired April 30, 1977, said he was entitled to serve until his successor was sworn in.

Staebler said that the Federal Election Campaign Act did not provide for a recess appointment to the commission. The Constitution, however, empowered the president to make recess appointments.

Staebler also said such an appointment could be damaging to the commission. "It affects the conditions under which the president and Congress are elected," he told an Oct. 26 news conference. "If you get a person on the commission who is beholden, it could influence decisions one way or another."

White House press secretary Jody Powell said the Justice Department had cleared the recess appointment of McGarry as valid.

Besides a renewed fight over McGarry's nomination in 1979, Carter faced other FEC problems: The terms of two commissioners, Chairman Vernon W. Thomson, R, and Thomas E. Harris, D, were to expire April 30, 1979.

Civiletti: Justice Department

By a 72-22 vote, the Senate confirmed the nomination of Assistant Attorney General Benjamin A. Civiletti to be deputy attorney general. The vote came May 9 after the Senate Judiciary Committee reported the nomination on April 19. *(Vote 156, p. 26-S)*

Civiletti replaced former Pittsburgh Mayor Peter Flaherty in the Justice Department's second highest post. Flaherty resigned to make an unsuccessful race for the Pennsylvania governorship.

Judiciary Committee hearings on Civiletti quickly turned into a discussion of the so-called "Marston affair." Committtee Republicans demanded to know the role of Civiletti and of Attorney General Griffin B. Bell in the firing of David Marston, U.S. attorney for the eastern district of Pennsylvania (Philadelphia).

Marston, a Republican, had been told to leave by Carter, upon Bell's recommendation. Carter acted following a Nov. 4, 1977, telephone call from Rep. Joshua M. Eilberg, D-Pa. Marston charged that Carter and Bell had succumbed to political pressure in an effort to stop an investigation into criminal charges against Eilberg and Rep. Daniel J. Flood, D-Pa. Judiciary Republicans quizzed Civiletti about the sequence of events.

Though the controversy continued on the Senate floor, Civiletti eventually won Senate confirmation over GOP protests. Marston tried to capitalize on the publicity he received by running for the Republican gubernatorial nomination in Pennsylvania, but finished third in a field of six.

To replace Marston, Carter nominated Peter F. Vaira, a Democrat. He was confirmed easily and continued the Marston investigations on Eilberg and Flood — producing indictments in the fall of 1978 against both men. *(Eilberg, Flood indictments, see Congress and Government chapter)*

Morris: LEAA

Opposition led by the National Rifle Association (NRA) helped block action by the Senate Judiciary Committee on the nomination of law professor Norval Morris to head the Justice Department's Law Enforcement Assistance Administration (LEAA).

Judgeships

The prestige of a federal judgeship is high, and appointment to the judiciary is considered by most attorneys and politicians to be the apex of a legal and public career.

Federal judgeships are lifetime appointments and pay $57,500 in the circuit court and $54,500 in the district court annually. There is no mandatory retirement age, but judges may retire at full salary at age 65 after 15 years or at 70 after 10 years on the bench.

The following list gives the number of confirmed federal circuit and district court judges appointed by President Carter in 1977-78 and by his seven immediate predecessors.

	Democrats	Republicans
Roosevelt	188	6
Truman	116	9
Eisenhower	9	165
Kennedy[1]	111	11
Johnson	159	9
Nixon[2]	15	198
Ford	12	52
Carter (1977)	26	0
Carter (1978)[3]	26	2

1 One New York liberal also was appointed.

2 No party affiliation was available for one judge from Puerto Rico, and one independent was chosen.

3 No party affiliation was available for six judges, and one independent was chosen. The 1978 figures do not include a Democrat who failed to win Senate confirmation to a district court judgeship.

Morris, 54, dean of the University of Chicago law school since 1975, had criticized the LEAA for its overemphasis on "hardware." But the NRA objected to his stands favoring gun control.

The argument over Morris also delayed committee consideration of two proposed deputy LEAA administrators. None of the three men was given a recess appointment.

Gartner: Commodities Commission

One Carter nominee ran into trouble after his Senate confirmation. David G. Gartner, a former aide to Minnesota Democratic Sens. Hubert and Muriel Humphrey, was confirmed to a seat on the Commodity Futures Trading Commission (CFTC) on May 17.

Gartner had been recommended for the post by a fellow Minnesotan, Vice President Walter F. Mondale. During his confirmation hearings, however, some other Minnesota ties got him in trouble. Gartner voluntarily told the Senate Agriculture Committee that over a period of four years, Minneapolis grain magnate Dwayne Andreas had given $72,000 worth of stock to Gartner's four children. The stock was in Archer Davis Midland Inc., a major grain dealer regulated by the CFTC and chaired by Andreas, a longtime Humphrey financial supporter.

During questioning by the panel, Gartner agreed to sell the stock and to disqualify himself from any CFTC decisions involving Andreas' firm. The committee unanimously reported his nomination May 17 and the Senate confirmed it by voice vote the same day.

Criticism of the stockholdings and questions of conflict-of-interest rose when Gartner took his CFTC seat. The Agriculture Committee called him back for more hearings, and Carter reversed course and decided Gartner had to go. On June 26, he and Mondale took the unusual step of publicly asking Gartner to resign his CFTC seat. Gartner, pointing out that he had sold the stock and put the proceeds in trust for the children, refused to leave. He remained a CFTC member.

Judgeships

Nominations for judgeships caused three controversies in the Senate in 1977-78.

McKay. The first occurred in November 1977, after the judicial nominating commission for the 10th Circuit Court of Appeals presented five names to President Carter. Among them was that of Monroe G. McKay of Provo, Utah, a law professor at Brigham Young University, and brother of Rep. Gunn McKay, D-Utah.

Carter's nomination of McKay angered Sen. Orrin G. Hatch, R-Utah, who got the Senate Judiciary Committee to approve the nomination but not report it, pending further hearings. After the hearings were held, the panel reported McKay's name and the Senate confirmed it Nov. 29, 1977.

O'Brien. Longtime Iowa Democratic official Donald E. O'Brien was confirmed to an Iowa district judgeship on Oct. 4, but not before drawing fire from the American Bar Association (ABA).

The ABA opposed O'Brien's nomination on both political and judicial grounds. Its statement referred to incidents in his service as Woodbury County (Iowa) attorney from 1955-58. Politically, the ABA felt he was too partisan: O'Brien, once a member of the Democratic National Committee, was a twice-beaten Democratic congressional nominee, U.S. attorney for the northern district of Iowa from 1961-67, and a special counsel to the House Small Business Committee at the request of Chairman Neal Smith, D-Iowa, in 1978.

However, the Iowa Bar Association, represented by former Rep. Wiley T. Mayne, R-Iowa (1967-75), backed O'Brien, according to an aide to Sen. John C. Culver, D-Iowa. The aide added that the Iowa Judicial Selection Commission — a panel established by the two Iowa senators at President Carter's request to provide for merit selection of judges — had recommended O'Brien as well.

Following a six-hour hearing in which the Senate Judiciary Committee grilled the ABA on its opposition, the panel voted to report O'Brien's name. After putting a temporary "hold" on the nomination pending further evidence, Sen. Dennis DeConcini, D-Ariz., withdrew his objections. The Senate then approved O'Brien by voice vote Oct. 4.

Clauss. However, Carin Ann Clauss, nominated for a vacant district judgeship in the District of Columbia, was not so lucky. Numerous objections caused the Judiciary Committee to refuse to report her name before Congress adjourned.

Prior to the Sept. 20 nomination, the ABA attempted to block the consideration of Clauss, who was solicitor of the Labor Department. The ABA charged that Clauss' admitted lack of trial experience disqualified her for the job. The ABA screening panel for judicial nominees unanimously rejected her name when it was first offered in the spring of 1978.

(Continued on p. 16-A)

Membership of Federal Regulatory Agencies, 1978

Civil Aeronautics Board

(Five members appointed for six-year terms; not more than three members from one political party; agency due to expire Jan. 1, 1985)

Member	Party	Term Expires	Nominated	Confirmed by Senate
Vacancy				
Gloria Schaffer*	D	12/31/84	7/13/78	9/13/78
Marvin S. Cohen (C)	D	12/31/79	9/12/78	10/10/78
Richard J. O'Melia	R	12/31/80	5/16/74	9/19/74
Elizabeth E. Bailey*	R	12/31/83	7/8/77	7/28/77

Commodity Futures Trading Commission

(Five members appointed for five-year terms; not more than three members from one political party.)

Member	Party	Term Expires	Nominated	Confirmed by Senate
Vacancy (C)				
Gary L. Seevers (VC)	I	4/15/79	3/19/75	4/10/75
Read P. Dunn Jr.‡	D	4/15/78	3/18/75	4/10/75
Robert L. Martin	R	6/19/81	6/3/76	6/17/76
David G. Gartner*	D	5/19/83	5/10/78	5/17/78

Consumer Product Safety Commission

(Five members appointed for seven-year terms; not more than three members from one political party.)

Member	Party	Term Expires	Nominated	Confirmed by Senate
Susan B. King (C)*	D	10/26/84	1/20/78	2/28/78
Barbara H. Franklin	R	10/26/79	4/9/73	5/10/73
R. David Pittle**	D	10/26/82	1/20/78	2/1/78
Edith B. Sloan*	D	10/26/83	1/20/78	2/28/78
Samuel D. Zagoria*	R	10/26/85	9/29/78	10/10/78

Federal Communications Commission

(Seven members appointed for seven-year terms; not more than four members from one political party.)

Member	Party	Term Expires	Nominated	Confirmed by Senate
Charles D. Ferris (C)*	D	6/30/84	9/12/77	10/10/77
Tyrone Brown*	D	6/30/79	10/17/77	11/9/77
James H. Quello	D	6/30/80	1/22/74	4/22/74
Robert E. Lee	R	6/30/81	5/17/74	6/27/74
Abbott Washburn	R	6/30/82	6/18/75	9/26/75
Joseph R. Fogarty	D	6/30/83	6/21/76	9/8/76
Vacancy				

Federal Election Commission

(Six members appointed for six-year terms; not more than three members from one political party)

Member	Party	Term Expires	Nominated	Confirmed by Senate
William L. Springer†	R	4/30/77	5/17/76	5/21/76
Neil Staebler†	D	4/30/77	5/17/76	5/18/76
Thomas E. Harris	D	4/30/79	5/17/76	5/18/76
Vernon W. Thomson (C)	R	4/30/79	5/17/76	5/18/76
Joan D. Aikens	R	4/30/81	5/17/76	5/18/76
Robert O. Tiernan	D	4/30/81	5/17/76	5/18/76

† Members sitting on commission pending Senate confirmation of their replacements. John W. McGarry, D, was given a recess appointment by President Carter for the Staebler seat, but Staebler questioned the legality of the move.

Federal Energy Regulatory Commission

(Five members appointed to staggered four-year terms; not more than three members from one party.)

Member	Party	Term Expires	Nominated	Confirmed by Senate
Charles B. Curtis (C)*	I	6/22/80	9/30/77	10/20/77
Don S. Smith**	D	6/22/79	9/30/77	10/20/77
George R. Hall*	D	6/22/80	9/13/77	10/20/77
Georgiana R. Sheldon*	R	6/22/80	9/13/77	10/20/77
Matthew Holden Jr.*	D	6/22/81	9/26/77	10/20/77

Federal Reserve System Governors

(Seven members appointed for 14-year terms; no statutory limitation on political party membership.)

Member	Party	Term Expires	Nominated	Confirmed by Senate
G. William Miller (C)*	D	1/31/92	1/25/78	3/3/78
Philip E. Caldwell	D	1/31/80	9/26/74	10/9/74
Nancy H. Teeters*	D	1/31/84	8/28/78	9/15/78
J. Charles Partee	I	1/31/86	12/8/75	12/19/75
Henry C. Wallich	R	1/31/88	1/11/74	2/8/74
Two vacancies				

Federal Trade Commission

(Five members appointed for seven-year terms; not more than three members from one party.)

Member	Party	Term Expires	Nominated	Confirmed by Senate
Michael J. Pertschuk (C)*	D	9/25/84	3/25/77	4/6/77
Mary E. Hanford-Dole	I	9/25/80	9/5/73	11/20/73
Paul Rand Dixon	D	9/25/81	9/5/74	9/26/74
Robert Pitofsky*	D	9/25/82	5/25/78	6/28/78
David A. Clanton	R	9/25/83	7/20/76	7/29/76

Interstate Commerce Commission

(Eleven members appointed for seven-year terms; not more than six members from one political party; President Carter and Chairman O'Neal decided to cut the commission's size by not filling vacancies.)

Member	Party	Term Expires	Nominated	Confirmed by Senate
Virginia Mae Brown	D	12/31/77	4/14/71	6/30/71
Betty Jo Christian	D	12/31/79	12/8/75	3/18/76
A. Daniel O'Neal Jr. (C)	D	12/31/79	3/6/73	4/6/73
George M. Stafford	R	12/31/80	1/15/74	2/27/74
Charles L. Clapp	R	12/31/80	1/22/74	2/27/74
Robert C. Gresham	R	12/31/81	6/3/74	9/19/74
Five vacancies				

Nuclear Regulatory Commission

(Five members appointed for five-year terms; not more than three members from one political party.)

Member	Party	Term Expires	Nominated	Confirmed by Senate
Joseph M. Hendrie (C)*	R	6/30/81	6/29/77	8/3/77
Victor Gilinsky	D	6/30/79	12/12/74	12/19/74
Richard T. Kennedy	R	6/30/80	12/12/74	12/19/74
Peter A. Bradford*	D	6/30/82	6/12/77	8/3/77
James F. Ahearne*	—	6/30/83	5/18/78	7/21/78

Securities and Exchange Commission

(Five members appointed for five-year terms; not more than three members from one political party.)

Member	Party	Term Expires	Nominated	Confirmed by Senate
Harold M. Williams (C)*	D	6/5/82	3/30/77	4/7/77
John R. Evans‡	R	6/5/78	5/29/73	6/1/73
Philip A. Loomis Jr.	R	6/5/79	7/15/74	8/8/74
Irving M. Pollack	D	6/5/80	7/1/75	8/1/75
Roberta S. Karmel*	D	6/5/81	8/1/77	9/22/77

* Carter appointment.
** Reappointed by Carter; first appointed by a previous administration.
‡ Continuing to serve pending filling of vacancy.

The ABA decision threw the nomination into limbo as Clauss attempted to gain further trial experience. The administration pledged to stand by her nomination, citing President Carter's desire to name more women and minority representatives to federal judgeships.

The administration, according to one official, also was determined to stand by its nominees and not let the ABA have a veto over them. Citing a judicial screening commission finding that "she is abundantly qualified despite the lack of trial experience," the official added that Carter would stand by the Clauss nomination "unless the ABA panel comes up with convincing evidence otherwise."

Clauss' trial experience during the summer of 1978 later caused the ABA panel to reverse its rejection of her, according to news reports — but that same trial experience cast another cloud over her nomination.

In a September 1978 opinion, the U.S. Court of Appeals for the Third Circuit criticized Clauss' office for its handling of an occupational safety case. The three-judge panel first criticized Labor Department lawyers — lawyers under Clauss' supervision — for filing a brief in August that was due in late April. The judges then added, "we register our most vigorous disapproval of the contumacious conduct of counsel in this case." They questioned the "competence of [government] counsel appearing in federal courts." The strong opinion damaged one of Clauss' main arguments for the nomination, namely that she ran an efficient and effective staff in the solicitor's office.

Energy Department Nominations

Two nomination fights from 1977 over Energy Department posts carried over into 1978. Both ended in confirmation of the controversial officials.

Coleman. Following the defeat of a motion to recommit his name to the Energy Committee, the Senate by voice vote May 9 approved the nomination of Lynn R. Coleman to be general counsel of the department.

Coleman had been under fire for his close ties to the energy industry. He had been a lawyer in the Washington office of Vinson and Elkins, a Texas law firm that included former Treasury Secretary and Texas Gov. John B. Connally among its partners and that represented many of the largest energy companies. Citing possible conflicts of interest, Sen. Howard M. Metzenbaum, D-Ohio, moved to kill Coleman's nomination by sending it back to committee. His motion was defeated 20-75. *(Vote 157, p. 26-S)*

Thorne. The controversy surrounding the nomination of Robert D. Thorne to be assistant secretary for energy technology ended much more quietly. The Senate confirmed his nomination by voice vote on May 4.

Thorne's nomination had run into trouble in 1977 over his role in an anti-nuclear power referendum in California in 1976. Environmentalists charged that he was too pro-nuclear power to be put into the technology post. They claimed that he used his position as head of the Energy Research and Development Administration's San Francisco office to put out pro-nuclear and anti-referendum material. *(1977 controversy over Thorne and Coleman, 1977 Almanac p. 607)*

Mendelsohn Withdrawn

Following allegations of fiscal irregularities in an unsuccessful political campaign, President Carter on Nov. 14, 1977, withdrew the nomination of San Francisco supervisor Robert Mendelsohn as assistant interior secretary for management, program and budget.

After Mendelsohn was cleared of charges brought against him by the California Fair Political Practices Commission, Carter appointed him on June 5 to a post as assistant to Interior Secretary Cecil D. Andrus. Mendelsohn's new post did not require Senate confirmation.

Stewart: SBA

By an 88-11 vote, the Senate July 18 confirmed the nomination of Milton D. Stewart as chief counsel for advocacy in the Small Business Administration. *(Vote 214, p. 35-S)*

Proponents of the nomination pointed to Stewart's long record of concern for small businesses, especially minority small businesses. They also stressed the wide range of his support and his familiarity with the needs of the SBA's constituents.

Opponents, led by Sen. Lowell P. Weicker Jr., R-Conn., conceded these points about Stewart, but they questioned his role in the 1974 collapse of one small company, which was then taken over by another firm in which Stewart, Weicker said, had an interest.

Cottine: OSHA

By a 56-33 vote, the Senate on April 27 confirmed Carter's nomination of Bertram R. Cottine to be a member of the Occupational Safety and Health Review Commission. *(Vote 141, p. 24-S)*

Opposition to Cottine was led by Senate conservatives who had declared war on the Occupational Safety and Health Administration (OSHA). Pointing to Cottine's position as policy assistant in the office of Eula T. Bingham, assistant labor secretary for occupational safety, they claimed Cottine would not be objective in his decisions.

Turner: Public Broadcasting

On Oct. 19, 1977, Carter nominated Irby Turner Jr. of Belzoni, Miss., to a seat on the board of directors of the Corporation for Public Broadcasting (CBP). But the Senate refused to act on his nomination before the end of the 1977 session and, unlike other such nominees, his name was not resubmitted in 1978.

Turner's nomination drew fire from national civil rights groups. They charged that during his service on the Mississippi Authority for Educational Television he had been insensitive to the need for minority-oriented programming on the state's public television stations.

Four 1978 Carter nominees for the CPB board were not acted upon by the Commerce Committee before adjournment: Geoffrey Cowan, Paul S. Friedlander, Kathleen Nolan and Howard A. White.

Sayre: Brazil

By a vote of 62-27, the Senate on April 27 tabled a motion to recommit the nomination of career diplomat Robert M. Sayre as ambassador to Brazil. The nomination was then confirmed by voice vote. The Sayre nomination was the only ambassadorial nomination to draw Senate fire in 1978. *(Vote 143, p. 24-S)*

The controversy around Sayre centered on his role in a 1972 incident in Panama. Sayre, who was U.S. ambassador at the time, received information that American drug enforcement agents were preparing to arrest Panamanian official Moises Torrijos on drug-smuggling charges when his plane landed in the Canal Zone. An arrest warrant had been issued in New York for Torrijos in connection with a smuggling ring.

Torrijos, the brother of Gen. Omar Torrijos, ruler of Panama, was then Panama's ambassador to Spain. Moises Torrijos' activities were questioned by senators opposed to the Panama Canal treaties earlier in 1978. They asked how a treaty could be concluded with a ruler whose brother was engaged in smuggling drugs.

Many of the senators who opposed the treaties opposed the Sayre nomination. They claimed that Sayre obstructed execution of the warrant by informing Gen. Torrijos of the fact that the United States knew his brother's destination. Torrijos informed his brother, the opponents added, who changed his landing place to one outside American jurisdiction, thus avoiding arrest.

Sayre told the Foreign Relations Committee that he had been informed of the plans regarding Moises Torrijos by the CIA Panama station chief. When he sought advice from his State Department superiors, they told him to communicate with Gen. Torrijos, as part of the U.S. campaign to soothe then-ruffled Panamanian feelings over the slow pace of negotiations on the treaties.

1978 Confirmations

Listed below are 163 persons named to major federal posts and confirmed by the Senate in 1978. Several major confirmations that occurred after the 1977 CQ Almanac went to press also are included. Information is given in the following order: name of office, salary, appointee, voting residence, last occupation before appointment, previous political or policy posts if any, date and place of birth, party affiliation (where available), confirmation date.

Also included are names of one person whose nomination was withdrawn (and later submitted for another agency), six who were not confirmed, one who was not confirmed but given a recess appointment by Carter, one who had been given a recess appointment prior to submission of his name for confirmation, and one whose post did not need confirmation.

Ambassadorial confirmations are listed only if the appointment was of more than routine interest.

EXECUTIVE OFFICE OF THE PRESIDENT

Central Intelligence Agency

Deputy director, $52,500 —**Frank Charles Carlucci III;** Bear Creek, Pa.; ambassador to Portugal (1974-78); under secretary of HEW (1972-74), associate and then deputy director, Office of Management and Budget (1971-72); director, Office of Economic Opportunity (1969-71); Oct. 18, 1930, in Scranton, Pa.; Feb. 9.

Council on Environmental Quality

Member, $50,000 — **Jane Hurt Yarn;** Atlanta, Ga.; chair, Charles A. Lindbergh Fund (1977-78); chair, Georgia Coastal Islands Committee (1969-70); Oct. 15, 1924, in Greenville, S.C.; Dem.; Aug. 18.

Office of Management and Budget

Director, $57,500 — **James T. McIntyre Jr.;** Alpharetta, Ga.; deputy director, OMB (1977-78); deputy Georgia revenue commissioner (1970-72); Dec. 17, 1940, in Vidalia, Ga.; Dem.; March 21.

Deputy director, $52,500 — **John Patrick White;** McLean, Va.; assistant secretary of defense for manpower and reserve affairs (1977-78); Feb. 27, 1938, in Syracuse, N.Y.; nominated Oct. 7; nomination not reported by Senate Governmental Affairs Committee before adjournment; recess appointment announced by Carter Nov. 1.

CABINET DEPARTMENTS

Agriculture Department

Assistant secretary for marketing and services and member of the board of directors of the Commodity Credit Corporation, $50,000 — **P. R. "Bobby" Smith;** Winder, Ga.; special assistant to the agriculture secretary (1977-78); national director, "Farmers for Carter" (1976); Feb. 25, 1925, in Winder; Dem.; Feb. 24 (assistant secretary) March 20 (CCC post).

Administrator, Rural Electrification Administration (terms expiring Oct. 30, 1988), $47,500 — **Robert W. Ferguson;** Reston, Va.; deputy REA administrator (1978); Jan. 28, 1925, in Minot, N.D.; Dem.; Oct. 15.

Commerce Department

Assistant secretary for congressional liaison, $50,000 — **Andrew E. Manatos;** Bethesda, Md.; counselor to the secretary of commerce for congressional liaison (1977); associate staff director, Senate District of Columbia Committee and legislative assistant to Sen. Thomas F. Eagleton, D-Mo. (1973-76); Dec. 7, 1944, in Washington, D.C.; Dem.; Dec. 15, 1977.

Assistant secretary for communications and information, $50,000 — **Henry Geller;** Alexandria, Va.; consultant to the Commerce Department (1977-78); special assistant to the chairman, Federal Communications Commission (FCC) (1970-73); FCC general counsel (1964-70); FCC deputy general counsel (1962-64); FCC associate general counsel (1961); March 14, 1924, in Springfield, Mass.; Dem.; June 28.

National Oceanographic and Atmospheric Administration

Deputy administrator, $50,000 — **James P. Walsh;** Washington, D.C.; general counsel, Senate Commerce Committee (1977-78); staff counsel, Commerce Committee (1972-77); assistant attorney general, Washington state (1971-72); Dec. 28, 1944, in North Bend, Ore.; Dem.; March 7.

Associate administrator, $47,500 — **George S. Benton;** Baltimore, Md.; assistant administrator for oceanic and atmospheric services, NOAA (1977-78); Sept. 24, 1917, in Oak Park, Ill.; June 28.

National Bureau of Standards

Director, $47,500 — **Ernest Ambler;** Bethesda, Md.; acting director, NBS (1975-78) and deputy director (1973-78); Nov. 20, 1923, in Yorkshire, England; Dem.; Feb. 1.

Patent and Trademark Office

Commissioner, $47,500 — **Donald Witte Banner;** Aurora, Ill.; General patent counsel, Borg-Warner Corp. (1964-78); Feb. 23, 1924, in Chicago, Ill.; Independent; May 24.

Defense Department

Under secretary for policy, $52,500 — **Stanley R. Resor;** New Canaan, Conn.; United States representative to the Mutual and Balanced Force Reduction negotiations (1973-78), secretary of the Army (1965-71), under secretary of the Army (1965); Dec. 5, 1917, in New York City; Rep.; Aug. 7.

Chairman, Defense Military Liaison Committee to the Department of Energy, $47,500 — **James P. Wade Jr.**; Reston, Va.; assistant to the defense secretary for atomic energy (1978 — concurrent post); Dec. 26, 1930, in Richmond Heights, Mo.; Aug. 7.

Air Force

Assistant secretary for financial management, $50,000 — **John Arnot Hewitt Jr.**; Princeton, N.J.; vice president for trust and fiduciary investment, Chase Manhattan Bank (1974-78); July 20, 1943, in Van Nuys, Calif.; Dem.; Feb. 24.

Joint Chiefs of Staff

Chairman (term expiring June 30, 1980), $47,500 — Gen. **David C. Jones**; Minot, N.D.; chief of staff, Air Force (1974-78); July 9, 1921, in Aberdeen, S.D.; May 24.

Air Force chief of staff (four-year term), $47,500 — Gen. **Lew Allen Jr.**; Gainesville, Texas; vice chief of staff, Air Force (1978); director, National Security Agency (1973-77); Sept. 30, 1925, in Miami, Fla.; May 24.

Chief of naval operations (four-year term), $47,500 — Adm. **Thomas B. Hayward**; Glendale, Calif.; commander-in-chief, U.S. Pacific Fleet (1976-78); May 3, 1924, in Glendale; May 24.

Department of Energy

Assistant secretary for conservation and solar applications, $50,000 — **Omi G. Walden**; Atlanta, Ga.; director, Georgia Office of Energy Resources (1976-78); policy adviser and federal-state relations coordinator for energy and environmental issues, office of the governor of Georgia (1973-76); Dec. 25, 1945 in Alma, Ga.; Dem.; July 26.

Assistant secretary for defense programs, $50,000 — **Duane C. Sewell**; Livermore, Calif.; Lawrence Livermore Laboratory, University of California since 1956, deputy director (1973-78); Aug. 15, 1918, in Oakland, Calif.; Dem.; Aug. 7.

Director of energy research (assistant secretary level), $50,000 — **John M. Deutch**; Lexington, Mass.; chairman, department of chemistry, Massachusetts Institute of Technology (1976-77); July 27, 1938, in Brussels, Belgium; Dec. 6, 1977.

Assistant secretary for resource applications, $50,000 — **George S. McIsaac**; Washington, D.C.; principal and director, McKinsey and Co. (consulting firm) (1962-78); July 25, 1930 in Auburn, N.Y.; Dem.; Feb. 10.

Assistant secretary for energy technology, $50,000 — **Robert D. Thorne**; Walnut Creek, Calif.; manager, San Francisco operations office, Energy Research and Development Administration (ERDA) (1978); acting assistant administrator for nuclear programs, ERDA (1977); July 22, 1938, in Laramie, Wyo.; Independent; May 4.

Assistant secretary for environment, $50,000 — **Ruth C. Clusen**; Green Bay, Wis.; president, League of Women Voters of U.S. (1974-78); member, U.S. delegation to U.S.-U.S.S.R. joint committee on environmental protection (1974); June 11, 1922, in Bruce, Wis.; Dem.; Aug. 25.

General counsel, $50,000 — **Lynn R. Coleman**; Washington, D.C.; lawyer, Vinson and Elkins (Texas law firm) (1965-78); campaign director, Barefoot Saunders for Senate (Texas Democratic primary candidate) (1972); Aug. 17, 1939, in Vernon, Texas; Dem.; May 9.

Inspector general, $50,000 — **John K. Mansfield**; Farmington, Conn.; special assistant to the assistant secretary of state for oceans and international environmental and scientific affairs (1974-78); inspector general of foreign assistance, State Department (1962-69); Oct. 8, 1921, in Chicago, Ill.; Dem.; May 3.

Deputy inspector general, $47,500 — **Thomas S. Williamson Jr.**; Washington, D.C.; associate with law firm of Covington and Burling (1974-78); July 14, 1946, in Plainfield, N.J.; Oct. 10.

Administrator, Energy Information Administration (assistant secretary level), $50,000 — **Lincoln E. Moses**; Stanford, Calif.; professor of statistics, Stanford University (1959-77); Dec. 21, 1921, in Kansas City, Mo.; Dem.; Dec. 15, 1977.

Department of Health, Education and Welfare

Administration on Aging

Commissioner, $47,500 — **Robert C. Benedict**; Mechanicsburg, Pa.; commissioner, Office of the Aging, Pennsylvania Department of Public Welfare (1972-78); Nov. 29, 1940, in Randolph, Vt.; Dem.; Feb. 10.

Alcohol, Drug Abuse and Mental Health Administration

Administrator, $50,000 — **Gerald L. Klerman**; Chestnut Hill, Mass.; professor of psychiatry, Harvard Medical School and director, Stanley Cobb Laboratories, Massachusetts General Hospital (1976-77); Dec. 29, 1928, in New York City; Dem.; Oct. 29, 1977.

Social Security Administration

Commissioner, $50,000 — **Stanford G. Ross**; Washington, D.C.; partner in D.C. law firm of Caplin and Drysdale (1969-78); Transportation Department general counsel (1968-69), White House staff assistant (1967-68), Treasury Department assistant counsel (1963-67); Oct. 9, 1931, in St. Louis, Mo.; Dem.; Sept. 27.

Institute of Museum Services

Director, $47,500 — **Leila I. Kimche**; Bethesda, Md.; executive director, Association of Science Technology Centers (1974-77); June 21, 1934, in New York City; Dec. 15, 1977.

Department of Housing and Urban Development

Federal Insurance Administration

Administrator, $50,000 — **Gloria Cusumano Jimenez**; Durham, N.C.; deputy commissioner and general counsel, North Carolina Department of Insurance (1975-78), director of housing and urban programs, N.C. Department of Local Affairs (1968-70); district aide to Rep. Richard L.,Ottinger, D-N.Y. (1965-66); July 1, 1932, in New York City; Dem.; March 9.

Department of Interior

Director, Office of Surface Mining, $50,000 — **Walter N. Heine**; Newville, Pa.; associate deputy secretary for mines and land protection, Pennsylvania Department of Environmental Resources (1971-77); Feb. 21, 1934, in New York City; Rep.; Dec. 6, 1977.

Director, Bureau of Mines, $47,500 — **Roger A. Markle**; Salt Lake City, Utah; president, western division, Valley Camp Coal Co. (1974-78); Dec. 12, 1933, in Sidney, Mont.; Aug. 25.

Director, Bureau of Land Management, $47,500 — **Frank Gregg**; Hingham, Mass.; chairman, New England River Basins Commission (1967-78); staff assistant to the Interior secretary (1961-63); Dec. 12, 1925, in Denver, Colo.; Aug. 25.

United States Geological Survey

Director, $47,500 — **Harry William Menard**; La Jolla, Calif.; professor of geology, Scripps Institution of Oceanography (1955-78); Dec. 10, 1920, in Fresno, Calif.; March 23.

Department of Justice

Deputy attorney general, $57,500 — **Benjamin Civiletti**; Baltimore, Md.; assistant attorney general, Criminal Division (1977-78); assistant U.S. attorney for Maryland (1962-64); July 17, 1935, in Peekskill, N.Y.; Dem.; May 9.

Director, Federal Bureau of Investigation (10-year term) $57,500 — **William H. Webster;** Ladue, Mo.; judge, eighth U.S. Circuit Court of Appeals (1973-78); U.S. district judge, eastern Missouri (1971-73), U.S. attorney, eastern Missouri (1960-61); March 6, 1924, in Webster Groves, Mo.; Rep.; Feb. 9.

Assistant attorney general, Criminal Division, $50,000 — **Philip Benjamin Heymann;** Belmont, Mass.; professor of law, Harvard University (1969-78); associate Watergate special prosecutor (1973-75); Oct. 30, 1932, in Pittsburgh, Pa.; June 23.

Director, Community Relations Service, $50,000 — **Gilbert G. Pompa;** San Antonio, Texas; acting director, CRS (1977-78) and deputy director (1976-78); assistant district attorney, Bexar County (San Antonio) (1963-67) and assistant city attorney, San Antonio (1960-63); Oct. 1, 1931, in Devine, Texas; Dem.; May 26.

Law Enforcement Assistance Administration

Administrator, $52,500 — **Norval Morris;** Chicago, Ill.; dean of the University of Chicago law school (1975-); director of the UN Institute for Prevention of Crime and the Treatment of Offenders (1962-64); Oct. 1, 1923, in Auckland, New Zealand; nomination submitted to Judiciary Committee Sept. 19, but not reported before adjournment of Congress.

(Two assistant administrators also were nominated by Carter, but the names were not formally sent to the Judiciary Committee due to the delay in the Morris nomination.)

U.S. Parole Commission

Commissioner for term expiring Nov. 21, 1983, $47,500 — **Audrey A. Kaslow;** Pacoima, Calif.; probation director (not department chief), Los Angeles County probation department (1950-77); Sept. 9, 1921, in Miami, Ariz.; Nov. 15, 1977.

Commissioner for term expiring Oct. 17, 1984, $47,500 — **Richard T. Mulcrone;** Shakopee, Minn.; chairman of Minnesota Corrections Board (1973-78); May 23, 1934, in St. Paul, Minn.; Sept. 30.

Commissioner for term expiring Aug. 31, 1984, $47,500 — **Oliver James Keller Jr.;** Gainesville, Fla.; visiting professor of criminal justice studies at the University of Florida (1975-78); secretary of the Florida Department of Health and Rehabilitative Services (1973-75); April 21, 1923, in Lancaster, Pa.; July 14.

Department of Labor

Assistant secretary for mine safety and health, $50,000 — **Robert B. Lagather;** Arlington, Va.; deputy solicitor for regional operations, Labor Department (1975-78); deputy assistant secretary for labor-management relations administration, Labor Department (1973-75); Dec. 8, 1925, in Chisholm, Minn.; Dem.; Feb. 10.

Department of State

Under secretary for political affairs, $52,500 — **David D. Newsom;** Berkeley, Calif.; ambassador to the Philippines (1977-78); ambassador to Indonesia (1974-77); assistant secretary of state for African affairs (1969-74); ambassador to Libya (1965-69); Jan. 6, 1918, in Richmond, Calif.; April 12.

Assistant secretary for Near Eastern and South Asian Affairs, $50,000 — **Harold H. Saunders;** Falls Church, Va.; director, Bureau of Intelligence and Research, State Department (1975-78); deputy assistant secretary for Near Eastern and South Asian affairs (1974-75); Dec. 27, 1930, in Philadelphia, Pa.; April 6.

Assistant secretary for Inter-American Affairs, $50,000 — **Viron P. Vaky;** Corpus Christi, Texas; ambassador to Venezuela (1976-78); ambassador to Colombia (1974-76); ambassador to Costa Rica (1972-74); acting assistant secretary for Inter-American Affairs (1968-69); Sept. 13, 1926, in Corpus Christi; July 12.

Assistant secretary for oceans and international environmental and scientific affairs, $50,000 — **Thomas R. Pickering;** Rutherford, N.J.; ambassador to Jordan (1974-78); special assistant to the secretary of state and executive secretary, State Department (1974); Nov. 5, 1931, in Orange, N.J.; Sept. 22.

Assistant secretary for educational and cultural affairs, $50,000 — **Alice Stone Ilchman;** Wellesley, Mass.; dean of the college and professor of economics and education, Wellesley College (1973-78); April 18, 1935, in Cincinnati, Ohio; Dem.; March 17. *(Post abolished April 1; see "International Communication Agency.")*

Agency for International Development

Assistant administrator for private and development cooperation, $50,000 — ***Calvin H. Raullerson;*** Lubbock, Texas; executive director, International Center for Arid and Semi-arid Land Studies, Texas Tech University (1973-78); Feb. 18, 1920, in Utica, N.Y.; Aug. 11.

Assistant administrator for intragovernmental and international affairs, $50,000 — **Donald Bromheim;** Washington, D.C.; vice-president, The Futures Group (part of Dreyfus Corp.) (1978); deputy coordinator, Alliance for Progress (1960-67); April 28, 1932, in New York; Dem.; May 2.

Ambassadors

(Salaries listed are those attached to the posts involved, according to the State Department.)

Chief of protocol (ambassadorial rank), $50,000 — **Edith Huntington Jones "Kit" Dobelle;** Pittsfield, Mass.; educational consultant, Massachusetts Education Department, Bureau of Equal Education Opportunity (1972-73); (1977-78: wife of Evan S. Dobelle, whom she succeeded as chief of protocol, and with whom she shared the office's duties); Sept. 2, 1944, in Hamden, Conn.; Dem.; Sept. 13.

Ambassador-at-large for Middle East peace negotiations, $57,500 — **Alfred L. "Roy" Atherton Jr.;** Palm Beach Gardens, Fla.; assistant secretary for Near Eastern and South Asian affairs (1974-78); deputy assistant secretary for Near Eastern and South Asian affairs (1973-74); Nov. 22, 1921, in Pittsburgh, Pa.; April 6.

Brazil, $57,500 — **Robert M. Sayre;** Falls Church, Va.; inspector general of the Foreign Service (1975-78); ambassador to Panama (1969-74) and Uruguay (1968-69); Aug. 18, 1924, in Hillsboro, Ore.; April 27.

Denmark, $47,500 — **Warren Demian Manshel;** New York City; editor and publisher, *Foreign Policy* magazine (1970-78) and *The Public Interest* magazine (1965-78); Jan. 26, 1924, in Berlin, Germany; June 22.

Ethiopia, $50,000 — **Frederic L. Chapin;** North Brunswick Township, N.J.; U.S. consul general, Sao Paulo, Brazil (1972-78); deputy executive secretary, AID (1965-68); July 13, 1929, in New York City; June 23.

Greece, $52,500 — **Robert J. McCloskey;** Chevy Chase, Md.; ambassador to Holland (1976-78); assistant secretary of state for congressional relations (1975-76); Nov. 25, 1922, in Philadelphia, Pa.; unaffiliated; March 1.

Jordan, $50,000 — **Nicholas A. Veliotes;** McLean, Va.; deputy assistant secretary, Bureau of Near Eastern and South Asian Affairs (1977-78); Oct. 28, 1928 in Oakland, Calif.; Aug. 18.

Korea, $57,500 — **William H. Gleysteen Jr.;** Jenkintown, Pa.; deputy assistant secretary for East Asian and Pacific affairs (1977-78 and 1974-76); May 8, 1926, in Peking, China; June 23.

Lebanon, $52,500 — **John Gunther Dean;** New York state; ambassador to Denmark (1975-78) and to Cambodia (1974-75); Feb. 26, 1926, in Germany; Sept. 30.

Netherlands, $50,000 — **Geri M. Joseph;** Minneapolis, Minn.; contributing editor and columnist, *Minneapolis Tribune* (1972-78); June 19, 1923, in St. Paul, Minn.; July 14.

Panama, $50,000 — **Ambler Holmes Moss Jr.,** Alexandria, Va.; attorney, Coudert Brothers, Washington, D.C. (1978); deputy assistant secretary for congressional relations (1977-78), member, Panama Canal treaty negotiating team (1977); Sept. 1, 1937, in Baltimore, Md.; Sept. 22.

Poland, $52,500 — **William E. Schaufele;** Avon Lake, Ohio; ambassador to Greece (1977-78); assistant secretary for African affairs (1975-77), deputy U.S. representative to the U.N. Security Council (1973-75); Dec. 7, 1923, in Lakewood, Ohio; Feb. 1.

Singapore, $47,500 — **Richard F. Kneip;** Pierre, S.D.; governor of South Dakota (D 1971-78); S.D. state senator (D 1965-71); Jan. 7, 1933, in Tyler, Minn.; Dem.; May 24.

South Africa, $52,500 — **William B. Edmondson;** Peru, Neb.; deputy assistant secretary for African affairs (1976-78); Feb. 26, 1927 in St. Joseph, Mo.; May 2.

Spain, $57,500 — **Terence A. Todman;** St. Thomas, Virgin Islands; assistant secretary for Inter-American Affairs (1977-78); March 13, 1926, in St. Thomas; Independent; May 24.

Vatican City (president's personal representative; does not need Senate confirmation), unpaid — **Robert F. Wagner;** New York City; senior partner, Finley, Kumble, Wagner, Heine and Underberg (New York law firm) (1975-78); ambassador to Spain (1968-69); mayor of New York City (D 1954-65); Manhattan borough president (D 1949-53); New York City planning commission chairman (1948), city housing commissioner (1947), city tax commissioner (1946), New York state assemblyman (D 1938-41); Dem.; does not require confirmation.

Transportation Department

Assistant secretary for budget and programs, $50,000 — **Mortimer L. Downey III;** Reston, Va.; deputy under secretary of transportation (1977); supervisor of rail public services for New York Port Authority (1973-75; worked for Port Authority since 1953); Aug. 9, 1936, in Springfield, Mass.; Dem.; Nov. 22, 1977.

Administrator, Federal Highway Administration, $57,500 — **Karl Smith Bowers;** Estill, S.C.; deputy FHA administrator (1977-78); Member and chairman (1976-77), South Carolina Highway Commission (1974-77); Oct. 13, 1941, in Estill; Dem.; Aug. 18.

Treasury Department

Assistant secretary for tax policy, $50,000 — **Donald C. Lubick;** Chevy Chase, Md.; deputy assistant secretary and acting (since December 1977) assistant secretary for tax policy (1977-78); April 29, 1926, in Buffalo, N.Y.; June 23.

INDEPENDENT AGENCIES

Civil Aeronautics Board

Member for term expiring Dec. 31, 1979, $50,000 — **Marvin S. Cohen;** Tucson, Ariz.; partner in law firm of Bilby, Shoenhair, Warnock and Dolph (1963-78); special assistant to the solicitor, Interior Department (1961-63); Oct. 16, 1931, in Akron, Ohio; Dem.; Oct. 10.

Member for term expiring Dec. 31, 1984, and term expiring Dec. 31, 1978, $50,000 — **Gloria Schaffer;** Woodbridge, Conn.; Connecticut secretary of state (D 1971-78); unsuccessful Democratic nominee for U.S. Senate (1976); Connecticut state senator (D 1959-71); Oct. 3, 1930 in New London, Conn.; Dem.; Sept. 13.

Commodity Futures Trading Commission

Commissioner for term expiring May 21, 1983, $50,000 — **David Gay Gartner;** Arlington, Va.; administrative assistant to Sens. Hubert H. and Muriel B. Humphrey (1971-78 and 1961-69); Sept. 27, 1935, in Des Moines, Iowa; Dem.; May 17.

Consumer Product Safety Commission

Chairman and commissioner for term expiring Oct. 26, 1984, $52,500 — **Susan B. King;** Washington, D.C.; special assistant to the chairman, Federal Election Commission (1975-77); April 29, 1940, in Sioux City, Iowa; Dem.; Feb. 28.

Commissioner for terms expiring Oct. 26, 1978, and Oct. 26, 1985, $50,000 — **Samuel D. Zagoria;** College Park, Md.; director, labor-management relations service, U.S. Conference of Mayors (1970-78); Member, National Labor Relations Board (1965-69); administrative assistant to Sen. Clifford L. Case, R-N.J. (1955-65); April 9, 1919, in Somerville, N.J.; Rep.; Oct. 10.

Commissioner for term expiring Oct. 26, 1982, $50,000 — **R. David Pittle;** Rockville, Md.; CPSC commissioner since Oct. 10, 1973; Oct. 7, 1938, in Washington, D.C.; Dem.; Feb. 1.

Commissioner for term expiring Oct. 26, 1983, $50,000 — **Edith B. Sloan;** Washington, D.C.; director, Washington, D.C., office of consumer protection (1976-78); New York City; Dem.; Feb. 28.

Equal Employment Opportunity Commission

Commissioner for term expiring July 1, 1982, $50,000 — **J. Clay Smith Jr.;** Washington, D.C.; associate general counsel, Federal Communications Commission (1976-78); April 15, 1942, in Omaha, Neb.; Rep.; Oct. 10.

Commissioner for term expiring July 1, 1983, $50,000 — **Armando M. Rodriguez,** Whittier, Calif.; president, East Los Angeles College (1973-78); assistant commissioner for regional office coordination, Office of Education (HEW) (1971-73); Sept. 30, 1921, in Mexico; Dem.; Oct. 10.

Environmental Protection Agency

Assistant administrator for research and development, $50,000 — **Stephen John Gage;** Bethesda, Md.; deputy assistant EPA administrator for minerals and industry, Office of Research and Development (1975-78); Sept. 27, 1940, in Palisade, Neb.; Independent; March 14.

Export-Import Bank

First vice-president and vice-chairman, $50,000 — **H. K. Allen;** Temple, Texas; chairman, Temple National Bank (1953-78); July 24, 1926, in Dallas, Texas; Dem.; March 23.

Federal Communications Commission

Commissioner, $50,000 — **Anne P. Jones;** Arlington, Mass.; general counsel for the Federal Home Loan Bank Board (1977-78); Feb. 9, 1935, in Somerville, Mass.; Rep.; not confirmed before Congress adjourned; no recess appointment.

Federal Deposit Insurance Corporation

Member of the board of directors for term expiring March 15, 1984, $50,000 — **William M. Isaac;** Louisville, Ky.; vice-president and general counsel, Kentucky National Corp. (bank holding company) (1974-78); Dec. 21, 1943 in Bryan, Ohio; Rep.; March 14.

Federal Election Commission

Commissioner, $50,000 — **John W. McGarry;** Boston, Mass.; partner, McGarry and Rovner (Boston law firm) (1977-78); special counsel on elections to the House Administration Committee (1973-77); June 11, 1922, in Boston; Dem.; nomination blocked in Senate; given recess (interim) appointment to FEC by President Carter on Oct. 25, 1978.

Commissioner, $50,000 — **Max L. Friedersdorf;** Alexandria, Va.; staff director, Senate Republican Policy Committee (1977-); assistant to the president for legislative affairs (1975-77); deputy assistant to the president (1973-75) and special assistant to the president (1971-73); July 7, 1929, in Grammer, Ind.; Rep.; not confirmed before Congress adjourned.

Commissioner, $50,000 — **Samuel D. Zagoria;** College Park, Md.; director of labor-management relations service, U.S. Conference of Mayors (1970-78); Member, National Labor Relations Board (1965-69); administrative assistant to Sen. Clifford L. Case, R-N.J. (1955-65); April 9, 1919, in Somerville, N.J.; Rep.; Nomination submitted April 7 and withdrawn Aug. 12.

Federal Home Loan Bank Board

Member for term expiring June 30, 1978, and term expiring June 30, 1982, $50,000 — **Anita Miller;** Ridgewood, N.J.; senior program officer, Ford Foundation (1972-78); April 20, 1931, in New York City; Dem.; April 25.

Federal Maritime Commission

Commissioner for term expiring June 30, 1983, $50,000 — **Thomas F. Moakley;** Whitman, Mass.; FMC commissioner since 1977 (reappointment); director of the Port of Boston for the Massachusetts Port Authority (1975-77); Nov. 3, 1921, in Boston; Dem. (cousin of Rep. Joe Moakley, D-Mass.); Aug. 11.

Commissioner for term expiring June 30, 1981, $50,000 — **Leslie Lazar Kanuk;** Englewood Cliffs, N.J.; professor and chairman, department of marketing, Baruch College, City University of New York (1967-78); Aug. 9, 1929, in New York City; Dem.; April 19.

Federal Reserve System

Chairman of the board of governors for term expiring Feb. 1, 1992, $57,500 — **G. William Miller;** Providence, R.I.; chief executive officer (1968-78) and chairman of the board (1974-78), Textron Inc.; Democratic National Convention delegate (1968); March 9, 1925, in Sapulpa, Okla.; Dem.; March 3.

Member of the board of governors for term expiring Feb. 1, 1984 — **Nancy Hays Teeters;** Washington, D.C.; assistant staff director and chief economist, House Budget Committee (1975-78); July 29, 1930, in Marion, Ind.; Dem.; Sept. 15.

Federal Trade Commission

Commissioner for term expiring Sept. 26, 1982, $50,000 — **Robert Pitofsky;** Chevy Chase, Md.; professor of law, Georgetown University and counsel, Arnold and Porter (both 1973-78); director, Bureau of Consumer Protection, FTC (1970-73); Dec. 27, 1929, in Patterson, N.J.; Dem.; June 28.

International Communication Agency

(New agency, combining old United States Information Agency and the State Department's Bureau of Educational and Cultural Affairs)

Director, $57,500 — **John E. Reinhardt;** Bethesda, Md.; director, USIA (1977-78); assistant secretary of state for public affairs (1975-77); March 8, 1920, in Glade Spring, Va.; March 17.

Deputy director, $52,500 — **Charles W. Bray III;** Bethesda, Md.; deputy director, USIA (1977-78); deputy assistant secretary of state for inter-American affairs (1976-77), for public affairs (1974-76) and for press relations (1973-74); Oct. 24, 1933, in New York City; March 17.

Associate director for educational and cultural affairs, $50,000 — **Alice Stone Ilchman;** Wellesley, Mass.; assistant secretary of state for educational and cultural affairs (1978); April 18, 1935, in Cincinnati, Ohio; Dem.; March 17.

Associate director for management, $50,000 — **James David Isbister;** Potomac, Md.; vice-president, Orkand Corp. (1977-78); administrator, Alcohol, Drug Abuse and Mental Health Administration, HEW (1974-77); March 31, 1937, in Mt. Clemens, Mich.; non-partisan; Aug. 18.

Associate director for programs, $50,000 — **Harold Frederick Schneidman;** Hazelton, Pa.; director, USIA Information Center Service (1971-78); June 23, 1922 in Hazelton; Aug. 18.

Associate director for the Voice of America, $50,000 — **R. Peter Straus;** New York City; assistant director, USIA and director of the Voice of America (1977-78); chairman, New York State Democratic Campaign Committee (1964); Feb. 15, 1923, in New York City; Dem.; July 14.

Interstate Commerce Commission

Director, Office of Rail Public Counsel, $47,500 — **Howard A. Heffron;** Bethesda, Md.; self-employed attorney, Washington, D.C. (1969-77); chief counsel, Federal Highway Administration (1967-69); Oct. 3, 1927, in New York City; Dec. 15, 1977.

National Labor Relations Board

Member for term expiring Aug. 27, 1983, $50,000 — **Howard Jenkins Jr.;** Kensington, Md.; member, NLRB since 1963 (reappointment); June 16, 1915, in Denver, Colo.; Rep.; Sept. 15.

National Mediation Board

Member for term expiring July 1, 1981, $50,000 — **George S. Ives;** Bethesda, Md.; member of board since 1969; administrative assistant to his father, Sen. Irving Ives, R-N.Y. (1953-58); Jan. 10, 1922 in Brooklyn, N.Y.; Rep.; Oct. 10.

National Science Foundation

Assistant director, $47,500 — **James A. Krumhansl;** Trumansburg, N.Y.; professor of physics, Cornell University; Aug. 2, 1919, in Cleveland, Ohio; Dec. 6, 1977.

National Transportation Safety Board

Chairman, $52,500 — **James B. King;** Boston, Mass.; member of the board (since 1977, chairmanship required separate confirmation); White House personnel assistant (1977); vice-president in charge of marketing for the Massachusetts Bay Transportation Authority (1975-76), administrative assistant to Sen. Edward M. Kennedy, D-Mass. (1967-75); March 27, 1935, in Ludlow, Mass.; Dem.; March 20.

Vice-chairman and member for term expiring Dec. 31, 1980, $50,000 — **Elwood T. Driver;** Reston, Va.; acting associate administrator, National Highway Traffic Safety Administration; Aug. 20, 1921, in Trenton, N.J.; Dem.; March 20.

Member for term expiring Dec. 31, 1982, $50,000 — **Francis H. McAdams;** Washington, D.C.; NTSB member since 1967 (reappointment); Dec. 27, 1915, in Brooklyn, N.Y.; Dem.; Aug. 11.

Nuclear Regulatory Commission

Commissioner for terms expiring June 30, 1978, and June 30, 1983, $52,500 — **John Francis Ahearne;** McLean, Va.; deputy assistant energy secretary for power applications (1977-78); staffer, White House Energy Policy and Planning Office (1977); June 14, 1934, in New Britain, Conn.; July 21.

Occupational Safety and Health Review Commission

Commissioner for term expiring April 27, 1983, $50,000 — **Bertram Robert Cottine;** Alexandria, Va.; special assistant for policy in office of the assistant secretary of labor for occupational safety and health (1977-78); April 2, 1947, in Kingston, N.Y.; unaffiliated; April 27.

Overseas Private Investment Corporation

President, $52,500 — **James Bruce Llewellyn;** The Bronx, N.Y.; president, Fedco Foods Corp. (1969-78); Small Business Administration regional director in New York (1965-66); July 16, 1927, in New York City; Dem.; Oct. 11.

United States Postal Service

Postal Rate Commission

Commissioner for the term expiring Oct. 14, 1982, $52,500 — **Alvin Harry Gandal;** Chevy Chase, Md.; director of the office of contract analysis of the Postal Service since 1976; Feb. 8, 1932, in Cleveland, Ohio; nomination submitted to Senate Governmental Affairs Committee Jan. 26, but not reported; not given a recess appointment.

Railroad Retirement Board

Chairman and member for the term expiring Aug. 29, 1982, $52,500 — **William P. Adams;** Naperville, Ill.; vice-president of the Motion Picture Association of America (1977-78); counsel, House Commerce Committee (1974-76) and in the Office of the Legislative Counsel of the House of Representatives (1955-74); Aug. 2, 1926, in Danville, Ill.; Independent; Feb. 10.

Member for the term expiring Aug. 28, 1983, $50,000 — **Earl Oliver;** Chicago, Ill.; member of the board since 1977 (reappointment); Feb. 25, 1917, in Monticello, Ky.; Dem.; Oct. 15.

Securities and Exchange Commission

Commissioner for term expiring June 5, 1981, $50,000 — **Roberta S. Karmel;** Potomac, Md.; partner in the New York City law firm of Rogers and Wells (1972-77); May 4, 1937 in Chicago, Ill.; Dem.; Sept. 22, 1977.

Small Business Administration

Chief counsel for advocacy, $47,500 — **Milton David Stewart;** Staten Island, New York; chairman of the Research Council for Small Business and the Professions (1975-78); research director, President's Committee on Civil Rights (1946), staff economist for the Senate Small Business Committee (1946-50); executive assistant administrator of the Small Defense Plants Administration (1950-52) and special counsel to Gov. Averell Harriman, D-N.Y. (1955-58); March 5, 1922, in Brooklyn, N.Y.; Dem.; July 18.

Tennessee Valley Authority

Member of the board for term expiring May 18, 1987, $50,000 — **Richard Merrell Freeman;** Glencoe, Ill.; vice-president, law, Chicago and Northwestern Transportation Co. (1967-78); July 2, 1941, in Crawfordsville, Ind.; Oct. 13.

United States Arms Control and Disarmament Agency

Director, $57,000 — Gen. (Ret.) **George M. Seignious II;** Charleston, S.C.; president of The Citadel (university) (1974-79); deputy assistant defense secretary for security assistance and director of the Defense Security Assistance Agency (1971-72); director of the Joint Staff of the Joint Chiefs of Staff (1972-74); June 21, 1921 in Orangeburg, S.C.; President Carter announced his "intention to nominate" Seignious to the post on Oct. 20 and gave him a recess appointment, beginning Dec. 1.

United States International Trade Commission

Commissioner for term expiring June 16, 1987, $50,000 — **Paula Stern;** Washington, D.C.; executive with Carnegie Endowment for International Peace (1977-78); legislative assistant to Sen. Gaylord Nelson, D-Wis. (1972-74, 1976); March 31, 1945, in Chicago, Ill.; Dem.; Sept. 27.

LEGISLATIVE BRANCH

Government Printing Office

Public Printer, $50,000 — **John P. Boyle;** Silver Spring, Md.; deputy public printer, GPO (1973-77); Jan. 25, 1919, in Honesdale, Pa.; Dem.; Oct. 27, 1977.

JUDICIARY

U.S. Circuit Courts of Appeals

Judge for the fourth circuit, $57,500 — **James Dickson Phillips Jr.;** Chapel Hill, N.C.; professor and dean of the law school (1964-74) at the University of North Carolina (1960-78); Sept. 23, 1922, in Scotland County, N.C.; Dem.; Aug. 11.

Judge for the fifth circuit, $57,500 — **Robert S. Vance;** Birmingham, Ala.; partner in the Birmingham law firm of Vance, Thompson and Brown (1964-77) and chairman of the Alabama Democratic Party (1966-77); chairman of the Alabama 1968 Democratic National Convention delegation, and delegate to the 1972 Democratic National Convention; May 10, 1931, in Talladega, Ala.; Dem.; Nov. 15, 1977.

Judge for the eighth circuit, $57,500 — **Theodore McMillian;** St. Louis, Mo.; judge on the Missouri Court of Appeals (1972-78); St. Louis circuit court judge (1956-72) and assistant circuit attorney (1952-56); Jan. 28, 1919, in St. Louis; Dem.; Sept. 22.

Judge for the tenth circuit, $57,500 — **James K. Logan;** Olathe, Kan.; senior partner in the Olathe law firm of Payne and Jones (1968-77); special assistant Kansas attorney general for antitrust programs (1971); Aug. 21, 1929, in Quenemo, Kan.; Dem.; Nov. 15, 1977.

Judge for the tenth circuit, $57,500 — **Monroe G. McKay;** Provo, Utah; professor at the Brigham Young University Law School (1974-77); May 30, 1928, in Huntsville, Utah; Dem.; Nov. 29, 1977.

U.S. Court of Claims

Chief judge, $57,500 — **Daniel M. Friedman;** Washington, D.C.; first deputy solicitor general, Justice Department (1968-78); Feb. 8, 1916, in New York City; Independent; May 17.

Associate judge, $57,500 — **Edward S. Smith;** Baltimore, Md.; member of the Baltimore law firm of Piper and Marbury (1963-78); supervisor of civil tax litigation, Justice Department (1961-63); March 27, 1919, in Birmingham, Ala.; Dem.; July 26.

U.S. Tax Court

Judge (15-year term), $54,500 — **Herbert L. Chabot;** Rockville, Md.; deputy chief of staff of the Joint Committee on Taxation (1977-78; with the committee since 1965); July 17, 1931, in New York City; Dem.; March 20.

U.S. District Courts

Judge for the eastern and western districts of Arkansas, $54,000 — **Richard S. Arnold;** Texarkana, Ark.; legislative assistant to Sen. Dale Bumpers, D-Ark. (1975-78); delegate to the Arkansas constitutional convention (1969-70), delegate to the Democratic National Convention from Arkansas (1968), candidate for Democratic nomination in the Fourth Congressional District of Arkansas (1966, 1972), member of the Arkansas Democratic state executive committee (1972-74), legislative secretary to then-Gov. Dale Bumpers, D-Ark. (1973-74); March 26, 1936, in Texarkana, Texas; Dem.; Sept. 20.

Judge for the central district of California, $54,500 — **Mariana R. Pfaelzer;** Los Angeles, Calif.; senior partner in the Los Angeles firm of Wyman, Bautzer, Rothman and Kuchel (1957-78); member, Los Angeles Board of Police Commissioners (1974-78); Feb. 4, 1926, in Wilmar, Calif.; Dem.; Sept. 22.

Judge for the district of Colorado, $54,500 — **John L. Kane Jr.;** Denver, Colo.; partner in Denver law firm of Holme, Robert and Owen (1972-77); Feb. 14, 1937, in Tucumcari, N.M.; Dem.; Nov. 15, 1977.

Judge for the district of Connecticut, $54,500 — **Ellen Bree Burns;** Hamden, Conn.; judge of the Connecticut Superior Court (1976-78); judge of the Connecticut Court of Common Pleas (1974-76), Connecticut circuit court judge (1973-74); Dec. 13, 1923, in New Haven, Conn.; Independent; May 17.

Judge for the district court of the District of Columbia, $54,500 — **Harold H. Greene;** Washington, D.C.; chief judge, D.C. Court of General Sessions (1965-71) and its successor, D.C. Superior Court (1971-78); associate judge, Court of General Sessions (1965-66); Feb. 6, 1923, in Frankfort, Germany; May 17.

Judge for the district court of the District of Columbia, $54,500 — **Carin Ann Clauss;** Alexandria, Va.; solicitor of the Labor Department (1977-); associate solicitor, fair labor standards division, Labor Department (1972-77); Jan. 24, 1939, in Knoxville, Tenn.; Dem.; Not confirmed by the Senate before end of 95th Congress.

Judge for the southern district of Florida, $54,500 — **Jose A. Gonzalez Jr.;** Fort Lauderdale, Fla.; judge of the 17th Florida judicial circuit (1964-78); assistant state's attorney for the 15th Florida circuit (1961-64); Nov. 26, 1931, in Tampa, Fla.; July 26.

Judge for the middle district of Florida, $54,500 — **George C. Carr;** Lakeland, Fla.; partner in the Lakeland law firm of Peterson, Carr and Harris (1957-77); part-time county attorney, Polk County, Fla. (1973-77); Lakeland municipal judge (1965-66); July 26, 1929, in Lakeland; Dem.; Dec. 15, 1977.

Judge for the southern district of Georgia, $54,500 — **B. Avant Edenfield;** Statesboro, Ga.; partner in Statesboro law firm of Allen, Edenfield, Brown and Wright (1958-78); deputy assistant state attorney general (1970-78), Georgia state senator (D 1965-67); Aug. 2, 1934, in Bullock County, Ga.; Dem.; Oct. 10.

Judge for the eastern district of Illinois, $54,500 — **Harold A. Baker;** Champaign, Ill.; partner in Champaign law firm of Hatch and Baker (1956-78); senior counsel to the President's Commission on CIA Activities in the United States (Rockefeller Commission) (1975); Oct. 4, 1929, in Mount Kisco, N.Y.; Dem.; Sept. 22.

Judge for the northern and southern districts of Iowa, $54,500 — **Donald E. O'Brien;** Sioux City, Iowa; special counsel to the House Small Business Committee (1978); member of the Democratic National Committee (1977-78); director, Carter for President Michigan campaign (1976); director of McGovern for President Texas campaign (1972), U.S. attorney for the northern district of Iowa (1961-67), Sioux City municipal judge (1959-60) and Woodbury County attorney (1955-58), unsuccessful candidate for Congress (D 1958, 1960); Sept. 30, 1923, in Marcus, Iowa; Dem.; Oct. 4.

Judge for the eastern district of Louisiana, $54,500 — **Adrian G. Duplantier;** New Orleans, La.; judge in Division B of the Orleans Parish civil district court (1974-78); first assistant district attorney for Orleans Parish (1954-56); March 5, 1929, in New Orleans; Dem.; May 26.

Judge for the eastern district of Louisiana, $54,500 — **Robert F. Collins;** New Orleans, La.; magistrate-judge of the Louisiana criminal district court in New Orleans (1972-78); judge-ad-hoc of New Orleans traffic court (1969-72); Jan. 27, 1931, in New Orleans; Dem.; May 17.

Judge for the district of Massachusetts, $54,500 — **Armando David Mazzone;** Wakefield, Mass.; Massachusetts superior court judge (1975-78); assistant U.S. attorney for Massachusetts (1961-65); June 3, 1928, in Everett, Mass.; Dem.; Feb. 7.

Judge for the eastern district of Michigan, $54,500 — **Patricia Jean Ehrhardt Boyle;** Detroit, Mich.; Detroit Recorder's Court judge (1976-78); assistant Wayne County prosecutor (1968-76) and assistant U.S. attorney for the eastern district (1964-68); March 31, 1937, in Detroit; Sept. 22.

Judge for the eastern district of Michigan, $54,500 — **Julian A. Cook Jr.;** Oak Park, Mich.; partner in the Pontiac, Mich., law firm of Cook and Curry (1974-78); chairman of the Michigan Civil Rights Commission (1968-71); June 22, 1930, in Washington, D.C.; Dem.; Sept. 22.

Judge for the district of Nevada, $54,500 — **Harry E. Claiborne;** Las Vegas, Nev.; self-employed attorney in Las Vegas (1946-78); special counsel to the Senate Rules Committee for Rockefeller confirmation hearings (1974); Nevada state assemblyman and assistant majority leader (D 1948-50); July 2, 1917, in McRae, Ark.; Dem.; Aug. 11.

Judge for the district of New Hampshire, $54,500 — **Shane Devine;** Manchester, N.H.; partner in Manchester law firm of Devine, Millimet, Stahl and Branch (1955-78); Feb. 1, 1926, in Manchester; Dem.; June 23.

Judge for the district of New Mexico, $54,500 — **Santiago Eloy Campos;** Santa Fe, N.M.; self-employed attorney in Santa Fe (1975-78) and judge of the New Mexico district court (1972-78); assistant to the state attorney general (1955-57); Dec. 25, 1926, in Santa Rosa, N.M.; Dem.; July 10.

Judge for the southern district of New York, $54,500 — **Robert W. Sweet;** New York City; partner in New York City firm of Skadden, Arps, Slate, Meagher and Flom (1970-78); deputy mayor of New York under John V. Lindsay (1966-69), executive assistant to Lindsay (1965-66); assistant U.S. attorney for the southern district (1955-57); Oct. 15, 1922, in Yonkers, N.Y.; Rep.; April 25.

Judge for the southern district of New York, $54,500 — **Mary Johnson Lowe;** The Bronx, N.Y.; justice in Bronx County state supreme court (1975-78); acting justice, Bronx County state supreme court (1973-75); New York City criminal court judge (1971-73); June 10, 1924, in New York City; Dem.; June 23.

Judge for the southern district of New York, $54,500 — **Leonard Burke Sand;** New York City; partner in the New York City law firm of Robinson, Silverman, Pearce, Aronsohn, Sand and Berman (1959-78); state constitutional convention delegate (1967); assistant to the solicitor general of the United States (1956-59); assistant U.S. attorney for the southern district (1953-55); May 24, 1928, in New York City; May 17.

Judge for the eastern district of Pennsylvania, $54,500 — **Norma Levy Shapiro;** Narberth, Pa.; partner in the Philadelphia law firm of Deckert, Price and Rhoads (1973-78); July 28, 1928, in Philadelphia, Pa.; Rep.; Aug. 11.

Judge for the eastern district of Pennsylvania, $54,500 — **Louis H. Pollak;** Philadelphia, Pa.; dean of the University of Pennsylvania law school (1975-78); special assistant to the ambassador-at-large, State Department (1951-53); Dec. 7, 1922, in New York City; Dem.; July 10.

Judge for the western district of Pennsylvania, $54,500 — **Paul A. Simmons;** Monongahela, Pa.; state judge, Washington County Court of Common Pleas (1973-78; appointed 1973, then elected to full term with nominations from both parties 1975); member, Washington County Redevelopment Authority (1968-73), and commissioner, Pennsylvania Human Relations Commission (1963-68); Aug. 21, 1931, in Monongahela; Dem.; April 6.

Judge for the western district of Pennsylvania, $54,500 — **Gustave Diamond;** McMurray, Pa.; self-employed attorney in Washington, Pa. (1976-78); assistant U.S. attorney (1961-63) and U.S. attorney (1963-69) for the western district; Jan. 29, 1928, in Burgettstown, Pa.; Dem.; May 1.

Judge for the western district of Pennsylvania, $54,500 — **Donald E. Ziegler;** Pittsburgh, Pa.; judge of the criminal division of the Allegheny County Court of Common Pleas (1974-78); member of the Pennsylvania Unemployment Compensation Board of Review (1962); Oct. 1, 1936, in Pittsburgh; Dem.; May 1.

Judge for the middle district of Tennessee, $54,500 — **Thomas A. Wiseman Jr.;** Nashville, Tenn.; partner in the Nashville firm of Chambers and Wiseman (1974-78); unsuccessful candidate for the Democratic gubernatorial nomination (1974); Tennessee state treasurer (D 1971-73); Nov. 3, 1930, in Tullahoma, Tenn.; Dem.; Aug. 11.

Judge for the district of Utah, $54,500 — **Bruce Sterling Jenkins;** Salt Lake City, Utah; U.S. bankruptcy referee (1965-78); state senator (D 1958-65), minority leader (1963-65) and senate president (1965); May 27, 1927, in Salt Lake City; Dem.; Sept. 20.

Judge for the western district of Washington $54,500 — **Jack E. Tanner;** Tacoma, Wash.; self-employed attorney in Tacoma (1955-78); Jan. 28, 1919, in Tacoma; Dem.; May 17.

Judge for the district of the Canal Zone (eight-year term), $54,500 — **Robert H. McFarland;** Bay Springs, Miss.; partner in the Bay Springs firm of Roberts and McFarland; chairman of the Mississippi Oil and Gas Board (1962-70); Feb. 25, 1919, in Bay Springs, July 10.

Judge for the district of Guam (eight-year term), $54,500 — **Cristobal Camacho Duenas;** Agana, Guam; judge for the district of Guam since 1969 (reappointment to seat); judge of the Guam Island Court (1960-69); Sept. 12, 1920, in Agana, Guam; May 17.

Judge for the district of the Northern Mariana Islands (eight-year term), $54,500 — **Alfred Laureta;** Kapaa, Hawaii; Fifth Hawaii circuit court judge (1969-78); First Hawaii circuit judge (1967-69); Hawaii state director of labor and industrial relations (1963-67); administrative assistant to then-Rep. Daniel K. Inouye, D-Hawaii; May 21, 1924, in Ewa, Hawaii; Dem.; May 17.

Judge for the district of the Virgin Islands (eight-year term), $54,500 — **Almeric L. Christian;** St. Thomas, V.I.; U.S. district judge for the Virgin Islands since 1969, and chief judge since 1970 (reappointment); U.S. attorney for the Virgin Islands (1962-69); Nov. 23, 1919, in Christiansted, St. Thomas, V.I.; Dem.; April 6.

District of Columbia Superior Courts

Associate judge, $49,050 — **Carlisle Edward Pratt;** Washington, D.C.; member of law firm of Pratt and Queen (1975-77); Jan. 26, 1923, in Washington; Dem.; Dec. 15, 1977.

Associate judge, $49,050 — **Frederick Howard Weisberg;** Washington, D.C.; chief of the appellate division of the D.C. public defender service (1974-77); March 22, 1944, in Buffalo, N.Y.; Independent; Dec. 15, 1977.

Associate judge, $49,050 — **Peter Henry Wolf;** Washington, D.C.; partner in Washington law firm of Wolf and Kovner (1974); May 5, 1935, in New Jersey; Dem.; nomination sent to Senate Governmental Affairs Committee Sept. 18, 1978, but not reported by panel before adjournment of Congress.

POLITICAL REPORT

CQ

The New Congress: A Small Step to the Right

The American electorate nudged Congress a step to the right Nov. 7, adding three Republicans in the Senate and 11 in the House, and allowing the GOP at least to entertain the notion that it is on the way back in national politics.

The numbers themselves are not exactly the stuff of which a renaissance is normally made. Free to campaign in opposition to the White House as well as Congress for the first time in 10 years, Republicans ought to have gained a few House seats, as they did. But for a party that suffered so badly in congressional voting four years ago, and failed to gain any of its strength back in 1976, 11 new House seats mark a beginning.

And the three new Senate seats may represent something more than a beginning. As important as the numerical change is the fact that Republicans managed to gain Senate strength in a year when they were defending half the seats at stake — a far higher proportion than they hold in the chamber as a whole. Taking incumbents and newcomers together, the GOP elected 20 people to the Senate this year — more than in any year since 1952.

So the congressional returns, combined with the news that six more Republican governors will supplement the current hardcore group of 12, allowed GOP leaders to claim an overall success in the 1978 election, even as the White House was pointing out — correctly — that the combined Democratic losses were relatively small compared with what has frequently happened to the party in power in midterm elections.

The Carter administration, which did not exactly exercise dictatorial control over the 95th Congress, can live with the probable new lineup of 59-41 in the Senate, and 276-157 (with two vacancies*) in the House. But it may have some reason to be disturbed about Republican gains at the statehouse level.

Gubernatorial Results

The Republican Party appears, for the time being at least, to have checked the startling erosion in its gubernatorial strength that began in 1970, when the GOP controlled 32 statehouses, and still raged in 1976, when it had sunk to a compact but embarrassing 12.

Six new Republican governorships will not cause an earthquake in the presidential politics of 1980, but they will change the outlines somewhat. This is mainly because of the election of two men — William Clements in Texas and Richard L. Thornburgh in Pennsylvania. Republicans entered the 1978 campaign holding statehouses in only three of the 10 largest states. When the 1980 campaign begins, if it hasn't already, there will be GOP governors in half the "megastates," with the advantages in national media attention, fund raising and organization that they can provide. And while statehouse control may be an overrated factor in presidential elections, there is an undeniable psychological advantage to being in charge in the states that draw most of the attention.

*Rep. Leo J. Ryan, D-Calif., was killed Nov. 18, 1978, and Rep. William A. Steiger, R-Wis., died Dec. 4, 1978.

—George L. Rebh

Possible Schism

Curiously, though, the separate gains for Republicans at the Senate and statehouse levels raised the possibility of a new split within the party between its congressional and gubernatorial factions.

On the gubernatorial side, it was the moderate Republicans who were the clear winners. Of the new "big five" Republican governors, Thornburgh and re-elected Govs. James R. Thompson in Illinois and William G. Milliken in Michigan are clearly identified with the party's left. James A. Rhodes, the veteran Republican narrowly returned in Ohio, is generally concerned with state issues, but has always sided with the moderates in national politics. Only Clements, still a political novice as he takes office in Texas, will add conservative influence at the big-state level.

The Republican left also re-elected Robert Ray of Iowa, the highly respected dean of American governors, to his fifth term. The right lost Meldrim Thomson Jr. of New Hampshire, who became nationally known for his outspoken extreme conservatism. It failed to elect Ted Strickland of Colorado, who would have been one of its leading spokesmen among the governors if he had won.

Congressional Results

The congressional picture is different. Moderate and liberal Republicans probably held even in Senate elections, gaining William S. Cohen in Maine, David Durenberger and Rudy Boschwitz in Minnesota, and Larry Pressler in South Dakota, all of whom replaced Democrats. But they lost national figures in Clifford P. Case in the New Jersey primary, Edward W. Brooke in the Massachusetts general election, and James B. Pearson of Kansas, who retired.

As published in the CQ Weekly Report, Nov. 11, 1978.

Pearson's replacement, Republican Nancy Landon Kassebaum, may also join the moderates. But Case and Brooke will be replaced by Democrats.

Conservative Republicans, on the other hand, lost virtually nothing. They won unexpected victories by ousting liberal Democrats Dick Clark of Iowa and Thomas J. McIntyre of New Hampshire, and gained a potential national leader in William L. Armstrong of Colorado. Thad Cochran of Mississippi, that state's first GOP senator ever chosen by popular vote, is certain to join the right on fiscal and defense issues, although he is likely to be a moderate on many social and some race-related questions.

Gordon Humphrey, R
New Hampshire Senator

Bill Bradley, D
New Jersey Senator

New Right Gains

In general, the Senate returns represented a modest victory for the complex of conservative organizations loosely labeled the New Right. Groups like the Committee for the Survival of a Free Congress and the National Conservative Political Action Committee were major backers of Roger Jepsen against Clark and Gordon Humphrey against McIntyre, and were able to claim considerable credit for these two upsets that seemed to symbolize for many disappointed Democrats the small but significant rightward trend of the 1978 election.

The Humphrey and Jepsen triumphs were not won primarily on the Kemp-Roth tax cutting issue or other economic proposals most Republican candidates chose to emphasize, but on more emotional topics that national Republican strategists generally tried to avoid. Jepsen reduced Clark's vote in normally Democratic Catholic areas because Clark declined to endorse anti-abortion measures or support tuition tax credits for parochial schools. Humphrey made McIntyre's vote in favor of the Panama Canal treaties a centerpiece of his campaign. *(Kemp-Roth tax amendment, p. 219; Panama Canal treaties, p. 379)*

In fact, it is difficult to find any Republican Senate candidate in the country who appears to owe his victory largely to his endorsement of a massive tax cut. New Jersey's Jeffrey Bell, who campaigned as hard and as effectively on this issue as anyone — "California had Proposition 13; New Jersey has Jeff Bell" — turned in a respectable showing but still found himself unable to overcome the personal popularity of his celebrity opponent, Democrat Bill Bradley, a former New York Knicks basketball player.

These results, scattered as they are, may strengthen the position of those conservatives centered around fundraiser Richard Viguerie, who believes social issues can be the basic vehicle for conservative success. The failure of the Kemp-Roth tax cut approach as a national campaign tool is likely to work against Rep. Jack Kemp, R-N.Y., and others who insist that a national majority can only be built on economic issues.

The Midwest

Perhaps as encouraging as anything else for Republicans in the election was the hint of recovery in the Midwest, the region which Republicans once monopolized but which has been systmatically torn from them by Democrats in the past decade. A party without a regional base is a minority party, and since 1970, Republicans have had no stronghold they could use to counter Democratic successes in other parts of the country.

They probably still do not have one, but Republicans did show surprising appeal in the farm states, where they have lost so badly in recent years. The GOP took eight of nine governorships contested in the Midwest, won two Democratic Senate seats in Minnesota and one each in South Dakota and Iowa, and gained House seats in Iowa, Kansas, Illinois, Indiana and Wisconsin.

Whether this phenomenon stems from problems with President Carter's farm policy, or whether it simply shows that the Democratic resurgence in the early 1970s in these states is petering out, the results will encourage midwestern Republicans at a point when some of them had begun to lose hope.

The South

For Republicans in the South, nothing can erase the legacy of 1974 and 1976, when first Watergate and then the Carter presidential candidacy wiped out the modest gains they had been making in the region since the early 1960s. Voting in 1978 still left the GOP far weaker than it was in 1972, the last time it made any overall progress in southern congressional representation. But there were a few signs that the Republican Party might still be able to grow in the South if it tries again.

Republicans took Democratic House seats in Arkansas, Georgia and South Carolina, the first such gains in six years. Cochran's election in a three-way contest as Mississippi's first popularly chosen Republican senator may have been a fluke, as Cochran himself has described it, but it is also a potent party-building tool for the GOP in that state.

Clements' election as governor of Texas gives Republicans an even more important boost there. And they needed it. Despite the victory of Clements and the re-election of incumbent Republican Sen. John G. Tower, GOP House candidates failed to take advantage of opportunities in several Texas House districts, capturing the seat of only one of eight departing Democrats after hoping earlier in this year to replace as many as six.

In Florida it was even worse. Presented with excellent opportunities to elect Republicans in two conservative districts Democrats vacated, Republicans not only lost both of those seats by embarrassing margins but failed to re-elect one of their own incumbents.

So the South offers conflicting evidence — glimmers of hope for a Republican future and obvious indications that the party is not even competitive yet in areas where it will have to be in order to win nationally. And in that respect, the results from the South simply offer in sharper focus a picture that applies to the rest of the country as well.

CQ Senate

Senate: Slightly More Conservative

The Senate that begins work in 1979, influenced by the second largest freshman class class in the history of popular elections, will have a slightly more conservative cast and a few more Republicans than its predecessor.

Barring a change in the outcome of the Virginia contest apparently won by Republican John Warner, the new Senate will have 59 Democrats and 41 Republicans. That is a gain of three Republicans from the 95th Congress, in which the party split was 62-to-38. The Democratic totals include Harry F. Byrd Jr. of Virginia, elected as an independent.

While the GOP increase was not overwhelming, it was slightly greater than what GOP officials themselves expected a year before. Oregon Sen. Bob Packwood, National Republican Senatorial Committee chairmen, then predicted a gain of one or two seats.

The GOP newcomers included Nancy Landon Kassebaum of Kansas, the first woman elected to the Senate without being preceded in Congress by her husband, and Thad Cochran, the first Republican senator elected in Mississippi since 1875, when Blanche K. Bruce, a black, represented the state. The only black senator currently serving — Edward W. Brooke of Massachusetts — was among the GOP losers Nov. 7.

The contests for 35 seats produced 20 winners who will be taking places in the Senate for the first time in January. Since the popular election of senators began in 1914, that number of freshmen has been exceeded only in the 80th Congress, which convened in January 1947. There were 23 freshmen that year.

The 20 newcomers are the result of 10 retirements, the most in the post-World War II era; three incumbents

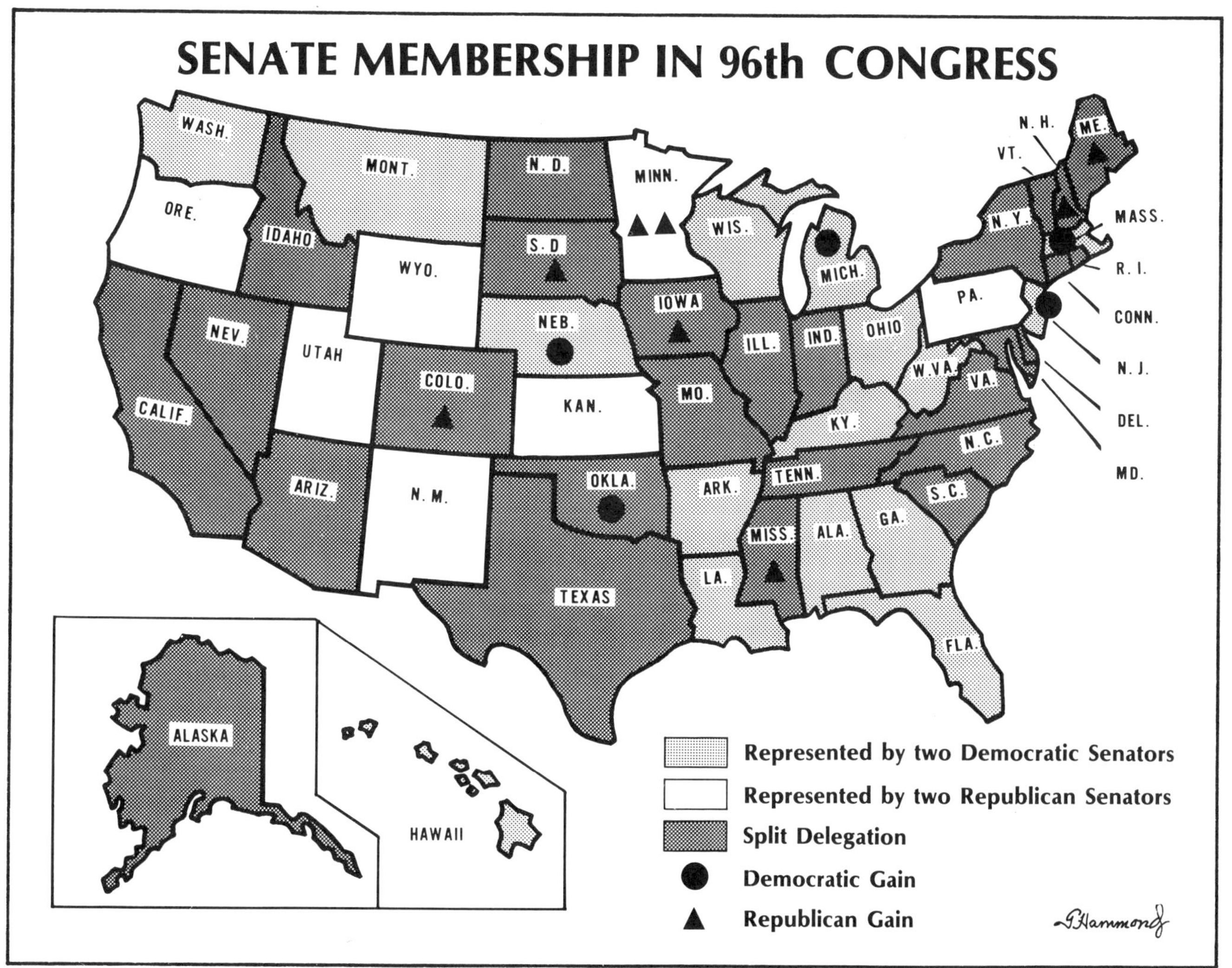

defeated in primary elections, the most in a decade; and seven incumbents defeated on Nov. 7. The number of incumbents ousted in 1978 in the general election was not as large as in 1976 when nine incumbents lost, but it was still more than in any other Senate election since 1958.

The large freshman classes of 1976 and 1978 differ markedly from their counterparts of a generation ago. The recent freshman classes represent no distinct national trends. The 1976 class of 18 was composed of eight Republicans and 10 Democrats, and the 1978 newcomers include 11 Republicans and nine Democrats.

In 1946, 17 of the 23 freshmen were Republicans, reflecting anti-Truman administration sentiment. Two years later, a Democratic tide gave that party 14 of the 18 freshmen. In 1958, 15 of the 18 newcomers were Democratic.

The large Senate turnover in recent years means that nearly half of the members — 48 — will have been chosen in the last three elections and will be in their first terms.

The most notable conservative gains in the Senate occurred in Iowa, where Republican Roger Jepsen unseated incumbent Dick Clark, and in New Hampshire where incumbent Democrat Thomas J. McIntyre lost to Gordon Humphrey, a 37-year-old airline pilot.

In addition to McIntyre and Clark, four other incumbents defeated Nov. 7 generally were regarded as liberal voters in the Senate on most issues. Five of the seven ousted incumbents were Democrats. But the loss of the six liberal incumbents was partly offset by shifts away from the right in such states as Alabama, Michigan and Arkansas.

The 1978 election had been regarded as an unusually vulnerable one for Republicans because they were forced to defend 17 of the 38 seats they held in the 95th Congress.

Eleven of those 17 GOP senators were first elected either in 1966, when a national Republican trend took place, or in 1972, the year of the Nixon landslide. The GOP managed to hold on to most of them, losing only Brooke and Robert P. Griffin of Michigan, first elected in 1966, and the seat of retiring Dewey F. Bartlett of Oklahoma, who won his post in 1972.

The Republican Party thus can enter the 1980 and 1982 Senate campaigns with a solid base of 19 GOP senators who will not be up for election until 1984. One of the three Republican pickups in the general election was for an unexpired Minnesota term which ends in 1982. In 1980, Republicans will have to defend 10 seats. In 1982 there will be 12 Republican positions at stake.

The Democratic class of 1972 turned out to be much more vulnerable than the Republican group. Democrats lost Clark, William D. Hathaway of Maine and Floyd K. Haskell of Colorado, incumbents first elected in 1972 over complacent Republicans whose political bases had become shaky. In addition to their defeats, the seat of retiring Democratic Sen. James Abourezk of South Dakota, a member of the class of '72, was captured by the Republicans.

Abourezk's successor will be U.S. Rep. Larry Pressler, who entered the House in 1975. Pressler won the Senate election with two-thirds of the vote. He is unlikely to come close to matching the fiery populism of Abourezk, but has shown at least as much flair for attracting publicity during his years in the House. Pressler is likely to occupy a place at or slightly to the left of the center of the Republican spectrum in the Senate.

Clark's foe, Jepsen, is a former Iowa lieutenant governor and a favorite of conservative pressure groups throughout the nation. He hounded Clark with the charge that the Democrat was "the most liberal member of the United States Senate." Clark's views earned the strident opposition of the National Right to Work Committee and national anti-abortion groups.

Paul E. Tsongas

Roger Jepsen

Jepsen achieved his victory despite strained relations within his own party. He defeated a GOP primary foe who had the tacit support of moderate Gov. Robert Ray. Jepsen also was able to fend off Clark's charges that he was "redbaiting" and guilty of "McCarthyism."

Senate watchers will have to become accustomed to hearing militant conservative views from a senator with the name of Humphrey. New Hampshire's Humphrey shares little of the political philosophy of the Minnesota Humphreys and probably will be a like-minded colleague of Jepsen.

Humphrey prevailed over two less conservative candidates in the Republican primary, rarely interrupting his criticism of McIntyre for straying too far left and ignoring local concerns. As in past elections, McIntyre followed a strategy of warning that the choice was between him and extremism. This time it failed.

In a more widely publicized Senate race in New Jersey, New Right forces fell short of electing Jeffrey Bell, a former political director of the American Conservative Union. Although he unseated veteran incumbent Clifford P. Case in the GOP primary, he could not match the personal appeal of Bill Bradley, the former professional basketball star and Rhodes scholar. Bell keyed most of his campaign to his perception of a public tax revolt and his support of the Kemp-Roth tax cut proposal.

Hathaway and Haskell were replaced by Republicans with more conservative records — in Haskell's case, considerably more conservative. But neither of the new senators from Colorado or Maine is likely to be a Jepsen or a Humphrey.

William L. Armstrong, a three-term U.S. representative, defeated Haskell in Colorado. In 1977 Armstrong had a "zero" rating from the liberal Americans for Democratic Action (ADA), while Haskell received a score of 85. But Armstrong's poor showing in the eyes of the ADA does not reflect his occasional moderate votes and reluctance to be strident in his approach. Armstrong supported President Gerald Ford for the 1976 GOP nomination over Ronald Reagan. His victory was particularly well received by business groups, such as the Business Industry Political Action Committee (BIPAC).

In Maine, William S. Cohen, another three-term U.S. representative, won over Democrat Hathaway — the most decisive defeat of a Senate incumbent in the 1978 general election. Slightly more conservative than Hathaway, Cohen will find a place in the moderate group of Senate Republicans, who will be especially happy to receive him in the wake of departures by Brooke and Case.

Republican losses from their classes of 1966 and 1972 produced little ideological change. U.S. Rep. Paul E. Tsongas, a Massachusetts Democrat, is likely to differ little from his predecessor, Brooke. A series of *Boston Globe* stories disclosing that Brooke had lied about his financial worth during divorce proceedings damaged him, but Tsongas did not mention the incumbent's personal and financial problems during the campaign.

In a departure from his past custom, Sen. Edward M. Kennedy campaigned actively against Brooke. Brooke tried to win back liberal support, telling voters that perhaps he has been a symbol of progress for both whites and blacks.

While Massachusetts traded a liberal Republican for a liberal Democrat, Oklahoma was replacing a retiring conservative Republican with a Democrat who has done little to offend conservatives at home.

Democratic Gov. David Boren had little trouble with Republican Robert Kamm for the seat of Oklahoma's Bartlett, who stepped aside for health reasons.

Boren acquired a reformer's reputation in his gubernatorial campaign four years ago. In his Senate campaign he played on decidedly conservative themes. He quarreled openly with President Carter's energy policy, which he said would hurt the state's oil and gas industry. He also endorsed the Kemp-Roth tax cut plan, the centerpiece of the Republican congressional campaign.

Business groups were disappointed in the loss of Michigan's Griffin to Democrat Carl Levin, a former Detroit City Council president. Griffin always has been an effective vote-getter, but the retirement decision he announced and then took back convinced many voters that he had grown weary of the Senate. Levin will be a decidedly more liberal voice in the Senate.

Republicans will be watching closely as the records of three Senate freshmen from the Midwest unfold. Kassebaum in Kansas and Rudy Boschwitz and David Durenberger in Minnesota will enter the Senate with moderate images, but none has an extensive public record by which an ideology can be judged accurately. Neither Boschwitz nor Durenberger has held public office and Kassebaum has served only on a small-town school board. Kassebaum once was a staff aide for Republican Sen. James B. Pearson, whose retirement opened the way for her Senate bid.

The Kassebaum campaign played heavily on the Landon name, which is revered among Kansans. Alf Landon, Kassebaum's father, was the state's governor in the 1930s and the 1936 GOP presidential nominee. The Landon connection gave Kassebaum the recognition necessary to emerge from a nine-person Republican primary field and to establish herself as a formidable contender against former U.S. Rep. Bill Roy, a Democrat who was making his second bid for the Senate. He lost by 13,500 votes to Sen. Bob Dole in 1974.

The Republicans' most dramatic gains came in Minnesota where both Senate seats, previously held by Democrats, fell into GOP hands. Boschwitz defeated incumbent Wendell Anderson, the former governor who had himself appointed to fill the last two years of Walter Mondale's Senate term when Mondale became vice president in 1977. Although he is a wealthy plywood manufacturer, Boschwitz used little of his own money in his Senate bid. Instead he built a broadly-based campaign that capitalized on voter resentment to Anderson's having arranged his own appointment. Of the nine governors who have tried it, Kentucky's Albert B. (Happy) Chandler is the only one to win election to the Senate in his own right after arranging his Senate appointment. That occurred in 1940.

Durenberger overcame massive personal spending by Bob Short, a hotel and trucking firm owner, to win the

Senate: Newcomers, Switched Seats, Losers

State	Old	New	Winner	Loser	Incumbent
Alabama (six-year term)	D	D	Howell Heflin	No Republican candidate	John Sparkman[1]
Alabama (two-year term)	D	D	Donald Stewart	James D. Martin	Maryon P. Allen[3]
Arkansas	D	D	David Pryor	Thomas Kelly Jr.	Kaneaster Hodges Jr.[2]
Colorado	D	R	William L. Armstrong	Floyd K. Haskell	Haskell
Iowa	D	R	Roger Jepsen	Dick Clark	Clark
Kansas	R	R	Nancy Landon Kassebaum	Bill Roy	James B. Pearson[1]
Maine	D	R	William S. Cohen	William D. Hathaway	Hathaway
Massachusetts	R	D	Paul E. Tsongas	Edward W. Brooke	Brooke
Michigan	R	D	Carl Levin	Robert P. Griffin	Griffin
Minnesota (six-year term)	D	R	Rudy Boschwitz	Wendell R. Anderson	Anderson
Minnesota (four-year term)	D	R	David Durenberger	Robert E. Short	Muriel Humphrey[1]
Mississippi	D	R	Thad Cochran	Maurice Dantin	James O. Eastland[1]
Montana	D	D	Max Baucus	Larry Williams	Paul Hatfield[3]
Nebraska	R	D	J. J. Exon	Donald E. Shasteen	Carl T. Curtis[1]
New Hampshire	D	R	Gordon Humphrey	Thomas J. McIntyre	McIntyre
New Jersey	R	D	Bill Bradley	Jeffrey Bell	Clifford P. Case[3]
Oklahoma	R	D	David L. Boren	Robert B. Kamm	Dewey F. Bartlett[1]
South Dakota	D	R	Larry Pressler	Don Barnett	James Abourezk[1]
Virginia	R	R	John W. Warner	Andrew P. Miller	Bill Scott[1]
Wyoming	R	R	Alan K. Simpson	Raymond B. Whitaker	Clifford P. Hansen[1]

[1] Retiring. [2] Appointee, ineligible to run. [3] Defeated in primary.

remaining four years of the late Hubert H. Humphrey's term. Since Humphrey's death in January, his seat had been held by his widow, Muriel, who was appointed to the post. She decided against running for the remainder of the term.

In the South, the trend toward more moderate senators continued. In Alabama, Democrat Howell Heflin, a former state supreme court chief justice, had opposition only from the Prohibition Party and will take over the post of retiring Democratic Sen. John Sparkman. State Sen. Donald Stewart, another Democrat, turned back the belated GOP effort of former U.S. Rep. James D. Martin and will serve the last two years of the term of the late James B. Allen, who died June 1. In the Democratic primary Stewart defeated Allen's widow, Maryon, who was appointed to the seat. Stewart was sworn into office Nov. 11, Minnesota's Durenberger on Nov. 9.

The Heflin-Stewart pair will be far less conservative in its outlook than the Sparkman-Allen team. Stewart received the enthusiastic support of organized labor.

Progressives also gained with the election in Arkansas of Gov. David Pryor, a Democrat, over token Republican opposition. Pryor challenged Sen. John L. McClellan unsuccessfully in the Democratic primary six years ago. When McClellan announced his retirement in 1977, Pryor quickly entered the race and went on to defeat two U.S. representatives in the Democratic primary. McClellan died in November 1977. Kaneaster Hodges Jr., appointed to succeed McClellan, was not eligible under state law to run for the full term.

Although Pryor lost much of the union support he had in 1972 because of arguments with labor during his tenure as governor, Pryor is likely to be a more pleasing senator to labor and liberal interests than McClellan.

It was a political oddity rather than a Republican resurgence that gave the GOP its first U.S. Senate seat in Mississippi in a century. Republican Cochran received only 45 percent of the vote, but the opposition was splintered between Democrat Maurice Dantin and black independent Charles Evers, who drew votes away from Dantin. Although Cochran had a "zero" ADA rating in 1977, he might find it politically necessary to move to the left a bit to attract black votes in 1984.

In Virginia, official returns gave former U.S. Navy Secretary John Warner, a Republican, a 4,721-vote victory lead for the seat of retiring GOP Sen. Bill Scott. But apparent discrepancies in the official count were cited by Democrat Andrew P. Miller, a former state attorney general, who sought a recount.

Warner initially lost the Republican nomination to Richard Obenshain, but was named the nominee after Obenshain was killed in a plane crash in August.

In the West, conservative Republicans held the seat of a retiring Republican in Wyoming, but failed to pick up a Democratic-held seat in Montana. Alan K. Simpson, a former state representative, will assume the Wyoming Senate position given up by his father, Milward L. Simpson, 12 years ago. Since then the seat has been occupied by Republican Clifford P. Hansen, who is retiring.

U.S. Rep. Max Baucus, a Democrat, withstood the conservative drive of Larry Williams, an investment counselor, in Montana. At one point, Williams seemed to have closed the gap on Baucus, but his campaign was hurt by the publication of a picture of him with long hair and a bead necklace, taken when he worked in California several years before. The seat had belonged to Democrat Lee Metcalf, who died in January, and then to Paul Hatfield, a Democrat who was appointed to replace Metcalf. Baucus swamped Hatfield in the Democratic primary by a more than 3-to-1 margin.

Senate Freshmen, 1940-1978

Year	Freshman Senators	Demo-crats	Repub-licans	Others
1940	12	5	7	
1942	13	3	10	
1944	14	8	6	
1946	23	6	17	
1948	18	14	4	
1950	14	6	8	
1952	16	6	10	
1954	14	7	7	
1956	10	6	4	
1958	10	15	3	
1960	9	7	2	
1962	12	9	3	
1964	8	6	2	
1966	7	2	5	
1968	15	5	10	
1970	11	5	5	1
1972	13	8	5	
1974	11	9	2	
1976	18	10	8	
1978	20	9	11	

One of the easiest winning campaigns was waged by Nebraska Gov. J. J. Exon for the post of retiring incumbent Carl T. Curtis, a Republican. Exon, a two-term governor, defeated Donald E. Shasteen, a former executive assistant to Curtis, by a 2-to-1 margin. This is the first time in history that both the state's senators are Democrats.

Republican incumbents withstood tough challenges in Illinois, Texas, North Carolina and South Carolina. The Illinois race was supposed to be easy for incumbent Charles H. Percy, but Democrat Alex Seith poured significant amounts of his personal money into his campaign and conducted a highly critical advertising drive against Percy. That paid off at first in the face of Percy's low-key re-election effort; one poll showed Seith with a healthy lead a week before the election. Percy responded quickly with his own hard-hitting advertising blitz and won going away.

Texans also witnessed a bitter Senate campaign, highlighted by personal charges between Republican incumbent John G. Tower and his Democratic challenger, U.S. Rep. Robert Krueger. Tower was hurt politically when he refused to shake hands with Krueger at a public gathering. The senator then aired television ads alleging that Krueger had insulted Tower's family.

The North Carolina campaign of Jesse Helms, a Republican incumbent, spent more than $6 million, but it produced a victory of only about 95,000 votes out of 1.1 million cast over Democrat John Ingram. Ingram's campaign spent well under $500,000.

South Carolina incumbent Strom Thurmond, Democrat turned Dixiecrat turned Republican, overcame Democrat Charles D. (Pug) Ravenel, who contended that Thurmond was not representative of the state's interests. ∎

Senate Membership in the 96th Congress

Democrats 59* **Republicans 41**

Seats Switched Parties D to R - 8
Seats Switched Parties R to D - 5

Freshman Senators - 20

> Senators elected in 1978 are *italicized*
> *#Freshman Senators*
> *✓Seat switched parties*

ALABAMA
Howell Heflin (D)#
Donald Stewart (D)#

ALASKA
Mike Gravel (D)
Ted Stevens (R)

ARIZONA
Dennis DeConcini (D)
Barry Goldwater (R)

ARKANSAS
Dale Bumpers (D)
David Pryor (D)#

CALIFORNIA
Alan Cranston (D)
S. I. Hayakawa (R)

COLORADO
Gary Hart (D)
✓William L. Armstrong (R)#

CONNECTICUT
Abraham Ribicoff (D)
Lowell P. Weicker Jr. (R)

DELAWARE
Joe Biden (D)
William V. Roth Jr. (R)

FLORIDA
Lawton Chiles (D)
Richard (Dick) Stone (D)

GEORGIA
Sam Nunn (D)
Herman E. Talmadge (D)

HAWAII
Daniel K. Inouye (D)
Spark M. Matsunaga (D)

IDAHO
Frank Church (D)
James A. McClure (R)

ILLINOIS
Adlai E. Stevenson III (D)
Charles H. Percy (R)

INDIANA
Birch Bayh (D)
Richard G. Lugar (R)

IOWA
John C. Culver (D)
✓Roger Jepsen (R)#

KANSAS
Robert Dole (R)
Nancy Landon Kassebaum (R)#

KENTUCKY
Wendell H. Ford (D)
Walter (Dee) Huddleston (D)

LOUISIANA
J. Bennett Johnston Jr. (D)
Russell B. Long (D)

MAINE
Edmund S. Muskie (D)
✓William S. Cohen (R)#

MARYLAND
Paul S. Sarbanes (D)
Charles McC. Mathias Jr. (R)

MASSACHUSETTS
Edward M. Kennedy (D)
✓Paul E. Tsongas (D)#

MICHIGAN
✓Carl Levin (D)#
Donald W. Riegle Jr. (D)

MINNESOTA
✓David Durenberger (R)#
✓Rudy Boschwitz (R)#

MISSISSIPPI
John C. Stennis (D)
✓Thad Cochran (R)#

MISSOURI
Thomas F. Eagleton (D)
John C. Danforth (R)

MONTANA
Max Baucus (D)#
John Melcher (D)

NEBRASKA
✓J. J. Exon (D)#
Edward Zorinsky (D)

NEVADA
Howard W. Cannon (D)
Paul Laxalt (R)

NEW HAMPSHIRE
John A. Durkin (D)
✓Gordon Humphrey (R)#

NEW JERSEY
✓Bill Bradley (D)#
Harrison A. Williams Jr. (D)

NEW MEXICO
Pete V. Domenici (R)
Harrison H. Schmitt (R)

NEW YORK
Daniel Patrick Moynihan (D)
Jacob K. Javits (R)

NORTH CAROLINA
Robert Morgan (D)
Jesse Helms (R)

NORTH DAKOTA
Quentin N. Burdick (D)
Milton R. Young (R)

OHIO
John Glenn (D)
Howard M. Metzenbaum (D)

OKLAHOMA
✓David L. Boren (D)#
Henry Bellmon (R)

OREGON
Mark O. Hatfield (R)
Robert W. Packwood (R)

PENNSYLVANIA
H. John Heinz III (R)
Richard S. Schweiker (R)

RHODE ISLAND
Claiborne Pell (D)
John H. Chafee (R)

SOUTH CAROLINA
Ernest F. Hollings (D)
Strom Thurmond (R)

SOUTH DAKOTA
George McGovern (D)
✓Larry Pressler (R)#

TENNESSEE
Howard H. Baker Jr. (R)
Jim Sasser (D)

TEXAS
Lloyd Bentsen (D)
John G. Tower (R)

UTAH
Jake Garn (R)
Orrin G. Hatch (R)

VERMONT
Patrick J. Leahy (D)
Robert T. Stafford (R)

VIRGINIA
Harry F. Byrd Jr. (Ind)
John Warner (R)#

WASHINGTON
Henry M. Jackson (D)
Warren G. Magnuson (D)

WEST VIRGINIA
Robert C. Byrd (D)
Jennings Randolph (D)

WISCONSIN
Gaylord Nelson (D)
William Proxmire (D)

WYOMING
Alan K. Simpson (R)#
Malcolm Wallop (R)

*Includes Byrd (Va.), elected as an independent in 1970 and 1976.

Years of Expiration of Senate Terms

1980

(34 Senators: 24 Democrats, 10 Republicans)

Bayh, Birch (D Ind.)
Bellmon, Henry (R Okla.)
Bumpers, Dale (D Ark.)
Church, Frank (D Idaho)
Cranston, Alan (D Calif.)
Culver, John C. (D Iowa)
Dole, Robert (R Kan.)
Durkin, John A. (D N.H.)
Eagleton, Thomas F. (D Mo.)
Ford, Wendell H. (D Ky.)
Garn, Jake (R Utah)
Glenn, John (D Ohio)
Goldwater, Barry (R Ariz.)
Gravel, Mike (D Alaska)
Hart, Gary (D Colo.)
Hollings, Ernest F. (D S.C.)
Inouye, Daniel K. (D Hawaii)
Javits, Jacob K. (R N.Y.)
Laxalt, Paul (R Nev.)
Leahy, Patrick J. (D Vt.)
Long, Russell B. (D La.)
McGovern, George (D S.D.)
Magnuson, Warren G. (D Wash.)
Mathias, Charles McC. Jr. (R Md.)
Morgan, Robert (D N.C.)
Nelson, Gaylord (D Wis.)
Packwood, Robert W. (R Ore.)
Ribicoff, Abraham (D Conn.)
Schweiker, Richard S. (R Pa.)
Stevenson, Adlai E. III (D Ill.)
Stewart, Donald (D Ala.)
Stone, Richard (Dick) (D Fla.)
Talmadge, Herman E. (D Ga.)
Young, Milton R. (R N.D.)

1982

(33 Senators: 20 Democrats, 12 Republicans, one Independent)

Bentsen, Lloyd (D Texas)
Burdick, Quentin N. (D N.D.)
Byrd, Harry F. Jr. (Ind Va.)
Byrd, Robert C. (D W.Va.)
Cannon, Howard W. (D Nev.)
Chafee, John H. (R R.I.)
Chiles, Lawton (D Fla.)
Danforth, John C. (R Mo.)
DeConcini, Dennis (D Ariz.)
Durenberger, David (R Minn.)
Hatch, Orrin G. (R Utah)
Hayakawa, S. I. (R Calif.)
Heinz, H. John III (R Pa.)
Jackson, Henry M. (D Wash.)
Kennedy, Edward M. (D Mass.)
Lugar, Richard G. (R Ind.)
Matsunaga, Spark M. (D Hawaii)
Melcher, John (D Mont.)
Metzenbaum, Howard M. (D Ohio)
Moynihan, Daniel P. (D N.Y.)
Muskie, Edmund S. (D Maine)
Proxmire, William (D Wis.)
Riegle, Donald W. Jr. (D Mich.)
Roth, William V. Jr. (R Del.)
Sarbanes, Paul S. (D Md.)
Sasser, James R. (D Tenn.)
Schmitt, Harrison H. (R N.M.)
Stafford, Robert T. (R Vt.)
Stennis, John C. (D Miss.)
Wallop, Malcolm (R Wyo.)
Weicker, Lowell P. Jr. (R Conn.)
Williams, Harrison A. Jr. (D N.J.)
Zorinsky, Edward (D Neb.)

1984

(33 Senators: 14 Democrats; 19 Republicans)

Armstrong, William L. (R Colo.)
Baker, Howard H. Jr. (R Tenn.)
Baucus, Max (D Mont.)
Biden, Joe (D Del.)
Boren, David L. (D Okla.)
Boschwitz, Rudy (R Minn.)
Bradley, Bill (D N.J.)
Cochran, Thad (R Miss.)
Cohen, William S. (R Maine)
Domenici, Pete V. (R N.M.)
Exon, J. J. (D Neb.)
Hatfield, Mark O. (R Ore.)
Heflin, Howell (D Ala.)
Helms, Jesse (R N.C.)
Huddleston, Walter (Dee) (D Ky.)
Humphrey, Gordon (R N.H.)
Jepsen, Roger (R Iowa)
Johnston, J. Bennett Jr. (D La.)
Kassebaum, Nancy Landon (R Kan.)
Levin, Carl (D Mich.)
McClure, James A. (R Idaho)
Nunn, Sam (D Ga.)
Pell, Claiborne (D R.I.)
Percy, Charles H. (R Ill.)
Pressler, Larry (R S.D.)
Pryor, David (D Ark.)
Randolph, Jennings (D W.Va.)
Simpson, Alan K. (R Wyo.)
Stevens, Ted (R Alaska)
Thurmond, Strom (R S.C.)
Tower, John G. (R Texas)
Tsongas, Paul E. (D Mass.)
Warner, John W. (R Va.)

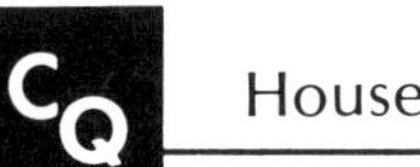

House

House: Modest Gains For the Minority

Republicans made modest inroads on the lopsided Democratic majority in the House Nov. 7, picking up an apparent net gain of 11 seats. But Democrats will remain in firm control with 276 seats to 157 for the GOP.. There are two vacancies, created by the deaths of Democrat Leo J. Ryan of California and Republican William A. Steiger of Wisconsin.

Democrats picked up one seat which first appeared to have gone Republican, when Tom Daschle was certified the winner by 139 votes over Republican Leo Thorsness, who had requested a recount.

With a record 58 open seats in the House because of retirement, desire to seek other office, death or primary defeat, Republicans hoped to make their biggest gains in the 39 open districts held by Democrats. But that strategy brought only a net gain of two, as Republicans captured eight Democratic-held open seats but lost six of their 19 vacant seats to the Democrats.

Campaigning against incumbents, usually a harder task, proved surprisingly successful for the GOP this time, as 14 Democratic House members were defeated, compared to five Republicans. It was the largest number of Democratic defeats since 1966, when 39 House Democrats, many of them brought in during the 1964 presidential landslide, lost their jobs.

The most surprising Democratic defeats came from the "Class of '74."

Republicans made a concerted effort to oust most of these Democratic newcomers in 1976, but defeated only two of them. This time GOP strategists chose not to target most of the 1974 group, given the two added years of incumbency its members had built up. But when the returns were in, seven of these Democrats had lost.

Representatives Defeated

	Terms
John J. McFall (D Calif.)	11
John Krebs (D Calif.)	2
Mark W. Hannaford (D Calif.)	2
J. Herbert Burke (R Fla.)	6
David L. Cornwell (D Ind.)	1
Michael T. Blouin (D Iowa)	2
Martha Keys (D Kan.)	2
Newton I. Steers Jr. (R Md.)	1
Garry Brown (R Mich.)	6
Elford A. Cederberg (R Mich.)	13
Helen Meyner (D N.J.)	2
Edward W. Pattison (D N.Y.)	2
Charles J. Carney (D Ohio)	4
Joshua Eilberg (D Pa.)	6
Fred B. Rooney (D Pa.)	8
Joseph S. Ammerman (D Pa.)	1
Bob Gammage (D Texas)	1
John E. Cunningham (R Wash.)	1
Robert J. Cornell (D Wis.)	2

The main reason for the defeats was lower turnout. In Wisconsin, where Democrat Robert J. Cornell won re-election in 1976 by a narrow margin, there were 42,000 fewer Democratic votes. The Republican vote declined, but only by 5,000 allowing state Rep. Tobias Roth to put the seat back in the Republican column.

In several cases, Republicans put up stronger candidates than in 1976. One was Charles "Chip" Pashayan, a wealthy businessman from Fresno, California, who knocked off Democrat John Krebs with 55 percent. In 1976 Krebs breezed to an easy victory over a poorly financed challenger.

In a rematch, Republican lawyer Daniel E. Lungren learned from his past mistakes, and beat another second-term California Democrat, Mark W. Hannaford.

Republicans and Conservatives got together in New York and turned out Troy Democrat Edward W. Pattison. In 1976 Pattison won with 47 percent because a Conservative Party candidate received 7 percent of the vote.

Democrat Michael T. Blouin in Iowa was also the victim of newly united opposition. State Rep. Tom Tauke, who won 53 percent of the vote, co-opted Blouin's anti-abortion position. Blouin's opponent in his two previous victories took a pro-abortion stand, alienating some party workers and losing votes in heavily Catholic areas.

Two women elected in 1974, Democrats Martha Keys in Kansas and Helen S. Meyner in New Jersey, were both defeated by well-financed candidates with no previous political experience. Keys lost by 5,000 votes to Jim Jeffries, an investment banker, and Meyner was overcome by James A. Courter, a former assistant county prosecutor. In each case the Republican emerged from a tough primary contest as the stronger candidate, and was able to heal the wounds within his party.

This kind of political Darwinism, in which a competitive primary guarantees an effective nominee, was actually more apparent among Democrats than among Republicans. In many states, it explains the GOP's inability to make significant gains among Democratic-held open seats. In the contest to succeed retiring Texas Democrat Omar Burleson, Charles W. Stenholm, a rancher, proved to be the strongest of seven Democratic primary contenders, surviving a tough primary and then winning a runoff against a well-financed opponent. Billy Lee Fisher was the only Republican to enter the contest. He was swamped in the general election, winning only 32 percent.

The failure of the Republican strategy of going after open seats was particularly apparent in Texas and California, where there were a dozen districts held by departing Democratic incumbents. A Republican carried only one of these — the Texas district Robert Krueger vacated.

These results challenged the GOP theory that Texas districts long held by personally popular Democrats would turn Republican when the aging incumbents retired. Krueger had held his seat for a shorter time than any of the other departing Texas or California Democrats, all of whom were replaced by Democrats.

Democrats won more than a fourth of the open Republican-held seats. In five districts, popular Republicans with safe seats decided that being a member of the minority party in the House offered too few rewards. Two decided to retire — Charles W. Whalen Jr. in Ohio and Gary A. Myers in Pennsylvania. Three others left to run for another office: Ronald A. Sarasin in Connecticut, Louis Frey Jr. in Florida and Bruce F. Caputo in New York. All three lost those bids, and Democrats were elected to seats that would have stayed in GOP control.

A second element of the Republican strategy, to benefit from the Korean bribery scandal and other assorted misdeeds and indictments, had a mixed effect on House results. *(Story, see Congress and Government chapter)*

The Korean probe, once touted by Republicans as a potential Watergate, brought down only California's John J. McFall, while two others who received mild reprimands from the House won easily.

Joshua Eilberg, the Pennsylvania Democrat indicted Oct. 25 on conflict-of-interest charges, was soundly defeated by state Sen. Charles Dougherty in a traditionally Democratic district. But Daniel J. Flood, also indicted in Pennsylvania on 13 counts including bribery and perjury, survived his challenge from a Hazleton attorney, though his 54 percent showing was far below what Flood was accustomed to receiving.

The conviction of Michigan Democratic Rep. Charles C. Diggs Jr. apparently had little impact on his constituents. They returned him for a 13th term with 80 percent of the vote.

One Republican in legal trouble, Florida's J. Herbert Burke, was soundly defeated by a Democrat, 68-year-old Broward County Sheriff Edward J. Stack. Burke was arrested in the parking lot of a nightclub in May and later pleaded guilty to misdemeanor charges of being disorderly and resisting arrest. Stack, who ran against Burke twice before as a Republican, will be the oldest House freshman in more than a decade.

Turnover in the House continues at a rapid pace. Including the 77 freshmen elected Nov. 7 — 41 Democrats and 36 Republicans — nearly half the members of the House will have been elected since 1974. The 96th Congress will also be younger, as six of the eight most senior members retired in 1978. With 78-year-old Claude Pepper of Florida the oldest member, the 96th Congress will be the first to have no House members born in the 19th century.

East

Republicans scored a net gain of only two seats in the 13 eastern states, and are still outnumbered by better than a two-to-one margin. The biggest changes occurred in Pennsylvania, New York and New Jersey.

Daniel Lungren

Charles Pashayan

California Newcomers

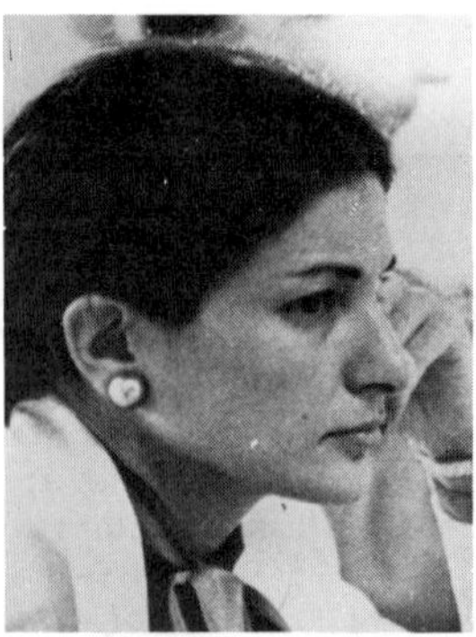

Olympia Snowe

Beverly Byron

Women Elected

Pennsylvania Republicans toppled three Democratic incumbents, but lost a GOP-held open seat, for a net rebound of two seats from the disaster of 1976 when they lost four House seats in the state. Pennsylvania has seen substantial turnover recently in its 25-member delegation. Thirteen members have been chosen in the last two elections, including five in 1978.

The state's biggest upset was the defeat of eight-term Democrat Fred B. Rooney, who lost to Donald L. Ritter, a political novice. Rooney, the chairman of the Transportation and Commerce Subcommittee, had been routinely reelected in the past.

Republicans gained one seat in the heavily Democratic New York delegation, defeating Pattison, while swapping Bruce Caputo's Republican seat for the Democrat-held district of retiring Otis G. Pike. Republican William Carney, a Suffolk county legislator, took 63 percent of the vote in Pike's district. Caputo was replaced by former Rep. Peter A. Peyser, who held the seat as a Republican until his unsuccessful 1976 Senate primary race against then-Sen. James L. Buckley. Peyser switched parties in 1977.

Democrat Geraldine A. Ferraro, a 43-year-old Forest Hills lawyer, maintained the party's hold on the seat of retiring Rep. James J. Delaney despite a strong GOP campaign in a district many thought would turn Republican once the 30-year incumbent left.

Ferraro joins Republican state Sen. Olympia J. Snowe in Maine and Maryland Democrat Beverly Byron, the widow of Rep. Goodloe E. Byron, as the only new women House members. Snowe, running for the seat of Republican Senate winner William S. Cohen, was aided by Cohen's strong showing in the northern part of the state. She defeated Secretary of State Markham L. Gartley, who was making his second try for the seat.

Byron's election gives Maryland its fourth woman member, more than any other state has.

Maryland and Connecticut each gained one Democratic seat. In Maryland, Democrat Michael D. Barnes ousted freshman Republican Newton I. Steers in a close 52-48 election. In Connecticut, Democrat William R. Ratchford took Sarasin's open seat by 9,000 votes. Ratchford nearly beat Sarasin in 1974.

A few Democratic incumbents in the East had close calls. Rhode Island Democrat Edward P. Beard was held to 53 percent by Claudine Schneider, a Republican housewife with no previous electoral experience. And in New Jersey, while Meyner was losing, 73-year-old Democratic incum-

Women in Congress

Nancy Landon Kassebaum became the first woman in 12 years to win a seat in the U.S. Senate, but the number of women senators will decline, as both Alabama's Maryon Allen and Muriel Humphrey in Minnesota will not return. Both were appointed to fill the vacancies caused by their husbands' deaths. Mrs. Humphrey chose not to run again, but Mrs. Allen tried and failed to win her party's nomination.

In the House, three of the 18 women in the 95th Congress retired, two others were beaten and only three of 31 women challengers who received major party nominations were victorious. The net result was two fewer women House members.

Democrats Martha Keys of Kansas and Helen Meyner of New Jersey both lost close races trying to win third terms in the House. Both had been major targets of national Republican strategists and fund raisers.

bent Edward J. Patten held on by just 3,000 votes. He was cleared in the House Korean investigation, but faced new difficulties with financial disclosure requirements. Patten's opponent ran against him in 1976 and only received 30 percent of the vote.

In Massachusetts, three open seats were filled by Democrats, keeping intact the 10-2 split in favor of the Democrats. Twenty-six-year-old James Shannon easily won the seat held by Sen.-elect Paul E. Tsongas. He was helped by Tsongas' heavy vote in the district. Shannon will be the youngest member of the House when he is sworn in in January.

South

Republicans made their largest advances in the South, with a net gain of four seats, but missed opportunities in Florida and Texas to pick up additional strength.

In Florida, Democrats not only ousted Burke, but held the seats of retiring members Robert L. F. Sikes and Paul G. Rogers, and captured Frey's seat, as state Rep. Bill Nelson thwarted a comeback effort from former U.S. Sen. Edward J. Gurney. Gurney won only 39 percent of the vote.

Elsewhere in the South, however, the GOP resumed the gradual resurgence halted by Watergate in 1974 and by Jimmy Carter in 1976. The open seat stategy enjoyed more success in the South than in other regions. Republicans took open seats from Democrats in Arkansas, Georgia, Kentucky and South Carolina.

Republican Ed Bethune's victory in central Arkansas over state Rep. Doug Brandon was a surprise and makes Bethune only the second Republican elected to the House from that state in this century.

In Georgia, Republican Newt Gingrich managed to win on his third try. He defeated Democratic state Sen. Virginia Shapard, considered one of the stronger women candidates in the country, to take the seat vacated by retiring Democrat John M. Flynt.

Kentucky Republicans proved agile in switching to a stronger candidate, Larry Hopkins, after Democratic incumbent John B. Breckinridge lost in the primary. Hopkins defeated Democratic state Sen. Tom Easterly by more than 4,000 votes, giving the state its third Republican House member.

With strong help from the national GOP operation, South Carolina state Sen. Carroll A. Campbell took the seat of retiring Democrat James R. Mann, defeating Max M. Heller, the Democrat who was favored to win.

The South will have more new faces in the House (23) than any other region. Texas alone will have nine. Republicans doubled their small Texas delegation, winning four House seats in the wake of narrow victories for governor and Senate. Along with two previously held, the GOP carried Krueger's seat, and former Republican Rep. Ron Paul took back the seat that Democrat Bob Gammage won from him in 1976 by 287 votes. This marked the third Gammage-Paul contest in the last three years. As in the April 1976 special election, which Paul also won, turnout was low. Nearly twice as many people voted in November 1976, when Gammage won.

Except in the Krueger district, however, Republican performance in the Texas open seats was disappointing. Several GOP candidates came within a few thousand votes of winning, including George W. Bush, son of the veteran Republican politician and presidential contender. But none made it. Bush lost to Democratic state Sen. Kent Hance, who took the seat held for 44 years by retiring Democrat George H. Mahon.

Midwest

Republicans managed to win back four midwestern seats they lost in 1974, knocking out incumbents in each case. Though the net Republican gain in the 12-state region was only two GOP strategists were relieved to see the gains come in districts which they feared might be slipping permanently into the Democratic column.

But several seats which changed hands in 1974 may now be out of Republican reach. In Michigan, Bob Carr, who won by 647 votes four years ago, drew a comfortable 58 percent against a supposedly strong challenger. Iowa Democrats Berkley Bedell and Tom Harkin, who took Republican districts in 1974 both scored a second round of substantial victories.

Along with the Democratic losses of Blouin in Iowa, Keys in Kansas, and Cornell in Wisconsin, Indiana freshman David L. Cornwell was defeated by former state Rep. H. Joel Deckard. Cornwell narrowly kept his southern Indiana district on the Democratic side in 1976, after Philip H. Hayes left it to run for the U.S. Senate.

Ed Stack

Bill Nelson

Florida Winners

In Illinois, Republican Daniel B. Crane, a dentist and the brother of Rep. Philip M. Crane, won the seat of retiring Democrat George E. Shipley. But a third Crane brother, David, lost his bid in Indiana to oust incumbent Democrat David W. Evans.

For the third consecutive election, Democratic Rep. Abner J. Mikva won a narrow victory in the Chicago suburbs. Mikva, who has had only one easy election since first coming to the House in 1968, beat state Rep. John E. Porter by just over 1,000 votes.

In the closest House race of the year, former state GOP chairman Leo K. Thorsness appeared to have lost Sen. elect Larry Pressler's House seat. Official totals showed Thorsness a 14-vote loser to Democrat Tom Daschle. A recount confirmed Daschle's victory.

Michigan provided the main source of joy for House Democrats in the Midwest. Although Democrats were unable to capture the seat of retiring Rep. Philip E. Ruppe, they took advantage of Carl Levin's strong Senate campaign to edge Republicans in two rematches. Former state Rep. Howard Wolpe overcame a deficit of nearly 4,000 votes from his 1976 race against incumbent Republican Garry Brown, and beat Brown by nearly 5,000. Democrat Donald J. Albosta made up even more ground against 13-term incumbent Republican Elford A. Cederberg, moving from 43 percent to 52 percent. Albosta was closely identified with the farmers' anger over a PBB chemical contamination scandal.

Freshman Harold S. Sawyer, a Republican who was helped by the strong showing of Gerald R. Ford two years ago, nearly lost Ford's old district to a little known challenger, Dale Sprik. Sprik fell 2,000 votes short of toppling Sawyers.

In Ohio, the defeat of Charles J. Carney was less surprising, though most thought the Youngstown Democrat's 1976 opponent had been stronger than the winner this year, Lyle Williams, a Trumbull County commissioner. Carney's image suffered when he was unable to prevent the closing of several local steel plants, and declined further when it was disclosed he had acquired more than 60,000 surplus books free from the Library of Congress.

The loss of Carney in Ohio was offset by the election of Democratic state Sen. Tony P. Hall to replace retiring Republican Charles W. Whalen Jr.

West

There were few changes in the western states except in California, where more than a quarter of the 43-member delegation will be new. Along with the eight new members who replaced retiring members from the same party — four Democrats and four Republicans — there will be three Republican freshmen, who defeated incumbent Democrats McFall, Krebs and Hannaford.

Republicans, while pleased with the defeat of the Democratic incumbents, missed several opportunities to further reduce the 26-17 Democratic edge in the California delegation. Sandy Smoley, the GOP choice to take the seat of retiring Democrat John E. Moss, was beaten by Sacramento city councilman Robert T. Matsui.

Democrat Tony Coelho, the longtime administrative assistant to retiring Rep. B. F. Sisk, had no trouble holding Sisk's seat. Coelho joined two other former House aides — Dan Mica in Florida and J. Marvin Leath in Texas — who will replace their bosses.

Freshman Democrat Leon E. Panetta soundly defeated a conservative challenger to keep the seat he took in 1976 from Republican Burt L. Talcott. Panetta won 62 percent over Eric Seastrand. But Republican freshman Robert K. Dornan was much less convincing in his race against Carey Peck. He won by just 2,500 votes, far less than his 55 percent victory for the open seat in 1976.

In other western states, Democrats picked up one seat in Washington, as 1977 special election winner John E. Cunningham fell to King County Councilman Mike Lowry. Of the four Republicans who won surprising victories in 1977 and 1978 special elections in usually Democratic districts, Cunningham was the only loser this year.

The Democratic gain in Washington was offset in the West by the victory of Richard Cheney, Gerald Ford's White House chief-of-staff, for the at-large seat in Wyoming left open by the retirement of Democrat Teno Roncalio. ▮

House: Newcomers, Switched Seats, Losers

State	District	Old	New	Winner	Loser	Incumbent
Alabama	7	D	D	Richard C. Shelby	James L. Scruggs	Walter Flowers[1]
Arkansas	2	D	R	Ed Bethune	Doug Brandon	Jim Guy Tucker[1]
	4	D	D	Beryl F. Anthony	No Republican candidate	Ray Thornton[1]
California	3	D	D	Robert T. Matsui	Sandy Smoley	John E. Moss[2]
	4	D	D	Vic Fazio	Rex Hime	Robert L. Leggett[2]
	14	D	R	Norman D. Shumway	John J. McFall	McFall
	15	D	D	Tony Coelho	Chris Patterakis	B. F. Sisk[2]
	17	D	R	Charles (Chip) Pashayan Jr.	John Krebs	Krebs
	18	R	R	William Thomas	Bob Sogge	William M. Ketchum[3]
	28	D	D	Julian C. Dixon	No Republican candidate	Yvonne Brathwaite Burke[4]
	33	R	R	Wayne Grisham	Dennis S. Kazarian	Del Clawson[2]
	34	D	R	Daniel E. Lungren	Mark W. Hannaford	Hannaford
	37	R	R	Jerry Lewis	Dan Corcoran	Shirley N. Pettis[2]
	39	R	R	William E. Dannemeyer	William E. Farris	Charles E. Wiggins[2]
Colorado	3	D	D	Ray Kogovsek	Harold L. McCormick	Frank E. Evans[2]
	5	R	R	Ken Kramer	Gerry Frank	William L. Armstrong[1]

State	District	Old	New	Winner	Loser	Incumbent
Connecticut	5	R	D	William R. Ratchford	George C. Guidera	Ronald A. Sarasin[5]
Florida	1	D	D	Earl D. Hutto	Warren Briggs	Robert L. F. Sikes[2]
	9	R	D	Bill Nelson	Edward J. Gurney	Louis Frey Jr.[5]
	11	D	D	Dan Mica	Bill James	Paul G. Rogers[2]
	12	R	D	Edward J. Stack	J. Herbert Burke	Burke
Georgia	6	D	R	Newt Gingrich	Virginia Shapard	John J. Flynt Jr.[2]
Illinois	1	D	D	Bennett Stewart	A. A. Rayner	Ralph H. Metcalfe[3]
	22	D	R	Daniel B. Crane	Terry L. Bruce	George E. Shipley[2]
Indiana	8	D	R	H. Joel Deckard	David L. Cornwell	Cornwell
Iowa	2	D	R	Tom Tauke	Michael T. Blouin	Blouin
Kansas	2	D	R	Jim Jeffries	Martha Keys	Keys
	5	R	R	Robert Whittaker	Donald L. Allegrucci	Joe Skubitz[2]
Kentucky	6	D	R	Larry J. Hopkins	Tom Easterly	John B. Breckinridge[6]
Louisiana	4	D	D	Claude (Buddy) Leach	Jimmy Wilson	Joe D. Waggonner Jr.[2]
Maine	2	R	R	Olympia J. Snowe	Markham L. Gartley	William S. Cohen[1]
Maryland	6	D	D	Beverly Byron	Melvin Perkins	Goodloe E. Byron[3]
	8	R	D	Michael D. Barnes	Newton I. Steers Jr.	Steers
Massachusetts	5	D	D	James M. Shannon	John L. Buckley	Paul E. Tsongas[1]
	6	D	D	Nicholas Mavroules	William E. Bronson	Michael J. Harrington[2]
	11	D	D	Brian J. Donnelly	No Republican candidate	James A. Burke[2]
Michigan	3	R	D	Howard Wolpe	Garry Brown	Brown
	10	R	D	Donald J. Albosta	Elford A. Cederberg	Cederberg
	11	R	R	Robert W. Davis	Keith McLeod	Philip E. Ruppe[2]
Minnesota	1	R	R	Arlen Erdahl	Gerry Sikorski	Albert H. Quie[5]
	5	D	D	Martin Olav Sabo	Michael Till	Donald M. Fraser[1]
Mississippi	4	R	R	Jon C. Hinson	John Hampton Stennis	Thad Cochran[1]
Montana	1	D	D	Pat Williams	Jim Waltermire	Max Baucus[1]
Nebraska	1	R	R	Douglas K. Bereuter	Hess Dyas	Charles Thone[5]
New Jersey	13	D	R	James A. Courter	Helen Meyner	Meyner
	14	D	D	Frank J. Guarini	Henry J. Hill	Joseph A. LeFante[2]
New York	1	D	R	William Carney	John F. Randolph	Otis G. Pike[2]
	9	D	D	Geraldine A. Ferraro	Alfred A. DelliBovi	James J. Delaney[2]
	23	R	D	Peter A. Peyser	Angelo R. Martinelli	Bruce F. Caputo[7]
	29	D	R	Gerald B. Solomon	Edward W. Pattison	Pattison
	33	R	R	Gary A. Lee	Roy A. Bernardi	William F. Walsh[2]
Ohio	3	R	D	Tony P. Hall	Dudley P. Kircher	Charles W. Whalen Jr.[2]
	19	D	R	Lyle Williams	Charles J. Carney	Carney
Oklahoma	2	D	D	Mike Synar	Gary L. Richardson	Ted Risenhoover[6]
Pennsylvania	2	D	D	William H. Gray III	Roland J. Atkins	Robert N. C. Nix[6]
	4	D	R	Charles F. Dougherty	Joshua Eilberg	Eilberg
	15	D	R	Donald L. Ritter	Fred B. Rooney	Rooney
	21	D	D	Don Bailey	Robert H. Miller	John H. Dent[2]
	23	D	R	William F. Clinger Jr.	Joseph S. Ammerman	Ammerman
	25	R	D	Eugene V. Atkinson	Tim Shaffer	Gary A. Myers[2]
South Carolina	4	D	R	Carroll A. Campbell Jr.	Max M. Heller	James R. Mann[2]
South Dakota	1	R	R	Thomas A. Daschle	Leo K. Thorsness[8]	Larry Pressler[1]
Tennessee	5	D	D	Bill Boner	Bill Goodwin	Clifford Allen[3]
Texas	6	D	D	Phil Gramm	Wesley H. Mowrey	Olin E. Teague[2]
	11	D	D	J. Marvin Leath	Jack Burgess	W.R. Poage[2]
	14	D	D	Joe Wyatt	Joy Yates	John Young[6]
	17	D	D	Charles W. Stenholm	Billy Lee Fisher	Omar Burleson[2]
	18	D	D	Mickey Leland	No Republican candidate	Barbara C. Jordan[2]
	19	D	D	Kent Hance	George W. Bush	George Mahon[2]
	21	D	R	Tom Loeffler	Nelson W. Wolff	Robert Krueger[1]
	22	D	R	Ron Paul	Bob Gammage	Gammage
	24	D	D	Martin Frost	Leo Berman	Dale Milford[6]
Washington	2	D	D	Al Swift	John Nance Garner	Lloyd Meeds[2]
	7	R	D	Mike Lowry	John E. Cunningham	Cunningham
Wisconsin	8	D	R	Tobias A. Roth	Robert J. Cornell	Cornell
	9	R	R	F. James Sensenbrenner Jr.	Matthew J. Flynn	Robert W. Kasten Jr.[5]
Wyoming	AL	D	R	Richard Cheney	Bill Bagley	Teno Roncalio[2]

1. Ran for Senate. 2. Retiring. 3. Deceased. 4. Ran for state attorney general. 5. Ran for governor. 6. Defeated in primary. 7. Ran for lieutenant governor. 8. Challenge possible.

House Membership in the 96th Congress

HOUSE LINEUP†

Democrats 276	Republicans 159
Freshman Democrats - 41	Freshman Republicans - 36
*Freshman Representative	#Former Representative
†election results	

ALABAMA
1. Jack Edwards (R)
2. William L. Dickinson (R)
3. Bill Nichols (D)
4. Tom Bevill (D)
5. Ronnie G. Flippo (D)
6. John Buchanan (R)
7. Richard C. Shelby (D)*

ALASKA
AL Don Young (R)

ARIZONA
1. John J. Rhodes (R)
2. Morris K. Udall (D)
3. Bob Stump (D)
4. Eldon Rudd (R)

ARKANSAS
1. Bill Alexander (D)
2. Ed Bethune (R)*
3. John Paul Hammerschmidt (R)
4. Beryl Anthony (D)*

CALIFORNIA
1. Harold T. Johnson (D)
2. Don H. Clausen (R)
3. Robert T. Matsui (D)*
4. Vic Fazio (D)*
5. John L. Burton (D)
6. Phillip Burton (D)
7. George Miller (D)
8. Ronald V. Dellums (D)
9. Fortney H. (Pete) Stark (D)
10. Don Edwards (D)
11. Leo J. Ryan (D)
12. Paul N. McCloskey Jr. (R)
13. Norman Y. Mineta (D)
14. Norman D. Shumway (R)*
15. Tom Coelho (D)*
16. Leon E. Panetta (D)
17. Charles (Chip) Pashayan Jr. (R)*
18. William Thomas (R)*
19. Robert J. Lagomarsino (R)
20. Barry M. Goldwater Jr. (R)
21. James C. Corman (D)
22. Carlos J. Moorhead (R)
23. Anthony C. (Tony) Beilenson (D)
24. Henry A. Waxman (D)
25. Edward R. Roybal (D)
26. John H. Rousselot (R)
27. Robert K. Dornan (R)
28. Julian C. Dixon (D)*
29. Augustus F. Hawkins (D)
30. George E. Danielson (D)
31. Charles H. Wilson (D)
32. Glenn M. Anderson (D)
33. Wayne Grisham (R)*
34. Dan Lungren (R)*
35. Jim Lloyd (D)
36. George E. Brown Jr. (D)
37. Jerry Lewis (R)*
38. Jerry M. Patterson (D)
39. William E. Dannemeyer (R)*
40. Robert E. Badham (R)
41. Bob Wilson (R)
42. Lionel Van Deerlin (D)
43. Clair W. Burgener (R)

COLORADO
1. Patricia Schroeder (D)
2. Timothy E. Wirth (D)
3. Ray Kogovsek (D)*
4. James P. Johnson (R)
5. Ken Kramer (R)*

CONNECTICUT
1. William R. Cotter (D)
2. Christopher J. Dodd (D)
3. Robert N. Giaimo (D)
4. Stewart B. McKinney (R)
5. William Ratchford (D)*
6. Toby Moffett (D)

DELAWARE
AL Thomas B. Evans Jr. (R)

FLORIDA
1. Earl Hutto (D)*
2. Don Fuqua (D)
3. Charles E. Bennett (D)
4. Bill Chappell Jr. (D)
5. Richard Kelly (R)
6. C. W. Bill Young (R)
7. Sam Gibbons (D)
8. Andy Ireland (D)
9. Bill Nelson (D)*
10. L. A. (Skip) Bafalis (R)
11. Don Mica (D)*
12. Edward J. Stack (D)*
13. William Lehman (D)
14. Claude Pepper (D)
15. Dante B. Fascell (D)

GEORGIA
1. Bo Ginn (D)
2. Dawson Mathis (D)
3. Jack Brinkley (D)
4. Elliott H. Levitas (D)
5. Wyche Fowler (D)
6. Newt Gingrich (R)*
7. Larry P. McDonald (D)
8. Billy Lee Evans (D)
9. Ed Jenkins (D)
10. Doug Barnard (D)

HAWAII
1. Cecil (Cec) Heftel (D)
2. Daniel K. Akaka (D)

IDAHO
1. Steven D. Symms (R)
2. George Hansen (R)

ILLINOIS
1. Bennett Stewart (D)*
2. Morgan F. Murphy (D)
3. Marty Russo (D)
4. Edward J. Derwinski (R)
5. John G. Fary (D)
6. Henry J. Hyde (R)
7. Cardiss Collns (D)
8. Dan Rostenkowski (D)
9. Sidney R. Yates (D)
10. Abner J. Mikva (D)
11. Frank Annunzio (D)
12. Philip M. Crane (R)
13. Robert McClory (R)
14. John N. Erlenborn (R)
15. Tom Corcoran (R)
16. John B. Anderson (R)
17. George M. O'Brien (R)
18. Robert H. Michel (R)
19. Tom Railsback (R)
20. Paul Findley (R)
21. Edward R. Madigan (R)
22. Daniel B. Crane (R)*
23. Melvin Price (D)
24. Paul Simon (D)

INDIANA
1. Adam Benjamin Jr. (D)
2. Floyd Fithian (D)
3. John Brademas (D)
4. Dan Quayle (R)
5. Elwood Hillis (R)
6. David W. Evans (D)
7. John T. Myers (R)
8. H. Joel Deckard (R)*
9. Lee H. Hamilton (D)
10. Phil Sharp (D)
11. Andy Jacobs Jr. (D)

IOWA
1. Jim Leach (R)
2. Tom Tauke (R)*
3. Charles E. Grassley (R)
4. Neal Smith (D)
5. Tom Harkin (D)
6. Berkley Bedell (D)

KANSAS
1. Keith G. Sebelius (R)
2. Jim Jeffries (R)*
3. Larry Winn Jr. (R)
4. Dan Glickman (D)
5. Robert Whittaker (R)*

KENTUCKY
1. Carroll Hubbard Jr. (D)
2. William H. Natcher (D)
3. Romano L. Mazzoli (D)
4. Gene Snyder (R)
5. Tim Lee Carter (R)
6. Larry J. Hopkins (R)*
7. Carl D. Perkins (D)

LOUISIANA
1. Robert L. Livingston (R)
2. Lindy Boggs (D)
3. David C. Treen (R)
4. Claude (Buddy) Leach (D)*
5. Jerry Huckaby (D)
6. W. Henson Moore (R)
7. John B. Breaux (D)
8. Gillis W. Long (D)

MAINE
1. David F. Emery (R)
2. Olympia J. Snowe (R)*

MARYLAND
1. Robert E. Bauman (R)
2. Clarence D. Long (D)
3. Barbara A. Mikulski (D)
4. Marjorie S. Holt (R)
5. Gladys Noon Spellman (D)
6. Beverly Byron (D)*
7. Parren J. Mitchell (D)
8. Michael D. Barnes (D)*

MASSACHUSETTS
1. Silvio O. Conte (R)
2. Edward P. Boland (D)
3. Joseph D. Early (D)
4. Robert F. Drinan (D)
5. James M. Shannon (D)*
6. Nicholas Mavroules (D)*
7. Edward J. Markey (D)
8. Thomas P. O'Neill Jr. (D)
9. Joe Moakley (D)
10. Margaret M. Heckler (R)
11. Brian J. Donnelly (D)*
12. Gerry E. Studds (D)

MICHIGAN
1. John Conyers Jr. (D)
2. Carl D. Pursell (R)
3. Howard Wolpe (D)*
4. Dave Stockman (R)
5. Harold S. Sawyer (R)
6. Bob Carr (D)
7. Dale E. Kildee (D)
8. Bob Traxler (D)
9. Guy Vander Jagt (R)
10. Don Albosta (D)*
11. Robert W. Davis (R)*
12. David E. Bonior (D)
13. Charles C. Diggs Jr. (D)
14. Lucien N. Nedzi (D)
15. William D. Ford (D)
16. John D. Dingell (D)
17. William M. Brodhead (D)
18. James J. Blanchard (D)
19. William S. Broomfield (R)

MINNESOTA
1. Arlen Erdahl (R)*
2. Tom Hagedorn (R)
3. Bill Frenzel (R)
4. Bruce F. Vento (D)
5. Martin Olav Sabo (D)*
6. Richard Nolan (D)
7. Arlan Stangeland (R)
8. James L. Oberstar (D)

House Membership in the 96th Congress

MISSISSIPPI
1. Jamie L. Whitten (D)
2. David R. Bowen (D)
3. G. V. (Sonny) Montgomery (D)
4. Jon C. Hinson (R)*
5. Trent Lott (R)

MISSOURI
1. William (Bill) Clay (D)
2. Robert A. Young (D)
3. Richard A. Gephardt (D)
4. Ike Skelton (D)
5. Richard Bolling (D)
6. E. Thomas Coleman (R)
7. Gene Taylor (R)
8. Richard H. Ichord (D)
9. Harold L. Volkmer (D)
10. Bill D. Burlison (D)

MONTANA
1. Pat Williams (D)*
2. Ron Marlenee (R)

NEBRASKA
1. Douglas K. Bereuter (R)*
2. John J. Cavanaugh (D)
3. Virginia Smith (R)

NEVADA
AL Jim Santini (D)

NEW HAMPSHIRE
1. Norman E. D'Amours (D)
2. James C. Cleveland (R)

NEW JERSEY
1. James J. Florio (D)
2. William J. Hughes (D)
3. James J. Howard (D)
4. Frank Thompson Jr. (D)
5. Millicent Fenwick (R)
6. Edwin B. Forsythe (R)
7. Andrew Maguire (D)
8. Robert A. Roe (D)
9. Harold C. Hollenbeck (R)
10. Peter W. Rodino Jr. (D)
11. Joseph G. Minish (D)
12. Matthew J. Rinaldo (R)
13. Jim Courter (R)*
14. Frank J. Guarini (D)*
15. Edward J. Patten (D)

NEW MEXICO
1. Manuel Lujan Jr. (R)
2. Harold Runnels (D)

NEW YORK
1. William Carney (R)*
2. Thomas J. Downey (D)
3. Jerome A. Ambro (D)
4. Norman F. Lent (R)
5. John W. Wydler (R)
6. Lester L. Wolff (D)
7. Joseph P. Addabbo (D)
8. Benjamin S. Rosenthal (D)
9. Geraldine A. Ferraro (D)*
10. Mario Biaggi (D)
11. James H. Scheuer (D)
12. Shirley Chisholm (D)
13. Stephen J. Solarz (D)
14. Frederick Richmond (D)
15. Leo C. Zeferetti (D)
16. Elizabeth Holtzman (D)
17. John M. Murphy (D)
18. S. William Green (R)
19. Charles B. Rangel (D)
20. Ted Weiss (D)
21. Robert Garcia (D)
22. Jonathan B. Bingham (D)
23. Peter A. Peyser (D)#*
24. Richard L. Ottinger (D)
25. Hamilton Fish Jr. (R)
26. Benjamin A. Gilman (R)
27. Matthew F. McHugh (D)
28. Samuel S. Stratton (D)
29. Gerald B. Solomon (R)*
30. Robert C. McEwen (R)
31. Donald J. Mitchell (R)
32. James M. Hanley (D)
33. Gary A. Lee (R)*
34. Frank Horton (R)
35. Barber B. Conable Jr. (R)
36. John J. LaFalce (D)
37. Henry J. Nowak (D)
38. Jack F. Kemp (R)
39. Stanley N. Lundine (D)

NORTH CAROLINA
1. Walter B. Jones (D)
2. L. H. Fountain (D)
3. Charlie Whitley (D)
4. Ike F. Andrews (D)
5. Stephen L. Neal (D)
6. Richardson Preyer (D)
7. Charlie Rose (D)
8. W. G. (Bill) Hefner (D)
9. James G. Martin (R)
10. James T. Broyhill (R)
11. Lamar Gudger (D)

NORTH DAKOTA
AL Mark Andrews (R)

OHIO
1. Bill Gradison (R)
2. Thomas A. Luken (D)
3. Tony P. Hall (D)*
4. Tennyson Guyer (R)
5. Delbert L. Latta (R)
6. William H. Harsha (R)
7. Clarence J. Brown (R)
8. Thomas N. Kindness (R)
9. Thomas L. Ashley (D)
10. Clarence E. Miller (R)
11. J. William Stanton (R)
12. Samuel L. Devine (R)
13. Don J. Pease (D)
14. John F. Seiberling (D)
15. Chalmers P. Wylie (R)
16. Ralph S. Regula (R)
17. John M. Ashbrook (R)
18. Douglas Applegate (D)
19. Lyle Williams (R)*
20. Mary Rose Oakar (D)
21. Louis Stokes (D)
22. Charles A. Vanik (D)
23. Ronald M. Mottl (D)

OKLAHOMA
1. James R. Jones (D)
2. Mike Synar (D)*
3. Wes Watkins (D)
4. Tom Steed (D)
5. Mickey Edwards (R)
6. Glenn English (D)

OREGON
1. Les AuCoin (D)
2. Al Ullman (D)
3. Robert Duncan (D)
4. James Weaver (D)

PENNSYLVANIA
1. Michael (Ozzie) Myers (D)
2. William H. Gray III (D)*
3. Raymond F. Lederer (D)
4. Charles F. Dougherty (R)*
5. Richard T. Schulze (R)
6. Gus Yatron (D)
7. Robert W. Edgar (D)
8. Peter H. Kostmayer (D)
9. Bud Shuster (R)
10. Joseph M. McDade (R)
11. Daniel J. Flood (D)
12. John P. Murtha (D)
13. Lawrence Coughlin (R)
14. William S. Moorhead (D)
15. Donald L. Ritter (R)*
16. Robert S. Walker (R)
17. Allen E. Ertel (D)
18. Doug Walgren (D)
19. Bill Goodling (R)
20. Joseph M. Gaydos (D)
21. Don Bailey (D)*
22. Austin J. Murphy (D)
23. William F. Clinger Jr. (R)*
24. Marc L. Marks (R)
25. Eugene V. Atkinson (D)*

RHODE ISLAND
1. Fernand J. St Germain (D)
1. Edward P. Beard (D)

SOUTH CAROLINA
1. Mendel J. Davis (D)
2. Floyd Spence (R)
3. Butler Derrick (D)
4. Carroll Campbell (R)*
5. Ken Holland (D)
6. John W. Jenrette Jr. (D)

SOUTH DAKOTA
†1. Tom Daschle (D)*
2. James Abdnor (R)

TENNESSEE
1. James H. (Jimmy) Quillen (R)
2. John J. Duncan (R)
3. Marilyn Lloyd (D)
4. Albert Gore Jr. (D)
5. Bill Boner (D)*
6. Robin L. Beard Jr. (R)
7. Ed Jones (D)
8. Harold E. Ford (D)

TEXAS
1. Sam B. Hall Jr. (D)
2. Charles Wilson (D)
3. James M. Collins (R)
4. Ray Roberts (D)
5. Jim Mattox (D)
6. Phil Gramm (D)*
7. Bill Archer (R)
8. Bob Eckhardt (D)
9. Jack Brooks (D)
10. J. J. Pickle (D)
11. J. Marvin Leath (D)*
12. Jim Wright (D)
13. Jack Hightower (D)
14. Joe Wyatt (D)*
15. E. (Kika) de la Garza (D)
16. Richard C. White (D)
17. Charles Stenholm (D)*
18. Mickey Leland (D)*
19. Kent Hance (D)*
20. Henry B. Gonzalez (D)
21. Tom Loeffler (R)*
22. Ron Paul (R)#*
23. Abraham Kazen Jr. (D)
24. Martin Frost (D)*

UTAH
1. Gunn McKay (D)
2. Dan Marriott (R)

VERMONT
AL James M. Jeffords (R)

VIRGINIA
1. Paul S. Trible Jr. (R)
2. G. William Whitehurst (R)
3. David E. Satterfield III (D)
4. Robert W. Daniel (R)
5. Dan Daniel (D)
6. M. Caldwell Butler (R)
7. J. Kenneth Robinson (R)
8. Herbert E. Harris II (D)
9. William C. Wampler (R)
10. Joseph L. Fisher (D)

WASHINGTON
1. Joel Pritchard (R)
2. Al Swift (D)*
3. Don Bonker (D)
4. Mike McCormack (D)
5. Thomas S. Foley (D)
6. Norman D. Dicks (D)
7. Mike Lowry (D)*

WEST VIRGINIA
1. Robert H. Mollohan (D)
2. Harley O. Staggers (D)
3. John M. Slack (D)
4. Nick J. Rahall (D)

WISCONSIN
1. Les Aspin (D)
2. Robert W. Kastenmeier (D)
3. Alvin Baldus (D)
4. Clement J. Zablocki (D)
5. Henry S. Reuss (D)
6. William A. Steiger (R)
7. David R. Obey (D)
8. Tobias A. Roth (R)*
9. F. James Sensenbrenner Jr. (R)*

WYOMING
AL Richard Cheney (R)*

† Challenge possible.

CQ Governors

Six More Republican Governors in 1979

Republicans moved a step closer to respectability in gubernatorial politics Nov. 7, increasing the number of statehouses under their control from 12 to 18, and taking power in two more of the nation's largest states.

William Clements' upset election in Texas, Richard L. Thornburgh's come-from-behind triumph in Pennsylvania and James A. Rhodes' narrow survival in Ohio guaranteed that the GOP will enter the 1980 election year with governors in five of the ten "megastates". That news diluted the Republican disappointment at failing to oust Democratic Gov. Hugh L. Carey in New York, or even to come close against incumbent Democrat Edmund G. Brown Jr. in California.

In all, sixteen of 21 incumbents were re-elected. The losers were Republicans Meldrim Thomson Jr. of New Hampshire and Robert F. Bennett of Kansas, and Democrats Rudy Perpich of Minnesota, Martin J. Schreiber of Wisconsin and Robert Straub of Oregon.

Perpich and Schreiber were unelected governors, having succeeded to office when their predecessors resigned to take other government positions. Perpich succeeded Wendell Anderson and Schreiber succeeded Patrick Lucey, who was appointed ambassador to Mexico.

The gubernatorial returns were a boost for the moderate wing of the Republican Party. Incumbents James R. Thompson of Illinois, Robert Ray of Iowa and William G. Milliken of Michigan won easy re-election, and U.S. Rep. Albert H. Quie, who compiled a moderate voting record in 11 terms in the House, won an unexpectedly decisive victory in Minnesota over Perpich.

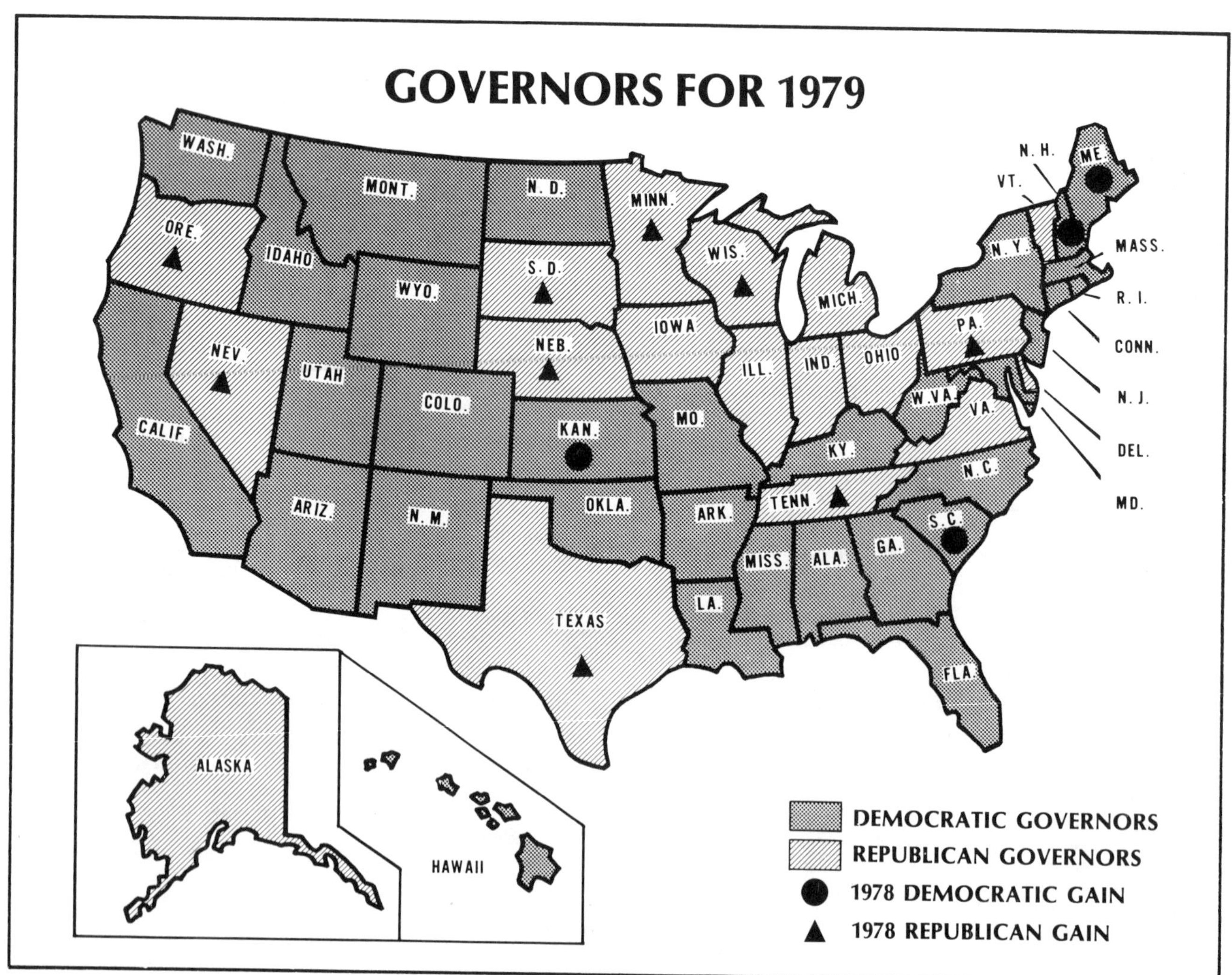

Republican moderates were encouraged most by the election of Thornburgh, a former Justice Department official in the Ford administration, and Lamar Alexander, a former aide to Sen. Howard H. Baker Jr., who won in Tennessee.

Thornburgh won a come-from-behind victory over former Pittsburgh Mayor Pete Flaherty. He was helped by a wide range of newspaper endorsements and a well-financed media campaign that cited corruption in the administration of outgoing Democratic Gov. Milton J. Shapp and sharply questioned Flaherty's effectiveness as mayor of Pittsburgh. Thornburgh was well behind in the polls in October but rallied to win with a plurality of 220,000 votes.

The more conservative wing of the Republican Party suffered the unexpected defeat of Thomson, who was turned out of office after six years. Democrat Hugh J. Gallen charged Thomson was not the hard-line tax opponent he claimed to be. Conservatives were also disappointed by the resounding rejection of GOP candidate Ted Strickland in his campaign for governor of Colorado. Strickland lost overwhelmingly to incumbent Democrat Richard Lamm.

But those losses were overshadowed for most conservatives by the good news from Texas, where Clements held on to defeat Democrat John Hill and bring the statehouse in Austin under Republican control for the first time since Reconstruction. Clements, who was deputy secretary of defense under Presidents Nixon and Ford, spent more than $1 million of his own money, effectively denouncing Hill as a liberal. Hill had beaten incumbent Dolph Briscoe in a Democratic primary, and Briscoe's family and other statehouse loyalists openly supported Clements.

Midwest

In numerical terms, the highlight of election day for Republicans was their showing in the Midwest, where the party captured eight of nine gubernatorial elections. Republicans held on to governorships in the industrial Great Lakes states — Illinois, Michigan and Ohio — while winning four states away from the Democrats in the farm areas farther west. Ray of Iowa capped the GOP's impressive performance in the region by easily winning a fifth term.

The Republican newcomers include two U.S. House members — Quie and four-term Rep. Charles Thone of Nebraska. Thone broke an eight-year Democratic hold on the governorship engineered by popular J.J. Exon, who was elected to the Senate.

Republican challengers easily defeated Perpich and Schreiber, the two non-elected Democratic governors in the upper Midwest. While Quie was beating Perpich by 100,000 votes in Minnesota, flamboyant college official Lee Sherman Dreyfus was making a memorable political debut in neighboring Wisconsin, overwhelming Schreiber by nearly 140,000 votes.

A polished orator whose trademark is a red vest, Dreyfus caught the fancy of Wisconsin voters with his wit and appeal to the progressive Republican tradition of the late Gov. Robert M. La Follette. Dreyfus upset party-backed Rep. Robert W. Kasten Jr. in the September primary, building up momentum that resulted in his comfortable general election victory.

The other midwestern Republican pickup was in South Dakota, where state Attorney General William J. Janklow recorded the first GOP gubernatorial victory in the state since 1968.

The only Republican loser in the region was Bennett, a suburban Kansas City lawyer who lost to Democratic state House Speaker John W. Carlin, a dairy farmer, by 15,000 votes.

Outside the Midwest, Republican victories were scattered, as Democrats won the wide majority of gubernatorial elections in other regions.

Democratic incumbents won impressively in the nation's two largest states, with Carey posting a victory margin of 230,000 votes and California's Brown overwhelming his Republican challenger by more than 1.3 million.

East

Democrats showed resilience in Maryland and Massachusetts, where they retained the statehouses after the incumbents were upset in September primaries. The two winners — Edward J. King in Massachusetts and Harry R. Hughes in Maryland — ran far different campaigns. Hughes won his primary and general election largely on a reputation as a reformer who had cut his ties to shady Democratic politics in Maryland. King ran as a tightfisted conservative both on money matters and social issues, easily ousting Gov. Michael S. Dukakis in the primary and overcoming liberal Republican Francis Hatch Nov. 7. Hughes had no trouble in the general election against former U.S. Sen. J. Glenn Beall Jr., the Republican nominee.

The Republican failures in Maryland and Massachusetts, coupled with Thomson's defeat in New Hampshire, left Republicans little to cheer about in the East as a whole. Except for Thornburgh's election, and the re-election of Richard A. Snelling in Vermont, Republicans were unable to win anywhere.

The Democrats picked up a new governorship in Maine, where state Attorney General Joseph E. Brennan won the chair of retiring Gov. James B. Longley, an independent. Fundamentalist minister Herman "Buddy" Frankland tried to follow in Longley's independent footsteps, but finished far behind the two major party candidates with about 18 percent of the vote.

Democrats swept the other governorships along the eastern seaboard, with incumbents Ella T. Grasso in Connecticut, J. Joseph Garrahy in Rhode Island and Carey in New York winning handily, along with newcomers King in Massachusetts and Hughes in Maryland. Victory totals ranged from 53 percent for Carey and King to 71 percent for Hughes.

South

Democrats took six of the eight gubernatorial contests in the South, losing only in Texas and Tennessee.

Two of the Democratic winners were 1976 state Carter campaign chairmen, Bill Clinton in Arkansas and Richard W. Riley in South Carolina.

Clinton has another distinction. At age 32, he will be the youngest governor anywhere since Harold Stassen was elected in Minnesota at age 31 in 1938.

Wealthy candidates squared off against each other in Florida and Tennessee, and each state chose the candidate who had tried to soften his moneyed image by striking a blue-collar theme.

In Florida, state Sen. Robert Graham, worth more than $4 million through a family dairy business and real estate development, worked at a variety of blue-collar jobs en route to a surprise primary win and a general election victory over drug store chain owner Jack M. Eckerd. Among jobs Graham tried during the primary campaign were citrus fruit picking and bellhopping. Graham beat Eckerd by about 280,000 votes.

Lamar Alexander, a Nashville lawyer, won the Tennessee governorship on his second try thanks in part to his walk across the state early in the year. Alexander felt that voter perception of him as a "country club" Republican was partially responsible for his 1974 loss to Democrat Ray Blanton. In an effort to remold his image Alexander made a 1,022-mile trek across Tennessee attired in khakis, work shirt and hiking boots. The walk, along with Alexander's success at keeping millionaire Democrat Jake Butcher on the defensive about Butcher's complex banking practices, helped produce a 140,000-vote Republican victory.

Other Democratic winners in the South were former college football star Forrest (Fob) James, a millionaire manufacturer of plastic dumbbells, in Alabama, Lt. Gov. George Nigh in Oklahoma, and Gov. George Busbee in Georgia. Busbee was the only incumbent governor in the South to run for re-election. He won with an impressive 80 percent of the vote, the highest percentage taken by any gubernatorial candidate in 1978.

Nigh was the only candidate to successfully make the jump from lieutenant governor to governor. Two other Democratic lieutenant governors, Gerald T. Whelan in Nebraska and Richard F. Celeste in Ohio, failed in their bids to win governorships.

West

Democrats entered the 1978 election holding every governorship in the West except Alaska, and they were able to hold onto their large majority. They lost Nevada and Oregon, but Democratic incumbents rolled to comfortable victories in six other states including California. A former governor, Bruce King, held a seventh state for the Democrats — New Mexico. The Democratic showing was impressive in the face of Carter's failure in the region in 1976 and the negative reaction to many of his programs there since then.

While Brown won re-election in California by the highest plurality for any gubernatorial candidate in the country, Lamm's victory in Colorado was nearly as impressive.

Lamm was opposed by Republican state Sen. Ted Strickland, who had put together what was supposed to be one of the finest organizations in Colorado history. Polls showed the GOP candidate ahead in late September, but a series of gaffes, including a statement by Strickland that he would not object to the closing of a major air base near Denver, brought an erosion in his support. Lamm won with 60 percent of the vote while Democratic incumbent Floyd K. Haskell was losing decisively.

The lone Democratic incumbent to lose in the West was Oregon's Straub, beaten in his rematch with Republican state Sen. Victor Atiyeh. Straub beat Atiyeh easily four years ago, but this time the Republican prevailed by more than 80,000 votes.

The other governor's chair to switch parties was in Nevada, where Republican state Attorney General Robert List won his bid to succeed popular Democratic incumbent Mike O'Callaghan.

The Republicans' lone western winner in 1974, Alaska's Jay S. Hammond, won a second term easily. In contrast to his narrow and disputed primary victory over former Republican Gov. Walter J. Hickel earlier in the year, Hammond won re-election by a 2-1 margin over his Democratic challenger. A late write-in drive for Hickel, though, netted 27 percent of the vote and enabled the former governor to finish second.

William Clements

Richard L. Thornburgh

Governors Defeated

	Terms
Robert F. Bennett (R Kan.)	1
Rudy Perpich (D Minn.)	1 (2 years)
Meldrim Thomson Jr. (R N.H.)	3
Robert Straub (D Ore.)	1
Martin J. Schreiber (D Wis.)	1 (1 year)

Newcomers

Twenty of the 36 governors elected Nov. 7 were non-incumbents. Five of the Democrats' 11 newcomers will be in the South, while four of the Republicans' nine new governors will be in the Midwest.

Most of the new governors are in their 40s or early 50s. Only four are under age 40 — Democrats Clinton (32) and Carlin (38), and Republicans Alexander (38) and Janklow (39).

The oldest of the incoming governors is Clements, who is 61. Ohio's Rhodes, who has already served 12 years in the Columbus statehouse, retains his status as the nation's oldest governor. He is 69.

The new governors come from a wide variety of backgrounds, although all but James and Dreyfus have held positions in government. The post of attorney general was a direct launching pad for four of the new governors — Democrats Brennan and Clinton, and Republicans Janklow and List.

Independent candidates did not fare well, taking 5 percent of the vote or more in only five states. Excluding Hickel's write-in effort, the most successful was Frankland in Maine, with 18 percent, according to unofficial returns, followed by Tom Kelly in Alaska with 17 percent, former Providence Mayor Joseph A. Doorley in Rhode Island with 7 percent and former Gov. Wesley Powell in New Hampshire with 5 percent.

VOTING STUDIES

CQ

The Year in Review:

Foreign Policy, Economics, Defense Top 1978 Key Votes

Foreign policy, defense and economic issues dominated key congressional votes during the 1978 session.

Domestic social issues played a small part in the key votes selected by Congressional Quarterly. This reflected the nature of the session, and of the entire 95th Congress.

Limited by a shortage of funds and restrained by a public more concerned about inflation than new government initiatives, Congress and President Carter made little effort to enact broad new social programs.

President Carter, like presidents before him beset by lack of a strong domestic base and lagging in popular acclaim, put much emphasis on foreign policy issues, and that produced a number of key votes.

Economy and Labor

In an election year dominated by controversy over government spending, several key votes involved fiscal policy issues.

In May, House Democrats narrowly defeated a Republican substitute for the first fiscal 1979 budget resolution that called for curbs on federal spending and a larger tax cut than the Carter administration and the Democratic majority had proposed.

A month later, shortly after California voters approved a state constitutional amendment slashing property taxes, the House voted the first of a series of across-the-board cuts in federal spending by approving a 2 percent cut in the appropriations bill for the Labor and Health, Education and Welfare departments. Similar cuts were offered to several other appropriations bills, but most were dropped in conference.

Riding the crest of a middle-class taxpayers' revolt, Congress enacted a tax bill that differed sharply from those of recent years by skewing the tax cuts much more toward the upper end of the income scale. An eleventh-hour liberal effort to provide larger tax cuts for persons earning less than $50,000 failed in the House. Although the Senate approved a proposal to tilt the tax cuts toward persons earning between $10,000 and $30,000, most of the extra cuts were dropped in conference.

On issues of particular interest to organized labor, the House in March narrowly rejected an effort to attach a specific anti-inflation goal to the Humphrey-Hawkins full employment bill, but an inflation target was later added to the measure in the Senate. In a bitter defeat for labor, the Senate failed by two votes to halt a filibuster against the labor law "reform" bill, thus dooming organized labor's No. 1 legislative priority.

Defense

The 1978 session of Congress appeared to be more content than many in recent years with the administration's defense budget. All attempts during the year to significantly alter — either up or down — the spending level for defense recommended by the White House were rejected handily.

Attempts in the Senate to make changes in the defense category of the annual congressional budget resolution were turned back in April, and the fiscal 1979 defense procurement and appropriations bills remained immune to the budget-cutting fever that swept Congress.

Amendments to make across-the-board cuts in defense as well as to cancel some expensive weapons systems sought by the Pentagon failed in both houses.

Carter also succeeded in making his own imprint on defense policy. Congress backed him in his refusal to continue the B-1 bomber project or add another $2 billion nuclear aircraft carrier to the Navy fleet. On the latter issue, Carter had to veto the defense authorization bill to back up his intention to set his own priorities for national security.

Foreign Affairs

President Carter had remarkably good success in Congress with foreign policy issues in 1978. He won the bulk of what he wanted.

The tone was set early in the year when the Senate consented to the ratification of the two Panama Canal treaties that will end U.S. control of the canal by the end of the century. Then Carter persuaded Congress to let him sell sophisticated jet fighter planes to Saudi Arabia, against the vigorous opposition of the politically potent coalition of groups supporting Israel.

Carter also got Congress to lift the arms sale embargo on Turkey — an embargo the administration argued was hurting relations with a key NATO ally.

Another victory, not entirely of the administration's doing, was won when Congress refused to lift economic sanctions against Rhodesia immediately. There was considerable sentiment, particularly among congressional conser-

How Votes Were Selected

Congressional Quarterly each year selects a series of key votes on major issues.

Selection of Issues. An issue is judged by the extent it represents one or more of the following:

- A matter of major controversy.
- A test of presidential or political power.
- A decision of potentially great impact on the nation and lives of Americans.

Selection of Votes. For each series of related votes on an issue, only one key vote is ordinarily chosen. This vote is the Senate roll call, or House recorded vote, that in the opinion of Congressional Quarterly was important in determining the outcome.

In the descriptions of the key votes, the designation ND denotes northern Democrats and SD denotes southern Democrats.

vatives, to lift the ban quickly to aid the troubled white minority government of Rhodesia. This was prevented when a more middle-of-the-road provision on sanctions was approved.

Senate Key Votes

1. NATURAL GAS PRICING. Months after House and Senate conferees took up two vastly different versions of natural gas pricing legislation, they narrowly approved a complicated compromise (HR 5289). The stalemate, broken in May 1978, had held up passage of other sections of President Carter's energy program.

But by August, just as final signatures were being placed on the conference report, a coalition of 24 senators announced their opposition to the compromise.

The bipartisan group of opponents included Democrats who were staunch supporters of price regulation and Republicans who wanted price controls lifted. Neither side liked the complicated scheme to raise prices gradually until 1985, when price controls on newly discovered gas would be lifted. The compromise established more than 18 categories of gas based on where the gas was found and who was using it.

Rather than trying to defeat the conference report, the coalition sought to recommit it with instructions that the disputed sections on gas pricing be removed and that other sections giving the president authority to allocate gas in emergencies be retained.

Determined to prevent what would have been a fatal blow for the energy bill, the administration launched a sophisticated lobbying campaign for the compromise, enlisting special support from Vice President Walter F. Mondale.

When, on Sept. 19, Sen. Howard M. Metzenbaum, D-Ohio, offered the motion to recommit, it failed, 39-59: R 21-15; D 18-44 (ND 13-30; SD 5-14).

On Sept. 27, President Carter won a major victory when the Senate approved the conference report, 57-42.

2. PANAMA CANAL TREATIES. No other single foreign policy issue of 1978 attracted as much attention, aroused as many emotions and consumed as much time and effort of the administration, the Senate and outside lobbying groups as did approval of two Panama Canal treaties. In the end, President Carter won a major victory when the Senate consented to ratification of the two pacts by identical 68-32 votes (R 16-22; D 52-10; ND 39-4; SD 13-6). The votes were just one over the constitutionally required two-thirds majority.

The treaties were the product of negotiations that formally began in 1964 but had in fact gone on intermittently ever since the original pact was signed in 1903. The basic treaty would turn over the U.S.-constructed, owned and operated Panama Canal to Panama by the year 2000. A second treaty — the neutrality treaty — would guarantee the United States and Panama the right to defend the canal after Dec. 31, 1999. The neutrality treaty was approved March 16, the transfer treaty on April 18.

The victory was especially significant for President Carter because opponents of the treaties had mounted a major nationwide grassroots lobbying campaign to defeat the pacts. Carter also had staked his administration's ability to conduct foreign policy on their ratification.

3. MIDEAST JET SALES. Given its first major role in shaping events in the Middle East, the Senate May 15 went along with the Carter administration's controversial plan to sell $4.8 billion worth of jet fighters to Saudi Arabia, Israel and Egypt.

The Senate's 44-54 vote (R 11-26; D 33-28; ND 26-17; SD 7-11) to turn down a resolution to block the sales was a victory for the Carter administration but a bitter defeat for Israel and U.S. Jewish organizations strongly opposed to the weapons package.

The package contained 60 F-15 fighters for Saudi Arabia, 50 F-5Es for Egypt and 15 F-15s and 75 F-16s for Israel. The major issue was the sale of the F-15s — America's most sophisticated fighter — to Saudi Arabia because of Israel's fears over its security.

Under arms sales procedures, House action was not required because the contracts automatically go through in 30 days unless rejected by both chambers.

Supporters of the sale argued the administration must be "evenhanded" in its relations with Israel and the Arab states because of the complex weave of U.S. economic and strategic interests in the Middle East.

4. RHODESIAN POLICY. In the fiscal 1979 military aid authorization bill (S 3075) Congress permitted the president to drop economic sanctions against Rhodesia after Dec. 31, 1978, if he determined that the Salisbury government had demonstrated a willingness to negotiate in good faith at an all-parties peace conference that included guerrilla factions, and a new government had been installed after being chosen in free elections under international supervision.

This final provision was close to a proposal adopted in the Senate that was sponsored by two Republicans: Sens. Clifford P. Case, N.J., and Jacob K. Javits, N.Y. That proposal was approved July 26 by a 59-36 vote. But prior to that in the key vote that set the stage for approval, the Senate refused by a 39-57 vote (R 27-11; D 12-46; ND 2-38; SD 10-8) to table and thereby kill the Case-Javits plan.

Unlike most other important foreign policy issues, the Carter administration's position on the Rhodesia moves was never publicly made clear. Many members of Congress had strongly criticized the administration for what they felt was too favorable U.S. treatment toward the black guerrillas fighting the coalition of moderate blacks and the minority white government.

But Senate sources said Carter lobbyists passed the word that the Case-Javits plan was acceptable when it became clear that nothing better could be obtained. Moreover, these sources told reporters, it was evident to participants in the debate that had the Case-Javits plan not prevailed, some other proposal to lift sanctions completely stood a good chance of winning Senate approval.

The importance of the administration's willingness to go along with Case-Javits was seen when the House later approved an amendment to the same bill that would have dramatically changed U.S. policy toward Rhodesia in a manner much more favorable to the minority white government. Conferees acceptance of the Senate approach put Congress on record favoring a more middle-of-the-road policy toward Rhodesia.

5, 6. DEFENSE SPENDING. In the face of conflicting concerns about a Soviet military buildup in Eastern

Europe, on the one hand, and the ever expanding federal budget and its impact on inflation, on the other, the Senate decided to approve basically the amount recommended by President Carter for national defense in fiscal 1979.

In the first concurrent resolution on the budget (S Con Res 80), the Senate Budget Committee recommended a national defense spending level of $129.8 billion, which was only slightly higher than the $128.4 billion requested by the administration.

By nearly identical votes, the Senate rejected an amendment that would have increased the defense spending level and another that would have decreased it.

A $1.6 billion increase proposed by John G. Tower, R-Texas, was rejected April 26 by a vote of 21-74: R 17-17; D 4-57 (ND 0-42; SD 4-15).

On April 25 Thomas F. Eagleton, D-Mo., had recommended a $1.4 billion reduction in the defense level, but his proposal was rejected 21-70: R 4-31; D 17-39 (ND 17-20; SD 0-19).

7. AIRLINE DEREGULATION. During Senate consideration of legislation — actively promoted by the Carter administration — to increase competition in the commercial passenger airline industry, Edward M. Kennedy, D-Mass., offered an amendment to strengthen the bill.

In 1977, the Senate Commerce Committee had voted to weaken Carter's plan by requiring any airline company seeking to offer a new service to prove to the Civil Aeronautics Board (CAB) that the service was "consistent with the public convenience and necessity."

Under Kennedy's amendment, the CAB was ordered to presume a new service to be in the public interest unless an opponent of the new service could convince the board that it was not.

Supporters of the amendment argued that it would increase competition by giving a company's applications an important procedural advantage. But its opponents argued that the Kennedy amendment went too far in deregulating the industry and predicted it would harm the airline companies' financial stability and, ultimately, the level of service they offered the nation.

The Kennedy amendment prevailed on a vote of 69-23: R 28-6; D 41-17 (ND 30-9; SD 11-8), and it subsequently was incorporated in the enacted version of the bill.

8. WATERWAY USER FEES. A controversial measure to impose fees on the users of the nation's inland waterways for the first time had been before Congress for 38 years and once again was endangered by Senate inaction. The legislation had been considered throughout the 95th Congress, and in May Sens. Pete V. Domenici, R-N.M., and Adlai E. Stevenson III, D-Ill., proposed a compromise that had the administration's backing. Their proposal called for an authorization for construction of a new lock and dam on the Mississippi River at Alton, Ill., with a phased-in tax on barge fuel plus a user charge sufficient to recover 10 percent of the capital costs of any newly constructed waterway within the first 10 years of the waterway's operation. In the administration's opinion, Transportation Secretary Brock Adams informed the Senate, the scheme offered "the minimum acceptable basis from which to develop an adequate House-Senate conference bill." Anything less, and Carter would veto the bill, Adams said.

Finance Committee Chairman Russell B. Long, D-La., however, was not happy with the plan. He proposed a substitute bill delaying the tax's imposition — in order to ensure that construction of the Alton lock and dam would be under way before the tax was collected — and eliminating the provision that new waterway projects be required to recover a portion of their construction costs through a user charge.

In a direct challenge to Adams' and President Carter's credibility, the Senate rejected the Domenici-Stevenson version of the bill — which would have been much more expensive for the barge industry — and opted for Long's alternative. The vote May 3 rejecting the Domenici-Stevenson version was 43-47: R 16-19; D 27-28 (ND 22-15; SD 5-13).

9. D.C. VOTING RIGHTS. Supporters of the long struggle for voting rights in the District of Columbia achieved a milestone Aug. 22 when the Senate passed a constitutional amendment giving added voting rights and full representation in Congress to D.C. residents.

A coalition of reform groups led by Majority Leader Robert C. Byrd, D-W. Va., and Sen. Edward M. Kennedy, D-Mass., led the fight for the amendment (H J Res 554) which passed by a vote of 67-32. This was just one over the required two-thirds majority for constitutional amendments.

The House passed the amendment March 2 by a 289-127 but the significant battle came in the Senate. There was relatively little opposition to allowing the District additional voting rights in the House based on population. The District already had a non-voting delegate in that chamber.

But opponents of the amendment contended that the Senate was based on states and the District wasn't the same as a state and never would be.

The vote in the Senate was considered a symbolic milestone for both the Republican Party and black voters. Though the District's predominantly black population was expected to elect Democrats for the foreseeable future, the Republican leadership actively lobbied for the amendments as part of its effort to win the support of black voters.

The amendment must be ratified by 38 states within seven years before it becomes part of the Constitution.

10. EQUAL RIGHTS AMENDMENT. The Senate gave final approval to a resolution (H J Res 638) granting states 39 additional months to ratify the proposed Equal Rights Amendment to the Constitution.

Passage of the resolution Oct. 6 by a 60-36 vote capped a year-long lobbying effort by backers of the ERA and marked the first time Congress had extended the ratification period for a constitutional amendment since it began setting time limits in 1917.

The key vote, however, was not the passage. The crucial vote came two days earlier when the Senate rejected a proposal which, had it succeeded, would have forced the extension's supporters to pull the resolution off the floor and probably would have ended any hope of extending the deadline. That proposal, sponsored by Sen. Jake Garn, R-Utah, would have allowed states that already ratified ERA to rescind their actions during the extension period. Garn's rescission amendment was rejected 44-54 (R 24-13; D 20-41; ND 5-37; SD 15-4).

Supporters of the rescission argued that it would be unfair to give state legislatures that have rejected ERA additional time to ratify without at the same time giving those that had ratified the choice of reconsidering their votes. Opponents said rescission would be unconstitutional and that states would not take ratification seriously if they could rescind their decision later.

The extension resolution was approved by the House Aug. 15. It did not require the president's signature and took effect upon Senate approval.

11. HOSPITAL COST CONTROL. The Senate Oct. 12 handed President Carter a surprise victory on hospital cost containment, but the bill (HR 5285) that passed was far weaker than the president's 1977 request to cap all hospital revenue increases at 9 percent annually.

Opposed by the medical and hospital establishment and by organized labor, the bill had languished in three of four congressional health committees in 1977, as administration negotiators stiffly resisted compromise.

By fall 1978, most observers had written off the legislation as dead. One Senate committee favored a different, industry-backed bill and a House committee had gutted a bill that included significant compromises, reluctantly accepted by the administration. The compromises included a wage "pass-through" to protect blue-collar hospital workers, and a built-in delay for the revenue controls, intended to let hospitals themselves try to cut costs.

The wage provision brought labor on board but hospitals still complained that a "meat ax" revenue control — even on a standby basis — would destroy an industry with widely varying and unpredictable costs. Instead they endorsed a Senate committee proposal to revise Medicare and Medicaid reimbursement procedures by providing for fixed reimbursement rates, tailored to different hospital types.

Days before adjournment, administration allies forced a dramatic floor fight, compelling senators to choose between the narrower Medicare-Medicaid bill and an administration hybrid that combined the federal reimbursement reforms, standby revenue controls for all hospitals, and numerous exemptions. Opponents charged that the administration had shot its bill full of exemptions to buy votes, but backers argued that support for the bill would be a meaningful anti-inflation vote. Timing may also have brought some senators on board because few expected the House to act on the measure in the last crowded days of the session.

In a key vote the Senate by a 42-47 vote (R 25-6; D 17-41 (ND 4-35; SD 13-6) refused to table (kill) the hybrid administration substitute for the narrower Medicare-Medicaid proposal.

12. COURT-ORDERED BUSING. By only a two-vote margin, the Senate Aug. 23 rejected an amendment to restrict the authority of the courts to order busing of school children as a remedy in desegregation cases.

Leading busing opponent Joe Biden, D-Del., said the closeness of the vote signaled the "death knell" of the pro-busing position in the Senate. The amendment, to the Elementary and Secondary Education Act (ESEA) extension bill (S 1753), was rejected only after Majority Leader Robert C. Byrd, D-W.Va., urged his colleagues not to plunge the Senate into an extremely controversial issue near the end of the session.

The amendment, offered by Biden and William V. Roth Jr., R-Del., was tabled by a 49-47 vote: R 12-26; D 37-21 (ND 34-8; SD 3-13).

Incorporating the substance of S 1651, the first bill ever reported by a congressional committee that sought to restrict court busing authority, the amendment would have barred any court from ordering busing without first determining that a "discriminatory purpose in education was a principal motivating factor" for the violation the busing was designed to correct.

All previous congressional attempts to limit busing had restricted only the authority of the Department of Health, Education and Welfare to require busing.

13. EMERGENCY FARM AID. Stampeded by three months of angry and unrelenting pressure from a militant new farm group, the Senate March 21 passed a multi-part farm bill that one opponent called a "three-headed monster."

The bill (HR 6782) combined three strategies for raising farm income — paid land diversion, boosts in price supports for corn, wheat and cotton, and a controversial "flexible parity" plan that permitted a farmer to set his own price support level by deciding how much land to take out of production.

Farmers of the ad hoc American Agriculture Movement (AAM) had camped out on Capitol Hill since January, demanding relief from financial problems caused by record grain surpluses, high production costs, widespread drought and heavy borrowing.

Opponents warned that the unwieldy Senate package combined contradictory methods of hiking farm income and that even if the Agriculture Department could figure out how to administer it, the various components would cancel each other out. Land diversion is intended to raise market prices by shrinking surplus production, while price supports tend to encourage production while supplementing farm income.

There were also heated warnings from Senate Budget Committee Chairman Edmund S. Muskie, D-Maine, that the bill was far too expensive — both in terms of federal payments to farmers and the overall impact on inflation. No cost estimates for the total package had been prepared because no one had anticipated that the Senate would adopt all options.

As senators voted 67-26 (R 26-11; D 41-15; ND 23-14; SD 18-1) to pass the the multi-part bill, farmer-lobbyists watched from crowded galleries. Members later said privately that some of their colleagues were exasperated with the farmers and apparently expected the urban-dominated House, or conferees, to extract a workable farm program from the flawed bill.

14. SENATE TAX BILL. When the tax bill reached the Senate floor, the Senate Finance Committee had already changed it to be more generous to people earning less than $11,000 (as well as providing additional tax breaks for the generally wealthy people who claim capital gains). But liberals, led by Dale Bumpers, D-Ark., and Edward M. Kennedy, D-Mass., argued that the bill still provided insufficient help to people earning between $10,000 and $30,000.

Bumpers and Kennedy thus proposed pumping $4.5 billion more into the bill (the Finance Committee had already added $6.3 billion), earmarking the extra funds for people in those middle income ranges. An aggressive effort paid off, as the Bumpers-Kennedy amendment was approved, 52-43 on Oct. 6: R 13-23; D 39-20 (ND 32-9; SD 7-11).

That success was short-lived, however. Most of the extra tax cuts provided by the amendment were removed from the bill in conference committee in an effort to meet budgetary standards imposed by the Carter administration.

15. LABOR LAW REFORM. Organized labor's legislative high-water mark in 1978 came June 14, when it struggled to within two Senate votes of the 60 needed to end a conservative filibuster against legislation (HR 8410) revising federal labor law.

The 58-41 defeat of a cloture motion offered by Majority Leader Robert C. Byrd, D-W.Va., represented the fourth in a series of six attempts to cut off a five-week filibuster against the bill, which was labor's overriding legislative goal for the year.

The cloture motion picked up substantial support from Republicans, who opposed it by a 14-24 margin. But labor lobbyists could make scarcely a dent in opposition among southern Democrats, whose 3-15 vote against the motion was in sharp contrast to the near-unanimous 41-2 vote among northern Democrats.

After two more unsuccessful cloture tries, bill sponsors were finally forced to recommit the bill to the Human Resources Committee, in hopes of coming up with a new version that could overcome a renewed filibuster. But a final "bare-bones" version of the bill, stripped of most of the controversial provisions of HR 8410, died when it became clear that opponents were prepared to resist the bill in any form.

The target of one of the most intense grassroots lobbying campaigns in history, HR 8410 would have amended the 1935 National Labor Relations Act by increasing the penalties for labor law violations, speeding up the process of settling unfair labor practice cases, and strengthening union rights during organizing campaigns.

House Key Votes

1. WATER POLICY. Despite opposition from the Democratic leadership in both the House and Senate, President Carter successfully vetoed a bill (HR 12928) funding several dams and other water projects he opposed.

The confrontation was a rehash of a 1977 battle over a similar public works appropriations bill, but this time Carter carried through his veto threat. The House Oct. 5 refused to override the veto. The vote was 223-190, 53 votes short of the two-thirds needed for an override. Carter's characterization of the expenditures as wasteful won important support from Republicans, who split on the issue, 73-62. A majority of Democrats also voted against Carter, 150-128 (ND 92-99; SD 58-29).

Later, Carter signed a version of the bill modified to meet his objections (H J Res 1139). But congressional leaders made it clear that the compromise was for fiscal 1979 appropriations only. The same conflict promised to resurface in the 96th Congress.

The dispute was part of a continuing battle between Carter and Congress over national water policy. Carter wanted to base funding on strict economic and environmental criteria, while Congress preferred to consider politics and other so-called "pork barrel" factors.

At issue in the public works bill were six projects from Carter's 1977 "hit list" that had been deleted in fiscal 1978 funding but restored by Congress for fiscal 1979. The president complained that taxpayers would pay about $1.8 billion over the next several years to complete those six projects and 26 other new ones added by Congress. He also opposed provisions mandating the hiring of 2,300 new government employees by the water development agencies and deleting funds for the Water Resources Council.

2. NATIONAL ENERGY BILL. From the earliest stages of congressional action on President Carter's energy program, the strategy of House Speaker Thomas P. O'Neill Jr. had been to keep the five-part package intact. He wanted to give members only one vote on energy so they would be forced to swallow the bill whole and would be unable to pick off, and possibly to defeat, individual pieces.

By the end of the session, Carter's original bill had survived the House, had been gutted by the Senate and had been rewritten in conference. As a result, O'Neill's strategy appeared all the wiser. The most controversial section, on natural gas pricing (HR 5289), would be sheltered by the more popular provisions, such as one giving homeowners tax credits for insulation (HR 5263).

Opponents of the natural gas bill realized their best chance at defeating it was to split the package and force a separate vote on the gas pricing section.

The odd coalition of opponents included members who preferred tough price controls to protect consumers and those who wanted an immediate end to price controls, instead of the gradual decontrol the bill provided.

The crucial vote was on a parliamentary maneuver leading to adoption of the rule (H Res 1434), which called for a single vote on the five-part package. The House floor was jammed Oct. 13 for what all knew would be a close vote. When time ran out, the tally was 200-200. But last minute votes by several members and switches by others gave the administration and the Democratic leadership the 207-206 victory: R 8-127; D 199-79 (ND 136-55; SD 63-24). The rule itself was adopted by voice vote.

Two days later, after an all-night session, the House voted 231-168 for the package, sending the measure to the president.

3. EMERGENCY FARM AID. The stunning lobbying success of the militant American Agriculture Movement (AAM) came to a grinding halt April 12 when the House emphatically rejected the conference report on a "flexible parity" farm bill (HR 6782) that would have allowed a farmer to idle up to half his land in return for sharply boosted support payments.

The margin of defeat (150-268) surprised observers almost as much as the longevity of the flexible parity concept, which had survived House, Senate and conference scrutiny despite veto threats from the president and repudiation by farm economists. (Conferees had discarded more modest price supports and land diversions from a grab-bag Senate bill, retaining only the flexible parity program.)

By shrinking production, the program would push food prices to intolerable heights, while payments to farmers would deplete the U.S. Treasury, critics warned.

But AAM farmer-lobbyists insisted that the expensive program was all that stood between them and bankruptcy. Soaring production costs, price-depressing surpluses, drought losses and meager support from the Carter administration had pushed them to the wall, producers said. Hardest hit were younger grain producers, whose high land and equipment costs had pushed them deeply into debt.

Established farm groups had failed to wring adequate support from Congress in 1977, so AAM members had left their farms to press their needs in Washington, they said. But the four months of unrelenting pressure from the gloomy farmers built countervailing pressures that finally showed in the House vote on the conference agreement.

Urban members, more concerned with inflated food prices than farm economics, apparently heeded administration warnings that the scheme was highly inflationary. Republican spokesmen characterized the vote as "anti-inflation."

Probably the most important element in the defeat was the fact that the flexible parity scheme benefited one segment of agriculture at the expense of another. Livestock and dairy producers feared sharply higher feed grain prices, and let their representatives know it. With the farm community divided, rural members themselves divided their votes and reportedly did little to recruit urban support for the measure. With majorities of both Republicans and Democrats voting no, the House by a 150-268 vote (R 70-75; D 80-193; ND 26-160; SD 54-33) defeated the bill. Congress later passed a pared-down version of HR 6782 that gave the president authority to raise grain and cotton target prices.

4. PUBLIC FINANCING OF ELECTIONS. Twice in 1978 a coalition of Republicans and southern Democrats succeeded in blocking House floor consideration of a proposal to extend public financing to congressional elections.

The clearest vote on the issue came in July on an attempt to open the fiscal 1979 Federal Election Commission (FEC) authorization bill (HR 11983) to a public financing amendment. An earlier effort was scuttled in March when the House refused to consider a controversial campaign financing bill (HR 11315) that was to have served as a vehicle for a public financing amendment. The Democratic leadership promoted the bill, which included controversial limits on party and political action committee (PAC) spending.

The extent of the public financing proposal was limited — applying only to House general elections and providing funds to candidates on a matching basis without any direct subsidies. Participation by candidates would have been voluntary.

Newer House members along with Common Cause and the Democratic Study Group led the major thrust for public financing in July. Without a majority on the Rules Committee, they were forced to try a complex set of parliamentary maneuvers to even bring their proposal to a floor vote. They failed, as the House voted 213-196 on July 19 not to allow a public financing amendment to the $8.6 million FEC authorization bill. A large majority of Republicans (106-30) and southern Democrats (62-22) joined to block consideration of the amendment.

5. TURKISH ARMS EMBARGO. By a three-vote margin, the House gave President Carter one of several significant foreign policy victories by permitting the president to drop the U.S. arms embargo against Turkey.

The issue had been troublesome since Congress in 1974 approved a total ban on military aid and arms shipments to Turkey in reaction to that country's invasion of Greek-populated sections of Cyprus in which U.S.-supplied armaments, intended for the defense of Turkey, were employed in violation of U.S. foreign aid laws. The ban took effect in 1975 and was somewhat modified later after a tough fight in the House.

The Carter administration's decision to ask the 95th Congress to repeal the embargo was prompted by fears that Turkey, a U.S. ally, would reduce its commitment to NATO, thus threatening the alliance's southeastern line of defense.

In the Senate, Carter's request passed with less trouble —57-42. But in the House, the margin on the vote July 26 was only 208-205: R 78-64; D 130-141 (ND 64-123; SD 66-18).

Paving the way for Carter's victory were at least three factors: an intense, two-month lobbying campaign by the White House and the State and Defense Departments; a last-minute compromise proposal on which the vote came; and the willingness of two members — Butler Derrick, D-S.C., and Richard T. Schulze, R-Pa. — to switch their votes when they were desperately needed by the administration. But the key element in the victory for Carter was the Republican Party. A majority of the GOP backed the repeal, while a majority of Carter's own party members went against the president.

6. FOREIGN AID CUTS. The House, in a signifcant and surprising turnaround from 1977, refused to make deep cuts in foreign aid appropriations. The U.S. foreign aid program — which almost always is in some sort of trouble in Congress — was thought particularly vulnerable in 1978 to the budget-cutting fever that swept through the House in mid-year. However, an effective lobbying campaign by the Carter administration and a coalition of House members, plus some outside groups devoted to foreign aid, prevented major cuts in the aid funding bill.

The key action came on a proposal by Rep. Clarence E. Miller, R-Ohio, to cut the appropriations bill (HR 12931) by 8 percent across-the-board except for funds for Israel and Egypt. The House rejected this by a 15-vote margin, 184-199. In 1977, the House approved a Miller 5-percent cut, 214-168. On this issue, there was a turnaround of 44 members who supported Miller in 1977 and opposed him in 1978: 25 Republicans and 19 Democrats. On the 1978 vote the breakdown was R 88-43; D 96-156 (ND 42-133; SD 54-23).

The House did accept a smaller cut in the aid funding: 2 percent except for allocations for Israel, Egypt, Jordan and Syria. However, conferees on the bill deleted these cuts.

7. BANK CURBS. Another dramatic House turnaround on foreign aid *(see previous item)* came on efforts to tell international lending institutions, such as the World Bank, how they could use U.S. contributions. In 1977 an amendment by Rep. C. W. Bill Young, R-Fla., to prohibit funds in the appropriations bill from being used by the banks in Uganda, Cambodia, Laos or Vietnam was approved overwhelmingly, 295-115. In 1978, the same Young amendment to the appropriations bill (HR 12931) was rejected 198-203: R 101-35; D 97-168 (ND 52-134; SD 45-34).

Eighty-eight members switched their position from support of Young in 1977 to opposition in 1978. Those switches, plus the addition of some members who didn't vote in 1978, were enough to give the administration a major victory. Of the total, 63 members were Democrats and 25 Republicans.

Opponents of the Young amendment argued that the restriction would play havoc with international lending programs and probably would destroy the banks. They argued that the charters of the multinational lending institutions did not permit the banks to accept funds with conditions. Consequently, the banks would have to refuse American funding, probably crippling their operations.

The Carter administration strongly opposed the Young amendment as it had in 1977.

8. B-1 BOMBER. Prodded by lobbying of rare intensity by the Carter administration, the House Feb. 22 finally acceded to the president's decision to cancel the controversial B-1 bomber project.

Carter had announced in June 1977 that he was canceling the $23 billion program to produce 244 planes, and Congress subsequently canceled all new funding for the program. But on Dec. 6 of that year the House voted 166-191 against a Carter request to also rescind $462 million that had been previously appropriated to build the first two production versions of the bomber.

House opponents of the rescission argued that production of the two planes would preserve for a time the option of reversing Carter's decision, should the Soviet military buildup continue.

But the White House was adamantly opposed to going forward with the program, and the administration gradually won more and more Democrats to the president's side of the argument. On Feb. 22 the rescission was approved on a 234-182 vote: R 30-106; D 204-76 (ND 155-38; SD 49-38).

9. AIRCRAFT CARRIER VETO. In a major victory for the administration on defense policy, the House Sept. 7 by a surprisingly wide margin rejected an attempt to override President Carter's Aug. 17 veto of the fiscal 1979 weapons procurement bill (HR 10929) that contained a $2 billion authorization for another nuclear aircraft carrier for the Navy. Carter insisted on setting his own defense priorities and argued that another giant, 1,000-foot-long carrier was wasteful and unnecessary. And he maintained the money for the ship would have diverted funds from important defense programs that he preferred.

Only 31 days earlier, on Aug. 7, the House had voted 156-218 against an amendment that would have deleted the appropriation for the carrier from the Pentagon's annual funding bill. But in September, carrier supporters could not even muster a majority of the House in favor of overridding the veto (a two-thirds vote would have been needed to override). The vote was 191-206: R 107-23; D 84-183 (ND 34-150; SD 50-33).

Subsequently, Congress, in a revised arms procurement measure for fiscal 1979, agreed to drop the carrier authorization.

10. CONSUMER PROTECTION AGENCY. Legislation to establish an agency within the federal government to represent the interests of the consumer had been actively sought by consumer groups since 1961, but the bill had died at the end of four successive Congresses. The Senate had approved a bill establishing such an agency in 1970. The House approved similar legislation in 1971 and 1974. Both houses approved a bill in 1975, but the bill was never sent to the White House because President Ford threatened to veto it.

In the 95th Congress, however, President Carter made establishment of a consumer agency his top consumer priority. When the bill (HR 6805) became stalled in the House in 1977, consumer groups showered potential swing votes with nickels — five cents representing what supporters of the idea said would be the cost per capita of the proposed agency. A compromise proposal, establishing a scaled-down Office of Consumer Representation, was unveiled in October 1977. But it barely squeaked through the House Rules Committee as consumer activists found their intense lobbying efforts surpassed by a coalition of business interests.

On Nov. 1, 1977, House Speaker Thomas P. O'Neill Jr., D-Mass., pulled the bill from the House calendar when his vote count indicated the legislation probably would lose.

Early in 1978, Carter reiterated his support for the bill and it was once again scheduled for House floor action.

On Feb. 8 the House finally voted on the measure, but it lost on a 189-227 vote: R 17-126; D 172-101 (ND 147-40; SD 25-61), ending consumers' hopes of enacting the bill in the 95th Congress. "I have been around here for 25 years," O'Neill remarked. "I have never seen such extensive lobbying."

11. LOBBY DISCLOSURE. Critics of existing lobby disclosure laws won a battle in 1978 but eventually lost the war. Legislation to impose strict new registration requirements on groups that lobby Congress was approved by the House in April by a 259-140 vote (R 75-67; D 184-73; ND 143-39; SD 41-34). But that was as far as supporters could go. When the bill (HR 8494) got to the Senate, the Governmental Affairs Committee was not able to resolve differences between different versions.

The bill passed by the House was far stronger than the version sent to the floor by the Judiciary Committee. The final bill required disclosure of grassroots lobbying activities such as computerized mass mailings and disclosure of the names of organizations contributing $3,000 or more to a lobby group.

The major debates on the issue during the 95th Congress focused on whether to require disclosure of grassroots lobbying efforts such as organized letter-writing campaigns, and disclosure of the names of major organizations contributing to registered lobby groups.

12. FISCAL POLICY. In an election year dominated by the issue of government spending, Republicans in the House mounted a united — and nearly successful — assault on the fiscal policy proposals of the president and the Democratic Congress.

The Republican critique hit not only at the specific spending and tax proposals of the administration and the Democratic majority, but it was directed also at the approach to budget-writing followed by the House Budget Committee.

Specifically, GOP leaders in the House complained that the majority party had failed to use the four-year-old congressional budget process as originally intended. They said that the Democrats, rather than making overall fiscal policy decisions first and only then setting specific spending and tax policies to fit the macroeconomic pie, merely used the budget process to add up a series of smaller decisions made without reference to the big picture.

The result, they said, was that the Democrats had failed to control the growth of federal spending. That, in turn, according to the Republican view, kept the federal deficit at unacceptably high levels and prevented the Democrats from proposing a tax cut as large as the GOP would like.

As an alternative, House Republicans rallied behind a proposal by Marjorie S. Holt, R-Md., to set overall spending goals that would allow all federal programs to grow only enough to keep pace with inflation — about 8 percent, compared to the 11 percent growth rate provided by the committee recommendation. Republicans said the Holt proposal, offered as a substitute to the House Budget Committee's proposed first fiscal 1979 budget resolution (H Con Res 559), would be the first step in a Republican plan to balance the federal budget in five years.

Democrats scoffed at the proposal, questioning whether it was economically realistic and suggesting that it failed to make the difficult decisions about where to limit federal spending.

The key test of the Republican approach came May 3, when the Holt amendment, supported by all House Republicans but one and by 58 Democratic defectors, fell only six votes short of winning, 197-203: R 139-1; D 58-202 (ND 24-155; SD 34-47).

13. SPENDING CUTS. One week after California voters approved their tax-cutting Proposition 13, the House adopted the first of a series of across-the-board cuts in federal spending.

The annually unsuccessful efforts of Clarence E. Miller, R-Ohio, to propose across-the-board cuts in controllable spending in appropriations bills were finally rewarded June 13, when the House adopted his amendment to reduce controllable spending in the fiscal 1979 Labor-Health, Education and Welfare (HEW) bill (HR 12929) by a total of 2 percent. The amendment limited reductions in individual programs to no more than 5 percent.

The amendment, which would have cut spending in the $56.6 billion bill by an estimated $380 million, was adopted on a 220-181 vote: R 122-18; D 98-163 (ND 47-133; SD 51-30).

Inspired by a report of the HEW Inspector General that up to $7 billion a year was lost by the department to waste, fraud and abuse, the House also approved a Robert H. Michel, R-Ill., amendment to cut HEW spending by $1 billion, with the reductions to come out of the programs identified as having serious losses.

But while it embraced the overall cuts, the House solidly rejected requests from the Carter administration to make specific reductions in Appropriations Committee-approved totals for health and education programs.

The Miller amendment was quietly dropped in conference with the Senate, but the $1 billion waste, fraud and abuse cut was enacted.

Across-the-board cut amendments were introduced on several other appropriations bills, but most of them did not survive in the final versions.

14. TUITION TAX CREDITS. The chances for enactment of separate legislation providing federal tax breaks for education expenses ended Oct. 12, when the House refused to accept a tuition tax credit bill (HR 12050) that included credits for college, but not private elementary and secondary school, tuition.

The surprise adoption of a Bill Gradison, R-Ohio, motion to recommit the conference report on HR 12050 with instructions to restore the House-passed elementary and secondary credits effectively killed the bill, since Senate opposition to credits below the college level was insurmountable. The motion was agreed to 207-185: R 100-23; D 107-152 (ND 91-86; SD 16-66).

The key factor in the approval of the Gradison motion, and the resulting death of the bill, was the presence of a large block of House members who were more interested in parochial school tuition credits than in the college aid. Feeling that they would have a better chance of overcoming the serious constitutional obstacles to the parochial credits if they were coupled with the college credits, supporters decided that they would be better off waiting until 1979, when they could try again to overcome Senate opposition to credits at all levels.

15. INFLATION TARGET. Spurred by growing congressional concern over inflation, the House March 9 came within a few votes of adding a specific anti-inflation target to the Humphrey-Hawkins full employment bill (HR 50).

By a 198-223 vote the House rejected an amendment sponsored by James M. Jeffords, R-Vt., to set a new national goal calling for a reduction in the rate of inflation to 3 percent a year by 1983, in addition to the bill's original goal of a reduction in the unemployment rate to 4 percent by 1983.

House Democratic leaders had to offer their own broad anti-inflation language, without the specific 3 percent target, in order to defuse support for the Jeffords amendment, which had picked up substantial Democratic backing during the days preceding the vote.

Republicans supported the Jeffords amendment overwhelmingly, 142-2, while Democrats voted 56-221 (ND 26-168; SD 30-53) against.

Despite its House victory, however, the coalition of labor and civil rights groups supporting HR 50 eventually had to accept the anti-inflation goal in order to forestall a threatened Senate filibuster in the last days of the 95th Congress.

16. HOUSE TAX BILL. Congressional consideration of tax legislation in 1978 marked a sharp departure from that of recent years.

In January, President Carter proposed a fairly traditional tax cut — one which offered the relatively largest benefits to lower income people, while tightening up on tax "loopholes" which benefited the well-to-do.

But Carter and liberal Democrats in Congress were caught off-guard when a coalition of Republicans and conservative Democrats seized the initiative and pushed through the House Ways and Means Committee a bill that took a very different approach. It directed relatively larger benefits to middle and upper income individuals, and — most controversially — it included a substantial reduction in the tax on capital gains.

The liberals, disunited and lacking direction from the president, were slow to respond to the conservative movement on taxes. But at almost the last moment they did come up with an alternative tax proposal. Sponsored by Reps. James C. Corman, D-Calif., and Joseph L. Fisher, D-Va., and written in consultation with the administration, the alternative reduced the proposed tax cuts for people earning more than $50,000 and provided larger tax cuts to people earning less than that amount. It also called for stricter treatment of capital gains than the committee bill did.

The conservative coalition saw the Corman-Fisher proposal as the key test of their tax philosophy. A vote for the alternative, they warned, would amount to upholding the traditional belief that tax bills should "redistribute income," while a vote for the committee bill would support the philosophy that tax cuts should be uniform for all income groups.

Despite the strong support of the House's Democratic leadership, the Corman-Fisher proposal was defeated in a key vote Aug. 10, 193-225: R 8-134; D 185-91 (ND 164-27; SD 21-64).

	1	2	3	4	5	6	7	8
ALABAMA								
Allen, M.[1]	N	N			?		Y	N
Sparkman	N	Y	N	N	N	N	N	N
ALASKA								
Gravel	N	Y	N	N	N	N	Y	N
Stevens	N	N	N	Y	N	N	N	N
ARIZONA								
DeConcini	N	Y	Y	N	N	N	Y	N
Goldwater	Y	N	N	Y	N	N	?	Y
ARKANSAS								
Bumpers	N	Y	N	N	N	N	Y	N
Hodges	N	Y	N	N	N	N	Y	N
CALIFORNIA								
Cranston	N	Y	Y	N	Y	N	Y	Y
Hayakawa	Y	Y	N	Y	N	Y	Y	Y
COLORADO								
Hart	N	Y	Y	N	N	N	Y	?
Haskell	Y	Y	Y	N	?	N	?	?
CONNECTICUT								
Ribicoff	N	Y	N	N	N	N	Y	Y
Weicker	Y	Y	Y	Y	Y	N	Y	Y
DELAWARE								
Biden	Y	Y	Y	N	?	N	Y	Y
Roth	Y	N	Y	N	N	Y	Y	N
FLORIDA								
Chiles	N	Y	Y	N	N	N	Y	Y
Stone	N	Y	Y	N	N	N	Y	Y
GEORGIA								
Nunn	N	Y	Y	Y	N	N	Y	Y
Talmadge	N	Y	Y	Y	N	N	N	Y
HAWAII								
Inouye	N	Y	N	N	?	N	Y	?
Matsunaga	N	Y	Y	N	N	N	Y	N
IDAHO								
Church	N	Y	Y	N	Y	N	Y	?
McClure	N	N	N	Y	N	Y	Y	Y
ILLINOIS								
Stevenson	N	Y	N	N	Y	N	N	Y
Percy	N	Y	N	N	N	?	Y	Y
INDIANA								
Bayh	Y	Y	Y	N	?	N	Y	Y
Lugar	Y	N	N	Y	N	Y	Y	Y
IOWA								
Clark	N	Y	Y	N	Y	N	Y	Y
Culver	N	Y	N	N	Y	N	Y	Y
KANSAS								
Dole	Y	N	Y	Y	N	Y	Y	N
Pearson	N	Y	N	N	?	?	Y	?
KENTUCKY								
Ford	N	N	Y	N	N	Y	Y	N
Huddleston	N	Y	?	N	N	N	Y	N
LOUISIANA								
Johnston	Y	N	N	Y	N	Y	Y	N
Long	Y	Y	N	Y	N	N	N	N
MAINE								
Hathaway	N	Y	Y	N	N	N	Y	Y
Muskie	N	Y	N	N	N	N	Y	Y
MARYLAND								
Sarbanes	Y	Y	Y	N	Y	N	Y	Y
Mathias	N	Y	N	N	Y	N	Y	Y
MASSACHUSETTS								
Kennedy	Y	Y	Y	N	Y	N	Y	Y
Brooke	?	Y	Y	N	N	N	Y	Y
MICHIGAN								
Riegle	Y	Y	Y	?	Y	N	Y	Y
Griffin	N	N	N	Y	N	N	N	?
MINNESOTA								
Anderson	Y	Y	Y	-	†	N	Y	N
Humphrey, M.	Y	Y	N	N	Y	N	Y	N
MISSISSIPPI								
Eastland	N	N	N	Y	N	N	N	N
Stennis	N	N	N	Y	N	N	N	N
MISSOURI								
Eagleton	N	Y	N	N	Y	N	Y	N
Danforth	N	Y	N	Y	N	N	N	N
MONTANA								
Melcher	N	N	Y	N	Y	N	N	Y
Hatfield, P.	N	Y	N	N	?	N	N	N
NEBRASKA								
Zorinsky	N	N	Y	N	N	N	N	Y
Curtis	Y	N	N	Y	N	Y	Y	Y
NEVADA								
Cannon	N	Y	N	Y	N	N	Y	?
Laxalt	Y	N	?	Y	N	Y	Y	N
NEW HAMPSHIRE								
Durkin	N	Y	Y	N	N	N	Y	N
McIntyre	N	Y	Y	N	N	N	?	†
NEW JERSEY								
Williams	N	Y	Y	N	Y	N	Y	N
Case	N	Y	Y	N	N	N	†	N
NEW MEXICO								
Domenici	N	N	Y	N	N	N	Y	Y
Schmitt	Y	N	N	Y	N	Y	N	Y
NEW YORK								
Moynihan	N	Y	Y	N	N	N	Y	N
Javits	N	Y	Y	N	N	N	Y	Y
NORTH CAROLINA								
Morgan	N	Y	N	Y	N	N	Y	?
Helms	?	N	N	Y	N	Y	Y	?
NORTH DAKOTA								
Burdick	N	N	Y	N	N	N	N	N
Young	N	N	N	Y	N	N	N	N
OHIO								
Glenn	N	Y	N	N	N	N	Y	Y
Metzenbaum	Y	Y	Y	N	Y	N	Y	Y
OKLAHOMA								
Bartlett	Y	N	N	Y	N	Y	Y	N
Bellmon	Y	Y	N	Y	N	N	Y	Y
OREGON								
Hatfield, M.	N	Y	Y	N	Y	N	†	N
Packwood	Y	Y	Y	Y	N	N	†	N
PENNSYLVANIA								
Heinz	N	Y	Y	Y	Y	N	Y	N
Schweiker	Y	N	Y	Y	N	Y	Y	N
RHODE ISLAND								
Pell	N	Y	Y	N	Y	N	Y	Y
Chafee	N	Y	N	N	N	N	Y	Y
SOUTH CAROLINA								
Hollings	Y	Y	N	Y	N	N	Y	N
Thurmond	Y	N	N	Y	N	Y	Y	N
SOUTH DAKOTA								
Abourezk	Y	Y	N	?	Y	?	?	Y
McGovern	Y	Y	N	N	Y	N	?	N
TENNESSEE								
Sasser	N	Y	Y	N	N	N	Y	N
Baker	Y	Y	N	Y	?	?	Y	N
TEXAS								
Bentsen	Y	Y	N	Y	N	N	N	N
Tower	Y	N	N	Y	N	Y	Y	N
UTAH								
Garn	Y	N	N	Y	?	?	Y	N
Hatch	Y	N	N	Y	N	Y	Y	N
VERMONT								
Leahy	N	Y	N	N	N	N	Y	Y
Stafford	N	Y	N	N	N	N	Y	Y
VIRGINIA								
*Byrd, H.	Y	N	N	Y	N	Y	N	Y
Scott	Y	N	N	Y	N	Y	N	N
WASHINGTON								
Jackson	N	Y	Y	N	N	N	N	N
Magnuson	N	Y	N	N	N	N	N	N
WEST VIRGINIA								
Byrd, R.	N	Y	N	N	N	N	N	N
Randolph	N	N	N	Y	N	N	N	Y
WISCONSIN								
Nelson	Y	Y	Y	N	N	N	Y	Y
Proxmire	Y	Y	Y	N	Y	N	Y	Y
WYOMING								
Hansen	Y	N	N	Y	N	Y	Y	N
Wallop	Y	N	N	Y	N	Y	Y	Y

Democrats ***Republicans***

1. Sen. Maryon P. Allen (D Ala.) sworn in June 12, 1978, succeeding her husband James B. Allen (D) who died June 1, 1978.

**Byrd elected as independent.*

KEY

- Y Voted for (yea).
- ✓ Paired for.
- † Announced for.
- N Voted against (nay).
- X Paired against.
- \- Announced against.
- P Voted "present."
- ● Voted "present" to avoid possible conflict of interest.
- ? Did not vote or otherwise make a position known.

1. **HR 5289. Natural Gas Pricing.** Metzenbaum, D-Ohio, motion to recommit the conference report to the conference committee with instructions to delete all pricing provisions except those related to Alaska gas and to grant certain emergency powers to the president and the Federal Energy Regulatory Commission. Rejected 39-59: R 21-15; D 18-44 (ND 13-40; SD 5-14), Sept. 19, 1978. A "nay" was a vote supporting the president's position.

2. **Exec N, 95th Congress, First Session, Panama Canal Treaties.** Adoption of the resolution of ratification to the neutrality treaty guaranteeing that the Panama Canal will be permanently neutral and remain secure and open to vessels of all nations. Adopted 68-32: R 16-22; D 52-10 (ND 39-4; SD 13-6), March 16, 1978. A "yea" was a vote supporting the president's position.

3. **S Con Res 86. Mideast Fighter Plane Sales.** Adoption of the resolution to disapprove the sale of $4.5 billion worth of jet fighter planes to Israel, Saudi Arabia and Egypt. Rejected 44-54: R 11-26; D 33-28 (ND 26-17; SD 7-11), May 15, 1978. A "nay" was a vote supporting the president's position.

4. **S 3075. Foreign Military Aid.** Baker, R-Tenn., motion to table (kill) the Case, R-N.J., amendment providing that U.S. sanctions against Rhodesia could not be lifted until the president determined that the Rhodesian government of Ian Smith had committed itself to a conference of all the groups contending for power in the country and free elections for a new government, supervised by international observers, were held. Tabling motion rejected 39-57: R 27-11; D 12-46 (ND 2-38; SD 10-8), July 26, 1978.

5. **S Con Res 80. Fiscal 1979 Budget Targets.** Eagleton, D-Mo., amendment to reduce national defense spending by $1.4 billion in budget authority and $900 million in outlays. Rejected 21-70: R 4-31; D 17-39 (ND 17-20; SD 0-19), April 25, 1978.

6. **S Con Res 80. Fiscal 1979 Budget Targets.** Tower, R-Texas, amendment to increase national defense spending by $1.6 billion in budget authority and $1.2 billion in outlays. Rejected 21-74: R 17-17; D 4-57 (ND 0-42; SD 4-15), April 26, 1978.

7. **S 2493. Airline Deregulation.** Kennedy, D-Mass., amendment to direct the Civil Aeronautics Board to authorize a proposed air transportation service unless it determined that the service was not consistent with the public convenience and necessity. Adopted 69-23: R 28-6; D 41-17 (ND 30-9; SD 11-8), April 19, 1978. A "yea" was a vote supporting the president's position.

8. **HR 8309. Waterway User Fees/Water Projects.** Domenici, R-N.M., amendment to phase in over 10 years a tax on inland waterway barge fuel of 12 cents per gallon, beginning with a 4 cent tax per gallon on Oct. 1, 1977; to require the secretary of transportation to recommend to Congress by Jan. 15, 1981, various ways to pay for the nation's future inland waterway needs, and to require that the Army Corps of Engineers recover, through user charges, 10 percent of the capital costs of any newly authorized water project within the first 10 years of the project's operation. Rejected 43-47: R 16-19; D 27-28 (ND 22-15; SD 5-13), May 3, 1978. A "yea" was a vote supporting the president's position.

(Senate votes continued on p. 16-C)

1. HR 12928. Public Works — Energy Appropriations, Fiscal 1979. Passage, over the president's Oct. 5 veto, of the bill to appropriate $10,160,483,000 for energy and water development programs of the Corps of Engineers and the Interior and Energy Departments. Rejected 223-190: R 73-62; D 150-128 (ND 92-99; SD 58-29), Oct. 5, 1978. A two-thirds majority vote (276 in this case) is required to override a veto. The president had requested $11,039,449,000. A "nay" was a vote supporting the president's position.

2. H Res 1434. National Energy Act. Bolling, D-Mo., motion to order the previous question (thus ending debate on adoption of the resolution to waive all points of order so that the House could consider en bloc the conference reports on the five pieces of the National Energy Act—(HR 5263, HR 5037, HR 5289, HR 5146, HR 4018). (The vote prevented a separate vote on the natural gas pricing section of the bill, which had been sought by its opponents.) Motion agreed to 207-206: R 8-127; D 199-79 (ND 136-55; SD 63-24), Oct. 13, 1978. A "yea" was a vote supporting the president's position.

3. HR 6782. Emergency Farm Bill. Adoption of the conference report on the bill to provide a one-year flexible parity program with graduated land diversion and target price levels for wheat, corn and cotton, and to raise loan rates for these commodities beginning Oct. 1, 1979 (with retroactive payments for 1978 crops). Rejected 150-268: R 70-75; D 80-193 (ND 26-160; SD 54-33), April 12, 1978. A "nay" was a vote supporting the president's position.

4. HR 11983. Federal Election Commission-Public Financing. Sisk, D-Calif., motion to order the previous question (thus ending debate) on the adoption of the rule (H Res 1172) providing for House floor consideration of the fiscal 1979 authorization bill for the Federal Election Commission. (Opponents of the rule sought to defeat the previous question in order to permit drafting an alternative rule that would allow a House vote on public financing of House general elections.) Motion agreed to 213-196: R 106-30; D 107-166 (ND 45-144; SD 62-22), July 19, 1978. The rule subsequently was adopted by voice vote.

5. HR 12514. Foreign Military Aid. Wright, D-Texas, amendment, to the Fascell, D-Fla., amendment, to lift the U.S. arms embargo against Turkey when the president certified to Congress that the action was in the national interest of the United States and NATO and that Turkey was acting in good faith to achieve a settlement of the Cyprus problem. Adopted 208-205: R 78-64; D 130-141 (ND 64-123; SD 66-18), Aug. 1, 1978. A "yea" was a vote supporting the president's position. (The Fascell amendment, as amended, was adopted subsequently by voice vote.)

6. HR 12931. Foreign Aid Appropriations, Fiscal 1979. Miller, R-Ohio, amendment, to the Young, R-Fla., amendment to reduce all appropriations in the bill by 8 percent except funds for Israel and Egypt. Rejected 184-199: R 88-43; D 96-156 (ND 42-133; SD 54-23), Aug. 14, 1978. A "nay" was a vote supporting the president's position.

7. HR 12931. Foreign Aid Appropriations, Fiscal 1979. Young, R-Fla., amendment to prohibit indirect U.S. aid to Uganda, Cambodia, Laos and Vietnam. Rejected 198-203: R 101-35; D 97-168 (ND 52-134; SD 45-34), Aug. 3, 1978. A "nay" was a vote supporting the president's position.

8. HR 9375. Fiscal 1978 Supplemental Appropriations. Mahon, D-Texas, motion that the House recede and concur in the Senate amendment, to the bill, rescinding $462 million appropriated in fiscal 1977 for the Defense Department for production of three B-1 bombers. Motion agreed to 234-182: R 30-106; D 204-76 (ND 155-38; SD 49-38), Feb. 22, 1978. A "yea" was a vote supporting the president's position.

KEY

- Y Voted for (yea).
- ✓ Paired for.
- † Announced for.
- N Voted against (nay).
- X Paired against.
- \- Announced against.
- P Voted "present."
- ● Voted "present" to avoid possible conflict of interest.
- ? Did not vote or otherwise make a position known.

	1	2	3	4	5	6	7	8
ALABAMA								
1 Edwards	Y	N	Y	Y	Y	Y	Y	Y
2 Dickinson	Y	?	Y	Y	Y	Y	Y	N
3 Nichols	Y	Y	Y	Y	Y	Y	Y	N
4 Bevill	Y	Y	Y	Y	Y	Y	Y	Y
5 Flippo	Y	Y	Y	Y	Y	Y	Y	Y
6 Buchanan	Y	Y	N	Y	N	N	Y	N
7 Flowers	N	Y	Y	?	N	?	?	Y
ALASKA								
AL Young	Y	Y	Y	Y	N	?	?	N
ARIZONA								
1 Rhodes	Y	N	Y	Y	Y	N	N	N
2 Udall	Y	Y	✓	N	Y	?	N	Y
3 Stump	Y	Y	N	Y	Y	Y	Y	N
4 Rudd	Y	X	Y	Y	Y	Y	Y	N
ARKANSAS								
1 Alexander	Y	Y	Y	Y	Y	N	Y	N
2 Tucker	N	Y	Y	Y	Y	N	N	Y
3 Hammerschmidt	Y	N	Y	Y	Y	Y	Y	N
4 Thornton	Y	Y	Y	Y	Y	Y	N	N
CALIFORNIA								
1 Johnson	Y	Y	Y	N	N	N	N	N
2 Clausen	Y	N	Y	Y	N	Y	Y	N
3 Moss	Y	N	N	N	Y	?	N	Y
4 Leggett	Y	Y	N	Y	Y	N	N	N
5 Burton, J.	N	N	?	N	N	N	N	Y
6 Burton, P.	N	N	N	N	N	N	N	Y
7 Miller	N	N	N	N	N	X	N	Y
8 Dellums	N	N	N	N	N	N	N	Y
9 Stark	N	N	N	N	N	N	N	Y
10 Edwards	N	Y	N	N	N	N	N	Y
11 Ryan	Y	Y	N	N	Y	N	N	Y
12 McCloskey	N	N	Y	N	Y	N	N	Y
13 Mineta	Y	Y	N	N	N	N	N	Y
14 McFall	Y	Y	N	Y	Y	N	N	N
15 Sisk	Y	Y	N	Y	Y	?	Y	N
16 Panetta	N	Y	N	N	N	N	Y	Y
17 Krebs	Y	Y	N	N	N	N	N	Y
18 Ketchum[1]								N
19 Lagomarsino	Y	N	N	Y	Y	Y	Y	N
20 Goldwater	Y	N	N	Y	Y	Y	Y	N
21 Corman	Y	Y	N	N	Y	N	N	Y
22 Moorhead	N	N	N	Y	N	Y	Y	N
23 Beilenson	N	Y	N	N	N	N	N	Y
24 Waxman	N	N	N	N	N	N	N	Y
25 Roybal	N	Y	N	N	N	N	N	Y
26 Rousselot	Y	N	N	Y	N	Y	Y	N
27 Dornan	N	N	Y	Y	N	N	Y	N
28 Burke	?	✓	?	N	N	N	N	N
29 Hawkins	Y	Y	N	Y	Y	X	N	?
30 Danielson	Y	Y	N	N	Y	N	N	N
31 Wilson, C.H.	N	Y	N	Y	Y	Y	Y	N
32 Anderson	Y	Y	N	N	N	Y	Y	N
33 Clawson	Y	N	?	?	N	?	Y	?
34 Hannaford	N	Y	N	N	N	Y	N	N
35 Lloyd	Y	Y	●	N	Y	N	Y	N
36 Brown	N	Y	N	N	Y	N	N	N
37 Pettis	?	?	Y	Y	Y	N	N	N
38 Patterson	N	Y	N	N	N	?	N	N
39 Wiggins	?	N	N	Y	Y	N	Y	N
40 Badham	Y	✓	N	Y	Y	Y	Y	X
41 Wilson, B.	Y	N	Y	Y	Y	Y	Y	N
42 Van Deerlin	Y	Y	X	N	Y	N	N	Y
43 Burgener	Y	N	Y	Y	Y	Y	Y	N
COLORADO								
1 Schroeder	N	N	N	N	N	N	N	Y
2 Wirth	Y	Y	N	N	Y	N	N	Y
3 Evans	Y	Y	Y	N	Y	?	N	Y
4 Johnson	Y	N	Y	N	N	Y	Y	Y
5 Armstrong	Y	N	Y	Y	N	Y	Y	N
CONNECTICUT								
1 Cotter	Y	Y	N	Y	N	Y	N	Y
2 Dodd	Y	Y	N	N	N	N	N	Y
3 Giaimo	Y	Y	N	N	N	N	N	Y
4 McKinney	Y	N	N	N	N	N	N	Y
5 Sarasin	✓	?	N	Y	?	?	N	Y
6 Moffett	N	N	N	N	N	N	N	Y
DELAWARE								
AL Evans	Y	Y	N	N	N	N	Y	N
FLORIDA								
1 Sikes	Y	Y	Y	Y	Y	✓	Y	N
2 Fuqua	Y	Y	Y	Y	N	Y	Y	N
3 Bennett	N	Y	N	Y	Y	Y	Y	N
4 Chappell	Y	N	N	Y	Y	Y	Y	N
5 Kelly	Y	N	N	✓	N	Y	Y	N
6 Young	Y	N	N	Y	Y	Y	Y	N
7 Gibbons	N	Y	N	?	Y	N	Y	Y
8 Ireland	Y	Y	N	N	N	Y	Y	Y
9 Frey	N	?	Y	?	N	Y	?	N
10 Bafalis	Y	N	N	Y	Y	Y	Y	N
11 Rogers	N	Y	N	N	Y	N	Y	Y
12 Burke	Y	N	N	Y	N	Y	Y	?
13 Lehman	N	Y	N	N	Y	N	N	Y
14 Pepper	N	Y	N	Y	Y	N	N	Y
15 Fascell	Y	Y	N	N	N	N	N	Y
GEORGIA								
1 Ginn	Y	Y	Y	Y	Y	Y	Y	Y
2 Mathis	Y	Y	Y	Y	?	Y	?	Y
3 Brinkley	Y	Y	Y	N	Y	Y	Y	Y
4 Levitas	N	Y	N	N	N	?	Y	Y
5 Fowler	N	Y	N	N	N	Y	N	Y
6 Flynt	Y	Y	Y	?	Y	Y	Y	N
7 McDonald	?	N	N	Y	Y	✓	Y	N
8 Evans	Y	Y	Y	Y	Y	N	Y	Y
9 Jenkins	Y	Y	Y	Y	?	Y	?	Y
10 Barnard	Y	Y	Y	Y	N	Y	?	Y
HAWAII								
1 Heftel	Y	Y	N	-	Y	N	N	Y
2 Akaka	Y	Y	N	N	Y	N	N	N
IDAHO								
1 Symms	Y	N	Y	Y	Y	?	Y	N
2 Hansen, G.	Y	N	Y	Y	N	Y	Y	?
ILLINOIS								
1 Metcalfe[2]	N		N	N	N	?	N	✓
2 Murphy	Y	Y	N	Y	N	Y	N	Y
3 Russo	N	Y	N	N	N	?	Y	Y
4 Derwinski	N	N	N	Y	N	N	N	N
5 Fary	Y	Y	N	Y	N	N	N	Y
6 Hyde	N	N	N	Y	Y	N	N	N
7 Collins	Y	N	N	Y	?	N	X	✓
8 Rostenkowski	Y	Y	N	X	Y	N	N	Y
9 Yates	Y	N	N	N	N	N	N	Y
10 Mikva	N	N	N	N	N	N	N	Y
11 Annunzio	Y	Y	N	Y	N	N	N	Y
12 Crane	?	X	?	?	N	Y	Y	N
13 McClory	Y	N	N	Y	Y	N	N	N
14 Erlenborn	N	N	N	Y	Y	N	N	N
15 Corcoran	Y	N	N	✓	N	Y	Y	N
16 Anderson	N	N	N	N	Y	N	N	N
17 O'Brien	N	N	N	Y	N	Y	N	N
18 Michel	N	N	Y	Y	Y	N	N	N
19 Railsback	N	N	N	N	Y	N	N	N
20 Findley	Y	N	N	Y	Y	?	N	N
21 Madigan	N	N	N	Y	Y	?	N	N
22 Shipley	✓	?	Y	✓	Y	X	Y	Y
23 Price	Y	Y	N	N	Y	N	N	Y
24 Simon	N	Y	N	N	Y	N	N	Y
INDIANA								
1 Benjamin	Y	N	N	Y	N	Y	Y	Y
2 Fithian	N	Y	N	N	N	Y	N	Y
3 Brademas	Y	Y	N	N	N	N	N	Y
4 Quayle	N	N	Y	Y	Y	Y	Y	Y
5 Hillis	Y	N	Y	N	Y	Y	Y	N
6 Evans	N	Y	N	N	N	Y	Y	Y
7 Myers, J.	Y	N	Y	Y	N	Y	Y	N
8 Cornwell	N	Y	N	N	Y	Y	N	Y
9 Hamilton	N	Y	N	N	Y	N	N	Y
10 Sharp	N	Y	N	N	Y	N	N	Y
11 Jacobs	N	Y	N	N	N	Y	N	Y
IOWA								
1 Leach	N	N	N	N	Y	Y	N	Y
2 Blouin	?	Y	N	N	N	N	N	Y
3 Grassley	Y	N	N	Y	N	Y	Y	N
4 Smith	Y	Y	Y	N	Y	Y	N	N
5 Harkin	N	N	Y	N	N	N	N	Y
6 Bedell	N	N	N	N	Y	N	N	Y

Democrats ***Republicans***

	1	2	3	4	5	6	7	8
KANSAS								
1 Sebelius	Y	N	Y	Y	Y	Y	Y	Y
2 Keys	N	Y	Y	N	Y	N	N	Y
3 Winn	Y	N	Y	Y	Y	N	Y	N
4 Glickman	N	Y	Y	N	Y	N	Y	Y
5 Skubitz	Y	Y	Y	Y	Y	N	Y	Y
KENTUCKY								
1 Hubbard	Y	Y	Y	N	Y	Y	Y	N
2 Natcher	Y	Y	Y	Y	Y	Y	N	Y
3 Mazzoli	Y	Y	N	N	Y	Y	N	Y
4 Snyder	Y	N	Y	Y	Y	Y	Y	N
5 Carter	Y	N	Y	Y	Y	Y	Y	N
6 Breckinridge	Y	Y	Y	N	Y	N	N	X
7 Perkins	Y	N	Y	Y	Y	Y	N	Y
LOUISIANA								
1 Livingston	Y	N	N	Y	Y	Y	Y	N
2 Boggs	Y	N	N	Y	N	N	N	N
3 Treen	Y	N	Y	Y	Y	Y	Y	?
4 Waggonner	Y	N	N	Y	Y	Y	Y	N
5 Huckaby	Y	N	Y	Y	Y	Y	Y	N
6 Moore	Y	N	Y	Y	Y	Y	Y	N
7 Breaux	Y	N	Y	Y	✓	✓	Y	N
8 Long	Y	N	Y	Y	Y	N	N	Y
MAINE								
1 Emery	N	N	Y	N	N	Y	Y	N
2 Cohen	N	N	N	N	N	?	Y	Y
MARYLAND								
1 Bauman	N	N	Y	Y	N	Y	Y	N
2 Long	Y	Y	N	N	N	N	N	N
3 Mikulski	Y	N	N	N	N	N	N	Y
4 Holt	N	N	Y	Y	N	Y	Y	N
5 Spellman	Y	N	?	N	N	N	N	Y
6 Byron[3]	N		N	Y	N	Y	Y	N
7 Mitchell	Y	N	N	N	N	X	N	Y
8 Steers	N	N	N	N	N	N	N	Y
MASSACHUSETTS								
1 Conte	N	Y	N	N	N	N	N	Y
2 Boland	Y	N	N	N	N	N	N	Y
3 Early	N	Y	N	Y	N	N	Y	Y
4 Drinan	N	N	N	N	N	N	N	Y
5 Tsongas	N	Y	N	?	N	X	X	Y
6 Harrington	N	Y	N	N	N	?	?	Y
7 Markey	N	N	N	N	N	N	N	Y
8 O'Neill								
9 Moakley	Y	Y	N	N	N	N	N	Y
10 Heckler	N	N	N	N	N	Y	N	Y
11 Burke	Y	N	Y	Y	X	N	X	Y
12 Studds	N	N	N	N	N	N	N	Y
MICHIGAN								
1 Conyers	N	N	N	N	?	N	X	Y
2 Pursell	Y	N	N	N	N	N	N	Y
3 Brown	N	N	Y	Y	Y	N	N	N
4 Stockman	N	N	N	N	Y	Y	Y	N
5 Sawyer	N	N	N	Y	Y	N	N	Y
6 Carr	N	Y	Y	N	N	N	N	Y
7 Kildee	N	N	Y	N	N	N	N	Y
8 Traxler	Y	Y	Y	N	N	N	Y	Y
9 Vander Jagt	?	N	Y	Y	Y	Y	Y	?
10 Cederberg	N	N	Y	Y	Y	N	Y	N
11 Ruppe	N	N	N	N	Y	?	N	Y
12 Bonior	N	N	N	N	N	N	N	Y
13 Diggs	X	?	Y	Y	N	?	X	Y
14 Nedzi	N	Y	N	N	N	N	N	Y
15 Ford	Y	Y	N	N	N	N	N	Y
16 Dingell	N	Y	N	Y	N	N	N	Y
17 Brodhead	N	Y	N	N	N	N	N	Y
18 Blanchard	N	Y	N	N	N	N	N	Y
19 Broomfield	N	N	Y	Y	Y	N	Y	N
MINNESOTA								
1 Quie	Y	?	Y	?	N	?	?	Y
2 Hagedorn	Y	N	Y	Y	Y	Y	Y	N
3 Frenzel	N	N	N	Y	Y	N	N	Y
4 Vento	N	N	N	N	N	N	N	Y
5 Fraser	N	N	Y	N	?	?	?	Y
6 Nolan	N	Y	Y	N	N	N	N	Y
7 Stangeland	Y	N	Y	Y	N	Y	Y	N
8 Oberstar	Y	Y	Y	N	N	N	N	Y
MISSISSIPPI								
1 Whitten	Y	Y	Y	Y	Y	Y	N	N
2 Bowen	Y	Y	N	Y	Y	Y	N	N
3 Montgomery	Y	Y	Y	Y	Y	Y	N	N
4 Cochran	✓	X	Y	N	N	Y	?	N
5 Lott	Y	N	Y	Y	Y	Y	Y	N
MISSOURI								
1 Clay	Y	N	N	Y	N	?	N	Y
2 Young	N	N	N	Y	Y	Y	N	N
3 Gephardt	N	Y	N	N	Y	Y	N	Y

	1	2	3	4	5	6	7	8
4 Skelton	N	Y	Y	Y	Y	N	?	N
5 Bolling	N	Y	N	N	Y	N	N	Y
6 Coleman	N	N	Y	Y	Y	Y	Y	N
7 Taylor	Y	N	Y	Y	Y	Y	Y	N
8 Ichord	Y	Y	Y	Y	Y	Y	Y	N
9 Volkmer	N	N	N	N	Y	N	Y	Y
10 Burlison	Y	Y	Y	N	?	N	N	N
MONTANA								
1 Baucus	Y	Y	Y	N	N	Y	N	Y
2 Marlenee	Y	N	Y	Y	N	Y	Y	N
NEBRASKA								
1 Thone	✓	N	Y	Y	Y	Y	?	N
2 Cavanaugh	Y	Y	Y	N	N	N	N	Y
3 Smith	Y	N	Y	Y	Y	Y	Y	N
NEVADA								
AL Santini	N	N	N	N	N	N	Y	Y
NEW HAMPSHIRE								
1 D'Amours	N	Y	N	N	N	Y	N	Y
2 Cleveland	N	N	N	N	Y	Y	Y	N
NEW JERSEY								
1 Florio	N	N	N	N	N	Y	Y	Y
2 Hughes	N	Y	N	N	N	Y	N	Y
3 Howard	Y	Y	X	N	N	N	N	Y
4 Thompson	Y	Y	N	N	N	N	N	Y
5 Fenwick	N	✓	N	N	Y	N	N	Y
6 Forsythe	N	N	N	Y	N	N	Y	Y
7 Maguire	N	N	N	N	?	N	N	Y
8 Roe	Y	Y	N	N	N	N	Y	N
9 Hollenbeck	N	Y	N	N	N	N	N	N
10 Rodino	N	Y	?	?	?	N	?	Y
11 Minish	N	Y	N	N	N	Y	Y	Y
12 Rinaldo	Y	N	N	N	N	Y	Y	N
13 Meyner	N	N	N	N	N	N	N	Y
14 LeFante	N	Y	N	X	X	?	✓	Y
15 Patten	N	Y	N	X	Y	N	N	Y
NEW MEXICO								
1 Lujan	?	?	Y	Y	N	Y	?	N
2 Runnels	N	N	✓	Y	Y	Y	Y	Y
NEW YORK								
1 Pike	N	Y	N	N	N	Y	Y	Y
2 Downey	N	Y	N	N	N	N	N	Y
3 Ambro	N	Y	N	N	N	N	Y	Y
4 Lent	N	N	N	Y	N	Y	Y	N
5 Wydler	N	N	N	Y	N	Y	Y	N
6 Wolff	N	Y	N	N	N	N	Y	Y
7 Addabbo	Y	Y	N	N	N	N	Y	Y
8 Rosenthal	Y	N	N	N	N	N	N	Y
9 Delaney	N	Y	N	Y	N	N	Y	Y
10 Biaggi	N	Y	N	Y	N	N	Y	N
11 Scheuer	Y	Y	N	N	N	N	N	Y
12 Chisholm	Y	N	N	N	N	N	N	Y
13 Solarz	N	Y	N	N	Y	N	N	Y
14 Richmond	Y	Y	N	N	N	X	N	Y
15 Zeferetti	Y	Y	N	Y	N	Y	Y	N
16 Holtzman	N	N	N	N	N	N	N	Y
17 Murphy	Y	Y	N	Y	N	?	Y	Y
18 Green	N	Y	N	N	N	N	N	Y
19 Rangel	Y	Y	N	N	N	N	N	Y
20 Weiss	N	N	N	N	N	N	N	Y
21 Garcia	N	Y	N	N	Y	N	N	Y
22 Bingham	N	Y	N	N	Y	N	N	Y
23 Caputo	?	N	N	?	N	?	Y	Y
24 Ottinger	N	N	N	N	N	N	N	Y
25 Fish	N	N	N	Y	N	N	Y	N
26 Gilman	Y	N	N	N	N	N	Y	N
27 McHugh	N	Y	N	N	Y	N	N	Y
28 Stratton	N	Y	N	Y	Y	Y	Y	N
29 Pattison	N	N	N	N	N	N	N	Y
30 McEwen	Y	N	Y	Y	Y	Y	Y	N
31 Mitchell	N	N	Y	N	Y	N	Y	N
32 Hanley	N	Y	N	N	N	?	Y	Y
33 Walsh	Y	N	N	Y	Y	Y	Y	N
34 Horton	Y	N	N	Y	N	N	N	Y
35 Conable	N	N	N	N	Y	N	N	Y
36 LaFalce	N	Y	N	N	N	N	N	Y
37 Nowak	Y	Y	N	N	N	N	N	Y
38 Kemp	Y	N	N	Y	Y	?	Y	N
39 Lundine	Y	Y	N	N	Y	N	N	Y
NORTH CAROLINA								
1 Jones	Y	Y	Y	Y	Y	Y	Y	N
2 Fountain	N	Y	Y	Y	Y	Y	Y	N
3 Whitley	Y	Y	✓	Y	N	Y	Y	N
4 Andrews	Y	Y	N	Y	Y	Y	Y	Y
5 Neal	N	Y	N	Y	Y	Y	N	Y
6 Preyer	N	Y	N	N	Y	N	N	Y
7 Rose	N	Y	Y	?	N	Y	N	Y
8 Hefner	N	Y	Y	Y	Y	Y	Y	Y

	1	2	3	4	5	6	7	8
9 Martin	N	N	Y	Y	N	Y	Y	N
10 Broyhill	N	N	Y	Y	Y	Y	Y	N
11 Gudger	N	Y	N	N	N	Y	Y	N
NORTH DAKOTA								
AL Andrews	Y	N	Y	Y	N	Y	Y	N
OHIO								
1 Gradison	N	N	N	Y	Y	N	Y	N
2 Luken	N	N	N	N	N	N	Y	N
3 Whalen	X	N	N	N	✓	N	?	Y
4 Guyer	N	N	Y	Y	N	Y	Y	N
5 Latta	N	N	Y	Y	Y	Y	Y	N
6 Harsha	Y	N	Y	Y	N	Y	Y	N
7 Brown	N	N	Y	Y	Y	Y	Y	?
8 Kindness	N	N	Y	Y	Y	Y	Y	N
9 Ashley	?	Y	N	N	N	N	N	Y
10 Miller	N	N	Y	Y	N	Y	Y	N
11 Stanton	Y	N	Y	Y	Y	N	N	N
12 Devine	N	N	Y	Y	N	Y	Y	N
13 Pease	N	Y	N	N	Y	N	N	Y
14 Seiberling	N	N	N	N	N	N	N	Y
15 Wylie	N	N	N	Y	N	Y	Y	N
16 Regula	N	N	N	Y	Y	Y	Y	N
17 Ashbrook	N	N	N	?	N	Y	Y	?
18 Applegate	Y	N	N	Y	Y	Y	Y	N
19 Carney	Y	Y	N	Y	N	N	N	Y
20 Oakar	Y	N	N	N	N	N	N	Y
21 Stokes	Y	N	N	N	N	?	N	Y
22 Vanik	N	N	N	N	N	N	N	Y
23 Mottl	N	Y	N	N	N	Y	Y	Y
OKLAHOMA								
1 Jones	Y	N	Y	Y	Y	Y	Y	N
2 Risenhoover	N	Y	Y	Y	✓	?	Y	N
3 Watkins	Y	N	Y	Y	Y	Y	Y	N
4 Steed	Y	Y	Y	Y	Y	Y	Y	N
5 Edwards	Y	N	Y	Y	N	Y	Y	?
6 English	N	Y	Y	Y	Y	Y	Y	N
OREGON								
1 AuCoin	Y	Y	N	N	N	Y	Y	Y
2 Ullman	Y	Y	Y	Y	Y	N	N	Y
3 Duncan	Y	Y	N	Y	Y	N	N	N
4 Weaver	N	Y	N	N	Y	Y	Y	Y
PENNSYLVANIA								
1 Myers, M.	Y	Y	N	Y	N	N	Y	Y
2 Nix	N	Y	N	X	Y	N	N	Y
3 Lederer	Y	Y	N	N	N	N	Y	Y
4 Eilberg	Y	N	N	N	X	N	Y	Y
5 Schulze	✓	N	Y	Y	Y	Y	Y	N
6 Yatron	Y	Y	N	Y	N	Y	Y	N
7 Edgar	N	N	N	N	N	N	N	Y
8 Kostmayer	N	N	N	N	N	N	N	Y
9 Shuster	Y	N	Y	Y	Y	?	Y	N
10 McDade	Y	N	N	Y	?	Y	?	N
11 Flood	Y	Y	N	Y	N	N	Y	Y
12 Murtha	Y	Y	N	Y	Y	Y	Y	N
13 Coughlin	N	N	N	Y	Y	N	Y	N
14 Moorhead	N	Y	N	N	Y	N	N	Y
15 Rooney	Y	Y	N	N	N	N	N	Y
16 Walker	N	N	N	Y	N	Y	Y	N
17 Ertel	Y	Y	N	Y	N	Y	Y	Y
18 Walgren	N	Y	N	N	N	N	N	Y
19 Goodling, W.	N	N	N	Y	?	?	Y	N
20 Gaydos	Y	Y	N	Y	N	Y	Y	Y
21 Dent	Y	Y	X	Y	X	Y	✓	✓
22 Murphy	N	Y	N	N	N	Y	Y	N
23 Ammerman	X	X	N	N	Y	Y	Y	Y
24 Marks	N	N	N	N	N	N	N	Y
25 Myers, G.	Y	Y	N	N	N	N	N	N
RHODE ISLAND								
1 St Germain	N	N	N	N	N	Y	Y	Y
2 Beard	Y	Y	N	N	N	N	Y	Y
SOUTH CAROLINA								
1 Davis	N	N	Y	Y	N	Y	Y	Y
2 Spence	Y	N	Y	Y	N	Y	Y	N
3 Derrick	N	Y	N	N	Y	Y	N	Y
4 Mann	N	Y	N	Y	Y	Y	N	Y
5 Holland	N	Y	Y	Y	Y	Y	Y	Y
6 Jenrette	Y	Y	Y	N	Y	Y	N	Y
SOUTH DAKOTA								
1 Pressler	Y	N	Y	Y	N	Y	?	Y
2 Abdnor	Y	N	Y	Y	Y	?	Y	N
TENNESSEE								
1 Quillen	Y	N	N	Y	Y	Y	Y	Y
2 Duncan	Y	N	N	Y	N	Y	Y	Y
3 Lloyd	Y	Y	N	Y	Y	✓	✓	Y
4 Gore	Y	N	Y	N	Y	N	N	Y
5 Allen[4]								Y
6 Beard	Y	N	N	Y	Y	Y	Y	N

	1	2	3	4	5	6	7	8
7 Jones	Y	Y	Y	Y	Y	Y	✓	Y
8 Ford	N	Y	N	N	N	N	X	Y
TEXAS								
1 Hall	Y	N	Y	Y	Y	Y	Y	N
2 Wilson, C.	Y	Y	Y	Y	Y	N	N	N
3 Collins	N	N	N	Y	Y	Y	Y	N
4 Roberts	Y	N	Y	Y	Y	Y	Y	N
5 Mattox	N	Y	N	N	N	N	Y	Y
6 Teague	Y	?	✓	Y	✓	✓	✓	X
7 Archer	N	N	N	Y	Y	Y	Y	N
8 Eckhardt	N	Y	?	N	N	N	N	Y
9 Brooks	Y	Y	N	Y	Y	Y	N	Y
10 Pickle	Y	Y	Y	Y	Y	Y	N	N
11 Poage	Y	Y	Y	Y	Y	Y	Y	N
12 Wright	Y	Y	N	N	Y	N	N	Y
13 Hightower	Y	N	Y	Y	Y	Y	N	Y
14 Young	Y	Y	Y	?	Y	?	?	Y
15 de la Garza	Y	N	Y	Y	Y	Y	Y	N
16 White	Y	N	Y	Y	Y	Y	Y	N
17 Burleson	N	N	Y	Y	Y	Y	Y	N
18 Jordan	Y	N	N	N	Y	N	N	Y
19 Mahon	Y	N	Y	Y	Y	N	N	Y
20 Gonzalez	Y	✓	Y	Y	Y	N	N	N
21 Krueger	✓	N	Y	Y	Y	?	✓	X
22 Gammage	N	N	Y	Y	N	✓	Y	Y
23 Kazen	Y	Y	Y	Y	Y	Y	Y	N
24 Milford	N	Y	N	Y	Y	?	N	Y
UTAH								
1 McKay	Y	Y	N	Y	Y	Y	N	N
2 Marriott	Y	N	N	Y	N	Y	Y	?
VERMONT								
AL Jeffords	N	N	Y	N	Y	N	N	✓
VIRGINIA								
1 Trible	Y	N	Y	Y	N	Y	Y	N
2 Whitehurst	Y	N	N	Y	N	Y	Y	N
3 Satterfield	Y	N	N	Y	Y	Y	Y	N
4 Daniel	Y	N	Y	Y	Y	Y	Y	N
5 Daniel	Y	Y	N	Y	Y	Y	Y	N
6 Butler	Y	N	N	Y	Y	Y	Y	N
7 Robinson	Y	N	Y	Y	Y	Y	Y	N
8 Harris	N	N	N	N	N	N	N	Y
9 Wampler	Y	N	Y	Y	Y	Y	Y	N
10 Fisher	N	Y	N	N	N	N	N	Y
WASHINGTON								
1 Pritchard	N	N	N	N	Y	N	N	Y
2 Meeds	Y	Y	N	N	Y	N	N	Y
3 Bonker	Y	Y	N	N	Y	N	N	Y
4 McCormack	Y	Y	Y	N	Y	Y	N	Y
5 Foley	Y	Y	Y	N	N	N	N	Y
6 Dicks	Y	Y	N	N	Y	N	N	Y
7 Cunningham	N	N	N	Y	N	Y	Y	N
WEST VIRGINIA								
1 Mollohan	Y	Y	N	Y	N	Y	N	N
2 Staggers	N	Y	N	Y	Y	Y	Y	N
3 Slack	Y	Y	Y	Y	N	Y	Y	N
4 Rahall	Y	Y	X	Y	Y	N	N	N
WISCONSIN								
1 Aspin	N	Y	N	N	Y	N	N	Y
2 Kastenmeier	Y	N	N	N	N	N	N	Y
3 Baldus	Y	Y	Y	N	Y	N	N	Y
4 Zablocki	Y	Y	N	Y	Y	N	N	N
5 Reuss	N	N	N	N	N	N	N	Y
6 Steiger	N	N	N	Y	Y	N	N	N
7 Obey	N	Y	N	N	Y	N	N	Y
8 Cornell	N	N	N	N	N	N	N	Y
9 Kasten	N	N	N	✓	N	?	?	N
WYOMING								
AL Roncalio	Y	Y	Y	N	N	?	N	Y

1. Rep. William M. Ketchum (R Calif.), died June 24, 1978.

2. Rep. Ralph H. Metcalfe (D Ill.), died Oct. 10, 1978.

3. Rep. Goodloe E. Byron (D Md.), died Oct. 11, 1978.

4. Rep. Clifford Allen (D Tenn.), died June 18, 1978.

Democrats ***Republicans***

9. HR 10929. Defense Procurement Authorization. Passage, over the president's Aug. 17 veto, of the bill to authorize $36,956,969,000 for Defense Department weapons procurement and military research programs in fiscal 1979. Rejected 191-206: R 107-23; D 84-183 (ND 34-150; SD 50-33), Sept. 7, 1978. A two-thirds majority vote (265 in this case) is required for passage over a veto. A "nay" was a vote supporting the president's position.

10. HR 6805. Consumer Protection Agency. Passage of the bill to establish an independent Office of Consumer Representation within the Executive Branch to represent the interests of consumers before federal agencies and courts. Rejected 189-227: R 17-126; D 172-101 (ND 147-40; SD 25-61), Feb. 8, 1978. A "yea" was a vote supporting the president's position.

11. HR 8494. Lobbying Disclosure. Passage of the bill to require annual registration and quarterly reporting by major lobbying organizations as well as disclosure of grass-roots (indirect) lobbying activities by reporting organizations and the names and addresses of major groups contributing to reporting organizations. Passed 259-140: R 75-67; D 184-73 (ND 143-39; SD 41-34), April 26, 1978. A "yea" was a vote supporting the president's position.

12. H Con Res 559. Fiscal 1979 Budget Targets. Holt, R-Md., amendment to set aggregate budget targets as follows: revenues of $440.1 billion, budget authority of $546.8 billion, outlays of $488.3 billion and a deficit of $48.2 billion. Rejected 197-203: R 139-1; D 58-202 (ND 24-155; SD 34-47), May 3, 1978.

13. HR 12929. Labor-HEW Appropriations, Fiscal 1979. Miller, R-Ohio, amendment to reduce controllable spending in the bill by 2 percent. Adopted 220-181: R 122-18; D 98-163 (ND 47-133; SD 51-30), June 13, 1978.

14. HR 12050. Tuition Tax Credits. Gradison, R-Ohio, motion to recommit the conference report on the bill to provide income tax credits for college and vocational school tuitions to the conference committee, with instructions that House conferees insist on a provision making tuitions paid to private elementary and secondary schools eligible for a credit. Motion agreed to 207-185: R 100-33; D 107-152 (ND 91-86; SD 16-66), Oct. 12, 1978. A "nay" was a vote supporting the president's position.

15. HR 50. Full Employment Act. Jeffords, R-Vt., substitute amendment, to the Sarasin, R-Conn., amendments, to require the president, beginning with the third year after passage of the bill, to include in his annual economic report goals for reasonable price stability, and to formulate policies for the reduction of inflation; and to define reasonable price stability as reduction of inflation to 3 percent within five years of enactment. Rejected 198-223: R 142-2; D 56-221 (ND 26-168; SD 30-53), March 9, 1978. (The Sarasin amendments, as amended by the Wright amendments, were adopted subsequently by voice vote.)

16. HR 13511. Revenue Act of 1978. Corman, D-Calif., amendment to provide an $18.1 billion tax cut including more benefits to taxpayers earning less than $50,000, and less to those earning more. Rejected 193-225: R 8-134; D 185-91 (ND 164-27; SD 21-64), Aug. 10, 1978. A "yea" was a vote supporting the president's position.

KEY

- Y Voted for (yea).
- ✓ Paired for.
- † Announced for.
- N Voted against (nay).
- X Paired against.
- \- Announced against.
- P Voted "present."
- ● Voted "present" to avoid possible conflict of interest.
- ? Did not vote or otherwise make a position known.

	9	10	11	12	13	14	15	16
ALABAMA								
1 Edwards	N	N	N	Y	Y	Y	Y	N
2 Dickinson	Y	N	N	Y	Y	N	Y	N
3 Nichols	Y	N	Y	Y	Y	N	Y	N
4 Bevill	Y	N	N	N	Y	N	Y	N
5 Flippo	N	N	Y	N	Y	N	Y	N
6 Buchanan	Y	N	Y	Y	Y	N	?	N
7 Flowers	N	N	Y	Y	Y	N	N	N
ALASKA								
AL Young	✓	N	?	Y	Y	N	Y	N
ARIZONA								
1 Rhodes	Y	N	N	Y	Y	N	Y	N
2 Udall	N	Y	N	N	N	N	N	Y
3 Stump	Y	N	N	Y	Y	N	Y	N
4 Rudd	Y	N	N	Y	Y	✓	Y	X
ARKANSAS								
1 Alexander	Y	N	Y	N	N	N	N	N
2 Tucker	N	Y	?	?	?	N	?	Y
3 Hammerschmidt	Y	N	N	Y	Y	N	Y	N
4 Thornton	N	Y	?	?	?	N	?	N
CALIFORNIA								
1 Johnson	Y	Y	Y	N	N	Y	N	Y
2 Clausen	Y	N	N	Y	Y	Y	Y	N
3 Moss	N	Y	?	N	?	?	N	Y
4 Leggett	N	Y	N	N	N	?	N	Y
5 Burton, J.	N	Y	Y	N	N	N	N	Y
6 Burton, P.	N	Y	Y	N	N	N	N	Y
7 Miller	?	Y	Y	?	N	?	N	✓
8 Dellums	N	Y	Y	N	N	N	N	Y
9 Stark	N	Y	Y	N	N	N	N	Y
10 Edwards	N	Y	N	N	?	?	N	Y
11 Ryan	N	N	N	N	Y	Y	N	Y
12 McCloskey	N	Y	Y	Y	N	N	Y	N
13 Mineta	N	Y	Y	N	N	N	N	Y
14 McFall	N	✓	Y	N	N	N	N	Y
15 Sisk	?	N	?	N	Y	N	N	?
16 Panetta	N	N	Y	Y	Y	N	Y	Y
17 Krebs	N	Y	N	N	Y	N	N	Y
18 Ketchum[1]		N	N	Y	Y		Y	
19 Lagomarsino	Y	N	N	Y	Y	Y	Y	N
20 Goldwater	Y	N	N	✓	Y	Y	Y	N
21 Corman	N	Y	N	N	N	N	N	Y
22 Moorhead	Y	N	Y	Y	Y	Y	Y	N
23 Beilenson	X	Y	N	N	N	N	N	Y
24 Waxman	N	Y	?	X	N	N	N	Y
25 Roybal	N	Y	N	N	N	N	N	Y
26 Rousselot	Y	N	N	Y	Y	Y	Y	N
27 Dornan	Y	N	N	Y	Y	Y	Y	N
28 Burke	X	✓	Y	X	?	X	N	✓
29 Hawkins	X	Y	Y	N	N	N	N	Y
30 Danielson	N	Y	Y	N	N	N	N	Y
31 Wilson, C.H.	Y	Y	N	X	N	N	N	Y
32 Anderson	N	Y	Y	N	N	N	N	Y
33 Clawson	✓	X	N	Y	?	Y	Y	N
34 Hannaford	Y	Y	Y	N	N	N	N	Y
35 Lloyd	Y	Y	N	N	N	N	N	Y
36 Brown	N	Y	N	N	N	N	N	Y
37 Pettis	✓	N	N	Y	Y	?	Y	N
38 Patterson	N	Y	Y	N	N	N	N	Y
39 Wiggins	?	N	N	Y	?	N	Y	N
40 Badham	Y	N	N	Y	Y	?	Y	N
41 Wilson, B.	Y	N	Y	✓	Y	Y	Y	N
42 Van Deerlin	N	Y	N	X	N	Y	N	Y
43 Burgener	Y	N	N	Y	Y	Y	Y	N
COLORADO								
1 Schroeder	N	N	Y	N	Y	N	N	Y
2 Wirth	N	Y	Y	X	Y	N	Y	Y
3 Evans	N	Y	N	N	Y	?	N	N
4 Johnson	Y	N	N	Y	Y	N	Y	N
5 Armstrong	Y	N	N	Y	Y	Y	Y	N
CONNECTICUT								
1 Cotter	N	Y	Y	N	Y	Y	N	N
2 Dodd	N	Y	N	N	N	N	N	Y
3 Giaimo	N	N	N	N	Y	Y	N	N
4 McKinney	N	Y	Y	Y	N	N	Y	N
5 Sarasin	Y	N	Y	Y	Y	?	Y	N
6 Moffett	N	Y	Y	N	N	N	N	Y
DELAWARE								
AL Evans	Y	N	N	Y	Y	Y	Y	N
FLORIDA								
1 Sikes	Y	N	N	N	Y	N	N	N
2 Fuqua	Y	N	Y	Y	Y	N	N	N
3 Bennett	Y	N	Y	Y	Y	N	N	N
4 Chappell	Y	N	N	Y	Y	X	Y	N
5 Kelly	Y	N	N	Y	Y	Y	Y	N
6 Young	Y	N	Y	Y	Y	N	Y	N
7 Gibbons	?	N	Y	Y	Y	Y	Y	N
8 Ireland	Y	N	Y	Y	Y	?	N	N
9 Frey	✓	N	?	✓	Y	?	Y	N
10 Bafalis	Y	N	Y	Y	Y	Y	Y	N
11 Rogers	N	Y	Y	Y	N	N	Y	Y
12 Burke	✓	N	Y	Y	Y	Y	Y	N
13 Lehman	X	Y	Y	N	N	N	N	Y
14 Pepper	Y	Y	Y	N	N	N	N	Y
15 Fascell	N	Y	Y	N	N	N	N	Y
GEORGIA								
1 Ginn	Y	N	N	Y	Y	N	N	N
2 Mathis	Y	N	N	Y	Y	Y	Y	N
3 Brinkley	N	N	Y	Y	Y	Y	Y	N
4 Levitas	N	N	Y	Y	Y	Y	Y	Y
5 Fowler	N	Y	Y	?	Y	N	N	N
6 Flynt	Y	N	N	Y	Y	Y	Y	N
7 McDonald	Y	X	N	Y	Y	Y	Y	X
8 Evans	N	N	N	N	Y	Y	Y	N
9 Jenkins	N	N	Y	Y	Y	N	Y	N
10 Barnard	Y	N	N	Y	Y	Y	Y	N
HAWAII								
1 Heftel	N	Y	Y	N	Y	Y	Y	N
2 Akaka	N	Y	Y	N	N	N	N	N
IDAHO								
1 Symms	✓	N	N	Y	Y	Y	Y	N
2 Hansen, G.	✓	N	N	Y	Y	Y	Y	N
ILLINOIS								
1 Metcalfe[2]	N	Y	Y	N	N		N	Y
2 Murphy	N	Y	N	X	N	Y	N	Y
3 Russo	N	Y	Y	Y	Y	Y	N	N
4 Derwinski	Y	N	Y	Y	Y	Y	Y	N
5 Fary	✓	Y	Y	N	N	Y	X	Y
6 Hyde	Y	N	N	Y	Y	Y	Y	N
7 Collins	N	✓	Y	N	N	N	N	Y
8 Rostenkowski	N	✓	Y	N	N	Y	N	Y
9 Yates	N	Y	N	N	N	N	N	Y
10 Mikva	X	Y	Y	X	?	N	N	Y
11 Annunzio	N	Y	✓	N	N	Y	N	Y
12 Crane	Y	N	N	Y	Y	✓	Y	N
13 McClory	Y	N	N	Y	Y	N	Y	N
14 Erlenborn	X	N	N	Y	Y	Y	Y	N
15 Corcoran	Y	N	Y	Y	Y	Y	Y	N
16 Anderson	N	N	Y	Y	N	N	?	N
17 O'Brien	Y	N	N	Y	N	Y	Y	N
18 Michel	Y	N	N	Y	Y	Y	Y	N
19 Railsback	Y	N	Y	Y	Y	Y	Y	N
20 Findley	Y	N	Y	Y	Y	N	Y	N
21 Madigan	N	N	Y	Y	?	?	Y	N
22 Shipley	✓	X	N	N	Y	?	N	N
23 Price	Y	Y	Y	N	N	Y	N	Y
24 Simon	N	Y	Y	N	?	N	N	Y
INDIANA								
1 Benjamin	N	Y	Y	N	N	Y	N	Y
2 Fithian	N	N	Y	N	Y	N	Y	Y
3 Brademas	N	Y	Y	N	N	N	N	Y
4 Quayle	Y	N	Y	Y	Y	Y	Y	N
5 Hillis	Y	N	Y	Y	Y	?	Y	N
6 Evans	Y	N	Y	Y	Y	N	Y	Y
7 Myers, J.	Y	N	N	Y	Y	Y	Y	N
8 Cornwell	N	N	N	Y	Y	N	Y	N
9 Hamilton	N	N	Y	N	Y	N	Y	Y
10 Sharp	N	Y	Y	Y	Y	N	Y	Y
11 Jacobs	N	N	Y	N	Y	?	Y	Y
IOWA								
1 Leach	N	N	Y	Y	Y	Y	Y	N
2 Blouin	N	Y	Y	N	N	Y	N	Y
3 Grassley	Y	N	N	Y	Y	Y	Y	N
4 Smith	Y	Y	Y	N	N	N	N	N
5 Harkin	N	Y	Y	N	Y	Y	Y	Y
6 Bedell	N	N	Y	N	N	N	Y	Y

Democrats ***Republicans***

	9	10	11	12	13	14	15	16
KANSAS								
1 Sebelius	Y	N	N	Y	Y	Y	Y	N
2 Keys	N	N	Y	N	N	N	N	Y
3 Winn	Y	N	N	Y	Y	Y	Y	N
4 Glickman	Y	N	Y	Y	N	N	Y	Y
5 Skubitz	N	N	N	Y	Y	N	Y	N
KENTUCKY								
1 Hubbard	N	N	N	N	Y	N	N	Y
2 Natcher	N	N	Y	N	N	Y	N	N
3 Mazzoli	N	N	Y	Y	Y	Y	N	N
4 Snyder	Y	N	N	Y	Y	Y	Y	N
5 Carter	Y	N	N	Y	N	N	Y	N
6 Breckinridge	Y	Y	Y	N	Y	N	N	Y
7 Perkins	N	N	Y	N	N	N	N	N
LOUISIANA								
1 Livingston	Y	N	Y	Y	Y	Y	Y	N
2 Boggs	Y	Y	Y	N	N	Y	N	N
3 Treen	Y	N	Y	Y	Y	Y	Y	N
4 Waggonner	Y	N	N	Y	Y	N	Y	N
5 Huckaby	✓	N	N	Y	Y	N	Y	N
6 Moore	Y	N	Y	Y	Y	Y	Y	N
7 Breaux	Y	N	Y	Y	Y	Y	Y	N
8 Long	Y	Y	Y	N	N	Y	N	N
MAINE								
1 Emery	Y	N	Y	Y	Y	Y	Y	N
2 Cohen	N	Y	Y	Y	Y	Y	Y	N
MARYLAND								
1 Bauman	Y	N	N	Y	Y	Y	Y	N
2 Long	Y	Y	N	Y	Y	N	Y	N
3 Mikulski	N	Y	Y	N	N	Y	N	Y
4 Holt	Y	N	N	Y	Y	Y	Y	N
5 Spellman	N	Y	Y	N	?	N	N	Y
6 Byron[3]	Y	N	Y	Y	Y		Y	N
7 Mitchell	N	Y	N	N	N	?	N	Y
8 Steers	N	Y	Y	Y	N	Y	N	Y
MASSACHUSETTS								
1 Conte	N	Y	Y	Y	N	Y	Y	N
2 Boland	N	Y	Y	N	N	Y	N	Y
3 Early	N	Y	Y	Y	N	Y	N	Y
4 Drinan	N	Y	Y	N	N	N	N	Y
5 Tsongas	X	Y	?	N	N	N	N	Y
6 Harrington	N	Y	Y	N	N	✓	N	Y
7 Markey	N	Y	N	N	N	Y	N	Y
8 O'Neill								
9 Moakley	N	Y	Y	N	N	Y	N	Y
10 Heckler	?	Y	Y	Y	Y	Y	Y	Y
11 Burke	N	Y	N	N	N	Y	N	Y
12 Studds	N	Y	Y	N	N	N	N	Y
MICHIGAN								
1 Conyers	N	Y	X	?	?	Y	N	Y
2 Pursell	Y	Y	Y	Y	N	N	Y	N
3 Brown	Y	N	N	Y	Y	Y	Y	N
4 Stockman	N	N	Y	Y	Y	Y	Y	N
5 Sawyer	Y	N	?	Y	Y	Y	Y	?
6 Carr	N	Y	Y	N	N	N	N	Y
7 Kildee	N	Y	Y	N	N	Y	N	Y
8 Traxler	N	Y	Y	N	N	Y	N	Y
9 Vander Jagt	Y	N	Y	Y	Y	Y	Y	N
10 Cederberg	Y	N	N	Y	Y	Y	Y	N
11 Ruppe	N	X	N	Y	Y	Y	Y	N
12 Bonior	N	Y	Y	N	N	N	N	Y
13 Diggs	N	Y	N	N	N	?	N	Y
14 Nedzi	N	Y	Y	N	?	Y	N	Y
15 Ford	N	Y	Y	N	N	N	N	Y
16 Dingell	N	Y	Y	N	N	N	N	Y
17 Brodhead	N	Y	Y	N	N	N	N	Y
18 Blanchard	N	Y	Y	N	N	N	N	Y
19 Broomfield	Y	N	Y	Y	Y	Y	Y	N
MINNESOTA								
1 Quie	?	N	Y	Y	?	?	Y	N
2 Hagedorn	Y	N	Y	Y	Y	Y	Y	N
3 Frenzel	Y	N	Y	Y	?	Y	Y	N
4 Vento	N	Y	Y	N	N	Y	N	Y
5 Fraser	?	Y	Y	N	N	N	N	?
6 Nolan	N	Y	Y	N	?	N	N	Y
7 Stangeland	Y	N	Y	Y	Y	Y	Y	N
8 Oberstar	N	Y	Y	N	N	N	N	Y
MISSISSIPPI								
1 Whitten	Y	?	Y	N	N	Y	N	Y
2 Bowen	Y	N	N	Y	Y	N	N	N
3 Montgomery	Y	N	N	Y	Y	?	Y	N
4 Cochran	Y	N	?	✓	Y	?	Y	N
5 Lott	Y	N	Y	Y	Y	?	Y	N
MISSOURI								
1 Clay	N	Y	Y	N	N	N	N	Y
2 Young	N	N	Y	N	Y	Y	N	Y
3 Gephardt	N	N	Y	N	Y	Y	N	Y
4 Skelton	Y	N	Y	N	?	N	Y	Y
5 Bolling	N	Y	Y	N	N	N	N	Y
6 Coleman	Y	N	Y	Y	Y	Y	Y	N
7 Taylor	Y	N	N	Y	Y	N	Y	N
8 Ichord	Y	N	Y	Y	Y	N	N	N
9 Volkmer	N	N	Y	N	Y	Y	N	Y
10 Burlison	N	N	Y	N	N	N	N	Y
MONTANA								
1 Baucus	N	Y	?	N	Y	N	N	Y
2 Marlenee	Y	N	Y	Y	Y	N	Y	N
NEBRASKA								
1 Thone	✓	N	Y	✓	Y	Y	Y	N
2 Cavanaugh	N	N	Y	Y	Y	Y	N	Y
3 Smith	Y	N	Y	Y	Y	Y	Y	N
NEVADA								
AL Santini	Y	N	N	Y	Y	Y	Y	Y
NEW HAMPSHIRE								
1 D'Amours	N	Y	Y	N	N	Y	N	Y
2 Cleveland	Y	N	Y	Y	Y	Y	Y	N
NEW JERSEY								
1 Florio	N	Y	Y	N	N	Y	N	Y
2 Hughes	N	Y	Y	Y	?	Y	N	Y
3 Howard	N	Y	?	X	N	Y	N	Y
4 Thompson	N	Y	Y	N	N	N	N	Y
5 Fenwick	N	Y	Y	Y	Y	N	Y	N
6 Forsythe	N	N	N	Y	Y	Y	Y	N
7 Maguire	N	Y	Y	N	N	Y	N	Y
8 Roe	N	Y	Y	N	N	Y	N	Y
9 Hollenbeck	N	Y	Y	Y	N	✓	Y	Y
10 Rodino	N	Y	?	X	?	Y	N	✓
11 Minish	N	Y	Y	N	N	Y	N	Y
12 Rinaldo	Y	Y	Y	Y	N	Y	Y	Y
13 Meyner	N	Y	Y	N	N	Y	N	Y
14 LeFante	N	Y	Y	N	?	Y	N	✓
15 Patten	N	Y	Y	N	N	Y	N	Y
NEW MEXICO								
1 Lujan	Y	N	Y	Y	Y	Y	Y	N
2 Runnels	Y	N	?	✓	?	Y	Y	N
NEW YORK								
1 Pike	Y	N	Y	Y	Y	N	Y	N
2 Downey	Y	Y	Y	N	Y	N	N	Y
3 Ambro	Y	Y	Y	Y	Y	Y	Y	Y
4 Lent	Y	N	Y	Y	?	Y	Y	N
5 Wydler	Y	N	Y	Y	Y	Y	Y	N
6 Wolff	Y	Y	Y	N	N	Y	N	Y
7 Addabbo	N	Y	Y	N	N	Y	N	Y
8 Rosenthal	N	Y	Y	N	N	N	N	Y
9 Delaney	N	Y	Y	N	Y	Y	N	Y
10 Biaggi	N	Y	Y	N	?	Y	N	Y
11 Scheuer	N	Y	N	N	N	Y	N	Y
12 Chisholm	N	Y	Y	N	N	N	N	Y
13 Solarz	N	Y	Y	N	N	Y	N	Y
14 Richmond	N	Y	N	N	N	N	N	Y
15 Zeferetti	Y	Y	Y	N	N	Y	N	Y
16 Holtzman	N	Y	N	N	N	N	N	Y
17 Murphy	?	Y	N	N	N	Y	N	Y
18 Green[5]	N		Y	Y	Y	Y	Y	N
19 Rangel	N	Y	N	N	N	N	N	Y
20 Weiss	N	Y	N	N	N	N	N	Y
21 Garcia[5]	N		N	N	N	Y	N	Y
22 Bingham	N	✓	Y	N	N	Y	N	Y
23 Caputo	Y	N	Y	Y	?	Y	Y	Y
24 Ottinger	N	Y	Y	N	N	Y	N	Y
25 Fish	Y	N	N	Y	Y	Y	Y	N
26 Gilman	Y	Y	Y	Y	N	Y	Y	Y
27 McHugh	N	Y	Y	N	N	N	N	Y
28 Stratton	Y	N	N	N	Y	Y	Y	N
29 Pattison	N	Y	Y	Y	N	Y	N	Y
30 McEwen	N	N	N	Y	Y	Y	Y	N
31 Mitchell	Y	N	Y	Y	N	N	Y	N
32 Hanley	Y	N	Y	N	N	Y	N	Y
33 Walsh	Y	N	N	Y	N	Y	Y	N
34 Horton	Y	Y	Y	Y	N	Y	Y	N
35 Conable	N	N	Y	✓	Y	Y	Y	N
36 LaFalce	N	Y	Y	Y	N	N	Y	Y
37 Nowak	N	Y	Y	N	N	Y	N	Y
38 Kemp	Y	N	N	Y	Y	Y	Y	N
39 Lundine	N	N	Y	N	N	?	N	Y
NORTH CAROLINA								
1 Jones	Y	N	?	N	N	N	N	N
2 Fountain	Y	N	?	Y	Y	N	Y	N
3 Whitley	Y	N	?	?	Y	N	Y	N
4 Andrews	N	N	Y	?	Y	N	N	N
5 Neal	N	N	Y	Y	Y	N	Y	N
6 Preyer	N	Y	Y	N	N	N	N	Y
7 Rose	N	N	Y	N	N	N	N	Y
8 Hefner	N	N	N	Y	Y	N	N	N
9 Martin	Y	N	Y	Y	Y	N	Y	N
10 Broyhill	Y	N	N	Y	Y	N	Y	N
11 Gudger	Y	N	?	N	Y	N	N	N
NORTH DAKOTA								
AL Andrews	Y	N	Y	Y	Y	Y	Y	N
OHIO								
1 Gradison	Y	N	Y	Y	Y	Y	Y	N
2 Luken	Y	N	?	N	Y	Y	N	N
3 Whalen	N	Y	Y	N	N	N	N	Y
4 Guyer	Y	N	Y	Y	Y	Y	Y	N
5 Latta	Y	N	Y	Y	Y	Y	Y	N
6 Harsha	Y	N	N	Y	Y	Y	Y	N
7 Brown	Y	N	N	Y	Y	Y	?	N
8 Kindness	Y	N	N	Y	Y	Y	Y	N
9 Ashley	N	Y	Y	N	N	Y	N	Y
10 Miller	Y	N	Y	Y	Y	Y	Y	N
11 Stanton	Y	N	Y	Y	Y	Y	Y	N
12 Devine	Y	N	N	Y	Y	Y	Y	X
13 Pease	N	Y	Y	N	N	Y	N	Y
14 Seiberling	N	Y	N	N	N	Y	N	Y
15 Wylie	N	Y	Y	Y	Y	Y	Y	N
16 Regula	Y	N	Y	Y	Y	Y	Y	N
17 Ashbrook	Y	N	N	✓	Y	Y	Y	N
18 Applegate	N	Y	Y	Y	Y	Y	Y	Y
19 Carney	N	Y	Y	N	N	Y	N	Y
20 Oakar	Y	Y	Y	N	N	Y	N	Y
21 Stokes	N	Y	Y	N	N	N	N	Y
22 Vanik	N	Y	Y	N	N	Y	N	Y
23 Mottl	Y	Y	Y	Y	Y	Y	Y	Y
OKLAHOMA								
1 Jones	Y	N	N	N	Y	N	Y	N
2 Risenhoover	Y	N	N	N	Y	N	?	N
3 Watkins	Y	N	Y	Y	Y	N	Y	N
4 Steed	Y	N	N	N	N	N	N	N
5 Edwards	Y	N	N	Y	Y	Y	Y	N
6 English	Y	N	Y	Y	Y	N	Y	N
OREGON								
1 AuCoin	N	Y	Y	Y	Y	?	Y	N
2 Ullman	N	N	Y	N	?	N	N	N
3 Duncan	?	N	N	?	N	N	N	N
4 Weaver	N	Y	Y	?	Y	N	N	Y
PENNSYLVANIA								
1 Myers, M.	N	Y	Y	N	N	Y	N	Y
2 Nix	N	Y	?	?	N	Y	N	Y
3 Lederer	N	Y	Y	N	N	Y	N	N
4 Eilberg	N	Y	?	N	N	Y	N	Y
5 Schulze	Y	N	Y	Y	Y	?	Y	?
6 Yatron	Y	Y	Y	Y	Y	Y	N	Y
7 Edgar	N	Y	Y	N	N	Y	N	Y
8 Kostmayer	N	Y	Y	Y	Y	Y	?	Y
9 Shuster	Y	N	N	Y	Y	Y	Y	N
10 McDade	Y	N	Y	Y	N	Y	Y	N
11 Flood	N	Y	Y	N	N	Y	N	Y
12 Murtha	Y	N	Y	N	Y	Y	N	N
13 Coughlin	Y	N	Y	Y	Y	Y	Y	N
14 Moorhead	N	Y	Y	N	N	N	N	Y
15 Rooney	N	Y	Y	?	N	Y	N	Y
16 Walker	Y	N	Y	Y	Y	Y	Y	N
17 Ertel	N	X	Y	N	Y	Y	N	Y
18 Walgren	N	Y	Y	N	N	Y	Y	Y
19 Goodling, W.	Y	N	?	Y	Y	Y	Y	N
20 Gaydos	N	Y	Y	N	N	Y	N	Y
21 Dent	Y	?	?	N	?	Y	N	Y
22 Murphy	N	Y	Y	Y	N	Y	N	Y
23 Ammerman	X	Y	Y	N	N	?	N	Y
24 Marks	N	N	Y	Y	Y	Y	Y	Y
25 Myers, G.	Y	Y	Y	Y	Y	N	Y	N
RHODE ISLAND								
1 St Germain	N	Y	Y	N	N	Y	N	Y
2 Beard	N	✓	?	N	N	Y	N	Y
SOUTH CAROLINA								
1 Davis	Y	Y	N	N	Y	N	N	N
2 Spence	Y	N	N	Y	Y	N	Y	N
3 Derrick	Y	N	?	N	Y	N	N	Y
4 Mann	Y	N	?	?	?	N	Y	N
5 Holland	N	N	N	N	?	N	N	N
6 Jenrette	N	Y	N	N	?	N	N	✓
SOUTH DAKOTA								
1 Pressler	?	N	Y	Y	Y	Y	Y	N
2 Abdnor	✓	N	N	Y	Y	N	Y	N
TENNESSEE								
1 Quillen	✓	N	N	Y	Y	N	Y	N
2 Duncan	Y	N	N	Y	Y	N	Y	N
3 Lloyd	Y	N	Y	Y	Y	N	N	X
4 Gore	Y	Y	Y	N	N	N	N	Y
5 Allen[4]		Y	Y	?	?		N	
6 Beard	Y	N	N	Y	Y	Y	Y	N
7 Jones	Y	X	N	N	N	N	N	N
8 Ford	N	Y	?	N	N	N	N	Y
TEXAS								
1 Hall	Y	N	N	Y	Y	N	N	N
2 Wilson, C.	Y	N	N	N	N	N	N	N
3 Collins	Y	N	N	Y	Y	Y	Y	N
4 Roberts	Y	N	?	N	Y	N	N	N
5 Mattox	N	Y	Y	N	Y	N	N	Y
6 Teague	✓	N	X	N	?	?	?	X
7 Archer	Y	N	Y	Y	Y	Y	Y	N
8 Eckhardt	N	Y	Y	N	N	N	N	Y
9 Brooks	N	Y	N	N	N	Y	N	N
10 Pickle	N	Y	Y	N	N	N	N	N
11 Poage	Y	N	?	N	N	N	N	N
12 Wright	N	✓	Y	N	N	N	N	Y
13 Hightower	Y	N	N	N	N	N	N	N
14 Young	?	Y	?	N	?	?	N	N
15 de la Garza	Y	N	Y	N	?	Y	N	N
16 White	Y	N	Y	✓	N	X	N	N
17 Burleson	Y	N	N	N	Y	N	Y	N
18 Jordan	N	Y	N	N	N	N	N	Y
19 Mahon	N	N	N	N	N	N	?	N
20 Gonzalez	Y	Y	N	N	N	N	N	Y
21 Krueger	✓	N	?	Y	Y	X	✓	N
22 Gammage	Y	N	✓	Y	Y	N	Y	N
23 Kazen	Y	N	N	?	N	N	Y	N
24 Milford	N	N	N	Y	Y	N	N	N
UTAH								
1 McKay	N	N	Y	N	Y	?	N	N
2 Marriott	Y	N	N	Y	Y	Y	Y	N
VERMONT								
AL Jeffords	Y	Y	Y	Y	N	Y	Y	N
VIRGINIA								
1 Trible	Y	N	Y	Y	Y	N	Y	N
2 Whitehurst	Y	N	Y	Y	Y	N	Y	N
3 Satterfield	Y	N	N	Y	Y	N	?	N
4 Daniel	Y	N	N	Y	Y	Y	Y	N
5 Daniel	Y	N	N	Y	Y	N	Y	N
6 Butler	Y	N	N	Y	Y	N	Y	N
7 Robinson	Y	N	N	Y	Y	N	Y	N
8 Harris	N	Y	Y	N	N	N	N	Y
9 Wampler	Y	N	N	Y	Y	N	Y	N
10 Fisher	N	Y	Y	N	Y	N	Y	Y
WASHINGTON								
1 Pritchard	N	Y	Y	Y	Y	Y	Y	N
2 Meeds	N	Y	Y	N	N	?	N	Y
3 Bonker	N	N	Y	N	N	?	N	Y
4 McCormack	Y	N	Y	N	Y	N	N	N
5 Foley	N	N	N	N	Y	Y	N	Y
6 Dicks	Y	Y	Y	N	N	N	N	Y
7 Cunningham	Y	N	N	Y	Y	Y	Y	N
WEST VIRGINIA								
1 Mollohan	Y	N	N	N	N	N	N	N
2 Staggers	Y	Y	Y	N	N	Y	N	Y
3 Slack	Y	N	N	N	N	Y	?	N
4 Rahall	N	N	Y	N	N	N	N	N
WISCONSIN								
1 Aspin	N	Y	Y	N	Y	N	N	Y
2 Kastenmeier	N	Y	Y	N	N	N	N	Y
3 Baldus	N	Y	Y	?	N	N	N	Y
4 Zablocki	Y	Y	Y	N	N	Y	N	Y
5 Reuss	N	Y	Y	N	N	?	N	Y
6 Steiger	N	X	N	Y	Y	Y	Y	N
7 Obey	N	N	Y	N	N	N	N	Y
8 Cornell	N	Y	Y	N	N	Y	N	Y
9 Kasten	✓	N	Y	Y	Y	Y	Y	N
WYOMING								
AL Roncalio	N	Y	Y	?	N	Y	N	Y

1. Rep. William M. Ketchum (R Calif.), died June 24, 1978.

2. Rep. Ralph H. Metcalfe (D Ill.), died Oct. 10, 1978.

3. Rep. Goodloe E. Byron (D Md.), died Oct. 11, 1978.

4. Rep. Clifford Allen (D Tenn.), died June 18, 1978.

5. Reps. S. William Green, R-N.Y., and Robert Garcia, D-N.Y., were sworn in on Feb. 21, 1978.

Democrats ***Republicans***

	9	10	11	12	13	14	15
ALABAMA							
Allen, M.[1]	N	Y	Y	N		?	N
Sparkman	Y	N	N	N	Y	Y	N
ALASKA							
Gravel	Y	N	N	Y	?	N	Y
Stevens	N	Y	Y	N	Y	Y	Y
ARIZONA							
DeConcini	Y	N	Y	N	Y	Y	Y
Goldwater	Y	Y	Y	N	N	N	N
ARKANSAS							
Bumpers	Y	N	N	Y	Y	Y	N
Hodges	N	N	N	Y	Y	Y	N
CALIFORNIA							
Cranston	Y	N	N	Y	N	Y	Y
Hayakawa	N	Y	Y	N	Y	N	N
COLORADO							
Hart	Y	N	N	Y	Y	Y	Y
Haskell	Y	N	?	Y	✓	?	Y
CONNECTICUT							
Ribicoff	Y	N	N	Y	N	N	Y
Weicker	Y	N	?	Y	Y	N	Y
DELAWARE							
Biden	Y	N	N	N	N	Y	Y
Roth	N	Y	Y	N	N	N	N
FLORIDA							
Chiles	N	Y	N	N	Y	N	N
Stone	Y	N	N	N	Y	Y	N
GEORGIA							
Nunn	Y	Y	Y	N	Y	N	N
Talmadge	Y	Y	Y	N	Y	N	N
HAWAII							
Inouye	Y	N	Y	Y	Y	Y	Y
Matsunaga	Y	N	N	Y	?	N	Y
IDAHO							
Church	Y	Y	Y	Y	Y	Y	Y
McClure	N	Y	†	N	Y	Y	N
ILLINOIS							
Stevenson	Y	Y	N	Y	N	Y	Y
Percy	Y	N	Y	Y	Y	Y	Y
INDIANA							
Bayh	Y	N	N	Y	Y	Y	Y
Lugar	Y	Y	Y	N	Y	N	N
IOWA							
Clark	Y	N	?	Y	Y	Y	Y
Culver	Y	N	N	Y	Y	Y	Y
KANSAS							
Dole	Y	Y	Y	N	Y	Y	N
Pearson	Y	†	Y	Y	Y	N	Y
KENTUCKY							
Ford	Y	Y	Y	N	Y	Y	Y
Huddleston	Y	Y	Y	N	Y	Y	Y
LOUISIANA							
Johnston	N	Y	Y	?	Y	N	N
Long	N	Y	Y	?	Y	N	N
MAINE							
Hathaway	Y	N	?	Y	Y	Y	Y
Muskie	Y	N	N	Y	N	N	Y
MARYLAND							
Sarbanes	Y	N	N	N	Y	Y	Y
Mathias	Y	N	?	Y	N	N	Y
MASSACHUSETTS							
Kennedy	Y	N	N	Y	Y	Y	Y
Brooke	Y	N	N	Y	Y	Y	Y
MICHIGAN							
Riegle	Y	N	N	Y	✓	Y	Y
Griffin	Y	N	X	N	Y	Y	N
MINNESOTA							
Anderson	Y	N	N	?	Y	?	Y
Humphrey, M.	Y	N	N	Y	Y	Y	Y
MISSISSIPPI							
Eastland	?	Y	Y	?	Y	N	N
Stennis	N	Y	Y	N	Y	N	N
MISSOURI							
Eagleton	Y	?	N	Y	Y	N	Y
Danforth	Y	Y	Y	N	Y	N	N
MONTANA							
Melcher	N	N	Y	Y	Y	Y	Y
Hatfield, P.	N	N	N	Y	Y	Y	Y
NEBRASKA							
Zorinsky	N	Y	N	N	Y	Y	N
Curtis	N	Y	Y	N	Y	N	N
NEVADA							
Cannon	N	Y	N	N	X	N	N
Laxalt	N	Y	Y	N	Y	N	N
NEW HAMPSHIRE							
Durkin	Y	N	N	Y	N	Y	Y
McIntyre	Y	N	?	Y	N	Y	Y
NEW JERSEY							
Williams	Y	N	N	Y	X	Y	Y
Case	Y	N	N	Y	N	Y	Y
NEW MEXICO							
Domenici	N	Y	?	N	Y	Y	N
Schmitt	N	N	Y	N	Y	N	N
NEW YORK							
Moynihan	Y	N	N	Y	N	N	Y
Javits	Y	N	N	Y	N	N	Y
NORTH CAROLINA							
Morgan	N	Y	Y	Y	Y	N	-
Helms	N	Y	Y	N	Y	Y	N
NORTH DAKOTA							
Burdick	N	N	N	Y	Y	Y	Y
Young	N	Y	Y	N	Y	N	N
OHIO							
Glenn	Y	N	N	Y	N	N	Y
Metzenbaum	Y	N	N	Y	N	Y	Y
OKLAHOMA							
Bartlett	N	Y	Y	N	?	N	N
Bellmon	N	Y	N	Y	N	N	N
OREGON							
Hatfield, M.	Y	N	Y	Y	Y	Y	Y
Packwood	Y	N	Y	N	Y	Y	Y
PENNSYLVANIA							
Heinz	Y	N	Y	Y	N	Y	Y
Schweiker	N	Y	Y	N	Y	N	Y
RHODE ISLAND							
Pell	Y	N	N	Y	N	Y	Y
Chafee	Y	N	N	Y	N	N	Y
SOUTH CAROLINA							
Hollings	Y	Y	Y	N	Y	N	N
Thurmond	Y	Y	Y	N	Y	Y	N
SOUTH DAKOTA							
Abourezk	Y	N	N	Y	Y	Y	Y
McGovern	Y	N	N	Y	Y	Y	Y
TENNESSEE							
Sasser	Y	Y	N	N	Y	Y	Y
Baker	Y	Y	Y	N	Y	N	N
TEXAS							
Bentsen	Y	Y	Y	N	Y	N	N
Tower	N	Y	✓	N	Y	?	N
UTAH							
Garn	N	Y	Y	N	N	N	N
Hatch	N	Y	Y	N	Y	N	N
VERMONT							
Leahy	Y	N	N	N	N	Y	Y
Stafford	Y	N	N	Y	N	N	Y
VIRGINIA							
*Byrd, H.	N	Y	Y	N	N	N	N
Scott	N	Y	?	N	N	?	N
WASHINGTON							
Jackson	Y	Y	N	Y	Y	Y	Y
Magnuson	Y	N	N	Y	Y	Y	Y
WEST VIRGINIA							
Byrd, R.	Y	N	N	Y	N	N	Y
Randolph	Y	N	N	N	Y	Y	Y
WISCONSIN							
Nelson	Y	N	N	Y	Y	Y	Y
Proxmire	Y	N	N	N	N	Y	Y
WYOMING							
Hansen	N	Y	Y	N	Y	N	N
Wallop	N	Y	Y	N	Y	N	N

KEY

- Y Voted for (yea).
- ✓ Paired for.
- † Announced for.
- N Voted against (nay).
- X Paired against.
- \- Announced against.
- P Voted "present."
- ● Voted "present" to avoid possible conflict of interest.
- ? Did not vote or otherwise make a position known.

Democrats ***Republicans***

1. Sen. Maryon P. Allen (D Ala.), sworn in June 12, 1978, succeeding her husband James B. Allen (D) who died June 1, 1978.

**Byrd elected as independent.*

9. H J Res 554. D.C. Voting Representation. Passage of the joint resolution to propose an amendment to the Constitution to provide for full voting representation in Congress (both in the House and the Senate) for the District of Columbia and to retain the right granted District residence by the 23rd Amendment to vote for the election of the president and vice president (the resolution would repeal the 23rd Amendment). Passed 67-32: R 19-19; D 48-13 (ND 38-5; SD 10-8), Aug. 22, 1978. A two-thirds majority vote (66 in this case) is required for passage of a joint resolution proposing an amendment to the Constitution. A "yea" was a vote supporting the president's position.

10. H J Res 638. ERA Deadline Extension. Garn, R-Utah, amendment to allow a state to rescind its ratification of the proposed amendment extending the time for ratification of the ERA at any time after the resolution became effective. Rejected 44-54: R 24-13; D 20-41 (ND 5-37; SD 15-4), Oct. 4, 1978. A "nay" was a vote supporting the president's position.

11. HR 5285. Medicare-Medicaid and Hospital Cost Containment. Talmadge, D-Ga., motion to table (kill) the Nelson, D-Wis., substitute amendment to authorize prospective reimbursement of hospitals by Medicare and Medicaid, to endorse a voluntary effort by hospitals to cut costs, and to authorize national hospital revenue limits if goals of the voluntary effort were not met. Motion rejected 42-47: R 25-6; D 17-41 (ND 4-35; SD 13-6), Oct. 12, 1978. A "nay" was a vote supporting the president's position. (The Nelson substitute for the bill was adopted subsequently by voice vote.)

12. S 1753. Elementary and Secondary Education Act Amendments. Pell, D-R.I., motion to table (kill) the Roth, R-Del., amendment to limit court-ordered busing of students only when there was a discriminatory purpose for segregated education; to require courts to determine whether a greater degree of racial segregation resulted because of the segregation policy; and to delay federal busing orders to provide time for appeals, unless the Supreme Court or a three-member appellate court denied such a delay. Motion agreed to 49-47: R 12-26; D 37-21 (ND 34-8; SD 3-13), Aug. 23, 1978.

13. HR 6782. Emergency Farm Bill. Passage of the bill to provide, for 1978 only, for a paid land diversion program for farmers, an increase in target price and loan levels for wheat, corn and cotton programs, and a flexible parity program of graduated target prices for wheat, corn and cotton. Passed 67-26: R 26-11; D 41-15 (ND 23-14; SD 18-1), March 21, 1978.

14. HR 13511. Revenue Act of 1978. Bumpers, D-Ark., amendment to cut individual income taxes in 1979 $4.5 billion more than the $16 billion recommended by the Finance Committee, with the extra relief going to persons with incomes below $50,000 and especially to those in the $10,000-$30,000 range. Adopted 52-43: R 13-23; D 39-20 (ND 32-9; SD 7-11), Oct. 6, 1978.

15. HR 8410. Labor Law Revision. Byrd, D-W.Va., motion to invoke cloture (cut off debate) on the Byrd, D-W.Va., substitute to the bill to amend the National Labor Relations Act. Motion rejected 58-41: R 14-24; D 44-17 (ND 41-2; SD 3-15), June 14, 1978. A three-fifths majority vote (60) of the total Senate membership is required to invoke cloture.

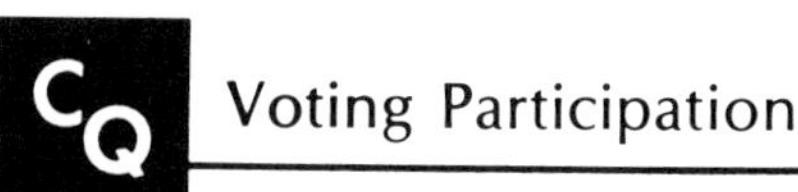

Voting Participation

Roll-Call Record:

Attendance During Votes Dropped Slightly in 1978

Congress set an all-time record for the number of votes taken in 1978, but as is traditional in election years, attendance at these votes fell off.

The 1978 attendance figure was 87 percent, three percentage points below the 1977 figure of 90 percent. The drop was primarily attributable to members' absences as they campaigned for re-election. In the 1976 election year attendance fell to 86 percent from its 1975 level of 91 percent.

Voting participation is the closest approach to an attendance record for Congress, but it is only an approximation. *(Definition, box, p. 3375)*

Republicans took part in voting slightly more often than Democrats in the House. One senator and five representatives had perfect scores for voting participation in 1978 and 12 representatives and two senators voted less than 50 percent of the time.

Chamber, Party Figures

An all-time record 1,350 recorded votes were taken in the House and Senate in 1978, one more than the 1,349 votes in 1976. In 1977 the Congress took 1,341 votes. There were 516 Senate votes in 1978, 119 fewer than in 1977 and 172 fewer than the record 688 taken in 1976. The House in 1978 set a new record of 834 votes, topping by 128 votes its previous high of 706 set in 1977. Twenty years ago the second session of the 85th Congress, in 1958, took 293 votes (200 in the Senate, 93 in the House). *(For a complete listing of congressional roll-call votes, see appendix pp. 1-H ff and 1-S ff.)*

For the first time since 1962, House members failed to vote more often than senators. The average score for members in each chamber in 1978 was 87 percent.

House Republicans voted 88 percent of the time in 1978, Democrats 87. In 1977 House Republicans led Democrats 91 to 90. In the Senate, each party scored 87 percent, compared with 1977 scores of 88 each. For the two chambers together, the 1978 scores were 88 percent for Republicans and 87 percent for Democrats. In 1977, Republicans led Democrats 91 to 90.

In the House, eastern Republicans led members from all regions, with a 91 percent participation score. In the Senate, eastern Democrats and eastern Republicans had the highest scores — 89 percent each.

High Scores

Democrat William Proxmire of Wisconsin was the only senator to answer every one of the 516 votes during the year. Proxmire extended his string of consecutive votes that began in 1966, when he last missed one, and reached a Senate record of 5,997 by the end of 1978.

Democratic Senators Edward Zorinsky of Nebraska, Henry M. Jackson of Washington and Majority Leader Robert C. Byrd of West Virginia scored 99 percent, as did Republican Richard G. Lugar of Indiana and Harry F. Byrd Jr. of Virginia, elected as an independent. Fifteen other senators scored 95 to 98 percent.

There were five perfect scores in the House in 1978, recorded by Democrats Adam Benjamin Jr. of Indiana, William H. Natcher of Kentucky and Republicans Robert J. Lagomarsino of California, Charles E. Grassley of Iowa and Ralph S. Regula of Ohio. Natcher had not missed a vote since he came to Congress in 1954, and in 1978 extended his record to 6,925 consecutive votes.

Low Scores

Twelve House members and two senators voted less than 50 percent of the time. Only three House members, and no senators, were in this category in 1977. *(1977 scores, 1977 Almanac p. 28-B)*

Of the twelve House members, only three were re-elected. Five ran for other offices, three retired and one was defeated in a primary. Scoring lowest in 1978 were Democrats Olin E. Teague of Texas, 9 percent; Yvonne Brathwaite Burke of California, 34; Peter W. Rodino Jr. of New Jersey, 36; and Robert (Bob) Krueger of Texas, 38. Teague had been seriously ill during the year and was retiring. Rodino had been ill and had illness in his family. Burke lost a bid for election as California attorney general and Krueger lost a race for the Senate. The lowest scoring Republican House member was Louis Frey Jr. of Florida, 40 percent, who lost a race for the gubernatorial nomination.

Lowest scoring senators were Democrats James Abourezk of South Dakota, 44 percent and Wendell R.

Absences

Failure to vote often is due to illness or conflicting duties. Members frequently have to be away from Washington on official business. Leaves of absence are granted members for these purposes.

Among those absent for a day or more in 1978 because they were sick or because of illness or death in their families were:

Senate Republican: Bartlett (Okla.).

House Democrats: Rodino (N.J.), Gonzalez (Texas), Dent (Pa.), Milford (Texas), Ottinger (N.Y.), Lloyd (Tenn.), Meyner (N.J.), Addabbo (N.Y.), Pepper (Fla.), Gibbons (Fla.), LeFante (N.J.), Roberts (Texas), Cotter (Conn.), Pike (N.Y.), Dellums (Calif.), Spellman (Md.), Runnels (N.M.), Whitley (N.C.), Udall (Ariz.), Foley (Wash.), Akaka (Hawaii), Satterfield (Va.), Mikulski (Md.), Holtzman (N.Y.), Fountain (N.C.), Ammerman (Pa.), Traxler (Mich.), Teague (Texas).

House Republicans: Rhodes (Ariz.), Corcoran (Ill.), McDade (Pa.), Michel (Ill.), Miller (Ohio), Hyde (Ill.), Pressler (S.D.), Young (Fla.), Young (Alaska), McKinney (Conn.), Pettis (Calif.).

Anderson of Minnesota, 49 percent. Abourezk retired after one term and Anderson was defeated for election to the seat to which he was appointed in 1976. John G. Tower of Texas had the lowest score among Senate Republicans, 69 percent. Tower was engaged in a hard-fought race for re-election against Krueger.

On the Record

In addition to scores on each member's participation in recorded votes, Congressional Quarterly also records, in its On the Record study, how often each member made public his position on issues that were brought to record votes. *(See Definitions.)*

Senators in 1978, on the average, made their position known on 90 percent of the roll-call votes (Democrats 90 percent; Republicans 89 percent). Representatives, on the average, made public their position on 92 percent of the votes (Democrats 92 percent; Republicans 92 percent).

Party Scores

Composites of Democratic and Republican voting participation scores for 1978 and 1977:

	1978		1977	
	Dems.	Reps.	Dems.	Reps.
Senate	87%	87%	88%	88%
House	87	88	90	91

Regional Scores

Regional voting participation breakdowns for 1978 with 1977 scores in parentheses:

DEMOCRATS

	East	West	South	Midwest
Senate	89% (91)	87% (87)	86% (86)	86% (89)
House	88 (89)	84 (89)	85 (91)	89 (91)

REPUBLICANS

	East	West	South	Midwest
Senate	89% (89)	87% (87)	84% (87)	87% (87)
House	91 (91)	84 (88)	90 (84)	88 (91)

Highest Scorers

SENATE

Democrats		Republicans	
Proxmire (Wis.)	100%	Lugar (Ind.)	99%
Zorinsky (Neb.)	99	Danforth (Mo.)	96
Byrd (Va.)*	99	Schweiker (Pa.)	96
Jackson (Wash.)	99	Hatch (Utah)	96
Byrd (W.Va.)	99	Hansen (Wyo.)	96
Glenn (Ohio)	98	Roth (Del.)	95
Metzenbaum (Ohio)	98	Dole (Kan.)	95
		Schmitt (N.M.)	95

* *Byrd (Va.) elected as an independent.*

HOUSE

Democrats. Those scoring 100 percent were Benjamin (Ind.), Natcher (Ky.). Scoring 99 percent were Johnson (Calif.), Krebs (Calif.), Bennett (Fla.), Hamilton (Ind.), Sharp (Ind.), Studds (Mass.), Kildee (Mich.), Oberstar (Minn.), Volkmer (Mo.), Murtha (Pa.), Harris (Va.), Zablocki (Wis.), Cornell (Wis.). Scoring 98 percent were Mineta (Calif.), Ginn (Ga.), Yates (Ill.), Price (Ill.), Glickman (Kan.), Blanchard (Mich.), Ertel (Pa.), Fisher (Va.).

Republicans. Those scoring 100 percent were Lagomarsino (Calif.), Grassley (Iowa), Regula (Ohio). Scoring 99 percent were Moore (La.), Bauman (Md.), Miller (Ohio), Daniel (Va.). Scoring 98 percent were Kelly (Fla.), Derwinski (Ill.), Snyder (Ky.), Steers (Md.), Conte (Mass.), Fenwick (N.J.), Rinaldo (N.J.), Shuster (Pa.), Marks (Pa.), Myers (Pa.), Spence (S.C.), Collins (Texas).

Definition

Voting Participation. Percentage of recorded votes on which a member voted "yea" or "nay." Failures to vote "yea" or "nay" lower scores — even if the member votes "present," enters a live pair, announces his stand in the *Congressional Record* or answers the CQ Poll. Only votes of "yea" or "nay" directly affect the outcome of a vote. Voting participation is the closest approach to an attendance record, but it is only an approximation. A member may be present and nevertheless decline to vote "yea" or "nay" — usually because he has entered a live pair with an absent member.

On the Record. Percentage of recorded votes on which congressman makes his position known by voting "yea" or "nay," entering a live pair, announcing his stand or answering the CQ Poll. Scores are lowered by general pairs as well as by complete silence on the issue. On the Record does not measure the effectiveness of a congressman in determining the outcome of votes, but it does show how frequently he tells his constituents and the general public where he stands on specific issues.

The CQ Poll gives absent congressmen the opportunity to announce their stands on recorded votes. On all recorded votes, CQ sends out ballots asking congressmen how they would have voted if they had been present.

Lowest Scorers

SENATE

Democrats		Republicans	
Abourezk (S.D.)	44%	Tower (Texas)	69%
Anderson (Minn.)	49	Brooke (Mass.)	72
Haskell (Colo.)	51	Goldwater (Ariz.)	73

HOUSE

Democrats		Republicans	
Teague (Texas)	9%	Frey (Fla.)	40%
Burke (Calif.)	34	Quie (Minn.)	45
Rodino (N.J.)	36	Cochran (Miss.)	50
Krueger (Texas)	38		
Shipley (Ill.)	41		
Conyers (Mich.)	45		
Dent (Pa.)	45		
Tucker (Ark.)	48		
Young (Texas)	48		
Diggs (Mich.)	49		
Tsongas (Mass.)	50		

	1	2	3	4
ALABAMA				
Allen[1]	56†	56*	56†	56*
Sparkman	81	83	87	93
ALASKA				
Gravel	81	80	83	92
Stevens	89	89	97	99
ARIZONA				
DeConcini	92	90	94	94
Goldwater	73	69	74	71
ARKANSAS				
Bumpers	86	88	87	89
Hodges	92	92*	92	92*
CALIFORNIA				
Cranston #	94	93	94	93
Hayakawa	92	87	93	87
COLORADO				
Hart	94	94	94	94
Haskell	51	69	53	78
CONNECTICUT				
Ribicoff	89	90	93	96
Weicker	87	84	94	95
DELAWARE				
Biden	87	86	87	87
Roth	95	95	95	95
FLORIDA				
Chiles	97	97	97	97
Stone	97	95	97	99
GEORGIA				
Nunn	93	94	93	94
Talmadge	88	86	91	93
HAWAII				
Inouye	75	79	82	92
Matsunaga	92	94	93	97
IDAHO				
Church	91	90	96	98
McClure	74	81	75	82
ILLINOIS				
Stevenson	91	89	92	96
Percy	84	84	85	86
INDIANA				
Bayh	91	93	91	95
Lugar	99	99	99	99
IOWA				
Clark	89	93	96	98
Culver	94	93	96	96
KANSAS				
Dole	95	96	96	98
Pearson	78	81	79	90
KENTUCKY				
Ford	94	93	94	94
Huddleston	82	83*	82	84*
LOUISIANA				
Johnston	68	79	71	82
Long	84	85	85	86
MAINE				
Hathaway	71	82	83	92
Muskie	93	85	93	90
MARYLAND				
Sarbanes	95	96	95	96
Mathias	79	83	80	83
MASSACHUSETTS				
Kennedy	89	89	93	93
Brooke	72	83	73	85
MICHIGAN				
Riegle	93	89	98	98
Griffin	75	70	78	72
MINNESOTA				
Anderson	49	71	65	84
Humphrey[2]	74†	74*	92†	92*
MISSISSIPPI				
Eastland	63	74	64	75
Stennis	76	79	76	79
MISSOURI				
Eagleton	89	91	89	92
Danforth	96	97	98	98
MONTANA				
Melcher	93	91	96	92
Hatfield, P.[3]	80†	80*	81†	81*
NEBRASKA				
Zorinsky	99	98	100	99
Curtis	84	89	86	94
NEVADA				
Cannon	93	91	96	93
Laxalt	84	86	84	87
NEW HAMPSHIRE				
Durkin	93	94	93	94
McIntyre	72	83	77	86
NEW JERSEY				
Williams	95	95	99	99
Case	90	90	96	98
NEW MEXICO				
Domenici	74	84	77	85
Schmitt	95	95*	97	98*
NEW YORK				
Moynihan	91	90	94	96
Javits	92	90	93	92
NORTH CAROLINA				
Morgan	93	85	98	96
Helms	87	91	88	95
NORTH DAKOTA				
Burdick	91	95	98	99
Young	83	81	87	93
OHIO				
Glenn	98	98	98	99
Metzenbaum	98	98	99	99
OKLAHOMA				
Bartlett #	92	82	92	82
Bellmon	88	90	89	91
OREGON				
Hatfield, M.	83	84	97	99
Packwood	92	90	93	91
PENNSYLVANIA				
Heinz	91	92	94	96
Schweiker	96	97	96	97
RHODE ISLAND				
Pell	90	91	95	96
Chafee	94	91	94	92
SOUTH CAROLINA				
Hollings	94	94	95	97
Thurmond	91	92	99	100
SOUTH DAKOTA				
Abourezk	44	55	70	85
McGovern	80	80	94	87
TENNESSEE				
Sasser	90	93	90	94
Baker	79	87	81	88
TEXAS				
Bentsen	92	91	93	92
Tower	69	81	76	85
UTAH				
Garn	92	91	92	96
Hatch	96	92	97	93
VERMONT				
Leahy	97	93	97	97
Stafford	88	81	95	87
VIRGINIA				
Byrd, H.[4]	99	99	99	99
Scott	82	80	83	80
WASHINGTON				
Jackson	99	99	100	100
Magnuson	94	93	98	98
WEST VIRGINIA				
Byrd, R.	99	99	99	99
Randolph	89	92	100	99
WISCONSIN				
Nelson	97	96	97	96
Proxmire	100	100	100	100
WYOMING				
Hansen	96	97	97	99
Wallop	90	91	94	96

- KEY -

† Not eligible for all recorded votes in 1978.
* Not eligible for all recorded votes in 95th Congress.
# Member absent a day or more in 1978 due to illness or illness or death in family.

Democrats ***Republicans***

1. Sen. Maryon P. Allen (D Ala.) sworn in June 12, 1978, succeeding her husband James B. Allen (D) who died June 1, 1978. His voting participation score for 1978 was 100 percent; for the 95th Congress his score was 99 percent. His On the Record score for 1978 was 100 percent; for the 95th Congress it was 99 percent.

2. Sen. Muriel Humphrey (D Minn.) sworn in Feb. 6, 1978, succeeding her husband Hubert H. Humphrey (D) who died Jan. 13, 1978. He was not eligible for any votes in 1978.

3. Sen. Paul Hatfield (D Mont.) sworn in Jan. 23, 1978, succeeding Lee Metcalf (D) who died Jan. 12, 1978. Metcalf was not eligible for any votes in 1978.

4. Sen. Byrd (Va.) elected as an independent.

Voting Participation and On the Record Scores: Senate

1. Voting Participation, 1978. Percentage of 516 roll calls in 1978 on which senator voted "yea" or "nay."

2. Voting Participation, 95th Congress. Percentage of 1,151 roll calls in 1977 and 1978 on which senator voted "yea" or "nay."

3. On the Record, 1978. Percentage of 516 roll calls in 1978 on which senator made his position known by voting "yea" or "nay," entering a live pair, announcing his stand or answering the CQ Poll.

4. On the Record, 95th Congress. Percentage of 1,151 roll calls in 1977 and 1978 on which senator made his position known by voting "yea" or "nay," entering a live pair, announcing his stand or answering the CQ Poll.

Voting Participation and On the Record Scores:

House

1. **Voting Participation, 1978.** Percentage of 834 recorded votes in 1978 on which representative voted "yea" or nay."

2. **Voting Participation, 95th Congress.** Percentage of 1,540 recorded votes in 1977 and 1978 on which representative voted "yea" or "nay."

3. **On the Record, 1978.** Percentage of 834 recorded votes in 1978 on which representative made his position known by voting "yea" or "nay," entering a live pair, announcing his stand or answering the CQ Poll.

4. **On the Record, 95th Congress.** Percentage of 1,540 recorded votes in 1977 and 1978 on which representative made his position known by voting "yea" or "nay," entering a live pair, announcing his stand or answering the CQ Poll.

KEY

† Not eligible for all recorded votes in 1978.
* Not eligible for all recorded votes in 95th Congress.
# Member absent a day or more in 1978 due to illness or illness or death in family.

	1	2	3	4
ALABAMA				
1 Edwards	95	92	95	93
2 Dickinson	84	84	85	91
3 Nichols	87	89	98	99
4 Bevill	94	95	95	96
5 Flippo	95	81	95	81
6 Buchanan	89	93	90	94
7 Flowers	55	72	55	72
ALASKA				
AL Young	65	70	90	94
ARIZONA				
1 Rhodes	78	82*	78	83*
2 Udall	87	88	98	99
3 Stump	83	88	94	97
4 Rudd	79	87	83	90
ARKANSAS				
1 Alexander	80	84	82	85
2 Tucker	48	67	96	97
3 Hammerschmidt	96	95	96	95
4 Thornton	55	72	56	72
CALIFORNIA				
1 Johnson	99	89	99	99
2 Clausen	88	88	89	89
3 Moss	70	72	71	80
4 Leggett	72	79	83	91
5 Burton, J.	77	79	79	80
6 Burton, P.	88	89	88	92
7 Miller	70	80	74	83
8 Dellums#	81	86	97	98
9 Stark	87	89	96	98
10 Edwards	93	94	94	96
11 Ryan	85	86	96	92
12 McCloskey	81	83	82	84
13 Mineta	98	95	99	97
14 McFall	93	95	94	95
15 Sisk	71	76	72	80
16 Panetta	96	96	99	99
17 Krebs	99	99	99	99
18 Ketchum[1]	94†	92*	69†	86*
19 Lagomarsino	100	100	100	100
20 Goldwater	84	83	85	86
21 Corman	91	89	96	97
22 Moorhead	96	97	99	99
23 Beilenson	85	86*	96	97*
24 Waxman	79	82	95	96
25 Roybal	91	92	95	94
26 Rousselot	89	89	90	91
27 Dornan	89	89	93	96
28 Burke	34	57	85	91
29 Hawkins	84	82	88	86
30 Danielson	87	91	97	99
31 Wilson, C.H.	59	69	87	92
32 Anderson	93	94	98	97
33 Clawson	73	73	76	77
34 Hannaford	92	94	98	99
35 Lloyd	97	96*	97	98*
36 Brown	81	82	82	88
37 Pettis	77	81	77	81
38 Patterson	91	87	97	97
39 Wiggins	68	74	95	97
40 Badham	82	86*	95	97*
41 Wilson, B.	91	87	94	91
42 Van Deerlin	89	87	90	92
43 Burgener	92	90	93	92
COLORADO				
1 Schroeder	95	97	98	99
2 Wirth	88	90	96	97
3 Evans	81	86	88	94
4 Johnson	84	84	84	84
5 Armstrong	60	75	61	76
CONNECTICUT				
1 Cotter#	80	79	92	95
2 Dodd	90	86	90	87
3 Giaimo	84	83	84	83*
4 McKinney #	86	76	96	96
5 Sarasin	51	68	88	94
6 Moffett	90	91	92	95
DELAWARE				
AL Evans	94	94	96	98
FLORIDA				
1 Sikes	87	88	90	91
2 Fuqua	88	88	97	98
3 Bennett	99	99	99	99
4 Chappell	85	85	94	91
5 Kelly	98	96*	99	97
6 Young#	97	94	98	96
7 Gibbons#	73	81	74	81
8 Ireland	81	87	82	87
9 Frey	40	60	45	64
10 Bafalis	97†	97*	97†	97*
11 Rogers	93	94	95	97
12 Burke	82	87	84	89
13 Lehman	83	86	95	97
14 Pepper#	78	77	92	96
15 Fascell	93	94	99	99
GEORGIA				
1 Ginn	98	97	100	99
2 Mathis	76	81	76	82
3 Brinkley	95	96	95	97
4 Levitas	97	97	98	97
5 Fowler	89	91*	89	91*
6 Flynt	77	86	79	87
7 McDonald	85	90	99	99
8 Evans	88	89*	98	99*
9 Jenkins	79	85	97	98
10 Barnard	86	89	88	90
HAWAII				
1 Heftel	95	92	96	93
2 Akaka#	94	94	99	99
IDAHO				
1 Symms	90	89	91	91
2 Hansen, G.	85	87	87	89
ILLINOIS				
1 Metcalfe[2]	78†	75*	80†	78*
2 Murphy	88	89*	96	95*
3 Russo	90	89	98	98
4 Derwinski	98	97	99	97
5 Fary	89	92	92	94
6 Hyde#	95	95	99	99
7 Collins	73	77	87	88
8 Rostenkowski	82	83	85	87
9 Yates	98	97	99	99
10 Mikva	81	84	93	95
11 Annunzio	95	95	99	99
12 Crane	72	80	94	93
13 McClory	93	92	99	99
14 Erlenborn	89	90	97	98
15 Corcoran#	95	96	98	99
16 Anderson	71	77	93	95
17 O'Brien	88†	91*	97†	96*
18 Michel#	90	88	97	98
19 Railsback	90	85	93	94
20 Findley	93	94	93	94
21 Madigan	89	90	90	91
22 Shipley	41	60	50	66
23 Price	98	88	99	99
24 Simon	84	90	90	94
INDIANA				
1 Benjamin	100	99*	100	100*
2 Fithian	95	93	96	96
3 Brademas	97	92	99	96
4 Quayle	90	90	90	90
5 Hillis	90	88	90	89
6 Evans	95	93	95	94
7 Myers, J.	96	95	97	96
8 Cornwell	82	86	88	92
9 Hamilton	99	98	99	98
10 Sharp	99	99*	99	99*
11 Jacobs	94	95	97	98
IOWA				
1 Leach	97	97	98	99
2 Blouin	90	93	93	96
3 Grassley	100	100	99	99
4 Smith	96	95	97	97
5 Harkin	96	93	97	97
6 Bedell	94†	94*	98†	99*

Democrats ***Republicans***

1. Rep. William M. Ketchum (R Calif.) died June 24, 1978.
2. Rep. Ralph H. Metcalfe (D Ill.) died Oct. 10, 1978.
3. Rep. Goodloe E. Byron (D Md.) died Oct. 11, 1978.
4. Rep. Thomas P. O'Neill Jr. (D Mass.), as Speaker, votes at his own discretion.
5. Rep. S. William Green (R N.Y.) sworn in Feb. 21, 1978, succeeding Edward I. Koch (D) who resigned Dec. 31, 1977.
6. Rep. Robert Garcia (D N.Y.) sworn in Feb. 21, 1978, succeeding Herman Badillo (D) who resigned Dec. 31, 1977.
7. Rep. Clifford Allen (D Tenn.) died June 18, 1978.

	1	2	3	4
KANSAS				
1 Sebelius	89	87	97	98
2 Keys	94	96	98	99
3 Winn	90	91	97	98
4 Glickman	98	98	99	99
5 Skubitz	78	82	80	86
KENTUCKY				
1 Hubbard	91	93	93	96
2 Natcher	100	100	100	100
3 Mazzoli	93	93	99	99
4 Snyder	98	98	98	98
5 Carter	93	93	93	94
6 Breckinridge	80	85	88	91
7 Perkins	97	97	99	99
LOUISIANA				
1 Livingston	91	90*	92	92*
2 Boggs	91	89	97	98
3 Treen	91	93	91	94
4 Waggonner	92	93	98	99
5 Huckaby	81	88	83	90
6 Moore	99	99	99	99
7 Breaux	80	84	84	88
8 Long	92	93	92	93
MAINE				
1 Emery	96	96	99	99
2 Cohen	78	86	81	90
MARYLAND				
1 Bauman	99	99	99	99
2 Long	96	96	96	96
3 Mikulski#	96	95	97	96
4 Holt	97	96	97	98
5 Spellman#	89	91	98	99
6 Byron[3]	91†	92*	91†	93*
7 Mitchell	89	90	97	98
8 Steers	98	90	99	98
MASSACHUSETTS				
1 Conte	98	97	98	99
2 Boland	92	91	97	98
3 Early	91	90	91	90
4 Drinan	97	98	99	99
5 Tsongas	50	70	59	76
6 Harrington	59	70	86	92
7 Markey	96	97	97	98
8 O'Neill[4]				
9 Moakley	93	93	99	99
10 Heckler	86	88	89	90
11 Burke	92	84	95	96
12 Studds	99	99	99	99
MICHIGAN				
1 Conyers	45	59	92	96
2 Pursell	84	84*	85	85*
3 Brown	90	91	95	97
4 Stockman	86	86	96	98
5 Sawyer	86	86	95	95
6 Carr	97	98	99	99
7 Kildee	99	99*	99	99*
8 Traxler#	88	89	97	98
9 Vander Jagt	86	85	87	86
10 Cederberg	92	91	93	93
11 Ruppe	70	75	82	87
12 Bonior	92	93*	97	98*
13 Diggs	49	56	82	90
14 Nedzi	92	95	94	96
15 Ford	79	78	81	84
16 Dingell	86	87	87	88
17 Brodhead	97	97	97	98
18 Blanchard	98	98	99	99
19 Broomfield	89	92	98	98
MINNESOTA				
1 Quie	45	66	61	79
2 Hagedorn	88	92	90	94
3 Frenzel	91	90	93	96
4 Vento	94	95	96	97
5 Fraser	63	72	80	86
6 Nolan	85	86	85	87
7 Stangeland	95	95*	99	99*
8 Oberstar	99	99	99	99
MISSISSIPPI				
1 Whitten	81	86	97	98
2 Bowen	91	91	91	91
3 Montgomery	93	93	96	97
4 Cochran	50	71	53	74
5 Lott	95	95	98	98
MISSOURI				
1 Clay	83	80*	84	81
2 Young	95	94	99	99
3 Gephardt	95	96	99	99

	1	2	3	4
4 Skelton	90	92*	94	97*
5 Bolling	80	76	97	98
6 Coleman	96	96*	97	98*
7 Taylor	96	96	96	96
8 Ichord	93	92	94	92
9 Volkmer	99	98*	99	99*
10 Burlison	97	97	97	97
MONTANA				
1 Baucus	77	85	96	98
2 Marlenee	91	89	91	90
NEBRASKA				
1 Thone	65	79	75	85
2 Cavanaugh	93	93	94	96
3 Smith	91	93	92	94
NEVADA				
AL Santini	82	84	98	98
NEW HAMPSHIRE				
1 D'Amours	95	96	98	98
2 Cleveland	91	92	93	96
NEW JERSEY				
1 Florio	94	84	99	89
2 Hughes	97	96	99	99
3 Howard	81	82	98	99
4 Thompson	88	87	95	97
5 Fenwick	98	99	99	99
6 Forsythe	94	84	98	97
7 Maguire	89	92	91	94
8 Roe	95	78	99	98
9 Hollenbeck	92	91	96	97
10 Rodino#	36	63	89	94
11 Minish	94	94	94	95
12 Rinaldo	98	98	99	99
13 Meyner#	87	89	98	99
14 LeFante#	63	76*	97	96*
15 Patten	92	94	99	99
NEW MEXICO				
1 Lujan	78	83	80	85
2 Runnels#	56	72	78	87
NEW YORK				
1 Pike#	89	92*	96	98*
2 Downey	94	93	98	99
3 Ambro	87	88	87	89
4 Lent	93	91	96	98
5 Wydler	88	88	88	88
6 Wolff	90	84	98	98
7 Addabbo#	84	86	93	96
8 Rosenthal	90	88	98	99
9 Delaney	90	92	90	92
10 Biaggi	84	83	92	95
11 Scheuer	91	92	94	96
12 Chisholm	83	83	95	95
13 Solarz	93	95	98	99
14 Richmond	79	83	86	93
15 Zeferetti	81	82	97	98
16 Holtzman#	94	94	96	97
17 Murphy	76	76	88	93
18 Green[5]	96†	96*	99†	99*
19 Rangel	86	88	89	94
20 Weiss	93	95	97	97
21 Garcia[6]	79†	79*	91†	91*
22 Bingham	91	92	99	99
23 Caputo	68	81	69	83
24 Ottinger#	94	96	97	98
25 Fish	92	90	92	91
26 Gilman	94	94	98	99
27 McHugh	97	93	98	97
28 Stratton	95	95*	98	99*
29 Pattison	91	93	98	98
30 McEwen	89	88	89	88
31 Mitchell	93	95	98	99
32 Hanley	95	95	99	99
33 Walsh	89	91	90	92
34 Horton	88	89	96	97
35 Conable	92	92*	93	93*
36 LaFalce	92	93	96	98
37 Nowak	97	97	99	99
38 Kemp	86	87	87	89
39 Lundine	92	91	99	96
NORTH CAROLINA				
1 Jones	88	91	99	99
2 Fountain#	90	92	98	99
3 Whitley#	82	90	85	92
4 Andrews	88	88	92	90
5 Neal	93	92	98	98
6 Preyer	95	96	97	98
7 Rose	87	85	94	90
8 Hefner	95	95	96	96

	1	2	3	4
9 Martin	91	93	99	99
10 Broyhill	94	94	95	94
11 Gudger	91	93*	99	99*
NORTH DAKOTA				
AL Andrews	94	94	96	98
OHIO				
1 Gradison	97†	96*	99†	99*
2 Luken	90	91	93	93
3 Whalen	80	78	99	99
4 Guyer	89	90	94	97
5 Latta	95	94	96	95
6 Harsha	93	92	93	92
7 Brown	81	86*	82	88*
8 Kindness	93	94	93	95
9 Ashley	84	87	86	89
10 Miller#	99	99	100	100
11 Stanton	97	97	98	99
12 Devine	97	95	99	99
13 Pease	97	98	98	99
14 Seiberling	95	95	98	99
15 Wylie	94	96	95	97
16 Regula	100	100	99	99
17 Ashbrook	83	87	97	98
18 Applegate	88	91	89	92
19 Carney	79	85	86	92
20 Oakar	81	87	81	88
21 Stokes	83	86	92	95
22 Vanik	95	92	99	99
23 Mottl	91	93	97	98
OKLAHOMA				
1 Jones	96	96	99	99
2 Risenhoover	71	81	76	86
3 Watkins	92	93*	97	97*
4 Steed	91	91	98	98
5 Edwards	90	93	90	93
6 English	96	97	98	99
OREGON				
1 AuCoin	83	88	95	97
2 Ullman	87	90*	97	99*
3 Duncan	82	86	87	89
4 Weaver	88	88	91	92
PENNSYLVANIA				
1 Myers, M.	88	88	88	88
2 Nix	59	74	67	82
3 Lederer	95	94	97	97
4 Eilberg	82	87	95	97
5 Schulze	91	94	92	94
6 Yatron	97	95	99	99
7 Edgar	95	96	99	99
8 Kostmayer	97	98	97	99
9 Shuster	98	98	98	98
10 McDade#	87	90	93	95
11 Flood	87	91	95	96
12 Murtha	99	96	99	96
13 Coughlin	95	96	98	98
14 Moorhead	91	93	98	99
15 Rooney	94	94	94	97
16 Walker	95	95	98	99
17 Ertel	98	96	98	97
18 Walgren	94	94	95	96
19 Goodling, W.	87	89	88	90
20 Gaydos	94	95	94	95
21 Dent#	45	37	89	92
22 Murphy	93	94	98	99
23 Ammerman#	72	84*	75	86*
24 Marks	98	98	98	98
25 Myers, G.	98	97	99	99
RHODE ISLAND				
1 St Germain	87	86	89	88
2 Beard	91	93	94	95
SOUTH CAROLINA				
1 Davis	91	92	92	93
2 Spence	98	96	98	97
3 Derrick	92	89	98	99
4 Mann	70	77	70	84
5 Holland	72	70	84	85
6 Jenrette	78	84	93	96
SOUTH DAKOTA				
1 Pressler#	73	79	74*	80
2 Abdnor	92	90	99	95
TENNESSEE				
1 Quillen	89	87*	98	98*
2 Duncan	97	98	99	99
3 Lloyd#	88	93	98	99
4 Gore	95	97	99	99
5 Allen[7]	75†	75*	51†	75*
6 Beard	85	88	94	96

	1	2	3	4
7 Jones	89	90	99	99
8 Ford	85	90	86	92
TEXAS				
1 Hall	97	96	99	97
2 Wilson, C.	80	81	96	98
3 Collins	98	98	99	99
4 Roberts#	82	86	85	89
5 Mattox	96	97	96	97
6 Teague#	9	13	29	38
7 Archer	95	97	96	97
8 Eckhardt	80	81	81	82
9 Brooks	95	92	95	92
10 Pickle	94	92	98	98
11 Poage	92	84	92	84
12 Wright	86	88	87	89
13 Hightower	94	94	94	95
14 Young	48	67	48	67
15 de la Garza	89	92	89	92
16 White	92	94	98	98
17 Burleson	95	96	97	98
18 Jordan	96	95	98	98
19 Mahon	94	95	99	99
20 Gonzalez#	95	91	96	95
21 Krueger	38†	55*	85†	92*
22 Gammage	80	81*	87	92*
23 Kazen	86	91	87	93
24 Milford#	62	68	62	70
UTAH				
1 McKay	91	92	98	98
2 Marriott	92	93	98	97
VERMONT				
AL Jeffords	90	90*	97	98*
VIRGINIA				
1 Trible	97	97	97	98
2 Whitehurst	94	93	98	98
3 Satterfield#	95	97	95	97
4 Daniel	99	99	99	99
5 Daniel	96	98	97	98
6 Butler	90	93	91	94
7 Robinson	97	98	99	99
8 Harris	99	99	99	99
9 Wampler	94	92	94	92
10 Fisher	98	98	99	99
WASHINGTON				
1 Pritchard	86	87	97	98
2 Meeds	76	84	87	92
3 Bonker	83	84	96	98
4 McCormack	90	90	92	93
5 Foley#	94	94	96	97
6 Dicks	93	92	94	95
7 Cunningham	95	89*	98	99*
WEST VIRGINIA				
1 Mollohan	92	93	99	99
2 Staggers	96	89	97	91
3 Slack	89	91	90	92
4 Rahall	85	89	99	99
WISCONSIN				
1 Aspin	91	89	91	89
2 Kastenmeier	99	98	99	99
3 Baldus	96	93	99	96
4 Zablocki	99	98	99	99
5 Reuss	93	94	99	99
6 Steiger	87	90	97	98
7 Obey	95	94	95	94
8 Cornell	99	99	100	100
9 Kasten	53	72	79	88
WYOMING				
AL Roncalio	70	76	80	86

Democrats ***Republicans***

Voting Support for Carter Remained Low During 1978 For Democratic President

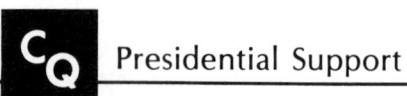

President Carter's congressional support in 1978 showed a slight improvement, but still lagged behind the success record a president usually enjoys when his own party controls Capitol Hill.

The Democratic dominated Congress supported Carter on 78.3 percent of the votes on which he indicated a clear position. That was a small rise from the 75.4 percent success rate he posted in 1977, when relations between the newcomer from Georgia, who had run against Washington, and Congress got off to a poor start. *(1977 presidential support study, 1977 Almanac p. 21-B)*

For the second year, Carter's performance in Congress fell in the middle range. Since 1953, the highest support score was 93 percent, received by Lyndon B. Johnson in 1965, and the lowest was 50.6 percent, by Richard M. Nixon in 1973.

Congressional Quarterly selected the votes using the same method it has employed every year since 1953, when it started analyzing presidential support. *(Ground rules, box, p. 24-C)*

By mid-1978, the administration had acquired a measure of sophistication in dealing with Congress and was able to rack up several significant legislative victories — passage of an energy bill by both houses, revisions in the Civil Service system, approval of a Panama Canal agreement. Carter even got the House to sustain his veto of the sacrosanct water projects bill, which he deemed inflationary.

But the White House still suffered its share of defeats, especially at the beginning of the year.

Carter Support Below Predecessors'

Carter's rating paled in comparison with those of his two Democratic predecessors during their second years in office. John F. Kennedy had an 85.4 percent score in 1962 and Johnson 93 percent in 1965. Republican Dwight D. Eisenhower, who had a GOP Congress in 1954, got his way with legislation on 82.8 percent of the votes that year.

In fact, Carter's tally was only a little better than the second-year record of Nixon, a Republican who had a 77 percent success rating from a Democratic Congress in 1970.

To be sure, Carter generally did better than Gerald R. Ford. He also outpaced Eisenhower's record from 1955 onward, when the Democrats made a comeback in Congress, and was significantly better than the performance of the post-Watergate Nixon.

The Carter support score was based on 151 votes in the Senate and 112 in the House. His position was defeated in the Senate 23 times and in the House 34 times.

He appeared to have greater support in the Senate, which backed him with 84.8 percent, than in the House where his victory level was 69.4 percent. However the difference reflects the large number of Senate votes taken on proposed changes in the Panama Canal treaties. The Senate support figure was inflated by the 55 votes taken on this single issue, which pro-treaty forces — and President Carter — won each time.

Administration lobbyists and supporters in the Senate beat down virtually all the amendments that would have revised the treaties and probably required renegotiation with Panama — an event that many observers feared would kill the long-sought transfer of the canal to that nation.

Carter's Defeats

Carter suffered losses on a broad range of issues, encompassing such areas as economic policy and federal public works. One of his most significant defeats in early 1978 was the House's surprise rejection of the proposed consumer protection agency.

Several of the president's defeats concerned legislation he later ended up vetoing. The House, for instance, tacked on money to the weapons procurement bill for a fifth nuclear aircraft carrier, over Carter's opposition. Terming the carrier unnecessary, he vetoed the entire procurement measure.

Carter also vetoed a bill limiting his authority to allow generally cheaper foreign beef into the country — legislation he failed to stop on the floor. The long list of water projects passed over strenuous White House objections drew a veto as well.

Among the first presidential losses in the Senate were two out of three votes that sought to couple waterway user

Success Rates

Following are the annual percentages of presidential victories since 1953 on congressional votes where the Presidents took clear-cut positions:

Eisenhower	
1953	89.0%
1954	82.8
1955	75.0
1956	70.0
1957	68.0
1958	76.0
1959	52.0
1960	65.0
Kennedy	
1961	81.0%
1962	85.4
1963	87.1
Johnson	
1964	88.0%
1965	93.0
1966	79.0
1967	79.0
1968	75.0
Nixon	
1969	74.0%
1970	77.0
1971	75.0
1972	66.0
1973	50.6
1974	59.6
Ford	
1974	58.2%
1975	61.0
1976	53.8
Carter	
1977	75.4%
1978	78.3

fees, which Carter favored, with water project authorizations, which he did not.

In addition, Congress went against Carter by ignoring his objections to limiting veterans preference for government jobs and authorizing sugar import quotas to keep up domestic prices for the commodity. It brushed aside his desire to curb special tax benefits for business.

Party Differences

As usual, the president attracted more support from his own party than from the opposition.

In the Senate, the average Democrat was behind Carter 66 percent of the time, with the GOP supporting him, on the average, only 41 percent of the time. Democrats opposed him just 23 percent of the time, while the Republicans went against him on 46 percent of the votes. (Absentees make up the remainder of the percentage points.)

In the House, Carter was backed by the average Democrat on 60 percent of the votes and by the average Republican on 36 percent. Democrats opposed him 29 percent of the time and Republicans, 53 percent.

Regional Differences

Members from the West and the South were Carter's most consistent opponents, with the bulk of his support coming from the East and the Midwest.

In the 1976 election, Carter did poorly in the West, a problem that he did not help by his effort to revise federal water project policy. The fact that, for the second year, members from the traditionally conservative South gave the southern president little help suggested the president could face additional re-election problems in 1980 if the low support reflects voter discontent in that region.

In the Senate, the average eastern senator supported Carter 77 percent of the time, midwestern senators 70 percent and western senators 66 percent. Southern Democratic senators were in the Carter column on just 53 percent of the votes.

The geographical pattern held true for Republican senators. His support was 64 percent from the East and 44 from the Midwest, yet a mere 29 percent from the West and 28 from the South.

The same regional variations held sway in the House, although Carter's support figures were a bit lower across-the-board.

The president's most diehard opposition, according to the tabulations, came from the South. Southern Democrats in the Senate deserted him 34 percent of the time and in the House 40 percent. Southern Republican senators went against Carter 56 percent of the time and southern House members 63 percent. Indeed, southern opposition to Carter grew in 1978, as compared to the year before.

Individual Support Scores

Carter's biggest supporters among individual senators were Democrats Alan Cranston of California, Paul S. Sarbanes of Maryland, John Glenn of Ohio and Patrick J. Leahy of Vermont — all at 87 percent. Among Republicans, his best backers were Jacob K. Javits of New York (86 percent), Robert T. Stafford of Vermont (81), Charles H. Percy of Illinois (79) and Clifford P. Case of New Jersey (79).

In the House, Carter's chief Democratic allies were clustered in the mid-80's percentile range. The top scorer was Democrat Paul Simon of Illinois (88 percent), followed by Gerry E. Studds of Massachusetts (87). Another consis-

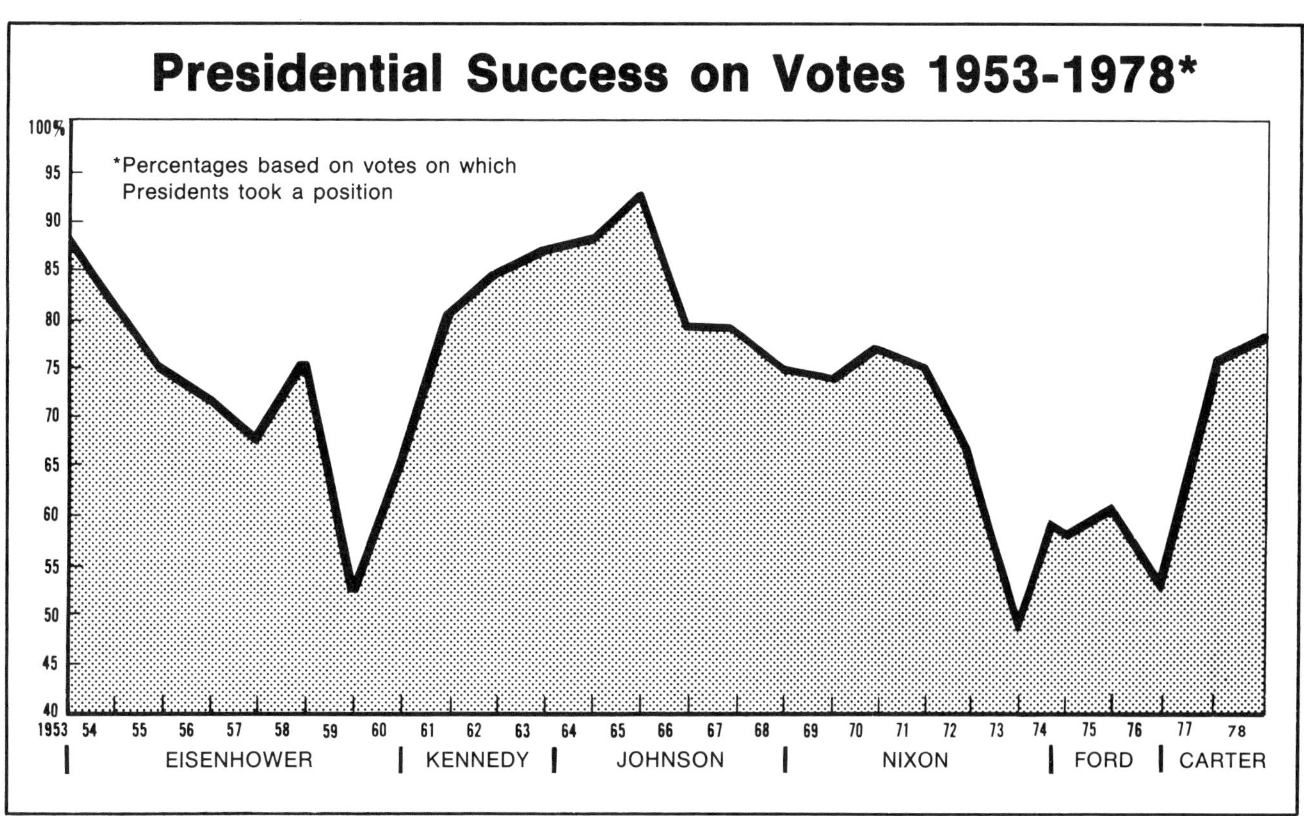

Ground Rules for CQ Presidential Support-Opposition

Presidential Issues—CQ tries to determine what the President personally, as distinct from other administration officials, does and does not want in the way of legislative action by analyzing his messages to Congress, press conference remarks and other public statements and documents.

Borderline Cases—By the time an issue reaches a vote, it may differ from the original form on which the President expressed himself. In such cases, CQ analyzes the measure to determine whether, on balance, the features favored by the President outweigh those he opposed or vice versa. Only then is the vote classified.

Some Votes Excluded—Occasionally, important measures are so extensively amended on the floor that it is impossible to characterize final passage as a victory or defeat for the President.

Procedural Votes—Votes on motions to recommit, to reconsider or to table often are key tests that govern the legislative outcome. Such votes are necessarily included in the presidential support tabulations.

Appropriations—Generally, votes on passage of appropriation bills are not included in the tabulation, since it is rarely possible to determine the President's position on the overall revisions Congress almost invariably makes in the sums allowed. Votes on amendments to cut or increase specific funds requested in the President's budget, however, are included.

Failures to Vote—In tabulating the support or opposition scores of members on the selected presidential-issue votes, CQ counts only "yea" and "nay" votes on the ground that only these affect the outcome. Most failures to vote reflect absences because of illness or official business. Failures to vote lower both support and opposition scores equally.

Weighting—All presidential-issue votes have equal statistical weight in the analysis.

Changed Positions—Presidential support is determined by the position of the President at the time of a vote, even though that position may be different from an earlier position, or may have been reversed after the vote was taken.

tent Democratic backer was John Brademas of Indiana, the majority whip (85). Carter's best Republican supporter in the House was, for the second year in a row, Silvio O. Conte of Massachusetts (80 percent), with second place going to Millicent Fenwick of New Jersey (77).

Individual Opposition Scores

In the Senate, Carter's leading opponents were Republicans Paul Laxalt of Nevada and Jake Garn of Utah (both 82 percent) and Clifford P. Hansen of Wyoming (79). Among Democratic senators, the biggest anti-Carter voter was James O. Eastland of Mississippi (54 percent), with Edward Zorinsky of Nebraska (53) and Dennis DeConcini of Arizona (48) coming next.

Independent Harry F. Byrd Jr. of Virginia, who caucuses with the Democrats, opposed the president on 68 percent of the votes.

In the House, the leading Carter opponents were Republicans Robert E. Bauman of Maryland and James M. Collins of Texas, who voted against his positions 79 percent of the time. Leading the list of Democrats against Carter was David E. Satterfield III of Virginia (78 percent), followed by Dan Daniel of the same state (75 percent).

State Rankings

By state, Carter's highest Senate support in 1978 came from eastern and midwestern states. Another characteristic of these states was that their two senators were liberals, whether Democratic or Republican. Backing on the average was most consistent from Ohio, 85 percent; Vermont, 84; Iowa, 82; New Jersey, 82; Rhode Island, 82; New York, 81; and Illinois, 80.

Opposition was centered in the Senate in states with conservative senators who mostly were Republican: Utah, 78 percent; Virginia, 70; Wyoming, 70; Nevada, 63; Nebraska, 61; and New Mexico, 60.

House delegations with two or more members that averaged the most faithful support of the president were: Wisconsin, 71 percent; Hawaii, 69; Massachusetts, 66; Iowa, 63; New Jersey, 63; New York, 62; and Rhode Island,62.

Opposition in the House ran the highest in: Idaho, 70 percent; Virginia, 60; Oklahoma, 55; Louisiana, 54; Mississippi, 54; South Dakota, 54; and Utah, 54.

New Approach to Hill

Both Carter's legislative program and his public esteem, as measured in the polls, were faring so badly in the beginning of 1978 that he called a conclave of his staff at Camp David on April 16-17. Out of that grew a new effort to coordinate activities better and focus on which of the many items on the agenda deserved the strongest emphasis.

The White House congressional liaison effort was bolstered by the addition of three lobbyists to its force of four, as well as by an augmented support staff. Several of the new lobbyists had Hill experience, which helped close the breach that had developed between many in Congress and the administration.

Average Scores

Following are composites of Democratic and Republican scores for 1978 and 1977:

	1978		1977	
	Dem.	Rep.	Dem.	Rep.
		SUPPORT		
Senate	66%	41%	70%	52%
House	60	36	63	42
		OPPOSITION		
Senate	23	46	21	38
House	29	53	28	50

1978 Presidential Position Votes

Following is a list of all Senate and House recorded votes in 1978 on which President Carter took a position. The votes, listed by CQ vote number, appear in the vote charts beginning on p. 2-S.

Senate Votes (151)

Presidential Victories (128) — 24, 25, 26, 30, 34, 35, 36, 37, 38, 39, 40, 41, 42, 43, 44, 45, 46, 47, 48, 49, 50, 51, 52, 53, 54, 55, 56, 57, 58, 63, 64, 65, 66, 67, 68, 73, 74, 75, 76, 77, 79, 80, 81, 82, 83, 86, 87, 88, 89, 90, 91, 92, 93, 94, 95, 96, 97, 98, 116, 119, 120, 125, 127, 141, 142, 143, 144, 156, 157, 161, 169, 196, 197, 204, 207, 212, 214, 215, 223, 240, 254, 267, 305, 307, 313, 314, 320, 346, 347, 361, 363, 374, 378, 381, 385, 386, 388, 389, 390, 404, 407, 416, 418, 420, 421, 422, 432, 433, 435, 436, 437, 438, 446, 451, 455, 457, 462, 463, 472, 475, 476, 480, 482, 491, 501, 508, 511, 512

Presidential Defeats (23) — 85, 149, 151, 153, 170, 180, 185, 224, 264, 319, 380, 406, 419, 427, 449, 453, 458, 459, 470, 479, 484, 485, 515.

House Votes (112)

Presidential Victories (78) — 11, 12, 36, 42, 43, 57, 58, 61, 78, 120, 135, 141, 160, 176, 180, 181, 182, 183, 210, 216, 278, 285, 286, 290, 297, 318, 371, 466, 469, 519, 532, 548, 549, 550, 555, 559, 560, 563, 564, 565, 566, 587, 601, 609, 612, 613, 614, 615, 620, 634, 639, 642, 643, 646, 647, 648, 654, 662, 676, 687, 719, 723, 746, 751, 760, 766, 771, 774, 783, 786, 792, 794, 799, 805, 824, 826, 827.

Presidential Defeats (34) — 41, 88, 156, 315, 317, 338, 377, 400, 448, 474, 480, 556, 561, 567, 569, 575, 600, 611, 640, 653, 657, 658, 675, 720, 755, 784, 785, 791, 798, 801, 802, 817, 831, 833.

Regional Averages

SUPPORT

Regional presidential support scores for 1978; scores for 1977 are in parentheses:

	East		West		South		Midwest	
DEMOCRATS								
Senate	77%	(77)	66%	(69)	53%	(64)	70%	(71)
House	66	(69)	62	(66)	47	(53)	68	(69)
REPUBLICANS								
Senate	64	(63)	29	(46)	28	(44)	44	(55)
House	45	(51)	29	(35)	28	(36)	37	(42)

OPPOSITION

Regional presidential opposition scores for 1978; scores for 1977 are in parentheses:

	East		West		South		Midwest	
DEMOCRATS								
Senate	14%	(17)	22%	(19)	34%	(26)	17%	(20)
House	24	(21)	24	(25)	40	(38)	23	(23)
REPUBLICANS								
Senate	26	(28)	59	(45)	56	(44)	43	(35)
House	45	(40)	55	(54)	63	(57)	51	(50)

High Scorers - Support

Highest individual scorers in presidential support — those who voted for the president's position most often in 1978:

SENATE

Democrats		Republicans	
Cranston (Calif.)	87%	Javits (N.Y.)	86%
Sarbanes (Md.)	87	Stafford (Vt.)	81
Glenn (Ohio)	87	Percy (Ill.)	79
Leahy (Vt.)	87	Case (N.J.)	79
Culver (Iowa)	85	Chafee (R.I.)	78
Williams (N.J.)	85	Danforth (Mo.)	74
Pell (R.I.)	85	Heinz (Pa.)	71
Nelson (Wis.)	85		

HOUSE

Democrats		Republicans	
Simon (Ill.)	88%	Conte (Mass.)	80%
Studds (Mass.)	87	Fenwick (N.J.)	77
Hamilton (Ind.)	86	Green (N.Y.)	74
Brodhead (Mich.)	86	Whalen (Ohio)	73
Kastenmeier (Wis.)	86	Steers (Md.)	72
Obey (Wis.)	86	McCloskey (Calif.)	71
Brademas (Ind.)	85	Marks (Pa.)	71
Fisher (Va.)	85	Pritchard (Wash.)	64
Reuss (Wis.)	85		

High Scorers - Opposition

Highest individual scorers in Carter opposition — those who voted most often against the president's position in 1978:

SENATE

Democrats		Republicans	
Byrd (Va.)*	68%	Laxalt (Nev.)	82%
Eastland (Miss.)	54	Garn (Utah)	82
Zorinsky (Neb.)	53	Hansen (Wyo.)	79
DeConcini (Ariz.)	48	Hatch (Utah)	75
Nunn (Ga.)	46	Scott (Va.)	72
Stennis (Miss.)	46	Schmitt (N.M.)	70
Cannon (Nev.)	44	Curtis (Neb.)	69
Ford (Ky.)	42	Helms (N.C.)	68

** Elected as an independent, but caucuses with Democrats*

HOUSE

Democrats		Republicans	
Satterfield (Va.)	78%	Bauman (Md.)	79%
Daniel, D. (Va.)	75	Collins (Tex.)	79
McDonald (Ga.)	72	Holt (Md.)	77
Stump (Ariz.)	65	Daniel, R. (Va.)	77
Montgomery (Miss.)	65	Kelly (Fla.)	76
Hall (Texas)	64	Robinson (Va.)	76
Burleson (Texas)	64	Taylor (Mo.)	74

Presidential Support and Opposition: House

1. **Carter Support Score, 1978.** Percentage of 112 Carter-issue recorded votes in 1978 on which representative voted "yea" or "nay *in agreement* with the President's position. Failures to vote lower both Support and Opposition scores.

2. **Carter Opposition Score, 1978.** Percentage of 112 Carter-issue recorded votes in 1978 on which representative voted "yea" or "nay" *in disagreement* with the President's position. Failures to votes lower both Support and Opposition scores.

3. **Carter Support Score, 95th Congress.** Percentage of 191 Carter-issue roll calls in 1977 and 1978 on which representative voted "yea" or "nay" *in agreement* with the President's position. Failures to vote lower both Support and Opposition scores.

4. **Carter Opposition Score, 95th Congress.** Percentage of 191 Carter-issue roll calls in 1977 and 1978 on which representative voted "yea" or "nay" *in disagreement* with the President's position. Failures to vote lower both Support and Opposition scores.

- KEY -

† Not eligible for all recorded votes in 1978.
* Not eligible for all recorded votes in 95th Congress.

	1	2	3	4
ALABAMA				
1 Edwards	38	61	39	54
2 Dickinson	21	62	26	59
3 Nichols	32	59	37	53
4 Bevill	45	52	49	48
5 Flippo	44	52	43	37
6 Buchanan	43	52	50	47
7 Flowers	34	28	46	29
ALASKA				
AL Young	13	44	24	41
ARIZONA				
1 Rhodes	32	49	36	48
2 Udall	71	15	72	16
3 Stump	20	65	24	63
4 Rudd	13	61	21	62
ARKANSAS				
1 Alexander	57	26	58	29
2 Tucker	47	21	55	23
3 Hammerschmidt	25	71	30	65
4 Thornton	41	23	49	27
CALIFORNIA				
1 Johnson	68	31	64	28
2 Clausen	33	63	37	57
3 Moss	55	10	56	15
4 Leggett	60	17	61	19
5 Burton, J.	63	21	65	20
6 Burton, P.	71	17	72	16
7 Miller	48	12	57	16
8 Dellums	76	17	75	20
9 Stark	75	13	71	17
10 Edwards	79	14	81	15
11 Ryan	64	27	66	23
12 McCloskey	71	20	66	21
13 Mineta	81	19	80	19
14 McFall	70	21	71	24
15 Sisk	28	25	40	26
16 Panetta	68	28	68	28
17 Krebs	71	29	71	28
18 Ketchum [1]	23†	74†	28*	61*
19 Lagomarsino	32	68	36	64
20 Goldwater	29	60	30	57
21 Corman	80	16	78	15
22 Moorhead	29	65	29	65
23 Beilenson	76	12	72	16
24 Waxman	75	14	74	17
25 Roybal	77	21	75	20
26 Rousselot	22	73	23	71
27 Dornan	26	63	28	62
28 Burke	22	09	36	15
29 Hawkins	63	15	61	16
30 Danielson	77	17	75	20
31 Wilson, C.H.	29	32	39	30
32 Anderson	63	36	63	35
33 Clawson	18	51	20	57
34 Hannaford	64	31	67	30
35 Lloyd	62†	36†	63*	34*
36 Brown	76	13	73	14
37 Pettis	28	36	31	39
38 Patterson	76	17	70	18
39 Wiggins	29	32	34	36
40 Badham	19	55	24	56
41 Wilson, B.	35	57	38	51
42 Van Deerlin	72	17	68	20
43 Burgener	33	59	34	57
COLORADO				
1 Schroeder	68	27	66	30
2 Wirth	71	21	71	22
3 Evans	58	21	66	20
4 Johnson	36	52	38	50

	1	2	3	4
5 Armstrong	15	47	21	53
CONNECTICUT				
1 Cotter	66	21	62	18
2 Dodd	71	23	72	20
3 Giaimo	70	18	71	15
4 McKinney	60	27	53	20
5 Sarasin	28	20	37	27
6 Moffett	71	20	75	19
DELAWARE				
AL Evans	39	57	46	50
FLORIDA				
1 Sikes	38	42	42	41
2 Fuqua	41	42	45	39
3 Bennett	48	52	53	47
4 Chappell	25	52	30	49
5 Kelly	23	76	27	71
6 Young	31	68	37	60
7 Gibbons	56	20	60	21
8 Ireland	39	44	49	38
9 Frey	13	38	23	39
10 Bafalis	29	70	34*	64*
11 Rogers	70	26	68	28
12 Burke	28	47	30	51
13 Lehman	63	13	68	15
14 Pepper	67	17	65	18
15 Fascell	78	13	78	15
GEORGIA				
1 Ginn	53	46	58	40
2 Mathis	31	45	39	42
3 Brinkley	43	54	48	48
4 Levitas	58	41	61	39
5 Fowler	70	25	71*	25*
6 Flynt	26	50	30	55
7 McDonald	14	72	18	73
8 Evans	44	46	49	41
9 Jenkins	44	34	47	34
10 Barnard	40	46	45	42
HAWAII				
1 Heftel	69	28	69	26
2 Akaka	70	27	69	25
IDAHO				
1 Symms	13	71	17	69
2 Hansen, G.	13	69	18	70
ILLINOIS				
1 Metcalfe [2]	63†	14†	60*	14*
2 Murphy	64	26	66	25
3 Russo	57	37	60	32
4 Derwinski	47	50	46	52
5 Fary	66	21	70	22
6 Hyde	43	54	45	53
7 Collins	54	14	57	17
8 Rostenkowski	71	21	71	20
9 Yates	81	16	79	18
10 Mikva	61	10	65	13
11 Annunzio	68	26	71	25
12 Crane	09	60	15	62
13 McClory	46	50	46	50
14 Erlenborn	43	46	42	49
15 Corcoran	38	54	39	56
16 Anderson	54	24	53	28
17 O'Brien	41	53	43*	51*
18 Michel	42	56	43	51
19 Railsback	51	38	51	37
20 Findley	61	31	54	39
21 Madigan	44	44	48	43
22 Shipley	24	09	34	20
23 Price	74	24	67	25
24 Simon	88	07	82	14
INDIANA				
1 Benjamin	62	38	61	39
2 Fithian	64	33	63	30
3 Brademas	85	13	82	13
4 Quayle	43	47	39	50
5 Hillis	33	52	40	48
6 Evans	45	52	48	46
7 Myers, J.	29	67	31	63
8 Cornwell	56	25	61	24
9 Hamilton	86	14	80	18
10 Sharp	80	20	77	23
11 Jacobs	62	31	61	35
IOWA				
1 Leach	56	43	54*	46*
2 Blouin	73	16	73	20
3 Grassley	30	70	32	68
4 Smith	71	27	67	27
5 Harkin	69	28	65	28
6 Bedell	79	20	73*	21*

Democrats ***Republicans***

1. Rep. William M. Ketchum (R Calif.) died June 24, 1978.
2. Rep. Ralph H. Metcalfe (D Ill.) died Oct. 10, 1978.
3. Rep. Goodloe E. Byron (D Md.) died Oct. 11, 1978.
4. Rep. Thomas P. O'Neill Jr. (D Mass.), as Speaker, votes at his own discretion.
5. Rep. S. William Green (R N.Y.) sworn in Feb. 21, 1978 to succeed Edward I. Koch (D) who resigned Dec. 31, 1977.
6. Rep. Robert Garcia (D N.Y.) sworn in Feb. 21, 1978 to succeed Herman Badillo (D) who resigned Dec. 31, 1977.
7. Rep. Clifford Allen (D Tenn.) died June 18, 1978.

	1	2	3	4
KANSAS				
1 Sebelius	33	59	33	56
2 Keys	70	24	72	24
3 Winn	34	56	38	52
4 Glickman	65	34	65	34
5 Skubitz	37	45	39	47
KENTUCKY				
1 Hubbard	46	49	49	47
2 Natcher	66	34	65	35
3 Mazzoli	66	26	68	25
4 Snyder	28	69	32	63
5 Carter	38	57	42	52
6 Breckinridge	52	30	55	32
7 Perkins	69	28	71	26
LOUISIANA				
1 Livingston	30	67	32*	65*
2 Boggs	64	32	61	32
3 Treen	30	61	32	61
4 Waggonner	31	61	29	63
5 Huckaby	28	52	36	52
6 Moore	31	69	35	65
7 Breaux	25	54	31	50
8 Long	59	34	59	34
MAINE				
1 Emery	43	49	50	45
2 Cohen	39	37	51	34
MARYLAND				
1 Bauman	20	79	23	76
2 Long	62	36	65	32
3 Mikulski	78	21	77	21
4 Holt	21	77	25	69
5 Spellman	67	22	72	22
6 Byron [3]	39†	48†	45*	44*
7 Mitchell	72	18	72	19
8 Steers	72	27	68	27
MASSACHUSETTS				
1 Conte	80	20	77	23
2 Boland	70	16	66	17
3 Early	69	29	67	26
4 Drinan	74	22	74	24
5 Tsongas	37	08	54	11
6 Harrington	46	07	55	11
7 Markey	79	18	77	20
8 O'Neill [4]				
9 Moakley	74	21	73	22
10 Heckler	58	26	60	27
11 Burke	54	29	52	24
12 Studds	87	13	83	17
MICHIGAN				
1 Conyers	49	11	53	16
2 Pursell	58	35	54	38
3 Brown	41	50	42	51
4 Stockman	35	53	38	47
5 Sawyer	38	50	41	43
6 Carr	75	23	74	25
7 Kildee	75	25	74	26
8 Traxler	66	25	62	26
9 Vander Jagt	32	57	36	51
10 Cederberg	40	56	39	53
11 Ruppe	40	31	39	34
12 Bonior	79	15	79	18
13 Diggs	42	08	48	10
14 Nedzi	76	19	77	20
15 Ford	69	15	66	14
16 Dingell	63	25	66	24
17 Brodhead	86	13	83	16
18 Blanchard	80	17	79	19
19 Broomfield	36	50	42	48
MINNESOTA				
1 Quie	19	21	31	28
2 Hagedorn	22	62	30	60
3 Frenzel	52	43	49	40
4 Vento	76	17	78	18
5 Fraser	54	8	62	10
6 Nolan	70	21	71	18
7 Stangeland	27	70	31*	63*
8 Oberstar	75	25	74	26
MISSISSIPPI				
1 Whitten	40	48	42	48
2 Bowen	38	61	41	54
3 Montgomery	30	65	31	61
4 Cochran	13	30	19	45
5 Lott	29	66	30	65
MISSOURI				
1 Clay	70	13	63	13
2 Young	54	43	60	37
3 Gephardt	74	26	73	27
4 Skelton	48	41	54	38
5 Bolling	74	8	71	10
6 Coleman	32	65	37	61
7 Taylor	26	74	27	71
8 Ichord	30	62	33	58
9 Volkmer	59	40	62	36
10 Burlison	73	24	75	21
MONTANA				
1 Baucus	52	26	58	27
2 Marlenee	25	65	29	62
NEBRASKA				
1 Thone	21	39	30	45
2 Cavanaugh	71	25	73	23
3 Smith	29	59	35	58
NEVADA				
AL Santini	46	45	46	39
NEW HAMPSHIRE				
1 D'Amours	61	37	65	34
2 Cleveland	31	58	35	54
NEW JERSEY				
1 Florio	66	29	62	26
2 Hughes	71	27	68	29
3 Howard	71	13	75	12
4 Thompson	72	13	72	13
5 Fenwick	77	21	72	27
6 Forsythe	42	50	42	44
7 Maguire	74	18	73	19
8 Roe	63	31	54	26
9 Hollenbeck	56	29	57	31
10 Rodino	31	07	50	13
11 Minish	70	27	71	25
12 Rinaldo	55	40	59	38
13 Meyner	75	20	73	20
14 LeFante	47	15	57	17
15 Patten	79	20	78	20
NEW MEXICO				
1 Lujan	18	53	25	52
2 Runnels	24	52	26	53
NEW YORK				
1 Pike	63	29	65	28
2 Downey	76	20	77	18
3 Ambro	62	37	68	30
4 Lent	41	55	43	49
5 Wydler	34	58	36	54
6 Wolff	61	34	62	29
7 Addabbo	68	25	67	23
8 Rosenthal	76	16	75	16
9 Delaney	63	24	70	20
10 Biaggi	57	31	61	27
11 Scheuer	73	20	76	18
12 Chisholm	74	18	71	19
13 Solarz	79	13	80	14
14 Richmond	63	14	68	15
15 Zeferetti	46	34	54	27
16 Holtzman	77	22	75	24
17 Murphy	57	24	57	20
18 Green [5]	74†	25†	74*	25*
19 Rangel	79	12	75	17
20 Weiss	79	17	77	19
21 Garcia [6]	66†	15†	66*	15*
22 Bingham	80	14	82	14
23 Caputo	28	31	40	34
24 Ottinger	79	18	78	19
25 Fish	50	41	50	39
26 Gilman	54	46	58	41
27 McHugh	84	15	79	17
28 Stratton	54	39	58	36
29 Pattison	81	14	80	16
30 McEwen	34	58	36	50
31 Mitchell	45	49	49	46
32 Hanley	67	27	70	25
33 Walsh	33	57	39	51
34 Horton	49	43	51	40
35 Conable	51	32	48	38
36 LaFalce	81	13	77	16
37 Nowak	78	21	75	24
38 Kemp	33	53	34	54
39 Lundine	73	18	71	21
NORTH CAROLINA				
1 Jones	42	48	49	42
2 Fountain	41	54	47	50
3 Whitley	38	52	47	46
4 Andrews	58	35	59	35
5 Neal	66	31	66	29
6 Preyer	75	21	75	21
7 Rose	63	33	62	27
8 Hefner	56	44	59	40
9 Martin	35	60	39	57
10 Broyhill	34	63	38	58
11 Gudger	46	47	54	42
NORTH DAKOTA				
AL Andrews	35	60	38	55
OHIO				
1 Gradison	48	48	47	45
2 Luken	45	46	51	39
3 Whalen	73	8	71	12
4 Guyer	32	55	35	55
5 Latta	29	66	31	62
6 Harsha	29	67	35	58
7 Brown	34	50	36	52
8 Kindness	22	69	27	66
9 Ashley	79	12	79	12
10 Miller	31	68	33	66
11 Stanton	49	47	53	45
12 Devine	24	71	27	69
13 Pease	79	17	76	20
14 Seiberling	82	14	81	14
15 Wylie	47	48	51	47
16 Regula	46	54	49	51
17 Ashbrook	16	73	21	70
18 Applegate	46	46	54	40
19 Carney	56	26	59	24
20 Oakar	60	28	62	30
21 Stokes	76	15	76	17
22 Vanik	79	18	72	18
23 Mottl	36	51	44	46
OKLAHOMA				
1 Jones	52	46	47	50
2 Risenhoover	22	48	30	48
3 Watkins	34	62	37	58
4 Steed	47	44	50	41
5 Edwards	22	71	25	71
6 English	35	63	35	64
OREGON				
1 AuCoin	59	27	59	29
2 Ullman	64	24	69	21
3 Duncan	56	29	57	31
4 Weaver	65	23	66	24
PENNSYLVANIA				
1 Myers, M.	67	29	66	27
2 Nix	57	13	65	16
3 Lederer	71	27	69	26
4 Eilberg	62	24	65	25
5 Schulze	24	64	35	57
6 Yatron	51	45	54	40
7 Edgar	76	21	75	19
8 Kostmayer	74	26	75	25
9 Shuster	22	73	29	68
10 McDade	42	41	51	37
11 Flood	65	23	65	27
12 Murtha	59	40	62	36
13 Coughlin	51	45	52	43
14 Moorhead	82	13	80	16
15 Rooney	69	23	67	26
16 Walker	29	71	32	65
17 Ertel	51	48	59	40
18 Walgren	70	24	69	24
19 Goodling, W.	36	54	38	53
20 Gaydos	57	40	62	34
21 Dent	26	23	24	18
22 Murphy	47	51	57	41
23 Ammerman	42	15	57	18
24 Marks	71	29	69	28
25 Myers, G.	46	52	51	47
RHODE ISLAND				
1 St Germain	65	25	62	21
2 Beard	59	33	62	31
SOUTH CAROLINA				
1 Davis	42	54	48	47
2 Spence	30	68	33	65
3 Derrick	56	33	57	32
4 Mann	58	30	52	36
5 Holland	53	32	48	29
6 Jenrette	51	35	54	32
SOUTH DAKOTA				
1 Pressler	29	46	34	47
2 Abdnor	27	61	30	59
TENNESSEE				
1 Quillen	31	54	32	50
2 Duncan	32	66	40	59
3 Lloyd	37	46	46	45
4 Gore	68	28	72	26
5 Allen [7]	69†	17†	62*	30*
6 Beard	28	64	29	60
7 Jones	40	48	50	41
8 Ford	66	17	69	18
TEXAS				
1 Hall	34	64	32	64
2 Wilson, C.	54	35	52	34
3 Collins	19	79	23	75
4 Roberts	30	54	33	55
5 Mattox	65	29	65	31
6 Teague	4	3	4	7
7 Archer	28	69	29	68
8 Eckhardt	76	13	75	15
9 Brooks	54	39	53	38
10 Pickle	54	41	52	42
11 Poage	32	60	28	57
12 Wright	68	22	72	20
13 Hightower	41	53	45	50
14 Young	25	17	35	29
15 de la Garza	36	56	39	56
16 White	35	54	42	51
17 Burleson	30	64	29	66
18 Jordan	79	11	76	16
19 Mahon	58	37	52	43
20 Gonzalez	56	39	53	35
21 Krueger	15	19	27	28
22 Gammage	31	50	32	48
23 Kazen	38	55	39	55
24 Milford	35	30	32	39
UTAH				
1 McKay	47	45	50	40
2 Marriott	27	64	29	62
VERMONT				
AL Jeffords	60	33	63	30
VIRGINIA				
1 Trible	31	66	36	61
2 Whitehurst	34	62	34	59
3 Satterfield	22	78	25	75
4 Daniel	23	77	26	73
5 Daniel	22	75	27	71
6 Butler	31	63	34	63
7 Robinson	23	76	26	73
8 Harris	77	23	77	23
9 Wampler	28	65	31	61
10 Fisher	85	13	81	17
WASHINGTON				
1 Pritchard	64	29	60	31
2 Meeds	64	09	67	15
3 Bonker	71	16	68	19
4 McCormack	55	39	58	35
5 Foley	64	30	67	28
6 Dicks	69	24	68	24
7 Cunningham	23	71	23*	67*
WEST VIRGINIA				
1 Mollohan	56	42	59	38
2 Staggers	65	29	64	25
3 Slack	43	48	48	46
4 Rahall	62	29	64	28
WISCONSIN				
1 Aspin	81	12	76	15
2 Kastenmeier	86	14	82	18
3 Baldus	81	17	75	19
4 Zablocki	73	27	71	29
5 Reuss	85	11	80	16
6 Steiger	49	36	48	38
7 Obey	86	14	81	17
8 Cornell	77	22	76	23
9 Kasten	21	29	30	38
WYOMING				
AL Roncalio	56	20	58	23

Democrats ***Republicans***

	1	2	3	4
ALABAMA				
Allen, M.[1]	22†	29†	22*	29*
Sparkman	68	10	69	13
ALASKA				
Gravel	67	13	66	14
Stevens	28	64	37	54
ARIZONA				
DeConcini	44	48	53	38
Goldwater	14	62	21	54
ARKANSAS				
Bumpers	70	17	69	17
Hodges	74	18	74*	18*
CALIFORNIA				
Cranston	87	13	84	14
Hayakawa	54	36	50	42
COLORADO				
Hart	84	9	80	15
Haskell	43	7	46	12
CONNECTICUT				
Ribicoff	81	9	79	12
Weicker	66	18	64	22
DELAWARE				
Biden	71	17	73	16
Roth	32	62	42	54
FLORIDA				
Chiles	66	30	67	28
Stone	64	32	68	30
GEORGIA				
Nunn	52	46	60	38
Talmadge	51	38	57	35
HAWAII				
Inouye	72	11	71	10
Matsunaga	82	14	82	15
IDAHO				
Church	76	19	73	18
McClure	18	60	27	56
ILLINOIS				
Stevenson	81	14	82	11
Percy	79	11	73	14
INDIANA				
Bayh	74	14	73	16
Lugar	35	64	40	59
IOWA				
Clark	79	9	80	13
Culver	85	7	82	12
KANSAS				
Dole	32	65	40	57
Pearson	63	11	64	15
KENTUCKY				
Ford	49	42	58	33
Huddleston	68	17	70	16
LOUISIANA				
Johnston	34	38	46	33
Long	57	32	58	32
MAINE				
Hathaway	69	7	70	12
Muskie	80	11	79	10
MARYLAND				
Sarbanes	87	12	85	14
Mathias	66	10	65	13
MASSACHUSETTS				
Kennedy	80	12	79	14
Brooke	41	40	53	34
MICHIGAN				
Riegle	74	17	69	20
Griffin	30	46	38	39
MINNESOTA				
Anderson	46	10	58	11
Humphrey, M.[2]	74†	10†	74*	10*
MISSISSIPPI				
Eastland	20	54	35	43
Stennis	31	46	40	40
MISSOURI				
Eagleton	76	13	78	13
Danforth	74	24	69	26
MONTANA				
Melcher	53	40	60	34
Hatfield, P.	54	28	54*	28*
NEBRASKA				
Zorinsky	45	53	53	46
Curtis	15	69	26	62
NEVADA				
Cannon	46	44	54	35
Laxalt	11	82	20	69
NEW HAMPSHIRE				
Durkin	78	18	75	20
McIntyre	59	16	64	16
NEW JERSEY				
Williams	85	11	83	12
Case	79	12	77	15
NEW MEXICO				
Domenici	25	50	37	46
Schmitt	26	70	32*	65*
NEW YORK				
Moynihan	75	16	75	16
Javits	86	9	79	14
NORTH CAROLINA				
Morgan	64	27	61	28
Helms	20	68	28	62
NORTH DAKOTA				
Burdick	54	39	62	34
Young	25	55	36	46
OHIO				
Glenn	87	11	86	13
Metzenbaum	83	16	82	18
OKLAHOMA				
Bartlett	24	62	23	53
Bellmon	44	41	47	41
OREGON				
Hatfield	62	18	64	22
Packwood	53	33	54	34
PENNSYLVANIA				
Heinz	71	24	65	29
Schweiker	36	58	45	50
RHODE ISLAND				
Pell	85	7	82	11
Chafee	78	13	70	18
SOUTH CAROLINA				
Hollings	66	23	66	26
Thurmond	30	61	39	53
SOUTH DAKOTA				
Abourezk	38	9	38	14
McGovern	68	11	65	15
TENNESSEE				
Sasser	63	30	67	27
Baker	53	27	54	30
TEXAS				
Bentsen	60	28	61	29
Tower	15	62	24	59
UTAH				
Garn	15	82	26	70
Hatch	19	75	27	65
VERMONT				
Leahy	87	10	84	13
Stafford	81	11	77	15
VIRGINIA				
Byrd, H.[3]	31	68	41	57
Scott	11	72	21	64
WASHINGTON				
Jackson	80	19	79	21
Magnuson	72	23	73	22
WEST VIRGINIA				
Byrd, R.	82	15	83	15
Randolph	54	35	62	30
WISCONSIN				
Nelson	85	13	81	17
Proxmire	74	26	70	30
WYOMING				
Hansen	19	79	28	69
Wallop	30	61	36	56

Democrats ***Republicans***

- KEY -

† Not eligible for all recorded votes in 1978.

* Not eligible for all recorded votes in 95th Congress.

1. Sen. Maryon P. Allen (D Ala.) sworn in June 12, 1978 succeeding her husband, James B. Allen (D) who died June 1, 1978. His presidential support score for 1978 was 14 percent; opposition was 86 percent. For the 95th Congress his support score was 39 percent; opposition was 61 percent.

2. Sen. Muriel Humphrey (D Minn.) sworn in Feb. 6, 1978 succeeding her husband, Hubert H. Humphrey (D) who died Jan. 13, 1978. He was not eligible for any presidential-issue votes in 1978.

3. Sen. Byrd (Va.) elected as an independent.

Presidential Support and Opposition: Senate

1. Carter Support Score, 1978. Percentage of 151 Carter-issue roll calls in 1978 on which senator voed "yea" or "nay" *in agreement* with the President's position. Failures to vote lower both Support and Opposition scores.

2. Carter Opposition Score, 1978. Percentage of 151 Carter-issue roll calls in 1978 on which senator voted "yea" or "nay" *in disagreement* with the President's position. Failures to vote lower both Support and Opposition scores.

3. Carter Support Score, 95th Congress. Percentage of 239 Carter-issue roll calls in 1977 and 1978 on which senator voted "yea" or "nay" *in agreement* with the President's position. Failures to vote lower both Support and Opposition scores.

4. Carter Opposition Score, 95th Congress. Percentage of 239 Carter-issue roll calls in 1977 and 1978 on which senator voted "yea" or "nay" *in disagreement* with the President's position. Failures to vote lower both Support and Opposition scores.

CQ Party Unity

Party Unity Down in House, Up in Senate

The reputation of members of the House of Representatives as a youthful and increasingly independent group showed up in 1978 as a significant drop in the number of partisan votes.

A majority of House Democrats opposed a majority of House Republicans only 33 percent of the time in 1978. This was substantially lower than in 1977, when party unity voting occurred on 42 percent of all recorded House votes. The figure was the lowest since 1974, when partisan voting in the House dropped to 29 percent.

Partisanship was considerably more evident in the Senate, where party unity votes occurred on 45 percent of the 516 recorded votes. This was slightly higher than the average incidence of partisan voting in the Senate over the previous two years and a 3 percentage point gain over 1977.

Party unity voting occurred in both chambers on 510 of 1,350 recorded votes in 1978, or 38 percent of the time. This was slightly less than the five-year average. The tendency for partisan voting to decline slightly in the second year of a session was also evident in 1978; the two parties split on 42 percent of all recorded votes in 1977.

Democrats in both chambers won substantially more of the partisan votes in 1978 than did Republicans, continuing a trend that began with the 83rd Congress (1953-54), the last time the Republicans had majorities in either chamber.

In votes that split the parties, the average Republican voted with his party 67 percent of the time, slightly more often than the average Democrat, who sided with his party 64 percent of the time.

In the Senate, the typical Democrat stuck with his party 66 percent of the time compared to 59 percent for the average Republican. This was 3 percentage points higher than the 1977 figure of 63 percent for Senate Democrats and 7 percentage points lower than the 1977 figure of 66 percent for Senate Republicans.

In the House, the average Democrat voted with his party 63 percent of the time, down 5 percentage points from 1977, while the typical Republican sided with his party 69 percent of the time, a 2 percentage point drop.

Opposition to Party Increases

Opposition to the party majority among Senate Republicans increased from 22 percent in 1977 to 30 percent in 1978. Opposition among House Republicans was the same in both years — 21 percent.

While Senate Democrats opposed their party 22 percent of the time, House Democrats voted against their party's majority 26 percent of the time.

Overall, Democrats in both chambers had an edge — 25 percent compared to 23 percent for Republicans — in the incidence of voting against their party's majority.

Southern Democrats in the Senate supported their party majority more often in 1978 — 48 percent compared to 41 percent in 1977 — while partisan voting among southern Democrats in the House declined from 51 percent to 46 percent in 1978.

Northern Democrats in the Senate voted with the majority 75 percent of the time and voted in opposition 15 percent of the time. Northern Democrats in the House followed a similar pattern with 71 percent support and 19 percent opposition.

The small band of southern Republicans in the House and Senate were strongly partisan on party unity votes, sticking with their party 72 percent of the time in the Senate and 77 percent of the time in the House.

Northern Republicans opposed their party's majority somewhat more often, with a 56-to-34 percent support-to-opposition ratio in the Senate and 66-to-23 percent ratio in the House.

Definitions

Party Unity Votes. Recorded votes in the Senate and House that split the parties, a majority of voting Democrats opposing a majority of voting Republicans. Votes on which either party divides evenly are excluded.

Party Unity Scores. Percentage of party unity votes on which a member votes "yea" or "nay" *in agreement* with a majority of his party. Failure to vote, even if a member announced his stand, lowers his score.

Opposition-to-Party Scores. Percentage of party unity votes on which a member votes "yea" or "nay" *in disagreement* with a majority of his party. A member's party unity and opposition-to-party scores add up to 100 percent only if he voted on all party unity votes.

Party Unity Scoreboard

The table below shows the proportion of party unity roll calls in 1978, 1977, 1976, 1975, 1974, 1973:

	Total Recorded Votes	Party Unity Recorded Votes	Percent of Total
1978			
Both Chambers	1,350	510	38
Senate	516	233	45
House	834	277	33
1977			
Both Chambers	1,341	567	42
Senate	635	269	42
House	706	298	42
1976			
Both Chambers	1,349	493	37
Senate	688	256	37
House	661	237	36
1975			
Both Chambers	1,214	584	48
Senate	602	288	48
House	612	296	48

	Total Recorded Votes	Party Unity Recorded Votes	Percent of Total
1974			
Both Chambers	1,081	399	37
Senate	544	241	44
House	537	158	29
1973			
Both Chambers	1,135	463	41
Senate	594	237	40
House	541	226	42

Victories, Defeats on Party Unity Votes

	Senate	House	Total
Democrats won, Republicans lost	191	188	379
Republicans won, Democrats lost	42	89	131
Democrats voted unanimously	1	0	1
Republicans voted unanimously	3	1	4

Party Scores

Party unity and opposition-to-party scores below are composites of individual scores and show the percentage of time the average Democrat and Republican voted with his party majority in disagreement with the other party's majority. Failures to vote lower both party unity and opposition-to-party scores. Averages are closer to House figures because individual votes are counted and the House has more members.

	1978		1977	
	DEM.	REP.	DEM.	REP.
Party Unity	64%	67%	67%	70%
Senate	66	59	63	66
House	63	69	68	71
Opposition to Party	25%	23%	24%	21%
Senate	22	30	25	22
House	26	21	24	21

Sectional Support, Opposition

SENATE	Support	Opposition
Northern Democrats	75%	15%
Southern Democrats	48	40
Northern Republicans	56	34
Southern Republicans	72	15

HOUSE	Support	Opposition
Northern Democrats	71%	19%
Southern Democrats	46	41
Northern Republicans	66	23
Southern Republicans	77	14

Individual Scores

Highest party unity scores — those who in 1978 most consistently voted with their party majority against the majority of the other party.

SENATE

Democrats		Republicans	
Sarbanes (Md.)	94%	Hatch (Utah)	93%
Culver (Iowa)	92	Garn (Utah)	90
Clark (Iowa)	91	Hansen (Wyo.)	90
Leahy (Vt.)	90	Lugar (Ind.)	85
Nelson (Wis.)	89	Curtis (Neb.)	84
Cranston (Calif.)	88	Laxalt (Nev.)	84
Matsunaga (Hawaii)	88	Helms (N.C.)	84
Stevenson (Ill.)	88		
Kennedy (Mass.)	88		
Williams (N.J)	88		

HOUSE

Democrats		Republicans	
Brodhead (Mich.)	93%	Collins (Texas)	94%
Brademas (Ind.)	91	Archer (Texas)	94
Kastenmeier (Wis.)	91	Moorhead (Calif.)	93
Mineta (Calif.)	90	Bauman (Md.)	92
Yates (Ill.)	89	Devine (Ohio)	92
Oberstar (Minn.)	89	Kelly (Fla.)	90
		Shuster (Pa.)	90
		Daniel R.W. (Va.)	90

Highest opposition-to-party scores — those who in 1978 most consistently voted against their party majority.

SENATE

Democrats		Republicans	
Byrd (Va.)*	83%	Javits (N.Y.)	84%
Nunn (Ga.)	60	Case (N.J.)	82
Zorinsky (Neb.)	60	Stafford (Vt.)	70
Eastland (Miss.)	52	Chafee (R.I.)	65
Stennis (Miss.)	52	Mathias (Md.)	65
Cannon (Nev.)	50	Heinz (Pa.)	64
		Weicker (Conn.)	64
		Percy (Ill.)	64

**Byrd elected as an Independent.*

HOUSE

Democrats		Republicans	
Satterfield (Va.)	87%	Steers (Md.)	71%
McDonald (Ga.)	82	Whalen (Ohio)	69
Daniel, D. (Va.)	81	Conte (Mass.)	68
Ichord (Mo.)	75	Green (N.Y.)	66†
Stump (Ariz.)	74	Hollenbeck (N.J.)	60
Hall (Texas)	74	Marks (Pa.)	56
Montgomery (Miss.)	73		

† Not eligible for all roll calls in 1978.

Party Unity History

Composite party unity scores showing the percentage of time the average Democrat and Republican voted with his party majority in partisan votes in recent years.

Year	Democrats	Republicans
1978	64%	67%
1977	67	70
1976	65	66
1975	69	70
1974	63	62
1973	68	68

	1	2	3	4
ALABAMA				
Allen [1]	21†	40†	21*	40*
Sparkman	71	14	56	26
ALASKA				
Gravel	70	13	59	25
Stevens	71	20	68	21
ARIZONA				
DeConcini	47	46	51	40
Goldwater	74	4	69	4
ARKANSAS				
Bumpers	69	21	69	19
Hodges	67	26	67	26
CALIFORNIA				
Cranston	88	8	84	9
Hayakawa	62	29	69	16
COLORADO				
Hart	87	8	83	12
Haskell	55	7	63	12
CONNECTICUT				
Ribicoff	79	12	81	9
Weicker	25	64	33	52
DELAWARE				
Biden	67	22	70	18
Roth	82	14	81	14
FLORIDA				
Chiles	63	34	52	45
Stone	59	37	49	46
GEORGIA				
Nunn	36	60	39	56
Talmadge	45	45	41	46
HAWAII				
Inouye	71	8	73	9
Matsunaga	88	7	85	10
IDAHO				
Church	76	17	74	17
McClure	75	6	78	5
ILLINOIS				
Stevenson	88	8	77	14
Percy	23	64	33	54
INDIANA				
Bayh	83	9	83	10
Lugar	85	14	88	11
IOWA				
Clark	91	3	90	5
Culver	92	3	88	5
KANSAS				
Dole	77	19	81	15
Pearson	30	53	42	40
KENTUCKY				
Ford	46	46	48	44
Huddleston	63	21	60*	25*
LOUISIANA				
Johnston	26	45	34	47
Long	52	36	45	41
MAINE				
Hathaway	78	4	79	8
Muskie	84	10	76	11
MARYLAND				
Sarbanes	94	5	93	5
Mathias	17	65	21	62
MASSACHUSETTS				
Kennedy	88	5	86	5
Brooke	39	38	26	59
MICHIGAN				
Riegle	86	5	80	8
Griffin	65	17	61	13
MINNESOTA				
Anderson	47	6	66	6
Humphrey [2]	78†	3†	78*	3*
MISSISSIPPI				
Eastland	17	52	23	53
Stennis	27	52	27	52
MISSOURI				
Eagleton	82	10	77	15
Danforth	41	57	60	37
MONTANA				
Melcher	57	37	55	36
Hatfield, P.	56	22	56*	22*
NEBRASKA				
Zorinsky	39	60	39	58
Curtis	84	2	86	4
NEVADA				
Cannon	45	50	51	43
Laxalt	84	6	84	6
NEW HAMPSHIRE				
Durkin	84	12	81	15
McIntyre	67	13	73	14
NEW JERSEY				
Williams	88	6	87	8
Case	12	82	14	77
NEW MEXICO				
Domenici	60	18	73	13
Schmitt	80	13	84*	9*
NEW YORK				
Moynihan	82	10	80	11
Javits	11	84	17	76
NORTH CAROLINA				
Morgan	50	44	41	43
Helms	84	6	87	6
NORTH DAKOTA				
Burdick	61	31	60	35
Young	69	15	66	15
OHIO				
Glenn	86	12	74	25
Metzenbaum	86	12	87	11
OKLAHOMA				
Bartlett	82	7	78	5
Bellmon	54	35	65	25
OREGON				
Hatfield, M.	21	62	37	47
Packwood	48	45	55	37
PENNSYLVANIA				
Heinz	27	64	37	56
Schweiker	71	25	69	29
RHODE ISLAND				
Pell	84	9	82	12
Chafee	29	65	42	49
SOUTH CAROLINA				
Hollings	61	33	63	31
Thurmond	78	15	79	13
SOUTH DAKOTA				
Abourezk	43	4	48	8
McGovern	76	4	76	5
TENNESSEE				
Sasser	62	29	69	24
Baker	50	33	62	26
TEXAS				
Bentsen	51	39	46	45
Tower	73	3	79	5
UTAH				
Garn	90	4	89	4
Hatch	93	3	90	2
VERMONT				
Leahy	90	7	82	11
Stafford	22	70	27	55
VIRGINIA				
Byrd, H. [3]	16	83	17	82
Scott	82	7	75	8
WASHINGTON				
Jackson	87	13	87	13
Magnuson	79	15	81	13
WEST VIRGINIA				
Byrd, R.	79	19	73	25
Randolph	55	34	54	38
WISCONSIN				
Nelson	89	10	87	11
Proxmire	66	34	74	26
WYOMING				
Hansen	90	6	91	6
Wallop	79	11	82	10

- KEY -

† Not eligible for all recorded votes in 1978

* Not eligible for all recorded votes in 95th Congress.

Democrats ***Republicans***

1. Sen. Maryon P. Allen (D Ala.) sworn in June 12, 1978 to succeed her husband, James B. Allen (D) who died June 1, 1978. His Party Unity score for 1978 was 9 percent; opposition was 91 percent. For the 95th Congress, his Party Unity score was 19 percent; opposition was 79 percent.

2. Sen. Muriel Humphrey (D Minn.) sworn in Feb. 7, 1978 to succeed her husband Hubert H. Humphrey (D) who died Jan. 13, 1978. He was not eligible for any votes in 1978.

3. Sen. Byrd (Va.) elected as an independent.

Party Unity and Party Opposition: Senate

1. **Party Unity, 1978.** Percentage of 233 Senate Party Unity votes in 1978, on which senator voted "yea" or "nay" *in agreement* with a majority of his party. (Party Unity roll calls are those on which a majority of voting Democrats opposed a majority of voting Republicans. Failures to vote lower both Party Unity and Party Opposition scores.)

2. **Party Opposition, 1978.** Percentage of 233 Senate Party Unity votes in 1978 on which senator voted "yea" or "nay" *in disagreement* with a majority of his party.

3. **Party Unity, 95th Congress.** Percentage of 502 Senate Party Unity roll calls in 1977 and 1978 on which senator voted "yea" or "nay" *in agreement* with a majority of his party.

4. **Party Opposition, 95th Congress.** Percentage of 502 Senate Party Unity roll calls in 1977 and 1978 on which senator voted "yea" or "nay" *in disagreement* with a majority of his party.

Party Unity and Party Opposition: House

1. Party Unity, 1978. Percentage of 277 House Party Unity recorded votes in 1978 on which representative voted "yea" or "nay" *in agreement* with a majority of his party. (Party unity roll calls are those on which a majority of voting Democrats opposed a majority of voting Republicans. Failures to vote lower both Party Unity and Party Opposition scores.)

2. Party Opposition, 1978. Percentage of 277 House Party Unity recorded votes in 1978 on which representative voted "yea" or "nay" *in disagreement* with a majority of his party.

3. Party Unity, 95th Congress. Percentage of 575 House Party Unity recorded votes in 1977 and 1978 on which representative voted "yea" or "nay" *in agreement* with the majority of his party.

4. Party Opposition, 95th Congress. Percentage of 575 House Party Unity recorded votes in 1977 and 1978 on which representative voted "yea" or "nay" *in disagreement* with a majority of his party.

1. Rep. William M. Ketchum (R Calif.) died June 24, 1978.
2. Rep. Ralph H. Metcalfe (D Ill.) died Oct. 10, 1978.
3. Rep. Goodloe E. Byron (D Md.) died oct. 11, 1978.
4. Rep. Thomas P. O'Neill Jr. (D Mass.), as Speaker, votes at his own discretion.
5. Rep. S. William Green (R N.Y.) sworn in Feb. 21, 1978 to succeed Edward I. Koch (D) who resigned Dec. 31, 1977.
6. Rep. Robert Garcia (D N.Y.) sworn in Feb. 21, 1978 to succeed Herman Badillo (D) who resigned Dec. 31, 1977.
7. Rep. Clifford Allen (D Tenn.) died June 18, 1978.

- KEY -

† Not eligible for all recorded votes in 1978

* Not eligible for all recorded votes in 95th Congress.

	1	2	3	4
ALABAMA				
1 Edwards	78	20	70	22
2 Dickinson	74	12	74	12
3 Nichols	29	60	30	61
4 Bevill	48	47	48	48
5 Flippo	47	50	42	37
6 Buchanan	53	37	54	40
7 Flowers	32	32	44	36
ALASKA				
AL Young	50	16	55	18
ARIZONA				
1 Rhodes	63	14	67*	16*
2 Udall	81	10	84	8
3 Stump	14	74	15	75
4 Rudd	76	5	84	5
ARKANSAS				
1 Alexander	65	18	67	20
2 Tucker	36	11	59	11
3 Hammerschmidt	83	14	79	16
4 Thornton	34	17	53	20
CALIFORNIA				
1 Johnson	86	14	77	11
2 Clausen	71	18	73	16
3 Moss	62	7	66	7
4 Leggett	64	15	72	12
5 Burton, J.	73	12	73	12
6 Burton, P.	83	6	84	5
7 Miller	65	8	74	9
8 Dellums	83	6	84	8
9 Stark	81	12	83	10
10 Edwards	88	6	90	5
11 Ryan	66	20	72	15
12 McCloskey	36	53	34	54
13 Mineta	90	8	89	6
14 McFall	82	13	85	11
15 Sisk	43	23	51	25
16 Panetta	69	28	68	27
17 Krebs	80	20	82	18
18 Ketchum[1]	83†	12†	80*	11*
19 Lagomarsino	88	12	90	10
20 Goldwater	81	8	79	7
21 Corman	86	6	86	4
22 Moorhead	93	4	93	4
23 Beilenson	81	9	82	8
24 Waxman	80	6	82	5
25 Roybal	88	5	89	5
26 Rousselot	87	5	85	5
27 Dornan	84	10	85	8
28 Burke	34	3	60	3
29 Hawkins	75	3	75	3
30 Danielson	84	7	87	7
31 Wilson, C.H.	39	17	51	18
32 Anderson	75	21	71	24
33 Clawson	68	3	71	3
34 Hannaford	74	19	75	19
35 Lloyd	74	25	75*	23*
36 Brown	74	9	77	6
37 Pettis	56	21	61	21
38 Patterson	84	9	81	8
39 Wiggins	54	21	59	21
40 Badham	75	7	80	7
41 Wilson, B.	67	27	65	24
42 Van Deerlin	79	12	79	11
43 Burgener	77	17	79	14
COLORADO				
1 Schroeder	75	23	75	23
2 Wirth	71	19	74	18
3 Evans	66	16	73	15
4 Johnson	61	28	58	30
5 Armstrong	62	6	76	7
CONNECTICUT				
1 Cotter	66	21	66	17
2 Dodd	80	12	78	10
3 Giaimo	70	18	72	15
4 McKinney	38	52	30	47
5 Sarasin	36	24	46	29
6 Moffett	79	16	80	14
DELAWARE				
AL Evans	74	21	70	24
FLORIDA				
1 Sikes	39	46	38	49
2 Fuqua	49	41	48	42
3 Bennett	42	58	40	60
4 Chappell	30	57	30	57
5 Kelly	90	8	89	7
6 Young	83	14	84	11
7 Gibbons	40	40	47	39
8 Ireland	30	56	36	54
9 Frey	35	5	58	6
10 Bafalis	84†	12†	88*	9*
11 Rogers	66	27	60	35
12 Burke	66	17	73	16
13 Lehman	74	10	79	9
14 Pepper	77	9	74	9
15 Fascell	88	6	89	7
GEORGIA				
1 Ginn	53	46	53	45
2 Mathis	31	48	33	52
3 Brinkley	38	60	40	57
4 Levitas	50	49	49	49
5 Fowler	62	30	62*	32*
6 Flynt	19	59	22	66
7 McDonald	3	82	4	88
8 Evans	40	51	44	47
9 Jenkins	36	44	39	45
10 Barnard	32	57	40	52
HAWAII				
1 Heftel	70	26	75	19
2 Akaka	84	9	87	7
IDAHO				
1 Symms	85	4	86	3
2 Hansen, G.	78	4	84	4
ILLINOIS				
1 Metcalfe[2]	77†	4†	71*	3*
2 Murphy	71	19	73*	19*
3 Russo	49	44	54	38
4 Derwinski	68	31	73	25
5 Fary	75	14	79	14
6 Hyde	75	19	76	20
7 Collins	71	5	75	5
8 Rostenkowski	71	17	73	15
9 Yates	89	10	87	11
10 Mikva	70	9	75	9
11 Annunzio	77	19	78	19
12 Crane	73	4	81	4
13 McClory	69	24	67	24
14 Erlenborn	68	23	69	22
15 Corcoran	79	16	83	13
16 Anderson	38	37	42	38
17 O'Brien	63	26	68*	24*
18 Michel	77	14	76	12
19 Railsback	54	40	50	38
20 Findley	56	39	56	40
21 Madigan	62	26	61	30
22 Shipley	34	10	47	18
23 Price	82	15	77	12
24 Simon	77	10	80	12
INDIANA				
1 Benjamin	72	28	73	27
2 Fithian	60	39	60	34
3 Brademas	91	5	88	4
4 Quayle	80	13	81	11
5 Hillis	71	20	68	22
6 Evans	40	57	41	53
7 Myers, J.	87	11	84	11
8 Cornwell	65	24	68	23
9 Hamilton	74	26	77	22
10 Sharp	71	28	72	27
11 Jacobs	48	47	51	45
IOWA				
1 Leach	68	30	67	30
2 Blouin	75	19	77	20
3 Grassley	88	12	90	10
4 Smith	79	18	78	17
5 Harkin	73	25	72	22
6 Bedell	78†	18†	74*	21*

Democrats ***Republicans***

	1	2	3	4
KANSAS				
1 Sebelius	75	15	76	12
2 Keys	69	27	72	25
3 Winn	71	18	77	15
4 Glickman	54	44	55	43
5 Skubitz	49	27	57	26
KENTUCKY				
1 Hubbard	43	50	45	50
2 Natcher	77	23	73	27
3 Mazzoli	60	34	66	28
4 Snyder	83	14	84	13
5 Carter	57	35	60	33
6 Breckinridge	55	26	59	29
7 Perkins	81	16	82	15
LOUISIANA				
1 Livingston	82	11	82*	11*
2 Boggs	71	25	70	23
3 Treen	78	14	81	14
4 Waggonner	26	65	27	67
5 Huckaby	24	58	29	61
6 Moore	86	14	86	14
7 Breaux	19	67	29	57
8 Long	67	26	69	25
MAINE				
1 Emery	70	26	68	30
2 Cohen	58	27	54	36
MARYLAND				
1 Bauman	92	8	93	7
2 Long	68	28	70	27
3 Mikulski	85	12	87	9
4 Holt	85	11	86	9
5 Spellman	77	14	79	14
6 Byron[3]	37†	54†	38*	56*
7 Mitchell	86	6	87	5
8 Steers	27	71	26	64
MASSACHUSETTS				
1 Conte	32	68	33	65
2 Boland	75	15	78	14
3 Early	68	26	66	25
4 Drinan	82	16	85	13
5 Tsongas	49	6	68	8
6 Harrington	60	8	70	8
7 Markey	83	13	85	12
8 O'Neill[4]				
9 Moakley	81	12	82	11
10 Heckler	41	51	40	53
11 Burke	72	19	67	15
12 Studds	88	12	89	11
MICHIGAN				
1 Conyers	47	6	60	8
2 Pursell	47	40	47*	39*
3 Brown	68	25	69	24
4 Stockman	73	14	74	13
5 Sawyer	66	24	63	25
6 Carr	79	18	81	17
7 Kildee	85	15	84	16
8 Traxler	75	18	72	19
9 Vander Jagt	71	17	70	16
10 Cederberg	71	23	70	22
11 Ruppe	57	20	56	25
12 Bonior	86	10	85	12
13 Diggs	50	5	59	4
14 Nedzi	77	15	79	15
15 Ford	79	5	78	5
16 Dingell	74	18	77	15
17 Brodhead	93	6	91	6
18 Blanchard	85	12	86	12
19 Broomfield	76	16	75	17
MINNESOTA				
1 Quie	36	18	49	26
2 Hagedorn	79	8	83	9
3 Frenzel	67	24	65	26
4 Vento	86	9	88	7
5 Fraser	61	6	72	5
6 Nolan	78	9	81	8
7 Stangeland	86	9	85*	10*
8 Oberstar	89	11	90	9
MISSISSIPPI				
1 Whitten	39	45	40	49
2 Bowen	32	63	39	55
3 Montgomery	23	73	21	72
4 Cochran	45	8	64	13
5 Lott	86	12	86	11
MISSOURI				
1 Clay	84	4	79	3
2 Young	63	33	68	29
3 Gephardt	64	33	70	29
4 Skelton	49	44	52	41
5 Bolling	75	8	74	4
6 Coleman	81	16	81	17
7 Taylor	86	12	89	9
8 Ichord	21	75	20	75
9 Volkmer	54	45	56	42
10 Burlison	84	14	84	14
MONTANA				
1 Baucus	55	23	68	18
2 Marlenee	68	25	68	22
NEBRASKA				
1 Thone	60	10	69	14
2 Cavanaugh	64	29	69	26
3 Smith	82	11	83	12
NEVADA				
AL Santini	42	44	50	40
NEW HAMPSHIRE				
1 D'Amours	58	38	66	30
2 Cleveland	77	18	75	19
NEW JERSEY				
1 Florio	75	22	67	19
2 Hughes	60	38	60	36
3 Howard	81	5	81	5
4 Thompson	83	4	85	3
5 Fenwick	48	51	45	55
6 Forsythe	73	23	63	22
7 Maguire	77	16	79	15
8 Roe	74	22	62	16
9 Hollenbeck	34	60	38	55
10 Rodino	34	3	63	5
11 Minish	70	26	73	22
12 Rinaldo	45	53	45	52
13 Meyner	82	9	85	8
14 LeFante	52	10	68	10
15 Patten	80	13	82	14
NEW MEXICO				
1 Lujan	63	14	69	15
2 Runnels	10	46	15	60
NEW YORK				
1 Pike	53	39	59	35
2 Downey	83	12	83	11
3 Ambro	61	34	65	30
4 Lent	71	23	72	21
5 Wydler	72	21	72	19
6 Wolff	69	22	68	18
7 Addabbo	83	8	84	7
8 Rosenthal	87	4	86	4
9 Delaney	68	26	75	19
10 Biaggi	65	23	66	21
11 Scheuer	83	10	86	8
12 Chisholm	84	6	86	4
13 Solarz	84	9	89	7
14 Richmond	80	4	84	4
15 Zeferetti	57	32	59	29
16 Holtzman	85	12	83	13
17 Murphy	65	16	65	14
18 Green[5]	30†	66†	30*	66*
19 Rangel	84	3	85	3
20 Weiss	87	8	88	8
21 Garcia[6]	78†	6†	78*	6*
22 Bingham	85	6	88	6
23 Caputo	42	27	49	35
24 Ottinger	84	12	87	11
25 Fish	57	37	57	35
26 Gilman	42	53	46	49
27 McHugh	84	13	79	15
28 Stratton	52	43	53*	43*
29 Pattison	79	16	82	14
30 McEwen	72	19	70	19
31 Mitchell	61	33	61	34
32 Hanley	72	25	75	21
33 Walsh	66	26	66	28
34 Horton	48	42	44	47
35 Conable	66	25	67	25
36 LaFalce	71	26	71	25
37 Nowak	81	19	83	16
38 Kemp	79	11	82	10
39 Lundine	83	13	81	11
NORTH CAROLINA				
1 Jones	48	45	49	44
2 Fountain	29	62	34	61
3 Whitley	33	49	40	51
4 Andrews	50	42	50	43
5 Neal	49	45	52	41
6 Preyer	76	19	78	19
7 Rose	68	22	66	21
8 Hefner	51	47	53	44
9 Martin	76	16	81	15
10 Broyhill	80	15	80	15
11 Gudger	45	48	49	47
NORTH DAKOTA				
AL Andrews	69	27	69	25
OHIO				
1 Gradison	74	24	75	22
2 Luken	48	47	53	41
3 Whalen	13	69	13	66
4 Guyer	74	12	76	13
5 Latta	88	8	87	8
6 Harsha	75	21	73	21
7 Brown	73	13	77	12
8 Kindness	84	10	86	10
9 Ashley	71	16	78	13
10 Miller	88	10	89	11
11 Stanton	71	29	68	31
12 Devine	92	6	91	6
13 Pease	76	22	82	17
14 Seiberling	88	9	89	8
15 Wylie	72	23	71	26
16 Regula	77	23	78	22
17 Ashbrook	79	7	84	6
18 Applegate	54	40	61	33
19 Carney	69	14	76	13
20 Oakar	65	20	71	19
21 Stokes	81	4	84	4
22 Vanik	80	16	79	13
23 Mottl	36	57	40	55
OKLAHOMA				
1 Jones	39	59	38	60
2 Risenhoover	30	40	41	43
3 Watkins	30	62	31	65
4 Steed	60	34	60	33
5 Edwards	80	11	85	9
6 English	25	71	28	70
OREGON				
1 AuCoin	57	29	66	24
2 Ullman	71	18	77*	15*
3 Duncan	58	26	64	23
4 Weaver	73	18	78	12
PENNSYLVANIA				
1 Myers, M.	73	16	75	15
2 Nix	54	8	71	8
3 Lederer	78	18	80	16
4 Eilberg	71	13	75	14
5 Schulze	82	8	83	11
6 Yatron	49	47	56	40
7 Edgar	81	16	82	14
8 Kostmayer	69	29	71	27
9 Shuster	90	8	90	9
10 McDade	49	40	48	44
11 Flood	71	13	76	14
12 Murtha	66	33	64	30
13 Coughlin	66	31	64	32
14 Moorhead	87	6	89	7
15 Rooney	79	13	79	15
16 Walker	86	11	86	10
17 Ertel	51	47	54	42
18 Walgren	71	23	73	22
19 Goodling, W.	74	15	77	14
20 Gaydos	64	32	66	30
21 Dent	29	17	23	11
22 Murphy	58	35	64	31
23 Ammerman	59	17	71	16
24 Marks	43	56	46	52
25 Myers, G.	60	39	59	39
RHODE ISLAND				
1 St Germain	74	14	73	15
2 Beard	77	15	78	15
SOUTH CAROLINA				
1 Davis	49	43	51	41
2 Spence	80	18	83	13
3 Derrick	66	27	63	28
4 Mann	43	33	45	39
5 Holland	53	24	49	25
6 Jenrette	58	26	63	26
SOUTH DAKOTA				
1 Pressler	46	31	54	28
2 Abdnor	75	16	79	12
TENNESSEE				
1 Quillen	69	19	68	17
2 Duncan	82	16	82	17
3 Lloyd	36	50	38	55
4 Gore	75	21	76	22
5 Allen[7]	60†	17†	60*	21*
6 Beard	79	10	81	10
7 Jones	48	42	54	37
8 Ford	80	7	83	9
TEXAS				
1 Hall	25	74	26	71
2 Wilson, C.	59	27	62	24
3 Collins	94	4	94	4
4 Roberts	31	52	33	55
5 Mattox	63	34	67	30
6 Teague	5	3	6	6
7 Archer	94	4	95	3
8 Eckhardt	81	6	83	6
9 Brooks	62	34	63	28
10 Pickle	55	42	53	41
11 Poage	31	62	25	59
12 Wright	77	12	79	10
13 Hightower	45	51	47	49
14 Young	33	14	44	25
15 de la Garza	36	52	41	53
16 White	38	54	41	53
17 Burleson	25	71	22	75
18 Jordan	86	10	86	10
19 Mahon	54	40	50	47
20 Gonzalez	73	23	66	25
21 Krueger	21	20	35	27
22 Gammage	22	61	29*	54*
23 Kazen	40	49	42	51
24 Milford	25	45	24	51
UTAH				
1 McKay	55	37	58	34
2 Marriott	86	9	86	9
VERMONT				
AL Jeffords	48	46	45*	49*
VIRGINIA				
1 Trible	81	17	81	17
2 Whitehurst	78	17	76	17
3 Satterfield	9	87	11	87
4 Daniel	90	9	88	11
5 Daniel	16	81	18	81
6 Butler	82	11	82	14
7 Robinson	88	8	90	8
8 Harris	82	18	84	15
9 Wampler	74	20	73	21
10 Fisher	82	17	83	16
WASHINGTON				
1 Pritchard	50	43	49	44
2 Meeds	72	7	81	6
3 Bonker	73	10	76	10
4 McCormack	65	26	70	22
5 Foley	69	25	75	18
6 Dicks	79	16	77	15
7 Cunningham	84	13	78*	11*
WEST VIRGINIA				
1 Mollohan	65	31	67	29
2 Staggers	78	18	74	15
3 Slack	56	33	62	30
4 Rahall	69	16	69	20
WISCONSIN				
1 Aspin	84	10	82	9
2 Kastenmeier	91	9	89	11
3 Baldus	87	10	84	10
4 Zablocki	78	22	79	20
5 Reuss	86	8	87	8
6 Steiger	56	34	59	33
7 Obey	88	9	88	9
8 Cornell	81	18	81	19
9 Kasten	44	11	61	14
WYOMING				
AL Roncalio	66	11	68	14

Democrats ***Republicans***

CQ Conservative Coalition

Conservative Coalition Loses Strength

The conservative congressional coalition of Republicans and southern Democrats lost strength in 1978. The voting alliance showed up in fewer congressional roll call votes in 1978 than in 1977. And the coalition won fewer times when it did form.

Its major loss was on the Panama Canal treaties, although that did not fully explain its lower success rate.

But any conclusion that this decline meant a weakening of the nationwide trend to the right was undercut by the fact that several leading liberal opponents of the coalition lost their re-election bids.

The coalition, as used by Congressional Quarterly in analyzing congressional votes, means a voting alliance of a majority of Republicans and southern Democrats against a majority of northern Democrats.

In 1978, the coalition was successful on only 52 percent of the votes on which it opposed a majority of northern Democrats — a 16 percentage point drop from 1977. And it formed on only 21 percent of the recorded votes, a five percentage point dropoff from the year before. In 1977, the coalition was successful on 68 percent of the votes on which it opposed a majority of northern Democrats, a 10 percentage point jump from 1976.

Conservative coalition support scores of individual members dipped as well. Average Republican support scores were down from 1977, to 61 percent from 72 percent in the Senate, and to 72 percent from 76 percent in the House. Senate northern Democrats voted with the coalition on 21 percent of the roll calls, down from 23 percent in 1977. *(1977 conservative coalition votes, 1977 Almanac p. 15-B)*

One minor factor contributing to the apparent loss of coalition voting strength may have been a dropoff in overall voting participation by members who missed votes because they were campaigning for re-election. *(Voting participation, p. 17-C)*

Definitions

Conservative Coalition. As used in this study, the term "conservative coalition" means a voting alliance of Republicans and southern Democrats against the northern Democrats in Congress. This meaning, rather than any philosophic definition of the "conservative" position, provides the basis for CQ's selection of coalition votes.

Conservative Coalition Vote. Any vote in the Senate or the House on which a majority of voting southern Democrats and a majority of voting Republicans oppose the stand taken by a majority of voting northern Democrats. Votes on which there is an even division within the ranks of voting northern Democrats, southern Democrats or Republicans are not included.

Southern States. The southern states are Alabama, Arkansas, Florida, Georgia, Kentucky, Louisiana, Mississippi, North Carolina, Oklahoma, South Carolina, Tennessee, Texas and Virginia. The other 37 states are grouped as the North in the study.

Conservative Coalition Support Score. Percentage of conservative coalition votes on which a member votes "yea" or "nay" *in agreement* with the position of the conservative coalition. Failures to vote, even if a member announces a stand, lower the score.

Conservative Coalition Opposition Score. Percentage of conservative coalition votes on which a member votes "yea" or "nay" *in disagreement* with the position of the conservative coalition.

Panama Canal, Other Issues

The coalition's biggest defeat was on ratification of the Panama Canal treaties where it lost on 19 votes, virtually every vote on the issue on which the alliance showed up. President Carter had made ratification of the treaties a top priority and administration lobbyists had pressed members hard for "aye" votes.

But even disregarding the block of Panama Canal votes, the voting record still showed a significant decrease in coalition voting strength. Its success rate in the Senate, including the canal votes, was only 46 percent, compared with a 1977 figure of 74 percent. Excluding the canal votes, the coalition still won only 54 percent of the Senate votes, a drop of 20 percentage points compared with the previous year.

The coalition lost three out of five Senate votes on revisions in the criminal code.

However, on labor law reform legislation, target of an intense grass-roots lobbying campaign, the coalition won six out of seven Senate votes, thus sustaining a filibuster of the measure that led to its defeat for the year.

Individual Scores

Half of Senate Republicans voting most often with the coalition were from western states, continuing a trend that showed up in 1977. Orrin G. Hatch, Utah, and Clifford P. Hansen, Wyo., each supported the coalition on 93 percent of the votes, and a second Utah Republican, Jake Garn, had the second highest support score (88 percent) in this group.

The three northern Democrats voting most often with the alliance also represented western or midwestern states: Edward Zorinsky, Neb. (69 percent), Howard W. Cannon, Nev. (62 percent) and Dennis DeConcini, Ariz. (60).

In the House, the western connection was less clear among the coalition's leading supporters. Western Republicans Robert J. Lagomarsino, Calif., and Dan Marriott, Utah, each voted with the alliance 94 percent of the time. This figure placed them below six leading southern Republican supporters of the coalition. But their scores were only four percentage points below top-scoring Republican Robert W. Daniel Jr., Va. (98 percent). Northern House Democrats supporting the coalition were mixed regionally, with only one of the top dozen from a western state (Gunn McKay of Utah, 57 percent support).

Five members who had been leading opponents of the conservative alliance lost at the polls. In three out of the five cases, liberal voting records of the losers were considered a major element in their defeat. Sens. Floyd K. Haskell, D-Colo., Dick Clark, D-Iowa, and Clifford P. Case, R-N.J., all failed to defeat conservative opponents. Case had been second only to Massachusetts Republican Edward W. Brooke in 1977 in his opposition to the conservative coalition in the Senate. Clark had the highest opposition score in the Senate in 1978 (93 percent). And Haskell had drawn attention in 1977 for a dramatically increased conservative support score, attributed to his tough re-election fight.

Two other leading coalition opponents, Brooke and Rep. Newton I. Steers Jr., R-Md., also lost in 1978, but to liberal opponents.

The highest opposition score, for the House and for the entire Congress, was that of Michigan Democrat William M. Brodhead, who voted against the alliance 98 percent of the time.

Texas Rep. Bob Eckhardt opposed the coalition 82 percent of the time, more often than any other southern Democrat in the House.

In the Senate, the Republican voting most often against the coalition was Jacob K. Javits, N.Y. (84 percent), and the southern Democrat with the highest opposition rating was John Sparkman, Ala. (57 percent).

Senate Majority Leader Robert C. Byrd, W. Va., was among the seven northern Democrats voting most often with the conservative alliance. But his 40 percent support score was 15 percentage points below his 1977 score.

Coalition Appearances, 1961-78

Following is the percentage of the recorded votes for both houses of Congress on which the coalition appeared:

1961	28%	1970	22%
1962	14	1971	30
1963	17	1972	27
1964	15	1973	23
1965	24	1974	24
1966	25	1975	28
1967	20	1976	24
1968	24	1977	26
1969	27	1978	21

Coalition Victories, 1961-78

	Total	Senate	House
1961	55%	48%	74%
1962	62	71	44
1963	50	44	67
1964	51	47	67
1965	33	39	25
1966	45	51	32
1967	63	54	73
1968	73	80	63
1969	68	67	71
1970	66	64	70
1971	83	86	79
1972	69	63	79
1973	61	54	67
1974	59	54	67
1975	50	48	52
1976	58	58	59
1977	68	74	60
1978	52	46	57

Average Scores

Following are the composite conservative coalition support and opposition scores for 1978 (scores for 1977 are in parentheses):

	Southern Democrats	Republicans	Northern Democrats
Coalition Support			
Senate	62% (64)	61% (72)	21% (23)
House	59 (63)	72 (76)	23 (23)
Coalition Opposition			
Senate	26% (21)	28% (18)	68% (67)
House	28 (29)	19 (17)	66 (69)

Regional Scores

The parties' coalition support and opposition scores, by region, for 1978 (scores for 1977 are in parentheses):

SUPPORT

	East	West	South	Midwest
Democrats				
Senate	17% (19)	29% (30)	62% (64)	18% (21)
House	22 (21)	23 (23)	59 (63)	24 (25)
Republicans				
Senate	33% (43)	72% (84)	75% (85)	63% (76)
House	59 (62)	74 (79)	84 (88)	72 (77)

OPPOSITION

	East	West	South	Midwest
Democrats				
Senate	74% (74)	59% (59)	26% (21)	69% (69)
House	68 (70)	63 (69)	28 (29)	67 (68)
Republicans				
Senate	57% (46)	17% (7)	11% (5)	25% (12)
House	34 (31)	13 (11)	7 (7)	18 (16)

Individual Scores

SUPPORT

Highest Coalition Support Scores. Those who voted with the conservative coalition most consistently in 1978:

SENATE

Southern Democrats		Republicans	
Byrd (Va.)*	92%	Hatch (Utah)	93%
Nunn (Ga.)	83	Hansen (Wyo.)	93
Talmadge (Ga.)	75	Garn (Utah)	88
Bentsen (Texas)	70	Bartlett (Okla.)	85
Johnston (La.)	68	Thurmond (S.C.)	85
Eastland (Miss.)	68	Dole (Kan.)	83

* *Byrd elected as an independent.*

Northern Democrats

Zorinsky (Neb.)	69%
Cannon (Nev.)	62
DeConcini (Ariz.)	60
Randolph (W.Va.)	47
Melcher (Mont.)	44
Burdick (N.D.)	41
Byrd (W.Va.)	40

HOUSE

Southern Democrats		Republicans	
Daniel (Va.)	95%	Daniel (Va.)	98%
Hall (Texas)	94	Lott (Miss.)	96
Satterfield (Va.)	95	Taylor (Mo.)	96
Montgomery (Miss.)	91	Moore (La.)	95
English (Okla.)	90	Bauman (Md.)	95
Burleson (Texas)	90	Robinson (Va.)	95
Waggonner (La.)	88	Lagomarsino (Calif.)	94
Fountain (N.C.)	88	Marriott (Utah)	94
Bowen (Miss.)	87		

Northern Democrats

Ichord (Mo.)	88%
Stump (Ariz.)	82
Byron (Md.)	74†
Evans (Ind.)	67
Ertel (Pa.)	62
Skelton (Mo.)	60
Mottl (Ohio)	58
Runnels (N.M.)	57
Applegate (Ohio)	57
Yatron (Pa.)	57
McKay (Utah)	57
Slack (W.Va.)	57

† Byron not eligible for all votes in 1978.

OPPOSITION

Highest Coalition Opposition Scores. Those who voted against the conservative coalition most consistently in 1978:

SENATE

Southern Democrats		Republicans	
Sparkman (Ala.)	51%	Javits (N.Y.)	84%
Bumpers (Ark.)	42	Case (N.J.)	78
Hodges (Ark.)	40	Mathias (Md.)	69
Sasser (Tenn.)	38	Chafee (R.I.)	65
		Weicker (Conn.)	63
		Stafford (Vt.)	62

Northern Democrats

Clark (Iowa)	93%
Culver (Iowa)	92
Sarbanes (Md.)	91
Kennedy (Mass.)	88
Cranston (Calif.)	87
Metzenbaum (Ohio)	84
Leahy (Vt.)	84
Nelson (Wis.)	84

1978 Coalition Votes

Following is a list of all 1978 Senate and House votes on which the conservative coalition appeared. The votes are listed by CQ vote number and may be found in the roll-call vote charts beginning on p. 2-H.

SENATE VOTES (120)

Coalition Victories (55) — 4, 5, 6, 71, 84, 85, 145 148, 149, 150, 158, 161, 162, 163, 165, 166, 167, 168, 169, 174, 179, 183, 187, 190, 191, 222, 224, 225, 240, 247, 256, 263, 266, 270, 287, 290, 291, 292, 294, 295, 315, 357, 380, 387, 412, 419, 444, 445, 450, 453, 461, 467, 471, 488, 490.

Coalition Defeats (65) — 12, 13, 16, 34, 39, 42, 43, 46, 48, 51, 53, 68, 75, 83, 86, 91, 93, 95, 96, 106, 108, 115, 122, 124, 129, 134, 137, 139, 164, 170, 186, 199, 209, 212, 242, 244, 251, 252, 253, 288, 305, 334, 337, 345, 348, 349, 350, 366, 367, 385, 390, 391, 394, 400, 409, 410, 423, 433, 435, 436, 442, 446, 448, 480, 512.

HOUSE VOTES (164)

Coalition Victories (93) — 17, 19, 26, 32, 41, 63, 73, 88, 101, 102, 132, 142, 175, 215, 221, 224, 242, 246, 247, 263, 265, 282, 288, 301, 302, 313, 315, 317, 330, 331, 332, 345, 367, 376, 377, 378, 383, 384, 389, 391, 393, 411, 412, 448, 461, 474, 480, 493, 505, 522, 525, 534, 540, 548, 550, 552, 554, 556, 557, 563, 572, 575, 576, 578, 581, 582, 584, 591, 592, 593, 594, 596, 598, 600, 611, 623, 638, 640, 652, 647, 679, 680, 699, 727, 738, 750, 755, 777, 784, 791, 801, 813, 820.

Coalition Defeats (71) — 11, 18, 22, 23, 28, 38, 60, 62, 108, 109, 110, 123, 129, 133, 160, 193, 208, 219, 231, 249, 254, 258, 260, 266, 267, 271, 297, 324, 333, 342, 371, 385, 390, 407, 413, 417, 445, 468, 470, 519, 549, 555, 559, 560, 566, 586, 590, 595, 609, 613, 614, 617, 618, 619, 620, 621, 626, 642, 646, 647, 653, 661, 706, 707, 744, 774, 778, 786, 787, 799, 800.

HOUSE

Southern Democrats		Republicans	
Eckhardt (Texas)	82%	Steers (Md.)	78%
Fascell (Fla.)	80	Green (N.Y.)	77†
Harris (Va.)	80	Conte (Mass.)	71
Fisher (Va.)	78	Hollenbeck (N.J.)	65
Jordan (Texas)	74	Whalen (Ohio)	65
Pepper (Fla.)	70	Fenwick (N.J.)	62
Lehman (Fla.)	69	McCloskey (Calif.)	57
Ford (Tenn.)	67	McKinney (Conn.)	57
		Heckler (Mass.)	57

† Green not eligible for all votes in 1978.

Northern Democrats

Brodhead (Mich.)	98%
Seiberling (Ohio)	95
Yates (Ill.)	93
Markey (Mass.)	93
Studds (Mass.)	93
Ottinger (N.Y.)	93
Kastenmeier (Wis.)	93
Holtzman (N.Y.)	93

	1	2	3	4
ALABAMA				
Allen [1]	52†	13†	52*	13*
Sparkman	33	51	50	31
ALASKA				
Gravel	23	61	40	45
Stevens	68	21	74	17
ARIZONA				
DeConcini	60	33	54	37
Goldwater	75	8	73	5
ARKANSAS				
Bumpers	46	42	34	55
Hodges	49	40	49*	40*
CALIFORNIA				
Cranston	11	87	16	79
Hayakawa	68	23	76	10
COLORADO				
Hart	20	76	20	74
Haskell	9	49	18	59
CONNECTICUT				
Ribicoff	16	75	11	82
Weicker	28	63	42	46
DELAWARE				
Biden	28	68	19	73
Roth	80	15	84	11
FLORIDA				
Chiles	61	37	73	24
Stone	62	35	69	26
GEORGIA				
Nunn	83	13	81	14
Talmadge	75	18	72	14
HAWAII				
Inouye	15	61	17	65
Matsunaga	13	80	21	75
IDAHO				
Church	31	59	25	66
McClure	72	10	79	6
ILLINOIS				
Stevenson	13	83	23	70
Percy	30	58	41	46
INDIANA				
Bayh	14	78	9	86
Lugar	80	20	89	10
IOWA				
Clark	3	93	3	93
Culver	6	92	3	92
KANSAS				
Dole	83	14	87	10
Pearson	38	46	55	29
KENTUCKY				
Ford	65	28	68	24
Huddleston	47	37	50*	35*
LOUISIANA				
Johnston	68	8	75	10
Long	58	28	66	19
MAINE				
Hathaway	2	75	7	79
Muskie	13	78	13	73
MARYLAND				
Sarbanes	6	91	5	93
Mathias	16	69	25	64
MASSACHUSETTS				
Kennedy	5	88	3	88
Brooke	26	48	17	67
MICHIGAN				
Riegle	8	82	6	83
Griffin	58	18	59	12
MINNESOTA				
Anderson	8	38	7	67
Humphrey [2]	7†	69†	7*	69*
MISSISSIPPI				
Eastland	68	8	72	7
Stennis	65	12	69	7
MISSOURI				
Eagleton	20	69	32	61
Danforth	62	37	75	23
MONTANA				
Melcher	44	53	49	44
Hatfield, P.	28	52	—	—
NEBRASKA				
Zorinsky	69	29	73	25
Curtis	78	5	87	3
NEVADA				
Cannon	62	30	60	32
Laxalt	76	10	83	06
NEW HAMPSHIRE				
Durkin	20	77	21	75
McIntyre	13	63	17	67
NEW JERSEY				
Williams	8	83	10	85
Case	12	78	12	77
NEW MEXICO				
Domenici	66	14	80	7
Schmitt	77	16	86	9
NEW YORK				
Moynihan	18	70	19	72
Javits	11	84	16	77
NORTH CAROLINA				
Morgan	63	29	59	23
Helms	82	05	89	3
NORTH DAKOTA				
Burdick	41	50	55	41
Young	77	5	76	5
OHIO				
Glenn	18	83	43	57
Metzenbaum	13	84	9	89
OKLAHOMA				
Bartlett	85	3	81	2
Bellmon	58	30	72	18
OREGON				
Hatfield, M.	31	51	49	38
Packwood	50	44	64	30
PENNSYLVANIA				
Heinz	36	56	45	48
Schweiker	65	28	73	24
RHODE ISLAND				
Pell	9	83	11	83
Chafee	29	65	49	43
SOUTH CAROLINA				
Hollings	58	35	47	47
Thurmond	85	08	88	4
SOUTH DAKOTA				
Abourezk	4	45	9	54
McGovern	11	68	6	76
TENNESSEE				
Sasser	52	38	38	55
Baker	64	21	75	15
TEXAS				
Bentsen	70	22	75	18
Tower	70	3	85	2
UTAH				
Garn	88	7	90	4
Hatch	93	3	92	2
VERMONT				
Leahy	13	84	16	79
Stafford	29	62	29	43
VIRGINIA				
Byrd, H. [3]	92	8	95	5
Scott	83	8	77	5
WASHINGTON				
Jackson	30	69	22	77
Magnuson	34	63	24	72
WEST VIRGINIA				
Byrd, R.	40	58	49	50
Randolph	47	43	57	36
WISCONSIN				
Nelson	14	84	11	85
Proxmire	38	63	25	75
WYOMING				
Hansen	93	3	95	2
Wallop	80	10	88	6

- KEY -

† Not eligible for all recorded votes in 1978.
* Not eligible for all recorded votes in 95th Congress.

Democrats ***Republicans***

1. Sen. Maryon P. Allen (D Ala.) sworn in June 12, 1978 succeeding her husband James B. Allen (D) who died June 1, 1978. His conservative coalition support score for 1978 was 95 percent; opposition was 5 percent. For the 95th Congress his support score was 94 percent; opposition was 6 percent.

2. Sen. Muriel Humphrey (D Minn.) sworn in Feb. 7, 1978 succeeding her husband Hubert H. Humphrey (D) who died Jan. 13, 1978. He was not eligible for any votes in 1978.

3. Sen. Byrd (Va.) elected as an independent.

Conservative Coalition Support and Opposition: Senate

1. Conservative Coalition Support, 1978. Percentage of 120 conservative coalition votes in 1978 on which senator voted "yea" or "nay" *in agreement* with the position of the conservative coalition. Failures to vote lower both Support and Opposition scores.

2. Conservative Coalition Opposition, 1978. Percentage of 120 conservative coalition votes in 1978 on which senator voted "yea" or "nay" *in disagreement* with the position of the conservative coalition. Failures to vote lower both Support and Opposition scores.

3. Conservative Coalition Support, 95th Congress. Percentage of 307 conservative coalition roll calls in 1977 and 1978 on which senator voted "yea" or "nay" *in agreement* with the position of the conservative coalition. Failures to vote lower both Support and Opposition scores.

4. Conservative Coalition Opposition, 95th Congress. Percentage of 307 conservative coalition roll calls in 1977 and 1978 on which senator voted "yea" or "nay" *in disagreement* with the position of the conservative coalition. Failures to vote lower both Support and Opposition scores.

Conservative Coalition Support and Opposition: House

1. Conservative Coalition Support, 1978. Percentage of 164 conservative coalition recorded votes in 1978 on which representative voted "yea" or "nay" *in agreement* with the position of the conservative coalition. Failures to vote lower both Support and Opposition scores.

2. Conservative Coalition Opposition, 1978. Percentage of 164 conservative coalition recorded votes in 1978 on which representative voted "yea" or "nay" *in disagreement* with the position of the conservative coalition. Failures to vote lower both Support and Opposition scores.

3. Conservative Coalition Support, 95th Congress. Percentage of 320 conservative coalition recorded votes in 1977 and 1978 on which representative voted "yea" or "nay" *in agreement* with the position of the conservative coalition. Failures to vote lower both Support and Opposition scores.

4. Conservative Coalition Opposition, 95th Congress. Percentage of 320 conservative coalition recorded votes in 1977 and 1978 on which representative voted "yea" or "nay" *in disagreement* with the position of the conservative coalition. Failures to vote lower both Support and Opposition scores.

- KEY -

† Not eligible for all recorded votes in 1978.
* Not eligible for all recorded votes in 95th Congress.

	1	2	3	4
ALABAMA				
1 Edwards	88	10	84	9
2 Dickinson	84	5	83	5
3 Nichols	84	5	86	6
4 Bevill	77	19	76	19
5 Flippo	80	15	63	15
6 Buchanan	61	30	60	34
7 Flowers	44	11	57	16
ALASKA				
AL Young	58	8	65	9
ARIZONA				
1 Rhodes	62	10	69	10
2 Udall	14	80	12	83
3 Stump	82	4	87	3
4 Rudd	82	2	89	1
ARKANSAS				
1 Alexander	33	51	41	47
2 Tucker	16	36	22	50
3 Hammerschmidt	93	4	91	5
4 Thornton	34	26	43	34
CALIFORNIA				
1 Johnson	27	73	25	65
2 Clausen	77	15	79	10
3 Moss	9	59	11	61
4 Leggett	25	58	21	67
5 Burton, J.	7	79	7	82
6 Burton, P.	4	82	3	85
7 Miller	4	67	6	74
8 Dellums	5	86	5	88
9 Stark	4	87	4	88
10 Edwards	4	88	4	92
11 Ryan	27	63	21	69
12 McCloskey	35	57	33	56
13 Mineta	9	89	8	87
14 McFall	24	74	23	75
15 Sisk	35	24	43	28
16 Panetta	31	64	33	62
17 Krebs	26	74	27	73
18 Ketchum [1]	91†	4†	85*	5*
19 Lagomarsino	94	6	94	6
20 Goldwater	85	4	86	4
21 Corman	12	80	8	83
22 Moorhead	92	4	92	5
23 Beilenson	5	80	4	85
24 Waxman	5	78	4	84
25 Roybal	7	90	8	88
26 Rousselot	87	4	89	3
27 Dornan	84	10	86	8
28 Burke	1	41	2	63
29 Hawkins	7	74	7	72
30 Danielson	14	79	17	78
31 Wilson, C.H.	26	29	31	35
32 Anderson	26	71	28	68
33 Clawson	70	2	71	3
34 Hannaford	30	66	29	68
35 Lloyd	40	60	38*	60*
36 Brown	7	79	7	78
37 Pettis	58	22	69	18
38 Patterson	15	81	13	79
39 Wiggins	62	13	63	13
40 Badham	82	4	86	3
41 Wilson, B.	76	18	76	15
42 Van Deerlin	13	79	14	76
43 Burgener	84	10	83	7
COLORADO				
1 Schroeder	19	81	19	81
2 Wirth	20	71	19	73
3 Evans	29	55	26	63
4 Johnson	60	28	61	27
5 Armstrong	60	7	75	6
CONNECTICUT				
1 Cotter	28	61	27	60
2 Dodd	13	82	14	76
3 Giaimo	26	62	23	65
4 McKinney	34	57	28	47
5 Sarasin	39	22	52	26
6 Moffett	13	81	12	83
DELAWARE				
AL Evans	78	18	74	20
FLORIDA				
1 Sikes	74	13	77	11
2 Fuqua	70	20	71	18
3 Bennett	79	21	75	25
4 Chappell	77	12	80	10
5 Kelly	93	5	93	4
6 Young	92	7	88	6
7 Gibbons	49	32	47	40
8 Ireland	74	12	73	17
9 Frey	41	2	61	4
10 Bafalis	92	7	93*	4*
11 Rogers	45	50	53	43
12 Burke	74	11	78	11
13 Lehman	13	69	12	75
14 Pepper	18	70	20	65
15 Fascell	14	80	14	83
GEORGIA				
1 Ginn	82	18	79	18
2 Mathis	63	10	71	10
3 Brinkley	82	15	83	14
4 Levitas	62	35	66	32
5 Fowler	43	48	47*	46*
6 Flynt	74	5	85	3
7 McDonald	80	1	88	2
8 Evans	70	24	72	21
9 Jenkins	59	12	68	12
10 Barnard	77	12	78	14
HAWAII				
1 Heftel	44	52	38	56
2 Akaka	24	70	21	73
IDAHO				
1 Symms	85	1	88	1
2 Hansen, G.	77	3	85	2
ILLINOIS				
1 Metcalfe [2]	6†	77†	6*	70*
2 Murphy	30	62	31	60
3 Russo	51	41	47	44
4 Derwinski	73	26	77	22
5 Fary	26	65	28	66
6 Hyde	73	20	77	18
7 Collins	7	64	8	69
8 Rostenkowski	26	63	26	62
9 Yates	7	93	8	91
10 Mikva	7	73	6	78
11 Annunzio	34	62	35	61
12 Crane	79	2	84	3
13 McClory	69	24	70	23
14 Erlenborn	66	26	70	23
15 Corcoran	77	16	85	11
16 Anderson	38	43	42	41
17 O'Brien	67	22	75*	18*
18 Michel	80	12	81	8
19 Railsback	57	37	54	36
20 Findley	59	38	57	39
21 Madigan	68	20	68	23
22 Shipley	20	24	32	33
23 Price	24	74	21	66
24 Simon	12	73	14	76
INDIANA				
1 Benjamin	34	66	32	67
2 Fithian	52	46	48	47
3 Brademas	8	90	6	88
4 Quayle	79	13	81	12
5 Hillis	75	15	76	14
6 Evans	67	28	63	30
7 Myers, J.	90	7	90	5
8 Cornwell	33	61	33	59
9 Hamilton	33	67	33	66
10 Sharp	29	71	31	69
11 Jacobs	51	45	46	51
IOWA				
1 Leach	67	30	66	32
2 Blouin	20	74	22	74
3 Grassley	93	7	92	8
4 Smith	33	65	31	64
5 Harkin	24	73	24	70
6 Bedell	17†	79†	24*	69*

Democrats ***Republicans***

1. Rep. William M. Ketchum (R Calif.) died June 24, 1978.
2. Rep. Ralph H. Metcalfe (D Ill.) died Oct. 10, 1978.
3. Rep. Goodloe E. Byron (D Md.) died Oct. 11, 1978.
4. Rep. Thomas P. O'Neill Jr. (D Mass.) as Speaker, votes at his own discretion.
5. Rep. S. William Green (R N.Y.) sworn in Feb. 21, 1978, succeeding Edward I. Koch (D) who resigned Dec. 31, 1977.
6. Rep. Robert Garcia (D N.Y.) sworn in Feb. 21, 1978, succeeding Herman Badillo (D) who resigned Dec. 31, 1977.
7. Rep. Clifford Allen (D Tenn.) died June 18, 1978.

	1	2	3	4
KANSAS				
1 Sebelius	81	8	82	7
2 Keys	27	69	28	69
3 Winn	79	14	84	11
4 Glickman	52	46	51	47
5 Skubitz	60	20	68	16
KENTUCKY				
1 Hubbard	78	18	79	18
2 Natcher	43	57	52	48
3 Mazzoli	41	55	39	56
4 Snyder	90	7	90	6
5 Carter	66	26	72	21
6 Breckinridge	41	39	47	39
7 Perkins	35	62	35	61
LOUISIANA				
1 Livingston	88	5	88*	5*
2 Boggs	42	54	41	50
3 Treen	85	7	88	6
4 Waggonner	88	5	89	5
5 Huckaby	74	10	85	6
6 Moore	95	5	96	4
7 Breaux	80	5	78	9
8 Long	46	48	46	48
MAINE				
1 Emery	71	27	70	27
2 Cohen	59	24	54	34
MARYLAND				
1 Bauman	95	5	94	5
2 Long	38	60	37	61
3 Mikulski	9	91	11	88
4 Holt	90	7	91	5
5 Spellman	18	73	19	74
6 Byron [3]	74†	20†	76*	18*
7 Mitchell	5	88	4	89
8 Steers	20	78	22	68
MASSACHUSETTS				
1 Conte	29	71	30	67
2 Boland	18	74	20	71
3 Early	18	78	18	75
4 Drinan	9	88	10	88
5 Tsongas	4	46	6	66
6 Harrington	4	62	3	75
7 Markey	3	93	7	91
8 O'Neill [4]				
9 Moakley	10	84	11	83
10 Heckler	34	57	36	57
11 Burke	23	62	22	54
12 Studds	7	93	8	91
MICHIGAN				
1 Conyers	4	48	5	62
2 Pursell	46	41	48	40
3 Brown	71	21	71	21
4 Stockman	70	15	69	15
5 Sawyer	71	18	67	20
6 Carr	10	87	12	86
7 Kildee	9	91	11	89
8 Traxler	26	68	29	63
9 Vander Jagt	78	13	74	13
10 Cederberg	74	23	76	17
11 Ruppe	57	23	59	26
12 Bonior	7	86	8	87
13 Diggs	5	55	6	61
14 Nedzi	22	70	23	71
15 Ford	10	76	11	73
16 Dingell	27	63	25	64
17 Brodhead	2	98	3	96
18 Blanchard	15	82	16	82
19 Broomfield	74	14	76	16
MINNESOTA				
1 Quie	39	9	52	19
2 Hagedorn	84	5	87	5
3 Frenzel	71	21	68	24
4 Vento	7	89	6	91
5 Fraser	4	65	4	74
6 Nolan	9	75	7	78
7 Stangeland	90	6	89*	6*
8 Oberstar	15	85	13	87
MISSISSIPPI				
1 Whitten	73	13	79	12
2 Bowen	87	9	85	10
3 Montgomery	91	6	90	5
4 Cochran	47	5	70	5
5 Lott	96	3	95	3
MISSOURI				
1 Clay	4	82	3	78
2 Young	46	48	47	48
3 Gephardt	40	55	38	59
4 Skelton	60	27	63	27
5 Bolling	12	70	8	70
6 Coleman	90	9	88	11
7 Taylor	96	4	95	3
8 Ichord	88	9	87	9
9 Volkmer	55	43	52	47
10 Burlison	26	70	29	68
MONTANA				
1 Baucus	29	51	27	60
2 Marlenee	77	20	77	17
NEBRASKA				
1 Thone	66	6	77	8
2 Cavanaugh	29	63	27	68
3 Smith	88	6	90	7
NEVADA				
AL Santini	52	31	52	36
NEW HAMPSHIRE				
1 D'Amours	43	54	39	58
2 Cleveland	80	16	76	18
NEW JERSEY				
1 Florio	29	68	23	64
2 Hughes	41	55	42	54
3 Howard	10	77	9	79
4 Thompson	8	80	6	84
5 Fenwick	37	62	33	66
6 Forsythe	63	32	56	28
7 Maguire	7	82	6	86
8 Roe	30	66	22	56
9 Hollenbeck	28	65	36	57
10 Rodino	2	33	3	61
11 Minish	30	66	28	65
12 Rinaldo	41	56	44	53
13 Meyner	7	83	8	84
14 LeFante	13	40	15	57
15 Patten	20	75	23	74
NEW MEXICO				
1 Lujan	66	12	72	12
2 Runnels	57	3	72	4
NEW YORK				
1 Pike	46	49	45	51
2 Downey	11	84	10	85
3 Ambro	41	55	37	59
4 Lent	70	27	74	21
5 Wydler	71	23	69	23
6 Wolff	30	61	23	64
7 Addabbo	13	79	11	80
8 Rosenthal	4	87	3	88
9 Delaney	34	56	30	64
10 Biaggi	30	56	29	59
11 Scheuer	8	86	6	89
12 Chisholm	5	82	3	86
13 Solarz	5	88	4	92
14 Richmond	2	80	2	85
15 Zeferetti	48	42	43	44
16 Holtzman	4	92	4	93
17 Murphy	23	58	24	56
18 Green [5]	16†	77†	16*	77*
19 Rangel	5	80	3	84
20 Weiss	4	90	3	93
21 Garcia [6]	5†	77†	5*	77*
22 Bingham	4	87	4	91
23 Caputo	38	26	43	36
24 Ottinger	4	93	4	94
25 Fish	55	38	57	36
26 Gilman	41	54	47	49
27 McHugh	12	87	16	77
28 Stratton	51	45	56*	40*
29 Pattison	12	84	13	82
30 McEwen	80	15	79	12
31 Mitchell	70	26	73	23
32 Hanley	36	61	38	59
33 Walsh	76	16	78	15
34 Horton	57	34	55	37
35 Conable	66	24	68	24
36 LaFalce	25	71	28	67
37 Nowak	19	80	18	81
38 Kemp	83	9	84	8
39 Lundine	14	82	14	78
NORTH CAROLINA				
1 Jones	77	18	76	18
2 Fountain	88	5	88	7
3 Whitley	80	9	81	13
4 Andrews	66	25	69	25
5 Neal	66	28	61	33
6 Preyer	39	58	39	57
7 Rose	40	52	41	48
8 Hefner	77	19	73	22
9 Martin	80	9	85	9
10 Broyhill	84	9	86	8
11 Gudger	70	20	75	19
NORTH DAKOTA				
AL Andrews	79	18	80	15
OHIO				
1 Gradison	73	24	76	21
2 Luken	54	41	52	43
3 Whalen	10	65	11	66
4 Guyer	78	9	82	8
5 Latta	93	5	91	5
6 Harsha	83	13	83	13
7 Brown	74	13	78	12
8 Kindness	90	5	88	6
9 Ashley	21	65	21	70
10 Miller	86	12	87	12
11 Stanton	74	26	73	26
12 Devine	93	6	92	5
13 Pease	20	77	19	80
14 Seiberling	4	95	4	94
15 Wylie	70	26	69	28
16 Regula	82	18	85	15
17 Ashbrook	81	4	84	5
18 Applegate	57	37	51	44
19 Carney	25	59	25	63
20 Oakar	21	62	23	66
21 Stokes	4	84	4	88
22 Vanik	10	87	11	83
23 Mottl	58	37	56	40
OKLAHOMA				
1 Jones	82	15	83	15
2 Risenhoover	61	10	67	18
3 Watkins	85	9	87	8
4 Steed	59	37	59	35
5 Edwards	86	6	90	5
6 English	90	7	91	8
OREGON				
1 AuCoin	31	52	27	60
2 Ullman	33	55	32*	59*
3 Duncan	43	43	40	50
4 Weaver	18	74	13	76
PENNSYLVANIA				
1 Myers, M.	26	66	25	67
2 Nix	13	51	14	66
3 Lederer	29	70	27	70
4 Eilberg	18	65	22	68
5 Schulze	82	9	85	9
6 Yatron	57	38	56	39
7 Edgar	7	90	8	90
8 Kostmayer	18	80	19	80
9 Shuster	91	7	93	6
10 McDade	50	37	53	37
11 Flood	26	62	29	61
12 Murtha	55	43	55	41
13 Coughlin	68	29	65	33
14 Moorhead	14	81	14	81
15 Rooney	20	74	28	68
16 Walker	85	12	86	11
17 Ertel	62	34	56	40
18 Walgren	26	72	25	71
19 Goodling, W.	76	12	78	13
20 Gaydos	49	49	47	49
21 Dent	24	20	18	17
22 Murphy	41	53	42	55
23 Ammerman	22	57	20	68
24 Marks	44	54	48	50
25 Myers, G.	54	45	58	40
RHODE ISLAND				
1 St Germain	17	70	17	70
2 Beard	22	73	24	71
SOUTH CAROLINA				
1 Davis	61	30	63	29
2 Spence	93	6	92	4
3 Derrick	48	47	48	43
4 Mann	50	24	59	23
5 Holland	46	35	44	30
6 Jenrette	47	38	49	40
SOUTH DAKOTA				
1 Pressler	46	30	55	28
2 Abdnor	79	8	85	5
TENNESSEE				
1 Quillen	76	8	76	7
2 Duncan	90	7	92	6
3 Lloyd	73	7	80	9
4 Gore	30	66	32	65
5 Allen [7]	26†	47†	37*	52*
6 Beard	85	4	87	3
7 Jones	67	22	65	27
8 Ford	14	67	17	72
TEXAS				
1 Hall	94	5	92	6
2 Wilson, C.	48	37	46	39
3 Collins	93	5	93	5
4 Roberts	76	7	83	6
5 Mattox	46	52	40	58
6 Teague	5	2	8	2
7 Archer	93	2	94	3
8 Eckhardt	5	82	5	85
9 Brooks	55	39	52	38
10 Pickle	63	33	68	27
11 Poage	85	7	77	6
12 Wright	33	57	30	61
13 Hightower	79	16	79	17
14 Young	27	16	45	21
15 de la Garza	75	16	79	15
16 White	82	12	86	11
17 Burleson	90	6	93	5
18 Jordan	23	74	20	75
19 Mahon	64	30	75	22
20 Gonzalez	41	56	42	51
21 Krueger	29	15	40	23
22 Gammage	77	9	73	12
23 Kazen	74	16	80	14
24 Milford	59	13	63	11
UTAH				
1 McKay	57	37	56	38
2 Marriott	94	3	91	4
VERMONT				
AL Jeffords	39	56	38*	57*
VIRGINIA				
1 Trible	91	6	91	7
2 Whitehurst	89	7	85	8
3 Satterfield	94	3	94	3
4 Daniel	98	2	95	4
5 Daniel	95	2	96	3
6 Butler	87	6	88	7
7 Robinson	95	2	96	2
8 Harris	19	80	18	81
9 Wampler	86	7	88	6
10 Fisher	21	78	23	77
WASHINGTON				
1 Pritchard	49	43	47	46
2 Meeds	13	68	14	74
3 Bonker	18	65	17	68
4 McCormack	42	50	39	53
5 Foley	40	55	33	61
6 Dicks	29	64	30	60
7 Cunningham	88	9	83*	7*
WEST VIRGINIA				
1 Mollohan	52	41	53	42
2 Staggers	34	62	31	56
3 Slack	57	34	54	39
4 Rahall	27	60	34	57
WISCONSIN				
1 Aspin	11	85	12	80
2 Kastenmeier	7	93	10	89
3 Baldus	15	83	16	77
4 Zablocki	33	67	34	66
5 Reuss	7	90	8	89
6 Steiger	54	37	59	33
7 Obey	13	85	15	83
8 Cornell	15	83	17	82
9 Kasten	38	12	58	13
WYOMING				
AL Roncalio	15	59	20	62

Democrats ***Republicans***

LOBBY REGISTRATIONS

CQ

CQ Lobby Registrations

Lobby Registrations Filed With Congress

Following is a list of persons and organizations that filed lobby registrations from October 1977 through October 1978. An index of lobby registrations begins on p. 46-D.

October 1977

Agriculture and Environment

LOREN BERGH et. al., Seattle, Wash. Lobbyist—Hageman, Prout, Kirkland & Coughlin, Seattle, Wash. Filed 10/11/77. Legislative interest—"...Seeking compensation through legislation...for losses due to the installation of a Munitions Pier by the Department of the Navy to the Commercial Pacific Cod Set Net Fishery...."

ENVIRONMENTAL POLICY CENTER, Washington, D.C. Lobbyist—Garry J. DeLoss, Washington, D.C. Filed 10/20/77. Legislative interest—"...Energy conservation and renewable sources of energy."

NATURAL RESOURCES DEFENSE COUNCIL INC., Washington, D.C. Lobbyist—Richard E. Ayres, Washington, D.C. Filed 10/31/67. Legislative interest—"Clean Air Act Amendments (S 251, 252, 3, HR 4151)."

Citizens' Groups

AD HOC COMMITTEE OF CONCERNED PARENTS, Lexington, Mass. Lobbyist—Francis J. O'Rourke, Boston, Mass. Filed 10/18/77. Legislative interest—"Contempt of Congress citation of P. G. Feffeman."

AMERICAN ETHICAL UNION, New York, N.Y. Lobbyist—Raymond Nathan, Washington, D.C. Filed 10/27/77. Legislative interest—"For arms reduction, separation of church and state, human needs programs, and civil liberties. Specific bills to be evaluated in terms of these goals."

CENTER FOR THE STUDY OF CONGRESS, Washington, D.C. Filed for self 10/25/77. Legislative interest: "Enactment of HR 3345, relating to simplified tax forms for wage-earning taxpayers." Lobbyist — Richard Halberstein, Washington, D.C.

COMMON CAUSE, Washington, D.C. Lobbyist—Robert Rodriguez, Washington, D.C. Filed 10/7/77. Legislative interest—"...Open government, campaign financing, consumer protection, freedom of information, ERA, energy policy, environmental protection, defense spending, tax reform, waste in government, voting rights, Presidential nomination and confirmation process, administration of justice and reform of the criminal code, merit selection of federal judges, intelligence policy, public participation in federal agency proceedings, the congressional budget process and congressional reform."

NATIONAL ASSOCIATION OF LATINO DEMOCRATIC OFFICIALS INC., Washington, D.C. Filed for self 10/6/77. Legislative interest—"Legislation which will benefit the health, social and economic welfare of Americans of Spanish origin or descent and other disadvantaged groups...."

NATIONAL ASSOCIATION OF RAILROAD PASSENGERS, Washington, D.C. Filed for self 10/28/77. Legislative interest—"...Railroad policy and administration."

NATIONAL RIFLE ASSOCIATION OF AMERICA, Washington, D.C. Lobbyist—William P. Crewe, Washington, D.C. Filed 10/28/77. Legislative interest—"Conservation, recreation and firearms legislation."

NOT ONE SQUARE INCH, Los Alamitos, Calif. Filed for self 10/28/77. Legislative interest—"Panama Canal Treaties."

Corporations and Businesses

ALCI INTERNATIONAL INC., New York, N.Y. Filed for self 10/7/77. Legislative interest—"Legislation affecting international and domestic trade and related areas." Lobbyist—John M. Damgard, Washington, D.C. Filed 10/7/77.

ALCAN PIPELINE CO., Washington, D.C. Lobbyist—Akin, Gump, Hauer & Feld, Washington, D.C. Filed 10/21/77. Legislative interest—"Hearings and any related legislation concerning natural gas policy."

ALLIED CHEMICAL CORP., Morristown, N.J. Lobbyist—John T. Estes, Washington, D.C. Filed 10/6/77. Legislative interest—"Energy, employee relations, taxes, environmental and other related matters affecting Allied Chemical Corp."

AMERICAN CAN CO., Greenwich, Conn. Lobbyist—Edward DeW. Kratovil, Greenwich, Conn. Filed 10/4/77. Legislative interest—"S 276, S 252, S 1952, S 1469, S 1883, S 1472, S 1785, S 1281, S 1811, S 37, S 1750, HR 936, HR 6161, HR 3199, HR 8444, HR 8410, HR 8494, HR 6796, HR 7599, PL 94-580."

AMERICAN NATURAL SERVICE CO., Washington, D.C. Lobbyist—Margaret Bryant, Washington, D.C. Filed 10/28/77. Legislative interest—"All matters of interest to the natural gas industry."

BANKAMERICA CORP., San Francisco, Calif. Lobbyist—H. Brent Egbert, Washington, D.C. Filed 10/7/77. Legislative interest—"Legislation affecting financial institutions, particularly banks and bank holding companies generally."

BECHTEL CORP., San Francisco, Calif. Lobbyist—John M. Mooney, San Francisco, Calif. Filed 10/27/77. Legislative interest—"Taxation of foreign operations (Title 26, U.S. Code)."

BENDIX CORP., Arlington, Va. Lobbyist—Nancy C. Reynolds, Arlington, Va. Filed 10/5/77. Legislative interest—"All matters of interest pertaining to aerospace, electronics, automotive, industrial energy and shelter."

BI-A-ROBI, Hamlin, Pa. Lobbyist—Donald W. Whitehead, Washington, D.C. Filed 10/6/77. Legislative interest—"Amendments to Federal Water Pollution Control Act of 1972, esp. sections 104, 201 and 205, re: alternative waste water systems."

THE BOEING CO., Seattle, Wash. Lobbyist—Gilbert W. Keyes, Seattle, Wash., filed 10/7/77; Ronald E. McWilliams, Washington, D.C., filed 10/25/77. Legislative interest—"Government procurement—funding and policies, revenue issues, regulation of transportation—air, surface and water, industrial relations issues, international trade regulation, energy resources."

CALIFORNIA & HAWAII SUGAR CO., San Francisco, Calif. Lobbyist—E. A. Jaenke & Associates Inc., Washington, D.C. Filed 10/17/77. Legislative interest—"None."

CATERPILLAR TRACTOR CO., Peoria, Ill. Lobbyist—Michael C. Maibach, Peoria, Ill. Filed 10/13/77. Legislative interest—"Present or future proposed legislation of interest to Caterpillar Tractor Co. and its subsidiary or affiliated companies."

CENTRAL AMERICAN PIPELINE CO., St. Peter Port, Guernsey, Channel Islands. Lobbyist—Rogers & Wells, Washington, D.C. Filed 10/6/77. Legislative interest—"All matters concerning energy legislation."

CENTRAL AND SOUTH WEST CORPORATION, Wilmington, Del. Lobbyist—Richard D. Cudahy, Washington, D.C. Filed 10/11/77. Legislative interest—"...Matters dealing with interconnection of electric utilities to insure supplying electrical energy with greater economy and with regard to proper utilization and conservation of natural resources. Specifically interested in legislation which promotes general objectives of Section 202 of the Federal Power Act."

CHROMALLOY AMERICAN CORP., St. Louis, Mo. Lobbyist—Judith A. Lorenson, St. Louis, Mo., Richard A. Paysor, Creve Coeur, Mo. Filed 10/19/77. Legislative interest—"To oppose HR 5959, to support HR 8403."

CITIES SERVICE GAS CO., Oklahoma City, Okla. Lobbyist—James R. Winnie, Oklahoma City, Okla. Filed 10/28/77. Legislative interest—"Legislation impacting the natural gas transmission industry."

COASTAL STATES GAS CORP., Houston, Texas. Lobbyist—Birch, Horton, Bittner & Monroe, Washington, D.C. Filed 10/11/77. Legislative interest—"All legislation relating to natural resources, financing or tax matters."

CONTINENTAL OIL CO., Stamford, Conn. Lobbyist—Michael O. Ware, Washington, D.C. Filed 10/11/77. Legislative interest—"...Any and all measures affecting the employer."

DAMON CORP., Needham Heights, Mass. Filed for self 10/11/77. Legislative interest—"Legislation affecting clinical laboratories." Lobbyist—Bruce G. Goodman, Needham Heights, Mass. Filed 10/11/77.

DRESSER INDUSTRIES INC., Dallas, Texas. Lobbyist—Seyfarth, Shaw, Fairweather & Geraldson, Washington, D.C. Filed 10/7/77. Legislative interest—"...Legislation relating to employer-employee relations, such as Labor Reform Act of 1977 (HR 8410/S 1883), Pregnancy Benefits Bill (HR 6075/S 995), Fair Labor Standards Amendment of 1977 (HR 3744/S 1871), Age Discrimination Bill (HR 5383/S 1784)."

FLORIDA GAS TRANSMISSION CO., Longwood, Fla. Lobbyist—David L. Turley, Longwood, Fla. Filed 10/14/77. Legislative interest—"Legislation affecting the regulation of natural gas and other energy forms, including but not limited to, pending bills such as S 826, HR 6804, HR 6831."

GENERAL ELECTRIC CO., Washington, D.C. Lobbyist—Robert M. Ketchel, Warren W. Walkley, Washington, D.C. Filed 10/6/77. Legislative interest—"Any legislation directly or indirectly affecting General Electric components manufacturing equipment for the public and private sectors of the electric utility industry, domestic and international."

GENERAL ELECTRIC CO., Schenectady, N.Y. Lobbyist—Leva, Hawes, Symington, Martin & Oppenheimer, Washington, D.C. Filed 10/11/77. Legislative interest—"...Pending legislation being considered in response to Presidential energy proposals (S 1469, S 1472 and HR 6831). Bills include S 977, HR 8444."

HARRIS CORP., Cleveland, Ohio. Lobbyist—Al William R. Tolley Jr., Washington, D.C. Filed 10/28/77. Legislative interest—"All legislation affecting this company's business interests and its relationship with the federal government. In particular...proposed amendments (S 1594 and HR 5959) to the Renegotiation Act of 1951. Opposed."

HOLLY CORP., Dallas, Texas. Lobbyist—Edward L. Merrigan, Washington, D.C. Filed 10/31/77. Legislative interest—"Protection of small refiners' competitive position in the event of enactment of crude oil equalization tax."

THE HORMEL FOUNDATION, Austin, Minn. Lobbyist—Dawson, Riddell, Taylor, Davis & Holroyd, Washington, D.C. Filed 10/31/77. Legislative interest—"Legislation of interest to and affecting the Foundation."

KANSAS CITY LIFE INSURANCE CO., Kansas City, Mo. Lobbyist—C. Bryan Cox, Kansas City, Mo. Filed 10/28/77. Legislative interest—"S 1710—Federal Insurance Act—Against tax reform legislation."

KOCH REFINING CO., Wichita, Kan. Filed for self 10/12/77. Legislative interest—"Energy Transportation Security Act of 1977, HR 1037, S 61." Lobbyist—Kominers, Fort, Schlefer & Boyer, Washington, D.C. Filed 10/12/77.

KOLLMORGAN CORP., Hartford, Conn. Lobbyist—Jones, Day, Reavis & Pogue. Filed 10/12/77. Legislative interest—"To determine application, if any, of Section 620B of the Foreign Assistance Act of 1961, as amended by the International Security Assistance Act of 1977."

LEGAL SERVICES CORP., Washington, D.C. Lobbyist—Mary M. Bourdette, Washington, D.C. Filed 10/25/77. Legislative interest—"...Legislation directly affecting the activities of the corporation."

McDONNELL DOUGLAS CORP., St. Louis, Mo. Lobbyist—R. J. Maglione, Arlington, Va. Filed 10/5/77. Legislative interest—"Defense authorization and appropriations bills."

McNAMARA CONSTRUCTION OF MANITOBA LTD., Ontario, Canada. Lobbyist—Lucas, Friedman & Mann, Washington, D.C. Filed 10/25/77. Legislative interest—"Passage of private relief legislation, HR 8532 and H Res 726, a resolution referring HR 8532 to the Chief Commissioner of the Court of Claims."

MARTIN OIL SERVICE, Blue Island, Ill. Lobbyist—Batzell, Nunn & Bode, Washington, D.C. Filed 10/12/77. Legislative interest—"To amend Section 613A of the Internal Revenue Code to allow independent oil and gas producers with limited marketing activities to claim percentage depletion by amendment to the Energy Bill (HR 8444) or the Technical Amendment Act to the Tax Reform Act of 1976."

MEDICAL AREA SERVICE CORP., Cambridge, Mass. Lobbyist—Miller & Chevalier, Washington, D.C. Filed 10/12/77. Legislative interest—"Insure that provisions of section 2061 of the National Energy Act, HR 8444, denying the investment credit and accelerated depreciation for combusters fueled by petroleum do not apply to cogeneration properly, and that the business energy credit available for cogeneration properly installed to replace an existing facility."

MONTGOMERY WARD & CO. INC., Chicago, Ill. Lobbyist—Michael B. Green, Washington, D.C. Filed 10/11/77. Legislative interest—"...Those bearing on the retail industry, including relations with federal agencies, manufacturers, suppliers, employees and customers."

MORGAN GUARANTY TRUST CO. OF NEW YORK, New York, N.Y. Lobbyist—Miller & Chevalier, Washington, D.C. Filed 10/11/77. Legislative interest—"In support of legislation which will amend the Internal Revenue Code of 1954 to provide rules for the tax treatment of employees under certain profit-sharing plans (HR 8136) and/or amend the Employee Retirement Income Security Act of 1974 to provide additional time to study salary reduction and cash and deferred option profit-sharing plans (HR 8938)."

THE NATIONAL SMALL BUSINESS INDEX, Aitkin, Minn. Filed for self 10/21/77. Legislative interest—"...General legislation proposed or enacted as respects the small business community." Lobbyist—Arthur I. Mindrum, Aitkin, Minn. Filed 10/21/77.

NORTHERN HELEX CO., Omaha, Neb. Lobbyist—Miller & Chevalier, Washington, D.C. Filed 10/25/77. Legislative interest—"Favoring the passage of helium conservation legislation such as H Res 91 and S 2109."

NORWICH-EATON PHARMACEUTICALS, Norwich, N.Y. Lobbyist—Frank M. Ault, South Otselic, N.Y. Filed 10/17/77. Legislative interest—"Anything pertaining to pharmaceutical industry."

REPUBLIC STEEL CORP., Cleveland, Ohio. Lobbyist—Thomas L. Adams Jr., Kathryn L. Newman, Washington, D.C. Filed 10/10/77. Legislative interest—"Legislation affecting employer steel company and related interests."

SHAMROCK FOODS CO., Phoenix, Ariz. Lobbyist—Jennings, Strouss & Salmon, Phoenix, Ariz. Filed 10/11/77. Legislative interest—"S 1874 and HR 8359."

SOUTHERN CALIFORNIA EDISON CO., Rosemead, Calif. Lobbyist—Charles E. Cooke, Washington, D.C. Filed 10/14/77. Legislative interest—"Legislation affecting Southern California Edison Co. or the electric utility industry."

SOUTHERN CALIFORNIA GAS CO., Los Angeles, Calif. Lobbyist—Gay H. Friedman, Washington, D.C. Filed 10/25/77. Legislative interest—"Legislation of interest to the energy industries, particularly regarding natural gas, LNG, SNG and energy siting."

TRANS UNION CORP., Lincolnshire, Ill. Lobbyist—Seyfarth, Shaw, Fairweather & Geraldson, Washington,

D.C. Filed 10/7/77. Legislative interest—"Legislation relating to employer-employee relations, such as Labor Reform Act of 1977 (HR 8410/S 1883), Pregnancy Benefits Bill (HR 6075/S 995), Fair Labor Standards Amendments of 1977 (HR 3744/S 1871), Age Discrimination Bill (HR 5383/S 1784)."

VICKERS PETROLEUM CORP., Wichita, Kan. Lobbyist—Akin, Gump, Hauer & Feld, Washington, D.C. Filed 10/11/77. Legislative interest—"Hearings and any related legislation concerning U.S. energy policy."

Labor Groups

AMERICAN POSTAL WORKERS UNION, AFL-CIO, Washington, D.C. Lobbyist—Emmet Andrews, Washington, D.C. Filed 10/25/77. Legislative interest—"All legislation pertaining to postal service and the welfare of postal employees."

LABORERS' INTERNATIONAL UNION OF N.A., AFL-CIO, Washington, D.C. Lobbyist—Donald Kaniewski, Washington, D.C. Filed 10/25/77. Legislative interest—"Legislation affecting the interest of working people."

MARINE ENGINEERS BENEFICIAL ASSOCIATION, New York, N.Y. Lobbyist—Robert J. Keefe, Washington, D.C. Filed 10/20/77. Legislative interest—"Cargo Equity legislation and related matters."

NATIONAL FEDERATION OF FEDERAL EMPLOYEES, Washington, D.C. Lobbyist—Robert C. Beverly, Washington, D.C. Filed 10/3/77. Legislative interest—"Legislation affecting federal employees. Specifically this will include bills before the Post Office and Civil Service Committee and other committees of the Senate and House, relating to the working conditions and welfare of federal employees."

PROFESSIONAL AIR TRAFFIC CONTROLLERS ORGANIZATION, Washington, D.C. Lobbyist—Joseph S. Miller, Washington, D.C. Filed 10/13/77. Legislative interest—"Legislation that deals with aviation, air traffic controllers and with civil service employees in general, HR 7292, HR 8600, HR 10."

UNITED MINE WORKERS OF AMERICA, Washington, D.C. Lobbyist—Joseph Jurczak, Matthew Miller, Washington, D.C. Filed 10/19/77. Legislative interest—"Promote legislation that in UMWA opinion benefits workers in the coal mining industry and conversely oppose legislation felt to be detrimental to workers."

UNITED PLANT GUARD WORKERS OF AMERICA, Roseville, Mich. Lobbyist—Patton, Boggs & Blow, Washington, D.C. Filed 10/11/77. Legislative interest—"Legislation amending the National Labor Relations Act and general legislative interest, Labor Reform Act of 1977, HR 8410."

Military and Veterans' Groups

THE RETIRED OFFICERS ASSOCIATION, Washington, D.C. Lobbyist—Henry S. Palau, Washington, D.C. Filed 10/11/77. Legislative interest—"Any and all legislation pertinent to the rights, benefits, privileges and obligations of retired officers, male and female, regular and reserve, and their dependents and survivors, of whatever nature, dealing with personnel matters, pay and retirement benefits and pensions, studying and analyzing bills, preparing statements for presentation to the cognizant committees, and principally the committees on Armed Services, the committees on Veterans' Affairs, and the committees dealing with various privileges, opportunities and obligations of the personnel involved."

State and Local Governments

STATE OF LOUISIANA, Washington, D.C. Lobbyist—Patton, Boggs & Blow, Washington, D.C. Filed 10/11/77. Legislative interest—"Federal legislation affecting State of Louisiana (i.e. Outer Continental Shelf Lands Act of 1977), HR 1614."

Trade Associations

ALLIANCE OF AMERICAN INSURERS, Chicago, Ill. Lobbyist—Donald L. Jordan, Washington, D.C. Filed 10/5/77. Legislative interest—"Legislation affecting property or casualty insurance companies or their policyholders."

AMERICAN BUS ASSOCIATION, Washington, D.C. Lobbyist—Dawson, Riddell, Taylor, Davis & Holroyd, Washington, D.C. Filed 10/31/77. Legislative interest—"Any legislation affecting the Association."

AMERICAN CHAMBER OF COMMERCE IN ITALY INC., Washington, D.C. Lobbyist—Nicholson & Carter, Washington, D.C. Filed 10/25/77. Legislative interest—"...To foster good business relationships between the United States and Italy. ...To support the provisions regarding international social security amendments in the House social security financing legislation, HR 9356."

AMERICAN INSURANCE ASSOCIATION, Washington, D.C. Lobbyist—George K. Bernstein, Washington, D.C. Filed 10/12/77. Legislative interest—"Air bag disapproval resolutions, H Con Res 273, S Con Res 31, 1977 housing legislation, HR 6655."

AMERICAN LAND TITLE ASSOCIATION, Washington, D.C. Lobbyist—Pierson Semmes Crolius and Finley, Washington, D.C. Filed 10/12/77. Legislative interest—"All legislation relating to Indian tribal claims to real estate, or to damages for trespasses committed on such lands, especially legislation relating to claims arising out of the alleged failure of the Congress to approve transfers of tribal lands in accordance with the Nonintercourse Act of 1790 (25 U.S.C. Section 177), including S J Res 86 and H J Res 612 and similar measures."

AMERICAN MINING CONGRESS, Washington, D.C. Lobbyist—Edward M. Green, Washington, D.C. Filed 10/21/77. Legislative interest—"Measures affecting mining, such as income taxation, social security, public lands, stockpiling, monetary policy, mine safety, environmental quality control."

AMERICAN PSYCHIATRIC ASSOCIATION, Washington, D.C. Lobbyist—Theodore Fine, Edmund J. Perret III, Jay B. Cutler, Washington, D.C. Filed 10/11/77. Legislative interest—"All health legislation affecting psychiatry."

AMERICAN RETAIL FEDERATION, Washington, D.C. Lobbyist—Jerry G. Udell, Washington, D.C. Filed 10/12/77. Legislative interest—"FTC Improvements Act, HR 3816; Product Liability, S 403; Federal Funding of Consumer Witnesses, S 270; Debt Collection Practices, HR 29; Fair Credit Reporting Act Amendments, HR 3875; Minimum Wage, HR 3744; Labor Reform Act, HR 77; Common Situs Picketing, HR 4250; Full Employment Act, HR 50, S 50; National Health Insurance, HR 21, S 3; Civil Aeronautics Board Reform, S 689; Consumer Communications Reform, HR 8, S 530, S J Res 30; Clean Air Act, S 251, S 252, S 253, HR 4151, HR 2380; Successor Employer Responsibility, HR 3501, S 528; Consumer Product Standards, S 825; ERISA Administration, HR 4340; Tax Reform Bill, HR 3477 and other similar legislation affecting the retail industry."

AMERICAN SOCIETY FOR PERSONNEL ADMINISTRATION, Berea, Ohio. Lobbyist—James H. Ferguson, Washington, D.C. Filed 10/18/77. Legislative interest—"Labor Law Reform (HR 8410 and S 1883), Pregnancy Disability (HR 5055 and S 995), Mandatory Retirement (HR 5383), Minimum Wage, Hatch Act (HR 10)."

AMERICAN VETERINARY MEDICAL ASSOCIATION, Washington, D.C. Lobbyist—John W. Thomas, Washington, D.C. Filed 10/11/77. Legislative interest—"The advancement of veterinary medical science."

ASSOCIATION OF AMERICAN CHAMBERS OF COMMERCE, EUROPE AND MEDITERRANEAN INC., Washington, D.C. Lobbyist—Nicholson & Carter, Washington, D.C. Filed 10/25/77. Legislative interest—"...To foster good business relationships between the United States and Europe. ...To support the provisions regarding international social security agreements in the House social security financing legislation, HR 9356."

ASSOCIATION OF AMERICAN RAILROADS, Washington, D.C. Lobbyist—Joseph S. Miller, Washington, D.C. Filed 10/13/77. Legislative interest—"Legislation dealing with coal slurry pipelines; HR 1324, HR 1609, HR 6248, HR 6643, S 707, S 1492."

ASSOCIATION OF AMERICAN VETERINARY MEDICAL COLLEGES, Washington, D.C. Lobbyist—John W. Thomas, Washington, D.C. Filed 10/11/77. Legislative interest—"Bills which would provide funding for teaching and/or research at schools of veterinary medicine."

AUTOMOTIVE PARTS & ACCESSORIES ASSOCIATION, Washington, D.C. Filed for self 10/20/77. Legislative interest—"Any legislation affecting the automotive aftermarket industry." Lobbyist—Linda J. Hoffman, Washington, D.C. Filed 10/20/77.

BUILDING OWNERS AND MANAGERS ASSOCIATION INTERNATIONAL, Washington, D.C. Lobbyist—Winston & Strawn, Washington, D.C. Filed 10/21/77. Legislative interest—"Legislation concerning the Internal Revenue Code, energy, the Clean Air Act and other environmental laws affecting real estate, including office and apartment buildings."

COMMERCIAL LAW LEAGUE OF AMERICA, Chicago, Ill. Lobbyist—Gordon L. Calvert, Washington, D.C. Filed 10/3/77. Legislative interest—"Bankruptcy law revision (HR 8200), debt collection practices, reporting commercial credit."

COUNCIL OF ACTIVE INDEPENDENT OIL & GAS PRODUCERS, Washington, D.C. Lobbyist—Richard A. Kline, Washington, D.C. Filed 10/12/77. Legislative interest—"Oil and gas legislation."

COUNCIL FOR INTER-AMERICAN SECURITY, Washington, D.C. Filed for self 10/6/77. Legislative interest—"Legislation affecting U.S. relations with the other nations of the western hemisphere and the political and military security of the western hemisphere. The Council opposes ratification of the proposed treaties transferring control of the U.S. Isthmian Canal to the Republic of Panama."

DEALER BANK ASSOCIATION, Washington, D.C. Lobbyist—Carl A. S. Coan Jr., Washington, D.C. Filed 10/14/77. Legislative interest—"...Any current or future legislation affecting the public finance activities of member banks, specifically, in support of HR 7485 and HR 8171."

FOOD MARKETING INSTITUTE, Washington, D.C. Lobbyist—Dennis M. Devaney, William S. Kies, Washington, D.C. Filed 10/17/77. Legislative interest—"Matters affecting the food distribution industry through trade regulation or otherwise."

FRIENDSHIP VILLA INC., Bismarck, N.D. Lobbyist—Nelson, Harding & Yeutter, Washington, D.C. Filed 10/12/77. Legislative interest—"Generally opposes Bellmon amendment to HR 3387 or other legislation. The Bellmon amendment would delay implementation of Section 249(a) cost-related reimbursement requirements for nursing homes for one year."

INDEPENDENT INSURANCE AGENTS OF AMERICA INC., New York, N.Y. Lobbyist—Roger N. Levy, Washington, D.C. Filed 10/6/77. Legislative interest—"Any legislation which affects, directly or indirectly, local property insurance agents; social security legislation; other legislation, e.g. tax and finance legislation."

INDEPENDENT PETROLEUM ASSOCIATION OF AMERICA, Washington, D.C. Lobbyist—Martha Williams Gray, Washington, D.C. Filed 10/19/77. Legislative interest—"...Maintaining surveillance of legislation that might affect the petroleum industry and taking such action with respect to such legislation as directed by the association."

INDEPENDENT U.S. TANKER OWNERS, Washington, D.C. Lobbyist—William J. Colley, Washington, D.C. Filed 10/11/77. Legislative interest—"Cargo equity legislation, HR 1037, S 61."

MANUFACTURED HOUSING INSTITUTE, Arlington, Va. Lobbyists—Judith Lynne Crain, Alexandria,Va., filed 10/11/77; John R. Maguire, Great Falls, Va., filed 10/11/77. Legislative interest—"HR 6655, HR 1523."

NATIONAL ASSOCIATION OF FEDERAL CREDIT UNIONS, Washington, D.C. Lobbyist—Roger H. Barnard, Washington, D.C. Filed 10/3/77. Legislative interest—"Financial institution and consumer credit legislation."

NATIONAL ASSOCIATION OF MUTUAL SAVINGS BANKS, New York, N.Y. Lobbyist—Saul B. Klaman, New York, N.Y. Filed 10/12/77. Legislative interest—"Legislation directly or indirectly affecting mutual savings banks, such as HR 3816, the Federal Trade Commission Amendments of 1977; HR 5675, a bill that would reform the administration of the Treasury's Tax and Loan Account System; HR 7179, the Federal Mutual Savings Bank Act of 1977; S 71 and HR 9086, to strengthen the supervisory authority of the federal banking agencies over financial institutions; HR 6655, the Housing and Community Development Act of 1977; S 1312, S 1501 and S 1846, the Truth-in-Lending Simplification Act of 1977, and S 665, Young Families Housing Act."

NATIONAL ASSOCIATION OF STEVEDORES, Washington, D.C. Lobbyist—Thevenot, Murray and Scheer, Washington, D.C. Filed 10/13/77. Legislative interest—"Generally to support such pending or proposed legislation believed to be in the interest of the National Association of Stevedores and to oppose legislation to such interest."

NATIONAL CABLE TELEVISION ASSOCIATION INC., Washington, D.C. Lobbyist—Vivian Goodier, Michael Lemov, Washington, D.C. Filed 10/14/77. Legislative interest—"Legislation affecting cable television, specifically S 1547 and HR 7442 (pole attachment legislation) in a desire to monitor and affect legislation favorable to the CATV industry."

NATIONAL CATTLEMEN'S ASSOCIATION, Denver, Colo. Lobbyist—Thomas A. Davis, Washington, D.C. Filed 10/12/77. Legislative interest—"Tax legislation and other matters affecting the beef cattle industry."

NATIONAL COTTON COUNCIL OF AMERICA, Memphis, Tenn. Lobbyist—Randall T. Jones, Washington, D.C. Filed 10/19/77. Legislative interest—"...Any legislation affecting the raw cotton industry as will promote the purpose for which the Council is organized."

NATIONAL COUNCIL OF COAL LESSORS INC., Washington, D.C. Lobbyist—Paige Wooldridge, Bluefield, W.Va. Filed 10/10/77. Legislative interest—"...Any bills which would abolish or modify Sec. 631C of the IRC or otherwise adversely affect the capital gains treatment of coal royalty income."

NATIONAL FEDERATION OF INDEPENDENT BUSINESS, Washington, D.C. Lobbyist—Frank S. Swain, Kathleen Ann Clarken, Washington, D.C. Filed 10/11/77. Legislative interest—"All legislation affecting small business and the economic well-being of the country."

NATIONAL LIMESTONE INSTITUTE INC., Fairfax, Va. Lobbyist—Michael P. deBlois, Fairfax, Va. Filed 10/11/77. Legislative interest—"All legislation which directly or indirectly affects the interest of limestone producers."

NATIONAL PEST CONTROL ASSOCIATION, Vienna Va. Filed for self 10/11/77. Legislative interest—"Proposed legislation to amend the Federal Insecticide, Fungicide and Rodenticide Act, as amended, including specifically HR 8681 and S 1678. The NPCA is generally in support of both bills." Lobbyists—Philip J. Spear; Berry Epstein, Sandstrom & Blatchford, Washington, D.C. Filed 10/12/77.

RADIOACTIVE WASTE MANAGEMENT GROUP, Washington, D.C. Lobbyist—Shaw, Pittman, Potts & Trowbridge, Washington, D.C. Filed 10/5/77. Legislative interest—"Authorization of U.S. government to develop and provide spent nuclear fuel storage capacity."

RADWASTE MANAGEMENT GROUP, Washington, D.C. Lobbyist—Ron M. Linton, Washington, D.C. Filed 10/19/77. Legislative interest—"Disposal of radioactive waste."

REDWOOD INDUSTRY PARK COMMITTEE, Arcata, Calif. Lobbyist—Patton, Boggs & Blow, Washington, D.C. Filed 10/11/77. Legislative interest—"Legislation affecting lumber industry, HR 3813."

RESILIENT FLOOR COVERING INSTITUTE, Washington, D.C. Lobbyist—Robert L. Koob, Washington, D.C. Filed 10/13/77. Legislative interest—"Legislation concerning general business interests; specifically the Age Discrimination Act (HR 5383); Asbestos Health Hazard Compensation Act of 1977; OSHA & Consumer Product Safety Commission legislation."

UNITED ACTION FOR ANIMALS INC., New York, N.Y. Filed for self 10/3/77. Legislative interest—"Legislation to promote the use of modern research methods, thereby reducing or eliminating the use of live animals in laboratory research for a variety of purposes." Lobbyist—Dunnells, Duvall & Porter, Washington, D.C. Filed 10/3/77.

UNITED FRESH FRUIT & VEGETABLE ASSOCIATION, Washington, D.C. Lobbyist—Robert C. Keeney, Washington, D.C. Filed 10/26/77. Legislative interest—"...Transportation and regulation thereof, labor and related matters, agricultural chemicals, nutrition, packaging and labeling. Specific interest...S 1188 (support) Cargo Claims Adjustment Act of 1977; HR 7768 (oppose) Motor Carrier Act of 1977; HR 2443 (oppose) to include independent owner-operator truckers as an exempted class under the ICC Act; HR 6805 and S 1262 (oppose) dealing with consumer protection; HR 4773 (oppose); HR 4777 (support), S 976 (support); Amendments to Perishable Agricultural Commodities Act; Amendments to Farm Labor Contractor Registration Act; HR 3744 (oppose) Minimum Wage; legislation dealing with illegal aliens; HR 4394, agricultural research; amendments to the FIFRA; HR 8410 and S 1883 (oppose) amendments to the Labor Reform Act of 1977."

Miscellaneous

AK CHIN INDIAN COMMUNITY, Maricopa, Ariz. Lobbyist—Rebecca D. Shapiro & Associates, Washington, D.C. Filed 10/20/77. Legislative interest—"HR 8099, S 1882, relating to Ak Chin water claim (for)."

ALL INDIAN PUEBLO COUNCIL INC., Albuquerque, N.M. Lobbyist—Rebecca D. Shapiro & Associates, Washington, D.C. Filed 10/20/77. Legislative interest—"Monitoring of legislation affecting Indian tribes, pursuing appropriations interests: HR 3787 and S 482, Zuni Pueblo (for); HR 2719, relating to Middle Rio Grande Conservary (for); and S 1509, to transfer land to all Indian Pueblo Council (for)."

GOVERNMENT OF THE STATE OF ANTIGUA, St. John, Antigua, West Indies. Lobbyist — Danzansky, Dickey, Tydings, Quint & Gordon, Washington, D.C. Filed 8/12/77. Legislative interest — "General legal representation, including the rendering of legal opinions, counsel and assistance on matters relating to relations between the Government of the United States and the Government of Antigua including international agreements and economic assistance programs."

EUGENE C. CASHMAN, Chicago, Ill. Lobbyist—Thomas A. Davis, Washington, D.C. Filed 10/3/77. Legislative interest—"Legislation pertaining to regulation of natural gas prices, including HR 8444 and S 2104."

COUSHATTA TRIBE OF LOUISIANA, Elton, La. Lobbyist—Lucas, Friedman & Mann, Washington, D.C. Filed 10/25/77. Legislative interest—"Passage of private relief legislation HR 9424 (a bill for the relief of Fulton Battise, chief of the Tribal Council of the Alabama Coushatta Tribes of Texas, and Ernest Sickey, chairman of the Tribal Council of the Coushatta Tribe of Louisiana, and all other enrolled members of the Alabama Coushatta Tribes of Texas and the Coushatta Tribe of Louisiana, respectively), and H Res 806 referring to HR 9424 to the Chief Commissioner of the Court of Claims."

ROBERT D. DEBRODT, Ann Arbor, Mich. Lobbyist—Michael A. Nemeroff, Washington, D.C. Filed 10/18/77. Legislative interest—"Concern with regulatory impact of HR 41."

FAMILY LEISURE CENTERS INC., Cincinnati, Ohio. Lobbyist—Taft, Stettinius & Hollister, Cincinnati, Ohio. Filed 10/13/77. Legislative interest—"Advice on legislative matters relating to broadcasting."

JOHN L. HARMER, Los Angeles, Calif. Filed for self 10/28/77. Legislative interest—"Reclamation Law Revision, Omnibus Flood Control Act of 1944—Section 10."

HARTKE AND BRINSMADE, Washington, D.C. Filed for self 10/27/77. Legislative interest—"Energy bill."

GARY D. HAWKS, Ypsilanti, Mich. Lobbyist—Michael A. Nemeroff, Washington, D.C. Filed 10/18/77. Legislative interest—"Concern with regulatory impact of HR 41."

HOPI INDIAN TRIBE, Oraibi, Ariz. Lobbyist—Boyden, Kennedy, Romney & Howard, Salt Lake City, Utah. Filed 10/11/77. Legislative interest—"All tribal-related matters."

BARBARA JANES, Ann Arbor, Mich. Lobbyist—Michael A. Nemeroff, Washington, D.C. Filed 10/18/77. Legislative interest—"Concern with regulatory inpact of HR 41."

KARTH-BEST ASSOCIATES, Washington, D.C. Lobbyist—Will E. Leonard, Washington, D.C. Filed 10/8/77. Legislative interest—"To provide legal and consulting services in connection with foreign agricultural trade including fair and equitable trade for U.S. agriculture and viable domestic sweetener industries, support for price support program for domestic cane and beet sugar industries embodied in the de la Garza amendment; Food and Agricultural Act of 1977, HR 7171, S 275, PL 95-113."

NELSON, HARDING & YEUTTER, Washington, D.C. Lobbyist—The Washington Group Inc., Washington, D.C. Filed 10/12/77. Legislative interest—"Generally oppose Bellmon amendment to HR 3387, or other legislation. The proposed Bellmon amendment would delay implementation of Section 249 (a) cost-related reimbursements for nursing homes for one year."

GILBERT E. SMITH, Chicago, Ill. Lobbyist—Michael A. Nemeroff, Washington, D.C. Filed 10/18/77. Legislative interest—"Concern with regulatory impact of HR 41."

VRANESH AND MUSICK, Boulder, Colo. Lobbyist—Bonneville Associates, Salt Lake City, Utah. Filed 10/25/77. Legislative interest—"Funding of advanced technology for water sharing between agriculture and municipal uses."

DON WALLACE ASSOCIATES INC., Washington, D.C. Filed for self 10/10/77. Legislative interest—"...Legislation and executive branch policy affecting its clients."

November 1977

Citizens' Groups

CITIZENS FOR MANAGEMENT OF ALASKA LANDS, Anchorage, Alaska. Lobbyist—Richard L. Sinnott & Co., Washington, D.C. Filed 11/18/77. Legislative interest—"Legislation pertaining to Par. 17D-2 of Alaska Native Claim Settlement Act of 1971."

CONSUMER ACTION NOW, Washington, D.C. Filed for self 11/27/77. Legislative interest—"...Any and all bills which may contain provisions having an impact on consumer products, health services or the environment. ...HR 6831, relating to the President's Energy Plan, HR 3982, relating to energy conservation and solar use in federal buildings, HR 3981, relating to low-interest loans for solar installations, HR 3985, relating to tax credits for energy conservation and solar." Lobbyist—Joan Porte, Washington, D.C. Filed 11/27/77.

NATIONAL RIFLE ASSOCIATION, Washington, D.C. Filed for self 11/23/77. Legislative interest—"All legislation as it relates to the acquisition/possession of firearms and ammunition as well as legislation relating to hunting and wildlife conservation." Lobbyist—Theodore A. Lattanzio, Washington, D.C. Filed 11/23/77.

THIRTY-NINTH CONGRESSIONAL DISTRICT ACTION COMMITTEE, Allegany, N.Y. Filed for self 11/7/77. Legislative interest—"Labor-HEW appropriations bill: Hyde Amendment (for)." Lobbyist—Mrs. John H. Hever, Allegany, N.Y. Filed 11/7/77.

TOM TOBIN, Winner, S.D. Filed for self 11/23/77. Legislative interest: "American Indian Legislation. HR 7259, S 1560, ...HR 9950, HR 9951. Support bills."

Corporations and Businesses

AIRLIFT INTERNATIONAL INC., Miami, Fla. Filed for self 11/30/77. Legislative interest—"HR 6010 and other congressional bills dealing with deregulation of all cargo air carriers." Lobbyists—Paul J. Finazzo, Miami, Fla., filed 11/30/77; James Lawrence Smith, Lipman Redman, Washington, D.C., filed 11/30/77.

ALASKA INTERNATIONAL AIR INC., Fairbanks, Alaska. Lobbyist—Martin, Whitfield, Thaler & Bebchick, Washington, D.C. Filed 11/10/77. Legislative interest—"...Interests are those affecting airlines and in particular those which seek to amend the Federal Aviation Act of 1958 such as various pending efforts to effect 'deregulation' of the airline industry."

AMERICAN EXPRESS CO., New York, N.Y. Lobbyist—Cole Corette & Bradfield, Washington, D.C. Filed 11/2/77. Legislative interest—"In favor of legislation removing income tax discrimination against foreign conventions."

AVON PRODUCTS INC., New York, N.Y. Filed for self 11/7/77. Legislative interest—"All legislation related to employer's business including government regulation of the manufacture and distribution of products, the environment and taxation. Specifically including withholding federal income taxes, and withholding and paying taxes of the Federal Insurance Contributions Act and the Federal Unemployment Tax Act." Lobbyists—Robert J. Grimm, New York, N.Y., filed 11/7/77; Jones, Day, Reavis & Pogue, Washington, D.C. Filed 11/7/77.

BECHTEL POWER CORP., San Francisco, Calif. Lobbyists—Isaac R. Caraco, Calabasas Park, Calif.; Harry O. Reinsch, Harvey F. Brush, San Francisco, Calif.; Miles H. Bresee Jr., Greenbrae, Calif.; Robert D. Allen, Hillsborough, Calif.; John H. Barnard Jr., Orinda, Calif.; Michael P. Cole, Berkeley, Calif.; Ashton J. O'Donnell, Atherton, Calif.; Charles D. Statton, Rockville, Md.; Stuart L. Hill, Potomac, Md., filed 11/7/77. Legislative interest—"...All matters which may be of special interest to an international engineering and construction enterprise."

THE BENDIX CORP., Arlington, Va. Filed for self 11/1/77. Legislative interest—"All legislative matters relating to the Bendix Corp." Lobbyist—Jay Bonitt, Arlington, Va. Filed 11/1/77.

CENTEX CORP., Dallas, Texas. Lobbyist—Leighton & Conklin, Washington, D.C. Filed 11/12/77. Legislative interest—"Representation regarding proposed ruling of the Financial Accounting Standards Board and the Securities Exchange Commission prohibiting use of successful efforts accounting method by Centex Corp."

CHAMPION INTERNATIONAL CORP., Stamford, Conn. Lobbyist—Silverstein and Mullens, Washington, D.C. Filed 11/1/77. Legislative interest—"...Concerned with all federal tax bills generally relating to the business and affairs of the employer."

CITIES SERVICE CO., Washington, D.C. Filed for self 11/30/77. Legislative interest—"Legislation impacting the following industries: petroleum, minerals, petrochemicals, chemicals, plastics and metal fabrication." Lobbyist—Lynn Kay Utzinger, Washington, D.C. Filed 11/30/77.

COMMODITY EXCHANGE INC., New York, N.Y. Lobbyist—John F. O'Neal, Washington, D.C. Filed 11/16/77. Legislative interest—"All legislation affecting commodities futures markets, generally, with specific interest in matters relating to the metals markets; opposed to Section 2(u), HR 6715, the 'Technical Corrections Act of 1977' which proposes to amend Sec. 1222 of the Internal Revenue Code."

ENTEX INC., Houston, Texas. Filed for self 11/25/77. Legislative interest—"National Energy Act, HR 8444, S 5289, S 4018, S 5146, S 5037, S 5263." Lobbyist—Saunders Gregg, Houston, Texas. Filed 11/25/77.

FEDERAL PACIFIC ELECTRIC CO., Newark, N.J. Lobbyist—Patton, Boggs & Blow, Washington, D.C. Filed 11/21/77. Legislative interest—"HR 5263—oppose provision giving investment tax credit for heat pumps."

THE FIRESTONE TIRE & RUBBER CO., Akron, Ohio. Lobbyist—Harry L. Downey Jr., Washington, D.C. Filed 11/16/77. Legislative interest—"Legislation relating to employer's interest in trade, tax policy, labor, consumer, environmental, health, welfare and other issues."

GENERAL ELECTRIC CO., Fairfield, Conn. Filed for self 11/3/77. Legislative interest—"Support of position of Aerospace Industries Association with respect to recommendation for Senate consent to ratification of Montreal Protocols to the Warsaw Convention." Lobbyist—William F. Kennedy, Fairfield, Conn. Filed 11/3/77.

GETTY OIL CO., Los Angeles, Calif. Lobbyist—DeLaney & Patrick, Washington, D.C. Filed 11/14/77. Legislative interest—"...Support for pending income tax convention, dated December 31, 1975, between the United States and the United Kingdom."

INDEPENDENT CONSULTANTS INC., Washington, D.C. Filed for self 11/11/77. Legislative interest—"Agriculture: Agriculture Act, PL 480, Commodity Credit Corp., export agriculture matters, commodities trading; Transportation: as it affects domestic agriculture and foreign trade in agricultural products; Appropriations: as it affects agriculture and funding for agriculture programs; generally, for increasing trade in agricultural products, U.S. agriculture exports." Lobbyist—Craig Hackler, Kearneysville, W.Va. Filed 11/11/77.

IRVING TRUST CO., New York, N.Y. Filed for self 11/8/77. Legislative interest—"Any legislation related to the operations of a major commercial bank including, but not limited to, S 71, HR 9600, HR 9251, S 2055." Lobbyist—L. Thomas Block, New York, N.Y. Filed 11/8/77.

IU INTERNATIONAL, Philadelphia, Pa. Lobbyist—Swift & Swift, Washington, D.C. Filed 11/10/77. Legislative interest—"Legislative matters of interest to the company and its subsidiaries."

KENNECOTT COPPER CORP., New York, N.Y. Lobbyist—Richard N. Sharood, Washington, D.C. Filed 11/23/77. Legislative interest—"For enactment of HR 3350—Deep Seabed Hard Minerals Act."

MONSANTO CO., St. Louis, Mo. Lobbyist—Earl C. Spurrier, Washington, D.C. Filed 11/2/77. Legislative interest—"...Any legislation affecting employer's business."

NORTHWEST PIPELINE CORP., Salt Lake City, Utah. Lobbyist—Akin, Gump, Hauer & Feld, Washington, D.C. Filed 11/29/77. Legislative interest—"Hearings and any related legislation concerning natural gas policy."

THOMSON-CSF, Malakoff, France, Lobbyists—DGA International Inc., Washington, D.C.; Alan Woods, Seymour N. Ross, Alexandria, Va.; Thomas T. Scambos, Washington, D.C. Filed 11/25/77. Legislative interest—"Military authorizations and appropriations on aircraft attack systems."

Labor Groups

AIR LINE PILOTS ASSOCIATION, Fort Walton Beach, Fla. Filed for self 11/22/77. Legislative interest—"Aviation safety." Lobbyist—C. A. Barker Jr., Fort Walton Beach, Fla. Filed 11/22/77.

UNITED MINE WORKERS OF AMERICA, Washington, D.C. Filed for self 11/3/77. Legislative interest—"Promote legislation that in UMWA opinion benefits workers in the coal mining industry and conversely oppose legislation felt to be detrimental to workers." Lobbyist—Frank Clements, Washington, D.C. Filed 11/3/77.

State and Local Governments

PORT OF OAKLAND, Oakland, Calif. Lobbyist—Richard L. Sinnott & Co., Washington, D.C. Filed 11/18/77. Legislative interest—"Any legislation pertaining to port activities, airport management and air carrier regulation."

Trade Associations

AD HOC COMMITTEE OF ZONAL ELECTRIC HEATING MANUFACTURERS, Newark, N.J. Lobbyist—Patton, Boggs & Blow, Washington, D.C. Filed 11/21/77. Legislative interest—HR 5263—favor tax credit for automatic set back thermostats."

AMERICAN AUTOMOBILE ASSOCIATION, Falls Church, Va. Filed for self 11/21/77. Legislative interest—"Legislation relating to American motorists and travel generally." Lobbyist—John Archer, Falls Church, Va. Filed 11/21/77.

THE AMERICAN INSTITUTE OF ARCHITECTS, Washington, D.C. Filed for self 11/21/77. Legislative interest—"All legislation affecting the practice of architecture, including housing, community development, land use, historic preservation, federal procurement procedures for architectural services, energy conservation, others." Lobbyist—John M. Devaney, Washington, D.C. Filed 11/21/77.

AMERICAN MINING CONGRESS, Washington, D.C. Filed for self 11/7/77. Legislative interest—"Measures affecting mining such as income taxation, social security, public lands, stockpiling, monetary policy, mine safety, environmental quality control, etc." Lobbyist—John D. Austin Jr., Washington, D.C. Filed 11/7/77.

CALORIE CONTROL COUNCIL, Atlanta, Ga. Filed for self 11/7/77. Legislative interest—"Legislation and committee hearings relating to proposed ban on saccharin by FDA. Interest in HR 8518 and S 1750." Lobbyist—Robert H. Kellen Co., Atlanta, Ga. Filed 11/7/77.

CHICAGO BOARD OF TRADE, Chicago, Ill. Lobbyist—Douglas P. Bennett, Washington, D.C. Filed 11/14/77. Legislative interest—"Legislation affecting the commodity futures industry."

INDEPENDENT GASOLINE MARKETERS COUNCIL, Washington, D.C. Lobbyist—Blum, Parker & Nash, Washington, D.C. Filed 11/25/77. Legislative interest—"Legislation relating to gasoline marketing including relevant tax and trade regulation proposals."

INDEPENDENT REFINERS ASSOCIATION OF AMERICA, Washington, D.C. Lobbyist—Baker & Daniels, Washington, D.C. Filed 11/28/77. Legislative interest—"Energy legislation—National Energy Act, HR 8444, HR 5263."

NATIONAL ASSOCIATION OF CORPORATE DIRECTORS, Washington, D.C. Filed for self 11/28/77. Legislative interest—"All legislation affecting corporate directors and the corporate structure, with particular emphasis on the duties, responsibilities and liabilities of same."

NATIONAL ASSOCIATION OF FEDERAL CREDIT UNIONS, Washington, D.C. Filed for self 11/29/77. Legislative interest—"Financial institution and consumer credit legislation." Lobbyist—Karl T. Hoyle, Washington, D.C. Filed 11/29/77.

NATIONAL ASSOCIATION OF HOME BUILDERS OF THE UNITED STATES, Washington, D.C. Filed for self 11/9/77. Legislative interest—"...All legislation affecting that industry and its members." Lobbyist—Bruce N. Rogers, Washington, D.C. Filed 11/9/77.

NATIONAL ASSOCIATION OF MANUFACTURERS, Washington, D.C. Lobbyist—Loomis, Owen, Fellman & Coleman, Washington, D.C. Filed 11/2/77. Legislative interest—"Interested in matters and legislation affecting labor relations."

NATIONAL BARREL AND DRUM ASSOCIATION, Washington, D.C. Lobbyist—Clarence W. Moore, Miami Beach, Fla. Filed 11/28/77. Legislative interest—"Bills concerning energy and natural resources conservation, looking toward the greater use of standard-gauge 55-gallon steel drums, as against drums with limited use capability."

NATIONAL CONSUMER FINANCE ASSOCIATION, Washington, D.C. Filed for self 11/4/77. Legislative interest—"All bills pertaining to, directly or indirectly, the consumer credit industry, including HR 6, HR 29, HR 1180, HR 3816, HR 5294, HR 5578, HR 5795, HR 6805, HR 6875, HR 7330, HR 8200, HR 8753, S 71, S 656, S 918, S 1130, S 1262, S 1288, S 1312, S 1501, S 1653, S 1846, S 2065." Lobbyist—Walter R. Kurth, Washington, D.C. Filed 11/4/77.

NATIONAL FOREST PRODUCTS ASSOCIATION, Washington, D.C. Filed for self 11/2/77. Legislative interest—"...All bills affecting forestry, appropriations, labor relations, transportation, technical, housing and other matters affecting the forest products industry; Dredge/Fill Section 404, S 381, 594; HR 3199; Dept. of Energy and Natural Resources S 591; Natural Gas Regulation S 256, HR 2088; Pesticide Regulations S 275; Endangered American Wilderness Act HR 3454; Endangered Species Act Amdts. S 363; President's Reorganization Authority S 626, HR 3131, 3407; Extension of Reg. Q S 21, HR 3365." Lobbyist—Evie Jarvis, Scott Shotwell, Washington, D.C. Filed 11/2/77.

NATIONAL REALTY COMMITTEE, Washington, D.C. Lobbyist—Carl F. Arnold, Washington, D.C. Filed 11/14/77. Legislative interest—"Legislation affecting the real estate industry."

NATIONAL VENTURE CAPITAL ASSOCIATION, Washington, D.C. Lobbyist—Deaver & Hannaford Inc., Washington, D.C. Filed 11/21/77. Legislative interest—"Taxation, security regulation, small business legislation; specific interest in S 1815, amendments to Small Business Investment Act."

PACIFIC NORTHWEST UTILITIES CONFERENCE COMMITTEE, Wenatchee, Wash. Lobbyist—Culp, Dwyer, Guterson & Grader, Seattle, Wash. Filed 11/15/77. Legislative interest—"Pacific Northwest Electric Power Supply and Conservation Act."

RADIATION WASTE MANAGEMENT GROUP, Washington, D.C. Lobbyist—Leighton & Conklin, Washington, D.C. Filed 11/12/77. Legislative interest—"...Legal and legislative advice regarding proposals to establish a federal intermediate term spent fuel storage facility for nuclear waste."

RECORDING INDUSTRY ASSOCIATION OF AMERICA, New York, N.Y. Lobbyist—John Jay Daly, Washington, D.C. Filed 11/21/77. Legislative interest—"HR 7700 plus related bills affecting postal rates and postal reorganization; and Senate studies and hearings on postal reorganization. Keenest interest is in status of the Special Fourth Class postal rate."

Miscellaneous

EUGENE C. CASHMAN, Chicago, Ill. Lobbyist—Douglas P. Bennett, Washington, D.C. Filed 11/14/77. Legislative interest—"Legislation pertaining to regulation of natural gas prices, including HR 8444 and S 2104."

COMMITTEE OF AMERICANS FOR THE CANAL TREATIES, Washington, D.C. Filed for self 11/1/77. Legislative interest—"The organization will support ratification of the Treaties as being in the best interest of the United States."

MAKAH TRIBAL COUNCIL, Neah Bay, Wash. Lobbyist—Rebecca D. Shapiro & Associates, Washington, D.C. Filed 11/2/77. Legislative interest—"General legislation affecting Indian tribes; pursuing appropriations interests."

NORMAN, LAWRENCE, PATTERSON AND FARRELL, New York, N.Y. Lobbyist—Cramer, Haber and Becker, Washington, D.C. Filed 11/4/77. Legislative interest—"Matters of interest to the Fur Conservation Institute of America Inc. (trapping, export-import of furs and fur products, etc.)."

QUILEUTE INDIAN TRIBE, LaPush, Wash. Lobbyist—Ziontz, Pirtle, Morisset, Ernstoff & Chestnut, Seattle, Wash. Filed 11/4/77. Legislative interest—"All bills relating to native American interest, land use planning, environmental protection, mining, water rights and welfare."

READING IS FUNDAMENTAL INC., Washington, D.C. Filed for self 11/7/77. Legislative interest—"All legislation affecting education of children—especially fundamentals of reading." Lobbyist—Ruth P. Graves, Mrs. Robert S. McNamara, Washington, D.C. Filed 11/7/77.

MARVIN I. THOMPSON, Knoxville, Tenn. Filed for self 11/7/77. Legislative interest—"Welfare legislation of intended general application, social security legislation."

YAKIMA TRIBAL COUNCIL, Toppenish, Wash. Lobbyist—Rebecca D. Shapiro & Associates, Washington, D.C. Filed 11/10/77. Legislative interest—Legislation affecting Indian tribes; pursuing appropriations interests."

December 1977

Agriculture and Environment

Cliffside Corp., Great Falls, Va. Filed for self 12/19/77. Legislative interest — "Solar energy (energy bill)."

Environmental Policy Center, Washington, D.C. Lobbyist Peter Carlson, Washington, D.C. Filed 12/19/77. Legislative interest—"...Water resources management, rivers and wetlands preservation."

Citizens' Groups

Citizens for Government Fairness, El Centro, Calif. Filed for self 12/9/77. Legislative Interest—"Exemption of the Imperial Valley from the 1902 Reclamation Act."

Fifth Pro-Life Congressional District Action Committee, Dunedin, Fla. Filed for self 12/2/77. Legislative interest — "All proposed human life amendments."

First Pro-Life Congressional District Action Committee, Cumberland, R.I. Filed for self 12/19/77. Legislative interest—"All proposed Human Life Amendments."

National Rifle Association of America, Washington, D.C. Lobbyist—Benjamin R. Fern, Washington, D.C. Filed 12/6/77. Legislative interest—"Conservation, recreation and firearms legislation."

National Taxpayers Union, Washington, D.C. Filed for self 12/5/77. Legislative interest—Health care legislation: HR 54, HR 8891, HR 6894, HR 3330, HR 6982, HR 3329, S 1683, S 1391, S 1470, S 3." Lobbyist—Sally F. Cromwell, Washington, D.C.

Public Citizen-Congress Watch, Washington, D.C. Lobbyist—Robert F. Furniss, Washington, D.C. Filed 12/1/77. Legislative interest—"Airline Regulatory Reform: S 689-support, HR 8813-support."

Second Pro-Life Congressional District Action Committee, Narragansett, R.I. Filed for self 12/19/77. Legislative interest—"All proposed Human Life Amendments, HJ Res 121, HJ Res 405, HJ Res 132, SJ Res 178, SJ Res 140."

Corporations and Businesses

American Sign and Indicator Corp., Spokane, Wash. Lobbyist—Gwen A. Anderson, Washington, D.C. Filed 12/12/77. Legislative interest—"Legislation relating to small business legislation, environmental matters, Highway Beautification Act (USC Title 23) and energy matters."

Burlington Northern Inc., St. Paul, Minn. Lobbyist—John C. Knott, Casper, Wyo. Filed 12/27/77. Legislative interest—"Generally to support such pending or proposed legislation as Burlington Northern Inc. believes to be in its interest and in the interest of a sound national transportation policy; and to oppose legislation that they believe to be contrary to such interest."

Calista Corp., Anchorage, Alaska. Lobbyist—Birch, Horton, Bittner & Monroe, Washington, D.C. Filed 12/6/77. Legislative interest—"All legislation affecting Alaska natives."

Clearfield Bituminous Coal Corp., Indiana, Pa. Lobbyist—O'Melveny & Myers, Washington, D.C. Filed 12/15/77. Legislative interest—"Bills amending federal black lung statutes: HR 4544, S 1538 and possibly others."

Continental Air Lines Inc., Los Angeles, Calif. Lobbyist—James T. Lloyd, Washington, D.C. Filed 12/13/77. Legislative interest—"S 689, HR 8813, Aviation Reform Legislation; supporting modifications in pending legislation."

The Dow Chemical Co., Midland, Mich. Lobbyist—Lynette B. Lenard, Washington, D.C. Filed 12/7/77. Legislative interest—"Legislation affecting or of interest to the Dow Chemical Co."

International Paper Inc., Washington, D.C. Lobbyist—Beveridge, Fairbanks & Diamond, Washington, D.C. Filed 12/5/77. Legislative interest—"Congressional action which would clarify congressional intent regarding accounting procedures under the Energy Policy and Conservation Act. Interest centers upon section 141 of HR 4018, the Electric Utility Rate Reform legislation within the proposed National Energy Plan."

Mt. Airy Refining Co., Houston, Texas. Lobbyist—Blum, Parker & Nash, Washington, D.C. Filed 12/16/77. Legislative interest—"...Preserving small refiner bias treatment under pending energy legislation, for Haskell, Dole amendment to HR 8444."

Texas Eastern Transmission Corp., Houston, Texas. Lobbyist—Vinson & Elkins, Washington, D.C. Filed 12/6/77. Legislative interest—"...Natural gas industry, including interests in the National Energy Act, HR 8444."

Texas International Airlines, Houston, Texas. Lobbyist—Verner, Liipfert, Bernhard and McPherson, Washington, D.C. Filed 12/1/77. Legislative interest—"Tax legislation; specifically, investment tax credit availability to air carriers."

Union Oil Co. of Calif., Los Angeles, Calif. Lobbyist—Thomas F. Hairston, Los Angeles, Calif. Filed 12/16/77. Legislative interest—"Legislation affecting petroleum industry."

U.S. Industries Inc., New York, N.Y. Lobbyist—Olwine, Connelly, Chase, O'Donnell & Weyher, New York, N.Y. Filed 12/7/77. Legislative interest—"1977 Technical Corrections Bill (HR 6715)."

Zantop International Airlines, Yipsilanti, Mich. Lobbyists—Douglas E. MacArthur, St. Louis, Mo., Sellers, Conner & Cuneo, Washington, D.C., filed 12/14/77. Legislative interest—"...Air cargo deregulation; in favor of HR 9851, a bill to amend the Federal Aviation Act of 1958 to improve air cargo service."

International Relations

Committee to Save the Panama Canal, Reston, Va. Filed for self 12/8/77. Legislative interest—"Against the ratification by the Senate of the Panama Canal Treaty."

Japan Atomic Industrial Forum, Tokyo, Japan. Lobbyist—Danzansky, Dickey, Tydings, Quint & Gordon, Washington, D.C. Filed 12/8/77. Legislative interest—"Legislation in the field of civil nuclear energy policy and programs. ...Nuclear Nonproliferation Act of 1977, S 897."

Labor Groups

Department for Professional Employees, AFL-CIO, Washington, D.C. Filed for self 12/19/77. Legislative interest—"All legislation affecting union organizations and their members, particularly those in scientific, cultural and other professional fields." Lobbyist—Jack Golodner, Washington, D.C.

State and Local Governments

State of Hawaii, Honolulu, Hawaii. Lobbyist—Wilkinson, Cragun & Barker, Washington, D.C. Filed 12/6/77. Legislative interest—"...The passage of legislation in matters involving telecommunications which will place the state on an equal footing with the other states of the Union. ...Secure the passage of S 1866 and HR 9640 which, if enacted, will amend 47 U.S.C. Section 222 (1970)."

Trade and Professional Associations

Ad Hoc Committee for Competitive Telecommunicators, Washington, D.C. Lobbyist—Sharon West Coffey, Washington, D.C. Filed 12/2/77. Legislative interest—"Opposition to 'Bell Bill,' HR 12323, HR 13091, HR 13243, S 3192, S 3403."

American Automobile Association, Falls Church, Va. Filed for self 12/20/77. Legislative interest—"Legislation relating to American motorists and travel generally." Lobbyist—William R. Berman, Falls Church, Va.

American Bakers Association, Washington, D.C. Lobbyist—Van Ness, Feldman & Sutcliffe, Washington, D.C. Filed 12/8/77. Legislative interest—"...Legislation affecting the baking industry with specific interest in comprehensive energy regulatory and tax proposal ...HR 6831 and S 1469 and similar and related bills; in favor of legislation with constructive amendments."

American Footwear Industries Association Inc., Arlington, Va. Filed for self 12/5/77. Legislative interest—"Matters affecting the footwear industry, favor Orderly Marketing Act." Lobbyist—Norman V. Germany, Arlington, Va.

American Meat Institute, Washington, D.C. Filed for self 12/9/77. Legislative interest—"Legislation affecting the food industry in general, and particularly the livestock and meat industry, including, but not limited to: livestock production and feeding, animal diseases, meat inspection, food additives, labeling, transportation, environmental protection, safety, trade practices, consumer protection, energy." Lobbyist—Michael E. Brunner, Washington, D.C.

American Petroleum Institute, Washington, D.C. Lobbyists—Rutherford C. Harris, Atlanta, Ga., filed 12/12/77; Dickstein, Shapiro & Morin, Washington, D.C., filed 12/7/77. Legislative interest—"All legislation pertaining to vertical divestiture in the oil and natural gas industry and horizontal divestiture of alternative sources of energy, legislation affecting the petroleum industry."

American Petroleum Institute, Washington, D.C. Lobbyist — Connecticut Petroleum Council, Hartford, Conn. Filed 12/27/77. Legislative interest — "Legislation affecting the petroleum industry."

The Business Roundtable, Washington, D.C. Filed for self 12/8/77. Legislative interest—"Legislative matters, generally, which may affect business and industry operations—including, but not limited to proposals in the fields of labor relations, employment, antitrust and consumerism." Lobbyist—Harriett Perkins Hackney, Washington, D.C.

Chain Saw Manufacturers Association, Washington, D.C. Filed for self 12/3/77. Legislative interest—"Matters relating to the chain saw industry."

Chamber of Commerce of the United States, Washington, D.C. Filed for self 12/1/77. Legislative interest—"Legislation to establish an independent Agency for Consumer Protection and related consumer legislative issues (HR 6805, HR 3816). Opposed to both bills." Lobbyist — Jeffrey H. Joseph, Washington, D.C.

Communications Attorney Service, Van Nuys, Calif. Filed for self 12/23/77. Legislative interest — "...Interested in all bills dealing with personal radio communications, presently very opposed to S 1547."

National Audio-Visual Association Inc., Fairfax, Va. Filed for self 12/16/77. Legislative interest—"In support of multiple-award government contracting as opposed to single-source awards. S 1264, the Federal Acquisition Act of 1977. To support legislation increasing the efficiency of the Postal Service's Bulk Mail Centers, especially in the processing of film cases." Lobbyist—Richard G. Fuller, Fairfax, Va.

National Committee on Hospital Capital Expenditures, New York, N.Y. Lobbyist—O'Connor & Hannan, Washington, D.C. Filed 12/6/77. Legislative interest—"All legislation dealing with hospital capital expenditures, including but not limited to the following: S 1391, S 1470, HR 6575, HR 8121 and HR 9717."

National Limestone Institute Inc., Fairfax, Va. Filed for self 12/12/77. Legislative interest—"All legislation which directly or indirectly affects the interest of limestone producers." Lobbyist—Francis J. Boyd Jr., Richard J. Haas, Steven B. Hellem, Phillip G. Hough, Fairfax, Va. Filed 12/12/77.

National Machine Tool Builders Association, McLean, Va. Filed for self 12/9/77. Legislative interest—"Legislation affecting the machine tool industry." Lobbyist—Sheffield C. Richey Jr.

National Sporting Goods Association, Chicago, Ill. Lobbyist—Webster & Chamberlain, Washington, D.C. Filed 12/21/77. Legislative interest—"Legislation affecting product liability."

National Swimming Pool Institute, Washington, D.C. Filed for self 12/1/77. Legislative interest—"...Matters affecting construction, recreation, health, and small business. Specific interest in S 382 (con), Swimming Pool Act of 1977; and HR 8444, Title II, against discriminatory wording on swimming pools as an integrated part of a solar system."

Southern Forest Products Association, New Orleans, La. Lobbyist—Clark R. Cosse III, New Orleans, La., filed 12/19/77; Barry W. Zander, Metairie, La., filed 12/19/77. Legislative interest—"...In support of forestry exemptions under HR 3199 from the Army Corps of Engineers dredge and fill regulatory permit program. ...Supported strengthening of the Federal Forestry Incentives Program and initiation of a national private forestry program calling for tax incentives for small landowners."

Tuna Research Foundation, Washington, D.C. Filed for self 12/13/77. Legislative interest—"...Legislation affecting interests of tuna canners. Specific legislative interest: Marine Mammal Protection Act; Fishery Conservation and Management Act; Fishery Conservation Zone Transition Act; Fisherman's Protective Act; Tuna Conventions Act; amendments to these acts; similar legislation. Support reasonable legislation relating to tuna." Lobbyist—John P. Mulligan, Washington, D.C.

Miscellaneous

Communications Lobby Service, Van Nuys, Calif. Lobbyist—Joe Cargile, Escondido, Calif. Filed 12/27/77. Legislative interest—"Generally will lobby on behalf of all Citizen Band Radio Operators."

John L. Harmer, Los Angeles, Calif. Lobbyist—Irvin M. Kipnes, McLean, Va. Filed 12/13/77. Legislative interest—"Reclamation Law Revision, Omnibus Flood Control Act, 1944."

Seven Months Session for Congress, Austin, Texas. Filed for self 12/8/77. Legislative interest—"An amendment to the United States Constitution to provide for one seven months session for Congress."

January 1978

Agriculture and Environment

Citizens for the Management of Alaska Lands, Anchorage, Alaska. Lobbyist — Edward D. Heffernan, Washington, D.C. Filed 1/18/78. Legislative interest — "HR 39 and any and all legislation dealing with Alaska D-2 lands issues."

Energy Action Educational Foundation, Washington D.C. Lobbyist — Edwin Rothschild, McLean, Va. Filed 1/26/78. Legislative interest — "...Any and all legislation relating to the nation's supply of and demand for energy resources.Specific legislative interests include support for amendments to the Outer Continental Shelf Amendments Act (HR 1614, S 9), and support for various parts of the National Energy Act (HR 5289, HR 5263) and other legislation of similar content."

Natural Resources Defense Council Inc., New York, N.Y. Filed for self 1/6/78. Legislative interest — "HR 4759: Recombinant DNA Research Act of 1977, (new HR 7897); S 1217: Recombinant DNA Regulation Act." Lobbyist — Marcia Cleveland, New York, N.Y.

Steering Council for Alaska Lands, Anchorage, Alaska. Lobbyists — Moss, Frink & Franklin, Washington, D.C., filed 1/19/78; Media Group, San Francisco, Calif., filed 1/27/78. Legislative interest — "All pending legislation affecting public lands in Alaska, with particular emphasis on any bills concerning section 17 (d) (2) of the Alaska Native Claims Settlement Act."

Citizens' Groups

Citizens Committee for the Right to Keep and Bear Arms, Bellevue, Wash. Lobbyist — Anita Korten, John M. Snyder, Washington, D.C. Filed 1/27/78. Legislative interest — "Conservation, recreation and firearms legislation."

Citizens for Management of Alaska Lands, Anchorage, Alaska. Lobbyist — Langhorne A. Motley, Anchorage, Alaska. Filed 1/6/78. Legislative interest — "Determination of National Interest Lands — against HR 39, S 499, S 1500; for S 1787."

Committee of Americans for the Canal Treaties Inc., Washington, D.C. Lobbyist — Fraser/Associates Inc. Filed 1/30/78. Legislative interest — "Ratification of the Panama Canal Treaties."

Committee Concerned with the Safe Banking Act, Metairie, La. Lobbyist — Patton, Boggs & Blow, Washington, D.C. Filed 1/17/78. Legislative interest — "HR 9600, Safe Banking Act — against provision of Title II dealing with restrictions on activities by attorneys representing financial institutions."

Committee for Consumers No-Fault, Washington, D.C. Filed for self 1/10/78. Legislative interest — "Is in the favorable action on HR 6601 and S 1381, bills to provide basic standards for state no-fault vehicle accident victims."

Healthy America, Washington, D.C. Filed for self 1/26/78. Legislative interest — "... The advancement of health promotion and disease prevention." Lobbyist — Deborah Drudge, Washington, D.C.

NAACP Legal Defense and Educational Fund Inc., Washington, D.C. Filed for self 1/11/78. Legislative interest — "Will focus on education issues in the second session of 95th Congress. Specific legislative interest is Title I of the Elementary and Secondary Education Act.... HR 15-for; HR 9968-for; HR 7571-against, S 1780-against." Lobbyist — Phyllis McClure, Washington, D.C.

National Abortion Rights Action League, Washington, D.C. Filed for self 1/26/78. Legislative interest — "Opposed to all restrictive legislation dealing with abortion, constitutional and statutory, including: S J Res 6, 14, 15; H J Res 5, 89, 198; and all similar constitutional amendments; and all restrictive anti-abortion amendments to legislation." Lobbyist — Therese Ogle, Washington, D.C.

National Congress of Hispanic American Citizens, Washington, D.C. Filed for self 1/30/78. Legislative interest — ". . . Education programs such as the ESE Act; economic programs such as CETA and related eclated economic issues, civil rights legislation such as S 35." Lobbyist — A. Mike Romo, Washington, D.C.

National Rifle Association of America, Washington, D.C. Filed for self 1/11/78. Legislative interest — "...Activity relating to all aspects of the acquisition, possession and use of firearms and ammunition, as well as legislation relating to hunting and wildlife conservation." Lobbyist — Randal Bowman, Wilhelm Pickens, Washington, D.C.

Seminole Indian Tribe of Florida, Hollywood, Fla. Lobbyist — Sonosky, Chambers & Sachse, Washington, D.C. Filed 1/6/78. Legislative interest — "To seek a fair division and distribution of the final award of the Indian Claims Commission to the Seminole Indian Nation."

Sioux Nation, Rosebud, S.D. Lobbyist — Sonosky, Chambers & Sachse, Washington, D.C. Filed 1/6/78. Legislative interest — "To obtain a jurisdictional act."

Twenty-third Pro-Life Congressional District Action Committee, Yonkers, N.Y. Filed for self 1/4/78. Legislative interest — "All proposed Human Life Amendments; H J Res 121; H J Res 405; H J Res 132; S J Res 178; S J Res 140."

Corporations and Businesses

Air Products Chemical Co., Washington, D.C. Lobbyist — Patton, Boggs and Blow, Washington, D.C. Filed 1/10/78. Legislative interest — "Various amendments to tax code. Technical Tax Amendments to Tax Reform Act of 1976, HR 6715."

Allied Chemical Corp., Morristown, N.J. Lobbyist — Albert A. Fox Jr., Washington, D.C. Filed 1/11/78. Legislative interest — "Energy, employee relations, taxes, environmental and other matters affecting Allied Chemical Corp."

AMAX Coal Co., Indianapolis, Ind. Filed for self 1/19/78. Legislative interest — "Energy, Tax, environment, labor, mining, agriculture. Surface Mining Control Reclamation Act of 1977 (support w/amendments); Black Lung Benefits Reform Act of 1977 (S 1538 and HR 4544); Federal Coal Leasing Amendments Act of 1977 (support w/amendments); Energy Leasing Amendments of 1977; Horizontal Divestiture (S 1469, S 1927, HR 7816) oppose; Clean Air (support w/amendments); Federal Water Pollution Control Act Amendments of 1977; Federal Mine Safety Health Amendments Act of 1977; Labor Reform Act of 1977."

American Paratransit Institute Inc., Washington, D.C. Lobbyist — National Counsel Associates Inc., Washington, D.C. Filed 1/18/78. Legislative interest — "HR 8444 and HR 5263. Interest is in gasoline excise taxes as affecting taxis."

Associated General Contractors, Washington, D.C. Lobbyist — Fraser/Associates, Washington, D.C. Filed 1/30/78. Legislative interest — "Ratification of the Labor Law 'Reform' Bill - S 1883."

Board of Trade Clearing Corp., Chicago, Ill. Lobbyist — Alston, Miller & Gaines, Washington, D.C. Filed 1/20/78. Legislative interest — "Proponent of legislation providing for tax deduction for additions to reserves for clearing losses by commodity clearing organizations; participation in connection with the sunset hearings on the Commodity Futures Trading Commission pursuant to the Commodity Futures."

Boeing Vertol Co., Philadelphia, Pa. Filed for self 1/16/78. Legislative interest — "Legislation of interest to the laws that affect operation of the Boeing Co.; ...1) authorization and appropriation laws of all departments of the government; 2) tax and revenue; 3) regulation control of transportation, air, land, water; 4) labor and management issues; and 5) international trade regulation and control." Lobbyist — W. Thomas H. MacNew, Philadelphia, Pa.

The Brooklyn Union Gas Co., Brooklyn, N.Y. Filed for self 1/27/78. Legislative interest — "Legislation relating to the natural gas industry and national energy program." Lobbyist — Richard A. Plata, Brooklyn, N.Y.

Cargill Inc., Minneapolis, Minn. Lobbyist — DeLaney & Patrick, Washington, D.C. Filed 1/12/78. Legislative interest — "International tax and trade considerations."

Caterpillar Tractor Co., Peoria, Ill. Filed for self 1/9/78. Legislative interest — "Present or future proposed legislation of interest to Caterpillar Tractor Co. and its subsidiary or affiliated companies." Lobbyist — Rita L. Castle, Peoria, Ill.

CENEX (Farmers Union Central Exchange Inc.), St. Paul, Minn. Lobbyist — E. A. Jaenke Associates, Washington, D.C. Filed 1/13/78. Legislative interest"Pesticide legislation."

Certain Teed Corp., Valley Forge, Pa. Lobbyist — Daniel M. Kush, Washington, D.C.,Filed 1/27/78. Legislative interest — "Matters as to which Certain Teed Corp. may wish to make recommendations or comments."

Chicago Mercantile Exchange, Chicago, Ill. Lobbyist — C. Dayle Henington, Washington, D.C. Filed 1/24/78. Legislative interest — "Legislation affecting commodity futures industry."

CNA Financial Corp., Chicago, Ill. Filed for self 1/11/78. Legislative interest — "Legislation relating to the regulation and chartering of insurance companies — S 1710." Lobbyist — Berman and Associates, Washington, D.C.

Delhi International Oil Corp., Dallas, Texas. Lobbyist — Edward Falck & Co., Washington, D.C. Filed 1/6/78. Legislative interest — "All material of interest to Delhi International Oil Co., an independent oil and gas producer."

Dow Chemical Co., Midland, Mich. Lobbyist — Charles T. Marck, Washington, D.C. Filed 1/17/78. Legislative interest — "Legislation affecting and/or of interest to Dow Chemical."

El Paso Natural Gas Co., Houston, Texas. Lobbyist — Frank W. Calhoun, Houston, Texas. Filed 1/17/78. Legislative interest — "National energy legislation including HR 5289 and HR 8444."

Encyclopaedia Britannica Inc., Chicago, Ill. Lobbyist — Wickham & Craft, Washington, D.C. Filed 1/23/78. Legislative interest — "For legislation (like HR 6880) to terminate enforcement of discriminatory, anti-competitive, affirmative requirements of FTC orders."

Exxon Corp., New York, N.Y. Lobbyist — Nicholas J. Bush, Washington, D.C. Filed 1/26/78. Legislative interest — "...Legislation affecting the employer."

First National Bank of Boston, Boston, Mass. Lobbyist — Bingham, Dana & Gould, Boston, Mass. Filed 1/13/78. Legislative interest — "...In clarifications, and/or changes, in income and employment tax provisions of Internal Revenue Code of 1954 affecting meals provided by employers for employees, including but not limited to IRC sections 61, 119, 3121 and 3401."

General Electric Co., Fairfield, Conn. Lobbyist — Peter E. Holmes, Washington, D.C. Filed 1/10/78. Legislative interest — "Government procurement, labor law, patent law, antitrust law, tax law, tariffs and interstate and foreign commerce, and other legislative matters."

Georgia Power Co., Atlanta, Ga. Lobbyist — W. Robert Worley, Atlanta, Ga. Filed 1/16/78. Legislative interest — "...Interests affecting the electric utility industry including energy, environmental and regulatory issues."

International Air Leases Inc., Miami, Fla. Lobbyist — Paul Reiber, Washington, D.C. Filed 1/30/78. Legislative interest — "Amendment of the Federal Aviation Act of 1958, Sec. 901 (b)."

J.C. Penney Co. Inc., New York, N.Y. Filed for self 1/27/78. Legislative interest — "Bills affecting the retailing industry including HR 8753, HR 2482, HR 8359, S 1653, S 957 and S 1874."

Kikkoman Foods Inc., Walworth, Wis. Filed for self 1/23/78. Legislative interest — "...Proposed legislation relating to food and requirements for food safety." Lobbyist — Milton E. Neshek, Elkhorn, Wis.

Laclede Gas Co., St. Louis, Mo. Lobbyist — James J. Murphy, Washington, D.C. Filed 1/9/78. Legislative interest — "Legislation affecting the operation of a gas distribution company, specifically, the proposed Natural Energy Act and related legislation."

Land O'Lakes Inc., Minneapolis, Minn. Lobbyist — E. A. Jaenke & Associates, Washington, D.C. Filed 1/13/78. Legislative interest — "Energy legislation."

Lear Siegler Inc., Santa Monica, Calif. Lobbyist — William D. Thompson, Washington, D.C. Filed 1/27/78. Legislative interest — "HR 4082, Renegotiation Reform Act of 1977; HR 5128, National Labor Relations Act Amendments; HR 1561, Export Administration Act; HR 77, Labor Reform Act of 1977; HR 5747, International Security Assistance and Arms Export Control Act of 1977; HR 314, Service Contract Act; and HR 7047, National Employment Priority Act of 1977."

Long Island Lighting Co., Mineola, N.Y. Filed for self 1/17/78. Legislative interest — "All legislation directly or indirectly affecting the operations of a regulated public utility." Lobbyist — Kevin Michael Rooney, Mineola, N.Y.

Lonza Inc., Fair Lawn, N.J. Lobbyist — Alfred R. McCauley, Washington, D.C. Filed 1/6/78. Legislative interest — "In favor of enactment of HR 10224, a bill to temporarily suspend the rate of duty on 2-methyl 5-ethyl pyridine."

Marion Laboratories Inc., Kansas City, Mo. Lobbyist — Sullivan & Worcester, Washington, D.C. Filed 1/10/78. Legislative interest — "Legislative activity in areas of pharmaceuticals, health and consumer product safety."

Meredith Corp., Washington, D.C. Filed for self 1/6/78. Legislative interest — "...Broad range of potential legislative activity as it may affect the interests of Meredith Corp." Lobbyist — Robert F. Goodwin, Washington, D.C.

National Limestone Institute Inc., Fairfax, Va. Filed for self 1/13/78. Legislative interest — "All legislation which directly or indirectly affects the interests of limestone producers." Lobbyist — Kevin D. MacAfee, Fairfax, Va.

Pacific Power and Light Co., Portland, Ore. Filed for self 1/18/78. Legislative interest — "Any and all legislation concerning sources, manufacture, transmission and distribution of electric power." Lobbyist — Alyce D. Canaday, Washington, D.C.

People's Drugstores Inc., Alexandria, Va. Lobbyist — Richard H. Fary, Washington, D.C. Filed 1/6/78. Legislative interest — "Interested in clarifications of HR 8410, "Labor Reform Act of 1977."

Pontchartrain Bank, Metairie, La. Lobbyist — Paul Corbin, Washington, D.C. Filed 1/23/78. Legislative interest — "Against further regulations against banks."

Printing Industries of America Inc., Arlington, Va. Filed for self 1/5/78. Legislative interest — "...Legislation of interest to commercial printers." Lobbyist — T. Randolph Shingler, Arlington, Va.

Reader's Digest Association Inc., Pleasantville, N.Y. Filed for self 1/25/78. Legislative interest — "Postal Service Act of 1977. HR 7700." Lobbyist — Kent Rhodes, Pleasantville, N.Y.

Standard Oil Co., Cleveland, Ohio. Lobbyist — Nancy J. Risque, Bruce A. McCrodden, Washington, D.C. Filed 1/10/78. Legislative interest — "...Matters pertaining to the interests of the company respecting petroleum products, refining, and distribution, petrochemicals and coal."

Stencel Aero Engineering Corp., Asheville, N.C. Lobbyist — Hydeman, Mason Goodell, Washington, D.C. Filed 1/10/78. Legislative interest — "Congressional reference bill."

Thiokol Corp., Newton, Pa. Lobbyist — Moss, Frink & Franklin, Washington, D.C. Filed 1/19/78. Legislative interest — "Passive restraint."

Trailways Inc., Dallas, Texas. Lobbyist — National Counsel Associates, Inc., Washington, D.C. Filed 1/18/78. Legislative interest — "HR 8444 and HR 5263. Interest is in gasoline excise taxes as affecting buses."

Union Mutual Life Insurance Co., Portland, Maine. Filed for self 1/19/78. Legislative interest — "Investment Policy, etc." Lobbyist — David Emery Hughes, Portland, Maine.

United Airlines, Chicago, Ill. Filed for self 1/19/78. Legislative interest — "All phases of the airline industry. Lobbyist — George J. Aste, Washington, D.C.

United States Steel Corp., Pittsburgh, Pa. Filed for self 1/13/78. Legislative interest — "Any legislation affecting interests of United States Steel Corp." Lobbyist — C. John Vermilye, Carl E. Atkinson, Washington, D.C.

Utah Power & Light Co., Salt Lake City, Utah. Lobbyist — Moss, Frink & Franklin, Washington, D.C. Filed 1/19/78. Legislative interest — "Energy legislation."

Warner Cable Corp., New York, N.Y. Lobbyist — Fleischman & Walsh, Washington, D.C. Filed 1/23/78. Legislative interest — "In favor of legislation favorably affecting the cable television industry."

Wometco Enterprises Inc., Miami, Fla. Lobbyist — Cohen and Uretz, Washington, D.C. Filed 1/24/78. Legislative interest — "Any tax legislation which may effect the present law on tax deductions for attendance at conventions."

Zenith Radio Corp., Glenview, Ill. Lobbyist — Bernard Nash, Washington, D.C. Filed 1/12/78. Legislative interest — "Legislation affecting the television and other consumer electronic product industries, including but not limited to, legislation affecting imports, the customs and tariff statutes, HR 8149 and HR 8367."

International Relations

Committee of Americans for the Canal Treaties Inc., Washington, D.C. Lobbyists — John O. Mongoven, Hugh O'Neill, Alexandria, Va.; Richard A. Brown, George Moffett, Washington, D.C.; William Jay Slosberg, Chevy Chase, Md. Filed 1/31/78. Legislative interest — "COACT seeks to fully air all views on the proposed Panama Canal Treaties."

Council for a Livable World, Washington, D.C. Filed for self 1/25/78. Legislative interest — "Legislation on arms control and Disarmament FY 1978 Authorizations and DOD, State, AEC, ACDA, etc." Lobbyist — John Isaacs, Washington, D.C.

Department of Information, Republic of South Africa. Lobbyist — deKieffer and Associates, Washington, D.C. Filed 1/19/78. Legislative interest — "Matters affecting American foreign policy toward the Republic of South Africa."

Deutsche Bank AG, Frankfort, West Germany. Lobbyist — Sullivan & Worcester, Washington, D.C. Filed 1/13/78. Legislative interest — "Opposing changes in existing law re: international banking in U.S.; HR 7325, The International Banking Act."

Labor Unions

American Federation of Teachers, Washington, D.C. Lobbyist — James G. O'Hara, Washington, D.C. Filed 1/16/78. Legislative interest — "Promotion of legislative interests of teachers generally in authorization and appropriations bills and in other pertinent legislative proposals that may be made."

Industrial Union Department, AFL-CIO, Washington, D.C. Filed for self 1/17/78. Legislative interest — "All bills affecting the welfare of the country generally, and specifically bills affecting workers." Lobbyist — Joseph Uehlein, Washington, D.C.

International Association of Machinists and Aerospace Workers, Washington, D.C. Filed for self 1/11/78. Legislative interest — "...All legislation affecting the socio-economic and political interests of the American workingman including all pending legislation dealing with Social Security, national health, aid to the physically handicapped, labor relations, displaced persons, etc." Lobbyist — Dorothy A. Ellsworth, Washington, D.C.

Oil, Chemical & Atomic Workers International Union, Denver, Colo. Lobbyist — L. Calvin Moore, Washington, D.C. Filed 1/12/78. Legislative interest — "Support all legislation favorable to the national peace, security, democracy, prosperity and general welfare — oppose legislation detrimental to those objectives."

Retail Store Employees Union, Clinton, Md. Filed for self 1/30/78. Legislative interest — "General social legislation and all matters relating to the interests of labor organizations." Lobbyist — Rosann Fuhrman, Clinton, Md.

Seafarers International Union, Washington, D.C. Filed for self 1/9/78. Legislative interest — "Legislation affecting the interest of working people." Lobbyist — David Dolgen, Washington, D.C.

Trade Associations

Alaska Movers Association, Bellevue, Wash. Lobbyist — Beveridge, Fairbanks and Diamond, Washington, D.C. Filed 1/16/78. Legislative interest — "General matters relating to the business of the moving and storage of household goods. Specifically, DOD bidding policies as such."

American Gas Association, Arlington, Va. Filed for self 1/13/78. Legislative interest — "OCS Lands Act Amendments, HR 1614, S 9; ERDA '78 budget, S 1811; Tax Provisions, S 1472; Natural Gas Act Amendments of HR 5289; Public Utility Regulatory Policy Act, HR 4018; Coal Conversion, HR 5146; Conservation, HR 5037." Lobbyist — William T. McCormick Jr.

American Hardware Manufacturers Association, Palatine, Ill. Lobbyist — London & Goldberg, Washington, D.C. Filed 1/24/78. Legislative interest — "All legislative matters affecting the membership generally, and in particular, legislation which relates to tax policy, labor, consumer, product liability, environmental, and other issues."

American Paper Institute Inc., New York, N.Y. Lobbyists — John L. Festa, Lauren Kim Schryver, Doreen Eisinger, Katherine Robinson, Washington, D.C. Filed 1/30/78. Legislative interest — "Those affecting the pulp, paper and paperboard industry, its operation, practices and properties."

American Petroleum Institute, Washington, D.C. Lobbyist — Vincent D. Brown, Lincoln, Neb. Filed 1/30/78. Legislative interest — "Legislation affecting the petroleum industry."

American Public Power Association, Washington, D.C. Filed for self 1/6/78. Legislative interest — "HR 8444, HR 4018, S 1469, S 2114, National Energy Act and other legislation relating to energy matters." Lobbyist — Carl Goldfield, Washington, D.C.

American Retail Federation, Washington, D.C. Lobbyists — Patton, Boggs & Blow; O'Connor & Hannan, Washington, D.C. Filed 1/17/78. Legislative interest — "Seeking amendments to S 1883, Labor Reform Act."

American Textile Manufacturers Institute, Charlotte, N.C. Filed for self 1/6/78. Legislative interest — "...All legislation affecting the welfare of the textile industry — such as domestic and foreign trade policy, tax policy, labor policy, government controls, raw cotton and wool policy, consumer, environmental control, energy policy, and lobbying legislation." Lobbyist — Ronald L. Floor, Washington, D.C.

Associated Gas Distributors, Washington, D.C. Filed for self 1/9/78. Legislative interest — "Legislation affecting the natural gas distribution industry, such as, National Energy Act (HR 4018, HR 5289) and the Outer Continental Shelf Lands Act Amendments, S 9 and HR 1614." Lobbyist — Dana Contratto, Washington, D.C.

Associated General Contractors of America, Washington, D.C. Filed for self 1/10/78. Legislative interest — "...Matters of federal legislation...." Lobbyist — George Stockton, Washington, D.C.

Associated Industries of Florida, Tallahassee, Fla. Lobbyist — Alcalde, Henderson, O'Bannon & Kline, Rosslyn, Va. Filed 1/25/78. Legislative interest — "All issues affecting the business community."

Associated Third Class Mail Users, Washington, D.C. Lobbyist — J. Edward Day, Washington, D.C. Filed 1/5/78. Legislative interest — "Any legislation relating to postal matters and to business users of the mail and mail advertisers."

Association of Executive Recruiting Consultants Inc., New York, N.Y. Lobbyist — Douglas P. Bennett, Washington, D.C. Filed 1/18/78. Legislative interest — "Fair Credit Reporting Act Amendments and privacy legislation."

Association of General Merchandise Chains, Washington, D.C. Lobbyists — O'Connor & Hannan, Patton, Boggs & Blow, Washington, D.C. Filed 1/19/78. Legislative interest — "Seeking amendments to S 1883."

Association of Independent Corrugated Converters, Evanston, Ill. Filed for self 1/12/78. Legislative interest — "Legislation affecting the paper and corrugated paper converting industries." Lobbyist — Blum, Parker & Nash, Washington, D.C.

Association of Oil Pipe Lines, Washington, D.C. Filed for self 1/24/78. Legislative interest — "Legislation affecting petroleum pipelines, S 9 and S 1879." Lobbyist — Patrick H. Corcoran, Washington, D.C.

Cast Iron Pipe Research Association, Washington, D.C. Filed for self 1/18/78. Legislative interest — "Any legislation affecting ... producers of cast and ductile iron pressure pipe." Lobbyist — Edward D. Heffernan, Washington, D.C.

Chamber of Commerce of the United States, Washington, D.C. Lobbyist — Fraser/Associates Inc., Washington, D.C. Filed 1/30/78. Legislative interest — "Ratification of the Labor Law 'Reform' Bill - S 1883."

Community Antenna Television Association Inc., Oklahoma City, Okla. Lobbyist — Stephen R. Effros, Washington, D.C. Filed 1/27/78. Legislative interest — "Communications and small business-related matters, including regulatory reform."

Cosmetic, Toiletry and Fragrance Association, Inc., Washington, D.C. Filed for self 1/23/78. Legislative interest — "Legislation affecting the cosmetic industry, including S 2365."

Direct Selling Association, Washington, D.C. Filed for self 1/27/78. Legislative interest — "Legislation of interest to the direct selling industry." Lobbyist - Jared O. Blum, Washington, D.C.

Electronic Industries Association, Washington, D.C. Lobbyist — J. Edward Day, Washington, D.C. Filed 1/5/78. Legislative interest — "Any legislation affecting manufacturers of consumer electronics products including consumer legislation, legislation relating to advertising and trade legislation."

Food Marketing Institute, Washington, D.C. Filed for self 1/18/78. Legislative interest — "Matters affecting the food distribution industry through trade regulation or otherwise." Lobbyist — John W. Farquhar, Washington, D.C.

Imperial Resources Association, Brawley, Calif. Lobbyist — Brownstein Zeidman Schomer & Chase, Washington, D.C. Filed 1/30/78. Legislative interest — "Legislation affecting Reclamation Acts."

Magazine Publishers Association Inc., New York, N.Y. Lobbyist — John M. Burzio, Washington, D.C. Filed 1/19/78. Legislative interest — "HR 7700 and other legislation affecting the postal rates of the magazine industry, supporting HR 7700."

Moving and Storage Association of Hawaii, Honolulu, Hawaii. Lobbyist — Beveridge, Fairbanks and Diamond, Washington, D.C. Filed 1/16/78. Legislative interest — "...Matters regarding the business of the moving and storage of household goods. Specifically, DOD bidding policies relating to such."

National Association of Farmworker Organizations, Washington, D.C. Filed for self 1/24/78. Legislative interest — "In support of legislation favorably affecting farmworkers, including but not limited to, HR 9030 — Welfare Reform; Comprehensive Employment and Training Act, Farm Labor Contractor Registration Act, Elementary and Secondary Education Act, Fair Labor Standards Act, Health Act of 1975."

National Association of Manufacturers, Washington, D.C. lobbyist — Fraser/Associates Inc., Washington, D.C. Filed 1/30/78. Legislative interest — "Ratification of the Labor Law 'Reform' Bill - S 1883."

National Association of Retired Federal Employees, Washington, D.C. Filed for self 1/31/78. Legislative interest — "Legislation affecting retired civil employees of U.S. government." Lobbyist — Robert M. Beers, Charles L. Merin, John F. McClelland, Judy E. Park, Stephen L. Skardon Jr., Washington, D.C.

National Cable Television Association, Washington, D.C. Lobbyist — Fleischman and Walsh, Bruce Collins, Washington, D.C. Filed 1/23/78. Legislative interest — "Legislation favorably affecting the CATV industry, HR 7442, S 1547."

National Conference of Bankruptcy Judges, New York, N.Y. Lobbyist — Webster & Sheffield, Washington, D.C. Filed 1/27/78. Legislative interest — "To establish a uniform law on bankruptcies."

National Federation of Independent Business, Washington, D.C. Filed for self 1/9/78. Legislative interest — "All legislation affecting small business and the economic well-being of the country." Lobbyist — Janet E. Munroe, Washington, D.C.

National Forest Products Association, Washington, D.C. Lobbyist — Patton, Boggs & Blow, Washington, D.C., filed 1/30/78; Souther, Spaulding, Kinsey, Williamson Schwabe, Portland, Ore., filed 1/27/78. Legislative interest — "Forest service, oral bidding bill, HR 6362, S 1360, in favor of said bills."

National Home Furnishings Association, Chicago, Ill. Filed for self 1/10/78. Legislative interest — "Legislation affecting retailing." Lobbyist — Gerald P. Nagy, Washington, D.C.

National Product Liability Council, Cincinnati, Ohio. Filed for self 1/10/78. Legislative interest — "Legislation dealing with product liability. S 403, S 527, S 1706, HR 6300 and HR 7711."

National Product Liability Council, Cincinnati, Ohio. Lobbyist — Lund Levin & O'Brien, Washington, D.C. Legislative interest — "Legislation dealing with product liability. S 403, S 527, S 1706, and HR 6300."

National Restaurant Association, Washington, D.C. Lobbyist — Douglas P. Bennett, Washington, D.C. Filed 1/18/78. Legislative interest — "1978 tax proposals."

National Retail Merchants Association, Washington, D.C. Lobbyist — Patton, Boggs & Blow; O'Connor & Hannan, Washington, D.C. Filed 1/17/78. Legislative interest — "Seeking amendments to S 1883, Labor Reform Act."

National Society of Professional Engineers, Washington, D.C. Filed for self 1/17/78. Legislative interest — "All legislation affecting interests of professional engineers." Lobbyist — Michael M. Schoor, Washington, D.C.

National Soft Drink Association, Washington, D.C. Filed for self 1/9/78. Legislative interest — "Legislation affecting the soft drink industry in the United States." Lobbyist — H. Christopher Nolde, Washington, D.C.

Oklahoma Association of Electric Cooperatives, Oklahoma City, Okla. Lobbyist — Ed Edmondson, Muskogee, Okla. Filed 1/31/78. Legislative interest — "Interests involve electric cooperative interests in current energy legislation, including HR 5263, HR 8444."

Outdoor Power Equipment Institute, Inc., Washington, D.C. Filed for self 1/12/78. Legislative interest — "Legislation affecting the production and marketing of outdoor power equipment."

Railway Progress Institute, Alexandria, Va. Filed for self 1/11/78. Legislative interest — "Interested in matters affecting the railroads and railway and mass transit supply industries." Lobbyist — Robert William Smith, Alexandria, Va.

Scientific Apparatus Makers Association, Washington, D.C. Filed for self 1/27/78. Legislative interest — "Hospital cost containment, product liability and other bills affecting makers of scientific apparatus." Lobbyist — John F. Rodgers, Alice V. Leaderman, Graydon R. Powers Jr., Washington, D.C.

Sheet Metal Air Condition Contractors National Association, Vienna, Va. Lobbyist — Gregg Ward, Alexandria, Va. Filed 1/23/78. Legislative interest — "Labor reform, social security, small business."

Tennessee Valley Public Power Association, Chattanooga, Tenn. Filed for self 1/11/78. Legislative interest — "Any legislation affecting the municipally and/or cooperatively owned electric power systems of the Tennessee Valley and TVA." Lobbyist — Jerry L. Campbell, Chattanooga, Tenn.

Miscellaneous

Ad Hoc 602 Committee, Washington, D.C. Lobbyist — William J. Colley, Washington, D.C. Filed 1/10/78. Legislative interest — "Various amendments to tax code, HR 6715."

Allison Technical Services, Santa Monica, Calif. Lobbyist — Timmons and Company Inc., Washington, D.C. Filed 1/12/78. Legislative interest — "...Matters concerning the procurement by the federal government of fighter aircraft, particularly the F-18 and other attack aircraft."

American Arts Alliance, Washington, D.C. Filed for self 1/13/78. Legislative interest — "Arts-related legislation of all kinds."

Meyer L. Aron, Brooklyn, N.Y. Filed for self 1/5/78. Legislative interest — "Lobbying for senior citizens re: airline fares and regulation; S 3364 and S 2551."

The Arthritis Foundation, Washington, D.C. Lobbyist — Smathers, Symington & Herlong, Washington, D.C. Filed 1/24/78. Legislative interest — "Interest dealing with arthritis programs as well as legislation dealing with programs under the Department of Health, Education and Welfare."

Carnegie Corporation of New York, New York, N.Y. Lobbyist — Sutherland, Asbill & Brennan, Washington, D.C. Filed 1/16/78. Legislative interest — "In support of HR 112 and S 2204."

Chicago Metropolitan Higher Education Council, et al, Chicago, Ill. Lobbyist — Dow, Lohnes & Albertson, Washington, D.C. Filed 1/30/78. Legislative interest — "Amendments to public broadcasting act sections of the Communications Act, HR 9620."

Congaree Limited Partnership, Chicago, Ill. Lobbyist — Wickham & Craft, Washington, D.C. Filed 1/23/78. Legislative interest — "For appropriations for land acquisition authorized under PL 94-455."

Stephen Junkunc III, Ft. Lauderdale, Fla. Filed for self 1/23/78. Legislative interest — "Renegotiation bills, Vinso-Trammell Act (against); Minish bill, HR 5959 (for); Cranston bill, S 1594 and Proxmire bill (for)."

Mark Kleinman, Washington, D.C. Filed for self 1/27/78. Legislative interest — "Mostly process questions under the broad title of: Government Operations."

Harvey Marshall Berg, Miami, Fla. Filed for self 1/3/78. Legislative interest — "Veterans Benefits Compensation; United States Postal Service Changes, international trade and tariffs, saber gas turbine automobile engine research, African development and commerce, metrics measurement systems."

New Foundations for Tax Justice Inc., Jenkintown, Pa. Filed for self 1/25/78. Legislative interest — "To amend tax laws so as to produce genuine progressivity, taking into account all federal, state and local taxes." Lobbyist — Milton A. Dauber, Jenkintown, Pa.

Public Service Research Council, Vienna, Va. Filed for self 1/30/78. Legislative interest — "Issues dealing with public sector unionism — HR 10, S 80 — opposed, S 274 — favor, HR 9094 — opposed." Lobbyist — Jon Minarik, Vienna, Va.

Q Enterprises, Washington, D.C. Filed for self 1/10/78. Legislative interest — "Domestic and foreign trade."

Tax Equity for Americans Abroad, Washington, D.C. Filed for self 1/31/78. Legislative interest — "...The amendment of inequitable tax laws as such laws relate to Americans living abroad. The specific legislative interest is the passage of amendments to the foreign income provisions of the Tax Reform Act of 1976."

Trade Adjustment Assistance Coordinating Committee, Washington, D.C. Lobbyist — Delaney Patrick, Washington, D.C. Filed 1/27/78. Legislative interest — "Possible amendments to Trade Act of 1974 and related administrative considerations."

February

Agriculture and Environment

ALASKA COALITION, Washington, D.C. Filed for self 2/6/78. Legislative interest — "Alaska National Interest Lands Conservation Act" and related legislation; HR 39 and S 1500, and all those bills pertaining to Alaskan lands." Lobbyist — J. Dee Frankfourth, Stephen Hiniker, Washington, D.C.

ENVIRONMENTAL DEFENSE FUND, Washington, D.C. Filed for self 2/23/78. Legislative interest — ". . . Such environmental issues as toxic substances regulation, energy, water, transportation and wilderness legislation; HR 8309, HR 39, HR 5263, HR 4018." Lobbyist — Charlene Dougherty, Washington, D.C.

ENVIRONMENTAL POLICY CENTER, Washington, D.C. Filed for self 2/1/78. Legislative interest — "Legislative interests relate to energy, land and water resources issues." Lobbyist — Lynn Coddington, Washington, D.C.

FRIENDS OF THE EARTH, Washington, D.C. Filed for self 2/9/78. Legislative interest — "...Legislation to preserve, restore and insure rational use of the ecosphere — generally, all environmental legislation." Lobbyist — Cathy Smith, Washington, D.C.

INTERNATIONAL AGRICULTURAL DEVELOPMENT SERVICE, New York, N.Y. Lobbyist — Vorys, Sater, Seymour & Pease, Washington, D.C. Filed 2/24/78. Legislative interest — ". . . Reconsideration of Section 911 of the Internal Revenue Code and any other matter of interest."

SIERRA CLUB, San Francisco, Calif. Lobbyists — Jonathan Carl Gibson, Washington, D.C., filed 2/28/78; Patricia S. Record, Madison, Wis., filed 2/20/78. Legislative interest — ". . . Issues of environmental concern."

Citizens' Groups

COALITION FOR NEW YORK INC., New York, N.Y. Filed for self 2/6/78. Legislative interest — "Problems confronting the city of New York."

COMMON CAUSE, Washington, D.C. Filed for self 2/20/78. Legislative interest — "Promotion of social and physical improvement in the United States." Lobbyist — Albert Winchester, Washington, D.C.

NATIONAL ASSOCIATION OF FARMER ELECTED COMMITTEEMEN, Darlington, S.C. Filed for self 2/15/78. Legislative interest — "All farm legislation." Lobbyist — Edward Bowman, Darlington, S.C.

NATIONAL COALITION TO BAN HANDGUNS, Washington, D.C. Filed for self 2/23/78. Legislative interest — "Legislation relating to handguns." Lobbyist — Michael K. Beard, Samuel S. Fields, Washington, D.C.

TWELFTH CONGRESSIONAL DISTRICT ACTION COMMITTEE, Mountain View, Calif. Filed for self 2/28/78. Legislative interest — "All proposed Human Life Amendments."

Corporations and Businesses

ALLEGHENY AIRLINES, Washington, D.C. Lobbyist — John L. Zorack, Washington, D.C. Filed 2/27/78. Legislative interest — "Legislation pertaining to local service air carriers compensation."

AMERICAN AIRLINES INC., New York, N.Y. Lobbyist — Charls E. Walker, Washington, D.C. Filed 2/27/78. Legislative interest — "Tax proposals relating to items of capital recovery and capital formation which affect airline companies."

AMERICAN SIGN AND INDICATOR CORP., Spokane, Wash. Lobbyist — Cramer, Visser, Lipsen & Smith, Washington, D.C. Filed 2/13/78. Legislative interest — "Legislation that might affect the industry and in particular federal aid highway authority and/or legislation."

BASIN INC., Midland, Texas. Lobbyist — Van Ness, Feldman & Sutcliffe, Washington, D.C. Filed 2/8/78. Legislative interest — "Federal legislation, if any, promoting competition and facilitating new market entry in the crude oil gathering and resale business."

BELCO PETROLEUM CORP., New York, N.Y. Lobbyist — National Counsel Associates Inc., Washington, D.C. Filed 2/21/78. Legislative interest — ". . . A provision made in the energy bill which would adjust fair rates for gas pricing rollover gas from expired contracts."

BOARD OF TRADE CLEARING CORP., Chicago, Ill. Lobbyists — Michael G. Wasserman, G. Conley Ingram, Atlanta, Ga., filed 2/3/78; Timothy J. Kincaid, Washington, D.C., filed 2/1/78. Legislative interest — "Proponent of legislation providing for tax deduction for additions to reserves for clearing losses by commodity clearing organizations. Proponent of changes in S 2266, Bankruptcy Act."

BONSIB INC., Washington, D.C. Filed for self 2/3/78. Legislative interest — "No specific legislative interests at this time."

CITIBANK, N.A., New York, N.Y. Lobbyist — Kutak Rock & Huie, Washington, D.C. Filed 2/6/78. Legislative interest — "Any legislation affecting national banks or bank holding companies."

CONSOLIDATION COAL CO., Pittsburgh, Pa. Filed for self 2/8/78. Legislative interest — ". . . Any and all measures affecting the employer." Lobbyist — J. K. Holman, Washington, D.C.

CRUM & FORSTER CORP., Morristown, N.J. Filed for self 2/2/78. Legislative interest — "All statutes and bills affecting the corporate and insurance interests of affiliates of Crum & Forster Corporation." Lobbyist — Leslie Cheek III, Washington, D.C.

THE DOW CHEMICAL CO., Midland, Mich. Filed for self 2/10/78. Legislative interest — "Legislation affecting and/or of interest to the Dow Chemical Co." Lobbyist — Richard M. Patterson, R.S. Chamberlin, Thomas E. Jones, Washington, D.C.

EASTERN AIRLINES INC., New York, N.Y. Lobbyist — Charls E. Walker, Washington, D.C. Filed 2/27/78. Legislative interest — "Tax proposals relating to items of capital recovery and capital formation which affects airline companies."

FM SCHAEFER CORP., New York, N.Y. Lobbyist — Rogers & Wells, Washington, D.C. Filed 2/6/78. Legislative interest — "Tax legislation."

THE FIRST NATIONAL BANK OF BOSTON, Boston, Mass. Filed for self 2/3/78. Legislative interest — "Any and all matters affecting the First National Bank of Boston."

FORD MOTOR CO., Dearborn, Mich. Filed for self 2/21/78. Legislative interest — "...To analyze federal plans, policies and trends and proposed legislation and regulations in relation to the interests of the Company." Lobbyist — Joseph G. Gerard, Washington, D.C.

FRONTIER AIRLINES, Denver, Colo. Lobbyist — John L. Zorack, Washington, D.C. Filed 2/27/78. Legislative interest — "Legislation pertaining to local service air carriers compensation."

GENERAL ATOMIC CO., San Diego, Calif. Lobbyist — Sheryl Brinson, Washington, D.C. Filed 2/20/78. Legislative interest — "Atomic and electrical energy, environmental legislation, federally supported research and development, general legislation related to U.S. industry."

GENERAL ELECTRIC CO., Fairfield, Conn. Filed for self 2/2/78. Legislative interest — "Any legislation . . . affecting General Electric Co. components providing products and services to health care professionals and institutions, domestic and international." Lobbyist — Robert M. Moliter, Washington, D.C.

HARRIS CORP., Washington, D.C. Lobbyist — Irving W. Swanson, Rockville, Md. Filed 2/14/78. Legislative interest — "All matters pending in Congress of interest to the Harris Corporation."

HOUSEHOLD FINANCE CORP., Chicago, Ill. Lobbyist — J. T. Nelson, Gibson Island, Md. Filed 2/10/78. Legislative interest — "Matters relating to consumer credit, merchandising, manufacturing, leasing and insurance."

THE KROGER CO., Cincinnati, Ohio. Lobbyist — Arnold Porter, Washington, D.C. Filed 2/7/78. Legislative interest — "HR 8359, S 1873 and related measures.

LEHMAN BROTHERS, New York, N.Y. Lobbyist — Patton, Boggs & Blow, Washington, D.C. Filed 2/28/78. Legislative interest — "Energy tax legislation relating to industrial revenue bonds."

LOUISIANA-PACIFIC CORP., Portland, Ore. Lobbyist — Patton, Boggs & Blow, Washington, D.C. Filed 2/28/78. Legislative interest — "Legislation affecting the classification of federal lands in Alaska."

MOCATTA METALS CORP., New York, N.Y. Filed for self 2/17/78. Legislative interest — "Legislation to extend the Commodity Futures Trading Commission, S 2391, and other legislation related to commodity options and futures, including HR 10901." Lobbyists — Patton, Boggs & Blow, Washington, D.C., filed 2/28/78; Cadwalader, Wickersham & Taft, Washington, D.C., filed 2/17/78.

MILES LABORATORIES INC., Elkhart, Ind. Lobbyist — David M. Jenkins, Washington, D.C. Filed 2/2/78. Legislative interest — "Legislation affecting the pharmaceutical industry and legislation relating to health and/or nutrition."

NATIONWIDE INSURANCE CO., Columbus, Ohio. Lobbyist — Williams & Jensen, Washington, D.C. Filed 2/17/78. Legislative interest — "Tax legislative matters of general interest to the corporation."

OCEAN MINERALS CO., Mountain View, Calif. Lobbyist —Patton, Boggs & Blow, Washington, D.C. Filed 2/28/78. Legislative interest — "Legislation and agency actions relating to deep seabed mining; HR 3350 and S 2053."

PAN AMERICAN WORLD AIRWAYS INC., New York, N.Y. Lobbyist — Charls E. Walker, Washington, D.C. Filed 2/27/78. Legislative interest — "Tax proposals relating to items of capital recovery and capital formation which affect airline companies."

REYNOLDS METALS CO., Richmond, Va. Lobbyist — William H. Darden, Washington, D.C. Filed 2/14/78. Legislative interest — "Legislation affecting the mining of bauxite; the production of alumina and aluminum; the price and availability of electric power, natural gas and crude oil; taxation; and the aluminum industry generally.

ROCKRESORTS INC., New York, N.Y. Lobbyist — Ragan & Mason, Washington, D.C. Filed 2/8/78. Legislative interest — "...Matters involving concessions on federal lands, private land acquisition, tourism and energy."

SEDCO INC., Dallas, Texas. Lobbyist — Alan H. Kaufman, Cambridge, Mass. Filed 2/27/78. Legislative interest — "All interests related to Deep Seabed Hard Minerals Act (proposed), S 2053 and HR 3350."

SEYFORTH LABORATORIES INC., Dallas, Texas. Lobbyist — Rogers & Wells, Washington, D.C. Filed 2/2/78. Legislative interest — "All matters relating to the regulation of food."

SUN PIPE LINE CO., Tulsa, Okla. Lobbyist — Akin, Gump, Hauer & Feld, Washington, D.C. Filed 2/3/78. Legislative interest — "Hearings and any related legislation concerning U.S. energy policy."

TRANS WORLD AIRLINES INC., New York, N.Y. Lobbyist — Charls E. Walker, Washington, D.C. Filed 2/27/78. Legislative interest — ". . . Tax proposals relating to items of capital recovery and capital formation which affect airline companies."

UNION CARBIDE CORP., New York, N.Y. Filed for self 2/13/78. Legislative interest — "Legislation of interest to Union Carbide Corp." Lobbyist — Thomas D. Finnigan, Washington, D.C.

UNITED PARCEL SERVICE OF AMERICA INC., Greenwich, Conn. Lobbyist — Moss, Frink & Franklin, Washington, D.C. Filed 2/24/78. Legislative interest — "Legislation affecting postal rates."

International Relations

THE FASTENERS INSTITUTE OF JAPAN, Tokyo, Japan. Lobbyist — H. William Tanaka, Washington, D. C. Filed 2/28/78. Legislative interest — ". . . H Con Res 483."

THE JAPAN MACHINERY EXPORTERS ASSOCIATION, Tokyo, Japan. Lobbyist — H. William Tanaka, Washington, D. C. Filed 2/28/78. Legislative interest — ". . . H Con Res 483."

U. S. - JAPAN TRADE COUNCIL, Washington, D. C. Filed for self 2/27/78. Legislative interest — "Legislation affecting U. S.-Japan trade." Lobbyist — Robert Angel, Washington, D.C.

VIRGIN ISLANDS GIFT FASHION SHOP ASSOCIATION, St. Thomas, V. I. Lobbyist — Dawson, Riddell, Taylor, Davis & Holroyd, Washington, D.C. Filed 2/8/78. Legislative interest — "Any legislation of interest and affecting the Association."

Labor Unions

AMERICAN FEDERATION OF GOVERNMENT EMPLOYEES, Washington, D.C. Lobbyist — Moss, Frink & Franklin, Washington, D.C. Filed 2/24/78. Legislative interest — "Legislation affecting government employees."

D. C. FEDERATION OF MUSICIANS LOCAL 161-710, Washington, D.C. Lobbyist — Moss, Frink & Franklin, Washington, D. C. Legislative interest — "Against HR 9713, legislation imposing certain restrictions on enlisted members of Armed Forces and on members of military bands."

NATIONAL LEAGUE OF POSTMASTERS, Arlington, Va. Lobbyist — Eugene B. Dalton, Arlington, Va. Filed 2/3/78. Legislative interest — ". . . To promote legislation for the benefit of postmasters throughout the United States . . . to promote legislation regarding postal matters that affect citizens of the United States; HR 7700."

NATIONAL RURAL LETTER CARRIERS' ASSOCIATION, Washington, D. C. Filed for self 2/15/78. Legislative interest — "All legislation under consideration in the Congress affecting postal employees." Lobbyist — Dean King, Wilbur S. Wood, Washington, D. C.

State and Local Government

CITY OF BIRMINGHAM, Birmingham, Ala. Lobbyist — Patton, Boggs & Blow, Washington, D.C. Filed 2/28/78. Legislative interest — "For certain provisions in the air transportation regulatory reform bills (HR 8813, S 2493)."

PUERTO RICO MAYORS ASSOCIATION, Santuree, Puerto Rico. Lobbyist — Nazario & Ortiz-Daliot, Washington, D.C. Filed 2/1/78. Legislative interest — "Any legislation which may affect the Commonwealth of Puerto Rico, with specific interest on local governments."

STATE OF OREGON, Salem, Ore. Lobbyist — Ron M. Linton, Washington, D.C. Filed 2/7/78. Legislative interests — "All legislation relating to transportation, energy, environment and recreation."

Trade Associations

AGRI-BUSINESSMEN INC., Chicago, Ill. Lobbyist — Robert W. Blanchette, Washington, D. C. Filed 2/21/78. Legislative interest — "Proponent changes in Commodity Exchange Act in connection with the reauthorization hearings of the Commodity Futures Trading Commission."

ALASKAN MOVERS ASSOCIATION, Bellevue, Wash. Filed for self 2/17/78. Legislative interest — "General matters relating to the business of the moving and storage of household goods. Specifically, DOD bidding policies on such." Lobbyist — Lawrence H. Landry, Leister L. Richards, Peter W. Sorenson, Bellevue, Wash.

ALTERNATIVE WASTEWATER MANAGEMENT ASSOCIATION, Washington, D. C. Lobbyist — Donald W. Whitehead, Washington, D. C. Filed 2/15/78. Legislative interest — "Legislation dealing with the treatment and disposition of wastes and wastewater."

AMERICAN BAKERS ASSOCIATION, Washington, D. C. Lobbyist — Marcus W. Sisk Jr., Washington, D. C. Filed 2/6/78. Legislative interest — "Legislation affecting the baking industry with specific interest in comprehensive energy regulatory and tax proposals such as those contained in HR 5289 and HR 5263."

AMERICAN BUS ASSOCIATION, Washington, D. C. Filed for self 2/2/78. Legislative interest — "Energy Conservation and Conversion Act of 1977 (HR 8444) with amendments." Lobbyist — Norman R. Sherlock, Washington, D.C.

AMERICAN IMPORTERS ASSOCIATION, New York, N.Y. Lobbyist — Barnes, Richardson & Colburn, Washington, D. C. Filed 2/24/78. Legislative interest — "Legislation attempting to override presidential determination of 2/10/78 on bolts, nuts large screws or iron or steel, H Con Res 483 and similar bills..."

AMERICAN PAPER INSTITUTE INC., New York, N. Y. Filed for self 2/1/78. Legislative interest — ". . . Those affecting the pulp, paper and paperboard industry, its operation, practices and properties." Lobbyist — Louis F. Laun, New York, N.Y.

ANIMAL HEALTH INSTITUTE, Washington, D. C. Lobbyist — Frederick A. Kessinger, Bethesda, Md. Filed 2/24/78. Legislative interest — "Amendments to the Federal Food, Drug Cosmetic Act...."

BOARD OF TRADE CLEARING CORP., Chicago, Ill. Lobbyist — Robert W. Blanchette, Washington, D.C. Filed 2/2/78. Legislative interest — "Proponent of changes in S 2266 (Bankruptcy Act).

CHAMBER OF COMMERCE OF THE UNITED STATES, Washington, D. C. Filed for self 2/6/78. Legislative interest — "Matters . . . particularly relating to labor, banking, budget and science issues." Lobbyist — Robert J. Aagre, Ted Heydinger, Margaret Gehres, Washington, D.C.

GUAYULE RUBBER GROWERS ASSOCIATION, San Marino, Calif. Filed for self 2/1/78. Legislative interest — "Support of S 1167 — Native Latex Commercialization Act of 1977."

INDEPENDENT BANKERS ASSOCIATION OF AMERICA, Sauk Centre, Minn. Lobbyist — Terrence H. Klasky, Washington, D.C. Filed 2/9/78. Legislative interest — "Banking, taxation, housing."

LEAD-ZINC PRODUCERS COMMITTEE, Washington, D. C. Filed for self 2/6/78. Legislative interest — "Any legislation pertaining to the lead and zinc industry, HR 9911; in support of this legislation." Lobbyist — Seth M. Bodner, Washington, D.C.

NATIONAL ASSOCIATION OF HOME BUILDERS OF THE UNITED STATES, Washington, D. C. Filed for self 2/17/78. Legislative interest — ". . . All legislation affecting the industry and its members." Lobbyist — Gary Paul Kane, Washington, D. C.

NATIONAL INSULATORS ASSOCIATION, Washington, D. C. Filed for self 2/22/78. Legislative interest — National Energy Act and other bills affecting industry or members." Lobbyist — John F. Lillard III, Washington, D. C.

NATIONAL PEST CONTROL ASSOCIATION, Vienna, Va. Filed for self 2/77/78. Legislative interest — "Federal pesticide legislation; S 1678, HR 8681." Lobbyist — Tom E. Persky, Vienna, Va.

NATIONAL RURAL ELECTRIC COOPERATIVE ASSOCIATION, Washington, D. C. Filed for self 2/13/78. Legislative interest — "All legislation affecting the RE Act of 1936, as amended." Lobbyist — Carolyn Herr, Washington, D.C.

UNITED STATES FASTENER MANUFACTURING GROUP, Cleveland, Ohio. Filed for self 2/27/78. Legislative interest — ". . . Support the enactment of H Con Res 483 and 485 and S Con Res 66." Lobbyists — Jones, Day, Reavis and Pogue; McClure and Trotter, Washington, D.C.

UNITED STATES INDUSTRIAL COUNCIL, Nashville, Tenn. Lobbyist — The Management Group, Washington, D. C. Filed 2/27/78. Legislative interest — "Legislation affecting our free enterprise system, our national defense and utilization of natural resources."

UNITED STATES MERCHANT MARINE ACADEMY ALUMNI ASSOCIATION INC., Kings Point, N.Y. Lobbyist — International Services Corp., Washington, D. C. Filed 2/16/78. Legislative interest — "Maritime related legislation."

Miscellaneous

ABERRANT BEHAVIOR CENTER, Dallas, Texas. Lobbyist — DK Consultants Inc., Washington, D.C. Filed 2/1/78. Legislative interest — "Matters pertaining to the psychological causes of criminal behavior."

AMERICAN CANCER SOCIETY, New York, N. Y. Filed for self 2/27/78. Legislative interest — "Health research appropriations." Lobbyist — Marvella Bayh, Washington, D.C.

BENJAMIN E. BARCKLOW, Washington, D. C. Filed for self 2/1/78 Legislative interest — "The Panama Canal Treaty."

COALITION FOR NEW YORK INC., New York, N.Y. Lobbyist — Swerdloff Associates Inc., New York, N.Y. Filed 2/6/78. Legislative interest — "...All aspects of the problems confronting the City of New York. The extension of PL 94-236 and outcome of the Energy Bill (HR 8444, S 2104, S 1469, S 2114, S 977, S 2057)."

HIGHWAY USERS FEDERATION FOR SAFETY MOBILITY, Washington, D. C. Filed for self 2/28/78. Legislative interest — ". . . Highway development and highway traffic safety legislation." Lobbyist — Victor J. Perini Jr., Washington, D.C.

INDIA CYCLONE INFORMATION CENTER, Washington, D.C. Filed for self 2/9/78. Legislative interest — "To promote passage of legislation for Indian Cyclone Rehabilitation and reconstruction."

INTERNATIONAL COUNCIL OF AIRSHOWS, Springfield, Va. Filed for self 2/3/78. Legislative interest — ". . . To educate government about benefits of air shows and related aviation enterprises, particularly as means or promoting and fostering the growth and safety of aviation; civil and military." Lobbyist — William F. Clarken, Springfield, Va.

MARLENE C. McGUIRL, Washington, D. C. Lobbyist — Shaw, Pittman, Potts and Trowbridge, Washington, D.C. Filed 2/4/78. Legislative interest — "House and Senate appropriations bill funding the Library of Congress for Fiscal 1979; support separate appropriations provisions for the Law Library of Congress."

NATIONAL ASSOCIATION FOR FREE ENTERPRISE, Washington, D. C. Filed for self 2/2/78. Legislative interest — All legislation affecting free enterprise." Lobbyist — John Edward Hurley, Washington, D.C.

NATIONAL COLLEGIATE ATHLETIC ASSOCIATION, Washington, D.C. Lobbyist — Cox, Langford & Brown, Washington, D.C. Filed 2/22/78. Legislative interest — "Investigation by Subcommittee on Oversight and Investigations, Committee on Interstate and Foreign Commerce, oversight only."

THE NAVAJO NATION, Window Rock, Ariz. Lobbyist — Joseph S. Miller, Washington, D.C. Filed 2/17/78. Legislative interest — "Legislation that affects Indians and Indian tribes, S 1714, HR 9810, S 1214 — for."

MARTINA NAVRATILOVA, Dallas, Texas. Lobbyist — Rogers & Wells, Washington, D.C. Filed 2/6/78. Legislative interest — "Support passage of private naturalization bills for the relief of Martina Navratilova, S 1524, HR 10109 and HR 10210."

OFFICE OF GOVERNMENT AND COMMUNITY AFFAIRS, Cambridge, Mass. Lobbyist — Nan Fielding Nixon, Washington, D. K. Filed 2/28/78. Legislative interest — "S 1217, HR 7418, S 1893, S 2159, HR 8444."

March

Citizens' Groups

AMERICANS FOR ALASKA INC., Elderwood, Md. Filed for self 3/9/78. Legislative interest — "...All of the Alaska land bills and any modifications thereto."

COMMITTEE FOR FULL FUNDING OF EDUCATION PROGRAMS, Washington, D.C. Filed for self 3/6/78. Legislative interest — "Educational funding, particularly those items contained in the Education Division Labor-HEW Appropriations for FY '78 and FY '79, and as contained in the function 500 series of the first and second budget resolutions." Lobbyist — Charles W. Lee, Washington, D.C.

COMMITTEE FOR RATIFICATION OF THE PANAMA CANAL TREATIES, Washington, D.C. Filed for self 3/28/78. Legislative interest — ". . . For the ratification of the Panama Canal Treaties." Lobbyist — Terry D. Garcia, Washington, D.C.

COMMITTEE FOR A UNIFORM INVESTMENT TAX CREDIT, Washington, D.C. Filed for self 3/3/78. Legislative interest — "To secure legislation to allow the full investment tax credit for qualifying assets with lives of at least three but less than seven years." Lobbyists — Shea, Gould, Climenko & Casey; Wickham, Craft & Cihlar, Washington, D.C.; filed 3/10/78.

COMMON CAUSE, Washington, D.C. Filed for self 3/29/78. Legislative interest — ". . . Open government, campaign financing, consumer protection, freedom of information, ERA, energy policy, environmental protection, defense spending, tax reform, waste in government, voting rights, presidential nomination and confirmation process, administration of justice and reform of the criminal code, merit selection of federal judges, intelligence policy, public participation in federal agency proceedings, the congressional budget process and congressional reform." Lobbyist — Kathryn Kavanagh, Washington, D.C.

CONSUMER ACTION NOW, Washington, D.C. Lobbyist — Lola Redford, New York, N.Y. Filed 3/20/78. Legislative interest — "...Any bills which may contain provisions having an impact on consumer products, health services or the environment."

FULL EMPLOYMENT ACTION COUNCIL, Washington, D.C. Filed for self 3/24/78. Legislative interest — "Full employment legislation — Humphrey-Hawkins Bill; HR 50, S 50." Lobbyist — John L. Carr, Washington, D.C.

LEAGUE OF WOMEN VOTERS OF THE UNITED STATES, Washington, D.C. Lobbyist — Arent, Fox, Kintner, Plotkin & Kahn, Washington, D.C. Filed 3/3/78. Legislative interest — "...Right to continue to engage in voter education activities under the Federal Election Campaign Act."

SECOND CONGRESSIONAL DISTRICT ACTION COMMITTEE, Tallahassee, Fla. Filed for self 3/6/78. Legislative interest — "Human life amendment."

Corporations and Businesses

ALLSTATE INSURANCE, Northbrook, Ill. Lobbyist — Van Ness, Feldman & Sutcliffe, Washington, D.C. Filed 3/16/78. Legislative interest — "Support for appropriations to purchase airbag-equipped vehicles for use by the federal government."

AMERICAN AIRLINES, New York, N.Y. Lobbyist — Wickham, Craft & Cihlar, Washington, D.C. Filed 3/22/78. Legislative interest — "For enactment of legislation similar to S 1270 to provide for refund of investment tax credits, or which would otherwise assure the availability of investment tax credits."

AMERICAN INVESTMENT CO., St. Louis, Mo. Filed for self 3/21/78. Legislative interest — "Monitor legislation and committee hearings relating to finance and insurance." Lobbyist — H. Radford Bishop, St. Louis, Mo.

ARCTIC SLOPE REGIONAL CORP., Barrow, Alaska. Lobbyist — Wickwire, Lewis, Goldmark, Dystel & Schorr, Seattle, Wash. Filed 3/27/78. Legislative interest — "Amendments generally to Alaska Native Claims Settlement Act, including Alaska National Interest Lands Conservation Act legislation."

BEACON OIL CO., Hanford, Calif. Lobbyist — Akin, Gump, Hauer & Feld, Washington, D.C. Filed 3/6/78. Legislative interest — "...Any related legislation concerning HR 130, the Petroleum Marketing Practices Act."

BLUE RIBBON SPORTS, Beaverton, Ore. Lobbyist — Jonathan W. Edwards, Washington, D.C. Filed 3/20/78. Legislative interest — "Legislation relating to international trade, customs, and the footwear industry."

COMBINED INSURANCE CO. OF AMERICA, Chicago, Ill. Lobbyist — Arent, Fox, Kintner, Plotkin & Kahn, Washington, D.C. Filed 3/1/78. Legislative interest — "No-fault legislation."

CONSOLIDATED NATURAL GAS CO., Pittsburgh, Pa. Lobbyist — Cook & Henderson, Washington, D.C. Filed 3/30/78. Legislative interest — "All matters which may affect national energy policy."

DOW CHEMICAL, U.S.A., Midland, Mich. Lobbyist — James E. Gentel, Washington, D.C. Filed 3/15/78. Legislative interest — "Energy legislation."

EASTERN AIRLINES, Miami, Fla. Lobbyist — Wickham, Craft & Cihlar, Washington, D.C. Filed 3/22/78. Legislative interest — "For enactment of legislation similar to S 1270 to provide for refund of investment tax credits, or which would otherwise assure the availability of investment tax credits."

EKLUTNA INC., Anchorage, Alaska. Lobbyist — Wyman, Bautzer, Rothman & Kuchel, Washington, D.C. Filed 3/23/78. Legislative interest — "Legislation affecting Alaska Native Corporations."

FIRST FEDERAL SAVINGS & LOAN ASSOCIATION OF PUERTO RICO, Santurce, P.R. Lobbyist — Anderson, Pendleton, McMahon, Peet & Donovan, Washington, D.C. Filed 3/30/78. Legislative interest — "Equal tax treatment for savings and loan associations and commercial banks."

THE FIRST NATIONAL BANK OF BOSTON, Boston, Mass. Filed for self 3/16/78. Legislative interest — "Any and all matters affecting the First National Bank of Boston." Lobbyist — Herbert R. Waite, Boston, Mass.

FISHER STOVES INTERNATIONAL INC., Eugene, Oregon. Lobbyist — Hogan & Hartson, Washington, D.C. Filed 3/20/78. Legislative interest — "HR 5263, Energy Production and Conservation Tax Incentive Act; in favor of tax credit for wood-burning stoves."

FORD MOTOR CO., Dearborn, Mich. Filed for self 3/19/78. Legislative interest — "...To analyze federal plans, policies, and trends and proposed legislation and regulations in relation to the interests of the company." Lobbyist — Wendell M. Holloway, Washington, D.C.

GREATER SOUTHEAST COMMUNITY HOSPITAL, Washington, D.C. Lobbyist — Frank C. Frantz, Washington, D.C. Filed 3/14/78. Legislative interest — "Advocating amendment — Labor-HEW Appropriations, FY 1979."

HARTFORD FIRE INSURANCE CO., Hartford, Conn. Filed for self 3/20/78. Legislative interest — "Insurance matters." Lobbyist — Melvin L. Stark, Washington, D.C.

H. J. HEINZ CO., Pittsburgh, Pa. Lobbyist — Timmons and Co. Inc., Washington, D.C. Filed 3/24/78. Legislative interest — "...Bills relating to the food processing industry, tuna fishing, sugar and sweeteners, and relevant tax proposals including treaties."

INTERNATIONAL PRECIOUS METALS CORP., Fort Lauderdale, Fla. Lobbyist — Smith, Miro, Hirsch and Brody, Detroit, Mich. Filed 3/20/78. Legislative interest — "S 2391 and other legislation affecting the CFTC. Support of S 2391."

KYUKUYO CO. LTD., Seattle, Wash. Lobbyist — Preston, Thorgrimson, Ellis, Holman & Fletcher, Washington, D.C. Filed 3/20/78. Legislative interest — "Legislation regulating whether and under what circumstances an American company, which is a subsidiary of a foreign corporation...may utilize American fisheries, HR 2564."

McDONALD'S SYSTEMS INC., Oak Brook, Ill. Filed for self 3/8/78. Legislative interest — "Matters of legislative interest to McDonald's Corp. and its subsidiaries." Lobbyist — Clayton C. Taylor, Oak Brook, Ill.

MELEX U.S.A. INC., Raleigh, N.C. Lobbyist — Metzger, Shadyac & Schwarz, Washington, D.C. Filed 3/21/78. Legislative interest — "Antidumping Act of 1921...as amended by the Trade Act of 1974...."

MOORE McCORMACK RESOURCES INC., Stamford, Conn. Lobbyist — Preston, Thorgrimson, Ellis, Holman & Fletcher, Washington, D.C. Filed 3/22/78. Legislative interest — "General education functions in connection with the fees and charges for Great Lakes navigation."

MOTOROLA INC., Washington, D.C. Lobbyist — Charlotte Reid, Arlington, Va. Filed 3/10/78. Legislative interest — "...Legislation pertaining to communications, taxation, commerce and trade, foreign affairs, labor, health, consumer affairs and other legislation affecting the electronics industry."

JOHN NUVEEN & CO., Chicago, Ill. Lobbyist — O'Connor & Hannan, Washington, D.C. Filed 3/20/78. Legislative interest — "...The taxable bond option issue."

OCEAN MINERALS CO., Mountain View, Calif. Lobbyist — David P. Stang, Washington, D.C. Filed 3/21/78. Legislative interest — "Deep Seabed Hard Mineral Resources Mining legislation and related multi-national treaties."

OCEAN MINING ASSOCIATES, Gloucester Point, Va. Lobbyist — Northcutt Ely, Washington, D.C. Filed 3/9/78. Legislative interest — "In favor of passage of HR 3350, The Deep Seabed Hard Minerals Act, or similar legislation."

PAN AMERICAN WORLD AIRWAYS INC., New York, N.Y. Lobbyist — Verner, Liipfert, Bernhard and McPherson, Washington, D.C. Filed 3/24/78. Legislative interest — "Legislation affecting air carriers, including regulatory reform and noise abatement legislation."

PAN AMERICAN WORLD AIRWAYS, New York, N.Y. Lobbyist — Wickham, Craft & Cihlar, Washington, D.C. Filed 3/22/78. Legislative interest — "For enactment of legislation similar to S 1270 to provide for refund of investment tax credits, or which would otherwise assure the availability of investment tax credits."

PEPSICO INC., Purchase, N.Y. Lobbyist — Patton, Boggs & Blow, Washington, D.C. Filed 3/27/78. Legislative interest — "Legislation to continue existing income tax treatment of nonqualified deferred compensation plans such as HR 11542...."

JACK PHILIP & SON INC., Miami, Fla. Lobbyist — Patton, Boggs & Blow, Washington, D.C. Filed 3/27/78. Legislative interest — "S 2575 and S 2632 amending the Strategic and Critical Stockpile Materials Act with particular reference to the authorization for disposal of excess industrial commodities."

PUBLIC SERVICE ELECTRIC AND GAS CO., Newark, N.J. Lobbyist — Berlack, Israels & Liberman, New York, N.Y. Filed 3/10/78. Legislative interest — "...Bills dealing with LNG; specifically the Liquefied Natural Gas Facility Safety Act, HR 6844."

REYNOLDS METAL CO., Richmond, Va. Lobbyist — Harry V. Helton, Portland, Ore. Filed 3/13/78. Legislative interest — "Price and availability of electric power in the Northwest."

RYDER SYSTEM INC., Miami, Fla. Lobbyist — Wickham, Craft & Cihlar, Washington, D.C. Filed 3/22/78. Legislative interest — "For enactment of legislation similar to S 1270 to provide for refund of investment tax credits, or which would otherwise assure the availability of investment tax credits."

SEARS, ROEBUCK AND CO., Chicago, Ill. Lobbyist — Joanne E. Mattiace, Washington, D.C. Filed 3/9/78. Legislative interest — "Legislation affecting the operation of Sears...as a part of the retail industry, its employees and customers."

SEATRAIN LINES INC., New York, N.Y. Lobbyist — Butler, Binion, Rice, Cook & Knapp, Washington, D.C. Legislative interest — "Defense authorization bill for FY 1979."

SEATRAIN LINES INC., New York, N.Y. Lobbyist — Preston, Thorgrimson, Ellis, Holman & Fletcher, Washington, D.C. Filed 3/22/78. Legislative interest — "General education functions to revise the tariff laws to permit duty free treatment of certain shipping expenses."

STANDARD OIL CO., Chicago, Ill. Lobbyist — Richard L. Fischer, Washington, D.C. Filed 3/24/78. Legislative interest — "Any legislation affecting the oil industry."

TENNESSEE GAS PIPELINE CO., Houston, Texas. Filed for self 3/20/78. Legislative interest — "General educational functions in connection with the natural gas pricing provisions of the pending energy legislation." Lobbyist — Preston, Thorgrimson, Ellis, Holman & Fletcher, Washington, D.C.

TRANS WORLD AIRLINES, New York, N.Y. Lobbyist — Wickham, Craft & Cihlar, Washington, D.C. Filed 3/22/78. Legislative interest — "For enactment of legislation similar to S 1270 to provide for refund of investment tax credits, or which would otherwise assure the availability of investment tax credits."

UNITED AIRLINES INC., Chicago, Ill. Lobbyist — Wickham, Craft & Cihlar, Washington, D.C. Filed 3/22/78. Legislative interest — "For enactment of legislation similar to S 1270 to provide for refund of investment tax credits, or which would otherwise assure the availability of investment tax credits."

UNITED NATIONS UNIVERSITY, New York, N.Y. Lobbyist — Francis R. Valeo, Washington, D.C. Filed 3/15/78. Legislative interest — "Legislation affecting the University (HR 10691, S 2420) — for."

UNITED REFINING CO., Warren, Pa. Lobbyist — Akin, Gump, Hauer & Feld, Washington, D.C. Filed 3/6/78. Legislative interest — "...Any related legislation concerning HR 130, the Petroleum Marketing Practices Act."

WAGNER ELECTRIC CORP., Parsippany, N.J. Lobbyist — Carella, Bain, Gilfillan & Rhodes, Newark, N.J. Filed 3/2/78. Legislative interest — "Legislation regarding vehicle safety standards, specifically antilock braking requirements."

Energy and Environment

FRIENDS OF THE EARTH, Washington, D.C. Filed for self 3/1/78. Legislative interest — "...Legislation to preserve, restore, and insure rational use of the ecosphere — generally, all environmental legislation." Lobbyist — David E. Ortman, Elizabeth R. Kaplan, Washington, D.C.

SIERRA CLUB, San Francisco, Calif. Filed for self 3/31/78. Legislative interest — "Outer Continental Shelf Lands Act Amendments, HR 1614; Federal Aid to Highways Act and Urban Mass Transit Act, HR 10578; Redwood National Park Expansion Act, HR 3813; Chattahoochee NRA, HR 8336; and related legislation on environmental protection and natural resources."

International Relations

ASSOCIACAO BRASILEIRA DE PRODUTORES DE FERRO LIGAS, Rio de Janeiro, Brazil. Lobbyist — Daniels, Houlihan & Palmeter, Washington, D.C. Filed 3/20/78. Legislative interest — "Oppose passage of H Con Res 469 to override the president's decision on ferrochrome."

COMMITTEE OF AMERICANS FOR THE CANAL TREATIES INC., Washington, D.C. Lobbyist — John O. Marsh Jr., Washington, D.C.; S. Lee Kling, St. Louis, Mo. Filed 3/23/78. Legislative interest — "COACT seeks to fully air all views on the proposed Panama Canal Treaties now pending before the Senate for ratification."

GOVERNMENT OF COLOMBIA, South America. Lobbyist — Kirkwood, Kaplan, Russin & Vecchi, Washington, D.C. Filed 3/29/78. Legislative interest — "Antitrust legislation relating to the right of purchasers, and particularly foreign sovereigns, to sue for damages relating to direct and indirect purchases."

THE ROYAL EMBASSY OF SAUDI ARABIA. Lobbyists — J. Crawford Cook Inc., Columbia, S.C., filed 3/20/78; Frederick G. Dutton, Washington, D.C., filed 3/27/78. Legislative interest — "For approval of F-15 airplanes to Saudi Arabia."

Labor Unions

INTERNATIONAL UNION OF ELECTRICAL, RADIO AND MACHINE WORKERS, Washington, D.C. Filed for self 3/10/78. Legislative interest — "All legislation affecting workers engaged in the electrical, electronics, machine and optical products manufacturing industries." Lobbyist — George Collins, Washington, D.C.

Military and Veterans' Groups

VIETNAM VETERAN COALITION INC., Washington, D.C. Filed for self 3/28/78. Legislative interest — "...Legislation affecting war veterans, their dependents and survivors." Lobbyists — Stuart F. Feldman, Washington, D.C.; Robert O. Muller, Dix Hills, N.Y.

State and Local Governments

NORTH SLOPE BOROUGH, Barrow, Alaska. Lobbyist — Van Ness, Feldman & Sutcliffe, Washington, D.C. Filed 3/29/78. Legislative interest — "Support for legislation appropriating funds for upgrading local utility system, distributing oil and gas revenues from National Wildlife Refuges to local governments (HR 8394) and other related legislation and amendments."

STATE OF ALASKA, Juneau, Alaska. Lobbyist — Robert H. Loeffler, Washington, D.C. Filed 3/31/78. Legislative interest — "Natural gas provisions of bills (HR 8444, HR 5289, S 1469) as they affect the proposed Alaska Natural Gas Transportation System and the State of Alaska's royalty gas interests."

AIR TRANSPORT ASSOCIATION OF AMERICA, Washington, D.C. Filed for self 3/7/78. Legislative interest — "...Proper advancement of airline industry." Lobbyist — Larry P. Barnett, Washington, D.C.

AMERICAN GAS ASSOCIATION, Arlington, Va. Lobbyist — Miller & Chevalier, Washington, D.C. Filed 3/10/78. Legislative interest — "...Enactment of HR 9380 with modifications."

AMERICAN HOSPITAL ASSOCIATION, Washington, D.C. Lobbyist — Randolph J. Stayin, Robert Taft Jr., Washington, D.C. Filed 3/2/78. Legislative interest — "...Legislative matters relating to hospitals."

CIGAR ASSOCIATION OF AMERICA INC., Washington, D.C. Filed for self 3/30/78. Legislative interest — "Customs legislation HR 8179 and labor reform legislation S 1883 and HR 8410." Lobbyist — Michael J. Kowalsky, Washington, D.C.

COMMITTEE FOR CONSUMERS NO-FAULT, Washington, D.C. Lobbyist — Van Ness, Feldman & Sutcliffe, Washington, D.C. Filed 3/23/78. Legislative interest — "National Standards for No-Fault Automobile Insurance, S 1381/HR 6601."

FURNITURE RENTAL ASSOCIATION OF AMERICA, Washington, D.C. Filed for self 3/2/78. Legislative interest — "Legislation affecting the furniture leasing industry...consumer leasing, consumer protection, trade regulation, investment tax credit and small business." Lobbyist — Spencer A. Johnson, Washington, D.C.

INDEPENDENT LOCAL NEWSPAPER ASSOCIATION, Washington, D.C. Filed for self 3/1/78. Legislative interest — "Legislation affecting newspapers." Lobbyist — Morris J. Levin, Washington, D.C.

INDEPENDENT PETROLEUM ASSOCIATION OF AMERICA, Washington, D.C. Filed for self 3/8/78. Legislative interest — "...Legislation that might effect the petroleum industry." Lobbyist — Lawrence E. Siegel, Washington, D.C.

INTERBANK CARD ASSOCIATION, New York, N.Y. Lobbyist — Covington & Burling, Washington, D.C. Filed 3/1/78. Legislative interest — "Legislation affecting bank card programs and services, electronic fund transfers, franchising, consumer credit, other similar aspects of banking."

LOUISIANA BANKERS ASSOCIATION, Baton Rouge, La. Filed for self 3/10/78. Legislative interest — "Legislation affecting the banking industry." Lobbyist — Allie G. Kleinpeter Jr., Baton Rouge, La.

MORTGAGE BANKERS ASSOCIATION OF AMERICA, Washington, D.C. Filed for self 3/3/78. Legislative interest — "Any legislation affecting the mortgage banking industry." Lobbyist — Burton C. Wood, Mark J. Riedy, Washington, D.C.

NATIONAL ASSOCIATION OF FARMER ELECTED COMMITTEEMEN, Darlington, S.C. Filed for self 3/24/78. Legislative interest — "All farm legislation." Lobbyist — Ralph Lubeck, Darlington, S.C.

NATIONAL ASSOCIATION OF OUTDOOR RECREATION, Richmond, Va. Lobbyist — Ragan & Mason, Washington, D.C. Filed 3/27/78. Legislative interest — "Interior and related agencies appropriation acts."

NATIONAL ASSOCIATION OF PERSONNEL CONSULTANTS, Washington, D.C. Lobbyist — O'Connor & Hannan, Washington, D.C. Filed 3/20/78. Legislative interest — "General legislative interests to the client."

NATIONAL CLUB ASSOCIATION, Washington, D.C. Lobbyist — Webster & Chamberlain, Washington, D.C. Filed 3/17/78. Legislative interest — "Legislation affecting taxation."

NATIONAL NEWSPAPER ASSOCIATION, Washington, D.C. Filed for self 3/31/78. Legislative interest — "Legislation affecting newspaper business, ranging from First Amendment considerations to the business issues." Lobbyist — Patricia Gallagher, Washington, D.C.

NATIONAL RESTAURANT ASSOCIATION, Chicago, Ill. Lobbyist — A. Kolbet Schrichte, Peter J. Hapworth, Washington, D.C. Filed 3/23/78. Legislative interest — "Any legislation affecting the restaurant and food service industries...small business, labor laws, wages and hours, taxation, consumer protection, food marketing and economic stabilization."

NATIONAL RETIRED TEACHERS ASSOCIATION, Washington, D.C. Filed for self 3/20/78. Legislative interest — "Support of improved Social Security and Medicare/Medicaid laws; Older Americans Act amendments; improved tax treatment of older Americans; improved nursing home standards; consumer protection legislation; employment of older workers; national health insurance; transportation for the elderly; no-fault insurance; housing for the elderly." Lobbyist — Fred W. Wegner, Washington, D.C.

NATIONAL SOCIETY OF PROFESSIONAL ENGINEERS, Washington, D.C. Filed for self 3/17/78. Legislative interest — "All legislation affecting interests of professional engineers." Lobbyist — Michael K. Blevins, Washington, D.C.

SECURITIES INDUSTRY ASSOCIATION, Washington, D.C. Filed for self 3/21/78. Legislative interest — "Legislation affecting the securities industry." Lobbyist — Stephan K. Small, Washington, D.C.

SOCIETY OF INDEPENDENT GASOLINE MARKETERS OF AMERICA, Washington, D.C. Lobbyist — Collier, Shannon, Rill, Edwards & Scott, Washington, D.C. Filed 3/3/78. Legislative interest — "...Availability and price of motor gasoline in the United States."

SOUTHWEST HOME FURNISHING ASSOCIATION, Dallas, Texas. Filed for self 3/20/78. Legislative interests — "...All statutes and bills that will relate to the home furnishings industry." Lobbyist — Frank Northcutt, Dallas, Texas.

Miscellaneous

THE ADHERENCE GROUP INC., New York, N.Y. Lobbyist — Billig, Sher & Jones, Washington, D.C. Filed 3/17/78. Legislative interest — "...Legislation to amend Shipping Act of 1916...."

ALEUTIAN/PRIBILOF ISLANDS ASSOCIATION INC., Anchorage, Alaska. Lobbyist — Cook & Henderson, Washington, D.C. Filed 3/30/78. Legislative interest — "All matters which might affect the economic well-being of the Aleut People...."

ALLIANCE OF ARTS & ARTISTS, Washington, D.C. Lobbyist — International Management Consultants Ltd., Washington, D.C. Filed 3/17/78. Legislative interest — "Opposition to administration's 1978 tax reform proposals to eliminate current business expense treatment of theatre tickets and to treat limited theatrical financing partnership with more than 15 limited partners as a corporation."

THE AMERICAN RADIO RELAY LEAGUE, Newington, Conn. Filed for self 3/20/78. Legislative interest — "...Revisions of the Communications Act of 1934...."

CAPITAL FORMATION THROUGH DIVIDEND REINVESTMENT, Washington, D.C. Filed for self 3/3/78. Legislative interest — "President's tax proposals." Lobbyist — Morgan, Lewis & Bockius, Washington, D.C.

CHARLES E. CAPRON, Washington, D.C. Filed for self 3/15/78. Legislative interest — "Acquisition and leasing of federal government real estate."

COMMITTEE FOR 806.30 AND 807 INC., Arlington, Va. Filed for self 3/2/78. Legislative interest — "Amend the Tariff Schedules by repealing Items 806.30 and 807."

COMMUNITY SERVICE SOCIETY, New York, N.Y. Filed for self 3/14/78. Legislative interest — "Extension of the Older Americans Act." Lobbyist — Florence K. Kallan, New York, N.Y.

CONTICOMMODITY SERVICES INC., Chicago, Ill. Lobbyist — Sidley & Austin, Chicago, Ill. Filed 3/2/78. Legislative Interest — "Tax legislation, including the president's 1978 Tax Proposals, and other legislation of interest to the above-named employer."

ESTATE OF SOL ATLAS, New York. N.Y. Lobbyist — Robert J. Casey, New York, N.Y. Filed 3/30/78. Legislative interest — "In favor of the Technical Corrections Bill."

FOOD DISTRIBUTORS TASK FORCE, Washington, D.C. Lobbyist — Cook & Henderson, Washington, D.C. Filed 3/30/78. Legislative interest — "Support of S 1699 and companion legislation in the House, the 'Diesel Fuel and Gasoline Conservation Act of 1977.' "

INTELLECTUAL PROPERTY OWNERS INC., Washington, D.C. Lobbyist — T. L. Bowes, Leesburg, Va. Filed 3/15/78. Legislative interest — "Intellectual property."

NATIONAL SKI PATROL, Denver, Colo. Lobbyist — John Stobierski, Washington, D.C. Filed 3/29/78. Legislative interest — "Incorporating the Ski Patrol, S 1571."

NEW YORK COFFEE AND SUGAR EXCHANGE INC., New York, N.Y. Filed for self 3/23/78. Legislative interest — "Legislation regarding the Commodity/Futures Trading Commission."

PAINE, WEBBER, JACKSON & CURTIS INC., New York, N.Y. Lobbyist — Sidley & Austin, Chicago, Ill. Filed 3/2/78. Legislative interest — "Tax legislation, including the president's 1978 tax proposals, and other legislation of interest to the above-named employer."

PUBLIC EMPLOYEES BENEFIT SERVICE CORP., Oklahoma City, Okla. Lobbyist — International Management Consultants Ltd., Washington, D.C. Filed 3/17/78. Legislative interest — "Matters dealing with the taxation of deferred compensation."

FRED J. RUSSELL, Los Angeles, Calif. Lobbyist — David P. Stang, Washington, D.C. Filed 3/21/78. Legislative interest — "Energy legislation."

73 INC., Peterborough, N.H. Lobbyist — Wayne Green, Peterborough, N.H. Filed 3/30/78. Legislative interest — "No specific bills."

April

Citizens' Groups

AMERICAN CONSERVATIVE UNION, Washington, D.C. Filed for self 4/17/78. Legislative interest — "All issues generating sufficient public interest to warrant involvement by conservatives and expression of a conservative point of view." Lobbyist — Yvonne Chicoine, Washington, D.C.

AMERICAN CONSTITUENCY OVERSEAS, Irvine, Calif. Lobbyist — Thomas M. Rees, Washington, D.C. Filed 4/13/78. Legislative interest — "Section 911 of the Tax Reform Act of 1976."

AMERICANS FOR ALASKA, Riderwood, Md. Lobbyist — George S. Wills, Charles W. Mitchell, Ruxton, Md. Filed 4/14/78. Legislative interest — "All of the Alaska land bills and any modifications thereto."

CITIZENS FOR MANAGEMENT OF ALASKA LANDS INC., Anchorage, Alaska. Filed for self 4/17/78. Legislative interest — "Determination of National Interest Lands — Alaska. Against — HR 39, Alaska National Interest Lands Conservation Act; S 499, Alaska Conservation Act; S 1500, Alaska National Interest Lands Conservation Act. For — S 1787, Alaska National Interest Lands Act."

CITIZENS FOR TAX REFORM IN 1978 INC., Washington, D.C. Filed for self 4/24/78. Legislative interest — ". . . Support the president's proposals for tax reform."

CITIZENS FOR TAX REFORM IN 1978 INC., Washington, D.C. Filed for self 4/24/78. Legislative interest — ". . . All views on tax reform; the organization will support the president's proposals for tax reform."

COMMON CAUSE, Washington, D.C. Filed for self 4/18/78. Legislative interest — ". . . Open government, campaign financing, consumer protection, freedom of information, ERA, energy policy, environmental protection, defense spending, tax reform, waste in government, voting rights, presidential nomination and confirmation process, administration of justice and reform of the criminal code, merit selection of federal judges, intelligence policy, public participation in federal agency proceedings, the congressional budget process and congressional reform." Lobbyist — Maureen Aspin, Washington, D.C.

CONCERNED CITIZENS AGAINST THE PANAMA CANAL GIVE-AWAY, Washington, D.C. Filed for self 4/1/78. Legislative interest — "Panama Canal Treaties." Lobbyist — Donald Baldwin, Washington, D.C.

NINETEENTH PRO-LIFE CONGRESSIONAL DISTRICT ACTION COMMITTEE, St. Lompoc, Calif. Filed for self 4/18/78. Legislative interest — "All proposed Human Life amendments."

THIRTIETH PRO-LIFE CONGRESSIONAL DISTRICT ACTION COMMITTEE, Bell, Calif. Filed for self 4/25/78. Legislative interest — "All proposed Human Life Amendments."

TWENTY-SIXTH PRO-LIFE CONGRESSIONAL DISTRICT ACTION COMMITTEE, Alhambra, Calif. Filed for self 4/18/78. Legislative interest — "All proposed Human Life amendments."

Corporations and Businesses

ALLEGHENY AIRLINES INC., Washington, D.C. Lobbyists — Charls E. Walker, Washington, D.C., filed 4/10/78; Wickham, Craft & Cihlar, Washington, D.C., filed 4/3/78. Legislative interest — ". . . Tax proposals relating to items of capital recovery and capital formation which affect airline companies; . . . for the enactment of legislation similar to S 1270. . . ."

ALTER CO., Davenport, Iowa. Filed for self 4/24/78. Legislative interest — "Legislation affecting waterways user charges; S 3132, HR 923, HR 8309 and companion bills — against discriminatory imposition of user taxes on the nation's waterways, against improper implementation of the Ports and Waterways Safety Act and concern for amendments thereto." Lobbyist — Robert L. Gardner, Davenport, Iowa.

AMERICAN QUASAR PETROLEUM CO., Fort Worth, Texas. Lobbyist — Williams & Jensen, Washington, D.C. Filed 4/26/78. Legislative interest — "Tax matters of interest to the company and its subsidiaries."

AMERICAN SUBSCRIPTION TELEVISION COS. Lobbyist — Seymour M. Chase, Washington, D.C. Filed 4/17/78. Legislative interest — ". . . Efforts to rewrite the Communications Act of 1934, . . . S 2728 and HR 11623, regarding television blackouts of sporting events, and HR 8804 regarding the licensing of subscription television. . . ."

AMEX COMMODITIES EXCHANGE INC., New York, N.Y. Lobbyist — Cadwalder, Wickersham & Taft, Washington, D.C. Filed 4/10/78. Legislative interest — "Legislation to extend the Commodities Futures Trading Commission, S 2391 and other legislation related to commodity options."

AVCO CORP., New York, N.Y. Lobbyist — Clifford, Glass, McIlwain & Finney, Washington, D.C. Filed 4/12/78. Legislative interest — "In support of adequate appropriations for mineral and energy research."

BALCOR CO., Skokie, Ill. Lobbyist — Francis O. McDermott, Washington, D.C. Filed 4/24/78. Legislative interest — "Amendments to the Internal Revenue Code of 1954 regarding partnerships, particularly HR 12078, "Revenue Act of 1978."

EARL BENHAM & CO. INC., New York, N.Y. Lobbyist — Edward L. Merrigan, Washington, D.C. Filed 4/14/78. Legislative interest — "Obtaining payment of valid U.S. citizen inheritance claims against Romania."

BOARD OF TRADE CLEARING CORP., Chicago, Ill. Lobbyist — Alston, Miller & Gaines, Atlanta, Ga. Filed 4/10/78. Legislative interest — "Proponent of changes in Commodity Exchange Act in connection with the reauthorization hearings of the Commodity Futures Trading Commission."

BOISE CASCADE CORP., Washington, D.C. Filed for self 4/7/78. Legislative interest — "All matters of interest to forest products based industry." Lobbyist — Jacqueline Balk-Tusa, Washington, D.C.

THE CARBORUNDUM CO., Washington, D.C. Filed for self 4/17/78. Legislative interest — "All legislation of interest to Carborundum Co. and Kennecott Copper Corp." Lobbyist — Jane K. Anderson, Washington, D.C.

CERTAINTEED CORP., Valley Forge, Pa. Filed for self 4/21/78. Legislative interest — "Matters on which CertainTeed may wish to make comments and recommendations." Lobbyist — W. R. Werner, Washington, D.C.

CHAMPLIN PETROLEUM CO., Fort Worth, Texas. Lobbyist — Hogan & Hartson, Washington, D.C. Filed 4/24/78. Legislative interest — "Dept. of Energy Funding Authorization for FY 1979, S 2692 and companion bills in the House of Representatives."

COMMONWEALTH EDISON CO., Chicago, Ill. Filed for self 4/12/78. Legislative interest — "Legislation to amend the Internal Revenue Code of 1954 and related statutes." Lobbyist — Frederic W. Hickman, Chicago, Ill.

DELTA AIR LINES INC., Atlanta, Ga. Lobbyist — Mervin E. Dullum, Washington, D.C. Filed 4/7/78. Legislative interest — "Any legislation affecting air transportation directly or indirectly."

E.I. du PONT DE NEMOURS & CO., Wilmington, Del. Lobbyist — Mark D. Nelson, Washington, D.C. Filed 4/4/78. Legislative interest — "All legislation directly related to employer's business, especially bills related to energy, the environment, taxation, economic policy, government regulation and programs supported by employer contributions."

DYNAMIC INSTRUMENT CORP., Hauppauge, N.Y. Lobbyist — DeLaney & Patrick, Washington, D.C. Filed 4/8/78. Legislative interest — "Possible amendments to Trade Act of 1974 and related administrative considerations."

ELECTRO SIGNAL LAB INC., Rockland, Mass. Lobbyist — Tyler & Reynolds & Craig, Boston, Mass. Filed 4/17/78. Legislative interest — "Proponent of legislation to prohibit or restrict the sale of ionization type smoke detector devices."

FIREMAN'S FUND AMERICAN LIFE INSURANCE CO., San Rafael, Calif. Lobbyist — Leighton and Conklin, Washington, D.C. Filed 4/7/78. Legislative interest — "Legislation relating to taxation of deferred annuities and life insurance."

THE FIRST NATIONAL BANK OF BOSTON, Boston, Mass. Filed for self 4/19/78. Legislative interest — "Any and all matters affecting the Bank." Lobbyist — Leonard F. O'Connor, Boston, Mass.

FLORIDA GAS TRANSMISSION CO., Winter Park, Fla. Filed for self 4/10/78. Legislative interest — "Legislation affecting the regulation of natural gas and other energy forms . . . S 826, HR 6804 and HR 6831." Lobbyist — Royston C. Hughes, Winter Park, Fla.

FLUOR CORP., Washington, D.C. Lobbyist — Thomas M. Rees, Washington, D.C. Filed 4/13/78. Legislative interest — ". . . Taxation of U.S. citizens working abroad."

FORT HOWARD PAPER CO., Green Bay, Wis. Lobbyist — Foley, Lardner, Hollabaugh & Jacobs, Washington, D.C. Filed 4/27/78. Legislative interest — "Dredging of Green Bay Harbor."

GENERAL ATOMIC CO., Washington, D.C. Lobbyist — Leighton & Conklin, Washington, D.C. Filed 4/7/78. Legislative interest — ". . . Matters relating to nuclear power and high temperature gas cooled reactors."

GLOBAL SEAFOODS INC., Portland, Maine. Lobbyist — Birch, Horton, Bittner & Monroe, Washington, D.C. Filed 4/19/78. Legislative interest — "All legislation pertaining to the fishing industry and vocational education for United States fishermen."

HEINOLD COMMODITIES INC., Chicago, Ill. Lobbyist — Sidley & Austin, Chicago, Ill. Filed 4/28/78. Legislative interest — "Reauthorization of the Commodity Futures Trading Commission under the Commodity Exchange Act, as amended; S 2391."

HERCULES INC., Wilmington, Del. Lobbyist — Miller & Chevalier, Washington, D.C. Filed 4/14/78. Legislative interest — ". . . Amending section 3121 of the Internal Revenue Code."

HOUDAILLE INDUSTRIES INC., Fort Lauderdale, Fla. Filed for self 4/21/78. Legislative interest — "Modification of NHTSA bumper standards. . . ."

HOUDAILLE INDUSTRIES INC., Fort Lauderdale, Fla. Filed for self 4/21/78. Legislative interest — "Modifications of NHTSA bumber standards...." Lobbyist — Phillip A. O'Reilly, Leonard Barstis, John Latona, Thomas Norton, Fort Lauderdale, Fla.

HUGHES AIRWEST, San Francisco, Calif. Lobbyist — Charls E. Walker; Wickham, Craft & Cihlar; Washington, D.C. Filed 4/10/78. Legislative interest — " . . . Tax proposals relating to items of capital recovery and capital formation which affect airline companies."

HUNT INTERNATIONAL RESOURCES, Dallas, Texas. Lobbyist — Claud Fleet, Denver, Colo. Filed 4/25/78. Legislative interest — "Commodities trading, sugar manufacturing."

N.B. HUNT, Dallas, Texas. Lobbyist — Claud Fleet, Denver, Colo. Filed 4/25/78. Legislative interest — "Commodity trading, silver, horse racing."

E.F. HUTTON & CO., New York, N.Y. Lobbyist — Kutak Rock & Huie, Omaha, Neb. Filed 4/7/78. Legislative interest — "1978 tax reform legislation as it relates to the securities industry."

IDS LIFE INSURANCE CO., Minneapolis, Minn. Lobbyist — Miller & Chevalier, Washington, D.C. Filed 4/14/78. Legislative interest — ". . . The president's 1978 Tax Program."

INTERNATIONAL PAPER CO., Washington, D.C. Filed for self 4/11/78. Legislative interest — "All matters of interest to forest products based industry." Lobbyist — J. Stephen Larkin, Washington, D.C.

INTERNATIONAL PRECIOUS METALS CORP., Fort Lauderdale, Fla. Lobbyist — John F. O'Neal, Washington, D.C. Filed 4/24/78. Legislative interest — "Opposed to repeal of Sec. 217 of P.L. 93-463."

JMB REALTY CORP., Chicago, Ill. Lobbyists — Francis O. McDermott, Washington, D.C. filed 4/24/78; Frederic W. Hickman, Chicago, Ill., filed 4/12/78. Legislative interest — "Amendments to the Internal Revenue Code of 1954 and related statutes."

MARATHON OIL CO., Findlay, Ohio. Lobbyist — Paula A. Dilley, Washington, D.C. Filed 4/10/78. Legislative interest — ". . . All legislative matters that would affect the oil and gas industry."

MARS INC., McLean, Va. Lobbyist — Patton, Boggs & Blow, Washington, D.C. Filed 4/20/78. Legislative interest — "General farm legislation affecting rice, sugar, cocoa, peanuts, petfoods. . . ."

MFA MUTUAL INSURANCE CO., Columbia, Mo. Lobbyist — Arnold & Porter, Washington, D.C. Filed 4/13/78. Legislative interest — "Supporting proposed amendments to . . . the Internal Revenue Code and . . . The Social Security Act."

MOORE McCORMACK RESOURCES INC., Stamford, Conn. Filed for self 4/3/78. Legislative interest — "Education functions in connection with fees and charges for Great Lakes navigation." Lobbyist — Preston, Thorgrimson, Ellis, Holman & Fletcher, Washington, D.C.

MOTOROLA INC., Schaumburg, Ill. Lobbyist — Lewis B. Hastings; Peabody, Rivlin, Lambert & Meyers; Washington, D.C. Filed 4/3/78. Legislative interest — ". . .Legislation pertaining to communications, taxation, commerce and trade, foreign affairs, labor health, consumer affairs, and other legislation affecting the electronics industry; . . . in support of HR 7102 — Investment Policy Act of 1977."

NORTHROP CORP., Los Angeles, Calif. Lobbyist — Timmons and Co. Inc., Washington, D.C. Filed 4/4/78. Legislative interest — "". . .All legislative matters concerning the procurement by the U.S. and other countries of aircraft...."

NORTHWEST PIPELINE CO., Salt Lake City, Utah. Lobbyist — Jack Ferguson Associates, Washington, D.C. Filed 4/10/78. Legislative interest — "Legislation relating to the Northwest Alaska Pipeline."

NORTHWEST PIPELINE CO., Salt Lake City, Utah. Lobbyist — Jack Ferguson Associates, Washington, D.C. Filed 4/17/78. Legislative interest — "Legislation relating to the Northwest Alaska Pipeline."

OGLETHORPE ELECTRIC MEMBERSHIP CORP., Decatur, Ga. Lobbyist — Sutherland, Asbill & Brennan, Washington, D.C. Filed 4/24/78. Legislative interest — "HR 3630, HR 7581, HR 4018, HR 8444, S 2114 and other bills of interest to electric utility industry."

OWENS-CORNING FIBERGLAS CORP., Toledo, Ohio. Filed for self 4/18/78. Legislative interest — "Energy legislation." Lobbyist — Bradford C. Oelman, Washington, D.C.

PAN AMERICAN WORLD AIRWAYS INC., Washington, D.C. Filed for self 4/10/78. Legislative interest — "Matters affecting civil aviation . . . HR 11145, Fill-Up Rights, HR 10877 and companion Senate bills." Lobbyist — Marvin Roy Osburn, Washington, D.C.

PIEDMONT AIRLINES, Winston Salem, N.C. Lobbyist — Wickham, Craft & Cihlar; Charls E. Walker; Washington, D.C., filed 4/3/78. Legislative interest — ". . . Tax proposals relating to items of capital recovery and capital formation which affect airline companies; . . . for enactment of legislation similar to S 1270 to provide for refund of investment tax credits. . . ."

PFIZER INC., Washington, D.C.,Lobbyists — Hughes Hubbard & Reed; Stephen R. Conafay, Washington, D.C., filed 4/25/78. Legislative interest — ". . . Issues regarding antitrust legislation. . . ."

THE PILLSBURY CO., Minneapolis, Minn. Lobbyist — Williams & Jensen, Washington, D.C. Filed 4/26/78. Legislative interest — "Tax matters of interest to the company and its subsidiaries."

ROSENTHAL & CO., Chicago, Ill. Lobbyists — Alston, Miller & Gaines, Atlanta, Ga., filed 4/12/78; Leonard Cohen, James T. Devine, Washington, D.C., filed 4/13/78. Legislative interest — ". . . Proponent of changes in Commodity Exchange Act in connection with reauthorization hearings of the Commodity Futures Trading Commission."

SANTA FE INDUSTRIES INC., Chicago, Ill. Filed for self 4/7/78. Legislative interest — ". . . Legislation affecting the interest of Santa Fe Industries Inc." Lobbyist — Gregory M. Pensabene, Washington, D.C.

JOS. SCHLITZ BREWING CO., Milwaukee, Wis. Filed for self 4/19/78. Legislative interest — ". . . Consumer fraud, lobbying controls, wage/price controls, alcoholism rehabilitation, environmental concerns, energy, ingredient labeling and health warnings on labels, OSHA, Humphrey-Hawkins, federal deposit legislation." Lobbyist — James M. Bennett, Daniel T. Coughlin, Milwaukee, Wis.

SECURITY PACIFIC NATIONAL BANK, Los Angeles, Calif. Lobbyist — Richard F. McAdoo, Myra J. DeLapp, Washington, D.C. Filed 4/4/78. Legislative interest — "Any legislation related to or affecting financial institutions."

TELEPROMPTER CORP., New York, N.Y. Lobbyist — Shea Gould Climenko & Casey, New York, N.Y. Filed 4/12/78. Legislative interest — "In favor of HR 9251, the Tax Treatment Extension Act of 1977."

TEXAS INTERNATIONAL AIRLINES, Houston, Texas. Lobbyist — Verner, Liipfert, Bernhard and McPherson, Washington, D.C. Filed 4/7/78. Legislative interest — "Tax legislation, specifically investment tax credit availability to air carriers."

TRANS UNION CORP., Lincolnshire, Ill. Lobbyist — Mays, Valentine, Davenport & Moore, Washington, D.C. Filed 4/11/78. Legislative interest — "Legislation relating to the transportation of hazardous materials with special attention given to those transported by rail. . . ."

TRANS WORLD AIRLINES INC., New York, N.Y. Filed for self 4/10/78. Legislative interest — "All legislation affecting operation of domestic and international airlines." Lobbyist — R. S. Tribbe, Washington, D.C.

UNITED EGG PRODUCERS, Decatur, Ga. Filed for self 4/5/78. Legislative interest — "Matters affecting the shell egg industry. . . ." Lobbyist — Betty Vorhies, Washington, D.C.

WOMETCO ENTERPRISES INC., Miami, Fla. Lobbyist — Preston, Thorgrimson, Ellis, Holman & Fletcher, Washington, D.C. Filed 4/10/78. Legislative interest — ". . . The adverse consequences certain provisions of the Canadian tax code have on U.S. broadcasters."

Energy and Environment

ENVIRONMENTAL POLICY CENTER, Washington, D.C. Filed for self 4/27/78. Legislative interest — ". . . Nuclear energy; . . . B.I.A. portion of Dept. of the Interior appropriations for FY 1979." Lobbyist — Cary Ridder, David Berick, Washington, D.C.

PRESERVATION ACTION, Washington, D.C. Filed for self 4/28/78. Legislative interest — "All legislation affecting historic preservation and neighborhood conservation." Lobbyist — Julia Churchman, Marie Louise P. Friendly, Washington, D.C.

SMALL PRODUCERS FOR ENERGY INDEPENDENCE, Wichita, Kansas. Lobbyist — Verner, Liipfert, Bernhard and McPherson, Washington, D.C. Filed 4/7/78. Legislative interest — "Representation of small oil and gas producers in both Senate and House on oil pricing and natural gas legislation."

SOCIETY OF AMERICAN WOOD PRESERVERS INC., Arlington, Va. Filed for self 4/11/78. Legislative interest — "International trade, construction/housing, business regulation, mining regulation, environmental legislation, product liability, labor law reform, Humphrey-Hawkins." Lobbyist — C. Wickliffe Caldwell, Arlington, Va.

International Relations

AUSTRALIAN MEAT AND LIVE-STOCK CORP., New York, N.Y. Lobbyist — Clifford, Glass, McIlwain & Finney, Washington, D.C. Filed 4/19/78. Legislative interest — "S 2895, Beef Import Act of 1978, and amendments to the Meat Import Act of 1964 and related legislation."

CONSTRUCTORA NACIONAL DE CARROS DE FERROCARRIL, Mexico. Lobbyist — Arent, Fox, Kintner, Plotkin and Kahn, Washington, D.C. Filed 4/11/78. Legislative interest — "Legislation for suspension of duty on railway freight cars."

HELLENIC REPUBLIC OF GREECE, Washington, D.C. Lobbyist — Verner, Liipfert, Bernhard and McPherson, Washington, D.C. Filed 4/7/78. Legislative interest — "Legislation affecting U.S. aid policy in the Eastern Mediterranean."

HOLT INTERNATIONAL CHILDREN'S SERVICES INC., Eugene, Ore. Filed for self 4/19/78. Legislative interest — ". . . Immigration laws relating to intercountry adoptions and naturalization of such children; laws restricting adoptions; foster care, child abuse and other related child welfare matters of U.S. born children. . . ."

JOINT COUNCIL ON INTERNATIONAL CHILDRENS' SERVICES, Washington, D.C. Filed for self 4/13/78. Legislative interest — ". . . Increasing the number of foreign born orphan children that can be adopted by families."

ROYAL EMBASSY OF SAUDI ARABIA. Lobbyists — Milton F. Capps, Columbia, S.C.; Stephen N. Conner, Easton, Md.; filed 4/5/78. Legislative interest — "Legislative activities concerning press relations; . . . proposed sale by the U.S. of F-15 fighter aircraft to the Kingdom of Saudi Arabia."

WABANEX ENERGY CORP. LTD., Montreal, Canada. Lobbyist — Casey, Lane & Mittendorf, Washington, D.C. Filed 4/17/78. Legislative interest — "All legislation affecting petroleum or petroleum product storage. . . ."

Labor Groups

MARINE ENGINEERS' BENEFICIAL ASSOCIATION, AFL-CIO, Washington, D.C. Filed for self 4/27/78. Legislative interest — "To support legislation pertaining to the maritime industry, other transportation industries, and labor generally, and oppose legislation detrimental to the preceding categories." Lobbyist — Charles J. Caldwell, Washington, D.C.

UNITED MINE WORKERS OF AMERICA, Washington, D.C. Filed for self 4/11/78. Legislative interest — ". . . Legislation that in UMWA opinion benefits workers in the coal mining industry and conversely oppose legislation believed to be detrimental to coal miners." Lobbyist — John J. Kelly, Washington, D.C.

Military and Veterans

ASSOCIATION OF NORTHEASTERN VETERANS COUNSELING ORGANIZATIONS, New York, N.Y. Lobbyist — Keith Snyder, Washington, D.C. Filed 4/7/78. Legislative interest — "Veterans' affairs, S 2384, HR 10173, S 364, S 1688 — for; S 274 — against."

State and Local Government

BUCKINGHAM TOWNSHIP SUPERVISOR, Buckingham, Pa. Filed for self 4/6/78. Legislative interest — "Aviation affairs, land use matters. . . ." Lobbyist — Alan P. Agle, Buckingham, Pa.

COMMONWEALTH OF PUERTO RICO. Lobbyist — Stroock & Stroock & Lavan, Washington, D.C. Filed 4/12/78. Legislative interest — "In favor of passage of HR 7200."

THE METROPOLITAN DISTRICT, Hartford, Conn. Lobbyist — Linton, Mields, Reisler & Cotton, Washington, D.C. Filed 4/24/78. Legislative interest — "All legislation dealing with water pollution and water resources."

TEXAS MUNICIPAL LEAGUE WORKERS' COMPENSATION JOINT INSURANCE FUND, Austin, Texas. Lobbyist — Tony Korioth, G. Sue Lowe, Austin, Texas. Filed 4/17/78. Legislative interest — ". . . HR 8470, to amend section 501 of the Internal Revenue Code of 1954 to provide tax exemption for an association operated exclusively to provide worker's compensation for state and local employees."

Trade Associations

AMERICAN BUS ASSOCIATION, Washington, D.C. Filed for self 4/25/78. Legislative interest — ". . . Highway and Mass Transit legislation, HR 11733 and S 2440; Urban Mass Transit legislation, S 2441; No-Fault Auto Insurance, HR 6601, S 1381, Tax Reform legislation, HR 12078 and Amtrak FY 79 budget, HR 11493." Lobbyist — E. Douglas Frost, Washington, D.C.

AMERICAN FOOTWEAR INDUSTRIES ASSOCIATION INC., Arlington, Va. Filed for self 4/11/78. Legislative interest — "Matters affecting the footwear industry; favor Orderly Marketing Act." Lobbyist — Frederick A. Meister Jr., Arlington, Va.

THE AMERICAN INSTITUTE OF ARCHITECTS, Washington, D.C. Filed for self 4/7/78. Legislative interest — ". . . Legislation relating to the practice of architecture, including housing, community development, historic preservation, federal procurement procedures for architectural services, energy conservation. . . ." Lobbyist — David O. Meeker, Washington, D.C.

AMERICAN MINING CONGRESS, Washington, D.C. Filed for self 4/13/78. Legislative interest — "Measures affecting mining such as income taxation, social security, public lands, stockpiling, monetary policy, mine safety, environmental quality control etc." Lobbyist — David G. Todd, Washington, D.C.

AMERICAN PETROLEUM INSTITUTE, Washington, D.C. Lobbyist — Alabama Petroleum Council, Montgomery, Ala. Filed 4/10/78. Legislative interest — "Legislation affecting the petroleum industry."

AMERICAN SPEECH AND HEARING ASSOCIATION, Rockville, Md. Filed for self 4/21/78. Legislative interest — "All legislation concerning health, education and environmental matters, especially pertaining to the communicatively handicapped and professional interests of speech-language pathologists and audiologists." Lobbyist — Richard Morgan Downey, Morrison G. Cain, Rockville, Md.

AMUSEMENT AND MUSIC OPERATORS ASSOCIATION, Chicago, Ill. Lobbyist — Herrick, Allen & Davis, Washington, D.C. Filed 4/7/78. Legislative interest — ". . . Matters pertaining to the Copyright Act of 1976 and legislation to amend the Act."

THE ASSOCIATED GENERAL CONTRACTORS OF AMERICA, Washington, D.C. Filed for self 4/12/78. Legislative interest — ". . . Measures which affect the general contracting business. . . ." Lobbyist — Ingrid A. Voorhees, Andrea I. Semmes, Robert D. Kimball, Donald A. Scott, James R. Baxter, Douglas A. Cowley, Washington, D.C.

ASSOCIATION OF AMERICAN RAILROADS, Washington, D.C. Filed for self 4/10/78. Legislative interest — ". . . Legislation believed to be in the interest of a sound national transportation policy. . . ." Lobbyist — Francis J. Duggan, Washington, D.C.

BUSINESS ROUNDTABLE, New York, N.Y. Lobbyist — Williams & Connolly, Washington, D.C. Filed 4/6/78. Legislative interest — ". . . S 1437, HR 6869 and HR 2311, bills to revise the federal criminal code."

CALIFORNIA SAVINGS & LOAN LEAGUE, Los Angeles, Calif. Lobbyist — Thomas M. Rees, Washington, D.C. Filed 4/13/78. Legislative interest — "Banking legislation."

CHAMBER OF COMMERCE OF THE UNITED STATES, Washington, D.C. Filed for self 4/5/78. Legislative interest — "Matters as to which the Chamber may wish to make recommendations or comments, particularly relating to federal election laws." Lobbyist — Harold R. Mayberry Jr., Linda M. Anzalone, Talbott C. Smith, Washington, D.C.

CHAMPLIN PETROLEUM CO., Fort Worth, Texas. Lobbyist — Hogan & Hartson, Washington, D.C. Filed 4/24/78. Legislative interest — "Department of Energy Funding Authorization for FY 1979."

COMMITTEE OF PRODUCERS OF HIGH CARBON FERROCHROMIUM, Niagara Falls, N.Y. Lobbyists — Leva, Hawes, Symington, Martin & Oppenheimer, Washington, D.C.; Airco Inc., Montvale, N.J.,; Airco Alloys, Niagara Falls, N.Y., filed 4/26/78. Legislative interest — "Proposed legislation affecting imports of high carbon ferrochromium."

COUNCIL OF AMERICAN-FLAG SHIP OPERATORS, Washington, D.C. Filed for self 4/5/78. Legislative interest — ". . . Matters relating to Merchant Marine Act of 1936. . . ." Lobbyist — Edmund T. Sommer Jr., Albert E. May, Washington, D.C.

CREDIT UNION NATIONAL ASSOCIATION INC., Washington, D.C. Filed for self 4/13/78. Legislative interest — ". . . Laws affecting credit unions and banking; tax; privacy and consumer affairs. . . ." Lobbyist — Joseph L. Gibson, James Cousins, David H. Miller, Washington, D.C.

GROCERY MANUFACTURERS OF AMERICA, Washington, D.C. Filed for self 4/11/78. Legislative interest — ". . . Legislation affecting the production of processing of grocery and related products." Lobbyist — Matthew O'Hara, Washington, D.C.

IMPERIAL RESOURCES ASSOCIATION, Brawley, Calif. Lobbyist — Thomas M. Rees, Washington, D.C. Filed 4/13/78. Legislative interest — "Legislation affecting Reclamation Acts."

INDEPENDENT PETROLEUM ASSOCIATION OF AMERICA, Washington, D.C. Filed for self 4/11/78. Legislative interest — ". . . Legislation that might affect the petroleum industry. . . ." Lobbyist — Howard S. Useem, Washington, D.C.

INSTITUTE OF SIGNAGE RESEARCH, Palo Alto, Calif. Lobbyist — Cramer, Visser, Lipsen & Smith, Washington, D.C. Filed 4/28/78. Legislative interest — "Legislation that might affect the industry and in particular federal aid highway authority and/or legislation."

INTERNATIONAL FRANCHISE ASSOCIATION, Washington, D.C. Filed for self 4/10/78. Legislative interest — ". . . HR 5016 and HR 9144 and S 2135. All three are franchise related bills. . . ." Lobbyist — Jerry C. Wilkerson, Washington, D.C.

MIDWEST ELECTRIC CONSUMERS' ASSOCIATION INC., Evergreen, Colo. Lobbyist — Duncan, Brown, Weinberg, Washington, D.C. Filed 4/7/78. Legislative interest — "Legislation affecting the organization."

MINERAL KING DISTRICT ASSOCIATION, Three Rivers, Calif. Lobbyist — Jerome R. Waldie, Washington, D.C. Filed 4/21/78. Legislative interest — "Support of legislation transferring Mineral King to National Park System."

NATIONAL ASSOCIATION OF MANUFACTURERS, Washington, D.C. Lobbyist — Robert P. Fogarty, Columbus, Ohio. Filed 4/3/78. Legislative interest — "Legislation affecting business and industry."

NATIONAL ASSOCIATION FOR MILK MARKETING REFORM, Washington, D.C. Lobbyist — Donald A. Randall, Washington, D.C. Filed 4/10/78. Legislative Interest — "Agricultural bills related to Capper-Volstead Act."

NATIONAL ASSOCIATION OF PENSION CONSULTANTS AND ADMINISTRATORS INC., Atlanta, Ga. Filed for self 4/18/78. Legislative interest — ". . . Particular interest in matters effecting the Internal Revenue Code of 1954 . . . and the Employee Retirement Income Security Act of 1974." Lobbyist — Henkel & Lamon, Atlanta, Ga.

NATIONAL ASSOCIATION OF PENSION CONSULTANTS & ADMINISTRATORS INC., Atlanta, Ga. Lobbyist —

Henkel & Lamon, Atlanta, Ga. Filed 4/21/78. Legislative Interest — " . . . All legislative matters relating to employee benefits, generally, including pension and welfare benefit plans, Social Security; and small business."

NATIONAL ASSOCIATION OF REALTORS, Chicago, Ill. Filed for self 4/10/78. Legislative interest — "Any legislation affecting the real estate industry." Lobbyist — William L. Warfield, Washington, D.C.

NATIONAL ASSOCIATION OF SMALL BUSINESS INVESTMENT COMPANIES, Washington, D.C. Filed for self 4/8/78. Legislative interest — ". . . Legislation relating to small business in general. . . ." Lobbyist — Eileen M. Biermann, Karen L. Stevens, Washington, D.C.

NATIONAL FOREST PRODUCTS ASSOCIATION, Washington, D.C. Lobbyist — Souther, Spaulding, Kinsey, Williamson & Schwabe, Portland, Ore. Legislative interest — "House and Senate Interior Appropriation and related bills. In favor of."

NATIONAL LIMESTONE INSTITUTE INC., Fairfax, Va. Filed for self 4/7/78. Legislative interest — "All legislation which directly or indirectly affects the interest of limestone producers." Lobbyist — Craig G. Thibaudeau, Fairfax, Va.

NATIONAL MANUFACTURED HOUSING FEDERATION, Washington, D.C. Lobbyist — Leighton & Conklin, Washington, D.C. Filed 4/7/78. Legislative interest — ". . . Matters relating to mobile homes and mobile home parks."

NATIONAL PEST CONTROL ASSOCIATION, Vienna, Va. Filed for self 4/10/78. Legislative interest — "Federal Pesticide Legislation, Federal Insecticide, Fungicide and Rodenticide Act, S 1678, HR 8681, support." Lobbyist — Jefferson D. Keith, Vienna, Va.

NATIONAL RURAL ELECTRIC COOPERATIVE ASSOCIATION, Washington, D.C. Filed for self 4/17/78. Legislative interest — "All legislative interests affecting the RE Act of 1936, as amended." Lobbyist — Tony Perkins, Washington, D.C.

NATIONAL SAVINGS AND LOAN LEAGUE, Washington, D.C. Filed for self 4/12/78. Legislative interest — "Support of bills to improve facilities of savings and loan associations for encouragement of thrift and home financing. . . ." Lobbyist — James L. Pledger, Washington, D.C.

PACIFIC SEAFOOD PROCESSORS ASSOCIATION, Seattle, Wash. Filed for self 4/25/78. Legislative interest — "Interest in assuring that inspection and regulation requirements for certain vessels utilized in the fishing industry accurately reflect operational and safety needs." Lobbyist — Preston, Thorgrimson, Ellis, Holman & Fletcher, Washington, D.C.

PALM BEACH-BROWARD FARMERS COMMITTEE FOR LEGISLATIVE ACTION, Boynton Beach, Fla. Lobbyist — Van Ness, Feldman & Sutcliffe, Washington, D.C. Filed 4/20/78. Legislative interest — "In favor of legislation such as HR 11349, permitting Florida winter vegetable farmers to compete with imports."

RAILWAY PROGRESS INSTITUTE, Alexandria, Va. Filed for self 4/7/78. Legislative interest — ". . . Matters affecting the railroads, railway and mass transit supply industries." Lobbyist — Phillip W. Jones, Alexandria, Va.

SCIENTIFIC APPARATUS MAKERS ASSOCIATION, Washington, D.C. Filed for self 4/11/78. Legislative interest — "Legislation concerning the welfare of the Scientific Apparatus Industry from the standpoint of international trade, business and commercial policy as well as domestic issues having a bearing on the industry's ability to compete in international markets." Lobbyist — St. Clair J. Tweedie, Washington, D.C.

SECURITIES INDUSTRY ASSOCIATION, New York, N.Y..Lobbyist — Carl F. Arnold, Washington, D.C. Filed 4/18/78. Legislative interest — "Legislation affecting the securities industry."

SOUTH FLORIDA TOMATO AND VEGETABLE GROWERS ASSOCIATION, Homestead, Fla. Lobbyist — Van Ness, Feldman & Sutcliffe, Washington, D.C. Filed 4/20/78. Legislative interest — "In favor of legislation such as HR 11349. . . ."

SOUTHWEST WINTER VEGETABLE GROWERS ASSOCIATION, Immokalee, Fla. Lobbyist — Van Ness, Feldman & Sutcliffe, Washington, D.C. Filed 4/20/78. Legislative interest — "In favor of legislation such as HR 11349. . . ."

THE TEXAS MEDICAL ASSOCIATION, Austin, Texas. Lobbyist — Ace Pickens, Jack D. Maroney, Will G. Barber, Austin, Texas. Filed 4/3/78. Legislative interest — "Health legislation, particularly that affecting the Texas Medical Association members."

TRIS INDEMNITY CORPORATE GROUP, Washington, D.C. Lobbyist — Stroock & Stroock & Lavan, Washington, D.C. Filed 4/12/78. Legislative interest — "In favor of Tris Indemnification Bill, S 1507. . . ."

UNITED STATES FASTENER MANUFACTURING GROUP, Washington, D.C. Lobbyist — Collier, Shannon, Rill, Edwards & Scott, Washington, D.C. Filed 4/5/78. Legislative interest — ". . . All legislation relating to the International Trade Commission in the nuts, bolts and large screws case, S Con Res 66 and H Con Res 497."

WESTERN COTTON GROWERS' ASSOCIATION, Arvin, Calif. Filed for self 4/21/78. Legislative interest — ". . . Farm program legislation relative to cotton." Lobbyist — Kenneth E. Frick, Arvin, Calif.

WESTERN REGIONAL COUNCIL, Salt Lake City, Utah. Lobbyist — Bonneville Associates Inc., Salt Lake City, Utah. Filed 4/21/78. Legislative interest — "Issues involving business interests in the Western states. . . ."

WHEY PRODUCTS INSTITUTE, Chicago, Ill. Lobbyist — Leighton & Conklin, Washington, D.C. Filed 4/12/78. Legislative interest — "Interests relating to whey product production and marketing."

Miscellaneous

THE ADHERENCE GROUP, New York, N.Y. Filed for self 4/3/78. Legislative interest — "Legislation to amend Shipping Act of 1916. . . ."

THE AMERICAN RADIO RELAY LEAGUE INC., Newington, Conn. Filed for self 4/5/78. Legislative interest — ". . . Revisions of the Communications Act of 1934. . . ."

CHEROKEE NATION, Tahlequah, Okla. Lobbyist — Ed Edmondson, Muskogee, Okla. Filed 4/8/8/78. Legislative interest — "Interests involve Cherokee rights to Arkansas Riverbed minerals. . . ."

CHEYENNE RIVER SIOUX TRIBE, Eagle Butte, S.D. Lobbyist — Rebecca D. Shapiro & Associates, Washington, D.C. 4/13/78. Legislative interest — "Legislation affecting Indian tribes, pursuing appropriations interests."

CHIPPEWA-CREE TRIBE, Box Elder, Mont. Lobbyist — Patton, Boggs & Blow, Washington, D.C. Filed 4/13/78. Legislative interest — "Representation of the tribe before the Appropriations Committee of the House and Senate."

CLIENT-PROJECT ORBIS INC., Houston, Texas. Lobbyist — Surrey, Karasik and Morse, Washington, D.C. Filed 4/10/78. Legislative interest — ". . . Legislation for AID under the Foreign Assistance Act. . . ."

RICHARD COLVIN, Michigan City, Ind. Filed for self 4/6/78. Legislative interest — "S 1437, against."

COMMITTEE CONCERNED WITH SAFE BANKING ACT, Washington, D.C. Lobbyist — Patton, Boggs & Blow, Washington, D.C. Filed 4/10/78. Legislative interest — HR 9600, Safe Banking Act. . . ."

COMMUNITY NUTRITION INSTITUTE, Washington, D.C. Filed for self 4/12/78. Legislative interest — "Interest is in the area of consumer, nutrition, food and drug, and agricultural oriented legislation." Lobbyist — Ellen Haas, Rodney E. Leonard, Washington, D.C.

CONSET, Washington, D.C. Filed for self 4/19/78. Legislative interest — "Social and economic development of rural communities." Lobbyist — Stanley Zimmerman, Washington, D.C.

FOOD RESEARCH AND ACTION CENTER, Washington, D.C. Filed for self 4/18/78. Legislative interest — "Federal domestic food programs and related programs for low-income people. . . ." Lobbyist — Paula Roberts, Edward Cooney, Lynn Parker, Michael Sandifer, Washington, D.C.

G-4 CHILDRENS' COALITION, Chevy Chase, Md. Filed for self 4/13/78. Legislative interest — "Rights of G-4 visa holders who are children, surviving spouses, and retirees to obtain permanent U.S. resident status." Lobbyist — Muir & Stolper, Washington, D.C.

HOLT INTERNATIONAL CHILDREN'S SERVICES INC., Eugene, Ore. Filed for self 4/19/78. Legislative interest — "Immigration laws relating to intercountry adoptions and naturalization of such children; laws relating to adoptions, foster care, child abuse, and other related child welfare matters of U.S. born children; tax laws relating to the adoption process and adopted children."

NATIONAL PUBLIC RADIO, Washington, D.C. Filed for self 4/19/78. Legislative interest — "Legislation which is consistent with the public interest, First Amendment, and full development goals of public radio." Lobbyist Walda W. Roseman, Washington, D.C.

PUBLIC BROADCASTING SERVICE, Washington, D.C. Lobbyist — Anne G. Murphy, Arlington, Va. Filed 4/11/78. Legislative interest — ". . . Matters directly affecting public television stations.

QUINAULT INDIAN NATION, Taholah, Wash. Lobbyist — Rebecca D. Shapiro & Associates, Washington, D.C. Legislative interest — " . . . Legislation affecting Indian tribes. . . ."

ROYAL EMBASSY OF SAUDI ARABIA. Lobbyist — Cook, Reuf, Spann & Weiser Inc. Columbia, S.C. Filed 4/17/78. Legislative interest — "Legislative activities concerning press relations."

May

Citizens' Groups

ALASKA FEDERATION OF NATIVES, Anchorage, Alaska. Lobbyist — Donald Craig Mitchell, Anchorage, Alaska. Filed 5/10/78. Legislative interest — ". . . National Interest Alaska Lands bill (HR 39/S 1500); other Alaska native concerns. . . ."

THIRTY-FOURTH PRO-LIFE CONGRESSIONAL DISTRICT ACTION COMMITTEE, Lakewood, Calif. Filed for self 5/24/78. Legislative interest — "All proposed Human Life Amendments."

Corporations and Businesses

ALLIED CAPITAL CORP., Washington, D.C. Lobbyist — McClure & Trotter, Washington, D.C. Filed 5/1/78. Legislative interest — "Tax legislation of interest to the corporation."

AMERICAN HONDA MOTOR CO. INC., Washington, D.C. Filed for self 5/1/78. Legislative interest — "All legislation affecting products imported and sold by the company."

ANCHOR NATIONAL LIFE INSURANCE CO., Phoenix, Ariz. Lobbyist — Covington & Burling, Washington, D.C. Filed 5/3/78. Legislative interest — "Taxation of annuities; 'Revenue Act of 1978,' HR 12078, section 246; against."

BECHTEL CORP., Washington, D.C. Filed for self 5/4/78. Legislative linterest — "All matters which may be of special interest to an international engineering and construction enterprise." Lobbyist — R. Eric Miller, Washington, D.C.

BUREAU OF NATIONAL AFFAIRS INC., Washington, D.C. Lobbyist — Hydeman, Mason & Goodell, Washington, D.C. Filed 5/5/78. Legislative interest — "Amendments to Postal Reorganization Act of 1970."

CAMPBELL SOUP CO., Camden, N.J. Lobbyist — Covington & Burling, Washington, D.C. Filed 5/26/78. Legislative interest — "Amendments proposed to Meat Import Act of 1964."

CHEVRON U.S.A. INC., Washington, D.C. Filed for self 5/23/78. Legislative interest — "Legislation affecting Chevron U.S.A. Inc.; its parent, Standard Oil Co. of California; and other subsidiaries of Standard Oil Co. of California. Lobbyist — Dale E. Brooks, Washington, D.C.

CHROMALLOY AMERICAN CORP., St. Louis, Mo. Lobbyist — Peter H. Hahn, Washington, D.C. Filed 5/17/78. Legislative interest — "Waterways user tax, tax reform act, renegotiation reform, lobby law reform."

CBS INC., Washington, D.C. Lobbyist — Williams & Connolly, Washington, D.C. Filed 5/26/78. Legislative interest — "Legislation of interest to CBS Inc."

EL PASO NATURAL GAS CO., El Paso, Texas. Lobbyist — Terrance M. Adlhock, Washington, D.C. Filed 5/22/78. Legislative interest — ". . . Pending and on-going congressional actions relative to the concerns of the above-mentioned company."

GENERAL MILLS INC., Minneapolis, Minn. Lobbyists — Robert Bird; Wilner & Scheiner, Washington, D.C. Filed 5/12/78. Legislative interest — "Supports ban on any rulemaking proceeding designed to prohibit advertising of food products which have not been declared unsafe by Food & Drug Administration."

GENERAL MOTORS CORP., Detroit, Mich. Filed for self 5/30/78. Legislative interest — ". . . Proposed and anticipated action by . . . Congress and agencies of the federal government. . . ." Lobbyist — William J. Way, Washington, D.C.

LOCKHEED CORP., Burbank, Calif. Lobbyist — Miller & Chevalier, Washington, D.C. Filed 5/8/78. Legislative interest — "Amendment of section 911 of Internal Revenue Code of 1954 to allow income exclusions for excessive cost of housing, education, and other specific costs incurred by U.S. citizens employed abroad."

MOORE McCORMACK RESOURCES INC., Stamford, Conn. Lobbyist — Preston, Thorgrimson, Ellis, Holman & Fletcher, Washington, D.C. Filed 5/15/78. Legislative interest — "Legislation affecting the business of the company or its subsidiaries."

KUTV INC., Salt Lake City, Utah. Lobbyist — Moss, Frink & Franklin, Washington, D.C. Filed 5/22/78. Legislative interest — "Dual ownership of TV and newspaper."

NATIONAL MOTORSPORTS COMMITTEE OF ACCUS, Washington, D.C. Filed for self 5/2/78. Legislative interest — "Legislation affecting the Motorsports industry, including H Res 111." Lobbyist — William H. G. France, Washington, D.C.

NEW YORK COFFEE AND SUGAR EXCHANGE INC., New York, N.Y. Filed for self 5/17/78. Legislative interest — "Legislation regarding the Commodity Futures Trading Commission and sugar legislation." Lobbyist — Joseph L. Fraites, New York, N.Y.

P & O FALCO INC., Shreveport, La. Lobbyist — Ginsburg, Feldman and Bress, Washington, D.C. Filed 5/31/78. Legislative interest — "DOE Authorization Act for FY 1979; energy legislation affecting independent crude oil resellers."

PEPSICO INC., Purchase, N.Y. Lobbyist — Douglas P. Bennett, Washington, D.C. Filed 5/17/78. Legislative Interest — "Tax legislation."

SMITHKLINE CORP., Philadelphia, Pa. Lobbyist — Thomas M. Landin, Washington, D.C. Filed 5/18/78. Legislative interest — "Proposals and matters relating to business and industry."

A.E. STALEY MANUFACTURING CO., Decatur, Ill. Lobbyist — Dale Sherwin, Washington, D.C. Filed 5/26/78. Legislative interest — ". . . Commodities of corn, soybeans and sugar. . . ."

SUN CO. INC., Radnor, Pa. Lobbyists — Baker, Hostetler, Frost & Towers; Mary W. Haught; Washington, D.C. Filed 5/22/78. Legislative interest — ". . . Amendment of the Internal Revenue code of 1954; petroleum and petroleum related matters."

TRUE OIL PURCHASING CO., Casper, Wyo. Lobbyist — Ginsburg, Feldman and Bress, Washington, D.C. Filed 5/31/78. Legislative interest — "DOE Authorization Act for FY 1979 — energy legislation affecting independent crude oil resellers."

WESTERN CRUDE OIL, Denver, Colo. Lobbyist — Ginsburg, Feldman and Bress, Washington, D.C. Filed 5/31/78. Legislative interest — "DOE Authorization Act for FY 1979 — energy legislation affecting independent crude oil resellers."

WESTWAY TRADING CORP., Englewood Cliffs, N.J. Lobbyist — Surrey, Karasik & Morse, Washington, D.C. Filed

5/23/78. Legislative interest — "Legislation concerning sugar; in particular S 2990 (against); HR 12486 (against); and HR 12492 (against)."

Energy and Environment

NATURAL RESOURCES DEFENSE COUNCIL INC., Palo Alto, Calif. Filed for self 5/1/78. Legislative interest — "Pacific Northwest Electric Power Supply & Conservation Act (HR 9664; HR 9020; S 2080) - (for and against various sections); Columbia Basin Energy Corporation Act (HR 5862) - (for and against various sections); various radioactive waste legislation." Lobbyist — Terry R. Lash, John Roger Beers, Palo Alto, Calif.

PRESERVATION ACTION, Washington, D.C. Filed for self 5/1/78. Legislative interest — "All legislation affecting historic preservation and neighborhood conservation." Lobbyist — Marie Louise P. Friendly, Julia Churchman, Washington, D.C.

SIERRA CLUB, Washington, D.C. Lobbyist — George Alderson, Washington, D.C. Filed 5/8/78. Legislative interest — "HR 39 and related bills concerning Alaska National Interest Lands."

THE WILDERNESS SOCIETY, Washington, D.C. Filed for self 5/30/78. Legislative interest — "HR 39; Alaska National Lands Conservation Act; HR 9292, reform of the 1872 mining law; HR 7970, Wilderness Designation within the National Forest System; HR 11063, Wilderness designation within Kistachic National Forest; HR 11437, wilderness lands in Wisconsin; HR 6625, Pine Barrens National Ecological Reserve, New Jersey; S 2306, natural Reserve System Act; HR 1614 and S 9, Outer Continental Shelf Act; HR 4167, Endangered Species Act Amendment; support all of the above." Lobbyists — Stanley E. Senner, Fairbanks, Alaska; Perry Moyle, Grand Junction, Colo.; Randall D. Snodgrass, Atlanta, Ga.; Grace Pierce, Denise Schlener, Dave Foreman, Celia Hunter, Deborah K. Sease, Washington, D.C.

International Relations

SWAZILAND SUGAR ASSOCIATION, Mbabane, Swaziland. Lobbyist — International Management Consultants, Ltd., Washington, D.C. Filed 5/5/78. Legislative interest — ". . . To protect the interests of the Swaziland Sugar Association."

State and Local Government

CITY OF BRIDGEPORT, CONN. Lobbyist — Krivit & Krivit, Washington, D.C. Filed 5/8/78. Legislative interest — "HR 12453, Comprehensive Employment and Training Act of 1978 and identical or related House and Senate measures."

CITY OF CAMDEN, N.J. Lobbyist — Krivit & Krivit, Washington, D.C. Filed 5/8/78. Legislative interest — "HR 12453, Comprehensive Employment and Training Act of 1978 and identical or related House and Senate measures."

CITY OF DETROIT, MICH. Lobbyist — Hudson & Leftwich, Washington, D.C. Filed 5/9/78. Legislative interest — "General legislation."

GLOUCESTER COUNTY, N.J. Lobbyist — Krivit & Krivit, Washington, D.C. Filed 5/8/78. Legislative interest — "HR 12453, Comprehensive Employment and Training Act of 1978 and identical or related House and Senate measures."

KANSAS CITY, MO. Lobbyist — Hudson & Leftwich, Washington, D.C. Filed 5/9/78. Legislative interest — "General legislation."

CITY OF PONTIAC, MICH. Filed for self 5/24/78. Legislative interest — "General legislature matters affecting municipalities." Lobbyist — Beer, Boltz & Bennia, Bloomfield Hill, Mich.

STATE TROOPERS FRATERNAL ASSOCIATION OF NEW JERSEY INC., Howell, N.J. Lobbyist — Battle, Fowler, Jaffin, Pierce & Kheel, New York, N.Y. Filed 5/1/78. Legislative interest — "Legislation relating to the federal income taxation of meal allowances paid to state police officials."

Trade Associations

AMERICAN ADVERTISING FEDERATION, Washington, D.C. Filed for self 5/16/78. Legislative interest — "Legislation of interest to advertisers, advertising agencies and advertising media." Lobbyist — Howard H. Bell, Jonah Gitlitz, Washington, D.C.

AMERICAN PAPER INSTITUTE INC., New York, N.Y. Filed for self 5/25/78. Legislative interest — "Those affecting the pulp, paper and paperboard industry, its operation, practices and properties." Lobbyist — Jeffrey M. Duke, New York, N.Y.

AMERICAN PETROLEUM INSTITUTE, Washington, D.C. Lobbyist — Mississippi Petroleum Council, Jackson, Miss. Filed 5/5/78. Legislative interest — "Legislation affecting the petroleum industry."

AMERICAN PETROLEUM REFINERS ASSOCIATION, Washington, D.C. Filed for self 5/8/78. Legislative interest — "All legislative issues affecting small refiners such as Petroleum Marketing Practices Act (S 743); toxic substances legislation; Crude Oil Equalization Tax, and other measures including but not limited to the president's energy proposal." Lobbyist — Scott P. Anger, Raymond F. Bragg Jr., Washington, D.C.

AMERICAN PSYCHIATRIC ASSOCIATION, Washington, D.C. Lobbyist — Bregman, Abell, Solter & Kay, Washington, D.C. Filed 5/5/78. Legislative interest — "All legislative matters of interest to the client."

AMERICAN SUGAR CANE LEAGUE OF THE U.S.A. INC., New Orleans, La. Lobbyist — Don Wallace Associates Inc., Washington, D.C. Filed 5/25/78. Legislative interest — '...Legislation and executive branch policy affecting its clients."

FINANCIAL ACCOUNTING STANDARDS BOARD, Stamford, Conn. Filed for self 5/4/78. Legislative interest — "...Legislation affecting or otherwise relating to the establishment or improvement of standards of financial accounting and reporting." Lobbyist — Patricia Pride, Washington, D.C.

FLORIDA SUGAR CANE LEAGUE INC., Clewiston, Fla. Lobbyist — Michael R. McLeod, Washington, D.C. Filed 5/12/78. Legislative interest — "All legislation affecting sugar cane growers."

GLASS PACKAGING INSTITUTE, Washington, D.C. Lobbyist — Leva, Hawes, Symington, Martin & Oppenheimer, Washington, D.C. Filed 5/19/78. Legislative interest — "...Solid Waste Disposal Act...and bills dealing with solid waste and litter problems."

GROCERY MANUFACTURERS OF AMERICA, Washington, D.C. Lobbyists — Andrews, Kurth, Campbell & Jones; A. Everette MacIntyre; Mays, Valentine, Davenport & Moore, Washington, D.C. Legislative interest — "...Matters regulating or affecting the production and sale of grocery and related products, including appropriations for agencies regulating such matters; ...any Federal Trade Commission action limiting advertising of food products with particular attention to pending appropriations legislation...."

GROUP HEALTH ASSOCIATION OF AMERICA INC., Washington, D.C. Filed for self 5/2/78. Legislative interest — "All bills relating to prepayment of health care, comprehensive health care, group practice medicine and matters relating to consumer health care services." Lobbyist — Gibson Kingren, Washington, D.C.

INDUSTRIAL FASTENERS GROUP, New York, N.Y. Lobbyist — Daniels, Houlihan & Palmeter, Washington, D.C. Filed 5/3/78. Legislative interest — "Oppose H Con Res 485 to override the president's decision on industrial fasteners."

INLAND FOREST RESOURCE COUNCIL, Missoula, Mont. Lobbyist — Scootch Pankonin, Washington, D.C. Filed 5/25/78. Legislative interest — "Legislation pertaining to forest products industry."

LIVESTOCK MARKETING ASSOCIATION, Kansas City, Mo. Filed for self 5/16/78. Legislative interest — "Freedom in Livestock Marketing Act, S 2275; Bumpers bill — S 2195; Thornton bill — HR 9482; Supporting each of the above, subject to certain amendments." Lobbyist — Robert M. Cook, Kansas City, Mo.

NATIONAL ASSOCIATION OF ELECTRIC COMPANIES, Washington, D.C. Filed for self 5/1/78. Legislative interest — "The association is interested in all developments in federal legislation that might affect its members as going electric utilities." Lobbyist — Edward J. Milne Jr., Washington, D.C.

NATIONAL ASSOCIATION OF FARMER ELECTED COMMITTEEMEN, Darlington, S.C. Filed for self 5/1/78. Legislative interest — "All farm legislation."

NATIONAL ASSOCIATION OF HOME BUILDERS OF THE U.S., Washington, D.C. Filed for self 5/10/78. Legislative interest — "...All legislation affecting the industry and its members." Lobbyist — Mark Fitzgerald, Washington, D.C.

NATIONAL COUNCIL OF FARMER COOPERATIVES, Washington, D.C. Filed for self 5/24/78. Legislative interest — "Legislation in the interest to the National Council of Farmer Cooperatives." Lobbyist — Charles D. Hartman, Washington, D.C.

PAPERBOARD PACKAGING COUNCIL, Washington, D.C. Filed for self 5/12/78. Legislative interest — "Legislation affecting the welfare of the paperboard packaging industry, ...domestic trade and commerce policy, labor policy, government controls, consumer and environmental legislation." Lobbyist — Spencer A. Johnson, Washington, D.C.

THE PROPRIETARY ASSOCIATION, Washington, D.C. Lobbyist — Clifford, Glass, McIlwain & Finney, Washington, D.C. Filed 5/26/78. Legislative interest — "S 2755 and HR 11611 and similar legislation concerning proprietary or over-the-counter drugs."

SLURRY TRANSPORT ASSOCIATION, Washington, D.C. Lobbyist — Scootch Pankonin, Washington, D.C. Filed 5/25/78. Legislative interest — "Coal slurry pipeline, HR 1609, for."

TIME-CRITICAL SHIPMENT COMMITTEE, Washington, D.C. Lobbyist — Cleary, Gottlieb, Steen & Hamilton, Washington, D.C. Filed 5/11/78. Legislative interest — "Support of section 19 of HR 7700 or similar legislation."

UNITED EGG PRODUCERS, Decatur, Ga. Lobbyist — Michael R. McLeod, Washington, D.C. Filed 5/12/78. Legislative interest — "All legislation affecting egg producers."

Miscellaneous

COMMITTEE TO COMBAT HUNTINGTON'S DISEASE, New York, N.Y. Filed for self 5/22/78. Legislative interest — "...Influencing support for National Health Insurance; services for the chronic diseased patients; the National Genetics Diseases Act; support for those institutes at NIH whose concerns include aging, genetics, metabolic disorders, neurologic disorders." Lobbyist — Marjorie Guthrie, New York, N.Y.

ESTATE OF SYLVIA S. BURING, Memphis, Tenn. Lobbyist — Cohen and Uretz, Washington, D.C. Filed 5/11/78. Legislative interest — "Amendment of Internal Revenue Code relating to estate tax alternate valuation date election."

ELMER W. KNEIP, Chicago, Ill. Lobbyist — Gardner, Carton & Douglas, Washington, D.C. Filed 5/11/78. Legislative interest — "Any tax laws relating to foreign trusts."

NATIONAL BOARD OF YOUNG MEN'S CHRISTIAN ASSOCIATIONS, New York, N.Y. Filed for self 5/16/78. Legislative interest — "All legislation having a financial effect on the YMCAs." Lobbyist — Robert K. Jenkins Jr., Washington, D.C.

NATIONAL HEALTH LAW PROGRAM INC., Santa Monica, Calif. Filed for self 5/31/78. Legislative interest — "Health access issues relating to eligible legal services clients including poor persons and minorities." Lobbyist — Andy Schneider, Sheila H. Boykin, Washington, D.C.

PASS 1010 COMMITTEE, New York, N.Y. Filed for self 5/25/78. Legislative interest — "...Passage of S 1010, HR 2777."

SERVICEMASTER INDUSTRIES INC., Downers Grove, Ill. Lobbyist — Louis C. Kramp and Associates, Washington, D.C. Filed 5/11/78. Legislative interest — "Legislation pertaining to franchising — HR 5016 — against."

SURREY, KARASIK & MORSE, Washington, D.C. Lobbyist — Phillip W. Moery, Washington, D.C. Filed 5/23/78. Legislative interest — "Legislation concerning sugar, in particular S 2990 (against), HR 12486 (against), and HR 12492 (against)."

THE THIRTEENTH REGIONAL CORPORATION, Seattle, Wash. Filed for self 5/3/78. Legislative interest — "Legislation affecting the 13th Regional Corporation and non-resident Alaska Natives, legislation to award land to the 13th Regional Corporation." Lobbyist — Billy B. Johnson, Seattle, Wash.

U.S. BORAX, Los Angeles, Calif. Lobbyist — Jack Ferguson Associates, Washington, D.C. Filed 5/30/78. Legislative interest — "Alaska Lands Bill."

June

Citizens' Groups

AD HOC COMMITTEE OF CONCERNED PARENTS, Lexington, Mass. Filed for self 6/12/78. Legislative interest — "Contempt of Congress citation of D. G. Fefferman." Lobbyist — Francis J. O'Rourke, Boston, Mass.

COMMON CAUSE, Washington, D.C. Filed for self 6/15/78. Legislative interest — ". . . Open government, campaign financing, environmental protection, defense spending, tax reform, waste in government, voting rights, Presidential nomination and confirmation process, administration of justice and reform of the criminal code, merit selection of federal judges, intelligence policy, public participation in federal agency proceedings, civil service reform, regulatory reform, the Congressional budget process and congressional reform." Lobbyist — Randy Huwa, Jane Wishner, Washington, D.C.

CONSUMER ACTION NOW, Washington, D.C. Lobbyist — Lola Redford, New York, N.Y. Filed 6/17/78. Legislative interest — ". . . Any and all bills which may contain provisions having an impact on consumer products, health services or the environment; HR 6831, HR 3982, HR 3981, HR 3985 and S 800, S 805, S 806."

CONSUMER FEDERATION OF AMERICA, Washington, D.C. Filed for self 6/26/78. Legislative interest — "Generally for all issues of benefit to consumers. Specifically for: S 1010 National Consumer Cooperative Bank bill; S 1874 and HR 11942 — Overrule Supreme Court decision in *Illinois v. Brick*; United Kingdom Trade Treaty; bank secrecy and privacy act." Lobbyist — Peter Ginsberg, Gerald Hogan, Washington, D.C.

LEAGUE OF WOMEN VOTERS OF THE UNITED STATES, Washington, D.C. Lobbyist — Arent, Fox, Kintner, Plotkin & Kahn, Washington, D.C. Filed 6/30/78. Legislative interest — ". . . To clarify their rights to continue to engage in voter education activities under the Federal Election Campaign Act."

NATIONAL ACTION COMMITTEE ON LABOR LAW REFORM, Washington, D.C. Lobbyist — Fraser/Associates Inc., Washington, D.C. Filed 6/14/78. Legislative interest — ". . . S 1883, Labor 'reform' bill."

NATIONAL ORGANIZATION FOR WOMEN, Washington, D.C. Filed for self 6/8/78. Legislative interest — ". . . H J Res 638/S J Res 134; HEW/Labor Appropriations bill; welfare reform bills; displaced homemaker legislation; pregnancy discrimination bill; federal Criminal Code revision; legislation to mint a new U.S. dollar coin; battered women legislation." Lobbyist — Margaret Mason, Jean Marshall Clarke, Christy Klein, Phyllis West, Kristine Blackwood, Washington, D.C.

NATIONAL RIFLE ASSOCIATION OF AMERICA, Washington, D.C. Filed for self 6/7/78. Legislative interest — "Conservation, recreation and firearms legislation." Lobbyist — John D. Anquilino Jr., Washington, D.C.

NINETEENTH PRO-LIFE CONGRESSIONAL DISTRICT ACTION COMMITTEE, Lompoc, Calif. Filed for self 6/26/78. Legislative interest — "All proposed Human Life Amendments."

SELF-DETERMINATION FOR D.C.: A COALITION, Washington, D.C. Lobbyist — P. Melanie Woolston, Washington, D.C. Filed 6/19/78. Legislative interest — "H J Res 554; a constitutional amendment."

THIRTY-SECOND CONGRESSIONAL DISTRICT ACTION COMMITTEE, Harbor City, Calif. Filed for self 6/13/78. Legislative interest — "All proposed Human Life Amendments."

UNITED STATES OLYMPIC COMMITTEE, New York, N.Y. Lobbyist — John A. McCahill; Michael T. Harrigan, Washington, D.C. Filed 6/6/78. Legislative interest — "In support of the Amateur Athletic Act of 1978; HR 12626 and S 2727."

WOMEN'S LOBBY INC., Washington, D.C. Lobbyists — Kristine Blackwood, Karen Johnson, Pamela MacEwan, Anne Reginstein, Carolyn Woolley, Washington, D.C.; Carolyn Bode, Hyattsville, Md.; Kristina Kiehl, Silver Spring, Md.; Ann Schmitt, Great Falls, Va. Legislative interest — "H J Res 638, SJ Res 134 (for); welfare reform; women and poverty; National Health Insurance S 3, HR 21, Labor/HEW appropriations bill; HR 12299, S 2759 — battered women; pregnancy disability, HR 6075."

ZERO POPULATION GROWTH, Washington, D.C. Filed for self 6/9/78. Legislative interest — "Oppose legislation limiting the availability of abortion such as constitutional amendments (HR Res 5) and funding restrictions (amendments to the fiscal 1979 Labor-HEW Appropriations bill and other bills such as HR 6075, the pregnancy disability legislation)." Lobbyist — Susan Alexander, Phyllis Eisen, Washington, D.C.

Corporations and Businesses

AIR SUNSHINE, Key West, Fla. Lobbyist — Alcalde, Henderson, O'Bannon & Kline, Rosslyn, Va. Filed 6/19/78. Legislative interest — "All matters affecting commuter airlines."

ALASKA AIRLINES, Seattle, Wash. Lobbyist — Daniel J. Edelman Inc., Washington, D.C. Filed 6/26/78. Legislative interest — "CAB Docket No. 30170."

BASKAHEGAN CO., New York, N.Y. Lobbyist — Pierce, Atwood, Scribner, Allen, Smith & Lancaster, Portland, Maine. Filed 6/21/78. Legislative interest — "Legislation affecting the Maine Indian claims."

BOARD OF TRADE CLEARING CORP., Chicago, Ill. Lobbyist — Alston, Miller & Gaines, Washington, D.C. Filed 6/19/78. Legislative interest — "Proponent of amendments to HR 10285 and S 2391."

THE BOEING CO., Seattle, Wash. Lobbyist — Garry C. Porter, Olalla, Wash. Filed 6/23/78. Legislative interest — ". . . Government procurement — funding and policies; revenue issues; regulation of transportation: air, surface and water; industrial relations issues; international trade regulation; energy resources."

BUFFALO BROADCASTING CO. INC., Buffalo, N.Y. Lobbyist — Cordon & Jacob, Washington, D.C. Filed 6/7/78. Legislative interest — ". . . The tax bill now under preparation by the House of Representatives Committee on Ways and Means, and particularly with respect to an expected provision on foreign conventions."

THE CARBORUNDUM CO., Washington, D.C. Filed for self 6/7/78. Legislative interest — "All legislation of interest to Carborundum Co. and Kennecott Copper Corp." Lobbyist — Robert E. Duffy, Washington, D.C.

CATERPILLAR TRACTOR CO., Peoria, Ill. Filed for self 6/6/78. Legislative interest — "Present or future proposed legislation of interest to Caterpillar Tractor Co. and its subsidiary or affiliated companies." Lobbyist — Timothy L. Elder, Peoria, Ill.

CITRONELLE-MOBILE GATHERING INC., Mobile, Ala. Filed for self 6/20/78. Legislative interest — "General educational functions in connection with the oil pricing provisions of pending energy legislation." Lobbyist — Preston, Thorgrimson, Ellis, Holman & Fletcher, Washington, D.C.

THE CONTINENTAL GROUP INC., New York, N.Y. Lobbyist — Alcalde, Henderson, O'Bannon & Kline, Rosslyn, Va. Filed 6/18/78. Legislative interest — "All legislation relating to corporate business activities."

DEAD RIVER CO., Bangor, Maine. Lobbyist — Pierce, Atwood, Scribner, Allen, Smith & Lancaster, Portland, Maine. File 6/21/78. Legislative interest — "Legislation affecting the Maine Indian claims."

DOW CORNING CORP., Midland, Mich. Filed for self 6/30/78. Legislative interest — "Legislation affecting and/or of interest to Dow Corning, particularly environmental and technological issues." Lobbyist — Mary Eileen O'Brien, Arthur E. Klauser, Washington, D.C.

THE FIRST NATIONAL BANK OF BOSTON, Boston, Mass. Filed for self 6/12/78. Legislative interest — ". . . Clarifications and/or changes in income and employment tax provisions of Internal Revenue Code of 1954 affecting meals provided by employers for employees; for: a proposal to amend section 119 and any related proposals." Lobbyist — Joseph L. Duran, Morton A. Geller, Boston, Mass.

FORD MOTOR CO., Dearborn, Mich. Filed for self 6/30/78. Legislative interest — ". . . To analyze federal plans, policies, and trends and proposed legislation and regulations in relation to the interests of the company. . . ." Lobbyist — Jay T. Scheck Jr., Washington, D.C.

GENERAL MILLS CORP., Minneapolis, Minn. Lobbyist — Patton, Boggs & Blow, Washington, D.C. Filed 6/21/78. Legislative interest — ". . . Matters before the Congress including tax matters."

GENERAL MOTORS CORP., Detroit, Mich. Filed for self 6/1/78. Legislative interest — ". . . Proposed and anticipated action by state and national business organizations, state legislatures, Congress and agencies of the federal government. . . ." Lobbyist — Herman C. Witthaus, Washington, D.C.

GETTY OIL CO., Los Angeles, Calif. Lobbyist — Charls E. Walker Associates Inc., Washington, D.C. Filed 6/12/78. Legislative interest — ". . . Senate approval of the 1975 Tax Convention between the United States and the United Kingdom."

GOULD INC., Rolling Meadows, Ill. Lobbyist — Snyder & Ball, Arlington, Va. Filed 6/7/78. Legislative interest — "Defense authorization and appropriation bills."

GREAT NORTHERN PAPER CO., Stamford, Conn. Lobbyist — Pierce, Atwood, Scribner, Allen, Smith & Lancaster, Portland, Maine. Filed 6/21/78. Legislative interest — "Legislation affecting the Maine Indian claims."

GULF OIL CORP., Pittsburgh, Pa. Lobbyist — Alan G. Macdonald, Washington, D.C. Filed 6/1/78. Legislative interest — "Legislative matters pertaining to the oil and gas industry."

HALLIBURTON CO., Dallas, Texas. Filed for self 6/13/78. Legislative interest — ". . . Legislation which will affect oil field services, engineering and construction, manufacturing of oil field equipment and related areas." Lobbyist — Stephen T. DeLaMater, Dallas, Texas.

ITT, New York, N.Y. Lobbyist — Charls E. Walker, Washington, D.C. Filed 6/12/78. Legislative interest — ". . . Senate approval of the 1975 Tax Convention between the United States and the United Kingdom."

JOHNSON CONTROLS INC., Milwaukee, Wis. Lobbyist — Foley, Lardner, Hollabaugh & Jacobs, Washington, D.C. Filed 6/2/78. Legislative interest — "Legislation assuring investment tax credit for investment in automatic energy control and fire detection systems."

MARS INC., Washington, D.C. Lobbyist — Patton, Boggs & Blow, Washington, D.C. Filed 6/13/78. Legislative interest — "General farm legislation affecting rice, sugar, cocoa, peanuts, petfoods; HR 7171; S 275 and HR 7558."

M & M/MARS INC., Hackettstown, N.J. Lobbyist — Martin Ryan Haley & Associates Inc., Washington, D.C. Filed 6/22/78. Legislative interest — "Affairs of legislative interest."

MEMOREX CORP., Santa Clara, Calif. Filed for self 6/8/78. Legislative interest — "Export administration, tax, anti-trust, science and technology, government EDP procurement." Lobbyist — Allen W. Wills, McLean, Va.

NATIONAL DISTILLERS AND CHEMICAL CORP., New York, N.Y. Lobbyist — Wakefield Washington Associates Inc., Washington, D.C. Filed 6/26/78. Legislative interest — "Energy, Health, safety, environmental matters...."

NATIONAL DISTILLERS AND CHEMICAL CORP., New York, N.Y. Lobbyist — Wakefield Washington Associates Inc., Washington, D.C. Filed 6/28/78. Legislative interest — "Energy, health, safety, environmental matters and the Toxic Substances Control Act."

NEW YORK COFFEE AND SUGAR EXCHANGE INC., New York, N.Y. Filed for self 6/30/78. Legislative interest — "Legislation regarding the Commodity Futures Trading Commission and sugar legislation." Lobbyist — John M. Schobel Jr., Joseph L. Fraites, James J. Garry, Bennett J. Corn, New York, N.Y.

NORFOLK AND WESTERN RAILWAY CO., Washington, D.C. Lobbyist — Thomas C. Williams, Washington, D.C. Filed 6/1/78. Legislative interest — "Matters relating to the Norfolk and Western Railway."

PFIZER INC., Washington, D.C. Lobbyist — Charles J. Micoleau, Portland, Maine. Filed 6/1/78. Legislative interest — "All legislation as their interests may appear, including HR 11942."

PILLSBURY CORP., Minneapolis, Minn. Lobbyist — Patton, Boggs & Blow, Washington, D.C. Filed 6/21/78. Legislative interest — "Matters before the Congress including tax matters."

ST. JOE MINERALS CORP., Washington, D.C. Lobbyist — Patton, Boggs & Blow, Washington, D.C. Filed 6/21/78. Legislative interest — ". . . Matters before the Congress including international trade matters."

SEALED POWER CORP., Muskegon, Mich. Lobbyist — Gardner, Carton & Douglas, Washington, D.C. Filed 6/13/78. Legislative interest — "Tax laws relating to recapture of foreign losses."

STATES STEAMSHIP CO., San Francisco, Calif. Filed for self 6/7/78. Legislative interest — "Merchant Marine Act, 1936." Lobbyist — Robert E. Mayer, San Francisco, Calif.

TADCO ENTERPRISES, Washington, D.C. Lobbyist — Mark A. Siegel, Silver Spring, Md. Filed 6/2/78. Legislative interest — "The Sugar Stabilization Act of 1979."

UNION BANK OF BAVARIA, Munich, Germany. Lobbyist — Arent, Fox, Kintner, Plotkin & Kahn, Washington, D.C. Filed 6/26/78. Legislative interest — "International Banking Act of 1978 and related legislation of interest to a multi-national commercial bank."

Energy and Environment

SIERRA CLUB, San Francisco, Calif. Filed for self 6/8/78. Legislative interest — ". . . Environmental concerns, energy legislation, including: National Energy Act (HR 8444, HR 5037, HR 4018, HR 5263); DOE authorization act (HR 10969, S 2692)." Lobbyist — Keith LeVern Kline, Washington, D.C.; Jonathan P. Ela, Madison, Wis.

THE WILDERNESS SOCIETY, Washington, D.C. Filed for self 6/30/78. Legislative interest — "Boundary Waters Wilderness Act, HR 12250." Lobbyist — Steve Payne, Duluth, Minn.

International Relations

AMALGAMATED WIRELESS LTD., Sydney, Australia. Lobbyist — Judith Marty, Ernest C. Marty, Cremorne, Australia. Filed 6/21/78. Legislative Interest — "Buy America Act, Australian Industry Participation Agreement."

EMBASSY OF BOLIVIA, Washington, D.C. Lobbyist — Vance & Joyce, Washington, D.C. Filed 6/28/78. Legislative interest — ". . . Opposing the current legislative proposals to authorize the sale of tin from the U.S. Strategic Stockpile (e.g. HR 2723, HR 5258, HR 6632, HR 9486, HR 11430, HR 11448, HR 12704, S 2167, S 2181, S 2635 and S 2702."

GOVERNMENT OF REPUBLIC OF LIBERIA, Monrovia, Liberia. Lobbyist — Carl A. Parker, Port Arthur, Texas. Filed 6/7/78. Legislative interest — "All statutes and bills affecting U.S. relations with Liberia."

Military and Veterans

COUNCIL OF VIETNAM VETERANS INC., Washington, D.C. Filed for self 6/7/78. Legislative interest — "Veterans' affairs." Lobbyist — Steven M. Champlin, Washington, D.C.

State and Local Government

CITY OF NORTHGLEN, COLO. Lobbyist — Webster & Sheffield, New York, N.Y. Filed 6/7/78. Legislative interest — "Proposed Environmental Research Development, and Demonstration Authorization Act of 1979."

STATE OF ALASKA. Lobbyist — Jack Ferguson Associates, Washington, D.C. Filed 6/30/78. Legislative interest — "Reservation to Article 9.4 of the U.S.-U.K. Tax Treaty."

Trade Associations

AMERICAN ACADEMY OF DERMATOLOGY, Evanston, Ill. Lobbyist — John T. Grupenhoff, Bethesda, Md. Filed 6/2/78. Legislative interest — "All health/medical legislation in the Senate and in the House, including authorizations and appropriations."

AMERICAN BUS ASSOCIATION, Washington, D.C. Filed for self 6/22/78. Legislative interest — "Highway and Mass Transit legislation, HR 11733 and S 2440; Urban mass transit legislation, S 2441; no-fault auto insurance, HR 6601 and S 1381; tax reform legislation, HR 12078, Amtrak FY '79 budget, HR 11493. Lobbyist — E. Douglas Frost, Washington, D.C.

AMERICAN GASTROENTEROLOGICAL ASSOCIATION, Thorofare, N.J. Lobbyist — John T. Grupenhoff, Bethesda, Md. Filed 6/2/78. Legislative interest — "All health/medical legislation in the Senate and the House, including authorizations and appropriations."

AMERICAN HEALTH PLANNING ASSOCIATION, Alexandria, Va. Filed for self 6/2/78. Legislative interest — "HR 11488 — Health Planning and Resources Development Act of 1978; HR 9717, HR 6575 — Hospital Cost Containment Proposals; HR 10553 — Health Services Amendments." Lobbyist — Elliot J. Stern, Alexandria, Va.

AMERICAN HOSPITAL ASSOCIATION, Chicago, Ill. Filed for self 6/6/78. Legislative interest — ". . . All legislation which may affect the ability of hospitals to render good care or which may affect the health care of the American people." Lobbyist — Robert Glavin, Walter McHugh, Washington, D.C.

AMERICAN LEAGUE FOR INTERNATIONAL SECURITY ASSISTANCE INC., Washington, D.C. Filed for self 6/6/78. Legislative interest — "Matters dealing with U.S. export policy and practices relating to the interest of ALISA." Lobbyist — Herbert Y. Schandler, Washington, D.C.

AMERICAN OSTEOPATHIC ASSOCIATION, Arlington, Va. Filed for self 6/28/78. Legislative interest — "Legislation relating to health, particularly cost containment, health planning, health maintenance organizations, drug regulation reform." Lobbyist — Karen Winterbottom, John P. Perrin, Arlington, Va.; Rosemarie Sweeney, Washington, D.C.

AMERICAN PSYCHIATRIC ASSOCIATION, Washington, D.C. Lobbyist — Bregman, Abell, Solter & Kay, Washington, D.C. Filed 6/20/78. Legislative interest — "All legislative matters of interest to the client."

CHAMBER OF COMMERCE OF THE U.S., Washington, D.C. Filed for self 6/2/78. Legislative interest — "Legislation affecting labor-management relations, specifically the Labor Law Reform Act (S 2467/HR 8410). Opposed to both bills." Lobbyist — Betty Jane Clark, Harold P. Coxson Jr., Richard L. Lesher, G. John Tysse, Washington, D.C.

FURNITURE RENTAL ASSOCIATION OF AMERICA, Washington, D.C. Filed for self 6/23/78. Legislative interest — ". . . Legislation confirming the applicability of the investment tax credit provisions of the Internal Revenue Code to furniture purchased by furniture rental companies for business purposes." Lobbyist — A. Stephens Clay, Joseph W. Dorn, Washington, D.C.

GROCERY MANUFACTURERS OF AMERICA INC., Washington, D.C. Lobbyist — Taft, Stettinius & Hollister, Cincinnati, Ohio. Filed 6/13/78. Legislative interest — ". . . Federal Trade Commission investigation and proposed rulemaking."

INLAND FOREST RESOURCE COUNCIL, Missoula, Mont. Lobbyist — Forest Land Services Inc., Elkins, W. Va. Filed 6/9/78. Legislative interest — "Legislation pertaining to forest products industry."

INVESTMENT COMPANY INSTITUTE, Washington, D.C. Lobbyist — Sullivan & Cromwell, New York, N.Y. Filed 6/21/78. Legislative interest — "Legislation affecting registered investment companies, their investment advisers and underwriters. In particular, the ERISA Improvements Act of 1978, S 3017; oppose in part and favor in part."

INVESTMENT COUNCIL ASSOCIATION OF AMERICA, New York, N.Y. Lobbyist — Hill, Christopher and Phillips, Washington, D.C. Filed 6/29/78. Legislative interest — "To oppose certain amendments of the Securities Exchange Act of 1934, as amended."

MOTION PICTURE ASSOCIATION OF AMERICA INC., Washington, D.C. Filed for self 6/21/78. Legislative interest — "HR 13015; obscenity and violence legislation generally; and HR 4452, HR 4571 and S 1188." Lobbyist — John E. Giles, Washington, D.C.

NATIONAL ASSOCIATION OF PRIVATE PSYCHIATRIC HOSPITALS, Washington, D.C. Filed for self 6/12/78. Legislative interest — "Issues affecting mental health, hospitals, hospital employees, health care delivery, HR 9717, HR 6575, S 2410." Lobbyist — Joy Midman, Robert L. Thomas, Washington, D.C.

NATIONAL CATTLEMEN'S ASSOCIATION, Denver, Colo. Lobbyist — Michael R. McLeod, Washington, D.C. Filed 6/26/78. Legislative interest — "Tax legislation and other matters affecting the beef cattle industry."

NATIONAL LIMESTONE INSTITUTE INC., Fairfax, Va. Filed for self 6/2/78. Legislative interest — "All legislation which directly or indirectly affects the interest of limestone producers." Lobbyist — Eric D. Lindeman, Gordon H. Fry, Washington, D.C.

NEW YORK MERCHANTILE EXCHANGE, New York, N.Y. Lobbyist — Blum, Parker & Nash, Washington, D.C. Filed 6/29/78. Legislative interest — "Developing trade in fuel oil futures markets."

TRANSPORTATION INSTITUTE, Washington, D.C. Filed for self 6/30/78. Legislative interest — "General educational functions concerning legislation affecting the American maritime industry." Lobbyist — Preston, Thorgrimson, Ellis, Holman & Fletcher, Washington, D.C.

WESTERN ASSOCIATION OF CHRISTIAN SCHOOLS, Whittier, Calif. Lobbyist — John B. Conlan, Washington, D.C. Filed 6/8/78. Legislative interest — "S 2142 or any similar legislation affecting non-government schools."

Miscellaneous

ADFAST SYSTEMS INC., Denver, Colo. Filed for self 6/30/78. Legislative interest — "Capital gain taxation on securities, HR 12111 and other unspecified bills, for legislation to reduce or eliminate taxation on securities transactions." Lobbyist — Walter G. Asmus, Littleton, Colo.

CAPITOL HILL HOSPITAL, Washington, D.C. Lobbyist — Taft, Stettinius & Hollister, Cincinnati, Ohio. Filed 6/13/78. Legislative interest — "Matters relating to financing capital improvements."

DECQ COMMITTEE, Beverly Hills, Calif. Lobbyist — Miller & Chevalier, Washington, D.C. Filed 6/26/78. Legislative interest — "In support of legislation which will amend the Internal Revenue Code of 1954 to allow a retirement savings deduction for persons covered by certain pension plans (HR 12561)."

EATON ASSOCIATES INC., Washington, D.C. Filed for self 6/30/78. Legislative interest — "Legislation pertaining to energy programs, space programs and national defense." Lobbyist — James M. McGarry Jr., Robert E. L. Eaton, Washington, D.C.

THE FUND FOR CONSTITUTIONAL GOVERNMENT, Washington, D.C. Lobbyist — William A. Dobrovir; Andra N. Oakes; Joseph D.Gebhardt; David L. Scull, Washington, D.C. Filed 6/30/78. Legislative interest — ". . . For certain provisions of Carter's civil service reorganization and against certain other provisions, HR 11280 and S 2640."

ROBERT N. PITNER, Washington, D.C. Filed for self 6/21/78. Legislative interest — "None at present time."

TUNA RESEARCH FOUNDATION, Washington, D.C. Lobbyist — Peabody, Rivlin, Lambert & Meyers, Washington, D.C. Filed 6/30/78. Legislative interest — "HR 12805 and related legislation to amend the Fishery Conservation and Management Act of 1976."

UNITED EFFORT TRUST, Washington, D.C. Filed for self 6/27/78. Legislative interest — ". . . Native Americans, HR 9950 and HR 9951 and efforts to amend the Indian Reorganization Act." Lobbyist — Charles Trimble, Washington, D.C.

July

Citizens' Groups

AMERICAN BROTHERHOOD FOR THE BLIND, Des Moines, Iowa. Lobbyist — Millman Broder and Curtis, Washington, D.C. Filed 7/8/78. Legislative interest — "HUD Appropriations Act, 1979; Housing and Community Development Act of 1978, S 2691."

AMERICAN CONSERVATIVE UNION, Washington, D.C. Filed for self 7/13/78. Legislative interest — "All issues generating sufficient public interest to warrant involvement by Conservatives and expression of a Conservative point of view." Lobbyist — Caren C. Steadman, Washington, D.C.

COALITION FOR NEW YORK, New York, N.Y. Lobbyist — Kurrus Dyer Jacobi & Mooers, Washington, D.C. Filed 7/28/78. Legislative interest — "Legislation introduced in either House having an effect on the Real Estate Industry (residential) in New York, HR 12426 — for."

COMMITTEE FOR RATIFICATION OF THE PANAMA CANAL TREATIES INC., Washington, D.C. Filed for self 7/13/78. Legislative interest — ". . .Lobbying for the ratification of the Panama Canal Treaties."

COMMON CAUSE, Washington, D.C. Filed for self 7/7/78. Legislative interest — "Open government, campaign financing, consumer protection, freedom of information, ERA, energy policy, environmental protection, defense spending, tax reform, waste in government, voting rights, presidential nomination and confirmation process, administration of justice and reform of the criminal code, merit selection of federal judges, intelligence policy, public participation in federal agency proceedings, civil service reform, regulatory reform, the congressional budget process and congressional reform." Lobbyist — Sr. Carol Coston, Washington, D.C.

DOCTORS FOR THE EQUAL RIGHTS AMENDMENT, Dallas, Texas. Filed for self 7/10/78. Legislative interest — "E.R.A. to the U.S. Constitution; H J Res 638." Lobbyist — Vanessa Lea Chiapetta, Martha Hardee, Candace Sue Kasper, Ruth G. McGill, Dallas, Texas.

ELEVENTH PRO-LIFE CONGRESSIONAL DISTRICT ACTION COMMITTEE, San Carlos, Calif. Filed for self 7/13/78. Legislative interest — "All proposed Human Life Amendments and any bills related to abortion and euthanasia."

NATIONAL ASSOCIATION OF ARAB AMERICANS, Washington, D.C. Filed for self 7/6/78. Legislative interest — "Congressional legislation pertaining to the Middle East." Lobbyist — John P. Richardson, Washington, D.C.

NATIONAL RIFLE ASSOCIATION OF AMERICA, Washington, D.C. Filed for self 7/25/78. Legislative interest — "All legislation as it relates to the acquisition/possession of firearms and ammunition as well as legislation relating to hunting and wildlife conservation." Lobbyist — Thomas G. Geiler, Washington, D.C.

PUBLIC CITIZEN'S TAX REFORM RESEARCH GROUP, Washington, D.C. Filed for self 7/19/78. Legislative interest — "General legislation concerning the Internal Revenue Code and federal fiscal tax policy." Lobbyist — Diane Fuchs, Washington, D.C.

THIRTIETH PRO-LIFE CONGRESSIONAL DISTRICT ACTION COMMITTEE, Bell, Calif. Filed for self 7/6/78. Legislative interest — ". . .Human life amendment to the U.S. Constitution . . . and against the enactment of any law that would permit publicly or tax supported abortions."

UNION OF CONCERNED SCIENTISTS, Cambridge, Mass. Filed for self 7/12/78. Legislative interest — "Nuclear Siting and Licensing — S 2775, HR 11704; Nuclear Waste Management — S 3146, S 2761, S 2804; Department of Energy Authorization — S 2692." Lobbyist — James M. Cubie, Washington, D.C.

WOMEN'S LOBBY, Washington, D.C. Lobbyist — Lynne Revo Cohen, Reston, Va. Filed 7/17/78. Legislative interest — "Career part-time HR 10126; S 518 Comprehensive Child Care."

Corporations and Businesses

AGRI-BUSINESS INC., San Antonio, Texas. Lobbyist — Martin Ryan Haley & Associates Inc., Washington, D.C. Filed 7/14/78. Legislative interest — "Affairs of legislative interest."

ALLEGHENY LUDLUM INDUSTRIES INC., Pittsburgh, Pa. Lobbyist — Collier, Shannon, Rill, Edwards & Scott, Washington, D.C. Filed 7/12/78. Legislative interest — "All legislation affecting the worldwide interests of Allegheny Ludlum Industries Inc."

ALLSTATE INSURANCE CO., Washington, D.C. Lobbyist — Johnson, Hoar & Co. Inc., Washington, D.C. Filed 7/11/78. Legislative interest — "Dept. of Transportation Appropriations bill HR 12933; in favor of appropriations related to DOT Federal Motor Vehicle Safety Standard 208."

ATLANTIC RICHFIELD CO., Dallas, Texas. Lobbyist — Gary Bushnell, Corpus Christi, Texas. Filed 7/19/78. Legislative interest — "Tertiary Recovery Incentives Act, S 2623 and similar legislation."

ATLAS MINERALS, Denver, Colo. Lobbyist — Shaw, Pittman, Potts & Trowbridge, Washington, D.C. Filed 7/28/78. Legislative interest — "S 3078, HR 12535, HR 12229, HR 13049 and similar bills dealing with the cleanup of mill tailings at operating mills."

BACHE HALSEY STUART SHIELDS INC., New York, N.Y. Filed for self 7/26/78. Legislative interest — ". . .Proposals affecting the taxation of capital gains and losses, dividend income, interest income, option income and any and all investment mediums that Bache offers for sale to its customers." Lobbyist — Edward T. Fergus, New York, N.Y.

BIXBY RANCH CO., Los Angeles, Calif. Lobbyist — Shaw, Pittman, Potts & Trowbridge, Washington, D.C. Filed 7/28/78. Legislative interest — "S 2273 and HR 11622 and similar legislation dealing with siting standards for liquid natural gas terminal facilities and related matters and responsibility and authority of various government agencies and departments to develop such standards."

CIBA-GEIGY CORP., Summit, N.J. Filed for self 7/19/78. Legislative interest — "Legislation affecting manufacturers, specifically pharmaceutical manufacturers. Specific legislation at present include Drug Regulatory Reform Bill, S 2755 and HR 11611." Lobbyist — J. L. Disque, Summit, N.J.

CITIES SERVICE CO., Washington, D.C. Filed for self 7/12/78. Legislative interest — "Legislation impacting the following industries: petroleum, minerals, petrochemicals, chemicals, plastics and metal fabrication." Lobbyist — Lawrence C. Laser, Washington, D.C.

COLT INDUSTRIES INC., New York, N.Y. Lobbyist — Charles G. Botsford, Washington, D.C. Filed 7/12/78. Legislative interest — "Tax bills, DOD authorizations and appropriations and Public Works authorizations and appropriations."

CONTICOMMODITY SERVICES INC., Chicago, Ill. Lobbyist — Frank V. Battle Jr., Chicago, Ill. Filed 7/26/78. Legislative interest — "Tax legislation, including the president's 1978 tax proposals."

COOK, RUEF, SPANN & WEISER INC., Columbia, S.C. Lobbyist — Milton F. Capps, Columbia, S.C. Filed 7/3/78. Legislative interest — "Legislative activities concerning press relations."

DeKALB AGRICULTURAL RESEARCH INC., DeKalb, Ill. Lobbyist — O'Connor & Hannan, Washington, D.C. Filed 7/25/78. Legislative interest — "All legislation as their interests may appear."

DGA INTERNATIONAL INC., Washington, D.C. Filed for self 7/3/78. Legislative interest — "Legislation regarding foreign commercial aircraft, Airport and Aircraft Noise Reduction Act, HR 4539." Lobbyist — Howard S. Goldberg, Washington, D.C.

DR. PEPPER CO., Dallas, Texas. Filed for self 7/5/78. Legislative interest — "...Nutrition, health, food safety, franchise matters, container matters, etc." Lobbyist — William F. Massmann, Dallas, Texas.

EKLUTNA INC., Anchorage, Alaska. Lobbyist — Burr, Pease & Kurtz Inc., Anchorage, Alaska. Filed 7/28/78. Legislative interest — "Legislative matters of interest to Alaska Native Corporations, including without limitation pending PL 92-203 amendments, S 3016, HR 39 and the like."

FEDERAL EXPRESS CORP., Memphis Tenn. Lobbyist — Martin Ryan Haley & Associates Inc., Washington, D.C. Filed 7/14/78. Legislative interest — "Affairs of legislative interest."

THE FIRST BOSTON CORP., New York, N.Y. Lobbyist — Williams & Jensen, Washington, D.C. Filed 7/25/78. Legislative interest — "Legislative matters of interest to the corporation."

FLORIDA POWER AND LIGHT CO., Miami, Fla. Lobbyist — Beveridge, Fairbanks & Diamond, Washington, D.C. Filed 7/13/78. Legislative interest — ". . .Proposed DOE rulemaking on residual fuel oil imports."

GREAT WESTERN SUGAR CO., Denver, Colo. Filed for self 7/12/78. Legislative interest — "Sugar legislation, S 3055, S 2990, HR 12709, HR 12486 — bills establishing national sugar program." Lobbyists — Allan Auger, Art Stewart, Clarence Davan, Denver, Colo.; Berry, Epstein, Sandstrom & Blatchford, Washington, D.C.

HEINOLD COMMODITIES INC., Chicago, Ill. Lobbyist — George E. Crapple, Chicago, Ill. Filed 7/26/78. Legislative interest — "Tax legislation, including the president's 1978 tax proposals."

INVESTMENT ANNUITIES INSTITUTE INC., Washington, D.C. Filed for self 7/25/78. Legislative interest — "Tax legislation affecting annuities and life insurance." Lobbyist — W. Thomas Kelly, Washington, D.C.

KAISER STEEL CORP., Washington, D.C. Filed for self 7/3/78. Legislative interest — "Various matters relating to interests of employer, trade matters, coal leasing, domestic preference." Lobbyist — Christie K. Bohner, John W. Feist, Washington, D.C.

KOLLSMAN INSTRUMENT CO., Merrimack, N.H. Lobbyist—Robert McVicker, Alexandria, Va. Filed 7/17/78. Legislative interest — "Defense authorization bills; appropriations bills."

LINCOLN NATIONAL LIFE INSURANCE CO., Fort Wayne, Ind. Lobbyist — Sutherland, Asbill & Brennan, Washington, D.C. Filed 7/19/78. Legislative interest — "In support of legislation to rescind, or defer the effective date of Prop. Treas. Reg. section 1.61-16, published Feb. 3, 1978."

LITTON INDUSTRIES, Beverly Hills, Calif. Lobbyist — Williams & Jensen, Washington, D.C. Filed 7/13/78. Legislative interest — "Tax legislative matters of interest to the corporation and its subsidiaries."

MAGNATEX CORP., Midland, Texas. Lobbyist — Baker & McKenzie, Washington, D.C. Filed 7/24/78. Legislative interest — "To add an amendment to HR 13511 which would liberalize investment tax credit for shorter-lived assets."

MOCATTA METALS, Washington, D.C. Lobbyist — Patton, Boggs and Blow, Washington, D.C. Filed 7/10/78. Legislative interest — "Legislation to extend the Commodity Futures Trading Commission, S 2391 and other legislation related to commodity options."

MORRISON-KNUDSEN, Boise, Idaho. Lobbyist — Mays, Valentine, Davenport & Moore, Washington, D.C. Filed 7/12/78. Legislative interest — ". . .Seabrook Nuclear plant including, but not limited to S 2775."

NATIONAL AIRLINES INC., Miami, Fla. Filed for self 7/18/78. Legislative interest — ". . .Phases of the airline industry." Lobbyist — James B. Magnor, Washington, D.C.

NATIONAL FUEL GAS DISTRIBUTION CORP., Buffalo, N.Y. Filed for self 7/24/78. Legislative interest — "Pertaining to production, transmission, storage and distribution of energy." Lobbyist — Charles A. Wood, Buffalo, N.Y.

NEW ENGLAND FISH CO., Seattle, Wash. Filed for self 7/5/78. Legislative interest — "Matters affecting U.S. processors, particularly as they affect foreign processors; amendment of the

Fisheries Conservation and Management Act (HR 12805, S 3050)." Lobbyist — Beveridge, Fairbanks and Diamond, Washington, D.C.

NORTHVILLE INDUSTRIES CORP., Huntington Station, N.Y. Lobbyist — McNutt, Dudley, Easterwood & Losch, Washington, D.C. Filed 7/3/78. Legislative interest — "HR 13059, Water Resources Development Act of 1978."

NORTHWESTERN MUTUAL LIFE INSURANCE CO., Milwaukee, Wis. Lobbyist — Sutherland, Asbill & Brennan, Washington, D.C. Filed 7/19/78. Legislative interest — "Support legislation to rescind, or defer effective date of Prop. Treas. Reg. section 1.61-16, published Feb. 3, 1978."

PAINE, WEBBER, JACKSON & CURTIS INC., New York, N.Y. Lobbyist — Lawrence H. Hunt, Chicago, Ill. Filed 7/26/78. Legislative interest — "Tax legislation, including the president's 1978 tax proposals."

PFIZER INC., New York, N.Y. Lobbyist — Raymond R. Krause, Washington, D.C. Filed 7/10/78. Legislative interest — ". . .Legislative matters related to the business interests of the organization. . . ."

PHELPS DODGE CORP., New York, N.Y. Filed for self 7/10/78. Legislative interest — "Measures affecting mining and manufacturing. . . ." Lobbyist — Joan Eazarsky, Washington, D.C.

JACK PHILIP & SON INC., Washington, D.C. Lobbyist — Patton, Boggs and Blow, Washington, D.C. Filed 7/10/78. Legislative interest — "S 2575 and S 2632 amending Strategic and Critical Stockpile Materials Act with particular reference to authorization for disposal of excess industrial commodities."

PIONEER HI-BRED INTERNATIONAL INC., Des Moines, Iowa. Lobbyist — O'Connor & Hannan, Washington, D.C. Filed 7/25/78. Legislative interest — "All legislation as their interests may appear."

SEATRAIN LINES INC., New York, N.Y. Lobbyist — Preston, Thorgrimson, Ellis, Holman & Fletcher, Washington, D.C. Filed 7/18/78. Legislative interest — "General education functions to revise tariff laws to permit duty free treatment of certain shipping expenses; seek congressional oversight and appropriations as necessary to encourage more effective use of merchant marine in national defense, particularly tactical employment of supertankers."

SIKES CORP., Lakeland, Fla. Lobbyist — Holland & Knight, Tampa, Fla. Filed 7/5/78. Legislative interest — "Oppose efforts to delay effective date of implementation of the New IRC section 382."

SQUIBB CORP., New York, N.Y. Lobbyist — Rogers & Wells, Washington, D.C. Filed 7/12/78. Legislative interest — "Legislation pertaining to drug manufacturers including HR 11611 and S 2755."

TEXAS OIL & GAS CO., Dallas, Texas. Lobbyist — O'Neill & Forgotson, Washington, D.C. Filed 7/24/78. Legislative interest — "Energy and environmental legislation."

TEXAS UTILITIES CO., Dallas, Texas. Lobbyist — O'Neill & Forgotson, Washington, D.C. Filed 7/24/78. Legislative interest — "Energy and environmental legislation."

UNICARE SERVICES INC., Milwaukee, Wis. Lobbyist — Berman and Associates, Washington, D.C. Filed 7/10/78. Legislative interest — "Health care and health care financing; national health insurance; Title XX financing."

UNION OIL CO. OF CALIFORNIA, Los Angeles, Calif. Filed for self 7/3/78. Legislative interest — "Legislation affecting the petroleum industry."

UNITED STATES PHARMACOPEIAL CONVENTION INC., Rockville, Md. Lobbyist — William J. Skinner, Washington, D.C. Filed 7/3/78. Legislative interest — "Drug Regulation Reform Act of 1978."

UNIVERSAL LEAF TOBACCO CO. INC., Richmond, Va. Lobbyist — Will E. Leonard, Washington, D.C. Filed 7/11/78. Legislative interest — "Agricultural and international trade legislation affecting tobacco. . . ."

YANDELL & HILLER INC., Fort Worth, Texas. Lobbyist — Martin Ryan Haley & Associates Inc., Washington, D.C. Filed 7/14/78. Legislative interest — "Affairs of legislative interest."

ZACHRY INC., San Antonio, Texas. Lobbyist — Robert J. Bird, Washington, D.C. Filed 7/12/78. Legislative interest — "Any tax legislation affecting employees. . . ."

Energy and Environment

THE AMERICAN LEAGUE OF ANGLERS, Washington, D.C. Filed for self 7/13/78. Legislative interest — "Legislation pertaining to sport fishing." Lobbyist — Eileen Barthelmy, Washington, D.C.

ENVIRONMENTAL DEFENSE FUND, Washington, D.C. Filed for self 7/21/78. Legislative interest — "Environmental legislation; food and drug legislation especially S 2755 and HR 11611." Lobbyist — Anita Johnson, Washington, D.C.

PRESERVATION ACTION, Washington, D.C. Filed for self 7/17/78. Legislative interest — "All legislation affecting historic preservation and neighborhood conservation." Lobbyist — Julia Churchman, Washington, D.C.

RESOURCE ASSOCIATES OF ALASKA, Fairbanks, Alaska. Lobbyist — Cook & Henderson, Washington, D.C. Filed 7/12/78. Legislative interest — "HR 39."

International Relations

CONSTRUCTORA NACIONAL DE CARROS DE FERROCARRIL, Miguel Laurent, Mexico. Lobbyist — Berry, Epstein, Sandstrom & Blatchford, Washington, D.C. Filed 7/12/78. Legislative interest — "In support of legislation which would provide duty suspension on railroad cars."

MITSUBISHI INTERNATIONAL CORP., Washington, D.C. Lobbyist — Dickstein, Shapiro & Morin, Washington, D.C. Filed 7/5/78. Legislative interest — "Legislation concerning mining in Alaska; Alaska National Interest Lands Conservation Act; HR 39; S 499; S 1500; S 1546; S 1787 and S 2465."

REPUBLIC OF CHINA, Taipei, Taiwan. Lobbyist — Collier, Shannon, Rill, Edwards & Scott, Washington, D.C. Filed 7/19/78. Legislative interest — "Legislative matters relating to the Republic of China, including legislation concerning treaties and diplomatic recognition, but excluding legislation concerning trade or investment."

REPUBLIC OF HAITI/EMBASSY OF HAITI, Washington, D.C. Lobbyist — Edelman International Corp., Washington, D.C. Filed 7/11/78. Legislative interest — "None at the time."

Military and Veterans' Groups

SOCIETY OF MILITARY WIDOWS, Coronado, Calif. Lobbyist — Robert H. Doyle, Washington, D.C. Filed 7/3/78. Legislative interest — "Legislation to secure survivor benefits for widows of servicemen who died prior to 1972."

Labor Groups

AMERICAN FEDERATION OF LABOR AND CONGRESS OF INDUSTRIAL ORGANIZATIONS, Washington, D.C. Filed for self 7/18/78. Legislative interest — "All bills affecting the welfare of the country generally, and specifically bills affecting workers." Lobbyist — Michael Gildea, Washington, D.C.

State and Local Governments

HURON-CLINTON METROPOLITAN AUTHORITY, Detroit, Mich. Lobbyist — Duncan, Brown, Weinberg & Palmer, Washington, D.C. Filed 7/14/78. Legislative interest — "S 3163 — Urban Recreation and Recovery Act."

Trade Associations

ALUMINUM ASSOCIATION, Washington, D.C. Filed for self 7/13/78. Legislative interest — "None." Lobbyist — Robert L. Harris, Washington, D.C.

AMERICAN ADVERTISING FEDERATION, Washington, D.C. Filed for self 7/11/78. Legislative interest — "Legislation of interest to advertisers, advertising agencies and advertising media." Lobbyist — Jonah Gitlitz, Howard H. Bell, Washington, D.C.

AMERICAN ASSOCIATION OF COLLEGES OF PHARMACY, Bethesda, Md. Lobbyist — William J. Skinner, Washington, D.C. Filed 7/3/78. Legislative interest — "HR 11611, S 2755."

AMERICAN BANKERS ASSOCIATION, Washington, D.C. Filed for self 7/11/78. Legislative interest — "Matters affecting banking, housing and community development including — the Federal Reserve Act, the national banking laws, the National Housing Act, the Bank Holding Company Act, the Interest Rate Control Act." Lobbyist — J. Denis O'Toole, Washington, D.C.

AMERICAN CONSULTING ENGINEERS COUNCIL, Washington, D.C. Filed for self 7/11/78. Legislative interest — "Matters relating to public works, transportation, the environment, pollution control, housing, equal employment opportunity, public health and safety, economy and efficiency in government, and energy legislation." Lobbyist — David Seldner, Richard L. Corrigan, Scott M. Jackson, Kenneth W. Butler, Washington, D.C.

AMERICAN DENTAL ASSOCIATION, Washington, D.C. Filed for self 7/17/78. Legislative interest — "Matters relating to health legislation." Lobbyist — Sheila K. Hixson, Washington, D.C.

AMERICAN FARM BUREAU FEDERATION, Park Ridge, Ill. Filed for self 7/20/78. Legislative interest — ". . .Monopoly, taxation, public health, agricultural credit, electoral college reform, insurance legislation, ERA." Lobbyist — Dave Hill, Washington, D.C.

AMERICAN FOOTWEAR INDUSTRIES ASSOCIATION, Arlington, Va. Filed for self 7/17/78. Legislative interest — "Trade related legislative issues." Lobbyist — Rena S. Pies, Arlington, Va.

AMERICAN GAS ASSOCIATION, Arlington, Va. Filed for self 7/17/78. Legislative interest — "National Energy Act, HR 8444; Conservation, HR 5037; Coal Conversion, HR 5146; Gas Pricing, HR 5289; Utility Rate Reform, HR 4018; Energy Taxes, HR 5263; OCS Lands Act Amendments, HR 1614; Tax Reform, HR 12078; Contributions in Aid of Construction, HR 11997; OPSO/LNG, HR 16112; DOE Authorization, HR 12163, S 2692, and any other proposed legislation affecting gas industry interests." Lobbyist — David A. Skedgell, Arlington, Va.

AMERICAN MINING CONGRESS, Washington, D.C. Filed for self 7/12/78. Legislative interest — ". . .Income taxation, social security, public lands, stockpiling, monetary policy, mine safety, environmental quality control, etc." Lobbyist — Henry Chajet, Washington, D.C.

AMERICAN RETAIL FEDERATION, Washington, D.C. Filed for self 7/20/78. Legislative interest — "FTC Improvements Act, HR 3816; Product Liability, S 403; Federal Funding of Consumer Witnesses, S 270; Fair Credit Reporting Act Amendments, HR 3875; Fair Fund Transfer Act of 1978, S 2470; EFT Consumer Protection Act, S 2546; Labor Reform Act, HR 8410; Full Employment Act, HR 50, S 50; National Health Insurance, HR 21, S 3; Civil Aeronautics Board Reform, S 689; Consumer Communications Reform, HR 8, S 530, S J Res 30; Successor Employer Responsibility, HR 3501, S 528; Consumer Product Standards, S 825; ERISA Administration, HR 4340; Tax Reform Bill, HR 3477; Customs Procedure Reform Legislation, HR 8149; Postal Service Act of 1978, HR 7700, and other similar legislation affecting the retail industry." Lobbyist — Lee Williams, Washington, D.C.

AMERICAN SOCIETY FOR MEDICAL TECHNOLOGY, Washington, D.C. Filed for self 7/10/78. Legislative interest — ". . .Health legislation, labor relations legislation, civil service legislation, armed services legislation." Lobbyist — Kim Alan Benjamin, Washington, D.C.

AMERICAN WATCH ASSOCIATION, New York, N.Y. Lobbyist — Covington & Burling, Washington, D.C. Filed 7/24/78. Legislative interest — "Legislation affecting customs and tariff treatment of watches, watch movements, and parts thereof, and other legislation affecting the manufacture, importation, assembly and sale of such products."

AMUSEMENT AND MUSIC OPERATORS ASSOCIATION, Chicago, Ill. Lobbyist — Herrick, Allen & Davis, Washington, D.C. Filed 7/11/78. Legislative interest — ". . . Matters pertaining to Copyright Act of 1976 and legislation to amend the Act."

ASSOCIATED BUILDERS AND CONTRACTORS, Washington, D.C. Filed for self 7/24/78. Legislative interest — "Legislation of interest to building and construction industry." Lobbyist — Gregory N. Friberg, Washington, D.C.

ASSOCIATED ELECTRIC COOPERATIVE INC., Springfield, Mo. Lobbyist — Northcutt Ely, Washington, D.C. Filed 7/12/78. Legislative interest — "In favor of passage of S 2249 and HR 12600, 'to prohibit discrimination in rates charged by the Southwestern Power Administration' or similar legislation, with amendments."

ASSOCIATED GAS DISTRIBUTORS, Washington, D.C. Lobbyist — Jones, Day, Reavis & Pogue, Washington, D.C. Filed 7/8/78. Legislative interest — "S 9; HR 4018; HR 5146; HR 5037; HR 5289; and any other legislation affecting the natural gas industry."

BUNDESVERBAND DEUTSCHER BANKEN, Cologne, Germany. Lobbyist — Chapman, Duff and Paul, Washington, D.C. Filed 7/6/78. Legislative interest — "Legislation affecting foreign banks; International Banking Act of 1978, HR 10899."

CHAMBER OF COMMERCE OF THE UNITED STATES, Washington, D.C. Filed for self 7/10/78. Legislative interest — "Legislation affecting labor-management relations, specifically the Labor Law Reform Act (S 2467/HR 8410); opposed to both bills." Lobbyist — Richard L. Lesher, Washington, D.C.

DIRECT MAIL/MARKETING ASSOCIATION, New York, N.Y. Filed for self 7/11/78. Legislative interest — "HR 7700 — The Postal Service Act of 1978; S 3229 — Postal Service Amendments Act of 1978; S 2173 — Interstate Taxation; S 2193 — Telephone Privacy Act; HR 9505 — Telephone Privacy Act." Lobbyist — Richard A. Barton, Washington, D.C.

FLORIDA FRUIT AND VEGETABLE ASSOCIATION, Orlando, Fla. Lobbyist — Barnett, Alagia & Carey, Washington, D.C. Filed 7/10/78. Legislative interest — ". . .Agricultural and horticultural industries."

GROCERY MANUFACTURERS OF AMERICA INC., Washington, D.C. Filed for self 7/24/78. Legislative interest — ". . .Matters affecting the grocery industry." Lobbyist — Steven J. Rukavina, Washington, D.C.

GROUP HEALTH ASSOCIATION OF AMERICA INC., Washington, D.C. Filed for self 7/11/78. Legislative interest — "All bills relating to prepayment of health care, comprehensive health care, group practice medicine, and matters relating to consumer health care services." Lobbyist — Gibson Kingren, Washington, D.C.

GUAYULE RUBBER GROWERS ASSOCIATION, San Marino, Calif. Filed for self 7/10/78. Legislative interest — "Support of S 1167 — Native Latex Commercialization Act of 1977."

HEALTH INSURANCE ASSOCIATION OF AMERICA INC., Washington, D.C. Filed for self 7/11/78. Legislative interest — "All matters pertaining to business of health and accident insurance companies and their policyholders." Lobbyist — Linda Jenckes, Washington, D.C.

INDEPENDENT REFINERS' ASSOCIATION OF CALIFORNIA, Los Angeles, Calif. Lobbyist — Pierson Semmes Crolius and Finley, Washington, D.C. Filed 7/17/78. Legislative interest — "All legislation relating to the level of production from naval petroleum reserves, including HR 11392, HR 12557 and similar measures."

INTERNATIONAL ASSOCIATION OF MACHINISTS AND AEROSPACE WORKERS, Washington, D.C. Filed for self 7/11/78. Legislative interest — ". . .All pending legislation dealing with Social Security, national health, aid to the physically handicapped, labor relations, displaced people, energy." Lobbyist — Barbara J. Shailor, Washington, D.C.

INTERSTATE NATURAL GAS ASSOCIATION OF AMERICA, Washington, D.C. Filed for self 7/12/78. Legislative interest — "Any legislation pertaining to natural gas." Lobbyist — Jerome J. McGrath, Washington, D.C.

INVESTMENT COUNSEL ASSOCIATION OF AMERICA INC., New York, N.Y. Lobbyist — David L. Babson & Co. Inc., Boston, Mass. Legislative interest — ". . .Securities matters, Investment Advisers Act and related subjects."

MANUFACTURED HOUSING INSTITUTE, Arlington, Va. Filed for self 7/12/78. Legislative interest — ". . .Housing, land use, community development legislation and all legislation generally concerning manufacturing industries and manufactured products." Lobbyist — Paul Edward Finger III, Arlington, Va.

MEAT IMPORTERS COUNCIL OF AMERICA INC., New York, N.Y. Lobbyists — Barnes, Richardson & Colburn, Washington, D.C. John E. Ward, White Plains, N.Y. Filed 7/18/78. Legislative interest — "Legislation affecting imports of meat and meat products; S 237 — for; S 239 — against; S 297 — against; S 727 — against; HR 1500 — for; HR 2526 — against; HR 12752 — for."

MEAT PRICE INVESTIGATORS ASSOCIATION, Des Moines, Iowa. Filed for self 7/12/78. Legislative interest — "Legislation to overturn the ruling called *Illinois-Brick* which was handed down by the Supreme Court in 1977 and remedial legislation to correct meat marketing practices; S 1874 and HR 11942." Lobbyist — Glenn Freie, Des Moines, Iowa.

MID-CONTINENT OIL & GAS ASSOCIATION, Tulsa, Okla. Filed for self 7/12/78. Legislative interest — "Legislation of interest to the petroleum industry." Lobbyist — Tom Biery, Washington, D.C.

MOTOR VEHICLE MANUFACTURERS ASSOCIATION, Detroit, Mich. Filed for self 7/17/78. Legislative interest — "All legislation affecting the motor vehicle industry." Lobbyist — V. J. Adduci, A. Edlund, J. Moller, T. MacCarthy, N. Lofgren, R. Kaplar, Detroit, Mich.

NATIONAL ASSOCIATION OF CHAIN DRUG STORES INC., Arlington, Va. Filed for self 7/14/78. Legislative interest — "All legislation affecting retail drug stores." Lobbyist — Patrick Donoho, Arlington, Va.

NATIONAL ASSOCIATION OF HOME BUILDERS OF THE UNITED STATES, Washington, D.C. Filed for self 7/10/78. Legislative interest — ". . .All legislation affecting the industry and its members." Lobbyist — Robert D. Bannister, Washington, D.C.

NATIONAL ASSOCIATION FOR HOSPITAL DEVELOPMENT, Washington, D.C. Lobbyist — Leva, Hawes, Symington, Martin & Oppenheimer, Washington, D.C. Filed 7/12/78. Legislative interest — "All pending legislation affecting community hospitals; S 1470, HR 6575 and all national health insurance proposals."

NATIONAL ASSOCIATION OF INDEPENDENT LUMBERMEN, Washington, D.C. Lobbyist — O'Connor & Hannan, Washington, D.C. Filed 7/12/78. Legislative interest — "All legislative matters affecting the forest products industry, forestry policy and small business."

NATIONAL ASSOCIATION OF REAL ESTATE INVESTMENT TRUSTS, Washington, D.C. Filed for self 7/18/78. Legislative interest — "Promotion of a broad program of legislation in furtherance of the best interests of real estate investment trusts including bankruptcy legislation (S 2266) and certain tax legislation." Lobbyist — Walter B. Laessig, Gary A. Brown, John B. Nicholson, Washington, D.C.

NATIONAL HOME FURNISHINGS ASSOCIATION, Chicago, Ill. Filed for self 7/12/78. Legislative interest — "Legislation affecting home furnishings retailing." Lobbyist — Paula C. Treat, Washington, D.C.

NATIONAL FRANCHISE ASSOCIATION COALITION, Fox Lake, Ill. Lobbyist — Leva, Hawes, Symington, Martin & Oppenheimer, Washington, D.C. Filed 7/25/78. Legislative interest — "HR 5016 — Franchise Termination Practices Reform Act of 1977."

NATIONAL NEWSPAPER ASSOCIATION, Washington, D.C. Filed for self 7/11/78. Legislative interest — "Legislation affecting newspaper business, ranging from First Amendment considerations to the business issues; S 3229 — Postal Reform — for; HR 6869, HR 2311 — Criminal Code Revision; HR 8494 — Lobbying reform; S 1281 — Newsprint tax bill; HR 12952, S 3162, S 3164 — bills to overturn *Stanford Daily* case; S 2266 - Bankruptcy reform." Lobbyist — W. Terry Maguire, Washington, D.C.

NATIONAL PARKS AND CONSERVATION ASSOCIATION, Washington, D.C. Lobbyist — T. Destry Jarvis, Alexandria, Va. Filed 7/17/78. Legislative interest — ". . .Natural resource conservation and national park system management and development. HR 39, S 1500 — Alaska National Interest Land Conservation Act; HR 12536 — National Park and Recreation Act of 1978; HR 12001, S 2866 — New River Gorge National River Act; for all of above."

NATIONAL PARKS AND CONSERVATION ASSOCIATION, Washington, D.C. Lobbyist — William C. Lienesch, Alexandria, Va. Filed 7/14/78. Legislative interest — ". . .Natural resource conservation and national park system management and development; National Parks and Recreation Act of 1978, HR 12536 — for; National Park Omnibus Act — S 2816 — for; Channel Islands and Santa Monica Mountains National Park and Seashore, S 1906, HR 7264, for; Lowell National Historical Park, S 2817, HR 11662, for; Jean Lafitte National Historical Park — S 1829, HR 8290 — for; Chattahoochee River National Recreation Area, S 1791, HR 8336 — for."

OUTDOOR ADVERTISING ASSOCIATION OF AMERICA INC., Washington, D.C. Lobbyist — Kaler, Lefkoff, Pike & Fox, Atlanta, Ga. Filed 7/10/78. Legislative interest — ". . .All legislation affecting standardized outdoor advertising."

PHYSICIANS NATIONAL HOUSESTAFF ASSOCIATION, Washington, D.C. Filed for self 7/17/78. Legislative interest — ". . .Supporting HR 2222 and S 1884." Lobbyist — Paula V. McMartin, Washington, D.C.

PRINTING INDUSTRIES OF AMERICA INC., Arlington, Va. Filed for self 7/20/78. Legislative interest — ". . .Legislation of interest to commercial printers." Lobbyist — John F. Grant, Benjamin Y. Cooper, Margaret Rogers, Arlington, Va.

PYROTECHNIC SIGNAL MANUFACTURERS ASSOCIATION, Washington, D.C. Lobbyist — Patton, Boggs & Blow, Washington, D.C. Filed 7/10/78. Legislative interest — "Legislation proposing the partial suspension of the duty on strontium nitrate."

RECORDING INDUSTRY ASSOCIATION OF AMERICA INC., New York, N.Y. Lobbyist — DeHart Associates Inc., Washington, D.C. Filed 7/13/78. Legislative interest — "Copyright and other legislation of interest to the recording industry."

REINSURANCE ASSOCIATION OF AMERICA, Washington, D.C. Filed for self 7/3/78. Legislative interest — "Legislation affecting the reinsurance industry." Lobbyist — Franklin W. Nutter, Washington, D.C.

SCIENTIFIC APPARATUS MAKERS ASSOCIATION, Washington, D.C. Filed for self 7/6/78. Legislative interest — "Legislation affecting the scientific apparatus industry." Lobbyist — Daniel Patrick Murphy II, Washington, D.C.

TANNERS' COUNCIL OF AMERICA INC., New York, N.Y. Lobbyist — Collier, Shannon, Rill, Edwards & Scott, Washington, D.C. Filed 7/28/78. Legislative interest — ". . .Measures affecting the tanning industry."

TEACHERS INSURANCE & ANNUITY ASSOCIATION, New York, N.Y. Lobbyist — Rogers & Wells, Washington, D.C.. Filed 7/6/78. Legislative interest — "All ERISA and pension-related legislation and all tax legislation."

TOBACCO TAX COUNCIL, Richmond, Va. Lobbyist — Martin Ryan Haley & Associates Inc., Washington, D.C. Filed 7/14/78. Legislative interest — ". . .Matters that pertain to the federal tax aspects of cigarettes."

Miscellaneous

AMERICAN CHILDRENS' CITIZENSHIP RIGHTS LEAGUE, Geneva, Switzerland. Filed for self 7/10/78. Legislative interest — "To encourage passage of legislation amending the Immigration and Nationality Act of 1952 (INA), so as to eliminate the statutory conditions on retention of citizenship imposed by

Section 301(b); eliminate or reduce the statutory requirements for transmission of citizenship imposed by Section 301(a); and eliminate or amend various other provisions of the INA which have been held to be unconstitutional." Lobbyist — Shaw, Pittman, Potts & Trowbridge, Washington, D.C.

COMMITTEE TO ASSURE THE AVAILABILITY OF CASEIN, Washington, D.C. Filed for self 7/12/78. Legislative interest — ". . .Legislation which intends to restrict imports of casein or caseinates." Lobbyist — Berry, Epstein, Sandstrom & Blatchford, Washington, D.C.

FACTS AND COMPARISONS, St. Louis, Mo. Lobbyist — Kurrus Dyer Jacobi & Mooers, Washington, D.C. Filed 7/28/78. Legislative interest — "HR 11611 — against."

CHARLES L. FISHMAN, Washington, D.C. Filed for self 7/28/78. Legislative interest — "DOD Authorization and appropriations bill in Senate — S 2692."

FOLEY, LARDNER, HOLLABAUGH & JACOBS, Washington, D.C. Filed for self 7/25/78. Legislative interest — ". . .Certain sections of S 1874 and HR 11942. . . ." Lobbyist — Michael D. Fischer, Douglas V. Rigler, John W. Byrnes, Robert C. Houser Jr., Catherine B. Klarfeld, Washington, D.C.

G-4 CHILDREN'S COALITION, Chevy Chase, Md. Filed for self 7/13/78. Legislative interest — "Rights of G-4 visa holders who are children, surviving spouses, and retirees to obtain permanent U.S. resident status." Lobbyist — Edward E. Wright, Washington, D.C.

GADSBY & HANNAH, Boston, Mass. Filed for self 7/13/78. Legislative interest — ". . .Changes in proposed international banking legislation, particularly the proposed International Banking Act of 1978, HR 10899." Lobbyist — Harry R. Hauser, Boston, Mass.

MARJORIE GUTHRIE, New York, N.Y. Filed for self 7/10/78. Legislative interest — ". . .Support for National Health Insurance; services for the chronic diseased patients; the National Genetics Diseases Act; support for those Institutes at NIH whose concerns include aging, genetics, metabolic disorders, neurologic disorders."

HALT INC., Washington, D.C. Filed for self 7/18/78. Legislative interest — "Legal reform in consumer-related areas." Lobbyist — Paul T. Hasse, Washington, D.C.

IVA MAY HARVEY, Blythe, Calif. Lobbyist — Duncan, Brown, Weinberg & Palmer, Washington, D.C. Filed 7/14/78. Legislative interest — "Legislative relief regarding alleged government usurpation of private property - S 2590 and HR 7101."

HOLT INTERNATIONAL CHILDREN'S SERVICES INC., Eugene, Ore. Filed for self 7/17/78. Legislative interest — "Immigration laws relating to intercountry adoptions and naturalization of such children; laws relating to adoptions, foster care, child abuse and other related child welfare matters of U.S. born children; tax laws relating to the adoption process and adopted children." Lobbyist — John E. Adams, Eugene, Ore.

BUNKER HUNT, Washington, D.C. Lobbyist — Vinson & Elkins, Washington, D.C. Filed 7/11/78. Legislative interest — ". . .Procedural amendments to the authority of the Commodity Futures Trading Commission."

JEFFERSON/YOUNG & ASSOCIATES, Honolulu, Hawaii. Lobbyist — Dewey, Ballantine, Bushby, Palmer & Wood, Washington, D.C. Filed 7/14/78. Legislative interest — "National Parks and Recreation Area Act of 1978, HR 12536."

LUCAS, FRIEDMAN & MANN, Washington, D.C. Filed for self 7/25/78. Legislative interest — ". . .Certain sections of S 1874 and HR 11942." Lobbyist — James H. Mann, Joseph B. Friedman, Washington, D.C.

MAJOR LEAGUE BASEBALL, New York, N.Y. Lobbyist — Timmons and Company Inc., Washington, D.C. Filed 7/6/78. Legislative interest — "All legislative activities affecting professional sports generally, and professional baseball in particular, with special attention to bills and proposals dealing with the deductibility of business expenses for entertainment activities and facilities."

PATTON, BOGGS & BLOW, Washington, D.C. Lobbyist — Godfrey Associates Inc., Washington, D.C. Filed 7/12/78. Legislative interest — "Authorizing legislation and appropriations for State, Justice, Commerce and Judiciary."

PATSY PERRY, Roslyn Heights, N.Y. Lobbyist — Stroock & Stroock & Lavan, Washington, D.C. Filed 7/17/78. Legislative interest — "Proponent of private bill to provide compensation for wrongful death."

SISSETON-WAHPETON SIOUX TRIBE, Sisseton, S.D. Lobbyist — Bertram E. Hirsch, Bellerose, N.Y. Filed 7/20/78. Legislative interest — ". . .To promote the enactment of S 3069 and HR 13096."

TIME-CRITICAL SHIPMENT COMMITTEE, Washington, D.C. Lobbyist — Cook & Henderson, Washington, D.C. Filed 7/13/78. Legislative interest — ". . .An amendment which would amend the Private Express Statutes."

August

Citizens' Groups

AMERICAN BROTHERHOOD FOR THE BLIND, Des Moines, Iowa. Lobbyist — Millman Broder and Curtis, Washington, D.C. Filed 8/18/78. Legislative interest — "HUD Appropriations Act, 1979; Housing and Community Development Act of 1978; S 2691."

COMMITTEE FOR THE DEATH PENALTY, Brooklyn, N.Y. Lobbyist — Annie O. Massey, Uniondale, N.Y. Filed 8/18/78. Legislative interest — ". . .Crime bills from 1978 to 1984."

MEN FOR ERA, New York, N.Y. Filed for self 8/9/78. Legislative interest — "ERA amendment to the Constitution; extension of ERA ratification H J Res 638; we are for these bills."

NATIONAL JAPANESE AMERICAN CITIZENS LEAGUE, San Francisco, Calif. Filed for self 8/17/78. Legislative interest — "District of Columbia full representation, H J Res 554, for; Internment Credit Bill, HR 9471/S 224, for; Pacific Asian American Heritage Week, H J Res 1007, S J Res 72, for; U.S. Atomic Bomb Survivors Medical Payment Bill, HR 8440, HR 5150, HR 10502, for." Lobbyist — Ronald K. Ikejiri, Washington, D.C.

NATIONAL RIFLE ASSOCIATION OF AMERICA, Washington, D.C. Filed for self 8/2/78. Legislative interest — ". . .Acquisition, possession, and use of firearms and ammunition as well as legislation relating to hunting and wildlife conservation."

SIXTH PRO-LIFE CONGRESSIONAL DISTRICT ACTION COMMITTEE, St. Petersburg, Fla. Filed for self 8/8/78. Legislative interest — "All proposed Human Life amendments, HR 6075 and HR 12929."

TRANSAFRICA, Washington, D.C. Filed for self 8/23/78. Legislative interest — "All legislation with implication for Africa and the Caribbean including . . . the Export-Import bank authorization bill and the Foreign Aid authorization and appropriations bills."

Corporations and Businesses

AIR PRODUCTS & CHEMICALS INC., Allentown, Pa. Filed for self 8/17/78. Legislative interest — ". . .All bills relating to energy, the environment, product distribution and procurement, research and development, and general corporate administration." Lobbyist — Carl F. Emde, Washington, D.C.

THE JOHN AKRIDGE CO., Washington, D.C. Lobbyist — Akin, Gump, Hauer & Feld, Washington, D.C. Filed 8/7/78. Legislative interest — "Hearings and any related legislation concerning real estate development."

AMERICAN STOCK EXCHANGE, New York, N.Y. Lobbyist — Silverstein and Mullens, Washington, D.C. Filed 8/25/78. Legislative interest — ". . .Tax reform legislation. . . ."

ATLANTIC CONTAINER LINE, New York, N.Y. Filed for self 8/30/78. Legislative interest — "Postal reform legislation, HR 7700, S 3229; against certain provisions in HR 7700." Lobbyists — Daniel Kerrigan, New York, N.Y.; Galland, Kharasch, Calkins & Short, Washington, D.C.

KENNETH D. BECK & C. C. PRUITT JR. CO. Lobbyist — Vorys, Sater, Seymour & Pease, Washington, D.C. Filed 8/21/78. Legislative interest — "Wording of capital gains proposed language (HR 13511)."

THE BUREAU OF NATIONAL AFFAIRS INC., Washington, D.C. Filed for self 8/14/78. Legislative interest — "Amendments to Postal Reorganization Act of 1970." Lobbyist — Duncan L. Lane Jr., Washington, D.C.

BURLINGTON NORTHERN, St. Paul, Minn. Lobbyist — Smathers, Symington & Herlong, Washington, D.C. Filed 8/17/78. Legislative interest — ". . .Support legislation required to preserve and protect the railroad industry in the United States."

THE DETROIT EDISON CO., Detroit, Mich. Lobbyist — Robert Jack Horn, Washington, D.C. Filed 8/15/78. Legislative interest — "Legislation affecting the electric utility industry including energy, the environment and regulatory issues."

DISCOVER AMERICA TRAVEL ORGANIZATION, Washington, D.C. Filed for self 8/2/78. Legislative interest — ". . .Federal programs to promote and facilitate travel to and within the United States and for fair and equitable tax and energy programs."

FARM BUREAU MUTUAL INSURANCE CO. OF ARKANSAS, Little Rock, Ark. Lobbyist — Sutherland, Asbill & Brennan, Washington, D.C. Filed 8/18/78. Legislative interest — "To support enactment of S 3007. . . ."

FOREMOST-McKESSON INC., San Francisco, Calif. Lobbyist — Perito, Duerk and Carlson, Washington, D.C. Filed 8/11/78. Legislative interest — "Drug legislation, S 2755 and HR 12980."

GENERAL FOODS, Washington, D.C. Filed for self 8/11/78. Legislative interest — "Quota provision — Sugar Stabilization legislation." Lobbyist — Beth Peacock, Washington, D.C.

GRAHAM-WHITE MANUFACTURING CO., Salem, Va. Lobbyist — Fortescue W. Hopkins, Daleville, Va. Filed 8/11/78. Legislative interest — "Minimum tax, capital gains, patent royalties, installment sales for HR 13511."

HOUSTON LIGHTING & POWER CO., Houston, Texas. Filed for self 8/25/78. Legislative interest — "National Energy Act, (S 977, HR 5146, S 2104, HR 5289, S 2114, HR 4018, HR 5263, S 701, S 2057, HR 5037); Coal Pipeline Act of 1977 (HR 1609); Nuclear Siting and Licensing Act of 1978 (S 2775, HR 11704), and related matters." Lobbyist — Craig L. McNeese, Houston, Texas.

ICX AVIATION INC., Washington, D.C. Filed for self 8/7/78. Legislative interest — "Deregulation of airline trafficking — CETA reauthorization." Lobbyist — Charles P. Collins, Falls Church, Va.

INTERNATIONAL PROCESSORS, New Orleans, La. Lobbyist — Cladouhos & Brashares, New York, N.Y. Filed 8/2/78. Legislative interest — ". . .Legislation relating to the Federal Energy Administration, the Energy Policy and Conservation Act and issues concerning the importation of crude oil and finished products and decontrol."

INTERNATIONAL RECTIFIER, Los Angeles, Calif. Lobbyist — National Counsel Associates, Washington, D.C. Filed 8/2/78. Legislative interest — ". . .Proposed FDA regulation on antibiotics in animal feed; these actions are opposed."

KANSAS FARM BUREAU LIFE INSURANCE CO., Manhattan, Kan. Lobbyist — Sutherland, Asbill & Brennan, Washington, D.C. Filed 8/18/78. Legislative interest — "To support enactment of S 3007."

KENNECOTT COPPER CORP., Washington, D.C. Filed for self 8/25/78. Legislative interest — "All legislation affecting the copper industry." Lobbyist — Melissa A. Nielson, Washington, D.C.

KENTUCKY FARM BUREAU MUTUAL INSURANCE CO., Louisville, Ky. Lobbyist — Sutherland, Asbill & Brennan, Washington, D.C. Filed 8/18/78. Legislative interest — "To support enactment of S 3007."

LYDALL INC., Manchester, Conn. Lobbyist — Covington & Burling, Washington, D.C. Filed 8/10/78. Legislative interest — "Legislation affecting nontoxic steel shot program of the Fish and Wildlife Service, Department of Interior including HR 12932; against Section 306 of HR 12932."

MOUNTAIN FUEL SUPPLY CO., Salt Lake City, Utah. Filed for self 8/2/78. Legislative interest — "Energy legislation and also natural gas and natural gas pricing." Lobbyist — Clyde M. Heiner, David N. Rose, R. L. Cox, Salt Lake City, Utah.

MUTUAL OF OMAHA INSURANCE CO., Omaha, Neb. Lobbyist — Sutherland, Asbill & Brennan, Washington, D.C. Filed 8/18/78. Legislative interest — "To support enactment of S 3007."

NATIONAL UNION ELECTRIC CORP., Philadelphia, Pa. Lobbyist — Blum, Parker & Nash, Washington, D.C. Filed 8/8/78. Legislative interest — "Legislation affecting the television and other consumer product industries, including but not limited to legislation affecting trade practices, imports, and customs and tariff statutes, HR 8149 and S 3127."

NATIONWIDE INSURANCE COMPANIES, Columbus, Ohio. Lobbyist — Sandra L. LaFevre, Washington, D.C. Filed 8/10/78. Legislative interest — "All statutes and bills affecting the corporate and insurance interests of affiliates of Nationwide Insurance Companies."

NORTHROP CORP., Arlington, Va. Lobbyist — James R. Calloway, Washington, D.C. Filed 8/28/78. Legislative interest — "Legislation affecting defense matters."

OGDEN TRANSPORTATION CORP., New York, N.Y. Lobbyist — Silverstein and Mullens, Washington, D.C. Filed 8/25/78. Legislative interest — ". . .Tax reform legislation generally as it relates to the business and affairs of the employer."

PATAGONIA CORP., Tucson, Ariz. Lobbyist — Hogan & Hartson, Washington, D.C. Filed 8/10/78. Legislative interest — "In support of legislation relating to bank holding company activities."

ST. JOE MINERALS CORP., New York, N.Y. Lobbyist — Patricia S. Ebaugh, Washington, D.C. Filed 8/25/78. Legislative interest — "Measures affecting mining, manufacturing and oil and gas production such as income taxation, tariff and trade legislation, stockpiling, public lands and environmental and safety regulations."

SOUTH CAROLINA FARM BUREAU MUTUAL INSURANCE CO., Cayce, S.C. Lobbyist — Sutherland, Asbill & Brennan, Washington, D.C. Filed 8/18/78. Legislative interest — "To support enactment of S 3007."

SOUTHERN FARM BUREAU LIFE INSURANCE CO., Jackson, Miss. Lobbyist — Sutherland, Asbill & Brennan, Washington, D.C. Filed 8/18/78. Legislative interest — "To support enactment of S 3007."

STANDARD BRANDS INC., New York, N.Y. Lobbyist — Covington & Burling, Washington, D.C. Filed 8/22/78. Legislative interest — "HR 13047, relating to tax accounting rules for redemption or coupons; HR 3050, relating to methods of accounting for publishers and distributors of magazines, books and records."

TERROS INC., Phoenix, Ariz. Filed for self 8/21/78. Legislative interest — ". . .Bills that affect HEW, and the field of health care and social services." Lobbyist — William K. Ponder, Phoenix, Ariz.

UNITED FARM BUREAU FAMILY LIFE INSURANCE CO., Indianapolis, Ind. Lobbyist — Sutherland, Asbill & Brennan, Washington, D.C. Filed 8/18/78. Legislative interest — "To support enactment of S 3007."

U.S. BORAX, Los Angeles, Calif. Lobbyist — Jack Ferguson Associates, Washington, D.C. Filed 8/11/78. Legislative interest — "Alaska Lands Bill."

VISA U.S.A. INC., San Francisco, Calif. Lobbyist — Marjorie J. Josiah, Washington, D.C. Filed 8/3/78. Legislative interest — ". . .Legislation and regulations affecting bank cards."

WATKINS JOHNSON CO., N. Springfield, Va. Filed for self 8/2/78. Legislative interest — ". . .Manufacture, export, sale or use of electronic equipment including computers." Lobbyist — Joseph A. Zielezienski, N. Springfield, Va.

Energy and Environment

SIERRA CLUB, San Francisco, Calif. Filed for self 8/11/78. Legislative interest — "Alaska National Interest Lands Conservation Act, HR 39 and S 1500; other assorted Alaska legislation and other wilderness and public land issues." Lobbyist — Barbara A. Blake, Washington, D.C.

THIRTEENTH REGIONAL CORPORATION, Seattle, Wash. Lobbyist — G. G. Reckley Associates, Washington, D.C. Filed 8/7/78. Legislative interest — ". . .HR 12529 to amend the Alaska Native Claims settlement act to provide for a distribution of land to the 13th Regional Corporation."

International Relations

SWAZILAND SUGAR ASSOCIATION, Mbabane, Swaziland. Lobbyist — Thevenot, Murray and Scheer, Washington, D.C. Filed 8/2/78. Legislative interest — "In support of ratification by Senate of International Sugar Agreement and other legislation affecting the increased importation of sugar."

Labor Groups

RETAIL CLERKS INTERNATIONAL UNION, AFL-CIO, Washington, D.C. Filed for self 8/14/78. Legislative interest — "General social legislation and all matters relating to the interests of labor organizations." Lobbyist — Lois M. Felder, W. J. Olwell, Washington, D.C.

Trade Associations

AMERICAN CAR RENTAL ASSOCIATION, Washington, D.C. Lobbyist — Bregman, Abell, Solter & Kay, Washington, D.C. Filed 8/16/78. Legislative interest — "All legislative matters of interest to the client."

AMERICAN DENTAL ASSOCIATION, Washington, D.C. Filed for self 8/18/78. Legislative interest — ". . .Matters relating to health legislation." Lobbyist — Sheila K. Hixson, Washington, D.C.

AMERICAN GREYHOUND TRACK OPERATORS ASSOCIATION, Miami, Fla. Lobbyist — Souther, Spaulding, Kinsey, Williamson & Schwabe, Portland, Ore. Filed 8/15/78. Legislative interest — "All matters relating to and of interest to parimutuel greyhound racing."

AMERICAN HARDWARE MANUFACTURERS ASSOCIATION, Palatine, Ill. Lobbyist — Sheldon I. London, Washington, D.C. Filed 8/3/78. Legislative interest — "Legislation which relates to tax policy, labor, consumer, product liability, environmental and other issues."

AMERICAN HOSPITAL ASSOCIATION, Chicago, Ill. Filed for self 8/14/78. Legislative interest — ". . .All legislation which may affect the ability of hospitals to render good care or which may affect the health care of the American people." Lobbyist — Daniel I. Zwick, Gilda Ventresca, Sarah Massengale Billock, Washington, D.C.

AMERICAN INSURANCE ASSOCIATION, Washington, D.C. Filed for self 8/4/78. Legislative interest — "Legislation affecting our membership of stock, property casualty and surety companies." Lobbyist — Geoffrey G. Peterson, Washington, D.C.

AMERICAN PAPER INSTITUTE INC., New York, N.Y. Lobbyist — Kelly Holley, Washington, D.C. Filed 8/4/78. Legislative interest — ". . .Pulp, paper and paperboard industry, its operation, practices and properties."

AMERICAN PETROLEUM INSTITUTE, Washington, D.C. Lobbyist — Prather Seeger Doolittle & Farmer, Washington, D.C. Filed 8/4/78. Legislative interest — ". . .All matters relating to horizontal or vertical divestiture proposals for the petroleum industry."

AMERICAN SOCIETY FOR MEDICAL TECHNOLOGY, Washington, D.C. Filed for self 8/15/78. Legislative interest — "Legislation with potential effect on medical laboratory services and personnel such as: health legislation, labor relations legislation, civil service legislation, armed services legislation." Lobbyist — Kim Alan Benjamin, Washington, D.C.

AMERICAN SUBCONTRACTORS ASSOCIATION, Washington, D.C. Lobbyist — Charles B. Lavin Jr., Laurel, Md. Filed 8/14/78. Legislative interest — "Construction related and small business related legislation."

ASSOCIATED BUILDERS AND CONTRACTORS INC., Washington, D.C. Filed for self 8/21/78. Legislative interest — "All activities in the U.S. Congress affecting labor-management relations including: Labor Law Reform (S 2467); Davis-Bacon Reform (HR 6100, S 1540); Humphrey-Hawkins; Criminal Code Reform (HR 6869)." Lobbyist — John H. Reed, Washington, D.C.

FAR WEST SKI ASSOCIATION, Los Angeles, Calif. Filed for self 8/1/78. Legislative interest — "Federal land use legislation." Lobbyist — Robert L. Jordan, Los Angeles, Calif.

NATIONAL ASSOCIATION OF CREDIT MANAGEMENT, New York, N.Y. Lobbyist — Lobel, Novins & Lamont, Washington, D.C. Filed 8/16/78. Legislative interest — "Bankruptcy legislation, S 2266, HR 8200; for passage, with amendments."

NATIONAL ASSOCIATION OF MANUFACTURERS, Washington, D.C. Filed for self 8/18/78. Legislative interest — "Legislation affecting business and industry." Lobbyist — Pamela K. Young, Tom E. Persky, Washington, D.C.

NATIONAL ASSOCIATION OF MARINE SERVICES INC., Silver Spring, Md. Lobbyist — Quinn, Jacobs, Barry & Dick, Washington, D.C. Filed 8/21/78. Legislative interest — "To amend the Internal Revenue Code of 1954 to provide an exemption from withholding of tax on nonresident aliens for ship suppliers in respect of certain commissions paid to nonresident aliens."

NATIONAL ASSOCIATION OF RAILROAD PASSENGERS, Washington, D.C. Filed for self 8/11/78. Legislative interest — ". . Railroad policy and administration." Lobbyist — Joseph Zucker, Washington, D.C.

NATIONAL DISTRICT ATTORNEYS ASSOCIATION, Chicago, Ill. Lobbyist — Perito, Duerk and Carlson, Washington, D.C. Filed 8/3/78. Legislative interest — ". . .Law enforcement and prosecution related criminal law procedures and any other legislative initiatives which affect state prosecutors and district attorneys in performing the functions and responsibilities of office."

NATIONAL REALTY COMMITTEE INC., Washington, D.C. Filed for self 8/3/78. Legislative interest — ". . .Revisions of laws affecting the interest of real estate owners and investors and particularly, their ability to provide or assist in providing a decent home in a suitable living environment for every American family." Lobbyist — Carl F. Arnold, Washington, D.C.

NATIONAL TIRE DEALERS & RETREADERS ASSOCIATION, Washington, D.C. Filed for self 8/21/78. Legislative interest — ". . .Those which affect the interests of independent tire dealers and retreaders. . . , bills to amend regulations concerning tire identification and recordkeeping, the Internal Revenue Code provisions dealing with the excise tax on tread rubber, the Motor Vehicle Safety Act, regulations promulgated under the Occupational Safety and Health Act, and the issue of allowing post exchanges to retail and service new tires." Lobbyist — Mark E. Grayson, Russell MacCleery, Washington, D.C.

PROFESSIONAL INSURANCE AGENTS, Alexandria, Va. Filed for self 8/17/78. Legislative interest — ". . .Insurance matters and any bills related to the welfare of local fire and casualty insurance agents." Lobbyist — Duward F. Sumner Jr., Alexandria, Va.

PUBLIC POWER COUNCIL, Vancouver, Wash. Filed for self 8/18/78. Legislative interest — "All legislation affecting the Bonneville Power Administration and any northwest regional power program." Lobbyists — David E. Piper, Vancouver, Wash.; Souther, Spaulding, Kinsey, Williamson & Schwabe, Portland, Ore.

TRUCK RENTING & LEASING ASSOCIATION, Washington, D.C. Lobbyist — Bregman, Abell, Solter & Kay, Washington, D.C. Filed 8/16/78. Legislative interest — "All legislative matters of interest to the client."

Miscellaneous

BRADFORD T. DEMPSEY, Vienna, Va. Filed for self 8/28/78. Legisltive interest — "All matters related to forestry, lumber and wood products."

FELLOWSHIP SQUARE FOUNDATION INC., Reston, Va. Filed for self 8/18/78. Legislative interest — "Housing subsidy for elderly and disabled." Lobbyist — Lloyd A. Nelson, Silver Spring, Md.

FRIENDS COMMITTEE ON NATIONAL LEGISLATION, Washington, D.C. Filed for self 8/18/78. Legislative interest — "Support steps toward world disarmament, support cutbacks in military spending and an end to military aid and sales, support growth of world law and strengthening of U.N., increase U.S. contributions to U.N. development and assistance programs, peacekeeping operations, food and relief programs, support proposal for human rights and peaceful development of seabeds and oceans; support development of more equitable taxation, food distribution, criminal justice and health care systems. . . ." Lobbyist — Don T. Reeves, Washington, D.C.

THE FUND FOR ANIMALS INC., New York, N.Y. Filed for self 8/28/78. Legislative interest — "Marine mammal and endangered species conservation and related habitat and ecological areas." Lobbyist — Milton M. Kaufmann, Gaithersburg, Md.

HEALTHY AMERICA, Washington, D.C. Filed for self 8/15/78. Legislative interest — ". . .The advancement of health promotion." Lobbyist — Deborah Drudge, Washington, D.C.

HILL AND KNOWLTON INC., New York, N.Y. Filed for self 8/3/78. Legislative interest — ". . .Amateur sports legislation, HR 12626, The Amateur Sports Act of 1978, and related legislation." Lobbyist — Linda Walker-Hill, Washington, D.C.

KETCHIKAN INDIAN CORP., Ketchikan, Alaska. Lobbyist — G. G. Reckley Associates, Washington, D.C. Filed 8/7/78. Legislative interest — ". . .Legislation to merge BIA Indian education programs into a new Department of Education."

JAMES H. LAKE, Washington, D.C. Filed for self 8/3/78. Legislative interest — "HR 4773 — to amend the Perishable Agriculture Commodities Act. . . ."

LEGAL SERVICES CORP., Washington, D.C. Filed for self 8/3/78. Legislative interest — ". . .Legislation directly affecting the activities of the corporation." Lobbyist — Quentin L. Burgess, Washington, D.C.

NATIONAL BLACKS INVESTMENTS ASSOCIATION, Brooklyn, N.Y. Filed for self 8/18/78. Legislative, interest — "Legislation to help investments in stocks or bonds or real estate; crime bills; legislation to help small business." Lobbyist — Grady O'Cummings, Brooklyn, N.Y.; Annie O. Massey, Uniondale, N.Y.

RAILWAY PROGRESS INSTITUTE TANK CAR SAFETY COMMITTEE, Alexandria, Va. Lobbyist — Carl Byoir & Associates Inc., Washington, D.C. Filed 8/21/78. Legislative interest — ". . .Tank car safety and transportation of hazardous materials."

SERENITY ARABIAN STUD INC., Citra, Fla. Lobbyist — John B. Fisher, Washington, D.C. Filed 8/3/78. Legislative interest — "Support of S 2786, a private bill for the relief of Hanna-Luise Heck."

MARK SHARFMAN, Phoenix, Ariz. Filed for self 8/21/78. Legislative interest — ". . .Bills related to health and mental health industry."

SISSETON-WAHPETON SIOUX TRIBE, Sisseton, S.D. Lobbyist — Bertram E. Hirsch, Bellerose, N.Y. Filed 8/23/78. Legislative interest — ". . .Promote enactment of S 3069 and HR 13096."

SPECIAL COMMITTEE FOR U.S. EXPORTS, Washington, D.C. Filed for self 8/2/78. Legislative interest — "Export trade and tax matters. . . ." Lobbyist — Joseph E. Karth, Washington, D.C.

UNIVERSITY OF HAWAII AT MANOA, Honolulu, Hawaii. Lobbyist — Vorys, Sater, Seymour & Pease, Washington, D.C. Filed 8/21/78. Legislative interest — "Limited work in connection with congressional appropriation for the College of Tropical Agriculture (HR 13125)."

September

Citizens' Groups

COMMON CAUSE, Washington, D.C. Filed for self 9/21/78. Legislative interest — "Open government, campaign financing, consumer protection, freedom of information, ERA, energy policy, environmental protection, defense spending, tax reform, waste in government, voting rights, presidential nomination and confirmation process, administration of justice and reform of the criminal code, merit selection of federal judges, intelligence policy, public participation in federal agency proceedings, civil service reform, regulatory reform, the congressional budget process and congressional reform." Lobbyist — Kirk L. Gray, Washington, D.C.

CONGRESS WATCH, Washington, D.C. Filed for self 9/8/78. Legislative interest — "Sunset, small claims court, public participation, consumer class actions, reauthorization of Consumer Product Safety Commission, legislative veto, airport noise bill, broadcasting bill." Lobbyist — Howard Symons, Washington, D.C.

NATIONAL RIFLE ASSOCIATION OF AMERICA, Washington, D.C. Filed for self 9/25/78. Legislative interest — "Conservation, recreation and firearms legislation." Lobbyist — Harlon B. Carter, Washington, D.C.

Corporations and Business

ACLI INTERNATIONAL INC., New York, N.Y. Lobbyist — Camp, Carmouche, Palmer, Barsh & Hunter, Washington, D.C. Filed 9/13/78. Legislative interest — "Supporting tax legislation relative to commodity transactions."

AMERICAN FAMILY LIFE ASSURANCE CO. OF GEORGIA, Columbus, Ga. Lobbyist — Caplin & Drysdale, Washington, D.C. Filed 9/18/78. Legislative interest — "Seek passage of HR 13828 or HR 13722 and S 3007 . . . provide relief to taxpayers who have been subjected to IRS reclassification in employment tax cases."

AMERICAN EXPRESS CO., Washington, D.C. Lobbyist — Leighton and Conklin, Washington, D.C. Filed 9/30/78. Legislative interest — "Tax legislation — HR 13511."

AMERICAN HONDA MOTOR CO. INC., Gardena, Calif. Lobbyist — William C. Triplett II, Toni Harrington, Washington, D.C. Filed 9/15/78. Legislative interest — "All legislation affecting products imported and sold by the Company."

BALTIMORE GAS AND ELECTRIC CO., Baltimore, Md. Filed for self 9/8/78. Legislative interest — ". . . All legislation affecting the generation, transmission and distribution of electricity, gas and steam to a 2,300 square mile territory in Central Maryland...legislation affecting the investor-owned utility on a nationwide basis." Lobbyist — E. John Neumann, Washington, D.C.

BESSEMER SECURITIES CORP., New York, N.Y. Lobbyists — Hogan & Hartson, Washington, D.C.; Dunnington, Bartholow & Miller, New York, N.Y. Filed 9/22/78. Legislative interest — "Representation in connection with tax legislation regarding section 2 of HR 12578 relating to personal holding companies."

J. G. BOSWELL CO., Los Angeles, Calif. Lobbyist — H. Wesley McAden, Washington, D.C. Filed 9/30/78. Legislative interest — "Legislation affecting Reclamation (a) to remove residency requirements and acreage limitations applicable to land subject to Reclamation Law (b) S 2867 and HR 12708."

BRUNSWICK CORP., Skokie, Ill. Lobbyists — Mayer, Brown & Platt, Washington, D.C.; Alcalde, Henderson, O'Bannon & Kline, Rosslyn, Va. Filed 9/29/78. Legislative interest — "All legislation affecting corporate activities and particularly S 3466 and HR 6853; . . . Amendments to the Internal Revenue Code of 1954, Revenue Act of 1978, HR 13511."

CALIFORNIA PLANTING COTTON SEED DISTRIBUTORS, Bakersfield, Calif. Lobbyist — H. Wesley McAden, Washington, D.C. Filed 9/30/78. Legislative interest — ". . . Agricultural research; Agriculture Appropriations Act, HR 13125."

CHICAGO COMMUNITY TRUST, Chicago, Ill. Lobbyist — Sidley & Austin, Chicago, Ill. Filed 9/13/78. Legislative interest — ". . . Legislation to amend the Internal Revenue Code to provide that charitable distribution of certain trusts are not items of tax preference subject to the Minimum Tax for Tax Preferences."

CLARK OIL & REFINING CORP., Milwaukee, Wis. Lobbyist — Caplin & Drysdale, Washington, D.C. Filed 9/18/78. Legislative interest — "... HR 13828 or HR 13722 and S 3007 ... provide tax relief to taxpayers who have been subjected to IRS reclassification in employment tax cases."

COMMUNICATIONS SATELLITE CORP., Washington, D.C. Lobbyist — Jones, Day, Reavis & Pogue, Washington, D.C. Filed 9/30/78. Legislative interest — "... Investment tax credit provisions of the Internal Revenue Code of 1954."

ENSERCH CORP., Dallas, Texas. Lobbyist — Candice J. Shy, Washington, D.C. Filed 9/14/78. Legislative interest — "Legislation of interest to energy industries."

GENERAL ELECTRIC CO., Fairfield, Conn. Filed for self 9/6/78. Legislative interest — "... Labor law, national economic planning, mediation and arbitration ...." Lobbyist — K. Richard Cook, Washington, D.C.

GOULD INC., St. Louis, Mo. Lobbyist — Burson-Marsteller, Washington, D.C. Filed 9/27/78. Legislative interest — "... Business energy tax credits for energy-conserving properties and equipment, HR 5263. ..."

GENERAL TIME CORP., Mesa, Ariz. Lobbyist — Steptoe & Johnson, Washington, D.C. Filed 9/26/78. Legislative interest — "... Amendments to General Headnote 3 (a) of the Tariff Schedules of the United States."

INDIANAPOLIS WATER CO., Indianapolis, Ind. Lobbyist — Doub, Purcell, Muntzing & Hansen, Washington, D.C. Filed 9/22/78. Legislative interest — "... Drinking water regulations."

INTERNATIONAL NICKEL CO. OF CANADA, Toronto, Ontario, Canada. Lobbyist — Sullivan & Cromwell, Washington, D.C. Filed 9/7/78. Legislative interest — "Tax legislation affecting foreign corporations and their domestic subsidiaries, Revenue Bill of 1978, HR 13511."

INTERNATIONAL PAPER CO., New York, N.Y. Lobbyist — Cadwalader, Wickersham & Taft, Washington, D.C. Filed 9/20/78. Legislative interest — "... Sections 103 and 169 of the Internal Revenue Code of 1954."

LACLEDE STEEL CO., St. Louis, Mo. Lobbyist — Lewis Rice Tucker Allen & Chubb, St. Louis, Mo. Filed 9/15/78. Legislative interest — "Antitrust Enforcement Act of 1978, S 1874; Clayton Act Amendments of 1978, HR 11942, against both bills."

MEGO CORP., New York, N.Y. Lobbyist — John T. Grupenhoff, Bethesda, Md. Filed 9/18/78. Legislative interest — "... Toy manufacturing, shipping, sales, advertising, taxation. ..."

NEEDHAM, HARPER & STEERS INC., New York, N.Y. Lobbyist — Dewey, Ballantine, Bushby, Palmer & Wood, New York, N.Y. Filed 9/19/78. Legislative interest — "ERISA legislation, S 3316, regarding profit sharing and 'floor' pension plans."

NORTHWEST ALASKA PIPELINE CO., Washington, D.C. Lobbyist — Cramer, Visser, Lipsen & Smith, Washington, D.C. Filed 9/12/78. Legislative interest — "Support of conference report in Senate of HR 5289, natural gas bill."

NORTHWEST EXPLORATION CO., Salt Lake City, Utah. Lobbyist — Akin, Gump, Hauer & Feld, Washington, D.C. Filed 9/8/78. Legislative interest — "... Crude oil and natural gas policy."

NORTHWEST PIPELINE CO., Salt Lake City, Utah. Lobbyist — Boyden, Kennedy, Romney & Howard, Salt Lake City, Utah. Filed 9/14/78. Legislative interest — "... Legislation of interest to Northwest Pipeline."

PROCTER & GAMBLE MANUFACTURING CO., Cincinnati, Ohio. Lobbyist — Walter A. Hasty, Washington, D.C. Filed 9/25/78 Legislative interest — "Matters generally of interest to employer."

REVERE COPPER & BRASS, New York, N.Y. Lobbyist Cyron T. Anderson, Washington, D.C. Filed 9/14/78. Legislative interest "... Legislation of interest to employer."

SALYER LAND CO., Corcoran, Calif. Lobbyist H. Wesley McAden, Washington, D.C. Filed 9/30/78. Legislative interest "... Remove residency requirements and acreage limitations applicable to land subject to Reclamation Law, S 2867 and HR 12708."

SONY CORP. OF AMERICA, New York, N.Y. Lobbyist Tanaka Walders & Ritger, Washington, D.C. Filed 9/22/78. Legislative interest "... Administration of the Anti-dumping Act of 1921. ..."

SOUTHLAND CORP., Dallas, Texas. Lobbyist — Simon & Twambly, Dallas, Texas. Filed 9/12/78. Legislative interest — "... Employee/independent contractor (for employment tax purposes) question."

UNION OIL CO. OF CALIFORNIA, Los Angeles, Calif. Filed for self 9/29/78. Legislative interest — "Matters relating to federal energy legislation." Lobbyist — Karen Sikkema, Los Angeles, Calif.

WORLD WIDE PRODUCTS, Santa Barbara, Calif. Filed for self 9/8/78. Legislative interest — "... Direct sales organizations."

Energy and Environment

FRIENDS OF THE EARTH, Washington, D.C. Filed for self 9/7/78. Legislative interest — "... Legislation to preserve, restore and insure rational use of the ecosphere, all environmental legislation." Lobbyist — David Masselli, Washington, D.C.

PACIFIC RESOURCES, INC., Honolulu, Hawaii. Filed for self 9/7/78. Legislative interest — "Energy related legislation such as the National Energy Act." Lobbyist — Frederick C. Spreyer, Washington, D.C.

International Relations

REPUBLIC OF THE PHILIPPINES. Lobbyists — Lucas, Friedman & Mann, Washington, D.C.; Foley, Lardner, Hollabaugh & Jacobs, Washington, D.C. Filed 9/12/78. Legislative interest — "Certain sections of S 1874 and HR 11942 as now proposed would reverse or limit the Supreme Court's decision in *Pfizer Inc. v. India,* which upheld the standing of foreign governments to maintain suit pursuant to Section 4 of the Clayton Act,... oppose such legislation. ..."

UNITED STATES-JAPAN TRADE COUNCIL, Washington, D.C. Filed for self 9/13/78. Legislative interest — "Legislation affecting U.S.-Japan trade." Lobbyist — Edward J. Lincoln, Washington, D.C.

State and Local Government

THE STATE OF ALASKA, Juneau, Alaska. Lobbyist — Wilmer, Cutler & Pickering, Washington, D.C. Filed 9/28/78. Legislative interest — "... Tax cut bill, HR 13511, and the enactment of other legislation necessary for the creation of a general stock ownership corporation. ..."

Trade Associations

AD HOC MOBILE HOME FINANCE GROUP, Washington, D.C. Lobbyist — Witkowski, Weiner, McCaffrey and Brodsky, Washington, D.C. Filed 9/21/78. Legislative interest — "Legislation impacting on the mobile home and manufactured housing industry particularly relating to finance and land development."

AMERICAN OCCUPATIONAL MEDICAL ASSOCIATION, Washington, D.C. Filed for self 9/18/78. Legislative interest — "Health, Education and Welfare; Labor." Lobbyist — Dennis J. Barbour, Washington, D.C.

AMERICAN HEALTH CARE ASSOCIATION, Washington, D.C. Filed for self 9/8/78. Legislative interest — "Legislation affecting infirm aged persons, disabled persons, long-term health care institutions. ..." Lobbyist — Bruce D. Thevenot, Washington, D.C.

AMERICAN NUCLEAR ENERGY COUNCIL, Washington, D.C. Filed for self 9/7/78. Legislative interest — "... To promote the enactment or maintenance of such legislation relating to the development and use of nuclear energy as will benefit its members and the public. ..." Lobbyist — John T. Conway, Washington, D.C.

AMERICAN PYROTECHNICS ASSOCIATION, Chestertown, Md. Lobbyist — Houger, Garvey & Schubert, Washington, D.C. Filed 9/13/78. Legislative interest — "Anti-Terrorism Act, S 2236."

AMERICAN TEXTILE MANUFACTURERS INSTITUTE, Washington, D.C. Lobbyist — Williams & Jensen, Washington, D.C. Filed 9/22/78. Legislative interest — "Tax, tariff, and related matters of interest to the association...."

ASSOCIATION OF MAXIMUM SERVICE TELECASTERS INC., Washington, D.C. Lobbyist — Covington & Burling, Washington, D.C. Filed 9/20/78. Legislative interest — ". . . Revision of the Communications Act of 1934, including HR 13105 and other similar legislation. MST opposes HR 13015."

BOWLING PROPRIETORS ASSOCIATIONS OF AMERICA, Arlington, Texas. Filed for self 9/8/78. Legislative interest — "All legislative proposals which may reasonably be expected to increase the cost of doing business as a bowling proprietor."

GUAYULE RUBBER GROWERS ASSOCIATION, San Marino, Calif. Filed for self 9/25/78. Legislative interest — "Support of S 1167, Native Latex Commercialization Act of 1977."

NATIONAL ASSOCIATION OF PLUMBING, Washington, D.C. Filed for self 9/18/78. Legislative interest — "Legislative efforts of interest to the industry." Lobbyist — Dennis Lavallee, Washington, D.C.

NATIONAL ASSOCIATION OF PRIVATE PSYCHIATRIC HOSPITALS, Washington, D.C. Filed for self 9/1/78. Legislative interest — "Issues effecting mental health, hospitals, hospital employees, health care delivery, HR 9717, HR 6575, S 2410." Lobbyist — Robert L. Thomas, Washington, D.C.

NATIONAL ASSOCIATION OF REAL ESTATE INVESTMENT TRUSTS INC., Washington, D.C. Lobbyist — Latham, Watkins & Hills, Washington, D.C. Filed 9/12/78. Legislative interest — "The Revenue Act of 1978, HR 13511."

NATIONAL FISHERIES INSTITUTE, Washington, D.C. Lobbyist — Gustave Fritschie, Washington, D.C. Filed 9/21/78. Legislative interest — ". . . In favor of legislation of interest to the fishing industry, including fisheries assistance, amendments to Food & Drug Act, fisheries and marine mammal management.

Miscellaneous

AGENCY FOR INSTRUCTIONAL TELEVISION, Bloomington, Ind. Lobbyist — Chalmers H. Marquis, Falls Church, Va. Filed 9/22/78. Legislative interest — "Legislation affecting uses of telecommunications for education, especially HR 15 and S 1753, Education Amendments of 1978."

CAMBRIDGE RESEARCH AND DEVELOPMENT GROUP, Westport Conn. Lobbyist — Baker & McKenzie, Washington, D.C. Filed 9/11/78. Legislative interest — "Modification of section 201 of HR 13511."

CHILD WELFARE LEAGUE OF AMERICA, Washington, D.C. Filed for self 9/20/78. Legislative interest — "International Development Assistance Authorization and Appropriation, HR 12222; Adolescent Pregnancy and Prevention Act, S 2910; Title X of the Public Health Services Act, HR 12370." Lobbyist — Nancy McConnell, Washington, D.C.

COOK, RUEF, SPANN & WEISER INC., Columbia, S.C. Filed for self 9/18/78. Legislative interest — "Legislative activities concerning press relations." Lobbyist — J. C. Cook, M. F. Capps, Columbia, S.C.

BRADFORD T. DEMPSEY, Vienna, Va. Filed for self 9/20/78. Legislative interest — "All subject matter related to forestry, lumber and wood products."

ROBERT W. GALVIN, Barrington, Ill. Lobbyist — Winston & Strawn, Washington, D.C. Filed 9/26/78. Legislative interest — "Amendments to the Internal Revenue Code eliminating or limiting the application of the minimum tax on preference income to charitable deductions, including the Technical Corrections Act of 1978, HR 6715 and The Revenue Act of 1978, HR 13511."

HEALTH RESEARCH GROUP, Washington, D.C. Filed for self 9/7/78. Legislative interest — ". . . Occupational Safety and Health Act of 1970 and related enactments." Lobbyist — Robert B. Stulberg, Washington, D.C.

JAMES H. LAKE, Washington, D.C. Filed for self 9/1/78. Legislative interest — "S 2391, a bill to extend the Commodity Exchange Act."

NORTHWESTERN UNIVERSITY, Evanston, Ill. Lobbyist — Sidley & Austin, Chicago, Ill. Filed 9/13/78. Legislative interest — ". . . Supporting legislation to amend the Internal Revenue Code to provide that charitable distribution of certain trusts are not items of tax preference subject to Minimum Tax for Tax Preferences."

BOB PERRY, Houston, Texas. Lobbyist — John S. Brunson, Houston, Texas. Filed 9/12/78. Legislative interest — "HJ Res 638 and SJ Res 134, against."

ROBERT V. SHIRLEY, Washington, D.C. Filed for self 9/1/78. Legislative interest — ". . . Energy bill. . . ."

TAX EQUITY FOR AMERICANS ABROAD, London, England. Lobbyist — Rogers & Wells, Washington, D.C. Filed 9/28/78. Legislative interest — "Tax legislation including HR 13488."

UNITED STATES OLYMPIC COMMITTEE, New York, N.Y. Lobbyist — John S. Monagan, Washington, D.C. Filed 9/25/78. Legislative interest — "Support S 2727 and HR 12626 — Amateur Sports Act of 1978."

CHARLS E. WALKER ASSOCIATES INC., Washington, D.C. Filed for self 9/13/78. Legislative interest — ". . . Deregulation of natural gas. . . ."

October

Citizens' Groups

CONSUMER ACTION NOW, Washington, D.C. Lobbyist — Barbara Gross, Washington, D.C. Filed 10/2/78. Legislative interest — ". . . Any and all bills which may contain provisions having an impact on consumer products, health services or the environment. . . ."

THE LEAGUE OF WOMEN VOTERS OF THE UNITED STATES, Washington, D.C. Filed for self 10/13/78. Legislative interest — "Human resources, natural resources, international relations and representative government." Lobbyist — Laureen E. Andrews, Washington, D.C.

NATIONAL CITIZENS COMMUNICATIONS, Washington, D.C. Filed for self 10/24/78. Legislative interest — "Opposition to legislation restricting the ability of citizens to affect public interest policies of and obtain responsive service from broadcast stations, S 22; support legislation designed to enhance citizens' ability. . . ., S 270, HR 3361."

NATIONAL COMMUNITY ACTION AGENCY EXECUTIVE DIRECTORS ASSOCIATION, Washington, D.C. Lobbyist — David A. Bradley, Fredericksburg, Va. Filed 10/9/78. Legislative interest — "Appropriations and legislation affecting community action agencies and the 20 million poor they serve."

POPULATION RESOURCE CENTER INC., New York, N.Y. Filed for self 10/15/78. Legislative interest — "Increased resources towards population and reproductive research, Labor-HEW appropriations bill, Title X of the Public Health Service Act reauthorization for HR 11007, HR 12370, HR 6075, S 2522 — Against S 2614." Lobbyist — Anne Harrison Clark, Washington, D.C.

THIRTY-FIFTH CONGRESSIONAL DISTRICT ACTION COMMITTEE, Perry, N.Y. Filed for self 10/4/78. Legislative interest — "An amendment to the U.S. Constitution which would limit and/or preclude abortion."

THIRTY-SECOND CONGRESSIONAL DISTRICT ACTION COMMITTEE, Harbor City, Calif. Filed for self 10/9/78. Legislative interest — "All proposed Human Life Amendments."

Corporations and Businesses

A.R.F. PRODUCTS INC., Raton, N.M. Lobbyist — Sullivan, Beauregard, Clarkson, Moss, Brown & Johnson, Washington, D.C. Filed 10/4/78. Legislative interest — "In support of legislation providing preferences for small businesses in government procurement."

AMERICAN CAN CO., Greenwich, Conn. Lobbyist — Endicott Peabody, Washington, D.C. Filed 10/20/78. Legislative interest — "HR 5289, National Gas Policy Act of 1978.'

AMERICAN BANKERS INSURANCE CO. OF FLORIDA, Miami, Fla. Lobbyist — M. Ray Niblack, Washington, D.C. Filed 10/4/78. Legislative interest — "HR 13471, Financial Institutions Regulatory Act of 1978; anything that would affect the insurance industry."

AMERICAN ELECTRIC POWER CORP., New York, N.Y. Filed for self 10/4/78. Legislative interest — "National energy legislation and other legislation involving the electric power industry generally. Lobbyist — Bruce A. Beam, McLean, Va.

AMERICAN FAMILY CORP., Columbus, Ga. Lobbyist — Carl F. Arnold, Washington, D.C. Filed 10/4/78. Legislative interest — "Legislation affecting the insurance business."

AMERICAN FAMILY LIFE INSURANCE CO., Columbus, Ga. Lobbyist — The Keefe Co., Washington, D.C. Filed 10/5/78. Legislative interest — "Support for bills relating to the interim treatment of controversies involving whether certain individuals are employees for purposes of employment taxes, HR 14159."

AMERICAN KITCHEN FOODS INC., Roslyn, N.Y. Lobbyist — Birch, Horton, Bittner & Monroe, Washington, D.C. Filed 10/10/78. Legislative interest — "All legislation relating to vegetable processing industry. . . ."

AMERICAN SEATING CO., Grand Rapids, Mich. Lobbyist — Richard F. Vander Veen, Grand Rapids, Mich. Filed 10/4/78. Legislative interest — "Amendment to HR 11733, specifically, the Urban Mass Transit Act of 1964."

APPALACHIAN POWER CO., Roanoke, Va. Filed for self 10/24/78. Legislative interest — "National energy legislation and other legislation involving the electric power industry." Lobbyist — James E. Jones, Roanoke, Va.

ARLINGTON RED TOP CAB CO., Arlington, Va. Lobbyist — Akin, Gump, Hauer & Feld, Washington, D.C. Filed 10/6/78. Legislative interest — "Surface Transportation Act of 1978."

ASARCO INC., New York, N.Y. Lobbyist — George W. Beatty, Washington, D.C. Filed 10/16/78. Legislative interest — "HR 13511."

BAYBANKS INC., Boston, Mass. Lobbyist — Timothy D. Naegele, Washington, D.C. Filed 10/15/78. Legislative interest — "Legislation relating to banks and financial institutions, specifically, HR 14072."

BULOVA WATCH CO., INC., Flushing, N.Y. Lobbyist — Leva, Hawes, Symington, Martin & Oppenheimer, Washington, D.C. Filed 10/17/78. Legislative interest — "Guidelines for duty-free imports from U.S. Virgin Islands to prevent discrimination against U.S. watch manufacturers; Amend HR 8222."

COLT INDUSTRIES INC., New York, N.Y. Lobbyist — Scott C. Whitney, Washington, D.C. Filed 10/3/78. Legislative interest — ". . . Tax policy, foreign trade policy, environmental interests. . . ."

CONTROL DATA CORP., Rockville, Md. Lobbyist — Jones, Day, Reavis & Pogue, Washington, D.C. Filed 10/16/78. Legislative interest — "Revisions to the Export Administration Act of 1969."

DeKALB AGRESEARCH, DeKalb, Ill. Lobbyist — Margaret R. Murray, Washington, D.C. Filed 10/12/78. Legislative interest — "S 976 - Perishable Agricultural Commodities Act; HR 5263-Energy tax bill."

THE DOW CHEMICAL CO., Midland, Mich. Lobbyist — J.J. Panella, Washington, D.C. Filed 10/10/78. Legislative interest — "Legislation affecting energy programs which are of interest to Dow, i.e., HR 8444, S 5037, S 5289, S 5263, S 5146."

EXXON CORP., New York, N.Y. Lobbyist — Mary A. Tobin, Washington, D.C. Filed 10/10/78. Legislative interest — ". . . Legislation affecting the employer. . . ."

FIREMAN'S FUND INSURANCE COMPANIES, San Rafael, Calif. Lobbyist — Leighton Conklin & Lemov, Washington, D.C. Filed 10/4/78. Legislative interest — "Tax legislation, HR 13511, Employee Retirement Plan provisions."

FLORIDA SUGAR CANE LEAGUE INC., Clewiston, Fla. Lobbyist — Thomas A. Davis, Washington, D.C. Filed 10/6/78. Legislative interest — "All legislation affecting sugar cane growers."

GATX CORP., Chicago, Ill. Lobbyist — Adams, Duque & Hazeltine, Washington, D.C. Filed 10/2/78. Legislative interest — "Amendments to the provisions of the Internal Revenue Code of 1954 to increase investment credits."

GENERAL MOTORS CORP., Detroit, Mich. Lobbyist — Bruce N. Rogers, Washington, D.C. Filed 10/25/78. Legislative interest —" . . .Proposed and anticipated action by state and national business organizations, state legislatures, Congress and agencies of the federal government. . . ."

HEINOLD COMMODITIES INC., Chicago, Ill. Filed for self 10/12/78. Legislative interest — "S 2391, Commodity Futures Trading Commission Reauthorizatin Act; S 2266, Bankruptcy Reform Act." Lobbyist — Margaret R. Murray, Washington, D.C.

THE KROGER CO., Cincinnati, Ohio. Filed for self 10/12/78. Legislative interest — "Antitrust legislation - S 1894 and HR 11942." Lobbyist — Manly Molpus, Cincinnati, Ohio.

NABISCO INC., East Hanover, N.J. Filed for self 10/11/78. Legislative interest — "Business-related legislation of interest to employer." Lobbyist — Wayne C. Anderson, East Hanover, N.J.

THE NEW YORK STATE URBAN DEVELOPMENT CORP., New York, N.Y. Lobbyist — Barrett Smith Schapiro Simon & Armstrong, New York, N.Y. Filed 10/19/78. Legislative interest — "Amendment to Section 103 of the Internal Revenue Code of 1954 to permit the advance refunding (through issuance of tax exempt bonds) of outstanding tax exempt obligations substantially all proceeds of which were used to finance low and moderate income housing under state housing finance agency programs, including a proposed revision of Sec. 332 of the Revenue Bill of 1978 (HR 13511).

NORTHWEST ALASKAN PIPELINE CO., Washington, D.C. Lobbyist — Moss, Frink & Franklin, Washington, D.C. Filed 10/23/78. Legislative interest — ". . . Natural gas pricing and regulation bill, HR 5289."

OCEAN MINERALS CO., Washington, D.C. Lobbyist — Patton, Boggs and Blow, Washington, D.C. Filed 10/10/78. Legislative interest — "Legislation relating to deep seabed mining, HR 3350 and S 2053."

PHILADELPHIA GAS WORKS, Philadelphia, Pa. Lobbyist — Obermayer, Rebmann, Maxwell and Hippel, Washington, D.C. Filed 10/6/78. Legislative interest — "Energy legislation, specifically that affecting natural gas."

POTLATCH CORP., San Francisco, Calif. Lobbyist — Birch, Horton, Bittner & Monroe, Washington, D.C. Filed 10/10/78. Legislative interest — "Legislation relating to truck safety."

PROVIDENT INDEMNITY LIFE INSURANCE CO., Norristown, Pa. Filed for self 10/30/78. Legislative interest — "Insurance." Lobbyist — Samuel C. Corey, Samuel C. Corey Jr., M. Warren Bolton, Stephen M. Belikoff, Norristown, Pa.

SHELL OIL CO., Houston, Texas. Filed for self 10/10/78. Legislative interest — "Legislation relating to the business affairs of the Shell Oil Co. and its affiliated companies." Lobbyist — William C. Lowrey, David B. Gross, Washington, D.C.

SOUTHERN NATURAL GAS CO., Birmingham, Ala. Filed for self 10/19/78. Legislative interest — ". . . The natural gas industry and related matters." Lobbyist — Martin R. Tilson Jr., Birmingham, Ala.

TITLE ASSOCIATES INC., Columbia, Tenn. Filed for self 10/18/78. Legislative interest — ". . . Lawyers and the practice of law, title insurance, real estate, an economic system based upon the free enterprise system." Lobbyist — Donald T. Chunn, Columbia, Tenn.

UNION OIL CO. OF CALIFORNIA, Los Angeles, Calif. Filed for self 10/10/78. Legislative interest — "Legislation affecting the petroleum industry." Lobbyist — Mary Frances Shlagel, Karen Sikkema, Los Angeles, Calif.

UNITED EGG PRODUCERS, Decatur, Ga. Lobbyist — Thomas A. Davis, Washington, D.C. Filed 10/6/78. Legislative interest — "All legislation affecting egg producers."

THE WESTERN CO. OF NORTH AMERICA, Forth Worth, Texas. Filed for self 10/13/78. Legislative interest — "All legislation as our interest may appear." Lobbyist — J.F. Godfrey, Forth Worth, Texas.

WEIN AIR ALASKA INC., Anchorage, Alaska. Filed for self 10/2/78. Legislative interest — "Airline deregulation bill. . . ." Lobbyist — Dennis Maconey, Anchorage, Alaska.

Energy and Environment

CONSUMER ENERGY COUNCIL OF AMERICA, Washington, D.C. Filed for self 10/31/78. Legislative interest — "All energy legislation affecting the public interest, particularly legislation affecting the pricing and supply of energy. Lobbyist — Ellen Berman, Washington, D.C.

ENERGY COOPERATIVE INC., Long Grove, Ill. Filed for self 10/24/78. Legislative interest — "Energy, fertilizer, farm cooperative, and related agricultural issues." Lobbyist — Bill Brier, Rosemary L. O'Brien, Washington, D.C.

NATIONAL AUDUBON SOCIETY, New York, N.Y. Filed for self 10/25/78. Legislative interest — "Legislation dealing with natural resource protection and conservation, HR 39, S 1500; HR 10255, S 1140; S 2899; HR 10587, S 2475; HR 8161." Lobbyist — Dr. Michael D. Zagata, Rockville, Md.; Stephen Young, Marcia Ann Graham, Washington, D.C.

SIERRA CLUB, Anchorage, Alaska. Filed for self 10/30/78. Legislative interest — ". . .Conservation legislation affecting Alaska, particularly HR 39 and S 1500, "The Alaska National Interest Land Conservation Act."

International Relations

AIRBUS INDUSTRIE, Blagnac, France. Lobbyist — DGA International Inc., Washington, D.C. Filed 10/11/78. Legislative interest — "Legislation regarding foreign commercial aircraft, Airport and Aircraft Noise Reduction Act, HR 4539; support certain aspects of bill and oppose restrictions on marketing European commercial airplanes."

GOVERNMENT OF MOROCCO, Rabat, Morocco. Lobbyist — DGA International Inc., Washington, D.C. Filed 10/17/78. Legislative interest — "Legislation regarding Morocco."

INTERNATIONAL SIX LTD., Alexandria, Va. Lobbyist — Cole Corette & Bradfield, Washington, D.C. Filed 10/18/78. Legislative interest — "Section 202, HR 13511 — Attempt to prevent enactment of provision or modify provision so that it will not be applicable to closely held leasing companies."

NERATOOM, The Hague, Holland. Filed for self 10/5/78. Legislative interest — "U.S. civilian nuclear power policies." Lobbyist — LeBoeuf, Lamb, Leiby & MacRae, Washington, D.C.

Labor Unions

NATIONAL TREASURY EMPLOYEES UNION, Washington, D.C. Filed for self 10/10/78. Legislative interest — "General legislation dealing with employment conditions, compensation, retirement, etc. of federal employees."

UNITED MINE WORKERS OF AMERICA, Washington, D.C. Filed for self 10/11/78. Legislative interest — "Promote legislation that in UMWA opinion benefits workers in the coal mining industry and conversely to oppose legislation believed to be detrimental to coal miners." Lobbyist — Michael W. Buckner, Washington, D.C.

DISABLED AMERICAN VETERANS, Cold Spring, Ky. Filed for self 10/13/78. Legislative interest — "All legislation affecting war veterans, their dependents, and survivors of deceased veterans." Lobbyist — Norman B. Hartnett, Stephen L. Edmiston, Washington, D.C.

NONCOMMISSIONED OFFICERS ASSOCIATION OF THE U.S.A. San Antonio, Texas. Filed 10/11/78. Legislative interest — "Military affairs, some veterans and Civil Service issues." Lobbyist — John R. Butz, Washington, D.C.

PARALYZED VETERANS OF AMERICA INC., Washington, D.C. Filed for self 10/4/78. Legislative interest — "Legislative matters of interest to the corporation and its subsidiaries." Lobbyist — Gerald Jones, John A. Lancaster, Washington, D.C.

State and Local Government

CENTRAL LINCOLN PEOPLE'S UTILITY DISTRICT, Newport, Oregon. Lobbyist — R. Ken Dyar, Vancouver, Wash. Filed 10/4/78. Legislative interest — "Pacific Northwest Electric Planning and Conservation Act, S 3418 and HR 13931."

MICHIGAN STATE DEMOCRATIC PARTY, Lansing, Mich. Lobbyist — Mark A. Siegel, Washington, D.C. Filed 10/10/78. Legislative interest — "HR 8533."

PITKIN COUNTY (CITY OF ASPEN), Colo. Lobbyist — Webster & Sheffield, New York, N.Y. Filed 10/10/78. Legislative interest — "HR 7971, environmental protection."

Trade Associations

AIR TRANSPORT ASSOCIATION OF AMERICA, Washington, D.C. Lobbyist — Williams & Connolly, Washington, D.C. Filed 10/10/78. Legislative interest — ". . .Noise pollution, aircraft passenger taxation, and other matters of interest to the airline industry."

AMERICAN ACADEMY OF ACTUARIES, Washington, D.C. Filed for self 10/4/78. Legislative interest — "All legislation having actuarial impact, especially in the areas of pensions, casualty, life, and health insurance." Lobbyist — Frederick D. Hunt Jr., Washington, D.C.

AMERICAN COUNCIL OF LIFE INSURANCE INC., Washington, D.C. Filed for self 10/4/78. Legislative interest — "Proposed legislation which would affect the life insurance industry." Lobbyist — A. Linwood Holton Jr., Gary E. Hughes, Robert S. McConnaughery, Ilbert Phillips, Washington, D.C.

AMERICAN FOOTWEAR INDUSTRIES ASSOCIATION, Arlington, Va. Filed for self 10/21/78. Legislative interest — "Trade related legislative issues." Lobbyist — Rena S. Pies, Arlington, Va.

AMERICAN INSURANCE ASSOCIATION, Washington, D.C. Filed for self 10/12/78. Legislative interest — "Tax legislation affecting our membership of stock property and surety companies." Lobbyist — Brenda R. Viehe-Naess, Washington, D.C.

AMERICAN RETAIL FEDERATION, Washington, D.C. Lobbyist — Patton, Boggs and Blow, Washington, D.C. Filed 10/10/78. Legislative interest — "Seeking amendments to president's tax bill — in favor of investment tax credit extension to retail structures."

AMERICAN WATERWAYS OPERATORS INC., Arlington, Va. Filed for self 10/17/78. Legislative interest — "All legislation of interest to the barge and towing industry." Lobbyist — James B. Potter Jr., Arlington, Va.

THE ASSOCIATED GENERAL CONTRACTORS OF AMERICA, Washington, D.C. Filed for self 10/23/78. Legislative interest — ". . .Measures which affect the general contracting business." Lobbyist — James H. Cromwell Sr., Washington, D.C.

CHAMBER OF COMMERCE OF THE U.S., Washington, D.C. Filed for self 10/10/78. Legislative interest — "Toxic substances legislation, cancer issues legislation, land use legislation," Lobbyist — Tatiana Roodkowsky, Washington, D.C.

CHEMICAL SPECIALTIES MANUFACTURERS ASSOCIATION, Washington, D.C. Filed for self 10/27/78. Legislative interest — " . . .Household, industrial and personal care chemical specialty products." Lobbyist — Daniel J. Cassidy, Washington, D.C.

CHICAGO BOARD OF TRADE, Chicago, Ill. Lobbyist — Davis & McLeod, Washington, D.C. Filed 10/12/78. Legislative interest — "All legislation affecting the Commodity Futures Industry."

THE CONSUMER BANKERS ASSOCIATION, Washington, D.C. Lobbyist — Baker & Daniels, Washington, D.C. Filed 10/6/78. Legislative interest — "Consumer credit legislation, S 2802, S 3156, HR 13007."

DEALER BANK ASSOCIATION, Washington, D.C. Lobbyist — Coan and Couture, Washington, D.C. Filed 10/23/78. Legislative interest — ". . .Public finance activities of members banks, specifically in support of HR 7485 and HR 8171."

DIRECT MAIL MARKETING ASSOCIATION, New York, N.Y. Filed for self 10/10/78. Legislative interest — ". . .Postal, communications, tax and privacy legislation." Lobbyist — Richard A. Barton, Washington, D.C.

EDISON ELECTRIC INSTITUTE, Washington, D.C. Filed for self 10/18/78. Legislative interest — ". . .General legislative interests." Lobbyist — Frederick K. Alderson, Washington, D.C.

FOOD MARKETING INSTITUTE, Washington, D.C. Filed for self 10/15/78. Legislative interest — . . .Consumer legislation, energy legislation, antitrust legislation, proposed amendments to the Food, Drug and Cosmetic Act, Wholesome Meat Act, Poultry Products Inspection Act, Egg Products Inspection Act, transportation legislation and packaging and labeling legislation." Lobbyist — Vicki Erickson, Washington, D.C.

INTERNATIONAL FRANCHISE ASSOCIATION, Washington, D.C. Filed for self 10/16/78. Legislative interest — "HR 5016, HR 9144, HR 11445, S 2135, . . . franchise related bills." Lobbyist — Carl E. Zwisler III, Washington, D.C.

INTERNATIONAL TAXICAB ASSOCIATION, Rockville, Md. Lobbyist — Akin, Gump, Hauer & Feld, Washington, D.C. Filed 10/6/78. Legislative interest — "Surface Transportation Act of 1978."

MANUFACTURING CHEMISTS ASSOCIATION, Washington, D.C. Filed for self 10/12/78. Legislative interest — "Safety and health legislation affecting the chemical manufacturing industry, OSHA carcinogen standards, toxic substances." Lobbyist — H. Christopher Nolde, Washington, D.C.

NATIONAL ASSOCIATION OF PENSION CONSULTANTS & ADMINISTRATORS INC., Atlanta, Ga. Filed for self 10/13/78. Legislative interest — " . . . Employee benefits, pension and welfare benefit plans, Social Security and small business, HR 4340, S 901, S 2342, S 3140 and S 3193." Lobbyist — Henkel & Lamon, Atlanta, Ga.

NATIONAL COUNCIL OF AGRICULTURAL EMPLOYERS, Washington, D.C. Filed for self 10/12/78. Legislative interest — "HR 7892, 8894, 10053, 10922, 10631, 10810 and 11250 — for; S 2467 — against." Lobbyist — Perry R. Ellsworth, Washington, D.C.

NATIONAL ELECTRICAL MANUFACTURERS ASSOCIATION, Washington, D.C. Lobbyist — Patton, Boggs & Blow, Washington, D.C. Filed 10/2/78. Legislative interest — "Promotion of legislative interests of the division generally."

NATIONAL FOOD PROCESSORS ASSOCIATION, Washington, D.C. Filed for self 10/12/78. Legislative interest — "All legislation directly affecting fruit, vegetable, seafood, and meat processing for human consumption." Lobbyist — Richard W. Murphy, Washington, D.C.

NATIONAL LIMESTONE INSTITUTE INC., Fairfax, Va. Filed for self 10/18/78. Legislative interest — "All legislation which directly or indirectly affects the interest of limestone producers." Lobbyist — Jerome J. Breiter, Fairfax, Va.

NATIONAL MOTORSPORTS COMMITTEE OF ACCUS, Washington, D.C. Filed for self 10/5/78. Legislative interest — "Legislation affecting the motorsports industry, HR 13511." Lobbyist — William C. France, Washington, D.C.

NATIONAL RURAL ELECTRIC COOPERATIVE ASSOCIATION, Washington, D.C. Filed for self 10/13/78. Legislative interest — "All legislation affecting the rural electrification program provided for under the RE Act of 1936, as amended." Lobbyist — Michael J. Molony, Washington, D.C.

NATIONAL SOCIETY OF PROFESSIONAL ENGINEERS, Washington, D.C. Filed for self 10/14/78. Legislative interest — "All legislation affecting interests of professional engineers." Lobbyist — Donald G. Weinert, Washington, D.C.

NORTH AMERICAN GAME BREEDERS AND SHOOTING PRESERVE ASSOCIATION, Gooselake, Iowa. Lobbyist — Williams & Jensen, Washington, D.C. Filed 10/23/78. Legislative interest — "Legislative matters of interest to the Association and its members."

PROFESSIONAL AIR TRAFFIC CONTROLLERS, Washington, D.C. Filed for self 10/10/78. Legislative interest — "All legislation pertaining to federal employees and specifically to air traffic controllers," HR 7292, HR 9219, HR 8503, HR 9279, HR 10." Lobbyist — Vincent J. Ferri, Washington, D.C.

SOCIETY OF AMERICAN FLORISTS, Alexandria, Va. Filed for self 10/18/78. Legislative interest — "All legislation affecting the floral industry, retail, wholesale and grower." Lobbyist — Timothy F. Burns, Alexandria, Va.

SOCIETY OF AMERICAN WOOD PRESERVERS INC., Arlington, Va. Filed for self 10/16/78. Legislative interest — "Environmental issues, construction/housing, product liability, labor, OSHA legislation, business regulation, forestry and timber supply, S 1874 — opposed; S 2 — support; S 1264 — support." Lobbyist — E. David Lewis, Arlington, Va.

SOUTHERN FURNITURE MANUFACTURERS ASSOCIATION, Washington, D.C. Filed for self 10/28/78. Legislative interest — "All matters pertaining to the furniture industry." Lobbyist — M. Elizabeth Powell, Washington, D.C.

WESTERN FUELS ASSOCIATION INC., Washington, D.C. Lobbyist — Duncan, Brown, Weinberg & Palmer, Washington, D.C. Filed 10/12/78. Legislative interest — "Endangered Species Act of 1978, HR 14104."

Miscellaneous

AD HOC LOW INCOME HOUSING COALITION, Washington, D.C. Filed for self 10/26/78. Legislative interest — "Increased quality and scope of programs providing housing for low income Americans, HR 12433 and S 3084, HR 12936." Lobbyist — Cushing N. Dolbeare, Washington, D.C.

AGENCY FOR INSTRUCTIONAL TELEVISION, Bloomington, Ind. Filed for self 10/2/78. Legislative interest — " . . . Uses of telecommunications for education, HR 15 and S 1753. . . ." Lobbyist — Edwin G. Cohen, Chalmers H. Marquis, Bloomington, Ind.

BUSINESS & PROFESSIONAL WOMEN'S CLUBS INC., Washington, D.C. Lobbyist — Cook & Henderson, Washington, D.C. Filed 10/30/78. Legislative interest — " . . . Validity of a state rescinding ratification of a constitutional amendment."

CHILD WELFARE LEAGUE OF AMERICA, Washington, D.C. Lobbyist — American Parents Committee, Washington, D.C. Filed 10/25/78. Legislative interest — "International Development Assistance Authorization and Appropriations HR 12222, Adolescent Pregnancy and Prevention Act, S 2910; Title X of the Public Health Services Act, HR 12370."

ROBERT D. GORDON, Bryans Road, Md. Filed for self 10/26/78. Legislative interest — "Legislation affecting police officers."

EDWARD J. KIERNAN, Congers, N.Y. Filed for self 10/26/78. Legislative interest — "Legislation affecting police officers."

KRIVIT & KRIVIT, Washington, D.C. Lobbyist — Dewey, Ballantine, Bushby, Palmer & Wood, Washington, D.C. Filed 10/3/78. Legislative interest — "Comprehensive Employment and Training Amendment of 1978, HR 12452."

NATIONAL HOUSING CONFERENCE INC., Washington, D.C. Lobbyist — Coan and Couture, Washington, D.C. Filed 10/23/78. Legislative interest — " . . . Housing and community development, HR 6655 and S 1523."

ZYGMUNT J. B. PLATER, Ann Arbor, Mich. Filed for Self 10/3/78. Legislative interest —"Conservation—endangered species."

PUEBLO OF ZIA, San Ysidro, N.M. Lobbyist — Rebecca D. Shapiro & Associates, Washington, D.C. Filed 10/10/78. Legislative interest — "HR 10240, S 2358, land for the Zia Pueblo, for."

THE ST. LOUIS MERCANTILE LIBRARY, St. Louis, Mo. Filed for self 10/13/78. Legislative interest — "To amend Internal Revenue Code of 1954 to treat as public charities certain institutions which operate libraries, S 3465 and HR 13951, for both bills." Lobbyists — John L. Davidson Jr.; Lewis, Rice, Tucker, Allen & Chubb, St. Louis, Mo.

UNION MINES, New York, N.Y. Lobbyist — Beveridge, Fairbanks & Diamond, Washington, D.C. Filed 10/12/78. Legislative interest — " . . . Disposal and storage of uranium mill tailings, S 3078."

LOBBY REGISTRATION INDEX

A

Associated Gas Distributors - 14-D, 35-D
Associated General Contractors of America - 12-D, 14-D, 25-D, 44-D
Associated Industries of Florida - 14-D
Associated Third Class Mail Users - 14-D
Association of American Chambers of Commerce, Europe and Mediterranean Inc. - 15-D
Association of American Railroads - 5-D, 25-D
Association of American Veterinary Medical Colleges - 6-D
Association of Executive Recruiting Consultants Inc. - 14-D
Association of General Merchandise Chains - 14-D
Association of Independent Corrugated Converters - 14-D
Association of Maximum Service Telecasters Inc. - 42-D
Association of Northeastern Veterans Counseling Organizations - 24-D
Association of Oil Pipe Lines - 14-D
Aste, George A. - 13-D
Atkinson, Carl E. - 13-D
Atlantic Container Line - 37-D
Atlantic Richfield Co. - 33-D
Atlas Minerals - 33-D
Auger, Allan - 33-D
Ault, Frank M. - 4-D
Austin, John D. Jr. - 9-D
Australian Meat and Livestock Corp. - 24-D
Automotive Parts & Accessories Association - 6-D
Avco Corp. - 22-D
Avon Products Inc. - 8-D
Ayres, Richard E. - 3-D

B

Bache Halsey Stuart Shields Inc. - 33-D
Baker & Daniels
Consumer Bankers Association - 44-D
Independent Refiners Association of America - 9-D
Baker, Hostetler, Frost & Towers
Sun Co. Inc. - 27-D
Baker & McKenzie
Cambridge Research and Development Group - 42-D
Magnatex Corp. - 33-D
Balcor Co. - 2-D
Baldwin, Donald - 22-D
Balk-Tusa, Jacqueline - 22-D
Baltimore Gas & Electric Co. - 40-D
Bankamerica Corp. - 3-D
Bannister, Robert D. - 36-D
Barber, Will G. - 26-D
Barbour, Dennis J. - 41-D
Barcklow, Benjamin E. - 18-D
Barker, C.A. Jr. - 8-D
Barnard, John H. Jr. - 8-D
Barnard, Roger H. - 6-D
Barnes, Richardson & Colburn - 17-D
Meat Importers Council of America - 36-D
Barnett, Alagia & Carey
Florida Fruit and Vegetable Association - 35-D
Barnett, Larry P. - 20-D
Barret, Smith, Schapiro, Simon & Armstrong
New York State Urban Development Corp. - 43-D
Barstis, Leonard - 23-D
Barthelmy, Eileen - 34-D
Barton, Richard A. - 35-D, 45-D
Baskahegan Co. - 30-D
Basin Inc. - 16-D
Battle, Fowler, Jaffin, Pierce & Kneel
State Troopers Fraternal Association of New Jersey Inc. - 28-D
Battle, Frank V. Jr. - 33-D
Batzell, Nunn & Bode
Martin Oil Service - 4-D
Baxter, James R. - 25-D
Baybanks Inc. - 43-D
Bayh, Marvella - 18-D
Beacon Oil Co. - 19-D
Beam, Bruce A. - 43-D
Beard, Michael K. - 16-D
Beatty, George W. - 43-D
Bechtel Corp - 3-D, 27-D
Bechtel Power Corp. - 8-D
Beer, Boltz & Bennia
City of Pontiac, Mich. - 28-D
Beers, John R. - 28-D
Beers, Robert M. - 15-D
Belco Petroleum Corp. - 16-D
Belikoff, Stephen M. - 43-D
Bell, Howard H. - 28-D, 35-D
Bendix Corp. - 3-D, 8-D
Benjamin, Kim A. - 35-D, 39-D
Bennett, Douglas P. - 9-D, 14-D, 15-D, 27-D
Bennett, James M. - 24-D
Berg, Harvey Marshall - 15-D
Berick, David - 24-D
Berlack, Israels & Liberman
Public Service Electric and Gas Co. - 20-D
Berman & Associates
CNA Financial Corp. - 12-D
Unicare Services Inc. - 34-D
Berman, Ellen - 44-D
Berman, William R. - 10-D
Bernstein, George K. - 5-D
Berry, Epstein, Sandstrom & Blatchford
Committee to Assure the Availability of Casein - 37-D
Constructora Nacional de Carros de Ferrocarril - 34-D
Great Western Sugar Co. - 33-D
National Pest Control Association - 6-D
Bessemer Securities Corp. - 40-D
Beveridge, Fairbanks & Diamond
Alaska Movers Association - 14-D
Florida Power & Light Co. - 33-D
International Paper Inc. - 10-D
Moving and Storage Association of Hawaii - 14-D
New England Fish Co. - 34-D
Union Mines - 46-D
Beverly, Robert C. - 5-D
Bi-a-robi - 3-D
Bierman, Eileen M. - 26-D
Biery, Tom - 36-D
Billig, Sher & Jones
Adherence Group Inc. - 21-D
Billock, Sarah M. - 39-D
Bingham, Dana & Gould
First National Bank of Boston - 12-D
Birch, Horton, Bittner & Monroe
American Kitchen Foods Inc. - 43-D
Calista Corp. - 10-D
Coastal States Gas Corp. - 4-D
Global Seafoods Inc. - 23-D
Potlatch Corp. - 43-D
Bird, Robert - 27-D, 34-D
Birmingham, City of - 17-D
Bishop, H. Radford - 19-D
Bixby Ranch Co. - 33-D
Blackwood, Kristine - 29-D, 30-D
Blake, Barbara A. - 39-D
Blanchette, Robert W. - 17-D, 18-D
Blevins, Michael K. - 21-D
Block, L. Thomas - 8-D
Blue Ribbon Sports - 19-D
Blum, Jared O. - 14-D
Blum, Parker & Nash
Association of Independent Corrugated Converters - 14-D
Independent Gasoline Marketers Council - 9-D
Mt. Airy Refining Co. - 10-D
National Union Electric Corp. - 38-D
New York Mercantile Exchange - 32-D
Board of Trade Clearing Corp. - 12-D, 16-D, 18-D, 22-D, 30-D
Bode, Carolyn - 30-D
Bodner, Seth M. - 18-D
Boeing Co. - 3-D, 30-D
Boeing Vertol Co. - 12-D
Bohner, Christie K. - 33-D
Boise Cascade Corp. - 22-D
Bolivia, Embassy of - 31-D
Bolton, M. Warren - 43-D
Bonitt, Jay - 8-D
Bonneville Associates Inc.
Vranesh and Muslick - 7-D
Western Regional Council - 26-D
Bonsib Inc. - 16-D
Botsford, Charles G. - 33-D
Bourdette, Mary M. - 4-D
Bowes, T.L. - 21-D
Bowling Proprietors Associations of America - 42-D
Bowman, Edward - 16-D
Bowman, Randal - 12-D
Boyd, Francis J. Jr. - 11-D
Boyden, Kennedy, Romney & Howard
Hopi Indian Tribe - 7-D
Northwest Pipeline Co. - 41-D
Boykin, Sheila H. - 29-D
Bradley, David A. - 42-D
Bragg, Raymond F. Jr. - 28-D
Bregman, Abell, Solter & Kay
American Car Rental Association - 39-D
American Psychiatric Association - 28-D, 31-D
Truck Renting and Leasing Association - 39-D
Breiter, Jerome J. - 45-D
Bresee, Miles H. Jr. - 8-D
Bridgeport, Conn., City of - 28-D
Brier, Bill - 44-D
Brinson, Sheryl - 16-D
Brooklyn Union Gas Co. - 12-D
Brooks, Dale E. - 27-D
Brown, Gary A. - 36-D
Brown, Richard A. - 13-D
Brown, Vincent D. - 14-D
Brownstein, Zeidman, Schomer & Chase
Imperial Resources Association - 14-D
Brunner, Michael E. - 11-D
Brunson, John S. - 42-D
Brunswick Corp. - 40-D
Brush, Harvey F. - 8-D
Bryant, Margaret - 3-D
Buckingham Township Supervisor - 24-D
Buckner, Michael E. - 44-D
Buffalo Broadcasting Co. Inc. - 30-D
Building Owners and Managers Association International - 6-D
Bulova Watch Co. Inc. - 43-D
Bundesverband Deutscher Banken - 35-D
Bureau of National Affairs - 27-D, 38-D
Burgess, Quentin L. - 40-D
Burlington Northern Inc. - 10-D, 38-D
Burns, Timothy F. - 45-D
Burr, Pease & Kurtz Inc.
Eklutna Inc. - 33-D
Burson-Marsteller
Gould Inc. - 41-D
Burzio, John M. - 14-D
Bush, Nicholas J. - 12-D
Bushnell, Gary - 33-D
Business and Professional Women's Clubs Inc. - 45-D
Business Roundtable - 11-D, 25-D
Butler, Binion, Rice, Cook & Knapp
Seatrain Lines Inc. - 20-D
Butler, Kenneth W. - 35-D
Butz, John R. - 44-D
Byrnes, John W. - 37-D

C

CBS Inc. - 27-D
CENEX (Farmers Union Central Exchange Inc.) - 12-D
Cadwalader, Wickersham & Taft
Amex Commodities Exchange Inc. - 22-D
International Paper Co. - 41-D
Mocatta Metals Corp. - 17-D
Cain, Morrison G. - 25-D
Caldwell, C. Wickliffe - 24-D
Caldwell, Charles D. - 24-D
Calhoun, Frank W. - 12-D
California & Hawaii Sugar Co. - 3-D
California Planting Cotton Seed Distributors - 40-D
California Savings & Loan League - 25-D
Calista Corp. - 10-D
Calloway, James R. - 38-D
Calorie Control Council - 9-D
Calvert, Gordon L. - 6-D
Cambridge Research and Development Group - 42-D
Camden, N.J., City of - 28-D
Camp, Carmouche, Palmer, Barsh & Hunter
ACLI International Inc. - 40-D
Campbell, Jerry L. - 15-D
Campbell Soup Co. - 27-D
Canaday, Alyce D. - 13-D
Capital Formation Through Dividend Reinvestment - 21-D
Capitol Hill Hospital - 32-D
Caplin & Drysdale
American Family Life Assurance Co. of Georgia - 40-D
Clark Oil & Refining Corp. - 41-D
Capps, Milton F. - 24-D, 33-D, 42-D
Capron, Charles E. - 21-D
Caraco, Isaac R. - 8-D
Carborundum Co. - 22-D, 30-D
Carella, Bain, Gilfillan & Rhodes
Wagner Electric Corp. - 20-D
Cargile, Joe - 11-D
Cargill Inc. - 12-D
Carl Byoir & Associates Inc. - 40-D
Carlson, Peter - 9-D
Carnegie Corp. of New York - 15-D
Carr, John L. - 19-D
Carte, Harlon B. - 40-D
Casey, Lane & Mittendorf
Wabanex Energy Corp. Ltd. - 24-D
Casey, Robert J. - 21-D
Cashman, Eugene C. - 7-D, 9-D
Cassidy, Daniel J. - 44-D
Cast Iron Pipe Research Association - 14-D
Castle, Rita L. - 12-D
Caterpillar Tractor Co. - 3-D, 12-D, 30-D
Center for the Study of Congress - 3-D
Centex Corp. - 8-D
Central American Pipeline Co. - 3-D
Central Lincoln People's Utility District - 44-D
Central and Southwest Corp. - 3-D

Certainteed Corp. - 12-D, 22-D
Chain Saw Manufacturers Association - 11-D
Chajet, Henry - 35-D
Chamber of Commerce of the U. S. - 11-D, 14-D, 18-D, 25-D, 31-D, 35-D, 44-D
Chamberlin, R.S. - 16-D
Champion International Corp. - 8-D
Champlin Petroleum Co. - 22-D, 25-D
Champlin, Steven M. - 31-D
Chapman, Duff & Paul
Bundesverband Deutscher Banken - 35-D
Charls E. Walker Associates Inc. - 42-D
Allegheny Airlines Inc. - 22-D
American Airlines Inc. - 16-D
Eastern Airlines Inc. - 16-D
Getty Oil - 30-D
Hughes Airwest - 23-D
ITT - 30-D
Pan American World Airways Inc. - 17-D
Piedmont Airlines - 24-D
Trans World Airlines Inc. - 17-D
Chase, Seymour M. - 22-D
Cheek, Leslie III - 16-D
Chemical Specialties Manufacturers Association - 44-D
Cherokee Nation - 26-D
Chevron U.S.A. Inc. - 27-D
Cheyenne River Sioux Tribe - 26-D
Chiapetta, Vanessa L. - 32-D
Chicago Board of Trade - 9-D, 44-D
Chicago Community Trust - 40-D
Chicago Mercantile Exchange - 12-D
Chicago Metropolitan Higher Education Council et. al. - 15-D
Chicoine, Yvonne - 2-D
Child Welfare League of America - 42-D, 45-D
China, Republic of - 34-D
Chippewa-Cree Tribe - 26-D
Chromalloy American Corp. - 4-D, 27-D
Chunn, Donald T. - 43-D
Churchman, Julia - 24-D, 28-D, 34-D
Ciba-Geigy Corp. - 33-D
Cigar, Association of America Inc. - 21-D
Citibank, N.A. - 16-D
Cities Service Co. - 8-D, 33-D
Cities Services Gas Co. - 4-D
Citizens Committee for the Right to Keep and Bear Arms - 11-D
Citizens for Government Fairness - 10-D
Citizens for Management of Alaska Lands - 7-D, 11-D, 22-D
Citizens for Tax Reform in 1978 Inc. - 22-D
Citronelle-Mobile Gathering Co. - 30-D
City of Birmingham - 17-D
City of Bridgeport, Conn. - 28-D
City of Camden, N.J. - 28-D
City of Detroit, Mich. - 28-D
City of Northglen, Ohio - 31-D
City of Pontiac, Mich. - 28-D
Cladouhos & Brashares
International Processors - 38-D
Clark, Anne H. - 42-D
Clark, Betty J. - 31-D
Clark Oil & Refining Corp. - 41-D
Clarke, Jean M. - 29-D
Clarken, William F. - 18-D
Clay, A. Stephens - 31-D
Clearfield Bituminous Coal Corp. - 10-D
Cleary, Gottlieb, Steen & Hamilton
Time Critical Shipment Committee - 29-D
Clements, Frank - 8-D
Cleveland, Marcia - 11-D
Client-Project Orbis Inc. - 26-D
Clifford, Glass, McIlwain & Finney
Australian Meat and Live-Stock Corp. - 24-D
Avco Corp. - 22-D
Proprietary Association - 29-D
Cliffside Corp. - 9-D
CNA Financial Corp. - 12-D
Coalition for New York Inc. - 16-D, 18-D, 32-D
Coan & Couture
Dealer Bank Association - 45-D
National Housing Conference Inc. - 45-D
Coan, Carl A.S. - 6-D
Coastal States Gas Corp. - 4-D
Coddington, Lynn - 16-D
Coffey, Sharon West - 10-D
Cohen, Edwin G. - 45-D
Cohen, Leonard - 24-D
Cohen, Lynne R. - 33-D
Cohen & Uretz
Estate of Sylvia S. Buring - 29-D
Wometco Enterprise Inc. - 13-D
Cole, Corette & Bradfield
American Express Co. - 8-D
International Six Ltd. - 44-D
Cole, Michael P. - 8-D
Colley, William J. - 6-D, 15-D
Collier, Shannon, Rill, Edwards & Scott
Allegheny Ludlum Industries Inc. - 33-D
Society of Independent Gasoline Marketers of America - 21-D
Republic of China - 34-D
Tanners' Council of America Inc. - 36-D
United States Fastener Manufacturing Group - 26-D
Collins, Bruce - 15-D
Collins, Charles P. - 38-D
Collins, George - 20-D
Columbia, Government of - 20-D
Colt Industries Inc. - 33-D, 43-D
Colvin, Richard - 26-D
Combined Insurance Co. of America - 19-D
Commercial Law League of America - 6-D
Commodity Exchange Inc. - 8-D
Common Cause - 3-D, 16-D, 18-D, 22-D, 29-D, 32-D, 40-D
Commonwealth Edison Co. - 22-D
Commonwealth of Puerto Rico - 25-D
Communications Attorney Service - 11-D
Communications Lobby Service - 11-D
Communications Satellite Corp. - 41-D
Community Antenna Television Association Inc. - 14-D
Community Nutrition Institute - 26-D
Community Service Society - 21-D
Conafay, Stephen R. - 24-D
Concerned Citizens Against the Panama Canal Give-Away - 22-D
Congaree Limited Partnership - 15-D
Congress Watch - 40-D
Conlan, John B. - 32-D
Connecticut Petroleum Council - 11-D
Conner, Stephen N. - 24-D
Conset - 26-D
Consolidation Coal Co. - 16-D
Consolidated Natural Gas Co. - 19-D
Constructora Nacional de Carros de Ferrocarril - 24-D, 34-D
Consumer Action Now - 7-D, 19-D, 29-D, 42-D
Consumer Bankers Association - 44-D
Consumer Energy Council - 44-D
Consumer Federation of America - 29-D
Conticommodity Services Inc. - 21-D, 33-D
Continental Airlines Inc. - 10-D
Continental Group Inc.- 30-D
Continental Oil Co. - 4-D
Contratto, Dana - 14-D
Control Data Corp. - 43-D
Conway, John T. - 41-D
Cook & Henderson
Aleutian/Pribilof Islands Association Inc. - 21-D
Business and Professional Women's Clubs Inc. - 45-D
Consolidated Natural Gas Co. - 19-D
Food Distributors Task Force - 21-D
Resource Associates of Alaska - 34-D
Time-Critical Shipment Committee - 37-D
Cook, J.C. - 42-D
Cook, K. Richard - 41-D
Cook, Reuf, Spann & Weiser Inc. - 33-D, 42-D
Royal Embassy of Saudi Arabia - 27-D
Cook, Robert M. - 28-D
Cooke, Charles E. - 4-D
Cooney, Edward - 27-D
Cooper, Benjamin Y. - 36-D
Corbin, Paul - 13-D
Corcoran, Patrick H. - 14-D
Cordon & Jacon
Buffalo Broadcasting Co. Inc. - 30-D
Corey, Samuel C. - 43-D
Corey, Samuel C. Jr. - 43-D
Corn, Bennett J. - 31-D
Corrigan, Richard L. - 35-D
Cosmetic, Toiletry and Fragrance Association Inc. - 14-D
Coston, Sr. Carol - 32-D
Cosse, Clark L. III - 11-D
Coughlin, Daniel T. - 24-D
Council of Active Independent Oil & Gas Producers - 6-D
Council of American-Flag Ship Operators - 25-D
Council for Inter-American Security - 6-D
Council for a Livable World - 13-D
Council of Vietnam Veterans - 31-D
Coushatta Tribe of Louisiana - 7-D
Cousins, James - 25-D
Covington & Burling
American Watch Association - 35-D
Anchor National Life Insurance Co. - 27-D
Association of Maximum Service Telecasters Inc. - 42-D
Campbell Soup Co. - 27-D
Interbank Card Association - 21-D
Lydall Inc. - 38-D
Cowley, Douglas A. - 25-D
Cox, C. Bryan - 4-D
Cox, Langford & Brown
National Collegiate Athletic Association - 18-D
Cox, R.L. - 38-D
Coxson, Harold P. - 31-D
Crain, Judith L. - 6-D
Cramer, Haber & Becker
Norman, Lawrence, Patterson & Farrell - 9-D
Cramer, Visser, Lipsen & Smith
American Sign and Indicator Corp. - 16-D
Institute of Signage Research - 25-D
Northwest Alaska Pipeline Co. - 41-D
Crapple, George E. - 33-D
Credit Union National Association Inc. - 25-D
Crewe, William P. - 3-D
Cromwell, James H. Sr. - 44-D
Cromwell, Sally F. - 10-D
Crum & Foster Corp. - 16-D
Cubie, James M. - 32-D
Cudahy, Richard D. - 3-D
Culp, Dwyer, Guterson & Grader
Pacific Northwest Utilities Conference Committee - 9-D
Cutler, Jay B. - 5-D

D

DECQ Committee - 32-D
DGA International Inc.
Airbus Industrie - 44-D
Government of Morocco - 44-D
Thomson-CSF - 8-D
DK Consultants Inc.
Aberrant Behavior Center - 18-D
Damgard, John M. - 3-D
Damon Corp. - 4-D
Dalton, Eugene B. - 17-D
Daly, John J. - 9-D
Daniel J. Edelman Inc.
Alaska Airlines - 30-D
Daniels, Houlihan & Palmeter
Associacao Brasileira de Productores de Ferro Ligas - 20-D
Industrial Fasteners Group - 28-D
Danzansky, Dickey, Tydings, Quint & Gordon
Government of the State of Antigua - 7-D
Japan Atomic Industrial Forum - 10-D
Darden, William H. - 17-D
Dauber, Milton A. - 15-D
Davan, Clarence - 33-D
David L. Babson & Co. Inc.
Investment Counsel Association of America - 36-D
Davidson, John L. - 45-D
Davis & McLeod
Chicago Board of Trade - 44-D
Davis, Thomas A. - 7-D, 43-D
Davis, Thomas N. - 6-D
Dawson, Riddell, Taylor, Davis & Holyrod
American Bus Association - 5-D
Hormel Foundation, The - 4-D
Virgin Islands Gift Fashion Shop Association - 17-D
Day, J. Edward - 14-D
Dead River Co. - 30-D
Dealer Bank Association - 6-D, 45-D
Deaver & Hannaford Inc.
National Venture Capital Association - 9-D
deBlois, Michael P. - 6-D
Debrodt, Robert D. - 7-D
DeHart Associates Inc.
Recording Industry Association of America Inc. - 36-D
DeKalb Agricultural Research Inc. - 33-D, 43-D
deKieffer & Associates
Department of Information, Republic of South Africa - 13-D
DeLaney & Patrick
Cargill Inc. - 12-D
Dynamic Instrument Corp. - 23-D
Getty Oil Co. - 8-D
DeLaMater, Stephen T. - 30-D
DeLapp, Myra J. - 24-D
Delhi International Oil Corp. - 12-D
DeLoss, Garry J. - 3-D
Delta Airlines Inc. - 23-D
Dempsey, Bradford T. - 39-D, 42-D
Department of Information, Republic of South Africa - 13-D
Department for Professional Employees - 10-D
Detroit Edison Co. - 38-D
Detroit, Mich., City of - 28-D
Deutsche Bank AG - 13-D
Devaney, Dennis M. - 6-D
DeVaney, John M. - 9-D
Devine, James T. - 24-D
Dewey, Ballantine, Bushby, Palmer & Wood

N

O

P

Q

R

U

V

XYZ

PRESIDENTIAL MESSAGES

CQ

Jimmy Carter's State of the Union Message

Following is the White House transcript of President Carter's State of the Union address, as delivered to a joint session of Congress Jan. 19, 1978:

Thank you very much.

Mr. President, Mr. Speaker, Members of the 95th Congress, ladies and gentlemen:

Two years ago today we had the first Caucus in Iowa and one year ago tomorrow, I walked from here to the White House to take up the duties of President of the United States. I didn't know it then when I walked, but I have been trying to save energy ever since. I return tonight to fulfill one of those duties of the Constitution: To "give to the Congress"—and to the Nation—"information on the state of the Union."

Militarily, politically, economically and in spirit, the state of our Union is sound.

We are a great country, a strong country, a vital and a dynamic country—and so we will remain.

We are a confident people and a hard-working people, a decent and a compassionate people—and so we will remain.

I want to speak to you tonight about where we are and where we must go, about what we have done and what we must do. And I want to pledge to you my best efforts and ask you to pledge yours.

Each generation of Americans has to face circumstances not of its own choosing, but by which its character is measured and its spirit is tested.

There are times of emergency, when a nation and its leaders must bring their energies to bear on a single urgent task. That was a duty Abraham Lincoln faced when our land was torn apart by conflict in the War Between the States. That was the duty faced by Franklin Roosevelt when he led America out of an economic depression and again when he led America to victory in war.

There are other times when there is no single overwhelming crisis—yet profound national interests are at stake.

At such times the risk of inaction can be equally great. It becomes the task of leaders to call forth the vast and restless energies of our people to build for the future.

That is what Harry Truman did in the years after the Second World War, when we helped Europe and Japan rebuild themselves and secured an international order that has protected freedom from aggression.

We live in such time now—and we face such duties.

We have come through a long period of turmoil and doubt, but we have once again found our moral course and with a new spirit, we are striving to express our best instincts to the rest of the world.

There is all across our land, a growing sense of peace and a sense of common purpose. This sense of unity cannot be expressed in programs or in legislation, or in dollars.

It is an achievement that belongs to every individual American. This unity ties together and it towers over all our efforts here in Washington, and it serves as an inspiring beacon for all of us who are elected to serve. This new atmosphere demands a new spirit, a partnership between those of us who lead and those who elect. The foundations of this partnership are truth, the courage to face hard decisions; concern for one another and the common good over special interests; and a basic faith and trust in the wisdom and strength and judgment of the American people.

For the first time in a generation, we are not haunted by a major international crisis or by domestic turmoil, and we now have a rare and a priceless opportunity to address persistent problems and burdens which come to us as a Nation—quietly and steadily getting worse over the years.

As President, I have had to ask you—the Members of Congress, and you, the American people—to come to grips with some of the most difficult and hard questions facing our society.

We must make a maximum effort—because if we do not aim for the best, we are very likely to achieve little.

I see no benefit to the country if we delay because the problems will only get worse.

We need patience and good will, but we really need to realize that there is a limit to the role and the function of government.

Government cannot solve all our problems, it can't set our goals, it cannot define our vision. Government cannot eliminate poverty, or provide a bountiful economy or reduce inflation or save our cities or cure illiteracy or provide energy, and government cannot mandate goodness. Only a true partnership between government and the people can ever hope to reach these goals.

Those of us who govern can sometimes inspire, and we can identify needs and marshal resources, but we simply cannot be the managers of everything and everybody.

We here in Washington must move away from crisis management, and we must establish clear goals for the immediate future and the distant future which will let us work together and not in conflict.

Never again should we neglect a growing crisis like the shortage of energy, where further delay will only lead to more harsh and painful solutions.

Every day we spend more than $120 million for foreign oil. This slows our economic growth. It lowers the value of the dollar overseas, and it aggravates unemployment and inflation here at home.

Now we know what we must do, increase production—

We must cut down on waste. And we must use more of those fuels which are plentiful and more permanent.

We must be fair to people and we must not disrupt our Nation's economy and our budget.

Now that sounds simple. But I recognize the difficulties involved. I know that it is not easy for the Congress to act. But the fact remains that on the energy legislation, we have failed the American people. Almost five years after the oil embargo dramatized the problem for us all, we still do not have a national energy program.

Not much longer can we tolerate this stalemate. It undermines our national interest both at home and abroad. We must succeed, and I believe we will.

Our main task at home this year, with energy a central element, is the Nation's economy. We must continue the recovery and further cut unemployment and inflation.

Last year was a good one for the United States. We reached all of our major economic goals for 1977. Four million new jobs were created—an all-time record—and the number of unemployed dropped by more than a million. Unemployment right now is the lowest it has been since 1974, and not since World War II has such a high percentage of American people been employed.

The rate of inflation went down. There was a good growth in business profits and investments, the source of more jobs for our workers, and a higher standard of living for all our people. After taxes and inflation, there was a healthy increase in workers' wages.

This year, our country will have the first two trillion dollar economy in the history of the world.

Now we are proud of this progress the first year, but we must do even better in the future.

We still have serious problems on which all of us must work together. Our trade deficit is too large. Inflation is still too high, and too many Americans still do not have a job. Now, I didn't have any simple answers for all these problems. But we have developed an economic policy that is working, because it is simple, balanced and fair. It is based on four principles:

First, the economy must keep on expanding to produce new jobs and better income which our people need. The fruits of growth must be widely shared. More jobs must be made available to those who have been by-passed until now, and the tax system must be made fairer and simpler.

Secondly, private business and not the government must lead the expansion in the future.

Third, we must lower the rate of inflation and keep it down. Inflation slows down economic growth, and it is the most cruel to the poor and also to the elderly and others who live on fixed incomes.

And fourth, we must contribute to the strength of the world economy.

I will announce detailed proposals for improving our tax system later this week. We can make our tax laws fairer, we can make them simpler and easier to understand; and at the same time, we can—and we will—reduce the tax burden on American citizens by $25 billion.

The tax reforms and the tax reductions go together. Only with the long overdue reforms will the full tax cut be advisable.

Almost $17 billion in income tax cuts **will go to individuals. Ninety-six per cent** of all American taxpayers will see their taxes go down. For a typical family of four, this means an annual saving of more than $250 a year, or a tax reduction of about 20 per cent.

A further $2 billion cut in excise taxes will give more relief and also contribute directly to lowering the rate of inflation.

We will also provide strong additional incentives for business investment and growth through substantial cuts in the corporate tax rates and improvement in the investment tax credit.

These tax proposals will increase opportunity everywhere in the Nation. But additional jobs for the disadvantaged deserve special attention.

We have already passed laws to assure equal access to the voting booth, and to restaurants, and to schools, to housing; and laws to permit access to jobs. But job opportunity—the chance to earn a decent living—is also a basic human right which we cannot and will not ignore.

A major priority for our Nation is the final elimination of the barriers that restrict the opportunities available to women, and also to black people, Hispanics and other minorities. We have come a long way toward that goal. But there is still more to do.

What we inherited from the past must not be permitted to shackle us in the future.

I will be asking you for a substantial increase in funds for public jobs for our young people, and I also am recommending that the Congress continue the Public Service Employment Programs at more than twice the level of a year ago.

When welfare reform is completed, we will have more than a million additional jobs so that those on welfare who are able to work can work.

However, again, we know that in our free society, private business is still the best source of new jobs.

Therefore, I will propose a new program to encourage businesses to hire young and disadvantaged Americans. Those people only need skills and a chance, in order to take their place in our economic system. Let's give them the chance they need.

A major step in the right direction would be the early passage of a greatly improved Humphrey-Hawkins Bill.

My budget for 1979 addresses these national needs, but it is lean and tight. I have cut waste wherever possible.

I am proposing an increase of less than 2 per cent after adjusting for inflation—the smallest increase in the Federal budget in four years.

Lately, Federal spending has taken a steadily increasing portion of what Americans produce. Our new budget reverses that trend, and later I hope to bring the Government's toll down even further. And with your help, we will do that.

In time of high employment and a strong economy, deficit spending should not be a feature of our budget.

As the economy continues to gain strength and as our unemployment rates continue to fall, revenues will grow. With careful planning, efficient management and proper restraint on spending, we can move rapidly toward a balanced budget—and we will.

Next year the budget deficit will be only slightly less than this year. But one-third of the deficit is due to the necessary tax cuts that I have proposed. This year the right choice is to reduce the burden on taxpayers and provide more jobs for our people.

The third element in our program is a renewed attack on inflation. We have learned the hard way that high unemployment will not prevent or cure inflation. **Government can help us by stimulating private investment and by maintaining a responsible economic policy. Through a new top level review process, we will do a better job of reducing government regulation that drives up costs and drives up prices.**

But again, government alone cannot bring down the rate of inflation. When a level of high inflation is expected to continue, then companies raise prices to protect their profit margins against the prospective increases in wages and other costs; while workers demand higher wages as protection against the expected price increases. It's like an escalation in the arms race, and understandably, no one wants to disarm alone.

Voluntary Anti-inflation Program

No one firm or a group of workers can halt this process. It is an effort that we must all make together. I am therefore asking government, business, labor, and other groups to join in a voluntary program to moderate inflation by holding wage and price increases in each sector of the economy during 1978 below the average increases of the last two years.

I do not believe in wage and price controls. **A sincere commitment to voluntary constraints provides a way, perhaps the only way to fight inflation without government interference.**

As I came into the Capitol tonight, I saw the farmers, my fellow farmers, standing out in the snow. I am familiar with their problem and I know from Congress' action that you are, too. When I was running Carter's Warehouse, we had spread on our own farms five, ten, fifteen fertilizers for about $40 a ton. The last time I was home, the price was about $100 a ton. The cost of nitrogen has gone up 150 per cent, and the price of products that farmers sell has either stayed the same or gone down a little. Now this past year in 1977, you the Congress and I together passed a new Agricultural Act. It went into effect October 1. It will have its first impact on the 1978 crops. It will help a great deal. It will add $8.5 billion or more to help the farmers with their price supports and target prices.

Last year we had the highest level of exports of farm products in the history of our country, $24 billion. We expect to have more this year. We will be working together. But I think it is incumbent on us to monitor very carefully the farm situation and continue to work harmoniously with the farmers of our country. What is best for the farmer, the farm families, in the long run is best for the consumers of our country.

Economic success at home is also the key to success in our international economic policy. An effective energy program, strong investment and productivity and controlled inflation will improve our trade balance and balance it, and it will help to protect the integrity of the dollar overseas.

By working closely with our friends abroad, we can promote the economic health of the whole world. With fair and balanced agreements lowering the barriers to trade.

Despite the inevitable pressures that build up when the world economy suffers from high unemployment, we must firmly resist the demands for self-defeating protectionism. But free trade must also be fair **trade. And I am determined to protect the American industry and American workers against the foreign trade practices which are unfair or illegal.**

In a separate written message to Congress, I have outlined other domestic initiatives, such as welfare reform, consumer protection, basic education skills, urban policy, reform of our labor laws and national health care later on this year. I will not repeat those tonight. But there are several other points that I would like to make directly to you.

During these past years, Americans have seen our government grow far from us.

Government Reorganization

For some citizens the government has almost become like a foreign country, so strange and distant that we have often had to deal with it through trained ambassadors who have sometimes become too powerful and too influential—lawyers, accountants and lobbyists. This cannot go on.

We must have what Abraham Lincoln wanted, a government for the people.

We have made progress toward that kind of government. You have given me the authority requested to reorganize the Federal bureaucracy. And I am using that authority.

We have already begun a series of reorganization plans which will be completed over a period of three years. We have also proposed abolishing almost 500 Federal advisory and other commissions and boards. But I know that the American people are still sick and tired of Federal **paperwork and red tape. Bit by bit we are chopping down the thicket of unnecessary Federal regulations by which government too often interferes in our personal lives and our personal business. We have cut the public's Federal paperwork load by more than 12 percent in less than a year. And we are not through cutting.**

We have made a good start on turning the gobbledygook of Federal regulations into plain English that people can understand. But we know that we still have a long way to go. We have brought together parts of eleven government agencies to create a new Department of Energy. And now it is time to take another major step by creating a separate Department of Education.

But even the best-organized government will only be as effective as the people who carry out its policies. For this reason, I consider Civil Service reform to be absolutely vital. Worked out with the civil servants themselves, this reorganization plan will restore the merit principle to a system which has grown into a bureaucratic maze. It will provide greater management flexibility and better rewards for better performance without compromising job security.

Then and only then can we have a government that is efficient, open, and truly worthy of our people's understanding and respect. I have promised that we will have such a government and I intend to keep that promise.

In our foreign policy, the separation of people from government has been in the past a source of weakness and error. In a democratic system like ours, foreign policy decisions must be able to stand the test of public examination and public debate. If we make a mistake in this Administration, it will be on the side of frankness and openness with the American people.

In our modern world when the deaths of literally millions of people can result from a few terrifying seconds of destruction, the path of national strength and security is identical to the path of peace. Tonight, I am happy to report that because we are strong, our Nation is at peace with the world.

Human Rights and Defense

We are a confident Nation. We have restored a moral basis for our foreign policy. The very heart of our identity as a Nation is our firm commitment to human rights.

We stand for human rights because we believe that government has as a purpose, to promote the well-being of its citizens. This is true in our domestic policy, it is also true in our foreign policy. The world must know that in support of human rights, the United States will stand firm.

We expect no quick or easy results, but there has been significant movement toward greater freedom and humanity in several parts of the world.

Thousands of political prisoners have been freed. The leaders of the world—even our ideological adversaries—now see that their attitude toward fundamental human rights affects their standing in the international community and it affects their relations with the United States.

To serve the interests of every American, our foreign policy has three major goals. The first and prime concern is and will remain the security of our country.

Security is based on our national will and security is based on the strength of our armed forces. We have the will, and militarily, we are very strong. Security also comes through the strength of our alliances. We have reconfirmed our commitment to the defense of Europe, and this year, we will demonstrate that commitment by further modernizing and strengthening our military capabilities there.

Security can also be enhanced by agreements with potential adversaries which reduce the threat of nuclear disaster while maintaining our own relative strategic capability.

In areas of peaceful competition with the Soviet Union, we will continue to more than hold our own.

At the same time, we are negotiating with quiet confidence, without haste, with careful determination, to ease the tension between us and to ensure greater stability and security.

The Strategic Arms Limitation Talks have been long and difficult. We want a mutual limit on both the quality and quantity of the giant nuclear arsenals of both nations—and then we want actual reductions in strategic arms as a major step toward the ultimate elimination of nuclear weapons from the face of the earth.

If those talks result in an agreement this year—and I trust they will—I pledge to you that the agreement will maintain and enhance the stability of the world's strategic balance and the security of the United States.

For 30 years, concerted but unsuccessful efforts have been made to ban the testing of atomic explosives—both military weapons and peaceful nuclear devices.

We are hard at work with Great Britain and the Soviet Union on an agreement which will stop testing and will protect our national security and provide for adequate verification of compliance.

We are now making progress, I believe good progress, toward this comprehensive ban on nuclear explosions.

We are also working vigorously to halt the proliferation of nuclear weapons among the nations of the world which do not now have them and to reduce the deadly global traffic in conventional arms sales. Our stand for peace is suspect if we are also the principal arms merchant of the world. So we have decided to cut down our arms transfers abroad on a year-by-year basis, and to work with other major arms exporters to encourage their similar restraint.

Every American has a stake in our second major goal—a world at peace. In a nuclear age, each of us is threatened when peace is not secured everywhere. We are trying to promote harmony in those parts of the world where major differences exist among other nations and threaten international peace.

In the Middle East, we are contributing our good offices to maintain the momentum of the current negotiations—and to keep open the lines of communication among the Middle Eastern leaders. The whole world has a great stake in the success of these efforts. This is a precious opportunity for a historic settlement of a longstanding conflict—an opportunity which may never come again in our lifetime.

Our role has been difficult and sometimes thankless and controversial. But it has been constructive and it has been necessary, and it will continue.

Our third major foreign policy goal is one that touches the life of every American citizen everyday: world economic growth and stability.

This requires strong economic performance by the industrialized democracies like ourselves and progress in resolving the global energy crisis. Last fall, with the help of others, we succeeded in our vigorous efforts to maintain the stability of the price of oil. But as many foreign leaders have emphasized to me personally, and I am sure to you, the greatest future contribution that America can make to the world economy would be an effective energy conservation program here at home.

We will not hesitate to take the actions needed to protect the integrity of the American dollar.

We are trying to develop a more just international system. And in this spirit, we are supporting the struggle for human development; in Africa, in Asia, and in Latin America.

Panama Canal Treaties

Finally, the world is watching to see how we act on one of our most important and controversial items of business: approval of the Panama Canal Treaties.

The treaties now before the Senate are the result of the work of four Administrations—two Democratic, two Republican.

They guarantee that the Canal will be open always for unrestricted use by the ships of the world. Our ships have the right to go to the head of the line for priority of passage in times of emergency or need.

We retain the permanent right to defend the Canal with our own military forces, if necessary, to guarantee its openness and its neutrality.

The treaties are to the clear advantage of ourselves, the Panamanians, and the other users of the Canal. Ratifying the Panama Canal Treaties will demonstrate our good faith to the world, discourage the spread of hostile ideologies in this hemisphere and directly contribute to the economic well-being and the security of the United States.

I have to say that that is very welcome applause.

There were two moments on my recent journey which, for me, confirmed the final aims of our foreign policy and what it always must be.

One was a little village in India, where I met a people as passionately attached to their rights and liberties as we are—but whose children have a far smaller chance for good health or food or education or human fulfillment than a child born in this country.

The other moment was in Warsaw, capital of a nation twice devastated by war in this century. Their people have rebuilt the city which war's destruction took from them; but what was new only emphasized clearly what was lost.

What I saw in those two places crystalized for me the purposes of our own Nation's policy: to ensure economic justice, to advance human rights, to resolve conflicts without violence, and to proclaim in our great democracy our constant faith in the liberty and dignity of human beings everywhere.

We Americans have a great deal of work to do together. In the end, how well we do that work will depend on the spirit in which we approach it.

We must seek fresh answers, unhindered by the stale prescriptions of the past.

It has been said that our best years are behind us. But I say again that America's best is still ahead. We have emerged from bitter experiences chastened but proud, confident once again, ready to face challenges once again, and united once again.

A Solemn Time

We come together tonight at a solemn time. Last week the Senate lost a good and honest man, Lee Metcalf of Montana.

And today, the flag of the United States flew at half-mast from this Capitol and from American installations and ships all over the world, in mourning for Senator Hubert Humphrey.

Because he exemplified so well the joy and the zest of living, his death reminds us not so much of our own mortality but of the possibilities offered to us by life. He always looked to the future with a special American kind of confidence, of hope and enthusiasm.

The best way that we can honor him is by following his example. Our task—to use the words of Senator Humphrey—is "reconciliation, rebuilding, and rebirth."

Reconciliation of private needs and interests into a higher purpose.

Rebuilding the old dreams of justice and liberty, and country and community.

Rebirth of our faith in the common good.

Each of us here tonight—and all who are listening in your homes—must rededicate ourselves to serving the common good.

We are a community, a beloved community, all of us; our individual fates are linked; our futures intertwined; and if we act in that knowledge and in that spirit, together, as the Bible says, we can move mountains.

Thank you very much.

Accompanying Message

Following is the text of President Carter's message to Congress that accompanied his State of the Union address Jan. 19, 1978. The accompanying message was sent to Congress with the State of the Union address but was not delivered by Carter.

TO THE CONGRESS
OF THE UNITED STATES:

Tonight's State of the Union Address concentrates on this year's highest priorities—a strong energy bill; a coordinated economic program of job creation, tax reduction, tax reform and anti-inflation measures; making the government more effective and efficient; maintaining the peace through a strong national defense; and ratifying both the Panama Canal Treaties and, if completed, the SALT II treaty.

It is important that the Congress and the Nation also understand what our other important initiatives and goals will be for 1978. I am therefore sending to Congress this separate, more detailed State of the Union Message, which describes Administration priorities in the areas not fully covered in the Address.

DOMESTIC AFFAIRS

A number of serious domestic problems faced the Nation when I took office one year ago. The economy had not yet fully recovered from the recession; our country had no sound energy policy; the Federal government was operating inefficiently and ineffectively in many areas; concerns about the openness and integrity of our government remained in the aftermath of Watergate; and many of our most pressing social problems had not been addressed.

In 1977, my Administration did not solve all of those problems. But Congress joined us in tackling many of these issues, and together we made progress. Now that a year has passed, I believe we are a more confident people, with more trust in our institutions. We are a country on the move again, prepared to address our problems with boldness and confidence, at home and abroad. We have reasserted our concern for the problems of people here at home and reaffirmed our position of moral leadership in the world.

This year, my domestic goals will continue to reflect those concerns that guided my actions in 1977: restoring economic prosperity; meeting our Nation's human needs; making the government more efficient and more responsive; and developing and protecting our natural resources.

RESTORING ECONOMIC PROSPERITY

I am devoting a substantial part of my State of the Union Address to the need for a comprehensive economic program, and I will devote the bulk of my Economic Report to Congress, to be delivered tomorrow, to a complete description of my Administration's economic goals and objectives. In this Message, therefore, I will not repeat those statements but I want to set forth briefly the key elements of those proposals:

—a $23 billion income tax cut in 1979, with $17 billion going to individuals and their families and $6 billion going to businesses;

—a tax reform program designed to make our tax laws fairer and simpler;

—an anti-inflation program, designed to reduce annual increases in wages and prices, with the cooperation of labor and business and with the Federal government setting an example; reductions of $2 billion in excise and payroll taxes will also make a contribution to reducing inflation;

—an extension of the funding for 725,000 public service (CETA) jobs, and a $700 million increase in spending for our youth employment efforts;

—a major new $400 million private sector jobs initiative, designed primarily to encourage businesses to hire unemployed minorities and youth.

I plan to work very closely with Congress to secure prompt action on these economic proposals. Their adoption will help achieve the kind of economic prosperity for our Nation that all of us want. Along with a sound energy bill, enactment of these economic proposals will be my highest domestic priority for 1978.

Energy

There can be no higher priority than prompt enactment of comprehensive energy legislation along the lines submitted to the Congress last spring.

Huge oil price increases in 1973-74 contributed to the double-digit inflation of 1974, and to the worst recession in 40 years. These price hikes were also the principal cause of our foreign trade deficit, which has contributed to the weakness of the dollar abroad.

Unless we act now, our energy problems will rapidly get worse. Failure to act will fuel inflation, erode the value of the dollar, render us vulnerable to disruptions in our oil supply, and limit our economic progress in the years to come.

I am confident that the Congress will respond to the Nation's clear need, by enacting responsible and balanced energy legislation early this year.

Employment

Last year we made considerable progress in our efforts to reduce unemployment. The unemployment rate decreased from 7.8% to 6.4%. During the year, 4.1 million new jobs were created. Unemployment fell by 1.1 million workers. The actions we took as part of our $21 billion economic stimulus package substantially helped us achieve these favorable results.

In 1978, the Administration will continue its efforts to reduce unemployment still further and to increase employment opportunities for all Americans. As part of the budget I will propose:

—additional funds to increase youth programs 260 per cent above the 1976 level, providing $2.3 billion in outlays and 450,000 man-years of employment and training for young workers;

—a $400 million private sector employment program focused on youth and other disadvantaged workers and aimed at mobilizing private industry to work with government in finding jobs. It will be implemented through business councils established throughout the country;

—maintenance of the 725,000 CETA jobs through 1979, while tying them in future years to national unemployment rates;

—beginning of a demonstration program for the jobs component of the Better Jobs and Income Program.

Humphrey-Hawkins Legislation

The Administration will seek passage of the Humphrey-Hawkins Full Employment and Balanced Growth Act.

This Act will help the Administration and the Congress in planning our efforts to reduce unemployment and to create jobs, while maintaining reasonable price stability. Its enactment would serve as a living memorial to the late Senator Hubert Humphrey.

Private Sector Jobs

The Administration plans a major $400 million effort to involve business and labor in the training and hiring of the hard-core unemployed.

The program will closely tie the Federal employment system with the private sector, through the use of business councils. I am confident that the private sector will respond positively to the call to help the Nation solve one of its most serious problems—the employment of our youth and minorities.

Inflation

Although inflation is lower now than in the recent past, we still must do more to keep it down. The steps my Administration will take include:

—incentives for business investment, contained in our tax proposals, which will increase production investment, and thereby help us hold down prices and costs;

—reduction in excise and unemployment taxes, proposed in the new budget;

—continuing reductions in needlessly complex Federal regulations. We have established a high-level inter-agency committee to review the effects of regulation in our economy, and we will continue our efforts for regulatory reform in the airline industry and elsewhere;

—a special effort to hold down the soaring costs of health care, through enactment of the Hospital Cost Containment Act.

But the government cannot solve this problem alone—especially once business, labor, and consumers have accepted inflation as a fact of life, and adjusted their behavior accordingly. I have therefore asked business and labor to undertake, voluntarily, a new program to reduce inflation. I will ask each industry to aim for smaller price and wage increases in 1978 than it averaged over the last two years. As a major employer the Federal government should take the lead in this effort. Voluntary cooperation is one way—perhaps the only way—to reduce inflation without unacceptable government interference and coercion.

Urban Assistance and Community Development

The Administration and Congress took major steps last year to meet the needs of our cities. We increased funding for Community Development Block Grants by $2.7 billion over three years, and provided an alternative formula for allocating funds that was more responsive to the needs of distressed urban areas. Next year we will recommend an increase of $150 million over the 1978 level for the Community Development Block Grant program. We enacted a new program of Urban Development Action Grants at an annual level of $400 million, and extended and expanded Anti-Recession Fiscal Assistance (ARFA).

I am proposing that the ARFA program, which expires September 30, 1978, be extended. We are evaluating possible revisions in programs and funding, and will make our recommendations to the Congress within two months.

The Administration is also studying closely the possible need for extended Federal lending to New York City. The current legislation expires on June 30, 1978. We are committed, along with the State and City, to preserving the City's solvency. If such extended lending is necessary for that purpose, we will propose it. However, all the interested parties must contribute to a permanent solution.

This spring I will submit to Congress a message outlining this Administration's urban policy, based on the work of the Urban and Regional Policy Group, chaired by the Secretary of Housing and Urban Development. It will be designed to make existing Federal programs more effective, and will involve new initiatives and resources to address our urban needs. The long-standing problems of our cities are structural in nature and cannot be corrected by short-term or one-time efforts. This Administration is committed to a long-term and continuing effort to meet stubborn problems and changing needs. Our urban policy proposals will:

—build a more effective partnership between the Federal government, State and local governments, the private sector, neighborhood groups and concerned citizens;

—be sufficiently flexible to meet the diverse needs of our urban areas and to respond to particular problems of distressed areas;

—address the fiscal needs of hard-pressed urban governments, as well as the economic and social needs of city residents;

—improve the urban physical environment and strengthen urban communities;

—use Federal assistance to stimulate job-creating investments by the private sector and to encourage innovative actions by the State and local governments.

Agriculture and Rural Development

Decent farm income and a strong family farm system are vital to our national economic stability and strength. For too long farm prices for many commodities have been severely depressed. Working with the Congress in the past year, we have adopted new programs and policies designed to strengthen farm income and to ensure abundant, reasonably priced food for consumers. Partially as a result of these policies and programs, farm prices are now improving. Nevertheless, we cannot be satisfied with the economic condition of many American farmers today. We will continue to monitor our agricultural economy and to work with Congressional and farm leaders to make certain that Federal programs and policies are carried out effectively.

Food and Agriculture Act

In the past year we have worked with the Congress to enact a new comprehensive Food and Agriculture Act, which will protect producers and consumers. We have also exercised set-aside authority for wheat and feed grains, which will protect farm income. This year we expect to pay farmers $7.3 billion for all price support programs. The new farm bill which became effective October 1, 1977, achieves long-needed changes in our agricultural policies, including:

—minimal governmental intervention in markets and in the decisions farmers make;

—price support loans for major commodities that permit us to remain competitive in world markets;

—a grain reserve designed to remove excess products from the market and hold them until supplies are short;

—income support levels based on cost-of-production.

Grain Reserve

Last year we initiated a plan to place 30-35 million metric tons of food and feed grains in reserve. Establishing this reserve will add further strength and stability to the market and provide a hedge against export control on grain. Most of this grain will be owned and controlled by farmers. To strengthen farmer control of the grain and to help keep the grain out of government ownership, terms of the farmer storage facility loan program were liberalized. In 1978, the Administration will propose an international emergency grain reserve of up to 6 million metric tons to help us meet our food aid commitments abroad.

Agricultural Disaster and Drought Aid

Because of the record droughts in 1977, I worked with Congress to pass an $844 million Emergency Drought Assistance Program. This year we will ask Congress to eliminate the many inconsistencies and inequities in existing disaster aid programs, and we will continue to give high priority to addressing the effects of the drought, which has begun to abate.

We are taking other steps to improve life in rural America. I recently signed a law to encourage better delivery of health services in rural communities. We will continue to expand the assignment of the National Health Service Corps' doctors, dentists and other health professionals to underserved rural areas. We will shortly be announcing methods to improve the effectiveness of rural housing programs with greater emphasis on home ownership for rural Americans.

Agricultural Exports

I want to increase our agricultural exports. To do so we need competitive prices, high quality products, and reserve supplies to meet all contingencies. We must remove unnecessary barriers to exports. And we must have an affirmative export policy. In 1977, the Administration more than doubled (to $1.7 billion) the short-term export credit program, increased Soviet grain purchase authorization to 15 million tons, developed a risk assurance program, and expanded efforts to develop export markets around the world.

This year we will continue these efforts, especially to reduce barriers to agricultural trade.

Sugar

To stabilize world sugar prices and to protect domestic sugar-producers, we negotiated an international sugar agreement this year with the major sugar-producing countries. We will seek Congressional ratification of the agreement early in 1978. The sugar program required by the 1977 Food and Agricultural Act will protect the domestic sugar industry in the meantime.

Rural Development and Credit Policy

In fiscal year 1977, the Farmers Home Administration provided nearly $7 billion in loans in four areas: farming, housing, community facilities and business and industrial development. We expect to provide at least $1 billion more in the current fiscal year.

Small Business

This Administration took several steps in 1977 to strengthen small business. The Small Business Administration expanded its financial and management assistance to these firms and developed an advocacy program to represent small business interests before all Federal departments and agencies. In 1978, we will continue efforts to support small business through tax cuts and special tax incentives, reduced regulations and other programmatic reforms, and expanded SBA loan authority.

MEETING OUR NATION'S HUMAN NEEDS

The Administration's constant concern has been with meeting the human needs of all Americans. Over the past year, we have moved on a number of fronts to make certain our citizens will be well housed, better educated, and properly cared for when they are in need. This year we will pursue our current initiatives in these areas and launch new ones.

Health

This past year we were very active in the effort to improve the health of our citizens and to restrain skyrocketing health care costs, through:

—Establishment of a Mental Health Commission to help develop a national mental health program. The Commission will issue its final report later this year, and I expect to carefully consider the Commission's findings.

—A campaign to immunize the more than 20 million children not yet protected against communicable childhood diseases.

—Reorganization of part of HEW to allow more efficient delivery of Medicare/Medicaid services. The cost savings from the reorganizations will be realized more fully this year.

—Signing legislation to attack fraud and abuse in Medicare/Medicaid programs.

—Signing legislation to make Medicare/Medicaid reimbursement available to physician extenders in rural clinics. The beneficial effects of that bill will be felt in our Nation's rural areas for the first time this year.

In 1978, the Administration will continue these and other efforts to bring us better and less costly health care.

Hospital Cost Containment

One of my main legislative goals for this year is the Hospital Cost Containment Bill. That bill, which would save hospital users more than $7 billion in the first two years after enactment, is our principal weapon in the effort to decrease health care costs, which now double every five years.

National Health Insurance

I will submit to Congress later this year a National Health Insurance proposal. While Congress will not have the time to complete action on this proposal in 1978, it is important to begin the national debate on the many complex issues involved in National Health Insurance.

National Health Insurance will not solve all our health problems. A sensible national health policy also requires more effective delivery of preventive services, better nutrition, vigorous abatement of environmental and occupational threats to health, and efforts to change individual lifestyles that endanger health.

But National Health Insurance is a crucial step. It will protect our people from ruinous medical bills and provide each citizen with better access to sound and balanced health insurance coverage.

Medicaid Improvements for Children

Last year I proposed the Child Health Assessment Program to improve the early and preventive screening, diagnosis and treatment program for lower-income children under Medicaid. The Administration will press for enactment of this measure, and will urge its expansion to make an additional 1.7 million lower-income children eligible.

Teenage Pregnancy Proposal

I will propose legislation to establish networks of community based services to prevent unwanted adolescent pregnancies. We need and will urge expansion of existing family planning services to reach an additional 280,000 teenagers.

Drug Abuse

Drug Abuse threatens the health and safety of our children, here and abroad. We will continue the efforts begun last year to make our drug abuse prevention and control programs more effective and efficient.

World Health

This year I will present a strategy for working directly with other nations and through international organizations to raise the standards of health and nutrition around the world.

Education

Last year the Congress adopted with our cooperation a 15 per cent increase in education funding—the largest increase since enactment of the Elementary and Secondary Education Act.

This year we will continue to demonstrate our commitment to improving the Nation's education programs. HEW's education budget expenditures will be increased by 14 per cent, with the most significant increases coming in education of the disadvantaged, assistance to State programs for education of the handicapped, and college student financial aid.

The Administration will also work with the Congress for the creation of a separate Cabinet-level Department of Education, and for legislation to replace and reform expiring Federal education acts.

These legislative proposals will concentrate on:

—increasing basic literacy;

—ensuring that students are prepared for jobs;

—supporting post-secondary education and lifelong learning; and,

—strengthening the partnership between Federal, State, and local governments.

To augment existing programs, I will propose legislation to help low and middle-income families meet rising college tuition costs, and will also support a significant expansion of student aid programs.

Income Assistance

Over the past year we have made many far-reaching improvements in the programs that provide income assistance to the needy. My Administration will continue to assign great importance to this area in 1978.

Welfare Reform

I proposed last year a reform of the Nation's welfare system, through the Better Jobs and Income Act. This Act would fundamentally reform current programs to assist the poor by:

—consolidating the Aid to Families with Dependent Children, Supplemental Security Income and Food Stamps programs into a single consolidated cash assistance program that provides a basic nationally uniform Federal benefit;

—improving efforts to find jobs for the poor in the private sector, and creating up to 1.4 million public service jobs for heads of families who cannot be placed in unsubsidized employment; and

—improving work incentives by expanding the Earned Income Tax Credit.

We will work actively with the Congress in the coming year to pass the Better Jobs and Income Act, and we will provide in this year's budget for pilot employment programs so we will be ready to implement the welfare reform program.

Family and Children

My Administration will continue its strong commitment to strengthening the American family and to expanding programs for children.

The Administration will propose this year that the school breakfast program be made mandatory in schools with high concentrations of needy children. Further, we will propose a major expansion in special supplemental food programs for women, infants, and children.

Among other major actions in 1978 will be:

—convening a White House Conference on Families;

—pressing for enactment of our proposed reforms in foster care programs including new financial assistance to aid in the adoption of hard-to-place children;

—more than doubling the budget outlays for child welfare services, with an emphasis on services that help keep families together;

—continuing $200 million in special funding for day care under Title XX of the Social Security Act.

We will also depend upon the revitalized Community Services Administration to develop new approaches to assist the poor.

The Elderly

Last year saw the enactment of Social Security financing legislation that will assure the system's financial integrity into the next century. This year the Administration will continue to work for strengthened legislation against unwarranted age discrimination in the Federal and private sector. We will propose legislation to extend and strengthen the Older Americans Act and we will seek a 13 per cent increase in funding for programs providing daily meals to the elderly, raising the total of daily meals served to 385,000. In addition, the Administration will work to assure that the contributions of older Americans are sought in our efforts to meet national needs.

Housing

Last year we made progress toward our national goal of a decent home in a suitable environment for every American family. 1977 was a good year for housing, generally, with total new starts exceeding two million. And we have renewed the Federal government's commitment to housing for the needy.

Early last year, the Administration proposed major new intiatives to meet the housing needs of low- and moderate-income Americans—initiatives which are central to our urban development strategy. We had about 118,000 starts under section 8 and public housing subsidized programs in 1977. We look forward to another 30 per cent increase in subsidized housing starts in these programs for 1978, and 92,000 starts in the Assisted Housing Rehabilitation Loan Programs. We will reassess our national housing needs and goals and our current housing and credit policies designed to meet those needs.

In 1978, the Administration will strengthen its commitment to meet the housing needs of all communities with a variety of expanded programs and new initiatives:

—Rental housing assistance to an additional 400,000 low-income families, and help to enable an additional 50,000 moderate-income families to own their own homes. The total number of families receiving housing assistance will increase from 2.6 million in 1977 to 3.1 million in 1979.

—More funds for the rehabilitation loan program under section 312, with an expansion of existing programs for substantial renovations and the creation of a new moderate rehabilitation program under section 8.

—A major new operating subsidy program for 1979. This new program, coupled with improved management controls and the monitoring of troubled projects, is intended to reduce the inventory of defaulted projects and aid in restoring distressed urban areas. The Department of Housing and Urban Development has made substantial progress in 1977 in reducing the stock of defaulted projects. This new program will give the Department additional tools. Outlays for this program are estimated to total $52 million in 1979.

—A Federal financing mechanism for assisted housing projects through use of the GNMA Tandem program.

—A targeted GNMA Tandem program which will provide subsidies designed to bring middle-income families back to the cities.

—Targeting of rural housing programs to lower-income residents, including a special program to help very poor families own their own homes.

—Continuing high levels of production of housing for the elderly and handicapped.

Transportation

This year we will build on the efforts we made last year to strengthen the Nation's transportation system by decreasing consumer costs, pursuing increased energy efficiency, and improving safety:

—negotiation of a new US-UK bilateral air services agreement;

—approval of new international air routes from a number of American cities;

—requiring passive restraint systems on all new automobiles by 1984;

—setting new fuel efficiency standards for 1981-1984 model automobiles;

—beginning work on the Northeast Corridor Railroad Improvement Program;

—passing an all-cargo airline deregulation bill.

We will also continue our policy of increasing competition and reducing airfares in international flights, and pursue additional bilateral agreements. Consumers have already benefited from reduced international fares and improved service.

Highway and Transit Programs

We will soon propose a comprehensive highway and transit program, which will provide more than $45 billion in total authorizations in the 1979-1982 period. The program will give states and localities more flexibility in planning and programming their highway and transit funding, by reducing the number of narrow, categorical accounts and by using consolidated accounts for a wider range of potential transportation projects.

In addition, we will make funding of transportation programs more uniform and give localities more control over highway and mass transit funds in large urban areas.

Highway Safety

The Administration will propose legislation to strengthen our efforts for highway safety and to reduce restrictions on the states' use of Federal highway safety grant funds. That legislation will earmark funds for the Department of Transportation to support important highway safety projects, such as the 55 mile per hour speed limit program.

Inland Waterway User Fees

Users of Federal inland waterways should pay fees which will pay a substantial part of the cost of constructing, operating and maintaining those waterways. My Administration will continue to work closely with Congress toward passage of a bill that will, for the first time, establish inland waterway user fees.

Aircraft Noise Abatement

My Administration will again seek passage of legislation to control aircraft noise.

No-Fault Automobile Insurance

We continue to support legislation to establish Federal minimum standards for no-fault automobile insurance.

Veterans

In 1977, we took a number of steps to make certain that the country continues to meet the special needs of our millions of veterans. Legislation was passed to increase compensation benefits for service-connected disabilities, benefits under the G.I. Bill, and veterans pension benefits. Millions of veterans will feel the effects of these increases this year.

In 1978, we will further improve our veterans programs by:

—initiating a government-wide review of the problems of Vietnam veterans and the means by which current programs can be made more effective in meeting their needs;

—beginning new programs to deal with problems of alcohol, drug abuse and psychological readjustment;

—proposing increased benefits for service-connected disabilities, and improvements in the veterans pension program;

—continuing special employment programs for Vietnam-era veterans.

Arts and Humanities

Americans are increasingly aware that the arts and humanities preserve and transmit our heritage, enrich our lives, and contribute significantly to the social and economic well-being of our Nation. This Administration is committed to fostering the highest standards of creativity and scholarship in an open partnership between public and private sectors—and we believe that the products of this commitment must be available to the many Americans who wish to share in them. This year's substantial increases in the budgets for the Arts and Humanities Endowments demonstrate my strong belief in the value of these programs.

MAKING THE GOVERNMENT MORE EFFICIENT AND MORE RESPONSIVE

Government Employees

Civil Service Reform

The Civil Service System is too often a bureaucratic maze which stifles the initiative of our dedicated Government employees while inadequately protecting their rights. Our 2.8 million civil servants are governed by outdated rules and institutions that keep them from being as efficient as they would like to be. No one is more frustrated by this system than hardworking public servants. Therefore, one of my major priorities in 1978 will be to ensure passage of the first comprehensive reform of the system since its creation nearly a century ago—reforms developed with the direct involvement of civil servants. Early this year, Congress will receive legislation and a reorganization plan to:

—restructure the institutions that run the Civil Service;

—increase safeguards against abuses of official power;

—provide greater incentives for managers to improve the Government's efficiency and responsiveness;

—reduce the system's red tape and delays;

—speed the procedures for dealing with employee grievances and disciplinary actions;

—make equal employment opportunities more effective.

Last year the Administration acted to protect Federal employees from the loss of a job due to reorganization. Such protection will be maintained.

Hatch Act Reform

I will continue to support reform of the Hatch Act, which would restore the right of most Civil Service employees to participate in the political process.

Part-time and Flexi-time Employment

To help obtain Federal jobs for the elderly, the handicapped, women, and others with family responsibilities, all Federal agencies will carry forward renewed efforts to increase part-time and flexi-time employment opportunities.

Reorganization, Management and Regulatory Reform

The Government Reorganization Project will keep working to make the Government more responsive and efficient. Last year we combined parts of 11 agencies into one Department of Energy, streamlined the Executive Office of the President and reduced the White House Staff, and proposed the abolition of nearly 500 advisory committees and small agencies.

In addition to the upcoming Civil Service and education reform efforts, we will soon submit proposals:

—to restructure our equal employment programs to provide better protection for the rights of minorities and women, and to ease the burden of compliance on State and local government as well as business;

—to improve the administration of justice; and

—to reorganize our disaster assistance programs.

Additional studies are under way in many other areas, and several of these will result in reorganization proposals later this year. Efforts to improve Federal cash management continue.

We are also vigorously pursuing the effort begun last year to reduce the burden of outdated, ineffective, and nit-picking regulations. For example, the Department of Health, Education and Welfare eliminated 5 per cent of their regulations, the Federal Trade Commission rescinded 111 outdated sets of rules on trade practices and both the Civil Aeronautics Board and the Interstate Commerce Commission have moved to allow more competition, which has led to lower prices. In 1978, we will continue these efforts.

Worker Health and Safety

The Occupational Health and Safety Administration has already slashed its paperwork requirements by 50 per cent and eliminated 1,100 unnecessary regulations, while improving its capacity to protect workers. This spring the Task Force on Worker Safety will make further recommendations to increase protection for workers and minimize employer cost.

Airline Regulatory Reform

Last year, I signed legislation deregulating all cargo air transportation. This year, I will continue to work for passage of the airline regulatory reform bill for passengers. That bill will allow air carriers to compete through lower fares, new services, and new markets, without excessive government interference or disruption of service to small communities.

Trucking Regulatory Reform

Forty years of tight government controls have not done enough to bring us competitive prices, good services, and efficient use of fuel. We will consider measures to bring more competition into the motor carrier area.

Drugs

We will propose legislation to reform regulation of the drug industry, which will protect the consumer and make regulations fairer and less burdensome.

Regulatory Process

Early in 1978, I will issue an Executive Order to improve the regulatory process. This Order will require officials responsible for regulations to sign them; assure that policy-level officials are fully involved in the process; require that regulations be written in plain English; make it easier for the public to participate in the process; increase coordination between agencies with overlapping responsibilities; require a closer look at the cost of regulations before they are issued; and require "sunset" reviews of existing regulations.

I have also set up an interagency committee to help regulatory agencies review the economic effects of major regulations, so that we can be sure that the costs of each proposed regulation have been fully considered. In this way we will be able to identify the least costly means of achieving our regulatory goals.

Paperwork Reduction

In 1977, my Administration decreased by 12 per cent the paperwork burden that the Government imposes on the people. This was done by eliminating, consolidating, simplifying, and decreasing the frequency of reports. That savings is the equivalent of 50,000 full-time workers filling out Federal forms for a full year. All departments and agencies are currently setting goals for further substantial reductions in 1978. All reporting requirements associated with grant-in-aid programs will be subject to "sunset" reviews, and ended unless they are found necessary. In addition, we are reviewing the recommendations of the Commission on Federal Paperwork.

Labor Law Reform

Last year we proposed legislation to reform our Nation's labor laws, in order to streamline the conduct of elections for employee representation and strengthen the enforcement powers of the National Labor Relations Board. We will work closely with Congress to ensure early passage of this bill, which is one of my highest legislative goals this year.

Election Reform

Last year, I supported proposals to make our elections fairer and more honest. These included public financing of Congressional campaigns, amendments to the Federal Election Campaign Act and other election reforms. The Administration will continue to support Congressional action on these measures.

Consumer Reform

We have taken many actions to benefit consumers by reducing the costs and improving the quality and safety of products. But one consumer initiative merits separate emphasis—the creation of the Office of Consumer Representation. We supported legislation last year to create such an Office, so that the interests of consumers could be represented in one government agency. The Office would not require additional government employees or expenditures since it would merely consolidate the consumer offices that already exist throughout the government. I am strongly committed to this legislation, and regard its enactment as one of the year's primary legislative priorities.

Public Broadcasting Reform

I proposed legislation last year to strengthen the public broadcasting service by providing increased long-term Federal support, insulation from political pressure, better coordination among the national organizations that run public broadcasting, and more opportunity for citizens to participate at the local level. My Administration will work with Congress this year to pass these reforms.

Openness and Integrity

One of our primary goals is to make certain that the government's ethical standards are high, and they they are fully observed. And we must ensure that our government is open and responsive to the American people.

Last year, I took steps in that direction by requiring that the senior officials of my Administration publicly disclose their income and assets and pledge not to do business with their agencies for two years after leaving government service. To increase the government's openness, we took steps to make certain that the spirit as well as the letter of the Freedom of Information Act was observed. And we tried to bring the Presidency to the people with citizen forums and discussion panels throughout the country.

This year, we will continue these efforts, concentrating our primary attention on these areas:

Lobby Reform

The Administration will press for legislation requiring registration of lobbyists and thorough public disclosure of their lobbying activities. This long-overdue legislation will help reestablish confidence and trust in government.

Ethics

I applaud the strong ethical codes adopted last year by the House and Senate. I believe those codes and the standards established for my Administration's officials should be made law, so that they will clearly apply to public officials in the future. I urge Congress to pass the Public Officials Integrity Act this year.

Classification

We are completing a study of classification systems for government documents and I will shortly issue an Executive Order designed to eliminate improper and unnecessary classification and to ensure that documents are declassified more rapidly.

Justice

Civil Rights and Equal Opportunity

All Americans have fundamental civil rights requiring government protection, and all must be afforded equal opportunities to participate as full members in our society. In 1977, this principle guided my Administration in numerous areas, and I plan to make certain that this year our efforts on behalf of civil rights and equal opportunities continue unabated. Our Nation's concern for human rights must be heard as clearly at home as abroad.

Educational Opportunities

In 1977, my Administration vigorously attacked educational discrimination on the elementary, secondary and higher education levels. A major suit was pursued to ensure non-discrimination at the university level. At the same time, we recognized and reaffirmed the importance of affirmative action programs to ensure equal opportunities at educational institutions through our brief in the *Bakke* case. Our efforts to eliminate discrimination and promote affirmative action programs, relying on flexible goals rather than on quotas, will continue in full force.

Handicapped

HEW issued regulations and guidelines to implement legislation guaranteeing equal access to programs receiving financial assistance from HEW. This year the other Cabinet Departments will issue similar regulations, so that the rights of handicapped Americans will begin to be fully observed. We are providing a $50 million loan fund to States and institutions to enable them to comply with these regulations and to eliminate barriers which prevent access by our handicapped citizens to federally assisted programs and activities. We are proposing a major increase in funding under the Education of all Handicapped Children Act.

Equal Opportunity

This past year the Administration reaffirmed Executive Order 11375, which prohibits discrimination on the basis of sex in Federal employment. In addition, I voluntarily placed the Executive Office of the President under Title VII of the Civil Rights Act. This year, as part of our effort to eliminate sex discrimination in unemployment *[sic]* and education, I will continue to urge the ratification of the Equal Rights Amendment to the Constitution.

This past year the Equal Employment Opportunity Commission was reorganized to increase its efficiency. As a result, the Commission made substantial progress on reducing its backlog of complaints. With the more than 40 per cent increase in funding that will be proposed in the 1979 budget, the EEOC will be able to further reduce its backlog. Early this year I will propose to Congress a reorganization plan concerning equal opportunity enforcement which will strengthen the EEOC.

Anti-Foreign Boycott

I strongly supported, and signed, legislation to prohibit American participation in secondary economic boycotts by foreign countries. That law will be strictly enforced by my Administration this year through the regulations just issued by the Department of Commerce.

Minority Business

Last year, we started a number of programs to make more opportunities available for minority-owned businesses. That effort will be continued and strengthened this year:

—We are half way toward our two-year goal of $2 billion in Federal purchases of services and goods from minority-owned firms. We will reach that goal by the end of the year.

—We will raise the goal for Federal deposits in minority-owned banks above the 1977 level of $100 billion.

—We will continue to enforce the $400 million minority business set-aside provision in the local public works act, and may exceed that target.

—We will continue to implement the minority business set-aside policy established for contracts let in the Northeast Corridor Railroad Improvement Program.

Undocumented Aliens

Last year, I proposed legislation to impose sanctions on employers who hire undocumented aliens and to change the legal status of the many undocumented aliens now residing in this country. That legislation would afford undocumented aliens residing here continuously since before 1970 the opportunity to apply for permanent resident status. It would create a new five-year temporary resident status for those undocumented aliens who resided here continuously from 1970 to January 1, 1977. I want to work with Congress this year toward passage of an undocumented aliens bill, for this social and economic problem can no longer be ignored.

Native Americans

The Administration has acted consistently to uphold its trusteeship responsibility to Native Americans. We also have elevated the post of Commissioner of Indian Affairs to the level of Assistant Secretary of Interior. In 1978, the Administration will review Federal Native American policy and will step up efforts to help Indian tribes assess and manage their natural resources.

Legal and Judicial Reform

Last year, my Administration began a number of major efforts to improve our Nation's legal and judicial system, and we intend to pursue those and related efforts fully this year.

Criminal Code Reform

We have worked closely with members of Congress to develop a proposed revision of the Nation's Criminal Code. That revision will codify in one part of the U.S. Code all Federal crime laws and will reform many outdated and inconsistent criminal laws. My Administration will work closely with Congress this year to seek passage of the first complete codification of the Nation's criminal laws.

Judicial Reform

The Federal judicial system has suffered for many years from an inadequate number of judges, and we will continue to work with Congress on an Omnibus Judgeship Bill to correct this problem. We will also continue our efforts to use our judges more effectively, through legislation which we have proposed to expand significantly the authority of magistrates, to increase the use of arbitration, and to tighten Federal jurisdiction. We will work this year to complete Congressional action on these bills.

Wiretap Reform

Last year we proposed legislation reforming our approach to electronic surveillance for foreign intelligence purposes, and affording greater protection to our citizens. Essentially, that legislation would require the government to obtain a court order before beginning any foreign intelligence wiretaps in this country. My Administration supports early passage of this much needed legislation.

Anti-trust Enforcement and Competition

Our Nation's anti-trust laws must be vigorously enforced. Therefore, I recently established a Presidential Commission to review Federal anti-trust enforcement, and to make its recommendations this year.

Last year, we initiated a new program, administered by the Department of Justice, to provide grant funds to State Attorneys General in order to strengthen anti-trust enforcement at the State level. We expect to see the results of this program this year.

By reducing government regulation, we can increase competition and thereby lower consumer costs. This year we will continue our deregulatory efforts in the legislative and administrative areas in order to reduce anti-competitive practices and abuses.

Crime Reduction and Criminal Justice

This past year the Reorganization Project and the Justice Department have been developing proposals to reorganize and to improve our Nation's criminal justice system, in order to strengthen enforcement and ensure equal justice. This year I will be sending a Message to Congress on criminal justice and crime reduction. My Message will include proposals to:

—reorganize the Federal Law Enforcement Assistance Administration;

—improve our criminal research efforts;

—develop better law enforcement methods against organized crime, white collar crime, drug abuse, and public corruption; and

—develop minimum standards for Federal correctional institutions.

FBI and Intelligence Agencies' Charters

I plan to issue a comprehensive Executive Order to govern the intelligence activities of the FBI, CIA, NSA and the Defense Department. That Executive Order will be the basis for the Administration's recommendations on legislative charters governing the activities of the FBI and various intelligence agencies.

Privacy

The Privacy Protection Study Committee recently proposed an extensive list of new legislative and regulatory safeguards. My Administration is analyzing these recent proposals and will develop this year a program to ensure that personal privacy is adequately protected.

District of Columbia

We proposed last year a series of reforms, including full voting representation in Congress, designed to give the residents of the District significantly greater control over their local affairs. My Administration will continue to work for the passage of those reforms this year.

DEVELOPING AND PROTECTING OUR NATURAL RESOURCES

National Energy Policy

In April 1977, I proposed to the Nation a comprehensive national energy policy. That policy is based on three principles, which will continue to guide our progress in 1978:

—we must learn to use energy more efficiently and more carefully, through conservation measures, including retrofitting our buildings, factories and homes;

—we must shift from oil and natural gas, which are becoming more scarce, to coal and renewable sources of energy which we have in abundance;

—we must provide fair prices to producers of energy, so as to encourage development of new supplies without permitting windfall profits.

The debate on this comprehensive policy has been long and arduous. A number of difficult, contentious issues remain to be settled. I am confident, however, that the Congress recognizes the seriousness of our energy problem and will act expeditiously on this program early this year. Securing passage of an acceptable energy bill—one which is fair to consumers, provides needed energy savings, and is prudent from a fiscal and budgetary standpoint—will continue as our highest and most urgent national priority in 1978.

Energy Statutes and Actions

We have already begun to lay a strong foundation for implementation of a national energy policy. In 1977 we took steps to put in place important policies and structural reforms needed to meet our energy goals:

—Creation of a new Department of Energy which combines, for the first time, major governmental functions of energy research, regulation, pricing policy, information collection and dissemination, and overall policy development. Without a strong organization, we would not hope to implement a comprehensive national policy.

—Congress has approved our proposed route for a pipeline to bring natural gas from the North Slope of Alaska to the lower 48 states.

—Passage of the Emergency Natural Gas Act to cope with the hardships of last winter's freeze and assure that high priority gas users were not cut off during supply emergencies.

—Funding of more than $4 billion to store the first 500 million barrels of oil in a strategic petroleum reserve. We have already begun to fill that reserve, and we remain committed to a 1 billion barrel strategic reserve by 1985.

Outer Continental Shelf Legislation

Legislation to improve the management of the Outer Continental Shelf for oil and gas development is a major item of unfinished business pending before Congress. Prompt passage is necessary so that we can have the benefit of the new law as we move to open more offshore areas to development and production. This bill mandates long-needed reforms in the leasing program to provide for the necessary development of offshore oil and gas while enhancing competition among oil companies, assuring that the public receives a fair return for the sale of the public's oil and gas resources, and protecting our marine and coastal resources.

Nuclear Energy

The United States has also advanced a policy to prevent the proliferation of nuclear weapons around the world. An International Nuclear Fuel Cycle Evaluation has been established with wide international participation to examine alternatives to existing proliferation-prone technologies. In addition, legislation was proposed last year to establish better controls on export of nuclear fuels and technologies. We will work with Congress to secure passage of that legislation early in 1978.

Our commitment to preventing the spread of nuclear weapons has led us to reorient our own domestic nuclear policies. I have deferred indefinitely the commercial reprocessing of spent nuclear fuel and plutonium recycling.

The Clinch River Plant itself would waste more than $2 billion while teaching us little that we do not already know, or cannot learn from our existing nuclear research and development program. I have recommended that the Clinch River Breeder Project be stopped, because it represents a premature and unwise commitment to commercialization of technology that we do not now need.

However, we intend to continue to develop the nuclear energy the Nation needs.

We will continue to move forward with a major research program on breeder technology.

We will begin to implement our program for government management of spent fuel from nuclear reactors.

In 1978, my Administration will work towards a policy for safe, permanent disposal of nuclear wastes.

In 1978 and beyond, we will carry on a vigorous nuclear research and development program designed to give us safe technologies that will reduce the danger of nuclear proliferation and will be environmentally responsible. We will also seek to improve the current system of licensing nuclear power reactors in order to cut bureaucratic delays, while firmly maintaining and strengthening health, safety and environmental requirements. I will propose nuclear licensing legislation to the Congress this year.

Environment

One of my deepest personal commitments is to a clean, healthy environment for all of our citizens. Last May, I outlined this Administration's environmental priorities and policies in a comprehensive Environmental Message. Working closely with the Congress, we have made good progress on many of the measures contained in that Message; it will continue to guide our administrative and legislative actions in 1978. Overall, we will:

—increase our environmental outlays by more than 10 per cent, and provide the new staff resources necessary to ensure that the Nation's environmental laws are obeyed;

—determine the best way of enforcing the landmark environmental statutes enacted in 1977, taking considerations of science and public policy into account;

—pursue several important initiatives, including a National Heritage program and designation of national interest lands in Alaska, to manage our precious natural resources better and to preserve our heritage.

Environmental Statutes

In 1977, we worked closely with Congress to enact three of the most significant environmental statutes in recent years:

—The Surface Mining Control and Reclamation Act establishes a joint Federal-State program to make sure we use economically and environmentally sound strip-mining practices. It also sets up a fund to reclaim lands which have been ravaged by uncontrolled, careless mining, and provides clear, stable policy direction for operators.

—The Clean Air Act Amendments establish strict but achievable standards for auto emissions and ensure continued progress in reducing pollution from stationary air pollution sources.

—The Clean Water Act authorizes many of our most important water clean-up programs and will protect our Nation's wetlands without unnecessary Federal requirements. The Act also reforms the sewage treatment construction grant program and gives strong emphasis to the control of toxic chemicals in our environment.

We will provide the leadership and the funding necessary to carry out these new laws.

Water Policy

In 1977, an effort was begun to ensure that Federal programs and policies provide sound and fair management of our limited and valuable water resources. We began a complete review of Federal water policy, which will be completed this year. After close consultation with the Congress, the States, and the public, we will propose measures needed to carry out the recommendations of that study.

We will also continue with the strong dam safety inspection program which was initiated late last year to make sure our dams, public or private, are safe.

Alaska Lands

Last year, I sent Congress a proposal for use of Federal lands in Alaska. This proposal will protect 92 million acres for the public, will create or expand 13 national parks and reserves, 13 national wildlife refuges, and will confer wild and scenic river status on 33 waterways. I hope Congress will adopt these measures, which are needed this year to preserve the unique natural treasures of Alaska and, at the same time, permit the orderly development of Alaskan resources.

Redwood National Park

Redwood National Park contains some of the Nation's largest and oldest trees. Last year, to protect these trees from destruction by commercial logging at the edges of the Park, legislation was proposed to expand its boundaries. We will press for Congressional action on this bill in 1978.

National Heritage Program

We will shortly be proposing a Federal-State program to preserve unique elements of our natural and cultural heritage. This program, modeled after successful ones in several states, will be administered by the Department of the Interior. Although many of the necessary steps can be taken administratively, we will seek some new legislative authority in 1978.

Federal Compliance with Environmental Laws

My Administration is committed to the principle that the Federal government must set a good example of compliance with those environmental laws and regulations which have been established for the private sector. So far, unfortunately, the Federal record has been found wanting. My 1979 budget includes money to bring Federal facilities into compliance with existing environmental laws and regulations.

Federal Reclamation

In 1977, we began a thorough review of the 1902 Reclamation Act. After the study has been completed and reviewed this year, I will propose to Congress any changes needed to modernize the law.

Mining Law Reform

Last year the Administration proposed legislation to replace the archaic 1872 Mining Law with a modern leasing system for publicly-owned mineral resources. The 1872 system has resulted in withdrawal of large areas of land from mineral exploration as the only tool for environmental protection. The Administration's proposal would establish a balanced system where the public interests in mineral development, environmental protection and revenue to the U.S. Treasury will all be accomplished. Special provisions would minimize burdens on small operators and provide incentives for exploration.

Oil Spills

Last year I proposed to Congress legislation which would establish strict liability standards for oil tanker spills and would improve regulations aimed at preventing future oil spills. That legislation is still needed.

Science and Technology

The health of American science and technology and the creation of new knowledge is important to our economic well-being, to our national security, to our ability to help solve pressing national problems in such areas as energy, environment, health, natural resources. I am recommending a program of real growth of scientific research and other steps that will strengthen the Nation's research centers and encourage a new surge of technological innovation by American industry. The budget increase of 11 per cent for basic research will lead to improved opportunities for young scientists and engineers, and upgraded scientific equipment in the Nation's research centers. I am determined to maintain our Nation's leadership role in science and technology.

We will continue America's progress in the field of space exploration with continued development of the space shuttle system and procurement of four shuttle orbiters for operations from both East and West coasts, development of a spacecraft to study for the first time the polar regions of the Sun, and increased outlays for demonstrations of the practical applications of space-based systems and development of space technology.

FOREIGN AFFAIRS

A year ago I set five goals for United States foreign policy in the late 1970s and early 1980s: to reassert America's moral leadership; to strengthen our traditional ties with friends and allies; to work toward a more just international system; to promote regional reconciliation; and to preserve peace through preparedness and arms control. These goals continue to underlie my agenda for 1978.

MORAL LEADERSHIP

During the past year, we have placed American foreign policy on a new course consistent with the values and highest ideals of the American people. We are trying to limit the worldwide sale of arms; we are trying to prevent nuclear explosives—and the ability to make them—from spreading to more countries; we are building a new relationship with the developing countries, and we are promoting human rights throughout the world.

Human Rights

Virtually everywhere, human rights have become an important issue—especially in countries where they are systematically violated. There has been real progress, and for that the United States can take some credit.

We have taken the lead among Western nations at the Belgrade Review Conference on Security and Cooperation in Europe. Working closely with our Allies, and with neutral and non-aligned nations, our delegation—led by Ambassador Arthur Goldberg—has conducted a thorough review of implementation of the Helsinki Final Act, in all its aspects. We have made clear the United States is committed to the full implementation of the Final Act in this and other areas. We will seek a further Review Conference in two years; meanwhile, we will press for better implementation of the Helsinki Final Act.

Non-Proliferation

We must not ignore the enormous dangers posed by the unrestrained spread of nuclear weapons technology. We recognize the benefits of commercial nuclear power, but we also must acknowledge the risks. We believe that all countries can enjoy the benefits, while the risks are minimized, by developing safer technologies and creating new institutions to manage and safeguard all phases of the nuclear fuel cycle. Meanwhile, we have decided to postpone a premature commitment to technologies we cannot yet safely manage on a commercial scale; and we are seeking to persuade others that there are sound economic and energy reasons for them to do likewise.

Arms Sales

The world is threatened by the spiraling increase in trade of conventional arms. Not only do these arms increase the likelihood of conflict, they also divert resources from other human needs. It will not be easy to slow this spiral. We will begin to cut back on our own sales in recognition of the fact that, as the world's principal seller, we have a duty to take the first step. But we know that our efforts can only succeed if other major arms suppliers and recipients cooperate.

TIES WITH FRIENDS AND ALLIES

The energy crisis has underscored the reality of interdependence among nations and the need for a stable international financial and trading system. Our own actions reflect the belief that consultations with traditional friends and dialogue with developing nations are the only way that the United States can provide the economic and political leadership which the world expects of us.

Working with the Allies

During the past year, the United States restored our traditional friends and allies to the center of our foreign policy. Within days after his inauguration, the Vice President visited Brussels, Rome, Bonn, Paris, Reykjavik, and Tokyo. I met frequently in Washington with European and Japanese leaders. I participated in the Economic Summit in London, the 1977 NATO Summit, and a Four-Power Summit with leaders of Britain, Germany, and France. At the beginning of 1978, I visited France and Belgium—and while in Brussels, made the first visit by an American President to the headquarters of the European Community. We have also consulted with our European Allies on such diverse subjects as SALT, MBFR, the Middle East, Africa, human rights, the Belgrade Conference, energy, non-proliferation, the global economy, and North-South relations. We will intensify these efforts this year, expanding the list to include close consultations with the Allies on major arms control issues.

On May 30-31, we will host a NATO Summit in Washington, and we are also planning another Economic Summit this year.

We have shown in our dealings with Japan that close allies can find solutions to shared problems. Early in the year, we were concerned about nuclear reprocessing in Japan, but through flexibility and goodwill on both sides a suitable accommodation was reached on the building of a nuclear reprocessing plant there. Most recently, we reached agreement with the Japanese on ways to deal with their large current account surplus. Our trade and economic talks are another example of constructive action.

International Economic Cooperation

We are working to improve and extend the international economic system, to strengthen international economic institutions, and to ensure that international economic competition takes place in an orderly fashion. We will seek to improve cooperation among nations in the IMF, the GATT, the World Bank, the OECD, and other international organizations which have enabled us to maintain an open, liberal, trade and payments system.

The American economy remains strong. Our competitive position in international trade is excellent. In 1977 our merchandise exports exceeded imports (except for oil) by a large amount. Our inflation rate is among the lowest in the industrial world.

But our balance of trade and payments incurred a large and worrisome deficit. There were two main causes:

—In 1977, $45 billion flowed out to pay for imported oil. This wiped out what would otherwise have been a trade surplus.

—The demand here for foreign goods was much greater than the demand for American goods abroad. In 1977, American GNP increased roughly twice as fast in real terms as the GNP of our main trading partners.

Against this background, the exchange rate of the dollar declined relative to the currencies of Japan, Germany, Switzerland, and other European countries. These developments led to disorderly conditions in the exchange markets. In December I made clear that the United States would intervene to counter these disorders, and we have done so.

To assure the integrity of the dollar we must act now:

—We need a healthy and growing United States economy, with adequate investment, a prudent budget, and declining inflation. This will make us more competitive and more attractive to foreign investors.

—We need to conserve energy and develop alternative sources of supply. This will reduce our dependence on imported oil, and cut the outflow of dollars.

—We need to see a more vigorous world economy. Stronger growth, particularly in countries like Germany, Japan, Switzerland, and the Netherlands, can help reduce our own deficits and bring stability to international payments.

Factors already at work will reduce our trade deficit. Economic activity in Europe and elsewhere should rise. Our oil imports should level off this year. The effect of new exchange rates that have already occurred will, when their full effect is realized, improve our trade balance by several billions of dollars. While our trade and payments deficit in 1978 will be large, our external position should show some improvement.

We must also augment our capacity to deal with possible strains and pressures by strengthening our international trade and monetary system. I urge the Congress to act promptly to approve United States participation in the IMF's Supplementary Financing Facility.

The trading nations of the world are engaged in negotiations to reduce barriers and improve the international trading system by a reciprocal and balanced opening of markets. Freer trade will enable us all to use the world's resources more efficiently and will contribute to economic growth.

We will also attempt to strengthen the rules that have regulated international trade during the last 30 years. International competition must take place within a framework of agreed rules that are recognized as appropriate and fair.

THE DEVELOPING COUNTRIES

One of the most critical issues facing the United States is our economic and political relationship with developing countries. Our economy has become visibly dependent on the developing world for supplies and markets.

North-South Dialogue

Throughout 1975 and 1976 the United States and other developed countries worked with a group of developing nations in the Conference of International Economic Cooperations (CIEC). That "North-South Dialogue" reached agreement on some issues in June 1977, but there remain a number of unresolved questions. The United States will continue to consult and negotiate with developing countries on questions like commodity price stabilization, technology, and a common fund for international buffer stocks. We will pursue the North-South dialogue in the months ahead, confident that the developed nations and the developing nations can agree upon measures that will let all nations participate more fully in the management of the world economy.

Africa

Our relations with Africa involve energy, human rights, economic development, and the North-South dialogue. The Maputo and Lagos Conferences demonstrated that African countries can discuss difficult problems with us, to mutual advantage. Our relations with Nigeria have improved dramatically.

The Administration's FY 79 budget substantially increases development assistance to Africa, including continued support for the African Development Fund, and other programs to help African governments meet their people's basic human needs. The growth of African regional institutions like the Sahel Development Fund is important to African development.

Latin-America/Caribbean

The Administration's approach to Latin America and the Caribbean recognizes this region's diversity. We have placed great importance on the protection and defense of human rights, on halting the proliferation of nuclear weapons capabilities, on restraining conventional arms sales, on contributing to the settlement of disputes, and on engaging Latin governments in global economic negotiations.

We are now seeking Senate ratification of Protocol I of the Treaty of Tlatelolco, and the American Convention on Human Rights. Through the Caribbean Group, we are trying to promote regional development. And we intend to help several nations develop alternative energy sources.

Panama

General Torrijos and I signed the two Panama Canal Treaties on September 9, 1977. These treaties meet the legitimate interests of Panama and the United States and guarantee our permanent right to protect and defend the Canal. They will contribute importantly to regional stability.

Asia

The United States has sought to underline our desire for a close relationship with the developing countries of Asia through my visit to that continent and through regular contacts with the member countries of the Association of Southeast Asian Nations. We welcome the cooperation with ASEAN of the developed countries of the region, such as Japan and Australia.

PROMOTING REGIONAL RECONCILIATION

The greatest danger to world peace and stability is not war among the great powers, but war among small nations. During the past year, the United States has helped to promote productive negotiations in two troubled regions: the Middle East and Southern Africa. We have also tried to settle conflicts in the Horn of Africa and on Cyprus. And we have negotiated two Panama Canal Treaties that will enhance our country's relations with all the nations of Latin America.

The Middle East

In an effort to break with the rigid approaches of the past and bring about an overall peace settlement, I have looked to three basic principles: normalization of political, economic and cultural relations through peace treaties; withdrawal of armed forces from occupied territory to recognized and secure borders and the establishment of effective security measures; and a resolution of the Palestinian question.

Significant progress toward peace in the Middle East was made last year; we particularly applaud President Sadat's courageous initiative, reciprocated by Prime Minister Begin, in launching direct negotiations. The United States will continue this year to encourage all parties to resolve this deep-seated conflict.

Southern Africa

The entering Administration inherited problems in Rhodesia, Namibia, and South Africa.

—With the British, the United States launched new Rhodesian discussions last year. The Anglo-American Plan of September 1 sets forth fair and workable principles for majority rule: a transition period leading to free elections, a UN presence, a constitution with a judicially protected bill of rights, and a Zimbabwe Development Fund.

—The five-power Contact Group, in which the United States participates, has held discussions with South Africa and with the Southwest Africa Peoples Organization and other interested parties on an internationally acceptable settlement for an independent Namibia under majority rule. This effort has produced wide agreement, including provisions for a substantial UN presence.

—The United States has told the South African Prime Minister that unless his nation begins a progressive transformation toward full political participation for all its people, our relations will suffer. We supported a United Nations arms embargo on South Africa, prohibited "gray area" sales, and began a review of US/South African economic relations.

The Horn of Africa

Arms supplied by the Soviet Union now fuel both sides of a conflict in the Horn of Africa between Somalia and Ethiopia. There is a danger that the Soviet Union and Cuba will commit their own soldiers in this conflict, transforming it from a local war to a confrontation with broader strategic implications.

We deplore the fact that disagreements in this region have grown—with the assistance of outside powers—into bloody conflict. We have made clear to both sides that we will supply no arms for aggressive purposes. We will not recognize forcible changes in boundaries. We want to see the fighting end and the parties move from the battlefield to the negotiating table.

Cyprus

We hope that the groundwork was laid in 1977 for a permanent settlement in Cyprus and we are encouraging movement in that direction.

PRESERVING PEACE

During the past year, the Administration has assessed the threats to our own and our Allies' security, as well as our collective strength to combat these threats. We have sought to promote responsible arms control efforts and to reduce competition in arms. Recognizing that a strong defense is the foundation of our security, we have made certain that our defense spending will be sufficient and used to maximum effect.

Arms Control

The fundamental purposes of our arms limitations efforts are to promote our own national security and to strengthen international stability, thereby enhancing the prospects for peace everywhere.

—We are trying to move the Strategic Arms Limitation Talks toward more ambitious objectives. We want to reduce, not just contain, the competition in the number of strategic weapons possessed by the United States and the Soviet Union, and to limit qualitative improvements in weapons which merely raise the risks to all of us. Precisely because of our determination to obtain both of these objectives negotiations have been difficult and prolonged. However, I am confident that the agreement that we will present to the Congress will meet them.

—We have also made solid progress toward an objective that the United States has pursued for many years: a comprehensive treaty banning all nuclear explosions. This treaty will be open to all nations of the world. It will be a major step toward reduced reliance on these weapons and toward halting their further spread in the world.

—At the same time we are seeking arms limitations agreements with the Soviet Union that will contribute to security and stability in various regions of the world. In Europe we and our NATO Allies are seeking a mutual and balanced force reductions agreement that will achieve greater stability and balance at lower levels of forces. In the Indian Ocean, where neither we nor the Soviet Union has yet deployed military power on a large scale, we are working for an agreement to prevent a major military competition.

—For the first time, we have begun to negotiate with the Soviet Union the outlines of a treaty banning chemical warfare.

—An essential element of American security is the maintenance of stability in the Western Pacific, where the United States plays a major role in maintaining a balance of power. We are seeking to readjust our military presence in Korea by reducing our ground forces on the Peninsula and undertaking compensatory measures to ensure that an adequate balance of forces remain. We are talking with the Filipino government about the future of our military bases there.

—We are continuing the process of normalization of our relations with the People's Republic of China within the framework of the Shanghai Communique.

—In the last year, we have sought to halt the worldwide spread of nuclear weapons capacity. Nearly 40 nations have joined with us in an effort to find nuclear power sources that cannot be readily used for building nuclear weapons.

Defense Posture/Budget

The defense budget that I am recommending to Congress will fulfill our most pressing defense needs. I am requesting increases in defense spending that more than compensate for inflation. They are needed to maintain an adequate military balance in the face of continued Soviet military efforts.

—As we negotiate with the Soviets over strategic arms, we are continuing to preserve essential equivalence in strategic nuclear strength. Here our technological advantage over the Soviet Union is most apparent. We are building cruise missiles, which together with upgraded B-52s will assure the capability of this element of our Triad. We are continuing to develop the M-X missile system in case we need to deploy them. In this budget, I am requesting funds for continued increase in our Trident submarine force, which is our most important strategic program because submarines are so hard for any enemy to destroy.

—With our NATO Allies we are trying to improve the initial combat capability of NATO forces. We will improve the readiness of critical combat units, enhance American capability to send ground and tactical air forces reinforcements, and increase our permanent forces there. To lay the foundation for future improvements, the budget I propose requests 18 per cent increases in the procurement of equipment for the Army. The United States is not taking these steps alone; we are participating in a mutual effort.

—The importance of sea forces to United States national security is undisputed. The Navy receives the largest share of the defense budget, and I am requesting funds to continue its modernization. But, we need to examine the appropriate size and mix of United States naval forces in the future. Therefore, I have deferred spending for new aircraft carriers until a current Defense Department study is completed early this year. While we maintain our naval strength, we should have the capability to deploy rapidly a light but effective combat force worldwide, if necessary, without overseas base support. To this end, I am requesting funds for a vigorous airlift enhancement program.

In these and other ways, we are seeking to develop a foreign policy which is wider in scope; a foreign policy which recognizes global diversity; and a foreign policy which builds a more just and stable international system.

JIMMY CARTER

The White House,
January 19, 1978

Economic Message

Following is the text of President Carter's economic message to Congress Jan. 20, 1978:

TO THE CONGRESS
OF THE UNITED STATES:

I will be working closely with the Congress in 1978 to enact a program addressed to the immediate and the long-term needs of our economy. I am proposing tax reductions and reforms to continue our strong economic recovery, to encourage increased investment by American businesses, and to create a simpler and fairer tax system. I am seeking legislation to address the special problems of the disadvantaged and the unemployed. And I am taking new steps to combat inflation.

This report to the Congress on the condition of the economy sets forth the overall framework within which my economic proposals were formulated. It outlines, for you and for the Nation, my economic priorities for the years ahead and my strategies for achieving them.

I have begun from the premise that our economy is basically healthy, but that well-chosen Government policies will assure continued progress toward our economic goals.

Last year more than four million new jobs were created in our country—an all-time record—and unemployment was reduced by more than one million persons. Output rose by almost 6 per cent, and the benefits of this large increase were widely shared. The after-tax income of consumers, adjusted for inflation, rose substantially during 1977. Wages of the typical American worker increased by more than the rise of prices, and business profits also advanced.

The American economy is completing three years of recovery from the severe recession of 1974-75. Recovery in most other nations has lagged far behind our own. In the economies of our six major trading partners, seven million persons were unemployed at year's end—more than at the depths of the 1974-75 recession. Our inflation rate is also lower than in most other nations around the world. We have a great many accomplishments. But much progress remains to be made, and there are problems to be dealt with along the way.

The recession of 1974-75 was the worst in 40 years, and the substantial increase in output over the past three years still leaves the economy operating below its productive potential. We cannot be content when almost 6½ million people actively seeking jobs cannot find work, when 3¼ million workers take part-time jobs because they cannot find fulltime employment, and when one million people have stopped looking for a job because they have lost hope of finding one. We cannot be content when a substantial portion of our industrial plant stands idle, as it does today.

We cannot be satisfied with an economic recovery that bypasses significant segments of the American people. Unemployment among minorities is more than twice as high as that among whites—and unemployment among minority teenagers is tragically high. Women have fewer satisfying job opportunities than men, and older Americans often find their access to the job market blocked. Farm incomes have dropped precipitously.

We must also address other problems if we are to assure full restoration of prosperity. Inflation is a serious economic concern for all Americans. The inflation rate is too high and must be brought down. Moreover, a residue of unease and caution about the future still pervades the thinking of some of our people. Businesses are still hesitant in their long-term investment planning, and the stock market remains depressed despite the substantial increase in business profits.

The economic difficulties that we face in the United States also confront most nations around the world. Our mutual problems are the legacy of the trauma suffered by the world economy during the early 1970s. The massive escalation of oil prices since 1973 continues to impose great burdens on the world economy. Oil imports drain away the purchasing power of oil-importing nations and upset the international balance of payments.

Many foreign governments have been reluctant to adopt policies needed to stimulate economic growth because they are concerned that inflationary pressures might be renewed or that their balance of international payments might be worsened. Abroad, as well as at home, concerns about the future have deterred business investment in new plants and equipment. As a consequence, economic growth has stagnated in many countries, and the rise in the capital stock needed to increase productivity, raise standards of living, and avoid future inflationary bottlenecks is not occurring.

The problems we face today are more complex and difficult than those of an earlier era. We cannot concentrate just on inflation, or just on unemployment, or just on deficits in the Federal budget or our international payments. Nor can we act in isolation from other countries. We must deal with all of these problems simultaneously and on a worldwide basis.

Our problems cannot be solved overnight. But we can resolve them if we fix our sights on long-term objectives, adopt programs that will help us to realize our goals, and remain prepared to make adjustments as basic circumstances change.

In making my decisions on tax and budget policies for fiscal 1979, and in planning more generally for our Nation's future, I have been guided by four objectives for our economy that I believe our Nation should pursue.

We must continue to move steadily toward a high-employment economy in which the benefits of prosperity are widely shared. Progress in reducing unemployment of our labor and capital resources must be sure and sustainable. Over the next several years I believe we can increase our real output by 4½ to 5 per cent per year, and reduce unemployment by about one-half of a percentage point each year. An especially high priority is to increase job opportunities for the disadvantaged, particularly for black and Spanish-speaking Americans, and to deal more effectively with local pockets of unemployment, such as those in urban areas. We should eliminate unfair advantages through reform of the tax system, and restructure our welfare system to assure that the fruits of economic growth are enjoyed by all Americans.

We should rely principally on the private sector to lead the economic expansion and to create new jobs for a growing labor force. Five out of every six new jobs in the economy are created in the private sector. There are good reasons for continuing to rely mainly on the private sector in the years ahead. By emphasizing the creation of private jobs, our resources will be used more efficiently, our future capacity to produce will expand more rapidly, and the standard of living for our people will rise faster. Reliance upon the private sector does not mean neglecting the tasks that government can and must perform. The Federal Government can be an active partner to help achieve progress toward meeting national needs and, through competent management, still absorb a declining portion of the Nation's output.

We must contain and reduce the rate of inflation as we move toward a more fully employed economy. Inflation extracts a heavy toll from all Americans, and particularly from the poor and those on fixed incomes. Reducing inflation would benefit us all. A more stable price environment would make it easier for business firms and consumers to plan for the future. Thus, reduced inflation would substantially enhance our chances to maintain a strong economic expansion and return to a high-employment economy. In the years ahead we must seek to unwind the inflation we have inherited from the past and take the steps necessary to prevent new inflationary pressures as we approach high employment.

We must act in ways that contribute to the health of the world economy. As the strongest economy in the world, the United States has unique responsibilities to improve the international economic climate. The well-being of the United States depends on the condition of other nations around the world. Their economic destiny is, in turn, shaped by ours. The United States can retain its stature in the world only by pursuing policies that measure up to its role as a leader in international economic affairs.

These four economic objectives are sufficiently ambitious to constitute a serious challenge, but sufficiently realistic to be within our reach. A well-designed program will permit us to achieve them. The principal elements of my economic strategy are:

- Adopting promptly an effective national energy program;
- Managing Federal budget expenditures carefully and prudently, so that we can meet national needs while gradually reducing the share of our national output devoted to Federal spending;
- Using tax reductions to ensure steady growth of the private economy and reforming the tax system to make it fairer, simpler, and more progressive;
- Working to reduce the Federal deficit and balance the budget as rapidly as the developing strength of the economy allows;
- Improving existing programs and developing new ones to attack the problem of structural unemployment among the disadvantaged;
- Promoting greater business capital formation in order to enhance productivity gains, increase standards of living, and reduce the chances that capacity shortages would inhibit expansion later on;
- Adopting more effective programs to reduce the current rate of inflation and prevent a reacceleration of inflation as we approach high employment; and
- Pursuing international economic policies that promote economic recovery throughout the world, encourage an expansion of world trade, and maintain a strong international monetary system.

National Energy Plan

It has now been over four years since our economy was buffeted by the oil embargo and its aftermath of sharply increased oil prices. The massive oil price increase in 1973-74 contributed to the double-digit inflation of 1974 and to the worst recession in 40 years. It is a primary factor today behind the large deficit in our international balance of payments. Yet the United States still has not enacted a comprehensive and effective energy policy.

Our dependence on imported oil is sapping the strength of the American economy. Last year our imports of oil reached a total of about $45 billion, compared with $8½ billion in 1973. The increased expenditures on those imports have been like a sudden and massive tax imposed on the American people. Only part of the revenues have been returned to the United States in the form of higher exports of American goods to oil-producing countries. As a consequence, that "tax" has become a major obstacle to economic growth.

The huge deficit in foreign trade arising from our oil imports has contributed to the fall in the value of the dollar abroad. The dollar's decline has raised the cost of the goods we import and contributed to inflation. Our deficit also has unsettled international monetary markets, with adverse consequences for our international trading partners. Our response to the energy crisis is therefore a central element in our international and domestic economic policy. The energy program will not solve our problems at once, but it will pave the way for a balanced foreign trade position and a strong and sound dollar.

Our energy problems will worsen in the years to come unless we curb our appetite for oil and gas. Without decisive action, we will put additional pressure on the world oil market, aggravate inflationary pressures at home, and increase our vulnerability to the threat of oil supply disruptions. Together, these forces could severely limit the potential for continued economic progress over the coming decade.

The United States has no choice but to adjust to the new era of expensive energy. We can only choose when and how. If we act today, we have time to make a gradual transition to more efficient energy use—by conserving energy, increasing domestic energy production, and developing alternative sources of energy. If we delay, adjustment later will be harsh and painful, requiring draconian measures to accomplish what can now be done gradually and with far less anguish.

The energy problem we face is enormously complex. Finding an acceptable and effective solution has not been easy for me or for the Congress. I look forward to working closely with the Congress early this year to assure a speedy resolution. An acceptable bill must satisfy the following principles:

- First, the program must effectively reduce our consumption of limited energy supplies—oil and gas—while encouraging energy production and promoting a transition to the use of resources that are more abundant.
- Second, the program must be fair. No segment of the population should bear a disproportionate share of the cost or burden of adjustment, and no industry should reap unnecessary and undeserved windfall gains.
- Third, the program must be consistent with our overall economic strategy. It must neither undermine our efforts to continue the recovery nor obstruct achievement of our long-term budgetary goals.

Dealing with the energy problem is a difficult test for our Nation. It is a test of our economic and political maturity. Our people would surely react if there were an immediate crisis. But I am asking them to undertake sacrifices to *prevent* a crisis. If we fail to act today, we will bring a crisis upon ourselves and our children in years to come.

Federal Budget Expenditures

My Administration has given high priority to making more effective use of limited Federal resources. In fiscal 1976, Federal outlays amounted to 22½ per cent of the Nation's gross national product. This is considerably higher than the share devoted to government spending that prevailed for many years. To some degree, the recent higher share reflects the fact that the economy is still performing below its capacity, and that Federal programs to support the unemployed and the needy are larger than they would be in a high-employment economy. But it also stems from very rapid growth in a number of Federal programs instituted over the past 10 to 15 years.

Most of our Federal expenditure programs are designed to achieve important national goals that the private sector of the economy cannot accomplish. Only the government can provide for the national defense, and government resources are essential to cushion the hardships created by economic recession, to preserve our national resources, to protect the environment, and to meet other critical needs.

The Federal Government has a particular obligation to provide assistance to those who remain in need even during good times. Last year I presented to the Congress a program to reform the welfare system—the Better Jobs and Income Act of 1977—that is a concrete example of our commitment to devote resources to the most pressing national needs. My program will cost money. But it also will establish a more easily understood welfare system that is less costly to administer, less subject to abuse, and more responsive to the true needs of those who receive a helping hand from government. This program will create up to 1.4 million jobs for those able to work, and it will replace the patchwork of Federal, State, and local programs with a consistent income-support system that will relieve much of the enormous burden now placed on State and local governments.

In the management of a business enterprise, efficiency is enforced by the discipline of the market place. The collective judgments of millions of consumers establish an environment in which waste and efficiency are eventually penalized. The government, however, is not subject to that discipline. We in government must therefore impose stringent controls on ourselves to ensure greater efficiency and to make better choices among the possible uses of the taxpayers' money.

To assist us in this endeavor, I have adopted methods of budgetary control that have been tested in the business community. Early last year I asked the Office of Management and Budget to inaugurate a system of zero-based budgeting throughout the Federal Government. Within this budgetary system, every Federal program is given careful scrutiny—no matter how large or how small it may be, no matter how long it has been in existence or how recently established. This new system of budgetary planning helped to hold down less essential outlays in the budget for fiscal 1979 and focus our resources on our important national needs. It will produce even greater savings in subsequent years. A process of multi-year budgeting also has been inaugurated within the Federal Government that will require tentative budget plans to be developed and reviewed for three years ahead. With this system we can more effectively control future expenditures—by avoiding commitments now to endeavors that would grow in the future beyond the proportions we desire.

In formulating my recommendations for the 1979 budget, I have exercised very strict controls over spending. Adjusted for inflation, the increase in outlays has been held to less than 2 percent. I intend to continue prudent expenditure controls in the future. With good management we can, I believe, achieve our Nation's important social goals and still reduce over time the share of gross national product committed to Federal expenditures to about 21 percent.

Tax Reductions

I propose to rely principally upon growth in the private sector of the economy to reduce unemployment and raise incomes. Special Federal efforts will, of course, be necessary to deal with such problems as structural unemployment, but tax reductions will be the primary means by which Federal budget policy will promote growth. Careful management of budget outlays and a growing economy should permit substantial reductions in the years ahead. Tax reductions will be needed to strengthen consumer purchasing power and expand consumer markets. Stable growth in markets, together with added tax incentives for business, will lead to rising business investment and growing productivity.

As inflation and real economic growth raise the incomes of most Americans, they are pushed into higher income tax brackets. The tax burden on individuals is raised just as if higher rates had been enacted. The payroll taxes levied on workers and business firms for social security and unemployment insurance will also increase substantially over the year ahead. These are very large increases, but they are needed to keep our social security and unemployment insurance systems soundly financed.

Between 1977 and 1979, taxes on businesses and individuals will rise very sharply as a result of these several factors. Even though our economy is basically healthy, this increasingly heavy tax burden would exert a mounting drag on economic growth. It must, therefore, be counteracted by tax reductions. The magnitude and timing of the reductions should be designed to maintain economic growth at a steady pace, taking into account the effects both of the growing tax burden and of other factors at work in the economy.

Consistent with this strategy, I am proposing a $25 billion program of net tax reductions accompanied by substantial tax reforms.

Individual income taxes will be reduced primarily through across-the-board reductions in personal tax rates, with special emphasis on low- and middle-income taxpayers. Personal taxes also will be simplified by my proposal to replace the existing personal exemption and credit with a tax credit of $240 for each person in the taxpayer's family.

There also will be important reforms that will improve the individual income tax system and raise substantial revenues, enabling me to recommend larger personal tax reductions.

Overall, I am proposing personal tax reductions of $24 billion, offset by $7 billion in tax reforms. These tax cuts, which will take effect next October 1, will significantly improve the progressivity of the tax system. The typical four-person family with $15,000 in income will receive a tax cut of $258—or more than 19 percent. As a result of the changes I am recommending, filling out tax returns will be simpler for many people.

Individuals also will benefit from reductions I have proposed in the Federal excise tax on telephone bills, and in the Federal payroll tax for unemployment insurance. These two proposals will add about $2 billion to consumers' purchasing power that will be realized principally through lower prices.

Business taxes will be reduced by more than $8 billion in 1979 under my tax program, offset partially by more than $2 billion in business tax reforms for a net tax reduction of nearly $6 billion. I have recommended that the overall corporate tax rate be reduced on October 1 from the current 48 percent to 45 percent, and be cut further to 44 percent in 1980. I also recommend that the existing 10-percent investment tax credit be made permanent, and that the benefits of this credit be extended to investments in industrial and utility structures. My proposal will enable businesses to use the investment tax credit to offset up to 90 percent of their Federal tax liability, compared with the 50-percent limit now imposed.

Important new tax reforms also will affect businesses. I am, for example, proposing to reduce the deductibility of a large class of business entertainment expenses. I have also proposed changes in the tax status of international business transactions that are of significant cost to taxpayers but that benefit the public insufficiently.

Because tax reform measures will raise $9 billion in revenue, it has been possible for me to recommend $34 billion in overall tax reductions while keeping the net loss in revenues to $25 billion, the level I believe is appropriate given the state of our economy and the size of the budget deficit.

These proposals do not include any adjustment to take account of congressional action on my energy proposals. I proposed last April that the Congress pass a wellhead tax and rebate the proceeds of that tax directly to the American people. This is the best course to follow because it protects the real incomes of consumers and avoids a new source of fiscal drag. If the final energy bill includes a full rebate of the net proceeds of the wellhead tax, no further action on my part will be necessary. However, if the final bill allows for a rebate only for 1978—as provided in the House version—I will send a supplemental message to the Congress recommending that the individual tax reduction I am now proposing be increased by the amount of the net proceeds of the wellhead tax.

These tax reductions are essential to healthy economic recovery during 1978 and 1979. Prospects for continuation of that recovery in the near term are favorable. Consumers have been spending freely, and many other economic indicators recently have been moving up strongly. Without the tax reductions I have proposed, however, the longer-term prospects for economic growth would become increasingly poor. Because of the fiscal drag imposed by rising payroll taxes and inflation, economic growth would slow substantially in late 1978, and fall to about 3½ percent in 1979. The unemployment rate would stop declining and might begin to rise again, and the growth of investment outlays for new plant and equipment would slow significantly.

With the reductions in taxes I have proposed, on the other hand, the economy should grow by 4½ to 5 percent in both 1978 and 1979. Nearly one million new jobs would be created. Unemployment would therefore continue to fall and by late 1979 should be down to around 5½ to 6 percent. Capacity utilization and after-tax business profits would both improve, and thus the rate of investment in new plants and equipment should increase significantly.

Success in keeping a firm rein on spending will permit further tax reductions in years to come. Our ability to foresee the future course of the economy is not good enough, however, to enable us to know when additional reductions will be needed or how large they should be. It would therefore be imprudent to plan specific policy measures now for more than the current and the next fiscal year. But I will make recommendations for budget and tax policies for 1980 and beyond that are in keeping with our objectives of steady growth in the economy, more stable prices, and principal reliance on the private sector to achieve economic expansion.

Federal Deficit

Federal budgetary policy can play a constructive role in maintaining the health of the economy. There are times when large deficits in the Federal budget must be tolerated because they are needed to bolster the purchasing power of consumers and businesses. A budget deficit that persisted during a period of high employment and strong further growth of private demand, however, would put upward pressures on prices and would aggravate our inflationary problem. Under those circumstances, a budget deficit would also absorb savings that would be better used by the private sector to build new factories and offices and to purchase new machines. In order to assure that our economic progress remains on a solid footing and is not undermined by inflation, we must reduce the Federal budget deficit and achieve a balanced budget as soon as the developing strength in the economy allows.

The first requisite is careful management and control of Federal spending. The second is a prudent weighing of the need for tax reductions against the goal of budget balance.

This year I have proposed budgets that call for a deficit of $62 billion in 1978, and one only slightly smaller in 1979. Had I decided not to recommend a tax cut to put additional purchasing power in the hands of consumers and businesses, the deficit in 1979 could have been $15 to $20 billion smaller. But I believe that tax reduction is essential to continued progress in an economy still characterized by substantial unemployment and idle plant capacity.

How rapidly we can restore budget balance depends on the strength of the private economy. Over the next few years, two factors will be of particular importance.

The first is the financial condition of State and local governments. In the past, the aggregate budget of these governments tended to be approximately in balance. Today the State and local sector as a whole is in surplus. In 1977, for example, aggregate State and local receipts from all sources exceeded expenditures by nearly $30 billion. This overall surplus does not mean that every State and local government is in good financial condition. Many are hard pressed. Moreover, a large part of the aggregate surplus represents accumulations of pension funds for the 13 million employees of State and local governments.

Substantial surpluses in the State and local sector are likely to continue in the future. They absorb the incomes of consumers and business, and so act as a drag on the economy.

The second factor affecting the pace at which we can expect to move toward budget balance is the large deficit in America's foreign trade in goods and services. Imports into the United States have been swollen by the enormous quantity of oil we buy abroad to drive our cars, heat our homes, and fuel our industry. Our exports have grown only slowly, in large measure because economic growth abroad has been much slower than in the United States. As a result, the United States last year recorded a deficit of close to $18 billion in our current international accounts. This deficit has the same general effect on economic activity as a multibillion dollar increase in taxes.

Enactment of an effective energy program ultimately will reverse our growing dependence on oil imports. Moreover, economic growth in other countries should be improving over the next few years. But we may expect a current account deficit of some size to continue in the near future.

If strong economic expansion is to be maintained in the face of these major drains on the economy, additional tax reductions may be necessary beyond those I have proposed for 1979. But we will be better able to judge this question in a year or two, and we should not prejudge it now.

In formulating my budgetary decisions thus far, I have been careful to avoid commitments that would make it impossible for us to balance the budget by 1981. With unusually strong growth in the private economy, we would need a balanced Federal budget. In an economy growing less strongly, however, balancing the budget by 1981 would be possible only by forgoing tax reductions needed to reach our goal of high employment. In those circumstances, the date for reaching the goal of budget balance would have to be deferred.

What is important is that the planning and execution of Federal fiscal policies proceed in a prudent manner. Every decision on spending and taxes during my Administration has been, and will continue to be, made in the context of long-run budgetary planning that avoids the creation of excess demand during periods of high employment. That is an essential ingredient of responsible budgetary policy.

Structural Unemployment

Meaningful job opportunities ought to be available for all Americans who wish to work. But overall fiscal and monetary policy alone will not provide employment to many in our Nation. If we are to reduce unemployment satisfactorily, we must do more.

Eleven percent of adult American workers from minority groups are now jobless—close to the rate a year ago, and over twice as high as the unemployment rate for white adults. About 17 percent of our teenagers are unemployed today; among black teenagers the unemployment rate is nearly 40 percent. These intolerably high rates of unemployment must be brought down. This is an important goal, but achieving it will be a difficult task.

A generally healthy and growing economy is a prerequisite for dealing effectively with structural unemployment, but it is not enough. Even in good times some groups suffer from very high unemployment, which adds to the difficulty of achieving low unemployment and low inflation simultaneously. As the economy moves toward high employment, employers try to fill job vacancies from those groups of workers with substantial training and experience. Wage rates are bid up and prices follow, while large numbers from other groups are still looking unsuccessfully for work. Efforts to reduce unemployment among the unskilled and otherwise disadvantaged can be frustrated by inflationary pressures set off in those sectors of the labor market already fully employed.

To reach high levels of employment while maintaining reasonable price stability, we must take effective and adequate measures now to increase the employment opportunities of the disadvantaged. This principle is a key element of the Humphrey-Hawkins Bill—The Full Employment and Balanced Growth Act. I support this legislation and hope the Congress will enact it.

We have already taken several significant steps in this direction. Last year I proposed and the Congress appropriated $8.4 billion to expand the Public Service Employment Program to 725,000 jobs. These jobs are more sharply targeted on the long-term unemployed and the poor than previous programs under the Comprehensive Employment and Training Act. Direct opportunities for youth also have been expanded. The Youth Employment and Demonstration Projects Act of 1977, which is providing job experience and training in skills to unemployed youths, also was proposed by my Administration and enacted in 1977, providing 166,000 work and training positions for unemployed youths.

Several further measures are proposed in my 1979 budget. I have recommended that Public Service Employment be continued at the 725,000 job level throughout 1979, and that the number of jobs be phased down gradually in subsequent years as progress is made in reducing the overall level of unemployment. I have also recommended an expansion to $1.2 billion of the Youth Employment and Demonstration Projects Act to provide work opportunities and skill training for the unemployed youth who most need help. The Better Jobs and Income Program that I sent to the Congress in mid-1977 will create up to 1.4 million jobs, supplemented by cash allowances, for poor people who are able to work. An initial demonstration project for this program that will create 50,000 jobs is proposed in my 1979 budget, and more jobs will be phased in gradually once the welfare reform program is enacted.

Government programs can provide valuable assistance to the unemployed. In the end, however, we must turn to the private sector for the bulk of permanent job opportunities for the disadvantaged. It is in private industry that most productive jobs with opportunity for advancement are found. For this reason, I am requesting $400 million in my 1979 budget to begin a major new initiative for private sector hiring of the disadvantaged. Details of this proposal will be submitted to the Congress shortly. I am requesting the fullest cooperation of the business community in this initiative and have been assured by business leaders that it will be forthcoming.

Capital Formation

Over a broad expanse of years, improvement of the standard of living in this Nation depends primarily on growth in the productivity of the American work force. During the first two decades of the postwar period, the productivity of American labor increased at an average annual rate of about 3 percent. Over the past ten years, however, productivity growth has slowed markedly—to about 2 percent or less a year.

The reasons for this break with past trends are complex, but one factor that clearly stands out is the relatively slow growth in the stock of business plant and equipment. Historically, improvements in productivity have been linked closely to investment in plant and equipment. Investment in new facilities has embodied new and more productive technology and has provided our work force with more and better tools.

Business investment has lagged during the recovery for several reasons. Some of the fears engendered by the steep recession and severe inflation of 1973-75 have remained and have reduced the incentive for business to invest. Uncertainties about energy supplies and energy prices have also been a deterrent to investment, and so have concerns about governmental regulations in a variety of areas. Finally, high costs of capital goods and a depressed stock market have diminished the incentives and raised the costs to businesses of investment in new plant and equipment.

Industrial capacity is ample now. But without a substantial increase in investment over the next few years, problems would build for the future. Rapid growth of capacity is needed to assure that shortages of particular products do not emerge before we regain high employment. If capacity is not sufficient, bottlenecks may develop in some sectors, forcing up prices of industrial commodities. Inadequate rates of capital formation will also hold back the gains in productivity needed to improve standards of living and to avoid further aggravation of our inflation problem.

My tax and other economic proposals will encourage a greater rate of business investment in several ways. By promoting a sustainable rate of economic recovery, they will assure businesses of an expanding market for the output from new factories and equipment. The specific tax reductions for business I have proposed will increase after-tax profits and so directly provide additional incentives for investment.

We must also have conditions in financial markets that permit businesses to raise the funds they need for investment. Prudent Federal budgetary policies will contribute significantly to that end, as will policies that deal effectively with inflation. Both will ease the Federal Reserve's task of pursuing monetary policies that support full recovery.

Rate of Inflation

We cannot achieve full prosperity unless we deal effectively with inflation. We must take steps to reduce the high rate of inflation inherited from the past and to guard against a renewed outbreak of inflation as we regain a high-employment economy.

Our economy is not suffering at present from excess demand. Monetary growth in recent years has not been excessive, and Federal budget deficits have occurred in an economy with high unemployment and excess capacity. Yet prices continue to rise as a result of an inflationary process that has been under way for a decade.

Our present inflation began back in the late 1960s and accelerated sharply in the early years of the 1970s. Since 1974 the rate of consumer price inflation has declined substantially—from 12 percent to between 6 and 6½ percent at present. But that improvement is due largely to the termination of special influences affecting prices during 1974—the sharp rise of food and fuel prices, and the bulge in prices following the removal of wage and price controls.

Recent experience has demonstrated that the inflation we have inherited from the past cannot be cured by policies that slow growth and keep unemployment high. Since 1975, inflation has persisted stubbornly at a 6 to 6½ percent rate—even though unemployment went as high as 9 percent and still stands above 6 percent, and even though a substantial proportion of our industrial capacity has been idle. The human tragedy and waste of resources associated with policies of slow growth are intolerable, and the impact of such policies on the current inflation is very small Moreover, by discouraging investment in new capacity, slow growth sows the seeds of future inflationary problems when the economy does return to high employment. Economic stagnation is not the answer to inflation.

Our first task in combating inflation is to guard against a renewed outbreak of higher price increases in the future. Firm discipline over the Federal budget and a prudent monetary policy are the most important steps that can be taken. Programs to attack structural pockets of unemployment among our people will make it possible to achieve higher levels of employment without exerting pressures on prices. Greater investment also will make a major contribution toward assuring that the capacity of our industry will be adequate to meet the needs of a high-employment economy.

Enactment of an energy program will eventually reduce the demand for oil imports—contributing to market conditions that discourage substantial oil price increases, and combating the inflation that results from a decline in the exchange value of the dollar. The programs I have inaugurated to build a 30- to 35-million metric ton grain reserve will provide a buffer against sudden upward movements in food prices in the event of bad weather.

Our second task—reducing the current rate of inflation—will be harder. Yet we must tackle the problem. Unless the inflation rate is brought down, the rate of price increase may well rise as unemployment falls to lower levels in later years, with consequences that would thwart our efforts to bring about full recovery.

The government has an obligation to set an example for the private sector, and we can play an important role in moderating inflation by reducing the effects of our own actions on prices. By adopting tax incentives and other policies to improve the growth of investment and productivity, we will help reduce the rise in costs and hence in prices.

The excise tax reductions I have proposed in my 1979 budget also will contribute moderately to lower costs and prices.

Government regulations also add to costs and raise prices. To some extent, this is the inevitable cost of much needed improvements in the environment and in the health and safety of workers and consumers. But there is no question that the scope of regulation has become excessive and that too little attention is given to its economic costs. We should not, and will not, give up our efforts to achieve cleaner air and water and a safer workplace. But, wherever possible, the extent of regulation should be reduced. We have eliminated hundreds of unneeded regulations already and will continue to pare down the remainder.

I also intend to put a high priority on minimizing the adverse effects of governmental regulations on the economy. To this end, I have established a high-level interagency committee that—together with the relevant regulatory agency—will review the economic effects of major regulations. This committee will seek to assure that the costs of each regulation have been fully considered, and that all alternatives have been explored, so that we may find and apply the least costly means of achieving our regulatory objectives. I have also directed my advisers to explore ways in which we can undertake an assessment of the impact of regulation on the economy as a whole and within each major sector. We need to find a way to set priorities among regulatory objectives and understand more fully the combined effects of our regulatory actions on the private economy.

Where regulation of economic activity has become outmoded and substantial overhaul is called for, I will pursue effective legislation. For example, I have supported actively congressional efforts to reform regulation of the airline industry, and I am considering proposals to reform the regulation of other industries.

I have given special attention to reducing the runaway costs of health care. The cost of a day in the hospital has more than doubled since 1970. Continuing escalation in the charges for hospital care can no longer be tolerated. I have submitted legislation, the Hospital Cost Containment Act of 1977, that would limit sharply the rate of growth in hospital spending, and I urge the Congress to enact this legislation in 1978.

The States can also play a role in moderating the current inflation. In 1976, State governments collected $50 billion in sales taxes. For the most part, these taxes enter directly into the cost of goods we buy and thus increase the price level. Today, State governments with significant surpluses are considering tax reductions. I urge those in a position to do so to consider the advantages to the national economy of reducing sales taxes, thereby helping to slow inflation.

Government alone cannot unwind the current inflation, however. Today's inflationary process is largely the consequence of self-fulfilling expectations. Businessmen, expecting inflation to continue, are less resistant to cost increases than they might be, since they have come to believe that, with all prices rising, their own increased costs can be passed on to consumers through higher prices. Wage increases are based on the expectation that prices will continue to rise. Wage gains in one sector spur similar demands in others.

There are gainers and losers in this process, since some groups in the economy are more successful than others at defending themselves against inflation. On the whole, however, the main result is continued inflation. No one group—neither business, nor labor, nor government—can stop this spiral on its own. What is needed is a joint effort.

Since the current inflation has developed strong momentum, it cannot be brought to a sudden halt. But we can achieve a gradual but sustained deceleration—having each succeeding year's inflation lower than the previous one. The benefits of slower growth of prices and wages would be broadly shared. Everyone would be better off. A conscious effort should be made by those who make wage and price decisions to take the individual actions necessary to bring about an economy-wide deceleration of inflation.

I am therefore asking the business community and American workers to participate in a voluntary program to decelerate the rate of price and wage increase. This program is based on the initial presumption that prices and wages in each industry should rise significantly less in 1978 than they did on average during the past two years.

I recognize that not all wages and prices can be expected to decelerate at the same pace. For example, where profit margins have been particularly squeezed, or where wages are lagging seriously, deceleration in 1978 would be less than for other firms or groups of workers. In exceptional cases deceleration may not be possible at all. Conversely, firms or groups that have done exceptionally well in the recent past may be expected to do more.

To enhance the prospects for success of this deceleration program, I have asked that major firms and unions respond to requests from members of my Administration to discuss with them on an informal basis steps that can be taken during the coming year to achieve deceleration in their industries. In reviewing the economic situation prior to making my recommendations to the Congress on the size of the pay raise for Federal workers, due to take effect next October, I will keep this objective of deceleration in mind.

This program does not establish a uniform set of numerical standards against which each price or wage action is to be measured. The past inflation has introduced too many distortions into the economy to make that possible or desirable. But it does establish a standard of behavior for each industry for the coming year: every effort should be made to reduce the rate of wage and price increase in 1978 to below the average rate of the past two years.

I have chosen this approach after reviewing extensively all of the available options. There is no guarantee that establishing a voluntary deceleration standard will unwind the current inflation. I believe, however, that with the cooperation of business and labor, this proposal will work. Deceleration is a feasible standard of behavior, for it seeks restraint in wage and price actions in exchange for a general reduction in inflation. It is also a fair standard. Industries and workers with far different histories and current situations will not be asked to fit within the constraint of a single numerical guideline.

The inflation problem will not be easy to overcome. It will take time and patience. But the importance of these efforts cannot be overestimated. Unless we gain better control over the inflation rate, the prospects for regaining a fully employed economy will be seriously reduced. My Administration cannot and will not pursue policies in the future that threaten to trigger a new and more virulent round of inflation in this country. To do so would be the surest way of destroying the hopes of our citizens for a long-lasting prosperity.

International Economic Policies

Outside the United States, the world economy has seen a hesitant recovery from the deep recession of 1974-75. The rapid pace of economic growth that was widespread over most of the postwar years has all but disappeared. Unemployment is high, and in most industrial countries except the United States it is rising. Inflation is at high levels and declining only very slowly.

The imbalances in the international economic system continue to strain the world economy. Because of the surpluses of oil-exporting countries, many countries have sizable deficits, including the United States. Some industrial nations are also running large and persistent surpluses—thus increasing the pressures on countries in deficit. These imbalances have been a major factor contributing to disorder in exchange markets in recent months.

The condition of the world economy requires above all that nations work together to develop mutually beneficial solutions to global problems. If we fail to work together, we will lose the gains in living standards arising from the expansion of world commerce over the past three decades. If the world economy becomes a collection of isolated and weak nations, we will all lose.

The first priority in our international economic policy is continued economic recovery throughout the industrial world. Growth of the U.S. economy—the largest and strongest in the world—is of vital importance. The economic program that I have proposed will ensure that America remains a leader and a source of strength in the world economy. It is important that other strong nations join with us to take direct actions to spur demand within their own economies. World recovery cannot proceed if nations rely upon exports as the principal source of economic expansion.

At the same time all countries must continue the battle against inflation. This will require prudent fiscal and monetary policies. Such policies must be supplemented by steps to reduce structural unemployment, measures to avoid bottlenecks by encouraging investment, and cooperation in the accumulation of commodity reserves to insulate the world from unforeseen shocks.

Reducing the widespread imbalances in international payments will require several parallel steps. To begin with, each individual country must ensure that its own policies help relieve the strains. The United States will do its part. In 1977 we had a current account deficit of about $18 billion. While not a cause for alarm, this is a matter of concern. We can take a most constructive step toward correcting this deficit by moving quickly to enact the National Energy Plan.

Countries in surplus should also do their part. Balance of payments surpluses in some countries have contributed to the economic stagnation among their trading partners. Where their own economies have slack, it is appropriate for nations in surplus to stimulate the growth of domestic demand—thereby increasing their imports and improving the prospects for growth in deficit countries. In some countries, lifting restraints on imports from abroad and reducing excessive government efforts to promote exports would be useful. After consultations with the United States, the Japanese have indicated they will take a series of steps toward reducing their large surplus.

The system of flexible exchange rates for currencies also can be helpful in correcting unsustainable imbalances in payments among countries. Since its inception in 1973, this system has operated well under unprecedented strains.

During 1977 the U.S. dollar has fallen in value against several key currencies. The decline in the dollar's value has occurred primarily against the currencies of those nations that have large trade and payments surpluses, and was not surprising in view of our large payments deficit and their surpluses. Late in 1977, however, movements in our exchange rate became both disorderly and excessively rapid. The United States reaffirmed its intention to step in when conditions in exchange markets become disorderly and to work in close cooperation with our friends abroad in this effort.

Under the flexible exchange rate system basic economic forces must continue to be the fundamental determinant of the value of currencies. However, we will not permit speculative activities in currency markets to disrupt our economy or those of our trading partners. We recognize fully our obligation in this regard, and we have taken steps to fulfill it.

Although substantial progress can be made toward a balanced world economy, some imbalances will persist for a substantial period of time. Financing requirements will remain large while adjustments occur. The private markets can and will continue to channel the bulk of the financing from surplus to deficit countries. But it is essential that adequate official financing also be available, in case of need, to encourage countries with severe payments problems to adopt orderly and responsible corrective measures. To meet this critical need the United States has strongly supported a proposal to strengthen the International Monetary Fund by the establishment of a new Supplementary Financing Facility.

The United States also will continue to contribute resources to promote growth in the economies of the developing nations. International assistance efforts—through bilateral aid and multilateral institutions—must continue to expand. We must also keep our doors open to imports from developing countries, so that their economies can grow and prosper through expanded trade.

A keystone of our international economic policy is to work with our trading partners to protect a free and open trading system. The American economy benefits by exporting those products that we make efficiently, and by importing those that we produce least efficiently. An open trading system increases our real incomes, strengthens competition in our markets, and contributes to combating inflation.

The United States will firmly resist the demands for protection that inevitably develop when the world economy suffers from high unemployment. The ensuing decline in world trade would worsen our problem of inflation, create inefficiencies in American enterprise, and lead to fewer jobs for American workers. But international competition must be fair. We have already taken and we will, when necessary, continue to take steps to ensure that our businesses and workers do not suffer from unfair trade practices.

I place great importance on the Multilateral Trade Negotiations now under way in Geneva. I believe our negotiators will bring home agreements that are fair and balanced and that will benefit our economy immensely over the years to come. The importance of these discussions can hardly be overemphasized. The trading system that emerges from the negotiations will set the tone for international commerce well into the 1980s. Our commitment to a successful conclusion to these talks underscores our long-term emphasis on the retention and expansion of open and fair trade among nations.

The Challenge Before Us

In this message I have outlined my fundamental economic goals and the strategy for attaining them. It is an ambitious, but I believe a realistic, agenda for the future. It calls for a broad range of actions to improve the health and fairness of the American economy. And it calls upon the American people to participate actively in many of these efforts.

I ask the Congress and the American people to join with me in a sustained effort to achieve a lasting prosperity. We all share the same fundamental goals. We can work together to reach them.

Jimmy Carter

January 20, 1978

Tax Reform Proposals

Following is the text of President Carter's Jan. 20 message to Congress proposing changes in the nation's tax system:

TO THE CONGRESS
OF THE UNITED STATES:

I recommend that Congress enact a series of proposals that will reform our tax system and provide $25 billion in net tax reductions for individuals and businesses.

Fundamental reform of our tax laws is essential and should begin now. Tax relief and the maintenance of a strong economy are essential as well. The enactment of these proposals will constitute a major step towards sustaining our economic recovery and making our tax system fairer and simpler.

The Need for Tax Reduction

I propose net tax reductions consisting of:

—$17 billion in net income tax cuts for individuals, through across-the-board rate reductions and a new personal credit, focused primarily on low- and middle-income taxpayers.

—$6 billion in net income tax cuts for small and large corporations, through reductions in the corporate tax rates and extensions of the investment tax credit.

—$2 billion for elimination of the excise tax on telephone calls and a reduction in the payroll tax for unemployment insurance.

These tax reductions are a central part of the administration's overall economic strategy, which will rely principally upon growth in the private sector to create the new jobs we need to achieve our high-employment objective. The tax reductions will more than offset the recent increase in social security taxes and will provide the consumer purchasing power and business investment strength we need to keep our economy growing strongly and unemployment moving down.

Together with the programs that I will outline in my Budget Message, these tax cuts should assure that our economy will grow at a 4½ to 5 per cent pace through 1979, with unemployment declining to between 5½ and 6 per cent by the end of 1979. Without the tax cuts, economic growth would slow markedly toward the end

Summary of Revenue Effects of Income Tax Reductions, Tax Reforms and Telephone Excise and Unemployment Insurance Tax Reductions

($ billions)

	Fiscal Years				
	1979	1980	1981	1982	1983
Individual Income Tax:					
Tax reductions	−22.5	−25.7	−29.2	−33.4	−38.5
Tax reforms	4.2	7.4	8.9	10.6	12.3
Net change	−18.3	−18.2	−20.3	−22.8	−26.2
Corporation Income Tax:					
Tax reductions	−6.3	−9.4	−11.1	−11.8	−12.8
Tax reforms	1.1	3.0	4.3	5.0	5.2
Net change	−5.1	−6.5	−6.8	−6.8	−7.6
Telephone excise and unemployment insurance tax reductions	−1.6	−2.0	−1.6	−1.2	−1.1
Total	**−25.0**	**−26.6**	**−28.6**	**−30.8**	**−34.9**

SOURCE: Treasury Department

of 1978 and fall to about 3½ per cent in 1979. Unemployment would be unlikely to fall below 6 per cent and, by the end of 1979, might be moving upward.

This tax program will mean up to one million additional jobs for American workers. It should lead to a pattern of economic growth which is steady, sustainable, and noninflationary.

In addition, I believe that our taxpayers, particularly those in the low- and middle-income brackets, *deserve* significant tax relief—I am determined to reduce federal taxes and expenditures as a share of our Gross National Product.

The Need for Tax Reform

The $25 billion in tax reductions are net reductions, *after* taking account of $9 billion in revenue-raising reforms which I am also proposing. Indeed, the full cuts in personal and corporate tax rates which I recommend would not be desirable in the absence of significant reform.

But these reforms stand on their own merits and would be long overdue even if I were not proposing any net tax reductions to accompany them. They focus on simplification for the individual taxpayer and the elimination of some of the most glaring tax preferences and loopholes.

Guided by the need for tax simplification and tax equity, I propose that Congress adopt reforms that would:

—Sharply curtail tax shelters.

—Eliminate the deductions claimed by businesses for theater and sporting tickets, yachts, hunting lodges, club dues, and first-class airfare and limit the deduction for the cost of meals to 50 per cent.

—Provide a taxable bond option for local governments and modify the tax treatment of industrial development bonds.

—Strengthen the minimum tax on items of preference income for individuals.

—Repeal the special alternative tax on capital gains, which only benefits individuals in the highest tax brackets.

—Replace the personal exemption and general tax credits with a $240 per person credit.

—Simplify return preparation and recordkeeping by:

- eliminating the deductions for sales, personal property, gasoline, and miscellaneous taxes;
- combining the separate medical and casualty deductions and allowing them only to the extent they exceed 10 per cent of adjusted gross income;
- repealing the deduction for political contributions but retaining the credit; and
- liberalizing and modifying the Subchapter S and depreciation rules applicable to small businesses.

—Include unemployment compensation benefits in the taxable income of taxpayers above certain income levels.

—Ensure that the tax preferences available for fringe benefits assist rank-and-file workers as well as executive officers.

—Eliminate the special bad debt deduction for commercial banks, reduce the bad debt deduction available to savings and loan associations, and remove the tax exemption for credit unions.

—**Phase out the tax subsidies for** Domestic International Sales Corporations (DISCs) and the deferral of tax on foreign profits.

These reforms will make our tax system both fairer and simpler. Many of them are targeted at tax preferences and subsidies for activities that do not deserve special treatment and that largely benefit those who have no need for financial assistance. The average working man and woman pay for the loopholes and the special provisions in our tax laws—because when some do not pay their fair share, the majority must pay higher taxes to make up the difference.

Low- and middle-income workers, struggling to make ends meet, are discouraged by tax laws that permit a few individuals to live extravagantly at the expense of government tax revenues. The privileged few are being subsidized by the rest of the taxpaying public when they routinely deduct the cost of country club dues, hunting lodges, elegant meals, theater and sports tickets, and night club shows. But the average worker's rare "night on the town" is paid for out of his *own* pocket with *after-tax* dollars.

Likewise, individuals who pay taxes on nearly every penny of earnings are treated unfairly compared to the few who are able to "shelter" their high incomes from taxes. Some persons with incomes exceeding $200,000 have little or no tax liability, while other high-income individuals return to the federal government nearly 60 cents of every dollar received. There is no good reason for next-door neighbors, in the same economic circumstances, to have vastly different tax bills because one has found tax shelters and loopholes.

In addition to the preferences for expense account items and tax shelter activities, there are a number of equally inappropriate and inefficient corporate tax subsidies. For example, there is no justification for the DISC export subsidy under which we pay over $1 billion a year in foregone tax revenue (mostly to our largest corporations) to encourage our firms to do what they would do anyway—export to profitable foreign markets. Nor can we rationalize proposals to reduce business taxes to increase investment at home while the deferral subsidy encourages multinational corporations to invest overseas by letting them pay lower taxes on their foreign profits than they pay on money earned in the United States.

I ask Congress to join with me to end these unwarranted subsidies and return the revenue to the vast majority of our taxpayers who want no more or less than to pay their fair share.

The tax reforms and tax reductions which I am proposing have been carefully balanced to coordinate with our overall economic and budgetary strategy. Large tax reductions are premised on substantial reforms.

I must, therefore, caution that fiscal prudence will require significantly reduced tax cuts for low- and middle-income taxpayers if we cannot help finance the reductions I have proposed through enactment of these revenue-raising reforms. I am proposing a balanced tax program, and I urge Congress to consider these recommendations as an integrated package.

Tax Reduction and Simplification for Individuals

Under this tax program, virtually all Americans will receive substantial tax relief, principally through a simple, across-

Income Tax and FICA Tax Changes Four-Person, One-Earner Families*

Wage Income	Income Tax[1]	FICA TAX[2]	Total Tax
$ 5,000	$ 0	$ 14	$ 14
10,000	−312	28	−284
15,000	−258	42	−216
20,000	−270	261	−9
25,000	−320	439	119
30,000	−322	439	117
40,000	−218	439	221
50,000	−80	439	359
100,000	590	439	1,029

1. Assumes deductible expenses equal to 23 percent of income under present law and 20 percent under the proposal.

2. Change in FICA tax calculated assuming present law rate and base for 1979 (6.13 per cent and $22,900), employees' share only; and assuming prior law rate and base for 1977 (5.85 per cent and $16,500), employees' share only.

** The above table was modified from the way it originally appeared in the President's tax message to conform to revised estimates released by the Treasury Department.*

SOURCE: Treasury Department

Income Tax Liabilities: Present Law and Administration Proposal (Personal Income Only)

(1976 Levels of Income)

Expanded Income Class	Present Law		Administration Proposal		Tax Change	
	Tax Liability	Percentage Distribution	Tax Liability	Percentage Distribution	Tax Liability	Change as Per Cent of Present Law Tax
($000)	($ millions)	(per cent)	($ millions)	(per cent)	($ millions)	(per cent)
Less than 5	$ 141	0.1%	$ −251	−0.2%	$ −392	−278.0%
5 - 10	8,227	6.1	6,368	5.2	−1,859	−22.6
10 - 15	18,071	13.4	15,361	12.4	−2,710	−15.0
15 - 20	23,009	17.0	20,148	16.3	−2,861	−12.4
20 - 30	32,778	24.2	29,593	23.9	−3,185	−9.7
30 - 50	22,017	16.3	20,971	17.0	−1,046	−4.8
50 - 100	16,492	12.2	16,344	13.2	−148	−0.9
100 - 200	8,084	6.0	8,261	6.7	177	2.2
200 and over	6,476	4.8	6,838	5.5	362	5.6
Total	$135,293	100.0%	$123,633	100.0%	$−11,660	− 8.6%

Note: Details may not add to totals due to rounding.

SOURCE: Office of the Secretary of the Treasury, Office of Tax Analysis

the-board reduction in personal tax rates. Lower withholding rates will be put into effect October 1, 1978, and taxpayers will experience an increase in take-home pay and purchasing power as of that date.

The typical taxpayer in all income classes up to $100,000 will pay lower taxes. But the bulk of relief has been targeted to low and middle-income taxpayers.

The $240 credit will be especially beneficial for low- and middle-income families. It will remove millions of Americans at or near the poverty level from the income tax rolls. No longer will the tax savings for dependents be worth more to high income than low income families. Instead, the credit will be worth just as much to the moderate income blue-collar worker as to the wealthy executive.

Over 94 per cent of the net individual tax relief will be provided to individuals and families earning less than $30,000 per year, and every income class up to $30,000 will bear a smaller share of the overall tax burden than it does now. *(See table above)*

Under my proposals, the typical family of four that earns $15,000 a year will save almost $260, a 19 per cent tax reduction.

For most persons in the low- and middle-income brackets, there will be a sizeable net reduction in combined income and payroll taxes even after the scheduled social security tax increases are taken into account. *(See table, previous page)*

Without this cut in income taxes, the social security tax increases would cause a reduction in the take-home pay of American workers. With this tax program, we will have restored the integrity of the Social Security system—returning that system to a sound financial basis and assuring the stability of future benefits for retired workers—without increasing total taxes for most working people or causing a slowdown in our economic recovery.

We must also act to ease the burdens of tax return preparation and recordkeeping. We have a tax system that requires millions of individuals to compute their own tax liability. The government relies upon the good faith and conscientiousness of our taxpayers to an extent unparalleled in the rest of the world. But in order for our system to remain successful, it must be comprehensible to the average taxpayer.

Judged by this standard, the current tax structure is seriously defective. Millions of honest and intelligent Americans find themselves confused and frustrated by its complexity. The cost of this complexity is enormous in terms of hours and dollars spent.

Accordingly, tax simplification has been a goal of this administration from the outset. The tax return individuals will file between now and April 15 has been simplified as a result of the Tax Reduction and Simplification Act which I proposed and Congress enacted last year. The short form 1040A has been reduced from 25 lines to 15 lines. Form 1040 has been restructured so that it can be completed more systematically. Tax tables have been revised to reduce arithmetic computations. The language of the tax forms and the instructions has been made more understandable.

The simplification efforts that were begun in 1977 will be continued and expanded in the tax program I am presenting today. The replacement of the existing personal exemption and general tax credits by the $240 personal credit will simplify return preparation for taxpayers and enable millions of individuals at or below the poverty level to file no tax return. Changes in itemized deductions (which will be more than offset by the rate cuts) will increase the number of nonitemizers to 84 per cent of all taxpayers. Six million Americans will be able to switch to the standard deduction and avoid keeping detailed records for tax purposes. The preparation of returns by itemizers will be simplified, and the tax program will reduce recordkeeping burdens on small businesses.

Business and Anti-Inflation Tax Reductions

Our Nation's employment and anti-inflation goals cannot be met without a strengthening of private business investment. In recent years, capital spending in the United States has been inadequate. Capacity growth in manufacturing has declined from a growth rate of about 4.5 per cent during the period 1948-1969, to 3.5 per cent from 1969-1973, and to 3 per cent from 1973-1976. Real business fixed investment in the third quarter of 1977 was 5 per cent below its 1974 peak.

In order to encourage needed capital outlays in the period ahead, my tax program contains annual net business tax reductions of approximately $6 billion. The corporate tax rate will be reduced on October 1, 1978, from 20 per cent to 18 per cent on the first $25,000 of income and from 22 per cent to 20 per cent on the second $25,000—this will result in a 10 per cent reduction in tax liability for most small corporations. The tax rate for large corporations will be cut from 48 per cent to 45 per cent on October 1, 1978, and to 44 per cent on January 1, 1980.

I also recommend several important changes in the existing 10 per cent investment tax credit: the 10 per cent credit should be made permanent; liberalized to cover up to 90 per cent of tax liability; made fully applicable to qualified pollution control facilities; and extended to investments in industrial and utility structures (including rehabilitation of existing structures). These changes should be particularly beneficial to developing businesses that are seeking to expand their productive facilities and should help to increase expenditures for the construction of new factories.

The corporate rate reductions and extensions of the investment tax credit which I am proposing will encourage capital formation by providing an immediate increase in cash flow to business and by enhancing the after-tax rewards of investment.

All small businesses will receive significant cuts in their tax rates under my program: reducing the bottom as well as the top corporate rates will be of special benefit to small corporations; small business proprietorships and partnerships will benefit from the individual rate cuts. In addition to these tax reductions, my program will simplify the depreciation rules applicable to small business and liberalize the provisions governing the deductions of losses on stock held in small companies.

Vigorous business investment will help ease inflationary pressure by averting capacity shortages that might otherwise occur as our economy continues to grow. The $2 billion reduction in telephone excise taxes and employer payroll taxes should provide additional relief from inflation by reducing costs and prices. These tax measures, applied in conjunction with other anti-inflation policies announced in my Economic Report, will support the objective of reducing and containing the rate of inflation.

The combination of these tax cuts and needed business tax reforms will result in a tax system that meets the needs of the broad spectrum of U.S. businesses more efficiently and equitably.

A detailed description of my program follows.

RECOMMENDATIONS TO REDUCE TAXES AND SIMPLIFY RETURNS FOR THE AVERAGE TAXPAYER

Tax Reductions for Individuals

Individual taxes will be reduced through across-the-board rate cuts and substitution of a single $240 personal credit for the existing personal exemption and alternative general credits. This tax relief will be reflected in decreased withholding rates for employees as of October 1, 1978.

The tax reductions I am now recommending do not include adjustments for congressional action on the National Energy Plan. In April, I proposed that Congress pass the crude oil equalization tax and rebate the proceeds to the American people on a per capita basis. This course is essential if we are to protect the real incomes of consumers. If the final energy bill includes a full rebate of the net proceeds of the crude oil tax, no further action on my part will be required. However, if the final bill contains a rebate provision only for 1978—as provided in the House version—I intend to send a supplemental message to Congress recommending that the individual tax reductions proposed in this message be increased by the net proceeds of the crude oil tax.

(1) **Rate Cuts.** The proposed rate schedule will range from a lowest bracket of 12 per cent to a top bracket of 68 per cent, compared with the current 14 to 70 per cent range. As under current law, the top rate bracket will apply with respect to income in excess of $200,000 for joint returns and $100,000 for single returns. The entire schedules are set forth in Tables 11 and 12. *(Tables, pp. 29-E, 30-E)*

This new rate structure will, in and of itself, increase the overall progressivity of the individual income tax because the cuts are proportionately larger in the low- and middle-income brackets.

(2) **Per Capita Tax Credit.** The tax benefits for dependents currently favor the wealthy over persons with modest incomes. A taxpayer is now entitled to a $750 exemption for each family member in addition to a general tax credit, which is equal to the greater of $35 per family member or 2 per cent of the first $9,000 of taxable income. The net effect of the complicated series of exemptions and credits is this: a family of four in the 50 per cent tax bracket enjoys a tax savings of $1,680 for dependents while families earning $10,000 save about one-third of that amount.

I propose that the existing exemption and general credits be replaced with a single credit of $240 per family member. Unlike the current structure, the new credit will provide the same benefit at all income levels; for a family with four members, the per capita credit will be worth $960 whether that family is middle class or wealthy. The $240 credit will ensure that most families at or near the poverty level will pay no taxes. Also, a single tax credit will simplify tax return preparation by eliminating the confusion caused by the existing combination of exemptions and alternative credits.

Changes in Itemized Deductions

The primary source of complexity in the tax laws for many middle-income individuals is itemized deductions. Average taxpayers have to maintain burdensome records in order to substantiate the deductions and are required to decipher complex tax rules to complete their tax returns. Restructuring of itemized deductions is essential if the tax laws are to be simplified for typical, middle-class individuals and families.

I am recommending changes in itemized deductions that will enable approximately 6 million taxpayers to switch to the simple standard deduction. The number of taxpayers who use the standard deduction will be increased from 77 per cent to 84 per cent. And the calculation of the deductions for itemizers will be simplified greatly.

The deductions that will be curtailed are ones that add complexity and inequity to the tax system without advancing significant objectives of public policy. We will have a simpler, more efficient tax system if we eliminate these deductions and return the revenue directly to taxpayers through the rate cuts I propose.

(1) **State and Local Taxes.** The special deduction will be eliminated for general sales taxes, taxes on personal property (but not on residences or buildings), gasoline taxes, and miscellaneous taxes. These itemized deductions are claimed at nearly uniform rates by all itemizers and result in a relatively small tax benefit. For those taxpayers who do not use the published deduction tables, the recordkeeping burden can be substantial.

Moreover, a deduction for these types of taxes cannot be defended on public policy grounds. A deduction for gasoline taxes runs counter to our national effort to conserve energy. And the present level of state sales taxes cannot be said to depend upon the fact that those state taxes are deductible for federal income tax purposes.

(2) **Political Contributions Deduction.** Political contributions are now deductible as an itemized deduction in an amount not exceeding $200 for a joint return. Alternatively, a taxpayer may claim a credit against his tax for one-half of his political contributions, with a maximum credit of $50 on a joint return.

The reform proposal will repeal the political contribution deduction but retain the credit. The deduction is undesirable because it provides a larger subsidy to high-bracket contributors. Due to the present deduction, the wealthiest individuals can contribute $200 at an after-tax cost to them of only $60; middle-income Americans incur a cost of $150 for the same contribution. Elimination of the deduction will enhance tax equity and diminish the confusing complexity of the current scheme of deductions and credits.

(3) **Medical and Casualty Deductions.** The medical expense deduction is one of the most complicated items on the tax forms. Currently, one-half of the first $300 of health insurance premiums is deductible outright for those who itemize. Other medical expenses (including additional health insurance premiums) are deductible to the extent they are in excess of 3 per cent of adjusted gross income. The latter category of deductibility also includes medicines and drugs to the extent they exceed 1 per cent of adjusted gross income. And there is a separate deduction for

damage to property from a casualty (such as theft or fire) if the loss exceeds $100 and is not reimbursed by insurance.

I recommend substantial simplification of these provisions. The deductions for medical and casualty expenses will be combined, and a new "extraordinary expense" deduction will be available for medical and casualty expenses in excess of 10 per cent of adjusted gross income. In the case of casualty losses, the excess over $100 will be included in this computation. Medical insurance premiums and medicines will be treated the same as other medical expenses.

Medical and casualty expenditures should properly be deductible only when they are unusually large and have a significant impact on the taxpayer's ability to pay. The medical expense deduction originally met that standard. But, as a result of the changing relationship between medical costs and income, that standard is no longer satisfied. Substantial recordkeeping burdens and administrative problems can be eliminated through the proposed simplification of the deduction and the redefinition of "extraordinary" in the light of current experience among taxpayers.

Proposals to Curtail Inappropriate Subsidies, Special Privileges, Inequities and Abuses of the Tax System

Entertainment and Other Expenditures for Personal Consumption

One feature of the current tax system that is most disheartening to average taxpayers is the favorable tax treatment accorded extravagant entertainment expenses that are claimed to be business-related. Some individuals are able to deduct expenditures that provide personal enjoyment with little or no business benefit. And, even where entertainment expenditures may have some relationship to the production of income, they provide untaxed personal benefits to the participants. More than $2 billion of tax revenue is lost every year through these tax preferences.

For example, one person claimed a deduction of $17,000 for the cost of entertaining other members of his profession at his home, at a country club, at sporting events, at restaurants, and at a rental cottage. Another individual wrote off the cost of business lunches 338 days of the year at an average cost far exceeding $20 for each lunch. But there is no deduction in the tax laws for the factory worker's ticket to a football game or the secretary's lunch with fellow workers.

These special tax advantages for the privileged few undermine confidence in our Nation's tax system. The disparity must be eliminated by denying a deduction for expenditures to the extent they provide the participants with such untaxed personal enjoyment and benefits.

(1) **Theater and Sporting Events.** No deduction will be permitted for purchases of tickets to theater and sporting events. Present law, by allowing a deduction for the purchase of such tickets, provides a "two for the price of one" bargain to some taxpayers. As long as an individual is in the 50 per cent tax bracket or above, he may be able to invite a business friend at no cost to himself by having the Federal government pay for at least one-half of the total ticket costs. The overwhelming majority of our citizens pay for their theater and sports tickets out of their own after-tax dollars. No taxpayer should be asked to help subsidize someone else's personal entertainment.

(2) **Other Entertainment Expenses.** The tax reform program will also deny deductibility of any expenses of maintaining facilities such as yachts, hunting lodges and swimming pools and for fees paid to social, athletic, or sporting clubs. During a recent tax year, one small corporation deducted $67,000 for yacht expenses incurred in entertaining customers and potential customers on cruises and fishing trips. Another small company deducts over $100,000 a year to maintain hunting and fishing lodges to entertain employees of customers. Asking taxpayers to subsidize these kinds of activities for a tiny minority of our citizens strikes at the fairness and integrity of the tax system.

(3) **Business Meals.** Fifty per cent of currently deductible business entertainment expenses for food and beverages will remain deductible, and 50 percent will be disallowed. A substantial portion of business meal expenses represents the cost of personal consumption that must be incurred regardless of the business connection. The millions of Americans who work on farms, in factories and in offices should not be required to provide their tax dollars to support the high-priced lunches and dinners of a relatively small number of taxpayers. The 50 percent disallowance represents a reasonable and fair approach to compensate for the untaxed personal benefit involved.

(4) **Foreign Conventions.** Many professional, business, and trade organizations can furnish their members with tax-deductible foreign vacations. The method of conferring such tax-subsidized luxury is to sponsor a foreign convention or seminar. A brochure for one professional organization provides the appropriate atmosphere in promoting its foreign seminars:

> "Decide where you would like to go this year: Rome. The Alps. The Holy Land. Paris and London. The Orient. Cruise the Rhine River or the Mediterranean. Visit the islands in the Caribbean. Delight in the art treasures of Florence."

The Tax Reform Act of 1976 placed some limits on the deductibility of foreign convention expenses. But the rules still permit taxpayers to take two foreign vacations a year partially at public expense—an exception that did not escape the attention of the organization whose 1977 brochure I have quoted.

I am proposing that the deductibility rules for foreign conventions be modified in a manner that will curb abuses while relaxing the current restrictions on conventions held in foreign countries for legitimate business purposes. The two convention rule will be stricken. In its place will be a rule that denies deductibility for foreign convention expenses unless factors such as the purpose and membership of the sponsor make it as reasonable to hold the convention outside the United States and possessions as within.

(5) **First Class Air Fare.** Another example of public support for private extravagance is the deductibility of first class air fare. Business travel constitutes a legitimate cost of producing income. However, the business purpose is served by purchasing a ticket at coach fare. The undue generosity of a deduction for first class air fare was recognized by Congress in 1976 when a deduction was denied for first class flights to foreign conventions. I propose that the rule be extended to tickets for domestic business travel.

Tax Shelters

Through tax shelters, persons can use "paper" losses to reduce taxes on high incomes from other sources. These shelter devices can slash the effective tax rate for many affluent individuals far below that of average income Americans. Moreover, such shelters attract investment dollars away from profit-seeking businesses and into ventures designed only for tax write-offs; legitimate businesses suffer competitive disadvantages as a result.

In the Tax Reform Act of 1976, Congress enacted reforms intended to restrict tax shelter abuses. The principal methods used in that legislation were revisions of the minimum tax and the adoption of an "at risk" rule to limit the deductibility of certain tax shelter losses.

However, some promoters have now adapted their operations to provide shelters in forms that were not specifically covered by the 1976 Act. In fact, shelter activity in 1977 may have surpassed the level reached in 1976. Form letters, addressed to "All of Us Who Wish to Reduce Our Taxes," boldly promise tax write-offs several times larger than the amount invested, and persons are urged to pass the message along "to anyone you think may have interest in tax reduction." Tax shelter experts promote their services in large and expensive advertisements in the financial sections of our Sunday papers.

Such flagrant manipulation of the tax laws should not be tolerated. I recommend action that will build upon the 1976 reforms and further reduce tax shelter abuses.

(1) **Strengthening of the Minimum Tax.** The minimum tax has proved to be one of the most useful devices to limit the attractiveness of tax shelter schemes, and it should be made still more effective. In its current form, the minimum tax is imposed at a rate of 15 per cent on the amount of certain tax preference items enjoyed by a tax-

payer. But the total amount of tax preferences can be reduced by the greater of $10,000 or one-half of regular liability (in the case of individuals) before the minimum tax is applied.

I recommend that the minimum tax for individuals be strengthened by eliminating the offset of one-half of regular tax liability against preference income. This change will make the minimum tax more progressive and a more sharply focused deterrent to the use of tax shelters. Persons making excessive use of preferences will be taxed on their preference income without regard to regular tax liability. On the other hand, those individuals with modest preference income will still be totally exempted from the minimum tax by the $10,000 preference offset, and the minimum tax will not be applied to capital gain realized on the sale of a personal residence. Ninety-eight per cent of the $284 million in revenue raised by this proposal will come from taxpayers with incomes exceeding $100,000 and more than 77 per cent will come from the income class over $200,000.

(2) **Extension of "at risk" Rule.** One of the 1976 reforms that should be toughened is the "at risk" rule. That rule denies deductibility for a shelter investor's paper losses that exceed his cash investment and indebtedness for which he has personal liability. My tax reform plan will generally extend the "at risk" provisions to cover all activities (except real estate) carried on individually, through partnerships, or by corporations controlled by five or fewer persons.

(3) **Changes in Real Estate Depreciation.** Reform of real estate depreciation practices is needed to reduce much of the wasteful tax shelter investment that has led to overbuilding of commercial real estate in such forms as shopping centers and office buildings. Real estate shelters were left virtually untouched by the 1976 Act. Consequently, these shelters have continued to thrive.

It is time to move depreciation for tax purposes more closely into line with a measurement of actual economic decline. The reform program will generally require taxpayers to base their depreciation for buildings on the straight-line method, using the present average tax lives claimed by taxpayers for different classes of property. Exceptions from the general rule will be granted until 1983 for new multi-family housing, which will be permitted to use a 150 per cent declining balance method; new low-income housing will remain eligible for a 200 per cent declining balance method until 1983, and for 150 per cent thereafter. Needed investment in industrial plants will be encouraged by an extension of the investment credit, as explained below. The investment credit is a more efficient and straight-forward means to provide a tax subsidy for such construction.

(4) **Taxation of Deferred Annuities.** Another flourishing tax shelter gimmick is the deferred annuity contract. Currently, a person can generally invest in an annuity contract and postpone taxation on the interest build-up until the annuity is actually received. Although originally designed primarily to provide a safe flow of retirement income, the deferred annuity contract is now used commonly as a convenient tax dodge for a wide range of investment opportunities. The shelter benefits are aptly described by the promotional literature:

> "HOW TO POSTPONE TAXES LEGALLY AND EARN INTEREST ON UNCLE SAM'S MONEY.... With An Investment That Never Goes Down, Always Goes Up, And Is Guaranteed Against Loss."

I recommend that this tax abuse be eliminated. Under my proposal, the earnings of most deferred annuities will be taxed currently to the purchaser. However, in order that an individual may still use a deferred annuity with guaranteed interest as a means to provide retirement income, the proposal will allow each person to designate a single contract, contributions to which may not exceed $1,000 annually, as a contract that will remain eligible for tax deferral. Also unaffected will be the tax treatment of qualified employee annuities.

(5) **Classification of Nominal Partnerships as Corporations for Tax Purposes.** In many cases, tax shelter schemes can offer the desired tax benefits to investors only if the shelter vehicle is organized as a partnership rather than a corporation. At the same time, limited partnerships can now provide traditional non-tax attributes of a corporation, such as limited personal liability, centralized management, and transferability of interests without sacrificing partnership tax benefits.

Promoters should not obtain the non-tax attributes of a corporation for their shelters while using technicalities to avoid corporate tax treatment. I recommend that new limited partnerships with more than 15 limited partners be treated as corporations for tax purposes; however, partnerships engaged primarily in housing activities will be excepted from this classification rule.

(6) **Tax Audit of Partnerships.** Tax shelter partnerships are not themselves subject to the tax assessment mechanism of the Internal Revenue Service; therefore, each individual partner must be audited separately even though the same substantive determinations may be involved. I recommend that legislation be enacted to permit a partnership to be treated as an entity for the purpose of determining tax issues. Tax shelters based on illegitimate deductions should not be permitted to succeed merely because of the difficulties involved in conducting an IRS examination of their activities.

Termination of Alternative Tax For Capital Gains

The wages of most workers are fully subject to tax at the rates contained in the published tax tables. But persons whose income arises from the sale of assets such as stock or land generally receive preferred treatment; a deduction for long-term capital gains has the effect of taxing these gains at a rate that is one-half of the rate for ordinary income. This preference results in an annual revenue loss to the Treasury of $8 billion.

Taxpayers in the highest income brackets are granted an additional tax preference over and above the special capital gains deduction. Individuals above the 50 per cent tax bracket can take advantage of a 25 per cent tax ceiling on the first $50,000 of capital gains, a provision known as the "alternative tax." The benefits of this provision go exclusively to persons with taxable incomes exceeding $52,000 (if filing a joint return) or $38,000 (if filing a single return)—less than one per cent of all taxpayers.

Through the alternative tax, a wealthy investor can shield nearly 65 per cent of his capital gains from taxation—a benefit that is grossly inequitable when middle-class investors are taxed on one-half of such gains, and most workers are taxed on every cent of their wages and salaries. The alternative tax costs the Treasury over $100 million every year, almost 90 per cent of which goes to taxpayers in income classes above $100,000. I propose the repeal of this unfair and complicated tax benefit.

Fringe Benefits Unavailable to Rank-and-File Workers

Our tax system generally operates under the principle that employees should be taxed on their compensation no matter what form that compensation assumes. A worker who receives cash wages that he uses to provide benefits for his family should not ordinarily be taxed more heavily than the employee who receives those benefits directly from his employer. There are now exceptions to this general rule for certain types of employee benefits. I urge Congress to act so that these tax preferences benefit rank-and-file workers as well as the executive officers.

(1) **Non-discrimination Requirement for Health and Group Life Plans.** An example of a tax-preferred employee benefit is a health or group life insurance plan. If an individual purchases medical insurance, the premiums are deductible only within the limits applicable to the medical expense deduction. However, if an employer establishes a medical insurance program for its employees, the premium payments by the employer are deductible while neither the premiums nor the benefits are taxable to the employee.

Although this tax preference was designed in theory to secure basic protections for a wide range of employees, it often serves instead to subsidize expenses of only the high-level corporate managers. It is now possible for a businessman, through his controlled corporation, to establish a health plan that covers only one employee—himself—and permits all of his medical and dental expenses to be deducted. Meanwhile, that corporation's other employees have to provide health care

Individual Tax Rate Schedules for Joint Returns

Taxable Income Bracket[1]	Present Law: Tax at Low End of Bracket	Present Law: Tax Rate on Income In Bracket	Tax Proposal: Tax at Low End of Bracket	Tax Proposal: Tax Rate on Income In Bracket
$ 0 - $ 500	$ 0	14%	$ 0	12%
500 - 1,000	70	14	60	12
1,000 - 2,000	140	15	120	14
2,000 - 3,000	290	16	260	16
3,000 - 4,000	450	17	420	17
4,000 - 8,000	620	19	590	18
8,000 - 12,000	1,380	22	1,310	19
12,000 - 16,000	2,260	25	2,070	20
16,000 - 20,000	3,250	28	2,870	23
20,000 - 24,000	4,380	32	3,790	27
24,000 - 28,000	5,660	36	4,870	32
28,000 - 32,000	7,100	39	6,150	36
32,000 - 36,000	8,660	42	7,590	39
36,000 - 40,000	10,340	45	9,150	42
40,000 - 44,000	12,140	48	10,830	44
44,000 - 48,000	14,060	50	12,590	48
48,000 - 52,000	16,060	50	14,510	48
52,000 - 54,000	18,060	53	16,430	51
54,000 - 62,000	19,120	53	17,450	51
62,000 - 64,000	23,360	53	21,530	51
64,000 - 76,000	24,420	55	22,550	54
76,000 - 88,000	31,020	58	29,030	57
88,000 - 90,000	37,980	60	35,870	57
90,000 - 100,000	39,180	60	37,010	60
100,000 - 110,000	45,180	62	43,010	60
110,000 - 120,000	51,380	62	49,010	62
120,000 - 130,000	57,580	64	55,210	62
130,000 - 140,000	63,980	64	61,410	64
140,000 - 150,000	70,380	66	67,810	64
150,000 - 160,000	76,980	66	74,210	65
160,000 - 175,000	83,580	68	80,710	65
175,000 - 180,000	98,780	68	90,460	66
180,000 - 200,000	97,180	69	93,760	66
200,000 and over	110,980	70	106,960	68

1. The zero bracket is not shown in this table. To include the zero bracket, increase all taxable incomes shown by $3,200.

SOURCE: Office of the Secretary of the Treasury, Office of Tax Analysis

for their families with nondeductible expenditures.

To curb this abuse, I recommend denial of the tax exemption for employer-established medical, disability, and group life insurance plans if those plans discriminate in favor of officers, shareholders, and higher-paid employees. Preferential tax treatment is now available to pension plans only if non-discrimination standards are met. The tax law should require similar non-discriminatory treatment for workers in the case of medical, disability, and group life insurance plans.

(2) **Employee Death Benefits.** Current law provides an exclusion for the first $5,000 of payments made by an employer on account of the death of an employee. I recommend the repeal of this exclusion. Typically, these death benefits are in the nature of deferred wages that would have been paid to employees in high tax brackets. Adequate tax relief for an employee's heirs is provided through a complete tax exemption for insurance proceeds.

(3) **Integration of Qualified Retirement Plans and Social Security.** Certain employer-sponsored retirement plans have a preferred tax status. Employer contributions to a qualified plan are currently deductible while the employee can defer taxation until retirement benefits are received. Although qualification for this special treatment is generally dependent upon non-discriminatory coverage of employees, the tax laws now permit a qualified plan to cover only employees who earn amounts exceeding the social security wage base—a base that will rise to $25,900 by 1980 under the recently enacted social security financing legislation.

Individual Tax Rate Schedules for Single Returns

Taxable Income Bracket[1]	Present Law: Tax at Low End of Bracket	Present Law: Tax Rate on Income In Bracket	Tax Proposal: Tax at Low End of Bracket	Tax Proposal: Tax Rate on Income In Bracket
$ 0 - $ 500	$ 0	14%	$ 0	12%
500 - 1,000	70	15	60	13
1,000 - 1,500	145	16	125	15
1,500 - 2,000	225	17	200	15
2,000 - 3,000	310	19	275	18
3,000 - 4,000	500	19	455	19
4,000 - 6,000	690	21	645	20
6,000 - 8,000	1,110	24	1,045	20
8,000 - 10,000	1,590	25	1,445	22
10,000 - 12,000	2,090	27	1,885	23
12,000 - 14,000	2,630	29	2,345	25
14,000 - 16,000	3,210	31	2,845	25
16,000 - 18,000	3,830	34	3,345	29
18,000 - 20,000	4,510	36	3,925	29
20,000 - 22,000	5,230	38	4,505	33
22,000 - 24,000	5,990	40	5,165	33
24,000 - 26,000	6,790	40	5,825	38
26,000 - 28,000	7,590	45	6,585	38
28,000 - 32,000	8,490	45	7,345	41
32,000 - 36,000	10,290	50	8,985	46
36,000 - 38,000	12,290	50	10,825	50
38,000 - 40,000	13,290	55	11,825	50
40,000 - 44,000	14,390	55	12,825	51
44,000 - 48,000	16,590	60	14,865	57
48,000 - 50,000	18,990	60	17,145	58
50,000 - 52,000	20,190	62	18,305	58
52,000 - 54,000	21,430	62	19,465	60
54,000 - 60,000	22,670	62	20,665	60
60,000 - 62,000	26,390	64	24,265	60
62,000 - 64,000	27,670	64	25,465	63
64,000 - 70,000	28,950	64	26,725	63
70,000 - 76,000	32,790	66	30,505	63
76,000 - 80,000	36,750	66	34,285	66
80,000 - 88,000	39,390	68	36,925	66
88,000 - 90,000	44,830	68	42,205	66
90,000 - 100,000	46,190	69	43,525	67
100,000 and over	53,090	70	50,225	68

1. The zero bracket is not shown in this table. To include the zero bracket, increase all taxable incomes shown by $2,200.

SOURCE: Office of the Secretary of the Treasury, Office of Tax Analysis

It is unfair to grant tax preferences for private pension plans that bar all low- and middle-income employees from participation. I propose that a new integration formula be enacted so that a qualified pension plan cannot provide benefits to supplement social security for highly compensated employees unless all employees receive some coverage under the plan.

Unemployment Compensation

Unemployment compensation is a substitute for wages that generally provides needed relief to persons in financial distress. But, in some cases, the unemployment compensation system discourages work for taxable income. Since unemployment benefits are tax-free, they are more valuable than an equivalent amount of wages. This means that if two individuals have the same total income, the one who remains idle several months and receives unemployment compensation will be better off financially than his colleague who works the whole year. There can be no justification for conferring this tax-free benefit upon middle- and upper-income workers.

I propose that the current tax exemption for unemployment compensation benefits be phased out as an individual's income rises above $20,000 for single persons or $25,000 for married couples.

Taxable Bond Option and Industrial Development Bonds

Present law exempts from federal taxation the interest on certain bonds issued by state and local governments. There are now two general categories of tax-exempt bonds: obligations issued for the benefit of the state and local government itself, and industrial development bonds issued by the government to provide facilities such as pollution control equipment, sports facilities, waste disposal facilities, industrial parks, and facilities (including hospitals) of private, non-profit organizations. Also, there is a "small issue" exemption for certain industrial development bonds with face amounts that do not exceed $1 million, or $5 million where the total cost of capital expenditures on the financed facility does not exceed the $5 million amount.

My tax program preserves the freedom of state and local governments to issue tax-exempt bonds. I am recommending reforms that will restrict the tax avoidance opportunities available to the wealthy in the tax-exempt market while, at the same time, increasing the ability of state and local governments to obtain low-cost financing. In particular, I propose the following:

(1) **Option for Bonds Benefitting Governmental Units.** State and local governments will be given the option of continuing to issue tax-exempt bonds or issuing fully taxable bonds, accompanied by a direct federal interest subsidy to the governmental units. For bonds issued in 1979 and 1980, the subsidy will be equal to 35 per cent of the interest cost; the subsidy will rise to 40 per cent for bonds issued after 1980. The federal government will exercise no control over the purposes for which state and local governments use subsidized financing. State and local governments will benefit under the taxable bond option regardless of whether they decide to issue taxable or tax-exempt bonds: those issuing taxable bonds will benefit directly from the interest subsidy, and those continuing to issue tax-exempt bonds will benefit because the reduced supply of such bonds will allow governments to sell them at lower interest rates.

(2) **Pollution Control Bonds, Bonds for the Development of Industrial Parks, and Private Hospital Bonds.** The tax exemption will be removed for interest on pollution control bonds and bonds for the development of industrial parks. Also, the exemption will be removed for bonds issued to finance construction of hospital facilities for private, non-profit institutions unless there is a certification by the state that a new hospital is needed. These activities are essentially for the benefit of private users, and the tax exemption for the bonds has the effect of undermining the financing of governmental functions. Moreover, the general exemption for hospital bonds encourages excessive expansion of unneeded hospital facilities and runs counter to the administration's Hospital Cost Containment proposal.

(3) **Small Issue Exemption.** The existing "small issue" exemptions will be retained only for economically distressed areas; and, with respect to those areas, the $5 million exemption will be raised to $10 million.

(4) **Option for Certain Industrial Development Bonds.** Industrial development bonds which continue to enjoy tax-exempt status (such as those to finance sports facilities, housing, airports and convention facilities and small issues for economically distressed areas) will be eligible for the taxable bond option on the same terms as obligations issued for the benefit of state and local governments.

Accrual Accounting for Large Corporate Farms

Most taxpayers that are in the business of selling products must use an accrual method of accounting so that income is reflected accurately for tax purposes. However, farmers have historically been permitted to use the simpler cash method on the grounds that they lack the accounting and bookkeeping expertise required by the accrual system.

Congress acted in 1976 to deny the cash accounting privilege to most large corporate farms (with annual gross receipts exceeding $1 million), but retained an exception for large corporations that are "family owned." This distinction between family and non-family corporations bears no relationship to the rationale of preserving simple bookkeeping methods for small farmers. It has resulted in severe competitive imbalances between large corporations now required to use accrual accounting and those that are equally large but happen to fall within the definition of a "family farm."

This inequitable exception should now be eliminated. Corporate farms with gross receipts exceeding $1 million cannot fairly claim that they lack the sophistication necessary to comply with accrual accounting standards. Nor can lack of financial sophistication be claimed by farm syndicates used as investment vehicles by non-farmers. Therefore, I recommend that the accrual accounting requirement cover corporations with gross receipts greater than $1 million, regardless of their ownership, and all farm syndicates.

Tax Treatment of Financial Institutions

Financial institutions now have a favored tax status that is based largely on outmoded concepts regarding the nature of these businesses. Commercial banks, mutual savings banks and savings and loan associations were permitted to deduct artificially inflated reserves for bad debts in order to protect the banking system from catastrophic losses that were prevalent prior to the extensive banking legislation of the 1930s. Credit unions were exempted from taxation in the days when these institutions were small entities with close bonds among the members and few powers to provide extensive financial services. I am recommending changes that will recognize the contemporary practices of financial institutions and will bring the tax treatment of commercial banks, savings and loan associations and credit unions more in line with the taxation of other businesses. These reforms will raise $300 million per year in revenue.

(1) **Commercial Banks.** Commercial banks may now claim bad debt deductions that greatly exceed their actual losses. Under legislation enacted in 1969, this special bad debt deduction is scheduled for elimination after 1987. I propose that the effective date for repeal be accelerated so that beginning in 1979 banks, like other businesses, will base their bad debt reserves on their own experience in the current and 5 preceding years.

(2) **Mutual Savings Banks and Savings and Loan Associations.** Mutual savings banks and savings and loan associations are also permitted a special bad debt deduction that bears no relationship to actual experience. These thrift institutions are generally entitled to deduct 40 per cent of their net income (this percentage is scheduled to apply in 1979) as a bad debt reserve as long as a significant portion of their deposits is invested in real estate loans. My tax program will reduce the percentage to 30 per cent over a 5-year period.

(3) **Credit Unions.** Credit unions are tax-exempt. Yet, their powers and functions are defined so broadly that the term "credit union" can include financial institutions that are functionally identical to a savings and loan association. The tax exemption provides them with an unfair financial advantage over their competitors. I propose that the percentage of exempt income be phased out over a 4-year period, and that credit unions be taxed in the same manner as mutual savings banks and savings and loan associations after 1982.

Domestic International Sales Corporation (DISC)

Business incentives form an integral part of my tax program. I am recommending measures that will encourage American businesses to invest in productive facilities and to create jobs. However, adoption of those incentives must be accompanied by the elimination of tax preferences that have proved to be wasteful. The so-called "DISC" provision is a prime example.

In 1971, Congress enacted a special tax program for exports. This program permitted tax benefits for exports channeled through a company's specially created subsidiary, usually a paper organization, known as a domestic international sales corporation (DISC). Artificial pricing rules on transactions between the parent company and its DISC permit a favorable allocation of export profits to the DISC, and the taxation of one-half of eligible DISC income is deferred as long as these profits are invested in export related assets.

DISC has proved to be a very inefficient and wasteful export subsidy in the current international monetary system. A recent Treasury study indicates that DISC may have contributed only $1 to $3 billion to U.S. exports in 1974—an increase of less than 3 per cent in total exports—at a tax revenue cost of $1.2 billion. In the long run, even these increased exports are probably offset by rising imports that result from the operation of the flexible exchange rate system. DISC does nothing for, and may even disadvantage, our import sensitive industries and our exporters not using the DISC provision. Independent experts believe that DISC may have had *no* positive effect on our balance of payments.

Congress has recognized the wasteful nature of DISC and, in 1976, limited its applicability. However, DISC continues to cost U.S. taxpayers over $1 billion per year, with 65 per cent of DISC benefits going to corporations with more than $250 million in assets.

I propose the elimination of one-third of DISC benefits in 1979, two-thirds in 1980, and all DISC benefits in 1981 and thereafter.

Foreign Tax Deferral

Domestic corporations can now avoid paying a U.S. tax on the earnings of their foreign subsidiaries as long as those earnings remain overseas. A U.S. tax is generally deferred until dividends are paid by the subsidiary to its domestic parent, and then U.S. tax liability is offset by a tax credit for foreign income taxes paid on those remitted earnings. Fifty per cent of all the benefits of tax deferral is obtained by 30 large multinational corporations.

I recommend that this deferral privilege be phased out over a 3-year period. At least one-third of a foreign subsidiary's earnings will be taxed to the U.S. parent in 1979, at least two-thirds in 1980, and all the subsidiary's earnings after 1980. The tax reform program is designed to create incentives for investment in the United States and the creation of jobs for American workers. Tax deferral runs counter to these objectives. By providing a preference for foreign source income, the current deferral provision provides an incentive for investing abroad rather than in the United States, thereby having the effect of reducing job opportunities for Americans. Moreover, deferral can encourage multinational corporations to manipulate internal transfer prices in order to allocate income to low-tax countries.

There is no reason to defer the imposition of a U.S. tax just because business operations are conducted abroad rather than in the United States, regardless of the motivation for creating a foreign subsidiary. Congress eliminated in 1969 certain special tax preferences for businesses conducted in the United States through multi-layered corporations. I propose that Congress act in a similar manner to end the present preference for business operations conducted internationally through such multinational corporate structures.

The foreign tax credit will be retained in its present form. Therefore, elimination of deferral will not result in a double taxation of overseas earnings. And, in the event it appears to be in the national interest to permit tax deferral with respect to specific countries, such treatment can be provided selectively under negotiated tax treaties involving mutual concessions.

SPECIAL TAX REDUCTIONS PROPOSED TO REDUCE COSTS FOR CONSUMERS AND BUSINESSES

I propose two tax reduction measures—outside the income tax system—that will assist our efforts to attain price stability.

Repeal of Excise Tax on Telephone Services

The present 4 per cent excise tax on amounts paid for telephone services is now being phased out at the rate of 1 percentage point a year, with full repeal scheduled as of January 1, 1982.

I recommend complete repeal of this tax as of October 1, 1978. This action will reduce the cost of living directly. It will also lower consumer prices indirectly through a reduction of the business cost associated with telephone services.

Federal Unemployment Insurance Tax

I recommend a reduction in the federal unemployment insurance tax to reduce the payroll costs of employers. On January 1, 1978, the unemployment insurance tax rate rose from 0.5 per cent to 0.7 per cent of an employer's taxable wage base. This tax increase was instituted in order to replenish general revenue funds that have been loaned to the unemployment insurance trust fund during recent periods of high unemployment. But the issue of unemployment compensation financing requires a thorough reexamination to determine the best means of providing future benefits. To this end, I will soon appoint the National Commission on Unemployment Insurance which the Congress established to make this study and to offer recommendations. In the meantime, I am guided by my concerns about inflation. I propose that the tax rate be reduced to the 0.5 per cent level as of January 1, 1979.

RECOMMENDED BUSINESS INCENTIVES TO FOSTER GROWTH OF THE ECONOMY

Corporate Rate Cut

I recommend a corporate rate cut that will reduce business taxes by $6 billion. Tax relief in this form is sizable, easily understood by taxpayers, and applicable across the board.

The corporate tax rate is now 20 per cent on the first $25,000 of income, 22 per cent on the next $25,000, and 48 per cent on corporate income exceeding $50,000. Effective October 1, 1978, this program will reduce the first two rate brackets to 18 and 20 per cent, respectively, and the rate to 45 per cent on taxable income in excess of $50,000. The top rate will be reduced an additional point, to 44 per cent, on January 1, 1980. Small as well as large corporations will benefit from these rate cuts.

A corporate rate reduction of this magnitude will increase capital formation and help to assure a sustained economic recovery. In recent years, the level of business fixed investment has been unsatisfactory. One of the primary causes of this inadequate investment performance has been the low rate of return businesses receive on their investments—after tax liability is taken into consideration. The lower tax rates I recommend will enhance the anticipated after-tax profits on corporate investment projects and increase cash flow immediately. Businesses will thereby be encouraged to increase capital spending and to create jobs for American workers. Corporate rate cuts this large are made possible by, and depend upon, passage of the revenue-raising business tax reforms I have described earlier.

Liberalization of Investment Tax Credit

The investment tax credit has proven to be one of the most potent tax incentives for capital formation. It provides a direct reduction in tax liability generally equal to 10 per cent of a business' qualifying investments. But there are now several limitations that restrict its effectiveness.

I recommend changes that will make the investment credit a stronger, more efficient, and more equitable incentive. These changes will reduce business taxes by approximately $2.5 billion per year.

(1) **Permanent 10 Per Cent Credit.** The present 10 per cent investment credit is not a permanent feature of the Internal Revenue Code. On January 1, 1981, the credit level is scheduled to revert to 7 per cent. I propose that the credit be extended permanently at a 10 per cent rate so that businesses can plan ahead with greater certainty of the tax benefits that will be associated with projected capital expenditures.

(2) **Increased Tax Liability Ceiling.** The investment credit claimed during any taxable year cannot generally exceed $25,000 plus 50 per cent of tax liability in excess of that amount (with excess credits being eligible for a 3-year carryback and a 7-year carry-forward). My tax program will provide a ceiling of 90 per cent of tax liability (including the first $25,000) and will thereby increase the incentive for those businesses with relatively high investment needs and low taxable incomes. Developing

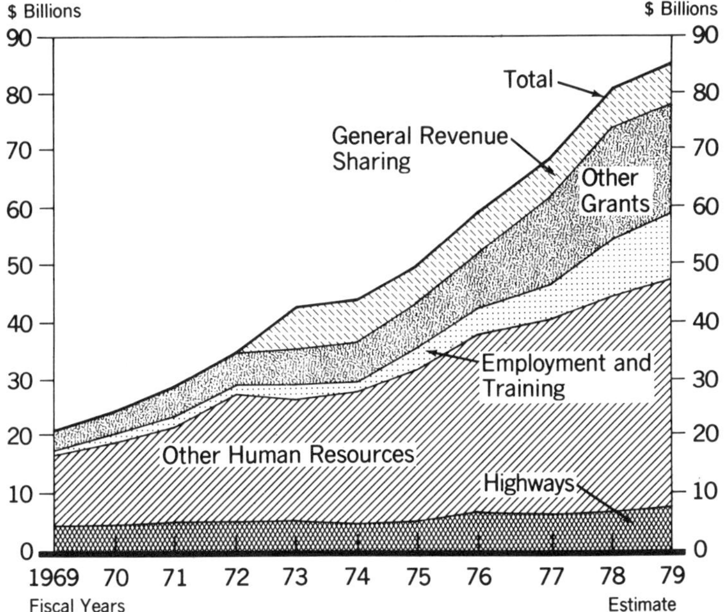

businesses and firms suffering from temporary business reversals will be helped to compete more effectively with their larger or more stable competitors.

(3) **Eligibility of Structures.** The investment credit now applies only to machinery and equipment. My tax program will extend eligibility for the credit to utility and industrial structures, where investments have been especially sluggish. Investment in these structures reached its peak over 4 years ago and is now 16 per cent below that level. It is important that we act to remedy the existing tax bias against structures and encourage balanced industrial expansion. In order to ensure that this provision has no anti-urban bias, I propose that the investment credit be available for both new structures and the rehabilitation of existing structures.

I recommend that this provision apply to construction costs incurred after December 31, 1977. In the case of new structures, there will be an additional requirement that the facility be placed in service after that date.

(4) **Liberalized Credit for Pollution Control Facilities.** I propose that pollution abatement facilities placed in service after December 31, 1977, be allowed to qualify for a full 10 per cent credit even if special 5-year amortization is claimed under the provisions of existing law. Currently, only a 5 per cent credit may be combined with rapid amortization. This proposal will provide significant tax relief for industries that are forced to make pollution control expenditures in order to comply with environmental regulations.

Revision and Simplification of Regulations Under the Asset Depreciation Range System

The asset depreciation range (ADR) system provides substantial tax benefits to businesses. Under ADR, generous class lives are prescribed for categories of assets, and a taxpayer can select useful lives for depreciation purposes within a range that extends from 20 per cent below to 20 per cent above the designated class life. However, certain complexities in the ADR regulations discourage most businesses, especially small ones, from electing this depreciation system and impose administrative burdens on those businesses that do use ADR.

I recommend legislation expressly permitting the Treasury Department to issue regulations that will simplify the ADR system. Included among the changes will be a termination of the annual reporting requirement.

Proposals Focused on Small Business

The tax reductions I recommend will provide significant benefits for small businesses. For example, a small corporation with annual income of $50,000 will save $1,000 in taxes due to corporate rate reductions. For that corporation, tax liability will be reduced by nearly 10 per cent. Moreover, those small businesses conducted in partnership or sole proprietorship form will benefit substantially from the rate cuts I have proposed for individuals.

But in addition to providing these general tax incentives, I recommend three proposals designed specifically to assist small businesses. First, my tax program will simplify and liberalize the rules (Subchapter S) that treat certain small corporations as partnerships; the number of permissible shareholders will generally be increased from 10 to 15, and the rules governing subchapter S elections will be made less stringent. Second, a simplified method of depreciation will be authorized for small businesses that will provide tax benefits similar to the current ADR system without complex recordkeeping requirements. And third, risk-taking will be encouraged by doubling the amount of a small corporation's stock (from $500,000 to $1 million) that can qualify for special ordinary loss treatment and by eliminating several technical requirements that needlessly restrict the ability of small businesses to use this provision.

Conclusion

Enactment of these recommendations will effect major reform of our tax laws, provide significant tax relief, and sustain our economic recovery.

This program will eliminate a number of the inequities that undermine the integrity of the tax system. It will make preparation of returns simpler and more understandable for millions of taxpayers. Prompt passage will strengthen the confidence of consumers and businesses in our growing economy and lead to the creation of up to one million new jobs for workers who need them.

I look forward to working in partnership with Congress to enact this program of tax reform and tax reduction.

JIMMY CARTER

The White House,
January 20, 1978

Budget Message

Following is the text of President Carter's fiscal 1979 budget message to Congress on January 23, 1978.

BUDGET MESSAGE OF THE PRESIDENT

To the Congress of the United States:

The first complete budget of any new administration is its most important. It is the administration's first full statement of its priorities, policies, and proposals for meeting our national needs. Last February, after just one month in office, I submitted a revised budget to the Congress. That revision changed the direction of the prior administration's budget, but was—of necessity—based upon a review of limited scope. I promised then that future budgets would reflect detailed, zero-based reviews of Federal spending programs, reform of the tax system, and reorganization of the government. This budget is my first major step in meeting that promise. It reflects, I believe, a determination to face and make difficult decisions in a manner that places the common good above that of any particular interest.

This budget represents a careful balancing of several considerations:

—The importance of a fiscal policy that provides for a continuing recovery of the nation's economy from the 1974-75 recession;

—The obligation of the government to meet the critical needs of the nation and its people;

—The fact that resources are limited and that government must discipline its choices and its scope; and

—The need for careful and prudent management of the taxpayers' resources.

My budget provides for total outlays of $500 billion, an increase of $38 billion, or 8 per cent, over the 1978 target, and receipts of $400 billion. This budget total is a restrained one that:

—Meets essential national needs;

—Imposes strict priorities upon federal expenditures; and

—Decreases the share of the nation's gross national product taken by the federal government from 22.6 per cent to 22.0 per cent.

This budget places us on a path that will permit a balanced budget in the future if the private economy continues its recovery over the coming years.

At the same time, my budget embodies a fiscal policy that will strengthen the economic recovery. I propose a progressive tax reduction of $25 billion to help assure continued economic recovery and reduction in unemployment. An integral part of this tax reduction proposal is a set of recommendations for tax reform that will make the tax system simpler and more equitable. Without the reduction, I would have been able to announce a decline in the deficit of $15 to $20 billion between 1978 and 1979. With the reduction, the budget deficit will still decline slightly, because of careful restraints on expenditures. But I judged that the most important priority this year was to reduce the burdens on taxpayers. Only in this way can we ensure a vigorous economy, a declining unemployment rate, a strong expansion of private investment, and a stable budget balance in future years.

While the expenditures I recommend in this budget are restrained, they are, nevertheless, directed toward overcoming our nation's crucial problems. I have looked carefully at existing approaches to these problems and improved those approaches where possible. The spending priorities of the past are now being shifted toward long-neglected areas. These new priorities are based on the following judgments:

Energy Plan

—*An effective national energy plan is essential to reduce our increasingly critical dependence upon diminishing supplies of oil and gas, to encourage conservation of scarce energy resources, to stimulate conversion to more abundant fuels, and to reduce our large trade deficit.*

The national energy plan I proposed last spring defined these goals. This budget includes the programs and initiatives designed to meet those objectives. Included are increased emphases on conservation and nonnuclear research and development, energy grants and technical assistance to states and localities, accelerated acquisition of the strategic petroleum reserve, and greater emphases on nuclear waste management. I continue in the unswerving belief that the nation's leaders have the obligation to plan for the future, and that the national energy plan is essential to the future health and vigor of the American economy. The United States also must take the lead in minimizing the risks of nuclear weapons proliferation as we advance nuclear power technology. Thus, this budget increases research and development funding for systems that present fewer risks than the plutonium-fueled liquid metal fast breeder reactor.

Human Needs

—*The essential human needs of our citizens must be given high priority.*

In the spring of 1977 I proposed a long-overdue reform of the nation's welfare system. This reform recognizes that this is a nation of men and women who do not wish to be wards of the government but who want to work and to be self-sufficient. It includes a combination of employment opportunities and incentives for those who should work, and a basic income for those who cannot. This budget anticipates that Congress will pass the program for better jobs and income, and begins the process of careful planning for the implementation of an efficient and equitable system.

The budget also recognizes that ensuring the opportunity to compete and excel remains very important to our people. To give all children the healthiest possible start in life, I propose major expansion of medical care and nutritional supplements for low-income expectant mothers and infants. In addition, I propose major increases in educational assistance at all levels. Because of the continued high level of unemployment, particularly among minorities, I believe public employment programs should be continued at high levels for another year. Major increases in programs stressing employment for unemployed youth are recommended. A new effort will be mounted to place more disadvantaged persons in private sector jobs by increasing the involvement of the business community in local employment and training programs.

I view a workable urban strategy as an important link in a well-articulated domestic program and essential to the continuing recovery of the national economy. This budget includes increases for many programs benefiting urban areas and supports several efforts to improve these programs. I anticipate sending to the Congress early in the spring a set of further proposals dealing with the nation's urban problems.

Defense

—*The nation's armed forces must always stand sufficiently strong to deter aggression and to assure our security.*

My request for defense provides for the steady modernization of our strategic forces, and for substantial improvements in the combat readiness of our tactical forces. To parallel commitments made by our European allies, I am proposing significant increases in our overall defense effort, with special emphasis on those forces and capabilities most directly related to our NATO commitments. The defense budget I recommend also emphasizes modernization and research and development to meet future challenges to our security. But at the same time, I am restraining defense expenditures by introducing important efficiencies and by placing careful priorities upon our defense needs. The 1979 defense budget is prudent and tight, but consists of a real growth in outlays of 3 per cent above the cur-

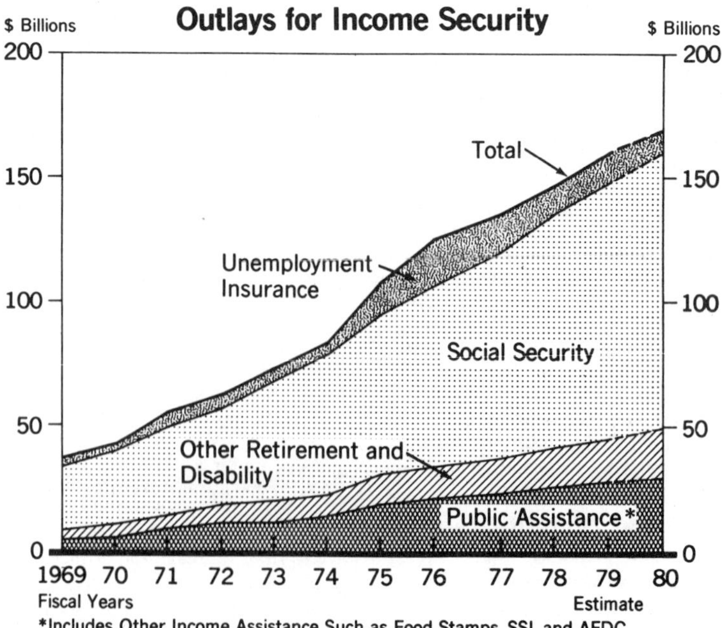

rent year's budget. Consistent with campaign pledges to the American people, it is $8 billion below the defense budget projected for 1979 by the previous administration.

Environment

—*The Federal Government has an obligation to nurture and protect our environment—the common resource, birthright and sustenance of the American people.*

This budget provides for substantially increased emphasis on protection of all our environmental resources, for new attention to our common heritage, and for substantial additions to our system of public lands. Planned use of our natural resources has been designed so that the most important of our unspoiled areas can remain forever in the hands of the people.

Technology

—*The Federal Government must lead the way in investing in the nation's technological future.*

Shortly after taking office, I determined that investment in basic research on the part of the federal government had fallen far too low over the past decade. Accordingly, I directed that a careful review be undertaken of appropriate basic research opportunities. As a result of that review, this budget proposes a real rate of growth of almost 5 per cent for basic research in 1979. I believe this emphasis is important to the continued vitality of our economy.

Government Operations

This budget also reflects this administration's commitment to two important approaches to making government work more efficiently and responsively: reorganization and zero-base budgeting.

The reorganization effort I have launched seeks more than just a streamlining of organization structure and the elimination of overlaps and duplication. It seeks to make our government more responsive, more efficient, and more clearly focused on the most pressing needs of our society. In 1977 I proposed—and the Congress accepted—a Cabinet-level Department of Energy, a streamlined Executive Office of the President, and a consolidation of our international information activities. In 1978 I will propose further reorganizations in such areas as the federal government's civil rights activities and the federal civil service system to make it more responsive and effective.

As I promised during my campaign, zero-base budgeting systems have been applied throughout the federal government. This budget is the product of a comprehensive zero-base review of all federal programs, both existing and new. In reviewing each agency's proposals, I have used zero-base budget alternatives and agency rankings to compare and evaluate the many requests competing for resources. As a result of the first year's effort, we have gained a better understanding of federal programs and have made better, more evenhanded judgments. Because of this system the budget includes dollar savings, and improvements in the way programs are operated. With experience, zero-based budgeting should be even more effective in future years.

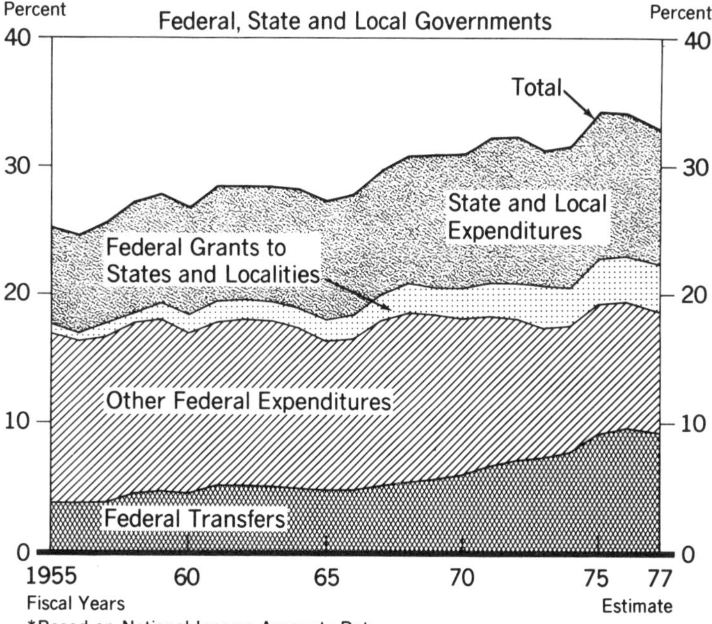

Other significant changes in the budget process are reflected in this document. First: I have directed the Office of Management and Budget to establish a multi-year budget planning system using longer range budget projections. This will ensure that budget decisions are made with full awareness of their longer range implications. Second: we are using better techniques for estimating outlays so as to avoid the chronic "shortfalls" of recent years. Third: we have explicitly related the classification of the budget in terms of functions performed by government programs to the national needs and agency missions served, as called for in the Congressional Budget Act of 1974.

In formulating this budget I have been made acutely aware once more of the overwhelming number of demands upon the budget and of the finite nature of our resources. Public needs are critically important; but private needs are equally valid, and the only resources the government has are those it collects from the taxpayer. The competition for these resources and my belief and commitment that we must firmly limit what the government taxes and expends have led me to the premises on which my first budget is based.

—Critical national needs exist—particularly human and social ones—to which resources must be directed.

—Government resources are scarce; their use must be planned with the full awareness that they come from the earnings of workers and profits of business firms.

—The span of government is not infinite. Priorities must be set and some old priorities changed. If we are to meet adequately the most critical needs, some demands must also be deferred. Government action must be limited to those areas where its intervention is more likely to solve problems than to compound them.

—We have an obligation to manage with excellence, and to maintain proper priorities within the $500 billion proposed in this budget. We all know that in a budget of this scale—larger than the gross national product of all but three nations in the world—there are dollars wasted and dollars misspent. These must be minimal.

These premises are unexceptionable in general, but difficult and controversial to apply. They have guided my actions in formulating this budget and they will continue to do so in the future. But to be successful I will need, and will work for, the help and cooperation of the Congress. Both the Congress and the Executive have a clear, joint interest in an approach that helps us to meet the demands of the future. In recent years the Congress has taken important steps—through the establishment of the congressional budget process—to improve its own means of establishing priorities. This administration has worked closely with the congressional appropriations and budget committees and has found them invaluable sources of advice. We will continue in this spirit of cooperation, and I look forward to working with the Congress and its leadership to obtain adoption of my budget for fiscal year 1979.

Jimmy Carter

January 20, 1978

Transportation Programs

Following is the text of President Carter's Jan. 26 message to Congress, transmitting his proposals to improve the federal highway and transit programs:

TO THE CONGRESS
OF THE UNITED STATES:

I am today transmitting to Congress proposed legislation that will significantly improve the organization and operation of the Federal Government's highway and transit programs.

One of the Administration's important goals is to develop a well balanced national transportation policy, one which takes account of our increased sensitivity to the effects of transportation on the social and economic life of our cities and rural communities. The reforms which are proposed in this legislation are designed to make certain that the nation has an effective transportation system, which uses energy more efficiently, enhances the quality of life in our urban and rural areas, and helps expand our economy.

The program I am proposing will intensify the Federal effort to complete the Interstate System and provide flexible assistance for highway construction and transit development. The legislation would authorize more than $50 billion over the next five years and proposes the following changes to meet national transportation needs:

—a comprehensive transportation planning program;

—measures to speed completion of the Interstate System and to improve maintenance;

—consolidation of more than 30 highway and public transportation grant programs into fewer and more flexible programs for both rural and urban areas;

—a uniform Federal share for all grant programs except Interstate construction and Interstate transfer projects;

—focusing the transit discretionary program on major investments;

—an expanded bridge replacement and rehabilitation program;

—a unified safety program; and

—greater flexibility for states and local governments to pursue their own priorities.

To achieve our objectives in this area, we propose a reorganization of a variety of highway and transit programs into a simpler and more manageable system of federal assistance. Certain aspects of our new approach to these programs should be emphasized.

Transportation Planning

To promote more efficient short-range and long-range planning by state and local officials, I propose to consolidate highway and transit planning funds and to distribute these funds as a single grant, under a formula to be determined by the Secretary of Transportation.

Planning grants will be made directly to designated metropolitan planning organizations in urbanized areas over one million in population. The Secretary will review transportation plans for such areas to ensure that they take reasonable account of such issues as air quality, energy conservation, environmental quality, accessibility to employment, effect on minorities, housing, land use and future development. The planning process for other areas will be strengthened as well.

Interstate System

Our first priority will be to complete the essential gaps in the Interstate System. Fifty per cent of the apportionment formula will be based on the cost to complete the essential gaps and 50 per cent on the cost to complete the total system. Highway projects substituted after an Interstate withdrawal will be funded from a state's Interstate apportionment, and substitute mass transit projects will be funded from the General Fund. Interstate substitute projects, both highway and transit, will be eligible for a ninety per cent federal share.

States will be required to have completed the Environmental Impact Statement process or to have submitted an application for an Interstate withdrawal on all uncompleted segments of the Interstate by September 30, 1982. Segments which have not met either requirement will be removed from the system. All incomplete Interstate segments must be under contract for construction and initial construction must have commenced by September 30, 1986.

Federal-Aid Primary System

To simplify an unduly restrictive funding structure, seven highway categories will be consolidated into a single Primary program. Funds will be apportioned by a formula specified in the legislation and the federal share will be eighty per cent. Up to 50 per cent of a state's primary system funds may be transferred to the urban highway or the small urban and rural transportation programs.

Urban Formula Grants

Two compatible programs will be established, one for highways and one for transit, for all urbanized areas with a population of 50,000 or more. The highway program will consolidate five categorical programs, and all urban roads not on the Interstate or primary systems will be eligible for assistance. The transit program will provide assistance for the acquisition, construction and improvement of facilities and equipment for use in public transportation services and the payment of operating expenses, including commuter rail operating expenses.

Funds will be apportioned by formula and the federal share for capital projects will be 80 per cent. The highway formula will be based on urbanized area population. Up to 50 per cent of the urban highway funds may be transferred to the Primary program or to the small urban and rural program. Up to 50 per cent of the transit funds may be transferred to the highway program. Highway funds will continue to be available for transit capital projects.

Governors and local officials will be required to designate a recipient or recipients for urban highway funds in urbanized areas with a population of one million or more. By this step we will significantly improve the opportunity for large cities to become more involved in the planning and programming of their highway systems. Urban highway funds for areas with small populations will go to the State.

Urban Discretionary Grant

This transit grant program will be focused on major expansion of bus fleets and new fixed guideway projects, including extensions of existing systems, and joint development projects.

Small Urban and Rural Formula Grant

To meet the unique needs of small cities and rural communities, we propose a consolidated grant program for highways and transit for all areas with a population below 50,000, with the state as the recipient.

Nine categorical highway programs will be consolidated into this new program, and all public roads not on the Interstate or primary systems will be eligible for assistance. The new program will provide assistance for both capital and operating expenses for public transportation in small urban and rural communities. Authorization for this program would come out of the Highway Trust Fund, but the Trust Fund would be reimbursed out of the General Fund for transit operating expenses.

Safety Program

To allow more flexible and rational use of funds, six highway safety programs will be consolidated into a single safety grant to states, with the federal share at 80 per cent.

Bridge Program

For the first time states will be able to use substantially increased funds for rehabilitation as well as replacements of deteriorating bridges. The federal share will be 80 per cent, and up to 30 per cent of the funds will be available for bridges not on the Federal-aid highway systems.

Authorizations

The proposed authorizations are designed to permit better long-term planning by those responsible for both highway and transit development. The Highway Trust Fund will be extended for an additional four years. The formula grant programs will be authorized for a four-year period, and the urban discretionary grant program will be authorized for a five-year period.

In proposing the reforms contained in this legislation I recognize the critical relationship between transportation, energy and development in urban and rural areas. I believe that these proposals will lead toward energy conservation and better land use. The enactment of this legislation will bring new opportunities and responsibilities to state and local officials, will respond to the problems of the present programs, and will help to place the surface transportation system on a sound financial basis.

I ask the Congress to move promptly to pass this highway and transit legislation.

JIMMY CARTER

The White House,
January 26, 1978

Arms Sales Cut

Following is the text of a statement by President Carter, issued Feb. 1, announcing reductions in the ceiling on arms sales abroad:

The United States Government, the Executive Branch and the Congress, are pledged to bring about a reduction in the trade in conventional arms. Last year, I promised to begin reducing U.S. arms sales as a necessary first step. I will continue that policy this year.

In the last fiscal year, the previous Administration and my Administration made sales commitments totaling many billions of dollars. While high, however, the total was considerably less than it would have been in the absence of new restraints we introduced, particularly in sales commitments to the developing countries of the world. Between January 20 and the close of the fiscal year, I approved and sent to Congress arms sales totaling $5.7 billion, which is less than half the total approved during the same period in 1976.

Today, I am announcing that arms transfer agreements covered by the ceiling which I have established will be reduced by $740 million in Fiscal Year 1978. This means that for the fiscal year which began on October 1, 1977, and which will end on September 30, 1978, new commitments under the Foreign Military Sales and Military Assistance programs for weapons and weapons-related items to all countries except NATO, Japan, Australia and New Zealand will not exceed $8.6 billion. The comparable figure for Fiscal Year 1977 was $9.3 billion. This is a reduction of 8 percent, figured on constant Fiscal Year 1976 dollars.

A larger cut in the ceiling would violate commitments already made, including our historic interest in the security of the Middle East, and would ignore the continuing realities of world politics and risk the confidence and security of those nations with whom the United States has vital and shared foreign policy and security interests. A smaller reduction would neglect our responsibility to set an example of restraint that others might follow.

I intend to make further reductions in the next fiscal year. The extent of next year's reduction will depend upon the world political situation and upon the degree of cooperation and understanding of other nations.

I want to emphasize that the restraint policy I announced on May 19, 1977, was not aimed exclusively at the volume of arms transfers. Equally important is restraint in the sophistication of arms being transferred and on the spreading capability to produce armaments. Therefore, in addition to the ceiling, I established five specific controls applicable to all transfers except those to our NATO allies, Japan, Australia, and New Zealand. These controls included: (1) a control on the first introduction of certain advanced systems into an area; (2) a prohibition on advanced systems for export only; (3) a prohibition on various types of coproduction arrangements; (4) tighter controls on retransfer; and (5) special controls on sales promotions.

These guidelines are at the heart of my decisions to approve or disapprove an arms transfer.

As I stated in my October 4 speech to the United Nations, genuine progress in this area will require multilateral efforts. But, we are committed to taking the first steps alone to stop the spiral of increasing arms transfers. I call upon suppliers and recipients alike to join us in a determined effort to make the world a safer place in which to live.

Nuclear Safeguards

Following is President Carter's Feb. 9 message to the Senate accompanying a proposed treaty with the International Atomic Energy Agency concerning safeguards for nuclear facilities:

TO THE SENATE
OF THE UNITED STATES:

I submit herewith, for Senate advice and consent to ratification, the Agreement between the United States of America and the International Atomic Energy Agency ("Agency") for the Application of Safeguards in the United States of America, with attached Protocol, approved by the Board of Governors of the Agency on September 17, 1976. This agreement provides for application of Agency safeguards to nuclear facilities in the United States, other than those having direct national security significance. The Agreement will enter into force when the United States notifies the Agency that its constitutional and statutory requirements for entry into force have been met.

The United States, as a nuclear weapons state party to the Treaty on the Non-Proliferation of Nuclear Weapons ("NPT"), is not obligated to accept Agency safeguards on its peaceful nuclear activities. On December 2, 1967, President Johnson offered to place United States nuclear facilities, except those with direct national security significance, under Agency safeguards in an effort to demonstrate that the application of those safeguards would not work to any nation's commercial disadvantage. Specifically, President Johnson stated:

"...I want to make it clear to the world that we in the United States are not asking any country to accept safeguards that we are unwilling to accept ourselves.

"So I am, today, announcing that when such safeguards are applied under the treaty, the United States will permit the International Atomic Energy Agency to apply its safeguards to all nuclear activities in the United States—excluding only those with direct national security significance.

"Under this offer the agency will be able to inspect a broad range of U.S. nuclear activities, both governmental and private, including the fuel in nuclear power reactors owned by utilities for generating electricity, and the fabrication, and chemical reprocessing of such fuel...."

Over the next ten years, both Presidents Nixon and Ford reaffirmed that offer.

I also transmit, for the information of the Senate, the report of the Department of State concerning the Agreement.

Universal participation in the NPT is a central goal of our non-proliferation policy. The entry into force of this Agreement would encourage that participation, and would fulfill our long-standing commitment to accept safeguards. I urge the Senate to act favorably on this Agreement at an early date and give its advice and consent to ratification.

JIMMY CARTER

The White House
Feb. 9, 1978

Jobs Program Renewal

Following is President Carter's Feb. 22 message to Congress requesting extension of the Comprehensive Employment and Training Act (CETA).

TO THE CONGRESS
OF THE UNITED STATES:

I am submitting today legislation to extend an improved Comprehensive Employment and Training Act through 1982.

This legislation is an essential complement to the balanced economic program I presented to the Congress last month. While our tax and budget proposals ensure that steady growth continues without inflation, the CETA legislation I am proposing today will make sure that more of our people share in the benefits of growth. With its training programs and direct job creation, this legislation is critical to reaching our employment goals.

In Fiscal Year 1979 we expect to spend $11.4 billion in this effort, providing jobs and training support for more than 4 million people under the CETA program.

This legislation will combine public and private efforts to attack the problem of *structural* unemployment, which affects groups, such as minorities and young people, who have difficulty finding work even when over-all economic prospects are good. Last year, for example, our employment situations improved markedly; 4.1 million more people held jobs at the end of 1977 than at the end of 1976, and the unemployment rate fell by 1.4 per cent. But even while unemployment was falling to 4 per cent among white males above the age of 20, it was rising—from 35 to 38 percent—among black teenagers.

Major Elements

The Comprehensive Employment and Training Act will enable us to concentrate on these groups that suffer structural problems, without putting inflationary pressures on the rest of the economy. Its major elements are:

—Public service jobs for the unemployed. In the last year, we have more than doubled the size of this program, increasing it from about 300,000 jobs to 725,000.

—The broad range of youth programs authorized by the Youth Employment and Demonstration Projects Act of 1977. Spending for youth programs has increased from about $660 million in Fiscal Year 1976 to about $2.3 billion in Fiscal Year 1979.

—The Administration's new Private Sector Initiative, which will provide opportunity for the private and public sectors to work together to provide jobs and training for the unemployed and disadvantaged.

—Other important related programs, such as the Job Corps, welfare reform demonstration projects, and the federal government's job training efforts.

These CETA programs have already played a role in reducing the unemployment rate from 7.8 per cent to 6.3 per cent in the last 13 months.

The bill I am submitting today, which will reauthorize the Comprehensive Employment and Training Act for an additional four years, from 1979 to 1982, will sustain the current programs, establish the foundation for future growth, and improve the operation of the CETA system.

A countercyclical program under Title VI, will maintain the 725,000 public service employment slots that were part of my stimulus program through Fiscal 1979. We are rapidly approaching the 700,000 mark in that effort, and I fully expect that the 725,000 goal will be reached in the month of March.

Also, I am recommending to the Congress that we adopt a trigger formula, beginning in 1980, to insure that countercyclical public service employment is activated quickly when needed and is reduced as unemployment declines.

When the unemployment rate falls below four and three-quarters per cent, the triggering formula will reduce the number of slots to 100,000, targeted on areas that still have high unemployment. For each half percentage point that unemployment exceeds that 4.75 percent level, 100,000 public service employment positions will be added in Title VI.

Recent evidence indicates the effectiveness of countercyclical public service employment. Just last week, the National Commission on Manpower Policy released a study done by the Brookings Institution showing that the substitution problem, which limits the usefulness of public service employment when federal dollars are used to replace local funds, is not as serious as had previously been feared.

To reduce substitution, I am encouraging the use of a special project approach which, according to recent evidence, has been successful in meeting this problem.

I am also proposing strict limits on the use of these funds to support higher-wage public employment.

This new bill takes further steps to target jobs on those most in need and sharply limit substitution.

Only for Disadvantaged

In order to target more effectively, I am recommending that funds given out under the CETA system be used only for the economically disadvantaged—defined as those whose family income is no greater than 70 percent of the Bureau of Labor Statistics' lower-income family budget standard. I am also recommending that young people whose parents claimed them as income tax deductions in the previous year include their parents' income in establishing their eligibility for the current year.

This year, I propose that we demonstrate the jobs component of my welfare reform proposal by creating 50,000 positions in selected cities. Beginning in Fiscal 1980, with the passage of the welfare reform bill, we will increase the structural unemployment program until it can accommodate the 1.4 million people I anticipate will be served in the welfare reform plan. That should ensure that, for every family containing children and parents who want to work, there will be a job. Most families containing an employable person will see their income rise substantially above the poverty line.

The purpose of the Public Service Employment program will remain what it has been—to provide *useful* jobs. For example:

—Major parks in urban centers, such as Boston, that were once abandoned to overgrowth and vandalism have been reclaimed for the enjoyment of the public.

—In North Carolina, elderly people are being cared for, in their homes, by public service employment workers, rather than being forced to leave home and spend their last years in expensive, sometimes impersonal nursing homes.

—In Portland, Oregon, CETA workers install locks, window grates and other security devices in the homes of senior citizens and low-income families living in high-crime areas.

—In Memphis, workers are building ramps for the handicapped in five areas of the city used heavily by the handicapped and elderly.

—In Humboldt County, California, CETA workers help to staff day care centers serving low-income families.

—In Worthington, Minnesota, workers are providing home insulation and energy conservation assistance to low-income households in a four-county area.

As the economy improves, employment and training programs should shift their emphasis from creating jobs in the public sector to providing training and finding jobs in the private sector.

New Program

To help place CETA participants in private-sector jobs, to provide an opportunity for cooperation between the local CETA programs and the private sector, and to tap the goodwill and commitment of private-sector businessmen, large and small, as well as labor leaders, I am asking Congress for authority to establish a new Private Sector Employment Initiative, under a new Title VII. In the budget, I have set aside $400 million for this activity in 1979.

Private Industry Councils—made up of representatives of large and small businesses and union organizations—will be responsible for developing on-the-job training and other placement opportunities with private firms for young workers and other participants in the CETA system.

The CETA legislation that I am presenting today provides Congress with a plan for a rational, efficient and targeted structural and countercyclical employment program.

We need an employment and training system which is administratively clear, that helps those most in need, that creates needed jobs and provides maximum opportunity for cooperation between the public and private sectors. To reach the goal of full employment, and price stability which we have set in the Humphrey-Hawkins bill, we must make these programs work. The legislation I am sending to Congress today can provide a framework within which we can all work together to achieve that commitment.

JIMMY CARTER

The White House,
February 22, 1978

Equal Employment Plan

Following is President Carter's Feb. 23 message to Congress on

Reorganization Plan No. 1 of 1978, consolidating the federal government's equal employment opportunity activities.

TO THE CONGRESS
OF THE UNITED STATES:

I am submitting to you today Reorganization Plan No. 1 of 1978. This Plan makes the Equal Employment Opportunity Commission the principal Federal agency in fair employment enforcement. Together with actions I shall take by Executive Order, it consolidates Federal equal employment opportunity activities and lays, for the first time, the foundation of a unified, coherent Federal structure to combat job discrimination in all its forms.

In 1940 President Roosevelt issued the first Executive Order forbidding discrimination in employment by the Federal government. Since that time the Congress, the courts and the Executive Branch — spurred by the courage and sacrifice of many people and organizations — have taken historic steps to extend equal employment opportunity protection throughout the private as well as public sector. But each new prohibition against discrimination unfortunately has brought with it a further dispersal of Federal equal employment opportunity responsibility. This fragmentation of authority among a number of Federal agencies has meant confusion and ineffective enforcement for employees, regulatory duplication and needless expense for employers.

Fair employment is too vital for haphazard enforcement. My Administration will aggressively enforce our civil rights laws. Although discrimination in any area has severe consequences, limiting economic opportunity affects access to education, housing and health care. I, therefore, ask you to join with me to reorganize administration of the civil rights laws and to begin that effort by reorganizing the enforcement of those laws which ensure an equal opportunity to a job.

Streamlining Proposal

Eighteen government units now exercise important responsibilities under statutes, Executive Orders and regulations relating to equal employment opportunity:

- The Equal Employment Opportunity Commission (EEOC) enforces Title VII of the Civil Rights Act of 1964, which bans employment discrimination based on race, national origin, sex or religion. The EEOC acts on individual complaints and also initiates private sector cases involving a "pattern or practice" of discrimination.
- The Department of Labor and other agencies enforce Executive Order 11246. This prohibits discrimination in employment on the basis of race, national origin sex, or religion and requires affirmative action by government contractors. While the Department now coordinates enforcement of this "contract compliance" program, it is actually administered by eleven other departments and agencies. The Department also administers those statutes requiring contractors to take affirmative action to employ handicapped people, disabled veterans and Vietnam veterans.

In addition, the Labor Department enforces the Equal Pay Act of 1963, which prohibits employers from paying unequal wages based on sex, and the Age Discrimination in Employment Act of 1967, which forbids age discrimination against persons between the ages of 40 and 65.

- The Department of Justice litigates Title VII cases involving public sector employers — State and local governments. The Department also represents the Federal government in lawsuits against Federal contractors and grant recipients who are in violation of Federal nondiscrimination prohibitions.
- The Civil Service Commission (CSC) enforces Title VII and all other nondiscrimination and affirmative action requirements for Federal employment. The CSC rules on complaints filed by individuals and monitors affirmative action plans submitted annually by other Federal agencies.
- The Equal Employment Opportunity Coordinating Council includes representatives from EEOC, Labor, Justice, CSC and the Civil Rights Commission. It is charged with coordinating the Federal equal employment opportunity enforcement effort and with eliminating overlap and inconsistent standards.
- In addition to these major government units, other agencies enforce various equal employment opportunity requirements which apply to specific grant programs. The Department of Treasury, for example, administers the anti-discrimination prohibitions applicable to recipients of revenue sharing funds.

These programs have had only limited success. Some of the past deficiencies include:

— inconsistent standards of compliance;
— duplicative, inconsistent paperwork requirements and investigative efforts;
— conflicts within agencies between their program responsibilities and their responsibility to enforce the civil rights laws;
— confusion on the part of workers about how and where to seek redress;
— lack of accountability.

I am proposing today a series of steps to bring coherence to the equal employment enforcement effort. These steps, to be accomplished by the Reorganization Plan and Executive Orders, constitute an important step toward consolidation of equal employment opportunity enforcement. They will be implemented over the next two years, so that the agencies involved may continue their internal reform.

EEOC Progress

Its experience and broad scope make the EEOC suitable for the role of principal Federal agency in fair employment enforcement. Located in the Executive Branch and responsible to the President, the EEOC has developed considerable expertise in the field of employment discrimination since Congress created it by the Civil Rights Act of 1964. The Commission has played a pioneer role in defining both employment discrimination and its appropriate remedies.

While it has had management problems in past administrations, the EEOC's new leadership is making substantial progress in correcting them. In the last seven months the Commission has redesigned its internal structures and adopted proven management techniques. Early experience with these procedures indicates a high degree of success in reducing and expediting new cases. At my direction, the Office of Management and Budget is actively assisting the EEOC to ensure that these reforms continue.

The Reorganization Plan I am submitting will accomplish the following:

- On July 1, 1978, abolish the Equal Employment Opportunity Coordinating Council (42 U.S.C. 2000e-14) and transfer its duties to the EEOC (no positions or funds shifted).
- On October 1, 1978, shift enforcement of equal employment opportunity for Federal employees from the CSC to the EEOC (100 positions and $6.5 million shifted).
- On July 1, 1979, shift responsibility for enforcing both the Equal Pay Act and the Age Discrimination in Employment Act from the Labor Department to the EEOC (198 positions and $5.3 million shifted for Equal Pay; 119 positions and $3.5 million for Age Discrimination).
- Clarify the Attorney General's authority to initiate "pattern or practice" suits under Title VII in the public sector.

In addition, I will issue an Executive Order on October 1, 1978, to consolidate the contract compliance program — now the responsibility of Labor and eleven "compliance agencies" — into the Labor Department (1,517 positions and $33.1 million shifted).

These proposed transfers and consolidations reduce from fifteen to three the number of Federal agencies having important equal employment opportunity responsibilities under Title VII of the Civil Rights Act of 1964 and Federal contract compliance provisions.

Each element of my Plan is important to the success of the entire proposal.

By abolishing the Equal Employment Opportunity Coordinating Council and transferring its responsibilities to the EEOC, this plan places the Commission at the center of equal employment opportunity enforcement. With these new responsibilities, the EEOC can give coherence and direction to the government's efforts by developing strong uniform enforcement standards to apply throughout the government: standardized data collection procedures, joint training programs, programs to ensure the sharing of enforcement related data among agencies, and methods and priorities for complaint and compliance reviews. Such direction has been absent in the Equal Employment Opportunity Coordinating Council.

It should be stressed, however, that affected agencies will be consulted before EEOC takes any action. When the Plan has been approved, I intend to issue an Executive Order which will provide for consultation, as well as a procedure for reviewing major disputed issues within the Executive Office of the President. The Attorney General's responsibility to advise the Executive Branch on legal issues will also be preserved.

Federal Employees

Transfer of the Civil Service Commission's equal employment opportunity responsibilities to EEOC is needed to ensure that: (1) Federal employees have the same rights and remedies as those in the private sector and in State and local government; (2) Federal agencies meet the same standards as are required of other employers; and (3) potential conflicts between an agency's equal employment opportunity and personnel management functions are minimized. The Federal government must not fall below the standard of performance it expects of private employers.

The Civil Service Commission has in the past been lethargic in enforcing fair employment requirements within the Federal government. While the Chairman and other Commissioners I have appointed have already demonstrated their personal commitment to expanding equal employment opportunity, responsibility for ensuring fair employment for Federal employees should rest ultimately with the EEOC.

We must ensure that the transfer in no way undermines the important objectives of the comprehensive civil service reorganization which will be submitted to Congress in the near future. When the two plans take effect, I will direct the EEOC and the CSC to coordinate their procedures to prevent any duplication and overlap.

The Equal Pay Act, now administered by the Labor Department, prohibits employers from paying unequal wages based on sex. Title VII of the Civil Rights Act, which is enforced by EEOC, contains a broader ban on sex discrimination. The transfer of Equal Pay responsibility from the Labor Department to the EEOC will minimize overlap and centralize enforcement of statutory prohibitions against sex discrimination in employment.

The transfer will strengthen efforts to combat sex discrimination. Such efforts would be enhanced still further by passage of the legislation pending before you, which I support, that would prohibit employers from excluding women disabled by pregnancy from participating in disability programs.

There is now virtually complete overlap in the employers, labor organizations, and employment agencies covered by Title VII and by the Age Discrimination in Employment Act. This overlap is burdensome to employers and confusing to victims of discrimination. The proposed transfer of the age discrimination program from the Labor Department to the EEOC will eliminate the duplication.

The Plan I am proposing will not affect the Attorney General's responsibility to enforce Title VII against State or local governments or to represent the Federal government in suits against Federal contractors and grant recipients. In 1972, the Congress determined that the Attorney General should be involved in suits against State and local governments. This proposal reinforces that judgment and clarifies the Attorney General's authority to initiate litigation against State or local governments engaged in a "pattern or practice" of discrimination. This in no way diminishes the EEOC's existing authority to investigate complaints filed against State or local governments and, where appropriate, to refer them to the Attorney General. The Justice Department and the EEOC will cooperate so that the Department sues on valid referrals, as well as on its own "pattern or practice" cases.

Contractors' Compliance

A critical element of my proposals will be accomplished by Executive Order rather than by the Reorganization Plan. This involves consolidation in the Labor Department of the responsibility to ensure that Federal contractors comply with Executive Order 11246. Consolidation will achieve the following: promote consistent standards, procedures, and reporting requirements; remove contractors from the jurisdiction of multiple agencies; prevent an agency's equal employment objectives from being outweighed by its procurement and construction objectives; and produce more effective law enforcement through unification of planning, training and sanctions. By 1981, after I have had an opportunity to review the manner in which both the EEOC and the Labor Department are exercising their new responsibilities, I will determine whether further action is appropriate.

Finally, the responsibility for enforcing grant-related equal employment provisions will remain with the agencies administering the grant programs. With the EEOC acting as coordinator of Federal equal employment programs, we will be able to bring overlap and duplication to a minimum. We will be able, for example, to see that a university's employment practices are not subject to duplicative investigations under both Title IX of the Education Amendments of 1972 and the contract compliance program. Because of the similarities between the Executive Order program and those statutes requiring Federal contractors to take affirmative action to employ handicapped individuals and disabled and Vietnam veterans, I have determined that enforcement of these statutes should remain in the Labor Department.

Each of the changes set forth in the Reorganization Plan accompanying this message is necessary to accomplish one or more of the purposes set forth in Section 901(a) of Title 5 of the United States Code. I have taken care to determine that all functions abolished by the Plan are done only under the statutory authority provided by Section 903(b) of Title 5 of the United States Code.

I do not anticipate that the reorganizations contained in this Plan will result in any significant change in expenditures. They will result in a more efficient and manageable enforcement program.

The Plan I am submitting is moderate and measured. It gives the Equal Employment Opportunity Commission — an agency dedicated solely to this purpose — the primary Federal responsibility in the area of job discrimination, but it is designed to give this agency sufficient time to absorb its new responsibilities. This reorganization will produce consistent agency standards, as well as increased accountability. Combined with the intense commitment of those charged with these responsibilities, it will become possible for us to accelerate this nation's progress in ensuring equal job opportunities for all our people.

JIMMY CARTER

The White House,
February 23, 1978

Education Proposals

Following is President Carter's Feb. 28 message to Congress outlining his proposals for federal programs to aid elementary and secondary education.

TO THE CONGRESS
OF THE UNITED STATES:

I am submitting today my proposals to strengthen our major elementary and secondary education programs. These are one part of a concerted effort to re-establish education in the forefront of our domestic priorities. The other parts are major increases in the Federal education budget, establishment of a Cabinet-level Department of Education, and our proposal for a significant expansion of eligibility for college student assistance.

The proposals which I am now submitting for elementary and secondary education seek to enhance the primary role of the states and local communities in educating our Nation's children and reaffirm the need for a strong and supportive Federal commitment to education. They will:

— strengthen our commitment to basic skills education in Title I of the Elementary and Secondary Education program; and add a new provision to concentrate a major share of increased Title I funding on those school systems most in need;

— create a new program to encourage state implementation of their own compensatory education programs;

— provide additional flexibility in the Emergency School Aid Act, designed to assist in desegregation, so that funds can be retargeted from areas where they are no longer needed to areas of greater need;

— create a new research and demonstration effort in the area of basic skills, and enhance our efforts to link schools with employers and other community resources;

— implement a phased, gradual but substantial reform of the Impact Aid Program;

— strengthen the bilingual education program with emphasis on teaching English as a primary and overriding goal but permitting flexibility in use of first language and culturally sensitive approaches to help achieve this goal;

— strengthen participation of private schools in existing grant programs.

We can be justly proud of the accomplishments of our system of education. Education has promoted understanding among a diverse people; it has been the springboard to advancement for generations of our citizens; and it has produced the skills and knowledge required for this country to have the most advanced economy in the world.

Yet our schools face many important challenges. We must do a better job of teaching the basic skills of reading, writing and mathematics. We must remain committed to full and equal educational opportunity for all children. We must help students achieve educational excellence. We must responsibly reduce the financial barriers that limit access to higher education. And we must give education a more prominent and visible role in the Federal government.

We will face these challenges and overcome them. No asset is of greater value to our Nation and no commitment is so characteristic of the American people as our strong commitment to educate all our children.

Education Budget

The Administration's budget proposals for the coming year show the priority we give to education. Our FY 1979 budget contains $12.9 billion in appropriations for the Education Division of the Department of Health, Education and Welfare. That represents an increase of 24 percent above the FY 1978 level and a total increase of 46 percent and $4 billion in the last two fiscal years.

I have requested appropriations of $6.9 billion for elementary and secondary education, an increase of fifteen percent over FY 1978. This increase is the largest since the creation of the program and exceeds the FY 1977 budget by $1.7 billion. Along with these increases goes a forty percent increase in student assistance programs for higher education and a new effort to expand the reach of these programs to moderate income families hard-pressed by escalating tuition costs. Funding for these student assistance programs will rise from $3.8 billion in FY 1978 to $5.2 billion in FY 1979.

This budget reflects the judgment, widely shared by the Congress, that improving the education of our children is a wise investment in our future.

Department of Education

I have instructed the Office of Management and Budget and the Department of Health, Education and Welfare to work with Congress on legislation needed to establish a Department of Education which will:

— let us focus on Federal educational policy, at the highest levels of our government;

— permit closer coordination of Federal education programs and other related activities;

— reduce Federal regulations and reporting requirements and cut duplication;

— assist school districts, teachers, and parents to make better use of local resources and ingenuity.

A separate Cabinet-level department will enable the federal government to be a true partner with State, local and private education institutions in sustaining and improving the quality of our education system.

College Student Assistance

I recently proposed a major expansion of the programs providing financial assistance to students in higher education. Average college costs have increased by seventy-seven percent in the last ten years. At average costs of $4,500 per year in private higher education and $2,500 in public universities low and middle income families are finding it difficult to send their children to college. No able student should be denied a college education because his or her family cannot afford tuition, room and board.

My proposals will increase the number of students receiving assistance from three million to more than five million at a cost of $1.46 billion. The proposals would:

— expand the Basic Educational Opportunity Grants program to serve students from families with incomes up to $25,000 and increase the maximum grant to $1,800;

— make interest-subsidized Guaranteed Student Loans available to families with incomes up to $45,000;

— provide part-time jobs to college students through an expanded college Work-Study program.

This coordinated program is the best way to meet the needs of our students and their families. I strongly oppose the enactment of a tuition tax credit.

A college tuition tax credit would cost too much, would provide benefits to those without need, would provide less benefit to genuinely hard-pressed families than the proposals we have advanced, and would fragment educational policy within the executive and legislative branches of the Federal government.

A choice must be made. We cannot afford — and I will not accept — both a tuition tax credit and the increased student aid I have proposed. I strongly urge the Congress to act responsibly on the Administration's proposals.

Elementary and Secondary Education Amendments of 1978

The legislation I am submitting today involves the major elementary and secondary education programs. Since the Administration of Lyndon Johnson the primary role of these Federal programs has been to support improvements in educational quality for all children and improve the educational opportunities and achievements of the disadvantaged, the handicapped, those with limited English language skills, Native Americans and other minorities. I propose to continue and strengthen the use of Federal resources to meet special needs, and Federal leadership in research and innovation.

These programs must focus on the mastery of the basic skills necessary to function in our highly complex society. Every child should obtain the basic skills of reading, writing and mathematics early in his or her educational career. This should be the fundamental goal for our entire education system, and I hope that Federal leadership will help us meet that goal at every level of our school system.

Special Programs for Disadvantaged Children

I propose to improve Title I of the Elementary and Secondary Education Act which provides supplemental educational services to economically disadvantaged children.

1. Concentration of Resources

Recent evaluations show that Title I is beginning to raise the achievement levels of low-income students. I propose to build upon this success by incorporating in the reauthorization of the Act a separate authority to increase help for school districts with high concentrations of poor children. The amendments I propose will target additional Title I funds to school districts with large numbers of poor children (5,000 or more) or large proportions of poor children (20 percent or more), for use in programs with a strong emphasis on basic skills. I have requested $400 million in the 1979 budget for this proposal, which would aid 3,500 school districts and could increase the number of Title I eligible children served to 6.5 million.

This targeting of additional funds on areas of greatest need will be of special benefit to urban school systems with concentrations of low-income children. It is an important part of our efforts to help meet the needs of our cities. Yet the problems of educational disadvantage are not unique to cities; therefore, while 67 percent of the funds will flow to center-city school systems, 33 percent will flow to rural and suburban school systems which have similar needs.

2. State Programs for Disadvantaged Children

Strong State efforts are clearly necessary to fully meet the needs of disadvantaged children. Currently, however, fewer than twenty States have special programs to aid disadvantaged students. To encourage the creation of compensatory education programs at the State level, I recommend that a share of future increases in the Title I program be allocated, on the basis of one Federal dollar for every two State dollars, to States with qualified compensatory education programs of their own. In fiscal year 1980 twenty percent of any increases would be devoted to this matching program. In future years an increasing percentage would be made available. I hope this Federal incentive program will encourage a response at the State level which will give greater opportunities to millions of children.

Emergency School Aid Act

We must move aggressively to end the last vestiges of racial and ethnic mistrust and disharmony in our schools and in our society as a whole. Great progress toward that goal has been made, particularly in the South, but much remains to be done.

The Emergency School Aid Act has helped numerous local school districts respond to the problems of racial isolation and improve education for all their children. I recommend amendments to that legislation which would:

— encourage voluntary local initiatives to overcome the adverse effects of minority group isolation;

— offer flexibility to meet the needs of desegregating districts;

— and encourage multi-year planning and implementation of desegregation.

To give us more flexibility in meeting changing needs, I propose to increase the share of discretionary funds from 22 percent to 42 percent. This will permit allocation of resources to areas of greatest need. At the same time I am recommending a new system of multi-year grants which will sharply reduce paperwork and will help local school systems plan for the future.

Basic Skills

The Federal government can play an important role in funding research and demonstration projects which will show us how to improve the quality and effectiveness of our educational system. Student achievement can be improved through innovation, and a concentration on basic skills. I propose several improvements in this area:

— the creation of a new Basic Skills and Educational Quality title in the Elementary and Secondary Education Act which would encourage state and local demonstration efforts to improve basic skills in reading, writing and mathematics, including increased use of achievement testing and the participation by parents in teaching their children;

— the creation of a new Special Projects title in the Elementary and Secondary Education Act to consolidate educational quality developmental programs and provide greater flexibility; and strengthen our efforts, through the Community Schools program, to link the school with employers and other resources in the surrounding community;

— changes in the Adult Education Act to put more emphasis on competency in basic skills and on obtaining high school credentials, and to increase sponsorship of adult education programs by business, labor and other community organizations.

Impact Aid

Reform of Impact Aid is a challenge which must be faced. The purpose of the program is to compensate school districts for the cost of educating children when local revenues are reduced by tax-exempt federally-owned land and when local school enrollments are increased by children whose parents live and/or work on that land. Yet Impact Aid, as currently structured, has strayed far from that purpose.

The legislation I propose makes realistic and responsible reforms;

— elimination of payments for children whose parents work on Federal property outside the county in which the school district is located;

— two-year cap on payments which are based on public housing at the 1978 level followed by a phase out of the payments;

— an "absorption" provision which will reduce funding for lightly impacted districts by eliminating payments for children of Federal employees below three percent of non-federal enrollment.

To ease the adjustment to these changes I recommend a gradually declining "hold-harmless" provision under which no district will receive less than seventy-five percent of its previous year's payments over the next three years. I also propose that advance funding be made so that districts can be notified early of their allocations.

These proposals will save $76 million in FY 1979 and $336 million in FY 1982. I believe they are a realistic way to start bringing the Impact Aid program into line with the actual Federal burden on local school districts.

Bilingual Education

Three million children today lack equal access to education in our schools because of their limited English-speaking ability. The Bilingual Education Act is designed to help local school systems develop and implement programs to help these children. The proposals I am submitting today will improve the bilingual education program by:

— emphasizing the overriding goal of achieving proficiency in English;

— permitting the flexible use of instructional materials and teaching techniques appropriate and sensitive to the language, background and needs of the child;

— making parents more involved;

— requiring that individual programs be of sufficient scope and duration to have a substantial educational impact;

— allowing English speaking children to take part in bilingual education programs;

— providing more money for teacher training and emphasizing the use of bilingual teachers; and

— increasing research in new teaching techniques.

Because the Bilingual Education Program is a demonstration program, every effort must be made to ensure that funds are used to help local school districts to establish and maintain programs of their own. To ensure that Federal demonstration funds benefit as many children as possible, I am proposing that program grants ordinarily be limited to 5 years. Districts will be required to show how they will ensure that educational progress is maintained following the phase-out of grant monies.

In addition, I am proposing that the Office of Bilingual Education be made responsible for coordinating bilingual education aspects of other programs administered by the Office of Education.

Private Schools

Private schools — particularly parochial schools — are an important part of our diverse educational system. Federal education programs have long required benefits to go to eligible students in both public and private schools. But this requirement has not been effective in practice. I am committed to doing all that the Constitution allows to ensure students in private schools benefit from Federal programs.

I propose the following changes to improve services to private school students:

— States will be required to develop plans for ensuring the equitable participation of private school students in all Federal educational programs.

— The Title I program will be changed to require that economically disadvantaged children in private schools receive comparable funds to those received by public school students, with similar needs.

— Where a school district fails to provide appropriate Federal educational benefits under any program to eligible private school children, authority will be used to by-pass the district and use another agency to provide constitutionally permissible services.

Private school children must receive fair treatment under Federal education programs. However I cannot support a tax credit for private elementary and secondary school tuition. First, there is grave doubt that such a tax credit program can meet Constitutional requirements concerning separation of church and State. Second, the Federal government provides funding primarily to help meet the needs of public school children who are disadvantaged, or handicapped, or bilingual, or who have some other form of special need. We do not provide general support for public schools and it would be unfair to extend such support, through a general tax credit, to private schools.

I will continue to do all I can, within Constitutional limits, to provide for full and equitable participation of private schools and their students in Federal education efforts.

Women's Educational Equity Act

In order to assist in the elimination of sexual discrimination in education I propose to make the Women's Educational Equity Act an independent authority and expand its role in assisting local school districts.

Conclusion

The proposals I have outlined today — to strengthen our basic education laws, substantially increase the education budget and undertake major organizational reform aimed at creating a Cabinet-level Department of Education — set forth a far-reaching agenda for education. These proposals are important not only for what they offer to all of us in the future: a country that is stronger, more united and better equipped to meet the challenges that lie before us.

JIMMY CARTER

The White House,
February 28, 1978

Civil Service Reform

Following is President Carter's March 2 message to Congress outlining his proposals to revise the federal government's civil service system:

TO THE CONGRESS
OF THE UNITED STATES:

I am transmitting to the Congress today a comprehensive program to reform the Federal Civil Service system. My proposals are intended to increase the government's efficiency by placing new emphasis on the quality of performance of Federal workers. At the same time, my recommendations will ensure that employees and the public are protected against political abuse of the system.

Nearly a century has passed since enactment of the first Civil Service Act — the Pendleton Act of 1883. That Act established the United States Civil Service Commission and the merit system it administers. These institutions have served our Nation well in fostering development of a Federal workforce which is basically honest, competent, and dedicated to constitutional ideals and the public interest.

But the system has serious defects. It has become a bureaucratic maze which neglects merit, tolerates poor performance, permits abuse of legitimate employee rights, and mires every personnel action in red tape, delay and confusion.

Civil Service reform will be the centerpiece of government reorganization during my term in office.

I have seen at first hand the frustration among those who work within the bureaucracy. No one is more concerned at the inability of government to deliver on its promises than the worker who is trying to do a good job.

Most Civil Service employees perform with spirit and integrity. Nevertheless, there is still widespread criticism of Federal government performance. The public suspects that there are too many government workers, that they are underworked, overpaid, and insulated from the consequences of incompetence.

Such sweeping criticisms are unfair to dedicated Federal workers who are conscientiously trying to do their best, but we have to recognize that the only way to restore public confidence in the vast majority who work well is to deal effectively and firmly with the few who do not.

For the past 7 months, a task force of more than 100 career civil servants has analyzed the Civil Service, explored its weaknesses and strengths and suggested how it can be improved.

The objectives of the Civil Service reform proposals I am transmitting today are:

—To strengthen the protection of legitimate employee rights;

—To provide incentives and opportunities for managers to improve the efficiency and responsiveness of the Federal Government;

—To reduce the red tape and costly delay in the present personnel system;

—To promote equal employment opportunity;

—To improve labor-management relations.

My specific proposals are these:

1. Replacing the Civil Service Commission with an Office of Personnel Management and a Merit Protection Board

Originally established to conduct Civil Service examinations, the Civil Service Commission has, over the years, assumed additional and inherently conflicting responsibilities. It serves simultaneously both as the protector of employee rights and as the promoter of efficient personnel management policy. It is a manager, rule-maker, prosecutor and judge. Consequently, none of these jobs are being done as effectively as they should be.

Acting under my existing reorganization authority, I propose to correct the inherent conflict of interest within the Civil Service Commission by abolishing the Commission and replacing it with a Merit Protection Board and Office of Personnel Management.

The Office of Personnel Management will be the center for personnel administration (including examination, training, and administration of pay and benefits); it will not have any prosecutorial or adjudicative powers against individuals. Its Director will be appointed by the President and confirmed by the Senate. The Director will be the government's management spokesman on Federal employee labor relations and will coordinate Federal personnel matters, except for Presidential appointments.

The Merit Protection Board will be the adjudicatory arm of the new personnel system. It will be headed by a bipartisan board of three members, appointed for 7 years, serving non-renewable overlapping terms, and removable only for cause. This structure will guarantee independent and impartial protection to employees. I also propose to create a Special Counsel to the Board, appointed by the President and confirmed by the Senate, who will investigate and prosecute political abuses and merit system violations. This will help safeguard the rights of Federal employees who "blow the whistle" on violations of laws or regulations by other employees, including their supervisors.

In addition, these proposals will write into law for the first time the fundamental principles of the merit system and enumerate prohibited personnel practices.

2. A Senior Executive Service

A critical factor in determining whether Federal programs succeed or fail is the ability of the senior managers who run them. Throughout the Executive Branch, these 9,200 top administrators carry responsibilities that are often more challenging than comparable work in private industry. But under the Civil Service system, they lack the incentives for first-rate performance that managers in private industry have. The Civil Service system treats top managers just like the 2.1 million employees whose activities they direct. They are equally insulated from the risks of poor performance, and equally deprived of tangible rewards for excellence.

To help solve these problems I am proposing legislation to create a Senior Executive Service affecting managers in grades GS-16 through non-Presidentially appointed Executive Level IV or its equivalent. It would allow:

—Transfer of executives among senior positions on the basis of government need;

—Authority for agency heads to adjust salaries within a range set by law with the result that top managers would no longer receive automatic pay increases based on longevity;

—Annual performance reviews, with inadequate performance resulting in removal from the Senior Executive Service (back to GS-15) without any right of appeal to the Merit Protection Board.

Agency heads would be authorized to distribute bonuses for superior performance to not more than 50 percent of the senior executives each year. These would be allocated according to criteria prescribed by the Office of Personnel Management, and should average less than five percent of base salary per year. They would not constitute an increase in salary but rather a one-time payment. The Office of Personnel Management also would be empowered to award an additional stipend directly to a select group of senior executives, approximately five percent of the total of the Senior Executive Service, who have especially distinguished themselves in their work. The total of base salary, bonus, and honorary stipend should in no case exceed 95 percent of the salary level for an Executive Level II position.

No one now serving in the "supergrade" managerial positions would be required to join the Senior Executive Service. But all would have the opportunity to join. And the current percentage of non-career supergrade managers — approximately 10 percent — would be written into law for the first time, so that the Office of Personnel Management would not retain the existing authority of the Civil Service Commission to expand the proportion of political appointees.

This new Senior Executive Service will provide a highly qualified corps of top managers with strong incentives and opportunities to improve the management of the Federal government.

3. Incentive Pay for Lower Level Federal Managers and Supervisors

The current Federal pay system provides virtually automatic "step" pay increases as well as further increases to keep Federal salaries comparable to those in private business. This may be appropriate for most Federal employees, but performance — not merely endurance — should determine the compensation of Federal managers and supervisors. I am proposing legislation to let the Office of Personnel Management establish an incentive pay system for government managers, starting with those in grades GS-13 through GS-15. Approximately 72,000 managers and supervisors would be affected by such a system which could later be extended by Congress to other managers and supervisors.

These managers and supervisors would no longer receive automatic "step" increases in pay and would receive only 50 percent of their annual comparability pay increase. They would, however, be eligible for "performance" pay increases of up to 12 percent of their existing salary. Such a change would not increase payroll costs, and it should be insulated against improprieties through the use of strong audit and performance reviews by the Office of Personnel Management.

4. A Fairer and Speedier Disciplinary System

The simple concept of a "merit system" has grown into a tangled web of complicated rules and regulations.

Managers are weakened in their ability to reward the best and most talented people — and to fire those few who are unwilling to work.

The sad fact is that it is easier to promote and transfer incompetent employees than to get rid of them.

It may take as long as 3 years merely to fire someone for just cause, and at the same time the protection of legitimate rights is a costly and time-consuming process for the employee.

A speedier and fairer disciplinary system will create a climate in which managers may discharge non-performing employees — using due process — with reasonable assurance that their judgment, if valid, will prevail.

At the same time, employees will receive a more rapid hearing for their grievances.

The procedures that exist to protect employee rights are absolutely essential.

But employee appeals must now go through the Civil Service Commission, which has a built-in conflict of interest by serving simultaneously as rule-maker, prosecutor, judge, and employee advocate.

The legislation I am proposing today would give all competitive employees a statutory right of appeal. It would spell out fair and sensible standards for the Merit Protection Board to apply in hearing appeals. Employees would be provided with attorneys' fees if they prevail and the agency's action were found to have been wholly without basis. Both employees and managers would have, for the first time, subpoena power to ensure witness participation and document submission. The subpoena power would expedite the appeals process, as would new provisions for prehearing discovery. One of the three existing appeal levels would be eliminated.

These changes would provide both employees and managers with speedier and fairer judgments on the appeal of disciplinary actions.

5. Improved Labor-Management Relations

In 1962, President John F. Kennedy issued Executive Order 10988, establishing a labor-management relations program in the Executive Branch. The Executive Order has demonstrated its value through five Administrations. However, I believe that the time has come to increase its effectiveness by abolishing the Federal Labor Relations Council created by Executive Order 10988 and transferring its functions, along with related functions of the Assistant Secretary of Labor for Labor Relations, to a newly established Federal Labor Relations Authority. The Authority will be composed of three full-time members appointed by the President with the advice and consent of the Senate.

I have also directed members of my Administration to develop, as part of Civil Service reform, a Labor-Management Relations legislative proposal by working with the appropriate Congressional Committees, Federal employees and their representatives. The goal of this legislation will be to make Executive Branch labor relations more comparable to those of private business, while recognizing the special requirements of the Federal Government and the paramount public interest in the effective conduct of the public's business. This will facilitate Civil Service reform of the managerial and supervisory elements of the Executive Branch, free of union involvement, and, at the same time, improve the collective bargaining process as an integral part of the personnel system for Federal workers.

It will permit the establishment through collective bargaining of grievance and arbitration systems, the cost of which will be borne largely by the parties to the dispute. Such procedures will largely displace the multiple appeals systems which now exist and which are unanimously perceived as too costly, too cumbersome and ineffective.

6. Decentralized Personnel Decisionmaking

Examining candidates for jobs in the career service is now done almost exclusively by the Civil Service Commission, which now may take as long as six or eight months to fill important agency positions.

In addition, many routine personnel management actions must be submitted to the Civil Service Commission for prior approval. Much red tape and delay are generated by these requirements; the public benefits little, if at all. My legislative proposals would authorize the Office of Personnel Management to delegate personnel authority to departments and agencies.

The risk of abuse would be minimized by performance agreements between agencies and the Office of Personnel Management, by requirements for reporting, and by follow-up evaluations.

7. Changes in the Veterans Preference Law

Granting preference in Federal employment to veterans of military service has long been an important and worthwhile national policy. It will remain our policy because of the debt we owe those who have served our nation. It is especially essential for disabled veterans, and there should be no change in current law which would adversely affect them. But the Veterans Preference Act of 1944 also conferred a *lifetime benefit* upon the nondisabled veteran, far beyond anything provided by other veterans readjustment laws like the GI Bill, the benefits of which are limited to 10 years following discharge from the service. Current law also severely limits agency ability to consider qualified applicants by forbidding consideration of all except the three highest-scoring applicants — the so-called rule of three. As a result of the 5-point lifetime preference and the "rule of three," women, minorities and other qualified non-veteran candidates often face insuperable obstacles in their quest for Federal jobs.

Similarly, where a manager believes a program would benefit from fewer employees, the veterans preference provides an absolute lifetime benefit to veterans. In any Reduction in Force, all veterans may "bump" all non-veterans, even those with far greater seniority. Thus women and minorities who have recently acquired middle management positions are more likely to lose their jobs in any cutback.

Therefore I propose:

—Limiting the 5-point veterans preference to the 10 year period following their discharge from the service, beginning 2 years after legislation is enacted;

—Expanding the number of applicants who may be considered by a hiring agency from three to seven, unless the Office of Personnel Management should determine that another number or category ranking is more appropriate;

—Eliminating the veterans preference for retired military officers of field grade rank or above and limiting its availability for other military personnel who have retired after at least 20 years in service to 3 years following their retirement;

—Restricting the absolute preference now accorded veterans in Reductions in Force to their first 3 years of Federal employment, after which time they would be granted 5 extra years of seniority for purposes of determining their rights when Reduction in Force occurs.

These changes would focus the veterans preference more sharply to help disabled veterans and veterans of the Viet Nam conflict. I have already proposed a 2-year extension of the Veterans Readjustment Appointment Authority to give these veterans easier entry into the Federal workforce; I support amendments to waive the educational limitation for disabled veterans and to expand Federal job openings for certain veterans in grades GS-5 to GS-7 under this authority. I propose that veterans with 50 percent or higher disability be eligible for non-competitive appointments.

These changes are intended to let the Federal Government meet the needs of the American people more effectively. At the same time, they would make the Federal work place a better environment for Federal employees. I ask the Congress to act promptly on Civil Service Reform and the Reorganization Plan which I will shortly submit.

JIMMY CARTER

The White House
March 2, 1978

Urban Policy

Following is President Carter's March 27 message to Congress, submitting his proposals for a comprehensive national urban policy:

TO THE CONGRESS
OF THE UNITED STATES:

I submit today my proposals for a comprehensive national urban policy. These proposals set a policy framework for actions my Administration has already taken, for proposed new initiatives, and for our efforts to assist America's communities and their residents in the years to come. The policy represents a comprehensive, long-term commitment to the Nation's urban areas.

The urban policy I am announcing today will build a *New Partnership* involving all levels of government, the private sector, and neighborhood and voluntary organizations in a major effort to make America's cities better places in which to live and work. It is a comprehensive policy aimed both at making cities more healthy and improving the lives of the people who live in them.

The major proposals will:

- Improve the effectiveness of existing Federal programs by coordinating these programs, simplifying planning requirements, reorienting resources, and reducing paperwork. And the proposals will make Federal actions more supportive of the urban policy effort and develop a process for analyzing the urban and community impact of all major Federal initiatives.
- Provide employment opportunities, primarily in the private sector, to the long-term unemployed and the disadvantaged in cities. This will be done through a labor-intensive public works program and tax and other incentives for business to hire the long-term unemployed.
- Provide fiscal relief to the most hard-pressed communities.
- Provide strong incentives to attract private investment to distressed communities, including the creation of a National Development Bank, expanded grant programs and targeted tax incentives.
- Encourage states to become partners in assisting urban areas through a new incentive grant program.
- Stimulate greater involvement by neighborhood organizations and voluntary associations through funding neighborhood development projects and by creating an Urban Volunteer Corps. These efforts will be undertaken with the approval of local elected officials.
- Increase access to opportunity for those disadvantaged by economic circumstance or a history of discrimination.
- Provide additional social and health services to disadvantaged people in cities and communities.
- Improve the urban physical environment and the cultural and aesthetic aspects of urban life by providing additional assistance for housing rehabilitation, mass transit, the arts, culture, parks and recreation facilities.

America's communities are an invaluable national asset. They are the center of our culture, the incubators of new ideas and inventions, the centers of commerce and finance, and the homes of our great museums, libraries and theatres. Cities contain trillions of dollars of public and private investments — investments which we must conserve, rehabilitate and fully use.

The New Partnership I am proposing today will focus the full energies of my Administration on a comprehensive, long-term effort. It will encourage States to redirect their own resources to support their urban areas more effectively. It will encourage local governments to streamline and coordinate their own activities. It will offer incentives to the private sector to make new investments in economically depressed communities. And it will involve citizens and neighborhood and voluntary organizations in meeting the economic and social needs of their communities.

The New Partnership will be guided by these principles:

- Simplifying and improving programs and policy at all levels of government.
- Combining the resources of federal, state and local government, and using them as a lever to involve the even greater strength of our private economy to conserve and strengthen our cities and communities.
- Being flexible enough to give help where it is most needed and to respond to the particular needs of each community.
- Increasing access to opportunity for those disadvantaged by economic circumstances or history of discrimination.
- And above all, drawing on the sense of community and voluntary effort that I believe is alive in America, and on the loyalty that Americans feel for their neighborhoods.

The need for a New Partnership is clear from the record of the last fifteen years. During the 1960s, the federal government took a strong leadership role in responding to the problems of the cities. The federal government attempted to identify the problems, develop the solutions and implement the programs. State and local governments and the private sector were not sufficiently involved. While many of these programs were successful, we learned an important lesson: that the federal government alone has neither the resources nor the knowledge to solve all urban problems.

An equally important lesson emerged from the experience of the early 1970s. During this period, the federal government retreated from its responsibilities, leaving states and localities with insufficient resources, interest or leadership to accomplish all that needed to be done. We learned that states and localities cannot solve the problems by themselves.

These experiences taught us that a successful urban policy must build a partnership that involves the leadership of the federal government and the participation of all levels of government, the private sector, neighborhood and voluntary organizations and individual citizens.

Prior Actions

The problems of our Nation's cities are complex and deep-seated. They have developed gradually over a generation as a result of private market and demographic forces and inadvertent government action; and the problems worsened markedly during the early 1970s.

These problems will not be solved immediately. They can be solved only by the long-term commitment which I offer today, and by the efforts of all levels of government, the private sector and neighborhood and voluntary organizations.

For my Administration, this commitment began on the day I took office and it will continue throughout my Presidency. With the cooperation of Congress, my Administration has already provided substantial increases in funding in many of the major urban assistance programs. Total assistance to state and local governments has increased by 25 percent, from $68 billion in FY 1977 to $85 billion in FY 1979. These increases are the direct result of actions we have taken during the past 14 months. They are as much a part of my Administration's urban policy as the initiatives which I am announcing today. Some of the most important programs have already been enacted into law or proposed to the Congress. These include:

- A $2.7 billion increase over three years in the Community Development Block Grant Program, accompanied by a change in the formula to provide more assistance to the older and declining cities.
- A $400 million a year Urban Development Action Grant Program providing assistance primarily to distressed cities.
- An expansion of youth and training programs and an increase in the number of public service employment jobs, from 325,000 to 725,000. Expenditures for employment and training doubled from FY '77 to FY '79 to over $12 billion.
- A $400 million private sector jobs proposal has been included in my proposal to reauthorize the CETA legislation. This initiative will encourage private businesses to hire the long-term unemployed and the disadvantaged.
- A sixty-five percent increase in grants provided by the Economic Development Administration to urban areas.
- A thirty percent increase in overall federal assistance to education, including a $400 million increase in the Elementary and Secondary Education Act, targeted in substantial part to large city school systems with a concentration of children from low-income families.
- An economic stimulus package enacted last year, (Anti-Recession Fiscal Assistance, Local Public Works and CETA) which provided almost $9 billion in additional aid to states and cities.
- A welfare reform proposal which, upon passage, will provide immediate fiscal relief to state and local governments.
- A doubling of outlays for the Section 312 housing rehabilitation loan program.
- Creation of a consumer cooperative bank which would provide financing assistance to consumer cooperatives which have difficulty obtaining conventional financing.

Improvements in Existing Programs

The Administration's Urban and Regional Policy Group (URPG) has examined all of the major urban assistance programs and proposed improvements. It also has worked with agencies traditionally not involved in urban policy, such as the Defense Department, the General Services Administration, and the Environmental Protection Agency, and has developed proposals to make their actions more supportive of urban areas. As a result of this massive effort, the federal government has become more sensitive to urban problems and more committed to their solutions.

The review of existing federal programs has resulted in more than 150 improvements in existing programs. Most of these improvements can be undertaken immediately through administrative action. Some will require legislation. None will increase the federal budget.

A few examples of the improvements are:

- All agencies will develop goals and timetables for minority participation in their grants and contracts — five major agencies have already begun.
- The Defense Department will set up a new program to increase procurement in urban areas.
- EPA will modify its water and sewer program to discourage wasteful sprawl.
- HUD has retargeted the Tandem Mortgage Assistance Program to provide greater support for urban housing.
- The existing countercyclical fiscal assistance program will be retargeted to help governments with unemployment rates above the national average.
- HUD and EDA are developing common planning and application requirements.
- The General Services Administration will attempt to locate federal facilities in cities whenever such a location is not inconsistent with the agency's mission.
- The Department of Transportation has proposed legislation to consolidate many categories of urban highway and transit grants, and to standardize the local matching share. These steps will provide local governments with greater flexibility to develop transportation systems suited to their needs.
- The Environmental Protection Agency will amend its regulations to accommodate new economic development in high pollution areas. Localities will be permitted to "bank" reductions in pollution which result from firms going out of business. These reductions then can be transferred to new firms locating in the community.

The effect of all these changes may be greater than even the substantial new initiatives which I have proposed in this message.

New Initiatives

The new initiatives which I am announcing today address five major urban needs:

1) Improving the operation of federal, state and local governments

2) Employment and Economic Development

3) Fiscal Assistance

4) Community and Human Development

5) Neighborhoods and Voluntary Associations

These initiatives require $4.4 billion in budget authority, $1.7 billion in new tax incentives, and $2.2 billion in guaranteed loan authority in FY 1979. For FY 1980 the budget authority will be $6.1 billion, the tax incentives $1.7 billion and the guaranteed loan authority $3.8 billion.

I. Improving the Operation of Federal, State and Local Governments

Federal Programs

Over the long run, reorganization of the economic and community development programs may be necessary. Last June, I directed my reorganization project staff in the Office of Management and Budget to begin exploring the reorganization options. They have completed the first stages of this work. During the next several months, they will consult with the Congress, state and local officials and the public to develop the best solution.

There are several actions I will take immediately.

- **Urban and Community Impact Analysis.** I am implementing a process through my Domestic Policy Staff (DPS) and Office of Management and Budget (OMB) to ensure that we do not inadvertently take actions which contradict the goals of the urban policy. Each agency submitting a major domestic initiative must include its own urban and community impact analysis. DPS and OMB will review these submissions and will ensure that any anti-urban impacts of proposed federal policies will be brought to my attention.
- **Interagency Coordinating Council.** To improve program coordination, I will form an Interagency Coordinating Council, composed of the Assistant Secretaries with major program responsibilities in the key urban departments. The Council will have two functions:

It will serve as a catalyst for operational improvements which cut across Departments (for example, instituting uniform grant applications); and it will encourage interagency cooperation on projects which are too large or too complex to be funded by one agency. This Council will, for the first time, provide a coordinated federal response to communities which develop comprehensive and multi-year projects. It will have direction from the Executive Office of the President.

- **Consolidating Planning Requirements and Other Management Improvements.** We soon will announce the consolidation of intra-agency planning requirements. I have asked the Director of the Office of Management and Budget to direct an interagency task force to improve the management of federal grant-in-aid programs and consolidate the numerous planning requirements in the community and economic development grant programs.
- **Improved Data and Information.** I have asked the Secretary of Commerce, in her capacity as Chair of the Statistical

Policy Coordination Committee, to design an improved urban data and information system. At the present time much of this data is inadequate or out of date.

• **The Role of State Governments.** State government policies, even more than federal policies, are important to the fiscal and economic health of cities. States affect their cities in a number of ways, including setting taxation and annexation powers, determining the placement of major development investments and apportioning the financial responsibility for welfare and education expenditures.

The federal government has little or no control over these developments, all of which clearly affect the economic and fiscal health of cities and communities.

These state responsibilities underscore the need for an urban policy which includes the states as full and equal partners. The effectiveness of our urban policy will be enhanced if the states can be encouraged to complement the federal effort.

To encourage states to support their urban areas, I will offer a new program of state incentive grants. These grants will be provided, on a discretionary basis, to states which adopt approved plans to help their cities and communities. The plans must be developed with the participation and approval of communities within the state. The grants will be provided to the states to finance a portion of the plan. The State Incentive Grant Program will be administered by HUD and will provide $400 million over two years.

• **Local Government Role.** Many communities and cities can improve management and planning improvements by reforming fiscal management practices, streamlining local regulatory procedures, and coordinating local community and economic development activities.

The federal government provides planning and technical assistance to communities through HUD and Commerce to help cities improve their management and planning practices. These funds will be used increasingly to build the local government's capacity to undertake the necessary fiscal and management reforms.

The federal government will offer special consideration in discretionary programs to cities which achieve coordinated action at the local level.

II. Employment and Economic Development

There is a serious shortage of jobs for many residents of our urban areas and a lack of investment to build the tax base of our cities.

The urban policy will address this issue in two ways.

In the short run, it will provide additional employment opportunities through a labor-intensive public works program, a targeted employment tax credit, and a private sector training and jobs initiative to encourage businesses to hire the hardcore unemployed, together with the extension I have already proposed in employment and training opportunities under the CETA Act.

In the long run, the policy attempts to rebuild the private sector economic base of these communities through a National Development Bank, a special tax incentive, an increase in economic development grants and other incentives.

Labor-intensive Public Works. I ask Congress for $1 billion a year for a program of labor-intensive public works, targeted on communities with high unemployment. Half of the estimated 60,000 full-time equivalent jobs created annually by this program will be reserved for the disadvantaged and the long-term unemployed. These workers will be paid at Davis-Bacon trainee wage levels.

This program will enable cities to make needed repairs on buildings, streets, parks, and other public facilities.

In contrast to the Local Public Works program — which involves projects requiring large equipment, material expenditures and a prolonged planning period — more of the funds under this labor-intensive program will go to job creation.

Targeted Employment Tax Credit. I also propose a Targeted Employment Tax Credit to encourage business to hire disadvantaged young workers between the ages of 18 and 24 who suffer the highest unemployment rates in the Nation.

Under my proposal, private employers of young and disadvantaged, or handicapped, workers would be entitled to claim a $2,000 tax credit for each eligible worker during the first year of employment and a $1,500 credit for each eligible worker during the second year.

I am proposing this Targeted Employment Tax Credit as a substitute for the expiring Employment Tax Credit. The current program costs $2.5 billion a year and has had little influence on hiring decisions. The Administration's targeted program will cost approximately $1.5 billion a year, with far greater impact.

Location of Federal Facilities. I will sign a new Executive Order directing the General Services Administration to give first priority to cities in locating new federal facilities or consolidating or relocating existing facilities. Under my Administration, federal facilities will be located in cities, unless such a location is inconsistent with the agency's mission.

Federal buildings and facilities can be an important source of jobs and of rental payments and, in many cities, a principal stabilizing force preventing decline.

The federal government should set an example for the private sector to invest in urban areas.

Federal Government Procurement. To assure that federal procurement is used to strengthen the economic base of our Nation's cities and communities, I will:

• strengthen the implementation of the existing procurement set-aside program for labor surplus areas, by directing the General Services Administration to work with each agency to develop specific procurement targets and to monitor their implementation. GSA will report to me every six months on the progress of each Agency;

• direct the Defense Department to implement an experimental program to target more of its procurement to high unemployment areas.

National Development Bank. I propose the creation of a National Development Bank, which would encourage businesses to locate or expand in economically distressed urban and rural areas. The Bank would be authorized to guarantee investments totaling $11 billion through 1981.

To lower operating costs in urban areas, the Bank would provide long-term, low-cost financing which, in conjunction with expanded grant programs administered by HUD and EDA, will reduce a firm's financing costs by up to 60 percent.

The Bank uses four major financing tools:

• Grants of up to 15 percent of a firm's total capital cost, to a maximum $3 million, for fixed assets of a project. The grants, which would be made under expanded EDA and HUD authorities, would cover expenditures for land assembly, site preparation, rehabilitation, and equipment.

• Loan guarantees, provided by the Bank to cover three-quarters of the remaining capital costs up to a maximum of $15 million per project. The Bank could, at its discretion, reduce the interest rate down to two and one-half percent for particularly desirable projects. Bank financing would be conditioned on obtaining 21 percent of the project's total costs from private lenders.

• The ceiling for industrial reserve bonds in economically distressed areas would be increased from $5 to $20 million with the approval of the Bank. A business which used this financing for a project could also receive a grant.

• The Bank also will provide a secondary loan market for private loans in eligible areas to finance capital expenditures. This will be particularly beneficial to small businesses.

Bank projects will require the approval of state or local government economic development entities, which would be responsible to the elected local leadership. Distressed urban and rural areas would be eligible. Additional employment would be a key test of project eligibility.

The Bank will be an interagency corporation, governed by a Board composed of the Secretaries of HUD, Commerce and the Treasury. This will ensure coordination between the major economic, community development and urban finance agencies of the government.

The Office of Management and Budget is currently assessing the organization of the federal economic and community development activities. The Bank will function on an interagency basis pending recommendations in this area.

Economic Development Grants. I propose substantial increases of $275 million each in the UDAG grant program and the EDA Title IX program. These increases will be used in conjunction with the financing incentives available from the National Development Bank.

Taken together these major increases will help leverage substantial new private sector investment in urban areas and address the long-term economic deterioration experienced by certain urban and rural areas.

Differential Investment Tax Credit. I propose that firms that locate or expand in economically distressed areas be eligible for a differential 5 percent investment tax credit, to a total of 15 percent for both structures and equipment. The credit would be available only to firms awarded "Certificates of Necessity" by the Commerce Department based on financing need and employment potential.

Commerce will be authorized to issue up to $200 million in certificates for each of the next two years.

Air Quality Planning Grants. I propose a $25 million planning grant program to help cities and communities comply with the Clean Air Act without limiting severely new, private sector investment within their areas.

I have also asked EPA, HUD and EDA to provide technical assistance to help local governments reconcile potential conflicts between air pollution and economic development goals.

Minority Business. Minority businesses are a critical part of the private sector economic base of many cities, communities and neighborhoods, and provide important employment opportunities to city residents.

I propose today two important initiatives which will increase the role of minority businesses in our economy. First, in comparison with FY 1977 levels, we will triple federal procurement from minority businesses by the end of FY 1979 — an increase over our earlier commitment to double minority procurement.

In addition, I intend to ask all federal agencies to include goals for minority business participation in their contract and grant-in-aid programs. Five agencies — HUD, Commerce, EPA, Interior and DOT — already have proposed improvements in minority business programs. These programs all build on our successful experience with the Local Public Works Program.

Finally, I intend to facilitate greater interaction between the minority business community and the leaders of our Nation's largest corporations.

Community Development Corporations. I propose that an additional $20 million be appropriated to the Community Services Administration as venture capital for the most effective Community Development Corporations. This assistance will help them have a substantial impact on their designated areas.

The funding will be made available for projects that receive support from local elected officials, involve leveraging private sector funds and are coordinated with HUD, EDA or the Small Business Administration.

Role of Private Financial Institutions. An effective urban strategy must involve private financial institutions. I am asking the independent financial regulatory agencies to develop appropriate actions, consistent with safe, sound and prudent lending practices, to encourage financial institutions to play a greater role in meeting the credit needs of their communities.

First, I am requesting that financial regulatory agencies determine what further actions are necessary to halt the practice of redlining — the refusal to extend credit without a sound economic justification. I will encourage those agencies to develop strong, consistent and effective regulations to implement the Community Reinvestment Act.

Second, I propose the creation of an Institute for Community Investment, under the Federal Home Loan Bank Board. The Institute will bring together appraisers, realtors, lenders, building and insurance companies to develop a consistent approach toward urban lending and to train urban lending specialists.

Third, I propose a pilot program to create Neighborhood Commercial Reinvestment Centers under the Comptroller of the Currency. This proposal is an adaptation of the highly successful Urban Reinvestment Task Force housing credit concept to the commercial credit area. Neighborhood Commercial Reinvestment Centers will be local organizations, comprised of merchants and neighborhood residents, local government officials, and commercial banks which will provide business credit in urban neighborhoods. SBA, EDA, and HUD will work with the financial regulatory agencies to revitalize specific commercial areas.

Finally, I have asked the Secretary of Housing and Urban Development to chair an interagency task force to evaluate the availability of credit in urban areas and recommend appropriate further action. I have asked the task force to examine and make recommendations with respect to the following areas:

- The availability of mortgage and commercial credit in urban areas, and the impacts of the activities of federal agencies on such credit;
- Existing mortgage insurance, casualty insurance and business credit insurance programs;
- The full range of urban credit and insurance risk reduction techniques.

III. Fiscal Assistance

While the fiscal condition of many state and local governments has improved dramatically over the last three years, many cities and communities still are experiencing severe problems. These cities and communities require fiscal assistance from the federal government, if they are to avoid severe service cutbacks or tax increases.

Supplemental Fiscal Assistance. Cities and communities currently receive fiscal assistance through the Anti-Recession Fiscal Assistance Act (ARFA), which expires on September 30, 1978. This program has been an effective tool for helping states and local governments withstand the fiscal impact of high unemployment.

Current unemployment projections, however, suggest that even if the ARFA program were extended in its current form, it would phase out by mid-FY 1979, when unemployment is expected to drop below six percent. If the program is permitted to phase out, many cities and communities will experience severe fiscal strain.

I propose today that ARFA be replaced with a Supplemental Fiscal Assistance Program, which will provide $1 billion of fiscal assistance annually for the next two fiscal years to local governments experiencing significant fiscal strain. Further extension of this program will be considered together with General Revenue Sharing.

Fiscal Relief in Welfare Proposal. In addition, I propose to phase in the fiscal relief component of the Better Jobs and Income Act as soon as Congress passes this legislation, rather than in 1981 as originally planned.

IV. Community and Human Development

A comprehensive program to revitalize America's cities must provide for community and human needs. This involves both physical facilities, such as parks, recreation facilities, housing and transportation systems, and the provision of health and social services.

Housing Rehabilitation. The conservation and upgrading of our housing stock is important to maintaining the strength of urban areas. Housing and rehabilitation improves the quality of community life and provides construction jobs in areas of high unemployment.

I propose an additional $150 million in FY 1979 for the Section 312 rehabilitation loan program, which will more than double the existing program. This expanded effort will permit the rehabilitation of small multi-family housing projects in distressed neighborhoods, for which financing presently is inadequate. In addition, expanded Section 312 funding will be used to strengthen the Urban Homesteading program.

Urban Transportation. In many cities, public transportation is inadequately financed. The federal government has begun to make substantial investments to rehabilitate, revitalize and construct urban transportation systems.

I have already submitted to Congress my proposals to extend and strengthen the highway and mass transit programs.

To supplement these efforts I today propose an additional $200 million for capital investments in intermodal urban transportation projects. These funds will be used to link existing transportation facilities in selected cities.

Resource Recovery Planning. Solid waste disposal is a growing problem in the many urban areas which face a shortage of landfill sites. At the same time, techniques to recover valuable resources and energy from solid waste have emerged.

I will request $15 million for the EPA to provide grants of $300,000 to $400,000 to cities for feasibility studies of solid waste recovery systems.

Arts and Culture. Cities are centers of culture and art, which thrive on the vitality of the urban environment.

To help renew and develop this artistic and cultural spirit, I propose a new Livable Cities program administered by the Department of Housing and Urban Development, with the participation of the National Endowment for the Arts. This program will provide up to $20 million in grants to states and communities for neighborhood- and community-based arts programs, urban design and planning, and the creation and display of art in public spaces. Historic preservation of buildings should also be encouraged.

Urban Parks and Recreation. The quality of life in urban areas is critically affected by the availability of open spaces and recreation facilities. Yet hard pressed communities often lack the resources to maintain and invest adequately in these amenities.

To address this problem, I propose a major new federal grant program. Urban communities will compete for funds to revive and rebuild parks and recreation facilities. Challenge grants totalling $150 million will be provided for construction and major rehabilitation of urban recreation systems, such as parks, tennis and basketball courts, swimming pools, bicycle paths, and other facilities. Cities will be awarded grants based on the quality of their planning, the degree of need and their ability to match the federal funds with private and local contributions.

Social Services. Urban revitalization efforts must be accompanied by efforts to help those in need to improve their own lives. A variety of income support and social service programs are designed to do this. Since 1974, however, the support given to state social service programs by the federal government has declined in real terms.

I propose an additional $150 million of new budget authority for the Title XX programs. These funds will be used to improve the delivery of social services in urban areas — ranging from Meals on Wheels for the elderly to day care for children of working mothers — and to develop greater coordination between local, public and private agencies.

Health Services. Nearly 50 million Americans live in areas without adequate health services. These areas, many of which are in inner cities, suffer from higher infant mortality rates, greater poverty and shortages of health care personnel.

In underserved areas, emergency room and outpatient departments of city hospitals are used as the routine source of medical care by the poor, primarily due to the lack of private physicians. As these departments were not designed to provide comprehensive medical care, the hospital resources are strained and the poor often go without adequate care.

To help meet the primary health care needs of the urban poor and reduce the strain on city hospitals, I propose to expand federally-supported Community Health Centers and to fund city-sponsored programs which provide comprehensive, but less costly, primary care services. The city-sponsored programs will enroll the medically indigent in existing health systems, such as HMOs. They also will help expand locally-supported centers, reform hospital outpatient departments and provide comprehensive health services.

Education. Schools are the focus of community activities in many places. Yet they are seldom fully used or linked to other community and social services.

I intend to provide $1.5 million to expand the experimental Cities in Schools program which seeks to bridge the gap by uniting a number of social services within schools to better serve both students and their families. We intend to expand this promising new program to 10 pilot schools.

In addition, I urge the Congress to enact the $600 million increase in the Title I program of the Elementary and Secondary Education Act, which I recently proposed, including my recommendation that $400 million of these funds be targeted to cities and other areas with high concentrations of low-income families.

V. Neighborhoods and Volunteer Organizations

No resource of our urban communities is more valuable than the commitment of our citizens.

Volunteer groups, which gain strength from the selfless efforts of many individuals, make an indispensable contribution to their cities.

Urban Volunteer Corps. I propose a $40 million program in ACTION to increase the effectiveness of voluntary activities at the local level. With the agreement of local government, the program will create a corps of volunteers at the local level and match their skills with the needs of local governments and community and neighborhood organizations.

It also will provide small grants averaging $5,000 for voluntary improvement and beautification projects.

ACTION would select, with the concurrence of local government, a lead agency in each city to administer the Urban Volunteer Corps.

Self-Help Development Program. Neighborhood associations are playing a key role in housing and neighborhood revitalization. We must strengthen that role.

I will request $15 million in FY 1979 for a self-help development program to be administered by the Office for Neighborhoods in HUD.

This new program will provide funds for specific housing and revitalization projects in poor and low-income areas. Each project would involve the participation of local residents, the private sector and local government and would require the concurrence of the mayor.

Crime Prevention. Street crime is a serious problem in America's cities and communities. Over the last few years a number of promising initiatives have been undertaken by community groups and local law enforcement agencies to combat street crime. Escort services for the elderly, centers to help the victims of crime, and neighborhood watchers are examples of promising developments.

I propose a program which will add $10 million in new resources to existing efforts in the Law Enforcement Assistance Administration for a program operated jointly by ACTION and LEAA. Under this program, mayors and local neighborhood groups will develop community crime prevention programs based on successful pilot models. My reorganization proposals for LEAA and the legislation I will submit to extend the Law Enforcement Assistance Act will strengthen our efforts at crime prevention.

Community Development Credit Unions. Some urban communities are not served by any financial institutions. Community Development Credit Unions address this problem by investing their assets in the communities in which they are established. This type of credit union was first established under the poverty programs in the 1960s. About 225 exist today, and many are the only financial institutions in their communities.

I am proposing a $12 million program to provide $200,000 seed capital for new Community Development Credit Unions, to provide them with an operating subsidy for staff, training and technical assistance.

* * *

The job of revitalizing the urban communities of our country will not be done overnight. Problems which have accumulated gradually over generations cannot be solved in a year or even in the term of a President.

But I believe that a New Partnership — bringing together in a common effort all who have a stake in the future of our communities — can bring us closer to our long-term goals. We can make America's cities more attractive places in which to live and work; we can help the people of urban America lead happier and more useful lives. But we can only do it together.

JIMMY CARTER

The White House,
March 27, 1978

Civil Service Commission Reorganization

Following is the text of President Carter's May 23 message to Congress accompanying his plan on reorganization of the Civil Service Commission.

TO THE CONGRESS
OF THE UNITED STATES:

On March 2 I sent to Congress a Civil Service reform proposal to enable the Federal Government to improve its service to the American people.

Today I am submitting another part of my comprehensive proposal to reform the Federal personnel management system through Reorganization Plan No. 2 of 1978. The plan will reorganize the Civil Service Commission and thereby create new institutions to increase the effectiveness of management and strengthen the protection of employee rights.

The Civil Service Commission has acquired inherently conflicting responsibilities: to help manage the Federal Government and to protect the rights of Federal employees. It has done neither job well. The plan would separate the two functions.

Office of Personnel Management

The positive personnel management tasks of the government — such as training, productivity programs, examinations, and pay and benefits administration — would be the responsibility of an Office of Personnel Management. Its director, appointed by the President and confirmed by the Senate, would be responsible for administering federal personnel matters except for presidential appointments. The director would be the government's principal representative in federal labor relations matters.

Merit Systems Protection Board

The adjudication and prosecution responsibilities of the Civil Service Commission will be performed by the Merit Systems Protection Board. The board will be headed by a bipartisan panel of three members appointed to 6-year, staggered terms. This board would be the first independent and institutionally impartial federal agency solely for the protection of federal employees.

The plan will create, within the board, a Special Counsel to investigate and prosecute political abuses and merit system violations. Under the civil service reform legislation now being considered by the Congress, the counsel would have power to investigate and prevent reprisals against employees who report illegal acts — the so-called "whistle-blowers." The counsel would be appointed by the President and confirmed by the Senate.

Federal Labor Relations Authority

An Executive Order now vests existing labor-management relations in a part-time Federal Labor Relations Council, comprised of three top government managers; other important functions are assigned to the Assistant Secretary of Labor for Labor-Management Relations. This arrangement is defective because the Council members are part-time, they come exclusively from the ranks of management and their jurisdiction is fragmented.

The plan I submit today would consolidate the central policymaking functions in labor-management relations now divided between the Council and the Assistant Secretary into one Federal Labor Relations Authority. The Authority would be composed of three full-time members appointed by the President with the advice and consent of the Senate. Its General Counsel, also appointed by the President and confirmed by the Senate, would present unfair labor practice complaints. The plan also provides for the continuance of the Federal Service Impasses Panel within the Authority to resolve negotiating impasses between federal employee unions and agencies.

The cost of replacing the Civil Service Commission can be paid by our present resources. The reorganization itself would neither increase nor decrease the costs of personnel management throughout the government. But taken together with the substantive reforms I have proposed, this plan will greatly improve the government's ability to manage programs, speed the delivery of federal services to the public, and aid in executing other reorganizations I will propose to the Congress, by improving federal personnel management.

Each of the provisions of this proposed reorganization would accomplish one or more of the purposes set forth in 5 U.S.C. 901 (a). No functions are abolished by the plan, but the offices referred to in 5 U.S.C. 5109 (b) and 5 U.S.C. 1103 (d) are abolished. The portions of the plan providing for the appointment and pay for the head and one or more officers of the Office of Personnel Management, the Merit Systems Protection Board, the Federal Labor Relations Authority and the Federal Service Impasses Panel, are necessary to carry out the reorganization. The rates of compensation are comparable to those for similar positions within the executive branch.

I am confident that this plan and the companion civil service reform legislation will both lead to more effective protection of federal employees' legitimate rights and a more rewarding workplace. At the same time the American people will benefit from a better managed, more productive and more efficient federal government.

JIMMY CARTER

The White House,
May 23, 1978

Water Policy

Following is the text of President Carter's June 6 message to Congress outlining his new water policy:

TO THE CONGRESS
OF THE UNITED STATES:

I am today sending to Congress water policy initiatives designed to:

— improve planning and efficient management of Federal water resource programs to prevent waste and to permit necessary water projects which are cost-effective, safe and environmentally sound to move forward expeditiously;

— provide a new, national emphasis on water conservation;

— enhance Federal-State cooperation and improved State water resources planning; and

— increase attention to environmental quality.

None of the initiatives would impose any new federal regulatory program for water management.

Last year, I directed the Water Resources Council, the Office of Management and Budget and the Council on Environmental Quality, under the chairmanship of Secretary [of the Interior] Cecil Andrus, to make a comprehensive review of Federal water policy and to recommend proposed reforms.

This new water policy results from their review, the study of water policy ordered by the Congress in Section 80 of the Water Resources Planning Act of 1974 and our extensive consultations with members of Congress, State, county, city and other local officials and the public.

Water is an essential resource, and over the years, the programs of the Bureau of Reclamation, the Corps of Engineers, the Soil Conservation Service and the Tennessee Valley Authority have helped permit a dramatic improvement in American agriculture, have provided irrigation water essential to the development of the West, and have developed community flood protection, electric power, navigation and recreation throughout the Nation.

I ordered this review of water policies and programs because of my concern that while Federal water resources programs have been of great benefit to our Nation, they are today plagued with problems and inefficiencies. In the course of this water policy review we found that:

— Twenty-five separate Federal agencies spend more than $10 billion per year on water resources projects and related programs.

— These projects often are planned without a uniform, standard basis for estimating benefits and costs.

— States are primarily responsible for water policy within their boundaries, yet are not integrally involved in setting priorities and sharing in Federal project planning and funding.

— There is a $34 billion backlog of authorized or uncompleted projects.

— Some water projects are unsafe or environmentally unwise and have caused losses of natural streams and rivers, fish and wildlife habitat and recreational opportunities.

The study also found that water conservation has not been addressed at a national level even though we have pressing water supply problems. Of 106 watershed subregions in the country, 21 already have severe water shortages. By the year 2000 this number could increase to 39 subregions. The Nation's cities are also beginning to experience water shortage problems which can only be solved at very high cost. In some areas, precious groundwater supplies are also being depleted at a faster rate than they are replenished. In many cases an effective water conservation program could play a key role in alleviating these problems.

These water policy initiatives will make the Federal government's water programs more efficient and responsive in meeting the Nation's water-related needs. They are designed to build on fundamentally sound statutes and on the Principles and Standards which govern the planning and development of Federal water projects, and also to enhance the role of the States, where the primary responsibilities for water policy must lie. For the first time, the Federal government will work with State and local governments and exert needed national leadership in the effort to conserve water. Above all, these policy reforms will encourage water projects which are economically and environmentally sound and will avoid projects which are wasteful or which benefit a few at the expense of many.

Across the Nation there is remarkable diversity in the role water plays. Over most of the West, water is scarce and must be managed carefully — and detailed traditions and laws have grown up to govern the use of water. In other parts of the country, flooding is more of a problem than drought, and in many areas, plentiful water resources have offered opportunities for hydroelectric power and navigation. In the urban areas of our Nation, water supply systems are the major concern — particularly where antiquated systems need rehabilitation in order to conserve water and assure continued economic growth.

Everywhere, water is fundamental to environmental quality. Clean drinking water, recreation, wildlife and beautiful natural areas depend on protection of our water resources.

Given this diversity, Federal water policy cannot attempt to prescribe water use patterns for the country. Nor should the Federal government preempt the primary responsibility of the States for water management and allocation. For those reasons, these water policy reforms will not preempt State or local water responsibilities. Yet water policy is an important national concern, and the Federal government has major responsibilities to exercise leadership, to protect the environment and to develop and maintain hydroelectric power, irrigated agriculture, flood control and navigation.

The primary focus of the proposals is on the water resources programs of the Corps of Engineers, the Bureau of Reclamation, the Soil Conservation Service and the Tennessee Valley Authority, where annual water program budgets total approximately $3.75 billion. These agencies perform the federal government's water resource development programs. In addition, a number of Federal agencies with water-related responsibilities will be affected by this water policy.

I am charging Secretary Andrus with the lead responsibility to see that these initiatives are carried out promptly and fully. With the assistance of the Office of Management and Budget and the Council on Environmental Quality, he will be responsible for working with the other Federal agencies, the Congress, State and local governments and the public to assure proper implementation of this policy and to make appropriate recommendations for reform in the future.

Specific Initiatives Improving Federal Water Resource Programs

The Federal government has played a vital role in developing the water resources of the United States. It is essential that Federal water programs be updated and better coordinated if they are to continue to serve the nation in the best way possible. The reforms I am proposing are designed to modernize and improve the coordination of federal water programs. In addition, in a few days, I will also be sending to the Congress a Budget amendment proposing funding for a number of new water project construction and planning starts. These projects meet the criteria I am announcing today. This is the first time the Executive Branch has proposed new water project starts since Fiscal Year 1975, four years ago.

The actions I am taking include:

- A directive to the Water Resources Council to improve the implementation of the Principles and Standards governing the planning of Federal water projects. The basic planning objectives of the Principles and Standards — national economic development and environmental quality — should be retained and given equal emphasis. In addition, the implementation of the Principles and Standards should be improved by:

— adding water conservation as a specific component of both the economic and environmental objectives;

— requiring the explicit formulation and consideration of a primarily non-structural plan as one alternative whenever structural water projects or programs are planned;

— instituting consistent, specific procedures for calculating benefits and costs in compliance with the Principles and Standards and other applicable planning and evaluation requirements. Benefit-cost analyses have not been uniformly applied by Federal agencies, and in some cases benefits have been improperly recognized, "double-counted" or included when inconsistent with federal policy or sound economic rationale. I am directing the Water Resources Council to prepare within 12 months a manual which ensures that benefits and costs are calculated using the best techniques and provides for consistent application of the Principles and Standards and other requirements;

— ensuring that water projects have been planned in accordance with the Principles and Standards and other planning requirements by creating, by Executive Order, a project review function located in the Water Resources Council. A professional staff will ensure an impartial review of pre-construction project plans for their consistency with established planning and benefit-cost analysis procedures and applicable requirements. They will report on compliance with these requirements to agency heads, who will include their report, together with the agency recommendations, to the Office of Management and Budget. Project reviews will be completed within 60 days, before the Cabinet officer makes his or her Budget request for the coming fiscal year. Responsibility will rest with the Cabinet officer for Budget requests to the Office of Management and Budget, but timely independent review will be provided. This review must be completed within the same budget cycle in which the Cabinet officer intends to make Budget requests so that the process results in no delay.

— The manual, the Principles and Standards requirements and the independent review process will apply to all authorized projects (and separable project features) not yet under construction.

- Establishment of the following criteria for setting priorities each year among the water projects eligible for funding or authorization, which will form the basis of my decisions on specific water projects:

— Projects should have net national economic benefits unless there are environmental benefits which clearly more than compensate for any economic deficit. Net adverse environmental consequences should be significantly outweighed by economic benefits. Generally, projects with higher benefit/cost ratios and fewer adverse environmental consequences will be given priority within the limits of available funds.

— Projects should have widely distributed benefits.

— Projects should stress water conservation and appropriate non-structural measures.

— Projects should have no significant safety problems involving design, construction or operation.

— There should be evidence of active public support including support by State and local officials.

— Projects will be given expedited consideration where State governments assume a share of costs over and above existing cost-sharing.

— There should be no significant international or inter-governmental problems.

— Where vendible outputs are involved preference should be given to projects which provide for greater recovery of Federal and State costs, consistent with project purposes.

— The project's problem assessment, environmental impacts, costs and benefits should be based on up-to-date conditions (planning should not be obsolete).

— Projects should be in compliance with all relevant environmental statutes.

— Funding for mitigation of fish and wildlife damages should be provided concurrently and proportionately with construction funding.

• Preparation of a legislative proposal for improving cost-sharing for water projects. Improved cost-sharing will allow States to participate more actively in project decisions and will remove biases in the existing system against non-structural flood control measures. These changes will help assure project merit. This proposal, based on the study required by Section 80 of P.L. 93-251, has two parts:

— participation of States in the financing of federal water project construction. For project purposes with vendible outputs (such as water supply or hydroelectric power), States would contribute 10% of the costs, proportionate to and phased with federal appropriations. Revenues would be returned to the States proportionate to their contribution. For project purposes without vendible outputs (such as flood control), the State financing share would be 5%. There would be a cap on State participation per project per year of 1/4 of 1% of the State's general revenues so that a small State would not be precluded from having a very large project located in it. Where project benefits accrue to more than one State, State contributions would be calculated accordingly, but if a benefiting State did not choose to participate in cost-sharing, its share could be paid by other participating States. This State cost-sharing proposal would apply on a mandatory basis to projects not yet authorized. However, for projects in the authorized backlog, States which voluntarily enter into these cost-sharing arrangements will achieve expedited Executive Branch consideration and priority for project funding, as long as other project planning requirements are met. Soil Conservation Service projects will be completely exempt from this State cost-sharing proposal.

— equalizing cost-sharing for structural and non-structural flood control alternatives. There is existing authority for 80%-20%-Federal/non-Federal cost-sharing for non-structural flood control measures (including in-kind contributions such as land and easements). I will begin approving non-structural flood control projects with this funding arrangement and will propose that a parallel cost-sharing requirement (including in-kind contributions) be enacted for structural flood control measures, which currently have a multiplicity of cost-sharing rules.

Another policy issue raised in Section 80 of P.L. 93-251 is that of the appropriate discount rate for computing the present value of future estimated economic benefits of water projects. After careful consideration of a range of options I have decided that the currently legislated discount rate formula is reasonable, and I am therefore recommending that no change be made in the current formula. Nor will I recommend retroactive changes in the discount rate for currently authorized projects.

Water Conservation

Managing our vital water resources depends on a balance of supply, demand and wise use. Using water more efficiently is often cheaper and less damaging to the environment than developing additional supplies. While increases in supply will still be necessary, these reforms place emphasis on water conservation and make clear that this is now a national priority.

In addition to adding the consideration of water conservation to the Principles and Standards, the initiatives I am taking include:

• Directives to all Federal agencies with programs which affect water supply or consumption to encourage water conservation, including:

— making appropriate community water conservation measures a condition of the water supply and wastewater treatment grant and loan programs of the Environmental Protection Agency, the Department of Agriculture and the Department of Commerce;

— integrating water conservation requirements into the housing assistance programs of the Department of Housing and Urban Development, the Veterans Administration and the Department of Agriculture;

— providing technical assistance to farmers and urban dwellers on how to conserve water through existing programs of the Department of Agriculture, the Department of Interior and the Department of Housing and Urban Development;

— requiring development of water conservation programs as a condition of contracts for storage or delivery of municipal and industrial water supplies from federal projects;

— requiring the General Services Administration, in consultation with affected agencies, to establish water conservation goals and standards in Federal buildings and facilities;

— encouraging water conservation in the agricultural assistance programs of the Department of Agriculture and the Department of Interior which affect water consumption in water-short areas; and

— requesting all Federal agencies to examine their programs and policies so that they can implement appropriate measures to increase water conservation and re-use.

• A directive to the Secretary of the Interior to improve the implementation of irrigation repayment and water service contract procedures under existing authorities of the Bureau of Reclamation. The Secretary will:

— require that new and renegotiated contracts include provisions for recalculation and renegotiation of water rates every five years. This will replace the previous practice of 40-year contracts which often do not reflect inflation and thus do not meet the beneficiaries' repayment obligations;

— under existing authority add provisions to recover operation and maintenance costs when existing contracts are renegotiated, or earlier where existing contracts have adjustment clauses;

— more precisely calculate and implement the "ability to pay" provision in existing law which governs recovery of a portion of project capital costs.

• Preparation of legislation to allow States the option of requiring higher prices for municipal and industrial water supplies from Federal projects in order to promote conservation, provided that State revenues in excess of Federal costs would be returned to municipalities or other public water supply entities for use in water conservation or rehabilitation of water supply systems.

Federal-State Cooperation

States must be the focal point for water resource management. The water reforms are based on this guiding principle. Therefore, I am taking several initiatives to strengthen Federal-State relations in the water policy area and to develop a new, creative partnership. In addition to proposing that States increase their roles and responsibilities in water resources development through cost-sharing, the actions I am taking include:

• Proposing a substantial increase from $3 million to $25 million annually in the funding of State water planning under the existing 50%-50% matching program administered by the Water Resources Council. State water planning would integrate water management and implementation programs which emphasize water conservation and which are tailored to each State's needs including assessment of water delivery system rehabilitation needs and development of programs to protect and manage groundwater and instream flows.

• Preparation of legislation to provide $25 million annually in 50%-50% matching grant assistance to States to implement water conservation technical assistance programs. These funds could be passed through to counties and cities for use in urban or rural water conservation programs. This program will be administered by the Water Resources Council in conjunction with matching grants for water resources planning.

• Working with Governors to create a Task Force of Federal, State, county, city and other local officials to continue to address water-related problems. The administrative actions and legislative proposals in this Message are designed to initiate sound water management policy at the national level. However, the Federal government must work closely with the States, and with local governments as well, to continue identifying and examining water-related problems and to help implement the initiatives I am announcing today. This Task Force will be a continuing guide as we implement the water policy reforms and will ensure that the State and local role in our Nation's water policy is constant and meaningful.

- An instruction to Federal agencies to work promptly and expeditiously to inventory and quantify Federal reserved and Indian water rights. In several areas of the country, States have been unable to allocate water because these rights have not been determined. This quantification effort should focus first on high priority areas, should involve close consultation with the States and water users and should emphasize negotiations rather than litigation wherever possible.

Environmental Protection

Water is a basic requirement for human survival, is necessary for economic growth and prosperity, and is fundamental to protecting the natural environment. Existing environmental statutes relating to water and water projects generally are adequate, but these laws must be consistently applied and effectively enforced to achieve their purposes. Sensitivity to environmental protection must be an important aspect of all water-related planning and management decisions. I am particularly concerned about the need to improve the protection of instream flows and to evolve careful management of our nation's precious groundwater supplies, which are threatened by depletion and contamination.

My initiatives in this area include the following:

- A directive to the Secretary of the Interior and other Federal agency heads to implement vigorously the Fish and Wildlife Coordination Act, the Historic Preservation Act and other environmental statutes. Federal agencies will prepare formal implementing procedures for the Fish and Wildlife Coordination Act and other statutes where appropriate. Affected agencies will prepare reports on compliance with environmental statutes on a project-by-project basis for inclusion in annual submissions to the Office of Management and Budget.
- A directive to agency heads requiring them to include designated funds for environmental mitigation in water project appropriation requests to provide for concurrent and proportionate expenditure of mitigation funds.
- Accelerated implementation of Executive Order No. 11988 on floodplain management. This Order requires agencies to protect floodplains and to reduce risks of flood losses by not conducting, supporting or allowing actions in floodplains unless there are no practicable alternatives. Agency implementation is behind schedule and must be expedited.
- A directive to the Secretaries of Army, Commerce, Housing and Urban Development and Interior to help reduce flood damages through acquisition of flood-prone land and property, where consistent with primary program purposes.
- A directive to the Secretary of Agriculture to encourage more effective soil and water conservation through watershed programs of the Soil Conservation Service by:

— working with the Fish and Wildlife Service to apply fully the recently-adopted stream channel modification guidelines;

— encouraging accelerated land treatment measures prior to funding of structural measures on watershed projects, and making appropriate land treatment measures eligible for Federal cost-sharing;

— establishing periodic post-project monitoring to ensure implementation of land treatment and operation and maintenance activities specified in the work plan and to provide information helpful in improving the design of future projects.

- A directive to Federal agency heads to provide increased cooperation with States and leadership in maintaining instream flows and protecting groundwater through joint assessment of needs, increased assistance in the gathering and sharing of data, appropriate design and operation of Federal water facilities, and other means. I also call upon the Governors and the Congress to work with Federal agencies to protect the fish and wildlife and other values associated with adequate instream flows. New and existing projects should be planned and operated to protect instream flows, consistent with State law and in close consultation with States. Where prior commitments and economic feasibility permit, amendments to authorizing statutes should be sought in order to provide for streamflow maintenance.

Conclusion

These initiatives establish the goals and the framework for water policy reform. They do so without impinging on the rights of States and by calling for a closer partnership among the Federal, State, county, city and other local levels of government. I want to work with the Congress, State and local governments and the public to implement this policy. Together we can protect and manage our nation's water resources, putting water to use for society's benefit, preserving our rivers and streams for future generations of Americans, and averting critical water shortages in the future through adequate supply, conservation and wise planning.

JIMMY CARTER

The White House,
June 6, 1978

Disaster Aid Plan

Following is President Carter's June 19 message to Congress outlining his proposal to reorganize the federal disaster aid structure, along with a copy of the plan itself, Reorganization Plan No. 3 of 1978:

TO THE CONGRESS
OF THE UNITED STATES:

Today I am transmitting Reorganization Plan No. 3 of 1978. The Plan improves Federal emergency management and assistance. By consolidating emergency preparedness, mitigation and response activities, it cuts duplicative administrative costs and strengthens our ability to deal effectively with emergencies.

The Plan, together with changes I will make through executive action, would merge five agencies from the Departments of Defense, Commerce, HUD [Housing and Urban Development] and GSA [General Services Administration] into one new agency.

For the first time, key emergency management and assistance functions would be unified and made directly accountable to the President and Congress. This will reduce pressures for increased costs to serve similar goals.

The present situation has severely hampered Federal support of State and local emergency organizations and resources, which bear the primary responsibility for preserving life and property in times of calamity. This reorganization has been developed in close cooperation with State and local governments.

If approved by the Congress, the Plan will establish the Federal Emergency Management Agency, whose Director shall report directly to the President. The National Fire Prevention and Control Administration (in the Department of Commerce), the Federal Insurance Administration (in the Department of Housing and Urban Development) and oversight responsibility for the Federal emergency broadcast system (now assigned in the Executive Office of the President) would be transferred to the Agency. The Agency's Director, its Deputy Director, and its five principal program managers would be appointed by the President with the advice and consent of the Senate.

If the Plan takes effect, I will assign to the Federal Emergency Management Agency all authorities and functions vested by law in the President and presently delegated to the Defense Civil Preparedness Agency (in the Department of Defense). This will include certain engineering and communications support functions for civil defense now assigned to the U.S. Army.

I will also transfer to the new Agency all authorities and functions under the Disaster Relief Acts of 1970 and 1974 now delegated to the Federal Disaster Assistance Administration in the Department of Housing and Urban Development.

I will also transfer all Presidential authorities and functions now delegated to the Federal Preparedness Agency in the General Services Administration, including the establishment of policy for the National Stockpile. The stockpile disposal function, which is statutorily assigned to the General Services Administration, would remain there. Once these steps have been taken by Executive Order, these three agencies would be abolished.

Several additional transfers of emergency preparedness and mitigation functions would complete the consolidation. These include:

- Oversight of the Earthquake Hazards Reduction Program, under Public Law 95-124, now carried out by the Office of Science and Technology Policy in the Executive Office of the President.
- Coordination of Federal activities to promote dam safety, carried by the same Office.
- Responsibility for assistance to communities in the development of readiness plans for severe weather-related emergencies, including floods, hurricanes, and tornadoes.
- Coordination of natural and nuclear disaster warning systems.
- Coordination of preparedness and planning to reduce the consequences of major terrorist incidents. This would not alter the present responsibility of the Executive Branch for reacting to the incidents themselves.

This reorganization rests on several fundamental principles. First, Federal authorities to anticipate, prepare for, and respond to major civil emergencies should be supervised by one official responsible to the President and given attention by other officials at the highest levels.

The new Agency would be in this position. To increase White House oversight and involvement still further, I shall establish by Executive Order an Emergency Management Committee, to be chaired by the Federal Emergency Management Agency Director. Its membership shall be comprised of the Assistants to the President for National Security, Domestic Affairs and Policy and Intergovernmental Relations, and the Director, Office of Management and Budget. It will advise the President on ways to meet national civil emergencies. It will also oversee and provide guidance on the management of all Federal emergency authorities, advising the President on alternative approaches to improve performance and avoid excessive costs.

Second, an effective civil defense system requires the most efficient use of all available emergency resources. At the same time, civil defense systems, organization, and resources must be prepared to cope with any disasters which threaten our people. The Congress has clearly recognized this principle in recent changes in the civil defense legislation.

The communications, warning, evacuation, and public education processes involved in preparedness for a possible nuclear attack should be developed, tested, and used for major natural and accidental disaster as well. Consolidation of civil defense functions in the new Agency will assure that attack readiness programs are effectively integrated into the preparedness organizations and programs of State and local government, private industry, and volunteer organizations.

While serving an important "all-hazards" readiness and response role, civil defense must continue to be fully compatible with and be ready to play an important role in our Nation's overall strategic policy. Accordingly, to maintain a link between our strategic nuclear planning and our nuclear attack preparedness planning, I will make the Secretary of Defense and the National Security Council responsible for oversight of civil defense related programs and policies of the new Agency. This will also include appropriate Department of Defense support in areas like program development, technical support, research, communications, intelligence and emergency operations.

Third, whenever possible, emergency responsibilities should be extensions of the regular missions of Federal agencies. The primary task of the Federal Emergency Management Agency will be to coordinate and plan for the emergency deployment of resources that have other routine uses. There is no need to develop a separate set of Federal skills and capabilities for those rare occasions when catastrophe occurs.

Fourth, Federal hazard mitigation activities should be closely linked with emergency preparedness and response functions. This reorganization would permit more rational decisions on the relative costs and benefits of alternative approaches to disasters by making the Federal Emergency Management Agency the focal point of all Federal hazard mitigation activities and by combining these with the key Federal preparedness and response functions.

The affected hazard mitigation activities include the Federal Insurance Administration which seeks to reduce flood losses by assisting states and local governments in developing appropriate land uses and building standards and several agencies that presently seek to reduce fire and earthquake losses through research and education.

Most State and local governments have consolidated emergency planning, preparedness and response functions on an "all hazard" basis to take advantage of the similarities in preparing for and responding to the full range of potential emergencies. The Federal Government can and should follow this lead.

Each of the changes set forth in the plan is necessary to accomplish one or more of the purposes set forth in Section 901(a) of Title 5 of the United States Code. The Plan does not call for abolishing any functions now authorized by law. The provisions in the Plan for the appointment and pay of any head or officer of the new agency have been found by me to be necessary.

I do not expect these actions to result in any significant changes in program expenditures for those authorities to be transferred. However, cost savings of between $10-$15 million annually can be achieved by consolidating headquarters and regional facilities and staffs. The elimination (through attrition) of about 300 jobs is also anticipated.

The emergency planning and response authorities involved in this Plan are vitally important to the security and well-being of our Nation. I urge the Congress to approve it.

JIMMY CARTER

The White House,

June 19, 1978

Reorganization Plan Number 3 of 1978

Prepared by the President and transmitted to the Senate and the House of Representatives in Congress assembled, June 19, 1978, pursuant to the provisions of Chapter 9 of Title 5 of the United States Code.

Part I. Federal Emergency Management Agency

Section 101. *Establishment of the Federal Emergency Management Agency.*

There is hereby established as an independent establishment in the Executive Branch, the Federal Emergency Management Agency (the "Agency").

Section 102. *The Director.*

The Agency shall be headed by a Director, who shall be appointed by the President, by and with the advice and consent of the Senate, and shall be compensated at the rate now or hereafter prescribed by law for level II of the Executive Schedule.

Section 103. *The Deputy Director.*

There shall be within the Agency a Deputy Director, who shall be appointed by the President, by and with the advice and consent of the Senate, and shall be compensated at the rate now or hereafter prescribed by law for level IV of the Executive Schedule. The Deputy Director shall perform such functions as the Director may from time to time prescribe and shall act as Director during the absence or disability of the Director or in the event of a vacancy in the Office of the Director.

Section 104. *Associate Directors.*

There shall be within the Agency not more than four Associate Directors, who shall be appointed by the President, by and with the advice and consent of the Senate, two of whom shall be compensated at the rate now or hereafter prescribed by law for level IV of the Executive Schedule, one of whom shall be compensated at the rate now or hereafter prescribed by law for level V of the Executive Schedule and one of whom shall be compensated at the rate now or hereafter prescribed by law for GS-18 of the General Schedule. The Associate Directors shall perform such functions as the Director may from time to time prescribe.

Section 105. *Regional Directors.*

There shall be within the Agency ten regional directors who shall be appointed by the Director in the excepted service and shall be compensated at the rate now or hereafter prescribed by law for GS-16 of the General Schedule.

Section 106. *Performance of Functions.*

The Director may establish bureaus, offices, divisions, and other units within the Agency. The Director may from time to time make provision for the performance of any function of the Director by any officer, employee, or unit of the Agency.

Part II. Transfer of Functions

Section 201. *Fire Prevention.*

There are hereby transferred to the Director all functions vested in the Secretary of Commerce, the Administrator and Deputy Administrator of the National Fire Prevention and Control Administration, and the Superintendent of the National Academy for Fire Prevention and Control pursuant to the Federal Fire Prevention and Control Act of 1974, as amended, (15 U.S.C. 2201 through 2219); exclusive of the functions set forth at Sections 18 and 23 of the Federal Fire Prevention and Control Act (15 U.S.C. 278 (f) and 1511).

Section 202. *Flood and Other Matters.*

There are hereby transferred to the Director all functions vested in the Secretary of Housing and Urban Development pursuant to the National Flood Insurance Act of 1968, as amended, and the Flood Disaster Protection Act of 1973, as amended, (42 U.S.C. 2414 and 42 U.S.C. 4001 through 4128), and Section 1 of the National Insurance Development Act of 1975, as amended, (89 Stat. 68).

Section 203. *Emergency Broadcast System.*

There are hereby transferred to the Director all functions concerning the Emergency Broadcast System, which were transferred to the President and all such functions transferred to the Secretary of Commerce, by Reorganization Plan Number 1.

Part III. General Provisions

Section 301. *Transfer and Abolishment of Agencies and Officers.*

The National Fire Prevention and Control Administration and the National Academy for Fire Prevention and Control and the positions of Administrator of said Administration and Superintendent of said Academy are hereby transferred to the Agency. The position of Deputy Administrator of said Administration (established by 15 U.S.C. 2204(c)) is hereby abolished.

Section 302. *Incidental Transfers.*

So much of the personnel, property, records, and unexpended balances of appropriations, allocations and other funds employed, used, held, available, or to be made available in connection with the functions transferred under this Plan, as the Director of the Office of Management and Budget shall determine, shall be transferred to the appropriate agency, or component at such time or times as the Director of the Office of Management and Budget shall provide, except that no such unexpended balances transferred shall be used for purposes other than those for which the appropriation was originally made. The Director of the Office of Management and Budget shall provide for terminating the affairs of any agencies abolished herein and for such further measures and dispositions as such Director deems necessary to effectuate the purposes of this Reorganization Plan.

Section 303. *Interim Officers.*

The President may authorize any persons who, immediately prior to the effective date of this Plan, held positions in the Executive Branch to which they were appointed by and with the advice and consent of the Senate, to act as Director, Deputy Director, and Associate Directors of the Agency, until those offices are for the first time filled pursuant to the provisions of this Reorganization Plan or by recess appointment, as the case may be. The President may authorize any such person to receive the compensation attached to the Office in respect of which that person so serves, in lieu of other compensation from the United States.

Section 304. *Effective Date.*

The provisions of this Reorganization Plan shall become effective at such time or times, on or before April 1, 1979, as the President shall specify, but not sooner than the earliest time allowable under Section 906 of title 5, United States Code. ■

Firefighters' Workweek Veto

Following is President Carter's June 19 message to Congress explaining his veto of HR 3161, a bill to shorten the workweek of federal firefighters. It was Carter's third veto.

TO THE HOUSE
OF REPRESENTATIVES:

I am returning, without my approval, H.R. 3161, a bill which would substantially reduce the work week for Federal firefighters, while maintaining their pay at nearly the present level. I have three principal objections to this bill.

First, this measure would reduce firefighters' work week without reducing the premium pay which was designed for a longer standby schedule. In effect, it would raise firefighters' total hourly pay by more than 15 percent. If only the basic hourly pay is considered, without overtime pay, the increase is almost 30 percent. I do not believe this is justified, particularly in light of the 5.5 percent pay cap I have recommended for Federal employees as part of my efforts to hold down inflation. Moreover, the length of the work week for Federal firefighters must be considered in light of the nature of their duty. Fires tend to be less frequent at Federal installations than in urban areas. Comparatively, there is a very low incidence of fire and there are very few severe fires.

Second, H.R. 3161 would impair the ability of agency heads to manage the work force and regulate the work week.

Third, H.R. 3161 would require the Department of Defense alone to hire 4,600 additional employees, at an annual cost of $46.7 million, just to maintain existing fire protection. These additional personnel and payroll measures are unacceptable.

I am very proud of the superb record of Federal firefighters at our military installations. I know them to be hard-working and dedicated. The evidence is not compelling, however, that they are unfairly treated in matters of pay and length of work week. And in extending unwarranted advantages to them, H.R. 3161 offends the ideals of fairness that should guide this Administration. I am not prepared to accept its preferential approach.

JIMMY CARTER

The White House,
June 19, 1978 ■

Legislative Veto Power

Following is President Carter's June 21 message to Congress opposing the legislative veto:

TO THE CONGRESS
OF THE UNITED STATES:

In recent years, the Congress has strengthened its oversight of Executive Branch decisions. I welcome that effort. Unfortunately, there has been increasing use of one oversight device that can do more harm than good — the "legislative veto."

In the past four years at least 48 of these provisions have been enacted — more than in the preceding twenty years. This proliferation threatens to upset the constitutional balance of responsibilities between the branches of government of the United States. It represents a fundamental departure from the way the government has been administered throughout American history. Unnecessary and unwarranted legislative veto procedures obstruct the efforts of my Administration and most members of Congress to make the administrative process quicker and simpler and divert attention from our common task of improving Federal programs and regulations.

Since taking office, I have several times expressed my deep reservations about legislative veto provisions in bills presented to me for signature. Herbert Hoover and every subsequent President have taken this position. The purpose of this message is to underscore and explain the concern and to propose alternatives.

The legislative veto was first used in the 1932 statute which authorized the President to reorganize the Executive Branch. The provision was repeated in subsequent reorganization acts, including the statute in effect today. This kind of legislative veto does not involve Congressional intrusion into the administration of on-going substantive programs, and it preserves the President's authority because he decides which proposals to submit to Congress. The Reorganization Act jeopardizes neither the President's responsibilities nor the prerogatives of Congress.

'Intrusive Device'

As employed in some recent legislation, however, the legislative veto injects the Congress into the details of administering substantive programs and laws. These new provisions require the President or an administrator of a Government agency to submit to Congress each decision or regulation adopted under a program. Instead of the decision going into effect, action is blocked for a set time — typically 60 congressional working days — while Congress studies it. A majority of both Houses, or either House, or even a single committee, is authorized to veto the action during that period.

Such intrusive devices infringe on the Executive's constitutional duty to faithfully execute the laws. They also authorize congressional action that has the effect of legislation while denying the President the opportunity to exercise his veto. Legislative vetoes thereby circumvent the President's role in the legislative process established by Article I, Section 7 of the Constitution.

These are fundamental constitutional issues. The Attorney General is seeking a definitive judgment on them from the courts, but no immediate resolution is in prospect. Pending a decision by the Supreme Court, it is my view, and that of the Attorney General, that these legislative veto provisions are unconstitutional.

Moreover, the legislative veto raises serious, practical policy problems.

Federal agencies issue thousands of complex regulations each year. Many are adopted after months or years of hearings and are based on many volumes of evidence. To act responsibly under a typical legislative veto provision, Congress would have to examine all of this evidence, hold its own hearings, and decide whether to overrule the agency — all in a few weeks. This task would add an additional burden to Congress' legislative agenda.

Causes Delay, Uncertainty

The regulatory process is rightly criticized for being slow and creating uncertainty which cripples planning by business, state, and local governments, and many others. The legislative veto greatly compounds both problems. At best, it prolongs the period of uncertainty for each regulation by several months. At worst, it can mean years of delay. Under the legislative veto procedure, Congress can only block an agency's rules, not rewrite them. If the House and Senate agree that a regulation is needed but disagree with the agency or each other on the specifics, exercise of the veto can lead to indefinite deadlock.

This danger is illustrated by the regulations concerning President Nixon's papers. Three versions of these regulations were vetoed, and it took three years to reach agreement on them. Whatever the merits of the issues, this is clearly an unsatisfactory way to decide them. Such lengthy, expensive procedures could easily become commonplace under legislative veto statutes.

In addition to causing delay, legislative veto provisions can seriously harm the regulatory process. Regulators operating under such laws would seek to avoid vetoes. They would therefore tend to give more weight to the perceived political power of affected groups and less to their substantive arguments. Meetings of regulatory commissions could degenerate into speculation about how to write rules so they would escape future disapproval of future Congressional reviewers who are not present nor represented when the rules are being drafted. Many regulations would be evolved in negotiations between agency officials and Congressional staff members, subverting requirements in present law for public notice and comment and for decisions based on the record. Parties to regulatory proceedings, never knowing when a decision might be vetoed, would have to reargue each issue in Congress.

These problems would lead many regulators to reverse the constructive trend toward adopting uniform rules. They would revert to acting on a case-by-case basis, because the legislative veto cannot be applied to such decisions. This lack of uniformity would not reduce the scope of regulation, but it would reduce clarity and certainty. Those affected would have to determine how dozens of decisions on individual fact situations might apply to their own cases, instead of abiding by a single rule.

Treating Symptoms, Not Causes

The most troubling problem, however, is that the legislative veto treats symptoms, not causes. The vast effort required to second-guess individual regulatory decisions could impede the crucial task of revising the underlying statutes.

Agencies issue regulations because Congress passes laws authorizing them, or — frequently — mandating them. Many of these laws have not been seriously reexamined for years and need change. This year, Congress is working on key bills to reform airline regulation, encourage public participation in the regulatory process, require lobbyists to work more openly, and adopt "sunset" procedures. Next year's agenda may be even fuller. We need legislation to speed up and simplify regulatory procedures, and we must reform a number of individual regulatory programs. We must deregulate where appropriate, make regulation easier to understand and to honor, and control the costs which regulations impose on our economy.

The President and the agency heads are responsible for improving the management of regulation, and we are doing so by administrative action encouraged by my Executive Order on improving the regulatory process. Only Congress through regulatory reform can deal with the underlying problems caused by a multitude of individual legislative mandates.

Regulation provides just one example of the problems caused by legislative vetoes; similarly severe problems arise in other areas of government. Thus, excessive use of legislative vetoes and other devices to restrict foreign policy actions can impede our ability to respond to rapidly changing world conditions. Reasonable flexibility is essential to effective government.

Overreaction to Abuses

In sum, for both constitutional and policy reasons I strongly oppose legislative vetoes over the execution of programs. The inclusion of such a provision in a bill will be an important factor in my decision to sign or to veto it.

I urge Congress to avoid including legislative veto provisions in legislation so that confrontations can be avoided. For areas where Congress feels special oversight of regulations or other actions is needed, I urge the adoption of "report-and-wait" provisions instead of legislative vetoes. Under such a provision, the Executive "reports" a proposed action to Congress and "waits" for a specified period before putting it into effect. This waiting period permits a dialogue with Congress to work out disagreements and gives Congress the opportunity to pass legislation, subject to my veto, to block or change the Executive action. Legislation establishing "report-and-wait" procedures has been introduced. Even these procedures consume resources and cause delays, however, so they should be used sparingly.

As for legislative vetoes over the execution of programs already described in legislation and in bills I must sign for other reasons, the Executive Branch will generally treat them as "report-and-wait" provisions. In such a case, if Congress subsequently adopts a resolution to veto an Executive action, we will give it serious consideration, but we will not, under our reading of the Constitution, consider it legally binding.

The desire for the legislative veto stems in part from Congress' mistrust of the Executive, due to the abuses of years past. Congress responded to those abuses by enacting constructive safeguards in such areas as war powers and the budget process. The legislative veto, however, is an overreaction which increases conflict between the branches of government. We need, instead, to focus on the future. By working together, we can restore trust and make the government more responsive and effective.

JIMMY CARTER

The White House
June 21, 1978

Earthquake Hazards Reduction

Following is the text of President Carter's message to Congress June 22, transmitting his plan to reduce the hazards of earthquakes:

TO THE CONGRESS
OF THE UNITED STATES:

Throughout its history, the human race has faced the threat of earthquakes, but in the last few years advances in science and technology have taught us more about earthquakes, and reduced the mystery of their origin and effects. These advances now permit us to anticipate earthquakes and to mitigate their potentially disastrous consequences. Today there is hope that we may eventually be able to predict earthquakes reliably.

Through the Earthquake Hazards Reduction Act of 1977 (Public Law 95-124), the Congress seeks to apply these advances by "the establishment and maintenance of an effective earthquake hazards reduction program." I am transmitting today a plan for a National Earthquake Hazards Reduction Program. This program is designed to meet the objectives of the important legislation you have passed. It deals with: predicting and preparing for earthquakes; ways in which government, industry, and the public can apply knowledge of seismic risk when making land-use decisions; and achieving earthquake-resistant design and construction.

As this program emphasizes, the Federal government must set a strong example in developing guidelines and standards for its own facilities. But Federal effort alone is not enough; to succeed in this effort, we must have the cooperative efforts of State and local governments, industry and business, professional and volunteer organizations, and the public.

JIMMY CARTER

The White House,
June 22, 1978

LEAA Overhaul

Following is President Carter's July 10 message to Congress, outlining his proposals to reorganize the programs being administered by the Law Enforcement Assistance Administration:

TO THE CONGRESS
OF THE UNITED STATES:

I am today sending to Congress the "Justice System Improvement Act of 1978," which will make significant changes in programs now being administered by the Law Enforcement Assistance Administration ("LEAA") and will revitalize our efforts to help State and local governments improve their justice systems.

For the past 10 years, Federal efforts to control crime through LEAA have been uncoordinated and ineffective. In providing financial assistance to State and local governments, the LEAA program has never been as efficient or effective as originally intended. A complex bureaucratic structure has enveloped the Federal effort, involving State and local law enforcement officials in excessive regulation, complexity, and mountains of redtape — rather than providing them with needed financial and technical assistance. Compliance with procedural guidelines has often overshadowed substantive accomplishments. Further, Federal research and statistics programs have not provided the types of information needed for sound management decisions by those involved in controlling crime and improving our justice system.

With the counsel and assistance of State and local officials and of Congressional leaders, particularly Senator Kennedy and Congressman Rodino, we have devoted more than a year to an intensive, thorough review of the LEAA program. Through that review, we sought to remedy the deficiencies in the LEAA program, while at the same time building upon the program's basic strengths. The Act which I am proposing today meets that goal: it effectively addresses LEAA's weaknesses and furthers our efforts, enhanced by our urban policy, to develop an effective partnership among the Federal government, State and local governments and community organizations.

Enactment of this bill will be a major step forward in our nation's efforts to control crime and improve the administration of justice. The bill contains the following major initiatives:

- It will streamline and redirect the LEAA program by simplifying the grant process and eliminating unnecessary paperwork; by targeting funds to areas of greatest need; by eliminating wasteful uses of LEAA funds; by strengthening the role of local governments; and by increasing community and neighborhood participation in program decisions.
- It will also consolidate within the Department of Justice civil and criminal research efforts in a new National Institute of Justice; and civil and criminal statistical programs in a new Bureau of Justice Statistics.

Law Enforcement Assistance Administration Eliminating Paperwork

The current statute authorizing LEAA imposes 25 broad planning requirements. Implementation of these requirements has resulted in annual State plans of uncertain value and extraordinary length. Each year, State plans total about 55,000 pages often filled with needless and repetitive narrative. Over the program's history, about 500 plans filling some one-half million pages have been submitted to LEAA. Countless staff time has been devoted to plan development and review at the Federal, State and local level.

My proposal will reverse this trend. Statutorily mandated requirements regarding content of plans will be reduced from 25 to 8. Annual State plans — now averaging about 1,000 pages — will be replaced by simplified applications submitted once every three years. This change alone will decrease paperwork by as much as 75 percent.

In addition, under the Act, major local government units will be able to submit single applications for funding of all projects covering a three-year period. The impact of this change will be significant. Presently, cities like Atlanta, Denver, Detroit, Chicago, Los Angeles and Newark fill out on the average 40 project applications each year. Under the Act, they will be required to complete only one.

Targeting Funds

Under the existing statute, LEAA funds are distributed to States solely on the basis of population. There is no requirement that funds be distributed according to an area's need to fight crime.

Under the Act, a priority will be placed on focusing funds to the areas with the most severe crime problems, in line with the Administration's general policy of targeting funds from government programs to areas of greatest need.

At present 17 States have about 55 percent of the nation's serious crime and about 45 percent of the total population. Under our proposals, those 17 States would receive additional funds to distribute to their local areas with the greatest crime problems.

Wasteful Use of Funds

The existing LEAA statute does not place any meaningful limits on how funds are to be used, or incentives for efficient use. In recent years, it has become obvious that some LEAA funds have been wasted on useless equipment, hardware, projects and programs.

To avoid future wasteful use, and to insure that LEAA funds are spent in the most productive ways, my proposal contains reasonable limits on the use of LEAA funds.

Strict limitations will be placed on the use of funds for equipment, hardware, administrative expenses, and general salary expenses. These limitations should result in additional LEAA funds for programs which will directly impact on the fight against crime and which will improve our judicial system.

Local Governments

Under the current LEAA statute, local crime prevention and control efforts have frequently been undercut by uncertainty about funding levels, as well as by disagreements over State and local roles and responsibilities.

My proposal will eliminate the uncertainty concerning the funding level for local governments and will more clearly establish the relationship between State and local governments. Rather than having to file innumerable applications with their State governments, my proposal will enable municipalities of over 100,000 population and counties of over 250,000 population for the first time to receive a fixed allocation of LEAA funds each year.

In addition, decisions regarding funding are now made at the State level, often without adequate local consultation. Under my proposal, these cities and counties will be given greater discretion to select projects and programs particularly suited to their own crime reduction and criminal justice needs.

Community and Neighborhood Participation

All too often, a wide gulf separates law enforcement officials from the communities and people they protect. This has been particularly true of the LEAA program.

My proposal recognizes that crime prevention and justice system improvement are not solely the tasks of government or justice agencies. Private citizens and neighborhood and community organizations will have a vital role to play. The participation of neighborhood and community groups in the development and approval of State and local applications will be assured. Not only will public hearings be required before State and local LEAA funding decisions are made, but those groups will be fully represented on the State and local advisory boards that will be established to determine how LEAA funds are spent locally. These actions will reenforce the neighborhood anti-crime proposal announced recently in our urban policy.

National Institute of Justice

Although the Federal, State, and local governments spend billions of dollars each year in their effort to combat crime and improve their criminal justice systems, we do not have adequate tools to assess the impact of these dollars in reducing crime or improving our justice system.

To date, Federal leadership in developing the necessary tools has been uncoordinated, fragmented, and has generally lacked focus.

My proposal will remedy this problem by creating a National Institute of Justice within the Justice Department. The Institute will replace two existing units, the National Institute for Law Enforcement and Criminal Justice and the National Institute of Corrections, and part of a third unit, the Institute of Juvenile Development and Research. The National Institute of Justice will be authorized to undertake basic and applied research and to conduct evaluations and sponsor demonstrations in the civil and criminal justice areas.

It will centralize the Federal effort to determine how the Federal, State and local governments can most effectively attack the crime problem and strengthen their justice system.

To ensure the independence and integrity of the Institute's efforts, its Director will have final authority for all grants and contracts made by the Institute.

An advisory board to the Institute will be composed of a broadly based group of academic experts, State and local officials, neighborhood and community leaders and citizens. The board will have authority to develop, in conjunction with the Director, policies and priorities for the National Institute of Justice.

Bureau of Justice Statistics

One of the most valuable services provided by the Federal government in the criminal justice area is the compilation of statistics. However, the Federal effort here has also lacked a central focus and direction.

Under my proposal, a Bureau of Justice Statistics will be created in the Department of Justice. The Bureau will be authorized to collect, analyze and disseminate statistics on criminal and civil justice matters. As a result, the Federal government will be able to provide crime statistics which are reliable and uniform.

An advisory board to the Bureau will consist of researchers, statisticians, State and local officials and citizens. The board would have authority to recommend to the Director policies and priorities for the Bureau of Justice Statistics.

To coordinate the operation of the streamlined LEAA, the National Institute of Justice and the Bureau of Justice Statistics, the Department of Justice will establish the Office of Justice Assistance, Research and Statistics. That Office will be responsible for ensuring that each of these three organizations attacks our criminal and civil justice problems in a focused and complementary way.

The "Justice System Improvement Act of 1978" lays the foundation for an effective Federal program of financial assistance, research and statistics and is vitally important to assist States, local governments and citizens groups in combating and improving the quality of the justice programs. I urge the Congress to give this proposal prompt and favorable consideration.

JIMMY CARTER

The White House
July 10, 1978

Sikes Act Veto

Following is President Carter's message to Congress giving his reasons for vetoing HR 10882. It was his fourth veto of a public bill.

TO THE HOUSE
OF REPRESENTATIVES:

I am returning without my approval H.R. 10882, the "Sikes Act Amendments of 1978."

The Sikes Act authorizes Federal-State cooperative programs for fish and wildlife conservation and public outdoor recreation on military reservations, National Forests, National Aeronautics and Space Administration sites, and certain Energy and Interior Department lands. It is intended to foster cooperation between the States and Federal land management agencies. H.R. 10882 would extend and increase appropriation authorizations under the act through 1981.

I am strongly committed to the wise management and conservation of fish and wildlife on public lands; I have recommended appropriations of approximately $35 million for fish and wildlife management on public lands subject to the Sikes Act. This total includes nearly $14.4 million for Federal/State cooperative programs of the type authorized by that Act, programs I believe are valuable and important.

However, these amendments are objectionable in two respects. First, the bill would more than double the current appropriation authorizations for Sikes Act programs — from $23.5 million in 1978 to $51 million in 1979, and $61 million in 1980 and 1981. These funds would be in addition to authorizations under other, more general, land management programs which are now used for carrying out most Sikes Act activities. I insist on adequate attention to the management of fish and wildlife resources on public lands, but the appropriations for these programs must be determined in the context of an effective and efficient management program encompassing all public land resources. These amendments provide unneeded authorization levels for Sikes Act programs.

Second, and more importantly, I object to the requirement in H.R. 10882 that directs the Secretaries of the Interior, Agriculture, and Defense to report to congressional authorizing committees whenever the President's budget request for Sikes Act activities is less than the amount authorized, and requires them to state specifically why the higher amount was not requested. This requirement is designed to bring pressure on the Administration to seek separate additional funds for Sikes Act programs and invites agencies to undercut the President's annual budget he has presented to the Congress. This is an unacceptable intrusion on the President's obligations and authority as Chief Executive. This approach would limit the President's ability to make his annual budget recommendations a positive, comprehensive, and balanced statement of the Administration's policies and budget priorities.

Disapproval of H.R. 10882 will not affect planned Federal expenditures for fish and wildlife management on public lands for 1979 which may be carried out under other more general land management authorities. This Administration will continue to move vigorously ahead in cooperation with the States to implement programs for the conservation and enhancement of fish and wildlife on public lands.

JIMMY CARTER

The White House,
July 10, 1978

Pension Regulation Plan

Following is President Carter's Aug. 10 message to Congress accompanying his Reorganization Plan No. 4 of 1978, which revises federal regulation of private pension and employee benefit plans:

TO THE CONGRESS
OF THE UNITED STATES:

Today I am submitting to the Congress my fourth Reorganization Plan for 1978. This proposal is designed to simplify and improve the unnecessarily complex administrative requirements of the Employee Retirement Income Security Act of 1974 (ERISA). The new plan will eliminate overlap and duplication in the administration of ERISA and help us achieve our goal of well regulated private pension plans.

ERISA was an essential step in the protection of worker pension rights. Its administrative provisions, however, have resulted in bureaucratic confusion and have been justifiably criticized by employers and unions alike. The biggest problem has been overlapping jurisdictional authority.

Under current ERISA provisions, the Departments of Treasury and Labor both have authority to issue regulations and decisions.

This dual jurisdiction has delayed a good many important rulings and, more importantly, produced bureaucratic runarounds and burdensome reporting requirements.

The new plan will significantly reduce these problems. In addition, both Departments are trying to cut red tape and paperwork, to eliminate unnecessary reporting requirements, and to streamline forms wherever possible.

Both Departments have already made considerable progress, and both will continue the effort to simplify their rules and their forms.

The Reorganization Plan is the most significant result of their joint effort to modify and simplify ERISA. It will eliminate most of the jurisdictional overlap between Treasury and Labor by making the following changes:

1) Treasury will have statutory authority for minimum standards. The new plan puts all responsibility for funding, participation, and vesting of benefit rights in the Department of Treasury. These standards are necessary to ensure that employee benefit plans are adequately funded and that all beneficiary rights are protected. Treasury is the most appropriate Department to administer these provisions; however, Labor will continue to have veto power over Treasury decisions that significantly affect collectively bargained plans.

2) Labor will have statutory authority for fiduciary obligations. ERISA prohibits transactions in which self-interest or conflict of interest could occur, but allows certain exemptions from these prohibitions. Labor will be responsible for overseeing fiduciary conduct under these provisions.

3) Both Departments will retain enforcement powers. The Reorganization Plan will continue Treasury's authority to audit plans and levy tax penalties for any deviation from standards. The plan will also continue Labor's authority to bring civil action against plans and fiduciaries. These provisions are retained in order to keep the special expertise of each Department available. New coordination between the Departments will eliminate duplicative investigations of alleged violations.

This reorganization will make an immediate improvement in ERISA's administration. It will eliminate almost all of the dual and overlapping authority in the two Departments and dramatically cut the time required to process applications for exemptions from prohibited transactions.

This plan is an interim arrangement. After the Departments have had a chance to administer ERISA under this new plan, the Office of Management and Budget and the Departments will jointly evaluate that experience. Based on that evaluation, early in 1980, the Administration will make appropriate legislative proposals to establish a long-term administrative structure for ERISA.

Each provision in this reorganization will accomplish one or more of the purposes in Title 5 of U.S.C. 901(a). There will be no change in expenditure or personnel levels, although a small number of people will be transferred from the Department of Treasury to the Department of Labor.

We all recognize that the administration of ERISA has been unduly burdensome. I am confident that this reorganization will significantly relieve much of that burden.

This plan is the culmination of our effort to streamline ERISA. It provides an administrative arrangement that will work. ERISA has been a symbol of unnecessarily complex government regulation. I hope this new step will become equally symbolic of my Administration's commitment to making government more effective and less intrusive in the lives of our people.

JIMMY CARTER

August 10, 1978

Weapons Procurement Veto

Following is President Carter's Aug. 17 message to Congress giving his reasons for vetoing HR 10929, the Defense Department weapons procurement bill. It was his fifth veto of a public bill.

TO THE HOUSE
OF REPRESENTATIVES:

I am returning without my approval HR 10929, the "Department of Defense Appropriation Authorization Act, 1979." I am doing so because I cannot, consistently with my constitutional responsibilities, sign into law a bill that in my view would weaken our national security in certain critical areas and wastes scarce defense dollars. The Congress' inclusion in this bill of a number of lower priority programs would force out of our defense budget certain central elements of our program, items needed now to modernize and bolster our military forces.

I believe that the defense of the United States needs to be strengthened. An adequate defense is the single most important concern I have as President. Accordingly, I submitted to the Congress in January of this year a budget request for the Department of Defense which would if enacted provide the defense we need. It requested $126.0 billion for the Department of Defense for Fiscal Year 1979. That amount was judged by me and by the Secretary of Defense to be adequate to provide for the military security of this country in Fiscal Year 1979, provided it was wisely spent.

The bill I am returning does not spend wisely. Instead, it actually would lead to less defense capability than I have requested. It does this by eliminating funds for high priority defense requirements and adding funds for purposes which do not meet our defense needs. Most notably, it would take nearly $2 billion from the total and set it aside for purchase of a nuclear-powered aircraft carrier — a ship which in the end would cost at least $2.4 billion, plus additional billions for its aircraft and the additional ships needed to defend and escort it.

We need more immediate improvements in our defense forces. A new nuclear-powered aircraft carrier would not be commissioned until 1987.

To spend $2 billion in defense dollars in that way would ignore much more serious and immediate defense needs. Other programs have been cut, during the appropriation process as well, to stay within Congressional budget limits. The effect would thus be to take away funds urgently needed by the Army, Navy, Air Force and Marine Corps for high priority programs — and to use those funds to build the most expensive ship in history. The result would be to weaken our military security in several critical areas, particularly during the next two years, at a time when we should be strengthening it. Within the $126.0 billion allocated for defense, we cannot have both an adequately balanced defense program and the luxury of an unneeded nuclear-powered aircraft carrier.

In pushing a nuclear-powered aircraft carrier into a $126.0 billion defense budget, HR 10929 would result in reduction or elimination of these essential programs, and a consequent weakening of our defense posture:

• **Weapons and equipment for the Army.** I requested a $1 billion increase to strengthen our ground forces, particularly our NATO-oriented forces, by providing more helicopters, combat vehicles and ammunition for our front-line forces. Adding the nuclear-powered aircraft carrier means eliminating $800 million of that increase.

• **Weapons and equipment for the Air Force.** I requested more funds for airlift, electronic warfare equipment and electronically guided ordnance. Adding the nuclear-powered aircraft carrier means eliminating $200 million of this increase.

• **Readiness funds.** It makes no sense to have military forces if their equipment is not in condition to fight. I requested an increase of $1 billion for items which are not glamorous, but which provide the immediate fighting capability of our forces — funds (requiring appropriation but not prior authorization) for repairs of weapons, spare parts for vehicles and aircraft, ship overhauls, training of personnel, communications, and logistical support to move equipment to where it is needed. Adding the nuclear-powered aircraft carrier means eliminating half of that increase in fighting capability — some $500 million.

• **Research and development.** To sustain our position of excellence in a world of weapons increasingly dependent on technology, I requested a 3% real growth in defense research and development. Adding the nuclear-powered aircraft carrier leads to an actual reduction in research and development. The bill also shifts some R&D funds from high priority programs to less important ones.

Our Navy has for a decade been moving in the direction of larger and larger, more-and-more-costly ships, and fewer of them. As a consequence our fleet today is smaller than at any time since 1940. We need a fleet that includes more vessels that can perform our Navy's mission but that are not, as this one would be, so designed as to be prohibitively expensive to build. The Navy does not need a fifth nuclear-powered aircraft carrier. It can maintain a twelve-carrier fleet and maintain the fighting capability it needs from a conventionally powered carrier, which I shall request in my budget for next year, at a saving of $1 billion for that single ship. Without this kind of discipline and control of the cost of ships, our Navy will not long be able to carry out its missions.

For these reasons, I must withhold my approval from HR 10929. I adhere firmly to my request that the Congress provide $126.0 billion for defense in Fiscal Year 1979. But I ask that the Congress delete the authorization for the nuclear-powered aircraft carrier, and use that essential $2 billion of that $126.0 billion instead for as many of our programs as possible from the following critical areas:

• **$1 billion for Army and Air Force equipment** — For helicopters, transport aircraft, combat vehicles, electronic equipment, ammunition and ordnance and other weapons and equipment.

• **$500 million for improving readiness in all the armed services** — For a wide variety of items, ranging from repair of weapons to spare parts stockage to improved training and logistical support.

• **Up to $500 million for research and development** — For programs proposed in my FY 79 budget but deleted by one or another Congressional action.

• **Naval Ships** — It is crucial to maintain an appropriate overall annual level of ship construction. The Congress should return all of the general purpose ships requested in our budget.

These are the ways in which our defense dollars need to be spent. These are the ways in which they will add to our military security, by obtaining the greatest military capability for each dollar and by focusing the effort where more effort is needed.

In light of the continuing Soviet buildup, we must not reduce our own real defense capability, either by cutting the budget amount I have requested, or by substituting for high priority defense requirements programs which are less urgent or less effective.

If we do not spend our defense dollars wisely, we do not provide adequately for the security of our country. I know that the Congress and I share common goals. I ask the Congress to cooperate with me to help our armed forces use their funds in ways which produce the greatest fighting power, and to provide the men and women of our armed forces with the kinds of weapons, equipment and other items of support which they need to do their jobs.

JIMMY CARTER

The White House,
August 17, 1978

Public Works Bill Veto

Following is President Carter's Oct. 5 veto message on HR 12928, public works appropriations. It was his sixth veto of a public bill.

TO THE HOUSE
OF REPRESENTATIVES:

Today I am returning HR 12928, the Energy and Water Development Appropriations bill, to the Congress without my approval. This bill would hamper the nation's ability to control inflation, eliminate waste and make the government more efficient.

I respect the hard work and good intentions of the members of Congress who have prepared this legislation. I share with the Congress a commitment to a strong program of water resource development. Wise development and management of water resources are vital to American agriculture's continued prosperity, and to community and economic development in key areas of our nation. I have proposed $2.5 billion this year to support nearly 300 water projects — including twenty-six project starts, the first proposed by any president in four years. Much of the water development funding in this bill is sensible and necessary.

HR 12928 also contains energy research and development programs which are important to our nation's energy future. These appropriations are generally in accord with national needs, and I support them.

But this bill also contains provisions for excessive, wasteful water projects and ill-advised limitations on efficient program management; these require that I disapprove HR 12928 in its present form.

The bill would require expenditures on water projects which have already been evaluated objectively and found to be unsound or to fall short of planning, design and environmental assessment requirement. These requirements are essential to ensure that tax dollars are well spent and that future cost over-runs and litigation are avoided. The bill attempts to mandate an unnecessary major increase in the size of the federal bureaucracy. And it uses funding procedures which conceal from the taxpayers the true size of excessive federal spending commitments.

In its present form, this bill appears to appropriate less than my FY 1979 Budget. In fact, however, it commits the federal government to 27 additional new projects and reinstates six projects halted last year — three for construction and three for planning. These added water projects represent a total long-term commitment, including inflation, $1.8 billion in excess of those I proposed. Yet only a little more than $100 million is appropriated in this bill for these projects. *(Chart, next page)*

Purchasing water projects on the installment plan does not reduce their cost to American taxpayers. Nor does it justify funding projects which fail to meet reasonable standards. We can achieve an efficient budget only if we are prepared to admit the true costs of the actions we take.

No challenge the Congress and the Executive Branch must face together is more painful than the exercise of budgetary discipline in each individual case. But only consistent, determined discipline will enable us to achieve our shared objectives of controlling inflation, balancing the budget and making government more efficient. The action I am taking today is part of that effort.

This appropriations bill is a true and difficult test of our resolve to discipline the

Administration's 1979 Request for Water Resource Projects Compared with Amounts Contained in HR 12928
($ in millions)

	President's Request	Bill	Difference
Number of Projects			
New Construction Starts	$ 26	$ 53	$ + 27
Six projects halted [in 1977]*	—	6	+ 6
Total	26	59	+ 33
1979 Appropriation for Projects			
New Construction Starts	640	104	− 536
Six projects halted [in 1977]*	—	8	+ 8
Total	640	112	− 528
Actual Total Cost of Projects			
New Construction Starts	640	1,821	+1,181
Six projects halted [in 1977]*	—	586	+ 586
Total	$640	$2,407	$ 1,767

* *Includes three projects funded for construction (total cost: $302 million) and three projects funded for further study (total cost: $284 million).*

federal budget. Each bit of additional spending always looks small and unimportant against the total federal budget. The temptation to look the other way in each case is always great. But both Congress and the Executive Branch must recognize that there is no one single dramatic act which will control the budget. Budgetary control must be achieved by the cumulative impact of hard choices such as the one I am presenting to the Congress today.

Following are my specific objections to this bill:

— *Funding is reinstated in this bill for unsound water projects.* Six projects not funded last year by the Congress after thorough review determined them to be unwise investments would receive funding this year. The six projects would cost more than $580 million to complete. Three of these would be funded for construction and three for further study, even though no additional analysis is needed to augment the exhaustive information now available. One of the projects funded for further study would require an investment of over $1 million per farm family served. The majority of another "study" project's water supply "benefits" are to serve one catfish farm and several "potential" catfish farms. One project funded for construction, whose major benefit category is flatwater recreation, would be the sixth Corps of Engineers reservoir in a 50-mile radius. American taxpayers simply should not be forced to fund projects which provide such questionable public benefits.

— The bill commits the Federal government to excessive new water project construction starts. I requested funds for 26 new water project construction starts costing a total of $640 million, including an allowance for inflation. This is the first time a president has recommended new starts in four years. This request was well-considered and reflects my commitment to a strong continued program of water resource development. I believe these initiatives are of high priority in meeting agricultural, flood damage reduction, economic development, environmental and other needs. However, the bill goes far beyond this large request. It includes initial funding for an additional 27 projects which, allowing for inflation, would add $1.2 billion in total costs. In addition to unacceptable long-term budgetary impact, many of these projects lack required planning or engineering information, present unresolved economic or environmental problems, fail to meet legal requirements or meet low-priority needs.

There are competing uses for every federal dollar and difficult choices must be faced. Every program in government, no matter how vital, must focus first on matters of highest priority. The president and the Congress must join in this difficult effort. Particularly with taxes and inflation a major concern of every American, I cannot support undertaking expenditures such as a $412 million project where planning is incomplete, or a $117 million project which, without adequate consideration of the concerns of local farmers or of the availability of less damaging alternatives, would take large amounts of valuable farm, pasture and forest land out of production and displace 140 people. Other projects funded in excess of my recommendations pose similar serious problems.

— *I would be forced to enlarge the federal bureaucracy substantially and unnecessarily.* This bill would mandate the hiring of more than 2,300 additional federal employees in the Corps of Engineers and the Bureau of Reclamation — far exceeding actual need. This requirement is inconsistent with efficient program management and would cause growth in this segment of the federal workforce that would be difficult to reverse.

— *The true costs of the bill far exceed the amounts appropriated.* I believe that funds to meet the full cost of all new water projects should be appropriated when the decision to go forward is made so that the true cost to the taxpayer is known and considered. Appropriating the full amount also helps ensure that, once a project is begun, funds are available to permit speedy, efficient completion. This bill continues the practice of committing the government to major financial investments for what appears on the surface to be very small appropriations. Thus, in making a relatively small appropriation of $103.6 million for new water project construction, HR 12928 is actually committing the government to total expenditures of $1.8 billion. At the same time, adding new starts each year without taking their full costs into account greatly increases the risk that budget pressures in the future will cause costly delays.

— *By eliminating funding for the Water Resources Council, the bill would seriously impair efforts to better coordinate water resources programs.* The Water Resources Council, composed of all the agencies with water programs, is our best assurance of consistent and efficient implementation of water programs throughout the government and close working relationships with other levels of government. The administration's new water policy stresses the need for systematic management of water resource programs and for increased coordination with state and local governments, and Congress recognized the importance of these objectives and of the Water Resources Council in reauthorizing the Council and its small staff this year.

I am pleased to note that the energy research and development portions of the bill are acceptable and meet important national needs. In a constructive step, this bill provides that decisions on the Clinch River Breeder Reactor project — or possible alternatives — will be determined in the Department of Energy authorization bill, the appropriate place to resolve this issue.

Vital energy programs and sound water development investments are important and shared goals of the Congress and my administration.

Yet the American people have the right to expect that their government will pursue these goals effectively, efficiently and with the budgetary discipline and careful planning essential to reduce inflation and continue economic growth. Citizens rightly demand sound programs to meet their needs. They rightly demand restraint and judgment in the allocation of public funds. And they expect those of us in public office to demonstrate the courage needed to face hard choices.

I call upon the Congress to join me in meeting our shared responsibility to the American people. I urge you to revise this bill expeditiously so that vital water and energy programs can continue unhampered by waste and inefficiency.

JIMMY CARTER

The White House,
October 5, 1978

Vietnam-Era Veterans

Following is President Carter's Oct. 10 message to Congress, outlining his proposals to assist veterans of the Vietnam War era:

TO THE CONGRESS
OF THE UNITED STATES:

I am submitting this message to report on the progress of Veterans of the Vietnam-era, and to describe the actions I will take to respond to the special problems a number of these Veterans still face.

Veterans of World War I, World War II and Korea have received the recognition and gratitude they deserve. They are honored and remembered as men and women who served their country. This has not always been the case for those who served during the War in Vietnam. In many ways, their service was more painful than in other eras: the selection process was often arbitrary; the war was long and brutal; the changes in warfare and innovations in medicine meant that fewer soldiers were killed than in other wars, but a far greater percentage survived with disabling injuries.

Because the war did not have the full backing of the American public, neither did those who fought in Vietnam. Many civilians came to confuse their view of the war with their view of those who were called upon to fight it. They confused the war with the warrior. Yet I know that all Americans join me in stating that the courage and patriotism of those who served in Vietnam have earned them full measure of honor and respect.

It is a tribute to the caliber of those who served that most Vietnam-era Veterans have already adjusted very successfully to civilian life. Still, in many ways, the effects of the war in Vietnam linger on. We have only begun to understand the full impact of the conflict. As part of healing its wounds, we have recognized our obligation to forget many harsh words and rash acts, and to forgive those who resisted the war. Of even greater importance is our determination to recognize those who did serve and to show our appreciation for the sacrifices they made.

I have directed the Secretary of Defense to honor the memory of all those who fought and died as well as those who are missing in action in Southeast Asia in ceremonies this fall at Arlington Cemetery.

As for those who did return, our review has found their personal and family median incomes are substantially higher than similar-aged non-Veterans, and their unemployment rates have been lowered. For the third quarter of 1978, Vietnam-era Veterans aged 20-34 had a 4.7 percent unemployment rate as compared to a 6.7 percent rate for the third quarter of 1977. Although rates vary from month to month, it is fair to say that most Vietnam-era Veterans have moved into the mainstream of economic life. Vietnam-era Veterans are making comparable or better use of their Veteran benefits than Veterans of previous wars. To date, nearly 65 percent have utilized their GI Bill benefits, which is far greater than under the World War II or Korean programs. We should not fail to recognize the hard work and determination that typify most Vietnam-era Veterans who have been successful in their military to civilian transition.

But for many Veterans — especially minority and disadvantaged Veterans — the transition to civilian life has led to unemployment, poverty and frustrations. The key to making our Veterans' programs successful — and efficient — is to target them carefully on those who continue to need help. By using our resources more skillfully and coordinating our efforts more closely, we can aid those ex-servicemen and women who are most in need of government assistance.

In my written State of the Union message to you last January, I indicated that my Administration would undertake a government-wide review of the status of the Vietnam-era Veteran and the programs designed to serve them. Since that time, the Veterans Administration, the Department of Labor, the Department of Defense, the Department of Justice, the Department of Health, Education and Welfare, the Community Services Administration, the Council of Economic Advisers, the Office of Management and Budget, and the Domestic Policy Staff have reviewed the status of these ex-servicemen and women and have prepared recommendations for improved government performance. On the basis of that policy review, I have ordered improvements in four areas of Veteran affairs:

- Employment Opportunities
- Educational Opportunities
- Other Veterans Services and Benefits
- Military Status

In order to implement my decisions in these areas and improve delivery of services to veterans, I have established an interagency Veterans Federal Coordinating Committee, composed of representatives of eight agencies, operating under the direction of the Executive Office of the President.

I am also conferring upon the Veterans Administration the status of a Cabinet Agency, for the purpose of attending Cabinet meetings. The Veterans Administration is a large and important part of our government. Its presence at Cabinet meetings will be useful for other departments with overlapping responsibilities, and for the Veterans Administration itself, which will have a stronger voice.

To better understand some of the issues that will continue to confront the Vietnam-era Veteran, I am instituting a survey of public attitudes toward those Veterans. This study will help us identify the real areas of concern, as well as accurately portray the public's overall support of Veterans' benefit programs generally.

I. Employment Opportunities

Most Vietnam-era Veterans are now doing better economically than non-veterans of the same age and background. In 1977, Vietnam-era Veterans aged 20-39 had median personal incomes of $12,680 compared to $9,820 for similar-aged non-veterans. When compared by family income, the figures are $15,040 and $12,850 respectively. For Vietnam-era Veterans aged 20-34, the unemployment rate of 7.4 percent for September one year ago declined to 4.9 percent in September 1978. As in all other sectors, unemployment rates for Veterans are substantially lower than they were when this Administration took office. We have hired nearly 98,000 Vietnam-era Veterans in public service jobs as part of the Administration's Economic Stimulus Package. Jobs and training assistance for Veterans became a top domestic priority when the Administration took office; the results are now clearly visible.

But if the overall employment picture for Vietnam-era Veterans is encouraging, the unemployment problems of minority, disabled, and disadvantaged Vietnam-era Veterans are cause for continued concern and attention. Black Vietnam-era Veterans, a significant percentage of whom saw active combat, face unemployment rates of 11.2 percent for the third quarter of 1978 compared to 15.9 percent for the third quarter of 1977. For the more seriously disabled Veterans, the unemployment rate is estimated to range as high as 50 percent. We have made great strides in every area of employment since the beginning of my Administration, but these jobless rates are still far too high. There is a clear need to better coordinate employment and employment assistance programs so that they are targeted on those Veterans most in need.

With that in mind, I have ordered a comprehensive review of the overall system for delivery of employment services to veterans. The review will yield further suggestions for improvement, but I have already initiated action to:

- improve the participation of Veterans in all Comprehensive Employment and Training Act (CETA) programs. We have designed a number of ways of making sure CETA prime sponsors take account of the special needs of Veterans. They include: inspecting grant plans and monitoring local prime sponsor systems to assure consideration of the Vietnam-era Veteran and seeking to have better Veterans representation on prime sponsor councils.
- continue operation of a national Help Through Industry Retraining and Employment (HIRE) program at a $40 million level, and supplement it with a $90 million HIRE II program, paid for with carry-over funds from the original HIRE effort. HIRE I is a national contract program operated through State Employment Services across the country, and through the National Alliance for Business. It hires and trains Veterans, members of Veterans' families eligible

for Veterans' preference, and disadvantaged non-veteran youth for jobs in the private sector. HIRE II will decentralize sponsors to contract for and operate it in cooperation with State Employment Security agencies. HIRE II will be available exclusively for Veterans. Participants will also have access to all of the training, public employment and outreach services available through other CETA programs.

- secure from Congress authority to spend in Fiscal 1979 HIRE funds appropriated in 1977. Without this extension the unobligated funds would have reverted to the Treasury.
- continued support will be given for the special outreach programs for Veterans operated by the National Alliance for Business and selected community organizations. One of the most important contributions government can make to Vietnam-era Veterans is to support outreach programs. They extend Veterans services to those who are unaware of the availability of assistance or intimidated by the idea of seeking it. We have extended our outreach efforts through HIRE II program and Veterans organizations. The National Alliance for Business and 13 other private programs funded by the Department of Labor must have continued backing.
- maintain current funding levels for the Disabled Veterans Outreach Program (DVOP). DVOP was originally funded as part of the economic stimulus package, but the program deserves to continue at its current level of $30 million. DVOP employs 2,000 disabled Veterans to help find jobs for other disabled Veterans. So far, 26,000 disabled Veterans have found work through the program and it continues to be targeted at those Veterans with the severest employment problems.
- improve coordination between Department of Labor and Veterans Administration employment programs. These programs will become more efficient as departmental policy links are clarified by a new high-level joint committee appointed by the Secretary of Labor and the Veterans Administrator. Money-wasting duplication of effort will be ended.
- order all Federal agencies to make greater use of the Veterans Readjustment Appointment (VRA) authority to bring Vietnam-era Veterans, especially the disabled, into government service. I have already submitted legislation to liberalize and extend the authority to June 30, 1980. The bill has passed both Houses of Congress and is now in conference.

II. Educational Opportunities

Vietnam-era Veterans are in the process of becoming the best educated group of Veterans in our history. Already, 65 percent of Vietnam-era Veterans have taken advantage of the GI Bill. That compares to a final rate of some 51 percent for World War II Veterans and 43 percent for Veterans of the Korean War. The Nation has spent nearly $25 billion on the GI Bill for Vietnam-era Veterans compared with $14 billion for those who served in World War II and $4.5 billion for Veterans of the Korean conflict.

But these readjustment assistance benefits often have not been utilized by those Vietnam-era Veterans who need them the most. Many members of minority groups and those lacking a high school diploma have not taken full advantage of the GI Bill. For them, outreach efforts must be intensified and eligibility expanded. At present, eligibility for most benefits under the GI Bill generally ends ten years after discharge. Although these provisions are more liberal than for Veterans of previous wars, we will:

—submit legislation to the Congress that would extend eligibility beyond ten years for these Veterans the Veterans Administration defines as in need or educationally disadvantaged.

—continue a VA program called "Operation Boost" designed to seek out Veterans who are unaware of the time limit that is fast approaching for many of them.

III. Other Veterans Services and Benefits

In general, Veterans benefits have been generous for Vietnam-era Veterans, but these and other benefits to which they are entitled need to be targeted better on those who really need them. Among those benefits and services requiring improvement are ones relating to:

- Disabled Veterans
- Incarcerated Veterans
- Readjustment counseling and substance abuse treatment.

Disabled Veterans. Individuals with service-connected disabilities are especially in need of greater assistance from the government. This is particularly true for Vietnam-era Veterans, who suffered a 300 percent greater loss of lower extremities than Veterans of any other war. Altogether, 512,000 have sustained some kind of disability.

Our vocational rehabilitation programs must reflect our paramount concern for those Veterans who have service-connected disabilities. The current VA program is based on a 1943 model and requires major updating. I will submit legislation to the next Congress that will modernize and improve that program.

Readjustment Counseling and Substance Abuse Treatment. The frequent image of the Vietnam Veteran as unbalanced, unstable and drug-dependent is simply not borne out by available information. Most Veterans have adjusted well and the incidence of drug abuse, although greatly increased while in service, has for the most part declined to pre-Vietnam levels or lower. Nevertheless, there is evidence that suggests a significant minority of Vietnam Veterans have experienced problems of readjustment which continue even today.

Vietnam-era Veterans under age 34 have a suicide rate 23 percent higher than non-Veterans of the same age group. The number of hospitalized Vietnam-era Veterans identified as alcoholics or problem drinkers more than doubled from 13 percent in 1970 to 31 percent in 1977. And, although the drug abuse problems has declined, Vietnam-era Veterans account for 39 percent of all inpatients and 55 percent of all outpatients being treated by the VA for drug dependence problems.

The government is addressing these concerns, but more must be done:

—The Administration has already proposed legislation which would authorize psychological readjustment counseling to Vietnam-era Veterans and their families. The proposal is aimed at those Veterans who are not classified as mentally ill but nevertheless need some kind of counseling. I urge Congress to enact this proposal prior to adjournment.

The Administration also requested legislative authority to contract for halfway houses in the treatment of Vietnam-era Veterans with substance abuse problems. This authority, together with the activation of 20 new VA substance abuse treatment units in this coming fiscal year, should provide needed resources to treat those with continuing alcohol and drug abuse problems.

—Finally, more research needs to be done into the problems of Vietnam-era Veterans. I am directing both the Veterans Administration and the National Institute of Mental Health to initiate studies in this area. A major study contracted for by the Veterans Administration to be submitted next year should enable us to better identify the nature and extent of problems being experienced by Vietnam-era Veterans.

Incarcerated Veterans. Like Veterans of all wars, a certain percentage of Vietnam-era Veterans end up in prison after returning home. Available data suggest that there are about 29,000 Vietnam-era Veterans in State and Federal prisons. Many of these Veterans received discharges which entitle them to VA benefits. Unfortunately, we lack comprehensive information about imprisoned Veterans.

I have directed the Law Enforcement Assistance Administration (LEAA) to compile accurate data about incarcerated Veterans. I have also asked the LEAA and the Bureau of Prisons to develop an information dissemination program for criminal justice system officials aimed at informing Veterans of the benefits available to them.

IV. Military Status

Ninety-seven percent of all Vietnam-era Veterans received discharges under honorable conditions after completing service. It is only fair that those few individuals with discharges under other than honorable conditions be presented with the fullest possible justification for the action taken against them. Because of the serious harm such a discharge can do to a Veteran seeking a responsible place in society, the government must assure that discharge review is readily available to insure fair and humane treatment.

In this connection the Administration will:

—grant assistance to Veterans seeking discharge review. The Department of Defense has agreed to provide indices of discharge review/correction board cases to selective regional offices of the VA.

—submit legislation to modify the provisions of PL 95-196 which automatically barred VA benefits for combat Veterans discharged because of unauthorized absences of 180 days or more.

Conclusion

No steps we take can undo all the damage done by the war. There is no legislation that can bring those who died back to life, nor restore arms, legs, eyes to those who lost them in service. What we can do is to acknowledge our debt to those who sacrificed so much when their country asked service of them, and to repay that debt fully, gladly, and with a deep sense of respect.

JIMMY CARTER

The White House,
Oct. 10, 1978

Aquaculture Pocket Veto

Following is President Carter's Oct. 18 message to Congress explaining his decision to withhold approval of HR 9370, the aquaculture assistance bill. It was Carter's first use of the pocket veto and his seventh veto of a public bill:

I have withheld approval from HR 9370, "A bill to establish new Federal programs and assistance for the development of aquaculture in the United States."

While the underlying purpose of the bill, development of an active aquaculture industry, is sound, I am concerned that the numerous broad-reaching programs established under the bill are premature. HR 9370 would establish a National Aquaculture Council to assess the state of aquaculture in the U.S. and to prepare a National Aquaculture Development Plan — a detailed set of Federal activities to expand the commercial potential of certain aquatic species. It would establish substantial new programs of Federal assistance to carry out the plan and undertake demonstration projects in aquaculture. The bill also would create a Federal Aquaculture Assistance Fund to provide financial assistance and support to the aquaculture industry through a new Federal loan guarantee program and a new Federal insurance program.

The Administration recognizes the importance of aquaculture, the need for effective programs to support this, and the concept of an assessment of the aquaculture industry. In fact, many of the actions that the bill would require are already underway. Federal agencies are now involved in a wide variety of aquaculture activities, and they already have the legislative authorities they need to provide research and technical and financial assistance to the aquaculture industry. For example, the Small Business Administration can assist small business concerns which are engaged in aquaculture. The Department of Commerce, through its aquaculture research activities and the Sea Grant program, is supporting marine research, development, and advisory services. The Department of the Interior spends about $15 million yearly on freshwater aquaculture at its fish hatcheries, research and development laboratories, and cooperative fishery units. The Agriculture Department provides a complete range of information and technical assistance related to aquaculture. Additionally, the Farm Credit Administration is authorized to extend credit to harvesters of aquatic products.

We also have in place a way to coordinate the aquaculture programs of the Federal Government — namely, the Interagency Subcommittee on Aquaculture of the Federal Council on Science and Technology.

Given this array of Federal activities, I believe we should more carefully assess the need for additional programs in this area. In particular, I am concerned about offering major new government subsidies such as the loan guarantee and insurance programs unless and until a clear need for them has been established. Accordingly, I must withhold my approval of the bill.

My Administration will continue to assess the needs of aquaculture and the effectiveness and adequacy of the Federal programs in this area. We look forward to reviewing these programs next year with the sponsors of this measure in the hope we can agree on additional improvements in the government's aquaculture programs.

JIMMY CARTER

The White House,
October 18, 1978

SBA Amendments Veto

Following is President Carter's Oct. 23 statement giving his reasons for refusing to sign HR 11445, Small Business Act amendments. It was his second use of the pocket veto and his eighth veto of a public bill.

I am withholding my approval of HR 11445, omnibus amendments to the Small Business Act and the Small Business Investment Act. Because I recognize very personally the needs of the small business community and the dedication of Congressman Neal Smith and Senator Gaylord Nelson, chairmen of the respective House and Senate small business committees, in developing this legislation, it is with great regret that I must take this action.

Having spent most of my adult life as a small businessman, I share with the Congress a strong commitment to the small business people of our country and I recognize the need for greater attention to small business needs by the federal government. Since I took office we have reduced the burden of federal regulations on small business, proposed significant tax reductions and increased lending under the guaranteed loan program by 40%. In May of this year I signed an Executive Order calling for a White House Conference on Small Business to be held in January 1980. This conference will involve over 25,000 small business people throughout the country helping us to develop a small business policy for this country. I intend to work with the Congress and particularly with Chairmen Smith and Nelson to develop and implement such a policy.

This legislation does have beneficial features. However, it is precisely because of my commitment to small business and an effective Small Business Administration, that I must withhold my approval from HR 11445. This bill, in its present form, is not the best we can do for small business in the United States and is inconsistent with the tight budget situation we will face in the next few years. Disapproval of the bill would not interrupt any existing SBA program since SBA programs are already authorized for fiscal year 1979, nor would it interfere with administration plans regarding the White House Conference on Small Business, since $4,000,000 has already been appropriated for the conference in fiscal year 1979. This conference is an important priority of mine and of my administration.

The bill authorizes over $2 billion in expenditures in excess of our budget projections through 1982. It continues a duplicative program of farm disaster lending by the SBA with excessively deep interest subsidies and terms which we believe to be wasteful. This has led to an unwarranted amount of farm disaster lending which should be done by the Farmers Home Administration. This administration has proposed that farm lending be consolidated in the Department of Agriculture which has the farm credit expertise and extensive field network necessary to operate the program effectively and efficiently. The Congress has failed to act on this recommendation.

Even more important is the effect this bill would have on the operations of the Small Business Administration. The bill virtually mandates significant staff increases. It would also interfere with the ability of the administrator of the SBA, my primary small business advisor and representative, to effectively run that agency. The legislation imposes specific titles and responsibilities upon agency officials and specifies funding and personnel levels for activities throughout SBA down to the smallest detail. These legislative strictures run counter to my efforts to better manage the federal government.

The bill also distorts the role of SBA's Chief Counsel for Advocacy. I supported the establishment of this office as a means to insure that the views of small business were adequately reflected in the policy-making processes of the government. But the legislation tends to move the Chief Counsel for Advocacy into policy and administrative areas more properly those of the administrator of the SBA. This bill also might begin to isolate the Chief Counsel for Advocacy from the executive policy-making process by calling for an annual report to Congress which could not be reviewed or coordinated with any other agency of the Executive Branch. Current statutes provide the Chief Counsel with sufficient authorities to evalute small business issues and serve as an ombudsman to small business interests.

I am also concerned by the loan pooling provision in this bill that would authorize private dealers to issue a new class of 100 percent federally guaranteed securities which would compete directly with the Treasury and other federally-backed securities in the bond markets.

I look forward to working with the Congress and the small business community who worked on this bill to develop a program to meet the needs of small business. It is my great hope that early in the next Congress an approach will be fashioned to meet the needs of the small business community, with the full involvement of my administration.

JIMMY CARTER

The White House,
October 25, 1978

Legionville Historic Site Veto

Following is President Carter's Nov. 2 statement giving his reasons for refusing to sign (pocket veto) S 1104:

I am withholding my approval from S 1104, a bill that would authorize the establishment of the Legionville National Historic Site in the State of Pennsylvania. I am withholding my signature because I do not believe the Legionville site is of sufficient national significance to merit the cost of establishing and maintaining it as a national historic site.

The site does not meet the national significance criteria for historical areas established by the Department of the Interior. The Pennsylvania State Historic Preservation Office judged the site of only local significance. A National Park Service report made in June 1977 agreed. Further, the site has been altered by such modern intrusions as a railroad and an interstate highway.

The career of General "Mad" Anthony Wayne has been amply commemorated at other designated sites and I do not believe the added expense of acquiring and developing this site is a worthwhile expenditure of Federal funds.

JIMMY CARTER

The White House,
November 2, 1978

Navajo-Hopi Relocation Veto

Following is President Carter's Nov. 2 statement giving his reasons for refusing to sign (a pocket veto) HR 11092.

I am withholding my approval of HR 11092, the "Navajo and Hopi Relocation Amendments of 1978." I have no objection to the authorization in this bill to fund the important and difficult work being performed by the Relocation Commission to administer the partitioning of land which has been jointly used by the Navajo and Hopi Tribes. My failure to approve this bill will not affect the ability of the Commission to continue its work, because appropriations for this fiscal year have already been approved.

My objections to the bill center on section 4, which would provide for a one-house veto of the relocation plan which is finally adopted by the Relocation Commission. I have previously informed the Congress of my view that such legislative veto devices are unconstitutional intrusions into the day-to-day administration of the law by the Executive Branch, including independent agencies such as the Relocation Commission. Congress is constitutionally empowered to overrule agency decisions executing the law only by enacting legislation subject to the veto power of the President under Article I, section 7 of the Constitution.

Where either Congress or the President is dissatisfied with the execution of the law by an independent agency of commission, legislation agreeable to both or enacted over the President's veto is an appropriate and constitutional means for overturning the result reached by that independent agency. If the Constitution required less, there would in fact be no true independence for agencies such as the Relocation Commission. This principle was adhered to by the Ninety-third Congress when it enacted the Navajo and Hopi Indian Relocation Commission Act in 1974 and is one from which we should not depart.

The bill also contains a provision which would oust incumbent members of the Navajo and Hopi Indian Relocation Commission if they happened to be Federal, State or local elected officials. This provision in section 2 has constitutional implications since it would allow for Congressional removal of officers in the Executive Branch. Further, as a matter of fairness and equity, interruption of the tenure of appointed officials by the imposition of new "qualifications" should not be lightly undertaken. Accordingly, I would suggest that the Ninety-sixth Congress, in any consideration of a similar bill, give due consideration to these problems.

The Administration will work with the Congress next year to develop any needed legislation to improve the operations of the Relocation Commission. The Commission needs to operate more effectively and I look forward to working with congressional leaders such as Senator DeConcini and Congressman Udall toward this end.

JIMMY CARTER

The White House,
November 4, 1978

Navy-Commerce Meetings Veto

Following is President Carter's Nov. 2 statement giving his reasons for refusing to sign (a pocket veto) HR 11861.

I am withholding my signature from HR 11861, which would require the Secretaries of Commerce and the Navy to meet at least four times a year with representatives of the maritime industry and to submit an annual report to the President and Congress on their activities and recommendations.

Both the Maritime Administration of the Commerce Department (MARAD) and the Navy already have numerous contacts with the maritime industry and with each other to study, develop, and implement the goals of the Merchant Marine Act. Navy and MARAD are currently working to improve their cooperation in this area by adding the Secretaries of Commerce and Navy to an existing inter-agency advisory board on maritime matters. They are also arranging to have the board meet at least four times a year, and at least one of these meetings will be open to maritime industry representatives.

In addition, in order to assure that the concerns that generated this bill are fully addressed, I am directing both Secretaries to consult regularly with maritime industry officials to discuss issues of mutual concern.

In light of these actions, I see no reason for this legislation. It is not necessary to achieve our goal of an adequate merchant marine. It would mandate a change in administrative functions which are currently satisfactory. It is an undue legislative intrusion into administrative activities which are the appropriate responsibility of the Executive Branch, and the required report would be an additional and unnecessary government expense. For these reasons, I am disapproving this bill.

The White House, November 2, 1978 — JIMMY CARTER

D.C. Employees' Pensions

Following is President Carter's Nov. 4 statement giving his reasons for refusing to sign (a pocket veto) the District of Columbia Employees' Pension bill. It was his 10th veto.

I am withholding my approval from HR 6536 which would make certain changes in the retirement program for police, firefighters, teachers and judges of the District of Columbia.

This action today in no way alters my commitment to the basic principles of fairness and self-determination which must be the cornerstone of Federal-District relations. Included among our actions to fulfill this commitment have been (1) support of full voting representation, (2) support for expansion of "Home Rule" for the District and (3) support of efforts to provide greater equity and predictability to the financial relationship between the Federal government and the District.

I have also proposed removal of the Federal government from the District's Budgetary process by 1982, as well the development of an equitable Federal payment process on the District's revenues. This process must rest on an objective, equitable basis and not be used as a device to balance the District's budget. To achieve movement toward that goal, I recommended a Federal payment for Fiscal year 1979 totaling $317 million — the highest total ever recommended by a President.

It is against that background that my Administration last year expressed its willingness to work with the Congress and the District to develop a sound, reasonable solution to the District's current financial difficulties with its pension program for police, firemen, teachers and judges. Previous Administrations have declined to acknowledge any Federal responsibility for the District's current pension funding problems. In the bill that passed the House of Representatives, my Administration announced its willingness to assume sixty percent of the cost of making a transition to an actuarially sound system. This would have obligated the Federal government to make payments of $462 million over 25 years. Instead, the Congress ultimately adopted a different method of funding which identified the Federal responsibility as that portion of the unfunded liability attributable to employees who retired prior to Home Rule. This would require the Federal government to pay more than $1.6 billion over that same period.

This proposal fails to recognize that a large part of that liability derives from abuses of the disability retirement statutes which were permitted to flourish by those responsible for their effective administration. It undervalues or ignores the significance of Federal assistance through the Federal funding of benefits for thousands of District employees who participate in the Federal Civil Service Retirement System. I am therefore of the view that the enrolled bill overstates the degree of Federal responsibility.

Although the bill's benefit and disability retirement reforms are desirable, its failure to apply these reforms to current employees constitutes a serious and costly deficiency. While the bill contains a penalty clause, the purpose of which is to refuse the Federal payment if abuse persists, the application of basic statutory reforms to all employees would be a far more effective and efficient means of preventing a recurrence of the abuses which have prevailed in recent years.

Accordingly, I am compelled to withhold my approval from this bill.

I realize that many members of Congress have worked long and hard with the Administration on this question. I agree with them that there is indeed a Federal responsibility to see that this program is converted to one which is actuarially sound and which minimizes opportunity for abuse.

I look forward to working with the Congress and the elected representatives of session to develop acceptable retirement funding and reform legislation. We are prepared to consider a reasonable Federal financial contribution, providing that provisions are included that fully remedy the problem of retirement abuses. Working together, I am sure we can place the District retirement programs on a sound basis in a manner which both limits the extent of Federal financial responsibility, while also recognizing the Federal responsibility in this area.

JIMMY CARTER

The White House, November 4, 1978

Shipping Rebates Veto

Following is President Carter's Nov. 4 statement giving his reasons for refusing to sign the Ocean Shipping Rebating bill.

I have decided not to sign into law HR 9518. This legislation, which would impose severe enforcement measures in the area of ocean shipping rebating, reflects concern with the possible disparity in enforcement of our anti-rebating laws against U.S.-flag carriers but not against foreign flag operators. I share that concern, and any disparity that exists must be eliminated.

The United States is currently engaged in important discussions with several European countries and Japan in an attempt to reach cooperative agreements involving a number of shipping problems, including rebating. Rather than taking immediate unilateral action undermining these efforts, I have directed the Secretary of State, in cooperation with the Federal Maritime Commission and other agencies to pursue these talks vigorously and to report to me on their progress. I am also directing the Administration's Maritime Policy Task Force to provide, by an early date, a set of recommendations that will address both the substance of our rebating laws as well procedures for enforcement, taking into account the inherently international character of ocean shipping.

In the interim, I am asking the Federal Maritime Commission to step up its enforcement efforts against illegal rebating under the authority now provided in the Shipping Act of 1916. The Administration is committed to assist the FMC in these efforts, and I urge the FMC to seek the assistance of the Department of State in obtaining any necessary cooperation from foreign governments.

Although I am withholding my signature on HR 9518 I believe the bill represents an important signal to foreign countries that we must work together to secure a cooperative shipping regime. I commit my Administration to work with the next Congress to develop a comprehensive maritime policy for the United States, in which the concerns reflected by this bill as well as broader policy issues can be fully addressed.

JIMMY CARTER

The White House, November 4, 1978

Guam, Virgin Island Payments Veto

Following is President Carter's Nov. 8 statement giving his reasons for refusing to sign (a pocket veto) HR 13719:

I have withheld my approval of HR 13719, which would have authorized special Federal payments to Guam and the Virgin Islands to offset the local revenue losses during calendar years 1978 through 1982 caused by the Revenue Act of 1978.

Because income taxes paid by territorial residents to the governments of Guam and the Virgin Islands are based on the U.S. Internal Revenue Code, tax changes intended to reduce Federal income tax liabilities in the United States have a corresponding effect in reducing territorial tax liabilities. HR 13719 would have authorized direct grants to the territories to offset revenue losses associated with the 1978 tax Act.

While recognizing the defects in the current territorial tax structures which HR 13719 was designed to alleviate, particularly the effects of periodic Federal tax reductions on local revenues, I do not believe the bill provides an acceptable long-range solution. By replacing reasonable local tax efforts with direct Federal payments, the bill is simply another attempt to manage territorial deficits without addressing the underlying economic and financial problems which have led to those deficits. We can no longer afford a piecemeal approach to the growing revenue problems of the territories.

Accordingly, although I am disapproving HR 13719, I am directing the Secretaries of the Interior and the Treasury to study the financial situation of both the Virgin Islands and Guam to recommend a plan designed to help those governments achieve a higher degree of financial stability without perpetuating a piecemeal system which is costly to the Federal government and which does not sufficiently encourage responsible fianancial management in these territories.

JIMMY CARTER

The White House,
November 8, 1978

Tris Bill Veto

Following is President Carter's Nov. 8 statement giving reasons for refusing to sign S 1503.

I am withholding my approval of S 1503, a bill which would authorize Government indemnification, upon a judgment by the U.S. Court of Claims, of businesses which sustained losses as a result of the ban on the use of the chemical Tris in children's sleepwear.

In 1971 and 1974 the Government established strict fabric flammability standards on children's sleepwear to protect children against burns. To meet these flammability standards, the clothing industry treated fabric by using substantial quantities of the flame-retardant chemical Tris. In 1975, information became available that Tris was a carcinogenic risk to humans. Some firms stopped using Tris after this test information became available, but other firms did not.

On April 8, 1977, the Consumer Product Safety Commission ruled that children's sleepwear containing Tris was banned as a "hazardous substance" under the Federal Hazardous Substances Act. This led to the removal of Tris-treated children's sleepwear from the marketplace. Both the imposition of flammability standards and the subsequent ban on Tris-treated fabrics have caused expenditures and losses by industry.

The imposition of strict flammability standards to protect the Nation's children was fully justified. After it was discovered that Tris was hazardous to health, the removal of Tris-treated sleepwear from the marketplace, again to protect the Nation's children, was also fully justified.

S 1503 would establish an unprecedented and unwise use of taxpayer's funds to indemnify private companies for losses incurred as a result of compliance with a federal standard. The Government could be placed in the position in the future of having to pay industry each time new information arises which shows that a product used to meet regulatory standards is hazardous. This would be wrong. Producers and retailers have a basic responsibility for insuring the safety of the consumer goods they market.

If this bill became law the potential would exist for compensation of firms who marketed Tris-treated material after they knew, or should have known, that such products constituted a hazard to the health of children. Extensive, costly, and time-consuming litigation would be required to determine, in each instance, the liability involved and the loss attributable to the ban action in April 1977, without regard to profits the claimants may have earned on Tris-treated garments in earlier years.

While it is most regrettable that losses have resulted from the regulatory actions taken to protect the safety and health of the Nation's children, no basis exists to require a potential Federal expenditure of millions of dollars when the actions of the Government were fully justified. Accordingly, I am compelled to withhold my approval from this bill.

JIMMY CARTER

The White House,
November 8, 1978

Textile Tariff, Meat Import, Nurse Training Vetoes

Following are President Carter's Nov. 10 statements giving his reasons for refusing to sign (pocket veto) HR 9937, HR 11545 and S 2416.

I have decided not to sign into law HR 9937. This bill is an amendment to the Bank Holding Company Act which would authorize the General Services Administration to sell certain silver dollar coins at negotiated prices. I have determined that this legislation would not be in the national interest because of an unrelated amendment which exempts all textile and apparel items from any tariff reductions in the Multilateral Trade Negotiations (MTN) now underway in Geneva.

I am determined to assist the beleaguered textile industy. We are committed to a healthy and growing textile and apparel industry. This legislation would not advance that cause, and could even harm the entire U.S. economy.

This bill would not address the real causes of the industry's difficulties. In return for any transient benefits, the bill would prompt our trading partners to retaliate by withdrawing offers in areas where our need for export markets is the greatest — products such as tobacco, grains, citrus, raw cotton, paper, machinery, poultry, and textile-related areas such as mill products and fashion clothing. The loss of these export areas is too high a price for our Nation to pay.

The cost of this bill might be even higher; at best, it would cost us many opportunities for export; at worst, it could cause the collapse of the trade talks and further restrict the growth of the world economy. If the two and a quarter million workers in the textile and apparel industry are to survive in their jobs, we must work to keep the world economy strong and international trade free.

Just within the last year we have taken a number of steps to improve the condition of the U.S. textile and apparel industry:

—We negotiated a renewal of the international Multifiber Arrangement through 1981, providing more responsive controls over disruptive imports.

—We have negotiatged 15 new bilateral export restraint agreements which are firmer and fairer than earlier versions, covering 80 percent of all imports from low-cost suppliers. And we are negotiating more.

—We have improved our monitoring of imports and implementation of restraints, through steps such as the new legislative initiatives I have approved.

—We have, despite the proposed small reduction in tariffs, the highest textile and apparel tariffs in the developed world.

—We have begun discussions with exporting countries not now under restraint to seek appropriate levels for their shipments.

—We have established a pilot program to improve productivity in the men's tailored clothing industry, and we have begun an export promotion program for the entire textile and apparel complex.

—And we have begun a review of existing and proposed Federal regulations affecting this industry to assess their impact.

This, however, is not enough. I pledge that we will do more:

—We will intensify our review of existing bilateral restraint agreements to be sure they really work, and if there are harmful surges we will work promptly to remedy them.

—We will not allow the effectiveness of our restraint agreements to be undermined by significant increases in shipments from uncontrolled suppliers, and we will maintain a world-wide evaluation of the imports of textile and apparel into the U.S. and seek appropriate action, country-by-country, where warranted.

—We will be prepared to expand the pilot project underway in the men's tailored clothing industry so that other sectors may benefit from that experience, and we will speed proposals for a similar program in the ladies apparel industry.

—We will negotiate strenuously for removal of non-tariff barriers to U.S. textile and apparel exports, including restrictive "rules of origin."

—The Office of the Special Representative for Trade Negotiations will begin a new policy review and report to me quarterly on developments in the domestic textile and apparel industry, with special emphasis on imports and exports, so that appropriate actions can be taken more promptly.

These steps, like those of the past year, will not be the limit of our assistance to this vital industry. But each step that we take must be directed toward the long-term health of this industry and the United States economy as a whole — unlike HR 9937 which on balance is detrimental to the textile industry, to its to million workers, and to the Nation as a whole.

JIMMY CARTER

The White House,
November 10, 1978

MEAT IMPORTS VETO

I have withheld my approval of HR 11545, the Meat Import Act of 1978.

I do so because the bill would severely restrict Presidential authority to increase meat imports and would place a floor or minimum access level for meat imports that I believe is too low. It deprives a President of the only anti-inflationary tool available in this area.

Current law allows the President substantial flexibility to increase meat imports when, in his judgment, domestic supplies are inadequate to meet demand at reasonable prices. I am convinced that this flexibility must be preserved, as a weapon against inflation.

Under this bill, however, authority to increase meat imports would be tied to declaration of a national emergency or natural disaster, or to a restrictive price formula. Under this formula, the farm price of cattle would have to increase faster than the retail meat price by more than ten percent during the first two calendar quarters of a year. Under this formula, quotas could have been relaxed only once in the last ten years.

I also believe that the United States must avoid imposing excessive restrictions on our trading partners who supply us with meat. HR 11545 would impose those restrictions by stipulating a minimum access level for meat imports of 1.2 billion pounds, instead of the 1.3 billion my Administration recommended. I am concerned that the bill's lower level could harm our trade relations with the meat exporting countries and thus impair their long-term reliability as souces of additional meat supplies when our own production is low, particularly at a time when we are negotiating for greater access to foreign markets for both our industrial and agricultural products.

If the Congress had enacted HR 11545 without these objectionable provisions, I would have been pleased to sign it, as my advisers make clear repeatedly. The bill would have amended the Meat Import Act of 1964 to provide a new formula for determining meat import quotas. The new formula would have adjusted meat import quotas up when domestic production of meats subject to the quota went down. Under the 1964 meat import law, quotas are adjusted in the opposite way, so that as domestic production declines, the limits on meat imports are tightened, at exactly the wrong time. This defect has often compelled Presidents to increase or suspend the meat import quota, in order to ensure supplies of meat at reasonable prices. The new counter-cyclical formula would, in most years, automatically make the necessary adjustment in the meat import quota, without involving the President in the normal operation of the meat trade.

This Administration supports such counter-cyclical management of meat imports; in fact, the Department of Agriculture was instrumental in developing the formula which the Congress approved. But for all the advantages of the new formula, it is still an untested mechanical formula which may not respond ideally to all future situations. This is why I find the restrictions on the President's discretion to increase meat imports so objectionable and why my Administration's support for HR 11545 was so clearly conditioned upon removal of those restrictions and on increasing the minimum access level for meat imports to 1.3 billion pounds annually.

I am prepared to work with the Congress next year to pass a counter-cyclical meat import bill which will provide the stability and certainty the cattle industry requires, while preserving the President's existing discretionary authority and setting an acceptable minimum access level for imports.

JIMMY CARTER

The White House,
November 10, 1978

NURSE TRAINING ACT VETO

I am withholding my approval from S 2416, a bill that would extend a series of programs authorizing special Federal support for the training of nurses.

Although I support a number of its provisions, this bill would continue several Federal nurse training programs whose objectives have been accomplished and for which there is no longer a need. Moreover, the funding authorizations are excessive and unacceptable if we are to reduce the budget deficit to help fight inflation.

For the past 22 years, the Federal government has provided substantial financial support for nursing education. From 1956 through 1977, almost $1.4 billion was awarded for student traineeships, loans, and scholarships; for construction and basic support for nursing education programs; and for projects to improve nursing education and recruitment.

With the help of this support, the number of active nurses has more than doubled since 1957 to over 1,000,000 in 1978. Ten years ago, in 1968, there were 300 active nurses per 100,000 population in the United States. By the beginning of 1977, this ratio had risen to 395 per 100,000 population.

The outlook is also good for adequate, sustained growth in the supply of nurses. There is, therefore, no reason for the government to provide special support to increase the total supply of professional nurses.

This year the Administration proposed to extend only the authorities for special projects in nursing education and for nurse practitioner training programs, in order to focus Federal nurse training support on areas of greatest national need. This proposal was based on the concept that future Federal assistance should be limited to geographic and specialty areas that need nurses most.

S 2416 would authorize more than $400 million for fiscal years 1979 and 1980, mostly for continued Federal funding of a number of unnecessary special nurse training programs, at a potential cost to the taxpayer far above my budget. At a time of urgent need for budget restraint, we cannot tolerate spending for any but truly essential purposes.

I must point out that nursing training is primarily undergraduate education, and nursing students are eligible for the assistance made available by the government to all students, based on need. I recently signed into law the Middle Income Student Assistance Act, which will significantly expand our basic grant and student loan guarantee programs. Nursing students are also eligible for National Health Service Corps scholarships.

Disapproval of this bill will not cause an abrupt termination of funding of the nurse training programs, since funds are available for fiscal year 1979 under the continuing resolution.

If the Nation is to meet its health care needs at reasonable cost, Federal nursing and other health professions programs must make the greatest contribution to adequate health care at the most reasonable cost. This bill does not meet that test.

The Administration is now conducting a major review of its support for all health professions training, including nursing. Legislative proposals in this area will be made to the 96th Congress. These proposals will recognize the key role of nurses in our society and the need for nurses to play an even greater role in the efficient delivery of health care services.

JIMMY CARTER

The White House,
November 10, 1978

PUBLIC LAWS

CQ

Public Laws, 95th Congress, 2nd Session

PL 95-224 (HR 7691)—Distinguish federal grant and cooperation agreement relationships from federal procurement relationships. BROOKS (D Texas), HORTON (R N.Y.) and STEED (D Okla.)—6/9/77—House Government Operations reported July 1, 1977 (H Rept 95-481). House passed Sept. 27. Senate passed, amended, Oct. 1. House agreed to Senate amendment Jan. 19, 1978. President signed Feb. 3, 1978.

PL 95-225 (S 1585)—Make unlawful the use of minors engaged in sexually explicit conduct for the purpose of promoting any film or printed material. MATHIAS (R Md.) and CULVER (D Iowa)—5/23/77—Senate Judiciary reported Sept. 16, 1977 (S Rept 95-438). Senate passed Oct. 10. House passed, amended, Oct. 25. Conference report filed in House Nov. 4 (H Rept 95-811). Conference report filed in Senate Nov. 4 (S Rept 95-601). Senate agreed to conference report Nov. 4. House agreed to conference report Jan. 24, 1978. President signed Feb. 6, 1978.

PL 95-226 (HR 10532)—Provide temporary authority to the Secretary of the Interior to facilitate measures to mitigate the effect of the drought of 1976-77. UDALL (D Ariz), SISK (D Calif.), ULLMAN (D Ore.), EVANS (D Colo.), JOHNSON (D Calif.), McFALL (D Calif.), MEEDS (D Wash.) and SMITH (R Neb.)—1/24/78—House Interior and Insular Affairs reported Jan. 30, 1978 (H Rept 95-854). House passed Jan. 30. Senate passed Jan. 31. President signed Feb. 7, 1978.

PL 95-227 (HR 5322)—Impose an excise tax on the sale of coal by the producer, and to establish a Black Lung Disability Trust Fund. FRENZEL (R Minn.)—3/22/77—House Ways and Means reported June 16, 1977 (H Rept 95-438). House passed July 18. Senate Finance reported Nov. 1 (S Rept 95-572). Senate passed, amended, Dec. 15. House agreed to Senate amendments Jan. 24, 1978. President signed Feb. 10, 1978.

PL 95-228 (HR 5054)—Repeal the statutory requirement that appointments to the competitive service positions in executive branch agencies in the Washington, D.C., area be apportioned among the states on the basis of population. HARRIS (D Va.), FAUNTROY (D D.C.), FISHER (D Va.), SPELLMAN (D Md.) and STEERS (R Md.)—3/15/77—House Post Office and Civil Service reported Sept. 7, 1977 (H Rept 95-593). House passed Sept. 19. Senate Governmental Affairs reported Dec. 15 (S Rept 95-614). Senate passed Jan. 26, 1978. President signed Feb. 10, 1978.

PL 95-229 (H J Res 386)—Provide for the striking of a medal to be issued annually in commemoration of the bicentennials of outstanding historical events and personalities from 1777 to 1789. FAUNTROY (D D.C.), BOGGS (D La.), CONABLE (R N.Y.), LEACH (R Iowa), PICKLE (D Texas), RHODES (R Ariz.) and WRIGHT (D Texas)—4/6/77—House passed Sept. 27, 1977. Senate Banking, Housing and Urban Affairs reported Dec. 8 (S Rept 95-611). Senate passed, amended, Jan. 23, 1978. House agreed to Senate amendments Jan. 31. President signed Feb. 14, 1978.

PL 95-230 (HR 2719)—Authorize the Secretary of the Interior to contract with the Middle Rio Grande Conservancy District of New Mexico for payments of maintenance charges on certain Pueblo Indian lands. LUJAN (R N.M.)—1/31/77—House Interior and Insular Affairs reported Aug. 4, 1977 (H Rept 95-570). House passed Sept. 19. Senate Indian Affairs reported Nov. 1 (S Rept 95-575). Senate passed, amended, Nov. 3. House agreed to Senate amendments Jan. 31, 1978. President signed Feb. 15, 1978.

PL 95-231 (HR 5798)—Authorize funds for the Office of Rail Public Counsel for fiscal year 1978. ROONEY (D Pa.)—3/30/77—House Interstate and Foreign Commerce reported May 16, 1977 (H Rept 95-334). House passed Jan. 30, 1978. Senate passed Jan. 31. President signed Feb. 15, 1978.

PL 95-232 (S 1509)—Return to the United States title to certain lands previously conveyed to certain Indian pueblos in New Mexico. DOMENICI (R N.M.) and SCHMITT (R N.M.)—5/13/77—Senate Indian Affairs reported Sept. 21, 1977 (S Rept 95-445). Senate passed Sept. 29. House Interior and Insular Affairs reported Jan. 23, 1978 (H Rept 95-846). House passed Feb. 6. President signed Feb. 17, 1978.

PL 95-233 (S 1360)—Amend the National Forest Management Act with regard to the role of the Secretary of Agriculture in selecting bidding methods for timber sales. CHURCH (D Idaho), McCLURE (R Idaho), HATFIELD (R Ore.), PACKWOOD (R Ore.), MELCHER (D Mont.) and HANSEN (R Wyo.)—4/22/77—Senate Energy and Natural Resources reported July 6, 1977 (S Rept 95-333). Senate passed Sept. 14. House passed Feb. 6, 1978. President signed Feb. 20, 1978.

PL 95-234 (HR 7442) — Assure that those providing communication services are able to use existing space on poles which are owned by regulated utilities, and to simplify Federal Communications Commission forfeiture procedures. WIRTH, D-Colo., BROYHILL, R-N.C., BROWN, R-Ohio, BROWN, D-Calif., FLORIO, D-N.J., GUDGER, D-N.C., LEGGETT, D-Calif., MARKEY, D-Mass., MURPHY, D-N.Y., NEAL, D-N.C., PATTISON, D-N.J., PEASE, D-Ohio, PREYER, D-N.C., ROONEY, D-N.Y., ROSE, D-N.C., WAXMAN, D-Calif. and WILSON, D-Calif. — 5/25/77 — House Interstate and Foreign Commerce reported Oct. 19, 1977 (H Rept 95-721). Supplemental report filed Oct. 25. House passed Oct. 25. Senate passed, amended, Jan. 31, 1978. House agreed to Senate amendment with amendments Feb. 1. Senate disagreed to House amendments Nos. 1, 2 and 3 Feb. 6. Senate agreed to House amendment No. 4 with an amendment Feb. 6. House receded from its amendments Nos. 1, 2 and 3 Feb. 6. House concurred in Senate amendment to House amendment No. 4 Feb. 6. President signed Feb. 21, 1978.

PL 95-235 (HR 7766) — Authorize the mayor of the District of Columbia to enter into an agreement with the U.S. Postal Service with respect to the use of certain public air space in the District of Columbia. DIGGS, D-Mich. — 6/14/77 — House District of Columbia reported Sept. 20, 1977 (H Rept 95-611). House passed Sept. 26. Senate Governmental Affairs reported Jan. 30, 1978 (H Rept 95-622). Senate passed Feb. 6. President signed Feb. 21, 1978.

PL 95-236 (S 266) — Authorize funds for the Energy Research and Development Administration to render financial assistance to limit radiation exposure from uranium mill tailings used for construction. JACKSON, D-Wash. and BAKER, R-Tenn. — 1/14/77 — Senate Energy and Natural Resources reported March 29, 1977 (H Rept 95-72). Senate passed April 4. House Interstate and Foreign Commerce reported Part I Sept. 29 (H Rept 95-649). House Interior and Insular Affairs reported Part II Oct. 17. House passed, amended, Jan. 24, 1978. Senate agreed to House amendments Feb. 7. President signed Feb. 21, 1978.

PL 95-237 (HR 3454) — Designate certain endangered public lands for preservation as wilderness areas. UDALL, D-Ariz. — 2/9/77 — House Interior and Insular Affairs reported July 27, 1977 (H Rept 95-540). House passed Sept. 12. Senate Energy and Natural Resources reported Oct. 11 (S Rept 95-490). Senate passed, amended, Oct. 20. Conference report filed in House Jan. 31, 1978 (H Rept 95-861). Conference report filed in Senate Jan. 31, 1978 (S Rept 95-626). Senate agreed to conference report Feb. 8. House agreed to conference report Feb. 9. House agreed to Senate amendment to the title of the bill Feb. 9. President signed Feb. 24, 1978.

PL 95-238 (S 1340) — Authorize funds for fiscal year 1978 for energy research and development programs of the Department of Energy. JACKSON, D-Wash. — 4/21/77 — Senate Energy and Natural Resources reported May 16, 1977 (S Rept 95-179). Senate passed June 13. House passed, amended, Dec. 7. Senate agreed to House amendment Feb. 8, 1978. President signed Feb. 25, 1978.

PL 95-239 (HR 4544) — Make reforms in the administration of the black lung benefits program. DENT, D-Pa. and PERKINS, D-Ky. — 3/7/77 — House Education and Labor reported March 31, 1977 (H Rept 95-151). House passed Sept. 19. Senate passed, amended, Sept. 20. Conference report filed in House Feb. 2, 1978 (H Rept 95-864). Senate agreed to conference report Feb. 6. House agreed to conference report Feb. 15. President signed March 1, 1978.

PL 95-240 (HR 9375) — Make supplemental appropriations for fiscal year 1978. MAHON, D-Texas — 9/28/77 — House Appropriations reported Sept. 28, 1977 (H Rept 95-644). House passed Oct. 25. Senate Appropriations reported Oct. 28 (S Rept 95-564). Senate passed, amended, Nov. 1. Conference report filed in House Nov. 8 (H Rept 95-812). House recommitted conference report Nov. 30. Conference report filed in House Dec. 1 (H Rept 95-829). House agreed to conference report Dec. 6. House receded and concurred in Senate amendments Nos. 2, 5, 8, 10, 15, 25, 28, 29, 31, 32, 35, 44, 48 through 51 and 53 Dec. 6. House receded and concurred with amendments in Senate amendments Nos. 1, 7, 16, 22, 23, 37 and 52 Dec. 6. House insisted on its disagreement to Senate amendment No. 43 Dec. 6. Senate agreed to conference report Dec. 7. Senate agreed to House amendments to Senate amendments Nos. 1, 7, 16, 22, 23, 37 and 52 Dec. 7. Senate further insisted on its amendment No. 43 Feb. 1, 1978. Senate asked for further conference Feb. 1. House receded and concurred in Senate amendment No. 43 Feb. 22. President signed March 7, 1978.

PL 95-241 (HR 10368) — Clarify that aircraft registered by "citizens of the United States" are not required to be based primarily in the U.S. in order to be eligible for U.S. registry. ANDERSON, D-Calif. — 12/15/77 — House Public Works and Transportation reported Feb. 9, 1978 (H Rept 95-868). House passed Feb. 21. Senate passed Feb. 23. President signed March 8, 1978.

PL 95-242 (HR 8638) — Strengthen U.S. policies on nuclear nonproliferation and to reorganize certain nuclear export functions. BINGHAM,

D-N.Y., ZABLOCKI, D-Wis., FINDLEY, R-Ill., WHALEN, R-Ohio, STUDDS, D-Mass., FOWLER, D-Ga., CAVANAUGH, D-Neb., BEILENSON, D-Calif. and WINN, R-Kan. — 7/29/77 — House International Relations reported Aug. 5, 1977 (H Rept 95-587). House passed Sept. 28. Senate passed, amended, Feb. 7, 1978. House agreed to Senate amendment Feb. 9. President signed March 10, 1978.

PL 95-243 (S 838) — Request the Court of Claims to review the Indian Claims Commission finding in the case affecting the Black Hills portion of the Great Sioux Reservation, South Dakota, ABOUREZK, D-S.D. — 3/1/77 — Senate Indian Affairs reported April 29, 1977 (S Rept 95-112). Senate passed May 3. House passed, amended, Feb. 9, 1978. Senate agreed to House amendment Feb. 27. President signed March 13, 1978.

PL 95-244 (S 2076) — Authorize the secretary of the interior to transfer franchise fees from certain Grand Canyon National Park concessions to the Grand Canyon Unified School District, Arizona. DeCONCINI, D-Ariz., GOLDWATER, R-Ariz., and HANSEN, R-Wyo. — 9/9/77 — Senate passed Sept. 9, 1977. House Interior and Insular Affairs reported Jan. 23, 1978 (H Rept 95-847). House passed, amended, Feb. 6. Senate agreed to House amendments Feb. 28. President signed March 14, 1978.

PL 95-245 (HR 9851) — Improve air cargo service by permitting supplemental air carriers to obtain certificates to provide scheduled all cargo service. ANDERSON, D-Calif., SYNDER, R-Ky., HAMMERSCHMIDT, R-Ark., and JOHNSON, D-Calif. — 10/31/77 — House Public Works and Transportation reported Nov. 2, 1977 (H Rept 95-798). House passed Jan. 31, 1978. Senate Commerce, Science and Transportation reported Feb. 21 (H Rept 95-638). Senate passed, amended, Feb. 24. House agreed to Senate amendments March 1. President signed March 14, 1978.

PL 95-246 (H J Res 746) — Make urgent supplemental appropriations for fiscal year 1978 for the Southwestern Power Administration, Department of Energy. MAHON, D-Texas — 2/22/78 — House Appropriations reported Feb. 28, 1978 (H Rept 95-914). House passed March 7. Senate passed March 9. President signed March 15, 1978.

PL 95-247 (S 773) — Authorize the Wichita Indian tribe of Oklahoma to file claims against the United States for lands taken without adequate compensation. BARTLETT, R-Okla. — 2/24/77 — Senate Indian Affairs reported May 3, 1977 (S Rept 95-119). Senate passed May 5. House passed, amended, Feb. 24, 1978. Senate agreed to House amendment March 8. President signed March 21, 1978.

PL 95-248 (HR 8803) — Authorize the secretary of the interior to acquire additional lands in order to protect the Appalachian Trail. BYRON, D-Md., BINGHAM, D-N.Y., BURTON, P. D-Calif., and SEIBERLING, D-Ohio — 8/4/77 — House Interior and Insular Affairs reported Oct. 21, 1977 (H Rept 95-734). House passed Oct. 25. Senate Energy and Natural Resources reported Feb. 10, 1978 (S Rept 95-636). Senate passed, amended, Feb. 22. House agreed to Senate amendment March 7. President signed March 21, 1978.

PL 95-249 (S 1671)—Designate the Absaroka-Beartooth Wilderness area within Custer and Gallatin National Forest, Mont. METCALF, D-Mont. — 6/10/77 — Senate Energy and Natural Resources reported Jan. 31, 1978 (S Rept 95-624). Senate passed Feb. 10. House Interior and Insular Affairs reported March 6 (H Rept 95-927). House passed March 14. President signed March 27, 1978.

PL 95-250 (HR 3813)—Add certain lands to the Redwood National Park, Calif. BURTON, P., D-Calif., UDALL, D-Ariz., KASTENMEIER, D-Wis., KAZEN, D-Texas, BINGHAM, D-N.Y., SEIBERLING, D-Ohio, RUNNELS, D-N.M., ECKHARDT, D-Texas, BYRON, D-Md., TSONGAS, D-Mass., CARR, D-Mich., MILLER, D-Calif., FLORIO, D-N.J., KREBS, D-Calif., KOSTMAYER, D-Pa., RAHALL, D-W.Va., BURTON, J., D-Calif., DELLUMS, D-Calif., EDWARDS, D-Calif., ROYBAL, D-Calif., STARK D-Calif., PATTERSON, D-Calif., WAXMAN, D-Calif., WON PAT, D-Gaum and MURPHY, D-Pa. — 2/22/78 — House Interior and Insular Affairs reported Aug. 5, 1977 (H Rept 95-581). House Appropriations reported Part II Sept. 23. House passed Feb. 9, 1978. Senate passed, amended, Feb. 28. Conference report filed in House March 8 (H Rept 95-931). House agreed to conference report March 14. Senate agreed to conference report March 21. President signed March 27, 1978.

PL 95-251 (HR 6975)—Provide that hearing examiners be known as administrative law judges, and to increase by 100, to a total of 340, the number of such positions which the Civil Service Commission may establish at a GS-16 level. SCHROEDER, D-Colo. — 5/5/77 — House Post Office and Civil Service reported May 16, 1977 (H Rept 95-321). House passed July 18. Senate Governmental Affairs reported March 9, 1978 (H Rept 95-697). Senate passed March 14. President signed March 27, 1978.

PL 95-252 (HR 11518)—Extend through July 31, 1978, the present $752 billion legal limit on the federal public debt. ULLMAN, D-Ore. — 3/14/78 — House Ways and Means reported March 17, 1978 (H Rept 95-984). House passed March 21. Senate passed March 22. President signed March 27, 1978.

PL 95-253 (H J Res 715)—Request the President to proclaim May 3, 1978, as "Sun Day." RYAN, D-Calif., JEFFORDS, R-Vt., OTTINGER, D-N.Y., ADDABBO, D-N.Y., ALEXANDER, D-Ark., ALLEN, D-Tenn., AMBRO, D-N.Y., ANDREWS, R-N.D., ANNUNZIO, D-Ill., ASHLEY, D-Ohio, ASPIN, D-Wis., AuCOIN, D-Ore., BALDUS, D-Wis., BAUCUS, D-Mont., BEDELL, D-Iowa, BEILENSON, D-Calif., BENJAMIN, D-Ind., BENNETT, D-Fla., BIAGGI, D-N.Y., BINGHAM, D-N.Y., BLANCHARD, D-Mich., BLOUIN, D-Iowa, BOGGS, D-La., BOLAND, D-Mass., and BONIOR, D-Mich. — 2/6/78 — House Post Office and Civil Service reported March 3, 1978 (H Rept 95-919). House passed March 6. Senate Judiciary reported March 9 (S Rept 95-686). Senate passed March 14. President signed March 27, 1978.

PL 95-254 (HR 10982) — Rescind certain budget authorities totaling $55,225,000 contained in the presidential message of Jan. 27, 1978. MAHON, D-Texas — 2/15/78 — House Appropriations reported Feb. 23, 1978 (H Rept 95-896). House passed March 10. Senate passed March 22. President signed April 4, 1978.

PL 95-255 (H J Res 796) — Make urgent supplemental appropriations for disaster relief for fiscal year 1978. MAHON, D-Texas — 3/16/78 — House Appropriations reported March 20, 1978 (H Rept 95-990). House passed March 22. Senate passed March 23. President signed April 4, 1978.

PL 95-256 (HR 5385) — Increase from 65 to 70 years the age limit for retirement under the Age Discrimination in Employment Act. PEPPER, D-Fla. and FINDLEY, R-Ill. — 3/22/77 — House Education and Labor reported July 25, 1977 (H Rept 95-527). House passed Sept. 23. Senate Human Resources reported Oct. 12 (S Rept 95-493). Senate passed, amended, Oct. 19. Conference report filed in House March 14, 1978 (H Rept 95-950). House agreed to conference report March 21. Senate agreed to conference report March 23. President signed April 6, 1978.

PL 95-257 (HR 9169) — Permit the guarantee of obligations for financing fishing vessels in an amount not exceeding 87.5 percent of the actual or depreciated actual cost of each vessel. LOTT, R-Miss., EDWARDS, R-Ala., EMERY, R-Maine, COCHRAN, R-Miss., WILSON, D-Texas, WHITEHURST, R-Va., BOGGS, D-La., DOWNEY, D-N.Y., AuCOIN, D-Ore., CLEVELAND, R-N.H., CORRADA, New Prog.-P.R., TRIBLE, R-Va., LEGGETT, D-Calif., HUGHES, D-N.J. and YOUNG, R-Alaska — 9/16/77 — House Merchant Marine and Fisheries reported Oct. 25, 1977 (H Rept 95-740). House passed Jan. 28, 1978. Senate Commerce, Science and Transportation reported March 16 (S Rept 95-703). Senate passed March 22. President signed April 7, 1978.

PL 95-258 (HR 11055) — Allow farmers to treat as 1977 income crop disaster or target price payments made in 1978 which are attributed to 1977 losses. ULLMAN, D-Ore., and FOLEY, D-Wash. — 2/22/78 — House Ways and Means reported March 7, 1978 (H Rept 95-929). House passed March 13. Senate passed March 22. President signed April 7, 1978.

PL 95-259 (HR 5981) — Authorize funds through fiscal year 1981 for the American Folklife Center at the Library of Congress. THOMPSON, D-N.J., NEDZI, D-Mich. and BRADEMAS, D-Ind. — 4/4/77 — House Administration reported Feb. 3, 1978 (H Rept 95-865). House passed Feb. 28. Senate Rules and Administration reported March 22 (H Rept 95-712). Senate passed April 4. President signed April 17, 1978.

PL 95-260 (HR 2960) — Authorize the Secretary of the Interior to memorialize the 56 signers of the Declaration of Independence in Constitution Gardens in Washington, D.C. BOGGS, D-La. and BUTLER, R-Va. — 2/2/77 — House Administration reported Part I June 24, 1977 (H Rept 95-462). House passed July 11. Senate Rules and Administration reported Jan. 25, 1978 (S Rept 95-621). Senate passed, amended, Jan. 27. House agreed to Senate amendment April 4. President signed April 17, 1978.

PL 95-261 (HR 8358) — Provide for the designation of libraries of accredited law schools as depository libraries of federal government publications. NEDZI, D-Mich., AMMERMAN, D-Pa., HAWKINS, D-Calif., PATTISON. D-N.J., PANETTA, D-Calif., STOCKMAN, R-Mich. and THOMPSON, D-N.J. — 7/15/77 — House Administration reported Sept. 30, 1977 (H Rept 95-650). House passed Oct. 25. Senate Rules and Administration reported March 3, 1978 (S Rept 95-670). Senate passed, amended, March 6. House agreed to Senate amendment April 4. President signed April 17, 1978.

PL 95-262 (H J Res 770) — Authorize the President to issue a proclamation designating April 18, 1978, as "Education Day, U.S.A." ROSENTHAL, D-N.Y. — 3/1/78 — House passed April 12, 1978. Senate passed April 13. President passed April 17, 1978.

PL 95-263 (S J Res 124) — Authorize the President to proclaim the week of April 16-22 as "National Oceans Week." STEVENS, R-Alaska, KENNEDY, D-Mass., MAGNUSON, D-Wash. and HOLLINGS, D-S.C. — 3/20/78 — Senate passed March 20, 1978. House passed April 4. President signed April 17, 1978.

PL 95-264 (HR 2540) — Modify federal law in order to reduce the amount of land leaving Indian ownership on the Umatilla Reservation in Oregon. ULLMAN, D-Ore. — 1/26/77 — House Interior and Insular Affairs reported Nov. 22, 1977 (H Rept 95-820). House passed Feb. 6, 1978. Senate Indian Affairs reported March 22 (S Rept 95-718). Senate passed April 5. President signed April 18, 1978.

PL 95-265 (HR 4979) — Direct the Secretary of the Interior to convey certain public lands to Mineral County, Nev. SANTINI, D-Nev. — 3/14/77 — House Interior and Insular Affairs reported July 26, 1977 (H Rept 95-530). House passed Aug. 1. Senate Energy and Natural Resources reported Oct. 20 (S Rept 95-522). Senate passed, amended, Oct. 28. House agreed to Senate amendment with an amendment Feb. 24, 1978. Senate agreed to House amendment April 12. President signed April 14, 1978.

PL 95-266 (HR 6693) — Authorize funds for programs administered under the Child Abuse Prevention and Treatment Act. BRADEMAS, D-Ind., JEFFORDS, R-Vt., PERKINS, D-Ky., QUIE, R-Minn., BEARD, D-R.I., PRESSLER, R-S.D., MILLER, D-Calif., KILDEE, D-Mich., HEFTEL, D-Hawaii, HAWKINS, D-Calif., and BIAGGI, D-N.Y. — 4/27/77 — House Education and Labor reported Sept. 26, 1977 (H Rept 95-609). House passed Sept. 26. Senate passed, amended, Oct. 27. House agreed to Senate amendments with amendments April 10, 1978. Senate agreed to House amendments April 12. President signed April 24, 1978.

PL 95-267 (H J Res 578) — Authorize the President to proclaim the third weeks of May of 1978 and 1979 as "National Architectural Barrier Awareness Week." NOLAN, D-Minn., ADDABBO, D-N.Y., ANDERSON, D-Calif., BADILLO, D-N.Y., BALDUS, D-Wis., BAUCUS, D-Mont., BEVILL, D-Ala., BINGHAM, D-N.Y., BLOUIN, D-Iowa, BOLAND, D-Mass., BONIOR, D-Mich., BRADEMAS, D-Ind., BRECKINRIDGE, D-Ky., BRODHEAD, D-Mich., BROWN, D-Calif., BURGENER, R-Calif., BURKE, D-Calif., BURTON, P., D-Calif., CARNEY, D-Ohio, CAVANAUGH, D-Neb., CHISHOLM, D-N.Y., CLEVELAND, R-N.H., COHEN, R-Maine, CONTE, R-Mass., and CORMAN, D-Calif. — 8/5/77 — House Post Office and Civil Service reported March 3, 1978 (H Rept 95-918). House passed March 6. Senate Judiciary reported April 6 (S Rept 95-727). Senate passed April 11. President signed April 24, 1978.

PL 95-268 (HR 9179) — Extend until Sept. 30, 1981, the basic operating authority of the Overseas Private Investment Corp. BINGHAM, D-N.Y., WHALEN, R-Ohio, CAVANAUGH, D-Neb., IRELAND, D-Fla., and SOLARZ, D-N.Y. — 9/19/77 — House International Relations reported Oct. 7, 1977 (H Rept 95-670). House passed Feb. 23, 1978. Senate passed, amended, March 6. Conference report filed in House April 5 (H Rept 95-1043). Senate agreed to conference report April 6. House agreed to conference report April 11. President signed April 24, 1978.

PL 95-269 (HR 7744) — Establish a policy with regard to the respective roles of the Corps of Engineers and private industry in meeting the national dredging needs. JOHNSON, D-Calif., HARSHA, R-Ohio, ROBERTS, D-Texas, HOWARD, D-N.J., and COCHRAN, R-Miss. — 6/13/77 — House Public Works and Transportation reported Sept. 15, 1977 (H Rept 95-605). House passed Sept. 27. Senate Environment and Public Works reported March 23, 1978 (S Rept 95-722). Senate passed, amended, April 5. House agreed to Senate amendments April 13. President signed April 26, 1978.

PL 95-270 (S 2452) — Authorize $5 million to develop the Hubert H. Humphrey Institute of Public Affairs at the University of Minnesota and $2.5 million for the Everett Dirksen Center in Pekin, Ill. ANDERSON, D-Minn. — 1/30/78 — Senate Human Resources reported March 20, 1978 (S Rept 95-706). Senate passed March 22. House passed, amended, April 18. Senate agreed to House amendment April 19. President signed April 27, 1978.

PL 95-271 (S 2697) — Move the location for holding court for the U.S. district court for the eastern district of New York to Brooklyn and Hempstead. MOYNIHAN, D-N.Y. — 2/27/78 — Senate Judiciary reported April 7, 1978 (S Rept 95-728). Senate passed April 12. House passed April 25. President signed April 28, 1978.

PL 95-272 (H J Res 649) — Authorize the President to call a White House Conference on the Arts and a White House Conference on the Humanities. BRADEMAS, D-Ind., THOMPSON, D-N.J., JEFFORDS, R-Vt., PERKINS, D-Ky., QUIE, R-Minn., DENT, D-Pa., HAWKINS, D-Calif., FORD, D-Mich., CLAY, D-Mo., BIAGGI, D-N.Y., BLOUIN, D-Iowa, SIMON, D-Ill., BEARD, D-R.I., ZEFERETTI, D-N.Y., MILLER, D-Calif., MEYERS, D-Pa., MURPHY, D-Pa., LE FANTE, D-N.J., WEISS, D-N.Y., HEFTEL, D-Hawaii, CORRADA, New Prog-P.R. and KILDEE, D-Mich. — 11/3/77 — House Education and Labor reported Feb. 17, 1978 (H Rept 95-887). House passed Feb. 21. Senate Human Resources reported April 12 (S Rept 95-736). Senate passed April 18. President signed May 3, 1978.

PL 95-273 (S 1617) — Enact the Ocean Pollution Research Program Act. MAGNUSON, D-Wash. — 5/27/77 — Senate passed Aug. 3, 1977. House Science and Technology reported Part I Sept. 26 (H Rept 95-626). House passed, amended, Feb. 28, 1978. Senate agreed to House amendment April 24. President signed May 8, 1978.

PL 95-274 (S J Res 106) — Reappoint Leon Higginbotham Jr. as a citizen regent of the Smithsonian Institution Board of Regents. JACKSON, D-Wash., PELL, D-R.I., and GOLDWATER, R-Ariz. — 1/27/78 — Senate Rules and Administration reported March 3, 1978 (S Rept 95-662). Senate passed March 6. House Administration reported April 18 (H Rept 95-1064). House passed May 1. President signed May 10, 1978.

PL 95-275 (S J Res 107) — Reappoint John Paul Austin as a citizen regent of the Smithsonian Institution Board of Regents. JACKSON, D-Wash., PELL, D-R.I. and GOLDWATER, R-Ariz. — 1/27/78 — Senate Rules and Administration reported March 3, 1978 (S Rept 95-663). Senate passed March 6. House Administration reported April 18 (H Rept 95-1065). House passed May 1. President signed May 10, 1978.

PL 95-276 (S J Res 108) — Reappoint Anne Legendre Armstrong as a citizen regent of the Smithsonian Institution Board of Regents. JACKSON, D-Wash., PELL, D-R.I. and GOLDWATER R-Ariz. — 1/27/78 — Senate Rules and Administration reported March 3, 1978 (S Rept 95-664). Senate passed March 6. House Administration reported April 18 (H Rept 95-1066). House passed May 1. President signed May 10, 1978.

PL 95-277 (S 2220) — Authorize the Secretary of the Treasury to designate an Assistant Secretary to serve in his place as a member of the Library of Congress Trust Fund Board. CANNON, D-Nev. — 10/19/77 — Senate Rules and Administration reported Jan. 25, 1978 (S Rept 95-616). Senate passed Jan. 27. House Administration reported April 18 (H Rept 95-1067). House passed May 1. President signed May 12, 1978.

PL 95-278 (S 917) — Convey to the University of Nevada certain lands adjacent to the Gund Ranch, Grass Valley, Nevada, LAXALT, R-Nev. and CANNON, D-Nev. — 3/4/77 — Senate Energy and Natural Resources reported Oct. 20, 1977 (S Rept 95-521). Senate passed Oct. 27. House Interior and Insular Affairs reported March 30, 1978 (H Rept 95-1006). House passed May 1. President signed May 12, 1978.

PL 95-279 (HR 6782) — Enact the Emergency Agricultural Act of 1978. KREBS, D-Calif., SISK, D-Calif., and JENRETTE, D-S.C. — 4/29/77 — House Agriculture reported Sept. 29, 1977 (H Rept 95-641). House passed Oct. 31. Senate Agriculture, Nutrition and Forestry reported March 13, 1978 (S Rept 95-699). Senate Appropriations reported March 17 (H Rept 95-705). Senate passed, amended, March 21. Conference report filed in House April 6 (H Rept 95-1044). Senate agreed to conference report April 10, 1978. House rejected conference report April 12. House asked for further conference April 24. Senate agreed to further conference April 25. Conference report filed in House May 1 (H Rept 95-1103). Senate agreed to conference report May 2. House agreed to conference report May 4. President signed May 15, 1978.

PL 95-280 (S 482) — Direct the Secretary of the Interior to purchase and hold certain lands in trust for the Zuni Indian Tribe of New Mexico. DOMENICI, R-N.M., and SCHMITT, R-N.M. — 1/28/77 — Senate Indian Affairs reported April 29, 1977 (S Rept 95-111). Senate passed May 3. House passed, amended, April 18, 1978. Senate agreed to House amendments May 2. President signed May 15, 1978.

PL 95-281 (S 661) — Restore federal recognition of certain Indian tribes. BARTLETT, R-Okla. and BELLMON, R-Okla. — 2/7/77 — Senate Indian Affairs reported Nov. 1, 1977 (S Rept 95-574). Senate passed Nov. 3. House passed, amended, April 11, 1978. Senate agreed to House amendments May 2. President signed May 15, 1978.

PL 95-282 (H J Res 859) — Make supplemental appropriations for fiscal year 1978 for the U.S. Railway Association. MAHON, D-Texas — 4/19/78 — House Appropriations reported April 25, 1978 (H Rept 95-1083). House passed April 27. Senate Appropriations reported May 10 (S Rept 95-800). Senate passed May 11. President signed May 19, 1978.

PL 95-283 (HR 8331) — Provide the federal courts and the Securities Investor Protection Corporation with improved procedures to protect customers from insolvent brokers and dealers. ECKHARDT, D-Texas —

7/14/77 — House Interstate and Foreign Commerce reported Oct. 26, 1977 (H Rept 95-746). House passed Nov. 1. Senate Banking, Housing and Urban Affairs reported April 25, 1978 (S Rept 95-763). Senate passed, amended, April 26. House agreed to Senate amendments Nos. 1 through 7 May 2. House disagreed to Senate amendment No. 8 May 2. House agreed to Senate amendment No. 9 with an amendment May 2. Senate agreed to House amendment to Senate amendment No. 9 with an amendment May 4. Senate insisted on its amendment No. 8 May 4. House receded and concurred in Senate amendment No. 8 with an amendment May 9. House agreed to Senate amendment to House amendment to Senate amendment No. 9 May 9. Senate agreed to House amendment to Senate amendment No. 8 May 10. President signed May 21, 1978.

PL 95-284 (H J Res 873) — Make urgent supplemental appropriations for the disaster loan program of the Small Business Administration for fiscal year 1978. MAHON, D-Texas — 4/26/78 — House Appropriations reported May 2, 1978 (H Rept 95-1105). House passed May 8. Senate Appropriations reported May 10 (S Rept 95-801). Senate passed, amended, May 11. House agreed to Senate amendments May 12. President signed May 21, 1978.

PL 95-285 (S 1568) — Name the lake located behind Lower Mountain Lock and Dam, Washington, "Lake Herbert G. West, Senior." JACKSON, D-Wash., and MAGNUSON, D-Wash — 5/19/77 — Senate Environment and Public Works reported March 23, 1978 (S Rept 95-721). Senate passed April 5. House passed May 15. President signed May 25, 1978.

PL 95-286 (HR 10392) — Establish a Hubert H. Humphrey Fellowship in Social and Political Thought at the Woodrow Wilson International Center for Scholars at the Smithsonian Institution. NEDZI, D-Mich., THOMPSON, D-N.J., BRADEMAS, D-Ind., WRIGHT, D-Texas, FRENZEL, R-Minn., QUIE, R-Minn., FRASER, D-Minn., OBERSTAR, D-Minn., HAGEDORN, R-Minn., NOLAN, D-Minn., VENTO, D-Minn., STANGELAND, R-Minn., ABDNOR, R-S.D., PRESSLER, R-S.D., SIMON, D-Ill., FORD, D-Mich., WILSON, D-Calif., PRICE, D-Ill., FOLEY, D-Wash., BONIOR, D-Mich., BLANCHARD, D-Mich., ROSTENKOWSKI, D-Ill., FASCELL, D-Fla., MIKVA, D-Ill. and SCHROEDER, D-Colo. — 12/15/77 — House Administration reported April 18, 1978 (H Rept 95-1062). House passed May 15. Senate passed May 16. President signed May 26, 1978.

PL 95-287 (S J Res 137) — Reaffirm the North Atlantic Alliance as a vital commitment of U.S. foreign policy. BYRD, D-W.Va., BAKER, R-Tenn., STENNIS, D-Miss., SPARKMAN, D-Ala., KENNEDY, D-Mass., NUNN, D-Ga., GRIFFIN, R-Mich., TOWER, R-Texas, PERCY, R-Ill. and DANFORTH, R-Mo. — 5/24/78 — Senate passed May 24, 1978. House passed May 25. President signed May 30, 1978.

PL 95-288 (HR 9005) — Make appropriations for the District of Columbia for fiscal year 1978. NATCHER, D-Ky. — 9/8/77 — House Appropriations reported Sept. 8, 1977 (H Rept 95-596). House passed Sept. 16. Senate Appropriations reported Sept. 19 (S Rept 95-439). Senate passed, amended, Oct. 4. Conference report filed in House May 11, 1978 (H Rept 95-1139). House agreed to conference report May 16. House receded and concurred with amendments in Senate amendments Nos. 2, 22, 28, 36 and 39 May 16. House receded and concurred with amendments in Senate amendments Nos. 20, 26 and 37 May 16. Senate agreed to conference report May 23. Senate agreed to House amendments to Senate amendments Nos. 20, 26 and 37 May 23. President signed June 5, 1978.

PL 95-289 (S 2370) — Remove the $100,000 limitation on the amount authorized annually under the Volunteers in the National Forests Act of 1977. JACKSON, D-Wash. and MAGNUSON, D-Wash. — 12/15/77 — Senate Agriculture, Nutrition and Forestry reported March 3, 1978 (S Rept 95-671). Senate passed March 8. House Agriculture reported May 15 (H Rept 95-1180). House passed May 22. President signed June 5, 1978.

PL 95-290 (HR 11662) — Establish the Lowell National Historical Park, Mass. TSONGAS, D-Mass., WRIGHT, D-Texas, UDALL, D-Ariz., REUSS, D-Wis., SEBELIUS, R-Kan., RODINO, D-N.J., MOAKLEY, D-Mass., DRINAN, D-Mass., BURKE, D-Mass., CONTE, R-Mass., HECKLER, R-Mass., BOLAND, D-Mass., MARKEY, D-Mass., HARRINGTON, D-Mass., EARLY, D-Mass., STUDDS, D-Mass., MILLER, D-Calif., BINGHAM, D-N.Y., MITCHELL, D-Md., PATTISON, D-N.J., WAXMAN, D-Calif., MOFFETT, D-Conn., FENWICK, D-N.J., NEAL, D-N.C. and DODD, D-Conn. — 3/20/78 — House Interior and Insular Affairs reported March 30, 1978 (H Rept 95-1023). House passed April 11. Senate Energy and Natural Resources reported May 12 (S Rept 95-813). Senate passed, amended, May 18. House agreed to Senate amendments May 22. President signed June 5, 1978.

PL 95-291 (HR 11370) — Authorize funds to reimburse the states for certain expenditures for social services incurred prior to Oct. 1, 1975. CORMAN, D-Calif., VANDER JAGT, R-Mich., RANGEL, D-N.Y., STARK, D-Calif., FISHER, D-Va., BURKE, D-Mass., BRODHEAD, D-Mich., TUCKER, D-Ark. and GRADISON, D-Ohio — 3/8/78 — House Judiciary reported Part I May 4, 1978 (H Rept 95-1114). House Ways and Means reported Part II May 9. House passed May 23. Senate passed May 25. President signed June 12, 1978.

PL 95-292 (HR 8423) — Make improvements in the Medicare end stage renal disease program. ROSTENKOWSKI, D-Ill., VANIK, D-Ohio, CORMAN, D-Calif., COTTER, D-Conn., KEYS, D-Kan., FORD, D-Tenn., BRODHEAD, D-Mich., DUNCAN, R-Tenn., MARTIN, D-N.C., and GRADISON, R-Ohio — 7/19/77 — House Ways and Means reported July 29, 1977 (H Rept 95-549). House passed Sept. 12. Senate Finance reported March 22, 1978 (S Rept 95-714). Senate passed, amended, April 10. House agreed to Senate amendment with an amendment May 1. Senate agreed to House amendment May 24. President signed June 13, 1978.

PL 95-293 (S 1792) — Remove the annual authorization ceiling on the Administrative Conference of the United States. ABOUREZK, D-S.D. — 6/30/77 — Senate Judiciary reported Nov. 2, 1977 (S Rept 95-583). Senate passed Nov. 4. House passed, amended, Jan. 24, 1978. Senate agreed to House amendment with amendments May 22. House agreed to Senate amendments May 25. President signed June 13, 1978.

PL 95-294 (S J Res 140) — Request the president proclaim June 11, 1978, as "American University Press Day." MATHIAS, R-Md. — 6/8/78 — Senate passed June 8, 1978. House passed June 9. President signed June 14, 1978.

PL 95-295 (HR 11657) — Authorize funds through fiscal year 1982, for the Central, Western and South Pacific Fisheries Development Act. MURPHY, D-N.Y. — 3/20/78 — House Merchant Marine and Fisheries reported April 21, 1978 (H Rept 95-1079). House passed May 1. Senate Commerce, Science and Transportation reported May 12 (S Rept 95-818). Senate passed, amended, May 18. House agreed to Senate amendments May 31. President signed June 16, 1978.

PL 95-296 (S 1640) — Designate the Federal Aviation Administration Aeronautical Center, Oklahoma City, as the "Mike Monroney Aeronautical Center." BARTLETT, R-Okla. and BELLMON, R-Okla. — 6/8/77 — Senate passed June 8, 1977. House passed June 5, 1978. President signed June 19, 1978.

PL 95-297 (HR 130) — Enact the Petroleum Marketing Practices Act. DINGELL, D-Mich. — 1/4/77 — House Interstate and Foreign Commerce reported April 5, 1977 (H Rept 95-161). House passed April 5. Senate Energy and Natural Resources reported April 10, 1978 (S Rept 95-731). Senate passed, amended, May 9. House agreed to Senate amendment June 6. President signed June 19, 1978.

PL 95-298 (S 2553) — Authorize funds for fiscal year 1979 for certain maritime programs of the Department of Commerce. CANNON, D-Nev., and PEARSON, R-Kan. — 2/21/78 — Senate Commerce, Science and Transportation reported April 19, 1978 (S Rept 95-741). Senate passed April 24. House passed, amended, May 23. Senate agreed to House amendment June 12. President signed June 26, 1978.

PL 95-299 (HR 5493) — Authorize additional funds for acquisition of lands for certain wildlife refuges. LEGGETT, D-Calif., FORSYTHE, R-N.J., BIAGGI, D-N.Y., McCLOSKEY, R-Calif., ANDERSON, D-Calif., EMERY, R-Maine. STUDDS, D-Mass., DORNAN, R-Calif., OBERSTAR, D-Minn., TRIBE, R-Va., HUGHES, D-N.J. and HANNAFORD, D-Calif. — 3/23/77 — House Merchant Marine and Fisheries reported May 13, 1977 (H Rept 95-317). House passed May 16. Senate passed, amended, May 24. House agreed to Senate amendment with an amendment May 31, 1978. Senate agreed to House amendment June 8. President signed June 26, 1978.

PL 95-300 (HR 10884) — Authorize funds through fiscal year 1981 for the Council on Environmental Quality. MURPHY, D-N.Y., LEGGETT, D-Calif., FORSYTHE, R-N.J., ROGERS, D-Fla., HUBBARD, D-Ky., TRIBLE, R-Va., MIKULSKI, D-Md. and HUGHES, D-N.J. — 2/9/78 — House Merchant Marine and Fisheries reported March 31, 1978 (H Rept 95-1027). House passed April 10. Senate Environment and Public Works reported May 15 (S Rept 95-876). Senate passed, amended, May 25. House agreed to Senate amendment June 12. President signed June 26, 1978.

PL 95-301 (H J Res 944) — Make urgent supplemental appropriations in the amount of $6,488,000 for the Federal Grain Inspection Service, Department of Agriculture. MAHON, D-Texas — 5/25/78 — House Appropriations reported May 31, 1978 (H Rept 95-1223). House passed June 16. Senate passed June 19. President signed June 26, 1978.

PL 95-302 (S 2380) — Implement the protocol relating to intervention on the high seas in cases of marine pollution by substances other than oil. BYRD, D-W.Va., MAGNUSON, D-Wash., and PEARSON, R-Kan. — 12/15/77 — Senate Commerce, Science and Transportation reported May 8, 1978 (H Rept 95-785). Senate passed May 11. House passed, amended, June 5. Senate agreed to House amendment June 13. President signed June 26, 1978.

PL 95-303 (HR 5176) — Lower the duty on levulose until June 30, 1980. CORMAN D-Calif. and STARK, D-Calif. — 3/17/77 — House Ways and Means reported June 16, 1977 (H Rept 95-434). House passed July 18. Senate Finance reported May 10, 1978 (S Rept 95-796). Senate passed, amended, June 9. House agreed to Senate amendment June 14. President signed June 29, 1978.

PL 95-304 (HR 10823) — Authorize funds for fiscal year 1979 for the National Advisory Committee on Oceans and Atmosphere. MURPHY, D-N.Y., BREAUX, D-La., PRITCHARD, R-Wash., AuCOIN, D-Ore., GINN, D-Ga., FORSYTHE, R-N.J., ZEFERETTI, D-N.Y., OBERSTAR, D-Minn., HUGHES, D-N.J., AKAKA, D-Hawaii and MIKULSKI, D-Md. — 2/7/78 — House Merchant Marine and Fisheries reported March 30, 1978 (H Rept 95-1013). House passed April 17. Senate Commerce, Science and Transportation reported May 15 (H Rept 95-862). Senate passed, amended, June 5. House agreed to Senate amendment June 14. President signed June 29, 1978.

PL 95-305 (S 2973) — Authorize funds for services necessary to the nonperforming arts functions of the John F. Kennedy Center for Performing Arts. MOYNIHAN, D-N.Y., and McCLURE, R-Idaho — 4/24/78 — Senate Environment and Public Works reported May 15, 1978 (S Rept 95-831). Senate passed May 23. House passed June 21. President signed June 29, 1978.

PL 95-306 (HR 11779) — Authorize funds through fiscal year 1988 for the Secretary of Agriculture to expand comprehensive extension programs concerning forest and rangeland renewable resources. WEAVER, D-Ore., FOLEY, D-Wash., AMMERMAN, D-Pa., AuCOIN, D-Ore., BAUCUS, D-Mont., BOWEN, D-Miss., BROWN, D-Calif., BURKE, D-Calif., BURTON, P., D-Calif., DUNCAN, D-Ore., FRASER, D-Minn., JEFFORDS, R-Vt., JENRETTE, D-S.C., JONES, D-Tenn., KREBS, D-Calif., LOTT, R-Miss., MATHIS, D-Ga., NOLAN, D-Minn., OBERSTAR, D-Minn., RICHMOND, D-N.Y., SYMMS, R-Idaho, THORNTON, D-Ark. and UDALL, D-Ariz. — 3/22/78 — House Agriculture reported May 15, 1978 (H Rept 95-1184). House passed May 22. Senate passed, amended, June 7. House agreed to Senate amendment June 16. President signed June 30, 1978.

PL 95-307 (HR 11778) — Authorize funds through fiscal year 1988 for the Secretary of Agriculture to carry out forest and rangeland renewable resources research, and to provide cooperative forest resources assistance to states. WEAVER, D-Ore., AMMERMAN, D-Pa., AuCOIN, D-Ore., BAUCUS, D-Mont., BOWEN, D-Miss., BROWN, D-Calif., BURKE, D-Calif., BURTON, P., D-Calif., DUNCAN, D-Ore., FRASER, D-Minn., KREBS, D-Calif., OBERSTAR, D-Minn., SYMMS, R-Idaho and UDALL, D-Ariz. — 3/22/78 — House Agriculture reported May 15, 1978 (H Rept 95-1179). House passed May 22. Senate passed, amended, June 7. House agreed to Senate amendments June 16. President signed June 30, 1978.

PL 95-308 (HR 11465) — Authorize funds for fiscal year 1979 for the Coast Guard. BIAGGI, D-N.Y., MURPHY, D-N.Y., TREEN, R-La., RUPPE, R-Mich., JONES, D-N.C., DE LA GARZA, D-Texas, YOUNG, R-Alaska, ROONEY, D-Pa., GINN, D-Ga., LENT, R-N.Y., STUDDS, D-Mass., EILBERG, D-Pa., EVANS, R-Del., DE LUGO, D-V.I., PRITCHARD, D-Wash., HUBBARD, D-Ky., BONKER, D-Wash., D'AMOURS, D-N.H., PATTERSON, D-N.J., OBERSTAR, D-Minn., HUGHES, D-N.J., BAUMAN, R-Md., MIKULSKI, D-Md., BONIOR, D-Mich. and AKAKA, D-Hawaii — 3/13/778 — House Merchant Marine and Fisheries reported March 31, 1978 (H Rept 95-1030). House passed April 17. Senate Commerce, Science and Transportation reported May 12 (S Rept 95-817). Senate passed, amended, May 19. House agreed to Senate amendments June 14. President signed June 30, 1978.

PL 95-309 (H J Res 995) — Designate June 25, 1978, as "National Brotherhood Day." CONTE, R-Mass. — 6/14/78 — House passed June 23, 1978. Senate passed June 23. President signed June 30, 1978.

PL 95-310 (S 2033) — Authorize the Secretary of Agriculture to convey certain lands in the Wenatchee National Forest, Wash. JACKSON, D-Wash. and MAGNUSON, D-Wash. — 8/5/77 — Senate Energy and Natural Resources reported Oct. 20, 1977 (S Rept 95-519). Senate passed Oct. 28. House Interior and Insular Affairs reported June 13, 1978 (H Rept 95-1291). House passed June 21. President signed June 30, 1978.

PL 95-311 (S 2351) — Name the new Veterans Administration hospital in Little Rock, Ark., the John L. McClellan Hospital. BUMPERS, D-Ark. — 12/8/77 — Senate passed Dec. 15, 1977. House passed, amended, June 19, 1978. Senate agreed to House amendments June 23. President signed June 30, 1978.

PL 95-312 (S J Res 128) — Request the President proclaim July 1, 1978, as Free Enterprise Day. BARTLETT, R-Okla. — 4/20/78 — Senate passed Feb. 20, 1978. House passed June 26. President signed June 30, 1978.

PL 95-313 (HR 11777) — Authorize funds through fiscal year 1988 for the Secretary of Agriculture to provide cooperative forestry assistance to states. WEAVER, D-Ore., AMMERMAN, D-Pa., AuCOIN, D-Ore., BAUCUS, D-Mont., BOWEN, D-Miss., BROWN, D-Calif., BURKE, D-Calif., BURTON, P., D-Calif., DUNCAN, D-Ore., FRASER, D-Minn., OBERSTAR, D-Minn., RICHMOND, D-N.Y. and UDALL, D-Ariz. — 3/22/78 — House Agriculture reported May 15, 1978 (H Rept 95-1183). House passed May 22. Senate passed, amended, June 7. House agreed to Senate amendments June 16. President signed July 1, 1978.

PL 95-314 (HR 12571) — Provide for the implementation of the 1978 Reciprocal Fisheries Agreement between the United States and Canada. LEGGETT, D-Calif., FORSYTHE, R-N.J., TRIBLE, R-Va. — 5/4/78 — House Merchant Marine and Fisheries reported May 24, 1978 (H Rept 95-1215). House passed May 25. Senate Foreign Relations reported June 26 (S Rept 95-955). Senate passed June 29. President signed July 1, 1978.

PL 95-315 (HR 11713) — Authorize grants to individuals and small business concerns for development of solar energy equipment and energy-related inventions. BEDELL, D-Iowa and BALDUS, D-Wis. — 3/22/78 — House Small Business reported April 19, 1978 (H Rept 95-1071). House passed May 2. Senate Small Business reported May 15 (S Rept 95-828). Senate passed, amended May 24. House agreed to Senate amendment with amendments June 16. Senate agreed to House amendments June 19. President signed July 4, 1978.

PL 95-316 (HR 10730) — Authorize funds through fiscal year 1981 to carry out programs administered under the Marine Mammal Protection Act. MURPHY, D-N.Y., LEGGET, D-Calif., RUPPE, R-Mich., BIAGGI, D-N.Y., ANDERSON, D-Calif., FORSYTHE, R-N.J., DE LA GARZA, D-Texas, METCALFE, D-Ill., BREAUX, D-La., ROONEY, D-Pa., GINN, D-Ga., STUDDS, D-Mass., BOWEN, D-Miss., McCLOSKEY, R-Calif., PRITCHARD, R-Wash., LENT, D-N.Y., DE LUGO, D-V.I., HUBBARD, D-Ky., EMERY, R-Maine, BONKER, D-Wash., AuCOIN, D-Ore., BAUMAN, R-Md., D'AMOURS, D-N.H., PATTERSON, D-N.J., ZEFERETTI, D-N.Y. and OBERSTAR, D-Minn. — 2/2/78 — House Merchant Marine and Fisheries reported March 31, 1978 (H Rept 95-1028). House passed April 10. Senate, Commerce, Science and Transportation reported May 15 (S Rept 95-888). Senate passed, amended, June 7. House agreed to Senate amendment June 28. President signed July 10, 1978.

PL 95-317 (HR 3447) — Grant an annuitant under the civil service retirement system the right to elect within one year after remarriage whether such annuitant's new spouse shall be entitled to a survivor annuity. SPELLMAN, D-Md. — 2/9/77 — House Post Office and Civil Service reported May 10, 1977 (H Rept 95-283). House passed June 6. Senate Governmental Affairs reported May 18, 1978 (S Rept 95-904). Senate passed, amended, June 19. House agreed to Senate amendment June 26. President signed July 10, 1978.

PL 95-318 (HR 3755) — Restore survivor annunities under the civil service retirement system to certain surviving spouses whose annuities were terminated because of remarriage prior to July 18, 1966. LEHMAN, D-Fla. and SPELLMAN, D-Md. — 2/22/77 — House Post Office and Civil Service reported June 30, 1977 (H Rept 95-475). House passed July 18. Senate Governmental Affairs reported May 18, 1978 (S Rept 95-905). Senate passed, amended, June 19. House agreed to Senate amendment June 26. President signed July 10, 1978.

PL 95-319 (S 2401) — Establish consumer product safety rules governing standards for flammable and corrosive cellulose insulation. FORD, D-Ky. — 1/23/78 — Senate passed Jan. 23, 1978. House passed, amended, May 16. Conference report filed in House June 28 (H Rept 95-1322). House agreed to conference report June 29. Senate agreed to conference report June 29. President signed July 11, 1978.

PL 95-320 (HR 2176) — Authorize the Comptroller General to conduct an audit of the Federal Reserve System, the Office of the Comptroller of the Currency and the Federal Deposit Insurance Corporation. ROSENTHAL, D-N.Y. — 1/19/77 — House Government Operations reported July 12, 1977 (H Rept 95-492). House passed Oct. 14. Senate Governmental Affairs reported March 23, 1978 (S Rept 95-723). Senate passed, amended, May 10. House agreed to Senate amendments June 29. President signed July 21, 1978.

PL 95-321 (HR 9757) — Place a moratorium on increases in public lands grazing fees for the 1978 grazing year pending an appropriate review of such fees. RONCALIO, D-Wyo., ARMSTRONG, R-Colo., BAUCUS, D-Mont., EVANS, D-Colo., FOLEY, D-Wash., HANSEN, R-Idaho, JOHNSON, D-Calif., JOHNSON, R-Colo., LUJAN, R-N.M., McKAY, D-Utah, MARLENEE, R-Mont., MARRIOTT, R-Utah, RISENHOOVER, D-Okla., RUDD, R-Ariz., RUNNELS, D-N.M., SANTINI, D-Nev., STUMP, D-Ariz., SYMMS, R-Idaho and ULLMAN, D-Ore. — 10/26/77 — House Interior and Insular Affairs reported Jan. 31, 1978 (H Rept 95-859). House passed Feb. 24. Senate Energy and Natural Resources reported April 25 (S Rept 95-761). Senate passed, amended, May 19. House agreed to Senate amendment with an amendment June 16. House agreed to Senate amendment to the title of the bill June 16. Senate agreed to House amendment June 29. President signed July 21, 1978.

PL 95-322 (HR 11232) — Authorize funds for fiscal years 1979-81 to carry out programs administered under the Standard Reference Data Act. TEAGUE, D-Texas — 3/1/78 — House Science and Technology reported March 16, 1978 (H Rept 95-977). House passed April 4. Senate Commerce, Science and Transportation reported May 8 (S Rept 95-786). Senate passed, amended, May 15. House agreed to Senate amendments with amendments June 28. Senate agreed to House amendments July 10. President signed July 21, 1978.

PL 95-323 (HR 3489) — Entitle the Delegates in the Congress from the District of Columbia, Guam and the Virgin Islands to make nominations for appointments to the Merchant Marine Academy. DE LUGO, D-V.I. — 2/16/77 — House Merchant Marine and Fisheries reported March 30, 1978 (H Rept 95-1012). House passed April 17. Senate Commerce, Science and Transportation reported July 10 (S Rept 95-971). Senate passed July 14. President signed July 28, 1978.

PL 95-324 (HR 4270) — Designate the federal building and U.S. courthouse in Hato Rey, Puerto Rico, the "Federico Degetau Federal Building." CORRADA, New Prog.-P.R. — 3/2/77 — House Public Works and Transportation reported May 19, 1978 (H Rept 95-1208). House passed June 5. Senate Environment and Public Works reported July 12 (S Rept 95-979). Senate passed July 14. President signed July 28, 1978.

PL 95-325 (H J Res 613) — Request the President to designate the first Sunday of September after Labor Day, 1978, as National Grandparents' Day. FLYNT, D-Ga., ADDABBO, D-N.Y., BARNARD, D-Ga., BRINKLEY, D-Ga., EVANS, D-Ga., GINN, D-Ga., JENKINS, D-Ga. and McDONALD, D-Ga. — 10/5/77 — House Post Office and Civil Service reported June 29, 1978 (H Rept 95-1327). House passed July 10. Senate passed July 14. President signed July 28, 1978.

PL 95-326 (HR 12637) — Implement Protocol of the International Convention of the High Seas Fisheries of the North Pacific Ocean. MURPHY, D-N.Y., LEGGETT, D-Calif. and FORSYTHE, R-N.J. — 5/9/78 — House Merchant Marine and Fisheries reported May 15, 1978 (H Rept 95-1194). House passed June 6. Senate passed, amended, June 14. House agreed to Senate amendments Nos. 1 through 8 and No. 11 June 28. House agreed to Senate amendments Nos. 9 and 10 with amendments June 28. Senate agreed to House amendments July 13. President signed July 28, 1978.

PL 95-327 (S 1291) — Hold in trust for the Cheyenne-Arapaho Tribes certain lands in Oklahoma. BARTLETT, R-Okla. — 4/19/77 — Senate Indian Affairs reported June 6, 1977 (S Rept 95-239). Senate passed June 9. House Interior and Insular Affairs reported June 19, 1978 (S Rept 95-1306). House passed July 17. President signed July 28, 1978.

PL 95-328 (S 1582) — Provide for the settlement of water claims of the Ak-chin Indian community. DeCONCINI, D-Ariz. — 5/23/77 — Senate Indian Affairs reported Sept. 30, 1977 (S Rept 95-460). Senate passed Oct. 11. House passed, amended, June 29, 1978. Senate agreed to House amendment July 13. President signed July 28, 1978.

PL 95-329 (S 947) — Hold in trust for the Creek Nation of Oklahoma land known as the Yardeka School land. BARTLETT, R-Okla. — 3/9/77 — Senate Indian Affairs reported June 6, 1977 (S Rept 95-238). Senate passed June 9. House Interior and Insular Affairs reported June 19, 1978 (H Rept 95-1305). House passed July 17. President signed July 28, 1978.

PL 95-330 (H J Res 1024) — Make urgent supplemental appropriations for the Agricultural Stabilization and Conservation Service of the Department of Agriculture. MAHON, D-Texas — 5/23/78 — House Appropriations reported June 28, 1978 (H Rept 95-1326). House passed July 11. Senate Appropriations reported July 19 (S Rept 95-1021). Senate passed July 24. President signed July 31, 1978.

PL 95-331 (HR 11877) — Authorize funds for fiscal year 1979 for the Peace Corps. HARRINGTON, D-Mass., WINN, R-Kan., BONKER, D-Ore., PEASE, D-Ohio, NIX, D-Pa. and GILMAN, R-N.Y. — 4/5/78 — House International Relations reported April 11, 1978 (H Rept 95-1049). House passed April 25. Senate Foreign Relations reported May 12 (S Rept 95-807). Senate passed, amended, June 8. Conference report filed in the House June 29 (H Rept 95-1333). Senate agreed to conference report June 29. House agreed to conference report July 25. President signed Aug. 2, 1978.

PL 95-332 (H J Res 945) — Make urgent supplemental appropriations for the Black Lung program, emergency rail transportation and emergency school aid. MAHON, D-Texas — 5/31/78 — House Appropriations reported June 1, 1978 (H Rept 95-1236). House passed June 9. Senate Appropriations reported June 19 (S Rept 95-937). Senate passed, amended, June 23. House agreed to Senate amendments Nos. 1 and 3 July 19. House agreed to Senate amendment No. 2 with an amendment July 19. House agreed to Senate amendment to the title of the bill July 19. Senate agreed to House amendment to Senate amendment No. 2 July 20. President signed Aug. 2, 1978.

PL 95-333 (HR 13385) — Set the public debt limit at $798 billion through March 31, 1979. ULLMAN, D-Ore. — 7/10/78 — House Ways and Means reported July 13, 1978 (H Rept 95-1349). House passed July 19. Senate Finance reported July 27 (S Rept 95-1042). Senate passed Aug. 2. President signed Aug. 3, 1978.

PL 95-334 (HR 11504) — Improve federal credit assistance programs for farmers, ranchers and rural communities and businesses. JONES, D-Tenn., FOLEY, D-Wash., SEBELIUS, R-Kan., DE LA GARZA, D-Texas, JONES, D-N.C., MATHIS, D-Ga., BROWN, D-Calif., BOWEN, D-Miss., JOHNSON, D-Colo., ROSE, D-N.C., RICHMOND, D-N.Y., NOLAN, D-Minn., WEAVER, D-Ore., BALDUS, D-Wis., JEFFORDS, R-Vt., KREBS, D-Calif., HARKIN, D-Iowa, HIGHTOWER, D-Texas, ENGLISH, D-Okla., FITHIAN, D-Ind., HAGEDORN, R-Minn., JENRETTE, D-S.C., THORNTON, D-Ark., SKELTON, D-Mo. and HUCKABY, D-La. — 3/13/78 — House Agriculture reported March 18, 1978 (H Rept 95-986). House passed April 24. Senate passed, amended, May 2. Conference report filed in House July 11 (H Rept 95-1344). House agreed to conference report July 19. Senate agreed to conference report July 20. President signed Aug. 4, 1978.

PL 95-335 (HR 12933) — Make appropriations for the Department of Transportation and related agencies for fiscal year 1979. McFALL, D-Calif. — 6/1/78 — House Appropriations reported June 1, 1978 (H Rept 95-1252). House passed June 12. Senate Appropriations reported June 19 (S Rept 95-938). Senate passed, amended, June 23. Conference report filed in the House June 29 (H Rept 95-1329). House agreed to conference report July 19. House receded and concurred in Senate amendments Nos. 27, 40 and 49 July 19. House receded and concurred with amendments in Senate amendments Nos. 14, 31, 32 and 33, July 19. Senate agreed to conference report July 20. Senate agreed to House amendments to Senate amendments Nos. 14, 31, 32 and 33 July 20. President signed Aug. 4, 1978.

PL 95-336 (HR 10569) — Authorize funds through fiscal year 1981 for programs administered under the Alcohol and Drug Abuse Education Act. BRADEMAS, D-Ind., JEFFORDS, R-Vt., PERKINS, D-Ky., QUIE, R-Minn., BEARD, D-R.I., PRESSLER, R-S.D., MILLER, D-Calif., KILDEE, D-Mich., HEFTEL, D-Hawaii, HAWKINS, D-Calif. and BIAGGI, D-N.Y. — 1/25/78 — House Education and Labor reported Feb. 16, 1978 (H Rept 95-884). House passed Feb. 21. Senate Human Resources reported May 15 (S Rept 95-821). Senate passed, amended, May 23. House agreed to Senate amendment July 24. House passed Aug. 4, 1978.

PL 95-337 (S 785) — Declare that certain land be held in trust for the Paiute and Shoshone Tribes of the Fallon Indian Reservation, Nevada. CANNON, D-Nev. and LAXALT, R-Nev. — 2/24/77 — Senate Indian Affairs reported Sept. 9, 1977 (S Rept 95-417). Senate passed Oct. 17. House Interior and Insular Affairs reported June 15, 1978 (H Rept 95-1298). House passed, amended, July 17. Senate agreed to House amendments July 21. President signed Aug. 4, 1978.

PL 95-338 (HR 11832) — Authorize $18.4 million for fiscal year 1979 for the Arms Control and Disarmament Agency. ZABLOCKI, D-Wis., FOUNTAIN, D-N.C., BINGHAM, D-N.Y., STUDDS, D-Mass., BEILENSON, D-Calif., BROOMFIELD, R-Mich. and WINN, R-Kan. — 4/3/78 — House International Relations reported April 11, 1978 (H Rept 95-1048). House passed April 26. Senate Foreign Relations reported May 15 (S Rept 95-843). Senate passed, amended, June 8. House agreed to Senate amendments Nos. 2 through 6 June 16. House agreed to Senate amendment No. 1 with an amendment June 16. House agreed to Senate amendment to title of bill June 16. Senate agreed to House amendment No. 1 July 27. President signed Aug. 8, 1978.

PL 95-339 (HR 12426) — Authorize funds for long-term loan guarantees for New York City. MOORHEAD, D-Pa., ASHLEY, D-Ohio, BARNARD, D-Ga., CAPUTO, R-N.Y., FAUNTROY, D-D.C., GARCIA, D-N.Y., GREEN, R-N.Y., LaFALCE, D-N.Y., LUNDINE, D-N.Y., McKINNEY, R-Conn., PATTISON, D-N.J., REUSS, D-Wis. and VENTO, D-Minn. — 4/27/78 — House Banking, Finance and Urban Affairs reported Part I May 10, 1978 (H Rept 95-1129). House Ways and Means reported Part II May 22. House passed June 8. Senate Banking, Housing and Urban Affairs reported June 23 (S Rept 95-952). Senate passed, amended, June 29. Conference report filed in House July 18 (H Rept 95-1369). House agreed to conference report July 25. Senate agreed to conference report July 27. President signed Aug. 8, 1978.

PL 95-340 (HR 12138) — Name the federal building located at 2400 Avila Road, Laguna Niguel, Calif., the "Chet Holifield Building." JOHNSON, D-Calif. — 4/13/78 — House Public Works and Transportation reported May 19, 1978 (H Rept 95-1210). House passed June 5. Senate Environment and Public Works reported July 25 (S Rept 95-1038). Senate passed July 28. President signed Aug. 11, 1978.

PL 95-341 (S J Res 102) — Re-evaluate U.S. policy to protect and preserve American Indian religious cultural rites and practices. ABOUREZK,

D-S.D., HUMPHREY, D-Minn., KENNEDY, D-Mass., INOUYE, D-Hawaii, MATSUNAGA, D-Hawaii, HATFIELD, R-Ore., STEVENS, R-Alaska, GRAVEL, D-Alaska and GOLDWATER, R-Ariz. — 12/15/77 — Senate Indian Affairs reported March 21, 1978 (S Rept 95-709). Senate passed April 3. House passed, amended, July 18. Senate agreed to House amendment July 27. President signed August 11, 1978.

PL 95-342 (S 920) — Allow oil and gas leases within the Lake Murray Recreational Demonstration Area project, Okla. BARTLETT, R-Okla. — 3/4/77 — Senate Energy and Natural Resources reported Oct. 20, 1977 (S Rept 95-523). Senate passed Oct. 28. House passed, amended, May 15, 1978. Senate agreed to House amendment with an amendment July 21. House agreed to Senate amendment July 28. President signed Aug. 11, 1978.

PL 95-343 (S 2463) — Authorize funds to implement the Federal Surface Mining Control and Reclamation Act. JACKSON, D-Wash. — 1/31/78 — Senate Energy and Natural Resources reported May 9, 1978 (S Rept 95-788). Senate passed May 16. House passed, amended, July 11. Senate agreed to House amendment July 28. President signed Aug. 11, 1978.

PL 95-344 (HR 8336) — Establish the Chattahoochee River National Recreation Area in Georgia. LEVITAS, D-Ga., UDALL, D-Ariz., BURTON, P., D-Calif., MATHIS, D-Ga., BRINKLEY, D-Ga., GINN, D-Ga., BARNARD, D-Ga., EVANS, D-Ga., FOWLER, D-Ga., SEIBERLING, D-Ohio, DE LUGO, D-V.I., WON PAT, D-Guam, SANTINI, D-Nev., CORRADA, New Prog-P.R., LAGOMARSINO, R-Calif., CARR, D-Mich. and MILLER D-Calif. — 7/14/77 — House Interior and Insular Affairs reported Sept. 8, 1977 (H Rept 95-598). House passed Feb. 14, 1978. Senate Energy and Natural Resources reported May 12 (S Rept 95-812). Senate passed, amended, July 21. House agreed to Senate amendments with an amendment July 31. Senate agreed to House amendment Aug. 3. President signed Aug. 15, 1978.

PL 95-345 (HR 7581) — Clarify the income source requirement which must be satisfied by a mutual or cooperative telephone company as a condition for exemption from federal income taxation. HOLLAND, D-S.C., — 6/2/78 — House Ways and Means reported Oct. 25, 1977 (H Rept 95-742). House passed Jan. 24, 1978. Senate Finance reported April 25 (S Rept 95-762). Senate passed, amended, April 27. House agreed to Senate amendments with amendments June 14. Senate agreed to House amendments Aug. 2. President signed Aug. 15, 1978.

PL 95-346 (S 2424) — Amend the act incorporating the American Legion so as to redefine eligibility for membership therein. BAYH, D-Ind., CRANSTON, D-Calif., THURMOND, R-S.C. and ABOUREZK, D-S.D. — 1/25/78 — Senate Judiciary reported April 6, 1978 (S Rept 95-726). Senate passed April 11. House Judiciary reported Aug. 2 (S Rept 95-1416). House passed Aug. 7. President Aug. 17, 1978.

PL 95-347 (H J Res 946) — Request the president to proclaim October 7, 1978, as "National Guard Day." BROWN, R-Ohio — 5/31/78 — House Post Office and Civil Service reported July 18, 1978 (H Rept 95-1372). House passed July 24. Senate Judiciary reported Aug. 10 (S Rept 95-1102). Senate passed Aug. 11. President signed Aug. 18, 1978.

PL 95-348 (S 2821) — Authorize $8.8 million for grants to the government of Guam for construction of public facilities. JACKSON, D-Wash. — 4/4/78 — Senate Energy and Natural Resources reported May 5, 1978 (S Rept 95-784). Senate passed May 10. House passed, amended, June 5. Senate agreed to House amendments with an amendment Aug. 3. House agreed to Senate amendment Aug. 4. President signed Aug. 18, 1978.

PL 95-349 (H J Res 963) — Request the president to proclaim July 18, 1979, as "National POW-MIA Recognition Day." MOORHEAD, D-Pa. — 6/7/78 — House Post Office and Civil Service reported July 19, 1978 (H Rept 95-1377). House passed Aug. 1. Senate Judiciary reported Aug. 10 (S Rept 95-1099). Senate passed Aug. 11. President signed Aug. 18, 1978.

PL 95-350 (H J Res 682) — Request the president to proclaim the week of Sept. 17, 1978, as "National Lupus Week." ANDERSON, D-Calif. — 1/19/78 — House Post Office and Civil Service reported July 18, 1978 (H Rept 95-1370). House passed July 24. Senate Judiciary reported Aug. 10 (S Rept 95-1101). Senate passed Aug. 11. President signed Aug. 18, 1978.

PL 95-351 (HR 2777) — Establish a National Consumer Cooperative Bank to make loan guarantees to eligible consumer cooperatives. ST GERMAIN, D-R.I., REUSS, D-Wis. and WYLIE, R-Ohio — 2/1/77 — House Banking, Finance and Urban Affairs reported May 13, 1977 (H Rept 95-311) House passed July 14. Senate Banking, Housing and Urban Affairs reported May 10, 1978 (S Rept 95-795). Senate passed, amended, July 13. Senate agreed to conference report July 27. Conference report filed in House July 28 (H Rept 95-1399). House agreed to conference report Aug. 9. President signed Aug. 20, 1978.

PL 95-352 (HR 10787) — Authorize funds for the Bureau of Land Management through fiscal year 1982. UDALL, D-Ariz. and RONCALIO, D-Wyo. — 2/6/78 — House Interior and Insular Affairs reported May 10, 1978 (H Rept 95-1121). House passed July 11. Senate passed, amended, July 27. House agreed to Senate amendment with an amendment Aug. 2. Senate agreed to House amendment Aug. 8. President signed Aug. 20, 1978.

PL 95-353 (HR 11579) — Designate the Olin E. Teague Veterans' Center, Temple, Texas; the James A. Haley Veterans' Hospital, Tampa; the Edith Nourse Rogers Memorial Veterans' Hospital, Bedford, Mass.; and the William Jennings Bryan Dorn Veterans' Hospital, Columbia, S.C. ROBERTS, D-Texas, MAHON, D-Texas, POAGE, D-Texas, BURLESON, D-Texas, BROOKS, D-Texas, WRIGHT, D-Texas, YOUNG, D-Texas, GONZALEZ, D-Texas, PICKLE, D-Texas, DE LA GARZA, D-Texas, WHITE, D-Texas, COLLINS, R-Texas, ECKHARDT, D-Texas, KAZEN, D-Texas, ARCHER, R-Texas, JORDAN, D-Texas, MILFORD, D-Texas, WILSON, D-Texas, HALL, D-Texas, HIGHTOWER, D-Texas, KRUEGER, D-Texas, GAMMAGE, D-Texas and MATTOX, D-Texas — 3/15/78 — House Veterans' Affairs reported Aug. 2, 1978 (H Rept 95-1411). House passed Aug. 7. Senate passed, amended, Aug. 11. House agreed to Senate amendments Aug. 15. President signed Aug. 28, 1978.

PL 95-354 (HR 10732) — Authorize funds for fiscal year 1979 to carry out programs administered under the Fishery Conservation and Management Act. MURPHY, D-N.Y., LEGGETT, D-Calif., FORSYTHE, R-N.J., BIAGGI, D-N.Y., METCALFE, D-Ill., McCLOSKEY, R-Calif., BREAUX, D-La., GINN, D-Ga., PRITCHARD, R-Wash., STUDDS, D-Mass., BOWEN, D-Miss., YOUNG, R-Alaska, DE LUGO, D-V.I., HUBBARD, D-Ky., LENT, D-N.Y., BONKER, D-Wash., AuCOIN, D-Ore., EMERY, R-Maine, D'AMOURS, D-N.H., PATTERSON, D-Calif., DORNAN, R-Calif., ZEFERETTI, D-N.Y., OBERSTAR, D-Minn., BAUMAN, R-Md. and HUGHES, D-N.J. — 2/2/78 — House Merchant Marine and Fisheries reported March 31, 1978 (H Rept 95-1024). House passed April 10. Senate Commerce, Science and Transportation reported May 12 (S Rept 95-815). Senate passed, amended, June 14. House agreed to Senate amendments with an amendment July 11. Senate agreed to House amendment with an amendment Aug. 4. House agreed to Senate amendment Aug. 10. President signed Aug. 28, 1978.

PL 95-355 (HR 13467) — Make supplemental appropriations for fiscal year 1978. MAHON, D-Texas — 7/13/78 — House Appropriations reported July 13, 1978 (H Rept 95-1350). House passed July 20. Senate Appropriations reported Aug. 1 (S Rept 95-1061). Senate passed, amended, Aug. 7. Conference report filed in House Aug. 10 (H Rept 95-1475). House agreed to conference report Aug. 17. House receded and concurred in Senate amendments Nos. 9, 15, 32 through 43, 44, 47, 49, 52, 53, 58, 64, 70, 79 and 83 Aug. 17. House receded and concurred with amendments in Senate amendments Nos. 18, 29, 51, and 62 Aug. 17. House insisted on its disagreement to Senate amendments Nos. 48 and 82 Aug. 17. Senate agreed to conference report Aug. 25. Senate receded from its amendments Nos. 48 and 82 Aug. 25. Senate agreed to House amendments to Senate amendments Nos. 18, 29, 51 and 62 Aug. 25. President signed Sept. 8, 1978.

PL 95-356 (HR 12602) — Authorize funds for military construction for fiscal year 1979. NEDZI, D-Mich. and WHITEHURST, R-Va. — 5/8/78 — House Armed Services reported May 12, 1978 (H Rept 95-1147). House passed May 22. Senate passed, amended, July 12. Conference report filed in House Aug. 7 (H Rept 95-1448). House agreed to conference report Aug. 16. Senate agreed to conference report Aug. 17. President signed Sept. 8, 1978.

PL 95-357 (HR 3532) — Authorize the Secretary of the Navy to change the name of the Naval Observatory publication "The American Ephemeris and Nautical Almanac" to the "Astronomical Ephemeris." PRICE, D-Ill. and WILSON, R-Calif. — 2/16/77 — House Armed Services reported July 19, 1978 (H Rept 95-1379). House passed Aug. 7. Senate Armed Services reported Aug. 22 (S Rept 95-1134). Senate passed Aug. 24. President signed Sept. 8, 1978.

PL 95-358 (HR 7161) — Authorize the establishment of a Junior Reserve Officers' Training Corps in America Samoa. WHITE, D-Texas — 5/12/77 — House Armed Services reported July 25, 1978 (H Rept 95-1390). House passed Aug. 7. Senate Armed Services reported Aug. 22 (S Rept 95-1135). Senate passed Aug. 25. President signed Sept. 8, 1978.

PL 95-359 (HR 8471) — Provide for the exhibition at the Wyoming State Museum of the nameplate, the ship's bell, and the silver service of the battleship U.S.S. Wyoming. RONCALIO, D-Wyo. — 7/21/77 — House Armed Services reported July 19, 1978 (H Rept 95-1380). House passed Aug. 7. Senate Armed Services reported Aug. 22 (S Rept 95-1136). Senate passed Aug. 25. President signed Sept. 8, 1978.

PL 95-360 (S 2543) — Amend Title 29 of the U.S. Code to provide better enforcement procedures for preventing fraudulent solicitations through the mails. GLENN, D-Ohio and SASSER, D-Tenn. — 2/10/78 — Senate Governmental Affairs reported Aug. 9, 1978 (S Rept 95-1077). Senate passed Aug. 14. House passed Aug. 17. President signed Sept. 9, 1978.

PL 95-361 (HR 8397) — Declare certain lands in Arizona a part of the Papago Indian Reservation. UDALL, D-Ariz. — 7/18/77 — House Interior and Insular Affairs reported March 30, 1978 (H Rept 95-1020). House passed April 17. Senate Indian Affairs reported Aug. 22 (S Rept 95-1133). Senate passed Aug. 25. President signed Sept. 10, 1978.

PL 95-362 (HR 185) — Authorize the Secretary of the Department in which the Coast Guard is operating to transport Coast Guard employees to and from certain places of employment. BIAGGI, D-N.Y. — 1/4/77 — House Merchant Marine and Fisheries reported June 1, 1978 (H Rept 95-1237). House passed June 5. Senate Commerce, Science and Transportation reported Aug. 17 (S Rept 95-1122). Senate passed Aug. 21. President signed Sept. 11, 1978.

PL 95-363 (HR 12106) — Authorize funds for the National Transportation Safety Board for fiscal year 1979. ANDERSON, D-Calif. and SNYDER, R-Ky. — 4/13/78 — House Public Works and Transportation reported Part I May 15, 1978 (H Rept 95-1169). House passed July 10. Senate passed, amended, Aug. 14. House agreed to Senate amendment Aug. 17. President signed Sept. 11, 1978.

PL 95-364 (H J Res 773) — Request the President to proclaim the seven calendar days beginning Sept. 17, 1978, as "National Port Week." MURPHY, D-N.Y. — 3/1/78 — House Post Office and Civil Service reported June 29, 1978 (H Rept 95-1328). House passed July 10. Senate Judiciary reported Aug. 24 (S Rept 95-1150). Senate passed Aug. 25. President signed Sept. 15, 1978.

PL 95-365 (HR 8342) — Extend application of law relating to the withholding of city or county income or employment taxes to federal employees who are residents of (but are employed outside of) cities or counties with which the secretary of the treasury has entered into tax withholding agreement. CLAY, D-Mo., FORD, D-Mich., HARRIS, D-Va., LOTT, R-Miss., SOLARZ, D-N.Y., TAYLOR, R-Mo., UDALL, D-Ariz., and WILSON, D-Calif. — 7/15/78 — House Post Office and Civil Service reported Sept. 7, 1978 (H Rept 95-594). House passed Sept. 19. Senate Governmental Affairs reported Aug. 10 (S Rept 95-1083). Senate passed Aug. 18. President signed Sept. 15, 1978.

PL 95-366 (HR 8771) — Authorize the Civil Service Commission to comply with the terms of a court order or property settlement in connection with the divorce, annulment, or legal separation of a federal employee who is entitled to civil service retirement annuities. SPELLMAN, D-Md., HEFTEL, D-Hawaii, FORD, D-Mich., HARRIS, D-Va., HOWARD, D-N.J., LEACH, R-Iowa, and ROUSSELOT, R-Calif. — 8/4/77 — House Post Office and Civil Service reported Oct. 17, 1977 (H Rept 95-713). House passed Jan. 23, 1978. Senate Governmental Affairs reported Aug. 10 (S Rept 95-1084). Senate passed Aug. 16. President signed Sept. 15, 1978.

PL 95-367 (HR 6669) — Establish a national climate program. BROWN, D-Calif., TEAGUE, D-Texas, WINN, R-Kan., AMBRO, D-N.Y., WIRTH, D-Colo., WALKER, D-Pa., LUJAN, R-N.M., SCHEUER, D-N.Y., WATKINS, D-Okla., WALGREN, D-Pa., BEILENSON, D-Calif., BROWN, R-Ohio, BLANCHARD, D-Mich., BURGENER, R-Calif., EDWARDS, D-Calif., FREY, R-Fla., FUQUA, D-Fla., HARKIN, D-Iowa, JEFFORDS, R-Vt., McCORMACK, D-Wash., Mikulski, D-Md., MILFORD, D-Texas, OBERSTAR, D-Minn., PATTEN, D-N.J., and PATTERSON, D-Calif. — 4/27/77 — House Science and Technology reported May 6, 1977 (H Rept 95-206). House passed Sept. 9. Senate Commerce, Science and Transportation reported April 18 (S Rept 95-740). Senate passed, amended, April 24. Conference report filed in House Aug. 14 (H Rept 95-1489). Senate agreed to conference report Aug. 17. House agreed to conference report Sept. 6. President signed Sept. 17, 1978.

PL 95-368 (HR 2931) — Establish uniformity in benefits and coverage under federal employees' health benefits programs. SPELLMAN, D-Md. — 2/1/77 — House Post Office and Civil Service reported May 10, 1977 (H Rept 95-282). House passed June 20. Senate Governmental Affairs reported May 18, 1978 (S Rept 95-903). Senate passed, amended, June 5. House agreed to Senate amendments Nos. 1 and 2 Aug. 10. House agreed to Senate amendments Nos. 3 and 4 with amendments Aug. 10. House agreed to Senate amendment to title of bill with an amendment Aug. 10. Senate agreed to House amendments Aug. 25. President signed Sept. 17, 1978.

PL 95-369 (HR 10899) — Provide for federal regulation of participation by foreign banks in domestic financial markets. ST GERMAIN, D-R.I. — 2/9/78 — House Banking, Finance and Urban Affairs reported Feb. 28, 1978 (H Rept 95-910). House passed April 6. Senate Banking, Housing and Urban Affairs reported Aug. 8 (S Rept 95-1073). Senate passed, amended, Aug. 15. House agreed to Senate amendment Aug. 17. President signed Sept. 17, 1978.

PL 95-370 (HR 12240) — Authorize funds for fiscal year 1979 for government intelligence activities. BOLAND, D-Mass. — 4/19/78 — House Intelligence reported Part I April 20, 1978 (H Rept 95-1075). House Armed Service reported Part II May 9. House passed June 6. Senate passed, amended, July 20. Conference report filed in House Aug. 2 (H Rept 95-1420). House agreed to conference report Aug. 17. Senate agreed to conference report Aug. 22. President signed Sept. 17, 1978.

PL 95-371 (H J Res 1014) — Designate April 28 and 29, 1979, as "Days of Remembrance of Victims of the Holocaust." WRIGHT, D-Texas, RHODES, R-Ariz., ROSENTHAL, D-N.Y., and VANDER JAGT, R-Mich. — 6/22/78 — House passed Aug. 17, 1978. Senate passed Aug. 25. President signed Sept. 18, 1978.

PL 95-372 (S 9) — Establish a policy for the management of oil and natural gas in the Outer Continental Shelf. JACKSON, D-Wash., and METCALFE, D-Mont. — 1/10/77 — Senate Energy and Natural Resources reported June 21, 1977 (S Rept 95-284). Senate passed July 15. House passed, amended, Feb. 2, 1978. Conference report filed in House Aug. 10 (H Rept 95-1474). Conference report filed in Senate Aug. 10 (S Rept 95-1091). House agreed to conference report Aug. 17. Senate agreed to conference report Aug. 22. President signed Sept. 18, 1978.

PL 95-373 (HR 13468) — Make appropriations for the District of Columbia for fiscal year 1979. NATCHER, D-Ky. — 7/13/78 — House Appropriations reported July 13, 1978 (H Rept 95-1351). House passed July 21. Senate Appropriations reported Aug. 9 (S Rept 95-1076). Senate passed, amended, Aug. 14. Conference report filed in House Aug. 16 (H Rept 95-1500). House agreed to conference report Aug. 17. House receded and concurred in Senate amendments Nos. 2, 4, 6, 11, 13, 18, 21, 25, 29, 30, 31 and 32 Aug. 17. House receded and concurred with amendments in Senate amendments Nos. 1, 5, 19, 20 and 33 Aug. 17. Senate agreed to conference report Aug. 17. Senate agreed to House amendments to Senate amendments Nos. 1, 5, 19, 20 and 33 Aug. 17. President signed Sept. 18, 1978.

PL 95-374 (HR 12927) — Make appropriations for military construction for fiscal year 1979. McKAY, D-Utah — 6/1/78 — House Appropriations reported June 1, 1978 (H Rept 95-1246). House passed June 16. Senate Appropriations reported July 19 (S Rept 95-1019). Senate passed, amended, Aug. 3. Conference report filed in House Aug. 15 (H Rept 95-1495). House agreed to conference report Aug. 17. House receded and concurred in Senate amendment No. 21 Aug. 17. House receded and concurred in Senate amendments Nos. 3, 5, 7, 8, 9, 15, 17 and 20 Aug. 21. Senate agreed to House amendments to Senate amendments Nos. 3, 5, 7, 8, 9, 15, 17 and 20 Aug. 21. President signed Sept. 18, 1978.

PL 95-375 (S 1633) — Extend certain federal benefits, services and assistance to the Pascua Yaqui Indians of Arizona. DECONCINI, D-Ariz. and ABOUREZK, D-S.D. — 6/7/78 — Senate Indian Affairs reported March 22, 1978 (S Rept 95-719). Senate passed April 5. House passed, amended, April 17. Conference report filed in House July 11 (H Rept 95-1339). House agreed to conference report Aug. 16. Senate agreed to conference report Aug. 25. President signed Sept. 18, 1978.

PL 95-376 (HR 10878) — Extend until Oct. 1, 1981, the voluntary insurance program provided by the Fishermen's Protective Act. MURPHY, D-N.Y., LEGGETT, D-Calif., FORSYTHE, R-N.J., ROGERS, D-Fla., BOWEN, D-Miss., TRIBLE, R-Va., HUBBARD, D-Ky., HUGHES, D-N.J., and DORNAN, R-Calif. — 2/9/78 — House Merchant Marines and Fisheries reported March 31, 1978 (H Rept 95-1029). House passed April 10. Senate Commerce, Science and Transportation reported May 12 (S Rept 95-816). Senate passed, amended, May 22. House agreed to Senate amendments with amendments Aug. 10. Senate agreed to House amendments with amendments Aug. 17. House agreed to Senate amendments Aug. 17. President signed Sept. 18, 1978.

PL 95-377 (S 3454) — Extend for one year authorized numbers for the grades of Lieutenant Colonel and Colonel in the Air Force and to extend certain other current military practices. NUNN, D-Ga. — 8/23/78 — Senate Armed Services reported Aug. 23, 1978 (S Rept 95-1144). Senate passed Sept. 7. House passed Sept. 12. President signed Sept. 19, 1978.

PL 95-378 (HR 8112) — Abolish the Federal Records Council. PREYER, D-N.C. — 6/29/77 — House Government Operations reported Aug. 1, 1978 (H Rept 95-1407). House passed Aug. 7. Senate Governmental Affairs reported Aug. 25 (S Rept 95-1160). Senate passed Sept. 11. President signed Sept. 22, 1978.

PL 95-379 (HR 12915) — Modify the membership of the National Archives Trust Fund by replacing congressional members with executive branch officials. BROOKS, D-Texas — 6/1/78 — House Government Operations reported Aug. 1, 1978 (H Rept 95-1408). House passed Aug. 7. Senate Governmental Affairs reported Aug. 25 (S Rept 95-1161). Senate passed Sept. 11. President signed Sept. 22, 1978.

PL 95-380 (HR 13087) — Authorize the issuance of substitute Treasury checks without undertakings of indemnity, except as the Secretary of the Treasury may require. REUSS, D-Wis., MITCHELL, D-Md., ANNUNZIO, D-Ill., LaFALCE, D-N.Y., D'AMOURS, D-N.H., LUNDINE, D-N.Y., VENTO, D-Minn., STANTON, R-Ohio, BROWN, R-Mich., WYLIE, R-Ohio, HANSEN, R-Idaho, HYDE, R-Ill., EVANS, R-Del. and HOLLENBECK, R-N.J. — 6/12/78 — House

Banking, Finance and Urban Affairs reported June 23, 1978 (H Rept 95-1320). House passed July 10. Senate Governmental Affairs reported Sept. 6 (S Rept 95-1176). Senate passed Sept. 12. President signed Sept. 22, 1978.

PL 95-381 (S 2928) — Authorize funds through fiscal years 1981 for programs administered under the International Investment Survey Act for collection and dissemination of information on foreign investments in the U.S. and American investments overseas. INOUYE, D-Hawaii — 4/17/78 — Senate Commerce, Science and Transportation reported May 15, 1978 (S Rept 95-863). Senate passed May 22. House passed, amended, June 28. Senate agreed to House amendments Sept. 7. President signed Sept. 22, 1978.

PL 95-382 (HR 9471) — Provide that Japanese-Americans be allowed civil service retirement credit for time spent in World War II internment camps. MINETTA, D-Calif., NIX, D-Pa., SPELLMAN, D-Md., UDALL, D-Ariz., WILSON, D-Calif., FORD, D-Mich., LEHMAN, D-N.Y., HARRIS, D-Va., SOLARZ, D-N.Y., HEFTEL, D-Hawaii, HOWARD, D-N.J., RYAN, D-Calif., LEACH, R-Iowa, ROUSSELOT, R-Calif. and GILMAN, R-N.Y. — 10/6/77 — House Post Office and Civil Service reported Nov. 1, 1977 (H Rept 95-789). House passed Jan. 23, 1978. Senate Governmental Affairs reported Aug. 10, 1978 (S Rept 95-1085). Senate passed, amended, Aug. 18. House agreed to Senate amendment Sept. 11. President signed Sept. 22, 1979.

PL 95-383 (S 3107) — Provide for uniform supervision and control of employees of referees in bankruptcy. DeCONCINI, D-Ariz. — 5/19/78 — Senate Judiciary reported July 13, 1978 (S Rept 95-984). Senate passed July 19. House passed Sept. 8. President signed Sept. 22, 1978.

PL 95-384 (S 3075) — Authorize funds for international security assistance programs for fiscal year 1979. SPARKMAN, D-Ala. — 5/15/78 — Senate Foreign Relations reported May 15, 1978 (S Rept 95-841). Senate passed July 26. House passed, amended, Aug. 2. Conference report filed in House Sept. 7 (H Rept 95-1546). Senate agreed to conference report Sept. 11. House agreed to conference report Sept. 12. President signed Sept. 26, 1978.

PL 95-385 (S 3119) — Transfer certain real property of the United States to the District of Columbia Redevelopment Land Agency. EAGLETON, D-Mo. — 5/19/78 — Senate Governmental Affairs reported July 31, 1978 (S Rept 95-1050). Senate passed Aug. 4. House passed Sept. 12. President signed Sept. 26, 1978.

PL 95-386 (S 3120) — Give the Temporary Commission on Financial Oversight greater flexibility of contractual authority so as to facilitate an audit of the District of Columbia government. EAGLETON, D-Mo. — 5/19/78 — Senate Governmental Affairs reported July 31, 1978 (S Rept 95-1051). Senate passed Aug. 4. House District of Columbia reported Aug. 17 (H Rept 95-1504). House passed Sept. 12. President signed Sept. 26, 1978.

PL 95-387 (S 1103) — Allow several states to sue for taxes in D.C. Superior Court. EAGLETON, D-Mo. — 3/23/77 — Senate Governmental Affairs reported May 23, 1977 (S Rept 95-228). Senate passed May 26. House District of Columbia reported July 18, 1978 (H Rept 95-1366). House passed, amended, Sept. 12. Senate agreed to House amendments Sept. 13. President signed Sept. 27, 1978.

PL 95-388 (S 2556) — Change the name of the District of Columbia Bail Agency to the District of Columbia Pretrial Service Agency. EAGLETON, D-Mo. — 2/22/78 — Senate Governmental Affairs reported May 16, 1978 (S Rept 95-895). Senate passed May 26. House District of Columbia reported July 18 (H Rept 95-1368). House passed, amended, Sept. 12. Senate agreed to House amendments Sept. 13. President signed Sept. 27, 1978.

PL 95-389 (S J Res 133) — Authorize the President to proclaim Sept. 24, 1978, as "National Good Neighbors Day." HATFIELD, D-Mont. — 5/3/78 — Senate Judiciary reported June 22, 1978 (S Rept 95-942). Senate passed June 23. House passed Sept. 20. President signed Sept. 29, 1978.

PL 95-390 (HR 7814) — Authorize federal employees and agencies to experiment with flexible and compressed work schedules. SOLARZ, D-N.Y., BAUCUS, D-Mont., DOWNEY, D-N.Y., DRINAN, D-Mass., EDWARDS, D-Calif., FENWICK, R-N.J., FRENZEL, R-Minn., GEPHARDT, D-Mo., HAWKINS, D-Calif., HUGHES, D-N.J., MEYNER, D-N.J., RYAN, D-Calif., SCHEUER, D-N.Y., SIMON, D-Ill., STEERS, R-Md., WAXMAN, D-Calif., WEISS, D-N.Y. and WIRTH, D-Colo. — 6/15/78 — House Post Office and Civil Service reported Feb. 28, 1978 (H Rept 95-912). House passed May 25. Senate Governmental Affairs reported Aug. 24 (no written report). Senate passed Sept. 15. President signed Sept. 29, 1978.

PL 95-391 (HR 12935) — Make appropriations for the Legislative Branch for fiscal year 1979. SHIPLEY, D-Ill. — 6/1/78 — House Appropriations reported June 1, 1978 (H Rept 95-1254). House passed June 14. Senate Appropriations reported July 19 (S Rept 95-1024). Senate passed, amended, Aug. 7. Conference report filed in House Aug. 9 (H Rept 95-1457). House agreed to conference report Aug. 17. House receded and concurred in Senate amendments Nos. 1 through 39, 45, 46, 47 and 52 Aug. 17. Senate agreed to conference report Sept. 19. President signed Sept. 30, 1978.

PL 95-392 (HR 12936) — Make appropriations for the Department of Housing and Urban Development and certain independent agencies for fiscal year 1979. BOLAND, D-Mass. — 6/1/78 — House Appropriations reported June 1, 1978 (H Rept 95-1255). House passed June 19. Senate Appropriations reported Aug. 1 (S Rept 95-1060). Senate passed, amended, Aug. 7. Conference report filed in House Sept. 13 (H Rept 95-1569). House agreed to conference report Sept. 19. House receded and concurred with amendments in Senate amendments Nos. 8, 47 and 48 Sept. 19. House receded and concurred with amendments in Senate amendments Nos. 6, 9, 32, and 42 Sept. 19. Senate agreed to conference report Sept. 20. Senate agreed to House amendments to Senate amendments Nos. 6, 9, 32 and 42 Sept. 20. President signed Sept. 30, 1978.

PL 95-393 (HR 7819) — Complement the Vienna Convention on Diplomatic Relations so that the diplomatic community understands clearly that its members are expected to obey the laws and regulations of the United States and local jurisdictions. FASCELL, D-Fla., DIGGS, D-Mich., BUCHANAN, R-Ala., FISHER, D-Va., WOLFF, D-N.Y., RYAN, D-Calif., MEYNER, D-N.J. and SOLARZ, D-N.Y. — 6/16/77 — House International Relations reported July 25, 1977 (H Rept 95-526). House passed July 27. Senate Foreign Relations reported June 26, 1978 (S Rept 95-958). Senate Judiciary reported Aug. 11 (S Rept 95-1108). Senate passed, amended, Aug. 17. House agreed to Senate amendments Sept. 18. President signed Sept. 30, 1978.

PL 95-394 (HR 12772) — Facilitate the exchange of certain lands in Oregon. AuCOIN — 5/17/78 — House Interior and Insular Affairs reported Aug. 8, 1978 (H Rept 95-1455). House passed Aug. 15. Senate passed Sept. 15. President signed Sept. 30, 1978.

PL 95-395 (HR 12860) — Provide for the settlement of Indian claims in Rhode Island and Providence Plantations. BEARD, D-R.I., and ST GERMAIN, D-R.I. — 5/25/78 — House Interior and Insular Affairs reported Aug. 8, 1978 (H Rept 95-1453). House passed Sept. 12. Senate passed Sept. 15. President signed Sept. 30, 1978.

PL 95-396 (S 1678) — Amend and extend for two years through fiscal year 1979 the Federal Insecticide, Fungicide, and Rodenticide Act. LEAHY, D-Vt. — 6/10/77 — Senate Agriculture, Nutrition and Forestry reported July 6, 1977 (S Rept 95-334). Senate passed July 29. House passed, amended, Oct. 31. Conference report filed in House Sept. 12, 1978 (H Rept 95-1560). Conference report filed in Senate Sept. 12 (S Rept 95-1188). Senate agreed to conference report Sept. 18. House agreed to conference report Sept. 19. President signed Sept. 30, 1978.

PL 95-397 (HR 3702) — Make certain changes in the Retired Serviceman's Family Protection Plan and the Survivor Benefit Plan. STRATTON, D-N.Y., and WILSON, D-Calif. — 2/17/77 — House Armed Services reported March 14, 1977 (H Rept 95-72). House passed Sept. 12. Senate Armed Services Reported Aug. 22, 1978 (S Rept 95-1138). Senate passed, amended, Aug. 24. House agreed to Senate amendment with an amendment Sept. 19. Senate agreed to House amendment Sept. 22. President signed Sept. 30, 1978.

PL 95-398 (S 3069) — Provide that the Siseton-Wahpeton Sioux Tribe shall have a preference right to purchase certain North and South Dakota lands held in trust by the United States for tribal members. ABOUREZK, D-S.D., and McGOVERN, D-S.D. — 5/15/78 — Senate Indian Affairs reported July 13, 1978 (S Rept 95-983). Senate passed July 21. House passed Sept. 18. President signed Sept. 30, 1978.

PL 95-399 (S 3002) — Modify a portion of the south boundary of the Salt River Pima-Maricopa Indian Reservation in Arizona. GOLDWATER, R-Ariz. — 4/27/78 — Senate Indian Affairs reported Aug. 25 (S Rept 95-1170). Senate passed Sept. 11. House passed Sept. 19. President signed Sept. 30, 1978.

PL 95-400 (S 3271) — Extend the time for reporting to the Congress on pilot projects involving public service work for food stamps. TALMADGE, D-Ga. — 7/10/78 — Senate Agriculture, Nutrition and Forestry reported July 31, 1978 (S Rept 95-1053). Senate passed Aug. 4. House passed Sept. 19. President signed Sept. 30, 1978.

PL 95-401 (HR 11401) — Authorize funds for fiscal year 1979 for the National Aeronautics and Space Administration. TEAGUE, D-Texas, FUQUA, D-Fla., FLOWERS, D-Ala., BROWN, D-Calif., MILFORD, D-Texas, HARKIN, D-Iowa, LLOYD, D-Calif., AMBRO, D-N.J., KRUEGER, D-Texas, LLOYD, D-Tenn., WIRTH, D-Colo., DOWNEY, D-N.Y., WALGREN, D-Pa., FLIPPO, D-Ala., GLICKMAN, D-Kan., GAMMAGE, D-Texas, BEILENSON, D-Calif., GORE, D-Tenn., WATKINS, D-Okla., YOUNG, D-Mo., WYDLER, R-N.Y., WINN, R-Kan., FREY, R-Fla., GOLDWATER, R-Calif. and PURSELL, R-Mich. — 3/8/78 — House Science and Technology reported March 15, 1978 (H Rept 95-973). House passed April 25. Senate Commerce, Science and Transportation reported May 10 (S Rept 95-799). Senate passed, amended, May 18. Conference report filed in

House Aug. 17 (H Rept 95-1509). Conference report filed in Senate Aug. 17 (S Rept 95-1123). Senate agreed to conference report Aug. 17. House agreed to conference report Sept. 19. President signed Sept. 30, 1978.

PL 95-402 (S 3468) — Insure that interest rates on price support loans for upland cotton are not less favorable to producers than the interest rates for such loans on other commodities. TALMADGE, D-Ga. — 8/25/78 — Senate Agriculture, Nutrition and Forestry reported Aug. 25, 1978 (S Rept 95-1154). Senate passed Sept. 8. House passed Sept. 18. President signed Sept. 30, 1978.

PL 95-403 (S 1896) — Authorize funds for fiscal year 1979 for programs administered under the Hazardous Materials Transportation Act. FORD, D-Ky. and PEARSON, R-Kan. — 7/19/78 — Senate Commerce, Science and Transportation reported May 12, 1978 (S Rept 95-814). Senate passed May 18. House passed Sept. 19. President signed Sept. 30, 1978.

PL 95-404 (S 2701) — Authorize funds for fiscal year 1979 for the Water Resources Planning Council. GRAVEL, D-Alaska and DOMENICI, R-N.M. — 3/9/78 — Senate Environment and Public Works reported May 15, 1978 (S Rept 95-835). Senate passed May 25. House passed, amended, July 11. Conference report filed in House Aug. 15 (H Rept 95-1494). House agreed to conference report Sept. 15. Senate agreed to conference report Sept. 18. President signed Sept. 30, 1978.

PL 95-405 (S 2391) — Extended through fiscal year 1984 the life of the Commodity Futures Trading Commission. HUDDLESTON, D-Ky. — 1/19/78 — Senate Agriculture, Nutrition and Forestry reported May 15, 1978 (S Rept 95-850). Senate passed July 12. House passed, amended, July 26. Conference report filed in House Sept. 25 (H Rept 95-1628). Conference report filed in Senate Sept. 25 (S Rept 95-1239). Senate agreed to conference report Sept. 28. House agreed to conference report Sept. 29. President signed Sept. 30, 1978.

PL 95-406 (S J Res 165) — Extended for an additional month, through Nov. 1, 1978, Federal Housing Administration mortgage insurance authorities. PROXMIRE, D-Wis., SPARKMAN, D-Ala., WILLIAMS, D-N.J., McINTYRE, D-N.H. and BROOKE, R-Mass. — 9/26/78 — Senate passed Sept. 29, 1978. House passed Sept. 29. President signed Sept. 30, 1978.

PL 95-407 (H J Res 1140) — Extend through Dec. 31, 1978, operating authority of the Export-Import Bank. NEAL, D-N.C. — 9/20/78 — House passed Sept. 28, 1978. Senate passed Sept. 29. President signed Sept. 30, 1978.

PL 95-408 (S 3375) — Make certain changes in the places of holding federal district courts, in the divisions within judicial districts and in judicial districts dividing lines. DeCONCINI, D-Ariz. — 8/3/78 — Senate Judiciary reported Aug. 17, 1978 (S Rept 95-1121). Senate passed Aug. 21. House passed, amended, Sept. 12. Senate agreed to House amendment Sept. 19. President signed Oct. 2, 1978.

PL 95-409 (S 3272) — Allow firms selling livestock to base their charges for sales on a percentage of the gross sale price of the livestock as well as a per head charge. TALMADGE, D-Ga. — 7/10/78 — Senate Agriculture, Nutrition and Forestry reported July 31, 1978 (S Rept 95-1053). Senate passed Aug. 4. House passed Sept. 19. President signed Oct. 2, 1978.

PL 95-410 (HR 8149) — Enact the Customs Procedural and Simplification Act of 1978. JONES, D-Okla., VANIK, D-Ohio, HOLLAND, D-S.C., JENKINS, D-Ga. and FRENZEL, R-Minn. — 6/30/77 — House Ways and Means reported Sept. 23, 1977 (H Rept 95-621). House passed Oct. 17. Senate Finance reported May 2, 1978 (S Rept 95-778). Senate passed, amended, June 7. Conference report filed in House Aug. 17 (H Rept 95-1517). Senate agreed to conference report Aug. 25. House agreed to conference report Sept. 19. President signed Oct. 3, 1978.

PL 95-411 (S J Res 154) — Authorize the president to invite the states and foreign nations to participate in the International Petroleum Exposition to be held in Tulsa, Okla., Sept. 10-13, 1979. BARTLETT, R-Okla., and BELLMON, R-Okla. — 9/18/78 — Senate Foreign Relations reported Aug. 24, 1978 (S Rept 95-1145). Senate passed Sept. 7. House passed Sept. 25. President signed Oct. 5, 1978.

PL 95-412 (HR 12443) — Amend in several aspects the Immigration and Naturalization Act, and to establish a Select Commission on Immigration and Refugee Policy. EILBERG, D-Pa., HOLTZMAN, D-N.Y., HARRIS, D-Va., EVANS, D-Ga., FISH, R-N.Y. and CONABLE, R-N.Y. — 5/1/78 — House Judiciary reported May 18, 1978 (H Rept 95-1206). House passed July 18. Senate passed Sept. 20. President signed Oct. 5, 1978.

PL 95-413 (S 3342) — Name a lake which has been completed as part of the Papillion Creek basin project as the "Standing Bear Lake." RANDOLPH, D-W.Va. — 7/25/78 — Senate Environment and Public Works reported July 25, 1978 (S Rept 95-1037). Senate passed July 28. Senate requested return July 31. Returned Aug. 1. Senate passed Sept. 20. House passed Sept. 25. President signed Oct. 5, 1978.

PL 95-414 (S 2507) — Authorize the Smithsonian Institution to acquire the Museum of African Art. ANDERSON, D-Minn., HUMPHREY, D-Minn., BROOKE, R-Mass., KENNEDY, D-Mass., BAYH, D-Ind., FORD, D-Ky., GRAVEL, D-Alaska, CHURCH, D-Idaho, STEVENSON, D-Ill., CLARK, D-Iowa, WILLIAMS, D-N.J., McGOVERN, D-S.D., HOLLINGS, D-S.C., GLENN, D-Ohio, THURMOND, R-S.C., LAXALT, R-Nev., RANDOLPH, D-W.Va., WEICKER, D-Conn., JACKSON, D-Wash., JAVITS, R-N.Y., HAYAKAWA, R-Calif., LEAHY, D-Vt., MORGAN, D-N.C., and HASKELL, D-Colo. — 2/7/78 — Senate Rules and Administration reported May 9, 1978 (S Rept 95-793). Senate passed May 16. House passed, amended, Sept. 18. Senate agreed to House amendment Sept. 22. President signed Oct. 5, 1978.

PL 95-415 (H J Res 1088) — Provided for loan guarantee authority for New York City, and appropriations in case of any eventual default. MAHON, D-Texas — 7/26/78 — House Appropriations reported Aug. 1, 1978 (H Rept 95-1404). House passed Sept. 6. Senate Appropriations reported Sept. 14 (S Rept 95-1192). Senate passed Sept. 20. President signed Oct. 5, 1978.

PL 95-416 (S 1265) — Amend the law governing the acceptance and use of records transferred to the custody of the Administrator of General Services. PERCY, R-Ill. — 4/6/77 — Senate Governmental Affairs reported March 21, 1978 (S Rept 95-710). Senate passed April 3. House Government Operations reported Aug. 21 (H Rept 95-1522). House passed Sept. 25. President signed Oct. 5, 1978.

PL 95-417 (HR 12508) — Facilitate the admission into the United States of more than two adopted children, and to provide for the expeditious naturalization of adopted children. HARRIS, D-Va., SISK, D-Calif., EILBERG, D-Pa., EDWARDS, D-Calif., HALL, D-Texas, EVANS, D-Ga., FISH, R-N.Y., SAWYER, R-Mich., FRENZEL, R-Minn., and FENWICK, R-N.J. — 5/2/78 — House Judiciary reported June 16, 1978 (H Rept 95-1301). House passed July 18. Senate passed Sept. 20. President signed Oct. 5, 1978.

PL 95-418 (HR 8812) — Name a federal building in Jonesboro, Ark., the "E. C. 'Took' Gathings Building." ALEXANDER, D-Ark. — 8/5/77 — House Public Works and Transportation reported Aug. 10, 1978 (H Rept 95-1468). House passed Sept. 18. Senate passed Sept. 22. President signed Oct. 5, 1978.

PL 95-419 (H J Res 1007) — Request that the President proclaim the 7-day period beginning on May 4, 1979, as Asian/Pacific American Heritage Week. HORTON, R-N.Y., and MINETA, D-Calif. — 6/19/78 — House Post Office and Civil Service reported July 10, 1978 (H Rept 95-1335). House passed July 10. Senate passed Sept. 19. President signed Oct. 5, 1978.

PL 95-420 (HR 13745) — Authorize funds to administer conservation programs on military reservations and other public lands during fiscal years 1979-81. MURPHY, D-N.Y., LEGGETT, D-Calif., FORSYTHE, R-N.J., DINGELL, D-Mich., YOUNG, R-Alaska, HUBBARD, D-Ky., HUGHES, D-N.J., TRIBLE, R-Va., AKAKA, D-Hawaii, TREEN, R-La., LENT, R-N.Y., and SIKES, D-Fla. — 8/4/78 — House Merchant Marine and Fisheries reported Aug. 18, 1978 (H Rept 95-1519). House passed Sept. 19. Senate passed Sept. 25. President signed Oct. 5, 1978.

PL 95-421 (S 3040) — Authorize funds for the National Railroad Passenger Corporation for fiscal year 1979, and calling for a review of the Amtrak route system. LONG, D-La. — 5/4/78 — Senate Commerce, Science and Transportation reported May 4, 1978 (S Rept 95-782). Senate passed May 10. House passed, amended, June 23. Conference report filed in House Aug. 11 (H Rept 95-1478). House agreed to conference report Sept. 19. Senate agreed to conference report Sept. 23. President signed Oct. 5, 1978.

PL 95-422 (HR 11291) — Authorize funds for fiscal year 1979 for the U.S. Fire Administration. TEAGUE, D-Texas, FLIPPO, D-Ala., and HOLLENBECK, R-N.J. — 3/3/78 — House Science and Technology reported March 20, 1978 (H Rept 95-992). House passed May 15. Senate passed, amended, June 13. House agreed to Senate amendment with an amendment Sept. 21. Senate agreed to House amendment Sept. 22. President signed Oct. 5, 1978.

PL 95-423 (HR 1920) — Provide for a refund of taxes on alcoholic beverages which have been lost or rendered unmarketable due to fire or other disaster or vandalism. WAGGONNER, D-La. — 1/13/77 — House Ways and Means reported April 5, 1978 (H Rept 95-1038). House passed May 8. Senate Finance reported Aug. 11 (S Rept 95-1112). Senate passed, amended, Aug. 25. House agreed to Senate amendment with amendments Sept. 19. Senate agreed to House amendments Sept. 25. President signed Oct. 6, 1978.

PL 95-424 (HR 12222) — Authorize funds for the International Development Assistance programs for fiscal year 1979. ZABLOCKI, D-Wis., FASCELL, D-Fla., DIGGS, D-Mich., NIX, D-Pa., FRASER, D-Minn., ROSENTHAL, D-N.Y., HAMILTON, D-Ind., WOLFF, D-N.Y., BINGHAM, D-N.Y., HARRINGTON, D-Mass., RYAN, D-

Calif., COLLINS, D-Ill., SOLARZ, D-N.Y., MEYNER, D-N.J., BONKER, D-Wash., STUDDS, D-Mass., PEASE, D-Ohio, BEILENSON, D-Calif., CAVANAUGH, D-Neb., FINDLEY, R-Ill., BUCHANAN, R-Ala., WHALEN, R-Ohio, WINN, R-Kan., and GILMAN, R-N.Y. — 4/19/78 — House International Relations reported April 25, 1978 (H Rept 95-1087). House passed May 15. Senate passed, amended, June 26. Conference report filed in House Sept. 7 (H Rept 95-1545). House agreed to conference report Sept. 19. Senate agreed to conference report Sept. 20. President signed Oct. 6, 1978.

PL 95-425 (HR 11567) — Authorize funds for the Securities and Exchange Commission for fiscal years 1979 and 1980. ECKHARDT, D-Texas — 3/15/78 — House Interstate and Foreign Commerce reported March 30, 1978 (H Rept 95-1010). House passed April 4. Senate Banking, Housing and Urban Affairs reported July 31 (S Rept 95-1057). Senate passed, amended, Aug. 9. House agreed to Senate amendments with an amendment Sept. 7. Senate agreed to House amendment Sept. 20. President signed Oct. 6, 1978.

PL 95-426 (HR 12598) — Authorize funds for fiscal year 1979 for the Department of State, the International Communication Agency, and the Board for International Broadcasting. FASCELL, D-Fla., BEILENSON, D-Calif., BINGHAM, D-N.Y., BONKER, D-Wash., BUCHANAN, R-Ala., CAVANAUGH, D-Neb., DIGGS, D-Mich., FRASER, D-Minn., HAMILTON, D-Ind., HARRINGTON, D-Mass., MEYNER, D-N.J., PEASE, D-Ohio, ROSENTHAL, D-N.Y., RYAN, D-Calif., SOLARZ, D-N.Y., WHALEN, R-Ohio, WINN, R-Kan., WOLFF, D-N.Y., and ZABLOCKI, D-Wis. — 5/8/78 — House International Relations reported May 15, 1978 (H Rept 95-1160). House passed May 31. Senate passed, amended, June 28. Conference report filed in House Sept. 6 (H Rept 95-1535). House agreed to conference report Sept. 19. Senate agreed to conference report Sept. 20. President signed Oct. 7, 1978.

PL 95-427 (HR 12841) — Prohibit the issuance of regulations on the taxation of fringe benefits. ULLMAN, D-Ore. — 5/24/78 — House Ways and Means reported May 31, 1978 (H Rept 95-1232). House passed June 28. Senate passed, amended, Aug. 2. Proceedings of Aug. 2 vacated Aug. 4. Senate passed, amended, Aug. 4. House agreed to Senate amendments Sept. 19. President signed Oct. 7, 1978.

PL 95-428 (HR 10822) — Authorize funds for fiscal years 1979 and 1980 for the National Sea Grant College Program. MURPHY, D-N.Y., BREAUX, D-La., RUPPE, R-Mich., ROGERS, D-Fla., ANDERSON, D-Calif., PRITCHARD, R-Wash., METCALFE, D-Ill., GINN, D-Ga., STUDDS, D-Mass., BOWEN, D-Miss., BONKER, D-Wash., AuCOIN, D-Ore., PATTERSON, D-Calif., ZEFERETTI, D-N.Y., OBERSTAR, D-Minn., HUGHES, D-N.J., MIKULSKI, D-Md., BONIOR, D-Mich., and AKAKA, D-Hawaii — 2/7/78 — House Merchant Marine and Fisheries reported March 30, 1978 (H Rept 95-1011). House passed April 17. Senate Commerce, Science and Transportation and Human Resources reported May 15 (S Rept 95-887). Senate passed, amended, June 7. House agreed to Senate amendment with amendments June 29. Senate agreed to House amendments Sept. 25. President signed Oct. 7, 1978.

PL 95-429 (HR 12930) — Make appropriations for the Treasury Department, the U.S. Postal Service, the Executive Office of the President, and certain independent agencies for the fiscal year 1979. STEED, D-Okla. — 6/1/78 — House Appropriations reported June 1, 1978 (H Rept 95-1249). House passed June 7. Senate Appropriations reported June 19 (S Rept 95-939). Senate passed, amended, June 27. Conference report filed in House Sept. 29 (H Rept 95-1673). House agreed to conference report Oct. 4. House receded and concurred in Senate amendments Nos. 14 and 15 Oct. 4. House receded and concurred with amendments in Senate amendments Nos. 30 and 31 Oct. 4. Senate agreed to conference report Oct. 4. Senate agreed to House amendments to Senate amendments Nos. 30 and 31 Oct. 4. President signed Oct. 10, 1978.

PL 95-430 (HR 11005) — Authorize funds for the International Trade Commission for fiscal year 1979. VANIK, D-Ohio — 2/20/78 — House Ways and Means reported April 18, 1978 (H Rept 95-1060). House passed May 15. Senate Finance reported May 25 (S Rept 95-914). Senate passed, amended, June 28. House agreed to Senate amendment with an amendment Sept. 19. Senate agreed to House amendment Sept. 28. President signed Oct. 10, 1978.

PL 95-431 (HR 12934) — Make appropriations for the Departments of Justice, State and Commerce, the Judiciary and certain related agencies. SLACK, D-W.Va. — 6/1/78 — House Appropriations reported June 1, 1978 (H Rept 95-1253). House passed June 14. Senate Appropriations reported July 28 (S Rept 95-1043). Senate passed, amended, Aug. 3. Proceedings of Aug. 3 vacated Aug. 7. Senate passed, amended, Aug. 7. Conference report filed in House Sept. 12 (H Rept 95-1565). House agreed to conference report Sept. 28. House receded and concurred in Senate amendments Nos. 1, 3 through 8, 10 through 19, 23, 26 through 29, 33, 35 through 38, 40, 41, 56, 73, 78, 88, 91, 92, 101 through 105, and 114 Sept. 28. House receded and concurred with amendments to Senate amendments Nos. 2, 22, 24, 25, 30, 31, 34, 51, 66, 67, 90, 100, 106, 109, 111, 113, 115 through 117 and 124 Sept. 28. House receded and concurred in Senate amendments Nos. 9 and 123 Sept. 29. Senate agreed to conference report Sept. 30. Senate agreed to House amendments to Senate amendments Nos. 2, 22, 24, 25, 30, 31, 34, 51, 66, 67, 90, 100, 106, 109, 111, 113, 115 through 117, 123 and 124 Sept. 30. President signed Oct. 10, 1978.

PL 95-432 (HR 13349) — Repeal certain sections of Title III of the Immigration and Nationality Act. EILBERG, D-Pa., McCLORY, R-Ill., HOLTZMAN, D-N.Y., HALL, D-Texas, HARRIS, D-Va., EVANS, D-Ga., FISH, R-N.Y., and SAWYER, R-Mich. — 6/29/78 — House Judiciary reported Aug. 15, 1978 (H Rept 95-1493). House passed Sept. 19. Senate passed Sept. 28. President signed Oct. 10, 1978.

PL 95-433 (HR 10581) — Provide for the distribution of certain judgment funds to the Confederated Tribes and Bands of the Yakima Indian Nation. McCORMACK, D-Wash. — 1/26/78 — House Interior and Insular Affairs reported June 19, 1978 (H Rept 95-1304). House passed July 17. Senate Indian Affairs reported Sept. 14 (H Rept 95-1193). Senate passed, amended, Sept. 20. House agreed to Senate amendments Sept. 26. President signed Oct. 10, 1978.

PL 95-434 (HR 11400) — Authorize funds for the National Science Foundation for fiscal year 1979. TEAGUE, D-Texas — 3/8/78 — House Science and Technology reported March 20, 1978 (H Rept 95-993). House passed April 18. Senate Human Resources reported May 15 (S Rept 95-853). Senate passed, amended, June 28. House agreed to Senate amendment with an amendment Sept. 19. Senate agreed to House amendment Sept. 29. President signed Oct. 10, 1978.

PL 95-435 (HR 9214) — Authorize approximately $1.7 billion for U.S. participation in the so-called Witteveen Financing Facility of the International Monetary Fund. NEAL, D-N.C. — 9/20/77 — House Banking, Finance and Urban Affairs reported Jan. 27, 1978 (H Rept 95-853). House passed Feb. 23. Senate passed, amended, July 31. Conference report filed in House Sept. 22 (H Rept 95-1613). Senate agreed to conference report Sept. 25. House agreed to conference report Sept. 28. President signed Oct. 10, 1978.

PL 95-436 (S 409) — Designate the Meat Animal Research Center near Clay Center, Neb., as the "Roman L. Hruska Meat Animal Research Center." CURTIS, R-Neb. and ZORINSKY, D-Neb. — 1/24/77 — Senate Agriculture, Nutrition and Forestry reported June 30, 1977 (S Rept 95-321). Senate passed July 12. House Agriculture reported Sept. 7 (H Rept 95-1547). House passed Sept. 26. President signed Oct. 10, 1978.

PL 95-437 (HR 10126) — Provide for increased employment opportunity by federal agencies for persons unable to work standard working hours. BURKE, D-Calif., SCHROEDER, D-Colo., LEHMAN, D-N.Y., SPELLMAN, D-Md., GILMAN, R-N.Y., CORCORAN, R-Ill., NIX, D-Pa., SOLARZ, D-N.Y., METCALFE, D-Ill., RYAN, D-Calif., DICKS, D-Wash. and CLAY, D-Mo. — 11/29/77 — House Post Office and Civil Service reported March 8, 1978 (H Rept 95-932). House passed March 13. Senate Governmental Affairs reported Aug. 24 (no written report). Senate passed, amended, Aug. 25. House agreed to Senate amendments with an amendment Sept. 22. Senate agreed to House amendment Sept. 26. President signed Oct. 10, 1978.

PL 95-438 (S 425) — Authorize the President to present on behalf of the Congress a special gold medal to Lieutenant General Ira S. Baker USAF (retired). GOLDWATER, R-Ariz. — 1/25/77 — Senate Banking, Housing and Urban Affairs reported May 12, 1977 (S Rept 95-139). Senate passed May 13. House Banking, Finance and Urban Affairs reported Sept. 21, 1978 (H Rept 95-1603). House passed Sept. 26. President signed Oct. 10, 1978.

PL 95-439 (S 286) — Repeal certain requirements for publication of notice to railroads and other carriers during business in areas quarantined by the Secretary of Agriculture for reasons of animal disease or insect infestation. DOLE, R-Kan. — 1/18/77 — Senate Agriculture, Nutrition and Forestry reported May 11, 1978 (S Rept 95-804). Senate passed May 18. House Agriculture reported Sept. 21 (H Rept 95-1606). House passed Sept. 26. President signed Oct. 10, 1978.

PL 95-440 (S 1267) — Require mandatory application of the General Records Schedules to all federal agencies. PERCY, R-Ill. — 4/6/77 — Senate Governmental Affairs reported March 21, 1978 (S Rept 95-711). Senate passed April 3. House Appropriations reported June 5 (S Rept 95-1263). House passed Sept. 26. President signed Oct. 10, 1978.

PL 95-441 (S 2946) — Authorize the Secretary of Agriculture to relinquish exclusive legislative jurisdiction over lands or interests under his control. TALMADGE, D-Ga. — 4/19/78 — Senate Agriculture, Nutrition and Forestry reported May 15 (S Rept 95-882). Senate passed June 8. House Agriculture reported Sept. 7 (H Rept 95-1552). House passed Sept. 26. President signed Oct. 10, 1978.

PL 95-442 (S 2951) — Authorize the Secretary of Agriculture to accept and administer on behalf of the United States gifts or devises of real or personal property for the benefit of the Department of Agriculture. TALMADGE, D-Ga. — 4/19/78 — Senate Agriculture, Nutrition and

Forestry reported May 15, 1978 (S Rept 95-883). Senate passed May 26. House Agriculture reported Sept. 7 (H Rept 95-1553). House passed Sept. 26. President signed Oct. 10, 1978.

PL 95-443 (S 3045) — Extend to 15 years the term for production credit association loans to producers or harvesters of aquatic products. ALLEN, D-Ala. — 5/5/78 — Senate Agriculture, Nutrition and Forestry reported May 15, 1978 (S Rept 95-849). Senate passed May 22. House passed Sept. 26. President signed Oct. 10, 1978.

PL 95-444 (S 3067) — Extend for three years the Commission on Civil Rights. BAYH, D-Ind. — 5/11/78 — Senate passed June 27, 1978. House passed, amended, Sept. 6. Conference report filed in House Sept. 25 (H Rept 95-1626). House agreed to conference report Sept. 28. Senate agreed to House amendment to the title Sept. 28. Senate agreed to conference report Sept. 28. President signed Oct. 10, 1978.

PL 95-445 (S 3092) — Prohibit inhumane slaughtering of livestock within the United States and the importation of any meat or meat products unless such livestock are slaughtered in a humane manner. DOLE, R-Kan. — 5/17/78 — Senate Agriculture, Nutrition and Forestry reported Aug. 1, 1978 (S Rept 95-1059). Senate passed Aug. 7. House passed, amended, Sept. 19. Senate agreed to House amendments Sept. 28. President signed Oct. 10, 1978.

PL 95-446 (S 3274) — Designate the Federal Bee Research Laboratory in Tuscon, Ariz., as the "Carl Hayden Bee Research Center." DeCONCINI, D-Ariz. and GOLDWATER, R-Ariz. — 7/11/78 — Senate Agriculture, Nutrition and Forestry reported Aug. 14, 1978 (S Rept 95-1115). Senate passed Aug. 18. House passed Sept. 26. President signed oct. 10, 1978.

PL 95-447 (S 3036) — Provide for the minting of a smaller size one-dollar coin to bear the likeness of Susan B. Anthony. PROXMIRE, D-Wis., WILLIAMS, D-N.J., CRANSTON, D-Calif., RIEGLE, D-Mich. and LUGAR, R-Ind. — 5/3/78 — Senate Banking, Housing and Urban Affairs reported Aug. 16, 1978 (S Rept 95-1120). Senate passed Aug. 22. House passed Sept. 26. President signed Oct. 10, 1978.

PL 95-448 (HR 13125) — Make appropriations for the Department of Agriculture and related agencies. WHITTEN, D-Miss. — 6/13/78 — House Appropriations reported June 13, 1978 (H Rept 95-1290). House passed June 22. Senate Appropriations reported Aug. 1 (S Rept 95-1058). Senate passed, amended, Aug. 10. Conference report filed in House Sept. 18 (H Rept 95-1579). House agreed to conference report Sept. 26. House receded and concurred in Senate amendment No. 83 Sept. 26. House receded and concurred with amendments in Senate amendments Nos. 10, 14, 82 and 84 Sept. 26. Senate agreed to conference report Sept. 27. Senate agreed to House amendments to Senate amendments Nos. 10, 14, 82 and 84 Sept. 27. President signed Oct. 11, 1978.

PL 95-449 (S J Res 29) — Authorize the President to designate that week in Nov., 1978, which includes Thanksgiving Day, as "National Family Week." BURDICK, D-N.D. — 2/24/77 — Senate Judiciary reported Sept. 25, 1978 (S Rept 95-1238). Senate passed Sept. 27. House passed Sept. 29. President signed Oct. 11, 1978.

PL 95-450 (HR 12026) — Create the Indian Peaks Wilderness Area and the Arapaho National Recreational Area, and to authorize a feasibility study of revising boundaries of the Rocky Mountain National Park. WIRTH, D-Colo. and JOHNSON, R-Colo. — 4/11/78 — House Interior and Insular Affairs reported Aug. 9, 1978 (H Rept 95-1460). House passed Sept. 12. Senate passed Sept. 27. President signed Oct. 11, 1978.

PL 95-451 (S 3467) — Designate the USDA Pecan Field Station in Brownwood, Texas, as the "W. R. 'Bob' Poage Pecan Field Station." TALMADGE, D-Ga. — 8/25/78 — Senate Agriculture, Nutrition and Forestry reported Aug. 25, 1978 (S Rept 95-1153). Senate passed Sept. 7. House passed, amended, Sept. 26. Senate agreed to House amendments Oct. 2. President signed Oct. 11, 1978.

PL 95-452 (HR 8588) — Establish offices of inspector general in certain federal departments and agencies. FOUNTAIN, D-N.C., BROOKS, D-Texas, FUQUA, D-Fla., ENGLISH, D-Okla., LEVITAS, D-Ga., WAXMAN, D-Calif., JENRETTE, D-S.C., BLOUIN, D-Iowa, HORTON, R-N.Y., WYDLER, R-N.Y., BROWN, R-Ohio and CUNNINGHAM, R-Wash. — 7/27/77 — House Government Operations reported Aug. 5, 1977 (H Rept 95-584). House passed April 18. Senate Governmental Affairs reported Aug. 8, 1978 (S Rept 95-1071). Senate passed, amended, Sept. 22. House agreed to Senate amendment Sept. 27. President signed Oct. 12, 1978.

PL 95-453 (HR 9945) — Repeal those provisions of the Indian Claims Commission Act which limit the activities of commissioners during the two years following their terms of office. QUILLEN, R-Tenn. — 11/3/77 — House Interior and Insular Affairs reported Aug. 17, 1978 (H Rept 95-1510). House passed Sept. 18. Senate passed Sept. 28. President signed Oct. 12, 1978.

PL 95-454 (S 2640) — Reform the Civil Service laws. RIBICOFF, D-Conn., SASSER, D-Tenn., PERCY, R-Ill. and JAVITS, R N.Y. — 3/3/78 — Senate Governmental Affairs reported July 10, 1978 (S Rept 95-969). Senate passed Aug. 24. House passed, amended, Sept. 13. Conference report filed in Senate Oct. 4 (S Rept 95-1272). Senate agreed to conference report Oct. 4. Conference report filed in House Oct. 5 (H Rept 95-1717). House agreed to conference report Oct. 6. House receded from its amendment to the title of the bill Oct. 6. President signed Oct. 13, 1978.

PL 95-455 (HR 12603) — Relieve the restrictive qualification standards for U.S. registered pilots on the Great Lakes. RUPPE, R-Mich., KEMP, R-N.Y., OBERSTAR, D-Minn. and McEWEN, R-N.Y. — 5/8/78 — House Merchant Marine and Fisheries reported Aug. 25, 1978 (H Rept 95-1526). House passed Sept. 25. Senate passed Sept. 28. President signed Oct. 13, 1978.

PL 95-456 (S 2249) — Prohibit rate discrimination among customers of the Southwest Power Administration. EAGLETON, D-Mo. — 10/27/77 — Senate Energy and Natural Resources reported May 9, 1978 (S Rept 95-792). Senate passed May 15. House passed Sept. 26. Senate agreed to House amendments Sept. 29. President signed Oct. 13, 1978.

PL 95-457 (HR 13635) — Make appropriations for the defense establishment for fiscal year 1979. MAHON, D-Texas — 7/27/78 — House Appropriations reported July 27, 1978 (H Rept 95-1398). House passed Aug. 9. Senate Appropriations reported Oct. 2 (S Rept 95-1264). Senate passed, amended, Oct. 5. Conference report filed in House Oct. 11 (H Rept 95-1764). House agreed to conference report Oct. 12. House receded and concurred in Senate amendments Oct. 12. House receded and concurred with amendments in Senate amendments Oct. 12. Senate agreed to conference report Sept. 12. Senate agreed to House amendments to Senate amendments Oct. 4. President signed Oct. 13, 1978.

PL 95-458 (HR 1337) — Prohibit the use of manufacturer's cost as the constructive sale price for purposes of the 10 percent manufacturer's excise tax on trucks, buses, highway tractors and trailers. STEIGER, R-Wis. — 1/4/77 — House Ways and Means reported March 16, 1978 (H Rept 95-976). House passed May 16. Senate Finance reported Aug. 21 (S Rept 95-1127). Senate passed, amended, Aug. 25. House agreed to Senate amendments with amendments Sept. 12. Senate agreed to House amendments Sept. 28. President signed Oct. 14, 1978.

PL 95-459 (HR 13991) — Provide that the United States holds in trust for the Susanville Indian Rancheria of Lassen County, Calif., approximately 120 acres of land. JOHNSON, D-Calif. — 9/6/78 — House Interior and Insular Affairs reported Sept. 26, 1978 (H Rept 95-1631). House passed Oct. 2. Senate passed Oct. 4. President signed Oct. 14, 1978.

PL 95-460 (S 3384) — Require foreign persons who acquire, transfer, or hold interests in agricultural land to report such transactions and holdings to the Secretary of Agriculture. TALMADGE, D-Ga. — 8/8/78 — Senate Agriculture, Nutrition and Forestry reported Aug. 8, 1978 (S Rept 95-1072). Senate passed Aug. 11. House passed, amended, Sept. 26. Senate agreed to House amendments Oct. 2. President signed Oct. 14, 1978.

PL 95-461 (S 2916) — Authorize $223 million for fiscal year 1979 for the Office of Drug Abuse for drug treatment programs. HATHAWAY, D-Maine, WILLIAMS, D-N.J., HATCH, R-Utah, JAVITS, R-N.Y. and RIEGLE, D-Mich. — 4/13/78 — Senate Human Resources reported May 15, 1978 (S Rept 95-820). Senate agreed to House amendment Oct. 2. President signed Oct. 14, 1978.

PL 95-462 (HR 13692) — Grant consent of the Congress to the Historic Chattahoochee Compact between Alabama and Georgia. DICKINSON, R-Ala., NICHOLS, D-Ala., BRINKLEY, D-Ga., MATHIS, D-Ga., FLOWERS, D-Ala., EDWARDS, R-Ala., BUCHANAN, R-Ala., BEVILL, D-Ala., FLIPPO, D-Ala. and BARNARD, D-Ga. — 8/2/78 — House Judiciary reported Sept. 27, 1978 (S Rept 95-1636). House passed Oct. 2. Senate passed Oct. 3. President signed Oct. 14, 1978.

PL 95-463 (H J Res 685) — Designate Oct. 7, 1979, as Firefighters' Memorial Sunday. TEAGUE, D-Texas — 1/23/77 — House Post Office and Civil Service reported July 19, 1978 (H Rept 95-1376). House passed Sept. 29. Senate passed, amended, Oct. 4. House agreed to Senate amendments Oct. 10. President signed Oct. 14, 1978.

PL 95-464 (S 415) — Make Vermont and New York eligible for funds to study fish in Lake Champlain that ascend streams to spawn. LEAHY, D-Vt. and STAFFORD, R-Vt. — 1/24/77 — Senate Environment and Public Works reported May 19, 1978 (S Rept 95-907). Senate passed May 25. House passed, amended, Sept. 25. Senate agreed to House amendment Oct. 3. President signed Oct. 17, 1978.

PL 95-465 (HR 12932) — Make appropriations for the Department of Interior and related agencies for fiscal year 1979. YATES, D-Ill. — 6/1/78 — House Appropriations reported June 1, 1978 (H Rept 95-1251). House passd June 21. Senate Appropriations reported Aug. 2 (S Rept 95-1063). Senate passed, amended, Aug. 9. Conference report filed in House Sept. 29 (H Rept 95-1672). House agreed to conference report Oct. 5. House receded and concurred in Senate amendments

Oct. 5. House receded and concurred with amendments in Senate amendments Oct. 5. Senate agreed to conference report Oct. 7. Senate agreed to House amendments to Senate amendments Oct. 7. President signed Oct. 17, 1978.

PL 95-466 (S J Res 16) — Restore posthumously full rights of citizenship to Jefferson F. Davis. HATFIELD, R-Ore — 1/25/77 — Senate Judiciary reported April 22, 1977 (S Rept 95-100). Senate passed April 27. House passed, amended, Sept. 26. Senate agreed to House amendments Oct. 3. President signed Oct. 17, 1978.

PL 95-467 (S 2704) — Promote a more adequate and responsive national program of water research and development. GRAVEL, D-Alaska and DOMENICI, R-N.M. — 3/9/78 — Senate Environment and Public Works reported May 15, 1978 (S Rept 95-836). Senate passed May 25. House passed, amended, July 11. Senate agreed to House amendment with amendments Sept. 25. House agreed to Senate amendments Oct. 2. President signed Oct. 17, 1978.

PL 95-468 (S 2801) — Designate a building known as the Ozark National Forest Headquarters Building in Russellville, Ark., as the "Henry R. Koen Forest Service Building." BUMPERS, D-Ark. — 3/23/78 — Senate Environment and Public Works reported July 11, 1978 (S Rept 95-974). Senate passed July 14. House passed Oct. 4. President signed Oct. 17, 1978.

PL 95-469 (HR 8394) — Provide for payments to local governments based upon acreage of the National Wildlife Refuge System which is within their boundaries. STEIGER, R-Wis. and GINN, D-Ga. — 7/18/77 — House Merchant Marine and Fisheries reported May 15, 1978 (H Rept 95-1197). House passed June 6. Senate Environment and Public Works reported Aug. 31 (S Rept 95-1174). Senate passed, amended, Sept. 25. House agreed to Senate amendments Sept. 29. President signed Oct. 17, 1978.

PL 95-470 (S 2376) — Authorize the Offices of the Secretary of the Senate and the Architect of the Capitol to withhold from salaries contributions to certain charitable organizations. BAKER, R-Tenn., MATHIAS, R-Md. and SARBANES, D-Md. — 12/15/77 — Senate Governmental Affairs reported Aug. 25, 1978 (S Rept 95-1162). Senate passed Sept. 11. House passed Oct. 3. President signed Oct. 17, 1978.

PL 95-471 (S 1215) — Provide grants to Indian-controlled post-secondary education institutions. ABOUREZK, D-S.D., BURDICK, D-N.D., GRAVEL, D-Alaska, DeCONCINI, D-Ariz. and JACKSON, D-Wash. — 4/1/77 — Senate Indian Affairs reported Nov. 2, 1977 (S Rept 95-582). Senate passed Nov. 4. House passed, amended, Sept. 26. Senate agreed to House amendment Oct. 3. President signed Oct. 17, 1978.

PL 95-472 (HR 8811) — Allow the Tax Court judges seeking to qualify for Civil Service retirement benefits to revoke their election to receive benefits under the Tax Court retirement system prior to receiving any such benefits. ULLMAN, D-Ore. and CONABLE, R-N.Y. — 8/5/77 — House Ways and Means reported Oct. 25, 1977 (H Rept 95-744). House passed Jan. 24, 1978. Senate Finance reported Aug. 11 (S Rept 95-1113). Senate passed, amended, Aug. 23. House agreed to Senate amendments with amendments Sept. 19. Senate agreed to House amendments Sept. 28. President signed Oct. 17, 1978.

PL 95-473 (HR 10965) — Revise and codify the Interstate Commerce Act and related transportation laws. RODINO, D-N.J. — 2/15/78 — House Judiciary reported July 26, 1978 (H Rept 95-1395). House passed Sept. 19. Senate passed, amended, Sept. 25. House agreed to Senate amendment Sept. 26. President signed Oct. 17, 1978.

PL 95-474 (S 682) — Expand and strengthen regulations concerning vessel safety standards. MAGNUSON, D-Wash. — 2/10/77 — Senate Commerce, Science and Transportation reported May 16, 1977 (S Rept 95-176). Senate passed May 26. House passed, amended, Sept. 12. Senate agreed to House amendment with an amendment Sept. 30. House agreed to Senate amendment Oct. 3. President signed Oct. 17, 1978.

PL 95-475 (HR 6503) — Alter the power of the Federal Maritime Commission to suspend general rate increases or decreases in the domestic offshore trade. MURPHY, D-N.Y., DINGELL, D-Mich., BREAUX, D-La., PATTERSON, D-Calif., ZEFERETTI, D-N.Y., OBERSTAR, D-Minn., RUPPE, R-Mich., McCLOSKEY, R-Calif., TREEN, R-La. and PRITCHARD, R-Wash. — 4/21/77 — House Merchante Marine and Fisheries reported June 30, 1977 (H Rept 95-474). House passed May 8, 1978. Senate Commerce, Science and Transportation reported Sept. 26 (S Rept 95-1240). Senate passed Oct. 3. President signed Oct. 18, 1978.

PL 95-476 (HR 12028) — Improve certain housing programs administered by the Veterans' Administration. BRINKLEY, D-Ga., ABDNOR, R-S.D., ROBERTS, D-Texas, HAMMERSCHMIDT, R-Ark., EDWARDS, D-Calif., CORNELL, D-Wis., BARNARD, D-Ga., CARNEY, D-Ohio and WALSH, R-N.Y. — 4/11/78 — House Veterans' Affairs reported June 29, 1978 (H Rept 95-1332). House passed July 17. Senate Veterans' Affairs reported July 31 (S Rept 95-1055). Senate passed, amended, Aug. 7. House agreed to Senate amendments with amendments Sept. 28. Senate agreed to House amendments Oct. 2. President signed Oct. 18, 1978.

PL 95-477 (HR 11302) — Authorize funds for fiscal year 1979 for research and development programs of the Environmental Protection Agency. BROWN, D-Calif., WORTH, D-Colo., WALKER, R-Pa., AMBRO, D-N.Y., WINN, R-Kan., WALGREN, D-Pa., FORSYTHE, R-N.J. and BEILENSON, D-Calif. — 3/6/78 — House Science and Technology reported March 17, 1978 (H Rept 95-985). House passed April 27. Senate Environment and Public Works reported May 15 (S Rept 95-877). Senate passed, amended, May 26. Conference report filed in House Sept. 20 (H Rept 95-1593). Senate agreed to conference report Sept. 26. House agreed to conference report Oct. 4. President signed Oct. 18, 1978.

PL 95-478 (HR 12255) — Enact the Older Americans Act Amendments of 1978. BRADEMAS, D-Ind., JEFFORDS, R-Vt., PERKINS, D-Ky., QUIE, R-Minn., BEARD, D-R.I., PRESSLER, R-S.D., MILLER, D-Calif., KILDEE, D-Mich., HEFTEL, D-Hawaii, HAWKINS, D-Calif., BIAGGI, D-N.Y., SARASIN, R-Conn., THOMPSON, D-N.J., GOODLING, R-Pa., DENT, D-Pa., PURSELL, R-Mich., FORD, D-Mich., BURTON, P., D-Calif., GAYDOS, D-Pa., CLAY, D-Mo., ANDREWS, D-N.C., BLOUIN, D-Iowa, CORNELL, D-Wis., SIMON, D-Ill. and ZEFFERETTI, D-N.Y. — 4/20/78 — House Education and Labor reported May 13, 1978 (H Rept 95-1150). House passed May 15. Senate passed, amended, July 24. Conference report filed in House Sept. 22 (H Rept 95-1618). Conference report filed in Senate Sept. 23 (S Rept 95-1236). House agreed to conference report Oct. 4. Senate agreed to conference report Oct. 6. President signed Oct. 18, 1978.

PL 95-479 (HR 11886) — Increase rates of compensation paid to disabled veterans and their survivors. MONTGOMERY, D-Miss., WYLIE, R-Ohio, ROBERTS, D-Texas, HAMMERSCHMIDT, R-Ark., TEAGUE, D-Texas, BRINKLEY, D-Ga., HEFNER, D-N.C., HALL, D-Texas, EGER, D-Pa. and GUYER, R-Ohio — 4/5/78 — House Veterans' Affairs reported May 31, 1978 (H Rept 95-1226). House passed June 28. Senate passed, amended, Aug. 7. House agreed to Senate amendments with amendments Sept. 26. Senate agreed to House amendments Oct. 2. President signed Oct. 18, 1978.

PL 95-480 (HR 12929) — Make appropriations for the Departments of Labor and Health, Education and Welfare for fiscal year 1979. FLOOD, D-Pa. — 6/1/78 — House Appropriations reported June 1, 1978 (H Rept 95-1248). House passed June 13. Senate Appropriations reported Aug. 16 (S Rept 95-1119). Senate passed, amended, Sept. 27. Conference report filed in House Oct. 6 (H Rept 95-1746). House agreed to conference report Oct. 12. House receded and concurred in Senate amendments Oct. 12. House receded and concurred with amendments in Senate amendments Oct. 12. House insisted on its amendment to Senate amendment No. 103 Oct. 12. Senate agreed to conference report Oct. 12. Senate agreed to House amendments to Senate amendments Oct. 12. Senate receded from its amendment No. 103 Oct. 12. Senate agreed to the bill with a further amendment Oct. 12. Senate requested bill returned Oct. 13. Returned Oct. 13. House agreed to Senate amendment Oct. 14. President signed Oct. 18, 1978.

PL 95-481 (HR 12931) — Make appropriations for foreign aid programs for fiscal year 1979. LONG, D-Md. — 6/1/78 — House Appropriations reported June 1, 1978 (H Rept 95-1250). House passed Aug. 14. Senate Appropriations reported Sept. 15 (S Rept 95-1194). Senate passed, amended, Sept. 22. Conference report filed in House Oct. 10 (H Rept 95-1754). House agreed to conference report Oct. 12. House receded and concurred in Senate amendments Oct. 12. House receded and concurred with amendments in Senate amendments Oct. 12. House insisted on its disagreement to Senate amendment No. 63 Oct. 12. Senate agreed to conference report Oct. 13. Senate agreed to House amendments to Senate amendments Oct. 13. Senate receded from its amendment No. 63. President signed Oct. 18, 1978.

PL 95-482 (H J Res 1139) — Make continuing appropriations for fiscal year 1979. MAHON, D-Texas — 9/19/78 — House Appropriations reported Sept. 21, 1978 (H Rept 95-1599). House passed Sept. 26. Senate Appropriations reported Sept. 28 (S Rept 95-1317). Senate passed, amended, Oct. 15. House agreed to Senate amendments Oct. 15. President signed Oct. 18, 1978.

PL 95-483 (HR 9998) — Provide for the regulation of rates or charges by certain state-owned carriers in the foreign commerce of the United States. MURPHY, D-N.Y., LEGGETT, D-Calif., BIAGGI, D-N.Y., TRIBLE, R-Va., ANDERSON, D-Calif., DE LUGO, D-V.I., ZEFERETTI, D-N.Y. and AKAKA, D-Hawaii — 11/3/77 — House Merchant Marine and Fisheries reported July 19, 1978 (H Rept 95-1381). House passd July 31. Senate Commerce, Science and Transportation reported Sept. 298 (S Rept 95-1260). Senate passed Oct. 3. President signed Oct. 18, 1978.

PL 95-484 (HR 13797) — Authorize establishment of the Fort Scott National Historic Site. SKUBITZ, R-Kan. — 8/8/78 — House Interior and Insular Affairs reported Sept. 28, 1978 (H Rept 95-1644). House passed Sept. 29. President signed Oct. 19, 1978.

PL 95-485 (S 3486) — Authorize funds for military procurement for fiscal year 1979. STENNIS, D-Miss. — 9/7/78 — Senate Armed Services reported Sept. 15, 1978 (S Rept 95-1197). Senate passed Sept. 26. House passed, amended, Oct. 4. Senate agreed to House amendment Oct. 7. President signed Oct. 20, 1978.

PL 95-486 (HR 7843) — Provide for the appointment of additional federal circuit and district court judges. RODINO, D-N.J., BROOKS, D-Texas, SEIBERLING, D-Ohio, JORDAN, D-Texas, MAZZOLI, D-Ky., HUGHES, D-N.J., McCLORY, R-Ill., WIGGINS, R-Calif. and COHEN, R-Maine — 6/16/77 — House Judiciary reported Jan. 31, 1978 (H Rept 95-858). House passed Feb. 7. Senate passed, amended, Feb. 7. Conference report filed in disagreement in the House Sept. 28 (H Rept 1643). Conference report filed in Senate Sept. 28 (S Rept 95-1257). House receded and concurred in Senate amendment with an amendment Oct. 4. Senate agreed to conference report Oct. 7. Senate agreed to House amendment Oct. 7. President signed Oct. 20, 1978.

PL 95-487 (HR 14026) — Provide means for acquisition and retention of title to certain lands for natives of Kake, Alaska. JOHNSON, R-Col. and YOUNG, R-Alaska —9/8/78 — House Interior and Insular Affairs reported Sept. 22, 1978 (S Rept 95-1615). House passed Oct. 2. Senate passed Oct. 4. President signed Oct. 20, 1978.

PL 95-488 (HR 13167) — Insure that the tax deduction for contributions to a black lung benefit trust be allowed for any such contributions which are made for the purpose of satisfying unfunded future liability. DUNCAN, R-Tenn. — 6/16/78 — House Ways and Means reported Sept. 29, 1978 (H Rept 95-1656). House passed Oct. 3. Senate passed Oct. 10. President signed Oct. 20, 1978.

PL 95-489 (HR 13803) — Terminate the authorization of the navigation project on the Columbia Slough, Ore. DUNCAN, D-Ore. — 8/9/78 — House passed Oct. 4, 1978. Senate passed Oct. 7. President signed Oct. 20, 1978.

PL 95-490 (S 1318) — Remove a federal restriction on the use of certain state-owned land on Sand Island, Hawaii, so that it may be leased or sold for public purposes. MATSUNAGA, D-Hawaii — 4/20/77 — Senate Energy and Natural Resources reported Oct. 20, 1977 (S Rept 95-515). Senate passed Oct. 28. House passed Oct. 10, 1978. President signed Oct. 20, 1978.

PL 95-491 (S 3259) — Authorize funds to establish a system of Federal Information Centers. CHILES, D-Fla., McINTYRE, D-N.H. and NUNN, D-Ga. — 6/28/78 — Senate Governmental Affairs reported Aug. 22, 1978 (S Rept 95-1129). Senate passed Sept. 12. House passed, amended, Sept. 25. Senate agreed to House amendments Oct. 5. President signed Oct. 20, 1978.

PL 95-492 (S 3373) — Authorize the Secretary of Defense to provide transportation at no cost to the taxpayers to the Girl Scouts of America in connection with certain events held in foreign countries. McINTYRE, D-N.H. — 8/3/78 — Senate Armed Services reported Aug. 22, 1978 (S Rept 95-1137). Senate passed Aug. 24. House Armed Services reported Sept. 15 (H Rept 95-1572). House passed Oct. 10. President signed Oct. 20, 1978.

PL 95-493 (HR 11035) — Incorporate the United States Capitol Historical Society. PICKLE, D-Texas, CONABLE, R-N.Y., WRIGHT, D-Texas, RHODES, R-Ariz., BRADEMAS, D-Ind. and McCLORY, R-Ill. — 2/21/78 — House Judiciary reported Sept. 28, 1978 (H Rept 95-1638). House passed Oct. 2. Senate passed Oct. 5. President signed Oct. 20, 1978.

PL 95-494 (HR 12264) — Designate certain lands in Wisconsin as wilderness. CORNELL, D-Wis., KASTENMEIER, D-Wis., ZABLOCKI, D-Wis., OBEY, D-Wis., ASPIN, D-Wis., BALDUS, D-Wis. and REUSS, D-Wis. — 4/20/78 — House Interior and Insular Affairs reported June 28, 1978 (H Rept 95-1323). House passed Sept. 25. Senate passed Oct. 9. President signed Oct. 21, 1978.

PL 95-495 (HR 12250) — Designate the Boundary Waters Canoe Areas Wilderness and establish the Boundary Waters Canoe Mining Protection Areas. BURTON, P., D-Calif., VENTO, D-Minn., NOLAN, D-Minn., UDALL, D-Ariz., KASTENMEIER, D-Wis., BINGHAM, D-N.Y., BYRON, D-Md., TSONGAS, D-Mass., FLORIO, D-N.J., KREBS, D-Calif., KOSTMAYER, D-Pa., SEIBERLING, D-Ohio, WEAVER, D-Ore., CARR, D-Mich., MILLER, D-Calif., HOWARD, D-N.J., RONCALIO, D-Wyo., BLOUIN, D-Iowa., BRODHEAD, D-Mich., HARKIN, D-Iowa, BROWN, D-Calif., PEASE, D-Ohio, OTTINGER, D-N.Y., BEILENSON, D-Calif. and CONYERS, D-Mich. — 4/20/78 — House Interior and Insular Affairs reported Part I May 4, 1978 (H Rept 95-1171). House passed June 5. Senate Energy and Natural Resources reported Oct. 4 (S Rept 95-1274). Senate passed, amended, Oct. 9. Conference report filed in House (H Rept 95-1790). Conference report filed in Senate Oct. 12 (S Rept 95-1327). House agreed to conference report Oct. 15. Senate agreed to conference report Oct. 15. President signed Oct. 21, 1978.

PL 95-496 (S 1081) — Amend certain laws relating to the Osage Tribe in Oklahoma. BARTLETT, R-Okla. and BELLMON, R-Okla. — 3/22/77 — Senate Indian Affairs reported Aug. 25, 1978 (S Rept 95-1157). Senate passed Sept. 8. House passed, amended, Oct. 3. Senate agreed to House amendments Oct. 7. President signed Oct. 21, 1978.

PL 95-497 (HR 12051) — Related to the application of certain provisions of the Internal Revenue Code of 1954 to specific transactions by certain public employee retirement systems created by New York State or any of its political subdivisions. RANGEL, D-N.Y. and CONABLE, R-N.Y. — 4/12/78 — House Ways and Means reported Sept. 21, 1978 (H Rept 95-1605). House passed Oct. 3. Senate passed Oct. 4. President signed Oct. 21, 1978.

PL 95-498 (S 2588) — Declare that the United States hold in trust for the Pueblo of Santa Ana certain public domain lands. DOMENICI, R-N.M., and SCHMITT, R-N.M. — 2/24/78 — Senate Indian Affairs reported Aug. 22, 1978 (S Rept 95-1132). Senate passsed Sept. 6. House passed, amended, Oct. 4. Senate agreed to House amendment Oct. 7. President signed Oct. 21, 1978.

PL 95-499 (S 2358) — Declare that the United States holds in trust for the Pueblo of Zia certain public domain lands. DOMENICI, R-N.M. — 12/15/77 — Senate Indian Affairs reported Aug. 22, 1978 (S Rept 95-1131). Senate passed Sept. 6. House passed, amended, Oct. 3. Senate agreed to House amendment Oct. 7. President signed Oct. 21, 1978.

PL 95-500 (HR 8755) — Make specific provisions for ball or roller bearing pillow block, flange, take-up, cartridge, and hanger units in the Tariff Schedules of the United States. COTTER, D-Conn., ROSTENKOWSKI, D-Ill. and VANDER JAGT, R-Mich. — 8/4/77 — House Ways and Means reported July 14, 1978 (H Rept 95-1356). House passed Sept. 18. Senate Finance reported Sept. 26 (S Rept 95-1241). Senate passed, amended, Sept. 30. House agreed to Senate amendments Oct. 10. President signed Oct. 21, 1978.

PL 95-501 (S 3447) — Enact the Agricultural Trade Act of 1978. STONE, D-Fla. — 8/23/78 — Senate Agriculture, Nutrition and Forestry reported Aug. 23, 1978 (S Rept 95-1142). Senate passed Sept. 8. House passed, amended, Sept. 25. Conference report filed in Senate Oct. 10 (S Rept 95-1315). Conference report filed in House Oct. 11 (H Rept 95-1755). Senate agreed to conference report Oct. 11. House agreed to conference report Oct. 15. President signed Oct. 21, 1978.

PL 95-502 (HR 8533) — Amend the Internal Revenue Code of 1954 to provide that income from the conducting of certain bingo games by certain tax-exempt organizations will not be subject to tax. BRODHEAD, D-Mich. — 7/25/77 — House Ways and Means reported Sept. 22, 1978 (H Rept 95-1608). House passed Sept. 25. Senate passed, amended, Oct. 10. House agreed to Senate amendment Oct. 13. President signed Oct. 21, 1978.

PL 95-503 (S 2411) — Amend Chapter 315 of Title 18 of the United States Code to authorize payment of transportation expenses for persons released from custody pending their appearance to face criminal charges before that court, any division of that court, or any court of the United States in another federal judicial district. DeCONCINI, D-Ariz. — 1/23/78 — Senate Judiciary reported April 25, 1978 (S Rept 95-760). Senate passed April 27. House Judiciary reported Sept. 28 (H Rept 95-1653). House passed Oct. 10. President signed Oct. 24, 1978.

PL 95-504 (S 2493) — Enact the Airline Deregulation Act of 1978. CANNON, D-Nev. — 2/6/78 — Senate Commerce, Science and Transportation reported Feb. 6, 1978 (S Rept 95-631). Senate passed April 19. House passed, amended, Sept. 21. Conference report filed in House Oct. 12 (H Rept 95-1779). Senate agreed to conference report Oct. 14. House agreed to conference report Oct. 15. President signed Oct. 24, 1978.

PL 95-505 (HR 11658) — Amend Title XI of the Merchant Marine Act of 1936 to permit the guarantee of obligations for financing Great Lakes vessels in an amount not exceeding 87| per centum of the actual or depreciated actual cost of each vessel. MURPHY, D-N.Y., ASHLEY, D-Ohio, DINGELL, D-Mich., LEGGETT, D-Calif., EILBERG, D-Pa., OBERSTAR, D-Minn., MIKULSKI, D-Md., BONIOR, D-Mich., AKAKA, D-Hawaii and RUPPE, R-Mich. — 3/20/78 — House Merchant Marine and Fisheries reported Aug. 25, 1978 (H Rept 95-1528). House passed Oct. 3. Senate passed Oct. 6. President signed Oct. 24, 1978.

PL 95-506 (HR 13767) — Amend the Federal Property and Administrative Services Act of 1949 to permit the recovery of replacement cost of motor vehicles and other related equipment and supplies. BURTON, J., D-Calif., BROOKS, D-Texas, HORTON, R-N.Y., WALKER, R-Pa. and STANGELAND, R-Minn. — 8/7/78 — House Government Operations reported Aug. 25, 1978 (H Rept 95-1529). House passed Sept. 25. Senate passed Oct. 10. President signed Oct. 24, 1978.

PL 95-507 (HR 11318) — Amend the Small Business Act and the Small Business Investment Act of 1958. ADDABBO, D-N.Y., McDADE, R-Pa., SMITH, D-Iowa, CONTE, R-Mass., STEED, D-Okla., CORMAN, D-Calif., FENWICK, R-N.J., GONZALEZ, D-Texas, HANLEY, D-N.Y., PRESSLER, R-S.D., BRECKINRIDGE, D-Ky., LaFALCE, D-N.Y., RICHMOND, D-N.Y., NOWAK, D-N.Y., LeFANTE, D-N.J., KILDEE, D-Mich. and MITCHELL D-Md. — 3/7/78 — House Small Business reported March 13, 1978 (H Rept 95-949). House passed March 20. Senate Small Business reported Aug. 8 (S

Rept 95-1070). Senate Governmental Affairs reported Aug. 23 (S Rept 95-1140). Senate passed, amended, Sept. 15. Conference report filed in House Oct. 4 (H Rept 95-1714). House agreed to conference report Oct. 6. Senate agreed to conference report Oct. 10. President signed Oct. 24, 1978.

PL 95-508 (HR 12165) — Extend until the close of June 30, 1981, the existing suspension of duties on certain metal waste and scrap, unwrought metal, and other articles of metal. VANDER JAGT, R-Mich. — 4/17/78 — House Ways and Means reported July 14, 1978 (H Rept 95-1361). House passed Sept. 12. Senate Finance reported Sept. 26 (S Rept 95-1243). Senate passed, amended, Sept. 30. House agreed to Senate amendments Oct. 10. President signed Oct. 24, 1978.

PL 95-509 (HR 11686) — Enact the Department of Energy National Security and Military Applications of Nuclear Energy Authorization Act of 1979. PRICE, D-Ill. — 3/21/78 — House Armed Services reported May 3, 1978 (H Rept 95-1108). House passed May 17. Senate passed, amended, Sept. 30. House agreed to Senate amendment Oct. 11. President signed Oct. 24, 1978.

PL 95-510 (HR 13418) — Amend the Small Business Act by transferring thereto those provisions of the Domestic Volunteer Service Act of 1973 affecting the operation of volunteer programs to assist small business, to increase the maximum allowable compensation and travel expenses for experts and consultants. SMITH, D-Iowa, CONTE, R-Mass., STEED, D-Okla., DINGELL, D-Mich., ADDABBO, D-N.Y., GONZALEZ, D-Texas, HANLEY, D-N.Y., BRECKINRIDGE, D-Ky., RICHMOND, D-N.Y., RUSSO, D-Ill., BALDUS, D-Wis., NOLAN, D-Minn., IRELAND, D-Fla., KILDEE, D-Mich., LaFALCE, D-N.Y., McDADE, R-Pa., CARTER, R-Ky., BUTLER, R-Va., COHEN, R-Maine, FENWICK, R-N.J. and PRESSLER, R-S.D. — 7/11/78 — House Small Business reported July 19, 1978 (H Rept 95-1375). House passed Sept. 25. Senate passed Oct. 11. President signed Oct. 24, 1978.

PL 95-511 (S 1566) — Enact the Foreign Intelligence Surveillance Act of 1978. KENNEDY, D-Mass., EASTLAND, D-Miss., McCLELLAN, D-Ark., NELSON, D-Wis., INOUYE, D-Hawaii, MATHIAS, R-Md., BAYH, D-Ind. and THURMOND, R-S.C. — 5/18/77 — Senate Judiciary reported Nov. 15, 1977 (S Rept 95-604). Supplemental report filed Nov. 22. Senate Select Intelligence reported March 14, 1978 (S Rept 95-701). Senate passed April 20. House passed, amended, Sept. 7. Senate disagreed to House amendments Sept. 12. Conference report filed in House Oct. 5 (H Rept 95-1720). Senate agreed to conference report Oct. 9. House agreed to conference report Oct. 12. President signed Oct. 24, 1978.

PL 95-512 (S 3412) — Enact the Comptroller General Annuity Adjustment Act of 1978. GLENN, D-Ohio — 8/14/78 — Senate Governmental Affairs reported reported Oct. 3, 1978 (S Rept 95-1267). Senate passed Oct. 9. House passed Oct. 11. President signed Oct. 24, 1978.

PL 95-513 (H J Res 1147) — Authorize and request the President to designate the seven-day period beginning on May 28, 1979, as "Vietnam Veterans Week." BONIOR, D-Mich., AKAKA, D-Hawaii, ALEXANDER, D-Ark., AMBRO, D-N.Y., AMMERMAN, D-Pa., ANDERSON, R-Ill., BALDUS, D-Wis., BARNARD, D-Ga., BAUCUS, D-Mont., BEARD, D-R.I., BEARD, R-Tenn., BEDELL, D-Iowa, BEILENSON, D-Calif., BENJAMIN, D-Ind., BEVILL, D-Ala., BINGHAM, D-N.Y., BLANCHARD, D-Mich., BOGGS, D-La., BONKER, D-Wash., BOWEN, D-Miss., BRADEMAS, D-Ind., BRINKLEY, D-Ga., BRODHEAD, D-Mich., BURGENER, R-Calif. and BURKE, R-Fla. — 10/14/78 — House passed Oct. 10, 1978. Senate passed Oct. 12. President signed Oct. 25, 1978.

PL 95-514 (HR 10587) — Enact the Public Rangelands Improvement Act of 1978. RONCALIO, D-Wyo., BAUCUS, D-Mont., EVANS, D-Colo., JOHNSON, R-Colo., LUJAN, R-N.M., McKAY, D-Utah, MARLENEE, R-Mont., MARRIOTT, R-Utah, RUDD, R-Ariz., RUNNELS, D-N.M., SANTANI, D-Nev., SYMMS, R-Idaho, DUNCAN, D-Ore. and ULLMAN, D-Ore. — 1/26/78 — House Interior and Insular Affairs reported May 10, 1978 (H Rept 95-1122). House passed June 29. Senate Energy and Natural Resources reported Sept. 23 (S Rept 95-1237). Senate passed, amended, Sept. 30. Conference report filed in House Oct. 6 (H Rept 95-1737). House agreed to conference report Oct. 10. Senate agreed to conference report Oct. 11. President signed Oct. 25, 1978.

PL 95-515 (S 1185) — Enact the Interstate Horseracing Act of 1978. MAGNUSON, D-Wash., BIDEN, D-Del., CHILES, D-Fla., DURKIN, D-N.H., FORD, D-Ky., HUDDLESTON, D-Ky., McINTYRE, D-N.H., MATHIAS, R-Md., STONE, D-Fla. and WILLIAMS, D-N.J. — 3/30/77 — Senate Commerce, Science and Transportation reported Oct. 27, 1977 (S Rept 95-554). Senate Judiciary reported Aug. 14, 1978 (S Rept 95-1117). Senate passed Sept. 26. House passed Oct. 10. President signed Oct. 25, 1978.

PL 95-516 (HR 10161) — For the relief of the Eastern Telephone Supply and Manufacturing, Inc. ST GERMAIN, D-R.I. — 11/29/78 — House Ways and Means reported July 14, 1978 (H Rept 95-1363). House passed Aug. 1. Senate Finance reported Aug. 11 (S Rept 95-1114). Senate passed, amended, Aug. 23. House agreed to Senate amendment to the title of the bill Oct. 10. House disagreed to Senate amendment No. 2 Oct. 10. Senate receded from its amendment No. 2 Oct. 12. President signed Oct. 25, 1978.

PL 95-517 (HR 11945) — Authorize the Secretary of the Army to return to the Federal Republic of Germany ten paintings of the German Navy seized by the United States Army at the end of World War II. WHITEHURST, R-Va. — 4/6/78 — House Armed Services reported Sept. 18, 1978 (H Rept 95-1575). House passed Oct. 2. Senate Armed Services reported Oct. 13 (no written report). Senate passed Oct. 14. President signed Oct. 25, 1978.

PL 95-518 (HR 12112) — Designate Gathright Lake on the Jackson River, Va., as Gathright Dam and Lake Moomaw. BUTLER, R-Va. — 4/13/78 — House Public Works and Transportation reported May 1, 1978 (H Rept 95-1094). House passed May 15. Senate Environment and Public Works reported Aug. 25 (S Rept 95-1165). Senate passed, amended, Sept. 6. House agreed to Senate amendments Oct. 15. President signed Oct. 25, 1978.

PL 95-519 (S 1626) — Clarify the status of certain legislative and judicial officers under the provisions of Title 5, United States Code, relating to annual and sick leave. RIBICOFF, D-Conn. — 6/6//77 — Senate Governmental Affairs reported Aug. 5, 1977 (S Rept 95-403). Senate passed Sept. 9. House Post Office and Civil Service reported Aug. 16 (H Rept 95-1496). House passed, amended, Sept. 18. Senate agreed to House amendments Oct. 10. President signed Oct. 25, 1978.

PL 95-520 (HR 5029) — Enact the Veterans Administration Programs Extension Act of 1978. SATTERFIELD, D-Va., HAMMERSCHMIDT, R-Ark., ROBERTS, D-Texas, EDWARDS, D-Calif., MONTGOMERY, D-Miss., CARNEY, D-Ohio, DANIELSON, D-Calif., HEFNER, D-N.C., HANNAFORD, C-Calif., HALL, D-Texas, APPLEGATE, D-Ohio, BARNARD, D-Ga., EDGAR, D-Pa., HECKLER, R-Mass., HILLIS, R-Ind., ABDNOR, R-S.D., GUYER, R-Ohio, HANSEN, R-Idaho, SAWYER, R-Mich., TEAGUE, D-Texas, BRINKLEY, D-Ga., CORNELL, D-Wis., BEARD, D-R.I., WYLIE, R-Ohio and WALSH, R-N.Y. — 3/14/77 — House Veterans' Affairs reported March 23, 1977 (H Rept 95-111). House passed April 4. Senate Veterans' Affairs reported May 15, 1978 (S Rept 95-825). Senate passed, amended, May 26. House agreed to Senate amendments with amendments Oct. 13. Senate agreed to House amendments Oct. 15. President signed Oct. 26, 1978.

PL 95-521 (S 555) — Enact the Ethics in Government Act of 1978. RIBICOFF, D-Conn., PERCY, R-Ill., JAVITS, R-N.Y., WEICKER, R-Conn., ABOUREZK, D-S.D., KENNEDY, D-Mass., CHAFEE, R-R.I., CHILES, D-Fla., CLARK, D-Iowa, GLENN, D-Ohio, HUMPHREY, D-Minn., LUGAR, R-Ind., MATSUNAGA, D-Hawaii, METCALF, D-Mont., MUSKIE, D-Maine, NUNN, D-Ga., SARBANES, D-Md., STEVENS, R-Alaska and ZORINSKY, D-Neb. — 2/1/77 — Senate Governmental Affairs reported May 16, 1977 (S Rept 95-170). Senate Judiciary reported June 15, 1977 (S Rept 95-273). Senate passed June 27. House passed, amended, Sept. 27, 1978. Senate agreed to conference report Oct. 7. Conference report filed in House Oct. 11 (H Rept 95-1756). House agreed to conference report Oct. 12. President signed Oct. 26, 1978.

PL 95-522 (HR 3481) — Name the post office and federal building in Portland, Maine, the "Frederick G. Payne Building." EMERY, R-Maine — 7/14/78 — House Public Works and Transportation reported Aug. 10, 1978 (H Rept 95-1471). House passed Sept. 18. Senate passed Oct. 15. President signed Oct. 27, 1978.

PL 95-523 (HR 50) — Enact the Full Employment and Balanced Growth Act of 1978. HAWKINS, D-Calif. and PERKINS, D-Ky. — 1/4/77 — House Education and Labor reported Part I Feb. 22, 1978 (H Rept 95-895). House Rules reported Part II March 3. House passed March 16. Senate passed, amended, Oct. 13. House agreed to Senate amendments Oct. 15. President signed Oct. 27, 1978.

PL 95-524 (S 2570) — Enact the Comprehensive Employment and Training Act Amendments of 1978. NELSON, D-Wis., WILLIAMS, D-N.J., JAVITS, R-N.Y., HATHAWAY, D-Maine, RIEGLE, D-Mich., KENNEDY, D-Mass. and CRANSTON, D-Calif. — 2/23/78 — Senate Human Resources reported May 15, 1978 (S Rept 95-891). Senate passed Aug. 25. House passed, amended, Sept. 22. Conference report filed in House Oct. 11 (H Rept 95-1765). Conference report filed in Senate Oct. 11 (S Rept 95-1325). Senate agreed to conference report Oct. 13. House agreed to conference report Oct. 15. President signed Oct. 27, 1978.

PL 95-525 (HR 7296) — Designate the new Terminal Radar Approach Control Federal Building in Hempstead, Long Island, New York, as the "Charles A. Lindbergh Federal Building." WYDLER, R-N.Y. — 5/18/78 — House Public Works and Transportation reported Aug. 10, 1978 (H Rept 95-1465). House passed Sept. 18. Senate passed Oct. 15. President signed Oct. 27, 1978.

PL 95-526 (HR 12116) — Amend the District of Columbia Self-Government and Reorganization Act to repeal the authority of the President to sustain vetoes by the Mayor of the District of Columbia of acts passed by the Council of the District of Columbia and repassed by two-thirds of the Council, and to change the period during which acts of the Council are subject to congressional review. DELLUMS, D-Calif., DIGGS, D-Mich., McKINNEY, R-Conn. and FAUNTROY, D-D.C. — 4/13/78 — House District of Columbia reported May 1, 1978 (H Rept 95-1104). House passed Sept. 12. Senate Governmental Affairs reported Oct. 6 (S Rept 95-1291). Senate passed Oct. 12. President signed Oct. 27, 1978.

PL 95-527 (HR 7305) — Designate a certain federal building in Champaign, Ill., the "William L. Springer Building." MADIGAN, R-Ill., ANDERSON, R-Ill., ANNUNZIO, D-Ill., DERWINSKI, R-Ill., ERLENBORN, R-Ill., FINDLEY, R-Ill., HYDE, R-Ill., METCALFE, D-Ill., MICHEL, R-Ill., MIKVA, D-Ill., O'BRIEN, R-Ill., RAILSBACK, R-Ill., SHIPLEY, D-Ill., SIMON, D-Ill. and STAGGERS, D-W.Va. — 5/18/77 — House Public Works and Transportation reported Aug. 10, 1978 (S Rept 95-1466). House passed Sept. 18. Senate passed, amended, Oct. 13. House agreed to Senate amendments Oct. 14. President signed Oct. 27, 1978.

PL 95-528 (HR 13808) — Designate the "Omar Burleson Federal Building." ROBERTS, D-Texas, BROOKS, D-Texas, HIGHTOWER, D-Texas, WILSON, D-Texas, POAGE, D-Texas, WRIGHT, D-Texas and PICKLE, D-Texas — 8/9/78 — House Public Works and Transportation reported Aug. 17, 1978 (H Rept 95-1514). House passed Sept. 18. Senate passed Oct. 15. President signed Oct. 27, 1978.

PL 95-529 (HR 13809) — Designate the "George Mahon Federal Building." ROBERTS, D-Texas, BROOKS, D-Texas, HIGHTOWER, D-Texas, WILSON, D-Texas, POAGE, D-Texas, WRIGHT, D-Texas and PICKLE, D-Texas — 8/9/78 — House Public Works and Transportation reported Aug. 17, 1978 (H Rept 95-1515). House passed Sept. 18. Senate passed Oct. 15. President signed Oct. 27, 1978.

PL 95-530 (HR 13892) — Amend Title 28 of the U.S. Code to provide that the requirement that each United States attorney and United States marshall reside in the district for which he is appointed shall not apply to an individual appointed to such a position for the Northern Mariana Islands if such individual is at the same time serving in the same capacity in another district. KASTENMEIER, D-Wis. — 8/16/78 — House Judiciary reported Sept. 28, 1978 (H Rept 95-1650). House passed Oct. 10. Senate passed Oct. 13. President signed Oct. 27, 1978.

PL 95-531 (HR 14223) — Designate a certain federal building in Bloomington, Ill., the "Leslie C. Arends Building." MADIGAN, D-Ill. — 10/4/78 — House passed Oct. 14. Senate passed Oct. 15. President signed Oct. 27, 1978.

PL 95-532 (HR 14295) — Designate the "Paul G. Rogers Federal Building." FASCELL, D-Fla. — 10/12/78 — House passed Oct. 14, 1978. Senate passed Oct. 15. President signed Oct. 27, 1978.

PL 95-533 (H J Res 747) — Consent to an amendment of the constitution of the state of New Mexico to provide a method for executing leases and other contracts for the development and operation of geothermal steam and waters on lands granted or confirmed to such state. RUNNELS, D-N.M. and LUJAN, R-N.M. — 2/22/78 — House Interior and Insular Affairs reported Sept. 26, 1978 (H Rept 95-1630). House passed Oct. 10. Senate passed Oct. 13. President signed Oct. 27, 1978.

PL 95-534 (H J Res 816) — Extend the authority of Federal Reserve banks to buy and sell certain obligations. MITCHELL, D-Md. — 4/3//78 — House Banking, Finance and Urban Affairs reported April 26, 1978 (H Rept 95-1088). House passed May 1. Senate passed Oct. 15. President signed Oct. 27, 1978.

PL 95-535 (S 2049) — Establish fees and allow per diem and mileage expenses for witnesses before United States courts. DeCONCINI, D-Ariz. and WALLOP, R-Wyo. — 8/5/77 — Senate Judiciary reported April 25, 1978 (S Rept 95-756). Senate passed April 27. House Judiciary reported Sept. 28 (H Rept 95-1651). House passed, amended, Oct. 12. Senate agreed to House amendment Oct. 13. President signed Oct. 27, 1978.

PL 95-536 (S 2403) — Consent to certain amendments to the New Hampshire-Vermont Interstate School Compact approved by PL 91-21. STAFFORD, R-Vt., McINTYRE, D-N.H., DURKIN, D-N.H. and LEAHY, D-Vt. — 1/23/78 — Senate Judiciary reported July 10, 1978 (S Rept 95-968). Senate passed July 14. House Judiciary reported Oct. 5 (H Rept 95-1722). House passed Oct. 12. President signed Oct. 27, 1978.

PL 95-537 (S 3336) - Enact the contract services for the "Drug Dependent Federal Offenders Act of 1978." HATFIELD, D-Mont., DeCONCINI, D-Ariz. and MATHIAS, R-Md. — 7/24/78 — Senate Judiciary reported Aug. 11, 1978 (S Rept 95-1110). Senate passed Aug. 17. House Judiciary reported Sept. 28 (H Rept 95-1649). House passed, amended, Oct. 10. Senate agreed to House amendments Oct. 13. President signed Oct. 27, 1978.

PL 95-538 (S 3540) — Rename the U.S. federal building in Yakima, Wash., the "Justice William O. Douglas Federal Building." JACKSON, D-Wash. and MAGNUSON, D-Wash. — 9/30/78 — Senate passed Oct. 2. House passed Oct. 12. President signed Oct. 27, 1978.

PL 95-539 (S 1315) — Enact the Court Interpreters Act. DeCONCINI, D-Ariz., ALLEN, D-Ala., BAYH, D-Ind. and KENNEDY, D-Mass. — 4/20/77 — Senate Judiciary reported Nov. 11, 1977 (S Rept 95-569). Senate passed Nov. 4. House passed, amended, Oct. 10. Senate agreed to House amendment Oct. 13. President signed Oct. 28, 1978.

PL 95-540 (HR 4727) — Amend the Federal Rules of Evidence to provide for the protection of the privacy of rape victims. HOLTZMAN, D-N.Y., D'AMOURS, D-N.H., DAVIS, D-S.C., DELLUMS, D-Calif., DIGGS, D-Mich., DODD, D-Conn., EDGAR, D-Pa., EDWARDS, D-Calif., ERTEL, D-Pa., EVANS, D-Ga., FENWICK, R-N.J., FISH, R-N.Y., FITHIAN, D-Ind., FLOOD, D-Pa., FLORIO, D-N.J., FORD, D-Tenn., FRASER, D-Minn., FRENZEL, R-Minn., GAMMAGE, D-Texas, GEPHARDT, D-Mo. and HANNAFORD, D-Calif. — 3/9/77 — House passed Oct. 10, 1978. Senate passed Oct. 12. President signed Oct 28, 1978.

PL 95-541 (HR 7749) — Enact the Antarctic Conservation Act of 1978. MURPHY, D-N.Y., LEGGETT, D-Calif., FORSYTHE, R-N.J., AuCOIN, D-Ore., HUGHES, D-N.J., McCLOSKEY, R-Calif., MIKULSKI, D-Md., TRIBLE, R-Va. and AKAKA, D-Hawaii — 6/13/77 — House Merchant Marine and Fisheries reported Part I March 31, 1978 (H Rept 95-1031). House Science and Technology reported Part II May 18. House passed Sept. 25. Senate passed, amended, Oct. 13. House agreed to Senate amendment Oct. 14. President signed Oct. 28, 1978.

PL 95-542 (HR 11671) — Designate a certain federal building in Big Stone Gap, Va., the "C. Bascome Slemp Building." WAMPLER, R-Va. — 3/20/78 — House Public Works and Transportation reported Aug. 10, 1978 (H Rept 95-1469). House passed Sept. 18. Senate passed Oct. 15. President signed Oct. 28, 1978.

PL 95-543 (HR 12634) — Designate a certain building in Pittsburg, Kan., as the "Joe Skubitz Social Security Administration Center." HARSHA, R-Ohio — 5/9/78 —House Public Works and Transportation reported Aug. 10, 1978 (H Rept 95-1467). House passed Sept. 18. Senate passed Oct 15. President signed Oct. 28, 1978.

PL 95-544 (HR 13187) — Designate the U.S. Post Office and Federal Building in Griffin, Ga., the "John J. Flynt Jr. Federal Building," GINN, D-Ga., BRINKLEY, D-Ga., MATHIS, D-Ga., LEVITAS, D-Ga., McDONALD, D-Ga., BARNARD, D-Ga., EVANS, D-Ga., JENKINS, D-Ga. and FOWLER, D-Ga. — 5/19/78 — House Public Works and Transportation reported Aug. 10, 1978 (H Rept 95-1470). House passed Sept. 18. Senate passed Oct. 15. President signed Oct. 28, 1978.

PL 95-545 (HR 13514) — Name a certain federal building in Shreveport, La., the "Joe Waggonner Federal Building." BREAUX, D-La. — 7/17/78 — House Public Works and Transportation reported Aug. 10, 1978 (H Rept 95-1472). House passed Sept. 18. Senate passed Oct. 15. President signed Oct. 28, 1978.

PL 95-546 (HR 13972) — Designate the Great Bear Wilderness, Flathead National Forest, and enlarge the Bob Marshall Wilderness, Flathead and Lewis and Clark National Forests in Montana. UDALL, D-Ariz. — 8/17/78 — House Interior and Insular Affairs reported Sept. 22, 1978 (H Rept 95-1616). House passed Oct. 3. Senate passed, amended, Oct. 6. House agreed to Senate amendments Oct. 14. President signed Oct. 28, 1978.

PL 95-547 (HR 13989) — Amend section 1145(b) of the Food and Agriculture Act of 1977 to modify the formula for distribution of funds authorized thereunder for agricultural research. DE LA GARZA, D-Texas — 9/6/78 — House Agriculture Sept. 22, 1978 (H Rept 95-1619). House passed Oct. 2. Senate passed Oct. 13. President signed Oct. 28, 1978.

PL 95-548 (S 3112) — Amend the Act of Oct. 19, 1965, to provide additional authorization for the Library of Congress James Madison Memorial Building. PELL, D-R.I. — 5/19/78 — Senate Rules and Administration reported May 19, 1978 (S Rept 95-906). Senate passed June 13. House passed, amended, Oct. 14. Senate Agreed to House amendment Oct. 15. President signed Oct. 28, 1978.

PL 95-549 (HR 12509) — Amend the Immigration and Nationality Act to exclude from admission into, and to deport from, the United States all aliens who persecuted any person on the basis of race, religion, national origin, or political opinion, under the direction of the Nazi government of Germany. HOLTZMAN, D-N.Y., EILBERG, D-Pa., HALL, D-Texas, HARRIS, D-Va., EVANS, D-Ga., FISH, R-N.Y. and SAWYER, R-Mich. — 5/2/78 — House Judiciary reported Aug. 8, 1978 (H Rept 95-1452). House passed Sept. 26. Senate passed, amended, Oct. 10. House agreed to Senate amendment Oct. 13. President signed Oct. 30, 1978.

PL 95-550 (S 1403) — Provide for conveyance of certain lands near Dixon, New Mexico, to the University of New Mexico. DOMENICI, R-N.M. and SCHMITT, R-N.M. — 4/22/77 — Senate Energy and Natural Resources reported Oct. 9, 1978 (S Rept 95-1301). Senate passed Oct. 13. House passed Oct. 14. President signed Oct. 30, 1978.

PL 95-551 (HR 13416) — Amend Title 10 of the U.S. Code to modernize the permanent faculty structure at the United States Military Academy. PRICE, D-Ill. and WILSON, R-Calif. — 7/11/78 — House Armed Services reported Sept. 29, 1978 (H Rept 95-1657). House passed Oct. 2. Senate Armed Services reportd Oct. 13 (no written report). Senate passed Oct. 14. President signed Oct. 30, 1978.

PL 95-552 (HR 13372) — Increase the price of migratory-bird hunting and conservation stamps and to provide for consultation by the Secretary of the Interior with state and local authorities before migratory bird areas are recommended for purchase or rental. DINGELL, D-Mich., AKAKA, D-Hawaii, ASHLEY, D-Ohio, BEILENSON, D-Calif., BONIOR, D-Mich., CONTE, R-Mass., ECKHARDT, D-Texas, EDGAR, D-Pa., EILBERG, D-Pa., FORSYTHE, R-N.J., KILDEE, D-Mich., LONG, D-Md., MOAKLEY, D-Mass., PREYER, D-N.C., RODINO, D-N.J., RUPPE, R-Mich., SEIBERLING, D-Ohio, SPELLMAN, D-Md., STOCKMAN, R-Mich., STUDDS, D-Mass., UDALL, D-Ariz., VENTO, D-Minn. and WAXMAN, D-Calif. — 6/29/78 — House Merchant Marine and Fisheries reported Aug. 18, 1978 (H Rept 95-1518). House passed Sept. 25. Senate passed, amended, Oct. 6. House agreed to Senate amendments Oct. 14. President signed Oct. 30, 1978.

PL 95-553 (S 3551) — Make technical corrections in the North Pacific Fisheries Act of 1954. STEVENS, R-Alaska — 10/4/78 — Senate passed Oct. 5. House passed Oct. 14. President signed Oct. 30, 1978.

PL 95-554 (S 3189) — Further amend the Mineral Leasing Act of 1920 to authorize the Secretary of the Interior to exchange federal coal leases and to encourage recovery of certain coal deposits. HASKELL, D-Colo. and HANSEN, R-Wyo. — 6/9/78 — Senate Energy and Natural Resources reported Aug. 25, 1978 (S Rept 95-1169). Senate passed Sept. 20. House passed, amended, Oct. 3. Senate agreed to House amendment Oct. 13. President signed Oct. 30, 1978.

PL 95-555 (S 995) — Amend title VII of the Civil Rights Act of 1964 to prohibit sex discrimination on the basis of pregnancy. WILLIAMS, D-N.J., BAYH, D-Ind., BROOKE, R-Mass., PELL, D-R.I., CLARK, D-Iowa, HEINZ, R-Pa., JAVITS, R-N.Y., KENNEDY, D-Mass., MATHIAS, R-Md., McINTYRE, D-N.H. and RIEGLE, D-Mich. — 3/15/77 — Senate Human Resources reported July 6, 1977 (S Rept 95-331). Senate passed Sept. 16. House passed, amended, July 18, 1978. Conference report filed in House Oct. 13 (H Rept 95-1786). Senate agreed to conference report Oct. 15. President Signed Oct. 31, 1978.

PL 95-556 (HR 13702) — Provide that American Samoa be represented by a nonvoting Delegate to the U.S. House of Representatives. BURTON, P., D-Calif., MEEDS, D-Wash., UDALL, D-Ariz., CLAUSEN, R-Calif., RONCALIO, D-Wyo., LAGOMARSINO, R-Calif., BINGHAM, D-N.Y., SKUBITZ, R-Kan., SEIBERLING, D-Ohio, LUJAN, R-N.M., RUNNELS, D-N.M., SEBELIUS, R-Kan., ECKHARDT, D-Texas, JOHNSON, R-Colo., BYRON, D-Md., YOUNG, R-Alaska, SANTINI, D-Nev., MARRIOTT, R-Utah, WEAVER, D-Ore., CARR, D-Mich., DUNCAN, D-Ore., McKAY, D-Utah, MOAKLEY, D-Mass., CHISHOLM, D-N.Y. and DODD, D-Conn. — 8/2/78 — House Interior and Insular Affairs reported Aug. 9, 1978 (H Rept 95-1458). House passed Oct. 3. Senate passed Oct. 13. President signed Oct. 31, 1978.

PL 95-557 (S 3084) — Enact the Housing and Community Development Amendments of 1978. PROXMIRE, D-Wis. — 5/15/78 — Senate Banking, Housing and Urban Affairs reported May 15, 1978 (S Rept 95-871). Senate passed July 20. House passed, amended, July 24. Conference report filed in House Oct. 14 (H Rept 95 1792). Senate agreed to conference report Oct. 14. House agreed to conference report Oct. 15. President signed Oct. 31, 1978.

PL 95-558 (S 3595) — Amend section 202(d) of the Magnuson-Moss Warranty Federal Trade Commission Improvement Act to extend the deadline for filing a report of rulemaking procedures. CANNON, D-Nev. — 10/12/78 — Senate passed Oct. 12, 1978. House passed Oct. 13. President signed Nov. 1, 1978.

PL 95-559 (S 2534) — Enact the Health Maintenance Organization Amendments of 1978. SCHWEICKER, R-Pa., KENNEDY, D-Mass., WILLIAMS, D-N.J., JAVITS, R-N.Y., PELL, D-R.I. and CHAFEE, R-R.I. — 2/10/78 — Senate Human Resources reported May 15, 1978 (S Rept 95-837). Senate passed July 21. House passed, amended, Sept. 25. Conference report filed in House Oct. 13 (H Rept 95-1784). House agreed to conference report Oct. 13. Senate agreed to conference report Oct. 14. President signed Nov. 1, 1978.

PL 95-560 (HR 8389) — Authorize the President to present a gold medal to the widow of Robert F. Kennedy. PEPPER, D-Fla. — 7/18/77 — House Banking, Finance and Urban Affairs reported Sept. 21, 1978 (H Rept 95-1601). House passed Sept. 26. Senate Banking, Housing and Urban Affairs reported Oct. 10 (S Rept 95-1316). Senate passed, amended, Oct. 15. House disagreed to Senate amendment Oct. 15. Senate receded from its amendment Oct. 15. President signed Nov. 1, 1978.

PL 95-561 (HR 15) — Enact the Education Amendments of 1978. PERKINS, D-Ky. — 1/4/77 — House Education and Labor reported May 11, 1978 (H Rept 95-1137). House passed July 13. Senate passed, amended, Aug. 24. Conference report filed in House Oct. 10 (H Rept 95-1753). Senate agreed to conference report Oct. 12. House agreed to conference report Oct. 15. President signed Nov. 1, 1978.

PL 95-562 (S 976) — Amend the Perishable Agricultural Commodities Act. HUDDLESTON, D-Ky. — 3/10/77 — Senate Agriculture, Nutrition and Forestry reported Aug. 25, 1978 (S Rept 95-1156). Senate passed Sept. 8. House passed, amended, Oct. 4. Senate agreed to House amendment with an amendment Oct. 13. House agreed to Senate amendment Oct. 14. President signed Nov. 1, 1978.

PL 95-563 (HR 11002) — Enact the Contract Disputes Act of 1978. HARRIS, D-Va. and KINDNESS, R-Ohio — 2/20/78 — Senate Judiciary reported Sept. 8, 1978 (H Rept 95-1556). House passed Sept. 26. Senate passed, amended, Oct. 13. House agreed to Senate amendment Oct. 14. President signed Nov. 1, 1978.

PL 95-564 (HR 11209) — Provide for the establishment, ownership, operation and governmental oversight and regulation of international maritime satellite telecommunications services. STAGGERS, D-W.Va., VAN DEERLIN, D-Calif., MURPHY, D-N.Y., BIAGGI, D-N.Y., DEVINE, R-Ohio and FREY, R-Fla. — 2/28/78 — House Interstate and Foreign Commerce reported Part I May 11, 1978 (H Rept 95-1134). House Merchant Marine and Fisheries reported Part II May 11. House passed May 15. Senate Commerce, Science and Transportation reported July 25 (S Rept 95-1036). Senate passed, amended, Aug. 7. House agreed to Senate amendment with an amendment Oct. 13. Senate agreed to House amendment Oct. 13. President signed Nov. 1, 1978.

PL 95-565 (S 2788) — Enact the U.S. Railway Association Amendments Act of 1978. LONG, D-La., MAGNUSON, D-Wash. and STEVENSON, D-Ill. — 3/22/78 — Senate Commerce, Science and Transportation reported May 15, 1978 (S Rept 95-885). Senate passed Aug. 1. House passed Oct. 15. President signed Nov. 1, 1978.

PL 95-566 (S 2539) — Enact the Middle Income Student Assistance Act. PELL, D-R.I., WILLIAMS, D-N.J., JAVITS, R-N.Y. and STAFFORD, R-Vt. — 2/10/78 — Senate Human Resources reported Feb. 28, 1978 (S Rept 95-643). Senate passed Aug. 16. House passed, amended, Oct. 14. Senate agreed to House amendments Oct. 15. President signed Nov. 1, 1978.

PL 95-567 (HR 12605) — Enact the Public Telecommunications Financing Act of 1978. VAN DEERLIN, D-Calif., FREY, R-Fla., CARNEY, D-Ohio, WIRTH, D-Colo., RUSSO, D-Ill., MARKEY, D-Mass., GORE, D-Tenn., MIKULSKI, D-Md., WAXMAN, D-Calif., MOORE, R-La., MOORHEAD, R-Calif. and MARKS, R-Pa. — 5/8/78 — House Interstate and Foreign Commerce reported May 15, 1978 (H Rept 95-1178). House passed July 10. Senate passed, amended, Sept. 19. Conference report filed in House Oct. 12 (H Rept 95-1774). House agreed to conference report Oct. 13. Senate agreed to conference report Oct. 14. President signed Nov. 2, 1978.

PL 95-568 (HR 7577) — Enact the Economic Opportunity Amendments of 1978. ANDREWS, D-N.C. and PERKINS, D-Ky. — 6/2/77 — House Education and Labor reported May 15, 1978 (H Rept 95-1151). House passed July 26. Senate passed, amended, Aug. 2. Conference report filed in House Oct. 11 (H Rept 95-1766). House agreed to conference report Oct. 15. Senate agreed to conference report Oct. 15. President signed Nov. 2, 1978.

PL 95-569 (S 1029) — Authorize the Smithsonian Institution to construct support museum facilities. JACKSON, D-Wash., PELL, D-R.I. and GOLDWATER, R-Ariz. — 3/17/77 — Senate Rules and Administration reported May 4, 1978 (S Rept 95-783). Senate passed May 9. House Public Works and Transportation reported Sept. 12 (H Rept 95-1559). House passed, amended, Sept. 25. Senate agreed to House amendment with an amendment Oct. 2. House agreed to Senate amendment Oct. 14. President signed Nov. 2, 1978.

PL 95-570 (HR 11003) — Clarify the authority for employment of personnel in the White House Office and the Executive Residence at the White House and to clarify the authority for employment of personnel by the President to meet unanticipated needs. HARRIS, D-Va., UDALL, D-Ariz., SCHROEDER, D-Colo., DERWINSKI, R-Ill., LEHMAN, D-Fla., SPELLMAN, D-Md., NIX, D-Pa. and STEED, D-Okla. — 2/20/78 — House Post Office and Civil Service reported March 16, 1978 (H Rept 95-979). House passed April 13. Senate Governmental Affairs reported May 15 (S Rept 95-868). Senate passed, amended, July 14. Conference report filed in Senate Sept. 28 (S Rept 95-1258). Conference report filed in House Sept. 29 (H Rept 95-1639). Senate agreed to conference report Oct. 7. House agreed to conference report Oct. 15. President signed Nov. 2, 1978.

PL 95-571 (HR 14224) — Authorize and direct the Secretary of the Interior to acquire certain lands for the benefit of the Mille Laes Band of the Minnesota Chippewa Indians. NOLAN, D-Minn. — 10/4/78 — House passed Oct. 14, 1978. Senate passed Oct. 15. President signed Nov. 2, 1978.

PL 95-572 (S 2075) — Enact the Jury System Improvements Act of 1978. DeCONCINI, D-Ariz. and WALLOP, R-Wyo. — 9/8/77 — Senate Judiciary reported April 25, 1978 (S Rept 95-757). Senate passed April 27. House Judiciary reported Sept. 28 (H Rept 95-1652). House passed, amended, Oct. 12. Senate agreed to House amendment Oct. 13. President signed Nov. 2, 1978.

PL 95-573 (HR 14145) — Amend title 28 of the U.S. Code to make certain changes in the divisions within judicial districts and in the places of holding court, and to require the Director of the Administrative Office of the U.S. Courts to conduct a study of the judicial business of the Central District of California and the Eastern District of New York. KASTENMEIER, D-Wis., DANIELSON, D-Calif., SANTINI, D-Nev., RAILSBACK, R-Ill., BUTLER, R-Va. and COHEN, R-Maine — 9/21/78 — House Judiciary reported Oct. 11, 1978 (H Rept 95-1763). House passed Oct. 12. Senate passed Oct. 15. President signed Nov. 2, 1978.

PL 95-574 (S 3081) — Enact the Federal Railroad Safety Authorization Act of 1978. CANNON, D-Nev. — 5/15/78 — Senate Commerce, Science and Transportation reported May 15, 1978 (S Rept 95-865). Senate passed May 25. House passed, amended, Oct. 15. Senate agreed to House amendment Oct. 15. President signed Nov. 2, 1978.

PL 95-575 (S 1487) — Amend title 18 of the U.S. Code to eliminate racketeering in the sale and distribution of cigarettes. BELLMON, R-Okla. and ANDERSON, D-Minn. — 5/11/77 — Senate Judiciary reported June 28, 1978 (S Rept 95-962). Senate passed Sept. 29. House passed, amended, Oct. 3. Conference report filed in House Oct. 12 (H Rept 95-1778). Senate agreed to conference report Oct. 15. House agreed to conference report Oct. 15. President signed Nov. 2, 1978.

PL 95-576 (HR 12140) — Amend the Federal Water Pollution Control Act to provide additional authorizations for certain operating programs under the Act. JOHNSON, D-Calif., ROBERTS, D-Texas and CLAUSEN, R-Calif. — 4/13/78 — House Public Works and Transportation reported May 1, 1978 (H Rept 95-1097). House passed June 5. Senate passed, amended, Oct. 15. House agreed to Senate amendment Oct. 15. President signed Nov. 2, 1978.

PL 95-577 (HR 13597) — Authorize the Architect of the Capitol to install solar collectors for furnishing a portion of the energy needs of the Rayburn House Office Building Annex No. 2. MINETA D-Calif., JOHNSON, D-Calif., WALSH, R-N.Y., PICKLE, D-Texas, HOWARD, D-N.J., CLEVELAND, R-N.H., ROE, D-N.J., GOLDWATER, R-Calif., AMBRO, D-N.Y., EDGAR, D-Pa., RISENHOOVER, D-Okla., BONIOR, D-Mich., OTTINGER, D-N.Y., ROSE, D-N.C. and BAUCUS, D-Mont. — 7/25/78 — House Public Works and Transportation reported Aug. 17, 1978 (H Rept 95-1513). House passed Sept. 25. Senate passed Oct. 15. President signed Nov. 2, 1978.

PL 95-578 (S 2820) — Enact the Reclamation Safety of Dams Act of 1978. JACKSON, D-Wash. — 4/4/78 — Senate Energy and Natural Resources reported May 12, 1978 (S Rept 95-810). Senate passed July 28. House passed, amended, Oct. 14. Senate agreed to House amendments Oct. 15. President signed Nov. 2, 1978.

PL 95-579 (S 2247) — Amend section 312 of the Immigration and Nationality Act. SCHWEIKER, R-Pa. — 10/27/78 — Senate Judiciary reported May 17, 1978 (S Rept 95-897). Senate passed May 23. House Judiciary reported Oct. 3 (H Rept 95-1683). House passed, amended, Oct. 14. Senate agreed to House amendment Oct. 15. President signed Nov. 2, 1978.

PL 95-580 (S 1835) — Establish a Rural Transportation Advisory Task Force. HUDDLESTON, D-Ky., McGOVERN, D-S.D. and DOLE, R-Kan. — 7/11/77 — Senate Agriculture, Nutrition and Forestry reported May 31, 1978 (S Rept 95-923). Senate passed June 8. House passed, amended, Oct. 4. Senate agreed to House amendment Oct. 15. President signed Nov. 2, 1978.

PL 95-581 (HR 10343) — Provide for recalculation of the retired pay of individuals who served as sergeant major of the Marine Corps before Dec. 16, 1967. NICHOLS, D-Ala., MITCHELL, R-N.Y., DAVIS, D-S.C., BEARD, D-R.I., SCHROEDER, D-Colo., TRIBLE, R-Va., WON PAT, D-Guam, BADHAM, R-Calif., LLOYD, D-Calif. and DOWNEY, D-N.Y. — 12/15/77 — House Armed Services reported Jan. 30, 1978 (H Rept 95-857). House passed June 5. Senate Armed Services reported Oct. 13 (no written report). Senate passed Oct. 14. President signed Nov. 2, 1978.

PL 95-582 (HR 12393) — Provide for nationwide service of subpoenas in all suits involving the False Claims Act. RODINO, D-N.J. — 4/26/78 — House Judiciary reported Aug. 7, 1978 (H Rept 95-1447). House passed Sept. 18. Senate passed, amended, Oct. 13. House agreed to Senate amendment Oct. 15. President signed Nov. 2, 1978.

PL 95-583 (HR 4319) — Amend subchapter III of chapter 83 of title 5 of the U.S. Code to provide that employees who retire after 5 years of service in certain instances may be eligible to retain their life and health insurance benefits. SPELLMAN, D-Md. — 3/2/77 — House Post Office and Civil Service reported May 10, 1977 (H Rept 95-284). House passed July 18. Senate Governmental Affairs reported Aug. 10, 1978 (S Rept 95-1080). Senate passed, amended, Aug. 18. House agreed to Senate amendment with an amendment Oct. 10. Senate agreed to House amendment Oct. 13. President signed Nov. 2, 1978.

PL 95-584 (S 3371) — Repeal certain provisions of the law establishing limits on the amount of land certain religious corporations may hold in any territory of the United States. DeCONCINI, D-Ariz., CANNON, D-Nev. and CHURCH, D-Idaho. — 8/2/78 — Senate Energy and Natural Resources reported Oct. 5, 1978 (S Rept 95-1275). Senate passed Oct. 11. House passed, amended, Oct. 12. Senate agreed to House amendment Oct. 13. President signed Nov. 2, 1978.

PL 95-585 (HR 3185) — Amend the Act commonly known as the Miller Act to raise the dollar amount of contracts to which such Act applies from $2,000 to $25,000. MOORHEAD, D-Pa. — 2/7/77 — House Judicary reported Sept. 29, 1978 (H Rept 95-1666). House passed Oct. 10. Senate passed Oct. 13. President signed Nov. 2, 1978.

PL 95-586 (HR 7971) — Validate certain land conveyances in California by the South Pacific Transportation Company. McFALL, D-Calif. — 6/22/77 — House Interior and Insular Affairs reported March 30, 1978 (H Rept 95-1008). House passed April 18. Senate Energy and Natural Resources reported Oct. 6 (S Rept 95-1287). Senate passed, amended, Oct. 12. House agreed to Senate amendments Oct. 14. President signed Nov. 3, 1978.

PL 95-587 (HR 7101) — Amend Certain provisions of law relating to land claims by the United States in Riverside County, Calif., based upon the accretion or avulsion. PETTIS, R-Calif. — 5/11/77 — House Interior and Insular Affairs reported March 30, 1978 (H Rept 95-1018). House passed April 11. Senate Energy and Natural Resources reported Oct. 6 (S Rept 95-1286). Senate passed Oct. 12. President signed Nov. 3, 1978.

PL 95-588 (HR 10173) — Enact the Veterans' and Survivors' Pension Improvement Act of 1978. MONTGOMERY, D-Miss., ROBERTS, D-Texas, HAMMERSCHMIDT, R-Ark., BRINKLEY, D-Ga., HEFNER, D-N.C., HALL, D-Texas, EDGAR, D-Pa. and GUYER, R-Ohio. — 11/30/77 — House Veterans' Affairs reported May 31, 1978 (H Rept 95-1225). House passed June 28. Senate passed, amended, July 31. Conference report filed in House Oct. 12 (H Rept 95-1768). Conference report filed in Senate Oct. 12 (S Rept 95-1329). Senate agreed to conference report Oct. 12. House agreed to conference report Oct. 14. President signed Nov. 4, 1978.

PL 95-589 (HR 13903) — Amend Title 10 of the U.S. Code to provide that a member of the Board of Regents of the Uniformed Services University of the Health Sciences whose term of office has expired shall continue to serve until a successor is appointed. STRATTON, D-N.Y. — 8/16/78 — House Armed Services reported Oct. 3, 1978 (H Rept 95-1685). House passed Oct. 10. Senate passed Oct. 15. President signed Nov. 4, 1978.

PL 95-590 (HR 12874) — Enact the Solar Photovoltaic Energy Research, Development and Demonstration Act of 1978. McCORMACK, D-Wash., TEAGUE, D-Texas and GOLDWATER, R-Calif. — 5/25/78 — House Science and Technology reported June 9, 1978 (H Rept 95-1285). House passed June 28. Senate passed, amended, Oct. 10. House agreed to Senate amendment Oct. 13. President signed Nov. 4, 1978.

PL 95-591 (HR 13500) — Enact the Presidential Records Act of 1978. PREYER, D-N.C., BRADEMAS, D-Ind., ERTEL, D-Pa., BROOKS, D-Texas, FOUNTAIN, D-N.C., HARRINGTON, D-Mass., JORDAN, D-Texas, MOSS, D-Calif., RYAN, D-Calif., WEISS, D-N.Y., HORTON, R-N.Y., ERLENBORN, R-Ill., McCLOSKEY, R-Calif. and QUAYLE, R-Ind. — 7/17/78 — House Government Operations reported Part I Aug. 14, 1978 (H Rept 95-1487). House passed Oct. 10. Senate passed, amended, Oct. 13. House agreed to Senate amendments Oct. 15. President signed Nov. 4, 1978.

PL 95-592 (S 1816) — Enact the Native Latex Commercialization and Economic Development Act of 1978. DOMENICI, R-N.M. — 6/30/77 — Senate Environment and Public Works reported May 15, 1978 (H Rept 95-829). Senate passed May 26. House passed, amended, Sept. 19. Senate agreed to House amendment with an amendment Oct. 7. House agreed to Senate amendment with an amendment Oct. 14. Senate agreed to House amendment Oct. 15. President signed Nov. 4, 1978.

PL 95-593 (S 703) — Improve the administration and operation of the Overseas Citizen Voting Rights Act of 1975. PELL, D-R.I., GOLDWATER, R-Ariz. and MATHIS, R-Md. — 2/10/77 — Senate Rules and Administration reported May 4, 1977 (S Rept 95-121). Senate passed May 9. House Administration reported Sept. 13, 1978 (H Rept 95-1568). House passed, amended, Sept. 19. Senate agreed to House amendment Oct. 13. President signed Nov. 4, 1978.

PL 95-594 (H J Res 1173) — Relative to the convening of the first session of the Ninety-sixth Congress. WRIGHT, D-Texas — 10/14/78 — House passed Oct. 15, 1978. Senate passed Oct. 15. President signed Nov. 4, 1978.

PL 95-595 (HR 9701) — Amend the Budget and Accounting Procedures Act of 1950. DENT, D-Pa. and ERLENBORN, R-Ill. — 10/20/77 — House

Government Operations reported Oct. 2, 1978 (H Rept 95-1678). House passed Oct. 10. Senate passed Oct. 15. President signed Nov. 4, 1978.

PL 95-596 (S J Res 160) — Initiate preliminary studies for the restoration and renovation of the Pension Building in Washington, D.C., to house a Museum of the Building Arts. MOYNIHAN, D-N.Y. — 9/11/78 — Senate Environment and Public Works reported Sept. 11, 1978 (S Rept 95-1181). Senate passed Sept. 15. House Public Works and Transportation reported Oct. 12 (H Rept 95-1776). House passed Oct. 14. President signed Nov. 4, 1978.

PL 95-597 (HR 5646) — Amend the Regional Rail Reorganization Act of 1973. ROONEY, D-Pa., METCALFE, D-Ill., MIKULSKI, D-Md., FLORIO, D-N.J., SANTINI, D-Nev., MURPHY, D-N.Y., SKUBITZ, R-Kan., MADIGAN, R-Ill., LENT, D-N.Y., RUSSO, D-Ill. and CARNEY, D-Ohio — 3/28/77 — House Interstate and Foreign Commerce reported June 1, 1977 (H Rept 95-37). House passed Jan. 30, 1978. Senate Commerce, Science and Transportation reported July 27 (S Rept 95-1041). Senate passed, amended, Aug. 2. House agreed to Senate amendment with amendments Oct. 11. Senate agreed to House amendments Oct. 13. President signed Nov. 4, 1978.

PL 95-598 (HR 8200) — Establish a uniform law on bankruptcy. EDWARDS, D-Calif., BUTLER, R-Va., SEIBERLING, D-Ohio, DRINAN, D-Mass., VOLKMER, D-Mo., BEILENSON, D-Calif. and McCLORY, R-Ill. — 7/11/77 — House Judiciary reported Sept. 8, 1977 (H Rept 95-595). House passed Feb. 1, 1978. House passed Feb. 1. Senate passed, amended, Sept. 7. Proceedings of Sept. 7 vacated Sept. 22. Senate passed, amended, Sept. 22. House agreed to Senate amendment with an amendment Sept. 28. Senate agreed to House amendment with amendments Oct. 5. House agreed to Senate amendments Oct. 6. President signed Nov. 6, 1978.

PL 95-599 (HR 11733) — Enact the Surface Transportation Assistance Act of 1978. HOWARD, D-N.J., SHUSTER, R-Pa., JOHNSON, D-Calif., CLEVELAND, R-N.Y., ANDERSON, D-Calif., ROE, D-N.J., CLAUSEN, R-Calif., McCORMACK, D-Wash., HAGEDORN, R-Minn., BREAUX, D-La., MINETA, D-Calif., ABDNOR, R-S.D., NOWAK, D-N.Y., EDGAR, D-Pa., HEFNER, D-N.C., FARY, D-Ill., RAHALL, D-W.Va., APPLEGATE, D-Ohio, EVANS, D-Ga., ROBERTS, D-Texas, RONCALIO, D-Wyo., GINN, D-Ga., OBERSTAR, D-Minn., AMBRO, D-N.Y. and HAMMERSCHMIDT, R-Ark. — 3/22/78 — House Public Works and Transportation reported Aug. 11, 1978 (H Rept 95-1485). House passed Sept. 28. Senate passed, amended, Oct. 3. Conference report filed in House Oct. 14 (H Rept 95-1797). Senate agreed to conference report Oct. 15. House agreed to conference report Oct. 15. President signed Nov. 6, 1978.

PL 95-600 (HR 13511) — Enact the Revenue Act of 1978. ULLMAN, D-Ore., JONES, D-Okla. and CONABLE, R-N.Y. — 7/18/78 — House Ways and Means reported Aug. 4, 1978 (H Rept 95-1445). House passed Aug. 10. Senate Finance reported Oct. 1 (S Rept 95-1263). Senate passed, amended, Oct. 10. Conference report filed in House Oct. 15 (H Rept 95-1800). Senate agreed to conference report Oct. 15. House agreed to conference report Oct. 15. President signed Nov. 6, 1978.

PL 95-601 (S 2584) — Authorize appropriations to the Nuclear Regulatory Commission for fiscal year 1979. HART, D-Colo. — 3/24/78 — Senate Environment and Public Works reported May 15, 1978 (S Rept 95-848). Senate passed Sept. 18. House passed, amended, Oct. 4. Conference report filed in House Oct. 14 (H Rept 95-1796). House agreed to conference report Oct. 14. Senate agreed to conference report Oct. 15. President signed Nov. 6, 1978.

PL 95-602 (HR 12467) — Enact the Rehabilitation, Comprehensive Services, and Development Disabilities Amendments of 1978. BRADEMAS, D-Ind., JEFFORDS, R-Vt., PERKINS, D-Ky., QUIE, R-Minn., BEARD, D-R.I., PRESSLER, R-S.D., MILLER, D-Calif., KILDEE, D-Mich., HEFTEL, D-Hawaii, HAWKINS, D-Calif., BIAGGI, D-N.Y., SARASIN, R-Conn., THOMPSON, D-N.J., DENT, D-Pa., FORD, D-Mich., GAYDOS, D-Pa., CLAY, D-Mo., BLOUIN, D-Iowa, CORNELL, D-Wis., SIMON, D-Ill., ZEFERETTI, D-N.Y., MOTTL, D-Ohio, MEYERS, D-Pa., MURPHY, D-Pa. and LeFANTE, D-N.J. — 5/1/78 — House Education and Labor reported May 13, 1978 (H Rept 95-1149). House passed May 16. Senate passed, amended, Sept. 21. House agreed to Senate amendments with amendments Sept. 26. Conference report filed in House Oct. 13 (H Rept 95-1780). Senate agreed to conference report Oct. 15. House agreed to conference report Oct. 15. President signed Nov. 6, 1978.

PL 95-603 (S 990) — Enact the Federal Physicians, Comparability Allowance Act of 1978. MATHIAS, R-Md. — 3/14/77 — Senate Governmental Affairs reported May 15, 1978 (S Rept 95-864). Senate passed May 25. House passed, amended, Oct. 3. Senate agreed to House amendments Oct. 13. President signed Nov. 6, 1978.

PL 95-604 (HR 13650) — Enact the Uranium Mill Tailings Radiation Control Act of 1978. UDALL, D-Ariz., LUJAN, R-N.M., SHARP, D-Ind., MARRIOTT, R-Utah, JOHNSON, R-Colo., McKAY, D-Utah, VENTO, D-Minn., KAZEN, D-Texas, RONCALIO, D-Wyo., BAUMAN, R-Md. and RHODES, R-Ariz. — 7/28/78 — House Interior and Insular Affairs reported Part I Aug. 11, 1978 (H Rept 95-1480). House Interstate and Foreign Commerce reported Part II Sept. 30. House passed Oct. 3. Senate passed, amended, Oct. 13. House agreed to Senate amendment with amendments Oct. 14. Senate agreed to House Amendments Oct. 15. President signed Nov. 8, 1978.

PL 95-605 (S 2774) — Extend the boundaries of the Toiyabe National Forest in Nevada. LAXALT, R-Nev. — 3/21/78 — Senate Energy and Natural Resources reported Oct. 7, 1978 (S Rept 95-1298). Senate passed Oct. 9. House passed Oct. 14. President signed Nov. 6, 1978.

PL 95-606 (S 2727) — Enact the Amateur Sports Act of 1978. STEVENS, R-Alaska, CULVER, D-Iowa, STONE, D-Fla., CANNON, D-Nev., PEARSON, R-Kan., GRIFFIN, R-Mich., GOLDWATER, R-Ariz., HAYAKAWA, R-Calif., MATSUNAGA, D-Hawaii, KENNEDY, D-Mass. — 3/10/78 — Senate Commerce, Science and Transportation reported April 27, 1978 (S Rept 95-770). Senate passed May 8. House Judiciary reported Sept. 25 (H Rept 95-1627). House passed, amended, Oct. 14. Senate agreed to House amendment Oct. 15. President signed Nov. 8, 1978.

PL 95-607 (S 2981) — Amend section 5 of the Department of Transportation Act relating to rail service assistance. CANNON, D-Nev., PEARSON, R-Kan. and CLARK, D-Iowa — 4/25/78 — Senate Commerce, Science and Transportation reported Aug. 25, 1978 (S Rept 95-1159). Senate passed Sept. 23. House passed, amended, Oct. 13. Senate agreed to House amendments Oct. 15. President signed Nov. 8, 1978.

PL 95-608 (S 1214) — Enact the Indian Child Welfare Act of 1978. ABOUREZK, D-S.D., HUMPHREY, D-Minn. and McGOVERN, D-S.D. — 4/1/77 — Senate Indian Affairs reported Nov. 3, 1977 (S Rept 95-597). Senate passed Nov. 4. House passed, amended, Oct. 14, 1978. Senate agreed to House amendments Oct. 15. President signed Nov. 8, 1978.

PL 95-609 (S 3083) — Enact the Quiet Communities Act of 1978. CULVER, D-Iowa — 5/15/78 — Senate Environment and Public Works reported May 15, 1978 (S Rept 95-875). Senate passed July 19. House passed, amended, Oct. 10. Senate agreed to House amendments Oct. 13. President signed Nov. 8, 1978.

PL 95-610 (S 274) — Amend Title 10 of the U.S. Code to prohibit union organization of the armed forces, membership in military labor organizations by members of the armed forces and recognition of military labor organizations by the federal government. THURMOND, R-S.C., ALLEN, D-Ala., BAKER, R-Tenn., BARTLETT, R-Okla., BELLMON, R-Okla., BENTSEN, D-Texas, BYRD, Ind-Va., CHILES, D-Fla., CURTIS, R-Neb., DANFORTH, R-Mo., DOLE, R-Kan., DOMENICI, R-N.M., EASTLAND, D-Miss., GARN, R-Utah, GOLDWATER, R-Ariz., HANSEN, R-Wyo., HATCH, R-Idaho, HAYAKAWA, R-Calif., HELMS, R-N.C., HOLLINGS, D-S.C., LAXALT, R-Nev., LUGAR, R-Ind., McCLELLAN, D-Ark., McCLURE, R-Idaho, MORGAN, D-N.C., NUNN, D-Ky., SCHMITT, R-N.M., SCOTT, R-Va., STEVENS, R-Alaska, STONE, D-Fla., TALMADGE, D-Ga., TOWER, R-Texas, WALLOP, R-Wyo., YOUNG, R-N.D. and ZORINSKY, D-Neb. — 1/18/77 — Senate Armed Services reported Aug. 18, 1977 (S Rept 96-411). Senate passed Sept. 16. House Post Office and Civil Service reported Part I Feb. 22, 1978 (H Rept 95-894). House Post Office and Civil Service reported Part II Aug. 4. House passed, amended, Sept. 26. Senate agreed to House amendment Oct. 15. President signed Nov. 8, 1978.

PL 95-611 (HR 10898) — Amend the Regional Rail Reorganization Act of 1973 to authorize appropriations for the U.S. Railway Association for fiscal year 1979. ROONEY, D-Pa. — 2/9/78 — House Interstate and Foreign Commerce reported May 15, 1978 (H Rept 95-1198). House passed Aug. 17. Senate passed, amended, Sept. 14. House agreed to Senate amendments Nos. 1, 2 and 4 Oct. 13. House agreed to Senate amendments Nos. 3 and 5 with amendments Oct. 13. Senate agreed to House amendments Oct. 15. President signed Nov. 8, 1978.

PL 95-612 (S 2093) — Provide that the exchange Stabilization Fund shall not be available for payment of administrative expenses. STEVENSON, D-Ill. and PROXMIRE, D-Wis. — 9/14/77 — Senate Banking, Housing and Urban Affairs reported March 2, 1978 (S Rept 95-661). Senate passed March 8. House Banking, Finance and Urban Affairs reported May 10 (H Rept 95-1126). House passed, amended, May 16. Senate agreed to House amendment with amendment Oct. 10. House agreed to Senate amendment No. 1 with an amendment Oct. 11. Senate agreed to House amendment Oct. 13. President signed Nov. 8, 1978.

PL 95-613 (S 2522) — Extend the programs of assistance under Title X and part B of Title XI of the Public Health Service Act. CRANSTON, D-Calif., WILLIAMS, D-N.J., JAVITS, R-N.Y., and RIEGLE, D-Mich. — 2/9/78 — Senate Human Resources reported May 15, 1978 (S Rept 95-822). Senate passed June 7. House passed, amended, Oct. 13. Senate agreed to House amendment Oct. 15. President signed Nov. 8, 1978.

PL 95-614 (S 553) — Amend the boundary of the Cibola National Forest and designate an intended wilderness area. DOMENICI, R-N.M. — 2/1/77

— Senate Energy and Natural Resources reported Oct. 20, 1977 (S Rept 95-516). Senate passed Oct. 28. House passed, amended, Oct. 3, 1978. Senate agreed to House amendments with amendments Oct. 14. House agreed to Senate amendments Oct. 14. President signed Nov. 8, 1978.

PL 95-615 (HR 9251) — Enact the Tax Treatment Extension Act of 1977. JONES, D-Okla., ULLMAN, D-Ore., WAGGONNER, D-La., BRODHEAD, D-Mich., DUNCAN, D-Ore., ARCHER, R-Texas, CRANE, R-Ill. and MARTIN, R-N.C. — 9/22/77 — House Ways and Means reported Oct. 12, 1977 (H Rept 95-697). House passed Oct. 25. Senate Finance reported April 19, 1978 (S Rept 95-746). Senate passed, amended, May 11. House disagreed to Senate amendments Nos. 1, 2 and 4 through 8 Sept. 25. House agreed to Senate amendment No. 3 with amendments Sept. 25. House disagreed to Senate amendment to the title of the bill Sept. 25. Senate insisted on its amendment Nos. 1, 2 and 4 through 8 Sept. 28. Senate disagreed to House amendments to Senate amendment No. 3 Sept. 28. Senate insisted on its amendment to the title of the bill Sept. 28. Conference report filed in House Oct. 15 (H Rept 95-1798). Senate agreed with conference report Oct. 15. House agreed to conference report Oct. 15. President signed Nov. 8, 1978.

PL 95-616 (HR 2329) — Enact the Fish and Wildlife Improvement Act of 1978. LEGGETT, D-Calif. — 1/24/77 — House Merchant Marine and Fisheries reported Feb. 28, 1977 (H Rept 95-29). House passed Jan. 19, 1978. Senate Environment and Public Works reported Aug. 31 (S Rept 95-1175). Senate passed, amended, Sept. 25. Proceedings of Sept. 25 vacated Sept. 26. Senate passed, amended, Sept. 26. Conference report filed in House Oct. 5 (H Rept 95-1730). Conference report filed in Senate Oct. 5 (S Rept 95-1277). Senate agreed to conference report Oct. 5. House agreed Oct. 15. President signed Nov. 8, 1978.

PL 95-617 (HR 4018) — Suspend until June 30, 1979, the duty on certain doxorubicin hydrochloride antibiotics. EVANS, R-Del. — 2/24/77 — (National Energy Act, Public Utility Rates) House Ways and Means reported June 16, 1977 (H Rept 95-429). House passed July 18. Senate passed, amended, Oct. 6. House agreed to Senate amendments with an amendment Oct. 13. Conference report filed in Senate Oct. 6 (S Rept 95-1292). Senate agreed to conference report Oct. 9. Conference report filed in House Oct. 10 (H Rept 95-1750). House agreed to conference report Oct. 15. President signed Nov. 9, 1978.

PL 95-618 (HR 5263) — Suspend until the close of June 30, 1979, the duty on certain bicycle parts. ROSTENKOWSKI, D-Ill. — 3/21/77 — (National Energy Act, Energy Tax) House Ways and Means reported June 16, 1977 (H Rept 95-435). House passed July 18. Senate Finance reported Oct. 21 (S Rept 95-529). Senate passed, amended, Oct. 31. Conference report filed in Senate Oct. 11, 1978 (S Rept 95-1324). Conference report filed in House Oct. 12 (H Rept 95-1773). Senate agreed to conference report Oct. 15. House agreed to conference report Oct. 15. President signed Nov. 9, 1978.

PL 95-619 (HR 5037) — Private bill (National Energy Act, Energy Conservation). House Ways and Means reported June 17, 1977 (H Rept 95-431). House passed July 18. Senate Finance reported Sept. 9 (S Rept 95-424). Senate passed, amended, Sept. 13. Conference report filed in Senate Oct. 6, 1978 (S Rept 95-1294). Senate agreed to conference report Oct. 9. Conference report filed in House (H Rept 95-1751). House agreed to conference report Oct. 15. President signed Nov. 9, 1978.

PL 95-620 (HR 5146) — Amend the Tariff Schedules of the United States to provide for the duty-free entry of competition bobsleds and luges. McEWEN, R-N.Y., CONABLE, R-N.Y., YOUNG, R-Alaska, RANGEL, D-N.Y. and PIKE, D-N.Y. — 3/16/77 — (National Energy Act, Coal Conversion) House Ways and Means reported June 16, 1977 (H Rept 95-433). House passed July 18. Senate passed, amended, Sept. 8. House agreed to Senate amendments Nos. 1 through 5 Oct. 13. House agreed to Senate amendment No. 6 with an amendment Oct. 13. Conference report filed in Senate July 14, 1978 (S Rept 95-988). Senate agreed to conference report July 18. Conference report filed in House Oct. 10 (H Rept 95-1749). House agreed to conference report Oct. 15. President signed Nov. 9, 1978.

PL 95-621 (HR 5289) — Private bill (National Energy Act, Natural Gas Policy) House Ways and Means reported June 16, 1977 (H Rept 95-437). House passed July 18. Senate Finance reported Sept. 9 (S Rept 95-423). Senate passed, amended, Oct. 4. House agreed to Senate amendments Nos. 1 through 7 Oct. 13. House agreed to Senate amendment No. 8 with an amendment Oct. 13. Conference report filed in Senate Aug. 18, 1978 (S Rept 95-1126). Senate agreed to conference report Sept. 27. Senate agreed to House amendment to Senate amendment No. 8 Sept. 27. Conference report filed in House Oct. 10 (H Rept 95-1752). House agreed to conference report Oct. 15. President signed Nov. 9, 1978.

PL 95-622 (S 2450) — Amend the Community Mental Health Centers Act. KENNEDY, D-Mass., SCHWEIKER, R-Pa., WILLIAMS, D-N.J. and JAVITS, R-N.Y. — 1/27/78 — Senate Human Resources reported May 15, 1978 (S Rept 95-838). Senate passed June 26. House passed, amended, Oct. 15. Senate agreed to House amendments Oct. 15. President signed Nov. 9, 1978.

PL 95-623 (S 2466) — Enact the Health Services Research, Health Statistics, and Health Care Technology Act of 1978. KENNEDY, D-Mass., SCHWEIKER, R-Pa., WILLIAMS, D-N.J. and JAVITS, R-N.Y. — 1/31/78 — Senate Human Resources reported May 15, 1978 (S Rept 95-839). Failed passage June 26. Reconsidered and passed Senate Aug. 9. House passed, amended, Sept. 25. Conference report filed in House Oct. 13 (H Rept 95-1783). House agreed to conference report Oct. 13. Senate agreed Oct. 15. President signed Nov. 9, 1978.

PL 95-624 (S 3151) — Authorize appropriations for the Department of Justice for fiscal year 1979. EASTLAND, D-Miss. — 5/21/78 — Senate Judiciary reported May 25, 1978 (S Rept 95-911). Senate passed July 10. House passed, amended, Sept. 28. Conference report filed in House Oct. 12 (H Rept 95-1777). Senate agreed to conference report Oct. 13. House agreed Oct. 14. President signed Nov. 9, 1978.

PL 95-625 (S 791) — Enact the National Parks and Recreation Act of 1978. CHURCH, D-Idaho and McCLURE, R-Idaho — 2/24/77 — Senate Energy and Natural Resources reported Oct. 20, 1977 (S Rept 95-514). Senate passed Oct. 27. House passed, amended, Oct. 4, 1978. Senate agreed to House amendment with amendments Oct. 12. House agreed to Senate amendments Oct. 13. President signed Nov. 10, 1978.

PL 95-626 (S 2474) — Enact the Health Services and Centers Amendments of 1978. KENNEDY, D-Mass., SCHWEIKER, R-Pa., WILLIAMS, D-N.J., JAVITS, R-N.Y., PELL, D-R.I. and HATHAWAY, D-Maine, — 2/1/78 — Senate Human Resources reported May 15, 1978 (S Rept 95-860). Senate passed Sept. 29. House passed, amended, Oct. 13. Conference report filed in House Oct. 15 (H Rept 95-1799). Senate agreed to conference report Oct. 15. House agreed to conference report Oct. 15. President signed Nov. 10, 1978.

PL 95-627 (S 3085) — Enact the Child Nutrition Amendments of 1978. McGOVERN, D-S.D. — 5/15/78 — Senate Agriculture, Nutrition and Forestry reported May 15, 1978 (S Rept 95-884). Senate Appropriations reported July 19 (S Rept 95-1020). Senate passed July 21. House passed, amended, Oct. 15. Senate agreed to House amendment Oct. 15. President signed Nov. 10, 1978.

PL 95-628 (HR 7320) — Revise miscellaneous timing requirements of the revenue laws. ULLMAN, D-Ore. and WAGGONNER, D-La. — 5/20/77 — House Ways and Means reported Sept. 29, 1977 (H Rept 95-645). House passed Nov. 1. Senate Finance reported May 10, 1978 (S Rept 95-797). Senate passed, amended, Aug. 23. House disagreed to Senate amendments with amendments Oct. 10. Senate concurred Oct. 14. President signed Nov. 10, 1978.

PL 95-629 (S 1829) — Amend the Pennsylvania Avenue Development Corporation Act of 1972 and to provide for the establishment of the San Antonio Missions National Historical Park, JOHNSTON, D-La. — 7/11/77 — Senate Energy and Natural Resources reported April 19, 1978 (S Rept 95-743). Senate passed April 24. House Interior and Insular Affairs reported Sept. 6 (H Rept 95-1544). House passed, amended, Oct. 14. Senate agreed to House amendments with amendments Oct. 15. House agreed Oct. 15. President signed Nov. 10, 1978.

PL 95-630 (HR 14279) — Enact the Financial Institutions Regulatory and Interest Rate Control Act of 1978. ST GERMAIN, D-R.I., REUSS, D-Wis. and ANNUNZIO, D-Ill. — 10/10/78 — House passed Oct. 11, 1978, Senate passed, amended, Oct. 12. House agreed to Senate amendments with amendments Oct. 15. Senate agreed to House amendments Oct. 15. President signed Nov. 10, 1978.

PL 95-631 (S 2796) — Amend the Consumer Product Safety Act to extend the authorization of appropriations. FORD, D-Ky. and MAGNUSON, D-Wash. — 3/23/78 — Senate Commerce, Science and Transportation reported May 15, 1978 (S Rept 95-889). Senate passed Aug. 4. House passed, amended, Oct. 15. Senate agreed to House amendment Oct. 15. President signed Nov. 10, 1978.

PL 95-632 (S 2899) — Enact the Endangered Species Act Amendments of 1978, CULVER, D-Iowa, BAKER, R-Tenn., RANDOLPH, D-W.Va., WALLOP, R-Wyo., GRAVEL, D-Alaska and HODGES, D-Ark. — 4/12/78 — Senate Environment and Public Works reported May 15, 1978 (S Rept 95-874). Senate passed July 19. House passed, amended, Oct. 14. Conference report filed in House Oct. 15 (H Rept 95-1804). House agreed to conference report Oct. 15. Senate agreed to conference report Oct. 15. President signed Nov. 10, 1978.

PL 95-633 (S 2399) — Enact the Psychotropic Substances Act of 1978. CULVER, D-Iowa, BAYH, D-Ind., EASTLAND, D-Miss., THURMOND, R-S.C., KENNEDY, D-Mass., McGOVERN, D-S.D., PERCY, D-Ill., CRANSTON, D-Calif., MATHIAS, R-Md., ABOUREZK, D-S.D., HATHAWAY, D-Maine, METZENBAUM, D-Ohio, DeCONCINI, D-Ariz. and MELCHER, D-Mont. — 1/20/78 — Senate Judiciary reported June 27, 1978 (S Rept 95-959). Senate passed July 27. House passed, amended, Sept. 18. Senate agreed to House amendment with amendments Oct. 7. House agreed to Senate amendments Oct. 13. President signed Nov. 10, 1978.

SENATE ROLL-CALL VOTES

CQ

	1	2	3	4	5	6	7	8
ALABAMA								
Allen	Y	N	N	N	Y	N	N	Y
Sparkman	Y	Y	N	N	Y	N	Y	Y
ALASKA								
Gravel	Y	Y	Y	Y	N	Y	Y	Y
Stevens	Y	Y	†	N	Y	N	Y	Y
ARIZONA								
DeConcini	Y	Y	Y	N	Y	N	Y	Y
Goldwater	?	?	?	?	?	?	?	?
ARKANSAS								
Bumpers	?	?	?	?	?	?	Y	Y
Hodges	Y	Y	Y	?	?	?	Y	Y
CALIFORNIA								
Cranston	N	Y	Y	Y	N	N	Y	Y
Hayakawa	Y	Y	Y	N	Y	N	Y	Y
COLORADO								
Hart	N	Y	Y	Y	N	N	Y	Y
Haskell	N	Y	Y	Y	N	Y	Y	Y
CONNECTICUT								
Ribicoff	Y	#	#	Y	N	Y	Y	Y
Weicker	Y	Y	Y	Y	N	Y	N	N
DELAWARE								
Biden	N	Y	Y	Y	N	Y	N	N
Roth	Y	Y	Y	N	Y	N	Y	Y
FLORIDA								
Chiles	?	Y	Y	N	Y	N	Y	Y
Stone	Y	Y	Y	Y	N	N	Y	Y
GEORGIA								
Nunn	Y	Y	Y	N	Y	N	Y	Y
Talmadge	Y	Y	N	N	Y	N	Y	Y
HAWAII								
Inouye	Y	Y	Y	Y	N	Y	Y	Y
Matsunaga	Y	Y	Y	Y	N	Y	Y	Y
IDAHO								
Church	Y	Y	Y	N	Y	N	#	Y
McClure	?	?	?	N	Y	N	Y	Y
ILLINOIS								
Stevenson	Y	Y	Y	Y	N	N	Y	Y
Percy	N	Y	Y	Y	N	N	Y	Y
INDIANA								
Bayh	Y	Y	Y	Y	N	Y	Y	Y
Lugar	Y	Y	Y	Y	Y	N	Y	Y
IOWA								
Clark	Y	Y	Y	Y	N	Y	Y	Y
Culver	Y	Y	Y	Y	N	Y	?	Y
KANSAS								
Dole	Y	N	Y	N	Y	N	Y	Y
Pearson	Y	Y	Y	N	Y	N	Y	Y
KENTUCKY								
Ford	Y	Y	Y	N	Y	N	Y	?
Huddleston	N	Y	Y	N	Y	N	N	Y
LOUISIANA								
Johnston	Y	Y	Y	N	Y	N	Y	Y
Long	Y	Y	Y	?	?	N	?	Y
MAINE								
Hathaway	?	Y	?	Y	N	Y	Y	Y
Muskie	Y	Y	Y	Y	N	N	Y	Y
MARYLAND								
Sarbanes	Y	Y	Y	Y	N	N	Y	Y
Mathias	N	Y	Y	Y	N	Y	Y	Y
MASSACHUSETTS								
Kennedy	Y	Y	Y	Y	N	Y	Y	Y
Brooke	N	Y	Y	Y	N	Y	Y	?
MICHIGAN								
Riegle	N	†	†	Y	N	N	Y	Y
Griffin	Y	Y	Y	N	Y	N	Y	?
MINNESOTA								
Anderson	Y	Y	Y	N	Y	N	?	?
Vacancy[2]								
MISSISSIPPI								
Eastland	Y	Y	?	N	Y	Y	Y	Y
Stennis	Y	Y	N	?	Y	N	Y	Y
MISSOURI								
Eagleton	Y	Y	Y	Y	N	N	Y	Y
Danforth	Y	Y	Y	N	Y	N	Y	#
MONTANA								
Melcher	Y	Y	Y	N	Y	Y	Y	Y
Hatfield, P.[1]		Y	Y	Y	N	Y	Y	Y
NEBRASKA								
Zorinsky	Y	Y	Y	N	Y	N	Y	Y
Curtis	Y	N	Y	N	Y	N	Y	Y
NEVADA								
Cannon	Y	Y	Y	N	Y	N	Y	Y
Laxalt	Y	N	N	?	?	?	?	?
NEW HAMPSHIRE								
Durkin	?	Y	Y	N	Y	N	Y	Y
McIntyre	Y	Y	Y	Y	Y	N	Y	Y
NEW JERSEY								
Williams	Y	†	Y	Y	N	Y	Y	Y
Case	N	Y	Y	Y	N	Y	Y	Y
NEW MEXICO								
Domenici	Y	Y	Y	N	Y	N	Y	Y
Schmitt	Y	N	Y	?	Y	N	Y	Y
NEW YORK								
Moynihan	Y	Y	Y	?	?	?	?	Y
Javits	N	Y	Y	Y	N	Y	Y	Y
NORTH CAROLINA								
Morgan	Y	Y	Y	N	Y	N	Y	Y
Helms	Y	N	N	N	Y	N	Y	Y
NORTH DAKOTA								
Burdick	Y	Y	Y	Y	N	N	Y	Y
Young	?	Y	Y	?	?	?	?	?
OHIO								
Glenn	Y	Y	Y	Y	N	Y	Y	Y
Metzenbaum	Y	Y	Y	Y	N	N	Y	Y
OKLAHOMA								
Bartlett	Y	Y	Y	N	Y	N	N	Y
Bellmon	Y	N	N	N	Y	N	Y	Y
OREGON								
Hatfield, M.	X	Y	Y	N	Y	N	Y	Y
Packwood	Y	Y	Y	Y	N	N	Y	Y
PENNSYLVANIA								
Heinz	Y	Y	Y	▮	#	▮	Y	Y
Schweiker	Y	Y	Y	?	?	?	Y	Y
RHODE ISLAND								
Pell	Y	Y	Y	Y	N	Y	Y	Y
Chafee	Y	Y	Y	Y	N	Y	Y	Y
SOUTH CAROLINA								
Hollings	?	Y	Y	N	Y	N	Y	Y
Thurmond	#	Y	Y	Y	Y	N	Y	Y
SOUTH DAKOTA								
Abourezk	N	Y	Y	Y	N	Y	#	Y
McGovern	Y	Y	Y	Y	N	N	Y	Y
TENNESSEE								
Sasser	?	Y	Y	Y	Y	N	Y	Y
Baker	Y	N	Y	N	Y	N	Y	Y
TEXAS								
Bentsen	?	?	?	N	Y	N	Y	Y
Tower	Y	Y	Y	N	Y	N	?	?
UTAH								
Garn	?	Y	Y	N	Y	N	N	Y
Hatch	✓	Y	Y	N	Y	N	Y	Y
VERMONT								
Leahy	Y	Y	Y	Y	N	Y	Y	Y
Stafford	Y	Y	Y	N	N	N	Y	Y
VIRGINIA								
*Byrd, H.	Y	Y	Y	N	Y	N	Y	Y
Scott	Y	N	N	N	Y	N	Y	Y
WASHINGTON								
Jackson	Y	Y	Y	Y	N	N	Y	Y
Magnuson	Y	Y	Y	Y	N	Y	Y	?
WEST VIRGINIA								
Byrd, R.	Y	Y	Y	N	Y	N	Y	Y
Randolph	Y	Y	Y	N	Y	N	Y	Y
WISCONSIN								
Nelson	N	Y	Y	Y	N	Y	Y	Y
Proxmire	Y	Y	Y	Y	N	Y	Y	Y
WYOMING								
Hansen	Y	Y	Y	N	Y	N	Y	Y
Wallop	?	Y	Y	N	Y	Y	Y	Y

KEY

- Y Voted for (yea).
- ✓ Paired for.
- † Announced for.
- # CQ Poll for.
- N Voted against (nay).
- X Paired against.
- \- Announced against.
- ▮ CQ Poll against.
- P Voted "present."
- ● Voted "present" to avoid possible conflict of interest.
- ? Did not vote or otherwise make a position known.

Democrats ***Republicans***

1. Paul G. Hatfield (D Mont.) was sworn in Jan. 23, 1978, to fill vacancy created by the death of Sen. Lee Metcalf (D), Jan. 11, 1978. The first vote Sen. Hatfield was eligible for was CQ 2.

2. Hubert H. Humphrey died Jan. 13, 1978.

**Byrd elected as independent.*

1. S 1437. Criminal Code. Kennedy (D Mass.) motion to table (kill) the Hart (D Colo.) amendment to prohibit imprisonment of a convicted defendant for the "sole" purpose of rehabilitation. Motion agreed to 70-13: R 25-5; D 45-8 (ND 32-7; SD 13-1), Jan. 23, 1978.

2. S 1437. Criminal Code. Kennedy (D Mass.) motion to table (kill) Scott (R Va.) amendment to delete from the bill a section that would allow a convicted defendant or the government to appeal sentences imposed on persons convicted of crimes. Motion agreed to 83-9: R 28-8; D 55-1 (ND 39-0; SD 16-1), Jan. 24, 1978.

3. S 1437. Criminal Code. Kennedy (D Mass.) motion to table (kill) the Scott (R Va.) amendment to delete from the bill a provision establishing a U.S. Sentencing Commission. Motion agreed to 82-8: R 31-4; D 51-4 (ND 39-0; SD 12-4), Jan. 24, 1978.

4. S 1437. Criminal Code. Kennedy (D Mass.) motion to table (kill) the Dole (R Kan.) amendment regarding obscenity prosecutions *(see vote 5, below).* Motion rejected 44-44: R 10-22; D 34-22 (ND 32-9; SD 2-13), Jan. 25, 1978.

5. S 1437. Criminal Code. Dole (R Kan.) amendment to specify that in federal prosecutions for distribution of obscene materials the concept of "community," under which a jury would determine whether such materials appeal to the prurient interest and were "patently offensive," means "the state or local community in which the obscene material is disseminated," and not the nation as a whole. Adopted 49-41: R 24-9; D 25-32 (ND 10-31; SD 15-1), Jan. 25, 1978.

6. S 1437. Criminal Code. Kennedy (D Mass.) motion to table (kill) the Dole (R Kan.) amendment to expand the list of violent crimes for which pretrial release may be denied by a judge. Motion rejected 29-62: R 7-26; D 22-36 (ND 21-20; SD 1-16), Jan. 25, 1978. (The Dole amendment was adopted subsequently by voice vote.)

7. S 1437. Criminal Code. Byrd (D W.Va.) motion to instruct the sergeant at arms to request the attendance of absent senators. Motion agreed to 83-6: R 31-3; D 52-3 (ND 36-1; SD 16-2), Jan. 25, 1978.

8. S 1437. Criminal Code. Byrd (D W.Va.) motion to instruct the sergeant at arms to request the attendance of absent senators. Motion agreed to 87-2: R 30-1; D 57-1 (ND 39-1; SD 18-0), Jan. 25, 1978.

CQ Senate Votes 9-13

Corresponding to Congressional Record Votes 9, 10, 11, 12, 13

	9	10	11	12	13
ALABAMA					
Allen	N	Y	Y	Y	N
Sparkman	Y	Y	Y	Y	N
ALASKA					
Gravel	Y	Y	Y	▮	Y
Stevens	N	Y	N	Y	N
ARIZONA					
DeConcini	Y	Y	N	N	Y
Goldwater	?	?	?	?	?
ARKANSAS					
Bumpers	Y	Y	Y	N	N
Hodges	Y	?	?	N	N
CALIFORNIA					
Cranston	Y	Y	N	N	Y
Hayakawa	Y	Y	Y	Y	N
COLORADO					
Hart	Y	Y	Y	N	Y
Haskell	Y	Y	Y	N	Y
CONNECTICUT					
Ribicoff	Y	#	#	▮	#
Weicker	Y	Y	N	N	Y
DELAWARE					
Biden	?	Y	Y	N	Y
Roth	N	Y	Y	Y	N
FLORIDA					
Chiles	Y	Y	Y	Y	N
Stone	Y	Y	Y	Y	N
GEORGIA					
Nunn	Y	Y	Y	Y	N
Talmadge	Y	Y	Y	Y	N
HAWAII					
Inouye	Y	Y	Y	N	Y
Matsunaga	Y	Y	N	N	Y
IDAHO					
Church	Y	Y	Y	N	Y
McClure	N	Y	Y	Y	N
ILLINOIS					
Stevenson	Y	Y	Y	N	Y
Percy	Y	Y	N	N	Y
INDIANA					
Bayh	Y	Y	N	N	Y
Lugar	N	Y	Y	Y	N
IOWA					
Clark	Y	Y	N	N	Y
Culver	Y	Y	N	N	Y
KANSAS					
Dole	N	Y	Y	Y	N
Pearson	Y	Y	N	N	Y
KENTUCKY					
Ford	?	Y	Y	Y	N
Huddleston	N	Y	Y	N	N
LOUISIANA					
Johnston	Y	Y	Y	Y	N
Long	Y	Y	Y	Y	N
MAINE					
Hathaway	Y	Y	Y	N	Y
Muskie	Y	Y	Y	N	Y
MARYLAND					
Sarbanes	Y	Y	Y	N	Y
Mathias	Y	Y	N	N	Y
MASSACHUSETTS					
Kennedy	Y	Y	Y	N	Y
Brooke	?	Y	?	?	?
MICHIGAN					
Riegle	Y	Y	N	N	Y
Griffin	?	Y	Y	Y	N
MINNESOTA					
Anderson	?	†	Y	N	Y
Vacancy					
MISSISSIPPI					
Eastland	N	Y	Y	Y	N
Stennis	N	?	?	?	?
MISSOURI					
Eagleton	Y	Y	Y	N	Y
Danforth	#	Y	N	N	Y
MONTANA					
Melcher	Y	Y	Y	N	Y
Hatfield, P.	Y	Y	Y	N	Y
NEBRASKA					
Zorinsky	N	Y	Y	Y	N
Curtis	N	?	?	?	?
NEVADA					
Cannon	Y	Y	Y	N	Y
Laxalt	?	?	?	?	?
NEW HAMPSHIRE					
Durkin	Y	Y	Y	Y	Y
McIntyre	Y	Y	N	N	?
NEW JERSEY					
Williams	Y	Y	N	N	Y
Case	Y	Y	N	N	Y
NEW MEXICO					
Domenici	N	Y	Y	Y	N
Schmitt	Y	Y	N	N	Y
NEW YORK					
Moynihan	Y	Y	N	N	Y
Javits	Y	Y	N	N	Y
NORTH CAROLINA					
Morgan	Y	Y	Y	N	N
Helms	N	Y	Y	Y	N
NORTH DAKOTA					
Burdick	Y	Y	Y	Y	N
Young	?	?	?	?	?
OHIO					
Glenn	Y	Y	Y	N	Y
Metzenbaum	Y	Y	N	N	Y
OKLAHOMA					
Bartlett	N	Y	Y	Y	N
Bellmon	N	Y	Y	Y	N
OREGON					
Hatfield, M.	Y	Y	Y	Y	N
Packwood	Y	Y	Y	Y	N
PENNSYLVANIA					
Heinz	Y	Y	Y	Y	Y
Schweiker	N	Y	Y	?	?
RHODE ISLAND					
Pell	Y	Y	Y	N	Y
Chafee	Y	Y	N	N	Y
SOUTH CAROLINA					
Hollings	N	Y	Y	Y	N
Thurmond	N	Y	Y	Y	N
SOUTH DAKOTA					
Abourezk	Y	Y	▮	N	Y
McGovern	Y	#	▮	▮	#
TENNESSEE					
Sasser	Y	Y	Y	Y	Y
Baker	N	Y	N	Y	N
TEXAS					
Bentsen	Y	?	?	?	Y
Tower	?	?	?	?	?
UTAH					
Garn	N	Y	Y	Y	N
Hatch	N	Y	Y	Y	N
VERMONT					
Leahy	Y	Y	N	N	Y
Stafford	Y	Y	Y	N	N
VIRGINIA					
*Byrd, H.	N	Y	N	Y	N
Scott	N	Y	N	Y	N
WASHINGTON					
Jackson	Y	Y	Y	N	Y
Magnuson	Y	Y	Y	N	Y
WEST VIRGINIA					
Byrd, R.	Y	Y	Y	N	Y
Randolph	Y	Y	Y	Y	N
WISCONSIN					
Nelson	Y	Y	Y	N	Y
Proxmire	Y	Y	Y	N	Y
WYOMING					
Hansen	N	Y	Y	Y	N
Wallop	Y	Y	N	Y	N

Democrats ***Republicans***

*Byrd elected as independent.

KEY

- Y Voted for (yea).
- ✔ Paired for.
- † Announced for.
- # CQ Poll for.
- N Voted against (nay).
- X Paired against.
- \- Announced against.
- ▮ CQ Poll against.
- P Voted "present."
- ● Voted "present" to avoid possible conflict of interest.
- ? Did not vote or otherwise make a position known.

9. S 1437. Criminal Code. Kennedy (D Mass.) motion to table (kill) the Scott (R Va.) amendment to expand the list of crimes for which the death penalty may be imposed to include murder, treason and kidnaping. Motion agreed to 65-24: R 14-17; D 51-7 (ND 39-1; SD 12-6), Jan. 25, 1978.

10. S 1437. Criminal Code. Culver (D Iowa) amendment to incorporate in the bill the Protection of Children Against Sexual Exploitation Act of 1977 which makes it a federal crime to use or permit the use of a child under 16 years old in the production of pornography. Adopted 88-0: R 33-0; D 55-0 (ND 39-0; SD 16-0), Jan. 26, 1978.

11. S 1437. Criminal Code. Thurmond (R S.C.) motion to table (kill) the Mathias (R Md.) amendment to allow a defendant in an obscenity case to request that the trial for the alleged offense be conducted in the district in which he had his primary place of business at the time of the alleged offense. Motion agreed to 61-26: **R 19-13; D 42-13 (ND 27-12; SD 15-1), Jan. 26, 1978.**

12. S 1437. Criminal Code. Allen (D Ala.) motion to table (kill) the committee amendment *(see vote 13, below)*, to allow obscenity prosecutions only in the district from which the material was disseminated or in which the offense was completed. Motion rejected 38-49: R 21-10; D 17-39 (ND 4-35; SD 13-4), Jan. 26, 1978.

13. S 1437. Criminal Code. Adoption of the committee amendment to allow obscenity prosecutions only in the district from which the material was disseminated or in which the offense was completed. Adopted 48-40: R 10-21; D 38-19 (ND 36-3; SD 2-16), Jan. 26, 1978.

	14	15	16	17	18	19	20	21
ALABAMA								
Allen	Y	Y	N	Y	N	N	N	N
Sparkman	Y	Y	N	Y	Y	N	#	#
ALASKA								
Gravel	N	Y	Y	Y	Y	Y	Y	Y
Stevens	X	Y	Y	Y	Y	Y	Y	Y
ARIZONA								
DeConcini	N	Y	Y	Y	Y	Y	Y	Y
Goldwater	?	?	?	?	?	Y	Y	Y
ARKANSAS								
Bumpers	N	Y	Y	Y	Y	Y	Y	Y
Hodges	?	?	?	?	?	Y	Y	Y
CALIFORNIA								
Cranston	?	?	?	?	?	Y	Y	N
Hayakawa	✓	Y	N	Y	N	Y	Y	Y
COLORADO								
Hart	N	Y	Y	Y	Y	Y	Y	Y
Haskell	?	?	?	?	?	Y	Y	Y
CONNECTICUT								
Ribicoff	N	Y	Y	Y	Y	Y	Y	Y
Weicker	N	N	Y	Y	Y	Y	Y	Y
DELAWARE								
Biden	N	N	Y	Y	Y	Y	Y	Y
Roth	Y	Y	N	Y	Y	Y	Y	Y
FLORIDA								
Chiles	N	Y	N	Y	Y	N	?	?
Stone	N	Y	N	Y	Y	N	Y	Y
GEORGIA								
Nunn	?	Y	N	Y	Y	N	Y	Y
Talmadge	N	#	▮	Y	Y	N	Y	Y
HAWAII								
Inouye	N	Y	Y	Y	Y	Y	Y	Y
Matsunaga	?	Y	Y	Y	Y	Y	Y	Y
IDAHO								
Church	N	Y	Y	Y	Y	Y	Y	Y
McClure	N	Y	N	Y	Y	N	N	N
ILLINOIS								
Stevenson	Y	Y	N	Y	Y	Y	Y	Y
Percy	N	Y	Y	Y	Y	Y	Y	Y
INDIANA								
Bayh	N	Y	Y	Y	Y	Y	?	?
Lugar	N	Y	Y	Y	Y	Y	Y	Y
IOWA								
Clark	N	Y	Y	Y	Y	Y	Y	Y
Culver	N	Y	Y	†	?	Y	Y	Y
KANSAS								
Dole	†	†	-	†	-	N	Y	N
Pearson	N	Y	Y	Y	Y	Y	Y	Y
KENTUCKY								
Ford	?	?	?	?	?	Y	Y	Y
Huddleston	Y	Y	N	Y	Y	Y	Y	Y
LOUISIANA								
Johnston	?	▮	?	?	?	Y	Y	Y
Long	N	Y	Y	Y	Y	?	?	✓
MAINE								
Hathaway	N	Y	Y	Y	Y	Y	Y	Y
Muskie	N	Y	Y	Y	Y	Y	Y	Y
MARYLAND								
Sarbanes	N	Y	Y	Y	Y	Y	Y	Y
Mathias	N	Y	Y	Y	Y	Y	Y	Y
MASSACHUSETTS								
Kennedy	N	Y	Y	Y	Y	Y	Y	Y
Brooke	N	Y	Y	Y	Y	Y	Y	Y
MICHIGAN								
Riegle	N	Y	Y	Y	Y	Y	Y	N
Griffin	Y	Y	N	?	Y	Y	Y	N
MINNESOTA								
Anderson	N	Y	Y	Y	Y	Y	?	†
Vacancy								
MISSISSIPPI								
Eastland	Y	Y	N	Y	Y	N	Y	N
Stennis	?	?	?	?	?	N	?	?
MISSOURI								
Eagleton	?	?	?	?	?	Y	Y	Y
Danforth	▮	#	#	#	#	Y	Y	Y
MONTANA								
Melcher	?	?	?	?	?	Y	Y	Y
Hatfield, P.	▮	Y	#	#	#	Y	Y	Y
NEBRASKA								
Zorinsky	Y	Y	N	Y	N	N	Y	Y
Curtis	N	Y	N	Y	N	N	-	†
NEVADA								
Cannon	N	Y	Y	Y	Y	Y	Y	Y
Laxalt	?	?	?	?	?	N	?	?
NEW HAMPSHIRE								
Durkin	?	?	?	?	?	Y	?	?
McIntyre	N	Y	Y	?	?	?	Y	Y
NEW JERSEY								
Williams	N	Y	Y	Y	Y	Y	Y	Y
Case	N	Y	Y	Y	Y	Y	Y	Y
NEW MEXICO								
Domenici	N	Y	Y	Y	Y	Y	Y	N
Schmitt	Y	Y	N	Y	?	Y	Y	Y
NEW YORK								
Moynihan	-	?	†	†	†	Y	Y	Y
Javits	N	Y	Y	Y	Y	Y	Y	Y
NORTH CAROLINA								
Morgan	N	Y	N	Y	Y	N	†	Y
Helms	Y	Y	N	Y	N	N	N	N
NORTH DAKOTA								
Burdick	N	Y	Y	Y	Y	Y	Y	Y
Young	?	?	?	?	?	Y	?	?
OHIO								
Glenn	N	Y	Y	Y	Y	Y	Y	Y
Metzenbaum	N	Y	Y	Y	Y	Y	Y	Y
OKLAHOMA								
Bartlett	Y	Y	N	Y	N	Y	Y	N
Bellmon	?	?	?	?	?	N	Y	N
OREGON								
Hatfield, M.	N	Y	Y	Y	Y	Y	Y	Y
Packwood	N	Y	?	Y	Y	Y	?	?
PENNSYLVANIA								
Heinz	▮	#	#	#	#	Y	Y	Y
Schweiker	Y	Y	N	Y	N	Y	Y	Y
RHODE ISLAND								
Pell	N	Y	Y	Y	Y	Y	Y	Y
Chafee	N	Y	Y	Y	Y	Y	Y	Y
SOUTH CAROLINA								
Hollings	Y	Y	N	Y	N	Y	Y	Y
Thurmond	Y	Y	N	Y	N	Y	Y	Y
SOUTH DAKOTA								
Abourezk	N	Y	Y	Y	Y	#	#	X
McGovern	▮	#	#	#	#	?	Y	Y
TENNESSEE								
Sasser	N	Y	Y	Y	Y	Y	Y	Y
Baker	N	Y	N	Y	Y	Y	Y	Y
TEXAS								
Bentsen	N	Y	Y	Y	?	Y	Y	Y
Tower	?	?	?	?	?	N	Y	N
UTAH								
Garn	Y	N	N	Y	N	Y	Y	N
Hatch	Y	Y	N	Y	N	N	Y	Y
VERMONT								
Leahy	?	?	?	?	?	Y	Y	Y
Stafford	▮	#	#	#	#	Y	Y	Y
VIRGINIA								
*Byrd, H.	N	Y	Y	Y	Y	N	Y	Y
Scott	Y	Y	N	Y	N	N	N	N
WASHINGTON								
Jackson	N	Y	N	Y	Y	Y	Y	Y
Magnuson	N	?	Y	Y	Y	Y	Y	Y
WEST VIRGINIA								
Byrd, R.	Y	Y	N	Y	N	Y	Y	Y
Randolph	Y	Y	N	Y	Y	Y	Y	Y
WISCONSIN								
Nelson	N	Y	Y	Y	Y	Y	Y	Y
Proxmire	N	Y	Y	Y	Y	Y	Y	Y
WYOMING								
Hansen	Y	Y	N	Y	N	Y	Y	N
Wallop	N	Y	Y	Y	Y	Y	Y	Y

Democrats ***Republicans***

*Byrd elected as independent.

KEY

- Y Voted for (yea).
- ✓ Paired for.
- † Announced for.
- # CQ Poll for.
- N Voted against (nay).
- X Paired against.
- \- Announced against.
- ▮ CQ Poll against.
- P Voted "present."
- ● Voted "present" to avoid possible conflict of interest.
- ? Did not vote or otherwise make a position known.

14. S 1437. Criminal Code. Allen (D Ala.) motion to table (kill) the committee amendment *(see vote 18, below)*, to provide that it is a defense to prosecution for dissemination of "obscene" materials that dissemination of the material was legal in the state in which it was disseminated. Motion rejected 20-53: R 11-16; D 9-37 (ND 4-28; SD 5-9), Jan. 27, 1978.

15. S 1437. Criminal Code. Abourezk (D S.D.) motion to instruct the sergeant at arms to request the attendance of absent senators. Motion agreed to 73-3: R 27-2; D 46-1 (ND 32-1; SD 14-0), Jan. 27, 1978.

16. S 1437. Criminal Code. Abourezk (D S.D.) motion to table (kill) the Allen (D Ala.) amendment to the committee amendment *(see vote 18, below)*, to provide as a defense to prosecution for dissemination of "obscene" materials if dissemination of such materials had been legalized by a statute in the state in which the material was disseminated. Motion agreed to 46-29: R 13-15; D 33-14 (ND 28-5; SD 5-9), Jan. 27, 1978.

17. S 1437. Criminal Code. Allen (D Ala.) amendment to the committee amendment *(see vote 18, below)* to provide as a defense to prosecution for dissemination of "obscene" materials if dissemination was legal in the "political subdivision" (locality) in which it was disseminated rather than in the "state" as was provided in the committee bill. Adopted 74-0: R 28-0; D 46-0 (ND 31-0; SD 15-0), Jan. 27, 1978.

18. S 1437. Criminal Code. Adoption of the committee amendment, as amended by Allen (D Ala.) amendment, to provide a defense to prosecution for dissemination of "obscene" materials that the dissemination was legal in the "political subdivision" (locality) in which the material was disseminated. Adopted 59-14: R 18-10; D 41-4 (ND 29-2; SD 12-2), Jan. 27, 1978.

19. S 1437. Criminal Code. Kennedy (D Mass.) motion to table (kill) the Allen (D Ala.) amendment to delete a section of the bill dealing with federal jurisdiction over an offense which stated that "the existence of federal jurisdiction is not an element of the offense" that would have to be proved to a jury in making a determination of guilt or innocence. Motion agreed to 75-20: R 29-9; D 46-11 (ND 38-1; SD 8-10), Jan. 30, 1978.

20. S 1437. Criminal Code. Kennedy (D Mass.) amendment to make numerous technical and conforming amendments to the bill en bloc. Adopted 82-4: R 31-3; D 51-1 (ND 38-0; SD 13-1), Jan. 30, 1978.

21. S 1437. Criminal Code. Passage of the bill to provide for consolidation and revision of the entire U.S. criminal code, including creation of a U.S. Sentencing Commission, expansion of the civil rights statutes, creation of a program to compensate victims of violent crimes, and stiffer penalties for organized and white collar crime. Passed 72-15: R 23-11; D 49-4 (ND 36-2; SD 13-2), Jan. 31, 1978.

CQ Senate Votes 22-26

Corresponding to Congressional Record Votes 22, 23, 24, 25, 26

	22	23	24	25	26
ALABAMA					
Allen	Y	Y	N	N	N
Sparkman	N	Y	Y	Y	Y
ALASKA					
Gravel	N	N	Y	Y	Y
Stevens	Y	Y	N	N	N
ARIZONA					
DeConcini	Y	N	Y	Y	Y
Goldwater	Y	Y	N	N	N
ARKANSAS					
Bumpers	N	N	Y	Y	Y
Hodges	N	N	Y	Y	Y
CALIFORNIA					
Cranston	N	N	Y	N	N
Hayakawa	Y	Y	N	N	N
COLORADO					
Hart	N	N	Y	Y	Y
Haskell	N	N	Y	?	?
CONNECTICUT					
Ribicoff	N	N	Y	Y	Y
Weicker	Y	N	Y	N	N
DELAWARE					
Biden	N	N	Y	Y	Y
Roth	Y	Y	N	Y	Y
FLORIDA					
Chiles	?	N	Y	Y	Y
Stone	?	?	?	N	N
GEORGIA					
Nunn	N	Y	Y	Y	Y
Talmadge	Y	N	Y	Y	Y
HAWAII					
Inouye	Y	N	Y	?	?
Matsunaga	N	N	Y	Y	Y
IDAHO					
Church	N	N	Y	Y	Y
McClure	Y	Y	N	?	N
ILLINOIS					
Stevenson	N	N	Y	Y	Y
Percy	Y	N	Y	Y	Y
INDIANA					
Bayh	N	N	Y	Y	Y
Lugar	Y	Y	N	N	N
IOWA					
Clark	N	N	Y	Y	Y
Culver	N	N	Y	Y	Y
KANSAS					
Dole	Y	Y	N	N	N
Pearson	Y	Y	Y	Y	Y
KENTUCKY					
Ford	N	N	Y	Y	Y
Huddleston	Y	N	Y	Y	Y
LOUISIANA					
Johnston	N	N	Y	N	N
Long	?	N	Y	N	?
MAINE					
Hathaway	N	N	Y	Y	Y
Muskie	Y	N	Y	Y	Y
MARYLAND					
Sarbanes	N	N	Y	Y	Y
Mathias	?	?	?	Y	Y
MASSACHUSETTS					
Kennedy	N	N	Y	Y	Y
Brooke	N	N	Y	Y	Y
MICHIGAN					
Riegle	N	N	Y	Y	Y
Griffin	Y	Y	Y	N	N
MINNESOTA					
Anderson	?	?	?	Y	Y
Vacancy					
MISSISSIPPI					
Eastland	N	N	Y	Y	Y
Stennis	N	N	Y	Y	Y
MISSOURI					
Eagleton	N	N	Y	Y	Y
Danforth	Y	N	Y	Y	Y
MONTANA					
Melcher	N	N	Y	Y	Y
Hatfield, P.	N	N	Y	Y	Y
NEBRASKA					
Zorinsky	N	N	Y	N	N
Curtis	Y	Y	N	N	N
NEVADA					
Cannon	N	N	Y	N	N
Laxalt	Y	Y	N	N	N
NEW HAMPSHIRE					
Durkin	N	N	Y	Y	Y
McIntyre	N	N	Y	N	N
NEW JERSEY					
Williams	N	N	Y	Y	Y
Case	N	N	Y	Y	Y
NEW MEXICO					
Domenici	Y	N	Y	N	?
Schmitt	Y	Y	Y	N	N
NEW YORK					
Moynihan	?	-	†	Y	Y
Javits	N	N	Y	Y	Y
NORTH CAROLINA					
Morgan	Y	Y	Y	†	Y
Helms	Y	Y	N	N	N
NORTH DAKOTA					
Burdick	N	N	Y	Y	Y
Young	Y	Y	Y	N	N
OHIO					
Glenn	N	N	Y	N	N
Metzenbaum	N	N	Y	Y	Y
OKLAHOMA					
Bartlett	Y	Y	N	N	N
Bellmon	Y	Y	N	Y	Y
OREGON					
Hatfield, M.	N	N	Y	Y	Y
Packwood	Y	N	Y	Y	Y
PENNSYLVANIA					
Heinz	N	N	Y	Y	Y
Schweiker	Y	Y	N	N	N
RHODE ISLAND					
Pell	N	N	Y	Y	Y
Chafee	Y	?	†	Y	Y
SOUTH CAROLINA					
Hollings	N	N	Y	N	N
Thurmond	Y	Y	Y	N	N
SOUTH DAKOTA					
Abourezk	N	N	Y	Y	Y
McGovern	N	N	Y	Y	Y
TENNESSEE					
Sasser	N	N	Y	N	N
Baker	Y	?	N	N	N
TEXAS					
Bentsen	N	N	Y	N	N
Tower	Y	Y	N	N	N
UTAH					
Garn	Y	Y	N	N	N
Hatch	Y	Y	N	N	N
VERMONT					
Leahy	N	N	Y	Y	Y
Stafford	N	N	Y	N	N
VIRGINIA					
*Byrd, H.	N	Y	N	N	N
Scott	N	Y	N	N	N
WASHINGTON					
Jackson	N	N	Y	Y	Y
Magnuson	N	N	Y	Y	Y
WEST VIRGINIA					
Byrd, R.	N	N	Y	Y	Y
Randolph	N	N	Y	N	N
WISCONSIN					
Nelson	N	N	Y	Y	Y
Proxmire	N	N	Y	Y	Y
WYOMING					
Hansen	N	N	Y	N	N
Wallop	Y	Y	Y	N	N

Democrats ***Republicans***

*Byrd elected as independent.

KEY

- Y Voted for (yea).
- ✓ Paired for.
- † Announced for.
- # CQ Poll for.
- N Voted against (nay).
- X Paired against.
- \- Announced against.
- ▮ CQ Poll against.
- P Voted "present."
- ● Voted "present" to avoid possible conflict of interest.
- ? Did not vote or otherwise make a position known.

22. S 1976. Redwood Park Expansion. Hayakawa (R Calif.) amendment to continue jurisdiction over compensation for land acquisition within the U.S. Court of Claims rather than in federal district courts as provided in the bill. Rejected 36-57: R 29-8; D 7-49 (ND 3-37; SD 4-12), Jan. 31, 1978.

23. S 1976. Redwood Park Expansion. Hayakawa (R Calif.) amendment to delete from the bill terms permitting the Secretary of the Interior to take over some or all of a 30,000-acre designated zone bordering the Redwood National Park if necessary to protect the park. Rejected 28-65: R 23-12; D 5-53 (ND 0-40; SD 5-13), Jan. 31, 1978.

24. S 1976. Redwood Park Expansion. Passage of the bill to mandate immediate acquisition of 48,000 privately owned acres of timberland to expand the Redwood National Park in northern California. Passed 74-20: R 18-18; D 56-2 (ND 40-0; SD 16-2), Jan. 31, 1978. A "yea" was a vote supporting the President's position.

25. HR 9375. Fiscal 1978 Supplemental Appropriations. Stennis (D Miss.) motion to table (kill) the Hayakawa (R Calif.) motion that the Senate recede from its position that the conference report on the bill rescind $462 million appropriated in fiscal 1977 for continued production of the B-1 bomber. Motion agreed to 57-38: R 13-24; D 44-14 (ND 34-6; SD 10-8), Feb. 1, 1978. A "yea" was a vote supporting the President's position.

26. HR 9375. Fiscal 1978 Supplemental Appropriations. Stennis (D Miss.) motion that the Senate insist on its position rescinding $462 million appropriated in fiscal 1977 for continued production of the B-1 bomber and requesting a new conference with the House to resolve the issue. Motion agreed to 58-37: R 13-24; D 45-13 (ND 34-6; SD 11-7), Feb. 1, 1978. A "yea" was a vote supporting the President's position.

	27	28	29	30	31	32	33
ALABAMA							
Allen	N	Y	N	Y	Y	Y	N
Sparkman	Y	Y	N	Y	Y	Y	Y
ALASKA							
Gravel	?	#	#	†	#	Y	Y
Stevens	N	Y	N	Y	N	Y	N
ARIZONA							
DeConcini	Y	Y	Y	Y	Y	Y	Y
Goldwater	N	Y	N	Y	N	Y	N
ARKANSAS							
Bumpers	Y	Y	Y	Y	Y	Y	Y
Hodges	Y	Y	Y	Y	?	Y	Y
CALIFORNIA							
Cranston	Y	Y	Y	Y	Y	Y	Y
Hayakawa	N	Y	N	Y	N	Y	Y
COLORADO							
Hart	Y	Y	Y	Y	Y	Y	Y
Haskell	Y	Y	Y	Y	Y	?	?
CONNECTICUT							
Ribicoff	Y	Y	Y	Y	Y	Y	Y
Weicker	N	Y	Y	Y	Y	N	Y
DELAWARE							
Biden	N	Y	Y	Y	Y	Y	?
Roth	?	?	?	?	Y	?	Y
FLORIDA							
Chiles	Y	Y	N	Y	Y	Y	Y
Stone	N	Y	Y	Y	Y	Y	Y
GEORGIA							
Nunn	N	Y	Y	Y	Y	Y	Y
Talmadge	Y	Y	Y	Y	Y	Y	Y
HAWAII							
Inouye	Y	Y	Y	Y	Y	Y	Y
Matsunaga	Y	Y	Y	Y	?	Y	Y
IDAHO							
Church	N	Y	Y	Y	Y	Y	Y
McClure	N	Y	N	Y	N	Y	N
ILLINOIS							
Stevenson	Y	Y	Y	Y	Y	?	Y
Percy	Y	Y	Y	Y	Y	Y	Y
INDIANA							
Bayh	Y	Y	Y	?	Y	Y	Y
Lugar	?	?	N	Y	Y	Y	N
IOWA							
Clark	Y	Y	Y	Y	Y	Y	Y
Culver	†	†	†	†	†	Y	Y
KANSAS							
Dole	N	Y	N	Y	Y	Y	N
Pearson	N	Y	N	Y	Y	Y	Y
KENTUCKY							
Ford	Y	Y	Y	Y	Y	Y	N
Huddleston	Y	Y	Y	Y	Y	Y	Y
LOUISIANA							
Johnston	N	Y	N	Y	Y	Y	N
Long	Y	Y	N	Y	Y	Y	Y
MAINE							
Hathaway	Y	Y	Y	Y	Y	Y	Y
Muskie	Y	Y	Y	Y	Y	Y	Y
MARYLAND							
Sarbanes	Y	Y	Y	Y	Y	Y	Y
Mathias	Y	Y	N	Y	Y	Y	Y
MASSACHUSETTS							
Kennedy	Y	Y	Y	Y	#	Y	Y
Brooke	N	Y	Y	Y	?	Y	Y
MICHIGAN							
Riegle	Y	Y	Y	Y	Y	Y	Y
Griffin	N	Y	N	Y	Y	Y	N
MINNESOTA							
Anderson	Y	Y	Y	Y	Y	Y	Y
Humphrey, M.[1]	Y	Y	Y	Y	Y	?	Y
MISSISSIPPI							
Eastland	Y	Y	Y	Y	Y	Y	N
Stennis	Y	Y	Y	Y	?	?	N
MISSOURI							
Eagleton	Y	Y	Y	Y	Y	Y	Y
Danforth	N	Y	N	Y	Y	Y	Y
MONTANA							
Melcher	N	Y	Y	Y	N	Y	N
Hatfield, P.	Y	Y	Y	Y	Y	Y	Y
NEBRASKA							
Zorinsky	N	Y	N	Y	Y	Y	N
Curtis	N	Y	?	?	Y	Y	N
NEVADA							
Cannon	Y	Y	Y	Y	Y	Y	N
Laxalt	N	Y	N	Y	Y	Y	N
NEW HAMPSHIRE							
Durkin	N	Y	Y	Y	Y	?	Y
McIntyre	Y	Y	Y	Y	Y	Y	Y
NEW JERSEY							
Williams	Y	Y	Y	Y	Y	Y	Y
Case	N	Y	Y	Y	Y	Y	Y
NEW MEXICO							
Domenici	N	Y	N	Y	Y	Y	N
Schmitt	N	Y	N	Y	Y	Y	N
NEW YORK							
Moynihan	Y	Y	Y	Y	Y	Y	Y
Javits	N	Y	Y	Y	Y	Y	Y
NORTH CAROLINA							
Morgan	N	Y	Y	Y	Y	Y	Y
Helms	N	Y	N	N	Y	#	N
NORTH DAKOTA							
Burdick	Y	Y	Y	Y	Y	Y	N
Young	N	Y	N	Y	?	?	N
OHIO							
Glenn	Y	Y	Y	Y	Y	Y	Y
Metzenbaum	N	Y	Y	Y	Y	Y	Y
OKLAHOMA							
Bartlett	N	Y	N	Y	?	Y	N
Bellmon	N	Y	N	Y	Y	Y	Y
OREGON							
Hatfield, M.	N	Y	Y	Y	Y	Y	Y
Packwood	?	?	?	?	?	Y	Y
PENNSYLVANIA							
Heinz	N	Y	N	Y	Y	Y	Y
Schweiker	N	Y	N	Y	Y	Y	N
RHODE ISLAND							
Pell	Y	Y	Y	Y	Y	Y	Y
Chafee	Y	Y	Y	Y	Y	Y	Y
SOUTH CAROLINA							
Hollings	Y	Y	N	Y	Y	Y	Y
Thurmond	N	Y	N	N	Y	Y	N
SOUTH DAKOTA							
Abourezk	#	#	#	#	#	#	Y
McGovern	#	#	#	#	Y	Y	Y
TENNESSEE							
Sasser	Y	Y	N	Y	Y	Y	Y
Baker	-	†	-	†	Y	Y	Y
TEXAS							
Bentsen	Y	Y	Y	Y	Y	Y	Y
Tower	N	Y	N	Y	Y	?	N
UTAH							
Garn	?	?	N	Y	Y	Y	N
Hatch	N	Y	N	Y	Y	?	-
VERMONT							
Leahy	Y	Y	Y	Y	Y	Y	Y
Stafford	Y	Y	Y	Y	Y	Y	Y
VIRGINIA							
*Byrd, H.	N	Y	N	Y	Y	Y	N
Scott	N	Y	N	N	Y	?	N
WASHINGTON							
Jackson	N	Y	Y	Y	Y	Y	Y
Magnuson	N	Y	Y	Y	Y	Y	Y
WEST VIRGINIA							
Byrd, R.	Y	Y	Y	Y	Y	Y	Y
Randolph	Y	Y	N	Y	Y	Y	Y
WISCONSIN							
Nelson	Y	Y	Y	Y	?	Y	Y
Proxmire	N	Y	Y	Y	Y	Y	Y
WYOMING							
Hansen	N	Y	N	Y	Y	Y	N
Wallop	N	Y	N	Y	Y	Y	N

Democrats ***Republicans***

*Byrd elected as independent.

1. Muriel Buck Humphrey (D Minn.) was sworn in on February 6, 1977, to fill vacancy created by the death of Sen. Hubert Humphrey (D), Jan. 13, 1978. The first vote Sen. Muriel Humphrey was eligible for was CQ 27.

KEY

- Y Voted for (yea).
- ✓ Paired for.
- † Announced for.
- # CQ Poll for.
- N Voted against (nay).
- X Paired against.
- - Announced against.
- ▮ CQ Poll against.
- P Voted "present."
- ● Voted "present" to avoid possible conflict of interest.
- ? Did not vote or otherwise make a position known.

27. HR 8638. Nuclear Nonproliferation. Glenn (D Ohio) substitute amendment, for McClure (R Idaho) amendment *(see vote 28, below)*, to allow Congress to veto by concurrent resolution any proposal to store in the United States spent fuel from other nations' nuclear reactors (as originally proposed, the amendment would have allowed either house to veto such a proposal). Adopted 47-44: R 4-29; D 43-15 (ND 30-9; SD 13-6), Feb. 7, 1978.

28. HR 8638. Nuclear Nonproliferation. McClure (R Idaho) amendment as amended by Glenn (D Ohio) amendment *(see vote 27, above)*. Adopted 91-0: R 33-0; D 58-0 (ND 39-0; SD 19-0), Feb. 7, 1978.

29. HR 8638. Nuclear Nonproliferation. Glenn (D Ohio) motion to table (kill) the Domenici (R N.M.) amendment to require full-scale reviews of nuclear export requests by regular customers only every five years. Motion agreed to 56-36: R 8-26; D 48-10 (ND 37-2; SD 11-8), Feb. 7, 1978.

30. HR 8638. Nuclear Nonproliferation. Passage of the bill to impose stricter standards on the export of nuclear material to prevent its unauthorized use for manufacturing nuclear explosives. Passed 88-3: R 31-3; D 57-0 (ND 38-0; SD 19-0), Feb. 7, 1978. A "yea" was a vote supporting the president's position.

31. HR 3454. Endangered Wilderness Act. Adoption of the conference report on the bill to designate as wilderness 1.3 million acres in 10 western states. Adopted 83-5: R 30-4; D 53-1 (ND 36-1; SD 17-0), Feb. 8, 1978.

32. Exec N, 95th Congress, First Session, Panama Canal Treaties. During a closed session of the Senate called to debate aspects of the canal treaties, a motion was made to compel the attendance of absent senators. The motion was approved 87-1: R 31-1; D 56-0 (ND 38-0; SD 18-0), Feb. 22, 1978.

33. Exec N, 95th Congress, First Session, Panama Canal Treaties. Byrd, D-W.Va., motion to table (kill) the Allen, D-Ala., motion to consider the approval of the Panama Canal treaty before the neutrality treaty. (The majority of members opposed this action because they wanted to consider U.S. rights to defend the canal before taking up the Panama Canal treaty giving the Republic of Panama control of the waterway after Dec. 31, 1999.) Motion agreed to 67-30: R 17-20; D 50-10 (ND 37-4; SD 13-6), Feb. 22, 1978.

CQ Senate Votes 34-41

Corresponding to Congressional Record Votes 34, 35, 36, 37, 38, 39, 40, 41

	34	35	36	37	38	39	40	41
ALABAMA								
Allen	N	N	Y	N	N	N	Y	Y
Sparkman	Y	Y	N	Y	Y	Y	N	N
ALASKA								
Gravel	Y	Y	N	Y	Y	Y	-	-
Stevens	N	N	Y	N	N	N	Y	N
ARIZONA								
DeConcini	N	Y	N	N	N	N	N	N
Goldwater	N	?	Y	?	N	?	Y	?
ARKANSAS								
Bumpers	?	?	?	Y	Y	Y	N	N
Hodges	Y	Y	N	Y	Y	N	N	N
CALIFORNIA								
Cranston	Y	?	N	Y	Y	Y	N	N
Hayakawa	Y	Y	N	Y	Y	Y	Y	N
COLORADO								
Hart	Y	Y	N	Y	?	?	N	N
Haskell	Y	Y	N	Y	Y	Y	N	N
CONNECTICUT								
Ribicoff	Y	Y	N	Y	Y	Y	N	N
Weicker	#	#	N	Y	#	Y	N	N
DELAWARE								
Biden	Y	Y	N	Y	Y	Y	N	?
Roth	N	Y	Y	N	Y	N	Y	N
FLORIDA								
Chiles	Y	N	N	Y	Y	Y	N	N
Stone	Y	N	N	Y	Y	Y	N	N
GEORGIA								
Nunn	N	Y	N	N	N	N	N	Y
Talmadge	N	#	N	N	N	N	N	#
HAWAII								
Inouye	Y	Y	N	Y	Y	?	?	?
Matsunaga	Y	Y	N	Y	Y	Y	N	N
IDAHO								
Church	Y	Y	N	Y	Y	Y	N	N
McClure	N	N	Y	N	N	N	Y	Y
ILLINOIS								
Stevenson	Y	Y	N	Y	Y	Y	N	N
Percy	Y	Y	N	Y	Y	Y	N	N
INDIANA								
Bayh	Y	Y	N	?	Y	Y	N	N
Lugar	N	N	Y	N	N	N	Y	Y
IOWA								
Clark	Y	Y	N	Y	†	Y	N	N
Culver	Y	Y	N	Y	Y	Y	N	N
KANSAS								
Dole	N	N	Y	N	N	N	N	N
Pearson	Y	?	N	Y	Y	Y	?	?
KENTUCKY								
Ford	N	?	N	?	N	N	N	Y
Huddleston	Y	Y	N	Y	Y	Y	N	N
LOUISIANA								
Johnston	N	Y	N	N	N	N	N	N
Long	N	Y	N	N	Y	N	N	N
MAINE								
Hathaway	Y	Y	N	Y	Y	Y	N	N
Muskie	Y	Y	N	Y	Y	Y	N	N
MARYLAND								
Sarbanes	Y	Y	N	Y	Y	Y	N	N
Mathias	?	?	?	Y	Y	Y	N	N
MASSACHUSETTS								
Kennedy	Y	Y	N	Y	Y	Y	N	N
Brooke	N	N	N	N	N	N	?	?
MICHIGAN								
Riegle	Y	Y	N	Y	Y	Y	?	?
Griffin	N	N	Y	N	N	?	?	?
MINNESOTA								
Anderson	†	Y	N	Y	Y	Y	N	N
Humphrey, M.	Y	Y	N	Y	Y	Y	N	-
MISSISSIPPI								
Eastland	N	N	Y	N	N	N	Y	?
Stennis	N	N	?	?	N	N	Y	Y
MISSOURI								
Eagleton	Y	Y	N	Y	Y	Y	N	N
Danforth	Y	Y	N	Y	Y	Y	N	N
MONTANA								
Melcher	N	Y	N	N	N	N	N	N
Hatfield, P.	X	#	N	N	Y	Y	Y	N
NEBRASKA								
Zorinsky	N	Y	N	N	N	N	N	N
Curtis	N	N	Y	N	N	N	Y	Y
NEVADA								
Cannon	N	N	N	N	Y	N	N	N
Laxalt	N	N	Y	N	N	N	Y	Y
NEW HAMPSHIRE								
Durkin	Y	Y	N	Y	Y	Y	N	N
McIntyre	Y	Y	N	Y	Y	Y	N	?
NEW JERSEY								
Williams	#	#	N	Y	Y	Y	N	N
Case	Y	Y	N	Y	Y	Y	N	N
NEW MEXICO								
Domenici	N	Y	Y	N	N	N	N	N
Schmitt	?	Y	Y	N	N	N	N	N
NEW YORK								
Moynihan	Y	Y	N	Y	Y	Y	N	N
Javits	Y	Y	N	Y	Y	Y	N	N
NORTH CAROLINA								
Morgan	✓	✓	X	Y	Y	Y	N	N
Helms	N	N	Y	N	N	N	Y	#
NORTH DAKOTA								
Burdick	-	N	N	N	N	N	N	N
Young	N	?	Y	N	N	N	Y	#
OHIO								
Glenn	Y	Y	N	Y	?	Y	N	N
Metzenbaum	Y	Y	N	Y	?	Y	N	N
OKLAHOMA								
Bartlett	N	N	Y	N	N	N	Y	Y
Bellmon	Y	N	Y	N	Y	Y	Y	N
OREGON								
Hatfield, M.	Y	Y	N	Y	Y	Y	N	N
Packwood	Y	?	N	Y	Y	Y	?	?
PENNSYLVANIA								
Heinz	Y	Y	N	Y	Y	Y	N	N
Schweiker	N	N	Y	N	N	N	N	N
RHODE ISLAND								
Pell	Y	Y	N	Y	Y	Y	N	?
Chafee	Y	Y	N	Y	Y	Y	?	?
SOUTH CAROLINA								
Hollings	Y	Y	N	Y	Y	Y	N	N
Thurmond	X	X	✓	N	N	N	Y	Y
SOUTH DAKOTA								
Abourezk	Y	Y	N	Y	Y	Y	N	▮
McGovern	✓	#	#	#	#	Y	N	▮
TENNESSEE								
Sasser	Y	Y	N	Y	Y	Y	N	N
Baker	Y	Y	N	Y	Y	Y	?	?
TEXAS								
Bentsen	Y	Y	N	N	Y	?	?	?
Tower	N	N	Y	N	N	N	Y	Y
UTAH								
Garn	N	N	Y	N	N	N	?	?
Hatch	N	N	Y	N	N	N	Y	Y
VERMONT								
Leahy	Y	Y	N	Y	Y	Y	N	N
Stafford	Y	Y	N	Y	Y	Y	N	N
VIRGINIA								
*Byrd, H.	N	N	Y	N	N	N	Y	Y
Scott	N	N	Y	N	N	N	Y	Y
WASHINGTON								
Jackson	Y	Y	N	Y	Y	Y	N	N
Magnuson	Y	Y	N	Y	Y	Y	N	N
WEST VIRGINIA								
Byrd, R.	Y	Y	N	Y	Y	Y	N	N
Randolph	N	N	N	N	Y	N	N	N
WISCONSIN								
Nelson	Y	?	N	Y	Y	Y	N	N
Proxmire	Y	Y	N	Y	Y	Y	N	N
WYOMING								
Hansen	N	N	#	N	N	N	Y	Y
Wallop	Y	Y	Y	N	N	Y	N	N

Democrats ***Republicans***

Byrd elected as independent.

KEY

- Y Voted for (yea).
- ✓ Paired for.
- † Announced for.
- # CQ Poll for.
- N Voted against (nay).
- X Paired against.
- - Announced against.
- ▮ CQ Poll against.
- P Voted "present."
- ● Voted "present" to avoid possible conflict of interest.
- ? Did not vote or otherwise make a position known.

34. Exec N, 95th Congress, First Session, Panama Canal Treaties. Byrd, D-W.Va., motion to table (kill) the Allen, D-Ala., amendment to allow the United States to maintain a military force in the Panama Canal Zone until 2019, if the president certified the troops were needed to defend the canal or maintain its neutrality. Motion agreed to 55-34: R 14-20; D 41-14 (ND 33-5; SD 8-9), Feb. 27, 1978. A "yea" was a vote supporting the president's position.

35. Exec N, 95th Congress, First Session, Panama Canal Treaties. Church, D-Idaho, motion to table (kill) the Hatch, R-Utah, amendment to make the English text the legally binding version of the treaties. Motion agreed to 58-26: R 14-17; D 44-9 (ND 35-3; SD 9-6), Feb. 27, 1978. A "yea" was a vote supporting the president's position.

36. Exec N, 95th Congress, First Session, Panama Canal Treaties. Scott, R-Va., amendment to prevent the neutrality treaty from taking effect without ratification of the Panama Canal treaty. Rejected 24-69: R 21-14; D 3-55 (ND 0-42; SD 3-13), Feb. 28, 1978. A "nay" was a vote supporting the president's position.

37. Exec N, 95th Congress, First Session, Panama Canal Treaties. Church, D-Idaho, motion to table (kill) the Allen, D-Ala., amendment to allow U.S. military bases in the Canal Zone area after Dec. 31, 1999, if the United States was at war with a nation that might send its warships through the neutral canal. Motion agreed to 57-38: R 14-23; D 43-15 (ND 34-7; SD 9-8), March 1, 1978. A "yea" was a vote supporting the president's position.

38. Exec N, 95th Congress, First Session, Panama Canal Treaties. Church, D-Idaho, motion to table (kill) the Allen, D-Ala., amendment to allow the United States to intercept enemy warships to prevent them from reaching the neutral canal. Motion agreed to 60-34: R 15-22; D 45-12 (ND 34-4; SD 11-8), March 1, 1978. A "yea" was a vote supporting the president's position.

39. Exec N, 95th Congress, First Session, Panama Canal Treaties. Church, D-Idaho, motion to table (kill) the Allen, D-Ala., amendment to allow U.S. bases in the Canal Zone area after Dec. 31, 1999, if the president stated that Panama was dominated by a foreign power. Motion agreed to 59-36: R 16-20; D 43-16 (ND 35-6; SD 8-10), March 2, 1978. A "yea" was a vote supporting the president's position.

40. Exec N, 95th Congress, First Session, Panama Canal Treaties. Hatch, R-Utah, amendment to provide that Panama respect and abide by the provisions of the Monroe Doctrine. Rejected 22-67: R 17-14; D 5-53 (ND 1-39; SD 4-14), March 2, 1978. A "nay" was a vote supporting the president's position.

41. Exec N, 95th Congress, First Session, Panama Canal Treaties. Allen, D-Ala., amendment to require that any other canal built in Panama also be neutral. Rejected 15-63: R 10-18; D 5-45 (ND 0-34; SD 5-11), March 2, 1978. A "nay" was a vote supporting the president's position.

	42	43	44	45	46
ALABAMA					
Allen	N	N	N	N	N
Sparkman	Y	Y	Y	Y	Y
ALASKA					
Gravel	Y	Y	Y	Y	#
Stevens	N	N	N	N	N
ARIZONA					
DeConcini	N	-	-	-	N
Goldwater	N	?	N	?	N
ARKANSAS					
Bumpers	Y	Y	Y	Y	Y
Hodges	Y	Y	Y	Y	?
CALIFORNIA					
Cranston	Y	Y	Y	Y	Y
Hayakawa	Y	Y	N	?	?
COLORADO					
Hart	Y	Y	Y	Y	Y
Haskell	Y	Y	Y	Y	Y
CONNECTICUT					
Ribicoff	Y	Y	Y	Y	Y
Weicker	Y	Y	Y	Y	Y
DELAWARE					
Biden	N	Y	Y	?	Y
Roth	N	N	N	N	N
FLORIDA					
Chiles	Y	N	Y	Y	N
Stone	Y	N	Y	Y	Y
GEORGIA					
Nunn	N	N	Y	N	N
Talmadge	N	N	Y	Y	N
HAWAII					
Inouye	Y	Y	Y	Y	Y
Matsunaga	Y	Y	Y	Y	Y
IDAHO					
Church	Y	Y	Y	Y	Y
McClure	N	N	N	N	N
ILLINOIS					
Stevenson	Y	Y	Y	Y	Y
Percy	Y	Y	Y	Y	Y
INDIANA					
Bayh	Y	Y	Y	?	Y
Lugar	N	N	N	N	N
IOWA					
Clark	Y	Y	Y	Y	Y
Culver	?	Y	Y	Y	Y
KANSAS					
Dole	N	N	N	N	N
Pearson	Y	Y	Y	Y	?
KENTUCKY					
Ford	N	N	Y	N	?
Huddleston	Y	Y	Y	Y	Y
LOUISIANA					
Johnston	N	N	N	N	N
Long	N	N	N	Y	N
MAINE					
Hathaway	Y	Y	Y	Y	Y
Muskie	Y	Y	Y	Y	Y
MARYLAND					
Sarbanes	Y	Y	Y	Y	Y
Mathias	Y	Y	Y	Y	Y
MASSACHUSETTS					
Kennedy	#	Y	Y	Y	Y
Brooke	N	N	N	N	N
MICHIGAN					
Riegle	Y	Y	Y	Y	Y
Griffin	N	N	N	N	N
MINNESOTA					
Anderson	Y	Y	Y	Y	?
Humphrey, M.	Y	Y	Y	Y	Y
MISSISSIPPI					
Eastland	N	N	N	N	N
Stennis	N	N	N	N	?
MISSOURI					
Eagleton	?	Y	Y	Y	Y
Danforth	Y	Y	Y	Y	Y
MONTANA					
Melcher	N	N	?	N	N
Hatfield, P.	#	#	Y	Y	N
NEBRASKA					
Zorinsky	N	N	Y	Y	N
Curtis	N	N	N	N	N
NEVADA					
Cannon	N	N	N	X	N
Laxalt	N	N	N	N	N
NEW HAMPSHIRE					
Durkin	Y	Y	?	?	Y
McIntyre	Y	Y	Y	Y	?
NEW JERSEY					
Williams	Y	#	Y	Y	Y
Case	Y	Y	Y	Y	Y
NEW MEXICO					
Domenici	N	N	N	N	N
Schmitt	N	N	N	N	N
NEW YORK					
Moynihan	†	Y	Y	Y	Y
Javits	Y	Y	Y	Y	Y
NORTH CAROLINA					
Morgan	Y	Y	Y	Y	X
Helms	N	N	N	N	X
NORTH DAKOTA					
Burdick	N	▮	-	▮	▮
Young	N	?	N	N	?
OHIO					
Glenn	Y	Y	N	Y	Y
Metzenbaum	Y	Y	Y	Y	Y
OKLAHOMA					
Bartlett	N	N	N	N	N
Bellmon	?	N	N	N	?
OREGON					
Hatfield, M.	Y	Y	Y	Y	✓
Packwood	Y	Y	?	?	Y
PENNSYLVANIA					
Heinz	Y	Y	Y	Y	N
Schweiker	N	N	N	N	N
RHODE ISLAND					
Pell	Y	Y	Y	Y	Y
Chafee	Y	Y	Y	Y	Y
SOUTH CAROLINA					
Hollings	Y	Y	Y	Y	N
Thurmond	N	N	N	N	N
SOUTH DAKOTA					
Abourezk	#	Y	✓	#	#
McGovern	Y	Y	Y	Y	Y
TENNESSEE					
Sasser	Y	Y	Y	Y	Y
Baker	Y	Y	Y	Y	Y
TEXAS					
Bentsen	N	Y	N	Y	?
Tower	N	N	N	N	N
UTAH					
Garn	N	N	N	N	N
Hatch	N	N	N	N	N
VERMONT					
Leahy	Y	Y	Y	Y	Y
Stafford	Y	Y	Y	Y	#
VIRGINIA					
*Byrd, H.	N	N	N	N	N
Scott	N	N	N	N	N
WASHINGTON					
Jackson	†	Y	Y	Y	N
Magnuson	Y	Y	Y	Y	Y
WEST VIRGINIA					
Byrd, R.	Y	Y	Y	Y	Y
Randolph	N	Y	X	✓	✓
WISCONSIN					
Nelson	Y	Y	Y	Y	Y
Proxmire	Y	Y	Y	Y	Y
WYOMING					
Hansen	N	N	N	N	N
Wallop	N	N	N	N	N

Democrats ***Republicans***

*Byrd elected as independent.

KEY

- Y Voted for (yea).
- ✓ Paired for.
- † Announced for.
- # CQ Poll for.
- N Voted against (nay).
- X Paired against.
- \- Announced against.
- ▮ CQ Poll against.
- P Voted "present."
- ● Voted "present" to avoid possible conflict of interest.
- ? Did not vote or otherwise make a position known.

42. Exec N, 95th Congress, First Session, Panama Canal Treaties. Church, D-Idaho, motion to table (kill) the Allen, D-Ala., amendment to prevent ships of nations at war with the United States to use the otherwise neutral canal. Motion agreed to 52-40: R 14-23; D 38-17 (ND 29-7; SD 9-10), March 6, 1978. A "yea" was a vote supporting the president's position.

43. Exec N, 95th Congress, First Session, Panama Canal Treaties. Church, D-Idaho, motion to table (kill) the Helms, R-N.C., amendment to allow the United States to maintain the Galeta Island Base in the Panama Canal Zone after Dec. 31, 1999. Motion agreed to 58-36: R 14-22; D 44-14 (ND 36-3; SD 8-11), March 7, 1978. A "yea" was a vote supporting the president's position.

44. Exec N, 95th Congress, First Session, Panama Canal Treaties. Church, D-Idaho, motion to table (kill) the Stevens, R-Alaska, amendment to prohibit ships of any nation "in a state of belligerency" with either Panama or the United States from using the canal. Motion agreed to 59-34: R 12-25; D 47-9 (ND 35-2; SD 12-7), March 8, 1978. A "yea" was a vote supporting the president's position.

45. Exec N, 95th Congress, First Session, Panama Canal Treaties. Sarbanes, D-Md., motion to table (kill) the Allen, D-Ala., amendment to delete article III of the neutrality treaty entitling warships of all nations to use the canal. Motion agreed to 58-31: R 12-23; D 46-8 (ND 34-1; SD 12-7), March 8, 1978. A "yea" was a vote supporting the president's position.

46. Exec N, 95th Congress, First Session, Panama Canal Treaties. Church, D-Idaho, motion to table the Dole, R-Kan., amendment, to the Byrd, D-W.Va., amendment *(see vote 49, p. 10-S)* to permit either the United States or Panama to determine when defense of the canal could be initiated. Motion agreed to 45-37: R 9-22; D 36-15 (ND 31-6; SD 5-9), March 9, 1978. A "yea" was a vote supporting the president's position.

CQ Senate Votes 47-54

Corresponding to Congressional Record Votes 47, 48, 49, 50, 51, 52, 53, 54

	47	48	49	50	51	52	53	54
ALABAMA								
Allen	N	N	Y	N	N	N	N	Y
Sparkman	Y	Y	Y	Y	Y	Y	Y	Y
ALASKA								
Gravel	#	#	†	#	#	Y	Y	Y
Stevens	N	N	Y	N	N	X	X	X
ARIZONA								
DeConcini	Y	N	Y	N	N	N	N	Y
Goldwater	N	N	N	N	N	N	N	Y
ARKANSAS								
Bumpers	Y	Y	Y	Y	Y	Y	Y	Y
Hodges	?	?	?	?	?	Y	Y	Y
CALIFORNIA								
Cranston	Y	Y	Y	Y	Y	Y	Y	Y
Hayakawa	?	?	?	?	?	Y	Y	Y
COLORADO								
Hart	Y	Y	Y	Y	Y	Y	Y	Y
Haskell	Y	Y	Y	Y	Y	?	?	?
CONNECTICUT								
Ribicoff	#	†	Y	Y	Y	Y	Y	Y
Weicker	Y	Y	Y	Y	Y	Y	Y	Y
DELAWARE								
Biden	Y	Y	Y	Y	Y	?	Y	Y
Roth	N	N	Y	N	N	N	N	Y
FLORIDA								
Chiles	Y	Y	Y	?	?	Y	Y	Y
Stone	N	Y	Y	Y	N	Y	N	Y
GEORGIA								
Nunn	Y	N	Y	N	N	N	N	Y
Talmadge	Y	N	Y	N	N	N	N	Y
HAWAII								
Inouye	Y	Y	Y	Y	Y	?	?	?
Matsunaga	?	Y	Y	Y	Y	Y	Y	Y
IDAHO								
Church	Y	Y	Y	Y	Y	Y	Y	Y
McClure	N	N	Y	N	N	N	N	Y
ILLINOIS								
Stevenson	Y	Y	Y	†	†	Y	Y	Y
Percy	Y	Y	Y	Y	Y	Y	Y	Y
INDIANA								
Bayh	Y	Y	Y	Y	Y	Y	Y	Y
Lugar	N	N	Y	N	N	N	N	Y
IOWA								
Clark	Y	Y	Y	Y	Y	Y	Y	Y
Culver	Y	Y	Y	Y	Y	Y	Y	Y
KANSAS								
Dole	N	N	Y	N	N	N	N	Y
Pearson	Y	Y	Y	Y	Y	Y	Y	Y
KENTUCKY								
Ford	?	?	?	?	?	N	N	Y
Huddleston	Y	Y	Y	Y	Y	Y	Y	?
LOUISIANA								
Johnston	Y	N	Y	▮	▮	▮	▮	#
Long	?	N	Y	N	N	Y	Y	Y
MAINE								
Hathaway	Y	Y	Y	Y	Y	Y	Y	Y
Muskie	Y	Y	Y	Y	Y	Y	Y	Y
MARYLAND								
Sarbanes	Y	Y	Y	Y	Y	Y	Y	Y
Mathias	Y	Y	Y	Y	Y	Y	Y	Y
MASSACHUSETTS								
Kennedy	Y	Y	Y	Y	Y	Y	Y	Y
Brooke	N	N	Y	N	N	N	N	Y
MICHIGAN								
Riegle	Y	Y	Y	Y	Y	Y	Y	Y
Griffin	N	N	N	N	N	N	N	N
MINNESOTA								
Anderson	†	†	†	†	†	Y	Y	Y
Humphrey, M.	Y	Y	Y	Y	Y	Y	Y	Y
MISSISSIPPI								
Eastland	N	N	Y	N	N	N	N	Y
Stennis	N	?	?	?	?	N	N	Y
MISSOURI								
Eagleton	Y	Y	Y	Y	Y	Y	Y	Y
Danforth	Y	Y	Y	Y	Y	Y	Y	Y
MONTANA								
Melcher	✓	N	Y	N	N	N	N	Y
Hatfield, P.	Y	Y	Y	N	N	#	#	#
NEBRASKA								
Zorinsky	Y	Y	Y	N	N	N	N	Y
Curtis	N	N	N	N	N	N	N	N
NEVADA								
Cannon	Y	X	Y	N	N	N	N	Y
Laxalt	N	N	Y	N	N	N	N	Y
NEW HAMPSHIRE								
Durkin	Y	Y	Y	Y	Y	Y	Y	Y
McIntyre	Y	Y	Y	Y	Y	Y	Y	Y
NEW JERSEY								
Williams	Y	Y	Y	Y	Y	Y	Y	Y
Case	Y	Y	Y	Y	Y	Y	Y	Y
NEW MEXICO								
Domenici	N	N	Y	N	N	N	N	Y
Schmitt	N	N	Y	N	N	N	N	Y
NEW YORK								
Moynihan	Y	Y	Y	Y	Y	?	?	?
Javits	Y	Y	Y	?	?	Y	Y	Y
NORTH CAROLINA								
Morgan	N	N	Y	Y	N	Y	N	Y
Helms	N	N	N	N	N	N	N	Y
NORTH DAKOTA								
Burdick	Y	N	Y	N	N	N	N	Y
Young	?	N	Y	N	N	N	N	Y
OHIO								
Glenn	Y	Y	Y	Y	Y	Y	Y	Y
Metzenbaum	Y	Y	Y	Y	Y	Y	Y	Y
OKLAHOMA								
Bartlett	?	?	?	?	?	N	N	Y
Bellmon	?	?	?	?	?	?	?	?
OREGON								
Hatfield, M.	†	†	†	†	†	✓	✓	✓
Packwood	Y	Y	Y	Y	N	Y	Y	Y
PENNSYLVANIA								
Heinz	Y	Y	Y	N	N	Y	N	Y
Schweiker	N	N	Y	N	N	N	N	Y
RHODE ISLAND								
Pell	Y	Y	Y	Y	Y	Y	Y	Y
Chafee	Y	Y	Y	Y	Y	Y	Y	Y
SOUTH CAROLINA								
Hollings	Y	Y	Y	Y	Y	?	?	?
Thurmond	N	N	Y	N	X	N	N	Y
SOUTH DAKOTA								
Abourezk	#	#	#	✓	✓	#	Y	Y
McGovern	Y	Y	Y	Y	Y	Y	#	Y
TENNESSEE								
Sasser	Y	Y	Y	Y	Y	?	?	?
Baker	Y	Y	Y	Y	✓	Y	Y	Y
TEXAS								
Bentsen	?	?	?	?	?	?	?	?
Tower	N	N	Y	N	N	N	N	Y
UTAH								
Garn	N	N	Y	N	N	N	N	Y
Hatch	N	N	Y	N	N	N	N	Y
VERMONT								
Leahy	Y	Y	Y	Y	Y	Y	Y	Y
Stafford	Y	Y	Y	Y	Y	Y	Y	Y
VIRGINIA								
*Byrd, H.	N	N	Y	N	N	N	N	Y
Scott	N	N	N	N	N	N	N	N
WASHINGTON								
Jackson	Y	Y	Y	Y	Y	Y	Y	Y
Magnuson	Y	Y	Y	Y	Y	Y	Y	Y
WEST VIRGINIA								
Byrd, R.	Y	Y	Y	Y	Y	Y	Y	Y
Randolph	X	✓	Y	X	X	Y	Y	Y
WISCONSIN								
Nelson	Y	Y	Y	Y	Y	Y	Y	Y
Proxmire	Y	Y	Y	Y	Y	Y	Y	Y
WYOMING								
Hansen	N	N	Y	N	N	N	N	Y
Wallop	N	N	Y	Y	N	N	N	Y

Democrats ***Republicans***

Byrd elected as independent.

KEY

- Y Voted for (yea).
- ✓ Paired for.
- † Announced for.
- # CQ Poll for.
- N Voted against (nay).
- X Paired against.
- - Announced against.
- ▮ CQ Poll against.
- P Voted "present."
- ● Voted "present" to avoid possible conflict of interest.
- ? Did not vote or otherwise make a position known.

47. Exec N, 95th Congress, First Session, Panama Canal Treaties. Church, D-Idaho, motion to table (kill) the Helms, R-N.C., amendment to give the United States and Panama the right to take whatever economic, diplomatic or military measures necessary to defend the canal if it were threatened. Motion agreed to 58-27: R 12-21; D 46-6 (ND 37-0; SD 9-6), March 10, 1978. A "yea" was a vote supporting the president's position.

48. Exec N, 95th Congress, First Session, Panama Canal Treaties. Clark, D-Iowa, motion to table (kill) the Allen, D-Ala., amendment stating that any U.S. action to defend the canal "be directed at" keeping the canal open, secure and accessible. Motion agreed to 53-33: R 12-22; D 41-11 (ND 34-3; SD 7-8), March 10, 1978. A "yea" was a vote supporting the president's position.

49. Exec N, 95th Congress, First Session, Panama Canal Treaties. Byrd, D-W.Va., amendment to ensure that the United States and Panama have the right to defend the canal against any threat to its neutrality. Adopted 84-5: R 29-5; D 55-0 (ND 40-0; SD 15-0), March 10, 1978. A "yea" was a vote supporting the president's position.

50. Exec N, 95th Congress, First Session, Panama Canal Treaties. Sarbanes, D-Md., motion to table (kill) the Dole, R-Kan., amendment to provide that U.S. troops could remain in Panama until Dec. 31, 2009, if the United States and Panama failed to reach an agreement allowing U.S. troops to remain after the year 2000. Motion agreed to 50-34: R 11-22; D 39-12 (ND 32-6; SD 7-6), March 10, 1978. A "yea" was a vote supporting the president's position.

51. Exec N, 95th Congress, First Session, Panama Canal Treaties. Sarbanes, D-Md., motion to table (kill) the Dole, R-Kan., amendment to provide that only Panama could maintain troops and military installations in that country "except as Panama and the United States might otherwise agree." Motion agreed to 45-37: R 8-23; D 37-14 (ND 32-6; SD 5-8), March 10, 1978. A "yea" was a vote supporting the president's position.

52. Exec N, 95th Congress, First Session, Panama Canal Treaties. Church, D-Idaho, motion to table (kill) the Allen, D-Ala., amendment, to the Byrd, D-W. Va., amendment *(see vote 54, below)*, to provide that the United States be the only judge of whether there was a need or emergency for its ships to go to the head of the line. Motion agreed to 53-34: R 13-22; D 40-12 (ND 32-5; SD 8-7), March 13, 1978. A "yea" was a vote supporting the president's position.

53. Exec N, 95th Congress, First Session, Panama Canal Treaties. Sarbanes, D-Md., motion to table (kill) the Dole, R-Kan., amendment, to the Byrd, D-W. Va., amendment *(see vote 54, below)*, to provide that Panama and the United States each determine whether an emergency existed for allowing its ships to go to the head of the line. Motion agreed to 51-37: R 12-23; D 39-14 (ND 33-5; SD 6-9), March 13, 1978. A "yea" was a vote supporting the president's position.

54. Exec N, 95th Congress, First Session, Panama Canal Treaties. Byrd, D-W.Va., amendment to provide that warships and auxiliary vessels of the United States and Panama have the right to go to the head of the line of ships waiting to transit the canal during emergencies. Adopted 85-3: R 32-3; D 53-0 (ND 39-0; SD 14-0), March 13, 1978. A "yea" was a vote supporting the president's position.

Corresponding to Congressional Record Votes 55, 56, 57, 58, 59, 60

	55	56	57	58	59	60
ALABAMA						
Allen	N	N	N	Y	Y	Y
Sparkman	Y	Y	Y	Y	Y	Y
ALASKA						
Gravel	Y	Y	Y	Y	N	N
Stevens	X	N	N	N	N	Y
ARIZONA						
DeConcini	N	N	N	N	Y	Y
Goldwater	N	N	N	N	N	Y
ARKANSAS						
Bumpers	Y	?	Y	Y	Y	Y
Hodges	Y	Y	Y	Y	Y	Y
CALIFORNIA						
Cranston	Y	Y	Y	Y	Y	Y
Hayakawa	Y	Y	Y	Y	Y	Y
COLORADO						
Hart	Y	Y	Y	Y	Y	Y
Haskell	?	N	Y	Y	Y	Y
CONNECTICUT						
Ribicoff	Y	Y	Y	Y	Y	Y
Weicker	Y	Y	Y	Y	Y	Y
DELAWARE						
Biden	Y	Y	Y	Y	Y	Y
Roth	N	N	N	N	Y	Y
FLORIDA						
Chiles	Y	Y	N	Y	Y	Y
Stone	Y	Y	N	Y	Y	Y
GEORGIA						
Nunn	Y	N	N	Y	Y	Y
Talmadge	Y	N	N	Y	Y	Y
HAWAII						
Inouye	?	Y	Y	Y	Y	Y
Matsunaga	Y	Y	Y	Y	Y	Y
IDAHO						
Church	Y	Y	Y	Y	Y	Y
McClure	N	N	N	N	N	Y
ILLINOIS						
Stevenson	Y	Y	Y	Y	Y	Y
Percy	Y	Y	Y	Y	Y	Y
INDIANA						
Bayh	Y	?	Y	Y	Y	Y
Lugar	N	N	N	N	N	Y
IOWA						
Clark	Y	Y	Y	Y	Y	Y
Culver	Y	Y	Y	Y	Y	Y
KANSAS						
Dole	N	N	N	N	N	Y
Pearson	Y	Y	Y	Y	Y	Y
KENTUCKY						
Ford	N	N	Y	Y	Y	Y
Huddleston	?	Y	Y	Y	Y	Y
LOUISIANA						
Johnston	▮	▮	▮	?	Y	Y
Long	Y	?	Y	Y	Y	Y
MAINE						
Hathaway	Y	Y	Y	Y	Y	Y
Muskie	Y	Y	Y	?	Y	Y
MARYLAND						
Sarbanes	Y	Y	Y	Y	Y	Y
Mathias	Y	Y	Y	Y	Y	Y
MASSACHUSETTS						
Kennedy	#	Y	Y	Y	Y	Y
Brooke	N	N	N	N	Y	Y
MICHIGAN						
Riegle	Y	Y	Y	Y	Y	Y
Griffin	N	N	N	N	N	Y
MINNESOTA						
Anderson	Y	Y	Y	Y	Y	Y
Humphrey, M.	Y	Y	Y	Y	Y	Y
MISSISSIPPI						
Eastland	N	N	N	N	Y	Y
Stennis	N	N	N	?	Y	Y
MISSOURI						
Eagleton	Y	Y	Y	Y	Y	Y
Danforth	Y	Y	Y	Y	Y	Y
MONTANA						
Melcher	Y	N	N	Y	Y	Y
Hatfield, P.	#	▮	▮	#	Y	#
NEBRASKA						
Zorinsky	Y	N	Y	Y	Y	Y
Curtis	N	N	N	N	N	Y
NEVADA						
Cannon	Y	N	N	Y	Y	Y
Laxalt	N	N	N	N	N	Y
NEW HAMPSHIRE						
Durkin	N	Y	Y	Y	Y	Y
McIntyre	N	Y	Y	Y	Y	Y
NEW JERSEY						
Williams	Y	Y	Y	Y	Y	Y
Case	#	Y	Y	Y	#	#
NEW MEXICO						
Domenici	Y	N	?	N	Y	Y
Schmitt	Y	N	N	N	N	Y
NEW YORK						
Moynihan	Y	Y	Y	Y	Y	Y
Javits	Y	Y	Y	Y	Y	Y
NORTH CAROLINA						
Morgan	N	Y	N	N	Y	Y
Helms	N	N	N	N	N	Y
NORTH DAKOTA						
Burdick	Y	N	N	Y	Y	Y
Young	N	N	N	N	Y	Y
OHIO						
Glenn	Y	Y	Y	Y	Y	Y
Metzenbaum	Y	Y	Y	Y	Y	Y
OKLAHOMA						
Bartlett	N	N	N	N	Y	Y
Bellmon	?	N	N	N	Y	Y
OREGON						
Hatfield, M.	✓	Y	Y	Y	Y	Y
Packwood	Y	N	N	N	Y	Y
PENNSYLVANIA						
Heinz	Y	N	Y	Y	Y	Y
Schweiker	N	N	N	N	Y	Y
RHODE ISLAND						
Pell	Y	Y	Y	Y	Y	Y
Chafee	Y	Y	Y	Y	Y	Y
SOUTH CAROLINA						
Hollings	Y	Y	Y	Y	Y	Y
Thurmond	N	N	N	N	Y	Y
SOUTH DAKOTA						
Abourezk	#	#	#	#	▮	#
McGovern	Y	Y	Y	Y	Y	Y
TENNESSEE						
Sasser	?	N	Y	Y	Y	Y
Baker	Y	Y	Y	N	Y	Y
TEXAS						
Bentsen	?	Y	Y	Y	Y	Y
Tower	?	N	N	N	N	Y
UTAH						
Garn	N	N	N	N	N	Y
Hatch	N	N	N	N	N	Y
VERMONT						
Leahy	Y	Y	Y	Y	Y	Y
Stafford	Y	Y	Y	Y	Y	Y
VIRGINIA						
*Byrd, H.	N	N	N	N	Y	Y
Scott	N	N	N	N	N	Y
WASHINGTON						
Jackson	Y	Y	Y	Y	Y	Y
Magnuson	Y	Y	Y	Y	Y	Y
WEST VIRGINIA						
Byrd, R.	Y	Y	Y	Y	Y	Y
Randolph	Y	N	N	Y	Y	Y
WISCONSIN						
Nelson	Y	Y	Y	Y	Y	Y
Proxmire	Y	Y	Y	Y	Y	Y
WYOMING						
Hansen	N	N	N	N	N	Y
Wallop	N	N	N	N	Y	Y

Democrats ***Republicans***

Byrd elected as independent.

KEY

- Y Voted for (yea).
- ✓ Paired for.
- † Announced for.
- # CQ Poll for.
- N Voted against (nay).
- X Paired against.
- \- Announced against.
- ▮ CQ Poll against.
- P Voted "present."
- ● Voted "present" to avoid possible conflict of interest.
- ? Did not vote or otherwise make a position known.

55. Exec N, 95th Congress, First Session, Panama Canal Treaties. Sarbanes, D-Md., motion to table (kill) the Helms, R-N.C., amendment to give U.S. warships toll-free transit of the canal. Motion agreed to 58-28: R 14-19; D 44-9 (ND 35-3; SD 9-6), March 13, 1978. A "yea" was a vote supporting the president's position.

56. Exec N, 95th Congress, First Session, Panama Canal Treaties. Sarbanes, D-Md., motion to table (kill) the Allen, D-Ala., amendment to negotiate a later agreement for stationing U.S. troops in Panama after the year 2000. Motion agreed to 53-41: R 12-26; D 41-15 (ND 33-7; SD 8-8), March 14, 1978. A "yea" was a vote supporting the president's position.

57. Exec N, 95th Congress, First Session, Panama Canal Treaties. Church, D-Idaho, motion to table (kill) the Thurmond, R-S.C., amendment to authorize the American Battle Monuments Commission to arrange for the removal of the remains of U.S. citizens from Mount Hope Cemetery to the American sector of Corozal Cemetery. Motion agreed to 58-38: R 13-24; D 45-14 (ND 36-5; SD 9-9), March 14, 1978. A "yea" was a vote supporting the president's position.

58. Exec N, 95th Congress, First Session, Panama Canal Treaties. Church, D-Idaho, motion to table (kill) the Schmitt, R-N.M., substitute amendment to the treaty to place the canal under an international operating organization composed of Western Hemisphere nations. Motion agreed to 65-30: R 12-26; D 53-4 (ND 39-1; D 14-3), March 14, 1978. A "yea" was a vote supporting the president's position.

59. Exec N, 95th Congress, First Session, Panama Canal Treaties. Nunn, D-Ga., reservation to the resolution of ratification to the neutrality treaty to provide that nothing in the pact precludes the United States and Panama from reaching an agreement for basing U.S. troops in Panama after 1999. Adopted 82-16: R 22-15; D 60-1 (ND 41-1; SD 19-0), March 15, 1978.

60. Exec N, 95th Congress, First Session, Panama Canal Treaties. Randolph, D-W.Va., reservation to the resolution of ratification providing that before the treaty becomes effective the United States and Panama negotiate an agreement whereby the American Battle Monuments Commission would administer after 1999 the section of the Corozal Cemetery where U.S. citizens were buried. Adopted 96-1: R 37-0; D 59-1 (ND 40-1; SD 19-0), March 15, 1978.

CQ Senate Votes 61-66

Corresponding to Congressional Record Votes 61, 62, 63, 64, 65, 66

	61	62	63	64	65	66
ALABAMA						
Allen	N	N	N	Y	N	N
Sparkman	Y	N	Y	Y	Y	Y
ALASKA						
Gravel	Y	Y	Y	N	Y	Y
Stevens	N	Y	N	N	N	N
ARIZONA						
DeConcini	N	N	N	Y	Y	Y
Goldwater	N	N	N	N	N	N
ARKANSAS						
Bumpers	Y	N	Y	Y	Y	Y
Hodges	Y	N	Y	Y	Y	Y
CALIFORNIA						
Cranston	Y	N	Y	N	Y	Y
Hayakawa	Y	N	Y	Y	Y	Y
COLORADO						
Hart	Y	N	Y	N	Y	Y
Haskell	Y	N	Y	Y	Y	Y
CONNECTICUT						
Ribicoff	Y	N	Y	Y	Y	Y
Weicker	Y	N	Y	N	Y	Y
DELAWARE						
Biden	Y	N	Y	Y	Y	Y
Roth	N	N	N	Y	N	N
FLORIDA						
Chiles	Y	N	N	Y	Y	Y
Stone	Y	N	Y	Y	Y	Y
GEORGIA						
Nunn	N	N	N	Y	Y	Y
Talmadge	Y	N	Y	Y	Y	Y
HAWAII						
Inouye	Y	N	Y	Y	Y	Y
Matsunaga	?	N	Y	Y	Y	Y
IDAHO						
Church	Y	N	Y	Y	Y	Y
McClure	N	Y	N	N	N	N
ILLINOIS						
Stevenson	Y	N	Y	Y	Y	Y
Percy	Y	N	Y	Y	Y	Y
INDIANA						
Bayh	Y	N	Y	Y	Y	Y
Lugar	N	N	N	Y	N	N
IOWA						
Clark	Y	N	Y	N	Y	Y
Culver	Y	N	Y	N	Y	Y
KANSAS						
Dole	N	N	N	Y	N	N
Pearson	Y	N	Y	Y	Y	Y
KENTUCKY						
Ford	N	N	N	Y	N	N
Huddleston	Y	N	Y	Y	Y	Y
LOUISIANA						
Johnston	N	N	N	Y	N	N
Long	Y	N	Y	Y	Y	Y
MAINE						
Hathaway	Y	N	Y	Y	Y	Y
Muskie	Y	N	Y	Y	Y	Y
MARYLAND						
Sarbanes	Y	N	Y	Y	Y	Y
Mathias	?	?	?	?	Y	Y
MASSACHUSETTS						
Kennedy	Y	Y	Y	N	Y	Y
Brooke	N	N	N	Y	N	Y
MICHIGAN						
Riegle	Y	Y	Y	Y	Y	Y
Griffin	N	N	N	N	N	N
MINNESOTA						
Anderson	Y	N	Y	Y	Y	Y
Humphrey, M.	Y	N	Y	Y	Y	Y
MISSISSIPPI						
Eastland	N	N	N	Y	N	N
Stennis	N	N	N	Y	N	N
MISSOURI						
Eagleton	Y	N	Y	Y	Y	Y
Danforth	Y	N	Y	Y	Y	Y
MONTANA						
Melcher	N	N	N	Y	N	N
Hatfield, P.	Y	N	N	Y	Y	Y
NEBRASKA						
Zorinsky	Y	N	N	Y	N	N
Curtis	N	N	N	Y	N	N
NEVADA						
Cannon	Y	N	Y	Y	Y	Y
Laxalt	N	N	N	N	N	N
NEW HAMPSHIRE						
Durkin	Y	Y	Y	N	Y	Y
McIntyre	Y	N	Y	Y	Y	Y
NEW JERSEY						
Williams	Y	N	Y	Y	Y	Y
Case	Y	N	Y	N	Y	Y
NEW MEXICO						
Domenici	N	N	N	Y	N	N
Schmitt	N	N	N	N	N	N
NEW YORK						
Moynihan	Y	Y	Y	N	Y	Y
Javits	Y	N	Y	N	Y	Y
NORTH CAROLINA						
Morgan	N	N	Y	Y	Y	Y
Helms	N	N	N	Y	N	N
NORTH DAKOTA						
Burdick	N	N	N	Y	N	N
Young	N	N	N	Y	N	N
OHIO						
Glenn	?	N	Y	Y	Y	Y
Metzenbaum	Y	Y	Y	N	Y	Y
OKLAHOMA						
Bartlett	N	N	N	Y	N	N
Bellmon	N	N	Y	Y	N	Y
OREGON						
Hatfield, M.	Y	N	Y	Y	Y	Y
Packwood	Y	N	Y	Y	Y	Y
PENNSYLVANIA						
Heinz	Y	N	Y	Y	Y	Y
Schweiker	N	N	N	Y	N	N
RHODE ISLAND						
Pell	Y	N	Y	Y	Y	Y
Chafee	Y	N	Y	Y	Y	Y
SOUTH CAROLINA						
Hollings	Y	N	Y	Y	Y	Y
Thurmond	N	N	N	Y	N	N
SOUTH DAKOTA						
Abourezk	Y	Y	#	▮	Y	Y
McGovern	Y	Y	Y	N	Y	Y
TENNESSEE						
Sasser	Y	N	Y	Y	Y	Y
Baker	N	N	Y	Y	Y	Y
TEXAS						
Bentsen	Y	N	Y	Y	Y	Y
Tower	N	N	N	N	N	N
UTAH						
Garn	N	Y	N	N	N	N
Hatch	N	Y	N	N	N	N
VERMONT						
Leahy	Y	N	Y	Y	Y	Y
Stafford	Y	N	Y	Y	Y	Y
VIRGINIA						
*Byrd, H.	N	N	N	Y	N	N
Scott	N	Y	N	N	N	N
WASHINGTON						
Jackson	Y	N	Y	Y	Y	Y
Magnuson	Y	N	Y	Y	Y	Y
WEST VIRGINIA						
Byrd, R.	Y	N	Y	Y	Y	Y
Randolph	N	N	Y	Y	Y	N
WISCONSIN						
Nelson	Y	N	Y	Y	Y	Y
Proxmire	Y	N	Y	Y	Y	Y
WYOMING						
Hansen	N	N	N	Y	N	N
Wallop	N	N	N	Y	N	N

Democrats ***Republicans***

*Byrd elected as independent.

KEY

- Y Voted for (yea).
- ✓ Paired for.
- † Announced for.
- # CQ Poll for.
- N Voted against (nay).
- X Paired against.
- - Announced against.
- ▮ CQ Poll against.
- P Voted "present."
- ● Voted "present" to avoid possible conflict of interest.
- ? Did not vote or otherwise make a position known.

61. Exec N, 95th Congress, First Session, Panama Canal Treaties. Church, D-Idaho, motion to table (kill) the Bartlett, R-Okla., reservation to the resolution of ratification that the president must determine whether Panama has ratified the amended treaties by national plebiscite before the ratified treaties are turned over to Panama. Motion agreed to 60-37: R 12-25; D 48-12 (ND 37-4; SD 11-8), March 16, 1978.

62. Exec N, 95th Congress, First Session, Panama Canal Treaties. Allen, D-Ala., motion to table the DeConcini, D-Ariz., amendment to the resolution of ratification *(see vote 64, below)*. Motion rejected 13-86: R 5-32; D 8-54 (ND 8-35; SD 0-19), March 16, 1978.

63. Exec N, 95th Congress, First Session, Panama Canal Treaties. Church, D-Idaho, motion to table the Allen, D-Ala, amendment, to the DeConcini, D-Ariz., amendment *(see vote 64, below)*, to stipulate that the DeConcini amendment be considered as an amendment to the treaty, rather than to the resolution of ratification. Motion agreed to 62-36: R 14-23; D 48-13 (ND 37-5; SD 11-8), March 16, 1978. A "yea" was a vote supporting the president's position.

64. Exec N, 95th Congress, First Session, Panama Canal Treaties. DeConcini, D-Ariz., amendment to the resolution of ratification to grant the United States the right to use military force to open and operate the canal if the canal closed for any reason. Adopted 75-23: R 24-13; D 51-10 (ND 32-10; SD 19-0), March 16, 1978. A "yea" was a vote supporting the president's position.

65. Exec N, 95th Congress, First Session, Panama Canal Treaties. Church, D-Idaho, motion to table (kill) the Griffin, R-Mich., substitute for the resolution of ratification to withhold Senate consent to the neutrality treaty and to advise the president to renegotiate the treaty with the participation of all American nations. Motion agreed to 67-33: R 14-24; D 53-9 (ND 40-3; SD 13-6), March 16, 1978. A "yea" was a vote supporting the president's position.

66. Exec N, 95th Congress, First Session, Panama Canal Treaties. Adoption of the resolution of ratification to the neutrality treaty guaranteeing that the Panama Canal will be permanently neutral and remain secure and open to vessels of all nations. Adopted 68-32: R 16-22; D 52-10 (ND 39-4; SD 13-6), March 16, 1978. A two-thirds majority vote (67 in this case) is required for adoption of resolutions of ratification of treaties. A "yea" was a vote supporting the president's position.

KEY

- Y Voted for (yea).
- ✓ Paired for.
- † Announced for.
- # CQ Poll for.
- N Voted against (nay).
- X Paired against.
- \- Announced against.
- ▮ CQ Poll against.
- P Voted "present."
- ● Voted "present" to avoid possible conflict of interest.
- ? Did not vote or otherwise make a position known.

	67	68	69	70	71	72	73	74
ALABAMA								
Allen	N	Y	Y	Y	Y	Y	N	N
Sparkman	#	▮	Y	Y	Y	Y	Y	#
ALASKA								
Gravel	#	▮	#	#	▮	#	#	†
Stevens	N	Y	Y	N	Y	Y	Y	N
ARIZONA								
DeConcini	N	Y	N	Y	Y	Y	Y	N
Goldwater	?	?	N	N	N	N	?	?
ARKANSAS								
Bumpers	Y	N	Y	N	N	Y	Y	Y
Hodges	Y	N	Y	Y	Y	Y	Y	Y
CALIFORNIA								
Cranston	Y	N	N	Y	N	N	Y	Y
Hayakawa	Y	Y	N	Y	Y	Y	N	Y
COLORADO								
Hart	Y	N	Y	Y	Y	Y	Y	Y
Haskell	?	X	?	✓	✓	X	?	?
CONNECTICUT								
Ribicoff	Y	N	N	N	N	N	Y	Y
Weicker	Y	N	N	Y	Y	Y	?	Y
DELAWARE								
Biden	Y	N	N	N	N	N	Y	N
Roth	N	Y	N	N	N	N	N	Y
FLORIDA								
Chiles	N	N	Y	N	Y	Y	N	Y
Stone	Y	Y	Y	Y	Y	Y	Y	Y
GEORGIA								
Nunn	N	Y	Y	Y	Y	Y	Y	N
Talmadge	N	Y	Y	Y	Y	Y	Y	▮
HAWAII								
Inouye	Y	N	Y	Y	N	Y	Y	?
Matsunaga	Y	N	?	?	?	?	?	Y
IDAHO								
Church	Y	N	Y	Y	Y	Y	Y	Y
McClure	N	Y	Y	Y	Y	Y	N	N
ILLINOIS								
Stevenson	Y	N	Y	N	N	N	Y	Y
Percy	?	?	?	Y	N	Y	Y	Y
INDIANA								
Bayh	Y	N	Y	N	Y	Y	Y	Y
Lugar	N	Y	N	N	Y	Y	Y	N
IOWA								
Clark	Y	N	Y	Y	N	Y	Y	Y
Culver	Y	N	Y	Y	N	Y	Y	Y
KANSAS								
Dole	N	Y	Y	Y	Y	Y	N	N
Pearson	Y	?	Y	Y	Y	Y	?	Y
KENTUCKY								
Ford	N	✓	Y	Y	Y	Y	Y	N
Huddleston	?	?	Y	Y	Y	Y	Y	Y
LOUISIANA								
Johnston	Y	Y	Y	Y	Y	Y	Y	N
Long	Y	Y	Y	Y	Y	Y	Y	Y
MAINE								
Hathaway	?	X	N	Y	N	Y	Y	Y
Muskie	?	?	N	N	N	N	Y	Y
MARYLAND								
Sarbanes	Y	N	Y	Y	N	Y	Y	Y
Mathias	?	?	N	N	N	N	Y	Y
MASSACHUSETTS								
Kennedy	Y	▮	N	N	N	Y	Y	Y
Brooke	N	Y	N	N	N	Y	Y	N
MICHIGAN								
Riegle	Y	N	†	†	✓	✓	†	Y
Griffin	?	?	N	Y	Y	Y	Y	N
MINNESOTA								
Anderson	Y	N	Y	Y	Y	Y	Y	Y
Humphrey, M.	Y	N	Y	Y	Y	Y	Y	Y
MISSISSIPPI								
Eastland	N	Y	Y	Y	Y	Y	?	N
Stennis	?	Y	Y	Y	N	Y	N	N
MISSOURI								
Eagleton	Y	N	Y	N	N	Y	?	Y
Danforth	Y	N	Y	Y	Y	Y	Y	Y
MONTANA								
Melcher	N	Y	Y	Y	Y	Y	Y	Y
Hatfield, P.	N	Y	Y	Y	Y	Y	#	N
NEBRASKA								
Zorinsky	N	✓	Y	Y	Y	Y	Y	N
Curtis	N	Y	N	Y	Y	Y	N	?
NEVADA								
Cannon	N	Y	N	Y	N	X	Y	N
Laxalt	N	Y	N	Y	Y	Y	N	N
NEW HAMPSHIRE								
Durkin	Y	N	N	N	N	N	Y	Y
McIntyre	Y	N	N	Y	N	N	Y	†
NEW JERSEY								
Williams	Y	N	▮	X	X	✓	Y	Y
Case	Y	N	N	N	N	N	Y	Y
NEW MEXICO								
Domenici	N	Y	Y	Y	Y	Y	N	N
Schmitt	N	Y	Y	Y	Y	Y	N	N
NEW YORK								
Moynihan	Y	N	Y	Y	N	N	Y	Y
Javits	Y	N	N	N	N	N	Y	Y
NORTH CAROLINA								
Morgan	Y	N	Y	Y	Y	Y	N	Y
Helms	N	Y	N	Y	Y	Y	N	N
NORTH DAKOTA								
Burdick	N	Y	Y	Y	Y	Y	Y	N
Young	N	Y	Y	Y	Y	Y	N	N
OHIO								
Glenn	Y	N	N	N	N	N	Y	Y
Metzenbaum	Y	N	N	N	N	N	Y	Y
OKLAHOMA								
Bartlett	N	Y	Y	Y	Y	?	N	N
Bellmon	N	Y	N	N	N	N	N	Y
OREGON								
Hatfield, M.	N	N	Y	Y	Y	Y	Y	Y
Packwood	N	Y	Y	Y	Y	Y	Y	N
PENNSYLVANIA								
Heinz	Y	N	N	N	N	N	Y	Y
Schweiker	?	?	N	Y	Y	Y	N	N
RHODE ISLAND								
Pell	Y	N	N	N	N	N	Y	Y
Chafee	Y	N	N	N	N	N	Y	Y
SOUTH CAROLINA								
Hollings	Y	N	Y	Y	Y	Y	?	Y
Thurmond	N	Y	Y	Y	Y	Y	Y	N
SOUTH DAKOTA								
Abourezk	Y	N	Y	Y	Y	Y	Y	Y
McGovern	Y	▮	Y	Y	Y	Y	Y	#
TENNESSEE								
Sasser	Y	N	Y	Y	N	Y	Y	Y
Baker	?	N	Y	N	N	Y	N	Y
TEXAS								
Bentsen	Y	Y	Y	Y	Y	Y	N	Y
Tower	N	Y	Y	Y	Y	Y	N	N
UTAH								
Garn	N	Y	N	Y	Y	N	N	N
Hatch	N	Y	?	Y	Y	Y	N	N
VERMONT								
Leahy	Y	N	Y	Y	X	N	Y	Y
Stafford	Y	N	Y	Y	Y	N	Y	Y
VIRGINIA								
*Byrd, H.	N	Y	N	Y	N	N	N	N
Scott	N	Y	N	N	N	N	N	N
WASHINGTON								
Jackson	Y	N	Y	Y	Y	Y	Y	Y
Magnuson	Y	N	Y	Y	Y	Y	Y	Y
WEST VIRGINIA								
Byrd, R.	Y	N	N	Y	N	N	Y	Y
Randolph	N	Y	Y	N	N	Y	Y	N
WISCONSIN								
Nelson	Y	N	Y	Y	N	Y	Y	Y
Proxmire	Y	N	N	N	N	N	Y	Y
WYOMING								
Hansen	N	Y	Y	Y	Y	Y	N	N
Wallop	N	Y	Y	N	Y	Y	N	N

Democrats *Republicans*

*Byrd elected as independent.

67. Exec N, 95th Congress, First Session, Panama Canal Treaties. Durkin, D-N.H., motion to table (kill) the Wallop, R-Wyo., amendment to provide that if Panama abrogated any provision of the treaties, those treaties superseded by the new pacts would again become effective. Motion agreed to 50-37: R 9-23; D 41-14 (ND 32-7; SD 9-7), March 20, 1978. A "yea" was a vote supporting the president's position.

68. Exec N, 95th Congress, First Session, Panama Canal Treaties. Dole, R-Kan., amendment to prohibit troops of nations other than the United States or Panama to be stationed in Panama before the year 2000. Rejected 39-45: R 23-9; D 16-36 (ND 6-30; SD 10-6), March 20, 1978. A "nay" was a vote supporting the president's position.

69. HR 6782. Emergency Farm Bill. McGovern, D-S.D., amendment to raise 1978 target prices and loan levels for wheat, corn and cotton programs. Adopted 58-35: R 17-19; D 41-16 (ND 23-15; SD 18-1), March 21, 1978.

70. HR 6782. Emergency Farm Bill. Dole, R-Kan., motion to table (kill) the Bellmon, R-Okla., amendment to the Dole amendment *(see vote 71, below)*, to raise acreage set-aside requirements in the flexible parity program. Motion agreed to 66-29: R 24-14; D 42-15 (ND 25-13; SD 17-2), March 21, 1978.

71. HR 6782. Emergency Farm Bill. Dole, R-Kan., amendment to provide for a flexible parity program of graduated target prices for wheat, corn and cotton in 1978. Adopted 55-39: R 26-12; D 29-27 (ND 14-23; SD 15-4), March 21, 1978.

72. HR 6782. Emergency Farm Bill. Passage of the bill to provide, for 1978 only, for a paid land diversion program for farmers, an increase in target price and loan levels for wheat, corn and cotton programs, and a flexible parity program of graduated target prices for wheat, corn and cotton. Passed 67-26: R 26-11; D 41-15 (ND 23-14; SD 18-1), March 21, 1978.

73. HR 3813. Redwood National Park. Adoption of the conference report on the bill to provide for the immediate expansion of the Redwood National Park in northern California by 48,000 acres. Adopted (thus cleared for the president) 63-26: R 15-20; D 48-6 (ND 37-0; SD 11-6), March 21, 1978. A "yea" was a vote supporting the president's position.

74. Exec N, 95th Congress, First Session, Panama Canal Treaties. Sarbanes, D-Md., motion to table (kill) part 1 of the Allen, D-Ala., amendment to provide that nothing in the treaty forbids the United States from preventing the construction of a new canal in Panama by another nation. Motion agreed to 56-35: R 15-21; D 41-14 (ND 31-7; SD 10-7), March 22, 1978. A "yea" was a vote supporting the president's position.

CQ Senate Votes 75-78

Corresponding to Congressional Record Votes 75, 76, 77, 78

	75	76	77	78
ALABAMA				
Allen	N	Y	Y	Y
Sparkman	Y	▮	▮	#
ALASKA				
Gravel	†	-	▮	†
Stevens	N	Y	Y	Y
ARIZONA				
DeConcini	N	N	Y	Y
Goldwater	?	?	?	?
ARKANSAS				
Bumpers	Y	N	N	Y
Hodges	Y	N	N	Y
CALIFORNIA				
Cranston	Y	N	N	Y
Hayakawa	Y	N	N	N
COLORADO				
Hart	Y	N	N	Y
Haskell	?	?	?	?
CONNECTICUT				
Ribicoff	Y	N	N	#
Weicker	Y	N	N	Y
DELAWARE				
Biden	Y	N	N	Y
Roth	N	N	Y	Y
FLORIDA				
Chiles	N	N	N	?
Stone	N	N	N	Y
GEORGIA				
Nunn	N	N	Y	Y
Talmadge	N	N	N	Y
HAWAII				
Inouye	?	?	?	?
Matsunaga	Y	N	N	?
IDAHO				
Church	Y	N	N	†
McClure	N	Y	Y	N
ILLINOIS				
Stevenson	Y	N	N	N
Percy	Y	N	N	Y
INDIANA				
Bayh	Y	N	?	Y
Lugar	N	Y	Y	Y

	75	76	77	78
IOWA				
Clark	Y	N	N	Y
Culver	Y	N	N	Y
KANSAS				
Dole	N	N	Y	Y
Pearson	Y	N	N	?
KENTUCKY				
Ford	N	N	Y	Y
Huddleston	Y	N	N	Y
LOUISIANA				
Johnston	N	N	N	Y
Long	Y	N	N	†
MAINE				
Hathaway	Y	N	N	Y
Muskie	Y	N	N	Y
MARYLAND				
Sarbanes	Y	N	N	Y
Mathias	Y	N	?	?
MASSACHUSETTS				
Kennedy	Y	N	N	#
Brooke	N	N	Y	?
MICHIGAN				
Riegle	Y	N	N	Y
Griffin	N	N	N	N
MINNESOTA				
Anderson	Y	N	N	Y
Humphrey, M.	Y	N	N	†
MISSISSIPPI				
Eastland	N	Y	?	?
Stennis	N	N	?	Y
MISSOURI				
Eagleton	Y	N	N	Y
Danforth	Y	N	N	N
MONTANA				
Melcher	N	N	N	Y
Hatfield, P.	N	N	Y	Y
NEBRASKA				
Zorinsky	N	N	N	Y
Curtis	?	?	?	?
NEVADA				
Cannon	N	N	Y	Y
Laxalt	N	Y	Y	Y

	75	76	77	78
NEW HAMPSHIRE				
Durkin	Y	N	N	Y
McIntyre	Y	N	N	Y
NEW JERSEY				
Williams	Y	N	N	Y
Case	Y	N	N	▮
NEW MEXICO				
Domenici	N	N	Y	Y
Schmitt	N	Y	Y	Y
NEW YORK				
Moynihan	Y	N	N	Y
Javits	Y	N	N	Y
NORTH CAROLINA				
Morgan	N	N	N	Y
Helms	N	Y	Y	†
NORTH DAKOTA				
Burdick	N	N	N	Y
Young	N	?	N	Y
OHIO				
Glenn	Y	N	N	Y
Metzenbaum	N	N	N	N
OKLAHOMA				
Bartlett	N	Y	Y	Y
Bellmon	N	N	N	?
OREGON				
Hatfield, M.	Y	N	N	Y
Packwood	N	N	N	?
PENNSYLVANIA				
Heinz	Y	N	N	Y
Schweiker	N	N	Y	Y
RHODE ISLAND				
Pell	Y	N	N	Y
Chafee	Y	N	N	Y
SOUTH CAROLINA				
Hollings	Y	N	N	Y
Thurmond	N	Y	Y	Y
SOUTH DAKOTA				
Abourezk	Y	▮	N	#
McGovern	Y	N	N	Y
TENNESSEE				
Sasser	Y	?	?	?
Baker	Y	N	N	N

KEY

- Y Voted for (yea).
- ✓ Paired for.
- † Announced for.
- # CQ Poll for.
- N Voted against (nay).
- X Paired against.
- \- Announced against.
- ▮ CQ Poll against.
- P Voted "present."
- ● Voted "present" to avoid possible conflict of interest.
- ? Did not vote or otherwise make a position known.

	75	76	77	78
TEXAS				
Bentsen	Y	N	N	?
Tower	N	Y	Y	Y
UTAH				
Garn	N	Y	Y	Y
Hatch	N	Y	Y	Y
VERMONT				
Leahy	?	N	N	Y
Stafford	Y	N	▮	#
VIRGINIA				
*Byrd, H.	N	N	N	N
Scott	N	Y	Y	?
WASHINGTON				
Jackson	Y	N	N	Y
Magnuson	Y	N	N	†
WEST VIRGINIA				
Byrd, R.	Y	N	N	Y
Randolph	N	N	Y	#
WISCONSIN				
Nelson	Y	N	N	Y
Proxmire	Y	N	N	Y
WYOMING				
Hansen	N	Y	Y	N
Wallop	N	N	Y	N

Democrats ***Republicans***

**Byrd elected as independent.*

75. Exec N, 95th Congress, First Session, Panama Canal Treaties. Sarbanes, D-Md., motion to table (kill) part 2 of the Allen, D-Ala., amendment to provide that nothing in the treaty would prevent the United States from negotiating with any other nation for construction of a new canal. Motion agreed to 52-42: R 13-23; D 39-19 (ND 31-8; SD 8-11), March 22, 1978. A "yea" was a vote supporting the president's position.

76. Exec N, 95th Congress, First Session, Panama Canal Treaties. Bartlett, R-Okla., amendment to provide that Panama lease to the United States facilities relating to the canal for a 99-year period. Rejected 15-76: R 13-22; D 2-54 (ND 0-39; SD 2-15), March 22, 1978. A "nay" was a vote supporting the president's position.

77. Exec N, 95th Congress, First Session, Panama Canal Treaties. Hatch, R-Utah, amendment to provide that Panama shall not nationalize, expropriate or seize any U.S. property in Panama for the duration of the treaty. Rejected 26-62: R 19-15; D 7-47 (ND 4-35; SD 3-12), March 22, 1978. A "nay" was a vote supporting the president's position.

78. HR 5383. Mandatory Retirement Age. Adoption of the conference report on the bill to amend the Age Discrimination in Employment Act of 1967 to raise to 70, from 65, the age limit for protection of non-federal workers from age-based discriminatory practices, including mandatory retirement (except for certain high-level executives and tenured college and university faculty), and to eliminate the upper limit for most civilian federal employees. Adopted (thus clearing for the president) 62-10: R 20-7; D 42-3 (ND 30-2; SD 12-1), March 23, 1978.

	79	80	81	82
ALABAMA				
Allen	N	N	N	N
Sparkman	Y	Y	Y	Y
ALASKA				
Gravel	#	#	#	#
Stevens	N	N	N	N
ARIZONA				
DeConcini	N	N	N	Y
Goldwater	N	N	N	?
ARKANSAS				
Bumpers	Y	Y	?	?
Hodges	Y	Y	N	Y
CALIFORNIA				
Cranston	Y	Y	Y	Y
Hayakawa	Y	Y	?	?
COLORADO				
Hart	Y	Y	Y	Y
Haskell	Y	Y	Y	Y
CONNECTICUT				
Ribicoff	Y	Y	Y	Y
Weicker	Y	Y	#	#
DELAWARE				
Biden	Y	?	Y	?
Roth	N	N	N	N
FLORIDA				
Chiles	†	?	Y	Y
Stone	N	N	Y	N
GEORGIA				
Nunn	N	N	Y	Y
Talmadge	N	N	Y	▮
HAWAII				
Inouye	Y	Y	Y	Y
Matsunaga	?	Y	Y	Y
IDAHO				
Church	Y	Y	Y	Y
McClure	N	N	N	N
ILLINOIS				
Stevenson	Y	Y	Y	Y
Percy	Y	Y	Y	Y
INDIANA				
Bayh	Y	Y	Y	?
Lugar	N	N	N	N

	79	80	81	82
IOWA				
Clark	Y	Y	†	†
Culver	Y	Y	Y	Y
KANSAS				
Dole	N	N	?	?
Pearson	Y	Y	?	?
KENTUCKY				
Ford	Y	N	Y	N
Huddleston	Y	Y	Y	Y
LOUISIANA				
Johnston	N	N	N	N
Long	Y	Y	Y	Y
MAINE				
Hathaway	Y	Y	Y	Y
Muskie	Y	Y	Y	Y
MARYLAND				
Sarbanes	Y	Y	Y	Y
Mathias	Y	Y	Y	Y
MASSACHUSETTS				
Kennedy	Y	Y	Y	Y
Brooke	N	N	?	?
MICHIGAN				
Riegle	Y	Y	Y	Y
Griffin	N	N	N	?
MINNESOTA				
Anderson	Y	Y	Y	Y
Humphrey, M.	Y	Y	Y	Y
MISSISSIPPI				
Eastland	N	N	N	N
Stennis	N	?	N	N
MISSOURI				
Eagleton	Y	Y	Y	?
Danforth	Y	Y	Y	Y
MONTANA				
Melcher	N	N	N	N
Hatfield, P.	N	Y	#	#
NEBRASKA				
Zorinsky	X	N	N	N
Curtis	N	N	N	N
NEVADA				
Cannon	N	N	N	?
Laxalt	N	N	N	N

	79	80	81	82
NEW HAMPSHIRE				
Durkin	Y	Y	Y	Y
McIntyre	Y	Y	Y	Y
NEW JERSEY				
Williams	Y	Y	Y	Y
Case	Y	Y	Y	Y
NEW MEXICO				
Domenici	N	N	N	Y
Schmitt	N	N	N	N
NEW YORK				
Moynihan	Y	Y	Y	Y
Javits	Y	Y	Y	Y
NORTH CAROLINA				
Morgan	Y	Y	N	Y
Helms	N	N	N	N
NORTH DAKOTA				
Burdick	Y	N	N	Y
Young	N	?	N	N
OHIO				
Glenn	Y	Y	Y	Y
Metzenbaum	Y	Y	Y	Y
OKLAHOMA				
Bartlett	N	N	N	N
Bellmon	Y	Y	Y	Y
OREGON				
Hatfield, M.	Y	Y	Y	Y
Packwood	N	Y	N	Y
PENNSYLVANIA				
Heinz	N	Y	Y	Y
Schweiker	N	N	N	N
RHODE ISLAND				
Pell	Y	Y	Y	Y
Chafee	Y	Y	Y	?
SOUTH CAROLINA				
Hollings	Y	Y	Y	Y
Thurmond	N	N	N	N
SOUTH DAKOTA				
Abourezk	Y	#	#	#
McGovern	Y	Y	Y	Y
TENNESSEE				
Sasser	Y	Y	Y	Y
Baker	Y	Y	?	?

KEY

- Y Voted for (yea).
- ✓ Paired for.
- † Announced for.
- # CQ Poll for.
- N Voted against (nay).
- X Paired against.
- - Announced against.
- ▮ CQ Poll against.
- P Voted "present."
- ● Voted "present" to avoid possible conflict of interest.
- ? Did not vote or otherwise make a position known.

	79	80	81	82
TEXAS				
Bentsen	✓	?	Y	Y
Tower	N	N	N	?
UTAH				
Garn	N	N	N	N
Hatch	N	N	-	-
VERMONT				
Leahy	Y	Y	Y	Y
Stafford	Y	Y	Y	Y
VIRGINIA				
*Byrd, H.	N	N	N	N
Scott	N	N	N	N
WASHINGTON				
Jackson	Y	Y	Y	Y
Magnuson	Y	†	†	†
WEST VIRGINIA				
Byrd, R.	Y	Y	Y	Y
Randolph	Y	N	N	N
WISCONSIN				
Nelson	Y	Y	Y	Y
Proxmire	Y	Y	Y	Y
WYOMING				
Hansen	N	N	N	N
Wallop	N	N	Y	Y

Democrats ***Republicans***

79. Exec N, 95th Congress, First Session, Panama Canal Treaties. Church, D-Idaho, motion to table (kill) the Hatch, R-Utah, amendment to provide that the Panama Canal treaty not take effect until the House had authorized disposal of U.S. property in the Canal Zone. Motion agreed to 58-37: R 13-25; D 45-12 (ND 36-4; SD 9-8), April 4, 1978. A "yea" was a vote supporting the president's position.

80. Exec N, 95th Congress, First Session, Panama Canal Treaties. Church, D-Idaho, motion to table (kill) the Allen, D-Ala., amendment to permit U.S. citizens employed by the Panama Canal Co. to hold their jobs until they reach retirement age or resign. Motion agreed to 56-36: R 15-22; D 41-14 (ND 33-6; SD 8-8), April 5, 1978. A "yea" was a vote supporting the president's position.

81. Exec N, 95th Congress, First Session, Panama Canal Treaties. Sarbanes, D-Md., motion to table (kill) the Helms, R-N.C., amendment to permit the United States and Panama to act independently to defend and preserve the security of the canal in cases of international war. Motion agreed to 54-33: R 11-20; D 43-13 (ND 32-6; SD 11-7), April 6, 1978. A "yea" was a vote supporting the president's position.

82. Exec N, 95th Congress, First Session, Panama Canal Treaties. Church, D-Idaho, motion to table (kill) the Allen, D-Ala., amendment to require the Senate to confirm all nine members (including the four Panamanian members) appointed to the Panama Canal Commission that would manage and operate the canal. Motion agreed to 53-25: R 12-15; D 41-10 (ND 31-3; SD 10-7), April 6, 1978. A "yea" was a vote supporting the president's position.

CQ Senate Votes 83-90

Corresponding to Congressional Record Votes 83, 84, 85, 86, 87, 88, 89, 90

	83	84	85	86	87	88	89	90
ALABAMA								
Allen	N	Y	Y	N	N	N	N	N
Sparkman	Y	Y	Y	Y	Y	Y	Y	Y
ALASKA								
Gravel	#	N	▮	Y	Y	Y	Y	Y
Stevens	-	N	Y	N	N	N	N	N
ARIZONA								
DeConcini	N	?	?	X	X	Y	N	N
Goldwater	N	N	N	N	N	N	N	?
ARKANSAS								
Bumpers	?	Y	Y	Y	Y	Y	Y	Y
Hodges	Y	Y	Y	Y	Y	Y	Y	Y
CALIFORNIA								
Cranston	Y	N	N	Y	Y	Y	Y	Y
Hayakawa	Y	Y	Y	Y	Y	?	Y	Y
COLORADO								
Hart	Y	Y	Y	Y	Y	Y	Y	Y
Haskell	Y	Y	Y	Y	Y	Y	Y	Y
CONNECTICUT								
Ribicoff	Y	N	N	Y	Y	Y	Y	Y
Weicker	#	N	N	Y	Y	Y	Y	Y
DELAWARE								
Biden	Y	N	N	Y	Y	Y	Y	Y
Roth	N	N	N	N	N	N	N	N
FLORIDA								
Chiles	N	N	Y	N	Y	Y	Y	Y
Stone	N	Y	Y	N	Y	Y	Y	Y
GEORGIA								
Nunn	N	Y	Y	N	Y	Y	Y	N
Talmadge	Y	Y	Y	N	N	Y	Y	Y
HAWAII								
Inouye	Y	N	N	Y	Y	Y	Y	Y
Matsunaga	Y	N	X	Y	Y	Y	Y	Y
IDAHO								
Church	Y	Y	Y	Y	Y	Y	Y	Y
McClure	N	Y	Y	N	N	N	N	N
ILLINOIS								
Stevenson	Y	N	N	Y	Y	Y	Y	Y
Percy	Y	N	N	Y	Y	Y	Y	Y
INDIANA								
Bayh	?	Y	Y	Y	Y	Y	Y	Y
Lugar	N	N	N	N	N	N	N	N
IOWA								
Clark	†	N	N	Y	Y	Y	Y	Y
Culver	Y	N	N	Y	Y	Y	Y	Y
KANSAS								
Dole	N	Y	Y	N	N	N	N	N
Pearson	?	Y	Y	Y	Y	Y	Y	Y
KENTUCKY								
Ford	N	Y	Y	N	X	N	N	N
Huddleston	?	Y	Y	Y	Y	Y	Y	Y
LOUISIANA								
Johnston	N	Y	Y	N	N	N	Y	Y
Long	Y	Y	Y	Y	Y	Y	Y	Y
MAINE								
Hathaway	?	?	?	?	Y	Y	Y	Y
Muskie	?	N	N	Y	Y	?	?	?
MARYLAND								
Sarbanes	Y	N	N	Y	Y	Y	Y	Y
Mathias	Y	N	N	?	Y	?	?	?
MASSACHUSETTS								
Kennedy	Y	N	N	Y	Y	Y	Y	Y
Brooke	?	N	N	N	N	N	N	N
MICHIGAN								
Riegle	Y	Y	Y	Y	Y	†	†	✓
Griffin	?	Y	Y	N	N	N	N	N
MINNESOTA								
Anderson	†	✓	✓	†	✓	†	†	†
Humphrey, M.	Y	N	N	Y	Y	†	Y	Y
MISSISSIPPI								
Eastland	N	Y	N	N	N	N	N	N
Stennis	?	Y	N	N	N	N	N	N
MISSOURI								
Eagleton	?	?	?	?	?	Y	Y	Y
Danforth	Y	Y	Y	Y	?	Y	Y	Y
MONTANA								
Melcher	X	Y	Y	N	Y	Y	Y	X
Hatfield, P.	▮	Y	Y	N	Y	N	Y	Y
NEBRASKA								
Zorinsky	N	Y	Y	Y	Y	Y	Y	N
Curtis	?	Y	Y	N	?	N	N	N
NEVADA								
Cannon	X	X	X	N	N	N	N	N
Laxalt	N	Y	Y	N	N	N	N	N
NEW HAMPSHIRE								
Durkin	Y	N	N	Y	Y	Y	Y	Y
McIntyre	N	N	N	Y	†	Y	Y	Y
NEW JERSEY								
Williams	Y	N	N	Y	Y	Y	Y	Y
Case	Y	N	N	Y	Y	Y	Y	Y
NEW MEXICO								
Domenici	N	Y	Y	N	N	N	N	N
Schmitt	N	Y	Y	N	N	Y	N	N
NEW YORK								
Moynihan	Y	N	N	Y	Y	Y	Y	Y
Javits	Y	N	N	Y	?	Y	Y	Y
NORTH CAROLINA								
Morgan	Y	N	Y	N	Y	Y	Y	Y
Helms	N	Y	Y	N	N	N	N	N
NORTH DAKOTA								
Burdick	N	Y	Y	N	N	Y	Y	Y
Young	N	Y	Y	N	N	N	N	N
OHIO								
Glenn	Y	N	N	Y	Y	Y	Y	Y
Metzenbaum	Y	N	N	Y	Y	Y	Y	Y
OKLAHOMA								
Bartlett	N	?	?	?	?	?	?	?
Bellmon	?	N	N	Y	Y	Y	Y	N
OREGON								
Hatfield, M.	Y	Y	Y	Y	Y	Y	Y	Y
Packwood	N	Y	Y	N	Y	Y	Y	N
PENNSYLVANIA								
Heinz	N	N	N	N	Y	Y	Y	Y
Schweiker	N	?	?	?	N	N	Y	N
RHODE ISLAND								
Pell	?	N	N	Y	Y	Y	Y	Y
Chafee	?	N	N	?	?	Y	Y	Y
SOUTH CAROLINA								
Hollings	Y	†	✓	✓	✓	?	?	?
Thurmond	-	Y	Y	-	X	N	N	N
SOUTH DAKOTA								
Abourezk	#	Y	Y	#	#	Y	Y	#
McGovern	Y	Y	Y	Y	#	Y	Y	Y
TENNESSEE								
Sasser	N	Y	N	N	N	Y	Y	N
Baker	Y	Y	N	N	✓	Y	Y	Y
TEXAS								
Bentsen	Y	Y	Y	Y	Y	Y	Y	Y
Tower	-	Y	Y	N	N	N	N	N
UTAH								
Garn	N	N	Y	N	N	N	N	N
Hatch	N	Y	Y	N	N	N	N	N
VERMONT								
Leahy	Y	N	N	Y	Y	Y	Y	Y
Stafford	Y	N	N	Y	Y	Y	Y	Y
VIRGINIA								
*Byrd, H.	N	N	N	N	X	Y	N	N
Scott	N	N	N	N	N	N	N	N
WASHINGTON								
Jackson	Y	Y	Y	Y	Y	Y	Y	Y
Magnuson	✓	Y	Y	Y	Y	Y	Y	Y
WEST VIRGINIA								
Byrd, R.	✓	N	N	Y	✓	Y	Y	Y
Randolph	N	Y	Y	N	N	Y	Y	Y
WISCONSIN								
Nelson	Y	N	N	Y	Y	Y	Y	Y
Proxmire	Y	N	N	Y	Y	Y	Y	Y
WYOMING								
Hansen	N	Y	Y	N	N	N	N	N
Wallop	N	Y	Y	N	N	N	N	Y

Democrats ***Republicans***

*Byrd elected as independent.

KEY

- Y Voted for (yea).
- ✓ Paired for.
- † Announced for.
- # CQ Poll for.
- N Voted against (nay).
- X Paired against.
- \- Announced against.
- ▮ CQ Poll against
- P Voted "present."
- ● Voted "present" to avoid possible conflict of interest.
- ? Did not vote or otherwise make a position known.

83. Exec N, 95th Congress, First Session, Panama Canal Treaties. Church, D-Idaho, motion to table (kill) the Bartlett, R-Okla., amendment providing that the treaty did not commit the United States to pay Panama the balance of annual $10 million contingency payments upon termination of the treaty. Motion agreed to 40-33: R 9-19; D 31-14 (ND 24-5; SD 7-9), April 7, 1978. A "yea" was a vote supporting the president's position.

84. HR 6782. Emergency Farm Bill. Talmadge, D-Ga., motion to waive, for the emergency farm bill, a section (303) of the 1974 Budget Act (PL 93-344) that bars consideration of legislation affecting spending for a fiscal year before Congress has adopted its first budget resolution for that year. Motion agreed to 49-43: R 20-16; D 29-27 (ND 14-24; SD 15-3), April 10, 1978.

85. HR 6782. Emergency Farm Bill. Adoption of the conference report on the bill to provide a one-year flexible parity program with graduated land diversion and target price levels for wheat, corn and cotton, and to raise loan rates for these commodities beginning Oct. 1, 1979 (with retroactive payments for 1978 crops). Adopted 49-41: R 21-15; D 28-26 (ND 14-22; SD 14-4), April 10, 1978. A "nay" was a vote supporting the president's position.

86. Exec N, 95th Congress, First Session, Panama Canal Treaties. Church, D-Idaho, motion to table (kill) the Dole, R-Kan., amendment deleting from the Panama Canal Treaty Article XII, which barred the construction in Panama of a new canal by a third nation and negotiations by the United States with third nations in Latin America for a new canal through its territory unless agreed to by the United States and Panama. Motion agreed to 49-40: R 10-23; D 39-17 (ND 33-5; SD 6-12), April 10, 1978. A "yea" was a vote supporting the president's position.

87. Exec N, 95th Congress, First Session, Panama Canal Treaties. Sarbanes, D-Md., motion to table (kill) the Hatch, R-Utah, amendment providing that operating revenues of the Panama Canal Commission be deposited in the U.S. treasury and that the United States, rather than the Panama Canal Commission, reimburse Panama for public services provided in the Canal Zone. Motion agreed to 54-29: R 11-20; D 43-9 (ND 33-3; SD 10-6), April 10, 1978. A "yea" was a vote supporting the president's position.

88. Exec N, 95th Congress, First Session, Panama Canal Treaties. Church, D-Idaho, motion to table (kill) the Helms, R-N.C., amendment providing for the free movement of U.S. personnel and equipment in Panama for the duration of the Panama Canal Treaty. Motion agreed to 64-28: R 14-21; D 50-7 (ND 37-2; SD 13-5), April 11, 1978. A "yea" was a vote supporting the president's position.

89. Exec N, 95th Congress, First Session, Panama Canal Treaties. Church, D-Idaho, motion to table (kill) the Helms, R-N.C., amendment providing that nothing in the Panama Canal Treaty prevented Panama or the United States from conducting military operations that each country felt was needed to protect and defend the canal. Motion agreed to 66-28: R 15-21; D 51-7 (ND 38-2; SD 13-5), April 11, 1978. A "yea" was a vote supporting the president's position.

90. Exec N, 95th Congress, First Session, Panama Canal Treaties. Church, D-Idaho, motion to table (kill) the Helms, R-N.C., amendment giving the United States the authority to transport any type of nuclear weapons through the canal or on military bases in the Canal Zone. Motion agreed to 59-32: R 13-22; D 46-10 (ND 35-3; SD 11-7), April 11, 1978. A "yea" was a vote supporting the president's position.

Corresponding to Congressional Record Votes 91, 92, 93, 94, 95, 96

	91	92	93	94	95	96
ALABAMA						
Allen	N	N	N	N	N	N
Sparkman	Y	Y	Y	Y	✓	#
ALASKA						
Gravel	Y	Y	Y	Y	Y	Y
Stevens	N	N	N	N	N	N
ARIZONA						
DeConcini	N	N	N	N	N	N
Goldwater	N	Y	N	?	N	N
ARKANSAS						
Bumpers	Y	Y	Y	Y	N	Y
Hodges	Y	Y	N	Y	N	Y
CALIFORNIA						
Cranston	Y	Y	Y	Y	Y	Y
Hayakawa	Y	Y	Y	Y	Y	Y
COLORADO						
Hart	Y	Y	Y	Y	Y	Y
Haskell	Y	Y	Y	Y	Y	Y
CONNECTICUT						
Ribicoff	Y	Y	Y	Y	Y	Y
Weicker	Y	Y	Y	#	Y	Y
DELAWARE						
Biden	Y	Y	Y	Y	Y	Y
Roth	N	N	N	N	N	N
FLORIDA						
Chiles	Y	Y	N	Y	N	N
Stone	N	N	N	N	Y	N
GEORGIA						
Nunn	N	Y	N	N	N	N
Talmadge	N	Y	N	Y	N	N
HAWAII						
Inouye	Y	Y	Y	Y	Y	Y
Matsunaga	Y	Y	?	Y	Y	Y
IDAHO						
Church	Y	Y	Y	Y	Y	Y
McClure	N	N	N	N	N	N
ILLINOIS						
Stevenson	Y	Y	Y	Y	Y	Y
Percy	Y	Y	Y	Y	Y	Y
INDIANA						
Bayh	Y	Y	Y	Y	Y	Y
Lugar	N	N	N	N	N	N
IOWA						
Clark	Y	Y	Y	Y	Y	Y
Culver	Y	Y	Y	Y	Y	Y
KANSAS						
Dole	N	N	N	N	N	N
Pearson	Y	Y	Y	Y	Y	Y
KENTUCKY						
Ford	N	?	N	N	N	N
Huddleston	Y	Y	Y	Y	Y	Y
LOUISIANA						
Johnston	N	▮	Y	▮	N	N
Long	Y	Y	Y	Y	Y	Y
MAINE						
Hathaway	Y	Y	Y	Y	Y	Y
Muskie	?	?	Y	Y	Y	Y
MARYLAND						
Sarbanes	Y	Y	Y	Y	Y	Y
Mathias	Y	Y	Y	Y	Y	Y
MASSACHUSETTS						
Kennedy	Y	Y	Y	Y	Y	Y
Brooke	N	N	N	N	N	N
MICHIGAN						
Riegle	†	†	†	†	†	†
Griffin	N	N	N	N	N	N
MINNESOTA						
Anderson	†	†	†	†	†	Y
Humphrey, M.	Y	Y	Y	Y	Y	Y
MISSISSIPPI						
Eastland	N	N	N	?	X	N
Stennis	N	N	N	Y	N	N
MISSOURI						
Eagleton	Y	Y	Y	Y	Y	Y
Danforth	Y	Y	Y	Y	Y	Y
MONTANA						
Melcher	Y	Y	N	N	N	Y
Hatfield, P.	N	Y	Y	Y	Y	N
NEBRASKA						
Zorinsky	N	N	Y	N	N	N
Curtis	N	N	N	N	N	N
NEVADA						
Cannon	N	N	N	Y	N	N
Laxalt	N	N	N	N	N	N
NEW HAMPSHIRE						
Durkin	Y	Y	Y	Y	Y	Y
McIntyre	N	Y	†	†	Y	Y
NEW JERSEY						
Williams	Y	Y	Y	Y	Y	Y
Case	Y	Y	Y	Y	Y	Y
NEW MEXICO						
Domenici	N	N	N	?	N	N
Schmitt	N	N	N	N	N	N
NEW YORK						
Moynihan	Y	?	Y	Y	Y	Y
Javits	Y	Y	Y	Y	Y	Y
NORTH CAROLINA						
Morgan	Y	Y	Y	Y	Y	Y
Helms	N	N	N	N	N	N
NORTH DAKOTA						
Burdick	N	Y	N	N	N	N
Young	N	N	N	N	N	N
OHIO						
Glenn	Y	Y	Y	Y	Y	Y
Metzenbaum	Y	Y	Y	Y	Y	Y
OKLAHOMA						
Bartlett	?	?	?	?	?	?
Bellmon	Y	Y	Y	N	Y	Y
OREGON						
Hatfield, M.	Y	Y	N	Y	Y	Y
Packwood	N	Y	N	N	?	?
PENNSYLVANIA						
Heinz	Y	Y	Y	#	N	Y
Schweiker	N	N	N	N	N	N
RHODE ISLAND						
Pell	Y	Y	Y	Y	Y	Y
Chafee	Y	Y	Y	Y	Y	Y
SOUTH CAROLINA						
Hollings	?	?	Y	Y	Y	Y
Thurmond	N	N	N	N	N	N
SOUTH DAKOTA						
Abourezk	#	#	#	#	#	#
McGovern	Y	Y	Y	Y	Y	Y
TENNESSEE						
Sasser	N	N	N	N	N	N
Baker	Y	Y	Y	Y	Y	Y
TEXAS						
Bentsen	Y	Y	Y	Y	Y	Y
Tower	N	N	N	N	N	N
UTAH						
Garn	N	N	N	N	N	N
Hatch	N	N	N	N	N	N
VERMONT						
Leahy	Y	Y	Y	Y	Y	Y
Stafford	Y	Y	Y	Y	Y	Y
VIRGINIA						
*Byrd, H.	N	Y	N	N	N	N
Scott	N	N	N	N	N	N
WASHINGTON						
Jackson	Y	Y	Y	Y	Y	Y
Magnuson	N	Y	Y	?	Y	Y
WEST VIRGINIA						
Byrd, R.	Y	Y	Y	Y	Y	Y
Randolph	N	N	N	N	N	N
WISCONSIN						
Nelson	Y	Y	Y	Y	Y	Y
Proxmire	N	Y	Y	Y	Y	Y
WYOMING						
Hansen	N	N	N	N	N	N
Wallop	N	Y	N	N	N	N

Democrats ***Republicans***

*Byrd elected as independent.

KEY

- Y Voted for (yea).
- ✓ Paired for.
- † Announced for.
- # CQ Poll for.
- N Voted against (nay).
- X Paired against.
- \- Announced against.
- ▮ CQ Poll against.
- P Voted "present."
- ● Voted "present" to avoid possible conflict of interest.
- ? Did not vote or otherwise make a position known.

91. Exec N, 95th Congress, First Session, Panama Canal Treaties. Church, D-Idaho, motion to table (kill) the Cannon, D-Nev., amendment reducing from $10 million to $5 million the amount the United States was to pay Panama annually for public services. Motion agreed to 52-42: R 14-23; D 38-19 (ND 30-9; SD 8-10), April 11, 1978. A "yea" was a vote supporting the president's position.

92. Exec N, 95th Congress, First Session, Panama Canal Treaties. Church, D-Idaho, motion to table (kill) the Hatch, R-Utah, amendment calling for Panama to respect freedom of speech and press. Motion agreed to 62-29: R 17-20; D 45-9 (ND 34-4; SD 11-5), April 11, 1978. A "yea" was a vote supporting the president's position.

93. Exec N, 95th Congress, First Session, Panama Canal Treaties. Sarbanes, D-Md., motion to table (kill) the Helms, R-N.C., amendment guaranteeing the civil rights of U.S. citizens in the Canal Zone by Panama. Motion agreed to 54-40: R 14-24; D 40-16 (ND 33-5; SD 7-11), April 12, 1978. A "yea" was a vote supporting the president's position.

94. Exec N, 95th Congress, First Session, Panama Canal Treaties. Sarbanes, D-Md., motion to table (kill) the Hatch, R-Utah, amendment calling for the placement of U.S. employees of the Panama Canal Company, who would lose their jobs as a result of the treaty, in U.S. government positions with no reduction in grade. Motion agreed to 55-33: R 11-22; D 44-11 (ND 33-5; SD 11-6), April 12, 1978. A "yea" was a vote supporting the president's position.

95. Exec N, 95th Congress, First Session, Panama Canal Treaties. Sarbanes, D-Md., motion to table (kill) the Stevens, R-Alaska, amendment providing that if either the United States or Panama abrogated any provision of the treaties, the treaties superseded by the agreements under debate would remain in full force and effect. Motion agreed to 53-40: R 13-23; D 40-17 (ND 34-6; SD 6-11), April 12, 1978. A "yea" was a vote supporting the president's position.

96. Exec N, 95th Congress, First Session, Panama Canal Treaties. Matsunaga, D-Hawaii, motion to table (kill) the Thurmond, R-S.C., amendment requiring that all operating expenses of the Panama Canal Commission be paid before any payments were made to Panama. Motion agreed to 56-39: R 14-22; D 42-17 (ND 35-6; SD 7-11), April 12, 1978. A "yea" was a vote supporting the president's position.

CQ Senate Votes 97-98

Corresponding to Congressional Record Votes 97 and 98

	97	98
ALABAMA		
Allen	N	N
Sparkman	#	#
ALASKA		
Gravel	Y	Y
Stevens	N	N
ARIZONA		
DeConcini	N	Y
Goldwater	N	N
ARKANSAS		
Bumpers	Y	Y
Hodges	Y	Y
CALIFORNIA		
Cranston	Y	Y
Hayakawa	Y	Y
COLORADO		
Hart	Y	Y
Haskell	Y	Y
CONNECTICUT		
Ribicoff	Y	Y
Weicker	Y	Y
DELAWARE		
Biden	Y	Y
Roth	N	N
FLORIDA		
Chiles	Y	Y
Stone	Y	Y
GEORGIA		
Nunn	N	N
Talmadge	▮	Y
HAWAII		
Inouye	Y	Y
Matsunaga	Y	Y
IDAHO		
Church	Y	Y
McClure	N	N
ILLINOIS		
Stevenson	Y	Y
Percy	?	Y
INDIANA		
Bayh	?	?
Lugar	N	N
IOWA		
Clark	Y	Y
Culver	†	Y
KANSAS		
Dole	N	N
Pearson	Y	Y
KENTUCKY		
Ford	N	N
Huddleston	Y	Y
LOUISIANA		
Johnston	Y	Y
Long	?	?
MAINE		
Hathaway	Y	Y
Muskie	Y	Y
MARYLAND		
Sarbanes	Y	Y
Mathias	Y	Y
MASSACHUSETTS		
Kennedy	Y	Y
Brooke	N	N
MICHIGAN		
Riegle	Y	Y
Griffin	N	?
MINNESOTA		
Anderson	Y	Y
Humphrey, M.	Y	Y
MISSISSIPPI		
Eastland	N	N
Stennis	N	N
MISSOURI		
Eagleton	?	?
Danforth	Y	Y
MONTANA		
Melcher	N	N
Hatfield, P.	Y	Y
NEBRASKA		
Zorinsky	N	N
Curtis	N	N
NEVADA		
Cannon	N	Y
Laxalt	N	N
NEW HAMPSHIRE		
Durkin	Y	Y
McIntyre	Y	Y
NEW JERSEY		
Williams	Y	#
Case	Y	Y
NEW MEXICO		
Domenici	N	-
Schmitt	N	N
NEW YORK		
Moynihan	Y	Y
Javits	Y	Y
NORTH CAROLINA		
Morgan	Y	Y
Helms	N	N
NORTH DAKOTA		
Burdick	Y	N
Young	N	?
OHIO		
Glenn	Y	Y
Metzenbaum	Y	Y
OKLAHOMA		
Bartlett	?	?
Bellmon	Y	Y
OREGON		
Hatfield, M.	Y	Y
Packwood	?	?
PENNSYLVANIA		
Heinz	Y	Y
Schweiker	N	N
RHODE ISLAND		
Pell	Y	Y
Chafee	Y	Y
SOUTH CAROLINA		
Hollings	Y	Y
Thurmond	N	N
SOUTH DAKOTA		
Abourezk	#	#
McGovern	Y	Y
TENNESSEE		
Sasser	N	Y
Baker	?	?
TEXAS		
Bentsen	Y	Y
Tower	N	N
UTAH		
Garn	N	N
Hatch	N	N
VERMONT		
Leahy	Y	Y
Stafford	Y	Y
VIRGINIA		
*Byrd, H.	N	N
Scott	N	N
WASHINGTON		
Jackson	Y	Y
Magnuson	Y	Y
WEST VIRGINIA		
Byrd, R.	Y	Y
Randolph	N	N
WISCONSIN		
Nelson	Y	Y
Proxmire	Y	Y
WYOMING		
Hansen	N	N
Wallop	N	N

Democrats ***Republicans***

*Byrd elected as independent.

KEY

- Y Voted for (yea).
- ✓ Paired for.
- † Announced for.
- # CQ Poll for.
- N Voted against (nay).
- X Paired against.
- \- Announced against.
- ▮ CQ Poll against.
- P Voted "present."
- ● Voted "present" to avoid possible conflict of interest.
- ? Did not vote or otherwise make a position known.

97. Exec N, 95th Congress, First Session, Panama Canal Treaties. Sarbanes, D-Md., motion to table (kill) the Schmitt, R-N.M., amendment calling for Panama to grant in perpetuity to the United States that part of Corozal Cemetery encompassing the remains of U.S. citizens. Motion agreed to 55-34: R 12-22; D 43-12 (ND 34-5; SD 9-7), April 13, 1978. A "yea" was a vote supporting the president's position.

98. Exec N, 95th Congress, First Session, Panama Canal Treaties. Matsunaga, D-Hawaii, motion to table (kill) the Allen, D-Ala., amendment calling for Panamanians to approve the treaty by national plebiscite within six months of the date the ratified treaties were exchanged by Panama and the United States. Motion agreed to 59-29: R 13-19; D 46-10 (ND 35-4; SD 11-6), April 13, 1978. A "yea" was a vote supporting the president's position.

	99	100	101	102	103	104	105	106
ALABAMA								
Allen	Y	Y	N	Y	Y	N	Y	N
Sparkman	Y	Y	#	#	#	Y	N	Y
ALASKA								
Gravel	N	N	Y	Y	Y	Y	N	Y
Stevens	†	†	-	†	†	N	Y	N
ARIZONA								
DeConcini	Y	Y	N	Y	Y	N	Y	N
Goldwater	Y	Y	N	Y	Y	N	Y	N
ARKANSAS								
Bumpers	Y	Y	Y	Y	Y	Y	N	Y
Hodges	Y	Y	Y	Y	Y	Y	N	Y
CALIFORNIA								
Cranston	N	Y	Y	Y	Y	Y	N	Y
Hayakawa	N	Y	Y	Y	Y	Y	N	Y
COLORADO								
Hart	N	Y	Y	N	N	Y	N	Y
Haskell	N	Y	Y	Y	Y	Y	N	Y
CONNECTICUT								
Ribicoff	†	†	†	†	†	Y	N	Y
Weicker	Y	Y	Y	Y	Y	Y	N	Y
DELAWARE								
Biden	?	?	?	?	?	Y	N	Y
Roth	Y	Y	N	Y	Y	N	Y	N
FLORIDA								
Chiles	Y	Y	Y	Y	Y	Y	N	Y
Stone	Y	Y	N	Y	Y	Y	N	N
GEORGIA								
Nunn	Y	Y	N	Y	Y	N	N	Y
Talmadge	Y	Y	Y	Y	Y	▮	Y	N
HAWAII								
Inouye	Y	Y	Y	Y	Y	Y	N	Y
Matsunaga	Y	Y	Y	Y	Y	?	N	Y
IDAHO								
Church	Y	Y	Y	Y	Y	Y	N	Y
McClure	Y	Y	N	Y	Y	N	Y	N
ILLINOIS								
Stevenson	N	Y	Y	Y	Y	Y	N	Y
Percy	Y	Y	Y	Y	Y	Y	N	Y
INDIANA								
Bayh	Y	Y	Y	Y	Y	Y	N	Y
Lugar	Y	Y	N	Y	Y	N	Y	N
IOWA								
Clark	N	Y	Y	Y	Y	Y	N	Y
Culver	N	Y	Y	Y	Y	Y	N	Y
KANSAS								
Dole	?	?	N	Y	Y	N	Y	N
Pearson	Y	Y	Y	Y	Y	Y	N	Y
KENTUCKY								
Ford	Y	Y	N	Y	Y	N	Y	N
Huddleston	N	Y	Y	Y	Y	Y	N	Y
LOUISIANA								
Johnston	Y	Y	N	Y	Y	N	Y	N
Long	Y	Y	Y	Y	Y	Y	N	Y
MAINE								
Hathaway	?	?	?	?	?	Y	N	Y
Muskie	Y	Y	Y	Y	Y	Y	N	Y
MARYLAND								
Sarbanes	Y	Y	Y	Y	Y	Y	N	Y
Mathias	Y	Y	Y	Y	Y	Y	N	Y
MASSACHUSETTS								
Kennedy	N	Y	#	#	#	Y	N	Y
Brooke	Y	Y	N	Y	Y	N	N	N
MICHIGAN								
Riegle	N	Y	Y	Y	Y	Y	N	Y
Griffin	N	N	N	Y	Y	N	N	N
MINNESOTA								
Anderson	N	Y	Y	Y	Y	Y	N	N
Humphrey, M.	Y	Y	Y	Y	Y	Y	N	Y
MISSISSIPPI								
Eastland	?	?	?	?	?	N	Y	N
Stennis	Y	Y	?	?	?	N	Y	N
MISSOURI								
Eagleton	Y	Y	Y	Y	Y	Y	N	Y
Danforth	Y	Y	Y	Y	Y	Y	N	Y
MONTANA								
·Melcher	Y	Y	N	Y	Y	N	N	N
Hatfield, P.	Y	Y	Y	Y	Y	N	N	Y
NEBRASKA								
Zorinsky	N	Y	N	Y	Y	N	Y	N
Curtis	Y	Y	N	Y	Y	N	Y	N
NEVADA								
Cannon	Y	Y	N	Y	Y	N	Y	N
Laxalt	Y	Y	N	Y	Y	N	Y	N
NEW HAMPSHIRE								
Durkin	N	Y	Y	N	N	Y	N	Y
McIntyre	Y	Y	Y	Y	Y	Y	N	Y
NEW JERSEY								
Williams	N	Y	Y	Y	Y	#	N	Y
Case	N	Y	Y	Y	Y	Y	N	Y
NEW MEXICO								
Domenici	Y	Y	N	Y	Y	N	N	N
Schmitt	Y	Y	N	Y	Y	N	Y	N
NEW YORK								
Moynihan	Y	Y	Y	Y	Y	Y	N	Y
Javits	N	Y	Y	Y	Y	Y	N	Y
NORTH CAROLINA								
Morgan	Y	Y	Y	N	Y	N	Y	N
Helms	Y	Y	N	Y	Y	N	Y	N
NORTH DAKOTA								
Burdick	Y	Y	N	Y	Y	N	Y	N
Young	Y	Y	?	?	?	N	Y	N
OHIO								
Glenn	N	Y	Y	Y	Y	Y	Y	Y
Metzenbaum	N	Y	Y	Y	Y	Y	N	Y
OKLAHOMA								
Bartlett	Y	Y	N	Y	Y	N	Y	N
Bellmon	Y	Y	Y	Y	N	Y	N	Y
OREGON								
Hatfield, M.	N	Y	Y	Y	Y	Y	N	Y
Packwood	Y	Y	Y	Y	Y	N	N	N
PENNSYLVANIA								
Heinz	Y	Y	Y	Y	Y	Y	N	Y
Schweiker	Y	Y	N	Y	Y	N	Y	N
RHODE ISLAND								
Pell	†	†	†	†	†	?	?	?
Chafee	N	Y	Y	Y	Y	Y	N	Y
SOUTH CAROLINA								
Hollings	N	Y	Y	Y	Y	Y	N	Y
Thurmond	Y	Y	N	Y	Y	N	Y	N
SOUTH DAKOTA								
Abourezk	N	Y	#	#	#	#	▮	#
McGovern	N	Y	#	#	#	Y	N	Y
TENNESSEE								
Sasser	Y	Y	Y	Y	Y	Y	N	N
Baker	Y	Y	Y	Y	Y	Y	N	Y
TEXAS								
Bentsen	Y	Y	Y	Y	Y	Y	N	Y
Tower	Y	Y	N	Y	Y	N	Y	N
UTAH								
Garn	Y	Y	N	Y	Y	N	Y	N
Hatch	Y	Y	N	Y	Y	N	Y	N
VERMONT								
Leahy	N	Y	Y	Y	Y	Y	N	Y
Stafford	N	Y	Y	Y	Y	Y	N	Y
VIRGINIA								
*Byrd, H.	Y	Y	N	Y	Y	N	Y	N
Scott	Y	Y	N	Y	Y	N	Y	N
WASHINGTON								
Jackson	Y	Y	Y	Y	Y	Y	N	Y
Magnuson	Y	Y	Y	Y	Y	Y	N	Y
WEST VIRGINIA								
Byrd, R.	Y	Y	Y	Y	Y	Y	N	Y
Randolph	Y	Y	Y	Y	Y	N	Y	N
WISCONSIN								
Nelson	Y	Y	Y	Y	Y	Y	N	Y
Proxmire	Y	Y	Y	Y	Y	Y	N	N
WYOMING								
Hansen	Y	Y	N	Y	Y	N	Y	N
Wallop	?	?	?	?	?	N	N	N

Democrats ***Republicans***

*Byrd elected as independent.

KEY

- Y Voted for (yea).
- ✓ Paired for.
- † Announced for.
- # CQ Poll for.
- N Voted against (nay).
- X Paired against.
- \- Announced against.
- ▮ CQ Poll against.
- P Voted "present."
- ● Voted "present" to avoid possible conflict of interest.
- ? Did not vote or otherwise make a position known.

99. Exec N, 95th Congress, First Session, Panama Canal Treaties. Long, D-La., reservation to allow Panama and the United States to waive their treaty rights giving each the authority to block the other from contracting with third countries for building any new canal. Adopted 65-27: R 28-7; D 37-20 (ND 21-18; SD 16-2), April 17, 1978.

100. Exec N, 95th Congress, First Session, Panama Canal Treaties. Hollings, D-S.C., reservation to provide that the treaty could not obligate the United States to pay Panama any carryover balance in 1999 resulting from the accumulation of annual funds — up to $10 million — available to Panama from toll surpluses not required to cover operating expenses. Adopted 90-2: R 34-1; D 56-1 (ND 38-1; SD 18-0), April 17, 1978.

101. Exec N, 95th Congress, First Session, Panama Canal Treaties. Sarbanes, D-Md., motion to table (kill) the McClure, R-Idaho, reservation to require enactment of implementing legislation before the exchange between Panama and the United States of instruments of ratification. Motion agreed to 56-31: R 15-20; D 41-11 (ND 31-5; SD 10-6), April 17, 1978.

102. Exec N, 95th Congress, First Session, Panama Canal Treaties. Brooke, R-Mass., reservation to provide that the exchange of instruments of ratification not be effected earlier than March 31, 1979, and that the treaties not enter into force before Oct. 1, 1979, unless implementing legislation was enacted before March 31, 1979. Adopted 84-3: R 35-0; D 49-3 (ND 34-2; SD 15-1), April 17, 1978.

103. Exec N, 95th Congress, First Session, Panama Canal Treaties. Brooke, R-Mass., reservation to provide that the United States and Panama agree to what public services Panama would provide relating to canal operations for which it would receive $10 million annually from the Panama Canal Commission. Adopted 84-3: R 34-1; D 50-2 (ND 34-2; SD 16-0), April 17, 1978.

104. Exec N, 95th Congress, First Session, Panama Canal Treaties. Church, D-Idaho, motion to table (kill) the Helms, R-N.C., reservation to obligate the Panama Canal Commission to pay Panama income only when operating revenues of the canal exceed expenditures of the commission. Motion agreed to 56-39: R 14-24; D 42-15 (ND 32-7; SD 10-8), April 18, 1978.

105. Exec N, 95th Congress, First Session, Panama Canal Treaties. Curtis, R-Neb., reservation to provide that economic assistance to Panama would be suspended until Panama compensated U.S. citizens for any property it had expropriated. Rejected 33-65: R 19-19; D 14-46 (ND 6-35; SD 8-11), April 18, 1978.

106. Exec N, 95th Congress, First Session, Panama Canal Treaties. Church, D-Idaho, motion to table (kill) the Dole, R-Kan., reservation to condition Senate ratification on the requirement that the fixed $10 million annual payment to Panama would cease during any period when the canal was inoperable. Motion agreed to 56-42: R 14-24; D 42-18 (ND 33-8; SD 9-10), April 18, 1978.

CQ Senate Votes 107-114

Corresponding to Congressional Record Votes 107, 108, 109, 110, 111, 112, 113, 114

KEY

- Y Voted for (yea).
- ✓ Paired for.
- † Announced for.
- # CQ Poll for.
- N Voted against (nay).
- X Paired against.
- \- Announced against.
- ▮ CQ Poll against.
- P Voted "present."
- ● Voted "present" to avoid possible conflict of interest.
- ? Did not vote or otherwise make a position known.

	107	108	109	110	111	112	113	114
ALABAMA								
Allen	N	N	Y	N	Y	N	N	Y
Sparkman	Y	Y	Y	Y	Y	Y	Y	N
ALASKA								
Gravel	Y	Y	Y	Y	Y	Y	Y	N
Stevens	N	N	Y	N	N	N	N	N
ARIZONA								
DeConcini	N	N	Y	Y	N	N	Y	N
Goldwater	N	N	Y	N	N	N	N	Y
ARKANSAS								
Bumpers	Y	Y	Y	Y	?	Y	Y	N
Hodges	Y	Y	Y	Y	Y	Y	Y	N
CALIFORNIA								
Cranston	Y	Y	Y	Y	Y	Y	Y	N
Hayakawa	Y	Y	Y	N	Y	Y	Y	N
COLORADO								
Hart	Y	Y	N	Y	Y	Y	Y	N
Haskell	Y	Y	N	Y	Y	Y	Y	N
CONNECTICUT								
Ribicoff	Y	Y	Y	Y	Y	Y	Y	N
Weicker	Y	Y	Y	Y	Y	Y	N	N
DELAWARE								
Biden	Y	Y	Y	Y	Y	Y	Y	N
Roth	N	N	Y	N	N	N	N	N
FLORIDA								
Chiles	Y	Y	Y	Y	Y	N	Y	N
Stone	Y	N	Y	Y	Y	Y	Y	N
GEORGIA								
Nunn	N	N	Y	N	Y	N	Y	N
Talmadge	N	N	Y	Y	Y	N	Y	N
HAWAII								
Inouye	Y	Y	Y	Y	Y	Y	Y	N
Matsunaga	Y	Y	Y	Y	Y	Y	Y	N
IDAHO								
Church	Y	Y	Y	Y	Y	Y	Y	N
McClure	N	N	Y	N	N	N	N	Y
ILLINOIS								
Stevenson	Y	Y	Y	Y	Y	Y	Y	N
Percy	Y	Y	Y	Y	Y	Y	Y	N
INDIANA								
Bayh	Y	Y	Y	Y	Y	Y	Y	N
Lugar	N	N	Y	N	N	N	N	Y
IOWA								
Clark	Y	Y	Y	Y	Y	Y	N	N
Culver	Y	Y	Y	Y	Y	Y	N	N
KANSAS								
Dole	N	N	Y	N	?	N	N	Y
Pearson	Y	Y	Y	Y	Y	Y	Y	N
KENTUCKY								
Ford	N	N	Y	N	Y	N	N	Y
Huddleston	Y	Y	Y	Y	Y	Y	Y	N
LOUISIANA								
Johnston	N	N	Y	Y	Y	N	Y	Y
Long	Y	N	Y	Y	Y	Y	Y	N
MAINE								
Hathaway	Y	Y	Y	Y	Y	Y	Y	N
Muskie	Y	Y	Y	Y	Y	Y	Y	N
MARYLAND								
Sarbanes	Y	Y	Y	Y	Y	Y	Y	N
Mathias	Y	Y	Y	Y	Y	Y	Y	N
MASSACHUSETTS								
Kennedy	Y	Y	N	Y	Y	Y	N	N
Brooke	N	N	Y	N	N	N	N	N
MICHIGAN								
Riegle	Y	Y	Y	Y	Y	Y	Y	N
Griffin	N	N	Y	N	N	N	N	N
MINNESOTA								
Anderson	Y	Y	Y	Y	Y	Y	Y	N
Humphrey, M.	Y	Y	Y	Y	Y	Y	Y	N
MISSISSIPPI								
Eastland	N	N	Y	N	Y	N	N	Y
Stennis	N	N	Y	N	Y	N	N	N
MISSOURI								
Eagleton	Y	Y	Y	Y	Y	Y	Y	N
Danforth	Y	Y	Y	Y	Y	Y	Y	N
MONTANA								
Melcher	N	Y	Y	N	Y	?	N	N
Hatfield, P.	N	N	Y	N	Y	N	Y	N
NEBRASKA								
Zorinsky	N	N	Y	Y	Y	N	N	N
Curtis	N	N	Y	N	N	N	N	Y
NEVADA								
Cannon	N	N	Y	N	Y	N	N	N
Laxalt	N	N	Y	N	N	Y	N	Y
NEW HAMPSHIRE								
Durkin	Y	Y	N	Y	Y	Y	N	N
McIntyre	Y	Y	Y	Y	Y	Y	Y	N
NEW JERSEY								
Williams	Y	Y	Y	Y	Y	Y	Y	N
Case	Y	Y	Y	Y	Y	Y	Y	N
NEW MEXICO								
Domenici	N	N	Y	N	N	N	N	Y
Schmitt	N	N	Y	N	N	N	N	Y
NEW YORK								
Moynihan	Y	Y	Y	Y	Y	Y	Y	N
Javits	Y	Y	Y	Y	Y	Y	Y	N
NORTH CAROLINA								
Morgan	N	N	Y	N	Y	Y	N	N
Helms	N	N	Y	N	Y	N	N	Y
NORTH DAKOTA								
Burdick	N	Y	Y	N	Y	N	N	N
Young	N	N	Y	N	Y	N	N	N
OHIO								
Glenn	Y	Y	Y	Y	Y	Y	Y	N
Metzenbaum	Y	Y	N	Y	Y	Y	N	N
OKLAHOMA								
Bartlett	N	N	Y	N	N	N	N	Y
Bellmon	Y	Y	Y	Y	Y	Y	Y	N
OREGON								
Hatfield, M.	Y	Y	Y	Y	Y	Y	Y	N
Packwood	Y	Y	Y	Y	N	N	N	N
PENNSYLVANIA								
Heinz	N	Y	Y	Y	Y	Y	Y	N
Schweiker	N	N	Y	N	N	N	N	Y
RHODE ISLAND								
Pell	?	?	?	Y	Y	Y	Y	N
Chafee	Y	Y	Y	Y	Y	Y	Y	N
SOUTH CAROLINA								
Hollings	Y	Y	Y	Y	Y	Y	Y	N
Thurmond	N	N	Y	N	N	N	N	Y
SOUTH DAKOTA								
Abourezk	#	#	#	#	#	#	Y	N
McGovern	Y	Y	Y	Y	#	Y	N	N
TENNESSEE								
Sasser	Y	N	Y	Y	Y	Y	Y	N
Baker	Y	Y	Y	Y	Y	Y	Y	N
TEXAS								
Bentsen	Y	N	Y	Y	Y	Y	Y	N
Tower	N	N	Y	N	N	N	N	Y
UTAH								
Garn	N	N	Y	N	N	N	N	Y
Hatch	N	N	Y	N	N	N	N	Y
VERMONT								
Leahy	Y	Y	Y	Y	Y	Y	Y	N
Stafford	Y	Y	Y	Y	Y	Y	Y	N
VIRGINIA								
*Byrd, H.	N	N	Y	N	Y	N	Y	N
Scott	N	N	Y	N	N	N	N	N
WASHINGTON								
Jackson	Y	Y	Y	Y	Y	Y	Y	N
Magnuson	Y	N	Y	Y	Y	Y	Y	N
WEST VIRGINIA								
Byrd, R.	Y	Y	Y	Y	Y	Y	Y	N
Randolph	N	N	Y	N	Y	N	N	N
WISCONSIN								
Nelson	Y	Y	Y	Y	Y	Y	Y	N
Proxmire	Y	Y	Y	Y	Y	Y	Y	N
WYOMING								
Hansen	N	N	Y	N	N	N	N	Y
Wallop	N	N	N	?	N	N	N	Y

Democrats *Republicans*

**Byrd elected as independent.*

107. Exec N, 95th Congress, First Session, Panama Canal Treaties. Church, D-Idaho, motion to table (kill) the Dole, R-Kan.-Thurmond, R-S.C., reservation to provide that the treaty be resubmitted to the Senate for its approval if Panama adds any amendments or reservations binding on the United States. Motion agreed to 58-40: R 14-24; D 44-16 (ND 34-7; SD 10-9), April 18, 1978.

108. Exec N, 95th Congress, First Session, Panama Canal Treaties. Church, D-Idaho, motion to table (kill) the Thurmond, R-S.C., reservation to require the United States to consider the economic impact on U.S. ports when exercising its rights to establish and modify canal tolls. Motion agreed to 56-42: R 15-23; D 41-19 (ND 35-6; SD 6-13), April 18, 1978.

109. Exec N, 95th Congress, First Session, Panama Canal Treaties. DeConcini, D-Ariz., reservation to provide that the $10 million annual payment due Panama from surplus canal revenues will not accumulate over the life of the basic treaty. Adopted 92-6: R 37-1; D 55-5 (ND 36-5; SD 19-0), April 18, 1978.

110. Exec N, 95th Congress, First Session, Panama Canal Treaties. Church, D-Idaho, motion to table (kill) the Bartlett, R-Okla., reservation to withhold Senate consent to ratification until the president determined that the people of Panama approved all changes to the treaty. Motion agreed to 63-35: R 14-23; D 49-12 (ND 37-5; SD 12-7), April 18, 1978.

111. Exec N, 95th Congress, First Session, Panama Canal Treaties. Byrd, D-W.Va., motion to table (kill) the Stevens, R-Alaska, appeal after the Chair ruled against his point of order that the Byrd reservation *(see vote 116, p. 21-S)* dealt with a subject not before the Senate. Motion agreed to 74-22: R 16-21; D 58-1 (ND 40-1; SD 18-0), April 18, 1978.

112. Exec N, 95th Congress, First Session, Panama Canal Treaties. Sarbanes, D-Md., motion to table (kill) the Allen, D-Ala., amendment to provide that the Byrd, D-W.Va., reservation *(see vote 116, p. 21-S)* would not limit the rights of the United States outlined in the DeConcini, D-Ariz., reservation *(see vote 64, p. 12-S)* to the neutrality treaty to take military action in Panama to keep the canal open if closed for any reason. Motion agreed to 60-38: R 15-23; D 45-15 (ND 34-6; SD 11-9), April 18, 1978.

113. Exec N, 95th Congress, First Session, Panama Canal Treaties. Sarbanes, R-Md., motion to table (kill) the Allen, D-Ala., amendment to the Byrd, D-W.Va., reservation *(see vote 116, p. 21-S)* that would limit the rights of the United States outlined in the DeConcini, D-Ariz., reservation *(see vote 64, p. 12-S)* to the neutrality treaty to take military action in Panama to keep the canal open if closed for any reason. Motion agreed to 59-41; R 13-25; D 46-16 (ND 32-11; SD 14-5), April 18, 1978.

114. Exec N, 95th Congress, First Session, Panama Canal Treaties. Allen, D-Ala., motion to table (kill) the Byrd, D-W.Va., reservation *(see vote 116, p. 21-S)*. Rejected 21-79: R 17-21; D 4-58 (ND 0-43; SD 4-15), April 18, 1978.

	115	116	117	118	119
ALABAMA					
Allen	N	N	N	Y	N
Sparkman	Y	Y	Y	Y	Y
ALASKA					
Gravel	Y	Y	Y	N	Y
Stevens	N	N	N	Y	N
ARIZONA					
DeConcini	Y	Y	Y	Y	Y
Goldwater	N	N	N	Y	N
ARKANSAS					
Bumpers	N	Y	Y	Y	Y
Hodges	Y	Y	Y	Y	Y
CALIFORNIA					
Cranston	Y	Y	Y	Y	Y
Hayakawa	Y	Y	Y	Y	Y
COLORADO					
Hart	Y	Y	Y	N	Y
Haskell	Y	Y	Y	Y	Y
CONNECTICUT					
Ribicoff	Y	Y	Y	Y	Y
Weicker	Y	Y	Y	N	Y
DELAWARE					
Biden	Y	Y	Y	Y	Y
Roth	N	Y	N	Y	N
FLORIDA					
Chiles	Y	Y	Y	Y	Y
Stone	Y	Y	Y	Y	Y
GEORGIA					
Nunn	N	Y	Y	Y	Y
Talmadge	N	Y	Y	Y	Y
HAWAII					
Inouye	Y	Y	Y	Y	Y
Matsunaga	Y	Y	Y	Y	Y
IDAHO					
Church	Y	Y	Y	Y	Y
McClure	N	N	N	Y	N
ILLINOIS					
Stevenson	Y	Y	Y	Y	Y
Percy	Y	Y	Y	Y	Y
INDIANA					
Bayh	Y	Y	Y	Y	Y
Lugar	N	N	N	Y	N
IOWA					
Clark	Y	Y	Y	N	Y
Culver	Y	Y	Y	N	Y
KANSAS					
Dole	N	N	N	Y	N
Pearson	Y	Y	Y	Y	Y
KENTUCKY					
Ford	N	N	N	Y	N
Huddleston	Y	Y	Y	Y	Y
LOUISIANA					
Johnston	N	N	N	Y	N
Long	Y	Y	Y	N	Y
MAINE					
Hathaway	Y	Y	Y	Y	Y
Muskie	Y	Y	Y	Y	Y
MARYLAND					
Sarbanes	Y	Y	Y	Y	Y
Mathias	Y	Y	Y	Y	Y
MASSACHUSETTS					
Kennedy	Y	Y	Y	N	Y
Brooke	N	Y	N	Y	Y
MICHIGAN					
Riegle	Y	Y	Y	Y	Y
Griffin	N	N	N	N	N
MINNESOTA					
Anderson	Y	Y	Y	Y	Y
Humphrey, M.	Y	Y	Y	Y	Y
MISSISSIPPI					
Eastland	?	N	N	Y	N
Stennis	N	Y	N	Y	N
MISSOURI					
Eagleton	Y	Y	Y	Y	Y
Danforth	Y	Y	Y	Y	Y
MONTANA					
Melcher	N	Y	N	Y	N
Hatfield, P.	Y	Y	Y	Y	Y
NEBRASKA					
Zorinsky	N	N	N	Y	N
Curtis	N	N	N	Y	N
NEVADA					
Cannon	N	Y	Y	Y	Y
Laxalt	N	N	N	Y	N
NEW HAMPSHIRE					
Durkin	Y	Y	Y	N	Y
McIntyre	N	Y	Y	Y	Y
NEW JERSEY					
Williams	Y	Y	Y	Y	Y
Case	Y	Y	Y	Y	Y
NEW MEXICO					
Domenici	N	N	N	Y	N
Schmitt	N	N	N	Y	N
NEW YORK					
Moynihan	Y	Y	Y	Y	Y
Javits	Y	Y	Y	Y	Y
NORTH CAROLINA					
Morgan	N	Y	N	Y	Y
Helms	N	N	N	Y	N
NORTH DAKOTA					
Burdick	N	N	N	Y	N
Young	N	N	N	Y	N
OHIO					
Glenn	Y	Y	Y	Y	Y
Metzenbaum	Y	Y	Y	Y	Y
OKLAHOMA					
Bartlett	N	N	N	Y	N
Bellmon	Y	Y	N	Y	Y
OREGON					
Hatfield, M.	Y	Y	Y	Y	Y
Packwood	N	Y	N	Y	Y
PENNSYLVANIA					
Heinz	Y	Y	Y	Y	Y
Schweiker	N	N	N	Y	N
RHODE ISLAND					
Pell	Y	Y	Y	Y	Y
Chafee	Y	Y	Y	Y	Y
SOUTH CAROLINA					
Hollings	N	Y	Y	Y	Y
Thurmond	N	N	N	Y	N
SOUTH DAKOTA					
Abourezk	Y	Y	Y	N	Y
McGovern	Y	Y	Y	Y	Y
TENNESSEE					
Sasser	Y	Y	Y	Y	Y
Baker	Y	Y	Y	Y	Y
TEXAS					
Bentsen	Y	Y	Y	Y	Y
Tower	N	N	N	Y	N
UTAH					
Garn	N	N	N	Y	N
Hatch	N	N	N	Y	N
VERMONT					
Leahy	Y	Y	Y	Y	Y
Stafford	Y	Y	Y	Y	Y
VIRGINIA					
*Byrd, H.	N	Y	N	Y	N
Scott	N	N	N	Y	N
WASHINGTON					
Jackson	N	Y	Y	Y	Y
Magnuson	N	Y	Y	Y	Y
WEST VIRGINIA					
Byrd, R.	Y	Y	Y	Y	Y
Randolph	Y	Y	N	Y	N
WISCONSIN					
Nelson	Y	Y	Y	Y	Y
Proxmire	Y	Y	Y	Y	Y
WYOMING					
Hansen	N	N	N	Y	N
Wallop	N	N	N	Y	N

Democrats ***Republicans***

*Byrd elected as independent.

KEY

- Y Voted for (yea).
- ✓ Paired for.
- † Announced for.
- # CQ Poll for.
- N Voted against (nay).
- X Paired against.
- \- Announced against.
- ▮ CQ Poll against.
- P Voted "present."
- ● Voted "present" to avoid possible conflict of interest.
- ? Did not vote or otherwise make a position known.

115. Exec N, 95th Congress, First Session, Panama Canal Treaties. Byrd, D-W.Va., motion to table (kill) the Cannon, D-Nev., amendment to delete wording from the Byrd reservation *(see vote 116, below)* stating that it could not be "interpreted as a right of" the United States to intervene in Panama's internal affairs. Motion agreed to 58-41: R 14-24; D 44-17 (ND 36-7; SD 8-10), April 18, 1978.

116. Exec N, 95th Congress, First Session, Panama Canal Treaties. Byrd, D-W.Va., reservation to state that any action taken by the United States in Panama "shall not have as its purpose or be interpreted as a right of intervention in the internal affairs of Panama...." Adopted 73-27: R 17-21; D 56-6 (ND 41-2; SD 15-4), April 18, 1978. A "yea" was a vote supporting the president's position.

117. Exec N, 95th Congress, First Session, Panama Canal Treaties. Church, D-Idaho, motion to table (kill) the Griffin, R-Mich., substitute amendment to require the Senate to return to the president the treaty with advice that negotiations be initiated to develop a new treaty. Motion agreed to 64-36: R 13-25; D 51-11 (ND 39-4; SD 12-7), April 18, 1978.

118. Exec N, 95th Congress, First Session, Panama Canal Treaties. Cannon, D-Nev., reservation to provide that no interest payments to the United States from the Panama Canal Commission be waived unless approved by Congress. Adopted 90-10: R 36-2; D 54-8 (ND 36-7; SD 18-1), April 18, 1978.

119. Exec N, 95th Congress, First Session, Panama Canal Treaties. Adoption of the resolution of ratification to the treaty providing for the transfer of the Panama Canal to Panama on Dec. 31, 1999. Adopted 68-32: R 16-22; D 52-10 (ND 39-4; SD 13-6), April 18, 1978. A two-thirds majority vote (67 in this case) is required for adoption of resolutions of ratification of treaties. A "yea" was a vote supporting the president's position.

CQ Senate Votes 120-127

Corresponding to Congressional Record Votes 120, 121, 122, 123, 124, 125, 126, 127

KEY

- Y Voted for (yea).
- ✓ Paired for.
- † Announced for.
- # CQ Poll for.
- N Voted against (nay).
- X Paired against.
- - Announced against.
- ▮ CQ Poll against.
- P Voted "present."
- ● Voted "present" to avoid possible conflict of interest.
- ? Did not vote or otherwise make a position known.

	120	121	122	123	124	125	126	127
ALABAMA								
Allen	Y	Y	N	N	Y	N	N	Y
Sparkman	N	Y	X	N	Y	N	N	Y
ALASKA								
Gravel	N	Y	N	N	Y	Y	N	Y
Stevens	N	Y	N	N	N	N	N	Y
ARIZONA								
DeConcini	N	Y	N	N	Y	Y	N	Y
Goldwater	Y	Y	Y	N	?	?	?	?
ARKANSAS								
Bumpers	N	Y	N	N	Y	Y	N	Y
Hodges	Y	N	N	Y	Y	Y	N	Y
CALIFORNIA								
Cranston	N	Y	Y	N	N	Y	N	Y
Hayakawa	N	Y	N	Y	Y	Y	Y	Y
COLORADO								
Hart	N	Y	Y	N	N	Y	N	Y
Haskell	?	?	?	?	?	?	?	?
CONNECTICUT								
Ribicoff	N	Y	Y	N	N	Y	N	Y
Weicker	N	Y	N	N	N	Y	N	Y
DELAWARE								
Biden	N	Y	N	N	N	Y	N	Y
Roth	N	Y	N	N	Y	Y	Y	Y
FLORIDA								
Chiles	Y	Y	Y	N	N	Y	N	N
Stone	Y	Y	Y	N	N	Y	N	N
GEORGIA								
Nunn	Y	Y	N	N	Y	Y	N	N
Talmadge	Y	Y	N	N	Y	N	N	N
HAWAII								
Inouye	Y	N	Y	N	N	Y	N	N
Matsunaga	Y	N	Y	N	N	Y	N	N
IDAHO								
Church	N	Y	N	N	N	Y	N	Y
McClure	N	Y	N	N	Y	Y	N	Y
ILLINOIS								
Stevenson	N	Y	N	N	Y	N	N	Y
Percy	N	Y	N	N	Y	Y	Y	Y
INDIANA								
Bayh	N	Y	Y	N	N	Y	N	Y
Lugar	N	Y	N	Y	Y	Y	Y	Y
IOWA								
Clark	N	Y	Y	N	N	Y	N	Y
Culver	N	Y	Y	N	N	Y	N	Y
KANSAS								
Dole	N	Y	Y	N	Y	Y	Y	Y
Pearson	N	Y	N	N	Y	Y	Y	Y
KENTUCKY								
Ford	N	Y	N	N	N	Y	N	Y
Huddleston	N	Y	Y	N	N	Y	N	Y
LOUISIANA								
Johnston	N	Y	N	N	Y	Y	N	Y
Long	Y	Y	N	N	Y	N	N	Y
MAINE								
Hathaway	N	N	N	N	N	Y	Y	Y
Muskie	N	N	N	N	N	Y	Y	Y
MARYLAND								
Sarbanes	N	Y	Y	N	N	Y	N	Y
Mathias	N	?	N	N	N	Y	Y	Y
MASSACHUSETTS								
Kennedy	N	Y	Y	N	N	Y	N	Y
Brooke	N	Y	Y	N	N	Y	N	Y
MICHIGAN								
Riegle	N	Y	Y	N	N	Y	N	Y
Griffin	?	Y	N	N	N	N	N	Y
MINNESOTA								
Anderson	Y	N	Y	N	N	Y	N	Y
Humphrey, M.	N	N	Y	N	N	Y	N	Y
MISSISSIPPI								
Eastland	Y	Y	N	N	Y	N	N	Y
Stennis	Y	Y	N	N	Y	N	N	Y
MISSOURI								
Eagleton	N	Y	Y	N	N	Y	Y	Y
Danforth	N	Y	Y	N	N	N	N	Y
MONTANA								
Melcher	Y	N	Y	N	N	N	N	N
Hatfield, P.	Y	N	Y	N	N	N	N	N
NEBRASKA								
Zorinsky	N	Y	N	N	Y	N	N	Y
Curtis	N	Y	N	Y	Y	Y	N	Y
NEVADA								
Cannon	N	Y	N	N	N	Y	N	Y
Laxalt	N	Y	N	N	N	Y	Y	Y
NEW HAMPSHIRE								
Durkin	N	Y	Y	N	N	Y	N	Y
McIntyre	?	?	?	?	?	?	?	†
NEW JERSEY								
Williams	N	Y	Y	N	N	Y	N	Y
Case	✓	#	✓	✓	X	†	▮	†
NEW MEXICO								
Domenici	N	Y	Y	N	N	Y	N	Y
Schmitt	N	Y	N	Y	Y	N	N	Y
NEW YORK								
Moynihan	N	Y	✓	✓	✓	Y	N	Y
Javits	N	Y	Y	N	N	Y	Y	Y
NORTH CAROLINA								
Morgan	N	Y	N	N	Y	Y	N	Y
Helms	N	Y	N	N	Y	Y	Y	Y
NORTH DAKOTA								
Burdick	Y	Y	Y	N	N	N	N	Y
Young	Y	Y	N	N	Y	N	N	Y
OHIO								
Glenn	N	Y	N	N	Y	Y	N	Y
Metzenbaum	N	Y	Y	N	N	Y	N	Y
OKLAHOMA								
Bartlett	N	Y	N	N	Y	Y	Y	Y
Bellmon	Y	N	Y	N	Y	Y	Y	Y
OREGON								
Hatfield, M.	✓	†	X	✓	✓	†	✓	†
Packwood	X	†	?	?	?	†	?	†
PENNSYLVANIA								
Heinz	N	Y	Y	N	N	Y	Y	Y
Schweiker	N	Y	Y	N	N	Y	Y	Y
RHODE ISLAND								
Pell	N	Y	Y	N	N	Y	N	Y
Chafee	N	Y	N	N	Y	Y	N	Y
SOUTH CAROLINA								
Hollings	N	Y	N	N	Y	Y	N	Y
Thurmond	N	Y	N	N	Y	Y	Y	Y
SOUTH DAKOTA								
Abourezk	▮	#	▮	▮	#	#	▮	#
McGovern	Y	N	#	▮	#	#	▮	▮
TENNESSEE								
Sasser	N	Y	Y	N	Y	Y	N	Y
Baker	N	Y	N	N	Y	Y	Y	Y
TEXAS								
Bentsen	Y	Y	N	N	Y	N	N	Y
Tower	N	Y	N	N	Y	Y	N	Y
UTAH								
Garn	N	Y	N	Y	Y	Y	N	Y
Hatch	N	Y	N	Y	Y	Y	N	Y
VERMONT								
Leahy	N	Y	N	N	N	Y	N	Y
Stafford	N	Y	N	N	N	Y	N	Y
VIRGINIA								
*Byrd, H.	N	Y	N	N	Y	N	N	Y
Scott	N	?	N	N	N	N	Y	Y
WASHINGTON								
Jackson	N	Y	N	N	N	N	N	Y
Magnuson	N	Y	Y	N	N	N	N	Y
WEST VIRGINIA								
Byrd, R.	N	Y	N	N	Y	N	N	Y
Randolph	Y	N	Y	N	Y	N	N	N
WISCONSIN								
Nelson	N	Y	N	N	N	Y	N	Y
Proxmire	N	Y	N	N	N	Y	N	Y
WYOMING								
Hansen	N	Y	N	N	Y	Y	N	Y
Wallop	N	Y	Y	N	Y	Y	N	Y

Democrats ***Republicans***

*Byrd elected as independent.

120. S 2493. Airline Deregulation. McGovern, D-S.D., amendment to provide a limited automatic market entry program with a termination date of June 30, 1985. Rejected 21-72: R 3-31; D 18-41 (ND 8-32; SD 10-9), April 19, 1978. A "nay" was a vote supporting the president's position.

121. S 2493. Airline Deregulation. Cannon, D-Nev., motion to table (kill) the McGovern, D-S.D., amendment to establish minimum standards for a substitute for discontinued "essential" air transportation service. Motion agreed to 80-12: R 32-1; D 48-11 (ND 30-10; SD 18-1), April 19, 1978.

122. S 2493. Airline Deregulation. Danforth, R-Mo., substitute amendment, to the Zorinsky, D-Neb., amendment *(see vote 124, below)*, to broaden the coverage of the airline employee protection plan. Rejected 37-54: R 10-25; D 27-29 (ND 23-15; SD 4-14), April 19, 1978.

123. S 2493. Airline Deregulation. Hatch, R-Utah, substitute amendment, to the Zorinsky, D-Neb., amendment *(see vote 124, below)*, to delete the airline employee protection plan from the bill. Rejected 7-85: R 6-29; D 1-56 (ND 0-38; SD 1-18), April 19, 1978.

124. S 2493. Airline Deregulation. Zorinsky, D-Neb., amendment to provide that airline employees dislocated because of the provisions of the bill be given hiring priority with other airlines rather than compensation. Rejected 43-48: R 21-13; D 22-35 (ND 7-31; SD 15-4), April 19, 1978.

125. S 2493. Airline Deregulation. Kennedy, D-Mass., amendment to direct the Civil Aeronautics Board to authorize a proposed air transportation service unless it determined that the service was not consistent with the public convenience and necessity. Adopted 69-23: R 28-6; D 41-17 (ND 30-9; SD 11-8), April 19, 1978. A "yea" was a vote supporting the president's position.

126. S 2493. Airline Deregulation. Heinz, R-Pa., amendment to require federal pre-emption of state regulation of any air carrier authorized to serve interstate routes. Rejected 20-72: R 17-17; D 3-55 (ND 3-36; SD 0-19), April 19, 1978.

127. S 2493. Airline Deregulation. Passage of the bill to encourage airline industry competition by increasing airlines' flexibility to set fares and enter additional routes. Passed 83-9: R 34-0; D 49-9 (ND 34-5; SD 15-4), April 19, 1978. A "yea" was a vote supporting the president's position.

	128	129	130	131	132	133	134	135
ALABAMA								
Allen	Y	Y	N	N	Y	Y	Y	N
Sparkman	Y	N	N	N	N	N	N	N
ALASKA								
Gravel	Y	N	Y	N	N	N	▮	N
Stevens	Y	N	N	N	N	N	N	Y
ARIZONA								
DeConcini	Y	Y	N	N	Y	N	Y	N
Goldwater	Y	Y	N	N	N	?	?	?
ARKANSAS								
Bumpers	Y	N	N	N	N	N	Y	N
Hodges	Y	Y	N	N	N	N	N	N
CALIFORNIA								
Cranston	Y	N	Y	Y	N	N	N	Y
Hayakawa	Y	Y	N	N	Y	Y	Y	Y
COLORADO								
Hart	Y	N	N	N	Y	N	N	N
Haskell	?	N	?	?	Y	N	Y	N
CONNECTICUT								
Ribicoff	Y	✓	N	N	N	N	N	N
Weicker	Y	▮	Y	Y	N	N	N	N
DELAWARE								
Biden	Y	N	?	?	?	?	?	?
Roth	Y	Y	N	N	Y	Y	Y	Y
FLORIDA								
Chiles	Y	?	N	N	N	N	N	N
Stone	Y	?	N	N	Y	Y	Y	N
GEORGIA								
Nunn	Y	Y	N	N	Y	Y	Y	N
Talmadge	Y	Y	N	N	N	Y	Y	N
HAWAII								
Inouye	Y	N	?	?	?	N	N	N
Matsunaga	Y	N	N	N	N	N	N	N
IDAHO								
Church	Y	N	N	Y	Y	N	Y	N
McClure	?	Y	N	N	Y	N	Y	Y
ILLINOIS								
Stevenson	Y	N	N	Y	N	N	N	N
Percy	Y	N	N	N	N	N	Y	Y
INDIANA								
Bayh	Y	N	?	?	?	?	?	?
Lugar	Y	Y	N	N	Y	Y	Y	Y
IOWA								
Clark	Y	N	Y	Y	N	N	N	N
Culver	Y	N	N	Y	N	N	N	N
KANSAS								
Dole	Y	Y	N	N	N	N	N	N
Pearson	Y	?	?	?	?	?	?	?
KENTUCKY								
Ford	Y	Y	N	N	Y	N	Y	Y
Huddleston	Y	?	N	N	Y	N	Y	N
LOUISIANA								
Johnston	Y	▮	N	N	N	N	Y	N
Long	Y	?	N	N	N	N	N	Y
MAINE								
Hathaway	Y	?	N	N	N	N	N	N
Muskie	Y	N	N	N	N	N	N	N
MARYLAND								
Sarbanes	Y	N	N	Y	N	N	N	N
Mathias	Y	N	N	Y	N	N	N	N
MASSACHUSETTS								
Kennedy	Y	N	Y	Y	N	N	N	N
Brooke	Y	?	N	N	N	N	N	N
MICHIGAN								
Riegle	Y	N	Y	Y	N	N	N	N
Griffin	Y	Y	N	N	?	?	?	?
MINNESOTA								
Anderson	Y	✓	✓	†	N	N	N	N
Humphrey, M.	Y	N	Y	Y	N	N	N	✓
MISSISSIPPI								
Eastland	Y	Y	N	N	N	N	Y	?
Stennis	Y	N	N	N	N	N	N	N
MISSOURI								
Eagleton	Y	?	Y	Y	N	N	Y	N
Danforth	Y	N	N	N	Y	N	Y	Y
MONTANA								
Melcher	Y	N	N	Y	N	N	N	N
Hatfield, P.	Y	▮	▮	▮	#	▮	#	▮
NEBRASKA								
Zorinsky	Y	Y	N	N	Y	Y	Y	N
Curtis	Y	?	N	N	Y	Y	Y	?
NEVADA								
Cannon	Y	N	N	N	N	N	N	N
Laxalt	Y	Y	N	N	N	Y	Y	Y
NEW HAMPSHIRE								
Durkin	Y	N	N	N	Y	N	Y	N
McIntyre	†	?	N	N	Y	N	N	Y
NEW JERSEY								
Williams	Y	▮	Y	Y	N	N	N	N
Case	Y	N	N	N	N	N	N	N
NEW MEXICO								
Domenici	Y	?	N	N	Y	N	Y	N
Schmitt	Y	Y	N	N	N	N	Y	N
NEW YORK								
Moynihan	Y	N	N	N	N	N	Y	N
Javits	Y	?	N	N	N	N	N	N
NORTH CAROLINA								
Morgan	Y	Y	N	N	N	N	Y	N
Helms	Y	Y	N	N	Y	Y	Y	Y
NORTH DAKOTA								
Burdick	Y	✓	N	N	N	N	N	N
Young	Y	Y	N	N	N	N	Y	?
OHIO								
Glenn	Y	N	N	N	N	N	N	N
Metzenbaum	†	N	Y	Y	Y	N	Y	N
OKLAHOMA								
Bartlett	Y	Y	N	N	N	Y	N	N
Bellmon	Y	N	N	N	N	N	N	N
OREGON								
Hatfield, M.	Y	N	Y	Y	Y	N	Y	N
Packwood	Y	N	N	N	?	N	N	Y
PENNSYLVANIA								
Heinz	Y	N	N	Y	N	N	Y	Y
Schweiker	Y	N	N	N	Y	N	Y	Y
RHODE ISLAND								
Pell	Y	N	N	Y	N	N	N	N
Chafee	Y	N	N	N	N	N	Y	N
SOUTH CAROLINA								
Hollings	Y	N	N	N	N	N	N	N
Thurmond	Y	Y	N	N	Y	Y	Y	Y
SOUTH DAKOTA								
Abourezk	Y	▮	Y	Y	▮	▮	?	▮
McGovern	Y	▮	Y	Y	Y	N	Y	N
TENNESSEE								
Sasser	Y	N	N	N	Y	N	Y	N
Baker	Y	?	?	?	?	?	?	?
TEXAS								
Bentsen	Y	?	N	N	N	N	Y	N
Tower	Y	Y	N	N	N	N	N	Y
UTAH								
Garn	Y	?	?	?	?	?	?	?
Hatch	Y	Y	N	N	Y	Y	Y	Y
VERMONT								
Leahy	Y	N	N	N	Y	N	N	N
Stafford	Y	N	N	N	N	N	N	N
VIRGINIA								
*Byrd, H.	Y	Y	N	N	Y	Y	Y	N
Scott	N	Y	N	N	Y	Y	Y	N
WASHINGTON								
Jackson	Y	N	N	N	N	N	N	N
Magnuson	Y	N	N	N	N	N	N	N
WEST VIRGINIA								
Byrd, R.	Y	N	N	N	N	N	N	N
Randolph	Y	N	N	N	N	N	N	N
WISCONSIN								
Nelson	Y	N	N	N	Y	N	?	N
Proxmire	Y	Y	Y	Y	Y	Y	Y	Y
WYOMING								
Hansen	Y	Y	N	N	N	Y	N	Y
Wallop	Y	N	N	N	Y	Y	Y	Y

Democrats ***Republicans***

**Byrd elected as independent.*

KEY

- Y Voted for (yea).
- ✓ Paired for.
- † Announced for.
- # CQ Poll for.
- N Voted against (nay).
- X Paired against.
- \- Announced against.
- ▮ CQ Poll against.
- P Voted "present."
- ● Voted "present" to avoid possible conflict of interest.
- ? Did not vote or otherwise make a position known.

128. S 1566. Foreign Intelligence Surveillance. Passage of the bill to establish judicial certification procedures for the authorization of electronic surveillance against agents of foreign powers operating within the United States. Passed 95-1: R 36-1; D 59-0 (ND 40-0; SD 19-0), April 20, 1978.

129. S Con Res 80. Fiscal 1979 Budget Targets. Byrd, Ind-Va., amendment to reduce by $5.6 billion budget authority and outlays for Health, Education and Welfare (HEW) Department programs, to make up for funds reported misspent by HEW in 1977. Rejected 28-48: R 17-13; D 11-35 (ND 3-30; SD 8-5), April 24, 1978.

130. S Con Res 80. Fiscal 1979 Budget Targets. McGovern, D-S.D., amendment to transfer $4.6 billion in budget authority and $1.5 billion in outlays from national defense to certain domestic programs. Rejected 14-77: R 2-33; D 12-44 (ND 12-25; SD 0-19), April 25, 1978.

131. S Con Res 80. Fiscal 1979 Budget Targets. Eagleton, D-Mo., amendment to reduce national defense spending by $1.4 billion in budget authority and $900 million in outlays. Rejected 21-70: R 4-31; D 17-39 (ND 17-20; SD 0-19), April 25, 1978.

132. S Con Res 80. Fiscal 1979 Budget Targets. Proxmire, D-Wis., amendment to reduce total budget authority to $540 billion from $566.1 billion. Rejected 33-57: R 14-19; D 19-38 (ND 12-26; SD 7-12), April 25, 1978.

133. S Con Res 80. Fiscal 1979 Budget Targets. Curtis, R-Neb., motion to recommit the resolution to the Budget Committee with instructions to report back with a balanced budget. Rejected 19-72: R 12-21; D 7-51 (ND 2-37; SD 5-14), April 25, 1978.

134. S Con Res 80. Fiscal 1979 Budget Targets. Proxmire, D-Wis., amendment to reduce total budget authority to $561.1 billion from $566.1 billion. Rejected 43-46: R 20-13; D 23-33 (ND 10-27; SD 13-6), April 25, 1978.

135. S Con Res 80. Fiscal 1979 Budget Targets. Roth, R-Del., amendment to reduce revenues to $438.4 billion from $443.3 billion to accommodate a $25 billion tax cut, effective Oct. 1, 1978. Rejected 22-65: R 17-14; D 5-51 (ND 3-35; SD 2-16), April 25, 1978.

CQ Senate Votes 136-143

Corresponding to Congressional Record Votes 136, 137, 138, 139, 140, 141, 142, 143

	136	137	138	139	140	141	142	143
ALABAMA								
Allen	Y	Y	Y	Y	N	N	Y	N
Sparkman	N	N	N	N	Y	Y	Y	Y
ALASKA								
Gravel	N	N	N	N	Y	Y	Y	Y
Stevens	N	N	N	N	Y	N	N	N
ARIZONA								
DeConcini	Y	Y	N	Y	N	Y	Y	Y
Goldwater	Y	Y	N	Y	N	N	N	N
ARKANSAS								
Bumpers	N	Y	N	N	Y	Y	Y	Y
Hodges	N	Y	N	N	Y	Y	Y	Y
CALIFORNIA								
Cranston	N	N	N	N	Y	Y	Y	Y
Hayakawa	Y	Y	Y	Y	N	N	Y	Y
COLORADO								
Hart	N	N	N	N	Y	Y	Y	Y
Haskell	Y	N	N	N	Y	?	?	?
CONNECTICUT								
Ribicoff	N	N	N	N	Y	Y	Y	Y
Weicker	N	N	N	N	Y	Y	Y	Y
DELAWARE								
Biden	Y	N	N	N	N	?	?	?
Roth	Y	Y	Y	Y	N	N	Y	N
FLORIDA								
Chiles	N	N	N	N	Y	N	Y	Y
Stone	N	Y	N	N	Y	N	Y	N
GEORGIA								
Nunn	Y	Y	N	Y	N	N	Y	Y
Talmadge	N	Y	N	Y	N	N	Y	Y
HAWAII								
Inouye	N	N	N	N	Y	Y	Y	Y
Matsunaga	N	N	N	N	Y	Y	Y	Y
IDAHO								
Church	Y	N	N	N	Y	Y	Y	Y
McClure	Y	Y	Y	Y	N	N	N	N
ILLINOIS								
Stevenson	N	N	N	N	Y	Y	Y	Y
Percy	?	?	?	?	Y	Y	Y	X
INDIANA								
Bayh	N	N	N	N	Y	Y	Y	Y
Lugar	N	Y	Y	N	Y	N	N	N
IOWA								
Clark	N	N	N	N	Y	Y	Y	Y
Culver	N	N	N	N	Y	?	?	†
KANSAS								
Dole	Y	Y	Y	Y	Y	N	Y	N
Pearson	?	?	?	?	?	Y	Y	Y
KENTUCKY								
Ford	Y	Y	Y	?	?	Y	Y	Y
Huddleston	N	Y	N	Y	Y	Y	Y	Y
LOUISIANA								
Johnston	Y	Y	Y	#	#	?	?	Y
Long	N	N	N	Y	Y	Y	?	Y
MAINE								
Hathaway	N	N	N	N	Y	Y	Y	Y
Muskie	N	N	N	N	Y	Y	Y	Y
MARYLAND								
Sarbanes	N	N	N	N	Y	Y	Y	Y
Mathias	N	N	N	N	Y	?	?	Y
MASSACHUSETTS								
Kennedy	N	N	N	N	Y	Y	Y	Y
Brooke	N	N	N	N	Y	Y	Y	Y
MICHIGAN								
Riegle	N	N	N	N	Y	Y	Y	Y
Griffin	Y	Y	N	Y	N	Y	N	N
MINNESOTA								
Anderson	N	N	N	N	Y	Y	Y	?
Humphrey, M.	N	N	N	N	Y	Y	Y	Y
MISSISSIPPI								
Eastland	N	Y	N	Y	Y	?	?	?
Stennis	N	N	N	Y	Y	N	Y	Y
MISSOURI								
Eagleton	Y	N	N	N	Y	Y	Y	Y
Danforth	Y	N	N	N	N	N	Y	Y
MONTANA								
Melcher	N	N	N	Y	Y	Y	Y	Y
Hatfield, P.	N	N	N	▮	#	#	#	#
NEBRASKA								
Zorinsky	Y	Y	N	Y	N	N	Y	N
Curtis	Y	Y	Y	Y	N	N	N	N
NEVADA								
Cannon	N	Y	N	Y	Y	Y	Y	Y
Laxalt	Y	Y	Y	Y	N	N	N	N
NEW HAMPSHIRE								
Durkin	N	N	N	N	Y	Y	Y	Y
McIntyre	Y	N	N	N	Y	Y	Y	N
NEW JERSEY								
Williams	N	N	N	N	Y	Y	Y	Y
Case	N	N	N	N	Y	Y	Y	Y
NEW MEXICO								
Domenici	Y	Y	N	Y	N	✓	?	?
Schmitt	?	Y	Y	Y	N	N	N	N
NEW YORK								
Moynihan	N	N	N	?	?	Y	Y	Y
Javits	N	N	N	N	Y	Y	Y	Y
NORTH CAROLINA								
Morgan	Y	Y	N	Y	Y	N	N	N
Helms	Y	Y	Y	Y	N	N	N	N
NORTH DAKOTA								
Burdick	N	N	N	Y	Y	Y	Y	Y
Young	N	Y	N	Y	Y	N	N	N
OHIO								
Glenn	N	N	N	N	Y	Y	Y	Y
Metzenbaum	Y	N	N	N	Y	Y	Y	Y
OKLAHOMA								
Bartlett	N	Y	Y	Y	N	N	N	N
Bellmon	N	N	N	N	Y	N	N	N
OREGON								
Hatfield, M.	Y	N	N	N	N	?	?	✓
Packwood	N	N	N	N	Y	Y	Y	Y
PENNSYLVANIA								
Heinz	N	N	N	N	Y	Y	Y	Y
Schweiker	Y	N	Y	N	Y	Y	Y	N
RHODE ISLAND								
Pell	N	N	N	N	Y	Y	Y	Y
Chafee	Y	N	N	N	Y	Y	Y	Y
SOUTH CAROLINA								
Hollings	Y	Y	N	N	Y	Y	Y	Y
Thurmond	Y	Y	Y	Y	N	N	Y	N
SOUTH DAKOTA								
Abourezk	N	▮	▮	#	#	?	?	#
McGovern	Y	N	N	▮	#	Y	Y	Y
TENNESSEE								
Sasser	Y	N	N	Y	Y	Y	Y	Y
Baker	?	?	?	?	?	N	N	N
TEXAS								
Bentsen	N	Y	N	N	Y	Y	Y	Y
Tower	N	Y	Y	Y	N	N	Y	N
UTAH								
Garn	?	?	?	?	?	N	N	N
Hatch	Y	Y	Y	Y	N	N	N	?
VERMONT								
Leahy	N	N	N	N	Y	Y	Y	Y
Stafford	N	N	N	N	Y	Y	Y	Y
VIRGINIA								
*Byrd, H.	Y	Y	Y	Y	N	N	Y	Y
Scott	Y	Y	Y	Y	N	N	N	N
WASHINGTON								
Jackson	N	N	N	N	Y	Y	Y	Y
Magnuson	N	N	N	N	Y	†	Y	Y
WEST VIRGINIA								
Byrd, R.	N	N	N	Y	Y	N	Y	Y
Randolph	N	N	N	Y	Y	Y	Y	Y
WISCONSIN								
Nelson	N	N	N	N	Y	Y	Y	Y
Proxmire	Y	Y	N	Y	N	Y	N	Y
WYOMING								
Hansen	N	Y	Y	Y	N	N	N	N
Wallop	Y	Y	Y	Y	N	N	Y	N

Democrats *Republicans*

*Byrd elected as independent.

KEY

- Y Voted for (yea).
- ✓ Paired for.
- † Announced for.
- # CQ Poll for.
- N Voted against (nay).
- X Paired against.
- - Announced against.
- ▮ CQ Poll against.
- P Voted "present."
- ● Voted "present" to avoid possible conflict of interest.
- ? Did not vote or otherwise make a position known.

136. S Con Res 80. Fiscal 1979 Budget Targets. Domenici, R-N.M., amendment to reduce budget authority by $2.2 billion and outlays by $2.1 billion. Rejected 36-59: R 18-15; D 18-44 (ND 10-33; SD 8-11), April 26, 1978.

137. S Con Res 80. Fiscal 1979 Budget Targets. Byrd, Ind-Va., amendment to reduce by $2.1 billion budget authority and outlays for Health, Education and Welfare (HEW) Department programs, to make up for funds reported to have been misspent by HEW in 1977. Rejected 38-57: R 20-14; D 18-43 (ND 4-38; SD 14-5), April 26, 1978.

138. S Con Res 80. Fiscal 1979 Budget Targets. Tower, R-Texas, amendment to increase national defense spending by $1.6 billion in budget authority and $1.2 billion in outlays. Rejected 21-74: R 17-17; D 4-57 (ND 0-42; SD 4-15), April 26, 1978.

139. S Con Res 80. Fiscal 1979 Budget Targets. Byrd, Ind-Va., amendment to reduce budget authority by $750 million by reducing funds for international financial institutions. Rejected 37-53: R 19-15; D 18-38 (ND 8-31; SD 10-7), April 26, 1978.

140. S Con Res 80. Fiscal 1979 Budget Targets. Adoption of the resolution setting the following fiscal 1979 budget targets: revenues of $443.3 billion, budget authority of $566.1 billion, outlays of $498.9 billion and a deficit of $55.6 billion. Adopted 64-27: R 16-19; D 48-8 (ND 35-4; SD 13-4), April 26, 1978.

141. Cottine Nomination. Confirmation of President Carter's nomination of Bertram R. Cottine of the District of Columbia to be a member of the Occupational Safety and Health (OSHA) Review Commission for a term expiring April 27, 1983. Confirmed 56-33: R 12-23; D 44-10 (ND 35-2; SD 9-8), April 27, 1978. A "yea" was a vote supporting the president's position.

142. Luna Nomination. Confirmation of President Carter's nomination of Charles Luna of Texas to be a member of the board of directors of the National Railroad Passenger Corporation for a term expiring July 18, 1980. Confirmed 70-19: R 18-17; D 52-2 (ND 37-1; SD 15-1), April 27, 1978. A "yea" was a vote supporting the president's position.

143. Sayre Nomination. Sparkman, D-Ala., motion to table (kill) the Helms, R-N.C., motion to recommit to the Foreign Relations Committee, and thus kill, President Carter's nomination of Robert Marion Sayre of Virginia to be the U.S. ambassador to Brazil. Motion agreed to 62-27: R 12-22; D 50-5 (ND 35-2; SD 15-3), April 27, 1978. A "yea" was a vote supporting the president's position. (Sayre was confirmed subsequently by voice vote.)

Corresponding to Congressional Record Votes 144, 145, 146, 147, 148, 149, 150, 151

	144	145	146	147	148	149	150	151
ALABAMA								
Allen	Y	N	Y	N	Y	N	Y	Y
Sparkman	Y	N	Y	Y	Y	N	Y	Y
ALASKA								
Gravel	Y	Y	Y	N	Y	N	Y	Y
Stevens	N	N	Y	N	N	N	Y	Y
ARIZONA								
DeConcini	Y	?	?	N	Y	N	Y	Y
Goldwater	N	N	Y	N	Y	Y	N	Y
ARKANSAS								
Bumpers	Y	N	Y	Y	N	N	Y	Y
Hodges	Y	N	Y	N	N	N	Y	Y
CALIFORNIA								
Cranston	Y	Y	Y	Y	Y	Y	N	Y
Hayakawa	N	N	Y	N	N	Y	N	Y
COLORADO								
Hart	Y	Y	Y	Y	Y	?	?	?
Haskell	?	?	?	?	?	?	?	?
CONNECTICUT								
Ribicoff	Y	N	Y	Y	Y	Y	N	Y
Weicker	Y	N	Y	Y	N	Y	N	Y
DELAWARE								
Biden	?	N	Y	Y	N	Y	N	Y
Roth	Y	N	Y	N	N	N	Y	Y
FLORIDA								
Chiles	Y	N	Y	N	N	Y	N	Y
Stone	N	Y	Y	?	N	Y	N	Y
GEORGIA								
Nunn	Y	N	Y	Y	N	Y	N	Y
Talmadge	Y	N	Y	Y	N	Y	Y	Y
HAWAII								
Inouye	Y	?	?	?	?	?	?	?
Matsunaga	Y	Y	Y	Y	Y	N	Y	Y
IDAHO								
Church	#	Y	Y	Y	Y	▮	#	#
McClure	N	N	Y	N	N	Y	N	Y
ILLINOIS								
Stevenson	N	Y	Y	Y	Y	Y	N	Y
Percy	N	Y	Y	Y	N	Y	N	Y
INDIANA								
Bayh	Y	N	Y	Y	Y	Y	N	Y
Lugar	N	N	Y	N	N	Y	N	Y
IOWA								
Clark	Y	Y	Y	Y	Y	Y	N	Y
Culver	?	Y	Y	Y	Y	Y	N	Y
KANSAS								
Dole	Y	N	Y	N	N	N	Y	Y
Pearson	N	?	?	?	?	?	?	?
KENTUCKY								
Ford	Y	Y	Y	Y	N	N	Y	Y
Huddleston	Y	Y	Y	Y	Y	N	Y	Y
LOUISIANA								
Johnston	Y	N	Y	Y	Y	N	Y	Y
Long	Y	N	Y	Y	Y	N	Y	Y
MAINE								
Hathaway	Y	Y	Y	Y	?	Y	N	Y
Muskie	Y	N	Y	Y	Y	Y	N	Y
MARYLAND								
Sarbanes	Y	Y	Y	Y	Y	Y	N	Y
Mathias	Y	N	Y	N	?	Y	N	Y
MASSACHUSETTS								
Kennedy	Y	Y	Y	Y	#	Y	N	Y
Brooke	Y	N	Y	Y	Y	Y	N	Y
MICHIGAN								
Riegle	Y	Y	Y	Y	Y	Y	N	Y
Griffin	N	N	Y	N	N	?	?	?
MINNESOTA								
Anderson	?	Y	Y	Y	Y	N	Y	Y
Humphrey, M.	†	Y	Y	Y	Y	N	Y	Y
MISSISSIPPI								
Eastland	?	?	Y	N	Y	N	Y	Y
Stennis	Y	N	Y	Y	Y	N	Y	Y
MISSOURI								
Eagleton	Y	N	Y	Y	Y	N	Y	Y
Danforth	N	N	Y	N	N	N	Y	Y
MONTANA								
Melcher	Y	N	Y	Y	Y	Y	N	Y
Hatfield, P.	#	#	†	#	Y	N	Y	Y
NEBRASKA								
Zorinsky	Y	N	Y	N	N	Y	N	Y
Curtis	N	N	Y	?	N	Y	N	Y
NEVADA								
Cannon	Y	?	?	?	?	?	?	?
Laxalt	N	N	Y	N	N	N	Y	Y
NEW HAMPSHIRE								
Durkin	Y	Y	Y	Y	Y	N	Y	Y
McIntyre	✓	N	Y	Y	?	†	-	†
NEW JERSEY								
Williams	Y	Y	Y	N	Y	N	Y	Y
Case	Y	N	Y	Y	N	N	Y	Y
NEW MEXICO								
Domenici	?	N	Y	N	N	Y	N	Y
Schmitt	N	N	Y	N	N	Y	N	Y
NEW YORK								
Moynihan	?	Y	Y	Y	Y	N	Y	Y
Javits	Y	N	Y	Y	Y	Y	N	Y
NORTH CAROLINA								
Morgan	N	Y	Y	Y	N	?	?	?
Helms	N	N	Y	N	N	?	?	Y
NORTH DAKOTA								
Burdick	Y	Y	Y	Y	N	N	Y	Y
Young	N	N	Y	?	N	N	Y	Y
OHIO								
Glenn	Y	N	Y	Y	N	Y	N	Y
Metzenbaum	Y	N	Y	Y	N	Y	N	Y
OKLAHOMA								
Bartlett	N	N	Y	N	N	N	Y	Y
Bellmon	N	N	Y	N	N	Y	N	Y
OREGON								
Hatfield, M.	?	-	†	†	Y	N	Y	N
Packwood	Y	N	Y	N	Y	N	Y	N
PENNSYLVANIA								
Heinz	Y	N	Y	N	N	N	Y	Y
Schweiker	N	N	Y	N	N	N	Y	Y
RHODE ISLAND								
Pell	Y	N	Y	Y	Y	Y	N	Y
Chafee	Y	N	Y	N	N	Y	N	Y
SOUTH CAROLINA								
Hollings	Y	Y	Y	Y	Y	N	Y	Y
Thurmond	Y	N	Y	N	N	N	Y	Y
SOUTH DAKOTA								
Abourezk	#	Y	Y	?	Y	Y	N	▮
McGovern	Y	Y	Y	Y	Y	N	Y	Y
TENNESSEE								
Sasser	Y	Y	Y	Y	Y	N	Y	Y
Baker	N	N	Y	N	N	N	Y	Y
TEXAS								
Bentsen	Y	Y	Y	Y	N	N	Y	Y
Tower	?	N	Y	N	N	N	Y	Y
UTAH								
Garn	N	N	Y	N	N	N	Y	Y
Hatch	?	N	Y	N	N	N	Y	Y
VERMONT								
Leahy	Y	N	Y	Y	N	Y	N	Y
Stafford	Y	N	Y	N	N	Y	N	Y
VIRGINIA								
*Byrd, H.	Y	N	Y	Y	N	Y	N	Y
Scott	N	N	Y	N	N	N	Y	Y
WASHINGTON								
Jackson	Y	N	Y	Y	Y	N	Y	Y
Magnuson	Y	N	Y	Y	Y	N	Y	Y
WEST VIRGINIA								
Byrd, R.	Y	N	Y	Y	N	N	Y	Y
Randolph	Y	-	†	-	Y	Y	N	Y
WISCONSIN								
Nelson	Y	Y	Y	Y	Y	Y	N	Y
Proxmire	Y	N	Y	Y	N	Y	N	Y
WYOMING								
Hansen	N	N	Y	N	N	N	Y	Y
Wallop	N	N	Y	N	N	Y	Y	Y

Democrats ***Republicans***

*Byrd elected as independent.

KEY

- Y Voted for (yea).
- ✓ Paired for.
- † Announced for.
- # CQ Poll for.
- N Voted against (nay).
- X Paired against.
- \- Announced against.
- ▮ CQ Poll against.
- P Voted "present."
- ● Voted "present" to avoid possible conflict of interest.
- ? Did not vote or otherwise make a position known.

144. Neel Nomination. Confirmation of President Carter's nomination of Frank H. Neel of Georgia to be a member of the board of directors of the National Railroad Passenger Corporation (Amtrak). Confirmed 61-25: R 12-22; D 49-3 (ND 33-1; SD 16-2), April 27, 1978. A "yea" was a vote supporting the president's position.

145. HR 11504. Farm Credit Revisions. Clark, D-Iowa, amendment to permit the Department of Agriculture to use certain revolving funds to upgrade and increase Farmers Home Administration (FmHA) staff. Rejected 29-62: R 1-35; D 28-27 (ND 21-16; SD 7-11), May 2, 1978.

146. HR 11504. Farm Credit Revisions. Passage of the bill to create a two-year, $4 billion "economic emergency" loan program permitting refinancing of existing farm debts; to raise individual loan levels and most interest rates for existing farm loan programs and to extend an emergency livestock credit program through Sept. 30, 1979. Passed 92-0: R 36-0; D 56-0 (ND 37-0; SD 19-0), May 2, 1978.

147. HR 8309. Waterway User Fees/Water Projects. Cranston, D-Calif., amendment, to the Gravel, D-Alaska, amendment, to delete a provision to exempt Kings River, Calif., water users from an acreage limitation imposed on them by federal reclamation law. Adopted 52-37: R 5-29; D 47-8 (ND 33-4; SD 14-4), May 2, 1978. (The Gravel amendment to authorize local flood control studies and projects was adopted subsequently by voice vote.)

148. HR 8309. Waterway User Fees/Water Projects. Gravel, D-Alaska, amendment to authorize $8 million for the establishment of an International Sea-Level Canal Study Commission. Rejected 43-49: R 5-31; D 38-18 (ND 29-8; SD 9-10), May 3, 1978.

149. HR 8309. Waterway User Fees/Water Projects. Domenici, R-N.M., amendment to phase in over 10 years a tax on inland waterway barge fuel of 12 cents per gallon, beginning with a 4 cent tax per gallon on Oct. 1, 1977; to require the secretary of transportation to recommend to Congress by Jan. 15, 1981, various ways to pay for the nation's future inland waterway needs, and to require that the Army Corps of Engineers recover, through user charges, 10 percent of the capital costs of any newly authorized water project within the first 10 years of the project's operation. Rejected 43-47: R 16-19; D 27-28 (ND 22-15; SD 5-13), May 3, 1978. A "yea" was a vote supporting the president's position.

150. HR 8309. Waterway User Fees/Water Projects. Long, D-La., motion to table (kill) the Baker, R-Tenn., motion to reconsider the vote rejecting the Domenici, R-N.M., amendment *(see vote 149, above)*. Motion agreed to 49-41: R 20-15; D 29-26 (ND 15-22; SD 14-4), May 3, 1978.

151. HR 8309. Waterway User Fees/Water Projects. Long, D-La., amendment to phase in over 10 years a tax on inland waterway barge fuel of 12 cents per gallon, beginning with a 4 cent tax per gallon on Jan. 1, 1982, or as of construction of a new Locks and Dam 26 at Alton, Ill., whichever came first; and to require the secretary of transportation to report to Congress within three years of the bill's enactment on the impact and need for waterway user charges and fuel taxes. Adopted 88-2: R 34-2; D 54-0 (ND 36-0; SD 18-0), May 3, 1978. A "nay" was a vote supporting the president's position.

CQ Senate Votes 152-157

Corresponding to Congressional Record Votes 152, 153, 154, 155, 156, 157

	152	153	154	155	156	157
ALABAMA						
Allen	Y	Y	Y	Y	Y	N
Sparkman	Y	Y	N	Y	Y	N
ALASKA						
Gravel	Y	Y	▮	▮	#	N
Stevens	N	Y	N	N	N	N
ARIZONA						
DeConcini	Y	Y	N	N	Y	Y
Goldwater	N	Y	N	N	N	N
ARKANSAS						
Bumpers	N	Y	?	?	Y	N
Hodges	Y	Y	N	N	Y	N
CALIFORNIA						
Cranston	Y	Y	N	N	Y	N
Hayakawa	N	Y	Y	N	N	N
COLORADO						
Hart	?	?	N	N	Y	N
Haskell	?	?	N	Y	Y	N
CONNECTICUT						
Ribicoff	Y	Y	N	Y	Y	N
Weicker	N	N	N	Y	N	N
DELAWARE						
Biden	Y	N	?	?	Y	Y
Roth	Y	N	N	N	N	N
FLORIDA						
Chiles	Y	Y	Y	Y	Y	N
Stone	Y	Y	N	N	Y	Y
GEORGIA						
Nunn	Y	Y	?	?	Y	N
Talmadge	Y	Y	N	Y	Y	N
HAWAII						
Inouye	?	?	?	?	Y	N
Matsunaga	Y	Y	?	N	Y	N
IDAHO						
Church	Y	Y	-	-	Y	N
McClure	N	Y	Y	N	N	N
ILLINOIS						
Stevenson	Y	Y	▮	?	Y	N
Percy	Y	Y	N	Y	N	N
INDIANA						
Bayh	Y	Y	N	N	Y	N
Lugar	N	Y	Y	Y	N	N
IOWA						
Clark	Y	Y	N	N	Y	Y
Culver	Y	Y	N	N	Y	N
KANSAS						
Dole	Y	Y	N	Y	N	N
Pearson	?	?	?	?	Y	N
KENTUCKY						
Ford	N	Y	?	?	Y	N
Huddleston	Y	Y	N	Y	Y	N
LOUISIANA						
Johnston	Y	Y	?	?	Y	N
Long	?	Y	?	?	Y	N
MAINE						
Hathaway	Y	Y	?	?	Y	Y
Muskie	Y	Y	N	Y	Y	N
MARYLAND						
Sarbanes	Y	Y	N	N	Y	N
Mathias	Y	Y	?	?	Y	N
MASSACHUSETTS						
Kennedy	Y	Y	N	N	Y	N
Brooke	N	N	?	?	Y	N
MICHIGAN						
Riegle	Y	Y	N	N	Y	Y
Griffin	N	Y	?	?	N	N
MINNESOTA						
Anderson	Y	Y	N	N	†	✓
Humphrey, M.	Y	Y	-	-	Y	Y
MISSISSIPPI						
Eastland	Y	Y	?	?	Y	N
Stennis	Y	Y	N	Y	Y	N
MISSOURI						
Eagleton	Y	Y	?	?	Y	N
Danforth	Y	Y	N	N	Y	N
MONTANA						
Melcher	Y	Y	Y	Y	Y	Y
Hatfield, P.	Y	Y	▮	#	#	▮
NEBRASKA						
Zorinsky	Y	Y	Y	Y	Y	Y
Curtis	Y	Y	Y	Y	N	N
NEVADA						
Cannon	?	?	?	?	Y	N
Laxalt	N	Y	?	?	?	?
NEW HAMPSHIRE						
Durkin	Y	Y	N	N	Y	Y
McIntyre	?	X	✓	†	Y	Y
NEW JERSEY						
Williams	Y	Y	N	N	Y	N
Case	N	Y	N	N	Y	N
NEW MEXICO						
Domenici	Y	N	?	?	Y	Y
Schmitt	N	N	Y	Y	Y	Y
NEW YORK						
Moynihan	Y	Y	N	Y	Y	N
Javits	N	Y	N	N	Y	N
NORTH CAROLINA						
Morgan	-	✓	?	Y	Y	N
Helms	N	N	Y	Y	N	N
NORTH DAKOTA						
Burdick	N	Y	▮	#	Y	N
Young	Y	Y	N	Y	N	N
OHIO						
Glenn	Y	Y	N	Y	Y	N
Metzenbaum	N	Y	N	Y	Y	Y
OKLAHOMA						
Bartlett	Y	Y	?	?	N	N
Bellmon	N	Y	?	?	N	N
OREGON						
Hatfield, M.	Y	Y	Y	N	Y	N
Packwood	Y	Y	Y	N	?	?
PENNSYLVANIA						
Heinz	Y	Y	Y	N	N	Y
Schweiker	N	Y	?	?	N	N
RHODE ISLAND						
Pell	Y	N	N	N	Y	Y
Chafee	Y	N	N	Y	Y	N
SOUTH CAROLINA						
Hollings	Y	Y	N	Y	Y	Y
Thurmond	N	Y	Y	Y	Y	N
SOUTH DAKOTA						
Abourezk	Y	Y	▮	#	Y	Y
McGovern	Y	Y	▮	#	Y	N
TENNESSEE						
Sasser	Y	Y	N	N	Y	N
Baker	Y	Y	N	N	N	N
TEXAS						
Bentsen	Y	Y	N	N	Y	N
Tower	N	Y	?	?	N	N
UTAH						
Garn	N	Y	?	?	N	N
Hatch	N	N	Y	Y	Y	N
VERMONT						
Leahy	N	N	N	Y	Y	N
Stafford	N	Y	N	Y	Y	N
VIRGINIA						
*Byrd, H.	N	N	N	Y	Y	N
Scott	N	Y	?	Y	Y	N
WASHINGTON						
Jackson	Y	Y	N	Y	Y	N
Magnuson	Y	Y	-	†	Y	Y
WEST VIRGINIA						
Byrd, R.	Y	Y	N	Y	Y	N
Randolph	Y	Y	N	Y	†	X
WISCONSIN						
Nelson	N	Y	N	Y	Y	N
Proxmire	N	N	N	Y	Y	Y
WYOMING						
Hansen	Y	Y	Y	Y	N	N
Wallop	Y	Y	?	N	N	N

Democrats ***Republicans***

**Byrd elected as independent.*

KEY

- Y Voted for (yea).
- ✓ Paired for.
- † Announced for.
- # CQ Poll for.
- N Voted against (nay).
- X Paired against.
- \- Announced against.
- ▮ CQ Poll against.
- P Voted "present."
- ● Voted "present" to avoid possible conflict of interest.
- ? Did not vote or otherwise make a position known.

152. HR 8309. Waterway User Fees/Water Projects. Gravel, D-Alaska, amendment to authorize $8 million for the establishment of an International Sea-Level Canal Study Commission to study the feasibility of a canal route through Panama. Adopted 63-29: R 16-21; D 47-8 (ND 33-5; SD 14-3), May 4, 1978. (A similar amendment offered by Gravel was rejected May 3. *See vote 148, p. 25-S)*

153. HR 8309. Waterway User Fees/Water Projects. Passage of the bill to authorize construction of a replacement for Locks and Dam 26 at Alton, Ill.; to impose a tax on barge fuel beginning at 6 cents per gallon and rising to 12 cents after 10 years; to establish a commission to study the feasibility of a sea-level canal in Panama; and to authorize approximately $2 billion for public works projects. Passed 80-13: R 29-8; D 51-5 (ND 34-4; SD 17-1), May 4, 1978. A "nay" was a vote supporting the president's position.

154. S Res 219. Senior Citizen Interns. Curtis, R-Neb., amendment to amend the Standing Rules of the Senate by requiring the attendance of 25 senators on the floor in order to transact any business. Rejected 16-48: R 12-13; D 4-35 (ND 2-25; SD 2-10), May 5, 1978.

155. S Res 219. Senior Citizen Interns. Allen, D-Ala., amendment to fund the Senate senior citizen intern program from the clerk-hire and travel allowance of individual senators employing the interns. Adopted 37-31: R 14-13; D 23-18 (ND 14-14; SD 9-4), May 5, 1978. (The resolution to establish a two-week Senate intern program for U.S. citizens 60 years or older was adopted subsequently by voice vote.)

156. Civiletti Nomination. Confirmation of President Carter's nomination of Benjamin R. Civiletti of Maryland to be deputy attorney general of the United States. Confirmed 72-22: R 14-22; D 58-0 (ND 39-0; SD 19-0), May 9, 1978. A "yea" was a vote supporting the president's position.

157. Coleman Nomination. Metzenbaum, D-Ohio, motion to recommit (kill) to the Energy and Natural Resources Committee President Carter's nomination of Lynn R. Coleman of the District of Columbia to be general counsel to the Department of Energy. Motion rejected 20-75: R 3-33; D 17-42 (ND 15-25; SD 2-17), May 9, 1978. A "nay" was a vote supporting the president's position. (The nomination was confirmed subsequently by voice vote.)

KEY

- Y Voted for (yea).
- ✓ Paired for.
- † Announced for.
- # CQ Poll for.
- N Voted against (nay).
- X Paired against.
- \- Announced against.
- ▌ CQ Poll against.
- P Voted "present."
- ● Voted "present" to avoid possible conflict of interest.
- ? Did not vote or otherwise make a position known.

	158	159	160	161	162	163	164
ALABAMA							
Allen [1]	Y	Y	Y	Y			
Sparkman	N	Y	Y	N	N	X	✓
ALASKA							
Gravel	Y	Y	Y	N	#	Y	Y
Stevens	Y	Y	Y	N	N	N	N
ARIZONA							
DeConcini	N	Y	Y	Y	Y	Y	N
Goldwater	Y	Y	Y	N	N	N	N
ARKANSAS							
Bumpers	Y	Y	Y	N	N	N	N
Hodges	Y	Y	Y	N	N	N	N
CALIFORNIA							
Cranston	N	Y	Y	Y	Y	Y	Y
Hayakawa	Y	?	Y	N	N	N	N
COLORADO							
Hart	N	Y	Y	Y	Y	Y	Y
Haskell	N	Y	Y	Y	Y	Y	Y
CONNECTICUT							
Ribicoff	N	Y	Y	N	Y	Y	Y
Weicker	Y	Y	Y	Y	Y	Y	Y
DELAWARE							
Biden	N	Y	?	Y	Y	?	Y
Roth	Y	Y	?	Y	N	N	N
FLORIDA							
Chiles	Y	Y	Y	Y	N	N	N
Stone	N	Y	Y	Y	N	N	N
GEORGIA							
Nunn	?	Y	Y	Y	N	N	N
Talmadge	Y	Y	Y	Y	N	N	N
HAWAII							
Inouye	Y	Y	Y	N	Y	Y	?
Matsunaga	N	Y	Y	Y	Y	Y	Y
IDAHO							
Church	Y	Y	Y	Y	Y	Y	Y
McClure	Y	Y	Y	N	N	N	N
ILLINOIS							
Stevenson	N	Y	#	N	Y	Y	Y
Percy	Y	Y	Y	N	N	N	N
INDIANA							
Bayh	N	Y	Y	Y	Y	Y	Y
Lugar	Y	Y	Y	N	N	N	N
IOWA							
Clark	N	Y	Y	Y	Y	Y	Y
Culver	N	Y	Y	N	Y	Y	Y
KANSAS							
Dole	Y	Y	Y	Y	N	N	N
Pearson	Y	Y	Y	N	Y	Y	N
KENTUCKY							
Ford	Y	Y	Y	Y	N	Y	Y
Huddleston	Y	Y	Y	?	N	Y	Y
LOUISIANA							
Johnston	Y	Y	Y	N	N	N	N
Long	Y	Y	Y	N	N	N	Y
MAINE							
Hathaway	N	Y	Y	Y	Y	Y	Y
Muskie	N	Y	Y	N	?	Y	Y
MARYLAND							
Sarbanes	N	Y	Y	Y	Y	Y	Y
Mathias	N	Y	Y	N	Y	Y	Y
MASSACHUSETTS							
Kennedy	N	Y	Y	Y	Y	Y	Y
Brooke	N	Y	Y	Y	†	?	Y
MICHIGAN							
Riegle	N	Y	Y	Y	Y	Y	Y
Griffin	N	Y	Y	N	N	N	N
MINNESOTA							
Anderson	-	Y	Y	Y	Y	Y	Y
Humphrey, M.	N	Y	Y	N	†	†	✓
MISSISSIPPI							
Eastland	Y	Y	Y	N	N	?	?
Stennis	Y	Y	Y	N	N	N	N
MISSOURI							
Eagleton	N	Y	Y	N	Y	Y	Y
Danforth	Y	Y	Y	N	N	N	N
MONTANA							
Melcher	N	Y	Y	Y	Y	Y	Y
Hatfield, P.	#	#	#	N	#	Y	Y
NEBRASKA							
Zorinsky	N	Y	Y	Y	N	N	X
Curtis	Y	Y	?	N	N	N	N
NEVADA							
Cannon	Y	Y	Y	N	X	N	N
Laxalt	?	?	?	?	N	N	N
NEW HAMPSHIRE							
Durkin	N	Y	Y	Y	Y	Y	Y
McIntyre	N	Y	Y	Y	N	Y	Y
NEW JERSEY							
Williams	N	Y	Y	Y	Y	Y	Y
Case	N	Y	?	Y	#	Y	Y
NEW MEXICO							
Domenici	Y	Y	Y	Y	N	?	?
Schmitt	Y	Y	Y	N	N	?	?
NEW YORK							
Moynihan	N	Y	Y	Y	Y	Y	Y
Javits	Y	Y	Y	Y	Y	Y	Y
NORTH CAROLINA							
Morgan	Y	Y	Y	N	N	N	X
Helms	Y	Y	Y	N	N	N	N
NORTH DAKOTA							
Burdick	Y	Y	Y	Y	Y	Y	Y
Young	Y	Y	Y	N	N	N	N
OHIO							
Glenn	Y	Y	Y	N	Y	Y	Y
Metzenbaum	X	Y	Y	Y	Y	Y	Y
OKLAHOMA							
Bartlett	Y	Y	Y	N	N	N	N
Bellmon	Y	Y	Y	N	N	N	N
OREGON							
Hatfield, M.	Y	Y	Y	Y	Y	†	✓
Packwood	?	?	Y	Y	Y	Y	Y
PENNSYLVANIA							
Heinz	Y	Y	Y	Y	N	N	Y
Schweiker	Y	Y	Y	Y	Y	Y	Y
RHODE ISLAND							
Pell	N	Y	Y	Y	Y	Y	Y
Chafee	Y	Y	Y	N	Y	Y	Y
SOUTH CAROLINA							
Hollings	Y	Y	Y	N	N	N	N
Thurmond	Y	Y	Y	N	N	N	N
SOUTH DAKOTA							
Abourezk	N	Y	#	N	#	Y	Y
McGovern	N	Y	Y	N	Y	Y	Y
TENNESSEE							
Sasser	N	Y	Y	Y	✓	Y	Y
Baker	Y	Y	Y	N	N	N	N
TEXAS							
Bentsen	Y	Y	Y	N	N	N	N
Tower	Y	Y	Y	N	N	N	N
UTAH							
Garn	Y	Y	Y	N	N	N	N
Hatch	Y	Y	Y	N	N	N	N
VERMONT							
Leahy	N	Y	Y	N	Y	Y	Y
Stafford	Y	Y	Y	N	N	N	Y
VIRGINIA							
*Byrd, H.	Y	Y	Y	N	N	N	N
Scott	Y	Y	Y	N	N	N	N
WASHINGTON							
Jackson	Y	Y	Y	Y	Y	Y	Y
Magnuson	N	Y	Y	N	†	✓	†
WEST VIRGINIA							
Byrd, R.	Y	Y	Y	N	Y	Y	Y
Randolph	✓	†	Y	N	Y	Y	Y
WISCONSIN							
Nelson	N	Y	Y	Y	Y	Y	Y
Proxmire	N	Y	Y	Y	Y	Y	Y
WYOMING							
Hansen	Y	Y	Y	N	N	N	X
Wallop	Y	Y	Y	N	N	N	N

Democrats ***Republicans***

1 *Sen. James B. Allen, D-Ala., died June 1, 1978.*

**Byrd elected as independent.*

158. HR 130. Petroleum Marketing Practices. Bumpers, D-Ark., motion to table (kill) the Kennedy, D-Mass., amendment to provide that any energy information acquired by the Energy Department under the act be shared with other specified government agencies. Motion agreed to 55-38: R 32-4; D 23-34 (ND 8-31; SD 15-3), May 9, 1978.

159. HR 130. Petroleum Marketing Practices. Passage of the bill to protect franchised distributors and retailers of motor fuel and to encourage competition. Passed 95-0: R 35-0; D 60-0 (ND 41-0; SD 19-0), May 9, 1978.

160. HR 2176. Banking Agency Audits. Brooke, R-Mass., amendment to delete language requiring the General Accounting Office (GAO) to disclose confidential financial information concerning individual banks or bank customers to congressional committees sitting in executive session. Adopted 92-0: R 34-0; D 58-0 (ND 39-0; SD 19-0), May 10, 1978. (The bill authorizing the GAO to audit records of the Federal Reserve Board and member banks, the Federal Deposit Insurance Corporation and the Office of the Comptroller of the Currency was passed subsequently by voice vote.)

161. S Con Res 86. Mideast Fighter Plane Sales. Adoption of the resolution to disapprove the sale of $4.5 billion worth of jet fighter planes to Israel, Saudi Arabia and Egypt. Rejected 44-54: R 11-26; D 33-28 (ND 26-17; SD 7-11) May 15, 1978. A "nay" was a vote supporting the president's position.

162. HR 8410. Labor Law Revision. Byrd, D-W.Va., motion to invoke cloture (cut off debate) on the bill to amend the National Labor Relations Act. Motion rejected 42-47: R 8-28; D 34-19 (ND 34-2; SD 0-17), June 7, 1978. A three-fifths majority vote (60) of the total Senate membership is required to invoke cloture.

163. HR 8410. Labor Law Revision. Byrd, D-W.Va., motion to invoke cloture (cut off debate) on the bill to amend the National Labor Relations Act. Rejected 49-41: R 8-26; D 41-15 (ND 38-2; SD 3-13), June 8, 1978. A three-fifths majority vote (60) of the total Senate membership is required to invoke cloture.

164. HR 8410. Labor Law Revision. Byrd, D-W.Va., motion to table (kill) the Baker, R-Tenn., motion to recommit the bill to the Human Resources Committee with instructions to the committee to conduct further hearings on amendments and the inflationary impact of the bill and to report the bill back to the Senate on July 17, 1978. Motion agreed to 51-37: R 10-24; D 41-13 (ND 37-2; SD 4-11), June 8, 1978.

CQ Senate Votes 165-168

Corresponding to Congressional Record Votes 165, 166, 167, 168

	165	166	167	168
ALABAMA				
Allen, M.†	N	N	N	N
Sparkman	N	N	N	N
ALASKA				
Gravel	Y	Y	Y	Y
Stevens	N	Y	Y	✓
ARIZONA				
DeConcini	Y	Y	Y	Y
Goldwater	N	N	N	N
ARKANSAS				
Bumpers	N	N	N	N
Hodges	N	N	N	N
CALIFORNIA				
Cranston	Y	Y	Y	N
Hayakawa	N	N	N	N
COLORADO				
Hart	Y	Y	Y	Y
Haskell	Y	Y	Y	Y
CONNECTICUT				
Ribicoff	Y	Y	Y	Y
Weicker	#	Y	Y	Y
DELAWARE				
Biden	Y	Y	Y	Y
Roth	N	N	N	N
FLORIDA				
Chiles	N	N	N	N
Stone	N	N	N	N
GEORGIA				
Nunn	N	N	N	N
Talmadge	N	N	N	N
HAWAII				
Inouye	Y	Y	Y	Y
Matsunaga	Y	Y	Y	Y
IDAHO				
Church	Y	Y	Y	Y
McClure	N	N	N	N
ILLINOIS				
Stevenson	Y	Y	Y	Y
Percy	N	Y	Y	N
INDIANA				
Bayh	Y	Y	Y	Y
Lugar	N	N	N	N
IOWA				
Clark	Y	Y	Y	Y
Culver	Y	Y	Y	Y
KANSAS				
Dole	N	N	N	N
Pearson	Y	Y	Y	Y
KENTUCKY				
Ford	Y	Y	Y	Y
Huddleston	Y	Y	Y	Y
LOUISIANA				
Johnston	N	N	N	N
Long	N	N	N	N
MAINE				
Hathaway	Y	Y	Y	Y
Muskie	Y	Y	Y	N
MARYLAND				
Sarbanes	Y	Y	Y	Y
Mathias	Y	Y	Y	Y
MASSACHUSETTS				
Kennedy	Y	Y	Y	Y
Brooke	Y	Y	Y	Y
MICHIGAN				
Riegle	Y	Y	Y	Y
Griffin	N	N	N	N
MINNESOTA				
Anderson	Y	Y	Y	Y
Humphrey, M.	Y	Y	Y	Y
MISSISSIPPI				
Eastland	N	N	N	N
Stennis	N	N	?	X
MISSOURI				
Eagleton	Y	Y	Y	Y
Danforth	N	N	N	N
MONTANA				
Melcher	Y	Y	Y	Y
Hatfield, P.	Y	Y	Y	Y
NEBRASKA				
Zorinsky	N	N	N	N
Curtis	N	N	N	N
NEVADA				
Cannon	N	N	N	N
Laxalt	N	N	-	N
NEW HAMPSHIRE				
Durkin	Y	Y	Y	Y
McIntyre	Y	Y	Y	Y
NEW JERSEY				
Williams	Y	Y	Y	Y
Case	Y	Y	Y	Y
NEW MEXICO				
Domenici	N	N	-	N
Schmitt	N	N	N	N
NEW YORK				
Moynihan	Y	Y	Y	Y
Javits	Y	Y	Y	Y
NORTH CAROLINA				
Morgan	N	-	N	N
Helms	N	N	N	N
NORTH DAKOTA				
Burdick	Y	Y	Y	Y
Young	N	N	N	N
OHIO				
Glenn	Y	Y	Y	Y
Metzenbaum	Y	Y	Y	Y
OKLAHOMA				
Bartlett	?	N	N	N
Bellmon	N	N	N	N
OREGON				
Hatfield, M.	Y	Y	Y	Y
Packwood	Y	Y	Y	Y
PENNSYLVANIA				
Heinz	N	Y	Y	Y
Schweiker	Y	Y	Y	Y
RHODE ISLAND				
Pell	Y	Y	Y	Y
Chafee	Y	Y	Y	Y
SOUTH CAROLINA				
Hollings	N	N	N	N
Thurmond	N	N	N	N
SOUTH DAKOTA				
Abourezk	Y	Y	Y	Y
McGovern	Y	Y	Y	Y
TENNESSEE				
Sasser	Y	Y	Y	Y
Baker	N	N	N	N
TEXAS				
Bentsen	N	N	N	N
Tower	N	N	N	N
UTAH				
Garn	N	N	N	N
Hatch	N	N	N	N
VERMONT				
Leahy	Y	Y	Y	Y
Stafford	Y	Y	Y	Y
VIRGINIA				
*Byrd, H.	N	N	N	N
Scott	N	N	N	N
WASHINGTON				
Jackson	Y	Y	Y	Y
Magnuson	Y	Y	Y	Y
WEST VIRGINIA				
Byrd, R.	Y	Y	Y	N
Randolph	Y	Y	Y	Y
WISCONSIN				
Nelson	Y	Y	Y	Y
Proxmire	Y	Y	Y	Y
WYOMING				
Hansen	▮	N	N	N
Wallop	N	N	N	N

KEY

- Y Voted for (yea).
- ✓ Paired for.
- † Announced for.
- # CQ Poll for.
- N Voted against (nay).
- X Paired against.
- \- Announced against.
- ▮ CQ Poll against.
- P Voted "present."
- ● Voted "present" to avoid possible conflict of interest.
- ? Did not vote or otherwise make a position known.

Democrats ***Republicans***

† Maryon Allen, D-Ala., was sworn in on June 12, 1978, to fill the vacancy created by the death of her husband.

**Byrd elected as independent.*

165. HR 8410. Labor Law Revision. Byrd, D-W.Va., motion to invoke cloture (cut off debate) on the Byrd, D-W.Va., substitute to the bill to amend the National Labor Relations Act. Motion rejected 54-43: R 10-25; D 44-18 (ND 41-2; SD 3-16), June 13, 1978. A three-fifths majority vote (60) of the total Senate membership is required to invoke cloture.

166. HR 8410. Labor Law Revision. Byrd, D-W.Va., motion to invoke cloture (cut off debate) on the Byrd, D-W.Va., substitute to the bill to amend the National Labor Relations Act. Motion rejected 58-41: R 14-24; D 44-17 (ND 41-2; SD 3-15), June 14, 1978. A three-fifths majority vote (60) of the total Senate membership is required to invoke cloture.

167. HR 8410. Labor Law Revision. Byrd, D-W.Va., motion to invoke cloture (cut off debate) on the Byrd, D-W.Va., substitute to the bill to amend the National Labor Relations Act. Motion rejected 58-39: R 14-22; D 44-17 (ND 41-2; SD 3-15), June 15, 1978. A three-fifths majority vote (60) of the total Senate membership is required to invoke cloture.

168. HR 8410. Labor Law Revision. Byrd, D-W.Va., motion to invoke cloture (cut off debate) on the Byrd, D-W.Va., substitute to the bill to amend the National Labor Relations Act. Motion rejected 53-45: R 12-25; D 41-20 (ND 38-5; SD 3-15), June 22, 1978. A three-fifths majority vote (60) of the total Senate membership is required to invoke cloture.

Corresponding to Congressional Record Votes 169, 170, 171, 172, 173, 174, 175, 176

	169	170	171	172	173	174	175	176
ALABAMA								
Allen, M.	Y	Y	Y	N	Y	N	Y	Y
Sparkman	X	Y	N	Y	Y	Y	N	Y
ALASKA								
Gravel	Y	Y	N	Y	#	#	▮	▮
Stevens	Y	N	N	Y	Y	N	Y	Y
ARIZONA								
DeConcini	Y	N	Y	Y	Y	N	Y	Y
Goldwater	N	N	Y	N	N	N	Y	Y
ARKANSAS								
Bumpers	N	Y	N	Y	Y	N	Y	Y
Hodges	Y	N	N	Y	?	?	?	?
CALIFORNIA								
Cranston	N	Y	N	Y	Y	Y	N	Y
Hayakawa	N	Y	Y	N	N	N	Y	Y
COLORADO								
Hart	Y	N	?	?	Y	N	Y	Y
Haskell	?	?	?	?	?	?	Y	Y
CONNECTICUT								
Ribicoff	N	Y	N	Y	Y	N	N	Y
Weicker	N	Y	N	Y	#	▮	▮	#
DELAWARE								
Biden	N	Y	Y	N	Y	N	Y	Y
Roth	N	Y	Y	N	Y	N	Y	Y
FLORIDA								
Chiles	N	Y	N	Y	Y	N	Y	Y
Stone	N	Y	Y	Y	Y	Y	Y	Y
GEORGIA								
Nunn	N	Y	?	?	Y	N	Y	Y
Talmadge	N	Y	Y	Y	Y	N	Y	Y
HAWAII								
Inouye	?	?	?	#	#	#	▮	#
Matsunaga	✓	Y	N	Y	Y	Y	N	Y
IDAHO								
Church	Y	N	N	Y	Y	Y	N	Y
McClure	Y	N	Y	N	N	N	Y	Y
ILLINOIS								
Stevenson	N	Y	N	#	Y	Y	N	Y
Percy	N	Y	N	Y	?	?	?	?
INDIANA								
Bayh	N	Y	N	Y	?	?	?	?
Lugar	N	Y	Y	N	Y	N	Y	Y
IOWA								
Clark	Y	N	N	Y	†	†	-	†
Culver	Y	N	N	Y	Y	Y	N	N
KANSAS								
Dole	N	Y	N	Y	Y	N	Y	Y
Pearson	N	Y	Y	Y	Y	N	Y	Y
KENTUCKY								
Ford	?	?	?	?	Y	N	Y	Y
Huddleston	N	Y	N	Y	Y	N	Y	Y
LOUISIANA								
Johnston	▮	#	?	?	Y	Y	Y	Y
Long	X	✓	?	?	?	?	?	?
MAINE								
Hathaway	?	?	?	?	?	?	?	?
Muskie	Y	X	N	Y	Y	N	Y	Y
MARYLAND								
Sarbanes	Y	N	N	Y	Y	Y	N	Y
Mathias	?	?	?	?	Y	Y	N	Y
MASSACHUSETTS								
Kennedy	Y	N	N	Y	Y	Y	N	N
Brooke	?	?	?	?	?	?	?	?
MICHIGAN								
Riegle	Y	N	N	Y	Y	Y	N	Y
Griffin	-	†	?	?	Y	N	Y	Y
MINNESOTA								
Anderson	†	?	?	†	?	?	?	?
Humphrey, M.	Y	N	N	Y	†	†	-	†
MISSISSIPPI								
Eastland	N	Y	?	?	?	?	?	?
Stennis	?	?	?	?	?	?	?	?
MISSOURI								
Eagleton	N	Y	N	Y	Y	Y	Y	Y
Danforth	N	Y	Y	?	Y	N	Y	Y
MONTANA								
Melcher	Y	N	N	Y	Y	Y	Y	Y
Hatfield, P.	Y	N	#	Y	Y	N	Y	Y
NEBRASKA								
Zorinsky	Y	N	Y	Y	Y	N	Y	Y
Curtis	N	Y	Y	Y	N	N	Y	Y
NEVADA								
Cannon	Y	N	?	?	Y	N	Y	Y
Laxalt	Y	N	Y	Y	?	?	?	?
NEW HAMPSHIRE								
Durkin	Y	N	N	N	Y	Y	Y	Y
McIntyre	Y	N	?	†	Y	Y	N	Y
NEW JERSEY								
Williams	N	Y	N	Y	Y	Y	N	Y
Case	N	Y	N	Y	Y	Y	N	Y
NEW MEXICO								
Domenici	Y	N	Y	Y	Y	N	Y	Y
Schmitt	Y	N	Y	Y	Y	N	Y	Y
NEW YORK								
Moynihan	N	Y	N	Y	Y	Y	Y	Y
Javits	N	Y	N	Y	?	?	?	?
NORTH CAROLINA								
Morgan	X	†	?	†	Y	N	N	Y
Helms	Y	Y	Y	N	N	N	Y	Y
NORTH DAKOTA								
Burdick	✓	✓	▮	†	Y	N	Y	Y
Young	?	?	?	?	Y	N	Y	Y
OHIO								
Glenn	N	Y	N	Y	Y	N	N	Y
Metzenbaum	Y	N	N	Y	Y	Y	N	Y
OKLAHOMA								
Bartlett	N	Y	Y	N	N	N	Y	Y
Bellmon	?	?	?	?	Y	N	N	Y
OREGON								
Hatfield, M.	Y	N	N	Y	Y	N	Y	Y
Packwood	Y	N	N	Y	Y	N	Y	Y
PENNSYLVANIA								
Heinz	N	Y	N	Y	Y	Y	Y	Y
Schweiker	N	Y	N	Y	Y	Y	Y	Y
RHODE ISLAND								
Pell	N	Y	?	?	Y	Y	N	Y
Chafee	N	Y	Y	Y	Y	Y	N	N
SOUTH CAROLINA								
Hollings	N	Y	N	Y	Y	N	Y	Y
Thurmond	N	Y	†	-	†	-	†	†
SOUTH DAKOTA								
Abourezk	✓	N	▮	#	Y	Y	Y	N
McGovern	Y	Y	N	Y	#	#	▮	▮
TENNESSEE								
Sasser	N	N	Y	Y	?	?	?	?
Baker	?	†	?	?	?	?	?	?
TEXAS								
Bentsen	X	✓	?	?	Y	Y	Y	Y
Tower	N	Y	?	?	N	N	Y	Y
UTAH								
Garn	Y	N	Y	N	?	?	?	?
Hatch	N	Y	Y	N	Y	N	Y	Y
VERMONT								
Leahy	Y	Y	N	Y	Y	Y	N	Y
Stafford	N	Y	N	Y	Y	Y	N	Y
VIRGINIA								
*Byrd, H.	N	Y	Y	N	Y	N	Y	Y
Scott	Y	N	?	?	N	N	Y	Y
WASHINGTON								
Jackson	N	Y	N	Y	Y	Y	Y	Y
Magnuson	Y	N	N	Y	Y	Y	Y	Y
WEST VIRGINIA								
Byrd, R.	✓	N	N	Y	Y	N	Y	Y
Randolph	N	Y	N	Y	Y	N	Y	Y
WISCONSIN								
Nelson	N	Y	?	?	Y	N	Y	Y
Proxmire	Y	N	Y	N	N	N	Y	Y
WYOMING								
Hansen	N	Y	Y	N	N	N	Y	Y
Wallop	?	?	?	Y	Y	N	Y	Y

Democrats ***Republicans***

Byrd elected as independent.

KEY

- Y Voted for (yea).
- ✓ Paired for.
- † Announced for.
- # CQ Poll for.
- N Voted against (nay).
- X Paired against.
- - Announced against.
- ▮ CQ Poll against.
- P Voted "present."
- ● Voted "present" to avoid possible conflict of interest.
- ? Did not vote or otherwise make a position known.

169. Exec K, 94th Cong, 2nd Sess. U.S.-U.K. Tax Convention. Church, D-Idaho, reservation to nullify an article that would prohibit states from using the unitary method of accounting in determining state tax liability of British corporations. Rejected 34-44: R 10-21; D 24-23 (ND 22-13; SD 2-10), June 23, 1978. A "nay" was a vote supporting the president's position.

170. Exec K, 94th Cong, 2nd Sess. U.S.-U.K. Tax Convention. Adoption of the resolution of ratification of the U.S.-U.K. Tax Convention and protocols (Exec Q, 94th Cong, 2nd Sess, and Exec J, 95th Cong, 1st Sess) to revise the relationship between the United States and the United Kingdom with respect to income taxes. Rejected 49-32: R 21-10; D 28-22 (ND 17-20; SD 11-2), June 23, 1978. A two-thirds majority vote (54 in this case) is required for adoption of resolutions of ratification. A "yea" was a vote supporting the president's position.

171. HR 12933. Transportation Appropriations, Fiscal 1979. Lugar, R-Ind., amendment to reduce the appropriation for the Urban Mass Transportation Administration by $170 million. Rejected 26-44: R 17-11; D 9-33 (ND 4-27; SD 5-6), June 23, 1978.

172. HR 12933. Transportation Appropriations, Fiscal 1979. Passage of the bill to appropriate $8,568,543,096 in new budget authority for the Transportation Department and related agencies for fiscal year 1979. Passed 55-15: R 18-10; D 37-5 (ND 28-3; SD 9-2), June 23, 1978. The president had requested $9,268,623,096 in new budget authority.

173. S 2579. Research on Human Subjects. Passage of the bill to extend for four years the National Commission for the Protection of Human Subjects of Biomedical and Behavioral Research and to broaden the commission's authority to review ethical, social and legal issues in research, and to authorize $24 million for the life of the commission. Passed 68-10: R 21-9; D 47-1 (ND 33-1; SD 14-0), June 26, 1978.

174. S 2466. National Institute of Health Care Research. Passage of the bill to create a National Institute of Health Care Research that would include separate centers or institutes for medical technology evaluation, health statistics, epidemiology and health services, and to authorize $440 million for the institute for fiscal 1979-81. Rejected 30-48: R 6-24; D 24-24 (ND 20-14; SD 4-10), June 26, 1978.

175. S 3074. Foreign Economic Aid. Byrd, Ind-Va., amendment to reduce the $1,860,504,000 Foreign Relations Committee-recommended authorization for fiscal 1979 foreign economic aid programs by 5 percent. Adopted 57-22: R 25-5; D 32-17 (ND 20-15; SD 12-2), June 26, 1978.

176. S 3074. Foreign Economic Aid. Helms, R-N.C., amendment to prohibit aid to Vietnam, Cambodia, Uganda and Cuba. Adopted 75-4: R 29-1; D 46-3 (ND 32-3; SD 14-0), June 26, 1978.

CQ Senate Votes 177-184

Corresponding to Congressional Record Votes 177, 178, 179, 180, 181, 182, 183, 184

	177	178	179	180	181	182	183	184
ALABAMA								
Allen, M.	N	Y	Y	N	Y	Y	N	Y
Sparkman	Y	Y	N	Y	N	Y	N	▮
ALASKA								
Gravel	#	▮	▮	†	#	?	▮	▮
Stevens	N	Y	Y	N	Y	Y	N	Y
ARIZONA								
DeConcini	N	Y	†	N	N	Y	Y	N
Goldwater	N	N	Y	N	N	Y	N	?
ARKANSAS								
Bumpers	Y	Y	Y	Y	N	Y	Y	N
Hodges	?	Y	N	Y	N	N	N	Y
CALIFORNIA								
Cranston	Y	Y	N	Y	N	Y	Y	N
Hayakawa	Y	?	?	?	?	?	?	?
COLORADO								
Hart	Y	Y	Y	Y	N	Y	N	N
Haskell	Y	Y	N	Y	N	Y	N	N
CONNECTICUT								
Ribicoff	Y	Y	N	N	N	Y	Y	N
Weicker	#	Y	N	N	N	Y	Y	?
DELAWARE								
Biden	Y	Y	Y	N	N	Y	N	Y
Roth	N	Y	Y	N	N	Y	N	Y
FLORIDA								
Chiles	Y	Y	N	N	N	Y	Y	N
Stone	Y	Y	Y	N	N	Y	Y	N
GEORGIA								
Nunn	N	Y	Y	Y	N	Y	N	Y
Talmadge	N	Y	N	Y	N	Y	Y	Y
HAWAII								
Inouye	#	#	#	#	#	#	#	▮
Matsunaga	Y	Y	N	Y	Y	Y	Y	N
IDAHO								
Church	Y	Y	Y	Y	N	Y	N	N
McClure	N	N	Y	N	N	Y	N	Y
ILLINOIS								
Stevenson	Y	Y	N	Y	N	Y	Y	N
Percy	✓	†	Y	Y	N	Y	?	Y
INDIANA								
Bayh	?	?	?	?	?	Y	Y	N
Lugar	Y	Y	Y	N	N	Y	N	Y
IOWA								
Clark	†	Y	N	Y	N	Y	N	N
Culver	Y	Y	N	Y	Y	Y	Y	N
KANSAS								
Dole	Y	Y	Y	N	Y	Y	N	Y
Pearson	Y	Y	N	N	N	Y	Y	N
KENTUCKY								
Ford	Y	Y	Y	N	N	Y	N	N
Huddleston	Y	Y	Y	Y	N	Y	N	N
LOUISIANA								
Johnston	N	Y	Y	Y	N	Y	N	N
Long	?	†	?	✓	?	?	?	?
MAINE								
Hathaway	?	Y	N	N	Y	Y	Y	N
Muskie	Y	Y	N	Y	N	Y	Y	N
MARYLAND								
Sarbanes	Y	Y	N	Y	Y	Y	Y	N
Mathias	Y	?	N	Y	Y	Y	Y	N
MASSACHUSETTS								
Kennedy	Y	Y	N	Y	Y	Y	Y	N
Brooke	?	?	?	?	?	?	?	Y
MICHIGAN								
Riegle	Y	Y	N	N	N	Y	Y	N
Griffin	Y	Y	Y	N	N	Y	N	Y
MINNESOTA								
Anderson	?	†	?	?	?	?	?	?
Humphrey, M.	†	Y	N	Y	N	Y	Y	?
MISSISSIPPI								
Eastland	?	?	?	?	?	?	N	?
Stennis	?	?	?	?	?	?	N	Y
MISSOURI								
Eagleton	Y	Y	Y	Y	N	Y	N	N
Danforth	Y	Y	Y	N	N	Y	N	N
MONTANA								
Melcher	N	Y	Y	N	N	Y	N	N
Hatfield, P.	Y	Y	Y	Y	N	Y	N	N
NEBRASKA								
Zorinsky	N	Y	Y	X	N	Y	N	Y
Curtis	N	N	Y	N	N	Y	N	?
NEVADA								
Cannon	N	Y	Y	Y	N	Y	Y	Y
Laxalt	?	Y	Y	?	N	Y	N	Y
NEW HAMPSHIRE								
Durkin	N	Y	Y	N	Y	Y	N	N
McIntyre	Y	Y	N	N	N	Y	N	N
NEW JERSEY								
Williams	Y	Y	N	Y	N	Y	Y	N
Case	Y	Y	N	Y	Y	Y	Y	N
NEW MEXICO								
Domenici	N	Y	Y	N	Y	Y	N	N
Schmitt	N	Y	Y	N	Y	Y	N	Y
NEW YORK								
Moynihan	Y	Y	N	Y	N	Y	Y	N
Javits	?	Y	N	Y	Y	Y	Y	N
NORTH CAROLINA								
Morgan	Y	N	Y	Y	N	Y	N	N
Helms	N	Y	Y	N	N	Y	N	Y
NORTH DAKOTA								
Burdick	N	Y	Y	N	N	Y	N	N
Young	N	Y	N	N	N	Y	N	N
OHIO								
Glenn	Y	Y	N	Y	N	Y	Y	N
Metzenbaum	Y	Y	Y	N	N	Y	Y	N
OKLAHOMA								
Bartlett	N	Y	Y	N	N	Y	N	Y
Bellmon	Y	Y	N	Y	N	Y	N	N
OREGON								
Hatfield, M.	Y	Y	Y	N	N	Y	N	?
Packwood	Y	Y	Y	N	N	Y	N	Y
PENNSYLVANIA								
Heinz	Y	Y	Y	N	Y	Y	N	#
Schweiker	Y	Y	Y	N	N	Y	N	Y
RHODE ISLAND								
Pell	Y	Y	Y	N	N	Y	Y	N
Chafee	Y	Y	Y	N	N	Y	Y	Y
SOUTH CAROLINA								
Hollings	N	Y	N	Y	N	Y	N	N
Thurmond	X	Y	Y	N	N	Y	N	Y
SOUTH DAKOTA								
Abourezk	N	#	N	N	N	N	Y	▮
McGovern	#	#	▮	#	▮	#	▮	▮
TENNESSEE								
Sasser	?	Y	Y	Y	Y	Y	N	N
Baker	?	Y	Y	N	Y	Y	N	Y
TEXAS								
Bentsen	Y	Y	Y	Y	N	Y	N	Y
Tower	N	Y	Y	N	N	Y	N	Y
UTAH								
Garn	?	Y	Y	N	N	Y	N	Y
Hatch	N	Y	Y	N	Y	Y	N	Y
VERMONT								
Leahy	Y	Y	Y	N	N	Y	N	N
Stafford	Y	Y	Y	N	N	Y	N	Y
VIRGINIA								
*Byrd, H.	N	Y	Y	N	N	Y	N	Y
Scott	N	N	Y	N	Y	Y	N	Y
WASHINGTON								
Jackson	Y	Y	N	Y	N	Y	N	N
Magnuson	Y	Y	N	Y	Y	Y	N	N
WEST VIRGINIA								
Byrd, R.	N	Y	N	Y	N	Y	N	N
Randolph	N	Y	Y	N	N	Y	N	N
WISCONSIN								
Nelson	Y	Y	N	Y	Y	Y	Y	N
Proxmire	N	Y	Y	Y	N	Y	N	N
WYOMING								
Hansen	N	Y	Y	N	N	Y	N	Y
Wallop	Y	Y	Y	N	N	Y	N	Y

Democrats ***Republicans***

*Byrd elected as independent.

KEY

- Y Voted for (yea).
- ✓ Paired for.
- † Announced for.
- # CQ Poll for.
- N Voted against (nay).
- X Paired against.
- \- Announced against.
- ▮ CQ Poll against.
- P Voted "present."
- ● Voted "present" to avoid possible conflict of interest.
- ? Did not vote or otherwise make a position known.

177. HR 12222. Foreign Economic Aid. Passage of the bill to authorize $1,767,478,800 for fiscal 1979 foreign economic aid programs. Passed 49-30: R 16-14; D 33-16 (ND 25-10; SD 8-6), June 26, 1978.

178. Exec K, 94th Cong, 2nd Sess. U.S.-U.K. Tax Convention. Adoption of the resolution of ratification *(see vote 170, p. 29-S)* and the Church, D-Idaho, reservation *(see vote 169, p. 29-S)*. Adopted 82-5: R 30-4; D 52-1 (ND 37-0; SD 15-1), June 27, 1978. A two-thirds majority vote (58 in this case) is required for adoption of resolutions of ratification.

179. HR 12930. Treasury, Postal Service Appropriations, Fiscal 1979. Roth, R-Del., amendment to reduce the appropriations for the Treasury Department, Executive Office of the President and independent agencies for fiscal 1979 by 2 percent. Adopted 55-34: R 29-7; D 26-27; (ND 15-22; SD 11-5), June 27, 1978.

180. HR 12930. Treasury, Postal Service Appropriations, Fiscal 1979. Talmadge, D-Ga., motion to table (kill) the Dole, R-Kan., amendment to prohibit use of funds appropriated in the bill to enforce the imposition of import fees on foreign oil. Motion rejected 39-49: R 5-30; D 34-19 (ND 23-14; SD 11-5), June 27, 1978. A "yea" was a vote supporting the president's position. (The Dole amendment subsequently was adopted by voice vote.)

181. HR 12930. Treasury, Postal Service Appropriations, Fiscal 1979. Stevens, R-Alaska, amendment to delete a committee amendment providing a 5.5 percent ceiling on wage increases for blue-collar federal workers. Rejected 21-69: R 11-25; D 10-44 (ND 8-30; SD 2-14), June 27, 1978.

182. HR 12930. Treasury, Postal Service Appropriations, Fiscal 1979. Chiles, D-Fla., motion to table (kill) the Abourezk, D-S.D., amendment, to the McClure, R-Idaho, amendment *(see vote 183, below)*, to prohibit payment of funds to any person or office staff allowance for any former president who had received a presidential pardon for crimes he committed. Motion agreed to 89-2: R 36-0; D 53-2 (ND 38-1; SD 15-1), June 27, 1978.

183. HR 12930. Treasury, Postal Service Appropriations, Fiscal 1979. Chiles, D-Fla., motion to table (kill) the McClure, R-Idaho, amendment to restore the House-passed figure of $131.3 million for the Bureau of Alcohol, Tobacco and Firearms. Motion rejected 31-61: R 6-29; D 25-32 (ND 21-18; SD 4-14), June 27, 1978. (The McClure amendment subsequently was adopted by voice vote, and the bill to appropriate $8.8 billion for fiscal 1979 was passed, also by voice vote.) The president had requested $9,203,-261,000 in new budget authority.

184. S 419. Oil Shale Research. Hansen, R-Wyo., amendment to prohibit formation of a federally owned government corporation to direct demonstration efforts to derive oil from oil shale. Rejected 34-51: R 24-8; D 10-43 (ND 3-34; SD 7-9), June 27, 1978.

Corresponding to Congressional Record Votes 185, 186, 187, 188, 189, 190, 191, 192

	185	186	187	188	189	190	191	192
ALABAMA								
Allen, M.	Y	N	Y	N	Y	N	Y	N
Sparkman	#	#	Y	Y	Y	▮	▮	#
ALASKA								
Gravel	#	#	#	#	▮	#	▮	#
Stevens	Y	Y	N	N	Y	N	Y	Y
ARIZONA								
DeConcini	Y	N	†	N	Y	N	Y	Y
Goldwater	?	N	N	N	Y	N	?	?
ARKANSAS								
Bumpers	Y	N	N	N	Y	N	Y	Y
Hodges	Y	Y	Y	N	Y	N	Y	Y
CALIFORNIA								
Cranston	Y	Y	Y	Y	N	Y	N	Y
Hayakawa	?	N	N	N	Y	N	Y	Y
COLORADO								
Hart	Y	Y	Y	Y	N	Y	N	N
Haskell	Y	Y	Y	N	Y	Y	N	?
CONNECTICUT								
Ribicoff	Y	Y	N	Y	N	Y	N	Y
Weicker	?	N	Y	N	Y	#	▮	#
DELAWARE								
Biden	N	Y	Y	Y	Y	N	Y	Y
Roth	N	Y	N	N	Y	N	Y	Y
FLORIDA								
Chiles	Y	N	Y	N	Y	N	Y	Y
Stone	Y	N	Y	N	Y	N	Y	Y
GEORGIA								
Nunn	Y	N	N	N	Y	N	Y	Y
Talmadge	Y	N	N	N	Y	N	Y	Y
HAWAII								
Inouye	#	#	#	▮	#	#	▮	#
Matsunaga	Y	Y	Y	N	Y	Y	N	Y
IDAHO								
Church	Y	#	▮	▮	#	#	▮	#
McClure	N	N	N	N	Y	N	Y	N
ILLINOIS								
Stevenson	Y	Y	N	N	Y	Y	N	Y
Percy	N	Y	N	N	Y	Y	N	?
INDIANA								
Bayh	Y	Y	N	N	Y	?	?	?
Lugar	N	N	Y	N	Y	N	Y	Y
IOWA								
Clark	Y	Y	Y	Y	Y	Y	N	Y
Culver	Y	Y	Y	Y	N	Y	N	Y
KANSAS								
Dole	N	N	N	N	Y	N	Y	Y
Pearson	N	Y	N	Y	N	Y	N	Y
KENTUCKY								
Ford	Y	Y	N	N	Y	N	Y	Y
Huddleston	Y	Y	N	N	Y	N	?	?
LOUISIANA								
Johnston	Y	N	?	N	Y	N	Y	Y
Long	?	?	?	?	?	?	?	?
MAINE								
Hathaway	Y	Y	Y	?	?	?	?	?
Muskie	Y	Y	†	?	X	?	?	?
MARYLAND								
Sarbanes	Y	Y	Y	N	Y	?	?	?
Mathias	Y	?	?	?	?	Y	N	Y
MASSACHUSETTS								
Kennedy	Y	Y	Y	Y	N	Y	N	Y
Brooke	N	Y	Y	N	Y	Y	N	Y
MICHIGAN								
Riegle	Y	Y	Y	Y	N	Y	N	Y
Griffin	Y	N	N	N	Y	N	?	Y
MINNESOTA								
Anderson	?	?	?	?	?	?	?	?
Humphrey, M.	✓	Y	Y	Y	N	Y	N	Y
MISSISSIPPI								
Eastland	?	N	N	N	Y	N	Y	?
Stennis	Y	N	Y	N	Y	Y	Y	?
MISSOURI								
Eagleton	Y	Y	Y	N	Y	Y	N	Y
Danforth	Y	N	N	N	Y	N	Y	Y
MONTANA								
Melcher	Y	Y	N	N	Y	Y	N	Y
Hatfield, P.	Y	#	Y	N	✓	Y	N	Y
NEBRASKA								
Zorinsky	Y	Y	N	N	Y	N	Y	Y
Curtis	?	N	N	N	Y	N	Y	N
NEVADA								
Cannon	Y	N	N	N	Y	N	Y	Y
Laxalt	N	N	N	N	Y	N	Y	N
NEW HAMPSHIRE								
Durkin	Y	Y	N	N	Y	N	Y	N
McIntyre	Y	Y	Y	N	Y	Y	Y	Y
NEW JERSEY								
Williams	Y	Y	Y	N	Y	Y	▮	Y
Case	Y	Y	Y	Y	N	Y	N	Y
NEW MEXICO								
Domenici	Y	N	N	N	Y	N	Y	Y
Schmitt	N	N	N	N	Y	N	Y	Y
NEW YORK								
Moynihan	Y	Y	Y	N	Y	Y	N	Y
Javits	Y	Y	Y	N	Y	Y	N	Y
NORTH CAROLINA								
Morgan	Y	N	N	N	Y	N	Y	†
Helms	N	N	N	N	Y	N	Y	N
NORTH DAKOTA								
Burdick	Y	Y	N	N	Y	N	Y	Y
Young	Y	N	N	?	Y	N	Y	Y
OHIO								
Glenn	Y	Y	Y	N	Y	Y	N	Y
Metzenbaum	Y	Y	Y	N	Y	Y	N	Y
OKLAHOMA								
Bartlett	N	N	N	N	Y	N	Y	Y
Bellmon	Y	N	N	N	Y	N	Y	Y
OREGON								
Hatfield, M.	?	-	-	Y	N	N	Y	Y
Packwood	Y	N	Y	N	Y	Y	N	Y
PENNSYLVANIA								
Heinz	#	Y	Y	N	#	N	#	Y
Schweiker	N	N	Y	N	Y	N	Y	Y
RHODE ISLAND								
Pell	Y	Y	N	Y	N	Y	N	Y
Chafee	Y	Y	N	N	Y	Y	N	Y
SOUTH CAROLINA								
Hollings	Y	N	N	N	Y	N	Y	N
Thurmond	N	N	N	N	Y	N	Y	N
SOUTH DAKOTA								
Abourezk	▮	Y	#	#	#	#	▮	#
McGovern	#	Y	Y	Y	N	Y	N	Y
TENNESSEE								
Sasser	Y	N	Y	N	Y	N	Y	Y
Baker	Y	N	N	Y	Y	N	Y	Y
TEXAS								
Bentsen	N	Y	N	N	Y	N	Y	Y
Tower	N	N	N	N	Y	N	Y	Y
UTAH								
Garn	N	?	N	N	Y	N	Y	N
Hatch	N	N	N	N	Y	N	Y	N
VERMONT								
Leahy	X	Y	Y	N	Y	Y	N	Y
Stafford	Y	Y	Y	N	Y	N	Y	Y
VIRGINIA								
*Byrd, H.	N	N	N	N	Y	N	Y	N
Scott	N	N	Y	N	Y	N	Y	N
WASHINGTON								
Jackson	Y	Y	N	N	Y	N	Y	Y
Magnuson	Y	Y	N	N	Y	N	Y	Y
WEST VIRGINIA								
Byrd, R.	Y	N	N	N	Y	N	Y	N
Randolph	Y	N	N	N	Y	N	Y	Y
WISCONSIN								
Nelson	Y	Y	Y	N	Y	Y	?	Y
Proxmire	N	Y	Y	N	Y	Y	N	N
WYOMING								
Hansen	N	N	N	N	Y	N	Y	N
Wallop	N	N	Y	N	Y	N	Y	N

Democrats ***Republicans***

*Byrd elected as independent.

KEY

- Y Voted for (yea).
- ✓ Paired for.
- † Announced for.
- # CQ Poll for.
- N Voted against (nay).
- X Paired against.
- - Announced against.
- ▮ CQ Poll against.
- P Voted "present."
- ● Voted "present" to avoid possible conflict of interest.
- ? Did not vote or otherwise make a position known.

185. S 419. Oil Shale Research. Passage of the bill to establish a new federal program to test the viability of several technologies aimed at deriving oil from oil shale. Passed 61-23: R 13-19; D 48-4 (ND 34-2; SD 14-2), June 27, 1978. A "nay" was a vote supporting the president's position.

186. S 3076. State Department Authorization. McGovern, D-S.D., motion to table (kill) the Helms, R-N.C., amendment to lift U.S. sanctions against Rhodesia until Sept. 30, 1979. Motion agreed to 48-42: R 10-25; D 38-17 (ND 34-4; SD 4-13), June 28, 1978.

187. S 3076. State Department Authorization. Case, R-N.J., amendment to require the president to consult with the Senate before making any international executive agreements. Rejected 41-48: R 11-25; D 30-23 (ND 23-13; SD 7-10), June 28, 1978.

188. S 3076. State Department Authorization. McGovern, D-S.D., motion to table (kill) the Byrd, Ind-Va., amendment *(see vote 189, below)* to delete a provision in the bill allowing for the re-writing of debts owed the United States by the Soviet Union from World War II. Motion rejected 16-74: R 4-32; D 12-42 (ND 11-25; SD 1-17), June 28, 1978.

189. S 3076. State Department Authorization. Byrd, Ind-Va., amendment *(see vote 188, above)*. Adopted 77-12: R 33-3; D 44-9 (ND 26-9; SD 18-0), June 28, 1978.

190. S 3076. State Department Authorization. McGovern, D-S.D., motion to table (kill) the Bartlett, R-Okla. amendment *(see vote 191, below)* expressing the sense of Congress that the president should sever diplomatic and economic relations with Cuba until the country removed its military forces from Africa. Motion rejected 33-55: R 8-29; D 25-26 (ND 24-10; SD 1-16), June 28, 1978.

191. S 3076. State Department Authorization. Bartlett, R-Okla., amendment expressing the sense of Congress that the president should sever diplomatic and economic relations with Cuba until Cuba removed its military forces from Africa. Adopted 53-29: R 26-8; D 27-21 (ND 11-21; SD 16-0), June 28, 1978.

192. HR 12598. State Department Authorization. Passage of the bill to authorize $1,897,195,000 for the State Department and related agencies for fiscal 1979. Passed 64-17: R 25-10; D 39-7 (ND 29-4; SD 10-3), June 28, 1978.

CQ Senate Votes 193-197

Corresponding to Congressional Record Votes 193, 194, 195, 196, 197

	193	194	195	196	197
ALABAMA					
Allen, M.	Y	N	Y	Y	N
Sparkman	N	N	N	N	Y
ALASKA					
Gravel	▮	▮	▮	▮	#
Stevens	N	Y	Y	N	Y
ARIZONA					
DeConcini	N	N	Y	N	N
Goldwater	Y	N	Y	Y	?
ARKANSAS					
Bumpers	N	N	N	?	✓
Hodges	N	N	N	N	Y
CALIFORNIA					
Cranston	N	N	N	N	Y
Hayakawa	Y	Y	Y	N	N
COLORADO					
Hart	N	N	N	N	Y
Haskell	?	?	?	?	?
CONNECTICUT					
Ribicoff	N	Y	N	N	Y
Weicker	N	Y	N	N	Y
DELAWARE					
Biden	N	N	N	N	Y
Roth	Y	N	Y	Y	N
FLORIDA					
Chiles	N	N	N	N	N
Stone	N	N	N	N	Y
GEORGIA					
Nunn	N	N	Y	Y	N
Talmadge	N	▮	▮	#	▮
HAWAII					
Inouye	▮	▮	N	N	Y
Matsunaga	?	N	N	N	Y
IDAHO					
Church	#	▮	#	#	▮
McClure	Y	Y	Y	Y	N
ILLINOIS					
Stevenson	N	N	N	N	Y
Percy	N	N	N	N	Y
INDIANA					
Bayh	N	N	N	N	Y
Lugar	N	N	N	N	Y
IOWA					
Clark	N	N	N	N	Y
Culver	N	N	N	N	Y
KANSAS					
Dole	N	Y	N	N	Y
Pearson	N	Y	N	N	Y
KENTUCKY					
Ford	Y	N	Y	N	Y
Huddleston	N	N	N	N	Y
LOUISIANA					
Johnston	N	N	N	N	Y
Long	?	?	?	?	?
MAINE					
Hathaway	N	N	N	N	Y
Muskie	?	Y	N	N	Y
MARYLAND					
Sarbanes	N	Y	N	N	Y
Mathias	N	Y	N	N	Y
MASSACHUSETTS					
Kennedy	N	Y	N	N	Y
Brooke	N	Y	N	N	Y
MICHIGAN					
Riegle	N	N	N	N	Y
Griffin	Y	Y	Y	Y	X
MINNESOTA					
Anderson	?	?	?	?	†
Humphrey, M.	N	N	N	-	†
MISSISSIPPI					
Eastland	Y	N	Y	Y	?
Stennis	Y	N	Y	Y	N
MISSOURI					
Eagleton	N	N	N	N	Y
Danforth	N	N	N	N	Y
MONTANA					
Melcher	N	X	-	-	†
Hatfield, P.	N	N	N	N	Y
NEBRASKA					
Zorinsky	N	N	N	N	N
Curtis	Y	Y	Y	Y	N
NEVADA					
Cannon	Y	✓	Y	Y	N
Laxalt	Y	Y	Y	Y	N
NEW HAMPSHIRE					
Durkin	N	N	N	N	Y
McIntyre	?	N	N	Y	Y
NEW JERSEY					
Williams	N	N	N	N	Y
Case	N	Y	N	N	Y
NEW MEXICO					
Domenici	N	Y	N	?	?
Schmitt	N	N	N	N	Y
NEW YORK					
Moynihan	N	N	N	N	Y
Javits	N	N	N	N	Y
NORTH CAROLINA					
Morgan	N	N	Y	N	✓
Helms	Y	N	Y	Y	N
NORTH DAKOTA					
Burdick	▮	#	#	#	X
Young	?	?	?	?	?
OHIO					
Glenn	N	Y	N	N	Y
Metzenbaum	N	Y	N	N	Y
OKLAHOMA					
Bartlett	Y	N	Y	Y	N
Bellmon	Y	N	N	?	-
OREGON					
Hatfield, M.	N	Y	N	N	Y
Packwood	N	Y	N	?	Y
PENNSYLVANIA					
Heinz	N	N	N	N	Y
Schweiker	N	N	Y	N	N
RHODE ISLAND					
Pell	N	N	N	?	Y
Chafee	N	N	N	N	Y
SOUTH CAROLINA					
Hollings	N	N	N	Y	N
Thurmond	Y	N	Y	Y	N
SOUTH DAKOTA					
Abourezk	▮	▮	▮	N	Y
McGovern	N	▮	▮	▮	†
TENNESSEE					
Sasser	N	?	N	N	N
Baker	N	Y	N	N	Y
TEXAS					
Bentsen	Y	N	Y	Y	N
Tower	Y	N	Y	Y	N
UTAH					
Garn	Y	N	Y	Y	N
Hatch	Y	Y	Y	Y	N
VERMONT					
Leahy	N	N	N	N	Y
Stafford	N	Y	N	N	Y
VIRGINIA					
*Byrd, H.	Y	N	Y	Y	N
Scott	Y	Y	Y	Y	N
WASHINGTON					
Jackson	N	N	N	N	Y
Magnuson	-	Y	N	?	X
WEST VIRGINIA					
Byrd, R.	N	N	N	N	Y
Randolph	N	N	N	N	Y
WISCONSIN					
Nelson	N	N	N	N	✓
Proxmire	N	N	N	N	N
WYOMING					
Hansen	Y	Y	Y	Y	N
Wallop	Y	Y	Y	Y	N

Democrats ***Republicans***

*Byrd elected as independent.

KEY

- Y Voted for (yea).
- ✓ Paired for.
- † Announced for.
- # CQ Poll for.
- N Voted against (nay).
- X Paired against.
- - Announced against.
- ▮ CQ Poll against.
- P Voted "present."
- ● Voted "present" to avoid possible conflict of interest.
- ? Did not vote or otherwise make a position known.

193. HR 12426. New York City Aid. Tower, R-Texas, amendment to terminate guarantees if the holder of guaranteed bonds failed to comply with terms of the city's long-term financing plan. Rejected 24-63: R 17-20; D 7-43 (ND 1-31; SD 6-12), June 29, 1978.

194. HR 12426. New York City Aid. Weicker, R-Conn., amendment to require a federal study to determine what other cities had financial problems similar to those that forced New York City to seek federal aid. Rejected 28-58: R 21-16; D 7-42 (ND 7-26; SD 0-16), June 29, 1978.

195. HR 12426. New York City Aid. Tower, R-Texas, amendment to require New York State to coinsure 10 percent, rather than 5 percent, of the value of guaranteed city bonds. Rejected 28-61: R 18-19; D 10-42 (ND 2-33; SD 8-9), June 29, 1978.

196. HR 12426. New York City Aid. Tower, R-Texas, amendment to reduce the total amount of city bonds that could be insured to $1 billion, from $1.5 billion. Rejected 24-59: R 15-19; D 9-40 (ND 2-31; SD 7-9), June 29, 1978. A "nay" was a vote supporting the president's position.

197. HR 12426. New York City Aid. Passage of the bill to provide up to $1.5 billion in long-term loan guarantees for New York City. Passed 53-27: R 18-15; D 35-12 (ND 29-4; SD 6-8), June 29, 1978. A "yea" was a vote supporting the president's position.

Corresponding to Congressional Record Votes 198, 199, 200, 201, 202, 203, 204, 209

	198	199	200	201	202	203	204	205
ALABAMA								
Allen, M.	N	Y	Y	Y	Y	Y	Y	N
Sparkman	N	N	Y	N	?	?	Y	Y
ALASKA								
Gravel	N	Y	Y	Y	Y	Y	Y	N
Stevens	N	N	Y	N	Y	Y	Y	N
ARIZONA								
DeConcini	N	Y	Y	Y	Y	Y	Y	N
Goldwater	N	N	Y	?	Y	Y	Y	Y
ARKANSAS								
Bumpers	Y	Y	Y	N	N	Y	Y	Y
Hodges	N	N	Y	N	N	Y	Y	N
CALIFORNIA								
Cranston	N	Y	Y	N	Y	Y	Y	Y
Hayakawa	N	Y	Y	Y	Y	Y	Y	Y
COLORADO								
Hart	Y	Y	Y	N	Y	Y	Y	Y
Haskell	?	?	?	?	N	Y	Y	Y
CONNECTICUT								
Ribicoff	Y	Y	Y	N	N	Y	Y	Y
Weicker	N	Y	Y	N	?	?	Y	N
DELAWARE								
Biden	N	Y	Y	N	N	Y	Y	N
Roth	Y	Y	Y	N	N	Y	Y	N
FLORIDA								
Chiles	N	Y	Y	N	N	Y	Y	Y
Stone	N	Y	Y	N	Y	Y	Y	Y
GEORGIA								
Nunn	Y	N	Y	N	N	Y	Y	Y
Talmadge	N	N	Y	N	N	Y	Y	Y
HAWAII								
Inouye	?	Y	Y	N	Y	Y	Y	Y
Matsunaga	?	Y	Y	Y	Y	Y	Y	Y
IDAHO								
Church	▮	?	?	?	?	?	?	?
McClure	N	Y	Y	Y	Y	Y	Y	Y
ILLINOIS								
Stevenson	Y	Y	Y	N	N	Y	Y	Y
Percy	N	N	Y	N	Y	Y	Y	Y
INDIANA								
Bayh	Y	Y	Y	N	Y	Y	Y	Y
Lugar	Y	Y	Y	N	N	Y	Y	Y
IOWA								
Clark	†	Y	Y	N	N	Y	Y	Y
Culver	Y	Y	Y	N	N	Y	Y	Y
KANSAS								
Dole	N	Y	Y	Y	N	Y	Y	Y
Pearson	N	N	Y	Y	N	Y	Y	Y
KENTUCKY								
Ford	N	Y	Y	Y	Y	Y	Y	Y
Huddleston	N	N	Y	N	Y	Y	Y	Y
LOUISIANA								
Johnston	N	N	Y	N	N	Y	Y	?
Long	N	N	Y	N	?	?	Y	Y
MAINE								
Hathaway	Y	Y	Y	N	N	Y	Y	Y
Muskie	Y	Y	Y	N	N	Y	Y	Y
MARYLAND								
Sarbanes	N	Y	Y	Y	Y	Y	Y	Y
Mathias	?	?	?	?	Y	Y	Y	Y
MASSACHUSETTS								
Kennedy	N	Y	Y	N	N	Y	Y	Y
Brooke	N	N	Y	Y	Y	Y	Y	Y
MICHIGAN								
Riegle	N	Y	Y	N	Y	Y	Y	Y
Griffin	N	N	Y	Y	Y	Y	Y	?
MINNESOTA								
Anderson	-	†	†	?	?	†	?	?
Humphrey, M.	Y	Y	Y	N	†	†	Y	Y
MISSISSIPPI								
Eastland	N	?	Y	N	N	Y	Y	Y
Stennis	N	N	Y	N	N	Y	Y	Y
MISSOURI								
Eagleton	N	Y	Y	N	N	Y	Y	N
Danforth	N	N	Y	N	N	Y	Y	Y
MONTANA								
Melcher	N	N	Y	N	Y	Y	Y	N
Hatfield, P.	N	Y	Y	N	Y	Y	Y	N
NEBRASKA								
Zorinsky	N	Y	Y	N	N	Y	Y	N
Curtis	-	-	†	-	†	†	Y	Y
NEVADA								
Cannon	N	N	Y	N	Y	Y	Y	Y
Laxalt	N	N	Y	Y	Y	Y	Y	Y
NEW HAMPSHIRE								
Durkin	N	Y	Y	P	†	?	Y	Y
McIntyre	N	N	Y	N	N	Y	Y	Y
NEW JERSEY								
Williams	Y	Y	Y	Y	Y	Y	Y	Y
Case	N	Y	Y	Y	Y	Y	Y	Y
NEW MEXICO								
Domenici	N	N	Y	Y	Y	Y	Y	Y
Schmitt	N	Y	Y	Y	N	Y	Y	Y
NEW YORK								
Moynihan	Y	Y	Y	N	N	Y	?	?
Javits	Y	Y	Y	N	N	Y	Y	Y
NORTH CAROLINA								
Morgan	N	N	Y	Y	Y	Y	Y	Y
Helms	N	N	Y	Y	Y	Y	Y	N
NORTH DAKOTA								
Burdick	N	N	Y	N	N	Y	Y	Y
Young	N	N	Y	N	N	Y	Y	Y
OHIO								
Glenn	-	Y	Y	N	N	Y	Y	Y
Metzenbaum	N	N	N	N	N	Y	Y	N
OKLAHOMA								
Bartlett	N	N	Y	N	Y	Y	Y	Y
Bellmon	N	N	Y	N	N	Y	Y	Y
OREGON								
Hatfield, M.	Y	N	N	N	N	N	Y	Y
Packwood	N	Y	Y	Y	Y	Y	Y	Y
PENNSYLVANIA								
Heinz	N	N	Y	N	?	?	Y	Y
Schweiker	N	N	Y	N	N	Y	Y	Y
RHODE ISLAND								
Pell	Y	Y	Y	Y	N	Y	Y	Y
Chafee	N	Y	Y	N	N	Y	Y	Y
SOUTH CAROLINA								
Hollings	N	Y	Y	Y	N	Y	Y	N
Thurmond	N	N	Y	Y	Y	Y	Y	N
SOUTH DAKOTA								
Abourezk	Y	Y	Y	N	?	?	?	?
McGovern	?	?	?	?	?	?	?	?
TENNESSEE								
Sasser	N	Y	Y	Y	N	Y	Y	Y
Baker	N	N	Y	Y	Y	Y	Y	N
TEXAS								
Bentsen	N	N	Y	N	Y	Y	Y	N
Tower	N	N	Y	N	Y	Y	Y	?
UTAH								
Garn	N	N	Y	N	Y	Y	Y	N
Hatch	N	N	Y	N	Y	Y	Y	N
VERMONT								
Leahy	Y	Y	Y	N	N	Y	Y	Y
Stafford	N	N	Y	Y	Y	Y	Y	Y
VIRGINIA								
*Byrd, H.	N	N	N	N	N	Y	Y	Y
Scott	N	N	Y	N	N	Y	Y	N
WASHINGTON								
Jackson	N	N	Y	N	Y	Y	Y	N
Magnuson	N	Y	Y	Y	Y	Y	Y	Y
WEST VIRGINIA								
Byrd, R.	Y	Y	Y	N	N	Y	Y	Y
Randolph	N	N	Y	Y	Y	Y	Y	Y
WISCONSIN								
Nelson	Y	Y	Y	N	N	Y	Y	Y
Proxmire	Y	N	N	N	N	N	Y	N
WYOMING								
Hansen	N	N	Y	N	Y	Y	Y	Y
Wallop	N	N	Y	N	N	Y	Y	Y

Democrats ***Republicans***

Byrd elected as independent.

KEY

- Y Voted for (yea).
- ✓ Paired for.
- † Announced for.
- # CQ Poll for.
- N Voted against (nay).
- X Paired against.
- - Announced against.
- ▮ CQ Poll against.
- P Voted "present."
- ● Voted "present" to avoid possible conflict of interest.
- ? Did not vote or otherwise make a position known.

198. S 2571. Defense Procurement Authorization. Hart, D-Colo., amendment to delete $983.1 million for development of the F-18 fighter plane and production of nine F-18s. Rejected 22-68: R 4-32; D 18-36 (ND 16-19; SD 2-17), July 11, 1978.

199. S 2571. Defense Procurement Authorization. Hart, D-Colo., amendment to authorize $5.5 million for development of the Harrier B+ fighter plane. Adopted 49-44: R 11-25; D 38-19 (ND 31-8; SD 7-11), July 11, 1978.

200. S 2571. Defense Procurement Authorization. Hart, D-Colo., amendment to authorize $25.2 million for five Navy research projects. Adopted 90-4: R 35-1; D 55-3 (ND 37-2; SD 18-1), July 11, 1978.

201. S 2571. Defense Procurement Authorization. Dole, R-Kan., amendment to increase to 95,900 the Naval Reserve force. Rejected 28-64: R 15-20; D 13-44 (ND 8-30; SD 5-14), July 11, 1978.

202. S 2571. Defense Procurement Authorization. Thurmond, R-S.C., amendment to revise the benefits program for survivors of military retirees. Rejected 43-46: R 21-14; D 22-32 (ND 16-21; SD 6-11), July 11, 1978.

203. HR 10929. Defense Procurement Authorization. Passage of the bill to authorize $36,099,534,000 for weapons procurement and military research in fiscal 1979. Passed 87-2: R 34-1; D 53-1 (ND 36-1; SD 17-0), July 11, 1978.

204. Treaties. Adoption en bloc of the resolutions of ratification of the following treaties: 1) Exec G, 95th Cong, 2nd Sess - Treaty with Bolivia on the Execution of Penal Sentences; 2) Exec O, 94th Cong, 2nd Sess - International Convention for the Safety of Life at Sea; 3) Exec L, 95th Cong, 1st Sess - Protocol Relating to Intervention on the High Seas in Cases of Marine Pollution by Substances other than Oil; 4) Exec O, 95th Cong, 1st Sess - Reciprocal Fisheries Agreement with the United Kingdom of Great Britain and Northern Ireland; 5) Exec K, 95th Cong, 1st Sess - Convention with the Union of Soviet Socialist Republics on the Conservation of Migratory Birds and their Environment. Adopted 95-0: R 38-0; D 57-0 (ND 38-0; SD 19-0), July 12, 1978. A two-thirds majority vote (64 in this case) is required for adoption of resolutions of ratification. A "yea" was a vote supporting the president's position.

205. S 2391. Commodity Futures Trading Commission. Leahy, D-Vt., motion to table (kill) the Melcher, D-Mont., amendment to replace the existing five-member Commodity Futures Trading Commission with a new, three-member Commodities Trading Commission. Motion agreed to 69-23: R 27-9; D 42-14 (ND 28-10; SD 14-4), July 12, 1978.

Corresponding to Congressional Record Votes 210, 211, 212, 213, 214, 215, 216

	206	207	208	209	210	211	212
ALABAMA							
Allen, M.	Y	Y	Y	Y	Y	Y	N
Sparkman	Y	N	Y	N	N	N	Y
ALASKA							
Gravel	Y	N	Y	N	N	N	Y
Stevens	Y	†	?	Y	Y	Y	Y
ARIZONA							
DeConcini	Y	N	Y	N	N	Y	Y
Goldwater	Y	Y	Y	Y	Y	Y	N
ARKANSAS							
Bumpers	?	Y	Y	N	N	N	N
Hodges	N	N	Y	N	Y	Y	N
CALIFORNIA							
Cranston	Y	N	Y	N	N	N	Y
Hayakawa	Y	N	Y	N	N	N	Y
COLORADO							
Hart	Y	N	Y	N	N	N	Y
Haskell	Y	N	Y	N	N	Y	Y
CONNECTICUT							
Ribicoff	Y	N	Y	N	N	N	Y
Weicker	Y	N	Y	N	N	N	Y
DELAWARE							
Biden	Y	N	Y	N	N	N	Y
Roth	Y	Y	Y	Y	Y	Y	N
FLORIDA							
Chiles	Y	Y	Y	Y	Y	Y	N
Stone	Y	N	Y	N	N	N	Y
GEORGIA							
Nunn	Y	Y	Y	Y	Y	Y	N
Talmadge	Y	N	Y	Y	N	Y	Y
HAWAII							
Inouye	Y	N	Y	N	N	N	Y
Matsunaga	Y	N	Y	N	N	N	Y
IDAHO							
Church	?	N	Y	N	N	Y	Y
McClure	N	Y	Y	?	?	?	?
ILLINOIS							
Stevenson	Y	N	Y	N	N	N	Y
Percy	Y	?	?	?	?	?	Y
INDIANA							
Bayh	Y	N	Y	Y	Y	N	Y
Lugar	Y	Y	Y	Y	Y	Y	N
IOWA							
Clark	Y	N	Y	N	N	N	Y
Culver	Y	N	Y	N	N	N	Y
KANSAS							
Dole	Y	Y	Y	Y	N	N	Y
Pearson	Y	N	Y	N	N	N	Y
KENTUCKY							
Ford	Y	N	Y	Y	Y	Y	Y
Huddleston	Y	Y	Y	Y	Y	N	N
LOUISIANA							
Johnston	?	?	?	?	?	?	?
Long	Y	N	Y	N	N	N	Y
MAINE							
Hathaway	Y	N	Y	N	N	N	Y
Muskie	Y	N	?	N	N	N	Y
MARYLAND							
Sarbanes	Y	N	Y	N	N	N	Y
Mathias	Y	Y	?	N	N	N	Y
MASSACHUSETTS							
Kennedy	Y	N	Y	N	N	N	Y
Brooke	Y	N	Y	?	?	?	?
MICHIGAN							
Riegle	Y	N	Y	N	N	N	Y
Griffin	Y	Y	Y	N	Y	N	Y
MINNESOTA							
Anderson	?	-	†	-	-	-	†
Humphrey, M.	Y	N	Y	N	N	N	Y
MISSISSIPPI							
Eastland	Y	Y	Y	Y	Y	N	N
Stennis	Y	Y	Y	Y	N	N	N
MISSOURI							
Eagleton	N	N	Y	N	N	N	Y
Danforth	Y	Y	Y	N	N	N	N
MONTANA							
Melcher	N	N	Y	N	N	N	Y
Hatfield, P.	Y	N	Y	?	N	N	Y
NEBRASKA							
Zorinsky	Y	N	Y	Y	Y	Y	N
Curtis	Y	Y	Y	Y	Y	Y	N
NEVADA							
Cannon	Y	N	Y	N	N	N	Y
Laxalt	Y	Y	Y	Y	Y	Y	N
NEW HAMPSHIRE							
Durkin	Y	N	Y	N	N	N	Y
McIntyre	Y	N	Y	N	N	N	Y
NEW JERSEY							
Williams	Y	N	Y	N	N	N	Y
Case	Y	N	Y	N	N	Y	Y
NEW MEXICO							
Domenici	Y	Y	Y	Y	Y	?	N
Schmitt	Y	Y	Y	Y	Y	Y	N
NEW YORK							
Moynihan	?	N	Y	N	N	N	Y
Javits	Y	N	Y	N	N	N	Y
NORTH CAROLINA							
Morgan	Y	N	Y	N	N	N	Y
Helms	Y	†	Y	Y	Y	Y	N
NORTH DAKOTA							
Burdick	Y	N	Y	N	N	N	Y
Young	Y	Y	Y	Y	Y	N	N
OHIO							
Glenn	Y	Y	Y	N	Y	Y	N
Metzenbaum	Y	N	Y	N	N	N	Y
OKLAHOMA							
Bartlett	Y	Y	Y	Y	Y	Y	N
Bellmon	Y	Y	Y	Y	Y	Y	N
OREGON							
Hatfield, M.	Y	N	?	N	N	N	Y
Packwood	Y	Y	Y	Y	Y	Y	N
PENNSYLVANIA							
Heinz	Y	N	Y	N	N	N	Y
Schweiker	?	N	Y	N	N	N	Y
RHODE ISLAND							
Pell	Y	N	Y	N	N	N	Y
Chafee	Y	Y	Y	N	Y	Y	N
SOUTH CAROLINA							
Hollings	?	N	Y	N	N	N	Y
Thurmond	Y	Y	Y	N	N	Y	Y
SOUTH DAKOTA							
Abourezk	?	N	N	?	?	?	Y
McGovern	?	-	?	-	-	-	†
TENNESSEE							
Sasser	Y	N	Y	Y	Y	Y	N
Baker	Y	N	Y	N	N	Y	†
TEXAS							
Bentsen	Y	Y	Y	Y	N	N	N
Tower	?	Y	Y	Y	Y	Y	?
UTAH							
Garn	Y	Y	Y	Y	Y	Y	N
Hatch	N	Y	Y	Y	Y	Y	N
VERMONT							
Leahy	Y	N	Y	N	N	N	Y
Stafford	Y	N	?	N	N	N	Y
VIRGINIA							
*Byrd, H.	Y	Y	Y	Y	Y	Y	N
Scott	Y	Y	Y	Y	Y	N	N
WASHINGTON							
Jackson	Y	N	Y	N	N	N	Y
Magnuson	Y	N	Y	N	N	N	Y
WEST VIRGINIA							
Byrd, R.	Y	N	Y	N	N	Y	Y
Randolph	Y	N	Y	Y	Y	Y	Y
WISCONSIN							
Nelson	Y	N	Y	N	N	N	Y
Proxmire	N	Y	Y	Y	Y	Y	N
WYOMING							
Hansen	Y	Y	Y	Y	Y	Y	N
Wallop	Y	Y	Y	Y	Y	Y	N

Democrats ***Republicans***

**Byrd elected as independent.*

KEY

- Y Voted for (yea).
- ✓ Paired for.
- † Announced for.
- # CQ Poll for.
- N Voted against (nay).
- X Paired against.
- \- Announced against.
- ▮ CQ Poll against.
- P Voted "present."
- ● Voted "present" to avoid possible conflict of interest.
- ? Did not vote or otherwise make a position known.

206. S 2391. Commodity Futures Trading Commission. Passage of the bill to extend through fiscal year 1984 authorization for funds as required for the operations of the Commodity Futures Trading Commission. Passed 84-6: R 34-2; D 50-4 (ND 35-3; SD 15-1), July 12, 1978.

207. HR 2777. National Consumer Cooperative Bank. Tower, R-Texas, substitute for the bill to provide for a two-year study of the need for a national consumer cooperative bank, and to fund a two-year pilot lending program for cooperatives. Rejected 35-59: R 24-11; D 11-48 (ND 2-39; SD 9-9), July 13, 1978. A "nay" was a vote supporting the president's position.

208. S Res 512. Nobel Prize for Soviet Dissidents. Adoption of the resolution expressing the Senate's support for the nomination for the 1978 Nobel Peace Prize of the 58 members of the Helsinki Watch Groups in the Soviet Union, who undertook to monitor USSR compliance with the 1975 Helsinki agreement on human rights. Adopted 90-1: R 33-0; D 57-1 (ND 39-1; SD 18-0), July 13, 1978.

209. HR 2777. National Consumer Cooperative Bank. Lugar, R-Ind., amendment to require the bank to determine, before making any loan, that the loan would not harm existing small businesses in the market area served by the cooperative borrower and that the area was not being adequately served by existing lending institutions. Rejected 35-57: R 20-15; D 15-42 (ND 4-35; SD 11-7), July 13, 1978.

210. HR 2777. National Consumer Cooperative Bank. Lugar, R-Ind., amendment to prohibit the bank from making a loan unless the cooperative borrower had been denied credit by at least two other lending institutions. Rejected 35-58: R 21-14; D 14-44 (ND 5-35; SD 9-9), July 13, 1978.

211. HR 2777. National Consumer Cooperative Bank. Lugar, R-Ind., amendment to increase to 50 percent from 35 percent the percentage of loans made by the bank to benefit low-income persons. Rejected 36-56: R 20-14; D 16-42 (ND 8-32; SD 8-10), July 13, 1978.

212. HR 2777. National Consumer Cooperative Bank. Passage of the bill to establish a national consumer cooperative bank; to establish within the bank an office to provide technical assistance to cooperatives; to authorize $300 million for the bank's first five years for capitalization and $75 million for the bank's first five years for technical assistance programs; to authorize $4 million for the programs' fiscal 1979 administrative costs; and to authorize additional sums, as necessary, for the programs' fiscal 1980 and 1981 administrative costs. Passed 60-33: R 15-19; D 45-14 (ND 38-3; SD 7-11), July 13, 1978. A "yea" was a vote supporting the president's position.

Corresponding to Congressional Record Votes 217, 218, 219, 220, 221, 222, 223, 224

	213	214	215	216	217	218	219	220
ALABAMA								
Allen, M.	N	Y	Y	Y	N	N	N	N
Sparkman	N	Y	Y	Y	N	N	N	N
ALASKA								
Gravel	N	Y	Y	N	N	N	N	N
Stevens	N	N	Y	Y	N	N	N	Y
ARIZONA								
DeConcini	N	Y	Y	Y	N	N	N	N
Goldwater	?	Y	N	Y	N	N	N	N
ARKANSAS								
Bumpers	?	Y	Y	N	N	N	N	N
Hodges	?	Y	Y	N	N	N	N	N
CALIFORNIA								
Cranston	N	Y	Y	N	N	N	N	N
Hayakawa	N	Y	Y	N	N	N	N	N
COLORADO								
Hart	N	Y	Y	N	N	N	N	N
Haskell	N	Y	Y	N	N	N	N	N
CONNECTICUT								
Ribicoff	N	Y	Y	N	N	?	Y	N
Weicker	?	N	Y	N	N	N	Y	N
DELAWARE								
Biden	N	Y	Y	N	N	N	Y	N
Roth	Y	N	Y	N	N	N	N	N
FLORIDA								
Chiles	N	Y	Y	N	N	?	N	N
Stone	?	Y	Y	N	N	N	Y	N
GEORGIA								
Nunn	N	Y	Y	N	N	N	N	Y
Talmadge	N	Y	Y	N	N	N	N	N
HAWAII								
Inouye	N	Y	Y	?	?	?	N	?
Matsunaga	N	Y	Y	N	N	N	Y	N
IDAHO								
Church	N	Y	Y	N	N	N	N	N
McClure	?	Y	Y	N	N	N	N	Y
ILLINOIS								
Stevenson	N	Y	Y	N	N	N	N	N
Percy	?	Y	Y	N	N	N	Y	N
INDIANA								
Bayh	N	Y	Y	N	N	N	Y	N
Lugar	N	Y	N	N	N	N	N	N
IOWA								
Clark	N	Y	Y	N	N	N	N	N
Culver	?	Y	Y	N	N	N	N	N
KANSAS								
Dole	N	Y	Y	N	N	N	N	N
Pearson	?	Y	Y	N	N	N	N	N
KENTUCKY								
Ford	N	Y	Y	Y	N	N	N	Y
Huddleston	?	Y	Y	Y	N	N	N	Y
LOUISIANA								
Johnston	?	Y	Y	N	N	N	N	Y
Long	N	Y	Y	Y	Y	N	N	Y
MAINE								
Hathaway	?	Y	Y	N	N	N	N	N
Muskie	?	Y	Y	N	N	N	N	N
MARYLAND								
Sarbanes	N	Y	Y	N	N	N	Y	N
Mathias	N	Y	Y	N	?	?	?	?
MASSACHUSETTS								
Kennedy	N	Y	Y	N	N	N	Y	N
Brooke	?	Y	Y	N	N	N	Y	N
MICHIGAN								
Riegle	N	Y	Y	N	N	N	Y	N
Griffin	?	Y	Y	N	N	N	N	N
MINNESOTA								
Anderson	?	Y	Y	N	N	N	N	N
Humphrey, M.	-	Y	Y	N	N	N	Y	N
MISSISSIPPI								
Eastland	?	Y	Y	Y	N	?	N	Y
Stennis	?	Y	Y	Y	Y	?	N	?
MISSOURI								
Eagleton	?	Y	Y	N	N	N	N	N
Danforth	Y	Y	Y	N	N	N	?	N
MONTANA								
Melcher	N	Y	Y	N	N	N	N	N
Hatfield, P.	N	Y	Y	N	N	N	N	?
NEBRASKA								
Zorinsky	N	Y	Y	N	N	N	N	N
Curtis	Y	Y	Y	Y	Y	?	N	Y
NEVADA								
Cannon	N	Y	Y	N	Y	N	?	Y
Laxalt	?	N	N	Y	Y	Y	N	Y
NEW HAMPSHIRE								
Durkin	N	Y	Y	N	N	N	Y	N
McIntyre	N	Y	Y	N	N	N	N	N
NEW JERSEY								
Williams	N	Y	Y	N	N	N	Y	N
Case	N	Y	Y	N	N	N	Y	N
NEW MEXICO								
Domenici	N	N	Y	N	N	N	N	?
Schmitt	Y	N	N	N	N	N	N	N
NEW YORK								
Moynihan	N	Y	Y	N	N	N	?	N
Javits	N	Y	Y	N	N	N	N	N
NORTH CAROLINA								
Morgan	N	Y	Y	Y	N	N	N	N
Helms	Y	Y	Y	Y	Y	N	N	Y
NORTH DAKOTA								
Burdick	?	Y	Y	Y	N	N	N	Y
Young	Y	Y	Y	Y	Y	?	N	Y
OHIO								
Glenn	N	Y	Y	N	N	N	N	N
Metzenbaum	?	Y	Y	N	N	N	Y	N
OKLAHOMA								
Bartlett	Y	Y	N	Y	N	N	N	Y
Bellmon	N	N	N	N	N	N	N	N
OREGON								
Hatfield, M.	Y	Y	Y	N	N	N	N	N
Packwood	N	Y	Y	N	N	N	Y	N
PENNSYLVANIA								
Heinz	N	Y	Y	N	N	N	Y	N
Schweiker	Y	Y	Y	N	N	N	N	N
RHODE ISLAND								
Pell	N	Y	Y	N	N	N	?	?
Chafee	N	Y	Y	N	N	N	Y	N
SOUTH CAROLINA								
Hollings	N	Y	Y	N	N	N	N	N
Thurmond	Y	Y	Y	Y	N	N	N	Y
SOUTH DAKOTA								
Abourezk	?	?	?	N	?	?	Y	?
McGovern	?	Y	Y	N	N	N	Y	?
TENNESSEE								
Sasser	N	Y	Y	N	N	N	N	Y
Baker	?	N	Y	N	N	N	N	N
TEXAS								
Bentsen	N	Y	Y	N	N	N	N	N
Tower	?	Y	Y	-	-	?	N	Y
UTAH								
Garn	Y	N	Y	Y	Y	N	N	Y
Hatch	N	Y	-	Y	Y	N	N	Y
VERMONT								
Leahy	-	Y	Y	N	N	N	Y	N
Stafford	Y	Y	Y	N	N	?	Y	N
VIRGINIA								
*Byrd, H.	Y	Y	Y	N	N	N	N	Y
Scott	Y	Y	Y	Y	Y	Y	N	Y
WASHINGTON								
Jackson	N	Y	Y	N	N	N	N	N
Magnuson	N	Y	Y	N	N	N	N	N
WEST VIRGINIA								
Byrd, R.	N	Y	Y	N	N	N	N	N
Randolph	N	Y	Y	N	N	N	N	N
WISCONSIN								
Nelson	N	Y	Y	N	N	N	Y	N
Proxmire	Y	Y	Y	N	N	N	Y	N
WYOMING								
Hansen	N	N	Y	Y	N	N	N	Y
Wallop	Y	N	Y	N	N	N	N	N

Democrats ***Republicans***

*Byrd elected as independent.

KEY

- Y Voted for (yea).
- ✓ Paired for.
- † Announced for.
- # CQ Poll for.
- N Voted against (nay).
- X Paired against.
- - Announced against.
- ▮ CQ Poll against.
- P Voted "present."
- ● Voted "present" to avoid possible conflict of interest.
- ? Did not vote or otherwise make a position known.

213. HR 11003. White House Staff Authorization. Helms, R-N.C., amendment to limit the authorization for the official expenses of the president to $219,700,000 for fiscal 1979, instead of the unlimited amount contained in the bill. Rejected 16-56: R 14-14; D 2-42 (ND 1-31; SD 1-11), July 14, 1978.

214. Stewart Nomination. Confirmation of President Carter's nomination of Milton D. Stewart of New York to be chief counsel for advocacy of the Small Business Administration. Confirmed 88-11: R 27-11; D 61-0 (ND 42-0; SD 19-0), July 18, 1978. A "yea" was a vote supporting the president's position.

215. HR 5146. Coal Conversion. Adoption of the conference report on the bill to grant the Department of Energy stronger regulatory powers to order electric utility power plants and major industrial facilities to cease burning oil and natural gas and to burn coal or other substitute fuels instead, subject to numerous restrictions. Adopted 92-6: R 31-6; D 61-0 (ND 42-0; SD 19-0), July 18, 1978. A "yea" was a vote supporting the president's position.

216. S 2899. Endangered Species. Stennis, D-Miss., amendment to exempt (from the law's requirement that endangered species not be harmed) any project under contract or for which construction funds had been appropriated at the time the act was passed in 1973 or any project 50 percent complete, and to give the heads of federal agencies authority to exempt any other project threatening an endangered species. Rejected 22-76: R 12-25; D 10-51 (ND 2-40; SD 8-11), July 18, 1978.

217. S 2899. Endangered Species. Scott, R-Va., amendment to protect endangered species only when "consistent with the welfare and national goals of the people of the United States." Rejected 10-86: R 7-29; D 3-57 (ND 1-40; SD 2-17), July 18, 1978.

218. S 2899. Endangered Species. Scott, R-Va., amendment to limit the definition of endangered species to those species that are of "substantial benefit to mankind." Rejected 2-87: R 2-31; D 0-56 (ND 0-40; SD 0-16), July 18, 1978.

219. S 2899. Endangered Species. Nelson, D-Wis., amendment to make eligible for exemption from the law only those projects for which a "substantial and irretrievable commitment of resources" had been made before the species was found. Rejected 25-70: R 8-28; D 17-42 (ND 16-24; SD 1-18), July 19, 1978.

220. S 2899. Endangered Species. Scott, R-Va., amendment to allow four members of the proposed seven-member Endangered Species Commission, instead of five, to vote an exemption from the law. Rejected 23-69: R 13-23; D 10-46 (ND 2-36; SD 8-10), July 19, 1978.

CQ Senate Votes 221-228

Corresponding to Congressional Record Votes 225, 226, 227, 228, 229, 230, 231, 232

	221	222	223	224	225	226	227	228
ALABAMA								
Allen, M.	Y	Y	Y	Y	Y	Y	Y	Y
Sparkman	Y	Y	N	Y	N	N	Y	N
ALASKA								
Gravel	Y	Y	N	Y	Y	N	Y	N
Stevens	Y	Y	Y	Y	Y	Y	Y	Y
ARIZONA								
DeConcini	Y	Y	Y	Y	Y	N	Y	N
Goldwater	Y	N	Y	Y	Y	Y	Y	Y
ARKANSAS								
Bumpers	Y	N	Y	Y	Y	N	Y	N
Hodges	Y	N	Y	Y	Y	N	Y	N
CALIFORNIA								
Cranston	Y	Y	N	Y	Y	N	Y	N
Hayakawa	Y	N	Y	Y	Y	Y	Y	Y
COLORADO								
Hart	Y	N	Y	Y	Y	N	Y	N
Haskell	Y	?	?	Y	Y	N	Y	Y
CONNECTICUT								
Ribicoff	Y	†	-	N	N	N	Y	N
Weicker	Y	Y	?	N	N	N	Y	N
DELAWARE								
Biden	Y	N	Y	N	N	N	Y	N
Roth	Y	N	Y	N	Y	Y	Y	Y
FLORIDA								
Chiles	Y	N	Y	?	Y	N	Y	N
Stone	Y	N	Y	Y	Y	N	Y	N
GEORGIA								
Nunn	Y	N	Y	Y	Y	Y	Y	Y
Talmadge	Y	Y	Y	N	Y	N	Y	N
HAWAII								
Inouye	Y	Y	Y	?	?	?	?	N
Matsunaga	Y	Y	N	?	?	N	Y	N
IDAHO								
Church	Y	N	Y	Y	Y	N	Y	N
McClure	Y	N	Y	Y	Y	Y	Y	Y
ILLINOIS								
Stevenson	Y	Y	N	N	N	N	Y	N
Percy	Y	N	Y	N	N	?	Y	N
INDIANA								
Bayh	Y	Y	N	?	?	Y	?	N
Lugar	Y	N	Y	N	Y	Y	Y	Y
IOWA								
Clark	Y	Y	?	N	N	N	Y	N
Culver	Y	?	?	N	N	N	Y	N
KANSAS								
Dole	Y	Y	✓	Y	Y	Y	Y	Y
Pearson	Y	N	Y	Y	Y	N	Y	N
KENTUCKY								
Ford	Y	N	Y	Y	Y	N	Y	N
Huddleston	Y	Y	Y	Y	Y	N	Y	?
LOUISIANA								
Johnston	Y	Y	Y	Y	Y	N	Y	N
Long	Y	Y	Y	Y	?	N	Y	N
MAINE								
Hathaway	Y	Y	Y	N	N	N	Y	N
Muskie	Y	N	Y	N	N	N	Y	N
MARYLAND								
Sarbanes	Y	Y	N	N	N	N	Y	N
Mathias	?	?	?	?	?	?	?	?
MASSACHUSETTS								
Kennedy	Y	Y	N	N	N	N	Y	N
Brooke	Y	Y	N	N	N	Y	Y	?
MICHIGAN								
Riegle	Y	Y	N	N	N	N	Y	N
Griffin	Y	N	Y	N	N	Y	Y	Y
MINNESOTA								
Anderson	†	?	-	?	?	?	?	?
Humphrey, M.	Y	Y	N	N	N	N	Y	N
MISSISSIPPI								
Eastland	Y	?	?	Y	Y	N	Y	N
Stennis	Y	N	Y	Y	Y	N	Y	N
MISSOURI								
Eagleton	Y	N	Y	N	N	N	Y	N
Danforth	Y	N	Y	N	N	Y	Y	N
MONTANA								
Melcher	Y	N	Y	Y	Y	N	Y	N
Hatfield, P.	?	?	?	?	?	?	?	?
NEBRASKA								
Zorinsky	Y	N	Y	Y	Y	N	Y	Y
Curtis	Y	?	?	Y	Y	Y	Y	Y
NEVADA								
Cannon	Y	N	Y	N	N	N	Y	N
Laxalt	Y	N	Y	Y	Y	Y	Y	Y
NEW HAMPSHIRE								
Durkin	Y	Y	N	N	N	N	Y	N
McIntyre	Y	N	Y	N	N	N	Y	N
NEW JERSEY								
Williams	Y	Y	N	-	N	N	Y	N
Case	Y	Y	N	?	N	N	Y	N
NEW MEXICO								
Domenici	Y	N	Y	Y	Y	Y	Y	Y
Schmitt	Y	Y	N	Y	Y	Y	Y	Y
NEW YORK								
Moynihan	Y	Y	N	N	N	N	Y	N
Javits	Y	Y	N	N	N	N	Y	N
NORTH CAROLINA								
Morgan	Y	Y	Y	Y	Y	Y	Y	N
Helms	Y	Y	Y	Y	Y	Y	Y	Y
NORTH DAKOTA								
Burdick	Y	N	Y	N	N	N	Y	N
Young	Y	?	?	Y	Y	N	Y	Y
OHIO								
Glenn	Y	Y	Y	N	N	N	Y	N
Metzenbaum	Y	Y	N	N	N	N	Y	N
OKLAHOMA								
Bartlett	Y	N	Y	Y	Y	Y	Y	N
Bellmon	Y	N	Y	Y	Y	N	Y	N
OREGON								
Hatfield, M.	Y	†	X	†	†	†	†	-
Packwood	Y	Y	?	Y	Y	Y	Y	Y
PENNSYLVANIA								
Heinz	Y	N	N	N	Y	Y	Y	N
Schweiker	Y	Y	Y	N	N	Y	Y	Y
RHODE ISLAND								
Pell	Y	Y	N	?	N	Y	Y	N
Chafee	Y	Y	Y	N	N	Y	Y	N
SOUTH CAROLINA								
Hollings	Y	?	?	Y	Y	N	Y	N
Thurmond	Y	N	Y	Y	Y	Y	Y	Y
SOUTH DAKOTA								
Abourezk	Y	Y	?	?	?	?	?	N
McGovern	Y	Y	X	?	N	N	Y	N
TENNESSEE								
Sasser	Y	N	Y	Y	Y	N	Y	N
Baker	Y	N	Y	Y	Y	Y	Y	Y
TEXAS								
Bentsen	Y	N	Y	Y	Y	N	Y	N
Tower	Y	N	Y	Y	Y	Y	Y	Y
UTAH								
Garn	Y	N	Y	Y	Y	Y	Y	Y
Hatch	Y	N	Y	?	?	Y	Y	Y
VERMONT								
Leahy	Y	N	Y	N	N	Y	Y	N
Stafford	Y	N	Y	N	N	Y	Y	N
VIRGINIA								
*Byrd, H.	Y	N	Y	Y	Y	Y	Y	Y
Scott	N	N	?	?	Y	Y	Y	Y
WASHINGTON								
Jackson	Y	N	Y	N	N	N	Y	N
Magnuson	Y	N	Y	Y	Y	N	Y	N
WEST VIRGINIA								
Byrd, R.	Y	Y	✓	Y	Y	N	Y	N
Randolph	Y	Y	Y	N	N	N	Y	N
WISCONSIN								
Nelson	N	Y	N	N	N	N	Y	N
Proxmire	N	N	Y	N	N	N	Y	N
WYOMING								
Hansen	Y	N	Y	Y	Y	Y	Y	Y
Wallop	Y	N	Y	N	Y	Y	Y	Y

Democrats ***Republicans***

Byrd elected as independent.

KEY

- Y Voted for (yea).
- ✓ Paired for.
- † Announced for.
- # CQ Poll for.
- N Voted against (nay).
- X Paired against.
- - Announced against.
- ▮ CQ Poll against.
- P Voted "present."
- ● Voted "present" to avoid possible conflict of interest.
- ? Did not vote or otherwise make a position known.

221. S 2899. Endangered Species. Passage of the bill to extend the Endangered Species Act of 1973 for three years, until 1981, and to establish a special commission that could exempt federal projects from the law's requirement that no project be built that would harm an endangered plant or animal species. Passed 94-3: R 36-2; D 58-1 (ND 39-1; SD 19-0), July 19, 1978.

222. S 3084. Housing and Community Development. Morgan, D-N.C., amendment, to the Chiles, D-Fla., amendment *(see vote 223, below)*, to reduce fiscal 1979 authorizations in the bill for assisted housing programs by $6.8 billion. Rejected 42-47: R 11-23; D 31-24 (ND 24-14; SD 7-10), July 19, 1978.

223. S 3084. Housing and Community Development. Chiles, D-Fla., amendment to reduce fiscal 1979 authorizations in the bill for assisted housing programs by $8 billion. Adopted 60-21: R 25-5; D 35-16 (ND 19-15; SD 16-1), July 19, 1978. A "yea" was a vote supporting the president's position.

224. S 3084. Housing and Community Development. Tower, R-Texas, amendment to allow cities with "distressed" areas to qualify for urban development action grants. Adopted 47-38: R 20-13; D 27-25 (ND 10-24; SD 17-1), July 20, 1978. A "nay" was a vote supporting the president's position.

225. S 3084. Housing and Community Development. Bentsen, D-Texas, motion to table (kill) the Tower, R-Texas, motion to reconsider the vote on the Tower amendment *(vote 224, above)*. Motion agreed to 52-38: R 25-10; D 27-28 (ND 10-27; SD 17-1), July 20, 1978.

226. S 3084. Housing and Community Development. Schmitt, R-N.M., amendment, to the Chiles, D-Fla., amendment *(see vote 227, below)*, to require the Department of Housing and Urban Development to publish in the *Federal Register* an economic impact analysis of each proposed regulation. Rejected 36-57: R 29-6; D 7-51 (ND 3-36; SD 4-15), July 20, 1978.

227. S 3084. Housing and Community Development. Chiles, D-Fla., amendment to require the secretary of Housing and Urban Development to analyze the amount of paperwork expected to result from new regulations and to require the results to be published in the *Federal Register.* Adopted 93-0: R 36-0; D 57-0 (ND 38-0; SD 19-0), July 20, 1978.

228. S 3084. Housing and Community Development. Schmitt, R-N.M., amendment to allow one house of Congress to veto proposed regulations issued by the Department of Housing and Urban Development. Rejected 29-65: R 24-11; D 5-54 (ND 2-39; SD 3-15), July 20, 1978.

	229	230	231	232	233	234	235	236
ALABAMA								
Allen, M.	Y	Y	?	?	Y	N	Y	Y
Sparkman	N	Y	Y	?	Y	N	Y	Y
ALASKA								
Gravel	?	?	†	†	Y	N	Y	Y
Stevens	N	Y	?	?	Y	N	Y	Y
ARIZONA								
DeConcini	N	Y	?	?	Y	N	Y	Y
Goldwater	Y	Y	Y	Y	Y	Y	N	Y
ARKANSAS								
Bumpers	N	Y	Y	Y	Y	Y	N	Y
Hodges	Y	Y	Y	Y	Y	N	Y	Y
CALIFORNIA								
Cranston	N	Y	Y	Y	?	?	?	?
Hayakawa	Y	?	?	?	Y	Y	N	Y
COLORADO								
Hart	N	Y	Y	Y	Y	N	Y	Y
Haskell	N	Y	?	?	Y	N	Y	Y
CONNECTICUT								
Ribicoff	N	Y	†	†	Y	N	Y	Y
Weicker	N	Y	?	?	?	?	?	?
DELAWARE								
Biden	?	?	Y	Y	Y	N	Y	Y
Roth	Y	Y	?	Y	Y	Y	N	Y
FLORIDA								
Chiles	N	Y	Y	Y	Y	N	Y	Y
Stone	N	Y	Y	Y	Y	N	Y	Y
GEORGIA								
Nunn	N	Y	Y	Y	Y	Y	N	Y
Talmadge	N	Y	Y	Y	Y	Y	N	Y
HAWAII								
Inouye	?	?	Y	Y	Y	N	Y	Y
Matsunaga	N	Y	?	Y	Y	N	Y	Y
IDAHO								
Church	N	Y	Y	Y	Y	N	Y	Y
McClure	Y	Y	Y	Y	Y	Y	N	Y
ILLINOIS								
Stevenson	N	Y	Y	?	Y	N	Y	Y
Percy	N	Y	†	?	?	?	?	?
INDIANA								
Bayh	N	Y	Y	Y	Y	N	Y	Y
Lugar	Y	Y	Y	Y	Y	Y	N	Y
IOWA								
Clark	N	Y	†	†	Y	N	Y	Y
Culver	N	Y	Y	Y	Y	N	Y	Y
KANSAS								
Dole	Y	Y	Y	Y	Y	N	Y	Y
Pearson	Y	Y	Y	Y	Y	Y	N	Y
KENTUCKY								
Ford	N	Y	Y	Y	Y	N	Y	Y
Huddleston	?	?	?	?	Y	N	Y	Y
LOUISIANA								
Johnston	Y	Y	?	?	Y	N	Y	Y
Long	Y	Y	Y	Y	Y	Y	N	Y
MAINE								
Hathaway	N	Y	?	?	Y	N	Y	Y
Muskie	N	Y	Y	?	Y	Y	N	Y
MARYLAND								
Sarbanes	N	Y	Y	Y	Y	N	Y	Y
Mathias	?	?	Y	Y	Y	N	Y	Y
MASSACHUSETTS								
Kennedy	N	Y	Y	Y	Y	N	Y	Y
Brooke	†	?	?	?	Y	N	Y	Y
MICHIGAN								
Riegle	N	Y	Y	Y	Y	N	Y	Y
Griffin	Y	Y	?	?	?	?	?	?
MINNESOTA								
Anderson	?	†	†	†	†	-	†	?
Humphrey, M.	N	Y	Y	Y	Y	N	Y	Y
MISSISSIPPI								
Eastland	Y	Y	Y	Y	Y	Y	N	Y
Stennis	?	Y	Y	?	Y	Y	N	Y
MISSOURI								
Eagleton	?	?	?	?	Y	Y	N	Y
Danforth	N	Y	Y	?	Y	Y	N	Y
MONTANA								
Melcher	Y	Y	Y	Y	Y	N	Y	Y
Hatfield, P.	?	?	?	?	Y	N	Y	Y
NEBRASKA								
Zorinsky	Y	Y	Y	Y	Y	N	Y	Y
Curtis	Y	Y	N	Y	Y	Y	N	Y
NEVADA								
Cannon	N	Y	Y	Y	Y	N	Y	Y
Laxalt	Y	N	?	?	Y	Y	N	Y
NEW HAMPSHIRE								
Durkin	N	Y	Y	Y	Y	N	Y	Y
McIntyre	?	?	?	?	Y	N	Y	Y
NEW JERSEY								
Williams	N	Y	Y	Y	Y	N	Y	Y
Case	N	Y	Y	Y	Y	N	Y	Y
NEW MEXICO								
Domenici	Y	Y	Y	Y	Y	N	Y	Y
Schmitt	Y	Y	Y	Y	Y	N	Y	Y
NEW YORK								
Moynihan	N	Y	†	†	Y	N	Y	Y
Javits	N	Y	Y	Y	Y	Y	N	Y
NORTH CAROLINA								
Morgan	N	Y	Y	Y	Y	N	Y	Y
Helms	Y	N	Y	Y	Y	N	Y	Y
NORTH DAKOTA								
Burdick	?	†	†	†	Y	N	Y	Y
Young	Y	Y	Y	Y	Y	Y	N	Y
OHIO								
Glenn	N	Y	Y	Y	?	?	?	?
Metzenbaum	N	Y	Y	Y	Y	N	Y	Y
OKLAHOMA								
Bartlett	Y	Y	Y	Y	Y	N	Y	Y
Bellmon	†	?	?	?	Y	Y	N	Y
OREGON								
Hatfield, M.	†	†	†	†	Y	N	Y	Y
Packwood	Y	Y	Y	Y	Y	Y	N	Y
PENNSYLVANIA								
Heinz	N	Y	Y	Y	Y	N	Y	Y
Schweiker	Y	Y	Y	Y	Y	N	Y	Y
RHODE ISLAND								
Pell	N	Y	Y	Y	Y	N	Y	Y
Chafee	N	Y	Y	Y	Y	Y	N	Y
SOUTH CAROLINA								
Hollings	Y	Y	Y	Y	?	N	Y	Y
Thurmond	N	Y	†	†	Y	N	✓	†
SOUTH DAKOTA								
Abourezk	?	?	Y	Y	Y	N	Y	Y
McGovern	N	Y	Y	Y	Y	N	Y	Y
TENNESSEE								
Sasser	N	Y	Y	†	Y	N	Y	Y
Baker	†	?	?	?	Y	N	Y	Y
TEXAS								
Bentsen	N	Y	Y	Y	?	?	?	?
Tower	Y	Y	Y	Y	†	-	†	†
UTAH								
Garn	Y	Y	Y	Y	Y	Y	N	Y
Hatch	Y	Y	Y	Y	Y	Y	N	Y
VERMONT								
Leahy	N	Y	Y	Y	Y	N	Y	Y
Stafford	N	Y	Y	Y	Y	N	Y	Y
VIRGINIA								
*Byrd, H.	Y	Y	Y	Y	Y	Y	N	Y
Scott	Y	N	Y	Y	Y	Y	X	Y
WASHINGTON								
Jackson	N	Y	Y	Y	Y	N	Y	Y
Magnuson	N	Y	Y	Y	†	?	?	†
WEST VIRGINIA								
Byrd, R.	Y	Y	Y	Y	Y	N	Y	Y
Randolph	Y	Y	Y	Y	†	-	†	†
WISCONSIN								
Nelson	N	Y	Y	Y	Y	Y	N	Y
Proxmire	N	Y	Y	Y	Y	Y	N	Y
WYOMING								
Hansen	Y	Y	Y	Y	Y	Y	N	Y
Wallop	Y	Y	Y	Y	Y	Y	N	Y

Democrats ***Republicans***

Byrd elected as independent.

KEY

- Y Voted for (yea).
- ✓ Paired for.
- † Announced for.
- # CQ Poll for.
- N Voted against (nay).
- X Paired against.
- - Announced against.
- ▌ CQ Poll against.
- P Voted "present."
- ● Voted "present" to avoid possible conflict of interest.
- ? Did not vote or otherwise make a position known.

229. S 3084. Housing and Community Development. Griffin, R-Mich. amendment to clarify the meaning of the term "expected to reside" in the Community Development Act of 1974. (The effect of the amendment was to block efforts by HUD to prod largely white, middle-class communities into increasing the number of low- and moderate-income residents.) Rejected 34-50: R 23-10; D 11-40 (ND 4-30; SD 7-10), July 20, 1978.

230. S 3084. Housing and Community Development. Passage of the bill to revise, extend and authorize $33.3 billion for certain housing and community development programs. Passed 81-3: R 29-3; D 52-0 (ND 34-0; SD 18-0), July 20, 1978.

231. S 2534. Health Maintenance Organization (HMO). Passage of the bill to authorize $185 million through fiscal 1981 for grants and loans to prepaid group medical practices (health maintenance organizations), and through fiscal 1983 for an HMO management training program. Passed 71-1: R 25-1; D 46-0 (ND 30-0; SD 16-0), July 21, 1978.

232. S 3085. Child Nutrition Programs. Passage of the bill to authorize $2.25 billion in fiscal years 1979-82 for the supplemental food program for women, infants and children (WIC), and to make changes in the child care food program and the school lunch and breakfast programs. Passed 68-0: R 26-0; D 42-0 (ND 29-0; SD 13-0), July 21, 1978.

233. S 2850. Older Americans Act. Melcher, D-Mont., amendment to allow the commissioner on aging to reimburse states for model project funds for social services supplied during a federally declared disaster. Adopted 89-0: R 34-0; D 55-0 (ND 38-0; SD 17-0), July 24, 1978.

234. S 2850. Older Americans Act. Eagleton, D-Mo., motion to table (kill) the Kennedy, D-Mass., amendment *(see vote 235, below)*. Rejected 30-60: R 19-15; D 11-45 (ND 4-34; SD 7-11), July 24, 1978.

235. S 2850. Older Americans Act. Kennedy, D-Mass., amendment to provide a separate authorization of $100 million in fiscal 1979 and $120 million in fiscal 1980 for home-delivered nutrition services (meals on wheels). Adopted 59-29: R 14-18; D 45-11 (ND 34-4; SD 11-7), July 24, 1978.

236. S 2850. Older Americans Act. Domenici, R-N.M., amendment to require that 1 percent of new authorizations be spent on a project for the transition to private employment of elderly public service job holders. Adopted 89-0: R 33-0; D 56-0 (ND 38-0; SD 18-0), July 24, 1978.

CQ Senate Votes 237-244

Corresponding to Congressional Record Votes 241, 242, 243, 244, 245, 246, 247, 248

	237	238	239	240	241	242	243	244
ALABAMA								
Allen, M.	Y	N	Y	N	Y	?	?	?
Sparkman	Y	N	Y	Y	Y	N	Y	N
ALASKA								
Gravel	Y	Y	Y	Y	Y	N	Y	N
Stevens	Y	N	Y	Y	Y	Y	Y	Y
ARIZONA								
DeConcini	Y	N	Y	N	Y	N	Y	N
Goldwater	Y	N	P	Y	Y	Y	N	Y
ARKANSAS								
Bumpers	Y	N	Y	Y	Y	N	Y	N
Hodges	Y	N	Y	Y	Y	N	Y	N
CALIFORNIA								
Cranston	?	?	?	N	Y	N	Y	N
Hayakawa	Y	Y	Y	Y	Y	Y	N	Y
COLORADO								
Hart	Y	?	Y	Y	Y	N	Y	N
Haskell	Y	N	Y	N	Y	N	Y	N
CONNECTICUT								
Ribicoff	Y	Y	Y	Y	Y	N	Y	N
Weicker	?	?	?	?	?	Y	N	Y
DELAWARE								
Biden	Y	N	Y	N	Y	N	Y	N
Roth	Y	N	Y	N	Y	N	Y	N
FLORIDA								
Chiles	Y	N	Y	Y	Y	N	Y	N
Stone	Y	N	Y	N	Y	N	Y	Y
GEORGIA								
Nunn	Y	N	Y	Y	Y	Y	N	Y
Talmadge	Y	N	Y	N	Y	Y	N	Y
HAWAII								
Inouye	Y	N	?	Y	Y	N	Y	N
Matsunaga	Y	N	Y	Y	Y	N	Y	N
IDAHO								
Church	Y	N	Y	Y	Y	N	Y	N
McClure	Y	N	Y	Y	Y	Y	N	Y
ILLINOIS								
Stevenson	Y	Y	Y	N	Y	N	Y	N
Percy	Y	Y	Y	N	Y	N	Y	N
INDIANA								
Bayh	Y	N	Y	N	Y	N	?	N
Lugar	Y	N	Y	Y	Y	Y	N	Y
IOWA								
Clark	Y	N	Y	N	Y	N	Y	N
Culver	Y	N	Y	Y	Y	N	Y	N
KANSAS								
Dole	Y	N	Y	N	Y	Y	N	Y
Pearson	Y	N	Y	Y	Y	N	Y	N
KENTUCKY								
Ford	Y	N	Y	Y	Y	N	Y	N
Huddleston	Y	N	Y	Y	Y	N	Y	N
LOUISIANA								
Johnston	Y	N	Y	N	Y	Y	Y	Y
Long	Y	N	Y	Y	Y	Y	N	Y
MAINE								
Hathaway	Y	N	Y	N	Y	N	Y	N
Muskie	Y	N	Y	N	Y	N	Y	N
MARYLAND								
Sarbanes	Y	Y	Y	N	Y	N	Y	N
Mathias	Y	Y	Y	Y	Y	N	Y	N
MASSACHUSETTS								
Kennedy	Y	Y	Y	N	Y	N	N	N
Brooke	Y	Y	Y	N	Y	N	Y	N
MICHIGAN								
Riegle	Y	Y	Y	N	Y	?	?	N
Griffin	?	?	?	Y	Y	Y	Y	Y
MINNESOTA								
Anderson	?	-	†	N	Y	-	†	-
Humphrey, M.	Y	N	Y	Y	Y	N	Y	-
MISSISSIPPI								
Eastland	Y	N	Y	N	Y	Y	N	Y
Stennis	Y	N	?	Y	?	Y	N	Y
MISSOURI								
Eagleton	Y	Y	Y	N	Y	N	Y	N
Danforth	Y	N	Y	Y	Y	Y	Y	Y
MONTANA								
Melcher	Y	N	Y	Y	Y	N	Y	N
Hatfield, P.	?	N	Y	Y	Y	N	Y	N
NEBRASKA								
Zorinsky	Y	N	Y	Y	Y	N	Y	N
Curtis	Y	N	X	Y	Y	Y	N	Y
NEVADA								
Cannon	Y	Y	Y	Y	Y	Y	N	Y
Laxalt	Y	N	Y	N	†	Y	N	Y
NEW HAMPSHIRE								
Durkin	Y	N	Y	N	Y	N	Y	-
McIntyre	Y	N	Y	N	Y	N	Y	N
NEW JERSEY								
Williams	Y	Y	Y	Y	Y	N	Y	N
Case	Y	Y	Y	N	Y	N	Y	N
NEW MEXICO								
Domenici	Y	N	Y	N	Y	N	Y	Y
Schmitt	Y	N	Y	Y	Y	Y	N	Y
NEW YORK								
Moynihan	Y	Y	Y	N	Y	N	Y	N
Javits	Y	Y	Y	N	Y	N	Y	N
NORTH CAROLINA								
Morgan	Y	N	Y	Y	†	Y	N	Y
Helms	Y	N	Y	Y	Y	Y	N	Y
NORTH DAKOTA								
Burdick	Y	N	Y	N	Y	N	Y	N
Young	Y	Y	?	Y	Y	Y	N	Y
OHIO								
Glenn	?	?	Y	Y	Y	N	Y	N
Metzenbaum	Y	Y	Y	N	Y	N	Y	N
OKLAHOMA								
Bartlett	Y	N	Y	Y	Y	Y	N	Y
Bellmon	Y	N	Y	Y	Y	Y	N	Y
OREGON								
Hatfield, M.	Y	N	Y	N	Y	N	Y	N
Packwood	Y	N	†	Y	Y	Y	N	Y
PENNSYLVANIA								
Heinz	Y	Y	Y	N	Y	Y	N	Y
Schweiker	Y	Y	Y	Y	Y	Y	N	Y
RHODE ISLAND								
Pell	Y	Y	Y	N	Y	N	Y	N
Chafee	Y	Y	Y	Y	Y	N	Y	N
SOUTH CAROLINA								
Hollings	Y	N	Y	N	Y	Y	N	Y
Thurmond	†	-	✓	Y	Y	Y	N	Y
SOUTH DAKOTA								
Abourezk	Y	N	?	N	?	?	?	N
McGovern	Y	N	Y	Y	Y	N	Y	N
TENNESSEE								
Sasser	Y	N	Y	Y	Y	N	Y	N
Baker	Y	N	Y	Y	Y	Y	N	Y
TEXAS								
Bentsen	?	N	Y	Y	Y	Y	Y	Y
Tower	Y	N	Y	Y	Y	Y	N	Y
UTAH								
Garn	Y	N	Y	Y	Y	Y	N	Y
Hatch	Y	N	Y	Y	Y	Y	N	Y
VERMONT								
Leahy	Y	N	Y	N	Y	N	Y	N
Stafford	Y	N	Y	Y	Y	N	Y	N
VIRGINIA								
*Byrd, H.	Y	N	N	Y	Y	Y	N	Y
Scott	Y	N	Y	Y	Y	Y	N	Y
WASHINGTON								
Jackson	Y	N	Y	N	Y	N	Y	N
Magnuson	†	?	†	N	Y	N	Y	N
WEST VIRGINIA								
Byrd, R.	Y	N	Y	Y	Y	N	N	Y
Randolph	†	N	Y	N	Y	Y	N	Y
WISCONSIN								
Nelson	Y	N	Y	Y	?	N	Y	N
Proxmire	Y	N	N	N	Y	N	Y	N
WYOMING								
Hansen	Y	N	Y	Y	Y	Y	N	Y
Wallop	Y	N	Y	Y	Y	Y	N	Y

Democrats ***Republicans***

*Byrd elected as independent.

KEY

- Y Voted for (yea).
- ✓ Paired for.
- † Announced for.
- # CQ Poll for.
- N Voted against (nay).
- X Paired against.
- \- Announced against.
- ▮ CQ Poll against.
- P Voted "present."
- ● Voted "present" to avoid possible conflict of interest.
- ? Did not vote or otherwise make a position known.

237. S 2850. Older Americans Act. Eagleton, D-Mo., amendment to discount Social Security and housing assistance payments when determining eligibility under the bill, to increase federal funding for programs for elderly Indians, to allow payment by recipients for meals provided under the bill, to require a report by the comptroller general on the relationship between the programs under the bill and other federal programs and to make other technical changes. Adopted 90-0: R 35-0; D 55-0 (ND 37-0; SD 18-0), July 24, 1978.

238. S 2850. Older Americans Act. Javits, R-N.Y., amendment, to the Domenici, R-N.M., amendment, to limit to one-half of 1 percent of appropriations or $5 million, whichever was greater, the amount that could be used for additional payments to states to meet the excess costs of providing services to older Americans in rural areas. Rejected 22-70: R 10-25; D 12-45 (ND 12-26; SD 0-19), July 24, 1978. (The Domenici amendment, to reallocate funds in the bill so as to provide extra assistance to states for the higher cost of delivering services to the rural elderly, was subsequently passed by voice vote.)

239. S 2850. Older Americans Act. Passage of the bill to amend the 1965 Older Americans Act to provide for improved programs for older persons. Passed 85-2: R 31-0; D 54-2 (ND 37-1; SD 17-1), July 24, 1978.

240. S 3075. Foreign Military Aid. Byrd, D-W.Va., amendment, to the Sparkman, D-Ala., amendment, to outline U.S. policy on settlement of the Cyprus dispute between Greece and Turkey as part of a repeal of the existing U.S. arms embargo against Turkey. Adopted 57-42: R 27-10; D 30-32 (ND 17-26; SD 13-6), July 25, 1978. A "yea" was a vote supporting the president's position. (The Sparkman amendment to lift the embargo, with the principles set forth by the Byrd amendment added, was adopted subsequently by voice vote.)

241. S 3075. Foreign Military Aid. Dole, R-Kan., amendment to state the sense of the Senate that any proposed policy changes in the 1954 U.S.-Republic of China Mutual Defense Treaty should be referred to the Senate. Adopted 94-0: R 36-0; D 58-0 (ND 41-0; SD 17-0), July 25, 1978.

242. S 3075. Foreign Military Aid. Baker, R-Tenn., motion to table (kill) the Case, R-N.J., amendment *(see vote 243, below)* to the Hayakawa, R-Calif., amendment *(see vote 245, p. 39-S)*. Motion rejected 39-57: R 27-11; D 12-46 (ND 2-38; SD 10-8), July 26, 1978.

243. S 3075. Foreign Military Aid. Case, R-N.J., amendment, to the Hayakawa, R-Calif., amendment *(see vote 245, p. 39-S)*, to provide that no U. S. sanctions against Rhodesia could be lifted until free elections for a new government were held under international observation. Adopted 59-36: R 14-24; D 45-12 (ND 35-4; SD 10-8), July 26, 1978.

244. S 3075. Foreign Military Aid. Danforth, R-Mo., amendment, to the Hayakawa, R-Calif., amendment *(see vote 245, p. 39-S)*, to lift U.S. sanctions against Rhodesia from Oct. 1 to Dec. 31, 1978. Rejected 42-54: R 28-10; D 14-44 (ND 3-37; SD 11-7), July 26, 1978.

	245	246	247	248	249	250
ALABAMA						
Allen, M.	?	?	?	?	?	?
Sparkman	?	N	Y	Y	†	†
ALASKA						
Gravel	Y	N	Y	Y	Y	Y
Stevens	Y	Y	N	Y	Y	Y
ARIZONA						
DeConcini	Y	Y	N	Y	Y	Y
Goldwater	N	Y	N	†	?	?
ARKANSAS						
Bumpers	Y	Y	Y	Y	Y	Y
Hodges	Y	Y	Y	Y	Y	Y
CALIFORNIA						
Cranston	Y	N	Y	Y	Y	Y
Hayakawa	Y	Y	N	Y	Y	Y
COLORADO						
Hart	Y	N	Y	Y	Y	Y
Haskell	Y	Y	Y	Y	?	Y
CONNECTICUT						
Ribicoff	Y	N	Y	Y	Y	Y
Weicker	Y	Y	N	N	Y	Y
DELAWARE						
Biden	Y	Y	Y	Y	Y	Y
Roth	Y	Y	N	Y	Y	Y
FLORIDA						
Chiles	Y	Y	N	Y	Y	Y
Stone	Y	Y	N	Y	Y	Y
GEORGIA						
Nunn	Y	Y	N	Y	Y	Y
Talmadge	Y	Y	N	Y	Y	N
HAWAII						
Inouye	Y	N	Y	Y	Y	?
Matsunaga	Y	N	Y	Y	Y	Y
IDAHO						
Church	Y	N	Y	Y	Y	Y
McClure	N	Y	N	Y	Y	Y
ILLINOIS						
Stevenson	Y	Y	Y	Y	Y	Y
Percy	Y	N	N	Y	Y	Y
INDIANA						
Bayh	Y	Y	Y	Y	Y	Y
Lugar	Y	Y	N	Y	Y	Y
IOWA						
Clark	Y	N	Y	Y	Y	Y
Culver	N	N	Y	Y	Y	Y
KANSAS						
Dole	Y	Y	Y	Y	Y	Y
Pearson	Y	?	?	?	?	?
KENTUCKY						
Ford	Y	Y	Y	Y	Y	Y
Huddleston	Y	Y	N	Y	Y	Y
LOUISIANA						
Johnston	Y	Y	N	Y	Y	Y
Long	Y	Y	N	N	Y	N
MAINE						
Hathaway	Y	N	Y	Y	Y	Y
Muskie	Y	Y	Y	Y	Y	Y
MARYLAND						
Sarbanes	Y	N	Y	Y	Y	?
Mathias	Y	N	?	?	Y	Y
MASSACHUSETTS						
Kennedy	N	N	Y	Y	Y	Y
Brooke	Y	N	N	?	?	?
MICHIGAN						
Riegle	Y	Y	Y	Y	Y	Y
Griffin	Y	Y	N	Y	Y	Y
MINNESOTA						
Anderson	†	?	?	?	†	†
Humphrey, M.	†	?	?	†	†	†
MISSISSIPPI						
Eastland	Y	Y	N	?	?	?
Stennis	Y	?	?	?	?	?
MISSOURI						
Eagleton	Y	N	Y	Y	Y	Y
Danforth	Y	Y	N	Y	Y	Y
MONTANA						
Melcher	Y	Y	Y	N	Y	N
Hatfield, P.	Y	Y	Y	N	Y	Y
NEBRASKA						
Zorinsky	Y	Y	Y	Y	Y	N
Curtis	Y	Y	N	Y	Y	N
NEVADA						
Cannon	Y	Y	Y	Y	Y	Y
Laxalt	Y	Y	N	Y	Y	Y
NEW HAMPSHIRE						
Durkin	Y	N	N	Y	Y	N
McIntyre	Y	N	Y	Y	Y	Y
NEW JERSEY						
Williams	Y	N	Y	Y	Y	Y
Case	Y	N	Y	Y	Y	Y
NEW MEXICO						
Domenici	Y	Y	N	Y	Y	Y
Schmitt	Y	Y	N	Y	Y	Y
NEW YORK						
Moynihan	Y	N	N	Y	Y	Y
Javits	Y	N	Y	Y	Y	Y
NORTH CAROLINA						
Morgan	Y	Y	N	Y	Y	Y
Helms	Y	Y	N	Y	Y	N
NORTH DAKOTA						
Burdick	Y	Y	Y	Y	Y	N
Young	Y	Y	?	?	?	?
OHIO						
Glenn	Y	Y	N	Y	Y	Y
Metzenbaum	Y	N	Y	Y	Y	Y
OKLAHOMA						
Bartlett	Y	Y	N	Y	Y	Y
Bellmon	Y	Y	N	Y	Y	Y
OREGON						
Hatfield, M.	Y	Y	N	N	Y	N
Packwood	Y	Y	N	Y	Y	Y
PENNSYLVANIA						
Heinz	Y	Y	N	Y	Y	Y
Schweiker	Y	Y	N	Y	Y	Y
RHODE ISLAND						
Pell	Y	Y	Y	Y	Y	Y
Chafee	Y	Y	Y	Y	Y	Y
SOUTH CAROLINA						
Hollings	Y	Y	N	Y	Y	N
Thurmond	Y	Y	N	Y	Y	N
SOUTH DAKOTA						
Abourezk	N	?	?	?	?	?
McGovern	Y	N	Y	N	Y	Y
TENNESSEE						
Sasser	Y	Y	Y	Y	Y	Y
Baker	Y	Y	N	Y	Y	Y
TEXAS						
Bentsen	Y	Y	N	Y	Y	Y
Tower	Y	Y	N	Y	Y	Y
UTAH						
Garn	Y	Y	N	Y	Y	Y
Hatch	Y	Y	N	Y	Y	Y
VERMONT						
Leahy	Y	Y	Y	Y	Y	Y
Stafford	Y	Y	Y	Y	Y	Y
VIRGINIA						
*Byrd, H.	Y	Y	N	Y	Y	N
Scott	N	Y	N	?	?	?
WASHINGTON						
Jackson	Y	Y	N	Y	Y	Y
Magnuson	Y	Y	N	Y	Y	Y
WEST VIRGINIA						
Byrd, R.	Y	Y	N	Y	Y	Y
Randolph	Y	Y	N	Y	Y	Y
WISCONSIN						
Nelson	Y	Y	Y	Y	Y	Y
Proxmire	Y	Y	Y	N	Y	N
WYOMING						
Hansen	Y	Y	N	Y	Y	Y
Wallop	Y	Y	N	Y	Y	Y

Democrats ***Republicans***

*Byrd elected as independent.

KEY

- Y Voted for (yea).
- ✓ Paired for.
- † Announced for.
- # CQ Poll for.
- N Voted against (nay).
- X Paired against.
- - Announced against.
- ▮ CQ Poll against.
- P Voted "present."
- ● Voted "present" to avoid possible conflict of interest.
- ? Did not vote or otherwise make a position known.

245. S 3075. Foreign Military Aid. Hayakawa, R-Calif., amendment, as amended by the Case, R-N.J., amendment *(see vote 243, p. 38-S)*, to provide that U.S. sanctions against Rhodesia could not be lifted until the president determined that the Rhodesian government had "committed itself" to a conference of all groups contending for power in the nation and that free elections involving all population groups have been held "with observation by impartial internationally recognized observers." Adopted 90-6: R 35-3; D 55-3 (ND 38-3; SD 17-0), July 26, 1978.

246. S 3075. Foreign Military Aid. Byrd, Ind-Va., amendment to delete $40 million from the $110 million authorization for southern Africa. Adopted 69-25: R 32-5; D 37-20 (ND 21-19; SD 16-1), July 26, 1978.

247. S 3075. Foreign Military Aid. McGovern, D-S.D., motion to table (kill) the Baker, R-Tenn., amendment to delete from existing law a requirement that the secretary of state automatically approve any application for a non-immigrant visa to a member of a communist organization seeking to enter the United States. Rejected 42-50: R 5-30; D 37-20 (ND 32-8; SD 5-12), July 26, 1978. (The Baker amendment was adopted subsequently by voice vote.)

248. S 3075. Foreign Military Aid. Percy, R-Ill., amendment to express the sense of Congress that U.S. troop withdrawals from South Korea could "seriously" upset the military balance of power in the region and "requires full advance consultation" with Congress. Adopted 81-7: R 30-2; D 51-5 (ND 36-4; SD 15-1), July 26, 1978.

249. S 3075. Foreign Military Aid. Baker, R-Tenn., amendment to express the sense of Congress that the United States continue to promote direct negotiations between Egypt and Israel, and that the United States provide additional advanced military aircraft to Israel. Adopted 87-0: R 33-0; D 54-0 (ND 39-0; SD 15-0), July 26, 1978.

250. S 3075. Foreign Military Aid. Passage of the bill to authorize $2,850,000,000 for foreign military assistance, arms sales and economic support programs of the State Department for fiscal 1979. Passed 73-13: R 29-4; D 44-9 (ND 33-5; SD 11-4), July 26, 1978.

CQ Senate Votes 251-258

Corresponding to Congressional Record Votes 255, 256, 257, 258, 259, 260, 261, 262

	251	252	253	254	255	256	257	258
ALABAMA								
Allen, M.	N	N	N	N	Y	Y	Y	Y
Sparkman	Y	N	N	Y	Y	N	Y	Y
ALASKA								
Gravel	N	Y	Y	Y	Y	N	Y	Y
Stevens	N	-	-	Y	Y	Y	Y	Y
ARIZONA								
DeConcini	N	N	N	N	Y	Y	Y	Y
Goldwater	N	N	N	N	?	?	?	?
ARKANSAS								
Bumpers	Y	N	Y	Y	Y	N	?	?
Hodges	N	N	N	Y	Y	Y	?	?
CALIFORNIA								
Cranston	Y	Y	Y	Y	?	?	?	?
Hayakawa	N	N	N	N	Y	Y	Y	Y
COLORADO								
Hart	Y	Y	Y	Y	Y	N	Y	Y
Haskell	Y	Y	Y	Y	?	?	?	?
CONNECTICUT								
Ribicoff	Y	Y	Y	Y	Y	Y	Y	Y
Weicker	Y	Y	Y	Y	Y	Y	Y	Y
DELAWARE								
Biden	Y	Y	Y	Y	?	?	?	?
Roth	N	N	N	N	Y	Y	Y	Y
FLORIDA								
Chiles	N	Y	Y	N	Y	N	Y	Y
Stone	Y	Y	Y	Y	Y	Y	Y	Y
GEORGIA								
Nunn	Y	Y	Y	N	Y	N	Y	?
Talmadge	Y	Y	Y	N	Y	Y	?	?
HAWAII								
Inouye	Y	Y	Y	Y	?	N	Y	Y
Matsunaga	Y	Y	Y	Y	?	N	Y	Y
IDAHO								
Church	Y	N	N	N	Y	N	Y	Y
McClure	N	N	N	N	Y	Y	Y	Y
ILLINOIS								
Stevenson	Y	Y	Y	Y	Y	N	Y	Y
Percy	Y	Y	Y	Y	Y	Y	Y	Y
INDIANA								
Bayh	Y	Y	Y	Y	Y	N	Y	Y
Lugar	Y	N	N	Y	Y	Y	Y	Y
IOWA								
Clark	Y	Y	Y	Y	Y	N	Y	Y
Culver	Y	Y	Y	Y	Y	N	N	Y
KANSAS								
Dole	N	N	N	Y	Y	Y	Y	Y
Pearson	Y	Y	Y	Y	Y	Y	Y	Y
KENTUCKY								
Ford	N	N	N	Y	Y	Y	Y	?
Huddleston	N	Y	N	Y	Y	Y	Y	?
LOUISIANA								
Johnston	N	N	N	Y	Y	?	?	?
Long	N	N	N	Y	Y	N	Y	Y
MAINE								
Hathaway	Y	Y	Y	Y	?	?	?	?
Muskie	Y	Y	Y	Y	Y	N	Y	Y
MARYLAND								
Sarbanes	Y	Y	Y	Y	Y	Y	Y	Y
Mathias	Y	Y	Y	Y	Y	N	Y	Y
MASSACHUSETTS								
Kennedy	Y	Y	Y	Y	Y	N	Y	?
Brooke	?	?	?	?	?	?	?	?
MICHIGAN								
Riegle	Y	Y	Y	Y	Y	Y	Y	Y
Griffin	N	N	N	N	?	?	?	?
MINNESOTA								
Anderson	?	?	?	?	†	-	†	†
Humphrey, M.	†	†	†	†	†	-	†	†
MISSISSIPPI								
Eastland	N	N	?	?	?	?	?	?
Stennis	N	N	N	N	Y	?	?	?
MISSOURI								
Eagleton	Y	Y	Y	Y	?	?	?	?
Danforth	Y	Y	Y	Y	Y	Y	Y	Y
MONTANA								
Melcher	N	N	N	Y	Y	Y	Y	Y
Hatfield, P.	Y	N	N	Y	Y	N	Y	Y
NEBRASKA								
Zorinsky	Y	Y	Y	N	Y	Y	Y	Y
Curtis	N	N	N	N	Y	Y	Y	Y
NEVADA								
Cannon	N	Y	Y	N	Y	Y	Y	Y
Laxalt	N	N	N	N	?	?	?	?
NEW HAMPSHIRE								
Durkin	Y	Y	Y	Y	Y	N	Y	Y
McIntyre	Y	Y	Y	Y	Y	?	?	?
NEW JERSEY								
Williams	Y	Y	Y	Y	Y	N	Y	Y
Case	Y	Y	Y	Y	†	-	†	†
NEW MEXICO								
Domenici	Y	N	N	N	Y	Y	Y	Y
Schmitt	N	N	N	Y	Y	Y	Y	Y
NEW YORK								
Moynihan	Y	Y	Y	Y	Y	N	Y	Y
Javits	Y	Y	Y	Y	Y	N	Y	Y
NORTH CAROLINA								
Morgan	N	N	N	Y	Y	Y	Y	Y
Helms	N	N	N	N	Y	Y	Y	Y
NORTH DAKOTA								
Burdick	Y	Y	Y	N	Y	N	Y	Y
Young	N	N	N	N	Y	Y	Y	Y
OHIO								
Glenn	Y	N	N	Y	Y	N	Y	Y
Metzenbaum	Y	Y	?	Y	Y	Y	Y	Y
OKLAHOMA								
Bartlett	N	N	N	N	Y	Y	Y	Y
Bellmon	Y	N	N	N	Y	Y	Y	Y
OREGON								
Hatfield, M.	Y	N	N	Y	Y	Y	Y	Y
Packwood	N	N	N	Y	Y	Y	Y	Y
PENNSYLVANIA								
Heinz	Y	Y	Y	Y	Y	Y	Y	Y
Schweiker	Y	Y	Y	N	Y	Y	Y	Y
RHODE ISLAND								
Pell	Y	Y	Y	Y	Y	N	Y	Y
Chafee	Y	Y	Y	Y	?	?	?	?
SOUTH CAROLINA								
Hollings	Y	N	N	N	Y	N	Y	Y
Thurmond	N	N	N	N	Y	Y	Y	Y
SOUTH DAKOTA								
Abourezk	Y	Y	Y	?	?	Y	Y	?
McGovern	Y	?	?	?	?	?	?	?
TENNESSEE								
Sasser	N	N	N	N	Y	N	Y	Y
Baker	N	N	N	Y	Y	Y	Y	?
TEXAS								
Bentsen	N	N	N	N	Y	?	?	?
Tower	N	N	N	N	?	?	?	†
UTAH								
Garn	N	N	N	N	Y	Y	Y	Y
Hatch	N	N	N	N	Y	Y	Y	?
VERMONT								
Leahy	Y	Y	Y	Y	Y	Y	Y	Y
Stafford	Y	Y	?	Y	Y	?	?	?
VIRGINIA								
*Byrd, H.	N	N	N	N	Y	Y	Y	Y
Scott	N	N	N	N	?	Y	Y	Y
WASHINGTON								
Jackson	Y	N	N	Y	Y	N	Y	Y
Magnuson	Y	Y	Y	N	Y	Y	Y	Y
WEST VIRGINIA								
Byrd, R.	N	Y	N	Y	Y	N	Y	Y
Randolph	Y	Y	Y	Y	Y	†	Y	Y
WISCONSIN								
Nelson	Y	Y	Y	Y	Y	N	Y	Y
Proxmire	Y	Y	Y	N	N	Y	Y	Y
WYOMING								
Hansen	N	N	N	N	†	?	?	?
Wallop	N	N	N	?	†	?	?	?

Democrats ***Republicans***

*Byrd elected as independent.

KEY

- Y Voted for (yea).
- ✓ Paired for.
- † Announced for.
- # CQ Poll for.
- N Voted against (nay).
- X Paired against.
- \- Announced against.
- ▮ CQ Poll against.
- P Voted "present."
- ● Voted "present" to avoid possible conflict of interest.
- ? Did not vote or otherwise make a position known.

251. S 2410. Health Planning. Kennedy, D-Mass., motion to table (kill) the Huddleston, D-Ky., amendment, part I, to permit states to treat health maintenance organizations (HMOs) separately from other providers of ambulatory health care with regard to legislation requiring certification (state approval of new or expanded services). Motion agreed to 57-40: R 15-22; D 42-18 (ND 36-5; SD 6-13), July 27, 1978.

252. S 2410. Health Planning. Kennedy, D-Mass., motion to table (kill) the Huddleston, D-Ky., amendment, part II, to permit states to decide the extent to which certification of major medical equipment should apply to non-institutional providers of health care. Motion agreed to 50-45: R 11-25; D 39-20 (ND 34-6; SD 5-14), July 27, 1978.

253. S 2410. Health Planning. Kennedy, D-Mass., motion to table (kill) the Javits, R-N.Y., motion to reconsider the vote by which the Huddleston, D-Ky., amendment, part II, was tabled *(see vote 252, above).* Motion agreed to 47-45: R 10-25; D 37-20 (ND 32-7; SD 5-13), July 27, 1978.

254. HR 12426. New York City Aid. Adoption of the conference report on the bill to authorize up to $1.65 billion in federal loan guarantees to New York City. Adopted (thus clearing for the president) 58-35: R 17-19; D 41-16 (ND 32-7; SD 9-9), July 27, 1978. A "yea" was a vote supporting the president's position.

255. S 2820. Safety of Reclamation Bureau Dams. Passage of the bill to authorize $100 million for safety modifications to Bureau of Reclamation dams and to give permanent authority to the secretary of the interior to order modifications. Passed 77-1: R 28-0; D 49-1 (ND 31-1; SD 18-0), July 28, 1978.

256. S 2152. IMF-Witteveen Facility. Hatfield, R-Ore., motion to table (kill) the Church, D-Idaho, substitute amendment, to the Weicker, R-Conn., amendment *(see vote 257, below)*, to urge the president to support international efforts, including economic restrictions, to condemn violations of human rights in Uganda. Motion agreed to 46-30: R 26-2; D 20-28 (ND 12-21; SD 8-7), July 28, 1978.

257. S 2152. IMF-Witteveen Facility. Weicker, R-Conn., amendment to prohibit trade with Uganda, other than U.S. food exports, until the president certified to Congress that the country was no longer committing gross violations of human rights. Adopted 73-1: R 28-0; D 45-1 (ND 33-1; SD 12-0), July 28, 1978.

258. S 2152. IMF-Witteveen Facility. Schweiker, R-Pa., amendment to require that U.S. participation in the Supplementary Financing Facility (Witteveen) of the IMF be subject to prior appropriation of funds by Congress for that purpose. Adopted 67-0: R 26-0; D 41-0 (ND 32-0; SD 9-0), July 28, 1978.

Corresponding to Congressional Record Votes 263, 264, 265, 266, 267, 268, 269, 270

	259	260	261	262	263	264	265	266
ALABAMA								
Allen, M.	Y	N	N	Y	N	N	N	Y
Sparkman	Y	Y	Y	N	Y	Y	Y	N
ALASKA								
Gravel	Y	Y	Y	N	Y	Y	Y	N
Stevens	Y	Y	N	Y	N	N	N	Y
ARIZONA								
DeConcini	Y	Y	N	Y	N	Y	Y	Y
Goldwater	?	?	?	?	?	?	?	?
ARKANSAS								
Bumpers	?	?	?	?	?	?	?	?
Hodges	Y	N	N	N	N	Y	Y	N
CALIFORNIA								
Cranston	Y	Y	Y	N	Y	Y	Y	N
Hayakawa	Y	Y	Y	N	Y	Y	Y	Y
COLORADO								
Hart	Y	Y	Y	N	Y	Y	Y	N
Haskell	?	?	?	?	?	?	?	?
CONNECTICUT								
Ribicoff	Y	Y	N	N	Y	Y	Y	N
Weicker	Y	N	N	N	N	Y	Y	N
DELAWARE								
Biden	Y	Y	N	N	Y	N	Y	Y
Roth	Y	Y	N	Y	Y	N	N	Y
FLORIDA								
Chiles	Y	Y	N	N	N	Y	Y	Y
Stone	Y	Y	N	N	N	Y	Y	Y
GEORGIA								
Nunn	?	?	?	?	?	?	Y	Y
Talmadge	Y	Y	N	Y	N	Y	Y	Y
HAWAII								
Inouye	?	?	?	?	?	?	?	?
Matsunaga	Y	Y	Y	N	N	Y	Y	Y
IDAHO								
Church	Y	Y	Y	N	Y	Y	Y	Y
McClure	Y	N	N	Y	N	N	N	Y
ILLINOIS								
Stevenson	Y	Y	Y	N	Y	Y	Y	N
Percy	Y	Y	Y	N	Y	Y	Y	Y
INDIANA								
Bayh	Y	N	N	N	N	Y	Y	Y
Lugar	Y	Y	Y	N	Y	Y	N	Y
IOWA								
Clark	Y	Y	Y	N	Y	Y	Y	N
Culver	Y	Y	Y	N	Y	Y	Y	N
KANSAS								
Dole	Y	N	N	Y	N	Y	N	Y
Pearson	Y	Y	N	N	Y	Y	N	N
KENTUCKY								
Ford	Y	Y	Y	N	Y	Y	Y	Y
Huddleston	Y	Y	Y	N	Y	Y	Y	Y
LOUISIANA								
Johnston	?	?	?	?	?	?	?	?
Long	Y	Y	N	N	N	Y	Y	N
MAINE								
Hathaway	?	?	?	?	?	?	?	?
Muskie	?	?	?	?	?	?	?	?
MARYLAND								
Sarbanes	Y	N	Y	N	Y	Y	Y	N
Mathias	Y	Y	Y	N	Y	Y	Y	N
MASSACHUSETTS								
Kennedy	Y	Y	Y	N	Y	Y	Y	N
Brooke	Y	N	N	N	N	Y	Y	Y
MICHIGAN								
Riegle	Y	N	N	N	Y	Y	Y	N
Griffin	?	?	?	?	?	?	?	?
MINNESOTA								
Anderson	†	?	?	?	?	?	?	?
Humphrey, M.	†	Y	Y	N	Y	Y	Y	N
MISSISSIPPI								
Eastland	Y	Y	Y	N	N	N	Y	Y
Stennis	Y	N	N	?	?	?	?	?
MISSOURI								
Eagleton	Y	Y	N	N	Y	Y	Y	N
Danforth	Y	Y	Y	N	Y	Y	N	Y
MONTANA								
Melcher	Y	N	N	N	N	Y	Y	Y
Hatfield, P.	Y	N	N	N	Y	Y	Y	N
NEBRASKA								
Zorinsky	Y	N	N	Y	N	N	Y	Y
Curtis	Y	Y	N	N	N	N	N	?
NEVADA								
Cannon	Y	Y	N	Y	N	N	Y	Y
Laxalt	Y	Y	N	Y	N	Y	N	Y
NEW HAMPSHIRE								
Durkin	Y	N	Y	N	Y	Y	Y	Y
McIntyre	Y	Y	Y	N	Y	Y	Y	Y
NEW JERSEY								
Williams	?	Y	Y	N	Y	Y	Y	N
Case	Y	N	N	N	Y	Y	Y	N
NEW MEXICO								
Domenici	Y	Y	N	Y	N	N	N	Y
Schmitt	Y	Y	Y	Y	Y	Y	N	Y
NEW YORK								
Moynihan	Y	Y	Y	N	Y	Y	N	Y
Javits	Y	Y	Y	N	Y	Y	Y	N
NORTH CAROLINA								
Morgan	Y	Y	N	Y	N	N	Y	Y
Helms	Y	N	N	Y	N	N	N	Y
NORTH DAKOTA								
Burdick	Y	N	N	Y	N	Y	Y	Y
Young	Y	Y	N	Y	N	Y	N	Y
OHIO								
Glenn	Y	Y	N	N	Y	Y	Y	N
Metzenbaum	Y	N	N	N	Y	Y	Y	N
OKLAHOMA								
Bartlett	Y	Y	N	Y	N	N	N	Y
Bellmon	Y	Y	N	N	Y	Y	N	Y
OREGON								
Hatfield, M.	Y	N	N	Y	N	Y	N	Y
Packwood	Y	Y	Y	N	N	N	N	Y
PENNSYLVANIA								
Heinz	Y	Y	Y	N	Y	Y	Y	Y
Schweiker	Y	N	N	N	N	Y	N	Y
RHODE ISLAND								
Pell	†	†	†	-	†	†	†	?
Chafee	Y	Y	Y	N	Y	Y	N	Y
SOUTH CAROLINA								
Hollings	Y	Y	N	Y	N	Y	Y	Y
Thurmond	Y	Y	N	Y	N	N	N	Y
SOUTH DAKOTA								
Abourezk	Y	N	?	?	?	?	?	?
McGovern	Y	N	N	N	Y	Y	Y	N
TENNESSEE								
Sasser	Y	N	?	?	?	?	?	?
Baker	Y	Y	N	N	N	Y	N	Y
TEXAS								
Bentsen	Y	Y	N	Y	N	Y	Y	Y
Tower	Y	Y	N	N	N	Y	N	Y
UTAH								
Garn	Y	Y	N	Y	N	Y	N	Y
Hatch	?	Y	N	Y	N	N	N	Y
VERMONT								
Leahy	Y	N	N	N	Y	Y	Y	Y
Stafford	Y	Y	N	N	Y	Y	Y	Y
VIRGINIA								
*Byrd, H.	Y	N	N	Y	N	N	N	Y
Scott	Y	N	N	Y	N	N	N	Y
WASHINGTON								
Jackson	Y	Y	N	Y	Y	Y	Y	N
Magnuson	Y	Y	N	Y	N	Y	Y	Y
WEST VIRGINIA								
Byrd, R.	Y	Y	N	N	N	Y	Y	N
Randolph	†	Y	N	Y	N	N	Y	Y
WISCONSIN								
Nelson	Y	Y	Y	N	Y	Y	Y	N
Proxmire	Y	N	N	Y	N	Y	Y	Y
WYOMING								
Hansen	Y	Y	N	Y	N	N	N	Y
Wallop	Y	Y	N	Y	N	N	N	Y

Democrats ***Republicans***

**Byrd elected as independent.*

KEY

- Y Voted for (yea).
- ✓ Paired for.
- † Announced for.
- # CQ Poll for.
- N Voted against (nay).
- X Paired against.
- \- Announced against.
- ▮ CQ Poll against.
- P Voted "present."
- ● Voted "present" to avoid possible conflict of interest.
- ? Did not vote or otherwise make a position known.

259. HR 10173. Veterans' and Survivors' Pensions. Passage of the bill to modify veterans' and survivors' pension systems to pay non-service-connected disabled veterans a pension sufficient to bring their total income to a specified minimum level. Passed 85-0: R 35-0; D 50-0 (ND 34-0; SD 16-0), July 31, 1978.

260. S 2152. IMF-Witteveen Facility. Church, D-Idaho, motion to table (kill) the Abourezk, D-S.D., amendment to ensure that no Witteveen Facility transaction contributes to the deprivation of human rights of citizens of a borrowing nation. Motion agreed to 62-27: R 27-9; D 35-18 (ND 24-13; SD 11-5), July 31, 1978.

261. S 2152. IMF-Witteveen Facility. Church, D-Idaho, motion to table (kill) the Dole, R-Kan., amendment to instruct the U.S. director of the Witteveen Facility to oppose loans to Cambodia or Uganda unless the president determined that these countries were "in compliance with internationally recognized human rights." Motion rejected 30-57: R 10-26; D 20-31 (ND 16-20; SD 4- 11), July 31, 1978. (The Dole amendment was adopted subsequently by voice vote.)

262. S 2152. IMF-Witteveen Facility. Helms, R-N.C., amendment to restrict the average salary levels of International Monetary Fund personnel by no more than 5 percent above levels of comparable U.S. Civil Service positions. Rejected 31-55: R 17-19; D 14-36 (ND 8-28; SD 6-8), July 31, 1978.

263. S 2152. IMF-Witteveen Facility. Church, D-Idaho, motion to table (kill) the Helms, R-N.C., amendment to instruct the U.S. executive director of the facility to oppose loans to nations providing aid to international terrorists. Motion rejected 42-44: R 14-22; D 28-22 (ND 25-11; SD 3-11), July 31, 1978. (The Helms amendment was adopted subsequently by voice vote.)

264. S 2152. IMF-Witteveen Facility. Church, D-Idaho, motion to table (kill) the Helms, R-N.C., amendment to limit U.S. participation in the facility to five years, through fiscal 1983. Motion agreed to 65-21: R 23-13; D 42-8 (ND 32-4; SD 10-4), July 31, 1978. A "nay" was a vote supporting the president's position.

265. S 2152. IMF-Witteveen Facility. Church, D-Idaho, substitute amendment, to the McClure, R-Idaho, amendment, to require an annual report to Congress from the secretary of the treasury on the observance of internationally recognized human rights in nations drawing funds from the Witteveen Facility. Adopted 57-30: R 9-27; D 48-3 (ND 35-1; SD 13-2), July 31, 1978. (The McClure amendment would have defined the term "human rights" to include free elections, rule by law, individual freedoms and minority rights.)

266. S 2152. IMF-Witteveen Facility. Byrd, Ind-Va., amendment to require a balanced federal budget beginning in fiscal 1981. Adopted 58-28: R 30-5; D 28-23 (ND 16-20; SD 12-3), July 31, 1978.

CQ Senate Votes 267-274

Corresponding to Congressional Record Votes 271, 272, 273, 274, 275, 276, 277, 278

	267	268	269	270	271	272	273	274
ALABAMA								
Allen, M.	N	Y	N	N	N	N	N	Y
Sparkman	Y	Y	N	N	Y	Y	N	Y
ALASKA								
Gravel	Y	Y	Y	Y	Y	Y	N	Y
Stevens	Y	Y	Y	N	N	N	N	Y
ARIZONA								
DeConcini	Y	Y	Y	N	Y	N	N	Y
Goldwater	?	Y	N	N	Y	N	N	Y
ARKANSAS								
Bumpers	?	Y	Y	N	N	Y	N	Y
Hodges	Y	Y	N	N	N	Y	N	Y
CALIFORNIA								
Cranston	Y	Y	N	Y	Y	Y	Y	Y
Hayakawa	Y	Y	N	N	Y	N	N	Y
COLORADO								
Hart	Y	Y	Y	N	N	Y	N	Y
Haskell	?	?	?	?	?	?	?	?
CONNECTICUT								
Ribicoff	Y	Y	Y	Y	Y	Y	N	Y
Weicker	Y	Y	Y	N	Y	Y	?	?
DELAWARE								
Biden	Y	Y	N	N	Y	Y	†	N
Roth	Y	N	N	N	Y	Y	Y	N
FLORIDA								
Chiles	Y	Y	Y	N	Y	Y	N	Y
Stone	Y	Y	Y	?	?	Y	Y	Y
GEORGIA								
Nunn	Y	Y	Y	N	N	N	N	Y
Talmadge	Y	Y	Y	Y	N	N	N	Y
HAWAII								
Inouye	?	?	?	?	?	?	?	?
Matsunaga	Y	?	Y	Y	Y	Y	N	Y
IDAHO								
Church	Y	Y	Y	N	Y	Y	Y	Y
McClure	N	Y	N	N	N	N	?	?
ILLINOIS								
Stevenson	Y	Y	Y	N	Y	Y	N	Y
Percy	Y	Y	Y	Y	Y	Y	N	Y
INDIANA								
Bayh	Y	Y	N	Y	N	Y	N	Y
Lugar	Y	Y	N	N	Y	Y	Y	Y
IOWA								
Clark	Y	Y	N	Y	N	Y	Y	Y
Culver	Y	Y	N	Y	N	Y	N	Y
KANSAS								
Dole	Y	Y	Y	N	Y	Y	Y	Y
Pearson	Y	Y	N	N	Y	Y	N	Y
KENTUCKY								
Ford	Y	Y	N	Y	N	N	N	Y
Huddleston	Y	Y	N	Y	Y	Y	N	Y
LOUISIANA								
Johnston	?	?	?	?	?	?	?	?
Long	N	Y	N	N	N	Y	N	Y
MAINE								
Hathaway	?	Y	Y	Y	N	Y	N	Y
Muskie	?	Y	Y	Y	Y	Y	N	Y
MARYLAND								
Sarbanes	Y	Y	N	Y	N	Y	N	Y
Mathias	Y	Y	Y	Y	Y	Y	N	Y
MASSACHUSETTS								
Kennedy	?	Y	Y	Y	N	Y	N	Y
Brooke	Y	?	Y	Y	N	Y	?	?
MICHIGAN								
Riegle	Y	Y	Y	Y	N	Y	Y	Y
Griffin	?	Y	N	N	Y	Y	Y	Y
MINNESOTA								
Anderson	?	?	?	†	-	?	?	?
Humphrey, M.	Y	Y	Y	Y	N	Y	N	Y
MISSISSIPPI								
Eastland	Y	Y	N	N	N	?	?	?
Stennis	?	?	Y	N	N	N	N	Y
MISSOURI								
Eagleton	Y	Y	Y	Y	Y	Y	Y	Y
Danforth	Y	Y	N	N	Y	Y	Y	Y
MONTANA								
Melcher	Y	Y	Y	Y	N	Y	Y	Y
Hatfield, P.	Y	Y	Y	Y	N	Y	N	Y
NEBRASKA								
Zorinsky	Y	Y	N	N	Y	N	N	Y
Curtis	-	Y	N	N	Y	Y	N	Y
NEVADA								
Cannon	Y	Y	N	N	Y	N	N	Y
Laxalt	N	Y	N	N	Y	N	Y	Y
NEW HAMPSHIRE								
Durkin	Y	?	Y	Y	N	N	N	Y
McIntyre	Y	Y	?	N	Y	Y	N	Y
NEW JERSEY								
Williams	Y	Y	Y	Y	Y	Y	N	Y
Case	Y	Y	Y	Y	Y	Y	N	Y
NEW MEXICO								
Domenici	N	Y	Y	N	Y	Y	N	Y
Schmitt	Y	Y	N	N	Y	Y	N	Y
NEW YORK								
Moynihan	Y	Y	Y	Y	Y	Y	N	Y
Javits	Y	Y	Y	Y	Y	Y	N	Y
NORTH CAROLINA								
Morgan	Y	Y	Y	N	Y	N	?	†
Helms	N	N	N	N	Y	N	Y	Y
NORTH DAKOTA								
Burdick	Y	Y	N	Y	N	Y	Y	Y
Young	N	Y	Y	N	N	Y	N	Y
OHIO								
Glenn	Y	Y	N	Y	Y	Y	N	Y
Metzenbaum	Y	Y	Y	Y	Y	N	Y	Y
OKLAHOMA								
Bartlett	Y	N	N	N	Y	N	N	Y
Bellmon	Y	Y	N	N	Y	Y	?	?
OREGON								
Hatfield, M.	N	Y	Y	N	Y	N	Y	N
Packwood	Y	Y	Y	?	Y	Y	N	Y
PENNSYLVANIA								
Heinz	Y	Y	N	Y	N	Y	N	Y
Schweiker	Y	Y	Y	Y	N	Y	N	Y
RHODE ISLAND								
Pell	†	Y	Y	Y	N	Y	Y	Y
Chafee	Y	Y	Y	Y	Y	N	Y	Y
SOUTH CAROLINA								
Hollings	Y	Y	N	N	Y	N	Y	Y
Thurmond	N	Y	N	N	N	N	-	†
SOUTH DAKOTA								
Abourezk	?	Y	?	?	N	?	?	?
McGovern	Y	?	Y	Y	N	Y	N	Y
TENNESSEE								
Sasser	?	?	Y	N	N	N	N	Y
Baker	Y	Y	Y	N	N	?	?	?
TEXAS								
Bentsen	Y	Y	Y	N	Y	Y	N	Y
Tower	Y	Y	N	N	Y	N	N	Y
UTAH								
Garn	N	Y	N	N	Y	N	N	Y
Hatch	N	Y	N	N	Y	N	Y	Y
VERMONT								
Leahy	Y	Y	N	Y	Y	N	N	Y
Stafford	Y	Y	N	Y	Y	Y	N	Y
VIRGINIA								
*Byrd, H.	Y	N	N	N	Y	N	Y	Y
Scott	N	Y	N	N	N	N	Y	Y
WASHINGTON								
Jackson	Y	Y	Y	Y	N	Y	N	Y
Magnuson	Y	Y	Y	Y	N	Y	N	Y
WEST VIRGINIA								
Byrd, R.	N	Y	Y	Y	N	Y	N	Y
Randolph	N	Y	†	N	N	Y	Y	Y
WISCONSIN								
Nelson	Y	Y	N	Y	Y	Y	Y	Y
Proxmire	Y	N	N	Y	Y	N	Y	N
WYOMING								
Hansen	N	Y	N	N	N	Y	N	Y
Wallop	N	Y	N	N	N	N	N	Y

Democrats ***Republicans***

*Byrd elected as independent.

KEY

- Y Voted for (yea).
- ✓ Paired for.
- † Announced for.
- # CQ Poll for.
- N Voted against (nay).
- X Paired against.
- - Announced against.
- ▮ CQ Poll against.
- P Voted "present."
- ● Voted "present" to avoid possible conflict of interest.
- ? Did not vote or otherwise make a position known.

267. HR 9214. IMF-Witteveen Facility. Passage of the bill to authorize U.S. participation in the new Supplementary Financing Facility (Witteveen) and authorize about $1.7 billion in U.S. contributions to the facility. Passed 69-16: R 23-12; D 46-4 (ND 33-2; SD 13-2), July 31, 1978. A "yea" was a vote supporting the president's position.

268. S 3243. Economic Development Administration. Passage of bill to authorize $3,788,000 for fiscal 1978 and $10,607,000 for fiscal 1979 to cover administrative expenses of the local public works programs of the Economic Development Administration of the Commerce Department. Passed 85-5: R 34-3; D 51-2 (ND 36-1; SD 15-1), Aug. 1, 1978.

269. S 2788. Consolidated Rail Corp. Ribicoff, D-Conn., amendment to authorize $9 million for the repair of a railroad bridge over the Hudson River at Poughkeepsie, N.Y. Adopted 48-45: R 15-23; D 33-22 (ND 24-13; SD 9-9), Aug. 1, 1978. (The bill to authorize $1.2 billion for fiscal 1979-83 for the Consolidated Rail Corp. was passed subsequently by voice vote.)

270. HR 11445. Small Business Administration. Nelson, D-Wis., motion to table (kill) the Bartlett, R-Okla., amendment to exempt from the requirements of the 1970 Occupational Safety and Health Act (PL 91-596) small businesses that employed 10 or fewer persons and were in an occupational category in which the injury or illness rate was less than 7 per 100 full-time workers based on the annual survey conducted by the Labor Department's Bureau of Labor Statistics. Motion rejected 42-51: R 9-28; D 33-23 (ND 30-9; SD 3-14), Aug. 2, 1978. (The Bartlett amendment was adopted subsequently by voice vote.)

271. HR 11445. Small Business Administration. Muskie, D-Maine, amendment to delete from the bill a provision permitting the federal government to subsidize the interest rate paid on Small Business Administration disaster loans (the effect was to set the interest rate for such loans at the federal government's cost of borrowing). Adopted 54-41: R 27-11; D 27-30 (ND 20-20; SD 7-10), Aug. 2, 1978. (The bill to authorize fiscal 1979 funds for Small Business Administration programs was passed subsequently by voice vote.)

272. HR 13385. Temporary Debt Limit. Passage of the bill to increase the temporary public debt limit to $798 billion through March 31, 1978. Passed (thus clearing for the president) 62-31: R 22-15; D 40-16 (ND 32-7; SD 8-9), Aug. 2, 1978.

273. HR 12927. Military Construction Appropriations, Fiscal 1979. Roth, R-Del., amendment to reduce by 2 percent the funds appropriated by the bill. Rejected 26-60: R 11-21; D 15-39 (ND 12-26; SD 3-13), Aug. 3, 1978.

274. HR 12927. Military Construction Appropriations, Fiscal 1979. Passage of the bill to appropriate $3,937,702,000 for military construction programs of the Defense Department in fiscal 1979. Passed 83-4: R 30-2; D 53-2 (ND 37-2; SD 16-0), Aug. 3, 1978. The president had requested $4,253,000,000.

	275	276	277	278	279	280	281	282
ALABAMA								
Allen, M.	?	?	?	?	?	?	?	?
Sparkman	N	N	Y	Y	Y	Y	N	Y
ALASKA								
Gravel	N	?	?	?	?	?	?	?
Stevens	Y	Y	Y	N	Y	Y	N	Y
ARIZONA								
DeConcini	N	N	Y	Y	Y	X	?	?
Goldwater	Y	N	Y	Y	?	?	Y	N
ARKANSAS								
Bumpers	N	N	Y	Y	Y	Y	N	Y
Hodges	N	N	Y	Y	Y	✓	N	Y
CALIFORNIA								
Cranston	N	N	Y	N	Y	Y	N	Y
Hayakawa	†	N	Y	Y	Y	N	Y	Y
COLORADO								
Hart	N	Y	Y	Y	?	Y	?	Y
Haskell	?	?	?	?	?	?	?	?
CONNECTICUT								
Ribicoff	N	Y	Y	N	?	?	?	?
Weicker	Y	Y	Y	N	Y	Y	N	Y
DELAWARE								
Biden	N	N	Y	Y	Y	N	N	N
Roth	Y	N	Y	Y	N	N	N	N
FLORIDA								
Chiles	N	N	Y	Y	Y	Y	N	Y
Stone	Y	N	Y	Y	Y	N	N	Y
GEORGIA								
Nunn	N	N	Y	Y	?	?	?	?
Talmadge	Y	Y	Y	Y	?	?	?	?
HAWAII								
Inouye	?	?	?	?	?	?	?	Y
Matsunaga	N	N	Y	Y	Y	Y	N	Y
IDAHO								
Church	N	?	?	?	?	?	?	?
McClure	?	?	?	?	?	?	?	?
ILLINOIS								
Stevenson	?	Y	Y	N	?	Y	N	Y
Percy	N	N	Y	N	Y	Y	Y	Y
INDIANA								
Bayh	N	N	Y	Y	Y	Y	N	?
Lugar	Y	N	Y	Y	Y	N	Y	Y
IOWA								
Clark	N	Y	Y	N	Y	†	-	†
Culver	N	Y	Y	Y	Y	Y	N	Y
KANSAS								
Dole	N	N	Y	Y	Y	N	Y	Y
Pearson	N	Y	Y	Y	Y	N	Y	Y
KENTUCKY								
Ford	Y	N	Y	Y	Y	Y	N	Y
Huddleston	Y	N	Y	Y	Y	Y	N	Y
LOUISIANA								
Johnston	?	?	?	?	?	?	?	?
Long	?	N	Y	Y	Y	Y	Y	Y
MAINE								
Hathaway	N	Y	Y	N	Y	?	?	?
Muskie	N	N	Y	Y	Y	Y	N	Y
MARYLAND								
Sarbanes	N	N	Y	N	?	Y	N	Y
Mathias	N	Y	Y	N	?	Y	N	Y
MASSACHUSETTS								
Kennedy	N	Y	Y	N	Y	Y	N	Y
Brooke	?	?	?	?	?	?	?	?
MICHIGAN								
Riegle	N	Y	Y	N	?	Y	N	Y
Griffin	Y	N	Y	Y	Y	Y	Y	Y
MINNESOTA								
Anderson	?	?	?	?	?	?	?	†
Humphrey, M.	N	Y	?	?	†	Y	N	Y
MISSISSIPPI								
Eastland	?	?	?	?	?	?	?	?
Stennis	Y	Y	?	?	?	Y	Y	Y
MISSOURI								
Eagleton	N	?	?	?	?	Y	N	Y
Danforth	Y	N	Y	Y	Y	N	Y	N
MONTANA								
Melcher	N	N	Y	Y	Y	Y	N	Y
Hatfield, P.	N	N	Y	Y	Y	?	N	Y
NEBRASKA								
Zorinsky	N	N	Y	Y	Y	N	N	Y
Curtis	Y	N	Y	Y	Y	?	?	?
NEVADA								
Cannon	Y	N	Y	Y	Y	Y	Y	Y
Laxalt	Y	N	Y	Y	N	N	Y	Y
NEW HAMPSHIRE								
Durkin	N	N	Y	Y	Y	Y	N	Y
McIntyre	N	N	Y	Y	Y	N	Y	Y
NEW JERSEY								
Williams	N	N	Y	N	Y	Y	N	Y
Case	N	N	Y	N	Y	Y	N	Y
NEW MEXICO								
Domenici	N	N	Y	Y	Y	?	?	?
Schmitt	Y	N	Y	Y	Y	N	Y	N
NEW YORK								
Moynihan	N	N	Y	N	Y	N	N	Y
Javits	N	Y	Y	N	Y	N	Y	Y
NORTH CAROLINA								
Morgan	N	N	Y	Y	Y	Y	N	Y
Helms	Y	N	Y	Y	N	N	Y	N
NORTH DAKOTA								
Burdick	Y	-	†	?	†	?	?	?
Young	Y	Y	Y	Y	Y	Y	Y	Y
OHIO								
Glenn	Y	Y	Y	Y	Y	Y	N	Y
Metzenbaum	N	N	Y	N	Y	Y	N	Y
OKLAHOMA								
Bartlett	Y	N	Y	Y	Y	N	Y	Y
Bellmon	?	?	?	?	?	?	?	?
OREGON								
Hatfield, M.	Y	Y	Y	Y	?	Y	Y	Y
Packwood	Y	Y	Y	Y	Y	N	Y	Y
PENNSYLVANIA								
Heinz	N	?	?	?	?	?	?	?
Schweiker	Y	N	Y	Y	Y	Y	Y	Y
RHODE ISLAND								
Pell	N	N	Y	N	Y	N	N	Y
Chafee	Y	N	Y	Y	Y	N	Y	N
SOUTH CAROLINA								
Hollings	N	N	Y	Y	Y	Y	N	Y
Thurmond	†	-	†	†	?	N	N	Y
SOUTH DAKOTA								
Abourezk	?	?	?	?	?	Y	N	Y
McGovern	N	N	Y	Y	Y	Y	N	Y
TENNESSEE								
Sasser	Y	?	?	?	?	?	Y	Y
Baker	?	?	?	?	?	?	?	?
TEXAS								
Bentsen	N	N	Y	Y	Y	Y	N	Y
Tower	Y	N	Y	Y	Y	N	Y	N
UTAH								
Garn	Y	N	Y	Y	N	N	Y	N
Hatch	Y	N	Y	Y	Y	N	Y	N
VERMONT								
Leahy	N	N	Y	Y	Y	N	N	Y
Stafford	Y	Y	Y	Y	Y	Y	N	Y
VIRGINIA								
*Byrd, H.	Y	N	Y	Y	N	N	Y	N
Scott	Y	N	Y	?	N	Y	Y	N
WASHINGTON								
Jackson	N	N	Y	Y	Y	Y	N	Y
Magnuson	Y	N	Y	Y	Y	Y	N	Y
WEST VIRGINIA								
Byrd, R.	N	N	Y	N	Y	Y	N	Y
Randolph	N	-	†	-	†	N	N	Y
WISCONSIN								
Nelson	N	N	Y	Y	?	Y	N	Y
Proxmire	Y	N	Y	Y	Y	N	Y	Y
WYOMING								
Hansen	Y	N	Y	Y	Y	N	Y	Y
Wallop	Y	N	Y	Y	Y	N	N	N

Democrats ***Republicans***

*Byrd elected as independent.

KEY

- Y Voted for (yea).
- ✓ Paired for.
- † Announced for.
- # CQ Poll for.
- N Voted against (nay).
- X Paired against.
- - Announced against.
- ▌ CQ Poll against.
- P Voted "present."
- ● Voted "present" to avoid possible conflict of interest.
- ? Did not vote or otherwise make a position known.

275. HR 12934. State, Justice, Commerce, Judiciary Appropriations, Fiscal 1979. Weicker, R-Conn., motion to table (kill) the Kennedy, D-Mass., amendment to increase appropriations for positions in the Justice Department Criminal Division. Motion rejected 36-49: R 24-8; D 12-41 (ND 5-33; SD 7-8), Aug. 3, 1978. (The Kennedy amendment was adopted subsequently by voice vote.)

276. HR 12934. State, Justice, Commerce, Judiciary Appropriations, Fiscal 1979. Weicker, R-Conn., motion to table (kill) the Roth, R-Del., amendment to reduce by 2 percent each line item in the bill. Motion rejected 21-60: R 9-23; D 12-37 (ND 10-24; SD 2-13), Aug. 3, 1978. (The Roth amendment, as amended by Hollings, D-S.C., was subsequently adopted by voice vote; *see votes 277 and 278, below*).

277. HR 12934. State, Justice, Commerce, Judiciary Appropriations, Fiscal 1979. Hollings, D-S.C., substitute amendment, division 1, to the Roth, R-Del., amendment *(see vote 276, above)*, to reduce by $26.1 million appropriations for several programs in the bill. Adopted 79-0: R 32-0; D 47-0 (ND 33-0; SD 14-0), Aug. 3, 1978.

278. HR 12934. State, Justice, Commerce, Judiciary Appropriations, Fiscal 1979. Hollings, D S.C., substitute amendment, division 2, to the Roth, R-Del., amendment *(see vote 276, above)*, to reduce by $150 million appropriations for Economic Development Assistance programs. Adopted 59-19: R 25-6; D 34-13 (ND 20-13; SD 14-0), Aug. 3, 1978. (The Roth amendment, as amended by the two Hollings amendments *(see vote 277, above)*, still represented a total 2 percent reduction and was subsequently adopted by voice vote.)

279. HR 12934. State, Justice, Commerce, Judiciary Appropriations, Fiscal 1979. Passage of the bill to appropriate $8,437,-130,000 for the Departments of State, Justice and Commerce, the federal judiciary and 20 related agencies for fiscal 1979. Passed 62-6: R 24-5; D 38-1 (ND 27-0; SD 11-1), Aug. 3, 1978. The president had requested $8,660,276,000.

280. HR 13467. Second Supplemental Appropriations, Fiscal 1978. Bumpers, D-Ark., motion to table (kill) the Chafee, R-R.I., amendment to rescind $54 million of the $85 million appropriated for the construction of the Hart Senate office building. Motion agreed to 45-29: R 11-19; D 34-10 (ND 24-8; SD 10-2), Aug. 4, 1978.

281. HR 13467. Second Supplemental Appropriations, Fiscal 1978. Schweiker, R-Pa., motion to table (kill) the Bumpers, D-Ark., amendment to appropriate an additional $8.2 million for the Center for Disease Control to conduct an influenza immunization program for high-risk persons (children under 12, elderly and the chronically ill). Motion rejected 30-47: R 23-8; D 7-39 (ND 3-29; SD 4-10), Aug. 4, 1978. (The Bumpers amendment was adopted subsequently by voice vote.)

282. HR 13467. Second Supplemental Appropriations, Fiscal 1978. Magnuson, D-Wash., amendment to appropriate $54,853,000 for construction of the Hart Senate office building with a $135 million ceiling on the total cost of the building. Adopted 65-13: R 20-11; D 45-2 (ND 32-1; SD 13-1), Aug. 4, 1978.

CQ Senate Votes 283-290

Corresponding to Congressional Record Votes 287, 288, 289, 290, 291, 292, 293, 294

	283	284	285	286	287	288	289	290
ALABAMA								
Allen, M.	?	P	Y	N	Y	N	N	N
Sparkman	Y	Y	Y	N	N	N	N	N
ALASKA								
Gravel	?	Y	Y	N	N	N	N	N
Stevens	Y	Y	Y	N	Y	N	N	N
ARIZONA								
DeConcini	?	Y	N	N	Y	N	Y	Y
Goldwater	Y	N	Y	Y	Y	Y	Y	Y
ARKANSAS								
Bumpers	?	Y	Y	N	Y	Y	N	Y
Hodges	Y	Y	Y	N	Y	Y	N	Y
CALIFORNIA								
Cranston	Y	Y	Y	N	N	N	N	N
Hayakawa	?	Y	Y	Y	Y	N	N	N
COLORADO								
Hart	Y	Y	Y	N	N	N	N	N
Haskell	?	?	?	?	?	?	Y	Y
CONNECTICUT								
Ribicoff	?	Y	Y	N	Y	N	N	N
Weicker	Y	Y	Y	N	N	N	N	N
DELAWARE								
Biden	Y	N	N	N	N	Y	Y	Y
Roth	Y	N	N	N	Y	Y	Y	Y
FLORIDA								
Chiles	Y	Y	Y	Y	Y	Y	N	Y
Stone	Y	Y	Y	N	Y	Y	Y	Y
GEORGIA								
Nunn	?	N	N	N	Y	Y	Y	Y
Talmadge	?	Y	Y	N	Y	Y	Y	Y
HAWAII								
Inouye	Y	Y	Y	Y	Y	?	?	?
Matsunaga	Y	Y	Y	N	N	N	N	N
IDAHO								
Church	?	Y	?	N	N	Y	N	Y
McClure	?	?	?	?	?	?	?	?
ILLINOIS								
Stevenson	Y	Y	Y	N	N	N	N	N
Percy	Y	Y	Y	N	Y	N	N	N
INDIANA								
Bayh	Y	Y	Y	N	N	N	N	N
Lugar	Y	N	N	N	N	Y	Y	Y
IOWA								
Clark	†	Y	Y	N	N	N	N	N
Culver	Y	Y	Y	N	Y	N	N	N
KANSAS								
Dole	Y	N	Y	N	Y	Y	N	Y
Pearson	Y	Y	Y	Y	Y	Y	N	Y
KENTUCKY								
Ford	Y	Y	Y	N	N	Y	N	Y
Huddleston	?	Y	Y	N	N	Y	N	Y
LOUISIANA								
Johnston	?	Y	Y	Y	Y	Y	Y	Y
Long	Y	Y	Y	Y	N	N	Y	Y
MAINE								
Hathaway	?	Y	Y	N	N	N	N	N
Muskie	Y	Y	Y	N	N	N	N	N
MARYLAND								
Sarbanes	Y	Y	Y	N	N	N	N	N
Mathias	Y	Y	Y	N	N	Y	N	Y
MASSACHUSETTS								
Kennedy	Y	Y	Y	N	Y	N	N	N
Brooke	?	?	?	?	?	-	?	?
MICHIGAN								
Riegle	Y	†	†	X	?	-	-	-
Griffin	?	?	?	?	?	?	?	?
MINNESOTA								
Anderson	?	†	†	?	?	-	-	-
Humphrey, M.	†	†	†	?	?	-	-	-
MISSISSIPPI								
Eastland	?	Y	Y	N	N	Y	Y	Y
Stennis	Y	Y	Y	N	N	Y	?	Y
MISSOURI								
Eagleton	Y	Y	Y	N	N	N	N	N
Danforth	Y	N	N	N	N	Y	Y	Y
MONTANA								
Melcher	Y	Y	Y	N	N	Y	?	Y
Hatfield, P.	Y	Y	Y	✓	Y	Y	?	N
NEBRASKA								
Zorinsky	Y	Y	N	N	Y	N	N	N
Curtis	?	?	?	?	?	?	?	?
NEVADA								
Cannon	Y	Y	Y	N	N	N	N	N
Laxalt	Y	N	N	N	Y	N	Y	N
NEW HAMPSHIRE								
Durkin	Y	N	Y	N	N	N	N	N
McIntyre	?	†	†	?	?	?	?	?
NEW JERSEY								
Williams	Y	Y	Y	N	N	N	N	N
Case	Y	Y	Y	N	Y	N	N	N
NEW MEXICO								
Domenici	?	?	?	?	?	?	?	?
Schmitt	Y	N	N	N	Y	Y	N	Y
NEW YORK								
Moynihan	Y	Y	Y	N	Y	N	N	N
Javits	Y	Y	Y	Y	Y	N	N	N
NORTH CAROLINA								
Morgan	Y	Y	Y	Y	Y	N	N	N
Helms	Y	N	N	N	Y	Y	Y	Y
NORTH DAKOTA								
Burdick	?	Y	Y	N	N	N	N	N
Young	Y	Y	Y	N	Y	Y	N	Y
OHIO								
Glenn	Y	Y	Y	N	Y	N	N	N
Metzenbaum	Y	Y	Y	N	N	N	N	N
OKLAHOMA								
Bartlett	Y	Y	N	Y	Y	Y	Y	Y
Bellmon	?	Y	Y	N	N	Y	N	Y
OREGON								
Hatfield, M.	Y	Y	Y	N	N	N	N	N
Packwood	Y	Y	Y	N	Y	N	N	Y
PENNSYLVANIA								
Heinz	?	?	Y	N	Y	N	N	N
Schweiker	Y	Y	Y	N	N	Y	Y	Y
RHODE ISLAND								
Pell	Y	Y	Y	N	N	N	N	N
Chafee	Y	N	Y	N	N	Y	Y	Y
SOUTH CAROLINA								
Hollings	Y	Y	Y	Y	Y	Y	Y	Y
Thurmond	Y	Y	N	N	Y	Y	Y	Y
SOUTH DAKOTA								
Abourezk	?	?	?	?	?	?	?	?
McGovern	Y	Y	Y	N	N	N	N	N
TENNESSEE								
Sasser	Y	Y	Y	N	Y	Y	Y	Y
Baker	?	Y	Y	N	Y	Y	N	Y
TEXAS								
Bentsen	Y	Y	Y	N	Y	Y	Y	Y
Tower	Y	?	?	?	?	?	?	?
UTAH								
Garn	Y	N	N	N	N	Y	Y	Y
Hatch	Y	N	N	N	Y	Y	Y	Y
VERMONT								
Leahy	Y	Y	N	N	Y	N	N	N
Stafford	Y	Y	Y	N	Y	Y	Y	Y
VIRGINIA								
*Byrd, H.	Y	N	N	N	N	Y	Y	Y
Scott	Y	N	N	Y	Y	Y	Y	Y
WASHINGTON								
Jackson	Y	Y	Y	N	Y	N	N	N
Magnuson	Y	Y	Y	N	N	Y	N	Y
WEST VIRGINIA								
Byrd, R.	Y	Y	Y	Y	N	Y	N	Y
Randolph	Y	Y	Y	Y	Y	N	N	N
WISCONSIN								
Nelson	Y	N	Y	N	N	N	N	N
Proxmire	Y	Y	N	N	N	Y	Y	Y
WYOMING								
Hansen	Y	Y	N	Y	Y	Y	Y	Y
Wallop	Y	Y	N	Y	N	N	Y	Y

Democrats ***Republicans***

Byrd elected as independent.

KEY

- Y Voted for (yea).
- ✓ Paired for.
- † Announced for.
- # CQ Poll for.
- N Voted against (nay).
- X Paired against.
- \- Announced against.
- ▌ CQ Poll against.
- P Voted "present."
- ● Voted "present" to avoid possible conflict of interest.
- ? Did not vote or otherwise make a position known.

283. HR 12935. Legislative Branch Appropriations, Fiscal 1979. Adoption of the Appropriations Committee amendment to reduce the total funds for fiscal 1979 legislative branch appropriations by 5 percent. Adopted 72-0: R 29-0; D 43-0 (ND 31-0; SD 12-0), Aug. 4, 1978.

284. HR 13467. Second Supplemental Appropriations, Fiscal 1978. Passage of the bill to appropriate $6,719,228,686 in supplemental funds for fiscal 1978 operations of the executive and legislative branches of the government. Passed 69-17: R 19-12; D 50-5 (ND 34-3; SD 16-2), Aug. 7, 1978. The president had requested $7,168,446,986 in supplemental new budget authority.

285. HR 12935. Legislative Branch Appropriations, Fiscal 1979. Passage of the bill to appropriate $1.118 billion (less a 5 percent reduction in payments not required by law) for operations of Congress and related agencies for fiscal 1979. Passed 67-20: R 19-13; D 48-7 (ND 31-5; SD 17-2), Aug. 7, 1978. The president had requested $1,143,824,100 in new budget authority.

286. HR 12936. HUD, Independent Agencies Appropriations, Fiscal 1979. Morgan, D-N.C., amendment to add $9,955,000 to the appropriation for the Selective Service System to begin registration of 18-year-old men in fiscal 1979. Rejected 16-71: R 8-24, D 8-47 (ND 3-33; SD 5-14), Aug. 7, 1978.

287. HR 12936. HUD, Independent Agencies Appropriations, Fiscal 1979. Dole, R-Kan., amendment to add $2,455,000 to the fiscal 1979 appropriation for the Selective Service System. Adopted 46-42: R 22-10; D 24-32 (ND 12-25; SD 12-7), Aug. 7, 1978.

288. HR 12936. HUD, Independent Agencies Appropriations, Fiscal 1979. Proxmire, D-Wis. substitute amendment, to the Roth, R-Del., amendment *(see vote 289, below)*, to reduce spending for fiscal 1979 by $810,205,000 in HUD and three independent agencies. Rejected 43-44: R 21-11; D 22-33 (ND 7-29; SD 15-4), Aug. 7, 1978.

289. HR 12936. HUD, Independent Agencies Appropriations, Fiscal 1979. Roth, R-Del., amendment to reduce spending in the bill by 2 percent, except for payments required by law. Rejected 30-55: R 16-16; D 14-39 (ND 4-31; SD 10-8), Aug. 7, 1978.

290. HR 12936. HUD, Independent Agencies Appropriations, Fiscal 1979. Long, D-La., motion to reconsider the vote by which the Proxmire, D-Wis., amendment *(vote 288, above)* was rejected. Motion agreed to 47-41: R 23-9; D 24-32 (ND 8-29; SD 16-3), Aug. 7, 1978.

	291	292	293	294	295	296	297	298
ALABAMA								
Allen, M.	N	N	Y	Y	Y	Y	N	Y
Sparkman	N	N	Y	Y	Y	Y	Y	Y
ALASKA								
Gravel	N	Y	Y	Y	Y	Y	Y	Y
Stevens	N	N	Y	Y	Y	Y	N	Y
ARIZONA								
DeConcini	Y	Y	Y	Y	Y	Y	?	Y
Goldwater	Y	Y	?	Y	Y	N	N	N
ARKANSAS								
Bumpers	Y	Y	Y	N	N	Y	Y	Y
Hodges	Y	Y	Y	N	N	Y	Y	Y
CALIFORNIA								
Cranston	N	N	Y	N	N	Y	Y	Y
Hayakawa	N	Y	Y	Y	Y	N	Y	N
COLORADO								
Hart	N	N	Y	Y	Y	Y	?	Y
Haskell	Y	Y	Y	Y	Y	Y	Y	N
CONNECTICUT								
Ribicoff	N	N	Y	N	N	Y	Y	Y
Weicker	N	N	Y	Y	Y	Y	Y	N
DELAWARE								
Biden	Y	Y	Y	N	N	N	Y	Y
Roth	Y	Y	Y	N	N	N	N	Y
FLORIDA								
Chiles	Y	Y	Y	Y	Y	Y	Y	Y
Stone	Y	Y	Y	N	N	N	Y	Y
GEORGIA								
Nunn	Y	Y	Y	?	?	?	Y	Y
Talmadge	Y	?	Y	Y	Y	N	Y	Y
HAWAII								
Inouye	N	N	?	Y	Y	Y	Y	Y
Matsunaga	N	N	Y	N	N	Y	Y	Y
IDAHO								
Church	Y	Y	Y	N	Y	Y	Y	Y
McClure	?	?	?	Y	Y	Y	N	N
ILLINOIS								
Stevenson	N	Y	Y	N	N	Y	Y	Y
Percy	?	N	Y	N	?	?	Y	Y
INDIANA								
Bayh	N	N	Y	N	N	Y	Y	N
Lugar	Y	Y	Y	Y	Y	N	N	N
IOWA								
Clark	N	N	Y	N	N	Y	Y	N
Culver	N	N	Y	N	N	Y	Y	Y
KANSAS								
Dole	Y	Y	Y	Y	Y	N	Y	Y
Pearson	Y	Y	Y	Y	Y	Y	Y	Y
KENTUCKY								
Ford	Y	Y	Y	Y	Y	Y	Y	Y
Huddleston	Y	Y	Y	N	Y	Y	?	Y
LOUISIANA								
Johnston	Y	Y	Y	Y	Y	Y	Y	Y
Long	Y	Y	Y	N	Y	N	Y	N
MAINE								
Hathaway	N	N	Y	N	N	Y	?	?
Muskie	N	N	Y	N	N	Y	Y	Y
MARYLAND								
Sarbanes	N	N	Y	N	N	Y	Y	Y
Mathias	Y	Y	Y	Y	Y	Y	Y	N
MASSACHUSETTS								
Kennedy	N	N	Y	N	N	Y	Y	Y
Brooke	?	?	?	N	N	Y	Y	Y
MICHIGAN								
Riegle	?	-	†	N	Y	Y	Y	Y
Griffin	?	?	?	?	?	?	Y	Y
MINNESOTA								
Anderson	?	-	†	N	N	Y	Y	N
Humphrey, M.	?	-	†	-	-	†	†	-
MISSISSIPPI								
Eastland	Y	Y	Y	Y	Y	N	Y	Y
Stennis	Y	Y	?	Y	Y	Y	Y	Y
MISSOURI								
Eagleton	N	N	Y	N	N	Y	Y	Y
Danforth	Y	Y	Y	Y	Y	N	Y	Y
MONTANA								
Melcher	Y	Y	Y	Y	Y	Y	Y	N
Hatfield, P.	N	N	Y	?	?	Y	Y	N
NEBRASKA								
Zorinsky	N	N	N	Y	Y	N	Y	Y
Curtis	?	?	?	Y	Y	N	N	N
NEVADA								
Cannon	N	N	Y	Y	Y	Y	Y	Y
Laxalt	N	N	N	Y	Y	N	N	N
NEW HAMPSHIRE								
Durkin	N	N	Y	Y	Y	Y	Y	Y
McIntyre	?	?	?	N	N	Y	Y	Y
NEW JERSEY								
Williams	N	N	Y	N	N	Y	Y	Y
Case	N	N	Y	N	N	Y	Y	Y
NEW MEXICO								
Domenici	?	?	?	Y	Y	Y	N	N
Schmitt	Y	Y	Y	Y	Y	Y	N	N
NEW YORK								
Moynihan	N	N	Y	?	?	?	Y	Y
Javits	N	N	Y	?	?	?	?	?
NORTH CAROLINA								
Morgan	N	Y	Y	Y	Y	N	Y	Y
Helms	Y	Y	N	Y	Y	N	N	N
NORTH DAKOTA								
Burdick	N	N	Y	Y	Y	Y	Y	Y
Young	Y	Y	Y	Y	Y	Y	Y	Y
OHIO								
Glenn	N	N	Y	N	N	Y	Y	Y
Metzenbaum	Y	N	Y	N	N	Y	Y	N
OKLAHOMA								
Bartlett	Y	Y	Y	Y	Y	Y	N	N
Bellmon	Y	Y	Y	Y	Y	Y	Y	N
OREGON								
Hatfield, M.	N	N	Y	Y	Y	Y	Y	Y
Packwood	N	N	Y	N	N	Y	Y	Y
PENNSYLVANIA								
Heinz	N	N	Y	N	N	Y	Y	Y
Schweiker	Y	Y	Y	Y	Y	N	Y	Y
RHODE ISLAND								
Pell	N	N	Y	N	N	Y	Y	Y
Chafee	N	Y	Y	Y	Y	N	Y	Y
SOUTH CAROLINA								
Hollings	Y	Y	Y	Y	Y	N	Y	N
Thurmond	Y	Y	Y	Y	Y	N	N	N
SOUTH DAKOTA								
Abourezk	?	?	?	?	?	?	?	Y
McGovern	N	N	Y	N	N	Y	Y	Y
TENNESSEE								
Sasser	Y	Y	Y	Y	Y	Y	Y	Y
Baker	Y	Y	Y	Y	Y	Y	Y	N
TEXAS								
Bentsen	Y	Y	Y	Y	Y	Y	Y	Y
Tower	?	?	?	Y	Y	Y	Y	N
UTAH								
Garn	Y	Y	N	Y	Y	N	N	N
Hatch	Y	Y	N	Y	Y	N	N	N
VERMONT								
Leahy	N	N	Y	N	N	Y	Y	Y
Stafford	Y	Y	Y	N	N	Y	Y	Y
VIRGINIA								
*Byrd, H.	Y	Y	Y	Y	Y	N	N	N
Scott	Y	Y	N	Y	Y	N	N	N
WASHINGTON								
Jackson	N	N	Y	N	Y	Y	Y	Y
Magnuson	Y	Y	Y	N	Y	Y	Y	Y
WEST VIRGINIA								
Byrd, R.	Y	Y	Y	Y	Y	Y	Y	N
Randolph	N	N	Y	N	N	Y	Y	Y
WISCONSIN								
Nelson	N	N	Y	N	N	Y	Y	Y
Proxmire	Y	Y	Y	N	N	N	N	Y
WYOMING								
Hansen	?	Y	Y	Y	Y	Y	N	N
Wallop	Y	Y	Y	Y	Y	Y	Y	?

Democrats ***Republicans***

*Byrd elected as independent.

KEY

- Y Voted for (yea).
- ✓ Paired for.
- † Announced for.
- # CQ Poll for.
- N Voted against (nay).
- X Paired against.
- \- Announced against.
- ▮ CQ Poll against.
- P Voted "present."
- ● Voted "present" to avoid possible conflict of interest.
- ? Did not vote or otherwise make a position known.

291. HR 12936. HUD, Independent Agencies Appropriations, Fiscal 1979. Reconsideration of the Proxmire, D-Wis., amendment *(vote 288, p. 44-S)* to cut $810,205,000 from fiscal 1979 appropriations for HUD and three independent agencies. Adopted 45-42: R 20-10; D 25-32 (ND 9-29; SD 16-3), Aug. 7, 1978.

292. HR 12936. HUD, Independent Agencies Appropriations, Fiscal 1979. Bentsen, D-Texas, motion to table (kill) the Metzenbaum, D-Ohio, motion to reconsider the vote by which the Proxmire amendment *(vote 291, above)* was adopted. Motion to table agreed to 49-39: R 23-9; D 26-30 (ND 10-28; SD 16-2), Aug. 7, 1978.

293. HR 12936. HUD, Independent Agencies Appropriations, Fiscal 1979. Passage of the bill to appropriate $67.7 billion for the Department of Housing and Urban Development and 17 independent federal agencies for fiscal 1979. Passed 80-6: R 26-5; D 54-1 (ND 36-1; SD 18-0), Aug. 7, 1978. The president had requested $69,517,534,000.

294. HR 12932. Interior Appropriations, Fiscal 1979. Ruling of the Senate as to whether the Cannon, D-Nev., amendment to allow continued construction on three Colorado River water projects was germane. Ruled germane 53-40: R 29-7; D 24-33 (ND 11-28; SD 13-5), Aug. 8, 1978. (The Cannon amendment was adopted subsequently by a division vote.)

295. HR 12932. Interior Appropriations, Fiscal 1979. Curtis, R-Neb., motion to table (kill) the Metzenbaum, D-Ohio, motion to reconsider the vote by which the Cannon, D-Nev., amendment regarding Colorado River water projects was adopted *(see vote 296, below)*. Motion to table agreed to 59-33: R 29-6; D 30-27 (ND 15-24; SD 15-3), Aug. 8, 1978.

296. HR 12932. Interior Appropriations, Fiscal 1979. Huddleston, D-Ky., motion to table (kill) the Roth, R-Del., amendment to cut funding for numerous items in the bill by 2 percent. Motion agreed to 68-25: R 20-15; D 48-10 (ND 37-3; SD 11-7), Aug. 8, 1978.

297. S 2466. Health Services Research. Passage of the bill to extend for three years, through fiscal 1981, and to authorize $318 million for programs of the National Center for Health Services Research and the National Center for Health Statistics, and to authorize an Office of Health Technology and a National Council for the Evaluation of Medical Technology. Passed 74-19: R 21-16; D 53-3 (ND 37-1; SD 16-2), Aug. 9, 1978.

298. HR 12932. Interior Appropriations, Fiscal 1979. Ruling of the Senate as to whether the Johnston, D-La., substitute amendment to the Johnston amendment *(see vote 299, p. 46-S)*, to force modifications in Energy Department plans to boost subsidies to certain oil refiners was germane. Ruled germane 65-31: R 16-20; D 49-11 (ND 33-8; SD 16-3), Aug. 9, 1978.

CQ Senate Votes 299-302

Corresponding to Congressional Record Votes 303, 304, 305, 306

KEY

- Y Voted for (yea).
- ✓ Paired for.
- † Announced for.
- # CQ Poll for.
- N Voted against (nay).
- X Paired against.
- - Announced against.
- ▮ CQ Poll against.
- P Voted "present."
- ● Voted "present" to avoid possible conflict of interest.
- ? Did not vote or otherwise make a position known.

	299	300	301	302
ALABAMA				
Allen, M.	Y	Y	Y	Y
Sparkman	Y	Y	Y	N
ALASKA				
Gravel	Y	Y	Y	N
Stevens	N	Y	Y	Y
ARIZONA				
DeConcini	Y	Y	Y	Y
Goldwater	N	Y	Y	?
ARKANSAS				
Bumpers	Y	Y	Y	N
Hodges	Y	Y	Y	N
CALIFORNIA				
Cranston	Y	Y	Y	N
Hayakawa	N	Y	N	Y
COLORADO				
Hart	Y	Y	Y	N
Haskell	N	Y	Y	N
CONNECTICUT				
Ribicoff	Y	Y	N	Y
Weicker	N	Y	Y	?
DELAWARE				
Biden	?	?	?	?
Roth	Y	N	?	Y
FLORIDA				
Chiles	Y	Y	N	N
Stone	Y	Y	Y	\
GEORGIA				
Nunn	Y	Y	Y	N
Talmadge	Y	Y	Y	N
HAWAII				
Inouye	Y	Y	?	?
Matsunaga	Y	Y	Y	N
IDAHO				
Church	Y	Y	Y	N
McClure	N	Y	Y	Y
ILLINOIS				
Stevenson	Y	?	Y	?
Percy	Y	Y	Y	N
INDIANA				
Bayh	N	Y	Y	N
Lugar	N	N	N	Y
IOWA				
Clark	Y	Y	Y	N
Culver	Y	Y	Y	N
KANSAS				
Dole	N	Y	Y	Y
Pearson	N	Y	N	?
KENTUCKY				
Ford	Y	Y	Y	N
Huddleston	Y	Y	N	N
LOUISIANA				
Johnston	Y	Y	Y	N
Long	Y	Y	Y	N
MAINE				
Hathaway	✓	✓	Y	N
Muskie	Y	Y	N	N
MARYLAND				
Sarbanes	Y	Y	Y	N
Mathias	N	Y	Y	Y
MASSACHUSETTS				
Kennedy	Y	Y	N	N
Brooke	Y	Y	Y	Y
MICHIGAN				
Riegle	N	Y	Y	N
Griffin	N	Y	N	?
MINNESOTA				
Anderson	N	Y	Y	N
Humphrey, M.	-	†	†	-
MISSISSIPPI				
Eastland	N	Y	Y	?
Stennis	N	?	?	?
MISSOURI				
Eagleton	Y	Y	N	N
Danforth	Y	Y	N	Y
MONTANA				
Melcher	N	Y	Y	N
Hatfield, P.	N	Y	Y	N
NEBRASKA				
Zorinsky	N	Y	Y	N
Curtis	N	Y	Y	Y
NEVADA				
Cannon	Y	Y	Y	Y
Laxalt	N	Y	?	?
NEW HAMPSHIRE				
Durkin	Y	Y	Y	N
McIntyre	Y	Y	Y	N
NEW JERSEY				
Williams	Y	Y	Y	N
Case	Y	Y	Y	Y
NEW MEXICO				
Domenici	N	Y	Y	Y
Schmitt	N	Y	Y	Y
NEW YORK				
Moynihan	Y	?	Y	N
Javits	?	?	?	?
NORTH CAROLINA				
Morgan	Y	Y	Y	N
Helms	N	N	N	Y
NORTH DAKOTA				
Burdick	Y	Y	Y	N
Young	N	Y	Y	N
OHIO				
Glenn	Y	Y	N	N
Metzenbaum	Y	Y	Y	N
OKLAHOMA				
Bartlett	N	Y	Y	Y
Bellmon	N	Y	N	N
OREGON				
Hatfield, M.	N	Y	Y	N
Packwood	N	Y	Y	N
PENNSYLVANIA				
Heinz	Y	Y	Y	Y
Schweiker	Y	Y	Y	Y
RHODE ISLAND				
Pell	Y	Y	N	N
Chafee	Y	Y	N	Y
SOUTH CAROLINA				
Hollings	N	Y	Y	N
Thurmond	N	Y	Y	Y
SOUTH DAKOTA				
Abourezk	?	?	?	?
McGovern	Y	Y	Y	N
TENNESSEE				
Sasser	N	Y	N	N
Baker	N	Y	Y	Y
TEXAS				
Bentsen	N	Y	Y	Y
Tower	N	Y	Y	Y
UTAH				
Garn	N	Y	N	Y
Hatch	N	Y	Y	Y
VERMONT				
Leahy	Y	Y	Y	N
Stafford	Y	Y	Y	Y
VIRGINIA				
*Byrd, H.	Y	N	N	Y
Scott	N	Y	N	Y
WASHINGTON				
Jackson	Y	Y	Y	N
Magnuson	N	Y	Y	N
WEST VIRGINIA				
Byrd, R.	X	X	N	N
Randolph	Y	Y	N	Y
WISCONSIN				
Nelson	Y	Y	Y	N
Proxmire	Y	N	N	Y
WYOMING				
Hansen	N	Y	Y	Y
Wallop	?	?	?	?

Democrats ***Republicans***

**Byrd elected as independent.*

299. HR 12932. Interior Appropriations, Fiscal 1979. Johnston, D-La., substitute amendment, to the Johnston, D-La., amendment, to force changes in the Energy Department plan to boost subsidies to certain refiners of imported refined oil products (the effect was to lower prices for East Coast consumers). Adopted 53-40: R 9-27; D 44-13 (ND 30-8; SD 14-5), Aug. 9, 1978. (The Johnston amendment, as amended, was subsequently adopted by voice vote.)

300. HR 12932. Interior Appropriations, Fiscal 1979. Passage of the bill to authorize $11,566,413,000 in fiscal 1979 for the programs and operations of the Department of the Interior, the Department of Energy and related agencies. Passed 85-5: R 33-3; D 52-2 (ND 35-1; SD 17-1), Aug. 9, 1978. The President had requested $12,830,946,000 in new budget authority.

301. HR 13125. Agriculture Appropriations, Fiscal 1979. Melcher, D-Mont., amendment to appropriate $20 million for animal health and disease research programs at veterinary colleges and veterinary research laboratories. Adopted 68-23: R 24-10; D 44-13 (ND 30-9; SD 14-4), Aug. 9, 1978.

302. HR 13125. Agriculture Appropriations, Fiscal 1979. Stevens, R-Alaska, amendment to delete $1.6 million for administrative expenses of the office of the secretary of agriculture from the bill to appropriate $23,365,764,000 for fiscal year 1979 programs of the Department of Agriculture and related agencies. Rejected 35-51: R 26-5; D 9-46 (ND 5-33; SD 4-13), Aug. 9, 1978.

	303	304	305	306	307	308	309	310
ALABAMA								
Allen, M.	Y	Y	Y	N	N	Y	Y	Y
Sparkman	Y	Y	N	Y	N	Y	Y	N
ALASKA								
Gravel	?	Y	N	N	N	Y	?	N
Stevens	N	N	Y	Y	N	Y	Y	Y
ARIZONA								
DeConcini	Y	Y	Y	Y	N	Y	Y	Y
Goldwater	N	Y	Y	Y	Y	N	Y	Y
ARKANSAS								
Bumpers	Y	Y	Y	Y	N	Y	Y	N
Hodges	Y	Y	Y	N	N	Y	Y	N
CALIFORNIA								
Cranston	Y	Y	N	Y	N	Y	Y	N
Hayakawa	N	Y	Y	Y	Y	Y	Y	N
COLORADO								
Hart	Y	Y	N	N	N	Y	Y	?
Haskell	?	N	N	Y	N	Y	Y	N
CONNECTICUT								
Ribicoff	N	Y	N	Y	N	N	Y	N
Weicker	N	N	N	Y	N	Y	Y	N
DELAWARE								
Biden	?	N	N	Y	N	Y	Y	Y
Roth	N	Y	Y	Y	Y	N	N	Y
FLORIDA								
Chiles	Y	Y	N	Y	N	Y	Y	N
Stone	Y	Y	N	N	N	Y	Y	N
GEORGIA								
Nunn	Y	Y	Y	Y	N	Y	Y	?
Talmadge	Y	Y	N	Y	N	Y	Y	Y
HAWAII								
Inouye	?	?	?	Y	N	Y	Y	N
Matsunaga	?	Y	N	Y	N	Y	Y	N
IDAHO								
Church	Y	N	N	Y	N	Y	Y	N
McClure	?	N	Y	N	Y	Y	Y	Y
ILLINOIS								
Stevenson	Y	Y	N	Y	N	Y	Y	N
Percy	Y	Y	Y	Y	N	Y	Y	N
INDIANA								
Bayh	Y	N	N	Y	N	Y	Y	N
Lugar	N	Y	Y	Y	N	Y	Y	Y
IOWA								
Clark	Y	Y	N	N	N	Y	Y	-
Culver	Y	Y	N	N	N	Y	Y	N
KANSAS								
Dole	Y	Y	N	Y	N	Y	Y	N
Pearson	N	Y	Y	Y	N	Y	Y	?
KENTUCKY								
Ford	Y	Y	N	N	N	Y	Y	?
Huddleston	Y	Y	N	N	N	Y	Y	N
LOUISIANA								
Johnston	?	Y	Y	Y	N	Y	Y	?
Long	Y	Y	Y	Y	N	Y	Y	N
MAINE								
Hathaway	Y	Y	N	N	N	Y	Y	Y
Muskie	Y	Y	N	Y	N	Y	Y	N
MARYLAND								
Sarbanes	Y	Y	N	Y	N	Y	Y	N
Mathias	?	N	N	Y	N	Y	Y	N
MASSACHUSETTS								
Kennedy	Y	Y	N	N	N	Y	Y	N
Brooke	N	N	N	N	N	Y	Y	?
MICHIGAN								
Riegle	Y	N	N	Y	N	Y	Y	N
Griffin	N	N	Y	Y	N	Y	Y	Y
MINNESOTA								
Anderson	Y	Y	N	Y	N	Y	Y	N
Humphrey, M.	†	†	-	†	-	†	†	-
MISSISSIPPI								
Eastland	?	Y	Y	Y	?	Y	?	?
Stennis	Y	Y	Y	N	N	Y	?	N
MISSOURI								
Eagleton	N	Y	N	Y	N	Y	Y	N
Danforth	N	Y	N	Y	N	Y	Y	N
MONTANA								
Melcher	?	Y	N	N	N	Y	Y	Y
Hatfield, P.	Y	Y	N	N	N	Y	Y	N
NEBRASKA								
Zorinsky	Y	Y	Y	N	N	Y	Y	N
Curtis	N	N	Y	Y	Y	Y	Y	Y
NEVADA								
Cannon	Y	Y	N	Y	N	Y	Y	N
Laxalt	N	N	Y	Y	Y	Y	Y	Y
NEW HAMPSHIRE								
Durkin	Y	Y	N	Y	N	Y	Y	Y
McIntyre	Y	Y	N	Y	N	Y	Y	Y
NEW JERSEY								
Williams	?	Y	N	Y	N	Y	Y	N
Case	Y	N	N	Y	N	N	Y	N
NEW MEXICO								
Domenici	†	N	N	N	N	Y	Y	N
Schmitt	Y	Y	Y	N	N	Y	Y	N
NEW YORK								
Moynihan	Y	Y	N	Y	N	Y	Y	N
Javits	?	?	?	?	?	?	?	N
NORTH CAROLINA								
Morgan	Y	Y	N	N	N	Y	Y	N
Helms	N	N	Y	Y	Y	N	N	Y
NORTH DAKOTA								
Burdick	Y	Y	N	N	N	Y	Y	N
Young	N	Y	Y	Y	N	Y	Y	N
OHIO								
Glenn	N	Y	N	Y	N	Y	Y	N
Metzenbaum	?	N	N	N	N	Y	Y	N
OKLAHOMA								
Bartlett	Y	N	Y	Y	Y	Y	Y	N
Bellmon	N	Y	N	Y	N	Y	Y	N
OREGON								
Hatfield, M.	N	Y	N	Y	N	Y	Y	N
Packwood	Y	N	Y	Y	N	Y	Y	N
PENNSYLVANIA								
Heinz	?	?	?	Y	N	Y	Y	N
Schweiker	Y	N	Y	Y	N	Y	Y	N
RHODE ISLAND								
Pell	N	Y	N	Y	N	N	Y	N
Chafee	Y	Y	N	Y	N	Y	Y	N
SOUTH CAROLINA								
Hollings	N	Y	N	Y	N	Y	Y	N
Thurmond	Y	Y	Y	Y	Y	Y	Y	Y
SOUTH DAKOTA								
Abourezk	Y	?	?	?	?	Y	?	?
McGovern	Y	Y	N	N	N	Y	Y	N
TENNESSEE								
Sasser	Y	Y	Y	Y	N	Y	Y	N
Baker	Y	N	Y	Y	N	Y	Y	N
TEXAS								
Bentsen	?	Y	N	Y	N	Y	Y	N
Tower	Y	N	Y	Y	Y	Y	Y	Y
UTAH								
Garn	N	Y	Y	Y	Y	Y	Y	Y
Hatch	Y	Y	Y	Y	Y	Y	Y	Y
VERMONT								
Leahy	Y	Y	N	Y	N	Y	N	N
Stafford	Y	Y	N	Y	N	Y	Y	N
VIRGINIA								
*Byrd, H.	N	Y	Y	Y	Y	N	Y	N
Scott	N	Y	Y	Y	Y	N	Y	N
WASHINGTON								
Jackson	Y	Y	N	Y	N	Y	Y	N
Magnuson	?	Y	N	Y	N	Y	Y	N
WEST VIRGINIA								
Byrd, R.	Y	Y	N	Y	N	Y	Y	N
Randolph	Y	Y	N	N	N	Y	Y	N
WISCONSIN								
Nelson	Y	Y	N	Y	N	Y	N	N
Proxmire	N	Y	Y	Y	Y	Y	N	N
WYOMING								
Hansen	N	N	Y	Y	Y	Y	Y	N
Wallop	?	N	Y	Y	N	Y	Y	N

Democrats ***Republicans***

*Byrd elected as independent.

KEY

- Y Voted for (yea).
- ✓ Paired for.
- † Announced for.
- # CQ Poll for.
- N Voted against (nay).
- X Paired against.
- \- Announced against.
- ▮ CQ Poll against.
- P Voted "present."
- ● Voted "present" to avoid possible conflict of interest.
- ? Did not vote or otherwise make a position known.

303. HR 13125. Agriculture Appropriations, Fiscal 1979. Hathaway, D-Maine, amendment to appropriate an additional $105 million, to the $85 million in the bill, for certain agricultural conservation programs. Adopted 55-26: R 13-19; D 42-7 (ND 28-5; SD 14-2), Aug. 10, 1978.

304. HR 13125. Agriculture Appropriations, Fiscal 1979. Eagleton, D-Mo., motion to table (kill) the Weicker, R-Conn., amendment to prohibit the use of appropriated funds to finance economic assistance to South Korea under the Food for Peace (PL 480) program in protest of the Korean government's lack of cooperation in the congressional influence-buying investigation. Motion agreed to 71-24: R 18-18; D 53-6 (ND 34-6; SD 19-0), Aug. 10, 1978.

305. HR 13125. Agriculture Appropriations, Fiscal 1979. Lugar, R-Ind., amendment to delete $250 million from the fiscal 1979 appropriation for the food stamp program. Rejected 38-57: R 25-11; D 13-46 (ND 3-37; SD 10-9), Aug. 10, 1978. A "nay" was a vote supporting the president's position.

306. HR 13125. Agriculture Appropriations, Fiscal 1979. Eagleton, D-Mo., amendment to reduce spending in 15 agriculture programs by a total of $126.5 million in agriculture appropriations for fiscal 1979. Adopted 73-24: R 33-4; D 40-20 (ND 28-13; SD 12-7), Aug. 10, 1978.

307. HR 13125. Agriculture Appropriations, Fiscal 1979. Curtis, R-Neb., amendment to delete $2 billion from the fiscal 1979 appropriation for the food stamp program. Rejected 16-80: R 14-23; D 2-57 (ND 1-40; SD 1-17), Aug. 10, 1978. A "nay" was a vote supporting the president's position.

308. HR 13125. Agriculture Appropriations, Fiscal 1979. Passage of the bill to appropriate $23,365,764,000 for fiscal 1979 operations and programs of the Department of Agriculture and related agencies. Passed 90-8: R 32-5; D 58-3 (ND 40-2; SD 18-1), Aug. 10, 1978. The president had requested $23,090,152,000 in new budget authority.

309. HR 12928. Public Works, Energy Appropriations, Fiscal 1979. Passage of the bill to appropriate $10,123,344,900 in fiscal 1979 for energy and water development programs of the Interior and Energy Departments. Passed 89-5: R 35-2; D 54-3 (ND 37-3; SD 17-0), Aug. 10, 1978. The president had requested $11,039,449,-000 in new budget authority.

310. HR 12050. Tuition Tax Credits. Goldwater, R-Ariz., amendment to allow a federal income tax credit of up to $150 a year for residential property taxes paid for the support of public schools. Rejected 21-69: R 13-23; D 8-46 (ND 6-33; SD 2-13), Aug. 14, 1978.

CQ Senate Votes 311-318

Corresponding to Congressional Record Votes 315, 316, 317, 318, 319, 320, 321, 322

KEY

- Y Voted for (yea).
- ✓ Paired for.
- † Announced for.
- # CQ Poll for.
- N Voted against (nay).
- X Paired against.
- \- Announced against.
- ▮ CQ Poll against.
- P Voted "present."
- ● Voted "present" to avoid possible conflict of interest.
- ? Did not vote or otherwise make a position known.

	311	312	313	314	315	316	317	318
ALABAMA								
Allen, M.	Y	Y	Y	N	N	Y	Y	Y
Sparkman	Y	Y	N	Y	Y	Y	Y	Y
ALASKA								
Gravel	Y	Y	N	Y	N	Y	N	Y
Stevens	Y	Y	Y	N	N	Y	Y	N
ARIZONA								
DeConcini	Y	N	Y	N	N	Y	Y	Y
Goldwater	Y	Y	Y	N	N	Y	Y	N
ARKANSAS								
Bumpers	Y	N	N	Y	Y	N	Y	N
Hodges	Y	N	N	Y	Y	Y	Y	N
CALIFORNIA								
Cranston	Y	N	N	Y	Y	Y	Y	N
Hayakawa	Y	Y	Y	N	N	N	N	Y
COLORADO								
Hart	?	N	?	?	Y	Y	Y	N
Haskell	Y	N	N	Y	Y	Y	Y	N
CONNECTICUT								
Ribicoff	Y	Y	Y	N	N	Y	N	Y
Weicker	Y	Y	N	Y	N	N	Y	N
DELAWARE								
Biden	Y	Y	Y	N	N	Y	N	Y
Roth	Y	Y	Y	N	N	Y	N	Y
FLORIDA								
Chiles	?	N	N	Y	Y	Y	Y	N
Stone	Y	Y	N	Y	Y	Y	Y	N
GEORGIA								
Nunn	?	Y	N	Y	N	Y	Y	N
Talmadge	Y	N	N	Y	Y	Y	N	Y
HAWAII								
Inouye	Y	N	N	Y	N	Y	Y	?
Matsunaga	Y	Y	Y	N	N	Y	N	Y
IDAHO								
Church	Y	Y	N	Y	Y	Y	Y	N
McClure	Y	Y	N	N	N	Y	Y	N
ILLINOIS								
Stevenson	Y	N	N	Y	N	Y	Y	N
Percy	Y	N	N	Y	N	Y	Y	N
INDIANA								
Bayh	Y	Y	N	Y	Y	Y	N	N
Lugar	Y	Y	Y	N	N	Y	Y	N
IOWA								
Clark	†	Y	N	Y	Y	Y	Y	N
Culver	Y	N	N	Y	Y	Y	Y	N
KANSAS								
Dole	Y	Y	Y	N	N	Y	Y	N
Pearson	?	Y	Y	N	N	Y	Y	N
KENTUCKY								
Ford	?	N	N	Y	N	Y	Y	N
Huddleston	Y	N	Y	N	N	N	Y	N
LOUISIANA								
Johnston	?	?	?	?	?	?	?	?
Long	Y	Y	Y	N	N	Y	N	Y
MAINE								
Hathaway	Y	Y	Y	N	Y	Y	Y	Y
Muskie	Y	N	Y	N	Y	Y	Y	N
MARYLAND								
Sarbanes	Y	Y	N	Y	Y	Y	Y	N
Mathias	Y	N	Y	N	N	Y	Y	Y
MASSACHUSETTS								
Kennedy	Y	N	N	Y	Y	?	Y	N
Brooke	?	Y	N	Y	N	Y	N	Y
MICHIGAN								
Riegle	Y	N	N	Y	Y	Y	Y	N
Griffin	Y	Y	Y	N	Y	Y	Y	N
MINNESOTA								
Anderson	Y	Y	Y	N	N	Y	Y	Y
Humphrey, M.	†	N	N	Y	Y	Y	Y	N
MISSISSIPPI								
Eastland	?	?	?	?	?	?	?	?
Stennis	Y	N	N	Y	N	N	Y	?
MISSOURI								
Eagleton	Y	N	N	Y	Y	Y	Y	N
Danforth	Y	Y	Y	N	N	Y	N	Y
MONTANA								
Melcher	Y	Y	Y	N	N	Y	N	Y
Hatfield, P.	Y	N	N	Y	N	Y	N	Y
NEBRASKA								
Zorinsky	Y	Y	Y	N	Y	Y	Y	N
Curtis	?	Y	Y	N	N	N	N	Y
NEVADA								
Cannon	Y	N	N	Y	Y	Y	Y	Y
Laxalt	?	Y	Y	N	N	Y	Y	N
NEW HAMPSHIRE								
Durkin	Y	N	Y	N	Y	?	?	?
McIntyre	Y	Y	Y	N	Y	Y	Y	Y
NEW JERSEY								
Williams	Y	Y	N	Y	Y	Y	Y	Y
Case	Y	N	N	Y	N	Y	Y	Y
NEW MEXICO								
Domenici	Y	Y	N	Y	N	Y	Y	N
Schmitt	Y	Y	Y	N	N	Y	N	Y
NEW YORK								
Moynihan	Y	Y	Y	N	N	Y	N	Y
Javits	Y	N	N	Y	Y	Y	Y	N
NORTH CAROLINA								
Morgan	Y	Y	N	Y	N	Y	Y	N
Helms	Y	Y	N	Y	N	Y	Y	N
NORTH DAKOTA								
Burdick	Y	N	N	Y	Y	Y	Y	N
Young	Y	Y	N	Y	N	Y	Y	N
OHIO								
Glenn	Y	N	N	Y	Y	N	Y	N
Metzenbaum	Y	N	N	Y	Y	N	Y	N
OKLAHOMA								
Bartlett	Y	Y	N	Y	N	Y	Y	N
Bellmon	Y	Y	N	Y	N	Y	Y	N
OREGON								
Hatfield, M.	Y	N	N	Y	Y	Y	Y	N
Packwood	Y	Y	Y	N	N	Y	N	Y
PENNSYLVANIA								
Heinz	Y	Y	Y	N	N	Y	N	Y
Schweiker	Y	Y	Y	N	N	Y	N	Y
RHODE ISLAND								
Pell	Y	N	N	Y	Y	Y	Y	N
Chafee	Y	N	N	Y	N	Y	Y	N
SOUTH CAROLINA								
Hollings	Y	N	N	Y	Y	Y	Y	N
Thurmond	Y	N	N	Y	N	Y	Y	N
SOUTH DAKOTA								
Abourezk	?	N	N	Y	Y	?	?	?
McGovern	Y	N	N	Y	?	Y	Y	N
TENNESSEE								
Sasser	Y	Y	N	Y	N	Y	Y	N
Baker	Y	Y	N	Y	N	Y	Y	N
TEXAS								
Bentsen	Y	Y	N	Y	N	Y	Y	Y
Tower	Y	Y	Y	N	N	Y	Y	N
UTAH								
Garn	Y	Y	Y	N	N	Y	Y	N
Hatch	Y	Y	Y	N	N	Y	N	Y
VERMONT								
Leahy	Y	N	N	Y	Y	Y	Y	N
Stafford	Y	N	N	Y	Y	Y	Y	N
VIRGINIA								
*Byrd, H.	Y	N	N	Y	N	N	Y	N
Scott	Y	N	N	Y	N	N	Y	?
WASHINGTON								
Jackson	Y	Y	Y	N	Y	Y	Y	N
Magnuson	Y	Y	Y	N	Y	Y	Y	N
WEST VIRGINIA								
Byrd, R.	Y	N	N	Y	N	Y	Y	N
Randolph	Y	N	N	Y	Y	Y	Y	N
WISCONSIN								
Nelson	Y	Y	Y	N	N	Y	Y	N
Proxmire	Y	Y	Y	N	N	Y	Y	N
WYOMING								
Hansen	Y	Y	Y	N	N	Y	N	Y
Wallop	Y	Y	Y	N	N	Y	Y	N

Democrats ***Republicans***

**Byrd elected as independent.*

311. HR 12050. Tuition Tax Credits. Moynihan, D-N.Y., amendment to add to the bill a finding of Congress that the maintenance of diversity was an important national goal. Adopted 87-0: R 34-0; D 53-0 (ND 39-0; SD 14-0), Aug. 14, 1978.

312. HR 12050. Tuition Tax Credits. Packwood, R-Ore., amendment to make clear that only the Supreme Court could render a decision as to the constitutionality of parochial school tuition tax credits. Adopted 56-42: R 29-9; D 27-33 (ND 19-24; SD 8-9), Aug. 15, 1978.

313. HR 12050. Tuition Tax Credits. Moynihan, D-N.Y., motion to table (kill) the Hollings, D-S.C., amendment *(see vote 314, below)*, to the Hodges, D-Ark., amendment, to delete credits for private and parochial elementary and secondary school tuitions. Motion rejected 40-57: R 21-17; D 19-40 (ND 16-26; SD 3-14), Aug. 15, 1978. A "nay" was a vote supporting the president's position.

314. HR 12050. Tuition Tax Credits. Hollings, D-S.C., amendment, to the Hodges, D-Ark., amendment, to delete credits for private and parochial elementary and secondary school tuitions. Adopted 56-41: R 16-22; D 40-19 (ND 26-16; SD 14-3), Aug. 15, 1978. A "yea" was a vote supporting the president's position. (The Hodges amendment, as amended, subsequently was adopted by voice vote.)

315. HR 12050. Tuition Tax Credits. Metzenbaum, D-Ohio, amendment to gradually phase out credits for taxpayers with annual incomes over $30,000 and to deny credits altogether to those with annual incomes over $40,000. Rejected 39-58: R 4-34; D 35-24 (ND 28-14; SD 7-10), Aug. 15, 1978.

316. HR 12050. Tuition Tax Credits. Domenici, R-N.M., amendment to increase participation by private school students in categorical aid programs authorized by the Elementary and Secondary Education Act. Adopted 85-10: R 34-4; D 51-6 (ND 38-2; SD 13-4), Aug. 15, 1978.

317. HR 12050. Tuition Tax Credits. Judgment of the Senate on the ruling of the Chair upholding a Long, D-La., point of order against the Long amendment to provide refundable tax credits, on the grounds that the amendment violated provisions of the 1974 budget control act. Ruling of the Chair sustained 75-21: R 27-11; D 48-10 (ND 33-8; SD 15-2), Aug. 15, 1978.

318. HR 12050. Tuition Tax Credits. Long, D-La., motion to waive provisions of the budget control act in order to allow consideration of a second Long amendment to provide refundable tax credits. Motion rejected 31-62: R 13-24; D 18-38 (ND 13-27; SD 5-11), Aug. 15, 1978.

Corresponding to Congressional Record Votes 323, 324, 325, 326, 327, 328, 329, 330

	319	320	321	322	323	324	325	326
ALABAMA								
Allen, M.	Y	Y	?	?	?	N	N	Y
Sparkman	?	Y	Y	Y	Y	Y	Y	Y
ALASKA								
Gravel	Y	Y	?	Y	Y	Y	N	Y
Stevens	Y	N	N	N	N	N	N	†
ARIZONA								
DeConcini	Y	N	Y	Y	Y	Y	N	Y
Goldwater	N	N	N	N	?	N	?	Y
ARKANSAS								
Bumpers	N	Y	Y	Y	Y	Y	Y	Y
Hodges	N	Y	Y	Y	Y	Y	Y	Y
CALIFORNIA								
Cranston	N	Y	Y	Y	Y	Y	Y	Y
Hayakawa	N	N	N	N	N	N	N	Y
COLORADO								
Hart	N	Y	?	?	?	Y	Y	Y
Haskell	Y	N	?	Y	Y	Y	Y	Y
CONNECTICUT								
Ribicoff	Y	Y	Y	Y	Y	Y	Y	Y
Weicker	Y	?	Y	N	Y	Y	Y	?
DELAWARE								
Biden	Y	Y	Y	Y	Y	?	?	?
Roth	Y	N	Y	N	Y	Y	N	N
FLORIDA								
Chiles	N	N	Y	Y	Y	Y	Y	Y
Stone	N	Y	Y	?	Y	Y	Y	Y
GEORGIA								
Nunn	Y	N	N	Y	Y	N	N	Y
Talmadge	Y	Y	Y	Y	Y	N	Y	Y
HAWAII								
Inouye	?	Y	Y	Y	Y	Y	Y	?
Matsunaga	Y	Y	Y	Y	Y	Y	Y	Y
IDAHO								
Church	Y	Y	Y	Y	Y	Y	Y	Y
McClure	Y	N	N	N	N	N	N	Y
ILLINOIS								
Stevenson	Y	Y	Y	Y	Y	Y	Y	Y
Percy	Y	Y	Y	Y	Y	Y	?	?
INDIANA								
Bayh	Y	Y	Y	Y	Y	Y	Y	Y
Lugar	Y	N	N	N	N	N	N	Y
IOWA								
Clark	N	Y	Y	Y	†	Y	Y	Y
Culver	N	Y	Y	Y	Y	?	Y	Y
KANSAS								
Dole	Y	Y	Y	N	Y	Y	Y	?
Pearson	Y	Y	Y	N	Y	?	?	?
KENTUCKY								
Ford	Y	Y	Y	Y	Y	Y	N	Y
Huddleston	Y	Y	Y	Y	Y	Y	Y	Y
LOUISIANA								
Johnston	?	?	?	?	?	?	?	?
Long	Y	Y	Y	Y	N	?	N	Y
MAINE								
Hathaway	Y	Y	Y	Y	Y	Y	Y	Y
Muskie	N	N	Y	Y	Y	Y	Y	Y
MARYLAND								
Sarbanes	N	Y	Y	Y	Y	Y	Y	Y
Mathias	Y	Y	Y	Y	Y	Y	Y	Y
MASSACHUSETTS								
Kennedy	N	Y	Y	Y	Y	Y	Y	Y
Brooke	Y	Y	Y	Y	Y	?	?	?
MICHIGAN								
Riegle	Y	Y	Y	Y	Y	Y	Y	Y
Griffin	Y	Y	Y	Y	Y	Y	Y	Y
MINNESOTA								
Anderson	Y	Y	Y	Y	Y	Y	?	?
Humphrey, M.	Y	Y	Y	Y	Y	Y	Y	Y
MISSISSIPPI								
Eastland	?	?	?	?	?	?	?	?
Stennis	?	N	N	Y	N	N	?	Y
MISSOURI								
Eagleton	Y	Y	Y	Y	Y	Y	Y	Y
Danforth	Y	Y	Y	Y	Y	Y	Y	Y
MONTANA								
Melcher	Y	Y	Y	Y	Y	Y	N	Y
Hatfield, P.	Y	Y	Y	Y	Y	Y	N	Y
NEBRASKA								
Zorinsky	Y	N	N	Y	Y	N	N	N
Curtis	Y	N	Y	N	N	N	N	N
NEVADA								
Cannon	Y	Y	Y	N	N	Y	N	Y
Laxalt	Y	N	Y	N	N	Y	N	N
NEW HAMPSHIRE								
Durkin	?	Y	Y	Y	Y	Y	Y	Y
McIntyre	Y	N	Y	Y	Y	Y	?	?
NEW JERSEY								
Williams	Y	Y	Y	?	Y	Y	Y	Y
Case	Y	Y	Y	Y	Y	Y	Y	Y
NEW MEXICO								
Domenici	Y	Y	Y	N	Y	Y	N	Y
Schmitt	Y	Y	Y	N	N	N	Y	Y
NEW YORK								
Moynihan	Y	Y	N	Y	Y	Y	?	Y
Javits	N	Y	Y	?	Y	Y	Y	Y
NORTH CAROLINA								
Morgan	N	N	N	N	N	Y	Y	N
Helms	Y	N	N	N	N	N	N	N
NORTH DAKOTA								
Burdick	N	Y	Y	Y	Y	Y	N	Y
Young	N	Y	Y	N	N	N	?	?
OHIO								
Glenn	N	Y	Y	Y	Y	Y	Y	Y
Metzenbaum	N	Y	Y	Y	Y	Y	Y	Y
OKLAHOMA								
Bartlett	N	N	Y	N	N	N	N	Y
Bellmon	N	N	N	N	N	Y	Y	Y
OREGON								
Hatfield, M.	N	Y	Y	Y	Y	†	†	?
Packwood	Y	N	Y	Y	Y	Y	Y	Y
PENNSYLVANIA								
Heinz	Y	Y	Y	Y	Y	Y	Y	Y
Schweiker	Y	Y	Y	N	Y	Y	Y	Y
RHODE ISLAND								
Pell	N	Y	Y	Y	Y	Y	N	Y
Chafee	N	Y	Y	Y	Y	Y	Y	Y
SOUTH CAROLINA								
Hollings	Y	Y	Y	Y	Y	Y	Y	Y
Thurmond	Y	Y	Y	Y	Y	Y	Y	Y
SOUTH DAKOTA								
Abourezk	?	?	?	?	?	?	?	?
McGovern	N	Y	Y	Y	Y	Y	Y	Y
TENNESSEE								
Sasser	Y	Y	Y	Y	Y	Y	Y	Y
Baker	Y	Y	Y	N	N	?	?	?
TEXAS								
Bentsen	Y	Y	Y	Y	Y	Y	N	Y
Tower	Y	N	N	N	N	N	N	Y
UTAH								
Garn	Y	N	Y	N	N	N	N	N
Hatch	Y	N	N	N	N	N	N	N
VERMONT								
Leahy	N	Y	Y	Y	Y	Y	Y	Y
Stafford	N	Y	Y	N	Y	Y	Y	Y
VIRGINIA								
*Byrd, H.	Y	N	N	Y	N	N	N	Y
Scott	?	N	N	N	N	N	N	Y
WASHINGTON								
Jackson	Y	Y	Y	Y	Y	Y	N	Y
Magnuson	Y	Y	Y	Y	Y	Y	Y	Y
WEST VIRGINIA								
Byrd, R.	Y	Y	Y	Y	Y	Y	Y	Y
Randolph	Y	Y	†	Y	Y	Y	N	Y
WISCONSIN								
Nelson	Y	Y	Y	Y	Y	Y	Y	Y
Proxmire	Y	N	Y	Y	Y	N	N	Y
WYOMING								
Hansen	Y	N	N	N	N	N	N	Y
Wallop	Y	Y	Y	N	Y	Y	N	Y

Democrats ***Republicans***

*Byrd elected as independent.

KEY

- Y Voted for (yea).
- ✓ Paired for.
- † Announced for.
- # CQ Poll for.
- N Voted against (nay).
- X Paired against.
- - Announced against.
- ▮ CQ Poll against.
- P Voted "present."
- ● Voted "present" to avoid possible conflict of interest.
- ? Did not vote or otherwise make a position known.

319. HR 12050. Tuition Tax Credits. Passage of the bill to provide a federal income tax credit equal to half the costs of college or vocational school tuitions, up to a maximum of $250 per student between Aug. 1, 1978, and Oct. 1, 1980, and $500 per student from Oct. 1, 1980, to Dec. 31, 1983. Passed 65-27: R 28-9; D 37-18 (ND 27-13; SD 10-5), Aug. 15, 1978. A "nay" was a vote supporting the president's position.

320. S 2539. Student Financial Aid. Passage of the bill to amend the 1965 Higher Education Act to expand existing federal programs of aid to college students by decreasing the family contribution in the basic grant program to 10.5 percent, from 20 percent, of disposable income; removing the income limit for interest subsidies on guaranteed student loans; and increasing funding for the college work-study and supplemental grant programs. Passed 68-28: R 20-17; D 48-11 (ND 36-6; SD 12-5), Aug. 16, 1978. A "yea" was a vote supporting the president's position.

321. S 2539. Student Financial Aid. Stafford, R-Vt., motion to table (kill) the Pell, D-R.I., motion to reconsider the vote *(vote 320, above)* by which the bill was passed. Motion to table agreed to 75-17: R 27-11; D 48-6 (ND 36-2; SD 12-4), Aug. 16, 1978.

322. H J Res 554. D.C. Voting Representation. Byrd, D-W.Va., motion to table (kill) the McClure, R-Idaho, appeal of the ruling of the chair that the Byrd motion to proceed to consideration of the joint resolution proposing a constitutional amendment granting congressional representation for the District of Columbia was in order. Motion to table agreed to 64-28: R 11-26; D 53-2 (ND 39-1; SD 14-1), Aug. 16, 1978.

323. H J Res 554. D.C. Voting Representation. Byrd, D-W.Va., motion to proceed to the consideration of the resolution proposing an amendment to the Constitution to provide for voting representation of the District of Columbia in both houses of Congress. Motion agreed to 71-22: R 20-17; D 51-5 (ND 39-1; SD 12-4), Aug. 16, 1978.

324. H J Res 554. D.C. Voting Representation. Byrd, D-W.Va., motion to table (kill) the Curtis, R-Neb., amendment to require a balanced federal budget. Motion agreed to 68-22: R 19-15; D 49-7 (ND 38-2; SD 11-5), Aug. 17, 1978.

325. H J Res 554. D.C. Voting Representation. Mathias, R-Md., motion to table (kill) the Melcher, D-Mont., amendment to provide that for purposes of representation in the House, the District of Columbia would be treated as though it were a state, and for purposes of representation in the Senate, the District would be treated as though it were part of Maryland. Motion agreed to 52-33: R 15-16; D 37-17 (ND 27-11; SD 10-6), Aug. 17, 1978.

326. HR 13468. District of Columbia Appropriations, Fiscal 1979. Adoption of the conference report on the bill to appropriate $255,200,900 in federal funds and establish a fiscal 1979 budget for the District of Columbia of $1,362,317,700. Adopted 76-8: R 23-6; D 53-2 (ND 37-1; SD 16-1), Aug. 17, 1978. The president had requested $457,090,000 in federal funds and a budget of $1,428,442,000.

CQ Senate Votes 327-334

Corresponding to Congressional Record Votes 331, 332, 333, 334, 335, 336, 337, 338

	327	328	329	330	331	332	333	334
ALABAMA								
Allen, M.	N	?	?	?	?	?	?	?
Sparkman	N	Y	?	Y	Y	Y	Y	Y
ALASKA								
Gravel	N	Y	Y	Y	N	Y	Y	Y
Stevens	?	?	N	N	N	N	Y	N
ARIZONA								
DeConcini	?	?	?	?	?	?	?	?
Goldwater	?	N	Y	N	N	Y	Y	N
ARKANSAS								
Bumpers	?	?	?	?	?	?	?	?
Hodges	N	Y	Y	Y	Y	Y	?	N
CALIFORNIA								
Cranston	?	?	?	?	?	?	Y	Y
Hayakawa	N	Y	Y	N	N	Y	Y	N
COLORADO								
Hart	N	Y	Y	Y	Y	Y	Y	N
Haskell	N	Y	Y	Y	Y	Y	Y	N
CONNECTICUT								
Ribicoff	?	Y	Y	Y	Y	Y	Y	N
Weicker	Y	Y	Y	Y	Y	Y	Y	N
DELAWARE								
Biden	N	N	Y	Y	Y	Y	Y	N
Roth	?	N	Y	N	N	N	Y	N
FLORIDA								
Chiles	Y	Y	Y	Y	Y	Y	Y	Y
Stone	N	N	Y	Y	Y	Y	Y	Y
GEORGIA								
Nunn	?	Y	Y	Y	N	Y	Y	N
Talmadge	?	?	?	?	?	?	?	?
HAWAII								
Inouye	N	?	Y	Y	Y	Y	Y	Y
Matsunaga	N	Y	Y	Y	Y	Y	Y	Y
IDAHO								
Church	?	N	Y	Y	Y	Y	Y	N
McClure	?	N	N	N	N	N	N	N
ILLINOIS								
Stevenson	?	?	Y	Y	Y	Y	Y	N
Percy	?	?	?	?	?	?	†	Y
INDIANA								
Bayh	N	?	?	Y	Y	Y	Y	Y
Lugar	N	Y	Y	N	N	Y	Y	Y
IOWA								
Clark	N	Y	Y	Y	Y	Y	Y	N
Culver	N	?	?	Y	Y	Y	Y	N
KANSAS								
Dole	N	?	?	?	?	?	?	?
Pearson	?	Y	Y	N	Y	Y	Y	N
KENTUCKY								
Ford	?	Y	Y	Y	Y	Y	Y	Y
Huddleston	?	Y	Y	Y	Y	Y	Y	Y
LOUISIANA								
Johnston	?	?	?	?	?	?	?	?
Long	N	Y	Y	N	N	Y	Y	Y
MAINE								
Hathaway	?	Y	Y	Y	Y	Y	Y	N
Muskie	?	Y	Y	Y	Y	Y	Y	N
MARYLAND								
Sarbanes	Y	?	?	Y	Y	Y	Y	Y
Mathias	Y	?	?	?	?	Y	Y	Y
MASSACHUSETTS								
Kennedy	?	Y	Y	Y	Y	Y	Y	Y
Brooke	?	Y	Y	Y	Y	Y	Y	N
MICHIGAN								
Riegle	N	Y	Y	Y	Y	Y	Y	Y
Griffin	-	?	?	?	?	?	†	-
MINNESOTA								
Anderson	?	?	?	?	?	?	?	?
Humphrey, M.	?	†	†	†	†	†	†	?
MISSISSIPPI								
Eastland	?	?	?	?	?	?	?	?
Stennis	?	Y	N	?	N	Y	Y	Y
MISSOURI								
Eagleton	N	N	Y	Y	Y	Y	Y	N
Danforth	?	Y	Y	Y	Y	Y	Y	N
MONTANA								
Melcher	N	Y	Y	N	N	Y	Y	Y
Hatfield, P.	N	?	?	?	?	?	?	?
NEBRASKA								
Zorinsky	N	Y	Y	Y	N	Y	Y	N
Curtis	N	N	Y	N	N	Y	Y	N
NEVADA								
Cannon	-	Y	Y	N	N	N	Y	N
Laxalt	?	N	Y	N	N	N	Y	N
NEW HAMPSHIRE								
Durkin	?	?	?	?	?	Y	Y	Y
McIntyre	?	?	?	?	?	?	?	N
NEW JERSEY								
Williams	N	Y	Y	Y	Y	Y	Y	Y
Case	✓	Y	Y	Y	Y	Y	Y	Y
NEW MEXICO								
Domenici	Y	?	Y	N	N	N	Y	Y
Schmitt	?	Y	Y	N	N	N	Y	N
NEW YORK								
Moynihan	?	Y	Y	Y	Y	Y	Y	N
Javits	Y	Y	Y	Y	Y	Y	Y	Y
NORTH CAROLINA								
Morgan	?	Y	Y	Y	N	Y	Y	Y
Helms	?	N	N	N	N	N	Y	N
NORTH DAKOTA								
Burdick	?	?	?	?	N	Y	Y	N
Young	N	Y	Y	N	N	Y	Y	N
OHIO								
Glenn	N	Y	Y	Y	Y	Y	Y	Y
Metzenbaum	N	Y	Y	Y	Y	Y	Y	Y
OKLAHOMA								
Bartlett	N	N	Y	N	N	N	Y	N
Bellmon	Y	?	?	N	N	Y	Y	N
OREGON								
Hatfield, M.	-	†	?	†	?	†	?	N
Packwood	N	Y	Y	N	N	N	Y	N
PENNSYLVANIA								
Heinz	?	?	?	?	Y	Y	Y	Y
Schweiker	N	N	Y	N	N	Y	Y	Y
RHODE ISLAND								
Pell	?	?	Y	Y	N	Y	Y	N
Chafee	N	?	?	?	Y	N	Y	N
SOUTH CAROLINA								
Hollings	?	Y	Y	Y	Y	Y	Y	N
Thurmond	X	Y	Y	Y	Y	Y	Y	N
SOUTH DAKOTA								
Abourezk	?	?	?	?	?	?	?	?
McGovern	N	Y	Y	Y	Y	Y	Y	Y
TENNESSEE								
Sasser	N	?	Y	Y	Y	N	Y	Y
Baker	N	N	Y	N	N	N	Y	Y
TEXAS								
Bentsen	N	Y	Y	Y	Y	Y	Y	N
Tower	?	N	Y	N	N	Y	Y	N
UTAH								
Garn	N	?	?	N	N	N	Y	N
Hatch	N	N	Y	N	N	N	Y	N
VERMONT								
Leahy	?	Y	Y	Y	Y	Y	Y	N
Stafford	N	?	?	Y	Y	Y	Y	N
VIRGINIA								
*Byrd, H.	N	N	Y	N	N	Y	Y	N
Scott	N	N	N	N	N	N	Y	Y
WASHINGTON								
Jackson	N	Y	Y	Y	Y	Y	Y	N
Magnuson	N	Y	Y	Y	Y	Y	Y	Y
WEST VIRGINIA								
Byrd, R.	Y	Y	Y	Y	Y	Y	Y	Y
Randolph	N	Y	Y	Y	Y	Y	Y	Y
WISCONSIN								
Nelson	?	N	Y	Y	Y	Y	Y	Y
Proxmire	N	Y	Y	Y	N	Y	Y	N
WYOMING								
Hansen	?	N	Y	N	N	Y	Y	N
Wallop	N	Y	Y	N	N	N	Y	N

Democrats ***Republicans***

*Byrd elected as independent.

KEY

- Y Voted for (yea).
- ✓ Paired for.
- † Announced for.
- # CQ Poll for.
- N Voted against (nay).
- X Paired against.
- - Announced against.
- ▌ CQ Poll against.
- P Voted "present."
- ● Voted "present" to avoid possible conflict of interest.
- ? Did not vote or otherwise make a position known.

327. S 3073. Surface Transportation Assistance Act. Mathias, R-Md., amendment to authorize the federal government to advance to a state 100 percent of the cost of construction for a toll tunnel or bridge necessary to complete an essential gap in the Interstate Highway System, and to provide the state with a schedule for the repayment of funds advanced in excess of the federal share of the project's final cost (this amendment applied to constructing tunnels in Baltimore and Boston). Rejected 8-45: R 5-15; D 3-30 (ND 2-22; SD 1-8), Aug. 18, 1978.

328. H J Res 554. D.C. Voting Representation. Kennedy, D-Mass., motion to table (kill) the Scott, R-Va., amendment to add to the proposed constitutional amendment an article to give states the power to regulate the circumstances under which abortions are performed. Motion agreed to 48-19: R 13-13; D 35-6 (ND 24-4; SD 11-2), Aug. 21, 1978.

329. H J Res 554. D.C. Voting Representation. Kennedy, D-Mass., motion to table (kill) the McClure, R-Idaho, amendment to prohibit states from rescinding their ratification of the amendment. Motion agreed to 67-5: R 24-4; D 43-1 (ND 31-0; SD 12-1), Aug. 21, 1978.

330. H J Res 554. D.C. Voting Representation. Kennedy, D-Mass., motion to table (kill) the McClure, R-Idaho, amendment to grant to District of Columbia residents the authority to implement the provisions of the amendment. Motion agreed to 50-28: R 7-24; D 43-4 (ND 32-2; SD 11-2), Aug. 21, 1978.

331. H J Res 554. D.C. Voting Representation. Kennedy, D-Mass., motion to table (kill) the McClure, R-Idaho, amendment to return the District of Columbia to Maryland. Motion agreed to 47-35: R 10-23; D 37-12 (ND 28-7; SD 9-5), Aug. 21, 1978.

332. H J Res 554. D.C. Voting Representation. Bayh, D-Ind., motion to table (kill) the McClure, R-Idaho, amendment to grant statehood to the District of Columbia. Motion agreed to 67-17: R 19-15; D 48-2 (ND 35-1; SD 13-1), Aug. 21, 1978.

333. HR 12927. Military Construction Appropriations, Fiscal 1979. Adoption of the conference report on the bill to appropriate $3,880,863,000 for construction projects of the Department of Defense in fiscal 1979. Adopted (thus clearing the bill for the president) 83-1: R 33-1; D 50-0 (ND 37-0; SD 13-0), Aug. 21, 1978. The president had requested $4,253,000,000.

334. S 3073. Surface Transportation Assistance Act. Huddleston, D-Ky., amendment to authorize $100 million annually from the Highway Trust Fund for fiscal years 1979 and 1980 for the rehabilitation of roads damaged by the extensive hauling of coal or other resource-recovery related activity. Rejected 37-51: R 10-26; D 27-25 (ND 18-20; SD 9-5), Aug. 21, 1978.

	335	336	337	338	339	340	341	342
ALABAMA								
Allen, M.	?	?	?	?	?	?	N	Y
Sparkman	Y	N	Y	Y	Y	Y	Y	Y
ALASKA								
Gravel	?	N	N	Y	Y	Y	Y	Y
Stevens	Y	N	N	N	N	N	N	Y
ARIZONA								
DeConcini	?	?	N	Y	Y	Y	Y	Y
Goldwater	Y	N	N	Y	?	?	?	?
ARKANSAS								
Bumpers	?	?	?	?	?	Y	Y	Y
Hodges	Y	N	N	Y	N	Y	Y	Y
CALIFORNIA								
Cranston	Y	Y	Y	Y	Y	Y	Y	Y
Hayakawa	Y	N	?	N	N	N	Y	Y
COLORADO								
Hart	Y	N	?	Y	Y	Y	Y	Y
Haskell	Y	N	Y	Y	Y	Y	Y	Y
CONNECTICUT								
Ribicoff	Y	N	Y	Y	Y	Y	Y	Y
Weicker	Y	Y	N	Y	Y	Y	Y	Y
DELAWARE								
Biden	Y	N	Y	Y	Y	Y	Y	Y
Roth	Y	N	N	Y	N	N	Y	Y
FLORIDA								
Chiles	Y	N	Y	Y	Y	Y	Y	Y
Stone	Y	N	Y	Y	Y	Y	Y	Y
GEORGIA								
Nunn	Y	N	N	Y	N	Y	Y	Y
Talmadge	?	?	?	Y	?	?	?	?
HAWAII								
Inouye	Y	?	?	?	?	Y	Y	Y
Matsunaga	Y	N	?	?	Y	Y	Y	Y
IDAHO								
Church	Y	N	Y	Y	Y	Y	Y	Y
McClure	Y	N	N	N	N	N	N	Y
ILLINOIS								
Stevenson	Y	N	Y	Y	Y	Y	Y	Y
Percy	Y	Y	Y	Y	Y	Y	Y	Y
INDIANA								
Bayh	Y	N	Y	Y	Y	Y	Y	Y
Lugar	Y	N	N	N	N	N	Y	Y
IOWA								
Clark	Y	N	Y	Y	Y	Y	Y	Y
Culver	Y	N	Y	?	Y	Y	Y	Y
KANSAS								
Dole	?	?	?	?	Y	Y'	Y	Y
Pearson	Y	N	Y	Y	Y	Y	Y	Y
KENTUCKY								
Ford	Y	N	Y	Y	Y	Y	Y	Y
Huddleston	Y	N	?	?	?	?	?	?
LOUISIANA								
Johnston	?	?	?	?	?	?	?	?
Long	Y	N	N	Y	N	Y	Y	?
MAINE								
Hathaway	Y	N	Y	Y	Y	Y	Y	Y
Muskie	Y	N	Y	Y	Y	Y	Y	Y
MARYLAND								
Sarbanes	Y	N	Y	Y	Y	Y	Y	Y
Mathias	Y	Y	Y	Y	Y	Y	Y	Y
MASSACHUSETTS								
Kennedy	Y	Y	Y	Y	Y	Y	Y	Y
Brooke	Y	Y	Y	Y	Y	Y	Y	Y
MICHIGAN								
Riegle	Y	N	Y	Y	Y	Y	Y	Y
Griffin	†	-	Y	Y	Y	Y	Y	Y
MINNESOTA								
Anderson	?	?	?	?	?	?	?	Y
Humphrey, M.	?	?	Y	Y	Y	Y	Y	Y
MISSISSIPPI								
Eastland	?	?	?	?	?	?	?	?
Stennis	Y	N	?	Y	N	N	N	Y
MISSOURI								
Eagleton	Y	N	Y	Y	Y	Y	Y	Y
Danforth	Y	N	Y	Y	Y	Y	Y	Y
MONTANA								
Melcher	Y	N	N	Y	Y	Y	Y	Y
Hatfield, P.	?	?	?	?	?	?	?	?
NEBRASKA								
Zorinsky	Y	N	N	Y	N	Y	Y	Y
Curtis	Y	N	N	Y	N	N	Y	Y
NEVADA								
Cannon	Y	N	N	Y	N	Y	Y	Y
Laxalt	Y	N	N	Y	N	N	Y	Y
NEW HAMPSHIRE								
Durkin	Y	N	Y	Y	Y	Y	Y	Y
McIntyre	Y	N	Y	Y	Y	Y	Y	Y
NEW JERSEY								
Williams	Y	N	Y	Y	Y	Y	Y	Y
Case	Y	N	?	?	Y	Y	Y	Y
NEW MEXICO								
Domenici	Y	N	N	Y	N	Y	N	Y
Schmitt	Y	N	N	Y	N	N	N	Y
NEW YORK								
Moynihan	Y	N	Y	Y	Y	Y	Y	Y
Javits	Y	Y	Y	Y	Y	Y	Y	Y
NORTH CAROLINA								
Morgan	Y	N	N	Y	N	N	Y	Y
Helms	Y	N	N	Y	N	N	N	Y
NORTH DAKOTA								
Burdick	Y	N	N	Y	N	Y	Y	Y
Young	?	?	N	Y	Y	N	Y	Y
OHIO								
Glenn	Y	N	Y	Y	Y	Y	Y	Y
Metzenbaum	Y	N	?	?	Y	Y	Y	Y
OKLAHOMA								
Bartlett	Y	N	N	Y	N	N	N	Y
Bellmon	Y	N	N	Y	Y	Y	N	Y
OREGON								
Hatfield, M.	Y	N	Y	Y	Y	Y	Y	Y
Packwood	Y	N	Y	Y	Y	Y	Y	Y
PENNSYLVANIA								
Heinz	Y	N	Y	Y	Y	Y	Y	Y
Schweiker	Y	N	N	Y	N	Y	Y	Y
RHODE ISLAND								
Pell	Y	Y	N	Y	Y	Y	Y	?
Chafee	Y	Y	Y	Y	Y	N	Y	Y
SOUTH CAROLINA								
Hollings	Y	N	Y	Y	Y	Y	Y	Y
Thurmond	Y	N	Y	Y	Y	Y	Y	Y
SOUTH DAKOTA								
Abourezk	?	?	?	?	?	?	?	Y
McGovern	Y	N	Y	Y	Y	Y	Y	Y
TENNESSEE								
Sasser	Y	?	?	?	?	Y	Y	Y
Baker	Y	N	N	Y	N	N	N	Y
TEXAS								
Bentsen	Y	N	N	Y	Y	Y	Y	Y
Tower	Y	N	N	Y	N	N	N	Y
UTAH								
Garn	Y	N	N	N	N	N	N	Y
Hatch	Y	N	N	Y	N	N	N	Y
VERMONT								
Leahy	Y	N	Y	Y	Y	Y	Y	Y
Stafford	Y	N	Y	Y	Y	N	Y	Y
VIRGINIA								
*Byrd, H.	Y	N	N	Y	N	Y	Y	Y
Scott	Y	N	N	N	N	N	N	?
WASHINGTON								
Jackson	Y	N	Y	Y	Y	Y	Y	Y
Magnuson	Y	N	Y	Y	Y	Y	Y	Y
WEST VIRGINIA								
Byrd, R.	Y	N	Y	Y	Y	Y	Y	Y
Randolph	Y	N	Y	Y	Y	Y	Y	Y
WISCONSIN								
Nelson	Y	N	Y	Y	Y	Y	Y	Y
Proxmire	Y	Y	N	Y	Y	Y	Y	Y
WYOMING								
Hansen	Y	N	N	Y	N	N	N	Y
Wallop	Y	N	N	Y	N	N	N	Y

Democrats ***Republicans***

*Byrd elected as independent.

KEY

- Y Voted for (yea).
- ✓ Paired for.
- † Announced for.
- # CQ Poll for.
- N Voted against (nay).
- X Paired against.
- \- Announced against.
- ▮ CQ Poll against.
- P Voted "present."
- ● Voted "present" to avoid possible conflict of interest.
- ? Did not vote or otherwise make a position known.

335. S 3073. Surface Transportation Assistance Act. Morgan, D-N.C., amendment to declare it to be the national policy that annual expenditures from the Highway Trust Fund be consistent with the fund's anticipated annual revenues. Adopted 86-0: R 35-0; D 51-0 (ND 37-0; SD 14-0), Aug. 21, 1978.

336. S 3073. Surface Transportation Assistance Act. Kennedy, D-Mass., amendment to terminate the Highway Trust Fund on Sept. 30, 1978. Rejected 10-75: R 6-29; D 4-46 (ND 4-33; SD 0-13), Aug. 21, 1978.

337. H J Res 554. D.C. Voting Representation. Leahy, D-Vt., motion to table (kill) the McClure, R-Idaho, amendment to treat the District of Columbia as part of Maryland for purposes of representation in the Senate. Motion agreed to 46-36: R 13-22; D 33-14 (ND 28-8; SD 5-6), Aug. 22, 1978.

338. H J Res 554. D.C. Voting Representation. Kennedy, D-Mass., motion to table (kill) the McClure, R-Idaho, amendment to grant voting representation in Congress to the 10 cities with populations larger than the District of Columbia. Motion agreed to 79-6: R 30-6; D 49-0 (ND 36-0; SD 13-0), Aug. 22, 1978.

339. H J Res 554. D.C. Voting Representation. Kennedy, D-Mass., motion to table (kill) the Scott, R-Va., amendment to treat the District of Columbia as a state for purposes of representation in the House, but not in the Senate. Motion agreed to 60-28: R 18-19; D 42-9 (ND 36-3; SD 6-6), Aug. 22, 1978.

340. H J Res 554. D.C. Voting Representation. Kennedy, D-Mass., motion to table (kill) the Scott, R-Va., amendment to provide for filling vacancies in the congressional delegation of the District of Columbia. Motion agreed to 69-22: R 17-20; D 52-2 (ND 40-0; SD 12-2), Aug. 22, 1978.

341. H J Res 554. D.C. Voting Representation. Kennedy, D-Mass., motion to table (kill) the Scott, R-Va., amendment to assure residents of the District of Columbia the right to implement provisions relating to representation in Congress. Motion agreed to 76-16: R 23-14; D 53-2 (ND 40-0; SD 13-2), Aug. 22, 1978.

342. S 2570. CETA Amendments. Domenici, R-N.M., amendment to establish a monitoring system in the Department of Labor and extend criminal penalties to CETA (Comprehensive Education and Training Act) contractors and subcontractors in order to reduce fraud in CETA programs. Adopted 91-0: R 36-0; D 55-0 (ND 41-0; SD 14-0), Aug. 22, 1978.

Corresponding to Congressional Record Votes 347, 348, 349, 350, 351, 352, 353, 354

	343	344	345	346	347	348	349	350
ALABAMA								
Allen, M.	N	N	N	N	Y	N	N	N
Sparkman	Y	Y	Y	Y	Y	N	Y	N
ALASKA								
Gravel	Y	Y	N	Y	Y	Y	Y	N
Stevens	N	N	N	N	N	N	N	N
ARIZONA								
DeConcini	N	Y	N	Y	Y	N	N	Y
Goldwater	?	?	?	Y	?	N	N	Y
ARKANSAS								
Bumpers	Y	Y	Y	Y	Y	Y	Y	Y
Hodges	N	N	N	N	Y	Y	Y	Y
CALIFORNIA								
Cranston	Y	Y	Y	Y	Y	Y	Y	Y
Hayakawa	N	N	N	N	Y	N	N	N
COLORADO								
Hart	Y	Y	Y	Y	?	Y	Y	Y
Haskell	Y	Y	Y	Y	Y	Y	Y	Y
CONNECTICUT								
Ribicoff	Y	Y	Y	Y	Y	Y	Y	Y
Weicker	N	Y	Y	Y	Y	Y	Y	N
DELAWARE								
Biden	Y	Y	Y	Y	Y	N	N	Y
Roth	Y	N	N	N	Y	N	N	N
FLORIDA								
Chiles	Y	Y	N	N	Y	N	N	Y
Stone	Y	Y	Y	Y	Y	N	N	Y
GEORGIA								
Nunn	N	Y	N	Y	Y	N	N	N
Talmadge	Y	?	?	Y	?	N	N	N
HAWAII								
Inouye	Y	Y	Y	Y	Y	Y	?	Y
Matsunaga	Y	Y	Y	Y	Y	Y	Y	N
IDAHO								
Church	Y	Y	Y	Y	Y	Y	Y	N
McClure	N	N	N	N	Y	N	N	N
ILLINOIS								
Stevenson	Y	Y	Y	Y	Y	Y	Y	Y
Percy	Y	Y	Y	Y	Y	Y	Y	Y
INDIANA								
Bayh	Y	Y	Y	Y	Y	Y	Y	Y
Lugar	N	N	Y	Y	Y	N	N	Y
IOWA								
Clark	Y	Y	Y	Y	Y	Y	Y	Y
Culver	Y	Y	Y	Y	Y	Y	Y	Y
KANSAS								
Dole	N	Y	Y	Y	Y	N	N	N
Pearson	Y	Y	Y	Y	?	Y	Y	Y
KENTUCKY								
Ford	Y	Y	Y	Y	Y	N	N	Y
Huddleston	?	Y	Y	Y	Y	N	N	Y
LOUISIANA								
Johnston	?	N	N	N	?	?	?	?
Long	Y	N	N	N	N	?	N	N
MAINE								
Hathaway	Y	Y	Y	Y	Y	Y	Y	N
Muskie	Y	Y	Y	Y	Y	Y	Y	Y
MARYLAND								
Sarbanes	Y	Y	Y	Y	Y	N	Y	Y
Mathias	Y	Y	Y	Y	Y	Y	Y	N
MASSACHUSETTS								
Kennedy	Y	Y	Y	Y	Y	Y	Y	Y
Brooke	Y	Y	Y	Y	Y	Y	Y	Y
MICHIGAN								
Riegle	Y	Y	Y	Y	Y	Y	Y	Y
Griffin	Y	Y	Y	Y	Y	N	N	Y
MINNESOTA								
Anderson	Y	Y	Y	Y	?	?	?	?
Humphrey, M.	Y	Y	Y	Y	Y	Y	Y	Y
MISSISSIPPI								
Eastland	?	?	?	?	?	?	?	?
Stennis	N	N	N	N	Y	N	N	Y
MISSOURI								
Eagleton	Y	Y	Y	Y	Y	Y	Y	Y
Danforth	Y	Y	Y	Y	Y	N	N	N
MONTANA								
Melcher	Y	N	N	N	Y	Y	Y	Y
Hatfield, P.	?	N	N	N	Y	Y	Y	Y
NEBRASKA								
Zorinsky	Y	N	N	N	Y	N	N	N
Curtis	N	N	N	N	?	N	N	N
NEVADA								
Cannon	N	N	N	N	Y	N	N	Y
Laxalt	N	N	N	N	?	N	N	Y
NEW HAMPSHIRE								
Durkin	Y	Y	Y	Y	Y	Y	Y	N
McIntyre	Y	Y	Y	Y	Y	Y	Y	Y
NEW JERSEY								
Williams	Y	Y	Y	Y	Y	Y	Y	N
Case	Y	Y	Y	Y	Y	Y	Y	N
NEW MEXICO								
Domenici	N	N	N	N	Y	N	N	Y
Schmitt	N	N	N	N	N	N	N	Y
NEW YORK								
Moynihan	Y	Y	Y	Y	Y	Y	Y	N
Javits	Y	Y	Y	Y	Y	Y	Y	Y
NORTH CAROLINA								
Morgan	N	N	N	N	Y	Y	Y	N
Helms	N	N	N	N	Y	N	N	N
NORTH DAKOTA								
Burdick	Y	N	N	N	Y	Y	Y	Y
Young	?	N	N	N	?	N	N	N
OHIO								
Glenn	Y	Y	Y	Y	Y	Y	Y	Y
Metzenbaum	Y	Y	Y	Y	Y	Y	Y	Y
OKLAHOMA								
Bartlett	N	N	N	N	N	N	N	N
Bellmon	N	N	N	N	N	Y	Y	N
OREGON								
Hatfield, M.	Y	Y	Y	Y	Y	Y	Y	N
Packwood	N	Y	Y	Y	Y	N	N	N
PENNSYLVANIA								
Heinz	Y	Y	Y	Y	Y	Y	Y	Y
Schweiker	N	N	N	N	Y	N	N	Y
RHODE ISLAND								
Pell	Y	Y	N	Y	Y	Y	Y	Y
Chafee	N	Y	Y	Y	Y	Y	Y	Y
SOUTH CAROLINA								
Hollings	Y	Y	Y	Y	Y	N	N	N
Thurmond	Y	Y	Y	Y	Y	N	N	N
SOUTH DAKOTA								
Abourezk	Y	Y	Y	Y	?	Y	Y	?
McGovern	Y	Y	Y	Y	Y	Y	Y	Y
TENNESSEE								
Sasser	Y	Y	Y	Y	Y	N	N	Y
Baker	N	Y	Y	Y	Y	N	N	N
TEXAS								
Bentsen	Y	Y	Y	Y	Y	N	N	N
Tower	N	N	N	N	N	N	N	N
UTAH								
Garn	N	N	N	N	Y	N	N	N
Hatch	N	N	N	N	N	N	N	N
VERMONT								
Leahy	Y	Y	Y	Y	Y	N	Y	Y
Stafford	Y	Y	Y	Y	Y	Y	Y	Y
VIRGINIA								
*Byrd, H.	N	N	N	N	Y	N	N	N
Scott	N	N	N	N	Y	N	N	N
WASHINGTON								
Jackson	Y	Y	Y	Y	Y	Y	Y	Y
Magnuson	Y	Y	Y	Y	Y	Y	Y	Y
WEST VIRGINIA								
Byrd, R.	Y	Y	Y	Y	Y	Y	Y	N
Randolph	Y	Y	Y	Y	Y	N	N	N
WISCONSIN								
Nelson	Y	Y	Y	Y	Y	Y	Y	Y
Proxmire	Y	Y	N	Y	Y	N	N	Y
WYOMING								
Hansen	N	N	N	N	Y	N	N	N
Wallop	N	N	N	N	Y	N	N	N

Democrats ***Republicans***

Byrd elected as independent.

KEY

- Y Voted for (yea).
- ✓ Paired for.
- † Announced for.
- # CQ Poll for.
- N Voted against (nay).
- X Paired against.
- \- Announced against.
- ▮ CQ Poll against.
- P Voted "present."
- ● Voted "present" to avoid possible conflict of interest.
- ? Did not vote or otherwise make a position known.

343. H J Res 554. D.C. Voting Representation. Kennedy, D-Mass., motion to table (kill) the Bartlett, R-Okla., amendment to prohibit establishment of any congressional committee having jurisdiction over District of Columbia legislative matters. Motion agreed to 63-31: R 13-23; D 50-8 (ND 40-2; SD 10-6), Aug. 22, 1978.

344. H J Res 554. D.C. Voting Representation. Byrd, D-W.Va., motion to table (kill) the Hatch, R-Utah, point of order that the proposed constitutional amendment was in violation of Article V of the Constitution, which provides for equal suffrage of the states in the Senate. Motion agreed to 65-32: R 17-20; D 48-12 (ND 38-5; SD 10-7), Aug. 22, 1978.

345. H J Res 554. D.C. Voting Representation. Kennedy, D-Mass., motion to table (kill) the Melcher, D-Mont., amendment to provide for direct representation in the House for the District of Columbia but representation in the Senate as though the District were a part of Maryland. Motion agreed to 60-37: R 18-19; D 42-18 (ND 34-9; SD 8-9), Aug. 22, 1978.

346. H J Res 554. D.C. Voting Representation. Passage of the joint resolution to propose an amendment to the Constitution to provide for full voting representation in Congress (both in the House and the Senate) for the District of Columbia and to retain the right granted District residents by the 23rd Amendment to vote for the election of the president and vice president (the resolution would repeal the 23rd Amendment). Passed 67-32: R 19-19; D 48-13 (ND 38-5; SD 10-8), Aug. 22, 1978. A two-thirds majority vote (66 in this case) is required for passage of a joint resolution proposing an amendment to the Constitution. A "yea" was a vote supporting the president's position.

347. S 9. Outer Continental Shelf Lands. Adoption of the conference report on the bill to revise leasing procedures, upgrade environmental standards and to increase state participation in federal decisions regarding the development of oil and gas on the Outer Continental Shelf. Adopted (thus clearing for the president) 82-7: R 27-6; D 55-1 (ND 40 0; SD 15-1), Aug. 22, 1978. A "yea" was a vote supporting the president's position.

348. S 1753. Elementary and Secondary Education Act Amendments. Pell, D-R.I., motion to table (kill) the Roth, R-Del., amendment to limit court-ordered busing of students only when there was a discriminatory purpose for segregated education; to require courts to determine whether a greater degree of racial segregation resulted because of the segregation policy; and to delay federal busing orders to provide time for appeals, unless the Supreme Court or a three-member appellate court denied such a delay. Motion agreed to 49-47: R 12-26; D 37-21 (ND 34-8; SD 3-13), Aug. 23, 1978.

349. S 1753. Elementary and Secondary Education Act Amendments. Javits, R-N.Y., motion to table (kill) the Biden, D-Del., motion to reconsider the vote *(vote 348, above)* by which the Roth, R-Del., amendment was tabled. Motion agreed to 51-45: R 12-26; D 39-19 (ND 35-6; SD 4-13), Aug. 23, 1978.

350. HR 112. Foundation Taxes/Energy Tax Credits. Hart, D-Colo., motion to table (kill) the Gravel, D-Alaska, amendment to add to the bill various tax breaks — previously approved by the Senate in other legislation that was stalled in conference — as incentives for producers of energy. Motion agreed to 53-43: R 14-24; D 39-19 (ND 31-10; SD 8-9), Aug. 23, 1978.

CQ Senate Votes 351-358

Corresponding to Congressional Record Votes 355, 356, 357, 358, 359, 360, 361, 362

	351	352	353	354	355	356	357	358
ALABAMA								
Allen, M.	N	Y	Y	N	N	N	Y	Y
Sparkman	Y	?	?	?	N	N	Y	Y
ALASKA								
Gravel	Y	Y	?	N	N	N	N	Y
Stevens	Y	Y	Y	N	N	N	Y	Y
ARIZONA								
DeConcini	N	Y	Y	N	N	Y	Y	Y
Goldwater	Y	Y	?	?	Y	Y	Y	N
ARKANSAS								
Bumpers	N	Y	Y	N	N	Y	Y	Y
Hodges	N	Y	Y	N	N	Y	N	Y
CALIFORNIA								
Cranston	Y	Y	?	N	N	N	Y	Y
Hayakawa	Y	N	N	N	Y	N	Y	Y
COLORADO								
Hart	N	Y	Y	N	N	N	Y	Y
Haskell	N	Y	Y	N	N	N	N	Y
CONNECTICUT								
Ribicoff	Y	N	N	N	N	N	N	Y
Weicker	Y	?	N	N	N	N	Y	Y
DELAWARE								
Biden	N	Y	Y	N	N	N	N	Y
Roth	Y	N	Y	N	Y	N	N	N
FLORIDA								
Chiles	N	Y	Y	N	N	Y	Y	Y
Stone	N	N	Y	N	N	N	Y	Y
GEORGIA								
Nunn	Y	Y	Y	N	Y	Y	N	Y
Talmadge	Y	Y	Y	?	N	Y	Y	Y
HAWAII								
Inouye	N	Y	Y	N	?	?	Y	Y
Matsunaga	N	N	N	N	?	N	N	Y
IDAHO								
Church	Y	N	Y	N	N	Y	N	Y
McClure	Y	N	Y	N	Y	N	N	N
ILLINOIS	⁄							
Stevenson	N	Y	N	N	N	N	N	Y
Percy	Y	N	N	N	N	N	N	Y
INDIANA								
Bayh	N	N	Y	N	N	N	Y'	Y
Lugar	Y	N	Y	Y	Y	Y	Y	Y
IOWA								
Clark	N	Y	†	Y	N	N	Y	Y
Culver	N	Y	Y	Y	N	N	Y	Y
KANSAS								
Dole	Y	Y	Y	N	Y	N	N	Y
Pearson	N	?	?	?	Y	N	Y	Y
KENTUCKY								
Ford	Y	N	Y	N	N	N	Y	Y
Huddleston	N	Y	Y	N	N	N	Y	Y
LOUISIANA								
Johnston	?	?	?	?	?	?	?	?
Long	Y	?	?	?	N	?	N	Y
MAINE								
Hathaway	Y	Y	Y	N	N	N	N	Y
Muskie	N	Y	Y	N	N	Y	Y	Y
MARYLAND								
Sarbanes	N	N	N	N	N	N	N	Y
Mathias	Y	N	N	N	N	N	N	Y
MASSACHUSETTS								
Kennedy	N	Y	N	N	N	N	N	Y
Brooke	N	Y	Y	N	N	N	N	Y
MICHIGAN								
Riegle	N	Y	N	N	N	N	Y	Y
Griffin	N	N	Y	Y	Y	N	Y	Y
MINNESOTA								
Anderson	?	-	?	?	?	?	?	†
Humphrey, M.	N	Y	Y	N	N	N	Y	Y
MISSISSIPPI								
Eastland	?	?	?	?	?	?	?	?
Stennis	N	Y	Y	?	?	Y	?	Y
MISSOURI								
Eagleton	N	Y	N	Y	N	N	Y	Y
Danforth	Y	N	N	Y	N	Y	Y	Y
MONTANA								
Melcher	Y	N	Y	N	N	N	N	Y
Hatfield, P.	N	N	Y	N	N	N	N	Y
NEBRASKA								
Zorinsky	Y	N	Y	N	N	N	N	Y
Curtis	Y	Y	?	?	Y	Y	N	Y
NEVADA								
Cannon	N	Y	?	N	N	N	N	Y
Laxalt	Y	?	?	?	?	?	?	?
NEW HAMPSHIRE								
Durkin	Y	N	N	N	N	Y	N	Y
McIntyre	N	N	N	N	N	N	N	Y
NEW JERSEY								
Williams	Y	N	N	N	N	N	N	Y
Case	Y	N	?	?	N	N	N	Y
NEW MEXICO								
Domenici	N	Y	Y	N	?	?	?	?
Schmitt	N	Y	Y	N	Y	Y	Y	Y
NEW YORK								
Moynihan	Y	N	N	N	N	N	Y	Y
Javits	N	N	N	N	N	N	Y	Y
NORTH CAROLINA								
Morgan	N	Y	Y	N	Y	Y	Y	Y
Helms	Y	Y	Y	N	Y	Y	Y	N
NORTH DAKOTA								
Burdick	N	Y	Y	N	N	N	Y	Y
Young	N	Y	Y	N	N	Y	Y	Y
OHIO								
Glenn	N	Y	Y	Y	N	Y	Y	Y
Metzenbaum	N	Y	N	Y	N	N	N	Y
OKLAHOMA								
Bartlett	Y	Y	Y	Y	Y	Y	Y	Y
Bellmon	N	Y	Y	Y	Y	Y	Y	Y
OREGON								
Hatfield, M.	Y	Y	Y	N	N	N	Y	Y
Packwood	Y	N	Y	Y	N	N	Y	Y
PENNSYLVANIA								
Heinz	N	N	N	N	N	N	N	Y
Schweiker	Y	N	N	N	N	N	N	Y
RHODE ISLAND								
Pell	N	N	N	N	N	N	N	Y
Chafee	N	N	Y	Y	N	N	Y	Y
SOUTH CAROLINA								
Hollings	N	Y	Y	Y	N	Y	Y	Y
Thurmond	Y	Y	Y	N	Y	N	Y	Y
SOUTH DAKOTA								
Abourezk	?	?	?	?	?	N	?	?
McGovern	N	Y	Y	N	N	N	Y	Y
TENNESSEE								
Sasser	N	Y	Y	N	N	Y	Y	Y
Baker	N	Y	Y	N	?	?	?	?
TEXAS								
Bentsen	Y	Y	Y	N	N	Y	Y	Y
Tower	Y	Y	Y	N	Y	N	N	Y
UTAH								
Garn	N	Y	Y	N	Y	N	Y	Y
Hatch	N	Y	Y	N	Y	N	Y	Y
VERMONT								
Leahy	N	Y	Y	Y	N	N	Y	Y
Stafford	N	Y	N	Y	N	N	Y	Y
VIRGINIA								
*Byrd, H.	N	Y	Y	N	Y	Y	Y	N
Scott	Y	?	?	?	Y	Y	Y	N
WASHINGTON								
Jackson	N	Y	Y	N	N	N	N	Y
Magnuson	N	Y	Y	N	N	Y	Y	Y
WEST VIRGINIA								
Byrd, R.	Y	Y	Y	Y	Y	Y	Y	Y
Randolph	Y	Y	Y	N	N	N	N	Y
WISCONSIN								
Nelson	N	Y	Y	Y	N	N	Y	Y
Proxmire	N	Y	Y	Y	Y	Y	Y	N
WYOMING								
Hansen	Y	Y	Y	Y	Y	N	Y	Y
Wallop	Y	N	Y	Y	Y	Y	Y	Y

Democrats ***Republicans***

*Byrd elected as independent.

KEY

- Y Voted for (yea).
- ✓ Paired for.
- † Announced for.
- # CQ Poll for.
- N Voted against (nay).
- X Paired against.
- - Announced against.
- ▮ CQ Poll against.
- P Voted "present."
- ● Voted "present" to avoid possible conflict of interest.
- ? Did not vote or otherwise make a position known.

351. HR 112. Foundation Taxes/Energy Tax Credits. Gravel, D-Alaska, amendment to add to the bill energy producer tax incentives plus tax credits for gasohol production and small hydro dams (a Gravel amendment with only the producer incentives was tabled previously, *see vote 350, p. 52-S*). Rejected 42-54: R 24-14; D 18-40 (ND 12-29; SD 6-11), Aug. 23, 1978. (The bill to reduce to 2 percent, from 4 percent, the excise tax imposed on the investment income of private foundations was passed subsequently by voice vote.)

352. S 1753. Elementary and Secondary Education Act Amendments. Hollings, D-S.C., amendment to delete Title XII of the bill to authorize $2.5 billion in fiscal 1979-83 for grants to private elementary and secondary schools for secular textbooks and instructional materials, counseling and diagnostic services and transportation. Adopted 60-30: R 19-15; D 41-15 (ND 28-13; SD 13-2), Aug. 23, 1978.

353. S 1753. Elementary and Secondary Education Act Amendments. Magnuson, D-Wash., amendment to authorize for each of fiscal years 1979-82 $120 million in impact aid to school districts in which there were federal public housing projects and to establish a presidential commission to study the impact aid program. Adopted 62-22: R 23-9; D 39-13 (ND 24-13; SD 15-0), Aug. 23, 1978.

354. S 1753. Elementary and Secondary Education Act Amendments. Eagleton, D-Mo., amendment to delete impact aid for all but so-called "A" students, children whose parents lived and worked on federal property. Rejected 20-66: R 10-22; D 10-44 (ND 9-32; SD 1-12), Aug. 23, 1978.

355. S 1753. Elementary and Secondary Education Act Amendments. Helms, R-N.C., amendment to maintain current law in the special projects program by deleting biomedical science education for disadvantaged students, and health and population education. Rejected 25-65: R 20-15; D 5-50 (ND 2-37; SD 3-13), Aug. 24, 1978.

356. S 1753. Elementary and Secondary Education Act Amendments. Morgan, D-N.C., amendment to delete $47 million to create a new grants program for basic skills education. Rejected 30-62: R 11-24; D 19-38 (ND 8-33; SD 11-5), Aug. 24, 1978.

357. S 1753. Elementary and Secondary Education Act Amendments. Bellmon, R-Okla., amendment to delete the tier system for funding the impact aid program of payments to school districts. Adopted 57-35: R 24-11; D 33-24 (ND 20-21; SD 13-3), Aug. 24, 1978.

358. HR 15. Elementary and Secondary Education Act Amendments. Passage of the bill to authorize approximately $55 billion in fiscal 1979-83 for federal elementary and secondary education programs. Passed 86-7: R 30-5; D 56-2 (ND 40-1; SD 16-1), Aug. 24, 1978.

CQ Senate Votes 359-364

Corresponding to Congressional Record Votes 363, 364, 365, 366, 367, 368

	359	360	361	362	363	364
ALABAMA						
Allen, M.	Y	Y	Y	Y	Y	Y
Sparkman	Y	Y	Y	?	?	?
ALASKA						
Gravel	Y	?	?	?	?	?
Stevens	N	Y	Y	N	Y	Y
ARIZONA						
DeConcini	Y	N	Y	N	Y	Y
Goldwater	N	P	?	N	?	?
ARKANSAS						
Bumpers	Y	Y	Y	Y	Y	Y
Hodges	Y	N	Y	Y	Y	Y
CALIFORNIA						
Cranston	Y	N	Y	Y	Y	Y
Hayakawa	N	N	Y	N	Y	Y
COLORADO						
Hart	Y	N	Y	Y	Y	Y
Haskell	N	N	Y	?	?	?
CONNECTICUT						
Ribicoff	Y	Y	Y	Y	Y	Y
Weicker	N	N	Y	Y	Y	Y
DELAWARE						
Biden	Y	N	?	N	Y	N
Roth	N	N	Y	N	N	N
FLORIDA						
Chiles	Y	Y	Y	Y	Y	Y
Stone	Y	Y	Y	Y	Y	Y
GEORGIA						
Nunn	Y	Y	Y	N	Y	?
Talmadge	N	Y	Y	Y	†	?
HAWAII						
Inouye	Y	Y	Y	Y	Y	Y
Matsunaga	Y	Y	Y	Y	Y	Y
IDAHO						
Church	Y	N	Y	Y	Y	Y
McClure	N	N	Y	N	Y	Y
ILLINOIS						
Stevenson	Y	Y	Y	Y	N	Y
Percy	N	N	Y	N	Y	Y
INDIANA						
Bayh	Y	N	Y	Y	Y	Y
Lugar	N	N	Y	N	Y	N
IOWA						
Clark	Y	Y	Y	Y	Y	Y
Culver	Y	Y	Y	Y	Y	Y
KANSAS						
Dole	N	N	Y	Y	Y	Y
Pearson	Y	N	Y	?	?	?
KENTUCKY						
Ford	Y	N	Y	Y	Y	Y
Huddleston	Y	Y	Y	N	Y	?
LOUISIANA						
Johnston	?	?	?	?	?	?
Long	Y	Y	Y	Y	Y	Y
MAINE						
Hathaway	Y	Y	Y	?	?	?
Muskie	Y	N	Y	?	?	?
MARYLAND						
Sarbanes	Y	Y	Y	Y	Y	Y
Mathias	N	Y	Y	?	?	?
MASSACHUSETTS						
Kennedy	Y	N	Y	?	?	?
Brooke	N	N	Y	?	?	?
MICHIGAN						
Riegle	Y	N	Y	Y	Y	Y
Griffin	N	N	Y	N	Y	?
MINNESOTA						
Anderson	?	?	?	?	†	?
Humphrey, M.	Y	Y	Y	†	†	†
MISSISSIPPI						
Eastland	?	?	?	?	?	?
Stennis	Y	Y	Y	N	?	Y
MISSOURI						
Eagleton	Y	N	Y	Y	Y	Y
Danforth	Y	N	Y	?	?	?
MONTANA						
Melcher	Y	N	Y	Y	Y	?
Hatfield, P.	Y	N	Y	?	?	?
NEBRASKA						
Zorinsky	Y	N	Y	Y	Y	Y
Curtis	N	N	Y	N	N	Y
NEVADA						
Cannon	Y	Y	Y	Y	Y	Y
Laxalt	?	?	?	N	N	N
NEW HAMPSHIRE						
Durkin	Y	Y	Y	N	Y	Y
McIntyre	N	Y	Y	Y	Y	Y
NEW JERSEY						
Williams	Y	N	Y	Y	Y	Y
Case	N	N	Y	Y	Y	Y
NEW MEXICO						
Domenici	?	?	?	?	?	?
Schmitt	?	?	?	?	?	?
NEW YORK						
Moynihan	Y	Y	Y	Y	Y	?
Javits	N	N	Y	Y	Y	Y
NORTH CAROLINA						
Morgan	†	N	Y	N	Y	Y
Helms	N	N	Y	N	N	N
NORTH DAKOTA						
Burdick	Y	N	Y	Y	Y	Y
Young	N	Y	Y	Y	Y	Y
OHIO						
Glenn	Y	Y	Y	Y	Y	Y
Metzenbaum	Y	N	Y	Y	Y	Y
OKLAHOMA						
Bartlett	N	N	Y	?	?	?
Bellmon	N	N	Y	N	Y	Y
OREGON						
Hatfield, M.	Y	Y	Y	N	Y	Y
Packwood	Y	N	Y	N	Y	Y
PENNSYLVANIA						
Heinz	N	N	Y	N	Y	Y
Schweiker	N	N	Y	N	Y	Y
RHODE ISLAND						
Pell	Y	N	Y	Y	Y	Y
Chafee	N	N	Y	N	Y	Y
SOUTH CAROLINA						
Hollings	Y	Y	Y	Y	Y	Y
Thurmond	Y	N	Y	N	Y	Y
SOUTH DAKOTA						
Abourezk	?	?	?	?	?	?
McGovern	Y	N	?	Y	Y	Y
TENNESSEE						
Sasser	Y	N	Y	?	?	?
Baker	?	?	?	?	?	?
TEXAS						
Bentsen	Y	N	Y	Y	Y	Y
Tower	N	N	Y	N	Y	Y
UTAH						
Garn	Y	N	Y	N	Y	N
Hatch	N	N	Y	N	Y	N
VERMONT						
Leahy	Y	N	Y	Y	Y	Y
Stafford	N	N	Y	Y	Y	Y
VIRGINIA						
*Byrd, H.	Y	Y	Y	N	N	N
Scott	N	N	N	N	N	N
WASHINGTON						
Jackson	Y	Y	Y	Y	Y	Y
Magnuson	Y	N	Y	Y	Y	Y
WEST VIRGINIA						
Byrd, R.	Y	Y	Y	Y	Y	Y
Randolph	Y	N	Y	Y	Y	Y
WISCONSIN						
Nelson	Y	N	Y	Y	Y	N
Proxmire	Y	N	Y	Y	N	N
WYOMING						
Hansen	N	N	Y	N	N	Y
Wallop	N	N	Y	N	N	Y

KEY

- Y Voted for (yea).
- ✓ Paired for.
- † Announced for.
- # CQ Poll for.
- N Voted against (nay).
- X Paired against.
- - Announced against.
- ▮ CQ Poll against.
- P Voted "present."
- ● Voted "present" to avoid possible conflict of interest.
- ? Did not vote or otherwise make a position known.

359. S 2640. Civil Service Reform. Chiles, D-Fla., motion to table (kill) the Percy, R-Ill., amendment to authorize the Merit System Protection Board to hear and make recommendations on charges that presidential appointees committed prohibited personnel practices. Motion agreed to 60-31: R 6-28; D 54-3 (ND 39-2; SD 15-1), Aug. 24, 1978.

360. S 2640. Civil Service Reform. Glenn, D-Ohio, motion to table (kill) the Heinz, R-Pa., amendment, to prevent military officers who retired after enactment of the bill and were appointed to federal jobs from drawing a federal salary and retired military pay totaling more than Executive Level V salaries. Motion rejected 32-58: R 4-29; D 28-29 (ND 16-24; SD 12-5), Aug. 24, 1978. (The Heinz amendment was adopted subsequently by voice vote.)

361. S 2640. Civil Service Reform. Passage of the bill to revise the federal civil service system. Passed 87-1: R 32-1; D 55-0 (ND 38-0; SD 17-0), Aug. 24, 1978. A "yea" was a vote supporting the president's position.

362. S 2570. CETA Amendments. Nelson, D-Wis., motion to table (kill) the Heinz, R-Pa., amendment to provide incentive grants to private employers to create job opportunities for individuals eligible for CETA programs. Motion agreed to 47-32: R 6-24; D 41-8 (ND 31-3; SD 10-5), Aug. 25, 1978.

363. S 2570. CETA Amendments. Passage of the bill to extend jobs programs under the Comprehensive Employment and Training Act for four years, through fiscal 1982, except for several youth programs, which were extended through fiscal 1980. Passed 66-10: R 22-7; D 44-3 (ND 32-2; SD 12-1), Aug. 25, 1978. A "yea" was a vote supporting the president's position.

364. HR 13467. Second Supplemental Appropriations, Fiscal 1978. Adoption of the conference report on the bill to appropriate $6,753,925,686 in supplemental funds for fiscal 1978 operations of the government, including $3.2 billion for federal employee pay raises. Adopted (thus clearing for the president) 61-11: R 21-7; D 40-4 (ND 29-3; SD 11-1), Aug. 25, 1978. The president had requested $7,168,446,986 in supplemental funds for fiscal 1978.

	365	366	367	368	369	370	371	372
ALABAMA								
Allen, M.	?	Y	Y	?	?	?	?	?
Sparkman	N	N	N	Y	Y	Y	Y	Y
ALASKA								
Gravel	?	?	N	Y	Y	Y	Y	Y
Stevens	▮	▮	▮	#	#	#	#	#
ARIZONA								
DeConcini	Y	Y	Y	N	Y	Y	Y	?
Goldwater	N	Y	Y	Y	Y	Y	Y	Y
ARKANSAS								
Bumpers	N	N	N	Y	Y	Y	Y	Y
Hodges	N	N	N	Y	N	Y	N	Y
CALIFORNIA								
Cranston	N	N	N	Y	N	N	N	Y
Hayakawa	Y	Y	Y	N	Y	Y	Y	Y
COLORADO								
Hart	N	N	N	Y	N	N	N	Y
Haskell	†	?	?	?	?	?	?	?
CONNECTICUT								
Ribicoff	N	N	N	Y	N	Y	Y	Y
Weicker	N	N	N	Y	Y	N	N	Y
DELAWARE								
Biden	?	Y	N	Y	?	Y	Y	?
Roth	Y	Y	Y	N	Y	Y	Y	Y
FLORIDA								
Chiles	N	N	N	Y	Y	Y	Y	Y
Stone	Y	Y	Y	Y	Y	Y	Y	Y
GEORGIA								
Nunn	Y	Y	Y	N	Y	Y	Y	Y
Talmadge	Y	Y	Y	N	Y	Y	Y	Y
HAWAII								
Inouye	N	N	N	Y	Y	N	N	#
Matsunaga	N	N	N	Y	Y	N	N	?
IDAHO								
Church	#	#	▮	Y	Y	N	N	Y
McClure	?	?	?	?	?	?	?	?
ILLINOIS								
Stevenson	?	?	?	?	?	?	?	?
Percy	N	N	N	Y	?	?	?	?
INDIANA								
Bayh	N	N	N	Y	N	N	N	Y
Lugar	Y	Y	N	Y	Y	N	N	Y
IOWA								
Clark	N	N	N	Y	N	Y	Y	Y
Culver	N	N	N	Y	N	Y	Y	Y
KANSAS								
Dole	N	Y	Y	Y	Y	▮	#	Y
Pearson	N	N	N	#	#	N	N	?
KENTUCKY								
Ford	Y	Y	Y	Y	Y	N	N	Y
Huddleston	Y	Y	Y	Y	Y	Y	N	Y
LOUISIANA								
Johnston	?	?	?	?	?	?	?	?
Long	N	N	Y	Y	N	Y	Y	Y
MAINE								
Hathaway	N	N	N	Y	N	N	N	#
Muskie	N	N	N	Y	N	N	N	Y
MARYLAND								
Sarbanes	?	N	N	Y	Y	N	N	Y
Mathias	N	N	N	Y	Y	N	N	?
MASSACHUSETTS								
Kennedy	?	?	?	?	?	?	#	#
Brooke	?	?	?	?	?	?	?	?
MICHIGAN								
Riegle	N	N	N	Y	Y	Y	Y	#
Griffin	Y	Y	Y	N	Y	N	N	†
MINNESOTA								
Anderson	?	?	?	?	?	?	?	?
Humphrey, M.	?	?	▮	†	?	?	?	†
MISSISSIPPI								
Eastland	?	?	?	?	?	?	?	?
Stennis	N	N	Y	Y	Y	Y	Y	Y
MISSOURI								
Eagleton	N	N	N	Y	N	N	N	Y
Danforth	Y	Y	N	N	N	Y	Y	Y
MONTANA								
Melcher	N	N	Y	Y	Y	N	N	Y
Hatfield, P.	?	?	?	?	?	?	?	?
NEBRASKA								
Zorinsky	Y	Y	Y	N	Y	Y	Y	Y
Curtis	#	Y	Y	N	Y	N	Y	Y
NEVADA								
Cannon	N	N	N	Y	Y	Y	Y	Y
Laxalt	?	?	?	?	?	?	?	?
NEW HAMPSHIRE								
Durkin	N	N	N	Y	N	?	?	?
McIntyre	?	?	?	?	?	?	?	?
NEW JERSEY								
Williams	N	N	N	Y	N	N	N	Y
Case	N	N	N	Y	?	N	N	Y
NEW MEXICO								
Domenici	N	Y	Y	N	?	?	?	Y
Schmitt	N	Y	Y	Y	Y	N	N	Y
NEW YORK								
Moynihan	▮	▮	N	Y	Y	N	N	Y
Javits	N	N	N	Y	N	N	?	?
NORTH CAROLINA								
Morgan	†	Y	Y	Y	Y	Y	Y	Y
Helms	?	?	?	?	?	?	†	†
NORTH DAKOTA								
Burdick	#	#	#	#	#	Y	Y	Y
Young	N	Y	Y	Y	Y	Y	Y	Y
OHIO								
Glenn	N	N	N	Y	Y	Y	Y	Y
Metzenbaum	Y	N	N	Y	N	N	Y	Y
OKLAHOMA								
Bartlett	N	Y	Y	N	Y	Y	Y	?
Bellmon	N	N	N	Y	Y	N	N	Y
OREGON								
Hatfield, M.	#	#	?	▮	†	#	†	†
Packwood	N	Y	N	Y	Y	Y	Y	Y
PENNSYLVANIA								
Heinz	N	N	N	Y	Y	N	N	Y
Schweiker	Y	Y	N	Y	Y	Y	Y	Y
RHODE ISLAND								
Pell	†	-	-	†	†	?	?	?
Chafee	?	?	?	?	?	N	N	Y
SOUTH CAROLINA								
Hollings	N	N	N	Y	Y	N	N	Y
Thurmond	Y	Y	Y	N	Y	Y	Y	Y
SOUTH DAKOTA								
Abourezk	▮	▮	?	?	?	N	N	Y
McGovern	Y	?	N	Y	N	N	?	Y
TENNESSEE								
Sasser	?	?	?	?	Y	Y	Y	Y
Baker	?	?	?	?	?	?	?	?
TEXAS								
Bentsen	Y	Y	N	Y	N	Y	Y	Y
Tower	?	?	?	?	?	?	?	?
UTAH								
Garn	Y	Y	Y	N	Y	Y	Y	Y
Hatch	Y	Y	Y	N	Y	Y	Y	Y
VERMONT								
Leahy	N	N	N	Y	Y	Y	Y	Y
Stafford	▮	#	▮	#	#	#	#	#
VIRGINIA								
*Byrd, H.	Y	Y	Y	N	Y	Y	Y	Y
Scott	Y	Y	Y	N	Y	N	N	?
WASHINGTON								
Jackson	N	N	N	Y	Y	Y	Y	Y
Magnuson	N	Y	Y	Y	Y	Y	Y	Y
WEST VIRGINIA								
Byrd, R.	N	N	N	Y	Y	Y	Y	Y
Randolph	N	N	Y	Y	†	N	N	Y
WISCONSIN								
Nelson	Y	Y	N	Y	N	Y	Y	Y
Proxmire	Y	Y	Y	N	N	N	N	N
WYOMING								
Hansen	Y	Y	Y	?	Y	Y	Y	Y
Wallop	Y	Y	Y	N	Y	Y	Y	Y

Democrats ***Republicans***

*Byrd elected as independent.

KEY

- Y Voted for (yea).
- ✓ Paired for.
- † Announced for.
- # CQ Poll for.
- N Voted against (nay).
- X Paired against.
- \- Announced against.
- ▮ CQ Poll against.
- P Voted "present."
- ● Voted "present" to avoid possible conflict of interest.
- ? Did not vote or otherwise make a position known.

365. S Con Res 104. Fiscal 1979 Binding Budget Levels. Proxmire, D-Wis., amendment to reduce budget authority to $540 billion — a level 5 percent below the president's January budget request. Rejected 25-44: R 12-15; D 13-29 (ND 6-22; SD 7-7), Sept. 6, 1978.

366. S Con Res 104. Fiscal 1979 Binding Budget Levels. Roth, R-Del., amendment to reduce the fiscal 1979 spending ceilings to $547 billion in budget authority and $479.4 billion in outlays. Rejected 35-38: R 20-8; D 15-30 (ND 6-23; SD 9-7), Sept. 6, 1978.

367. S Con Res 104. Fiscal 1979 Binding Budget Levels. Byrd, Ind-Va., amendment to cut budget authority for foreign aid by $2.4 billion, to $10.2 billion. Rejected 32-44: R 16-12; D 16-32 (ND 6-26; SD 10-6), Sept. 6, 1978.

368. H Con Res 683. Fiscal 1979 Binding Budget Levels. Adoption of the second budget resolution setting the following budget levels: budget authority, $557.7 billion; outlays, $489.5 billion; revenues, $447.2 billion; deficit, $42.3 billion. Adopted 56-18: R 14-12; D 42-6 (ND 30-3; SD 12-3), Sept. 6, 1978.

369. S 2266. Uniform Bankruptcy Law. Bartlett, R-Okla., amendment to allow a person discharged of an obligation to a creditor through bankruptcy to rescind any commitment made to reaffirm a debt to a creditor within 30 days of such reaffirmation. Adopted 51-20: R 22-2; D 29-18 (ND 16-15; SD 13-3), Sept. 7, 1978.

370. S 1423. Judicial Tenure. DeConcini, D-Ariz., motion to table (kill) the Bayh, D-Ind., motion to recommit to the Judiciary Committee the bill to establish within the judicial branch a system for investigating and resolving allegations that the condition or conduct of a federal judge is or has been inconsistent with the good behavior required by the Constitution. Motion agreed to 43-33: R 13-13; D 30-20 (ND 16-18; SD 14-2), Sept. 7, 1978.

371. S 1423. Judicial Tenure. Passage of the bill to establish within the federal judicial branch a system for investigating and resolving allegations that the condition or conduct of a federal judge is or has been inconsistent with the good behavior required by the Constitution. Passed 43-31: R 14-11; D 29-20 (ND 17-16; SD 12-4), Sept. 7, 1978.

372. S 3447. Agricultural Exports. Passage of the bill to promote the sale of U.S. agricultural commodities by providing intermediate term (3-10 year) credit under the Commodity Credit Corporation, to make the People's Republic of China eligible for short-term (up to three years) credit, and to establish from six to 25 agricultural trade offices overseas. Passed 65-1: R 22-0; D 43-1 (ND 27-1; SD 16-0), Sept. 8, 1978.

CQ Senate Votes 373-378

Corresponding to Congressional Record Votes 377, 378, 379, 380, 381, 382

	373	374	375	376	377	378
ALABAMA						
Allen, M.	?	N	Y	?	?	?
Sparkman	✓	N	N	N	?	?
ALASKA						
Gravel	N	N	N	N	Y	Y
Stevens	Y	N	N	N	Y	Y
ARIZONA						
DeConcini	Y	N	N	Y	Y	N
Goldwater	Y	Y	?	?	N	N
ARKANSAS						
Bumpers	Y	N	N	N	Y	Y
Hodges	N	N	N	N	Y	Y
CALIFORNIA						
Cranston	N	N	N	N	Y	Y
Hayakawa	Y	Y	Y	Y	?	N
COLORADO						
Hart	Y	N	N	N	Y	Y
Haskell	?	Y	?	N	Y	Y
CONNECTICUT						
Ribicoff	N	N	?	?	†	?
Weicker	Y	Y	N	N	Y	Y
DELAWARE						
Biden	Y	Y	?	?	Y	Y
Roth	Y	Y	N	Y	?	?
FLORIDA						
Chiles	Y	N	N	N	Y	N
Stone	Y	N	N	N	Y	Y
GEORGIA						
Nunn	Y	N	?	N	Y	N
Talmadge	N	N	N	Y	Y	N
HAWAII						
Inouye	Y	N	▮	▮	Y	Y
Matsunaga	Y	N	N	N	Y	Y
IDAHO						
Church	Y	N	N	Y	Y	N
McClure	Y	N	Y	Y	?	?
ILLINOIS						
Stevenson	N	N	N	N	Y	Y
Percy	Y	N	N	N	Y	Y
INDIANA						
Bayh	Y	Y	N	?	Y	Y
Lugar	Y	Y	N	N	Y	Y
IOWA						
Clark	?	N	-	Y	Y	Y
Culver	?	N	N	N	Y	Y
KANSAS						
Dole	Y	Y	Y	Y	Y	Y
Pearson	Y	N	?	?	?	?
KENTUCKY						
Ford	Y	N	N	N	Y	Y
Huddleston	Y	N	N	?	Y	Y
LOUISIANA						
Johnston	?	Y	N	N	?	?
Long	Y	Y	N	N	Y	Y
MAINE						
Hathaway	#	N	N	N	Y	Y
Muskie	Y	N	N	Y	Y	Y
MARYLAND						
Sarbanes	N	Y	N	N	Y	Y
Mathias	N	N	N	N	?	?
MASSACHUSETTS						
Kennedy	N	Y	N	N	Y	Y
Brooke	?	?	?	?	?	?
MICHIGAN						
Riegle	Y	Y	N	N	Y	Y
Griffin	?	N	Y	Y	Y	?
MINNESOTA						
Anderson	Y	Y	N	Y	?	?
Humphrey, M.	?	Y	-	-	†	†
MISSISSIPPI						
Eastland	Y	N	N	?	Y	?
Stennis	Y	N	?	?	Y	Y
MISSOURI						
Eagleton	Y	N	N	Y	Y	Y
Danforth	Y	N	N	Y	Y	Y
MONTANA						
Melcher	Y	N	N	N	Y	Y
Hatfield, P.	Y	N	N	N	Y	Y
NEBRASKA						
Zorinsky	Y	N	Y	Y	Y	N
Curtis	Y	Y	Y	Y	N	N
NEVADA						
Cannon	Y	N	N	N	Y	N
Laxalt	Y	Y	Y	Y	N	N
NEW HAMPSHIRE						
Durkin	Y	N	N	N	Y	Y
McIntyre	Y	N	?	?	Y	Y
NEW JERSEY						
Williams	X	N	N	N	Y	Y
Case	N	N	N	N	Y	Y
NEW MEXICO						
Domenici	Y	N	Y	Y	Y	N
Schmitt	Y	Y	Y	Y	Y	Y
NEW YORK						
Moynihan	N	N	N	N	Y	Y
Javits	N	N	N	N	Y	Y
NORTH CAROLINA						
Morgan	Y	N	N	Y	Y	Y
Helms	?	?	?	?	?	?
NORTH DAKOTA						
Burdick	N	N	N	N	Y	N
Young	Y	N	Y	#	Y	N
OHIO						
Glenn	Y	N	N	N	Y	Y
Metzenbaum	N	Y	N	Y	Y	Y
OKLAHOMA						
Bartlett	Y	Y	Y	N	Y	N
Bellmon	Y	Y	Y	Y	Y	N
OREGON						
Hatfield, M.	Y	N	N	Y	Y	Y
Packwood	Y	Y	Y	N	Y	Y
PENNSYLVANIA						
Heinz	N	N	N	Y	?	?
Schweiker	Y	Y	Y	Y	?	?
RHODE ISLAND						
Pell	Y	N	N	N	Y	Y
Chafee	Y	N	Y	Y	?	?
SOUTH CAROLINA						
Hollings	N	Y	N	N	Y	N
Thurmond	†	Y	N	Y	Y	N
SOUTH DAKOTA						
Abourezk	N	Y	?	?	?	#
McGovern	#	Y	N	N	Y	#
TENNESSEE						
Sasser	Y	N	N	Y	Y	N
Baker	?	Y	Y	Y	?	?
TEXAS						
Bentsen	N	Y	N	N	Y	N
Tower	Y	Y	?	?	Y	N
UTAH						
Garn	Y	Y	Y	Y	N	N
Hatch	Y	Y	Y	Y	N	N
VERMONT						
Leahy	Y	N	N	Y	Y	Y
Stafford	†	N	N	Y	Y	Y
VIRGINIA						
*Byrd, H.	Y	Y	N	Y	Y	N
Scott	Y	Y	?	?	N	N
WASHINGTON						
Jackson	N	N	N	N	Y	Y
Magnuson	N	N	N	N	Y	N
WEST VIRGINIA						
Byrd, R.	Y	N	N	N	Y	Y
Randolph	N	N	N	N	Y	Y
WISCONSIN						
Nelson	Y	Y	N	N	Y	Y
Proxmire	Y	Y	N	N	Y	N
WYOMING						
Hansen	Y	Y	?	?	Y	N
Wallop	Y	Y	Y	N	?	#

Democrats ***Republicans***

*Byrd elected as independent.

KEY

- Y Voted for (yea).
- ✓ Paired for.
- † Announced for.
- # CQ Poll for.
- N Voted against (nay).
- X Paired against.
- \- Announced against.
- ▮ CQ Poll against.
- P Voted "present."
- ● Voted "present" to avoid possible conflict of interest.
- ? Did not vote or otherwise make a position known.

373. H Con Res 683. Fiscal 1979 Binding Budget Levels. Adoption of the resolution (S Res 562) to instruct Senate conferees to insist that no funds be included in the second budget resolution (H Con Res 683) for new local public works programs. Adopted 63-21: R 28-4; D 35-17 (ND 23-13; SD 12-4), Sept. 14, 1978.

374. HR 5289. Natural Gas Pricing. Metzenbaum, D-Ohio, motion to recommit the conference report to the conference committee with instructions to delete all pricing provisions except those related to Alaska gas and to grant certain emergency powers to the president and the Federal Energy Regulatory Commission. Rejected 39-59: R 21-15; D 18-44 (ND 13-30; SD 5-14), Sept. 19, 1978. A "nay" was a vote supporting the president's position.

375. S 2883. Public Broadcasting Reorganization. Griffin, R-Mich., amendment to authorize federal funds for the public broadcasting system's Corporation for Public Broadcasting solely for fiscal 1981. Rejected 20-63: R 18-13; D 2-50 (ND 1-34; SD 1-16), Sept. 19, 1978.

376. S 2883. Public Broadcasting Reorganization. McClure, R-Idaho, amendment to limit the salaries of public broadcasting executives to that of a Cabinet-level officer. Rejected 33-48: R 20-10; D 13-38 (ND 9-27; SD 4-11), Sept. 19, 1978.

377. HR 12936. HUD-Independent Agencies Appropriations, Fiscal 1979. Adoption of the conference report on the bill to appropriate $67,911,419,000 in fiscal 1979 for programs of the Department of Housing and Urban Development and 17 independent federal agencies. Adopted (thus cleared for the president) 75-6: R 20-6; D 55-0 (ND 39-0; SD 16-0), Sept. 20, 1978. The president had requested $69,517,534,000 in new budget authority.

378. H J Res 1088. New York City Loan Guarantees. Adoption of the joint resolution to permit the secretary of the treasury to guarantee up to $1.65 billion in New York City bonds, as authorized under the 1978 New York City Loan Guarantee Act (PL 95-339) and to appropriate funds as necessary to pay guaranteed loans if the city defaulted on them. Passed (thus cleared for the president) 51-28: R 12-14; D 39-14 (ND 31-7; SD 8-7), Sept. 20, 1978. A "yea" was a vote supporting the president's position.

	379	380	381	382
ALABAMA				
Allen, M.	?	?	?	?
Sparkman	?	?	?	?
ALASKA				
Gravel	Y	Y	N	N
Stevens	Y	?	▮	▮
ARIZONA				
DeConcini	Y	N	Y	N
Goldwater	Y	N	?	?
ARKANSAS				
Bumpers	Y	?	?	?
Hodges	Y	N	N	N
CALIFORNIA				
Cranston	Y	Y	?	N
Hayakawa	Y	N	Y	N
COLORADO				
Hart	Y	Y	N	N
Haskell	?	?	?	?
CONNECTICUT				
Ribicoff	†	?	?	?
Weicker	Y	N	Y	N
DELAWARE				
Biden	Y	N	N	N
Roth	?	?	?	?
FLORIDA				
Chiles	Y	Y	?	?
Stone	Y	▮	#	?
GEORGIA				
Nunn	Y	N	Y	?
Talmadge	Y	Y	?	?
HAWAII				
Inouye	Y	Y	N	N
Matsunaga	Y	Y	N	N
IDAHO				
Church	Y	N	▮	N
McClure	Y	N	Y	Y
ILLINOIS				
Stevenson	Y	Y	N	N
Percy	Y	?	?	?
INDIANA				
Bayh	Y	Y	N	N
Lugar	Y	Y	N	N
IOWA				
Clark	Y	Y	N	N
Culver	Y	Y	N	N
KANSAS				
Dole	Y	N	N	N
Pearson	Y	?	?	?
KENTUCKY				
Ford	Y	Y	?	?
Huddleston	?	?	?	?
LOUISIANA				
Johnston	?	?	?	?
Long	Y	N	?	?
MAINE				
Hathaway	Y	†	N	N
Muskie	Y	Y	?	?
MARYLAND				
Sarbanes	Y	Y	N	N
Mathias	Y	?	?	?
MASSACHUSETTS				
Kennedy	Y	Y	▮	▮
Brooke	?	?	?	?
MICHIGAN				
Riegle	Y	Y	N	N
Griffin	?	?	?	?
MINNESOTA				
Anderson	?	?	?	?
Humphrey, M.	†	?	?	?
MISSISSIPPI				
Eastland	Y	N	?	?
Stennis	Y	?	?	?
MISSOURI				
Eagleton	Y	N	Y	N
Danforth	Y	Y	N	N
MONTANA				
Melcher	Y	Y	Y	Y
Hatfield, P.	Y	Y	Y	N
NEBRASKA				
Zorinsky	Y	N	Y	N
Curtis	Y	?	?	?
NEVADA				
Cannon	Y	N	?	?
Laxalt	Y	N	Y	N
NEW HAMPSHIRE				
Durkin	Y	?	?	?
McIntyre	?	?	?	?
NEW JERSEY				
Williams	Y	Y	N	?
Case	Y	Y	N	N
NEW MEXICO				
Domenici	Y	N	Y	N
Schmitt	Y	Y	Y	N
NEW YORK				
Moynihan	Y	N	N	N
Javits	Y	Y	N	N
NORTH CAROLINA				
Morgan	Y	Y	Y	N
Helms	?	?	?	?
NORTH DAKOTA				
Burdick	Y	N	Y	Y
Young	Y	▮	#	#
OHIO				
Glenn	Y	N	N	N
Metzenbaum	Y	N	▮	▮
OKLAHOMA				
Bartlett	Y	N	Y	N
Bellmon	Y	?	?	?
OREGON				
Hatfield, M.	Y	Y	N	Y
Packwood	Y	Y	N	N
PENNSYLVANIA				
Heinz	?	?	N	?
Schweiker	Y	N	N	N
RHODE ISLAND				
Pell	Y	Y	N	?
Chafee	?	?	?	?
SOUTH CAROLINA				
Hollings	Y	N	N	N
Thurmond	Y	-	#	#
SOUTH DAKOTA				
Abourezk	#	▮	▮	▮
McGovern	Y	▮	▮	▮
TENNESSEE				
Sasser	Y	N	N	N
Baker	?	?	?	?
TEXAS				
Bentsen	Y	N	N	?
Tower	Y	N	?	?
UTAH				
Garn	Y	N	Y	N
Hatch	Y	N	Y	Y
VERMONT				
Leahy	Y	Y	N	N
Stafford	Y	Y	N	▮
VIRGINIA				
*Byrd, H.	Y	N	Y	Y
Scott	Y	?	?	?
WASHINGTON				
Jackson	Y	N	N	N
Magnuson	Y	N	N	▮
WEST VIRGINIA				
Byrd, R.	Y	N	N	N
Randolph	Y	N	Y	N
WISCONSIN				
Nelson	Y	N	?	?
Proxmire	N	N	Y	Y
WYOMING				
Hansen	Y	N	Y	N
Wallop	#	#	?	?

KEY

- Y Voted for (yea).
- ✓ Paired for.
- † Announced for.
- # CQ Poll for.
- N Voted against (nay).
- X Paired against.
- \- Announced against.
- ▮ CQ Poll against.
- P Voted "present."
- ● Voted "present" to avoid possible conflict of interest.
- ? Did not vote or otherwise make a position known.

Democrats ***Republicans***

**Byrd elected as independent.*

379. HR 12467. Rehabilitation Act Amendments. Passage of the bill to extend the Rehabilitation Act of 1973 for three years, through fiscal 1981, and to authorize up to $3.9 billion for fiscal 1979-81 rehabilitation and service programs for the severely handicapped. Passed 81-1: R 30-0; D 51-1 (ND 36-1; SD 15-0), Sept. 21, 1978.

380. HR 12931. Foreign Aid Appropriations, Fiscal 1979. Morgan, D-N.C., amendment to delete language in the bill prohibiting the use of funds for a U.S. contribution to the United Nations University in Tokyo. Rejected 30-37: R 8-13; D 22-24 (ND 18-16; SD 4-8), Sept. 21, 1978. A "yea" was a vote supporting the president's position.

381. HR 12931. Foreign Aid Appropriations, Fiscal 1979. Melcher, D-Mont., amendment to delete $20 million from the economic support fund in the bill earmarked for Zambia. Rejected 21-34: R 10-10; D 11-24 (ND 8-20; SD 3-4), Sept. 21, 1978. A "nay" was a vote supporting the president's position.

382. HR 12931. Foreign Aid Appropriations, Fiscal 1979. Hatch, R-Utah, motion to table (kill) the committee provision to limit unobligated and deobligated amounts for fiscal 1978 and 1979 to $211,875,000. Vote invalid (because a quorum (51) was not present) 7-43: R 3-15; D 4-28 (ND 3-24; SD 1-4), Sept. 21, 1978. (The Senate agreed to take a second vote the next day, *see vote 384, p. 58-S.*)

CQ Senate Votes 383-390

Corresponding to Congressional Record Votes 387, 388, 389, 390, 391, 392, 393, 394

	383	384	385	386	387	388	389	390
ALABAMA								
Allen, M.	?	?	?	?	?	?	?	?
Sparkman	?	?	?	?	?	?	?	?
ALASKA								
Gravel	Y	N	Y	N	Y	Y	Y	Y
Stevens	#	▮	#	▮	▮	#	#	#
ARIZONA								
DeConcini	Y	N	Y	Y	N	N	Y	N
Goldwater	?	N	N	Y	N	N	N	N
ARKANSAS								
Bumpers	?	?	?	?	?	?	?	?
Hodges	?	?	?	?	?	?	?	?
CALIFORNIA								
Cranston	Y	N	Y	N	Y	Y	Y	Y
Hayakawa	Y	N	Y	N	?	?	?	?
COLORADO								
Hart	Y	N	Y	N	Y	?	Y	Y
Haskell	?	?	?	?	?	?	?	?
CONNECTICUT								
Ribicoff	?	-	?	?	?	?	?	?
Weicker	N	N	Y	Y	Y	N	Y	N
DELAWARE								
Biden	Y	N	Y	?	?	✓	N	N
Roth	?	?	?	?	?	?	?	?
FLORIDA								
Chiles	Y	N	Y	N	Y	Y	Y	Y
Stone	Y	N	N	N	N	Y	N	N
GEORGIA								
Nunn	Y	N	N	N	N	N	Y	N
Talmadge	Y	Y	N	Y	Y	N	N	N
HAWAII								
Inouye	Y	N	Y	N	Y	Y	Y	Y
Matsunaga	?	?	Y	N	Y	Y	Y	Y
IDAHO								
Church	Y	N	Y	N	N	Y	Y	Y
McClure	?	?	?	?	?	?	?	?
ILLINOIS								
Stevenson	Y	N	Y	N	Y	Y	Y	Y
Percy	?	?	?	?	?	?	?	?
INDIANA								
Bayh	Y	N	Y	N	Y	Y	Y	N
Lugar	Y	N	N	N	N	Y	Y	N
IOWA								
Clark	Y	N	Y	N	Y	Y	Y	Y
Culver	Y	N	Y	N	Y	Y	Y	Y
KANSAS								
Dole	Y	N	N	N	N	Y	N	N
Pearson	Y	N	Y	N	Y	Y	Y	Y
KENTUCKY								
Ford	Y	N	N	N	N	N	Y	N
Huddleston	?	?	?	?	?	?	?	?
LOUISIANA								
Johnston	Y	N	N	N	N	N	N	N
Long	Y	Y	?	N	N	X	N	N
MAINE								
Hathaway	#	▮	#	▮	#	#	#	#
Muskie	Y	N	Y	N	Y	Y	Y	Y
MARYLAND								
Sarbanes	Y	N	Y	N	Y	Y	Y	Y
Mathias	?	?	Y	N	Y	Y	Y	Y
MASSACHUSETTS								
Kennedy	Y	N	Y	N	Y	Y	Y	Y
Brooke	?	?	?	?	?	?	?	?
MICHIGAN								
Riegle	Y	N	Y	N	Y	Y	Y	Y
Griffin	?	?	?	?	?	?	?	?
MINNESOTA								
Anderson	?	?	?	?	?	?	?	?
Humphrey, M.	Y	N	Y	N	Y	Y	Y	Y
MISSISSIPPI								
Eastland	?	?	N	Y	?	?	?	?
Stennis	Y	N	?	?	?	?	?	?
MISSOURI								
Eagleton	Y	N	N	N	N	Y	Y	Y
Danforth	Y	N	N	N	N	Y	Y	Y
MONTANA								
Melcher	Y	N	N	N	N	N	N	N
Hatfield, P.	Y	N	Y	N	N	Y	Y	Y
NEBRASKA								
Zorinsky	Y	N	N	Y	N	N	N	N
Curtis	?	?	?	?	?	?	?	?
NEVADA								
Cannon	Y	N	N	Y	N	N	N	N
Laxalt	Y	N	N	Y	N	N	N	N
NEW HAMPSHIRE								
Durkin	Y	N	Y	N	N	Y	Y	Y
McIntyre	?	?	?	?	?	?	?	?
NEW JERSEY								
Williams	#	▮	#	N	Y	#	Y	Y
Case	#	▮	#	▮	#	#	#	#
NEW MEXICO								
Domenici	?	?	N	Y	N	N	N	N
Schmitt	Y	N	Y	▮	▮	▮	▮	▮
NEW YORK								
Moynihan	Y	N	Y	?	?	?	?	?
Javits	Y	N	Y	N	Y	Y	Y	Y
NORTH CAROLINA								
Morgan	Y	N	Y	-	†	†	†	†
Helms	?	?	?	?	?	?	?	?
NORTH DAKOTA								
Burdick	Y	Y	N	Y	▮	▮	▮	▮
Young	#	▮	#	▮	▮	▮	▮	#
OHIO								
Glenn	Y	N	Y	-	Y	Y	Y	Y
Metzenbaum	Y	N	Y	N	Y	Y	N	Y
OKLAHOMA								
Bartlett	Y	N	?	?	?	?	?	?
Bellmon	?	?	?	?	?	?	?	?
OREGON								
Hatfield, M.	Y	Y	Y	N	N	Y	Y	Y
Packwood	Y	N	Y	N	Y	Y	Y	Y
PENNSYLVANIA								
Heinz	Y	N	Y	N	N	Y	Y	N
Schweiker	Y	N	Y	N	N	Y	Y	N
RHODE ISLAND								
Pell	Y	N	N	N	?	†	†	?
Chafee	Y	N	N	N	Y	Y	Y	Y
SOUTH CAROLINA								
Hollings	Y	N	Y	?	?	?	?	?
Thurmond	#	†	N	Y	N	N	N	N
SOUTH DAKOTA								
Abourezk	#	▮	#	▮	#	#	#	#
McGovern	Y	N	Y	N	Y	Y	Y	Y
TENNESSEE								
Sasser	?	?	?	?	?	?	?	?
Baker	?	?	?	?	?	?	?	?
TEXAS								
Bentsen	Y	N	N	N	Y	Y	Y	N
Tower	?	?	?	?	?	?	?	?
UTAH								
Garn	Y	N	N	Y	N	N	N	N
Hatch	Y	Y	N	Y	N	N	N	N
VERMONT								
Leahy	Y	N	Y	N	Y	Y	Y	Y
Stafford	?	▮	Y	▮	#	#	#	▮
VIRGINIA								
*Byrd, H.	Y	N	N	Y	N	N	N	N
Scott	?	?	N	Y	N	N	N	N
WASHINGTON								
Jackson	Y	N	Y	N	Y	Y	Y	Y
Magnuson	?	▮	N	N	Y	Y	Y	N
WEST VIRGINIA								
Byrd, R.	Y	N	Y	N	N	Y	N	N
Randolph	Y	Y	N	Y	N	N	N	N
WISCONSIN								
Nelson	Y	N	N	N	N	Y	Y	Y
Proxmire	Y	Y	N	Y	N	N	N	N
WYOMING								
Hansen	Y	N	N	Y	N	N	N	N
Wallop	?	▮	#	#	#	▮	▮	#

Democrats ***Republicans***

*Byrd elected as independent.

KEY

- Y Voted for (yea).
- ✓ Paired for.
- † Announced for.
- # CQ Poll for.
- N Voted against (nay).
- X Paired against.
- \- Announced against.
- ▮ CQ Poll against.
- P Voted "present."
- ● Voted "present" to avoid possible conflict of interest.
- ? Did not vote or otherwise make a position known.

383. Procedural Motion. Byrd, D-W.Va., motion to instruct the sergeant at arms to request the attendance of absent senators. Motion agreed to 63-1: R 17-1; D 46-0 (ND 34-0; SD 12-0), Sept. 22, 1978.

384. HR 12931. Foreign Aid Appropriations, Fiscal 1979. Hatch, R-Utah, motion to table (kill) *(see vote 382, p. 57-S)* the Appropriations Committee amendment to limit unobligated and deobligated military aid appropriations for fiscal 1978 and 1979 to $211,875,000. Motion rejected 7-58: R 2-17; D 5-41 (ND 3-31; SD 2-10), Sept. 22, 1978. (The committee amendment subsequently was adopted by voice vote.)

385. HR 12931. Foreign Aid Appropriations, Fiscal 1979. Appropriations Committee amendment to delete House language reducing Title I assistance programs by 2 percent, except funding for Israel, Jordan, and Egypt. Adopted 40-30: R 11-12; D 29-18 (ND 26-10; SD 3-8), Sept. 22, 1978. A "yea" was a vote supporting the president's position.

386. HR 12931. Foreign Aid Appropriations, Fiscal 1979. DeConcini, D-Ariz., amendment to reduce to $500 million, from $1.8 billion, the level of U. S. participation in the Witteveen Facility of the International Monetary Fund. Rejected 18-47: R 9-12; D 9-35 (ND 6-28; SD 3-7), Sept. 22, 1978. A "nay" was a vote supporting the president's position.

387. HR 12931. Foreign Aid Appropriations, Fiscal 1979. Appropriations Committee amendment to delete language preventing use of Peace Corps funds for abortions. Rejected 30-32: R 6-14; D 24-18 (ND 21-12; SD 3-6), Sept. 22, 1978.

388. HR 12931. Foreign Aid Appropriations, Fiscal 1979. Appropriations Committee amendment to increase to $309.6 million, from $220 million provided by the House, funds for U.S. contributions to the Asian Development Bank. Adopted 39-20: R 11-9; D 28-11 (ND 25-6; SD 3-5), Sept. 22, 1978. A "yea" was a vote supporting the president's position.

389. HR 12931. Foreign Aid Appropriations, Fiscal 1979. Appropriations Committee amendment to increase to $500 million, from $421.4 million provided by the House, funds for U.S. contributions to the International Development Association. Adopted 41-22: R 11-9; D 30-13 (ND 26-8; SD 4-5), Sept. 22, 1978. A "yea" was a vote supporting the president's position.

390. HR 12931. Foreign Aid Appropriations, Fiscal 1979. Appropriations Committee amendment to delete House language prohibiting U.S. assistance to Vietnam through the International Development Association. Adopted 32-31: R 7-13; D 25-18 (ND 24-10; SD 1-8), Sept. 22, 1978. A "yea" was a vote supporting the president's position.

	391	392	393	394	395	396	397	398
ALABAMA								
Allen, M.	?	?	?	?	?	?	?	?
Sparkman	?	?	?	?	?	?	?	?
ALASKA								
Gravel	Y	Y	?	?	?	?	Y	?
Stevens	#	#	#	▮	#	#	#	#
ARIZONA								
DeConcini	N	N	N	N	Y	Y	Y	Y
Goldwater	N	N	?	?	?	?	?	?
ARKANSAS								
Bumpers	?	?	?	?	?	?	Y	?
Hodges	?	?	?	?	?	?	Y	Y
CALIFORNIA								
Cranston	Y	Y	?	?	?	?	?	Y
Hayakawa	?	?	?	?	?	?	Y	Y
COLORADO								
Hart	?	Y	Y	Y	Y	Y	Y	Y
Haskell	?	?	?	?	?	?	?	?
CONNECTICUT								
Ribicoff	?	✓	†	?	?	†	Y	?
Weicker	Y	Y	#	?	#	#	N	N
DELAWARE								
Biden	N	Y	Y	Y	N	N	Y	?
Roth	?	?	?	?	?	?	Y	Y
FLORIDA								
Chiles	Y	Y	Y	Y	Y	Y	Y	?
Stone	N	Y	Y	Y	Y	Y	Y	Y
GEORGIA								
Nunn	N	N	Y	Y	Y	N	?	Y
Talmadge	N	N	?	?	?	?	Y	Y
HAWAII								
Inouye	Y	Y	Y	N	Y	Y	#	#
Matsunaga	Y	Y	Y	N	Y	Y	Y	?
IDAHO								
Church	Y	Y	Y	Y	Y	Y	Y	Y
McClure	?	?	?	?	?	?	N	?
ILLINOIS								
Stevenson	Y	?	?	?	?	?	?	?
Percy	?	?	?	?	?	?	?	Y
INDIANA								
Bayh	N	Y	Y	N	Y	Y	Y	#
Lugar	N	Y	Y	Y	N	N	Y	#
IOWA								
Clark	Y	Y	Y	N	Y	Y	?	?
Culver	Y	†	Y	N	Y	Y	Y	Y
KANSAS								
Dole	N	N	Y	N	N	Y	Y	Y
Pearson	N	Y	Y	Y	Y	Y	Y	?
KENTUCKY								
Ford	N	Y	Y	Y	Y	Y	Y	Y
Huddleston	?	?	?	?	?	?	?	?
LOUISIANA								
Johnston	N	N	Y	Y	Y	Y	Y	?
Long	N	N	?	?	?	?	?	Y
MAINE								
Hathaway	#	#	#	▮	#	#	Y	#
Muskie	Y	Y	Y	N	Y	Y	Y	?
MARYLAND								
Sarbanes	Y	Y	Y	N	Y	Y	?	?
Mathias	Y	Y	Y	N	Y	Y	Y	?
MASSACHUSETTS								
Kennedy	Y	Y	#	▮	#	#	Y	#
Brooke	?	?	?	?	?	?	Y	Y
MICHIGAN								
Riegle	Y	Y	Y	N	Y	Y	Y	Y
Griffin	?	?	?	X	?	†	?	?
MINNESOTA								
Anderson	?	?	?	?	?	†	?	?
Humphrey, M.	Y	Y	Y	N	Y	Y	Y	Y
MISSISSIPPI								
Eastland	?	?	?	?	?	?	?	?
Stennis	?	?	?	?	?	?	Y	Y
MISSOURI								
Eagleton	N	Y	Y	N	Y	Y	Y	?
Danforth	Y	Y	N	Y	Y	Y	Y	?
MONTANA								
Melcher	N	N	Y	N	Y	Y	Y	Y
Hatfield, P.	Y	Y	Y	N	Y	Y	Y	Y
NEBRASKA								
Zorinsky	N	N	Y	N	Y	Y	Y	Y
Curtis	?	?	?	?	?	?	Y	Y
NEVADA								
Cannon	N	N	Y	Y	Y	Y	Y	?
Laxalt	N	N	?	?	?	?	Y	Y
NEW HAMPSHIRE								
Durkin	Y	Y	Y	N	Y	N	Y	?
McIntyre	?	?	?	?	?	?	?	?
NEW JERSEY								
Williams	Y	Y	Y	N	Y	Y	Y	#
Case	#	#	#	▮	#	#	Y	#
NEW MEXICO								
Domenici	N	N	-	?	?	✓	Y	Y
Schmitt	▮	▮	Y	Y	N	Y	Y	Y
NEW YORK								
Moynihan	?	?	Y	N	Y	Y	Y	Y
Javits	Y	Y	Y	N	Y	Y	?	?
NORTH CAROLINA								
Morgan	†	†	Y	Y	Y	Y	#	Y
Helms	?	?	?	?	?	?	?	?
NORTH DAKOTA								
Burdick	#	X	†	#	▮	†	#	Y
Young	▮	▮	Y	#	▮	#	Y	Y
OHIO								
Glenn	Y	Y	Y	N	Y	Y	Y	?
Metzenbaum	Y	Y	Y	N	Y	Y	Y	Y
OKLAHOMA								
Bartlett	?	?	?	?	?	?	Y	?
Bellmon	?	?	?	?	?	?	Y	Y
OREGON								
Hatfield, M.	Y	N	N	N	Y	Y	Y	Y
Packwood	Y	Y	Y	Y	N	Y	Y	?
PENNSYLVANIA								
Heinz	N	Y	?	?	?	?	Y	Y
Schweiker	N	Y	Y	Y	N	Y	Y	?
RHODE ISLAND								
Pell	?	†	Y	N	Y	Y	?	Y
Chafee	Y	Y	Y	N	N	Y	?	Y
SOUTH CAROLINA								
Hollings	?	?	Y	Y	N	N	Y	#
Thurmond	N	N	-	✓	X	X	#	Y
SOUTH DAKOTA								
Abourezk	#	▮	#	?	?	?	#	#
McGovern	Y	Y	#	▮	#	#	Y	Y
TENNESSEE								
Sasser	?	?	?	?	?	?	Y	Y
Baker	?	?	Y	N	Y	Y	?	Y
TEXAS								
Bentsen	N	Y	Y	Y	Y	N	Y	Y
Tower	?	?	?	?	?	?	?	Y
UTAH								
Garn	N	N	N	Y	N	Y	Y	Y
Hatch	N	N	N	Y	N	Y	Y	Y
VERMONT								
Leahy	Y	Y	Y	?	?	?	Y	Y
Stafford	▮	#	#	▮	#	#	Y	#
VIRGINIA								
*Byrd, H.	N	N	N	Y	N	N	Y	?
Scott	N	N	?	?	?	?	Y	?
WASHINGTON								
Jackson	Y	Y	Y	N	Y	Y	Y	Y
Magnuson	Y	Y	Y	N	Y	Y	Y	?
WEST VIRGINIA								
Byrd, R.	Y	N	Y	N	Y	Y	Y	Y
Randolph	N	N	†	-	†	†	Y	Y
WISCONSIN								
Nelson	Y	Y	Y	N	Y	Y	Y	Y
Proxmire	N	N	N	Y	N	N	Y	Y
WYOMING								
Hansen	N	N	?	?	?	?	Y	Y
Wallop	▮	▮	#	#	▮	#	Y	?

Democrats *Republicans*

*Byrd elected as independent.

KEY

- Y Voted for (yea).
- ✓ Paired for.
- † Announced for.
- # CQ Poll for.
- N Voted against (nay).
- X Paired against.
- - Announced against.
- ▮ CQ Poll against.
- P Voted "present."
- ● Voted "present" to avoid possible conflict of interest.
- ? Did not vote or otherwise make a position known.

391. HR 12931. Foreign Aid Appropriations, Fiscal 1979. Committee amendment to delete House language barring indirect U.S. assistance to Cuba. Adopted 32-30: R 7-13; D 25-17 (ND 24-9; SD 1-8), Sept. 22, 1978.

392. HR 12931. Foreign Aid Appropriations, Fiscal 1979. Passage of the bill to appropriate $9,203,806,072 for U.S. foreign assistance programs in fiscal 1979. Passed 39-22: R 10-10; D 29-12 (ND 25-7; SD 4-5), Sept. 22, 1978. The president had requested $10,387,760,919.

393. H Con Res 683. Fiscal 1979 Binding Budget Levels. Muskie, D-Maine, motion to approve the conference committee's version of the resolution setting the following binding budget levels for fiscal 1979: budget authority, $555.65 billion; outlays, $487.5 billion; revenues, $448.7 billion; deficit, $38.8 billion. Motion agreed to (thus completing congressional action) 47-7: R 11-4; D 36-3 (ND 28-2; SD 8-1), Sept. 23, 1978.

394. HR 2852. Anti-recession Fiscal Assistance. Chiles, D-Fla., amendment to eliminate the proposed supplementary fiscal assistance program for financially distressed cities. Rejected 22-30: R 8-6; D 14-24 (ND 5-24; SD 9-0), Sept. 23, 1978.

395. HR 2852. Anti-recession Fiscal Assistance. Moynihan, D-N.Y., motion to table (kill) the Lugar, R-Ind., amendment to require the national unemployment rate to exceed 7 percent before financial aid could be available. Motion agreed to 40-12: R 6-8; D 34-4 (ND 27-2; SD 7-2), Sept. 23, 1978.

396. HR 2852. Anti-recession Fiscal Assistance. Passage of the bill to extend the anti-recession fiscal assistance program (countercyclical revenue sharing) for two years, through fiscal 1980, and to establish a supplementary fiscal assistance program for cities with long-term financial difficulties. Passed 44-8: R 13-1; D 31-7 (ND 26-3; SD 5-4), Sept. 23, 1978.

397. HR 12929. Labor-HEW Appropriations, Fiscal 1979. Byrd, D-W.Va., motion to instruct the sergeant at arms to request the attendance of absent senators. Motion agreed to 70-2: R 26-2; D 44-0 (ND 32-0; SD 12-0), Sept. 25, 1978.

398. Procedural Motion. Byrd, D-W.Va., motion to instruct the sergeant at arms to request the attendance of absent senators. Motion agreed to 51-1: R 20-1; D 31-0 (ND 21-0; SD 10-0), Sept. 26, 1978.

CQ Senate Votes 399-406

Corresponding to Congressional Record Votes 403, 404, 405, 406, 407, 408, 409, 410

	399	400	401	402	403	404	405	406
ALABAMA								
Allen, M.	?	?	?	?	?	?	?	?
Sparkman	?	?	?	?	?	?	?	Y
ALASKA								
Gravel	N	Y	Y	Y	Y	N	Y	N
Stevens	N	Y	Y	Y	Y	N	Y	Y
ARIZONA								
DeConcini	Y	N	N	Y	Y	N	Y	N
Goldwater	?	?	?	†	?	?	?	?
ARKANSAS								
Bumpers	N	N	N	Y	Y	N	Y	N
Hodges	N	Y	N	Y	Y	N	Y	N
CALIFORNIA								
Cranston	N	N	N	Y	Y	N	Y	N
Hayakawa	N	Y	Y	Y	Y	Y	Y	N
COLORADO								
Hart	N	Y	N	Y	Y	N	?	Y
Haskell	?	?	?	?	?	?	?	?
CONNECTICUT								
Ribicoff	N	N	Y	Y	Y	N	?	N
Weicker	N	Y	Y	Y	?	?	#	N
DELAWARE								
Biden	Y	N	N	Y	Y	Y	Y	N
Roth	N	N	N	Y	Y	Y	Y	N
FLORIDA								
Chiles	N	Y	N	Y	Y	N	Y	N
Stone	N	Y	N	Y	Y	N	Y	N
GEORGIA								
Nunn	N	Y	Y	Y	Y	N	Y	Y
Talmadge	N	Y	Y	Y	Y	N	Y	N
HAWAII								
Inouye	N	Y	N	Y	?	N	Y	N
Matsunaga	N	Y	N	Y	Y	N	?	Y
IDAHO								
Church	N	N	N	Y	Y	N	Y	Y
McClure	N	Y	Y	Y	Y	N	Y	Y
ILLINOIS								
Stevenson	N	N	N	Y	?	N	N	N
Percy	N	N	N	Y	Y	N	N	Y
INDIANA								
Bayh	Y	N	N	Y	Y	Y	Y	Y
Lugar	N	Y	Y	Y	Y	Y	Y	N
IOWA								
Clark	Y	N	N	Y	Y	N	Y	N
Culver	N	Y	N	Y	Y	N	N	N
KANSAS								
Dole	N	N	N	Y	Y	Y	Y	N
Pearson	N	N	Y	Y	Y	N	Y	Y
KENTUCKY								
Ford	N	Y	N	Y	Y	N	Y	Y
Huddleston	N	Y	N	Y	Y	N	Y	N
LOUISIANA								
Johnston	N	Y	Y	Y	Y	Y	Y	N
Long	N	N	Y	Y	Y	✓	?	N
MAINE								
Hathaway	▮	#	▮	?	?	▮	#	Y
Muskie	Y	Y	N	Y	Y	N	N	N
MARYLAND								
Sarbanes	Y	N	N	Y	Y	Y	?	Y
Mathias	N	N	Y	Y	Y	N	Y	Y
MASSACHUSETTS								
Kennedy	N	N	N	Y	Y	Y	Y	N
Brooke	N	N	Y	Y	Y	Y	Y	Y
MICHIGAN								
Riegle	Y	N	N	Y	Y	Y	Y	N
Griffin	?	N	N	Y	Y	N	Y	Y
MINNESOTA								
Anderson	N	N	N	Y	?	Y	Y	Y
Humphrey, M.	N	N	N	Y	Y	Y	?	Y
MISSISSIPPI								
Eastland	N	Y	Y	Y	Y	N	Y	N
Stennis	N	Y	Y	Y	Y	N	?	?
MISSOURI								
Eagleton	N	N	N	Y	Y	N	Y	N
Danforth	N	Y	Y	Y	Y	N	Y	N
MONTANA								
Melcher	Y	N	N	Y	Y	N	Y	Y
Hatfield, P.	N	Y	Y	Y	Y	N	Y	Y
NEBRASKA								
Zorinsky	Y	N	N	Y	Y	N	Y	Y
Curtis	N	Y	Y	Y	Y	Y	Y	Y
NEVADA								
Cannon	N	Y	Y	Y	Y	N	N	N
Laxalt	N	Y	Y	Y	Y	Y	?	N
NEW HAMPSHIRE								
Durkin	N	N	N	Y	Y	N	Y	Y
McIntyre	?	?	?	?	?	N	Y	Y
NEW JERSEY								
Williams	N	N	Y	Y	Y	N	Y	Y
Case	N	N	Y	Y	Y	N	Y	Y
NEW MEXICO								
Domenici	Y	N	N	Y	Y	N	Y	N
Schmitt	N	N	Y	Y	Y	Y	Y	Y
NEW YORK								
Moynihan	N	N	N	Y	Y	N	Y	Y
Javits	N	N	N	Y	Y	N	Y	Y
NORTH CAROLINA								
Morgan	N	Y	N	Y	Y	N	Y	#
Helms	?	?	?	?	?	?	?	?
NORTH DAKOTA								
Burdick	Y	N	N	Y	Y	N	N	N
Young	N	Y	Y	Y	Y	N	#	N
OHIO								
Glenn	N	N	Y	Y	Y	N	Y	N
Metzenbaum	Y	N	N	Y	Y	Y	Y	Y
OKLAHOMA								
Bartlett	N	Y	Y	Y	Y	Y	Y	Y
Bellmon	N	Y	N	Y	Y	Y	Y	N
OREGON								
Hatfield, M.	Y	N	N	N	Y	N	Y	N
Packwood	N	N	N	Y	Y	Y	Y	N
PENNSYLVANIA								
Heinz	N	N	N	Y	Y	N	Y	?
Schweiker	N	N	N	Y	Y	Y	Y	Y
RHODE ISLAND								
Pell	N	Y	Y	Y	Y	N	Y	Y
Chafee	N	Y	Y	Y	Y	N	Y	N
SOUTH CAROLINA								
Hollings	N	N	N	Y	Y	Y	Y	N
Thurmond	N	Y	Y	Y	Y	Y	Y	Y
SOUTH DAKOTA								
Abourezk	Y	▮	▮	?	Y	Y	?	Y
McGovern	N	N	N	N	Y	Y	Y	N
TENNESSEE								
Sasser	N	Y	N	Y	Y	N	Y	Y
Baker	N	Y	Y	Y	Y	Y	Y	Y
TEXAS								
Bentsen	N	Y	Y	Y	Y	Y	Y	N
Tower	N	Y	Y	Y	Y	Y	Y	Y
UTAH								
Garn	N	N	Y	Y	Y	Y	Y	Y
Hatch	N	Y	N	Y	Y	Y	Y	Y
VERMONT								
Leahy	N	N	N	Y	Y	N	Y	N
Stafford	N	Y	Y	Y	Y	N	Y	Y
VIRGINIA								
*Byrd, H.	N	Y	Y	Y	Y	Y	Y	N
Scott	N	Y	Y	Y	Y	Y	Y	N
WASHINGTON								
Jackson	N	Y	N	Y	Y	N	Y	N
Magnuson	N	Y	N	Y	Y	N	Y	N
WEST VIRGINIA								
Byrd, R.	N	Y	N	Y	Y	N	?	N
Randolph	N	N	N	Y	?	X	†	N
WISCONSIN								
Nelson	?	N	N	Y	Y	Y	Y	N
Proxmire	Y	N	N	N	Y	Y	Y	N
WYOMING								
Hansen	N	Y	Y	Y	Y	Y	Y	N
Wallop	N	Y	Y	Y	Y	Y	Y	N

Democrats ***Republicans***

*Byrd elected as independent.

KEY

- Y Voted for (yea).
- ✓ Paired for.
- † Announced for.
- # CQ Poll for.
- N Voted against (nay).
- X Paired against.
- \- Announced against.
- ▮ CQ Poll against.
- P Voted "present."
- ● Voted "present" to avoid possible conflict of interest.
- ? Did not vote or otherwise make a position known.

399. S 3486. Defense Procurement Authorization. Proxmire, D-Wis., amendment to delete $209 million for shipbuilders' claims settlements. Rejected 15-76: R 2-33; D 13-43 (ND 13-26; SD 0-17), Sept. 26, 1978.

400. S 3486. Defense Procurement Authorization. Stennis, D-Miss., motion to table (kill) the Proxmire, D-Wis., amendment to abolish the Women's Army Corps. Rejected 46-46: R 20-16; D 26-30 (ND 12-27; SD 14-3), Sept. 26, 1978. (The Proxmire amendment subsequently was adopted by voice vote.)

401. S 3486. Defense Procurement Authorization. Stennis, D-Miss., motion to table (kill) the Proxmire, D-Wis., amendment to require a General Accounting Office (GAO) audit of proposed shipbuilding contract claims settlements. Rejected 39-53: R 24-12; D 15-41 (ND 7-32; SD 8-9), Sept. 26, 1978. (The Proxmire amendment subsequently was adopted by voice vote.)

402. S 3486. Defense Procurement Auhorization. Passage of the bill to authorize $35,235,969,000 for Defense Department weapons procurement and military research in fiscal 1979. Passed 89-3: R 35-1; D 54-2 (ND 37-2; SD 17-0), Sept. 26, 1978.

403. HR 5289. Natural Gas Pricing. Byrd, D-W.Va., motion to instruct the sergeant at arms to request the attendance of absent senators. Motion agreed to 88-0: R 35-0; D 53-0 (ND 36-0; SD 17-0), Sept. 26, 1978.

404. HR 5289. Natural Gas Pricing. Dole, R-Kan., motion to recommit the conference report on the natural gas pricing bill to the conference committee with instructions that conferees include authority for emergency allocation of gas, to give farmers using gas priority and to drop all pricing provisions except those relating to Alaskan gas. Motion rejected 36-55: R 20-15; D 16-40 (ND 12-28; SD 4-12), Sept. 26, 1978. A "nay" was a vote supporting the president's position.

405. S 1185. Interstate Parimutuel Wagering on Horseracing. Magnuson, D-Wash., motion to table (kill) the Stevenson, D-Ill., amendment to eliminate from the bill a provision requiring the consent of race tracks and horse owners associations before a state could permit off-track betting. Motion agreed to 75-6: R 32-1; D 43-5 (ND 28-5; SD 15-0), Sept. 26, 1978.

406. HR 12929. Labor-HEW Appropriations, Fiscal 1979. Mathias, R-Md. amendment to add $57.3 million to the appropriation in the bill for impact aid assistance to local school districts, for a total of $856.4 million. Rejected 41-52: R 19-16; D 22-36 (ND 18-24; SD 4-12), Sept. 27, 1978. A "yea" was a vote supporting the president's position.

Corresponding to Congressional Record Votes 411, 412, 413, 414, 415, 416, 417, 418

	407	408	409	410	411	412	413	414
ALABAMA								
Allen, M.	Y	?	?	?	?	?	?	?
Sparkman	Y	Y	Y	Y	Y	N	N	N
ALASKA								
Gravel	Y	Y	Y	Y	Y	Y	N	N
Stevens	Y	Y	N	N	Y	N	N	N
ARIZONA								
DeConcini	Y	Y	N	N	N	N	Y	Y
Goldwater	N	Y	N	N	N	N	Y	Y
ARKANSAS								
Bumpers	Y	Y	N	N	Y	N	N	N
Hodges	Y	Y	N	N	Y	N	N	N
CALIFORNIA								
Cranston	Y	Y	Y	Y	Y	Y	N	N
Hayakawa	N	Y	N	N	Y	N	N	N
COLORADO								
Hart	Y	Y	Y	Y	Y	Y	N	N
Haskell	N	Y	?	?	?	?	?	?
CONNECTICUT								
Ribicoff	Y	Y	Y	Y	Y	Y	N	N
Weicker	N	Y	Y	Y	N	Y	N	N
DELAWARE								
Biden	N	N	N	N	Y	N	Y	N
Roth	N	N	N	N	Y	N	Y	N
FLORIDA								
Chiles	Y	Y	N	N	Y	N	N	Y
Stone	Y	Y	N	N	Y	N	Y	Y
GEORGIA								
Nunn	Y	Y	N	N	Y	N	N	Y
Talmadge	Y	Y	N	Y	Y	N	Y	Y
HAWAII								
Inouye	Y	Y	Y	Y	Y	Y	N	N
Matsunaga	Y	Y	Y	Y	Y	Y	N	N
IDAHO								
Church	Y	Y	N	N	Y	Y	N	Y
McClure	Y	Y	N	N	N	N	Y	Y
ILLINOIS								
Stevenson	Y	Y	Y	Y	?	Y	N	N
Percy	Y	Y	N	Y	Y	Y	N	N
INDIANA								
Bayh	N	Y	Y	Y	Y	Y	N	N
Lugar	N	N	N	N	Y	N	Y	Y
IOWA								
Clark	Y	Y	Y	Y	Y	Y	N	N
Culver	Y	Y	Y	Y	Y	Y	N	N
KANSAS								
Dole	N	Y	N	N	Y	N	Y	Y
Pearson	Y	Y	N	N	Y	Y	?	?
KENTUCKY								
Ford	Y	Y	Y	Y	Y	N	Y	Y
Huddleston	Y	Y	?	Y	N	N	Y	N
LOUISIANA								
Johnston	N	Y	?	N	Y	N	Y	Y
Long	N	Y	Y	Y	Y	N	N	N
MAINE								
Hathaway	Y	Y	Y	Y	Y	#	▮	▮
Muskie	Y	Y	Y	Y	Y	Y	N	N
MARYLAND								
Sarbanes	N	Y	Y	Y	Y	N	N	N
Mathias	Y	Y	Y	Y	Y	Y	?	?
MASSACHUSETTS								
Kennedy	N	Y	Y	Y	Y	Y	N	N
Brooke	N	N	Y	Y	Y	Y	N	N
MICHIGAN								
Riegle	N	Y	Y	Y	Y	N	N	N
Griffin	Y	Y	N	N	Y	N	Y	Y
MINNESOTA								
Anderson	N	Y	Y	Y	?	?	?	?
Humphrey, M.	N	Y	Y	Y	Y	Y	N	N
MISSISSIPPI								
Eastland	N	Y	N	N	Y	N	?	?
Stennis	Y	Y	N	N	Y	N	?	?
MISSOURI								
Eagleton	Y	Y	Y	Y	Y	N	Y	N
Danforth	Y	Y	N	N	Y	N	Y	N
MONTANA								
Melcher	Y	Y	Y	Y	Y	Y	Y	N
Hatfield, P.	Y	Y	Y	Y	Y	N	Y	Y
NEBRASKA								
Zorinsky	N	Y	N	N	Y	N	Y	N
Curtis	N	Y	N	N	Y	N	Y	N
NEVADA								
Cannon	Y	Y	N	N	Y	N	N	N
Laxalt	N	Y	N	N	Y	N	Y	N
NEW HAMPSHIRE								
Durkin	N	Y	Y	Y	Y	Y	Y	N
McIntyre	Y	Y	Y	Y	Y	?	?	?
NEW JERSEY								
Williams	Y	Y	Y	Y	Y	Y	N	N
Case	Y	Y	Y	Y	Y	#	N	N
NEW MEXICO								
Domenici	Y	Y	N	N	Y	N	Y	N
Schmitt	N	Y	N	N	Y	N	N	N
NEW YORK								
Moynihan	Y	Y	Y	Y	Y	Y	N	N
Javits	Y	Y	Y	Y	Y	Y	N	N
NORTH CAROLINA								
Morgan	Y	Y	Y	N	Y	Y	N	N
Helms	?	?	?	?	?	?	?	?
NORTH DAKOTA								
Burdick	Y	Y	Y	Y	Y	N	N	N
Young	Y	Y	N	N	?	N	Y	N
OHIO								
Glenn	Y	Y	Y	Y	Y	Y	N	N
Metzenbaum	N	Y	Y	Y	Y	Y	N	N
OKLAHOMA								
Bartlett	N	Y	N	N	Y	N	Y	N
Bellmon	N	Y	N	N	Y	Y	N	N
OREGON								
Hatfield, M.	Y	#	▮	-	?	#	†	†
Packwood	Y	Y	N	N	Y	Y	N	N
PENNSYLVANIA								
Heinz	Y	Y	N	Y	Y	Y	N	N
Schweiker	N	Y	N	N	Y	N	Y	N
RHODE ISLAND								
Pell	Y	†	Y	Y	Y	Y	N	N
Chafee	Y	N	N	N	Y	Y	N	N
SOUTH CAROLINA								
Hollings	N	Y	N	N	?	?	?	?
Thurmond	Y	Y	N	N	Y	N	Y	Y
SOUTH DAKOTA								
Abourezk	N	?	?	?	?	?	?	?
McGovern	N	Y	Y	Y	Y	Y	N	N
TENNESSEE								
Sasser	N	Y	Y	Y	Y	N	N	N
Baker	N	Y	N	N	Y	N	N	N
TEXAS								
Bentsen	N	Y	N	N	Y	N	N	N
Tower	N	Y	N	N	Y	N	N	N
UTAH								
Garn	N	Y	N	N	Y	N	Y	N
Hatch	N	Y	N	N	Y	N	Y	N
VERMONT								
Leahy	Y	N	Y	Y	Y	Y	N	N
Stafford	Y	Y	Y	Y	Y	Y	N	N
VIRGINIA								
*Byrd, H.	N	N	N	N	Y	N	Y	Y
Scott	N	Y	N	N	Y	N	?	?
WASHINGTON								
Jackson	Y	Y	Y	Y	Y	N	N	N
Magnuson	Y	Y	Y	Y	Y	N	N	N
WEST VIRGINIA								
Byrd, R.	Y	Y	Y	Y	Y	N	N	Y
Randolph	Y	Y	Y	Y	Y	-	†	†
WISCONSIN								
Nelson	N	N	Y	Y	Y	N	N	N
Proxmire	N	N	Y	Y	Y	N	Y	Y
WYOMING								
Hansen	N	Y	N	N	Y	N	N	Y
Wallop	N	Y	N	N	Y	N	N	N

Democrats ***Republicans***

*Byrd elected as independent.

KEY

- Y Voted for (yea).
- ✓ Paired for.
- † Announced for.
- # CQ Poll for.
- N Voted against (nay).
- X Paired against.
- - Announced against.
- ▮ CQ Poll against.
- P Voted "present."
- ● Voted "present" to avoid possible conflict of interest.
- ? Did not vote or otherwise make a position known.

407. HR 5289. Natural Gas Pricing. Adoption of the conference report on the bill to lift price controls on newly discovered natural gas by 1985. Adopted 57-42: R 17-20; D 40-22 (ND 28-15; SD 12-7), Sept. 27, 1978. A "yea" was a vote supporting the president's position.

408. HR 12928. Public Works, Energy Appropriations, Fiscal 1979. Adoption of the conference report on the bill to appropriate $10,160,483,000 in fiscal 1979 for energy and water development programs of the Interior and Energy Departments. Adopted (thus cleared for the president) 86-9: R 32-4; D 54-5 (ND 37-4; SD 17-1), Sept. 27, 1978. The president had requested $11,039,449,000 in new budget authority.

409. HR 12929. Labor-HEW Appropriations, Fiscal 1979. Byrd, D-W.Va., motion to table (kill) the Bartlett, R-Okla., question to the Senate that the Bartlett amendment — to prohibit the Occupational Safety and Health Administration from making safety (but not health) inspections of businesses with 10 or fewer employees in non-hazardous industries, unless a serious injury had already occurred in the workplace or OSHA had received a safety complaint from an employee — was germane to the bill *(see vote 410, below)*. Motion agreed to 47-46: R 6-30; D 41-16 (ND 36-5; SD 5-11), Sept. 27, 1978.

410. HR 12929. Labor-HEW Appropriations, Fiscal 1979. Magnuson, D-Wash., motion to table (kill) the Bartlett, R-Okla., appeal of the chair's ruling that the Bartlett amendment *(see vote 409, above)* violated the Senate rule prohibiting legislation in an appropriation bill. Motion agreed to 50-45: R 8-28; D 42-17 (ND 36-5; SD 6-12), Sept. 27, 1978.

411. HR 12929. Labor-HEW Appropriations, Fiscal 1979. Byrd, D-W.Va., motion to instruct the sergeant at arms to request the attendance of absent senators. Motion agreed to 86-5: R 32-3; D 54-2 (ND 38-1; SD 16-1), Sept. 27, 1978.

412. HR 12929. Labor-HEW Appropriations, Fiscal 1979. Brooke, R-Mass., amendment to delete the provision barring use of funds in the bill to require the busing of schoolchildren beyond the school nearest their homes, including the use of pairing, clustering or reorganization of grade structures among schools. Rejected 35-54: R 11-24; D 24-30 (ND 23-14; SD 1-16), Sept. 27, 1978.

413. HR 12929. Labor-HEW Appropriations, Fiscal 1979. Hatch, R-Utah, amendment to prohibit use of funds in the bill to perform abortions, unless the life of the mother would be endangered if the fetus were carried to term. Rejected 30-55: R 16-17; D 14-38 (ND 8-29; SD 6-9), Sept. 27, 1978.

414. HR 12929. Labor-HEW Appropriations, Fiscal 1979. Thurmond, R-S.C., amendment to prohibit the use of funds in the bill to perform abortions, unless the life of the mother would be endangered if the fetus were carried to term,or in cases of rape, when reported to authorities within 48 hours of the incident, or in cases of incest, as defined by state law. Rejected 19-66: R 7-26; D 12-40 (ND 5-32; SD 7-8), Sept. 27, 1978.

CQ Senate Votes 415-422

Corresponding to Congressional Record Votes 419, 420, 421, 422, 423, 424, 425, 426

	415	416	417	418	419	420	421	422
ALABAMA								
Allen, M.	?	?	?	?	?	?	?	?
Sparkman	Y	Y	Y	Y	N	?	?	?
ALASKA								
Gravel	Y	N	Y	Y	N	Y	Y	?
Stevens	Y	Y	N	N	Y	N	N	Y
ARIZONA								
DeConcini	N	Y	Y	Y	Y	Y	Y	Y
Goldwater	N	Y	N	N	Y	N	N	X
ARKANSAS								
Bumpers	Y	Y	Y	Y	Y	Y	Y	Y
Hodges	Y	Y	Y	Y	?	Y	Y	Y
CALIFORNIA								
Cranston	Y	Y	Y	Y	Y	Y	Y	Y
Hayakawa	N	Y	N	N	Y	N	N	N
COLORADO								
Hart	Y	Y	Y	Y	Y	Y	Y	Y
Haskell	?	?	?	?	?	?	?	?
CONNECTICUT								
Ribicoff	Y	Y	Y	Y	N	Y	Y	Y
Weicker	Y	N	N	Y	Y	#	#	Y
DELAWARE								
Biden	Y	Y	Y	Y	N	Y	Y	Y
Roth	N	Y	N	N	N	Y	Y	Y
FLORIDA								
Chiles	Y	Y	Y	Y	Y	Y	Y	Y
Stone	Y	Y	Y	Y	Y	Y	Y	Y
GEORGIA								
Nunn	Y	Y	Y	Y	N	Y	Y	Y
Talmadge	Y	Y	Y	Y	N	Y	Y	Y
HAWAII								
Inouye	†	Y	Y	Y	Y	Y	Y	Y
Matsunaga	Y	Y	Y	Y	N	Y	Y	Y
IDAHO								
Church	Y	Y	Y	Y	Y	Y	Y	Y
McClure	Y	Y	N	?	†	?	?	?
ILLINOIS								
Stevenson	Y	N	Y	Y	N	N	Y	Y
Percy	Y	Y	N	Y	N	Y	Y	Y
INDIANA								
Bayh	Y	#	?	?	?	?	?	†
Lugar	N	Y	N	N	Y	N	Y	Y
IOWA								
Clark	Y	Y	Y	Y	N	Y	Y	Y
Culver	Y	Y	Y	Y	N	Y	Y	Y
KANSAS								
Dole	Y	Y	N	Y	Y	N	Y	Y
Pearson	?	?	?	?	?	?	?	?
KENTUCKY								
Ford	Y	?	Y	Y	Y	Y	Y	Y
Huddleston	Y	Y	Y	Y	N	Y	Y	Y
LOUISIANA								
Johnston	Y	?	?	?	?	?	?	?
Long	Y	Y	Y	Y	N	Y	Y	Y
MAINE								
Hathaway	#	#	Y	Y	N	Y	Y	Y
Muskie	Y	Y	Y	Y	N	Y	Y	Y
MARYLAND								
Sarbanes	Y	N	Y	Y	Y	Y	Y	Y
Mathias	?	Y	N	Y	?	?	?	Y
MASSACHUSETTS								
Kennedy	Y	N	Y	Y	Y	Y	Y	Y
Brooke	Y	N	N	Y	Y	N	Y	Y
MICHIGAN								
Riegle	Y	Y	Y	Y	N	Y	Y	Y
Griffin	Y	Y	?	N	Y	Y	Y	Y
MINNESOTA								
Anderson	?	?	?	?	?	?	?	†
Humphrey, M.	Y	Y	Y	Y	Y	Y	Y	Y
MISSISSIPPI								
Eastland	?	Y	Y	N	Y	N	?	?
Stennis	?	Y	Y	N	Y	Y	Y	Y
MISSOURI								
Eagleton	Y	Y	Y	Y	N	Y	Y	Y
Danforth	Y	Y	N	Y	N	Y	Y	Y
MONTANA								
Melcher	Y	Y	Y	Y	N	Y	Y	Y
Hatfield, P.	Y	Y	Y	Y	Y	Y	Y	Y
NEBRASKA								
Zorinsky	Y	Y	Y	Y	N	Y	Y	Y
Curtis	Y	Y	N	N	Y	?	?	?
NEVADA								
Cannon	Y	Y	Y	N	N	Y	Y	Y
Laxalt	N	Y	N	N	Y	N	N	N
NEW HAMPSHIRE								
Durkin	N	N	Y	Y	Y	Y	Y	Y
McIntyre	?	†	?	?	?	?	?	?
NEW JERSEY								
Williams	Y	N	Y	Y	N	Y	Y	Y
Case	Y	N	N	Y	N	Y	Y	Y
NEW MEXICO								
Domenici	Y	Y	N	Y	N	N	Y	Y
Schmitt	Y	N	N	N	Y	N	N	N
NEW YORK								
Moynihan	Y	N	Y	Y	N	Y	Y	N
Javits	Y	N	N	Y	N	Y	Y	Y
NORTH CAROLINA								
Morgan	Y	Y	Y	N	Y	N	Y	N
Helms	?	Y	N	N	Y	N	N	N
NORTH DAKOTA								
Burdick	Y	Y	Y	Y	Y	Y	Y	Y
Young	Y	Y	N	?	#	▮	▮	#
OHIO								
Glenn	Y	Y	Y	Y	N	Y	Y	Y
Metzenbaum	Y	Y	Y	Y	N	Y	Y	Y
OKLAHOMA								
Bartlett	N	Y	N	Y	Y	Y	Y	Y
Bellmon	Y	Y	N	Y	N	Y	Y	Y
OREGON								
Hatfield, M.	†	†	?	†	†	#	#	†
Packwood	Y	N	N	N	Y	N	Y	Y
PENNSYLVANIA								
Heinz	Y	N	N	Y	N	Y	Y	Y
Schweiker	Y	Y	N	Y	N	Y	Y	Y
RHODE ISLAND								
Pell	Y	Y	?	Y	N	Y	Y	Y
Chafee	Y	N	N	Y	Y	N	Y	Y
SOUTH CAROLINA								
Hollings	?	Y	Y	Y	Y	Y	Y	Y
Thurmond	Y	Y	N	N	Y	N	Y	Y
SOUTH DAKOTA								
Abourezk	?	?	?	#	-	#	#	#
McGovern	Y	Y	Y	Y	N	Y	Y	Y
TENNESSEE								
Sasser	Y	Y	Y	Y	Y	Y	Y	Y
Baker	Y	Y	N	?	?	N	N	Y
TEXAS								
Bentsen	Y	Y	Y	Y	N	Y	Y	Y
Tower	Y	Y	N	N	Y	N	N	N
UTAH								
Garn	N	Y	N	N	Y	N	N	✓
Hatch	N	Y	N	N	Y	N	N	Y
VERMONT								
Leahy	Y	Y	Y	Y	N	Y	Y	Y
Stafford	Y	Y	N	Y	Y	Y	Y	Y
VIRGINIA								
*Byrd, H.	N	Y	Y	N	Y	N	N	N
Scott	?	Y	N	N	Y	N	N	N
WASHINGTON								
Jackson	Y	Y	Y	Y	Y	Y	Y	Y
Magnuson	Y	Y	Y	Y	N	Y	Y	Y
WEST VIRGINIA								
Byrd, R.	Y	Y	Y	Y	Y	Y	Y	Y
Randolph	†	Y	Y	Y	N	Y	Y	Y
WISCONSIN								
Nelson	Y	Y	Y	Y	Y	Y	Y	Y
Proxmire	N	Y	Y	Y	N	Y	N	N
WYOMING								
Hansen	N	Y	N	N	Y	N	N	N
Wallop	Y	Y	N	N	Y	Y	Y	Y

Democrats ***Republicans***

Byrd elected as independent.

KEY

- Y Voted for (yea).
- ✓ Paired for.
- † Announced for.
- # CQ Poll for.
- N Voted against (nay).
- X Paired against.
- \- Announced against.
- ▮ CQ Poll against.
- P Voted "present."
- ● Voted "present" to avoid possible conflict of interest.
- ? Did not vote or otherwise make a position known.

415. HR 12929. Labor-HEW Appropriations, Fiscal 1979. Passage of the bill to appropriate $54.5 billion for the Departments of Labor and Health, Education and Welfare and related agencies in fiscal year 1979. Passed 71-13: R 24-9; D 47-4 (ND 33-3; SD 14-1), Sept. 27, 1978. The president had requested $57,432,676,000.

416. S 2441. Urban Mass Transportation. Muskie, D-Maine, amendment to delete from the bill a provision to authorize a federal subsidy of up to 50 percent of an urban mass transit system's operating deficits, so long as the total federal operating subsidy did not exceed one-third of total operating costs. Adopted 74-15: R 28-8; D 46-7 (ND 30-7; SD 16-0), Sept. 28, 1978. A "yea" was a vote supporting the president's position.

417. Procedural Motion. Byrd, D-W.Va., motion that the Senate adjourn temporarily. Motion agreed to 54-35: R 0-35; D 54-0 (ND 37-0; SD 17-0), Sept. 28, 1978.

418. S 991. Education Department. Ribicoff, D-Conn., motion to table (kill) the Schmitt, R-N.M., amendment to delete the provision transferring overseas military dependents' schools operated by the Defense Department to the proposed Education Department. Motion agreed to 65-23: R 15-18; D 50-5 (ND 37-1; SD 13-4), Sept. 28, 1978. A "yea" was a vote supporting the president's position.

419. S 991. Education Department. Stevens, R-Alaska, amendment to delete the provision transferring Indian education programs of the Bureau of Indian Affairs to the proposed Education Department. Adopted 47-39: R 23-9; D 24-30 (ND 14-24; SD 10-6), Sept. 28, 1978. A "nay" was a vote supporting the president's position.

420. S 991. Education Department. Ribicoff, D-Conn., motion to table (kill) the Schmitt, R-N.M., amendment to delete the provision transferring science education programs of the National Science Foundation to the proposed Education Department. Motion agreed to 62-23: R 12-19; D 50-4 (ND 37-1; SD 13-3), Sept. 28, 1978. A "yea" was a vote supporting the president's position.

421. S 991. Education Department. Ribicoff, D-Conn., motion to table (kill) the Hayakawa, R-Calif., substitute for the bill, to require the National Institute of Education to undertake a study of the need for a separate department of education. Motion agreed to 70-14: R 19-12; D 51-2 (ND 37-1; SD 14-1), Sept. 28, 1978. A "yea" was a vote supporting the president's position.

422. S 991. Education Department. Passage of the bill to establish a new Cabinet-level Department of Education. Passed 72-11: R 24-7; D 48-4 (ND 35-2; SD 13-2), Sept. 28, 1978. A "yea" was a vote supporting the president's position.

Corresponding to Congressional Record Votes 427, 428, 429, 430, 431, 432, 433, 434

	423	424	425	426	427	428	429	430
ALABAMA								
Allen, M.	?	?	?	?	?	?	?	?
Sparkman	Y	N	Y	Y	N	Y	Y	Y
ALASKA								
Gravel	Y	N	Y	N	Y	Y	Y	Y
Stevens	N	Y	Y	✓	N	Y	Y	Y
ARIZONA								
DeConcini	Y	Y	Y	X	?	?	?	?
Goldwater	N	Y	N	N	N	Y	Y	Y
ARKANSAS								
Bumpers	Y	Y	Y	N	N	Y	Y	N
Hodges	N	N	Y	N	N	Y	Y	Y
CALIFORNIA								
Cranston	Y	N	Y	N	Y	Y	Y	Y
Hayakawa	N	Y	N	Y	N	Y	Y	Y
COLORADO								
Hart	Y	Y	Y	N	Y	Y	Y	Y
Haskell	?	?	?	?	?	?	?	?
CONNECTICUT								
Ribicoff	Y	N	Y	N	Y	?	?	?
Weicker	N	N	Y	N	Y	Y	Y	?
DELAWARE								
Biden	N	Y	Y	N	N	Y	Y	Y
Roth	N	Y	Y	N	Y	N	Y	Y
FLORIDA								
Chiles	N	Y	Y	N	Y	Y	Y	Y
Stone	Y	Y	Y	N	Y	Y	Y	Y
GEORGIA								
Nunn	?	?	?	?	?	?	?	?
Talmadge	Y	Y	Y	Y	N	Y	Y	Y
HAWAII								
Inouye	Y	Y	Y	N	N	Y	Y	Y
Matsunaga	?	Y	Y	N	Y	Y	Y	Y
IDAHO								
Church	N	Y	Y	Y	N	Y	Y	Y
McClure	?	?	?	?	?	?	?	✓
ILLINOIS								
Stevenson	N	N	Y	Y	Y	Y	Y	Y
Percy	N	Y	Y	Y	N	?	?	?
INDIANA								
Bayh	Y	Y	Y	N	N	Y	Y	Y
Lugar	Y	Y	Y	Y	Y	Y	Y	Y
IOWA								
Clark	Y	Y	Y	N	?	†	†	?
Culver	Y	Y	Y	N	?	?	?	?
KANSAS								
Dole	N	Y	Y	N	N	Y	Y	Y
Pearson	?	?	?	?	?	?	?	?
KENTUCKY								
Ford	Y	Y	Y	Y	N	Y	Y	Y
Huddleston	N	Y	Y	Y	N	?	?	?
LOUISIANA								
Johnston	?	?	?	?	?	?	?	?
Long	N	Y	Y	?	?	Y	Y	Y
MAINE								
Hathaway	#	#	#	▮	▮	#	#	#
Muskie	N	Y	Y	N	N	Y	Y	X
MARYLAND								
Sarbanes	Y	Y	Y	N	N	?	?	?
Mathias	Y	N	Y	N	N	Y	Y	Y
MASSACHUSETTS								
Kennedy	Y	Y	Y	N	Y	#	#	#
Brooke	Y	N	Y	N	N	Y	Y	N
MICHIGAN								
Riegle	Y	N	Y	N	N	Y	Y	Y
Griffin	?	?	?	?	?	?	?	?
MINNESOTA								
Anderson	?	?	?	-	?	?	?	?
Humphrey, M.	Y	N	Y	N	Y	Y	Y	Y
MISSISSIPPI								
Eastland	Y	Y	Y	Y	N	Y	Y	Y
Stennis	Y	Y	Y	Y	N	Y	Y	Y
MISSOURI								
Eagleton	Y	Y	Y	N	?	?	?	?
Danforth	N	Y	Y	Y	✓	Y	Y	Y
MONTANA								
Melcher	Y	?	?	?	?	?	?	✓
Hatfield, P.	Y	?	?	N	N	Y	Y	Y
NEBRASKA								
Zorinsky	N	Y	Y	Y	N	Y	Y	Y
Curtis	N	Y	Y	N	N	Y	Y	Y
NEVADA								
Cannon	Y	Y	Y	Y	N	Y	Y	Y
Laxalt	N	?	Y	N	N	N	Y	Y
NEW HAMPSHIRE								
Durkin	Y	Y	Y	N	N	?	?	?
McIntyre	?	?	?	?	-	?	?	?
NEW JERSEY								
Williams	Y	N	Y	N	N	Y	Y	N
Case	Y	N	Y	N	N	Y	Y	X
NEW MEXICO								
Domenici	Y	Y	Y	N	N	?	?	?
Schmitt	N	N	Y	N	N	Y	Y	Y
NEW YORK								
Moynihan	Y	Y	Y	N	N	Y	Y	Y
Javits	Y	N	Y	N	Y	?	?	?
NORTH CAROLINA								
Morgan	N	Y	Y	N	N	Y	Y	Y
Helms	N	Y	Y	N	N	N	Y	Y
NORTH DAKOTA								
Burdick	Y	Y	Y	N	N	Y	Y	Y
Young	N	Y	Y	N	N	Y	Y	Y
OHIO								
Glenn	Y	Y	Y	Y	Y	Y	Y	N
Metzenbaum	Y	Y	Y	Y	N	Y	Y	N
OKLAHOMA								
Bartlett	N	Y	Y	N	N	Y	Y	Y
Bellmon	Y	Y	Y	N	Y	Y	Y	Y
OREGON								
Hatfield, M.	#	▮	#	-	-	†	†	†
Packwood	N	N	Y	Y	Y	Y	Y	Y
PENNSYLVANIA								
Heinz	Y	Y	Y	Y	N	Y	Y	Y
Schweiker	Y	Y	Y	Y	N	Y	Y	Y
RHODE ISLAND								
Pell	Y	Y	Y	N	N	†	†	†
Chafee	Y	N	Y	Y	N	Y	Y	Y
SOUTH CAROLINA								
Hollings	N	Y	Y	N	N	Y	Y	Y
Thurmond	N	Y	Y	N	X	Y	Y	Y
SOUTH DAKOTA								
Abourezk	#	Y	Y	N	N	#	#	#
McGovern	Y	Y	Y	N	Y	Y	Y	Y
TENNESSEE								
Sasser	N	Y	Y	N	N	?	?	?
Baker	N	Y	Y	N	?	?	?	?
TEXAS								
Bentsen	N	Y	Y	Y	Y	Y	Y	Y
Tower	?	?	?	?	-	?	?	?
UTAH								
Garn	N	Y	Y	N	N	N	Y	Y
Hatch	N	Y	Y	N	?	?	?	?
VERMONT								
Leahy	Y	N	Y	N	N	Y	Y	Y
Stafford	Y	N	Y	▮	N	Y	Y	Y
VIRGINIA								
*Byrd, H.	N	Y	Y	Y	N	N	Y	Y
Scott	N	Y	N	N	N	N	Y	Y
WASHINGTON								
Jackson	Y	Y	Y	Y	N	Y	Y	Y
Magnuson	Y	Y	Y	Y	N	Y	Y	Y
WEST VIRGINIA								
Byrd, R.	N	Y	Y	Y	N	Y	Y	Y
Randolph	Y	Y	Y	N	-	†	†	†
WISCONSIN								
Nelson	N	Y	Y	Y	Y	Y	Y	N
Proxmire	N	Y	N	Y	Y	Y	N	N
WYOMING								
Hansen	N	Y	Y	N	N	Y	Y	Y
Wallop	N	Y	Y	Y	N	N	Y	Y

Democrats ***Republicans***

**Byrd elected as independent.*

KEY

- Y Voted for (yea).
- ✓ Paired for.
- † Announced for.
- # CQ Poll for.
- N Voted against (nay).
- X Paired against.
- - Announced against.
- ▮ CQ Poll against.
- P Voted "present."
- ● Voted "present" to avoid possible conflict of interest.
- ? Did not vote or otherwise make a position known.

423. S 2474. Public Health Programs. Pell, D-R.I., motion to table (kill) the Proxmire, D-Wis., amendment to eliminate physical fitness promotion programs. Motion agreed to 47-39: R 11-22; D 36-17 (ND 29-8; SD 7-9), Sept. 29, 1978.

424. S 2474. Public Health Programs. Kennedy, D-Mass., motion to table (kill) the Stafford, R-Vt., amendment to require adolescent pregnancy centers to provide counseling to clients on all options open to them regarding their pregnancy or refer them to a conveniently accessible counseling agency. Motion agreed to 66-19: R 23-9; D 43-10 (ND 29-8; SD 14-2), Sept. 29, 1978.

425. S 2474. Public Health Programs. Passage of the bill to provide one-, two-, and three-year authorizations totaling $2,764,000,000 for 18 public health programs including categorical grants, community and migrant health centers, adolescent pregnancy services and health promotion programs. Passed 82-4: R 30-3; D 52-1 (ND 36-1; SD 16-0), Sept. 29, 1978.

426. S 3077. Export-Import Bank. Stevenson, D-Ill., motion to table (kill) the Abourezk, D-S.D., amendment to extend the Senate Select Committee on Indian Affairs two years. Motion rejected 28-55: R 9-22; D 19-33 (ND 11-26; SD 8-7), Sept. 29, 1978. (The Abourezk amendment subsequently was adopted by voice vote.)

427. S 3077. Export-Import Bank. Ribicoff, D-Conn., motion to table (kill) the Hollings, D-S.C., amendment to prohibit the elimination of protective tariffs on imported textiles. Motion rejected 21-56: R 6-23; D 15-33 (ND 12-21; SD 3-12), Sept. 29, 1978. (The Hollings amendment subsequently was adopted by voice vote.) A "yea" was a vote supporting the president's position.

428. HR 12934. State, Justice, Commerce, Judiciary Appropriations, Fiscal 1979. Adoption of the conference report on the bill to appropriate $8,515,354,000 for fiscal 1979 programs and operations of the Departments of State, Justice, Commerce, the federal judiciary and related agencies. Adopted (thus cleared for the president) 62-7: R 22-6; D 40-1 (ND 27-0; SD 13-1), Sept. 30, 1978. The president had requested $8,660,076,000.

429. HR 11686. Energy Department — National Security Programs. Passage of the bill to authorize $2,971,484,000 for the national security programs of the Department of Energy for fiscal 1979. Passed 68-1: R 28-0; D 40-1 (ND 26-1; SD 14-0), Sept. 30, 1978.

430. HR 10587. Public Rangelands Improvement. Passage of the bill to authorize $360 million for a 20-year Bureau of Land Management program, beginning in fiscal 1980, that would improve deteriorated federally owned rangelands, which would be financed by a new grazing fee schedule for ranchers. Passed 59-7: R 25-1; D 34-6 (ND 21-5; SD 13-1), Sept. 30, 1978.

CQ Senate Votes 431-438

Corresponding to Congressional Record Votes 435, 436, 437, 438, 439, 440, 441, 442

	431	432	433	434	435	436	437	438
ALABAMA								
Allen, M.	?	Y	?	N	Y	?	?	?
Sparkman	X	N	N	N	N	N	N	N
ALASKA								
Gravel	Y	N	N	N	N	N	N	N
Stevens	Y	N	N	N	Y	Y	N	N
ARIZONA								
DeConcini	Y	N	X	N	N	N	N	N
Goldwater	?	Y	Y	N	Y	Y	N	Y
ARKANSAS								
Bumpers	Y	N	Y	N	N	N	N	N
Hodges	Y	N	N	N	N	N	N	N
CALIFORNIA								
Cranston	N	N	N	N	N	N	N	N
Hayakawa	Y	N	Y	?	Y	Y	N	N
COLORADO								
Hart	Y	N	N	N	N	N	N	N
Haskell	?	?	?	N	N	N	?	?
CONNECTICUT								
Ribicoff	Y	N	N	N	N	N	N	N
Weicker	N	N	Y	N	N	N	N	N
DELAWARE								
Biden	Y	N	N	N	N	N	N	N
Roth	Y	N	Y	N	Y	Y	N	N
FLORIDA								
Chiles	?	N	N	N	Y	Y	N	N
Stone	N	N	Y	N	N	N	Y	N
GEORGIA								
Nunn	Y	Y	Y	N	Y	Y	N	N
Talmadge	N	Y	Y	N	Y	Y	Y	N
HAWAII								
Inouye	?	?	N	N	N	N	N	N
Matsunaga	Y	N	N	?	N	N	N	N
IDAHO								
Church	N	Y	N	N	Y	Y	N	N
McClure	N	Y	Y	N	Y	Y	Y	N
ILLINOIS								
Stevenson	N	N	N	Y	Y	N	N	N
Percy	Y	N	N	N	N	N	N	N
INDIANA								
Bayh	Y	N	N	N	N	N	N	N
Lugar	Y	N	Y	N	Y	Y	N	N
IOWA								
Clark	?	N	N	N	N	N	N	N
Culver	Y	N	N	N	N	?	N	N
KANSAS								
Dole	N	N	Y	N	Y	Y	N	N
Pearson	?	?	?	?	†	?	?	?
KENTUCKY								
Ford	N	Y	N	N	Y	Y	N	N
Huddleston	?	Y	Y	N	Y	Y	N	N
LOUISIANA								
Johnston	N	Y	Y	N	Y	Y	N	N
Long	Y	Y	Y	N	Y	Y	N	N
MAINE								
Hathaway	?	N	N	N	N	N	N	N
Muskie	N	N	N	N	N	N	N	N
MARYLAND								
Sarbanes	N	N	N	N	N	N	N	N
Mathias	Y	X	N	N	N	N	N	N
MASSACHUSETTS								
Kennedy	?	N	N	N	N	N	N	N
Brooke	N	N	N	N	N	N	N	N
MICHIGAN								
Riegle	N	N	N	N	N	N	N	N
Griffin	Y	N	N	N	N	N	N	N
MINNESOTA								
Anderson	?	N	N	N	N	N	N	N
Humphrey, M.	Y	N	N	N	N	N	N	-
MISSISSIPPI								
Eastland	N	Y	✓	N	Y	Y	✓	Y
Stennis	N	Y	Y	N	Y	Y	N	N
MISSOURI								
Eagleton	Y	N	N	?	?	?	?	?
Danforth	N	Y	Y	N	Y	Y	N	Y
MONTANA								
Melcher	Y	N	N	N	N	N	N	N
Hatfield, P.	Y	N	N	N	N	N	N	N
NEBRASKA								
Zorinsky	Y	Y	Y	N	Y	Y	Y	N
Curtis	Y	Y	?	N	Y	Y	Y	Y
NEVADA								
Cannon	✓	Y	Y	N	Y	Y	X	-
Laxalt	Y	Y	Y	N	Y	Y	Y	Y
NEW HAMPSHIRE								
Durkin	N	N	N	N	N	N	N	N
McIntyre	?	?	N	N	N	N	N	N
NEW JERSEY								
Williams	N	N	N	N	N	N	N	N
Case	N	N	N	N	N	N	N	N
NEW MEXICO								
Domenici	?	?	?	N	Y	N	N	N
Schmitt	Y	N	N	Y	N	?	N	N
NEW YORK								
Moynihan	N	-	N	N	N	N	N	N
Javits	†	N	N	N	N	N	N	N
NORTH CAROLINA								
Morgan	N	N	N	Y	Y	Y	N	N
Helms	Y	Y	Y	N	Y	Y	Y	Y
NORTH DAKOTA								
Burdick	Y	N	N	N	N	N	N	N
Young	N	N	Y	N	Y	N	N	N
OHIO								
Glenn	Y	N	N	N	N	N	N	N
Metzenbaum	N	N	N	N	N	N	N	N
OKLAHOMA								
Bartlett	Y	Y	Y	N	Y	Y	N	N
Bellmon	Y	N	Y	N	Y	N	Y	N
OREGON								
Hatfield, M.	N	-	?	N	N	N	N	N
Packwood	Y	N	N	N	N	N	N	N
PENNSYLVANIA								
Heinz	N	N	N	N	N	N	N	N
Schweiker	Y	N	Y	N	Y	Y	N	N
RHODE ISLAND								
Pell	Y	-	N	Y	N	N	N	N
Chafee	Y	N	N	N	N	N	N	N
SOUTH CAROLINA								
Hollings	Y	N	N	N	Y	Y	N	N
Thurmond	Y	✓	✓	N	Y	Y	Y	N
SOUTH DAKOTA								
Abourezk	?	N	N	N	N	?	?	N
McGovern	Y	N	N	N	N	N	N	N
TENNESSEE								
Sasser	N	N	Y	N	Y	Y	N	N
Baker	Y	N	Y	N	Y	Y	N	N
TEXAS								
Bentsen	Y	N	N	N	Y	Y	N	N
Tower	?	Y	Y	N	Y	Y	Y	Y
UTAH								
Garn	N	Y	Y	N	Y	Y	Y	Y
Hatch	?	Y	Y	N	Y	Y	Y	Y
VERMONT								
Leahy	?	N	N	N	N	N	N	N
Stafford	Y	N	X	N	N	N	N	N
VIRGINIA								
*Byrd, H.	N	Y	Y	N	Y	Y	N	N
Scott	N	Y	Y	N	Y	Y	Y	Y
WASHINGTON								
Jackson	N	N	N	N	Y	Y	N	N
Magnuson	N	N	N	N	N	N	N	N
WEST VIRGINIA								
Byrd, R.	N	N	N	N	N	N	N	N
Randolph	N	N	N	N	N	N	N	N
WISCONSIN								
Nelson	Y	N	N	N	N	N	N	N
Proxmire	N	N	N	N	N	N	N	N
WYOMING								
Hansen	Y	Y	Y	N	Y	Y	Y	N
Wallop	Y	Y	Y	N	Y	Y	N	N

Democrats ***Republicans***

Byrd elected as independent.

KEY

- Y Voted for (yea).
- ✓ Paired for.
- † Announced for.
- # CQ Poll for.
- N Voted against (nay).
- X Paired against.
- - Announced against.
- ▮ CQ Poll against.
- P Voted "present."
- ● Voted "present" to avoid possible conflict of interest.
- ? Did not vote or otherwise make a position known.

431. S 3077. Export-Import Bank. Chafee, R-R.I., amendment to allow the president to deny Export-Import Bank credits to nations that tolerate terrorism or violate human rights. Adopted 45-35: R 21-11; D 24-24 (ND 18-15; SD 6-9), Oct. 2, 1978.

432. H J Res 638. ERA Deadline Extension. Scott, R-Va., amendment to permit a state legislature to rescind a ratification of the equal rights amendment and to recognize any rescission of such ratification made before the date the ERA extension resolution became law. Rejected 26-64: R 13-20; D 13-44 (ND 3-35; SD 10-9), Oct. 3, 1978. A "nay" was a vote supporting the president's position.

433. H J Res 638. ERA Deadline Extension. Scott, R-Va., amendment to require that the resolution extending the date for ratification of the equal rights amendment be passed by two-thirds of both houses of the Congress in order to become effective. Rejected 33-57: R 21-11; D 12-46 (ND 2-39; SD 10-7), Oct. 3, 1978. A "nay" was a vote supporting the president's position.

434. H J Res 638. ERA Deadline Extension. Stevenson, D-Ill., substitute amendment to the Garn, R-Utah, amendment *(see vote 435, below)*, to provide that Congress expressed no opinion with respect to the effect of the action of any state legislature in rescinding its ratification of the proposed equal rights amendment to the Constitution. Rejected 4-92: R 1-35; D 3-57 (ND 2-39; SD 1-18), Oct. 4, 1978.

435. H J Res 638. ERA Deadline Extension. Garn, R-Utah, amendment to allow a state to rescind its ratification of the proposed amendment extending the time for ratification of the ERA at any time after the resolution became effective. Rejected 44-54: R 24-13; D 20-41 (ND 5-37; SD 15-4), Oct. 4, 1978. A "nay" was a vote supporting the president's position.

436. H J Res 638. ERA Deadline Extension. Scott, R-Va., amendment to permit a state legislature to rescind its ratification of the proposed equal rights amendment to the Constitution after March 22, 1979. Rejected 39-55: R 21-15; D 18-40 (ND 4-36; SD 14-4), Oct. 4, 1978. A "nay" was a vote supporting the president's position.

437. H J Res 638. ERA Deadline Extension. Scott, R-Va., substitute amendment to propose an amendment to the Constitution to provide that equality of rights not be denied on account of sex, except in the military where Congress and the president would control selection of individuals. Rejected 14-79: R 11-26; D 3-53 (ND 1-38; SD 2-15), Oct. 4, 1978. A "nay" was a vote supporting the president's position.

438. H J Res 638. ERA Deadline Extension. Scott, R-Va., amendment to establish Jan. 1, 1980, as the deadline for ratification of the proposed equal rights amendment to the Constitution. Rejected 10-84: R 9-28; D 1-56 (ND 0-39; SD 1-17), Oct. 4, 1978. A "nay" was a vote supporting the president's position.

Corresponding to Congressional Record Votes 443, 444, 445, 446, 447, 448, 449

	439	440	441	442	443	444	445
ALABAMA							
Allen, M.	?	?	?	Y	Y	N	Y
Sparkman	Y	N	Y	Y	Y	?	?
ALASKA							
Gravel	Y	N	Y	Y	Y	N	Y
Stevens	Y	N	Y	Y	Y	-	†
ARIZONA							
DeConcini	Y	N	Y	Y	N	N	Y
Goldwater	?	N	Y	Y	N	N	Y
ARKANSAS							
Bumpers	Y	N	Y	N	Y	Y	Y
Hodges	Y	N	Y	N	Y	N	Y
CALIFORNIA							
Cranston	Y	Y	Y	N	Y	Y	N
Hayakawa	Y	N	Y	N	Y	N	Y
COLORADO							
Hart	Y	N	Y	Y	Y	Y	N
Haskell	?	?	†	Y	?	?	?
CONNECTICUT							
Ribicoff	Y	N	Y	N	Y	N	Y
Weicker	Y	N	Y	Y	N	Y	N
DELAWARE							
Biden	N	N	Y	Y	Y	N	N
Roth	N	N	Y	N	Y	N	Y
FLORIDA							
Chiles	Y	N	Y	Y	Y	Y	N
Stone	Y	N	Y	Y	Y	N	Y
GEORGIA							
Nunn	Y	N	Y	N	Y	Y	N
Talmadge	Y	N	Y	N	Y	N	Y
HAWAII							
Inouye	?	N	Y	N	Y	▮	#
Matsunaga	Y	?	Y	Y	Y	N	Y
IDAHO							
Church	Y	Y	Y	#	#	▮	#
McClure	N	N	Y	Y	Y	Y	N
ILLINOIS							
Stevenson	Y	Y	Y	Y	Y	Y	N
Percy	Y	N	Y	N	Y	N	Y
INDIANA							
Bayh	Y	N	Y	Y	Y	Y	N
Lugar	N	N	Y	Y	Y	N	N
IOWA							
Clark	Y	N	Y	Y	Y	Y	N
Culver	Y	N	Y	Y	Y	Y	N
KANSAS							
Dole	N	N	Y	Y	Y	N	Y
Pearson	?	?	?	N	Y	N	Y
KENTUCKY							
Ford	Y	N	Y	Y	Y	N	Y
Huddleston	Y	N	Y	?	?	?	?
LOUISIANA							
Johnston	Y	?	?	N	Y	N	Y
Long	Y	N	Y	N	Y	N	Y
MAINE							
Hathaway	Y	?	#	Y	#	Y	N
Muskie	Y	N	Y	N	Y	N	N
MARYLAND							
Sarbanes	Y	N	Y	Y	Y	Y	N
Mathias	Y	?	Y	N	Y	Y	N
MASSACHUSETTS							
Kennedy	Y	N	Y	N	Y	Y	N
Brooke	Y	-	†	?	?	N	Y
MICHIGAN							
Riegle	Y	Y	Y	Y	Y	Y	N
Griffin	Y	Y	Y	Y	Y	N	Y
MINNESOTA							
Anderson	Y	N	Y	Y	Y	Y	N
Humphrey, M.	†	N	Y	Y	?	?	?
MISSISSIPPI							
Eastland	Y	N	Y	N	Y	?	Y
Stennis	Y	N	Y	N	Y	N	Y
MISSOURI							
Eagleton	?	?	?	?	?	?	?
Danforth	Y	N	Y	N	Y	N	Y
MONTANA							
Melcher	Y	N	Y	Y	Y	Y	N
Hatfield, P.	?	N	Y	Y	Y	N	Y
NEBRASKA							
Zorinsky	Y	N	Y	Y	Y	N	Y
Curtis	Y	N	Y	N	Y	N	Y
NEVADA							
Cannon	†	N	Y	Y	Y	N	Y
Laxalt	N	N	Y	Y	?	?	?
NEW HAMPSHIRE							
Durkin	N	N	Y	Y	Y	Y	N
McIntyre	Y	N	Y	Y	Y	Y	N
NEW JERSEY							
Williams	Y	N	Y	#	#	▮	#
Case	Y	N	Y	N	Y	Y	N
NEW MEXICO							
Domenici	?	?	?	?	?	?	?
Schmitt	N	N	Y	N	Y	N	Y
NEW YORK							
Moynihan	Y	N	Y	N	Y	N	Y
Javits	Y	N	Y	N	Y	Y	N
NORTH CAROLINA							
Morgan	Y	N	Y	Y	Y	N	N
Helms	N	N	Y	Y	Y	N	Y
NORTH DAKOTA							
Burdick	Y	N	Y	Y	Y	Y	N
Young	Y	N	Y	N	Y	N	Y
OHIO							
Glenn	Y	N	Y	N	Y	Y	N
Metzenbaum	Y	Y	Y	N	Y	Y	N
OKLAHOMA							
Bartlett	N	N	Y	Y	Y	N	Y
Bellmon	Y	N	Y	N	Y	Y	N
OREGON							
Hatfield, M.	N	Y	N	Y	Y	Y	N
Packwood	Y	N	Y	N	Y	N	Y
PENNSYLVANIA							
Heinz	Y	N	Y	Y	Y	N	Y
Schweiker	Y	N	Y	N	Y	N	Y
RHODE ISLAND							
Pell	Y	Y	Y	Y	Y	Y	N
Chafee	Y	N	Y	N	Y	N	Y
SOUTH CAROLINA							
Hollings	Y	N	Y	N	Y	Y	N
Thurmond	N	N	Y	Y	Y	N	Y
SOUTH DAKOTA							
Abourezk	Y	?	#	Y	#	Y	N
McGovern	Y	Y	N	Y	Y	Y	N
TENNESSEE							
Sasser	Y	N	Y	Y	Y	Y	N
Baker	N	N	Y	N	Y	Y	Y
TEXAS							
Bentsen	Y	N	Y	N	Y	N	Y
Tower	N	?	?	†	?	?	?
UTAH							
Garn	N	N	Y	Y	Y	N	Y
Hatch	N	N	Y	Y	Y	N	Y
VERMONT							
Leahy	Y	N	Y	Y	Y	Y	N
Stafford	Y	N	Y	Y	Y	Y	N
VIRGINIA							
*Byrd, H.	N	N	Y	N	Y	N	Y
Scott	N	?	Y	Y	Y	N	?
WASHINGTON							
Jackson	Y	N	Y	N	Y	N	Y
Magnuson	Y	?	Y	Y	Y	N	Y
WEST VIRGINIA							
Byrd, R.	Y	N	Y	N	Y	Y	N
Randolph	Y	-	†	N	#	-	†
WISCONSIN							
Nelson	Y	Y	Y	N	Y	Y	N
Proxmire	Y	Y	N	N	Y	Y	N
WYOMING							
Hansen	N	N	Y	N	Y	N	Y
Wallop	N	N	Y	N	Y	N	Y

Democrats ***Republicans***

Byrd elected as independent.

KEY

- Y Voted for (yea).
- ✓ Paired for.
- † Announced for.
- # CQ Poll for.
- N Voted against (nay).
- X Paired against.
- \- Announced against.
- ▮ CQ Poll against.
- P Voted "present."
- ● Voted "present" to avoid possible conflict of interest.
- ? Did not vote or otherwise make a position known.

439. HR 12930. Treasury, Postal Service Appropriations, Fiscal 1979. Adoption of the conference report on the bill to appropriate $8,983,261,000 for fiscal 1979 for the Treasury, Postal Service, the Executive Office of the President and various independent agencies. Adopted (thus cleared for the president) 70-20: R 18-17; D 52-3 (ND 35-2; SD 17-1), Oct. 4, 1978. The president had requested $9,203,261,000 in new budget authority.

440. HR 13635. Defense Department Appropriations, Fiscal 1979. McGovern, D-S.D., amendment to reduce the appropriation by 1 percent. Rejected 11-74: R 2-30; D 9-44 (ND 9-27; SD 0-17), Oct. 5, 1978.

441. HR 13635. Defense Department Appropriations, Fiscal 1979. Passage of the bill to appropriate $116,401,635,000 for the military programs of the Department of Defense for fiscal 1979. Passed 86-3: R 33-1; D 53-2 (ND 36-2; SD 17-0), Oct. 5, 1978. The president had requested $119,300,283,000.

442. HR 13511. Revenue Act of 1978. Haskell, D-Colo., amendment to extend the general jobs tax credit for two years, through Dec. 31, 1980, and to reduce the maximum corporate income tax rate to 47 percent, rather than 46 percent, between Jan. 1, 1979, and Oct. 1, 1979. Adopted 51-42: R 17-18; D 34-24 (ND 27-13; SD 7-11), Oct. 5, 1978.

443. HR 13511. Revenue Act of 1978. Byrd, D-W.Va., motion to instruct the sergeant at arms to request the attendance of absent senators. Motion agreed to 84-3: R 32-2; D 52-1 (ND 34-1; SD 18-0), Oct. 5, 1978.

444. HR 13511. Revenue Act of 1978. Long, D-La., appeal of the ruling of the chair sustaining the Muskie, D-Maine, point of order that the Roth, R-Del., amendment to provide phased individual income tax reductions violated provisions of the Congressional Budget Act. Ruling of the chair not sustained 38-48: R 9-25; D 29-23 (ND 24-12; SD 5-11), Oct. 5, 1978. (The Roth amendment subsequently was rejected by a 36-60 vote, *see vote 447, p. 66-S*)

445. HR 13511. Revenue Act of 1978. Moynihan, D-N.Y., motion to table (kill) the Long, D-La., motion to reconsider the vote (*see vote 444, above*) by which the ruling of the chair was not sustained. Motion agreed to 46-40: R 24-9; D 22-31 (ND 10-26; SD 12-5), Oct. 5, 1978.

CQ Senate Votes 446-453

Corresponding to Congressional Record Votes 450, 451, 452, 453, 454, 455, 456, 457

	446	447	448	449	450	451	452	453
ALABAMA								
Allen, M.	?	N	?	?	?	?	?	?
Sparkman	Y	Y	Y	Y	Y	?	?	?
ALASKA								
Gravel	Y	Y	N	Y	N	Y	Y	N
Stevens	Y	Y	Y	Y	Y	N	Y	N
ARIZONA								
DeConcini	Y	N	Y	Y	Y	N	Y	N
Goldwater	N	Y	N	Y	Y	N	N	N
ARKANSAS								
Bumpers	N	N	Y	Y	Y	Y	Y	Y
Hodges	Y	N	Y	Y	Y	Y	Y	Y
CALIFORNIA								
Cranston	Y	N	Y	N	N	Y	N	N
Hayakawa	N	Y	N	N	N	N	?	?
COLORADO								
Hart	Y	N	Y	N	Y	N	Y	Y
Haskell	?	?	?	?	?	?	?	?
CONNECTICUT								
Ribicoff	Y	N	N	Y	N	Y	N	N
Weicker	Y	N	N	Y	Y	Y	Y	N
DELAWARE								
Biden	Y	Y	Y	Y	Y	N	Y	Y
Roth	N	Y	N	Y	Y	N	N	N
FLORIDA								
Chiles	N	N	N	N	Y	Y	N	N
Stone	Y	N	Y	N	Y	Y	N	N
GEORGIA								
Nunn	N	Y	N	N	Y	Y	N	N
Talmadge	N	N	N	N	?	Y	N	N
HAWAII								
Inouye	Y	N	Y	Y	N	Y	N	N
Matsunaga	Y	N	N	Y	N	Y	N	N
IDAHO								
Church	N	N	Y	Y	Y	N	Y	Y
McClure	N	Y	Y	Y	Y	N	Y	N
ILLINOIS								
Stevenson	Y	N	Y	Y	N	Y	N	N
Percy	Y	Y	Y	Y	N	N	Y	N
INDIANA								
Bayh	Y	N	Y	Y	Y	Y	Y	Y
Lugar	N	Y	N	Y	Y	N	Y	N
IOWA								
Clark	Y	N	Y	N	Y	Y	Y	Y
Culver	Y	N	Y	N	Y	Y	Y	Y
KANSAS								
Dole	N	Y	Y	Y	N	N	Y	N
Pearson	Y	N	N	Y	Y	N	?	?
KENTUCKY								
Ford	N	N	Y	Y	Y	Y	N	N
Huddleston	N	N	Y	Y	?	?	?	?
LOUISIANA								
Johnston	Y	Y	N	Y	N	Y	?	?
Long	N	N	N	N	N	Y	N	N
MAINE								
Hathaway	Y	N	Y	Y	N	Y	Y	Y
Muskie	Y	N	N	N	Y	Y	Y	Y
MARYLAND								
Sarbanes	Y	N	Y	Y	N	Y	?	?
Mathias	Y	N	N	Y	N	Y	N	N
MASSACHUSETTS								
Kennedy	Y	N	Y	Y	N	Y	Y	Y
Brooke	Y	N	Y	Y	N	N	Y	N
MICHIGAN								
Riegle	Y	N	Y	Y	N	Y	#	▮
Griffin	Y	Y	Y	Y	N	N	Y	N
MINNESOTA								
Anderson	Y	?	?	?	?	?	?	?
Humphrey, M.	Y	N	Y	Y	N	Y	?	?
MISSISSIPPI								
Eastland	?	N	N	Y	Y	Y	?	?
Stennis	N	N	N	?	?	Y	N	N
MISSOURI								
Eagleton	Y	N	N	Y	Y	Y	Y	Y
Danforth	N	Y	N	Y	Y	N	Y	N
MONTANA								
Melcher	Y	N	Y	Y	N	Y	Y	Y
Hatfield, P.	Y	N	Y	Y	N	N	Y	N
NEBRASKA								
Zorinsky	N	Y	Y	Y	N	Y	Y	Y
Curtis	N	Y	N	N	N	N	N	N
NEVADA								
Cannon	N	N	N	Y	Y	Y	N	N
Laxalt	N	Y	N	Y	Y	N	Y	N
NEW HAMPSHIRE								
Durkin	Y	N	Y	Y	N	N	Y	N
McIntyre	Y	N	Y	Y	Y	N	N	Y
NEW JERSEY								
Williams	Y	N	Y	Y	N	Y	N	N
Case	Y	N	Y	Y	N	Y	N	N
NEW MEXICO								
Domenici	N	Y	Y	Y	?	?	?	?
Schmitt	Y	Y	N	Y	Y	N	Y	N
NEW YORK								
Moynihan	Y	N	N	Y	N	Y	Y	N
Javits	Y	N	N	N	N	Y	N	N
NORTH CAROLINA								
Morgan	N	N	N	N	N	Y	Y	Y
Helms	N	Y	Y	Y	Y	N	Y	N
NORTH DAKOTA								
Burdick	Y	N	Y	N	N	Y	Y	Y
Young	Y	Y	N	?	Y	N	?	?
OHIO								
Glenn	Y	N	N	N	N	Y	N	N
Metzenbaum	Y	N	Y	N	Y	Y	N	Y
OKLAHOMA								
Bartlett	N	Y	N	N	Y	N	Y	N
Bellmon	N	Y	N	N	Y	Y	Y	N
OREGON								
Hatfield, M.	Y	N	Y	Y	Y	N	N	N
Packwood	Y	Y	Y	Y	Y	N	Y	Y
PENNSYLVANIA								
Heinz	Y	Y	Y	Y	Y	N	Y	N
Schweiker	N	Y	N	Y	N	N	Y	N
RHODE ISLAND								
Pell	Y	N	Y	N	N	Y	Y	Y
Chafee	Y	Y	N	N	Y	Y	Y	N
SOUTH CAROLINA								
Hollings	N	N	N	Y	Y	Y	Y	Y
Thurmond	N	Y	Y	Y	Y	N	Y	N
SOUTH DAKOTA								
Abourezk	Y	N	Y	N	?	?	Y	Y
McGovern	Y	N	Y	N	Y	Y	Y	Y
TENNESSEE								
Sasser	N	N	Y	Y	Y	Y	N	N
Baker	N	Y	N	Y	Y	N	N	N
TEXAS								
Bentsen	Y	N	N	Y	Y	Y	N	N
Tower	-	✓	?	?	†	-	?	?
UTAH								
Garn	N	Y	N	Y	Y	N	Y	N
Hatch	N	Y	N	Y	?	?	?	?
VERMONT								
Leahy	Y	N	Y	Y	Y	Y	N	Y
Stafford	Y	X	N	N	Y	Y	N	N
VIRGINIA								
*Byrd, H.	N	N	N	Y	Y	Y	Y	Y
Scott	N	Y	?	?	Y	N	?	?
WASHINGTON								
Jackson	Y	N	Y	Y	N	N	N	N
Magnuson	Y	N	Y	Y	N	N	N	N
WEST VIRGINIA								
Byrd, R.	Y	N	N	N	N	Y	N	Y
Randolph	Y	N	Y	Y	†	†	-	-
WISCONSIN								
Nelson	Y	N	Y	Y	N	Y	N	Y
Proxmire	Y	Y	Y	Y	Y	N	Y	Y
WYOMING								
Hansen	N	Y	N	N	Y	Y	N	N
Wallop	N	Y	N	Y	Y	N	Y	N

Democrats ***Republicans***

*Byrd elected as independent.

KEY

- Y Voted for (yea).
- ✓ Paired for.
- † Announced for.
- # CQ Poll for.
- N Voted against (nay).
- X Paired against.
- - Announced against.
- ▮ CQ Poll against.
- P Voted "present."
- ● Voted "present" to avoid possible conflict of interest.
- ? Did not vote or otherwise make a position known.

446. H J Res 638. ERA Deadline Extension. Passage of the joint resolution to provide an additional 39 months, until June 30, 1982, for states to ratify the proposed Equal Rights Amendment to the Constitution under which discrimination on the basis of sex would be prohibited. Passed (thus completing congressional action) 60-36: R 16-21; D 44-15 (ND 39-3; SD 5-12), Oct. 6, 1978. A "yea" was a vote supporting the president's position.

447. HR 13511. Revenue Act of 1978. Roth, R-Del., amendment to cut individual income tax rates by 7 percent in 1979, 13 percent in 1980, and 10 percent in 1981 (the Roth-Kemp, R-N.Y., proposal). Rejected 36-60: R 29-7; D 7-53 (ND 4-37; SD 3-16), Oct. 6, 1978.

448. HR 13511. Revenue Act of 1978. Bumpers, D-Ark., amendment to cut individual income taxes in 1979 $4.5 billion more than the $16 billion recommended by the Finance Committee, with the extra relief going to persons with incomes below $50,-000 and especially to those in the $10,000-$30,000 range. Adopted 52-43: R 13-23; D 39-20 (ND 32-9; SD 7-11), Oct. 6, 1978.

449. HR 13511. Revenue Act of 1978. Packwood, R-Ore., amendment to provide a tuition tax credit equal to 35 percent of college tuition and fees up to a maximum of $100 in 1978, $150 in 1979 and $250 in 1980. Adopted 67-26: R 27-8; D 40-18 (ND 29-12; SD 11-6), Oct. 6, 1978. A "nay" was a vote supporting the president's position.

450. HR 13511. Revenue Act of 1978. Danforth, R-Mo., amendment to delete from the bill a section providing an estimated $400 million in fiscal relief to state and local governments to offset Aid to Families with Dependent Children (AFDC) costs. Adopted 52-37: R 25-10; D 27-27 (ND 15-24; SD 12-3), Oct. 6, 1978.

451. HR 13511. Revenue Act of 1978. Talmadge, D-Ga., motion to table (kill) the Griffin, R-Mich., amendment to index individual income taxes for inflation for four years, beginning in 1980. Motion agreed to 53-37: R 8-27; D 45-10 (ND 29-10; SD 16-0), Oct. 6, 1978. A "yea" was a vote supporting the president's position.

452. HR 13511. Revenue Act of 1978. Packwood, R-Ore., amendment-division one, to reduce the maximum corporate income tax rate (on corporate income above $100,000) to 46 percent on Jan. 1, 1979, to 45.5 percent on Oct. 1, 1979, and to 45 percent on Jan. 1, 1982. Adopted 48-34: R 21-10; D 27-24 (ND 22-15; SD 5-9), Oct. 6, 1978.

453. HR 13511. Revenue Act of 1978. Packwood, R-Ore., amendment-division two, to repeal special tax treatment for Domestic International Sales Corporations (DISCs). Rejected 28-54: R 1-30; D 27-24; (ND 22-15; SD 5-9), Oct. 6, 1978. A "yea" was a vote supporting the president's position.

	454	455	456	457	458	459	460	461
ALABAMA								
Allen, M.	Y	Y	Y	N	?	Y	Y	Y
Sparkman	N	Y	Y	Y	Y	N	Y	Y
ALASKA								
Gravel	Y	Y	Y	N	Y	Y	Y	Y
Stevens	Y	N	Y	N	Y	Y	Y	Y
ARIZONA								
DeConcini	?	†	?	?	?	Y	Y	Y
Goldwater	Y	N	Y	Y	Y	Y	Y	Y
ARKANSAS								
Bumpers	N	Y	Y	Y	?	?	?	?
Hodges	N	Y	Y	Y	X	N	Y	N
CALIFORNIA								
Cranston	Y	Y	Y	Y	Y	N	Y	N
Hayakawa	Y	Y	Y	N	Y	Y	Y	Y
COLORADO								
Hart	N	?	Y	Y	N	N	Y	N
Haskell	?	?	?	?	?	?	?	?
CONNECTICUT								
Ribicoff	Y	Y	Y	?	?	Y	Y	Y
Weicker	#	#	#	#	#	Y	Y	Y
DELAWARE								
Biden	N	Y	N	?	?	?	N	N
Roth	Y	N	N	N	Y	Y	Y	Y
FLORIDA								
Chiles	N	Y	Y	Y	Y	Y	Y	N
Stone	Y	Y	Y	?	?	Y	Y	Y
GEORGIA								
Nunn	Y	Y	Y	Y	Y	Y	Y	Y
Talmadge	Y	Y	Y	N	?	N	Y	Y
HAWAII								
Inouye	Y	Y	Y	N	Y	Y	Y	N
Matsunaga	N	Y	Y	Y	Y	Y	N	N
IDAHO								
Church	N	Y	Y	#	#	N	N	Y
McClure	?	?	?	?	?	?	?	?
ILLINOIS								
Stevenson	Y	Y	Y	Y	Y	Y	?	Y
Percy	Y	Y	Y	?	?	?	?	?
INDIANA								
Bayh	N	Y	Y	Y	?	N	Y	N
Lugar	N	N	Y	Y	Y	Y	N	Y
IOWA								
Clark	N	Y	Y	†	?	N	N	N
Culver	N	Y	Y	?	?	N	Y	N
KANSAS								
Dole	Y	N	Y	N	Y	Y	Y	Y
Pearson	Y	Y	Y	?	?	Y	Y	Y
KENTUCKY								
Ford	N	Y	Y	Y	Y	Y	Y	Y
Huddleston	?	?	?	?	?	?	Y	Y
LOUISIANA								
Johnston	?	?	?	?	?	?	Y	Y
Long	N	Y	Y	N	Y	Y	Y	Y
MAINE								
Hathaway	▮	#	#	#	▮	▮	?	#
Muskie	N	Y	Y	N	N	N	Y	N
MARYLAND								
Sarbanes	N	Y	Y	Y	?	N	Y	N
Mathias	N	Y	Y	Y	Y	?	Y	Y
MASSACHUSETTS								
Kennedy	N	Y	Y	Y	N	N	Y	N
Brooke	?	?	?	?	?	Y	N	N
MICHIGAN								
Riegle	N	Y	Y	Y	N	Y	N	N
Griffin	?	?	?	?	?	?	?	?
MINNESOTA								
Anderson	?	†	†	?	?	?	?	-
Humphrey, M.	N	Y	Y	Y	?	†	†	N
MISSISSIPPI								
Eastland	N	Y	Y	N	?	Y	Y	Y
Stennis	?	Y	Y	N	?	?	Y	Y
MISSOURI								
Eagleton	Y	Y	Y	N	Y	Y	N	Y
Danforth	Y	N	Y	N	Y	Y	Y	Y
MONTANA								
Melcher	Y	Y	Y	Y	Y	?	Y	Y
Hatfield, P.	Y	?	Y	N	X	Y	Y	N
NEBRASKA								
Zorinsky	N	Y	Y	Y	Y	Y	Y	Y
Curtis	Y	N	Y	N	Y	?	Y	Y
NEVADA								
Cannon	Y	Y	Y	N	✓	?	?	?
Laxalt	Y	Y	Y	?	?	Y	N	Y
NEW HAMPSHIRE								
Durkin	N	Y	Y	Y	Y	Y	Y	Y
McIntyre	N	Y	Y	Y	Y	Y	N	N
NEW JERSEY								
Williams	Y	Y	Y	Y	Y	Y	Y	N
Case	Y	Y	Y	Y	Y	Y	N	N
NEW MEXICO								
Domenici	?	?	?	?	?	?	?	?
Schmitt	Y	N	Y	N	Y	Y	N	Y
NEW YORK								
Moynihan	N	Y	Y	Y	Y	Y	Y	Y
Javits	N	Y	Y	Y	Y	†	N	N
NORTH CAROLINA								
Morgan	N	Y	Y	N	Y	Y	Y	N
Helms	Y	N	N	Y	Y	Y	N	Y
NORTH DAKOTA								
Burdick	N	Y	Y	N	N	N	Y	Y
Young	Y	Y	Y	?	?	Y	Y	Y
OHIO								
Glenn	N	Y	Y	Y	?	Y	Y	N
Metzenbaum	N	Y	Y	Y	N	N	Y	N
OKLAHOMA								
Bartlett	Y	Y	Y	N	Y	Y	Y	Y
Bellmon	Y	N	Y	N	Y	Y	Y	Y
OREGON								
Hatfield, M.	N	Y	Y	Y	Y	Y	N	Y
Packwood	N	Y	Y	N	Y	Y	Y	Y
PENNSYLVANIA								
Heinz	N	N	Y	Y	Y	Y	N	Y
Schweiker	?	?	?	?	?	Y	N	Y
RHODE ISLAND								
Pell	N	Y	Y	?	?	†	Y	Y
Chafee	N	N	Y	?	?	Y	Y	Y
SOUTH CAROLINA								
Hollings	N	Y	Y	▮	#	Y	Y	Y
Thurmond	Y	Y	Y	N	Y	Y	N	Y
SOUTH DAKOTA								
Abourezk	N	Y	Y	#	?	?	?	N
McGovern	N	Y	Y	N	N	Y	Y	N
TENNESSEE								
Sasser	N	Y	Y	Y	Y	Y	Y	Y
Baker	?	?	?	?	?	Y	N	Y
TEXAS								
Bentsen	Y	Y	Y	?	Y	Y	Y	Y
Tower	†	?	?	?	†	?	?	†
UTAH								
Garn	Y	Y	Y	Y	Y	Y	Y	Y
Hatch	Y	Y	Y	N	Y	Y	Y	Y
VERMONT								
Leahy	N	Y	Y	Y	Y	†	Y	Y
Stafford	Y	Y	Y	Y	Y	Y	Y	Y
VIRGINIA								
*Byrd, H.	Y	N	N	N	Y	Y	Y	Y
Scott	?	?	?	?	?	Y	N	Y
WASHINGTON								
Jackson	N	Y	Y	Y	Y	N	Y	Y
Magnuson	N	Y	Y	N	Y	Y	Y	Y
WEST VIRGINIA								
Byrd, R.	Y	Y	Y	N	Y	Y	Y	Y
Randolph	†	†	†	†	✓	Y	N	Y
WISCONSIN								
Nelson	N	Y	Y	Y	N	N	Y	N
Proxmire	N	Y	N	Y	N	N	Y	N
WYOMING								
Hansen	N	N	Y	N	Y	Y	Y	Y
Wallop	Y	N	Y	N	Y	Y	N	Y

Democrats ***Republicans***

Byrd elected as independent.

KEY

- Y Voted for (yea).
- ✓ Paired for.
- † Announced for.
- # CQ Poll for.
- N Voted against (nay).
- X Paired against.
- \- Announced against.
- ▮ CQ Poll against.
- P Voted "present."
- ● Voted "present" to avoid possible conflict of interest.
- ? Did not vote or otherwise make a position known.

454. HR 13511. Revenue Act of 1978. Glenn, D-Ohio, motion to table (kill) the Glenn "sunset" amendment, to the Muskie, D-Maine, amendment, to establish a schedule whereby all tax expenditures (deductions, credits, exclusions and others) would expire once every 10 years unless renewed. Motion rejected 38-45: R 21-8; D 17-37 (ND 11-27; SD 6-10), Oct. 7, 1978. (The Muskie amendment was also a sunset provision on direct spending programs; both the Muskie and Glenn amendments were ruled out of order subsequently.)

455. HR 7843. Omnibus Judgeships Bill. Eastland, D-Miss., motion to concur in the House amendment, to the Senate amendment to the bill, stipulating the areas of agreement between the House and Senate conferees on the bill to provide for the appointment of an additional 35 federal circuit court judges and 117 district court judges. Motion agreed to (thus cleared for the president) 67-15: R 15-14; D 52-1 (ND 36-0; SD 16-1), Oct. 7, 1978. A "yea" was a vote supporting the president's position.

456. HR 12932. Interior Appropriations, Fiscal 1979. Adoption of the conference report on the bill to appropriate $11,578,692,000 for fiscal 1979 for the Interior Department and various programs of the Energy Department and related agencies. Adopted (thus cleared for the president) 79-5: R 27-2; D 52-3 (ND 36-2; SD 16-1), Oct. 7, 1978. The president had requested $12,878,467,000.

457. HR 13511. Revenue Act of 1978. Metzenbaum, D-Ohio, amendment to allow investment tax credits for rehabilitation of commercial and industrial buildings at least 20 years old. Adopted 38-31: R 10-14; D 28-17 (ND 21-10; SD 7-7), Oct. 7, 1978. A "yea" was a vote supporting the president's position.

458. HR 13511. Revenue Act of 1978. Danforth, R-Mo., motion to table (kill) the Kennedy, D-Mass., amendment to phase in over three years a provision allowing tax deductions for only half instead of the total cost of business meals. Motion agreed to 49-9: R 24-0; D 25-9 (ND 16-9; SD 9-0), Oct. 7, 1978. A "nay" was a vote supporting the president's position.

459. HR 13511. Revenue Act of 1978. Long, D-La., motion to table (kill) the Church, D-Idaho, amendment to phase out the law allowing U.S.-controlled corporations to defer taxes on foreign-earned income until it is brought into the United States. Motion agreed to 61-17: R 30-0; D 31-17 (ND 19-14; SD 12-3), Oct. 9, 1978. A "nay" was a vote supporting the president's position.

460. HR 13511. Revenue Act of 1978. Heinz, R-Pa., appeal of the ruling of the chair sustaining the Muskie, D-Maine, point of order that the Heinz amendment to provide a $75 refundable "energy tax credit" for low-income elderly people violated the Congressional Budget Act by causing revenues to be less than set by the second budget resolution for fiscal 1979. Ruling of the chair sustained 65-22: R 19-14; D 46-8 (ND 28-8; SD 18-0), Oct. 9, 1978.

461. HR 13511. Revenue Act of 1978. Byrd, D-W.Va., motion to invoke cloture (thus ending debate) on the Finance Committee substitute amendment to the bill. Motion agreed to 62-28: R 30-3; D 32-25 (ND 17-22; SD 15-3), Oct. 9, 1978. A three-fifths majority of the total Senate (60) is necessary to invoke cloture.

CQ Senate Votes 462-469

Corresponding to Congressional Record Votes 466, 467, 468, 469, 470, 471, 472, 473

	462	463	464	465	466	467	468	469
ALABAMA								
Allen, M.	Y	Y	?	?	?	?	Y	?
Sparkman	Y	Y	?	Y	X	Y	Y	N
ALASKA								
Gravel	Y	Y	Y	?	Y	Y	Y	N
Stevens	Y	Y	Y	N	N	Y	Y	N
ARIZONA								
DeConcini	Y	Y	Y	N	Y	Y	Y	N
Goldwater	N	Y	?	Y	N	Y	Y	N
ARKANSAS								
Bumpers	?	?	?	?	?	N	Y	N
Hodges	Y	Y	Y	N	Y	Y	Y	Y
CALIFORNIA								
Cranston	Y	Y	Y	Y	N	N	Y	N
Hayakawa	Y	Y	Y	N	Y	Y	Y	N
COLORADO								
Hart	Y	Y	Y	N	Y	Y	?	Y
Haskell	?	?	?	?	?	?	?	?
CONNECTICUT								
Ribicoff	Y	Y	N	Y	N	Y	N	N
Weicker	Y	Y	N	N	Y	Y	Y	N
DELAWARE								
Biden	Y	Y	Y	N	Y	Y	Y	N
Roth	Y	Y	Y	N	N	Y	Y	N
FLORIDA								
Chiles	Y	Y	Y	Y	Y	Y	Y	N
Stone	Y	Y	Y	N	Y	Y	Y	N
GEORGIA								
Nunn	Y	Y	Y	Y	Y	Y	N	N
Talmadge	Y	Y	Y	Y	N	N	N	N
HAWAII								
Inouye	Y	Y	Y	Y	N	Y	Y	N
Matsunaga	Y	Y	Y	?	Y	N	N	N
IDAHO								
Church	Y	Y	Y	Y	Y	N	Y	N
McClure	?	?	?	?	?	?	?	?
ILLINOIS								
Stevenson	Y	Y	N	Y	?	N	N	N
Percy	†	†	Y	N	N	Y	Y	N
INDIANA								
Bayh	Y	Y	Y	Y	Y	N	Y	Y
Lugar	N	Y	Y	N	Y	Y	Y	N
IOWA								
Clark	Y	Y	N	Y	Y	N	Y	Y
Culver	Y	Y	N	Y	Y	N	Y	Y
KANSAS								
Dole	Y	Y	Y	N	Y	Y	Y	N
Pearson	Y	Y	Y	Y	N	Y	Y	N
KENTUCKY								
Ford	Y	Y	Y	N	Y	Y	Y	N
Huddleston	Y	Y	Y	Y	Y	N	Y	N
LOUISIANA								
Johnston	Y	Y	Y	Y	N	Y	Y	N
Long	Y	Y	Y	Y	N	N	N	N
MAINE								
Hathaway	#	#	N	#	#	▮	#	#
Muskie	Y	Y	N	Y	Y	N	Y	Y
MARYLAND								
Sarbanes	Y	Y	N	Y	Y	N	Y	N
Mathias	Y	Y	N	N	Y	Y	Y	N
MASSACHUSETTS								
Kennedy	Y	Y	N	Y	Y	N	Y	Y
Brooke	Y	Y	Y	N	Y	Y	Y	N
MICHIGAN								
Riegle	Y	Y	N	N	Y	Y	Y	N
Griffin	?	?	Y	-	Y	Y	Y	N
MINNESOTA								
Anderson	†	?	?	?	Y	Y	Y	N
Humphrey, M.	Y	Y	?	Y	†	N	Y	N
MISSISSIPPI								
Eastland	N	Y	?	?	N	N	N	N
Stennis	N	Y	Y	?	N	N	N	N
MISSOURI								
Eagleton	Y	Y	Y	Y	Y	Y	Y	N
Danforth	Y	Y	Y	N	N	Y	Y	N
MONTANA								
Melcher	Y	Y	✓	?	✓	†	†	?
Hatfield, P.	Y	Y	X	Y	Y	?	Y	N
NEBRASKA								
Zorinsky	Y	Y	Y	N	Y	Y	Y	N
Curtis	N	Y	N	N	N	Y	N	N
NEVADA								
Cannon	?	?	Y	Y	Y	Y	Y	N
Laxalt	N	N	Y	N	Y	Y	Y	N
NEW HAMPSHIRE								
Durkin	Y	Y	N	?	Y	Y	Y	N
McIntyre	Y	Y	Y	Y	Y	N	Y	N
NEW JERSEY								
Williams	Y	Y	Y	Y	Y	Y	Y	N
Case	Y	Y	?	N	Y	Y	Y	N
NEW MEXICO								
Domenici	†	†	†	?	?	?	†	?
Schmitt	N	Y	Y	N	Y	Y	Y	N
NEW YORK								
Moynihan	Y	Y	N	Y	N	Y	N	N
Javits	Y	Y	N	N	N	Y	Y	N
NORTH CAROLINA								
Morgan	Y	Y	Y	Y	N	N	Y	N
Helms	Y	Y	Y	N	Y	Y	Y	N
NORTH DAKOTA								
Burdick	Y	Y	Y	Y	Y	N	Y	N
Young	Y	Y	Y	N	Y	Y	N	N
OHIO								
Glenn	Y	Y	N	Y	Y	N	Y	N
Metzenbaum	Y	Y	N	Y	Y	N	Y	Y
OKLAHOMA								
Bartlett	N	Y	Y	N	N	Y	P	N
Bellmon	N	Y	Y	N	N	Y	N	N
OREGON								
Hatfield, M.	Y	Y	Y	N	Y	Y	Y	N
Packwood	✓	Y	Y	N	Y	Y	Y	N
PENNSYLVANIA								
Heinz	Y	Y	Y	N	Y	Y	Y	N
Schweiker	Y	Y	Y	N	Y	Y	Y	N
RHODE ISLAND								
Pell	Y	Y	Y	Y	Y	N	Y	N
Chafee	Y	Y	Y	N	Y	Y	Y	N
SOUTH CAROLINA								
Hollings	Y	Y	N	Y	Y	N	N	N
Thurmond	Y	Y	Y	-	Y	Y	Y	N
SOUTH DAKOTA								
Abourezk	Y	Y	N	Y	?	?	Y	Y
McGovern	Y	Y	Y	Y	Y	N	Y	Y
TENNESSEE								
Sasser	Y	Y	Y	Y	Y	Y	Y	N
Baker	Y	Y	Y	N	N	Y	N	N
TEXAS								
Bentsen	Y	Y	N	Y	N	Y	N	N
Tower	X	X	?	-	?	†	†	-
UTAH								
Garn	N	N	Y	N	Y	Y	Y	N
Hatch	N	N	Y	Y	Y	Y	Y	N
VERMONT								
Leahy	Y	Y	Y	Y	Y	Y	Y	N
Stafford	Y	✓	Y	N	Y	Y	Y	N
VIRGINIA								
*Byrd, H.	Y	Y	Y	Y	N	Y	N	N
Scott	N	Y	Y	?	N	Y	N	N
WASHINGTON								
Jackson	Y	Y	Y	Y	Y	N	Y	N
Magnuson	Y	Y	Y	#	Y	N	Y	N
WEST VIRGINIA								
Byrd, R.	Y	Y	Y	Y	Y	N	Y	N
Randolph	Y	Y	Y	Y	Y	N	Y	N
WISCONSIN								
Nelson	Y	Y	Y	Y	Y	N	Y	N
Proxmire	Y	Y	Y	N	Y	Y	Y	N
WYOMING								
Hansen	N	Y	Y	N	N	Y	N	N
Wallop	Y	Y	#	▮	#	#	#	▮

Democrats ***Republicans***

*Byrd elected as independent.

KEY

- Y Voted for (yea).
- ✓ Paired for.
- † Announced for.
- # CQ Poll for.
- N Voted against (nay).
- X Paired against.
- \- Announced against.
- ▮ CQ Poll against.
- P Voted "present."
- ● Voted "present" to avoid possible conflict of interest.
- ? Did not vote or otherwise make a position known.

462. HR 4018. National Energy Act — Public Utility Rates. Adoption of the conference report on the bill to revamp the method for setting utility rates to more accurately reflect the cost of providing electricity. Adopted 76-13: R 21-11; D 55-2 (ND 39-0; SD 16-2), Oct. 9, 1978. A "yea" was a vote supporting the president's position.

463. HR 5037. National Energy Act — Conservation. Adoption of the conference report on the bill to encourage conservation of energy by providing loans to homeowners, schools and hospitals to make energy-saving improvements, establishing energy consumption standards for home appliances and through other methods. Adopted 86-3: R 29-3; D 57-0 (ND 39-0; SD 18-0), Oct. 9, 1978. A "yea" was a vote supporting the president's position.

464. HR 13511. Revenue Act of 1978. Nunn, D-Ga. amendment to cut individual income taxes by about 5 percent annually in 1980-83 provided that federal outlays increased no more than 1 percent annually, in real terms, that the federal share of gross national product declined each year by specified amounts and that the federal budget was balanced by 1982. Adopted 65-20: R 28-4; D 37-16 (ND 24-14; SD 13-2), Oct. 9, 1978.

465. HR 13511. Revenue Act of 1978. Long, D-La., motion to table (kill) the Danforth, R-Mo., amendment to provide for a reduction in the maximum corporate income tax to 44 percent in 1981 and 1982 (under a Finance Committee provision, it would drop to 46 percent from 48 percent in 1979). Motion agreed to 44-37: R 3-28; D 41-9 (ND 29-6; SD 12-3), Oct. 10, 1978.

466. HR 13511. Revenue Act of 1978. Nelson, D-Wis., amendment to substitute, for the Finance Committee provision increasing the allowable range for asset depreciation under the Asset Depreciation Range (ADR) system, a provision allowing three-year straight-line depreciation on the first $25,000 of machinery and equipment purchased each year. Adopted 62-25: R 21-13; D 41-12 (ND 33-4; SD 8-8), Oct. 10, 1978.

467. HR 13511. Revenue Act of 1978. Danforth, R-Mo., amendment to reduce the maximum corporate income tax rate to 45 percent in 1980 and to 44 percent in 1981. Adopted 60-30: R 34-0; D 26-30 (ND 16-22; SD 10-8), Oct. 10, 1978.

468. HR 13511. Revenue Act of 1978. Church, D-Idaho, amendment to provide for a once-only complete capital gains tax exclusion for profits from the sale of personal homes priced up to $100,000 and a partial exclusion for more expensive homes, available only to people who are disabled or 55 years of age or older. (The provision replaced a Finance Committee proposal to allow a comparable reusable exclusion for houses priced at $50,000, available to all taxpayers.) Adopted 73-18: R 27-6; D 46-12 (ND 35-4; SD 11-8), Oct. 10, 1978.

469. HR 13511. Revenue Act of 1978. Kennedy, D-Mass., amendment to delete the Finance Committee provision increasing to 70 percent from 50 percent the amount of capital gains excluded from ordinary taxation. Rejected 10-82: R 0-34; D 10-48 (ND 9-31; SD 1-17), Oct. 10, 1978.

Corresponding to Congressional Record Votes 474, 475, 476, 477, 478, 479, 480

KEY

- Y Voted for (yea).
- ✓ Paired for.
- † Announced for.
- # CQ Poll for.
- N Voted against (nay).
- X Paired against.
- \- Announced against.
- ▮ CQ Poll against.
- P Voted "present."
- ● Voted "present" to avoid possible conflict of interest.
- ? Did not vote or otherwise make a position known.

	470	471	472	473	474	475	476
ALABAMA							
Allen, M.	?	Y	?	?	Y	?	?
Sparkman	Y	Y	Y	Y	Y	?	?
ALASKA							
Gravel	Y	Y	Y	Y	Y	Y	Y
Stevens	Y	Y	N	N	X	Y	Y
ARIZONA							
DeConcini	Y	N	N	N	Y	Y	Y
Goldwater	Y	Y	N	N	Y	Y	Y
ARKANSAS							
Bumpers	Y	N	N	N	Y	N	Y
Hodges	N	N	N	Y	Y	Y	Y
CALIFORNIA							
Cranston	Y	Y	N	N	Y	Y	Y
Hayakawa	Y	Y	N	N	Y	Y	Y
COLORADO							
Hart	N	N	Y	Y	Y	Y	Y
Haskell	?	?	?	?	?	†	?
CONNECTICUT							
Ribicoff	Y	Y	Y	Y	Y	Y	Y
Weicker	Y	Y	Y	Y	Y	Y	Y
DELAWARE							
Biden	Y	N	Y	Y	Y	Y	Y
Roth	Y	Y	N	N	Y	Y	Y
FLORIDA							
Chiles	Y	Y	N	N	Y	Y	Y
Stone	Y	Y	Y	Y	Y	Y	Y
GEORGIA							
Nunn	Y	Y	Y	Y	Y	Y	Y
Talmadge	Y	Y	Y	Y	Y	Y	Y
HAWAII							
Inouye	Y	Y	Y	Y	Y	Y	Y
Matsunaga	Y	Y	Y	Y	Y	Y	Y
IDAHO							
Church	N	N	N	N	Y	Y	Y
McClure	?	?	?	?	?	?	?
ILLINOIS							
Stevenson	N	N	Y	Y	Y	Y	Y
Percy	Y	Y	Y	Y	Y	Y	Y
INDIANA							
Bayh	Y	N	Y	Y	Y	Y	Y
Lugar	Y	N	N	N	Y	Y	Y
IOWA							
Clark	N	N	Y	Y	Y	Y	Y
Culver	N	N	Y	Y	Y	Y	Y
KANSAS							
Dole	Y	Y	N	N	Y	Y	Y
Pearson	Y	N	N	N	Y	?	?
KENTUCKY							
Ford	Y	N	N	N	Y	Y	Y
Huddleston	Y	Y	Y	Y	Y	Y	Y
LOUISIANA							
Johnston	N	Y	Y	Y	Y	Y	Y
Long	Y	Y	Y	Y	Y	Y	Y
MAINE							
Hathaway	#	▮	?	?	#	#	#
Muskie	Y	N	Y	Y	Y	Y	Y
MARYLAND							
Sarbanes	N	N	Y	Y	Y	Y	Y
Mathias	Y	N	N	N	Y	Y	Y
MASSACHUSETTS							
Kennedy	N	N	Y	Y	Y	Y	Y
Brooke	Y	N	N	N	Y	Y	Y
MICHIGAN							
Riegle	N	N	N	N	Y	Y	Y
Griffin	Y	N	N	N	Y	Y	Y
MINNESOTA							
Anderson	Y	N	Y	Y	Y	Y	Y
Humphrey, M.	N	N	Y	Y	Y	Y	Y
MISSISSIPPI							
Eastland	Y	Y	Y	Y	?	Y	Y
Stennis	Y	Y	Y	Y	Y	Y	Y
MISSOURI							
Eagleton	Y	Y	Y	Y	Y	Y	Y
Danforth	Y	Y	Y	Y	Y	Y	Y
MONTANA							
Melcher	?	✓	-	-	†	Y	Y
Hatfield, P.	Y	Y	N	N	Y	Y	Y
NEBRASKA							
Zorinsky	Y	N	N	N	Y	Y	Y
Curtis	Y	Y	Y	Y	Y	Y	?
NEVADA							
Cannon	Y	Y	N	Y	Y	Y	Y
Laxalt	Y	Y	N	N	Y	Y	Y
NEW HAMPSHIRE							
Durkin	N	N	N	N	Y	Y	Y
McIntyre	Y	Y	-	-	†	†	?
NEW JERSEY							
Williams	Y	X	Y	Y	Y	Y	Y
Case	Y	Y	N	N	Y	Y	Y
NEW MEXICO							
Domenici	?	?	?	?	†	†	?
Schmitt	Y	Y	N	N	Y	Y	Y
NEW YORK							
Moynihan	Y	Y	Y	Y	Y	Y	Y
Javits	Y	N	N	N	Y	†	?
NORTH CAROLINA							
Morgan	Y	N	N	N	Y	Y	Y
Helms	Y	Y	Y	N	Y	Y	Y
NORTH DAKOTA							
Burdick	N	N	Y	Y	Y	Y	Y
Young	Y	Y	N	N	Y	Y	Y
OHIO							
Glenn	Y	N	Y	Y	Y	Y	Y
Metzenbaum	N	N	Y	Y	N	Y	Y
OKLAHOMA							
Bartlett	Y	Y	N	N	Y	Y	Y
Bellmon	Y	Y	N	N	Y	Y	Y
OREGON							
Hatfield, M.	Y	N	N	N	N	Y	Y
Packwood	Y	N	N	N	Y	Y	?
PENNSYLVANIA							
Heinz	Y	N	N	N	Y	Y	Y
Schweiker	Y	Y	N	N	Y	Y	Y
RHODE ISLAND							
Pell	N	N	N	N	Y	Y	Y
Chafee	Y	N	Y	Y	Y	Y	Y
SOUTH CAROLINA							
Hollings	N	N	N	N	N	Y	Y
Thurmond	Y	Y	N	N	Y	Y	Y
SOUTH DAKOTA							
Abourezk	N	?	Y	Y	N	Y	Y
McGovern	N	N	Y	Y	Y	Y	Y
TENNESSEE							
Sasser	N	N	Y	Y	Y	Y	Y
Baker	Y	Y	N	N	Y	?	?
TEXAS							
Bentsen	Y	Y	Y	Y	Y	Y	Y
Tower	†	†	-	-	†	?	?
UTAH							
Garn	Y	Y	N	N	Y	Y	Y
Hatch	Y	Y	N	N	Y	Y	Y
VERMONT							
Leahy	N	N	Y	Y	Y	Y	Y
Stafford	Y	Y	N	N	Y	Y	Y
VIRGINIA							
*Byrd, H.	Y	Y	Y	Y	Y	Y	Y
Scott	Y	Y	N	N	Y	?	?
WASHINGTON							
Jackson	Y	N	Y	Y	Y	Y	Y
Magnuson	Y	Y	Y	Y	Y	Y	Y
WEST VIRGINIA							
Byrd, R.	N	Y	Y	Y	Y	Y	Y
Randolph	Y	Y	Y	Y	Y	Y	Y
WISCONSIN							
Nelson	N	N	Y	Y	Y	Y	Y
Proxmire	Y	N	Y	Y	Y	Y	Y
WYOMING							
Hansen	Y	Y	Y	Y	Y	Y	Y
Wallop	?	#	?	?	✓	Y	Y

Democrats ***Republicans***

**Byrd elected as independent.*

470. HR 13511. Revenue Act of 1978. Long, D-La., motion to table (kill) the Kennedy, D-Mass., amendment to prohibit tax deductions for excess of first-class over coach air fare for business trips, business-related purchase of sports and theater tickets, and business meals in excess of $25. Motion agreed to 70-22: R 34-0; D 36-22 (ND 22-18; SD 14-4), Oct. 10, 1978. A "nay" was a vote supporting the president's position.

471. HR 13511. Revenue Act of 1978. Long, D-La., motion to table (kill) the Glenn, D-Ohio, amendment to require periodic re-approval of all the tax expenditures in the bill ("sunset"). Motion agreed to 50-41: R 24-10; D 26-31 (ND 13-25; SD 13-6), Oct. 10, 1978.

472. HR 13511. Revenue Act of 1978. Helms, R-N.C., appeal of the ruling of the chair that the Helms amendment *(see vote 473, below)* to delete a Finance Committee amendment eliminating the tax deduction for state and local gas taxes was out of order because it violated the revenue floor established by the second budget resolution for fiscal 1979. Ruling of the chair sustained 49-41: R 7-27; D 42-15 (ND 30-9; SD 12-6), Oct. 10, 1978. A "yea" was a vote supporting the president's position.

473. HR 13511. Revenue Act of 1978. Byrd, Ind-Va., motion to table (kill) the Helms, R-N.C., motion to reconsider the vote by which the Helms, R-N.C., appeal of the chair's ruling was rejected *(see vote 472)*. Tabling motion agreed to 50-41: R 6-28; D 44-13 (ND 31-8; SD 13-5), Oct. 10, 1978.

474. HR 13511. Revenue Act of 1978. Passage of the bill to reduce taxes by $29.1 billion in 1979. Passed 86-4: R 32-1; D 54-3 (ND 37-2; SD 17-1), Oct. 10, 1978.

475. S 2. Sunset Bill. Passage of the bill to automatically terminate federal spending programs unless they were specifically re-authorized by Congress after a comprehensive review every 10 years. Passed 87-1: R 31-0; D 56-1 (ND 40-0; SD 16-1), Oct. 11, 1978. A "yea" was a vote supporting the president's position.

476. Exec J, 95th Cong, 2nd Sess. U.S.-Japan Fisheries Convention. Adoption of the resolution of ratification of the protocol, signed on April 25, 1978, to the International Convention for the High Seas Fisheries of the North Pacific to limit Japanese salmon fishing in the North Pacific and to organize joint Japanese-U.S.-Canadian research on Pacific salmon and mammals. Adopted 86-0: R 29-0; D 57-0 (ND 40-0; SD 17-0), Oct. 11, 1978. A "yea" was a vote supporting the president's position.

CQ Senate Votes 477-483

Corresponding to Congressional Record Votes 481, 482, 483, 484, 485, 486, 487

	477	478	479	480	481	482	483
ALABAMA							
Allen, M.	?	Y	Y	Y	?	?	?
Sparkman	Y	Y	Y	N	Y	Y	Y
ALASKA							
Gravel	?	Y	?	N	Y	Y	Y
Stevens	Y	Y	Y	Y	N	N	Y
ARIZONA							
DeConcini	Y	Y	Y	Y	Y	N	Y
Goldwater	N	N	Y	Y	N	N	†
ARKANSAS							
Bumpers	Y	Y	Y	N	Y	Y	Y
Hodges	Y	Y	Y	N	Y	Y	Y
CALIFORNIA							
Cranston	Y	Y	N	N	Y	Y	Y
Hayakawa	Y	Y	Y	Y	Y	N	Y
COLORADO							
Hart	Y	Y	Y	N	Y	Y	Y
Haskell	?	?	?	?	?	?	?
CONNECTICUT							
Ribicoff	Y	?	N	N	Y	Y	?
Weicker	N	Y	#	▮	#	#	#
DELAWARE							
Biden	?	?	Y	N	Y	Y	Y
Roth	Y	Y	Y	Y	Y	N	Y
FLORIDA							
Chiles	Y	Y	Y	N	Y	Y	Y
Stone	Y	Y	Y	N	Y	Y	Y
GEORGIA							
Nunn	Y	Y	Y	Y	Y	Y	Y
Talmadge	Y	Y	Y	Y	Y	Y	Y
HAWAII							
Inouye	#	Y	Y	Y	Y	Y	#
Matsunaga	?	?	Y	N	Y	Y	Y
IDAHO							
Church	Y	Y	Y	Y	Y	Y	Y
McClure	?	?	†	†	?	?	?
ILLINOIS							
Stevenson	?	Y	Y	N	Y	Y	Y
Percy	Y	Y	Y	Y	Y	Y	Y
INDIANA							
Bayh	Y	Y	Y	N	Y	Y	Y
Lugar	Y	Y	Y	Y	Y	N	Y
IOWA							
Clark	?	?	?	?	?	?	?
Culver	Y	Y	N	N	Y	Y	Y
KANSAS							
Dole	Y	Y	Y	Y	Y	N	Y
Pearson	Y	Y	Y	Y	Y	Y	Y
KENTUCKY							
Ford	Y	Y	Y	Y	N	N	Y
Huddleston	N	Y	Y	Y	Y	Y	Y
LOUISIANA							
Johnston	Y	Y	Y	Y	N	Y	Y
Long	Y	Y	Y	Y	N	Y	Y
MAINE							
Hathaway	#	?	▮	▮	#	#	#
Muskie	Y	Y	N	N	Y	Y	Y
MARYLAND							
Sarbanes	Y	Y	Y	N	Y	Y	Y
Mathias	?	?	?	?	?	?	?
MASSACHUSETTS							
Kennedy	Y	Y	N	N	Y	Y	Y
Brooke	Y	Y	Y	N	Y	Y	Y
MICHIGAN							
Riegle	Y	Y	Y	N	Y	Y	Y
Griffin	Y	N	†	X	†	✓	†
MINNESOTA							
Anderson	Y	Y	N	N	Y	Y	?
Humphrey, M.	Y	Y	N	N	Y	Y	Y
MISSISSIPPI							
Eastland	Y	Y	Y	Y	Y	Y	?
Stennis	Y	Y	Y	Y	Y	Y	Y
MISSOURI							
Eagleton	Y	Y	Y	N	Y	Y	Y
Danforth	Y	Y	Y	Y	Y	Y	Y
MONTANA							
Melcher	Y	Y	Y	Y	Y	Y	Y
Hatfield, P.	Y	Y	Y	N	Y	Y	Y
NEBRASKA							
Zorinsky	Y	Y	Y	N	Y	Y	Y
Curtis	Y	Y	Y	Y	N	N	Y
NEVADA							
Cannon	Y	Y	Y	N	Y	Y	Y
Laxalt	Y	Y	Y	Y	Y	N	†
NEW HAMPSHIRE							
Durkin	Y	Y	N	N	Y	Y	Y
McIntyre	?	?	?	?	?	?	†
NEW JERSEY							
Williams	Y	Y	N	N	Y	Y	Y
Case	#	?	N	N	Y	Y	Y
NEW MEXICO							
Domenici	?	?	?	?	?	?	†
Schmitt	Y	N	Y	Y	Y	N	Y
NEW YORK							
Moynihan	Y	Y	Y	N	Y	Y	Y
Javits	Y	Y	N	N	Y	Y	Y
NORTH CAROLINA							
Morgan	Y	Y	Y	Y	Y	Y	†
Helms	?	Y	Y	Y	N	N	Y
NORTH DAKOTA							
Burdick	Y	Y	Y	N	Y	Y	Y
Young	Y	Y	Y	Y	Y	N	Y
OHIO							
Glenn	Y	Y	Y	N	Y	Y	Y
Metzenbaum	Y	N	N	N	Y	Y	Y
OKLAHOMA							
Bartlett	Y	N	Y	Y	N	N	Y
Bellmon	Y	N	Y	N	Y	Y	Y
OREGON							
Hatfield, M.	Y	Y	Y	Y	Y	#	N
Packwood	?	?	Y	Y	Y	N	Y
PENNSYLVANIA							
Heinz	Y	Y	Y	Y	Y	Y	Y
Schweiker	Y	Y	Y	Y	Y	N	Y
RHODE ISLAND							
Pell	Y	Y	N	N	Y	Y	Y
Chafee	Y	Y	Y	N	Y	Y	Y
SOUTH CAROLINA							
Hollings	Y	Y	Y	Y	Y	Y	Y
Thurmond	Y	Y	Y	Y	Y	Y	Y
SOUTH DAKOTA							
Abourezk	Y	Y	N	N	Y	#	#
McGovern	Y	Y	N	N	Y	Y	N
TENNESSEE							
Sasser	Y	Y	Y	N	Y	Y	Y
Baker	?	?	Y	Y	N	N	Y
TEXAS							
Bentsen	Y	Y	Y	Y	Y	Y	Y
Tower	?	?	†	✓	?	X	†
UTAH							
Garn	Y	Y	Y	Y	Y	N	Y
Hatch	Y	Y	Y	Y	N	N	Y
VERMONT							
Leahy	Y	Y	Y	N	Y	Y	Y
Stafford	Y	Y	Y	N	Y	Y	Y
VIRGINIA							
*Byrd, H.	Y	Y	#	Y	Y	N	Y
Scott	?	?	?	?	?	?	?
WASHINGTON							
Jackson	Y	Y	Y	N	Y	Y	Y
Magnuson	Y	Y	Y	N	Y	Y	Y
WEST VIRGINIA							
Byrd, R.	Y	Y	N	N	Y	Y	Y
Randolph	Y	Y	N	N	Y	Y	Y
WISCONSIN							
Nelson	Y	Y	N	N	Y	Y	Y
Proxmire	Y	Y	Y	N	Y	Y	N
WYOMING							
Hansen	Y	N	Y	Y	Y	N	Y
Wallop	Y	N	Y	Y	Y	N	Y

Democrats ***Republicans***

Byrd elected as independent.

KEY

- Y Voted for (yea).
- ✓ Paired for.
- † Announced for.
- # CQ Poll for.
- N Voted against (nay).
- X Paired against.
- \- Announced against.
- ▮ CQ Poll against.
- P Voted "present."
- ● Voted "present" to avoid possible conflict of interest.
- ? Did not vote or otherwise make a position known.

477. Procedural Motion. Byrd, D-W.Va., motion to instruct the sergeant at arms to compel the attendance of absent senators. Motion agreed to 78-3: R 27-2; D 51-1 (ND 34-0; SD 17-1), Oct. 12, 1978.

478. HR 5263. Energy Taxes. Byrd, D-W.Va., motion that the Senate proceed to the consideration of the conference report on the Energy Tax Act of 1978. Motion agreed to 77-8: R 23-7; D 54-1 (ND 35-1; SD 19-0), Oct. 12, 1978.

479. HR 5285. Medicare-Medicaid and Hospital Cost Containment. Talmadge, D-Ga., motion to table (kill) the Kennedy, D-Mass., substitute amendment to authorize national revenue limits for hospitals. Motion agreed to 69-18: R 29-2; D 40-16 (ND 22-16; SD 18-0), Oct. 12, 1978. A "nay" was a vote supporting the president's position.

480. HR 5285. Medicare-Medicaid and Hospital Cost Containment. Talmadge, D-Ga., motion to table (kill) the Nelson, D-Wis., substitute amendment to authorize prospective reimbursement of hospitals by Medicare and Medicaid, to endorse a voluntary effort by hospitals to cut costs, and to authorize national hospital revenue limits if goals of the voluntary effort were not met. Motion rejected 42-47: R 25-6; D 17-41 (ND 4-35; SD 13-6), Oct. 12, 1978. A "nay" was a vote supporting the president's position. (The Nelson substitute for the bill subsequently was adopted by voice vote.)

481. HR 5285. Medicare-Medicaid and Hospital Cost Containment. Metzenbaum, D-Ohio, amendment, to the Nelson substitute, to revise Medicare-Medicaid reimbursements for services of hospital-based physicians, to ensure that professional rates were paid only for services performed by the physician and to exclude some charges for overhead. Adopted 78-10: R 24-7; D 54-3 (ND 39-0; SD 15-3), Oct. 12, 1978.

482. HR 5285. Medicare-Medicaid and Hospital Cost Containment. Passage of the bill to authorize prospective reimbursement of hospitals by Medicare and Medicaid, to endorse a voluntary effort by hospitals to cut costs, and to authorize national hospital revenue limits if goals of the voluntary effort were not met. Passed 64-22: R 11-19; D 53-3 (ND 37-1; SD 16-2), Oct. 12, 1978. A "yea" was a vote supporting the president's position.

483. HR 13635. Defense Appropriations, Fiscal 1979. Adoption of the conference report on the bill to appropriate $117,255,621,000 for the programs and operation of the Defense Department in fiscal 1979. Adopted (thus cleared for the president) 77-3: R 28-1; D 49-2 (ND 33-2; SD 16-0), Oct. 12, 1978. The president had requested $119,300,283,000 for fiscal 1979.

Corresponding to Congressional Record Votes 488, 489, 490, 491, 492, 493, 494, 495

	484	485	486	487	488	489	490	491
ALABAMA								
Allen, M.	?	?	?	?	?	?	?	?
Sparkman	?	?	Y	Y	N	?	Y	?
ALASKA								
Gravel	Y	Y	Y	Y	Y	Y	Y	Y
Stevens	#	#	Y	N	Y	N	N	N
ARIZONA								
DeConcini	Y	Y	N	Y	N	N	N	Y
Goldwater	?	?	N	N	Y	N	N	N
ARKANSAS								
Bumpers	Y	Y	Y	Y	Y	Y	N	Y
Hodges	Y	Y	Y	Y	N	Y	Y	Y
CALIFORNIA								
Cranston	Y	Y	Y	Y	N	Y	Y	Y
Hayakawa	Y	Y	Y	N	Y	N	N	N
COLORADO								
Hart	Y	Y	Y	Y	Y	N	N	Y
Haskell	?	?	?	?	?	✓	?	?
CONNECTICUT								
Ribicoff	?	?	Y	Y	N	N	Y	Y
Weicker	▮	▮	Y	Y	Y	N	N	N
DELAWARE								
Biden	?	?	Y	N	Y	Y	Y	N
Roth	N	N	N	N	Y	N	N	N
FLORIDA								
Chiles	Y	Y	Y	N	Y	N	N	Y
Stone	Y	Y	Y	N	Y	N	N	Y
GEORGIA								
Nunn	N	N	N	N	Y	N	N	Y
Talmadge	?	?	N	Y	Y	Y	N	Y
HAWAII								
Inouye	Y	Y	Y	Y	Y	Y	Y	Y
Matsunaga	Y	Y	Y	Y	N	Y	Y	Y
IDAHO								
Church	Y	Y	Y	Y	N	Y	Y	Y
McClure	?	?	?	?	?	?	?	?
ILLINOIS								
Stevenson	?	?	Y	Y	N	?	Y	Y
Percy	N	N	Y	N	Y	N	N	Y
INDIANA								
Bayh	N	Y	Y	Y	N	Y	Y	Y
Lugar	N	N	Y	N	Y	N	N	Y
IOWA								
Clark	Y	Y	Y	Y	N	Y	Y	Y
Culver	Y	Y	Y	Y	N	Y	Y	Y
KANSAS								
Dole	Y	Y	N	N	Y	N	N	Y
Pearson	?	?	Y	Y	Y	N	N	Y
KENTUCKY								
Ford	Y	Y	Y	Y	Y	Y	N	Y
Huddleston	Y	Y	Y	?	?	?	?	?
LOUISIANA								
Johnston	Y	Y	Y	Y	Y	Y	Y	Y
Long	Y	Y	?	Y	N	Y	?	Y
MAINE								
Hathaway	N	N	Y	Y	Y	Y	Y	Y
Muskie	N	N	Y	Y	Y	Y	Y	Y
MARYLAND								
Sarbanes	N	N	Y	Y	N	Y	?	Y
Mathias	N	N	Y	Y	N	N	N	Y
MASSACHUSETTS								
Kennedy	N	N	Y	Y	N	✓	✓	?
Brooke	N	N	Y	Y	Y	Y	Y	Y
MICHIGAN								
Riegle	Y	Y	Y	Y	N	Y	Y	Y
Griffin	?	?	Y	N	Y	N	N	Y
MINNESOTA								
Anderson	Y	Y	Y	Y	N	Y	Y	Y
Humphrey, M.	?	†	Y	Y	N	Y	Y	Y
MISSISSIPPI								
Eastland	?	?	N	Y	Y	X	X	N
Stennis	?	?	N	Y	Y	N	N	N
MISSOURI								
Eagleton	?	?	Y	Y	Y	N	Y	Y
Danforth	Y	Y	Y	N	N	Y	✓	Y
MONTANA								
Melcher	Y	Y	N	Y	N	X	N	Y
Hatfield, P.	Y	Y	Y	Y	N	N	N	Y
NEBRASKA								
Zorinsky	Y	Y	N	N	Y	N	N	Y
Curtis	Y	Y	N	N	Y	N	N	N
NEVADA								
Cannon	Y	Y	N	Y	Y	Y	Y	Y
Laxalt	?	?	N	N	Y	N	N	N
NEW HAMPSHIRE								
Durkin	N	N	Y	Y	N	Y	Y	Y
McIntyre	?	?	Y	Y	N	N	N	Y
NEW JERSEY								
Williams	N	Y	Y	Y	N	Y	Y	Y
Case	?	?	Y	Y	N	Y	Y	Y
NEW MEXICO								
Domenici	?	?	?	?	?	?	?	?
Schmitt	Y	Y	N	▮	#	-	?	?
NEW YORK								
Moynihan	?	?	Y	Y	Y	Y	Y	Y
Javits	N	N	Y	Y	N	N	N	Y
NORTH CAROLINA								
Morgan	Y	Y	#	N	Y	Y	N	Y
Helms	Y	N	N	N	Y	N	N	N
NORTH DAKOTA								
Burdick	Y	Y	N	Y	Y	Y	Y	Y
Young	Y	Y	N	N	#	#	X	?
OHIO								
Glenn	N	Y	Y	Y	N	Y	Y	Y
Metzenbaum	N	N	Y	Y	Y	Y	Y	Y
OKLAHOMA								
Bartlett	Y	Y	N	N	Y	N	N	N
Bellmon	Y	Y	Y	N	Y	N	N	N
OREGON								
Hatfield, M.	Y	Y	N	N	N	N	N	N
Packwood	?	?	Y	N	Y	N	N	Y
PENNSYLVANIA								
Heinz	N	N	?	?	?	Y	Y	Y
Schweiker	N	N	Y	N	N	N	N	Y
RHODE ISLAND								
Pell	N	N	Y	Y	N	Y	Y	Y
Chafee	N	N	Y	N	Y	N	N	Y
SOUTH CAROLINA								
Hollings	N	N	N	N	Y	N	N	Y
Thurmond	Y	Y	N	N	Y	N	N	Y
SOUTH DAKOTA								
Abourezk	?	N	N	#	N	Y	Y	Y
McGovern	▮	#	Y	Y	N	N	Y	Y
TENNESSEE								
Sasser	N	Y	Y	Y	Y	Y	Y	Y
Baker	N	N	Y	N	Y	N	N	Y
TEXAS								
Bentsen	Y	Y	Y	Y	Y	N	N	Y
Tower	?	?	?	?	?	?	?	?
UTAH								
Garn	Y	Y	N	N	Y	N	N	N
Hatch	Y	Y	N	N	Y	N	N	N
VERMONT								
Leahy	Y	Y	Y	Y	N	Y	Y	Y
Stafford	?	?	Y	Y	N	N	N	Y
VIRGINIA								
*Byrd, H.	Y	Y	N	N	Y	N	N	N
Scott	#	#	?	?	?	?	?	?
WASHINGTON								
Jackson	Y	Y	Y	Y	N	Y	Y	Y
Magnuson	Y	Y	Y	Y	N	Y	Y	Y
WEST VIRGINIA								
Byrd, R.	Y	Y	N	Y	N	Y	Y	Y
Randolph	Y	Y	N	Y	N	Y	Y	Y
WISCONSIN								
Nelson	N	?	N	Y	N	N	N	Y
Proxmire	N	N	N	N	Y	N	N	Y
WYOMING								
Hansen	Y	Y	N	N	Y	N	N	N
Wallop	Y	Y	N	N	N	N	?	N

Democrats ***Republicans***

*Byrd elected as independent.

KEY

- Y Voted for (yea).
- ✓ Paired for.
- † Announced for.
- # CQ Poll for.
- N Voted against (nay).
- X Paired against.
- \- Announced against.
- ▮ CQ Poll against.
- P Voted "present."
- ● Voted "present" to avoid possible conflict of interest.
- ? Did not vote or otherwise make a position known.

484. HR 7200. Sugar Stabilization Act. Long, D-La., motion to table (kill) the Metzenbaum, D-Ohio, amendment to set a support price for domestic sugar of 15 cents a pound, through fiscal 1983. Motion agreed to 47-25: R 15-10; D 32-15 (ND 21-12; SD 11-3), Oct. 12, 1978. A "nay" was a vote supporting the president's position.

485. HR 13750. Sugar Stabilization Act. Passage of the bill to authorize U.S. participation in the International Sugar Agreement, to set a 16 cents a pound support price for domestic sugar producers and authorize import quotas and fees to maintain that price, and to establish minimum wages and other benefits for sugar industry workers. Passed 50-22: R 14-11; D 36-11 (ND 24-9; SD 12-2), Oct. 12, 1978. A "nay" was a vote supporting the president's position.

486. HR 12931. Foreign Aid Appropriations, Fiscal 1979. Passage of the bill appropriating $9,135,031,948 for foreign aid programs in fiscal 1979. Passed (thus cleared for the president) 60-31: R 18-15; D 42-16 (ND 32-10; SD 10-6), Oct. 13, 1978. The president had requested $10,387,760,919.

487. HR 50. Full Employment Act. Muskie, D-Maine, amendment, to the Proxmire, D-Wis., amendment, to set a national goal of reducing federal spending, as a percentage of the gross national product, to the lowest possible level, consistent with national needs. Adopted 56-34: R 7-25; D 49-9 (ND 38-3; SD 11-6), Oct. 13, 1978. (The Proxmire amendment as modified by the Muskie amendment was subsequently adopted by voice vote.)

488. HR 50. Full Employment Act. Bellmon, R-Okla., amendment to give the Budget Committees discretion, if the president determined that the bill's unemployment goal could not be reached within the stated time period, as to whether to include in the subsequent first budget resolution a new date for achievement of the goal. Adopted 50-40: R 23-8; D 27-32 (ND 13-29; SD 14-3), Oct. 13, 1978.

489. HR 50. Full Employment Act. Muskie, D-Maine, and Humphrey, D-Minn., amendment to set a national goal of reducing the inflation rate to 3 percent as soon as possible. Rejected 41-45: R 4-28; D 37-17 (ND 29-10; SD 8-7), Oct. 13, 1978.

490. HR 50. Full Employment Act. Eagleton, D-Mo., motion to reconsider the vote *(vote 489, above)* by which the Muskie-Humphrey amendment was rejected. Motion rejected 39-46: R 3-27; D 36-19 (ND 32-8; SD 4-11), Oct. 13, 1978.

491. HR 50. Full Employment Act. Passage of the bill to set national goals of reducing the unemployment rate to 4 percent by 1983 and the inflation rate to 3 percent by 1983 and to 0 percent by 1988. Passed 70-19: R 17-15; D 53-4 (ND 40-1; SD 13-3), Oct. 13, 1978. A "yea" was a vote supporting the president's position.

CQ Senate Votes 492-499

Corresponding to Congressional Record Votes 496, 497, 498, 499, 500, 501, 502, 503

	492	493	494	495	496	497	498	499
ALABAMA								
Allen, M.	?	?	?	?	?	?	Y	Y
Sparkman	?	Y	Y	Y	Y	Y	Y	Y
ALASKA								
Gravel	Y	Y	?	Y	Y	Y	Y	Y
Stevens	N	N	Y	Y	Y	Y	?	?
ARIZONA								
DeConcini	Y	Y	Y	Y	Y	Y	Y	Y
Goldwater	?	?	?	?	?	?	?	?
ARKANSAS								
Bumpers	Y	Y	Y	Y	Y	Y	Y	Y
Hodges	Y	Y	?	Y	Y	Y	Y	Y
CALIFORNIA								
Cranston	Y	?	Y	Y	?	Y	Y	Y
Hayakawa	N	Y	N	?	N	Y	N	N
COLORADO								
Hart	?	Y	?	Y	Y	Y	Y	Y
Haskell	?	?	?	?	?	?	?	?
CONNECTICUT								
Ribicoff	?	Y	Y	Y	Y	Y	Y	Y
Weicker	N	N	N	N	N	Y	N	N
DELAWARE								
Biden	?	Y	Y	Y	Y	Y	Y	Y
Roth	N	Y	Y	Y	Y	Y	Y	N
FLORIDA								
Chiles	Y	Y	?	?	Y	Y	Y	Y
Stone	Y	Y	Y	Y	?	Y	Y	Y
GEORGIA								
Nunn	Y	Y	Y	Y	Y	Y	Y	Y
Talmadge	Y	Y	Y	Y	Y	Y	Y	Y
HAWAII								
Inouye	Y	Y	Y	Y	Y	Y	Y	Y
Matsunaga	Y	?	?	?	Y	Y	Y	Y
IDAHO								
Church	?	Y	Y	Y	Y	Y	Y	Y
McClure	?	?	?	?	?	?	?	?
ILLINOIS								
Stevenson	Y	Y	Y	Y	Y	Y	Y	?
Percy	N	?	?	?	?	?	?	?
INDIANA								
Bayh	Y	Y	Y	Y	Y	Y	Y	Y
Lugar	N	Y	Y	Y	Y	N	Y	N
IOWA								
Clark	Y	Y	Y	Y	Y	Y	Y	Y
Culver	Y	Y	Y	Y	Y	Y	Y	?
KANSAS								
Dole	N	Y	Y	Y	Y	N	Y	Y
Pearson	?	Y	Y	Y	Y	Y	N	N
KENTUCKY								
Ford	Y	Y	Y	Y	Y	Y	Y	Y
Huddleston	?	?	?	?	?	?	?	?
LOUISIANA								
Johnston	Y	Y	Y	Y	Y	Y	Y	Y
Long	Y	Y	?	?	?	?	Y	?
MAINE								
Hathaway	Y	?	?	?	?	?	?	?
Muskie	Y	Y	Y	Y	Y	Y	Y	Y
MARYLAND								
Sarbanes	Y	?	?	?	?	?	?	Y
Mathias	N	?	?	?	?	?	?	?
MASSACHUSETTS								
Kennedy	?	Y	Y	Y	Y	Y	Y	?
Brooke	?	N	Y	Y	Y	Y	N	N
MICHIGAN								
Riegle	Y	Y	Y	Y	Y	Y	Y	Y
Griffin	N	Y	Y	Y	Y	Y	N	N
MINNESOTA								
Anderson	Y	Y	Y	Y	Y	Y	Y	Y
Humphrey, M.	?	Y	?	Y	?	Y	Y	Y
MISSISSIPPI								
Eastland	?	?	?	?	?	?	?	?
Stennis	Y	Y	Y	Y	Y	Y	?	Y
MISSOURI								
Eagleton	Y	Y	Y	Y	Y	Y	Y	Y
Danforth	N	Y	Y	Y	Y	Y	Y	Y
MONTANA								
Melcher	Y	Y	Y	Y	Y	Y	Y	Y
Hatfield, P.	Y	Y	Y	?	Y	Y	Y	N
NEBRASKA								
Zorinsky	Y	Y	Y	Y	Y	Y	Y	Y
Curtis	N	Y	Y	?	Y	N	Y	N
NEVADA								
Cannon	Y	Y	Y	Y	Y	Y	Y	Y
Laxalt	?	Y	Y	Y	Y	N	N	N
NEW HAMPSHIRE								
Durkin	Y	Y	Y	Y	Y	Y	Y	Y
McIntyre	?	Y	Y	Y	Y	Y	Y	Y
NEW JERSEY								
Williams	Y	Y	Y	Y	Y	Y	Y	Y
Case	?	Y	Y	Y	Y	Y	Y	Y
NEW MEXICO								
Domenici	?	?	?	?	?	?	?	?
Schmitt	?	Y	Y	Y	Y	N	N	N
NEW YORK								
Moynihan	Y	Y	Y	?	Y	Y	Y	Y
Javits	N	Y	Y	Y	Y	Y	N	Y
NORTH CAROLINA								
Morgan	Y	Y	Y	Y	Y	Y	Y	Y
Helms	?	N	Y	Y	Y	Y	N	N
NORTH DAKOTA								
Burdick	Y	Y	Y	Y	Y	Y	Y	Y
Young	?	Y	Y	Y	Y	Y	Y	Y
OHIO								
Glenn	Y	Y	Y	Y	Y	Y	Y	Y
Metzenbaum	Y	N	Y	Y	Y	Y	Y	N
OKLAHOMA								
Bartlett	N	N	Y	Y	?	Y	N	N
Bellmon	N	N	Y	Y	Y	Y	N	N
OREGON								
Hatfield, M.	N	Y	Y	Y	Y	Y	N	Y
Packwood	N	Y	Y	Y	Y	Y	N	Y
PENNSYLVANIA								
Heinz	N	Y	Y	Y	Y	Y	N	Y
Schweiker	N	Y	Y	Y	Y	Y	Y	Y
RHODE ISLAND								
Pell	Y	Y	Y	Y	Y	Y	Y	Y
Chafee	N	Y	Y	Y	Y	Y	N	N
SOUTH CAROLINA								
Hollings	Y	Y	Y	Y	Y	Y	Y	Y
Thurmond	N	N	Y	Y	Y	Y	Y	N
SOUTH DAKOTA								
Abourezk	Y	N	Y	Y	Y	Y	N	N
McGovern	Y	Y	Y	Y	Y	Y	Y	Y
TENNESSEE								
Sasser	Y	Y	Y	Y	Y	Y	Y	Y
Baker	N	Y	Y	Y	Y	Y	N	Y
TEXAS								
Bentsen	Y	Y	Y	?	Y	Y	Y	Y
Tower	?	?	?	?	?	?	?	?
UTAH								
Garn	N	?	?	?	?	?	?	?
Hatch	N	N	Y	Y	Y	N	N	N
VERMONT								
Leahy	Y	Y	Y	Y	Y	Y	Y	Y
Stafford	?	Y	Y	Y	Y	Y	Y	?
VIRGINIA								
*Byrd, H.	Y	N	Y	?	Y	Y	Y	N
Scott	?	?	?	?	?	?	?	?
WASHINGTON								
Jackson	Y	Y	Y	Y	Y	Y	Y	Y
Magnuson	Y	Y	Y	Y	Y	Y	Y	Y
WEST VIRGINIA								
Byrd, R.	Y	Y	Y	Y	Y	Y	Y	Y
Randolph	Y	Y	Y	Y	Y	Y	Y	Y
WISCONSIN								
Nelson	Y	Y	Y	Y	Y	Y	Y	Y
Proxmire	Y	Y	Y	Y	Y	Y	N	N
WYOMING								
Hansen	N	N	Y	Y	Y	N	N	N
Wallop	N	N	Y	Y	Y	N	N	N

Democrats *Republicans*

*Byrd elected as independent.

KEY

- Y Voted for (yea).
- ✓ Paired for.
- † Announced for.
- # CQ Poll for.
- N Voted against (nay).
- X Paired against.
- - Announced against.
- ▮ CQ Poll against.
- P Voted "present."
- ● Voted "present" to avoid possible conflict of interest.
- ? Did not vote or otherwise make a position known.

492. McGarry Nomination. Byrd, D-W.Va., motion that the Senate go into closed session to consider President Carter's nomination of John W. McGarry of Massachusetts to be a member of the Federal Election Commission. Motion agreed to 50-25: R 0-25; D 50-0 (ND 35-0; SD 15-0), Oct. 13, 1978.

493. HR 5263. Energy Taxes. Byrd, D-W.Va., motion to invoke cloture (cut off debate) on the adoption of the conference report on the bill to provide tax incentives for the production and conservation of energy. Motion agreed to 71-13: R 20-10; D 51-3 (ND 36-2; SD 15-1), Oct. 14, 1978. A three-fifths majority of the total Senate (60) is necessary to invoke cloture.

494. HR 5263. Energy Taxes. Byrd, D-W.Va., motion to instruct the sergeant at arms to request the attendance of absent senators. Motion agreed to 77-2: R 28-2; D 49-0 (ND 36-0; SD 13-0), Oct. 14, 1978.

495. HR 5263. Energy Taxes. Byrd, D-W.Va., motion to instruct the sergeant at arms to request the attendance of absent senators. Motion agreed to 76-1: R 27-1; D 49-0 (ND 37-0; SD 12-0), Oct. 14, 1978.

496. HR 5263. Energy Taxes. Byrd, D-W.Va., motion to instruct the sergeant at arms to request the attendance of absent senators. Motion agreed to 79-2: R 27-2; D 52-0 (ND 38-0; SD 14-0), Oct. 14, 1978.

497. S 3084. Housing and Community Development. Adoption of the conference report on the bill to revise and extend certain federal housing and community development programs and to authorize $33.3 billion for their operation. Adopted 77-8: R 22-8; D 55-0 (ND 40-0; SD 15-0), Oct. 14, 1978.

498. HR 5263. Energy Taxes. Byrd, D-W.Va., motion to table (kill) the Weicker, R-Conn., appeal of the chair's ruling that the Weicker motion to recess until 5 p.m. was dilatory and thus out of order after cloture had been invoked. Motion to table agreed to 64-21: R 10-19; D 54-2 (ND 38-2; SD 16-0), Oct. 14, 1978.

499. HR 5263. Energy Taxes. Byrd, D-W.Va., motion to table (kill) the Abourezk, D-S.D., appeal of the chair's ruling that the denial of an unanimous consent request did not constitute the transaction of business for the purpose of requesting a second quorum call. Motion to table agreed to 59-23: R 10-18; D 49-5 (ND 34-4; SD 15-1), Oct. 14, 1978.

	500	501	502	503	504	505	506	507
ALABAMA								
Allen, M.	Y	Y	Y	?	?	?	?	?
Sparkman	Y	Y	?	?	?	?	?	?
ALASKA								
Gravel	?	Y	Y	Y	N	?	Y	Y
Stevens	Y	Y	Y	Y	N	?	?	?
ARIZONA								
DeConcini	Y	Y	Y	N	N	Y	Y	Y
Goldwater	?	?	?	?	?	?	?	?
ARKANSAS								
Bumpers	Y	Y	Y	Y	Y	Y	Y	Y
Hodges	Y	Y	Y	Y	N	Y	Y	Y
CALIFORNIA								
Cranston	Y	Y	Y	Y	N	Y	Y	Y
Hayakawa	N	Y	N	N	N	Y	Y	N
COLORADO								
Hart	Y	Y	Y	Y	N	Y	Y	Y
Haskell	?	?	?	?	?	?	?	?
CONNECTICUT								
Ribicoff	Y	Y	Y	Y	N	Y	Y	Y
Weicker	N	Y	N	N	Y	N	N	N
DELAWARE								
Biden	Y	Y	Y	?	?	?	?	?
Roth	Y	Y	Y	Y	N	?	Y	Y
FLORIDA								
Chiles	Y	N	Y	?	N	Y	Y	Y
Stone	Y	N	Y	Y	N	?	?	Y
GEORGIA								
Nunn	Y	Y	Y	Y	N	Y	Y	Y
Talmadge	Y	Y	Y	?	?	?	Y	?
HAWAII								
Inouye	Y	Y	Y	Y	N	Y	Y	Y
Matsunaga	Y	Y	Y	Y	N	?	Y	Y
IDAHO								
Church	Y	Y	Y	Y	N	Y	Y	Y
McClure	?	?	?	?	?	?	?	?
ILLINOIS								
Stevenson	Y	Y	Y	Y	N	?	?	Y
Percy	?	Y	Y	Y	N	Y	Y	Y
INDIANA								
Bayh	Y	Y	Y	Y	Y	Y	N	Y
Lugar	Y	Y	N	Y	N	Y	Y	Y
IOWA								
Clark	?	†	†	?	-	?	†	?
Culver	Y	Y	Y	Y	Y	Y	Y	Y
KANSAS								
Dole	Y	Y	Y	Y	Y	?	N	Y
Pearson	Y	Y	Y	Y	N	?	?	?
KENTUCKY								
Ford	Y	Y	Y	Y	N	Y	Y	Y
Huddleston	?	?	?	?	?	?	?	?
LOUISIANA								
Johnston	Y	Y	Y	Y	N	Y	Y	Y
Long	?	Y	Y	Y	N	?	Y	?
MAINE								
Hathaway	?	?	?	?	?	?	?	?
Muskie	Y	Y	Y	Y	N	Y	Y	Y
MARYLAND								
Sarbanes	Y	Y	Y	?	N	Y	Y	Y
Mathias	Y	Y	N	Y	N	Y	?	?
MASSACHUSETTS								
Kennedy	?	?	?	?	?	?	?	?
Brooke	Y	?	?	?	?	?	?	?
MICHIGAN								
Riegle	Y	Y	Y	Y	Y	Y	N	Y
Griffin	Y	Y	N	Y	N	?	Y	Y
MINNESOTA								
Anderson	Y	Y	Y	Y	Y	Y	Y	Y
Humphrey, M.	Y	Y	Y	Y	N	Y	Y	?
MISSISSIPPI								
Eastland	?	?	?	?	?	?	?	?
Stennis	Y	Y	Y	Y	N	Y	Y	Y
MISSOURI								
Eagleton	Y	Y	?	?	?	?	?	?
Danforth	Y	Y	Y	Y	N	Y	Y	Y
MONTANA								
Melcher	Y	N	Y	Y	N	Y	Y	Y
Hatfield, P.	Y	N	Y	Y	?	Y	Y	Y
NEBRASKA								
Zorinsky	Y	Y	Y	Y	N	Y	Y	Y
Curtis	?	Y	?	Y	Y	?	Y	?
NEVADA								
Cannon	Y	Y	Y	Y	N	Y	Y	Y
Laxalt	Y	Y	N	Y	N	N	?	?
NEW HAMPSHIRE								
Durkin	Y	Y	Y	Y	Y	Y	Y	Y
McIntyre	Y	Y	?	?	?	?	?	?
NEW JERSEY								
Williams	Y	Y	Y	Y	N	Y	Y	Y
Case	Y	Y	Y	Y	N	Y	Y	Y
NEW MEXICO								
Domenici	?	?	?	?	?	?	?	?
Schmitt	Y	Y	N	Y	Y	N	N	Y
NEW YORK								
Moynihan	Y	Y	Y	Y	N	Y	Y	Y
Javits	Y	Y	Y	?	?	Y	Y	?
NORTH CAROLINA								
Morgan	Y	Y	Y	?	N	Y	Y	Y
Helms	Y	Y	N	Y	N	N	Y	Y
NORTH DAKOTA								
Burdick	Y	Y	Y	Y	N	Y	Y	Y
Young	Y	Y	Y	Y	N	Y	Y	Y
OHIO								
Glenn	Y	Y	Y	Y	N	Y	Y	Y
Metzenbaum	Y	Y	N	Y	Y	N	N	Y
OKLAHOMA								
Bartlett	Y	Y	N	Y	Y	N	N	Y
Bellmon	Y	Y	Y	Y	Y	Y	N	Y
OREGON								
Hatfield, M.	Y	Y	Y	Y	N	Y	Y	Y
Packwood	Y	Y	N	Y	N	?	Y	Y
PENNSYLVANIA								
Heinz	Y	Y	N	Y	N	Y	Y	Y
Schweiker	Y	Y	Y	Y	N	Y	Y	Y
RHODE ISLAND								
Pell	Y	Y	Y	Y	N	Y	Y	Y
Chafee	Y	Y	N	Y	Y	Y	N	Y
SOUTH CAROLINA								
Hollings	Y	Y	Y	Y	N	Y	Y	Y
Thurmond	Y	Y	Y	Y	N	N	Y	Y
SOUTH DAKOTA								
Abourezk	Y	Y	N	Y	Y	N	N	Y
McGovern	Y	Y	Y	Y	Y	Y	N	Y
TENNESSEE								
Sasser	Y	Y	Y	Y	N	Y	Y	Y
Baker	Y	Y	N	Y	N	Y	Y	Y
TEXAS								
Bentsen	Y	Y	Y	Y	N	Y	Y	Y
Tower	?	?	?	?	?	?	?	?
UTAH								
Garn	?	?	?	?	?	?	N	Y
Hatch	Y	Y	N	Y	Y	N	N	Y
VERMONT								
Leahy	Y	Y	Y	Y	Y	Y	N	Y
Stafford	?	?	?	?	?	?	?	?
VIRGINIA								
*Byrd, H.	Y	Y	Y	Y	N	?	Y	Y
Scott	?	?	?	?	?	?	?	?
WASHINGTON								
Jackson	Y	Y	Y	Y	N	Y	Y	Y
Magnuson	Y	Y	Y	Y	N	Y	Y	Y
WEST VIRGINIA								
Byrd, R.	Y	Y	Y	Y	N	Y	Y	Y
Randolph	Y	Y	Y	Y	N	Y	Y	Y
WISCONSIN								
Nelson	Y	Y	Y	Y	Y	?	?	Y
Proxmire	Y	Y	N	Y	Y	N	N	Y
WYOMING								
Hansen	?	Y	N	Y	Y	?	N	N
Wallop	Y	Y	N	Y	Y	N	?	Y

Democrats ***Republicans***

*Byrd elected as independent.

KEY

- Y Voted for (yea).
- ✓ Paired for.
- † Announced for.
- # CQ Poll for.
- N Voted against (nay).
- X Paired against.
- \- Announced against.
- ▮ CQ Poll against.
- P Voted "present."
- ● Voted "present" to avoid possible conflict of interest.
- ? Did not vote or otherwise make a position known.

500. HR 5263. Energy Taxes. Byrd, D-W.Va., motion to instruct the sergeant at arms to request the attendance of absent senators. Motion agreed to 80-2: R 26-2; D 54-0 (ND 38-0; SD 16-0), Oct. 14, 1978.

501. S 2493. Airline Deregulation. Adoption of the conference report on the bill to introduce a measure of marketplace competition in the airline industry by gradually phasing out federal controls over a seven-year period and mandating the abolition of the Civil Aeronautics Board (CAB), unless Congress acted to retain it. Adopted 82-4: R 30-0; D 52-4 (ND 37-2; SD 15-2), Oct. 14, 1978. A "yea" was a vote supporting the president's position.

502. HR 5263. Energy Taxes. Byrd, D-W.Va., motion to table (kill) the Abourezk, D-S.D., appeal of the chair's ruling that the Abourezk motion to adjourn was dilatory after cloture had been invoked. Motion to table agreed to 63-19: R 13-17; D 50-2 (ND 34-2; SD 16-0), Oct. 14, 1978.

503. HR 5263. Energy Taxes. Cannon, D-Nev., motion to direct the sergeant at arms to request the attendance of absent senators. Motion agreed to 72-3: R 26-2; D 46-1 (ND 34-1; SD 12-0), Oct. 14, 1978.

504. HR 5263. Energy Taxes. Bellmon, R-Okla., motion to table the conference report on the bill. Motion rejected 22-56: R 10-19; D 12-37 (ND 11-24; SD 1-13), Oct. 14, 1978.

505. HR 5263. Energy Taxes. Byrd, D-W.Va., motion to table (kill) the Abourezk, D-S.D., appeal of the chair's ruling that the granting of unanimous consent to insert material in the *Congressional Record* did not constitute the transaction of business for the purpose of calling a quorum. Motion to table agreed to 54-11: R 14-8; D 40-3 (ND 29-3; SD 11-0), Oct. 14, 1978.

506. HR 5263. Energy Taxes. Cranston, D-Calif., motion to table the Abourezk, D-S.D., motion to recommit the conference report on the bill. Motion to table agreed to 58-16: R 17-9; D 41-7 (ND 27-7; SD 14-0), Oct. 14, 1978.

507. HR 5263. Energy Taxes. Byrd, D-W.Va., motion to instruct the sergeant at arms to compel the attendance of absent senators. Motion agreed to 70-3: R 22-3; D 48-0 (ND 35-0; SD 13-0), Oct. 14, 1978.

CQ Senate Votes 508-511

Corresponding to Congressional Record Votes 512, 513, 514, 515

	508	509	510	511
ALABAMA				
Allen, M.	?	?	?	?
Sparkman	?	?	?	?
ALASKA				
Gravel	Y	?	Y	Y
Stevens	?	Y	Y	Y
ARIZONA				
DeConcini	Y	Y	Y	Y
Goldwater	?	?	?	?
ARKANSAS				
Bumpers	Y	Y	Y	Y
Hodges	Y	Y	Y	Y
CALIFORNIA				
Cranston	Y	Y	Y	Y
Hayakawa	Y	Y	Y	Y
COLORADO				
Hart	Y	Y	Y	Y
Haskell	?	?	?	?
CONNECTICUT				
Ribicoff	Y	Y	Y	Y
Weicker	N	N	N	N
DELAWARE				
Biden	?	Y	Y	Y
Roth	Y	Y	Y	Y
FLORIDA				
Chiles	Y	Y	Y	Y
Stone	Y	Y	Y	Y
GEORGIA				
Nunn	Y	Y	Y	Y
Talmadge	?	?	?	†
HAWAII				
Inouye	Y	Y	Y	Y
Matsunaga	Y	Y	Y	Y
IDAHO				
Church	Y	Y	Y	Y
McClure	?	?	?	?
ILLINOIS				
Stevenson	?	Y	Y	Y
Percy	Y	Y	Y	Y
INDIANA				
Bayh	N	Y	N	Y
Lugar	Y	Y	Y	N
IOWA				
Clark	†	?	†	†
Culver	Y	Y	Y	Y
KANSAS				
Dole	Y	Y	Y	N
Pearson	?	?	?	?
KENTUCKY				
Ford	Y	Y	Y	Y
Huddleston	?	?	?	?
LOUISIANA				
Johnston	Y	Y	Y	Y
Long	?	?	?	Y
MAINE				
Hathaway	?	?	?	?
Muskie	Y	Y	Y	Y
MARYLAND				
Sarbanes	Y	Y	Y	Y
Mathias	?	?	?	?
MASSACHUSETTS				
Kennedy	?	?	?	?
Brooke	?	?	?	?
MICHIGAN				
Riegle	N	Y	N	Y
Griffin	Y	Y	Y	Y
MINNESOTA				
Anderson	Y	Y	Y	Y
Humphrey, M.	?	Y	Y	Y
MISSISSIPPI				
Eastland	?	?	?	?
Stennis	Y	Y	Y	?
MISSOURI				
Eagleton	?	?	Y	N
Danforth	Y	Y	Y	Y
MONTANA				
Melcher	Y	Y	Y	Y
Hatfield, P.	Y	Y	Y	Y
NEBRASKA				
Zorinsky	Y	Y	Y	Y
Curtis	?	Y	Y	Y
NEVADA				
Cannon	Y	Y	Y	Y
Laxalt	Y	Y	Y	Y
NEW HAMPSHIRE				
Durkin	Y	Y	Y	Y
McIntyre	?	?	?	†
NEW JERSEY				
Williams	Y	Y	Y	Y
Case	?	?	?	?
NEW MEXICO				
Domenici	?	?	?	?
Schmitt	N	Y	N	N
NEW YORK				
Moynihan	Y	Y	Y	Y
Javits	Y	Y	Y	Y
NORTH CAROLINA				
Morgan	Y	Y	Y	?
Helms	Y	?	?	?
NORTH DAKOTA				
Burdick	Y	Y	Y	Y
Young	Y	Y	Y	Y
OHIO				
Glenn	Y	Y	Y	Y
Metzenbaum	N	Y	N	N
OKLAHOMA				
Bartlett	N	N	N	N
Bellmon	Y	Y	Y	N
OREGON				
Hatfield, M.	Y	Y	Y	Y
Packwood	Y	Y	Y	Y
PENNSYLVANIA				
Heinz	Y	Y	Y	Y
Schweiker	Y	Y	Y	Y
RHODE ISLAND				
Pell	Y	Y	Y	Y
Chafee	Y	Y	Y	Y
SOUTH CAROLINA				
Hollings	Y	Y	Y	Y
Thurmond	Y	Y	Y	Y
SOUTH DAKOTA				
Abourezk	N	Y	N	N
McGovern	N	Y	N	N
TENNESSEE				
Sasser	Y	Y	Y	Y
Baker	Y	Y	Y	Y
TEXAS				
Bentsen	Y	Y	Y	Y
Tower	?	?	?	†
UTAH				
Garn	Y	Y	Y	N
Hatch	Y	Y	Y	N
VERMONT				
Leahy	N	Y	Y	N
Stafford	?	?	?	?
VIRGINIA				
*Byrd, H.	Y	Y	Y	Y
Scott	?	?	?	?
WASHINGTON				
Jackson	Y	Y	Y	Y
Magnuson	Y	Y	Y	Y
WEST VIRGINIA				
Byrd, R.	Y	Y	Y	Y
Randolph	Y	Y	Y	Y
WISCONSIN				
Nelson	Y	Y	Y	N
Proxmire	N	Y	N	N
WYOMING				
Hansen	N	N	N	N
Wallop	N	N	N	N

Democrats ***Republicans***

**Byrd elected as independent.*

KEY

- Y Voted for (yea).
- ✓ Paired for.
- † Announced for.
- # CQ Poll for.
- N Voted against (nay).
- X Paired against.
- \- Announced against.
- ▌ CQ Poll against.
- P Voted "present."
- ● Voted "present" to avoid possible conflict of interest.
- ? Did not vote or otherwise make a position known.

508. HR 5263. Energy Taxes. Byrd, D-W.Va., motion to table (kill) the Abourezk, D-S.D., motion to recommit the conference report with instructions to delete section 404 on encouragement of recycling of lubricating oil. Motion to table agreed to 61-12: R 21-5; D 40-7 (ND 27-7; SD 13-0), Oct. 14, 1978. A "yea" was a vote supporting the president's position.

509. HR 5263. Energy Taxes. Byrd, D-W.Va., motion to instruct the sergeant at arms to request the attendance of absent senators. Motion agreed to 72-4: R 23-4; D 49-0 (ND 36-0; SD 13-0), Oct. 15, 1978.

510. HR 5263. Energy Taxes. Byrd, D-W.Va., motion to table (kill) the Weicker, R-Conn., motion to recommit the conference report to the Finance Committee. Motion agreed to 67-11: R 22-5; D 45-6 (ND 32-6; SD 13-0), Oct. 15, 1978.

511. HR 5263. Energy Taxes. Adoption of the conference report on the bill to provide tax incentives to homeowners, businesses and industry for the production and conservation of energy. Adopted 60-17: R 17-10; D 43-7 (ND 31-7; SD 12-0), Oct. 15, 1978. A "yea" was a vote supporting the president's position.

CQ Senate Votes 512-516

Corresponding to Congressional Record Votes 516, 517, 518, 519, 520

	512	513	514	515	516
ALABAMA					
Allen, M.	?	?	?	?	?
Sparkman	?	N	Y	Y	Y
ALASKA					
Gravel	N	N	Y	N	Y
Stevens	N	Y	Y	Y	N
ARIZONA					
DeConcini	N	N	Y	Y	Y
Goldwater	?	?	?	?	?
ARKANSAS					
Bumpers	Y	N	Y	Y	?
Hodges	Y	N	Y	?	?
CALIFORNIA					
Cranston	N	N	Y	N	Y
Hayakawa	Y	Y	Y	Y	Y
COLORADO					
Hart	N	N	Y	N	Y
Haskell	?	?	?	?	?
CONNECTICUT					
Ribicoff	N	N	Y	?	?
Weicker	N	N	Y	?	?
DELAWARE					
Biden	Y	Y	Y	Y	?
Roth	Y	Y	Y	N	N
FLORIDA					
Chiles	Y	Y	Y	N	Y
Stone	Y	Y	Y	N	Y
GEORGIA					
Nunn	Y	Y	Y	Y	Y
Talmadge	?	N	Y	?	?
HAWAII					
Inouye	N	N	Y	Y	Y
Matsunaga	N	N	Y	Y	Y
IDAHO					
Church	Y	N	Y	Y	Y
McClure	?	?	?	?	?
ILLINOIS					
Stevenson	Y	N	Y	?	?
Percy	N	Y	Y	?	?
INDIANA					
Bayh	N	N	Y	Y	N
Lugar	Y	Y	Y	N	N
IOWA					
Clark	?	-	†	?	-
Culver	N	N	Y	N	N
KANSAS					
Dole	Y	Y	Y	Y	N
Pearson	?	?	?	?	?
KENTUCKY					
Ford	N	Y	Y	Y	?
Huddleston	?	?	?	?	?
LOUISIANA					
Johnston	Y	N	Y	Y	Y
Long	Y	N	Y	Y	Y
MAINE					
Hathaway	?	?	?	?	?
Muskie	Y	N	Y	Y	Y
MARYLAND					
Sarbanes	N	N	Y	Y	Y
Mathias	?	?	?	?	?
MASSACHUSETTS					
Kennedy	?	?	?	?	?
Brooke	?	?	?	?	?
MICHIGAN					
Riegle	N	N	Y	?	?
Griffin	N	Y	Y	?	?
MINNESOTA					
Anderson	?	?	†	?	?
Humphrey, M.	N	N	Y	Y	Y
MISSISSIPPI					
Eastland	?	?	?	?	?
Stennis	?	?	?	?	?
MISSOURI					
Eagleton	N	N	Y	Y	Y
Danforth	Y	Y	Y	?	?
MONTANA					
Melcher	N	Y	Y	Y	Y
Hatfield, P.	N	N	Y	Y	Y
NEBRASKA					
Zorinsky	N	Y	Y	Y	N
Curtis	Y	?	?	?	?
NEVADA					
Cannon	N	N	Y	Y	Y
Laxalt	Y	N	Y	?	?
NEW HAMPSHIRE					
Durkin	N	N	Y	Y	N
McIntyre	?	?	†	?	?
NEW JERSEY					
Williams	N	N	Y	Y	Y
Case	?	?	?	?	?
NEW MEXICO					
Domenici	?	?	†	?	?
Schmitt	Y	Y	Y	Y	N
NEW YORK					
Moynihan	N	N	Y	?	?
Javits	N	N	Y	N	Y
NORTH CAROLINA					
Morgan	Y	N	Y	Y	Y
Helms	?	?	?	?	?
NORTH DAKOTA					
Burdick	N	N	Y	Y	Y
Young	N	?	?	?	N
OHIO					
Glenn	N	N	Y	N	Y
Metzenbaum	N	N	Y	Y	Y
OKLAHOMA					
Bartlett	Y	Y	Y	Y	N
Bellmon	Y	?	?	?	?
OREGON					
Hatfield, M.	N	Y	N	Y	N
Packwood	Y	Y	Y	N	N
PENNSYLVANIA					
Heinz	N	Y	Y	Y	Y
Schweiker	Y	Y	Y	Y	N
RHODE ISLAND					
Pell	N	Y	Y	Y	N
Chafee	N	N	Y	Y	N
SOUTH CAROLINA					
Hollings	Y	Y	N	Y	Y
Thurmond	Y	Y	Y	Y	N
SOUTH DAKOTA					
Abourezk	N	N	N	Y	Y
McGovern	?	?	?	?	?
TENNESSEE					
Sasser	N	N	Y	Y	Y
Baker	N	Y	Y	?	?
TEXAS					
Bentsen	Y	N	Y	?	?
Tower	?	?	?	?	?
UTAH					
Garn	Y	Y	Y	Y	N
Hatch	N	Y	Y	Y	N
VERMONT					
Leahy	N	N	Y	?	?
Stafford	?	?	?	?	?
VIRGINIA					
*Byrd, H.	Y	N	Y	Y	?
Scott	?	?	?	?	?
WASHINGTON					
Jackson	N	N	Y	Y	Y
Magnuson	N	N	Y	Y	?
WEST VIRGINIA					
Byrd, R.	N	N	Y	Y	Y
Randolph	N	N	Y	Y	†
WISCONSIN					
Nelson	N	N	Y	N	Y
Proxmire	Y	Y	Y	N	Y
WYOMING					
Hansen	Y	N	Y	Y	Y
Wallop	Y	Y	Y	Y	N

Democrats ***Republicans***

*Byrd elected as independent.

KEY

- Y Voted for (yea).
- ✓ Paired for.
- † Announced for.
- # CQ Poll for.
- N Voted against (nay).
- X Paired against.
- \- Announced against.
- ▌ CQ Poll against.
- P Voted "present."
- ● Voted "present" to avoid possible conflict of interest.
- ? Did not vote or otherwise make a position known.

512. H J Res 1139. Continuing Appropriations, Fiscal 1979. Chiles, D-Fla., amendment to require a reduction of 68,000 public service jobs in fiscal 1979 in Comprehensive Employment and Training Act programs. Rejected 32-44: R 16-11; D 16-33 (ND 5-31; SD 11-2), Oct. 15, 1978. A "nay" was a vote supporting the president's positions.

513. HR 13511. Revenue Act of 1978. Roth, R-Del., motion to recommit the conference report on the bill with instructions to the Senate conferees to insist on a Senate amendment to schedule 5 percent across-the-board tax cuts annually between 1980 and 1983 provided spending was held within certain limits. Motion rejected 29-46: R 19-5; D 10-41 (ND 5-31; SD 5-10), Oct. 15, 1978.

514. HR 13511. Revenue Act of 1978. Adoption of the conference report on the bill to reduce taxes by $18.7 billion in 1979. Adopted 72-3: R 23-1; D 49-2 (ND 35-1; SD 14-1), Oct. 15, 1978.

515. HR 9937. Carson City Silver Dollars/Textile Negotiations. Adoption of the conference report on the bill to authorize the General Services Administration to dispose of $24 million worth of Carson City silver dollars and to prohibit the reduction or elimination in trade negotiations of duties or import restrictions on certain imported textiles and textile products. Adopted 48-13: R 14-4; D 34-9 (ND 24-7; SD 10-2), Oct. 15, 1978. A "nay" was a vote supporting the president's position.

516. HR 13750. Sugar Stabilization Act. Long, D-La., motion to table (kill) the Dole, R-Kan., motion to recommit the conference report on the bill to authorize, through fiscal 1983, U.S. participation in the International Sugar Agreement, maintain a minimum per-pound price for U.S. sugar producers through import quotas and fees and direct payments, establish minimum wages and other benefits for sugar industry workers, and to extend through Feb. 15, 1979, the president's authority to waive countervailing duties, and to authorize contributions to an international stockpile and sale of stockpiled U.S. tin. Motion to table agreed to 36-20: R 4-15; D 32-5 (ND 23-5; SD 9-0), Oct. 15, 1978.

HOUSE ROLL-CALL VOTES

CQ

1. **HR 2329. Fish and Wildlife Administration.** Weiss (D N.Y.) amendment to delete language allowing warrantless searches and seizures and to substitute language permitting such actions by enforcing officers when there were reasonable grounds to believe that a person had committed or was attempting to commit an offense in the officers' presence or view. Adopted 215-131: R 68-41; D 147-90 (ND 110-55; SD 37-35), Jan. 19, 1978.

2. **HR 2329. Fish and Wildlife Administration.** Passage of the bill to improve the enforcement of fish and wildlife laws by consolidating authority scattered in different statutes and expanding other authority. Passed 292-59: R 78-34; D 214-25 (ND 158-5; SD 56-20), Jan. 19, 1978.

3. **HR 9165. George C. Marshall Statue.** Fascell (D Fla.) motion to suspend the rules and pass the bill to authorize $10,000 for the Secretary of State to acquire a statue or bust of the late Secretary of State George C. Marshall (1947-49), to be displayed in the State Department. Motion agreed to 351-22: R 111-16; D 240-6 (ND 169-4; SD 71-2), Jan. 23, 1978. A two-thirds majority vote (249 in this case) is required for passage under suspension of the rules.

4. **HR 8771. Civil Service Retirement System.** Spellman (D Md.) motion to suspend the rules and pass the bill to authorize the Civil Service Commission to comply with the terms of state court orders or property settlements in connection with the divorce or legal separation of a Civil Service employee (the effect of the bill was to grant divorced or separated spouses of federal employees rights in Civil Service pensions). Motion agreed to 369-7: R 125-3; D 244-4 (ND 174-1; SD 70-3), Jan. 23, 1978. A two-thirds majority vote (251 in this case) is required for passage under suspension of the rules.

5. **HR 9471. Japanese-Americans' Retirement Credit.** Spellman (D Md.) motion to suspend the rules and pass the bill to provide Civil Service retirement credit for certain federal employees of Japanese-American descent who were interned in relocation camps during World War II. Motion agreed to 366-12: R 123-6; D 243-6 (ND 175-1; SD 68-5), Jan. 23, 1978. A two-thirds majority vote (252 in this case) is required for passage under suspension of the rules.

6. **HR 9169. Fishing Vessel Loan Guarantees.** Murphy (D N.Y.) motion to suspend the rules and pass the bill to amend the Merchant Marine Act to increase permissible federal loan guarantees for financing construction or rehabilitation of commercial fishing vessels to 87 1/2 per cent from 75 per cent of the cost of the vessel. Motion agreed to 309-68: R 93-36; D 216-32 (ND 157-18; SD 59-14), Jan. 23, 1978. A two-thirds majority vote (252 in this case) is required for passage under suspension of the rules.

7. **HR 8811. Tax Court Retirement System.** Ullman (D Ore.) motion to suspend the rules and pass the bill to amend the Internal Revenue Code to enable Tax Court judges to revoke their participation in the Tax Court retirement system so they might return to the Civil Service System. Motion agreed to 399-1: R 139-1; D 260-0 (ND 181-0; SD 79-0), Jan. 24, 1978. A two-thirds majority vote (267 in this case) is required for passage under suspension of the rules.

8. **HR 7662. Administrative Conference.** Danielson (D Calif.) motion to suspend the rules and pass the bill to authorize $6 million for fiscal 1979-81 for the operations of the Administrative Conference to study administrative procedures and make recommendations to improve efficiency. Motion agreed to 292-103: R 77-61; D 215-42 (ND 160-19; SD 55-23), Jan. 24, 1978. A two-thirds majority vote (264 in this case) is required for passage under suspension of the rules.

KEY

- Y Voted for (yea).
- ✓ Paired for.
- † Announced for.
- # CQ Poll for.
- N Voted against (nay).
- X Paired against.
- \- Announced against.
- ▮ CQ Poll against.
- P Voted "present."
- ● Voted "present" to avoid possible conflict of interest.
- ? Did not vote or otherwise make a position known.

	1	2	3	4	5	6	7	8
ALABAMA								
1 Edwards	Y	N	Y	Y	Y	Y	Y	Y
2 Dickinson	Y	N	Y	Y	Y	N	Y	Y
3 Nichols	N	N	Y	Y	Y	Y	Y	Y
4 Bevill	N	N	Y	Y	Y	Y	Y	Y
5 Flippo	N	N	Y	Y	N	Y	Y	Y
6 Buchanan	Y	N	Y	Y	Y	Y	Y	Y
7 Flowers	N	N	Y	Y	Y	Y	Y	Y
ALASKA								
AL Young	N	Y	Y	Y	Y	Y	Y	N
ARIZONA								
1 Rhodes	N	Y	Y	Y	Y	Y	Y	Y
2 Udall	Y	Y	Y	Y	Y	Y	Y	Y
3 Stump	Y	N	?	?	?	?	?	?
4 Rudd	▮	▮	N	Y	Y	N	Y	N
ARKANSAS								
1 Alexander	Y	Y	?	?	?	?	Y	Y
2 Tucker	#	#	#	#	#	▮	#	#
3 Hammerschmidt	Y	N	Y	Y	Y	N	Y	Y
4 Thornton	Y	Y	Y	Y	Y	N	Y	Y
CALIFORNIA								
1 Johnson	N	Y	Y	Y	Y	Y	Y	Y
2 Clausen	?	Y	Y	Y	Y	Y	Y	Y
3 Moss	Y	Y	Y	Y	Y	Y	Y	Y
4 Leggett	N	Y	Y	Y	Y	Y	Y	Y
5 Burton, J.	Y	Y	Y	Y	Y	Y	Y	Y
6 Burton, P.	Y	Y	Y	Y	Y	?	?	?
7 Miller	?	?	Y	Y	Y	Y	Y	Y
8 Dellums	Y	Y	#	#	#	?	Y	Y
9 Stark	#	#	Y	Y	Y	Y	Y	Y
10 Edwards	Y	Y	Y	Y	Y	Y	Y	Y
11 Ryan	#	?	Y	Y	Y	Y	Y	Y
12 McCloskey	N	Y	Y	Y	Y	Y	Y	Y
13 Mineta	Y	Y	Y	Y	Y	Y	Y	Y
14 McFall	N	Y	Y	Y	Y	Y	Y	Y
15 Sisk	Y	Y	Y	Y	Y	Y	Y	Y
16 Panetta	N	Y	Y	Y	Y	Y	Y	N
17 Krebs	Y	Y	Y	Y	Y	Y	Y	Y
18 Ketchum	N	Y	Y	Y	Y	Y	Y	Y
19 Lagomarsino	N	Y	Y	Y	Y	Y	Y	N
20 Goldwater	?	?	N	Y	Y	Y	Y	N
21 Corman	N	Y	Y	Y	Y	Y	Y	#
22 Moorhead	N	N	Y	Y	Y	Y	Y	Y
23 Beilenson	Y	Y	Y	Y	Y	Y	Y	Y
24 Waxman	Y	Y	Y	Y	Y	Y	Y	Y
25 Roybal	Y	Y	Y	Y	Y	Y	Y	Y
26 Rousselot	Y	N	N	Y	Y	N	Y	N
27 Dornan	?	?	?	Y	Y	Y	Y	?
28 Burke	Y	Y	#	#	#	#	Y	Y
29 Hawkins	Y	Y	Y	Y	Y	Y	Y	Y
30 Danielson	†	†	Y	Y	Y	Y	Y	Y
31 Wilson, C.H.	N	Y	Y	Y	Y	Y	Y	Y
32 Anderson	Y	Y	#	#	?	#	Y	Y
33 Clawson	?	?	Y	Y	Y	N	Y	N
34 Hannaford	Y	Y	Y	Y	Y	Y	Y	Y
35 Lloyd	Y	Y	Y	Y	Y	Y	Y	Y
36 Brown	Y	Y	Y	Y	Y	Y	Y	Y
37 Pettis	?	?	Y	Y	Y	Y	Y	Y
38 Patterson	N	Y	#	#	#	#	#	#
39 Wiggins	N	Y	Y	Y	Y	N	Y	Y
40 Badham	▮	#	Y	Y	Y	Y	Y	Y
41 Wilson, B.	N	Y	Y	Y	Y	Y	Y	Y
42 Van Deerlin	N	Y	Y	Y	Y	Y	Y	Y
43 Burgener	N	Y	Y	Y	Y	Y	Y	N
COLORADO								
1 Schroeder	Y	Y	Y	Y	Y	Y	Y	Y
2 Wirth	Y	Y	Y	Y	Y	Y	Y	Y
3 Evans	Y	Y	Y	Y	Y	Y	Y	Y
4 Johnson	?	?	Y	Y	Y	Y	Y	Y
5 Armstrong	?	?	Y	Y	Y	Y	Y	Y
CONNECTICUT								
1 Cotter	N	Y	Y	Y	Y	Y	?	#
2 Dodd	?	?	Y	Y	Y	Y	#	?
3 Giaimo	?	Y	?	?	?	?	?	?
4 McKinney	N	Y	Y	Y	Y	Y	Y	Y
5 Sarasin	N	Y	Y	Y	Y	Y	Y	Y
6 Moffett	Y	Y	Y	Y	Y	Y	Y	N
DELAWARE								
AL Evans	N	Y	Y	Y	Y	Y	Y	N
FLORIDA								
1 Sikes	N	Y	Y	Y	Y	Y	Y	Y
2 Fuqua	N	Y	Y	Y	Y	Y	Y	Y
3 Bennett	N	Y	Y	Y	Y	Y	Y	Y
4 Chappell	▮	#	#	?	#	#	#	#
5 Kelly	N	N	Y	Y	Y	Y	Y	N
6 Young	N	Y	N	Y	Y	Y	Y	N
7 Gibbons	Y	Y	Y	Y	Y	Y	Y	Y
8 Ireland	Y	Y	Y	Y	N	Y	Y	Y
9 Frey	?	?	?	?	?	?	Y	N
10 Bafalis	Y	Y	Y	Y	Y	Y	Y	N
11 Rogers	N	Y	Y	Y	Y	Y	Y	Y
12 Burke	?	?	Y	Y	Y	Y	Y	Y
13 Lehman	Y	Y	Y	Y	Y	Y	Y	Y
14 Pepper	#	#	#	#	#	#	#	#
15 Fascell	#	#	Y	Y	Y	Y	Y	Y
GEORGIA								
1 Ginn	N	Y	Y	Y	Y	Y	Y	N
2 Mathis	N	N	Y	Y	Y	Y	Y	N
3 Brinkley	?	Y	?	?	?	?	Y	Y
4 Levitas	Y	Y	Y	Y	Y	Y	Y	N
5 Fowler	Y	Y	Y	Y	Y	Y	Y	N
6 Flynt	?	?	N	N	N	N	Y	N
7 McDonald	#	X	N	Y	Y	N	Y	N
8 Evans	Y	N	Y	Y	Y	Y	▮	▮
9 Jenkins	Y	Y	Y	Y	N	N	Y	N
10 Barnard	Y	Y	Y	Y	Y	Y	?	?
HAWAII								
1 Heftel	Y	Y	Y	Y	Y	Y	Y	Y
2 Akaka	Y	Y	Y	Y	Y	Y	Y	Y
IDAHO								
1 Symms	Y	N	N	Y	Y	N	Y	N
2 Hansen, G.	?	N	N	Y	Y	N	Y	N
ILLINOIS								
1 Metcalfe	N	Y	Y	Y	Y	Y	Y	Y
2 Murphy	N	Y	Y	Y	Y	Y	Y	Y
3 Russo	N	Y	Y	Y	Y	Y	Y	Y
4 Derwinski	Y	Y	Y	Y	Y	Y	Y	N
5 Fary	N	Y	Y	Y	Y	Y	Y	Y
6 Hyde	N	Y	Y	Y	Y	Y	Y	Y
7 Collins	Y	Y	Y	Y	Y	Y	Y	Y
8 Rostenkowski	?	?	?	?	?	?	Y	Y
9 Yates	Y	Y	Y	Y	Y	N	Y	Y
10 Mikva	Y	Y	Y	Y	Y	N	Y	Y
11 Annunzio	N	Y	Y	Y	Y	Y	Y	Y
12 Crane	#	▮	N	Y	Y	N	Y	N
13 McClory	N	Y	Y	Y	Y	Y	Y	Y
14 Erlenborn	Y	Y	#	#	#	▮	#	#
15 Corcoran	N	Y	Y	Y	Y	Y	Y	N
16 Anderson	Y	Y	Y	Y	Y	Y	Y	Y
17 O'Brien	N	Y	Y	Y	Y	Y	Y	Y
18 Michel	N	Y	#	#	#	▮	Y	N
19 Railsback	N	Y	Y	Y	Y	Y	Y	Y
20 Findley	?	?	Y	Y	Y	Y	Y	Y
21 Madigan	?	?	?	Y	Y	Y	Y	Y
22 Shipley	?	?	Y	Y	Y	Y	Y	Y
23 Price	Y	Y	Y	Y	Y	Y	Y	Y
24 Simon	N	Y	Y	Y	Y	Y	Y	Y
INDIANA								
1 Benjamin	Y	Y	Y	Y	Y	Y	Y	Y
2 Fithian	N	Y	Y	Y	Y	Y	Y	N
3 Brademas	Y	Y	Y	Y	Y	Y	Y	Y
4 Quayle	Y	Y	N	Y	Y	N	Y	N
5 Hillis	N	Y	?	?	?	?	?	?
6 Evans	N	Y	?	?	?	?	Y	Y
7 Myers, J.	?	?	Y	Y	Y	Y	Y	N
8 Cornwell	N	Y	N	Y	Y	Y	#	#
9 Hamilton	N	Y	Y	Y	Y	N	Y	Y
10 Sharp	Y	Y	Y	Y	Y	Y	Y	N
11 Jacobs	Y	Y	N	Y	Y	N	Y	N
IOWA								
1 Leach	Y	Y	Y	Y	Y	Y	Y	Y
2 Blouin	Y	Y	Y	Y	Y	Y	Y	Y
3 Grassley	Y	N	Y	Y	Y	N	Y	N
4 Smith	Y	Y	Y	Y	Y	Y	Y	Y
5 Harkin	Y	Y	Y	Y	Y	Y	Y	Y
6 Bedell	Y	●	Y	Y	Y	●	Y	Y

Democrats ***Republicans***

	1	2	3	4	5	6	7	8
KANSAS								
1 Sebelius	Y	Y	Y	Y	Y	Y	Y	N
2 Keys	Y	Y	N	Y	Y	N	Y	Y
3 Winn	#	#	Y	Y	Y	N	Y	Y
4 Glickman	Y	Y	N	Y	Y	Y	Y	N
5 Skubitz	?	?	?	?	?	?	Y	Y
KENTUCKY								
1 Hubbard	Y	Y	Y	Y	Y	Y	Y	N
2 Natcher	N	Y	Y	Y	Y	Y	Y	Y
3 Mazzoli	Y	Y	Y	Y	Y	Y	Y	Y
4 Snyder	Y	Y	N	Y	Y	N	Y	Y
5 Carter	Y	Y	Y	Y	Y	N	Y	Y
6 Breckinridge	Y	Y	Y	Y	Y	Y	Y	Y
7 Perkins	Y	Y	Y	Y	Y	Y	Y	Y
LOUISIANA								
1 Livingston	Y	N	?	?	?	?	Y	Y
2 Boggs	Y	Y	Y	Y	Y	Y	Y	Y
3 Treen	N	N	Y	Y	Y	Y	Y	Y
4 Waggonner	?	N	Y	Y	Y	Y	Y	Y
5 Huckaby	Y	N	Y	Y	Y	Y	Y	Y
6 Moore	?	?	?	?	?	?	Y	Y
7 Breaux	?	Y	?	?	?	?	?	?
8 Long	Y	Y	Y	Y	Y	Y	Y	Y
MAINE								
1 Emery	N	Y	Y	Y	Y	Y	Y	Y
2 Cohen	Y	Y	Y	Y	Y	Y	Y	Y
MARYLAND								
1 Bauman	Y	N	N	Y	Y	Y	Y	N
2 Long	Y	Y	Y	Y	Y	N	Y	Y
3 Mikulski	Y	Y	Y	Y	Y	Y	Y	Y
4 Holt	Y	N	Y	Y	Y	Y	Y	N
5 Spellman	Y	Y	Y	Y	Y	Y	Y	Y
6 Byron	Y	Y	Y	Y	Y	Y	Y	Y
7 Mitchell	Y	Y	Y	Y	Y	Y	Y	Y
8 Steers	Y	Y	Y	Y	Y	Y	Y	Y
MASSACHUSETTS								
1 Conte	Y	Y	Y	Y	Y	Y	Y	Y
2 Boland	Y	Y	Y	Y	Y	Y	Y	Y
3 Early	Y	Y	?	?	?	?	Y	Y
4 Drinan	Y	Y	Y	Y	Y	Y	Y	Y
5 Tsongas	Y	Y	Y	Y	Y	Y	Y	Y
6 Harrington	Y	Y	Y	Y	Y	Y	Y	Y
7 Markey	Y	Y	Y	Y	Y	Y	Y	Y
8 O'Neill								
9 Moakley	Y	Y	Y	Y	Y	Y	Y	Y
10 Heckler	Y	Y	Y	Y	Y	Y	Y	Y
11 Burke	Y	Y	Y	Y	Y	Y	Y	Y
12 Studds	Y	Y	Y	Y	Y	Y	Y	?
MICHIGAN								
1 Conyers	#	#	#	N	Y	N	Y	Y
2 Pursell	Y	Y	Y	Y	Y	Y	Y	?
3 Brown	▮	#	Y	Y	Y	Y	Y	Y
4 Stockman	N	Y	Y	Y	Y	N	Y	Y
5 Sawyer	N	Y	Y	Y	Y	Y	Y	Y
6 Carr	Y	#	Y	Y	Y	N	Y	Y
7 Kildee	Y	Y	Y	Y	Y	Y	Y	Y
8 Traxler	N	Y	Y	Y	Y	Y	Y	Y
9 Vander Jagt	N	Y	Y	Y	Y	Y	Y	Y
10 Cederberg	N	Y	Y	Y	Y	Y	Y	Y
11 Ruppe	N	Y	#	#	#	#	Y	Y
12 Bonior	Y	Y	Y	Y	Y	Y	Y	Y
13 Diggs	#	#	#	Y	Y	Y	Y	Y
14 Nedzi	N	Y	Y	Y	Y	Y	Y	Y
15 Ford	N	Y	Y	Y	Y	Y	Y	Y
16 Dingell	N	Y	Y	Y	Y	Y	Y	Y
17 Brodhead	Y	Y	Y	Y	Y	Y	Y	Y
18 Blanchard	N	Y	Y	Y	Y	Y	#	?
19 Broomfield	#	#	Y	Y	Y	Y	Y	Y
MINNESOTA								
1 Quie	Y	Y	#	#	#	#	Y	Y
2 Hagedorn	Y	Y	Y	?	?	?	Y	Y
3 Frenzel	N	Y	Y	Y	Y	Y	Y	Y
4 Vento	Y	Y	Y	Y	Y	Y	Y	Y
5 Fraser	Y	Y	#	#	#	#	Y	Y
6 Nolan	Y	Y	Y	Y	Y	Y	Y	Y
7 Stangeland	Y	N	Y	Y	Y	Y	Y	N
8 Oberstar	N	Y	Y	Y	Y	Y	Y	Y
MISSISSIPPI								
1 Whitten	Y	N	Y	Y	Y	Y	Y	N
2 Bowen	Y	Y	?	?	?	?	Y	Y
3 Montgomery	N	N	Y	Y	Y	Y	Y	Y
4 Cochran	Y	Y	Y	Y	Y	Y	Y	Y
5 Lott	Y	N	Y	Y	Y	Y	Y	N
MISSOURI								
1 Clay	Y	Y	Y	Y	Y	Y	Y	Y
2 Young	Y	N	Y	Y	Y	Y	Y	Y
3 Gephardt	Y	Y	Y	Y	Y	Y	Y	Y
4 Skelton	Y	N	Y	Y	Y	Y	Y	N
5 Bolling	N	Y	Y	Y	Y	Y	Y	Y
6 Coleman	?	Y	Y	Y	Y	Y	Y	Y
7 Taylor	Y	N	Y	Y	Y	N	Y	N
8 Ichord	Y	Y	Y	Y	Y	N	Y	N
9 Volkmer	Y	Y	Y	Y	Y	Y	Y	Y
10 Burlison	N	Y	Y	Y	Y	Y	Y	Y
MONTANA								
1 Baucus	Y	Y	Y	Y	Y	Y	Y	Y
2 Marlenee	Y	N	Y	Y	Y	Y	Y	N
NEBRASKA								
1 Thone	Y	N	Y	Y	Y	Y	Y	N
2 Cavanaugh	?	?	Y	Y	Y	Y	Y	Y
3 Smith	Y	N	Y	Y	Y	Y	Y	N
NEVADA								
AL Santini	Y	Y	Y	Y	Y	Y	#	#
NEW HAMPSHIRE								
1 D'Amours	N	Y	Y	Y	Y	Y	Y	N
2 Cleveland	Y	Y	Y	Y	Y	Y	Y	N
NEW JERSEY								
1 Florio	N	Y	Y	Y	Y	Y	Y	Y
2 Hughes	N	Y	Y	Y	Y	Y	Y	Y
3 Howard	N	#	Y	Y	Y	Y	Y	Y
4 Thompson	Y	Y	Y	Y	Y	Y	Y	Y
5 Fenwick	Y	Y	Y	Y	Y	Y	Y	N
6 Forsythe	N	Y	Y	Y	Y	Y	Y	Y
7 Maguire	Y	Y	Y	Y	Y	Y	Y	Y
8 Roe	Y	Y	Y	Y	Y	Y	Y	Y
9 Hollenbeck	Y	Y	?	?	?	?	?	?
10 Rodino	Y	Y	#	#	#	#	Y	Y
11 Minish	Y	Y	Y	Y	Y	Y	Y	Y
12 Rinaldo	Y	Y	Y	Y	Y	Y	Y	Y
13 Meyner	#	#	#	#	#	#	Y	Y
14 LeFante	Y	Y	Y	Y	Y	Y	Y	Y
15 Patten	Y	Y	Y	Y	Y	Y	Y	Y
NEW MEXICO								
1 Lujan	Y	N	Y	Y	Y	N	Y	N
2 Runnels	Y	N	Y	Y	Y	Y	Y	N
NEW YORK								
1 Pike	N	Y	Y	Y	Y	Y	Y	Y
2 Downey	#	#	Y	Y	Y	Y	Y	Y
3 Ambro	N	Y	Y	Y	Y	Y	?	Y
4 Lent	N	Y	Y	Y	Y	Y	Y	N
5 Wydler	?	?	Y	Y	Y	N	Y	N
6 Wolff	#	#	Y	Y	Y	Y	Y	Y
7 Addabbo	#	#	#	#	#	#	Y	Y
8 Rosenthal	Y	Y	Y	Y	Y	Y	Y	Y
9 Delaney	Y	Y	Y	Y	Y	Y	Y	Y
10 Biaggi	#	#	Y	Y	Y	Y	Y	Y
11 Scheuer	#	#	Y	Y	Y	Y	Y	Y
12 Chisholm	Y	Y	Y	Y	Y	Y	Y	Y
13 Solarz	Y	Y	Y	Y	Y	Y	Y	Y
14 Richmond	N	Y	Y	Y	Y	Y	Y	Y
15 Zeferetti	▮	✓	#	#	#	#	Y	Y
16 Holtzman	?	†	Y	Y	Y	Y	Y	Y
17 Murphy	N	Y	Y	Y	Y	Y	Y	Y
18 Vacancy [1]								
19 Rangel	?	?	Y	Y	Y	Y	Y	Y
20 Weiss	Y	Y	Y	Y	Y	Y	Y	Y
21 Vacancy [1]								
22 Bingham	#	#	#	#	#	#	Y	Y
23 Caputo	Y	Y	Y	Y	Y	Y	Y	N
24 Ottinger	Y	Y	Y	Y	Y	N	Y	Y
25 Fish	Y	Y	Y	Y	Y	Y	Y	Y
26 Gilman	?	†	Y	Y	Y	Y	Y	Y
27 McHugh	Y	Y	Y	Y	Y	Y	Y	Y
28 Stratton	Y	Y	Y	Y	Y	N	Y	Y
29 Pattison	#	#	Y	Y	Y	N	Y	Y
30 McEwen	?	?	Y	Y	Y	Y	Y	Y
31 Mitchell	?	#	Y	Y	Y	Y	Y	Y
32 Hanley	N	Y	Y	Y	Y	Y	Y	Y
33 Walsh	?	?	?	?	?	?	?	?
34 Horton	Y	Y	Y	Y	Y	Y	Y	Y
35 Conable	N	Y	Y	Y	Y	N	Y	Y
36 LaFalce	Y	Y	Y	Y	Y	Y	Y	Y
37 Nowak	Y	Y	Y	Y	Y	Y	Y	Y
38 Kemp	?	?	?	?	?	#	Y	Y
39 Lundine	Y	Y	Y	Y	Y	Y	Y	Y
NORTH CAROLINA								
1 Jones	?	#	Y	Y	Y	Y	Y	N
2 Fountain	Y	N	#	#	#	#	Y	N
3 Whitley	#	#	Y	Y	Y	Y	Y	Y
4 Andrews	N	Y	Y	N	Y	N	Y	Y
5 Neal	Y	Y	Y	Y	Y	Y	N	N
6 Preyer	N	Y	Y	Y	Y	Y	Y	Y
7 Rose	N	Y	#	#	#	#	Y	Y
8 Hefner	N	Y	Y	Y	Y	Y	Y	N
9 Martin	Y	Y	Y	Y	Y	N	Y	N
10 Broyhill	Y	Y	Y	Y	Y	N	Y	Y
11 Gudger	N	Y	Y	Y	N	Y	Y	Y
NORTH DAKOTA								
AL Andrews	Y	Y	Y	Y	Y	Y	Y	Y
OHIO								
1 Gradison	Y	Y	Y	Y	Y	N	Y	N
2 Luken	Y	Y	Y	Y	Y	Y	Y	N
3 Whalen	Y	Y	Y	Y	Y	Y	Y	Y
4 Guyer	#	#	Y	Y	Y	Y	Y	Y
5 Latta	Y	N	?	?	?	?	Y	N
6 Harsha	N	N	N	N	Y	N	Y	N
7 Brown	Y	Y	Y	Y	Y	Y	?	?
8 Kindness	Y	N	Y	Y	Y	Y	Y	Y
9 Ashley	N	Y	?	?	?	?	Y	Y
10 Miller	Y	Y	N	Y	Y	N	Y	N
11 Stanton	Y	Y	Y	Y	Y	Y	Y	Y
12 Devine	N	N	Y	Y	N	N	Y	N
13 Pease	#	▮	Y	Y	N	Y	Y	Y
14 Seiberling	Y	Y	Y	Y	Y	Y	Y	Y
15 Wylie	N	Y	Y	Y	Y	Y	N	N
16 Regula	Y	Y	Y	Y	Y	Y	Y	Y
17 Ashbrook	Y	N	N	Y	N	N	Y	N
18 Applegate	N	Y	Y	Y	Y	Y	Y	Y
19 Carney	Y	Y	#	#	#	#	Y	Y
20 Oakar	Y	Y	Y	Y	Y	Y	Y	N
21 Stokes	Y	Y	Y	Y	Y	Y	Y	#
22 Vanik	Y	Y	Y	Y	Y	Y	Y	Y
23 Mottl	Y	Y	Y	Y	Y	Y	Y	N
OKLAHOMA								
1 Jones	Y	Y	Y	Y	Y	N	Y	N
2 Risenhoover	Y	N	Y	Y	Y	Y	?	?
3 Watkins	Y	N	Y	Y	Y	Y	Y	N
4 Steed	N	Y	Y	Y	Y	Y	Y	Y
5 Edwards	?	?	?	?	?	?	Y	N
6 English	Y	Y	Y	Y	Y	Y	Y	N
OREGON								
1 AuCoin	N	Y	#	#	#	#	#	▮
2 Ullman	#	#	Y	Y	Y	Y	Y	Y
3 Duncan	N	Y	Y	Y	Y	Y	Y	Y
4 Weaver	#	#	Y	Y	Y	Y	#	?
PENNSYLVANIA								
1 Myers, M.	N	Y	Y	?	Y	Y	?	?
2 Nix	▮	#	Y	Y	Y	Y	Y	Y
3 Lederer	Y	Y	Y	Y	Y	Y	?	?
4 Eilberg	Y	Y	Y	Y	Y	Y	Y	Y
5 Schulze	N	N	Y	Y	Y	N	Y	Y
6 Yatron	Y	Y	Y	Y	Y	Y	Y	Y
7 Edgar	Y	Y	Y	Y	Y	N	Y	Y
8 Kostmayer	Y	N	Y	Y	Y	Y	Y	N
9 Shuster	?	?	Y	Y	N	N	Y	N
10 McDade	?	?	Y	Y	Y	Y	Y	Y
11 Flood	N	Y	Y	Y	Y	Y	Y	Y
12 Murtha	N	Y	Y	Y	Y	Y	Y	Y
13 Coughlin	N	Y	#	#	Y	Y	Y	Y
14 Moorhead	Y	Y	Y	Y	Y	Y	Y	Y
15 Rooney	N	Y	Y	Y	Y	Y	Y	Y
16 Walker	Y	N	Y	Y	Y	N	Y	N
17 Ertel	Y	Y	Y	Y	Y	Y	Y	N
18 Walgren	N	Y	Y	Y	Y	N	Y	N
19 Goodling, W.	Y	Y	Y	Y	Y	Y	Y	N
20 Gaydos	N	Y	Y	Y	Y	Y	Y	Y
21 Dent	▮	#	#	#	#	#	#	#
22 Murphy	N	Y	#	Y	Y	Y	Y	Y
23 Ammerman	Y	Y	Y	Y	Y	N	Y	N
24 Marks	Y	Y	Y	Y	Y	Y	Y	Y
25 Myers, G.	Y	Y	N	Y	N	N	Y	N
RHODE ISLAND								
1 St Germain	Y	Y	Y	Y	Y	Y	Y	Y
2 Beard	Y	Y	Y	Y	Y	Y	Y	Y
SOUTH CAROLINA								
1 Davis	N	N	Y	Y	Y	Y	Y	Y
2 Spence	Y	Y	?	?	?	?	Y	N
3 Derrick	Y	Y	#	#	#	#	Y	Y
4 Mann	?	?	?	?	?	?	Y	Y
5 Holland	Y	Y	?	#	#	#	Y	Y
6 Jenrette	?	#	#	#	#	#	Y	N
SOUTH DAKOTA								
1 Pressler	?	?	Y	Y	Y	Y	Y	N
2 Abdnor	Y	N	Y	N	Y	Y	Y	N
TENNESSEE								
1 Quillen	Y	Y	Y	Y	Y	Y	Y	N
2 Duncan	Y	Y	Y	Y	Y	Y	Y	Y
3 Lloyd	Y	Y	Y	Y	Y	Y	Y	#
4 Gore	Y	Y	Y	Y	Y	N	Y	Y
5 Allen	Y	Y	Y	Y	Y	Y	Y	Y
6 Beard	N	Y	Y	Y	N	N	Y	N
7 Jones	N	Y	Y	Y	Y	Y	Y	N
8 Ford	#	#	Y	Y	Y	Y	Y	Y
TEXAS								
1 Hall	N	Y	Y	Y	Y	N	Y	N
2 Wilson, C.	#	#	Y	Y	Y	Y	Y	Y
3 Collins	N	N	N	N	N	N	N	N
4 Roberts	N	N	Y	N	Y	N	Y	N
5 Mattox	Y	Y	Y	Y	Y	Y	Y	Y
6 Teague	?	?	?	?	?	?	?	?
7 Archer	N	N	N	Y	Y	N	Y	N
8 Eckhardt	Y	Y	Y	Y	Y	Y	Y	Y
9 Brooks	N	Y	Y	Y	Y	Y	Y	Y
10 Pickle	N	N	Y	Y	Y	N	Y	Y
11 Poage	Y	Y	?	?	?	?	?	?
12 Wright	N	Y	Y	Y	Y	Y	Y	Y
13 Hightower	Y	Y	Y	Y	Y	Y	Y	Y
14 Young	N	Y	Y	Y	Y	Y	Y	Y
15 de la Garza	N	Y	Y	Y	Y	Y	Y	Y
16 White	N	Y	Y	Y	Y	Y	Y	Y
17 Burleson	N	N	Y	Y	Y	N	Y	N
18 Jordan	N	Y	Y	Y	Y	Y	Y	Y
19 Mahon	N	Y	Y	Y	Y	Y	Y	Y
20 Gonzalez	N	Y	?	?	?	?	?	?
21 Krueger	#	#	Y	Y	Y	Y	Y	Y
22 Gammage	N	Y	?	?	?	?	?	?
23 Kazen	N	N	Y	Y	Y	Y	Y	Y
24 Milford	N	Y	Y	Y	Y	N	Y	N
UTAH								
1 McKay	#	#	Y	Y	Y	Y	Y	Y
2 Marriott	Y	N	Y	Y	Y	Y	Y	N
VERMONT								
AL Jeffords	Y	Y	#	#	#	#	Y	Y
VIRGINIA								
1 Trible	N	Y	Y	Y	Y	Y	Y	N
2 Whitehurst	Y	Y	Y	Y	Y	Y	Y	Y
3 Satterfield	Y	N	Y	Y	Y	N	Y	N
4 Daniel	Y	N	Y	Y	Y	Y	Y	N
5 Daniel	Y	N	Y	Y	Y	Y	Y	Y
6 Butler	?	?	Y	Y	Y	Y	Y	Y
7 Robinson	Y	N	Y	Y	Y	Y	Y	N
8 Harris	Y	Y	Y	Y	Y	Y	Y	Y
9 Wampler	Y	Y	Y	Y	Y	Y	Y	Y
10 Fisher	#	Y	Y	Y	Y	Y	Y	Y
WASHINGTON								
1 Pritchard	#	#	Y	Y	Y	Y	Y	Y
2 Meeds	N	Y	Y	Y	Y	Y	Y	Y
3 Bonker	N	Y	Y	Y	Y	Y	Y	Y
4 McCormack	Y	Y	Y	Y	Y	Y	Y	Y
5 Foley	Y	Y	Y	Y	Y	Y	Y	Y
6 Dicks	Y	Y	Y	Y	Y	Y	Y	Y
7 Cunningham	#	▮	Y	Y	Y	Y	Y	N
WEST VIRGINIA								
1 Mollohan	N	Y	Y	Y	Y	Y	Y	N
2 Staggers	N	Y	Y	Y	Y	Y	Y	Y
3 Slack	N	Y	Y	Y	Y	Y	Y	Y
4 Rahall	#	#	Y	Y	Y	Y	Y	N
WISCONSIN								
1 Aspin	?	?	Y	Y	Y	Y	Y	Y
2 Kastenmeier	Y	Y	Y	Y	Y	N	Y	Y
3 Baldus	Y	Y	Y	Y	Y	Y	Y	Y
4 Zablocki	#	#	Y	Y	Y	Y	Y	Y
5 Reuss	N	Y	Y	Y	Y	N	Y	Y
6 Steiger	#	#	Y	Y	Y	N	#	#
7 Obey	N	Y	Y	Y	Y	N	Y	Y
8 Cornell	Y	Y	Y	Y	Y	Y	Y	Y
9 Kasten	Y	Y	Y	Y	Y	N	Y	Y
WYOMING								
AL Roncalio	N	Y	Y	Y	Y	Y	Y	Y

1 Reps. Edward I. Koch (D N.Y.) and Herman Badillo (D N.Y.) resigned Dec. 31, 1977.

Democrats ***Republicans***

9. S 1585. Child Pornography. Adoption of the conference report on the bill to prohibit the use of children under 16 in explicit sexual conduct for production of pornographic material for interstate or foreign commerce, the sale or distribution of obscene material depicting children in such conduct, and the interstate transportation of children under 18 for purposes of prostitution. Adopted (thus completing congressional action) 401-0: R 138-0; D 263-0 (ND 183-0: SD 80-0), Jan. 24, 1978.

10. HR 1614. Outer Continental Shelf. Adoption of the rule (H Res 964) providing for House floor consideration of a bill (HR 1614) to amend the Outer Continental Shelf Lands Act of 1953 to provide alternative bidding systems, grants to affected coastal states and environmental controls in federal leasing of offshore oil and gas reserves to private developers. Adopted 247-158: R 22-115; D 225-43 (ND 184-3; SD 41-40), Jan. 25, 1978.

11. HR 1614. Outer Continental Shelf. Breaux (D La.) substitute amendment to retain existing bidding systems at least 50 per cent of the time, provide sharing of federal offshore revenues with coastal states and restrict government involvement in exploratory drilling. Rejected 187-211: R 113-19; D 74-192 (ND 21-166; SD 53-26), Jan. 26, 1978. A "nay" was a vote supporting the President's position.

12. HR 1614. Outer Continental Shelf. Fish (R N.Y.) substitute amendment to limit the use of alternative bidding systems, channel revenue sharing through existing coastal zone programs and restrict government involvement in exploratory drilling. Rejected 143-229: R 101-21; D 42-208 (ND 4-168; SD 38-40), Jan. 26, 1978. A "nay" was a vote supporting the President's position.

KEY

- Y Voted for (yea).
- ✓ Paired for.
- † Announced for.
- # CQ Poll for.
- N Voted against (nay).
- X Paired against.
- \- Announced against.
- ▮ CQ Poll against.
- P Voted "present."
- ● Voted "present" to avoid possible conflict of interest.
- ? Did not vote or otherwise make a position known.

	9	10	11	12
ALABAMA				
1 Edwards	Y	N	Y	Y
2 Dickinson	Y	N	Y	Y
3 Nichols	Y	Y	✓	▮
4 Bevill	Y	Y	N	N
5 Flippo	Y	Y	Y	Y
6 Buchanan	Y	N	Y	Y
7 Flowers	Y	N	Y	?
ALASKA				
AL Young	Y	N	Y	Y
ARIZONA				
1 Rhodes	Y	N	Y	Y
2 Udall	Y	Y	N	N
3 Stump	?	Y	Y	Y
4 Rudd	Y	N	Y	Y
ARKANSAS				
1 Alexander	Y	Y	Y	N
2 Tucker	#	#	#	▮
3 Hammerschmidt	Y	N	Y	Y
4 Thornton	Y	?	?	?
CALIFORNIA				
1 Johnson	Y	Y	N	N
2 Clausen	Y	Y	Y	N
3 Moss	Y	Y	N	N
4 Leggett	Y	Y	N	?
5 Burton, J.	Y	?	N	N
6 Burton, P.	?	?	N	N
7 Miller	Y	Y	N	N
8 Dellums	Y	Y	N	N
9 Stark	Y	Y	N	N
10 Edwards	Y	Y	N	N
11 Ryan	Y	Y	X	X
12 McCloskey	?	Y	N	N
13 Mineta	Y	Y	N	N
14 McFall	Y	Y	N	N
15 Sisk	Y	Y	Y	?
16 Panetta	Y	Y	N	N
17 Krebs	Y	Y	N	N
18 Ketchum	Y	N	Y	?
19 Lagomarsino	Y	Y	Y	N
20 Goldwater	Y	N	Y	?
21 Corman	Y	Y	N	N
22 Moorhead	Y	N	Y	#
23 Beilenson	Y	Y	N	N
24 Waxman	Y	Y	N	N
25 Roybal	Y	Y	N	▮
26 Rousselot	Y	N	Y	Y
27 Dornan	Y	N	Y	✓
28 Burke	Y	Y	X	X
29 Hawkins	Y	Y	N	N
30 Danielson	Y	Y	N	-
31 Wilson, C.H.	#	Y	X	▮
32 Anderson	Y	Y	N	N
33 Clawson	Y	N	Y	Y
34 Hannaford	Y	Y	Y	N
35 Lloyd	Y	Y	N	N
36 Brown	Y	?	N	N
37 Pettis	Y	?	?	?
38 Patterson	#	Y	N	N
39 Wiggins	Y	N	Y	Y
40 Badham	Y	N	Y	Y
41 Wilson, B.	Y	#	#	▮
42 Van Deerlin	Y	Y	N	N
43 Burgener	Y	N	Y	?
COLORADO				
1 Schroeder	Y	Y	Y	N
2 Wirth	#	Y	N	▮
3 Evans	Y	Y	N	N
4 Johnson	Y	N	Y	Y
5 Armstrong	Y	?	?	?
CONNECTICUT				
1 Cotter	#	Y	N	X
2 Dodd	?	?	N	N
3 Giaimo	?	?	?	N
4 McKinney	Y	N	Y	Y
5 Sarasin	Y	N	Y	Y
6 Moffett	Y	Y	N	N
DELAWARE				
AL Evans	Y	Y	Y	Y
FLORIDA				
1 Sikes	?	N	✓	✓
2 Fuqua	Y	Y	Y	Y
3 Bennett	Y	Y	N	N
4 Chappell	#	N	Y	Y
5 Kelly	Y	N	Y	Y
6 Young	Y	Y	Y	Y
7 Gibbons	Y	N	?	N
8 Ireland	Y	N	✓	✓
9 Frey	Y	N	Y	Y
10 Bafalis	Y	N	Y	Y
11 Rogers	Y	Y	N	N
12 Burke	Y	N	Y	Y
13 Lehman	Y	Y	N	N
14 Pepper	#	#	X	▮
15 Fascell	Y	Y	N	N
GEORGIA				
1 Ginn	Y	Y	N	N
2 Mathis	Y	Y	Y	Y
3 Brinkley	Y	Y	Y	Y
4 Levitas	Y	Y	N	N
5 Fowler	Y	Y	N	N
6 Flynt	Y	N	Y	?
7 McDonald	Y	N	Y	Y
8 Evans	Y	Y	N	Y
9 Jenkins	Y	Y	Y	N
10 Barnard	Y	Y	Y	Y
HAWAII				
1 Heftel	Y	Y	Y	N
2 Akaka	Y	Y	N	N
IDAHO				
1 Symms	Y	N	?	✓
2 Hansen, G.	Y	N	Y	Y
ILLINOIS				
1 Metcalfe	Y	Y	N	N
2 Murphy	Y	Y	N	N
3 Russo	Y	Y	N	N
4 Derwinski	Y	N	Y	Y
5 Fary	Y	Y	N	N
6 Hyde	Y	N	Y	Y
7 Collins	Y	Y	N	N
8 Rostenkowski	Y	Y	N	N
9 Yates	Y	Y	N	N
10 Mikva	Y	Y	X	N
11 Annunzio	Y	Y	N	N
12 Crane	#	X	Y	Y
13 McClory	Y	N	Y	Y
14 Erlenborn	#	N	Y	Y
15 Corcoran	Y	N	Y	Y
16 Anderson	Y	Y	Y	Y
17 O'Brien	Y	Y	Y	Y
18 Michel	Y	N	Y	Y
19 Railsback	Y	N	Y	Y
20 Findley	Y	N	?	?
21 Madigan	Y	N	Y	Y
22 Shipley	Y	?	N	?
23 Price	Y	Y	N	N
24 Simon	Y	Y	N	N
INDIANA				
1 Benjamin	Y	Y	N	N
2 Fithian	Y	Y	N	N
3 Brademas	Y	Y	N	N
4 Quayle	Y	N	Y	Y
5 Hillis	?	?	?	?
6 Evans	Y	Y	N	N
7 Myers, J.	Y	Y	Y	Y
8 Cornwell	Y	Y	Y	N
9 Hamilton	Y	Y	N	N
10 Sharp	Y	Y	N	N
11 Jacobs	Y	Y	N	N
IOWA				
1 Leach	Y	N	Y	Y
2 Blouin	#	Y	N	N
3 Grassley	Y	N	Y	Y
4 Smith	Y	Y	N	N
5 Harkin	Y	Y	N	N
6 Bedell	Y	Y	N	N

Democrats ***Republicans***

	9	10	11	12
KANSAS				
1 Sebelius	Y	N	✓	✓
2 Keys	Y	Y	N	N
3 Winn	Y	N	Y	Y
4 Glickman	Y	Y	Y	N
5 Skubitz	Y	N	N	N
KENTUCKY				
1 Hubbard	Y	N	Y	Y
2 Natcher	Y	Y	N	N
3 Mazzoli	Y	Y	N	N
4 Snyder	Y	N	Y	Y
5 Carter	Y	Y	N	N
6 Breckinridge	Y	Y	N	N
7 Perkins	Y	Y	N	N
LOUISIANA				
1 Livingston	Y	N	Y	Y
2 Boggs	Y	N	Y	Y
3 Treen	Y	N	Y	Y
4 Waggonner	Y	#	Y	?
5 Huckaby	#	▮	Y	Y
6 Moore	Y	N	Y	Y
7 Breaux	?	N	Y	Y
8 Long	Y	N	Y	Y
MAINE				
1 Emery	Y	Y	N	N
2 Cohen	Y	Y	N	N
MARYLAND				
1 Bauman	Y	N	Y	Y
2 Long	Y	Y	Y	N
3 Mikulski	Y	Y	N	N
4 Holt	Y	N	Y	Y
5 Spellman	Y	Y	N	N
6 Byron	Y	Y	N	N
7 Mitchell	Y	Y	N	N
8 Steers	Y	Y	N	N
MASSACHUSETTS				
1 Conte	Y	Y	N	N
2 Boland	Y	Y	N	▮
3 Early	Y	Y	N	N
4 Drinan	Y	Y	N	N
5 Tsongas	Y	Y	N	N
6 Harrington	Y	Y	N	N
7 Markey	Y	Y	N	N
8 O'Neill				
9 Moakley	Y	Y	N	N
10 Heckler	Y	Y	N	N
11 Burke	Y	Y	N	N
12 Studds	Y	Y	N	N
MICHIGAN				
1 Conyers	Y	N	N	N
2 Pursell	Y	N	N	Y
3 Brown	Y	N	Y	Y
4 Stockman	Y	N	Y	Y
5 Sawyer	Y	N	Y	Y
6 Carr	Y	Y	N	N
7 Kildee	Y	Y	N	N
8 Traxler	Y	Y	N	N
9 Vander Jagt	Y	N	Y	Y
10 Cederberg	Y	N	Y	Y
11 Ruppe	Y	N	?	#
12 Bonior	Y	Y	N	N
13 Diggs	Y	#	N	▮
14 Nedzi	Y	Y	N	N
15 Ford	Y	Y	N	N
16 Dingell	Y	Y	N	N
17 Brodhead	Y	Y	N	N
18 Blanchard	#	Y	N	N
19 Broomfield	Y	N	✓	✓
MINNESOTA				
1 Quie	Y	N	Y	▮
2 Hagedorn	Y	N	Y	Y
3 Frenzel	Y	N	Y	Y
4 Vento	Y	Y	N	N
5 Fraser	Y	Y	N	N
6 Nolan	Y	Y	N	N
7 Stangeland	Y	N	Y	✓
8 Oberstar	Y	Y	N	N
MISSISSIPPI				
1 Whitten	Y	N	Y	Y
2 Bowen	Y	N	Y	Y
3 Montgomery	Y	N	Y	Y
4 Cochran	Y	N	Y	Y
5 Lott	#	N	Y	Y
MISSOURI				
1 Clay	Y	Y	N	N
2 Young	Y	Y	Y	N
3 Gephardt	Y	Y	N	N

	9	10	11	12
4 Skelton	Y	Y	Y	N
5 Bolling	Y	Y	N	N
6 Coleman	Y	N	Y	Y
7 Taylor	Y	N	Y	Y
8 Ichord	Y	Y	Y	Y
9 Volkmer	Y	Y	Y	N
10 Burlison	Y	Y	N	N
MONTANA				
1 Baucus	Y	Y	N	X
2 Marlenee	Y	N	Y	Y
NEBRASKA				
1 Thone	Y	N	Y	Y
2 Cavanaugh	Y	Y	N	N
3 Smith	Y	N	Y	Y
NEVADA				
AL Santini	Y	Y	Y	Y
NEW HAMPSHIRE				
1 D'Amours	Y	Y	N	N
2 Cleveland	Y	N	Y	Y
NEW JERSEY				
1 Florio	Y	Y	N	N
2 Hughes	Y	Y	N	N
3 Howard	Y	Y	N	N
4 Thompson	Y	Y	X	N
5 Fenwick	Y	N	N	N
6 Forsythe	Y	N	Y	Y
7 Maguire	Y	Y	N	N
8 Roe	Y	Y	N	▮
9 Hollenbeck	?	Y	N	N
10 Rodino	Y	✓	X	X
11 Minish	Y	Y	N	N
12 Rinaldo	Y	Y	N	N
13 Meyner	Y	Y	N	N
14 LeFante	Y	Y	N	N
15 Patten	Y	Y	N	N
NEW MEXICO				
1 Lujan	Y	N	Y	✓
2 Runnels	Y	N	Y	Y
NEW YORK				
1 Pike	Y	Y	N	N
2 Downey	Y	Y	N	N
3 Ambro	Y	Y	N	N
4 Lent	Y	N	N	N
5 Wydler	Y	Y	N	Y
6 Wolff	Y	Y	N	N
7 Addabbo	Y	Y	N	N
8 Rosenthal	Y	Y	N	N
9 Delaney	Y	Y	N	N
10 Biaggi	Y	Y	N	N
11 Scheuer	Y	Y	N	N
12 Chisholm	Y	Y	N	N
13 Solarz	Y	Y	N	N
14 Richmond	Y	Y	N	N
15 Zeferetti	Y	Y	N	N
16 Holtzman	Y	Y	N	N
17 Murphy	Y	Y	N	N
18 Vacancy				
19 Rangel	Y	Y	N	N
20 Weiss	Y	Y	N	N
21 Vacancy				
22 Bingham	Y	Y	N	N
23 Caputo	Y	N	Y	Y
24 Ottinger	Y	Y	N	N
25 Fish	Y	N	Y	Y
26 Gilman	Y	Y	N	N
27 McHugh	Y	Y	N	N
28 Stratton	Y	Y	N	N
29 Pattison	Y	Y	N	N
30 McEwen	Y	N	Y	Y
31 Mitchell	Y	N	Y	Y
32 Hanley	Y	Y	N	N
33 Walsh	?	?	?	?
34 Horton	Y	N	Y	Y
35 Conable	Y	N	Y	Y
36 LaFalce	Y	Y	N	N
37 Nowak	Y	Y	N	N
38 Kemp	Y	N	Y	Y
39 Lundine	Y	Y	Y	N
NORTH CAROLINA				
1 Jones	Y	Y	Y	Y
2 Fountain	Y	N	Y	N
3 Whitley	Y	N	Y	N
4 Andrews	Y	N	N	N
5 Neal	Y	Y	N	N
6 Preyer	Y	Y	N	N
7 Rose	Y	N	N	N
8 Hefner	Y	Y	N	N

	9	10	11	12
9 Martin	Y	#	Y	Y
10 Broyhill	Y	N	Y	Y
11 Gudger	Y	Y	Y	N
NORTH DAKOTA				
AL Andrews	Y	N	Y	Y
OHIO				
1 Gradison	Y	N	Y	Y
2 Luken	Y	Y	Y	N
3 Whalen	Y	Y	N	N
4 Guyer	Y	X	✓	✓
5 Latta	Y	N	Y	Y
6 Harsha	Y	N	Y	Y
7 Brown	Y	N	Y	Y
8 Kindness	Y	N	Y	Y
9 Ashley	Y	Y	N	N
10 Miller	Y	N	Y	Y
11 Stanton	Y	N	Y	Y
12 Devine	Y	N	Y	Y
13 Pease	Y	Y	N	N
14 Seiberling	Y	Y	N	N
15 Wylie	Y	N	Y	Y
16 Regula	Y	N	Y	Y
17 Ashbrook	Y	N	✓	✓
18 Applegate	Y	Y	Y	N
19 Carney	Y	Y	N	N
20 Oakar	Y	Y	N	N
21 Stokes	Y	Y	N	N
22 Vanik	Y	Y	N	N
23 Mottl	Y	Y	N	N
OKLAHOMA				
1 Jones	Y	N	Y	Y
2 Risenhoover	?	N	Y	Y
3 Watkins	Y	N	#	Y
4 Steed	Y	N	Y	Y
5 Edwards	Y	N	Y	Y
6 English	Y	▮	Y	Y
OREGON				
1 AuCoin	#	Y	N	N
2 Ullman	Y	Y	N	N
3 Duncan	Y	Y	N	N
4 Weaver	Y	Y	N	N
PENNSYLVANIA				
1 Myers, M.	?	Y	N	N
2 Nix	Y	Y	N	X
3 Lederer	Y	Y	N	N
4 Eilberg	Y	Y	N	N
5 Schulze	Y	N	Y	Y
6 Yatron	Y	Y	N	N
7 Edgar	Y	Y	N	N
8 Kostmayer	Y	Y	N	N
9 Shuster	Y	N	Y	Y
10 McDade	Y	N	Y	N
11 Flood	Y	Y	N	N
12 Murtha	Y	Y	N	N
13 Coughlin	Y	N	Y	Y
14 Moorhead	Y	Y	N	N
15 Rooney	Y	Y	N	N
16 Walker	Y	N	Y	Y
17 Ertel	Y	Y	N	N
18 Walgren	Y	Y	N	N
19 Goodling, W.	Y	N	Y	Y
20 Gaydos	Y	Y	N	N
21 Dent	#	✓	X	X
22 Murphy	Y	Y	N	#
23 Ammerman	Y	Y	N	N
24 Marks	Y	Y	N	N
25 Myers, G.	Y	Y	Y	Y
RHODE ISLAND				
1 St Germain	Y	Y	N	X
2 Beard	Y	Y	N	?
SOUTH CAROLINA				
1 Davis	Y	N	Y	N
2 Spence	Y	N	Y	Y
3 Derrick	Y	Y	N	N
4 Mann	Y	Y	Y	N
5 Holland	Y	Y	Y	N
6 Jenrette	Y	Y	N	N
SOUTH DAKOTA				
1 Pressler	Y	Y	N	N
2 Abdnor	Y	N	Y	Y
TENNESSEE				
1 Quillen	Y	N	Y	Y
2 Duncan	Y	N	Y	Y
3 Lloyd	Y	Y	Y	Y
4 Gore	Y	Y	N	N
5 Allen	Y	Y	N	N
6 Beard	Y	N	Y	Y

	9	10	11	12
7 Jones	Y	Y	Y	N
8 Ford	Y	Y	N	N
TEXAS				
1 Hall	Y	N	Y	Y
2 Wilson, C.	Y	#	Y	Y
3 Collins	Y	N	Y	Y
4 Roberts	Y	N	Y	N
5 Mattox	Y	N	Y	N
6 Teague	?	X	✓	N
7 Archer	Y	N	Y	Y
8 Eckhardt	Y	✓	N	N
9 Brooks	Y	Y	✓	?
10 Pickle	Y	N	Y	Y
11 Poage	?	N	Y	Y
12 Wright	Y	Y	Y	N
13 Hightower	Y	N	Y	?
14 Young	Y	N	Y	Y
15 de la Garza	Y	N	?	Y
16 White	Y	N	Y	Y
17 Burleson	Y	N	Y	Y
18 Jordan	Y	Y	Y	N
19 Mahon	Y	N	Y	Y
20 Gonzalez	Y	N	Y	?
21 Krueger	Y	N	Y	Y
22 Gammage	?	N	Y	Y
23 Kazen	Y	N	Y	Y
24 Milford	Y	N	Y	Y
UTAH				
1 McKay	Y	Y	Y	N
2 Marriott	Y	N	Y	Y
VERMONT				
AL Jeffords	Y	N	N	N
VIRGINIA				
1 Trible	Y	N	Y	?
2 Whitehurst	Y	N	Y	N
3 Satterfield	Y	N	Y	Y
4 Daniel	Y	N	Y	Y
5 Daniel	Y	Y	Y	Y
6 Butler	Y	N	Y	Y
7 Robinson	Y	N	Y	Y
8 Harris	Y	Y	N	N
9 Wampler	Y	N	?	?
10 Fisher	Y	Y	N	N
WASHINGTON				
1 Pritchard	Y	N	Y	Y
2 Meeds	Y	Y	N	N
3 Bonker	Y	Y	X	X
4 McCormack	Y	Y	N	N
5 Foley	Y	Y	N	N
6 Dicks	Y	Y	N	N
7 Cunningham	Y	N	Y	#
WEST VIRGINIA				
1 Mollohan	Y	N	Y	N
2 Staggers	Y	Y	N	X
3 Slack	Y	Y	Y	N
4 Rahall	Y	Y	N	N
WISCONSIN				
1 Aspin	Y	Y	N	N
2 Kastenmeier	Y	Y	N	N
3 Baldus	Y	Y	N	N
4 Zablocki	Y	Y	N	N
5 Reuss	Y	Y	N	▮
6 Steiger	#	N	Y	Y
7 Obey	Y	Y	N	N
8 Cornell	Y	Y	N	N
9 Kasten	Y	†	†	†
WYOMING				
AL Roncalio	Y	Y	Y	?

Democrats ***Republicans***

13. HR 5798. Office of Rail Public Counsel. Passage of the bill to authorize $1 million for fiscal 1978 for the Office of Rail Public Counsel in the Interstate Commerce Commission. Passed 318-44: R 89-31; D 229-13 (ND 156-5; SD 73-8), Jan. 30, 1978.

14. HR 5646. ConRail Insurance Payments. Passage of the bill to enable the U.S. Railway Association to loan funds to the Consolidated Rail Corporation for payment of medical and life insurance premiums for certain retired employees of currently bankrupt or reorganized railroads. Passed 314-50: R 85-34; D 229-16 (ND 164-1; SD 65-15), Jan. 30, 1978.

15. HR 9851. Air Cargo Service. Anderson (D Calif.) motion to suspend the rules and pass the bill to permit charter airlines to immediately seek certification to provide all-cargo air service under the provisions of a 1977 air cargo deregulation law (PL 95-173). Motion agreed to 403-0: R 137-0; D 266-0 (ND 182-0; SD 84-0), Jan. 31, 1978. A two-thirds majority vote (269 in this case) is required for passage under suspension of the rules.

16. HR 1614. Outer Continental Shelf. Studds (D Mass.) amendment to delete language authorizing any federal agency to do exploratory drilling for oil or gas. Adopted 328-77: R 135-2; D 193-75 (ND 118-65; SD 75-10), Jan. 31, 1978.

17. HR 1614. Outer Continental Shelf. Wiggins (R Calif.) amendment to replace the bill's formula for determining federal compensation to a lessee on the Outer Continental Shelf for losses incurred if the lease were cancelled with the statement that cancellation should not foreclose any claim for compensation as required by the Constitution or other law. Adopted 208-194: R 126-11; D 82-183 (ND 15-166; SD 67-17), Jan. 31, 1978.

18. HR 1614. Outer Continental Shelf. Brown (R Ohio) substitute amendment, to the Treen (R La.) amendment, to require use of alternative bidding systems in at least 10 per cent and not more than 30 per cent of lease sales for five years. (The Treen amendment would have removed the requirement for use of alternative bidding in 50 per cent of leases.) Rejected 196-207: R 130-7; D 66-200 (ND 14-168; SD 52-32), Jan. 31, 1978.

19. HR 1614. Outer Continental Shelf. Emery (R Maine) substitute amendment, to the Treen (R La.) amendment, to require use of alternative bidding in at least 20 per cent and not more than 50 per cent of lease sales. Adopted 219-188: R 135-4; D 84-184 (ND 23-160; SD 61-24), Jan. 31, 1978. (The Treen amendment as amended was adopted subsequently by voice vote. *See vote 18, above.*)

20. HR 8200. Bankruptcy Law Revision. Edwards (Calif.) motion that the House resolve itself into the Committee of the Whole to consider the bill to establish a uniform modern bankruptcy law; to provide cosumers with more adequate relief under the bankruptcy laws; and to create a separate federal bankruptcy court system. Motion agreed to 405-4: R 138-2; D 267-2 (ND 182-2; SD 85-0), Feb. 1, 1978.

KEY

- Y Voted for (yea).
- ✓ Paired for.
- † Announced for.
- # CQ Poll for.
- N Voted against (nay).
- X Paired against.
- \- Announced against.
- ▮ CQ Poll against
- P Voted "present."
- ● Voted "present" to avoid possible conflict of interest.
- ? Did not vote or otherwise make a position known.

	13	14	15	16	17	18	19	20
ALABAMA								
1 Edwards	Y	Y	Y	Y	Y	Y	Y	Y
2 Dickinson	Y	N	Y	Y	Y	Y	Y	Y
3 Nichols	Y	Y	Y	Y	Y	Y	Y	Y
4 Bevill	Y	Y	Y	N	N	N	N	Y
5 Flippo	Y	Y	Y	Y	Y	Y	Y	Y
6 Buchanan	Y	Y	Y	Y	Y	Y	Y	Y
7 Flowers	Y	Y	Y	Y	Y	Y	Y	Y
ALASKA								
AL Young	Y	▮	Y	Y	Y	Y	Y	Y
ARIZONA								
1 Rhodes	Y	?	Y	Y	Y	Y	Y	Y
2 Udall	Y	Y	Y	Y	N	N	N	Y
3 Stump	N	Y	Y	Y	Y	Y	Y	Y
4 Rudd	N	N	Y	Y	Y	Y	Y	Y
ARKANSAS								
1 Alexander	?	?	?	Y	Y	N	N	Y
2 Tucker	N	Y	Y	Y	N	Y	Y	Y
3 Hammerschmidt	Y	N	Y	Y	Y	Y	Y	Y
4 Thornton	Y	N	Y	Y	Y	Y	Y	Y
CALIFORNIA								
1 Johnson	Y	Y	Y	Y	N	N	N	Y
2 Clausen	N	Y	Y	Y	Y	Y	Y	Y
3 Moss	Y	Y	?	?	?	?	?	?
4 Leggett	Y	Y	Y	?	N	N	N	#
5 Burton, J.	Y	Y	?	N	?	N	N	?
6 Burton, P.	Y	Y	Y	N	N	N	N	Y
7 Miller	Y	Y	Y	N	N	N	N	Y
8 Dellums	Y	Y	#	N	N	N	N	Y
9 Stark	Y	Y	Y	N	N	N	N	Y
10 Edwards	Y	Y	Y	N	N	N	N	Y
11 Ryan	?	?	Y	Y	-	N	N	Y
12 McCloskey	?	?	Y	Y	Y	Y	Y	Y
13 Mineta	Y	Y	Y	Y	N	X	X	Y
14 McFall	Y	Y	Y	Y	N	N	N	Y
15 Sisk	Y	?	Y	Y	Y	N	Y	Y
16 Panetta	Y	Y	Y	Y	N	N	N	Y
17 Krebs	Y	Y	Y	Y	N	N	N	Y
18 Ketchum	Y	Y	Y	Y	Y	Y	Y	Y
19 Lagomarsino	N	N	Y	Y	Y	Y	Y	Y
20 Goldwater	?	?	Y	Y	Y	Y	Y	Y
21 Corman	Y	Y	Y	N	N	N	N	Y
22 Moorhead	▮	▮	#	#	✓	✓	✓	Y
23 Beilenson	Y	Y	Y	N	N	N	N	Y
24 Waxman	Y	Y	Y	Y	N	X	N	Y
25 Roybal	#	#	Y	Y	N	N	N	Y
26 Rousselot	N	N	Y	Y	Y	Y	Y	Y
27 Dornan	?	?	?	?	✓	✓	✓	Y
28 Burke	#	#	#	#	X	X	X	Y
29 Hawkins	Y	Y	Y	N	X	N	N	Y
30 Danielson	Y	Y	Y	Y	N	N	N	Y
31 Wilson, C.H.	Y	Y	Y	Y	X	N	X	Y
32 Anderson	N	Y	Y	Y	N	N	X	Y
33 Clawson	N	N	Y	Y	Y	Y	Y	Y
34 Hannaford	Y	Y	Y	Y	Y	N	N	Y
35 Lloyd	Y	Y	Y	Y	N	N	N	Y
36 Brown	Y	Y	?	?	?	?	?	?
37 Pettis	Y	Y	Y	Y	Y	Y	Y	Y
38 Patterson	Y	Y	Y	N	N	N	N	Y
39 Wiggins	▮	▮	Y	Y	Y	Y	Y	#
40 Badham	Y	Y	Y	Y	Y	Y	Y	Y
41 Wilson, B.	Y	Y	Y	Y	Y	Y	Y	N
42 Van Deerlin	?	?	Y	Y	N	N	N	Y
43 Burgener	Y	Y	Y	Y	Y	Y	Y	Y
COLORADO								
1 Schroeder	Y	Y	Y	Y	N	N	Y	Y
2 Wirth	Y	Y	Y	Y	N	Y	Y	Y
3 Evans	Y	Y	Y	N	Y	Y	Y	Y
4 Johnson	Y	Y	Y	Y	Y	Y	Y	Y
5 Armstrong	?	?	?	?	?	?	?	?
CONNECTICUT								
1 Cotter	#	#	Y	Y	N	N	N	Y
2 Dodd	Y	Y	Y	Y	N	N	N	Y
3 Giaimo	Y	Y	Y	Y	N	N	N	Y
4 McKinney	Y	Y	Y	Y	Y	Y	Y	Y
5 Sarasin	Y	Y	Y	Y	Y	Y	Y	Y
6 Moffett	Y	Y	Y	N	N	N	N	Y
DELAWARE								
AL Evans	Y	Y	Y	Y	Y	Y	Y	Y
FLORIDA								
1 Sikes	Y	Y	Y	Y	Y	Y	Y	Y
2 Fuqua	Y	Y	Y	Y	Y	Y	Y	Y
3 Bennett	Y	N	Y	Y	Y	N	N	Y
4 Chappell	Y	†	Y	Y	Y	Y	Y	Y
5 Kelly	Y	N	Y	Y	Y	Y	Y	Y
6 Young	N	N	Y	Y	Y	Y	Y	Y
7 Gibbons	Y	N	Y	N	Y	Y	Y	Y
8 Ireland	Y	Y	Y	Y	Y	Y	Y	Y
9 Frey	Y	Y	Y	Y	Y	Y	Y	Y
10 Bafalis	Y	N	Y	Y	Y	Y	Y	Y
11 Rogers	Y	Y	Y	?	X	N	N	Y
12 Burke	Y	Y	Y	Y	Y	Y	Y	Y
13 Lehman	#	#	#	#	X	X	X	#
14 Pepper	#	#	Y	Y	N	N	N	Y
15 Fascell	Y	Y	Y	Y	N	N	N	Y
GEORGIA								
1 Ginn	Y	Y	Y	Y	N	N	Y	Y
2 Mathis	Y	Y	Y	Y	Y	N	Y	Y
3 Brinkley	Y	Y	Y	Y	Y	Y	Y	Y
4 Levitas	Y	N	Y	Y	N	N	Y	Y
5 Fowler	Y	N	Y	Y	N	N	Y	Y
6 Flynt	Y	N	Y	Y	Y	Y	Y	Y
7 McDonald	N	N	#	#	✓	✓	✓	#
8 Evans	Y	Y	Y	Y	Y	N	Y	Y
9 Jenkins	Y	Y	Y	Y	Y	N	Y	Y
10 Barnard	Y	Y	Y	Y	Y	Y	Y	Y
HAWAII								
1 Heftel	Y	Y	Y	Y	N	N	N	Y
2 Akaka	Y	Y	Y	Y	N	N	N	Y
IDAHO								
1 Symms	N	N	Y	Y	Y	Y	Y	Y
2 Hansen, G.	N	N	Y	Y	Y	Y	Y	Y
ILLINOIS								
1 Metcalfe	?	?	Y	Y	N	N	N	Y
2 Murphy	#	#	Y	Y	N	N	N	Y
3 Russo	Y	Y	Y	Y	Y	Y	Y	Y
4 Derwinski	#	Y	Y	Y	Y	Y	Y	Y
5 Fary	Y	Y	Y	Y	N	N	N	Y
6 Hyde	N	Y	Y	Y	Y	Y	Y	Y
7 Collins	Y	Y	Y	N	N	N	N	Y
8 Rostenkowski	Y	Y	Y	Y	N	N	N	Y
9 Yates	Y	Y	Y	N	N	N	N	Y
10 Mikva	Y	Y	Y	N	N	N	N	Y
11 Annunzio	#	#	Y	Y	N	N	N	Y
12 Crane	▮	▮	Y	Y	Y	Y	Y	Y
13 McClory	N	N	Y	Y	Y	Y	Y	Y
14 Erlenborn	#	#	Y	Y	Y	Y	Y	Y
15 Corcoran	Y	Y	Y	Y	Y	Y	Y	Y
16 Anderson	#	#	Y	Y	Y	Y	Y	Y
17 O'Brien	Y	Y	Y	Y	Y	N	Y	Y
18 Michel	Y	Y	Y	Y	Y	Y	Y	Y
19 Railsback	Y	Y	Y	Y	Y	Y	Y	Y
20 Findley	Y	N	Y	Y	Y	Y	Y	Y
21 Madigan	Y	Y	Y	Y	Y	Y	Y	Y
22 Shipley	Y	Y	Y	Y	N	N	N	Y
23 Price	Y	Y	Y	Y	N	N	N	Y
24 Simon	Y	Y	Y	N	N	N	N	Y
INDIANA								
1 Benjamin	Y	Y	Y	Y	Y	N	N	Y
2 Fithian	Y	Y	Y	Y	N	N	N	Y
3 Brademas	#	#	Y	Y	N	N	N	Y
4 Quayle	N	Y	Y	Y	Y	Y	Y	Y
5 Hillis	Y	Y	Y	Y	Y	Y	Y	Y
6 Evans	Y	Y	Y	Y	N	N	N	Y
7 Myers, J.	Y	Y	Y	▮	Y	Y	Y	Y
8 Cornwell	Y	Y	Y	?	Y	Y	Y	Y
9 Hamilton	Y	Y	Y	Y	N	N	N	Y
10 Sharp	Y	Y	Y	Y	N	N	N	Y
11 Jacobs	N	Y	Y	Y	N	N	N	Y
IOWA								
1 Leach	Y	Y	Y	Y	Y	Y	Y	Y
2 Blouin	Y	Y	Y	N	N	N	N	Y
3 Grassley	Y	N	Y	Y	Y	Y	Y	Y
4 Smith	Y	Y	Y	Y	N	N	N	Y
5 Harkin	Y	Y	Y	N	N	N	N	Y
6 Bedell	Y	Y	Y	N	N	N	N	Y

Democrats ***Republicans***

	13	14	15	16	17	18	19	20
KANSAS								
1 Sebelius	#	#	Y	Y	Y	Y	Y	Y
2 Keys	Y	Y	Y	N	N	N	N	Y
3 Winn	Y	Y	Y	Y	Y	Y	Y	Y
4 Glickman	Y	Y	Y	Y	N	Y	Y	Y
5 Skubitz	?	?	?	?	✓	✓	✓	Y
KENTUCKY								
1 Hubbard	Y	Y	Y	Y	N	Y	Y	Y
2 Natcher	Y	Y	Y	Y	N	N	N	Y
3 Mazzoli	Y	Y	Y	Y	Y	N	N	Y
4 Snyder	N	N	Y	Y	Y	Y	Y	Y
5 Carter	Y	Y	Y	Y	Y	Y	Y	Y
6 Breckinridge	Y	Y	Y	Y	Y	N	N	Y
7 Perkins	Y	Y	Y	Y	Y	N	N	Y
LOUISIANA								
1 Livingston	N	N	Y	Y	Y	Y	Y	Y
2 Boggs	Y	Y	Y	Y	Y	Y	Y	Y
3 Treen	N	Y	Y	Y	Y	N	N	Y
4 Waggonner	Y	N	Y	Y	Y	Y	Y	Y
5 Huckaby	Y	Y	Y	Y	Y	Y	Y	Y
6 Moore	N	Y	Y	Y	Y	Y	Y	Y
7 Breaux	Y	N	Y	Y	Y	Y	Y	Y
8 Long	Y	Y	Y	Y	Y	Y	Y	Y
MAINE								
1 Emery	Y	Y	Y	Y	Y	Y	Y	Y
2 Cohen	?	?	Y	Y	N	Y	Y	Y
MARYLAND								
1 Bauman	Y	N	Y	Y	Y	Y	Y	Y
2 Long	Y	Y	Y	Y	N	N	N	Y
3 Mikulski	Y	Y	Y	Y	N	N	N	Y
4 Holt	N	Y	Y	Y	Y	Y	Y	Y
5 Spellman	Y	Y	Y	N	N	N	N	Y
6 Byron	Y	Y	Y	Y	Y	N	N	Y
7 Mitchell	Y	Y	Y	Y	N	N	N	#
8 Steers	Y	Y	Y	N	Y	Y	Y	Y
MASSACHUSETTS								
1 Conte	Y	Y	Y	N	N	Y	Y	Y
2 Boland	Y	Y	Y	Y	N	N	N	Y
3 Early	Y	Y	Y	N	N	N	N	Y
4 Drinan	Y	Y	Y	N	N	N	N	Y
5 Tsongas	Y	Y	Y	Y	N	N	N	Y
6 Harrington	Y	Y	Y	N	N	X	X	Y
7 Markey	Y	Y	Y	N	N	N	N	Y
8 O'Neill								
9 Moakley	Y	Y	Y	Y	N	N	N	Y
10 Heckler	?	?	Y	Y	N	Y	Y	?
11 Burke	Y	Y	Y	Y	N	N	N	Y
12 Studds	Y	Y	Y	Y	N	N	N	Y
MICHIGAN								
1 Conyers	Y	Y	Y	N	N	N	N	Y
2 Pursell	?	Y	Y	Y	?	Y	Y	Y
3 Brown	Y	Y	Y	Y	Y	Y	Y	Y
4 Stockman	Y	Y	Y	Y	Y	Y	Y	Y
5 Sawyer	Y	Y	Y	Y	Y	Y	Y	Y
6 Carr	Y	Y	Y	Y	N	N	N	Y
7 Kildee	Y	Y	Y	N	N	N	N	Y
8 Traxler	Y	Y	Y	Y	N	N	N	Y
9 Vander Jagt	?	?	Y	Y	Y	Y	Y	Y
10 Cederberg	Y	Y	Y	Y	Y	Y	Y	Y
11 Ruppe	#	#	#	Y	Y	Y	Y	Y
12 Bonior	Y	Y	Y	#	N	N	N	Y
13 Diggs	#	#	#	#	X	N	N	#
14 Nedzi	Y	Y	Y	Y	N	N	N	Y
15 Ford	Y	Y	Y	Y	N	N	N	Y
16 Dingell	?	Y	Y	Y	N	N	N	Y
17 Brodhead	Y	Y	Y	N	N	N	N	Y
18 Blanchard	Y	Y	Y	N	N	N	N	Y
19 Broomfield	Y	Y	Y	Y	Y	Y	Y	Y
MINNESOTA								
1 Quie	#	#	Y	Y	Y	Y	Y	Y
2 Hagedorn	?	?	Y	Y	Y	Y	Y	Y
3 Frenzel	N	Y	Y	Y	Y	Y	Y	Y
4 Vento	Y	Y	Y	N	N	N	N	Y
5 Fraser	#	?	Y	N	N	N	N	Y
6 Nolan	Y	Y	Y	N	N	N	N	Y
7 Stangeland	N	Y	Y	Y	Y	Y	Y	Y
8 Oberstar	Y	Y	Y	N	N	N	N	Y
MISSISSIPPI								
1 Whitten	Y	Y	Y	Y	Y	Y	Y	Y
2 Bowen	Y	Y	Y	Y	Y	Y	Y	Y
3 Montgomery	N	Y	Y	Y	Y	Y	Y	Y
4 Cochran	N	N	Y	Y	Y	Y	Y	Y
5 Lott	N	Y	Y	Y	Y	Y	Y	Y
MISSOURI								
1 Clay	Y	Y	Y	N	N	N	N	Y
2 Young	Y	Y	Y	Y	N	N	N	Y
3 Gephardt	#	#	Y	Y	N	N	N	Y
4 Skelton	Y	N	Y	Y	N	N	Y	Y
5 Bolling	#	#	#	N	■	N	N	Y
6 Coleman	Y	Y	Y	Y	Y	Y	Y	Y
7 Taylor	N	N	Y	Y	Y	Y	Y	Y
8 Ichord	N	?	Y	Y	Y	Y	Y	Y
9 Volkmer	Y	Y	Y	Y	N	N	Y	Y
10 Burlison	Y	Y	Y	Y	N	N	N	Y
MONTANA								
1 Baucus	Y	Y	Y	Y	N	N	N	Y
2 Marlenee	Y	Y	Y	Y	Y	Y	Y	Y
NEBRASKA								
1 Thone	Y	Y	Y	Y	Y	Y	Y	#
2 Cavanaugh	Y	Y	Y	N	N	N	N	Y
3 Smith	Y	Y	Y	Y	Y	Y	Y	Y
NEVADA								
AL Santini	Y	Y	Y	Y	N	N	N	Y
NEW HAMPSHIRE								
1 D'Amours	Y	Y	Y	N	N	N	N	N
2 Cleveland	Y	Y	Y	Y	Y	Y	Y	Y
NEW JERSEY								
1 Florio	Y	Y	Y	Y	N	N	N	Y
2 Hughes	Y	Y	Y	Y	N	N	N	Y
3 Howard	Y	Y	Y	Y	N	N	N	Y
4 Thompson	Y	Y	Y	Y	X	N	N	#
5 Fenwick	Y	Y	Y	Y	N	N	Y	Y
6 Forsythe	Y	Y	Y	Y	Y	Y	Y	Y
7 Maguire	?	?	Y	N	N	N	N	Y
8 Roe	Y	Y	Y	Y	N	N	N	Y
9 Hollenbeck	?	?	Y	Y	N	N	Y	N
10 Rodino	#	#	Y	N	N	N	N	Y
11 Minish	Y	Y	Y	Y	N	N	N	Y
12 Rinaldo	Y	Y	Y	Y	N	N	Y	Y
13 Meyner	Y	Y	Y	N	N	N	N	Y
14 LeFante	Y	Y	#	#	X	X	X	Y
15 Patten	Y	Y	Y	Y	N	N	N	Y
NEW MEXICO								
1 Lujan	Y	N	Y	Y	Y	Y	Y	Y
2 Runnels	Y	Y	Y	Y	Y	Y	Y	Y
NEW YORK								
1 Pike	Y	Y	Y	Y	N	N	N	Y
2 Downey	Y	Y	Y	#	■	■	■	#
3 Ambro	?	Y	Y	Y	Y	N	N	Y
4 Lent	Y	Y	Y	Y	Y	#	Y	Y
5 Wydler	?	?	?	?	✓	Y	Y	Y
6 Wolff	Y	Y	Y	N	N	N	N	#
7 Addabbo	#	#	Y	Y	N	N	N	Y
8 Rosenthal	Y	Y	Y	Y	N	N	N	Y
9 Delaney	Y	Y	Y	Y	N	N	N	Y
10 Biaggi	#	#	Y	Y	N	N	N	Y
11 Scheuer	Y	Y	Y	N	N	N	N	Y
12 Chisholm	Y	Y	Y	Y	N	N	N	Y
13 Solarz	Y	Y	Y	N	N	N	N	Y
14 Richmond	Y	Y	Y	Y	N	N	N	Y
15 Zeferetti	†	#	Y	Y	N	N	N	Y
16 Holtzman	?	Y	Y	N	N	N	N	Y
17 Murphy	Y	Y	Y	Y	N	N	N	Y
18 Vacancy								
19 Rangel	Y	Y	?	N	N	N	N	Y
20 Weiss	Y	Y	Y	N	N	N	N	Y
21 Vacancy								
22 Bingham	#	#	#	■	X	X	X	#
23 Caputo	Y	Y	Y	Y	Y	Y	Y	Y
24 Ottinger	#	#	Y	N	N	N	N	Y
25 Fish	Y	Y	Y	Y	Y	Y	Y	Y
26 Gilman	Y	Y	Y	Y	Y	N	Y	Y
27 McHugh	Y	Y	Y	Y	N	N	N	Y
28 Stratton	Y	Y	Y	Y	N	N	N	Y
29 Pattison	Y	Y	Y	#	N	#	N	Y
30 McEwen	Y	Y	Y	Y	Y	Y	Y	Y
31 Mitchell	Y	Y	Y	Y	N	Y	Y	Y
32 Hanley	Y	Y	Y	Y	N	N	N	Y
33 Walsh	?	?	Y	Y	N	Y	Y	Y
34 Horton	Y	Y	Y	#	Y	#	Y	Y
35 Conable	N	Y	Y	Y	Y	✓	✓	Y
36 LaFalce	Y	Y	Y	Y	N	N	N	Y
37 Nowak	Y	Y	Y	Y	N	N	N	Y
38 Kemp	N	Y	†	Y	Y	Y	Y	Y
39 Lundine	Y	Y	Y	Y	Y	N	N	Y
NORTH CAROLINA								
1 Jones	Y	Y	Y	Y	Y	Y	Y	Y
2 Fountain	Y	N	Y	Y	Y	Y	Y	Y
3 Whitley	Y	Y	Y	Y	Y	Y	Y	Y
4 Andrews	Y	Y	Y	Y	Y	Y	Y	Y
5 Neal	Y	N	Y	Y	Y	N	N	Y
6 Preyer	?	?	Y	Y	Y	Y	Y	Y
7 Rose	Y	Y	Y	Y	Y	Y	N	Y
8 Hefner	Y	Y	Y	Y	Y	Y	Y	Y
9 Martin	Y	Y	#	#	✓	✓	✓	#
10 Broyhill	Y	N	Y	Y	Y	Y	Y	Y
11 Gudger	Y	Y	Y	Y	Y	N	N	Y
NORTH DAKOTA								
AL Andrews	?	?	Y	Y	Y	Y	Y	Y
OHIO								
1 Gradison	N	Y	Y	Y	Y	Y	Y	Y
2 Luken	Y	Y	Y	Y	N	N	N	Y
3 Whalen	Y	Y	Y	Y	N	N	N	Y
4 Guyer	#	#	#	#	✓	✓	✓	Y
5 Latta	Y	N	Y	Y	Y	Y	Y	Y
6 Harsha	Y	Y	Y	?	Y	Y	Y	Y
7 Brown	Y	Y	Y	Y	✓	Y	Y	?
8 Kindness	Y	N	Y	Y	Y	Y	Y	Y
9 Ashley	Y	Y	Y	Y	N	N	N	Y
10 Miller	N	Y	Y	Y	Y	Y	Y	Y
11 Stanton	Y	Y	Y	Y	Y	Y	Y	Y
12 Devine	Y	N	Y	Y	Y	Y	Y	Y
13 Pease	Y	Y	Y	Y	N	N	N	Y
14 Seiberling	Y	Y	Y	Y	N	N	N	Y
15 Wylie	Y	Y	Y	Y	Y	Y	Y	Y
16 Regula	Y	Y	Y	Y	Y	Y	Y	Y
17 Ashbrook	N	N	Y	Y	Y	Y	Y	Y
18 Applegate	Y	Y	Y	Y	N	Y	Y	Y
19 Carney	Y	Y	Y	Y	N	N	N	Y
20 Oakar	Y	Y	Y	N	N	N	N	Y
21 Stokes	Y	Y	Y	N	N	N	N	Y
22 Vanik	Y	Y	Y	Y	N	N	N	Y
23 Mottl	N	Y	Y	N	N	X	X	Y
OKLAHOMA								
1 Jones	Y	N	Y	Y	Y	Y	Y	Y
2 Risenhoover	Y	Y	Y	Y	Y	Y	Y	?
3 Watkins	■	■	Y	Y	Y	Y	Y	Y
4 Steed	Y	Y	Y	Y	Y	Y	Y	Y
5 Edwards	N	N	Y	Y	Y	Y	Y	Y
6 English	N	Y	Y	Y	Y	Y	Y	Y
OREGON								
1 AuCoin	#	#	Y	Y	N	N	N	Y
2 Ullman	Y	Y	Y	Y	N	N	Y	Y
3 Duncan	Y	Y	Y	Y	Y	Y	Y	Y
4 Weaver	Y	Y	Y	N	N	N	N	Y
PENNSYLVANIA								
1 Myers, M.	Y	Y	Y	Y	N	N	N	Y
2 Nix	Y	Y	Y	Y	N	N	N	Y
3 Lederer	Y	Y	Y	Y	N	N	N	Y
4 Eilberg	Y	Y	Y	Y	N	N	N	Y
5 Schulze	Y	Y	Y	Y	Y	Y	Y	Y
6 Yatron	#	Y	Y	Y	N	N	Y	Y
7 Edgar	Y	Y	Y	N	N	N	N	Y
8 Kostmayer	?	Y	?	N	N	N	N	Y
9 Shuster	Y	Y	Y	Y	Y	Y	Y	Y
10 McDade	Y	Y	Y	Y	Y	Y	Y	Y
11 Flood	?	?	Y	Y	N	X	N	Y
12 Murtha	Y	Y	Y	Y	N	N	Y	Y
13 Coughlin	Y	Y	Y	Y	Y	Y	Y	Y
14 Moorhead	#	#	Y	Y	N	N	N	Y
15 Rooney	Y	Y	Y	Y	N	N	N	Y
16 Walker	Y	N	Y	Y	Y	Y	Y	Y
17 Ertel	Y	Y	Y	Y	N	N	N	Y
18 Walgren	Y	Y	Y	N	Y	N	Y	Y
19 Goodling, W.	Y	Y	Y	Y	Y	Y	Y	Y
20 Gaydos	Y	Y	Y	Y	N	N	N	Y
21 Dent	#	#	#	#	X	X	X	#
22 Murphy	#	#	Y	Y	N	N	N	Y
23 Ammerman	Y	Y	Y	N	N	N	N	Y
24 Marks	Y	Y	Y	Y	N	Y	Y	Y
25 Myers, G.	Y	Y	Y	Y	Y	Y	Y	Y
RHODE ISLAND								
1 St Germain	Y	Y	Y	N	N	N	N	Y
2 Beard	?	?	Y	Y	N	N	N	Y
SOUTH CAROLINA								
1 Davis	Y	Y	Y	Y	Y	N	N	Y
2 Spence	Y	Y	Y	Y	Y	Y	Y	Y
3 Derrick	Y	Y	Y	N	N	N	N	Y
4 Mann	?	?	Y	Y	Y	N	N	Y
5 Holland	Y	Y	Y	N	Y	N	N	Y
6 Jenrette	Y	Y	Y	N	N	N	N	Y
SOUTH DAKOTA								
1 Pressler	Y	?	Y	Y	N	Y	N	Y
2 Abdnor	Y	Y	Y	Y	Y	Y	Y	Y
TENNESSEE								
1 Quillen	Y	Y	Y	Y	Y	Y	Y	Y
2 Duncan	Y	Y	Y	Y	Y	Y	Y	Y
3 Lloyd	Y	Y	Y	Y	Y	Y	Y	Y
4 Gore	Y	Y	Y	N	N	N	N	Y
5 Allen	Y	Y	Y	N	N	N	N	Y
6 Beard	Y	N	Y	Y	Y	Y	Y	Y
7 Jones	Y	Y	#	#	✓	✓	✓	#
8 Ford	Y	Y	Y	Y	N	N	Y	Y
TEXAS								
1 Hall	Y	N	Y	Y	Y	Y	Y	Y
2 Wilson, C.	Y	Y	Y	Y	Y	Y	Y	Y
3 Collins	N	N	Y	Y	Y	Y	Y	Y
4 Roberts	N	Y	Y	Y	Y	Y	Y	Y
5 Mattox	Y	Y	Y	Y	Y	Y	Y	Y
6 Teague	?	?	?	Y	Y	✓	✓	Y
7 Archer	N	N	Y	Y	Y	Y	Y	Y
8 Eckhardt	Y	Y	Y	N	N	N	N	Y
9 Brooks	Y	Y	Y	Y	Y	Y	Y	Y
10 Pickle	Y	Y	Y	Y	Y	Y	Y	Y
11 Poage	N	Y	Y	Y	?	?	Y	Y
12 Wright	Y	Y	Y	Y	Y	N	Y	Y
13 Hightower	?	?	?	?	✓	✓	✓	?
14 Young	Y	Y	Y	Y	Y	Y	Y	Y
15 de la Garza	Y	Y	Y	Y	Y	Y	Y	Y
16 White	Y	Y	Y	Y	Y	Y	Y	Y
17 Burleson	N	N	Y	Y	Y	Y	Y	Y
18 Jordan	Y	Y	Y	Y	Y	N	N	Y
19 Mahon	Y	Y	Y	Y	Y	Y	Y	Y
20 Gonzalez	Y	Y	Y	Y	Y	N	N	Y
21 Krueger	#	#	Y	Y	Y	Y	Y	Y
22 Gammage	N	Y	Y	Y	Y	Y	Y	Y
23 Kazen	Y	Y	Y	Y	Y	Y	Y	Y
24 Milford	Y	Y	Y	Y	Y	Y	Y	Y
UTAH								
1 McKay	Y	Y	Y	Y	Y	Y	Y	Y
2 Marriott	Y	Y	Y	Y	Y	Y	Y	Y
VERMONT								
AL Jeffords	#	#	Y	Y	Y	Y	N	Y
VIRGINIA								
1 Trible	N	Y	Y	Y	Y	Y	Y	Y
2 Whitehurst	Y	Y	Y	Y	Y	Y	Y	Y
3 Satterfield	Y	N	Y	Y	Y	Y	Y	Y
4 Daniel	Y	N	Y	Y	Y	Y	Y	Y
5 Daniel	Y	Y	Y	Y	Y	Y	Y	Y
6 Butler	Y	N	Y	Y	Y	Y	Y	Y
7 Robinson	Y	N	Y	Y	Y	Y	Y	Y
8 Harris	Y	Y	Y	N	N	N	N	Y
9 Wampler	Y	Y	Y	Y	Y	Y	Y	Y
10 Fisher	Y	Y	Y	N	N	N	Y	Y
WASHINGTON								
1 Pritchard	Y	Y	Y	Y	Y	Y	Y	Y
2 Meeds	Y	Y	Y	N	N	N	N	Y
3 Bonker	Y	Y	Y	N	N	N	N	Y
4 McCormack	Y	Y	Y	N	N	Y	Y	Y
5 Foley	Y	Y	Y	N	N	Y	Y	Y
6 Dicks	Y	Y	Y	N	N	N	Y	Y
7 Cunningham	N	N	Y	Y	Y	Y	Y	Y
WEST VIRGINIA								
1 Mollohan	Y	Y	#	Y	N	Y	Y	Y
2 Staggers	Y	Y	Y	Y	N	N	N	Y
3 Slack	Y	Y	Y	Y	N	N	N	Y
4 Rahall	Y	Y	Y	Y	N	N	N	Y
WISCONSIN								
1 Aspin	Y	Y	Y	Y	N	N	N	N
2 Kastenmeier	Y	Y	Y	N	N	N	N	Y
3 Baldus	Y	Y	Y	N	N	N	N	Y
4 Zablocki	#	#	Y	Y	N	N	N	Y
5 Reuss	#	#	Y	N	N	N	N	Y
6 Steiger	Y	Y	Y	Y	Y	Y	Y	Y
7 Obey	?	Y	Y	N	N	N	N	Y
8 Cornell	Y	Y	Y	Y	N	N	N	Y
9 Kasten	-	†	Y	Y	Y	Y	Y	Y
WYOMING								
AL Roncalio	?	?	?	?	?	?	?	?

Democrats ***Republicans***

21. HR 8200. Bankruptcy Law Revision. Danielson (D Calif.) substitute amendment for the bill to retain the existing court structure for dealing with bankruptcies, expand the jurisdiction of bankruptcy courts and lengthen the term of bankruptcy judges from six to 15 years. Rejected 146-262: R 67-73; D 79-189 (ND 36-149; SD 43-40), Feb. 1, 1978. (The bill was passed subsequently by voice vote.)

22. HR 1614. Outer Continental Shelf. Dodd (D Conn.) amendment to authorize the Attorney General and the Federal Trade Commission to conduct antitrust investigations of any proposed lease. Adopted 241-162: R 30-106; D 211-56 (ND 171-14; SD 40-42), Feb. 1, 1978.

23. HR 1614. Outer Continental Shelf. Miller (D Calif.) amendment to delete the provision requiring that tracts sold by alternative bidding systems be randomly selected. Adopted 225-174: R 18-117; D 207-57 (ND 174-10; SD 33-47), Feb. 1, 1978.

24. Procedural Motion. Brademas (D Ind.) motion to approve the House *Journal* of Wednesday, Feb. 1, 1978. Motion agreed to 368-21: R 121-12; D 247-9 (ND 171-6; SD 76-3), Feb. 2, 1978.

25. HR 1614. Outer Continental Shelf. Whalen (R Ohio) substitute amendment, to the Murphy (D N.Y.) amendment *(see vote 26, below)*, to delete the section in the bill requiring that U.S. nationals be hired, if available, for OCS-related jobs. Rejected 118-280: R 52-80; D 66-200 (ND 45-137; SD 21-63), Feb. 2, 1978.

26. HR 1614. Outer Continental Shelf. Murphy (D N.Y.) amendment to require that U.S.-built equipment and nationals be used in offshore activities. Rejected 201-208: R 52-85; D 149-123 (ND 113-76; SD 36-47), Feb. 2, 1978.

27. HR 1614. Outer Continental Shelf. Hughes (D N.J.) amendment to provide that 20 per cent of federal OCS revenues, up to $200 million annually, be shared with coastal states. Adopted 279-120: R 90-41; D 189-79 (ND 120-68; SD 69-11), Feb. 2, 1978.

28. HR 1614. Outer Continental Shelf. Treen (R La.) amendment to delete the requirement that states have a federally approved coastal zone management plan in order to be eligible for the OCS revenue sharing. Rejected 159-230: R 97-31; D 62-199 (ND 12-171; SD 50-28), Feb. 2, 1978.

KEY

Y Voted for (yea).
✓ Paired for.
† Announced for.
# CQ Poll for.
N Voted against (nay).
X Paired against.
\- Announced against.
▮ CQ Poll against.
P Voted "present."
● Voted "present" to avoid possible conflict of interest.
? Did not vote or otherwise make a position known.

	21	22	23	24	25	26	27	28
ALABAMA								
1 Edwards	Y	N	N	Y	N	N	Y	Y
2 Dickinson	Y	N	N	Y	Y	?	?	✓
3 Nichols	Y	N	N	Y	N	Y	Y	Y
4 Bevill	Y	Y	Y	?	N	Y	N	N
5 Flippo	Y	Y	N	Y	N	Y	Y	Y
6 Buchanan	N	N	N	Y	N	Y	Y	Y
7 Flowers	Y	Y	N	Y	N	Y	Y	Y
ALASKA								
AL Young	N	Y	N	Y	N	Y	Y	Y
ARIZONA								
1 Rhodes	N	N	N	Y	?	N	?	?
2 Udall	Y	Y	Y	Y	N	N	N	N
3 Stump	N	N	N	Y	N	N	Y	Y
4 Rudd	N	N	N	Y	N	N	N	#
ARKANSAS								
1 Alexander	Y	N	Y	Y	Y	N	Y	?
2 Tucker	Y	#	#	#	▮	▮	#	▮
3 Hammerschmidt	Y	N	N	Y	N	N	N	Y
4 Thornton	Y	Y	N	Y	N	N	N	Y
CALIFORNIA								
1 Johnson	N	Y	Y	Y	Y	Y	Y	N
2 Clausen	Y	N	N	Y	N	Y	?	?
3 Moss	?	?	✓	?	?	?	?	?
4 Leggett	N	Y	Y	Y	N	Y	Y	N
5 Burton, J.	N	?	Y	Y	N	Y	Y	N
6 Burton, P.	N	Y	Y	Y	N	Y	Y	N
7 Miller	N	Y	Y	Y	N	Y	Y	N
8 Dellums	N	Y	Y	Y	N	Y	Y	N
9 Stark	N	Y	Y	Y	N	Y	Y	N
10 Edwards	N	Y	Y	Y	Y	N	Y	N
11 Ryan	N	Y	Y	Y	N	N	Y	N
12 McCloskey	N	N	N	Y	Y	N	Y	N
13 Mineta	N	Y	Y	Y	N	N	Y	N
14 McFall	N	Y	Y	Y	N	Y	Y	N
15 Sisk	N	Y	?	?	N	Y	Y	N
16 Panetta	N	Y	Y	#	▮	#	✓	X
17 Krebs	Y	Y	Y	Y	N	Y	Y	N
18 Ketchum	N	N	N	Y	N	N	Y	Y
19 Lagomarsino	Y	N	N	Y	Y	N	Y	N
20 Goldwater	N	N	N	Y	Y	N	Y	Y
21 Corman	N	Y	Y	Y	Y	N	Y	▮
22 Moorhead	Y	N	N	Y	N	N	Y	Y
23 Beilenson	N	Y	Y	Y	Y	N	Y	N
24 Waxman	N	Y	Y	Y	N	Y	Y	N
25 Roybal	N	Y	Y	Y	▮	Y	Y	N
26 Rousselot	N	N	N	Y	N	N	Y	Y
27 Dornan	Y	N	N	Y	N	Y	Y	Y
28 Burke	N	Y	Y	Y	N	Y	Y	N
29 Hawkins	N	Y	Y	Y	N	Y	Y	N
30 Danielson	Y	Y	Y	Y	N	N	N	N
31 Wilson, C.H.	N	Y	Y	Y	Y	N	✓	X
32 Anderson	N	Y	Y	Y	N	Y	Y	▮
33 Clawson	N	N	N	Y	N	N	Y	Y
34 Hannaford	N	N	N	Y	N	N	Y	Y
35 Lloyd	Y	N	Y	Y	N	N	Y	N
36 Brown	X	?	✓	Y	N	Y	Y	X
37 Pettis	N	N	N	Y	Y	N	Y	Y
38 Patterson	N	Y	Y	Y	N	Y	Y	N
39 Wiggins	N	N	N	#	Y	N	▮	Y
40 Badham	Y	N	N	Y	Y	N	Y	#
41 Wilson, B.	▮	#	#	▮	▮	#	✓	?
42 Van Deerlin	Y	Y	Y	Y	Y	N	Y	N
43 Burgener	Y	N	N	Y	Y	N	Y	Y
COLORADO								
1 Schroeder	N	Y	Y	Y	N	Y	N	N
2 Wirth	N	Y	Y	Y	Y	N	N	N
3 Evans	N	Y	Y	Y	Y	N	Y	Y
4 Johnson	N	Y	N	Y	Y	N	N	Y
5 Armstrong	?	?	?	?	?	?	?	?
CONNECTICUT								
1 Cotter	N	Y	Y	Y	N	Y	Y	N
2 Dodd	N	Y	Y	Y	N	Y	Y	N
3 Giaimo	N	Y	Y	Y	N	N	Y	N
4 McKinney	N	Y	N	Y	N	N	Y	Y
5 Sarasin	N	Y	Y	N	N	N	Y	Y
6 Moffett	N	Y	Y	Y	N	N	Y	N
DELAWARE								
AL Evans	Y	Y	N	Y	N	Y	Y	N
FLORIDA								
1 Sikes	N	N	Y	Y	Y	N	Y	N
2 Fuqua	N	Y	Y	#	Y	N	Y	N
3 Bennett	Y	Y	Y	Y	Y	N	Y	N
4 Chappell	N	Y	X	Y	N	Y	Y	N
5 Kelly	N	N	N	Y	Y	N	Y	Y
6 Young	Y	N	N	N	N	Y	Y	N
7 Gibbons	N	Y	Y	Y	Y	N	Y	N
8 Ireland	N	N	N	Y	N	Y	Y	Y
9 Frey	Y	N	N	Y	N	N	Y	Y
10 Bafalis	N	N	N	Y	N	Y	Y	Y
11 Rogers	N	Y	Y	Y	N	N	Y	N
12 Burke	Y	N	N	Y	Y	N	Y	Y
13 Lehman	▮	#	✓	#	▮	✓	X	X
14 Pepper	N	Y	Y	Y	N	Y	Y	N
15 Fascell	N	Y	Y	Y	N	Y	N	N
GEORGIA								
1 Ginn	N	N	Y	Y	N	Y	Y	N
2 Mathis	N	N	N	Y	Y	Y	Y	Y
3 Brinkley	N	Y	N	Y	N	N	Y	Y
4 Levitas	Y	N	N	Y	N	Y	Y	N
5 Fowler	N	N	Y	Y	N	N	Y	Y
6 Flynt	Y	N	N	Y	N	Y	Y	Y
7 McDonald	✓	▮	X	#	Y	N	Y	Y
8 Evans	N	N	N	Y	N	Y	Y	N
9 Jenkins	N	Y	Y	Y	N	N	Y	Y
10 Barnard	N	N	N	Y	N	N	Y	Y
HAWAII								
1 Heftel	N	Y	Y	Y	N	N	Y	N
2 Akaka	N	Y	Y	Y	N	Y	Y	N
IDAHO								
1 Symms	Y	N	N	Y	N	N	Y	Y
2 Hansen, G.	Y	?	?	Y	N	N	Y	Y
ILLINOIS								
1 Metcalfe	N	Y	Y	Y	N	Y	N	N
2 Murphy	N	Y	Y	#	N	Y	N	N
3 Russo	N	Y	Y	Y	N	Y	N	N
4 Derwinski	N	N	N	Y	N	Y	Y	Y
5 Fary	N	Y	Y	Y	N	Y	N	N
6 Hyde	Y	N	N	Y	Y	N	N	Y
7 Collins	N	Y	#	#	▮	Y	Y	N
8 Rostenkowski	X	?	✓	Y	N	N	N	N
9 Yates	Y	Y	Y	Y	Y	N	N	N
10 Mikva	N	Y	Y	Y	Y	N	N	N
11 Annunzio	Y	Y	Y	Y	N	Y	N	N
12 Crane	Y	N	N	Y	N	N	Y	✓
13 McClory	N	N	N	Y	Y	N	Y	Y
14 Erlenborn	Y	N	N	Y	Y	N	N	Y
15 Corcoran	N	N	N	Y	N	Y	Y	Y
16 Anderson	Y	Y	N	Y	Y	N	Y	Y
17 O'Brien	N	Y	N	Y	N	N	N	Y
18 Michel	Y	N	N	Y	Y	N	Y	Y
19 Railsback	Y	N	Y	Y	Y	N	N	Y
20 Findley	Y	N	?	Y	Y	N	Y	Y
21 Madigan	Y	N	N	Y	Y	N	Y	Y
22 Shipley	N	Y	N	Y	N	Y	Y	Y
23 Price	N	Y	Y	Y	N	N	N	N
24 Simon	Y	Y	Y	Y	Y	N	Y	N
INDIANA								
1 Benjamin	N	Y	Y	Y	N	Y	Y	N
2 Fithian	N	Y	Y	Y	N	Y	N	N
3 Brademas	N	Y	Y	Y	Y	N	N	N
4 Quayle	Y	N	N	N	Y	N	N	Y
5 Hillis	N	N	N	Y	Y	N	Y	Y
6 Evans	N	Y	Y	Y	N	Y	N	N
7 Myers, J.	Y	N	N	Y	Y	N	N	Y
8 Cornwell	N	Y	Y	Y	N	Y	N	N
9 Hamilton	Y	Y	Y	Y	Y	N	N	N
10 Sharp	N	Y	Y	Y	Y	N	N	N
11 Jacobs	Y	Y	N	N	N	Y	N	N
IOWA								
1 Leach	N	Y	N	Y	Y	N	Y	Y
2 Blouin	N	Y	Y	Y	Y	N	Y	N
3 Grassley	Y	N	N	Y	N	Y	Y	Y
4 Smith	Y	Y	Y	Y	Y	N	N	N
5 Harkin	Y	Y	Y	Y	Y	N	Y	N
6 Bedell	Y	Y	Y	Y	Y	N	Y	N

Democrats ***Republicans***

Corresponding to Congressional Record Votes 26, 27, 28, 29, 30, 31, 33, 34

	21	22	23	24	25	26	27	28
KANSAS								
1 Sebelius	Y	N	N	Y	N	N	N	Y
2 Keys	Y	Y	Y	Y	N	N	N	N
3 Winn	Y	N	N	#	N	Y	N	Y
4 Glickman	Y	Y	Y	N	N	N	N	N
5 Skubitz	Y	N	N	Y	N	N	N	N
KENTUCKY								
1 Hubbard	N	N	N	Y	N	Y	Y	Y
2 Natcher	N	Y	Y	Y	N	Y	N	N
3 Mazzoli	N	Y	N	Y	Y	N	Y	N
4 Snyder	Y	N	N	Y	N	Y	N	Y
5 Carter	N	Y	Y	Y	?	Y	N	N
6 Breckinridge	N	Y	N	Y	Y	N	X	X
7 Perkins	N	Y	Y	Y	Y	Y	?	?
LOUISIANA								
1 Livingston	N	N	N	Y	N	Y	Y	Y
2 Boggs	N	N	N	Y	N	N	Y	Y
3 Treen	Y	N	N	N	N	Y	Y	Y
4 Waggonner	Y	N	N	Y	N	N	Y	Y
5 Huckaby	Y	N	N	Y	N	Y	✓	✓
6 Moore	Y	N	N	Y	Y	N	Y	Y
7 Breaux	Y	N	N	Y	Y	N	Y	Y
8 Long	N	N	N	Y	N	Y	Y	Y
MAINE								
1 Emery	N	Y	N	Y	N	Y	Y	N
2 Cohen	N	Y	N	Y	Y	N	Y	N
MARYLAND								
1 Bauman	Y	N	N	Y	N	Y	Y	Y
2 Long	N	Y	Y	Y	Y	N	N	N
3 Mikulski	N	Y	Y	Y	N	Y	Y	N
4 Holt	Y	N	N	Y	N	Y	Y	Y
5 Spellman	N	Y	Y	Y	N	N	Y	N
6 Byron	Y	N	N	Y	N	Y	Y	N
7 Mitchell	N	Y	Y	N	N	Y	Y	N
8 Steers	N	Y	Y	Y	Y	N	Y	N
MASSACHUSETTS								
1 Conte	N	Y	Y	Y	N	Y	Y	N
2 Boland	N	Y	Y	Y	N	N	Y	N
3 Early	N	Y	Y	Y	Y	N	Y	N
4 Drinan	N	Y	Y	Y	Y	N	Y	N
5 Tsongas	N	Y	Y	Y	N	N	Y	N
6 Harrington	N	Y	Y	Y	Y	N	Y	N
7 Markey	N	Y	Y	Y	N	N	Y	N
8 O'Neill								
9 Moakley	N	Y	Y	Y	N	Y	Y	N
10 Heckler	?	?	?	?	N	N	Y	N
11 Burke	N	Y	Y	Y	N	Y	Y	N
12 Studds	N	Y	Y	Y	N	N	Y	N
MICHIGAN								
1 Conyers	N	#	Y	#	#	Y	Y	N
2 Pursell	N	N	Y	Y	?	Y	N	Y
3 Brown	N	N	N	N	Y	N	N	Y
4 Stockman	Y	▮	#	#	#	▮	▮	#
5 Sawyer	N	N	Y	Y	Y	N	Y	Y
6 Carr	▮	Y	Y	Y	Y	N	Y	N
7 Kildee	N	Y	Y	Y	N	Y	N	N
8 Traxler	N	Y	Y	N	N	Y	N	N
9 Vander Jagt	N	N	N	Y	Y	N	N	Y
10 Cederberg	N	N	Y	Y	Y	N	Y	Y
11 Ruppe	N	?	?	#	▮	?	#	?
12 Bonior	N	Y	Y	#	Y	N	Y	N
13 Diggs	N	#	Y	#	Y	✓	Y	N
14 Nedzi	Y	Y	Y	Y	N	N	N	N
15 Ford	N	Y	Y	?	?	Y	N	N
16 Dingell	Y	Y	Y	Y	N	Y	N	N
17 Brodhead	N	Y	Y	Y	N	Y	N	N
18 Blanchard	N	Y	Y	Y	N	Y	N	N
19 Broomfield	N	N	N	#	▮	X	X	✓
MINNESOTA								
1 Quie	N	N	N	Y	Y	N	Y	#
2 Hagedorn	N	N	N	Y	Y	N	N	Y
3 Frenzel	N	N	N	Y	Y	N	N	N
4 Vento	N	Y	Y	Y	N	Y	Y	N
5 Fraser	N	Y	Y	Y	Y	N	N	N
6 Nolan	N	Y	Y	Y	N	Y	Y	N
7 Stangeland	N	N	N	Y	Y	N	N	Y
8 Oberstar	N	Y	Y	Y	N	Y	Y	N
MISSISSIPPI								
1 Whitten	✓	N	N	Y	N	N	Y	Y
2 Bowen	Y	N	N	Y	N	N	Y	Y
3 Montgomery	Y	N	N	Y	N	Y	Y	Y
4 Cochran	N	N	N	Y	Y	N	Y	Y
5 Lott	N	N	N	Y	N	Y	Y	Y
MISSOURI								
1 Clay	N	Y	Y	Y	N	Y	N	N
2 Young	N	Y	Y	Y	N	Y	Y	N
3 Gephardt	N	Y	Y	Y	N	Y	Y	N
4 Skelton	N	Y	Y	Y	N	Y	Y	N
5 Bolling	N	Y	Y	#	Y	N	N	N
6 Coleman	Y	Y	N	Y	N	Y	Y	Y
7 Taylor	Y	N	N	Y	N	Y	N	Y
8 Ichord	Y	Y	Y	Y	N	Y	N	Y
9 Volkmer	N	N	Y	Y	N	Y	Y	Y
10 Burlison	N	Y	Y	Y	N	Y	N	N
MONTANA								
1 Baucus	N	Y	Y	Y	N	N	N	?
2 Marlenee	Y	Y	N	Y	N	N	Y	Y
NEBRASKA								
1 Thone	#	?	?	?	?	X	X	?
2 Cavanaugh	N	Y	Y	Y	N	N	N	N
3 Smith	Y	N	N	Y	N	N	N	Y
NEVADA								
AL Santini	N	N	N	Y	N	Y	Y	Y
NEW HAMPSHIRE								
1 D'Amours	Y	Y	Y	N	N	Y	Y	N
2 Cleveland	Y	Y	Y	Y	Y	N	Y	N
NEW JERSEY								
1 Florio	N	Y	Y	Y	N	Y	Y	N
2 Hughes	N	Y	Y	Y	N	Y	Y	N
3 Howard	N	Y	Y	Y	N	Y	Y	N
4 Thompson	X	#	✓	Y	N	Y	Y	N
5 Fenwick	N	Y	Y	Y	Y	N	Y	N
6 Forsythe	N	N	N	N	Y	N	Y	Y
7 Maguire	N	Y	Y	Y	Y	N	Y	N
8 Roe	N	Y	Y	Y	N	Y	Y	N
9 Hollenbeck	N	Y	Y	N	N	Y	Y	N
10 Rodino	N	Y	Y	Y	N	N	Y	N
11 Minish	N	Y	Y	Y	N	Y	Y	N
12 Rinaldo	N	Y	Y	Y	N	Y	Y	N
13 Meyner	N	Y	Y	Y	N	Y	Y	N
14 LeFante	N	Y	Y	#	N	Y	Y	N
15 Patten	N	Y	Y	Y	N	Y	Y	N
NEW MEXICO								
1 Lujan	Y	N	N	Y	?	Y	N	Y
2 Runnels	Y	N	N	Y	?	N	Y	Y
NEW YORK								
1 Pike	Y	Y	Y	Y	N	Y	Y	N
2 Downey	▮	#	#	Y	N	Y	Y	N
3 Ambro	N	Y	Y	?	N	Y	Y	N
4 Lent	Y	Y	Y	Y	N	Y	Y	N
5 Wydler	N	N	N	Y	N	Y	Y	N
6 Wolff	N	Y	Y	Y	N	Y	Y	N
7 Addabbo	N	Y	Y	Y	N	Y	Y	N
8 Rosenthal	N	Y	✓	Y	Y	N	Y	N
9 Delaney	N	Y	Y	Y	N	Y	Y	N
10 Biaggi	N	Y	Y	Y	N	Y	Y	N
11 Scheuer	N	Y	Y	Y	Y	N	Y	N
12 Chisholm	N	Y	Y	Y	N	Y	Y	N
13 Solarz	N	Y	Y	Y	N	Y	Y	▮
14 Richmond	X	Y	Y	?	?	✓	X	X
15 Zeferetti	N	Y	Y	Y	N	Y	Y	N
16 Holtzman	N	Y	Y	Y	Y	N	Y	N
17 Murphy	N	Y	Y	Y	N	Y	N	N
18 Vacancy								
19 Rangel	N	Y	Y	Y	N	Y	Y	N
20 Weiss	N	Y	Y	Y	Y	N	Y	N
21 Vacancy								
22 Bingham	X	#	✓	#	#	X	X	X
23 Caputo	N	N	N	Y	N	Y	Y	Y
24 Ottinger	N	Y	Y	Y	N	Y	Y	N
25 Fish	N	N	N	Y	N	Y	Y	Y
26 Gilman	N	N	Y	Y	N	Y	Y	N
27 McHugh	N	Y	Y	Y	N	N	Y	N
28 Stratton	Y	Y	Y	Y	N	Y	Y	N
29 Pattison	Y	Y	Y	Y	Y	N	Y	N
30 McEwen	Y	N	N	Y	Y	N	Y	Y
31 Mitchell	?	?	?	#	▮	✓	✓	▮
32 Hanley	N	Y	Y	Y	N	Y	N	N
33 Walsh	Y	N	N	Y	N	Y	Y	N
34 Horton	N	N	N	Y	N	N	Y	N
35 Conable	Y	N	N	Y	Y	N	Y	?
36 LaFalce	Y	Y	Y	Y	Y	N	N	N
37 Nowak	N	Y	Y	Y	N	Y	Y	N
38 Kemp	Y	N	N	Y	Y	N	Y	Y
39 Lundine	N	N	Y	#	N	Y	Y	N
NORTH CAROLINA								
1 Jones	Y	Y	Y	Y	N	N	Y	Y
2 Fountain	Y	Y	Y	Y	N	N	Y	Y
3 Whitley	Y	Y	Y	Y	N	N	Y	Y
4 Andrews	Y	Y	Y	Y	N	N	Y	Y
5 Neal	Y	Y	Y	Y	N	N	Y	Y
6 Preyer	Y	Y	Y	Y	N	N	Y	Y
7 Rose	N	Y	Y	Y	N	N	Y	Y
8 Hefner	Y	Y	Y	Y	N	N	Y	Y
9 Martin	Y	Y	N	#	▮	N	Y	Y
10 Broyhill	Y	Y	N	Y	N	N	Y	Y
11 Gudger	Y	Y	Y	Y	N	N	Y	Y
NORTH DAKOTA								
AL Andrews	N	N	N	Y	Y	N	N	Y
OHIO								
1 Gradison	N	N	N	Y	Y	N	#	N
2 Luken	Y	N	Y	Y	N	Y	N	N
3 Whalen	N	Y	Y	Y	Y	N	N	N
4 Guyer	Y	N	N	Y	N	N	Y	Y
5 Latta	Y	N	N	Y	N	N	?	?
6 Harsha	N	N	N	Y	Y	Y	Y	Y
7 Brown	?	?	?	?	?	X	?	✓
8 Kindness	N	N	N	Y	N	N	Y	Y
9 Ashley	N	Y	Y	Y	Y	N	N	N
10 Miller	Y	N	N	Y	N	Y	Y	Y
11 Stanton	N	N	N	Y	Y	N	N	Y
12 Devine	Y	N	N	Y	N	N	N	Y
13 Pease	N	Y	Y	Y	Y	N	N	N
14 Seiberling	N	Y	Y	Y	Y	N	N	N
15 Wylie	Y	N	N	Y	N	N	?	?
16 Regula	N	N	N	Y	N	Y	Y	Y
17 Ashbrook	Y	N	N	Y	N	Y	Y	Y
18 Applegate	N	Y	Y	Y	N	Y	N	Y
19 Carney	N	Y	Y	Y	N	Y	N	N
20 Oakar	N	Y	Y	Y	N	Y	N	N
21 Stokes	N	Y	Y	Y	N	Y	N	N
22 Vanik	N	Y	Y	Y	Y	N	N	N
23 Mottl	Y	Y	Y	Y	N	Y	N	N
OKLAHOMA								
1 Jones	N	N	N	N	Y	N	N	N
2 Risenhoover	?	?	X	?	?	✓	X	✓
3 Watkins	N	N	N	Y	N	Y	N	N
4 Steed	N	N	X	Y	N	Y	N	Y
5 Edwards	N	N	N	Y	N	N	N	Y
6 English	N	N	N	Y	N	N	N	Y
OREGON								
1 AuCoin	N	Y	Y	N	▮	N	Y	N
2 Ullman	N	N	N	Y	Y	N	N	N
3 Duncan	Y	N	N	Y	N	N	N	N
4 Weaver	N	Y	Y	Y	N	Y	Y	N
PENNSYLVANIA								
1 Myers, M.	N	Y	Y	Y	N	Y	Y	N
2 Nix	N	Y	Y	Y	N	Y	Y	N
3 Lederer	N	Y	Y	Y	N	Y	Y	N
4 Eilberg	N	Y	Y	Y	N	Y	Y	N
5 Schulze	Y	N	N	Y	Y	N	N	Y
6 Yatron	N	Y	Y	Y	N	Y	Y	Y
7 Edgar	N	Y	Y	Y	N	N	Y	N
8 Kostmayer	N	Y	Y	Y	N	N	Y	N
9 Shuster	Y	N	N	Y	N	Y	N	Y
10 McDade	N	Y	N	Y	N	Y	N	Y
11 Flood	N	Y	Y	Y	N	Y	Y	N
12 Murtha	N	Y	Y	Y	N	Y	Y	Y
13 Coughlin	Y	N	N	N	N	N	Y	N
14 Moorhead	N	Y	Y	Y	N	Y	N	N
15 Rooney	N	Y	Y	Y	N	Y	N	N
16 Walker	N	N	N	N	N	Y	N	N
17 Ertel	N	Y	Y	Y	N	Y	Y	Y
18 Walgren	N	Y	Y	Y	N	Y	Y	N
19 Goodling, W.	Y	N	N	N	N	Y	N	Y
20 Gaydos	Y	Y	Y	Y	N	Y	Y	N
21 Dent	✓	#	✓	#	▮	✓	✓	X
22 Murphy	Y	Y	Y	Y	N	Y	Y	N
23 Ammerman	N	Y	Y	Y	N	Y	Y	N
24 Marks	N	Y	Y	Y	N	Y	N	N
25 Myers, G.	N	Y	Y	Y	Y	N	N	N
RHODE ISLAND								
1 St Germain	Y	Y	Y	Y	N	Y	?	N
2 Beard	N	Y	Y	Y	N	Y	Y	N
SOUTH CAROLINA								
1 Davis	Y	Y	N	Y	N	Y	Y	Y
2 Spence	Y	N	N	Y	N	Y	Y	Y
3 Derrick	Y	Y	Y	Y	N	N	Y	N
4 Mann	Y	N	N	Y	N	N	Y	N
5 Holland	Y	Y	Y	Y	N	Y	Y	N
6 Jenrette	Y	Y	Y	Y	N	Y	Y	Y
SOUTH DAKOTA								
1 Pressler	N	Y	Y	Y	N	Y	N	N
2 Abdnor	Y	N	N	Y	N	Y	N	Y
TENNESSEE								
1 Quillen	Y	N	N	Y	N	Y	Y	Y
2 Duncan	N	N	N	Y	N	Y	N	Y
3 Lloyd	N	N	N	Y	N	Y	Y	Y
4 Gore	N	Y	Y	Y	Y	N	N	N
5 Allen	Y	Y	Y	Y	N	N	N	N
6 Beard	Y	▮	▮	#	▮	N	N	Y
7 Jones	X	▮	X	#	▮	X	✓	✓
8 Ford	N	Y	Y	Y	N	N	Y	▮
TEXAS								
1 Hall	Y	N	N	Y	N	N	Y	Y
2 Wilson, C.	Y	N	N	Y	N	Y	Y	Y
3 Collins	Y	N	N	Y	Y	N	Y	Y
4 Roberts	N	N	N	Y	N	Y	Y	Y
5 Mattox	Y	Y	Y	N	Y	N	Y	Y
6 Teague	✓	?	X	?	?	X	?	✓
7 Archer	Y	N	N	Y	N	N	Y	Y
8 Eckhardt	N	Y	Y	?	N	N	Y	N
9 Brooks	N	N	N	Y	N	Y	Y	N
10 Pickle	N	N	N	Y	Y	N	Y	N
11 Poage	Y	?	N	Y	Y	N	Y	Y
12 Wright	N	Y	N	?	?	?	?	?
13 Hightower	✓	?	X	?	N	Y	Y	Y
14 Young	N	N	N	Y	N	Y	Y	N
15 de la Garza	Y	N	N	Y	N	Y	Y	Y
16 White	Y	N	N	Y	N	N	Y	Y
17 Burleson	Y	N	N	Y	Y	N	Y	Y
18 Jordan	N	Y	N	Y	N	Y	Y	N
19 Mahon	Y	N	X	Y	Y	N	N	Y
20 Gonzalez	Y	Y	N	Y	N	Y	Y	Y
21 Krueger	N	N	N	N	Y	▮	#	#
22 Gammage	Y	N	N	Y	N	Y	Y	Y
23 Kazen	Y	N	N	Y	N	Y	Y	Y
24 Milford	Y	N	N	Y	N	N	Y	Y
UTAH								
1 McKay	N	N	N	Y	▮	N	N	▮
2 Marriott	N	N	N	Y	N	N	Y	Y
VERMONT								
AL Jeffords	N	Y	N	Y	Y	N	N	N
VIRGINIA								
1 Trible	N	N	N	Y	N	Y	Y	Y
2 Whitehurst	N	N	N	Y	N	Y	Y	Y
3 Satterfield	Y	N	N	Y	N	N	Y	Y
4 Daniel	N	N	N	Y	N	Y	Y	Y
5 Daniel	Y	N	N	Y	N	Y	Y	Y
6 Butler	N	N	N	Y	N	N	Y	Y
7 Robinson	N	N	N	Y	N	N	Y	Y
8 Harris	N	Y	Y	Y	Y	N	Y	N
9 Wampler	N	N	N	Y	N	Y	Y	Y
10 Fisher	N	Y	Y	Y	Y	N	Y	N
WASHINGTON								
1 Pritchard	N	N	N	N	Y	N	Y	Y
2 Meeds	#	Y	Y	Y	Y	N	Y	N
3 Bonker	N	Y	#	#	▮	Y	N	N
4 McCormack	N	Y	Y	Y	N	Y	Y	N
5 Foley	N	Y	Y	Y	Y	N	Y	N
6 Dicks	N	Y	Y	Y	N	Y	Y	N
7 Cunningham	Y	N	N	Y	N	Y	Y	Y
WEST VIRGINIA								
1 Mollohan	N	N	Y	Y	N	Y	N	N
2 Staggers	Y	Y	Y	Y	N	Y	N	N
3 Slack	Y	N	Y	Y	N	Y	N	N
4 Rahall	N	Y	Y	#	N	Y	N	N
WISCONSIN								
1 Aspin	Y	Y	Y	Y	Y	N	N	N
2 Kastenmeier	Y	Y	Y	Y	Y	N	N	N
3 Baldus	N	Y	Y	Y	N	N	N	N
4 Zablocki	N	Y	Y	Y	N	N	N	N
5 Reuss	N	Y	Y	Y	Y	N	N	N
6 Steiger	Y	Y	N	N	Y	N	Y	N
7 Obey	Y	Y	Y	Y	Y	N	N	N
8 Cornell	N	Y	Y	Y	N	N	N	N
9 Kasten	Y	Y	N	Y	N	Y	N	N
WYOMING								
AL Roncalio	✓	?	?	?	?	?	?	?

Democrats ***Republicans***

29. HR 1614. Outer Continental Shelf. Passage of the bill to amend the 1953 law governing oil and gas exploration on the Outer Continental Shelf by improving environmental controls, increasing state participation in federal leasing decisions, sharing federal revenues from leases with coastal states and broadening competition for lease sales by changing bidding procedures. Passed 291-91: R 70-56; D 221-35 (ND 176-7; SD 45-28), Feb. 2, 1978.

30. HR 9434. Medicaid Payment Ceilings. Rogers (D Fla.) motion to suspend the rules and pass the bill to raise ceilings for fiscal 1978 Medicaid payments to Puerto Rico, the Virgin Islands and Guam, to provide for cost-of-living increases in the ceilings thereafter, and to revise the matching formula for Medicaid payments to these jurisdictions. Motion agreed to 253-106: R 51-72; D 202-34 (ND 144-13; SD 58-21), Feb. 6, 1978. A two-thirds majority vote (240 in this case) is required for passage under suspension of the rules.

31. HR 8336. Chattahoochee River National Park. Adoption of the rule (H Res 982) providing for House floor consideration of a bill to establish the Chattahoochee River National Recreation Area in Georgia and authorize $73 million for the purchase of 6,300 acres of land and $500,000 in fiscal year 1979 to develop public facilities in the recreation area. Adopted 323-41: R 85-38; D 238-3 (ND 160-1; SD 78-2), Feb. 6, 1978.

32. HR 6362. Timber Bids. Krebs (D Calif.) substitute amendment, to the Foley (D Wash.) substitute for the bill *(see vote 33, below)*, directing the Secretary of Agriculture to require sealed bidding for national forest timber sales except where he determined otherwise by regulation. Rejected 136-239: R 26-101; D 110-138 (ND 94-74; SD 16-64), Feb. 6, 1978.

33. HR 6362. Timber Bids. Foley (D Wash.) substitute amendment to repeal a provision of the 1976 National Forest Management Act (PL 94-588) requiring sealed bids for national forest timber, allowing the Agriculture Secretary to select whatever bidding method he deemed necessary and setting certain conditions if oral bidding were chosen. Adopted 295-78: R 115-14; D 180-64 (ND 111-53; SD 69-11), Feb. 6, 1978. (The amended bill was subsequently passed by voice vote and cleared for the President.)

34. HR 7843. Federal Judgeships. Passage of the bill to create 110 new federal district court judgeships and 35 new appeals court judgeships, and to provide that the President promulgate non-binding procedures for the selection of new district court judges on the basis of merit. Passed 319-80: R 75-60; D 244-20 (ND 171-10; SD 73-10), Feb. 7, 1978.

35. HR 6805. Agency for Consumer Protection. Adoption of the rule (H Res 872) providing for House floor consideration of the bill (HR 6805) to establish an Agency for Consumer Protection. Adopted 271-138: R 37-101; D 234-37 (ND 181-5; SD 53-32), Feb. 7, 1978.

36. HR 6805. Agency for Consumer Protection. Glickman (D Kan.) substitute amendment, to the Brooks (D Texas) substitute for the bill, to establish an independent Office of Consumer Counsel within each of 23 major federal departments and agencies and a Division of Consumer Protection and Advocacy within the Justice Department. Rejected 93-313: R 49-89; D 44-224 (ND 18-165; SD 26-59), Feb. 7, 1978. A "nay" was a vote supporting the President's position.

KEY

- Y Voted for (yea).
- ✓ Paired for.
- † Announced for.
- # CQ Poll for.
- N Voted against (nay).
- X Paired against.
- \- Announced against.
- ▮ CQ Poll against.
- P Voted "present."
- ● Voted "present" to avoid possible conflict of interest.
- ? Did not vote or otherwise make a position known.

	29	30	31	32	33	34	35	36
ALABAMA								
1 Edwards	N	?	?	?	?	?	Y	Y
2 Dickinson	X	N	Y	N	Y	N	N	N
3 Nichols	#	N	Y	N	Y	Y	Y	Y
4 Bevill	Y	?	Y	N	Y	Y	Y	Y
5 Flippo	N	Y	Y	N	Y	Y	Y	Y
6 Buchanan	N	Y	Y	N	Y	Y	Y	N
7 Flowers	Y	N	Y	N	Y	Y	Y	N
ALASKA								
AL Young	N	N	▮	N	Y	Y	N	Y
ARIZONA								
1 Rhodes	?	N	Y	N	Y	Y	N	N
2 Udall	Y	Y	Y	N	Y	#	Y	N
3 Stump	N	N	Y	N	Y	Y	N	Y
4 Rudd	X	N	N	N	Y	Y	N	N
ARKANSAS								
1 Alexander	?	Y	Y	N	Y	Y	Y	Y
2 Tucker	#	Y	Y	N	Y	Y	Y	N
3 Hammerschmidt	N	Y	Y	N	Y	Y	N	N
4 Thornton	N	Y	Y	N	Y	Y	Y	N
CALIFORNIA								
1 Johnson	Y	Y	Y	N	Y	Y	Y	N
2 Clausen	?	Y	Y	N	Y	N	N	N
3 Moss	?	Y	Y	Y	?	Y	Y	N
4 Leggett	Y	Y	Y	N	Y	Y	Y	N
5 Burton, J.	Y	Y	?	?	?	Y	Y	N
6 Burton, P.	Y	Y	Y	Y	N	Y	Y	N
7 Miller	Y	Y	Y	Y	N	Y	Y	N
8 Dellums	Y	Y	Y	N	Y	Y	Y	N
9 Stark	Y	Y	Y	Y	N	Y	Y	N
10 Edwards	Y	Y	Y	Y	Y	Y	Y	N
11 Ryan	Y	Y	Y	Y	N	Y	N	Y
12 McCloskey	Y	Y	Y	N	Y	Y	Y	N
13 Mineta	Y	#	Y	Y	N	Y	Y	N
14 McFall	Y	Y	Y	N	Y	Y	Y	N
15 Sisk	Y	Y	Y	N	Y	Y	Y	N
16 Panetta	✓	Y	Y	Y	N	N	Y	N
17 Krebs	Y	Y	Y	Y	N	Y	Y	N
18 Ketchum	N	Y	Y	N	Y	N	N	N
19 Lagomarsino	Y	Y	Y	N	Y	N	N	Y
20 Goldwater	Y	?	Y	N	Y	N	N	?
21 Corman	#	Y	Y	Y	N	Y	Y	N
22 Moorhead	N	N	N	Y	Y	N	N	N
23 Beilenson	Y	Y	Y	Y	N	N	Y	N
24 Waxman	Y	Y	Y	Y	N	Y	Y	N
25 Roybal	Y	Y	Y	Y	N	Y	Y	N
26 Rousselot	N	N	N	N	Y	N	N	N
27 Dornan	N	N	N	N	Y	N	N	N
28 Burke	Y	#	#	#	▮	Y	Y	N
29 Hawkins	Y	Y	Y	Y	Y	Y	Y	N
30 Danielson	Y	Y	Y	Y	N	Y	Y	N
31 Wilson, C.H.	Y	N	#	▮	#	Y	Y	N
32 Anderson	✓	Y	Y	Y	Y	Y	Y	N
33 Clawson	N	N	N	N	Y	N	N	N
34 Hannaford	Y	Y	Y	Y	Y	Y	Y	N
35 Lloyd	Y	Y	Y	Y	Y	Y	Y	N
36 Brown	Y	Y	Y	Y	N	Y	Y	N
37 Pettis	Y	Y	Y	N	Y	Y	N	Y
38 Patterson	Y	#	#	Y	N	Y	Y	N
39 Wiggins	N	#	Y	Y	Y	Y	▮	N
40 Badham	▮	N	#	N	Y	N	N	N
41 Wilson, B.	#	#	#	▮	#	Y	N	Y
42 Van Deerlin	Y	Y	Y	Y	N	Y	Y	N
43 Burgener	Y	Y	Y	Y	N	N	N	N
COLORADO								
1 Schroeder	Y	Y	Y	Y	Y	Y	Y	Y
2 Wirth	Y	N	Y	Y	Y	Y	Y	N
3 Evans	Y	Y	Y	N	Y	Y	Y	N
4 Johnson	Y	Y	Y	N	Y	Y	N	N

	29	30	31	32	33	34	35	36
5 Armstrong	?	?	?	N	Y	N	?	N
CONNECTICUT								
1 Cotter	Y	#	#	#	#	#	#	▮
2 Dodd	Y	Y	Y	Y	N	Y	Y	N
3 Giaimo	Y	Y	Y	Y	Y	Y	N	N
4 McKinney	Y	#	#	Y	Y	Y	N	N
5 Sarasin	Y	Y	Y	N	Y	Y	N	N
6 Moffett	Y	Y	Y	N	Y	Y	Y	N
DELAWARE								
AL Evans	Y	#	Y	Y	N	N	N	Y
FLORIDA								
1 Sikes	?	Y	Y	N	Y	Y	N	N
2 Fuqua	Y	Y	Y	N	Y	Y	N	N
3 Bennett	Y	Y	Y	N	Y	Y	N	N
4 Chappell	Y	#	#	▮	#	Y	N	N
5 Kelly	N	N	N	N	Y	Y	Y	N
6 Young	Y	N	Y	N	Y	Y	Y	Y
7 Gibbons	Y	Y	Y	N	Y	Y	Y	N
8 Ireland	Y	Y	Y	N	Y	Y	N	N
9 Frey	Y	?	?	?	?	?	N	Y
10 Bafalis	Y	N	Y	N	Y	Y	N	N
11 Rogers	Y	Y	Y	N	Y	Y	Y	N
12 Burke	N	N	N	N	Y	Y	Y	N
13 Lehman	#	Y	Y	Y	N	Y	Y	N
14 Pepper	Y	#	#	▮	#	Y	Y	N
15 Fascell	Y	Y	Y	N	Y	Y	Y	N
GEORGIA								
1 Ginn	Y	Y	Y	N	Y	Y	Y	Y
2 Mathis	Y	Y	Y	N	Y	Y	N	N
3 Brinkley	Y	Y	Y	N	Y	N	N	Y
4 Levitas	Y	Y	Y	N	Y	Y	Y	N
5 Fowler	Y	Y	Y	N	Y	Y	Y	N
6 Flynt	N	N	Y	?	?	Y	N	N
7 McDonald	N	N	N	N	Y	-	-	-
8 Evans	Y	N	Y	N	Y	Y	Y	N
9 Jenkins	Y	Y	Y	N	Y	Y	Y	Y
10 Barnard	Y	N	Y	N	Y	Y	N	Y
HAWAII								
1 Heftel	Y	Y	Y	Y	Y	Y	Y	N
2 Akaka	Y	Y	Y	N	Y	Y	Y	N
IDAHO								
1 Symms	N	N	N	N	Y	N	N	N
2 Hansen, G.	N	N	N	N	Y	N	N	N
ILLINOIS								
1 Metcalfe	Y	?	Y	Y	Y	Y	Y	N
2 Murphy	Y	#	#	▮	#	Y	Y	N
3 Russo	Y	Y	Y	Y	Y	Y	Y	N
4 Derwinski	N	Y	Y	N	Y	N	N	Y
5 Fary	Y	Y	Y	N	Y	Y	Y	N
6 Hyde	Y	Y	Y	N	Y	Y	N	N
7 Collins	Y	#	Y	N	Y	Y	Y	N
8 Rostenkowski	Y	?	?	?	?	?	?	?
9 Yates	Y	Y	Y	Y	N	Y	Y	N
10 Mikva	Y	Y	Y	N	Y	Y	Y	N
11 Annunzio	Y	Y	Y	N	Y	Y	Y	N
12 Crane	X	N	N	N	Y	▮	N	N
13 McClory	N	Y	Y	N	Y	Y	N	N
14 Erlenborn	Y	Y	Y	N	Y	N	N	N
15 Corcoran	Y	N	N	N	Y	Y	N	N
16 Anderson	Y	#	#	▮	#	Y	N	N
17 O'Brien	Y	N	Y	N	Y	Y	N	Y
18 Michel	Y	Y	Y	N	Y	N	N	N
19 Railsback	Y	Y	Y	N	Y	Y	Y	Y
20 Findley	Y	N	Y	Y	N	N	N	Y
21 Madigan	Y	Y	Y	N	?	?	N	Y
22 Shipley	Y	?	?	?	?	?	?	?
23 Price	Y	Y	Y	N	Y	Y	Y	N
24 Simon	Y	Y	Y	Y	N	Y	Y	N
INDIANA								
1 Benjamin	Y	Y	Y	N	Y	Y	Y	N
2 Fithian	Y	N	Y	Y	Y	Y	Y	N
3 Brademas	Y	Y	Y	Y	N	Y	Y	N
4 Quayle	N	N	N	N	Y	Y	N	Y
5 Hillis	N	Y	Y	?	?	N	N	Y
6 Evans	Y	N	Y	Y	Y	N	Y	N
7 Myers, J.	N	N	Y	N	Y	N	N	Y
8 Cornwell	N	Y	Y	N	Y	Y	Y	N
9 Hamilton	Y	Y	Y	N	Y	Y	Y	N
10 Sharp	Y	Y	Y	Y	Y	Y	Y	N
11 Jacobs	Y	Y	Y	N	Y	N	Y	Y
IOWA								
1 Leach	Y	Y	Y	Y	N	Y	N	Y
2 Blouin	Y	#	#	#	▮	Y	Y	N
3 Grassley	N	N	N	N	Y	N	N	Y
4 Smith	Y	Y	Y	Y	N	Y	Y	N
5 Harkin	Y	Y	Y	Y	N	Y	Y	N
6 Bedell	Y	Y	Y	Y	N	Y	Y	N

Democrats ***Republicans***

	29	30	31	32	33	34	35	36
KANSAS								
1 Sebelius	N	Y	Y	N	Y	Y	N	Y
2 Keys	Y	Y	Y	N	Y	Y	Y	Y
3 Winn	N	Y	Y	N	Y	Y	N	N
4 Glickman	Y	Y	Y	Y	Y	Y	Y	Y
5 Skubitz	N	Y	Y	N	Y	Y	N	N
KENTUCKY								
1 Hubbard	N	Y	Y	N	Y	Y	N	Y
2 Natcher	Y	Y	Y	N	Y	Y	N	N
3 Mazzoli	Y	Y	Y	Y	Y	Y	N	N
4 Snyder	N	Y	Y	N	Y	Y	N	N
5 Carter	Y	Y	Y	N	Y	Y	Y	N
6 Breckinridge	✓	Y	Y	Y	N	Y	Y	N
7 Perkins	#	Y	Y	N	Y	Y	Y	?
LOUISIANA								
1 Livingston	N	N	Y	N	Y	Y	N	Y
2 Boggs	N	Y	Y	N	Y	Y	Y	N
3 Treen	N	N	Y	?	?	?	?	?
4 Waggonner	N	N	Y	N	Y	Y	N	Y
5 Huckaby	X	Y	Y	N	Y	Y	N	Y
6 Moore	N	N	Y	Y	Y	Y	Y	Y
7 Breaux	Y	N	Y	N	Y	Y	N	Y
8 Long	N	Y	Y	N	Y	Y	Y	N
MAINE								
1 Emery	Y	N	Y	N	Y	Y	Y	Y
2 Cohen	Y	N	Y	N	Y	Y	Y	N
MARYLAND								
1 Bauman	Y	-	-	-	†	N	N	N
2 Long	Y	N	Y	N	Y	Y	Y	N
3 Mikulski	Y	Y	Y	N	Y	Y	Y	N
4 Holt	Y	N	N	?	?	?	?	?
5 Spellman	Y	Y	Y	N	Y	Y	Y	N
6 Byron	Y	?	Y	N	Y	Y	Y	Y
7 Mitchell	Y	Y	Y	N	#	Y	Y	▮
8 Steers	Y	Y	Y	Y	Y	Y	Y	N
MASSACHUSETTS								
1 Conte	Y	Y	Y	Y	N	Y	Y	N
2 Boland	Y	Y	Y	N	Y	Y	Y	N
3 Early	Y	Y	Y	Y	N	Y	Y	N
4 Drinan	Y	Y	Y	Y	N	Y	Y	N
5 Tsongas	Y	Y	Y	Y	N	Y	Y	N
6 Harrington	Y	Y	Y	Y	N	Y	Y	N
7 Markey	Y	Y	Y	Y	N	Y	Y	N
8 O'Neill								
9 Moakley	Y	Y	Y	Y	▮	Y	Y	N
10 Heckler	Y	Y	Y	?	?	N	N	N
11 Burke	Y	Y	Y	?	?	Y	Y	N
12 Studds	Y	Y	Y	Y	N	Y	Y	N
MICHIGAN								
1 Conyers	Y	#	Y	Y	Y	Y	Y	N
2 Pursell	Y	?	Y	N	Y	Y	Y	N
3 Brown	N	▮	#	N	N	Y	N	Y
4 Stockman	#	N	N	N	Y	Y	N	Y
5 Sawyer	✓	Y	Y	N	Y	Y	Y	N
6 Carr	Y	†	†	Y	Y	Y	Y	N
7 Kildee	Y	Y	Y	Y	N	Y	Y	N
8 Traxler	Y	#	#	Y	N	Y	Y	N
9 Vander Jagt	Y	Y	Y	N	Y	Y	N	Y
10 Cederberg	Y	N	Y	N	Y	Y	N	N
11 Ruppe	#	#	#	?	?	#	#	?
12 Bonior	Y	Y	#	N	Y	Y	Y	N
13 Diggs	Y	#	#	▮	#	#	Y	▮
14 Nedzi	Y	Y	Y	Y	Y	Y	Y	N
15 Ford	Y	?	?	N	Y	?	Y	N
16 Dingell	Y	Y	?	Y	N	N	Y	N
17 Brodhead	Y	Y	Y	Y	N	Y	Y	N
18 Blanchard	Y	N	Y	N	Y	Y	Y	N
19 Broomfield	#	N	#	▮	#	N	N	#
MINNESOTA								
1 Quie	Y	#	#	▮	#	Y	Y	Y
2 Hagedorn	N	N	Y	N	Y	?	N	Y
3 Frenzel	Y	Y	Y	N	Y	Y	N	Y
4 Vento	Y	Y	Y	Y	Y	Y	Y	N
5 Fraser	Y	Y	#	Y	Y	Y	Y	N
6 Nolan	Y	Y	Y	N	Y	Y	Y	N
7 Stangeland	N	N	Y	N	Y	Y	N	Y
8 Oberstar	Y	Y	Y	N	Y	Y	Y	N
MISSISSIPPI								
1 Whitten	N	N	#	N	Y	#	▮	▮
2 Bowen	N	Y	Y	N	Y	N	N	N
3 Montgomery	N	N	Y	N	Y	N	N	N
4 Cochran	N	N	Y	N	Y	Y	N	N
5 Lott	N	N	Y	N	Y	N	N	N
MISSOURI								
1 Clay	Y	Y	Y	Y	Y	Y	Y	N
2 Young	Y	Y	Y	N	Y	Y	Y	N
3 Gephardt	Y	Y	Y	N	Y	Y	Y	Y
4 Skelton	Y	Y	Y	N	Y	Y	Y	Y
5 Bolling	Y	#	#	▮	#	Y	Y	N
6 Coleman	Y	N	N	N	Y	Y	N	Y
7 Taylor	N	N	Y	N	Y	N	N	N
8 Ichord	N	N	Y	N	Y	Y	N	N
9 Volkmer	Y	Y	Y	Y	Y	Y	Y	N
10 Burlison	Y	Y	Y	N	Y	Y	Y	N
MONTANA								
1 Baucus	#	Y	Y	N	Y	Y	Y	N
2 Marlenee	Y	N	Y	N	Y	N	N	Y
NEBRASKA								
1 Thone	?	Y	Y	Y	Y	Y	N	N
2 Cavanaugh	Y	Y	Y	N	Y	Y	Y	N
3 Smith	N	Y	Y	N	Y	Y	N	N
NEVADA								
AL Santini	#	#	#	▮	#	Y	Y	N
NEW HAMPSHIRE								
1 D'Amours	Y	?	Y	Y	N	Y	Y	N
2 Cleveland	Y	N	Y	Y	Y	N	N	Y
NEW JERSEY								
1 Florio	Y	Y	Y	N	Y	Y	Y	N
2 Hughes	Y	#	#	Y	N	Y	Y	N
3 Howard	Y	Y	Y	Y	N	Y	Y	N
4 Thompson	Y	Y	Y	N	Y	Y	Y	N
5 Fenwick	Y	Y	Y	Y	N	Y	Y	N
6 Forsythe	Y	N	N	N	Y	Y	N	N
7 Maguire	Y	?	?	?	?	Y	Y	N
8 Roe	Y	Y	Y	Y	N	Y	Y	N
9 Hollenbeck	Y	Y	Y	Y	N	Y	Y	N
10 Rodino	Y	#	#	Y	N	Y	Y	N
11 Minish	Y	?	#	Y	N	Y	Y	N
12 Rinaldo	Y	▮	#	Y	N	Y	Y	N
13 Meyner	Y	Y	Y	Y	N	Y	Y	N
14 LeFante	Y	#	#	▮	#	#	#	▮
15 Patten	Y	Y	Y	N	N	Y	Y	N
NEW MEXICO								
1 Lujan	N	Y	N	N	Y	Y	N	N
2 Runnels	N	N	Y	Y	Y	Y	N	Y
NEW YORK								
1 Pike	Y	Y	Y	Y	Y	Y	Y	Y
2 Downey	Y	Y	Y	Y	Y	Y	Y	N
3 Ambro	Y	?	?	?	?	Y	Y	N
4 Lent	Y	N	Y	Y	Y	Y	Y	Y
5 Wydler	Y	?	?	?	?	?	?	?
6 Wolff	Y	Y	Y	Y	Y	Y	Y	N
7 Addabbo	Y	Y	Y	Y	Y	Y	Y	N
8 Rosenthal	Y	Y	Y	Y	Y	Y	Y	N
9 Delaney	Y	Y	Y	Y	N	Y	Y	N
10 Biaggi	Y	#	#	▮	#	Y	Y	N
11 Scheuer	Y	Y	Y	Y	Y	Y	Y	N
12 Chisholm	Y	Y	Y	?	#	Y	Y	N
13 Solarz	Y	Y	Y	Y	Y	Y	Y	N
14 Richmond	✓	Y	Y	Y	N	Y	Y	N
15 Zeferetti	Y	#	#	▮	#	#	#	N
16 Holtzman	N	Y	Y	Y	N	Y	Y	N
17 Murphy	Y	Y	Y	N	Y	Y	Y	N
18 Vacancy								
19 Rangel	Y	Y	Y	Y	N	Y	Y	N
20 Weiss	Y	†	†	†	-	Y	Y	N
21 Vacancy								
22 Bingham	✓	Y	Y	#	▮	Y	Y	N
23 Caputo	N	?	?	Y	N	N	Y	Y
24 Ottinger	Y	Y	Y	N	Y	Y	Y	N
25 Fish	Y	Y	Y	N	Y	Y	N	N
26 Gilman	Y	†	†	Y	Y	Y	Y	N
27 McHugh	Y	Y	Y	Y	N	Y	Y	N
28 Stratton	Y	Y	Y	Y	Y	Y	Y	N
29 Pattison	Y	Y	Y	N	Y	Y	Y	N
30 McEwen	Y	N	Y	N	Y	N	N	Y
31 Mitchell	✓	Y	Y	Y	N	N	N	Y
32 Hanley	Y	Y	Y	N	Y	Y	Y	N
33 Walsh	Y	Y	Y	N	Y	N	N	Y
34 Horton	Y	Y	#	▮	Y	Y	Y	N
35 Conable	?	N	Y	N	Y	N	N	Y
36 LaFalce	?	?	?	?	?	?	?	?
37 Nowak	Y	Y	Y	N	Y	Y	Y	N
38 Kemp	N	?	#	?	Y	N	N	N
39 Lundine	Y	Y	Y	N	Y	Y	Y	N
NORTH CAROLINA								
1 Jones	Y	Y	Y	N	Y	Y	N	Y
2 Fountain	Y	N	Y	N	Y	Y	N	N
3 Whitley	Y	Y	Y	N	Y	Y	N	Y
4 Andrews	Y	Y	Y	▮	#	Y	Y	N
5 Neal	Y	Y	Y	N	Y	Y	Y	N
6 Preyer	Y	Y	Y	N	Y	Y	Y	N
7 Rose	Y	Y	Y	N	Y	Y	Y	N
8 Hefner	Y	Y	Y	N	Y	Y	Y	Y
9 Martin	Y	N	Y	N	Y	Y	N	Y
10 Broyhill	Y	?	?	?	?	Y	N	N
11 Gudger	Y	Y	Y	N	Y	Y	Y	Y
NORTH DAKOTA								
AL Andrews	N	N	Y	N	Y	Y	Y	N
OHIO								
1 Gradison	Y	Y	Y	Y	N	N	N	N
2 Luken	Y	N	Y	Y	Y	Y	Y	Y
3 Whalen	Y	Y	Y	Y	N	Y	Y	N
4 Guyer	N	Y	Y	N	Y	N	N	N
5 Latta	X	N	N	N	Y	N	N	N
6 Harsha	Y	N	Y	N	Y	N	N	N
7 Brown	?	N	N	N	Y	?	?	?
8 Kindness	N	N	N	?	Y	N	N	N
9 Ashley	Y	?	Y	N	Y	Y	Y	N
10 Miller	N	N	N	N	Y	N	Y	N
11 Stanton	Y	Y	Y	N	Y	N	N	Y
12 Devine	N	N	N	N	Y	N	N	N
13 Pease	Y	Y	Y	Y	N	Y	Y	N
14 Seiberling	Y	Y	Y	Y	Y	Y	Y	N
15 Wylie	?	N	Y	N	Y	N	Y	N
16 Regula	Y	Y	Y	N	Y	N	N	Y
17 Ashbrook	N	N	N	N	Y	N	N	N
18 Applegate	Y	Y	Y	Y	Y	Y	Y	Y
19 Carney	Y	Y	Y	Y	Y	Y	Y	N
20 Oakar	Y	Y	Y	Y	N	N	Y	?
21 Stokes	Y	Y	Y	Y	Y	Y	Y	N
22 Vanik	Y	Y	Y	Y	N	Y	Y	N
23 Mottl	✓	N	Y	Y	N	N	Y	▮
OKLAHOMA								
1 Jones	N	Y	Y	N	Y	Y	Y	Y
2 Risenhoover	X	?	Y	N	Y	Y	Y	N
3 Watkins	N	N	Y	N	Y	Y	Y	N
4 Steed	N	Y	Y	N	Y	Y	Y	N
5 Edwards	N	N	N	Y	Y	N	Y	N
6 English	N	N	Y	Y	N	Y	Y	N
OREGON								
1 AuCoin	Y	N	Y	N	Y	Y	Y	N
2 Ullman	Y	Y	Y	N	Y	Y	Y	N
3 Duncan	Y	Y	N	N	Y	Y	Y	N
4 Weaver	Y	Y	Y	N	Y	Y	Y	N
PENNSYLVANIA								
1 Myers, M.	Y	?	Y	N	Y	Y	Y	N
2 Nix	Y	#	#	▮	#	#	#	▮
3 Lederer	Y	Y	Y	N	Y	Y	Y	N
4 Eilberg	Y	Y	Y	Y	Y	Y	Y	N
5 Schulze	Y	N	N	Y	Y	N	N	Y
6 Yatron	Y	Y	Y	N	Y	Y	Y	Y
7 Edgar	Y	Y	Y	Y	Y	Y	Y	N
8 Kostmayer	Y	Y	Y	Y	N	N	Y	N
9 Shuster	N	N	Y	N	Y	Y	N	Y
10 McDade	Y	Y	Y	N	Y	Y	Y	N
11 Flood	Y	?	?	?	?	?	?	?
12 Murtha	Y	Y	Y	N	Y	Y	Y	N
13 Coughlin	Y	Y	Y	Y	Y	N	Y	N
14 Moorhead	Y	Y	Y	N	Y	Y	Y	N
15 Rooney	Y	Y	Y	N	Y	Y	Y	N
16 Walker	N	N	N	N	Y	N	N	Y
17 Ertel	Y	Y	Y	N	Y	Y	Y	Y
18 Walgren	Y	Y	Y	N	Y	Y	Y	Y
19 Goodling, W.	Y	?	?	?	?	?	?	?
20 Gaydos	Y	Y	Y	N	Y	Y	Y	N
21 Dent	X	#	#	▮	#	#	#	▮
22 Murphy	Y	#	#	#	▮	N	Y	N
23 Ammerman	Y	Y	Y	Y	N	N	Y	N
24 Marks	Y	?	?	?	?	?	Y	Y
25 Myers, G.	N	N	Y	N	Y	N	Y	N
RHODE ISLAND								
1 St Germain	Y	Y	Y	N	Y	Y	Y	N
2 Beard	Y	Y	Y	N	Y	Y	Y	?
SOUTH CAROLINA								
1 Davis	Y	Y	Y	N	Y	Y	Y	N
2 Spence	N	N	Y	N	Y	Y	N	N
3 Derrick	Y	Y	Y	Y	Y	Y	Y	N
4 Mann	Y	?	?	?	?	Y	Y	N
5 Holland	Y	#	#	▮	#	?	Y	N
6 Jenrette	Y	Y	Y	N	Y	Y	Y	N
SOUTH DAKOTA								
1 Pressler	Y	Y	Y	N	Y	Y	Y	N
2 Abdnor	N	Y	Y	N	Y	Y	Y	N
TENNESSEE								
1 Quillen	✓	N	N	N	Y	N	N	N
2 Duncan	✓	N	N	N	Y	N	N	Y
3 Lloyd	Y	Y	Y	N	Y	Y	Y	Y
4 Gore	Y	Y	Y	Y	N	Y	Y	N
5 Allen	Y	Y	Y	Y	Y	Y	Y	N
6 Beard	Y	N	N	N	Y	Y	N	N
7 Jones	X	Y	Y	▮	#	#	#	▮
8 Ford	#	Y	Y	Y	Y	Y	Y	N
TEXAS								
1 Hall	N	N	Y	N	Y	Y	N	N
2 Wilson, C.	N	Y	Y	Y	N	Y	Y	Y
3 Collins	N	N	N	N	Y	N	N	N
4 Roberts	Y	N	Y	N	Y	Y	N	N
5 Mattox	Y	Y	Y	Y	Y	Y	Y	N
6 Teague	X	?	?	N	Y	?	?	?
7 Archer	N	N	N	N	Y	N	N	N
8 Eckhardt	Y	?	?	?	?	Y	Y	N
9 Brooks	Y	N	Y	Y	N	N	Y	N
10 Pickle	X	Y	Y	N	Y	N	Y	N
11 Poage	N	N	Y	N	Y	N	N	Y
12 Wright	?	Y	Y	N	Y	Y	Y	N
13 Hightower	N	Y	Y	N	Y	Y	N	Y
14 Young	N	Y	Y	N	Y	Y	Y	N
15 de la Garza	Y	Y	Y	Y	N	Y	N	Y
16 White	N	N	Y	N	Y	Y	N	Y
17 Burleson	N	N	Y	N	Y	N	N	Y
18 Jordan	?	Y	Y	Y	N	Y	Y	N
19 Mahon	N	#	#	▮	#	#	N	N
20 Gonzalez	?	Y	P	Y	N	N	Y	N
21 Krueger	▮	#	#	▮	#	#	▮	Y
22 Gammage	N	Y	Y	N	Y	Y	N	Y
23 Kazen	N	Y	Y	Y	N	Y	N	Y
24 Milford	N	?	Y	N	Y	Y	N	N
UTAH								
1 McKay	#	N	Y	N	Y	Y	Y	Y
2 Marriott	N	N	N	N	Y	Y	N	N
VERMONT								
AL Jeffords	Y	Y	Y	Y	N	N	Y	N
VIRGINIA								
1 Trible	Y	N	N	N	Y	Y	N	Y
2 Whitehurst	Y	N	Y	Y	N	N	N	Y
3 Satterfield	N	N	N	N	Y	N	N	N
4 Daniel	Y	N	N	N	Y	N	N	N
5 Daniel	N	N	N	Y	N	Y	N	N
6 Butler	N	N	N	N	Y	Y	N	N
7 Robinson	N	N	N	N	Y	N	N	N
8 Harris	Y	Y	Y	Y	N	Y	Y	N
9 Wampler	N	N	Y	N	Y	N	Y	Y
10 Fisher	Y	Y	Y	N	Y	Y	Y	N
WASHINGTON								
1 Pritchard	Y	Y	Y	N	Y	Y	Y	N
2 Meeds	Y	Y	Y	N	Y	?	Y	N
3 Bonker	Y	Y	Y	N	Y	Y	#	Y
4 McCormack	Y	Y	Y	N	Y	Y	Y	N
5 Foley	Y	Y	Y	N	Y	†	Y	N
6 Dicks	Y	?	?	▮	#	Y	Y	N
7 Cunningham	Y	N	N	N	Y	N	N	N
WEST VIRGINIA								
1 Mollohan	N	Y	Y	N	Y	Y	Y	N
2 Staggers	Y	Y	Y	N	Y	Y	Y	N
3 Slack	N	Y	Y	N	Y	Y	Y	N
4 Rahall	Y	#	#	Y	#	Y	Y	N
WISCONSIN								
1 Aspin	Y	?	Y	Y	Y	Y	Y	N
2 Kastenmeier	Y	Y	Y	Y	N	Y	Y	N
3 Baldus	Y	#	Y	N	Y	Y	Y	N
4 Zablocki	Y	Y	Y	N	Y	Y	Y	N
5 Reuss	Y	Y	#	#	▮	Y	Y	N
6 Steiger	Y	Y	Y	N	Y	Y	N	N
7 Obey	Y	Y	Y	Y	?	Y	Y	N
8 Cornell	Y	Y	Y	N	Y	Y	Y	N
9 Kasten	N	-	†	Y	Y	Y	N	N
WYOMING								
AL Roncalio	?	Y	Y	N	Y	P	Y	N

Democrats ***Republicans***

37. HR 6805. Agency for Consumer Protection. Brooks (D Texas) motion that the House resolve itself into the Committee of the Whole for further consideration of the bill to establish a consumer protection agency. Motion agreed to 377-25: R 119-23; D 258-2 (ND 179-1; SD 79-1), Feb. 8, 1978.

38. HR 6805. Agency for Consumer Protection. Levitas (D Ga.) amendment to the Brooks (D Texas) substitute amendment (HR 9718) to require the proposed Office of Consumer Representation to give the President 30 days' advance notice of its intent to seek judicial review of an action by an independent federal regulatory agency. Rejected 195-219: R 112-28; D 83-191 (ND 27-162; SD 56-29), Feb. 8, 1978.

39. HR 6805. Agency for Consumer Protection. Quayle (R Ind.) amendment, to the Brooks (D Texas) substitute amendment (incorporating the provisions of HR 9718), to delete from the bill the exemption covering certain labor proceedings before the National Labor Relations Board and the activities of the Federal Mediation and Conciliation Service. Rejected 138-274: R 101-42; D 37-232 (ND 8-177; SD 29-55), Feb. 8, 1978.

40. HR 6805. Agency for Consumer Protection. Fenwick (R N.J.) amendment, to the Brooks (D Texas) substitute amendment, to delete from the bill the exemption covering Department of Agriculture proceedings concerning loans, price supports and the purchase of agricultural commodities, PL 480 programs, and the programs administered by the Soil Conservation Service, the Farmers Home Administration, the Rural Electrification Administration and the Federal Crop Insurance Corporation. Rejected 105-309: R 36-107; D 69-202 (ND 60-126; SD 9-76), Feb. 8, 1978.

41. HR 6805. Agency for Consumer Protection. Passage of the bill to establish an independent Office of Consumer Representation within the Executive Branch to represent the interests of consumers before federal agencies and courts. Rejected 189-227: R 17-126; D 172-101 (ND 147-40; SD 25-61), Feb. 8, 1978. A "yea" was a vote supporting the President's position.

42. HR 3813. Redwood National Park. Clausen (R Calif.) motion to recommit the bill to the Committee on Interior and Insular Affairs with instructions to cut back the acreage to be acquired from 48,000 to 14,000 and to delete terms providing a 30,000 acre park protection zone. Rejected 116-274: R 93-43; D 23-231 (ND 10-171; SD 13-60), Feb. 9, 1978. A "nay" was a vote supporting the President's position.

43. HR 3813. Redwood National Park. Passage of the bill providing for the immediate acquisition of 48,000 acres of privately owned timberland to be added to the existing Redwood National Park in northern California. Passed 328-60: R 91-43; D 237-17 (ND 174-8; SD 63-9), Feb. 9, 1978. A "yea" was a vote supporting the President's position.

44. HR 3454. Endangered Wilderness Act. Adoption of the conference report adding 1.3 million acres spread through 17 areas in 10 western states to the National Wilderness Preservation System. Adopted 333-44: R 98-33; D 235-11 (ND 172-2; SD 63-9), Feb. 9, 1978.

KEY

- Y Voted for (yea).
- ✓ Paired for.
- † Announced for.
- # CQ Poll for.
- N Voted against (nay).
- X Paired against.
- \- Announced against.
- ▮ CQ Poll against.
- P Voted "present."
- ● Voted "present" to avoid possible conflict of interest.
- ? Did not vote or otherwise make a position known.

	37	38	39	40	41	42	43	44
ALABAMA								
1 Edwards	Y	Y	Y	N	N	Y	Y	Y
2 Dickinson	Y	Y	Y	N	N	Y	N	N
3 Nichols	Y	Y	Y	N	N	N	Y	Y
4 Bevill	Y	Y	N	N	N	N	Y	Y
5 Flippo	Y	Y	N	N	N	N	Y	Y
6 Buchanan	Y	Y	Y	N	N	N	Y	Y
7 Flowers	Y	Y	N	N	N	N	?	Y
ALASKA								
AL Young	N	Y	N	N	N	Y	N	N
ARIZONA								
1 Rhodes	Y	Y	Y	N	N	Y	N	Y
2 Udall	Y	N	N	N	Y	N	Y	Y
3 Stump	Y	Y	Y	N	N	Y	N	N
4 Rudd	N	Y	Y	N	N	Y	N	N
ARKANSAS								
1 Alexander	Y	Y	Y	N	N	N	Y	Y
2 Tucker	Y	N	Y	N	Y	▮	#	#
3 Hammerschmidt	Y	Y	Y	N	N	Y	N	N
4 Thornton	Y	Y	N	N	Y	?	?	?
CALIFORNIA								
1 Johnson	Y	N	N	N	Y	Y	Y	Y
2 Clausen	Y	Y	Y	N	N	Y	N	N
3 Moss	Y	N	N	N	Y	N	Y	Y
4 Leggett	#	N	N	N	Y	N	Y	Y
5 Burton, J.	Y	N	N	N	Y	N	Y	Y
6 Burton, P.	Y	N	N	N	Y	N	Y	Y
7 Miller	Y	N	N	N	Y	N	Y	Y
8 Dellums	Y	N	N	Y	Y	N	Y	Y
9 Stark	Y	N	N	N	Y	N	Y	Y
10 Edwards	Y	N	N	N	Y	N	Y	Y
11 Ryan	Y	Y	Y	Y	N	N	Y	Y
12 McCloskey	Y	N	N	Y	Y	?	?	?
13 Mineta	Y	N	N	N	Y	N	Y	Y
14 McFall	Y	N	?	?	✓	?	?	?
15 Sisk	Y	Y	N	N	N	Y	Y	N
16 Panetta	Y	N	N	N	N	N	Y	Y
17 Krebs	Y	N	N	N	Y	N	Y	Y
18 Ketchum	Y	Y	Y	N	N	Y	N	N
19 Lagomarsino	Y	Y	Y	N	N	N	Y	Y
20 Goldwater	Y	Y	Y	N	N	N	Y	Y
21 Corman	Y	N	N	N	Y	N	Y	Y
22 Moorhead	Y	Y	Y	N	N	Y	Y	Y
23 Beilenson	Y	N	N	N	Y	N	Y	Y
24 Waxman	Y	N	N	N	Y	N	Y	Y
25 Roybal	Y	N	N	Y	Y	N	Y	Y
26 Rousselot	N	Y	Y	Y	N	Y	N	N
27 Dornan	N	Y	Y	N	N	Y	N	N
28 Burke	#	N	▮	▮	✓	▮	#	#
29 Hawkins	Y	N	N	N	Y	N	Y	Y
30 Danielson	Y	N	N	N	Y	N	Y	Y
31 Wilson, C.H.	#	N	N	N	Y	N	Y	Y
32 Anderson	Y	N	N	N	Y	N	Y	Y
33 Clawson	?	?	?	?	X	?	?	?
34 Hannaford	Y	Y	N	▮	Y	N	Y	Y
35 Lloyd	Y	N	N	N	Y	N	Y	Y
36 Brown	Y	?	N	N	Y	?	Y	?
37 Pettis	Y	N	Y	N	N	Y	N	Y
38 Patterson	Y	N	N	N	Y	N	Y	Y
39 Wiggins	Y	Y	Y	Y	N	#	▮	#
40 Badham	N	Y	Y	N	N	Y	N	N
41 Wilson, B.	N	Y	N	Y	N	Y	Y	Y
42 Van Deerlin	Y	N	N	Y	Y	N	Y	Y
43 Burgener	Y	Y	Y	N	N	N	Y	N
COLORADO								
1 Schroeder	Y	N	N	Y	N	N	Y	Y
2 Wirth	Y	N	Y	Y	Y	N	Y	Y
3 Evans	Y	N	N	N	Y	Y	N	Y
4 Johnson	Y	N	Y	N	N	Y	Y	Y
5 Armstrong	N	N	Y	N	N	?	?	?
CONNECTICUT								
1 Cotter	#	N	N	Y	Y	N	Y	Y
2 Dodd	Y	N	N	Y	Y	N	Y	Y
3 Giaimo	Y	Y	N	Y	N	N	N	Y
4 McKinney	Y	N	Y	Y	Y	N	Y	?
5 Sarasin	Y	Y	Y	Y	N	N	Y	Y
6 Moffett	Y	N	N	Y	Y	N	Y	Y
DELAWARE								
AL Evans	Y	Y	Y	Y	N	N	Y	?
FLORIDA								
1 Sikes	?	Y	Y	N	N	N	Y	?
2 Fuqua	Y	Y	Y	N	N	N	Y	Y
3 Bennett	Y	Y	Y	Y	N	N	Y	Y
4 Chappell	Y	Y	N	N	N	Y	Y	Y
5 Kelly	Y	Y	Y	N	N	Y	N	Y
6 Young	Y	Y	Y	N	N	Y	Y	Y
7 Gibbons	Y	Y	N	Y	N	N	Y	Y
8 Ireland	Y	Y	N	N	N	?	?	?
9 Frey	Y	Y	Y	N	N	Y	Y	Y
10 Bafalis	Y	Y	Y	N	N	Y	Y	Y
11 Rogers	Y	N	N	N	Y	N	Y	Y
12 Burke	Y	Y	Y	N	N	N	Y	Y
13 Lehman	Y	Y	N	Y	Y	N	Y	Y
14 Pepper	Y	N	N	N	Y	N	Y	Y
15 Fascell	Y	N	N	N	Y	N	Y	Y
GEORGIA								
1 Ginn	Y	Y	N	N	N	N	Y	Y
2 Mathis	?	Y	N	N	N	Y	Y	?
3 Brinkley	Y	Y	N	N	N	N	Y	Y
4 Levitas	Y	Y	Y	Y	N	N	Y	Y
5 Fowler	Y	Y	N	N	Y	N	Y	Y
6 Flynt	Y	Y	Y	N	N	?	?	?
7 McDonald	-	†	†	-	X	†	-	-
8 Evans	Y	N	N	N	N	N	Y	Y
9 Jenkins	Y	Y	N	N	N	N	Y	N
10 Barnard	Y	Y	Y	N	N	N	Y	Y
HAWAII								
1 Heftel	Y	Y	N	N	Y	N	Y	Y
2 Akaka	Y	N	N	N	Y	N	Y	Y
IDAHO								
1 Symms	N	Y	Y	N	N	Y	N	N
2 Hansen, G.	N	Y	Y	N	N	Y	N	N
ILLINOIS								
1 Metcalfe	Y	N	N	N	Y	N	Y	Y
2 Murphy	Y	N	N	N	Y	N	Y	Y
3 Russo	Y	N	N	Y	Y	N	Y	Y
4 Derwinski	Y	Y	N	N	N	N	Y	Y
5 Fary	Y	N	N	Y	Y	N	Y	Y
6 Hyde	Y	Y	Y	Y	N	N	Y	Y
7 Collins	Y	N	N	▮	✓	N	Y	?
8 Rostenkowski	?	?	?	?	✓	?	?	?
9 Yates	Y	N	N	Y	Y	N	Y	Y
10 Mikva	Y	N	N	Y	Y	N	Y	Y
11 Annunzio	Y	N	N	Y	Y	N	Y	Y
12 Crane	Y	Y	Y	N	N	Y	N	N
13 McClory	N	Y	Y	N	N	N	Y	Y
14 Erlenborn	N	Y	Y	Y	N	Y	N	Y
15 Corcoran	Y	Y	Y	N	N	Y	Y	Y
16 Anderson	Y	Y	Y	N	N	N	#	#
17 O'Brien	Y	N	N	N	N	Y	Y	Y
18 Michel	Y	Y	Y	Y	N	Y	N	Y
19 Railsback	Y	N	N	N	N	N	Y	Y
20 Findley	Y	Y	N	Y	N	N	Y	Y
21 Madigan	Y	Y	N	N	N	N	Y	Y
22 Shipley	?	?	?	?	X	?	?	?
23 Price	Y	N	N	Y	Y	N	Y	Y
24 Simon	Y	N	Y	Y	Y	N	Y	Y
INDIANA								
1 Benjamin	Y	N	N	N	Y	N	Y	Y
2 Fithian	Y	N	N	N	N	N	Y	Y
3 Brademas	Y	N	N	N	Y	N	Y	Y
4 Quayle	N	Y	Y	Y	N	Y	Y	Y
5 Hillis	Y	Y	N	N	N	Y	Y	Y
6 Evans	Y	Y	N	N	N	N	Y	Y
7 Myers, J.	Y	Y	Y	N	N	Y	Y	Y
8 Cornwell	Y	N	N	N	N	N	Y	Y
9 Hamilton	Y	N	Y	Y	N	N	Y	Y
10 Sharp	Y	N	Y	Y	Y	N	Y	Y
11 Jacobs	Y	N	N	N	N	N	Y	Y
IOWA								
1 Leach	Y	N	N	N	N	Y	Y	Y
2 Blouin	Y	N	N	N	Y	N	Y	Y
3 Grassley	Y	Y	Y	N	N	Y	Y	N
4 Smith	Y	N	N	N	Y	N	Y	Y
5 Harkin	#	N	N	N	Y	N	Y	Y
6 Bedell	Y	N	N	N	N	N	Y	Y

Democrats ***Republicans***

	37	38	39	40	41	42	43	44
KANSAS								
1 Sebelius	N	N	Y	N	N	Y	N	Y
2 Keys	#	N	N	N	N	N	Y	Y
3 Winn	N	Y	Y	N	N	Y	Y	Y
4 Glickman	Y	N	N	N	N	N	Y	Y
5 Skubitz	Y	Y	Y	N	N	Y	N	N
KENTUCKY								
1 Hubbard	Y	Y	N	N	N	N	Y	Y
2 Natcher	Y	N	N	N	N	N	Y	Y
3 Mazzoli	Y	Y	N	N	N	?	?	?
4 Snyder	Y	Y	Y	Y	N	Y	Y	Y
5 Carter	Y	Y	N	N	N	Y	Y	Y
6 Breckinridge	Y	N	N	N	Y	N	Y	Y
7 Perkins	Y	N	N	N	N	N	Y	Y
LOUISIANA								
1 Livingston	Y	Y	Y	Y	N	Y	Y	Y
2 Boggs	Y	N	N	N	Y	N	Y	Y
3 Treen	?	Y	Y	Y	N	Y	N	Y
4 Waggonner	Y	Y	Y	N	N	#	■	■
5 Huckaby	Y	Y	Y	N	N	N	Y	Y
6 Moore	Y	Y	N	N	N	Y	Y	Y
7 Breaux	Y	Y	Y	N	N	Y	Y	Y
8 Long	Y	N	N	N	Y	N	Y	Y
MAINE								
1 Emery	Y	Y	Y	Y	N	■	#	#
2 Cohen	Y	N	Y	Y	Y	N	Y	?
MARYLAND								
1 Bauman	N	Y	Y	N	N	Y	N	N
2 Long	Y	N	?	?	Y	N	Y	Y
3 Mikulski	Y	N	N	N	Y	N	Y	Y
4 Holt	N	Y	Y	N	N	Y	Y	N
5 Spellman	Y	N	N	Y	Y	■	#	#
6 Byron	Y	Y	N	N	N	N	Y	Y
7 Mitchell	N	N	N	Y	Y	N	Y	Y
8 Steers	Y	N	N	N	Y	N	Y	Y
MASSACHUSETTS								
1 Conte	Y	N	N	Y	Y	N	Y	Y
2 Boland	Y	N	N	Y	Y	N	Y	Y
3 Early	Y	N	N	Y	Y	N	Y	Y
4 Drinan	Y	N	N	Y	Y	N	Y	Y
5 Tsongas	Y	N	N	Y	Y	N	Y	Y
6 Harrington	Y	N	N	N	Y	■	#	#
7 Markey	Y	N	N	Y	Y	N	Y	Y
8 O'Neill								
9 Moakley	Y	N	■	Y	Y	N	Y	Y
10 Heckler	Y	N	Y	Y	Y	N	Y	Y
11 Burke	Y	N	N	N	Y	N	Y	Y
12 Studds	Y	N	N	Y	Y	N	Y	Y
MICHIGAN								
1 Conyers	Y	N	N	N	Y	N	Y	Y
2 Pursell	Y	N	N	N	Y	N	Y	Y
3 Brown	N	Y	Y	N	N	Y	Y	Y
4 Stockman	Y	#	Y	Y	N	Y	N	Y
5 Sawyer	Y	Y	N	N	N	N	Y	Y
6 Carr	Y	N	N	Y	Y	N	Y	Y
7 Kildee	Y	N	N	N	Y	N	Y	Y
8 Traxler	Y	N	N	N	Y	N	Y	Y
9 Vander Jagt	Y	Y	Y	N	N	Y	Y	Y
10 Cederberg	Y	Y	N	N	N	Y	Y	Y
11 Ruppe	#	?	?	?	X	?	#	#
12 Bonior	Y	N	N	N	Y	N	Y	Y
13 Diggs	#	■	N	N	Y	■	Y	?
14 Nedzi	Y	N	N	Y	Y	N	Y	Y
15 Ford	Y	N	N	N	Y	?	?	?
16 Dingell	Y	N	N	N	Y	N	Y	?
17 Brodhead	Y	N	N	N	Y	N	Y	Y
18 Blanchard	Y	N	N	N	Y	N	Y	Y
19 Broomfield	Y	Y	Y	N	N	N	Y	Y
MINNESOTA								
1 Quie	Y	Y	N	N	N	Y	Y	Y
2 Hagedorn	Y	Y	Y	N	N	Y	N	Y
3 Frenzel	Y	Y	Y	Y	N	Y	Y	Y
4 Vento	Y	N	N	N	Y	N	Y	Y
5 Fraser	Y	N	N	N	Y	N	Y	Y
6 Nolan	Y	N	N	Y	Y	N	Y	Y
7 Stangeland	Y	#	Y	N	N	Y	N	N
8 Oberstar	Y	N	N	N	Y	N	Y	Y
MISSISSIPPI								
1 Whitten	#	■	■	#	■	Y	Y	N
2 Bowen	Y	Y	N	N	N	Y	Y	Y
3 Montgomery	Y	Y	Y	N	N	Y	N	N
4 Cochran	Y	Y	Y	N	N	Y	Y	Y
5 Lott	Y	Y	Y	N	N	Y	Y	N
MISSOURI								
1 Clay	Y	N	N	N	Y	N	Y	Y
2 Young	Y	N	N	N	N	N	Y	Y
3 Gephardt	Y	N	N	N	N	N	Y	Y
4 Skelton	Y	N	N	N	N	Y	N	?
5 Bolling	Y	N	N	N	Y	N	Y	Y
6 Coleman	Y	Y	N	N	N	Y	Y	Y
7 Taylor	Y	Y	Y	N	N	Y	N	Y
8 Ichord	Y	N	N	N	N	Y	N	Y
9 Volkmer	Y	Y	N	N	N	N	Y	Y
10 Burlison	Y	N	N	N	N	N	Y	Y
MONTANA								
1 Baucus	Y	N	N	N	Y	N	Y	Y
2 Marlenee	Y	Y	N	N	N	Y	Y	Y
NEBRASKA								
1 Thone	Y	Y	Y	N	N	Y	Y	Y
2 Cavanaugh	Y	N	N	N	N	N	Y	Y
3 Smith	Y	Y	Y	N	N	Y	Y	Y
NEVADA								
AL Santini	Y	Y	N	N	N	N	Y	Y
NEW HAMPSHIRE								
1 D'Amours	Y	N	N	Y	Y	N	Y	Y
2 Cleveland	Y	Y	Y	Y	N	Y	Y	Y
NEW JERSEY								
1 Florio	Y	N	N	N	Y	N	Y	Y
2 Hughes	Y	N	N	Y	Y	N	Y	Y
3 Howard	Y	N	N	Y	Y	N	Y	Y
4 Thompson	Y	N	N	N	Y	N	Y	?
5 Fenwick	Y	N	N	Y	Y	N	Y	Y
6 Forsythe	Y	Y	Y	Y	N	Y	N	N
7 Maguire	Y	N	N	Y	Y	N	Y	Y
8 Roe	Y	N	N	Y	Y	N	Y	Y
9 Hollenbeck	Y	N	N	Y	Y	Y	Y	Y
10 Rodino	Y	N	N	Y	Y	N	Y	Y
11 Minish	Y	N	N	Y	Y	N	Y	Y
12 Rinaldo	Y	N	N	Y	Y	N	Y	Y
13 Meyner	Y	N	N	Y	Y	N	Y	Y
14 LeFante	Y	N	N	Y	Y	N	Y	Y
15 Patten	Y	N	N	Y	Y	N	Y	Y
NEW MEXICO								
1 Lujan	Y	Y	Y	N	N	N	Y	Y
2 Runnels	Y	Y	Y	N	N	Y	Y	Y
NEW YORK								
1 Pike	Y	Y	N	N	N	N	Y	Y
2 Downey	Y	N	N	Y	Y	N	Y	Y
3 Ambro	Y	Y	N	N	Y	N	Y	Y
4 Lent	Y	Y	N	Y	N	Y	Y	Y
5 Wydler	Y	Y	Y	Y	N	N	Y	Y
6 Wolff	Y	N	N	Y	Y	N	Y	Y
7 Addabbo	Y	N	N	N	Y	N	Y	Y
8 Rosenthal	Y	N	N	N	Y	N	Y	Y
9 Delaney	Y	N	N	N	Y	N	Y	Y
10 Biaggi	Y	N	N	N	Y	N	Y	Y
11 Scheuer	Y	N	N	Y	Y	N	Y	Y
12 Chisholm	#	N	N	N	Y	N	Y	Y
13 Solarz	Y	N	N	Y	Y	?	#	Y
14 Richmond	Y	N	N	N	Y	N	Y	Y
15 Zeferetti	Y	N	N	N	Y	N	Y	?
16 Holtzman	Y	N	N	Y	Y	N	Y	Y
17 Murphy	Y	N	N	N	Y	N	Y	Y
18 Vacancy								
19 Rangel	Y	N	N	Y	Y	N	Y	Y
20 Weiss	Y	N	N	Y	Y	N	Y	Y
21 Vacancy								
22 Bingham	#	■	■	?	✓	■	#	#
23 Caputo	Y	Y	N	N	N	N	Y	Y
24 Ottinger	Y	N	N	N	Y	N	Y	Y
25 Fish	Y	N	N	Y	N	N	Y	Y
26 Gilman	Y	N	N	Y	Y	N	Y	Y
27 McHugh	Y	N	N	N	Y	N	Y	Y
28 Stratton	Y	Y	N	N	N	N	Y	Y
29 Pattison	Y	N	N	Y	Y	N	Y	Y
30 McEwen	Y	Y	N	N	N	Y	N	N
31 Mitchell	Y	Y	N	N	N	N	Y	Y
32 Hanley	Y	N	N	N	N	N	Y	Y
33 Walsh	Y	Y	N	N	N	N	Y	Y
34 Horton	Y	N	N	N	Y	Y	Y	?
35 Conable	Y	Y	Y	Y	N	●	●	Y
36 LaFalce	Y	N	N	Y	Y	N	Y	Y
37 Nowak	Y	Y	N	N	Y	N	Y	Y
38 Kemp	Y	Y	Y	N	N	Y	N	Y
39 Lundine	Y	N	N	N	N	N	Y	Y
NORTH CAROLINA								
1 Jones	Y	Y	N	N	N	N	Y	Y
2 Fountain	Y	Y	N	N	N	N	Y	Y
3 Whitley	Y	Y	N	N	N	N	Y	Y
4 Andrews	#	Y	N	N	N	N	Y	Y
5 Neal	Y	Y	N	N	N	N	Y	Y
6 Preyer	Y	N	N	N	Y	N	Y	Y
7 Rose	Y	N	N	N	N	N	Y	Y
8 Hefner	Y	Y	N	N	N	N	Y	Y
9 Martin	Y	Y	Y	N	N	Y	Y	Y
10 Broyhill	Y	Y	Y	N	N	Y	N	Y
11 Gudger	Y	Y	N	N	N	N	Y	Y
NORTH DAKOTA								
AL Andrews	Y	Y	N	N	N	Y	Y	Y
OHIO								
1 Gradison	Y	Y	Y	Y	N	Y	Y	Y
2 Luken	Y	N	N	N	N	■	#	#
3 Whalen	Y	N	N	N	Y	N	Y	?
4 Guyer	Y	Y	Y	N	N	Y	Y	Y
5 Latta	Y	Y	Y	N	N	Y	Y	Y
6 Harsha	Y	N	Y	N	N	Y	Y	Y
7 Brown	Y	Y	Y	Y	N	Y	Y	Y
8 Kindness	N	Y	Y	N	N	Y	N	N
9 Ashley	Y	N	N	N	Y	N	Y	Y
10 Miller	Y	N	Y	N	N	N	Y	Y
11 Stanton	Y	Y	Y	N	N	Y	Y	Y
12 Devine	Y	Y	Y	N	N	Y	N	N
13 Pease	Y	N	N	Y	Y	N	Y	Y
14 Seiberling	Y	N	N	Y	Y	N	Y	Y
15 Wylie	Y	N	Y	N	Y	N	Y	Y
16 Regula	Y	Y	N	N	N	Y	Y	Y
17 Ashbrook	N	Y	Y	N	N	Y	N	N
18 Applegate	Y	Y	N	N	Y	N	Y	Y
19 Carney	Y	N	N	N	Y	N	Y	Y
20 Oakar	Y	N	N	Y	Y	N	Y	Y
21 Stokes	Y	N	N	Y	Y	N	Y	Y
22 Vanik	Y	N	N	Y	Y	N	Y	Y
23 Mottl	Y	Y	N	N	Y	Y	Y	Y
OKLAHOMA								
1 Jones	Y	Y	Y	Y	N	N	Y	Y
2 Risenhoover	Y	N	N	N	N	N	Y	N
3 Watkins	Y	Y	Y	N	N	N	Y	N
4 Steed	Y	N	N	N	N	■	Y	Y
5 Edwards	Y	Y	Y	N	N	Y	Y	N
6 English	Y	Y	Y	N	N	N	Y	Y
OREGON								
1 AuCoin	Y	N	N	N	Y	N	Y	Y
2 Ullman	Y	N	N	N	N	Y	Y	Y
3 Duncan	Y	Y	N	N	N	Y	N	Y
4 Weaver	Y	N	N	N	Y	N	Y	Y
PENNSYLVANIA								
1 Myers, M.	Y	N	N	N	Y	N	Y	?
2 Nix	Y	N	N	N	Y	N	Y	Y
3 Lederer	Y	N	N	N	Y	N	Y	Y
4 Eilberg	Y	N	N	N	Y	N	Y	Y
5 Schulze	N	Y	Y	N	N	?	?	?
6 Yatron	Y	Y	N	N	Y	N	Y	Y
7 Edgar	Y	N	N	Y	Y	N	Y	Y
8 Kostmayer	Y	N	N	Y	Y	N	Y	Y
9 Shuster	N	Y	Y	N	N	Y	N	N
10 McDade	Y	N	N	N	N	N	Y	Y
11 Flood	?	N	?	N	Y	N	Y	Y
12 Murtha	Y	Y	N	N	N	N	Y	Y
13 Coughlin	Y	N	N	N	N	N	Y	Y
14 Moorhead	Y	N	N	N	Y	N	Y	Y
15 Rooney	Y	N	N	N	Y	N	Y	Y
16 Walker	N	Y	Y	N	N	Y	Y	Y
17 Ertel	Y	Y	N	N	X	N	N	Y
18 Walgren	#	N	Y	Y	Y	N	Y	?
19 Goodling, W.	Y	Y	Y	N	N	Y	N	Y
20 Gaydos	Y	N	N	N	Y	N	Y	?
21 Dent	#	■	■	■	#	■	#	#
22 Murphy	Y	Y	N	N	Y	N	Y	Y
23 Ammerman	Y	N	N	N	Y	N	Y	Y
24 Marks	Y	Y	N	N	N	N	Y	Y
25 Myers, G.	Y	N	N	N	Y	N	Y	Y
RHODE ISLAND								
1 St Germain	Y	N	N	N	Y	N	Y	Y
2 Beard	?	?	?	?	✓	?	?	?
SOUTH CAROLINA								
1 Davis	Y	N	N	N	Y	N	Y	Y
2 Spence	Y	Y	Y	N	N	Y	Y	Y
3 Derrick	#	N	N	N	N	■	?	Y
4 Mann	Y	Y	N	N	N	N	Y	Y
5 Holland	Y	N	N	N	N	N	Y	Y
6 Jenrette	Y	Y	N	N	Y	N	Y	N
SOUTH DAKOTA								
1 Pressler	Y	Y	Y	N	N	N	Y	Y
2 Abdnor	Y	Y	Y	N	N	Y	N	N
TENNESSEE								
1 Quillen	Y	Y	N	N	N	Y	N	Y
2 Duncan	Y	Y	Y	N	N	Y	Y	Y
3 Lloyd	Y	Y	N	N	N	N	Y	Y
4 Gore	Y	Y	Y	N	Y	N	Y	Y
5 Allen	Y	N	N	N	Y	N	Y	Y
6 Beard	Y	Y	Y	N	N	Y	Y	Y
7 Jones	#	#	■	■	X	■	#	#
8 Ford	Y	N	N	N	Y	N	Y	Y
TEXAS								
1 Hall	Y	Y	Y	N	N	Y	N	Y
2 Wilson, C.	Y	Y	N	N	N	N	Y	Y
3 Collins	N	Y	Y	N	N	Y	N	N
4 Roberts	Y	Y	Y	N	N	Y	N	Y
5 Mattox	Y	N	Y	N	Y	N	Y	Y
6 Teague	?	?	?	?	N	?	?	?
7 Archer	Y	Y	Y	Y	N	Y	N	N
8 Eckhardt	Y	N	N	N	Y	?	?	?
9 Brooks	Y	N	N	N	Y	N	Y	Y
10 Pickle	Y	Y	N	N	Y	N	N	Y
11 Poage	P	Y	?	N	N	Y	N	N
12 Wright	?	?	?	?	✓	?	?	?
13 Hightower	Y	Y	Y	N	N	N	Y	Y
14 Young	Y	N	N	N	Y	?	?	?
15 de la Garza	Y	N	N	N	N	N	Y	Y
16 White	Y	Y	N	N	N	N	Y	Y
17 Burleson	Y	Y	Y	N	N	Y	N	N
18 Jordan	Y	N	N	N	Y	N	Y	Y
19 Mahon	Y	N	Y	N	N	■	#	#
20 Gonzalez	Y	Y	N	N	Y	N	Y	Y
21 Krueger	Y	Y	Y	N	N	N	#	#
22 Gammage	Y	Y	N	N	N	?	?	?
23 Kazen	Y	Y	Y	N	N	?	?	?
24 Milford	Y	Y	Y	Y	N	Y	N	Y
UTAH								
1 McKay	Y	Y	■	N	N	N	N	Y
2 Marriott	Y	Y	Y	N	N	#	■	#
VERMONT								
AL Jeffords	Y	#	N	Y	Y	N	Y	Y
VIRGINIA								
1 Trible	Y	Y	Y	N	N	Y	Y	Y
2 Whitehurst	Y	Y	Y	N	N	N	Y	Y
3 Satterfield	N	Y	Y	Y	N	Y	N	Y
4 Daniel	Y	Y	Y	N	N	Y	N	N
5 Daniel	Y	Y	Y	N	N	Y	N	N
6 Butler	Y	Y	Y	N	N	Y	N	N
7 Robinson	Y	Y	Y	N	N	Y	N	N
8 Harris	Y	N	N	Y	Y	N	Y	Y
9 Wampler	Y	Y	Y	N	N	Y	N	Y
10 Fisher	Y	N	Y	Y	Y	N	Y	Y
WASHINGTON								
1 Pritchard	Y	N	Y	Y	Y	N	#	Y
2 Meeds	#	N	N	N	Y	N	Y	Y
3 Bonker	Y	N	N	N	N	N	Y	Y
4 McCormack	Y	Y	N	N	N	N	Y	Y
5 Foley	Y	Y	N	N	N	-	†	†
6 Dicks	Y	N	N	N	Y	N	Y	Y
7 Cunningham	Y	Y	N	N	N	Y	N	N
WEST VIRGINIA								
1 Mollohan	Y	N	N	N	N	N	Y	Y
2 Staggers	Y	N	N	N	Y	N	Y	Y
3 Slack	Y	N	N	N	N	N	Y	Y
4 Rahall	Y	N	N	N	N	N	Y	Y
WISCONSIN								
1 Aspin	Y	N	N	N	Y	N	Y	Y
2 Kastenmeier	Y	N	N	N	Y	N	Y	Y
3 Baldus	Y	N	N	N	Y	N	Y	Y
4 Zablocki	Y	N	N	N	Y	N	Y	Y
5 Reuss	Y	N	N	Y	Y	N	Y	Y
6 Steiger	#	■	■	?	X	■	#	#
7 Obey	Y	Y	N	N	N	N	Y	Y
8 Cornell	Y	N	N	N	Y	N	Y	Y
9 Kasten	Y	Y	N	N	N	N	Y	Y
WYOMING								
AL Roncalio	Y	Y	N	Y	Y	N	?	Y

Democrats ***Republicans***

45. HR 2554. Sioux Land Claims. Udall (D Ariz.) motion that the House resolve itself into the Committee of the Whole to consider the bill to enable the U.S. Court of Claims to reconsider Sioux claims against the United States' taking of 7 million acres in the Black Hills in 1877 on the merits of the case rather than on procedural technicalities. Motion agreed to 337-17: R 110-15; D 227-2 (ND 161-2; SD 66-0), Feb. 9, 1978. (The bill was passed subsequently by voice vote.)

46. HR 7843. Federal Judgeships. McClory (R Ill.) motion to instruct House conferees to insist on a provision providing for merit selection of federal district court judges to fill new positions created by the bill. Motion agreed to 321-19: R 120-0; D 201-19 (ND 150-8; SD 51-11), Feb. 9, 1978.

47. HR 8336. Chattahoochee River National Park. P. Burton (D Calif.) motion that the House resolve itself into the Committee of the Whole to consider the bill to establish a Chattahoochee River National Park in Atlanta, Ga. Motion agreed to 325-7: R 116-3; D 209-4 (ND 144-4; SD 65-0), Feb. 14, 1978.

48. HR 8336. Chattahoochee River National Park. Sebelius (R Kan.) amendment to create a federal/state partnership to fund acquisition of the lands and to require that the state take over the park within two and a half years. Rejected 119-230: R 96-24; D 23-206 (ND 7-150; SD 16-56), Feb. 14, 1978.

49. HR 8336. Chattahoochee River National Park. Passage of the bill to authorize $73 million from the Land and Water Conservation Fund to purchase 6,300 acres along the Chattahoochee River for the national park system. Passed 273-79: R 64-56; D 209-23 (ND 149-10; SD 60-13), Feb. 14, 1978.

50. HR 5503. Military Officer Promotions. Passage of the bill to amend the U.S. Code to standardize the officer promotion procedures within the uniformed services and to reduce the number of higher grade officers. Passed 351-7: R 120-1; D 231-6 (ND 160-4; SD 71-2), Feb. 14, 1978.

51. HR 4544. Black Lung Benefits. Adoption of the conference report on the bill to liberalize the black lung benefits program. Adopted (thus completing congressional action) 264-113: R 45-88; D 219-25 (ND 160-5; SD 59-20), Feb. 15, 1978.

52. HR 9370. Aquaculture Development. Passage of the bill to authorize $72 million in fiscal 1979-81 for the Departments of Commerce, Agriculture and Interior to develop and implement programs to increase the production of aquatic species, such as shellfish and plants, for food, and also to establish a disaster loan program. Passed 234-130: R 60-66; D 174-64 (ND 125-36; SD 49-28), Feb. 15, 1978.

KEY

- Y Voted for (yea).
- ✓ Paired for.
- † Announced for.
- # CQ Poll for.
- N Voted against (nay).
- X Paired against.
- \- Announced against.
- ▮ CQ Poll against.
- P Voted "present."
- ● Voted "present" to avoid possible conflict of interest.
- ? Did not vote or otherwise make a position known.

	45	46	47	48	49	50	51	52
ALABAMA								
1 Edwards	Y	Y	Y	N	Y	Y	N	Y
2 Dickinson	Y	Y	Y	N	N	Y	N	Y
3 Nichols	#	Y	Y	N	Y	Y	Y	Y
4 Bevill	Y	?	Y	N	Y	Y	Y	N
5 Flippo	Y	?	Y	N	Y	Y	Y	N
6 Buchanan	Y	Y	?	X	?	?	Y	N
7 Flowers	Y	Y	Y	N	Y	Y	Y	Y
ALASKA								
AL Young	#	Y	Y	Y	N	Y	N	Y
ARIZONA								
1 Rhodes	Y	Y	?	?	?	?	?	?
2 Udall	Y	Y	Y	N	Y	Y	#	#
3 Stump	Y	Y	Y	N	N	Y	N	N
4 Rudd	Y	Y	Y	Y	N	Y	N	N
ARKANSAS								
1 Alexander	Y	?	Y	N	Y	Y	Y	N
2 Tucker	#	#	#	?	#	#	#	X
3 Hammerschmidt	Y	Y	Y	N	Y	Y	Y	Y
4 Thornton	?	?	?	?	?	?	?	?
CALIFORNIA								
1 Johnson	Y	#	Y	N	Y	Y	Y	Y
2 Clausen	Y	Y	Y	Y	Y	Y	Y	Y
3 Moss	Y	N	Y	N	Y	Y	Y	Y
4 Leggett	#	Y	Y	N	Y	Y	Y	Y
5 Burton, J.	Y	Y	Y	N	Y	Y	Y	?
6 Burton, P.	Y	Y	Y	N	Y	Y	Y	Y
7 Miller	Y	?	Y	N	Y	Y	Y	N
8 Dellums	Y	Y	Y	N	Y	Y	Y	N
9 Stark	Y	Y	Y	N	Y	Y	Y	N
10 Edwards	Y	Y	Y	N	Y	Y	Y	Y
11 Ryan	Y	Y	#	▮	#	?	?	?
12 McCloskey	?	?	?	?	?	?	Y	N
13 Mineta	Y	Y	Y	N	Y	Y	Y	Y
14 McFall	?	?	?	N	Y	Y	Y	Y
15 Sisk	?	N	Y	N	Y	Y	Y	Y
16 Panetta	Y	Y	Y	N	Y	Y	Y	Y
17 Krebs	Y	Y	Y	N	Y	Y	Y	N
18 Ketchum	Y	Y	Y	Y	N	Y	N	Y
19 Lagomarsino	Y	Y	Y	Y	Y	Y	N	Y
20 Goldwater	Y	Y	?	?	?	?	N	N
21 Corman	Y	Y	#	▮	#	#	#	#
22 Moorhead	Y	Y	Y	Y	Y	Y	N	N
23 Beilenson	Y	Y	#	▮	#	?	Y	Y
24 Waxman	#	Y	Y	N	Y	Y	Y	Y
25 Roybal	Y	Y	#	▮	#	#	#	#
26 Rousselot	N	Y	Y	Y	N	Y	N	?
27 Dornan	N	Y	Y	Y	N	Y	Y	Y
28 Burke	#	#	#	▮	✓	#	✓	X
29 Hawkins	Y	Y	Y	N	Y	Y	Y	Y
30 Danielson	Y	Y	Y	N	Y	Y	Y	Y
31 Wilson	#	#	#	▮	#	#	Y	Y
32 Anderson	Y	Y	Y	N	Y	Y	Y	Y
33 Clawson	?	?	Y	Y	N	Y	N	Y
34 Hannaford	Y	Y	Y	N	Y	Y	Y	N
35 Lloyd	Y	?	N	N	Y	Y	Y	Y
36 Brown	?	?	?	?	?	?	✓	Y
37 Pettis	Y	Y	?	?	?	?	?	?
38 Patterson	#	#	Y	N	Y	Y	Y	Y
39 Wiggins	#	▮	Y	Y	N	Y	N	▮
40 Badham	N	Y	Y	Y	N	Y	N	Y
41 Wilson	Y	Y	N	Y	#	Y	N	Y
42 Van Deerlin	Y	Y	Y	N	Y	Y	Y	Y
43 Burgener	Y	?	Y	Y	Y	Y	N	Y
COLORADO								
1 Schroeder	Y	Y	Y	N	Y	Y	Y	Y
2 Wirth	Y	Y	Y	N	Y	Y	Y	Y
3 Evans	Y	Y	Y	Y	N	Y	Y	N
4 Johnson	Y	Y	Y	Y	Y	Y	Y	N
5 Armstrong	?	?	?	?	?	?	?	?
CONNECTICUT								
1 Cotter	Y	Y	Y	N	Y	Y	N	Y
2 Dodd	Y	Y	?	N	Y	Y	Y	Y
3 Giaimo	?	Y	Y	N	Y	Y	?	?
4 McKinney	#	#	Y	N	Y	Y	N	Y
5 Sarasin	Y	†	Y	N	Y	Y	N	Y
6 Moffett	Y	#	Y	N	Y	Y	Y	N
DELAWARE								
AL Evans	Y	Y	Y	Y	N	Y	Y	✓
FLORIDA								
1 Sikes	?	?	Y	N	Y	Y	Y	Y
2 Fuqua	Y	Y	#	▮	#	#	Y	Y
3 Bennett	Y	Y	Y	Y	Y	Y	Y	Y
4 Chappell	Y	Y	#	▮	#	#	Y	Y
5 Kelly	Y	Y	Y	Y	N	Y	N	N
6 Young	Y	Y	Y	N	Y	Y	N	Y
7 Gibbons	Y	?	?	?	?	?	?	?
8 Ireland	?	?	?	?	?	?	N	N
9 Frey	Y	Y	Y	Y	Y	Y	N	?
10 Bafalis	Y	Y	Y	N	Y	Y	●	Y
11 Rogers	Y	Y	Y	N	Y	Y	Y	Y
12 Burke	Y	Y	Y	Y	Y	Y	N	Y
13 Lehman	Y	Y	Y	N	Y	Y	Y	Y
14 Pepper	Y	Y	#	▮	✓	#	Y	Y
15 Fascell	Y	#	Y	N	Y	Y	Y	Y
GEORGIA								
1 Ginn	Y	N	Y	N	Y	Y	Y	Y
2 Mathis	?	?	Y	N	Y	Y	?	?
3 Brinkley	P	Y	Y	N	Y	Y	N	✓
4 Levitas	Y	Y	Y	N	Y	Y	Y	N
5 Fowler	Y	?	Y	N	Y	Y	Y	N
6 Flynt	?	?	?	?	?	?	N	Y
7 McDonald	†	#	Y	Y	N	†	X	X
8 Evans	Y	Y	#	▮	✓	#	Y	Y
9 Jenkins	Y	Y	Y	N	Y	Y	Y	Y
10 Barnard	?	?	Y	N	Y	Y	Y	Y
HAWAII								
1 Heftel	Y	Y	#	▮	#	#	#	#
2 Akaka	Y	Y	Y	N	Y	Y	Y	Y
IDAHO								
1 Symms	N	Y	Y	Y	N	?	N	N
2 Hansen, G.	N	Y	?	?	X	?	X	X
ILLINOIS								
1 Metcalfe	Y	Y	Y	N	Y	Y	Y	Y
2 Murphy	Y	Y	#	▮	#	#	Y	Y
3 Russo	Y	Y	#	▮	#	#	#	#
4 Derwinski	Y	Y	Y	N	Y	Y	Y	N
5 Fary	Y	Y	Y	N	Y	Y	Y	Y
6 Hyde	Y	Y	Y	Y	N	Y	N	N
7 Collins	#	#	Y	X	Y	Y	Y	Y
8 Rostenkowski	?	?	?	?	?	?	Y	Y
9 Yates	Y	Y	Y	N	Y	N	Y	Y
10 Mikva	Y	Y	Y	N	Y	Y	Y	Y
11 Annunzio	Y	Y	Y	N	Y	Y	Y	Y
12 Crane	Y	Y	#	#	X	#	N	N
13 McClory	Y	Y	#	#	X	#	X	X
14 Erlenborn	Y	Y	Y	Y	Y	Y	N	N
15 Corcoran	Y	Y	Y	Y	N	Y	N	N
16 Anderson	#	#	#	#	#	#	▮	#
17 O'Brien	Y	#	#	#	#	#	Y	N
18 Michel	Y	Y	Y	Y	N	Y	N	N
19 Railsback	Y	Y	Y	Y	N	Y	Y	Y
20 Findley	Y	Y	Y	Y	Y	Y	Y	N
21 Madigan	Y	Y	Y	Y	Y	Y	Y	N
22 Shipley	?	?	?	N	Y	Y	Y	Y
23 Price	Y	Y	Y	N	Y	Y	Y	Y
24 Simon	Y	N	Y	N	Y	Y	Y	Y
INDIANA								
1 Benjamin	Y	Y	Y	N	Y	Y	Y	Y
2 Fithian	Y	Y	Y	N	Y	Y	Y	Y
3 Brademas	Y	Y	Y	N	Y	Y	✓	✓
4 Quayle	N	Y	Y	Y	Y	Y	N	N
5 Hillis	Y	?	Y	Y	Y	Y	N	Y
6 Evans	Y	Y	Y	N	Y	Y	?	?
7 Myers	N	Y	Y	Y	Y	Y	Y	N
8 Cornwell	#	Y	Y	N	Y	Y	Y	Y
9 Hamilton	Y	Y	Y	N	Y	Y	Y	Y
10 Sharp	Y	Y	Y	N	Y	Y	Y	N
11 Jacobs	Y	Y	Y	Y	N	Y	Y	N
IOWA								
1 Leach	Y	Y	Y	Y	N	Y	Y	N
2 Blouin	Y	Y	#	N	Y	Y	Y	N
3 Grassley	Y	Y	Y	Y	N	Y	N	N
4 Smith	Y	Y	Y	N	Y	Y	#	?
5 Harkin	Y	Y	Y	N	Y	Y	Y	N
6 Bedell	Y	Y	Y	N	Y	Y	Y	N

Democrats ***Republicans***

	45	46	47	48	49	50	51	52
KANSAS								
1 Sebelius	Y	Y	Y	Y	N	Y	N	N
2 Keys	Y	Y	Y	Y	Y	Y	Y	Y
3 Winn	Y	#	Y	Y	Y	Y	N	N
4 Glickman	Y	Y	#	✓	Y	Y	Y	N
5 Skubitz	Y	Y	Y	Y	Y	Y	Y	N
KENTUCKY								
1 Hubbard	Y	Y	?	Y	Y	Y	Y	Y
2 Natcher	Y	Y	Y	N	Y	Y	Y	Y
3 Mazzoli	†	†	†	-	†	†	Y	N
4 Snyder	Y	Y	Y	Y	Y	Y	N	N
5 Carter	Y	Y	Y	Y	N	Y	Y	Y
6 Breckinridge	?	Y	Y	N	Y	Y	Y	N
7 Perkins	Y	Y	Y	N	Y	Y	Y	Y
LOUISIANA								
1 Livingston	?	Y	Y	Y	Y	Y	N	Y
2 Boggs	Y	#	#	N	Y	Y	Y	Y
3 Treen	Y	Y	Y	Y	Y	Y	N	Y
4 Waggonner	#	#	Y	N	Y	Y	N	Y
5 Huckaby	Y	Y	Y	N	Y	Y	N	Y
6 Moore	Y	Y	Y	Y	Y	Y	N	Y
7 Breaux	Y	Y	Y	Y	Y	Y	N	Y
8 Long	Y	?	?	N	Y	Y	Y	Y
MAINE								
1 Emery	#	#	Y	X	#	Y	Y	Y
2 Cohen	?	?	Y	N	Y	Y	Y	Y
MARYLAND								
1 Bauman	Y	Y	N	Y	N	Y	N	Y
2 Long	Y	Y	Y	N	Y	Y	Y	Y
3 Mikulski	Y	Y	?	?	?	?	Y	Y
4 Holt	Y	Y	Y	Y	N	Y	N	✓
5 Spellman	#	#	#	■	Y	Y	Y	N
6 Byron	Y	Y	Y	N	Y	Y	N	Y
7 Mitchell	N	Y	N	N	Y	Y	Y	Y
8 Steers	Y	Y	Y	N	Y	Y	Y	Y
MASSACHUSETTS								
1 Conte	Y	Y	Y	N	Y	Y	N	N
2 Boland	Y	Y	Y	N	Y	Y	#	#
3 Early	Y	Y	?	?	?	?	Y	?
4 Drinan	Y	Y	Y	N	Y	Y	Y	Y
5 Tsongas	Y	Y	#	■	#	#	Y	Y
6 Harrington	#	#	Y	N	Y	Y	✓	✓
7 Markey	Y	Y	Y	N	Y	Y	Y	Y
8 O'Neill								
9 Moakley	Y	Y	†	■	†	†	✓	†
10 Heckler	Y	Y	Y	Y	Y	Y	Y	Y
11 Burke	Y	Y	Y	N	Y	Y	Y	Y
12 Studds	Y	Y	Y	N	Y	Y	Y	Y
MICHIGAN								
1 Conyers	Y	Y	#	■	#	Y	Y	■
2 Pursell	?	Y	Y	N	Y	Y	Y	Y
3 Brown	Y	Y	#	#	#	#	N	Y
4 Stockman	N	Y	Y	Y	Y	Y	N	N
5 Sawyer	Y	Y	Y	N	X	Y	Y	N
6 Carr	Y	Y	Y	N	Y	Y	Y	Y
7 Kildee	Y	Y	Y	N	Y	Y	Y	Y
8 Traxler	Y	N	Y	N	Y	Y	Y	Y
9 Vander Jagt	Y	Y	Y	Y	Y	Y	N	Y
10 Cederberg	Y	Y	Y	Y	Y	Y	N	Y
11 Ruppe	#	#	#	?	Y	Y	Y	#
12 Bonior	#	N	Y	N	Y	Y	Y	Y
13 Diggs	#	Y	#	■	#	#	#	#
14 Nedzi	Y	Y	Y	N	Y	Y	Y	Y
15 Ford	?	Y	Y	N	Y	Y	?	✓
16 Dingell	N	N	Y	N	Y	Y	Y	Y
17 Brodhead	Y	Y	Y	N	Y	Y	Y	Y
18 Blanchard	Y	Y	Y	N	Y	Y	#	?
19 Broomfield	Y	#	Y	Y	N	#	Y	Y
MINNESOTA								
1 Quie	Y	Y	Y	Y	Y	Y	N	X
2 Hagedorn	Y	Y	Y	Y	N	Y	N	N
3 Frenzel	Y	Y	Y	Y	Y	Y	N	N
4 Vento	Y	Y	Y	N	Y	Y	Y	N
5 Fraser	Y	Y	#	■	?	#	Y	Y
6 Nolan	?	?	?	?	?	?	Y	Y
7 Stangeland	Y	#	Y	Y	N	Y	N	N
8 Oberstar	Y	Y	Y	N	Y	Y	Y	Y
MISSISSIPPI								
1 Whitten	#	N	Y	N	N	Y	Y	N
2 Bowen	Y	Y	Y	N	Y	Y	Y	Y
3 Montgomery	Y	N	Y	Y	N	Y	N	N
4 Cochran	Y	Y	Y	Y	N	Y	N	N
5 Lott	Y	Y	Y	Y	N	Y	N	Y
MISSOURI								
1 Clay	Y	Y	Y	N	Y	Y	?	?
2 Young	Y	Y	#	■	#	Y	Y	Y
3 Gephardt	Y	Y	#	■	#	Y	Y	Y

	45	46	47	48	49	50	51	52
4 Skelton	?	#	Y	N	Y	Y	Y	N
5 Bolling	Y	#	Y	N	Y	Y	Y	Y
6 Coleman	Y	Y	Y	Y	N	Y	Y	N
7 Taylor	Y	Y	?	✓	X	?	X	?
8 Ichord	Y	Y	Y	Y	N	Y	N	N
9 Volkmer	Y	Y	Y	N	Y	Y	Y	Y
10 Burlison	Y	Y	Y	N	Y	Y	Y	Y
MONTANA								
1 Baucus	Y	#	#	■	#	#	✓	#
2 Marlenee	Y	Y	Y	Y	N	Y	Y	Y
NEBRASKA								
1 Thone	Y	Y	Y	Y	Y	Y	N	N
2 Cavanaugh	Y	Y	Y	N	Y	Y	Y	N
3 Smith	Y	Y	Y	Y	Y	Y	N	N
NEVADA								
AL Santini	Y	Y	#	X	✓	#	N	Y
NEW HAMPSHIRE								
1 D'Amours	Y	Y	Y	N	Y	Y	Y	Y
2 Cleveland	Y	Y	Y	N	Y	Y	N	Y
NEW JERSEY								
1 Florio	Y	Y	Y	N	Y	Y	Y	Y
2 Hughes	Y	Y	Y	N	Y	Y	Y	Y
3 Howard	Y	Y	Y	N	Y	Y	Y	Y
4 Thompson	Y	Y	Y	N	Y	Y	Y	Y
5 Fenwick	Y	Y	Y	Y	Y	Y	Y	N
6 Forsythe	Y	Y	Y	Y	N	Y	N	Y
7 Maguire	Y	Y	Y	N	Y	Y	Y	Y
8 Roe	Y	Y	Y	N	Y	Y	Y	#
9 Hollenbeck	Y	Y	Y	N	Y	Y	Y	N
10 Rodino	Y	Y	Y	N	Y	Y	Y	Y
11 Minish	Y	Y	Y	N	N	Y	Y	N
12 Rinaldo	Y	Y	Y	Y	N	Y	Y	N
13 Meyner	Y	#	Y	N	Y	Y	Y	Y
14 LeFante	Y	Y	Y	N	Y	Y	Y	Y
15 Patten	Y	Y	Y	N	Y	Y	Y	Y
NEW MEXICO								
1 Lujan	Y	Y	Y	Y	N	Y	Y	N
2 Runnels	Y	?	Y	N	N	Y	Y	N
NEW YORK								
1 Pike	Y	Y	Y	N	Y	N	Y	N
2 Downey	Y	Y	Y	N	Y	Y	Y	Y
3 Ambro	Y	Y	Y	N	Y	Y	Y	Y
4 Lent	Y	Y	#	✓	#	#	X	✓
5 Wydler	Y	Y	?	Y	Y	Y	N	Y
6 Wolff	Y	Y	Y	N	Y	Y	Y	N
7 Addabbo	Y	Y	#	■	✓	#	✓	✓
8 Rosenthal	Y	Y	Y	N	Y	Y	Y	Y
9 Delaney	Y	Y	Y	N	Y	Y	Y	Y
10 Biaggi	Y	Y	Y	N	Y	Y	Y	Y
11 Scheuer	Y	Y	Y	N	Y	N	Y	Y
12 Chisholm	Y	#	#	N	Y	Y	Y	Y
13 Solarz	Y	Y	Y	N	Y	Y	Y	N
14 Richmond	Y	Y	Y	N	Y	Y	Y	Y
15 Zeferetti	#	#	Y	N	Y	Y	Y	Y
16 Holtzman	Y	Y	Y	N	Y	Y	Y	N
17 Murphy	Y	Y	#	■	✓	#	✓	✓
18 Vacancy								
19 Rangel	Y	Y	Y	N	Y	Y	Y	Y
20 Weiss	Y	Y	Y	N	Y	Y	Y	Y
21 Vacancy								
22 Bingham	#	#	#	■	✓	#	✓	#
23 Caputo	Y	Y	Y	N	Y	Y	Y	Y
24 Ottinger	Y	Y	Y	N	Y	Y	Y	X
25 Fish	Y	Y	Y	Y	N	?	Y	Y
26 Gilman	Y	Y	Y	Y	N	Y	Y	Y
27 McHugh	Y	Y	Y	N	Y	Y	Y	Y
28 Stratton	Y	Y	Y	Y	N	Y	N	N
29 Pattison	Y	#	#	Y	Y	Y	Y	N
30 McEwen	Y	?	Y	Y	Y	Y	?	?
31 Mitchell	Y	Y	Y	Y	Y	Y	Y	Y
32 Hanley	Y	#	#	N	Y	Y	Y	Y
33 Walsh	Y	Y	Y	Y	Y	Y	N	N
34 Horton	#	#	#	■	#	#	X	✓
35 Conable	Y	Y	?	✓	N	Y	N	N
36 LaFalce	Y	Y	Y	N	Y	Y	Y	Y
37 Nowak	Y	Y	Y	N	Y	Y	Y	Y
38 Kemp	N	Y	#	?	N	Y	N	Y
39 Lundine	Y	Y	Y	N	Y	Y	Y	Y
NORTH CAROLINA								
1 Jones	Y	N	Y	N	Y	Y	Y	Y
2 Fountain	Y	Y	Y	N	N	Y	N	N
3 Whitley	Y	Y	Y	N	N	Y	Y	Y
4 Andrews	Y	Y	Y	N	Y	Y	Y	Y
5 Neal	Y	Y	Y	N	Y	Y	Y	Y
6 Preyer	Y	Y	Y	N	Y	Y	Y	Y
7 Rose	Y	Y	Y	N	Y	Y	Y	Y
8 Hefner	Y	Y	Y	N	Y	Y	Y	N

	45	46	47	48	49	50	51	52
9 Martin	Y	Y	Y	#	#	#	N	N
10 Broyhill	Y	?	Y	Y	N	Y	N	N
11 Gudger	Y	Y	Y	N	Y	Y	N	Y
NORTH DAKOTA								
AL Andrews	Y	Y	Y	N	Y	Y	N	N
OHIO								
1 Gradison	Y	Y	Y	N	Y	Y	N	N
2 Luken	#	#	Y	N	Y	Y	Y	N
3 Whalen	#	Y	Y	N	Y	Y	Y	N
4 Guyer	Y	Y	Y	Y	Y	Y	N	Y
5 Latta	Y	Y	Y	Y	N	N	N	N
6 Harsha	Y	Y	Y	Y	N	Y	Y	N
7 Brown	Y	Y	?	Y	Y	Y	Y	Y
8 Kindness	N	Y	N	Y	N	Y	N	N
9 Ashley	Y	Y	?	N	Y	Y	Y	?
10 Miller	Y	Y	Y	Y	N	Y	Y	N
11 Stanton	#	#	Y	Y	Y	Y	N	N
12 Devine	N	Y	#	#	X	#	N	N
13 Pease	Y	Y	Y	N	Y	Y	Y	N
14 Seiberling	Y	Y	Y	N	Y	Y	Y	Y
15 Wylie	Y	Y	Y	Y	Y	Y	N	N
16 Regula	Y	Y	Y	N	Y	Y	N	N
17 Ashbrook	N	Y	Y	Y	N	Y	N	X
18 Applegate	Y	Y	Y	N	Y	Y	Y	Y
19 Carney	Y	N	Y	N	Y	Y	Y	Y
20 Oakar	Y	Y	Y	N	Y	Y	Y	Y
21 Stokes	#	Y	#	■	✓	#	#	#
22 Vanik	Y	Y	#	■	■	#	Y	N
23 Mottl	#	#	Y	N	Y	Y	Y	N
OKLAHOMA								
1 Jones	#	Y	Y	Y	N	Y	N	N
2 Risenhoover	Y	Y	Y	N	N	Y	X	X
3 Watkins	Y	Y	#	N	N	Y	Y	N
4 Steed	Y	Y	Y	N	Y	Y	N	N
5 Edwards	Y	Y	Y	N	N	Y	N	N
6 English	Y	Y	#	Y	N	Y	Y	N
OREGON								
1 AuCoin	Y	Y	N	N	Y	Y	Y	Y
2 Ullman	Y	Y	Y	N	Y	Y	Y	Y
3 Duncan	Y	?	Y	Y	N	Y	Y	Y
4 Weaver	?	#	Y	N	Y	Y	Y	Y
PENNSYLVANIA								
1 Myers	?	?	?	?	?	?	?	?
2 Nix	Y	Y	Y	N	Y	Y	Y	#
3 Lederer	Y	Y	Y	N	Y	Y	Y	Y
4 Eilberg	Y	Y	Y	N	Y	Y	Y	Y
5 Schulze	?	?	?	?	X	?	N	Y
6 Yatron	Y	Y	Y	N	Y	Y	Y	Y
7 Edgar	Y	Y	Y	N	Y	Y	Y	Y
8 Kostmayer	Y	Y	?	?	?	?	Y	N
9 Shuster	N	Y	Y	Y	N	Y	Y	N
10 McDade	Y	Y	Y	Y	Y	Y	Y	Y
11 Flood	Y	Y	Y	N	Y	Y	Y	Y
12 Murtha	Y	Y	Y	N	Y	Y	Y	Y
13 Coughlin	Y	Y	Y	#	#	Y	Y	Y
14 Moorhead	Y	Y	#	■	#	#	#	#
15 Rooney	Y	Y	Y	N	Y	Y	Y	Y
16 Walker	N	Y	#	Y	N	Y	N	N
17 Ertel	Y	Y	Y	N	Y	Y	Y	Y
18 Walgren	Y	Y	Y	N	Y	Y	Y	Y
19 Goodling, W.	Y	?	Y	Y	N	Y	N	N
20 Gaydos	?	?	Y	N	Y	Y	Y	Y
21 Dent	#	#	#	■	#	#	#	#
22 Murphy	Y	Y	#	■	#	#	Y	Y
23 Ammerman	Y	Y	Y	N	N	N	Y	N
24 Marks	?	Y	Y	Y	Y	Y	Y	Y
25 Myers	Y	Y	Y	Y	N	Y	N	Y
RHODE ISLAND								
1 St Germain	Y	Y	Y	N	Y	Y	Y	Y
2 Beard	?	?	Y	N	Y	Y	Y	Y
SOUTH CAROLINA								
1 Davis	Y	N	Y	N	Y	N	Y	Y
2 Spence	Y	Y	?	?	?	?	X	?
3 Derrick	Y	Y	Y	■	#	Y	Y	Y
4 Mann	Y	?	?	?	?	?	N	Y
5 Holland	Y	N	#	■	#	#	Y	Y
6 Jenrette	Y	Y	Y	N	Y	Y	Y	Y
SOUTH DAKOTA								
1 Pressler	Y	Y	Y	Y	Y	Y	Y	Y
2 Abdnor	Y	Y	Y	Y	Y	Y	N	Y
TENNESSEE								
1 Quillen	Y	Y	Y	Y	N	Y	#	#
2 Duncan	Y	Y	Y	N	?	?	Y	Y
3 Lloyd	Y	Y	Y	N	Y	Y	Y	Y
4 Gore	Y	Y	Y	Y	Y	Y	Y	■
5 Allen	Y	Y	Y	Y	Y	Y	Y	N
6 Beard	Y	Y	#	Y	Y	Y	N	Y

	45	46	47	48	49	50	51	52
7 Jones	#	#	#	■	#	#	#	Y
8 Ford	Y	Y	#	Y	Y	Y	Y	Y
TEXAS								
1 Hall	Y	Y	Y	N	N	Y	N	N
2 Wilson	Y	Y	#	#	#	#	Y	#
3 Collins	N	Y	Y	Y	N	Y	N	N
4 Roberts	Y	N	Y	Y	N	Y	N	N
5 Mattox	Y	Y	Y	N	Y	Y	Y	Y
6 Teague	?	?	?	?	?	?	X	?
7 Archer	Y	Y	Y	Y	N	Y	N	N
8 Eckhardt	?	?	Y	N	Y	Y	Y	Y
9 Brooks	Y	N	Y	N	Y	Y	Y	N
10 Pickle	Y	N	Y	N	Y	Y	N	N
11 Poage	Y	N	Y	N	Y	Y	N	N
12 Wright	?	?	?	N	Y	Y	Y	Y
13 Hightower	Y	Y	Y	N	Y	Y	Y	Y
14 Young	?	?	?	?	?	?	Y	Y
15 de la Garza	Y	Y	Y	N	Y	Y	Y	Y
16 White	Y	Y	Y	N	Y	Y	Y	Y
17 Burleson	Y	Y	Y	Y	N	Y	N	N
18 Jordan	Y	N	?	N	Y	Y	Y	Y
19 Mahon	#	#	Y	N	Y	Y	N	N
20 Gonzalez	Y	Y	?	Y	Y	N	Y	Y
21 Krueger	#	#	Y	■	Y	Y	■	#
22 Gammage	?	?	Y	Y	Y	Y	?	?
23 Kazen	?	?	Y	N	Y	Y	Y	N
24 Milford	Y	Y	?	Y	N	Y	N	N
UTAH								
1 McKay	Y	Y	Y	N	Y	Y	#	Y
2 Marriott	?	#	Y	Y	N	Y	N	Y
VERMONT								
AL Jeffords	#	Y	Y	Y	Y	Y	N	Y
VIRGINIA								
1 Trible	Y	Y	Y	Y	N	Y	N	Y
2 Whitehurst	Y	#	Y	Y	N	Y	N	Y
3 Satterfield	Y	Y	Y	Y	N	Y	?	?
4 Daniel	Y	Y	Y	Y	N	Y	N	N
5 Daniel	Y	Y	Y	Y	N	Y	N	N
6 Butler	?	Y	?	?	X	?	N	N
7 Robinson	Y	Y	Y	Y	N	Y	N	N
8 Harris	Y	Y	Y	N	Y	Y	Y	N
9 Wampler	Y	Y	Y	Y	Y	Y	Y	Y
10 Fisher	Y	Y	Y	N	Y	Y	Y	Y
WASHINGTON								
1 Pritchard	Y	Y	Y	Y	N	Y	N	Y
2 Meeds	Y	?	Y	N	Y	Y	?	#
3 Bonker	Y	Y	#	■	#	#	Y	Y
4 McCormack	Y	#	#	■	#	#	?	?
5 Foley	†	†	Y	N	N	Y	Y	N
6 Dicks	Y	Y	Y	N	Y	Y	Y	Y
7 Cunningham	Y	Y	Y	Y	N	Y	N	N
WEST VIRGINIA								
1 Mollohan	#	Y	Y	N	Y	Y	Y	Y
2 Staggers	Y	Y	Y	N	Y	Y	Y	Y
3 Slack	Y	Y	Y	N	Y	Y	Y	Y
4 Rahall	Y	Y	#	■	#	#	Y	Y
WISCONSIN								
1 Aspin	Y	Y	N	N	Y	Y	Y	Y
2 Kastenmeier	Y	N	#	N	Y	Y	Y	Y
3 Baldus	Y	Y	Y	N	Y	Y	Y	N
4 Zablocki	Y	Y	Y	N	Y	Y	Y	Y
5 Reuss	Y	Y	Y	N	Y	Y	Y	Y
6 Steiger	#	■	Y	N	Y	Y	N	N
7 Obey	?	?	Y	N	Y	Y	Y	Y
8 Cornell	Y	Y	Y	N	Y	Y	Y	N
9 Kasten	Y	†	†	-	†	†	N	N
WYOMING								
AL Roncalio	Y	?	?	N	?	Y	?	Y

Democrats ***Republicans***

53. HR 10979. Emergency Highway and Transportation Repair. Howard, D-N.J., motion to suspend the rules and pass the bill to authorize $250 million from the Highway Trust Fund to reimburse the states for 100 percent of the cost of repairing weather-related damage to highways and the surface rails of urban mass transportation systems. Motion agreed to 274-137: R 71-71; D 203-66 (ND 158-29; SD 45-37), Feb. 21, 1978. A two-thirds majority vote (274 in this case) is required for passage under suspension of the rules.

54. H J Res 649. Arts and Humanities Conferences. Brademas, D-Ind., motion to suspend the rules and pass the joint resolution to appropriate the necessary funds for the president to hold White House Conferences on the Arts and Humanities in calendar year 1979 and to establish 15-member National Conference Planning Councils on the Arts and on the Humanities. Passed 341-65: R 96-43; D 245-22 (ND 176-9; SD 69-13), Feb. 21, 1978. A two-thirds majority vote (271 in this case) is required for passage under suspension of the rules.

55. HR 10569. Alcohol and Drug Abuse Education. Brademas, D-Ind., motion to suspend the rules and pass the bill to amend the 1970 Alcohol and Drug Abuse Education Act and authorize $67.6 million for fiscal 1979-83 to provide grants to state and local education agencies, through the U.S. Office of Education, to establish training programs for local educators to prevent drug and alcohol abuse by youths. Motion agreed to 409-0: R 141-0; D 268-0 (ND 186-0; SD 82-0), Feb. 21, 1978. A two-thirds majority vote (273 in this case) is required for passage under suspension of the rules.

56. HR 10606. Hubert H. Humphrey Institute. Ford, D-Mich., motion to suspend the rules and pass the bill to authorize $5 million for the Hubert H. Humphrey Institute of Public Affairs at the University of Minnesota-Twin Cities to honor the late Sen. Humphrey, D-Minn. Motion agreed to 356-53: R 106-34; D 250-19 (ND 178-9; SD 72-10), Feb. 21, 1978. A two-thirds majority vote (273 in this case) is required for passage under suspension of the rules.

57. HR 9375. Fiscal 1978 Supplemental Appropriations. Lloyd, D-Calif., motion to table (kill) the Mahon, D-Texas, motion *(see vote 58, below)* that the House recede and concur in the Senate amendment, to the bill, rescinding funds for the production of the B-1 bomber. Rejected 172-244: R 106-30; D 66-214 (ND 28-165; SD 38-49), Feb. 22, 1978. A "nay" was a vote supporting the president's position.

58. HR 9375. Fiscal 1978 Supplemental Appropriations. Mahon, D-Texas, motion that the House recede and concur in the Senate amendment, to the bill, rescinding $462 million appropriated in fiscal 1977 for the Defense Department for production of three B-1 bombers. Motion agreed to (thus completing congressional action) 234-182: R 30-106; D 204-76 (ND 155-38; SD 49-38), Feb. 22, 1978. A "yea" was a vote supporting the president's position.

59. HR 9214. International Monetary Fund. Adoption of the rule (H Res 990) providing for House floor consideration of the bill to authorize the United States to loan up to $1.8 billion to the Supplementary Financing Facility of the International Monetary Fund. Adopted 386-15: R 123-11; D 263-4 (ND 188-2; SD 75-2), Feb. 22, 1978.

KEY

- Y Voted for (yea).
- ✓ Paired for.
- † Announced for.
- # CQ Poll for.
- N Voted against (nay).
- X Paired against.
- \- Announced against.
- ▮ CQ Poll against.
- P Voted "present."
- ● Voted "present" to avoid possible conflict of interest.
- ? Did not vote or otherwise make a position known.

	53	54	55	56	57	58	59
ALABAMA							
1 Edwards	Y	Y	Y	Y	N	Y	Y
2 Dickinson	Y	N	Y	Y	Y	N	Y
3 Nichols	Y	Y	Y	Y	Y	N	Y
4 Bevill	Y	Y	Y	Y	N	Y	Y
5 Flippo	Y	Y	Y	Y	N	Y	?
6 Buchanan	N	Y	Y	Y	Y	N	Y
7 Flowers	N	Y	Y	Y	N	Y	Y
ALASKA							
AL Young	Y	N	Y	Y	Y	N	#
ARIZONA							
1 Rhodes	N	Y	Y	Y	Y	N	Y
2 Udall	N	Y	Y	Y	N	Y	Y
3 Stump	Y	N	Y	N	Y	N	N
4 Rudd	N	N	Y	N	Y	N	N
ARKANSAS							
1 Alexander	Y	Y	Y	Y	Y	N	?
2 Tucker	Y	Y	Y	Y	N	Y	#
3 Hammerschmidt	Y	Y	Y	Y	Y	N	Y
4 Thornton	Y	Y	Y	Y	N	N	Y
CALIFORNIA							
1 Johnson	Y	Y	Y	Y	Y	N	Y
2 Clausen	Y	Y	Y	Y	Y	N	?
3 Moss	Y	Y	Y	Y	N	Y	Y
4 Leggett	✓	#	#	#	Y	N	Y
5 Burton, J.	Y	Y	Y	Y	N	Y	Y
6 Burton, P.	Y	Y	Y	Y	N	Y	Y
7 Miller	Y	Y	Y	Y	N	Y	Y
8 Dellums	Y	Y	Y	Y	N	Y	Y
9 Stark	N	Y	Y	Y	N	Y	Y
10 Edwards	Y	Y	Y	Y	N	Y	Y
11 Ryan	N	Y	Y	Y	N	Y	Y
12 McCloskey	N	Y	Y	Y	N	Y	Y
13 Mineta	Y	Y	Y	Y	N	Y	Y
14 McFall	Y	Y	Y	Y	Y	N	Y
15 Sisk	Y	Y	Y	Y	Y	N	Y
16 Panetta	Y	Y	Y	Y	N	Y	Y
17 Krebs	Y	Y	Y	Y	N	Y	Y
18 Ketchum	N	N	Y	Y	Y	N	Y
19 Lagomarsino	N	Y	Y	Y	Y	N	Y
20 Goldwater	N	Y	Y	Y	Y	N	Y
21 Corman	Y	Y	Y	Y	N	Y	Y
22 Moorhead	N	N	Y	N	Y	N	Y
23 Beilenson	N	Y	Y	N	N	Y	Y
24 Waxman	Y	Y	Y	Y	N	Y	Y
25 Roybal	Y	Y	Y	Y	N	Y	Y
26 Rousselot	N	N	Y	Y	Y	N	Y
27 Dornan	N	?	Y	N	Y	N	Y
28 Burke	X	✓	#	#	Y	N	Y
29 Hawkins	Y	Y	Y	Y	?	?	Y
30 Danielson	-	-	†	†	N	N	Y
31 Wilson, C.H.	Y	Y	Y	Y	Y	N	Y
32 Anderson	Y	Y	Y	Y	Y	N	Y
33 Clawson	N	N	Y	N	?	?	?
34 Hannaford	N	Y	Y	Y	Y	N	Y
35 Lloyd	Y	Y	Y	Y	Y	N	Y
36 Brown	Y	Y	Y	Y	N	N	Y
37 Pettis	N	Y	Y	Y	Y	N	Y
38 Patterson	Y	Y	Y	Y	Y	N	Y
39 Wiggins	N	Y	Y	Y	Y	N	Y
40 Badham	N	N	Y	N	✓	X	#
41 Wilson, B.	Y	Y	Y	Y	Y	N	Y
42 Van Deerlin	N	Y	Y	Y	N	Y	Y
43 Burgener	N	Y	Y	Y	Y	N	Y
COLORADO							
1 Schroeder	Y	Y	Y	Y	N	Y	Y
2 Wirth	N	Y	Y	Y	N	Y	Y
3 Evans	N	Y	Y	Y	N	Y	#
4 Johnson	Y	Y	Y	Y	N	Y	Y
5 Armstrong	?	?	?	?	Y	N	Y
CONNECTICUT							
1 Cotter	Y	Y	Y	Y	N	Y	Y
2 Dodd	Y	Y	Y	Y	N	Y	Y
3 Giaimo	?	?	?	?	N	Y	Y
4 McKinney	Y	Y	Y	Y	N	Y	Y
5 Sarasin	Y	†	†	†	N	Y	Y
6 Moffett	Y	Y	Y	Y	N	Y	Y
DELAWARE							
AL Evans	Y	Y	Y	Y	Y	N	Y
FLORIDA							
1 Sikes	Y	Y	Y	Y	Y	N	Y
2 Fuqua	N	Y	Y	Y	Y	N	Y
3 Bennett	Y	N	Y	Y	Y	N	Y
4 Chappell	Y	Y	Y	Y	Y	N	Y
5 Kelly	N	N	Y	N	Y	N	N
6 Young	N	Y	Y	N	Y	N	Y
7 Gibbons	N	Y	Y	Y	N	Y	Y
8 Ireland	N	Y	Y	Y	N	Y	?
9 Frey	Y	Y	Y	Y	Y	N	Y
10 Bafalis	Y	Y	Y	Y	Y	N	Y
11 Rogers	N	Y	Y	Y	N	Y	Y
12 Burke	?	?	?	?	?	?	?
13 Lehman	N	Y	Y	Y	N	Y	Y
14 Pepper	✓	✓	Y	Y	N	Y	Y
15 Fascell	Y	Y	Y	Y	N	Y	Y
GEORGIA							
1 Ginn	Y	Y	Y	Y	N	Y	Y
2 Mathis	Y	Y	Y	Y	N	Y	Y
3 Brinkley	N	Y	Y	Y	N	Y	Y
4 Levitas	Y	Y	Y	N	Y	Y	Y
5 Fowler	N	Y	Y	N	N	Y	Y
6 Flynt	?	?	?	?	Y	N	Y
7 McDonald	-	X	†	-	Y	N	N
8 Evans	Y	N	Y	N	N	Y	#
9 Jenkins	N	Y	Y	N	N	Y	#
10 Barnard	Y	Y	Y	N	N	Y	Y
HAWAII							
1 Heftel	N	Y	Y	Y	N	Y	Y
2 Akaka	Y	Y	Y	Y	N	N	Y
IDAHO							
1 Symms	N	N	Y	N	Y	N	N
2 Hansen, G.	N	N	Y	N	?	?	?
ILLINOIS							
1 Metcalfe	Y	Y	Y	Y	X	✓	?
2 Murphy	Y	Y	Y	Y	N	Y	Y
3 Russo	Y	Y	Y	Y	N	Y	Y
4 Derwinski	N	N	Y	Y	Y	N	Y
5 Fary	Y	Y	Y	Y	N	Y	Y
6 Hyde	N	N	Y	N	Y	N	Y
7 Collins	✓	#	#	#	X	✓	#
8 Rostenkowski	?	?	?	?	N	Y	Y
9 Yates	Y	Y	Y	Y	N	Y	Y
10 Mikva	Y	Y	Y	Y	N	Y	Y
11 Annunzio	Y	Y	Y	Y	N	Y	Y
12 Crane	N	N	Y	N	Y	N	N
13 McClory	N	Y	Y	Y	Y	N	Y
14 Erlenborn	N	Y	Y	Y	Y	N	Y
15 Corcoran	N	Y	Y	Y	Y	N	Y
16 Anderson	N	Y	Y	Y	Y	N	Y
17 O'Brien	Y	N	Y	N	Y	N	Y
18 Michel	N	Y	Y	Y	Y	N	Y
19 Railsback	Y	Y	Y	Y	Y	N	Y
20 Findley	N	N	Y	Y	Y	N	Y
21 Madigan	Y	Y	Y	Y	Y	N	Y
22 Shipley	Y	Y	Y	Y	N	Y	N
23 Price	Y	Y	Y	Y	N	Y	Y
24 Simon	Y	Y	Y	Y	N	Y	Y
INDIANA							
1 Benjamin	Y	N	Y	Y	N	Y	Y
2 Fithian	Y	Y	Y	Y	N	Y	Y
3 Brademas	Y	Y	Y	Y	N	Y	Y
4 Quayle	Y	Y	Y	N	N	Y	Y
5 Hillis	Y	Y	Y	Y	Y	N	Y
6 Evans	N	Y	Y	Y	N	Y	Y
7 Myers, J.	Y	Y	Y	Y	Y	N	Y
8 Cornwell	Y	Y	Y	Y	N	Y	Y
9 Hamilton	Y	Y	Y	Y	N	Y	Y
10 Sharp	Y	Y	Y	Y	N	Y	Y
11 Jacobs	N	N	Y	N	N	Y	Y
IOWA							
1 Leach	N	Y	Y	Y	N	Y	Y
2 Blouin	Y	Y	Y	Y	N	Y	Y
3 Grassley	N	Y	Y	Y	Y	N	Y
4 Smith	Y	Y	Y	Y	N	N	Y
5 Harkin	N	Y	Y	Y	N	Y	Y
6 Bedell	Y	Y	Y	Y	N	Y	Y

Democrats ***Republicans***

	53	54	55	56	57	58	59
KANSAS							
1 Sebelius	N	Y	Y	Y	N	Y	Y
2 Keys	N	Y	Y	N	N	Y	Y
3 Winn	N	Y	Y	▮	Y	N	Y
4 Glickman	N	Y	Y	N	N	Y	Y
5 Skubitz	N	Y	Y	Y	?	Y	Y
KENTUCKY							
1 Hubbard	Y	Y	Y	Y	Y	N	Y
2 Natcher	Y	Y	Y	Y	N	Y	Y
3 Mazzoli	N	Y	Y	Y	N	Y	Y
4 Snyder	Y	N	Y	N	Y	N	N
5 Carter	Y	Y	Y	Y	Y	N	Y
6 Breckinridge	N	Y	Y	Y	✓	X	?
7 Perkins	#	?	#	#	N	Y	Y
LOUISIANA							
1 Livingston	Y	Y	Y	Y	Y	N	Y
2 Boggs	Y	Y	Y	Y	N	N	Y
3 Treen	N	N	Y	Y	?	?	?
4 Waggonner	Y	N	Y	N	Y	N	?
5 Huckaby	Y	Y	Y	Y	Y	N	#
6 Moore	N	Y	Y	Y	Y	N	Y
7 Breaux	Y	N	Y	Y	Y	N	Y
8 Long	Y	Y	Y	Y	N	Y	Y
MAINE							
1 Emery	N	Y	Y	Y	Y	N	Y
2 Cohen	N	Y	Y	Y	N	Y	Y
MARYLAND							
1 Bauman	N	N	Y	N	Y	N	N
2 Long	Y	Y	Y	Y	Y	N	Y
3 Mikulski	Y	Y	Y	Y	N	Y	Y
4 Holt	N	N	Y	N	Y	N	N
5 Spellman	Y	Y	Y	Y	N	Y	Y
6 Byron	Y	Y	Y	Y	Y	N	Y
7 Mitchell	Y	Y	Y	Y	N	Y	Y
8 Steers	Y	Y	Y	Y	N	Y	Y
MASSACHUSETTS							
1 Conte	Y	Y	Y	Y	N	Y	Y
2 Boland	Y	Y	Y	Y	N	Y	Y
3 Early	Y	Y	Y	Y	N	Y	Y
4 Drinan	Y	Y	Y	Y	N	Y	Y
5 Tsongas	Y	Y	Y	Y	N	Y	Y
6 Harrington	Y	Y	Y	Y	N	Y	Y
7 Markey	Y	Y	Y	Y	N	Y	Y
8 O'Neill							
9 Moakley	Y	Y	Y	Y	N	Y	Y
10 Heckler	Y	Y	Y	Y	N	Y	Y
11 Burke	Y	Y	Y	Y	N	Y	Y
12 Studds	Y	Y	Y	Y	N	Y	Y
MICHIGAN							
1 Conyers	Y	Y	#	Y	N	Y	Y
2 Pursell	Y	Y	Y	Y	N	Y	Y
3 Brown	Y	N	Y	Y	Y	N	Y
4 Stockman	Y	Y	Y	Y	Y	N	Y
5 Sawyer	N	Y	Y	Y	Y	Y	Y
6 Carr	Y	Y	Y	Y	N	Y	Y
7 Kildee	Y	Y	Y	Y	N	Y	Y
8 Traxler	Y	Y	Y	Y	N	Y	Y
9 Vander Jagt	Y	N	Y	Y	Y	?	Y
10 Cederberg	Y	Y	Y	Y	Y	N	Y
11 Ruppe	N	Y	Y	Y	N	Y	Y
12 Bonior	Y	Y	Y	Y	N	Y	Y
13 Diggs	Y	Y	Y	Y	N	Y	Y
14 Nedzi	Y	Y	Y	Y	N	Y	Y
15 Ford	Y	Y	Y	Y	N	Y	P
16 Dingell	Y	Y	Y	Y	N	Y	Y
17 Brodhead	Y	Y	Y	Y	N	Y	Y
18 Blanchard	Y	Y	Y	Y	N	Y	Y
19 Broomfield	Y	Y	Y	Y	Y	N	Y
MINNESOTA							
1 Quie	Y	Y	Y	Y	N	Y	Y
2 Hagedorn	Y	N	Y	Y	Y	N	Y
3 Frenzel	N	Y	Y	Y	N	Y	Y
4 Vento	Y	Y	Y	Y	N	Y	Y
5 Fraser	Y	#	Y	Y	N	Y	Y
6 Nolan	Y	Y	Y	Y	N	Y	Y
7 Stangeland	#	▮	#	#	Y	N	Y
8 Oberstar	Y	Y	Y	Y	N	Y	Y
MISSISSIPPI							
1 Whitten	Y	Y	Y	Y	Y	N	Y
2 Bowen	N	Y	Y	Y	Y	N	Y
3 Montgomery	N	N	Y	N	Y	N	Y
4 Cochran	N	Y	Y	N	Y	N	Y
5 Lott	N	N	Y	N	Y	N	Y
MISSOURI							
1 Clay	Y	Y	Y	Y	N	Y	Y
2 Young	Y	Y	Y	Y	Y	N	Y
3 Gephardt	N	Y	Y	Y	N	Y	Y
4 Skelton	Y	N	Y	Y	Y	N	Y
5 Bolling	Y	Y	Y	Y	N	Y	Y
6 Coleman	Y	Y	Y	Y	Y	N	Y
7 Taylor	Y	N	Y	N	Y	N	N
8 Ichord	N	N	Y	Y	Y	N	Y
9 Volkmer	Y	Y	Y	Y	N	Y	Y
10 Burlison	Y	Y	Y	Y	Y	N	Y
MONTANA							
1 Baucus	Y	Y	Y	Y	N	Y	Y
2 Marlenee	Y	Y	Y	Y	Y	N	Y
NEBRASKA							
1 Thone	N	Y	Y	Y	Y	N	Y
2 Cavanaugh	Y	Y	Y	Y	N	Y	Y
3 Smith	N	Y	Y	Y	Y	N	Y
NEVADA							
AL Santini	N	Y	Y	Y	N	Y	Y
NEW HAMPSHIRE							
1 D'Amours	N	Y	Y	Y	N	Y	Y
2 Cleveland	N	Y	Y	Y	Y	N	Y
NEW JERSEY							
1 Florio	Y	Y	Y	Y	N	Y	Y
2 Hughes	Y	Y	Y	Y	N	Y	Y
3 Howard	Y	Y	Y	Y	N	Y	Y
4 Thompson	Y	Y	Y	Y	N	Y	Y
5 Fenwick	N	Y	Y	Y	N	Y	Y
6 Forsythe	Y	Y	Y	Y	N	Y	Y
7 Maguire	N	Y	Y	N	N	Y	Y
8 Roe	Y	Y	Y	Y	Y	N	Y
9 Hollenbeck	Y	Y	Y	Y	Y	N	Y
10 Rodino	Y	Y	Y	Y	N	Y	Y
11 Minish	Y	Y	Y	Y	N	Y	Y
12 Rinaldo	Y	Y	Y	Y	Y	N	Y
13 Meyner	Y	Y	Y	Y	N	Y	Y
14 LeFante	Y	Y	Y	Y	N	Y	Y
15 Patten	Y	Y	Y	Y	N	Y	Y
NEW MEXICO							
1 Lujan	N	Y	Y	N	Y	N	Y
2 Runnels	N	Y	Y	Y	N	Y	Y
NEW YORK							
1 Pike	N	Y	Y	Y	N	Y	Y
2 Downey	Y	Y	Y	Y	N	Y	Y
3 Ambro	Y	Y	Y	Y	N	Y	Y
4 Lent	N	Y	Y	Y	Y	N	Y
5 Wydler	N	P	Y	Y	Y	N	Y
6 Wolff	Y	Y	Y	Y	N	Y	Y
7 Addabbo	Y	Y	Y	Y	N	Y	Y
8 Rosenthal	Y	Y	Y	Y	N	Y	Y
9 Delaney	Y	Y	Y	Y	N	Y	Y
10 Biaggi	Y	Y	Y	Y	N	N	Y
11 Scheuer	Y	Y	Y	Y	N	Y	Y
12 Chisholm	Y	Y	Y	Y	N	Y	Y
13 Solarz	Y	Y	Y	Y	N	Y	Y
14 Richmond	Y	Y	Y	Y	N	Y	Y
15 Zeferetti	✓	✓	#	#	N	N	Y
16 Holtzman	Y	Y	Y	Y	N	Y	Y
17 Murphy	✓	✓	#	#	N	Y	Y
18 Green[1]	Y	Y	Y	Y	N	Y	Y
19 Rangel	Y	Y	Y	Y	N	Y	Y
20 Weiss	Y	Y	Y	Y	N	Y	Y
21 Garcia[1]	Y	Y	Y	Y	N	Y	Y
22 Bingham	Y	Y	Y	Y	N	Y	Y
23 Caputo	Y	Y	Y	Y	N	Y	Y
24 Ottinger	Y	Y	Y	Y	N	Y	Y
25 Fish	Y	Y	Y	Y	Y	N	Y
26 Gilman	Y	Y	Y	Y	Y	N	Y
27 McHugh	Y	Y	Y	Y	N	Y	Y
28 Stratton	Y	Y	Y	Y	Y	N	Y
29 Pattison	Y	N	Y	Y	N	Y	Y
30 McEwen	Y	Y	Y	Y	Y	N	Y
31 Mitchell	Y	Y	Y	Y	Y	N	Y
32 Hanley	Y	Y	Y	Y	N	Y	Y
33 Walsh	Y	Y	Y	Y	Y	N	Y
34 Horton	Y	Y	Y	Y	N	Y	Y
35 Conable	N	Y	Y	Y	N	Y	Y
36 LaFalce	N	Y	Y	Y	N	Y	Y
37 Nowak	Y	Y	Y	Y	N	Y	Y
38 Kemp	N	Y	Y	Y	Y	N	Y
39 Lundine	N	Y	Y	Y	N	Y	Y
NORTH CAROLINA							
1 Jones	?	#	#	?	Y	N	Y
2 Fountain	N	Y	Y	Y	Y	N	Y
3 Whitley	N	Y	Y	Y	Y	N	Y
4 Andrews	Y	Y	Y	Y	N	Y	Y
5 Neal	N	Y	Y	Y	N	Y	Y
6 Preyer	Y	Y	Y	Y	N	Y	Y
7 Rose	N	Y	Y	Y	N	Y	Y
8 Hefner	Y	Y	Y	Y	N	Y	Y
9 Martin	Y	Y	Y	Y	Y	N	Y
10 Broyhill	N	Y	Y	Y	Y	N	Y
11 Gudger	N	Y	Y	Y	Y	N	Y
NORTH DAKOTA							
AL Andrews	Y	Y	Y	Y	Y	N	Y
OHIO							
1 Gradison	Y	Y	Y	Y	Y	N	Y
2 Luken	Y	Y	Y	Y	Y	N	Y
3 Whalen	Y	Y	Y	Y	N	Y	Y
4 Guyer	N	Y	Y	Y	Y	N	Y
5 Latta	Y	N	Y	N	Y	N	N
6 Harsha	Y	Y	Y	Y	Y	N	N
7 Brown	N	N	Y	Y	?	?	?
8 Kindness	Y	N	Y	Y	Y	N	Y
9 Ashley	Y	?	Y	Y	N	Y	Y
10 Miller	Y	N	Y	N	Y	N	Y
11 Stanton	Y	Y	Y	Y	Y	N	Y
12 Devine	N	N	Y	N	Y	N	N
13 Pease	Y	Y	Y	Y	N	Y	Y
14 Seiberling	Y	Y	Y	Y	N	Y	Y
15 Wylie	Y	Y	Y	Y	Y	N	Y
16 Regula	Y	Y	Y	Y	Y	N	Y
17 Ashbrook	#	▮	#	▮	▮	▮	#
18 Applegate	Y	Y	Y	Y	Y	N	Y
19 Carney	Y	Y	Y	Y	N	Y	Y
20 Oakar	Y	Y	Y	Y	N	N	Y
21 Stokes	Y	Y	Y	Y	N	Y	Y
22 Vanik	Y	Y	Y	Y	N	Y	Y
23 Mottl	Y	Y	Y	Y	N	Y	Y
OKLAHOMA							
1 Jones	N	N	Y	Y	Y	N	Y
2 Risenhoover	Y	Y	Y	Y	Y	N	Y
3 Watkins	Y	N	Y	Y	Y	N	Y
4 Steed	Y	N	Y	Y	Y	N	Y
5 Edwards	N	N	Y	N	?	?	?
6 English	N	Y	Y	N	Y	N	Y
OREGON							
1 AuCoin	Y	Y	Y	Y	N	Y	Y
2 Ullman	N	Y	Y	Y	N	Y	#
3 Duncan	N	N	Y	Y	Y	N	Y
4 Weaver	Y	Y	Y	Y	N	Y	Y
PENNSYLVANIA							
1 Myers, M.	Y	Y	Y	Y	N	Y	Y
2 Nix	Y	Y	Y	Y	N	Y	Y
3 Lederer	Y	Y	Y	Y	N	Y	Y
4 Eilberg	Y	Y	Y	Y	N	Y	Y
5 Schulze	Y	Y	Y	Y	Y	N	Y
6 Yatron	Y	Y	Y	Y	N	N	Y
7 Edgar	Y	Y	Y	Y	N	Y	Y
8 Kostmayer	Y	Y	Y	N	N	Y	Y
9 Shuster	Y	N	Y	N	Y	N	Y
10 McDade	Y	Y	Y	Y	Y	N	Y
11 Flood	Y	Y	Y	Y	N	Y	Y
12 Murtha	Y	Y	Y	Y	N	N	Y
13 Coughlin	Y	Y	Y	Y	Y	N	#
14 Moorhead	Y	Y	Y	Y	N	Y	Y
15 Rooney	Y	Y	Y	Y	N	Y	Y
16 Walker	N	N	Y	N	Y	N	Y
17 Ertel	Y	Y	Y	Y	N	Y	Y
18 Walgren	Y	N	Y	N	N	Y	Y
19 Goodling, W.	Y	N	Y	N	N	N	Y
20 Gaydos	Y	Y	Y	Y	N	Y	Y
21 Dent	✓	#	#	#	X	✓	#
22 Murphy	Y	Y	Y	Y	Y	N	Y
23 Ammerman	Y	Y	Y	Y	N	Y	Y
24 Marks	Y	Y	Y	Y	N	Y	Y
25 Myers, G.	N	Y	Y	Y	Y	N	Y
RHODE ISLAND							
1 St Germain	Y	Y	Y	Y	N	Y	Y
2 Beard	Y	Y	Y	Y	N	Y	?
SOUTH CAROLINA							
1 Davis	Y	Y	Y	Y	N	Y	Y
2 Spence	N	Y	Y	Y	Y	N	Y
3 Derrick	N	Y	Y	Y	N	Y	Y
4 Mann	N	Y	Y	Y	N	Y	Y
5 Holland	N	Y	Y	Y	N	Y	Y
6 Jenrette	N	Y	Y	Y	Y	Y	Y
SOUTH DAKOTA							
1 Pressler	Y	Y	Y	Y	N	Y	Y
2 Abdnor	Y	Y	Y	Y	Y	N	Y
TENNESSEE							
1 Quillen	Y	Y	Y	Y	N	Y	#
2 Duncan	Y	N	Y	Y	N	Y	Y
3 Lloyd	Y	Y	Y	Y	N	Y	Y
4 Gore	Y	Y	Y	Y	N	Y	Y
5 Allen	Y	Y	Y	Y	N	Y	Y
6 Beard	Y	Y	Y	Y	Y	N	Y
7 Jones	Y	Y	Y	Y	N	Y	Y
8 Ford	Y	Y	Y	Y	N	Y	Y
TEXAS							
1 Hall	Y	N	Y	N	Y	N	Y
2 Wilson, C.	N	Y	Y	Y	Y	N	#
3 Collins	N	N	Y	N	Y	N	Y
4 Roberts	Y	N	Y	Y	Y	N	Y
5 Mattox	N	Y	Y	Y	N	Y	Y
6 Teague	X	?	?	?	✓	X	?
7 Archer	N	N	Y	N	Y	N	Y
8 Eckhardt	Y	Y	Y	Y	N	Y	Y
9 Brooks	N	Y	Y	Y	N	Y	Y
10 Pickle	N	Y	Y	Y	Y	N	Y
11 Poage	N	N	?	?	Y	N	Y
12 Wright	Y	Y	Y	Y	N	Y	Y
13 Hightower	Y	Y	Y	Y	N	Y	Y
14 Young	Y	Y	Y	Y	N	Y	?
15 de la Garza	N	N	Y	Y	Y	N	Y
16 White	Y	Y	Y	Y	Y	N	Y
17 Burleson	▮	X	#	▮	Y	N	N
18 Jordan	N	Y	Y	Y	N	Y	Y
19 Mahon	N	Y	Y	Y	N	Y	Y
20 Gonzalez	Y	Y	Y	Y	Y	N	Y
21 Krueger	▮	#	#	#	✓	X	#
22 Gammage	N	Y	Y	Y	N	Y	Y
23 Kazen	Y	Y	Y	Y	Y	N	Y
24 Milford	Y	Y	Y	Y	N	Y	Y
UTAH							
1 McKay	N	N	Y	N	Y	N	Y
2 Marriott	N	N	Y	N	#	▮	?
VERMONT							
AL Jeffords	Y	Y	Y	Y	X	✓	Y
VIRGINIA							
1 Trible	N	N	Y	Y	Y	N	Y
2 Whitehurst	Y	Y	Y	Y	Y	N	Y
3 Satterfield	N	N	Y	N	Y	N	Y
4 Daniel	N	N	Y	N	Y	N	Y
5 Daniel	N	Y	Y	Y	Y	N	Y
6 Butler	N	N	Y	N	Y	N	Y
7 Robinson	N	N	Y	N	Y	N	Y
8 Harris	N	Y	Y	Y	N	Y	Y
9 Wampler	Y	Y	Y	Y	Y	N	Y
10 Fisher	N	Y	Y	Y	N	Y	Y
WASHINGTON							
1 Pritchard	N	Y	Y	Y	N	Y	Y
2 Meeds	Y	Y	Y	Y	N	Y	Y
3 Bonker	Y	Y	Y	Y	N	Y	Y
4 McCormack	Y	Y	Y	Y	N	Y	Y
5 Foley	Y	Y	Y	Y	N	Y	Y
6 Dicks	Y	Y	Y	Y	N	Y	Y
7 Cunningham	N	N	Y	N	N	N	Y
WEST VIRGINIA							
1 Mollohan	N	Y	Y	Y	Y	N	Y
2 Staggers	Y	Y	Y	Y	N	N	Y
3 Slack	N	Y	Y	Y	Y	N	Y
4 Rahall	Y	Y	Y	Y	Y	N	Y
WISCONSIN							
1 Aspin	Y	Y	Y	Y	N	Y	Y
2 Kastenmeier	Y	Y	Y	Y	N	Y	Y
3 Baldus	Y	Y	Y	Y	N	Y	Y
4 Zablocki	Y	Y	Y	Y	Y	N	Y
5 Reuss	Y	Y	Y	Y	N	Y	Y
6 Steiger	N	Y	Y	Y	Y	N	Y
7 Obey	Y	Y	Y	Y	N	Y	Y
8 Cornell	N	Y	Y	Y	N	Y	Y
9 Kasten	†	†	†	†	Y	N	Y
WYOMING							
AL Roncalio	?	?	?	?	N	Y	Y

1 Rep. S. William Green, R-N.Y., and Rep. Robert Garcia, D-N.Y., were sworn in on Feb. 21, 1978; the first vote for which they were eligible was CQ 53.

Democrats ***Republicans***

60. HR 9214. International Monetary Fund. Neal, D-N.C., amendment to limit the salary of the U.S. executive director to the new IMF facility to $50,000. Adopted 253-141: R 60-73; D 193-68 (ND 162-21; SD 31-47), Feb. 23, 1978.

61. HR 9214. International Monetary Fund. Passage of the bill to allow the United States to participate in a new $10 billion IMF (Witteveen) facility to make loans to nations with large balance-of-payments deficits, and set the U.S. share at $1.8 billion. Passed 267-125: R 65-68; D 202-57 (ND 162-23; SD 40-34), Feb. 23, 1978. A "yea" was a vote supporting the President's position.

62. HR 9179. Overseas Private Investment Corporation. Crane, R-Ill., amendment to prohibit the Overseas Private Investment Corporation (OPIC) from making any loans to or guaranteeing or insuring any borrowings of the National Finance Corporation of Panama unless such loans or guarantees were first approved by the House. Rejected 166-199: R 97-29; D 69-170 (ND 26-141; SD 43-29), Feb. 23, 1978.

63. HR 9179. Overseas Private Investment Corporation. Moore, R-La., amendment to prohibit OPIC from providing any insurance or financial support for any project to establish or expand production or processing of palm oil, sugar, or citrus crops for export. Adopted 191-167: R 95-30; D 96-137 (ND 42-121; SD 54-16), Feb. 23, 1978.

64. HR 9179. Overseas Private Investment Corporation. Passage of the bill to extend through Sept. 30, 1980, the operating authority of OPIC and repeal a requirement that OPIC transfer all its loan insurance operations to private financial institutions by Dec. 31, 1980. Passed 191-165: R 83-40; D 108-125 (ND 73-88; SD 35-37), Feb. 23, 1978.

KEY

- Y Voted for (yea).
- ✓ Paired for.
- † Announced for.
- # CQ Poll for.
- N Voted against (nay).
- X Paired against.
- \- Announced against.
- ▮ CQ Poll against.
- P Voted "present."
- ● Voted "present" to avoid possible conflict of interest.
- ? Did not vote or otherwise make a position known.

	60	61	62	63	64
ALABAMA					
1 Edwards	N	Y	Y	Y	N
2 Dickinson	N	N	Y	Y	Y
3 Nichols	N	N	✓	✓	X
4 Bevill	N	N	Y	Y	N
5 Flippo	N	N	Y	Y	N
6 Buchanan	N	Y	Y	N	Y
7 Flowers	N	?	?	?	?
ALASKA					
AL Young	N	N	Y	Y	N
ARIZONA					
1 Rhodes	?	?	?	?	?
2 Udall	Y	Y	N	N	Y
3 Stump	N	N	Y	Y	N
4 Rudd	N	N	Y	Y	Y
ARKANSAS					
1 Alexander	Y	Y	X	?	?
2 Tucker	#	#	▮	#	#
3 Hammerschmidt	N	Y	N	Y	Y
4 Thornton	?	?	?	?	?
CALIFORNIA					
1 Johnson	Y	Y	N	N	Y
2 Clausen	?	?	✓	✓	?
3 Moss	Y	Y	N	N	Y
4 Leggett	?	Y	N	N	Y
5 Burton, J.	?	?	?	?	?
6 Burton, P.	Y	Y	?	?	?
7 Miller	Y	Y	N	N	N
8 Dellums	Y	Y	N	N	N
9 Stark	Y	Y	N	N	N
10 Edwards	Y	Y	X	X	✓
11 Ryan	Y	Y	N	Y	N
12 McCloskey	Y	Y	N	N	Y
13 Mineta	Y	Y	▮	▮	#
14 McFall	Y	Y	N	Y	Y
15 Sisk	Y	Y	N	Y	Y
16 Panetta	Y	Y	N	Y	N
17 Krebs	Y	Y	N	Y	N
18 Ketchum	N	N	Y	N	N
19 Lagomarsino	N	N	Y	Y	Y
20 Goldwater	N	N	Y	Y	Y
21 Corman	Y	Y	N	N	Y
22 Moorhead	N	N	Y	Y	Y
23 Beilenson	Y	Y	N	N	Y
24 Waxman	Y	Y	N	N	Y
25 Roybal	Y	Y	N	X	▮
26 Rousselot	N	N	Y	Y	Y
27 Dornan	N	N	Y	Y	Y
28 Burke	Y	Y	X	X	X
29 Hawkins	Y	Y	X	X	?
30 Danielson	Y	Y	N	N	N
31 Wilson, C.H.	#	N	#	▮	N
32 Anderson	Y	Y	Y	Y	N
33 Clawson	?	X	✓	✓	?
34 Hannaford	#	✓	X	X	✓
35 Lloyd	Y	Y	Y	N	Y
36 Brown	Y	Y	N	N	Y
37 Pettis	Y	Y	N	Y	Y
38 Patterson	Y	Y	▮	▮	#
39 Wiggins	Y	Y	N	N	Y
40 Badham	▮	X	✓	✓	#
41 Wilson, B.	Y	Y	Y	Y	Y
42 Van Deerlin	Y	Y	X	X	?
43 Burgener	Y	N	✓	✓	?
COLORADO					
1 Schroeder	Y	Y	N	N	Y
2 Wirth	Y	Y	N	N	Y
3 Evans	Y	Y	N	N	Y
4 Johnson	Y	Y	N	Y	Y
5 Armstrong	Y	N	?	?	?
CONNECTICUT					
1 Cotter	Y	Y	N	N	▮
2 Dodd	Y	Y	N	N	Y
3 Giaimo	Y	Y	N	N	Y
4 McKinney	Y	✓	▮	N	Y
5 Sarasin	Y	Y	-	X	†
6 Moffett	Y	Y	N	N	N
DELAWARE					
AL Evans	Y	Y	Y	N	Y
FLORIDA					
1 Sikes	N	Y	Y	Y	N
2 Fuqua	N	N	Y	Y	N
3 Bennett	N	N	Y	Y	N
4 Chappell	N	N	Y	Y	N
5 Kelly	N	N	Y	Y	Y
6 Young	N	N	Y	Y	Y
7 Gibbons	Y	Y	Y	Y	N
8 Ireland	N	N	Y	Y	Y
9 Frey	N	N	Y	Y	Y
10 Bafalis	N	N	Y	Y	N
11 Rogers	N	N	Y	Y	N
12 Burke	?	?	✓	✓	?
13 Lehman	Y	Y	N	N	Y
14 Pepper	Y	✓	N	Y	Y
15 Fascell	Y	Y	N	N	Y
GEORGIA					
1 Ginn	N	Y	N	Y	N
2 Mathis	N	N	✓	?	?
3 Brinkley	N	N	N	Y	N
4 Levitas	N	N	N	N	N
5 Fowler	N	Y	N	Y	Y
6 Flynt	N	?	Y	Y	Y
7 McDonald	N	N	Y	Y	N
8 Evans	N	N	Y	Y	N
9 Jenkins	N	N	N	#	N
10 Barnard	Y	Y	N	Y	N
HAWAII					
1 Heftel	Y	Y	N	Y	Y
2 Akaka	Y	Y	X	X	✓
IDAHO					
1 Symms	N	N	Y	Y	N
2 Hansen, G.	N	N	Y	Y	N
ILLINOIS					
1 Metcalfe	?	?	X	X	?
2 Murphy	Y	N	N	N	N
3 Russo	Y	N	Y	N	X
4 Derwinski	Y	Y	Y	N	N
5 Fary	Y	Y	N	N	N
6 Hyde	Y	Y	N	N	Y
7 Collins	Y	Y	N	▮	Y
8 Rostenkowski	Y	Y	N	N	?
9 Yates	Y	Y	N	N	N
10 Mikva	Y	Y	N	N	Y
11 Annunzio	Y	Y	N	N	N
12 Crane	N	N	Y	Y	X
13 McClory	Y	Y	X	✓	✓
14 Erlenborn	▮	Y	N	N	Y
15 Corcoran	Y	N	†	✓	X
16 Anderson	▮	#	X	▮	✓
17 O'Brien	Y	Y	Y	Y	Y
18 Michel	#	Y	N	Y	Y
19 Railsback	Y	Y	N	Y	Y
20 Findley	Y	Y	N	N	Y
21 Madigan	N	Y	Y	Y	Y
22 Shipley	?	X	✓	?	X
23 Price	Y	Y	N	N	N
24 Simon	Y	Y	N	N	Y
INDIANA					
1 Benjamin	Y	N	N	Y	N
2 Fithian	Y	N	Y	Y	N
3 Brademas	Y	Y	N	N	Y
4 Quayle	N	Y	Y	Y	N
5 Hillis	Y	Y	Y	Y	N
6 Evans	Y	N	Y	Y	N
7 Myers, J.	Y	N	Y	Y	N
8 Cornwell	#	#	N	Y	N
9 Hamilton	Y	Y	N	N	Y
10 Sharp	Y	Y	N	N	N
11 Jacobs	Y	Y	N	N	N
IOWA					
1 Leach	Y	Y	Y	Y	Y
2 Blouin	Y	Y	N	Y	Y
3 Grassley	N	N	Y	Y	N
4 Smith	Y	Y	N	N	Y
5 Harkin	Y	Y	N	Y	N
6 Bedell	Y	Y	N	Y	●

Democrats ***Republicans***

	60	61	62	63	64
KANSAS					
1 Sebelius	N	N	Y	Y	Y
2 Keys	Y	Y	N	N	N
3 Winn	Y	Y	Y	#	#
4 Glickman	Y	Y	N	Y	N
5 Skubitz	Y	Y	N	Y	N
KENTUCKY					
1 Hubbard	Y	Y	Y	Y	N
2 Natcher	N	Y	Y	N	N
3 Mazzoli	Y	Y	N	N	N
4 Snyder	N	N	Y	Y	N
5 Carter	Y	Y	Y	Y	N
6 Breckinridge	?	✓	X	?	✓
7 Perkins	#	#	#	#	?
LOUISIANA					
1 Livingston	N	N	Y	Y	Y
2 Boggs	Y	✓	N	Y	Y
3 Treen	N	Y	Y	Y	Y
4 Waggonner	Y	Y	Y	Y	Y
5 Huckaby	N	N	Y	Y	N
6 Moore	N	Y	Y	Y	Y
7 Breaux	N	X	✓	✓	Y
8 Long	Y	Y	N	Y	Y
MAINE					
1 Emery	Y	N	Y	Y	N
2 Cohen	Y	Y	Y	Y	Y
MARYLAND					
1 Bauman	N	N	Y	Y	N
2 Long	Y	N	N	N	N
3 Mikulski	Y	Y	N	N	N
4 Holt	N	N	Y	Y	N
5 Spellman	Y	Y	N	N	N
6 Byron	N	N	Y	Y	N
7 Mitchell	Y	Y	N	N	N
8 Steers	Y	Y	N	N	Y
MASSACHUSETTS					
1 Conte	Y	Y	N	N	Y
2 Boland	Y	Y	N	N	N
3 Early	Y	N	?	?	?
4 Drinan	Y	Y	N	N	N
5 Tsongas	Y	Y	N	N	Y
6 Harrington	Y	Y	N	N	N
7 Markey	Y	Y	N	▮	N
8 O'Neill					
9 Moakley	Y	Y	N	N	N
10 Heckler	Y	✓	Y	N	Y
11 Burke	Y	Y	N	N	N
12 Studds	Y	Y	N	N	N
MICHIGAN					
1 Conyers	Y	Y	N	▮	N
2 Pursell	N	N	N	?	?
3 Brown	Y	Y	N	N	Y
4 Stockman	#	▮	#	▮	▮
5 Sawyer	N	N	N	Y	Y
6 Carr	Y	Y	N	N	Y
7 Kildee	Y	Y	N	N	N
8 Traxler	Y	N	N	Y	Y
9 Vander Jagt	Y	Y	Y	Y	Y
10 Cederberg	Y	Y	N	Y	Y
11 Ruppe	Y	Y	N	Y	Y
12 Bonior	#	✓	▮	▮	X
13 Diggs	Y	Y	X	N	Y
14 Nedzi	Y	Y	N	N	Y
15 Ford	?	Y	N	N	N
16 Dingell	Y	Y	N	N	N
17 Brodhead	Y	Y	N	N	N
18 Blanchard	Y	Y	N	N	Y
19 Broomfield	Y	Y	X	X	✓
MINNESOTA					
1 Quie	N	Y	Y	Y	Y
2 Hagedorn	N	N	Y	Y	Y
3 Frenzel	Y	Y	Y	Y	Y
4 Vento	Y	Y	N	N	N
5 Fraser	Y	Y	▮	?	#
6 Nolan	Y	Y	?	?	?
7 Stangeland	N	N	Y	Y	Y
8 Oberstar	Y	Y	N	Y	N
MISSISSIPPI					
1 Whitten	N	N	Y	#	✓
2 Bowen	N	N	Y	Y	Y
3 Montgomery	N	N	Y	Y	Y
4 Cochran	N	N	Y	Y	Y
5 Lott	N	N	Y	Y	Y
MISSOURI					
1 Clay	Y	?	N	N	N
2 Young	N	Y	N	Y	N
3 Gephardt	Y	Y	N	#	N
4 Skelton	Y	Y	Y	Y	N
5 Bolling	Y	?	▮	▮	#
6 Coleman	?	?	✓	✓	?
7 Taylor	N	N	Y	Y	N
8 Ichord	N	N	Y	Y	N
9 Volkmer	N	N	Y	Y	N
10 Burlison	Y	Y	N	Y	N
MONTANA					
1 Baucus	Y	Y	N	Y	N
2 Marlenee	Y	N	Y	Y	N
NEBRASKA					
1 Thone	N	N	Y	Y	Y
2 Cavanaugh	Y	Y	N	N	Y
3 Smith	N	N	Y	Y	Y
NEVADA					
AL Santini	Y	Y	Y	N	N
NEW HAMPSHIRE					
1 D'Amours	Y	Y	Y	N	Y
2 Cleveland	N	Y	Y	N	Y
NEW JERSEY					
1 Florio	Y	N	N	N	N
2 Hughes	Y	Y	Y	N	✓
3 Howard	N	Y	N	N	Y
4 Thompson	#	Y	N	N	Y
5 Fenwick	Y	Y	N	N	Y
6 Forsythe	Y	Y	N	N	Y
7 Maguire	Y	Y	N	N	Y
8 Roe	Y	Y	N	Y	Y
9 Hollenbeck	Y	Y	Y	N	N
10 Rodino	Y	Y	N	N	N
11 Minish	Y	Y	N	N	N
12 Rinaldo	Y	Y	Y	N	N
13 Meyner	Y	Y	N	N	Y
14 LeFante	#	✓	X	X	X
15 Patten	Y	Y	N	N	N
NEW MEXICO					
1 Lujan	N	N	Y	Y	N
2 Runnels	N	N	Y	Y	Y
NEW YORK					
1 Pike	N	Y	N	N	N
2 Downey	Y	Y	N	▮	#
3 Ambro	Y	Y	N	Y	Y
4 Lent	N	Y	Y	Y	Y
5 Wydler	N	Y	Y	Y	N
6 Wolff	Y	Y	N	Y	Y
7 Addabbo	Y	Y	N	Y	N
8 Rosenthal	Y	Y	X	X	?
9 Delaney	Y	Y	N	N	N
10 Biaggi	Y	Y	Y	Y	N
11 Scheuer	Y	Y	N	N	Y
12 Chisholm	?	Y	N	N	Y
13 Solarz	Y	Y	N	N	Y
14 Richmond	Y	Y	N	N	✓
15 Zeferetti	N	Y	Y	Y	N
16 Holtzman	Y	Y	N	N	N
17 Murphy	Y	Y	N	N	Y
18 Green	Y	Y	N	N	Y
19 Rangel	Y	Y	N	N	Y
20 Weiss	Y	Y	N	N	N
21 Garcia	Y	Y	N	N	Y
22 Bingham	Y	Y	N	N	Y
23 Caputo	N	N	Y	Y	N
24 Ottinger	Y	Y	N	N	Y
25 Fish	Y	Y	Y	N	Y
26 Gilman	N	N	Y	N	Y
27 McHugh	Y	Y	N	N	Y
28 Stratton	N	N	Y	N	Y
29 Pattison	Y	Y	N	N	Y
30 McEwen	Y	Y	Y	Y	Y
31 Mitchell	N	Y	Y	Y	Y
32 Hanley	Y	Y	N	Y	Y
33 Walsh	N	Y	Y	Y	Y
34 Horton	Y	Y	Y	Y	Y
35 Conable	Y	Y	N	N	Y
36 LaFalce	Y	Y	N	N	Y
37 Nowak	Y	Y	N	N	N
38 Kemp	N	N	Y	N	N
39 Lundine	Y	Y	N	N	Y
NORTH CAROLINA					
1 Jones	N	N	Y	Y	Y
2 Fountain	N	N	Y	Y	Y
3 Whitley	N	N	Y	Y	Y
4 Andrews	?	Y	N	N	Y
5 Neal	Y	Y	?	Y	Y
6 Preyer	Y	Y	N	N	Y
7 Rose	Y	Y	N	Y	Y
8 Hefner	Y	Y	N	Y	N
9 Martin	N	Y	Y	Y	N
10 Broyhill	N	N	Y	Y	Y
11 Gudger	Y	N	Y	Y	N
NORTH DAKOTA					
AL Andrews	N	N	Y	Y	Y
OHIO					
1 Gradison	Y	Y	Y	Y	Y
2 Luken	Y	Y	Y	N	N
3 Whalen	Y	Y	N	N	Y
4 Guyer	▮	X	✓	✓	X
5 Latta	N	N	Y	Y	N
6 Harsha	Y	N	?	?	?
7 Brown	Y	Y	Y	Y	Y
8 Kindness	N	N	Y	Y	Y
9 Ashley	Y	Y	N	N	Y
10 Miller	N	N	Y	Y	N
11 Stanton	Y	Y	N	N	Y
12 Devine	N	N	Y	Y	N
13 Pease	Y	Y	N	N	Y
14 Seiberling	Y	Y	N	N	N
15 Wylie	Y	Y	N	N	Y
16 Regula	Y	Y	Y	Y	Y
17 Ashbrook	N	N	Y	Y	N
18 Applegate	N	N	Y	Y	N
19 Carney	N	N	N	N	X
20 Oakar	Y	Y	?	Y	N
21 Stokes	Y	Y	X	X	#
22 Vanik	Y	Y	N	N	Y
23 Mottl	N	N	Y	Y	N
OKLAHOMA					
1 Jones	Y	Y	Y	N	N
2 Risenhoover	N	N	Y	Y	N
3 Watkins	Y	N	Y	Y	N
4 Steed	Y	#	N	N	Y
5 Edwards	?	X	✓	?	?
6 English	N	N	Y	Y	N
OREGON					
1 AuCoin	Y	Y	N	Y	Y
2 Ullman	Y	Y	N	N	Y
3 Duncan	Y	Y	?	?	✓
4 Weaver	N	N	N	N	N
PENNSYLVANIA					
1 Myers, M.	Y	Y	N	N	N
2 Nix	Y	Y	N	X	#
3 Lederer	Y	Y	N	N	N
4 Eilberg	Y	Y	N	N	N
5 Schulze	N	N	Y	Y	Y
6 Yatron	N	Y	Y	Y	Y
7 Edgar	Y	#	▮	▮	#
8 Kostmayer	Y	Y	N	N	N
9 Shuster	N	N	Y	Y	N
10 McDade	Y	Y	Y	Y	Y
11 Flood	Y	Y	Y	N	Y
12 Murtha	N	Y	N	Y	N
13 Coughlin	#	▮	#	✓	#
14 Moorhead	Y	Y	N	N	Y
15 Rooney	Y	Y	N	N	Y
16 Walker	N	N	Y	Y	N
17 Ertel	N	Y	Y	N	N
18 Walgren	Y	Y	N	N	N
19 Goodling, W.	N	N	Y	Y	N
20 Gaydos	N	N	Y	Y	N
21 Dent	▮	▮	#	#	▮
22 Murphy	N	N	Y	Y	N
23 Ammerman	Y	Y	Y	N	N
24 Marks	Y	Y	N	N	Y
25 Myers, G.	Y	Y	N	N	Y
RHODE ISLAND					
1 St Germain	Y	Y	X	X	X
2 Beard	Y	Y	X	N	N
SOUTH CAROLINA					
1 Davis	N	N	Y	Y	N
2 Spence	N	N	Y	Y	Y
3 Derrick	Y	N	Y	Y	N
4 Mann	N	Y	N	Y	Y
5 Holland	N	N	Y	Y	N
6 Jenrette	N	N	Y	Y	N
SOUTH DAKOTA					
1 Pressler	N	N	Y	Y	N
2 Abdnor	N	N	Y	Y	N
TENNESSEE					
1 Quillen	Y	N	Y	Y	Y
2 Duncan	N	N	Y	Y	N
3 Lloyd	N	N	Y	Y	N
4 Gore	Y	Y	N	N	Y
5 Allen	Y	Y	N	N	N
6 Beard	N	N	✓	✓	▮
7 Jones	N	N	Y	Y	N
8 Ford	Y	Y	N	Y	N
TEXAS					
1 Hall	N	Y	Y	Y	Y
2 Wilson, C.	#	X	✓	▮	✓
3 Collins	Y	N	Y	Y	Y
4 Roberts	?	Y	✓	?	?
5 Mattox	Y	Y	N	?	N
6 Teague	?	?	✓	✓	✓
7 Archer	N	N	Y	Y	Y
8 Eckhardt	Y	Y	N	N	N
9 Brooks	Y	Y	N	Y	Y
10 Pickle	N	Y	Y	Y	Y
11 Poage	N	?	Y	Y	N
12 Wright	?	Y	N	N	?
13 Hightower	N	Y	Y	Y	Y
14 Young	?	?	?	?	?
15 de la Garza	Y	Y	?	?	?
16 White	N	Y	Y	Y	Y
17 Burleson	N	Y	Y	Y	Y
18 Jordan	N	Y	N	Y	Y
19 Mahon	Y	Y	Y	Y	Y
20 Gonzalez	N	Y	Y	Y	N
21 Krueger	#	#	▮	#	#
22 Gammage	N	N	✓	?	✓
23 Kazen	?	?	?	?	?
24 Milford	Y	Y	N	N	Y
UTAH					
1 McKay	Y	Y	N	N	N
2 Marriott	#	X	✓	✓	X
VERMONT					
AL Jeffords	Y	Y	Y	Y	Y
VIRGINIA					
1 Trible	N	N	Y	Y	?
2 Whitehurst	N	Y	Y	Y	Y
3 Satterfield	N	N	Y	Y	Y
4 Daniel	N	N	Y	Y	Y
5 Daniel	N	N	Y	Y	Y
6 Butler	Y	N	Y	Y	Y
7 Robinson	N	N	Y	Y	N
8 Harris	Y	Y	N	N	Y
9 Wampler	N	N	Y	Y	N
10 Fisher	Y	Y	N	N	Y
WASHINGTON					
1 Pritchard	Y	Y	N	Y	Y
2 Meeds	Y	Y	N	N	Y
3 Bonker	Y	Y	N	N	Y
4 McCormack	?	Y	N	N	Y
5 Foley	Y	Y	N	N	Y
6 Dicks	Y	Y	N	N	Y
7 Cunningham	N	N	Y	Y	N
WEST VIRGINIA					
1 Mollohan	N	Y	N	N	N
2 Staggers	Y	Y	N	N	N
3 Slack	N	N	?	?	X
4 Rahall	Y	Y	▮	▮	X
WISCONSIN					
1 Aspin	Y	Y	N	N	Y
2 Kastenmeier	Y	Y	N	N	N
3 Baldus	Y	Y	N	Y	Y
4 Zablocki	Y	Y	N	N	Y
5 Reuss	Y	Y	N	N	Y
6 Steiger	Y	Y	N	N	Y
7 Obey	Y	Y	N	N	N
8 Cornell	Y	Y	N	N	N
9 Kasten	N	N	Y	Y	N
WYOMING					
AL Roncalio	Y	?	N	N	Y

Democrats ***Republicans***

65. HR 9757. Grazing Fee Moratorium. Adoption of the rule (H Res 1024) providing for House floor consideration of the bill to delay for one year any increases in grazing fees on public lands. Adopted 302-1: R 105-0; D 197-1 (ND 136-1; SD 61-0), Feb. 24, 1978.

66. HR 3377. Wichita Indian Land Claims. Adoption of the rule (H Res 1030) providing for House floor consideration of the bill to enable the Wichita tribe of Oklahoma to file land claims with the Indian Claims Commission. Adopted 295-6: R 100-4; D 195-2 (ND 137-0; SD 58-2), Feb. 24, 1978.

67. HR 9757. Grazing Fee Moratorium. Passage of the bill to prohibit the secretaries of interior and agriculture from raising, for one year, grazing fees on public lands to allow Congress to study the impact of the increase, which was scheduled to take effect March 1, 1978. Passed 257-47: R 92-12; D 165-35 (ND 106-32; SD 59-3), Feb. 24, 1978.

68. HR 3377. Wichita Indian Land Claims. Roncalio, D-Wyo., substitute amendment to the bill *(see vote 69, below)*. Adopted 293-1: R 99-1; D 194-0 (ND 133-0; SD 61-0), Feb. 24, 1978.

69. HR 3377. Wichita Indian Land Claims. Passage of the bill, as amended by Roncalio, D-Wyo. *(see vote 68, above)*, to waive the Indian Claims Commission Act statute of limitations to enable the Wichita, Keechi, Tawakonie and Waco tribes to file land claims with the Indian Claims Commission or the U.S. Court of Claims. Passed 226-68: R 66-35; D 160-33 (ND 112-21; SD 48-12), Feb. 24, 1978.

70. H Con Res 464. District of Columbia Initiative and Referendum. Adoption of the concurrent resolution to approve the action of the District of Columbia Council amending the District of Columbia Charter to allow D.C. voters to initiate laws and to disapprove council acts by referendum. Adopted 321-24: R 111-10; D 210-14 (ND 143-11; SD 67-3), Feb. 27, 1978.

71. H Con Res 471. Recall of D.C. Elected Officials. Adoption of the concurrent resolution to approve the action of the District of Columbia Council amending the District of Columbia Charter to allow D.C. voters to recall an elected official of the District. Adopted 350-4: R 122-2; D 228-2 (ND 157-1; SD 71-1), Feb. 27, 1978.

72. HR 9622. U.S. District Court Jurisdiction. Kastenmeier, D-Wis., motion to suspend the rules and pass the bill to abolish "diversity of citizenship" as a ground for requesting federal district court jurisdiction in most cases involving disputes between residents of different states. Motion agreed to 266-133: R 95-37; D 171-96 (ND 133-56; SD 38-40), Feb. 28, 1978. A two-thirds majority vote (266 in this case) is required for passage under suspension of the rules.

KEY

- Y Voted for (yea).
- ✓ Paired for.
- † Announced for.
- \# CQ Poll for.
- N Voted against (nay).
- X Paired against.
- \- Announced against.
- ▮ CQ Poll against.
- P Voted "present."
- ● Voted "present" to avoid possible conflict of interest.
- ? Did not vote or otherwise make a position known.

	65	66	67	68	69	70	71	72
ALABAMA								
1 Edwards	?	?	?	?	?	N	Y	Y
2 Dickinson	Y	Y	Y	Y	Y	Y	Y	N
3 Nichols	#	#	#	#	#	Y	Y	Y
4 Bevill	Y	Y	Y	Y	Y	Y	Y	Y
5 Flippo	?	Y	Y	Y	Y	Y	Y	Y
6 Buchanan	Y	Y	Y	Y	Y	Y	Y	Y
7 Flowers	?	?	?	?	?	?	Y	Y
ALASKA								
AL Young	#	#	Y	Y	#	Y	Y	Y
ARIZONA								
1 Rhodes	?	?	?	?	?	?	?	Y
2 Udall	Y	Y	Y	#	#	Y	Y	Y
3 Stump	Y	Y	Y	Y	Y	Y	Y	Y
4 Rudd	Y	Y	Y	Y	N	Y	Y	▮
ARKANSAS								
1 Alexander	?	?	?	?	?	Y	Y	N
2 Tucker	#	#	#	#	#	#	#	▮
3 Hammerschmidt	Y	Y	Y	Y	Y	N	Y	N
4 Thornton	?	?	?	?	?	?	?	N
CALIFORNIA								
1 Johnson	Y	Y	Y	Y	Y	Y	Y	Y
2 Clausen	?	?	?	?	?	?	?	Y
3 Moss	Y	Y	?	Y	Y	N	Y	N
4 Leggett	#	#	#	#	Y	Y	#	Y
5 Burton, J.	?	?	?	?	?	Y	Y	Y
6 Burton, P.	?	?	?	?	?	Y	Y	Y
7 Miller	?	?	?	?	?	Y	Y	Y
8 Dellums	Y	Y	Y	Y	Y	#	#	#
9 Stark	#	#	▮	#	#	Y	Y	N
10 Edwards	?	?	?	?	?	Y	Y	Y
11 Ryan	Y	Y	Y	Y	Y	Y	Y	N
12 McCloskey	Y	Y	Y	Y	Y	?	?	Y
13 Mineta	#	#	#	#	#	Y	Y	Y
14 McFall	Y	Y	Y	Y	Y	Y	Y	N
15 Sisk	Y	Y	Y	Y	Y	Y	Y	Y
16 Panetta	Y	Y	Y	Y	Y	Y	Y	N
17 Krebs	Y	Y	Y	Y	Y	Y	Y	N
18 Ketchum	Y	Y	Y	Y	Y	Y	Y	Y
19 Lagomarsino	Y	Y	Y	Y	N	Y	Y	Y
20 Goldwater	Y	Y	Y	Y	Y	Y	Y	Y
21 Corman	Y	Y	Y	Y	Y	Y	Y	Y
22 Moorhead	Y	Y	Y	Y	N	Y	Y	Y
23 Beilenson	Y	Y	N	Y	Y	Y	Y	Y
24 Waxman	Y	Y	Y	Y	Y	Y	Y	Y
25 Roybal	#	#	#	#	#	Y	Y	Y
26 Rousselot	Y	Y	Y	Y	N	Y	Y	?
27 Dornan	Y	N	Y	?	N	Y	Y	Y
28 Burke	#	#	#	#	#	✓	✓	Y
29 Hawkins	?	?	?	?	?	Y	Y	Y
30 Danielson	Y	Y	Y	Y	Y	Y	Y	Y
31 Wilson, C.H.	#	Y	Y	Y	N	#	#	N
32 Anderson	Y	Y	Y	Y	Y	#	?	Y
33 Clawson	?	?	?	?	?	Y	Y	N
34 Hannaford	#	#	#	#	#	Y	Y	Y
35 Lloyd	Y	Y	Y	Y	Y	N	Y	Y
36 Brown	Y	Y	Y	Y	Y	Y	Y	Y
37 Pettis	Y	Y	Y	Y	Y	Y	Y	Y
38 Patterson	#	#	#	#	#	#	#	Y
39 Wiggins	#	#	#	#	#	N	Y	Y
40 Badham	#	#	#	#	▮	Y	Y	Y
41 Wilson, B.	Y	Y	Y	Y	Y	#	#	Y
42 Van Deerlin	?	?	?	?	?	?	?	Y
43 Burgener	?	?	?	?	?	Y	Y	Y
COLORADO								
1 Schroeder	Y	Y	N	Y	Y	†	†	N
2 Wirth	Y	Y	Y	Y	Y	Y	Y	N
3 Evans	Y	Y	Y	Y	Y	Y	Y	Y
4 Johnson	Y	Y	Y	Y	Y	Y	Y	Y
5 Armstrong	?	?	?	?	?	?	?	?
CONNECTICUT								
1 Cotter	#	#	#	#	#	Y	Y	Y
2 Dodd	Y	Y	Y	Y	Y	Y	Y	Y
3 Giaimo	Y	Y	N	Y	Y	Y	Y	N
4 McKinney	#	#	#	Y	Y	Y	Y	Y
5 Sarasin	†	†	†	†	†	†	†	†
6 Moffett	Y	Y	N	Y	Y	Y	Y	N
DELAWARE								
AL Evans	Y	Y	Y	Y	N	Y	Y	Y
FLORIDA								
1 Sikes	Y	Y	Y	Y	Y	Y	Y	Y
2 Fuqua	Y	Y	Y	Y	Y	Y	Y	Y
3 Bennett	Y	Y	N	Y	Y	Y	Y	Y
4 Chappell	#	#	#	#	#	#	#	#
5 Kelly	Y	Y	Y	Y	N	Y	Y	N
6 Young	Y	Y	Y	Y	N	?	?	Y
7 Gibbons	Y	Y	Y	Y	Y	Y	Y	N
8 Ireland	?	?	?	?	?	?	?	Y
9 Frey	?	?	?	?	?	?	?	?
10 Bafalis	Y	Y	Y	Y	Y	Y	Y	Y
11 Rogers	Y	Y	Y	Y	Y	Y	Y	N
12 Burke	?	?	?	?	?	?	?	?
13 Lehman	Y	Y	Y	Y	Y	Y	Y	N
14 Pepper	Y	#	#	Y	Y	✓	✓	#
15 Fascell	#	#	#	#	#	Y	Y	Y
GEORGIA								
1 Ginn	Y	Y	Y	Y	Y	Y	Y	Y
2 Mathis	?	?	?	?	?	Y	Y	N
3 Brinkley	Y	Y	Y	Y	Y	Y	Y	?
4 Levitas	Y	Y	N	Y	Y	Y	Y	N
5 Fowler	Y	Y	Y	Y	Y	Y	Y	Y
6 Flynt	?	?	?	?	?	Y	Y	N
7 McDonald	Y	N	Y	Y	N	Y	Y	▮
8 Evans	#	#	#	#	#	Y	Y	N
9 Jenkins	Y	Y	Y	Y	#	Y	Y	Y
10 Barnard	Y	Y	Y	Y	Y	?	?	Y
HAWAII								
1 Heftel	Y	Y	Y	Y	Y	Y	Y	N
2 Akaka	#	#	#	#	#	#	#	N
IDAHO								
1 Symms	Y	Y	Y	Y	N	Y	Y	?
2 Hansen, G.	?	Y	Y	Y	N	Y	Y	N
ILLINOIS								
1 Metcalfe	?	?	?	?	?	Y	Y	Y
2 Murphy	#	#	#	?	#	#	#	N
3 Russo	Y	Y	N	Y	Y	N	Y	Y
4 Derwinski	Y	Y	Y	Y	N	Y	Y	Y
5 Fary	Y	Y	Y	Y	Y	Y	Y	Y
6 Hyde	Y	Y	Y	Y	Y	Y	Y	Y
7 Collins	#	#	#	#	#	#	#	Y
8 Rostenkowski	?	?	?	?	?	N	Y	Y
9 Yates	Y	Y	N	Y	Y	#	#	N
10 Mikva	†	†	†	†	†	N	Y	N
11 Annunzio	Y	Y	Y	Y	Y	Y	Y	Y
12 Crane	#	#	#	#	▮	#	#	#
13 McClory	#	#	#	#	#	N	N	Y
14 Erlenborn	Y	Y	Y	Y	Y	▮	#	#
15 Corcoran	Y	Y	Y	Y	Y	Y	Y	Y
16 Anderson	#	#	#	#	#	Y	Y	Y
17 O'Brien	Y	Y	#	Y	Y	Y	Y	N
18 Michel	Y	Y	Y	Y	N	N	Y	Y
19 Railsback	Y	Y	Y	Y	Y	Y	Y	Y
20 Findley	Y	?	?	?	Y	Y	Y	?
21 Madigan	Y	Y	Y	?	Y	Y	Y	Y
22 Shipley	?	?	?	?	?	?	?	Y
23 Price	Y	Y	Y	Y	Y	Y	Y	Y
24 Simon	Y	Y	Y	Y	Y	#	#	N
INDIANA								
1 Benjamin	Y	Y	N	Y	N	Y	Y	N
2 Fithian	Y	Y	Y	Y	Y	Y	Y	N
3 Brademas	Y	Y	Y	Y	Y	Y	Y	Y
4 Quayle	?	?	?	?	?	Y	Y	N
5 Hillis	Y	Y	Y	Y	N	Y	Y	Y
6 Evans	Y	Y	N	Y	N	Y	Y	N
7 Myers, J.	Y	Y	Y	Y	Y	Y	Y	Y
8 Cornwell	Y	Y	Y	Y	Y	Y	Y	#
9 Hamilton	Y	Y	Y	Y	N	Y	Y	Y
10 Sharp	Y	Y	Y	Y	Y	Y	Y	N
11 Jacobs	Y	Y	N	Y	Y	Y	Y	Y
IOWA								
1 Leach	Y	Y	Y	#	Y	Y	Y	Y
2 Blouin	Y	Y	N	Y	Y	Y	Y	N
3 Grassley	Y	Y	Y	Y	N	Y	Y	Y
4 Smith	Y	Y	N	Y	Y	Y	Y	Y
5 Harkin	Y	Y	N	Y	Y	Y	Y	Y
6 Bedell	Y	Y	N	Y	N	Y	Y	N

Democrats ***Republicans***

	65	66	67	68	69	70	71	72
KANSAS								
1 Sebelius	Y	Y	Y	Y	Y	Y	Y	N
2 Keys	Y	Y	Y	Y	Y	Y	Y	Y
3 Winn	#	#	#	#	#	Y	Y	N
4 Glickman	Y	Y	Y	Y	Y	Y	Y	N
5 Skubitz	Y	Y	Y	Y	Y	Y	?	Y
KENTUCKY								
1 Hubbard	Y	Y	Y	Y	N	Y	Y	Y
2 Natcher	Y	Y	Y	Y	Y	Y	Y	N
3 Mazzoli	Y	Y	Y	Y	Y	Y	Y	Y
4 Snyder	Y	Y	Y	Y	N	Y	Y	N
5 Carter	Y	Y	Y	Y	Y	Y	Y	Y
6 Breckinridge	?	?	?	?	†	X	X	N
7 Perkins	Y	Y	Y	Y	Y	Y	Y	Y
LOUISIANA								
1 Livingston	Y	Y	Y	Y	Y	?	?	N
2 Boggs	Y	Y	Y	Y	Y	Y	Y	N
3 Treen	Y	Y	N	Y	N	?	?	Y
4 Waggonner	Y	Y	Y	Y	N	N	Y	N
5 Huckaby	Y	Y	Y	Y	N	Y	Y	N
6 Moore	Y	Y	Y	Y	Y	Y	Y	Y
7 Breaux	Y	Y	Y	?	?	Y	Y	N
8 Long	Y	Y	Y	Y	Y	?	?	N
MAINE								
1 Emery	Y	Y	Y	Y	Y	Y	Y	Y
2 Cohen	?	?	?	?	?	Y	Y	Y
MARYLAND								
1 Bauman	Y	Y	Y	?	?	Y	Y	N
2 Long	Y	Y	N	Y	Y	Y	Y	Y
3 Mikulski	Y	Y	Y	Y	Y	Y	Y	N
4 Holt	Y	Y	Y	Y	Y	Y	Y	N
5 Spellman	Y	Y	Y	Y	Y	#	Y	Y
6 Byron	Y	Y	N	Y	Y	Y	Y	N
7 Mitchell	Y	Y	#	#	#	Y	Y	Y
8 Steers	Y	Y	Y	Y	Y	†	Y	Y
MASSACHUSETTS								
1 Conte	Y	Y	N	Y	Y	Y	Y	N
2 Boland	Y	Y	Y	Y	Y	Y	Y	Y
3 Early	?	?	?	?	?	Y	Y	Y
4 Drinan	Y	Y	Y	Y	Y	Y	Y	Y
5 Tsongas	Y	Y	N	Y	Y	Y	Y	Y
6 Harrington	Y	Y	N	#	#	Y	Y	Y
7 Markey	Y	Y	Y	Y	Y	Y	Y	N
8 O'Neill								
9 Moakley	Y	Y	Y	Y	Y	Y	Y	Y
10 Heckler	Y	Y	N	Y	Y	Y	Y	Y
11 Burke	Y	Y	Y	Y	Y	Y	Y	Y
12 Studds	Y	Y	N	Y	Y	Y	Y	Y
MICHIGAN								
1 Conyers	#	#	▮	#	#	#	#	Y
2 Pursell	?	?	?	?	?	Y	Y	Y
3 Brown	#	#	#	#	#	Y	Y	Y
4 Stockman	Y	#	▮	#	#	#	Y	#
5 Sawyer	#	#	#	#	#	#	Y	Y
6 Carr	Y	Y	Y	Y	N	Y	Y	N
7 Kildee	Y	Y	Y	Y	Y	Y	Y	Y
8 Traxler	Y	Y	Y	Y	Y	#	#	Y
9 Vander Jagt	Y	Y	Y	Y	Y	Y	Y	Y
10 Cederberg	Y	Y	Y	Y	Y	Y	Y	Y
11 Ruppe	Y	Y	N	Y	Y	Y	Y	?
12 Bonior	#	#	#	#	?	Y	Y	Y
13 Diggs	#	#	Y	#	Y	Y	Y	Y
14 Nedzi	?	?	?	?	?	Y	Y	Y
15 Ford	?	Y	?	?	?	?	Y	Y
16 Dingell	?	?	Y	Y	N	Y	Y	N
17 Brodhead	Y	Y	Y	Y	Y	Y	Y	Y
18 Blanchard	Y	Y	Y	Y	Y	Y	Y	Y
19 Broomfield	Y	Y	Y	#	#	Y	Y	Y
MINNESOTA								
1 Quie	Y	Y	Y	Y	Y	#	#	Y
2 Hagedorn	Y	Y	Y	Y	Y	Y	Y	N
3 Frenzel	Y	Y	Y	Y	Y	N	Y	Y
4 Vento	Y	Y	N	Y	Y	Y	Y	N
5 Fraser	#	#	#	#	#	?	?	Y
6 Nolan	?	?	?	?	?	?	?	Y
7 Stangeland	Y	Y	Y	Y	Y	Y	Y	Y
8 Oberstar	Y	Y	Y	Y	Y	Y	Y	Y
MISSISSIPPI								
1 Whitten	#	#	#	#	#	Y	Y	N
2 Bowen	?	?	?	?	?	Y	Y	?
3 Montgomery	Y	Y	Y	Y	N	Y	Y	#
4 Cochran	Y	Y	Y	Y	Y	Y	Y	Y
5 Lott	Y	Y	#	#	#	Y	Y	Y
MISSOURI								
1 Clay	?	?	?	?	?	Y	Y	Y
2 Young	Y	Y	Y	Y	Y	#	#	N
3 Gephardt	Y	Y	Y	Y	Y	Y	Y	N
4 Skelton	Y	Y	Y	Y	N	#	#	N
5 Bolling	#	#	#	#	#	Y	Y	#
6 Coleman	?	?	?	?	?	Y	Y	N
7 Taylor	?	?	?	?	?	Y	Y	Y
8 Ichord	Y	Y	Y	Y	N	Y	Y	Y
9 Volkmer	Y	Y	Y	Y	Y	Y	Y	N
10 Burlison	Y	Y	Y	Y	Y	Y	Y	Y
MONTANA								
1 Baucus	Y	Y	Y	Y	Y	#	Y	N
2 Marlenee	?	?	?	?	?	Y	Y	N
NEBRASKA								
1 Thone	#	#	?	#	?	?	?	Y
2 Cavanaugh	Y	Y	Y	?	?	Y	Y	N
3 Smith	Y	Y	Y	Y	#	Y	Y	Y
NEVADA								
AL Santini	Y	Y	Y	Y	Y	Y	Y	Y
NEW HAMPSHIRE								
1 D'Amours	Y	Y	Y	Y	Y	Y	Y	N
2 Cleveland	Y	Y	N	Y	Y	#	#	N
NEW JERSEY								
1 Florio	Y	Y	Y	Y	#	Y	Y	Y
2 Hughes	Y	Y	Y	Y	Y	Y	Y	Y
3 Howard	Y	Y	Y	Y	Y	#	#	Y
4 Thompson	#	#	#	#	#	Y	Y	Y
5 Fenwick	Y	Y	N	Y	Y	Y	Y	N
6 Forsythe	Y	Y	Y	Y	Y	Y	Y	Y
7 Maguire	?	?	?	?	?	Y	Y	Y
8 Roe	Y	Y	Y	Y	Y	Y	Y	#
9 Hollenbeck	Y	Y	Y	Y	Y	Y	Y	Y
10 Rodino	Y	Y	Y	Y	Y	#	#	Y
11 Minish	Y	Y	Y	Y	Y	Y	Y	Y
12 Rinaldo	Y	Y	N	Y	Y	Y	Y	Y
13 Meyner	Y	Y	Y	Y	Y	#	#	#
14 LeFante	#	#	#	#	#	#	#	#
15 Patten	Y	Y	Y	Y	Y	Y	Y	Y
NEW MEXICO								
1 Lujan	Y	Y	Y	Y	Y	Y	Y	Y
2 Runnels	Y	Y	Y	Y	Y	Y	Y	N
NEW YORK								
1 Pike	Y	Y	Y	Y	Y	Y	Y	N
2 Downey	Y	Y	N	Y	Y	Y	Y	Y
3 Ambro	Y	Y	N	Y	Y	N	Y	Y
4 Lent	Y	Y	Y	Y	N	Y	Y	N
5 Wydler	?	?	?	?	?	Y	Y	N
6 Wolff	Y	Y	N	Y	Y	Y	Y	Y
7 Addabbo	#	#	#	#	#	#	#	Y
8 Rosenthal	?	?	?	?	?	Y	Y	Y
9 Delaney	Y	Y	Y	Y	Y	Y	Y	Y
10 Biaggi	Y	Y	Y	Y	Y	#	#	Y
11 Scheuer	Y	Y	N	Y	Y	Y	Y	Y
12 Chisholm	#	#	#	#	#	#	#	Y
13 Solarz	Y	Y	Y	Y	Y	#	Y	Y
14 Richmond	?	?	?	?	?	Y	Y	Y
15 Zeferetti	#	#	#	?	#	#	#	Y
16 Holtzman	N	Y	N	Y	Y	†	Y	N
17 Murphy	Y	Y	Y	Y	Y	Y	Y	Y
18 Green	Y	Y	Y	Y	Y	Y	Y	Y
19 Rangel	?	?	?	?	?	Y	Y	Y
20 Weiss	Y	Y	N	Y	Y	?	?	N
21 Garcia	Y	Y	N	Y	Y	?	?	Y
22 Bingham	Y	Y	Y	Y	Y	Y	Y	Y
23 Caputo	Y	Y	N	Y	Y	Y	Y	N
24 Ottinger	Y	Y	N	Y	Y	Y	Y	Y
25 Fish	Y	Y	Y	Y	Y	Y	Y	?
26 Gilman	?	?	†	?	†	†	Y	Y
27 McHugh	Y	Y	Y	Y	Y	Y	Y	Y
28 Stratton	Y	Y	Y	Y	N	Y	Y	Y
29 Pattison	#	Y	N	Y	N	Y	Y	Y
30 McEwen	Y	Y	Y	Y	Y	?	?	Y
31 Mitchell	Y	Y	Y	Y	Y	Y	Y	Y
32 Hanley	Y	Y	Y	#	#	Y	Y	Y
33 Walsh	Y	Y	Y	?	?	Y	Y	Y
34 Horton	#	#	#	#	#	Y	#	Y
35 Conable	Y	Y	N	Y	Y	N	Y	Y
36 LaFalce	?	?	?	?	?	Y	Y	Y
37 Nowak	Y	Y	Y	Y	Y	Y	Y	Y
38 Kemp	#	?	#	?	?	Y	Y	Y
39 Lundine	Y	Y	Y	Y	Y	Y	Y	N
NORTH CAROLINA								
1 Jones	Y	Y	Y	Y	Y	Y	Y	Y
2 Fountain	#	#	#	#	#	Y	Y	Y
3 Whitley	Y	Y	Y	Y	Y	Y	Y	N
4 Andrews	Y	#	Y	Y	Y	N	Y	Y
5 Neal	Y	Y	Y	Y	N	Y	Y	N
6 Preyer	Y	Y	Y	Y	Y	?	?	Y
7 Rose	Y	Y	Y	Y	Y	Y	Y	#
8 Hefner	Y	Y	Y	Y	Y	Y	Y	Y
9 Martin	Y	Y	Y	Y	Y	Y	Y	N
10 Broyhill	Y	Y	Y	Y	N	Y	Y	Y
11 Gudger	Y	N	Y	Y	N	Y	Y	Y
NORTH DAKOTA								
AL Andrews	Y	Y	Y	Y	Y	?	?	?
OHIO								
1 Gradison	Y	Y	Y	Y	N	Y	Y	Y
2 Luken	Y	Y	Y	Y	Y	Y	Y	N
3 Whalen	Y	Y	N	Y	Y	Y	Y	Y
4 Guyer	#	#	#	#	#	Y	Y	N
5 Latta	Y	N	Y	Y	N	Y	Y	N
6 Harsha	?	?	?	?	?	Y	Y	N
7 Brown	?	?	Y	Y	Y	?	?	Y
8 Kindness	Y	Y	Y	Y	N	Y	Y	Y
9 Ashley	Y	Y	Y	Y	Y	Y	Y	Y
10 Miller	Y	Y	Y	Y	Y	Y	Y	N
11 Stanton	Y	Y	Y	Y	N	Y	Y	Y
12 Devine	Y	N	Y	Y	N	Y	Y	N
13 Pease	Y	Y	Y	Y	Y	Y	Y	N
14 Seiberling	Y	#	Y	Y	Y	Y	Y	Y
15 Wylie	?	?	?	?	?	Y	Y	N
16 Regula	Y	Y	Y	Y	Y	Y	Y	N
17 Ashbrook	Y	N	Y	Y	N	Y	Y	N
18 Applegate	Y	Y	Y	Y	Y	Y	Y	N
19 Carney	#	#	#	#	#	Y	Y	N
20 Oakar	Y	Y	Y	Y	Y	Y	Y	Y
21 Stokes	#	#	#	#	#	Y	Y	Y
22 Vanik	Y	Y	N	Y	Y	Y	Y	N
23 Mottl	Y	Y	N	Y	N	#	#	N
OKLAHOMA								
1 Jones	Y	Y	Y	Y	Y	Y	Y	N
2 Risenhoover	Y	Y	Y	Y	Y	Y	Y	N
3 Watkins	Y	Y	Y	Y	Y	#	#	N
4 Steed	Y	Y	Y	Y	Y	Y	Y	Y
5 Edwards	?	?	?	?	?	Y	Y	?
6 English	Y	Y	Y	Y	Y	Y	Y	Y
OREGON								
1 AuCoin	Y	Y	Y	Y	N	#	#	N
2 Ullman	#	#	#	#	#	#	Y	N
3 Duncan	?	?	?	?	?	Y	?	Y
4 Weaver	Y	Y	Y	Y	N	Y	Y	Y
PENNSYLVANIA								
1 Myers, M.	?	?	?	?	?	Y	Y	Y
2 Nix	#	#	#	#	#	#	#	Y
3 Lederer	?	?	?	?	?	Y	Y	Y
4 Eilberg	#	#	#	#	#	#	#	Y
5 Schulze	Y	Y	Y	Y	Y	Y	Y	Y
6 Yatron	#	#	#	#	#	Y	Y	Y
7 Edgar	#	#	#	#	#	Y	Y	Y
8 Kostmayer	Y	Y	Y	Y	Y	Y	Y	Y
9 Shuster	Y	Y	Y	Y	N	N	Y	Y
10 McDade	Y	Y	Y	Y	Y	Y	Y	Y
11 Flood	Y	Y	Y	Y	Y	Y	Y	Y
12 Murtha	Y	Y	Y	Y	N	Y	Y	Y
13 Coughlin	#	#	#	#	#	Y	Y	Y
14 Moorhead	Y	#	Y	Y	Y	Y	Y	Y
15 Rooney	Y	Y	Y	Y	Y	Y	Y	Y
16 Walker	#	#	#	#	▮	Y	Y	N
17 Ertel	Y	Y	Y	Y	N	Y	Y	Y
18 Walgren	Y	Y	Y	Y	Y	Y	Y	N
19 Goodling, W.	Y	Y	Y	Y	N	Y	Y	N
20 Gaydos	Y	Y	Y	Y	Y	Y	Y	Y
21 Dent	#	#	#	#	#	#	#	#
22 Murphy	#	#	#	#	#	N	Y	N
23 Ammerman	Y	Y	N	Y	Y	N	Y	N
24 Marks	Y	Y	Y	Y	Y	Y	Y	N
25 Myers, G.	Y	Y	N	Y	N	Y	Y	N
RHODE ISLAND								
1 St Germain	?	?	?	?	?	Y	Y	N
2 Beard	?	?	?	?	?	Y	Y	Y
SOUTH CAROLINA								
1 Davis	?	?	?	?	?	Y	Y	Y
2 Spence	Y	Y	Y	Y	N	Y	Y	Y
3 Derrick	Y	Y	Y	Y	Y	Y	Y	Y
4 Mann	Y	Y	Y	Y	Y	Y	?	Y
5 Holland	#	#	#	#	#	Y	Y	Y
6 Jenrette	Y	Y	Y	Y	Y	Y	Y	N
SOUTH DAKOTA								
1 Pressler	Y	Y	Y	Y	Y	Y	Y	Y
2 Abdnor	Y	Y	Y	Y	Y	Y	Y	Y
TENNESSEE								
1 Quillen	Y	Y	Y	Y	Y	Y	Y	Y
2 Duncan	Y	Y	Y	Y	Y	Y	Y	Y
3 Lloyd	Y	Y	Y	Y	N	Y	Y	N
4 Gore	Y	Y	Y	Y	Y	Y	Y	N
5 Allen	Y	Y	Y	Y	Y	Y	Y	N
6 Beard	#	#	#	#	#	Y	Y	Y
7 Jones	Y	Y	Y	Y	Y	Y	Y	N
8 Ford	Y	Y	Y	#	#	#	#	Y
TEXAS								
1 Hall	?	?	?	?	?	Y	Y	N
2 Wilson, C.	#	#	#	#	#	#	#	N
3 Collins	Y	Y	Y	Y	Y	N	N	Y
4 Roberts	?	?	?	?	?	?	?	?
5 Mattox	Y	Y	Y	Y	Y	Y	Y	?
6 Teague	?	?	?	?	?	?	?	?
7 Archer	Y	Y	Y	Y	N	Y	Y	Y
8 Eckhardt	Y	Y	Y	Y	Y	?	Y	Y
9 Brooks	Y	Y	N	Y	Y	Y	Y	Y
10 Pickle	Y	Y	Y	Y	Y	Y	Y	N
11 Poage	Y	Y	Y	Y	N	N	N	N
12 Wright	?	?	Y	Y	Y	Y	Y	Y
13 Hightower	Y	Y	Y	Y	Y	Y	Y	N
14 Young	?	?	?	?	?	?	?	Y
15 de la Garza	?	?	?	?	?	?	Y	N
16 White	Y	Y	Y	Y	Y	Y	Y	N
17 Burleson	Y	Y	Y	Y	N	Y	Y	Y
18 Jordan	Y	Y	Y	Y	Y	Y	Y	Y
19 Mahon	Y	Y	Y	Y	Y	Y	Y	N
20 Gonzalez	Y	Y	Y	Y	Y	Y	Y	N
21 Krueger	#	#	#	#	#	X	X	#
22 Gammage	?	?	?	?	?	?	?	N
23 Kazen	?	?	?	?	?	Y	Y	N
24 Milford	?	?	?	?	?	Y	Y	N
UTAH								
1 McKay	Y	Y	Y	Y	Y	N	N	Y
2 Marriott	#	#	#	#	#	Y	Y	Y
VERMONT								
AL Jeffords	Y	Y	N	Y	Y	#	#	N
VIRGINIA								
1 Trible	Y	Y	Y	Y	N	Y	Y	Y
2 Whitehurst	Y	Y	Y	Y	N	Y	Y	Y
3 Satterfield	Y	Y	Y	Y	N	Y	Y	N
4 Daniel	Y	Y	Y	Y	N	Y	Y	Y
5 Daniel	Y	Y	Y	Y	N	Y	Y	Y
6 Butler	Y	Y	Y	Y	N	N	Y	Y
7 Robinson	Y	Y	Y	Y	N	Y	Y	Y
8 Harris	Y	Y	Y	Y	Y	Y	Y	Y
9 Wampler	Y	Y	Y	Y	?	?	?	Y
10 Fisher	Y	Y	Y	Y	Y	Y	Y	Y
WASHINGTON								
1 Pritchard	#	#	#	#	#	Y	Y	Y
2 Meeds	Y	▮	Y	Y	N	Y	Y	Y
3 Bonker	Y	Y	Y	Y	#	Y	Y	Y
4 McCormack	Y	Y	Y	Y	N	Y	Y	Y
5 Foley	Y	Y	Y	Y	N	Y	Y	Y
6 Dicks	Y	Y	Y	Y	N	?	?	N
7 Cunningham	Y	Y	Y	N	N	Y	Y	N
WEST VIRGINIA								
1 Mollohan	Y	Y	Y	Y	Y	Y	Y	▮
2 Staggers	Y	Y	Y	Y	N	Y	Y	Y
3 Slack	?	?	?	?	?	Y	Y	N
4 Rahall	#	#	#	#	#	Y	Y	Y
WISCONSIN								
1 Aspin	Y	Y	Y	?	?	?	?	Y
2 Kastenmeier	Y	Y	N	Y	Y	Y	Y	Y
3 Baldus	Y	Y	Y	Y	Y	N	Y	Y
4 Zablocki	Y	Y	Y	Y	Y	Y	Y	Y
5 Reuss	Y	Y	▮	Y	Y	Y	Y	Y
6 Steiger	Y	Y	Y	Y	Y	Y	Y	Y
7 Obey	Y	Y	Y	?	?	N	Y	Y
8 Cornell	Y	Y	Y	Y	Y	Y	Y	Y
9 Kasten	†	†	†	†	†	Y	Y	Y
WYOMING								
AL Roncalio	Y	Y	Y	Y	Y	?	?	Y

Democrats ***Republicans***

73. HR 3816. FTC Act Amendments. Adoption of the conference report on the bill to amend the Federal Trade Commission Act to strengthen and expedite the Federal Trade Commission's powers for enforcing its rules and subpoenas and to authorize funds for the Federal Trade Commission for fiscal years 1978-81. Rejected 146-255: R 3-130; D 143-125 (ND 128-63; SD 15-62), Feb. 28, 1978.

74. HR 5981. American Folklife Preservation. Passage of the bill to authorize $3.1 million for fiscal 1979-81 for the American Folklife Center to preserve and present American folklife through research, documentation and presentation programs. Passed 306-80: R 72-54; D 234-26 (ND 173-12; SD 61-14), Feb. 28, 1978.

75. H J Res 554. D.C. Voting Representation. Adoption of the rule (H Res 1048) providing for House floor consideration of the joint resolution to amend the Constitution to provide for full voting representation in Congress for the District of Columbia. Adopted 386-21: R 123-16; D 263-5 (ND 186-1; SD 77-4), March 1, 1978.

76. H J Res 554. D.C. Voting Representation. Edwards, D-Calif., motion that the House resolve itself into the Committee of the Whole for consideration of the joint resolution to amend the Constitution to provide for full voting representation in Congress for the District of Columbia. Motion agreed to 369-15: R 120-10; D 249-5 (ND 179-1; SD 70-4), March 1, 1978.

77. H J Res 554. D.C. Voting Representation. Edwards, D-Calif., motion that the House resolve itself into the Committee of the Whole for further consideration of the joint resolution to amend the Constitution to provide for full voting representation in Congress for the District of Columbia. Motion agreed to 394-12: R 133-7; D 261-5 (ND 185-1; SD 76-4), March 2, 1978.

78. H J Res 554. D.C. Voting Representation. Passage of the joint resolution proposing an amendment to the Constitution to provide for full voting representation in Congress (both in the House and the Senate) and to retain the right granted by the 23rd Amendment to vote for the election of the president and vice president (the resolution would repeal the 23rd Amendment). Passed 289-127: R 61-79; D 228-48 (ND 172-19; SD 56-29), March 2, 1978. A two-thirds majority vote (278 in this case) is required to pass a resolution proposing an amendment to the Constitution. A "yea" was a vote supporting the president's position.

KEY

- Y Voted for (yea).
- ✓ Paired for.
- † Announced for.
- # CQ Poll for.
- N Voted against (nay).
- X Paired against.
- \- Announced against.
- ▮ CQ Poll against.
- P Voted "present."
- ● Voted "present" to avoid possible conflict of interest.
- ? Did not vote or otherwise make a position known.

	73	74	75	76	77	78
ALABAMA						
1 Edwards	N	Y	Y	Y	Y	Y
2 Dickinson	N	Y	Y	Y	Y	N
3 Nichols	N	Y	Y	#	Y	N
4 Bevill	N	Y	Y	Y	Y	Y
5 Flippo	N	N	Y	Y	Y	N
6 Buchanan	N	Y	Y	Y	Y	Y
7 Flowers	N	Y	Y	Y	Y	Y
ALASKA						
AL Young	N	#	Y	Y	Y	N
ARIZONA						
1 Rhodes	N	Y	Y	Y	Y	N
2 Udall	Y	Y	Y	Y	Y	Y
3 Stump	N	N	Y	Y	Y	N
4 Rudd	▮	▮	N	N	N	N
ARKANSAS						
1 Alexander	N	Y	Y	Y	Y	N
2 Tucker	#	#	Y	Y	Y	N
3 Hammerschmidt	N	Y	?	?	?	?
4 Thornton	?	?	Y	?	?	?
CALIFORNIA						
1 Johnson	Y	Y	Y	Y	Y	Y
2 Clausen	N	Y	Y	Y	Y	?
3 Moss	Y	Y	Y	Y	Y	Y
4 Leggett	Y	#	Y	#	Y	Y
5 Burton, J.	Y	Y	?	?	Y	Y
6 Burton, P.	Y	Y	Y	Y	Y	Y
7 Miller	Y	Y	Y	Y	Y	Y
8 Dellums	✓	#	#	#	Y	Y
9 Stark	Y	Y	Y	Y	Y	Y
10 Edwards	Y	Y	Y	Y	Y	Y
11 Ryan	N	Y	Y	Y	Y	N
12 McCloskey	N	Y	Y	Y	Y	Y
13 Mineta	N	Y	Y	Y	Y	Y
14 McFall	Y	Y	Y	Y	Y	N
15 Sisk	N	Y	Y	Y	Y	N
16 Panetta	Y	Y	Y	Y	Y	Y
17 Krebs	N	Y	Y	Y	Y	Y
18 Ketchum	N	N	Y	Y	Y	N
19 Lagomarsino	N	N	Y	Y	Y	N
20 Goldwater	?	?	Y	Y	Y	N
21 Corman	Y	Y	Y	Y	Y	Y
22 Moorhead	N	N	N	N	N	N
23 Beilenson	Y	Y	Y	Y	Y	Y
24 Waxman	Y	Y	Y	Y	Y	Y
25 Roybal	Y	Y	Y	Y	Y	Y
26 Rousselot	?	?	N	Y	Y	N
27 Dornan	N	Y	Y	N	Y	X
28 Burke	Y	Y	Y	Y	Y	Y
29 Hawkins	Y	Y	Y	Y	Y	Y
30 Danielson	Y	Y	Y	Y	Y	Y
31 Wilson, C.H.	N	Y	#	#	Y	Y
32 Anderson	N	Y	Y	Y	Y	N
33 Clawson	N	N	N	N	Y	N
34 Hannaford	N	Y	Y	Y	Y	Y
35 Lloyd	Y	Y	Y	Y	Y	Y
36 Brown	Y	Y	Y	Y	Y	Y
37 Pettis	N	Y	Y	Y	Y	N
38 Patterson	N	Y	Y	Y	Y	Y
39 Wiggins	N	#	Y	Y	Y	N
40 Badham	N	N	N	Y	Y	N
41 Wilson, B.	N	Y	Y	N	N	Y
42 Van Deerlin	Y	Y	Y	Y	Y	Y
43 Burgener	N	Y	Y	Y	Y	N
COLORADO						
1 Schroeder	N	Y	Y	Y	Y	Y
2 Wirth	Y	Y	Y	Y	Y	Y
3 Evans	Y	Y	Y	Y	Y	Y
4 Johnson	N	Y	Y	Y	Y	N
5 Armstrong	?	?	N	Y	Y	N
CONNECTICUT						
1 Cotter	Y	Y	Y	Y	Y	Y
2 Dodd	N	?	Y	Y	Y	Y
3 Giaimo	N	Y	Y	Y	?	Y
4 McKinney	N	Y	Y	Y	Y	Y
5 Sarasin	-	†	†	†	Y	Y
6 Moffett	Y	Y	Y	Y	Y	Y
DELAWARE						
AL Evans	N	Y	Y	Y	Y	Y
FLORIDA						
1 Sikes	N	Y	Y	Y	Y	N
2 Fuqua	N	Y	Y	Y	Y	Y
3 Bennett	N	N	Y	Y	Y	Y
4 Chappell	X	#	#	#	#	▮
5 Kelly	N	N	Y	Y	Y	N
6 Young	N	N	Y	Y	Y	N
7 Gibbons	Y	Y	N	Y	Y	N
8 Ireland	N	N	Y	Y	Y	Y
9 Frey	?	?	?	?	?	X
10 Bafalis	N	N	Y	Y	Y	N
11 Rogers	Y	?	Y	Y	Y	Y
12 Burke	?	?	?	?	Y	N
13 Lehman	Y	Y	Y	Y	Y	Y
14 Pepper	✓	#	Y	Y	Y	Y
15 Fascell	Y	Y	Y	Y	Y	Y
GEORGIA						
1 Ginn	N	Y	Y	Y	Y	Y
2 Mathis	?	Y	Y	?	Y	Y
3 Brinkley	?	?	?	?	?	Y
4 Levitas	N	Y	Y	Y	Y	Y
5 Fowler	N	Y	?	?	Y	Y
6 Flynt	N	N	Y	Y	Y	Y
7 McDonald	X	#	N	N	N	N
8 Evans	N	Y	Y	N	N	Y
9 Jenkins	N	Y	Y	Y	Y	N
10 Barnard	N	Y	Y	Y	Y	Y
HAWAII						
1 Heftel	N	Y	Y	Y	Y	Y
2 Akaka	Y	Y	Y	Y	Y	Y
IDAHO						
1 Symms	?	?	N	N	N	N
2 Hansen, G.	N	N	N	N	N	N
ILLINOIS						
1 Metcalfe	Y	Y	Y	Y	Y	Y
2 Murphy	Y	Y	Y	Y	Y	Y
3 Russo	N	Y	Y	#	#	✓
4 Derwinski	N	Y	Y	Y	Y	N
5 Fary	Y	Y	Y	Y	Y	Y
6 Hyde	N	N	Y	Y	Y	N
7 Collins	Y	Y	Y	Y	#	Y
8 Rostenkowski	Y	Y	Y	Y	Y	Y
9 Yates	Y	#	Y	Y	Y	Y
10 Mikva	Y	Y	Y	Y	Y	✓
11 Annunzio	Y	Y	Y	Y	Y	Y
12 Crane	▮	▮	N	Y	Y	N
13 McClory	N	Y	Y	Y	Y	Y
14 Erlenborn	▮	#	Y	Y	Y	Y
15 Corcoran	N	Y	Y	Y	Y	Y
16 Anderson	N	Y	#	#	#	✓
17 O'Brien	N	N	Y	Y	Y	Y
18 Michel	N	N	Y	Y	Y	N
19 Railsback	N	Y	Y	#	Y	Y
20 Findley	N	Y	Y	Y	Y	Y
21 Madigan	N	Y	Y	?	Y	Y
22 Shipley	Y	?	Y	Y	Y	N
23 Price	Y	Y	Y	Y	Y	Y
24 Simon	Y	Y	Y	Y	Y	Y
INDIANA						
1 Benjamin	N	Y	Y	Y	Y	Y
2 Fithian	N	Y	Y	Y	Y	Y
3 Brademas	Y	Y	Y	Y	Y	Y
4 Quayle	N	Y	Y	Y	Y	Y
5 Hillis	N	N	Y	Y	Y	Y
6 Evans	N	N	Y	Y	Y	Y
7 Myers, J.	N	N	Y	Y	Y	Y
8 Cornwell	✓	#	Y	Y	Y	Y
9 Hamilton	N	Y	Y	Y	Y	Y
10 Sharp	Y	Y	Y	?	Y	Y
11 Jacobs	N	N	Y	Y	Y	Y
IOWA						
1 Leach	N	Y	Y	Y	Y	Y
2 Blouin	Y	Y	Y	Y	Y	Y
3 Grassley	N	Y	Y	Y	Y	N
4 Smith	Y	Y	Y	Y	Y	Y
5 Harkin	N	Y	Y	Y	Y	Y
6 Bedell	Y	Y	Y	Y	Y	Y

Democrats ***Republicans***

	73	74	75	76	77	78
KANSAS						
1 Sebelius	N	N	Y	Y	Y	N
2 Keys	N	N	Y	Y	Y	Y
3 Winn	N	Y	Y	Y	Y	Y
4 Glickman	N	Y	Y	Y	Y	Y
5 Skubitz	N	Y	Y	Y	Y	N
KENTUCKY						
1 Hubbard	N	Y	Y	?	Y	Y
2 Natcher	N	Y	Y	Y	Y	Y
3 Mazzoli	N	Y	Y	Y	Y	Y
4 Snyder	N	N	Y	Y	Y	N
5 Carter	N	Y	Y	Y	Y	Y
6 Breckinridge	N	Y	Y	Y	Y	Y
7 Perkins	Y	Y	Y	Y	Y	Y
LOUISIANA						
1 Livingston	N	N	Y	Y	Y	N
2 Boggs	N	Y	Y	Y	Y	Y
3 Treen	N	N	Y	Y	Y	N
4 Waggonner	N	Y	Y	Y	Y	N
5 Huckaby	N	Y	Y	Y	Y	Y
6 Moore	N	Y	Y	Y	Y	N
7 Breaux	N	N	Y	Y	Y	N
8 Long	N	Y	Y	Y	Y	Y
MAINE						
1 Emery	N	Y	Y	Y	Y	Y
2 Cohen	N	Y	Y	Y	Y	Y
MARYLAND						
1 Bauman	N	N	N	N	N	N
2 Long	Y	Y	Y	Y	Y	N
3 Mikulski	Y	Y	Y	Y	Y	Y
4 Holt	N	N	Y	Y	Y	N
5 Spellman	N	Y	Y	Y	Y	Y
6 Byron	N	Y	Y	Y	Y	Y
7 Mitchell	Y	Y	Y	Y	N	Y
8 Steers	N	Y	Y	Y	Y	Y
MASSACHUSETTS						
1 Conte	N	Y	Y	Y	Y	Y
2 Boland	N	Y	Y	Y	Y	Y
3 Early	N	Y	Y	Y	Y	Y
4 Drinan	Y	Y	Y	Y	Y	Y
5 Tsongas	Y	Y	Y	Y	Y	Y
6 Harrington	Y	#	Y	Y	Y	Y
7 Markey	Y	Y	Y	Y	Y	Y
8 O'Neill						
9 Moakley	Y	Y	Y	Y	Y	Y
10 Heckler	N	Y	Y	Y	Y	Y
11 Burke	N	Y	Y	Y	Y	Y
12 Studds	Y	Y	Y	Y	Y	Y
MICHIGAN						
1 Conyers	Y	Y	Y	Y	Y	Y
2 Pursell	N	Y	Y	Y	Y	Y
3 Brown	N	N	Y	Y	Y	N
4 Stockman	N	Y	Y	Y	Y	Y
5 Sawyer	N	Y	Y	Y	Y	Y
6 Carr	Y	Y	Y	Y	Y	Y
7 Kildee	Y	Y	Y	Y	Y	Y
8 Traxler	Y	Y	Y	Y	Y	Y
9 Vander Jagt	N	Y	Y	Y	Y	N
10 Cederberg	N	Y	Y	#	Y	N
11 Ruppe	N	N	#	#	#	N
12 Bonior	Y	Y	#	Y	Y	Y
13 Diggs	Y	#	Y	Y	#	Y
14 Nedzi	N	Y	Y	Y	Y	Y
15 Ford	Y	Y	Y	Y	Y	N
16 Dingell	Y	Y	N	N	?	N
17 Brodhead	Y	Y	Y	Y	Y	Y
18 Blanchard	N	Y	Y	Y	Y	Y
19 Broomfield	N	#	Y	#	N	N
MINNESOTA						
1 Quie	N	#	Y	Y	Y	Y
2 Hagedorn	?	?	Y	Y	Y	N
3 Frenzel	N	N	Y	Y	Y	Y
4 Vento	Y	Y	Y	Y	Y	Y
5 Fraser	Y	Y	Y	Y	Y	Y
6 Nolan	Y	Y	Y	Y	Y	Y
7 Stangeland	N	N	Y	Y	Y	N
8 Oberstar	N	Y	Y	Y	Y	Y
MISSISSIPPI						
1 Whitten	N	#	Y	Y	Y	N
2 Bowen	?	?	Y	?	Y	N
3 Montgomery	▮	#	Y	Y	Y	N
4 Cochran	N	Y	Y	Y	Y	N
5 Lott	N	Y	N	Y	Y	N
MISSOURI						
1 Clay	Y	Y	Y	?	Y	Y
2 Young	N	Y	?	Y	Y	N
3 Gephardt	N	Y	Y	Y	#	Y
4 Skelton	N	Y	Y	Y	Y	Y
5 Bolling	Y	Y	Y	Y	Y	Y
6 Coleman	N	N	Y	Y	Y	Y
7 Taylor	N	N	Y	Y	Y	N
8 Ichord	N	N	Y	Y	Y	N
9 Volkmer	N	N	Y	Y	Y	Y
10 Burlison	Y	Y	Y	Y	Y	Y
MONTANA						
1 Baucus	N	Y	Y	Y	Y	Y
2 Marlenee	N	Y	Y	Y	Y	Y
NEBRASKA						
1 Thone	N	N	Y	Y	Y	Y
2 Cavanaugh	N	N	Y	Y	Y	Y
3 Smith	N	N	Y	Y	Y	N
NEVADA						
AL Santini	N	Y	Y	Y	Y	N
NEW HAMPSHIRE						
1 D'Amours	N	Y	#	#	Y	Y
2 Cleveland	N	Y	Y	Y	Y	N
NEW JERSEY						
1 Florio	N	Y	Y	Y	Y	Y
2 Hughes	N	Y	Y	Y	Y	Y
3 Howard	Y	Y	Y	Y	Y	Y
4 Thompson	Y	Y	Y	Y	Y	Y
5 Fenwick	N	Y	Y	Y	Y	N
6 Forsythe	N	Y	Y	Y	Y	Y
7 Maguire	Y	Y	Y	?	Y	Y
8 Roe	▮	#	Y	Y	Y	Y
9 Hollenbeck	N	Y	Y	Y	Y	Y
10 Rodino	Y	Y	Y	Y	Y	Y
11 Minish	Y	Y	Y	Y	Y	Y
12 Rinaldo	Y	Y	Y	Y	Y	Y
13 Meyner	Y	Y	#	#	Y	Y
14 LeFante	#	#	Y	Y	#	✓
15 Patten	Y	Y	Y	Y	Y	Y
NEW MEXICO						
1 Lujan	N	Y	Y	Y	Y	N
2 Runnels	N	N	Y	?	Y	N
NEW YORK						
1 Pike	Y	Y	Y	Y	Y	N
2 Downey	Y	Y	Y	Y	Y	Y
3 Ambro	N	Y	Y	Y	Y	N
4 Lent	N	Y	Y	Y	Y	Y
5 Wydler	N	N	Y	Y	Y	N
6 Wolff	N	Y	Y	Y	Y	Y
7 Addabbo	Y	Y	Y	Y	Y	Y
8 Rosenthal	Y	Y	Y	Y	Y	Y
9 Delaney	Y	Y	Y	Y	Y	Y
10 Biaggi	N	Y	Y	Y	Y	Y
11 Scheuer	Y	Y	Y	Y	Y	Y
12 Chisholm	Y	Y	Y	Y	#	Y
13 Solarz	Y	Y	Y	Y	Y	Y
14 Richmond	Y	Y	Y	Y	Y	Y
15 Zeferetti	N	Y	Y	Y	Y	Y
16 Holtzman	Y	Y	Y	Y	Y	Y
17 Murphy	Y	Y	Y	Y	Y	Y
18 Green	Y	Y	Y	Y	Y	Y
19 Rangel	Y	Y	Y	Y	Y	Y
20 Weiss	Y	Y	Y	Y	Y	Y
21 Garcia	Y	Y	Y	?	Y	Y
22 Bingham	Y	Y	Y	Y	Y	Y
23 Caputo	N	N	Y	Y	Y	Y
24 Ottinger	Y	Y	Y	Y	Y	Y
25 Fish	?	?	Y	Y	Y	Y
26 Gilman	N	Y	Y	Y	Y	Y
27 McHugh	Y	Y	Y	Y	Y	Y
28 Stratton	N	Y	Y	Y	Y	N
29 Pattison	Y	Y	Y	Y	Y	Y
30 McEwen	N	Y	Y	Y	Y	Y
31 Mitchell	N	Y	Y	Y	Y	Y
32 Hanley	N	Y	Y	Y	Y	Y
33 Walsh	N	Y	Y	Y	Y	Y
34 Horton	N	Y	Y	#	#	Y
35 Conable	N	N	Y	Y	Y	Y
36 LaFalce	Y	Y	Y	Y	Y	Y
37 Nowak	Y	Y	Y	Y	Y	Y
38 Kemp	N	Y	Y	Y	Y	Y
39 Lundine	Y	Y	#	Y	Y	Y
NORTH CAROLINA						
1 Jones	N	Y	#	#	Y	Y
2 Fountain	N	Y	Y	Y	Y	Y
3 Whitley	N	Y	Y	Y	Y	Y
4 Andrews	N	Y	Y	Y	Y	Y
5 Neal	N	Y	#	#	#	Y
6 Preyer	N	Y	Y	Y	Y	Y
7 Rose	▮	#	Y	Y	Y	Y
8 Hefner	N	Y	Y	Y	Y	Y
9 Martin	N	Y	Y	Y	Y	N
10 Broyhill	N	Y	Y	Y	Y	Y
11 Gudger	N	Y	Y	Y	Y	Y
NORTH DAKOTA						
AL Andrews	?	?	Y	Y	Y	N
OHIO						
1 Gradison	N	Y	Y	Y	Y	Y
2 Luken	Y	N	Y	Y	Y	Y
3 Whalen	N	Y	Y	Y	Y	Y
4 Guyer	N	Y	Y	Y	Y	Y
5 Latta	N	N	N	Y	Y	N
6 Harsha	N	N	Y	?	Y	N
7 Brown	N	Y	?	?	?	?
8 Kindness	N	N	Y	Y	Y	N
9 Ashley	Y	Y	Y	Y	Y	N
10 Miller	N	N	Y	Y	Y	N
11 Stanton	N	Y	Y	Y	Y	Y
12 Devine	N	N	Y	Y	Y	N
13 Pease	Y	Y	Y	Y	Y	Y
14 Seiberling	Y	Y	Y	Y	Y	Y
15 Wylie	N	N	Y	Y	Y	Y
16 Regula	N	Y	Y	Y	Y	Y
17 Ashbrook	N	▮	N	Y	Y	N
18 Applegate	N	Y	Y	Y	Y	Y
19 Carney	Y	Y	Y	Y	Y	Y
20 Oakar	Y	Y	Y	Y	Y	Y
21 Stokes	Y	Y	Y	Y	Y	Y
22 Vanik	Y	Y	Y	Y	Y	Y
23 Mottl	Y	Y	Y	Y	Y	Y
OKLAHOMA						
1 Jones	N	N	Y	#	Y	Y
2 Risenhoover	N	N	?	?	?	?
3 Watkins	N	N	Y	Y	Y	N
4 Steed	N	N	#	#	Y	N
5 Edwards	?	?	Y	Y	Y	N
6 English	N	Y	Y	Y	Y	N
OREGON						
1 AuCoin	N	N	Y	Y	Y	Y
2 Ullman	N	Y	Y	Y	Y	Y
3 Duncan	N	N	Y	Y	Y	Y
4 Weaver	Y	Y	Y	Y	Y	Y
PENNSYLVANIA						
1 Myers, M.	N	Y	Y	?	Y	Y
2 Nix	Y	Y	Y	#	#	#
3 Lederer	Y	Y	Y	Y	Y	Y
4 Eilberg	Y	Y	Y	Y	Y	Y
5 Schulze	N	N	Y	?	Y	N
6 Yatron	N	Y	Y	Y	Y	Y
7 Edgar	Y	Y	Y	Y	Y	Y
8 Kostmayer	Y	Y	Y	Y	Y	Y
9 Shuster	N	N	Y	?	Y	N
10 McDade	N	?	?	?	?	✓
11 Flood	Y	Y	Y	Y	Y	Y
12 Murtha	N	Y	Y	Y	Y	Y
13 Coughlin	N	N	Y	Y	Y	Y
14 Moorhead	Y	Y	Y	Y	Y	Y
15 Rooney	Y	Y	Y	Y	Y	Y
16 Walker	N	N	Y	Y	Y	N
17 Ertel	N	Y	Y	Y	Y	Y
18 Walgren	N	Y	Y	Y	Y	Y
19 Goodling, W.	N	N	Y	N	Y	Y
20 Gaydos	N	Y	Y	Y	?	Y
21 Dent	▮	#	#	#	#	#
22 Murphy	N	Y	Y	Y	Y	Y
23 Ammerman	Y	Y	Y	Y	Y	Y
24 Marks	N	Y	Y	Y	Y	Y
25 Myers, G.	Y	N	Y	Y	Y	N
RHODE ISLAND						
1 St Germain	Y	Y	Y	Y	Y	Y
2 Beard	Y	Y	Y	Y	Y	Y
SOUTH CAROLINA						
1 Davis	N	Y	Y	Y	Y	Y
2 Spence	N	Y	Y	Y	Y	N
3 Derrick	N	Y	Y	Y	Y	Y
4 Mann	N	Y	Y	Y	?	Y
5 Holland	N	Y	Y	Y	Y	Y
6 Jenrette	N	Y	Y	Y	Y	Y
SOUTH DAKOTA						
1 Pressler	N	Y	Y	Y	Y	N
2 Abdnor	N	N	Y	Y	Y	N
TENNESSEE						
1 Quillen	N	N	N	Y	Y	N
2 Duncan	N	N	Y	Y	Y	N
3 Lloyd	N	Y	Y	Y	Y	Y
4 Gore	Y	Y	Y	Y	Y	Y
5 Allen	Y	Y	Y	Y	Y	Y
6 Beard	N	N	Y	Y	Y	N
7 Jones	N	Y	Y	Y	Y	Y
8 Ford	Y	Y	Y	Y	Y	Y
TEXAS						
1 Hall	N	N	Y	Y	Y	Y
2 Wilson, C.	N	#	Y	Y	Y	N
3 Collins	N	N	N	N	Y	N
4 Roberts	?	?	?	?	?	X
5 Mattox	N	Y	Y	Y	Y	Y
6 Teague	?	?	?	?	?	N
7 Archer	N	N	N	Y	Y	N
8 Eckhardt	Y	Y	Y	Y	Y	Y
9 Brooks	Y	Y	Y	Y	?	N
10 Pickle	N	Y	Y	Y	Y	Y
11 Poage	N	N	N	N	N	N
12 Wright	Y	Y	Y	Y	Y	Y
13 Hightower	N	Y	Y	Y	Y	N
14 Young	N	Y	Y	Y	Y	N
15 de la Garza	N	Y	Y	Y	Y	N
16 White	N	Y	Y	Y	Y	N
17 Burleson	N	N	N	Y	Y	N
18 Jordan	Y	Y	Y	Y	Y	Y
19 Mahon	N	Y	Y	Y	#	▮
20 Gonzalez	Y	Y	Y	Y	Y	Y
21 Krueger	X	#	Y	#	Y	Y
22 Gammage	N	Y	Y	Y	Y	Y
23 Kazen	N	Y	Y	Y	Y	N
24 Milford	N	Y	Y	Y	Y	N
UTAH						
1 McKay	N	N	Y	Y	Y	N
2 Marriott	N	N	Y	Y	Y	N
VERMONT						
AL Jeffords	N	Y	Y	Y	Y	N
VIRGINIA						
1 Trible	N	N	Y	Y	Y	Y
2 Whitehurst	N	#	Y	Y	Y	N
3 Satterfield	N	N	Y	N	N	N
4 Daniel	N	N	Y	Y	Y	N
5 Daniel	N	N	Y	Y	Y	N
6 Butler	N	Y	Y	Y	Y	N
7 Robinson	N	N	Y	Y	Y	N
8 Harris	Y	Y	Y	Y	Y	Y
9 Wampler	N	Y	Y	Y	Y	N
10 Fisher	Y	Y	Y	Y	Y	Y
WASHINGTON						
1 Pritchard	N	Y	Y	Y	Y	Y
2 Meeds	Y	Y	Y	Y	Y	Y
3 Bonker	N	Y	Y	Y	Y	Y
4 McCormack	N	Y	Y	Y	Y	✓
5 Foley	Y	Y	Y	Y	Y	Y
6 Dicks	Y	Y	Y	?	Y	Y
7 Cunningham	N	N	Y	Y	Y	N
WEST VIRGINIA						
1 Mollohan	▮	#	Y	Y	Y	N
2 Staggers	Y	Y	Y	Y	Y	Y
3 Slack	Y	Y	Y	Y	Y	Y
4 Rahall	N	Y	Y	Y	Y	Y
WISCONSIN						
1 Aspin	Y	Y	Y	Y	Y	Y
2 Kastenmeier	Y	Y	Y	Y	Y	Y
3 Baldus	Y	Y	Y	Y	Y	Y
4 Zablocki	Y	Y	Y	Y	Y	Y
5 Reuss	Y	Y	Y	Y	Y	Y
6 Steiger	N	Y	Y	#	Y	Y
7 Obey	Y	Y	Y	Y	Y	Y
8 Cornell	Y	Y	Y	Y	Y	Y
9 Kasten	N	Y	Y	Y	Y	Y
WYOMING						
AL Roncalio	Y	Y	?	?	Y	Y

Democrats ***Republicans***

79. Procedural Motion. Bauman, R-Md., motion to approve the House *Journal* for Thursday, March 2, 1978. Motion agreed to 304-20: R 102-19; D 202-1 (ND 140-1; SD 62-0), March 3, 1978.

80. H Res 957. Veterans' Affairs Committee. Adoption of the resolution to authorize $400,000 for calendar year 1978 for expenses of investigations and studies of the House Committee on Veterans' Affairs. Adopted 336-1: R 122-1; D 214-0 (ND 149-0; SD 65-0), March 3, 1978.

81. H Res 953. District of Columbia Committee. Adoption of the resolution to authorize $275,000 for calendar year 1978 for expenses of investigations and studies of the House Committee on the District of Columbia. Adopted 318-15: R 111-11; D 207-4 (ND 146-2; SD 61-2), March 3, 1978.

82. H Res 1012. Rules Committee. Adoption of the resolution to authorize $49,500 for calendar year 1978 for expenses of investigations and studies of the House Committee on Rules. Adopted 321-13: R 120-3; D 201-10 (ND 139-8; SD 62-2), March 3, 1978.

83. Procedural Motion. Ashbrook, R-Ohio, motion to approve the House *Journal* for Friday, March 3, 1978. Motion agreed to 331-11: R 111-8; D 220-3 (ND 147-2; SD 73-1), March 6, 1978.

84. H J Res 715. Sun Day Designation. Lehman, D-Fla., motion to suspend the rules and pass the joint resolution to designate May 3, 1978, as "Sun Day" to promote and call attention to the possibilities of solar energy. Motion agreed to 348-7: R 120-3; D 228-4 (ND 154-4; SD 74-0), March 6, 1978. A two-thirds majority vote (237 in this case) is required for passage under suspension of the rules.

85. HR 10551. Education Act Waiver. Perkins, D-Ky., motion to suspend the rules and pass the bill to continue fiscal 1978 funding and waive some requirements of Title I of the 1974 Elementary and Secondary Education Act for 13 school districts that participated in demonstration programs to improve operation of Title I programs. Motion agreed to 404-0: R 140-0; D 264-0 (ND 182-0; SD 82-0), March 7, 1978. A two-thirds majority vote (270 in this case) is required for passage under suspension of the rules.

KEY

- Y Voted for (yea).
- ✓ Paired for.
- † Announced for.
- # CQ Poll for.
- N Voted against (nay).
- X Paired against.
- \- Announced against.
- ▮ CQ Poll against.
- P Voted "present."
- ● Voted "present" to avoid possible conflict of interest.
- ? Did not vote or otherwise make a position known.

	79	80	81	82	83	84	85
ALABAMA							
1 Edwards	Y	Y	Y	Y	Y	Y	Y
2 Dickinson	Y	Y	Y	Y	Y	Y	Y
3 Nichols	Y	Y	Y	Y	Y	Y	Y
4 Bevill	Y	Y	Y	Y	Y	Y	Y
5 Flippo	Y	Y	Y	Y	Y	Y	Y
6 Buchanan	Y	Y	Y	Y	Y	?	?
7 Flowers	Y	Y	Y	Y	Y	Y	Y
ALASKA							
AL Young	Y	Y	Y	Y	Y	Y	Y
ARIZONA							
1 Rhodes	?	?	?	?	?	?	Y
2 Udall	Y	Y	Y	Y	Y	Y	#
3 Stump	?	?	?	?	Y	Y	?
4 Rudd	#	#	▮	#	Y	Y	#
ARKANSAS							
1 Alexander	Y	Y	Y	Y	Y	Y	Y
2 Tucker	#	#	#	#	#	#	#
3 Hammerschmidt	?	?	?	?	Y	Y	Y
4 Thornton	?	?	?	?	?	?	?
CALIFORNIA							
1 Johnson	Y	Y	Y	Y	Y	Y	Y
2 Clausen	?	?	?	?	Y	Y	Y
3 Moss	?	?	Y	Y	Y	Y	Y
4 Leggett	#	#	#	#	Y	Y	Y
5 Burton, J.	Y	Y	Y	Y	N	Y	Y
6 Burton, P.	Y	Y	Y	Y	Y	Y	Y
7 Miller	Y	Y	Y	Y	Y	Y	Y
8 Dellums	#	Y	Y	Y	Y	Y	Y
9 Stark	Y	Y	Y	Y	Y	Y	Y
10 Edwards	Y	Y	Y	Y	Y	Y	Y
11 Ryan	Y	Y	Y	Y	Y	Y	Y
12 McCloskey	?	?	?	?	Y	Y	Y
13 Mineta	Y	Y	Y	Y	Y	Y	Y
14 McFall	?	Y	Y	N	Y	Y	Y
15 Sisk	Y	Y	Y	Y	Y	Y	Y
16 Panetta	Y	Y	Y	Y	Y	Y	Y
17 Krebs	Y	Y	Y	Y	Y	Y	Y
18 Ketchum	Y	Y	Y	Y	Y	Y	Y
19 Lagomarsino	Y	Y	Y	Y	Y	Y	Y
20 Goldwater	?	?	?	?	?	?	Y
21 Corman	Y	Y	Y	#	Y	Y	Y
22 Moorhead	Y	Y	Y	Y	Y	Y	Y
23 Beilenson	#	Y	Y	Y	Y	Y	Y
24 Waxman	Y	Y	Y	Y	Y	Y	Y
25 Roybal	Y	Y	Y	Y	#	#	Y
26 Rousselot	?	?	?	?	Y	Y	Y
27 Dornan	?	?	N	Y	Y	Y	?
28 Burke	#	#	#	#	#	#	#
29 Hawkins	Y	Y	Y	Y	Y	Y	Y
30 Danielson	Y	Y	Y	Y	Y	Y	Y
31 Wilson, C.H.	Y	Y	Y	Y	Y	Y	Y
32 Anderson	Y	Y	Y	Y	Y	Y	Y
33 Clawson	Y	Y	N	Y	Y	Y	Y
34 Hannaford	Y	Y	Y	Y	Y	Y	Y
35 Lloyd	?	?	?	?	?	?	Y
36 Brown	Y	Y	Y	Y	Y	Y	Y
37 Pettis	Y	Y	Y	Y	?	?	Y
38 Patterson	#	#	#	#	Y	Y	Y
39 Wiggins	#	Y	#	#	#	Y	Y
40 Badham	Y	Y	Y	Y	Y	N	Y
41 Wilson, B.	N	Y	Y	Y	▮	#	Y
42 Van Deerlin	?	?	?	?	?	?	Y
43 Burgener	Y	Y	Y	Y	?	Y	Y
COLORADO							
1 Schroeder	Y	Y	Y	Y	Y	Y	Y
2 Wirth	Y	Y	Y	Y	Y	Y	Y
3 Evans	Y	Y	Y	Y	#	Y	#
4 Johnson	Y	Y	Y	Y	Y	Y	Y
5 Armstrong	Y	Y	Y	N	?	?	Y
CONNECTICUT							
1 Cotter	#	#	#	#	Y	Y	Y
2 Dodd	?	?	?	?	?	?	Y
3 Giaimo	Y	Y	Y	Y	Y	Y	Y
4 McKinney	Y	Y	Y	Y	#	Y	#
5 Sarasin	N	Y	Y	Y	-	†	Y
6 Moffett	Y	Y	Y	Y	#	Y	Y
DELAWARE							
AL Evans	#	#	#	#	Y	Y	Y
FLORIDA							
1 Sikes	?	?	?	?	Y	Y	Y
2 Fuqua	#	#	#	#	Y	Y	Y
3 Bennett	Y	Y	Y	Y	Y	Y	Y
4 Chappell	#	#	#	#	Y	Y	Y
5 Kelly	Y	Y	Y	Y	Y	Y	Y
6 Young	Y	Y	Y	Y	Y	Y	Y
7 Gibbons	?	?	?	?	Y	Y	Y
8 Ireland	?	Y	Y	Y	Y	Y	Y
9 Frey	?	?	?	?	?	?	Y
10 Bafalis	Y	Y	Y	Y	Y	Y	Y
11 Rogers	?	?	?	?	Y	Y	Y
12 Burke	Y	Y	Y	Y	Y	Y	Y
13 Lehman	#	#	#	#	Y	Y	Y
14 Pepper	Y	Y	Y	Y	Y	Y	Y
15 Fascell	Y	Y	Y	Y	Y	Y	Y
GEORGIA							
1 Ginn	#	#	#	#	Y	Y	Y
2 Mathis	Y	Y	Y	Y	Y	?	Y
3 Brinkley	?	?	?	?	Y	Y	Y
4 Levitas	Y	Y	Y	Y	Y	Y	Y
5 Fowler	Y	Y	Y	Y	Y	Y	Y
6 Flynt	?	?	?	?	Y	Y	Y
7 McDonald	Y	Y	N	Y	Y	Y	Y
8 Evans	Y	Y	N	Y	Y	Y	Y
9 Jenkins	Y	Y	Y	Y	Y	Y	Y
10 Barnard	Y	Y	Y	Y	Y	Y	Y
HAWAII							
1 Heftel	Y	Y	Y	Y	#	#	Y
2 Akaka	Y	Y	Y	Y	#	#	Y
IDAHO							
1 Symms	?	?	?	?	Y	Y	Y
2 Hansen, G.	N	Y	N	Y	N	Y	Y
ILLINOIS							
1 Metcalfe	?	?	?	?	Y	Y	Y
2 Murphy	Y	Y	Y	N	#	#	Y
3 Russo	#	#	#	#	Y	Y	Y
4 Derwinski	Y	Y	Y	Y	Y	Y	Y
5 Fary	Y	Y	Y	Y	Y	Y	Y
6 Hyde	Y	Y	Y	Y	N	Y	Y
7 Collins	#	#	#	#	#	#	#
8 Rostenkowski	Y	Y	Y	Y	?	?	Y
9 Yates	Y	Y	Y	Y	Y	Y	Y
10 Mikva	Y	Y	Y	Y	Y	Y	Y
11 Annunzio	Y	Y	Y	Y	Y	Y	Y
12 Crane	#	#	#	#	Y	Y	Y
13 McClory	#	#	#	#	Y	Y	Y
14 Erlenborn	Y	Y	Y	Y	#	#	Y
15 Corcoran	Y	Y	Y	Y	Y	Y	Y
16 Anderson	#	#	#	#	Y	#	#
17 O'Brien	Y	Y	Y	Y	Y	Y	Y
18 Michel	Y	Y	Y	Y	Y	Y	Y
19 Railsback	Y	Y	Y	Y	Y	Y	Y
20 Findley	Y	Y	Y	Y	Y	Y	Y
21 Madigan	Y	Y	Y	Y	Y	Y	Y
22 Shipley	Y	Y	Y	Y	Y	Y	Y
23 Price	Y	Y	Y	Y	Y	Y	Y
24 Simon	Y	Y	Y	Y	Y	Y	Y
INDIANA							
1 Benjamin	Y	Y	Y	Y	Y	Y	Y
2 Fithian	Y	Y	Y	Y	#	#	Y
3 Brademas	Y	Y	Y	Y	Y	Y	Y
4 Quayle	N	N	N	Y	N	Y	Y
5 Hillis	Y	Y	Y	Y	Y	Y	Y
6 Evans	?	?	?	?	Y	Y	Y
7 Myers, J.	Y	Y	Y	Y	Y	Y	Y
8 Cornwell	#	Y	N	Y	Y	Y	Y
9 Hamilton	Y	Y	Y	Y	Y	Y	Y
10 Sharp	Y	Y	Y	Y	Y	Y	Y
11 Jacobs	N	Y	Y	Y	N	Y	Y
IOWA							
1 Leach	N	Y	Y	Y	#	#	Y
2 Blouin	#	#	#	#	Y	Y	Y
3 Grassley	Y	Y	Y	Y	Y	Y	Y
4 Smith	Y	Y	Y	Y	Y	Y	Y
5 Harkin	Y	Y	Y	Y	Y	Y	Y
6 Bedell	Y	Y	Y	Y	Y	Y	Y

Democrats ***Republicans***

	79	80	81	82	83	84	85
KANSAS							
1 Sebelius	Y	Y	Y	Y	P	Y	Y
2 Keys	Y	Y	Y	Y	Y	Y	Y
3 Winn	Y	Y	Y	Y	Y	Y	Y
4 Glickman	Y	Y	Y	Y	Y	Y	Y
5 Skubitz	Y	Y	Y	Y	?	Y	Y
KENTUCKY							
1 Hubbard	Y	Y	Y	Y	Y	Y	Y
2 Natcher	Y	Y	Y	Y	Y	Y	Y
3 Mazzoli	†	†	†	†	Y	Y	Y
4 Snyder	Y	Y	Y	Y	Y	Y	Y
5 Carter	Y	Y	Y	Y	Y	Y	Y
6 Breckinridge	Y	Y	Y	Y	Y	Y	Y
7 Perkins	Y	Y	Y	Y	Y	Y	Y
LOUISIANA							
1 Livingston	Y	Y	Y	Y	Y	Y	?
2 Boggs	Y	Y	Y	Y	Y	#	Y
3 Treen	N	Y	Y	Y	Y	N	Y
4 Waggonner	Y	#	#	Y	Y	Y	Y
5 Huckaby	Y	Y	Y	Y	Y	Y	Y
6 Moore	Y	Y	Y	Y	Y	Y	Y
7 Breaux	Y	Y	Y	Y	Y	Y	Y
8 Long	Y	Y	Y	N	?	?	Y
MAINE							
1 Emery	Y	Y	Y	Y	Y	Y	Y
2 Cohen	Y	Y	Y	Y	Y	?	Y
MARYLAND							
1 Bauman	Y	Y	N	Y	Y	Y	Y
2 Long	Y	Y	Y	Y	Y	Y	Y
3 Mikulski	Y	Y	Y	Y	?	Y	Y
4 Holt	Y	Y	Y	Y	Y	Y	Y
5 Spellman	Y	Y	Y	Y	Y	Y	Y
6 Byron	Y	Y	Y	Y	Y	Y	Y
7 Mitchell	Y	Y	Y	Y	■	Y	Y
8 Steers	Y	Y	Y	Y	Y	Y	#
MASSACHUSETTS							
1 Conte	Y	Y	Y	Y	Y	Y	Y
2 Boland	#	#	#	#	Y	Y	Y
3 Early	Y	Y	Y	Y	Y	Y	?
4 Drinan	Y	Y	Y	Y	Y	Y	Y
5 Tsongas	Y	Y	Y	Y	#	Y	Y
6 Harrington	#	#	#	#	#	#	#
7 Markey	Y	Y	Y	Y	Y	Y	Y
8 O'Neill							
9 Moakley	Y	Y	Y	Y	Y	Y	Y
10 Heckler	N	Y	Y	Y	?	Y	Y
11 Burke	?	Y	Y	Y	Y	Y	Y
12 Studds	Y	Y	Y	Y	Y	Y	Y
MICHIGAN							
1 Conyers	#	#	#	#	#	#	Y
2 Pursell	Y	Y	N	Y	?	Y	Y
3 Brown	N	Y	Y	Y	N	Y	Y
4 Stockman	N	Y	#	Y	#	Y	Y
5 Sawyer	#	#	#	#	Y	Y	Y
6 Carr	Y	Y	Y	Y	Y	Y	Y
7 Kildee	Y	Y	Y	Y	Y	Y	Y
8 Traxler	Y	Y	Y	Y	Y	Y	Y
9 Vander Jagt	Y	Y	Y	Y	Y	?	Y
10 Cederberg	Y	Y	Y	Y	#	Y	Y
11 Ruppe	#	#	#	#	#	#	Y
12 Bonior	Y	Y	Y	Y	Y	Y	Y
13 Diggs	Y	#	#	#	#	#	#
14 Nedzi	Y	Y	Y	Y	Y	Y	Y
15 Ford	?	?	?	?	?	?	Y
16 Dingell	?	?	?	?	Y	Y	?
17 Brodhead	Y	Y	Y	Y	Y	Y	Y
18 Blanchard	#	#	#	#	Y	Y	Y
19 Broomfield	Y	Y	Y	Y	Y	Y	Y
MINNESOTA							
1 Quie	#	#	#	#	#	#	Y
2 Hagedorn	Y	Y	Y	Y	Y	Y	Y
3 Frenzel	Y	Y	Y	Y	Y	Y	Y
4 Vento	Y	Y	Y	Y	Y	Y	Y
5 Fraser	Y	Y	Y	Y	#	#	Y
6 Nolan	Y	Y	Y	Y	Y	Y	Y
7 Stangeland	Y	Y	Y	Y	Y	Y	Y
8 Oberstar	Y	Y	Y	Y	Y	Y	Y
MISSISSIPPI							
1 Whitten	Y	Y	Y	Y	Y	Y	Y
2 Bowen	Y	Y	Y	Y	Y	Y	Y
3 Montgomery	Y	Y	Y	Y	Y	Y	Y
4 Cochran	#	#	#	#	Y	Y	Y
5 Lott	Y	Y	Y	N	Y	Y	Y
MISSOURI							
1 Clay	?	?	?	?	Y	Y	Y
2 Young	Y	Y	Y	Y	Y	Y	Y
3 Gephardt	Y	Y	#	Y	Y	#	#
4 Skelton	Y	Y	Y	Y	Y	Y	Y
5 Bolling	Y	Y	Y	N	Y	Y	Y
6 Coleman	Y	Y	Y	Y	Y	Y	Y
7 Taylor	N	Y	Y	Y	Y	Y	Y
8 Ichord	Y	Y	Y	Y	Y	Y	Y
9 Volkmer	Y	Y	Y	Y	Y	Y	Y
10 Burlison	Y	Y	Y	Y	Y	Y	Y
MONTANA							
1 Baucus	#	#	#	#	Y	Y	Y
2 Marlenee	Y	Y	Y	Y	Y	Y	Y
NEBRASKA							
1 Thone	Y	Y	Y	Y	Y	Y	Y
2 Cavanaugh	Y	Y	Y	Y	Y	Y	Y
3 Smith	Y	Y	Y	Y	Y	Y	Y
NEVADA							
AL Santini	#	#	#	#	#	#	Y
NEW HAMPSHIRE							
1 D'Amours	Y	Y	Y	Y	Y	Y	Y
2 Cleveland	Y	Y	Y	Y	#	#	Y
NEW JERSEY							
1 Florio	Y	Y	Y	Y	Y	Y	Y
2 Hughes	Y	Y	Y	Y	Y	Y	Y
3 Howard	#	#	#	#	#	#	Y
4 Thompson	Y	Y	Y	Y	Y	Y	Y
5 Fenwick	Y	Y	Y	Y	Y	Y	Y
6 Forsythe	N	Y	Y	Y	N	Y	Y
7 Maguire	Y	Y	Y	Y	Y	Y	Y
8 Roe	Y	Y	Y	Y	Y	Y	Y
9 Hollenbeck	Y	Y	Y	Y	Y	Y	Y
10 Rodino	Y	Y	Y	Y	Y	Y	Y
11 Minish	Y	Y	Y	Y	Y	Y	Y
12 Rinaldo	Y	Y	Y	Y	Y	Y	Y
13 Meyner	#	#	#	#	Y	Y	Y
14 LeFante	#	#	#	#	Y	Y	Y
15 Patten	Y	Y	Y	Y	#	#	Y
NEW MEXICO							
1 Lujan	Y	Y	Y	Y	Y	Y	Y
2 Runnels	?	?	?	?	?	?	Y
NEW YORK							
1 Pike	Y	Y	Y	Y	Y	N	Y
2 Downey	Y	Y	Y	Y	Y	Y	Y
3 Ambro	?	?	?	?	?	Y	Y
4 Lent	#	#	#	#	Y	Y	Y
5 Wydler	?	?	?	?	Y	?	Y
6 Wolff	Y	Y	Y	N	Y	Y	Y
7 Addabbo	#	#	#	#	#	#	Y
8 Rosenthal	Y	Y	Y	Y	Y	Y	Y
9 Delaney	Y	Y	Y	N	Y	Y	Y
10 Biaggi	Y	Y	Y	N	#	#	Y
11 Scheuer	Y	Y	Y	Y	Y	Y	Y
12 Chisholm	#	#	#	#	Y	Y	Y
13 Solarz	Y	Y	Y	Y	#	Y	Y
14 Richmond	?	?	?	?	?	?	Y
15 Zeferetti	#	#	#	#	#	#	Y
16 Holtzman	Y	Y	Y	Y	Y	Y	Y
17 Murphy	Y	Y	Y	Y	Y	#	Y
18 Green	Y	Y	Y	Y	Y	Y	Y
19 Rangel	Y	Y	Y	N	Y	Y	Y
20 Weiss	?	?	?	?	Y	Y	Y
21 Garcia	Y	Y	Y	Y	?	?	Y
22 Bingham	Y	Y	Y	Y	#	Y	Y
23 Caputo	Y	Y	Y	Y	Y	Y	Y
24 Ottinger	Y	Y	Y	Y	Y	Y	Y
25 Fish	Y	Y	Y	Y	?	?	Y
26 Gilman	?	†	†	†	Y	Y	Y
27 McHugh	Y	Y	Y	Y	Y	Y	Y
28 Stratton	Y	Y	Y	N	Y	N	Y
29 Pattison	#	#	#	#	Y	Y	Y
30 McEwen	Y	Y	Y	Y	?	?	Y
31 Mitchell	Y	Y	Y	Y	#	Y	Y
32 Hanley	#	#	#	#	Y	Y	Y
33 Walsh	Y	Y	Y	Y	Y	Y	Y
34 Horton	Y	Y	Y	Y	Y	Y	Y
35 Conable	N	Y	Y	Y	Y	?	Y
36 LaFalce	?	?	?	?	Y	Y	Y
37 Nowak	Y	Y	Y	Y	#	#	Y
38 Kemp	Y	Y	Y	Y	Y	Y	Y
39 Lundine	Y	Y	Y	#	Y	Y	Y
NORTH CAROLINA							
1 Jones	Y	Y	#	Y	#	#	Y
2 Fountain	Y	Y	Y	Y	Y	Y	Y
3 Whitley	Y	Y	Y	Y	Y	Y	Y
4 Andrews	Y	Y	Y	Y	Y	Y	Y
5 Neal	Y	Y	Y	Y	Y	Y	Y
6 Preyer	Y	Y	Y	Y	Y	Y	Y
7 Rose	Y	Y	Y	Y	Y	Y	Y
8 Hefner	Y	Y	Y	Y	Y	Y	Y
9 Martin	N	Y	Y	Y	Y	Y	Y
10 Broyhill	Y	Y	Y	Y	Y	Y	Y
11 Gudger	#	Y	Y	Y	#	#	Y
NORTH DAKOTA							
AL Andrews	Y	Y	Y	Y	Y	Y	Y
OHIO							
1 Gradison	Y	Y	Y	N	Y	Y	Y
2 Luken	#	Y	N	Y	#	#	Y
3 Whalen	Y	Y	Y	Y	Y	Y	Y
4 Guyer	Y	Y	Y	Y	#	#	Y
5 Latta	Y	Y	Y	Y	Y	Y	Y
6 Harsha	Y	Y	Y	Y	Y	Y	Y
7 Brown	Y	Y	Y	Y	Y	Y	Y
8 Kindness	Y	Y	Y	Y	Y	Y	Y
9 Ashley	?	Y	Y	Y	Y	Y	Y
10 Miller	Y	Y	N	Y	Y	Y	Y
11 Stanton	Y	Y	Y	Y	Y	Y	Y
12 Devine	Y	Y	Y	Y	Y	Y	Y
13 Pease	Y	Y	Y	Y	P	Y	Y
14 Seiberling	Y	Y	Y	Y	#	#	Y
15 Wylie	Y	Y	Y	Y	Y	Y	Y
16 Regula	Y	Y	Y	Y	Y	Y	Y
17 Ashbrook	N	Y	N	Y	Y	Y	Y
18 Applegate	Y	Y	Y	Y	Y	Y	Y
19 Carney	#	#	#	#	Y	Y	Y
20 Oakar	Y	Y	Y	Y	?	?	Y
21 Stokes	Y	Y	Y	Y	#	Y	Y
22 Vanik	Y	Y	Y	Y	Y	Y	Y
23 Mottl	Y	Y	Y	Y	#	#	Y
OKLAHOMA							
1 Jones	#	#	#	#	N	Y	Y
2 Risenhoover	?	?	?	?	Y	Y	Y
3 Watkins	Y	Y	Y	Y	Y	Y	Y
4 Steed	Y	Y	Y	Y	Y	Y	Y
5 Edwards	?	?	?	?	Y	Y	Y
6 English	Y	Y	Y	Y	Y	Y	Y
OREGON							
1 AuCoin	Y	Y	Y	Y	Y	Y	Y
2 Ullman	#	Y	Y	Y	Y	Y	Y
3 Duncan	Y	Y	Y	Y	?	?	?
4 Weaver	Y	Y	Y	Y	Y	Y	Y
PENNSYLVANIA							
1 Myers, M.	?	?	?	?	?	?	Y
2 Nix	Y	Y	Y	Y	#	#	#
3 Lederer	?	?	?	?	Y	Y	Y
4 Eilberg	#	#	#	#	Y	Y	Y
5 Schulze	Y	Y	Y	Y	Y	Y	Y
6 Yatron	Y	Y	Y	Y	Y	Y	Y
7 Edgar	#	#	#	#	Y	Y	Y
8 Kostmayer	†	†	†	†	Y	Y	Y
9 Shuster	N	Y	N	Y	Y	Y	Y
10 McDade	?	Y	Y	Y	Y	Y	Y
11 Flood	Y	Y	Y	?	Y	Y	Y
12 Murtha	Y	Y	Y	Y	Y	Y	Y
13 Coughlin	N	Y	Y	Y	N	Y	Y
14 Moorhead	Y	Y	Y	Y	Y	Y	Y
15 Rooney	Y	Y	Y	Y	Y	Y	Y
16 Walker	N	Y	Y	Y	N	Y	Y
17 Ertel	Y	Y	Y	Y	Y	Y	Y
18 Walgren	Y	Y	#	Y	Y	Y	Y
19 Goodling, W.	N	Y	Y	Y	?	?	Y
20 Gaydos	Y	Y	Y	Y	Y	Y	Y
21 Dent	#	#	#	#	Y	Y	Y
22 Murphy	Y	Y	Y	Y	#	#	Y
23 Ammerman	Y	Y	Y	Y	Y	Y	Y
24 Marks	Y	Y	Y	Y	Y	Y	Y
25 Myers, G.	Y	Y	Y	Y	Y	N	Y
RHODE ISLAND							
1 St Germain	?	?	?	?	?	?	Y
2 Beard	Y	Y	Y	Y	?	Y	Y
SOUTH CAROLINA							
1 Davis	Y	Y	Y	Y	Y	Y	Y
2 Spence	Y	Y	Y	Y	Y	Y	Y
3 Derrick	Y	Y	Y	Y	Y	Y	Y
4 Mann	Y	Y	Y	Y	?	?	Y
5 Holland	Y	Y	Y	Y	#	#	Y
6 Jenrette	Y	Y	Y	Y	?	#	Y
SOUTH DAKOTA							
1 Pressler	Y	Y	Y	Y	Y	Y	Y
2 Abdnor	Y	Y	Y	Y	Y	Y	Y
TENNESSEE							
1 Quillen	#	#	#	#	Y	Y	Y
2 Duncan	Y	Y	Y	Y	Y	Y	Y
3 Lloyd	Y	Y	Y	Y	Y	Y	Y
4 Gore	Y	Y	Y	Y	Y	Y	Y
5 Allen	Y	Y	Y	Y	Y	Y	Y
6 Beard	Y	Y	Y	Y	Y	Y	Y
7 Jones	#	#	#	#	Y	Y	Y
8 Ford	Y	Y	Y	Y	Y	Y	Y
TEXAS							
1 Hall	Y	Y	Y	Y	Y	Y	Y
2 Wilson, C.	Y	Y	Y	Y	Y	Y	Y
3 Collins	Y	Y	N	Y	Y	Y	Y
4 Roberts	?	?	?	?	Y	Y	Y
5 Mattox	Y	Y	Y	Y	Y	Y	Y
6 Teague	?	?	?	?	?	?	?
7 Archer	Y	Y	Y	Y	Y	?	Y
8 Eckhardt	Y	Y	Y	Y	?	?	Y
9 Brooks	Y	Y	Y	Y	Y	Y	Y
10 Pickle	Y	Y	Y	Y	Y	Y	Y
11 Poage	Y	Y	Y	Y	?	Y	Y
12 Wright	?	Y	?	?	Y	Y	Y
13 Hightower	Y	Y	Y	Y	Y	Y	Y
14 Young	?	?	?	?	?	?	?
15 de la Garza	?	?	?	?	Y	Y	Y
16 White	Y	Y	Y	Y	Y	Y	Y
17 Burleson	Y	Y	Y	Y	Y	Y	Y
18 Jordan	Y	Y	Y	Y	Y	Y	Y
19 Mahon	#	#	#	#	Y	Y	#
20 Gonzalez	Y	Y	Y	N	?	Y	P
21 Krueger	#	#	#	#	#	#	#
22 Gammage	?	?	?	?	?	?	Y
23 Kazen	?	?	?	?	Y	Y	Y
24 Milford	?	Y	Y	?	Y	Y	Y
UTAH							
1 McKay	Y	Y	Y	Y	Y	N	Y
2 Marriott	Y	Y	Y	Y	Y	Y	Y
VERMONT							
AL Jeffords	#	#	#	#	#	#	Y
VIRGINIA							
1 Trible	Y	Y	N	Y	Y	Y	Y
2 Whitehurst	Y	Y	Y	Y	Y	Y	Y
3 Satterfield	?	?	?	?	Y	Y	Y
4 Daniel	Y	Y	Y	Y	Y	Y	Y
5 Daniel	Y	Y	Y	Y	Y	Y	Y
6 Butler	Y	Y	Y	Y	Y	Y	Y
7 Robinson	Y	Y	Y	Y	Y	Y	Y
8 Harris	Y	Y	Y	Y	Y	Y	Y
9 Wampler	Y	Y	Y	Y	?	Y	Y
10 Fisher	Y	Y	Y	Y	?	†	-
WASHINGTON							
1 Pritchard	Y	Y	Y	Y	N	Y	Y
2 Meeds	Y	Y	Y	Y	Y	Y	Y
3 Bonker	Y	Y	Y	Y	Y	Y	#
4 McCormack	Y	Y	Y	Y	Y	Y	Y
5 Foley	?	Y	Y	Y	?	?	Y
6 Dicks	Y	Y	Y	Y	Y	Y	Y
7 Cunningham	Y	Y	Y	Y	Y	Y	Y
WEST VIRGINIA							
1 Mollohan	Y	Y	Y	Y	Y	Y	Y
2 Staggers	Y	Y	Y	Y	Y	Y	Y
3 Slack	Y	Y	Y	Y	Y	Y	?
4 Rahall	#	#	#	#	Y	Y	Y
WISCONSIN							
1 Aspin	Y	Y	Y	Y	Y	Y	Y
2 Kastenmeier	Y	Y	Y	Y	Y	Y	Y
3 Baldus	Y	Y	Y	Y	Y	Y	Y
4 Zablocki	Y	Y	Y	Y	Y	Y	#
5 Reuss	#	#	#	#	Y	Y	Y
6 Steiger	N	Y	Y	Y	Y	Y	Y
7 Obey	Y	Y	Y	Y	Y	N	Y
8 Cornell	Y	Y	Y	Y	Y	Y	Y
9 Kasten	Y	Y	Y	Y	Y	Y	Y
WYOMING							
AL Roncalio	?	?	?	?	?	?	Y

Democrats ***Republicans***

86. HR 11180. Debt Limit. Adoption of the rule (H Res 1056) providing for House floor consideration of the bill to increase the debt limit and revise procedures for establishing it in the future. Adopted 285-115: R 50-90; D 235-25 (ND 165-13; SD 70-12), March 7, 1978.

87. HR 11180. Debt Limit. Bolling, D-Mo., amendment to delete title II, which would establish the debt limit through concurrent budget resolutions in the future. Adopted 277-132: R 107-34; D 170-98 (ND 127-59; SD 43-39), March 7, 1978.

88. HR 11180. Debt Limit. Passage of the bill to increase the debt limit to $824 billion through March 1, 1979. Rejected 165-248: R 8-133; D 157-115 (ND 135-54; SD 22-61), March 7, 1978. A "yea" was a vote supporting the president's position.

89. H J Res 746. Power Supplemental Appropriations, Fiscal 1978. Passage of the joint resolution to appropriate $13.1 million for the operation of the Southwestern Power Administration for fiscal 1978. Passed 353-50: R 96-42; D 257-8 (ND 179-5; SD 78-3), March 7, 1978. The president had requested $13.1 million.

90. H Res 1003. Public Works and Transportation Committee. Adoption of the resolution to authorize $2 million for calendar year 1978 for expenses of investigations and studies of the House Committee on Public Works and Transportation. Adopted 399-1: R 140-0; D 259-1 (ND 178-0; SD 81-1), March 7, 1978.

91. Procedural Motion. Bauman, R-Md., demand for the yeas and nays on the question of dispensing with further proceedings under a quorum call. Proceedings dispensed with 372-34: R 107-32; D 265-2 (ND 185-1; SD 80-1), March 8, 1978.

92. Procedural Motion. Dickinson, R-Ala., motion to approve the House *Journal* of Tuesday, March 7, 1978. Motion agreed to 377-26: R 117-22; D 260-4 (ND 181-3; SD 79-1), March 8, 1978.

93. Procedural Motion. Bolling, D-Mo., motion to table (kill) the Zablocki, D-Wis., motion to reconsider the vote *(see vote 92, above)* approving the *Journal*. Motion agreed to 313-91: R 53-87; D 260-4 (ND 181-3; SD 79-1), March 8, 1978.

KEY

- Y Voted for (yea).
- ✓ Paired for.
- † Announced for.
- # CQ Poll for.
- N Voted against (nay).
- X Paired against.
- \- Announced against.
- ▮ CQ Poll against.
- P Voted "present."
- ● Voted "present" to avoid possible conflict of interest.
- ? Did not vote or otherwise make a position known.

	86	87	88	89	90	91	92	93
ALABAMA								
1 Edwards	Y	Y	N	Y	Y	Y	Y	N
2 Dickinson	Y	Y	N	Y	Y	Y	Y	Y
3 Nichols	Y	N	N	Y	Y	Y	Y	Y
4 Bevill	Y	N	N	Y	Y	Y	Y	Y
5 Flippo	Y	N	N	Y	Y	Y	Y	Y
6 Buchanan	#	?	X	?	?	?	?	?
7 Flowers	Y	N	N	Y	Y	Y	Y	Y
ALASKA								
AL Young	N	Y	N	Y	Y	Y	Y	▮
ARIZONA								
1 Rhodes	Y	N	N	Y	Y	Y	Y	Y
2 Udall	#	▮	#	#	#	Y	Y	Y
3 Stump	?	?	-	?	?	Y	Y	Y
4 Rudd	X	#	X	▮	?	N	N	N
ARKANSAS								
1 Alexander	Y	N	Y	Y	Y	Y	Y	Y
2 Tucker	#	#	#	?	#	#	#	#
3 Hammerschmidt	N	Y	N	Y	Y	Y	Y	Y
4 Thornton	?	?	?	?	?	?	?	?
CALIFORNIA								
1 Johnson	Y	Y	Y	Y	Y	Y	Y	Y
2 Clausen	N	Y	N	Y	Y	Y	Y	Y
3 Moss	Y	N	Y	Y	Y	Y	Y	Y
4 Leggett	#	Y	Y	Y	#	#	#	#
5 Burton, J.	Y	N	N	Y	Y	Y	Y	Y
6 Burton, P.	Y	N	Y	Y	Y	Y	Y	Y
7 Miller	Y	Y	N	Y	Y	Y	Y	Y
8 Dellums	Y	X	Y	Y	Y	Y	Y	Y
9 Stark	Y	N	Y	Y	Y	Y	Y	Y
10 Edwards	Y	N	Y	Y	?	Y	Y	Y
11 Ryan	Y	Y	Y	N	Y	Y	Y	Y
12 McCloskey	✓	N	Y	Y	Y	Y	?	?
13 Mineta	Y	Y	Y	Y	Y	Y	Y	Y
14 McFall	Y	N	Y	Y	Y	Y	Y	Y
15 Sisk	Y	Y	Y	Y	Y	?	?	?
16 Panetta	Y	Y	N	Y	Y	Y	Y	Y
17 Krebs	Y	Y	Y	Y	Y	Y	Y	Y
18 Ketchum	N	Y	N	Y	Y	Y	Y	N
19 Lagomarsino	N	Y	N	N	Y	Y	Y	N
20 Goldwater	N	Y	N	Y	Y	?	?	?
21 Corman	Y	N	Y	Y	Y	Y	Y	Y
22 Moorhead	N	Y	N	N	Y	Y	Y	N
23 Beilenson	Y	Y	Y	Y	Y	Y	Y	Y
24 Waxman	Y	N	Y	Y	Y	Y	#	?
25 Roybal	Y	N	Y	Y	Y	Y	Y	Y
26 Rousselot	N	Y	N	N	Y	N	Y	N
27 Dornan	X	?	X	?	?	Y	Y	N
28 Burke	#	X	#	#	#	#	#	#
29 Hawkins	Y	Y	Y	Y	Y	Y	Y	Y
30 Danielson	Y	Y	Y	Y	Y	Y	Y	Y
31 Wilson, C.H.	Y	Y	Y	Y	Y	Y	Y	Y
32 Anderson	Y	Y	N	Y	Y	Y	Y	Y
33 Clawson	N	Y	N	N	Y	Y	Y	N
34 Hannaford	Y	Y	Y	Y	Y	Y	Y	Y
35 Lloyd	Y	Y	N	Y	Y	Y	N	Y
36 Brown	?	Y	Y	Y	Y	Y	Y	Y
37 Pettis	Y	N	N	Y	Y	Y	Y	N
38 Patterson	Y	Y	Y	Y	Y	Y	Y	Y
39 Wiggins	Y	N	Y	Y	Y	Y	Y	Y
40 Badham	N	Y	N	Y	Y	Y	Y	N
41 Wilson, B.	Y	Y	N	Y	Y	▮	N	N
42 Van Deerlin	Y	N	Y	Y	Y	Y	Y	Y
43 Burgener	N	Y	N	Y	Y	Y	Y	N
COLORADO								
1 Schroeder	Y	N	N	Y	Y	Y	Y	Y
2 Wirth	Y	Y	N	Y	Y	Y	Y	Y
3 Evans	#	Y	Y	Y	Y	Y	Y	Y
4 Johnson	Y	Y	N	Y	Y	Y	Y	Y
5 Armstrong	N	Y	N	N	Y	N	N	N
CONNECTICUT								
1 Cotter	Y	N	Y	Y	Y	Y	Y	Y
2 Dodd	Y	Y	Y	Y	Y	Y	Y	Y
3 Giaimo	Y	N	Y	Y	Y	Y	Y	Y
4 McKinney	#	#	▮	#	#	Y	Y	Y
5 Sarasin	Y	N	N	Y	Y	Y	N	N
6 Moffett	Y	Y	N	Y	Y	Y	Y	Y
DELAWARE								
AL Evans	N	Y	N	Y	Y	Y	Y	N
FLORIDA								
1 Sikes	Y	Y	N	Y	Y	Y	Y	Y
2 Fuqua	Y	N	N	Y	Y	Y	Y	Y
3 Bennett	Y	N	N	Y	Y	Y	Y	Y
4 Chappell	#	N	N	#	Y	Y	Y	Y
5 Kelly	N	Y	N	Y	Y	N	Y	N
6 Young	N	Y	N	N	Y	N	?	N
7 Gibbons	Y	N	N	Y	Y	Y	Y	Y
8 Ireland	N	Y	N	Y	Y	Y	Y	Y
9 Frey	N	Y	N	N	Y	Y	Y	N
10 Bafalis	N	Y	N	N	Y	Y	Y	N
11 Rogers	N	N	N	Y	Y	Y	Y	Y
12 Burke	Y	Y	N	Y	Y	Y	Y	N
13 Lehman	Y	N	Y	Y	Y	Y	Y	Y
14 Pepper	Y	Y	Y	Y	Y	#	#	#
15 Fascell	Y	Y	Y	Y	Y	Y	Y	Y
GEORGIA								
1 Ginn	Y	N	N	Y	Y	Y	Y	Y
2 Mathis	Y	N	N	Y	Y	Y	Y	Y
3 Brinkley	N	N	N	Y	Y	Y	Y	Y
4 Levitas	Y	Y	N	Y	Y	Y	Y	Y
5 Fowler	Y	N	N	Y	Y	Y	Y	Y
6 Flynt	N	Y	N	Y	Y	Y	Y	Y
7 McDonald	N	Y	N	N	N	N	Y	N
8 Evans	Y	N	N	Y	Y	Y	Y	Y
9 Jenkins	Y	N	Y	Y	Y	Y	Y	Y
10 Barnard	Y	N	N	Y	Y	Y	Y	Y
HAWAII								
1 Heftel	Y	N	N	Y	Y	Y	Y	Y
2 Akaka	Y	Y	Y	Y	Y	Y	Y	Y
IDAHO								
1 Symms	N	Y	N	N	Y	N	N	N
2 Hansen, G.	N	Y	N	N	Y	N	N	N
ILLINOIS								
1 Metcalfe	Y	Y	Y	Y	Y	Y	Y	Y
2 Murphy	Y	Y	Y	Y	Y	Y	Y	Y
3 Russo	Y	Y	N	Y	Y	Y	Y	Y
4 Derwinski	N	N	Y	N	Y	Y	Y	Y
5 Fary	?	✓	✓	?	?	?	?	?
6 Hyde	Y	Y	N	Y	Y	Y	N	N
7 Collins	#	#	✓	#	#	Y	#	#
8 Rostenkowski	Y	N	Y	Y	Y	Y	Y	Y
9 Yates	Y	Y	Y	Y	Y	Y	Y	Y
10 Mikva	Y	N	Y	Y	Y	Y	Y	Y
11 Annunzio	Y	Y	Y	#	#	Y	Y	Y
12 Crane	N	Y	N	N	Y	Y	Y	N
13 McClory	N	Y	N	N	Y	Y	Y	Y
14 Erlenborn	Y	Y	N	Y	Y	Y	Y	N
15 Corcoran	N	Y	N	Y	Y	Y	Y	N
16 Anderson	✓	#	X	#	#	#	#	#
17 O'Brien	Y	Y	N	Y	Y	Y	N	N
18 Michel	N	Y	N	Y	Y	Y	Y	Y
19 Railsback	Y	Y	N	Y	Y	Y	Y	Y
20 Findley	Y	Y	Y	Y	Y	Y	Y	Y
21 Madigan	Y	N	N	Y	Y	Y	Y	Y
22 Shipley	Y	Y	Y	Y	Y	Y	Y	Y
23 Price	Y	Y	Y	Y	Y	Y	Y	Y
24 Simon	Y	N	Y	Y	Y	Y	Y	Y
INDIANA								
1 Benjamin	N	Y	N	Y	Y	Y	Y	Y
2 Fithian	Y	Y	N	Y	Y	Y	Y	Y
3 Brademas	Y	Y	Y	Y	Y	Y	Y	Y
4 Quayle	N	Y	N	N	Y	N	N	N
5 Hillis	N	Y	N	Y	Y	Y	Y	N
6 Evans	Y	Y	N	N	Y	Y	Y	Y
7 Myers, J.	N	Y	N	Y	Y	Y	Y	N
8 Cornwell	Y	Y	Y	Y	Y	Y	Y	Y
9 Hamilton	Y	N	Y	Y	Y	Y	Y	Y
10 Sharp	Y	N	Y	Y	Y	Y	Y	Y
11 Jacobs	Y	Y	N	Y	Y	Y	N	N
IOWA								
1 Leach	N	Y	N	Y	Y	Y	N	Y
2 Blouin	Y	N	Y	Y	Y	#	Y	Y
3 Grassley	N	Y	N	Y	Y	Y	Y	N
4 Smith	Y	Y	Y	Y	Y	Y	Y	Y
5 Harkin	Y	Y	N	Y	Y	Y	Y	Y
6 Bedell	Y	Y	Y	Y	Y	Y	Y	Y

Democrats ***Republicans***

Corresponding to Congressional Record Votes 108, 110, 111, 112, 113, 115, 116, 117

	86	87	88	89	90	91	92	93
KANSAS								
1 Sebelius	N	N	N	Y	Y	Y	Y	Y
2 Keys	Y	N	Y	Y	Y	Y	Y	Y
3 Winn	Y	Y	N	Y	Y	Y	Y	N
4 Glickman	N	Y	N	Y	Y	Y	Y	Y
5 Skubitz	Y	Y	N	Y	Y	Y	Y	Y
KENTUCKY								
1 Hubbard	Y	N	N	Y	Y	Y	Y	Y
2 Natcher	Y	Y	N	Y	Y	Y	Y	Y
3 Mazzoli	Y	Y	N	Y	Y	Y	Y	Y
4 Snyder	N	Y	N	Y	Y	Y	Y	N
5 Carter	Y	Y	N	Y	Y	Y	Y	Y
6 Breckinridge	Y	Y	Y	Y	Y	Y	Y	Y
7 Perkins	Y	Y	Y	Y	Y	Y	Y	Y
LOUISIANA								
1 Livingston	Y	Y	N	N	Y	N	Y	Y
2 Boggs	Y	Y	Y	Y	Y	Y	Y	Y
3 Treen	Y	?	?	Y	Y	Y	Y	Y
4 Waggonner	Y	N	Y	Y	Y	Y	Y	Y
5 Huckaby	Y	N	N	#	Y	Y	Y	Y
6 Moore	N	Y	N	Y	Y	Y	Y	Y
7 Breaux	Y	Y	N	Y	Y	Y	Y	Y
8 Long	Y	Y	Y	Y	Y	Y	Y	Y
MAINE								
1 Emery	N	Y	N	Y	Y	Y	Y	Y
2 Cohen	Y	Y	N	Y	Y	Y	Y	Y
MARYLAND								
1 Bauman	N	Y	N	N	Y	N	N	N
2 Long	Y	Y	Y	Y	?	Y	Y	Y
3 Mikulski	Y	Y	N	Y	Y	Y	Y	Y
4 Holt	N	Y	N	N	Y	Y	Y	N
5 Spellman	Y	N	Y	Y	Y	Y	Y	Y
6 Byron	N	Y	N	Y	Y	Y	Y	Y
7 Mitchell	Y	Y	Y	Y	Y	N	N	Y
8 Steers	Y	N	Y	Y	Y	Y	Y	Y
MASSACHUSETTS								
1 Conte	Y	N	Y	N	Y	Y	Y	Y
2 Boland	Y	Y	Y	Y	Y	Y	Y	Y
3 Early	?	?	?	?	?	Y	Y	Y
4 Drinan	Y	Y	Y	Y	Y	Y	Y	Y
5 Tsongas	Y	Y	Y	Y	Y	Y	Y	Y
6 Harrington	Y	N	Y	Y	Y	Y	Y	Y
7 Markey	Y	Y	Y	Y	Y	Y	Y	Y
8 O'Neill								
9 Moakley	Y	Y	Y	Y	Y	Y	Y	Y
10 Heckler	Y	N	N	?	Y	?	?	Y
11 Burke	Y	Y	Y	Y	Y	Y	Y	Y
12 Studds	Y	Y	Y	Y	Y	Y	Y	Y
MICHIGAN								
1 Conyers	Y	Y	Y	Y	#	Y	Y	Y
2 Pursell	?	Y	N	Y	Y	Y	Y	Y
3 Brown	N	N	N	Y	Y	Y	N	N
4 Stockman	N	Y	N	▮	Y	Y	Y	N
5 Sawyer	Y	Y	N	Y	Y	Y	Y	N
6 Carr	Y	N	N	Y	Y	Y	Y	Y
7 Kildee	†	Y	Y	Y	Y	Y	Y	Y
8 Traxler	Y	N	Y	Y	Y	Y	Y	Y
9 Vander Jagt	Y	N	N	Y	Y	Y	Y	N
10 Cederberg	Y	Y	N	Y	Y	Y	Y	N
11 Ruppe	Y	Y	N	N	Y	N	Y	N
12 Bonior	#	N	Y	?	Y	Y	Y	Y
13 Diggs	#	Y	Y	#	Y	Y	Y	Y
14 Nedzi	?	Y	Y	Y	Y	Y	Y	Y
15 Ford	Y	Y	Y	Y	Y	Y	Y	Y
16 Dingell	Y	Y	Y	Y	Y	Y	Y	Y
17 Brodhead	?	N	Y	Y	Y	Y	Y	Y
18 Blanchard	Y	Y	Y	Y	Y	Y	Y	Y
19 Broomfield	N	Y	N	N	Y	Y	Y	N
MINNESOTA								
1 Quie	Y	N	N	Y	Y	Y	Y	Y
2 Hagedorn	Y	Y	N	Y	Y	Y	Y	Y
3 Frenzel	Y	N	N	N	Y	Y	Y	N
4 Vento	Y	Y	Y	N	Y	Y	Y	Y
5 Fraser	Y	Y	Y	#	#	Y	Y	Y
6 Nolan	Y	Y	Y	Y	Y	Y	Y	Y
7 Stangeland	Y	Y	N	Y	Y	Y	Y	N
8 Oberstar	Y	N	Y	Y	Y	Y	Y	Y
MISSISSIPPI								
1 Whitten	Y	Y	N	Y	Y	Y	Y	Y
2 Bowen	Y	Y	N	Y	Y	Y	Y	Y
3 Montgomery	Y	Y	N	Y	Y	Y	Y	Y
4 Cochran	N	Y	N	Y	Y	Y	Y	N
5 Lott	N	Y	N	Y	Y	N	Y	N
MISSOURI								
1 Clay	Y	Y	Y	Y	Y	?	?	?
2 Young	Y	N	N	Y	Y	Y	Y	Y
3 Gephardt	Y	N	Y	Y	Y	Y	Y	Y
4 Skelton	Y	Y	N	Y	#	Y	Y	Y
5 Bolling	Y	Y	Y	Y	Y	Y	Y	Y
6 Coleman	N	Y	N	Y	Y	N	Y	Y
7 Taylor	N	Y	N	Y	Y	N	Y	N
8 Ichord	N	Y	N	Y	Y	Y	Y	N
9 Volkmer	Y	Y	N	Y	Y	Y	Y	Y
10 Burlison	Y	Y	Y	Y	Y	Y	Y	Y
MONTANA								
1 Baucus	Y	Y	N	Y	Y	Y	Y	Y
2 Marlenee	N	Y	N	N	Y	Y	Y	N
NEBRASKA								
1 Thone	N	N	N	Y	Y	Y	Y	Y
2 Cavanaugh	Y	Y	N	Y	Y	Y	Y	Y
3 Smith	N	N	N	Y	Y	Y	Y	Y
NEVADA								
AL Santini	Y	Y	N	Y	Y	Y	Y	Y
NEW HAMPSHIRE								
1 D'Amours	Y	Y	N	Y	Y	Y	Y	Y
2 Cleveland	Y	Y	N	Y	Y	Y	Y	N
NEW JERSEY								
1 Florio	Y	Y	N	Y	Y	Y	Y	Y
2 Hughes	N	Y	N	Y	Y	Y	Y	Y
3 Howard	Y	Y	Y	Y	Y	Y	Y	Y
4 Thompson	#	Y	Y	Y	Y	Y	Y	Y
5 Fenwick	N	Y	N	N	Y	Y	Y	N
6 Forsythe	Y	N	N	N	Y	Y	N	N
7 Maguire	Y	N	N	Y	Y	Y	Y	Y
8 Roe	Y	Y	N	Y	Y	Y	Y	Y
9 Hollenbeck	N	Y	N	Y	Y	Y	Y	Y
10 Rodino	Y	Y	Y	Y	Y	Y	Y	Y
11 Minish	Y	Y	N	Y	Y	Y	Y	Y
12 Rinaldo	N	Y	N	Y	Y	Y	Y	Y
13 Meyner	Y	Y	Y	Y	Y	Y	Y	Y
14 LeFante	Y	Y	N	Y	Y	Y	Y	Y
15 Patten	Y	N	Y	Y	Y	Y	Y	Y
NEW MEXICO								
1 Lujan	N	Y	N	Y	Y	N	Y	N
2 Runnels	N	Y	N	Y	Y	Y	Y	Y
NEW YORK								
1 Pike	Y	Y	N	Y	Y	Y	Y	Y
2 Downey	Y	Y	N	Y	Y	Y	Y	Y
3 Ambro	Y	Y	N	Y	Y	Y	Y	Y
4 Lent	N	N	N	Y	Y	Y	Y	Y
5 Wydler	N	Y	N	N	N	Y	Y	Y
6 Wolff	Y	Y	N	Y	Y	Y	Y	#
7 Addabbo	Y	Y	Y	Y	Y	Y	Y	Y
8 Rosenthal	Y	N	Y	Y	Y	Y	Y	Y
9 Delaney	Y	Y	Y	Y	Y	Y	Y	Y
10 Biaggi	Y	Y	Y	Y	Y	Y	Y	Y
11 Scheuer	Y	Y	Y	Y	Y	Y	Y	Y
12 Chisholm	Y	Y	Y	Y	Y	Y	Y	Y
13 Solarz	Y	Y	Y	Y	Y	Y	Y	Y
14 Richmond	Y	Y	Y	Y	Y	Y	Y	Y
15 Zeferetti	N	N	Y	Y	Y	Y	Y	Y
16 Holtzman	Y	Y	Y	Y	Y	Y	Y	Y
17 Murphy	Y	Y	Y	Y	Y	Y	Y	Y
18 Green	Y	Y	Y	Y	Y	N	Y	N
19 Rangel	Y	N	Y	Y	Y	Y	Y	Y
20 Weiss	Y	N	Y	Y	Y	Y	Y	Y
21 Garcia	?	Y	Y	Y	Y	?	Y	Y
22 Bingham	Y	Y	Y	Y	Y	Y	Y	Y
23 Caputo	N	Y	N	Y	Y	Y	Y	Y
24 Ottinger	Y	N	Y	N	Y	Y	Y	Y
25 Fish	Y	N	N	Y	Y	?	?	?
26 Gilman	Y	Y	N	Y	Y	Y	Y	Y
27 McHugh	Y	N	Y	Y	Y	Y	Y	Y
28 Stratton	Y	Y	Y	Y	Y	Y	Y	Y
29 Pattison	#	N	Y	Y	Y	Y	Y	Y
30 McEwen	Y	N	N	Y	Y	Y	Y	Y
31 Mitchell	Y	N	N	Y	Y	Y	Y	Y
32 Hanley	Y	Y	N	Y	Y	Y	Y	Y
33 Walsh	Y	Y	N	Y	Y	Y	Y	Y
34 Horton	N	Y	N	Y	Y	Y	Y	Y
35 Conable	Y	N	N	Y	Y	Y	N	N
36 LaFalce	Y	N	N	Y	Y	Y	Y	Y
37 Nowak	Y	Y	Y	Y	Y	Y	Y	Y
38 Kemp	Y	Y	N	Y	Y	N	N	Y
39 Lundine	Y	Y	Y	Y	#	Y	Y	Y
NORTH CAROLINA								
1 Jones	Y	N	N	Y	Y	Y	Y	Y
2 Fountain	Y	Y	N	Y	Y	Y	Y	Y
3 Whitley	Y	N	N	Y	Y	Y	Y	Y
4 Andrews	Y	Y	N	Y	Y	#	#	#
5 Neal	N	N	N	Y	Y	Y	Y	#
6 Preyer	Y	Y	Y	Y	Y	Y	Y	Y
7 Rose	Y	Y	Y	Y	Y	Y	Y	Y
8 Hefner	Y	N	N	Y	Y	Y	Y	Y
9 Martin	N	Y	N	N	Y	Y	Y	N
10 Broyhill	Y	N	N	N	Y	Y	Y	Y
11 Gudger	Y	Y	N	Y	Y	Y	Y	Y
NORTH DAKOTA								
AL Andrews	N	N	N	Y	Y	Y	Y	Y
OHIO								
1 Gradison	N	N	N	Y	Y	Y	Y	Y
2 Luken	N	N	N	Y	Y	Y	Y	Y
3 Whalen	Y	Y	Y	Y	Y	Y	Y	Y
4 Guyer	N	Y	N	Y	Y	N	Y	N
5 Latta	N	Y	N	N	Y	Y	Y	Y
6 Harsha	N	Y	N	Y	Y	Y	Y	N
7 Brown	N	N	N	Y	Y	Y	Y	N
8 Kindness	N	Y	N	N	Y	N	Y	N
9 Ashley	Y	N	Y	Y	?	Y	Y	Y
10 Miller	N	Y	N	N	Y	Y	Y	Y
11 Stanton	Y	Y	N	Y	Y	Y	Y	N
12 Devine	N	Y	N	N	Y	N	Y	N
13 Pease	Y	Y	Y	Y	Y	Y	Y	Y
14 Seiberling	Y	N	Y	Y	Y	Y	Y	Y
15 Wylie	N	Y	N	Y	Y	Y	Y	N
16 Regula	N	Y	N	N	Y	Y	N	Y
17 Ashbrook	N	Y	N	N	Y	N	Y	Y
18 Applegate	Y	Y	N	Y	Y	Y	Y	Y
19 Carney	Y	Y	Y	Y	Y	Y	Y	Y
20 Oakar	Y	?	Y	Y	Y	Y	Y	Y
21 Stokes	Y	N	Y	Y	Y	Y	Y	Y
22 Vanik	Y	N	Y	Y	Y	Y	Y	Y
23 Mottl	N	N	N	Y	Y	Y	Y	Y
OKLAHOMA								
1 Jones	Y	N	N	Y	Y	Y	Y	Y
2 Risenhoover	Y	Y	N	Y	Y	Y	Y	Y
3 Watkins	Y	Y	N	Y	Y	Y	Y	Y
4 Steed	Y	Y	Y	Y	Y	Y	Y	Y
5 Edwards	N	Y	N	Y	Y	Y	Y	N
6 English	Y	Y	N	Y	Y	Y	Y	Y
OREGON								
1 AuCoin	Y	Y	N	Y	Y	Y	Y	Y
2 Ullman	Y	N	Y	Y	Y	Y	Y	Y
3 Duncan	Y	N	Y	Y	?	Y	Y	Y
4 Weaver	Y	N	Y	Y	Y	Y	Y	Y
PENNSYLVANIA								
1 Myers, M.	Y	N	Y	Y	Y	Y	Y	Y
2 Nix	#	✓	#	Y	Y	Y	Y	Y
3 Lederer	Y	N	Y	Y	Y	Y	Y	?
4 Eilberg	Y	Y	Y	Y	Y	Y	Y	Y
5 Schulze	N	Y	N	Y	Y	N	Y	Y
6 Yatron	N	Y	N	Y	Y	Y	Y	Y
7 Edgar	Y	N	Y	Y	Y	Y	Y	Y
8 Kostmayer	N	Y	N	Y	Y	Y	Y	Y
9 Shuster	N	Y	N	N	Y	N	N	N
10 McDade	Y	Y	N	Y	Y	Y	Y	N
11 Flood	Y	Y	Y	Y	Y	Y	?	Y
12 Murtha	Y	Y	N	Y	Y	Y	Y	Y
13 Coughlin	N	Y	N	N	Y	N	N	N
14 Moorhead	Y	Y	Y	Y	Y	Y	Y	Y
15 Rooney	Y	N	Y	Y	Y	Y	Y	Y
16 Walker	N	Y	N	Y	Y	N	N	N
17 Ertel	Y	Y	N	Y	Y	Y	#	?
18 Walgren	Y	Y	N	Y	Y	Y	Y	Y
19 Goodling, W.	N	Y	N	N	Y	Y	Y	N
20 Gaydos	N	Y	N	Y	Y	Y	Y	Y
21 Dent	N	Y	N	#	#	Y	Y	Y
22 Murphy	Y	N	N	N	Y	Y	Y	Y
23 Ammerman	Y	Y	Y	Y	Y	?	?	Y
24 Marks	N	N	N	N	Y	N	Y	N
25 Myers, G.	N	N	N	N	Y	?	Y	Y
RHODE ISLAND								
1 St Germain	Y	N	Y	Y	Y	Y	Y	Y
2 Beard	Y	N	Y	Y	Y	Y	Y	Y
SOUTH CAROLINA								
1 Davis	N	Y	N	Y	Y	Y	Y	Y
2 Spence	N	Y	N	Y	Y	Y	Y	N
3 Derrick	Y	N	Y	Y	Y	Y	Y	Y
4 Mann	Y	N	N	Y	Y	Y	Y	Y
5 Holland	Y	Y	N	Y	Y	#	#	#
6 Jenrette	Y	Y	Y	Y	Y	Y	Y	Y
SOUTH DAKOTA								
1 Pressler	N	Y	N	Y	Y	N	Y	N
2 Abdnor	N	Y	N	Y	Y	N	Y	N
TENNESSEE								
1 Quillen	N	Y	N	Y	Y	Y	Y	N
2 Duncan	N	N	N	Y	Y	Y	Y	N
3 Lloyd	Y	Y	N	Y	Y	Y	Y	Y
4 Gore	Y	N	N	Y	Y	Y	Y	Y
5 Allen	Y	Y	N	Y	Y	Y	Y	Y
6 Beard	Y	Y	N	#	#	#	?	#
7 Jones	Y	Y	N	Y	Y	Y	Y	Y
8 Ford	Y	Y	Y	Y	Y	Y	Y	Y
TEXAS								
1 Hall	N	N	N	Y	Y	Y	Y	Y
2 Wilson, C.	Y	#	N	Y	Y	Y	Y	Y
3 Collins	N	Y	N	#	Y	N	N	N
4 Roberts	Y	N	N	Y	Y	Y	Y	Y
5 Mattox	Y	N	N	Y	Y	Y	Y	Y
6 Teague	?	X	✓	?	?	?	?	?
7 Archer	N	Y	N	Y	Y	Y	Y	N
8 Eckhardt	Y	Y	Y	Y	Y	Y	?	Y
9 Brooks	Y	Y	N	Y	Y	Y	Y	Y
10 Pickle	Y	N	Y	Y	Y	Y	Y	Y
11 Poage	N	Y	N	Y	Y	Y	Y	Y
12 Wright	Y	Y	Y	Y	Y	Y	Y	Y
13 Hightower	Y	N	N	Y	Y	Y	Y	Y
14 Young	?	?	?	?	?	?	?	?
15 de la Garza	Y	N	N	Y	Y	Y	Y	Y
16 White	Y	N	N	Y	Y	Y	Y	Y
17 Burleson	Y	N	Y	Y	Y	Y	Y	Y
18 Jordan	Y	N	Y	Y	Y	Y	Y	Y
19 Mahon	#	▮	#	#	#	#	#	#
20 Gonzalez	Y	Y	Y	Y	Y	Y	Y	Y
21 Krueger	▮	✓	✓	#	#	Y	N	Y
22 Gammage	N	Y	N	Y	Y	Y	Y	Y
23 Kazen	Y	Y	N	Y	Y	Y	Y	Y
24 Milford	N	N	N	Y	Y	Y	Y	Y
UTAH								
1 McKay	Y	Y	Y	Y	Y	Y	#	#
2 Marriott	N	Y	N	Y	Y	Y	Y	N
VERMONT								
AL Jeffords	N	Y	N	Y	Y	N	Y	N
VIRGINIA								
1 Trible	N	Y	N	N	Y	Y	Y	N
2 Whitehurst	N	Y	N	Y	Y	Y	Y	N
3 Satterfield	N	Y	N	N	Y	?	?	?
4 Daniel	N	Y	N	N	Y	Y	Y	N
5 Daniel	Y	Y	N	N	Y	Y	Y	Y
6 Butler	Y	N	N	Y	Y	N	Y	N
7 Robinson	N	Y	N	Y	Y	N	Y	N
8 Harris	Y	Y	N	Y	#	Y	Y	Y
9 Wampler	Y	N	N	Y	Y	Y	Y	N
10 Fisher	-	▮	†	†	†	Y	Y	Y
WASHINGTON								
1 Pritchard	Y	N	N	N	#	Y	N	N
2 Meeds	Y	Y	Y	Y	Y	Y	Y	Y
3 Bonker	Y	#	Y	Y	Y	Y	Y	Y
4 McCormack	Y	N	Y	Y	Y	Y	Y	Y
5 Foley	Y	Y	Y	Y	Y	Y	Y	Y
6 Dicks	Y	N	Y	Y	Y	Y	Y	Y
7 Cunningham	N	Y	N	N	Y	Y	Y	N
WEST VIRGINIA								
1 Mollohan	Y	Y	Y	Y	Y	Y	Y	Y
2 Staggers	Y	Y	Y	Y	Y	Y	Y	Y
3 Slack	?	?	?	?	?	?	?	?
4 Rahall	Y	Y	N	#	#	Y	Y	Y
WISCONSIN								
1 Aspin	Y	Y	Y	Y	Y	Y	Y	Y
2 Kastenmeier	Y	N	Y	Y	Y	Y	Y	Y
3 Baldus	Y	Y	Y	Y	Y	#	Y	Y
4 Zablocki	Y	Y	Y	Y	Y	Y	Y	N
5 Reuss	Y	Y	Y	Y	Y	Y	Y	Y
6 Steiger	N	N	N	Y	Y	Y	N	N
7 Obey	Y	Y	Y	Y	Y	?	?	?
8 Cornell	Y	Y	Y	Y	Y	Y	Y	Y
9 Kasten	N	Y	N	Y	Y	Y	Y	N
WYOMING								
AL Roncalio	Y	N	Y	Y	Y	Y	Y	Y

Democrats ***Republicans***

94. HR 50. Full Employment Act. Rousselot, R-Calif., demand for the yeas and nays on the Bolling, D-Mo., motion to order the previous question (ending further debate) on the adoption of the rule (H Res 1057) providing for House floor consideration of the bill to promote full employment, balanced growth and price stability by economic planning and employment programs. Motion agreed to 371-36: R 106-33; D 265-3 (ND 185-2; SD 80-1), March 8, 1978.

95. HR 50. Full Employment Act. Adoption of the rule (H Res 1057) providing for House floor consideration of the bill *(see vote 94, above).* Adopted 349-58: R 90-52; D 259-6 (ND 183-2; SD 76-4), March 8, 1978.

96. HR 50. Full Employment Act. Bolling, D-Mo., motion to table (kill) the Long, D-La., motion to reconsider the vote *(vote 95, above)* adopting the rule providing for House floor consideration of the bill. Motion agreed to 368-29: R 112-27; D 256-2 (ND 181-0; SD 75-2), March 8, 1978.

97. HR 50. Full Employment Act. Hawkins, D-Calif., motion that the House resolve into the Committee of the Whole to consider the bill to promote full employment, balanced growth and price stability. Motion agreed to 364-32: R 107-31; D 257-1 (ND 181-0; SD 76-1). March 8, 1978.

98. Procedural Motion. Ashbrook, R-Ohio, motion to approve the House *Journal* of Wednesday, March 8, 1978. Motion agreed to 386-15: R 124-13; D 262-2 (ND 178-2; SD 84-0), March 9, 1978.

KEY

- Y Voted for (yea).
- ✓ Paired for.
- † Announced for.
- # CQ Poll for.
- N Voted against (nay).
- X Paired against.
- \- Announced against.
- ▮ CQ Poll against.
- P Voted "present."
- ● Voted "present" to avoid possible conflict of interest.
- ? Did not vote or otherwise make a position known.

	94	95	96	97	98
ALABAMA					
1 Edwards	Y	Y	Y	Y	Y
2 Dickinson	N	N	Y	Y	Y
3 Nichols	Y	Y	Y	Y	Y
4 Bevill	Y	Y	Y	Y	Y
5 Flippo	Y	Y	Y	Y	Y
6 Buchanan	?	?	?	?	?
7 Flowers	Y	Y	Y	Y	Y
ALASKA					
AL Young	Y	N	#	Y	Y
ARIZONA					
1 Rhodes	Y	Y	Y	Y	Y
2 Udall	Y	Y	#	Y	#
3 Stump	Y	N	Y	Y	Y
4 Rudd	N	N	N	N	Y
ARKANSAS					
1 Alexander	Y	Y	Y	Y	Y
2 Tucker	#	#	#	#	#
3 Hammerschmidt	Y	N	Y	Y	Y
4 Thornton	?	?	?	?	Y
CALIFORNIA					
1 Johnson	Y	Y	Y	Y	Y
2 Clausen	Y	Y	Y	Y	Y
3 Moss	Y	Y	Y	Y	Y
4 Leggett	#	#	#	#	#
5 Burton, J.	Y	Y	Y	Y	Y
6 Burton, P.	Y	Y	Y	Y	Y
7 Miller	Y	Y	Y	Y	Y
8 Dellums	Y	Y	Y	Y	Y
9 Stark	Y	Y	Y	Y	Y
10 Edwards	Y	Y	Y	Y	Y
11 Ryan	Y	Y	Y	Y	Y
12 McCloskey	Y	Y	Y	Y	Y
13 Mineta	Y	Y	Y	Y	Y
14 McFall	Y	Y	Y	Y	Y
15 Sisk	?	?	?	?	Y
16 Panetta	Y	Y	Y	Y	Y
17 Krebs	Y	Y	Y	Y	Y
18 Ketchum	Y	N	Y	Y	Y
19 Lagomarsino	Y	Y	Y	Y	Y
20 Goldwater	?	?	?	?	Y
21 Corman	Y	Y	Y	Y	Y
22 Moorhead	N	N	N	N	Y
23 Beilenson	Y	Y	Y	Y	Y
24 Waxman	#	#	#	#	Y
25 Roybal	Y	Y	Y	Y	Y
26 Rousselot	Y	N	N	N	Y
27 Dornan	N	N	N	N	Y
28 Burke	#	#	#	#	Y
29 Hawkins	Y	Y	Y	Y	Y
30 Danielson	Y	Y	Y	Y	Y
31 Wilson, C.H.	Y	Y	Y	Y	Y
32 Anderson	Y	Y	Y	Y	Y
33 Clawson	Y	N	N	N	Y
34 Hannaford	Y	Y	Y	Y	Y
35 Lloyd	Y	Y	Y	Y	Y
36 Brown	?	?	?	?	Y
37 Pettis	?	N	Y	Y	?
38 Patterson	Y	Y	Y	Y	Y
39 Wiggins	Y	N	#	#	Y
40 Badham	N	N	N	N	Y
41 Wilson, B.	Y	Y	N	Y	N
42 Van Deerlin	Y	Y	Y	Y	Y
43 Burgener	Y	Y	Y	Y	Y
COLORADO					
1 Schroeder	Y	Y	Y	Y	Y
2 Wirth	Y	Y	Y	Y	Y
3 Evans	Y	Y	#	#	Y
4 Johnson	Y	Y	Y	Y	Y
5 Armstrong	?	N	N	N	N
CONNECTICUT					
1 Cotter	Y	Y	Y	Y	Y
2 Dodd	Y	Y	Y	Y	Y
3 Giaimo	Y	Y	Y	Y	Y
4 McKinney	Y	Y	N	Y	Y
5 Sarasin	Y	Y	Y	Y	N
6 Moffett	N	Y	Y	Y	Y
DELAWARE					
AL Evans	Y	Y	Y	Y	Y
FLORIDA					
1 Sikes	Y	Y	?	?	Y
2 Fuqua	Y	Y	Y	Y	Y
3 Bennett	Y	Y	Y	Y	Y
4 Chappell	Y	Y	Y	Y	Y
5 Kelly	N	Y	Y	N	Y
6 Young	Y	Y	Y	Y	Y
7 Gibbons	Y	Y	Y	Y	Y
8 Ireland	N	N	Y	Y	Y
9 Frey	Y	Y	Y	Y	Y
10 Bafalis	Y	N	Y	Y	Y
11 Rogers	Y	Y	Y	Y	Y
12 Burke	N	Y	Y	Y	Y
13 Lehman	Y	Y	#	Y	Y
14 Pepper	#	#	#	#	Y
15 Fascell	Y	Y	Y	Y	Y
GEORGIA					
1 Ginn	Y	Y	Y	Y	Y
2 Mathis	Y	Y	Y	Y	Y
3 Brinkley	Y	Y	Y	Y	Y
4 Levitas	Y	Y	Y	Y	Y
5 Fowler	Y	Y	Y	Y	Y
6 Flynt	Y	Y	Y	Y	Y
7 McDonald	Y	N	N	N	Y
8 Evans	Y	Y	Y	Y	Y
9 Jenkins	Y	Y	Y	Y	Y
10 Barnard	Y	Y	Y	Y	Y
HAWAII					
1 Heftel	Y	Y	Y	Y	Y
2 Akaka	Y	Y	Y	Y	Y
IDAHO					
1 Symms	N	N	N	N	Y
2 Hansen, G.	N	N	N	N	Y
ILLINOIS					
1 Metcalfe	Y	Y	Y	Y	Y
2 Murphy	Y	Y	Y	Y	Y
3 Russo	Y	Y	Y	Y	Y
4 Derwinski	Y	Y	Y	Y	Y
5 Fary	?	?	?	?	?
5 Hyde	N	Y	N	Y	Y
7 Collins	Y	Y	Y	Y	#
8 Rostenkowski	Y	Y	Y	Y	Y
9 Yates	Y	Y	Y	Y	Y
10 Mikva	Y	Y	Y	Y	Y
11 Annunzio	Y	Y	Y	Y	Y
12 Crane	N	N	N	N	#
13 McClory	Y	N	Y	N	Y
14 Erlenborn	Y	Y	Y	Y	Y
15 Corcoran	Y	Y	Y	Y	Y
16 Anderson	#	#	#	#	#
17 O'Brien	Y	Y	Y	Y	Y
18 Michel	Y	Y	Y	Y	Y
19 Railsback	Y	Y	Y	Y	Y
20 Findley	Y	Y	Y	Y	?
21 Madigan	Y	Y	?	Y	Y
22 Shipley	Y	Y	Y	Y	Y
23 Price	Y	Y	Y	#	Y
24 Simon	Y	Y	Y	Y	Y
INDIANA					
1 Benjamin	Y	Y	Y	Y	Y
2 Fithian	Y	Y	Y	Y	Y
3 Brademas	Y	Y	Y	Y	Y
4 Quayle	N	Y	Y	N	N
5 Hillis	Y	Y	Y	Y	Y
6 Evans	Y	Y	Y	Y	Y
7 Myers, J.	N	N	Y	N	Y
8 Cornwell	Y	Y	#	#	Y
9 Hamilton	Y	Y	Y	Y	?
10 Sharp	Y	Y	Y	Y	Y
11 Jacobs	N	Y	Y	Y	Y
IOWA					
1 Leach	Y	Y	Y	Y	N
2 Blouin	Y	Y	Y	Y	Y
3 Grassley	N	N	Y	Y	Y
4 Smith	Y	Y	Y	Y	Y
5 Harkin	Y	Y	Y	Y	Y
6 Bedell	Y	Y	#	Y	Y

Democrats ***Republicans***

	94	95	96	97	98
KANSAS					
1 ***Sebelius***	Y	Y	Y	Y	Y
2 Keys	Y	Y	Y	Y	Y
3 ***Winn***	Y	Y	Y	Y	Y
4 Glickman	Y	Y	Y	Y	Y
5 ***Skubitz***	Y	Y	Y	Y	?
KENTUCKY					
1 Hubbard	Y	Y	Y	Y	Y
2 Natcher	Y	Y	Y	Y	Y
3 Mazzoli	Y	Y	Y	Y	Y
4 ***Snyder***	Y	N	Y	Y	Y
5 ***Carter***	Y	Y	Y	Y	Y
6 Breckinridge	Y	Y	Y	Y	Y
7 Perkins	Y	Y	Y	Y	Y
LOUISIANA					
1 ***Livingston***	Y	Y	Y	Y	P
2 Boggs	Y	Y	Y	Y	Y
3 ***Treen***	Y	Y	Y	Y	N
4 Waggonner	Y	Y	Y	Y	Y
5 Huckaby	Y	Y	Y	Y	Y
6 ***Moore***	Y	Y	Y	Y	Y
7 Breaux	Y	Y	Y	Y	Y
8 Long	Y	Y	N	Y	Y
MAINE					
1 ***Emery***	Y	Y	Y	Y	Y
2 ***Cohen***	Y	Y	Y	Y	Y
MARYLAND					
1 ***Bauman***	N	N	N	N	Y
2 Long	Y	?	Y	Y	Y
3 Mikulski	Y	Y	Y	Y	Y
4 ***Holt***	N	N	Y	Y	Y
5 Spellman	Y	Y	Y	Y	Y
6 Byron	Y	Y	Y	Y	Y
7 Mitchell	Y	Y	Y	Y	N
8 ***Steers***	Y	Y	Y	Y	Y
MASSACHUSETTS					
1 ***Conte***	Y	Y	Y	Y	Y
2 Boland	Y	Y	Y	Y	Y
3 Early	Y	Y	Y	Y	Y
4 Drinan	Y	Y	Y	Y	Y
5 Tsongas	Y	Y	Y	Y	Y
6 Harrington	Y	Y	Y	Y	Y
7 Markey	Y	Y	Y	Y	Y
8 O'Neill					
9 Moakley	Y	Y	Y	Y	Y
10 ***Heckler***	Y	Y	N	?	Y
11 Burke	Y	Y	Y	Y	Y
12 Studds	Y	Y	Y	Y	Y
MICHIGAN					
1 Conyers	Y	#	Y	Y	#
2 ***Pursell***	Y	Y	Y	Y	?
3 ***Brown***	Y	Y	Y	Y	N
4 ***Stockman***	N	N	Y	N	Y
5 ***Sawyer***	Y	Y	Y	Y	Y
6 Carr	Y	Y	Y	Y	Y
7 Kildee	Y	Y	Y	Y	Y
8 Traxler	Y	Y	Y	Y	Y
9 ***Vander Jagt***	Y	N	Y	Y	Y
10 ***Cederberg***	Y	Y	Y	Y	Y
11 ***Ruppe***	Y	Y	Y	Y	Y
12 Bonior	Y	Y	Y	Y	Y
13 Diggs	Y	Y	Y	Y	#
14 Nedzi	Y	Y	Y	Y	Y
15 Ford	Y	Y	Y	Y	?
16 Dingell	Y	Y	Y	Y	?
17 Brodhead	Y	Y	Y	Y	Y
18 Blanchard	Y	Y	Y	Y	Y
19 ***Broomfield***	Y	Y	Y	Y	Y
MINNESOTA					
1 ***Quie***	Y	Y	Y	Y	Y
2 ***Hagedorn***	Y	Y	Y	Y	Y
3 ***Frenzel***	Y	Y	Y	Y	Y
4 Vento	Y	Y	Y	Y	Y
5 Fraser	Y	Y	Y	Y	Y
6 Nolan	Y	Y	Y	Y	Y
7 ***Stangeland***	Y	N	Y	Y	Y
8 Oberstar	Y	Y	Y	Y	Y
MISSISSIPPI					
1 Whitten	Y	Y	Y	Y	Y
2 Bowen	Y	Y	?	?	Y
3 Montgomery	Y	N	Y	Y	Y
4 ***Cochran***	Y	N	Y	Y	Y
5 ***Lott***	Y	N	Y	Y	Y
MISSOURI					
1 Clay	Y	Y	Y	Y	Y
2 Young	Y	Y	Y	Y	Y
3 Gephardt	Y	Y	Y	Y	Y
4 Skelton	Y	Y	Y	Y	Y
5 Bolling	Y	Y	Y	Y	Y
6 ***Coleman***	Y	N	N	N	Y
7 ***Taylor***	Y	N	N	Y	Y
8 Ichord	Y	N	Y	Y	P
9 Volkmer	Y	Y	Y	Y	Y
10 Burlison	Y	Y	Y	Y	Y
MONTANA					
1 Baucus	Y	Y	Y	Y	Y
2 ***Marlenee***	Y	N	Y	N	Y
NEBRASKA					
1 ***Thone***	Y	Y	Y	Y	Y
2 Cavanaugh	Y	Y	Y	Y	Y
3 ***Smith***	Y	Y	Y	Y	Y
NEVADA					
AL Santini	Y	Y	Y	Y	#
NEW HAMPSHIRE					
1 D'Amours	Y	Y	Y	Y	N
2 ***Cleveland***	Y	Y	Y	Y	Y
NEW JERSEY					
1 Florio	Y	Y	Y	Y	Y
2 Hughes	Y	Y	Y	Y	Y
3 Howard	Y	Y	Y	Y	Y
4 Thompson	Y	Y	Y	Y	Y
5 ***Fenwick***	Y	Y	Y	Y	Y
6 ***Forsythe***	Y	N	N	N	N
7 Maguire	Y	Y	Y	Y	Y
8 Roe	Y	Y	Y	Y	Y
9 ***Hollenbeck***	Y	Y	Y	Y	Y
10 Rodino	Y	Y	Y	Y	Y
11 Minish	Y	Y	Y	Y	Y
12 ***Rinaldo***	Y	Y	Y	Y	Y
13 Meyner	Y	Y	Y	Y	Y
14 LeFante	Y	Y	Y	Y	Y
15 Patten	Y	Y	Y	Y	Y
NEW MEXICO					
1 ***Lujan***	Y	Y	Y	Y	Y
2 Runnels	Y	Y	Y	Y	Y
NEW YORK					
1 Pike	Y	Y	Y	Y	Y
2 Downey	Y	Y	Y	Y	Y
3 Ambro	Y	Y	Y	Y	Y
4 ***Lent***	Y	Y	Y	Y	Y
5 ***Wydler***	N	N	Y	Y	Y
6 Wolff	Y	Y	Y	Y	Y
7 Addabbo	Y	Y	Y	Y	Y
8 Rosenthal	Y	Y	Y	Y	Y
9 Delaney	Y	Y	Y	Y	Y
10 Biaggi	Y	Y	Y	Y	Y
11 Scheuer	Y	Y	Y	Y	Y
12 Chisholm	Y	Y	Y	Y	Y
13 Solarz	Y	Y	Y	Y	Y
14 Richmond	Y	Y	Y	Y	Y
15 Zeferetti	Y	Y	Y	Y	Y
16 Holtzman	Y	Y	Y	Y	Y
17 Murphy	Y	Y	#	#	Y
18 ***Green***	Y	Y	Y	Y	Y
19 Rangel	Y	Y	Y	Y	Y
20 Weiss	Y	Y	Y	Y	Y
21 Garcia	Y	Y	Y	Y	Y
22 Bingham	Y	Y	Y	Y	Y
23 ***Caputo***	Y	Y	Y	Y	Y
24 Ottinger	Y	Y	Y	Y	Y
25 ***Fish***	?	?	?	?	Y
26 ***Gilman***	Y	Y	Y	Y	Y
27 McHugh	Y	Y	Y	Y	Y
28 Stratton	Y	Y	Y	Y	Y
29 Pattison	Y	Y	Y	Y	Y
30 ***McEwen***	Y	Y	Y	Y	Y
31 ***Mitchell***	Y	Y	Y	Y	Y
32 Hanley	Y	Y	Y	Y	Y
33 ***Walsh***	Y	Y	Y	Y	Y
34 ***Horton***	Y	Y	Y	Y	Y
35 ***Conable***	Y	N	Y	N	Y
36 LaFalce	Y	Y	Y	Y	P
37 Nowak	Y	Y	Y	Y	Y
38 ***Kemp***	Y	Y	Y	Y	Y
39 Lundine	Y	Y	#	Y	Y
NORTH CAROLINA					
1 Jones	Y	Y	Y	Y	Y
2 Fountain	Y	†	Y	Y	Y
3 Whitley	Y	Y	Y	Y	Y
4 Andrews	?	?	?	#	Y
5 Neal	Y	Y	Y	?	Y
6 Preyer	Y	Y	Y	Y	Y
7 Rose	Y	Y	Y	Y	Y
8 Hefner	Y	Y	Y	Y	Y
9 ***Martin***	N	N	N	Y	Y
10 ***Broyhill***	N	N	Y	N	Y
11 Gudger	Y	Y	Y	Y	Y
NORTH DAKOTA					
AL Andrews	Y	Y	Y	Y	Y
OHIO					
1 ***Gradison***	Y	Y	Y	Y	Y
2 Luken	Y	Y	Y	Y	Y
3 ***Whalen***	Y	Y	Y	#	Y
4 ***Guyer***	N	N	Y	Y	Y
5 ***Latta***	N	N	N	N	Y
6 ***Harsha***	Y	Y	Y	Y	Y
7 ***Brown***	Y	Y	Y	Y	?
8 ***Kindness***	?	Y	Y	Y	Y
9 Ashley	Y	Y	Y	Y	?
10 ***Miller***	Y	Y	Y	Y	Y
11 ***Stanton***	Y	Y	Y	Y	Y
12 ***Devine***	N	N	N	Y	Y
13 Pease	Y	Y	Y	Y	Y
14 Seiberling	Y	Y	Y	Y	Y
15 ***Wylie***	Y	Y	Y	Y	Y
16 ***Regula***	Y	Y	Y	Y	Y
17 ***Ashbrook***	N	N	Y	Y	Y
18 Applegate	Y	Y	Y	Y	Y
19 Carney	Y	Y	Y	Y	Y
20 Oakar	Y	Y	Y	Y	Y
21 Stokes	Y	Y	Y	Y	Y
22 Vanik	Y	Y	Y	Y	Y
23 Mottl	Y	Y	Y	Y	Y
OKLAHOMA					
1 Jones	Y	Y	Y	Y	Y
2 Risenhoover	Y	Y	Y	Y	Y
3 Watkins	Y	Y	Y	Y	Y
4 Steed	Y	Y	Y	Y	Y
5 ***Edwards***	Y	Y	Y	Y	Y
6 English	Y	Y	Y	Y	Y
OREGON					
1 AuCoin	Y	Y	Y	Y	#
2 Ullman	Y	Y	Y	Y	Y
3 Duncan	Y	Y	Y	?	Y
4 Weaver	Y	Y	Y	Y	Y
PENNSYLVANIA					
1 Myers, M.	Y	Y	Y	Y	Y
2 Nix	Y	Y	Y	Y	Y
3 Lederer	?	?	?	?	Y
4 Eilberg	Y	Y	Y	Y	Y
5 ***Schulze***	Y	N	N	N	Y
6 Yatron	Y	Y	Y	Y	Y
7 Edgar	Y	Y	Y	Y	Y
8 Kostmayer	Y	Y	Y	Y	Y
9 ***Shuster***	N	N	Y	N	Y
10 ***McDade***	Y	Y	Y	Y	Y
11 Flood	Y	Y	Y	Y	Y
12 Murtha	Y	Y	Y	Y	Y
13 ***Coughlin***	Y	Y	Y	Y	N
14 Moorhead	Y	Y	Y	Y	Y
15 Rooney	Y	Y	Y	Y	Y
16 ***Walker***	N	N	N	N	N
17 Ertel	Y	Y	Y	Y	Y
18 Walgren	Y	Y	Y	Y	Y
19 ***Goodling, W.***	Y	Y	Y	N	Y
20 Gaydos	Y	Y	Y	Y	Y
21 Dent	Y	Y	Y	Y	Y
22 Murphy	Y	Y	Y	Y	Y
23 Ammerman	Y	Y	Y	Y	Y
24 ***Marks***	Y	Y	N	Y	Y
25 ***Myers, G.***	Y	Y	Y	Y	Y
RHODE ISLAND					
1 St Germain	Y	Y	Y	Y	Y
2 Beard	Y	Y	Y	Y	Y
SOUTH CAROLINA					
1 Davis	Y	Y	Y	Y	Y
2 ***Spence***	N	N	Y	Y	Y
3 Derrick	Y	Y	Y	Y	Y
4 Mann	Y	Y	Y	Y	Y
5 Holland	#	#	#	#	Y
6 Jenrette	Y	Y	Y	Y	Y
SOUTH DAKOTA					
1 ***Pressler***	N	Y	Y	Y	Y
2 ***Abdnor***	N	N	Y	Y	Y
TENNESSEE					
1 ***Quillen***	N	N	Y	N	Y
2 ***Duncan***	Y	N	Y	Y	Y
3 Lloyd	Y	Y	Y	Y	Y
4 Gore	Y	Y	Y	Y	Y
5 Allen	Y	Y	Y	Y	Y
6 ***Beard***	#	#	#	#	Y
7 Jones	Y	Y	Y	Y	Y
8 Ford	Y	Y	Y	Y	Y
TEXAS					
1 Hall	Y	Y	Y	Y	Y
2 Wilson, C.	Y	Y	Y	Y	Y
3 ***Collins***	N	N	N	N	N
4 Roberts	Y	Y	Y	Y	Y
5 Mattox	Y	Y	Y	Y	Y
6 Teague	?	?	?	?	?
7 ***Archer***	N	N	N	Y	Y
8 Eckhardt	Y	Y	Y	Y	Y
9 Brooks	Y	Y	Y	Y	Y
10 Pickle	Y	Y	Y	Y	Y
11 Poage	Y	Y	Y	Y	Y
12 Wright	Y	Y	Y	?	Y
13 Hightower	Y	Y	Y	Y	Y
14 Young	Y	Y	Y	Y	?
15 de la Garza	Y	Y	Y	Y	Y
16 White	Y	Y	Y	Y	Y
17 Burleson	Y	N	Y	Y	Y
18 Jordan	Y	Y	Y	Y	Y
19 Mahon	#	[illegible]	#	#	#
20 Gonzalez	Y	Y	Y	Y	Y
21 Krueger	#	#	#	#	#
22 Gammage	Y	Y	Y	Y	Y
23 Kazen	Y	Y	Y	Y	Y
24 Milford	Y	Y	Y	Y	Y
UTAH					
1 McKay	Y	Y	Y	Y	Y
2 ***Marriott***	Y	Y	Y	Y	Y
VERMONT					
AL Jeffords	N	Y	N	Y	Y
VIRGINIA					
1 ***Trible***	Y	Y	Y	N	Y
2 ***Whitehurst***	Y	Y	Y	Y	Y
3 Satterfield	?	?	?	?	?
4 ***Daniel***	Y	N	Y	N	Y
5 Daniel	Y	Y	#	Y	Y
6 ***Butler***	Y	N	Y	N	P
7 ***Robinson***	Y	N	Y	Y	Y
8 Harris	Y	Y	Y	Y	Y
9 ***Wampler***	Y	Y	Y	Y	Y
10 Fisher	Y	Y	Y	Y	Y
WASHINGTON					
1 ***Pritchard***	Y	Y	Y	Y	N
2 Meeds	Y	Y	Y	Y	Y
3 Bonker	Y	Y	Y	Y	Y
4 McCormack	Y	Y	Y	Y	Y
5 Foley	Y	Y	Y	Y	Y
6 Dicks	Y	Y	Y	Y	Y
7 ***Cunningham***	Y	Y	Y	Y	Y
WEST VIRGINIA					
1 Mollohan	Y	Y	Y	Y	Y
2 Staggers	Y	Y	Y	Y	Y
3 Slack	?	?	?	?	?
4 Rahall	#	#	#	#	P
WISCONSIN					
1 Aspin	Y	Y	Y	Y	Y
2 Kastenmeier	Y	Y	Y	Y	Y
3 Baldus	Y	Y	Y	Y	Y
4 Zablocki	Y	Y	Y	Y	Y
5 Reuss	Y	Y	Y	Y	Y
6 ***Steiger***	Y	Y	Y	#	N
7 Obey	?	?	?	?	Y
8 Cornell	Y	Y	Y	Y	Y
9 ***Kasten***	Y	Y	Y	Y	Y
WYOMING					
AL Roncalio	Y	Y	Y	?	?

Democrats ***Republicans***

99. HR 50. Full Employment Act. Wright, D-Texas, amendments, to the Sarasin, R-Conn., amendments, to require the president, beginning with the third year after enactment of the bill, to include in his annual economic report goals for reasonable price stability, and to formulate policies to reduce inflation. Adopted 277-143: R 9-134; D 268-9 (ND 191-3; SD 77-6), March 9, 1978.

100. HR 50. Full Employment Act. Jeffords, R-Vt., substitute amendment, to the Sarasin, R-Conn., amendments, to require the president, beginning with the third year after passage of the bill, to include in his annual economic report goals for reasonable price stability, and to formulate policies for the reduction of inflation; and to define reasonable price stability as reduction of inflation to 3 percent within five years of enactment. Rejected 198-223: R 142-2; D 56-221 (ND 26-168; SD 30-53), March 9, 1978. (The Sarasin amendments, as amended by the Wright amendments, were adopted subsequently by voice vote.)

101. HR 50. Full Employment Act. Jeffords, R-Vt., amendment to require the president's economic report to differentiate between employment in the private and permanent public sector and employment in temporary public service programs. Adopted 239-177: R 138-5; D 101-172 (ND 50-140; SD 51-32), March 9, 1978.

102. HR 50. Full Employment Act. Quie, R-Minn., amendment to include maintenance of farm income at 100 percent of parity at the marketplace among the goals of the president's economic report. Adopted 264-150: R 124-19; D 140-131 (ND 74-117; SD 66-14), March 9, 1978.

KEY

- Y Voted for (yea).
- ✓ Paired for.
- † Announced for.
- # CQ Poll for.
- N Voted against (nay).
- X Paired against.
- \- Announced against.
- ▮ CQ Poll against.
- P Voted "present."
- ● Voted "present" to avoid possible conflict of interest.
- ? Did not vote or otherwise make a position known.

	99	100	101	102
ALABAMA				
1 Edwards	N	Y	Y	Y
2 Dickinson	N	Y	Y	Y
3 Nichols	Y	Y	N	Y
4 Bevill	Y	Y	N	Y
5 Flippo	Y	Y	Y	Y
6 Buchanan	?	?	?	?
7 Flowers	Y	N	Y	Y
ALASKA				
AL Young	Y	Y	Y	Y
ARIZONA				
1 Rhodes	N	Y	Y	Y
2 Udall	#	N	N	Y
3 Stump	Y	Y	Y	N
4 Rudd	N	Y	Y	Y
ARKANSAS				
1 Alexander	Y	N	N	Y
2 Tucker	#	▮	#	#
3 Hammerschmidt	Y	Y	Y	Y
4 Thornton	?	?	?	?
CALIFORNIA				
1 Johnson	Y	N	N	Y
2 Clausen	N	Y	Y	Y
3 Moss	Y	N	N	N
4 Leggett	Y	N	N	Y
5 Burton, J.	Y	N	N	N
6 Burton, P.	Y	N	N	Y
7 Miller	Y	N	N	N
8 Dellums	Y	N	N	N
9 Stark	Y	N	N	N
10 Edwards	Y	N	N	N
11 Ryan	Y	N	Y	N
12 McCloskey	N	Y	Y	Y
13 Mineta	Y	N	N	N
14 McFall	Y	N	N	Y
15 Sisk	Y	N	Y	Y
16 Panetta	Y	Y	N	Y
17 Krebs	Y	N	N	N
18 Ketchum	N	Y	?	?
19 Lagomarsino	N	Y	Y	Y
20 Goldwater	N	Y	Y	Y
21 Corman	Y	N	N	N
22 Moorhead	N	Y	Y	Y
23 Beilenson	Y	N	N	N
24 Waxman	Y	N	N	N
25 Roybal	Y	N	N	N
26 Rousselot	N	Y	Y	?
27 Dornan	N	Y	Y	Y
28 Burke	Y	N	N	N
29 Hawkins	Y	N	N	N
30 Danielson	Y	N	N	N
31 Wilson, C.H.	Y	N	#	N
32 Anderson	Y	N	N	Y
33 Clawson	N	Y	Y	Y
34 Hannaford	Y	N	N	N
35 Lloyd	Y	N	N	N
36 Brown	Y	N	N	N
37 Pettis	N	Y	?	Y
38 Patterson	Y	N	N	N
39 Wiggins	N	Y	Y	Y
40 Badham	N	Y	Y	Y
41 Wilson, B.	N	Y	N	Y
42 Van Deerlin	Y	N	N	?
43 Burgener	N	Y	Y	Y
COLORADO				
1 Schroeder	Y	N	N	N
2 Wirth	Y	Y	Y	Y
3 Evans	Y	N	Y	Y
4 Johnson	N	Y	Y	Y
5 Armstrong	N	Y	Y	Y
CONNECTICUT				
1 Cotter	Y	N	N	N
2 Dodd	Y	N	N	N
3 Giaimo	Y	N	N	N
4 McKinney	N	Y	Y	Y
5 Sarasin	N	Y	Y	N
6 Moffett	Y	N	N	Y
DELAWARE				
AL Evans	N	Y	Y	Y
FLORIDA				
1 Sikes	Y	N	Y	Y
2 Fuqua	Y	N	Y	Y
3 Bennett	Y	N	Y	Y
4 Chappell	Y	Y	Y	Y
5 Kelly	N	Y	Y	Y
6 Young	N	Y	Y	Y
7 Gibbons	Y	Y	Y	N
8 Ireland	Y	N	Y	N
9 Frey	N	Y	Y	Y
10 Bafalis	N	Y	Y	Y
11 Rogers	N	Y	Y	N
12 Burke	N	Y	Y	Y
13 Lehman	Y	N	▮	X
14 Pepper	Y	N	N	N
15 Fascell	Y	N	N	N
GEORGIA				
1 Ginn	Y	N	Y	Y
2 Mathis	Y	Y	Y	Y
3 Brinkley	Y	Y	Y	Y
4 Levitas	Y	Y	Y	Y
5 Fowler	Y	N	Y	Y
6 Flynt	N	Y	Y	Y
7 McDonald	N	Y	Y	Y
8 Evans	Y	Y	N	Y
9 Jenkins	Y	Y	Y	Y
10 Barnard	N	Y	Y	Y
HAWAII				
1 Heftel	Y	Y	Y	Y
2 Akaka	Y	N	N	Y
IDAHO				
1 Symms	N	Y	Y	Y
2 Hansen, G.	N	Y	Y	Y
ILLINOIS				
1 Metcalfe	Y	N	N	N
2 Murphy	Y	N	N	N
3 Russo	Y	N	Y	N
4 Derwinski	N	Y	Y	N
5 Fary	-	X	X	X
6 Hyde	N	Y	Y	Y
7 Collins	Y	N	N	N
8 Rostenkowski	Y	N	N	N
9 Yates	Y	N	N	N
10 Mikva	Y	N	N	N
11 Annunzio	Y	N	N	N
12 Crane	N	Y	Y	Y
13 McClory	N	Y	Y	Y
14 Erlenborn	N	Y	Y	Y
15 Corcoran	N	Y	Y	N
16 Anderson	#	#	#	#
17 O'Brien	N	Y	Y	Y
18 Michel	N	Y	Y	Y
19 Railsback	N	Y	Y	Y
20 Findley	N	Y	Y	Y
21 Madigan	N	Y	Y	Y
22 Shipley	Y	N	N	Y
23 Price	Y	N	N	N
24 Simon	Y	N	N	N
INDIANA				
1 Benjamin	Y	N	N	N
2 Fithian	Y	Y	Y	Y
3 Brademas	Y	N	N	N
4 Quayle	N	Y	Y	Y
5 Hillis	N	Y	Y	Y
6 Evans	Y	Y	Y	Y
7 Myers, J.	N	Y	Y	Y
8 Cornwell	Y	Y	N	N
9 Hamilton	N	Y	Y	Y
10 Sharp	Y	Y	Y	Y
11 Jacobs	Y	Y	Y	Y
IOWA				
1 Leach	N	Y	Y	Y
2 Blouin	Y	N	N	N
3 Grassley	N	Y	Y	Y
4 Smith	Y	N	N	Y
5 Harkin	Y	Y	Y	Y
6 Bedell	Y	Y	Y	N

Democrats ***Republicans***

	99	100	101	102
KANSAS				
1 Sebelius	N	Y	Y	Y
2 Keys	Y	N	Y	Y
3 Winn	N	Y	Y	Y
4 Glickman	Y	Y	Y	Y
5 Skubitz	N	Y	Y	Y
KENTUCKY				
1 Hubbard	Y	N	N	Y
2 Natcher	Y	N	N	Y
3 Mazzoli	Y	N	Y	N
4 Snyder	N	Y	Y	Y
5 Carter	N	Y	Y	Y
6 Breckinridge	Y	N	Y	Y
7 Perkins	Y	N	N	Y
LOUISIANA				
1 Livingston	N	Y	Y	Y
2 Boggs	Y	N	Y	Y
3 Treen	N	Y	Y	Y
4 Waggonner	Y	Y	Y	▮
5 Huckaby	Y	Y	Y	Y
6 Moore	N	Y	Y	Y
7 Breaux	N	Y	Y	Y
8 Long	Y	N	N	?
MAINE				
1 Emery	N	Y	Y	Y
2 Cohen	N	Y	Y	N
MARYLAND				
1 Bauman	N	Y	Y	Y
2 Long	N	Y	Y	N
3 Mikulski	Y	N	N	N
4 Holt	N	Y	Y	Y
5 Spellman	Y	N	Y	N
6 Byron	Y	Y	Y	Y
7 Mitchell	Y	N	N	N
8 Steers	Y	N	Y	Y
MASSACHUSETTS				
1 Conte	N	Y	N	N
2 Boland	Y	N	N	N
3 Early	Y	N	N	N
4 Drinan	Y	N	N	N
5 Tsongas	Y	N	Y	N
6 Harrington	Y	N	N	N
7 Markey	Y	N	N	N
8 O'Neill				
9 Moakley	Y	N	N	N
10 Heckler	Y	Y	Y	N
11 Burke	Y	N	N	N
12 Studds	Y	N	N	N
MICHIGAN				
1 Conyers	Y	N	N	N
2 Pursell	N	Y	Y	Y
3 Brown	N	Y	Y	Y
4 Stockman	▮	Y	Y	N
5 Sawyer	N	Y	Y	Y
6 Carr	Y	N	#	Y
7 Kildee	Y	N	N	Y
8 Traxler	Y	N	Y	Y
9 Vander Jagt	N	Y	Y	Y
10 Cederberg	N	Y	Y	Y
11 Ruppe	N	Y	Y	Y
12 Bonior	Y	N	N	Y
13 Diggs	Y	N	N	N
14 Nedzi	Y	N	N	N
15 Ford	Y	N	N	N
16 Dingell	Y	N	N	N
17 Brodhead	Y	N	N	N
18 Blanchard	Y	N	N	N
19 Broomfield	N	Y	Y	Y
MINNESOTA				
1 Quie	N	Y	Y	Y
2 Hagedorn	N	Y	Y	Y
3 Frenzel	N	Y	Y	Y
4 Vento	Y	N	N	Y
5 Fraser	Y	N	N	N
6 Nolan	Y	N	N	Y
7 Stangeland	N	Y	Y	Y
8 Oberstar	Y	N	N	Y
MISSISSIPPI				
1 Whitten	Y	N	Y	Y
2 Bowen	Y	N	Y	Y
3 Montgomery	Y	Y	Y	Y
4 Cochran	N	Y	Y	Y
5 Lott	N	Y	Y	Y
MISSOURI				
1 Clay	Y	N	N	N
2 Young	Y	N	N	Y
3 Gephardt	Y	N	Y	Y
4 Skelton	Y	Y	N	Y
5 Bolling	Y	N	N	N
6 Coleman	N	Y	Y	Y
7 Taylor	N	Y	Y	Y
8 Ichord	Y	N	Y	Y
9 Volkmer	Y	N	N	Y
10 Burlison	Y	N	N	Y
MONTANA				
1 Baucus	Y	N	Y	Y
2 Marlenee	N	Y	Y	Y
NEBRASKA				
1 Thone	N	Y	Y	Y
2 Cavanaugh	Y	N	N	Y
3 Smith	N	Y	Y	Y
NEVADA				
AL Santini	Y	Y	N	N
NEW HAMPSHIRE				
1 D'Amours	Y	N	Y	N
2 Cleveland	N	Y	Y	Y
NEW JERSEY				
1 Florio	Y	N	N	N
2 Hughes	Y	N	Y	Y
3 Howard	Y	N	N	N
4 Thompson	Y	N	N	N
5 Fenwick	Y	Y	Y	N
6 Forsythe	N	Y	Y	Y
7 Maguire	Y	N	N	N
8 Roe	Y	N	Y	Y
9 Hollenbeck	N	Y	Y	N
10 Rodino	Y	N	N	N
11 Minish	Y	N	N	N
12 Rinaldo	Y	Y	Y	N
13 Meyner	Y	N	N	Y
14 LeFante	Y	N	N	N
15 Patten	Y	N	N	N
NEW MEXICO				
1 Lujan	N	Y	Y	Y
2 Runnels	Y	Y	Y	Y
NEW YORK				
1 Pike	Y	Y	Y	N
2 Downey	Y	N	N	Y
3 Ambro	Y	Y	Y	Y
4 Lent	N	Y	Y	N
5 Wydler	N	Y	Y	Y
6 Wolff	Y	N	Y	N
7 Addabbo	Y	N	N	Y
8 Rosenthal	Y	N	N	Y
9 Delaney	Y	N	N	N
10 Biaggi	Y	N	Y	Y
11 Scheuer	Y	N	N	Y
12 Chisholm	Y	N	N	Y
13 Solarz	Y	N	N	N
14 Richmond	Y	N	N	N
15 Zeferetti	Y	N	Y	Y
16 Holtzman	Y	N	N	N
17 Murphy	Y	N	N	N
18 Green	N	Y	N	N
19 Rangel	Y	N	N	Y
20 Weiss	Y	N	N	N
21 Garcia	Y	N	N	Y
22 Bingham	Y	N	N	N
23 Caputo	N	Y	Y	Y
24 Ottinger	Y	N	N	N
25 Fish	N	Y	Y	N
26 Gilman	Y	Y	N	N
27 McHugh	Y	N	Y	N
28 Stratton	Y	Y	Y	N
29 Pattison	Y	N	N	N
30 McEwen	N	Y	Y	Y
31 Mitchell	N	Y	Y	Y
32 Hanley	Y	N	Y	N
33 Walsh	N	Y	Y	Y
34 Horton	N	Y	Y	Y
35 Conable	N	Y	Y	Y
36 LaFalce	N	Y	Y	N
37 Nowak	Y	N	Y	N
38 Kemp	N	Y	Y	N
39 Lundine	Y	N	N	N
NORTH CAROLINA				
1 Jones	Y	N	Y	Y
2 Fountain	Y	Y	Y	Y
3 Whitley	Y	Y	Y	Y
4 Andrews	Y	N	Y	Y
5 Neal	Y	Y	Y	Y
6 Preyer	Y	N	N	Y
7 Rose	Y	N	N	Y
8 Hefner	Y	N	Y	Y
9 Martin	N	Y	Y	Y
10 Broyhill	N	Y	Y	Y
11 Gudger	Y	N	Y	Y
NORTH DAKOTA				
AL Andrews	N	Y	Y	Y
OHIO				
1 Gradison	N	Y	Y	N
2 Luken	Y	N	Y	N
3 Whalen	Y	N	N	N
4 Guyer	N	Y	Y	Y
5 Latta	N	Y	Y	Y
6 Harsha	N	Y	Y	Y
7 Brown	?	?	Y	Y
8 Kindness	N	Y	Y	Y
9 Ashley	Y	N	Y	N
10 Miller	N	Y	Y	Y
11 Stanton	N	Y	Y	Y
12 Devine	N	Y	Y	Y
13 Pease	Y	N	Y	N
14 Seiberling	Y	N	N	N
15 Wylie	N	Y	Y	Y
16 Regula	N	Y	Y	Y
17 Ashbrook	N	Y	Y	Y
18 Applegate	Y	Y	Y	Y
19 Carney	Y	N	N	Y
20 Oakar	Y	N	?	X
21 Stokes	Y	N	N	N
22 Vanik	Y	N	N	N
23 Mottl	Y	Y	N	N
OKLAHOMA				
1 Jones	Y	Y	Y	Y
2 Risenhoover	?	?	N	Y
3 Watkins	Y	Y	Y	Y
4 Steed	Y	N	N	Y
5 Edwards	N	Y	Y	Y
6 English	Y	Y	Y	Y
OREGON				
1 AuCoin	Y	Y	Y	N
2 Ullman	Y	N	N	N
3 Duncan	Y	N	N	N
4 Weaver	Y	N	N	Y
PENNSYLVANIA				
1 Myers, M.	Y	N	N	N
2 Nix	Y	N	N	N
3 Lederer	Y	N	N	N
4 Eilberg	Y	N	N	N
5 Schulze	N	Y	Y	Y
6 Yatron	Y	N	Y	Y
7 Edgar	Y	N	N	N
8 Kostmayer	Y	?	N	N
9 Shuster	N	Y	Y	Y
10 McDade	N	Y	Y	Y
11 Flood	Y	N	N	Y
12 Murtha	Y	N	N	Y
13 Coughlin	N	Y	Y	N
14 Moorhead	Y	N	Y	N
15 Rooney	Y	N	N	Y
16 Walker	N	Y	Y	Y
17 Ertel	Y	N	Y	Y
18 Walgren	Y	Y	Y	N
19 Goodling, W.	N	Y	Y	Y
20 Gaydos	Y	N	Y	Y
21 Dent	Y	N	N	X
22 Murphy	Y	N	N	Y
23 Ammerman	Y	N	N	N
24 Marks	Y	Y	Y	Y
25 Myers, G.	N	Y	Y	N
RHODE ISLAND				
1 St Germain	Y	N	N	N
2 Beard	Y	N	N	N
SOUTH CAROLINA				
1 Davis	Y	N	N	Y
2 Spence	N	Y	Y	Y
3 Derrick	Y	N	N	N
4 Mann	Y	Y	N	Y
5 Holland	Y	N	N	Y
6 Jenrette	Y	N	N	Y
SOUTH DAKOTA				
1 Pressler	N	Y	Y	Y
2 Abdnor	N	Y	Y	Y
TENNESSEE				
1 Quillen	N	Y	Y	Y
2 Duncan	N	Y	Y	Y
3 Lloyd	Y	N	Y	Y
4 Gore	N	N	N	Y
5 Allen	Y	N	N	Y
6 Beard	N	Y	Y	Y
7 Jones	Y	N	N	Y
8 Ford	Y	N	N	N
TEXAS				
1 Hall	Y	N	Y	Y
2 Wilson, C.	Y	N	N	Y
3 Collins	N	Y	Y	Y
4 Roberts	Y	N	N	Y
5 Mattox	Y	N	Y	Y
6 Teague	?	?	✓	✓
7 Archer	N	Y	Y	Y
8 Eckhardt	Y	N	N	N
9 Brooks	Y	N	N	Y
10 Pickle	Y	N	Y	✓
11 Poage	Y	N	Y	Y
12 Wright	Y	N	N	Y
13 Hightower	Y	N	Y	Y
14 Young	Y	N	N	Y
15 de la Garza	Y	N	Y	Y
16 White	Y	N	Y	Y
17 Burleson	Y	Y	Y	Y
18 Jordan	Y	N	Y	N
19 Mahon	#	#	▮	#
20 Gonzalez	Y	N	N	N
21 Krueger	-	✓	✓	✓
22 Gammage	Y	Y	Y	Y
23 Kazen	Y	Y	Y	Y
24 Milford	Y	N	N	N
UTAH				
1 McKay	Y	N	Y	N
2 Marriott	N	Y	Y	Y
VERMONT				
AL Jeffords	N	Y	Y	Y
VIRGINIA				
1 Trible	N	Y	Y	Y
2 Whitehurst	N	Y	Y	Y
3 Satterfield	?	?	?	?
4 Daniel	N	Y	Y	Y
5 Daniel	Y	Y	Y	Y
6 Butler	N	Y	Y	Y
7 Robinson	N	Y	Y	Y
8 Harris	Y	N	N	N
9 Wampler	N	Y	Y	Y
10 Fisher	Y	Y	Y	N
WASHINGTON				
1 Pritchard	N	Y	Y	Y
2 Meeds	Y	N	N	N
3 Bonker	Y	N	Y	Y
4 McCormack	Y	N	N	Y
5 Foley	Y	N	N	Y
6 Dicks	Y	N	?	Y
7 Cunningham	N	Y	Y	Y
WEST VIRGINIA				
1 Mollohan	Y	N	X	✓
2 Staggers	Y	N	N	Y
3 Slack	?	?	?	?
4 Rahall	Y	N	N	Y
WISCONSIN				
1 Aspin	Y	N	N	Y
2 Kastenmeier	Y	N	N	Y
3 Baldus	Y	N	N	Y
4 Zablocki	Y	N	N	N
5 Reuss	Y	N	N	N
6 Steiger	N	Y	Y	Y
7 Obey	Y	N	N	Y
8 Cornell	Y	N	N	Y
9 Kasten	N	Y	Y	Y
WYOMING				
AL Roncalio	Y	N	N	N

Democrats ***Republicans***

103. HR 10982. First Budget Rescission, Fiscal 1978. Passage of the bill to rescind $55,255,000 in fiscal 1978 appropriations: $40,200,000 in military assistance; $10,055,000 (borrowing authority) for the Federal Home Loan Bank Board; and $5,000,000 in international peacekeeping activities. Passed 318-0: R 111-0; D 207-0 (ND 142-0; SD 65-0), March 10, 1978.

104. HR 6635. Retirement Bond Interest. Conable, R-N.Y., demand for a second on the Ullman, D-Ore., motion to suspend the rules and pass the bill to allow the interest rates paid on U.S. retirement plan and individual retirement bonds to be increased to the rate paid on U.S. series E savings bonds. Second ordered 372-1: R 127-0; D 245-1 (ND 173-1; SD 72-0), March 13, 1978. (The bill subsequently was passed by voice vote.)

105. HR 7814. Federal Employees' Flexible Work Schedules. Solarz, D-N.Y., motion to suspend the rules and pass the bill to authorize federal agencies to experiment with flexible and compressed work schedules. Motion rejected 242-141: R 68-64; D 174-77 (ND 153-24; SD 21-53), March 13, 1978. A two-thirds majority vote (256 in this case) is required for passage under suspension of the rules.

106. HR 10126. Federal Employees' Part-Time Employment. Schroeder, D-Colo., motion to suspend the rules and pass the bill to establish a program to increase part-time career employment within the U.S. Civil Service. Motion agreed to 294-84: R 98-33; D 196-51 (ND 152-22; SD 44-29), March 13, 1978. A two-thirds majority vote (252 in this case) is required for passage under suspension of the rules.

107. HR 9146. Postal Service Changes. Hanley, D-N.Y., motion to suspend the rules and pass the bill to provide for a one-house congressional veto within 60 days of proposed postal service changes submitted by the U.S. Postal Service. Motion agreed to 371-6: R 126-5; D 245-1 (ND 173-1; SD 72-0), March 13, 1978. A two-thirds majority vote (252 in this case) is required for passage under suspension of the rules.

108. H Res 1010. Judiciary Committee Funding. Ashbrook, R-Ohio, motion to recommit the resolution to the House Administration Committee with instructions to report it back with an amendment requiring that $300,000 of the $1,482,805 provided for the committee by the resolution for the remainder of the 95th Congress be earmarked for the committee's internal security functions. Motion rejected 161-216: R 106-24; D 55-192 (ND 15-159; SD 40-33), March 13, 1978.

109. H Res 956. Assassinations Committee Funding. Bauman, R-Md., motion to recommit the resolution to the House Administration Committee with instructions to report it back with an amendment cutting funding for the committee to $600,000, from $2.5 million, and instructing the House Administration Committee to justify further funding for the Select Committee on Assassinations. Motion rejected 182-198: R 98-33; D 84-165 (ND 41-135; SD 43-30), March 13, 1978.

110. H Res 956. Assassinations Committee Funding. Adoption of the resolution providing $2.5 million for the activities of the House Select Committee on Assassinations for the remainder of the 95th Congress. Adopted 204-175: R 41-89; D 163-86 (ND 129-47; SD 34-39), March 13, 1978.

KEY

- Y Voted for (yea).
- ✓ Paired for.
- † Announced for.
- # CQ Poll for.
- N Voted against (nay).
- X Paired against.
- \- Announced against.
- ■ CQ Poll against.
- P Voted "present."
- ● Voted "present" to avoid possible conflict of interest.
- ? Did not vote or otherwise make a position known.

	103	104	105	106	107	108	109	110
ALABAMA								
1 ***Edwards***	?	Y	Y	Y	Y	Y	Y	N
2 ***Dickinson***	Y	Y	Y	Y	Y	Y	N	Y
3 Nichols	Y	Y	N	N	Y	Y	Y	N
4 Bevill	Y	Y	N	N	Y	Y	N	Y
5 Flippo	Y	?	?	?	?	?	?	?
6 ***Buchanan***	#	Y	Y	Y	Y	Y	N	Y
7 Flowers	Y	Y	N	Y	Y	N	Y	N
ALASKA								
AL ***Young***	#	Y	N	Y	Y	Y	Y	N
ARIZONA								
1 ***Rhodes***	?	Y	N	N	Y	Y	Y	N
2 Udall	Y	Y	Y	Y	Y	N	N	Y
3 Stump	Y	Y	N	N	Y	Y	Y	N
4 ***Rudd***	Y	Y	N	N	Y	Y	Y	N
ARKANSAS								
1 Alexander	Y	Y	Y	Y	Y	N	N	Y
2 Tucker	#	#	#	#	#	■	■	#
3 ***Hammerschmidt***	Y	Y	N	?	Y	Y	Y	N
4 Thornton	?	Y	Y	Y	Y	N	Y	N
CALIFORNIA								
1 Johnson	Y	Y	Y	Y	Y	N	N	Y
2 ***Clausen***	?	Y	Y	Y	Y	Y	Y	N
3 Moss	Y	Y	Y	Y	Y	N	N	Y
4 Leggett	#	Y	N	Y	Y	N	N	Y
5 Burton, J.	Y	Y	Y	Y	Y	N	N	Y
6 Burton, P.	Y	Y	Y	Y	Y	N	N	Y
7 Miller	Y	?	Y	Y	Y	N	N	Y
8 Dellums	Y	Y	Y	Y	Y	N	N	Y
9 Stark	#	Y	Y	Y	Y	N	N	Y
10 Edwards	Y	Y	Y	Y	Y	N	N	Y
11 Ryan	#	#	#	Y	Y	N	Y	N
12 ***McCloskey***	Y	Y	Y	Y	Y	N	N	Y
13 Mineta	Y	Y	Y	Y	Y	N	N	Y
14 McFall	Y	Y	Y	Y	Y	N	N	Y
15 Sisk	Y	Y	?	?	?	?	N	Y
16 Panetta	Y	Y	N	Y	Y	N	N	Y
17 Krebs	Y	Y	N	N	Y	N	N	Y
18 ***Ketchum***	?	Y	N	N	Y	Y	Y	N
19 ***Lagomarsino***	Y	Y	Y	Y	Y	Y	Y	N
20 ***Goldwater***	Y	Y	Y	Y	Y	Y	Y	N
21 Corman	#	Y	Y	Y	Y	N	N	Y
22 ***Moorhead***	Y	Y	N	Y	Y	Y	Y	N
23 Beilenson	Y	Y	Y	Y	Y	N	N	Y
24 Waxman	Y	Y	Y	Y	Y	N	■	Y
25 Roybal	#	Y	Y	Y	Y	N	N	Y
26 ***Rousselot***	?	Y	N	Y	Y	Y	Y	N
27 ***Dornan***	?	Y	N	N	Y	Y	Y	N
28 Burke	#	Y	Y	Y	Y	N	N	Y
29 Hawkins	Y	Y	Y	Y	Y	X	N	Y
30 Danielson	Y	N	Y	Y	Y	N	N	Y
31 Wilson, C.H.	#	#	#	#	#	X	#	■
32 Anderson	#	Y	Y	Y	Y	N	N	Y
33 ***Clawson***	Y	Y	N	N	Y	Y	Y	N
34 Hannaford	Y	Y	Y	Y	Y	N	N	Y
35 Lloyd	Y	Y	Y	Y	Y	Y	Y	Y
36 Brown	Y	Y	Y	Y	Y	N	N	Y
37 ***Pettis***	Y	Y	Y	Y	Y	N	N	Y
38 Patterson	Y	Y	Y	Y	Y	N	N	Y
39 ***Wiggins***	Y	#	Y	N	N	N	Y	N
40 ***Badham***	Y	Y	N	N	Y	Y	Y	N
41 ***Wilson, B.***	#	Y	Y	Y	Y	N	Y	N
42 Van Deerlin	?	Y	Y	Y	Y	N	N	Y
43 ***Burgener***	Y	Y	N	Y	Y	Y	Y	N
COLORADO								
1 Schroeder	Y	Y	Y	Y	Y	N	Y	N
2 Wirth	Y	Y	Y	Y	Y	N	Y	N
3 Evans	#	Y	Y	Y	Y	N	N	Y
4 ***Johnson***	Y	Y	Y	Y	Y	N	N	Y
5 ***Armstrong***	Y	Y	N	?	Y	Y	Y	N
CONNECTICUT								
1 Cotter	#	Y	N	N	Y	N	N	Y
2 Dodd	Y	Y	Y	?	Y	N	N	Y
3 Giaimo	Y	Y	Y	Y	Y	N	N	?
4 ***McKinney***	#	#	Y	Y	Y	N	N	Y
5 ***Sarasin***	Y	Y	Y	Y	Y	Y	N	Y
6 Moffett	#	Y	Y	Y	Y	N	N	Y
DELAWARE								
AL ***Evans***	#	Y	Y	N	Y	Y	Y	N
FLORIDA								
1 Sikes	Y	Y	N	Y	Y	Y	Y	N
2 Fuqua	Y	Y	N	Y	Y	Y	N	Y
3 Bennett	Y	Y	N	Y	Y	Y	Y	Y
4 Chappell	Y	Y	N	N	Y	Y	N	Y
5 ***Kelly***	Y	Y	N	N	Y	Y	Y	N
6 ***Young***	Y	Y	N	Y	Y	Y	Y	N
7 Gibbons	?	Y	N	Y	Y	N	N	Y
8 Ireland	Y	?	?	?	?	?	?	?
9 ***Frey***	?	Y	N	Y	Y	Y	Y	N
10 ***Bafalis***	Y	Y	N	Y	Y	Y	Y	N
11 Rogers	Y	Y	N	Y	Y	Y	N	Y
12 ***Burke***	Y	Y	N	N	Y	Y	Y	N
13 Lehman	#	#	#	#	#	X	■	#
14 Pepper	Y	#	Y	Y	Y	N	N	Y
15 Fascell	Y	Y	Y	Y	Y	N	N	Y
GEORGIA								
1 Ginn	Y	Y	N	N	Y	Y	Y	Y
2 Mathis	Y	Y	?	?	?	?	?	?
3 Brinkley	Y	Y	N	N	Y	Y	Y	Y
4 Levitas	Y	Y	N	Y	Y	N	Y	Y
5 Fowler	?	?	✓	✓	?	?	?	?
6 Flynt	Y	Y	N	N	Y	Y	Y	N
7 McDonald	Y	Y	N	N	Y	Y	Y	N
8 Evans	Y	Y	N	N	Y	N	N	N
9 Jenkins	Y	#	■	#	#	■	#	■
10 Barnard	?	Y	N	Y	Y	Y	Y	N
HAWAII								
1 Heftel	Y	Y	Y	Y	Y	N	Y	N
2 Akaka	Y	Y	Y	Y	Y	N	N	Y
IDAHO								
1 ***Symms***	Y	Y	N	N	Y	Y	Y	N
2 ***Hansen, G.***	Y	?	N	N	Y	Y	Y	N
ILLINOIS								
1 Metcalfe	?	Y	Y	Y	Y	N	N	Y
2 Murphy	Y	Y	Y	Y	Y	N	N	Y
3 Russo	Y	Y	N	Y	Y	N	Y	N
4 ***Derwinski***	Y	Y	Y	Y	Y	Y	Y	N
5 Fary	?	Y	Y	Y	Y	N	N	Y
6 ***Hyde***	Y	Y	N	Y	Y	Y	Y	Y
7 Collins	†	#	#	#	#	X	?	?
8 Rostenkowski	Y	Y	Y	N	Y	N	Y	N
9 Yates	#	Y	Y	#	Y	N	N	Y
10 Mikva	†	Y	Y	Y	Y	N	N	N
11 Annunzio	Y	Y	Y	Y	Y	N	N	Y
12 ***Crane***	#	#	N	N	Y	✓	#	■
13 ***McClory***	Y	#	X	X	#	✓	#	■
14 ***Erlenborn***	Y	#	#	#	#	✓	#	■
15 ***Corcoran***	Y	Y	Y	Y	Y	N	Y	N
16 ***Anderson***	#	#	#	#	#	#	■	#
17 ***O'Brien***	#	Y	Y	Y	Y	Y	N	Y
18 ***Michel***	Y	Y	N	N	Y	Y	Y	N
19 ***Railsback***	Y	Y	Y	Y	Y	N	N	Y
20 ***Findley***	Y	Y	Y	Y	Y	N	Y	N
21 ***Madigan***	Y	?	?	?	?	✓	?	?
22 Shipley	?	?	✓	✓	?	?	?	?
23 Price	Y	Y	Y	Y	Y	N	N	Y
24 Simon	Y	Y	Y	Y	Y	N	Y	N
INDIANA								
1 Benjamin	Y	Y	N	N	Y	N	N	Y
2 Fithian	Y	Y	N	N	Y	N	N	Y
3 Brademas	Y	Y	Y	Y	Y	N	N	Y
4 ***Quayle***	Y	Y	N	Y	Y	N	Y	N
5 ***Hillis***	Y	Y	N	Y	Y	Y	N	Y
6 Evans	Y	Y	N	N	Y	Y	Y	N
7 ***Myers, J.***	Y	Y	N	Y	Y	Y	Y	N
8 Cornwell	Y	Y	N	N	Y	N	N	N
9 Hamilton	Y	Y	Y	Y	Y	Y	Y	Y
10 Sharp	Y	Y	Y	Y	Y	N	Y	N
11 Jacobs	#	Y	Y	Y	Y	N	Y	N
IOWA								
1 ***Leach***	Y	Y	Y	Y	Y	Y	N	Y
2 Blouin	Y	Y	Y	Y	Y	N	N	Y
3 ***Grassley***	Y	Y	Y	Y	Y	Y	Y	N
4 Smith	Y	Y	Y	Y	Y	N	N	Y
5 Harkin	Y	Y	Y	N	Y	N	N	Y
6 Bedell	Y	#	#	#	#	■	■	#

Democrats ***Republicans***

	103	104	105	106	107	108	109	110
KANSAS								
1 Sebelius	Y	Y	Y	Y	Y	Y	Y	N
2 Keys	†	Y	Y	Y	Y	N	Y	N
3 Winn	Y	Y	Y	Y	Y	Y	Y	N
4 Glickman	Y	Y	Y	Y	Y	N	Y	N
5 Skubitz	Y	Y	N	Y	Y	Y	Y	N
KENTUCKY								
1 Hubbard	Y	Y	N	N	Y	Y	Y	N
2 Natcher	Y	Y	N	Y	Y	N	N	Y
3 Mazzoli	†	Y	N	Y	Y	N	N	Y
4 Snyder	?	Y	N	N	Y	Y	N	Y
5 Carter	Y	Y	Y	Y	Y	Y	Y	N
6 Breckinridge	?	Y	N	?	?	N	Y	Y
7 Perkins	Y	Y	Y	Y	Y	N	Y	N
LOUISIANA								
1 Livingston	Y	Y	N	Y	Y	Y	Y	Y
2 Boggs	#	#	✓	✓	#	✓	▮	#
3 Treen	Y	Y	N	Y	Y	Y	Y	Y
4 Waggonner	#	Y	N	N	Y	Y	Y	N
5 Huckaby	Y	Y	N	Y	Y	Y	Y	N
6 Moore	Y	Y	Y	Y	Y	Y	Y	Y
7 Breaux	Y	?	X	X	?	✓	?	?
8 Long	Y	?	?	?	?	✓	?	?
MAINE								
1 Emery	Y	Y	Y	Y	Y	Y	N	Y
2 Cohen	Y	Y	Y	Y	Y	Y	N	Y
MARYLAND								
1 Bauman	Y	Y	N	N	Y	Y	Y	N
2 Long	Y	Y	Y	Y	Y	N	N	Y
3 Mikulski	Y	Y	Y	Y	Y	N	N	Y
4 Holt	Y	Y	N	Y	Y	Y	Y	N
5 Spellman	Y	Y	Y	Y	Y	N	N	Y
6 Byron	?	Y	N	N	Y	Y	Y	N
7 Mitchell	Y	Y	Y	Y	Y	N	N	Y
8 Steers	Y	Y	Y	Y	Y	N	N	Y
MASSACHUSETTS								
1 Conte	Y	Y	Y	Y	Y	N	N	Y
2 Boland	Y	Y	Y	Y	Y	N	N	Y
3 Early	Y	Y	Y	N	Y	N	N	Y
4 Drinan	Y	Y	Y	Y	Y	N	N	Y
5 Tsongas	Y	Y	Y	Y	Y	N	N	Y
6 Harrington	#	Y	Y	Y	Y	N	N	Y
7 Markey	Y	Y	Y	Y	Y	N	N	Y
8 O'Neill								
9 Moakley	#	Y	Y	Y	Y	N	N	Y
10 Heckler	?	?	Y	Y	Y	Y	N	Y
11 Burke	Y	Y	Y	Y	Y	N	N	Y
12 Studds	Y	Y	Y	Y	Y	N	N	Y
MICHIGAN								
1 Conyers	Y	#	Y	Y	Y	N	N	Y
2 Pursell	?	Y	Y	Y	Y	N	Y	N
3 Brown	Y	Y	Y	Y	Y	Y	Y	N
4 Stockman	Y	Y	N	N	Y	Y	Y	N
5 Sawyer	Y	Y	Y	Y	Y	N	N	Y
6 Carr	Y	Y	Y	Y	Y	N	N	Y
7 Kildee	Y	Y	Y	Y	Y	N	N	Y
8 Traxler	#	#	#	#	#	Y	N	N
9 Vander Jagt	?	?	?	?	?	✓	?	?
10 Cederberg	Y	Y	N	Y	Y	Y	N	Y
11 Ruppe	Y	#	▮	#	#	✓	▮	▮
12 Bonior	Y	Y	Y	Y	Y	N	N	Y
13 Diggs	#	#	Y	Y	Y	X	▮	Y
14 Nedzi	Y	Y	Y	Y	Y	N	Y	N
15 Ford	?	?	Y	Y	?	N	Y	N
16 Dingell	Y	Y	Y	N	Y	X	Y	N
17 Brodhead	?	Y	Y	Y	Y	N	N	Y
18 Blanchard	Y	Y	Y	Y	Y	N	N	Y
19 Broomfield	Y	#	X	▮	#	✓	#	▮
MINNESOTA								
1 Quie	#	#	X	#	#	#	#	#
2 Hagedorn	Y	Y	N	Y	Y	Y	Y	N
3 Frenzel	Y	Y	Y	Y	Y	Y	Y	N
4 Vento	Y	Y	Y	Y	Y	N	N	Y
5 Fraser	#	#	#	#	#	▮	▮	#
6 Nolan	Y	?	?	?	?	?	?	?
7 Stangeland	Y	Y	N	Y	Y	Y	Y	N
8 Oberstar	Y	Y	Y	Y	Y	N	Y	Y
MISSISSIPPI								
1 Whitten	Y	Y	N	N	#	Y	N	Y
2 Bowen	?	Y	N	Y	Y	Y	N	Y
3 Montgomery	Y	Y	N	N	Y	Y	Y	N
4 Cochran	Y	Y	N	Y	Y	Y	Y	N
5 Lott	Y	Y	N	Y	Y	Y	Y	N
MISSOURI								
1 Clay	?	Y	Y	Y	Y	N	N	Y
2 Young	Y	Y	N	Y	Y	N	N	Y
3 Gephardt	Y	Y	Y	Y	Y	N	Y	N

	103	104	105	106	107	108	109	110
4 Skelton	#	Y	N	N	Y	Y	Y	N
5 Bolling	#	Y	Y	#	#	N	N	Y
6 Coleman	Y	Y	Y	Y	Y	Y	Y	Y
7 Taylor	?	Y	N	Y	Y	Y	Y	N
8 Ichord	Y	Y	N	N	Y	Y	Y	N
9 Volkmer	Y	Y	Y	Y	Y	N	Y	N
10 Burlison	Y	Y	Y	Y	Y	N	N	Y
MONTANA								
1 Baucus	Y	Y	Y	Y	Y	N	N	N
2 Marlenee	Y	Y	N	Y	Y	N	Y	N
NEBRASKA								
1 Thone	#	Y	Y	Y	Y	Y	Y	Y
2 Cavanaugh	Y	Y	N	Y	Y	N	N	Y
3 Smith	Y	Y	Y	Y	Y	Y	Y	N
NEVADA								
AL Santini	#	#	Y	Y	Y	Y	▮	#
NEW HAMPSHIRE								
1 D'Amours	Y	Y	Y	N	Y	Y	N	N
2 Cleveland	Y	Y	Y	Y	Y	Y	Y	N
NEW JERSEY								
1 Florio	Y	#	Y	Y	Y	N	N	N
2 Hughes	Y	Y	Y	Y	Y	N	N	N
3 Howard	Y	Y	Y	Y	Y	N	N	Y
4 Thompson	#	Y	Y	Y	Y	N	N	Y
5 Fenwick	Y	Y	Y	Y	Y	N	N	Y
6 Forsythe	Y	Y	N	N	Y	Y	Y	N
7 Maguire	Y	Y	Y	Y	Y	N	N	Y
8 Roe	Y	Y	Y	Y	Y	N	N	Y
9 Hollenbeck	Y	Y	Y	Y	Y	N	Y	N
10 Rodino	Y	Y	Y	Y	Y	N	N	Y
11 Minish	Y	Y	N	Y	Y	N	Y	N
12 Rinaldo	Y	Y	Y	Y	Y	N	Y	N
13 Meyner	Y	Y	Y	Y	Y	N	N	Y
14 LeFante	Y	Y	Y	Y	Y	N	N	Y
15 Patten	Y	Y	Y	Y	Y	N	N	Y
NEW MEXICO								
1 Lujan	Y	?	X	X	?	✓	?	?
2 Runnels	?	Y	N	N	Y	Y	Y	N
NEW YORK								
1 Pike	Y	Y	Y	Y	Y	N	Y	N
2 Downey	Y	Y	Y	Y	Y	N	N	Y
3 Ambro	?	Y	Y	Y	Y	N	N	Y
4 Lent	#	Y	Y	Y	Y	Y	Y	N
5 Wydler	?	Y	N	N	Y	Y	Y	N
6 Wolff	#	Y	Y	Y	Y	N	N	Y
7 Addabbo	#	Y	Y	Y	Y	X	N	Y
8 Rosenthal	Y	Y	Y	Y	Y	N	N	Y
9 Delaney	Y	Y	Y	Y	Y	N	N	N
10 Biaggi	Y	Y	✓	▮	#	X	?	#
11 Scheuer	Y	Y	Y	Y	Y	N	N	Y
12 Chisholm	#	Y	Y	Y	Y	N	N	Y
13 Solarz	Y	Y	Y	Y	Y	N	N	#
14 Richmond	?	Y	Y	Y	Y	N	N	Y
15 Zeferetti	#	Y	Y	Y	Y	Y	Y	N
16 Holtzman	Y	Y	Y	Y	Y	N	N	Y
17 Murphy	#	#	✓	#	#	X	▮	#
18 Green	?	Y	Y	Y	N	N	N	Y
19 Rangel	Y	Y	Y	Y	Y	N	N	Y
20 Weiss	Y	Y	Y	Y	Y	N	N	Y
21 Garcia	?	?	?	?	?	X	?	?
22 Bingham	Y	Y	Y	Y	Y	N	N	Y
23 Caputo	Y	Y	Y	Y	Y	N	N	Y
24 Ottinger	#	Y	Y	Y	Y	N	N	Y
25 Fish	Y	Y	Y	Y	Y	Y	N	Y
26 Gilman	†	Y	Y	Y	Y	Y	N	Y
27 McHugh	Y	Y	Y	Y	N	N	N	Y
28 Stratton	Y	Y	Y	Y	Y	Y	Y	N
29 Pattison	Y	Y	Y	Y	Y	N	N	Y
30 McEwen	Y	Y	N	Y	Y	Y	Y	N
31 Mitchell	Y	Y	Y	Y	Y	Y	Y	N
32 Hanley	Y	Y	Y	Y	Y	N	Y	N
33 Walsh	Y	Y	Y	Y	Y	Y	Y	N
34 Horton	Y	Y	Y	Y	Y	Y	N	Y
35 Conable	Y	Y	Y	Y	Y	Y	Y	N
36 LaFalce	Y	Y	Y	Y	Y	N	N	Y
37 Nowak	Y	Y	Y	Y	Y	N	N	Y
38 Kemp	?	Y	N	N	Y	Y	Y	N
39 Lundine	Y	Y	Y	Y	Y	N	N	Y
NORTH CAROLINA								
1 Jones	Y	Y	N	N	Y	Y	Y	Y
2 Fountain	Y	Y	N	Y	Y	Y	Y	N
3 Whitley	Y	Y	N	N	Y	Y	Y	N
4 Andrews	Y	#	N	Y	Y	Y	Y	N
5 Neal	Y	Y	N	N	Y	Y	N	Y
6 Preyer	Y	Y	Y	Y	Y	N	N	Y
7 Rose	#	Y	Y	Y	Y	N	N	Y
8 Hefner	Y	Y	N	Y	Y	Y	N	N

	103	104	105	106	107	108	109	110
9 Martin	Y	#	▮	▮	#	✓	#	#
10 Broyhill	Y	Y	N	N	Y	?	?	?
11 Gudger	Y	Y	N	Y	Y	N	Y	Y
NORTH DAKOTA								
AL Andrews	Y	Y	Y	Y	Y	Y	N	Y
OHIO								
1 Gradison	Y	Y	Y	Y	N	Y	N	Y
2 Luken	Y	Y	Y	Y	N	N	Y	N
3 Whalen	Y	Y	Y	Y	Y	N	N	Y
4 Guyer	Y	Y	N	Y	Y	Y	N	Y
5 Latta	Y	Y	N	Y	Y	Y	Y	N
6 Harsha	Y	Y	Y	Y	Y	Y	Y	N
7 Brown	?	Y	N	Y	Y	Y	Y	N
8 Kindness	Y	Y	Y	Y	Y	✓	Y	N
9 Ashley	?	?	?	?	?	?	?	?
10 Miller	Y	Y	Y	N	Y	Y	Y	N
11 Stanton	Y	Y	Y	Y	Y	Y	Y	N
12 Devine	Y	Y	N	Y	Y	Y	N	Y
13 Pease	Y	Y	Y	Y	Y	N	Y	N
14 Seiberling	Y	Y	Y	Y	Y	N	N	Y
15 Wylie	?	Y	N	Y	Y	Y	Y	N
16 Regula	Y	Y	Y	Y	Y	Y	Y	N
17 Ashbrook	#	Y	N	N	Y	Y	Y	▮
18 Applegate	Y	Y	N	Y	Y	N	N	Y
19 Carney	#	Y	Y	Y	Y	N	N	Y
20 Oakar	?	Y	Y	†	†	N	N	Y
21 Stokes	Y	Y	Y	Y	Y	N	N	Y
22 Vanik	Y	Y	Y	Y	Y	N	N	Y
23 Mottl	#	Y	Y	N	Y	Y	Y	N
OKLAHOMA								
1 Jones	Y	Y	Y	Y	Y	Y	Y	N
2 Risenhoover	Y	?	?	?	?	?	?	?
3 Watkins	#	#	▮	#	#	#	#	▮
4 Steed	Y	Y	N	Y	Y	Y	Y	N
5 Edwards	Y	Y	N	N	Y	✓	?	?
6 English	Y	Y	N	Y	Y	Y	Y	N
OREGON								
1 AuCoin	#	#	#	#	#	▮	▮	#
2 Ullman	Y	Y	Y	Y	Y	N	N	Y
3 Duncan	Y	Y	Y	Y	Y	N	Y	N
4 Weaver	Y	?	#	#	#	▮	?	?
PENNSYLVANIA								
1 Myers, M.	#	Y	Y	Y	Y	N	N	Y
2 Nix	Y	#	✓	#	#	X	▮	#
3 Lederer	Y	Y	Y	Y	Y	N	N	Y
4 Eilberg	#	Y	Y	Y	Y	N	N	Y
5 Schulze	Y	Y	N	N	?	Y	Y	N
6 Yatron	Y	Y	N	Y	Y	Y	Y	N
7 Edgar	Y	Y	Y	Y	Y	N	N	Y
8 Kostmayer	Y	Y	Y	N	Y	N	N	Y
9 Shuster	Y	Y	N	Y	Y	Y	Y	N
10 McDade	?	?	?	?	?	N	N	Y
11 Flood	Y	Y	Y	Y	Y	N	N	Y
12 Murtha	Y	Y	N	Y	Y	N	N	Y
13 Coughlin	Y	Y	Y	Y	#	N	Y	N
14 Moorhead	#	#	#	✓	#	X	▮	#
15 Rooney	Y	Y	Y	Y	Y	N	N	Y
16 Walker	Y	Y	N	N	Y	Y	Y	N
17 Ertel	Y	Y	Y	Y	Y	N	Y	N
18 Walgren	Y	Y	Y	Y	Y	N	Y	Y
19 Goodling, W.	Y	Y	N	Y	Y	Y	Y	N
20 Gaydos	Y	Y	N	N	Y	N	Y	N
21 Dent	#	#	✓	#	#	X	▮	#
22 Murphy	Y	Y	N	N	Y	N	N	Y
23 Ammerman	Y	Y	Y	Y	Y	N	N	Y
24 Marks	Y	Y	Y	Y	Y	Y	Y	Y
25 Myers, G.	Y	Y	Y	N	Y	Y	N	Y
RHODE ISLAND								
1 St Germain	Y	Y	✓	✓	?	X	?	?
2 Beard	Y	Y	Y	Y	Y	N	N	?
SOUTH CAROLINA								
1 Davis	Y	Y	N	Y	Y	N	Y	Y
2 Spence	Y	Y	N	N	Y	Y	Y	N
3 Derrick	Y	Y	Y	Y	Y	N	N	Y
4 Mann	Y	Y	Y	N	Y	N	N	Y
5 Holland	Y	Y	Y	Y	Y	N	N	Y
6 Jenrette	#	Y	N	Y	Y	N	N	Y
SOUTH DAKOTA								
1 Pressler	?	Y	Y	Y	Y	Y	Y	N
2 Abdnor	#	Y	Y	N	Y	Y	Y	N
TENNESSEE								
1 Quillen	Y	#	▮	#	#	✓	#	▮
2 Duncan	Y	Y	Y	Y	Y	Y	Y	N
3 Lloyd	Y	Y	N	N	Y	Y	N	Y
4 Gore	Y	Y	Y	Y	Y	N	N	Y
5 Allen	Y	Y	Y	Y	Y	N	N	Y
6 Beard	#	#	▮	▮	#	✓	#	▮

	103	104	105	106	107	108	109	110
7 Jones	Y	Y	N	N	Y	N	Y	Y
8 Ford	Y	Y	Y	Y	Y	N	N	Y
TEXAS								
1 Hall	Y	Y	N	N	Y	N	Y	N
2 Wilson, C.	Y	Y	Y	Y	Y	N	N	N
3 Collins	Y	Y	N	Y	N	Y	Y	N
4 Roberts	Y	Y	N	N	Y	Y	Y	N
5 Mattox	Y	Y	N	Y	Y	N	N	N
6 Teague	?	?	N	N	Y	Y	Y	N
7 Archer	Y	Y	N	N	Y	Y	Y	N
8 Eckhardt	?	?	?	?	?	?	?	?
9 Brooks	?	Y	Y	Y	Y	N	N	Y
10 Pickle	#	Y	N	Y	Y	N	Y	N
11 Poage	Y	Y	N	N	Y	Y	Y	N
12 Wright	Y	Y	Y	Y	Y	N	N	Y
13 Hightower	?	Y	N	Y	Y	Y	Y	N
14 Young	Y	Y	N	Y	Y	Y	N	N
15 de la Garza	Y	Y	N	N	Y	Y	Y	N
16 White	#	Y	N	N	Y	Y	Y	N
17 Burleson	Y	Y	N	N	Y	Y	Y	N
18 Jordan	Y	Y	Y	Y	Y	N	N	Y
19 Mahon	#	Y	N	Y	Y	▮	▮	▮
20 Gonzalez	Y	Y	Y	N	Y	Y	Y	N
21 Krueger	#	#	✓	✓	#	X	#	▮
22 Gammage	?	?	✓	?	?	X	?	?
23 Kazen	Y	Y	N	N	Y	Y	Y	N
24 Milford	?	Y	N	N	Y	Y	Y	N
UTAH								
1 McKay	Y	Y	Y	N	Y	N	N	Y
2 Marriott	Y	Y	N	N	Y	Y	Y	N
VERMONT								
AL Jeffords	#	#	#	Y	Y	Y	Y	Y
VIRGINIA								
1 Trible	Y	Y	Y	Y	Y	Y	Y	N
2 Whitehurst	Y	Y	N	Y	Y	Y	Y	N
3 Satterfield	?	?	?	?	?	?	?	?
4 Daniel	Y	Y	N	N	Y	Y	Y	N
5 Daniel	Y	Y	N	N	Y	Y	Y	N
6 Butler	Y	Y	Y	Y	Y	Y	Y	N
7 Robinson	Y	Y	N	Y	Y	Y	Y	N
8 Harris	Y	Y	Y	Y	Y	N	N	Y
9 Wampler	Y	Y	N	Y	Y	Y	Y	N
10 Fisher	Y	Y	Y	Y	Y	N	Y	N
WASHINGTON								
1 Pritchard	Y	Y	Y	Y	Y	N	N	Y
2 Meeds	Y	Y	Y	Y	Y	N	N	Y
3 Bonker	Y	#	#	#	#	▮	#	▮
4 McCormack	Y	Y	Y	Y	Y	N	Y	N
5 Foley	Y	Y	Y	Y	Y	N	N	Y
6 Dicks	Y	Y	Y	Y	Y	N	N	Y
7 Cunningham	#	Y	N	N	Y	Y	Y	N
WEST VIRGINIA								
1 Mollohan	Y	Y	N	Y	Y	N	N	Y
2 Staggers	Y	Y	Y	Y	?	N	N	Y
3 Slack	?	Y	N	Y	Y	N	N	Y
4 Rahall	#	Y	Y	Y	Y	N	N	N
WISCONSIN								
1 Aspin	Y	Y	Y	Y	Y	N	N	Y
2 Kastenmeier	Y	Y	Y	Y	Y	N	N	Y
3 Baldus	Y	Y	Y	Y	Y	N	Y	Y
4 Zablocki	Y	Y	Y	Y	Y	Y	N	N
5 Reuss	Y	Y	Y	Y	Y	N	N	Y
6 Steiger	Y	Y	Y	Y	N	Y	Y	N
7 Obey	Y	Y	Y	Y	Y	N	N	Y
8 Cornell	Y	Y	Y	Y	Y	N	N	N
9 Kasten	Y	†	†	†	†	†	†	-
WYOMING								
AL Roncalio	?	Y	Y	Y	Y	?	?	Y

Democrats ***Republicans***

111. Procedural Motion. Michel, R-Ill., demand for the yeas and nays on the Sisk, D-Calif., motion that the House dispense with further proceedings under the quorum call. Motion agreed to 331-72: R 70-69; D 261-3 (ND 181-2; SD 80-1), March 14, 1978.

112. Procedural Motion. Bauman, R-Md., motion that the House *Journal* for Monday, March 13, 1978, be read in full. Motion rejected 99-301: R 94-43; D 5-258 (ND 3-180; SD 2-78), March 14, 1978.

113. Procedural Motion. Foley, D-Wash., motion to approve the House *Journal* for Monday, March 13, 1978. Motion agreed to 371-29: R 112-27; D 259-2 (ND 181-2; SD 78-0), March 14, 1978.

114. Procedural Motion. Foley, D-Wash., motion to table (kill) the Edwards, R-Okla., motion to reconsider the previous vote *(see vote 113, above)*. Motion agreed to 308-91: R 54-87; D 254-4 (ND 177-1; SD 77-3), March 14, 1978.

115. S 1671. Absaroka-Beartooth Wilderness. Johnson, R-Colo., demand for a second on the Roncalio, D-Wyo., motion to suspend the rules and pass the bill to designate 904,500 acres of the Custer and Gallatin National Forests in Montana as the Absaroka-Beartooth Wilderness. Second ordered 380-20: R 122-18; D 258-2 (ND 177-1; SD 81-1), March 14, 1978.

116. HR 810. Government Officials' Travel Expenses. Conable, R-N.Y., demand for a second on the Ullman, D-Ore., motion to suspend the rules and pass the bill *(see vote 119, p. 36-H)* to permit private foundations to pay foreign travel expenses of government officials under certain circumstances. Second ordered 387-2: R 133-1; D 254-1 (ND 174-1; SD 80-0), March 14, 1978.

117. HR 2028. Home Production of Beer and Wine. Conable, R-N.Y., demand for a second on the Ullman, D-Ore., motion to suspend the rules and pass the bill to permit individuals aged 18 and older to produce limited quantities of beer and wine for personal and family use without incurring excise taxes or penalties. Second ordered 388-3: R 136-3; D 252-0 (ND 173-0; SD 79-0), March 14, 1978. (The bill subsequently was passed by voice vote.)

118. S 1671. Absaroka-Beartooth Wilderness. Roncalio, D-Wyo., motion to suspend the rules and pass the bill to include 904,500 acres of national forest lands in the National Wilderness Preservation System and designate it the Absaroka-Beartooth Wilderness. Motion agreed to 405-7: R 137-4; D 268-3 (ND 187-1; SD 81-2), March 14, 1978. A two-thirds majority vote (275 in this case) is required for passage under suspension of the rules.

KEY

- Y Voted for (yea).
- ✓ Paired for.
- † Announced for.
- # CQ Poll for.
- N Voted against (nay).
- X Paired against.
- \- Announced against.
- ▮ CQ Poll against.
- P Voted "present."
- ● Voted "present" to avoid possible conflict of interest.
- ? Did not vote or otherwise make a position known.

	111	112	113	114	115	116	117	118
ALABAMA								
1 Edwards	Y	Y	Y	N	Y	Y	Y	Y
2 Dickinson	Y	Y	N	N	Y	Y	Y	Y
3 Nichols	Y	N	#	Y	Y	Y	Y	Y
4 Bevill	Y	N	Y	Y	Y	Y	Y	Y
5 Flippo	Y	N	Y	Y	Y	Y	?	Y
6 Buchanan	Y	Y	Y	N	Y	Y	Y	Y
7 Flowers	Y	N	?	?	Y	Y	Y	Y
ALASKA								
AL Young	N	#	Y	Y	Y	Y	Y	Y
ARIZONA								
1 Rhodes	Y	N	Y	Y	Y	Y	Y	Y
2 Udall	Y	N	Y	Y	Y	Y	Y	Y
3 Stump	N	Y	Y	Y	Y	Y	Y	N
4 Rudd	N	Y	Y	Y	Y	Y	Y	Y
ARKANSAS								
1 Alexander	Y	N	Y	Y	Y	Y	Y	Y
2 Tucker	#	▮	#	#	#	#	#	Y
3 Hammerschmidt	Y	Y	N	N	Y	N	Y	Y
4 Thornton	?	?	?	?	?	?	?	Y
CALIFORNIA								
1 Johnson	Y	N	Y	Y	Y	Y	Y	Y
2 Clausen	Y	N	Y	N	Y	Y	Y	Y
3 Moss	Y	N	?	?	?	?	?	?
4 Leggett	Y	▮	#	#	#	Y	#	Y
5 Burton, J.	Y	Y	Y	N	Y	Y	Y	Y
6 Burton, P.	Y	N	Y	Y	Y	Y	Y	Y
7 Miller	Y	N	Y	Y	Y	Y	Y	Y
8 Dellums	Y	N	Y	Y	Y	#	▮	Y
9 Stark	Y	N	Y	Y	Y	Y	Y	Y
10 Edwards	Y	N	Y	Y	Y	?	?	Y
11 Ryan	Y	▮	#	?	#	Y	Y	Y
12 McCloskey	?	?	?	?	?	?	?	?
13 Mineta	Y	N	Y	Y	Y	Y	Y	Y
14 McFall	Y	N	Y	?	?	Y	Y	Y
15 Sisk	Y	N	Y	Y	Y	Y	Y	Y
16 Panetta	Y	N	Y	Y	Y	Y	Y	Y
17 Krebs	Y	N	Y	Y	Y	Y	Y	Y
18 Ketchum	Y	Y	Y	Y	Y	Y	Y	Y
19 Lagomarsino	Y	Y	Y	N	Y	Y	Y	Y
20 Goldwater	Y	?	?	N	Y	Y	Y	?
21 Corman	Y	N	Y	Y	Y	Y	Y	Y
22 Moorhead	N	Y	Y	N	Y	Y	Y	Y
23 Beilenson	Y	N	Y	Y	#	#	#	Y
24 Waxman	Y	N	Y	Y	#	#	Y	Y
25 Roybal	Y	N	Y	Y	Y	Y	Y	Y
26 Rousselot	N	Y	Y	N	N	Y	Y	Y
27 Dornan	N	Y	Y	N	Y	Y	Y	Y
28 Burke	Y	N	Y	Y	Y	Y	Y	Y
29 Hawkins	Y	N	Y	Y	Y	Y	Y	Y
30 Danielson	Y	N	Y	Y	Y	Y	Y	Y
31 Wilson, C.H.	#	▮	#	#	#	#	#	#
32 Anderson	Y	N	Y	Y	Y	Y	Y	Y
33 Clawson	N	Y	Y	N	Y	Y	Y	Y
34 Hannaford	Y	N	Y	Y	#	Y	Y	Y
35 Lloyd	Y	N	N	Y	Y	Y	Y	Y
36 Brown	Y	N	Y	Y	Y	Y	Y	Y
37 Pettis	N	Y	N	N	N	Y	Y	Y
38 Patterson	Y	N	Y	Y	Y	Y	Y	Y
39 Wiggins	Y	N	Y	Y	#	#	#	Y
40 Badham	N	Y	Y	N	Y	Y	Y	Y
41 Wilson, B.	N	N	Y	N	N	Y	Y	Y
42 Van Deerlin	Y	N	Y	Y	Y	Y	Y	Y
43 Burgener	Y	N	Y	Y	Y	Y	Y	Y
COLORADO								
1 Schroeder	Y	N	Y	Y	Y	Y	Y	Y
2 Wirth	Y	N	Y	Y	Y	Y	Y	Y
3 Evans	Y	N	Y	Y	Y	P	#	Y
4 Johnson	Y	Y	Y	N	Y	Y	Y	Y
5 Armstrong	N	Y	N	N	Y	Y	Y	Y
CONNECTICUT								
1 Cotter	Y	N	Y	Y	Y	Y	Y	Y
2 Dodd	Y	N	Y	Y	Y	Y	Y	Y
3 Giaimo	Y	N	Y	Y	Y	Y	Y	Y
4 McKinney	Y	N	Y	Y	Y	Y	Y	Y
5 Sarasin	Y	N	Y	Y	Y	Y	Y	Y
6 Moffett	Y	N	Y	Y	Y	Y	Y	Y
DELAWARE								
AL Evans	Y	N	Y	N	Y	Y	Y	Y
FLORIDA								
1 Sikes	Y	N	Y	N	Y	Y	Y	Y
2 Fuqua	Y	N	Y	Y	Y	Y	Y	Y
3 Bennett	Y	N	Y	Y	Y	Y	Y	Y
4 Chappell	Y	N	Y	Y	Y	Y	Y	Y
5 Kelly	N	N	Y	N	N	Y	Y	Y
6 Young	N	N	Y	N	Y	Y	Y	Y
7 Gibbons	Y	N	Y	Y	Y	Y	Y	Y
8 Ireland	Y	N	Y	Y	Y	Y	?	Y
9 Frey	Y	Y	Y	Y	Y	Y	Y	Y
10 Bafalis	Y	Y	Y	N	Y	Y	Y	Y
11 Rogers	Y	N	Y	Y	Y	Y	Y	Y
12 Burke	N	N	Y	N	Y	Y	Y	Y
13 Lehman	Y	N	Y	Y	Y	Y	Y	Y
14 Pepper	Y	N	Y	Y	Y	Y	Y	Y
15 Fascell	Y	N	Y	Y	Y	Y	Y	Y
GEORGIA								
1 Ginn	Y	N	Y	Y	Y	Y	Y	Y
2 Mathis	Y	N	Y	Y	Y	Y	Y	Y
3 Brinkley	Y	N	Y	Y	Y	Y	Y	Y
4 Levitas	Y	N	Y	Y	N	Y	Y	Y
5 Fowler	Y	N	Y	Y	Y	Y	Y	Y
6 Flynt	Y	N	Y	Y	Y	Y	Y	Y
7 McDonald	N	Y	Y	N	Y	Y	Y	N
8 Evans	Y	N	Y	N	Y	Y	Y	Y
9 Jenkins	Y	N	Y	Y	Y	Y	Y	Y
10 Barnard	Y	N	Y	Y	Y	Y	Y	Y
HAWAII								
1 Heftel	Y	N	Y	Y	Y	Y	Y	Y
2 Akaka	Y	N	Y	Y	Y	Y	Y	Y
IDAHO								
1 Symms	N	Y	Y	N	Y	Y	Y	N
2 Hansen, G.	N	Y	Y	N	Y	Y	Y	N
ILLINOIS								
1 Metcalfe	?	?	?	?	?	?	?	?
2 Murphy	Y	N	Y	Y	Y	Y	Y	Y
3 Russo	Y	N	Y	Y	Y	Y	Y	Y
4 Derwinski	Y	Y	Y	Y	Y	Y	Y	Y
5 Fary	Y	N	Y	Y	Y	Y	Y	Y
6 Hyde	Y	Y	N	N	N	Y	Y	Y
7 Collins	?	?	?	?	?	?	?	?
8 Rostenkowski	?	?	?	?	?	?	?	?
9 Yates	Y	N	Y	Y	Y	Y	Y	Y
10 Mikva	Y	N	Y	Y	Y	#	?	Y
11 Annunzio	Y	N	Y	Y	Y	Y	Y	Y
12 Crane	N	Y	Y	N	N	Y	Y	N
13 McClory	N	Y	N	Y	Y	Y	Y	Y
14 Erlenborn	#	#	#	#	#	#	Y	Y
15 Corcoran	N	Y	Y	N	Y	Y	Y	Y
16 Anderson	#	▮	#	#	#	#	#	#
17 O'Brien	Y	Y	Y	N	Y	Y	Y	Y
18 Michel	N	Y	Y	N	N	#	Y	Y
19 Railsback	N	Y	N	Y	N	Y	Y	Y
20 Findley	Y	N	Y	Y	Y	Y	Y	Y
21 Madigan	Y	Y	Y	Y	Y	Y	Y	Y
22 Shipley	?	?	?	?	Y	Y	Y	Y
23 Price	Y	N	Y	Y	Y	Y	Y	Y
24 Simon	Y	N	Y	Y	Y	Y	Y	Y
INDIANA								
1 Benjamin	Y	N	Y	Y	Y	Y	Y	Y
2 Fithian	Y	N	Y	Y	Y	Y	Y	Y
3 Brademas	Y	-	Y	Y	Y	Y	Y	Y
4 Quayle	Y	Y	N	N	Y	Y	N	Y
5 Hillis	N	N	Y	N	Y	Y	Y	Y
6 Evans	Y	N	Y	Y	Y	Y	Y	Y
7 Myers, J.	Y	Y	N	N	N	Y	Y	?
8 Cornwell	Y	N	Y	#	P	N	Y	Y
9 Hamilton	Y	N	Y	Y	Y	Y	Y	Y
10 Sharp	Y	N	Y	?	Y	Y	Y	Y
11 Jacobs	N	N	N	Y	Y	Y	Y	Y
IOWA								
1 Leach	Y	N	N	Y	Y	Y	Y	Y
2 Blouin	Y	N	Y	Y	Y	Y	Y	Y
3 Grassley	N	Y	Y	Y	Y	Y	Y	Y
4 Smith	Y	N	Y	Y	Y	Y	Y	Y
5 Harkin	Y	N	Y	Y	Y	Y	Y	Y
6 Bedell	Y	N	Y	Y	Y	Y	Y	Y

Democrats ***Republicans***

	111	112	113	114	115	116	117	118
KANSAS								
1 ***Sebelius***	Y	Y	Y	N	Y	Y	Y	Y
2 Keys	Y	N	Y	Y	Y	Y	Y	Y
3 ***Winn***	N	N	Y	N	N	Y	Y	Y
4 Glickman	Y	N	Y	Y	Y	Y	Y	Y
5 ***Skubitz***	Y	Y	Y	Y	Y	Y	Y	Y
KENTUCKY								
1 Hubbard	?	?	?	?	?	?	?	?
2 Natcher	Y	N	Y	Y	Y	Y	Y	Y
3 Mazzoli	Y	N	Y	Y	Y	Y	Y	Y
4 ***Snyder***	N	N	Y	N	Y	Y	Y	Y
5 ***Carter***	Y	Y	Y	Y	Y	Y	Y	Y
6 Breckinridge	Y	N	Y	Y	Y	Y	Y	Y
7 Perkins	Y	N	Y	Y	Y	Y	Y	Y
LOUISIANA								
1 ***Livingston***	N	Y	N	Y	Y	Y	Y	Y
2 Boggs	Y	▮	Y	Y	Y	Y	Y	Y
3 ***Treen***	Y	?	Y	N	Y	Y	Y	Y
4 Waggonner	Y	N	Y	Y	Y	Y	Y	Y
5 Huckaby	Y	N	Y	Y	Y	Y	Y	#
6 ***Moore***	Y	N	Y	Y	Y	Y	Y	Y
7 Breaux	?	?	?	?	?	?	?	?
8 Long	Y	Y	Y	Y	Y	Y	Y	Y
MAINE								
1 ***Emery***	N	Y	Y	N	Y	Y	Y	Y
2 ***Cohen***	N	Y	Y	N	Y	Y	Y	Y
MARYLAND								
1 ***Bauman***	N	Y	Y	N	Y	Y	Y	Y
2 Long	Y	N	Y	Y	Y	Y	Y	Y
3 Mikulski	Y	N	Y	?	Y	Y	Y	Y
4 ***Holt***	Y	N	Y	Y	Y	Y	Y	Y
5 Spellman	Y	N	Y	Y	Y	Y	Y	Y
6 Byron	Y	N	Y	Y	Y	Y	Y	Y
7 Mitchell	Y	▮	▮	Y	Y	Y	Y	Y
8 ***Steers***	Y	Y	N	Y	Y	Y	Y	Y
MASSACHUSETTS								
1 ***Conte***	Y	N	Y	Y	Y	Y	Y	Y
2 Boland	Y	N	Y	Y	Y	Y	Y	Y
3 Early	Y	N	Y	Y	Y	Y	?	Y
4 Drinan	Y	N	Y	Y	Y	Y	Y	Y
5 Tsongas	#	N	Y	Y	Y	Y	Y	Y
6 Harrington	#	N	Y	Y	Y	Y	Y	Y
7 Markey	Y	N	Y	Y	Y	Y	Y	Y
8 O'Neill								
9 Moakley	Y	N	Y	Y	Y	Y	Y	Y
10 ***Heckler***	Y	Y	Y	Y	Y	Y	Y	Y
11 Burke	Y	N	Y	Y	Y	Y	Y	Y
12 Studds	Y	N	Y	Y	Y	Y	Y	Y
MICHIGAN								
1 Conyers	#	▮	#	#	#	#	#	Y
2 ***Pursell***	N	Y	?	N	N	Y	Y	Y
3 ***Brown***	N	N	N	N	Y	Y	#	Y
4 ***Stockman***	Y	Y	N	N	Y	Y	#	Y
5 ***Sawyer***	Y	Y	Y	N	Y	Y	Y	Y
6 Carr	Y	N	Y	Y	Y	Y	Y	Y
7 Kildee	Y	N	Y	Y	Y	Y	Y	Y
8 Traxler	Y	N	Y	Y	Y	Y	Y	Y
9 ***Vander Jagt***	N	Y	Y	N	Y	Y	Y	Y
10 ***Cederberg***	N	Y	Y	Y	Y	Y	Y	Y
11 ***Ruppe***	#	▮	#	#	#	#	#	#
12 Bonior	Y	N	Y	Y	Y	Y	Y	Y
13 Diggs	#	▮	#	Y	Y	Y	Y	Y
14 Nedzi	Y	N	Y	Y	Y	Y	Y	Y
15 Ford	Y	N	Y	Y	Y	Y	Y	Y
16 Dingell	Y	N	Y	Y	?	Y	Y	Y
17 Brodhead	Y	N	Y	Y	Y	Y	Y	Y
18 Blanchard	Y	N	Y	Y	Y	Y	Y	Y
19 ***Broomfield***	N	Y	Y	N	Y	Y	Y	Y
MINNESOTA								
1 ***Quie***	Y	N	Y	Y	Y	Y	Y	Y
2 ***Hagedorn***	Y	N	Y	Y	N	Y	Y	Y
3 ***Frenzel***	N	Y	Y	N	Y	Y	Y	Y
4 Vento	Y	N	Y	Y	Y	Y	Y	Y
5 Fraser	Y	N	Y	Y	Y	#	#	Y
6 Nolan	Y	N	Y	Y	Y	Y	Y	Y
7 ***Stangeland***	N	Y	N	N	Y	Y	Y	Y
8 Oberstar	Y	N	Y	Y	Y	Y	Y	Y
MISSISSIPPI								
1 Whitten	#	N	Y	Y	Y	Y	Y	Y
2 Bowen	Y	N	Y	Y	Y	Y	Y	Y
3 Montgomery	Y	N	#	#	Y	Y	Y	Y
4 ***Cochran***	N	Y	Y	N	Y	Y	Y	Y
5 ***Lott***	N	Y	Y	N	Y	Y	Y	Y
MISSOURI								
1 Clay	Y	N	Y	Y	Y	Y	Y	Y
2 Young	Y	N	Y	Y	Y	Y	Y	Y
3 Gephardt	Y	#	Y	Y	Y	Y	Y	Y

	111	112	113	114	115	116	117	118
4 Skelton	Y	N	Y	Y	Y	Y	Y	Y
5 Bolling	Y	N	#	Y	Y	Y	Y	Y
6 ***Coleman***	Y	Y	Y	N	Y	Y	Y	Y
7 ***Taylor***	Y	N	N	Y	N	Y	Y	Y
8 Ichord	Y	?	Y	Y	Y	?	Y	Y
9 Volkmer	Y	N	Y	Y	Y	Y	Y	Y
10 Burlison	Y	N	Y	Y	Y	Y	Y	Y
MONTANA								
1 Baucus	Y	N	Y	Y	Y	Y	Y	Y
2 ***Marlenee***	N	N	Y	N	Y	Y	Y	N
NEBRASKA								
1 ***Thone***	Y	Y	Y	Y	Y	Y	Y	Y
2 Cavanaugh	Y	N	Y	Y	Y	Y	Y	Y
3 ***Smith***	N	Y	Y	Y	Y	Y	Y	Y
NEVADA								
AL Santini	Y	N	Y	Y	Y	Y	Y	Y
NEW HAMPSHIRE								
1 D'Amours	Y	N	Y	Y	Y	Y	Y	Y
2 ***Cleveland***	N	Y	Y	N	Y	Y	Y	Y
NEW JERSEY								
1 Florio	Y	N	Y	Y	Y	Y	Y	Y
2 Hughes	Y	N	Y	Y	Y	Y	Y	Y
3 Howard	Y	N	Y	Y	Y	Y	Y	Y
4 Thompson	Y	N	Y	Y	#	Y	Y	Y
5 ***Fenwick***	N	Y	Y	N	Y	Y	Y	Y
6 ***Forsythe***	N	Y	N	N	Y	Y	Y	Y
7 Maguire	Y	N	Y	Y	Y	Y	Y	Y
8 Roe	Y	N	Y	Y	Y	Y	Y	Y
9 ***Hollenbeck***	N	Y	Y	Y	Y	Y	Y	Y
10 Rodino	Y	N	Y	Y	Y	Y	Y	Y
11 Minish	Y	N	Y	Y	Y	Y	Y	Y
12 ***Rinaldo***	Y	Y	Y	Y	Y	Y	Y	Y
13 Meyner	Y	N	#	#	Y	Y	Y	Y
14 LeFante	Y	N	Y	Y	Y	Y	Y	Y
15 Patten	Y	N	Y	Y	Y	Y	Y	Y
NEW MEXICO								
1 ***Lujan***	?	?	?	?	?	?	Y	Y
2 Runnels	Y	N	Y	Y	?	?	?	Y
NEW YORK								
1 Pike	Y	N	Y	Y	Y	Y	Y	Y
2 Downey	Y	N	Y	#	Y	Y	Y	Y
3 Ambro	Y	N	Y	Y	Y	?	?	Y
4 ***Lent***	N	Y	Y	Y	Y	Y	Y	Y
5 ***Wydler***	N	Y	N	Y	Y	Y	Y	Y
6 Wolff	Y	N	Y	Y	Y	Y	Y	Y
7 Addabbo	Y	N	Y	Y	Y	Y	Y	Y
8 Rosenthal	Y	N	Y	Y	Y	Y	Y	Y
9 Delaney	Y	N	Y	Y	Y	Y	Y	Y
10 Biaggi	Y	N	Y	Y	Y	Y	Y	Y
11 Scheuer	Y	N	Y	Y	Y	Y	Y	Y
12 Chisholm	Y	N	Y	Y	Y	Y	Y	Y
13 Solarz	Y	N	Y	Y	Y	Y	Y	Y
14 Richmond	Y	N	Y	Y	Y	Y	Y	Y
15 Zeferetti	Y	N	Y	Y	Y	Y	Y	Y
16 Holtzman	Y	N	Y	Y	†	Y	Y	Y
17 Murphy	Y	N	Y	Y	Y	Y	Y	Y
18 ***Green***	Y	N	Y	Y	Y	Y	Y	Y
19 Rangel	Y	N	Y	Y	Y	Y	Y	Y
20 Weiss	Y	N	Y	Y	Y	Y	Y	Y
21 Garcia	Y	N	Y	Y	Y	Y	Y	Y
22 Bingham	Y	N	Y	Y	Y	Y	Y	Y
23 ***Caputo***	N	N	Y	Y	Y	Y	Y	Y
24 Ottinger	Y	N	Y	Y	Y	Y	Y	Y
25 ***Fish***	N	N	Y	Y	Y	Y	Y	Y
26 ***Gilman***	Y	N	Y	Y	Y	Y	Y	Y
27 McHugh	?	N	Y	Y	Y	Y	Y	Y
28 Stratton	Y	N	Y	Y	Y	Y	Y	Y
29 Pattison	Y	N	Y	Y	Y	Y	Y	Y
30 ***McEwen***	N	N	Y	Y	Y	Y	Y	Y
31 ***Mitchell***	Y	Y	Y	N	Y	#	Y	Y
32 Hanley	Y	N	Y	Y	Y	Y	Y	Y
33 ***Walsh***	Y	Y	Y	Y	Y	Y	Y	Y
34 ***Horton***	Y	N	Y	Y	Y	#	Y	Y
35 ***Conable***	Y	N	Y	Y	Y	Y	Y	Y
36 LaFalce	Y	N	Y	Y	Y	Y	Y	Y
37 Nowak	Y	Y	N	N	Y	Y	Y	Y
38 ***Kemp***	N	N	Y	N	Y	Y	Y	Y
39 Lundine	Y	N	Y	Y	Y	Y	Y	Y
NORTH CAROLINA								
1 Jones	Y	N	Y	Y	Y	Y	Y	Y
2 Fountain	Y	N	Y	Y	Y	Y	Y	Y
3 Whitley	Y	N	Y	Y	Y	Y	Y	Y
4 Andrews	Y	N	Y	Y	Y	Y	Y	Y
5 Neal	Y	N	Y	Y	Y	#	#	Y
6 Preyer	Y	N	Y	Y	Y	Y	Y	Y
7 Rose	Y	N	Y	Y	Y	Y	Y	Y
8 Hefner	Y	N	Y	Y	?	Y	Y	Y

	111	112	113	114	115	116	117	118
9 ***Martin***	N	Y	N	N	Y	Y	Y	Y
10 ***Broyhill***	Y	Y	Y	Y	Y	Y	Y	Y
11 Gudger	Y	N	Y	Y	Y	Y	Y	Y
NORTH DAKOTA								
AL ***Andrews***	Y	N	Y	Y	Y	Y	Y	Y
OHIO								
1 ***Gradison***	Y	N	Y	Y	Y	Y	Y	Y
2 Luken	Y	N	Y	Y	Y	Y	Y	Y
3 ***Whalen***	Y	N	Y	Y	Y	Y	Y	Y
4 ***Guyer***	N	Y	Y	Y	Y	Y	Y	Y
5 ***Latta***	N	Y	Y	Y	Y	Y	Y	Y
6 ***Harsha***	Y	Y	Y	N	Y	Y	Y	Y
7 ***Brown***	Y	Y	N	N	Y	Y	Y	Y
8 ***Kindness***	?	N	N	N	Y	Y	?	Y
9 Ashley	Y	N	Y	Y	Y	Y	Y	Y
10 ***Miller***	N	Y	Y	Y	Y	Y	Y	Y
11 ***Stanton***	N	N	Y	Y	Y	Y	Y	Y
12 ***Devine***	Y	N	Y	Y	Y	Y	Y	Y
13 Pease	Y	N	Y	Y	Y	Y	Y	Y
14 Seiberling	Y	N	Y	#	Y	Y	Y	Y
15 ***Wylie***	Y	N	Y	Y	Y	Y	Y	Y
16 ***Regula***	N	N	Y	N	Y	Y	Y	Y
17 ***Ashbrook***	N	Y	Y	N	Y	Y	N	Y
18 Applegate	Y	N	Y	Y	Y	Y	Y	Y
19 Carney	Y	N	Y	Y	Y	#	#	#
20 Oakar	Y	N	Y	Y	Y	Y	Y	?
21 Stokes	Y	N	Y	Y	Y	Y	Y	Y
22 Vanik	Y	N	Y	Y	Y	Y	Y	Y
23 Mottl	Y	N	Y	Y	Y	Y	Y	Y
OKLAHOMA								
1 Jones	Y	N	Y	Y	Y	Y	Y	Y
2 Risenhoover	Y	N	Y	Y	Y	Y	Y	Y
3 Watkins	Y	N	Y	Y	Y	Y	Y	N
4 Steed	Y	N	Y	Y	Y	Y	#	Y
5 ***Edwards***	Y	N	Y	N	Y	Y	Y	Y
6 English	Y	N	#	Y	Y	Y	Y	Y
OREGON								
1 AuCoin	Y	N	Y	Y	Y	Y	Y	Y
2 Ullman	Y	N	Y	Y	Y	Y	Y	Y
3 Duncan	P	N	Y	Y	Y	Y	?	Y
4 Weaver	?	?	?	?	?	?	?	#
PENNSYLVANIA								
1 Myers, M.	Y	N	Y	Y	Y	Y	Y	Y
2 Nix	Y	N	Y	#	Y	Y	Y	Y
3 Lederer	Y	N	Y	Y	Y	Y	Y	Y
4 Eilberg	Y	N	Y	Y	Y	Y	Y	Y
5 ***Schulze***	N	Y	Y	N	Y	Y	Y	Y
6 Yatron	Y	N	Y	Y	Y	Y	Y	Y
7 Edgar	Y	N	Y	Y	Y	#	#	Y
8 Kostmayer	Y	N	Y	Y	Y	Y	Y	Y
9 ***Shuster***	N	Y	N	N	N	Y	Y	Y
10 ***McDade***	Y	?	Y	N	Y	Y	Y	Y
11 Flood	Y	N	Y	Y	Y	Y	Y	Y
12 Murtha	Y	N	Y	Y	Y	Y	Y	Y
13 ***Coughlin***	N	Y	Y	N	N	Y	Y	Y
14 Moorhead	Y	N	Y	Y	Y	Y	Y	Y
15 Rooney	Y	N	Y	Y	Y	Y	Y	Y
16 ***Walker***	Y	Y	Y	N	Y	Y	Y	Y
17 Ertel	Y	N	Y	Y	Y	Y	Y	Y
18 Walgren	Y	N	Y	Y	Y	Y	Y	Y
19 ***Goodling, W.***	N	Y	Y	Y	Y	Y	Y	Y
20 Gaydos	Y	N	Y	Y	Y	Y	Y	Y
21 Dent	#	Y	Y	Y	Y	#	#	Y
22 Murphy	Y	N	Y	Y	Y	Y	Y	Y
23 Ammerman	Y	N	Y	Y	Y	Y	Y	Y
24 ***Marks***	N	Y	N	Y	Y	Y	Y	Y
25 ***Myers, G.***	N	Y	N	N	Y	Y	Y	Y
RHODE ISLAND								
1 St Germain	Y	N	Y	Y	N	Y	Y	Y
2 Beard	Y	N	Y	Y	Y	Y	Y	Y
SOUTH CAROLINA								
1 Davis	Y	?	Y	Y	Y	Y	Y	Y
2 ***Spence***	Y	Y	Y	N	Y	Y	Y	Y
3 Derrick	Y	N	Y	#	Y	Y	Y	Y
4 Mann	Y	N	Y	Y	Y	Y	Y	Y
5 Holland	Y	N	Y	Y	Y	Y	Y	Y
6 Jenrette	Y	N	Y	Y	Y	Y	Y	Y
SOUTH DAKOTA								
1 ***Pressler***	?	?	?	?	?	?	?	?
2 ***Abdnor***	N	Y	Y	N	Y	Y	Y	Y
TENNESSEE								
1 ***Quillen***	Y	Y	N	N	Y	Y	Y	Y
2 ***Duncan***	Y	Y	Y	N	Y	Y	Y	Y
3 Lloyd	Y	N	Y	Y	Y	Y	Y	Y
4 Gore	Y	N	Y	Y	Y	Y	Y	Y
5 Allen	Y	N	Y	Y	Y	Y	Y	Y
6 ***Beard***	N	Y	Y	N	Y	Y	Y	Y

	111	112	113	114	115	116	117	118
7 Jones	Y	N	Y	Y	Y	Y	Y	Y
8 Ford	Y	N	Y	Y	Y	Y	Y	Y
TEXAS								
1 Hall	Y	N	Y	Y	Y	Y	Y	Y
2 Wilson, C.	Y	N	Y	Y	Y	Y	Y	Y
3 ***Collins***	Y	Y	Y	N	N	P	N	Y
4 Roberts	Y	N	Y	Y	Y	Y	Y	Y
5 Mattox	Y	N	Y	Y	Y	Y	Y	Y
6 Teague	?	?	?	?	?	?	?	?
7 ***Archer***	N	N	Y	N	N	?	Y	Y
8 Eckhardt	Y	N	Y	Y	Y	Y	Y	Y
9 Brooks	Y	N	Y	Y	Y	Y	Y	Y
10 Pickle	Y	N	Y	Y	Y	Y	Y	Y
11 Poage	Y	N	Y	Y	Y	Y	Y	Y
12 Wright	Y	N	Y	Y	Y	?	Y	Y
13 Hightower	Y	N	Y	Y	Y	Y	Y	Y
14 Young	?	?	?	?	?	?	?	?
15 de la Garza	Y	N	Y	Y	Y	Y	Y	Y
16 White	Y	N	Y	Y	Y	Y	Y	Y
17 Burleson	Y	N	Y	Y	Y	Y	Y	Y
18 Jordan	Y	N	Y	Y	Y	Y	Y	Y
19 Mahon	Y	N	Y	Y	Y	Y	Y	#
20 Gonzalez	Y	N	Y	Y	Y	Y	Y	Y
21 Krueger	#	▮	#	#	#	#	#	#
22 Gammage	?	?	?	Y	Y	Y	Y	Y
23 Kazen	Y	N	Y	Y	Y	Y	Y	Y
24 Milford	Y	N	Y	Y	Y	Y	Y	Y
UTAH								
1 McKay	Y	N	Y	Y	Y	Y	#	Y
2 ***Marriott***	Y	Y	Y	N	Y	Y	Y	Y
VERMONT								
AL ***Jeffords***	Y	Y	Y	N	Y	#	Y	Y
VIRGINIA								
1 ***Trible***	Y	Y	Y	N	Y	Y	Y	Y
2 ***Whitehurst***	Y	Y	Y	N	Y	Y	Y	Y
3 Satterfield	Y	N	Y	Y	Y	Y	Y	Y
4 ***Daniel***	Y	N	Y	N	Y	Y	Y	Y
5 Daniel	Y	N	Y	Y	Y	Y	Y	Y
6 ***Butler***	N	Y	Y	N	Y	Y	Y	Y
7 ***Robinson***	Y	Y	Y	Y	Y	Y	Y	Y
8 Harris	Y	N	Y	Y	Y	Y	Y	Y
9 ***Wampler***	N	Y	Y	N	Y	Y	Y	Y
10 Fisher	Y	N	Y	Y	Y	#	Y	Y
WASHINGTON								
1 ***Pritchard***	N	Y	N	N	N	Y	Y	Y
2 Meeds	Y	N	Y	Y	Y	Y	Y	Y
3 Bonker	#	N	Y	Y	Y	Y	Y	Y
4 McCormack	Y	N	Y	Y	Y	Y	#	Y
5 Foley	Y	N	Y	Y	Y	Y	Y	Y
6 Dicks	Y	N	Y	Y	Y	Y	Y	Y
7 ***Cunningham***	#	N	Y	Y	Y	Y	Y	Y
WEST VIRGINIA								
1 Mollohan	Y	N	Y	Y	Y	Y	Y	Y
2 Staggers	Y	N	Y	Y	?	Y	?	Y
3 Slack	Y	N	Y	Y	Y	Y	Y	Y
4 Rahall	Y	N	Y	Y	Y	Y	Y	Y
WISCONSIN								
1 Aspin	Y	N	Y	Y	Y	Y	Y	?
2 Kastenmeier	Y	N	Y	Y	Y	#	Y	Y
3 Baldus	Y	N	Y	Y	Y	Y	Y	Y
4 Zablocki	Y	N	Y	Y	Y	Y	Y	Y
5 Reuss	Y	N	Y	Y	Y	Y	Y	Y
6 ***Steiger***	Y	Y	N	N	Y	Y	Y	Y
7 Obey	Y	N	Y	?	Y	Y	Y	Y
8 Cornell	Y	N	Y	Y	Y	Y	Y	Y
9 ***Kasten***	N	Y	Y	N	Y	Y	Y	Y
WYOMING								
AL Roncalio	Y	N	Y	Y	Y	?	Y	Y

Democrats ***Republicans***

119. HR 810. Government Officials' Travel Expenses. Ullman, D-Ore., motion to suspend the rules and pass the bill to permit private foundations to pay foreign travel expenses of government officials under certain circumstances. Motion agreed to 372-38: R 124-16; D 248-22 (ND 170-17; SD 78-5), March 14, 1978. A two-thirds majority vote (274 in this case) is required for passage under suspension of the rules.

120. HR 3813. Redwood Park Expansion. Adoption of the conference report on the bill to provide for the immediate expansion of the Redwood National Park in northern California by 48,000 acres. Adopted 317-60: R 89-42; D 228-18 (ND 165-8; SD 63-10), March 14, 1978. A "yea" was a vote supporting the president's position.

121. Procedural Motion. Ashbrook, R-Ohio, motion to approve the House *Journal* of Tuesday, March 14, 1978. Motion agreed to 387-15: R 128-11; D 259-4 (ND 177-4; SD 82-0), March 15, 1978.

122. HR 50. Full Employment Act. Hawkins, D-Calif., motion that the House resolve into the Committee of the Whole to consider the bill to promote full employment, balanced growth and price stability. Motion agreed to 380-19: R 121-18; D 259-1 (ND 181-0; SD 78-1), March 15, 1978.

123. HR 50. Full Employment Act. Ashbrook, R-Ohio, amendment to the Baucus, D-Mont., substitute *(see vote 124, below)* for the Ashbrook amendment to the bill. The Ashbrook amendment to the Baucus substitute would provide alternative language for the original Ashbrook amendment to the bill. Both Ashbrook amendments aimed to achieve a balanced federal budget within five years. Rejected 205-215: R 134-9; D 71-206 (ND 24-167; SD 47-39), March 15, 1978.

124. HR 50. Full Employment Act. Baucus, D-Mont., substitute, to the Ashbrook, R-Ohio, amendment, to declare that one of the purposes of the act is achievement of a balanced budget consistent with achievement of the unemployment goals enumerated in the bill. Adopted 411-3: R 138-2; D 273-1 (ND 189-0; SD 84-1), March 15, 1978. (The Ashbrook amendment, as amended by the Baucus substitute, subsequently was adopted by voice vote.)

125. HR 50. Full Employment Act. Hawkins, D-Calif., motion to end debate at 5:45 p.m. on Title I of the bill and all amendments thereto. Motion agreed to 237-170: R 2-139; D 235-31 (ND 168-16; SD 67-15), March 15, 1978.

126. HR 50. Full Employment Act. Quie, R-Minn., amendment to make specified permanent reductions in individual and corporate taxes a medium-term goal to be included in the first Economic Report submitted by the president following enactment of the bill. Rejected 194-216: R 140-2; D 54-214 (ND 16-171; SD 38-43), March 15, 1978.

KEY

- Y Voted for (yea).
- ✓ Paired for.
- † Announced for.
- # CQ Poll for.
- N Voted against (nay).
- X Paired against.
- \- Announced against.
- ▮ CQ Poll against.
- P Voted "present."
- ● Voted "present" to avoid possible conflict of interest.
- ? Did not vote or otherwise make a position known.

	119	120	121	122	123	124	125	126
ALABAMA								
1 Edwards	Y	Y	Y	Y	Y	Y	N	Y
2 Dickinson	Y	Y	Y	N	Y	Y	N	Y
3 Nichols	Y	#	Y	Y	Y	Y	Y	Y
4 Bevill	Y	Y	Y	Y	Y	Y	N	N
5 Flippo	Y	Y	Y	Y	Y	Y	Y	N
6 Buchanan	Y	Y	?	?	✓	?	?	✓
7 Flowers	Y	Y	Y	Y	N	Y	Y	N
ALASKA								
AL Young	Y	▮	Y	Y	Y	Y	Y	Y
ARIZONA								
1 Rhodes	Y	Y	Y	Y	Y	Y	N	Y
2 Udall	Y	Y	Y	Y	N	Y	Y	N
3 Stump	N	N	Y	Y	Y	Y	Y	Y
4 Rudd	Y	N	Y	N	Y	Y	N	Y
ARKANSAS								
1 Alexander	Y	?	Y	Y	N	Y	Y	N
2 Tucker	Y	#	#	#	N	Y	#	▮
3 Hammerschmidt	Y	N	Y	N	Y	Y	N	Y
4 Thornton	Y	?	?	?	?	?	?	?
CALIFORNIA								
1 Johnson	Y	Y	Y	Y	N	Y	Y	N
2 Clausen	N	N	Y	Y	✓	?	N	Y
3 Moss	?	?	Y	Y	N	Y	Y	N
4 Leggett	Y	Y	#	#	N	Y	Y	N
5 Burton, J.	Y	Y	Y	Y	Y	Y	Y	Y
6 Burton, P.	Y	Y	Y	Y	N	Y	?	N
7 Miller	Y	Y	N	Y	N	Y	Y	N
8 Dellums	Y	#	Y	Y	N	Y	N	N
9 Stark	Y	Y	Y	Y	N	Y	Y	Y
10 Edwards	Y	Y	Y	Y	N	Y	Y	N
11 Ryan	Y	Y	Y	Y	N	Y	Y	N
12 McCloskey	?	?	?	Y	N	Y	N	N
13 Mineta	Y	Y	Y	Y	N	Y	Y	N
14 McFall	Y	Y	Y	?	N	?	Y	N
15 Sisk	Y	Y	Y	Y	N	Y	Y	N
16 Panetta	Y	Y	Y	Y	Y	Y	Y	N
17 Krebs	Y	Y	Y	Y	Y	Y	Y	N
18 Ketchum	Y	N	Y	Y	Y	Y	N	Y
19 Lagomarsino	Y	Y	Y	Y	Y	Y	N	Y
20 Goldwater	?	?	Y	N	Y	Y	N	Y
21 Corman	Y	Y	#	#	N	Y	Y	N
22 Moorhead	Y	Y	Y	Y	Y	Y	N	Y
23 Beilenson	Y	Y	Y	Y	N	Y	Y	N
24 Waxman	Y	Y	Y	Y	N	Y	Y	N
25 Roybal	Y	Y	Y	Y	N	Y	Y	N
26 Rousselot	Y	N	Y	N	Y	Y	N	Y
27 Dornan	Y	N	Y	Y	Y	Y	N	Y
28 Burke	Y	Y	Y	Y	N	Y	Y	N
29 Hawkins	Y	Y	Y	Y	N	Y	Y	N
30 Danielson	Y	Y	Y	Y	N	Y	Y	N
31 Wilson, C.H.	#	#	#	?	N	Y	Y	N
32 Anderson	Y	Y	Y	Y	N	Y	Y	N
33 Clawson	Y	N	Y	Y	Y	Y	N	Y
34 Hannaford	Y	Y	Y	Y	N	Y	Y	N
35 Lloyd	Y	Y	N	Y	N	Y	Y	Y
36 Brown	Y	Y	?	?	N	Y	Y	N
37 Pettis	Y	N	Y	Y	Y	Y	N	Y
38 Patterson	Y	Y	Y	Y	N	Y	Y	N
39 Wiggins	Y	N	Y	#	Y	Y	#	✓
40 Badham	Y	N	Y	N	Y	Y	N	Y
41 Wilson, B.	Y	Y	Y	N	Y	N	N	Y
42 Van Deerlin	Y	Y	Y	Y	N	Y	Y	N
43 Burgener	Y	Y	Y	Y	Y	Y	N	Y
COLORADO								
1 Schroeder	Y	#	Y	Y	N	Y	N	N
2 Wirth	Y	Y	Y	Y	N	Y	Y	N
3 Evans	Y	N	Y	#	N	Y	#	N
4 Johnson	Y	Y	Y	Y	Y	Y	N	Y
5 Armstrong	Y	Y	?	?	Y	Y	N	Y
CONNECTICUT								
1 Cotter	Y	Y	Y	Y	N	Y	Y	N
2 Dodd	Y	Y	Y	Y	N	Y	?	?
3 Giaimo	Y	N	Y	Y	N	Y	Y	N
4 McKinney	Y	Y	Y	#	N	Y	N	Y
5 Sarasin	Y	Y	N	Y	Y	Y	N	Y
6 Moffett	Y	Y	Y	Y	N	Y	Y	N
DELAWARE								
AL Evans	Y	Y	Y	Y	Y	Y	N	Y
FLORIDA								
1 Sikes	Y	Y	?	Y	Y	Y	Y	N
2 Fuqua	Y	Y	Y	Y	Y	Y	Y	N
3 Bennett	N	Y	Y	Y	Y	Y	Y	N
4 Chappell	Y	Y	Y	Y	Y	Y	Y	Y
5 Kelly	N	N	Y	Y	Y	Y	N	Y
6 Young	Y	Y	Y	Y	Y	Y	N	Y
7 Gibbons	Y	Y	Y	Y	Y	Y	Y	Y
8 Ireland	Y	Y	Y	Y	Y	Y	Y	Y
9 Frey	Y	Y	Y	Y	Y	Y	N	Y
10 Bafalis	Y	Y	Y	N	Y	Y	N	Y
11 Rogers	Y	Y	Y	Y	N	Y	Y	Y
12 Burke	Y	Y	Y	Y	Y	Y	N	Y
13 Lehman	Y	?	Y	Y	N	Y	Y	N
14 Pepper	Y	Y	Y	#	N	Y	Y	N
15 Fascell	Y	#	Y	#	N	Y	Y	N
GEORGIA								
1 Ginn	Y	Y	Y	Y	N	Y	Y	N
2 Mathis	Y	Y	Y	Y	Y	Y	Y	Y
3 Brinkley	Y	Y	Y	Y	Y	Y	Y	Y
4 Levitas	Y	Y	Y	Y	Y	Y	N	Y
5 Fowler	Y	Y	Y	Y	N	Y	Y	N
6 Flynt	Y	?	Y	Y	Y	Y	N	Y
7 McDonald	N	N	Y	N	Y	Y	N	Y
8 Evans	N	N	Y	Y	Y	Y	Y	N
9 Jenkins	Y	Y	Y	Y	Y	Y	Y	N
10 Barnard	Y	N	Y	Y	Y	Y	Y	Y
HAWAII								
1 Heftel	Y	Y	Y	Y	N	Y	Y	Y
2 Akaka	Y	Y	Y	Y	N	Y	Y	N
IDAHO								
1 Symms	Y	N	Y	N	Y	Y	N	Y
2 Hansen, G.	N	N	Y	N	Y	Y	N	Y
ILLINOIS								
1 Metcalfe	?	?	?	?	X	?	?	X
2 Murphy	Y	Y	Y	Y	N	Y	Y	N
3 Russo	N	Y	Y	Y	Y	Y	Y	Y
4 Derwinski	Y	Y	Y	Y	Y	Y	N	Y
5 Fary	Y	Y	Y	Y	N	Y	Y	N
6 Hyde	Y	Y	Y	Y	Y	Y	N	Y
7 Collins	?	?	?	?	X	?	?	X
8 Rostenkowski	✓	?	Y	Y	N	Y	Y	N
9 Yates	Y	Y	Y	Y	N	Y	Y	N
10 Mikva	Y	Y	Y	Y	N	Y	Y	N
11 Annunzio	Y	Y	Y	Y	N	Y	Y	N
12 Crane	Y	N	Y	N	Y	Y	N	Y
13 McClory	Y	Y	Y	N	Y	Y	N	Y
14 Erlenborn	Y	Y	Y	N	Y	Y	N	✓
15 Corcoran	Y	Y	Y	Y	Y	Y	N	Y
16 Anderson	#	#	#	#	#	#	?	#
17 O'Brien	Y	Y	Y	Y	Y	Y	N	Y
18 Michel	Y	N	Y	Y	Y	Y	N	Y
19 Railsback	Y	Y	Y	Y	Y	Y	N	Y
20 Findley	Y	Y	Y	Y	Y	Y	N	Y
21 Madigan	Y	Y	Y	Y	Y	Y	N	Y
22 Shipley	Y	Y	Y	Y	N	Y	Y	N
23 Price	Y	Y	Y	Y	N	Y	Y	N
24 Simon	Y	Y	Y	Y	N	Y	#	N
INDIANA								
1 Benjamin	Y	Y	Y	Y	N	Y	Y	N
2 Fithian	Y	Y	Y	Y	Y	Y	Y	N
3 Brademas	Y	Y	Y	Y	N	Y	Y	N
4 Quayle	N	Y	N	N	Y	Y	N	Y
5 Hillis	Y	Y	?	Y	Y	Y	N	Y
6 Evans	N	Y	Y	Y	Y	Y	N	Y
7 Myers, J.	?	?	N	Y	Y	Y	N	Y
8 Cornwell	Y	#	Y	Y	N	Y	#	N
9 Hamilton	N	Y	Y	Y	Y	Y	Y	N
10 Sharp	N	Y	Y	Y	Y	Y	N	N
11 Jacobs	N	Y	N	Y	Y	Y	P	N
IOWA								
1 Leach	Y	Y	N	Y	Y	Y	N	Y
2 Blouin	Y	Y	Y	Y	N	Y	Y	N
3 Grassley	Y	Y	Y	Y	Y	Y	N	Y
4 Smith	Y	Y	Y	Y	N	Y	Y	N
5 Harkin	Y	Y	Y	Y	N	Y	Y	N
6 Bedell	Y	Y	Y	Y	N	Y	Y	N

Democrats ***Republicans***

Corresponding to Congressional Record Votes 147, 148, 150, 151, 152, 153, 154, 155

	119	120	121	122	123	124	125	126
KANSAS								
1 ***Sebelius***	Y	Y	Y	Y	Y	Y	N	Y
2 Keys	Y	Y	Y	Y	Y	Y	Y	N
3 ***Winn***	Y	Y	Y	Y	Y	Y	N	Y
4 Glickman	N	Y	Y	Y	Y	Y	Y	N
5 ***Skubitz***	Y	Y	Y	Y	Y	?	N	Y
KENTUCKY								
1 Hubbard	?	?	Y	Y	N	Y	Y	Y
2 Natcher	Y	Y	Y	Y	N	Y	Y	N
3 Mazzoli	Y	Y	Y	Y	N	Y	Y	N
4 ***Snyder***	Y	N	Y	Y	Y	Y	N	Y
5 ***Carter***	Y	Y	Y	Y	Y	Y	N	Y
6 Breckinridge	Y	Y	Y	†	Y	Y	Y	N
7 Perkins	Y	Y	Y	Y	N	Y	Y	N
LOUISIANA								
1 ***Livingston***	Y	Y	Y	Y	Y	Y	N	Y
2 Boggs	Y	Y	Y	Y	N	Y	Y	N
3 ***Treen***	Y	N	N	Y	Y	Y	N	Y
4 Waggonner	Y	N	#	#	Y	Y	N	N
5 Huckaby	#	Y	Y	Y	Y	Y	N	Y
6 ***Moore***	Y	Y	Y	Y	Y	Y	N	Y
7 Breaux	?	?	Y	Y	Y	Y	N	Y
8 Long	Y	N	Y	Y	N	Y	Y	N
MAINE								
1 ***Emery***	Y	Y	Y	Y	Y	Y	N	Y
2 ***Cohen***	Y	?	Y	Y	Y	Y	N	Y
MARYLAND								
1 ***Bauman***	Y	N	Y	N	Y	Y	N	Y
2 Long	Y	Y	Y	Y	N	Y	Y	N
3 Mikulski	Y	Y	Y	Y	N	Y	Y	N
4 ***Holt***	Y	N	Y	Y	Y	Y	N	Y
5 Spellman	Y	Y	Y	Y	N	#	Y	N
6 Byron	Y	Y	Y	Y	Y	Y	Y	N
7 Mitchell	Y	Y	N	Y	N	Y	Y	N
8 ***Steers***	Y	Y	Y	Y	N	Y	N	Y
MASSACHUSETTS								
1 ***Conte***	Y	Y	Y	Y	N	Y	N	Y
2 Boland	Y	Y	Y	Y	N	Y	Y	N
3 Early	Y	Y	Y	Y	N	Y	Y	N
4 Drinan	Y	Y	Y	Y	N	Y	Y	N
5 Tsongas	Y	Y	Y	Y	N	Y	Y	N
6 Harrington	Y	#	Y	Y	N	Y	Y	N
7 Markey	Y	Y	Y	Y	N	Y	Y	N
8 O'Neill								
9 Moakley	Y	Y	Y	Y	N	Y	Y	N
10 ***Heckler***	Y	?	Y	Y	Y	Y	?	Y
11 Burke	Y	Y	Y	Y	N	Y	Y	N
12 Studds	Y	Y	Y	Y	N	Y	N	N
MICHIGAN								
1 Conyers	Y	Y	Y	Y	N	Y	Y	N
2 ***Pursell***	N	Y	Y	Y	Y	?	N	Y
3 ***Brown***	Y	Y	N	Y	Y	Y	N	Y
4 ***Stockman***	Y	N	Y	Y	Y	Y	N	Y
5 ***Sawyer***	Y	Y	Y	Y	Y	Y	N	Y
6 Carr	Y	Y	Y	Y	N	Y	N	N
7 Kildee	N	Y	Y	Y	N	Y	Y	N
8 Traxler	Y	Y	Y	Y	Y	Y	Y	N
9 ***Vander Jagt***	Y	Y	Y	Y	Y	Y	N	Y
10 ***Cederberg***	Y	#	Y	Y	Y	Y	N	Y
11 ***Ruppe***	#	#	Y	Y	Y	Y	N	Y
12 Bonior	Y	Y	Y	Y	N	Y	Y	N
13 Diggs	Y	Y	Y	Y	N	Y	Y	N
14 Nedzi	Y	Y	Y	Y	N	Y	Y	N
15 Ford	Y	?	?	Y	N	Y	Y	N
16 Dingell	Y	?	Y	Y	N	Y	Y	N
17 Brodhead	N	Y	?	?	N	Y	Y	N
18 Blanchard	N	Y	Y	Y	N	Y	Y	N
19 ***Broomfield***	Y	#	Y	Y	Y	Y	N	Y
MINNESOTA								
1 ***Quie***	Y	Y	Y	Y	Y	Y	N	Y
2 ***Hagedorn***	Y	?	Y	Y	Y	Y	N	Y
3 ***Frenzel***	Y	Y	Y	Y	Y	Y	N	Y
4 Vento	Y	Y	Y	Y	N	Y	Y	N
5 Fraser	Y	Y	Y	Y	N	Y	Y	N
6 Nolan	Y	Y	Y	Y	N	Y	Y	N
7 ***Stangeland***	Y	N	Y	Y	Y	Y	N	Y
8 Oberstar	Y	Y	Y	Y	N	Y	Y	N
MISSISSIPPI								
1 Whitten	Y	#	Y	#	Y	Y	Y	✓
2 Bowen	Y	Y	Y	Y	Y	Y	Y	Y
3 Montgomery	Y	Y	Y	Y	Y	Y	Y	Y
4 ***Cochran***	Y	Y	Y	Y	Y	Y	N	Y
5 ***Lott***	Y	Y	Y	Y	Y	Y	N	Y
MISSOURI								
1 Clay	Y	Y	Y	Y	N	Y	Y	N
2 Young	Y	Y	#	Y	N	Y	Y	N
3 Gephardt	Y	Y	#	Y	N	Y	Y	N
4 Skelton	N	N	Y	Y	Y	Y	Y	N
5 Bolling	Y	Y	#	Y	N	Y	Y	N
6 ***Coleman***	N	Y	Y	Y	Y	Y	N	Y
7 ***Taylor***	N	N	Y	Y	Y	Y	N	Y
8 Ichord	Y	N	Y	P	N	Y	N	Y
9 Volkmer	N	Y	Y	Y	N	Y	Y	N
10 Burlison	Y	Y	Y	Y	N	Y	Y	N
MONTANA								
1 Baucus	N	Y	Y	Y	N	Y	Y	N
2 ***Marlenee***	Y	Y	Y	Y	Y	Y	N	Y
NEBRASKA								
1 ***Thone***	Y	Y	Y	Y	Y	Y	N	Y
2 Cavanaugh	Y	Y	Y	Y	N	Y	Y	N
3 ***Smith***	Y	Y	Y	Y	Y	Y	N	Y
NEVADA								
AL Santini	Y	#	Y	Y	#	Y	#	N
NEW HAMPSHIRE								
1 D'Amours	Y	Y	Y	Y	N	Y	Y	N
2 ***Cleveland***	Y	Y	Y	Y	Y	Y	N	Y
NEW JERSEY								
1 Florio	N	Y	Y	Y	N	Y	Y	N
2 Hughes	Y	Y	Y	Y	Y	Y	N	N
3 Howard	Y	Y	Y	Y	N	Y	Y	N
4 Thompson	Y	Y	Y	Y	N	Y	Y	N
5 ***Fenwick***	Y	Y	Y	Y	Y	Y	N	Y
6 ***Forsythe***	Y	N	▮	Y	Y	N	N	Y
7 Maguire	Y	Y	Y	Y	N	Y	Y	?
8 Roe	Y	Y	Y	Y	N	Y	Y	N
9 ***Hollenbeck***	N	Y	Y	Y	N	Y	N	Y
10 Rodino	Y	Y	Y	Y	N	Y	Y	N
11 Minish	Y	Y	Y	Y	N	Y	Y	Y
12 ***Rinaldo***	Y	Y	Y	Y	N	Y	N	Y
13 Meyner	Y	Y	Y	Y	N	Y	Y	N
14 LeFante	Y	Y	Y	Y	N	Y	Y	N
15 Patten	Y	Y	Y	Y	N	Y	Y	X
NEW MEXICO								
1 ***Lujan***	N	Y	Y	Y	Y	Y	N	Y
2 Runnels	Y	?	Y	Y	Y	Y	Y	Y
NEW YORK								
1 Pike	Y	Y	Y	Y	Y	Y	N	N
2 Downey	Y	Y	Y	Y	N	Y	Y	N
3 Ambro	Y	Y	Y	?	N	Y	N	N
4 ***Lent***	Y	Y	Y	Y	Y	Y	N	Y
5 ***Wydler***	Y	Y	Y	Y	Y	Y	N	Y
6 Wolff	Y	Y	#	#	N	Y	Y	N
7 Addabbo	Y	Y	Y	Y	N	Y	Y	N
8 Rosenthal	Y	Y	Y	Y	N	Y	Y	N
9 Delaney	Y	Y	Y	Y	N	Y	Y	X
10 Biaggi	Y	#	Y	Y	N	Y	Y	Y
11 Scheuer	Y	Y	Y	Y	N	Y	N	Y
12 Chisholm	Y	Y	Y	Y	N	Y	Y	N
13 Solarz	Y	Y	Y	Y	N	Y	Y	N
14 Richmond	Y	Y	Y	Y	N	Y	Y	N
15 Zeferetti	Y	Y	Y	Y	N	Y	Y	Y
16 Holtzman	Y	†	Y	Y	N	Y	Y	N
17 Murphy	Y	#	#	#	X	#	#	X
18 ***Green***	?	?	Y	Y	N	Y	N	Y
19 Rangel	Y	Y	Y	Y	N	?	Y	N
20 Weiss	Y	Y	Y	Y	N	Y	Y	N
21 Garcia	Y	Y	Y	Y	N	Y	Y	N
22 Bingham	Y	Y	Y	Y	N	Y	Y	N
23 ***Caputo***	N	Y	Y	Y	Y	Y	N	Y
24 Ottinger	Y	Y	Y	Y	N	Y	Y	N
25 ***Fish***	Y	Y	Y	Y	Y	Y	N	Y
26 ***Gilman***	Y	Y	Y	Y	N	Y	N	Y
27 McHugh	Y	Y	Y	?	N	Y	Y	N
28 Stratton	Y	Y	Y	Y	N	Y	Y	N
29 Pattison	Y	Y	Y	Y	N	Y	Y	N
30 ***McEwen***	Y	N	Y	Y	Y	Y	N	Y
31 ***Mitchell***	Y	Y	Y	Y	Y	Y	N	Y
32 Hanley	Y	Y	Y	Y	N	Y	Y	N
33 ***Walsh***	Y	Y	Y	Y	Y	Y	N	Y
34 ***Horton***	Y	Y	Y	#	Y	Y	N	Y
35 ***Conable***	Y	P	Y	N	Y	Y	N	Y
36 LaFalce	Y	Y	Y	Y	N	Y	N	N
37 Nowak	Y	Y	Y	Y	N	Y	N	N
38 ***Kemp***	Y	Y	Y	Y	Y	Y	N	Y
39 Lundine	Y	#	Y	Y	N	Y	Y	N
NORTH CAROLINA								
1 Jones	Y	Y	Y	Y	Y	Y	Y	Y
2 Fountain	Y	#	Y	Y	Y	Y	N	Y
3 Whitley	Y	Y	Y	Y	Y	Y	Y	Y
4 Andrews	Y	Y	Y	Y	Y	Y	Y	Y
5 Neal	Y	Y	Y	Y	Y	Y	Y	Y
6 Preyer	Y	Y	Y	Y	N	Y	Y	N
7 Rose	Y	Y	Y	Y	N	Y	Y	N
8 Hefner	Y	Y	?	Y	Y	Y	Y	Y
9 ***Martin***	Y	Y	Y	#	Y	Y	N	Y
10 ***Broyhill***	Y	N	Y	Y	Y	Y	N	Y
11 Gudger	Y	Y	Y	Y	Y	Y	Y	Y
NORTH DAKOTA								
AL Andrews	Y	Y	Y	Y	Y	Y	N	Y
OHIO								
1 ***Gradison***	Y	Y	Y	Y	Y	Y	N	Y
2 Luken	Y	Y	Y	Y	N	Y	Y	Y
3 ***Whalen***	Y	Y	Y	Y	N	Y	N	N
4 ***Guyer***	Y	#	#	Y	Y	Y	Y	Y
5 ***Latta***	N	Y	Y	Y	Y	Y	N	Y
6 ***Harsha***	Y	Y	Y	Y	Y	Y	N	Y
7 ***Brown***	Y	Y	Y	Y	Y	Y	N	Y
8 ***Kindness***	Y	N	Y	Y	Y	Y	N	Y
9 Ashley	Y	Y	?	Y	N	Y	Y	N
10 ***Miller***	N	Y	Y	Y	Y	Y	N	Y
11 ***Stanton***	Y	Y	Y	Y	Y	Y	N	Y
12 ***Devine***	Y	▮	Y	Y	Y	Y	N	Y
13 Pease	Y	Y	Y	Y	N	Y	Y	N
14 Seiberling	Y	Y	Y	Y	N	Y	Y	N
15 ***Wylie***	Y	Y	Y	Y	Y	Y	?	Y
16 ***Regula***	Y	Y	Y	Y	Y	Y	N	Y
17 ***Ashbrook***	Y	N	Y	Y	Y	Y	N	Y
18 Applegate	Y	Y	Y	Y	Y	Y	Y	Y
19 Carney	✓	#	Y	Y	N	Y	Y	N
20 Oakar	?	?	Y	Y	N	Y	Y	N
21 Stokes	Y	Y	Y	Y	N	Y	Y	N
22 Vanik	Y	Y	Y	Y	N	Y	Y	N
23 Mottl	N	Y	Y	Y	Y	Y	Y	Y
OKLAHOMA								
1 Jones	Y	Y	Y	Y	Y	Y	Y	N
2 Risenhoover	Y	Y	Y	Y	N	Y	Y	X
3 Watkins	Y	Y	Y	Y	Y	Y	Y	Y
4 Steed	Y	Y	Y	Y	N	Y	#	N
5 ***Edwards***	N	N	Y	Y	Y	Y	N	Y
6 English	Y	Y	Y	Y	Y	Y	Y	Y
OREGON								
1 AuCoin	Y	Y	Y	Y	Y	Y	Y	N
2 Ullman	Y	Y	Y	Y	N	Y	Y	▮
3 Duncan	Y	N	Y	Y	N	Y	Y	N
4 Weaver	?	#	Y	Y	N	Y	Y	N
PENNSYLVANIA								
1 Myers, M.	Y	Y	Y	Y	N	Y	Y	N
2 Nix	Y	#	Y	Y	N	Y	Y	N
3 Lederer	Y	Y	Y	Y	N	Y	Y	N
4 Eilberg	Y	Y	Y	Y	N	Y	Y	N
5 ***Schulze***	Y	N	Y	N	Y	Y	N	Y
6 Yatron	Y	Y	Y	Y	Y	Y	Y	N
7 Edgar	Y	Y	Y	Y	N	Y	N	N
8 Kostmayer	N	Y	Y	Y	Y	Y	N	N
9 ***Shuster***	Y	N	N	Y	Y	Y	N	Y
10 ***McDade***	Y	Y	Y	Y	Y	Y	N	Y
11 Flood	Y	Y	Y	Y	N	Y	Y	N
12 Murtha	Y	Y	Y	Y	N	Y	Y	N
13 ***Coughlin***	Y	Y	N	Y	Y	Y	N	Y
14 Moorhead	Y	Y	Y	Y	N	Y	Y	N
15 Rooney	Y	Y	Y	Y	N	Y	Y	N
16 ***Walker***	N	N	N	Y	Y	Y	N	Y
17 Ertel	Y	N	Y	Y	Y	Y	Y	N
18 Walgren	Y	Y	Y	Y	N	Y	Y	N
19 ***Goodling, W.***	N	N	Y	Y	Y	?	N	Y
20 Gaydos	Y	Y	Y	Y	N	Y	Y	N
21 Dent	Y	Y	Y	Y	N	#	Y	N
22 Murphy	Y	Y	Y	Y	N	Y	Y	N
23 Ammerman	N	?	Y	Y	N	Y	Y	N
24 ***Marks***	Y	Y	Y	Y	Y	Y	N	Y
25 ***Myers, G.***	Y	Y	Y	Y	Y	Y	N	Y
RHODE ISLAND								
1 St Germain	Y	Y	Y	Y	N	Y	Y	N
2 Beard	Y	Y	Y	Y	N	Y	Y	N
SOUTH CAROLINA								
1 Davis	Y	Y	Y	Y	N	Y	Y	N
2 ***Spence***	Y	Y	Y	Y	Y	Y	N	Y
3 Derrick	Y	Y	Y	Y	N	Y	Y	N
4 Mann	Y	Y	Y	Y	N	Y	N	N
5 Holland	Y	Y	Y	P	Y	#	#	▮
6 Jenrette	Y	Y	Y	Y	N	Y	Y	N
SOUTH DAKOTA								
1 ***Pressler***	?	?	Y	Y	Y	Y	N	Y
2 ***Abdnor***	Y	N	Y	Y	Y	Y	N	Y
TENNESSEE								
1 ***Quillen***	Y	N	Y	Y	Y	Y	N	Y
2 ***Duncan***	Y	Y	Y	Y	Y	Y	N	Y
3 Lloyd	Y	Y	Y	Y	Y	Y	Y	Y
4 Gore	N	Y	Y	Y	N	Y	Y	N
5 Allen	Y	Y	Y	Y	N	Y	Y	N
6 ***Beard***	Y	Y	Y	Y	Y	Y	N	Y
7 Jones	Y	Y	Y	Y	Y	Y	Y	N
8 Ford	Y	Y	Y	Y	N	Y	Y	N
TEXAS								
1 Hall	Y	?	Y	Y	Y	Y	Y	Y
2 Wilson, C.	Y	Y	Y	Y	N	Y	N	N
3 ***Collins***	N	N	N	N	Y	Y	N	Y
4 Roberts	Y	Y	Y	Y	Y	Y	Y	Y
5 Mattox	Y	Y	Y	Y	N	Y	Y	Y
6 Teague	?	?	?	?	✓	?	?	✓
7 ***Archer***	Y	N	Y	Y	Y	Y	N	Y
8 Eckhardt	Y	Y	Y	Y	N	Y	Y	N
9 Brooks	Y	Y	Y	Y	N	Y	Y	N
10 Pickle	Y	N	Y	Y	N	Y	N	N
11 Poage	Y	Y	Y	Y	Y	Y	N	Y
12 Wright	Y	Y	Y	Y	N	Y	Y	N
13 Hightower	Y	Y	Y	Y	N	Y	Y	N
14 Young	?	?	?	?	?	?	?	?
15 de la Garza	N	Y	Y	Y	Y	Y	Y	Y
16 White	Y	Y	Y	Y	Y	Y	Y	Y
17 Burleson	Y	N	Y	Y	Y	Y	Y	Y
18 Jordan	Y	?	Y	Y	N	Y	Y	N
19 Mahon	#	#	Y	Y	Y	Y	#	▮
20 Gonzalez	Y	Y	Y	Y	N	Y	Y	N
21 Krueger	X	#	#	#	✓	#	#	✓
22 Gammage	Y	Y	Y	Y	Y	Y	Y	Y
23 Kazen	Y	Y	Y	Y	N	Y	N	Y
24 Milford	Y	N	Y	Y	N	N	Y	Y
UTAH								
1 McKay	Y	N	Y	Y	N	Y	#	N
2 ***Marriott***	Y	N	Y	Y	Y	Y	N	Y
VERMONT								
AL Jeffords	Y	Y	Y	Y	Y	Y	N	Y
VIRGINIA								
1 ***Trible***	Y	Y	Y	Y	Y	Y	N	Y
2 ***Whitehurst***	Y	Y	Y	Y	Y	Y	N	Y
3 Satterfield	Y	N	Y	Y	Y	Y	N	Y
4 ***Daniel***	Y	N	Y	Y	Y	Y	N	Y
5 Daniel	Y	N	Y	Y	Y	Y	N	Y
6 ***Butler***	Y	N	Y	Y	Y	Y	N	Y
7 ***Robinson***	Y	N	#	#	✓	#	▮	✓
8 Harris	Y	Y	Y	Y	N	Y	Y	N
9 ***Wampler***	Y	N	Y	Y	Y	Y	N	Y
10 Fisher	Y	Y	Y	Y	N	Y	Y	N
WASHINGTON								
1 ***Pritchard***	Y	Y	Y	Y	Y	Y	N	Y
2 Meeds	#	Y	Y	Y	N	Y	Y	N
3 Bonker	Y	Y	Y	Y	N	Y	Y	N
4 McCormack	Y	Y	Y	Y	N	Y	Y	N
5 Foley	Y	Y	Y	Y	X	Y	Y	N
6 Dicks	Y	Y	Y	Y	N	Y	Y	N
7 ***Cunningham***	Y	N	Y	Y	Y	Y	N	Y
WEST VIRGINIA								
1 Mollohan	Y	Y	Y	Y	N	Y	Y	N
2 Staggers	Y	Y	Y	Y	N	Y	Y	N
3 Slack	Y	Y	Y	Y	N	Y	Y	N
4 Rahall	Y	#	#	#	X	#	#	X
WISCONSIN								
1 Aspin	?	?	Y	Y	N	Y	Y	N
2 Kastenmeier	Y	Y	Y	Y	N	Y	Y	N
3 Baldus	Y	Y	Y	Y	N	Y	Y	N
4 Zablocki	Y	Y	Y	Y	N	Y	Y	N
5 Reuss	Y	Y	Y	Y	N	Y	Y	N
6 ***Steiger***	Y	Y	N	Y	Y	Y	N	Y
7 Obey	Y	Y	Y	Y	N	Y	Y	N
8 Cornell	Y	Y	Y	Y	N	Y	N	N
9 ***Kasten***	Y	Y	Y	Y	Y	Y	N	Y
WYOMING								
AL Roncalio	Y	Y	?	?	N	Y	?	?

Democrats ***Republicans***

127. **HR 50. Full Employment Act.** Hawkins, D-Calif., motion that the House resolve itself into the Committee of the Whole to further consider the bill to promote full employment, balanced growth and price stability. Motion agreed to 379-8: R 126-8; D 253-0 (ND 175-0; SD 78-0), March 16, 1978.

128. **HR 50. Full Employment Act.** Jeffords, R-Vt., amendment to make removal of architectural barriers to the handicapped one of the explicit national priorities under the bill. Adopted 398-0: R 133-0; D 265-0 (ND 182-0; SD 83-0), March 16, 1978.

129. **HR 50. Full Employment Act.** Pike, D-N.Y., amendment to exclude from the measurement of unemployment used under the bill persons unemployed because of strikes, those who have been unemployed less than four weeks, those who have jobs waiting but for their own convenience are not ready to enter employment, those who are not seeking full-time work, and those who voluntarily left their last jobs. Rejected 199-204: R 125-12; D 74-192 (ND 18-165; SD 56-27), March 16, 1978.

130. **HR 50. Full Employment Act.** Wiggins, R-Calif., motion to strike the enacting clause and thus kill the bill. Motion rejected 106-310: R 91-51; D 15-259 (ND 3-186; SD 12-73), March 16, 1978.

131. **HR 50. Full Employment Act.** Ashbrook, R-Ohio, amendment to require the president, in carrying out the purposes of the act, to consider the impact of all the provisions of the U.S. Code and Code of Federal Regulations on the national economy. Rejected 114-296: R 100-39; D 14-257 (ND 3-184; SD 11-73), March 16, 1978.

132. **HR 50. Full Employment Act.** Conable, R-N.Y., amendment, to the Rules Committee substitute to Title III of the bill, to permit the Joint Economic Committee to submit an amendment recommending economic goals to the first annual concurrent resolution on the budget, eliminating provisions that would permit the joint committee to report its own concurrent resolution each year. Adopted 259-153: R 132-7; D 127-146 (ND 70-119; SD 57-27), March 16, 1978. (The substitute, as amended, subsequently was adopted by voice vote.)

KEY

Y Voted for (yea).
✓ Paired for.
† Announced for.
# CQ Poll for.
N Voted against (nay).
X Paired against.
- Announced against.
■ CQ Poll against.
P Voted "present."
● Voted "present" to avoid possible conflict of interest.
? Did not vote or otherwise make a position known.

	127	128	129	130	131	132
ALABAMA						
1 Edwards	Y	Y	Y	Y	Y	Y
2 Dickinson	Y	Y	Y	Y	Y	Y
3 Nichols	Y	Y	Y	N	N	Y
4 Bevill	Y	Y	N	N	N	N
5 Flippo	Y	Y	Y	N	N	Y
6 Buchanan	?	?	?	?	?	?
7 Flowers	Y	Y	Y	N	N	Y
ALASKA						
AL Young	■	#	■	■	?	?
ARIZONA						
1 Rhodes	Y	Y	Y	Y	Y	Y
2 Udall	Y	Y	N	N	N	N
3 Stump	Y	Y	Y	Y	Y	Y
4 Rudd	Y	#	Y	Y	Y	Y
ARKANSAS						
1 Alexander	Y	Y	N	N	N	N
2 Tucker	#	#	■	■	■	#
3 Hammerschmidt	Y	Y	Y	Y	Y	Y
4 Thornton	?	?	?	?	?	?
CALIFORNIA						
1 Johnson	Y	Y	N	N	N	N
2 Clausen	?	?	Y	N	Y	?
3 Moss	Y	Y	N	N	N	N
4 Leggett	Y	Y	Y	N	N	Y
5 Burton, J.	?	Y	N	N	N	Y
6 Burton, P.	Y	Y	N	N	N	N
7 Miller	Y	Y	N	N	N	Y
8 Dellums	Y	Y	N	N	N	N
9 Stark	Y	Y	N	N	N	N
10 Edwards	Y	Y	N	N	?	N
11 Ryan	#	#	?	■	■	#
12 McCloskey	?	Y	N	N	N	Y
13 Mineta	#	Y	N	N	N	Y
14 McFall	Y	Y	N	N	N	N
15 Sisk	Y	Y	Y	N	N	N
16 Panetta	Y	Y	N	N	N	Y
17 Krebs	Y	Y	N	N	N	Y
18 Ketchum	Y	Y	Y	Y	Y	Y
19 Lagomarsino	Y	Y	Y	Y	Y	Y
20 Goldwater	Y	Y	Y	Y	Y	Y
21 Corman	Y	Y	N	N	N	N
22 Moorhead	Y	Y	Y	Y	Y	Y
23 Beilenson	#	#	■	N	N	Y
24 Waxman	Y	Y	N	N	N	N
25 Roybal	Y	Y	N	N	?	N
26 Rousselot	Y	Y	Y	Y	Y	Y
27 Dornan	Y	Y	Y	Y	Y	Y
28 Burke	Y	Y	N	N	N	N
29 Hawkins	Y	Y	N	N	N	N
30 Danielson	Y	Y	N	N	N	N
31 Wilson, C.H.	Y	Y	■	N	■	N
32 Anderson	Y	Y	N	N	N	N
33 Clawson	N	Y	Y	Y	?	Y
34 Hannaford	Y	Y	N	N	N	Y
35 Lloyd	Y	Y	Y	N	N	Y
36 Brown	Y	Y	N	N	N	N
37 Pettis	Y	Y	Y	Y	Y	Y
38 Patterson	#	Y	N	N	N	N
39 Wiggins	#	Y	Y	Y	N	Y
40 Badham	Y	Y	Y	Y	Y	Y
41 Wilson, B.	N	Y	Y	N	Y	Y
42 Van Deerlin	P	Y	N	N	N	N
43 Burgener	Y	Y	Y	Y	Y	Y
COLORADO						
1 Schroeder	Y	Y	N	N	N	N
2 Wirth	Y	Y	N	N	N	Y
3 Evans	Y	Y	N	N	N	Y
4 Johnson	Y	Y	Y	Y	N	Y
5 Armstrong	N	Y	Y	Y	Y	Y
CONNECTICUT						
1 Cotter	Y	Y	N	N	N	Y
2 Dodd	Y	Y	N	N	N	N
3 Giaimo	Y	Y	N	N	N	N
4 McKinney	Y	Y	Y	Y	N	Y
5 Sarasin	Y	Y	Y	N	N	Y
6 Moffett	#	Y	N	N	N	N
DELAWARE						
AL Evans	Y	Y	Y	Y	Y	Y
FLORIDA						
1 Sikes	Y	Y	Y	N	Y	✓
2 Fuqua	Y	Y	Y	N	N	Y
3 Bennett	Y	Y	Y	N	Y	Y
4 Chappell	Y	Y	Y	N	Y	Y
5 Kelly	Y	Y	Y	Y	Y	Y
6 Young	Y	Y	Y	N	Y	Y
7 Gibbons	?	?	Y	N	N	Y
8 Ireland	Y	Y	Y	N	Y	Y
9 Frey	?	?	?	?	?	?
10 Bafalis	Y	Y	Y	Y	Y	Y
11 Rogers	Y	Y	Y	N	N	Y
12 Burke	Y	Y	Y	Y	Y	Y
13 Lehman	Y	Y	Y	N	N	Y
14 Pepper	#	Y	N	N	N	N
15 Fascell	Y	Y	N	N	N	N
GEORGIA						
1 Ginn	Y	Y	N	N	N	N
2 Mathis	Y	Y	Y	N	N	Y
3 Brinkley	Y	Y	Y	N	N	Y
4 Levitas	Y	Y	Y	N	N	Y
5 Fowler	Y	Y	N	N	N	N
6 Flynt	Y	Y	Y	Y	Y	Y
7 McDonald	Y	Y	Y	Y	Y	Y
8 Evans	Y	Y	N	N	N	Y
9 Jenkins	Y	Y	Y	N	N	Y
10 Barnard	Y	Y	Y	Y	N	Y
HAWAII						
1 Heftel	Y	Y	Y	N	N	N
2 Akaka	Y	Y	N	N	■	X
IDAHO						
1 Symms	N	?	Y	Y	Y	Y
2 Hansen, G.	N	Y	Y	Y	Y	Y
ILLINOIS						
1 Metcalfe	?	?	X	N	N	N
2 Murphy	Y	Y	N	N	N	N
3 Russo	Y	Y	N	N	N	Y
4 Derwinski	Y	Y	Y	Y	N	Y
5 Fary	Y	Y	N	N	N	N
6 Hyde	Y	Y	Y	Y	N	Y
7 Collins	Y	Y	N	N	N	N
8 Rostenkowski	Y	Y	N	N	N	N
9 Yates	Y	Y	N	N	N	N
10 Mikva	Y	#	N	N	N	Y
11 Annunzio	Y	Y	N	N	N	N
12 Crane	Y	Y	Y	Y	Y	Y
13 McClory	Y	Y	Y	Y	Y	#
14 Erlenborn	Y	Y	Y	N	Y	Y
15 Corcoran	Y	Y	Y	Y	Y	Y
16 Anderson	#	#	#	■	■	#
17 O'Brien	Y	Y	Y	N	N	Y
18 Michel	Y	Y	✓	Y	Y	Y
19 Railsback	Y	Y	Y	N	N	Y
20 Findley	?	Y	Y	N	Y	Y
21 Madigan	Y	Y	Y	N	?	Y
22 Shipley	Y	Y	N	N	N	Y
23 Price	Y	Y	N	N	N	N
24 Simon	Y	Y	N	N	N	?
INDIANA						
1 Benjamin	Y	Y	N	N	N	N
2 Fithian	Y	Y	N	N	N	Y
3 Brademas	Y	Y	N	N	N	N
4 Quayle	Y	Y	Y	Y	Y	Y
5 Hillis	Y	Y	Y	N	N	Y
6 Evans	Y	Y	N	N	Y	Y
7 Myers, J.	Y	Y	Y	Y	Y	Y
8 Cornwell	Y	Y	Y	N	N	N
9 Hamilton	Y	Y	N	N	N	N
10 Sharp	Y	Y	N	N	N	Y
11 Jacobs	Y	Y	Y	N	N	N
IOWA						
1 Leach	Y	Y	Y	N	N	Y
2 Blouin	Y	Y	N	N	N	N
3 Grassley	Y	Y	Y	N	Y	Y
4 Smith	Y	Y	N	N	N	Y
5 Harkin	Y	Y	N	N	N	Y
6 Bedell	Y	Y	N	N	N	Y

Democrats **Republicans**

Corresponding to Congressional Record Votes 156, 157, 158, 159, 160, 161

	127	128	129	130	131	132
KANSAS						
1 Sebelius	Y	Y	Y	Y	N	N
2 Keys	Y	Y	N	N	N	N
3 Winn	Y	Y	Y	Y	Y	Y
4 Glickman	Y	Y	N	N	N	Y
5 Skubitz	Y	Y	Y	Y	N	Y
KENTUCKY						
1 Hubbard	Y	Y	Y	N	?	Y
2 Natcher	Y	Y	N	N	N	N
3 Mazzoli	Y	Y	Y	N	N	Y
4 Snyder	Y	Y	Y	Y	Y	Y
5 Carter	Y	Y	N	N	Y	Y
6 Breckinridge	†	Y	N	N	N	Y
7 Perkins	Y	Y	N	N	N	N
LOUISIANA						
1 Livingston	Y	Y	Y	Y	Y	Y
2 Boggs	Y	Y	Y	N	N	N
3 Treen	Y	Y	Y	N	?	Y
4 Waggonner	Y	Y	Y	Y	N	Y
5 Huckaby	Y	Y	Y	Y	N	?
6 Moore	Y	Y	Y	Y	Y	Y
7 Breaux	Y	Y	Y	Y	Y	Y
8 Long	Y	Y	N	N	N	N
MAINE						
1 Emery	Y	Y	Y	Y	Y	Y
2 Cohen	Y	Y	Y	N	Y	Y
MARYLAND						
1 Bauman	N	Y	Y	Y	Y	Y
2 Long	Y	Y	Y	N	N	Y
3 Mikulski	Y	Y	N	N	N	N
4 Holt	Y	Y	Y	Y	Y	Y
5 Spellman	Y	Y	N	N	N	Y
6 Byron	Y	Y	Y	N	N	N
7 Mitchell	#	#	X	N	N	N
8 Steers	Y	Y	N	N	N	Y
MASSACHUSETTS						
1 Conte	Y	Y	N	N	N	Y
2 Boland	Y	Y	N	N	N	N
3 Early	Y	Y	N	N	N	N
4 Drinan	Y	Y	N	N	N	N
5 Tsongas	Y	Y	N	N	N	Y
6 Harrington	Y	Y	N	N	N	N
7 Markey	Y	Y	■	N	N	N
8 O'Neill						
9 Moakley	Y	#	N	N	N	N
10 Heckler	Y	Y	N	N	Y	N
11 Burke	Y	Y	N	N	N	N
12 Studds	Y	Y	N	N	N	Y
MICHIGAN						
1 Conyers	#	Y	N	N	N	N
2 Pursell	Y	Y	Y	N	Y	?
3 Brown	Y	Y	Y	Y	Y	N
4 Stockman	#	#	#	Y	Y	Y
5 Sawyer	Y	Y	Y	N	N	Y
6 Carr	Y	Y	N	N	N	Y
7 Kildee	Y	Y	N	N	N	N
8 Traxler	Y	Y	N	N	N	N
9 Vander Jagt	Y	Y	Y	N	Y	Y
10 Cederberg	Y	Y	Y	N	N	Y
11 Ruppe	Y	Y	Y	Y	Y	Y
12 Bonior	Y	Y	N	N	N	N
13 Diggs	Y	Y	N	N	N	N
14 Nedzi	Y	Y	N	N	N	N
15 Ford	Y	Y	N	N	N	N
16 Dingell	Y	Y	N	N	N	N
17 Brodhead	Y	Y	N	N	N	N
18 Blanchard	Y	Y	N	N	N	N
19 Broomfield	Y	Y	Y	Y	Y	Y
MINNESOTA						
1 Quie	Y	Y	Y	N	N	Y
2 Hagedorn	Y	Y	Y	Y	Y	Y
3 Frenzel	Y	Y	Y	Y	Y	Y
4 Vento	Y	Y	N	N	N	N
5 Fraser	Y	Y	N	N	N	N
6 Nolan	Y	Y	N	N	N	?
7 Stangeland	Y	Y	Y	Y	Y	Y
8 Oberstar	Y	Y	N	N	N	N
MISSISSIPPI						
1 Whitten	Y	Y	✓	N	N	Y
2 Bowen	Y	Y	Y	N	N	Y
3 Montgomery	Y	Y	Y	Y	N	Y
4 Cochran	Y	Y	Y	Y	Y	Y
5 Lott	Y	Y	Y	Y	Y	Y
MISSOURI						
1 Clay	Y	Y	N	N	N	N
2 Young	Y	Y	N	N	N	N
3 Gephardt	Y	Y	N	N	N	N
4 Skelton	Y	Y	N	N	N	Y
5 Bolling	Y	Y	N	N	N	N
6 Coleman	?	?	Y	Y	Y	Y
7 Taylor	Y	Y	Y	Y	Y	Y
8 Ichord	Y	Y	Y	Y	N	Y
9 Volkmer	Y	Y	N	N	N	N
10 Burlison	Y	Y	N	N	N	N
MONTANA						
1 Baucus	#	#	?	■	■	✓
2 Marlenee	Y	Y	Y	Y	Y	Y
NEBRASKA						
1 Thone	Y	Y	Y	N	Y	Y
2 Cavanaugh	Y	Y	N	N	N	Y
3 Smith	Y	Y	Y	Y	Y	Y
NEVADA						
AL Santini	Y	Y	Y	N	N	Y
NEW HAMPSHIRE						
1 D'Amours	Y	Y	N	N	N	Y
2 Cleveland	Y	Y	Y	N	N	Y
NEW JERSEY						
1 Florio	Y	Y	N	■	N	N
2 Hughes	Y	Y	N	N	N	Y
3 Howard	Y	Y	N	N	N	N
4 Thompson	#	Y	N	N	N	N
5 Fenwick	Y	Y	Y	Y	N	Y
6 Forsythe	Y	Y	Y	Y	Y	Y
7 Maguire	Y	Y	N	N	N	N
8 Roe	Y	Y	N	N	N	N
9 Hollenbeck	Y	Y	N	N	N	Y
10 Rodino	Y	Y	N	N	N	N
11 Minish	Y	Y	N	N	N	Y
12 Rinaldo	Y	Y	N	N	N	N
13 Meyner	Y	#	N	N	N	N
14 LeFante	Y	Y	N	N	N	N
15 Patten	Y	Y	N	N	N	N
NEW MEXICO						
1 Lujan	Y	Y	Y	Y	Y	Y
2 Runnels	?	?	Y	?	Y	?
NEW YORK						
1 Pike	Y	Y	Y	Y	N	Y
2 Downey	Y	Y	N	N	N	Y
3 Ambro	?	Y	N	N	N	Y
4 Lent	Y	Y	Y	Y	Y	Y
5 Wydler	Y	?	Y	Y	Y	Y
6 Wolff	Y	Y	N	N	N	N
7 Addabbo	Y	Y	N	N	N	N
8 Rosenthal	Y	Y	N	N	N	N
9 Delaney	Y	Y	N	N	N	N
10 Biaggi	Y	Y	N	N	N	Y
11 Scheuer	Y	Y	N	N	N	N
12 Chisholm	Y	Y	N	N	N	N
13 Solarz	Y	Y	N	N	N	N
14 Richmond	Y	Y	N	N	N	N
15 Zeferetti	Y	Y	N	N	N	Y
16 Holtzman	Y	Y	N	N	N	N
17 Murphy	Y	Y	N	N	N	N
18 Green	Y	Y	N	N	N	Y
19 Rangel	Y	Y	N	N	N	N
20 Weiss	Y	Y	N	N	N	N
21 Garcia	Y	Y	N	N	N	N
22 Bingham	Y	Y	N	N	N	N
23 Caputo	Y	Y	N	N	Y	Y
24 Ottinger	Y	Y	N	N	N	Y
25 Fish	Y	Y	Y	N	N	Y
26 Gilman	Y	Y	Y	N	N	Y
27 McHugh	Y	Y	N	N	N	N
28 Stratton	Y	Y	Y	N	N	Y
29 Pattison	Y	Y	N	N	N	Y
30 McEwen	Y	Y	Y	Y	Y	Y
31 Mitchell	Y	Y	Y	N	N	Y
32 Hanley	Y	Y	N	N	N	Y
33 Walsh	Y	Y	Y	N	N	Y
34 Horton	#	Y	Y	N	N	Y
35 Conable	Y	Y	Y	Y	Y	Y
36 LaFalce	Y	Y	N	N	N	Y
37 Nowak	Y	Y	N	N	N	Y
38 Kemp	Y	Y	Y	Y	Y	Y
39 Lundine	Y	Y	N	N	N	Y
NORTH CAROLINA						
1 Jones	Y	Y	Y	N	N	Y
2 Fountain	Y	Y	Y	N	N	Y
3 Whitley	Y	Y	Y	N	N	Y
4 Andrews	Y	Y	Y	N	N	N
5 Neal	Y	Y	Y	N	N	Y
6 Preyer	Y	Y	Y	N	N	N
7 Rose	Y	Y	N	N	N	N
8 Hefner	P	Y	Y	N	N	Y
9 Martin	Y	Y	Y	Y	N	Y
10 Broyhill	Y	?	?	Y	N	Y
11 Gudger	Y	Y	Y	N	N	Y
NORTH DAKOTA						
AL Andrews	Y	Y	Y	N	N	Y
OHIO						
1 Gradison	Y	Y	Y	Y	Y	Y
2 Luken	Y	Y	N	N	N	Y
3 Whalen	Y	Y	N	N	N	N
4 Guyer	Y	Y	Y	Y	Y	Y
5 Latta	Y	Y	Y	Y	Y	Y
6 Harsha	Y	Y	Y	N	Y	Y
7 Brown	?	?	?	Y	Y	N
8 Kindness	Y	Y	Y	Y	Y	N
9 Ashley	?	?	?	N	N	Y
10 Miller	Y	Y	Y	N	Y	Y
11 Stanton	Y	Y	Y	N	N	Y
12 Devine	Y	Y	Y	Y	Y	Y
13 Pease	Y	Y	N	N	N	Y
14 Seiberling	Y	Y	N	N	N	N
15 Wylie	Y	Y	Y	N	N	Y
16 Regula	Y	Y	Y	N	Y	Y
17 Ashbrook	Y	Y	Y	Y	Y	Y
18 Applegate	Y	Y	Y	N	N	Y
19 Carney	Y	Y	N	N	N	Y
20 Oakar	Y	Y	N	N	N	N
21 Stokes	Y	Y	N	N	N	N
22 Vanik	Y	Y	N	N	N	N
23 Mottl	Y	Y	N	N	N	N
OKLAHOMA						
1 Jones	Y	Y	Y	N	N	Y
2 Risenhoover	?	Y	N	N	N	Y
3 Watkins	Y	Y	Y	N	N	Y
4 Steed	Y	Y	N	N	N	N
5 Edwards	Y	Y	Y	Y	Y	Y
6 English	Y	Y	Y	Y	N	Y
OREGON						
1 AuCoin	#	Y	N	N	N	Y
2 Ullman	Y	Y	N	N	N	Y
3 Duncan	Y	Y	N	N	N	Y
4 Weaver	Y	Y	N	N	N	N
PENNSYLVANIA						
1 Myers, M.	Y	Y	N	N	N	N
2 Nix	Y	Y	N	N	N	N
3 Lederer	Y	Y	N	N	N	Y
4 Eilberg	Y	Y	N	N	N	N
5 Schulze	Y	Y	Y	Y	Y	Y
6 Yatron	Y	Y	N	N	N	Y
7 Edgar	Y	Y	N	N	N	Y
8 Kostmayer	Y	Y	N	N	N	Y
9 Shuster	Y	Y	Y	Y	Y	Y
10 McDade	Y	Y	N	N	N	Y
11 Flood	?	?	X	?	■	X
12 Murtha	Y	Y	N	N	N	N
13 Coughlin	Y	Y	Y	N	N	Y
14 Moorhead	Y	Y	N	N	N	N
15 Rooney	Y	Y	N	N	N	N
16 Walker	Y	Y	Y	Y	Y	Y
17 Ertel	Y	Y	Y	N	N	Y
18 Walgren	Y	Y	N	N	N	Y
19 Goodling, W.	Y	Y	Y	Y	Y	Y
20 Gaydos	Y	Y	N	N	N	Y
21 Dent	#	Y	N	N	N	Y
22 Murphy	Y	Y	N	N	N	Y
23 Ammerman	Y	Y	N	N	N	Y
24 Marks	Y	Y	N	N	N	Y
25 Myers, G.	Y	Y	Y	Y	Y	N
RHODE ISLAND						
1 St Germain	Y	Y	N	N	N	N
2 Beard	Y	?	X	N	N	N
SOUTH CAROLINA						
1 Davis	Y	Y	Y	N	N	N
2 Spence	Y	Y	Y	Y	Y	Y
3 Derrick	Y	Y	N	N	N	Y
4 Mann	Y	Y	Y	N	N	Y
5 Holland	Y	Y	Y	N	N	Y
6 Jenrette	Y	Y	Y	N	N	N
SOUTH DAKOTA						
1 Pressler	Y	Y	Y	N	N	Y
2 Abdnor	Y	Y	Y	Y	Y	Y
TENNESSEE						
1 Quillen	Y	Y	Y	Y	Y	Y
2 Duncan	Y	?	?	Y	Y	Y
3 Lloyd	Y	#	#	N	N	Y
4 Gore	Y	Y	N	N	N	Y
5 Allen	Y	Y	N	N	N	N
6 Beard	Y	Y	Y	Y	Y	Y
7 Jones	Y	Y	N	N	#	N
8 Ford	Y	Y	N	N	N	N
TEXAS						
1 Hall	Y	Y	Y	N	N	Y
2 Wilson, C.	Y	Y	Y	N	N	N
3 Collins	N	Y	Y	Y	Y	Y
4 Roberts	Y	Y	Y	N	N	Y
5 Mattox	Y	Y	N	N	N	Y
6 Teague	?	?	✓	?	?	?
7 Archer	Y	Y	Y	Y	Y	Y
8 Eckhardt	?	Y	N	N	N	N
9 Brooks	Y	Y	N	N	N	N
10 Pickle	Y	Y	Y	N	N	Y
11 Poage	?	Y	Y	N	N	Y
12 Wright	Y	Y	N	N	N	N
13 Hightower	Y	Y	Y	N	N	Y
14 Young	?	?	?	?	N	N
15 de la Garza	Y	Y	Y	N	N	Y
16 White	Y	Y	Y	N	N	Y
17 Burleson	Y	Y	Y	Y	Y	Y
18 Jordan	Y	Y	N	N	N	N
19 Mahon	Y	Y	Y	N	N	Y
20 Gonzalez	Y	Y	N	N	N	N
21 Krueger	#	#	✓	■	#	✓
22 Gammage	Y	Y	Y	N	Y	Y
23 Kazen	Y	Y	Y	N	N	Y
24 Milford	Y	Y	Y	Y	N	Y
UTAH						
1 McKay	Y	Y	Y	N	N	Y
2 Marriott	Y	Y	Y	Y	Y	Y
VERMONT						
AL Jeffords	Y	Y	Y	N	N	Y
VIRGINIA						
1 Trible	Y	Y	Y	Y	Y	Y
2 Whitehurst	Y	Y	Y	Y	Y	Y
3 Satterfield	Y	Y	Y	Y	Y	Y
4 Daniel	Y	Y	Y	Y	Y	Y
5 Daniel	Y	Y	Y	Y	Y	Y
6 Butler	Y	Y	Y	Y	Y	Y
7 Robinson	#	#	✓	#	#	#
8 Harris	Y	Y	N	N	N	N
9 Wampler	Y	Y	Y	N	Y	Y
10 Fisher	Y	Y	N	N	N	Y
WASHINGTON						
1 Pritchard	N	Y	Y	N	N	Y
2 Meeds	Y	Y	N	N	N	N
3 Bonker	Y	Y	N	N	N	Y
4 McCormack	Y	Y	N	N	?	N
5 Foley	Y	Y	N	N	?	Y
6 Dicks	Y	Y	N	N	N	Y
7 Cunningham	Y	Y	Y	N	Y	Y
WEST VIRGINIA						
1 Mollohan	#	#	■	■	N	N
2 Staggers	?	?	?	N	N	N
3 Slack	Y	Y	N	N	N	Y
4 Rahall	#	#	X	■	■	X
WISCONSIN						
1 Aspin	Y	Y	N	N	N	N
2 Kastenmeier	Y	Y	N	N	N	N
3 Baldus	Y	Y	N	N	N	N
4 Zablocki	Y	Y	N	N	N	N
5 Reuss	Y	Y	N	N	N	N
6 Steiger	Y	Y	Y	Y	Y	Y
7 Obey	Y	Y	N	N	N	N
8 Cornell	Y	Y	N	N	N	N
9 Kasten	Y	Y	Y	N	Y	Y
WYOMING						
AL Roncalio	?	Y	?	?	N	N

Democrats ***Republicans***

133. HR 50. Full Employment Act. Bauman, R-Md., amendment to terminate the provisions of the act Sept. 30, 1983, unless extended beyond that date by act of Congress. Rejected 196-216: R 128-8; D 68-208 (ND 22-169; SD 46-39), March 16, 1978.

134. HR 50. Full Employment Act. Quie, R-Minn., substitute for the bill to set as national goals 4 percent unemployment and 3 percent inflation rates, 100 percent of parity in farm prices, a reduction in tax levels and a balanced federal budget; to prohibit use of public service jobs to meet the unemployment goal; and to establish a presidential task force on youth unemployment. Rejected 137-276: R 127-10; D 10-266 (ND 3-188; SD 7-78), March 16, 1978.

135. HR 50. Full Employment Act. Passage of the bill to promote full employment, balanced growth and price stability. Passed 257-152: R 24-111; D 233-41 (ND 181-9; SD 52-32), March 16, 1978. A "yea" was a vote supporting the president's position.

136. HR 11274. Middle-Income Student Assistance. Erlenborn, R-Ill., demand for a second on the Ford, D-Mich., motion to suspend the rules and pass the bill to expand educational grant and loan programs for middle-income students. Second not ordered (thus preventing consideration of the bill) 156-218: R 6-125; D 150-93 (ND 112-60; SD 38-33), March 20, 1978.

137. H Res 996. International Relations Committee Funding. Adoption of the resolution to provide $375,000 for the expenses of investigations and studies by the International Relations Subcommittee on International Organizations through Oct. 31, 1978. Adopted 367-13: R 121-10; D 246-3 (ND 174-1; SD 72-2), March 20, 1978.

138. HR 7700. Postal Service Act. Adoption of the rule (H Res 1078) providing for House floor consideration of the bill to reorganize the United States Postal Service. Adopted 387-0: R 134-0; D 253-0 (ND 176-0; SD 77-0), March 20, 1978.

139. H Res 1082. Aldo Moro Kidnaping. Adoption of the resolution to condemn the terrorist kidnaping of former Italian Premier Aldo Moro on March 16, 1978, and to express the sense of the House that the president press for consideration of anti-terrorism measures by the United Nations. Adopted 398-0: R 136-0; D 262-0 (ND 180-0; SD 82-0), March 21, 1978.

140. HR 11518. Debt Limit Extension. Adoption of the rule (H Res 1092) providing for House floor consideration of the bill to extend the public debt limit. Adopted 314-80: R 74-64; D 240-16 (ND 163-10; SD 77-6), March 21, 1978.

KEY

- Y Voted for (yea).
- ✓ Paired for.
- † Announced for.
- # CQ Poll for.
- N Voted against (nay).
- X Paired against.
- - Announced against.
- ▮ CQ Poll against.
- P Voted "present."
- ● Voted "present" to avoid possible conflict of interest.
- ? Did not vote or otherwise make a position known.

	133	134	135	136	137	138	139	140
ALABAMA								
1 Edwards	Y	Y	N	N	Y	Y	Y	Y
2 Dickinson	Y	Y	N	X	?	?	Y	Y
3 Nichols	Y	N	N	X	Y	Y	Y	Y
4 Bevill	N	N	Y	N	Y	Y	Y	Y
5 Flippo	N	N	Y	Y	Y	Y	Y	Y
6 Buchanan	?	X	?	Y	Y	Y	Y	N
7 Flowers	N	N	Y	?	?	?	Y	Y
ALASKA								
AL Young	?	X	?	X	?	?	Y	N
ARIZONA								
1 Rhodes	Y	Y	N	?	?	Y	Y	Y
2 Udall	N	N	Y	Y	Y	Y	Y	Y
3 Stump	Y	Y	N	N	Y	Y	Y	N
4 Rudd	Y	Y	N	N	N	Y	Y	N
ARKANSAS								
1 Alexander	N	N	Y	?	Y	Y	Y	Y
2 Tucker	▮	X	#	▮	#	#	#	#
3 Hammerschmidt	Y	Y	N	N	Y	Y	Y	N
4 Thornton	?	X	?	?	?	?	?	?
CALIFORNIA								
1 Johnson	N	N	Y	Y	Y	Y	Y	Y
2 Clausen	?	X	?	N	Y	Y	Y	N
3 Moss	N	N	Y	Y	Y	Y	Y	Y
4 Leggett	N	N	Y	✓	Y	Y	Y	Y
5 Burton, J.	N	N	Y	Y	Y	Y	Y	Y
6 Burton, P.	N	N	Y	Y	Y	Y	Y	Y
7 Miller	N	N	Y	Y	Y	Y	Y	Y
8 Dellums	N	N	Y	✓	#	#	#	#
9 Stark	N	N	Y	Y	Y	Y	Y	Y
10 Edwards	N	N	Y	Y	Y	Y	Y	Y
11 Ryan	▮	X	✓	#	#	#	#	#
12 McCloskey	Y	Y	Y	N	Y	Y	Y	Y
13 Mineta	N	N	Y	Y	Y	Y	#	Y
14 McFall	N	N	Y	Y	Y	Y	Y	Y
15 Sisk	N	N	Y	Y	Y	Y	Y	Y
16 Panetta	Y	N	Y	Y	Y	Y	Y	Y
17 Krebs	Y	N	N	Y	Y	Y	Y	Y
18 Ketchum	Y	Y	N	N	Y	Y	Y	Y
19 Lagomarsino	Y	Y	N	N	Y	Y	Y	Y
20 Goldwater	Y	Y	N	N	Y	Y	Y	N
21 Corman	N	N	Y	Y	Y	Y	Y	Y
22 Moorhead	Y	Y	N	N	Y	Y	Y	N
23 Beilenson	N	N	Y	Y	Y	Y	Y	Y
24 Waxman	N	N	Y	Y	Y	Y	Y	#
25 Roybal	N	N	Y	Y	Y	Y	Y	Y
26 Rousselot	Y	Y	N	N	Y	Y	Y	N
27 Dornan	Y	Y	N	N	Y	Y	Y	N
28 Burke	N	N	Y	✓	#	#	Y	Y
29 Hawkins	N	N	Y	Y	Y	?	Y	Y
30 Danielson	N	N	Y	Y	Y	Y	Y	Y
31 Wilson, C.H.	N	N	Y	Y	▮	Y	Y	Y
32 Anderson	N	N	Y	Y	Y	Y	Y	Y
33 Clawson	Y	Y	N	N	Y	Y	Y	N
34 Hannaford	N	N	Y	Y	Y	Y	Y	Y
35 Lloyd	Y	N	N	Y	Y	Y	Y	Y
36 Brown	N	N	Y	Y	Y	Y	Y	?
37 Pettis	Y	Y	N	N	Y	Y	Y	Y
38 Patterson	N	N	Y	Y	Y	Y	Y	Y
39 Wiggins	Y	Y	N	N	#	Y	Y	Y
40 Badham	Y	Y	N	N	Y	Y	Y	N
41 Wilson, B.	Y	Y	N	N	N	Y	Y	Y
42 Van Deerlin	N	N	Y	✓	#	?	Y	Y
43 Burgener	Y	Y	N	N	Y	Y	Y	Y
COLORADO								
1 Schroeder	N	N	Y	Y	Y	Y	Y	Y
2 Wirth	N	N	Y	Y	Y	Y	Y	Y
3 Evans	Y	N	Y	Y	Y	Y	Y	Y
4 Johnson	Y	Y	N	N	Y	Y	Y	Y
5 Armstrong	Y	Y	N	N	N	Y	Y	N
CONNECTICUT								
1 Cotter	N	N	Y	Y	Y	Y	Y	Y
2 Dodd	N	N	Y	Y	Y	Y	Y	Y
3 Giaimo	N	N	Y	Y	Y	Y	Y	Y
4 McKinney	Y	Y	N	X	Y	Y	Y	Y
5 Sarasin	Y	Y	Y	X	†	†	†	†
6 Moffett	N	N	Y	Y	Y	Y	Y	Y
DELAWARE								
AL Evans	Y	Y	N	N	Y	Y	Y	Y
FLORIDA								
1 Sikes	✓	?	X	N	Y	Y	Y	Y
2 Fuqua	N	N	N	Y	Y	Y	Y	Y
3 Bennett	Y	N	N	N	Y	Y	Y	Y
4 Chappell	Y	N	N	X	#	#	Y	Y
5 Kelly	Y	Y	N	N	Y	Y	Y	N
6 Young	Y	Y	N	N	Y	Y	Y	N
7 Gibbons	Y	N	N	Y	Y	Y	Y	Y
8 Ireland	Y	N	N	N	Y	Y	Y	Y
9 Frey	?	X	?	?	?	?	?	?
10 Bafalis	Y	Y	N	N	Y	Y	Y	N
11 Rogers	Y	N	N	N	Y	Y	Y	Y
12 Burke	Y	Y	N	N	N	Y	Y	N
13 Lehman	N	N	Y	Y	Y	Y	Y	Y
14 Pepper	N	N	Y	Y	Y	Y	Y	Y
15 Fascell	N	N	Y	Y	Y	Y	Y	Y
GEORGIA								
1 Ginn	N	N	Y	N	Y	Y	Y	Y
2 Mathis	Y	N	Y	N	Y	Y	?	Y
3 Brinkley	N	N	Y	N	Y	Y	Y	N
4 Levitas	Y	N	Y	N	Y	Y	Y	Y
5 Fowler	N	N	Y	?	?	?	Y	Y
6 Flynt	Y	N	N	N	Y	Y	Y	Y
7 McDonald	Y	Y	N	N	N	Y	Y	N
8 Evans	Y	N	Y	N	Y	Y	Y	Y
9 Jenkins	N	N	Y	✓	#	#	Y	Y
10 Barnard	Y	N	N	N	Y	Y	Y	Y
HAWAII								
1 Heftel	N	N	Y	Y	Y	Y	Y	Y
2 Akaka	X	▮	✓	✓	#	#	#	#
IDAHO								
1 Symms	Y	Y	N	N	N	Y	Y	N
2 Hansen, G.	Y	Y	N	N	N	Y	Y	?
ILLINOIS								
1 Metcalfe	N	N	Y	Y	Y	Y	?	?
2 Murphy	N	N	Y	N	Y	Y	#	Y
3 Russo	N	N	Y	N	Y	Y	Y	Y
4 Derwinski	Y	Y	N	N	Y	Y	Y	Y
5 Fary	N	N	Y	?	?	?	?	?
6 Hyde	Y	Y	N	N	Y	Y	Y	Y
7 Collins	N	N	Y	✓	?	?	?	?
8 Rostenkowski	N	N	Y	Y	Y	Y	Y	Y
9 Yates	N	N	Y	Y	Y	Y	Y	Y
10 Mikva	N	N	Y	Y	Y	Y	Y	Y
11 Annunzio	N	N	Y	N	Y	Y	#	#
12 Crane	Y	Y	N	N	N	Y	#	N
13 McClory	#	✓	X	#	#	#	Y	Y
14 Erlenborn	Y	Y	N	N	Y	#	#	#
15 Corcoran	Y	Y	N	N	Y	Y	Y	N
16 Anderson	#	X	#	▮	#	#	#	#
17 O'Brien	Y	Y	Y	N	Y	Y	#	#
18 Michel	Y	Y	N	N	Y	Y	Y	Y
19 Railsback	Y	Y	N	N	Y	Y	Y	Y
20 Findley	Y	Y	Y	?	?	?	?	?
21 Madigan	?	✓	✓	X	?	?	?	?
22 Shipley	Y	N	Y	✓	?	?	?	?
23 Price	N	N	Y	#	Y	Y	Y	Y
24 Simon	N	N	Y	Y	Y	Y	Y	Y
INDIANA								
1 Benjamin	N	N	Y	N	Y	Y	Y	N
2 Fithian	N	N	Y	Y	Y	Y	Y	Y
3 Brademas	N	N	Y	Y	Y	Y	Y	Y
4 Quayle	Y	Y	N	N	Y	Y	?	N
5 Hillis	Y	Y	Y	N	Y	Y	Y	Y
6 Evans	Y	N	Y	Y	Y	Y	Y	Y
7 Myers, J.	Y	Y	N	N	Y	Y	Y	N
8 Cornwell	N	N	Y	?	?	?	Y	Y
9 Hamilton	Y	N	Y	Y	Y	Y	Y	Y
10 Sharp	Y	N	Y	Y	Y	Y	Y	Y
11 Jacobs	N	N	Y	Y	Y	Y	Y	Y
IOWA								
1 Leach	Y	Y	N	N	Y	Y	Y	N
2 Blouin	N	N	Y	Y	Y	Y	Y	Y
3 Grassley	Y	Y	N	N	Y	Y	Y	N
4 Smith	N	N	Y	Y	Y	Y	Y	Y
5 Harkin	N	N	Y	Y	Y	Y	Y	Y
6 Bedell	N	N	Y	Y	Y	Y	Y	Y

Democrats *Republicans*

	133	134	135	136	137	138	139	140
KANSAS								
1 Sebelius	Y	Y	N	N	Y	Y	Y	Y
2 Keys	N	N	Y	Y	Y	Y	Y	Y
3 Winn	Y	Y	X	■	#	#	Y	Y
4 Glickman	Y	N	Y	N	Y	Y	Y	Y
5 Skubitz	Y	Y	N	N	Y	Y	Y	Y
KENTUCKY								
1 Hubbard	Y	N	Y	N	Y	Y	Y	Y
2 Natcher	N	N	Y	Y	Y	Y	Y	Y
3 Mazzoli	Y	N	Y	N	Y	Y	Y	Y
4 Snyder	Y	Y	N	N	Y	Y	Y	N
5 Carter	Y	N	Y	N	Y	Y	Y	Y
6 Breckinridge	Y	N	Y	N	Y	Y	Y	Y
7 Perkins	N	N	Y	Y	Y	Y	Y	Y
LOUISIANA								
1 Livingston	Y	Y	N	N	Y	Y	Y	N
2 Boggs	N	N	Y	N	Y	Y	Y	Y
3 Treen	Y	Y	N	N	Y	Y	Y	N
4 Waggonner	Y	N	N	N	Y	Y	†	Y
5 Huckaby	Y	N	N	Y	?	Y	Y	Y
6 Moore	Y	Y	N	N	Y	Y	Y	N
7 Breaux	Y	Y	N	Y	Y	Y	Y	Y
8 Long	N	N	?	Y	Y	Y	Y	Y
MAINE								
1 Emery	Y	Y	N	Y	Y	Y	Y	Y
2 Cohen	Y	Y	N	N	Y	Y	Y	Y
MARYLAND								
1 Bauman	Y	Y	N	N	Y	Y	Y	N
2 Long	N	N	Y	Y	Y	Y	Y	Y
3 Mikulski	N	N	Y	Y	Y	Y	Y	Y
4 Holt	Y	Y	N	N	Y	Y	Y	N
5 Spellman	N	N	Y	Y	Y	Y	Y	Y
6 Byron	N	N	Y	N	Y	Y	Y	Y
7 Mitchell	N	N	Y	Y	Y	Y	#	#
8 Steers	N	N	✓	Y	Y	Y	Y	Y
MASSACHUSETTS								
1 Conte	N	N	Y	Y	Y	Y	Y	Y
2 Boland	N	N	Y	N	Y	Y	Y	Y
3 Early	N	N	Y	N	Y	Y	Y	Y
4 Drinan	N	N	Y	†	Y	Y	Y	Y
5 Tsongas	N	N	Y	Y	Y	Y	Y	Y
6 Harrington	N	N	Y	#	#	#	Y	Y
7 Markey	N	N	Y	Y	Y	Y	Y	Y
8 O'Neill								
9 Moakley	N	N	Y	N	Y	Y	Y	Y
10 Heckler	Y	N	Y	N	Y	Y	Y	Y
11 Burke	N	N	Y	N	Y	Y	Y	Y
12 Studds	N	N	Y	Y	Y	Y	Y	Y
MICHIGAN								
1 Conyers	N	N	Y	Y	Y	Y	Y	Y
2 Pursell	Y	Y	N	X	?	?	Y	N
3 Brown	#	X	X	N	Y	Y	Y	Y
4 Stockman	#	Y	N	N	Y	Y	Y	N
5 Sawyer	Y	Y	N	N	Y	Y	Y	Y
6 Carr	N	N	Y	Y	Y	Y	Y	Y
7 Kildee	N	N	Y	Y	Y	Y	Y	Y
8 Traxler	N	N	Y	N	Y	Y	#	#
9 Vander Jagt	Y	Y	N	N	Y	Y	Y	Y
10 Cederberg	Y	Y	N	N	Y	Y	Y	Y
11 Ruppe	Y	Y	N	N	Y	Y	Y	#
12 Bonior	N	N	Y	Y	Y	Y	Y	Y
13 Diggs	N	N	Y	✓	?	Y	?	#
14 Nedzi	N	N	Y	Y	Y	Y	Y	Y
15 Ford	N	N	Y	Y	?	Y	Y	Y
16 Dingell	N	N	Y	Y	Y	Y	Y	Y
17 Brodhead	N	N	Y	Y	Y	Y	Y	Y
18 Blanchard	N	N	Y	Y	Y	Y	Y	Y
19 Broomfield	Y	Y	N	N	Y	Y	Y	N
MINNESOTA								
1 Quie	Y	Y	N	■	#	#	Y	Y
2 Hagedorn	Y	Y	N	N	Y	Y	Y	Y
3 Frenzel	?	✓	X	N	Y	Y	Y	Y
4 Vento	N	N	Y	Y	Y	Y	Y	Y
5 Fraser	N	N	Y	#	#	#	Y	Y
6 Nolan	N	N	Y	Y	Y	?	Y	Y
7 Stangeland	Y	Y	N	N	Y	Y	Y	Y
8 Oberstar	N	N	Y	Y	Y	Y	Y	Y
MISSISSIPPI								
1 Whitten	Y	N	Y	Y	Y	Y	Y	Y
2 Bowen	Y	N	N	Y	Y	Y	Y	Y
3 Montgomery	Y	Y	N	N	Y	Y	Y	Y
4 Cochran	Y	Y	N	N	Y	Y	Y	Y
5 Lott	Y	Y	N	N	Y	Y	Y	N
MISSOURI								
1 Clay	N	N	Y	Y	Y	Y	Y	Y
2 Young	N	N	Y	N	Y	Y	Y	Y
3 Gephardt	N	N	Y	N	Y	Y	Y	Y

	133	134	135	136	137	138	139	140
4 Skelton	N	N	Y	N	Y	Y	Y	Y
5 Bolling	N	N	Y	Y	Y	Y	Y	Y
6 Coleman	Y	Y	N	N	Y	Y	Y	N
7 Taylor	Y	Y	N	N	Y	Y	Y	N
8 Ichord	Y	N	N	N	Y	Y	Y	N
9 Volkmer	Y	N	Y	N	Y	Y	Y	Y
10 Burlison	N	N	Y	Y	Y	Y	Y	Y
MONTANA								
1 Baucus	X	#	#	N	Y	Y	Y	Y
2 Marlenee	Y	Y	N	N	Y	Y	Y	Y
NEBRASKA								
1 Thone	Y	Y	N	?	#	#	#	Y
2 Cavanaugh	N	N	Y	N	Y	Y	Y	Y
3 Smith	Y	Y	N	N	Y	Y	Y	Y
NEVADA								
AL Santini	N	N	Y	N	Y	Y	Y	Y
NEW HAMPSHIRE								
1 D'Amours	N	N	Y	Y	Y	Y	Y	Y
2 Cleveland	Y	Y	N	N	Y	Y	Y	N
NEW JERSEY								
1 Florio	Y	N	Y	N	Y	Y	Y	Y
2 Hughes	Y	N	Y	N	Y	Y	Y	Y
3 Howard	N	N	Y	Y	Y	Y	Y	Y
4 Thompson	N	N	Y	Y	Y	Y	Y	#
5 Fenwick	Y	Y	Y	N	Y	Y	Y	Y
6 Forsythe	Y	Y	N	N	Y	Y	Y	Y
7 Maguire	N	N	Y	N	Y	Y	Y	Y
8 Roe	N	N	Y	Y	Y	Y	Y	Y
9 Hollenbeck	Y	N	Y	N	Y	Y	Y	Y
10 Rodino	N	N	Y	Y	Y	Y	Y	Y
11 Minish	Y	N	Y	N	Y	Y	Y	Y
12 Rinaldo	Y	N	Y	N	Y	Y	Y	Y
13 Meyner	N	N	Y	Y	Y	Y	Y	Y
14 LeFante	N	N	Y	Y	Y	Y	Y	Y
15 Patten	N	N	Y	✓	#	Y	Y	Y
NEW MEXICO								
1 Lujan	Y	Y	N	N	Y	Y	Y	N
2 Runnels	✓	Y	N	?	#	#	Y	N
NEW YORK								
1 Pike	Y	N	N	Y	Y	Y	Y	Y
2 Downey	N	N	Y	N	Y	Y	Y	Y
3 Ambro	Y	N	Y	N	Y	Y	Y	?
4 Lent	Y	Y	N	N	Y	Y	Y	Y
5 Wydler	Y	Y	N	N	Y	Y	Y	N
6 Wolff	Y	N	Y	N	Y	Y	Y	Y
7 Addabbo	N	N	Y	N	Y	Y	Y	Y
8 Rosenthal	N	N	Y	Y	Y	Y	Y	Y
9 Delaney	N	N	Y	N	Y	Y	Y	Y
10 Biaggi	N	N	Y	Y	Y	Y	Y	Y
11 Scheuer	N	N	Y	?	#	#	#	#
12 Chisholm	N	N	Y	Y	Y	Y	Y	Y
13 Solarz	N	N	Y	Y	Y	Y	Y	Y
14 Richmond	N	N	Y	?	?	Y	Y	Y
15 Zeferetti	N	N	Y	N	Y	Y	Y	Y
16 Holtzman	N	N	Y	Y	Y	Y	Y	Y
17 Murphy	N	N	Y	N	Y	Y	Y	Y
18 Green	N	N	Y	N	Y	Y	Y	Y
19 Rangel	N	N	Y	Y	Y	?	Y	Y
20 Weiss	N	N	Y	Y	Y	?	Y	Y
21 Garcia	N	N	Y	Y	Y	Y	Y	?
22 Bingham	N	N	✓	Y	Y	Y	Y	Y
23 Caputo	Y	Y	Y	N	Y	Y	Y	N
24 Ottinger	N	N	Y	N	Y	Y	Y	Y
25 Fish	Y	Y	Y	N	Y	Y	Y	Y
26 Gilman	N	N	Y	N	Y	Y	Y	Y
27 McHugh	N	N	Y	Y	Y	Y	Y	Y
28 Stratton	N	N	Y	X	Y	Y	Y	Y
29 Pattison	N	N	Y	Y	Y	Y	Y	Y
30 McEwen	Y	Y	N	N	Y	Y	Y	Y
31 Mitchell	Y	Y	Y	N	Y	Y	Y	Y
32 Hanley	N	N	Y	N	Y	Y	Y	Y
33 Walsh	Y	Y	Y	X	Y	Y	Y	Y
34 Horton	Y	Y	Y	N	#	Y	Y	Y
35 Conable	Y	Y	N	N	Y	Y	Y	Y
36 LaFalce	N	N	Y	Y	Y	Y	Y	Y
37 Nowak	N	N	Y	N	Y	Y	Y	Y
38 Kemp	Y	Y	N	N	Y	Y	Y	N
39 Lundine	N	N	Y	Y	Y	Y	Y	Y
NORTH CAROLINA								
1 Jones	Y	N	Y	Y	Y	Y	Y	Y
2 Fountain	Y	N	Y	N	Y	Y	Y	Y
3 Whitley	Y	N	Y	?	?	?	?	?
4 Andrews	N	N	Y	Y	Y	Y	Y	Y
5 Neal	Y	N	Y	Y	Y	Y	Y	Y
6 Preyer	N	N	N	Y	Y	Y	Y	Y
7 Rose	N	N	Y	Y	Y	Y	Y	Y
8 Hefner	N	N	Y	N	Y	Y	Y	Y

	133	134	135	136	137	138	139	140
9 Martin	Y	Y	N	N	Y	Y	Y	Y
10 Broyhill	Y	Y	N	N	Y	Y	Y	N
11 Gudger	Y	N	Y	■	#	#	Y	Y
NORTH DAKOTA								
AL Andrews	Y	Y	N	N	Y	Y	Y	N
OHIO								
1 Gradison	Y	Y	N	N	Y	Y	Y	Y
2 Luken	N	N	Y	N	Y	Y	Y	N
3 Whalen	N	N	Y	Y	Y	Y	Y	Y
4 Guyer	Y	Y	N	N	Y	Y	Y	Y
5 Latta	Y	Y	N	N	Y	Y	Y	N
6 Harsha	N	Y	Y	N	Y	Y	Y	Y
7 Brown	Y	Y	N	N	Y	Y	Y	N
8 Kindness	Y	Y	N	N	Y	Y	Y	Y
9 Ashley	N	N	Y	N	Y	Y	Y	?
10 Miller	Y	Y	N	N	Y	Y	Y	N
11 Stanton	Y	Y	Y	N	Y	Y	Y	Y
12 Devine	Y	Y	N	N	Y	Y	Y	N
13 Pease	N	N	Y	N	Y	Y	Y	Y
14 Seiberling	N	N	Y	Y	#	Y	Y	Y
15 Wylie	Y	Y	N	N	Y	Y	Y	N
16 Regula	Y	Y	Y	N	Y	Y	Y	Y
17 Ashbrook	Y	Y	N	N	N	Y	Y	Y
18 Applegate	N	N	Y	N	Y	Y	Y	Y
19 Carney	N	N	Y	N	Y	Y	Y	Y
20 Oakar	N	N	Y	N	Y	Y	Y	Y
21 Stokes	N	N	Y	Y	Y	Y	Y	Y
22 Vanik	N	N	Y	N	Y	Y	Y	Y
23 Mottl	N	N	Y	Y	Y	Y	Y	Y
OKLAHOMA								
1 Jones	Y	N	N	N	Y	Y	Y	Y
2 Risenhoover	Y	N	N	✓	?	?	?	?
3 Watkins	Y	N	N	N	Y	Y	Y	Y
4 Steed	Y	N	N	Y	Y	Y	Y	Y
5 Edwards	Y	Y	N	N	Y	Y	Y	Y
6 English	Y	N	N	N	Y	Y	Y	Y
OREGON								
1 AuCoin	Y	N	N	N	Y	Y	Y	Y
2 Ullman	N	■	✓	Y	#	Y	Y	Y
3 Duncan	N	N	N	Y	Y	Y	Y	Y
4 Weaver	N	N	Y	Y	Y	Y	Y	Y
PENNSYLVANIA								
1 Myers, M.	N	N	Y	Y	Y	Y	?	?
2 Nix	N	N	Y	N	Y	Y	Y	?
3 Lederer	N	N	Y	Y	Y	Y	#	?
4 Eilberg	N	N	Y	N	Y	Y	Y	Y
5 Schulze	Y	Y	N	N	Y	Y	Y	Y
6 Yatron	N	N	Y	N	Y	Y	Y	N
7 Edgar	N	N	Y	N	Y	Y	Y	Y
8 Kostmayer	N	N	Y	N	Y	Y	Y	N
9 Shuster	Y	Y	N	N	Y	Y	Y	N
10 McDade	Y	N	Y	N	Y	Y	Y	Y
11 Flood	X	■	✓	✓	#	#	#	#
12 Murtha	N	N	Y	N	Y	Y	Y	Y
13 Coughlin	Y	Y	N	N	Y	Y	Y	Y
14 Moorhead	N	N	Y	Y	Y	Y	Y	Y
15 Rooney	N	N	Y	N	Y	Y	Y	Y
16 Walker	Y	Y	N	N	Y	Y	Y	N
17 Ertel	N	N	Y	X	Y	Y	Y	Y
18 Walgren	N	N	Y	N	Y	Y	Y	Y
19 Goodling, W.	Y	Y	N	N	Y	Y	Y	N
20 Gaydos	N	N	Y	N	Y	Y	Y	Y
21 Dent	N	N	Y	X	#	#	Y	N
22 Murphy	N	N	Y	N	Y	Y	Y	N
23 Ammerman	N	N	Y	N	Y	Y	Y	Y
24 Marks	N	Y	Y	N	Y	Y	Y	N
25 Myers, G.	N	Y	N	N	Y	Y	Y	N
RHODE ISLAND								
1 St Germain	N	N	Y	N	Y	Y	Y	Y
2 Beard	N	N	Y	N	Y	Y	Y	Y
SOUTH CAROLINA								
1 Davis	N	N	Y	Y	N	Y	Y	N
2 Spence	Y	Y	N	N	Y	Y	Y	N
3 Derrick	N	N	Y	N	Y	Y	Y	Y
4 Mann	Y	N	N	Y	Y	Y	Y	Y
5 Holland	N	N	Y	?	Y	Y	Y	Y
6 Jenrette	N	N	Y	Y	#	Y	Y	Y
SOUTH DAKOTA								
1 Pressler	Y	Y	N	Y	Y	Y	Y	N
2 Abdnor	Y	Y	N	N	Y	Y	Y	N
TENNESSEE								
1 Quillen	Y	Y	N	N	N	Y	Y	Y
2 Duncan	Y	Y	N	N	Y	Y	Y	N
3 Lloyd	N	N	Y	N	Y	Y	Y	Y
4 Gore	Y	N	Y	Y	Y	Y	Y	Y
5 Allen	N	N	Y	Y	Y	Y	Y	Y
6 Beard	Y	Y	N	N	Y	Y	Y	Y

	133	134	135	136	137	138	139	140
7 Jones	N	N	Y	Y	Y	Y	Y	Y
8 Ford	N	N	Y	Y	Y	Y	Y	Y
TEXAS								
1 Hall	Y	N	N	N	Y	Y	Y	Y
2 Wilson, C.	N	N	Y	■	#	#	#	#
3 Collins	Y	Y	N	N	N	Y	Y	N
4 Roberts	Y	N	N	Y	Y	Y	Y	Y
5 Mattox	N	N	Y	Y	Y	Y	Y	Y
6 Teague	✓	✓	X	X	?	?	?	?
7 Archer	Y	Y	N	N	Y	Y	Y	N
8 Eckhardt	N	N	Y	Y	Y	Y	Y	Y
9 Brooks	N	N	Y	Y	Y	Y	Y	Y
10 Pickle	Y	N	N	Y	Y	Y	Y	Y
11 Poage	Y	Y	N	Y	Y	Y	Y	?
12 Wright	N	N	Y	✓	?	Y	Y	Y
13 Hightower	Y	N	Y	Y	Y	Y	Y	Y
14 Young	N	N	Y	?	?	?	Y	Y
15 de la Garza	N	N	Y	N	Y	Y	Y	N
16 White	Y	N	N	N	Y	Y	Y	Y
17 Burleson	Y	Y	N	N	Y	Y	Y	Y
18 Jordan	N	N	Y	Y	Y	Y	Y	Y
19 Mahon	Y	N	N	Y	Y	Y	Y	Y
20 Gonzalez	N	N	Y	Y	Y	Y	Y	Y
21 Krueger	✓	✓	X	✓	#	#	Y	Y
22 Gammage	Y	N	Y	N	Y	Y	Y	N
23 Kazen	Y	N	Y	Y	Y	Y	Y	Y
24 Milford	Y	N	N	N	Y	Y	Y	N
UTAH								
1 McKay	Y	N	N	Y	Y	Y	Y	Y
2 Marriott	Y	Y	N	N	Y	Y	Y	N
VERMONT								
AL Jeffords	Y	Y	N	N	Y	Y	Y	N
VIRGINIA								
1 Trible	Y	Y	N	N	Y	Y	Y	N
2 Whitehurst	Y	Y	N	N	Y	Y	Y	Y
3 Satterfield	Y	Y	N	N	Y	Y	Y	Y
4 Daniel	Y	Y	N	N	Y	Y	Y	Y
5 Daniel	Y	Y	N	X	Y	Y	Y	Y
6 Butler	Y	Y	N	N	Y	Y	†	Y
7 Robinson	#	✓	X	N	Y	Y	Y	N
8 Harris	N	N	Y	Y	Y	Y	Y	Y
9 Wampler	Y	Y	N	N	Y	Y	Y	Y
10 Fisher	N	N	Y	#	Y	Y	Y	Y
WASHINGTON								
1 Pritchard	Y	Y	N	N	Y	Y	Y	Y
2 Meeds	N	N	Y	Y	Y	Y	Y	Y
3 Bonker	N	N	Y	Y	Y	Y	Y	#
4 McCormack	N	N	Y	†	Y	Y	Y	Y
5 Foley	Y	N	Y	Y	Y	Y	Y	Y
6 Dicks	N	N	Y	Y	Y	Y	Y	Y
7 Cunningham	Y	Y	N	N	Y	Y	Y	N
WEST VIRGINIA								
1 Mollohan	N	N	Y	Y	Y	Y	Y	#
2 Staggers	N	N	Y	N	Y	Y	Y	Y
3 Slack	N	N	Y	N	Y	Y	Y	Y
4 Rahall	X	■	✓	N	Y	Y	Y	Y
WISCONSIN								
1 Aspin	N	N	Y	Y	Y	Y	Y	Y
2 Kastenmeier	N	N	Y	Y	Y	Y	Y	Y
3 Baldus	N	N	Y	Y	Y	Y	Y	Y
4 Zablocki	N	N	Y	N	Y	Y	Y	Y
5 Reuss	N	N	Y	Y	Y	Y	Y	Y
6 Steiger	Y	Y	N	■	#	#	Y	Y
7 Obey	N	N	Y	Y	Y	Y	Y	Y
8 Cornell	N	N	Y	N	Y	Y	Y	Y
9 Kasten	Y	Y	N	N	Y	Y	Y	N
WYOMING								
AL Roncalio	Y	Y	Y	?	?	?	Y	Y

Democrats ***Republicans***

141. HR 11518. Debt Limit Extension. Passage of the bill to extend the public debt limit at its existing level of $752 billion through July 31, 1978. Passed 233-172: R 27-113; D 206-59 (ND 155-26; SD 51-33), March 21, 1978. A "yea" was a vote supporting the president's position.

142. HR 11315. Campaign Financing. Adoption of the rule (H Res 1093) providing for House floor consideration of the bill to amend the Federal Election Campaign Act, last amended in 1976, and to permit a floor amendment on the public financing of House general election campaigns. Rejected 198-209: R 0-140; D 198-69 (ND 163-20; SD 35-49), March 21, 1978.

143. HR 5383. Mandatory Retirement Age. Adoption of the conference report on the bill to amend the Age Discrimination in Employment Act of 1967 to raise to 70, from 65, the age limit for protection of non-federal workers from age-based discriminatory practices, including mandatory retirement (except for certain high-level executives and tenured college and university faculty), and to eliminate the upper limit for most civilian federal employees. Adopted 391-6: R 134-2; D 257-4 (ND 175-3; SD 82-1), March 21, 1978.

144. HR 7700. Postal Service Act. C. Wilson, D-Calif., motion that the House resolve into the Committee of the Whole to consider the bill to reorganize the United States Postal Service. Motion agreed to 364-2: R 123-2; D 241-0 (ND 163-0; SD 78-0), March 21, 1978.

145. H J Res 796. Disaster Relief Appropriations, Fiscal 1978. Passage of the joint resolution to appropriate $300 million for the remainder of fiscal 1978 for disaster relief programs caused by the severe winter weather conditions throughout the country. Passed 393-4: R 133-2; D 260-2 (ND 178-1; SD 82-1), March 22, 1978. The president had requested $150 million in supplemental appropriations.

KEY

- Y Voted for (yea).
- ✓ Paired for.
- † Announced for.
- # CQ Poll for.
- N Voted against (nay).
- X Paired against.
- - Announced against.
- ▮ CQ Poll against.
- P Voted "present."
- ● Voted "present" to avoid possible conflict of interest.
- ? Did not vote or otherwise make a position known.

	141	142	143	144	145
ALABAMA					
1 Edwards	Y	N	Y	Y	Y
2 Dickinson	N	N	Y	Y	Y
3 Nichols	Y	N	Y	P	Y
4 Bevill	Y	N	Y	Y	Y
5 Flippo	Y	N	Y	Y	Y
6 Buchanan	N	N	Y	Y	Y
7 Flowers	Y	N	Y	Y	Y
ALASKA					
AL Young	N	N	Y	Y	?
ARIZONA					
1 Rhodes	N	N	Y	Y	Y
2 Udall	Y	Y	#	Y	Y
3 Stump	N	N	Y	Y	Y
4 Rudd	N	N	Y	Y	Y
ARKANSAS					
1 Alexander	Y	N	Y	Y	Y
2 Tucker	#	#	#	#	#
3 Hammerschmidt	N	N	?	Y	Y
4 Thornton	?	?	?	?	?
CALIFORNIA					
1 Johnson	Y	Y	Y	Y	Y
2 Clausen	N	N	Y	Y	Y
3 Moss	Y	Y	Y	?	Y
4 Leggett	Y	Y	Y	Y	Y
5 Burton, J.	N	Y	Y	Y	Y
6 Burton, P.	Y	Y	Y	?	Y
7 Miller	Y	Y	Y	?	Y
8 Dellums	#	✓	#	#	#
9 Stark	Y	Y	Y	Y	Y
10 Edwards	Y	Y	Y	Y	Y
11 Ryan	#	#	#	#	Y
12 McCloskey	Y	N	Y	Y	Y
13 Mineta	Y	Y	Y	Y	Y
14 McFall	Y	N	Y	Y	Y
15 Sisk	Y	N	Y	?	Y
16 Panetta	N	Y	Y	Y	Y
17 Krebs	Y	Y	Y	Y	Y
18 Ketchum	N	N	Y	Y	Y
19 Lagomarsino	N	N	Y	Y	Y
20 Goldwater	N	N	Y	Y	Y
21 Corman	Y	Y	Y	Y	Y
22 Moorhead	N	N	Y	Y	Y
23 Beilenson	Y	Y	Y	Y	Y
24 Waxman	#	Y	Y	?	?
25 Roybal	Y	Y	Y	Y	Y
26 Rousselot	N	N	Y	Y	Y
27 Dornan	N	N	Y	Y	Y
28 Burke	Y	Y	Y	Y	Y
29 Hawkins	?	Y	Y	Y	Y
30 Danielson	Y	Y	Y	Y	Y
31 Wilson, C.H.	Y	N	Y	Y	Y
32 Anderson	N	Y	Y	Y	Y
33 Clawson	N	N	Y	?	Y
34 Hannaford	Y	Y	Y	Y	Y
35 Lloyd	N	Y	Y	Y	Y
36 Brown	Y	Y	Y	?	Y
37 Pettis	Y	N	Y	Y	Y
38 Patterson	Y	Y	Y	?	Y
39 Wiggins	Y	N	Y	Y	Y
40 Badham	N	N	Y	Y	Y
41 Wilson, B.	N	N	Y	N	Y
42 Van Deerlin	Y	Y	Y	Y	Y
43 Burgener	N	N	Y	Y	Y
COLORADO					
1 Schroeder	Y	Y	Y	Y	Y
2 Wirth	Y	Y	Y	Y	Y
3 Evans	?	Y	Y	Y	Y
4 Johnson	Y	N	Y	Y	Y
5 Armstrong	N	N	Y	Y	Y
CONNECTICUT					
1 Cotter	Y	N	Y	Y	Y
2 Dodd	Y	Y	Y	Y	Y
3 Giaimo	Y	Y	Y	?	Y
4 McKinney	Y	N	#	#	#
5 Sarasin	-	-	†	†	†
6 Moffett	Y	Y	Y	Y	Y
DELAWARE					
AL Evans	N	N	Y	Y	Y
FLORIDA					
1 Sikes	N	Y	Y	Y	Y
2 Fuqua	Y	Y	Y	Y	Y
3 Bennett	Y	Y	Y	Y	Y
4 Chappell	N	N	Y	Y	Y
5 Kelly	N	N	Y	Y	Y
6 Young	N	N	Y	Y	Y
7 Gibbons	Y	N	Y	Y	Y
8 Ireland	Y	Y	Y	Y	Y
9 Frey	X	?	?	?	?
10 Bafalis	N	N	Y	Y	Y
11 Rogers	Y	Y	Y	Y	Y
12 Burke	N	N	Y	Y	Y
13 Lehman	Y	Y	Y	#	Y
14 Pepper	Y	Y	Y	Y	Y
15 Fascell	Y	Y	Y	Y	Y
GEORGIA					
1 Ginn	N	N	Y	Y	Y
2 Mathis	Y	N	Y	Y	Y
3 Brinkley	N	N	Y	Y	Y
4 Levitas	N	Y	Y	Y	Y
5 Fowler	N	Y	Y	Y	Y
6 Flynt	N	N	Y	Y	Y
7 McDonald	N	N	Y	Y	N
8 Evans	N	N	Y	Y	Y
9 Jenkins	Y	N	Y	Y	Y
10 Barnard	N	Y	Y	Y	Y
HAWAII					
1 Heftel	Y	Y	Y	Y	Y
2 Akaka	#	✓	#	#	#
IDAHO					
1 Symms	N	N	Y	Y	Y
2 Hansen, G.	N	N	Y	Y	Y
ILLINOIS					
1 Metcalfe	?	✓	?	?	?
2 Murphy	Y	N	Y	Y	Y
3 Russo	N	Y	Y	Y	Y
4 Derwinski	Y	N	Y	Y	Y
5 Fary	?	?	?	Y	Y
6 Hyde	N	N	Y	#	Y
7 Collins	?	✓	?	?	?
8 Rostenkowski	Y	#	#	#	Y
9 Yates	Y	Y	Y	Y	Y
10 Mikva	Y	Y	Y	#	Y
11 Annunzio	✓	▮	#	#	#
12 Crane	N	N	Y	Y	Y
13 McClory	N	N	Y	Y	Y
14 Erlenborn	▮	▮	#	#	Y
15 Corcoran	N	N	Y	Y	Y
16 Anderson	▮	X	#	#	#
17 O'Brien	X	▮	#	#	#
18 Michel	N	N	Y	Y	Y
19 Railsback	Y	N	Y	Y	Y
20 Findley	✓	?	?	?	?
21 Madigan	X	X	?	?	?
22 Shipley	?	X	?	?	?
23 Price	Y	Y	Y	Y	Y
24 Simon	Y	Y	Y	Y	Y
INDIANA					
1 Benjamin	Y	Y	Y	Y	Y
2 Fithian	N	Y	Y	Y	Y
3 Brademas	Y	Y	Y	Y	Y
4 Quayle	N	N	Y	Y	Y
5 Hillis	N	N	Y	Y	Y
6 Evans	N	Y	Y	Y	Y
7 Myers, J.	N	N	Y	Y	Y
8 Cornwell	Y	Y	Y	Y	Y
9 Hamilton	Y	Y	Y	Y	Y
10 Sharp	Y	Y	Y	Y	Y
11 Jacobs	Y	Y	Y	Y	Y
IOWA					
1 Leach	N	N	Y	Y	Y
2 Blouin	Y	Y	Y	?	Y
3 Grassley	N	N	Y	Y	Y
4 Smith	Y	Y	Y	Y	Y
5 Harkin	Y	Y	Y	Y	Y
6 Bedell	Y	Y	N	Y	Y

Democrats ***Republicans***

	141	142	143	144	145
KANSAS					
1 Sebelius	N	N	Y	Y	Y
2 Keys	Y	Y	Y	Y	Y
3 Winn	N	N	Y	Y	Y
4 Glickman	N	Y	Y	Y	Y
5 Skubitz	N	N	Y	Y	Y
KENTUCKY					
1 Hubbard	Y	Y	Y	Y	Y
2 Natcher	Y	Y	Y	Y	Y
3 Mazzoli	Y	N	Y	Y	Y
4 Snyder	N	N	Y	Y	Y
5 Carter	N	N	Y	Y	Y
6 Breckinridge	Y	Y	Y	Y	Y
7 Perkins	Y	Y	Y	Y	Y
LOUISIANA					
1 Livingston	N	N	Y	Y	Y
2 Boggs	Y	Y	Y	#	#
3 Treen	Y	N	Y	Y	Y
4 Waggonner	Y	N	N	Y	Y
5 Huckaby	N	N	Y	Y	Y
6 Moore	N	N	Y	Y	Y
7 Breaux	N	N	Y	Y	Y
8 Long	Y	Y	Y	Y	Y
MAINE					
1 Emery	N	N	Y	Y	Y
2 Cohen	Y	N	Y	?	?
MARYLAND					
1 Bauman	N	N	Y	Y	Y
2 Long	Y	Y	Y	Y	Y
3 Mikulski	Y	Y	Y	Y	Y
4 Holt	N	N	Y	Y	Y
5 Spellman	Y	Y	Y	Y	Y
6 Byron	N	N	Y	Y	Y
7 Mitchell	Y	Y	Y	Y	Y
8 Steers	Y	N	Y	Y	Y
MASSACHUSETTS					
1 Conte	Y	N	Y	Y	Y
2 Boland	Y	Y	Y	Y	Y
3 Early	Y	Y	Y	Y	Y
4 Drinan	Y	Y	Y	Y	Y
5 Tsongas	Y	Y	Y	Y	Y
6 Harrington	Y	Y	Y	Y	Y
7 Markey	Y	Y	Y	Y	Y
8 O'Neill					
9 Moakley	Y	Y	Y	Y	Y
10 Heckler	N	N	Y	Y	Y
11 Burke	Y	Y	Y	Y	Y
12 Studds	Y	Y	Y	Y	Y
MICHIGAN					
1 Conyers	Y	Y	Y	Y	Y
2 Pursell	N	N	Y	?	Y
3 Brown	N	N	Y	Y	Y
4 Stockman	N	N	Y	Y	Y
5 Sawyer	N	N	Y	Y	Y
6 Carr	Y	Y	Y	Y	Y
7 Kildee	Y	Y	Y	Y	Y
8 Traxler	Y	Y	Y	Y	#
9 Vander Jagt	N	N	Y	Y	?
10 Cederberg	N	N	Y	Y	Y
11 Ruppe	Y	N	Y	Y	Y
12 Bonior	Y	Y	Y	Y	Y
13 Diggs	#	X	#	#	#
14 Nedzi	Y	Y	Y	Y	Y
15 Ford	Y	Y	Y	Y	Y
16 Dingell	Y	N	Y	Y	Y
17 Brodhead	Y	Y	Y	Y	Y
18 Blanchard	Y	Y	Y	Y	#
19 Broomfield	N	N	Y	#	Y
MINNESOTA					
1 Quie	N	N	Y	Y	Y
2 Hagedorn	Y	N	Y	Y	Y
3 Frenzel	Y	N	N	?	Y
4 Vento	Y	Y	Y	?	Y
5 Fraser	Y	Y	#	#	Y
6 Nolan	Y	Y	Y	Y	Y
7 Stangeland	N	N	Y	Y	Y
8 Oberstar	Y	Y	Y	Y	Y
MISSISSIPPI					
1 Whitten	N	N	Y	Y	Y
2 Bowen	N	N	Y	Y	Y
3 Montgomery	N	N	Y	Y	Y
4 Cochran	N	N	Y	Y	Y
5 Lott	N	N	Y	Y	Y
MISSOURI					
1 Clay	Y	Y	Y	Y	Y
2 Young	N	Y	Y	Y	Y
3 Gephardt	Y	Y	N	Y	Y
4 Skelton	Y	Y	Y	Y	Y
5 Bolling	Y	Y	Y	Y	Y
6 Coleman	N	N	Y	Y	Y
7 Taylor	N	N	Y	Y	Y
8 Ichord	N	N	Y	Y	Y
9 Volkmer	Y	Y	Y	Y	Y
10 Burlison	Y	Y	Y	Y	Y
MONTANA					
1 Baucus	N	Y	Y	Y	Y
2 Marlenee	N	N	Y	Y	Y
NEBRASKA					
1 Thone	N	N	Y	Y	Y
2 Cavanaugh	N	Y	Y	Y	Y
3 Smith	N	N	Y	Y	Y
NEVADA					
AL Santini	N	Y	Y	Y	Y
NEW HAMPSHIRE					
1 D'Amours	N	Y	Y	Y	Y
2 Cleveland	N	N	Y	Y	Y
NEW JERSEY					
1 Florio	Y	Y	Y	Y	#
2 Hughes	N	Y	Y	Y	Y
3 Howard	Y	Y	Y	Y	Y
4 Thompson	Y	Y	Y	Y	Y
5 Fenwick	Y	N	Y	Y	Y
6 Forsythe	N	N	Y	Y	Y
7 Maguire	Y	Y	Y	Y	?
8 Roe	Y	Y	Y	Y	Y
9 Hollenbeck	N	N	Y	Y	Y
10 Rodino	Y	Y	Y	Y	Y
11 Minish	Y	Y	Y	Y	Y
12 Rinaldo	N	N	Y	Y	Y
13 Meyner	Y	Y	Y	Y	Y
14 LeFante	Y	Y	Y	Y	Y
15 Patten	Y	Y	Y	Y	Y
NEW MEXICO					
1 Lujan	N	N	Y	Y	Y
2 Runnels	N	N	Y	Y	Y
NEW YORK					
1 Pike	Y	Y	Y	Y	Y
2 Downey	Y	Y	Y	Y	Y
3 Ambro	Y	Y	Y	Y	Y
4 Lent	N	N	Y	Y	Y
5 Wydler	N	N	Y	Y	N
6 Wolff	Y	Y	Y	#	Y
7 Addabbo	Y	Y	Y	Y	Y
8 Rosenthal	Y	Y	Y	#	Y
9 Delaney	Y	N	Y	Y	Y
10 Biaggi	Y	N	Y	Y	Y
11 Scheuer	#	✓	#	#	#
12 Chisholm	Y	Y	Y	Y	Y
13 Solarz	Y	Y	Y	#	Y
14 Richmond	Y	Y	Y	Y	Y
15 Zeferetti	Y	Y	#	#	Y
16 Holtzman	Y	Y	Y	Y	Y
17 Murphy	Y	Y	#	Y	Y
18 Green	Y	N	Y	Y	Y
19 Rangel	Y	Y	Y	Y	Y
20 Weiss	Y	Y	Y	Y	Y
21 Garcia	Y	Y	Y	Y	Y
22 Bingham	Y	Y	Y	#	Y
23 Caputo	N	N	Y	Y	Y
24 Ottinger	Y	Y	Y	Y	Y
25 Fish	Y	N	Y	Y	Y
26 Gilman	N	N	Y	Y	Y
27 McHugh	Y	Y	Y	#	Y
28 Stratton	Y	Y	Y	Y	Y
29 Pattison	Y	Y	N	Y	Y
30 McEwen	N	N	Y	Y	Y
31 Mitchell	N	N	Y	Y	Y
32 Hanley	Y	Y	Y	Y	Y
33 Walsh	N	N	Y	Y	Y
34 Horton	Y	N	Y	Y	Y
35 Conable	Y	N	Y	Y	Y
36 LaFalce	Y	Y	Y	Y	Y
37 Nowak	Y	Y	Y	Y	Y
38 Kemp	N	N	Y	Y	Y
39 Lundine	Y	Y	Y	Y	Y
NORTH CAROLINA					
1 Jones	Y	N	Y	Y	Y
2 Fountain	N	N	Y	Y	Y
3 Whitley	?	X	?	?	?
4 Andrews	Y	Y	Y	Y	Y
5 Neal	N	Y	Y	#	Y
6 Preyer	Y	Y	Y	Y	Y
7 Rose	Y	Y	Y	Y	Y
8 Hefner	Y	N	Y	Y	Y
9 Martin	Y	N	†	Y	Y
10 Broyhill	N	N	Y	Y	?
11 Gudger	N	Y	Y	Y	Y
NORTH DAKOTA					
AL Andrews	N	N	Y	Y	Y
OHIO					
1 Gradison	N	N	Y	Y	Y
2 Luken	N	Y	Y	Y	Y
3 Whalen	Y	N	Y	Y	Y
4 Guyer	N	N	Y	Y	Y
5 Latta	N	N	Y	Y	Y
6 Harsha	N	N	Y	Y	Y
7 Brown	N	N	Y	Y	Y
8 Kindness	N	N	Y	?	Y
9 Ashley	Y	Y	Y	Y	Y
10 Miller	N	N	Y	Y	Y
11 Stanton	Y	N	Y	Y	Y
12 Devine	N	N	Y	Y	Y
13 Pease	Y	Y	Y	Y	Y
14 Seiberling	Y	Y	Y	Y	Y
15 Wylie	N	N	Y	Y	Y
16 Regula	N	N	Y	Y	Y
17 Ashbrook	N	N	Y	Y	Y
18 Applegate	Y	N	Y	Y	Y
19 Carney	Y	Y	Y	Y	Y
20 Oakar	Y	Y	Y	Y	Y
21 Stokes	Y	Y	Y	Y	Y
22 Vanik	Y	Y	Y	Y	Y
23 Mottl	N	Y	Y	Y	Y
OKLAHOMA					
1 Jones	N	N	Y	Y	Y
2 Risenhoover	?	X	?	?	?
3 Watkins	N	N	Y	Y	Y
4 Steed	Y	N	Y	Y	Y
5 Edwards	N	N	Y	Y	Y
6 English	N	N	Y	Y	Y
OREGON					
1 AuCoin	N	Y	Y	Y	Y
2 Ullman	Y	Y	Y	Y	Y
3 Duncan	Y	Y	Y	?	Y
4 Weaver	Y	Y	Y	Y	#
PENNSYLVANIA					
1 Myers, M.	?	?	?	?	Y
2 Nix	Y	N	Y	Y	Y
3 Lederer	?	#	#	#	Y
4 Eilberg	Y	Y	Y	Y	Y
5 Schulze	N	N	Y	Y	Y
6 Yatron	N	N	Y	Y	Y
7 Edgar	Y	Y	Y	Y	Y
8 Kostmayer	N	Y	Y	Y	Y
9 Shuster	N	N	Y	Y	Y
10 McDade	N	N	Y	Y	Y
11 Flood	#	✓	#	#	#
12 Murtha	Y	N	Y	Y	Y
13 Coughlin	N	N	Y	?	Y
14 Moorhead	Y	Y	Y	Y	Y
15 Rooney	Y	Y	Y	Y	Y
16 Walker	N	N	Y	Y	Y
17 Ertel	Y	Y	Y	Y	Y
18 Walgren	Y	Y	Y	Y	Y
19 Goodling, W.	N	N	?	?	?
20 Gaydos	N	N	Y	Y	Y
21 Dent	N	N	Y	#	#
22 Murphy	N	Y	Y	Y	Y
23 Ammerman	Y	Y	Y	Y	Y
24 Marks	N	N	Y	?	Y
25 Myers, G.	N	N	N	Y	Y
RHODE ISLAND					
1 St Germain	Y	Y	Y	Y	Y
2 Beard	Y	Y	Y	Y	Y
SOUTH CAROLINA					
1 Davis	N	N	Y	Y	Y
2 Spence	N	N	Y	Y	Y
3 Derrick	N	Y	Y	Y	Y
4 Mann	Y	N	Y	Y	Y
5 Holland	Y	N	#	#	Y
6 Jenrette	N	Y	Y	Y	Y
SOUTH DAKOTA					
1 Pressler	N	N	Y	?	Y
2 Abdnor	N	N	Y	Y	Y
TENNESSEE					
1 Quillen	N	N	Y	Y	Y
2 Duncan	N	N	Y	Y	Y
3 Lloyd	N	N	Y	Y	Y
4 Gore	Y	Y	Y	Y	Y
5 Allen	Y	Y	Y	Y	Y
6 Beard	N	N	Y	?	Y
7 Jones	N	N	Y	Y	Y
8 Ford	Y	Y	Y	Y	Y
TEXAS					
1 Hall	N	N	Y	Y	Y
2 Wilson, C.	#	X	#	#	#
3 Collins	N	N	Y	N	N
4 Roberts	N	N	Y	Y	Y
5 Mattox	Y	Y	Y	Y	Y
6 Teague	✓	✓	?	?	?
7 Archer	N	N	Y	Y	Y
8 Eckhardt	Y	Y	Y	Y	Y
9 Brooks	Y	N	Y	Y	Y
10 Pickle	Y	N	Y	Y	Y
11 Poage	Y	N	Y	Y	Y
12 Wright	Y	Y	Y	Y	Y
13 Hightower	Y	N	Y	Y	Y
14 Young	Y	Y	Y	Y	Y
15 de la Garza	N	N	Y	Y	Y
16 White	Y	N	Y	Y	Y
17 Burleson	Y	N	Y	Y	Y
18 Jordan	Y	Y	Y	Y	Y
19 Mahon	Y	Y	Y	Y	Y
20 Gonzalez	Y	N	Y	Y	Y
21 Krueger	Y	N	Y	Y	Y
22 Gammage	N	N	Y	Y	Y
23 Kazen	Y	N	Y	Y	Y
24 Milford	N	N	Y	Y	Y
UTAH					
1 McKay	Y	Y	Y	Y	Y
2 Marriott	N	N	Y	Y	Y
VERMONT					
AL Jeffords	Y	N	Y	Y	Y
VIRGINIA					
1 Trible	N	N	Y	Y	Y
2 Whitehurst	Y	N	Y	Y	Y
3 Satterfield	N	N	Y	Y	Y
4 Daniel	N	N	Y	Y	Y
5 Daniel	N	N	Y	?	Y
6 Butler	Y	N	Y	?	Y
7 Robinson	N	N	Y	Y	Y
8 Harris	Y	Y	Y	Y	Y
9 Wampler	N	N	Y	Y	Y
10 Fisher	Y	Y	Y	Y	Y
WASHINGTON					
1 Pritchard	N	N	Y	#	Y
2 Meeds	Y	Y	Y	Y	#
3 Bonker	Y	Y	Y	Y	Y
4 McCormack	Y	Y	Y	Y	Y
5 Foley	Y	Y	Y	†	Y
6 Dicks	Y	Y	Y	Y	Y
7 Cunningham	N	N	Y	Y	Y
WEST VIRGINIA					
1 Mollohan	Y	N	Y	Y	Y
2 Staggers	Y	Y	?	Y	Y
3 Slack	Y	N	Y	Y	Y
4 Rahall	Y	Y	Y	Y	Y
WISCONSIN					
1 Aspin	Y	Y	Y	Y	Y
2 Kastenmeier	Y	Y	Y	Y	Y
3 Baldus	Y	Y	Y	Y	Y
4 Zablocki	Y	Y	Y	Y	Y
5 Reuss	Y	Y	Y	Y	#
6 Steiger	Y	N	Y	Y	Y
7 Obey	Y	Y	Y	Y	N
8 Cornell	Y	Y	Y	Y	Y
9 Kasten	N	N	Y	Y	Y
WYOMING					
AL Roncalio	Y	Y	Y	Y	Y

Democrats ***Republicans***

146. HR 9518. Shipping Act Amendments. Adoption of the rule (H Res 1074) providing for House floor consideration of the bill to increase the penalties for illegal merchant marine rebating and to expedite the enforcement of the rebating laws. Adopted 365-33: R 102-32; D 263-1 (ND 178-0; SD 85-1), March 22, 1978.

147. HR 9518. Shipping Act Amendments. Murphy, D-N.Y., motion that the House resolve itself into the Committee of the Whole to consider the bill to increase the penalties for illegal merchant marine rebating and to expedite the enforcement of the rebating laws. Adopted 376-0: R 129-0; D 247-0 (ND 165-0; SD 82-0), March 22, 1978.

148. HR 9518. Shipping Act Amendments. Passage of the bill to increase the penalties for illegal merchant marine rebating and to expedite the enforcement of the rebating laws. Passed 390-1: R 133-1; D 257-0 (ND 176-0; SD 81-0), March 22, 1978.

149. HR 6782. Emergency Farm Bill. Foley, D-Wash., motion to disagree with Senate amendments attaching emergency farm aid provisions to the House raisin promotion bill, and request a conference with the Senate. Motion agreed to 332-63: R 117-19; D 215-44 (ND 142-38; SD 73-6), March 22, 1978.

150. HR 6782. Emergency Farm Bill. Foley, D-Wash., motion to table (kill) the Moore, R-La., motion to instruct House conferees to support a Senate amendment providing a flexible parity program of graduated target prices for wheat, corn and cotton for 1978. Motion agreed to 224-167: R 13-123; D 211-44 (ND 163-13; SD 48-31), March 22, 1978.

KEY

Y	Voted for (yea).
✓	Paired for.
†	Announced for.
#	CQ Poll for.
N	Voted against (nay).
X	Paired against.
-	Announced against.
▮	CQ Poll against.
P	Voted "present."
●	Voted "present" to avoid possible conflict of interest.
?	Did not vote or otherwise make a position known.

	146	147	148	149	150
ALABAMA					
1 Edwards	Y	Y	Y	Y	N
2 Dickinson	Y	Y	Y	Y	N
3 Nichols	Y	Y	Y	Y	N
4 Bevill	Y	Y	Y	Y	N
5 Flippo	Y	Y	Y	Y	N
6 Buchanan	Y	Y	Y	Y	Y
7 Flowers	Y	Y	Y	Y	N
ALASKA					
AL Young	?	?	?	Y	N
ARIZONA					
1 Rhodes	Y	Y	Y	Y	N
2 Udall	Y	Y	#	Y	Y
3 Stump	Y	Y	Y	Y	Y
4 Rudd	?	?	?	?	?
ARKANSAS					
1 Alexander	Y	Y	Y	Y	Y
2 Tucker	Y	#	#	#	#
3 Hammerschmidt	N	Y	Y	Y	N
4 Thornton	?	?	?	?	?
CALIFORNIA					
1 Johnson	Y	Y	Y	Y	N
2 Clausen	Y	Y	Y	Y	N
3 Moss	Y	Y	Y	N	Y
4 Leggett	Y	#	Y	Y	#
5 Burton, J.	Y	Y	Y	Y	Y
6 Burton, P.	Y	Y	Y	Y	Y
7 Miller	Y	Y	Y	N	Y
8 Dellums	#	#	#	#	#
9 Stark	Y	Y	Y	N	#
10 Edwards	Y	Y	?	Y	Y
11 Ryan	Y	Y	Y	Y	Y
12 McCloskey	Y	Y	Y	Y	Y
13 Mineta	Y	Y	Y	N	Y
14 McFall	Y	#	Y	Y	Y
15 Sisk	Y	Y	Y	Y	Y
16 Panetta	Y	Y	Y	N	Y
17 Krebs	Y	Y	Y	N	Y
18 Ketchum	Y	Y	Y	Y	Y
19 Lagomarsino	Y	Y	Y	Y	N
20 Goldwater	Y	?	Y	Y	N
21 Corman	Y	Y	Y	N	Y
22 Moorhead	Y	Y	Y	N	N
23 Beilenson	Y	#	Y	N	Y
24 Waxman	#	?	Y	N	Y
25 Roybal	Y	Y	Y	Y	Y
26 Rousselot	N	Y	Y	N	N
27 Dornan	N	Y	Y	Y	N
28 Burke	Y	Y	Y	Y	Y
29 Hawkins	Y	Y	Y	Y	Y
30 Danielson	Y	Y	Y	Y	Y
31 Wilson, C.H.	#	#	#	#	#
32 Anderson	Y	Y	Y	N	Y
33 Clawson	Y	Y	Y	N	N
34 Hannaford	Y	Y	Y	N	Y
35 Lloyd	Y	Y	?	?	?
36 Brown	Y	Y	Y	N	N
37 Pettis	Y	Y	Y	Y	N
38 Patterson	Y	Y	Y	N	Y
39 Wiggins	Y	Y	Y	Y	N
40 Badham	Y	Y	Y	Y	N
41 Wilson, B.	Y	Y	Y	Y	N
42 Van Deerlin	Y	Y	Y	Y	Y
43 Burgener	Y	Y	Y	Y	N
COLORADO					
1 Schroeder	Y	Y	Y	N	Y
2 Wirth	Y	Y	Y	Y	Y
3 Evans	Y	Y	Y	Y	Y
4 Johnson	Y	Y	Y	Y	N

	146	147	148	149	150
5 Armstrong	N	Y	Y	Y	N
CONNECTICUT					
1 Cotter	Y	Y	Y	Y	Y
2 Dodd	Y	?	Y	Y	Y
3 Giaimo	Y	Y	Y	N	Y
4 McKinney	#	#	#	Y	N
5 Sarasin	†	†	†	†	-
6 Moffett	Y	Y	Y	Y	?
DELAWARE					
AL Evans	Y	Y	Y	Y	Y
FLORIDA					
1 Sikes	Y	Y	Y	Y	Y
2 Fuqua	Y	Y	Y	Y	Y
3 Bennett	Y	Y	Y	Y	Y
4 Chappell	Y	Y	Y	Y	N
5 Kelly	Y	Y	Y	Y	N
6 Young	N	Y	Y	N	N
7 Gibbons	Y	Y	Y	Y	Y
8 Ireland	Y	Y	Y	Y	Y
9 Frey	?	?	?	?	?
10 Bafalis	N	Y	Y	Y	N
11 Rogers	Y	Y	Y	Y	Y
12 Burke	Y	#	Y	Y	N
13 Lehman	Y	Y	Y	Y	Y
14 Pepper	Y	#	#	#	#
15 Fascell	Y	Y	Y	Y	Y
GEORGIA					
1 Ginn	Y	Y	Y	Y	N
2 Mathis	Y	Y	Y	Y	Y
3 Brinkley	Y	Y	Y	Y	N
4 Levitas	Y	Y	Y	Y	Y
5 Fowler	Y	Y	Y	Y	N
6 Flynt	Y	Y	Y	Y	N
7 McDonald	N	Y	Y	N	N
8 Evans	Y	Y	Y	Y	N
9 Jenkins	Y	Y	Y	Y	N
10 Barnard	Y	Y	Y	Y	?
HAWAII					
1 Heftel	Y	Y	?	Y	Y
2 Akaka	#	#	#	#	#
IDAHO					
1 Symms	N	Y	Y	Y	N
2 Hansen, G.	N	Y	Y	Y	N
ILLINOIS					
1 Metcalfe	?	?	?	?	?
2 Murphy	Y	Y	Y	Y	Y
3 Russo	Y	Y	Y	Y	Y
4 Derwinski	Y	Y	Y	Y	N
5 Fary	Y	Y	Y	Y	Y
6 Hyde	Y	Y	Y	Y	N
7 Collins	?	?	?	?	?
8 Rostenkowski	Y	Y	Y	Y	Y
9 Yates	Y	Y	Y	N	Y
10 Mikva	Y	Y	Y	Y	Y
11 Annunzio	#	#	#	#	#
12 Crane	N	#	Y	Y	N
13 McClory	Y	Y	Y	Y	N
14 Erlenborn	Y	Y	Y	N	N
15 Corcoran	Y	Y	Y	Y	N
16 Anderson	#	#	#	#	▮
17 O'Brien	#	#	Y	Y	N
18 Michel	N	Y	Y	Y	N
19 Railsback	Y	Y	Y	Y	N
20 Findley	?	?	?	?	?
21 Madigan	?	?	?	?	?
22 Shipley	?	?	?	?	?
23 Price	Y	Y	Y	Y	Y
24 Simon	Y	Y	Y	N	Y
INDIANA					
1 Benjamin	Y	Y	Y	Y	Y
2 Fithian	Y	Y	Y	Y	Y
3 Brademas	Y	Y	Y	Y	Y
4 Quayle	N	Y	Y	Y	N
5 Hillis	Y	Y	Y	Y	N
6 Evans	Y	Y	Y	?	?
7 Myers, J.	Y	Y	Y	Y	N
8 Cornwell	Y	Y	Y	Y	N
9 Hamilton	Y	Y	Y	Y	Y
10 Sharp	Y	Y	Y	Y	Y
11 Jacobs	Y	Y	Y	Y	Y
IOWA					
1 Leach	Y	Y	Y	Y	N
2 Blouin	Y	Y	Y	Y	Y
3 Grassley	Y	Y	Y	Y	N
4 Smith	Y	Y	Y	Y	Y
5 Harkin	Y	Y	Y	Y	Y
6 Bedell	Y	Y	Y	Y	Y

Democrats ***Republicans***

	146	147	148	149	150
KANSAS					
1 ***Sebelius***	Y	Y	Y	Y	N
2 Keys	Y	Y	†	Y	N
3 ***Winn***	Y	Y	Y	Y	N
4 Glickman	Y	Y	Y	Y	N
5 ***Skubitz***	Y	?	Y	Y	N
KENTUCKY					
1 Hubbard	Y	Y	Y	Y	Y
2 Natcher	Y	Y	Y	Y	N
3 Mazzoli	Y	Y	Y	N	Y
4 ***Snyder***	Y	Y	Y	N	N
5 ***Carter***	Y	Y	Y	Y	N
6 Breckinridge	Y	Y	Y	Y	Y
7 Perkins	Y	Y	Y	Y	Y
LOUISIANA					
1 ***Livingston***	Y	Y	Y	Y	N
2 Boggs	Y	Y	Y	Y	Y
3 ***Treen***	Y	Y	Y	Y	N
4 Waggonner	Y	Y	Y	Y	Y
5 Huckaby	Y	Y	Y	Y	N
6 ***Moore***	Y	Y	Y	Y	N
7 Breaux	Y	Y	Y	Y	N
8 Long	Y	Y	Y	Y	Y
MAINE					
1 ***Emery***	Y	Y	Y	Y	N
2 ***Cohen***	?	?	?	?	N
MARYLAND					
1 ***Bauman***	N	Y	Y	Y	N
2 Long	Y	Y	Y	Y	Y
3 Mikulski	Y	#	Y	Y	Y
4 ***Holt***	N	Y	Y	Y	N
5 Spellman	Y	Y	Y	Y	Y
6 Byron	?	Y	Y	Y	Y
7 Mitchell	Y	#	Y	Y	Y
8 ***Steers***	Y	Y	Y	Y	N
MASSACHUSETTS					
1 ***Conte***	Y	Y	Y	Y	Y
2 Boland	Y	Y	Y	Y	Y
3 Early	Y	Y	Y	N	Y
4 Drinan	Y	Y	Y	Y	Y
5 Tsongas	Y	Y	Y	Y	Y
6 Harrington	Y	Y	Y	N	Y
7 Markey	Y	Y	Y	Y	Y
8 O'Neill					
9 Moakley	Y	Y	Y	Y	Y
10 ***Heckler***	Y	Y	Y	Y	N
11 Burke	Y	Y	Y	Y	Y
12 Studds	Y	Y	Y	N	Y
MICHIGAN					
1 Conyers	Y	Y	Y	Y	Y
2 ***Pursell***	N	Y	Y	Y	N
3 ***Brown***	Y	Y	Y	Y	N
4 ***Stockman***	N	Y	N	Y	Y
5 ***Sawyer***	Y	Y	Y	Y	N
6 Carr	Y	Y	Y	N	Y
7 Kildee	Y	Y	Y	Y	Y
8 Traxler	#	#	#	#	#
9 ***Vander Jagt***	?	?	Y	Y	N
10 ***Cederberg***	Y	Y	Y	Y	N
11 ***Ruppe***	Y	#	Y	Y	N
12 Bonior	?	Y	Y	N	Y
13 Diggs	#	#	#	#	#
14 Nedzi	Y	Y	Y	Y	Y
15 Ford	Y	Y	Y	Y	Y
16 Dingell	Y	Y	Y	Y	Y
17 Brodhead	Y	?	Y	Y	Y
18 Blanchard	Y	Y	Y	N	Y
19 ***Broomfield***	Y	Y	Y	Y	N
MINNESOTA					
1 ***Quie***	Y	Y	Y	Y	N
2 ***Hagedorn***	Y	Y	Y	Y	N
3 ***Frenzel***	Y	Y	Y	Y	N
4 Vento	Y	Y	Y	Y	Y
5 Fraser	Y	Y	#	Y	N
6 Nolan	Y	Y	Y	Y	N
7 ***Stangeland***	Y	Y	Y	Y	N
8 Oberstar	Y	Y	Y	Y	Y
MISSISSIPPI					
1 Whitten	Y	Y	Y	Y	N
2 Bowen	Y	Y	Y	Y	Y
3 Montgomery	Y	Y	Y	Y	N
4 ***Cochran***	Y	Y	Y	Y	N
5 ***Lott***	Y	Y	Y	Y	N
MISSOURI					
1 Clay	Y	Y	Y	Y	Y
2 Young	Y	Y	Y	Y	Y
3 Gephardt	Y	Y	Y	Y	Y

	146	147	148	149	150
4 Skelton	Y	Y	Y	Y	N
5 Bolling	Y	Y	Y	Y	Y
6 ***Coleman***	Y	Y	Y	Y	N
7 ***Taylor***	Y	Y	Y	Y	N
8 Ichord	Y	Y	Y	Y	N
9 Volkmer	Y	Y	Y	Y	Y
10 Burlison	Y	Y	Y	Y	N
MONTANA					
1 Baucus	Y	Y	Y	Y	N
2 ***Marlenee***	N	Y	Y	Y	N
NEBRASKA					
1 ***Thone***	Y	Y	Y	Y	N
2 Cavanaugh	Y	Y	Y	Y	Y
3 ***Smith***	Y	Y	Y	Y	N
NEVADA					
AL Santini	Y	Y	Y	Y	Y
NEW HAMPSHIRE					
1 D'Amours	Y	Y	Y	N	Y
2 ***Cleveland***	Y	Y	Y	Y	N
NEW JERSEY					
1 Florio	#	#	#	Y	Y
2 Hughes	Y	Y	Y	N	N
3 Howard	Y	Y	#	N	Y
4 Thompson	Y	Y	Y	Y	Y
5 ***Fenwick***	Y	Y	Y	N	N
6 ***Forsythe***	Y	Y	Y	▮	#
7 Maguire	Y	Y	Y	Y	Y
8 Roe	Y	Y	Y	Y	Y
9 ***Hollenbeck***	Y	Y	Y	N	N
10 Rodino	Y	Y	Y	Y	Y
11 Minish	Y	Y	Y	Y	Y
12 ***Rinaldo***	Y	Y	Y	N	N
13 Meyner	Y	Y	Y	Y	Y
14 LeFante	Y	Y	Y	Y	Y
15 Patten	Y	Y	Y	N	Y
NEW MEXICO					
1 ***Lujan***	Y	Y	Y	Y	N
2 Runnels	Y	#	Y	Y	N
NEW YORK					
1 Pike	Y	Y	Y	N	Y
2 Downey	Y	Y	Y	N	Y
3 Ambro	Y	Y	Y	Y	Y
4 ***Lent***	Y	Y	Y	N	N
5 ***Wydler***	Y	Y	Y	N	N
6 Wolff	Y	#	Y	N	Y
7 Addabbo	Y	Y	Y	Y	Y
8 Rosenthal	Y	#	Y	Y	Y
9 Delaney	Y	Y	Y	Y	Y
10 Biaggi	Y	Y	Y	Y	Y
11 Scheuer	#	#	#	#	#
12 Chisholm	Y	#	Y	Y	Y
13 Solarz	Y	Y	Y	N	Y
14 Richmond	Y	Y	Y	Y	Y
15 Zeferetti	Y	Y	Y	Y	Y
16 Holtzman	Y	Y	Y	N	Y
17 Murphy	Y	Y	Y	Y	#
18 ***Green***	Y	Y	Y	Y	Y
19 Rangel	Y	Y	Y	Y	Y
20 Weiss	Y	Y	Y	N	Y
21 Garcia	Y	Y	Y	Y	Y
22 Bingham	Y	Y	Y	Y	Y
23 ***Caputo***	N	Y	Y	N	Y
24 Ottinger	Y	Y	Y	Y	Y
25 ***Fish***	Y	Y	Y	Y	Y
26 ***Gilman***	Y	Y	Y	Y	Y
27 McHugh	Y	Y	Y	Y	Y
28 Stratton	Y	Y	Y	N	Y
29 Pattison	Y	Y	Y	Y	Y
30 ***McEwen***	Y	Y	?	N	N
31 ***Mitchell***	Y	Y	Y	Y	N
32 Hanley	Y	Y	Y	Y	Y
33 ***Walsh***	Y	Y	Y	Y	N
34 ***Horton***	Y	Y	Y	Y	N
35 ***Conable***	N	Y	Y	N	Y
36 LaFalce	Y	Y	Y	N	Y
37 Nowak	Y	Y	Y	Y	Y
38 ***Kemp***	Y	Y	Y	N	N
39 Lundine	Y	Y	Y	Y	Y
NORTH CAROLINA					
1 Jones	Y	Y	Y	Y	Y
2 Fountain	Y	Y	Y	#	Y
3 Whitley	?	?	?	?	?
4 Andrews	Y	Y	Y	Y	Y
5 Neal	Y	Y	Y	Y	Y
6 Preyer	Y	Y	Y	Y	Y
7 Rose	Y	Y	Y	Y	Y
8 Hefner	Y	Y	Y	Y	Y

	146	147	148	149	150
9 ***Martin***	Y	Y	Y	Y	N
10 ***Broyhill***	?	?	?	?	?
11 Gudger	Y	Y	Y	Y	Y
NORTH DAKOTA					
AL Andrews	Y	Y	Y	Y	N
OHIO					
1 ***Gradison***	Y	Y	Y	Y	N
2 Luken	Y	Y	Y	Y	Y
3 ***Whalen***	Y	Y	Y	Y	Y
4 ***Guyer***	Y	Y	Y	Y	N
5 ***Latta***	N	Y	Y	Y	N
6 ***Harsha***	Y	Y	Y	Y	N
7 ***Brown***	N	Y	Y	N	N
8 ***Kindness***	Y	Y	Y	Y	N
9 Ashley	Y	Y	Y	Y	Y
10 ***Miller***	N	Y	Y	Y	N
11 ***Stanton***	Y	Y	Y	N	N
12 ***Devine***	N	Y	Y	Y	N
13 Pease	Y	Y	Y	Y	Y
14 Seiberling	Y	Y	Y	Y	Y
15 ***Wylie***	Y	Y	Y	Y	N
16 ***Regula***	Y	Y	Y	Y	N
17 ***Ashbrook***	N	Y	Y	Y	N
18 Applegate	Y	Y	Y	Y	Y
19 Carney	Y	Y	Y	Y	Y
20 Oakar	Y	Y	Y	Y	Y
21 Stokes	Y	Y	Y	Y	Y
22 Vanik	Y	Y	Y	Y	Y
23 Mottl	Y	Y	Y	#	#
OKLAHOMA					
1 Jones	Y	Y	Y	Y	Y
2 Risenhoover	?	?	?	?	?
3 Watkins	Y	Y	Y	#	#
4 Steed	Y	Y	Y	Y	Y
5 ***Edwards***	N	Y	?	?	?
6 English	Y	#	Y	Y	Y
OREGON					
1 AuCoin	Y	Y	Y	Y	Y
2 Ullman	Y	Y	Y	Y	Y
3 Duncan	Y	?	Y	Y	Y
4 Weaver	Y	#	Y	Y	Y
PENNSYLVANIA					
1 Myers, M.	Y	Y	Y	Y	Y
2 Nix	Y	?	Y	Y	Y
3 Lederer	Y	Y	Y	Y	Y
4 Eilberg	Y	Y	Y	Y	Y
5 ***Schulze***	Y	Y	Y	Y	N
6 Yatron	Y	Y	Y	Y	Y
7 Edgar	Y	Y	Y	N	Y
8 Kostmayer	Y	Y	Y	N	Y
9 ***Shuster***	N	Y	Y	Y	N
10 ***McDade***	Y	Y	Y	Y	N
11 Flood	#	#	#	#	#
12 Murtha	Y	Y	Y	Y	Y
13 ***Coughlin***	N	Y	Y	Y	N
14 Moorhead	Y	#	Y	Y	Y
15 Rooney	Y	Y	Y	Y	Y
16 ***Walker***	N	Y	Y	Y	N
17 Ertel	Y	Y	Y	Y	Y
18 Walgren	Y	Y	Y	Y	Y
19 ***Goodling, W.***	?	?	?	?	?
20 Gaydos	?	?	Y	Y	Y
21 Dent	Y	Y	Y	Y	Y
22 Murphy	Y	Y	Y	Y	Y
23 Ammerman	Y	Y	Y	N	Y
24 ***Marks***	Y	Y	Y	Y	N
25 ***Myers, G.***	Y	Y	Y	N	N
RHODE ISLAND					
1 St Germain	Y	Y	Y	Y	?
2 Beard	Y	Y	Y	Y	Y
SOUTH CAROLINA					
1 Davis	Y	Y	Y	Y	N
2 ***Spence***	Y	Y	Y	Y	N
3 Derrick	Y	Y	#	Y	Y
4 Mann	Y	Y	Y	Y	N
5 Holland	Y	Y	Y	Y	N
6 Jenrette	Y	#	Y	Y	Y
SOUTH DAKOTA					
1 ***Pressler***	Y	Y	Y	Y	N
2 ***Abdnor***	Y	Y	Y	Y	N
TENNESSEE					
1 ***Quillen***	N	Y	Y	Y	N
2 ***Duncan***	Y	Y	Y	Y	N
3 Lloyd	Y	Y	Y	Y	Y
4 Gore	Y	Y	Y	Y	Y
5 Allen	Y	Y	Y	Y	Y
6 ***Beard***	Y	Y	Y	Y	N

	146	147	148	149	150
7 Jones	Y	Y	Y	Y	Y
8 Ford	Y	Y	Y	Y	Y
TEXAS					
1 Hall	Y	Y	Y	Y	N
2 Wilson, C.	#	#	#	#	#
3 ***Collins***	N	Y	Y	Y	N
4 Roberts	Y	Y	?	?	?
5 Mattox	Y	Y	Y	N	Y
6 Teague	Y	Y	?	?	?
7 ***Archer***	N	Y	Y	N	N
8 Eckhardt	Y	Y	Y	N	Y
9 Brooks	Y	Y	Y	Y	Y
10 Pickle	Y	Y	Y	Y	N
11 Poage	Y	Y	Y	Y	Y
12 Wright	Y	Y	Y	Y	Y
13 Hightower	Y	Y	Y	Y	N
14 Young	Y	Y	Y	Y	N
15 de la Garza	Y	Y	Y	Y	Y
16 White	Y	Y	Y	Y	N
17 Burleson	Y	Y	Y	Y	N
18 Jordan	Y	Y	Y	Y	Y
19 Mahon	Y	Y	Y	Y	Y
20 Gonzalez	Y	Y	Y	Y	Y
21 Krueger	Y	Y	Y	Y	N
22 Gammage	Y	Y	Y	Y	N
23 Kazen	Y	Y	Y	Y	N
24 Milford	Y	Y	Y	?	?
UTAH					
1 McKay	Y	Y	Y	Y	Y
2 ***Marriott***	Y	Y	Y	Y	N
VERMONT					
AL Jeffords	N	Y	Y	Y	N
VIRGINIA					
1 ***Trible***	Y	Y	Y	Y	N
2 ***Whitehurst***	Y	Y	Y	Y	N
3 Satterfield	Y	Y	Y	Y	N
4 ***Daniel***	Y	Y	Y	Y	N
5 Daniel	Y	Y	Y	Y	N
6 ***Butler***	Y	Y	Y	Y	N
7 ***Robinson***	Y	Y	Y	Y	N
8 Harris	Y	Y	Y	N	Y
9 ***Wampler***	Y	Y	Y	Y	N
10 Fisher	Y	Y	Y	N	Y
WASHINGTON					
1 ***Pritchard***	Y	Y	Y	Y	#
2 Meeds	#	#	#	#	#
3 Bonker	Y	Y	Y	Y	Y
4 McCormack	Y	Y	Y	Y	Y
5 Foley	Y	Y	Y	Y	Y
6 Dicks	Y	Y	Y	Y	Y
7 ***Cunningham***	Y	Y	Y	Y	N
WEST VIRGINIA					
1 Mollohan	Y	Y	Y	Y	Y
2 Staggers	?	?	Y	Y	Y
3 Slack	Y	Y	Y	Y	Y
4 Rahall	Y	Y	Y	Y	Y
WISCONSIN					
1 Aspin	Y	Y	Y	Y	Y
2 Kastenmeier	Y	Y	Y	#	Y
3 Baldus	Y	Y	Y	Y	Y
4 Zablocki	Y	Y	Y	Y	Y
5 Reuss	#	Y	Y	Y	Y
6 ***Steiger***	N	Y	Y	Y	Y
7 Obey	Y	Y	Y	Y	Y
8 Cornell	Y	Y	Y	Y	Y
9 ***Kasten***	Y	Y	Y	Y	N
WYOMING					
AL Roncalio	Y	?	?	?	?

Democrats ***Republicans***

151. HR 10984. Albert Gallatin Historic Site. P. Burton, D-Calif., motion to suspend the rules and pass the bill to authorize $100,000 plus acquisition costs in fiscal 1979 to establish within the National Park system the Friendship Hill National Historic Site in Fayette County, Pa., to preserve the home and commemorate the life of Albert Gallatin, secretary of the treasury under President Thomas Jefferson. Motion agreed to 351-6: R 119-4; D 232-2 (ND 159-0; SD 73-2), April 3, 1978. A two-thirds majority vote (238 in this case) is required for passage under suspension of the rules.

152. H Con Res 359. Gen. Thaddeus Kosciuszko Memorials. P. Burton, D-Calif., motion to suspend the rules and pass the bill to recognize the contribution of Gen. Thaddeus Kosciuszko of Poland in the victory of the American forces at the Battle of Saratoga in 1777 by setting up markers at various National Park locations (the markers would be privately donated and the bill authorized no government expenditures). Motion agreed to 358-0: R 123-0; D 235-0 (ND 159-0; SD 76-0), April 3, 1978. A two-thirds majority vote (239 in this case) is required for passage under suspension of the rules.

153. HR 6900. Oregon National Trail. P. Burton, D-Calif., motion to suspend the rules and pass the bill to amend the 1968 National Trails System Act to provide two categories of national trails — historic and scenic — and to appropriate $5 million for the 2,000-mile Oregon Trail from Independence, Mo., to Portland, Ore., the first trail in the new historic category. Motion agreed to 353-4: R 120-2; D 233-2 (ND 159-0; SD 74-2), April 3, 1978. A two-thirds majority vote (238 in this case) is required for passage under suspension of the rules.

154. HR 11662. Lowell (Mass.) Historical Park. P. Burton, D-Calif., motion to suspend the rules and pass the bill to authorize $18.5 million for establishment of a historic park administered by the National Park Service at Lowell, Mass., to preserve the first planned industrial city in 19th century America. Motion rejected 228-132: R 33-91; D 195-41 (ND 150-9; SD 45-32), April 3, 1978. A two-thirds majority vote (240 in this case) is required for passage under suspension of the rules.

155. HR 11003. White House Personnel. Derwinski, R-Ill., demand for a second on the Schroeder, D-Colo., motion to suspend the rules and pass the bill to authorize an increase in White House personnel and to provide for congressional oversight of White House staffing. Second ordered 239-147: R 12-123; D 227-24 (ND 157-19; SD 70-5), April 4, 1978.

156. HR 11003. White House Personnel. Schroeder, D-Colo., motion to suspend the rules and pass the bill to amend the U.S. Code to authorize White House personnel and to provide for congressional oversight of White House staffing. Motion rejected 207-188: R 16-123; D 191-65 (ND 134-43; SD 57-22), April 4, 1978. A two-thirds majority vote (264 in this case) is required for passage under suspension of the rules. A "yea" was a vote supporting the president's position.

157. HR 7700. Postal Service Act. Hanley, D-N.Y., motion that the House resolve itself into the Committee of the Whole to consider the bill to reorganize the United States Postal Service. Motion agreed to 386-4: R 134-2; D 252-2 (ND 172-2; SD 80-0), April 5, 1978.

158. HR 7700. Postal Service Act. Allen, D-Tenn., substitute amendment, to the Simon, D-Ill., amendment *(see vote 159, p. 48-H)*, to prohibit the United States Postal Service from undercutting or discriminating against the rates of private parcel delivery services. Rejected 147-257: R 18-123; D 129-134 (ND 88-94; SD 41-40), April 5, 1978.

KEY

Y Voted for (yea).
✓ Paired for.
† Announced for.
# CQ Poll for.
N Voted against (nay).
X Paired against.
- Announced against.
▮ CQ Poll against.
P Voted "present."
● Voted "present" to avoid possible conflict of interest.
? Did not vote or otherwise make a position known.

	151	152	153	154	155	156	157	158
ALABAMA								
1 Edwards	Y	Y	Y	N	N	N	Y	N
2 Dickinson	Y	Y	Y	Y	Y	N	Y	N
3 Nichols	Y	Y	Y	N	Y	N	Y	Y
4 Bevill	?	Y	Y	N	Y	Y	Y	Y
5 Flippo	Y	Y	Y	N	Y	N	Y	N
6 Buchanan	Y	Y	Y	N	N	N	Y	N
7 Flowers	Y	Y	Y	N	Y	Y	Y	Y
ALASKA								
AL Young	?	?	?	?	N	N	Y	N
ARIZONA								
1 Rhodes	Y	Y	Y	N	N	N	Y	N
2 Udall	Y	Y	Y	Y	#	#	#	✓
3 Stump	Y	Y	Y	N	Y	N	Y	N
4 Rudd	?	?	?	?	N	N	Y	N
ARKANSAS								
1 Alexander	Y	Y	Y	Y	Y	Y	Y	?
2 Tucker	#	#	#	#	#	#	#	#
3 Hammerschmidt	Y	Y	Y	N	N	N	Y	N
4 Thornton	?	?	?	?	?	?	?	?
CALIFORNIA								
1 Johnson	Y	Y	Y	Y	Y	Y	Y	Y
2 Clausen	Y	Y	Y	N	N	N	Y	N
3 Moss	Y	Y	Y	Y	N	N	Y	Y
4 Leggett	Y	Y	Y	Y	▮	Y	Y	Y
5 Burton, J.	Y	Y	Y	Y	Y	Y	Y	Y
6 Burton, P.	Y	Y	Y	Y	Y	Y	Y	Y
7 Miller	Y	Y	Y	Y	Y	Y	Y	Y
8 Dellums	Y	Y	Y	Y	Y	Y	Y	Y
9 Stark	Y	Y	Y	Y	Y	Y	Y	Y
10 Edwards	Y	Y	Y	Y	Y	Y	Y	Y
11 Ryan	Y	Y	Y	Y	Y	N	Y	Y
12 McCloskey	?	?	?	?	?	X	Y	N
13 Mineta	Y	Y	Y	Y	Y	Y	Y	Y
14 McFall	Y	Y	Y	Y	Y	Y	Y	N
15 Sisk	Y	Y	Y	Y	Y	Y	Y	N
16 Panetta	Y	Y	Y	Y	Y	N	Y	N
17 Krebs	Y	Y	Y	Y	N	N	Y	N
18 Ketchum	Y	Y	Y	N	N	Y	Y	N
19 Lagomarsino	Y	Y	Y	N	N	N	Y	N
20 Goldwater	Y	Y	Y	N	N	N	Y	N
21 Corman	Y	Y	Y	Y	Y	?	Y	Y
22 Moorhead	Y	Y	Y	N	N	N	Y	N
23 Beilenson	Y	Y	Y	Y	Y	Y	Y	Y
24 Waxman	Y	Y	Y	Y	Y	Y	#	N
25 Roybal	Y	Y	Y	Y	Y	Y	Y	Y
26 Rousselot	Y	Y	Y	N	N	N	Y	N
27 Dornan	#	#	#	#	N	N	Y	N
28 Burke	#	#	#	#	#	✓	#	X
29 Hawkins	Y	Y	Y	Y	Y	Y	Y	N
30 Danielson	Y	Y	Y	Y	Y	Y	Y	Y
31 Wilson, C.H.	Y	Y	Y	Y	#	Y	Y	Y
32 Anderson	Y	Y	Y	Y	Y	Y	Y	N
33 Clawson	Y	Y	Y	N	N	X	Y	N
34 Hannaford	Y	Y	Y	Y	Y	Y	Y	N
35 Lloyd	Y	Y	Y	Y	Y	Y	Y	N
36 Brown	Y	Y	Y	Y	Y	Y	Y	Y
37 Pettis	Y	Y	Y	N	N	N	Y	N
38 Patterson	Y	Y	Y	Y	Y	Y	Y	Y
39 Wiggins	Y	Y	Y	N	Y	Y	#	N
40 Badham	Y	Y	Y	N	N	N	Y	N
41 Wilson, B.	Y	Y	Y	Y	N	N	N	N
42 Van Deerlin	Y	Y	Y	Y	Y	Y	Y	N
43 Burgener	Y	Y	Y	N	N	N	?	N
COLORADO								
1 Schroeder	Y	Y	Y	Y	Y	Y	Y	N
2 Wirth	Y	Y	Y	Y	N	N	Y	N
3 Evans	Y	Y	Y	Y	Y	Y	Y	Y
4 Johnson	Y	Y	Y	Y	N	N	Y	N
5 Armstrong	Y	Y	Y	N	N	N	Y	N
CONNECTICUT								
1 Cotter	Y	Y	Y	Y	Y	N	Y	N
2 Dodd	?	?	?	?	?	?	Y	N
3 Giaimo	Y	Y	Y	Y	Y	Y	Y	N
4 McKinney	#	#	#	#	#	▮	#	▮
5 Sarasin	†	†	†	†	-	-	Y	N
6 Moffett	Y	Y	Y	Y	Y	Y	Y	Y
DELAWARE								
AL Evans	Y	Y	Y	N	N	N	Y	N
FLORIDA								
1 Sikes	Y	Y	Y	Y	Y	Y	Y	Y
2 Fuqua	Y	Y	Y	Y	Y	N	Y	N
3 Bennett	Y	Y	Y	Y	Y	N	Y	Y
4 Chappell	#	#	#	#	#	✓	#	✓
5 Kelly	Y	Y	Y	N	N	N	Y	N
6 Young	Y	Y	Y	N	N	N	Y	Y
7 Gibbons	Y	Y	Y	N	Y	Y	Y	Y
8 Ireland	Y	Y	Y	Y	Y	Y	Y	N
9 Frey	?	?	?	?	?	N	Y	N
10 Bafalis	Y	Y	Y	N	N	N	Y	N
11 Rogers	Y	Y	Y	Y	?	N	Y	Y
12 Burke	Y	Y	Y	Y	N	N	Y	N
13 Lehman	#	#	#	#	#	#	#	▮
14 Pepper	#	#	#	#	Y	Y	Y	Y
15 Fascell	Y	Y	Y	Y	Y	Y	Y	N
GEORGIA								
1 Ginn	Y	Y	Y	N	Y	Y	Y	Y
2 Mathis	Y	Y	Y	Y	N	Y	?	N
3 Brinkley	Y	Y	Y	N	Y	Y	Y	Y
4 Levitas	Y	Y	Y	Y	Y	Y	Y	Y
5 Fowler	Y	Y	Y	N	Y	Y	Y	Y
6 Flynt	Y	Y	Y	N	?	Y	Y	N
7 McDonald	N	Y	N	N	N	N	Y	N
8 Evans	Y	Y	Y	N	Y	▮	Y	N
9 Jenkins	Y	Y	Y	N	Y	Y	Y	Y
10 Barnard	Y	Y	Y	Y	Y	Y	Y	Y
HAWAII								
1 Heftel	?	?	?	?	Y	Y	Y	N
2 Akaka	Y	Y	Y	Y	Y	Y	Y	Y
IDAHO								
1 Symms	Y	Y	Y	N	N	N	Y	N
2 Hansen, G.	Y	Y	Y	N	N	N	Y	N
ILLINOIS								
1 Metcalfe	?	?	?	?	Y	Y	Y	N
2 Murphy	#	#	#	#	#	?	Y	N
3 Russo	Y	Y	Y	N	Y	Y	Y	N
4 Derwinski	Y	Y	Y	Y	Y	Y	Y	Y
5 Fary	Y	Y	Y	Y	Y	Y	Y	N
6 Hyde	Y	Y	Y	N	N	N	Y	N
7 Collins	Y	Y	Y	Y	Y	Y	Y	N
8 Rostenkowski	#	#	#	#	Y	Y	Y	N
9 Yates	Y	Y	Y	Y	Y	N	Y	N
10 Mikva	Y	Y	Y	Y	Y	Y	Y	Y
11 Annunzio	Y	Y	Y	Y	Y	Y	Y	N
12 Crane	#	#	#	▮	N	N	Y	N
13 McClory	Y	Y	Y	N	N	N	Y	N
14 Erlenborn	Y	Y	Y	N	N	N	Y	N
15 Corcoran	Y	Y	Y	Y	N	Y	Y	N
16 Anderson	Y	Y	Y	Y	N	N	Y	N
17 O'Brien	#	#	#	▮	#	#	#	✓
18 Michel	#	#	#	▮	#	X	#	X
19 Railsback	Y	Y	Y	N	N	N	Y	N
20 Findley	?	?	?	?	N	N	Y	N
21 Madigan	?	?	?	?	Y	Y	Y	N
22 Shipley	Y	Y	Y	Y	Y	Y	Y	N
23 Price	Y	Y	Y	Y	Y	Y	Y	N
24 Simon	Y	Y	Y	Y	Y	Y	Y	N
INDIANA								
1 Benjamin	Y	Y	Y	Y	Y	Y	Y	N
2 Fithian	Y	Y	Y	Y	N	N	Y	N
3 Brademas	Y	Y	Y	Y	Y	Y	Y	N
4 Quayle	Y	Y	Y	N	N	N	Y	N
5 Hillis	Y	Y	Y	N	N	N	Y	N
6 Evans	Y	Y	Y	N	Y	N	Y	N
7 Myers, J.	Y	Y	Y	N	N	N	Y	N
8 Cornwell	Y	Y	Y	Y	Y	N	Y	N
9 Hamilton	Y	Y	Y	Y	Y	Y	Y	N
10 Sharp	Y	Y	Y	Y	Y	N	Y	N
11 Jacobs	Y	Y	Y	N	Y	N	Y	N
IOWA								
1 Leach	Y	Y	Y	N	N	N	Y	N
2 Blouin	?	?	?	?	Y	Y	?	Y
3 Grassley	Y	Y	Y	N	N	N	Y	N
4 Smith	Y	Y	Y	Y	Y	Y	Y	Y
5 Harkin	Y	Y	Y	Y	Y	Y	Y	Y
6 Bedell	Y	Y	Y	Y	N	N	Y	Y

Democrats ***Republicans***

	151	152	153	154	155	156	157	158
KANSAS								
1 Sebelius	Y	Y	Y	Y	N	N	Y	Y
2 Keys	Y	Y	Y	Y	Y	N	Y	N
3 Winn	Y	Y	Y	N	N	N	Y	Y
4 Glickman	Y	Y	Y	N	N	N	Y	N
5 Skubitz	Y	Y	Y	Y	N	N	Y	N
KENTUCKY								
1 Hubbard	Y	Y	Y	Y	Y	Y	Y	Y
2 Natcher	Y	Y	Y	Y	Y	Y	Y	Y
3 Mazzoli	Y	Y	Y	Y	Y	N	Y	N
4 Snyder	Y	Y	Y	N	N	N	Y	N
5 Carter	Y	Y	Y	Y	Y	Y	Y	N
6 Breckinridge	Y	Y	Y	Y	Y	Y	Y	Y
7 Perkins	Y	Y	Y	Y	Y	Y	Y	Y
LOUISIANA								
1 Livingston	Y	Y	Y	N	N	N	Y	N
2 Boggs	Y	Y	Y	Y	Y	Y	Y	N
3 Treen	Y	Y	Y	N	N	Y	Y	N
4 Waggonner	Y	Y	Y	N	Y	Y	Y	N
5 Huckaby	Y	Y	Y	N	Y	N	Y	N
6 Moore	Y	Y	Y	N	N	N	Y	N
7 Breaux	Y	Y	Y	N	Y	N	Y	N
8 Long	?	?	?	?	?	?	?	?
MAINE								
1 Emery	Y	Y	Y	Y	N	N	Y	N
2 Cohen	Y	Y	Y	Y	N	N	Y	N
MARYLAND								
1 Bauman	Y	Y	Y	N	N	N	Y	N
2 Long	Y	Y	Y	Y	N	N	Y	N
3 Mikulski	Y	Y	Y	Y	Y	Y	Y	Y
4 Holt	Y	Y	Y	N	N	N	Y	N
5 Spellman	#	#	#	#	#	✓	#	▮
6 Byron	Y	Y	Y	Y	N	N	Y	N
7 Mitchell	Y	Y	Y	Y	Y	Y	N	Y
8 Steers	Y	Y	Y	Y	N	N	Y	N
MASSACHUSETTS								
1 Conte	?	?	?	?	Y	Y	Y	N
2 Boland	#	#	#	#	Y	Y	Y	N
3 Early	?	?	?	?	Y	N	Y	Y
4 Drinan	Y	Y	Y	Y	Y	N	Y	N
5 Tsongas	Y	Y	Y	Y	?	Y	Y	N
6 Harrington	Y	Y	Y	Y	Y	Y	Y	N
7 Markey	Y	Y	Y	Y	Y	Y	Y	N
8 O'Neill								
9 Moakley	Y	Y	Y	Y	Y	Y	#	N
10 Heckler	Y	Y	Y	Y	N	Y	Y	N
11 Burke	Y	Y	Y	Y	Y	Y	Y	Y
12 Studds	Y	Y	Y	Y	Y	Y	Y	N
MICHIGAN								
1 Conyers	Y	Y	Y	Y	Y	Y	Y	Y
2 Pursell	Y	Y	Y	N	N	N	Y	N
3 Brown	Y	Y	Y	Y	N	N	Y	N
4 Stockman	Y	Y	Y	N	N	N	Y	N
5 Sawyer	Y	Y	Y	N	N	N	Y	N
6 Carr	Y	Y	Y	Y	Y	Y	Y	N
7 Kildee	Y	Y	Y	Y	Y	Y	Y	Y
8 Traxler	Y	Y	Y	Y	Y	Y	Y	Y
9 Vander Jagt	Y	Y	Y	Y	?	N	Y	N
10 Cederberg	Y	Y	Y	Y	Y	Y	?	N
11 Ruppe	Y	Y	Y	Y	#	▮	Y	N
12 Bonior	Y	Y	Y	Y	Y	Y	Y	N
13 Diggs	#	#	#	#	#	#	#	X
14 Nedzi	Y	Y	Y	Y	Y	Y	Y	Y
15 Ford	Y	Y	Y	Y	Y	Y	Y	Y
16 Dingell	?	?	?	?	?	N	Y	N
17 Brodhead	Y	Y	Y	Y	N	Y	Y	Y
18 Blanchard	Y	Y	Y	Y	Y	Y	Y	Y
19 Broomfield	Y	Y	Y	N	N	N	Y	N
MINNESOTA								
1 Quie	#	#	#	#	N	N	Y	N
2 Hagedorn	Y	Y	N	Y	N	N	Y	N
3 Frenzel	Y	Y	Y	N	N	N	Y	N
4 Vento	Y	Y	Y	Y	Y	Y	Y	Y
5 Fraser	#	#	#	#	Y	Y	Y	N
6 Nolan	Y	Y	Y	Y	N	Y	Y	Y
7 Stangeland	N	Y	N	N	N	N	Y	N
8 Oberstar	Y	Y	Y	Y	Y	Y	Y	Y
MISSISSIPPI								
1 Whitten	#	Y	Y	N	Y	Y	Y	N
2 Bowen	Y	Y	Y	N	Y	Y	Y	N
3 Montgomery	Y	Y	Y	N	Y	Y	Y	N
4 Cochran	Y	Y	Y	N	?	N	Y	N
5 Lott	Y	Y	Y	N	N	Y	Y	N
MISSOURI								
1 Clay	Y	Y	Y	Y	Y	Y	?	Y
2 Young	Y	Y	Y	Y	Y	Y	#	N
3 Gephardt	Y	Y	Y	Y	Y	Y	Y	▮
4 Skelton	Y	Y	Y	Y	Y	Y	Y	N
5 Bolling	#	#	#	#	#	#	Y	N
6 Coleman	Y	Y	Y	N	N	N	Y	N
7 Taylor	Y	Y	Y	N	N	Y	Y	N
8 Ichord	Y	Y	Y	N	N	N	Y	N
9 Volkmer	Y	Y	Y	Y	Y	N	Y	Y
10 Burlison	Y	Y	Y	Y	Y	Y	Y	N
MONTANA								
1 Baucus	Y	Y	Y	Y	Y	N	Y	N
2 Marlenee	Y	Y	Y	N	N	N	P	N
NEBRASKA								
1 Thone	#	#	#	?	N	N	Y	N
2 Cavanaugh	Y	Y	Y	Y	N	Y	Y	Y
3 Smith	Y	Y	Y	N	N	N	Y	Y
NEVADA								
AL Santini	Y	Y	Y	Y	Y	Y	Y	N
NEW HAMPSHIRE								
1 D'Amours	Y	Y	Y	Y	N	N	Y	N
2 Cleveland	#	#	#	▮	N	N	Y	N
NEW JERSEY								
1 Florio	Y	Y	Y	Y	Y	N	Y	Y
2 Hughes	Y	Y	Y	Y	N	N	Y	Y
3 Howard	#	#	#	#	Y	Y	Y	N
4 Thompson	Y	Y	Y	Y	Y	Y	Y	Y
5 Fenwick	Y	Y	Y	Y	N	N	Y	N
6 Forsythe	Y	Y	Y	N	N	N	Y	N
7 Maguire	Y	Y	Y	Y	Y	Y	Y	Y
8 Roe	Y	Y	Y	Y	Y	Y	Y	Y
9 Hollenbeck	Y	Y	Y	N	N	N	Y	N
10 Rodino	#	#	#	#	▮	✓	#	▮
11 Minish	Y	Y	Y	Y	Y	Y	Y	Y
12 Rinaldo	Y	Y	Y	Y	N	N	Y	Y
13 Meyner	Y	Y	Y	Y	Y	N	Y	N
14 LeFante	#	#	#	#	Y	N	Y	N
15 Patten	#	#	#	#	Y	Y	Y	Y
NEW MEXICO								
1 Lujan	Y	Y	Y	N	?	N	Y	N
2 Runnels	#	#	#	?	?	X	#	X
NEW YORK								
1 Pike	Y	Y	Y	Y	N	N	Y	N
2 Downey	Y	Y	Y	Y	Y	Y	Y	N
3 Ambro	Y	Y	Y	Y	Y	Y	?	Y
4 Lent	#	#	#	#	N	N	Y	N
5 Wydler	Y	Y	Y	N	N	N	Y	N
6 Wolff	Y	Y	Y	Y	Y	Y	Y	Y
7 Addabbo	Y	Y	Y	Y	Y	Y	Y	Y
8 Rosenthal	Y	Y	Y	Y	Y	Y	Y	N
9 Delaney	Y	Y	Y	Y	Y	Y	Y	N
10 Biaggi	Y	Y	Y	Y	Y	Y	?	N
11 Scheuer	Y	Y	Y	Y	Y	Y	Y	Y
12 Chisholm	Y	Y	Y	Y	Y	Y	Y	N
13 Solarz	#	#	#	#	#	✓	#	X
14 Richmond	Y	Y	Y	Y	Y	Y	?	✓
15 Zeferetti	#	#	#	#	Y	Y	Y	N
16 Holtzman	Y	Y	Y	Y	N	N	Y	Y
17 Murphy	Y	Y	Y	Y	Y	Y	#	X
18 Green	Y	Y	Y	Y	N	N	Y	N
19 Rangel	?	?	?	?	Y	Y	Y	Y
20 Weiss	Y	Y	Y	Y	Y	Y	Y	Y
21 Garcia	Y	Y	Y	Y	Y	?	Y	Y
22 Bingham	Y	Y	Y	Y	Y	Y	Y	Y
23 Caputo	Y	Y	Y	Y	N	N	Y	N
24 Ottinger	Y	Y	Y	Y	Y	Y	Y	Y
25 Fish	Y	Y	Y	Y	N	N	Y	N
26 Gilman	Y	Y	Y	Y	N	N	Y	N
27 McHugh	Y	Y	Y	Y	Y	N	Y	N
28 Stratton	Y	Y	Y	Y	N	N	Y	Y
29 Pattison	Y	Y	Y	Y	Y	Y	Y	N
30 McEwen	Y	Y	Y	N	N	N	Y	Y
31 Mitchell	#	#	#	Y	N	N	Y	N
32 Hanley	#	#	#	?	Y	Y	Y	Y
33 Walsh	?	?	?	?	N	N	Y	Y
34 Horton	Y	Y	Y	Y	#	N	Y	Y
35 Conable	Y	Y	Y	N	N	N	Y	N
36 LaFalce	#	#	#	#	Y	N	Y	N
37 Nowak	Y	Y	Y	Y	Y	Y	Y	N
38 Kemp	Y	Y	Y	N	N	N	Y	N
39 Lundine	Y	Y	Y	Y	Y	Y	Y	N
NORTH CAROLINA								
1 Jones	Y	Y	Y	Y	Y	Y	Y	N
2 Fountain	Y	Y	Y	N	Y	Y	Y	Y
3 Whitley	?	?	?	?	?	?	?	X
4 Andrews	Y	Y	Y	N	Y	Y	Y	N
5 Neal	Y	Y	Y	Y	N	Y	Y	N
6 Preyer	#	#	#	#	#	?	Y	N
7 Rose	Y	Y	Y	Y	Y	Y	Y	N
8 Hefner	Y	Y	Y	N	Y	Y	Y	N
9 Martin	Y	Y	Y	N	N	N	Y	N
10 Broyhill	Y	Y	Y	N	N	N	Y	N
11 Gudger	Y	Y	Y	Y	Y	Y	Y	N
NORTH DAKOTA								
AL Andrews	Y	Y	Y	N	N	N	Y	Y
OHIO								
1 Gradison	Y	Y	Y	N	N	N	Y	N
2 Luken	Y	Y	Y	Y	Y	Y	Y	N
3 Whalen	Y	Y	Y	Y	Y	Y	Y	N
4 Guyer	Y	Y	Y	N	N	N	Y	N
5 Latta	Y	Y	Y	N	N	N	Y	N
6 Harsha	Y	Y	Y	N	Y	N	?	N
7 Brown	?	?	?	?	N	N	Y	N
8 Kindness	?	?	?	?	N	N	Y	Y
9 Ashley	?	?	?	?	Y	?	Y	N
10 Miller	Y	Y	Y	N	N	N	Y	N
11 Stanton	Y	Y	Y	Y	N	N	Y	N
12 Devine	Y	Y	Y	N	N	N	Y	N
13 Pease	Y	Y	Y	Y	Y	Y	Y	N
14 Seiberling	Y	Y	Y	Y	Y	Y	Y	Y
15 Wylie	Y	Y	Y	Y	N	N	Y	N
16 Regula	Y	Y	Y	Y	N	N	Y	N
17 Ashbrook	Y	Y	Y	N	N	N	Y	N
18 Applegate	Y	Y	Y	Y	Y	Y	Y	Y
19 Carney	Y	Y	Y	Y	Y	Y	Y	Y
20 Oakar	?	?	?	?	Y	Y	?	Y
21 Stokes	?	?	?	?	?	✓	Y	Y
22 Vanik	#	#	#	#	#	#	#	Y
23 Mottl	Y	Y	Y	N	N	N	Y	Y
OKLAHOMA								
1 Jones	Y	Y	Y	N	Y	Y	Y	Y
2 Risenhoover	N	Y	N	N	Y	N	Y	N
3 Watkins	Y	Y	▮	N	Y	Y	Y	Y
4 Steed	#	#	#	#	#	#	Y	Y
5 Edwards	N	Y	Y	N	N	N	Y	Y
6 English	Y	Y	Y	N	Y	N	Y	Y
OREGON								
1 AuCoin	Y	Y	Y	Y	Y	N	Y	N
2 Ullman	Y	Y	Y	Y	Y	Y	Y	N
3 Duncan	Y	Y	Y	Y	Y	Y	Y	Y
4 Weaver	Y	Y	Y	Y	Y	Y	Y	Y
PENNSYLVANIA								
1 Myers, M.	?	?	?	?	Y	Y	Y	N
2 Nix	Y	Y	Y	Y	Y	Y	Y	Y
3 Lederer	#	#	#	#	Y	N	Y	N
4 Eilberg	Y	Y	Y	Y	Y	Y	Y	Y
5 Schulze	Y	Y	Y	N	N	N	Y	N
6 Yatron	Y	Y	Y	Y	Y	N	Y	Y
7 Edgar	Y	Y	Y	Y	Y	N	Y	N
8 Kostmayer	Y	Y	Y	Y	Y	N	Y	N
9 Shuster	Y	Y	Y	N	N	N	Y	N
10 McDade	#	#	#	#	N	N	Y	Y
11 Flood	#	#	#	#	#	✓	#	✓
12 Murtha	Y	Y	Y	Y	Y	Y	Y	N
13 Coughlin	Y	Y	Y	Y	N	N	Y	N
14 Moorhead	Y	Y	Y	Y	Y	Y	Y	Y
15 Rooney	Y	Y	Y	Y	Y	Y	Y	Y
16 Walker	Y	Y	Y	N	N	N	Y	N
17 Ertel	Y	Y	Y	N	Y	N	N	Y
18 Walgren	Y	Y	Y	Y	N	N	Y	N
19 Goodling, W.	Y	Y	Y	N	N	N	Y	Y
20 Gaydos	Y	Y	Y	Y	Y	Y	Y	Y
21 Dent	Y	Y	Y	Y	Y	#	Y	N
22 Murphy	Y	Y	Y	Y	Y	N	Y	Y
23 Ammerman	Y	Y	Y	Y	Y	Y	Y	Y
24 Marks	Y	Y	Y	N	N	Y	Y	Y
25 Myers, G.	N	Y	Y	N	Y	Y	Y	N
RHODE ISLAND								
1 St Germain	?	?	?	?	Y	Y	Y	Y
2 Beard	?	?	?	?	Y	Y	Y	N
SOUTH CAROLINA								
1 Davis	Y	Y	Y	Y	Y	N	Y	N
2 Spence	Y	Y	Y	N	N	N	Y	N
3 Derrick	Y	Y	Y	Y	Y	Y	Y	N
4 Mann	Y	Y	Y	N	Y	Y	Y	N
5 Holland	#	#	#	?	?	Y	Y	Y
6 Jenrette	Y	Y	Y	Y	▮	Y	Y	N
SOUTH DAKOTA								
1 Pressler	Y	Y	Y	N	N	N	?	?
2 Abdnor	Y	Y	Y	N	N	N	Y	N
TENNESSEE								
1 Quillen	Y	Y	Y	N	N	Y	Y	N
2 Duncan	Y	Y	Y	N	N	N	Y	N
3 Lloyd	Y	Y	Y	N	Y	N	Y	N
4 Gore	Y	Y	Y	Y	Y	N	Y	Y
5 Allen	Y	Y	Y	Y	Y	Y	Y	Y
6 Beard	N	Y	Y	N	N	N	Y	N
7 Jones	Y	Y	Y	Y	Y	N	Y	Y
8 Ford	Y	Y	Y	Y	Y	N	Y	Y
TEXAS								
1 Hall	Y	Y	Y	Y	▮	N	Y	N
2 Wilson, C.	Y	Y	Y	Y	Y	Y	Y	N
3 Collins	Y	Y	Y	N	N	N	N	N
4 Roberts	Y	Y	Y	Y	Y	Y	Y	N
5 Mattox	Y	Y	Y	Y	Y	Y	Y	N
6 Teague	?	?	?	?	?	✓	?	✓
7 Archer	Y	Y	Y	N	N	N	Y	N
8 Eckhardt	?	?	?	?	Y	Y	Y	Y
9 Brooks	Y	Y	Y	Y	Y	Y	Y	Y
10 Pickle	Y	Y	Y	Y	Y	N	Y	Y
11 Poage	Y	Y	Y	Y	Y	Y	Y	Y
12 Wright	Y	Y	Y	Y	Y	Y	Y	Y
13 Hightower	Y	Y	Y	Y	Y	N	Y	Y
14 Young	Y	Y	Y	Y	Y	Y	Y	Y
15 de la Garza	Y	Y	Y	Y	Y	Y	P	Y
16 White	Y	Y	Y	Y	Y	Y	Y	Y
17 Burleson	Y	?	Y	N	Y	Y	Y	N
18 Jordan	Y	Y	Y	Y	Y	Y	Y	N
19 Mahon	Y	Y	Y	Y	Y	Y	Y	N
20 Gonzalez	Y	Y	Y	Y	Y	Y	Y	Y
21 Krueger	#	#	#	#	#	▮	#	✓
22 Gammage	Y	Y	Y	N	Y	N	Y	N
23 Kazen	Y	Y	Y	Y	Y	Y	Y	Y
24 Milford	Y	Y	Y	N	Y	Y	Y	N
UTAH								
1 McKay	Y	Y	Y	Y	Y	Y	Y	N
2 Marriott	Y	Y	Y	N	N	N	Y	Y
VERMONT								
AL Jeffords	#	#	#	#	N	N	Y	N
VIRGINIA								
1 Trible	Y	Y	Y	N	N	N	Y	N
2 Whitehurst	Y	Y	Y	N	N	N	Y	N
3 Satterfield	Y	Y	Y	N	N	N	Y	N
4 Daniel	Y	Y	Y	N	N	N	Y	N
5 Daniel	Y	Y	Y	N	N	N	Y	N
6 Butler	Y	Y	Y	N	Y	N	Y	N
7 Robinson	Y	Y	Y	N	N	N	Y	N
8 Harris	Y	Y	Y	Y	Y	Y	Y	Y
9 Wampler	Y	Y	Y	Y	Y	N	Y	N
10 Fisher	Y	Y	Y	Y	Y	Y	Y	Y
WASHINGTON								
1 Pritchard	Y	Y	#	N	N	N	Y	Y
2 Meeds	#	#	#	#	#	#	#	▮
3 Bonker	Y	Y	Y	Y	#	Y	Y	Y
4 McCormack	Y	Y	Y	N	Y	Y	Y	Y
5 Foley	Y	Y	Y	Y	Y	Y	Y	Y
6 Dicks	Y	Y	Y	Y	Y	Y	Y	Y
7 Cunningham	Y	Y	Y	N	N	N	Y	Y
WEST VIRGINIA								
1 Mollohan	Y	Y	Y	Y	Y	Y	Y	N
2 Staggers	Y	Y	Y	Y	Y	Y	Y	Y
3 Slack	Y	Y	Y	Y	Y	Y	Y	N
4 Rahall	#	#	#	#	Y	Y	#	✓
WISCONSIN								
1 Aspin	?	?	?	?	?	?	?	?
2 Kastenmeier	Y	Y	Y	Y	Y	Y	Y	Y
3 Baldus	Y	Y	Y	Y	Y	Y	Y	Y
4 Zablocki	Y	Y	Y	Y	Y	Y	Y	N
5 Reuss	#	#	#	#	#	▮	#	▮
6 Steiger	#	#	#	#	#	▮	#	▮
7 Obey	Y	Y	Y	Y	Y	Y	Y	N
8 Cornell	Y	Y	Y	Y	Y	Y	Y	N
9 Kasten	Y	Y	Y	N	N	N	#	X
WYOMING								
AL Roncalio	?	?	?	?	Y	Y	Y	N

Democrats ***Republicans***

159. HR 7700. Postal Service Act. Simon, D-Ill., amendment to prohibit the United States Postal Service from subsidizing the rates of its parcel delivery service. Adopted 292-112: R 127-14; D 165-98 (ND 112-70; SD 53-28), April 5, 1978.

160. HR 7700. Postal Service Act. Ashbrook, R-Ohio, amendment to permit Congress, by concurrent resolution, to veto postal rate increases recommended by the Postal Rate Commission and to authorize additional sums of money to offset financial losses incurred as a result of a congressional veto of a rate increase. Rejected 180-218: R 82-58; D 98-160 (ND 51-127; SD 47-33), April 5, 1978. A "nay" was a vote supporting the president's position.

161. HR 7700. Postal Service Act. Hanley, D-N.Y., motion that the House resolve itself into the Committee of the Whole for further consideration of the bill to reorganize the U.S. Postal Service. Motion agreed to 386-1: R 136-0; D 250-1 (ND 172-1; SD 78-0), April 6, 1978.

162. HR 7700. Postal Service Act. Corcoran, R-Ill., amendment to require the Postal Service to spell out in detail how it would spend its annual public service subsidy, and to provide an open-ended authorization for that subsidy, but requiring that the amount equal or exceed the $920 million authorized under existing law. Adopted 203-189: R 127-8; D 76-181 (ND 39-139; SD 37-42), April 6, 1978.

163. HR 7700. Postal Service Act. Passage of the bill to establish criteria for the setting of postal rates, provide for presidential appointment of the postmaster general, abolish the postal board of governors, and provide for an open-ended annual public service subsidy for the Postal Service but with the requirement that it spell out for Congress in advance how it would spend the subsidy. Passed 384-11: R 136-3; D 248-8 (ND 171-7; SD 77-1), April 6, 1978.

164. HR 10899. International Banking Act. Passage of the bill to provide a system of federal regulation of the operations of foreign banks in the United States. Passed 367-2: R 128-1; D 239-1 (ND 167-1; SD 72-0), April 6, 1978.

KEY

Y Voted for (yea).
✓ Paired for.
† Announced for.
# CQ Poll for.
N Voted against (nay).
X Paired against.
\- Announced against.
▮ CQ Poll against.
P Voted "present."
● Voted "present" to avoid possible conflict of interest.
? Did not vote or otherwise make a position known.

	159	160	161	162	163	164
ALABAMA						
1 Edwards	Y	Y	Y	Y	Y	Y
2 Dickinson	Y	Y	Y	Y	Y	Y
3 Nichols	N	Y	P	Y	Y	Y
4 Bevill	N	N	Y	N	Y	Y
5 Flippo	Y	N	Y	N	Y	Y
6 Buchanan	Y	Y	Y	Y	Y	Y
7 Flowers	N	N	Y	Y	Y	Y
ALASKA						
AL Young	N	Y	Y	Y	Y	?
ARIZONA						
1 Rhodes	Y	N	Y	Y	Y	?
2 Udall	X	▮	#	X	#	#
3 Stump	Y	#	Y	N	Y	Y
4 Rudd	Y	Y	Y	Y	Y	Y
ARKANSAS						
1 Alexander	?	Y	Y	?	Y	Y
2 Tucker	#	#	#	#	#	#
3 Hammerschmidt	Y	Y	Y	Y	Y	Y
4 Thornton	?	?	?	?	?	?
CALIFORNIA						
1 Johnson	N	N	Y	N	Y	Y
2 Clausen	Y	N	Y	Y	Y	Y
3 Moss	N	?	Y	?	Y	Y
4 Leggett	Y	?	Y	N	Y	#
5 Burton, J.	N	Y	Y	N	Y	Y
6 Burton, P.	N	N	Y	N	Y	Y
7 Miller	N	N	Y	N	Y	Y
8 Dellums	N	N	Y	N	Y	Y
9 Stark	Y	N	Y	Y	Y	Y
10 Edwards	N	N	Y	N	Y	Y
11 Ryan	N	N	Y	N	Y	#
12 McCloskey	Y	N	Y	Y	Y	Y
13 Mineta	N	N	Y	N	Y	Y
14 McFall	N	N	#	N	Y	Y
15 Sisk	Y	?	Y	?	Y	Y
16 Panetta	Y	Y	Y	N	Y	Y
17 Krebs	Y	Y	Y	N	Y	Y
18 Ketchum	Y	Y	Y	Y	Y	?
19 Lagomarsino	Y	Y	Y	Y	Y	Y
20 Goldwater	Y	N	Y	Y	Y	Y
21 Corman	N	N	Y	N	#	Y
22 Moorhead	Y	Y	Y	Y	Y	Y
23 Beilenson	N	N	Y	N	Y	Y
24 Waxman	Y	N	Y	N	Y	Y
25 Roybal	N	N	Y	N	?	Y
26 Rousselot	Y	Y	Y	Y	Y	Y
27 Dornan	✓	Y	Y	Y	Y	Y
28 Burke	✓	▮	#	X	#	#
29 Hawkins	Y	N	Y	N	Y	Y
30 Danielson	N	N	Y	N	Y	Y
31 Wilson, C.H.	N	N	Y	N	Y	#
32 Anderson	Y	N	Y	N	Y	Y
33 Clawson	Y	Y	Y	Y	Y	Y
34 Hannaford	Y	Y	Y	N	Y	Y
35 Lloyd	Y	Y	Y	Y	Y	Y
36 Brown	N	N	?	N	Y	Y
37 Pettis	Y	Y	Y	Y	Y	Y
38 Patterson	Y	Y	Y	N	Y	Y
39 Wiggins	Y	N	#	#	Y	Y
40 Badham	Y	Y	Y	Y	Y	Y
41 Wilson, B.	Y	Y	Y	Y	Y	Y
42 Van Deerlin	N	N	Y	N	Y	?
43 Burgener	Y	N	Y	N	Y	Y
COLORADO						
1 Schroeder	Y	Y	Y	Y	N	Y
2 Wirth	Y	N	Y	N	Y	Y
3 Evans	N	N	Y	N	Y	Y
4 Johnson	Y	N	Y	Y	Y	Y
5 Armstrong	Y	N	Y	Y	Y	Y
CONNECTICUT						
1 Cotter	Y	N	Y	N	Y	Y
2 Dodd	Y	Y	Y	N	Y	?
3 Giaimo	Y	N	Y	Y	N	Y
4 McKinney	#	#	#	#	#	?
5 Sarasin	Y	Y	Y	Y	Y	Y
6 Moffett	N	Y	Y	N	Y	Y
DELAWARE						
AL Evans	Y	Y	Y	Y	Y	Y
FLORIDA						
1 Sikes	Y	N	Y	N	?	?
2 Fuqua	Y	Y	Y	N	Y	#
3 Bennett	Y	N	Y	Y	Y	Y
4 Chappell	✓	▮	#	✓	#	#
5 Kelly	Y	N	Y	Y	N	Y
6 Young	Y	Y	?	✓	?	?
7 Gibbons	Y	N	Y	Y	Y	Y
8 Ireland	Y	Y	Y	N	Y	Y
9 Frey	Y	Y	Y	Y	Y	Y
10 Bafalis	Y	Y	Y	Y	Y	Y
11 Rogers	N	Y	Y	Y	Y	Y
12 Burke	Y	Y	Y	Y	Y	Y
13 Lehman	#	N	Y	Y	Y	Y
14 Pepper	N	N	Y	N	†	Y
15 Fascell	Y	N	Y	N	Y	Y
GEORGIA						
1 Ginn	N	Y	Y	N	Y	Y
2 Mathis	Y	Y	Y	Y	Y	Y
3 Brinkley	N	Y	Y	Y	Y	Y
4 Levitas	Y	Y	Y	N	Y	Y
5 Fowler	Y	Y	Y	N	Y	Y
6 Flynt	Y	?	?	?	?	?
7 McDonald	Y	Y	Y	Y	N	Y
8 Evans	Y	Y	Y	N	Y	Y
9 Jenkins	Y	Y	Y	N	Y	Y
10 Barnard	N	Y	Y	N	Y	Y
HAWAII						
1 Heftel	Y	N	Y	Y	Y	Y
2 Akaka	N	N	Y	N	Y	Y
IDAHO						
1 Symms	Y	Y	Y	Y	Y	Y
2 Hansen, G.	Y	Y	Y	Y	Y	Y
ILLINOIS						
1 Metcalfe	Y	N	Y	N	Y	Y
2 Murphy	Y	N	Y	N	Y	Y
3 Russo	Y	N	Y	Y	Y	Y
4 Derwinski	N	N	Y	Y	Y	Y
5 Fary	Y	N	Y	N	Y	Y
6 Hyde	Y	Y	#	✓	Y	Y
7 Collins	Y	N	Y	N	Y	Y
8 Rostenkowski	Y	N	#	?	Y	Y
9 Yates	Y	N	Y	Y	Y	Y
10 Mikva	N	N	Y	Y	Y	Y
11 Annunzio	Y	N	Y	N	Y	Y
12 Crane	Y	Y	Y	Y	Y	Y
13 McClory	Y	N	Y	Y	Y	Y
14 Erlenborn	Y	Y	Y	Y	Y	Y
15 Corcoran	Y	N	Y	Y	Y	Y
16 Anderson	Y	#	#	#	Y	Y
17 O'Brien	Y	N	Y	Y	Y	●
18 Michel	✓	#	Y	Y	Y	Y
19 Railsback	Y	N	Y	Y	Y	Y
20 Findley	Y	Y	Y	Y	Y	Y
21 Madigan	Y	N	Y	?	Y	Y
22 Shipley	Y	N	Y	N	Y	Y
23 Price	Y	N	Y	N	Y	Y
24 Simon	Y	N	Y	Y	Y	Y
INDIANA						
1 Benjamin	Y	Y	Y	Y	Y	Y
2 Fithian	Y	Y	Y	N	Y	Y
3 Brademas	Y	N	†	-	†	Y
4 Quayle	Y	Y	Y	Y	Y	Y
5 Hillis	Y	Y	Y	Y	Y	Y
6 Evans	Y	Y	Y	N	Y	Y
7 Myers, J.	Y	Y	Y	Y	Y	Y
8 Cornwell	N	N	?	N	Y	Y
9 Hamilton	Y	N	Y	N	Y	Y
10 Sharp	Y	Y	Y	Y	Y	Y
11 Jacobs	Y	Y	Y	N	N	Y
IOWA						
1 Leach	Y	N	Y	Y	Y	Y
2 Blouin	Y	Y	Y	N	Y	Y
3 Grassley	Y	Y	Y	Y	Y	Y
4 Smith	N	Y	Y	N	Y	#
5 Harkin	N	Y	Y	N	Y	Y
6 Bedell	N	N	Y	Y	Y	Y

Democrats ***Republicans***

	159	160	161	162	163	164
KANSAS						
1 Sebelius	N	N	Y	Y	Y	Y
2 Keys	Y	Y	Y	N	Y	Y
3 Winn	Y	N	Y	Y	Y	Y
4 Glickman	Y	Y	Y	Y	Y	N
5 Skubitz	N	Y	Y	N	Y	Y
KENTUCKY						
1 Hubbard	Y	Y	Y	Y	Y	Y
2 Natcher	N	Y	Y	Y	Y	Y
3 Mazzoli	Y	N	Y	Y	Y	Y
4 Snyder	Y	Y	Y	Y	Y	Y
5 Carter	Y	N	Y	Y	Y	Y
6 Breckinridge	N	?	Y	Y	Y	?
7 Perkins	N	N	Y	N	Y	Y
LOUISIANA						
1 Livingston	Y	Y	Y	Y	Y	Y
2 Boggs	Y	Y	Y	N	Y	Y
3 Treen	Y	N	Y	Y	Y	Y
4 Waggonner	Y	Y	Y	#	#	Y
5 Huckaby	Y	Y	Y	N	Y	Y
6 Moore	Y	Y	Y	Y	Y	Y
7 Breaux	Y	Y	Y	N	Y	Y
8 Long	?	Y	Y	N	Y	Y
MAINE						
1 Emery	Y	Y	Y	Y	Y	Y
2 Cohen	Y	Y	Y	Y	Y	?
MARYLAND						
1 Bauman	Y	Y	Y	Y	Y	Y
2 Long	Y	Y	Y	Y	Y	Y
3 Mikulski	N	Y	Y	N	Y	Y
4 Holt	Y	Y	Y	Y	Y	Y
5 Spellman	X	#	#	X	#	#
6 Byron	N	N	Y	Y	Y	Y
7 Mitchell	Y	N	N	N	Y	Y
8 Steers	Y	Y	Y	N	Y	Y
MASSACHUSETTS						
1 Conte	Y	N	Y	Y	Y	Y
2 Boland	Y	N	Y	Y	Y	Y
3 Early	N	N	Y	N	Y	Y
4 Drinan	Y	N	Y	Y	Y	Y
5 Tsongas	Y	?	Y	N	Y	Y
6 Harrington	N	N	Y	N	Y	Y
7 Markey	Y	N	Y	Y	Y	Y
8 O'Neill						
9 Moakley	N	N	Y	N	Y	Y
10 Heckler	Y	N	Y	Y	Y	Y
11 Burke	N	Y	Y	N	Y	Y
12 Studds	Y	Y	Y	Y	Y	Y
MICHIGAN						
1 Conyers	N	N	Y	N	Y	Y
2 Pursell	Y	Y	Y	Y	Y	Y
3 Brown	Y	N	Y	Y	Y	Y
4 Stockman	Y	Y	Y	Y	Y	Y
5 Sawyer	Y	Y	Y	Y	Y	Y
6 Carr	Y	N	Y	Y	Y	Y
7 Kildee	N	N	Y	Y	Y	Y
8 Traxler	N	N	Y	N	Y	Y
9 Vander Jagt	Y	Y	Y	Y	Y	Y
10 Cederberg	Y	N	Y	✔	?	?
11 Ruppe	Y	N	Y	X	Y	Y
12 Bonior	Y	N	Y	N	Y	Y
13 Diggs	#	▮	#	▮	#	#
14 Nedzi	N	N	Y	Y	Y	Y
15 Ford	N	N	?	?	Y	Y
16 Dingell	Y	N	?	?	Y	Y
17 Brodhead	N	N	Y	N	Y	Y
18 Blanchard	N	N	Y	Y	Y	Y
19 Broomfield	Y	Y	Y	Y	Y	#
MINNESOTA						
1 Quie	Y	Y	Y	Y	Y	#
2 Hagedorn	Y	Y	Y	Y	Y	Y
3 Frenzel	Y	N	Y	Y	Y	Y
4 Vento	N	Y	Y	N	Y	Y
5 Fraser	Y	N	Y	N	Y	Y
6 Nolan	N	Y	Y	N	Y	Y
7 Stangeland	Y	Y	Y	Y	Y	Y
8 Oberstar	N	Y	Y	N	Y	Y
MISSISSIPPI						
1 Whitten	N	Y	Y	Y	Y	#
2 Bowen	Y	N	Y	Y	Y	Y
3 Montgomery	Y	N	Y	Y	Y	Y
4 Cochran	Y	?	?	✔	?	?
5 Lott	Y	N	Y	Y	Y	Y
MISSOURI						
1 Clay	N	N	Y	N	Y	?
2 Young	Y	N	Y	N	Y	Y
3 Gephardt	Y	N	Y	Y	Y	Y
4 Skelton	Y	Y	Y	N	Y	Y
5 Bolling	Y	N	Y	N	N	Y
6 Coleman	Y	Y	Y	Y	Y	Y
7 Taylor	Y	N	Y	Y	Y	?
8 Ichord	Y	N	Y	Y	Y	Y
9 Volkmer	N	N	Y	N	Y	Y
10 Burlison	Y	N	Y	N	N	Y
MONTANA						
1 Baucus	Y	Y	Y	Y	Y	Y
2 Marlenee	Y	N	?	Y	Y	Y
NEBRASKA						
1 Thone	Y	Y	Y	Y	Y	Y
2 Cavanaugh	N	N	Y	N	Y	Y
3 Smith	N	Y	Y	Y	Y	Y
NEVADA						
AL Santini	Y	Y	#	N	Y	#
NEW HAMPSHIRE						
1 D'Amours	Y	Y	Y	Y	Y	Y
2 Cleveland	Y	Y	Y	Y	Y	Y
NEW JERSEY						
1 Florio	Y	Y	Y	N	Y	Y
2 Hughes	Y	Y	Y	N	Y	Y
3 Howard	Y	Y	Y	N	Y	Y
4 Thompson	N	N	#	✔	#	#
5 Fenwick	Y	N	Y	Y	Y	Y
6 Forsythe	Y	N	Y	Y	Y	Y
7 Maguire	N	Y	Y	Y	Y	Y
8 Roe	Y	Y	Y	N	Y	Y
9 Hollenbeck	Y	N	Y	N	Y	Y
10 Rodino	▮	▮	#	▮	#	#
11 Minish	Y	Y	Y	N	Y	Y
12 Rinaldo	Y	N	Y	N	Y	Y
13 Meyner	Y	N	Y	N	Y	Y
14 LeFante	Y	N	Y	N	Y	Y
15 Patten	N	▮	Y	N	Y	Y
NEW MEXICO						
1 Lujan	Y	Y	Y	Y	Y	Y
2 Runnels	✔	?	#	✔	#	#
NEW YORK						
1 Pike	Y	N	Y	N	Y	Y
2 Downey	Y	N	Y	N	Y	Y
3 Ambro	N	Y	?	Y	Y	Y
4 Lent	Y	Y	Y	Y	Y	Y
5 Wydler	N	Y	Y	Y	Y	Y
6 Wolff	Y	Y	Y	N	Y	#
7 Addabbo	Y	N	Y	N	Y	#
8 Rosenthal	Y	N	Y	N	Y	Y
9 Delaney	Y	N	Y	N	Y	Y
10 Biaggi	Y	Y	Y	N	?	Y
11 Scheuer	Y	N	Y	Y	#	Y
12 Chisholm	Y	N	#	N	Y	#
13 Solarz	X	▮	Y	N	Y	Y
14 Richmond	X	?	?	X	?	?
15 Zeferetti	Y	N	Y	N	Y	#
16 Holtzman	N	N	Y	N	Y	Y
17 Murphy	✔	▮	Y	N	Y	Y
18 Green	Y	N	Y	N	Y	Y
19 Rangel	Y	N	Y	N	Y	?
20 Weiss	N	N	Y	N	Y	?
21 Garcia	N	N	Y	N	Y	Y
22 Bingham	N	N	Y	N	Y	Y
23 Caputo	Y	Y	Y	Y	Y	Y
24 Ottinger	N	N	Y	N	Y	Y
25 Fish	Y	N	Y	Y	Y	Y
26 Gilman	Y	N	Y	Y	Y	Y
27 McHugh	Y	N	Y	N	Y	Y
28 Stratton	Y	N	Y	Y	Y	Y
29 Pattison	Y	N	Y	N	Y	Y
30 McEwen	Y	N	Y	Y	Y	Y
31 Mitchell	Y	N	Y	Y	Y	Y
32 Hanley	N	N	Y	N	Y	Y
33 Walsh	Y	N	Y	Y	Y	Y
34 Horton	N	N	Y	Y	Y	Y
35 Conable	Y	N	Y	Y	Y	Y
36 LaFalce	Y	N	P	N	Y	Y
37 Nowak	Y	N	Y	N	Y	Y
38 Kemp	Y	Y	Y	Y	Y	?
39 Lundine	Y	N	P	N	Y	Y
NORTH CAROLINA						
1 Jones	Y	N	Y	N	Y	Y
2 Fountain	N	Y	Y	Y	Y	Y
3 Whitley	✔	?	?	X	?	?
4 Andrews	Y	Y	Y	Y	Y	Y
5 Neal	Y	Y	Y	N	Y	Y
6 Preyer	Y	N	Y	N	Y	Y
7 Rose	Y	Y	Y	N	Y	Y
8 Hefner	N	Y	Y	N	Y	Y
9 Martin	Y	Y	Y	Y	Y	Y
10 Broyhill	Y	N	Y	Y	Y	Y
11 Gudger	Y	N	Y	Y	Y	#
NORTH DAKOTA						
AL Andrews	Y	N	Y	N	Y	Y
OHIO						
1 Gradison	Y	N	Y	Y	N	Y
2 Luken	Y	Y	#	?	#	#
3 Whalen	Y	N	Y	N	Y	Y
4 Guyer	Y	Y	Y	Y	Y	Y
5 Latta	Y	Y	Y	Y	Y	Y
6 Harsha	Y	N	Y	Y	Y	Y
7 Brown	Y	N	Y	Y	Y	Y
8 Kindness	Y	Y	Y	Y	Y	Y
9 Ashley	Y	N	Y	Y	Y	Y
10 Miller	Y	Y	Y	Y	Y	Y
11 Stanton	Y	N	Y	Y	Y	Y
12 Devine	Y	Y	Y	Y	Y	Y
13 Pease	Y	N	Y	N	Y	Y
14 Seiberling	N	N	Y	N	Y	Y
15 Wylie	Y	Y	Y	Y	Y	Y
16 Regula	Y	N	Y	Y	Y	Y
17 Ashbrook	Y	Y	#	✔	#	#
18 Applegate	N	N	Y	N	Y	Y
19 Carney	N	N	Y	N	Y	Y
20 Oakar	N	Y	Y	N	Y	Y
21 Stokes	Y	N	Y	N	Y	Y
22 Vanik	Y	N	Y	N	Y	Y
23 Mottl	N	Y	Y	Y	N	Y
OKLAHOMA						
1 Jones	Y	Y	Y	N	Y	Y
2 Risenhoover	Y	Y	Y	N	Y	Y
3 Watkins	N	Y	Y	Y	Y	Y
4 Steed	Y	N	#	N	Y	Y
5 Edwards	N	Y	Y	Y	?	Y
6 English	N	Y	Y	Y	Y	Y
OREGON						
1 AuCoin	Y	Y	Y	N	Y	Y
2 Ullman	Y	Y	Y	#	#	Y
3 Duncan	N	N	Y	N	Y	Y
4 Weaver	N	N	Y	N	Y	Y
PENNSYLVANIA						
1 Myers, M.	Y	N	Y	N	Y	Y
2 Nix	Y	N	Y	N	Y	?
3 Lederer	Y	N	Y	N	Y	Y
4 Eilberg	N	N	Y	N	Y	#
5 Schulze	Y	Y	Y	Y	Y	Y
6 Yatron	Y	N	Y	N	Y	Y
7 Edgar	Y	N	Y	N	Y	Y
8 Kostmayer	Y	Y	Y	N	Y	Y
9 Shuster	Y	Y	Y	Y	Y	Y
10 McDade	N	Y	Y	Y	Y	Y
11 Flood	X	#	#	X	#	#
12 Murtha	Y	N	Y	N	Y	Y
13 Coughlin	Y	Y	Y	Y	Y	Y
14 Moorhead	N	N	Y	N	Y	Y
15 Rooney	N	N	Y	N	Y	Y
16 Walker	Y	N	Y	Y	Y	Y
17 Ertel	Y	Y	Y	N	Y	Y
18 Walgren	Y	N	Y	Y	Y	Y
19 Goodling, W.	Y	N	Y	Y	Y	Y
20 Gaydos	N	N	Y	N	?	Y
21 Dent	Y	N	Y	N	Y	#
22 Murphy	Y	N	Y	Y	Y	Y
23 Ammerman	N	Y	Y	N	Y	Y
24 Marks	Y	N	Y	Y	Y	Y
25 Myers, G.	Y	N	Y	Y	Y	N
RHODE ISLAND						
1 St Germain	N	N	Y	N	Y	Y
2 Beard	X	N	Y	N	Y	Y
SOUTH CAROLINA						
1 Davis	Y	Y	Y	Y	Y	Y
2 Spence	Y	Y	Y	Y	Y	Y
3 Derrick	Y	N	Y	N	Y	Y
4 Mann	Y	Y	Y	Y	Y	Y
5 Holland	N	N	Y	N	Y	#
6 Jenrette	Y	N	Y	N	Y	Y
SOUTH DAKOTA						
1 Pressler	?	?	Y	Y	Y	Y
2 Abdnor	Y	Y	Y	Y	Y	Y
TENNESSEE						
1 Quillen	Y	Y	Y	Y	Y	?
2 Duncan	N	Y	Y	Y	Y	Y
3 Lloyd	Y	Y	Y	N	Y	Y
4 Gore	N	Y	Y	Y	Y	Y
5 Allen	N	Y	Y	N	Y	Y
6 Beard	Y	N	?	Y	Y	Y
7 Jones	Y	N	Y	Y	Y	Y
8 Ford	Y	N	Y	N	Y	Y
TEXAS						
1 Hall	Y	Y	Y	Y	Y	Y
2 Wilson, C.	Y	N	Y	N	Y	Y
3 Collins	Y	Y	Y	Y	N	?
4 Roberts	Y	?	?	?	?	?
5 Mattox	Y	N	Y	Y	Y	Y
6 Teague	X	?	?	X	?	?
7 Archer	Y	Y	Y	Y	?	Y
8 Eckhardt	N	N	Y	N	Y	Y
9 Brooks	N	N	Y	Y	Y	Y
10 Pickle	N	Y	Y	Y	Y	Y
11 Poage	Y	N	Y	Y	Y	Y
12 Wright	N	?	Y	N	Y	Y
13 Hightower	N	Y	Y	N	Y	Y
14 Young	N	N	Y	N	Y	Y
15 de la Garza	Y	Y	Y	Y	Y	Y
16 White	Y	Y	Y	Y	Y	†
17 Burleson	Y	Y	Y	Y	Y	Y
18 Jordan	Y	N	Y	N	Y	Y
19 Mahon	Y	N	Y	Y	Y	Y
20 Gonzalez	N	Y	Y	N	Y	Y
21 Krueger	#	▮	#	X	#	#
22 Gammage	Y	Y	?	Y	Y	?
23 Kazen	N	Y	Y	N	Y	?
24 Milford	Y	N	?	?	?	?
UTAH						
1 McKay	Y	N	Y	Y	Y	Y
2 Marriott	Y	Y	Y	Y	Y	Y
VERMONT						
AL Jeffords	Y	N	Y	Y	Y	Y
VIRGINIA						
1 Trible	Y	Y	Y	Y	Y	Y
2 Whitehurst	Y	Y	Y	Y	Y	Y
3 Satterfield	Y	Y	Y	Y	Y	Y
4 Daniel	N	Y	Y	Y	Y	Y
5 Daniel	N	Y	Y	Y	Y	Y
6 Butler	N	N	Y	Y	Y	Y
7 Robinson	N	Y	Y	Y	Y	Y
8 Harris	Y	N	Y	N	Y	Y
9 Wampler	N	N	Y	Y	Y	Y
10 Fisher	Y	N	Y	N	Y	Y
WASHINGTON						
1 Pritchard	Y	N	Y	Y	Y	Y
2 Meeds	▮	▮	Y	N	Y	Y
3 Bonker	Y	Y	Y	N	Y	Y
4 McCormack	Y	Y	Y	Y	Y	Y
5 Foley	Y	Y	Y	N	Y	Y
6 Dicks	Y	Y	Y	Y	Y	Y
7 Cunningham	Y	Y	Y	Y	Y	#
WEST VIRGINIA						
1 Mollohan	N	N	Y	Y	Y	Y
2 Staggers	N	?	Y	N	N	Y
3 Slack	Y	N	Y	N	Y	Y
4 Rahall	X	N	Y	N	#	#
WISCONSIN						
1 Aspin	?	?	?	?	?	?
2 Kastenmeier	N	N	Y	N	Y	Y
3 Baldus	Y	N	Y	N	Y	Y
4 Zablocki	Y	N	Y	N	Y	Y
5 Reuss	#	N	Y	N	Y	Y
6 Steiger	#	▮	#	#	▮	#
7 Obey	Y	N	Y	N	Y	Y
8 Cornell	Y	N	Y	N	Y	Y
9 Kasten	✔	#	#	✔	Y	Y
WYOMING						
AL Roncalio	Y	N	?	?	Y	Y

Democrats ***Republicans***

165. HR 10730. Marine Mammal Protection. Murphy, D-N.Y., motion to suspend the rules and pass the bill to authorize $45.2 million for fiscal 1979-81 to carry out the Marine Mammal Protection Act of 1972. Motion agreed to 380-5: R 132-2; D 248-3 (ND 175-3; SD 73-0), April 10, 1978. A two-thirds majority vote (257 in this case) is required for passage under suspension of the rules.

166. HR 10878. Fishermen's Protective Act. Murphy, D-N.Y., motion to suspend the rules and pass the bill to extend the fishermen's cooperative insurance program from Oct. 1, 1978, until Oct. 1, 1981; to establish a compensation program for fishermen whose vessels or gear were damaged as a result of foreign seizure — considered illegal under U.S. law — and to authorize the president to embargo any or all fish and wildlife products of a nation certified by the Commerce Department to be jeopardizing the continued existence of an endangered or threatened wildlife species. Motion agreed to 365-14: R 129-4; D 236-10 (ND 167-8; SD 69-2), April 10, 1978. A two-thirds majority vote (253 in this case) is required for passage under suspension of the rules.

167. HR 10882. Military and Public Lands Conservation. Murphy, D-N.Y., motion to suspend the rules and pass the bill to authorize appropriations for three years (fiscal 1979-81) to carry out wildlife conservation and public outdoor recreation programs on military installations and public lands. Motion agreed to 377-8: R 131-3; D 246-5 (ND 173-5; SD 73-0), April 10, 1978. A two-thirds majority vote (257 in this case) is required for passage under suspension of the rules.

168. HR 10732. Fishery Conservation and Management. Murphy, D-N.Y., motion to suspend the rules and pass the bill to authorize $40 million for fiscal 1979 and $45 million for each of fiscal 1980-81 to provide for the conservation and management of fish within the United States' 200-mile offshore fishing zone under the 1976 Fishery Conservation and Management Act (PL 94-265). Motion agreed to 329-55: R 124-11; D 205-44 (ND 151-25; SD 54-19), April 10, 1978. A two-thirds majority vote (256 in this case) is required for passage under suspension of the rules.

169. HR 10884. Council on Environmental Quality. Murphy, D-N.Y., motion to suspend the rules and pass the bill to authorize $9 million for fiscal 1979-81 to carry out the programs of the Council on Environmental Quality. Motion agreed to 307-76: R 98-37; D 209-39 (ND 162-13; SD 47-26), April 10, 1978. A two-thirds majority vote (256 in this case) is required for passage under suspension of the rules.

170. HR 11445. Small Business Administration. Smith, D-Iowa, motion to suspend the rules and pass the bill to authorize appropriations of $8.443 billion for fiscal year 1980, $9.264 billion for 1981 and $10.267 billion for 1982, plus an open-ended authorization for natural disaster loans, for programs of the Small Business Administration (SBA); to increase interest rates for certain disaster loans; to authorize the financing of loans through SBA sales of notes to the secretary of the treasury and to authorize the president to convene a White House conference on small business. Motion agreed to 310-72: R 103-32; D 207-40 (ND 141-32; SD 66-8), April 10, 1978. A two-thirds majority vote (255 in this case) is required for passage under suspension of the rules.

171. HR 7101. Riverside County Land Claims. Roncalio, D-Wyo., motion to suspend the rules and pass the bill to amend the boundary limitation contained in a 1970 law to include approximately 340 acres within specified points along the Colorado River to permit an equitable settlement in court of a dispute between private individuals and the federal government regarding title to certain lands that had been combined or divided. Motion agreed to 390-14: R 135-3; D 255-11 (ND 174-9; SD 81-2), April 11, 1978. A two-thirds majority vote (270 in this case) is required for passage under suspension of the rules.

172. HR 2497. Recognition of Indian Tribes. Roncalio, D-Wyo., motion to suspend the rules and pass the bill to reinstate the Modoc, Wyandotte, Peoria and Ottawa Indian tribes of Oklahoma as federally supervised and recognized Indian tribes. Motion agreed to 368-33: R 114-21; D 254-12 (ND 176-7; SD 78-5), April 11, 1978. A two-thirds majority vote (268 in this case) is required for passage under suspension of the rules.

KEY

- Y Voted for (yea).
- ✓ Paired for.
- † Announced for.
- # CQ Poll for.
- N Voted against (nay).
- X Paired against.
- \- Announced against.
- ▮ CQ Poll against.
- P Voted "present."
- ● Voted "present" to avoid possible conflict of interest.
- ? Did not vote or otherwise make a position known.

	165	166	167	168	169	170	171	172
ALABAMA								
1 Edwards	?	?	?	?	?	?	Y	Y
2 Dickinson	Y	Y	Y	Y	Y	Y	Y	Y
3 Nichols	Y	Y	Y	Y	N	Y	Y	Y
4 Bevill	Y	Y	Y	Y	N	Y	Y	Y
5 Flippo	Y	Y	Y	N	N	Y	Y	Y
6 Buchanan	?	?	?	?	?	?	?	?
7 Flowers	Y	Y	Y	Y	Y	Y	Y	Y
ALASKA								
AL Young	Y	Y	?	Y	Y	Y	Y	?
ARIZONA								
1 Rhodes	?	?	?	?	?	?	?	?
2 Udall	?	?	?	?	?	?	✓	?
3 Stump	N	N	N	N	N	Y	Y	N
4 Rudd	Y	Y	N	Y	N	Y	Y	N
ARKANSAS								
1 Alexander	Y	Y	Y	Y	Y	Y	Y	Y
2 Tucker	#	#	#	#	#	#	Y	Y
3 Hammerschmidt	Y	Y	Y	Y	N	N	Y	Y
4 Thornton	?	?	?	?	?	?	Y	Y
CALIFORNIA								
1 Johnson	Y	Y	Y	Y	Y	Y	Y	Y
2 Clausen	Y	Y	Y	Y	Y	Y	Y	Y
3 Moss	Y	Y	Y	Y	Y	Y	Y	Y
4 Leggett	Y	Y	Y	Y	Y	Y	#	#
5 Burton, J.	Y	Y	Y	Y	Y	Y	Y	Y
6 Burton, P.	Y	Y	Y	Y	Y	Y	Y	Y
7 Miller	Y	Y	Y	Y	Y	N	Y	Y
8 Dellums	Y	Y	Y	Y	Y	Y	Y	Y
9 Stark	Y	Y	Y	Y	Y	N	Y	Y
10 Edwards	Y	Y	Y	Y	Y	N	Y	Y
11 Ryan	Y	Y	Y	Y	Y	Y	Y	Y
12 McCloskey	Y	Y	Y	Y	Y	Y	Y	Y
13 Mineta	Y	Y	Y	Y	Y	N	Y	Y
14 McFall	Y	?	Y	Y	Y	Y	Y	Y
15 Sisk	Y	Y	Y	Y	N	Y	Y	Y
16 Panetta	Y	Y	Y	Y	Y	Y	Y	Y
17 Krebs	Y	Y	Y	Y	Y	Y	Y	Y
18 Ketchum	Y	Y	Y	Y	N	N	Y	Y
19 Lagomarsino	Y	Y	Y	Y	Y	N	Y	Y
20 Goldwater	Y	Y	Y	Y	N	N	Y	Y
21 Corman	Y	Y	Y	Y	Y	Y	Y	Y
22 Moorhead	Y	Y	Y	Y	N	Y	Y	N
23 Beilenson	Y	Y	Y	Y	Y	N	Y	Y
24 Waxman	?	?	?	?	?	?	Y	Y
25 Roybal	Y	Y	Y	Y	Y	Y	Y	Y
26 Rousselot	Y	Y	Y	Y	N	N	Y	N
27 Dornan	Y	Y	Y	Y	N	Y	Y	Y
28 Burke	?	?	?	?	?	?	?	?
29 Hawkins	Y	Y	Y	Y	Y	Y	Y	Y
30 Danielson	Y	Y	Y	Y	Y	Y	Y	Y
31 Wilson, C.H.	Y	Y	Y	Y	N	Y	Y	N
32 Anderson	Y	Y	Y	Y	Y	Y	Y	Y
33 Clawson	Y	Y	Y	N	N	N	?	?
34 Hannaford	Y	Y	Y	Y	Y	N	Y	Y
35 Lloyd	Y	Y	Y	Y	Y	Y	Y	Y
36 Brown	?	?	?	?	?	?	Y	Y
37 Pettis	Y	Y	Y	Y	Y	Y	Y	Y
38 Patterson	Y	Y	Y	Y	Y	Y	Y	Y
39 Wiggins	Y	Y	Y	Y	Y	Y	Y	?
40 Badham	Y	Y	Y	Y	N	N	Y	N
41 Wilson, B.	N	Y	Y	Y	Y	Y	Y	Y
42 Van Deerlin	Y	Y	Y	Y	Y	Y	Y	Y
43 Burgener	Y	Y	Y	Y	Y	Y	Y	Y
COLORADO								
1 Schroeder	Y	Y	Y	Y	Y	Y	Y	Y
2 Wirth	Y	Y	Y	?	?	?	Y	Y
3 Evans	Y	Y	Y	Y	Y	Y	Y	Y
4 Johnson	Y	Y	Y	Y	N	Y	Y	Y
5 Armstrong	Y	Y	Y	Y	N	Y	Y	Y
CONNECTICUT								
1 Cotter	Y	Y	Y	N	Y	Y	Y	Y
2 Dodd	Y	Y	Y	Y	Y	N	Y	Y
3 Giaimo	Y	Y	Y	N	Y	N	Y	Y
4 McKinney	Y	Y	Y	Y	Y	Y	Y	Y
5 Sarasin	Y	Y	Y	Y	Y	Y	Y	Y
6 Moffett	Y	N	Y	Y	Y	N	Y	Y
DELAWARE								
AL Evans	Y	Y	Y	Y	Y	Y	Y	Y
FLORIDA								
1 Sikes	Y	Y	Y	Y	N	Y	Y	Y
2 Fuqua	?	?	?	?	?	?	Y	Y
3 Bennett	Y	Y	Y	Y	Y	Y	Y	Y
4 Chappell	#	#	#	#	#	#	Y	Y
5 Kelly	Y	Y	Y	Y	N	N	Y	N
6 Young	Y	Y	Y	Y	Y	Y	Y	N
7 Gibbons	Y	Y	Y	Y	Y	Y	Y	N
8 Ireland	Y	Y	Y	Y	Y	Y	Y	Y
9 Frey	Y	Y	Y	Y	Y	Y	Y	Y
10 Bafalis	Y	Y	Y	Y	Y	Y	Y	Y
11 Rogers	Y	Y	Y	N	Y	Y	Y	Y
12 Burke	Y	Y	Y	Y	Y	Y	Y	N
13 Lehman	Y	Y	Y	Y	Y	N	Y	Y
14 Pepper	#	#	#	#	#	#	Y	Y
15 Fascell	Y	Y	Y	Y	Y	Y	Y	Y
GEORGIA								
1 Ginn	Y	Y	Y	Y	Y	Y	Y	Y
2 Mathis	Y	Y	Y	Y	N	Y	Y	Y
3 Brinkley	Y	Y	Y	Y	Y	Y	Y	Y
4 Levitas	?	#	?	?	?	#	Y	Y
5 Fowler	Y	Y	Y	N	Y	Y	Y	Y
6 Flynt	Y	Y	Y	N	N	Y	Y	Y
7 McDonald	X	X	Y	N	N	N	Y	N
8 Evans	Y	Y	Y	N	N	Y	Y	Y
9 Jenkins	Y	Y	Y	N	N	Y	Y	Y
10 Barnard	Y	Y	Y	Y	N	Y	Y	Y
HAWAII								
1 Heftel	Y	?	Y	Y	Y	Y	Y	Y
2 Akaka	Y	Y	Y	Y	Y	Y	Y	Y
IDAHO								
1 Symms	Y	Y	Y	Y	N	N	?	?
2 Hansen, G.	Y	Y	Y	Y	N	N	Y	N
ILLINOIS								
1 Metcalfe	Y	Y	Y	Y	Y	Y	Y	Y
2 Murphy	Y	Y	Y	N	Y	Y	Y	Y
3 Russo	Y	Y	Y	N	Y	Y	Y	Y
4 Derwinski	Y	Y	Y	Y	Y	N	Y	Y
5 Fary	Y	Y	Y	Y	Y	Y	Y	Y
6 Hyde	Y	Y	Y	Y	Y	N	Y	Y
7 Collins	Y	Y	Y	Y	Y	Y	Y	Y
8 Rostenkowski	Y	Y	Y	N	Y	N	Y	Y
9 Yates	Y	N	Y	N	Y	N	Y	Y
10 Mikva	Y	Y	Y	N	Y	N	Y	Y
11 Annunzio	Y	Y	Y	Y	Y	Y	Y	Y
12 Crane	?	?	?	?	?	?	?	▮
13 McClory	Y	Y	Y	Y	Y	Y	Y	Y
14 Erlenborn	Y	Y	Y	Y	N	Y	Y	Y
15 Corcoran	Y	Y	Y	Y	Y	Y	Y	Y
16 Anderson	Y	Y	Y	Y	Y	Y	Y	Y
17 O'Brien	Y	Y	Y	Y	Y	Y	Y	Y
18 Michel	#	#	#	#	▮	#	Y	N
19 Railsback	Y	Y	Y	Y	Y	Y	Y	Y
20 Findley	Y	Y	Y	N	Y	Y	Y	Y
21 Madigan	Y	Y	Y	Y	Y	N	Y	Y
22 Shipley	Y	Y	Y	Y	Y	Y	Y	Y
23 Price	Y	Y	Y	Y	Y	Y	Y	Y
24 Simon	Y	N	Y	N	Y	N	Y	Y
INDIANA								
1 Benjamin	N	Y	Y	N	N	N	N	N
2 Fithian	?	?	?	?	?	?	Y	Y
3 Brademas	Y	Y	Y	Y	Y	Y	Y	Y
4 Quayle	Y	Y	Y	Y	Y	Y	Y	Y
5 Hillis	Y	Y	Y	Y	Y	Y	?	?
6 Evans	N	Y	N	N	N	Y	N	Y
7 Myers, J.	Y	Y	Y	Y	N	Y	Y	Y
8 Cornwell	?	?	?	?	?	?	Y	Y
9 Hamilton	Y	Y	Y	Y	Y	Y	Y	Y
10 Sharp	Y	Y	Y	N	N	Y	Y	Y
11 Jacobs	Y	Y	N	N	N	Y	N	N
IOWA								
1 Leach	Y	N	Y	Y	Y	Y	Y	Y
2 Blouin	Y	Y	Y	Y	Y	Y	Y	Y
3 Grassley	Y	N	Y	Y	Y	Y	Y	Y
4 Smith	Y	Y	Y	Y	Y	Y	Y	Y
5 Harkin	Y	Y	Y	#	#	#	Y	Y
6 Bedell	Y	N	Y	●	Y	Y	Y	Y

Democrats ***Republicans***

	165	166	167	168	169	170	171	172
KANSAS								
1 ***Sebelius***	?	?	?	?	?	?	Y	Y
2 Keys	Y	Y	Y	N	N	Y	Y	Y
3 ***Winn***	Y	Y	Y	Y	Y	Y	Y	Y
4 Glickman	Y	Y	Y	Y	?	?	Y	Y
5 ***Skubitz***	Y	Y	Y	Y	N	Y	Y	Y
KENTUCKY								
1 Hubbard	Y	Y	Y	Y	Y	Y	Y	Y
2 Natcher	Y	Y	Y	Y	Y	Y	Y	Y
3 Mazzoli	Y	Y	Y	Y	Y	Y	Y	Y
4 ***Snyder***	Y	Y	Y	Y	Y	Y	Y	Y
5 ***Carter***	?	?	?	?	?	?	N	Y
6 Breckinridge	Y	Y	Y	Y	Y	Y	Y	Y
7 Perkins	Y	Y	Y	Y	Y	Y	Y	Y
LOUISIANA								
1 ***Livingston***	Y	Y	N	Y	Y	Y	Y	Y
2 Boggs	✓	✓	?	?	?	?	Y	Y
3 ***Treen***	Y	Y	Y	Y	Y	N	Y	Y
4 Waggonner	Y	Y	Y	Y	N	Y	Y	Y
5 Huckaby	Y	Y	Y	Y	N	Y	Y	Y
6 ***Moore***	Y	Y	Y	Y	Y	N	Y	Y
7 Breaux	Y	Y	Y	Y	Y	Y	Y	Y
8 Long	Y	?	Y	Y	Y	Y	Y	Y
MAINE								
1 ***Emery***	Y	Y	Y	Y	Y	Y	Y	Y
2 ***Cohen***	?	?	Y	Y	Y	Y	?	?
MARYLAND								
1 ***Bauman***	Y	Y	Y	Y	N	Y	Y	N
2 Long	Y	?	Y	Y	Y	Y	Y	Y
3 Mikulski	Y	Y	Y	Y	Y	Y	Y	Y
4 ***Holt***	Y	Y	Y	Y	Y	N	Y	N
5 Spellman	?	?	?	?	?	?	X	?
6 Byron	Y	Y	Y	Y	Y	N	Y	Y
7 Mitchell	Y	Y	Y	Y	Y	Y	Y	Y
8 ***Steers***	Y	Y	Y	Y	Y	Y	Y	Y
MASSACHUSETTS								
1 ***Conte***	Y	Y	Y	Y	Y	Y	Y	Y
2 Boland	Y	Y	Y	Y	Y	Y	Y	Y
3 Early	Y	Y	Y	Y	Y	Y	Y	Y
4 Drinan	Y	Y	Y	N	Y	Y	Y	Y
5 Tsongas	Y	Y	Y	Y	Y	Y	Y	Y
6 Harrington	Y	Y	Y	Y	Y	Y	Y	Y
7 Markey	Y	Y	Y	Y	Y	Y	Y	Y
8 O'Neill								
9 Moakley	Y	Y	Y	Y	Y	Y	Y	Y
10 ***Heckler***	Y	Y	Y	Y	Y	Y	Y	?
11 Burke	Y	Y	Y	Y	Y	Y	Y	Y
12 Studds	Y	Y	Y	Y	Y	Y	Y	Y
MICHIGAN								
1 Conyers	?	?	?	?	?	?	?	?
2 ***Pursell***	Y	Y	Y	Y	Y	N	Y	Y
3 ***Brown***	Y	Y	Y	Y	Y	Y	Y	Y
4 ***Stockman***	Y	Y	Y	Y	Y	Y	Y	Y
5 ***Sawyer***	Y	Y	Y	Y	Y	Y	Y	Y
6 Carr	Y	Y	Y	Y	Y	Y	Y	Y
7 Kildee	Y	Y	Y	Y	Y	Y	Y	Y
8 Traxler	Y	Y	Y	Y	Y	Y	Y	Y
9 ***Vander Jagt***	Y	Y	Y	Y	Y	Y	Y	Y
10 ***Cederberg***	Y	Y	Y	Y	Y	Y	Y	Y
11 ***Ruppe***	Y	Y	Y	Y	Y	Y	Y	Y
12 Bonior	Y	N	Y	Y	Y	Y	Y	Y
13 Diggs	Y	Y	Y	Y	Y	Y	Y	Y
14 Nedzi	Y	Y	Y	Y	Y	Y	?	Y
15 Ford	Y	Y	Y	Y	Y	Y	Y	Y
16 Dingell	Y	Y	Y	Y	Y	Y	N	Y
17 Brodhead	Y	Y	Y	Y	Y	Y	Y	Y
18 Blanchard	Y	Y	Y	Y	Y	N	N	Y
19 ***Broomfield***	Y	Y	Y	Y	Y	Y	Y	Y
MINNESOTA								
1 ***Quie***	?	?	?	?	?	?	Y	Y
2 ***Hagedorn***	Y	Y	Y	Y	N	Y	Y	Y
3 ***Frenzel***	Y	Y	Y	Y	Y	Y	Y	Y
4 Vento	Y	Y	Y	Y	Y	Y	Y	Y
5 Fraser	?	#	?	?	?	?	Y	Y
6 Nolan	Y	Y	Y	Y	Y	Y	Y	Y
7 ***Stangeland***	Y	?	Y	Y	N	Y	Y	Y
8 Oberstar	Y	Y	Y	Y	Y	Y	Y	Y
MISSISSIPPI								
1 Whitten	Y	Y	Y	Y	N	Y	Y	Y
2 Bowen	Y	Y	Y	Y	Y	Y	Y	Y
3 Montgomery	Y	Y	Y	Y	N	Y	Y	Y
4 ***Cochran***	Y	Y	Y	Y	Y	Y	Y	Y
5 ***Lott***	Y	Y	Y	Y	N	Y	Y	Y
MISSOURI								
1 Clay	Y	Y	Y	Y	Y	Y	Y	Y
2 Young	Y	Y	Y	Y	Y	Y	Y	Y
3 Gephardt	Y	Y	Y	?	Y	Y	?	?

	165	166	167	168	169	170	171	172
4 Skelton	Y	Y	Y	N	Y	Y	Y	N
5 Bolling	Y	Y	Y	Y	Y	#	Y	Y
6 ***Coleman***	Y	Y	Y	Y	Y	Y	Y	Y
7 ***Taylor***	Y	Y	Y	N	N	Y	Y	Y
8 Ichord	Y	Y	Y	Y	N	Y	Y	Y
9 Volkmer	Y	Y	N	N	N	N	Y	Y
10 Burlison	Y	Y	Y	Y	Y	Y	Y	Y
MONTANA								
1 Baucus	Y	Y	Y	Y	Y	Y	Y	Y
2 ***Marlenee***	Y	N	Y	Y	Y	Y	Y	N
NEBRASKA								
1 ***Thone***	#	#	#	#	?	?	?	#
2 Cavanaugh	Y	Y	Y	Y	Y	Y	Y	Y
3 ***Smith***	Y	Y	Y	Y	N	Y	Y	Y
NEVADA								
AL Santini	?	?	?	?	?	?	Y	Y
NEW HAMPSHIRE								
1 D'Amours	Y	Y	Y	Y	Y	Y	Y	Y
2 ***Cleveland***	Y	Y	Y	N	Y	Y	Y	Y
NEW JERSEY								
1 Florio	Y	Y	Y	Y	Y	Y	Y	Y
2 Hughes	Y	Y	Y	Y	Y	Y	Y	Y
3 Howard	Y	Y	Y	Y	Y	Y	#	#
4 Thompson	Y	Y	Y	Y	Y	Y	✓	?
5 ***Fenwick***	Y	Y	Y	Y	Y	Y	Y	Y
6 ***Forsythe***	Y	Y	Y	Y	Y	Y	Y	Y
7 Maguire	Y	Y	Y	Y	Y	Y	Y	Y
8 Roe	Y	Y	Y	Y	Y	Y	Y	Y
9 ***Hollenbeck***	Y	Y	Y	Y	Y	Y	Y	Y
10 Rodino	?	?	?	?	?	?	?	?
11 Minish	Y	Y	Y	Y	Y	N	Y	Y
12 ***Rinaldo***	Y	Y	Y	Y	Y	Y	Y	Y
13 Meyner	Y	Y	Y	Y	Y	Y	Y	Y
14 LeFante	Y	Y	Y	Y	Y	Y	Y	Y
15 Patten	Y	Y	Y	Y	Y	Y	Y	Y
NEW MEXICO								
1 ***Lujan***	Y	Y	Y	Y	Y	Y	Y	Y
2 Runnels	?	?	?	?	?	?	?	?
NEW YORK								
1 Pike	Y	Y	Y	Y	Y	Y	Y	Y
2 Downey	Y	Y	Y	Y	?	?	Y	Y
3 Ambro	Y	Y	Y	Y	Y	Y	Y	Y
4 ***Lent***	Y	Y	Y	Y	Y	Y	Y	Y
5 ***Wydler***	Y	Y	Y	Y	Y	Y	Y	Y
6 Wolff	✓	✓	?	?	?	?	Y	Y
7 Addabbo	Y	Y	Y	Y	Y	Y	Y	Y
8 Rosenthal	Y	Y	Y	Y	Y	Y	Y	Y
9 Delaney	Y	Y	Y	Y	Y	Y	Y	Y
10 Biaggi	?	?	Y	Y	Y	Y	Y	Y
11 Scheuer	Y	Y	Y	Y	Y	Y	Y	Y
12 Chisholm	Y	Y	Y	Y	Y	Y	Y	Y
13 Solarz	Y	Y	Y	Y	Y	Y	Y	Y
14 Richmond	Y	Y	Y	Y	Y	Y	Y	Y
15 Zeferetti	Y	Y	Y	Y	Y	Y	Y	Y
16 Holtzman	Y	Y	Y	Y	Y	Y	N	Y
17 Murphy	Y	Y	Y	Y	Y	Y	Y	Y
18 ***Green***	Y	Y	Y	Y	Y	Y	Y	Y
19 Rangel	Y	Y	Y	Y	Y	?	Y	Y
20 Weiss	Y	N	Y	N	Y	Y	Y	Y
21 Garcia	Y	Y	Y	Y	Y	Y	Y	Y
22 Bingham	Y	Y	Y	Y	Y	N	Y	Y
23 ***Caputo***	Y	Y	Y	Y	Y	Y	Y	Y
24 Ottinger	Y	Y	Y	Y	Y	Y	Y	Y
25 ***Fish***	Y	Y	Y	Y	Y	Y	Y	Y
26 ***Gilman***	Y	Y	Y	Y	Y	Y	Y	Y
27 McHugh	Y	Y	Y	Y	Y	Y	Y	Y
28 Stratton	Y	Y	Y	Y	Y	Y	Y	Y
29 Pattison	Y	Y	Y	Y	Y	Y	Y	Y
30 ***McEwen***	Y	Y	Y	Y	Y	Y	Y	Y
31 ***Mitchell***	Y	Y	Y	Y	Y	Y	Y	Y
32 Hanley	Y	Y	Y	Y	Y	Y	Y	Y
33 ***Walsh***	Y	Y	Y	Y	Y	Y	Y	Y
34 ***Horton***	Y	Y	Y	Y	Y	Y	Y	Y
35 ***Conable***	Y	Y	Y	N	Y	N	?	?
36 LaFalce	Y	Y	Y	Y	Y	N	Y	Y
37 Nowak	Y	Y	Y	Y	Y	Y	Y	Y
38 ***Kemp***	Y	Y	Y	Y	Y	N	Y	Y
39 Lundine	Y	Y	Y	Y	Y	Y	Y	Y
NORTH CAROLINA								
1 Jones	?	?	?	#	?	#	?	?
2 Fountain	Y	Y	Y	Y	N	Y	Y	Y
3 Whitley	?	?	?	?	?	?	?	?
4 Andrews	Y	Y	Y	N	Y	Y	Y	Y
5 Neal	Y	Y	Y	N	Y	Y	Y	Y
6 Preyer	Y	Y	Y	Y	Y	Y	Y	Y
7 Rose	Y	Y	Y	Y	Y	Y	Y	Y
8 Hefner	Y	Y	Y	N	Y	Y	Y	Y

	165	166	167	168	169	170	171	172
9 ***Martin***	Y	Y	Y	Y	Y	Y	Y	Y
10 ***Broyhill***	Y	Y	Y	Y	N	Y	Y	Y
11 Gudger	Y	Y	Y	Y	Y	Y	#	#
NORTH DAKOTA								
AL Andrews	Y	Y	Y	Y	Y	Y	Y	Y
OHIO								
1 ***Gradison***	?	?	?	?	?	?	N	Y
2 Luken	Y	Y	Y	Y	Y	N	Y	Y
3 ***Whalen***	Y	Y	Y	Y	Y	Y	Y	Y
4 ***Guyer***	Y	Y	Y	Y	Y	Y	Y	Y
5 ***Latta***	Y	Y	Y	N	Y	Y	Y	N
6 ***Harsha***	Y	Y	Y	Y	N	Y	Y	Y
7 ***Brown***	Y	Y	Y	Y	Y	Y	Y	Y
8 ***Kindness***	Y	Y	Y	Y	Y	Y	Y	Y
9 Ashley	Y	Y	Y	Y	N	Y	N	?
10 ***Miller***	Y	Y	Y	Y	N	Y	Y	Y
11 ***Stanton***	Y	Y	Y	Y	Y	Y	Y	Y
12 ***Devine***	Y	Y	Y	N	Y	Y	Y	N
13 Pease	Y	Y	Y	Y	Y	Y	Y	Y
14 Seiberling	Y	Y	Y	Y	Y	N	Y	Y
15 ***Wylie***	Y	Y	Y	Y	Y	N	Y	Y
16 ***Regula***	Y	Y	Y	N	Y	Y	Y	Y
17 ***Ashbrook***	Y	Y	Y	N	N	Y	Y	N
18 Applegate	Y	Y	Y	Y	N	N	Y	Y
19 Carney	#	#	#	#	#	#	Y	Y
20 Oakar	Y	Y	Y	Y	Y	Y	Y	Y
21 Stokes	Y	Y	Y	Y	Y	Y	Y	Y
22 Vanik	Y	Y	Y	Y	Y	Y	Y	Y
23 Mottl	Y	Y	N	N	Y	N	N	Y
OKLAHOMA								
1 Jones	Y	N	Y	N	Y	N	N	Y
2 Risenhoover	Y	Y	Y	Y	N	Y	Y	Y
3 Watkins	Y	Y	Y	Y	N	Y	Y	Y
4 Steed	Y	Y	Y	Y	Y	Y	Y	Y
5 ***Edwards***	Y	N	N	N	N	N	Y	Y
6 English	Y	Y	Y	Y	N	Y	Y	Y
OREGON								
1 AuCoin	Y	Y	Y	Y	Y	Y	Y	Y
2 Ullman	Y	Y	Y	Y	Y	Y	Y	Y
3 Duncan	Y	Y	Y	Y	Y	Y	Y	Y
4 Weaver	Y	Y	Y	Y	Y	Y	Y	Y
PENNSYLVANIA								
1 Myers, M.	Y	Y	Y	Y	Y	Y	Y	Y
2 Nix	?	?	?	?	?	?	?	?
3 Lederer	Y	Y	Y	Y	Y	Y	N	Y
4 Eilberg	Y	Y	Y	Y	Y	Y	Y	Y
5 ***Schulze***	Y	Y	Y	Y	Y	N	Y	Y
6 Yatron	Y	Y	Y	Y	Y	Y	Y	Y
7 Edgar	Y	Y	Y	N	Y	Y	Y	Y
8 Kostmayer	Y	Y	Y	N	Y	Y	Y	Y
9 ***Shuster***	Y	Y	Y	Y	Y	Y	Y	N
10 ***McDade***	Y	Y	Y	Y	Y	Y	Y	Y
11 Flood	Y	Y	Y	Y	Y	N	Y	Y
12 Murtha	Y	Y	Y	Y	N	N	Y	Y
13 ***Coughlin***	Y	Y	Y	Y	Y	Y	Y	Y
14 Moorhead	Y	Y	Y	Y	Y	Y	Y	Y
15 Rooney	Y	Y	Y	Y	Y	Y	Y	Y
16 ***Walker***	Y	Y	Y	Y	N	N	Y	Y
17 Ertel	Y	Y	Y	N	Y	Y	Y	Y
18 Walgren	Y	Y	Y	N	Y	N	Y	Y
19 ***Goodling, W.***	Y	Y	Y	Y	N	Y	Y	N
20 Gaydos	Y	Y	Y	Y	N	N	Y	Y
21 Dent	?	?	?	?	?	?	?	?
22 Murphy	Y	Y	Y	Y	Y	Y	Y	Y
23 Ammerman	Y	Y	Y	N	Y	Y	Y	Y
24 ***Marks***	Y	Y	Y	Y	Y	Y	Y	Y
25 ***Myers, G.***	Y	Y	Y	Y	Y	N	N	Y
RHODE ISLAND								
1 St Germain	Y	Y	?	Y	Y	Y	Y	Y
2 Beard	Y	Y	Y	Y	Y	Y	Y	Y
SOUTH CAROLINA								
1 Davis	Y	Y	Y	Y	Y	Y	Y	Y
2 ***Spence***	Y	Y	Y	Y	Y	Y	Y	Y
3 Derrick	Y	Y	Y	N	Y	Y	Y	Y
4 Mann	?	?	?	?	?	?	?	?
5 Holland	Y	Y	Y	Y	Y	Y	Y	Y
6 Jenrette	Y	Y	Y	Y	Y	Y	Y	Y
SOUTH DAKOTA								
1 ***Pressler***	Y	Y	Y	Y	Y	Y	Y	Y
2 ***Abdnor***	Y	Y	Y	Y	N	Y	Y	Y
TENNESSEE								
1 ***Quillen***	?	?	?	?	?	?	Y	Y
2 ***Duncan***	Y	Y	Y	Y	Y	N	Y	Y
3 Lloyd	Y	Y	Y	Y	N	Y	Y	Y
4 Gore	Y	N	Y	Y	Y	Y	Y	Y
5 Allen	Y	Y	Y	Y	Y	N	Y	Y
6 ***Beard***	Y	Y	Y	Y	N	N	Y	N

	165	166	167	168	169	170	171	172
7 Jones	Y	Y	Y	Y	N	Y	Y	Y
8 Ford	Y	Y	Y	Y	Y	Y	Y	Y
TEXAS								
1 Hall	Y	Y	Y	N	N	Y	Y	N
2 Wilson, C.	Y	Y	Y	Y	Y	Y	Y	Y
3 ***Collins***	N	Y	Y	N	N	N	Y	N
4 Roberts	?	?	?	?	?	?	Y	Y
5 Mattox	Y	Y	Y	Y	Y	N	Y	N
6 Teague	?	?	?	?	?	?	?	?
7 ***Archer***	Y	Y	Y	Y	Y	Y	Y	N
8 Eckhardt	?	?	?	?	?	?	Y	Y
9 Brooks	Y	Y	Y	Y	Y	Y	Y	Y
10 Pickle	Y	Y	Y	N	Y	Y	Y	Y
11 Poage	Y	Y	Y	N	N	N	Y	Y
12 Wright	Y	Y	Y	Y	Y	Y	Y	Y
13 Hightower	Y	Y	Y	Y	Y	Y	Y	Y
14 Young	Y	Y	Y	Y	?	Y	Y	Y
15 de la Garza	Y	Y	Y	Y	Y	Y	Y	Y
16 White	Y	Y	Y	Y	Y	Y	Y	Y
17 Burleson	Y	Y	?	N	N	Y	Y	N
18 Jordan	Y	Y	Y	Y	Y	Y	Y	Y
19 Mahon	Y	Y	Y	N	Y	Y	Y	Y
20 Gonzalez	Y	Y	Y	Y	Y	Y	Y	Y
21 Krueger	?	?	?	?	?	?	?	?
22 Gammage	?	?	?	?	?	?	N	Y
23 Kazen	?	?	?	?	?	?	?	?
24 Milford	Y	?	Y	N	N	Y	Y	Y
UTAH								
1 McKay	Y	N	Y	Y	Y	N	Y	Y
2 ***Marriott***	Y	Y	Y	Y	N	Y	Y	Y
VERMONT								
AL Jeffords	Y	Y	Y	Y	Y	N	Y	Y
VIRGINIA								
1 ***Trible***	Y	Y	Y	Y	Y	N	Y	Y
2 ***Whitehurst***	Y	Y	Y	Y	Y	Y	Y	Y
3 Satterfield	Y	Y	Y	Y	N	N	Y	Y
4 ***Daniel***	Y	Y	Y	Y	N	N	Y	Y
5 Daniel	Y	Y	Y	Y	N	Y	Y	Y
6 ***Butler***	?	?	?	?	?	?	Y	Y
7 ***Robinson***	Y	Y	Y	Y	N	N	Y	Y
8 Harris	Y	Y	Y	N	Y	N	Y	Y
9 ***Wampler***	Y	Y	Y	Y	Y	Y	Y	Y
10 Fisher	Y	Y	Y	Y	Y	Y	Y	Y
WASHINGTON								
1 ***Pritchard***	Y	Y	Y	Y	Y	Y	Y	Y
2 Meeds	Y	Y	Y	Y	Y	Y	Y	Y
3 Bonker	Y	Y	Y	Y	Y	Y	Y	Y
4 McCormack	?	?	?	?	?	?	Y	Y
5 Foley	Y	Y	Y	Y	Y	Y	Y	N
6 Dicks	Y	Y	Y	Y	Y	Y	Y	N
7 ***Cunningham***	Y	Y	Y	Y	N	Y	Y	N
WEST VIRGINIA								
1 Mollohan	Y	Y	Y	Y	Y	Y	Y	Y
2 Staggers	Y	Y	Y	Y	Y	Y	Y	Y
3 Slack	Y	Y	Y	Y	Y	N	Y	Y
4 Rahall	Y	Y	Y	Y	Y	N	Y	Y
WISCONSIN								
1 Aspin	Y	Y	Y	Y	Y	Y	Y	Y
2 Kastenmeier	Y	Y	Y	Y	Y	Y	Y	Y
3 Baldus	Y	Y	Y	Y	Y	Y	Y	Y
4 Zablocki	Y	Y	Y	Y	Y	Y	Y	Y
5 Reuss	Y	Y	Y	Y	Y	Y	#	#
6 ***Steiger***	Y	Y	Y	Y	Y	N	Y	Y
7 Obey	Y	Y	Y	Y	Y	Y	Y	Y
8 Cornell	Y	Y	Y	Y	Y	Y	N	Y
9 ***Kasten***	Y	Y	Y	Y	Y	Y	Y	Y
WYOMING								
AL Roncalio	?	?	?	?	?	?	Y	Y

Democrats ***Republicans***

173. HR 11092. Navajo-Hopi Indians Relocation. Roncalio, D-Wyo., motion to suspend the rules and pass the bill to increase the authorization for the Navajo-Hopi Relocation Commission to $1 million from $500,000. Motion agreed to 361-43: R 115-23; D 246-20 (ND 175-8; SD 71-12), April 11, 1978. A two-thirds majority vote (270 in this case) is required for passage under suspension of the rules.

174. HR 11662. Lowell (Mass.) Historical Park. Passage of the bill to authorize $18.5 million for the establishment of a historical park administered by the National Park Service at Lowell, Mass., to preserve the first planned industrial city in 19th century America. Passed 326-76: R 79-60; D 247-16 (ND 177-5; SD 70-11), April 11, 1978.

175. HR 9179. Overseas Private Investment Corporation. Adoption of the conference report on the bill to extend the operating authority and programs of the Overseas Private Investment Corporation (OPIC) through Sept. 30, 1981. Adopted (thus cleared for the president) 216-185: R 91-48; D 125-137 (ND 83-96; SD 42-41), April 11, 1978.

176. HR 6782. Emergency Farm Bill. Adoption of the conference report on the bill to provide a one-year flexible parity program with graduated land diversion and target price levels for wheat, corn and cotton, and to raise loan rates for these commodities beginning Oct. 1, 1979 (with retroactive payments for 1978 crops). Rejected 150-268: R 70-75; D 80-193 (ND 26-160; SD 54-33), April 12, 1978. A "nay" was a vote supporting the president's position.

177. HR 3161. Federal Firefighters. Adoption of the rule (H Res 1067) providing for House floor consideration of the bill to reduce the basic workweek of firefighting personnel of federal government agencies from 72 hours to 56 hours. Adopted 374-5: R 131-3; D 243-2 (ND 167-1; SD 76-1), April 12, 1978.

178. HR 3161. Federal Firefighters. Passage of the bill to reduce the basic workweek of firefighting personnel of federal government agencies from 72 hours to 56 hours. Passed 241-129: R 63-68; D 178-61 (ND 131-31; SD 47-30), April 12, 1978.

KEY

- Y Voted for (yea).
- ✓ Paired for.
- † Announced for.
- # CQ Poll for.
- N Voted against (nay).
- X Paired against.
- \- Announced against.
- ▮ CQ Poll against.
- P Voted "present."
- ● Voted "present" to avoid possible conflict of interest.
- ? Did not vote or otherwise make a position known.

	173	174	175	176	177	178
ALABAMA						
1 Edwards	Y	N	N	Y	?	?
2 Dickinson	Y	Y	Y	Y	Y	Y
3 Nichols	Y	Y	N	Y	Y	Y
4 Bevill	Y	Y	N	Y	Y	Y
5 Flippo	Y	Y	N	Y	Y	Y
6 Buchanan	?	Y	Y	N	Y	Y
7 Flowers	Y	Y	N	Y	?	Y
ALASKA						
AL Young	Y	Y	N	Y	Y	Y
ARIZONA						
1 Rhodes	?	?	?	Y	Y	N
2 Udall	?	?	?	✓	?	?
3 Stump	N	N	N	N	Y	N
4 Rudd	Y	N	N	Y	Y	N
ARKANSAS						
1 Alexander	Y	Y	Y	Y	Y	Y
2 Tucker	Y	Y	N	Y	#	?
3 Hammerschmidt	Y	Y	Y	Y	Y	?
4 Thornton	Y	Y	N	Y	?	?
CALIFORNIA						
1 Johnson	Y	Y	Y	Y	Y	Y
2 Clausen	Y	Y	Y	Y	Y	Y
3 Moss	Y	Y	N	N	?	?
4 Leggett	#	Y	Y	N	Y	Y
5 Burton, J.	Y	Y	?	?	?	Y
6 Burton, P.	Y	Y	N	N	?	?
7 Miller	Y	?	?	N	Y	Y
8 Dellums	Y	Y	N	N	Y	Y
9 Stark	Y	Y	N	N	Y	Y
10 Edwards	Y	Y	Y	N	Y	Y
11 Ryan	Y	Y	N	N	Y	N
12 McCloskey	Y	Y	Y	Y	Y	Y
13 Mineta	Y	Y	Y	N	Y	Y
14 McFall	Y	Y	Y	N	?	Y
15 Sisk	Y	Y	Y	N	?	?
16 Panetta	Y	Y	N	N	Y	Y
17 Krebs	Y	Y	N	N	Y	Y
18 Ketchum	N	N	N	N	Y	Y
19 Lagomarsino	N	Y	Y	N	Y	Y
20 Goldwater	Y	Y	Y	N	Y	N
21 Corman	Y	Y	Y	N	Y	Y
22 Moorhead	N	N	Y	N	Y	N
23 Beilenson	N	Y	Y	N	Y	N
24 Waxman	Y	?	Y	N	Y	Y
25 Roybal	Y	Y	N	N	Y	Y
26 Rousselot	N	N	Y	N	Y	Y
27 Dornan	Y	N	Y	Y	Y	N
28 Burke	?	?	?	?	?	?
29 Hawkins	Y	Y	Y	N	Y	?
30 Danielson	Y	Y	Y	N	Y	Y
31 Wilson, C.H.	N	Y	▮	N	?	Y
32 Anderson	Y	Y	N	N	Y	Y
33 Clawson	?	?	?	?	?	?
34 Hannaford	Y	Y	Y	N	Y	?
35 Lloyd	Y	Y	N	●	Y	Y
36 Brown	Y	Y	?	N	?	?
37 Pettis	Y	Y	N	Y	Y	N
38 Patterson	Y	Y	N	N	Y	Y
39 Wiggins	Y	N	Y	N	Y	N
40 Badham	Y	N	Y	N	Y	N
41 Wilson, B.	Y	Y	Y	Y	Y	Y
42 Van Deerlin	Y	Y	Y	X	?	?
43 Burgener	Y	Y	Y	Y	Y	Y
COLORADO						
1 Schroeder	Y	Y	Y	N	Y	Y
2 Wirth	Y	Y	Y	N	Y	Y
3 Evans	Y	Y	Y	Y	?	?
4 Johnson	Y	Y	Y	Y	N	N
5 Armstrong	Y	Y	Y	Y	Y	N
CONNECTICUT						
1 Cotter	Y	Y	N	N	Y	Y
2 Dodd	Y	Y	Y	N	Y	Y
3 Giaimo	Y	Y	Y	N	Y	Y
4 McKinney	Y	Y	Y	N	Y	Y
5 Sarasin	Y	Y	Y	N	Y	†
6 Moffett	Y	Y	N	N	Y	?
DELAWARE						
AL Evans	Y	N	Y	N	#	▮
FLORIDA						
1 Sikes	Y	Y	N	Y	Y	?
2 Fuqua	Y	Y	N	Y	Y	Y
3 Bennett	Y	Y	N	N	Y	Y
4 Chappell	Y	Y	N	N	Y	N
5 Kelly	N	N	N	N	Y	N
6 Young	Y	Y	Y	N	Y	Y
7 Gibbons	Y	N	N	N	Y	Y
8 Ireland	Y	Y	Y	N	Y	N
9 Frey	Y	Y	Y	Y	Y	Y
10 Bafalis	Y	Y	N	N	Y	N
11 Rogers	Y	Y	N	N	Y	Y
12 Burke	N	Y	Y	N	Y	N
13 Lehman	Y	Y	Y	N	Y	Y
14 Pepper	Y	Y	Y	N	Y	Y
15 Fascell	Y	?	Y	N	?	Y
GEORGIA						
1 Ginn	Y	Y	N	Y	Y	Y
2 Mathis	Y	N	N	Y	Y	Y
3 Brinkley	N	Y	N	Y	Y	Y
4 Levitas	Y	Y	N	N	Y	N
5 Fowler	N	Y	Y	N	?	?
6 Flynt	Y	Y	Y	Y	Y	N
7 McDonald	N	N	N	N	N	N
8 Evans	Y	Y	N	Y	Y	Y
9 Jenkins	N	Y	N	Y	Y	N
10 Barnard	N	Y	N	Y	Y	N
HAWAII						
1 Heftel	Y	Y	Y	N	Y	Y
2 Akaka	Y	Y	Y	N	Y	Y
IDAHO						
1 Symms	?	?	?	Y	Y	N
2 Hansen, G.	N	N	N	Y	Y	?
ILLINOIS						
1 Metcalfe	Y	Y	Y	N	Y	Y
2 Murphy	Y	Y	N	N	Y	Y
3 Russo	Y	Y	N	N	Y	N
4 Derwinski	Y	Y	N	N	Y	N
5 Fary	Y	Y	N	N	Y	Y
6 Hyde	Y	N	Y	N	Y	N
7 Collins	Y	Y	Y	N	Y	Y
8 Rostenkowski	Y	Y	N	N	Y	N
9 Yates	Y	Y	N	N	Y	N
10 Mikva	Y	Y	N	N	Y	?
11 Annunzio	Y	Y	N	N	?	#
12 Crane	▮	▮	X	▮	▮	▮
13 McClory	Y	Y	Y	N	Y	Y
14 Erlenborn	Y	Y	Y	N	Y	N
15 Corcoran	Y	Y	N	N	Y	N
16 Anderson	Y	Y	Y	N	Y	Y
17 O'Brien	Y	N	Y	N	Y	N
18 Michel	N	Y	Y	Y	Y	N
19 Railsback	Y	Y	Y	N	Y	Y
20 Findley	Y	Y	Y	N	Y	N
21 Madigan	Y	Y	Y	N	Y	Y
22 Shipley	Y	Y	X	Y	Y	Y
23 Price	Y	Y	N	N	Y	Y
24 Simon	Y	Y	Y	N	Y	Y
INDIANA						
1 Benjamin	Y	Y	N	N	Y	N
2 Fithian	Y	Y	N	N	Y	N
3 Brademas	Y	Y	Y	N	?	?
4 Quayle	Y	N	N	Y	?	?
5 Hillis	?	Y	N	Y	Y	Y
6 Evans	N	N	N	N	Y	N
7 Myers, J.	Y	Y	N	Y	Y	Y
8 Cornwell	Y	Y	N	N	Y	N
9 Hamilton	Y	Y	Y	N	Y	N
10 Sharp	Y	Y	N	N	Y	N
11 Jacobs	Y	N	N	N	Y	N
IOWA						
1 Leach	Y	Y	Y	N	Y	Y
2 Blouin	Y	Y	Y	N	Y	Y
3 Grassley	Y	N	N	N	Y	N
4 Smith	Y	Y	Y	Y	Y	Y
5 Harkin	Y	Y	N	Y	Y	Y
6 Bedell	Y	Y	●	N	Y	N

Democrats ***Republicans***

	173	174	175	176	177	178
KANSAS						
1 ***Sebelius***	Y	Y	Y	Y	Y	N
2 Keys	Y	Y	N	Y	Y	N
3 ***Winn***	Y	N	Y	Y	Y	N
4 Glickman	Y	Y	N	Y	Y	N
5 ***Skubitz***	Y	Y	N	Y	Y	Y
KENTUCKY						
1 Hubbard	Y	Y	Y	Y	Y	Y
2 Natcher	Y	Y	N	Y	Y	Y
3 Mazzoli	Y	Y	N	N	Y	N
4 ***Snyder***	Y	N	N	Y	Y	N
5 ***Carter***	Y	Y	X	Y	Y	Y
6 Breckinridge	Y	Y	Y	Y	Y	Y
7 Perkins	Y	Y	N	Y	?	?
LOUISIANA						
1 ***Livingston***	Y	N	Y	N	Y	Y
2 Boggs	Y	Y	Y	N	Y	Y
3 ***Treen***	Y	N	Y	Y	?	?
4 Waggonner	N	N	Y	N	Y	N
5 Huckaby	Y	Y	N	Y	Y	N
6 ***Moore***	Y	N	Y	Y	Y	N
7 Breaux	Y	N	N	Y	?	?
8 Long	Y	Y	Y	Y	Y	Y
MAINE						
1 ***Emery***	Y	Y	N	Y	Y	Y
2 ***Cohen***	?	?	?	N	Y	N
MARYLAND						
1 ***Bauman***	N	N	N	Y	Y	Y
2 Long	Y	Y	N	N	?	?
3 Mikulski	Y	Y	N	N	Y	Y
4 ***Holt***	N	Y	N	Y	Y	Y
5 Spellman	?	?	X	▮	#	#
6 Byron	Y	Y	N	N	Y	?
7 Mitchell	Y	Y	N	N	Y	Y
8 ***Steers***	Y	Y	Y	N	Y	Y
MASSACHUSETTS						
1 ***Conte***	Y	Y	Y	N	Y	Y
2 Boland	Y	Y	Y	N	Y	Y
3 Early	Y	Y	N	N	Y	N
4 Drinan	Y	Y	Y	N	Y	Y
5 Tsongas	Y	Y	Y	N	Y	Y
6 Harrington	Y	Y	N	N	Y	Y
7 Markey	Y	Y	N	N	Y	Y
8 O'Neill						
9 Moakley	Y	Y	N	N	Y	Y
10 ***Heckler***	Y	Y	Y	N	?	Y
11 Burke	Y	Y	Y	Y	Y	Y
12 Studds	Y	Y	N	N	Y	Y
MICHIGAN						
1 Conyers	?	Y	N	N	Y	Y
2 ***Pursell***	Y	Y	Y	N	Y	?
3 ***Brown***	Y	Y	Y	Y	Y	N
4 ***Stockman***	Y	N	Y	N	#	▮
5 ***Sawyer***	Y	Y	Y	N	Y	Y
6 Carr	Y	Y	N	Y	Y	Y
7 Kildee	Y	Y	N	Y	Y	Y
8 Traxler	Y	Y	Y	Y	Y	Y
9 ***Vander Jagt***	Y	Y	Y	Y	Y	?
10 ***Cederberg***	Y	Y	Y	Y	Y	N
11 ***Ruppe***	Y	Y	Y	N	Y	Y
12 Bonior	Y	Y	N	N	?	Y
13 Diggs	Y	?	?	Y	?	?
14 Nedzi	Y	Y	Y	N	Y	Y
15 Ford	Y	?	?	N	Y	Y
16 Dingell	N	Y	N	N	Y	Y
17 Brodhead	Y	Y	N	N	Y	Y
18 Blanchard	Y	Y	Y	N	Y	Y
19 ***Broomfield***	Y	Y	Y	Y	Y	N
MINNESOTA						
1 ***Quie***	Y	Y	Y	Y	Y	Y
2 ***Hagedorn***	Y	Y	Y	Y	Y	N
3 ***Frenzel***	Y	N	Y	N	Y	N
4 Vento	Y	Y	N	N	Y	Y
5 Fraser	Y	Y	Y	Y	Y	Y
6 Nolan	Y	?	?	Y	Y	Y
7 ***Stangeland***	Y	N	Y	Y	Y	N
8 Oberstar	Y	Y	N	Y	Y	Y
MISSISSIPPI						
1 Whitten	Y	Y	Y	Y	Y	Y
2 Bowen	Y	Y	Y	N	Y	Y
3 Montgomery	N	N	Y	Y	Y	Y
4 ***Cochran***	Y	N	Y	Y	?	?
5 ***Lott***	Y	N	Y	Y	Y	Y
MISSOURI						
1 Clay	Y	Y	?	N	Y	Y
2 Young	Y	Y	N	N	Y	Y
3 Gephardt	Y	Y	N	N	Y	Y

	173	174	175	176	177	178
4 Skelton	N	N	N	Y	Y	N
5 Bolling	Y	Y	Y	N	#	#
6 ***Coleman***	Y	N	N	Y	Y	N
7 ***Taylor***	Y	N	N	Y	Y	N
8 Ichord	N	N	N	Y	Y	N
9 Volkmer	Y	Y	N	N	Y	N
10 Burlison	Y	Y	N	Y	Y	N
MONTANA						
1 Baucus	Y	Y	N	Y	Y	Y
2 ***Marlenee***	Y	N	N	Y	?	?
NEBRASKA						
1 ***Thone***	#	N	Y	Y	Y	?
2 Cavanaugh	Y	Y	Y	Y	Y	Y
3 ***Smith***	Y	N	Y	Y	Y	N
NEVADA						
AL Santini	Y	Y	N	N	Y	?
NEW HAMPSHIRE						
1 D'Amours	Y	Y	N	N	Y	Y
2 ***Cleveland***	Y	N	N	N	Y	N
NEW JERSEY						
1 Florio	Y	Y	N	N	Y	Y
2 Hughes	Y	Y	Y	N	Y	Y
3 Howard	#	#	✓	X	#	#
4 Thompson	?	Y	Y	N	Y	Y
5 ***Fenwick***	Y	Y	Y	N	Y	N
6 ***Forsythe***	Y	Y	Y	N	Y	Y
7 Maguire	?	Y	Y	N	?	?
8 Roe	Y	Y	Y	N	Y	Y
9 ***Hollenbeck***	Y	Y	N	N	Y	Y
10 Rodino	?	?	X	▮	?	?
11 Minish	Y	Y	N	N	Y	Y
12 ***Rinaldo***	Y	Y	N	N	Y	Y
13 Meyner	Y	Y	Y	N	Y	Y
14 LeFante	Y	Y	Y	N	Y	Y
15 Patten	Y	Y	Y	N	Y	Y
NEW MEXICO						
1 ***Lujan***	Y	Y	N	Y	Y	Y
2 Runnels	?	?	?	✓	?	?
NEW YORK						
1 Pike	Y	Y	N	N	Y	N
2 Downey	Y	Y	Y	N	Y	Y
3 Ambro	?	Y	N	N	Y	?
4 ***Lent***	Y	Y	N	N	Y	Y
5 ***Wydler***	Y	N	N	N	Y	N
6 Wolff	Y	?	Y	N	Y	Y
7 Addabbo	Y	Y	Y	N	Y	Y
8 Rosenthal	Y	Y	Y	N	#	#
9 Delaney	Y	Y	N	N	Y	Y
10 Biaggi	Y	Y	N	N	Y	Y
11 Scheuer	Y	Y	Y	N	Y	Y
12 Chisholm	Y	Y	Y	N	Y	Y
13 Solarz	Y	Y	Y	N	Y	Y
14 Richmond	Y	Y	N	N	Y	Y
15 Zeferetti	Y	Y	N	N	Y	Y
16 Holtzman	Y	Y	N	N	Y	Y
17 Murphy	Y	Y	N	N	Y	Y
18 ***Green***	Y	Y	Y	N	Y	Y
19 Rangel	Y	Y	Y	N	Y	Y
20 Weiss	Y	Y	N	N	Y	Y
21 Garcia	Y	Y	Y	N	Y	Y
22 Bingham	Y	Y	Y	N	Y	?
23 ***Caputo***	Y	Y	N	N	Y	N
24 Ottinger	Y	Y	Y	N	?	?
25 ***Fish***	Y	Y	Y	N	?	Y
26 ***Gilman***	Y	Y	Y	N	Y	Y
27 McHugh	Y	Y	Y	N	Y	N
28 Stratton	Y	Y	Y	N	Y	Y
29 Pattison	Y	Y	Y	N	Y	Y
30 ***McEwen***	Y	Y	Y	Y	Y	N
31 ***Mitchell***	Y	Y	Y	Y	Y	Y
32 Hanley	Y	Y	Y	N	Y	Y
33 ***Walsh***	Y	Y	Y	N	Y	Y
34 ***Horton***	Y	?	?	Y	N	Y
35 ***Conable***	?	?	✓	N	N	N
36 LaFalce	Y	Y	N	N	Y	N
37 Nowak	Y	Y	N	N	Y	Y
38 ***Kemp***	Y	N	N	N	Y	Y
39 Lundine	Y	Y	Y	N	Y	Y
NORTH CAROLINA						
1 Jones	#	?	✓	Y	Y	Y
2 Fountain	Y	Y	Y	Y	Y	N
3 Whitley	?	?	✓	✓	?	?
4 Andrews	Y	Y	Y	N	Y	N
5 Neal	Y	Y	Y	N	Y	N
6 Preyer	Y	Y	Y	N	Y	Y
7 Rose	Y	Y	Y	Y	Y	Y
8 Hefner	Y	Y	Y	Y	Y	N

	173	174	175	176	177	178
9 ***Martin***	Y	N	N	Y	Y	N
10 ***Broyhill***	Y	N	Y	Y	Y	N
11 Gudger	#	#	#	N	Y	N
NORTH DAKOTA						
AL ***Andrews***	Y	Y	Y	Y	Y	N
OHIO						
1 ***Gradison***	N	N	Y	N	Y	N
2 Luken	Y	Y	N	N	Y	Y
3 ***Whalen***	Y	Y	Y	N	Y	Y
4 ***Guyer***	Y	Y	Y	Y	Y	Y
5 ***Latta***	N	N	N	Y	Y	N
6 ***Harsha***	Y	N	Y	Y	Y	N
7 ***Brown***	Y	Y	Y	Y	Y	N
8 ***Kindness***	Y	Y	Y	Y	Y	Y
9 Ashley	Y	Y	Y	N	?	?
10 ***Miller***	Y	N	N	Y	Y	N
11 ***Stanton***	Y	Y	Y	Y	Y	N
12 ***Devine***	N	N	N	Y	Y	N
13 Pease	Y	Y	Y	N	Y	N
14 Seiberling	Y	Y	N	N	Y	Y
15 ***Wylie***	Y	Y	Y	Y	Y	N
16 ***Regula***	Y	Y	Y	N	Y	N
17 ***Ashbrook***	N	N	▮	N	Y	N
18 Applegate	Y	Y	N	N	Y	Y
19 Carney	Y	Y	Y	N	Y	Y
20 Oakar	Y	Y	N	N	Y	Y
21 Stokes	Y	Y	N	N	Y	Y
22 Vanik	Y	Y	Y	N	Y	#
23 Mottl	N	Y	N	N	Y	Y
OKLAHOMA						
1 Jones	Y	X	N	Y	Y	N
2 Risenhoover	Y	Y	N	Y	Y	N
3 Watkins	Y	Y	N	Y	Y	Y
4 Steed	Y	Y	Y	Y	Y	Y
5 ***Edwards***	Y	Y	N	Y	Y	Y
6 English	Y	Y	N	Y	Y	N
OREGON						
1 AuCoin	Y	Y	Y	N	Y	Y
2 Ullman	Y	Y	Y	Y	?	#
3 Duncan	Y	Y	Y	N	Y	?
4 Weaver	Y	Y	N	N	Y	Y
PENNSYLVANIA						
1 Myers, M.	Y	Y	Y	N	Y	Y
2 Nix	?	?	?	N	Y	Y
3 Lederer	Y	Y	N	N	Y	Y
4 Eilberg	Y	Y	N	N	Y	Y
5 ***Schulze***	Y	N	Y	Y	Y	Y
6 Yatron	Y	Y	Y	N	Y	Y
7 Edgar	Y	Y	Y	N	Y	Y
8 Kostmayer	Y	Y	N	N	Y	Y
9 ***Shuster***	N	N	N	Y	Y	N
10 ***McDade***	Y	Y	Y	N	Y	Y
11 Flood	Y	Y	N	N	Y	Y
12 Murtha	Y	Y	N	N	Y	N
13 ***Coughlin***	Y	Y	Y	N	?	Y
14 Moorhead	Y	Y	Y	N	Y	Y
15 Rooney	Y	Y	Y	N	Y	Y
16 ***Walker***	N	N	N	N	Y	Y
17 Ertel	Y	Y	Y	N	Y	N
18 Walgren	Y	Y	Y	N	Y	Y
19 ***Goodling, W.***	N	N	N	N	Y	Y
20 Gaydos	Y	Y	N	N	Y	Y
21 Dent	?	?	?	X	?	#
22 Murphy	Y	Y	N	N	N	N
23 Ammerman	Y	Y	N	N	Y	N
24 ***Marks***	Y	N	Y	N	Y	N
25 ***Myers, G.***	Y	N	Y	N	Y	N
RHODE ISLAND						
1 St Germain	Y	?	N	N	Y	Y
2 Beard	Y	Y	N	N	Y	Y
SOUTH CAROLINA						
1 Davis	Y	Y	N	Y	Y	Y
2 ***Spence***	Y	Y	N	Y	Y	Y
3 Derrick	Y	Y	Y	N	Y	N
4 Mann	?	?	?	N	Y	N
5 Holland	Y	Y	N	Y	Y	?
6 Jenrette	Y	Y	Y	Y	Y	Y
SOUTH DAKOTA						
1 ***Pressler***	Y	Y	N	Y	?	Y
2 ***Abdnor***	Y	N	N	Y	Y	N
TENNESSEE						
1 ***Quillen***	Y	N	Y	N	Y	Y
2 ***Duncan***	Y	Y	N	N	Y	Y
3 Lloyd	N	Y	N	N	Y	Y
4 Gore	Y	N	Y	Y	Y	N
5 Allen	N	Y	N	N	Y	Y
6 ***Beard***	N	N	N	N	Y	?

	173	174	175	176	177	178
7 Jones	Y	Y	N	Y	Y	?
8 Ford	Y	Y	N	N	Y	Y
TEXAS						
1 Hall	N	Y	Y	Y	Y	N
2 Wilson, C.	Y	Y	Y	Y	Y	Y
3 ***Collins***	N	N	Y	N	N	N
4 Roberts	Y	N	N	Y	Y	N
5 Mattox	N	Y	N	N	Y	?
6 Teague	?	?	✓	✓	?	?
7 ***Archer***	N	N	Y	N	Y	N
8 Eckhardt	Y	Y	N	?	?	?
9 Brooks	Y	Y	N	N	Y	N
10 Pickle	Y	Y	Y	Y	Y	Y
11 Poage	Y	Y	Y	Y	?	N
12 Wright	Y	Y	Y	N	Y	Y
13 Hightower	Y	Y	Y	Y	?	Y
14 Young	Y	Y	Y	Y	?	?
15 de la Garza	Y	Y	Y	Y	Y	Y
16 White	Y	Y	N	Y	Y	Y
17 Burleson	Y	N	Y	Y	Y	N
18 Jordan	Y	Y	Y	N	Y	Y
19 Mahon	Y	Y	Y	Y	Y	N
20 Gonzalez	Y	Y	N	Y	Y	Y
21 Krueger	?	?	?	Y	Y	Y
22 Gammage	Y	N	Y	Y	Y	Y
23 Kazen	?	?	?	Y	Y	Y
24 Milford	Y	Y	Y	N	Y	N
UTAH						
1 McKay	Y	Y	N	N	Y	Y
2 ***Marriott***	Y	N	Y	N	Y	Y
VERMONT						
AL ***Jeffords***	N	Y	Y	Y	Y	N
VIRGINIA						
1 ***Trible***	Y	N	N	Y	Y	Y
2 ***Whitehurst***	Y	Y	Y	Y	Y	Y
3 Satterfield	N	N	Y	N	Y	N
4 ***Daniel***	N	N	Y	Y	Y	Y
5 Daniel	Y	Y	Y	N	Y	N
6 ***Butler***	Y	N	Y	N	Y	N
7 ***Robinson***	N	N	N	Y	Y	N
8 Harris	Y	Y	Y	N	Y	Y
9 ***Wampler***	Y	Y	N	Y	Y	Y
10 Fisher	Y	Y	Y	N	Y	Y
WASHINGTON						
1 ***Pritchard***	Y	Y	Y	N	Y	N
2 Meeds	Y	Y	Y	N	Y	?
3 Bonker	Y	Y	Y	N	Y	Y
4 McCormack	Y	Y	N	Y	Y	Y
5 Foley	Y	Y	Y	Y	?	Y
6 Dicks	Y	Y	Y	N	Y	Y
7 ***Cunningham***	Y	N	N	N	#	#
WEST VIRGINIA						
1 Mollohan	Y	Y	N	N	Y	Y
2 Staggers	Y	Y	N	N	Y	Y
3 Slack	Y	Y	N	Y	Y	N
4 Rahall	Y	Y	N	X	#	#
WISCONSIN						
1 Aspin	Y	Y	Y	N	Y	Y
2 Kastenmeier	Y	Y	Y	N	Y	Y
3 Baldus	Y	Y	Y	Y	Y	Y
4 Zablocki	Y	Y	Y	N	Y	Y
5 Reuss	#	Y	Y	N	Y	Y
6 ***Steiger***	Y	✓	Y	N	Y	N
7 Obey	Y	Y	N	N	Y	N
8 Cornell	Y	Y	N	N	Y	Y
9 ***Kasten***	Y	N	N	N	Y	Y
WYOMING						
AL Roncalio	Y	Y	N	Y	Y	Y

Democrats ***Republicans***

179. HR 11003. White House Personnel. Adoption of the rule (H Res 1127) providing for House floor consideration of the bill to clarify the authority of the president to employ personnel in the White House office and the executive residence and to allow for congressional oversight. Adopted 395-1: R 138-1; D 257-0 (ND 177-0; SD 80-0), April 13, 1978.

180. HR 11003. White House Personnel. Bauman, R-Md., amendment to limit to 75 rather than 100 the number of Executive Office employees authorized to be compensated at levels above GS-16. Rejected 180-215: R 131-8; D 49-207 (ND 24-154; SD 25-53), April 13, 1978. A "nay" was a vote supporting the president's position.

181. HR 11003. White House Personnel. Gilman, R-N.Y., amendment to limit the authorization to four years by requiring the next president to submit a new personnel authorization request within one year of assuming office. Rejected 171-232: R 116-26; D 55-206 (ND 31-151; SD 24-55), April 13, 1978. A "nay" was a vote supporting the president's position.

182. HR 11003. White House Personnel. Symms, R-Idaho, amendment to prohibit use of any funds appropriated under the authorization to lobby state legislatures with regard to pending constitutional amendments. Rejected 85-320: R 67-74; D 18-246 (ND 4-179; SD 14-67), April 13, 1978. A "nay" was a vote supporting the president's position.

183. HR 11003. White House Personnel. Passage of the bill to clarify the authority of the president to employ personnel in the White House office and the executive residence and to allow for congressional oversight. Passed 265-134: R 49-91; D 216-43 (ND 160-20; SD 56-23), April 13, 1978. A "yea" was a vote supporting the president's position.

184. HR 5289. Natural Gas Pricing. Moffett, D-Conn., motion to require meetings between House and Senate conferees on the natural gas pricing portion of President Carter's national energy bill to be closed to the public. Rejected 6-371: R 0-135; D 6-236 (ND 3-166; SD 3-70), April 13, 1978.

185. HR 3489. Merchant Marine Academy Nominations. Murphy, D-N.Y., motion to suspend the rules and pass the bill to amend the U.S. Code to allow the U.S. delegates from Guam, the Virgin Islands and the District of Columbia to nominate candidates for admission to the U.S. Merchant Marine Academy, instead of appointed officials as under existing procedures, and to delete references to Alaska and Hawaii. Motion agreed to 357-1: R 121-1; D 236-0 (ND 167-0; SD 69-0), April 17, 1978. A two-thirds majority vote (239 in this case) is required for passage under suspension of the rules.

186. HR 10822. National Sea Grant Authorization. Murphy, D-N.Y., motion to suspend the rules and pass the bill to authorize $58 million for each of fiscal years 1977 and 1978, $63 million for fiscal year 1979 and $64.6 million for fiscal year 1980 for the operation of the national sea grant program. Motion agreed to 341-23: R 114-8; D 227-15 (ND 165-6; SD 62-9), April 17, 1978. A two-thirds majority vote (243 in this case) is required for passage under suspension of the rules.

KEY

Y Voted for (yea).
✓ Paired for.
† Announced for.
# CQ Poll for.
N Voted against (nay).
X Paired against.
\- Announced against.
▮ CQ Poll against.
P Voted "present."
● Voted "present" to avoid possible conflict of interest.
? Did not vote or otherwise make a position known.

	179	180	181	182	183	184	185	186
ALABAMA								
1 Edwards	Y	Y	Y	N	N	N	Y	Y
2 Dickinson	Y	Y	N	Y	N	N	Y	Y
3 Nichols	Y	Y	N	N	N	N	Y	Y
4 Bevill	Y	N	N	Y	Y	?	Y	Y
5 Flippo	Y	N	Y	N	N	N	Y	Y
6 Buchanan	Y	Y	Y	N	N	N	Y	Y
7 Flowers	Y	Y	Y	N	N	N	Y	Y
ALASKA								
AL Young	Y	Y	Y	Y	N	N	Y	?
ARIZONA								
1 Rhodes	Y	Y	N	Y	Y	N	Y	Y
2 Udall	?	▮	▮	▮	?	▮	Y	Y
3 Stump	Y	Y	Y	Y	N	Y	Y	N
4 Rudd	Y	Y	Y	Y	N	N	Y	Y
ARKANSAS								
1 Alexander	Y	N	N	N	Y	N	?	?
2 Tucker	?	?	?	?	?	?	?	?
3 Hammerschmidt	Y	Y	N	Y	N	N	Y	Y
4 Thornton	?	?	?	?	?	?	?	?
CALIFORNIA								
1 Johnson	Y	N	N	N	Y	N	Y	Y
2 Clausen	Y	N	Y	N	Y	N	?	?
3 Moss	Y	N	N	N	Y	N	Y	Y
4 Leggett	Y	▮	▮	▮	Y	N	Y	Y
5 Burton, J.	?	N	?	N	Y	?	Y	Y
6 Burton, P.	Y	N	N	N	Y	N	Y	Y
7 Miller	Y	N	N	N	Y	N	Y	Y
8 Dellums	Y	N	N	N	Y	N	Y	Y
9 Stark	Y	N	N	N	Y	N	Y	Y
10 Edwards	Y	N	N	N	Y	N	Y	Y
11 Ryan	Y	N	N	N	Y	?	Y	Y
12 McCloskey	Y	Y	Y	N	Y	N	?	?
13 Mineta	Y	N	N	N	Y	N	Y	Y
14 McFall	Y	N	N	N	Y	N	Y	Y
15 Sisk	Y	N	N	N	Y	N	Y	Y
16 Panetta	Y	Y	N	N	Y	N	#	#
17 Krebs	Y	N	N	N	Y	N	Y	Y
18 Ketchum	Y	Y	Y	Y	Y	?	Y	Y
19 Lagomarsino	Y	Y	Y	Y	N	N	Y	Y
20 Goldwater	Y	Y	Y	N	N	N	?	?
21 Corman	Y	N	N	N	Y	N	Y	Y
22 Moorhead	Y	Y	Y	Y	N	N	Y	Y
23 Beilenson	Y	N	N	N	Y	N	Y	Y
24 Waxman	Y	N	N	N	Y	N	?	Y
25 Roybal	Y	N	N	N	Y	N	Y	Y
26 Rousselot	Y	Y	Y	Y	Y	N	Y	Y
27 Dornan	#	Y	Y	Y	N	N	Y	Y
28 Burke	?	X	X	?	?	?	?	?
29 Hawkins	Y	?	N	N	Y	N	Y	Y
30 Danielson	Y	N	N	N	Y	N	Y	Y
31 Wilson, C.H.	Y	N	N	N	Y	▮	Y	Y
32 Anderson	Y	N	N	N	Y	N	Y	Y
33 Clawson	?	✓	✓	?	?	?	Y	Y
34 Hannaford	Y	N	N	N	Y	N	Y	Y
35 Lloyd	Y	Y	Y	N	Y	N	Y	Y
36 Brown	Y	N	N	N	Y	N	Y	Y
37 Pettis	Y	Y	N	N	Y	N	Y	Y
38 Patterson	Y	N	N	N	Y	N	Y	Y
39 Wiggins	Y	Y	Y	?	Y	N	?	?
40 Badham	Y	Y	N	Y	Y	N	Y	Y
41 Wilson, B.	Y	Y	N	Y	Y	N	Y	Y
42 Van Deerlin	?	?	?	?	?	?	Y	Y
43 Burgener	Y	Y	Y	Y	Y	?	Y	Y
COLORADO								
1 Schroeder	Y	N	N	N	Y	?	Y	Y
2 Wirth	Y	N	N	N	Y	?	Y	Y
3 Evans	Y	N	N	N	Y	N	Y	Y
4 Johnson	Y	Y	Y	N	Y	N	Y	Y

	179	180	181	182	183	184	185	186
5 Armstrong	Y	Y	Y	Y	N	?	Y	N
CONNECTICUT								
1 Cotter	Y	N	N	N	Y	N	Y	Y
2 Dodd	Y	N	Y	N	Y	N	?	Y
3 Giaimo	Y	N	N	?	?	?	Y	Y
4 McKinney	Y	Y	N	N	Y	N	Y	Y
5 Sarasin	†	✓	X	-	-	-	†	†
6 Moffett	Y	Y	Y	N	Y	N	?	Y
DELAWARE								
AL Evans	Y	Y	Y	N	N	N	Y	Y
FLORIDA								
1 Sikes	Y	N	N	N	Y	N	Y	Y
2 Fuqua	Y	N	N	N	Y	N	Y	Y
3 Bennett	Y	Y	Y	Y	Y	N	Y	Y
4 Chappell	Y	#	N	N	N	N	Y	Y
5 Kelly	N	Y	Y	Y	N	N	Y	Y
6 Young	Y	Y	N	N	N	N	Y	Y
7 Gibbons	Y	N	N	Y	Y	N	Y	Y
8 Ireland	Y	Y	Y	N	N	N	Y	Y
9 Frey	Y	Y	Y	Y	N	N	?	?
10 Bafalis	Y	Y	Y	Y	N	N	?	Y
11 Rogers	Y	N	N	N	Y	N	Y	Y
12 Burke	Y	Y	N	N	Y	N	Y	Y
13 Lehman	Y	N	N	N	Y	N	Y	Y
14 Pepper	Y	N	N	N	†	N	†	Y
15 Fascell	Y	N	N	N	Y	N	Y	Y
GEORGIA								
1 Ginn	Y	Y	N	N	Y	N	Y	Y
2 Mathis	Y	N	N	N	N	N	Y	Y
3 Brinkley	Y	N	N	N	Y	N	Y	N
4 Levitas	Y	Y	Y	N	Y	N	Y	Y
5 Fowler	Y	Y	Y	N	Y	?	Y	Y
6 Flynt	Y	N	N	N	Y	N	Y	Y
7 McDonald	Y	Y	Y	Y	N	N	Y	N
8 Evans	Y	N	Y	N	N	N	Y	N
9 Jenkins	?	Y	N	N	Y	N	Y	N
10 Barnard	Y	Y	?	?	?	?	Y	Y
HAWAII								
1 Heftel	Y	N	N	N	Y	N	Y	Y
2 Akaka	Y	N	N	N	Y	N	Y	Y
IDAHO								
1 Symms	Y	Y	Y	Y	N	N	Y	Y
2 Hansen, G.	Y	Y	Y	Y	N	N	Y	N
ILLINOIS								
1 Metcalfe	Y	?	N	N	Y	N	Y	Y
2 Murphy	Y	N	N	N	Y	N	Y	Y
3 Russo	Y	N	Y	N	Y	N	Y	Y
4 Derwinski	Y	N	N	N	Y	N	Y	Y
5 Fary	Y	N	N	N	Y	N	Y	Y
6 Hyde	Y	Y	Y	Y	Y	N	Y	Y
7 Collins	Y	N	N	N	Y	N	?	?
8 Rostenkowski	Y	N	N	N	Y	N	Y	Y
9 Yates	Y	N	N	N	N	N	Y	Y
. 10 Mikva	Y	N	Y	N	Y	N	Y	Y
11 Annunzio	Y	N	N	N	Y	N	Y	Y
12 Crane	#	✓	✓	#	▮	▮	#	#
13 McClory	Y	Y	Y	N	Y	N	Y	Y
14 Erlenborn	Y	Y	Y	Y	N	N	Y	Y
15 Corcoran	Y	Y	N	Y	Y	N	Y	Y
16 Anderson	Y	Y	Y	N	Y	N	?	?
17 O'Brien	Y	N	N	N	Y	N	Y	Y
18 Michel	Y	Y	N	Y	N	N	Y	Y
19 Railsback	#	Y	N	N	N	▮	Y	#
20 Findley	Y	Y	Y	N	Y	N	Y	Y
21 Madigan	Y	N	Y	Y	Y	N	Y	Y
22 Shipley	Y	N	N	N	Y	?	Y	Y
23 Price	Y	N	N	N	Y	N	Y	Y
24 Simon	Y	N	N	N	Y	N	Y	Y
INDIANA								
1 Benjamin	Y	N	N	N	Y	N	Y	Y
2 Fithian	Y	N	N	N	N	?	Y	Y
3 Brademas	Y	N	N	N	Y	-	Y	Y
4 Quayle	Y	Y	Y	N	N	N	Y	N
5 Hillis	Y	Y	Y	N	Y	N	Y	Y
6 Evans	Y	Y	N	N	N	N	Y	N
7 Myers, J.	Y	Y	Y	N	N	N	Y	Y
8 Cornwell	Y	X	?	?	?	?	Y	Y
9 Hamilton	Y	N	N	N	Y	N	Y	Y
10 Sharp	Y	N	Y	N	Y	N	Y	Y
11 Jacobs	Y	Y	Y	N	N	N	#	#
IOWA								
1 Leach	Y	Y	Y	N	N	▮	Y	Y
2 Blouin	Y	N	N	N	Y	N	Y	Y
3 Grassley	Y	Y	Y	Y	N	N	Y	Y
4 Smith	Y	N	N	N	Y	▮	Y	Y
5 Harkin	Y	N	Y	N	Y	N	Y	Y
6 Bedell	Y	N	Y	N	Y	N	Y	Y

Democrats ***Republicans***

	179	180	181	182	183	184	185	186
KANSAS								
1 ***Sebelius***	Y	Y	N	N	N	N	Y	Y
2 Keys	Y	N	Y	N	Y	N	Y	Y
3 ***Winn***	Y	Y	Y	Y	N	N	Y	Y
4 Glickman	Y	Y	N	N	N	N	Y	Y
5 ***Skubitz***	Y	Y	N	N	?	N	Y	Y
KENTUCKY								
1 Hubbard	Y	Y	N	Y	N	N	Y	Y
2 Natcher	Y	N	N	N	Y	N	Y	Y
3 Mazzoli	Y	Y	Y	N	†	N	Y	Y
4 ***Snyder***	Y	Y	N	Y	N	N	Y	Y
5 ***Carter***	Y	Y	N	N	N	N	Y	Y
6 Breckinridge	Y	N	Y	N	Y	?	?	?
7 Perkins	Y	N	N	N	Y	N	Y	Y
LOUISIANA								
1 ***Livingston***	Y	Y	Y	Y	N	N	?	Y
2 Boggs	Y	N	N	N	Y	▮	#	Y
3 ***Treen***	Y	Y	Y	Y	Y	N	Y	Y
4 Waggonner	Y	N	Y	N	Y	Y	Y	Y
5 Huckaby	Y	Y	Y	N	N	N	Y	Y
6 ***Moore***	Y	Y	Y	N	N	N	Y	Y
7 Breaux	?	X	✓	N	Y	N	Y	Y
8 Long	Y	N	N	N	Y	N	?	?
MAINE								
1 ***Emery***	Y	Y	Y	N	▮	N	Y	Y
2 ***Cohen***	Y	Y	Y	N	N	N	?	?
MARYLAND								
1 ***Bauman***	Y	Y	Y	Y	N	N	Y	Y
2 Long	Y	Y	N	N	N	N	Y	Y
3 Mikulski	Y	N	N	N	Y	N	Y	Y
4 ***Holt***	Y	Y	Y	N	N	N	Y	Y
5 Spellman	#	▮	▮	▮	#	▮	Y	Y
6 Byron	Y	N	Y	N	N	N	?	?
7 Mitchell	Y	N	N	N	?	N	Y	Y
8 ***Steers***	Y	Y	Y	N	Y	N	Y	Y
MASSACHUSETTS								
1 ***Conte***	Y	Y	N	N	Y	N	Y	Y
2 Boland	Y	N	N	N	Y	N	Y	Y
3 Early	Y	Y	Y	N	Y	?	Y	Y
4 Drinan	Y	N	N	N	Y	N	Y	Y
5 Tsongas	Y	N	N	N	Y	N	#	#
6 Harrington	Y	N	N	N	Y	N	#	#
7 Markey	Y	N	N	N	Y	N	Y	Y
8 O'Neill								
9 Moakley	Y	N	N	N	Y	▮	Y	Y
10 ***Heckler***	?	?	X	?	?	?	Y	Y
11 Burke	Y	N	N	N	Y	N	Y	Y
12 Studds	Y	N	N	N	Y	N	Y	Y
MICHIGAN								
1 Conyers	Y	N	N	N	Y	N	?	?
2 ***Pursell***	?	Y	Y	N	Y	N	Y	?
3 ***Brown***	Y	Y	Y	N	N	N	Y	Y
4 ***Stockman***	Y	Y	Y	N	Y	N	#	#
5 ***Sawyer***	Y	Y	Y	N	N	N	?	?
6 Carr	Y	N	N	N	Y	N	Y	Y
7 Kildee	Y	N	N	N	Y	N	Y	Y
8 Traxler	Y	N	N	N	Y	N	?	Y
9 ***Vander Jagt***	Y	Y	Y	Y	N	N	Y	Y
10 ***Cederberg***	Y	N	Y	N	Y	N	Y	Y
11 ***Ruppe***	Y	Y	Y	N	Y	N	Y	Y
12 Bonior	Y	?	N	N	Y	N	Y	Y
13 Diggs	Y	N	N	N	Y	?	Y	Y
14 Nedzi	Y	N	N	N	Y	N	Y	Y
15 Ford	Y	N	N	N	Y	N	?	?
16 Dingell	?	Y	N	N	Y	N	Y	Y
17 Brodhead	Y	N	N	N	Y	N	Y	Y
18 Blanchard	Y	N	N	N	Y	N	Y	Y
19 ***Broomfield***	Y	Y	Y	Y	Y	N	Y	Y
MINNESOTA								
1 ***Quie***	Y	Y	Y	N	Y	N	?	?
2 ***Hagedorn***	Y	Y	Y	Y	N	N	Y	Y
3 ***Frenzel***	Y	Y	Y	N	Y	N	Y	Y
4 Vento	Y	N	N	N	Y	N	Y	Y
5 Fraser	Y	N	?	N	Y	N	?	?
6 Nolan	Y	N	N	N	Y	N	Y	Y
7 ***Stangeland***	Y	Y	Y	Y	N	N	Y	Y
8 Oberstar	Y	N	N	N	Y	N	Y	Y
MISSISSIPPI								
1 Whitten	Y	N	Y	N	Y	?	Y	Y
2 Bowen	Y	N	Y	Y	Y	N	Y	Y
3 Montgomery	Y	N	Y	Y	Y	N	Y	Y
4 ***Cochran***	Y	Y	Y	Y	N	N	?	?
5 ***Lott***	Y	Y	Y	Y	Y	N	Y	Y
MISSOURI								
1 Clay	Y	N	N	N	?	N	?	?
2 Young	Y	▮	N	N	Y	N	Y	Y
3 Gephardt	Y	N	N	N	Y	N	Y	Y
4 Skelton	Y	Y	Y	N	Y	N	Y	N
5 Bolling	Y	N	N	N	Y	N	Y	Y
6 ***Coleman***	Y	Y	Y	N	N	N	Y	Y
7 ***Taylor***	Y	Y	N	Y	Y	N	Y	Y
8 Ichord	Y	N	N	Y	Y	N	Y	Y
9 Volkmer	Y	N	Y	N	Y	N	Y	N
10 Burlison	Y	N	N	N	Y	N	Y	Y
MONTANA								
1 Baucus	?	X	?	?	?	?	Y	Y
2 ***Marlenee***	Y	Y	Y	Y	N	N	Y	Y
NEBRASKA								
1 ***Thone***	#	✓	?	?	?	▮	#	#
2 Cavanaugh	Y	N	N	N	Y	N	Y	Y
3 ***Smith***	Y	Y	Y	N	N	N	Y	Y
NEVADA								
AL Santini	Y	?	Y	N	Y	N	Y	Y
NEW HAMPSHIRE								
1 D'Amours	Y	Y	N	N	N	N	Y	Y
2 ***Cleveland***	Y	Y	Y	N	N	N	Y	Y
NEW JERSEY								
1 Florio	Y	N	Y	N	Y	N	Y	Y
2 Hughes	Y	Y	Y	N	Y	N	Y	Y
3 Howard	#	▮	?	?	?	?	?	?
4 Thompson	Y	N	N	N	Y	N	?	?
5 ***Fenwick***	Y	Y	Y	N	N	N	N	Y
6 ***Forsythe***	Y	Y	Y	N	N	N	Y	#
7 Maguire	Y	Y	Y	N	Y	N	Y	Y
8 Roe	Y	N	N	N	Y	N	Y	Y
9 ***Hollenbeck***	Y	Y	Y	N	N	N	Y	Y
10 Rodino	?	▮	▮	▮	?	▮	?	?
11 Minish	Y	N	Y	N	Y	N	Y	Y
12 ***Rinaldo***	Y	Y	Y	N	N	N	Y	Y
13 Meyner	#	N	N	N	Y	N	Y	Y
14 LeFante	Y	N	N	N	N	N	Y	Y
15 Patten	Y	N	N	N	Y	N	Y	Y
NEW MEXICO								
1 ***Lujan***	Y	Y	Y	N	N	?	Y	Y
2 Runnels	?	?	?	?	?	▮	?	?
NEW YORK								
1 Pike	Y	Y	Y	N	Y	N	Y	Y
2 Downey	Y	Y	N	N	Y	N	Y	Y
3 Ambro	?	N	N	N	Y	N	?	?
4 ***Lent***	Y	Y	Y	Y	N	N	Y	Y
5 ***Wydler***	Y	Y	Y	Y	N	N	?	?
6 Wolff	Y	N	N	N	Y	N	Y	Y
7 Addabbo	Y	N	N	N	Y	N	Y	Y
8 Rosenthal	Y	N	N	N	Y	N	Y	Y
9 Delaney	Y	N	N	N	Y	N	Y	Y
10 Biaggi	Y	N	Y	N	Y	N	Y	Y
11 Scheuer	Y	N	N	N	Y	N	Y	Y
12 Chisholm	Y	N	N	N	Y	N	Y	Y
13 Solarz	Y	N	N	N	Y	N	Y	Y
14 Richmond	Y	N	N	N	Y	N	?	Y
15 Zeferetti	Y	N	N	Y	Y	N	Y	Y
16 Holtzman	Y	N	N	N	N	N	Y	Y
17 Murphy	?	?	?	?	?	?	Y	Y
18 ***Green***	Y	Y	Y	N	N	N	Y	Y
19 Rangel	Y	N	N	N	Y	N	Y	Y
20 Weiss	Y	N	N	N	Y	N	Y	Y
21 Garcia	Y	N	N	N	Y	N	?	?
22 Bingham	Y	N	N	N	Y	N	Y	Y
23 ***Caputo***	Y	Y	Y	N	N	N	Y	Y
24 Ottinger	Y	N	N	N	Y	N	Y	Y
25 ***Fish***	Y	Y	Y	N	N	N	?	Y
26 ***Gilman***	Y	Y	Y	Y	Y	N	Y	Y
27 McHugh	Y	N	N	N	Y	N	Y	Y
28 Stratton	Y	N	N	N	Y	Y	Y	Y
29 Pattison	Y	N	Y	N	Y	N	Y	Y
30 ***McEwen***	Y	Y	N	N	Y	N	Y	Y
31 ***Mitchell***	Y	Y	Y	N	N	N	Y	Y
32 Hanley	Y	N	N	N	Y	N	Y	Y
33 ***Walsh***	Y	Y	Y	Y	N	N	Y	Y
34 ***Horton***	Y	Y	Y	N	N	N	Y	Y
35 ***Conable***	Y	✓	Y	N	Y	N	?	?
36 LaFalce	Y	N	N	N	Y	N	Y	Y
37 Nowak	Y	N	N	N	Y	N	Y	Y
38 ***Kemp***	Y	Y	Y	Y	Y	N	Y	Y
39 Lundine	Y	N	N	N	Y	N	#	#
NORTH CAROLINA								
1 Jones	?	#	▮	#	#	▮	?	?
2 Fountain	Y	Y	N	N	Y	▮	Y	Y
3 Whitley	?	?	?	?	?	?	?	?
4 Andrews	Y	N	N	N	Y	N	?	?
5 Neal	Y	N	N	N	Y	N	Y	Y
6 Preyer	Y	N	N	N	Y	N	Y	Y
7 Rose	Y	N	N	N	Y	N	#	#
8 Hefner	Y	Y	Y	N	Y	N	Y	Y
9 ***Martin***	Y	Y	Y	N	N	N	Y	Y
10 ***Broyhill***	Y	Y	Y	N	N	N	Y	Y
11 Gudger	Y	N	N	N	Y	▮	#	#
NORTH DAKOTA								
AL Andrews	Y	Y	Y	N	N	N	Y	Y
OHIO								
1 ***Gradison***	Y	Y	Y	N	N	N	Y	N
2 Luken	Y	N	N	N	?	N	Y	N
3 ***Whalen***	Y	N	N	N	Y	N	Y	Y
4 ***Guyer***	Y	Y	Y	Y	N	N	Y	Y
5 ***Latta***	Y	Y	N	Y	N	N	Y	Y
6 ***Harsha***	Y	Y	Y	Y	N	N	Y	Y
7 ***Brown***	Y	Y	Y	Y	Y	N	Y	Y
8 ***Kindness***	Y	Y	N	Y	Y	N	Y	Y
9 Ashley	?	N	N	N	Y	N	?	?
10 ***Miller***	Y	Y	Y	Y	N	N	Y	N
11 ***Stanton***	Y	Y	Y	N	Y	N	?	?
12 ***Devine***	Y	Y	Y	Y	N	N	Y	Y
13 Pease	Y	▮	Y	N	Y	N	Y	Y
14 Seiberling	Y	N	N	N	Y	N	Y	Y
15 ***Wylie***	Y	Y	Y	N	N	N	Y	Y
16 ***Regula***	Y	Y	Y	N	N	N	Y	Y
17 ***Ashbrook***	Y	Y	Y	Y	N	N	?	?
18 Applegate	Y	N	N	N	Y	N	?	?
19 Carney	Y	N	N	N	Y	N	Y	Y
20 Oakar	Y	N	N	N	Y	N	Y	Y
21 Stokes	Y	N	N	N	Y	N	?	?
22 Vanik	Y	N	N	N	Y	N	Y	Y
23 Mottl	Y	Y	Y	Y	Y	N	Y	N
OKLAHOMA								
1 Jones	Y	N	N	N	Y	N	Y	N
2 Risenhoover	Y	Y	Y	Y	N	N	Y	N
3 Watkins	Y	N	N	Y	Y	N	Y	N
4 Steed	Y	▮	N	N	Y	N	Y	Y
5 ***Edwards***	Y	Y	Y	Y	N	N	Y	N
6 English	Y	Y	Y	Y	N	N	Y	N
OREGON								
1 AuCoin	Y	N	N	N	Y	N	Y	Y
2 Ullman	Y	N	N	N	Y	N	Y	Y
3 Duncan	Y	N	N	N	Y	N	Y	Y
4 Weaver	Y	N	N	N	Y	N	Y	Y
PENNSYLVANIA								
1 Myers, M.	Y	Y	N	N	N	N	Y	Y
2 Nix	Y	N	N	N	Y	N	Y	Y
3 Lederer	Y	Y	N	N	N	N	Y	Y
4 Eilberg	P	N	N	N	Y	N	?	?
5 ***Schulze***	Y	Y	Y	Y	N	N	Y	Y
6 Yatron	Y	Y	Y	N	N	N	Y	Y
7 Edgar	Y	Y	Y	N	N	N	Y	Y
8 Kostmayer	Y	Y	N	N	N	N	Y	Y
9 ***Shuster***	Y	Y	Y	Y	N	N	?	Y
10 ***McDade***	Y	Y	N	N	N	N	Y	Y
11 Flood	Y	N	N	N	Y	N	Y	Y
12 Murtha	Y	N	N	N	Y	Y	Y	Y
13 ***Coughlin***	Y	Y	Y	N	N	N	Y	Y
14 Moorhead	Y	N	N	N	Y	N	Y	Y
15 Rooney	Y	N	N	N	Y	N	Y	Y
16 ***Walker***	Y	Y	Y	N	N	N	Y	Y
17 Ertel	Y	Y	Y	N	N	N	Y	Y
18 Walgren	Y	N	N	N	Y	N	Y	Y
19 ***Goodling, W.***	Y	Y	Y	N	N	N	Y	Y
20 Gaydos	Y	N	N	N	Y	N	Y	?
21 Dent	#	▮	▮	▮	#	▮	Y	Y
22 Murphy	Y	Y	N	N	N	N	Y	Y
23 Ammerman	Y	N	N	N	Y	N	Y	Y
24 ***Marks***	Y	N	Y	N	Y	N	Y	Y
25 ***Myers, G.***	Y	N	N	Y	Y	N	Y	Y
RHODE ISLAND								
1 St Germain	Y	N	N	N	Y	?	Y	Y
2 Beard	Y	N	N	N	Y	N	Y	Y
SOUTH CAROLINA								
1 Davis	Y	Y	Y	N	N	N	Y	Y
2 ***Spence***	Y	Y	Y	Y	N	N	Y	Y
3 Derrick	Y	N	✓	Y	N	N	Y	Y
4 Mann	Y	N	N	Y	Y	N	?	?
5 Holland	?	?	?	?	?	?	?	?
6 Jenrette	Y	N	Y	N	N	N	?	?
SOUTH DAKOTA								
1 ***Pressler***	Y	Y	Y	N	N	N	?	?
2 ***Abdnor***	Y	Y	Y	Y	N	N	Y	Y
TENNESSEE								
1 ***Quillen***	Y	Y	Y	Y	Y	▮	Y	Y
2 ***Duncan***	Y	Y	Y	Y	N	N	Y	Y
3 Lloyd	Y	N	N	N	N	N	Y	Y
4 Gore	Y	Y	N	N	Y	N	Y	Y
5 Allen	Y	N	N	N	Y	N	Y	Y
6 ***Beard***	Y	Y	Y	N	N	N	Y	N
7 Jones	Y	Y	Y	N	N	N	Y	Y
8 Ford	Y	N	N	N	Y	N	Y	Y
TEXAS								
1 Hall	Y	Y	Y	N	N	N	Y	Y
2 Wilson, C.	Y	N	N	N	Y	N	Y	Y
3 ***Collins***	Y	Y	Y	Y	N	N	Y	N
4 Roberts	Y	N	N	N	N	?	Y	N
5 Mattox	Y	?	N	N	Y	N	Y	Y
6 Teague	?	?	?	?	?	?	?	?
7 ***Archer***	Y	Y	Y	Y	N	N	Y	Y
8 Eckhardt	Y	N	N	N	Y	N	Y	Y
9 Brooks	Y	N	N	N	Y	N	Y	Y
10 Pickle	Y	Y	N	N	Y	N	Y	Y
11 Poage	Y	N	N	N	Y	Y	Y	Y
12 Wright	Y	N	N	N	Y	N	Y	Y
13 Hightower	Y	Y	Y	Y	N	N	Y	Y
14 Young	Y	N	N	N	Y	N	?	?
15 de la Garza	?	N	N	N	Y	N	?	?
16 White	Y	N	N	N	Y	N	Y	Y
17 Burleson	Y	N	N	N	N	Y	Y	Y
18 Jordan	Y	N	N	N	Y	N	Y	Y
19 Mahon	Y	N	N	N	Y	N	Y	Y
20 Gonzalez	Y	N	N	N	Y	N	Y	Y
21 Krueger	?	X	X	?	✓	?	?	?
22 Gammage	Y	X	?	?	X	?	?	?
23 Kazen	Y	N	N	N	Y	N	?	?
24 Milford	Y	N	N	N	Y	N	Y	Y
UTAH								
1 McKay	Y	N	N	N	Y	N	Y	Y
2 ***Marriott***	Y	Y	Y	Y	N	N	Y	Y
VERMONT								
AL Jeffords	Y	Y	Y	N	N	N	?	?
VIRGINIA								
1 ***Trible***	Y	Y	Y	Y	N	N	Y	Y
2 ***Whitehurst***	Y	Y	Y	N	Y	N	Y	Y
3 Satterfield	Y	Y	Y	Y	N	N	Y	Y
4 ***Daniel***	Y	Y	Y	Y	N	N	Y	Y
5 Daniel	Y	Y	N	Y	N	N	Y	Y
6 ***Butler***	Y	✓	Y	Y	Y	N	?	?
7 ***Robinson***	Y	Y	Y	Y	N	N	Y	Y
8 Harris	Y	N	N	N	Y	N	Y	Y
9 ***Wampler***	Y	Y	Y	Y	Y	N	Y	Y
10 Fisher	Y	N	N	N	Y	N	Y	Y
WASHINGTON								
1 ***Pritchard***	Y	▮	Y	N	Y	N	Y	Y
2 Meeds	?	?	?	?	?	?	Y	Y
3 Bonker	Y	N	N	N	Y	N	Y	Y
4 McCormack	Y	N	Y	N	Y	N	Y	Y
5 Foley	?	N	Y	N	†	?	Y	Y
6 Dicks	Y	N	N	N	Y	N	Y	Y
7 ***Cunningham***	Y	Y	Y	N	N	N	Y	Y
WEST VIRGINIA								
1 Mollohan	Y	N	N	N	Y	N	Y	Y
2 Staggers	Y	N	N	N	Y	N	Y	Y
3 Slack	Y	N	N	N	Y	N	Y	Y
4 Rahall	#	N	N	N	Y	▮	#	?
WISCONSIN								
1 Aspin	Y	N	N	N	Y	N	?	?
2 Kastenmeier	Y	N	N	N	Y	N	Y	Y
3 Baldus	Y	N	N	N	Y	N	Y	Y
4 Zablocki	Y	N	N	N	Y	N	Y	Y
5 Reuss	Y	N	N	N	Y	N	Y	Y
6 ***Steiger***	Y	Y	Y	N	Y	N	Y	Y
7 Obey	Y	N	N	N	Y	N	Y	Y
8 Cornell	Y	N	N	N	Y	N	Y	Y
9 ***Kasten***	Y	Y	Y	N	N	N	Y	Y
WYOMING								
AL Roncalio	?	N	N	N	Y	N	?	?

Democrats ***Republicans***

187. HR 10823. National Advisory Committee on Oceans and Atmosphere. Murphy, D-N.Y., motion to suspend the rules and pass the bill to authorize $572,000 for fiscal 1979 for the National Advisory Committee on Oceans and Atmosphere, and to extend by one year the terms of the committee's members appointed in January 1978. Motion agreed to 317-47: R 94-26; D 223-21 (ND 163-11; SD 60-10), April 17, 1978. A two-thirds majority vote (243 in this case) is required for passage under suspension of the rules.

188. HR 11465. Coast Guard Authorization. Murphy, D-N.Y., motion to suspend the rules and pass the bill to authorize $1.4 billion for fiscal 1979 operations of the U.S. Coast Guard, including $960 million for operating expenses; $380 million for the acquisition and improvement of vessels, aircraft and shore facilities; $34.6 million for the alteration or removal of obstructive bridges, and $25 million for research and development. Motion agreed to 357-13: R 118-6; D 239-7 (ND 170-5; SD 69-2), April 17, 1978. A two-thirds majority vote (247 in this case) is required for passage under suspension of the rules.

189. HR 8588. Inspector General Offices. Fountain, D-N.C., motion to suspend the rules and pass the bill to establish offices of inspector general to conduct audits and investigations of the programs in the Departments of Agriculture, Commerce, Housing and Urban Development, Interior, Labor and Transportation and the Community Services Administration, Environmental Protection Agency, General Services Administration, National Aeronautics and Space Administration, Small Business Administration and Veterans Administration. Motion agreed to 388-6: R 137-1; D 251-5 (ND 175-4; SD 76-1), April 18, 1978. A two-thirds majority vote (263 in this case) is required for passage under suspension of the rules.

190. S 2452. Humphrey and Dirksen Institutes. Ford, D-Mich., motion to suspend the rules and pass the bill to authorize $7.5 million for the Hubert H. Humphrey Institute of Public Affairs at the University of Minnesota and the Everett McKinley Dirksen Congressional Leadership Research Center at Pekin, Ill. Motion agreed to 267-127: R 82-59; D 185-68 (ND 148-29; SD 37-39), April 18, 1978. A two-thirds majority vote (263 in this case) is required for passage under suspension of the rules.

191. HR 3787. Zuni Indian Claims. Passage of the bill to authorize the secretary of the interior to purchase from or exchange with the state of New Mexico 600 acres, valued at $30,000, containing the sacred Zuni Salt Lake and to allow the Zuni tribe to file claims with the Indian Claims Commission despite the 1951 cutoff date for such claims. Passed 347-48: R 111-30; D 236-18 (ND 167-12; SD 69-6), April 18, 1978.

192. HR 11400. National Science Foundation. Breaux, D-La., amendment to add $3.2 million to the fiscal 1979 National Science Foundation authorization for astronomical, atmospheric sciences and for Earth and ocean sciences to be used for a study of a deep sea drilling project. Rejected 111-291: R 58-85; D 53-206 (ND 36-145; SD 17-61), April 18, 1978.

193. HR 11400. National Science Foundation. Ashbrook, R-Ohio, amendment to reduce by $6 million, to $152 million, from $158 million, the fiscal 1979 authorization for biological, behavioral and social sciences programs. Rejected 174-229: R 99-43; D 75-186 (ND 33-149; SD 42-37), April 18, 1978.

194. HR 11400. National Science Foundation. Passage of the bill to authorize $934.4 million in fiscal 1979 for operations and programs of the National Science Foundation. Passed 364-37: R 119-23; D 245-14 (ND 174-6; SD 71-8), April 18, 1978.

KEY

Y Voted for (yea).
✓ Paired for.
† Announced for.
# CQ Poll for.
N Voted against (nay).
X Paired against.
\- Announced against.
▮ CQ Poll against.
P Voted "present."
● Voted "present" to avoid possible conflict of interest.
? Did not vote or otherwise make a position known.

	187	188	189	190	191	192	193	194
ALABAMA								
1 Edwards	Y	Y	Y	N	Y	Y	Y	Y
2 Dickinson	Y	Y	Y	N	Y	Y	Y	Y
3 Nichols	Y	Y	Y	N	Y	N	Y	Y
4 Bevill	Y	Y	Y	N	Y	N	Y	N
5 Flippo	Y	Y	Y	N	Y	N	N	Y
6 Buchanan	Y	Y	Y	Y	Y	N	Y	Y
7 Flowers	Y	Y	Y	N	Y	N	N	Y
ALASKA								
AL Young	Y	Y	Y	Y	Y	Y	?	N
ARIZONA								
1 Rhodes	Y	Y	Y	Y	Y	N	N	Y
2 Udall	?	Y	Y	Y	Y	▮	N	Y
3 Stump	Y	Y	Y	N	N	N	Y	N
4 Rudd	N	Y	Y	N	N	N	Y	N
ARKANSAS								
1 Alexander	?	?	?	?	Y	Y	N	Y
2 Tucker	?	?	?	?	?	?	?	?
3 Hammerschmidt	Y	Y	Y	Y	N	Y	Y	Y
4 Thornton	?	?	?	?	?	?	?	?
CALIFORNIA								
1 Johnson	Y	Y	Y	Y	Y	N	N	Y
2 Clausen	?	?	?	?	?	?	?	?
3 Moss	Y	Y	Y	Y	Y	N	N	Y
4 Leggett	Y	Y	#	#	#	Y	N	Y
5 Burton, J.	Y	Y	Y	Y	Y	Y	N	Y
6 Burton, P.	Y	Y	Y	Y	Y	?	?	?
7 Miller	Y	Y	Y	Y	Y	Y	N	Y
8 Dellums	Y	?	?	?	?	?	▮	?
9 Stark	Y	Y	Y	Y	Y	Y	N	Y
10 Edwards	Y	Y	Y	Y	Y	N	N	Y
11 Ryan	Y	Y	Y	Y	Y	N	N	Y
12 McCloskey	?	?	Y	Y	Y	N	N	Y
13 Mineta	Y	Y	Y	Y	Y	N	N	Y
14 McFall	Y	Y	Y	Y	Y	N	N	Y
15 Sisk	Y	Y	Y	Y	Y	?	?	?
16 Panetta	#	#	N	Y	Y	N	N	Y
17 Krebs	Y	Y	Y	Y	Y	N	N	Y
18 Ketchum	Y	?	Y	N	N	Y	Y	Y
19 Lagomarsino	Y	Y	Y	Y	Y	Y	Y	Y
20 Goldwater	?	?	?	Y	Y	Y	Y	Y
21 Corman	Y	Y	#	#	Y	N	N	Y
22 Moorhead	N	Y	Y	N	N	Y	Y	Y
23 Beilenson	Y	Y	Y	N	Y	N	N	Y
24 Waxman	Y	Y	Y	Y	Y	N	N	Y
25 Roybal	Y	Y	Y	Y	Y	Y	N	Y
26 Rousselot	N	Y	Y	?	N	Y	Y	N
27 Dornan	Y	Y	Y	N	Y	Y	Y	Y
28 Burke	?	?	?	?	?	?	?	?
29 Hawkins	Y	Y	Y	Y	Y	Y	N	Y
30 Danielson	Y	Y	Y	Y	Y	N	N	Y
31 Wilson, C.H.	Y	Y	?	?	▮	N	N	Y
32 Anderson	Y	Y	Y	N	Y	Y	N	Y
33 Clawson	N	Y	Y	N	Y	Y	Y	N
34 Hannaford	Y	Y	Y	Y	Y	Y	N	Y
35 Lloyd	Y	Y	Y	Y	Y	N	N	Y
36 Brown	Y	Y	Y	Y	Y	N	N	Y
37 Pettis	Y	Y	Y	Y	Y	Y	N	Y
38 Patterson	Y	Y	Y	Y	Y	Y	N	Y
39 Wiggins	?	?	Y	N	N	Y	N	Y
40 Badham	Y	Y	Y	N	N	Y	Y	Y
41 Wilson, B.	Y	?	Y	Y	Y	Y	N	Y
42 Van Deerlin	Y	Y	Y	Y	Y	Y	N	Y
43 Burgener	Y	Y	Y	Y	Y	Y	N	Y
COLORADO								
1 Schroeder	Y	Y	Y	Y	Y	Y	N	Y
2 Wirth	Y	Y	Y	N	Y	N	N	Y
3 Evans	Y	Y	?	?	?	N	N	Y
4 Johnson	Y	Y	Y	Y	Y	Y	N	Y
5 Armstrong	N	Y	?	?	Y	Y	Y	Y
CONNECTICUT								
1 Cotter	Y	Y	Y	Y	Y	Y	N	Y
2 Dodd	Y	Y	Y	Y	Y	Y	N	Y
3 Giaimo	Y	Y	Y	N	Y	N	N	Y
4 McKinney	Y	Y	Y	Y	Y	Y	N	Y
5 Sarasin	†	†	Y	Y	Y	Y	N	Y
6 Moffett	Y	Y	Y	Y	Y	N	N	Y
DELAWARE								
AL Evans	Y	Y	Y	Y	N	N	Y	Y
FLORIDA								
1 Sikes	Y	Y	Y	N	Y	N	N	Y
2 Fuqua	Y	Y	Y	Y	Y	N	N	Y
3 Bennett	Y	Y	Y	Y	Y	N	Y	N
4 Chappell	Y	Y	Y	N	Y	N	N	Y
5 Kelly	N	Y	Y	N	N	N	Y	Y
6 Young	Y	Y	Y	N	Y	Y	Y	N
7 Gibbons	Y	Y	Y	Y	Y	N	N	Y
8 Ireland	Y	Y	Y	N	Y	N	Y	Y
9 Frey	?	?	Y	N	Y	N	Y	Y
10 Bafalis	Y	Y	Y	N	Y	N	Y	N
11 Rogers	Y	Y	Y	Y	?	N	N	Y
12 Burke	Y	Y	Y	N	N	N	Y	Y
13 Lehman	Y	Y	Y	Y	Y	Y	N	Y
14 Pepper	Y	Y	Y	Y	Y	N	N	Y
15 Fascell	Y	Y	Y	Y	Y	Y	N	?
GEORGIA								
1 Ginn	Y	Y	Y	N	Y	Y	Y	Y
2 Mathis	Y	Y	Y	N	Y	Y	Y	N
3 Brinkley	N	Y	Y	N	Y	N	Y	Y
4 Levitas	Y	Y	Y	N	Y	N	Y	Y
5 Fowler	Y	Y	Y	N	Y	N	Y	Y
6 Flynt	Y	Y	Y	N	?	N	N	Y
7 McDonald	N	Y	Y	N	N	N	Y	N
8 Evans	N	Y	Y	N	Y	Y	Y	N
9 Jenkins	N	Y	Y	N	Y	N	Y	Y
10 Barnard	Y	Y	Y	N	Y	N	Y	N
HAWAII								
1 Heftel	Y	Y	Y	N	Y	N	Y	Y
2 Akaka	Y	Y	Y	Y	Y	N	N	Y
IDAHO								
1 Symms	N	Y	Y	N	Y	N	Y	N
2 Hansen, G.	N	Y	Y	N	N	N	Y	N
ILLINOIS								
1 Metcalfe	Y	Y	Y	Y	Y	N	N	Y
2 Murphy	Y	Y	Y	Y	Y	N	Y	Y
3 Russo	Y	Y	Y	N	Y	Y	Y	Y
4 Derwinski	Y	Y	Y	N	Y	Y	Y	Y
5 Fary	Y	Y	Y	Y	Y	N	N	Y
6 Hyde	Y	Y	Y	N	Y	N	Y	#
7 Collins	Y	Y	Y	Y	Y	N	N	Y
8 Rostenkowski	Y	Y	Y	Y	Y	N	N	Y
9 Yates	Y	Y	Y	N	Y	N	N	Y
10 Mikva	Y	Y	Y	N	Y	N	N	Y
11 Annunzio	Y	Y	Y	Y	Y	N	N	Y
12 Crane	▮	#	#	N	Y	N	Y	N
13 McClory	Y	Y	Y	Y	Y	Y	N	Y
14 Erlenborn	Y	Y	Y	N	Y	Y	N	Y
15 Corcoran	Y	Y	Y	Y	Y	N	Y	Y
16 Anderson	Y	Y	Y	Y	Y	N	N	Y
17 O'Brien	Y	Y	Y	N	Y	Y	Y	Y
18 Michel	Y	N	Y	Y	Y	N	Y	Y
19 Railsback	#	Y	Y	Y	#	Y	N	Y
20 Findley	Y	Y	Y	Y	N	N	Y	Y
21 Madigan	Y	Y	Y	Y	Y	N	Y	Y
22 Shipley	Y	Y	Y	Y	Y	N	?	?
23 Price	Y	Y	Y	Y	Y	N	N	Y
24 Simon	Y	Y	Y	Y	Y	N	N	Y
INDIANA								
1 Benjamin	Y	N	Y	Y	Y	N	Y	N
2 Fithian	Y	Y	Y	Y	Y	N	N	Y
3 Brademas	Y	Y	Y	Y	Y	N	N	Y
4 Quayle	N	N	Y	N	Y	N	Y	Y
5 Hillis	Y	Y	Y	Y	Y	N	Y	Y
6 Evans	N	Y	Y	Y	Y	N	Y	N
7 Myers, J.	Y	Y	Y	Y	Y	N	Y	Y
8 Cornwell	Y	Y	Y	Y	Y	N	Y	Y
9 Hamilton	N	Y	Y	N	Y	N	Y	Y
10 Sharp	Y	Y	Y	N	Y	N	Y	Y
11 Jacobs	▮	#	Y	N	Y	N	N	Y
IOWA								
1 Leach	Y	Y	Y	Y	Y	N	N	Y
2 Blouin	Y	Y	Y	Y	?	Y	N	Y
3 Grassley	N	Y	Y	Y	Y	N	Y	Y
4 Smith	Y	Y	Y	Y	Y	N	N	Y
5 Harkin	Y	Y	Y	Y	Y	N	N	Y
6 Bedell	Y	Y	Y	Y	Y	N	N	Y

Democrats ***Republicans***

	187	188	189	190	191	192	193	194
KANSAS								
1 Sebelius	Y	Y	Y	Y	Y	Y	Y	Y
2 Keys	N	Y	Y	N	Y	N	N	Y
3 Winn	Y	Y	Y	N	Y	N	N	Y
4 Glickman	N	N	Y	N	Y	N	Y	Y
5 Skubitz	Y	Y	Y	Y	Y	?	N	Y
KENTUCKY								
1 Hubbard	Y	Y	?	?	?	?	?	?
2 Natcher	Y	Y	Y	Y	Y	N	N	Y
3 Mazzoli	Y	Y	Y	Y	Y	N	N	?
4 Snyder	Y	Y	Y	N	N	N	Y	N
5 Carter	Y	Y	Y	Y	Y	Y	N	Y
6 Breckinridge	?	?	Y	Y	Y	N	N	Y
7 Perkins	Y	Y	Y	Y	Y	N	N	Y
LOUISIANA								
1 Livingston	N	Y	Y	N	Y	Y	Y	Y
2 Boggs	#	Y	Y	Y	Y	Y	N	Y
3 Treen	Y	Y	Y	Y	Y	Y	Y	Y
4 Waggonner	Y	Y	Y	N	■	Y	Y	Y
5 Huckaby	Y	Y	Y	N	Y	Y	Y	Y
6 Moore	Y	Y	Y	Y	Y	Y	N	Y
7 Breaux	Y	Y	Y	N	Y	Y	Y	Y
8 Long	?	?	Y	Y	Y	Y	N	Y
MAINE								
1 Emery	Y	Y	Y	Y	Y	N	N	Y
2 Cohen	?	?	Y	Y	Y	N	N	Y
MARYLAND								
1 Bauman	N	Y	Y	N	N	N	Y	N
2 Long	Y	Y	Y	N	Y	N	N	Y
3 Mikulski	Y	Y	Y	Y	Y	Y	N	Y
4 Holt	N	Y	Y	N	Y	N	N	Y
5 Spellman	Y	Y	Y	Y	Y	N	N	Y
6 Byron	?	?	Y	Y	Y	N	N	Y
7 Mitchell	Y	Y	Y	Y	Y	N	N	Y
8 Steers	Y	Y	Y	Y	Y	N	N	Y
MASSACHUSETTS								
1 Conte	Y	Y	Y	Y	Y	N	N	Y
2 Boland	Y	Y	Y	Y	Y	N	N	Y
3 Early	Y	Y	N	Y	Y	N	Y	Y
4 Drinan	Y	Y	Y	Y	Y	N	N	Y
5 Tsongas	#	#	Y	Y	Y	N	■	#
6 Harrington	#	Y	Y	Y	Y	N	N	Y
7 Markey	Y	Y	Y	Y	Y	N	N	Y
8 O'Neill								
9 Moakley	Y	Y	Y	Y	Y	N	Y	Y
10 Heckler	Y	Y	Y	Y	Y	N	Y	Y
11 Burke	Y	Y	Y	Y	Y	N	N	Y
12 Studds	Y	Y	Y	Y	Y	Y	N	Y
MICHIGAN								
1 Conyers	?	?	?	?	?	■	■	?
2 Pursell	Y	Y	Y	Y	Y	Y	?	?
3 Brown	Y	Y	Y	Y	Y	Y	Y	Y
4 Stockman	■	#	Y	Y	Y	N	Y	Y
5 Sawyer	?	?	Y	Y	Y	N	N	Y
6 Carr	Y	Y	Y	Y	N	N	N	Y
7 Kildee	Y	Y	Y	Y	Y	N	N	Y
8 Traxler	Y	Y	Y	Y	Y	N	N	Y
9 Vander Jagt	Y	Y	?	?	?	?	Y	Y
10 Cederberg	Y	Y	Y	Y	Y	N	N	Y
11 Ruppe	Y	Y	?	Y	Y	N	Y	Y
12 Bonior	Y	Y	Y	Y	Y	N	N	Y
13 Diggs	Y	Y	Y	Y	Y	N	N	Y
14 Nedzi	Y	Y	Y	Y	Y	N	N	Y
15 Ford	?	?	Y	Y	?	Y	N	?
16 Dingell	Y	Y	Y	N	Y	N	Y	Y
17 Brodhead	Y	Y	Y	Y	Y	N	N	Y
18 Blanchard	N	Y	Y	Y	Y	N	N	Y
19 Broomfield	N	Y	Y	N	Y	N	Y	Y
MINNESOTA								
1 Quie	?	?	Y	Y	Y	Y	N	Y
2 Hagedorn	?	Y	Y	Y	Y	Y	Y	Y
3 Frenzel	?	Y	Y	Y	Y	N	Y	Y
4 Vento	Y	Y	Y	Y	Y	N	N	Y
5 Fraser	?	?	Y	Y	Y	Y	N	Y
6 Nolan	Y	Y	Y	Y	Y	Y	N	Y
7 Stangeland	?	Y	Y	Y	N	Y	Y	Y
8 Oberstar	Y	Y	Y	Y	Y	Y	N	Y
MISSISSIPPI								
1 Whitten	Y	Y	Y	N	Y	N	Y	Y
2 Bowen	Y	Y	Y	Y	Y	N	Y	Y
3 Montgomery	Y	Y	Y	N	Y	N	Y	Y
4 Cochran	?	?	?	?	?	?	?	?
5 Lott	Y	Y	Y	N	Y	Y	Y	Y
MISSOURI								
1 Clay	?	?	Y	Y	Y	N	N	Y
2 Young	Y	Y	Y	Y	Y	N	N	Y
3 Gephardt	Y	Y	Y	N	Y	N	N	Y

	187	188	189	190	191	192	193	194
4 Skelton	Y	Y	Y	Y	N	N	Y	N
5 Bolling	Y	Y	Y	Y	#	N	N	Y
6 Coleman	Y	Y	Y	Y	Y	N	N	Y
7 Taylor	Y	Y	Y	N	N	N	Y	N
8 Ichord	N	Y	Y	N	N	N	Y	N
9 Volkmer	Y	Y	Y	N	Y	N	N	Y
10 Burlison	Y	Y	Y	Y	Y	N	N	Y
MONTANA								
1 Baucus	Y	Y	Y	Y	Y	N	N	Y
2 Marlenee	Y	Y	Y	Y	Y	N	Y	Y
NEBRASKA								
1 Thone	#	#	#	?	#	?	?	?
2 Cavanaugh	Y	Y	?	?	?	N	N	Y
3 Smith	Y	Y	Y	Y	Y	N	Y	Y
NEVADA								
AL Santini	Y	Y	Y	Y	Y	Y	Y	Y
NEW HAMPSHIRE								
1 D'Amours	Y	Y	Y	Y	Y	Y	Y	Y
2 Cleveland	Y	N	Y	N	Y	Y	Y	Y
NEW JERSEY								
1 Florio	Y	Y	Y	Y	Y	N	Y	Y
2 Hughes	Y	Y	Y	N	N	Y	Y	Y
3 Howard	?	?	?	?	?	?	?	?
4 Thompson	?	?	Y	Y	Y	N	N	Y
5 Fenwick	?	Y	Y	Y	N	N	N	Y
6 Forsythe	Y	Y	Y	Y	Y	Y	Y	Y
7 Maguire	Y	Y	Y	N	Y	N	N	Y
8 Roe	Y	Y	Y	Y	Y	N	N	Y
9 Hollenbeck	Y	Y	Y	Y	Y	N	N	Y
10 Rodino	?	?	?	?	?	?	■	?
11 Minish	Y	Y	Y	Y	Y	N	Y	Y
12 Rinaldo	Y	Y	Y	Y	Y	N	Y	Y
13 Meyner	Y	Y	Y	Y	Y	N	N	Y
14 LeFante	Y	N	Y	Y	Y	N	N	Y
15 Patten	Y	Y	Y	N	Y	N	N	Y
NEW MEXICO								
1 Lujan	Y	Y	Y	N	Y	Y	Y	Y
2 Runnels	?	?	?	?	?	?	?	?
NEW YORK								
1 Pike	Y	Y	Y	Y	Y	N	N	Y
2 Downey	Y	Y	Y	Y	Y	N	N	Y
3 Ambro	?	Y	Y	Y	Y	N	N	Y
4 Lent	Y	Y	Y	N	Y	Y	Y	Y
5 Wydler	?	?	Y	N	N	N	Y	Y
6 Wolff	Y	Y	Y	Y	Y	N	N	Y
7 Addabbo	Y	Y	Y	Y	Y	N	Y	Y
8 Rosenthal	Y	Y	Y	Y	Y	N	N	Y
9 Delaney	Y	Y	Y	Y	Y	N	N	Y
10 Biaggi	Y	Y	Y	Y	Y	N	N	Y
11 Scheuer	Y	Y	Y	N	Y	N	N	Y
12 Chisholm	Y	Y	Y	Y	Y	N	N	Y
13 Solarz	Y	Y	Y	Y	Y	N	N	Y
14 Richmond	Y	Y	Y	Y	Y	N	N	Y
15 Zeferetti	Y	Y	Y	Y	Y	Y	Y	Y
16 Holtzman	Y	Y	Y	?	Y	N	N	Y
17 Murphy	Y	Y	Y	Y	Y	Y	N	Y
18 Green	Y	Y	Y	Y	Y	N	N	Y
19 Rangel	Y	Y	Y	Y	Y	N	N	Y
20 Weiss	Y	Y	Y	Y	Y	N	N	Y
21 Garcia	Y	Y	Y	?	Y	Y	N	Y
22 Bingham	Y	Y	Y	Y	Y	N	N	Y
23 Caputo	Y	Y	Y	Y	Y	N	Y	Y
24 Ottinger	Y	Y	Y	Y	Y	N	N	Y
25 Fish	Y	Y	Y	Y	Y	Y	N	Y
26 Gilman	Y	Y	Y	Y	Y	Y	Y	Y
27 McHugh	Y	Y	Y	Y	Y	N	N	Y
28 Stratton	Y	Y	Y	Y	Y	Y	N	Y
29 Pattison	Y	Y	Y	Y	Y	N	N	Y
30 McEwen	Y	Y	Y	N	Y	Y	Y	Y
31 Mitchell	Y	Y	Y	Y	Y	N	Y	Y
32 Hanley	Y	Y	Y	Y	Y	N	N	Y
33 Walsh	Y	Y	Y	N	Y	Y	Y	Y
34 Horton	Y	Y	Y	Y	?	N	Y	Y
35 Conable	?	?	Y	N	Y	Y	N	Y
36 LaFalce	Y	Y	Y	Y	Y	N	N	Y
37 Nowak	Y	Y	Y	Y	Y	N	N	Y
38 Kemp	Y	Y	?	Y	Y	N	Y	Y
39 Lundine	#	#	Y	Y	Y	■	N	Y
NORTH CAROLINA								
1 Jones	?	?	?	#	?	N	Y	Y
2 Fountain	N	Y	Y	N	Y	N	Y	Y
3 Whitley	?	?	?	?	?	?	?	?
4 Andrews	?	?	Y	Y	Y	?	?	Y
5 Neal	Y	Y	Y	N	Y	N	Y	Y
6 Preyer	Y	Y	Y	Y	Y	N	N	Y
7 Rose	#	#	#	#	#	■	N	Y
8 Hefner	Y	Y	#	#	#	■	#	#

	187	188	189	190	191	192	193	194
9 Martin	#	Y	Y	Y	Y	N	N	Y
10 Broyhill	?	Y	Y	Y	Y	N	Y	N
11 Gudger	#	#	Y	Y	Y	N	N	Y
NORTH DAKOTA								
AL Andrews	Y	Y	Y	Y	Y	Y	Y	Y
OHIO								
1 Gradison	Y	Y	Y	Y	N	Y	N	Y
2 Luken	Y	Y	Y	N	Y	N	N	?
3 Whalen	Y	Y	Y	Y	Y	Y	N	Y
4 Guyer	Y	Y	Y	N	N	N	Y	Y
5 Latta	N	Y	Y	N	Y	N	Y	N
6 Harsha	Y	P	Y	N	N	Y	Y	N
7 Brown	Y	Y	Y	Y	Y	Y	Y	Y
8 Kindness	Y	Y	Y	Y	N	Y	Y	N
9 Ashley	?	?	Y	Y	Y	N	N	Y
10 Miller	N	Y	Y	N	Y	N	Y	Y
11 Stanton	?	?	Y	Y	Y	N	N	Y
12 Devine	N	N	Y	N	N	N	Y	N
13 Pease	Y	Y	Y	Y	Y	N	N	Y
14 Seiberling	Y	Y	Y	Y	Y	Y	N	Y
15 Wylie	Y	Y	Y	N	Y	N	N	Y
16 Regula	Y	Y	Y	Y	Y	N	Y	Y
17 Ashbrook	?	?	Y	N	N	N	Y	N
18 Applegate	Y	Y	Y	Y	Y	N	Y	Y
19 Carney	Y	Y	Y	Y	Y	Y	N	Y
20 Oakar	N	Y	Y	Y	Y	N	N	Y
21 Stokes	?	?	Y	Y	Y	N	N	Y
22 Vanik	Y	Y	Y	Y	Y	N	N	Y
23 Mottl	N	N	Y	Y	N	N	Y	N
OKLAHOMA								
1 Jones	N	N	Y	Y	Y	N	Y	Y
2 Risenhoover	N	Y	Y	N	Y	Y	Y	Y
3 Watkins	Y	Y	Y	N	Y	N	Y	Y
4 Steed	Y	Y	Y	Y	Y	N	Y	Y
5 Edwards	N	Y	Y	N	Y	N	Y	N
6 English	Y	Y	Y	N	Y	N	Y	Y
OREGON								
1 AuCoin	Y	Y	Y	N	N	N	Y	Y
2 Ullman	Y	Y	Y	Y	Y	N	N	Y
3 Duncan	Y	N	Y	?	N	N	N	Y
4 Weaver	Y	Y	Y	Y	Y	N	N	Y
PENNSYLVANIA								
1 Myers, M.	Y	Y	Y	Y	Y	N	N	Y
2 Nix	Y	Y	Y	Y	Y	?	?	?
3 Lederer	Y	Y	Y	Y	Y	N	Y	Y
4 Eilberg	?	?	?	?	?	?	?	?
5 Schulze	Y	Y	Y	Y	Y	N	Y	N
6 Yatron	Y	Y	Y	N	Y	N	Y	Y
7 Edgar	Y	Y	Y	Y	Y	N	N	Y
8 Kostmayer	N	Y	N	N	Y	N	N	Y
9 Shuster	Y	Y	Y	N	Y	N	Y	Y
10 McDade	Y	Y	Y	Y	Y	N	N	Y
11 Flood	Y	Y	Y	Y	Y	N	N	Y
12 Murtha	Y	Y	Y	Y	Y	N	Y	Y
13 Coughlin	Y	Y	Y	Y	Y	N	Y	Y
14 Moorhead	Y	Y	Y	Y	Y	Y	N	Y
15 Rooney	Y	Y	Y	Y	Y	Y	N	Y
16 Walker	N	Y	Y	N	Y	N	Y	Y
17 Ertel	N	Y	Y	N	Y	N	N	Y
18 Walgren	N	Y	#	#	?	?	?	?
19 Goodling, W.	N	Y	Y	N	N	N	Y	N
20 Gaydos	Y	Y	Y	Y	Y	N	Y	Y
21 Dent	Y	Y	Y	Y	Y	N	Y	Y
22 Murphy	Y	Y	Y	Y	Y	N	N	Y
23 Ammerman	Y	?	?	?	?	?	N	Y
24 Marks	Y	Y	Y	Y	Y	N	N	Y
25 Myers, G.	N	N	Y	Y	N	N	Y	Y
RHODE ISLAND								
1 St Germain	Y	Y	Y	Y	Y	N	N	Y
2 Beard	Y	Y	Y	Y	Y	N	N	Y
SOUTH CAROLINA								
1 Davis	Y	Y	Y	Y	Y	Y	Y	Y
2 Spence	Y	Y	Y	N	Y	Y	Y	Y
3 Derrick	Y	Y	Y	N	Y	N	Y	Y
4 Mann	?	?	Y	N	Y	N	N	Y
5 Holland	?	?	Y	Y	Y	N	N	Y
6 Jenrette	?	?	Y	N	Y	Y	Y	Y
SOUTH DAKOTA								
1 Pressler	?	?	Y	Y	Y	N	N	Y
2 Abdnor	Y	Y	Y	Y	Y	N	Y	Y
TENNESSEE								
1 Quillen	Y	Y	Y	Y	Y	N	Y	Y
2 Duncan	Y	Y	Y	Y	Y	N	Y	Y
3 Lloyd	Y	Y	Y	N	Y	N	N	Y
4 Gore	N	Y	N	Y	Y	N	N	Y
5 Allen	Y	N	Y	Y	N	N	Y	Y
6 Beard	N	Y	Y	N	Y	N	N	Y

	187	188	189	190	191	192	193	194
7 Jones	Y	Y	Y	Y	Y	N	N	Y
8 Ford	Y	Y	Y	Y	Y	N	N	Y
TEXAS								
1 Hall	Y	Y	Y	N	Y	N	Y	Y
2 Wilson, C.	Y	Y	Y	N	Y	Y	Y	Y
3 Collins	N	N	Y	N	Y	N	Y	N
4 Roberts	Y	Y	Y	Y	N	N	Y	Y
5 Mattox	Y	Y	Y	N	Y	N	Y	N
6 Teague	?	?	?	?	?	N	N	Y
7 Archer	N	Y	Y	N	N	Y	Y	Y
8 Eckhardt	Y	Y	Y	Y	?	N	N	Y
9 Brooks	Y	Y	Y	Y	Y	N	N	Y
10 Pickle	Y	Y	Y	Y	Y	N	?	Y
11 Poage	Y	Y	Y	Y	Y	N	Y	Y
12 Wright	Y	Y	Y	Y	Y	N	N	Y
13 Hightower	Y	Y	Y	Y	Y	N	Y	Y
14 Young	?	?	?	?	?	?	?	?
15 de la Garza	?	?	Y	Y	Y	Y	Y	Y
16 White	Y	Y	Y	Y	Y	N	N	Y
17 Burleson	Y	Y	Y	N	Y	N	Y	Y
18 Jordan	Y	Y	Y	Y	Y	N	N	Y
19 Mahon	Y	Y	Y	Y	Y	Y	Y	Y
20 Gonzalez	Y	Y	Y	?	Y	N	N	Y
21 Krueger	?	?	?	?	?	?	?	?
22 Gammage	?	?	?	?	?	?	?	?
23 Kazen	?	?	?	?	?	?	?	?
24 Milford	Y	Y	Y	N	Y	?	N	Y
UTAH								
1 McKay	Y	Y	N	N	Y	N	Y	Y
2 Marriott	Y	Y	Y	N	Y	N	Y	Y
VERMONT								
AL Jeffords	?	?	N	Y	Y	N	Y	Y
VIRGINIA								
1 Trible	Y	Y	Y	N	Y	N	Y	Y
2 Whitehurst	Y	Y	Y	Y	Y	N	Y	Y
3 Satterfield	N	Y	Y	N	N	N	Y	N
4 Daniel	N	Y	Y	N	N	N	Y	Y
5 Daniel	N	Y	Y	N	N	N	Y	Y
6 Butler	?	?	Y	N	N	N	Y	Y
7 Robinson	N	Y	Y	N	Y	N	Y	N
8 Harris	Y	Y	Y	Y	Y	N	N	Y
9 Wampler	Y	Y	Y	Y	Y	N	N	Y
10 Fisher	Y	Y	Y	N	Y	N	N	Y
WASHINGTON								
1 Pritchard	Y	Y	Y	Y	Y	Y	Y	Y
2 Meeds	Y	Y	Y	Y	N	Y	N	Y
3 Bonker	Y	Y	?	?	?	?	?	?
4 McCormack	Y	Y	Y	Y	N	N	N	Y
5 Foley	Y	Y	Y	Y	N	Y	N	Y
6 Dicks	Y	Y	Y	Y	N	Y	N	Y
7 Cunningham	Y	Y	Y	N	N	Y	Y	Y
WEST VIRGINIA								
1 Mollohan	Y	Y	?	?	Y	N	Y	Y
2 Staggers	Y	Y	Y	Y	Y	N	Y	Y
3 Slack	Y	Y	Y	Y	Y	N	Y	Y
4 Rahall	?	?	#	Y	Y	N	N	Y
WISCONSIN								
1 Aspin	?	?	?	?	?	?	?	?
2 Kastenmeier	Y	Y	Y	Y	Y	N	N	Y
3 Baldus	Y	Y	Y	Y	Y	N	N	Y
4 Zablocki	Y	Y	Y	Y	Y	N	N	Y
5 Reuss	Y	Y	Y	Y	Y	N	N	Y
6 Steiger	Y	Y	Y	Y	Y	N	N	Y
7 Obey	Y	Y	Y	Y	Y	N	N	Y
8 Cornell	Y	Y	Y	Y	Y	N	N	Y
9 Kasten	Y	Y	Y	N	Y	N	Y	Y
WYOMING								
AL Roncalio	?	?	Y	Y	Y	N	N	Y

Democrats ***Republicans***

195. HR 8494. Lobbying Disclosure. Adoption of the rule (H Res 1139) providing for House floor consideration of the bill to regulate lobbying before congressional members. Adopted 379-15: R 127-11; D 252-4 (ND 179-0; SD 73-4), April 19, 1978.

196. HR 8494. Lobbying Disclosure. Kindness, R-Ohio, amendment to expand the geographical exemption that applied to communications made by an organization or individual with its principal place of business in a district or county represented by a representative or a state represented by a senator. Rejected 195-212: R 122-17; D 73-195 (ND 37-149; SD 36-46), April 19, 1978.

197. HR 8494. Lobbying Disclosure. Flowers, D-Ala., amendment to require that registered lobbying organizations disclose mass mailings and other solicitations or "indirect lobbying" designed to bring constituent pressure on a representative or senator. Adopted 245-161: R 63-77; D 182-84 (ND 126-60; SD 56-24), April 19, 1978.

198. HR 8494. Lobbying Disclosure. Danielson, D-Calif., motion that the House resolve itself into the Committee of the Whole for further consideration of the Public Disclosure of Lobbying Act. Motion agreed to 369-15: R 129-7; D 240-8 (ND 162-8; SD 78-0), April 20, 1978.

199. HR 8494. Lobbying Disclosure. Danielson, D-Calif., motion to table (kill) the Downey, D-N.Y., motion to reconsider the Danielson motion *(see vote 198, above)*. Motion agreed to 362-26: R 126-10; D 236-16 (ND 158-15; SD 78-1), April 20, 1978.

200. HR 8494. Lobbying Disclosure. Pressler, R-S.D., amendment to include departments or agencies of the executive branch of the federal government and various White House offices under the provisions of the lobbying disclosure bill. Rejected 44-350: R 36-100; D 8-250 (ND 5-174; SD 3-76), April 20, 1978.

201. HR 8494. Lobbying Disclosure. Railsback, R-Ill., amendment to require registered lobbying organizations to report the name and address of any organization contributing $3,000 or more during the calendar year to the registered lobbying organization and the amount of the contribution given if spent in whole or in part by an organization that spends at least 1 percent of its time lobbying. Adopted 251-135: R 89-45; D 162-90 (ND 111-64; SD 51-26), April 20, 1978.

202. HR 8494. Lobbying Disclosure. Danielson, D-Calif., motion to end all debate on the bill and amendments to the bill at 5 p.m. Motion rejected 158-215: R 21-108; D 137-107 (ND 90-80; SD 47-27), April 20, 1978.

KEY

Y Voted for (yea).
✓ Paired for.
† Announced for.
# CQ Poll for.
N Voted against (nay).
X Paired against.
- Announced against.
▮ CQ Poll against.
P Voted "present."
● Voted "present" to avoid possible conflict of interest.
? Did not vote or otherwise make a position known.

	195	196	197	198	199	200	201	202
ALABAMA								
1 Edwards	Y	Y	Y	Y	Y	N	N	N
2 Dickinson	Y	Y	Y	Y	Y	Y	N	N
3 Nichols	Y	N	Y	Y	Y	N	Y	N
4 Bevill	Y	N	Y	Y	Y	N	N	N
5 Flippo	Y	N	Y	Y	Y	N	N	N
6 Buchanan	Y	Y	Y	Y	Y	N	Y	N
7 Flowers	Y	N	Y	Y	Y	N	N	N
ALASKA								
AL Young	Y	Y	Y	Y	?	Y	N	N
ARIZONA								
1 Rhodes	Y	Y	N	Y	N	N	?	?
2 Udall	Y	N	N	Y	Y	N	N	Y
3 Stump	Y	Y	N	Y	Y	N	N	N
4 Rudd	Y	Y	N	Y	N	N	N	N
ARKANSAS								
1 Alexander	Y	N	?	Y	Y	N	?	Y
2 Tucker	?	N	Y	?	?	?	?	?
3 Hammerschmidt	Y	Y	Y	Y	N	N	N	N
4 Thornton	?	?	?	?	?	?	?	?
CALIFORNIA								
1 Johnson	Y	N	Y	Y	Y	N	N	Y
2 Clausen	?	†	?	?	?	?	?	?
3 Moss	Y	N	N	N	Y	N	N	N
4 Leggett	Y	N	Y	Y	#	N	Y	Y
5 Burton, J.	Y	?	✓	?	?	?	✓	?
6 Burton, P.	?	N	N	Y	Y	N	Y	Y
7 Miller	Y	N	N	N	Y	N	Y	N
8 Dellums	?	X	X	?	▮	▮	X	▮
9 Stark	Y	N	N	Y	N	N	N	N
10 Edwards	Y	N	N	Y	N	N	N	N
11 Ryan	Y	Y	Y	Y	Y	N	Y	Y
12 McCloskey	Y	Y	Y	Y	Y	N	Y	N
13 Mineta	Y	N	N	Y	Y	N	Y	Y
14 McFall	Y	N	N	Y	Y	N	N	Y
15 Sisk	Y	N	N	?	?	N	N	Y
16 Panetta	Y	N	N	Y	Y	N	Y	N
17 Krebs	Y	N	N	Y	Y	N	N	Y
18 Ketchum	Y	Y	N	Y	Y	N	Y	N
19 Lagomarsino	Y	Y	N	Y	Y	N	N	N
20 Goldwater	?	Y	N	Y	Y	N	N	Y
21 Corman	Y	N	N	Y	Y	N	N	N
22 Moorhead	Y	Y	N	Y	Y	N	N	N
23 Beilenson	Y	N	N	Y	Y	N	N	N
24 Waxman	Y	N	Y	Y	Y	N	N	Y
25 Roybal	Y	N	N	Y	Y	N	N	Y
26 Rousselot	N	Y	N	Y	Y	Y	Y	N
27 Dornan	Y	Y	N	Y	Y	Y	Y	Y
28 Burke	?	X	X	?	?	?	X	?
29 Hawkins	Y	N	N	Y	Y	N	N	?
30 Danielson	Y	N	N	Y	Y	N	N	Y
31 Wilson, C.H.	Y	Y	?	?	?	Y	N	N
32 Anderson	Y	N	N	Y	Y	N	N	N
33 Clawson	N	Y	N	Y	Y	Y	N	N
34 Hannaford	Y	N	Y	Y	Y	N	Y	Y
35 Lloyd	Y	N	N	Y	Y	N	N	Y
36 Brown	Y	N	N	?	Y	N	N	?
37 Pettis	Y	?	Y	Y	Y	N	N	N
38 Patterson	Y	N	N	Y	Y	N	Y	N
39 Wiggins	N	Y	N	Y	Y	N	N	N
40 Badham	Y	Y	Y	Y	Y	Y	Y	N
41 Wilson, B.	Y	Y	Y	N	N	N	Y	Y
42 Van Deerlin	Y	N	Y	Y	Y	N	N	Y
43 Burgener	Y	Y	N	Y	Y	N	N	N
COLORADO								
1 Schroeder	Y	N	Y	Y	Y	N	Y	N
2 Wirth	Y	N	Y	N	Y	N	Y	Y
3 Evans	Y	Y	Y	Y	Y	N	N	Y
4 Johnson	Y	Y	N	Y	Y	N	N	N
5 Armstrong	N	Y	N	Y	Y	Y	N	N
CONNECTICUT								
1 Cotter	Y	Y	Y	Y	Y	N	Y	Y
2 Dodd	Y	Y	N	?	Y	N	N	N
3 Giaimo	Y	?	N	Y	Y	N	N	N
4 McKinney	Y	Y	Y	Y	Y	N	Y	N
5 Sarasin	Y	Y	Y	Y	Y	N	Y	N
6 Moffett	Y	N	Y	Y	N	N	Y	N
DELAWARE								
AL Evans	Y	Y	N	Y	Y	N	N	N
FLORIDA								
1 Sikes	Y	Y	Y	?	Y	N	N	Y
2 Fuqua	Y	N	Y	Y	Y	N	N	N
3 Bennett	Y	N	Y	Y	Y	N	Y	Y
4 Chappell	#	Y	Y	Y	Y	N	Y	Y
5 Kelly	Y	Y	N	Y	Y	N	N	N
6 Young	Y	N	Y	Y	Y	Y	Y	N
7 Gibbons	Y	Y	Y	Y	Y	N	Y	Y
8 Ireland	Y	N	N	Y	Y	N	Y	N
9 Frey	Y	Y	Y	?	?	?	?	?
10 Bafalis	Y	Y	N	Y	Y	N	Y	N
11 Rogers	Y	N	Y	Y	Y	N	Y	Y
12 Burke	Y	Y	Y	Y	Y	Y	Y	N
13 Lehman	Y	N	Y	Y	Y	▮	?	?
14 Pepper	Y	†	Y	Y	Y	N	N	Y
15 Fascell	Y	N	Y	Y	Y	N	Y	Y
GEORGIA								
1 Ginn	Y	Y	Y	Y	Y	N	Y	Y
2 Mathis	?	Y	Y	?	Y	N	Y	N
3 Brinkley	Y	N	Y	Y	Y	N	Y	Y
4 Levitas	Y	Y	N	Y	Y	N	Y	Y
5 Fowler	Y	N	N	Y	Y	N	Y	N
6 Flynt	Y	Y	N	Y	Y	N	N	Y
7 McDonald	N	Y	N	Y	Y	Y	Y	N
8 Evans	Y	Y	Y	#	Y	N	Y	N
9 Jenkins	Y	N	N	Y	Y	N	Y	Y
10 Barnard	Y	N	N	Y	Y	N	?	?
HAWAII								
1 Heftel	Y	N	Y	Y	Y	N	Y	N
2 Akaka	Y	N	N	Y	Y	N	N	Y
IDAHO								
1 Symms	Y	Y	N	N	Y	Y	Y	N
2 Hansen, G.	N	Y	N	N	Y	?	?	?
ILLINOIS								
1 Metcalfe	Y	N	Y	Y	Y	N	Y	Y
2 Murphy	Y	Y	Y	Y	Y	N	N	Y
3 Russo	Y	Y	Y	#	#	▮	#	▮
4 Derwinski	Y	N	N	Y	Y	N	Y	N
5 Fary	Y	Y	Y	Y	Y	N	N	Y
6 Hyde	Y	Y	N	Y	Y	N	N	N
7 Collins	Y	N	Y	Y	Y	N	Y	Y
8 Rostenkowski	Y	Y	Y	Y	Y	N	N	N
9 Yates	Y	N	Y	Y	Y	N	N	N
10 Mikva	Y	N	Y	Y	Y	N	Y	Y
11 Annunzio	Y	Y	Y	Y	Y	N	N	Y
12 Crane	Y	Y	N	Y	Y	Y	Y	N
13 McClory	Y	Y	N	Y	Y	N	N	▮
14 Erlenborn	Y	Y	N	Y	Y	N	Y	N
15 Corcoran	Y	Y	N	Y	Y	N	Y	N
16 Anderson	Y	N	Y	Y	Y	N	Y	N
17 O'Brien	Y	?	N	Y	Y	?	?	?
18 Michel	Y	Y	X	Y	Y	N	Y	▮
19 Railsback	Y	N	Y	Y	Y	N	Y	Y
20 Findley	Y	Y	N	Y	Y	N	Y	Y
21 Madigan	Y	Y	Y	Y	?	N	Y	Y
22 Shipley	Y	Y	Y	?	?	?	X	?
23 Price	Y	Y	Y	Y	Y	N	N	Y
24 Simon	Y	N	Y	Y	Y	N	?	?
INDIANA								
1 Benjamin	Y	Y	N	Y	Y	N	N	Y
2 Fithian	Y	N	Y	Y	Y	N	Y	Y
3 Brademas	Y	N	Y	Y	Y	N	Y	Y
4 Quayle	Y	Y	N	N	N	Y	Y	N
5 Hillis	Y	Y	N	Y	Y	N	Y	Y
6 Evans	Y	Y	Y	Y	Y	Y	Y	N
7 Myers, J.	Y	Y	N	Y	Y	N	Y	N
8 Cornwell	?	N	N	Y	Y	N	Y	N
9 Hamilton	Y	N	Y	Y	Y	N	Y	Y
10 Sharp	Y	N	Y	Y	Y	N	Y	N
11 Jacobs	Y	Y	Y	Y	Y	N	Y	N
IOWA								
1 Leach	Y	N	Y	Y	Y	Y	Y	N
2 Blouin	Y	N	Y	Y	Y	N	Y	Y
3 Grassley	Y	Y	N	Y	Y	N	N	N
4 Smith	Y	N	Y	Y	Y	N	Y	Y
5 Harkin	Y	N	Y	N	N	N	Y	N
6 Bedell	Y	N	Y	Y	Y	N	Y	N

Democrats ***Republicans***

	195	196	197	198	199	200	201	202
KANSAS								
1 Sebelius	Y	Y	N	Y	Y	N	N	N
2 Keys	Y	N	Y	Y	Y	N	Y	Y
3 Winn	Y	Y	Y	Y	Y	▮	#	▮
4 Glickman	Y	N	N	Y	Y	N	Y	Y
5 Skubitz	Y	Y	N	?	Y	Y	?	?
KENTUCKY								
1 Hubbard	Y	Y	Y	Y	Y	N	Y	N
2 Natcher	Y	N	Y	Y	Y	N	Y	N
3 Mazzoli	Y	N	Y	Y	Y	N	Y	Y
4 Snyder	Y	Y	Y	Y	Y	N	N	Y
5 Carter	Y	Y	Y	Y	Y	Y	N	N
6 Breckinridge	Y	N	Y	Y	?	N	?	?
7 Perkins	Y	N	Y	Y	Y	N	Y	Y
LOUISIANA								
1 Livingston	Y	Y	N	Y	Y	N	Y	N
2 Boggs	Y	N	Y	Y	Y	N	N	N
3 Treen	Y	Y	Y	Y	Y	N	Y	N
4 Waggonner	Y	Y	N	Y	Y	N	Y	N
5 Huckaby	Y	Y	N	Y	Y	N	Y	Y
6 Moore	Y	Y	N	Y	Y	N	Y	N
7 Breaux	Y	✓	Y	Y	Y	N	Y	Y
8 Long	Y	N	Y	Y	Y	N	N	Y
MAINE								
1 Emery	Y	N	Y	Y	Y	N	Y	N
2 Cohen	Y	N	Y	Y	Y	N	Y	N
MARYLAND								
1 Bauman	Y	Y	N	Y	Y	Y	Y	N
2 Long	Y	N	Y	Y	Y	Y	Y	Y
3 Mikulski	Y	N	N	?	?	?	X	?
4 Holt	Y	Y	N	Y	Y	N	N	N
5 Spellman	Y	N	Y	Y	Y	N	Y	Y
6 Byron	Y	N	Y	Y	Y	N	N	N
7 Mitchell	Y	N	N	N	?	N	N	N
8 Steers	Y	Y	Y	Y	Y	N	Y	N
MASSACHUSETTS								
1 Conte	Y	Y	N	Y	Y	N	N	Y
2 Boland	Y	N	N	Y	Y	N	Y	Y
3 Early	Y	N	Y	Y	Y	N	Y	N
4 Drinan	Y	N	Y	Y	Y	N	N	N
5 Tsongas	Y	N	Y	Y	Y	N	Y	N
6 Harrington	Y	N	N	Y	Y	N	Y	Y
7 Markey	Y	N	N	Y	N	N	N	N
8 O'Neill								
9 Moakley	Y	N	Y	#	Y	N	N	Y
10 Heckler	Y	N	Y	Y	Y	Y	Y	N
11 Burke	Y	N	Y	Y	Y	N	Y	Y
12 Studds	Y	N	N	Y	Y	N	Y	N
MICHIGAN								
1 Conyers	?	X	X	?	?	?	X	▮
2 Pursell	?	Y	N	?	Y	?	?	?
3 Brown	Y	Y	N	Y	Y	N	N	N
4 Stockman	Y	Y	N	Y	Y	Y	N	N
5 Sawyer	Y	Y	N	Y	Y	N	N	Y
6 Carr	Y	N	Y	Y	Y	N	Y	N
7 Kildee	Y	N	Y	Y	N	N	Y	N
8 Traxler	Y	N	N	Y	Y	N	✓	▮
9 Vander Jagt	Y	Y	N	Y	Y	N	Y	N
10 Cederberg	?	✓	?	?	?	?	?	?
11 Ruppe	Y	Y	N	Y	Y	N	N	N
12 Bonior	Y	N	N	N	N	N	Y	N
13 Diggs	?	N	Y	?	Y	N	Y	?
14 Nedzi	?	?	?	Y	Y	N	Y	Y
15 Ford	Y	N	Y	?	Y	N	N	Y
16 Dingell	Y	N	Y	Y	Y	N	Y	N
17 Brodhead	Y	N	Y	Y	Y	N	Y	Y
18 Blanchard	Y	N	Y	Y	Y	N	Y	Y
19 Broomfield	Y	Y	N	N	N	Y	Y	N
MINNESOTA								
1 Quie	Y	Y	N	Y	Y	Y	Y	N
2 Hagedorn	Y	Y	N	Y	Y	N	Y	N
3 Frenzel	Y	Y	Y	Y	Y	N	Y	N
4 Vento	Y	N	Y	Y	Y	N	Y	N
5 Fraser	?	N	Y	Y	Y	N	Y	Y
6 Nolan	Y	N	Y	N	N	N	Y	N
7 Stangeland	Y	Y	N	Y	Y	N	Y	N
8 Oberstar	Y	Y	N	Y	Y	N	Y	Y
MISSISSIPPI								
1 Whitten	Y	Y	?	Y	Y	N	Y	Y
2 Bowen	Y	Y	N	Y	Y	N	N	Y
3 Montgomery	Y	Y	N	Y	Y	N	N	Y
4 Cochran	?	?	?	?	?	?	?	?
5 Lott	Y	Y	Y	Y	Y	N	Y	N
MISSOURI								
1 Clay	Y	N	Y	Y	Y	N	N	N
2 Young	Y	N	Y	Y	Y	N	Y	N
3 Gephardt	Y	N	N	Y	Y	N	Y	N
4 Skelton	Y	N	Y	Y	Y	N	Y	N
5 Bolling	Y	N	Y	Y	Y	N	Y	Y
6 Coleman	Y	Y	Y	Y	Y	N	Y	N
7 Taylor	Y	Y	Y	Y	Y	N	N	Y
8 Ichord	Y	Y	Y	Y	Y	Y	Y	N
9 Volkmer	Y	N	N	Y	Y	N	Y	N
10 Burlison	Y	N	Y	Y	Y	N	Y	Y
MONTANA								
1 Baucus	Y	N	Y	Y	Y	N	Y	N
2 Marlenee	Y	N	Y	Y	N	Y	N	?
NEBRASKA								
1 Thone	#	?	?	#	?	▮	?	?
2 Cavanaugh	Y	N	Y	Y	Y	?	Y	Y
3 Smith	Y	Y	N	Y	Y	Y	N	N
NEVADA								
AL Santini	Y	N	N	Y	Y	?	N	N
NEW HAMPSHIRE								
1 D'Amours	Y	N	Y	Y	Y	N	Y	Y
2 Cleveland	Y	Y	Y	Y	Y	Y	Y	N
NEW JERSEY								
1 Florio	Y	N	Y	Y	Y	N	Y	Y
2 Hughes	Y	N	N	Y	Y	N	Y	N
3 Howard	?	?	✓	?	?	?	✓	?
4 Thompson	Y	N	Y	?	Y	N	Y	Y
5 Fenwick	Y	N	Y	Y	Y	N	Y	Y
6 Forsythe	Y	Y	N	Y	Y	Y	N	N
7 Maguire	Y	N	Y	Y	Y	N	Y	Y
8 Roe	Y	N	N	Y	Y	N	Y	Y
9 Hollenbeck	Y	N	Y	Y	Y	N	Y	Y
10 Rodino	?	X	X	?	?	▮	✓	?
11 Minish	Y	N	Y	Y	Y	N	Y	N
12 Rinaldo	Y	N	Y	Y	Y	N	Y	N
13 Meyner	Y	N	Y	Y	Y	N	Y	Y
14 LeFante	Y	N	Y	Y	Y	N	Y	Y
15 Patten	Y	N	Y	Y	Y	N	N	Y
NEW MEXICO								
1 Lujan	Y	Y	Y	Y	Y	N	Y	Y
2 Runnels	?	✓	✓	?	?	?	✓	#
NEW YORK								
1 Pike	Y	Y	Y	Y	Y	N	Y	N
2 Downey	Y	N	Y	Y	Y	N	N	N
3 Ambro	?	Y	Y	Y	Y	N	Y	?
4 Lent	Y	Y	Y	Y	Y	N	Y	Y
5 Wydler	Y	Y	Y	Y	Y	Y	Y	N
6 Wolff	Y	N	Y	Y	Y	N	Y	Y
7 Addabbo	Y	N	Y	Y	#	N	Y	N
8 Rosenthal	Y	N	Y	Y	Y	N	N	Y
9 Delaney	Y	Y	Y	Y	Y	N	N	N
10 Biaggi	Y	Y	N	Y	Y	N	Y	N
11 Scheuer	Y	N	Y	Y	Y	N	Y	N
12 Chisholm	Y	N	N	#	#	N	N	N
13 Solarz	?	N	N	Y	Y	N	Y	N
14 Richmond	Y	N	Y	Y	Y	N	N	N
15 Zeferetti	Y	Y	Y	Y	Y	N	Y	N
16 Holtzman	Y	N	N	Y	Y	N	N	N
17 Murphy	Y	Y	N	?	Y	N	N	N
18 Green	Y	N	Y	Y	Y	N	Y	N
19 Rangel	Y	N	Y	Y	N	N	N	N
20 Weiss	Y	N	N	Y	Y	N	N	N
21 Garcia	Y	N	N	Y	Y	N	N	N
22 Bingham	Y	N	Y	Y	Y	N	N	N
23 Caputo	Y	N	Y	Y	Y	Y	Y	N
24 Ottinger	Y	N	Y	Y	Y	N	Y	N
25 Fish	Y	Y	N	Y	Y	N	N	N
26 Gilman	Y	N	Y	Y	Y	N	Y	N
27 McHugh	Y	N	N	Y	Y	N	Y	N
28 Stratton	Y	Y	N	Y	Y	N	N	N
29 Pattison	Y	N	Y	Y	N	N	Y	N
30 McEwen	Y	Y	?	?	?	?	?	?
31 Mitchell	Y	Y	Y	Y	Y	N	Y	N
32 Hanley	Y	N	Y	Y	Y	N	Y	N
33 Walsh	N	Y	Y	Y	Y	N	Y	N
34 Horton	Y	Y	Y	Y	?	N	Y	▮
35 Conable	Y	Y	Y	Y	Y	N	Y	N
36 LaFalce	#	N	Y	Y	Y	N	N	N
37 Nowak	Y	N	Y	Y	Y	N	Y	Y
38 Kemp	Y	Y	N	Y	Y	N	Y	N
39 Lundine	Y	N	Y	Y	Y	N	Y	Y
NORTH CAROLINA								
1 Jones	Y	Y	Y	Y	Y	N	N	Y
2 Fountain	Y	N	N	Y	Y	N	N	Y
3 Whitley	?	?	✓	?	?	?	X	?
4 Andrews	Y	N	N	Y	Y	N	Y	Y
5 Neal	Y	N	Y	Y	Y	N	Y	Y
6 Preyer	Y	N	Y	Y	Y	N	Y	Y
7 Rose	#	N	Y	Y	Y	N	Y	Y
8 Hefner	#	N	N	Y	Y	N	Y	Y
9 Martin	Y	Y	N	Y	Y	N	Y	N
10 Broyhill	N	Y	N	Y	Y	N	N	N
11 Gudger	Y	N	N	Y	Y	N	N	▮
NORTH DAKOTA								
AL Andrews	Y	Y	N	Y	Y	N	Y	N
OHIO								
1 Gradison	Y	Y	Y	Y	Y	N	Y	N
2 Luken	Y	N	Y	Y	Y	N	Y	N
3 Whalen	Y	N	Y	Y	Y	N	Y	N
4 Guyer	Y	Y	N	Y	Y	Y	Y	N
5 Latta	Y	Y	N	Y	Y	N	Y	Y
6 Harsha	Y	Y	N	?	Y	N	N	Y
7 Brown	Y	✓	N	N	N	Y	Y	N
8 Kindness	Y	Y	N	Y	Y	N	N	N
9 Ashley	Y	Y	Y	Y	?	N	Y	N
10 Miller	Y	Y	N	Y	Y	Y	Y	N
11 Stanton	Y	Y	N	Y	Y	N	Y	N
12 Devine	Y	Y	N	Y	Y	N	Y	N
13 Pease	Y	N	Y	Y	Y	N	Y	N
14 Seiberling	Y	N	N	Y	Y	N	▮	Y
15 Wylie	Y	Y	Y	Y	Y	N	Y	N
16 Regula	Y	Y	N	Y	Y	N	Y	N
17 Ashbrook	N	Y	N	Y	Y	Y	Y	N
18 Applegate	Y	Y	Y	Y	Y	N	Y	Y
19 Carney	Y	Y	Y	Y	Y	N	Y	Y
20 Oakar	Y	N	Y	Y	Y	N	Y	Y
21 Stokes	Y	N	Y	Y	Y	N	X	?
22 Vanik	Y	N	Y	Y	Y	N	Y	Y
23 Mottl	Y	N	Y	Y	Y	Y	Y	Y
OKLAHOMA								
1 Jones	Y	Y	Y	Y	Y	N	N	N
2 Risenhoover	N	Y	?	Y	Y	Y	N	Y
3 Watkins	?	?	#	Y	Y	N	Y	N
4 Steed	Y	N	Y	Y	Y	▮	N	Y
5 Edwards	Y	Y	N	Y	Y	Y	Y	N
6 English	Y	N	Y	Y	Y	N	Y	Y
OREGON								
1 AuCoin	Y	N	Y	Y	Y	N	Y	Y
2 Ullman	Y	N	N	#	#	N	N	N
3 Duncan	Y	Y	N	?	?	?	?	?
4 Weaver	Y	N	N	N	Y	N	N	Y
PENNSYLVANIA								
1 Myers, M.	Y	N	Y	Y	N	N	Y	?
2 Nix	Y	N	N	?	?	?	?	?
3 Lederer	Y	N	Y	Y	Y	N	Y	Y
4 Eilberg	Y	N	Y	Y	Y	N	Y	Y
5 Schulze	Y	Y	Y	Y	Y	N	Y	N
6 Yatron	Y	N	N	Y	N	N	Y	N
7 Edgar	Y	N	Y	†	†	-	†	-
8 Kostmayer	?	N	N	Y	N	N	N	N
9 Shuster	Y	Y	Y	Y	Y	Y	N	N
10 McDade	Y	Y	Y	Y	Y	N	Y	Y
11 Flood	Y	Y	N	Y	Y	N	Y	Y
12 Murtha	Y	Y	Y	Y	Y	N	Y	Y
13 Coughlin	Y	Y	Y	Y	Y	N	Y	N
14 Moorhead	Y	N	Y	Y	Y	N	N	▮
15 Rooney	Y	N	Y	Y	Y	N	Y	N
16 Walker	Y	Y	Y	Y	Y	N	Y	N
17 Ertel	Y	N	Y	Y	Y	N	Y	Y
18 Walgren	?	X	✓	Y	N	N	Y	N
19 Goodling, W.	N	Y	N	Y	?	N	N	N
20 Gaydos	Y	Y	Y	Y	Y	N	Y	Y
21 Dent	Y	Y	Y	#	#	▮	✓	#
22 Murphy	Y	N	Y	Y	N	N	Y	N
23 Ammerman	Y	N	Y	Y	Y	N	Y	Y
24 Marks	Y	Y	Y	Y	Y	N	Y	Y
25 Myers, G.	Y	Y	Y	Y	Y	N	Y	N
RHODE ISLAND								
1 St Germain	Y	N	Y	Y	Y	N	N	N
2 Beard	Y	N	Y	Y	Y	N	N	Y
SOUTH CAROLINA								
1 Davis	Y	Y	N	Y	Y	N	Y	Y
2 Spence	Y	Y	Y	Y	Y	N	N	N
3 Derrick	Y	N	Y	Y	Y	N	Y	N
4 Mann	Y	Y	?	?	?	?	?	?
5 Holland	Y	Y	N	?	?	?	?	?
6 Jenrette	Y	Y	Y	?	?	?	X	?
SOUTH DAKOTA								
1 Pressler	Y	Y	Y	Y	Y	Y	Y	N
2 Abdnor	Y	Y	N	Y	Y	N	Y	N
TENNESSEE								
1 Quillen	N	Y	N	Y	Y	N	N	N
2 Duncan	Y	Y	N	Y	Y	N	Y	Y
3 Lloyd	Y	N	Y	Y	Y	N	Y	Y
4 Gore	Y	N	N	Y	Y	N	Y	N
5 Allen	Y	N	Y	Y	Y	N	Y	Y
6 Beard	?	Y	N	Y	Y	N	Y	N
7 Jones	Y	N	N	Y	Y	N	N	?
8 Ford	Y	N	Y	Y	Y	N	N	N
TEXAS								
1 Hall	Y	Y	Y	Y	?	N	Y	Y
2 Wilson, C.	?	N	Y	Y	Y	N	Y	Y
3 Collins	N	Y	Y	N	N	Y	Y	N
4 Roberts	Y	Y	Y	Y	Y	N	Y	Y
5 Mattox	Y	Y	Y	Y	Y	N	Y	Y
6 Teague	?	?	✓	?	?	?	✓	?
7 Archer	Y	Y	N	?	Y	Y	Y	Y
8 Eckhardt	Y	N	Y	Y	Y	N	Y	N
9 Brooks	Y	Y	N	Y	Y	N	N	N
10 Pickle	Y	N	Y	Y	Y	N	N	N
11 Poage	Y	Y	Y	Y	Y	N	N	Y
12 Wright	Y	N	Y	Y	Y	N	N	Y
13 Hightower	Y	Y	Y	Y	Y	N	Y	Y
14 Young	?	Y	Y	Y	Y	N	Y	Y
15 de la Garza	Y	Y	Y	Y	Y	N	Y	?
16 White	Y	Y	Y	Y	Y	N	Y	N
17 Burleson	Y	Y	N	Y	Y	N	Y	Y
18 Jordan	Y	N	N	Y	Y	N	N	N
19 Mahon	Y	Y	Y	Y	Y	N	N	Y
20 Gonzalez	N	N	Y	Y	Y	Y	Y	Y
21 Krueger	?	X	X	?	?	?	X	?
22 Gammage	Y	N	Y	Y	Y	N	Y	N
23 Kazen	?	?	?	?	?	?	✓	?
24 Milford	Y	Y	Y	Y	N	N	Y	Y
UTAH								
1 McKay	Y	N	Y	Y	Y	N	Y	Y
2 Marriott	Y	Y	N	?	?	?	?	?
VERMONT								
AL Jeffords	Y	N	Y	Y	N	Y	Y	▮
VIRGINIA								
1 Trible	Y	Y	Y	Y	Y	N	Y	N
2 Whitehurst	Y	Y	Y	Y	Y	N	Y	N
3 Satterfield	N	Y	N	Y	Y	N	N	N
4 Daniel	?	✓	?	Y	Y	N	Y	N
5 Daniel	Y	Y	N	Y	Y	N	Y	?
6 Butler	Y	Y	N	Y	Y	N	N	N
7 Robinson	Y	Y	N	Y	Y	N	N	N
8 Harris	Y	N	Y	Y	Y	N	Y	Y
9 Wampler	Y	Y	N	Y	Y	N	N	N
10 Fisher	Y	N	Y	Y	Y	N	Y	N
WASHINGTON								
1 Pritchard	Y	Y	Y	Y	Y	N	Y	N
2 Meeds	Y	N	Y	Y	Y	N	N	Y
3 Bonker	?	?	?	?	?	?	?	?
4 McCormack	Y	Y	Y	Y	Y	N	Y	Y
5 Foley	Y	Y	N	Y	Y	N	?	?
6 Dicks	Y	Y	Y	Y	Y	N	?	N
7 Cunningham	?	Y	Y	Y	Y	N	Y	N
WEST VIRGINIA								
1 Mollohan	Y	N	Y	Y	Y	N	Y	Y
2 Staggers	Y	N	Y	Y	Y	N	N	Y
3 Slack	Y	N	Y	Y	Y	N	Y	Y
4 Rahall	Y	N	Y	#	#	▮	✓	#
WISCONSIN								
1 Aspin	?	N	Y	Y	Y	N	Y	Y
2 Kastenmeier	Y	N	Y	Y	Y	N	Y	Y
3 Baldus	Y	N	Y	Y	Y	N	N	Y
4 Zablocki	Y	N	Y	Y	Y	N	N	Y
5 Reuss	Y	N	Y	Y	Y	N	Y	Y
6 Steiger	Y	Y	N	Y	Y	N	N	N
7 Obey	Y	Y	Y	Y	Y	N	Y	Y
8 Cornell	Y	N	Y	Y	Y	N	Y	Y
9 Kasten	Y	Y	N	Y	Y	N	N	N
WYOMING								
AL Roncalio	Y	N	N	Y	Y	N	N	?

Democrats ***Republicans***

203. HR 11401. NASA Authorization. Adoption of the rule (H Res 1143) providing for House floor consideration of the bill to authorize $4.4 billion in fiscal 1979 for programs and activities of the National Aeronautics and Space Administration. Adopted 332-0: R 123-0; D 209-0 (ND 148-0; SD 61-0), April 24, 1978.

204. HR 11504. Farm Credit Revisions. Madigan, R-Ill., substitute amendment to the bill to provide, through December 1979, loans for installment payments on existing debts and for farmer and rancher operating expenses. Rejected 151-215: R 103-22; D 48-193 (ND 37-130; SD 11-63), April 24, 1978.

205. HR 11504. Farm Credit Revisions. Passage of the bill to create a two-year, $4 billion "economic emergency" loan program permitting refinancing of existing farm debts; to raise individual loan levels and most interest rates for existing farm loan programs; to require two-year reauthorizations of loan programs beginning Oct. 1, 1979, and to extend an emergency livestock credit program through Sept. 30, 1979. Passed 347-23: R 108-19; D 239-4 (ND 165-3; SD 74-1), April 24, 1978.

206. HR 11401. NASA Authorization. Teague, D-Texas, motion that the House resolve itself into the Committee of the Whole for further consideration of the bill to authorize $4.4 billion in fiscal 1979 for the National Aeronautics and Space Administration. Motion agreed to 387-3: R 138-1; D 249-2 (ND 172-2; SD 77-0), April 25, 1978.

207. HR 11401. NASA Authorization. Passage of the bill to authorize $4,415,300,000 in fiscal 1979 for operations and programs of the National Aeronautics and Space Administration, including $1.4 billion for the space shuttle program, $292 million for aeronautical research and $6 million for energy research. Passed 345-54: R 133-8; D 212-46 (ND 136-44; SD 76-2), April 25, 1978.

208. HR 11877. Peace Corps. Young, R-Fla., amendment to prohibit funds authorized by the bill to be used for programs in the Central African Empire. Rejected 169-228: R 100-40; D 69-188 (ND 24-156; SD 45-32), April 25, 1978.

209. HR 11877. Peace Corps. Passage of the bill to authorize $96 million for fiscal 1979 programs of the Peace Corps, and to amend the Peace Corps Act to emphasize assistance to the poorest nations, the need to integrate women into the economies of the third world nations and to make various administrative changes. Passed 297-102: R 87-53; D 210-49 (ND 169-13; SD 41-36), April 25, 1978.

210. H Res 1049. Equal Employment Reorganization. Adoption of the resolution to disapprove Reorganization Plan No. 1 to consolidate various equal employment programs into the Equal Employment Opportunity Commission. Rejected 39-356: R 28-110; D 11-246 (ND 4-177; SD 7-69), April 25, 1978. A "nay" was a vote supporting the president's position.

KEY

- Y Voted for (yea).
- ✓ Paired for.
- † Announced for.
- # CQ Poll for.
- N Voted against (nay).
- X Paired against.
- \- Announced against.
- ▮ CQ Poll against.
- P Voted "present."
- ● Voted "present" to avoid possible conflict of interest.
- ? Did not vote or otherwise make a position known.

	203	204	205	206	207	208	209	210
ALABAMA								
1 Edwards	Y	N	Y	Y	Y	N	Y	N
2 Dickinson	Y	Y	Y	Y	Y	Y	N	N
3 Nichols	Y	N	Y	Y	Y	Y	N	N
4 Bevill	Y	N	Y	Y	Y	Y	N	N
5 Flippo	Y	N	Y	Y	Y	Y	N	N
6 Buchanan	Y	N	Y	Y	Y	N	Y	N
7 Flowers	?	N	Y	Y	Y	Y	N	N
ALASKA								
AL Young	Y	Y	Y	Y	Y	Y	N	Y
ARIZONA								
1 Rhodes	Y	Y	Y	Y	Y	Y	Y	N
2 Udall	Y	N	Y	Y	?	N	Y	N
3 Stump	Y	N	Y	Y	Y	Y	N	N
4 Rudd	Y	N	Y	Y	Y	Y	N	Y
ARKANSAS								
1 Alexander	Y	N	Y	Y	Y	N	Y	N
2 Tucker	?	?	?	?	?	?	?	?
3 Hammerschmidt	Y	N	Y	Y	Y	Y	N	N
4 Thornton	?	?	?	?	?	?	?	?
CALIFORNIA								
1 Johnson	Y	N	Y	Y	Y	N	Y	N
2 Clausen	?	Y	Y	Y	Y	Y	Y	N
3 Moss	?	?	?	?	?	?	?	?
4 Leggett	Y	N	Y	#	Y	N	Y	N
5 Burton, J.	Y	N	Y	Y	N	N	Y	N
6 Burton, P.	Y	N	Y	Y	Y	?	Y	N
7 Miller	Y	N	Y	Y	Y	N	Y	N
8 Dellums	Y	N	Y	Y	N	N	Y	N
9 Stark	Y	N	Y	Y	Y	N	Y	N
10 Edwards	Y	N	Y	Y	Y	N	Y	N
11 Ryan	Y	N	Y	Y	Y	Y	Y	N
12 McCloskey	Y	Y	Y	?	Y	?	Y	N
13 Mineta	Y	N	Y	Y	Y	N	Y	N
14 McFall	Y	N	Y	Y	Y	N	Y	N
15 Sisk	Y	N	Y	Y	Y	N	Y	N
16 Panetta	Y	N	Y	Y	Y	N	Y	N
17 Krebs	Y	N	Y	Y	N	N	Y	N
18 Ketchum	Y	Y	Y	Y	Y	Y	Y	N
19 Lagomarsino	Y	Y	Y	Y	Y	Y	N	Y
20 Goldwater	?	Y	N	Y	Y	N	N	Y
21 Corman	Y	N	Y	Y	Y	N	Y	N
22 Moorhead	Y	Y	Y	Y	Y	Y	N	Y
23 Beilenson	Y	N	?	Y	N	N	Y	N
24 Waxman	?	▮	?	?	?	▮	?	▮
25 Roybal	Y	N	Y	Y	N	N	Y	N
26 Rousselot	Y	Y	N	Y	Y	Y	N	Y
27 Dornan	Y	Y	Y	Y	Y	Y	N	Y
28 Burke	?	?	?	?	?	?	?	?
29 Hawkins	Y	N	Y	Y	Y	N	Y	N
30 Danielson	Y	N	Y	Y	Y	N	Y	N
31 Wilson, C.H.	Y	N	Y	?	Y	Y	Y	N
32 Anderson	#	▮	▮	Y	Y	N	Y	N
33 Clawson	Y	Y	N	Y	Y	Y	N	Y
34 Hannaford	?	▮	?	Y	Y	N	Y	N
35 Lloyd	?	?	Y	Y	Y	N	Y	N
36 Brown	Y	N	Y	Y	Y	N	Y	N
37 Pettis	?	?	?	Y	Y	N	Y	N
38 Patterson	Y	N	Y	Y	Y	N	Y	N
39 Wiggins	Y	N	Y	Y	Y	Y	N	N
40 Badham	?	?	?	Y	Y	Y	N	Y
41 Wilson, B.	Y	Y	Y	N	Y	N	Y	N
42 Van Deerlin	Y	N	Y	Y	Y	N	Y	N
43 Burgener	Y	Y	Y	Y	Y	Y	Y	N
COLORADO								
1 Schroeder	Y	Y	Y	Y	Y	N	Y	N
2 Wirth	?	?	?	Y	Y	N	Y	N
3 Evans	?	N	Y	Y	Y	N	Y	N
4 Johnson	Y	Y	Y	Y	Y	N	Y	N
5 Armstrong	Y	Y	Y	Y	Y	N	Y	N
CONNECTICUT								
1 Cotter	?	▮	?	?	Y	N	Y	N
2 Dodd	?	Y	Y	Y	Y	N	Y	N
3 Giaimo	Y	N	Y	Y	Y	N	Y	N
4 McKinney	Y	N	Y	Y	Y	Y	Y	N
5 Sarasin	†	-	†	Y	Y	-	†	-
6 Moffett	?	?	?	Y	Y	N	Y	N
DELAWARE								
AL Evans	Y	Y	Y	Y	Y	Y	Y	N
FLORIDA								
1 Sikes	Y	N	Y	Y	Y	?	N	N
2 Fuqua	Y	N	Y	Y	Y	Y	N	N
3 Bennett	Y	N	Y	Y	Y	Y	Y	N
4 Chappell	Y	Y	Y	Y	Y	Y	N	N
5 Kelly	Y	Y	N	Y	Y	Y	N	Y
6 Young	Y	Y	Y	Y	Y	Y	N	Y
7 Gibbons	?	?	Y	Y	Y	Y	Y	N
8 Ireland	?	?	?	Y	Y	Y	N	N
9 Frey	?	?	?	?	?	?	?	?
10 Bafalis	Y	Y	Y	Y	Y	Y	N	N
11 Rogers	Y	N	Y	Y	N	Y	N	N
12 Burke	Y	Y	Y	Y	Y	Y	N	N
13 Lehman	Y	N	Y	Y	Y	N	Y	N
14 Pepper	†	N	Y	Y	Y	N	Y	N
15 Fascell	Y	N	Y	Y	Y	N	Y	N
GEORGIA								
1 Ginn	Y	N	Y	Y	Y	Y	Y	N
2 Mathis	?	N	Y	?	Y	Y	N	N
3 Brinkley	Y	Y	Y	Y	Y	Y	Y	N
4 Levitas	Y	N	Y	Y	Y	Y	Y	N
5 Fowler	?	?	?	Y	Y	Y	Y	N
6 Flynt	Y	N	Y	Y	Y	Y	N	N
7 McDonald	Y	Y	N	Y	N	Y	N	Y
8 Evans	Y	N	Y	#	Y	Y	N	N
9 Jenkins	Y	N	Y	Y	Y	Y	N	N
10 Barnard	Y	N	Y	Y	Y	Y	N	N
HAWAII								
1 Heftel	Y	N	Y	Y	Y	N	Y	N
2 Akaka	Y	N	Y	Y	Y	N	Y	N
IDAHO								
1 Symms	?	Y	N	Y	Y	Y	N	Y
2 Hansen, G.	Y	Y	N	Y	Y	Y	N	Y
ILLINOIS								
1 Metcalfe	Y	N	Y	Y	N	N	Y	N
2 Murphy	?	Y	Y	Y	Y	N	Y	N
3 Russo	#	▮	#	#	▮	#	#	▮
4 Derwinski	Y	Y	N	?	?	?	?	?
5 Fary	Y	N	Y	Y	Y	N	Y	N
6 Hyde	Y	Y	Y	Y	Y	Y	N	Y
7 Collins	†	N	Y	Y	Y	N	Y	N
8 Rostenkowski	?	?	?	Y	Y	N	Y	N
9 Yates	Y	Y	N	Y	N	N	Y	N
10 Mikva	Y	N	Y	Y	N	N	Y	N
11 Annunzio	Y	Y	Y	Y	Y	N	Y	N
12 Crane	Y	Y	N	Y	Y	Y	N	Y
13 McClory	Y	Y	Y	Y	Y	Y	Y	N
14 Erlenborn	Y	N	Y	Y	Y	N	Y	N
15 Corcoran	Y	Y	Y	Y	Y	Y	Y	N
16 Anderson	?	?	?	Y	Y	N	Y	N
17 O'Brien	#	?	#	Y	#	Y	N	N
18 Michel	Y	Y	Y	Y	Y	Y	Y	N
19 Railsback	Y	Y	Y	Y	Y	N	Y	N
20 Findley	Y	Y	N	Y	N	N	Y	N
21 Madigan	Y	Y	N	Y	Y	Y	?	N
22 Shipley	Y	N	Y	Y	Y	N	Y	N
23 Price	Y	Y	Y	Y	Y	N	Y	N
24 Simon	?	Y	Y	Y	N	N	Y	N
INDIANA								
1 Benjamin	Y	N	Y	Y	Y	N	N	N
2 Fithian	Y	Y	Y	Y	Y	N	Y	N
3 Brademas	Y	N	Y	Y	Y	N	Y	N
4 Quayle	Y	Y	Y	Y	N	N	Y	N
5 Hillis	Y	Y	?	Y	Y	Y	N	N
6 Evans	Y	Y	Y	Y	N	N	Y	N
7 Myers, J.	Y	Y	Y	Y	Y	Y	N	N
8 Cornwell	Y	Y	Y	Y	Y	N	Y	N
9 Hamilton	Y	Y	Y	Y	Y	N	Y	N
10 Sharp	Y	Y	Y	Y	Y	N	Y	N
11 Jacobs	Y	Y	Y	Y	N	N	Y	N
IOWA								
1 Leach	Y	Y	Y	Y	Y	N	Y	N
2 Blouin	Y	N	Y	Y	Y	N	Y	N
3 Grassley	Y	Y	Y	Y	Y	Y	Y	N
4 Smith	Y	N	Y	Y	Y	N	Y	N
5 Harkin	Y	N	Y	Y	Y	N	Y	N
6 Bedell	Y	N	Y	Y	N	N	Y	N

Democrats ***Republicans***

	203	204	205	206	207	208	209	210
KANSAS								
1 Sebelius	Y	N	Y	Y	Y	Y	N	N
2 Keys	Y	N	Y	Y	Y	N	Y	N
3 Winn	Y	N	Y	Y	Y	N	Y	N
4 Glickman	Y	N	Y	Y	Y	N	Y	N
5 Skubitz	?	?	?	?	?	N	Y	N
KENTUCKY								
1 Hubbard	Y	N	Y	Y	Y	N	N	N
2 Natcher	Y	N	Y	Y	Y	N	Y	N
3 Mazzoli	Y	Y	Y	Y	Y	N	Y	N
4 Snyder	Y	Y	Y	Y	Y	Y	N	N
5 Carter	Y	N	Y	Y	Y	N	Y	N
6 Breckinridge	?	?	?	Y	Y	N	Y	N
7 Perkins	Y	N	Y	Y	Y	N	Y	N
LOUISIANA								
1 Livingston	Y	Y	Y	Y	Y	Y	N	N
2 Boggs	Y	N	Y	Y	Y	N	Y	N
3 Treen	Y	Y	Y	Y	Y	Y	Y	N
4 Waggonner	#	N	Y	Y	Y	Y	N	N
5 Huckaby	Y	N	Y	Y	Y	Y	Y	N
6 Moore	Y	Y	Y	Y	Y	Y	Y	N
7 Breaux	Y	N	Y	Y	Y	Y	N	N
8 Long	Y	N	Y	Y	Y	N	Y	N
MAINE								
1 Emery	Y	Y	Y	Y	Y	Y	Y	N
2 Cohen	Y	Y	Y	Y	Y	Y	Y	N
MARYLAND								
1 Bauman	Y	Y	Y	Y	Y	Y	N	Y
2 Long	Y	N	N	Y	Y	Y	Y	N
3 Mikulski	Y	N	Y	Y	Y	N	Y	N
4 Holt	Y	Y	Y	Y	Y	Y	N	N
5 Spellman	Y	N	Y	Y	Y	N	Y	N
6 Byron	?	Y	Y	Y	Y	Y	N	N
7 Mitchell	Y	N	Y	N	N	N	Y	N
8 Steers	Y	Y	Y	Y	Y	N	Y	N
MASSACHUSETTS								
1 Conte	Y	Y	N	Y	Y	N	Y	N
2 Boland	?	Y	Y	Y	Y	N	Y	N
3 Early	?	Y	Y	Y	Y	N	Y	N
4 Drinan	Y	N	Y	Y	Y	N	Y	N
5 Tsongas	Y	N	Y	Y	Y	N	Y	N
6 Harrington	Y	N	Y	Y	N	N	Y	N
7 Markey	Y	Y	Y	Y	N	N	Y	N
8 O'Neill								
9 Moakley	Y	N	Y	Y	Y	N	Y	N
10 Heckler	Y	Y	Y	Y	Y	N	Y	N
11 Burke	Y	N	Y	Y	Y	?	Y	N
12 Studds	Y	Y	Y	Y	N	N	Y	N
MICHIGAN								
1 Conyers	?	▮	?	?	X	▮	?	▮
2 Pursell	Y	Y	Y	Y	Y	Y	Y	?
3 Brown	Y	Y	Y	Y	Y	N	Y	N
4 Stockman	Y	Y	Y	Y	Y	Y	N	▮
5 Sawyer	Y	Y	Y	Y	Y	Y	Y	N
6 Carr	Y	N	Y	Y	Y	N	Y	N
7 Kildee	Y	Y	Y	Y	Y	N	Y	N
8 Traxler	Y	Y	Y	Y	Y	N	Y	N
9 Vander Jagt	Y	Y	Y	Y	Y	Y	Y	N
10 Cederberg	Y	Y	Y	Y	Y	Y	Y	N
11 Ruppe	#	?	?	#	?	▮	?	▮
12 Bonior	Y	N	Y	Y	N	N	Y	N
13 Diggs	?	?	?	?	Y	N	Y	N
14 Nedzi	Y	N	Y	Y	Y	N	Y	N
15 Ford	?	N	Y	Y	Y	N	Y	N
16 Dingell	?	?	?	Y	Y	N	Y	N
17 Brodhead	Y	N	Y	Y	N	N	Y	N
18 Blanchard	Y	Y	Y	Y	Y	N	Y	N
19 Broomfield	Y	Y	N	Y	Y	Y	Y	N
MINNESOTA								
1 Quie	Y	Y	Y	Y	Y	N	Y	N
2 Hagedorn	Y	Y	Y	Y	Y	Y	Y	N
3 Frenzel	Y	?	Y	Y	N	N	Y	N
4 Vento	Y	N	Y	Y	N	N	Y	N
5 Fraser	Y	N	Y	Y	N	N	Y	N
6 Nolan	?	N	Y	Y	N	N	Y	N
7 Stangeland	Y	Y	Y	Y	Y	Y	Y	N
8 Oberstar	Y	N	Y	Y	Y	N	Y	N
MISSISSIPPI								
1 Whitten	Y	N	Y	Y	Y	Y	N	N
2 Bowen	?	N	Y	Y	Y	N	Y	Y
3 Montgomery	Y	N	Y	Y	Y	Y	N	Y
4 Cochran	Y	N	Y	?	?	?	?	?
5 Lott	Y	N	Y	Y	Y	Y	N	Y
MISSOURI								
1 Clay	?	N	Y	Y	Y	N	Y	N
2 Young	Y	N	Y	Y	Y	Y	Y	N
3 Gephardt	Y	Y	Y	Y	N	N	N	N

	203	204	205	206	207	208	209	210
4 Skelton	Y	N	Y	Y	N	Y	N	N
5 Bolling	Y	▮	#	Y	Y	N	Y	N
6 Coleman	?	?	?	Y	Y	Y	Y	N
7 Taylor	Y	Y	Y	Y	Y	Y	N	Y
8 Ichord	Y	Y	Y	Y	Y	Y	N	N
9 Volkmer	Y	Y	Y	Y	N	Y	Y	N
10 Burlison	Y	N	Y	Y	Y	N	Y	N
MONTANA								
1 Baucus	?	?	?	?	✓	?	?	?
2 Marlenee	?	?	Y	Y	Y	Y	Y	Y
NEBRASKA								
1 Thone	#	?	?	Y	Y	Y	Y	?
2 Cavanaugh	Y	N	Y	Y	Y	N	Y	N
3 Smith	Y	N	Y	Y	Y	Y	Y	N
NEVADA								
AL Santini	Y	Y	Y	Y	Y	Y	Y	?
NEW HAMPSHIRE								
1 D'Amours	Y	Y	Y	Y	Y	N	Y	N
2 Cleveland	Y	Y	Y	Y	Y	Y	Y	N
NEW JERSEY								
1 Florio	#	▮	#	#	#	▮	#	▮
2 Hughes	Y	N	Y	Y	N	N	Y	N
3 Howard	?	N	Y	?	?	?	?	?
4 Thompson	Y	N	Y	Y	Y	N	Y	N
5 Fenwick	Y	Y	N	Y	N	N	Y	N
6 Forsythe	Y	Y	Y	Y	Y	N	Y	N
7 Maguire	Y	N	Y	Y	N	N	Y	N
8 Roe	Y	Y	Y	Y	Y	N	Y	N
9 Hollenbeck	Y	Y	Y	Y	Y	N	Y	N
10 Rodino	?	▮	?	?	✓	▮	?	▮
11 Minish	Y	N	Y	Y	N	N	N	N
12 Rinaldo	Y	N	Y	Y	Y	N	Y	N
13 Meyner	#	N	Y	Y	Y	N	Y	N
14 LeFante	Y	N	Y	Y	Y	Y	N	N
15 Patten	Y	N	Y	Y	Y	N	Y	N
NEW MEXICO								
1 Lujan	Y	Y	Y	Y	Y	Y	N	N
2 Runnels	?	?	?	?	?	?	?	?
NEW YORK								
1 Pike	Y	N	N	Y	Y	N	Y	N
2 Downey	Y	N	Y	Y	Y	N	Y	N
3 Ambro	Y	Y	Y	Y	Y	Y	Y	Y
4 Lent	Y	Y	Y	Y	Y	Y	Y	N
5 Wydler	Y	Y	N	Y	Y	Y	Y	N
6 Wolff	Y	N	Y	Y	Y	N	Y	N
7 Addabbo	Y	N	Y	Y	Y	N	Y	N
8 Rosenthal	Y	N	Y	Y	N	N	Y	N
9 Delaney	?	?	?	Y	Y	N	Y	N
10 Biaggi	?	N	Y	?	Y	N	Y	N
11 Scheuer	Y	N	Y	Y	Y	N	Y	N
12 Chisholm	#	N	Y	Y	N	N	Y	N
13 Solarz	Y	N	Y	Y	Y	N	Y	N
14 Richmond	Y	N	Y	Y	Y	N	Y	N
15 Zeferetti	?	N	Y	Y	Y	N	Y	N
16 Holtzman	†	-	†	Y	N	N	Y	N
17 Murphy	?	N	Y	Y	Y	N	Y	N
18 Green	?	Y	Y	Y	Y	N	Y	N
19 Rangel	Y	N	Y	Y	N	N	Y	N
20 Weiss	Y	N	Y	Y	N	N	Y	N
21 Garcia	?	N	Y	Y	Y	N	Y	N
22 Bingham	Y	N	Y	Y	Y	N	Y	N
23 Caputo	Y	Y	N	Y	Y	Y	Y	N
24 Ottinger	Y	N	Y	Y	N	N	Y	N
25 Fish	Y	Y	Y	Y	N	?	?	?
26 Gilman	?	†	†	Y	Y	Y	Y	N
27 McHugh	Y	N	?	N	Y	N	Y	N
28 Stratton	Y	Y	Y	Y	Y	N	Y	N
29 Pattison	Y	Y	Y	Y	Y	N	Y	N
30 McEwen	Y	Y	Y	Y	Y	N	Y	N
31 Mitchell	Y	N	Y	Y	Y	N	Y	N
32 Hanley	Y	N	Y	Y	Y	N	Y	N
33 Walsh	Y	Y	Y	Y	Y	Y	Y	N
34 Horton	Y	Y	Y	?	Y	Y	Y	N
35 Conable	Y	?	N	Y	Y	N	Y	N
36 LaFalce	Y	Y	Y	#	Y	N	Y	N
37 Nowak	Y	N	Y	?	Y	?	Y	N
38 Kemp	Y	?	?	Y	Y	Y	Y	N
39 Lundine	Y	N	Y	Y	Y	N	Y	N
NORTH CAROLINA								
1 Jones	?	#	?	?	?	#	#	▮
2 Fountain	Y	N	Y	Y	Y	Y	Y	N
3 Whitley	?	?	?	?	?	?	?	?
4 Andrews	Y	N	Y	Y	?	N	Y	?
5 Neal	Y	N	Y	Y	Y	Y	Y	N
6 Preyer	Y	N	Y	Y	Y	N	Y	N
7 Rose	Y	N	Y	Y	Y	N	Y	N
8 Hefner	Y	N	Y	Y	Y	Y	Y	N

	203	204	205	206	207	208	209	210
9 Martin	Y	#	#	#	Y	Y	Y	N
10 Broyhill	Y	Y	Y	Y	N	Y	Y	N
11 Gudger	#	▮	#	Y	Y	Y	Y	N
NORTH DAKOTA								
AL Andrews	Y	N	Y	Y	Y	N	Y	N
OHIO								
1 Gradison	Y	Y	N	Y	Y	Y	Y	N
2 Luken	Y	Y	Y	Y	Y	Y	Y	N
3 Whalen	Y	N	Y	Y	Y	N	Y	N
4 Guyer	Y	Y	Y	Y	Y	Y	Y	N
5 Latta	Y	?	?	Y	N	Y	N	Y
6 Harsha	Y	Y	Y	Y	Y	Y	N	N
7 Brown	Y	Y	Y	Y	Y	N	Y	N
8 Kindness	Y	Y	Y	Y	Y	Y	N	N
9 Ashley	Y	N	Y	Y	Y	N	Y	N
10 Miller	Y	Y	Y	Y	Y	Y	N	N
11 Stanton	Y	Y	Y	Y	Y	N	Y	N
12 Devine	Y	Y	Y	Y	Y	Y	N	Y
13 Pease	Y	Y	Y	Y	Y	N	Y	N
14 Seiberling	Y	N	Y	Y	N	N	Y	N
15 Wylie	Y	Y	Y	Y	Y	N	Y	N
16 Regula	Y	Y	Y	Y	Y	Y	Y	N
17 Ashbrook	?	▮	?	Y	Y	Y	N	Y
18 Applegate	?	N	Y	Y	Y	Y	Y	N
19 Carney	Y	N	Y	Y	Y	N	Y	N
20 Oakar	Y	N	Y	Y	Y	N	Y	N
21 Stokes	Y	N	Y	Y	Y	N	Y	N
22 Vanik	Y	N	Y	Y	Y	N	Y	N
23 Mottl	?	▮	?	Y	N	N	N	N
OKLAHOMA								
1 Jones	Y	N	Y	Y	Y	Y	N	N
2 Risenhoover	Y	N	Y	?	?	?	?	?
3 Watkins	?	N	Y	Y	Y	Y	N	N
4 Steed	Y	N	Y	Y	Y	N	N	N
5 Edwards	Y	N	Y	Y	Y	Y	N	N
6 English	Y	N	Y	Y	Y	Y	N	▮
OREGON								
1 AuCoin	Y	N	Y	Y	?	N	Y	N
2 Ullman	Y	N	Y	#	Y	N	Y	N
3 Duncan	?	?	?	Y	Y	N	Y	N
4 Weaver	Y	N	Y	Y	N	N	Y	N
PENNSYLVANIA								
1 Myers, M.	?	N	Y	Y	Y	Y	Y	N
2 Nix	?	?	?	?	?	?	?	?
3 Lederer	Y	N	Y	Y	Y	Y	Y	N
4 Eilberg	Y	N	Y	Y	Y	?	?	?
5 Schulze	Y	Y	Y	Y	Y	Y	Y	N
6 Yatron	Y	Y	Y	Y	Y	Y	Y	N
7 Edgar	Y	N	Y	Y	Y	N	Y	N
8 Kostmayer	Y	Y	Y	Y	N	N	Y	N
9 Shuster	Y	Y	Y	Y	Y	Y	N	N
10 McDade	Y	Y	Y	Y	Y	Y	Y	N
11 Flood	Y	N	Y	Y	Y	N	Y	N
12 Murtha	Y	N	Y	Y	Y	Y	N	N
13 Coughlin	Y	Y	Y	Y	Y	Y	Y	N
14 Moorhead	Y	N	Y	Y	Y	N	Y	N
15 Rooney	?	?	?	Y	Y	N	Y	N
16 Walker	Y	Y	Y	Y	Y	Y	N	N
17 Ertel	Y	N	Y	Y	Y	Y	Y	N
18 Walgren	Y	N	Y	Y	Y	N	Y	N
19 Goodling, W.	?	Y	Y	Y	N	N	Y	N
20 Gaydos	Y	?	Y	Y	Y	Y	N	Y
21 Dent	#	N	Y	Y	Y	Y	N	Y
22 Murphy	Y	Y	Y	Y	Y	Y	Y	N
23 Ammerman	Y	Y	Y	Y	?	Y	?	?
24 Marks	?	Y	Y	Y	Y	Y	Y	N
25 Myers, G.	Y	Y	N	Y	Y	Y	N	N
RHODE ISLAND								
1 St Germain	Y	N	Y	?	Y	N	Y	Y
2 Beard	Y	?	Y	Y	Y	N	Y	N
SOUTH CAROLINA								
1 Davis	Y	N	Y	Y	Y	Y	N	N
2 Spence	Y	N	Y	Y	Y	Y	N	N
3 Derrick	Y	N	Y	Y	Y	Y	N	N
4 Mann	?	?	?	?	?	?	?	?
5 Holland	?	N	Y	Y	Y	Y	?	N
6 Jenrette	Y	N	Y	Y	Y	Y	N	N
SOUTH DAKOTA								
1 Pressler	?	?	?	Y	Y	Y	Y	N
2 Abdnor	Y	N	Y	Y	Y	Y	Y	N
TENNESSEE								
1 Quillen	Y	Y	Y	Y	Y	Y	N	Y
2 Duncan	Y	Y	Y	Y	Y	Y	N	N
3 Lloyd	Y	N	Y	Y	Y	Y	N	N
4 Gore	Y	N	Y	Y	Y	N	Y	N
5 Allen	Y	Y	Y	Y	Y	N	Y	N
6 Beard	Y	N	Y	Y	Y	Y	N	N

	203	204	205	206	207	208	209	210
7 Jones	Y	N	Y	Y	Y	Y	N	N
8 Ford	?	N	Y	Y	Y	N	Y	N
TEXAS								
1 Hall	?	N	Y	Y	Y	Y	N	N
2 Wilson, C.	?	N	Y	Y	Y	N	Y	N
3 Collins	Y	Y	N	Y	Y	Y	N	Y
4 Roberts	?	?	?	?	?	?	?	?
5 Mattox	Y	N	Y	Y	Y	N	Y	N
6 Teague	?	?	?	Y	Y	?	?	?
7 Archer	Y	Y	Y	Y	Y	Y	N	Y
8 Eckhardt	?	?	?	Y	Y	N	Y	N
9 Brooks	Y	N	Y	Y	Y	N	Y	N
10 Pickle	Y	N	Y	Y	Y	N	Y	N
11 Poage	Y	Y	Y	Y	Y	Y	N	Y
12 Wright	Y	N	Y	Y	Y	N	Y	N
13 Hightower	Y	N	Y	Y	Y	N	N	N
14 Young	Y	N	Y	?	?	?	?	?
15 de la Garza	Y	N	Y	Y	Y	Y	Y	N
16 White	Y	N	Y	Y	Y	N	Y	N
17 Burleson	Y	N	Y	Y	Y	Y	N	Y
18 Jordan	#	N	Y	Y	Y	N	Y	N
19 Mahon	Y	N	Y	Y	Y	N	Y	N
20 Gonzalez	?	N	Y	Y	Y	N	Y	N
21 Krueger	?	?	?	?	?	?	?	?
22 Gammage	?	?	?	?	X	?	?	?
23 Kazen	?	?	?	?	?	?	?	?
24 Milford	?	Y	Y	Y	Y	Y	N	N
UTAH								
1 McKay	Y	?	Y	Y	Y	Y	Y	N
2 Marriott	Y	Y	Y	Y	Y	Y	N	N
VERMONT								
AL Jeffords	Y	N	Y	Y	Y	N	Y	N
VIRGINIA								
1 Trible	Y	Y	Y	Y	Y	Y	Y	N
2 Whitehurst	Y	Y	Y	Y	Y	Y	Y	N
3 Satterfield	Y	Y	Y	Y	Y	Y	N	Y
4 Daniel	Y	Y	Y	Y	Y	Y	N	Y
5 Daniel	Y	Y	Y	Y	Y	Y	N	Y
6 Butler	?	Y	Y	Y	Y	Y	N	N
7 Robinson	Y	Y	Y	Y	Y	Y	N	Y
8 Harris	Y	Y	Y	Y	Y	N	Y	N
9 Wampler	?	Y	Y	Y	Y	Y	Y	N
10 Fisher	Y	Y	Y	Y	Y	N	Y	N
WASHINGTON								
1 Pritchard	Y	Y	Y	Y	Y	N	Y	N
2 Meeds	Y	N	Y	Y	?	N	Y	N
3 Bonker	Y	N	Y	?	Y	N	Y	N
4 McCormack	Y	N	Y	Y	Y	?	?	?
5 Foley	Y	N	Y	Y	Y	N	Y	N
6 Dicks	Y	N	Y	Y	Y	N	Y	N
7 Cunningham	Y	P	P	Y	Y	Y	N	Y
WEST VIRGINIA								
1 Mollohan	?	▮	?	?	?	▮	▮	▮
2 Staggers	Y	N	Y	Y	Y	N	Y	N
3 Slack	Y	N	Y	Y	Y	N	N	N
4 Rahall	Y	N	?	Y	N	N	Y	N
WISCONSIN								
1 Aspin	Y	N	Y	Y	N	N	Y	N
2 Kastenmeier	Y	N	Y	Y	N	N	Y	N
3 Baldus	Y	N	Y	Y	N	N	Y	N
4 Zablocki	Y	N	Y	Y	Y	N	Y	N
5 Reuss	#	#	#	Y	N	N	Y	N
6 Steiger	?	?	?	Y	Y	N	Y	N
7 Obey	Y	N	Y	Y	N	N	Y	N
8 Cornell	?	N	Y	Y	N	N	Y	N
9 Kasten	#	#	#	Y	Y	N	Y	N
WYOMING								
AL Roncalio	?	N	Y	?	?	N	Y	N

Democrats ***Republicans***

211. H Con Res 573. Cambodia. Adoption of the concurrent resolution denouncing murders and atrocities committed by the Cambodian government. Adopted 388-0: R 139-0; D 249-0 (ND 173-0; SD 76-0), April 25, 1978.

212. Procedural Motion. Russo, D-Ill., motion to approve the House *Journal* of Tuesday, April 25, 1978. Motion agreed to 382-9: R 135-7; D 247-2 (ND 173-2; SD 74-0), April 26, 1978.

213. HR 11832. Arms Control and Disarmament Agency. Passage of the bill to authorize $18.4 million for the activities of the Arms Control and Disarmament Agency in fiscal 1979. Passed 332-74: R 100-44; D 232-30 (ND 180-5; SD 52-25), April 26, 1978.

214. HR 8494. Lobbying Disclosure. Santini, D-Nev., amendment to direct the General Accounting Office to study lobbying activities of organizations of state or local elected officials and to delay until Jan. 1, 1980, coverage of those organizations under the bill. Rejected 197-211: R 61-83; D 136-128 (ND 87-99; SD 49-29), April 26, 1978.

215. HR 8494. Lobbying Disclosure. Kindness, R-Ohio, amendment to exempt from coverage under the bill communications dealing only with the status, existence or subject of a legislative issue. Adopted 207-188: R 133-9; D 74-179 (ND 33-145; SD 41-34), April 26, 1978.

216. HR 8494. Lobbying Disclosure. Passage of the bill to require annual registration and quarterly reporting by major lobbying organizations as well as disclosure of grass-roots (indirect) lobbying activities by reporting organizations and the names and addresses of major groups contributing to reporting organizations. Passed 259-140: R 75-67; D 184-73 (ND 143-39; SD 41-34), April 26, 1978. A "yea" was a vote supporting the president's position.

217. HR 11302. EPA Authorization. Brown, D-Calif., motion that the House resolve itself into the Committee of the Whole for consideration of the bill to authorize $431.3 million for research, development and demonstration programs of the Environmental Protection Agency for fiscal 1979. Motion agreed to 384-5: R 140-2; D 244-3 (ND 170-2; SD 74-1), April 27, 1978.

218. HR 11302. EPA Authorization. Passage of the bill to authorize $432.9 million for research, development and demonstration programs of the Environmental Protection Agency for fiscal 1979. Passed 367-33: R 125-17; D 242-16 (ND 179-4; SD 63-12), April 27, 1978.

KEY

- Y Voted for (yea).
- ✓ Paired for.
- † Announced for.
- # CQ Poll for.
- N Voted against (nay).
- X Paired against.
- \- Announced against.
- ▮ CQ Poll against.
- P Voted "present."
- ● Voted "present" to avoid possible conflict of interest.
- ? Did not vote or otherwise make a position known.

	211	212	213	214	215	216	217	218
ALABAMA								
1 Edwards	Y	Y	N	N	Y	N	Y	Y
2 Dickinson	Y	Y	N	N	Y	N	Y	Y
3 Nichols	Y	Y	N	Y	Y	Y	Y	Y
4 Bevill	Y	Y	N	Y	Y	N	Y	Y
5 Flippo	Y	Y	N	N	Y	Y	Y	Y
6 Buchanan	Y	Y	Y	Y	Y	Y	Y	Y
7 Flowers	Y	Y	N	N	N	Y	Y	Y
ALASKA								
AL Young	Y	Y	N	N	?	?	Y	N
ARIZONA								
1 Rhodes	Y	Y	Y	Y	Y	N	Y	Y
2 Udall	Y	Y	Y	Y	N	N	Y	Y
3 Stump	Y	Y	N	Y	Y	N	Y	N
4 Rudd	Y	Y	N	N	Y	N	Y	N
ARKANSAS								
1 Alexander	Y	Y	Y	N	N	Y	Y	Y
2 Tucker	?	?	?	?	?	?	?	?
3 Hammerschmidt	Y	Y	N	Y	Y	N	Y	N
4 Thornton	?	?	?	?	?	?	?	?
CALIFORNIA								
1 Johnson	Y	Y	Y	Y	N	Y	Y	Y
2 Clausen	Y	Y	Y	Y	Y	N	Y	Y
3 Moss	?	?	?	?	?	?	Y	Y
4 Leggett	Y	#	#	N	Y	N	Y	Y
5 Burton, J.	?	Y	Y	N	N	Y	?	Y
6 Burton, P.	Y	Y	Y	N	?	Y	Y	Y
7 Miller	Y	Y	Y	N	N	Y	Y	Y
8 Dellums	?	Y	Y	Y	N	Y	Y	Y
9 Stark	Y	Y	Y	Y	?	Y	Y	Y
10 Edwards	Y	Y	Y	Y	N	N	?	Y
11 Ryan	Y	Y	Y	Y	Y	N	Y	Y
12 McCloskey	Y	Y	Y	N	Y	Y	Y	Y
13 Mineta	Y	?	Y	Y	N	Y	Y	Y
14 McFall	Y	Y	Y	Y	N	Y	Y	Y
15 Sisk	Y	Y	Y	Y	?	?	?	Y
16 Panetta	Y	Y	Y	N	N	Y	Y	Y
17 Krebs	Y	Y	Y	Y	N	N	Y	Y
18 Ketchum	Y	Y	Y	Y	Y	N	Y	Y
19 Lagomarsino	Y	Y	N	Y	Y	N	Y	Y
20 Goldwater	Y	Y	Y	N	Y	N	Y	Y
21 Corman	Y	Y	Y	Y	N	N	#	Y
22 Moorhead	Y	Y	N	N	Y	Y	Y	Y
23 Beilenson	Y	Y	Y	N	N	N	Y	Y
24 Waxman	?	?	?	X	X	?	?	?
25 Roybal	Y	Y	Y	Y	N	N	Y	Y
26 Rousselot	Y	Y	N	N	Y	N	Y	N
27 Dornan	Y	Y	Y	N	Y	N	Y	N
28 Burke	?	Y	Y	N	N	Y	Y	?
29 Hawkins	Y	Y	Y	N	N	Y	?	Y
30 Danielson	Y	Y	Y	N	N	Y	Y	Y
31 Wilson, C.H.	Y	?	Y	N	N	N	Y	Y
32 Anderson	Y	Y	Y	Y	N	Y	Y	Y
33 Clawson	Y	Y	N	N	Y	N	Y	N
34 Hannaford	Y	Y	Y	Y	N	Y	Y	Y
35 Lloyd	Y	Y	Y	Y	N	N	Y	Y
36 Brown	Y	Y	Y	N	N	N	Y	Y
37 Pettis	Y	Y	Y	N	Y	N	Y	Y
38 Patterson	Y	Y	Y	Y	N	Y	Y	Y
39 Wiggins	Y	Y	Y	N	Y	N	Y	Y
40 Badham	Y	?	N	N	Y	N	Y	N
41 Wilson, B.	Y	N	Y	Y	Y	Y	N	Y
42 Van Deerlin	Y	Y	Y	Y	N	N	Y	Y
43 Burgener	Y	Y	Y	N	Y	N	Y	Y
COLORADO								
1 Schroeder	Y	Y	Y	N	N	Y	Y	Y
2 Wirth	Y	Y	Y	Y	N	Y	Y	Y
3 Evans	Y	Y	Y	Y	N	N	Y	Y
4 Johnson	Y	Y	Y	Y	Y	N	Y	Y
5 Armstrong	Y	Y	Y	Y	Y	N	Y	Y
CONNECTICUT								
1 Cotter	Y	Y	Y	N	N	Y	Y	Y
2 Dodd	Y	Y	Y	Y	N	N	Y	Y
3 Giaimo	Y	Y	Y	N	N	N	?	Y
4 McKinney	Y	Y	Y	N	Y	Y	Y	Y
5 Sarasin	†	N	Y	N	Y	Y	Y	Y
6 Moffett	Y	Y	Y	N	N	Y	Y	Y
DELAWARE								
AL Evans	Y	Y	Y	Y	Y	N	Y	Y
FLORIDA								
1 Sikes	Y	Y	N	N	N	N	Y	Y
2 Fuqua	Y	Y	Y	N	N	Y	Y	Y
3 Bennett	Y	Y	Y	N	N	Y	Y	Y
4 Chappell	Y	Y	Y	N	N	N	Y	N
5 Kelly	Y	Y	N	N	Y	N	Y	N
6 Young	Y	Y	N	N	N	Y	Y	Y
7 Gibbons	Y	Y	Y	N	Y	Y	Y	Y
8 Ireland	Y	Y	N	Y	Y	Y	Y	Y
9 Frey	?	?	?	?	?	?	?	?
10 Bafalis	Y	Y	N	Y	N	Y	Y	Y
11 Rogers	Y	Y	Y	Y	N	Y	Y	Y
12 Burke	Y	P	N	Y	Y	Y	Y	Y
13 Lehman	Y	Y	Y	N	N	Y	Y	Y
14 Pepper	Y	#	Y	Y	N	Y	Y	Y
15 Fascell	Y	Y	Y	N	N	Y	Y	Y
GEORGIA								
1 Ginn	Y	Y	N	Y	Y	N	Y	Y
2 Mathis	Y	?	?	?	Y	N	Y	Y
3 Brinkley	Y	Y	Y	Y	Y	Y	Y	Y
4 Levitas	Y	Y	Y	Y	Y	Y	Y	Y
5 Fowler	Y	Y	Y	Y	Y	Y	Y	?
6 Flynt	Y	Y	N	Y	Y	N	Y	N
7 McDonald	Y	Y	N	N	Y	N	N	N
8 Evans	Y	Y	N	N	N	N	Y	N
9 Jenkins	Y	Y	N	Y	Y	Y	Y	Y
10 Barnard	Y	Y	N	Y	Y	N	Y	Y
HAWAII								
1 Heftel	Y	Y	Y	Y	N	Y	Y	Y
2 Akaka	Y	Y	Y	Y	N	Y	Y	Y
IDAHO								
1 Symms	Y	Y	N	N	Y	N	Y	N
2 Hansen, G.	Y	Y	N	N	Y	N	Y	N
ILLINOIS								
1 Metcalfe	Y	Y	Y	N	N	Y	Y	Y
2 Murphy	Y	Y	Y	N	N	N	Y	Y
3 Russo	#	Y	Y	Y	Y	Y	Y	Y
4 Derwinski	?	Y	Y	Y	Y	Y	Y	Y
5 Fary	Y	Y	Y	N	N	Y	Y	Y
6 Hyde	Y	Y	Y	N	Y	N	Y	Y
7 Collins	Y	Y	Y	N	N	Y	Y	Y
8 Rostenkowski	Y	Y	Y	N	N	Y	Y	Y
9 Yates	Y	Y	Y	Y	N	N	Y	Y
10 Mikva	Y	Y	Y	N	N	Y	Y	Y
11 Annunzio	Y	Y	Y	N	#	✓	Y	Y
12 Crane	Y	#	▮	▮	Y	N	Y	N
13 McClory	Y	Y	Y	N	Y	N	Y	Y
14 Erlenborn	Y	Y	Y	N	Y	N	Y	Y
15 Corcoran	Y	Y	Y	N	Y	Y	Y	Y
16 Anderson	Y	Y	Y	N	Y	Y	Y	Y
17 O'Brien	Y	Y	Y	N	Y	N	Y	Y
18 Michel	Y	Y	Y	Y	Y	N	#	Y
19 Railsback	Y	Y	Y	N	Y	Y	Y	#
20 Findley	Y	Y	Y	N	Y	Y	Y	Y
21 Madigan	Y	Y	Y	N	Y	Y	Y	Y
22 Shipley	?	?	Y	N	N	N	Y	Y
23 Price	Y	Y	Y	N	N	Y	Y	Y
24 Simon	Y	Y	Y	N	N	Y	Y	Y
INDIANA								
1 Benjamin	Y	Y	Y	Y	Y	Y	Y	Y
2 Fithian	Y	Y	Y	N	Y	Y	Y	Y
3 Brademas	Y	Y	Y	N	N	Y	Y	Y
4 Quayle	Y	N	Y	N	Y	Y	Y	Y
5 Hillis	Y	Y	N	N	Y	Y	Y	Y
6 Evans	Y	?	Y	N	Y	Y	Y	N
7 Myers, J.	Y	Y	Y	N	Y	N	Y	Y
8 Cornwell	Y	Y	Y	N	N	N	Y	Y
9 Hamilton	Y	Y	Y	N	N	Y	Y	Y
10 Sharp	Y	Y	Y	N	Y	Y	Y	Y
11 Jacobs	Y	N	Y	N	N	Y	Y	Y
IOWA								
1 Leach	Y	Y	Y	Y	Y	Y	Y	Y
2 Blouin	Y	Y	Y	N	N	Y	Y	Y
3 Grassley	Y	Y	N	Y	Y	N	Y	Y
4 Smith	Y	Y	Y	N	N	Y	Y	Y
5 Harkin	†	Y	Y	N	N	Y	Y	Y
6 Bedell	Y	Y	Y	N	N	Y	Y	Y

Democrats ***Republicans***

	211	212	213	214	215	216	217	218
KANSAS								
1 Sebelius	Y	Y	Y	Y	Y	N	Y	Y
2 Keys	Y	Y	Y	N	N	Y	Y	Y
3 Winn	Y	Y	Y	Y	Y	N	Y	Y
4 Glickman	Y	Y	Y	Y	Y	Y	Y	N
5 Skubitz	?	?	Y	Y	Y	N	Y	Y
KENTUCKY								
1 Hubbard	Y	Y	Y	Y	Y	N	Y	Y
2 Natcher	Y	Y	Y	N	N	Y	Y	Y
3 Mazzoli	Y	Y	Y	N	N	Y	Y	Y
4 Snyder	Y	Y	N	N	Y	N	Y	Y
5 Carter	Y	Y	Y	N	Y	N	Y	Y
6 Breckinridge	Y	?	?	Y	Y	Y	Y	Y
7 Perkins	Y	Y	Y	N	N	Y	Y	Y
LOUISIANA								
1 Livingston	Y	Y	N	Y	Y	Y	Y	Y
2 Boggs	Y	Y	Y	Y	N	Y	Y	Y
3 Treen	Y	Y	Y	Y	Y	Y	Y	Y
4 Waggonner	Y	Y	N	Y	Y	N	Y	N
5 Huckaby	Y	Y	N	Y	Y	N	Y	N
6 Moore	Y	Y	N	Y	Y	Y	Y	Y
7 Breaux	Y	Y	N	Y	Y	Y	Y	Y
8 Long	Y	Y	Y	Y	N	Y	Y	Y
MAINE								
1 Emery	Y	Y	Y	N	Y	Y	Y	Y
2 Cohen	Y	Y	Y	N	Y	Y	Y	Y
MARYLAND								
1 Bauman	Y	Y	N	N	Y	N	Y	N
2 Long	Y	Y	Y	N	Y	N	Y	Y
3 Mikulski	Y	Y	Y	N	N	Y	Y	Y
4 Holt	Y	Y	N	N	Y	N	Y	N
5 Spellman	Y	Y	Y	Y	N	Y	Y	Y
6 Byron	Y	Y	Y	Y	N	Y	Y	Y
7 Mitchell	Y	N	Y	N	N	N	N	Y
8 Steers	Y	Y	Y	N	Y	Y	Y	Y
MASSACHUSETTS								
1 Conte	Y	Y	Y	N	N	Y	Y	Y
2 Boland	Y	Y	Y	Y	N	Y	Y	Y
3 Early	Y	Y	Y	N	N	Y	Y	Y
4 Drinan	Y	Y	Y	N	N	Y	Y	Y
5 Tsongas	Y	Y	Y	N	▮	#	#	#
6 Harrington	Y	Y	Y	N	N	Y	Y	Y
7 Markey	Y	Y	Y	N	N	N	Y	Y
8 O'Neill								
9 Moakley	Y	Y	Y	N	N	Y	Y	Y
10 Heckler	Y	Y	Y	N	N	Y	Y	Y
11 Burke	Y	Y	Y	N	N	N	Y	Y
12 Studds	Y	Y	Y	Y	Y	Y	Y	Y
MICHIGAN								
1 Conyers	?	?	?	✓	▮	X	?	?
2 Pursell	?	Y	Y	Y	Y	Y	Y	Y
3 Brown	Y	N	?	N	Y	N	Y	Y
4 Stockman	Y	Y	Y	N	Y	Y	Y	Y
5 Sawyer	Y	Y	Y	Y	?	?	?	?
6 Carr	Y	#	Y	N	N	Y	Y	Y
7 Kildee	Y	Y	Y	N	Y	Y	Y	Y
8 Traxler	Y	Y	Y	Y	N	Y	Y	Y
9 Vander Jagt	Y	Y	Y	Y	Y	Y	Y	Y
10 Cederberg	Y	Y	Y	Y	Y	N	Y	Y
11 Ruppe	#	Y	Y	N	Y	N	Y	Y
12 Bonior	Y	Y	Y	N	N	Y	Y	Y
13 Diggs	Y	?	Y	N	N	N	?	Y
14 Nedzi	Y	Y	Y	Y	N	Y	Y	Y
15 Ford	Y	Y	Y	Y	N	Y	Y	Y
16 Dingell	Y	Y	Y	N	Y	Y	Y	Y
17 Brodhead	Y	Y	Y	N	N	Y	Y	Y
18 Blanchard	Y	Y	Y	Y	N	Y	Y	Y
19 Broomfield	Y	Y	Y	Y	Y	Y	Y	Y
MINNESOTA								
1 Quie	Y	Y	Y	Y	N	Y	Y	Y
2 Hagedorn	Y	Y	N	Y	Y	Y	Y	Y
3 Frenzel	Y	Y	Y	N	N	Y	Y	Y
4 Vento	Y	Y	Y	Y	N	Y	Y	?
5 Fraser	Y	?	?	N	N	Y	Y	Y
6 Nolan	Y	Y	Y	N	N	Y	?	Y
7 Stangeland	Y	Y	N	Y	Y	Y	Y	Y
8 Oberstar	Y	Y	Y	Y	N	Y	Y	Y
MISSISSIPPI								
1 Whitten	Y	Y	Y	Y	Y	Y	?	?
2 Bowen	Y	Y	Y	Y	Y	N	Y	Y
3 Montgomery	Y	Y	N	Y	Y	N	Y	Y
4 Cochran	?	Y	N	N	?	?	Y	Y
5 Lott	Y	Y	Y	Y	Y	Y	Y	N
MISSOURI								
1 Clay	?	Y	Y	Y	N	Y	Y	Y
2 Young	Y	Y	Y	N	N	Y	Y	Y
3 Gephardt	Y	Y	Y	Y	N	Y	Y	Y

	211	212	213	214	215	216	217	218
4 Skelton	Y	Y	N	Y	Y	Y	Y	Y
5 Bolling	Y	Y	Y	N	N	Y	Y	Y
6 Coleman	Y	Y	N	?	Y	Y	Y	Y
7 Taylor	Y	Y	N	N	Y	N	Y	Y
8 Ichord	Y	Y	N	N	Y	Y	Y	Y
9 Volkmer	Y	Y	N	N	N	Y	?	Y
10 Burlison	Y	Y	Y	N	N	Y	Y	Y
MONTANA								
1 Baucus	?	?	?	?	?	?	?	?
2 Marlenee	Y	Y	Y	Y	Y	Y	Y	Y
NEBRASKA								
1 Thone	Y	Y	Y	Y	Y	Y	Y	Y
2 Cavanaugh	Y	Y	Y	N	N	Y	Y	Y
3 Smith	Y	Y	Y	Y	Y	Y	Y	Y
NEVADA								
AL Santini	?	Y	Y	Y	Y	N	Y	Y
NEW HAMPSHIRE								
1 D'Amours	Y	Y	Y	Y	N	Y	Y	Y
2 Cleveland	Y	Y	Y	N	Y	Y	Y	Y
NEW JERSEY								
1 Florio	#	Y	Y	Y	N	Y	Y	Y
2 Hughes	Y	Y	Y	Y	Y	Y	Y	Y
3 Howard	?	?	?	?	?	?	?	?
4 Thompson	Y	Y	Y	N	N	Y	Y	Y
5 Fenwick	Y	Y	Y	N	Y	Y	Y	Y
6 Forsythe	Y	Y	Y	N	Y	N	Y	Y
7 Maguire	Y	Y	Y	N	N	Y	Y	Y
8 Roe	Y	#	#	Y	Y	Y	Y	Y
9 Hollenbeck	Y	Y	Y	N	N	Y	Y	Y
10 Rodino	?	?	?	▮	▮	?	?	?
11 Minish	Y	Y	Y	Y	N	Y	Y	Y
12 Rinaldo	Y	Y	Y	N	Y	Y	Y	Y
13 Meyner	Y	Y	Y	N	N	Y	Y	Y
14 LeFante	Y	Y	Y	Y	N	Y	Y	Y
15 Patten	Y	Y	Y	Y	N	Y	Y	Y
NEW MEXICO								
1 Lujan	Y	Y	Y	Y	Y	Y	Y	Y
2 Runnels	?	?	?	✓	?	?	?	?
NEW YORK								
1 Pike	Y	Y	Y	N	N	Y	Y	Y
2 Downey	Y	Y	Y	Y	N	Y	Y	Y
3 Ambro	Y	Y	Y	Y	N	Y	?	Y
4 Lent	Y	Y	Y	Y	Y	Y	Y	Y
5 Wydler	Y	Y	Y	N	Y	Y	Y	Y
6 Wolff	Y	Y	Y	Y	Y	Y	Y	Y
7 Addabbo	Y	Y	Y	Y	N	Y	Y	Y
8 Rosenthal	#	Y	Y	N	N	Y	Y	Y
9 Delaney	Y	Y	Y	Y	N	Y	Y	Y
10 Biaggi	Y	Y	Y	Y	N	Y	Y	Y
11 Scheuer	Y	Y	Y	Y	N	N	Y	Y
12 Chisholm	Y	Y	Y	N	N	Y	Y	Y
13 Solarz	Y	Y	Y	N	N	Y	Y	Y
14 Richmond	Y	Y	Y	Y	N	N	Y	Y
15 Zeferetti	Y	Y	Y	N	N	Y	Y	Y
16 Holtzman	Y	Y	Y	Y	Y	N	Y	Y
17 Murphy	Y	?	Y	?	Y	N	Y	Y
18 Green	Y	Y	Y	N	Y	Y	Y	Y
19 Rangel	Y	Y	Y	Y	N	N	?	Y
20 Weiss	Y	Y	Y	Y	N	N	Y	Y
21 Garcia	Y	?	Y	Y	N	N	Y	Y
22 Bingham	Y	Y	Y	Y	Y	Y	?	?
23 Caputo	Y	Y	Y	N	N	Y	Y	Y
24 Ottinger	Y	Y	Y	N	N	Y	Y	Y
25 Fish	?	Y	Y	N	Y	N	Y	Y
26 Gilman	Y	Y	Y	Y	Y	Y	Y	Y
27 McHugh	Y	Y	Y	Y	Y	Y	Y	Y
28 Stratton	Y	Y	N	N	Y	N	Y	Y
29 Pattison	Y	Y	Y	Y	N	Y	Y	Y
30 McEwen	Y	Y	Y	N	Y	N	Y	Y
31 Mitchell	Y	Y	Y	Y	Y	Y	Y	Y
32 Hanley	Y	Y	Y	N	N	Y	Y	Y
33 Walsh	Y	N	Y	Y	Y	N	Y	?
34 Horton	Y	Y	Y	N	Y	Y	Y	Y
35 Conable	Y	Y	Y	N	Y	Y	Y	Y
36 LaFalce	Y	Y	Y	Y	N	Y	Y	Y
37 Nowak	Y	Y	Y	Y	N	Y	Y	Y
38 Kemp	Y	Y	Y	N	Y	N	Y	Y
39 Lundine	Y	Y	Y	Y	N	Y	Y	Y
NORTH CAROLINA								
1 Jones	?	?	?	▮	#	▮	?	#
2 Fountain	Y	Y	Y	Y	?	?	Y	Y
3 Whitley	?	?	?	?	?	?	?	?
4 Andrews	?	Y	Y	N	N	Y	Y	Y
5 Neal	Y	Y	Y	Y	Y	Y	Y	Y
6 Preyer	Y	Y	Y	N	N	Y	Y	Y
7 Rose	Y	Y	Y	N	N	Y	Y	Y
8 Hefner	Y	#	Y	Y	Y	N	Y	Y

	211	212	213	214	215	216	217	218
9 Martin	Y	Y	Y	Y	Y	Y	Y	Y
10 Broyhill	Y	Y	Y	Y	Y	N	Y	Y
11 Gudger	Y	Y	Y	Y	#	#	#	#
NORTH DAKOTA								
AL Andrews	Y	Y	Y	N	Y	Y	Y	Y
OHIO								
1 Gradison	Y	Y	Y	N	Y	Y	Y	Y
2 Luken	Y	Y	Y	N	?	?	Y	Y
3 Whalen	Y	Y	Y	N	N	Y	Y	Y
4 Guyer	Y	Y	Y	Y	Y	Y	Y	Y
5 Latta	Y	Y	N	N	Y	Y	Y	N
6 Harsha	Y	Y	N	Y	Y	N	Y	Y
7 Brown	Y	Y	N	N	Y	N	Y	Y
8 Kindness	Y	Y	N	N	Y	N	Y	Y
9 Ashley	Y	Y	Y	N	N	Y	Y	Y
10 Miller	Y	Y	Y	N	Y	Y	Y	Y
11 Stanton	Y	Y	Y	Y	Y	Y	Y	Y
12 Devine	Y	Y	N	N	Y	N	Y	Y
13 Pease	Y	Y	Y	Y	Y	Y	Y	Y
14 Seiberling	Y	Y	Y	Y	N	N	Y	Y
15 Wylie	Y	Y	Y	N	Y	Y	Y	Y
16 Regula	Y	Y	Y	N	Y	Y	Y	Y
17 Ashbrook	Y	Y	N	N	Y	N	?	▮
18 Applegate	Y	Y	Y	Y	N	Y	Y	Y
19 Carney	Y	Y	Y	N	N	Y	Y	Y
20 Oakar	Y	Y	Y	Y	N	Y	Y	Y
21 Stokes	Y	Y	Y	N	?	Y	Y	Y
22 Vanik	Y	Y	Y	N	N	Y	Y	Y
23 Mottl	Y	Y	Y	Y	Y	Y	Y	N
OKLAHOMA								
1 Jones	Y	Y	N	N	Y	N	Y	Y
2 Risenhoover	?	?	?	Y	N	N	Y	Y
3 Watkins	Y	Y	N	Y	Y	Y	Y	Y
4 Steed	Y	Y	N	Y	N	N	Y	Y
5 Edwards	Y	Y	N	N	Y	N	Y	Y
6 English	Y	Y	N	Y	Y	Y	Y	Y
OREGON								
1 AuCoin	Y	Y	Y	N	N	Y	Y	Y
2 Ullman	Y	Y	Y	Y	#	Y	Y	Y
3 Duncan	Y	Y	Y	Y	Y	N	Y	Y
4 Weaver	Y	Y	Y	Y	N	Y	Y	Y
PENNSYLVANIA								
1 Myers, M.	Y	Y	Y	Y	N	Y	Y	Y
2 Nix	?	?	?	X	?	?	?	?
3 Lederer	Y	Y	Y	Y	N	Y	Y	Y
4 Eilberg	?	?	?	X	X	?	?	?
5 Schulze	Y	Y	Y	N	Y	Y	Y	Y
6 Yatron	Y	Y	Y	Y	Y	Y	Y	Y
7 Edgar	Y	Y	Y	N	N	Y	Y	Y
8 Kostmayer	Y	Y	Y	N	Y	Y	Y	Y
9 Shuster	Y	Y	N	N	Y	N	Y	N
10 McDade	Y	Y	Y	N	Y	Y	Y	Y
11 Flood	Y	Y	Y	N	N	Y	Y	Y
12 Murtha	Y	Y	Y	N	N	Y	Y	Y
13 Coughlin	Y	N	Y	N	Y	Y	Y	Y
14 Moorhead	Y	Y	Y	N	N	Y	Y	Y
15 Rooney	Y	Y	Y	N	N	Y	Y	Y
16 Walker	Y	Y	N	N	Y	Y	Y	Y
17 Ertel	Y	Y	Y	Y	Y	Y	Y	Y
18 Walgren	Y	Y	Y	N	Y	Y	Y	Y
19 Goodling, W.	Y	Y	N	N	?	?	Y	Y
20 Gaydos	Y	Y	Y	N	N	Y	Y	Y
21 Dent	#	#	Y	X	X	#	Y	Y
22 Murphy	Y	Y	Y	Y	N	Y	Y	Y
23 Ammerman	?	Y	Y	N	N	Y	Y	Y
24 Marks	Y	Y	Y	Y	Y	Y	Y	Y
25 Myers, G.	Y	Y	Y	N	Y	Y	Y	Y
RHODE ISLAND								
1 St Germain	Y	Y	Y	N	N	Y	Y	Y
2 Beard	Y	Y	Y	N	?	?	Y	Y
SOUTH CAROLINA								
1 Davis	Y	Y	Y	Y	N	N	Y	Y
2 Spence	Y	Y	Y	Y	Y	N	Y	Y
3 Derrick	Y	#	Y	✓	✓	?	Y	Y
4 Mann	?	?	?	?	?	#	?	?
5 Holland	Y	Y	Y	Y	N	N	Y	Y
6 Jenrette	Y	Y	Y	Y	N	N	Y	N
SOUTH DAKOTA								
1 Pressler	Y	Y	Y	Y	Y	Y	Y	Y
2 Abdnor	Y	Y	Y	Y	Y	N	Y	Y
TENNESSEE								
1 Quillen	Y	Y	Y	Y	Y	N	Y	Y
2 Duncan	Y	Y	Y	Y	Y	N	Y	Y
3 Lloyd	Y	Y	Y	Y	Y	Y	Y	N
4 Gore	Y	Y	Y	Y	N	Y	Y	Y
5 Allen	Y	Y	Y	N	N	Y	Y	?
6 Beard	Y	Y	Y	Y	Y	N	Y	Y

	211	212	213	214	215	216	217	218
7 Jones	Y	Y	Y	Y	N	N	Y	Y
8 Ford	Y	Y	Y	Y	?	?	?	?
TEXAS								
1 Hall	Y	Y	N	Y	Y	N	Y	N
2 Wilson, C.	Y	Y	Y	Y	N	N	Y	Y
3 Collins	Y	Y	N	N	Y	N	N	N
4 Roberts	?	?	?	?	?	?	?	?
5 Mattox	Y	Y	Y	Y	N	Y	?	Y
6 Teague	?	?	?	?	✓	X	?	?
7 Archer	Y	Y	N	N	Y	Y	Y	Y
8 Eckhardt	Y	Y	Y	N	N	Y	Y	Y
9 Brooks	Y	Y	Y	N	N	Y	Y	Y
10 Pickle	Y	Y	Y	Y	Y	Y	Y	Y
11 Poage	?	Y	N	Y	?	?	Y	N
12 Wright	Y	Y	Y	Y	N	Y	?	Y
13 Hightower	Y	Y	Y	N	Y	N	Y	Y
14 Young	?	?	?	?	?	?	?	?
15 de la Garza	Y	Y	Y	N	Y	Y	Y	Y
16 White	Y	Y	Y	Y	Y	Y	Y	Y
17 Burleson	Y	Y	N	Y	Y	N	Y	N
18 Jordan	Y	Y	Y	Y	N	N	Y	Y
19 Mahon	Y	Y	Y	N	Y	N	Y	Y
20 Gonzalez	Y	Y	Y	N	Y	N	Y	Y
21 Krueger	?	?	?	?	?	?	?	?
22 Gammage	?	?	?	✓	✓	✓	?	?
23 Kazen	?	Y	Y	Y	Y	N	Y	Y
24 Milford	Y	Y	Y	N	Y	N	Y	Y
UTAH								
1 McKay	Y	Y	Y	N	N	Y	?	?
2 Marriott	Y	Y	Y	N	Y	N	Y	Y
VERMONT								
AL Jeffords	Y	Y	Y	Y	Y	Y	?	Y
VIRGINIA								
1 Trible	Y	Y	Y	Y	Y	Y	Y	Y
2 Whitehurst	Y	Y	N	Y	Y	Y	Y	Y
3 Satterfield	Y	Y	N	Y	Y	N	Y	N
4 Daniel	Y	Y	N	Y	Y	N	Y	Y
5 Daniel	Y	Y	N	Y	Y	N	Y	Y
6 Butler	Y	Y	Y	Y	Y	N	Y	Y
7 Robinson	Y	Y	N	Y	Y	N	Y	Y
8 Harris	Y	Y	Y	N	N	Y	Y	Y
9 Wampler	Y	Y	Y	Y	Y	N	Y	Y
10 Fisher	Y	Y	Y	N	N	Y	Y	Y
WASHINGTON								
1 Pritchard	Y	Y	Y	Y	Y	Y	Y	Y
2 Meeds	Y	Y	Y	N	N	Y	?	Y
3 Bonker	Y	Y	Y	N	N	Y	Y	Y
4 McCormack	?	Y	Y	Y	N	Y	Y	Y
5 Foley	Y	Y	Y	Y	Y	N	Y	Y
6 Dicks	Y	Y	Y	Y	Y	Y	Y	Y
7 Cunningham	Y	Y	N	Y	Y	N	Y	Y
WEST VIRGINIA								
1 Mollohan	?	Y	Y	N	N	N	Y	Y
2 Staggers	Y	Y	Y	N	N	Y	Y	Y
3 Slack	Y	Y	Y	N	N	N	Y	Y
4 Rahall	Y	Y	Y	N	N	Y	#	#
WISCONSIN								
1 Aspin	Y	Y	Y	N	N	Y	Y	Y
2 Kastenmeier	Y	Y	Y	N	N	Y	Y	Y
3 Baldus	Y	Y	Y	N	N	Y	Y	Y
4 Zablocki	Y	Y	Y	N	N	Y	Y	Y
5 Reuss	Y	Y	Y	Y	N	Y	#	Y
6 Steiger	Y	N	Y	N	Y	N	Y	Y
7 Obey	?	Y	Y	Y	N	Y	Y	Y
8 Cornell	Y	Y	Y	Y	Y	Y	Y	Y
9 Kasten	Y	Y	Y	Y	Y	Y	Y	Y
WYOMING								
AL Roncalio	Y	?	Y	Y	Y	N	Y	N

Democrats ***Republicans***

219. H J Res 859. U.S. Railway Association Supplemental Appropriations, Fiscal 1978. Passage of the joint resolution to appropriate $13 million for fiscal 1978 operations of the U.S. Railway Association. Passed 202-196: R 44-98; D 158-98 (ND 127-53; SD 31-45), April 27, 1978. The president had requested $13 million in new budget authority.

220. HR 11657. Pacific Fisheries Development. Leggett, D-Calif., motion to suspend the rules and pass the bill to authorize an additional $3 million for fiscal 1979 and $6 million for each of fiscal 1980-83 for the development of the fishing industry in the Pacific waters of Samoa, Guam, and the Northern Marianas. Motion agreed to 326-23: R 111-11; D 215-12 (ND 146-10; SD 69-2), May 1, 1978. A two-thirds majority vote (233 in this case) is required for passage under suspension of the rules.

221. HR 10392. Hubert H. Humphrey Fellowship. Nedzi, D-Mich., motion to suspend the rules and pass the bill to authorize $1 million for a Hubert H. Humphrey fellowship at the Woodrow Wilson International Center for Scholars of the Smithsonian Institution. Motion rejected 219-137: R 40-84; D 179-53 (ND 146-14; SD 33-39), May 1, 1978. A two-thirds majority vote (238 in this case) is required for passage under suspension of the rules.

222. H J Res 816. Federal Reserve Draw Authority. Mitchell, D-Md., motion to suspend the rules and pass the joint resolution to extend for one year, through April 30, 1979, the authority of Federal Reserve banks to purchase up to $5 billion in U.S. public debt obligations directly from the treasury. Motion agreed to 278-77: R 55-68; D 223-9 (ND 156-4; SD 67-5), May 1, 1978. A two-thirds majority vote (237 in this case) is required for passage under suspension of the rules.

223. HR 9400. Civil Rights of Institutionalized Persons. Adoption of the rule (H Res 1150) providing for House floor consideration of the bill to allow the attorney general to file suit on behalf of persons in state-operated prisons, nursing homes, mental institutions and other facilities where a "pattern or practice" of violations of constitutional rights was found. Adopted 320-20: R 104-14; D 216-6 (ND 153-1; SD 63-5), May 1, 1978.

224. HR 9400. Civil Rights of Institutionalized Persons. Ertel, D-Pa., amendment to delete prisons and other correctional facilities from coverage under the bill, thereby preventing the attorney general from filing "pattern or practice" suits where violations of the constitutional rights of such inmates were found. Adopted 227-132: R 103-23; D 124-109 (ND 67-95; SD 57-14), May 1, 1978.

225. HR 11713. Solar Loan Program. Smith, D-Iowa, motion to suspend the rules and pass the bill to create a $75 million solar, renewable energy sources and energy conservation loan program within the Small Business Administration. Motion agreed to 375-17: R 123-13; D 252-4 (ND 179-2; SD 73-2), May 2, 1978. A two-thirds majority vote (262 in this case) is required for passage under suspension of the rules.

226. HR 8099. Ak-Chin Indian Claims. Roncalio, D-Wyo., motion to suspend the rules and pass the bill to authorize $43 million for fiscal 1979-83 to provide the Ak-Chin Indian community in Arizona with 85,000 acre-feet of water annually within 25 years of enactment and to attempt to provide the community with water in the interim. Motion rejected 256-138: R 46-92; D 210-46 (ND 165-17; SD 45-29), May 2, 1978. A two-thirds majority vote (263 in this case) is required for passage under suspension of the rules.

KEY

- Y Voted for (yea).
- ✓ Paired for.
- † Announced for.
- # CQ Poll for.
- N Voted against (nay).
- X Paired against.
- \- Announced against.
- ▮ CQ Poll against.
- P Voted "present."
- ● Voted "present" to avoid possible conflict of interest.
- ? Did not vote or otherwise make a position known.

	219	220	221	222	223	224	225	226
ALABAMA								
1 Edwards	Y	Y	N	Y	Y	Y	Y	N
2 Dickinson	N	Y	N	N	N	Y	Y	N
3 Nichols	Y	Y	N	Y	Y	Y	Y	N
4 Bevill	Y	Y	N	Y	Y	Y	Y	Y
5 Flippo	N	Y	N	Y	Y	Y	Y	N
6 Buchanan	N	?	?	?	?	N	Y	N
7 Flowers	N	Y	N	Y	Y	Y	Y	N
ALASKA								
AL Young	N	Y	N	N	Y	Y	Y	Y
ARIZONA								
1 Rhodes	N	?	?	?	?	?	Y	Y
2 Udall	Y	Y	Y	Y	Y	Y	Y	Y
3 Stump	N	X	X	?	?	?	N	N
4 Rudd	N	N	N	N	Y	Y	Y	Y
ARKANSAS								
1 Alexander	Y	Y	Y	Y	Y	N	Y	Y
2 Tucker	?	?	?	?	?	?	?	?
3 Hammerschmidt	N	Y	N	N	Y	Y	Y	N
4 Thornton	?	?	?	?	?	?	?	?
CALIFORNIA								
1 Johnson	Y	Y	Y	Y	Y	N	Y	Y
2 Clausen	N	?	?	?	?	✓	Y	Y
3 Moss	Y	?	?	?	?	?	Y	Y
4 Leggett	#	Y	?	?	?	Y	Y	Y
5 Burton, J.	N	Y	Y	Y	?	?	Y	Y
6 Burton, P.	N	Y	Y	Y	Y	N	Y	Y
7 Miller	N	?	Y	Y	Y	N	Y	Y
8 Dellums	N	?	?	?	?	X	?	?
9 Stark	N	Y	Y	Y	Y	N	Y	Y
10 Edwards	Y	Y	Y	Y	Y	N	Y	Y
11 Ryan	Y	Y	Y	Y	Y	N	Y	N
12 McCloskey	N	Y	Y	Y	Y	N	Y	Y
13 Mineta	Y	Y	Y	Y	Y	N	Y	Y
14 McFall	Y	Y	Y	Y	Y	N	Y	Y
15 Sisk	N	Y	Y	Y	?	N	Y	Y
16 Panetta	N	Y	Y	N	Y	N	Y	Y
17 Krebs	N	Y	Y	Y	Y	N	Y	Y
18 Ketchum	N	Y	N	N	Y	Y	Y	N
19 Lagomarsino	N	Y	N	N	Y	Y	Y	N
20 Goldwater	N	Y	N	N	?	Y	Y	Y
21 Corman	Y	Y	Y	Y	?	N	Y	Y
22 Moorhead	N	Y	N	N	Y	Y	Y	N
23 Beilenson	Y	Y	Y	Y	?	N	Y	Y
24 Waxman	?	?	?	?	?	▮	Y	Y
25 Roybal	N	Y	Y	Y	Y	N	Y	Y
26 Rousselot	N	Y	N	N	N	Y	Y	N
27 Dornan	N	Y	N	N	Y	Y	Y	N
28 Burke	?	?	?	?	?	X	Y	Y
29 Hawkins	Y	Y	Y	Y	Y	N	Y	Y
30 Danielson	Y	Y	Y	Y	Y	N	Y	Y
31 Wilson, C.H.	?	Y	Y	Y	?	Y	Y	N
32 Anderson	N	Y	Y	Y	Y	N	Y	Y
33 Clawson	N	?	N	N	N	Y	N	N
34 Hannaford	N	Y	Y	Y	Y	N	Y	Y
35 Lloyd	Y	Y	Y	Y	Y	Y	Y	Y
36 Brown	Y	Y	Y	Y	Y	?	Y	Y
37 Pettis	Y	?	?	?	?	?	?	?
38 Patterson	N	Y	Y	Y	Y	Y	Y	Y
39 Wiggins	N	Y	N	N	Y	Y	N	N
40 Badham	N	Y	N	N	Y	Y	Y	N
41 Wilson, B.	N	Y	N	N	Y	Y	Y	N
42 Van Deerlin	Y	Y	Y	Y	Y	?	Y	Y
43 Burgener	Y	Y	N	Y	Y	Y	Y	N
COLORADO								
1 Schroeder	N	Y	Y	Y	Y	N	Y	Y
2 Wirth	Y	Y	Y	Y	Y	X	Y	Y
3 Evans	Y	Y	Y	Y	Y	Y	Y	Y
4 Johnson	N	?	?	?	?	?	?	?
5 Armstrong	N	?	?	?	?	?	Y	N
CONNECTICUT								
1 Cotter	N	Y	Y	Y	Y	Y	Y	N
2 Dodd	N	?	?	?	?	Y	Y	Y
3 Giaimo	N	Y	Y	Y	Y	Y	Y	Y
4 McKinney	N	Y	Y	Y	Y	N	Y	N
5 Sarasin	Y	Y	Y	Y	Y	Y	Y	N
6 Moffett	N	Y	Y	Y	Y	N	Y	Y
DELAWARE								
AL Evans	Y	Y	N	Y	Y	Y	Y	N
FLORIDA								
1 Sikes	Y	Y	N	Y	Y	Y	Y	Y
2 Fuqua	N	Y	N	Y	Y	Y	Y	Y
3 Bennett	N	Y	Y	Y	Y	Y	Y	Y
4 Chappell	Y	Y	N	Y	Y	Y	Y	Y
5 Kelly	N	N	N	N	Y	Y	N	N
6 Young	N	Y	N	Y	Y	Y	Y	N
7 Gibbons	N	Y	Y	Y	Y	Y	Y	Y
8 Ireland	N	Y	Y	Y	?	Y	Y	N
9 Frey	?	?	?	?	?	✓	?	?
10 Bafalis	N	Y	N	N	Y	Y	Y	Y
11 Rogers	N	Y	Y	Y	Y	Y	Y	Y
12 Burke	N	Y	N	Y	#	Y	Y	N
13 Lehman	N	Y	Y	Y	?	N	Y	Y
14 Pepper	Y	Y	Y	Y	Y	Y	Y	Y
15 Fascell	Y	Y	Y	Y	Y	N	Y	Y
GEORGIA								
1 Ginn	N	Y	N	Y	Y	Y	Y	Y
2 Mathis	N	Y	N	N	Y	Y	Y	N
3 Brinkley	N	Y	N	Y	Y	Y	Y	N
4 Levitas	N	Y	N	Y	Y	Y	Y	Y
5 Fowler	N	Y	N	Y	Y	Y	Y	Y
6 Flynt	N	Y	N	Y	N	Y	Y	N
7 McDonald	N	N	N	N	N	Y	N	N
8 Evans	N	#	N	N	Y	Y	Y	N
9 Jenkins	N	Y	N	Y	#	Y	Y	N
10 Barnard	N	Y	N	Y	Y	Y	Y	Y
HAWAII								
1 Heftel	N	Y	Y	Y	?	Y	Y	Y
2 Akaka	Y	Y	Y	Y	Y	Y	Y	Y
IDAHO								
1 Symms	N	N	N	N	N	Y	N	N
2 Hansen, G.	N	N	N	N	N	Y	N	N
ILLINOIS								
1 Metcalfe	Y	Y	Y	Y	Y	N	Y	Y
2 Murphy	N	Y	Y	Y	Y	N	Y	Y
3 Russo	N	#	Y	Y	Y	Y	Y	Y
4 Derwinski	N	Y	Y	Y	Y	Y	Y	N
5 Fary	Y	Y	Y	Y	Y	Y	Y	Y
6 Hyde	N	#	▮	#	#	▮	Y	N
7 Collins	N	Y	Y	Y	Y	N	Y	Y
8 Rostenkowski	Y	Y	Y	Y	Y	N	Y	Y
9 Yates	Y	Y	Y	Y	Y	N	Y	Y
10 Mikva	N	?	?	?	Y	N	Y	Y
11 Annunzio	N	Y	Y	Y	Y	N	Y	Y
12 Crane	N	N	N	N	N	Y	N	N
13 McClory	Y	Y	Y	Y	Y	N	N	N
14 Erlenborn	N	Y	N	?	Y	N	Y	Y
15 Corcoran	N	Y	N	Y	Y	N	Y	N
16 Anderson	N	Y	Y	Y	Y	N	Y	Y
17 O'Brien	Y	Y	N	N	Y	Y	Y	N
18 Michel	N	Y	Y	N	Y	Y	Y	N
19 Railsback	N	Y	Y	Y	Y	N	Y	Y
20 Findley	N	Y	Y	Y	?	N	Y	N
21 Madigan	N	Y	Y	Y	Y	N	Y	N
22 Shipley	Y	✓	?	?	?	X	Y	Y
23 Price	Y	Y	Y	Y	Y	N	Y	Y
24 Simon	Y	Y	Y	Y	Y	N	Y	Y
INDIANA								
1 Benjamin	Y	N	N	Y	Y	N	Y	Y
2 Fithian	Y	Y	Y	Y	Y	Y	Y	Y
3 Brademas	Y	✓	†	†	†	X	Y	Y
4 Quayle	N	N	N	N	Y	Y	Y	N
5 Hillis	Y	?	?	?	?	?	Y	N
6 Evans	N	N	N	N	Y	Y	?	?
7 Myers, J.	N	Y	N	N	Y	Y	Y	N
8 Cornwell	Y	Y	N	Y	Y	Y	Y	N
9 Hamilton	Y	Y	N	Y	Y	N	Y	Y
10 Sharp	Y	Y	N	Y	Y	N	Y	Y
11 Jacobs	N	N	N	Y	Y	Y	Y	N
IOWA								
1 Leach	N	Y	Y	Y	Y	N	Y	N
2 Blouin	Y	Y	Y	Y	Y	N	Y	Y
3 Grassley	N	Y	N	N	Y	Y	Y	N
4 Smith	Y	Y	Y	Y	Y	Y	Y	Y
5 Harkin	N	Y	Y	Y	Y	N	Y	Y
6 Bedell	N	●	Y	Y	Y	Y	Y	Y

Democrats ***Republicans***

	219	220	221	222	223	224	225	226
KANSAS								
1 Sebelius	N	Y	N	Y	Y	Y	Y	Y
2 Keys	N	Y	Y	Y	Y	N	Y	Y
3 Winn	N	Y	N	N	Y	Y	Y	Y
4 Glickman	N	N	N	N	Y	Y	Y	Y
5 Skubitz	Y	Y	N	Y	Y	Y	Y	Y
KENTUCKY								
1 Hubbard	Y	Y	N	Y	Y	Y	Y	N
2 Natcher	Y	Y	Y	Y	Y	Y	Y	Y
3 Mazzoli	N	Y	N	Y	Y	N	Y	Y
4 Snyder	N	Y	N	N	Y	Y	Y	N
5 Carter	Y	Y	Y	Y	Y	Y	Y	N
6 Breckinridge	Y	?	?	?	?	?	Y	Y
7 Perkins	Y	Y	Y	Y	Y	N	Y	Y
LOUISIANA								
1 Livingston	N	?	?	?	?	?	Y	N
2 Boggs	Y	#	✓	#	#	✓	Y	Y
3 Treen	N	Y	N	Y	Y	Y	Y	N
4 Waggonner	N	Y	N	Y	N	Y	N	N
5 Huckaby	N	Y	N	Y	Y	Y	Y	N
6 Moore	N	Y	N	N	Y	Y	Y	N
7 Breaux	N	Y	N	Y	Y	Y	Y	N
8 Long	Y	Y	Y	Y	Y	Y	Y	Y
MAINE								
1 Emery	Y	Y	Y	Y	Y	Y	Y	Y
2 Cohen	Y	?	?	?	?	?	Y	Y
MARYLAND								
1 Bauman	N	Y	N	N	Y	Y	N	N
2 Long	Y	Y	Y	#	Y	Y	Y	Y
3 Mikulski	Y	Y	Y	Y	Y	N	Y	Y
4 Holt	Y	Y	N	Y	Y	Y	Y	N
5 Spellman	Y	Y	✓	?	Y	N	Y	Y
6 Byron	N	Y	N	Y	Y	Y	Y	Y
7 Mitchell	N	Y	Y	Y	Y	N	Y	Y
8 Steers	Y	Y	Y	Y	Y	N	Y	Y
MASSACHUSETTS								
1 Conte	Y	Y	Y	Y	Y	N	Y	Y
2 Boland	Y	Y	Y	Y	Y	N	Y	Y
3 Early	N	Y	Y	Y	Y	N	Y	Y
4 Drinan	Y	Y	Y	Y	Y	N	Y	Y
5 Tsongas	?	Y	Y	Y	Y	N	Y	Y
6 Harrington	Y	#	Y	Y	Y	N	Y	Y
7 Markey	Y	Y	Y	Y	Y	N	Y	Y
8 O'Neill								
9 Moakley	Y	Y	Y	Y	Y	N	Y	Y
10 Heckler	Y	?	?	?	?	?	Y	N
11 Burke	Y	Y	Y	Y	Y	N	Y	Y
12 Studds	Y	Y	Y	Y	Y	N	Y	Y
MICHIGAN								
1 Conyers	▮	?	?	?	?	▮	?	?
2 Pursell	N	?	?	?	?	?	?	?
3 Brown	Y	Y	N	Y	Y	Y	Y	Y
4 Stockman	▮	▮	?	?	?	?	?	?
5 Sawyer	?	Y	Y	Y	N	Y	Y	Y
6 Carr	Y	Y	Y	Y	Y	N	Y	Y
7 Kildee	Y	Y	Y	Y	Y	N	Y	Y
8 Traxler	Y	Y	Y	Y	Y	Y	Y	Y
9 Vander Jagt	N	Y	N	Y	Y	Y	Y	N
10 Cederberg	Y	Y	Y	Y	Y	Y	Y	N
11 Ruppe	Y	#	?	?	?	✓	?	?
12 Bonior	Y	Y	Y	Y	Y	N	Y	Y
13 Diggs	Y	?	?	?	?	?	Y	Y
14 Nedzi	Y	Y	Y	Y	Y	Y	Y	Y
15 Ford	Y	Y	Y	Y	Y	Y	Y	?
16 Dingell	Y	Y	Y	Y	Y	Y	Y	N
17 Brodhead	Y	Y	Y	Y	Y	N	Y	Y
18 Blanchard	Y	Y	Y	Y	Y	Y	Y	Y
19 Broomfield	N	Y	Y	Y	Y	Y	Y	Y
MINNESOTA								
1 Quie	N	?	?	?	?	?	Y	Y
2 Hagedorn	N	Y	Y	Y	Y	Y	Y	N
3 Frenzel	N	Y	Y	Y	Y	Y	Y	Y
4 Vento	Y	Y	Y	Y	Y	Y	Y	Y
5 Fraser	Y	?	?	?	#	N	Y	Y
6 Nolan	Y	Y	Y	Y	?	N	Y	Y
7 Stangeland	N	Y	Y	Y	Y	Y	Y	N
8 Oberstar	Y	Y	Y	Y	Y	N	Y	Y
MISSISSIPPI								
1 Whitten	?	Y	Y	Y	Y	Y	Y	Y
2 Bowen	N	?	?	?	?	?	Y	Y
3 Montgomery	N	Y	N	Y	Y	Y	Y	N
4 Cochran	N	?	?	?	?	?	?	?
5 Lott	N	Y	N	Y	Y	Y	Y	N
MISSOURI								
1 Clay	Y	Y	Y	Y	Y	N	Y	Y
2 Young	Y	#	Y	Y	Y	Y	Y	Y
3 Gephardt	Y	Y	Y	Y	#	Y	Y	Y

	219	220	221	222	223	224	225	226
4 Skelton	N	Y	Y	Y	N	Y	Y	N
5 Bolling	Y	Y	Y	Y	?	N	Y	Y
6 Coleman	N	Y	N	N	Y	Y	Y	N
7 Taylor	N	Y	N	N	Y	Y	Y	N
8 Ichord	N	N	N	Y	Y	Y	Y	N
9 Volkmer	N	N	N	Y	Y	Y	Y	Y
10 Burlison	Y	Y	Y	Y	Y	Y	Y	Y
MONTANA								
1 Baucus	?	Y	Y	Y	Y	N	Y	Y
2 Marlenee	Y	N	N	N	Y	Y	Y	Y
NEBRASKA								
1 Thone	N	?	▮	#	#	#	#	#
2 Cavanaugh	N	?	?	?	?	?	Y	Y
3 Smith	N	Y	N	N	Y	Y	Y	N
NEVADA								
AL Santini	?	Y	Y	Y	Y	?	Y	Y
NEW HAMPSHIRE								
1 D'Amours	Y	Y	Y	Y	Y	Y	Y	Y
2 Cleveland	Y	Y	N	N	Y	Y	Y	N
NEW JERSEY								
1 Florio	Y	Y	Y	Y	Y	Y	Y	Y
2 Hughes	Y	Y	Y	Y	Y	Y	Y	N
3 Howard	?	Y	Y	Y	#	▮	Y	Y
4 Thompson	Y	Y	Y	Y	Y	N	Y	Y
5 Fenwick	Y	Y	Y	Y	Y	N	Y	N
6 Forsythe	N	Y	Y	N	Y	Y	Y	N
7 Maguire	Y	N	Y	Y	Y	N	Y	Y
8 Roe	Y	Y	Y	Y	Y	N	Y	Y
9 Hollenbeck	Y	Y	Y	Y	Y	N	Y	Y
10 Rodino	?	?	?	?	?	X	?	?
11 Minish	N	?	?	?	?	?	Y	Y
12 Rinaldo	Y	Y	Y	Y	Y	Y	Y	Y
13 Meyner	Y	Y	Y	Y	Y	N	Y	Y
14 LeFante	Y	?	?	?	?	X	Y	Y
15 Patten	Y	?	?	Y	Y	N	Y	Y
NEW MEXICO								
1 Lujan	Y	?	?	?	?	Y	Y	Y
2 Runnels	?	?	?	?	?	?	?	?
NEW YORK								
1 Pike	N	Y	Y	Y	Y	Y	Y	Y
2 Downey	N	Y	Y	Y	Y	N	Y	Y
3 Ambro	Y	?	?	?	?	?	Y	Y
4 Lent	Y	Y	N	N	?	Y	Y	N
5 Wydler	N	Y	N	N	Y	Y	Y	N
6 Wolff	Y	Y	Y	Y	?	Y	Y	Y
7 Addabbo	Y	Y	Y	Y	Y	Y	Y	Y
8 Rosenthal	Y	#	?	?	Y	N	Y	Y
9 Delaney	Y	Y	Y	Y	Y	Y	Y	Y
10 Biaggi	Y	Y	Y	Y	Y	N	Y	N
11 Scheuer	Y	Y	Y	Y	Y	N	Y	Y
12 Chisholm	N	Y	Y	Y	Y	N	Y	Y
13 Solarz	N	Y	Y	Y	#	N	Y	Y
14 Richmond	Y	Y	Y	Y	Y	N	Y	Y
15 Zeferetti	Y	Y	Y	Y	Y	Y	Y	Y
16 Holtzman	N	Y	Y	Y	Y	N	Y	Y
17 Murphy	Y	Y	Y	Y	Y	?	?	?
18 Green	Y	Y	Y	Y	Y	N	Y	Y
19 Rangel	Y	Y	Y	Y	Y	X	Y	Y
20 Weiss	Y	Y	Y	Y	?	N	Y	Y
21 Garcia	Y	?	?	?	?	N	Y	Y
22 Bingham	?	Y	Y	Y	Y	N	Y	Y
23 Caputo	Y	Y	Y	N	Y	Y	Y	Y
24 Ottinger	Y	Y	Y	Y	Y	N	Y	Y
25 Fish	Y	Y	Y	Y	Y	Y	N	N
26 Gilman	Y	Y	Y	Y	?	N	Y	N
27 McHugh	Y	Y	Y	Y	Y	N	Y	N
28 Stratton	Y	?	#	#	Y	Y	Y	N
29 Pattison	Y	Y	Y	Y	Y	N	Y	Y
30 McEwen	Y	Y	N	Y	Y	Y	N	N
31 Mitchell	Y	Y	Y	N	Y	Y	Y	N
32 Hanley	Y	Y	Y	Y	Y	Y	Y	Y
33 Walsh	?	Y	N	N	Y	Y	Y	N
34 Horton	Y	Y	N	Y	?	Y	Y	Y
35 Conable	N	Y	N	Y	Y	Y	N	Y
36 LaFalce	Y	Y	Y	Y	Y	Y	N	Y
37 Nowak	Y	Y	Y	Y	Y	N	Y	Y
38 Kemp	N	Y	N	N	Y	Y	Y	Y
39 Lundine	Y	Y	Y	Y	Y	Y	Y	Y
NORTH CAROLINA								
1 Jones	▮	?	▮	#	#	#	#	▮
2 Fountain	N	?	?	?	?	?	?	?
3 Whitley	?	?	?	?	?	?	?	?
4 Andrews	N	?	?	?	#	?	#	?
5 Neal	N	Y	N	Y	Y	Y	Y	Y
6 Preyer	Y	Y	Y	Y	Y	Y	Y	Y
7 Rose	Y	Y	Y	Y	Y	Y	Y	Y
8 Hefner	N	Y	Y	Y	Y	Y	Y	Y

	219	220	221	222	223	224	225	226
9 Martin	N	Y	Y	N	Y	Y	Y	N
10 Broyhill	N	Y	N	N	Y	Y	Y	N
11 Gudger	▮	#	#	#	#	#	#	#
NORTH DAKOTA								
AL Andrews	N	Y	Y	Y	Y	Y	Y	Y
OHIO								
1 Gradison	Y	Y	N	Y	Y	Y	Y	N
2 Luken	N	?	Y	Y	Y	Y	Y	Y
3 Whalen	Y	Y	Y	Y	Y	N	Y	Y
4 Guyer	N	Y	N	N	Y	Y	Y	N
5 Latta	N	Y	N	N	N	Y	Y	N
6 Harsha	N	?	?	?	Y	Y	Y	N
7 Brown	N	Y	N	N	Y	Y	Y	N
8 Kindness	N	Y	N	N	N	Y	Y	N
9 Ashley	N	Y	Y	Y	Y	Y	Y	Y
10 Miller	N	Y	N	N	Y	Y	Y	N
11 Stanton	Y	Y	N	Y	Y	Y	Y	Y
12 Devine	N	Y	N	N	Y	Y	Y	N
13 Pease	Y	Y	Y	Y	Y	Y	Y	Y
14 Seiberling	Y	Y	Y	Y	Y	N	Y	Y
15 Wylie	N	Y	N	Y	Y	Y	?	?
16 Regula	N	Y	N	Y	Y	Y	Y	Y
17 Ashbrook	▮	Y	N	N	N	Y	Y	N
18 Applegate	Y	Y	Y	Y	Y	Y	Y	Y
19 Carney	Y	#	?	?	?	X	?	?
20 Oakar	N	?	?	?	?	?	Y	Y
21 Stokes	Y	Y	Y	Y	Y	N	Y	Y
22 Vanik	Y	Y	Y	Y	Y	#	Y	Y
23 Mottl	N	N	N	Y	Y	Y	Y	N
OKLAHOMA								
1 Jones	N	Y	N	Y	Y	N	Y	N
2 Risenhoover	N	Y	N	Y	Y	Y	?	?
3 Watkins	N	Y	N	Y	Y	Y	Y	Y
4 Steed	Y	Y	Y	Y	Y	Y	Y	Y
5 Edwards	N	Y	N	N	Y	Y	Y	Y
6 English	N	Y	N	Y	Y	Y	Y	Y
OREGON								
1 AuCoin	N	Y	Y	Y	Y	Y	?	Y
2 Ullman	Y	Y	Y	Y	Y	N	Y	Y
3 Duncan	Y	Y	Y	Y	Y	N	?	Y
4 Weaver	N	?	?	?	?	?	?	?
PENNSYLVANIA								
1 Myers, M.	Y	Y	Y	Y	Y	Y	Y	Y
2 Nix	?	?	?	?	?	✓	?	?
3 Lederer	Y	Y	Y	Y	Y	Y	Y	Y
4 Eilberg	?	?	?	?	?	X	?	?
5 Schulze	Y	Y	N	N	Y	Y	Y	N
6 Yatron	Y	Y	N	Y	Y	Y	Y	Y
7 Edgar	Y	N	Y	Y	Y	N	Y	Y
8 Kostmayer	N	N	Y	N	Y	N	Y	Y
9 Shuster	Y	Y	N	N	N	Y	?	N
10 McDade	Y	Y	Y	Y	Y	Y	Y	Y
11 Flood	Y	#	#	#	Y	Y	Y	Y
12 Murtha	Y	Y	Y	Y	Y	Y	Y	Y
13 Coughlin	Y	Y	N	Y	Y	Y	Y	N
14 Moorhead	Y	Y	Y	Y	Y	N	Y	Y
15 Rooney	Y	Y	Y	Y	Y	Y	Y	Y
16 Walker	N	N	N	N	Y	Y	Y	N
17 Ertel	N	Y	N	Y	Y	Y	Y	N
18 Walgren	Y	Y	Y	Y	Y	N	Y	Y
19 Goodling, W.	N	?	?	?	?	✓	Y	N
20 Gaydos	Y	Y	Y	Y	Y	Y	Y	Y
21 Dent	#	#	#	#	Y	Y	Y	Y
22 Murphy	Y	Y	Y	Y	Y	Y	Y	Y
23 Ammerman	Y	Y	Y	Y	Y	Y	Y	Y
24 Marks	N	Y	Y	Y	?	Y	Y	Y
25 Myers, G.	N	N	N	Y	Y	N	Y	N
RHODE ISLAND								
1 St Germain	Y	Y	Y	Y	Y	N	Y	Y
2 Beard	Y	Y	Y	Y	Y	N	Y	Y
SOUTH CAROLINA								
1 Davis	Y	Y	Y	Y	?	Y	Y	N
2 Spence	N	Y	N	N	Y	Y	Y	N
3 Derrick	Y	Y	Y	Y	Y	Y	Y	N
4 Mann	?	?	?	?	?	?	?	?
5 Holland	Y	Y	Y	Y	Y	Y	Y	N
6 Jenrette	Y	Y	Y	Y	Y	Y	Y	Y
SOUTH DAKOTA								
1 Pressler	Y	?	?	?	?	?	Y	Y
2 Abdnor	N	Y	Y	Y	Y	Y	Y	Y
TENNESSEE								
1 Quillen	N	Y	N	N	N	Y	Y	Y
2 Duncan	N	Y	N	N	Y	Y	Y	N
3 Lloyd	N	Y	N	Y	Y	Y	Y	N
4 Gore	Y	Y	Y	Y	Y	N	Y	Y
5 Allen	?	Y	Y	Y	Y	N	Y	N
6 Beard	N	Y	N	N	Y	Y	Y	N

	219	220	221	222	223	224	225	226
7 Jones	Y	Y	N	Y	Y	Y	Y	Y
8 Ford	?	Y	Y	Y	Y	N	Y	Y
TEXAS								
1 Hall	N	Y	N	Y	Y	Y	Y	N
2 Wilson, C.	Y	Y	Y	Y	Y	Y	Y	▮
3 Collins	N	N	N	N	N	Y	N	N
4 Roberts	?	Y	N	Y	Y	Y	Y	Y
5 Mattox	Y	Y	N	Y	Y	Y	Y	N
6 Teague	?	?	?	?	?	✓	?	?
7 Archer	N	N	N	N	N	Y	Y	N
8 Eckhardt	Y	?	?	?	?	?	Y	Y
9 Brooks	N	Y	Y	Y	Y	N	Y	N
10 Pickle	N	Y	Y	Y	Y	Y	Y	Y
11 Poage	N	Y	N	Y	N	Y	Y	Y
12 Wright	Y	Y	Y	Y	Y	Y	Y	Y
13 Hightower	Y	Y	N	Y	Y	?	Y	N
14 Young	?	Y	Y	Y	Y	Y	Y	Y
15 de la Garza	N	Y	N	Y	Y	Y	Y	Y
16 White	Y	†	†	?	†	-	†	†
17 Burleson	N	?	?	?	?	✓	?	?
18 Jordan	Y	Y	Y	Y	Y	N	Y	Y
19 Mahon	Y	Y	Y	Y	Y	Y	?	Y
20 Gonzalez	N	Y	Y	Y	Y	N	Y	Y
21 Krueger	?	?	?	?	?	?	?	?
22 Gammage	?	?	?	?	?	?	?	?
23 Kazen	N	?	?	?	?	✓	?	?
24 Milford	N	Y	N	Y	Y	Y	Y	N
UTAH								
1 McKay	?	Y	Y	Y	Y	Y	Y	Y
2 Marriott	N	Y	N	N	Y	Y	Y	Y
VERMONT								
AL Jeffords	Y	Y	Y	Y	Y	N	Y	Y
VIRGINIA								
1 Trible	N	Y	N	N	Y	Y	Y	N
2 Whitehurst	N	Y	N	N	Y	Y	Y	N
3 Satterfield	N	Y	N	N	N	Y	Y	N
4 Daniel	N	Y	N	N	Y	Y	Y	N
5 Daniel	N	Y	N	N	Y	Y	Y	N
6 Butler	N	Y	N	N	Y	N	N	N
7 Robinson	N	Y	N	N	Y	Y	Y	N
8 Harris	N	N	Y	Y	Y	N	Y	N
9 Wampler	N	?	?	?	?	✓	Y	Y
10 Fisher	Y	Y	Y	Y	Y	N	Y	Y
WASHINGTON								
1 Pritchard	N	?	Y	Y	Y	Y	Y	N
2 Meeds	Y	?	?	?	?	?	Y	Y
3 Bonker	Y	?	?	?	?	?	Y	Y
4 McCormack	Y	Y	Y	Y	Y	Y	?	?
5 Foley	Y	Y	Y	Y	Y	Y	Y	N
6 Dicks	Y	?	?	?	?	?	Y	N
7 Cunningham	N	Y	N	N	Y	Y	Y	N
WEST VIRGINIA								
1 Mollohan	N	?	▮	?	?	?	?	?
2 Staggers	Y	Y	Y	Y	Y	N	Y	Y
3 Slack	Y	Y	N	Y	Y	Y	Y	Y
4 Rahall	?	Y	Y	Y	Y	N	?	?
WISCONSIN								
1 Aspin	Y	Y	Y	Y	Y	N	Y	Y
2 Kastenmeier	Y	Y	Y	Y	Y	N	Y	Y
3 Baldus	Y	?	?	?	?	▮	?	?
4 Zablocki	Y	Y	Y	Y	Y	N	Y	Y
5 Reuss	Y	Y	Y	Y	Y	N	Y	Y
6 Steiger	Y	Y	Y	Y	Y	N	N	Y
7 Obey	Y	Y	Y	Y	Y	N	Y	Y
8 Cornell	N	Y	Y	Y	Y	N	Y	Y
9 Kasten	Y	Y	Y	N	Y	▮	Y	Y
WYOMING								
AL Roncalio	Y	?	?	?	?	?	Y	Y

Democrats ***Republicans***

227. HR 8331. Securities Investor Protection Act. Eckhardt, D-Texas, motion to suspend the rules and adopt H Res 1158 to amend the bill as passed by the Senate and to request a conference on the bill to amend the Securities Investors Protection Act of 1970 (in effect passing the bill). Motion agreed to 384-10: R 138-0; D 246-10 (ND 173-9; SD 73-1), May 2, 1978. A two-thirds majority (263 in this case) is required for adoption under suspension of the rules.

228. H Res 1159. Claude Powell Contempt Citation. Adoption of the resolution to request the U.S. attorney for the District of Columbia to prosecute Claude Powell Jr. for contempt of Congress for not responding to the House Select Committee on Assassinations subpoena to testify in the Martin Luther King Jr. assassination investigation. Adopted 367-16: R 133-1; D 234-15 (ND 166-11; SD 68-4), May 2, 1978.

229. H Con Res 559. Fiscal 1979 Budget Targets. Giaimo, D-Conn., motion that the House resolve itself into the Committee of the Whole to consider the resolution to set fiscal 1979 budget targets. Motion agreed to 383-4: R 133-2; D 250-2 (ND 175-1; SD 75-1), May 3, 1978.

230. H Con Res 559. Fiscal 1979 Budget Targets. Holt, R-Md., amendment to set aggregate budget targets as follows: revenues of $440.1 billion, budget authority of $546.8 billion, outlays of $488.3 billion and a deficit of $48.2 billion. Rejected 197-203: R 139-1; D 58-202 (ND 24-155; SD 34-47), May 3, 1978.

231. H Con Res 559. Fiscal 1979 Budget Targets. Stratton, D-N.Y., substitute amendment, to the Mitchell, D-Md., amendment *(see vote 232, below)*, to increase the budget authority target for national defense programs by $2.4 billion, to $129.8 billion. Rejected 142-262: R 71-67; D 71-195 (ND 16-167; SD 55-28), May 3, 1978.

232. H Con Res 559. Fiscal 1979 Budget Targets. Mitchell, D-Md., amendment to reduce targets for national defense programs by $4.8 billion in budget authority to $122.6 billion and $2.8 billion in outlays to $112.9 billion, and to make matching increases in targets for commerce and housing credit; transportation, community and regional development; education, training, employment and social services and health. Rejected 98-313: R 6-135; D 92-178 (ND 89-98; SD 3-80), May 3, 1978.

233. H Con Res 559. Fiscal 1979 Budget Targets. Conable, R-N.Y., amendment to reduce the target for revenues by $3.2 billion to $440.1 billion in order to allow for a larger tax cut. Rejected 163-239: R 136-3; D 27-236 (ND 11-171; SD 16-65), May 3, 1978.

234. H Con Res 559. Fiscal 1979 Budget Targets. Roberts, D-Texas, amendment to increase spending targets for veterans' programs by $1.1 billion in budget authority to $21.7 billion, and by $844 million in outlays to $21.3 billion. Adopted 362-33: R 131-6; D 231-27 (ND 150-26; SD 81-1), May 3, 1978.

KEY

- Y Voted for (yea).
- ✓ Paired for.
- † Announced for.
- # CQ Poll for.
- N Voted against (nay).
- X Paired against.
- \- Announced against.
- ▮ CQ Poll against.
- P Voted "present."
- ● Voted "present" to avoid possible conflict of interest.
- ? Did not vote or otherwise make a position known.

	227	228	229	230	231	232	233	234
ALABAMA								
1 Edwards	Y	Y	Y	Y	Y	N	Y	Y
2 Dickinson	Y	Y	Y	Y	Y	N	Y	Y
3 Nichols	Y	Y	Y	Y	Y	N	N	Y
4 Bevill	Y	Y	Y	N	Y	N	N	Y
5 Flippo	Y	Y	Y	N	Y	N	N	Y
6 Buchanan	Y	Y	Y	Y	Y	N	Y	Y
7 Flowers	Y	Y	Y	Y	Y	N	N	Y
ALASKA								
AL Young	Y	Y	Y	Y	#	N	Y	#
ARIZONA								
1 Rhodes	Y	Y	Y	Y	N	N	Y	Y
2 Udall	Y	Y	Y	N	N	Y	▮	Y
3 Stump	Y	Y	Y	Y	Y	N	N	Y
4 Rudd	Y	Y	?	Y	Y	N	Y	Y
ARKANSAS								
1 Alexander	Y	Y	Y	N	Y	N	N	Y
2 Tucker	?	?	?	?	?	?	?	?
3 Hammerschmidt	Y	?	Y	Y	N	N	Y	Y
4 Thornton	?	?	?	?	?	?	?	?
CALIFORNIA								
1 Johnson	Y	Y	Y	N	N	N	N	Y
2 Clausen	Y	Y	Y	Y	Y	N	Y	Y
3 Moss	Y	Y	Y	N	?	N	N	?
4 Leggett	Y	Y	Y	N	N	N	N	N
5 Burton, J.	N	?	?	N	N	Y	Y	Y
6 Burton, P.	N	N	Y	N	N	Y	N	Y
7 Miller	Y	N	?	?	N	Y	N	Y
8 Dellums	?	?	?	N	N	Y	N	Y
9 Stark	N	N	Y	N	N	Y	N	N
10 Edwards	Y	N	Y	N	N	Y	N	Y
11 Ryan	Y	Y	Y	N	N	Y	N	Y
12 McCloskey	Y	Y	Y	Y	N	Y	Y	Y
13 Mineta	Y	Y	Y	N	N	Y	N	Y
14 McFall	Y	Y	Y	N	N	N	N	Y
15 Sisk	Y	Y	Y	N	N	N	X	?
16 Panetta	Y	Y	Y	Y	N	Y	N	Y
17 Krebs	Y	Y	Y	N	N	N	N	Y
18 Ketchum	Y	Y	Y	Y	Y	N	Y	Y
19 Lagomarsino	Y	Y	Y	Y	Y	N	Y	Y
20 Goldwater	Y	Y	?	✓	Y	N	Y	Y
21 Corman	Y	Y	Y	N	N	Y	N	Y
22 Moorhead	Y	Y	Y	Y	Y	N	Y	Y
23 Beilenson	Y	N	Y	N	N	Y	N	N
24 Waxman	Y	Y	Y	X	N	Y	N	Y
25 Roybal	Y	N	Y	N	N	Y	N	Y
26 Rousselot	Y	Y	Y	Y	?	N	Y	Y
27 Dornan	Y	Y	Y	Y	Y	N	Y	Y
28 Burke	Y	Y	?	X	X	✓	X	X
29 Hawkins	Y	Y	Y	N	?	✓	X	✓
30 Danielson	Y	Y	Y	N	N	N	N	Y
31 Wilson, C.H.	Y	▮	Y	X	▮	▮	▮	?
32 Anderson	Y	Y	Y	N	N	Y	N	Y
33 Clawson	Y	Y	Y	Y	?	?	✓	?
34 Hannaford	Y	Y	Y	N	N	N	N	Y
35 Lloyd	Y	Y	Y	N	Y	N	N	Y
36 Brown	Y	Y	Y	N	N	Y	N	Y
37 Pettis	?	?	Y	Y	N	N	Y	Y
38 Patterson	Y	Y	Y	N	N	N	N	?
39 Wiggins	Y	?	?	Y	Y	N	Y	N
40 Badham	Y	Y	Y	Y	Y	N	Y	Y
41 Wilson, B.	Y	Y	N	✓	Y	N	Y	Y
42 Van Deerlin	Y	Y	?	X	?	?	?	Y
43 Burgener	Y	Y	Y	Y	Y	N	Y	Y
COLORADO								
1 Schroeder	Y	Y	Y	N	N	Y	N	†
2 Wirth	Y	Y	Y	X	X	X	X	?
3 Evans	Y	Y	Y	N	N	Y	N	#
4 Johnson	?	?	Y	Y	N	N	Y	Y
5 Armstrong	Y	Y	Y	Y	Y	N	Y	Y
CONNECTICUT								
1 Cotter	Y	Y	Y	N	N	N	N	Y
2 Dodd	Y	Y	Y	N	N	N	N	Y
3 Giaimo	Y	Y	Y	N	N	N	N	N
4 McKinney	Y	Y	Y	Y	N	Y	Y	Y
5 Sarasin	Y	Y	Y	Y	N	N	Y	Y
6 Moffett	Y	Y	?	N	N	Y	N	Y
DELAWARE								
AL Evans	Y	Y	Y	Y	Y	N	Y	Y
FLORIDA								
1 Sikes	Y	Y	Y	N	Y	N	N	Y
2 Fuqua	Y	Y	Y	Y	N	N	N	Y
3 Bennett	Y	Y	Y	Y	Y	N	N	Y
4 Chappell	Y	Y	Y	Y	Y	N	Y	Y
5 Kelly	Y	Y	Y	Y	Y	N	Y	Y
6 Young	Y	Y	Y	Y	Y	N	Y	Y
7 Gibbons	Y	Y	Y	Y	N	N	Y	Y
8 Ireland	Y	?	Y	Y	Y	N	N	Y
9 Frey	?	?	?	✓	?	?	✓	?
10 Bafalis	Y	Y	Y	Y	Y	N	✓	?
11 Rogers	Y	Y	Y	Y	N	N	N	Y
12 Burke	Y	Y	Y	Y	N	N	Y	Y
13 Lehman	Y	Y	Y	N	N	N	N	N
14 Pepper	Y	Y	Y	N	N	N	N	Y
15 Fascell	Y	?	Y	N	N	N	N	Y
GEORGIA								
1 Ginn	Y	Y	Y	Y	Y	N	N	Y
2 Mathis	Y	?	?	Y	Y	N	Y	Y
3 Brinkley	Y	Y	Y	Y	Y	N	N	Y
4 Levitas	Y	Y	Y	Y	Y	N	N	Y
5 Fowler	Y	Y	Y	?	Y	N	N	Y
6 Flynt	Y	Y	Y	Y	Y	N	Y	Y
7 McDonald	Y	Y	Y	Y	Y	N	Y	Y
8 Evans	Y	N	Y	N	Y	N	Y	Y
9 Jenkins	Y	Y	Y	Y	Y	N	N	Y
10 Barnard	Y	Y	Y	Y	Y	N	N	Y
HAWAII								
1 Heftel	Y	Y	Y	N	N	N	N	Y
2 Akaka	Y	Y	Y	N	N	N	N	Y
IDAHO								
1 Symms	Y	Y	Y	Y	Y	N	Y	Y
2 Hansen, G.	Y	Y	Y	Y	Y	N	Y	Y
ILLINOIS								
1 Metcalfe	Y	Y	Y	N	N	Y	N	Y
2 Murphy	Y	Y	Y	X	N	N	N	Y
3 Russo	Y	Y	Y	Y	N	N	Y	Y
4 Derwinski	Y	Y	Y	Y	Y	N	Y	Y
5 Fary	Y	Y	Y	N	N	N	N	Y
6 Hyde	Y	Y	Y	Y	N	N	Y	Y
7 Collins	Y	?	?	N	N	Y	N	Y
8 Rostenkowski	Y	Y	Y	N	N	N	N	N
9 Yates	Y	Y	Y	N	N	Y	N	N
10 Mikva	Y	N	†	X	X	✓	X	X
11 Annunzio	Y	Y	#	N	N	N	N	Y
12 Crane	Y	Y	Y	Y	Y	N	Y	Y
13 McClory	Y	Y	Y	Y	N	N	Y	Y
14 Erlenborn	Y	Y	Y	Y	N	N	Y	Y
15 Corcoran	Y	Y	Y	Y	Y	N	Y	Y
16 Anderson	Y	Y	Y	Y	N	N	Y	N
17 O'Brien	Y	Y	Y	Y	Y	N	Y	Y
18 Michel	Y	Y	Y	Y	Y	N	Y	Y
19 Railsback	Y	Y	Y	Y	N	N	Y	Y
20 Findley	Y	Y	Y	Y	Y	N	N	Y
21 Madigan	Y	?	Y	Y	Y	N	Y	Y
22 Shipley	Y	Y	Y	N	N	N	N	Y
23 Price	Y	Y	Y	N	Y	N	N	Y
24 Simon	Y	Y	Y	N	N	Y	N	N
INDIANA								
1 Benjamin	Y	Y	Y	N	N	Y	N	N
2 Fithian	Y	Y	Y	N	N	N	N	Y
3 Brademas	Y	Y	Y	N	N	N	N	Y
4 Quayle	Y	Y	Y	Y	N	N	Y	?
5 Hillis	Y	Y	?	Y	Y	N	Y	Y
6 Evans	?	?	Y	Y	Y	N	Y	Y
7 Myers, J.	Y	Y	Y	Y	N	N	Y	Y
8 Cornwell	Y	Y	Y	Y	N	N	N	Y
9 Hamilton	Y	Y	Y	N	N	N	N	Y
10 Sharp	Y	Y	Y	Y	N	N	N	Y
11 Jacobs	Y	Y	Y	N	N	N	N	N
IOWA								
1 Leach	Y	Y	Y	Y	N	N	Y	Y
2 Blouin	Y	Y	Y	N	N	Y	N	Y
3 Grassley	Y	Y	Y	Y	N	N	Y	Y
4 Smith	Y	Y	Y	N	N	Y	N	Y
5 Harkin	N	Y	Y	N	N	Y	N	Y
6 Bedell	N	Y	Y	N	N	Y	N	Y

Democrats ***Republicans***

	227	228	229	230	231	232	233	234
KANSAS								
1 Sebelius	Y	Y	Y	Y	N	N	Y	Y
2 Keys	Y	Y	Y	N	N	Y	N	N
3 Winn	Y	Y	Y	Y	Y	N	Y	Y
4 Glickman	Y	Y	?	Y	N	N	N	Y
5 Skubitz	Y	Y	Y	Y	?	?	✓	?
KENTUCKY								
1 Hubbard	Y	Y	Y	N	Y	N	N	Y
2 Natcher	Y	Y	Y	N	N	N	N	Y
3 Mazzoli	Y	Y	Y	Y	N	N	N	Y
4 Snyder	Y	Y	Y	Y	Y	N	N	Y
5 Carter	Y	Y	Y	Y	Y	N	Y	Y
6 Breckinridge	Y	Y	Y	N	Y	N	N	Y
7 Perkins	Y	Y	Y	N	N	N	N	Y
LOUISIANA								
1 Livingston	Y	Y	Y	Y	Y	N	Y	Y
2 Boggs	Y	Y	Y	N	Y	N	Y	Y
3 Treen	Y	Y	Y	Y	Y	N	Y	Y
4 Waggonner	Y	Y	Y	Y	Y	N	Y	Y
5 Huckaby	Y	Y	?	Y	Y	N	Y	Y
6 Moore	Y	Y	Y	Y	Y	N	Y	Y
7 Breaux	Y	Y	Y	Y	Y	N	Y	Y
8 Long	Y	Y	Y	N	N	N	N	Y
MAINE								
1 Emery	Y	Y	Y	Y	Y	N	Y	Y
2 Cohen	Y	Y	Y	Y	N	N	Y	Y
MARYLAND								
1 Bauman	Y	Y	Y	Y	Y	N	Y	Y
2 Long	Y	Y	Y	Y	N	N	N	?
3 Mikulski	Y	Y	Y	N	N	Y	N	Y
4 Holt	Y	Y	Y	Y	?	N	Y	Y
5 Spellman	Y	Y	#	N	N	Y	N	Y
6 Byron	Y	Y	Y	Y	Y	N	N	Y
7 Mitchell	Y	Y	N	N	N	Y	N	Y
8 Steers	Y	Y	Y	Y	N	Y	Y	Y
MASSACHUSETTS								
1 Conte	Y	Y	Y	Y	N	N	Y	Y
2 Boland	Y	Y	Y	N	N	N	N	Y
3 Early	Y	Y	Y	Y	N	Y	N	N
4 Drinan	Y	Y	Y	N	N	Y	N	Y
5 Tsongas	Y	Y	Y	N	N	Y	N	Y
6 Harrington	Y	P	Y	N	N	Y	N	N
7 Markey	Y	N	Y	N	N	Y	N	Y
8 O'Neill								
9 Moakley	Y	Y	Y	N	N	Y	N	Y
10 Heckler	Y	Y	Y	Y	N	Y	Y	Y
11 Burke	Y	Y	Y	N	N	N	Y	Y
12 Studds	Y	Y	Y	N	N	Y	N	Y
MICHIGAN								
1 Conyers	?	?	?	▮	▮	?	X	?
2 Pursell	?	?	Y	Y	N	N	Y	Y
3 Brown	Y	Y	Y	Y	N	N	Y	Y
4 Stockman	Y	Y	Y	Y	N	N	Y	Y
5 Sawyer	Y	Y	Y	Y	N	N	Y	Y
6 Carr	Y	Y	Y	N	N	Y	N	Y
7 Kildee	Y	Y	Y	N	N	Y	N	Y
8 Traxler	Y	Y	Y	N	N	N	N	Y
9 Vander Jagt	Y	Y	Y	Y	Y	N	Y	Y
10 Cederberg	Y	Y	?	Y	N	N	Y	Y
11 Ruppe	#	#	#	Y	N	N	Y	Y
12 Bonior	Y	P	Y	N	N	Y	N	Y
13 Diggs	Y	Y	?	N	N	Y	X	Y
14 Nedzi	Y	Y	Y	N	N	N	N	Y
15 Ford	?	Y	Y	N	?	N	N	Y
16 Dingell	Y	Y	Y	N	N	N	N	Y
17 Brodhead	Y	Y	Y	N	N	Y	N	Y
18 Blanchard	Y	Y	Y	N	N	Y	N	Y
19 Broomfield	Y	Y	Y	Y	N	N	Y	Y
MINNESOTA								
1 Quie	Y	Y	Y	Y	N	N	Y	Y
2 Hagedorn	Y	Y	Y	Y	N	N	Y	Y
3 Frenzel	Y	Y	Y	Y	N	N	Y	Y
4 Vento	Y	Y	Y	N	N	Y	N	Y
5 Fraser	Y	Y	Y	N	N	Y	N	Y
6 Nolan	N	Y	Y	N	N	Y	N	Y
7 Stangeland	Y	Y	Y	Y	N	N	Y	Y
8 Oberstar	Y	Y	?	N	N	Y	N	Y
MISSISSIPPI								
1 Whitten	Y	Y	P	N	Y	N	N	Y
2 Bowen	Y	Y	Y	Y	Y	N	Y	Y
3 Montgomery	Y	Y	Y	Y	Y	N	Y	Y
4 Cochran	?	?	?	✓	?	?	✓	?
5 Lott	Y	Y	Y	Y	Y	N	Y	Y
MISSOURI								
1 Clay	Y	Y	Y	N	N	Y	N	Y
2 Young	Y	Y	Y	N	Y	N	N	Y
3 Gephardt	Y	Y	Y	N	N	N	N	Y
4 Skelton	Y	Y	Y	N	Y	N	N	Y
5 Bolling	Y	Y	Y	N	N	N	N	N
6 Coleman	Y	Y	Y	Y	Y	N	Y	Y
7 Taylor	Y	Y	Y	Y	Y	N	Y	Y
8 Ichord	Y	Y	Y	Y	Y	N	N	Y
9 Volkmer	Y	Y	Y	N	N	N	N	Y
10 Burlison	Y	Y	Y	N	N	N	N	N
MONTANA								
1 Baucus	Y	Y	Y	N	N	N	N	Y
2 Marlenee	Y	Y	Y	Y	Y	N	Y	Y
NEBRASKA								
1 Thone	?	#	#	✓	?	?	✓	#
2 Cavanaugh	Y	Y	Y	Y	N	N	N	Y
3 Smith	Y	Y	Y	Y	Y	N	Y	Y
NEVADA								
AL Santini	Y	Y	Y	Y	N	N	N	Y
NEW HAMPSHIRE								
1 D'Amours	Y	Y	Y	N	N	N	N	Y
2 Cleveland	Y	Y	Y	Y	Y	N	Y	Y
NEW JERSEY								
1 Florio	Y	Y	Y	N	N	N	N	#
2 Hughes	Y	Y	Y	Y	N	N	N	Y
3 Howard	Y	#	Y	X	N	N	N	Y
4 Thompson	Y	Y	Y	N	N	N	N	N
5 Fenwick	Y	Y	Y	Y	N	N	Y	N
6 Forsythe	Y	Y	Y	Y	N	N	Y	Y
7 Maguire	Y	Y	Y	N	N	Y	N	N
8 Roe	Y	Y	Y	N	N	N	N	Y
9 Hollenbeck	Y	Y	Y	Y	N	N	Y	Y
10 Rodino	?	?	Y	X	N	Y	N	Y
11 Minish	Y	Y	Y	N	N	N	N	Y
12 Rinaldo	Y	Y	Y	Y	N	N	Y	Y
13 Mèyner	Y	Y	Y	N	N	N	N	Y
14 LeFante	Y	Y	Y	N	N	Y	N	Y
15 Patten	Y	Y	Y	N	N	N	N	Y
NEW MEXICO								
1 Lujan	Y	N	Y	Y	Y	N	Y	Y
2 Runnels	?	?	?	✓	✓	X	✓	#
NEW YORK								
1 Pike	Y	Y	Y	Y	N	N	N	N
2 Downey	Y	Y	Y	N	N	Y	N	Y
3 Ambro	Y	Y	Y	Y	Y	N	N	Y
4 Lent	Y	Y	Y	Y	Y	N	Y	Y
5 Wydler	Y	Y	Y	Y	N	N	Y	Y
6 Wolff	Y	Y	Y	N	N	Y	N	Y
7 Addabbo	Y	Y	Y	N	N	Y	N	Y
8 Rosenthal	Y	Y	Y	N	N	Y	N	Y
9 Delaney	Y	Y	Y	N	N	N	N	Y
10 Biaggi	Y	Y	Y	N	Y	Y	N	Y
11 Scheuer	Y	Y	?	N	N	Y	N	Y
12 Chisholm	Y	Y	Y	N	N	Y	N	Y
13 Solarz	Y	Y	Y	N	N	Y	N	Y
14 Richmond	N	Y	Y	N	N	Y	N	Y
15 Zeferetti	Y	Y	Y	N	Y	N	N	Y
16 Holtzman	N	Y	Y	N	N	Y	N	N
17 Murphy	?	?	Y	N	Y	N	N	Y
18 Green	Y	Y	Y	Y	N	N	Y	N
19 Rangel	Y	Y	Y	N	N	Y	N	Y
20 Weiss	Y	Y	Y	N	N	Y	N	N
21 Garcia	Y	Y	Y	N	N	Y	N	Y
22 Bingham	Y	Y	Y	N	N	Y	X	N
23 Caputo	Y	Y	Y	Y	N	Y	Y	Y
24 Ottinger	Y	Y	Y	N	N	Y	N	†
25 Fish	Y	?	Y	Y	N	N	Y	Y
26 Gilman	Y	Y	Y	Y	Y	N	Y	Y
27 McHugh	Y	Y	Y	N	N	Y	N	Y
28 Stratton	Y	Y	Y	N	Y	N	N	Y
29 Pattison	Y	Y	Y	Y	N	Y	N	N
30 McEwen	Y	Y	Y	Y	N	N	Y	Y
31 Mitchell	Y	Y	Y	Y	Y	N	Y	Y
32 Hanley	Y	Y	Y	N	N	N	N	Y
33 Walsh	Y	Y	Y	Y	N	N	Y	Y
34 Horton	Y	Y	Y	Y	N	N	Y	?
35 Conable	Y	Y	Y	✓	N	N	Y	N
36 LaFalce	Y	Y	Y	Y	N	N	Y	N
37 Nowak	Y	Y	Y	N	N	Y	Y	Y
38 Kemp	Y	Y	Y	Y	Y	N	Y	Y
39 Lundine	Y	Y	P	N	N	Y	N	N
NORTH CAROLINA								
1 Jones	#	#	Y	N	N	N	N	Y
2 Fountain	?	?	Y	Y	N	N	N	Y
3 Whitley	?	?	?	?	?	?	X	?
4 Andrews	#	#	#	?	?	▮	?	#
5 Neal	Y	Y	Y	Y	N	N	#	Y
6 Preyer	Y	Y	Y	N	N	N	N	Y
7 Rose	Y	Y	Y	N	N	N	N	Y
8 Hefner	Y	Y	Y	Y	N	N	N	Y
9 Martin	Y	Y	Y	Y	N	N	Y	Y
10 Broyhill	Y	Y	Y	Y	N	N	Y	Y
11 Gudger	#	#	Y	N	Y	N	N	Y
NORTH DAKOTA								
AL Andrews	Y	Y	Y	Y	Y	N	Y	Y
OHIO								
1 Gradison	●	Y	Y	Y	N	N	Y	Y
2 Luken	Y	Y	Y	N	N	N	Y	Y
3 Whalen	Y	Y	Y	N	N	Y	N	Y
4 Guyer	Y	Y	Y	Y	N	N	Y	Y
5 Latta	Y	Y	Y	Y	N	N	Y	Y
6 Harsha	Y	Y	Y	Y	Y	N	Y	Y
7 Brown	Y	Y	Y	Y	Y	N	Y	Y
8 Kindness	Y	Y	Y	Y	Y	N	Y	Y
9 Ashley	Y	Y	Y	N	N	N	N	?
10 Miller	Y	Y	Y	Y	N	N	Y	Y
11 Stanton	Y	Y	Y	Y	N	N	Y	Y
12 Devine	Y	Y	#	Y	N	N	Y	Y
13 Pease	Y	Y	Y	N	N	Y	N	Y
14 Seiberling	Y	Y	Y	N	N	Y	N	Y
15 Wylie	?	?	Y	Y	N	N	Y	Y
16 Regula	Y	Y	Y	Y	N	N	Y	Y
17 Ashbrook	Y	Y	?	✓	Y	N	Y	Y
18 Applegate	Y	Y	Y	Y	N	N	N	Y
19 Carney	?	?	Y	N	N	Y	N	Y
20 Oakar	Y	Y	Y	N	N	Y	Y	Y
21 Stokes	Y	Y	Y	N	N	Y	N	Y
22 Vanik	Y	Y	Y	N	N	Y	N	Y
23 Mottl	N	Y	Y	Y	N	N	Y	Y
OKLAHOMA								
1 Jones	Y	Y	Y	N	Y	N	N	Y
2 Risenhoover	?	?	Y	N	Y	N	Y	Y
3 Watkins	Y	Y	Y	Y	Y	N	N	Y
4 Steed	Y	Y	Y	N	Y	N	N	Y
5 Edwards	Y	Y	Y	Y	Y	N	Y	Y
6 English	Y	Y	Y	Y	Y	N	N	Y
OREGON								
1 AuCoin	Y	Y	Y	Y	N	N	N	N
2 Ullman	Y	N	Y	N	N	N	N	Y
3 Duncan	Y	N	Y	?	N	N	N	Y
4 Weaver	?	?	?	?	?	?	?	?
PENNSYLVANIA								
1 Myers, M.	Y	Y	Y	N	N	Y	N	?
2 Nix	?	?	?	?	?	?	X	?
3 Lederer	Y	Y	Y	N	N	Y	N	Y
4 Eilberg	?	?	Y	N	N	Y	N	Y
5 Schulze	Y	Y	Y	Y	Y	N	Y	Y
6 Yatron	Y	Y	Y	Y	N	N	N	Y
7 Edgar	Y	Y	Y	N	N	Y	N	Y
8 Kostmayer	Y	Y	Y	Y	N	Y	N	Y
9 Shuster	Y	Y	Y	Y	Y	N	Y	Y
10 McDade	Y	Y	Y	Y	N	N	Y	Y
11 Flood	Y	Y	Y	N	N	N	N	Y
12 Murtha	Y	Y	Y	N	N	N	N	Y
13 Coughlin	Y	Y	Y	Y	N	N	Y	Y
14 Moorhead	Y	Y	Y	N	N	N	N	N
15 Rooney	Y	Y	Y	?	N	N	N	Y
16 Walker	Y	Y	Y	Y	N	N	Y	Y
17 Ertel	Y	Y	Y	N	N	N	N	Y
18 Walgren	Y	N	Y	N	N	N	N	Y
19 Goodling, W.	Y	Y	Y	Y	N	N	Y	Y
20 Gaydos	Y	Y	Y	N	N	N	N	Y
21 Dent	Y	Y	Y	N	▮	N	N	#
22 Murphy	Y	Y	Y	Y	N	N	Y	Y
23 Ammerman	Y	Y	Y	N	N	N	N	Y
24 Marks	Y	Y	Y	Y	N	N	Y	Y
25 Myers, G.	Y	Y	Y	Y	N	N	Y	N
RHODE ISLAND								
1 St Germain	Y	Y	Y	N	N	Y	N	Y
2 Beard	Y	Y	?	N	N	N	N	Y
SOUTH CAROLINA								
1 Davis	Y	Y	N	N	Y	N	N	Y
2 Spence	Y	Y	Y	Y	Y	N	Y	Y
3 Derrick	Y	Y	Y	N	N	N	N	Y
4 Mann	?	?	?	?	?	?	?	?
5 Holland	Y	Y	?	N	N	N	N	Y
6 Jenrette	Y	Y	Y	N	N	N	N	Y
SOUTH DAKOTA								
1 Pressler	Y	Y	Y	Y	N	N	Y	Y
2 Abdnor	Y	Y	#	Y	Y	N	Y	Y
TENNESSEE								
1 Quillen	Y	Y	Y	Y	Y	N	Y	Y
2 Duncan	Y	Y	Y	Y	Y	N	Y	Y
3 Lloyd	Y	Y	Y	Y	Y	N	N	Y
4 Gore	Y	Y	Y	N	Y	N	N	Y
5 Allen	Y	Y	?	?	N	N	N	Y
6 Beard	Y	Y	Y	Y	Y	N	Y	Y
7 Jones	Y	Y	Y	N	Y	N	N	Y
8 Ford	Y	Y	Y	N	N	Y	N	Y
TEXAS								
1 Hall	Y	Y	Y	Y	Y	N	Y	Y
2 Wilson, C.	?	Y	Y	N	Y	N	N	Y
3 Collins	Y	Y	N	Y	Y	N	Y	Y
4 Roberts	Y	Y	Y	N	Y	N	N	Y
5 Mattox	Y	Y	Y	N	N	N	N	Y
6 Teague	?	?	?	N	Y	N	N	Y
7 Archer	Y	Y	Y	Y	Y	N	Y	Y
8 Eckhardt	Y	N	Y	N	N	Y	N	Y
9 Brooks	Y	Y	Y	N	N	N	N	Y
10 Pickle	N	Y	Y	N	N	N	N	Y
11 Poage	Y	Y	Y	N	Y	N	N	Y
12 Wright	Y	Y	Y	N	Y	N	N	Y
13 Hightower	Y	Y	Y	N	Y	N	N	Y
14 Young	Y	Y	Y	N	Y	N	N	Y
15 de la Garza	Y	Y	Y	N	Y	N	N	Y
16 White	†	†	?	✓	✓	X	✓	†
17 Burleson	?	?	Y	N	Y	N	N	Y
18 Jordan	Y	Y	Y	N	N	Y	N	Y
19 Mahon	Y	Y	Y	N	Y	N	N	Y
20 Gonzalez	Y	N	Y	N	Y	N	N	Y
21 Krueger	?	?	?	Y	Y	N	N	Y
22 Gammage	?	?	Y	Y	Y	N	?	?
23 Kazen	?	?	?	?	✓	?	?	✓
24 Milford	Y	N	Y	Y	Y	N	N	Y
UTAH								
1 McKay	Y	Y	Y	N	▮	N	N	Y
2 Marriott	Y	Y	Y	Y	Y	N	Y	Y
VERMONT								
AL Jeffords	Y	Y	Y	Y	N	N	✓	Y
VIRGINIA								
1 Trible	Y	Y	Y	Y	Y	N	Y	Y
2 Whitehurst	Y	Y	Y	Y	Y	N	Y	Y
3 Satterfield	Y	Y	Y	Y	Y	N	Y	Y
4 Daniel	Y	Y	Y	Y	Y	N	Y	Y
5 Daniel	Y	Y	Y	Y	Y	N	Y	Y
6 Butler	Y	Y	Y	Y	Y	N	Y	Y
7 Robinson	Y	Y	Y	Y	Y	N	Y	Y
8 Harris	Y	Y	Y	N	N	N	N	Y
9 Wampler	Y	?	Y	Y	Y	N	Y	Y
10 Fisher	Y	Y	Y	N	N	N	N	Y
WASHINGTON								
1 Pritchard	Y	Y	Y	Y	N	N	Y	Y
2 Meeds	Y	Y	Y	N	N	N	N	?
3 Bonker	Y	Y	Y	N	N	Y	?	Y
4 McCormack	?	?	Y	N	N	N	N	Y
5 Foley	Y	Y	Y	N	N	N	N	Y
6 Dicks	Y	Y	Y	N	N	N	N	Y
7 Cunningham	Y	Y	Y	Y	N	N	Y	Y
WEST VIRGINIA								
1 Mollohan	?	?	Y	N	Y	N	N	Y
2 Staggers	Y	Y	Y	N	Y	N	N	Y
3 Slack	Y	Y	Y	N	N	N	N	Y
4 Rahall	?	?	Y	N	N	Y	N	Y
WISCONSIN								
1 Aspin	Y	Y	Y	N	N	N	N	Y
2 Kastenmeier	Y	Y	Y	N	N	Y	N	Y
3 Baldus	?	?	?	▮	N	N	Y	Y
4 Zablocki	Y	Y	Y	N	Y	N	N	Y
5 Reuss	Y	Y	Y	N	N	N	N	Y
6 Steiger	Y	Y	Y	Y	N	N	Y	Y
7 Obey	Y	Y	Y	N	N	N	N	N
8 Cornell	Y	Y	Y	N	N	Y	N	Y
9 Kasten	Y	Y	Y	Y	#	▮	✓	#
WYOMING								
AL Roncalio	Y	Y	Y	?	N	Y	N	Y

Democrats ***Republicans***

235. H Con Res 559. Fiscal 1979 Budget Targets. Fraser, D-Minn., amendment to increase targets for budget authority by $435 million and outlays by $390 million for job training programs for youths and older Americans. Rejected 123-265: R 31-107; D 92-158 (ND 83-88; SD 9-70), May 3, 1978.

236. H Con Res 559. Fiscal 1979 Budget Targets. Mattox, D-Texas, amendment to reduce budget authority and outlay targets by $255 million, reflecting a reduction in the expected federal pay raise to 5.5 percent from 6 percent. Rejected 172-210: R 86-49; D 86-161 (ND 56-115; SD 30-46), May 3, 1978.

237. Procedural Motion. Russo, D-Ill., motion to approve the House *Journal* of Wednesday, May 3, 1978. Motion agreed to 360-13: R 127-8; D 233-5 (ND 156-5; SD 77-0), May 4, 1978.

238. HR 6782. Emergency Farm Aid. Adoption of the rule (H Res 1162) providing for House floor consideration of the conference report on the bill to authorize the secretary of agriculture to raise grain and cotton target prices when acreage set-asides are in effect; to revise the cotton loan level formula and establish a minimum loan of 48 cents a pound; to establish a federal marketing order for raisins; and to raise the limit on the Commodity Credit Corporation borrowing authority to $25 billion, from $14.5 billion. Adopted 241-148: R 40-96; D 201-52 (ND 131-43; SD 70-9), May 4, 1978.

239. HR 6782. Emergency Farm Aid. Adoption of the conference report on the bill to authorize the secretary of agriculture to raise grain and cotton target prices when acreage set-asides are in effect; to revise the cotton loan level formula and establish a minimum loan of 48 cents a pound; to establish a federal marketing order for raisins; and to raise the limit on the Commodity Credit Corporation borrowing authority to $25 billion, from $14.5 billion. Adopted 212-182: R 34-105; D 178-77 (ND 112-63; SD 66-14), May 4, 1978.

240. H Con Res 559. Fiscal 1979 Budget Targets. Luken, D-Ohio, substitute amendment, to the Coughlin, R-Pa. amendment *(see vote 241, below)*, to reduce the revenue target by $635 million to accommodate a tuition tax credit for college and elementary and secondary school costs. Adopted 199-173: R 103-33; D 96-140 (ND 76-89; SD 20-51), May 4, 1978. (The Coughlin amendment would have provided a credit for college costs only.)

241. H Con Res 559. Fiscal 1979 Budget Targets. Coughlin, R-Pa., amendment as amended by the Luken, D-Ohio, substitute amendment *(see vote 240, above)*. Adopted 227-136: R 111-21; D 116-115 (ND 85-76; SD 31-39), May 4, 1978.

KEY

- Y Voted for (yea).
- ✓ Paired for.
- † Announced for.
- # CQ Poll for.
- N Voted against (nay).
- X Paired against.
- \- Announced against.
- ▮ CQ Poll against.
- P Voted "present."
- ● Voted "present" to avoid possible conflict of interest.
- ? Did not vote or otherwise make a position known.

	235	236	237	238	239	240	241
ALABAMA							
1 ***Edwards***	N	N	Y	N	N	Y	Y
2 ***Dickinson***	N	N	Y	N	✓	N	Y
3 Nichols	N	N	Y	Y	Y	N	Y
4 Bevill	N	N	Y	Y	Y	Y	Y
5 Flippo	N	N	Y	Y	Y	N	N
6 ***Buchanan***	Y	N	Y	N	N	N	N
7 Flowers	N	N	Y	Y	Y	N	Y
ALASKA							
AL ***Young***	▮	▮	Y	Y	N	N	Y
ARIZONA							
1 ***Rhodes***	N	Y	Y	N	N	?	?
2 Udall	N	N	#	Y	N	N	N
3 Stump	N	Y	Y	N	N	▮	▮
4 ***Rudd***	N	Y	Y	N	N	Y	?
ARKANSAS							
1 Alexander	?	?	Y	Y	Y	?	?
2 Tucker	▮	#	#	#	#	▮	▮
3 ***Hammerschmidt***	Y	Y	Y	N	N	N	Y
4 Thornton	?	?	?	?	✓	?	?
CALIFORNIA							
1 Johnson	N	N	P	Y	Y	N	Y
2 ***Clausen***	N	Y	Y	?	N	Y	Y
3 Moss	N	N	?	N	N	?	?
4 Leggett	Y	Y	Y	N	N	N	N
5 Burton, J.	Y	N	?	Y	Y	N	N
6 Burton, P.	Y	N	Y	Y	Y	N	N
7 Miller	Y	N	Y	Y	N	N	N
8 Dellums	Y	N	Y	N	Y	N	N
9 Stark	Y	Y	Y	N	N	N	N
10 Edwards	Y	N	Y	N	N	N	N
11 Ryan	N	Y	Y	Y	N	Y	Y
12 ***McCloskey***	N	Y	Y	N	N	N	N
13 Mineta	N	N	Y	N	N	N	N
14 McFall	N	N	#	N	N	N	N
15 Sisk	?	?	Y	N	N	N	N
16 Panetta	N	Y	Y	N	N	N	N
17 Krebs	N	N	Y	N	N	N	N
18 ***Ketchum***	N	N	Y	N	N	Y	Y
19 ***Lagomarsino***	N	N	Y	N	N	Y	Y
20 ***Goldwater***	N	N	Y	N	N	Y	Y
21 Corman	Y	N	Y	N	N	▮	?
22 ***Moorhead***	N	Y	Y	N	N	Y	Y
23 Beilenson	N	N	Y	Y	N	N	N
24 Waxman	Y	N	Y	N	N	N	N
25 Roybal	Y	N	Y	Y	Y	N	N
26 ***Rousselot***	N	Y	Y	N	N	Y	Y
27 ***Dornan***	N	Y	Y	N	N	Y	Y
28 Burke	✓	▮	#	#	X	X	X
29 Hawkins	✓	?	?	?	?	X	X
30 Danielson	-	-	†	†	-	-	-
31 Wilson, C.H.	▮	▮	#	#	#	▮	#
32 Anderson	Y	N	#	▮	▮	▮	#
33 ***Clawson***	?	?	?	?	X	✓	✓
34 Hannaford	✓	▮	#	#	#	X	#
35 Lloyd	N	N	N	Y	Y	N	Y
36 Brown	N	?	Y	N	N	N	N
37 ***Pettis***	N	Y	Y	N	N	Y	Y
38 Patterson	?	?	?	?	?	?	?
39 ***Wiggins***	N	Y	#	#	N	N	N
40 ***Badham***	N	Y	Y	N	N	Y	✓
41 ***Wilson, B.***	N	N	N	N	N	Y	Y
42 Van Deerlin	Y	N	Y	N	N	N	N
43 ***Burgener***	N	N	Y	N	N	Y	Y
COLORADO							
1 Schroeder	-	†	†	†	-	-	-
2 Wirth	X	▮	#	▮	✓	X	X
3 Evans	▮	#	#	#	#	#	#
4 ***Johnson***	N	Y	Y	N	N	N	N
5 ***Armstrong***	N	Y	Y	N	N	Y	Y
CONNECTICUT							
1 Cotter	Y	N	Y	Y	N	Y	Y
2 Dodd	Y	Y	Y	Y	N	N	N
3 Giaimo	N	N	Y	Y	N	N	N
4 ***McKinney***	N	Y	Y	N	N	N	N
5 ***Sarasin***	Y	N	N	N	N	Y	Y
6 Moffett	Y	Y	Y	N	Y	N	N
DELAWARE							
AL ***Evans***	N	Y	Y	Y	N	N	Y
FLORIDA							
1 Sikes	N	?	Y	Y	Y	Y	Y
2 Fuqua	N	Y	Y	Y	Y	N	N
3 Bennett	N	N	Y	Y	N	N	N
4 Chappell	N	N	Y	N	Y	Y	Y
5 ***Kelly***	N	Y	Y	N	N	Y	Y
6 ***Young***	N	Y	Y	N	N	Y	Y
7 Gibbons	N	Y	Y	N	N	Y	Y
8 Ireland	N	Y	Y	Y	N	N	N
9 ***Frey***	?	?	?	?	?	✓	?
10 ***Bafalis***	?	?	?	?	X	✓	✓
11 Rogers	N	Y	Y	N	N	Y	Y
12 ***Burke***	N	N	Y	N	N	Y	Y
13 Lehman	N	Y	Y	Y	N	N	N
14 Pepper	Y	N	Y	N	N	N	N
15 Fascell	N	N	Y	N	N	N	N
GEORGIA							
1 Ginn	N	Y	Y	Y	Y	N	N
2 Mathis	N	N	Y	Y	Y	Y	Y
3 Brinkley	N	N	Y	Y	Y	N	Y
4 Levitas	N	Y	Y	Y	Y	Y	Y
5 Fowler	N	Y	Y	Y	Y	Y	Y
6 Flynt	N	?	Y	Y	Y	Y	Y
7 McDonald	N	Y	Y	N	N	Y	Y
8 Evans	N	N	Y	Y	Y	#	#
9 Jenkins	N	Y	Y	Y	Y	N	N
10 Barnard	N	N	Y	Y	Y	Y	#
HAWAII							
1 Heftel	N	N	Y	Y	Y	Y	Y
2 Akaka	Y	N	Y	Y	Y	Y	N
IDAHO							
1 ***Symms***	N	?	Y	N	N	Y	Y
2 ***Hansen, G.***	N	Y	Y	N	N	Y	Y
ILLINOIS							
1 Metcalfe	Y	N	Y	Y	Y	N	N
2 Murphy	Y	N	Y	Y	Y	Y	Y
3 Russo	Y	N	Y	Y	N	Y	Y
4 ***Derwinski***	Y	Y	Y	N	N	Y	Y
5 Fary	N	N	Y	Y	Y	Y	Y
6 ***Hyde***	N	N	Y	#	N	Y	Y
7 Collins	Y	N	Y	Y	N	N	N
8 Rostenkowski	N	N	Y	Y	Y	Y	Y
9 Yates	N	N	Y	N	N	N	N
10 Mikva	X	-	Y	N	N	▮	X
11 Annunzio	N	N	Y	Y	Y	Y	Y
12 ***Crane***	N	Y	#	N	N	Y	Y
13 ***McClory***	N	N	Y	N	N	N	Y
14 ***Erlenborn***	N	Y	Y	N	N	Y	✓
15 ***Corcoran***	N	Y	Y	N	N	Y	Y
16 ***Anderson***	N	Y	Y	N	N	N	Y
17 ***O'Brien***	N	N	Y	N	N	Y	Y
18 ***Michel***	N	Y	Y	N	N	Y	Y
19 ***Railsback***	Y	N	Y	N	N	Y	Y
20 ***Findley***	N	Y	Y	N	N	N	N
21 ***Madigan***	Y	N	Y	N	N	Y	P
22 Shipley	X	?	?	?	?	X	X
23 Price	N	N	Y	Y	N	Y	Y
24 Simon	Y	Y	?	Y	Y	N	N
INDIANA							
1 Benjamin	N	Y	Y	N	N	Y	Y
2 Fithian	N	Y	Y	Y	Y	N	?
3 Brademas	N	N	Y	Y	Y	N	N
4 ***Quayle***	?	?	N	N	Y	Y	Y
5 ***Hillis***	N	Y	Y	N	Y	N	N
6 Evans	N	Y	Y	Y	Y	N	N
7 ***Myers, J.***	N	Y	Y	N	Y	Y	Y
8 Cornwell	N	Y	?	Y	Y	N	N
9 Hamilton	N	Y	Y	Y	Y	N	N
10 Sharp	N	Y	Y	Y	Y	N	N
11 Jacobs	N	Y	N	Y	N	N	N
IOWA							
1 ***Leach***	N	Y	Y	N	Y	Y	Y
2 Blouin	Y	Y	Y	Y	Y	Y	Y
3 ***Grassley***	Y	Y	Y	✓	Y	Y	Y
4 Smith	Y	N	Y	N	Y	N	Y
5 Harkin	Y	Y	Y	N	Y	Y	Y
6 Bedell	N	Y	Y	Y	Y	N	N

Democrats ***Republicans***

	235	236	237	238	239	240	241
KANSAS							
1 Sebelius	N	Y	Y	Y	N	N	N
2 Keys	N	Y	Y	Y	Y	N	N
3 Winn	N	N	Y	Y	N	Y	Y
4 Glickman	N	Y	Y	Y	Y	N	Y
5 Skubitz	?	?	?	?	✓	?	?
KENTUCKY							
1 Hubbard	N	Y	Y	Y	Y	N	N
2 Natcher	N	N	Y	Y	Y	Y	Y
3 Mazzoli	N	Y	Y	Y	N	Y	Y
4 Snyder	N	N	Y	N	N	Y	Y
5 Carter	Y	Y	Y	N	Y	Y	Y
6 Breckinridge	N	N	Y	Y	Y	X	X
7 Perkins	Y	N	Y	Y	Y	N	N
LOUISIANA							
1 Livingston	Y	N	Y	N	N	Y	Y
2 Boggs	N	N	Y	Y	Y	Y	Y
3 Treen	N	Y	Y	Y	Y	Y	Y
4 Waggonner	N	Y	Y	Y	Y	N	N
5 Huckaby	N	Y	Y	Y	Y	N	N
6 Moore	N	Y	Y	Y	Y	Y	Y
7 Breaux	N	Y	Y	Y	Y	Y	Y
8 Long	N	N	Y	Y	Y	N	Y
MAINE							
1 Emery	N	N	Y	N	N	Y	Y
2 Cohen	Y	Y	Y	N	N	Y	Y
MARYLAND							
1 Bauman	N	Y	Y	N	N	Y	Y
2 Long	?	?	Y	N	N	N	Y
3 Mikulski	Y	Y	Y	Y	▮	Y	Y
4 Holt	N	N	Y	N	N	N	Y
5 Spellman	Y	N	Y	Y	N	Y	Y
6 Byron	N	N	Y	Y	N	N	Y
7 Mitchell	Y	N	N	Y	N	N	N
8 Steers	Y	N	Y	Y	N	Y	Y
MASSACHUSETTS							
1 Conte	Y	N	Y	N	N	Y	Y
2 Boland	N	N	Y	▮	N	Y	Y
3 Early	N	Y	Y	N	N	Y	Y
4 Drinan	Y	Y	Y	N	N	N	N
5 Tsongas	N	N	Y	Y	N	N	Y
6 Harrington	Y	N	Y	Y	N	Y	Y
7 Markey	Y	Y	Y	Y	▮	Y	Y
8 O'Neill							
9 Moakley	N	N	Y	Y	X	Y	Y
10 Heckler	N	N	Y	N	N	Y	Y
11 Burke	N	N	Y	Y	Y	Y	Y
12 Studds	Y	N	Y	N	N	N	N
MICHIGAN							
1 Conyers	#	▮	Y	▮	X	N	N
2 Pursell	Y	N	Y	Y	Y	N	Y
3 Brown	Y	N	N	N	Y	Y	Y
4 Stockman	N	Y	Y	N	N	Y	Y
5 Sawyer	N	Y	Y	N	N	Y	Y
6 Carr	Y	Y	Y	Y	Y	N	N
7 Kildee	Y	N	Y	Y	Y	Y	Y
8 Traxler	N	#	N	Y	Y	Y	Y
9 Vander Jagt	N	Y	?	?	?	Y	Y
10 Cederberg	N	Y	Y	N	N	Y	Y
11 Ruppe	N	N	Y	N	N	Y	Y
12 Bonior	Y	N	Y	Y	Y	N	N
13 Diggs	Y	N	#	Y	X	▮	▮
14 Nedzi	N	N	Y	Y	Y	Y	Y
15 Ford	Y	N	Y	Y	Y	N	N
16 Dingell	N	N	?	Y	Y	Y	Y
17 Brodhead	Y	N	Y	Y	Y	N	N
18 Blanchard	N	Y	Y	Y	Y	N	N
19 Broomfield	N	Y	Y	N	N	Y	Y
MINNESOTA							
1 Quie	N	Y	Y	Y	Y	✓	✓
2 Hagedorn	N	Y	Y	N	N	✓	✓
3 Frenzel	N	Y	Y	N	N	✓	✓
4 Vento	Y	N	Y	Y	Y	Y	Y
5 Fraser	Y	N	Y	Y	Y	▮	▮
6 Nolan	Y	N	?	Y	Y	Y	Y
7 Stangeland	N	Y	Y	Y	Y	Y	Y
8 Oberstar	Y	N	Y	Y	Y	N	N
MISSISSIPPI							
1 Whitten	N	N	#	Y	Y	Y	Y
2 Bowen	N	N	Y	Y	Y	N	N
3 Montgomery	N	Y	Y	Y	Y	N	Y
4 Cochran	?	?	?	?	?	?	?
5 Lott	N	Y	Y	Y	Y	Y	Y
MISSOURI							
1 Clay	Y	N	?	Y	N	N	X
2 Young	Y	N	Y	Y	Y	Y	Y
3 Gephardt	N	Y	#	Y	Y	Y	Y

	235	236	237	238	239	240	241
4 Skelton	N	N	Y	Y	Y	N	N
5 Bolling	N	N	Y	Y	Y	N	N
6 Coleman	N	N	Y	N	Y	N	N
7 Taylor	N	Y	Y	N	N	N	N
8 Ichord	N	Y	Y	Y	Y	N	N
9 Volkmer	N	Y	Y	Y	Y	Y	Y
10 Burlison	N	N	Y	Y	Y	N	N
MONTANA							
1 Baucus	N	N	Y	Y	Y	N	N
2 Marlenee	N	Y	Y	Y	Y	Y	Y
NEBRASKA							
1 Thone	?	?	?	Y	Y	N	Y
2 Cavanaugh	N	Y	Y	Y	Y	Y	Y
3 Smith	N	Y	Y	Y	Y	N	Y
NEVADA							
AL Santini	N	#	Y	Y	N	Y	Y
NEW HAMPSHIRE							
1 D'Amours	N	N	Y	Y	N	Y	Y
2 Cleveland	N	N	Y	N	N	Y	Y
NEW JERSEY							
1 Florio	#	▮	Y	Y	N	Y	Y
2 Hughes	Y	N	Y	N	N	Y	Y
3 Howard	Y	N	Y	Y	N	Y	Y
4 Thompson	N	N	Y	Y	Y	Y	Y
5 Fenwick	N	Y	Y	N	N	N	N
6 Forsythe	N	Y	N	N	N	Y	Y
7 Maguire	N	Y	Y	N	Y	P	Y
8 Roe	Y	N	Y	Y	Y	Y	Y
9 Hollenbeck	Y	N	Y	N	N	Y	Y
10 Rodino	N	N	#	#	X	✓	✓
11 Minish	Y	N	Y	N	N	Y	Y
12 Rinaldo	Y	N	Y	N	N	Y	Y
13 Meyner	N	Y	Y	Y	Y	N	Y
14 LeFante	Y	N	Y	Y	Y	✓	✓
15 Patten	Y	N	Y	Y	Y	Y	Y
NEW MEXICO							
1 Lujan	Y	Y	Y	Y	Y	Y	Y
2 Runnels	✓	?	#	?	?	✓	✓
NEW YORK							
1 Pike	N	Y	Y	N	N	N	N
2 Downey	Y	N	Y	Y	Y	Y	Y
3 Ambro	Y	Y	Y	N	Y	Y	Y
4 Lent	N	Y	Y	N	N	Y	Y
5 Wydler	N	Y	Y	N	N	Y	Y
6 Wolff	Y	N	Y	N	N	Y	Y
7 Addabbo	Y	N	Y	Y	Y	N	N
8 Rosenthal	#	N	Y	N	Y	N	N
9 Delaney	N	Y	Y	Y	Y	Y	Y
10 Biaggi	Y	N	Y	Y	Y	Y	Y
11 Scheuer	Y	N	Y	Y	Y	Y	Y
12 Chisholm	Y	N	Y	Y	Y	N	N
13 Solarz	Y	N	Y	Y	Y	N	N
14 Richmond	Y	N	Y	Y	Y	N	N
15 Zeferetti	Y	N	Y	Y	Y	Y	Y
16 Holtzman	Y	N	Y	Y	N	N	N
17 Murphy	N	N	#	Y	Y	Y	Y
18 Green	Y	Y	Y	N	N	Y	Y
19 Rangel	Y	N	Y	Y	Y	N	N
20 Weiss	Y	N	Y	Y	Y	N	N
21 Garcia	Y	N	Y	Y	Y	N	N
22 Bingham	Y	N	Y	N	Y	N	N
23 Caputo	Y	N	Y	N	N	Y	Y
24 Ottinger	-	-	Y	Y	Y	Y	Y
25 Fish	Y	?	Y	N	N	N	N
26 Gilman	Y	N	Y	Y	N	Y	Y
27 McHugh	N	Y	Y	Y	Y	N	N
28 Stratton	N	Y	Y	N	N	Y	Y
29 Pattison	N	Y	Y	Y	Y	N	N
30 McEwen	N	Y	Y	?	?	Y	Y
31 Mitchell	Y	N	Y	Y	Y	✓	✓
32 Hanley	N	N	Y	Y	Y	Y	Y
33 Walsh	N	N	Y	N	N	Y	Y
34 Horton	N	N	Y	N	N	Y	Y
35 Conable	N	Y	Y	N	N	Y	Y
36 LaFalce	N	Y	Y	Y	Y	Y	Y
37 Nowak	N	Y	Y	N	Y	Y	Y
38 Kemp	N	Y	Y	?	N	Y	Y
39 Lundine	#	Y	Y	Y	Y	N	N
NORTH CAROLINA							
1 Jones	N	N	Y	Y	Y	N	Y
2 Fountain	N	Y	Y	Y	Y	N	Y
3 Whitley	X	?	?	?	?	X	✓
4 Andrews	▮	?	#	Y	Y	N	Y
5 Neal	N	Y	Y	Y	Y	N	Y
6 Preyer	N	N	Y	Y	Y	N	N
7 Rose	N	▮	Y	Y	Y	X	X
8 Hefner	N	N	Y	Y	Y	N	N

	235	236	237	238	239	240	241
9 Martin	N	Y	Y	N	N	N	N
10 Broyhill	N	Y	Y	N	Y	N	N
11 Gudger	N	Y	Y	Y	Y	N	Y
NORTH DAKOTA							
AL Andrews	N	Y	Y	Y	Y	Y	Y
OHIO							
1 Gradison	N	Y	Y	N	N	Y	Y
2 Luken	N	Y	Y	N	N	Y	Y
3 Whalen	N	N	Y	Y	N	N	N
4 Guyer	N	N	Y	Y	Y	Y	Y
5 Latta	N	Y	Y	N	Y	Y	Y
6 Harsha	N	N	Y	Y	Y	Y	Y
7 Brown	N	N	Y	N	N	Y	Y
8 Kindness	N	?	Y	Y	N	Y	Y
9 Ashley	?	N	Y	Y	N	Y	Y
10 Miller	N	Y	Y	Y	Y	Y	Y
11 Stanton	N	Y	Y	N	N	Y	Y
12 Devine	N	Y	Y	N	N	Y	Y
13 Pease	N	Y	Y	Y	Y	Y	Y
14 Seiberling	Y	Y	#	N	N	Y	Y
15 Wylie	N	Y	Y	Y	N	Y	✓
16 Regula	N	Y	Y	Y	Y	Y	Y
17 Ashbrook	N	Y	Y	N	N	Y	Y
18 Applegate	Y	N	Y	Y	Y	Y	Y
19 Carney	Y	N	Y	Y	Y	Y	Y
20 Oakar	Y	N	Y	?	N	Y	Y
21 Stokes	Y	N	Y	Y	N	N	N
22 Vanik	N	Y	Y	N	N	#	X
23 Mottl	N	Y	Y	N	N	Y	Y
OKLAHOMA							
1 Jones	N	Y	Y	Y	Y	N	N
2 Risenhoover	X	?	?	?	?	X	X
3 Watkins	N	Y	Y	Y	Y	N	N
4 Steed	N	N	Y	Y	Y	N	N
5 Edwards	N	Y	Y	Y	Y	Y	Y
6 English	N	Y	Y	Y	Y	N	N
OREGON							
1 AuCoin	N	Y	N	N	Y	N	N
2 Ullman	N	Y	Y	Y	Y	N	N
3 Duncan	N	Y	?	?	?	?	?
4 Weaver	?	?	#	?	?	?	?
PENNSYLVANIA							
1 Myers, M.	?	?	?	?	Y	?	?
2 Nix	?	?	?	?	?	?	?
3 Lederer	Y	N	#	Y	Y	Y	Y
4 Eilberg	Y	N	Y	Y	Y	✓	✓
5 Schulze	N	Y	Y	N	N	Y	Y
6 Yatron	N	N	Y	Y	Y	Y	Y
7 Edgar	Y	N	Y	Y	N	Y	Y
8 Kostmayer	N	Y	Y	Y	N	Y	Y
9 Shuster	N	Y	Y	N	N	Y	Y
10 McDade	Y	N	#	N	N	Y	Y
11 Flood	N	N	Y	Y	Y	#	X
12 Murtha	N	N	Y	Y	Y	N	Y
13 Coughlin	N	N	N	N	N	Y	Y
14 Moorhead	N	N	Y	Y	Y	N	N
15 Rooney	Y	N	Y	Y	Y	Y	Y
16 Walker	N	Y	N	N	N	Y	Y
17 Ertel	N	N	Y	Y	Y	Y	Y
18 Walgren	N	Y	Y	Y	N	Y	Y
19 Goodling, W.	N	N	Y	N	N	Y	Y
20 Gaydos	Y	N	?	?	Y	Y	Y
21 Dent	▮	▮	#	N	Y	▮	▮
22 Murphy	N	N	#	N	N	N	Y
23 Ammerman	N	Y	Y	N	N	Y	Y
24 Marks	N	Y	Y	Y	N	Y	Y
25 Myers, G.	N	Y	Y	N	N	N	N
RHODE ISLAND							
1 St Germain	N	N	Y	Y	Y	Y	?
2 Beard	N	Y	Y	?	Y	Y	?
SOUTH CAROLINA							
1 Davis	N	N	Y	Y	Y	N	N
2 Spence	N	N	Y	Y	Y	N	Y
3 Derrick	N	N	Y	Y	Y	N	N
4 Mann	?	?	?	?	?	?	?
5 Holland	N	N	Y	#	Y	?	?
6 Jenrette	N	N	Y	Y	Y	N	N
SOUTH DAKOTA							
1 Pressler	Y	N	Y	Y	Y	Y	Y
2 Abdnor	N	Y	Y	Y	Y	N	N
TENNESSEE							
1 Quillen	Y	Y	Y	N	N	N	N
2 Duncan	Y	Y	Y	N	N	N	N
3 Lloyd	Y	N	Y	Y	Y	N	N
4 Gore	N	Y	Y	Y	Y	N	N
5 Allen	Y	N	?	?	Y	N	N
6 Beard	Y	Y	Y	Y	Y	Y	Y

	235	236	237	238	239	240	241
7 Jones	N	N	Y	Y	Y	N	N
8 Ford	Y	N	?	Y	Y	N	N
TEXAS							
1 Hall	N	N	Y	Y	Y	N	N
2 Wilson, C.	N	Y	Y	Y	Y	N	N
3 Collins	N	Y	Y	N	N	Y	Y
4 Roberts	N	N	Y	Y	Y	?	?
5 Mattox	N	Y	Y	N	Y	N	N
6 Teague	?	?	?	?	?	?	X
7 Archer	N	Y	Y	N	N	Y	Y
8 Eckhardt	Y	N	Y	Y	Y	N	N
9 Brooks	N	N	Y	Y	Y	Y	Y
10 Pickle	N	N	Y	Y	Y	N	N
11 Poage	N	N	Y	Y	Y	N	N
12 Wright	N	Y	Y	Y	Y	X	X
13 Hightower	N	Y	Y	Y	Y	?	?
14 Young	Y	N	Y	Y	?	?	?
15 de la Garza	N	N	Y	Y	Y	?	?
16 White	✓	†	?	†	†	X	✓
17 Burleson	N	Y	Y	Y	Y	N	N
18 Jordan	Y	N	Y	Y	Y	N	N
19 Mahon	N	Y	Y	Y	Y	N	N
20 Gonzalez	Y	N	Y	Y	Y	N	Y
21 Krueger	N	N	Y	Y	Y	N	N
22 Gammage	?	?	?	?	✓	?	?
23 Kazen	?	?	?	?	✓	?	?
24 Milford	N	N	Y	Y	N	Y	Y
UTAH							
1 McKay	N	N	Y	Y	Y	N	N
2 Marriott	N	N	Y	N	N	N	Y
VERMONT							
AL Jeffords	Y	Y	Y	Y	Y	Y	Y
VIRGINIA							
1 Trible	N	N	Y	Y	N	Y	Y
2 Whitehurst	N	N	Y	Y	N	Y	Y
3 Satterfield	N	Y	Y	N	N	Y	Y
4 Daniel	N	N	Y	Y	Y	Y	Y
5 Daniel	N	N	Y	Y	N	Y	Y
6 Butler	N	Y	Y	Y	N	N	N
7 Robinson	N	Y	Y	Y	N	Y	Y
8 Harris	N	N	Y	N	N	N	Y
9 Wampler	Y	Y	Y	Y	N	N	N
10 Fisher	N	N	Y	Y	N	N	N
WASHINGTON							
1 Pritchard	Y	Y	#	N	N	Y	Y
2 Meeds	#	▮	Y	Y	Y	N	N
3 Bonker	N	N	Y	Y	Y	N	N
4 McCormack	Y	N	Y	Y	Y	N	N
5 Foley	N	N	Y	Y	Y	Y	Y
6 Dicks	N	N	Y	Y	Y	N	?
7 Cunningham	Y	N	Y	N	N	Y	Y
WEST VIRGINIA							
1 Mollohan	Y	Y	Y	Y	Y	N	N
2 Staggers	Y	Y	Y	Y	Y	?	X
3 Slack	?	?	Y	Y	Y	N	Y
4 Rahall	Y	Y	#	#	✓	X	X
WISCONSIN							
1 Aspin	N	N	Y	Y	Y	Y	Y
2 Kastenmeier	Y	N	Y	Y	Y	N	N
3 Baldus	Y	N	Y	Y	Y	N	N
4 Zablocki	Y	N	Y	Y	N	Y	Y
5 Reuss	Y	N	Y	Y	N	N	N
6 Steiger	N	Y	N	N	N	✓	Y
7 Obey	N	N	Y	Y	Y	N	N
8 Cornell	N	N	Y	Y	Y	Y	Y
9 Kasten	▮	#	#	Y	Y	Y	Y
WYOMING							
AL Roncalio	Y	N	Y	Y	Y	?	?

Democrats ***Republicans***

242. HR 12481. U.S. Territories Authorization. P. Burton, D-Calif., motion to suspend the rules and pass the bill to authorize \$73 million for programs and projects in Guam, the Virgin Islands, the Northern Mariana Islands and the Trust Territory of the Pacific Islands. Motion rejected 203-170: R 47-80; D 156-90 (ND 121-47; SD 35-43), May 8, 1978. A two-thirds majority vote (249 in this case) is required for passage under suspension of the rules.

243. H Con Res 583. American MIAs in Vietnam. Wolff, D-N.Y., motion to suspend the rules and adopt the concurrent resolution to state the sense of Congress that the president, through the secretary of state, should request the United Nations secretary general to obtain a full accounting of the 2,300 Americans listed as missing in the Vietnam conflict. Motion agreed to 369-0: R 128-0; D 241-0 (ND 167-0; SD 74-0), May 8, 1978. A two-thirds majority vote (246 in this case) is required for adoption under suspension of the rules.

244. H J Res 873. SBA Disaster Loan Supplemental Appropriations, Fiscal 1978. Passage of the joint resolution to appropriate \$758 million for the disaster loan fund of the Small Business Administration for fiscal 1978. Passed 346-23: R 117-8; D 229-15 (ND 155-11; SD 74-4), May 8, 1978. The president had requested \$758 million.

245. H Con Res 559. Fiscal 1979 Budget Targets. Giaimo, D-Conn., motion that the House resolve itself into the Committee of the Whole for further consideration of the concurrent resolution to set fiscal 1979 budget targets. Motion agreed to 380-3: R 134-1; D 246-2 (ND 169-2; SD 77-0), May 9, 1978.

246. H Con Res 559. Fiscal 1979 Budget Targets. First vote on the Ashbrook, R-Ohio, amendment to reduce budget authority and outlays by \$3.15 billion for programs of the Department of Health, Education and Welfare. Adopted 198-189: R 123-11; D 75-178 (ND 28-149; SD 47-29), May 9, 1978. (The Ashbrook amendment subsequently was rejected by a 192-205 vote. *See vote 254, p. 72-H*)

247. H Con Res 559. Fiscal 1979 Budget Targets. Hansen, R-Idaho, amendment to adjust revenue and spending targets to reflect that Panama Canal tolls be funneled through the U.S. Treasury. Adopted 231-170: R 118-20; D 113-150 (ND 51-131; SD 62-19), May 9, 1978.

248. H Con Res 559. Fiscal 1979 Budget Targets. Fisher, D-Va., amendment to reduce budget authority by \$8 billion and outlays by \$7 billion. Rejected 195-203: R 122-15; D 73-188 (ND 33-147; SD 40-41), May 9, 1978.

249. H Con Res 559. Fiscal 1979 Budget Targets. Brown, R-Mich., amendment to reduce outlays by \$195.4 million and budget authority by \$178.2 million for various regulatory agencies. Rejected 196-196: R 121-12; D 75-184 (ND 20-160; SD 55-24), May 9, 1978.

KEY

- Y Voted for (yea).
- ✓ Paired for.
- † Announced for.
- # CQ Poll for.
- N Voted against (nay).
- X Paired against.
- \- Announced against.
- ▮ CQ Poll against.
- P Voted "present."
- ● Voted "present" to avoid possible conflict of interest.
- ? Did not vote or otherwise make a position known.

	242	243	244	245	246	247	248	249
ALABAMA								
1 Edwards	N	Y	Y	Y	Y	Y	Y	Y
2 Dickinson	Y	Y	Y	Y	Y	Y	Y	Y
3 Nichols	N	Y	Y	Y	Y	Y	Y	Y
4 Bevill	N	Y	Y	Y	Y	Y	Y	Y
5 Flippo	N	Y	Y	Y	Y	Y	Y	Y
6 Buchanan	N	Y	Y	Y	Y	Y	Y	Y
7 Flowers	N	Y	Y	Y	Y	Y	Y	Y
ALASKA								
AL Young	N	Y	Y	Y	Y	Y	N	Y
ARIZONA								
1 Rhodes	?	?	?	?	?	?	?	?
2 Udall	Y	Y	Y	Y	N	N	N	N
3 Stump	Y	Y	Y	Y	Y	Y	Y	Y
4 Rudd	N	Y	Y	Y	Y	Y	Y	Y
ARKANSAS								
1 Alexander	Y	Y	Y	Y	N	N	N	N
2 Tucker	#	#	#	#	▮	#	#	▮
3 Hammerschmidt	?	?	?	Y	Y	Y	Y	Y
4 Thornton	?	?	?	?	?	?	?	?
CALIFORNIA								
1 Johnson	Y	Y	Y	Y	N	Y	N	N
2 Clausen	Y	Y	Y	Y	Y	Y	Y	Y
3 Moss	Y	Y	Y	Y	N	N	N	N
4 Leggett	Y	Y	Y	?	N	Y	N	N
5 Burton, J.	Y	Y	Y	?	N	N	N	N
6 Burton, P.	Y	Y	Y	Y	N	N	?	?
7 Miller	Y	Y	Y	Y	N	N	N	N
8 Dellums	Y	Y	Y	Y	N	N	N	N
9 Stark	Y	Y	Y	Y	▮	N	N	N
10 Edwards	Y	Y	Y	Y	N	N	N	N
11 Ryan	Y	Y	N	Y	N	Y	N	N
12 McCloskey	Y	Y	Y	Y	N	N	N	N
13 Mineta	Y	Y	Y	Y	N	N	N	N
14 McFall	Y	Y	Y	Y	N	N	N	N
15 Sisk	?	?	?	Y	?	?	N	?
16 Panetta	Y	Y	Y	Y	N	N	Y	N
17 Krebs	Y	Y	Y	Y	N	N	N	Y
18 Ketchum	Y	Y	Y	Y	Y	Y	Y	Y
19 Lagomarsino	Y	Y	Y	Y	Y	Y	Y	Y
20 Goldwater	Y	Y	Y	Y	Y	Y	Y	Y
21 Corman	#	#	#	Y	N	N	N	N
22 Moorhead	N	Y	Y	Y	Y	Y	Y	Y
23 Beilenson	#	#	#	Y	N	N	N	N
24 Waxman	Y	Y	Y	Y	N	N	N	N
25 Roybal	Y	Y	Y	Y	N	N	N	N
26 Rousselot	Y	Y	Y	Y	Y	Y	Y	Y
27 Dornan	N	Y	Y	Y	Y	Y	Y	Y
28 Burke	#	#	#	Y	N	N	▮	▮
29 Hawkins	Y	Y	Y	Y	N	N	N	N
30 Danielson	Y	Y	Y	Y	N	N	N	N
31 Wilson, C.H.	Y	Y	Y	Y	▮	#	▮	N
32 Anderson	Y	Y	Y	Y	N	Y	Y	N
33 Clawson	?	?	?	?	✓	✓	?	✓
34 Hannaford	Y	Y	Y	Y	N	Y	N	N
35 Lloyd	Y	Y	Y	Y	Y	Y	N	Y
36 Brown	Y	Y	Y	?	N	N	N	N
37 Pettis	Y	Y	Y	Y	Y	N	Y	Y
38 Patterson	Y	Y	Y	Y	N	N	N	N
39 Wiggins	N	Y	N	#	Y	N	Y	Y
40 Badham	N	Y	Y	Y	Y	Y	Y	#
41 Wilson, B.	Y	Y	Y	N	Y	Y	N	Y
42 Van Deerlin	Y	Y	Y	Y	N	N	N	N
43 Burgener	Y	Y	Y	Y	Y	Y	Y	Y
COLORADO								
1 Schroeder	Y	Y	Y	Y	N	N	Y	N
2 Wirth	▮	#	#	Y	N	N	Y	N
3 Evans	Y	Y	Y	#	N	N	Y	N
4 Johnson	Y	Y	Y	Y	Y	N	Y	Y
5 Armstrong	Y	Y	Y	?	?	Y	Y	Y
CONNECTICUT								
1 Cotter	N	Y	Y	Y	N	N	N	N
2 Dodd	?	?	?	Y	N	N	N	N
3 Giaimo	N	Y	N	Y	N	N	N	N
4 McKinney	Y	Y	Y	Y	▮	N	Y	Y
5 Sarasin	-	†	†	†	N	Y	Y	Y
6 Moffett	N	Y	Y	Y	N	N	N	N
DELAWARE								
AL Evans	Y	Y	Y	Y	Y	Y	Y	Y
FLORIDA								
1 Sikes	N	Y	Y	Y	Y	Y	N	Y
2 Fuqua	N	Y	Y	Y	Y	Y	N	Y
3 Bennett	N	Y	N	Y	Y	Y	Y	Y
4 Chappell	Y	Y	Y	Y	Y	Y	N	Y
5 Kelly	N	Y	N	Y	Y	Y	Y	Y
6 Young	Y	Y	Y	Y	Y	Y	Y	Y
7 Gibbons	N	Y	Y	Y	Y	N	Y	Y
8 Ireland	N	Y	Y	Y	Y	Y	Y	Y
9 Frey	?	?	?	?	?	✓	?	✓
10 Bafalis	Y	Y	Y	Y	Y	Y	Y	Y
11 Rogers	N	Y	Y	Y	N	Y	N	N
12 Burke	N	Y	N	Y	Y	Y	Y	Y
13 Lehman	Y	#	N	Y	N	N	N	N
14 Pepper	†	†	Y	Y	N	N	N	N
15 Fascell	Y	Y	Y	Y	N	N	N	N
GEORGIA								
1 Ginn	N	Y	Y	Y	Y	Y	N	Y
2 Mathis	Y	Y	Y	Y	N	Y	N	Y
3 Brinkley	N	Y	Y	Y	Y	Y	Y	N
4 Levitas	N	Y	Y	Y	N	Y	N	Y
5 Fowler	N	Y	Y	Y	N	Y	Y	Y
6 Flynt	N	Y	Y	Y	Y	Y	Y	Y
7 McDonald	N	Y	N	Y	Y	Y	Y	Y
8 Evans	Y	Y	Y	Y	N	Y	#	#
9 Jenkins	N	Y	Y	Y	Y	Y	Y	Y
10 Barnard	N	Y	Y	#	#	#	#	#
HAWAII								
1 Heftel	Y	Y	Y	Y	N	N	N	Y
2 Akaka	Y	Y	Y	Y	N	N	N	N
IDAHO								
1 Symms	?	?	?	Y	Y	Y	Y	Y
2 Hansen, G.	N	Y	Y	Y	Y	Y	Y	Y
ILLINOIS								
1 Metcalfe	Y	Y	Y	Y	N	N	N	N
2 Murphy	Y	Y	Y	Y	N	Y	N	N
3 Russo	N	Y	Y	Y	Y	N	Y	Y
4 Derwinski	N	Y	N	Y	Y	Y	Y	Y
5 Fary	Y	Y	Y	Y	N	N	N	N
6 Hyde	Y	Y	Y	Y	N	N	Y	Y
7 Collins	Y	Y	Y	Y	X	N	N	N
8 Rostenkowski	N	Y	Y	Y	N	N	N	N
9 Yates	Y	Y	N	Y	N	N	N	N
10 Mikva	Y	Y	N	Y	N	N	N	N
11 Annunzio	N	Y	Y	Y	N	N	N	N
12 Crane	N	Y	Y	Y	Y	Y	Y	Y
13 McClory	Y	Y	Y	Y	Y	Y	Y	Y
14 Erlenborn	Y	Y	Y	Y	Y	N	Y	Y
15 Corcoran	Y	Y	Y	Y	Y	Y	Y	Y
16 Anderson	Y	Y	Y	Y	Y	N	Y	Y
17 O'Brien	N	Y	Y	Y	Y	Y	Y	Y
18 Michel	▮	#	#	Y	Y	Y	Y	Y
19 Railsback	Y	Y	Y	Y	Y	N	Y	Y
20 Findley	N	Y	Y	Y	Y	N	Y	Y
21 Madigan	?	Y	Y	Y	?	Y	Y	?
22 Shipley	Y	Y	Y	?	N	Y	N	N
23 Price	Y	Y	Y	Y	N	N	N	N
24 Simon	Y	Y	Y	Y	N	N	N	N
INDIANA								
1 Benjamin	Y	Y	Y	Y	N	N	N	N
2 Fithian	Y	Y	Y	Y	Y	Y	Y	Y
3 Brademas	Y	Y	Y	Y	N	N	N	N
4 Quayle	N	Y	Y	Y	Y	Y	Y	Y
5 Hillis	N	Y	Y	Y	Y	Y	Y	Y
6 Evans	N	Y	Y	Y	Y	Y	N	Y
7 Myers, J.	Y	Y	Y	Y	Y	Y	Y	Y
8 Cornwell	Y	Y	Y	Y	N	N	N	N
9 Hamilton	N	Y	Y	Y	N	N	Y	Y
10 Sharp	Y	Y	Y	Y	N	N	Y	N
11 Jacobs	N	Y	N	Y	Y	Y	Y	Y
IOWA								
1 Leach	N	Y	Y	Y	Y	Y	Y	Y
2 Blouin	N	Y	Y	Y	N	N	N	N
3 Grassley	N	Y	Y	Y	Y	Y	Y	Y
4 Smith	Y	Y	Y	Y	N	Y	N	N
5 Harkin	Y	Y	Y	Y	N	Y	Y	N
6 Bedell	N	Y	N	Y	N	N	N	N

Democrats ***Republicans***

	242	243	244	245	246	247	248	249
KANSAS								
1 Sebelius	Y	Y	Y	Y	Y	Y	Y	Y
2 Keys	N	Y	Y	Y	N	N	Y	N
3 Winn	N	Y	Y	Y	Y	Y	Y	Y
4 Glickman	N	Y	Y	Y	N	Y	Y	N
5 Skubitz	?	?	?	?	?	?	?	?
KENTUCKY								
1 Hubbard	N	Y	Y	Y	Y	Y	Y	Y
2 Natcher	Y	Y	Y	Y	N	Y	N	N
3 Mazzoli	Y	Y	Y	Y	Y	N	Y	N
4 Snyder	N	Y	Y	Y	Y	Y	Y	Y
5 Carter	Y	Y	Y	Y	N	Y	Y	Y
6 Breckinridge	?	?	?	Y	N	Y	N	N
7 Perkins	Y	Y	Y	Y	N	Y	N	N
LOUISIANA								
1 Livingston	N	Y	Y	Y	Y	Y	Y	Y
2 Boggs	Y	#	Y	Y	N	Y	N	N
3 Treen	N	Y	Y	Y	Y	Y	Y	Y
4 Waggonner	N	Y	Y	Y	✓	Y	Y	Y
5 Huckaby	N	Y	Y	Y	Y	Y	Y	Y
6 Moore	N	Y	Y	Y	Y	Y	Y	Y
7 Breaux	N	Y	Y	Y	Y	Y	Y	Y
8 Long	N	Y	Y	Y	N	Y	N	N
MAINE								
1 Emery	N	Y	Y	Y	Y	Y	Y	Y
2 Cohen	N	Y	Y	Y	Y	Y	Y	Y
MARYLAND								
1 Bauman	N	Y	Y	Y	Y	Y	Y	Y
2 Long	Y	Y	Y	Y	Y	Y	Y	N
3 Mikulski	Y	Y	Y	Y	N	N	N	N
4 Holt	N	Y	Y	Y	Y	Y	N	Y
5 Spellman	N	Y	Y	Y	N	N	N	N
6 Byron	Y	Y	Y	Y	Y	Y	Y	Y
7 Mitchell	Y	Y	Y	N	N	N	N	N
8 Steers	Y	Y	Y	Y	N	N	Y	N
MASSACHUSETTS								
1 Conte	Y	Y	Y	Y	N	N	N	Y
2 Boland	Y	Y	Y	Y	N	N	N	N
3 Early	N	Y	Y	Y	N	N	N	Y
4 Drinan	N	Y	Y	Y	N	N	N	N
5 Tsongas	Y	Y	#	Y	N	N	N	N
6 Harrington	Y	Y	Y	#	N	N	N	N
7 Markey	Y	Y	Y	Y	N	N	N	N
8 O'Neill								
9 Moakley	Y	Y	#	Y	N	N	N	N
10 Heckler	Y	Y	Y	Y	N	Y	Y	N
11 Burke	Y	Y	Y	Y	N	Y	N	N
12 Studds	N	Y	Y	Y	N	N	N	N
MICHIGAN								
1 Conyers	#	#	#	#	▮	▮	▮	X
2 Pursell	?	?	?	Y	N	Y	Y	?
3 Brown	Y	Y	Y	Y	Y	Y	Y	Y
4 Stockman	N	Y	N	Y	#	Y	Y	Y
5 Sawyer	Y	Y	Y	Y	Y	Y	Y	Y
6 Carr	Y	Y	Y	Y	Y	N	Y	N
7 Kildee	Y	Y	Y	Y	N	N	N	N
8 Traxler	Y	Y	Y	Y	N	Y	N	N
9 Vander Jagt	Y	Y	Y	Y	Y	Y	Y	Y
10 Cederberg	N	Y	Y	?	Y	Y	Y	Y
11 Ruppe	Y	Y	Y	Y	Y	Y	Y	Y
12 Bonior	Y	Y	Y	Y	N	N	N	N
13 Diggs	?	?	?	?	N	N	N	N
14 Nedzi	?	?	?	Y	N	N	N	N
15 Ford	Y	Y	Y	?	N	N	?	X
16 Dingell	N	Y	Y	Y	N	Y	N	X
17 Brodhead	Y	Y	Y	Y	N	N	N	N
18 Blanchard	Y	Y	N	Y	N	N	N	N
19 Broomfield	N	Y	Y	Y	Y	Y	Y	Y
MINNESOTA								
1 Quie	#	#	#	Y	Y	Y	Y	Y
2 Hagedorn	N	Y	Y	Y	Y	Y	Y	Y
3 Frenzel	N	Y	Y	Y	Y	Y	Y	Y
4 Vento	Y	Y	N	Y	N	N	N	N
5 Fraser	Y	Y	Y	#	▮	▮	N	N
6 Nolan	?	?	?	Y	N	N	N	N
7 Stangeland	N	Y	Y	Y	Y	Y	Y	Y
8 Oberstar	Y	Y	Y	Y	N	N	N	N
MISSISSIPPI								
1 Whitten	Y	#	Y	Y	Y	Y	N	Y
2 Bowen	Y	Y	Y	Y	Y	Y	N	Y
3 Montgomery	Y	Y	Y	Y	Y	Y	N	Y
4 Cochran	?	?	?	?	?	?	?	?
5 Lott	N	Y	Y	Y	Y	Y	N	Y
MISSOURI								
1 Clay	Y	Y	Y	Y	N	N	N	N
2 Young	Y	Y	Y	Y	N	Y	N	N
3 Gephardt	N	Y	Y	Y	N	Y	N	N
4 Skelton	N	Y	Y	Y	Y	Y	Y	Y
5 Bolling	N	Y	Y	Y	N	N	N	N
6 Coleman	N	Y	Y	Y	Y	Y	Y	Y
7 Taylor	N	Y	Y	Y	Y	Y	Y	Y
8 Ichord	N	Y	Y	Y	Y	Y	Y	Y
9 Volkmer	N	Y	N	Y	N	Y	Y	Y
10 Burlison	N	Y	Y	Y	N	N	N	N
MONTANA								
1 Baucus	▮	#	#	#	✓	X	Y	N
2 Marlenee	Y	Y	Y	Y	Y	Y	Y	Y
NEBRASKA								
1 Thone	?	#	#	#	#	?	#	#
2 Cavanaugh	N	Y	Y	?	?	X	✓	X
3 Smith	Y	Y	Y	Y	Y	Y	Y	Y
NEVADA								
AL Santini	#	#	#	Y	Y	Y	Y	Y
NEW HAMPSHIRE								
1 D'Amours	N	Y	Y	Y	N	Y	Y	N
2 Cleveland	N	Y	Y	Y	Y	Y	Y	Y
NEW JERSEY								
1 Florio	Y	Y	Y	Y	N	Y	N	N
2 Hughes	N	Y	Y	Y	Y	Y	Y	N
3 Howard	Y	Y	Y	Y	N	N	N	N
4 Thompson	Y	Y	Y	Y	N	N	N	N
5 Fenwick	N	Y	N	Y	Y	N	Y	N
6 Forsythe	N	Y	Y	Y	Y	Y	Y	Y
7 Maguire	Y	Y	Y	Y	N	N	N	N
8 Roe	Y	Y	Y	Y	N	Y	N	N
9 Hollenbeck	Y	Y	Y	Y	Y	Y	N	N
10 Rodino	#	#	#	#	▮	▮	▮	▮
11 Minish	N	Y	Y	Y	N	Y	N	N
12 Rinaldo	N	Y	Y	Y	Y	Y	N	N
13 Meyner	#	#	#	#	X	X	N	N
14 LeFante	Y	Y	Y	Y	N	N	N	N
15 Patten	Y	Y	Y	Y	N	N	N	N
NEW MEXICO								
1 Lujan	?	?	?	?	✓	?	?	✓
2 Runnels	?	#	#	#	✓	?	#	✓
NEW YORK								
1 Pike	N	Y	N	Y	Y	N	Y	Y
2 Downey	Y	Y	Y	#	N	N	N	N
3 Ambro	N	Y	Y	?	Y	N	N	N
4 Lent	Y	Y	Y	Y	Y	Y	Y	Y
5 Wydler	N	Y	Y	Y	N	Y	Y	Y
6 Wolff	Y	Y	Y	Y	N	Y	N	N
7 Addabbo	Y	Y	Y	Y	N	N	N	N
8 Rosenthal	Y	Y	Y	Y	N	N	N	N
9 Delaney	Y	Y	Y	Y	Y	Y	N	N
10 Biaggi	N	Y	Y	Y	Y	Y	N	N
11 Scheuer	Y	Y	Y	Y	N	N	N	N
12 Chisholm	Y	Y	Y	#	N	N	N	N
13 Solarz	Y	Y	Y	Y	N	N	N	N
14 Richmond	Y	Y	Y	Y	N	N	N	N
15 Zeferetti	N	Y	Y	Y	Y	Y	N	N
16 Holtzman	†	†	†	Y	N	N	N	N
17 Murphy	Y	Y	Y	#	N	N	N	N
18 Green	Y	Y	Y	Y	N	N	N	N
19 Rangel	Y	Y	Y	?	X	N	N	N
20 Weiss	Y	Y	Y	Y	N	N	N	N
21 Garcia	?	?	?	?	N	N	N	N
22 Bingham	Y	Y	Y	Y	N	N	N	N
23 Caputo	N	Y	Y	Y	Y	Y	Y	Y
24 Ottinger	Y	Y	Y	Y	N	N	N	N
25 Fish	N	Y	Y	Y	Y	Y	Y	Y
26 Gilman	Y	Y	Y	Y	Y	Y	N	N
27 McHugh	Y	Y	Y	Y	N	N	N	N
28 Stratton	Y	Y	Y	Y	Y	Y	N	N
29 Pattison	Y	#	N	Y	N	N	N	N
30 McEwen	N	Y	Y	Y	Y	Y	N	Y
31 Mitchell	Y	Y	Y	Y	Y	Y	N	Y
32 Hanley	Y	Y	Y	Y	N	N	N	Y
33 Walsh	N	Y	Y	Y	Y	Y	Y	Y
34 Horton	N	Y	Y	Y	Y	Y	N	N
35 Conable	N	Y	N	Y	Y	N	Y	Y
36 LaFalce	N	Y	Y	Y	N	N	Y	N
37 Nowak	N	Y	Y	Y	N	N	N	Y
38 Kemp	N	Y	Y	Y	Y	Y	Y	Y
39 Lundine	Y	Y	Y	Y	N	N	Y	N
NORTH CAROLINA								
1 Jones	Y	Y	Y	Y	Y	Y	Y	Y
2 Fountain	N	Y	Y	Y	Y	Y	Y	Y
3 Whitley	?	?	?	?	✓	?	✓	✓
4 Andrews	N	Y	Y	Y	Y	N	?	#
5 Neal	N	Y	Y	Y	Y	Y	Y	Y
6 Preyer	N	Y	Y	Y	N	N	Y	N
7 Rose	Y	Y	Y	Y	Y	Y	N	Y
8 Hefner	N	Y	Y	Y	Y	Y	Y	Y
9 Martin	N	Y	Y	Y	Y	Y	Y	Y
10 Broyhill	N	Y	?	Y	Y	N	Y	Y
11 Gudger	N	Y	Y	Y	Y	Y	Y	Y
NORTH DAKOTA								
AL Andrews	N	Y	Y	Y	Y	Y	Y	Y
OHIO								
1 Gradison	N	Y	Y	Y	Y	Y	Y	Y
2 Luken	N	Y	Y	Y	Y	Y	Y	N
3 Whalen	Y	Y	Y	Y	N	N	N	N
4 Guyer	N	Y	Y	Y	Y	Y	Y	Y
5 Latta	N	Y	Y	Y	Y	Y	Y	Y
6 Harsha	N	Y	Y	Y	Y	Y	Y	Y
7 Brown	?	?	?	Y	Y	Y	Y	Y
8 Kindness	N	Y	Y	Y	Y	Y	Y	Y
9 Ashley	?	?	?	Y	N	N	N	N
10 Miller	N	Y	Y	Y	Y	Y	Y	Y
11 Stanton	N	Y	Y	Y	Y	Y	Y	Y
12 Devine	N	Y	Y	Y	Y	Y	Y	Y
13 Pease	N	Y	Y	Y	N	N	N	N
14 Seiberling	#	#	#	Y	N	N	-	N
15 Wylie	N	Y	Y	Y	Y	Y	Y	Y
16 Regula	Y	Y	Y	Y	Y	Y	Y	Y
17 Ashbrook	N	Y	Y	Y	Y	Y	Y	Y
18 Applegate	N	Y	Y	Y	Y	Y	N	N
19 Carney	Y	Y	Y	Y	N	Y	N	N
20 Oakar	N	Y	Y	Y	N	Y	N	N
21 Stokes	Y	Y	Y	Y	N	N	N	N
22 Vanik	N	Y	Y	Y	N	N	N	N
23 Mottl	Y	Y	Y	Y	Y	Y	Y	N
OKLAHOMA								
1 Jones	N	Y	Y	Y	Y	Y	Y	Y
2 Risenhoover	?	?	?	?	✓	✓	?	✓
3 Watkins	N	Y	Y	Y	Y	Y	Y	Y
4 Steed	#	#	#	#	▮	N	N	Y
5 Edwards	N	Y	Y	Y	Y	Y	Y	Y
6 English	N	Y	Y	Y	Y	Y	Y	Y
OREGON								
1 AuCoin	N	Y	Y	N	N	N	Y	N
2 Ullman	Y	Y	Y	Y	N	▮	N	N
3 Duncan	N	Y	Y	Y	?	N	N	Y
4 Weaver	Y	Y	Y	Y	N	N	N	N
PENNSYLVANIA								
1 Myers, M.	Y	Y	Y	Y	N	N	?	?
2 Nix	?	?	?	?	X	X	?	X
3 Lederer	Y	Y	Y	Y	X	N	N	N
4 Eilberg	#	#	?	#	X	#	X	?
5 Schulze	N	Y	Y	Y	Y	Y	Y	Y
6 Yatron	N	Y	Y	Y	Y	Y	Y	N
7 Edgar	Y	Y	Y	Y	N	N	N	N
8 Kostmayer	Y	Y	Y	Y	N	N	N	N
9 Shuster	N	Y	Y	Y	Y	Y	Y	Y
10 McDade	N	Y	Y	Y	Y	Y	Y	Y
11 Flood	Y	Y	Y	Y	N	Y	▮	X
12 Murtha	N	Y	Y	Y	N	N	N	N
13 Coughlin	Y	Y	Y	Y	Y	Y	Y	Y
14 Moorhead	#	#	#	Y	N	N	N	N
15 Rooney	Y	Y	Y	Y	N	N	N	N
16 Walker	N	Y	Y	Y	Y	Y	Y	Y
17 Ertel	N	Y	Y	Y	N	Y	Y	Y
18 Walgren	Y	Y	Y	Y	Y	N	N	N
19 Goodling, W.	N	Y	Y	Y	Y	Y	Y	Y
20 Gaydos	Y	Y	Y	Y	Y	Y	N	N
21 Dent	#	#	#	#	X	X	▮	X
22 Murphy	N	Y	Y	Y	?	N	?	?
23 Ammerman	Y	Y	Y	Y	N	Y	N	N
24 Marks	N	Y	Y	Y	Y	Y	Y	Y
25 Myers, G.	Y	Y	Y	Y	Y	N	Y	N
RHODE ISLAND								
1 St Germain	Y	Y	Y	Y	N	Y	N	N
2 Beard	Y	Y	Y	Y	N	Y	N	N
SOUTH CAROLINA								
1 Davis	Y	Y	Y	Y	Y	Y	N	Y
2 Spence	N	Y	Y	Y	Y	Y	Y	Y
3 Derrick	N	Y	Y	Y	N	Y	N	N
4 Mann	?	?	?	?	?	?	?	?
5 Holland	Y	Y	Y	Y	?	Y	N	Y
6 Jenrette	#	#	#	Y	N	Y	N	Y
SOUTH DAKOTA								
1 Pressler	Y	Y	Y	Y	Y	Y	Y	Y
2 Abdnor	Y	Y	#	Y	Y	Y	Y	Y
TENNESSEE								
1 Quillen	#	#	#	Y	Y	Y	Y	Y
2 Duncan	Y	Y	#	Y	Y	Y	Y	Y
3 Lloyd	N	Y	Y	Y	Y	Y	N	Y
4 Gore	Y	Y	Y	Y	N	N	N	N
5 Allen	Y	Y	?	Y	Y	Y	N	N
6 Beard	N	Y	Y	Y	Y	Y	?	?
7 Jones	Y	Y	Y	Y	Y	Y	N	Y
8 Ford	Y	Y	Y	Y	N	N	N	N
TEXAS								
1 Hall	N	Y	Y	Y	Y	Y	Y	Y
2 Wilson, C.	Y	Y	Y	#	✓	N	N	▮
3 Collins	N	Y	N	Y	Y	Y	Y	Y
4 Roberts	?	?	?	?	?	?	?	✓
5 Mattox	Y	Y	N	Y	Y	Y	N	N
6 Teague	?	?	?	?	✓	✓	N	✓
7 Archer	N	Y	Y	Y	Y	Y	Y	Y
8 Eckhardt	Y	Y	Y	Y	X	N	N	N
9 Brooks	Y	Y	Y	Y	N	N	N	Y
10 Pickle	Y	Y	Y	Y	N	N	Y	Y
11 Poage	N	Y	Y	Y	Y	Y	Y	Y
12 Wright	Y	Y	Y	Y	N	N	N	N
13 Hightower	Y	Y	Y	Y	Y	Y	Y	Y
14 Young	Y	Y	Y	Y	Y	Y	N	Y
15 de la Garza	Y	Y	Y	Y	N	Y	Y	Y
16 White	Y	Y	Y	Y	Y	Y	Y	Y
17 Burleson	N	Y	Y	Y	Y	Y	N	Y
18 Jordan	Y	Y	Y	Y	N	N	N	N
19 Mahon	N	Y	Y	Y	N	Y	Y	Y
20 Gonzalez	Y	Y	Y	Y	N	Y	N	N
21 Krueger	N	Y	Y	Y	N	Y	Y	Y
22 Gammage	N	?	Y	Y	Y	Y	Y	Y
23 Kazen	Y	Y	Y	Y	N	Y	Y	Y
24 Milford	?	?	?	?	Y	Y	Y	Y
UTAH								
1 McKay	Y	Y	Y	Y	Y	N	N	N
2 Marriott	N	Y	Y	Y	Y	Y	Y	Y
VERMONT								
AL Jeffords	Y	Y	Y	Y	Y	Y	Y	Y
VIRGINIA								
1 Trible	N	Y	Y	Y	Y	Y	Y	Y
2 Whitehurst	N	Y	Y	Y	Y	N	N	#
3 Satterfield	N	Y	Y	Y	Y	Y	Y	Y
4 Daniel	N	Y	Y	Y	Y	Y	Y	Y
5 Daniel	N	Y	Y	?	?	?	Y	Y
6 Butler	N	Y	Y	Y	Y	?	?	?
7 Robinson	N	Y	Y	Y	Y	Y	Y	Y
8 Harris	N	Y	Y	#	Y	N	N	N
9 Wampler	N	Y	Y	Y	Y	Y	Y	Y
10 Fisher	Y	Y	Y	Y	N	N	Y	N
WASHINGTON								
1 Pritchard	#	#	#	#	▮	#	#	#
2 Meeds	#	#	#	#	▮	▮	▮	▮
3 Bonker	N	Y	Y	Y	N	N	N	N
4 McCormack	Y	Y	Y	Y	N	N	Y	N
5 Foley	?	?	?	Y	N	N	N	N
6 Dicks	?	?	?	Y	N	N	N	N
7 Cunningham	▮	#	#	Y	Y	Y	Y	Y
WEST VIRGINIA								
1 Mollohan	#	#	#	Y	Y	Y	N	N
2 Staggers	Y	Y	Y	Y	N	Y	N	N
3 Slack	Y	Y	Y	Y	Y	Y	N	N
4 Rahall	#	#	#	#	X	✓	X	X
WISCONSIN								
1 Aspin	N	Y	Y	Y	N	N	N	N
2 Kastenmeier	Y	Y	Y	Y	N	N	N	N
3 Baldus	Y	Y	Y	Y	N	N	N	N
4 Zablocki	Y	Y	Y	Y	N	N	N	N
5 Reuss	Y	Y	Y	Y	N	N	N	N
6 Steiger	#	#	#	Y	#	N	Y	N
7 Obey	Y	Y	Y	Y	N	N	N	N
8 Cornell	Y	Y	Y	Y	N	N	N	N
9 Kasten	▮	#	#	Y	Y	Y	Y	Y
WYOMING								
AL Roncalio	?	?	?	Y	N	N	N	N

Democrats ***Republicans***

250. H Con Res 559. Fiscal 1979 Budget Targets. Giaimo, D-Conn., motion that the House resolve itself into the Committee of the Whole to resume consideration of the resolution. Motion agreed to 392-4: R 135-1; D 257-3 (ND 178-2; SD 79-1), May 10, 1978.

251. H Con Res 559. Fiscal 1979 Budget Targets. Caputo, R-N.Y., amendment to reduce budget authority and outlays by $56 million representing cuts in aid to South Korea. Rejected 146-254: R 68-71; D 78-183 (ND 57-119; SD 21-64), May 10, 1978.

252. H Con Res 559. Fiscal 1979 Budget Targets. Jacobs, D-Ind., amendment to the Rousselot, R-Calif., substitute amendment *(see vote 253, below)* to the bill, to provide for a balanced budget and no new tax cut. Rejected 45-352: R 5-134; D 40-218 (ND 36-139; SD 4-79), May 10, 1978.

253. H Con Res 559. Fiscal 1979 Budget Targets. Rousselot, R-Calif., substitute amendment, to the bill, to provide for a balanced budget with revenues of $464.6 billion, budget authority of $520.4 billion and outlays of $464.6 billion, with no deficit. Rejected 170-226: R 115-24; D 55-202 (ND 14-161; SD 41-41), May 10, 1978.

254. H Con Res 559. Fiscal 1979 Budget Targets. Second vote on the Ashbrook, R-Ohio, amendment to reduce budget authority and outlays by $3.15 billion for programs of the Department of Health, Education and Welfare. Rejected 192-205: R 127-12; D 65-193 (ND 18-158; SD 47-35), May 10, 1978. (The Ashbrook amendment previously had been adopted in Committee of the Whole. *See vote 246, p. 70-H)*

255. H Con Res 559. Fiscal 1979 Budget Targets. Adoption of the concurrent resolution setting the following fiscal 1979 budget targets: revenues of $433 billion, budget authority of $569.5 billion, outlays of $500.9 billion and a deficit of $57.9 billion. Adopted 201-197: R 3-136; D 198-61 (ND 152-25; SD 46-36), May 10, 1978.

KEY

Y Voted for (yea).
✓ Paired for.
† Announced for.
# CQ Poll for.
N Voted against (nay).
X Paired against.
\- Announced against.
▮ CQ Poll against.
P Voted "present."
● Voted "present" to avoid possible conflict of interest.
? Did not vote or otherwise make a position known.

	250	251	252	253	254	255
ALABAMA						
1 Edwards	Y	N	N	Y	Y	N
2 Dickinson	Y	Y	N	Y	Y	N
3 Nichols	Y	N	N	Y	Y	N
4 Bevill	Y	Y	N	N	Y	Y
5 Flippo	Y	N	N	N	Y	N
6 Buchanan	Y	Y	N	Y	Y	N
7 Flowers	?	N	N	N	Y	N
ALASKA						
AL Young	Y	N	N	Y	Y	N
ARIZONA						
1 Rhodes	Y	Y	N	Y	Y	N
2 Udall	Y	Y	N	N	N	Y
3 Stump	Y	N	N	Y	Y	N
4 Rudd	Y	N	N	Y	Y	N
ARKANSAS						
1 Alexander	Y	N	N	N	N	Y
2 Tucker	#	▮	▮	▮	▮	#
3 Hammerschmidt	Y	N	N	Y	Y	N
4 Thornton	?	?	?	?	?	?
CALIFORNIA						
1 Johnson	Y	N	N	N	N	Y
2 Clausen	Y	Y	N	Y	Y	N
3 Moss	Y	N	N	N	N	Y
4 Leggett	Y	N	N	N	N	Y
5 Burton, J.	Y	Y	Y	P	N	N
6 Burton, P.	Y	Y	N	N	N	N
7 Miller	Y	Y	Y	Y	N	Y
8 Dellums	Y	Y	N	N	N	Y
9 Stark	Y	Y	Y	N	N	Y
10 Edwards	Y	N	N	N	N	Y
11 Ryan	Y	N	N	N	N	Y
12 McCloskey	Y	N	Y	Y	N	N
13 Mineta	Y	N	N	N	N	Y
14 McFall	Y	Y	N	N	N	Y
15 Sisk	Y	N	N	N	?	?
16 Panetta	Y	Y	Y	Y	N	Y
17 Krebs	Y	N	N	N	N	Y
18 Ketchum	Y	N	N	Y	Y	N
19 Lagomarsino	Y	Y	N	Y	Y	N
20 Goldwater	Y	N	N	Y	Y	N
21 Corman	Y	N	N	N	N	Y
22 Moorhead	Y	Y	N	Y	Y	N
23 Beilenson	Y	N	N	N	N	Y
24 Waxman	Y	N	N	N	N	Y
25 Roybal	Y	?	N	N	N	Y
26 Rousselot	Y	Y	N	Y	Y	N
27 Dornan	Y	Y	N	Y	Y	N
28 Burke	#	X	▮	▮	▮	#
29 Hawkins	Y	N	?	X	?	✓
30 Danielson	Y	N	N	N	N	Y
31 Wilson, C.H.	Y	N	N	N	N	Y
32 Anderson	Y	N	Y	N	Y	Y
33 Clawson	?	✓	#	✓	✓	X
34 Hannaford	Y	#	N	N	N	Y
35 Lloyd	Y	N	N	Y	N	N
36 Brown	Y	N	N	N	N	Y
37 Pettis	Y	N	N	Y	Y	N
38 Patterson	?	N	N	N	N	Y
39 Wiggins	Y	N	N	Y	Y	N
40 Badham	Y	Y	N	Y	Y	N
41 Wilson, B.	Y	Y	N	Y	Y	N
42 Van Deerlin	Y	N	N	N	N	Y
43 Burgener	Y	Y	N	Y	Y	N
COLORADO						
1 Schroeder	Y	Y	Y	N	N	Y
2 Wirth	Y	Y	Y	N	N	Y
3 Evans	Y	N	N	N	N	Y
4 Johnson	Y	Y	N	Y	Y	N
5 Armstrong	?	Y	N	Y	Y	N
CONNECTICUT						
1 Cotter	Y	N	N	N	N	Y
2 Dodd	Y	N	N	N	N	Y
3 Giaimo	Y	N	N	N	N	Y
4 McKinney	Y	N	N	Y	N	N
5 Sarasin	Y	Y	N	Y	N	N
6 Moffett	Y	Y	Y	Y	N	Y
DELAWARE						
AL Evans	Y	Y	N	N	Y	N
FLORIDA						
1 Sikes	Y	N	N	N	Y	Y
2 Fuqua	Y	Y	N	N	Y	Y
3 Bennett	Y	Y	N	Y	Y	N
4 Chappell	Y	N	N	Y	Y	N
5 Kelly	Y	Y	N	Y	Y	N
6 Young	Y	Y	N	Y	Y	N
7 Gibbons	Y	Y	N	N	Y	N
8 Ireland	Y	Y	N	Y	Y	N
9 Frey	?	✓	?	✓	?	X
10 Bafalis	Y	Y	N	Y	Y	N
11 Rogers	Y	Y	N	Y	N	Y
12 Burke	Y	N	N	Y	N	N
13 Lehman	Y	N	N	N	N	Y
14 Pepper	Y	N	N	N	N	Y
15 Fascell	Y	N	N	N	N	Y
GEORGIA						
1 Ginn	Y	N	N	Y	Y	Y
2 Mathis	Y	N	N	Y	Y	N
3 Brinkley	Y	N	N	Y	Y	N
4 Levitas	Y	N	N	Y	N	N
5 Fowler	Y	N	N	Y	N	Y
6 Flynt	Y	N	N	N	Y	N
7 McDonald	Y	N	N	Y	Y	N
8 Evans	Y	N	N	Y	Y	N
9 Jenkins	Y	N	N	Y	Y	Y
10 Barnard	Y	N	N	Y	Y	Y
HAWAII						
1 Heftel	Y	N	N	N	N	Y
2 Akaka	Y	N	N	N	N	Y
IDAHO						
1 Symms	Y	N	N	Y	Y	N
2 Hansen, G.	Y	N	N	Y	Y	N
ILLINOIS						
1 Metcalfe	Y	N	N	N	N	Y
2 Murphy	Y	N	N	N	N	Y
3 Russo	Y	Y	N	N	Y	N
4 Derwinski	Y	N	N	Y	Y	N
5 Fary	Y	N	N	N	N	Y
6 Hyde	Y	N	N	Y	Y	N
7 Collins	Y	N	N	N	N	Y
8 Rostenkowski	Y	N	N	N	N	Y
9 Yates	Y	N	N	N	N	Y
10 Mikva	Y	Y	Y	N	N	Y
11 Annunzio	Y	N	N	N	N	Y
12 Crane	Y	N	N	Y	Y	N
13 McClory	Y	N	N	Y	Y	N
14 Erlenborn	Y	N	N	Y	Y	N
15 Corcoran	Y	Y	N	Y	Y	N
16 Anderson	Y	N	N	Y	Y	N
17 O'Brien	Y	Y	N	Y	Y	N
18 Michel	Y	Y	N	Y	Y	N
19 Railsback	Y	Y	N	N	Y	N
20 Findley	Y	N	Y	N	Y	N
21 Madigan	Y	N	N	Y	Y	N
22 Shipley	Y	N	N	N	N	Y
23 Price	Y	N	N	N	N	Y
24 Simon	Y	N	N	N	N	Y
INDIANA						
1 Benjamin	Y	N	N	N	N	Y
2 Fithian	Y	Y	Y	Y	Y	N
3 Brademas	Y	Y	N	N	N	Y
4 Quayle	N	Y	N	Y	Y	N
5 Hillis	Y	N	N	Y	Y	N
6 Evans	Y	Y	Y	Y	Y	N
7 Myers, J.	?	N	N	Y	Y	N
8 Cornwell	?	N	N	N	N	Y
9 Hamilton	Y	Y	N	N	N	Y
10 Sharp	Y	Y	N	N	N	Y
11 Jacobs	Y	Y	Y	N	Y	N
IOWA						
1 Leach	Y	Y	N	Y	Y	N
2 Blouin	Y	Y	N	N	N	Y
3 Grassley	Y	Y	N	Y	Y	N
4 Smith	Y	Y	Y	N	N	Y
5 Harkin	Y	Y	Y	Y	N	Y
6 Bedell	Y	Y	Y	N	N	Y

Democrats ***Republicans***

	250	251	252	253	254	255
KANSAS						
1 *Sebelius*	Y	Y	N	Y	Y	N
2 Keys	Y	Y	Y	N	N	N
3 *Winn*	Y	N	N	Y	Y	N
4 Glickman	Y	N	Y	N	N	N
5 *Skubitz*	?	✓	?	?	?	X
KENTUCKY						
1 Hubbard	Y	N	N	Y	Y	Y
2 Natcher	Y	Y	N	N	N	Y
3 Mazzoli	#	†	-	-	†	†
4 *Snyder*	Y	N	Y	Y	Y	N
5 *Carter*	Y	N	N	N	N	N
6 Breckinridge	Y	N	N	N	X	✓
7 Perkins	Y	Y	N	N	N	Y
LOUISIANA						
1 *Livingston*	?	✓	?	✓	✓	X
2 Boggs	Y	N	N	N	N	Y
3 *Treen*	Y	N	N	Y	Y	N
4 Waggonner	Y	N	N	N	Y	N
5 Huckaby	Y	N	N	Y	Y	N
6 *Moore*	Y	N	N	Y	Y	N
7 Breaux	Y	N	N	Y	Y	N
8 Long	Y	N	N	N	N	Y
MAINE						
1 *Emery*	Y	Y	N	Y	Y	N
2 *Cohen*	Y	Y	N	N	Y	N
MARYLAND						
1 *Bauman*	Y	N	N	Y	Y	N
2 Long	Y	N	N	N	Y	Y
3 Mikulski	Y	N	N	N	N	Y
4 *Holt*	Y	N	N	Y	Y	N
5 Spellman	Y	N	Y	N	N	Y
6 Byron	Y	N	N	Y	N	N
7 Mitchell	N	Y	N	N	N	Y
8 *Steers*	Y	Y	N	N	N	Y
MASSACHUSETTS						
1 *Conte*	Y	N	N	N	N	Y
2 Boland	Y	N	N	N	N	Y
3 Early	Y	Y	N	N	N	Y
4 Drinan	Y	N	N	N	N	Y
5 Tsongas	Y	Y	N	N	N	Y
6 Harrington	Y	N	N	N	N	Y
7 Markey	Y	N	N	N	N	Y
8 O'Neill						
9 Moakley	Y	N	N	N	N	Y
10 *Heckler*	Y	Y	N	Y	N	N
11 Burke	Y	N	N	N	N	Y
12 Studds	Y	N	N	N	N	Y
MICHIGAN						
1 Conyers	#	✓	▮	▮	▮	X
2 *Pursell*	Y	N	N	N	N	N
3 *Brown*	Y	N	N	Y	Y	N
4 *Stockman*	Y	N	N	Y	Y	N
5 *Sawyer*	Y	N	N	N	Y	N
6 Carr	Y	Y	Y	Y	Y	N
7 Kildee	Y	N	Y	N	N	Y
8 Traxler	Y	N	Y	N	N	Y
9 *Vander Jagt*	Y	N	N	Y	Y	N
10 *Cederberg*	Y	N	N	Y	Y	N
11 *Ruppe*	Y	N	N	Y	Y	N
12 Bonior	?	N	N	N	N	Y
13 Diggs	?	N	?	?	N	Y
14 Nedzi	Y	Y	N	N	N	Y
15 Ford	?	?	?	?	?	✓
16 Dingell	Y	N	N	N	N	Y
17 Brodhead	Y	Y	Y	Y	N	Y
18 Blanchard	Y	N	Y	N	N	Y
19 *Broomfield*	Y	N	N	Y	Y	N
MINNESOTA						
1 *Quie*	Y	Y	N	N	Y	N
2 *Hagedorn*	Y	Y	N	Y	Y	N
3 *Frenzel*	Y	N	N	N	Y	N
4 Vento	Y	N	N	N	N	Y
5 Fraser	#	#	▮	▮	▮	#
6 Nolan	?	N	N	N	N	Y
7 *Stangeland*	Y	Y	N	Y	Y	N
8 Oberstar	Y	N	N	N	N	Y
MISSISSIPPI						
1 Whitten	Y	N	N	N	Y	Y
2 Bowen	Y	N	N	Y	Y	N
3 Montgomery	Y	N	N	Y	Y	N
4 *Cochran*	?	?	?	✓	?	?
5 *Lott*	Y	N	N	Y	Y	N
MISSOURI						
1 Clay	?	N	N	N	N	Y
2 Young	Y	N	N	N	N	Y
3 Gephardt	Y	Y	N	N	N	Y
4 Skelton	Y	N	N	N	Y	N
5 Bolling	#	N	N	N	N	Y
6 *Coleman*	Y	Y	N	Y	Y	N
7 *Taylor*	Y	N	N	Y	Y	N
8 Ichord	Y	Y	Y	Y	Y	N
9 Volkmer	Y	Y	N	N	N	Y
10 Burlison	Y	Y	N	N	N	Y
MONTANA						
1 Baucus	Y	N	N	N	N	N
2 *Marlenee*	Y	Y	N	Y	Y	N
NEBRASKA						
1 *Thone*	#	?	?	?	#	X
2 Cavanaugh	Y	N	N	N	N	N
3 *Smith*	Y	N	N	Y	Y	N
NEVADA						
AL Santini	Y	N	N	N	#	N
NEW HAMPSHIRE						
1 D'Amours	Y	Y	N	N	N	Y
2 *Cleveland*	Y	Y	N	Y	Y	N
NEW JERSEY						
1 Florio	Y	N	N	N	N	Y
2 Hughes	Y	N	N	N	Y	Y
3 Howard	Y	N	N	N	N	Y
4 Thompson	Y	#	N	N	N	Y
5 *Fenwick*	Y	Y	N	N	Y	N
6 *Forsythe*	Y	Y	Y	Y	Y	N
7 Maguire	Y	Y	N	N	N	Y
8 Roe	Y	N	N	N	N	Y
9 *Hollenbeck*	Y	Y	N	N	Y	N
10 Rodino	#	▮	▮	▮	▮	✓
11 Minish	Y	Y	N	N	N	Y
12 *Rinaldo*	Y	Y	N	N	Y	N
13 Meyner	Y	N	N	N	▮	Y
14 LeFante	Y	N	▮	X	X	✓
15 Patten	Y	N	N	N	N	Y
NEW MEXICO						
1 *Lujan*	?	✓	?	✓	✓	X
2 Runnels	#	✓	?	✓	✓	X
NEW YORK						
1 Pike	Y	N	N	N	Y	N
2 Downey	Y	Y	Y	Y	N	Y
3 Ambro	Y	Y	N	N	Y	Y
4 *Lent*	Y	Y	N	Y	Y	N
5 *Wydler*	Y	Y	N	Y	N	N
6 Wolff	Y	N	N	N	N	Y
7 Addabbo	Y	N	N	N	N	Y
8 Rosenthal	Y	▮	▮	▮	▮	#
9 Delaney	Y	N	N	N	N	Y
10 Biaggi	Y	N	N	N	N	Y
11 Scheuer	Y	Y	Y	N	N	?
12 Chisholm	Y	N	N	N	N	Y
13 Solarz	Y	N	N	N	N	Y
14 Richmond	Y	Y	N	N	N	Y
15 Zeferetti	Y	N	N	N	N	Y
16 Holtzman	Y	Y	N	N	N	Y
17 Murphy	Y	N	N	N	N	Y
18 *Green*	Y	N	N	N	N	N
19 Rangel	Y	N	?	N	N	Y
20 Weiss	Y	N	Y	N	N	Y
21 Garcia	Y	N	N	N	N	Y
22 Bingham	Y	N	N	N	N	Y
23 *Caputo*	Y	Y	N	Y	Y	N
24 Ottinger	Y	Y	Y	N	N	N
25 *Fish*	Y	Y	N	Y	Y	N
26 *Gilman*	Y	Y	N	N	Y	N
27 McHugh	Y	N	N	N	N	Y
28 Stratton	Y	N	N	N	N	Y
29 Pattison	Y	Y	N	N	N	Y
30 *McEwen*	Y	N	N	Y	Y	N
31 *Mitchell*	Y	N	N	Y	Y	N
32 Hanley	Y	N	N	N	N	Y
33 *Walsh*	Y	Y	N	Y	Y	N
34 *Horton*	Y	N	N	N	Y	N
35 *Conable*	Y	N	N	N	Y	N
36 LaFalce	Y	N	N	N	Y	N
37 Nowak	Y	N	N	N	N	Y
38 *Kemp*	Y	N	N	Y	Y	N
39 Lundine	Y	N	N	N	N	N
NORTH CAROLINA						
1 Jones	Y	N	N	N	Y	Y
2 Fountain	Y	Y	N	Y	Y	N
3 Whitley	?	X	?	?	✓	?
4 Andrews	Y	N	N	N	N	N
5 Neal	Y	Y	N	Y	Y	N
6 Preyer	Y	Y	N	N	N	Y
7 Rose	Y	N	N	Y	N	Y
8 Hefner	Y	Y	N	Y	Y	N
9 *Martin*	Y	✓	▮	✓	✓	X
10 *Broyhill*	Y	N	N	Y	Y	N
11 Gudger	Y	Y	N	Y	Y	Y
NORTH DAKOTA						
AL Andrews	Y	N	N	Y	Y	N
OHIO						
1 *Gradison*	Y	N	N	N	Y	N
2 Luken	Y	N	N	N	N	Y
3 *Whalen*	Y	N	N	N	N	Y
4 *Guyer*	Y	N	N	Y	Y	N
5 *Latta*	Y	Y	N	Y	Y	N
6 *Harsha*	Y	N	N	Y	Y	N
7 *Brown*	Y	N	N	Y	Y	N
8 *Kindness*	Y	Y	N	Y	Y	N
9 Ashley	Y	X	?	X	X	✓
10 *Miller*	Y	Y	Y	Y	Y	N
11 *Stanton*	Y	N	N	Y	Y	N
12 *Devine*	Y	N	N	Y	Y	N
13 Pease	Y	N	N	N	N	Y
14 Seiberling	Y	N	N	N	N	Y
15 *Wylie*	Y	Y	N	Y	Y	N
16 *Regula*	Y	N	N	Y	Y	N
17 *Ashbrook*	Y	N	N	Y	Y	N
18 Applegate	Y	N	N	N	N	Y
19 Carney	Y	X	?	X	X	✓
20 Oakar	Y	?	?	?	?	X
21 Stokes	Y	N	▮	N	N	Y
22 Vanik	Y	N	Y	N	N	Y
23 Mottl	Y	Y	Y	Y	Y	N
OKLAHOMA						
1 Jones	Y	N	Y	Y	Y	N
2 Risenhoover	?	X	?	?	?	✓
3 Watkins	Y	Y	N	Y	Y	Y
4 Steed	Y	N	N	N	N	Y
5 *Edwards*	Y	Y	N	Y	Y	N
6 English	Y	N	▮	#	#	?
OREGON						
1 AuCoin	N	N	Y	N	N	N
2 Ullman	Y	N	N	N	N	Y
3 Duncan	Y	N	Y	N	N	Y
4 Weaver	Y	Y	N	N	N	Y
PENNSYLVANIA						
1 Myers, M.	?	?	?	?	?	?
2 Nix	?	X	?	?	?	?
3 Lederer	Y	N	N	N	N	Y
4 Eilberg	#	▮	▮	X	X	✓
5 *Schulze*	Y	Y	N	Y	Y	N
6 Yatron	Y	Y	N	N	N	Y
7 Edgar	Y	Y	N	N	N	Y
8 Kostmayer	Y	Y	Y	N	N	N
9 *Shuster*	Y	Y	N	Y	Y	N
10 *McDade*	Y	Y	N	N	Y	N
11 Flood	Y	Y	N	N	N	Y
12 Murtha	Y	N	N	N	N	Y
13 *Coughlin*	Y	N	N	Y	Y	N
14 Moorhead	Y	N	N	N	N	Y
15 Rooney	Y	N	N	N	N	Y
16 *Walker*	Y	Y	N	Y	Y	N
17 Ertel	Y	Y	Y	N	N	N
18 Walgren	Y	N	Y	N	N	Y
19 *Goodling, W.*	?	N	N	Y	Y	N
20 Gaydos	Y	Y	N	N	N	Y
21 Dent	#	X	▮	▮	▮	#
22 Murphy	Y	?	▮	▮	?	?
23 Ammerman	Y	?	?	?	N	Y
24 *Marks*	Y	N	N	Y	Y	N
25 *Myers, G.*	Y	N	N	N	Y	N
RHODE ISLAND						
1 St Germain	Y	N	N	N	N	Y
2 Beard	Y	Y	N	N	N	Y
SOUTH CAROLINA						
1 Davis	N	Y	N	Y	Y	N
2 *Spence*	Y	Y	N	Y	Y	N
3 Derrick	Y	N	N	N	N	Y
4 Mann	?	N	N	N	Y	N
5 Holland	Y	Y	N	Y	Y	N
6 Jenrette	Y	N	N	Y	N	Y
SOUTH DAKOTA						
1 *Pressler*	Y	Y	N	Y	Y	N
2 *Abdnor*	Y	Y	N	Y	Y	N
TENNESSEE						
1 *Quillen*	Y	Y	N	Y	Y	N
2 *Duncan*	Y	Y	N	Y	Y	N
3 Lloyd	Y	N	N	Y	N	N
4 Gore	Y	Y	Y	N	N	Y
5 Allen	?	Y	N	?	N	Y
6 *Beard*	?	N	N	Y	Y	N
7 Jones	Y	N	N	Y	N	Y
8 Ford	Y	N	N	N	N	Y
TEXAS						
1 Hall	Y	Y	N	Y	Y	N
2 Wilson, C.	Y	N	N	N	N	Y
3 *Collins*	Y	Y	N	Y	Y	N
4 Roberts	Y	N	N	Y	Y	Y
5 Mattox	Y	N	N	Y	N	Y
6 Teague	?	N	?	?	?	?
7 *Archer*	Y	Y	N	Y	Y	N
8 Eckhardt	Y	N	N	N	N	Y
9 Brooks	Y	N	N	N	N	Y
10 Pickle	Y	Y	N	N	N	N
11 Poage	Y	N	N	N	Y	Y
12 Wright	Y	N	N	N	N	Y
13 Hightower	Y	N	N	Y	Y	Y
14 Young	Y	N	N	N	Y	Y
15 de la Garza	Y	N	N	Y	Y	Y
16 White	Y	N	N	Y	Y	N
17 Burleson	Y	N	Y	N	Y	Y
18 Jordan	Y	N	N	N	N	Y
19 Mahon	Y	N	N	N	N	Y
20 Gonzalez	Y	N	N	N	N	Y
21 Krueger	Y	N	N	Y	Y	N
22 Gammage	Y	Y	N	Y	Y	N
23 Kazen	Y	N	N	N	N	Y
24 Milford	Y	N	N	N	Y	Y
UTAH						
1 McKay	Y	N	N	N	N	Y
2 *Marriott*	Y	N	N	Y	Y	N
VERMONT						
AL Jeffords	Y	Y	N	N	Y	N
VIRGINIA						
1 *Trible*	Y	Y	N	Y	Y	N
2 *Whitehurst*	Y	N	N	Y	Y	N
3 Satterfield	?	N	N	Y	Y	N
4 *Daniel*	Y	N	N	Y	Y	N
5 Daniel	Y	N	N	Y	Y	N
6 *Butler*	Y	N	N	Y	Y	N
7 *Robinson*	Y	N	N	Y	Y	N
8 Harris	Y	N	Y	N	N	N
9 *Wampler*	Y	Y	N	Y	Y	N
10 Fisher	Y	N	N	N	N	N
WASHINGTON						
1 *Pritchard*	Y	Y	N	Y	Y	N
2 Meeds	Y	N	N	N	N	Y
3 Bonker	Y	N	N	N	N	Y
4 McCormack	Y	N	N	N	N	Y
5 Foley	Y	N	N	N	N	Y
6 Dicks	Y	N	N	N	N	Y
7 *Cunningham*	Y	Y	N	Y	Y	N
WEST VIRGINIA						
1 Mollohan	Y	▮	N	N	Y	Y
2 Staggers	Y	N	N	X	N	Y
3 Slack	Y	N	N	N	Y	Y
4 Rahall	Y	X	▮	X	X	✓
WISCONSIN						
1 Aspin	Y	Y	N	N	N	Y
2 Kastenmeier	Y	Y	N	N	N	Y
3 Baldus	Y	N	N	N	N	Y
4 Zablocki	Y	N	N	N	N	Y
5 Reuss	Y	N	N	N	N	Y
6 *Steiger*	Y	N	N	N	Y	N
7 Obey	Y	Y	N	N	N	Y
8 Cornell	Y	N	N	N	N	Y
9 *Kasten*	Y	Y	N	Y	Y	N
WYOMING						
AL Roncalio	Y	N	Y	N	N	Y

Democrats *Republicans*

256. Procedural Motion. Symms, R-Idaho, motion to approve the House *Journal* of Wednesday, May 10, 1978. Motion agreed to 377-15: R 125-11; D 252-4 (ND 174-4; SD 78-0), May 11, 1978.

257. H Con Res 617. Aldo Moro Assassination. Adoption of the concurrent resolution to denounce the murder of Italian Christian Democratic Party leader Aldo Moro by terrorists and to state the sense of Congress that the United States supports the Italian government in apprehending the terrorists and that the U.S. president should redouble efforts in gaining international cooperation in controlling such acts. Adopted 398-0: R 136-0; D 262-0 (ND 183-0; SD 79-0), May 11, 1978.

258. HR 12222. Foreign Economic Aid. Lott, R-Miss., amendment to make the following cuts in authorization levels: population planning, from $225.4 million to $205.4 million; American schools and hospitals abroad, from $25 million to $8 million; international organizations and programs, from $283.5 million to $282.2 million. Rejected 183-212: R 99-35; D 84-177 (ND 28-152; SD 56-25), May 11, 1978.

259. HR 12222. Foreign Economic Aid. Hagedorn, R-Minn., amendment to prohibit assistance to nations that do not make "reasonable progress" toward eliminating domestic impediments to agricultural production. Rejected 141-236: R 103-27; D 38-209 (ND 13-159; SD 25-50), May 11, 1978.

260. HR 12222. Foreign Economic Aid. Lagomarsino, R-Calif., amendment to limit U.S. economic aid to Panama to 25 percent of the amount of Panama Canal revenues provided under the 1977 canal transfer treaty that Panama used for Panamanian development programs. Rejected 187-187: R 95-31; D 92-156 (ND 39-131; SD 53-25), May 11, 1978.

KEY

Y Voted for (yea).
✓ Paired for.
† Announced for.
# CQ Poll for.
N Voted against (nay).
X Paired against.
- Announced against.
▮ CQ Poll against.
P Voted "present."
● Voted "present" to avoid possible conflict of interest.
? Did not vote or otherwise make a position known.

	256	257	258	259	260
ALABAMA					
1 Edwards	Y	Y	Y	Y	Y
2 Dickinson	Y	Y	Y	Y	Y
3 Nichols	Y	Y	Y	Y	Y
4 Bevill	Y	Y	Y	Y	Y
5 Flippo	Y	Y	Y	Y	Y
6 Buchanan	Y	Y	N	N	N
7 Flowers	Y	Y	Y	N	Y
ALASKA					
AL Young	#	#	✓	Y	Y
ARIZONA					
1 Rhodes	?	?	?	?	?
2 Udall	Y	Y	N	N	N
3 Stump	#	Y	Y	Y	Y
4 Rudd	Y	Y	Y	Y	Y
ARKANSAS					
1 Alexander	?	?	X	?	X
2 Tucker	#	#	#	#	#
3 Hammerschmidt	Y	Y	Y	Y	Y
4 Thornton	?	?	?	?	?
CALIFORNIA					
1 Johnson	Y	Y	N	N	Y
2 Clausen	Y	Y	Y	Y	Y
3 Moss	Y	Y	N	N	N
4 Leggett	Y	Y	N	?	?
5 Burton, J.	Y	Y	N	N	N
6 Burton, P.	Y	Y	N	N	N
7 Miller	Y	Y	N	N	N
8 Dellums	Y	Y	N	N	N
9 Stark	Y	Y	N	N	N
10 Edwards	Y	Y	N	N	N
11 Ryan	Y	Y	N	Y	N
12 McCloskey	Y	Y	N	N	N
13 Mineta	Y	Y	N	N	N
14 McFall	Y	Y	N	N	N
15 Sisk	Y	Y	N	N	Y
16 Panetta	Y	Y	N	N	Y
17 Krebs	Y	Y	N	N	N
18 Ketchum	Y	Y	Y	Y	?
19 Lagomarsino	Y	Y	Y	Y	Y
20 Goldwater	Y	Y	Y	Y	Y
21 Corman	Y	Y	N	N	N
22 Moorhead	Y	Y	Y	Y	Y
23 Beilenson	Y	Y	N	N	N
24 Waxman	Y	Y	N	▮	X
25 Roybal	Y	Y	N	N	N
26 Rousselot	Y	Y	Y	Y	Y
27 Dornan	Y	Y	Y	Y	Y
28 Burke	#	#	X	▮	X
29 Hawkins	?	?	X	-	X
30 Danielson	Y	Y	N	N	-
31 Wilson, C.H.	Y	Y	▮	▮	#
32 Anderson	Y	Y	N	N	Y
33 Clawson	Y	Y	Y	Y	Y
34 Hannaford	Y	Y	N	▮	X
35 Lloyd	N	Y	N	N	N
36 Brown	Y	Y	N	?	?
37 Pettis	Y	Y	Y	Y	N
38 Patterson	Y	Y	N	N	?
39 Wiggins	#	#	✓	✓	#
40 Badham	Y	Y	Y	Y	Y
41 Wilson, B.	N	Y	N	Y	Y
42 Van Deerlin	Y	Y	N	Y	N
43 Burgener	Y	Y	Y	Y	Y
COLORADO					
1 Schroeder	Y	Y	N	Y	N
2 Wirth	Y	Y	N	N	N
3 Evans	Y	Y	N	N	N
4 Johnson	Y	Y	Y	Y	N
5 Armstrong	Y	Y	Y	Y	?
CONNECTICUT					
1 Cotter	Y	Y	N	N	N
2 Dodd	Y	Y	N	N	N
3 Giaimo	Y	Y	N	N	N
4 McKinney	Y	Y	N	N	N
5 Sarasin	N	Y	N	Y	Y
6 Moffett	?	?	N	N	N
DELAWARE					
AL Evans	Y	Y	Y	#	#
FLORIDA					
1 Sikes	Y	Y	Y	N	Y
2 Fuqua	Y	Y	Y	N	Y
3 Bennett	Y	Y	Y	Y	Y
4 Chappell	Y	Y	N	Y	Y
5 Kelly	Y	Y	Y	Y	Y
6 Young	Y	Y	Y	Y	Y
7 Gibbons	Y	Y	N	N	N
8 Ireland	Y	Y	Y	Y	Y
9 Frey	?	?	✓	✓	✓
10 Bafalis	Y	Y	Y	Y	Y
11 Rogers	Y	?	N	N	Y
12 Burke	Y	Y	N	Y	Y
13 Lehman	Y	Y	N	N	N
14 Pepper	Y	Y	N	N	N
15 Fascell	Y	Y	N	▮	N
GEORGIA					
1 Ginn	Y	Y	Y	Y	Y
2 Mathis	?	Y	Y	?	Y
3 Brinkley	Y	Y	Y	Y	Y
4 Levitas	Y	Y	Y	Y	Y
5 Fowler	Y	Y	Y	N	Y
6 Flynt	Y	Y	Y	?	?
7 McDonald	Y	Y	Y	Y	Y
8 Evans	Y	Y	Y	#	Y
9 Jenkins	#	Y	Y	N	Y
10 Barnard	Y	Y	Y	N	Y
HAWAII					
1 Heftel	Y	Y	Y	N	Y
2 Akaka	Y	Y	N	N	N
IDAHO					
1 Symms	Y	Y	Y	Y	Y
2 Hansen, G.	Y	?	Y	Y	Y
ILLINOIS					
1 Metcalfe	Y	Y	N	N	N
2 Murphy	Y	Y	N	N	N
3 Russo	Y	Y	Y	N	N
4 Derwinski	Y	Y	Y	Y	N
5 Fary	Y	Y	N	N	N
6 Hyde	Y	Y	Y	Y	N
7 Collins	Y	Y	N	N	N
8 Rostenkowski	Y	Y	N	N	N
9 Yates	Y	Y	N	N	N
10 Mikva	Y	Y	N	N	N
11 Annunzio	Y	Y	N	N	N
12 Crane	Y	Y	Y	Y	Y
13 McClory	Y	Y	N	Y	N
14 Erlenborn	Y	Y	N	Y	N
15 Corcoran	Y	Y	Y	Y	Y
16 Anderson	Y	Y	Y	Y	N
17 O'Brien	Y	Y	✓	Y	N
18 Michel	Y	Y	Y	Y	N
19 Railsback	Y	Y	Y	N	N
20 Findley	Y	Y	Y	N	N
21 Madigan	Y	Y	Y	Y	N
22 Shipley	Y	Y	Y	N	Y
23 Price	Y	Y	N	N	N
24 Simon	Y	Y	N	N	N
INDIANA					
1 Benjamin	Y	Y	N	Y	Y
2 Fithian	Y	Y	Y	Y	Y
3 Brademas	Y	Y	N	N	N
4 Quayle	N	Y	Y	N	N
5 Hillis	Y	Y	Y	?	?
6 Evans	Y	Y	Y	N	Y
7 Myers, J.	Y	Y	Y	?	?
8 Cornwell	Y	Y	N	N	N
9 Hamilton	Y	Y	N	N	N
10 Sharp	Y	Y	N	N	N
11 Jacobs	N	Y	Y	N	N
IOWA					
1 Leach	Y	Y	Y	Y	Y
2 Blouin	Y	Y	N	N	N
3 Grassley	Y	Y	Y	Y	Y
4 Smith	Y	Y	N	N	N
5 Harkin	Y	Y	N	N	N
6 Bedell	Y	Y	N	N	N

Democrats ***Republicans***

	256	257	258	259	260
KANSAS					
1 ***Sebelius***	Y	Y	Y	N	Y
2 Keys	Y	Y	N	N	N
3 ***Winn***	Y	Y	Y	N	Y
4 Glickman	Y	Y	Y	N	N
5 ***Skubitz***	?	?	✓	X	✓
KENTUCKY					
1 Hubbard	Y	Y	Y	Y	Y
2 Natcher	Y	Y	N	N	Y
3 Mazzoli	Y	Y	Y	N	N
4 ***Snyder***	Y	Y	Y	Y	Y
5 ***Carter***	Y	Y	Y	Y	Y
6 Breckinridge	?	?	?	?	X
7 Perkins	Y	Y	Y	N	Y
LOUISIANA					
1 ***Livingston***	Y	Y	Y	Y	Y
2 Boggs	Y	Y	N	N	N
3 ***Treen***	Y	Y	Y	Y	N
4 Waggonner	Y	Y	Y	Y	Y
5 Huckaby	Y	Y	Y	N	Y
6 ***Moore***	Y	Y	Y	Y	Y
7 Breaux	Y	Y	Y	Y	Y
8 Long	Y	Y	Y	N	N
MAINE					
1 ***Emery***	Y	Y	Y	Y	Y
2 ***Cohen***	Y	Y	Y	Y	Y
MARYLAND					
1 ***Bauman***	Y	Y	Y	N	Y
2 Long	Y	Y	?	Y	Y
3 Mikulski	Y	Y	N	N	N
4 ***Holt***	Y	Y	Y	X	✓
5 Spellman	Y	Y	▮	N	N
6 Byron	Y	Y	Y	Y	Y
7 Mitchell	N	Y	N	N	N
8 ***Steers***	Y	Y	N	N	N
MASSACHUSETTS					
1 ***Conte***	Y	Y	N	N	N
2 Boland	Y	Y	N	N	N
3 Early	Y	Y	N	N	N
4 Drinan	Y	Y	N	N	N
5 Tsongas	#	Y	N	N	N
6 Harrington	Y	Y	N	N	N
7 Markey	Y	Y	N	N	N
8 O'Neill					
9 Moakley	Y	Y	N	N	N
10 ***Heckler***	Y	Y	N	Y	Y
11 Burke	Y	Y	N	N	N
12 Studds	Y	Y	N	N	N
MICHIGAN					
1 Conyers	#	#	X	▮	X
2 ***Pursell***	Y	Y	Y	?	?
3 ***Brown***	N	Y	Y	N	Y
4 ***Stockman***	Y	Y	Y	N	Y
5 ***Sawyer***	Y	Y	N	Y	Y
6 Carr	#	Y	N	N	N
7 Kildee	Y	Y	N	N	N
8 Traxler	N	Y	N	N	N
9 ***Vander Jagt***	Y	Y	N	Y	Y
10 ***Cederberg***	Y	Y	Y	Y	Y
11 ***Ruppe***	Y	Y	Y	Y	N
12 Bonior	Y	Y	N	N	N
13 Diggs	Y	Y	N	N	N
14 Nedzi	Y	Y	N	N	N
15 Ford	?	?	X	?	?
16 Dingell	Y	Y	Y	N	Y
17 Brodhead	Y	Y	N	N	N
18 Blanchard	Y	Y	N	N	N
19 ***Broomfield***	Y	Y	Y	Y	N
MINNESOTA					
1 ***Quie***	#	Y	N	Y	Y
2 ***Hagedorn***	Y	Y	Y	Y	Y
3 ***Frenzel***	Y	Y	N	Y	Y
4 Vento	Y	Y	N	N	N
5 Fraser	Y	Y	N	N	N
6 Nolan	Y	Y	N	N	N
7 ***Stangeland***	Y	Y	Y	Y	Y
8 Oberstar	Y	Y	N	N	N
MISSISSIPPI					
1 Whitten	Y	Y	Y	Y	N
2 Bowen	Y	Y	Y	Y	Y
3 Montgomery	Y	Y	Y	Y	Y
4 ***Cochran***	?	?	?	✓	?
5 ***Lott***	Y	Y	Y	Y	Y
MISSOURI					
1 Clay	Y	Y	N	N	N
2 Young	Y	Y	Y	N	Y
3 Gephardt	Y	Y	N	N	Y

	256	257	258	259	260
4 Skelton	Y	Y	Y	N	Y
5 Bolling	Y	Y	N	N	N
6 ***Coleman***	Y	Y	Y	N	Y
7 ***Taylor***	Y	Y	Y	Y	Y
8 Ichord	Y	Y	Y	Y	Y
9 Volkmer	Y	Y	Y	N	Y
10 Burlison	Y	Y	N	N	N
MONTANA					
1 Baucus	Y	Y	N	N	N
2 ***Marlenee***	Y	Y	Y	N	Y
NEBRASKA					
1 ***Thone***	#	#	#	X	✓
2 Cavanaugh	Y	Y	N	?	?
3 ***Smith***	Y	Y	Y	N	Y
NEVADA					
AL Santini	Y	Y	Y	?	?
NEW HAMPSHIRE					
1 D'Amours	Y	Y	N	?	#
2 ***Cleveland***	Y	Y	Y	Y	Y
NEW JERSEY					
1 Florio	Y	Y	Y	N	N
2 Hughes	Y	Y	Y	N	N
3 Howard	Y	Y	N	N	N
4 Thompson	Y	Y	N	▮	X
5 ***Fenwick***	Y	Y	N	N	N
6 ***Forsythe***	N	Y	Y	Y	Y
7 Maguire	Y	Y	N	N	N
8 Roe	Y	Y	N	N	Y
9 ***Hollenbeck***	Y	Y	N	N	Y
10 Rodino	#	Y	X	▮	▮
11 Minish	Y	Y	N	N	Y
12 ***Rinaldo***	Y	Y	N	Y	Y
13 Meyner	Y	Y	N	N	N
14 LeFante	Y	Y	N	N	Y
15 Patten	Y	Y	N	N	N
NEW MEXICO					
1 ***Lujan***	?	?	✓	?	✓
2 Runnels	#	#	✓	?	✓
NEW YORK					
1 Pike	Y	Y	Y	N	N
2 Downey	Y	Y	N	N	N
3 Ambro	Y	Y	Y	N	Y
4 ***Lent***	Y	Y	N	Y	Y
5 ***Wydler***	Y	Y	N	Y	Y
6 Wolff	Y	Y	N	N	N
7 Addabbo	Y	Y	N	N	N
8 Rosenthal	Y	Y	N	N	N
9 Delaney	Y	Y	N	N	N
10 Biaggi	Y	Y	N	N	Y
11 Scheuer	Y	Y	N	N	N
12 Chisholm	Y	Y	N	N	N
13 Solarz	Y	Y	N	N	N
14 Richmond	Y	Y	N	N	N
15 Zeferetti	Y	Y	N	N	Y
16 Holtzman	Y	Y	N	N	N
17 Murphy	Y	Y	N	N	N
18 ***Green***	Y	Y	N	Y	▮
19 Rangel	Y	Y	N	N	N
20 Weiss	Y	Y	N	N	N
21 Garcia	Y	Y	N	N	N
22 Bingham	Y	Y	N	N	N
23 ***Caputo***	Y	Y	N	Y	Y
24 Ottinger	Y	Y	N	N	N
25 ***Fish***	Y	Y	Y	Y	N
26 ***Gilman***	Y	Y	N	Y	Y
27 McHugh	Y	Y	N	N	X
28 Stratton	Y	Y	N	N	Y
29 Pattison	Y	Y	N	N	N
30 ***McEwen***	Y	Y	N	Y	Y
31 ***Mitchell***	Y	Y	N	Y	Y
32 Hanley	Y	Y	N	N	N
33 ***Walsh***	Y	Y	N	Y	Y
34 ***Horton***	Y	Y	X	▮	✓
35 ***Conable***	Y	Y	N	N	N
36 LaFalce	Y	Y	N	N	N
37 Nowak	Y	Y	N	N	N
38 ***Kemp***	Y	Y	Y	Y	Y
39 Lundine	Y	Y	N	N	N
NORTH CAROLINA					
1 Jones	Y	Y	N	N	N
2 Fountain	Y	Y	Y	N	Y
3 Whitley	?	?	X	?	X
4 Andrews	Y	Y	Y	N	N
5 Neal	Y	Y	N	Y	Y
6 Preyer	Y	Y	N	N	N
7 Rose	Y	Y	N	N	N
8 Hefner	Y	Y	N	N	N

	256	257	258	259	260
9 ***Martin***	Y	Y	Y	Y	Y
10 ***Broyhill***	Y	Y	Y	Y	Y
11 Gudger	Y	Y	Y	N	Y
NORTH DAKOTA					
AL Andrews	Y	Y	Y	N	Y
OHIO					
1 ***Gradison***	#	#	#	#	#
2 Luken	Y	Y	Y	N	Y
3 ***Whalen***	Y	Y	N	N	N
4 ***Guyer***	Y	Y	Y	Y	Y
5 ***Latta***	Y	Y	Y	Y	Y
6 ***Harsha***	Y	Y	Y	Y	Y
7 ***Brown***	Y	Y	N	N	Y
8 ***Kindness***	Y	Y	Y	Y	Y
9 Ashley	Y	Y	N	?	N
10 ***Miller***	Y	Y	Y	Y	Y
11 ***Stanton***	Y	Y	Y	N	N
12 ***Devine***	Y	Y	Y	Y	Y
13 Pease	Y	Y	N	N	N
14 Seiberling	Y	Y	N	N	N
15 ***Wylie***	Y	Y	Y	Y	Y
16 ***Regula***	Y	Y	Y	Y	Y
17 ***Ashbrook***	Y	Y	Y	N	Y
18 Applegate	Y	Y	N	?	?
19 Carney	?	?	X	?	X
20 Oakar	?	?	?	?	?
21 Stokes	Y	Y	N	N	N
22 Vanik	Y	Y	N	N	N
23 Mottl	Y	Y	Y	Y	Y
OKLAHOMA					
1 Jones	Y	Y	Y	N	Y
2 Risenhoover	?	?	✓	?	✓
3 Watkins	Y	Y	Y	Y	Y
4 Steed	Y	#	Y	N	Y
5 ***Edwards***	Y	Y	Y	N	Y
6 English	Y	Y	Y	Y	Y
OREGON					
1 AuCoin	#	Y	N	N	N
2 Ullman	Y	Y	N	N	N
3 Duncan	Y	?	N	N	N
4 Weaver	Y	Y	N	N	N
PENNSYLVANIA					
1 Myers, M.	Y	Y	N	?	?
2 Nix	?	?	X	?	?
3 Lederer	Y	Y	Y	N	Y
4 Eilberg	#	#	▮	▮	#
5 ***Schulze***	Y	Y	Y	Y	Y
6 Yatron	Y	Y	Y	N	Y
7 Edgar	Y	Y	N	N	N
8 Kostmayer	?	?	?	?	?
9 ***Shuster***	Y	Y	Y	Y	Y
10 ***McDade***	Y	Y	N	Y	Y
11 Flood	Y	Y	N	N	Y
12 Murtha	Y	Y	Y	N	Y
13 ***Coughlin***	N	Y	Y	Y	N
14 Moorhead	Y	Y	N	N	N
15 Rooney	Y	Y	N	N	N
16 ***Walker***	N	Y	Y	Y	Y
17 Ertel	Y	Y	N	N	Y
18 Walgren	Y	Y	N	N	N
19 ***Goodling, W.***	N	Y	Y	Y	Y
20 Gaydos	Y	Y	Y	Y	Y
21 Dent	#	#	✓	▮	✓
22 Murphy	#	#	?	▮	?
23 Ammerman	Y	Y	N	N	Y
24 ***Marks***	Y	Y	N	Y	Y
25 ***Myers, G.***	Y	Y	?	Y	N
RHODE ISLAND					
1 St Germain	Y	Y	N	N	Y
2 Beard	Y	Y	N	N	N
SOUTH CAROLINA					
1 Davis	Y	Y	Y	?	?
2 ***Spence***	Y	Y	Y	Y	Y
3 Derrick	Y	Y	N	N	Y
4 Mann	Y	Y	Y	N	N
5 Holland	Y	Y	Y	?	?
6 Jenrette	#	Y	N	N	Y
SOUTH DAKOTA					
1 ***Pressler***	Y	Y	?	?	?
2 ***Abdnor***	Y	Y	Y	Y	Y
TENNESSEE					
1 ***Quillen***	Y	Y	Y	Y	Y
2 ***Duncan***	Y	Y	Y	Y	Y
3 Lloyd	Y	Y	Y	N	Y
4 Gore	Y	Y	N	N	N
5 Allen	?	Y	Y	Y	Y
6 ***Beard***	?	?	?	✓	✓

	256	257	258	259	260
7 Jones	Y	Y	Y	N	Y
8 Ford	Y	Y	N	N	N
TEXAS					
1 Hall	Y	Y	Y	Y	Y
2 Wilson, C.	Y	Y	▮	N	N
3 ***Collins***	N	Y	Y	Y	Y
4 Roberts	Y	Y	Y	Y	Y
5 Mattox	Y	Y	Y	N	N
6 Teague	?	?	✓	?	✓
7 ***Archer***	Y	Y	Y	Y	Y
8 Eckhardt	Y	Y	N	N	N
9 Brooks	Y	Y	Y	N	Y
10 Pickle	Y	Y	Y	N	Y
11 Poage	Y	Y	Y	?	?
12 Wright	Y	?	N	N	N
13 Hightower	Y	Y	Y	N	Y
14 Young	Y	Y	N	N	Y
15 de la Garza	Y	Y	N	N	Y
16 White	Y	Y	Y	N	Y
17 Burleson	Y	Y	Y	N	Y
18 Jordan	Y	Y	N	N	N
19 Mahon	Y	Y	Y	N	N
20 Gonzalez	Y	Y	N	N	N
21 Krueger	#	#	▮	#	#
22 Gammage	Y	Y	Y	N	Y
23 Kazen	Y	Y	Y	N	Y
24 Milford	Y	Y	Y	Y	Y
UTAH					
1 McKay	Y	Y	Y	N	N
2 ***Marriott***	Y	Y	Y	Y	Y
VERMONT					
AL Jeffords	Y	Y	N	Y	N
VIRGINIA					
1 ***Trible***	Y	Y	Y	Y	Y
2 ***Whitehurst***	Y	Y	Y	Y	Y
3 Satterfield	Y	Y	Y	Y	Y
4 ***Daniel***	Y	Y	Y	Y	Y
5 Daniel	Y	Y	Y	Y	Y
6 ***Butler***	Y	Y	Y	Y	Y
7 ***Robinson***	Y	Y	Y	Y	Y
8 Harris	Y	Y	N	N	N
9 ***Wampler***	Y	Y	Y	Y	Y
10 Fisher	Y	Y	N	N	N
WASHINGTON					
1 ***Pritchard***	N	Y	N	N	N
2 Meeds	Y	Y	N	N	N
3 Bonker	Y	Y	N	N	N
4 McCormack	Y	Y	N	N	N
5 Foley	Y	Y	N	N	N
6 Dicks	Y	Y	N	N	N
7 ***Cunningham***	Y	Y	Y	Y	#
WEST VIRGINIA					
1 Mollohan	Y	Y	Y	N	Y
2 Staggers	Y	Y	N	N	Y
3 Slack	Y	Y	Y	N	Y
4 Rahall	Y	Y	Y	N	Y
WISCONSIN					
1 Aspin	Y	Y	N	N	N
2 Kastenmeier	Y	Y	N	N	N
3 Baldus	Y	Y	N	N	N
4 Zablocki	Y	Y	N	N	N
5 Reuss	Y	Y	N	N	N
6 ***Steiger***	N	Y	N	N	N
7 Obey	Y	Y	N	N	N
8 Cornell	Y	Y	N	N	N
9 ***Kasten***	Y	Y	Y	X	#
WYOMING					
AL Roncalio	?	Y	N	Y	N

Democrats ***Republicans***

261. HR 12222. Foreign Economic Aid. Zablocki, D-Wis., motion that the House resolve itself into the Committee of the Whole to further consider the bill to authorize $3.7 billion in aid for fiscal 1979. Motion agreed to 300-6: R 115-1; D 185-5 (ND 129-4; SD 56-1), May 12, 1978.

262. HR 12222. Foreign Economic Aid. Johnson, R-Colo., amendment to make tobacco and tobacco products ineligible for the Food for Peace (PL 480) program. Rejected 126-189: R 64-50; D 62-139 (ND 56-86; SD 6-53), May 12, 1978.

263. HR 12222. Foreign Economic Aid. Derwinski, R-Ill., substitute amendment, to the Ashbrook, R-Ohio, amendment, to prohibit only direct U.S. aid to Vietnam, Cambodia, Uganda or Cuba. Rejected 148-155: R 20-87; D 128-68 (ND 110-29; SD 18-39), May 12, 1978. (The Ashbrook amendment, to prohibit aid directly and indirectly to Vietnam, Cambodia, Uganda and Cuba, was adopted subsequently by voice vote.)

264. HR 11209. Maritime Satellite Communications. Van Deerlin, D-Calif., motion to suspend the rules and pass the bill to authorize the United States to join the United Nations International Maritime Satellite Organization; to designate the Communications Satellite Corp. (COMSAT) as the U.S. participant in the organization to provide a satellite communications system for merchant shipping; and to make COMSAT subject to federal supervision. Motion agreed to 350-0; R 121-0; D 229-0 (ND 157-0; SD 72-0), May 15, 1978. A two-thirds majority vote (234 in this case) is required for passage under suspension of the rules.

265. HR 12222. Foreign Economic Aid. Bauman, R-Md., amendment to reduce the $3,747,850,000 authorization in the bill by 5 percent, except for food aid and certain other programs. Adopted 200-172: R 116-14; D 84-158 (ND 28-140; SD 56-18), May 15, 1978.

266. HR 12222. Foreign Economic Aid. Passage of the bill to authorize $3,747,850,000 for U.S. foreign economic aid programs for fiscal 1979, less 5 percent for all programs except food and nutrition and certain other authorizations in the bill. Passed 225-148: R 55-75; D 170-73 (ND 147-21; SD 23-52), May 15, 1978.

267. HR 10392. Hubert H. Humphrey Fellowship. Passage of the bill to authorize $1 million for a Hubert H. Humphrey fellowship at the Woodrow Wilson International Center for Scholars of the Smithsonian Institution. Passed 222-152: R 40-90; D 182-62 (ND 154-14; SD 28-48), May 15, 1978.

268. HR 11291. Federal Fire Prevention Act. Passage of the bill to authorize $25,567,000 for fiscal 1979 for the programs of the Federal Fire Prevention and Control Administration, the Fire Research Center and for the renovation of the federal Fire Academy. Passed 360-11: R 124-5; D 236-6 (ND 165-2; SD 71-4), May 15, 1978.

KEY

- Y Voted for (yea).
- ✓ Paired for.
- † Announced for.
- # CQ Poll for.
- N Voted against (nay).
- X Paired against.
- \- Announced against.
- ▮ CQ Poll against.
- P Voted "present."
- ● Voted "present" to avoid possible conflict of interest.
- ? Did not vote or otherwise make a position known.

	261	262	263	264	265	266	267	268
ALABAMA								
1 Edwards	Y	N	N	Y	Y	N	N	Y
2 Dickinson	Y	N	N	Y	Y	N	?	Y
3 Nichols	#	X	X	Y	Y	N	N	Y
4 Bevill	Y	N	N	Y	Y	N	N	Y
5 Flippo	Y	N	N	Y	Y	N	N	Y
6 Buchanan	Y	Y	N	?	N	Y	Y	Y
7 Flowers	Y	N	?	Y	Y	N	N	Y
ALASKA								
AL Young	Y	N	#	Y	Y	N	N	Y
ARIZONA								
1 Rhodes	?	?	?	Y	Y	N	N	Y
2 Udall	Y	Y	Y	Y	N	Y	Y	Y
3 Stump	Y	N	N	Y	Y	N	N	Y
4 Rudd	Y	N	N	Y	Y	N	N	Y
ARKANSAS								
1 Alexander	?	?	✓	Y	N	Y	Y	Y
2 Tucker	#	#	▮	#	#	#	#	#
3 Hammerschmidt	Y	N	N	Y	Y	N	N	Y
4 Thornton	?	?	?	?	?	?	?	?
CALIFORNIA								
1 Johnson	Y	N	Y	Y	N	Y	Y	Y
2 Clausen	Y	Y	N	Y	Y	N	N	Y
3 Moss	Y	Y	Y	Y	N	Y	Y	Y
4 Leggett	?	?	?	?	N	Y	Y	Y
5 Burton, J.	Y	N	Y	Y	N	Y	?	Y
6 Burton, P.	Y	N	Y	Y	N	Y	Y	Y
7 Miller	Y	N	Y	Y	N	Y	Y	Y
8 Dellums	Y	N	Y	Y	N	Y	Y	Y
9 Stark	Y	N	Y	Y	N	Y	#	Y
10 Edwards	?	Y	Y	Y	N	Y	?	Y
11 Ryan	#	✓	#	Y	N	N	Y	Y
12 McCloskey	?	?	?	?	?	✓	?	?
13 Mineta	Y	Y	Y	#	N	Y	Y	Y
14 McFall	Y	N	Y	Y	N	Y	Y	Y
15 Sisk	?	?	?	Y	N	N	Y	Y
16 Panetta	Y	Y	N	Y	N	Y	Y	Y
17 Krebs	Y	Y	N	Y	N	Y	Y	Y
18 Ketchum	?	?	?	Y	Y	N	N	Y
19 Lagomarsino	Y	Y	N	Y	Y	N	N	Y
20 Goldwater	Y	N	N	?	?	X	?	?
21 Corman	#	#	?	Y	N	Y	Y	#
22 Moorhead	Y	Y	N	Y	Y	N	N	Y
23 Beilenson	Y	N	Y	Y	N	Y	Y	Y
24 Waxman	#	✓	✓	Y	N	Y	Y	Y
25 Roybal	Y	?	Y	Y	N	Y	Y	Y
26 Rousselot	Y	N	N	Y	Y	N	N	Y
27 Dornan	Y	Y	N	Y	Y	N	N	Y
28 Burke	#	#	▮	#	X	#	#	#
29 Hawkins	Y	N	Y	Y	N	Y	Y	Y
30 Danielson	†	†	†	Y	N	Y	Y	Y
31 Wilson, C.H.	#	▮	▮	#	#	#	#	#
32 Anderson	Y	Y	N	Y	N	Y	Y	Y
33 Clawson	Y	Y	N	Y	Y	N	N	Y
34 Hannaford	#	#	✓	Y	N	Y	Y	Y
35 Lloyd	N	N	Y	Y	N	Y	Y	Y
36 Brown	?	?	?	Y	N	Y	Y	Y
37 Pettis	Y	Y	Y	Y	Y	Y	N	Y
38 Patterson	?	?	?	Y	N	Y	Y	Y
39 Wiggins	#	▮	#	#	Y	Y	N	Y
40 Badham	Y	Y	N	Y	Y	N	N	Y
41 Wilson, B.	N	Y	Y	Y	Y	Y	N	Y
42 Van Deerlin	?	?	?	Y	N	Y	Y	Y
43 Burgener	Y	Y	N	Y	Y	N	N	Y
COLORADO								
1 Schroeder	Y	Y	Y	Y	Y	Y	Y	Y
2 Wirth	#	✓	#	Y	N	Y	Y	Y
3 Evans	#	▮	▮	Y	N	Y	Y	Y
4 Johnson	Y	Y	N	?	?	?	?	?
5 Armstrong	?	?	?	Y	Y	N	N	Y
CONNECTICUT								
1 Cotter	#	#	#	#	N	Y	Y	Y
2 Dodd	?	?	?	Y	N	Y	Y	Y
3 Giaimo	?	N	Y	Y	N	Y	Y	Y
4 McKinney	Y	Y	Y	Y	N	Y	Y	Y
5 Sarasin	†	†	†	†	-	✓	†	†
6 Moffett	Y	Y	Y	Y	N	Y	Y	Y
DELAWARE								
AL Evans	Y	Y	N	Y	Y	Y	N	Y
FLORIDA								
1 Sikes	?	X	X	Y	Y	N	N	Y
2 Fuqua	#	X	#	Y	Y	N	N	Y
3 Bennett	Y	Y	N	Y	Y	N	Y	Y
4 Chappell	Y	N	N	Y	N	N	N	Y
5 Kelly	Y	Y	N	Y	Y	N	N	N
6 Young	Y	Y	N	Y	Y	N	N	Y
7 Gibbons	?	?	?	Y	Y	Y	Y	Y
8 Ireland	?	?	?	Y	Y	N	N	Y
9 Frey	?	✓	?	?	?	X	?	?
10 Bafalis	Y	Y	N	Y	Y	N	N	Y
11 Rogers	?	✓	✓	Y	Y	Y	Y	Y
12 Burke	Y	Y	N	Y	✓	X	N	Y
13 Lehman	Y	Y	Y	Y	N	Y	N	Y
14 Pepper	#	▮	▮	Y	N	Y	Y	#
15 Fascell	Y	N	Y	Y	N	Y	Y	Y
GEORGIA								
1 Ginn	Y	N	N	Y	Y	N	N	Y
2 Mathis	Y	N	N	Y	Y	N	Y	Y
3 Brinkley	Y	N	N	Y	Y	N	N	Y
4 Levitas	Y	N	N	Y	Y	Y	N	Y
5 Fowler	Y	N	Y	Y	Y	Y	N	Y
6 Flynt	Y	N	N	Y	Y	N	N	Y
7 McDonald	Y	Y	N	Y	Y	N	N	N
8 Evans	N	N	N	Y	Y	Y	N	Y
9 Jenkins	Y	N	N	#	#	X	▮	#
10 Barnard	Y	N	N	Y	Y	N	N	Y
HAWAII								
1 Heftel	Y	N	Y	Y	N	Y	Y	Y
2 Akaka	Y	N	Y	Y	N	Y	Y	Y
IDAHO								
1 Symms	Y	Y	N	Y	Y	N	N	N
2 Hansen, G.	Y	Y	N	Y	Y	N	N	Y
ILLINOIS								
1 Metcalfe	?	?	?	?	X	?	?	?
2 Murphy	#	?	?	#	N	Y	Y	Y
3 Russo	Y	Y	N	Y	Y	N	Y	Y
4 Derwinski	Y	N	Y	Y	Y	N	Y	Y
5 Fary	Y	N	Y	Y	N	Y	Y	Y
6 Hyde	Y	Y	N	Y	Y	Y	N	Y
7 Collins	Y	N	Y	?	X	?	?	?
8 Rostenkowski	Y	N	Y	Y	N	Y	Y	Y
9 Yates	Y	Y	Y	Y	N	Y	Y	Y
10 Mikva	#	#	#	Y	N	Y	Y	Y
11 Annunzio	Y	N	Y	Y	N	Y	Y	Y
12 Crane	#	#	X	Y	Y	N	N	N
13 McClory	Y	Y	Y	Y	Y	Y	Y	Y
14 Erlenborn	Y	Y	Y	Y	Y	Y	N	Y
15 Corcoran	Y	Y	N	Y	Y	N	N	Y
16 Anderson	?	?	?	Y	Y	Y	Y	Y
17 O'Brien	Y	N	Y	#	✓	✓	▮	#
18 Michel	Y	N	N	Y	Y	Y	Y	Y
19 Railsback	Y	N	#	#	Y	Y	Y	Y
20 Findley	Y	N	Y	Y	Y	Y	Y	Y
21 Madigan	Y	N	N	Y	Y	Y	?	Y
22 Shipley	?	?	?	Y	N	N	Y	Y
23 Price	Y	N	Y	Y	N	Y	Y	Y
24 Simon	Y	Y	Y	Y	N	Y	Y	Y
INDIANA								
1 Benjamin	Y	N	Y	Y	N	Y	N	Y
2 Fithian	?	?	?	Y	Y	N	Y	Y
3 Brademas	Y	Y	Y	Y	N	Y	Y	Y
4 Quayle	?	?	?	Y	Y	N	N	Y
5 Hillis	?	?	?	Y	Y	N	N	Y
6 Evans	Y	N	N	Y	Y	N	N	Y
7 Myers, J.	Y	N	N	Y	Y	N	N	Y
8 Cornwell	Y	N	N	Y	Y	Y	Y	Y
9 Hamilton	Y	N	Y	Y	N	Y	N	Y
10 Sharp	Y	Y	Y	Y	Y	Y	Y	Y
11 Jacobs	Y	Y	Y	Y	Y	N	N	Y
IOWA								
1 Leach	Y	Y	Y	Y	Y	N	Y	Y
2 Blouin	Y	Y	Y	Y	N	Y	Y	Y
3 Grassley	Y	Y	N	Y	Y	N	N	Y
4 Smith	Y	N	N	Y	N	Y	Y	Y
5 Harkin	Y	N	Y	Y	Y	Y	Y	Y
6 Bedell	Y	Y	▮	Y	N	Y	Y	Y

Democrats ***Republicans***

	261	262	263	264	265	266	267	268
KANSAS								
1 Sebelius	Y	N	#	#	✓	X	▮	#
2 Keys	Y	Y	Y	Y	Y	Y	Y	Y
3 Winn	Y	N	N	Y	N	Y	N	Y
4 Glickman	#	#	▮	Y	Y	Y	N	Y
5 Skubitz	?	?	?	Y	Y	N	N	Y
KENTUCKY								
1 Hubbard	Y	N	N	Y	Y	N	N	Y
2 Natcher	Y	N	Y	Y	N	Y	Y	Y
3 Mazzoli	†	-	†	Y	N	Y	N	Y
4 Snyder	?	?	?	Y	Y	N	N	Y
5 Carter	?	?	?	?	?	✓	?	?
6 Breckinridge	?	X	?	?	?	?	?	?
7 Perkins	Y	N	Y	Y	N	Y	Y	Y
LOUISIANA								
1 Livingston	Y	?	?	Y	Y	N	N	Y
2 Boggs	Y	N	Y	Y	N	Y	Y	Y
3 Treen	Y	N	N	Y	Y	Y	N	Y
4 Waggonner	Y	N	N	Y	Y	N	N	Y
5 Huckaby	?	?	X	Y	Y	N	N	Y
6 Moore	Y	Y	N	Y	Y	N	N	Y
7 Breaux	Y	N	?	Y	Y	Y	N	Y
8 Long	?	?	?	?	?	?	?	?
MAINE								
1 Emery	Y	Y	N	Y	Y	Y	Y	Y
2 Cohen	?	?	?	?	Y	Y	Y	Y
MARYLAND								
1 Bauman	Y	N	N	Y	Y	N	N	Y
2 Long	Y	Y	N	Y	?	Y	N	Y
3 Mikulski	N	N	Y	Y	N	Y	Y	Y
4 Holt	?	?	?	Y	Y	N	N	Y
5 Spellman	Y	N	Y	Y	N	Y	Y	Y
6 Byron	Y	Y	N	Y	Y	N	Y	Y
7 Mitchell	N	N	Y	Y	N	Y	Y	Y
8 Steers	Y	Y	Y	Y	N	Y	Y	Y
MASSACHUSETTS								
1 Conte	Y	Y	Y	Y	N	Y	Y	Y
2 Boland	Y	N	▮	#	▮	Y	Y	Y
3 Early	Y	Y	N	Y	N	Y	Y	Y
4 Drinan	Y	Y	Y	Y	N	Y	Y	Y
5 Tsongas	Y	Y	Y	Y	N	Y	Y	Y
6 Harrington	Y	Y	Y	#	N	Y	Y	Y
7 Markey	Y	Y	Y	Y	N	Y	Y	Y
8 O'Neill								
9 Moakley	Y	Y	Y	Y	N	Y	Y	Y
10 Heckler	Y	Y	N	?	N	Y	Y	Y
11 Burke	Y	N	Y	Y	N	Y	Y	Y
12 Studds	Y	Y	Y	Y	N	Y	Y	Y
MICHIGAN								
1 Conyers	#	#	✓	#	X	#	#	#
2 Pursell	?	?	?	?	N	Y	Y	Y
3 Brown	Y	N	N	Y	Y	Y	N	Y
4 Stockman	Y	Y	#	Y	Y	Y	N	Y
5 Sawyer	#	#	#	Y	Y	Y	N	Y
6 Carr	Y	Y	Y	Y	N	Y	Y	Y
7 Kildee	Y	Y	Y	Y	N	Y	Y	Y
8 Traxler	#	▮	▮	Y	N	N	Y	Y
9 Vander Jagt	Y	?	?	Y	Y	Y	N	Y
10 Cederberg	Y	Y	N	Y	Y	N	Y	Y
11 Ruppe	Y	Y	N	#	Y	Y	N	#
12 Bonior	?	Y	Y	Y	N	Y	Y	Y
13 Diggs	Y	N	Y	#	N	Y	Y	#
14 Nedzi	Y	Y	Y	Y	N	Y	Y	Y
15 Ford	?	?	?	?	X	✓	?	?
16 Dingell	Y	N	Y	Y	N	Y	Y	Y
17 Brodhead	?	?	?	?	N	Y	Y	Y
18 Blanchard	Y	Y	Y	Y	N	Y	Y	Y
19 Broomfield	Y	N	N	Y	Y	Y	N	Y
MINNESOTA								
1 Quie	Y	Y	N	#	#	#	#	#
2 Hagedorn	Y	Y	N	Y	Y	N	Y	Y
3 Frenzel	Y	Y	N	Y	Y	Y	Y	Y
4 Vento	Y	N	Y	Y	N	Y	Y	Y
5 Fraser	#	Y	Y	#	▮	#	#	#
6 Nolan	Y	N	Y	?	?	?	?	?
7 Stangeland	Y	N	N	Y	Y	N	Y	Y
8 Oberstar	Y	N	Y	Y	N	Y	Y	Y
MISSISSIPPI								
1 Whitten	#	▮	▮	#	#	X	#	#
2 Bowen	?	?	?	Y	Y	N	N	Y
3 Montgomery	?	?	?	Y	Y	N	N	Y
4 Cochran	?	?	?	?	?	?	?	?
5 Lott	Y	Y	N	Y	Y	N	N	Y
MISSOURI								
1 Clay	?	?	?	?	N	Y	Y	Y
2 Young	Y	N	Y	Y	N	Y	Y	Y
3 Gephardt	Y	N	Y	Y	N	Y	Y	Y
4 Skelton	Y	N	N	#	#	#	#	#
5 Bolling	Y	N	▮	Y	N	Y	Y	Y
6 Coleman	Y	N	N	Y	Y	N	N	Y
7 Taylor	Y	N	N	Y	Y	N	N	Y
8 Ichord	Y	N	?	?	Y	N	N	Y
9 Volkmer	Y	N	N	Y	Y	Y	N	Y
10 Burlison	Y	N	Y	Y	N	Y	Y	Y
MONTANA								
1 Baucus	Y	N	Y	#	X	✓	#	#
2 Marlenee	Y	N	N	Y	Y	N	N	Y
NEBRASKA								
1 Thone	Y	Y	N	Y	Y	N	N	Y
2 Cavanaugh	?	?	?	Y	N	Y	Y	Y
3 Smith	Y	Y	N	Y	Y	N	N	Y
NEVADA								
AL Santini	#	#	X	#	?	?	#	#
NEW HAMPSHIRE								
1 D'Amours	#	?	#	Y	Y	Y	Y	Y
2 Cleveland	Y	Y	N	Y	Y	N	N	Y
NEW JERSEY								
1 Florio	#	Y	Y	Y	N	N	Y	Y
2 Hughes	Y	Y	Y	Y	Y	Y	Y	Y
3 Howard	Y	N	Y	#	N	Y	Y	Y
4 Thompson	Y	N	Y	Y	N	Y	Y	#
5 Fenwick	Y	Y	Y	Y	Y	Y	Y	N
6 Forsythe	Y	Y	Y	Y	Y	Y	Y	Y
7 Maguire	Y	Y	Y	Y	N	Y	Y	Y
8 Roe	Y	Y	N	Y	Y	Y	Y	Y
9 Hollenbeck	Y	N	N	Y	N	Y	Y	Y
10 Rodino	#	▮	▮	#	▮	#	#	#
11 Minish	Y	Y	N	Y	N	Y	Y	Y
12 Rinaldo	Y	Y	N	Y	N	Y	Y	Y
13 Meyner	Y	N	Y	Y	N	Y	Y	Y
14 LeFante	Y	N	N	Y	N	Y	Y	Y
15 Patten	Y	N	Y	Y	Y	Y	Y	Y
NEW MEXICO								
1 Lujan	?	?	?	Y	Y	Y	Y	Y
2 Runnels	#	?	?	#	✓	?	?	#
NEW YORK								
1 Pike	Y	Y	N	Y	Y	N	Y	Y
2 Downey	Y	N	Y	Y	N	Y	Y	Y
3 Ambro	Y	N	Y	Y	N	Y	Y	Y
4 Lent	#	#	▮	Y	Y	Y	N	Y
5 Wydler	?	?	?	Y	Y	Y	N	Y
6 Wolff	Y	N	Y	Y	N	Y	Y	Y
7 Addabbo	#	X	✓	Y	N	Y	Y	Y
8 Rosenthal	#	N	Y	Y	N	Y	Y	#
9 Delaney	Y	Y	Y	Y	Y	Y	Y	Y
10 Biaggi	#	▮	▮	Y	N	Y	Y	Y
11 Scheuer	Y	Y	Y	Y	N	Y	Y	Y
12 Chisholm	#	?	?	Y	N	Y	Y	Y
13 Solarz	Y	N	Y	Y	N	Y	Y	Y
14 Richmond	?	?	?	Y	N	Y	Y	Y
15 Zeferetti	Y	N	N	#	Y	Y	Y	Y
16 Holtzman	Y	Y	Y	Y	N	Y	Y	†
17 Murphy	Y	N	Y	Y	N	Y	Y	Y
18 Green	Y	N	Y	#	▮	✓	#	#
19 Rangel	?	X	✓	Y	N	Y	Y	Y
20 Weiss	Y	N	Y	Y	N	Y	Y	Y
21 Garcia	?	N	Y	?	N	Y	Y	Y
22 Bingham	Y	N	Y	#	N	Y	Y	Y
23 Caputo	Y	Y	N	Y	Y	N	Y	Y
24 Ottinger	Y	Y	Y	Y	N	Y	Y	Y
25 Fish	Y	Y	Y	?	Y	Y	N	Y
26 Gilman	Y	Y	N	Y	N	Y	Y	Y
27 McHugh	#	N	Y	Y	N	Y	Y	Y
28 Stratton	Y	Y	N	Y	N	Y	Y	Y
29 Pattison	Y	N	Y	Y	N	Y	Y	Y
30 McEwen	Y	Y	?	Y	Y	Y	N	Y
31 Mitchell	Y	N	N	Y	Y	Y	Y	Y
32 Hanley	Y	N	Y	#	N	Y	Y	Y
33 Walsh	Y	N	N	?	Y	N	N	Y
34 Horton	#	▮	#	#	▮	✓	N	#
35 Conable	Y	Y	Y	Y	Y	Y	Y	Y
36 LaFalce	Y	N	Y	Y	N	Y	Y	Y
37 Nowak	Y	N	Y	Y	N	Y	Y	Y
38 Kemp	Y	Y	N	Y	Y	N	N	Y
39 Lundine	Y	N	Y	Y	N	Y	Y	Y
NORTH CAROLINA								
1 Jones	Y	N	N	Y	Y	Y	N	Y
2 Fountain	Y	N	N	Y	Y	N	N	Y
3 Whitley	?	X	?	Y	Y	N	N	Y
4 Andrews	Y	N	N	#	?	?	N	Y
5 Neal	Y	N	Y	Y	Y	N	N	Y
6 Preyer	#	▮	?	Y	N	Y	Y	Y
7 Rose	Y	N	Y	Y	N	Y	Y	Y
8 Hefner	Y	N	N	Y	Y	N	N	Y
9 Martin	Y	N	N	Y	Y	Y	Y	Y
10 Broyhill	Y	N	N	?	✓	X	?	?
11 Gudger	Y	N	Y	Y	Y	N	Y	Y
NORTH DAKOTA								
AL Andrews	Y	N	N	Y	Y	N	Y	Y
OHIO								
1 Gradison	#	#	▮	Y	Y	Y	N	Y
2 Luken	Y	Y	N	Y	N	Y	Y	Y
3 Whalen	Y	Y	Y	Y	N	Y	Y	Y
4 Guyer	Y	N	N	Y	Y	Y	N	Y
5 Latta	Y	Y	N	Y	Y	N	N	Y
6 Harsha	Y	N	N	Y	Y	N	N	Y
7 Brown	Y	Y	N	Y	Y	N	N	Y
8 Kindness	Y	N	N	Y	Y	N	N	Y
9 Ashley	Y	N	N	Y	N	Y	Y	Y
10 Miller	Y	N	N	Y	Y	N	N	Y
11 Stanton	Y	Y	Y	Y	Y	Y	Y	Y
12 Devine	Y	Y	N	Y	Y	N	N	Y
13 Pease	Y	Y	Y	Y	N	Y	Y	Y
14 Seiberling	Y	N	Y	Y	N	Y	Y	Y
15 Wylie	Y	Y	N	Y	Y	Y	N	Y
16 Regula	Y	Y	N	Y	Y	N	N	Y
17 Ashbrook	Y	N	N	Y	Y	N	N	Y
18 Applegate	?	?	?	Y	Y	N	Y	Y
19 Carney	?	?	?	Y	X	Y	Y	Y
20 Oakar	?	?	?	Y	N	N	Y	Y
21 Stokes	#	▮	▮	Y	N	Y	Y	Y
22 Vanik	Y	Y	Y	Y	N	Y	#	Y
23 Mottl	#	✓	▮	Y	Y	N	N	Y
OKLAHOMA								
1 Jones	Y	N	N	Y	Y	N	N	Y
2 Risenhoover	?	X	✓	Y	Y	N	N	Y
3 Watkins	#	▮	?	#	#	N	N	Y
4 Steed	Y	N	Y	Y	N	N	Y	Y
5 Edwards	?	?	?	Y	Y	N	N	Y
6 English	Y	N	N	Y	Y	N	N	Y
OREGON								
1 AuCoin	#	✓	?	#	#	✓	?	#
2 Ullman	Y	N	Y	Y	N	#	Y	Y
3 Duncan	Y	N	Y	Y	?	?	N	N
4 Weaver	Y	N	Y	Y	N	Y	Y	Y
PENNSYLVANIA								
1 Myers, M.	?	?	?	?	?	?	?	?
2 Nix	?	?	?	?	X	?	?	?
3 Lederer	Y	N	N	Y	N	Y	Y	Y
4 Eilberg	#	▮	#	#	X	✓	#	#
5 Schulze	Y	N	N	?	✓	X	?	?
6 Yatron	Y	Y	N	#	#	#	#	#
7 Edgar	†	†	-	Y	N	Y	Y	Y
8 Kostmayer	Y	Y	Y	Y	N	Y	Y	Y
9 Shuster	Y	Y	N	Y	Y	N	N	Y
10 McDade	#	▮	▮	Y	Y	Y	Y	#
11 Flood	#	X	X	#	X	✓	#	#
12 Murtha	Y	N	N	#	✓	N	N	Y
13 Coughlin	Y	Y	N	Y	Y	Y	N	Y
14 Moorhead	Y	N	Y	Y	N	Y	Y	Y
15 Rooney	Y	N	Y	Y	N	Y	?	?
16 Walker	?	✓	?	Y	Y	N	N	Y
17 Ertel	N	Y	N	?	?	?	?	?
18 Walgren	?	#	✓	Y	Y	Y	Y	Y
19 Goodling, W.	Y	Y	N	Y	N	N	N	Y
20 Gaydos	Y	N	N	Y	Y	N	Y	Y
21 Dent	#	▮	X	#	✓	X	#	#
22 Murphy	#	?	?	Y	Y	Y	Y	Y
23 Ammerman	Y	Y	Y	Y	N	Y	Y	Y
24 Marks	Y	N	N	Y	Y	Y	Y	Y
25 Myers, G.	Y	Y	N	Y	N	Y	N	Y
RHODE ISLAND								
1 St Germain	Y	N	?	Y	N	Y	Y	Y
2 Beard	Y	N	Y	Y	N	Y	Y	Y
SOUTH CAROLINA								
1 Davis	?	X	?	Y	Y	N	Y	Y
2 Spence	Y	N	N	Y	Y	N	N	Y
3 Derrick	Y	Y	N	Y	Y	N	N	Y
4 Mann	Y	N	N	?	?	?	?	?
5 Holland	#	▮	?	#	#	▮	#	#
6 Jenrette	Y	N	Y	Y	Y	N	Y	Y
SOUTH DAKOTA								
1 Pressler	?	?	?	?	?	?	?	?
2 Abdnor	Y	N	N	Y	Y	N	Y	Y
TENNESSEE								
1 Quillen	Y	N	X	#	✓	X	▮	#
2 Duncan	Y	N	N	Y	Y	N	N	Y
3 Lloyd	Y	N	N	Y	Y	N	N	Y
4 Gore	Y	N	N	Y	N	Y	Y	Y
5 Allen	Y	N	Y	Y	Y	N	Y	Y
6 Beard	Y	N	N	?	Y	N	N	Y
7 Jones	Y	N	N	Y	Y	N	N	Y
8 Ford	?	?	?	?	?	?	?	?
TEXAS								
1 Hall	Y	N	N	Y	Y	N	N	N
2 Wilson, C.	Y	N	Y	#	▮	#	▮	#
3 Collins	Y	Y	N	Y	Y	N	N	N
4 Roberts	Y	N	N	Y	Y	N	N	Y
5 Mattox	Y	N	N	Y	Y	N	N	Y
6 Teague	?	?	X	?	✓	X	?	?
7 Archer	Y	Y	N	Y	Y	N	N	Y
8 Eckhardt	?	?	?	?	?	?	?	?
9 Brooks	Y	N	N	Y	N	Y	Y	Y
10 Pickle	Y	N	N	Y	Y	N	Y	Y
11 Poage	?	?	?	Y	Y	N	N	N
12 Wright	?	?	?	Y	N	Y	Y	Y
13 Hightower	Y	N	N	Y	Y	N	N	Y
14 Young	?	N	Y	?	?	?	?	?
15 de la Garza	Y	N	N	Y	Y	N	N	Y
16 White	Y	N	N	Y	Y	N	N	Y
17 Burleson	Y	N	N	Y	Y	N	N	N
18 Jordan	Y	N	Y	Y	N	Y	Y	Y
19 Mahon	?	N	N	Y	Y	N	Y	Y
20 Gonzalez	Y	N	Y	?	N	Y	Y	Y
21 Krueger	#	▮	#	#	▮	#	#	#
22 Gammage	?	✓	?	Y	Y	N	Y	Y
23 Kazen	?	?	?	?	Y	N	Y	Y
24 Milford	Y	N	N	Y	Y	N	N	Y
UTAH								
1 McKay	Y	Y	Y	Y	Y	Y	N	N
2 Marriott	Y	Y	N	Y	Y	N	N	Y
VERMONT								
AL Jeffords	#	✓	#	Y	Y	Y	Y	Y
VIRGINIA								
1 Trible	Y	N	N	Y	Y	N	N	Y
2 Whitehurst	Y	N	N	Y	Y	N	N	Y
3 Satterfield	Y	N	N	Y	Y	N	N	Y
4 Daniel	Y	N	N	Y	Y	N	N	Y
5 Daniel	Y	N	N	Y	Y	N	N	Y
6 Butler	Y	N	N	Y	Y	N	N	Y
7 Robinson	Y	N	N	Y	Y	N	N	Y
8 Harris	Y	Y	Y	Y	N	Y	Y	Y
9 Wampler	Y	N	?	Y	Y	N	Y	Y
10 Fisher	Y	Y	Y	Y	N	Y	Y	Y
WASHINGTON								
1 Pritchard	Y	Y	Y	Y	N	Y	Y	Y
2 Meeds	Y	N	Y	Y	N	Y	Y	Y
3 Bonker	#	#	#	Y	N	#	Y	Y
4 McCormack	Y	Y	Y	Y	N	?	Y	Y
5 Foley	Y	N	Y	Y	N	?	Y	Y
6 Dicks	Y	N	Y	Y	N	Y	Y	Y
7 Cunningham	#	#	▮	Y	Y	Y	N	Y
WEST VIRGINIA								
1 Mollohan	Y	N	N	Y	N	Y	Y	Y
2 Staggers	Y	N	Y	Y	N	N	Y	Y
3 Slack	Y	N	N	Y	Y	N	N	Y
4 Rahall	Y	N	N	Y	N	N	Y	Y
WISCONSIN								
1 Aspin	?	?	?	Y	N	Y	Y	Y
2 Kastenmeier	#	Y	Y	Y	N	Y	Y	Y
3 Baldus	Y	N	Y	Y	N	Y	Y	Y
4 Zablocki	Y	N	Y	Y	N	Y	Y	Y
5 Reuss	#	#	Y	#	▮	#	#	#
6 Steiger	Y	N	Y	Y	Y	Y	Y	Y
7 Obey	Y	N	Y	Y	N	Y	Y	Y
8 Cornell	Y	Y	Y	#	▮	#	#	#
9 Kasten	#	#	▮	Y	Y	N	Y	Y
WYOMING								
AL Roncalio	?	Y	Y	?	?	?	?	?

Democrats ***Republicans***

269. HR 4030. Private Foundations Stock Holdings. Frenzel, R-Minn., demand for a second on the Waggonner, D-La., motion to suspend the rules and pass the bill to increase the amount of stock that certain private foundations may hold in various public utilities without being subject to the excise tax on excess business holdings. Second ordered 334-16: R 116-6; D 218-10 (ND 147-9; SD 71-1), May 15, 1978.

270. HR 12255. Older Americans Act. Brademas, D-Ind., motion to suspend the rules and pass the bill to extend the 1965 Older Americans Act for three years until fiscal 1981 and Title II of the 1973 Domestic Volunteer Service Act until fiscal 1980, and to authorize $1.269 billion for fiscal 1979, $1.361 billion for fiscal 1980 and $1.583 billion for fiscal 1981 for programs authorized by the acts. Motion agreed to 361-6: R 124-4; D 237-2 (ND 165-0; SD 72-2), May 15, 1978. A two-thirds majority vote (245 in this case) is required for passage under suspension of the rules.

271. HR 4030. Private Foundations Stock Holdings. Waggonner, D-La., motion to suspend the rules and pass the bill to increase the amount of stock that certain private foundations may hold in various public utilities without being subject to the excise tax on excess business holdings. Motion rejected 218-145: R 115-12; D 103-133 (ND 46-116; SD 57-17), May 15, 1978. A two-thirds majority vote (242 in this case) is required for passage under suspension of the rules.

272. Procedural Motion. Steiger, R-Wis., motion to approve the House *Journal* of Monday, May 15, 1978. Motion agreed to 348-12: R 122-6; D 226-6 (ND 149-6; SD 77-0), May 16, 1978.

273. HR 12467. Comprehensive Rehabilitation Services. Brademas, D-Ind., motion to suspend the rules and pass the bill to authorize $6.9 billion through fiscal 1983 to extend certain rehabilitation programs, and to establish a community service employment program and an independent living program for handicapped individuals. Motion agreed to 382-12: R 129-7; D 253-5 (ND 173-1; SD 80-4), May 16, 1978. A two-thirds majority vote (263 in this case) is required for passage under suspension of the rules.

274. HR 9005. District of Columbia Appropriations, Fiscal 1978. Bauman, R-Md., motion to table (kill) the Natcher, D-Ky., motion *(see vote 275, below)* to concur in the Senate amendment to the conference report with an amendment adding $27 million for capital outlays for a civic center in Washington, D.C. Motion rejected 190-199: R 102-34; D 88-165 (ND 57-114; SD 31-51), May 16, 1978.

275. HR 9005. District of Columbia Appropriations, Fiscal 1978. Natcher, D-Ky., motion to concur in the Senate amendment to the conference report with an amendment adding $27 million for capital outlays for a civic center in Washington, D.C. Adopted 199-183: R 32-100; D 167-83 (ND 116-55; SD 51-28), May 16, 1978. (The House by voice vote subsequently adopted the conference report on the bill, appropriating $1,368,623,200 for the District of Columbia for fiscal 1978.) The president had requested $1,414,-561,100.

276. HR 11686. Energy Department — Military Programs. Adoption of the rule (H Res 1174) providing for House floor consideration of the bill to authorize $2.9 billion for military-related activities of the Energy Department for fiscal 1979, including research, development and production of military nuclear programs. Adopted 378-0: R 132-0; D 246-0 (ND 168-0; SD 78-0), May 16, 1978.

KEY

- Y Voted for (yea).
- ✓ Paired for.
- † Announced for.
- # CQ Poll for.
- N Voted against (nay).
- X Paired against.
- \- Announced against.
- ▮ CQ Poll against.
- P Voted "present."
- ● Voted "present" to avoid possible conflict of interest.
- ? Did not vote or otherwise make a position known.

	269	270	271	272	273	274	275	276
ALABAMA								
1 Edwards	Y	Y	Y	Y	Y	Y	N	Y
2 Dickinson	Y	Y	Y	Y	Y	Y	N	Y
3 Nichols	Y	Y	Y	Y	Y	Y	N	Y
4 Bevill	Y	Y	Y	Y	Y	N	Y	Y
5 Flippo	Y	Y	Y	Y	Y	N	N	Y
6 Buchanan	Y	Y	Y	Y	Y	N	Y	Y
7 Flowers	Y	Y	Y	Y	Y	N	Y	Y
ALASKA								
AL Young	#	Y	Y	Y	Y	Y	N	Y
ARIZONA								
1 Rhodes	Y	Y	Y	Y	Y	N	Y	?
2 Udall	Y	Y	N	Y	Y	N	Y	Y
3 Stump	Y	Y	Y	Y	Y	Y	N	Y
4 Rudd	Y	Y	Y	Y	Y	Y	N	Y
ARKANSAS								
1 Alexander	Y	Y	Y	Y	Y	N	Y	Y
2 Tucker	#	#	▮	#	#	▮	#	#
3 Hammerschmidt	Y	Y	Y	Y	Y	Y	N	Y
4 Thornton	?	?	?	?	?	?	?	?
CALIFORNIA								
1 Johnson	Y	Y	N	Y	Y	N	Y	Y
2 Clausen	Y	Y	Y	Y	Y	N	N	Y
3 Moss	Y	?	?	Y	Y	Y	N	Y
4 Leggett	?	Y	Y	Y	Y	N	Y	Y
5 Burton, J.	?	Y	N	Y	Y	N	Y	Y
6 Burton, P.	N	Y	N	Y	Y	N	Y	Y
7 Miller	?	Y	N	Y	Y	N	Y	Y
8 Dellums	Y	Y	N	#	Y	N	Y	Y
9 Stark	N	Y	N	Y	Y	Y	N	Y
10 Edwards	Y	Y	Y	Y	Y	N	Y	Y
11 Ryan	Y	Y	N	Y	Y	N	Y	Y
12 McCloskey	?	?	?	?	?	?	?	?
13 Mineta	Y	Y	N	Y	Y	N	Y	Y
14 McFall	Y	Y	Y	Y	Y	N	Y	Y
15 Sisk	?	?	?	Y	Y	N	Y	Y
16 Panetta	Y	Y	N	Y	Y	N	N	Y
17 Krebs	Y	Y	N	Y	Y	N	Y	Y
18 Ketchum	Y	Y	Y	Y	Y	Y	N	Y
19 Lagomarsino	Y	Y	Y	Y	Y	Y	N	Y
20 Goldwater	?	?	?	N	Y	N	N	Y
21 Corman	Y	Y	N	Y	Y	N	Y	Y
22 Moorhead	Y	Y	Y	Y	Y	Y	N	Y
23 Beilenson	#	Y	N	N	Y	Y	N	Y
24 Waxman	#	?	▮	Y	Y	N	Y	Y
25 Roybal	Y	Y	N	Y	Y	N	Y	Y
26 Rousselot	?	Y	Y	Y	Y	Y	N	Y
27 Dornan	Y	Y	Y	Y	Y	Y	N	Y
28 Burke	#	#	▮	#	#	X	✓	#
29 Hawkins	Y	Y	N	Y	Y	N	Y	Y
30 Danielson	Y	Y	N	Y	Y	N	Y	Y
31 Wilson, C.H.	#	#	#	#	#	▮	#	#
32 Anderson	Y	Y	N	Y	Y	N	Y	Y
33 Clawson	Y	Y	Y	Y	N	Y	N	Y
34 Hannaford	Y	Y	N	Y	Y	Y	Y	Y
35 Lloyd	?	Y	Y	N	Y	N	Y	Y
36 Brown	Y	Y	Y	?	?	X	✓	?
37 Pettis	Y	Y	Y	Y	Y	N	Y	Y
38 Patterson	N	Y	N	Y	Y	N	Y	Y
39 Wiggins	#	#	Y	Y	Y	N	▮	#
40 Badham	Y	Y	Y	Y	Y	Y	N	Y
41 Wilson, B.	N	Y	Y	N	Y	N	Y	Y
42 Van Deerlin	Y	Y	N	Y	Y	Y	N	Y
43 Burgener	Y	Y	Y	Y	Y	N	Y	Y
COLORADO								
1 Schroeder	Y	Y	N	Y	Y	Y	N	Y
2 Wirth	Y	Y	N	Y	Y	N	Y	Y
3 Evans	Y	Y	N	Y	Y	N	Y	Y
4 Johnson	?	?	?	Y	Y	Y	N	Y
5 Armstrong	Y	Y	Y	Y	Y	Y	N	Y
CONNECTICUT								
1 Cotter	Y	Y	Y	Y	Y	Y	N	Y
2 Dodd	Y	Y	N	Y	Y	Y	N	Y
3 Giaimo	Y	Y	Y	Y	Y	N	Y	Y
4 McKinney	Y	Y	N	#	Y	N	Y	Y
5 Sarasin	†	†	†	-	†	-	†	†
6 Moffett	Y	Y	N	?	Y	N	Y	Y
DELAWARE								
AL Evans	Y	Y	Y	Y	Y	Y	N	Y
FLORIDA								
1 Sikes	?	?	?	Y	Y	N	Y	Y
2 Fuqua	Y	Y	Y	Y	Y	N	Y	Y
3 Bennett	Y	Y	N	Y	Y	Y	N	Y
4 Chappell	Y	Y	Y	Y	Y	N	Y	Y
5 Kelly	Y	Y	Y	Y	N	Y	N	Y
6 Young	Y	Y	Y	Y	Y	Y	N	Y
7 Gibbons	Y	Y	N	Y	Y	Y	N	Y
8 Ireland	Y	Y	N	Y	Y	Y	N	Y
9 Frey	?	?	?	?	?	✓	?	?
10 Bafalis	Y	Y	Y	Y	Y	Y	N	Y
11 Rogers	Y	Y	Y	Y	Y	N	Y	Y
12 Burke	Y	Y	N	Y	Y	Y	N	Y
13 Lehman	Y	Y	N	Y	Y	N	Y	Y
14 Pepper	Y	Y	Y	Y	Y	N	Y	Y
15 Fascell	Y	Y	▮	Y	Y	N	Y	Y
GEORGIA								
1 Ginn	Y	Y	Y	Y	Y	N	Y	Y
2 Mathis	?	Y	Y	?	Y	N	Y	Y
3 Brinkley	Y	Y	Y	Y	Y	N	Y	Y
4 Levitas	Y	Y	N	Y	Y	N	Y	Y
5 Fowler	Y	Y	N	Y	Y	N	Y	Y
6 Flynt	Y	Y	Y	Y	Y	Y	N	Y
7 McDonald	Y	N	Y	Y	N	Y	N	Y
8 Evans	▮	Y	Y	Y	Y	Y	Y	Y
9 Jenkins	#	#	#	#	#	#	▮	#
10 Barnard	Y	Y	Y	Y	Y	N	Y	Y
HAWAII								
1 Heftel	Y	Y	N	?	Y	N	Y	Y
2 Akaka	Y	Y	N	Y	Y	N	Y	Y
IDAHO								
1 Symms	Y	Y	Y	Y	Y	Y	N	Y
2 Hansen, G.	Y	Y	Y	Y	N	Y	N	Y
ILLINOIS								
1 Metcalfe	?	?	?	?	Y	Y	?	Y
2 Murphy	Y	Y	N	Y	Y	Y	N	Y
3 Russo	Y	Y	N	Y	Y	Y	N	Y
4 Derwinski	Y	Y	Y	Y	Y	Y	N	Y
5 Fary	Y	Y	Y	Y	Y	Y	N	Y
6 Hyde	Y	Y	Y	Y	Y	Y	N	Y
7 Collins	?	?	?	Y	Y	Y	N	Y
8 Rostenkowski	Y	Y	Y	Y	Y	Y	N	Y
9 Yates	Y	Y	N	Y	Y	Y	N	Y
10 Mikva	N	Y	N	Y	Y	Y	N	Y
11 Annunzio	Y	Y	Y	Y	Y	N	Y	Y
12 Crane	Y	N	Y	Y	N	Y	N	Y
13 McClory	Y	Y	Y	Y	Y	Y	Y	Y
14 Erlenborn	N	Y	N	Y	Y	Y	N	Y
15 Corcoran	Y	Y	Y	Y	Y	N	Y	Y
16 Anderson	Y	Y	Y	Y	Y	N	Y	Y
17 O'Brien	#	#	#	#	Y	N	Y	Y
18 Michel	Y	Y	Y	Y	Y	N	Y	Y
19 Railsback	Y	Y	Y	Y	Y	Y	N	#
20 Findley	Y	Y	Y	Y	Y	N	Y	Y
21 Madigan	Y	Y	Y	Y	Y	Y	N	Y
22 Shipley	Y	Y	Y	Y	Y	Y	N	Y
23 Price	Y	Y	Y	Y	Y	N	Y	Y
24 Simon	Y	Y	N	Y	Y	N	Y	Y
INDIANA								
1 Benjamin	N	Y	N	Y	Y	N	Y	Y
2 Fithian	Y	Y	N	Y	Y	Y	N	Y
3 Brademas	Y	Y	Y	Y	Y	N	Y	Y
4 Quayle	N	Y	Y	Y	Y	Y	N	Y
5 Hillis	Y	Y	Y	Y	Y	Y	N	Y
6 Evans	Y	Y	N	Y	Y	N	N	Y
7 Myers, J.	Y	Y	Y	Y	Y	Y	N	Y
8 Cornwell	Y	Y	N	Y	Y	Y	N	Y
9 Hamilton	Y	Y	N	Y	Y	N	Y	Y
10 Sharp	Y	Y	N	Y	Y	N	Y	Y
11 Jacobs	Y	Y	N	N	Y	Y	N	Y
IOWA								
1 Leach	Y	Y	Y	Y	Y	Y	N	Y
2 Blouin	Y	Y	Y	Y	Y	N	Y	Y
3 Grassley	Y	Y	Y	Y	Y	Y	N	Y
4 Smith	Y	Y	Y	Y	Y	N	Y	Y
5 Harkin	Y	Y	N	Y	Y	N	Y	Y
6 Bedell	Y	Y	N	Y	N	N	N	Y

Democrats ***Republicans***

	269	270	271	272	273	274	275	276
KANSAS								
1 Sebelius	#	#	#	Y	Y	N	Y	Y
2 Keys	Y	Y	N	Y	Y	Y	Y	Y
3 Winn	Y	Y	Y	Y	Y	Y	N	Y
4 Glickman	Y	Y	N	Y	Y	Y	N	Y
5 Skubitz	Y	Y	Y	Y	Y	N	Y	Y
KENTUCKY								
1 Hubbard	Y	Y	Y	Y	Y	N	?	?
2 Natcher	Y	Y	Y	Y	Y	N	Y	Y
3 Mazzoli	Y	Y	N	Y	Y	N	Y	†
4 Snyder	Y	Y	Y	Y	Y	Y	N	Y
5 Carter	?	?	?	?	?	?	?	?
6 Breckinridge	?	?	?	?	?	?	?	?
7 Perkins	Y	Y	Y	Y	Y	N	Y	Y
LOUISIANA								
1 Livingston	Y	Y	Y	Y	Y	Y	N	Y
2 Boggs	Y	Y	Y	Y	Y	N	Y	Y
3 Treen	Y	Y	Y	Y	Y	Y	N	Y
4 Waggonner	Y	Y	Y	Y	N	Y	N	Y
5 Huckaby	Y	Y	Y	Y	Y	Y	N	Y
6 Moore	Y	Y	Y	Y	Y	Y	N	Y
7 Breaux	Y	Y	Y	Y	Y	Y	N	Y
8 Long	?	?	?	Y	Y	Y	Y	Y
MAINE								
1 Emery	Y	Y	Y	Y	Y	Y	N	Y
2 Cohen	Y	Y	Y	Y	Y	Y	N	Y
MARYLAND								
1 Bauman	N	Y	Y	Y	Y	Y	N	Y
2 Long	Y	Y	Y	Y	Y	Y	N	Y
3 Mikulski	Y	Y	N	Y	Y	Y	N	Y
4 Holt	Y	Y	Y	Y	Y	Y	N	Y
5 Spellman	Y	Y	N	Y	Y	Y	N	Y
6 Byron	Y	Y	Y	Y	Y	Y	N	Y
7 Mitchell	Y	Y	Y	N	Y	P	P	Y
8 Steers	Y	Y	Y	Y	Y	N	Y	Y
MASSACHUSETTS								
1 Conte	Y	Y	Y	Y	Y	N	Y	Y
2 Boland	Y	Y	N	Y	Y	N	Y	Y
3 Early	Y	Y	N	Y	Y	N	Y	Y
4 Drinan	N	Y	N	Y	Y	N	N	Y
5 Tsongas	Y	Y	N	Y	Y	N	Y	Y
6 Harrington	Y	#	▮	Y	Y	N	Y	Y
7 Markey	Y	Y	N	Y	Y	N	Y	Y
8 O'Neill								
9 Moakley	Y	Y	#	Y	Y	N	Y	Y
10 Heckler	Y	Y	N	Y	Y	N	N	Y
11 Burke	Y	Y	N	Y	Y	N	Y	Y
12 Studds	Y	Y	N	Y	Y	N	Y	Y
MICHIGAN								
1 Conyers	#	#	▮	#	Y	N	Y	Y
2 Pursell	?	Y	?	?	Y	Y	N	Y
3 Brown	Y	Y	Y	N	N	N	Y	Y
4 Stockman	Y	Y	Y	Y	Y	Y	N	Y
5 Sawyer	Y	Y	Y	Y	Y	Y	N	Y
6 Carr	Y	Y	N	Y	Y	N	Y	Y
7 Kildee	Y	Y	N	Y	Y	N	Y	Y
8 Traxler	Y	Y	N	N	Y	N	Y	Y
9 Vander Jagt	Y	Y	Y	Y	Y	Y	N	Y
10 Cederberg	Y	Y	Y	?	Y	N	Y	Y
11 Ruppe	Y	Y	Y	Y	Y	N	#	Y
12 Bonior	Y	Y	N	Y	Y	N	Y	Y
13 Diggs	Y	#	▮	#	Y	X	✓	#
14 Nedzi	Y	Y	N	Y	Y	N	Y	Y
15 Ford	?	?	?	?	?	X	✓	?
16 Dingell	Y	Y	N	Y	Y	Y	N	Y
17 Brodhead	?	Y	N	Y	Y	N	Y	Y
18 Blanchard	Y	Y	N	Y	Y	N	Y	Y
19 Broomfield	Y	Y	Y	Y	Y	Y	N	Y
MINNESOTA								
1 Quie	#	#	#	#	Y	Y	N	Y
2 Hagedorn	Y	Y	Y	Y	Y	Y	N	Y
3 Frenzel	Y	Y	Y	?	?	?	?	?
4 Vento	Y	Y	N	Y	Y	?	?	?
5 Fraser	#	#	▮	#	Y	N	Y	#
6 Nolan	?	?	?	?	Y	N	Y	Y
7 Stangeland	Y	Y	Y	Y	Y	Y	N	Y
8 Oberstar	Y	Y	N	Y	Y	N	Y	Y
MISSISSIPPI								
1 Whitten	#	#	#	#	#	▮	#	#
2 Bowen	Y	Y	Y	Y	Y	Y	N	Y
3 Montgomery	Y	Y	Y	Y	Y	Y	N	Y
4 Cochran	?	?	?	?	?	✓	?	?
5 Lott	Y	Y	Y	Y	Y	Y	N	Y
MISSOURI								
1 Clay	?	Y	Y	Y	Y	N	Y	Y
2 Young	Y	Y	Y	Y	Y	N	Y	Y
3 Gephardt	Y	Y	Y	Y	Y	Y	N	Y
4 Skelton	#	#	#	#	Y	Y	N	Y
5 Bolling	#	Y	N	Y	Y	N	Y	Y
6 Coleman	N	Y	Y	Y	Y	Y	N	Y
7 Taylor	Y	Y	Y	Y	Y	Y	N	Y
8 Ichord	Y	Y	N	Y	Y	Y	N	Y
9 Volkmer	N	Y	N	Y	Y	Y	Y	Y
10 Burlison	Y	Y	N	Y	Y	N	Y	Y
MONTANA								
1 Baucus	#	#	#	#	#	▮	▮	#
2 Marlenee	Y	Y	Y	Y	Y	Y	N	Y
NEBRASKA								
1 Thone	Y	Y	Y	Y	Y	Y	N	Y
2 Cavanaugh	Y	Y	N	Y	Y	Y	N	Y
3 Smith	Y	Y	Y	Y	Y	Y	N	Y
NEVADA								
AL Santini	#	#	▮	#	Y	Y	N	Y
NEW HAMPSHIRE								
1 D'Amours	Y	Y	N	Y	Y	Y	N	Y
2 Cleveland	Y	Y	N	Y	Y	Y	N	Y
NEW JERSEY								
1 Florio	Y	Y	N	Y	Y	Y	Y	Y
2 Hughes	#	#	▮	Y	Y	Y	N	Y
3 Howard	#	Y	N	Y	Y	N	Y	#
4 Thompson	#	#	#	Y	Y	N	Y	Y
5 Fenwick	Y	N	N	Y	N	N	Y	Y
6 Forsythe	Y	Y	Y	N	Y	Y	N	Y
7 Maguire	N	Y	N	Y	Y	N	Y	?
8 Roe	Y	Y	Y	Y	Y	N	Y	Y
9 Hollenbeck	Y	Y	Y	Y	Y	Y	N	Y
10 Rodino	#	#	#	#	#	▮	#	#
11 Minish	Y	Y	N	Y	Y	Y	N	Y
12 Rinaldo	Y	Y	N	Y	Y	Y	N	Y
13 Meyner	Y	Y	N	#	Y	N	Y	Y
14 LeFante	Y	Y	N	Y	Y	N	#	#
15 Patten	Y	Y	N	Y	Y	N	Y	Y
NEW MEXICO								
1 Lujan	Y	Y	Y	Y	Y	Y	N	Y
2 Runnels	#	#	#	#	?	✓	X	#
NEW YORK								
1 Pike	Y	Y	N	N	Y	N	Y	Y
2 Downey	Y	Y	N	†	†	N	Y	Y
3 Ambro	Y	Y	N	?	Y	Y	N	Y
4 Lent	Y	Y	Y	Y	Y	Y	N	Y
5 Wydler	Y	Y	Y	Y	Y	Y	N	Y
6 Wolff	Y	Y	N	Y	Y	N	Y	Y
7 Addabbo	Y	Y	N	Y	Y	N	Y	Y
8 Rosenthal	#	#	▮	Y	Y	N	Y	Y
9 Delaney	Y	Y	N	Y	Y	Y	N	Y
10 Biaggi	Y	Y	Y	Y	Y	N	Y	Y
11 Scheuer	Y	Y	N	Y	Y	N	Y	Y
12 Chisholm	Y	Y	N	#	Y	N	Y	Y
13 Solarz	Y	Y	N	Y	Y	X	Y	Y
14 Richmond	Y	Y	N	Y	Y	N	Y	Y
15 Zeferetti	Y	Y	N	Y	Y	Y	N	Y
16 Holtzman	†	†	-	Y	Y	N	Y	Y
17 Murphy	Y	Y	Y	Y	#	▮	✓	#
18 Green	#	#	#	Y	Y	N	Y	Y
19 Rangel	Y	Y	N	Y	Y	N	Y	Y
20 Weiss	Y	Y	N	Y	Y	N	Y	Y
21 Garcia	Y	Y	N	Y	Y	N	Y	Y
22 Bingham	Y	Y	N	Y	Y	N	Y	Y
23 Caputo	Y	Y	N	Y	Y	Y	N	Y
24 Ottinger	Y	Y	N	Y	Y	N	Y	Y
25 Fish	Y	Y	Y	Y	Y	Y	N	Y
26 Gilman	Y	Y	?	Y	Y	Y	N	Y
27 McHugh	Y	Y	N	Y	Y	?	?	Y
28 Stratton	Y	Y	Y	Y	Y	Y	N	Y
29 Pattison	#	Y	N	Y	Y	Y	N	Y
30 McEwen	?	Y	Y	Y	Y	Y	N	Y
31 Mitchell	Y	Y	Y	Y	Y	Y	▮	#
32 Hanley	Y	Y	Y	Y	Y	Y	Y	Y
33 Walsh	Y	Y	Y	Y	Y	Y	Y	Y
34 Horton	Y	Y	Y	Y	Y	N	Y	Y
35 Conable	Y	Y	Y	Y	Y	Y	N	Y
36 LaFalce	Y	Y	Y	Y	Y	N	N	Y
37 Nowak	Y	Y	N	#	Y	N	Y	Y
38 Kemp	Y	Y	Y	Y	Y	N	Y	Y
39 Lundine	Y	Y	N	#	Y	N	Y	Y
NORTH CAROLINA								
1 Jones	Y	Y	Y	Y	Y	N	Y	Y
2 Fountain	Y	Y	Y	Y	Y	Y	Y	Y
3 Whitley	Y	Y	Y	Y	Y	N	Y	Y
4 Andrews	Y	Y	Y	Y	Y	Y	N	Y
5 Neal	Y	Y	N	Y	Y	Y	X	#
6 Preyer	Y	Y	Y	Y	Y	N	Y	Y
7 Rose	Y	Y	N	Y	Y	N	Y	Y
8 Hefner	Y	Y	Y	Y	Y	N	Y	Y
9 Martin	#	#	#	#	Y	Y	N	Y
10 Broyhill	?	?	?	Y	Y	Y	N	Y
11 Gudger	Y	Y	Y	Y	Y	Y	N	Y
NORTH DAKOTA								
AL Andrews	Y	Y	Y	Y	Y	Y	N	Y
OHIO								
1 Gradison	Y	Y	Y	Y	Y	Y	N	Y
2 Luken	Y	Y	Y	Y	Y	N	N	Y
3 Whalen	Y	Y	Y	Y	Y	N	Y	Y
4 Guyer	Y	Y	Y	Y	Y	Y	Y	Y
5 Latta	Y	Y	Y	Y	Y	Y	N	Y
6 Harsha	Y	Y	Y	Y	Y	Y	N	Y
7 Brown	Y	Y	N	Y	Y	Y	N	Y
8 Kindness	Y	Y	Y	Y	Y	Y	?	Y
9 Ashley	Y	Y	Y	Y	Y	Y	Y	Y
10 Miller	Y	Y	Y	Y	Y	Y	N	Y
11 Stanton	Y	Y	Y	Y	Y	N	Y	Y
12 Devine	Y	Y	Y	Y	Y	Y	N	Y
13 Pease	Y	Y	N	Y	Y	Y	N	Y
14 Seiberling	Y	Y	Y	#	Y	N	Y	Y
15 Wylie	Y	Y	Y	Y	Y	Y	N	Y
16 Regula	Y	Y	Y	Y	Y	Y	Y	Y
17 Ashbrook	#	#	▮	Y	Y	Y	N	Y
18 Applegate	Y	Y	Y	Y	Y	N	Y	Y
19 Carney	Y	Y	N	Y	Y	Y	N	Y
20 Oakar	Y	Y	Y	?	?	?	?	?
21 Stokes	Y	Y	Y	#	Y	N	Y	#
22 Vanik	Y	Y	N	Y	Y	Y	N	Y
23 Mottl	N	Y	Y	Y	Y	Y	N	Y
OKLAHOMA								
1 Jones	Y	Y	Y	Y	Y	N	Y	Y
2 Risenhoover	Y	Y	Y	?	Y	N	Y	Y
3 Watkins	Y	Y	Y	Y	Y	Y	N	Y
4 Steed	Y	Y	Y	Y	Y	N	Y	Y
5 Edwards	Y	Y	Y	Y	Y	Y	N	Y
6 English	Y	Y	Y	Y	Y	Y	N	Y
OREGON								
1 AuCoin	#	#	?	#	#	?	?	#
2 Ullman	Y	Y	Y	Y	#	N	Y	Y
3 Duncan	Y	Y	Y	Y	Y	N	Y	Y
4 Weaver	Y	Y	N	Y	Y	Y	N	Y
PENNSYLVANIA								
1 Myers, M.	?	?	?	?	?	✓	X	?
2 Nix	?	?	?	?	?	?	?	?
3 Lederer	Y	Y	N	#	#	✓	X	?
4 Eilberg	▮	#	#	#	#	▮	#	#
5 Schulze	?	?	?	?	?	?	?	?
6 Yatron	#	#	#	Y	Y	Y	N	Y
7 Edgar	Y	Y	N	Y	Y	Y	N	Y
8 Kostmayer	Y	Y	N	Y	Y	Y	N	?
9 Shuster	Y	Y	Y	Y	Y	Y	N	Y
10 McDade	#	#	?	#	#	?	#	#
11 Flood	#	?	#	#	#	N	Y	Y
12 Murtha	Y	Y	Y	Y	Y	Y	N	Y
13 Coughlin	Y	Y	Y	?	Y	Y	N	Y
14 Moorhead	Y	Y	N	#	#	▮	#	#
15 Rooney	?	?	?	?	?	?	?	?
16 Walker	Y	Y	Y	?	?	?	?	?
17 Ertel	?	?	?	Y	Y	Y	N	Y
18 Walgren	Y	Y	N	?	?	?	?	?
19 Goodling, W.	?	Y	Y	N	Y	N	N	Y
20 Gaydos	Y	Y	N	?	?	?	?	?
21 Dent	#	#	#	#	#	#	▮	#
22 Murphy	Y	Y	#	#	#	?	?	#
23 Ammerman	Y	Y	N	Y	Y	N	Y	Y
24 Marks	Y	Y	Y	Y	Y	N	Y	Y
25 Myers, G.	Y	Y	N	Y	Y	N	Y	Y
RHODE ISLAND								
1 St Germain	Y	Y	N	?	Y	N	Y	Y
2 Beard	Y	Y	N	Y	Y	X	Y	Y
SOUTH CAROLINA								
1 Davis	Y	Y	Y	?	Y	✓	X	?
2 Spence	Y	Y	Y	Y	Y	Y	N	Y
3 Derrick	Y	Y	N	Y	Y	Y	N	Y
4 Mann	?	?	?	Y	Y	N	Y	Y
5 Holland	#	#	#	#	Y	N	Y	Y
6 Jenrette	Y	Y	N	Y	Y	N	Y	Y
SOUTH DAKOTA								
1 Pressler	?	?	?	?	?	?	?	?
2 Abdnor	Y	Y	Y	Y	Y	Y	N	Y
TENNESSEE								
1 Quillen	#	#	#	Y	Y	Y	N	Y
2 Duncan	Y	Y	Y	Y	Y	Y	N	Y
3 Lloyd	Y	Y	Y	Y	Y	N	Y	Y
4 Gore	Y	Y	N	Y	Y	Y	N	Y
5 Allen	Y	Y	Y	?	Y	N	Y	Y
6 Beard	?	Y	Y	Y	Y	Y	N	Y
7 Jones	Y	Y	Y	Y	Y	Y	N	Y
8 Ford	?	?	?	?	Y	N	Y	Y
TEXAS								
1 Hall	Y	Y	Y	Y	Y	Y	N	Y
2 Wilson, C.	#	#	▮	Y	Y	N	Y	Y
3 Collins	Y	N	Y	Y	N	Y	N	Y
4 Roberts	Y	Y	Y	Y	Y	Y	N	Y
5 Mattox	Y	Y	N	Y	Y	N	Y	Y
6 Teague	?	?	?	?	?	?	?	?
7 Archer	Y	Y	Y	Y	Y	Y	N	Y
8 Eckhardt	?	?	?	Y	Y	N	?	Y
9 Brooks	Y	Y	Y	Y	Y	Y	N	Y
10 Pickle	Y	Y	Y	Y	Y	N	Y	Y
11 Poage	N	Y	Y	Y	Y	?	?	?
12 Wright	Y	Y	Y	Y	Y	N	Y	Y
13 Hightower	Y	Y	Y	Y	Y	N	N	Y
14 Young	?	?	?	?	Y	N	Y	?
15 de la Garza	Y	Y	Y	Y	Y	Y	N	Y
16 White	Y	†	Y	Y	Y	N	Y	Y
17 Burleson	Y	Y	Y	Y	Y	Y	N	Y
18 Jordan	Y	Y	Y	Y	Y	N	Y	Y
19 Mahon	Y	Y	Y	Y	Y	N	Y	Y
20 Gonzalez	Y	Y	Y	Y	Y	N	Y	Y
21 Krueger	#	#	#	Y	Y	N	Y	Y
22 Gammage	Y	Y	Y	Y	Y	Y	N	Y
23 Kazen	Y	Y	Y	Y	Y	Y	N	Y
24 Milford	Y	Y	Y	Y	N	Y	N	Y
UTAH								
1 McKay	Y	Y	N	#	Y	Y	N	Y
2 Marriott	Y	Y	Y	Y	Y	Y	N	Y
VERMONT								
AL Jeffords	Y	Y	Y	Y	Y	Y	Y	Y
VIRGINIA								
1 Trible	Y	Y	Y	Y	Y	Y	N	Y
2 Whitehurst	Y	Y	Y	Y	Y	Y	N	Y
3 Satterfield	Y	N	N	Y	N	Y	N	Y
4 Daniel	Y	Y	Y	Y	Y	Y	N	Y
5 Daniel	?	Y	N	Y	Y	Y	N	Y
6 Butler	N	N	N	Y	Y	N	N	Y
7 Robinson	Y	Y	Y	#	Y	Y	N	Y
8 Harris	Y	Y	N	Y	Y	N	Y	Y
9 Wampler	Y	Y	Y	Y	Y	Y	N	Y
10 Fisher	Y	Y	N	Y	Y	N	Y	Y
WASHINGTON								
1 Pritchard	Y	Y	Y	Y	Y	N	Y	Y
2 Meeds	Y	Y	Y	Y	Y	N	Y	Y
3 Bonker	#	Y	#	#	Y	Y	Y	Y
4 McCormack	Y	Y	Y	Y	Y	Y	N	Y
5 Foley	Y	Y	Y	Y	Y	N	Y	Y
6 Dicks	Y	Y	Y	Y	Y	N	Y	?
7 Cunningham	Y	Y	Y	Y	Y	Y	N	Y
WEST VIRGINIA								
1 Mollohan	Y	Y	Y	Y	Y	N	Y	Y
2 Staggers	Y	Y	Y	Y	Y	N	Y	Y
3 Slack	Y	Y	Y	Y	Y	N	Y	Y
4 Rahall	Y	Y	N	Y	Y	N	Y	Y
WISCONSIN								
1 Aspin	Y	Y	N	Y	Y	N	Y	Y
2 Kastenmeier	Y	Y	N	Y	Y	N	Y	Y
3 Baldus	Y	Y	N	Y	Y	N	Y	Y
4 Zablocki	Y	Y	Y	Y	Y	N	Y	Y
5 Reuss	#	#	#	Y	Y	N	Y	Y
6 Steiger	Y	Y	N	N	Y	N	Y	Y
7 Obey	Y	Y	N	Y	Y	N	Y	Y
8 Cornell	#	Y	N	Y	Y	Y	N	Y
9 Kasten	Y	Y	Y	#	#	#	▮	#
WYOMING								
AL Roncalio	Y	Y	N	?	Y	N	Y	Y

Democrats ***Republicans***

277. HR 11686. Energy Department — Military Programs. Price, D-Ill., motion that the House resolve itself into the Committee of the Whole for further consideration of the bill to authorize funds for the military-related activities of the Energy Department for fiscal 1979. Motion agreed to 355-4: R 123-2; D 232-2 (ND 156-1; SD 76-1), May 17, 1978.

278. HR 11686. Energy Department — Military Programs. Weiss, D-N.Y., amendment to remove discretionary authorization for production of enhanced radiation weapons (neutron bombs) if the president met certain conditions. Rejected 90-306: R 5-130; D 85-176 (ND 81-98; SD 4-78), May 17, 1978. A "nay" was a vote supporting the president's position.

279. HR 11686. Energy Department — Military Programs. Passage of the bill to authorize $2,897,090,000 for the national security programs of the Energy Department for fiscal 1979. Passed 348-46: R 133-1; D 215-45 (ND 132-45; SD 83-0), May 17, 1978.

280. S Con Res 80. Fiscal 1979 Budget Targets. Giaimo, D-Conn., motion to approve the conference version of the resolution setting the following budget targets for fiscal 1979: revenues of $447.9 billion, budget authority of $568.85 billion, outlays of $498.8 billion, a deficit of $50.9 billion and a public debt limit of $849.1 billion. Motion agreed to 201-198: R 2-133; D 199-65 (ND 134-47; SD 65-18), May 17, 1978. (Approval of the conference version completed action on the resolution.)

281. HR 12641. Temporary Debt Limit. Adoption of the rule (H Res 1176) providing for House floor consideration of the bill to provide for a temporary increase in the public debt limit. Adopted 320-77: R 76-59; D 244-18 (ND 170-9; SD 74-9), May 17, 1978.

282. HR 12641. Temporary Debt Limit. Passage of the bill to raise the public debt limit to $849.1 billion through Sept. 30, 1979, thus making the statutory limit conform to the fiscal 1979 budget target set in S Con Res 80 *(see vote 280, above)*. Rejected 167-228: R 5-129; D 162-99 (ND 127-51; SD 35-48), May 17, 1978.

283. HR 39. Alaska Lands. Adoption of the rule (H Res 1186) providing for House floor consideration of the bill to designate certain federal land in Alaska as national park, national forest, wildlife refuge, wild and scenic rivers and wilderness lands. Adopted 354-42: R 104-30; D 250-12 (ND 178-2; SD 72-10), May 17, 1978.

KEY

Y Voted for (yea).
✓ Paired for.
† Announced for.
# CQ Poll for.
N Voted against (nay).
X Paired against.
- Announced against.
▮ CQ Poll against.
P Voted "present."
● Voted "present" to avoid possible conflict of interest.
? Did not vote or otherwise make a position known.

	277	278	279	280	281	282	283
ALABAMA							
1 Edwards	Y	N	Y	N	Y	N	Y
2 Dickinson	Y	N	Y	N	Y	N	N
3 Nichols	Y	N	Y	Y	Y	N	Y
4 Bevill	Y	N	Y	Y	Y	Y	?
5 Flippo	Y	N	Y	Y	Y	N	Y
6 Buchanan	Y	N	Y	N	Y	N	Y
7 Flowers	Y	N	Y	Y	Y	N	Y
ALASKA							
AL Young	#	N	Y	N	N	N	N
ARIZONA							
1 Rhodes	Y	N	Y	N	Y	N	N
2 Udall	Y	Y	Y	Y	Y	Y	Y
3 Stump	Y	N	Y	N	N	N	N
4 Rudd	Y	N	Y	N	N	N	N
ARKANSAS							
1 Alexander	Y	N	Y	Y	Y	Y	Y
2 Tucker	#	▮	#	#	#	#	#
3 Hammerschmidt	Y	N	Y	N	N	N	Y
4 Thornton	?	?	?	?	?	?	?
CALIFORNIA							
1 Johnson	Y	N	Y	Y	Y	Y	Y
2 Clausen	Y	N	Y	N	N	N	Y
3 Moss	Y	N	Y	Y	Y	Y	Y
4 Leggett	Y	N	Y	N	Y	Y	Y
5 Burton, J.	?	Y	N	N	Y	N	Y
6 Burton, P.	Y	Y	N	N	Y	Y	Y
7 Miller	Y	Y	N	N	N	Y	Y
8 Dellums	#	Y	N	N	Y	Y	Y
9 Stark	Y	Y	N	N	Y	Y	Y
10 Edwards	Y	Y	N	N	Y	Y	Y
11 Ryan	Y	N	Y	Y	Y	Y	Y
12 McCloskey	?	?	?	X	?	X	?
13 Mineta	Y	Y	Y	Y	Y	Y	Y
14 McFall	Y	N	Y	Y	Y	Y	Y
15 Sisk	Y	N	Y	Y	Y	Y	Y
16 Panetta	Y	Y	Y	Y	Y	N	Y
17 Krebs	Y	N	Y	Y	Y	Y	Y
18 Ketchum	Y	N	Y	N	Y	N	N
19 Lagomarsino	Y	N	Y	N	N	N	Y
20 Goldwater	?	?	?	N	N	N	Y
21 Corman	Y	N	Y	Y	Y	Y	Y
22 Moorhead	Y	N	Y	N	N	N	Y
23 Beilenson	#	Y	N	Y	Y	Y	Y
24 Waxman	Y	Y	Y	Y	Y	Y	Y
25 Roybal	?	Y	N	Y	Y	Y	Y
26 Rousselot	Y	N	Y	N	N	N	N
27 Dornan	Y	N	Y	N	Y	N	N
28 Burke	#	✓	#	X	#	✓	#
29 Hawkins	Y	Y	Y	Y	Y	Y	Y
30 Danielson	Y	N	Y	Y	Y	Y	Y
31 Wilson, C.H.	#	▮	#	✓	#	▮	#
32 Anderson	Y	Y	Y	Y	N	N	Y
33 Clawson	Y	N	Y	N	N	N	N
34 Hannaford	Y	Y	Y	Y	Y	Y	Y
35 Lloyd	Y	N	Y	Y	Y	N	Y
36 Brown	Y	Y	N	N	Y	Y	Y
37 Pettis	Y	N	Y	N	Y	N	Y
38 Patterson	Y	N	Y	Y	Y	Y	Y
39 Wiggins	#	N	Y	N	Y	N	N
40 Badham	Y	N	Y	N	N	N	N
41 Wilson, B.	N	N	Y	N	Y	N	N
42 Van Deerlin	Y	N	Y	Y	Y	Y	Y
43 Burgener	Y	N	Y	N	Y	N	Y
COLORADO							
1 Schroeder	Y	Y	N	N	Y	N	Y
2 Wirth	Y	Y	Y	Y	Y	Y	Y
3 Evans	Y	N	Y	Y	Y	Y	Y
4 Johnson	Y	N	Y	N	Y	N	Y
5 Armstrong	Y	N	Y	N	N	N	Y
CONNECTICUT							
1 Cotter	Y	N	Y	Y	Y	Y	Y
2 Dodd	Y	N	Y	Y	Y	Y	Y
3 Giaimo	Y	N	Y	Y	Y	Y	Y
4 McKinney	Y	N	Y	N	Y	Y	Y
5 Sarasin	†	-	†	-	#	X	#
6 Moffett	?	✓	X	N	Y	N	Y
DELAWARE							
AL Evans	Y	N	Y	N	Y	N	Y
FLORIDA							
1 Sikes	Y	N	Y	Y	Y	N	Y
2 Fuqua	Y	N	Y	Y	Y	N	Y
3 Bennett	Y	N	Y	Y	Y	Y	Y
4 Chappell	Y	N	Y	Y	Y	N	Y
5 Kelly	#	N	Y	N	N	N	Y
6 Young	Y	N	Y	N	N	N	N
7 Gibbons	Y	N	Y	N	Y	N	Y
8 Ireland	Y	N	Y	N	Y	N	Y
9 Frey	?	?	?	?	?	X	?
10 Bafalis	Y	N	Y	N	N	N	Y
11 Rogers	Y	N	Y	Y	Y	N	Y
12 Burke	Y	N	Y	N	N	N	Y
13 Lehman	Y	Y	Y	Y	Y	Y	Y
14 Pepper	Y	N	Y	Y	Y	Y	Y
15 Fascell	Y	N	Y	Y	Y	Y	Y
GEORGIA							
1 Ginn	Y	N	Y	Y	Y	N	Y
2 Mathis	Y	N	Y	N	N	N	Y
3 Brinkley	Y	N	Y	Y	Y	N	Y
4 Levitas	Y	N	Y	N	Y	N	Y
5 Fowler	Y	N	Y	Y	Y	N	Y
6 Flynt	Y	N	Y	Y	Y	N	Y
7 McDonald	Y	N	Y	N	N	N	N
8 Evans	Y	N	Y	N	N	N	Y
9 Jenkins	Y	N	Y	Y	Y	Y	Y
10 Barnard	Y	N	Y	Y	Y	N	Y
HAWAII							
1 Heftel	Y	N	Y	Y	Y	N	Y
2 Akaka	Y	N	Y	Y	Y	Y	Y
IDAHO							
1 Symms	Y	N	Y	N	N	N	N
2 Hansen, G.	Y	N	Y	N	N	N	N
ILLINOIS							
1 Metcalfe	Y	Y	N	Y	Y	Y	Y
2 Murphy	Y	N	Y	Y	Y	Y	Y
3 Russo	Y	N	Y	N	N	N	Y
4 Derwinski	Y	N	Y	N	Y	Y	Y
5 Fary	Y	N	Y	Y	Y	Y	Y
6 Hyde	Y	N	Y	N	Y	N	Y
7 Collins	Y	Y	N	Y	?	✓	?
8 Rostenkowski	Y	N	Y	Y	Y	Y	Y
9 Yates	Y	Y	Y	Y	Y	Y	Y
10 Mikva	†	†	-	✓	†	†	†
11 Annunzio	Y	N	Y	Y	Y	Y	Y
12 Crane	#	▮	#	X	▮	▮	N
13 McClory	Y	N	Y	N	Y	N	Y
14 Erlenborn	Y	N	Y	N	Y	N	Y
15 Corcoran	Y	N	Y	N	Y	N	Y
16 Anderson	Y	N	Y	N	Y	N	Y
17 O'Brien	#	N	Y	N	Y	N	Y
18 Michel	Y	N	Y	N	Y	N	N
19 Railsback	Y	N	Y	N	Y	N	Y
20 Findley	Y	N	Y	N	Y	Y	Y
21 Madigan	Y	N	Y	N	Y	N	Y
22 Shipley	Y	N	Y	Y	Y	Y	Y
23 Price	Y	N	Y	Y	Y	Y	Y
24 Simon	Y	Y	Y	Y	Y	Y	Y
INDIANA							
1 Benjamin	Y	N	Y	Y	Y	N	Y
2 Fithian	Y	N	Y	N	Y	N	Y
3 Brademas	Y	N	Y	Y	†	✓	†
4 Quayle	N	N	Y	N	N	N	Y
5 Hillis	Y	N	Y	N	N	N	Y
6 Evans	Y	N	Y	N	Y	N	Y
7 Myers, J.	Y	N	Y	N	N	N	Y
8 Cornwell	Y	N	Y	Y	Y	N	Y
9 Hamilton	Y	N	Y	Y	Y	Y	Y
10 Sharp	Y	Y	Y	Y	Y	Y	Y
11 Jacobs	Y	Y	Y	N	N	N	Y
IOWA							
1 Leach	Y	N	Y	N	N	N	Y
2 Blouin	Y	Y	Y	N	Y	N	Y
3 Grassley	Y	N	Y	N	N	N	N
4 Smith	Y	N	Y	Y	Y	Y	Y
5 Harkin	Y	Y	Y	N	Y	N	Y
6 Bedell	Y	Y	N	N	Y	Y	Y

Democrats ***Republicans***

	277	278	279	280	281	282	283
KANSAS							
1 Sebelius	Y	N	Y	N	Y	N	Y
2 Keys	Y	Y	Y	N	Y	N	Y
3 Winn	Y	N	Y	N	Y	N	Y
4 Glickman	Y	Y	Y	N	Y	N	Y
5 Skubitz	?	N	Y	N	Y	N	Y
KENTUCKY							
1 Hubbard	?	N	Y	Y	N	N	Y
2 Natcher	Y	N	Y	Y	Y	Y	Y
3 Mazzoli	Y	Y	Y	Y	Y	N	Y
4 Snyder	Y	N	Y	N	N	N	Y
5 Carter	?	?	?	X	?	X	?
6 Breckinridge	Y	N	Y	Y	Y	Y	Y
7 Perkins	Y	N	Y	Y	Y	Y	Y
LOUISIANA							
1 Livingston	?	N	Y	N	Y	N	Y
2 Boggs	#	N	Y	Y	Y	Y	Y
3 Treen	Y	N	Y	N	Y	N	Y
4 Waggonner	Y	N	Y	Y	Y	Y	N
5 Huckaby	?	X	?	X	?	✓	?
6 Moore	Y	N	Y	N	N	N	Y
7 Breaux	Y	N	Y	N	Y	N	N
8 Long	Y	N	Y	Y	Y	Y	Y
MAINE							
1 Emery	Y	N	Y	N	Y	N	Y
2 Cohen	Y	N	Y	N	Y	N	Y
MARYLAND							
1 Bauman	Y	N	Y	N	N	N	N
2 Long	Y	N	Y	Y	Y	Y	Y
3 Mikulski	#	Y	N	Y	Y	N	Y
4 Holt	Y	N	Y	N	N	N	N
5 Spellman	Y	N	Y	Y	Y	Y	Y
6 Byron	Y	N	Y	Y	Y	N	Y
7 Mitchell	N	Y	N	N	#	✓	Y
8 Steers	Y	Y	Y	Y	Y	Y	Y
MASSACHUSETTS							
1 Conte	Y	N	Y	Y	Y	Y	Y
2 Boland	Y	N	Y	Y	Y	Y	Y
3 Early	Y	Y	N	N	N	N	Y
4 Drinan	Y	Y	N	Y	Y	Y	Y
5 Tsongas	Y	Y	Y	Y	Y	Y	Y
6 Harrington	#	Y	N	Y	Y	Y	Y
7 Markey	Y	Y	N	N	Y	Y	Y
8 O'Neill							
9 Moakley	Y	Y	Y	Y	Y	Y	Y
10 Heckler	?	N	Y	N	Y	N	Y
11 Burke	Y	N	Y	Y	Y	Y	Y
12 Studds	Y	Y	N	Y	Y	Y	Y
MICHIGAN							
1 Conyers	#	✓	X	X	#	#	#
2 Pursell	Y	Y	Y	N	Y	N	Y
3 Brown	Y	N	Y	N	Y	N	Y
4 Stockman	Y	▮	#	▮	#	▮	#
5 Sawyer	Y	N	Y	N	Y	N	Y
6 Carr	Y	N	Y	N	Y	N	Y
7 Kildee	Y	Y	N	N	Y	Y	Y
8 Traxler	Y	N	#	Y	Y	N	Y
9 Vander Jagt	Y	N	Y	N	Y	N	Y
10 Cederberg	Y	N	Y	N	Y	N	Y
11 Ruppe	Y	N	#	N	Y	N	Y
12 Bonior	Y	Y	N	Y	Y	Y	Y
13 Diggs	#	Y	N	Y	#	✓	#
14 Nedzi	Y	N	Y	Y	Y	Y	Y
15 Ford	Y	N	?	Y	Y	Y	Y
16 Dingell	?	N	Y	Y	Y	Y	Y
17 Brodhead	Y	Y	?	Y	Y	Y	Y
18 Blanchard	Y	N	Y	Y	Y	Y	Y
19 Broomfield	Y	N	Y	N	N	N	Y
MINNESOTA							
1 Quie	Y	N	Y	N	Y	N	Y
2 Hagedorn	Y	N	Y	N	Y	N	N
3 Frenzel	Y	N	Y	N	Y	N	Y
4 Vento	?	N	Y	N	Y	?	Y
5 Fraser	Y	Y	Y	Y	Y	Y	Y
6 Nolan	Y	Y	N	N	Y	N	Y
7 Stangeland	Y	N	Y	N	N	N	N
8 Oberstar	Y	Y	Y	Y	Y	Y	Y
MISSISSIPPI							
1 Whitten	#	▮	#	#	#	▮	#
2 Bowen	Y	N	Y	Y	Y	N	N
3 Montgomery	Y	N	Y	Y	Y	N	N
4 Cochran	?	?	?	?	?	X	?
5 Lott	#	N	Y	N	N	N	N
MISSOURI							
1 Clay	?	Y	N	Y	Y	Y	Y
2 Young	Y	N	Y	Y	Y	N	Y
3 Gephardt	Y	N	Y	Y	Y	Y	Y
4 Skelton	Y	N	Y	Y	Y	N	Y
5 Bolling	Y	N	Y	Y	Y	Y	Y
6 Coleman	Y	N	Y	N	N	N	Y
7 Taylor	Y	N	Y	N	N	N	N
8 Ichord	Y	N	Y	N	N	N	Y
9 Volkmer	Y	Y	Y	Y	Y	N	Y
10 Burlison	Y	N	Y	Y	Y	Y	Y
MONTANA							
1 Baucus	#	X	✓	✓	▮	▮	#
2 Marlenee	Y	Y	Y	N	N	N	Y
NEBRASKA							
1 Thone	Y	N	Y	N	Y	N	Y
2 Cavanaugh	Y	Y	Y	N	Y	N	Y
3 Smith	Y	N	Y	N	Y	N	Y
NEVADA							
AL Santini	Y	N	Y	Y	Y	N	Y
NEW HAMPSHIRE							
1 D'Amours	Y	N	Y	Y	Y	N	Y
2 Cleveland	Y	N	Y	N	Y	N	Y
NEW JERSEY							
1 Florio	Y	N	Y	Y	Y	N	Y
2 Hughes	Y	N	Y	Y	Y	N	Y
3 Howard	Y	N	Y	Y	Y	Y	Y
4 Thompson	Y	Y	N	Y	Y	Y	Y
5 Fenwick	Y	N	Y	N	Y	N	Y
6 Forsythe	Y	Y	N	N	Y	N	Y
7 Maguire	Y	Y	N	Y	Y	N	Y
8 Roe	Y	N	Y	Y	Y	Y	Y
9 Hollenbeck	Y	N	Y	N	Y	N	Y
10 Rodino	#	▮	✓	✓	#	✓	†
11 Minish	Y	N	Y	Y	Y	N	Y
12 Rinaldo	#	N	Y	N	Y	N	Y
13 Meyner	Y	N	Y	Y	Y	Y	Y
14 LeFante	Y	N	Y	Y	Y	Y	Y
15 Patten	Y	N	Y	Y	Y	Y	Y
NEW MEXICO							
1 Lujan	Y	N	Y	N	N	N	Y
2 Runnels	#	?	?	X	?	X	#
NEW YORK							
1 Pike	Y	N	Y	N	Y	N	Y
2 Downey	Y	N	Y	N	Y	Y	Y
3 Ambro	?	N	Y	Y	Y	Y	Y
4 Lent	Y	N	Y	N	N	N	Y
5 Wydler	Y	N	Y	N	N	N	Y
6 Wolff	#	Y	Y	Y	Y	N	Y
7 Addabbo	Y	Y	Y	N	Y	Y	Y
8 Rosenthal	Y	Y	N	Y	Y	Y	Y
9 Delaney	Y	N	Y	Y	Y	Y	Y
10 Biaggi	Y	Y	Y	Y	Y	Y	#
11 Scheuer	?	?	?	?	?	?	?
12 Chisholm	#	Y	N	Y	Y	Y	Y
13 Solarz	Y	N	Y	Y	Y	Y	Y
14 Richmond	Y	Y	N	Y	Y	Y	Y
15 Zeferetti	Y	N	Y	Y	Y	N	Y
16 Holtzman	Y	Y	N	N	Y	Y	Y
17 Murphy	#	▮	#	✓	#	Y	Y
18 Green	Y	N	Y	N	Y	N	Y
19 Rangel	Y	Y	N	Y	?	✓	Y
20 Weiss	Y	Y	N	N	Y	Y	Y
21 Garcia	Y	Y	N	Y	Y	Y	Y
22 Bingham	Y	Y	Y	Y	Y	Y	Y
23 Caputo	Y	N	Y	N	N	N	Y
24 Ottinger	Y	Y	N	N	Y	Y	Y
25 Fish	Y	N	Y	N	Y	N	Y
26 Gilman	Y	N	Y	N	Y	N	Y
27 McHugh	Y	Y	Y	N	Y	Y	Y
28 Stratton	Y	N	Y	Y	Y	Y	Y
29 Pattison	#	N	N	Y	Y	#	#
30 McEwen	?	N	Y	N	Y	N	Y
31 Mitchell	Y	N	Y	N	Y	N	Y
32 Hanley	Y	N	Y	Y	Y	N	Y
33 Walsh	Y	N	Y	N	Y	N	Y
34 Horton	Y	N	Y	N	Y	N	Y
35 Conable	Y	N	Y	N	Y	N	Y
36 LaFalce	Y	N	Y	N	Y	N	Y
37 Nowak	Y	Y	Y	Y	Y	N	Y
38 Kemp	Y	N	Y	N	N	N	?
39 Lundine	#	Y	Y	N	Y	Y	Y
NORTH CAROLINA							
1 Jones	Y	N	Y	Y	Y	Y	Y
2 Fountain	Y	N	Y	N	Y	N	Y
3 Whitley	Y	N	Y	N	Y	N	Y
4 Andrews	Y	N	Y	Y	Y	N	Y
5 Neal	Y	N	Y	N	N	N	Y
6 Preyer	Y	N	Y	Y	Y	Y	Y
7 Rose	#	N	Y	Y	Y	Y	Y
8 Hefner	Y	N	Y	Y	Y	N	Y
9 Martin	Y	N	Y	N	Y	N	Y
10 Broyhill	Y	N	Y	N	N	N	N
11 Gudger	Y	N	Y	N	Y	N	Y
NORTH DAKOTA							
AL Andrews	Y	N	Y	N	N	N	Y
OHIO							
1 Gradison	Y	N	Y	N	Y	N	Y
2 Luken	Y	N	Y	Y	Y	N	Y
3 Whalen	#	▮	#	#	#	#	Y
4 Guyer	Y	N	Y	N	Y	X	#
5 Latta	Y	N	Y	N	N	N	Y
6 Harsha	Y	N	Y	N	N	N	Y
7 Brown	Y	N	Y	N	Y	N	N
8 Kindness	Y	X	?	X	?	X	?
9 Ashley	Y	N	Y	Y	Y	Y	Y
10 Miller	Y	N	Y	N	N	N	Y
11 Stanton	Y	N	Y	N	Y	N	Y
12 Devine	Y	N	Y	N	N	N	Y
13 Pease	Y	Y	Y	Y	Y	Y	Y
14 Seiberling	Y	Y	N	Y	Y	Y	Y
15 Wylie	Y	N	Y	N	N	N	Y
16 Regula	Y	N	Y	N	Y	N	Y
17 Ashbrook	Y	N	Y	N	N	N	N
18 Applegate	Y	N	Y	Y	Y	Y	Y
19 Carney	Y	N	Y	Y	Y	Y	Y
20 Oakar	?	Y	N	N	Y	N	?
21 Stokes	#	✓	X	✓	#	✓	#
22 Vanik	#	Y	Y	Y	Y	Y	Y
23 Mottl	Y	N	Y	N	N	N	Y
OKLAHOMA							
1 Jones	Y	N	Y	Y	Y	Y	Y
2 Risenhoover	Y	N	Y	Y	Y	N	N
3 Watkins	Y	N	Y	Y	Y	Y	N
4 Steed	Y	N	Y	Y	Y	Y	Y
5 Edwards	?	N	Y	N	N	N	N
6 English	Y	N	Y	Y	N	N	Y
OREGON							
1 AuCoin	#	#	?	X	#	▮	†
2 Ullman	Y	N	Y	Y	Y	Y	Y
3 Duncan	Y	N	Y	Y	Y	Y	Y
4 Weaver	Y	Y	N	N	Y	N	Y
PENNSYLVANIA							
1 Myers, M.	?	?	?	✓	Y	Y	Y
2 Nix	?	?	?	✓	?	✓	?
3 Lederer	Y	N	Y	Y	Y	Y	Y
4 Eilberg	#	Y	Y	Y	Y	Y	Y
5 Schulze	Y	N	Y	N	Y	N	Y
6 Yatron	Y	N	Y	Y	N	N	Y
7 Edgar	Y	Y	N	Y	Y	Y	Y
8 Kostmayer	?	Y	Y	N	Y	N	Y
9 Shuster	Y	N	Y	N	N	N	N
10 McDade	#	X	#	X	#	X	#
11 Flood	Y	N	Y	Y	Y	Y	Y
12 Murtha	Y	N	Y	Y	Y	Y	Y
13 Coughlin	Y	N	Y	N	N	N	Y
14 Moorhead	Y	N	Y	Y	Y	Y	Y
15 Rooney	Y	?	✓	Y	Y	Y	Y
16 Walker	Y	N	Y	N	N	N	Y
17 Ertel	Y	N	Y	N	Y	N	Y
18 Walgren	Y	Y	Y	Y	Y	N	Y
19 Goodling, W.	Y	N	Y	N	N	N	Y
20 Gaydos	?	?	?	Y	Y	N	Y
21 Dent	#	N	Y	✓	#	✓	Y
22 Murphy	#	▮	#	?	Y	Y	Y
23 Ammerman	Y	N	Y	Y	Y	Y	Y
24 Marks	Y	N	Y	N	Y	N	Y
25 Myers, G.	Y	N	Y	N	Y	N	Y
RHODE ISLAND							
1 St Germain	Y	Y	Y	Y	Y	Y	Y
2 Beard	Y	N	Y	Y	Y	Y	Y
SOUTH CAROLINA							
1 Davis	Y	N	Y	N	N	N	Y
2 Spence	Y	N	Y	N	N	N	Y
3 Derrick	Y	N	Y	Y	Y	N	Y
4 Mann	Y	N	Y	Y	Y	N	Y
5 Holland	Y	▮	#	?	#	?	Y
6 Jenrette	?	N	Y	Y	Y	N	Y
SOUTH DAKOTA							
1 Pressler	Y	Y	Y	-	N	N	Y
2 Abdnor	#	N	Y	N	Y	N	Y
TENNESSEE							
1 Quillen	Y	N	Y	N	N	N	Y
2 Duncan	Y	N	Y	N	N	N	#
3 Lloyd	Y	N	Y	Y	Y	N	Y
4 Gore	Y	N	Y	Y	Y	N	Y
5 Allen	Y	N	Y	N	Y	N	Y
6 Beard	Y	N	Y	N	?	X	?
7 Jones	Y	N	Y	Y	Y	N	Y
8 Ford	Y	Y	Y	Y	Y	Y	Y
TEXAS							
1 Hall	#	N	Y	Y	Y	N	N
2 Wilson, C.	Y	▮	Y	Y	Y	Y	Y
3 Collins	Y	N	Y	N	N	N	Y
4 Roberts	Y	N	Y	Y	Y	Y	?
5 Mattox	N	N	Y	Y	Y	Y	Y
6 Teague	?	?	?	✓	?	✓	?
7 Archer	Y	N	Y	N	N	N	Y
8 Eckhardt	Y	Y	Y	Y	Y	Y	Y
9 Brooks	Y	N	Y	Y	Y	Y	Y
10 Pickle	Y	N	Y	Y	Y	Y	Y
11 Poage	Y	N	Y	Y	Y	N	Y
12 Wright	?	N	Y	Y	Y	Y	Y
13 Hightower	Y	N	Y	Y	Y	N	Y
14 Young	?	?	?	?	?	?	?
15 de la Garza	Y	N	Y	Y	Y	N	Y
16 White	Y	N	Y	Y	Y	N	Y
17 Burleson	Y	N	Y	Y	Y	Y	N
18 Jordan	Y	N	Y	Y	Y	Y	Y
19 Mahon	Y	N	Y	Y	Y	Y	Y
20 Gonzalez	Y	N	Y	Y	Y	Y	Y
21 Krueger	#	N	Y	N	Y	Y	Y
22 Gammage	Y	N	Y	N	N	N	Y
23 Kazen	Y	N	Y	Y	Y	Y	Y
24 Milford	Y	N	Y	Y	Y	Y	Y
UTAH							
1 McKay	Y	N	Y	Y	Y	Y	Y
2 Marriott	Y	N	Y	N	Y	N	Y
VERMONT							
AL Jeffords	Y	N	Y	N	Y	N	Y
VIRGINIA							
1 Trible	Y	N	Y	N	Y	N	Y
2 Whitehurst	Y	N	Y	N	Y	N	Y
3 Satterfield	Y	N	Y	N	N	N	N
4 Daniel	Y	N	Y	N	N	N	Y
5 Daniel	Y	N	Y	N	Y	N	Y
6 Butler	Y	N	Y	N	Y	N	Y
7 Robinson	Y	N	Y	N	N	N	N
8 Harris	Y	N	Y	N	Y	N	Y
9 Wampler	Y	N	Y	N	N	N	N
10 Fisher	Y	N	Y	Y	Y	Y	Y
WASHINGTON							
1 Pritchard	Y	N	Y	N	Y	N	Y
2 Meeds	#	N	Y	Y	Y	Y	N
3 Bonker	Y	Y	Y	✓	Y	Y	Y
4 McCormack	Y	N	Y	Y	Y	Y	Y
5 Foley	Y	N	Y	Y	Y	Y	Y
6 Dicks	Y	N	Y	Y	Y	Y	Y
7 Cunningham	Y	N	Y	N	Y	N	Y
WEST VIRGINIA							
1 Mollohan	Y	N	Y	Y	Y	Y	Y
2 Staggers	?	N	Y	Y	Y	Y	Y
3 Slack	?	N	Y	Y	Y	Y	Y
4 Rahall	Y	Y	N	Y	Y	N	Y
WISCONSIN							
1 Aspin	?	N	Y	Y	Y	Y	Y
2 Kastenmeier	Y	Y	N	N	Y	Y	Y
3 Baldus	Y	Y	N	N	Y	Y	Y
4 Zablocki	Y	N	Y	Y	Y	Y	Y
5 Reuss	Y	Y	N	Y	Y	Y	Y
6 Steiger	Y	N	Y	N	Y	N	Y
7 Obey	Y	N	Y	N	Y	Y	Y
8 Cornell	Y	Y	N	N	Y	Y	Y
9 Kasten	#	▮	#	X	#	X	#
WYOMING							
AL Roncalio	Y	?	Y	Y	Y	Y	Y

Democrats ***Republicans***

284. H Con Res 624. Helsinki Accord Observance. Adoption of the concurrent resolution protesting the harassment and imprisonment of 22 Soviet citizens, including Dr. Yuri Orlov, who was sentenced May 18 to a total of 12 years in prison and exile from Moscow, who monitored the Soviet's compliance with the August 1975 Helsinki accord on respect for human rights; stating the sense of Congress that these citizens should be released; urging the U.S. government to continue protesting such imprisonments; and directing that copies of the resolution be sent to officials of the Soviet government. Adopted 399-0: R 137-0; D 262-0 (ND 182-0; SD 80-0), May 18, 1978.

285. HR 39. Alaska Lands. Young, R-Alaska, amendment, to the Udall, D-Ariz., amendment to the Meeds, D-Wash., substitute for the bill, to remove five million acres from the proposed additions to the nation's parks, refuges and forests in order to allow the state of Alaska to select the land. Rejected 141-251: R 89-43; D 52-208 (ND 18-163; SD 34-45), May 18, 1978. A "nay" was a vote supporting the president's position.

286. HR 39. Alaska Lands. Meeds, D-Wash., amendment, to the Udall, D-Ariz., substitute amendment to the Meeds, D-Wash., substitute for the bill, to reduce from 66 million acres to 33 million acres the land in proposed and existing parks, refuges and forests that would also be classified as wilderness, a designation that prohibited development. Rejected 119-240: R 62-57; D 57-183 (ND 27-137; SD 30-46), May 18, 1978. A "nay" was a vote supporting the president's position.

KEY

Y Voted for (yea).
✓ Paired for.
† Announced for.
# CQ Poll for.
N Voted against (nay).
X Paired against.
\- Announced against.
▮ CQ Poll against.
P Voted "present."
● Voted "present" to avoid possible conflict of interest.
? Did not vote or otherwise make a position known.

	284	285	286
ALABAMA			
1 Edwards	Y	N	Y
2 Dickinson	Y	Y	Y
3 Nichols	Y	Y	Y
4 Bevill	Y	N	N
5 Flippo	Y	N	N
6 Buchanan	Y	N	N
7 Flowers	Y	N	N
ALASKA			
AL Young	Y	Y	Y
ARIZONA			
1 Rhodes	Y	Y	Y
2 Udall	Y	N	N
3 Stump	Y	Y	Y
4 Rudd	Y	Y	Y
ARKANSAS			
1 Alexander	Y	N	N
2 Tucker	#	▮	▮
3 Hammerschmidt	Y	Y	Y
4 Thornton	?	?	?
CALIFORNIA			
1 Johnson	Y	Y	Y
2 Clausen	Y	Y	Y
3 Moss	Y	N	N
4 Leggett	Y	N	N
5 Burton, J.	?	N	N
6 Burton, P.	Y	N	N
7 Miller	Y	N	?
8 Dellums	Y	N	N
9 Stark	Y	N	▮
10 Edwards	Y	N	N
11 Ryan	Y	N	N
12 McCloskey	?	?	?
13 Mineta	Y	N	N
14 McFall	Y	Y	Y
15 Sisk	Y	Y	Y
16 Panetta	Y	N	N
17 Krebs	Y	N	N
18 Ketchum	Y	Y	Y
19 Lagomarsino	Y	Y	N
20 Goldwater	Y	Y	Y
21 Corman	Y	N	N
22 Moorhead	Y	Y	Y
23 Beilenson	Y	N	▮
24 Waxman	Y	N	N
25 Roybal	Y	N	N
26 Rousselot	Y	Y	Y
27 Dornan	Y	Y	▮
28 Burke	#	▮	▮
29 Hawkins	Y	N	N
30 Danielson	Y	N	N
31 Wilson, C.H.	#	#	▮
32 Anderson	Y	N	N
33 Clawson	Y	Y	Y
34 Hannaford	Y	N	N
35 Lloyd	Y	N	N
36 Brown	Y	N	N
37 Pettis	Y	Y	N
38 Patterson	Y	N	N
39 Wiggins	Y	#	#
40 Badham	Y	#	#
41 Wilson, B.	Y	Y	Y
42 Van Deerlin	Y	N	N
43 Burgener	Y	Y	Y
COLORADO			
1 Schroeder	Y	N	N
2 Wirth	Y	N	N
3 Evans	Y	N	N
4 Johnson	?	N	Y
5 Armstrong	Y	Y	N
CONNECTICUT			
1 Cotter	Y	N	N
2 Dodd	Y	N	?
3 Giaimo	Y	N	N
4 McKinney	Y	Y	N
5 Sarasin	#	▮	▮
6 Moffett	Y	N	N
DELAWARE			
AL Evans	Y	N	N
FLORIDA			
1 Sikes	Y	Y	Y
2 Fuqua	Y	N	▮
3 Bennett	Y	N	N
4 Chappell	Y	Y	Y
5 Kelly	Y	Y	Y
6 Young	Y	Y	Y
7 Gibbons	Y	N	N
8 Ireland	Y	N	N
9 Frey	?	?	?
10 Bafalis	Y	Y	Y
11 Rogers	Y	?	N
12 Burke	Y	N	N
13 Lehman	Y	N	N
14 Pepper	Y	-	N
15 Fascell	Y	N	▮
GEORGIA			
1 Ginn	Y	Y	N
2 Mathis	Y	Y	Y
3 Brinkley	Y	N	N
4 Levitas	Y	N	N
5 Fowler	Y	N	N
6 Flynt	Y	Y	Y
7 McDonald	Y	Y	Y
8 Evans	Y	N	N
9 Jenkins	Y	Y	N
10 Barnard	Y	N	N
HAWAII			
1 Heftel	Y	Y	N
2 Akaka	Y	N	N
IDAHO			
1 Symms	Y	Y	Y
2 Hansen, G.	Y	Y	Y
ILLINOIS			
1 Metcalfe	Y	N	?
2 Murphy	Y	N	Y
3 Russo	Y	N	Y
4 Derwinski	Y	Y	Y
5 Fary	Y	N	Y
6 Hyde	Y	Y	Y
7 Collins	Y	Y	?
8 Rostenkowski	Y	N	Y
9 Yates	Y	N	N
10 Mikva	Y	▮	▮
11 Annunzio	Y	N	Y
12 Crane	Y	Y	Y
13 McClory	Y	N	N
14 Erlenborn	Y	Y	#
15 Corcoran	Y	N	N
16 Anderson	Y	Y	N
17 O'Brien	Y	Y	Y
18 Michel	#	Y	Y
19 Railsback	Y	Y	N
20 Findley	Y	Y	N
21 Madigan	Y	N	N
22 Shipley	Y	N	?
23 Price	Y	N	Y
24 Simon	Y	N	N
INDIANA			
1 Benjamin	Y	N	N
2 Fithian	Y	N	N
3 Brademas	Y	N	N
4 Quayle	Y	?	?
5 Hillis	Y	Y	Y
6 Evans	Y	N	N
7 Myers, J.	Y	Y	N
8 Cornwell	?	?	?
9 Hamilton	Y	N	N
10 Sharp	Y	N	N
11 Jacobs	Y	N	N
IOWA			
1 Leach	Y	N	N
2 Blouin	Y	N	N
3 Grassley	Y	Y	N
4 Smith	Y	N	N
5 Harkin	Y	N	N
6 Bedell	Y	N	N

Democrats ***Republicans***

	284	285	286
KANSAS			
1 ***Sebelius***	Y	Y	N
2 Keys	Y	N	N
3 ***Winn***	Y	Y	N
4 Glickman	Y	N	N
5 ***Skubitz***	Y	N	?
KENTUCKY			
1 Hubbard	Y	Y	Y
2 Natcher	Y	N	N
3 Mazzoli	Y	Y	N
4 ***Snyder***	Y	Y	Y
5 ***Carter***	?	?	?
6 Breckinridge	†	-	-
7 Perkins	Y	N	N
LOUISIANA			
1 ***Livingston***	Y	Y	Y
2 Boggs	Y	Y	N
3 ***Treen***	Y	Y	Y
4 Waggonner	Y	Y	Y
5 Huckaby	Y	Y	Y
6 ***Moore***	Y	Y	Y
7 Breaux	Y	Y	Y
8 Long	Y	N	?
MAINE			
1 ***Emery***	Y	Y	N
2 ***Cohen***	Y	Y	N
MARYLAND			
1 ***Bauman***	Y	Y	Y
2 Long	Y	N	N
3 Mikulski	Y	N	N
4 ***Holt***	Y	Y	N
5 Spellman	Y	N	N
6 Byron	Y	N	N
7 Mitchell	#	N	N
8 ***Steers***	Y	N	N
MASSACHUSETTS			
1 ***Conte***	Y	N	N
2 Boland	Y	N	▮
3 Early	Y	N	N
4 Drinan	Y	N	N
5 Tsongas	#	▮	▮
6 Harrington	Y	N	N
7 Markey	Y	N	N
8 O'Neill			
9 Moakley	Y	N	N
10 ***Heckler***	Y	N	?
11 Burke	Y	N	N
12 Studds	Y	N	N
MICHIGAN			
1 Conyers	Y	▮	▮
2 ***Pursell***	Y	N	N
3 ***Brown***	Y	N	N
4 ***Stockman***	Y	Y	Y
5 ***Sawyer***	Y	N	▮
6 Carr	Y	N	N
7 Kildee	Y	N	N
8 Traxler	Y	N	N
9 ***Vander Jagt***	Y	Y	?
10 ***Cederberg***	Y	Y	Y
11 ***Ruppe***	Y	?	?
12 Bonior	Y	N	N
13 Diggs	Y	N	▮
14 Nedzi	Y	N	N
15 Ford	Y	N	N
16 Dingell	Y	N	?
17 Brodhead	Y	N	N
18 Blanchard	Y	N	N
19 ***Broomfield***	Y	Y	▮
MINNESOTA			
1 ***Quie***	Y	▮	▮
2 ***Hagedorn***	Y	Y	Y
3 ***Frenzel***	Y	N	N
4 Vento	Y	N	N
5 Fraser	Y	N	N
6 Nolan	Y	N	N
7 ***Stangeland***	Y	Y	Y
8 Oberstar	Y	N	Y
MISSISSIPPI			
1 Whitten	#	▮	#
2 Bowen	Y	Y	Y
3 Montgomery	Y	Y	Y
4 ***Cochran***	?	?	?
5 ***Lott***	Y	Y	Y
MISSOURI			
1 Clay	Y	N	N
2 Young	Y	Y	Y
3 Gephardt	Y	N	N

	284	285	286
4 Skelton	Y	N	N
5 Bolling	Y	▮	#
6 ***Coleman***	Y	N	N
7 ***Taylor***	Y	Y	Y
8 Ichord	Y	N	N
9 Volkmer	Y	Y	?
10 Burlison	Y	N	N
MONTANA			
1 Baucus	#	▮	▮
2 ***Marlenee***	Y	?	?
NEBRASKA			
1 ***Thone***	Y	N	N
2 Cavanaugh	Y	N	N
3 ***Smith***	Y	N	N
NEVADA			
AL Santini	Y	Y	Y
NEW HAMPSHIRE			
1 D'Amours	Y	N	N
2 ***Cleveland***	Y	?	?
NEW JERSEY			
1 Florio	Y	N	N
2 Hughes	Y	N	N
3 Howard	Y	N	N
4 Thompson	Y	N	N
5 ***Fenwick***	Y	N	N
6 ***Forsythe***	Y	Y	Y
7 Maguire	Y	N	N
8 Roe	Y	N	N
9 ***Hollenbeck***	Y	N	N
10 Rodino	Y	▮	▮
11 Minish	Y	N	N
12 ***Rinaldo***	Y	N	N
13 Meyner	Y	N	N
14 LeFante	Y	N	N
15 Patten	Y	N	Y
NEW MEXICO			
1 ***Lujan***	Y	Y	?
2 Runnels	#	?	?
NEW YORK			
1 Pike	Y	N	N
2 Downey	†	▮	N
3 Ambro	Y	N	N
4 ***Lent***	Y	Y	▮
5 ***Wydler***	Y	Y	?
6 Wolff	Y	N	N
7 Addabbo	Y	N	▮
8 Rosenthal	Y	N	N
9 Delaney	Y	N	Y
10 Biaggi	Y	N	▮
11 Scheuer	?	?	?
12 Chisholm	Y	N	N
13 Solarz	Y	▮	▮
14 Richmond	Y	N	?
15 Zeferetti	Y	Y	#
16 Holtzman	Y	N	N
17 Murphy	Y	Y	N
18 ***Green***	Y	N	N
19 Rangel	Y	N	N
20 Weiss	Y	N	-
21 Garcia	Y	N	N
22 Bingham	Y	N	N
23 ***Caputo***	Y	?	?
24 Ottinger	Y	N	N
25 ***Fish***	Y	N	N
26 ***Gilman***	Y	N	N
27 McHugh	Y	N	Y
28 Stratton	Y	N	N
29 Pattison	Y	N	N
30 ***McEwen***	Y	Y	?
31 ***Mitchell***	Y	Y	N
32 Hanley	Y	N	N
33 ***Walsh***	?	Y	Y
34 ***Horton***	Y	N	N
35 ***Conable***	Y	Y	N
36 LaFalce	Y	N	Y
37 Nowak	Y	N	Y
38 ***Kemp***	Y	Y	Y
39 Lundine	Y	N	N
NORTH CAROLINA			
1 Jones	Y	Y	Y
2 Fountain	Y	N	Y
3 Whitley	Y	N	Y
4 Andrews	Y	N	N
5 Neal	Y	N	N
6 Preyer	Y	N	N
7 Rose	Y	N	N
8 Hefner	Y	N	N

	284	285	286
9 ***Martin***	Y	Y	Y
10 ***Broyhill***	Y	Y	Y
11 Gudger	Y	N	N
NORTH DAKOTA			
AL ***Andrews***	Y	Y	#
OHIO			
1 ***Gradison***	Y	N	N
2 Luken	Y	N	N
3 ***Whalen***	Y	N	N
4 ***Guyer***	Y	Y	Y
5 ***Latta***	Y	Y	N
6 ***Harsha***	Y	N	N
7 ***Brown***	Y	Y	Y
8 ***Kindness***	Y	Y	Y
9 Ashley	Y	N	N
10 ***Miller***	Y	Y	Y
11 ***Stanton***	Y	Y	N
12 ***Devine***	Y	Y	Y
13 Pease	Y	N	N
14 Seiberling	Y	N	N
15 ***Wylie***	Y	N	N
16 ***Regula***	Y	N	N
17 ***Ashbrook***	Y	Y	Y
18 Applegate	Y	Y	N
19 Carney	Y	N	?
20 Oakar	Y	N	N
21 Stokes	#	N	N
22 Vanik	Y	N	N
23 Mottl	Y	N	N
OKLAHOMA			
1 Jones	#	N	N
2 Risenhoover	Y	Y	Y
3 Watkins	#	?	?
4 Steed	Y	Y	N
5 ***Edwards***	Y	Y	Y
6 English	Y	N	N
OREGON			
1 AuCoin	#	▮	▮
2 Ullman	Y	▮	▮
3 Duncan	Y	Y	Y
4 Weaver	Y	N	N
PENNSYLVANIA			
1 Myers, M.	Y	N	N
2 Nix	?	?	?
3 Lederer	Y	N	N
4 Eilberg	Y	N	N
5 ***Schulze***	?	Y	Y
6 Yatron	Y	N	N
7 Edgar	#	N	N
8 Kostmayer	Y	N	N
9 ***Shuster***	Y	Y	Y
10 ***McDade***	Y	N	N
11 Flood	Y	N	▮
12 Murtha	Y	N	N
13 ***Coughlin***	Y	N	N
14 Moorhead	Y	N	N
15 Rooney	Y	N	N
16 ***Walker***	Y	Y	Y
17 Ertel	Y	N	N
18 Walgren	Y	N	N
19 ***Goodling, W.***	Y	Y	Y
20 Gaydos	Y	N	N
21 Dent	#	N	Y
22 Murphy	Y	N	N
23 Ammerman	Y	N	N
24 ***Marks***	Y	N	N
25 ***Myers, G.***	Y	N	N
RHODE ISLAND			
1 St Germain	Y	N	N
2 Beard	Y	N	N
SOUTH CAROLINA			
1 Davis	Y	N	N
2 ***Spence***	Y	Y	N
3 Derrick	Y	N	N
4 Mann	Y	N	N
5 Holland	#	N	Y
6 Jenrette	Y	N	Y
SOUTH DAKOTA			
1 ***Pressler***	Y	-	-
2 ***Abdnor***	Y	N	N
TENNESSEE			
1 ***Quillen***	Y	N	N
2 ***Duncan***	Y	N	N
3 Lloyd	Y	Y	N
4 Gore	Y	N	N
5 Allen	Y	Y	Y
6 ***Beard***	Y	Y	Y

	284	285	286
7 Jones	Y	Y	N
8 Ford	Y	Y	N
TEXAS			
1 Hall	Y	Y	Y
2 Wilson, C.	Y	N	Y
3 ***Collins***	Y	Y	Y
4 Roberts	?	?	?
5 Mattox	Y	N	N
6 Teague	?	?	?
7 ***Archer***	Y	Y	Y
8 Eckhardt	Y	N	N
9 Brooks	Y	N	N
10 Pickle	Y	Y	N
11 Poage	Y	Y	Y
12 Wright	Y	?	?
13 Hightower	Y	Y	Y
14 Young	?	?	?
15 de la Garza	Y	Y	Y
16 White	Y	N	-
17 Burleson	Y	Y	Y
18 Jordan	Y	N	N
19 Mahon	Y	Y	N
20 Gonzalez	Y	N	N
21 Krueger	Y	N	Y
22 Gammage	Y	N	Y
23 Kazen	Y	Y	Y
24 Milford	Y	Y	?
UTAH			
1 McKay	Y	Y	Y
2 ***Marriott***	Y	Y	Y
VERMONT			
AL ***Jeffords***	Y	N	N
VIRGINIA			
1 ***Trible***	Y	N	N
2 ***Whitehurst***	Y	N	N
3 Satterfield	Y	Y	Y
4 ***Daniel***	Y	N	Y
5 Daniel	Y	Y	Y
6 ***Butler***	Y	Y	?
7 ***Robinson***	Y	Y	Y
8 Harris	Y	N	N
9 ***Wampler***	Y	Y	Y
10 Fisher	Y	N	N
WASHINGTON			
1 ***Pritchard***	Y	Y	Y
2 Meeds	Y	Y	Y
3 Bonker	Y	N	N
4 McCormack	Y	Y	Y
5 Foley	Y	Y	Y
6 Dicks	Y	Y	Y
7 ***Cunningham***	Y	Y	Y
WEST VIRGINIA			
1 Mollohan	Y	N	N
2 Staggers	Y	N	N
3 Slack	Y	N	Y
4 Rahall	Y	N	Y
WISCONSIN			
1 Aspin	Y	N	N
2 Kastenmeier	Y	N	N
3 Baldus	Y	N	N
4 Zablocki	Y	N	Y
5 Reuss	Y	N	N
6 ***Steiger***	Y	Y	N
7 Obey	Y	N	N
8 Cornell	Y	N	N
9 ***Kasten***	#	▮	▮
WYOMING			
AL Roncalio	Y	N	N

Democrats ***Republicans***

287. HR 39. Alaska Lands. Udall, D-Ariz., motion that the House resolve itself into the Committee of the Whole for further consideration of the bill to designate 102 million acres of federal land in Alaska as national park, national forest, wildlife refuge and wild and scenic rivers. Motion agreed to 280-8: R 94-4; D 186-4 (ND 131-3; SD 55-1), May 19, 1978.

288. HR 39. Alaska Lands. Santini, D-Nev., amendment, to the Udall, D-Ariz., substitute amendment to the Meeds, D-Wash., substitute for the bill, to direct the secretary of the interior to continue mineral assessment programs in Alaska and to direct the president to propose to Congress by Oct. 1, 1981, a procedure for evaluating applications from persons who wished to explore for or extract minerals from federal conservation lands in Alaska. Adopted 157-150: R 73-29; D 84-121 (ND 44-99; SD 40-22), May 19, 1978. (Both the Udall and Meeds substitute amendments were adopted subsequently by voice vote.)

289. HR 39. Alaska Lands. Young, R-Alaska, motion that the bill be recommitted to the Committees on Interior and Insular Affairs and Merchant Marine and Fisheries with instructions to report it back to the House containing the text of the Meeds, D-Wash., substitute to reduce the wilderness lands to 33 million instead of the 66 million acres in the bill. Motion rejected 67-242: R 38-64; D 29-178 (ND 10-135; SD 19-43), May 19, 1978.

290. HR 39. Alaska Lands. Passage of the bill to designate 102 million acres of federal land in Alaska as national park, national forest, wildlife refuge and wild and scenic rivers. Passed 277-31: R 87-15; D 190-16 (ND 140-5; SD 50-11), May 19, 1978. A "yea" was a vote supporting the president's position.

291. H Res 1072. Education Advisory Councils. Perkins, D-Ky., motion to suspend the rules and adopt the resolution to express the disapproval of the House to the proposal by the commissioner of education to consolidate certain education advisory councils. Motion agreed to 269-109: R 103-26; D 166-83 (ND 120-56; SD 46-27), May 22, 1978. A two-thirds majority vote (252 in this case) is required for adoption under suspension of the rules.

292. HR 11777. Cooperative Forestry Assistance. Weaver, D-Ore., motion to suspend the rules and pass the bill to consolidate several Agriculture Department cooperative forestry assistance programs. Motion agreed to 373-2: R 128-1; D 245-1 (ND 173-0; SD 72-1), May 22, 1978. A two-thirds majority vote (249 in this case) is required for passage under suspension of the rules.

293. HR 11778. Forest and Rangeland Resources. Weaver, D-Ore., motion to suspend the rules and pass the bill to authorize such sums as necessary for forest and rangeland renewable resource research in the Agriculture Department. Motion agreed to 373-3: R 127-1; D 246-2 (ND 174-1; SD 72-1), May 22, 1978. A two-thirds majority vote (251 in this case) is required for passage under suspension of the rules.

294. HR 11779. Renewable Resources. Weaver, D-Ore., motion to suspend the rules and pass the bill to authorize $150 million in fiscal 1979-88 for expansion of the Agriculture Department forest and rangeland renewable resources (such as fish, wildlife, forage, water and timber) education extension program. Motion agreed to 377-7: R 128-1; D 249-6 (ND 174-5; SD 75-1), May 22, 1978. A two-thirds majority vote (256 in this case) is required for passage under suspension of the rules.

KEY

Y Voted for (yea).
✓ Paired for.
† Announced for.
# CQ Poll for.
N Voted against (nay).
X Paired against.
- Announced against.
▮ CQ Poll against.
P Voted "present."
● Voted "present" to avoid possible conflict of interest.
? Did not vote or otherwise make a position known.

	287	288	289	290	291	292	293	294
ALABAMA								
1 Edwards	Y	Y	Y	Y	N	Y	Y	Y
2 Dickinson	Y	Y	Y	Y	Y	Y	Y	Y
3 Nichols	Y	Y	Y	Y	N	Y	Y	Y
4 Bevill	?	✓	?	†	Y	Y	Y	Y
5 Flippo	Y	Y	N	Y	N	Y	Y	Y
6 Buchanan	Y	Y	N	Y	Y	Y	Y	Y
7 Flowers	Y	Y	N	Y	Y	Y	Y	Y
ALASKA								
AL Young	Y	Y	Y	N	#	#	#	#
ARIZONA								
1 Rhodes	Y	Y	Y	Y	?	?	?	?
2 Udall	Y	N	N	Y	Y	Y	Y	Y
3 Stump	Y	Y	Y	N	#	#	#	?
4 Rudd	Y	Y	Y	N	Y	Y	Y	Y
ARKANSAS								
1 Alexander	?	N	N	Y	N	Y	Y	Y
2 Tucker	#	▮	▮	#	#	#	#	#
3 Hammerschmidt	Y	Y	Y	Y	Y	Y	Y	Y
4 Thornton	?	?	?	?	?	?	?	?
CALIFORNIA								
1 Johnson	Y	Y	Y	Y	Y	Y	Y	Y
2 Clausen	Y	Y	Y	Y	?	?	?	Y
3 Moss	?	N	N	Y	Y	Y	Y	Y
4 Leggett	Y	Y	N	Y	Y	Y	?	Y
5 Burton, J.	?	N	N	Y	N	Y	Y	Y
6 Burton, P.	Y	N	N	Y	N	Y	Y	Y
7 Miller	?	?	?	?	N	Y	Y	Y
8 Dellums	#	N	N	Y	#	#	#	#
9 Stark	#	▮	▮	#	N	Y	Y	Y
10 Edwards	Y	N	N	Y	N	Y	Y	Y
11 Ryan	Y	N	N	Y	N	Y	Y	Y
12 McCloskey	?	?	X	?	Y	Y	?	Y
13 Mineta	Y	N	N	Y	Y	Y	Y	Y
14 McFall	Y	Y	N	Y	Y	Y	Y	Y
15 Sisk	Y	Y	Y	N	Y	Y	Y	Y
16 Panetta	Y	Y	N	Y	N	Y	Y	Y
17 Krebs	Y	Y	N	Y	N	Y	Y	Y
18 Ketchum	Y	Y	Y	Y	Y	Y	Y	Y
19 Lagomarsino	Y	Y	N	Y	Y	Y	Y	Y
20 Goldwater	?	Y	N	Y	Y	Y	Y	Y
21 Corman	Y	N	N	Y	N	Y	Y	Y
22 Moorhead	Y	Y	Y	Y	Y	Y	Y	Y
23 Beilenson	#	▮	▮	#	Y	Y	Y	Y
24 Waxman	#	▮	N	Y	N	Y	Y	Y
25 Roybal	Y	N	N	Y	Y	Y	Y	Y
26 Rousselot	N	Y	Y	N	Y	Y	Y	Y
27 Dornan	#	✓	✓	#	Y	Y	Y	Y
28 Burke	#	▮	▮	#	#	#	#	#
29 Hawkins	Y	N	N	Y	?	?	?	?
30 Danielson	Y	N	N	Y	Y	Y	Y	Y
31 Wilson, C.H.	#	#	▮	#	Y	Y	Y	Y
32 Anderson	Y	N	N	Y	▮	#	?	#
33 Clawson	Y	Y	Y	N	Y	Y	Y	Y
34 Hannaford	Y	Y	N	Y	Y	Y	Y	Y
35 Lloyd	N	Y	N	Y	Y	Y	Y	Y
36 Brown	Y	N	N	Y	Y	Y	Y	Y
37 Pettis	Y	Y	N	Y	Y	Y	Y	Y
38 Patterson	Y	N	N	Y	Y	Y	Y	Y
39 Wiggins	#	#	#	▮	Y	Y	Y	Y
40 Badham	#	✓	#	▮	Y	Y	Y	Y
41 Wilson, B.	N	Y	N	Y	?	?	?	?
42 Van Deerlin	Y	N	N	Y	Y	Y	Y	Y
43 Burgener	Y	Y	N	Y	Y	Y	Y	Y
COLORADO								
1 Schroeder	Y	N	N	Y	N	Y	Y	Y
2 Wirth	Y	N	N	Y	N	Y	Y	Y
3 Evans	Y	N	N	Y	Y	Y	Y	Y
4 Johnson	Y	Y	N	Y	Y	Y	Y	Y
5 Armstrong	Y	N	N	Y	N	Y	Y	Y
CONNECTICUT								
1 Cotter	#	X	▮	#	Y	Y	Y	Y
2 Dodd	Y	Y	N	Y	Y	Y	Y	Y
3 Giaimo	Y	N	N	Y	Y	Y	Y	Y
4 McKinney	Y	N	N	Y	Y	Y	Y	Y
5 Sarasin	†	-	-	†	Y	Y	Y	Y
6 Moffett	Y	N	N	Y	N	Y	Y	Y
DELAWARE								
AL Evans	Y	N	N	Y	Y	Y	Y	Y
FLORIDA								
1 Sikes	Y	Y	Y	Y	Y	Y	Y	Y
2 Fuqua	#	▮	▮	#	#	#	#	#
3 Bennett	Y	N	N	Y	N	Y	Y	Y
4 Chappell	Y	Y	Y	Y	Y	Y	Y	Y
5 Kelly	Y	Y	Y	N	Y	Y	Y	Y
6 Young	Y	Y	Y	Y	Y	Y	Y	Y
7 Gibbons	?	?	?	?	?	?	?	?
8 Ireland	Y	N	N	Y	Y	Y	Y	Y
9 Frey	?	✓	?	?	?	?	?	?
10 Bafalis	Y	Y	Y	Y	Y	Y	Y	Y
11 Rogers	Y	N	N	Y	N	Y	Y	Y
12 Burke	Y	Y	N	Y	N	Y	Y	Y
13 Lehman	Y	N	N	Y	Y	Y	Y	Y
14 Pepper	Y	N	N	Y	Y	Y	Y	Y
15 Fascell	#	▮	▮	#	Y	Y	Y	Y
GEORGIA								
1 Ginn	Y	Y	N	Y	N	Y	Y	Y
2 Mathis	Y	Y	Y	Y	Y	Y	Y	Y
3 Brinkley	Y	N	N	Y	Y	Y	Y	Y
4 Levitas	Y	N	N	Y	Y	Y	Y	Y
5 Fowler	Y	N	N	Y	Y	Y	Y	Y
6 Flynt	Y	Y	Y	N	N	Y	Y	Y
7 McDonald	Y	Y	Y	N	N	N	N	N
8 Evans	Y	Y	N	Y	N	Y	Y	Y
9 Jenkins	Y	Y	N	Y	Y	Y	Y	Y
10 Barnard	Y	N	N	Y	Y	Y	Y	Y
HAWAII								
1 Heftel	?	?	?	?	Y	Y	Y	Y
2 Akaka	#	#	▮	#	Y	Y	Y	Y
IDAHO								
1 Symms	N	Y	Y	N	Y	Y	Y	Y
2 Hansen, G.	Y	Y	Y	N	Y	Y	Y	Y
ILLINOIS								
1 Metcalfe	?	?	?	?	Y	Y	Y	Y
2 Murphy	#	?	▮	#	Y	Y	Y	Y
3 Russo	Y	N	N	Y	Y	Y	Y	Y
4 Derwinski	Y	Y	N	Y	Y	Y	Y	Y
5 Fary	Y	Y	N	Y	Y	Y	Y	Y
6 Hyde	Y	Y	N	Y	Y	Y	Y	Y
7 Collins	?	?	?	?	Y	Y	Y	Y
8 Rostenkowski	Y	Y	Y	Y	Y	Y	Y	Y
9 Yates	Y	N	N	Y	Y	Y	Y	Y
10 Mikva	†	-	-	†	N	Y	Y	Y
11 Annunzio	Y	Y	Y	Y	Y	Y	Y	Y
12 Crane	#	✓	#	▮	▮	#	#	#
13 McClory	Y	N	N	Y	Y	Y	Y	Y
14 Erlenborn	#	✓	✓	X	N	Y	Y	Y
15 Corcoran	Y	N	N	Y	Y	Y	Y	Y
16 Anderson	Y	N	N	Y	Y	Y	Y	Y
17 O'Brien	Y	Y	N	Y	Y	Y	Y	Y
18 Michel	Y	Y	N	Y	Y	Y	Y	Y
19 Railsback	Y	Y	N	Y	Y	Y	Y	Y
20 Findley	Y	Y	N	Y	?	?	?	?
21 Madigan	Y	Y	N	Y	N	Y	Y	Y
22 Shipley	?	?	?	?	?	?	?	?
23 Price	Y	N	N	Y	Y	Y	Y	Y
24 Simon	Y	Y	N	Y	Y	Y	Y	Y
INDIANA								
1 Benjamin	Y	Y	N	Y	Y	Y	Y	N
2 Fithian	Y	Y	N	Y	N	Y	Y	Y
3 Brademas	Y	N	N	Y	Y	Y	Y	Y
4 Quayle	?	?	?	?	Y	Y	Y	Y
5 Hillis	Y	Y	N	Y	Y	Y	Y	Y
6 Evans	Y	Y	N	Y	N	Y	Y	N
7 Myers, J.	Y	✓	?	?	Y	Y	Y	Y
8 Cornwell	?	?	?	?	N	Y	Y	Y
9 Hamilton	Y	N	N	Y	N	Y	Y	Y
10 Sharp	Y	N	N	Y	N	Y	Y	Y
11 Jacobs	Y	✓	N	Y	N	Y	Y	Y
IOWA								
1 Leach	Y	N	N	Y	Y	Y	Y	Y
2 Blouin	Y	N	N	Y	Y	Y	Y	Y
3 Grassley	Y	Y	N	Y	Y	Y	Y	Y
4 Smith	Y	Y	N	Y	Y	Y	Y	Y
5 Harkin	Y	N	N	Y	N	Y	Y	Y
6 Bedell	Y	N	N	Y	N	Y	Y	Y

Democrats ***Republicans***

	287	288	289	290	291	292	293	294
KANSAS								
1 Sebelius	Y	Y	N	Y	Y	Y	Y	Y
2 Keys	#	X	-	†	N	Y	Y	Y
3 Winn	#	✓	▮	▮	Y	Y	Y	Y
4 Glickman	Y	Y	N	Y	N	Y	Y	Y
5 Skubitz	?	?	?	?	Y	Y	Y	Y
KENTUCKY								
1 Hubbard	?	?	?	?	N	Y	Y	Y
2 Natcher	Y	Y	N	Y	Y	Y	Y	Y
3 Mazzoli	†	†	-	†	N	Y	Y	Y
4 Snyder	Y	Y	Y	Y	Y	Y	Y	Y
5 Carter	?	?	?	?	?	?	?	?
6 Breckinridge	†	†	-	†	†	†	†	†
7 Perkins	Y	N	N	Y	Y	Y	Y	Y
LOUISIANA								
1 Livingston	Y	Y	Y	Y	?	?	?	?
2 Boggs	#	Y	N	Y	N	Y	Y	Y
3 Treen	?	✓	?	?	?	?	?	?
4 Waggonner	Y	Y	Y	N	N	Y	Y	Y
5 Huckaby	Y	Y	Y	N	N	Y	Y	Y
6 Moore	Y	Y	Y	Y	N	Y	Y	Y
7 Breaux	Y	Y	Y	N	N	Y	Y	Y
8 Long	?	?	?	?	N	Y	Y	Y
MAINE								
1 Emery	Y	N	N	Y	N	Y	Y	Y
2 Cohen	Y	N	N	Y	Y	Y	Y	Y
MARYLAND								
1 Bauman	Y	Y	Y	Y	Y	Y	Y	Y
2 Long	Y	N	N	Y	Y	Y	Y	Y
3 Mikulski	Y	N	N	Y	Y	Y	Y	Y
4 Holt	?	?	?	✓	Y	Y	Y	Y
5 Spellman	Y	N	N	Y	Y	Y	Y	Y
6 Byron	Y	N	N	Y	Y	Y	Y	Y
7 Mitchell	N	N	N	Y	Y	Y	Y	Y
8 Steers	Y	N	N	Y	Y	Y	Y	Y
MASSACHUSETTS								
1 Conte	Y	N	N	Y	Y	Y	Y	Y
2 Boland	#	X	▮	#	Y	Y	Y	Y
3 Early	Y	N	N	Y	N	Y	Y	Y
4 Drinan	Y	N	N	Y	Y	Y	Y	Y
5 Tsongas	#	▮	▮	#	Y	Y	Y	Y
6 Harrington	#	N	N	Y	Y	Y	Y	Y
7 Markey	#	N	N	Y	N	Y	Y	Y
8 O'Neill								
9 Moakley	Y	N	N	Y	Y	Y	Y	Y
10 Heckler	?	N	N	Y	N	Y	Y	Y
11 Burke	Y	N	N	Y	Y	Y	Y	Y
12 Studds	Y	N	N	Y	N	Y	Y	Y
MICHIGAN								
1 Conyers	#	▮	▮	#	#	#	#	#
2 Pursell	#	X	▮	#	?	?	?	?
3 Brown	#	X	X	#	Y	Y	Y	Y
4 Stockman	Y	Y	Y	N	Y	Y	Y	Y
5 Sawyer	#	X	▮	#	#	#	#	#
6 Carr	Y	N	N	Y	N	Y	Y	Y
7 Kildee	Y	N	N	Y	Y	Y	Y	Y
8 Traxler	Y	N	N	Y	Y	Y	Y	Y
9 Vander Jagt	?	N	N	Y	Y	Y	Y	Y
10 Cederberg	Y	Y	N	Y	Y	Y	Y	Y
11 Ruppe	#	#	?	#	N	Y	Y	Y
12 Bonior	Y	N	N	Y	Y	Y	Y	Y
13 Diggs	#	N	N	Y	Y	Y	Y	Y
14 Nedzi	Y	N	N	Y	Y	Y	Y	Y
15 Ford	?	N	N	Y	Y	Y	Y	?
16 Dingell	?	?	?	?	Y	Y	Y	Y
17 Brodhead	Y	N	N	Y	Y	Y	Y	Y
18 Blanchard	Y	N	N	Y	N	Y	Y	Y
19 Broomfield	#	X	▮	#	N	Y	Y	Y
MINNESOTA								
1 Quie	#	▮	▮	#	#	#	#	#
2 Hagedorn	?	#	#	▮	N	Y	Y	Y
3 Frenzel	Y	Y	N	Y	N	Y	Y	Y
4 Vento	Y	N	N	Y	Y	Y	Y	Y
5 Fraser	Y	N	N	Y	#	#	#	#
6 Nolan	Y	N	N	Y	N	Y	Y	Y
7 Stangeland	Y	Y	Y	N	Y	Y	Y	Y
8 Oberstar	Y	Y	N	Y	N	Y	Y	Y
MISSISSIPPI								
1 Whitten	#	#	▮	#	Y	Y	Y	Y
2 Bowen	?	?	?	?	Y	Y	Y	Y
3 Montgomery	Y	Y	Y	N	Y	Y	Y	Y
4 Cochran	?	?	?	?	?	?	?	?
5 Lott	Y	Y	Y	N	Y	Y	Y	Y
MISSOURI								
1 Clay	?	?	?	?	Y	Y	Y	Y
2 Young	Y	Y	N	Y	N	Y	Y	Y
3 Gephardt	Y	N	N	Y	N	Y	Y	N
4 Skelton	Y	N	▮	#	Y	Y	Y	Y
5 Bolling	#	▮	▮	#	Y	Y	Y	Y
6 Coleman	Y	Y	N	Y	Y	Y	Y	Y
7 Taylor	Y	Y	Y	Y	Y	Y	Y	Y
8 Ichord	Y	Y	N	Y	Y	Y	Y	Y
9 Volkmer	Y	Y	N	Y	N	Y	N	N
10 Burlison	Y	N	N	Y	N	Y	Y	Y
MONTANA								
1 Baucus	#	#	▮	#	#	#	#	#
2 Marlenee	?	?	?	?	Y	Y	Y	?
NEBRASKA								
1 Thone	#	?	?	#	Y	Y	Y	Y
2 Cavanaugh	?	?	?	?	N	Y	Y	Y
3 Smith	Y	Y	N	Y	Y	Y	Y	Y
NEVADA								
AL Santini	Y	Y	N	Y	Y	Y	Y	Y
NEW HAMPSHIRE								
1 D'Amours	Y	N	N	Y	Y	Y	Y	Y
2 Cleveland	?	X	?	?	N	Y	Y	Y
NEW JERSEY								
1 Florio	Y	N	N	Y	Y	Y	Y	Y
2 Hughes	Y	N	N	Y	Y	Y	Y	Y
3 Howard	Y	N	N	Y	Y	Y	Y	Y
4 Thompson	Y	N	N	Y	Y	Y	Y	Y
5 Fenwick	Y	N	N	Y	N	Y	Y	Y
6 Forsythe	Y	Y	N	Y	Y	Y	Y	Y
7 Maguire	Y	N	N	Y	Y	Y	Y	Y
8 Roe	Y	N	N	Y	Y	Y	Y	Y
9 Hollenbeck	Y	N	N	Y	#	#	#	#
10 Rodino	#	▮	▮	#	#	#	#	#
11 Minish	Y	N	N	Y	N	Y	Y	Y
12 Rinaldo	Y	N	N	Y	Y	Y	Y	Y
13 Meyner	#	N	N	Y	Y	Y	Y	Y
14 LeFante	Y	N	N	Y	Y	Y	Y	Y
15 Patten	Y	Y	N	Y	Y	#	Y	Y
NEW MEXICO								
1 Lujan	?	?	?	?	N	Y	Y	Y
2 Runnels	#	?	?	?	?	#	#	#
NEW YORK								
1 Pike	Y	N	N	Y	Y	Y	Y	Y
2 Downey	†	-	-	†	N	Y	Y	Y
3 Ambro	?	?	N	Y	Y	Y	Y	Y
4 Lent	#	X	▮	#	Y	Y	Y	Y
5 Wydler	?	X	?	?	Y	Y	Y	Y
6 Wolff	#	#	▮	#	N	Y	Y	Y
7 Addabbo	#	X	▮	✓	Y	Y	Y	Y
8 Rosenthal	#	▮	▮	#	Y	Y	Y	Y
9 Delaney	Y	N	N	Y	Y	Y	Y	Y
10 Biaggi	#	X	▮	✓	#	#	#	#
11 Scheuer	?	?	?	?	Y	?	Y	Y
12 Chisholm	#	?	▮	#	Y	Y	Y	Y
13 Solarz	Y	N	N	Y	Y	Y	Y	Y
14 Richmond	?	?	?	?	N	Y	Y	Y
15 Zeferetti	#	X	X	#	Y	Y	Y	Y
16 Holtzman	Y	N	N	Y	N	Y	Y	Y
17 Murphy	Y	Y	N	Y	#	#	#	Y
18 Green	Y	N	N	Y	Y	Y	Y	Y
19 Rangel	Y	N	N	Y	Y	Y	Y	Y
20 Weiss	†	-	X	†	Y	Y	Y	Y
21 Garcia	Y	N	N	Y	Y	Y	Y	Y
22 Bingham	#	N	N	Y	Y	Y	Y	Y
23 Caputo	Y	Y	N	Y	N	Y	Y	Y
24 Ottinger	Y	N	N	Y	N	Y	Y	Y
25 Fish	Y	N	N	Y	Y	Y	Y	Y
26 Gilman	Y	N	N	Y	Y	Y	Y	Y
27 McHugh	#	N	N	Y	Y	Y	Y	Y
28 Stratton	Y	N	N	Y	N	Y	Y	Y
29 Pattison	#	#	▮	#	Y	Y	Y	Y
30 McEwen	?	?	?	?	Y	Y	Y	Y
31 Mitchell	Y	Y	N	Y	Y	Y	Y	Y
32 Hanley	†	X	-	†	Y	Y	Y	Y
33 Walsh	?	✓	✓	X	Y	Y	Y	Y
34 Horton	#	X	▮	#	Y	Y	Y	Y
35 Conable	?	?	?	?	N	Y	Y	Y
36 LaFalce	Y	Y	N	Y	N	Y	Y	Y
37 Nowak	Y	Y	N	Y	N	Y	Y	Y
38 Kemp	Y	Y	Y	N	Y	Y	Y	Y
39 Lundine	#	▮	▮	#	Y	Y	Y	Y
NORTH CAROLINA								
1 Jones	Y	Y	N	Y	▮	#	#	#
2 Fountain	Y	Y	Y	Y	Y	Y	Y	Y
3 Whitley	Y	Y	N	Y	N	Y	Y	Y
4 Andrews	#	N	N	Y	?	#	#	Y
5 Neal	#	N	N	Y	Y	Y	Y	Y
6 Preyer	#	-	▮	#	Y	Y	Y	Y
7 Rose	#	▮	▮	#	Y	#	Y	Y
8 Hefner	Y	N	N	Y	Y	Y	Y	Y
9 Martin	#	✓	▮	#	N	Y	Y	Y
10 Broyhill	Y	Y	Y	Y	N	Y	Y	Y
11 Gudger	#	▮	▮	#	Y	Y	Y	Y
NORTH DAKOTA								
AL Andrews	#	X	▮	#	Y	Y	Y	Y
OHIO								
1 Gradison	Y	N	N	Y	Y	Y	Y	Y
2 Luken	Y	N	N	Y	?	#	#	#
3 Whalen	Y	N	N	Y	N	Y	Y	Y
4 Guyer	#	✓	▮	#	Y	Y	Y	Y
5 Latta	Y	Y	N	Y	Y	Y	Y	Y
6 Harsha	Y	N	N	Y	Y	Y	Y	Y
7 Brown	Y	Y	Y	N	Y	Y	Y	Y
8 Kindness	?	Y	Y	Y	N	Y	Y	Y
9 Ashley	?	?	N	Y	Y	?	Y	Y
10 Miller	Y	Y	Y	Y	N	Y	Y	Y
11 Stanton	Y	Y	N	Y	Y	Y	Y	Y
12 Devine	#	✓	#	▮	Y	Y	Y	Y
13 Pease	Y	N	N	Y	N	Y	Y	Y
14 Seiberling	Y	N	N	Y	N	Y	Y	Y
15 Wylie	?	?	?	?	Y	Y	Y	Y
16 Regula	Y	Y	N	Y	Y	Y	Y	Y
17 Ashbrook	#	✓	#	▮	Y	Y	Y	Y
18 Applegate	Y	Y	N	Y	?	?	?	Y
19 Carney	?	X	?	?	Y	Y	Y	Y
20 Oakar	?	?	?	?	?	?	?	?
21 Stokes	#	#	▮	#	#	#	#	#
22 Vanik	Y	N	N	Y	Y	Y	Y	Y
23 Mottl	#	#	▮	#	Y	Y	Y	Y
OKLAHOMA								
1 Jones	Y	Y	N	Y	N	Y	Y	N
2 Risenhoover	?	?	?	?	Y	Y	Y	Y
3 Watkins	#	?	▮	?	Y	Y	Y	Y
4 Steed	#	Y	N	Y	Y	Y	Y	Y
5 Edwards	Y	Y	Y	N	N	Y	Y	Y
6 English	Y	Y	N	Y	N	Y	Y	Y
OREGON								
1 AuCoin	#	?	▮	#	?	#	#	#
2 Ullman	#	▮	▮	#	#	#	#	#
3 Duncan	Y	Y	Y	N	N	Y	Y	Y
4 Weaver	Y	N	N	Y	Y	Y	Y	Y
PENNSYLVANIA								
1 Myers, M.	?	?	?	?	Y	Y	Y	Y
2 Nix	?	?	?	?	Y	Y	Y	Y
3 Lederer	Y	Y	N	Y	Y	Y	Y	Y
4 Eilberg	Y	Y	N	Y	Y	Y	Y	Y
5 Schulze	Y	Y	Y	Y	Y	Y	Y	Y
6 Yatron	Y	N	N	Y	Y	Y	Y	Y
7 Edgar	Y	N	N	Y	N	Y	Y	Y
8 Kostmayer	Y	N	N	Y	N	Y	Y	Y
9 Shuster	Y	Y	Y	N	Y	Y	Y	Y
10 McDade	Y	Y	N	Y	Y	Y	Y	Y
11 Flood	#	#	▮	#	Y	Y	Y	Y
12 Murtha	Y	Y	N	Y	Y	Y	Y	Y
13 Coughlin	Y	N	N	Y	Y	Y	Y	Y
14 Moorhead	Y	N	N	Y	Y	Y	Y	Y
15 Rooney	Y	N	N	Y	Y	Y	Y	Y
16 Walker	?	?	?	?	Y	Y	Y	Y
17 Ertel	Y	Y	N	Y	Y	Y	Y	Y
18 Walgren	Y	N	N	Y	N	Y	Y	Y
19 Goodling, W.	Y	Y	N	Y	Y	Y	Y	Y
20 Gaydos	Y	N	N	Y	Y	Y	Y	Y
21 Dent	#	Y	N	Y	#	#	#	Y
22 Murphy	Y	Y	N	Y	Y	Y	Y	Y
23 Ammerman	Y	N	N	Y	N	Y	Y	Y
24 Marks	Y	N	N	Y	N	Y	Y	Y
25 Myers, G.	Y	N	N	Y	N	Y	Y	Y
RHODE ISLAND								
1 St Germain	N	Y	?	?	Y	Y	Y	Y
2 Beard	Y	N	N	Y	Y	Y	Y	Y
SOUTH CAROLINA								
1 Davis	Y	N	N	Y	Y	Y	Y	Y
2 Spence	Y	N	N	Y	Y	Y	Y	Y
3 Derrick	Y	N	N	Y	Y	Y	Y	Y
4 Mann	?	?	?	?	Y	Y	Y	Y
5 Holland	Y	N	▮	#	Y	Y	Y	Y
6 Jenrette	Y	N	N	Y	?	?	?	?
SOUTH DAKOTA								
1 Pressler	†	-	-	†	Y	Y	Y	Y
2 Abdnor	#	▮	X	#	Y	Y	Y	Y
TENNESSEE								
1 Quillen	Y	N	N	Y	Y	Y	Y	Y
2 Duncan	Y	Y	N	Y	#	#	#	#
3 Lloyd	Y	Y	N	Y	?	?	?	?
4 Gore	Y	N	N	Y	#	#	#	#
5 Allen	Y	Y	N	Y	?	?	?	?
6 Beard	Y	Y	N	Y	Y	Y	Y	Y
7 Jones	Y	Y	N	Y	?	#	#	#
8 Ford	?	?	?	?	?	?	?	Y
TEXAS								
1 Hall	Y	Y	Y	N	N	Y	Y	Y
2 Wilson, C.	#	Y	N	Y	Y	Y	Y	Y
3 Collins	N	Y	Y	N	N	N	N	N
4 Roberts	?	✓	✓	X	Y	Y	Y	Y
5 Mattox	Y	Y	N	Y	N	Y	Y	Y
6 Teague	?	✓	✓	X	?	?	?	?
7 Archer	Y	Y	Y	Y	Y	Y	Y	Y
8 Eckhardt	?	?	?	?	N	Y	?	Y
9 Brooks	Y	N	N	Y	Y	Y	Y	Y
10 Pickle	Y	Y	N	Y	N	Y	Y	Y
11 Poage	Y	Y	Y	N	Y	Y	Y	Y
12 Wright	?	?	?	?	Y	Y	Y	Y
13 Hightower	Y	Y	N	?	Y	Y	Y	Y
14 Young	?	?	?	?	?	?	?	?
15 de la Garza	?	?	Y	Y	?	?	?	Y
16 White	?	†	-	†	Y	Y	Y	Y
17 Burleson	Y	Y	Y	N	N	Y	Y	Y
18 Jordan	Y	Y	N	Y	Y	Y	Y	Y
19 Mahon	Y	Y	N	Y	Y	Y	Y	Y
20 Gonzalez	Y	Y	N	Y	P	Y	Y	Y
21 Krueger	#	✓	▮	#	N	Y	Y	Y
22 Gammage	Y	Y	Y	Y	Y	Y	Y	Y
23 Kazen	Y	Y	Y	Y	N	Y	Y	Y
24 Milford	?	?	?	?	N	Y	Y	Y
UTAH								
1 McKay	Y	Y	Y	Y	N	Y	Y	Y
2 Marriott	Y	Y	Y	Y	Y	Y	Y	Y
VERMONT								
AL Jeffords	Y	N	N	Y	Y	Y	Y	Y
VIRGINIA								
1 Trible	Y	Y	N	Y	Y	Y	Y	Y
2 Whitehurst	Y	N	N	Y	Y	Y	Y	Y
3 Satterfield	N	Y	Y	N	Y	Y	Y	Y
4 Daniel	Y	Y	Y	Y	Y	Y	Y	Y
5 Daniel	Y	Y	Y	N	Y	Y	Y	Y
6 Butler	Y	Y	Y	Y	Y	Y	Y	Y
7 Robinson	Y	Y	Y	Y	Y	Y	Y	Y
8 Harris	Y	N	N	Y	Y	Y	Y	Y
9 Wampler	?	X	?	?	Y	Y	Y	Y
10 Fisher	Y	N	N	Y	Y	Y	Y	Y
WASHINGTON								
1 Pritchard	#	Y	N	Y	#	#	#	#
2 Meeds	Y	Y	Y	N	Y	Y	Y	Y
3 Bonker	Y	▮	▮	#	Y	Y	Y	Y
4 McCormack	Y	Y	Y	N	N	Y	Y	Y
5 Foley	Y	Y	Y	Y	N	Y	Y	Y
6 Dicks	Y	Y	N	Y	Y	Y	Y	Y
7 Cunningham	Y	Y	N	Y	Y	Y	Y	Y
WEST VIRGINIA								
1 Mollohan	Y	N	N	Y	Y	Y	Y	Y
2 Staggers	Y	N	N	Y	Y	Y	Y	Y
3 Slack	Y	N	N	Y	Y	Y	Y	Y
4 Rahall	Y	Y	N	Y	Y	Y	Y	Y
WISCONSIN								
1 Aspin	Y	N	N	Y	Y	Y	Y	Y
2 Kastenmeier	Y	N	N	Y	Y	Y	Y	Y
3 Baldus	Y	N	N	Y	N	Y	Y	Y
4 Zablocki	Y	Y	N	Y	Y	Y	Y	Y
5 Reuss	#	#	▮	#	Y	Y	Y	Y
6 Steiger	#	X	▮	✓	Y	Y	Y	Y
7 Obey	Y	N	N	Y	Y	Y	Y	Y
8 Cornell	Y	N	N	Y	Y	Y	Y	Y
9 Kasten	#	✓	▮	#	#	#	#	#
WYOMING								
AL Roncalio	?	?	?	?	?	?	?	?

Democrats ***Republicans***

295. S 2370. Forest Service Volunteers. Weaver, D-Ore., motion to suspend the rules and pass the bill to eliminate the $100,000 limitation in the 1972 Volunteers in National Forest Act for incidental expenses, such as transportation, uniforms and subsistence, to support the volunteers who assist in programs and services performed in the national forests. Motion agreed to 378-5: R 127-2; D 251-3 (ND 175-2; SD 76-1), May 22, 1978. A two-thirds majority vote (256 in this case) is required for passage under suspension of the rules.

296. HR 12353. Vietnam Veterans Readjustment. Roberts, D-Texas, motion to suspend the rules and pass the bill to extend the exemption of Vietnam-era and disabled veterans from federal Civil Service employment requirements until 1980; to expand the appointment grades to GS-7, from GS-1 through GS-5, and to eliminate the education limitation for disabled veterans. Motion agreed to 388-0: R 131-0; D 257-0 (ND 180-0; SD 77-0), May 22, 1978. A two-thirds majority vote (259 in this case) is required for passage under suspension of the rules.

297. H Con Res 555. U.S.-Hungarian Trade Agreement. Adoption of the concurrent resolution to approve the extension of nondiscriminatory treatment (most-favored nation status) to the Hungarian People's Republic in accordance with the trade agreement concluded by the United States and Hungary on March 17, 1978. Adopted 209-173: R 48-82; D 161-91 (ND 129-48; SD 32-43), May 22, 1978. A "yea" was a vote supporting the president's position.

298. HR 12602. Military Construction. Adoption of the rule (H Res 1193) providing for House floor consideration of the bill to authorize funds for military construction programs of the Department of Defense. Adopted 377-1: R 127-1; D 250-0 (ND 176-0; SD 74-0), May 22, 1978.

299. HR 12602. Military Construction. Passage of the bill to authorize $4.2 billion for various military construction programs of the Department of Defense for fiscal 1979, including nearly $600 million for NATO-related projects in Western Europe and $145.66 million for a space shuttle launching base at Vandenberg Air Force Base, California. Passed 363-18: R 123-3; D 240-15 (ND 164-15; SD 76-0), May 22, 1978.

300. HR 10729. Maritime Administration Authorization. McCloskey, R-Calif., amendment to preserve the debt ceiling of $7 billion on the government's ship construction loan guarantee program. Rejected 126-241: R 79-45; D 47-196 (ND 30-138; SD 17-58), May 22, 1978.

301. S J Res 4. Hawaiian Native Claims. Roncalio, D-Wyo., motion to suspend the rules and pass the joint resolution to establish a 15-member commission to study the claims of aboriginal Hawaiians resulting from the 1893 conspiracy to overthrow the Hawaiian government. Motion rejected 210-194: R 20-118; D 190-76 (ND 151-33; SD 39-43), May 23, 1978. A two-thirds majority vote (270 in this case) is required for passage under suspension of the rules.

302. HR 12299. Domestic Violence Assistance Act. Brademas, D-Ind., motion to suspend the rules and pass the bill to establish a domestic violence (spouse abuse) program and to authorize $125 million for fiscal 1979-83. Motion rejected 201-205: R 36-101; D 165-104 (ND 138-48; SD 27-56), May 23, 1978. A two-thirds majority vote (271 in this case) is required for passage under suspension of the rules.

KEY

- Y Voted for (yea).
- ✓ Paired for.
- † Announced for.
- # CQ Poll for.
- N Voted against (nay).
- X Paired against.
- \- Announced against.
- ▮ CQ Poll against.
- P Voted "present."
- ● Voted "present" to avoid possible conflict of interest.
- ? Did not vote or otherwise make a position known.

	295	296	297	298	299	300	301	302
ALABAMA								
1 Edwards	Y	Y	N	Y	Y	N	N	N
2 Dickinson	Y	Y	N	Y	Y	Y	N	N
3 Nichols	Y	Y	N	Y	Y	N	N	N
4 Bevill	Y	Y	Y	Y	Y	N	N	Y
5 Flippo	Y	Y	N	Y	Y	N	Y	N
6 Buchanan	Y	Y	N	Y	Y	N	N	Y
7 Flowers	Y	Y	N	Y	Y	N	N	N
ALASKA								
AL Young	#	?	X	?	?	?	?	?
ARIZONA								
1 Rhodes	?	?	?	?	?	?	N	N
2 Udall	Y	Y	Y	Y	Y	Y	Y	Y
3 Stump	#	#	▮	#	#	#	N	N
4 Rudd	Y	Y	N	Y	Y	Y	N	N
ARKANSAS								
1 Alexander	Y	Y	Y	Y	Y	N	Y	Y
2 Tucker	#	#	#	#	#	▮	▮	#
3 Hammerschmidt	Y	Y	N	Y	Y	N	N	N
4 Thornton	?	?	?	?	?	?	?	?
CALIFORNIA								
1 Johnson	Y	Y	Y	Y	Y	N	Y	Y
2 Clausen	Y	Y	N	Y	Y	N	N	N
3 Moss	Y	Y	Y	Y	Y	?	Y	Y
4 Leggett	Y	Y	?	Y	Y	N	Y	Y
5 Burton, J.	Y	Y	Y	Y	Y	N	Y	Y
6 Burton, P.	Y	Y	Y	Y	Y	N	Y	Y
7 Miller	Y	Y	Y	Y	Y	N	Y	Y
8 Dellums	#	#	#	#	▮	#	Y	Y
9 Stark	Y	Y	Y	Y	N	N	Y	Y
10 Edwards	Y	Y	Y	Y	N	N	Y	Y
11 Ryan	Y	Y	N	Y	Y	N	N	Y
12 McCloskey	Y	Y	Y	Y	Y	Y	Y	N
13 Mineta	Y	Y	Y	Y	Y	N	Y	Y
14 McFall	Y	Y	Y	Y	Y	N	Y	Y
15 Sisk	Y	Y	Y	Y	Y	?	Y	N
16 Panetta	Y	Y	Y	Y	Y	Y	N	Y
17 Krebs	Y	Y	N	Y	Y	N	Y	Y
18 Ketchum	Y	Y	N	N	Y	Y	N	N
19 Lagomarsino	Y	Y	N	Y	Y	Y	N	N
20 Goldwater	Y	Y	N	Y	Y	Y	Y	N
21 Corman	Y	Y	Y	Y	Y	N	Y	Y
22 Moorhead	Y	Y	N	Y	Y	Y	N	N
23 Beilenson	Y	Y	Y	Y	Y	Y	Y	Y
24 Waxman	Y	Y	Y	Y	Y	N	#	Y
25 Roybal	Y	Y	Y	Y	Y	N	Y	Y
26 Rousselot	Y	Y	N	Y	Y	Y	N	N
27 Dornan	Y	Y	N	Y	Y	N	N	N
28 Burke	#	#	✓	#	#	▮	✓	✓
29 Hawkins	?	?	✓	?	?	?	Y	Y
30 Danielson	Y	Y	Y	Y	Y	N	Y	Y
31 Wilson, C.H.	Y	Y	Y	Y	Y	▮	Y	Y
32 Anderson	#	#	#	#	#	▮	Y	Y
33 Clawson	Y	Y	N	Y	Y	Y	N	N
34 Hannaford	Y	Y	Y	Y	Y	N	Y	Y
35 Lloyd	Y	Y	Y	Y	Y	N	Y	Y
36 Brown	?	?	Y	Y	Y	Y	Y	N
37 Pettis	Y	Y	Y	Y	Y	Y	N	Y
38 Patterson	Y	Y	Y	Y	Y	N	Y	Y
39 Wiggins	Y	Y	Y	Y	Y	N	N	N
40 Badham	Y	Y	N	Y	Y	Y	N	N
41 Wilson, B.	?	?	?	?	?	?	Y	Y
42 Van Deerlin	Y	Y	Y	Y	Y	N	Y	Y
43 Burgener	Y	Y	N	Y	Y	N	Y	N
COLORADO								
1 Schroeder	Y	Y	Y	Y	Y	N	Y	Y
2 Wirth	Y	Y	Y	Y	N	Y	Y	Y
3 Evans	Y	Y	Y	Y	Y	N	N	N
4 Johnson	Y	Y	Y	Y	Y	Y	Y	N
5 Armstrong	Y	Y	N	Y	Y	N	N	N
CONNECTICUT								
1 Cotter	Y	Y	N	Y	Y	N	N	Y
2 Dodd	Y	Y	Y	Y	Y	N	Y	Y
3 Giaimo	Y	Y	Y	Y	Y	N	N	N
4 McKinney	Y	Y	N	Y	Y	Y	N	Y
5 Sarasin	Y	Y	N	Y	Y	Y	N	Y
6 Moffett	Y	Y	Y	?	Y	N	Y	Y
DELAWARE								
AL Evans	Y	Y	Y	Y	Y	N	N	N
FLORIDA								
1 Sikes	Y	Y	N	Y	Y	N	Y	N
2 Fuqua	#	#	▮	#	#	▮	Y	N
3 Bennett	Y	Y	N	Y	Y	Y	Y	N
4 Chappell	Y	Y	N	Y	Y	N	N	N
5 Kelly	Y	Y	N	Y	Y	Y	N	N
6 Young	Y	Y	N	Y	Y	N	N	N
7 Gibbons	?	?	?	Y	Y	Y	N	N
8 Ireland	Y	Y	N	Y	Y	Y	N	N
9 Frey	?	?	X	?	?	?	?	?
10 Bafalis	Y	Y	N	Y	Y	Y	N	N
11 Rogers	Y	Y	N	Y	Y	N	N	N
12 Burke	Y	Y	N	Y	Y	N	N	Y
13 Lehman	Y	Y	Y	Y	Y	N	Y	Y
14 Pepper	Y	Y	Y	Y	Y	N	Y	Y
15 Fascell	Y	Y	Y	Y	Y	N	Y	Y
GEORGIA								
1 Ginn	Y	Y	N	Y	Y	N	N	N
2 Mathis	Y	Y	N	Y	Y	N	Y	Y
3 Brinkley	Y	Y	N	Y	Y	Y	N	N
4 Levitas	Y	Y	N	Y	Y	N	N	N
5 Fowler	Y	Y	N	Y	Y	N	N	Y
6 Flynt	Y	Y	N	Y	Y	N	N	N
7 McDonald	N	Y	N	Y	Y	Y	N	N
8 Evans	Y	Y	N	Y	Y	N	Y	Y
9 Jenkins	Y	Y	N	Y	Y	Y	N	N
10 Barnard	Y	Y	N	Y	Y	N	N	N
HAWAII								
1 Heftel	Y	Y	Y	Y	Y	Y	Y	Y
2 Akaka	Y	Y	Y	Y	Y	N	Y	Y
IDAHO								
1 Symms	Y	Y	N	Y	Y	Y	N	N
2 Hansen, G.	Y	Y	N	Y	Y	Y	Y	N
ILLINOIS								
1 Metcalfe	Y	Y	Y	Y	Y	N	Y	Y
2 Murphy	Y	Y	N	Y	Y	N	N	N
3 Russo	Y	Y	N	Y	Y	N	N	N
4 Derwinski	Y	Y	N	Y	Y	N	N	N
5 Fary	Y	Y	Y	Y	Y	N	Y	Y
6 Hyde	Y	Y	N	Y	Y	N	N	Y
7 Collins	Y	Y	?	Y	Y	?	Y	Y
8 Rostenkowski	Y	Y	Y	Y	Y	N	Y	N
9 Yates	Y	Y	Y	Y	Y	Y	Y	N
. 10 Mikva	Y	Y	Y	Y	Y	N	Y	N
11 Annunzio	Y	Y	✓	#	Y	N	Y	N
12 Crane	#	#	X	#	#	✓	N	N
13 McClory	Y	Y	N	Y	Y	Y	N	Y
14 Erlenborn	Y	Y	X	#	#	✓	N	N
15 Corcoran	Y	Y	Y	Y	Y	Y	N	N
16 Anderson	Y	Y	Y	Y	Y	Y	N	N
17 O'Brien	Y	Y	Y	Y	Y	N	N	N
18 Michel	Y	Y	Y	Y	Y	Y	N	N
19 Railsback	Y	Y	Y	Y	Y	N	N	N
20 Findley	?	?	?	?	?	?	N	N
21 Madigan	Y	Y	N	Y	Y	Y	N	N
22 Shipley	?	?	✓	?	?	?	Y	Y
23 Price	Y	Y	Y	Y	Y	N	Y	Y
24 Simon	Y	Y	Y	Y	Y	Y	†	†
INDIANA								
1 Benjamin	Y	Y	N	Y	Y	N	N	Y
2 Fithian	Y	Y	Y	Y	Y	N	N	Y
3 Brademas	Y	Y	Y	Y	†	-	Y	Y
4 Quayle	Y	Y	Y	Y	Y	Y	N	N
5 Hillis	Y	Y	N	Y	Y	Y	N	N
6 Evans	Y	Y	N	Y	Y	N	N	N
7 Myers, J.	Y	Y	N	Y	Y	Y	N	Y
8 Cornwell	Y	Y	N	?	Y	N	Y	N
9 Hamilton	Y	Y	Y	Y	Y	Y	Y	N
10 Sharp	Y	Y	Y	Y	Y	Y	Y	Y
11 Jacobs	Y	Y	N	Y	Y	Y	N	N
IOWA								
1 Leach	Y	Y	Y	Y	Y	Y	N	N
2 Blouin	Y	Y	Y	Y	Y	N	Y	Y
3 Grassley	Y	Y	N	Y	Y	Y	N	N
4 Smith	Y	Y	Y	Y	Y	Y	Y	Y
5 Harkin	?	Y	Y	Y	Y	N	Y	N
6 Bedell	Y	Y	Y	Y	N	Y	Y	Y

Democrats ***Republicans***

	295	296	297	298	299	300	301	302
KANSAS								
1 Sebelius	Y	Y	Y	Y	Y	Y	Y	N
2 Keys	Y	Y	Y	Y	Y	Y	Y	Y
3 Winn	Y	Y	Y	Y	Y	N	N	N
4 Glickman	Y	Y	Y	Y	Y	Y	Y	N
5 Skubitz	Y	Y	Y	Y	Y	✓	Y	Y
KENTUCKY								
1 Hubbard	Y	Y	N	Y	Y	Y	N	N
2 Natcher	Y	Y	N	Y	Y	N	Y	Y
3 Mazzoli	Y	Y	#	#	#	#	■	#
4 Snyder	Y	Y	N	Y	Y	N	N	N
5 Carter	?	?	X	?	?	?	?	?
6 Breckinridge	†	†	†	†	†	-	†	-
7 Perkins	Y	Y	Y	Y	Y	N	N	Y
LOUISIANA								
1 Livingston	?	?	✓	?	?	X	N	N
2 Boggs	Y	Y	Y	Y	Y	N	Y	Y
3 Treen	?	?	✓	?	?	X	?	?
4 Waggonner	Y	Y	Y	Y	Y	N	N	N
5 Huckaby	Y	Y	Y	Y	Y	N	Y	N
6 Moore	Y	Y	Y	Y	Y	N	Y	N
7 Breaux	Y	Y	Y	Y	Y	N	N	N
8 Long	Y	Y	Y	Y	Y	N	N	Y
MAINE								
1 Emery	Y	Y	Y	Y	Y	N	N	N
2 Cohen	Y	Y	Y	Y	Y	N	N	N
MARYLAND								
1 Bauman	N	Y	N	Y	Y	N	N	N
2 Long	Y	Y	N	Y	Y	N	Y	N
3 Mikulski	Y	Y	Y	Y	Y	N	Y	Y
4 Holt	Y	Y	N	Y	Y	N	N	N
5 Spellman	Y	Y	Y	Y	Y	N	Y	Y
6 Byron	Y	Y	N	Y	Y	N	Y	N
7 Mitchell	Y	Y	Y	#	Y	Y	Y	Y
8 Steers	Y	Y	Y	Y	Y	Y	Y	#
MASSACHUSETTS								
1 Conte	Y	Y	Y	Y	Y	Y	Y	N
2 Boland	Y	Y	N	Y	Y	N	Y	N
3 Early	Y	Y	Y	Y	Y	N	Y	Y
4 Drinan	Y	Y	Y	Y	Y	Y	Y	N
5 Tsongas	Y	Y	Y	Y	Y	?	#	#
6 Harrington	Y	Y	Y	Y	N	#	Y	Y
7 Markey	Y	Y	Y	Y	Y	N	Y	Y
8 O'Neill								
9 Moakley	Y	Y	Y	Y	Y	N	Y	Y
10 Heckler	Y	Y	N	Y	Y	X	Y	Y
11 Burke	Y	Y	N	Y	Y	N	Y	Y
12 Studds	Y	Y	Y	Y	Y	N	Y	Y
MICHIGAN								
1 Conyers	#	#	#	#	■	#	#	#
2 Pursell	?	?	?	?	?	?	N	Y
3 Brown	Y	Y	N	Y	Y	Y	N	N
4 Stockman	Y	Y	Y	Y	Y	Y	N	N
5 Sawyer	Y	Y	Y	Y	Y	Y	N	Y
6 Carr	Y	Y	Y	Y	Y	N	Y	Y
7 Kildee	Y	Y	Y	Y	Y	N	Y	Y
8 Traxler	Y	Y	N	Y	Y	N	Y	Y
9 Vander Jagt	Y	Y	Y	Y	Y	Y	N	N
10 Cederberg	Y	Y	N	Y	Y	Y	?	?
11 Ruppe	Y	Y	Y	Y	Y	Y	N	N
12 Bonior	Y	Y	Y	Y	Y	N	Y	Y
13 Diggs	Y	Y	Y	#	Y	N	Y	Y
14 Nedzi	Y	Y	Y	Y	Y	N	Y	Y
15 Ford	Y	Y	Y	Y	Y	N	Y	Y
16 Dingell	Y	Y	N	Y	Y	N	N	Y
17 Brodhead	Y	Y	Y	Y	Y	N	Y	Y
18 Blanchard	Y	Y	N	Y	Y	N	Y	Y
19 Broomfield	Y	Y	N	Y	Y	Y	N	N
MINNESOTA								
1 Quie	#	#	✓	#	#	#	N	Y
2 Hagedorn	Y	Y	Y	Y	Y	Y	N	N
3 Frenzel	Y	Y	Y	Y	Y	Y	N	Y
4 Vento	Y	Y	Y	Y	Y	N	Y	Y
5 Fraser	#	#	#	#	■	■	Y	Y
6 Nolan	Y	Y	Y	Y	N	N	Y	Y
7 Stangeland	Y	Y	Y	Y	Y	Y	N	N
8 Oberstar	Y	Y	Y	Y	Y	N	Y	Y
MISSISSIPPI								
1 Whitten	Y	Y	N	Y	Y	N	N	N
2 Bowen	Y	Y	?	?	?	?	N	N
3 Montgomery	Y	Y	Y	Y	Y	N	N	N
4 Cochran	?	?	?	?	?	?	?	?
5 Lott	Y	Y	N	Y	Y	N	N	N
MISSOURI								
1 Clay	Y	Y	Y	Y	Y	N	Y	Y
2 Young	Y	Y	N	Y	Y	N	Y	N
3 Gephardt	N	Y	Y	Y	■	#	Y	N
4 Skelton	Y	Y	N	Y	Y	N	Y	N
5 Bolling	Y	Y	Y	Y	Y	■	Y	Y
6 Coleman	Y	Y	Y	Y	Y	N	N	N
7 Taylor	Y	Y	N	Y	Y	N	N	N
8 Ichord	Y	Y	N	Y	Y	Y	N	N
9 Volkmer	Y	Y	N	Y	N	Y	Y	N
10 Burlison	Y	Y	Y	Y	Y	N	Y	N
MONTANA								
1 Baucus	#	#	Y	Y	Y	N	Y	Y
2 Marlenee	Y	Y	N	Y	Y	Y	Y	Y
NEBRASKA								
1 Thone	Y	Y	Y	Y	Y	Y	N	Y
2 Cavanaugh	Y	Y	Y	Y	Y	N	Y	Y
3 Smith	Y	Y	Y	Y	Y	Y	N	Y
NEVADA								
AL Santini	Y	Y	N	Y	Y	N	Y	Y
NEW HAMPSHIRE								
1 D'Amours	Y	Y	N	Y	Y	N	N	N
2 Cleveland	Y	Y	N	Y	Y	Y	N	N
NEW JERSEY								
1 Florio	Y	Y	N	Y	Y	N	N	N
2 Hughes	Y	Y	N	Y	Y	N	N	N
3 Howard	Y	Y	Y	Y	Y	N	Y	Y
4 Thompson	Y	Y	Y	Y	Y	N	Y	Y
5 Fenwick	Y	Y	Y	Y	N	Y	N	N
6 Forsythe	Y	Y	Y	Y	N	Y	N	Y
7 Maguire	Y	Y	Y	Y	N	Y	Y	Y
8 Roe	Y	Y	N	Y	Y	N	Y	N
9 Hollenbeck	#	#	X	#	#	X	N	Y
10 Rodino	#	#	#	#	#	■	#	#
11 Minish	Y	Y	N	Y	Y	N	N	N
12 Rinaldo	Y	Y	N	Y	Y	N	N	Y
13 Meyner	Y	Y	Y	Y	Y	Y	Y	Y
14 LeFante	Y	Y	N	Y	Y	N	Y	Y
15 Patten	Y	Y	N	Y	Y	N	Y	Y
NEW MEXICO								
1 Lujan	Y	Y	Y	Y	Y	Y	N	N
2 Runnels	#	#	?	#	#	✓	X	X
NEW YORK								
1 Pike	Y	Y	Y	Y	Y	N	Y	N
2 Downey	Y	Y	Y	Y	Y	■	Y	Y
3 Ambro	Y	Y	N	Y	Y	N	Y	Y
4 Lent	?	Y	N	Y	?	Y	N	Y
5 Wydler	Y	Y	N	Y	Y	Y	N	N
6 Wolff	Y	Y	Y	Y	Y	N	Y	Y
7 Addabbo	Y	Y	N	Y	Y	N	Y	Y
8 Rosenthal	Y	Y	Y	Y	#	N	Y	Y
9 Delaney	Y	Y	N	Y	Y	N	N	Y
10 Biaggi	#	Y	#	Y	Y	N	Y	Y
11 Scheuer	Y	Y	Y	Y	N	N	Y	Y
12 Chisholm	Y	Y	Y	Y	Y	N	✓	✓
13 Solarz	Y	Y	Y	Y	Y	N	Y	Y
14 Richmond	Y	Y	Y	Y	N	N	Y	Y
15 Zeferetti	Y	Y	N	Y	Y	N	Y	Y
16 Holtzman	Y	Y	Y	Y	N	N	Y	Y
17 Murphy	Y	Y	Y	Y	Y	N	Y	Y
18 Green	Y	Y	Y	Y	Y	■	Y	Y
19 Rangel	Y	Y	Y	Y	N	✓	Y	Y
20 Weiss	Y	Y	Y	Y	N	N	Y	Y
21 Garcia	Y	Y	Y	Y	Y	N	Y	Y
22 Bingham	Y	Y	Y	Y	Y	N	Y	Y
23 Caputo	Y	Y	N	Y	N	Y	N	Y
24 Ottinger	N	Y	Y	Y	N	N	Y	Y
25 Fish	Y	Y	Y	Y	Y	Y	N	N
26 Gilman	Y	Y	N	Y	Y	N	Y	Y
27 McHugh	Y	Y	Y	#	Y	N	Y	Y
28 Stratton	Y	Y	N	Y	Y	N	N	N
29 Pattison	Y	Y	Y	Y	Y	Y	Y	Y
30 McEwen	Y	Y	N	Y	Y	N	N	N
31 Mitchell	Y	Y	N	Y	Y	N	N	N
32 Hanley	Y	Y	Y	Y	Y	N	Y	Y
33 Walsh	Y	Y	N	Y	Y	N	N	N
34 Horton	Y	Y	N	Y	Y	Y	N	N
35 Conable	Y	Y	Y	Y	Y	Y	N	N
36 LaFalce	Y	Y	Y	Y	Y	Y	Y	Y
37 Nowak	Y	Y	N	Y	Y	N	Y	Y
38 Kemp	Y	Y	N	Y	?	?	N	?
39 Lundine	Y	Y	N	Y	Y	N	Y	Y
NORTH CAROLINA								
1 Jones	#	#	■	#	#	■	■	■
2 Fountain	Y	Y	N	Y	Y	N	N	N
3 Whitley	Y	Y	N	Y	Y	Y	Y	N
4 Andrews	Y	Y	Y	Y	Y	Y	Y	N
5 Neal	Y	Y	Y	Y	Y	X	N	N
6 Preyer	Y	Y	Y	Y	Y	N	Y	Y
7 Rose	Y	Y	N	Y	Y	■	Y	Y
8 Hefner	Y	Y	N	Y	Y	N	N	N
9 Martin	Y	Y	N	Y	Y	Y	N	N
10 Broyhill	Y	Y	N	Y	Y	Y	N	N
11 Gudger	Y	Y	N	Y	Y	N	Y	N
NORTH DAKOTA								
AL Andrews	Y	Y	Y	Y	Y	N	Y	N
OHIO								
1 Gradison	Y	Y	Y	Y	Y	Y	N	N
2 Luken	#	#	■	#	#	?	N	N
3 Whalen	Y	Y	Y	Y	Y	N	#	#
4 Guyer	Y	Y	N	Y	Y	Y	N	N
5 Latta	Y	Y	N	Y	Y	Y	N	N
6 Harsha	Y	Y	N	Y	Y	N	N	N
7 Brown	Y	Y	Y	Y	Y	Y	N	N
8 Kindness	Y	Y	N	Y	Y	N	N	Y
9 Ashley	Y	Y	Y	Y	Y	N	Y	N
10 Miller	Y	Y	N	Y	Y	Y	N	N
11 Stanton	Y	Y	Y	Y	Y	N	N	N
12 Devine	Y	Y	N	Y	Y	Y	N	N
13 Pease	Y	Y	Y	Y	Y	N	#	N
14 Seiberling	Y	Y	Y	Y	Y	N	Y	Y
15 Wylie	Y	Y	N	Y	Y	Y	N	Y
16 Regula	Y	Y	Y	Y	Y	N	N	Y
17 Ashbrook	N	Y	N	Y	Y	Y	N	N
18 Applegate	Y	Y	N	Y	Y	N	Y	N
19 Carney	Y	Y	N	Y	Y	N	Y	Y
20 Oakar	?	?	?	?	?	?	?	?
21 Stokes	#	Y	Y	Y	Y	N	Y	Y
22 Vanik	Y	Y	Y	Y	Y	Y	Y	Y
23 Mottl	Y	Y	N	Y	Y	N	N	Y
OKLAHOMA								
1 Jones	Y	Y	Y	Y	Y	N	N	N
2 Risenhoover	Y	Y	N	Y	Y	?	Y	N
3 Watkins	Y	Y	N	Y	Y	Y	N	N
4 Steed	Y	Y	N	Y	Y	N	N	N
5 Edwards	Y	Y	N	Y	Y	Y	N	N
6 English	Y	Y	Y	Y	Y	Y	N	N
OREGON								
1 AuCoin	#	#	✓	#	?	X	✓	✓
2 Ullman	#	#	#	#	#	?	Y	Y
3 Duncan	Y	Y	Y	Y	Y	N	?	?
4 Weaver	Y	Y	Y	Y	Y	N	Y	Y
PENNSYLVANIA								
1 Myers, M.	Y	Y	N	Y	Y	N	Y	Y
2 Nix	Y	Y	Y	Y	Y	?	?	✓
3 Lederer	Y	Y	N	Y	Y	N	Y	Y
4 Eilberg	Y	Y	Y	Y	Y	N	Y	Y
5 Schulze	Y	Y	N	Y	Y	Y	N	Y
6 Yatron	Y	Y	Y	Y	Y	N	Y	N
7 Edgar	Y	Y	Y	Y	Y	N	Y	Y
8 Kostmayer	Y	Y	Y	Y	Y	Y	Y	Y
9 Shuster	Y	Y	N	Y	Y	Y	N	N
10 McDade	Y	Y	N	Y	#	N	N	Y
11 Flood	Y	Y	N	Y	Y	N	Y	Y
12 Murtha	Y	Y	N	Y	Y	N	Y	N
13 Coughlin	Y	Y	Y	Y	Y	Y	N	N
14 Moorhead	Y	Y	Y	Y	Y	N	Y	Y
15 Rooney	Y	Y	Y	Y	Y	?	Y	Y
16 Walker	Y	Y	N	Y	Y	Y	N	Y
17 Ertel	Y	Y	N	Y	Y	Y	Y	Y
18 Walgren	Y	Y	Y	Y	Y	Y	Y	Y
19 Goodling, W.	Y	Y	N	?	?	✓	N	Y
20 Gaydos	Y	Y	Y	Y	Y	N	N	Y
21 Dent	Y	Y	X	Y	Y	■	Y	N
22 Murphy	Y	Y	N	Y	Y	N	N	Y
23 Ammerman	Y	Y	Y	Y	Y	N	N	Y
24 Marks	Y	Y	Y	Y	Y	N	Y	Y
25 Myers, G.	Y	Y	Y	Y	Y	#	Y	Y
RHODE ISLAND								
1 St Germain	Y	Y	Y	Y	Y	N	Y	Y
2 Beard	Y	Y	Y	Y	Y	N	Y	Y
SOUTH CAROLINA								
1 Davis	Y	Y	N	Y	Y	N	N	N
2 Spence	Y	Y	N	Y	Y	N	N	N
3 Derrick	Y	Y	N	Y	Y	N	N	N
4 Mann	Y	Y	N	Y	Y	?	Y	Y
5 Holland	Y	Y	N	Y	Y	N	N	N
6 Jenrette	?	#	X	#	#	X	✓	Y
SOUTH DAKOTA								
1 Pressler	Y	Y	N	Y	Y	Y	N	Y
2 Abdnor	Y	Y	Y	Y	Y	Y	N	N
TENNESSEE								
1 Quillen	Y	Y	N	Y	Y	Y	N	N
2 Duncan	#	#	X	†	#	■	N	N
3 Lloyd	?	?	X	?	?	N	N	N
4 Gore	#	#	#	#	#	N	Y	Y
5 Allen	?	?	?	?	?	?	N	N
6 Beard	Y	Y	N	Y	Y	N	N	N
7 Jones	#	#	✓	#	#	N	Y	N
8 Ford	Y	Y	Y	Y	Y	N	Y	Y
TEXAS								
1 Hall	Y	Y	Y	Y	Y	N	N	N
2 Wilson, C.	Y	Y	Y	Y	Y	N	N	Y
3 Collins	Y	Y	N	Y	Y	Y	N	N
4 Roberts	Y	Y	N	Y	Y	N	N	N
5 Mattox	Y	Y	N	Y	Y	N	Y	N
6 Teague	?	?	X	?	?	✓	X	X
7 Archer	Y	Y	N	Y	Y	Y	N	N
8 Eckhardt	Y	Y	Y	Y	Y	N	Y	Y
9 Brooks	Y	Y	Y	Y	Y	N	Y	Y
10 Pickle	Y	Y	Y	Y	Y	N	Y	N
11 Poage	Y	Y	Y	Y	Y	Y	Y	N
12 Wright	Y	Y	Y	?	Y	N	Y	Y
13 Hightower	Y	Y	N	Y	Y	Y	Y	N
14 Young	?	?	?	?	?	?	?	?
15 de la Garza	Y	Y	Y	Y	Y	N	Y	N
16 White	Y	Y	N	Y	Y	N	Y	N
17 Burleson	Y	Y	N	Y	Y	Y	N	N
18 Jordan	Y	Y	Y	Y	Y	N	Y	Y
19 Mahon	Y	Y	Y	?	Y	Y	N	N
20 Gonzalez	Y	Y	Y	Y	Y	N	Y	Y
21 Krueger	Y	Y	N	Y	Y	N	Y	Y
22 Gammage	Y	Y	N	Y	Y	N	Y	N
23 Kazen	Y	Y	N	Y	Y	N	Y	N
24 Milford	Y	Y	Y	Y	Y	Y	N	N
UTAH								
1 McKay	Y	Y	N	Y	Y	N	Y	N
2 Marriott	Y	Y	N	Y	Y	Y	N	N
VERMONT								
AL Jeffords	Y	Y	Y	Y	Y	Y	Y	Y
VIRGINIA								
1 Trible	Y	Y	N	Y	Y	N	N	N
2 Whitehurst	Y	Y	N	Y	Y	N	N	N
3 Satterfield	Y	Y	N	Y	Y	N	N	N
4 Daniel	Y	Y	N	Y	Y	N	N	N
5 Daniel	Y	Y	N	Y	Y	N	N	N
6 Butler	Y	Y	N	Y	Y	Y	N	N
7 Robinson	?	Y	N	Y	Y	Y	N	N
8 Harris	Y	Y	Y	Y	Y	N	Y	Y
9 Wampler	Y	Y	N	Y	Y	N	N	N
10 Fisher	Y	Y	Y	Y	Y	Y	Y	Y
WASHINGTON								
1 Pritchard	#	#	✓	#	#	■	#	N
2 Meeds	Y	Y	Y	Y	Y	N	Y	Y
3 Bonker	Y	Y	Y	Y	Y	N	N	Y
4 McCormack	Y	Y	Y	Y	Y	N	N	N
5 Foley	Y	Y	Y	Y	Y	N	N	Y
6 Dicks	Y	Y	Y	Y	Y	N	N	Y
7 Cunningham	Y	Y	N	Y	Y	N	N	N
WEST VIRGINIA								
1 Mollohan	Y	Y	N	Y	Y	N	N	N
2 Staggers	Y	Y	N	Y	Y	N	N	N
3 Slack	Y	Y	N	Y	Y	N	N	N
4 Rahall	Y	Y	Y	Y	Y	N	Y	Y
WISCONSIN								
1 Aspin	Y	Y	Y	Y	Y	Y	Y	Y
2 Kastenmeier	Y	Y	Y	Y	N	Y	Y	Y
3 Baldus	Y	Y	Y	Y	Y	N	Y	Y
4 Zablocki	Y	Y	Y	Y	Y	N	Y	Y
5 Reuss	Y	Y	Y	Y	Y	Y	Y	N
6 Steiger	Y	Y	Y	#	Y	Y	Y	N
7 Obey	Y	Y	Y	Y	Y	N	N	N
8 Cornell	Y	Y	Y	Y	Y	N	Y	Y
9 Kasten	#	#	✓	#	#	#	#	#
WYOMING								
AL Roncalio	?	?	?	?	?	?	Y	Y

Democrats *Republicans*

303. HR 3050. Tax Treatment of Magazines, Paperbacks and Records. Ullman, D-Ore., motion to suspend the rules and pass the bill to amend the Internal Revenue Code to provide a new accounting method applicable to returns of unsold magazines, paperbacks and records. Motion agreed to 358-50: R 133-5; D 225-45 (ND 152-35; SD 73-10), May 23, 1978. A two-thirds majority vote (272 in this case) is required for passage under suspension of the rules.

304. HR 8535. Day Care Tax Credit. Ullman, D-Ore., motion to suspend the rules and pass the bill to revise eligibility requirements for a tax credit for expenses of certain dependent care services performed by relatives. Motion agreed to 363-44: R 132-6; D 231-38 (ND 154-32; SD 77-6), May 23, 1978. A two-thirds majority vote (272 in this case) is required for passage under suspension of the rules.

305. H Res 238. Dried Fruit Exports. Vanik, D-Ohio, motion to suspend the rules and adopt the resolution expressing the sense of the House that the president should take action to eliminate restrictions imposed by the European Economic Community on imports of U.S.-processed fruits, juices and vegetables, including dried prunes. Motion agreed to 407-0: R 137-0; D 270-0 (ND 187-0; SD 83-0), May 23, 1978. A two-thirds majority vote (272 in this case) is required for passage under suspension of the rules.

306. HR 11370. Social Services Reimbursement. Ullman, D-Ore., motion to suspend the rules and pass the bill to authorize $543 million for fiscal 1979 for the final settlement of a dispute between the Department of Health, Education and Welfare and 28 states over social services provided by the states before Oct. 1, 1975. Motion agreed to 377-25: R 131-4; D 246-21 (ND 174-11; SD 72-10), May 23, 1978. A two-thirds majority vote (268 in this case) is required for passage under suspension of the rules.

307. HR 10729. Maritime Administration Authorization. McCloskey, R-Calif., amendment to prevent the payment of federal ship construction subsidies to any organization that engages in lobbying activities. Rejected 168-227: R 95-43; D 73-184 (ND 46-131; SD 27-53), May 23, 1978.

308. HR 10729. Maritime Administration Authorization. McCloskey, R-Calif., amendment to prohibit the use of federal ship construction subsidy funds for the training of new entrants into the maritime industry. Rejected 111-289: R 80-55; D 31-234 (ND 16-168; SD 15-66), May 23, 1978.

309. HR 10729. Maritime Administration Authorization. McCloskey, R-Calif., amendment to prohibit the use of federal ship construction subsidy funds to subsidize the shipment of grain to Russia. Rejected 180-218: R 112-26; D 68-192 (ND 37-143; SD 31-49), May 23, 1978.

310. HR 10729. Maritime Administration Authorization. Passage of the bill to authorize $496,792,000 for fiscal 1979 programs of the Commerce Department Maritime Administration. Passed 326-82: R 86-53; D 240-29 (ND 168-18; SD 72-11), May 23, 1978.

KEY

Y Voted for (yea).
✓ Paired for.
† Announced for.
# CQ Poll for.
N Voted against (nay).
X Paired against.
- Announced against.
▮ CQ Poll against.
P Voted "present."
● Voted "present" to avoid possible conflict of interest.
? Did not vote or otherwise make a position known.

	303	304	305	306	307	308	309	310
ALABAMA								
1 ***Edwards***	Y	Y	Y	Y	N	N	Y	Y
2 ***Dickinson***	Y	Y	Y	Y	Y	Y	Y	Y
3 Nichols	N	Y	Y	Y	Y	N	Y	Y
4 Bevill	Y	Y	Y	Y	N	N	Y	Y
5 Flippo	Y	Y	Y	Y	N	N	N	Y
6 ***Buchanan***	Y	Y	Y	Y	N	N	Y	Y
7 Flowers	Y	Y	Y	Y	N	N	N	Y
ALASKA								
AL ***Young***	?	?	?	?	?	?	✓	?
ARIZONA								
1 ***Rhodes***	Y	Y	Y	Y	Y	Y	Y	Y
2 Udall	Y	Y	Y	Y	Y	N	Y	Y
3 Stump	Y	N	Y	Y	Y	N	Y	N
4 ***Rudd***	Y	Y	Y	Y	Y	?	Y	N
ARKANSAS								
1 Alexander	Y	Y	Y	Y	N	N	N	Y
2 Tucker	#	#	#	#	▮	▮	▮	#
3 ***Hammerschmidt***	Y	Y	Y	Y	Y	Y	Y	N
4 Thornton	?	?	?	?	?	?	?	?
CALIFORNIA								
1 Johnson	Y	Y	Y	Y	N	N	N	Y
2 ***Clausen***	Y	Y	Y	Y	Y	N	Y	Y
3 Moss	N	N	Y	N	?	?	?	N
4 Leggett	N	Y	Y	Y	N	N	N	Y
5 Burton, J.	N	Y	Y	Y	N	N	N	Y
6 Burton, P.	Y	Y	Y	Y	N	N	N	Y
7 Miller	Y	Y	Y	Y	N	N	N	Y
8 Dellums	Y	Y	Y	#	N	N	N	Y
9 Stark	N	N	Y	Y	N	N	N	Y
10 Edwards	Y	N	Y	Y	N	N	N	Y
11 Ryan	N	N	Y	Y	N	N	N	Y
12 ***McCloskey***	Y	Y	?	Y	Y	Y	Y	N
13 Mineta	Y	Y	Y	Y	N	N	N	Y
14 McFall	Y	Y	Y	Y	N	N	N	Y
15 Sisk	Y	N	Y	Y	N	Y	N	Y
16 Panetta	Y	Y	Y	Y	Y	N	Y	Y
17 Krebs	Y	N	Y	Y	Y	N	N	Y
18 ***Ketchum***	Y	Y	Y	Y	Y	Y	Y	N
19 ***Lagomarsino***	Y	Y	Y	Y	N	N	Y	Y
20 ***Goldwater***	Y	Y	Y	Y	Y	N	Y	Y
21 Corman	Y	Y	Y	Y	N	N	N	Y
22 ***Moorhead***	Y	Y	Y	Y	Y	Y	Y	Y
23 Beilenson	Y	N	Y	Y	Y	N	N	N
24 Waxman	Y	N	Y	#	N	N	N	Y
25 Roybal	Y	Y	Y	Y	N	N	N	Y
26 ***Rousselot***	Y	Y	Y	Y	Y	Y	Y	N
27 ***Dornan***	Y	Y	Y	Y	N	Y	Y	Y
28 Burke	#	#	#	#	▮	X	X	#
29 Hawkins	Y	Y	Y	Y	N	N	N	Y
30 Danielson	Y	N	Y	Y	N	N	N	Y
31 Wilson, C.H.	Y	Y	Y	Y	▮	▮	N	Y
32 Anderson	Y	Y	Y	Y	N	N	N	Y
33 ***Clawson***	Y	Y	Y	Y	Y	Y	Y	N
34 Hannaford	Y	Y	Y	Y	N	N	N	Y
35 Lloyd	Y	Y	Y	Y	N	N	N	Y
36 Brown	Y	Y	Y	Y	N	N	Y	Y
37 ***Pettis***	Y	Y	Y	Y	Y	Y	Y	Y
38 Patterson	Y	Y	Y	Y	Y	N	N	Y
39 ***Wiggins***	Y	Y	Y	Y	Y	Y	Y	Y
40 ***Badham***	Y	Y	Y	Y	Y	Y	Y	N
41 ***Wilson, B.***	Y	Y	Y	Y	N	N	N	Y
42 Van Deerlin	Y	N	Y	Y	N	N	Y	Y
43 ***Burgener***	Y	Y	Y	Y	N	N	Y	Y
COLORADO								
1 Schroeder	N	Y	Y	Y	N	N	N	N
2 Wirth	Y	N	Y	Y	Y	N	Y	Y
3 Evans	Y	Y	Y	Y	N	N	N	Y
4 ***Johnson***	Y	Y	Y	Y	Y	Y	Y	N
5 ***Armstrong***	Y	Y	Y	Y	Y	N	Y	N
CONNECTICUT								
1 Cotter	N	Y	Y	Y	N	N	N	Y
2 Dodd	Y	Y	Y	Y	N	N	N	Y
3 Giaimo	Y	N	Y	Y	N	N	N	Y
4 ***McKinney***	Y	Y	Y	Y	Y	Y	Y	N
5 ***Sarasin***	Y	Y	Y	Y	Y	Y	Y	Y
6 Moffett	N	Y	Y	Y	N	N	N	Y
DELAWARE								
AL ***Evans***	Y	Y	Y	Y	Y	Y	Y	Y
FLORIDA								
1 Sikes	N	Y	Y	Y	N	N	Y	Y
2 Fuqua	N	Y	Y	Y	N	N	Y	Y
3 Bennett	N	N	Y	N	Y	N	Y	Y
4 Chappell	Y	Y	Y	Y	N	N	Y	Y
5 ***Kelly***	Y	Y	Y	Y	Y	Y	Y	N
6 ***Young***	N	Y	Y	Y	Y	Y	Y	N
7 Gibbons	Y	Y	Y	Y	Y	N	Y	Y
8 Ireland	Y	Y	Y	Y	Y	N	Y	Y
9 ***Frey***	?	?	?	?	?	?	✓	?
10 ***Bafalis***	Y	Y	Y	Y	Y	Y	Y	N
11 Rogers	N	Y	Y	Y	N	N	Y	Y
12 ***Burke***	Y	Y	Y	Y	N	Y	Y	Y
13 Lehman	Y	Y	Y	Y	N	N	N	Y
14 Pepper	Y	Y	Y	Y	N	N	N	Y
15 Fascell	Y	Y	Y	Y	N	N	N	Y
GEORGIA								
1 Ginn	N	Y	Y	Y	N	N	N	Y
2 Mathis	Y	Y	Y	Y	Y	N	N	Y
3 Brinkley	Y	Y	Y	Y	Y	Y	Y	Y
4 Levitas	Y	Y	Y	Y	Y	N	N	Y
5 Fowler	N	Y	Y	Y	Y	Y	N	Y
6 Flynt	N	N	Y	Y	Y	N	N	Y
7 McDonald	Y	Y	Y	N	Y	Y	Y	N
8 Evans	Y	Y	Y	N	N	N	N	N
9 Jenkins	Y	Y	Y	Y	Y	Y	N	N
10 Barnard	N	Y	Y	Y	Y	N	N	Y
HAWAII								
1 Heftel	N	Y	Y	Y	N	N	Y	Y
2 Akaka	N	Y	Y	Y	N	N	N	Y
IDAHO								
1 ***Symms***	Y	Y	Y	Y	Y	Y	Y	N
2 ***Hansen, G.***	Y	Y	Y	?	N	N	Y	N
ILLINOIS								
1 Metcalfe	Y	Y	Y	Y	N	N	N	Y
2 Murphy	N	Y	Y	Y	N	N	N	Y
3 Russo	Y	Y	Y	Y	Y	N	N	Y
4 ***Derwinski***	Y	Y	Y	Y	Y	N	Y	Y
5 Fary	Y	Y	Y	Y	N	N	N	Y
6 ***Hyde***	Y	Y	Y	Y	Y	N	Y	Y
7 Collins	Y	Y	Y	Y	N	N	N	Y
8 Rostenkowski	Y	Y	Y	Y	N	N	N	Y
9 Yates	Y	N	Y	Y	N	Y	Y	N
10 Mikva	Y	Y	Y	Y	Y	N	N	N
11 Annunzio	Y	Y	Y	Y	N	N	N	Y
12 ***Crane***	Y	Y	Y	Y	Y	Y	Y	N
13 ***McClory***	Y	Y	Y	Y	Y	Y	Y	N
14 ***Erlenborn***	Y	Y	Y	Y	Y	Y	Y	N
15 ***Corcoran***	Y	Y	Y	Y	Y	N	Y	Y
16 ***Anderson***	Y	Y	Y	Y	Y	Y	Y	N
17 ***O'Brien***	Y	Y	Y	N	Y	N	N	Y
18 ***Michel***	Y	Y	Y	Y	Y	Y	Y	N
19 ***Railsback***	#	Y	Y	Y	Y	Y	Y	Y
20 ***Findley***	Y	Y	Y	Y	Y	N	Y	N
21 ***Madigan***	Y	Y	Y	Y	Y	N	✓	Y
22 Shipley	Y	Y	Y	Y	N	N	N	Y
23 Price	Y	Y	Y	Y	N	N	N	Y
24 Simon	†	†	†	†	?	?	?	?
INDIANA								
1 Benjamin	N	Y	Y	N	N	N	Y	Y
2 Fithian	N	Y	Y	Y	N	N	N	Y
3 Brademas	Y	Y	Y	Y	N	N	N	Y
4 ***Quayle***	N	Y	Y	Y	Y	Y	Y	N
5 ***Hillis***	Y	Y	Y	Y	Y	Y	Y	Y
6 Evans	N	Y	Y	N	Y	Y	Y	Y
7 ***Myers, J.***	Y	Y	Y	Y	Y	Y	Y	Y
8 Cornwell	N	Y	Y	N	N	N	N	Y
9 Hamilton	Y	Y	Y	Y	Y	Y	Y	N
10 Sharp	Y	Y	Y	Y	Y	N	Y	Y
11 Jacobs	Y	Y	Y	Y	Y	N	Y	N
IOWA								
1 ***Leach***	Y	Y	Y	Y	Y	Y	Y	N
2 Blouin	Y	Y	Y	Y	Y	N	N	Y
3 ***Grassley***	Y	Y	Y	Y	Y	N	Y	Y
4 Smith	Y	Y	Y	Y	Y	N	N	Y
5 Harkin	N	Y	Y	N	N	N	N	Y
6 Bedell	Y	N	Y	Y	Y	N	N	N

Democrats ***Republicans***

	303	304	305	306	307	308	309	310
KANSAS								
1 ***Sebelius***	Y	Y	Y	Y	Y	Y	Y	Y
2 Keys	Y	Y	Y	Y	Y	N	N	Y
3 ***Winn***	Y	Y	Y	Y	Y	Y	Y	Y
4 Glickman	Y	Y	Y	Y	Y	N	N	N
5 ***Skubitz***	Y	Y	Y	Y	Y	Y	Y	Y
KENTUCKY								
1 Hubbard	Y	Y	Y	Y	N	N	N	Y
2 Natcher	Y	Y	Y	Y	N	N	Y	Y
3 Mazzoli	#	#	#	#	#	#	#	▮
4 ***Snyder***	Y	N	Y	Y	N	N	N	Y
5 ***Carter***	?	?	?	?	?	?	?	?
6 Breckinridge	†	†	†	†	-	-	-	†
7 Perkins	Y	Y	Y	Y	N	N	N	Y
LOUISIANA								
1 ***Livingston***	Y	Y	Y	Y	N	N	N	Y
2 Boggs	Y	Y	Y	Y	N	N	N	Y
3 ***Treen***	?	?	?	?	?	?	Y	Y
4 Waggonner	Y	Y	Y	N	N	N	N	Y
5 Huckaby	Y	Y	Y	N	N	N	?	Y
6 ***Moore***	Y	Y	Y	Y	Y	N	N	Y
7 Breaux	Y	Y	Y	Y	N	N	N	Y
8 Long	Y	Y	Y	Y	N	N	N	Y
MAINE								
1 ***Emery***	Y	Y	Y	Y	Y	Y	Y	Y
2 ***Cohen***	Y	Y	Y	Y	Y	Y	Y	Y
MARYLAND								
1 ***Bauman***	Y	Y	Y	Y	N	N	Y	Y
2 Long	Y	Y	Y	Y	N	N	Y	Y
3 Mikulski	Y	Y	Y	Y	N	N	N	Y
4 ***Holt***	Y	Y	Y	Y	N	N	Y	Y
5 Spellman	Y	Y	Y	Y	N	N	N	Y
6 Byron	Y	?	Y	Y	N	N	N	Y
7 Mitchell	Y	Y	Y	Y	▮	N	X	Y
8 ***Steers***	Y	Y	Y	#	N	N	N	Y
MASSACHUSETTS								
1 ***Conte***	Y	Y	Y	Y	N	Y	Y	Y
2 Boland	Y	Y	Y	Y	N	N	Y	Y
3 Early	Y	N	Y	Y	Y	Y	Y	Y
4 Drinan	N	Y	Y	Y	Y	Y	Y	N
5 Tsongas	?	#	#	#	?	?	?	?
6 Harrington	Y	N	Y	Y	N	Y	Y	Y
7 Markey	Y	N	Y	Y	N	Y	N	Y
8 O'Neill								
9 Moakley	Y	Y	Y	Y	N	N	N	Y
10 ***Heckler***	Y	Y	Y	Y	N	N	Y	Y
11 Burke	Y	Y	Y	Y	N	N	N	Y
12 Studds	Y	Y	Y	Y	N	N	N	Y
MICHIGAN								
1 Conyers	Y	Y	Y	Y	N	N	▮	N
2 ***Pursell***	Y	Y	Y	Y	Y	Y	Y	Y
3 ***Brown***	Y	Y	Y	Y	Y	Y	N	Y
4 ***Stockman***	Y	Y	Y	Y	Y	Y	Y	N
5 ***Sawyer***	Y	Y	Y	Y	Y	Y	Y	Y
6 Carr	Y	N	Y	Y	Y	Y	Y	Y
7 Kildee	N	Y	Y	Y	Y	N	N	Y
8 Traxler	Y	Y	Y	Y	N	N	N	Y
9 ***Vander Jagt***	Y	Y	Y	Y	?	N	N	Y
10 ***Cederberg***	?	?	?	?	?	?	✓	?
11 ***Ruppe***	Y	Y	Y	Y	N	N	Y	Y
12 Bonior	Y	Y	Y	Y	N	N	N	Y
13 Diggs	Y	Y	Y	Y	▮	N	N	Y
14 Nedzi	Y	Y	Y	Y	N	N	N	Y
15 Ford	Y	Y	Y	Y	N	N	N	Y
16 Dingell	Y	Y	Y	Y	?	N	N	Y
17 Brodhead	Y	Y	Y	Y	N	N	N	Y
18 Blanchard	Y	Y	Y	Y	N	N	Y	Y
19 ***Broomfield***	Y	Y	Y	Y	Y	Y	Y	N
MINNESOTA								
1 ***Quie***	Y	Y	Y	Y	N	N	Y	Y
2 ***Hagedorn***	Y	Y	Y	Y	Y	Y	Y	N
3 ***Frenzel***	Y	Y	Y	Y	Y	Y	Y	N
4 Vento	Y	Y	Y	Y	N	?	N	Y
5 Fraser	Y	Y	Y	Y	N	N	N	Y
6 Nolan	N	Y	Y	Y	?	N	N	Y
7 ***Stangeland***	Y	Y	Y	Y	N	Y	Y	N
8 Oberstar	Y	Y	Y	Y	N	N	N	Y
MISSISSIPPI								
1 Whitten	Y	Y	Y	Y	▮	N	Y	Y
2 Bowen	Y	Y	Y	Y	N	N	Y	Y
3 Montgomery	Y	Y	Y	Y	Y	Y	Y	Y
4 ***Cochran***	?	?	?	?	?	?	✓	?
5 ***Lott***	Y	Y	Y	Y	Y	N	Y	Y
MISSOURI								
1 Clay	Y	Y	Y	Y	N	N	N	Y
2 Young	Y	Y	Y	Y	N	N	N	Y
3 Gephardt	N	Y	Y	Y	Y	N	Y	N
4 Skelton	Y	N	Y	Y	Y	N	N	Y
5 Bolling	Y	Y	Y	Y	N	N	Y	Y
6 ***Coleman***	Y	Y	Y	Y	Y	Y	N	Y
7 ***Taylor***	Y	N	Y	Y	Y	N	Y	Y
8 Ichord	N	Y	Y	Y	Y	Y	Y	Y
9 Volkmer	N	Y	Y	Y	Y	Y	N	Y
10 Burlison	N	Y	Y	Y	N	N	N	Y
MONTANA								
1 Baucus	Y	Y	Y	Y	N	N	N	Y
2 ***Marlenee***	Y	Y	Y	Y	Y	N	N	Y
NEBRASKA								
1 ***Thone***	Y	Y	Y	Y	N	Y	Y	Y
2 Cavanaugh	N	N	Y	Y	N	N	N	Y
3 ***Smith***	Y	Y	Y	Y	N	Y	Y	Y
NEVADA								
AL Santini	Y	Y	Y	N	Y	N	Y	Y
NEW HAMPSHIRE								
1 D'Amours	Y	Y	Y	Y	N	N	N	Y
2 ***Cleveland***	Y	Y	Y	Y	Y	Y	Y	N
NEW JERSEY								
1 Florio	N	Y	Y	Y	N	N	N	Y
2 Hughes	Y	N	Y	Y	N	N	N	Y
3 Howard	Y	Y	Y	Y	#	N	X	Y
4 Thompson	Y	Y	Y	Y	N	N	N	Y
5 ***Fenwick***	Y	Y	Y	Y	Y	Y	Y	N
6 ***Forsythe***	Y	Y	Y	Y	N	Y	N	Y
7 Maguire	Y	N	Y	Y	Y	N	N	N
8 Roe	Y	Y	Y	Y	N	N	Y	Y
9 ***Hollenbeck***	Y	Y	Y	Y	N	N	N	Y
10 Rodino	#	#	#	#	▮	▮	▮	#
11 Minish	Y	Y	Y	Y	N	N	Y	Y
12 ***Rinaldo***	Y	Y	Y	Y	N	N	N	Y
13 Meyner	Y	Y	Y	Y	N	N	N	Y
14 LeFante	Y	Y	Y	Y	N	N	N	Y
15 Patten	Y	Y	Y	Y	N	N	N	Y
NEW MEXICO								
1 ***Lujan***	N	?	Y	N	N	Y	Y	N
2 Runnels	X	#	#	X	?	✓	✓	X
NEW YORK								
1 Pike	Y	N	Y	Y	N	N	N	Y
2 Downey	Y	Y	Y	Y	N	N	N	Y
3 Ambro	Y	Y	Y	Y	Y	N	N	Y
4 ***Lent***	Y	Y	Y	Y	Y	N	Y	Y
5 ***Wydler***	N	Y	Y	Y	Y	N	Y	Y
6 Wolff	Y	Y	Y	Y	▮	N	Y	Y
7 Addabbo	Y	Y	Y	Y	N	N	N	Y
8 Rosenthal	Y	Y	Y	Y	N	N	N	Y
9 Delaney	Y	Y	Y	Y	N	N	N	Y
10 Biaggi	Y	Y	Y	Y	N	N	X	?
11 Scheuer	Y	Y	Y	Y	Y	N	Y	Y
12 Chisholm	✓	?	#	#	?	N	X	Y
13 Solarz	Y	Y	Y	Y	N	N	N	Y
14 Richmond	N	Y	Y	Y	N	N	N	Y
15 Zeferetti	Y	Y	Y	Y	N	N	N	Y
16 Holtzman	Y	Y	Y	Y	Y	Y	N	N
17 Murphy	Y	Y	Y	Y	N	N	N	Y
18 ***Green***	Y	N	Y	Y	Y	N	Y	Y
19 Rangel	Y	Y	Y	Y	Y	N	N	Y
20 Weiss	Y	N	Y	Y	N	N	N	Y
21 Garcia	Y	Y	Y	Y	N	N	N	Y
22 Bingham	Y	N	Y	Y	N	N	N	Y
23 ***Caputo***	Y	Y	Y	Y	Y	N	N	Y
24 Ottinger	N	Y	Y	Y	N	N	Y	Y
25 ***Fish***	Y	Y	Y	Y	N	Y	Y	Y
26 ***Gilman***	Y	Y	Y	Y	Y	N	Y	Y
27 McHugh	Y	Y	Y	Y	N	N	N	Y
28 Stratton	Y	N	Y	Y	N	N	Y	Y
29 Pattison	Y	Y	Y	Y	N	N	N	Y
30 ***McEwen***	Y	Y	Y	Y	N	?	N	Y
31 ***Mitchell***	Y	Y	Y	Y	N	N	Y	Y
32 Hanley	Y	Y	Y	Y	N	N	Y	Y
33 ***Walsh***	Y	Y	Y	Y	N	N	N	Y
34 ***Horton***	Y	Y	Y	Y	N	N	Y	Y
35 ***Conable***	Y	Y	Y	Y	Y	Y	Y	N
36 LaFalce	Y	Y	Y	Y	N	N	N	Y
37 Nowak	Y	Y	Y	Y	N	N	N	Y
38 ***Kemp***	Y	Y	Y	Y	N	N	Y	Y
39 Lundine	Y	Y	Y	Y	N	N	N	Y
NORTH CAROLINA								
1 Jones	#	#	#	Y	▮	N	N	Y
2 Fountain	Y	Y	Y	N	N	N	Y	Y
3 Whitley	Y	Y	Y	Y	N	N	N	Y
4 Andrews	Y	Y	Y	Y	N	N	N	N
5 Neal	Y	Y	Y	Y	Y	N	N	Y
6 Preyer	Y	Y	Y	Y	N	N	N	Y
7 Rose	Y	Y	Y	N	▮	N	N	Y
8 Hefner	Y	Y	Y	Y	Y	N	?	Y
9 ***Martin***	Y	Y	Y	Y	Y	N	Y	N
10 ***Broyhill***	Y	Y	Y	N	Y	P	Y	N
11 Gudger	Y	Y	Y	Y	N	N	N	Y
NORTH DAKOTA								
AL ***Andrews***	Y	Y	Y	Y	Y	N	N	Y
OHIO								
1 ***Gradison***	Y	Y	Y	Y	Y	Y	Y	N
2 Luken	Y	N	Y	N	N	N	N	Y
3 ***Whalen***	#	#	#	#	▮	▮	▮	#
4 ***Guyer***	Y	Y	Y	Y	Y	Y	Y	N
5 ***Latta***	Y	Y	Y	Y	Y	Y	Y	N
6 ***Harsha***	Y	Y	Y	Y	N	N	Y	Y
7 ***Brown***	Y	N	Y	Y	Y	Y	Y	N
8 ***Kindness***	Y	N	Y	Y	Y	Y	N	Y
9 Ashley	Y	N	Y	Y	N	N	N	Y
10 ***Miller***	Y	N	Y	Y	Y	Y	Y	Y
11 ***Stanton***	Y	Y	Y	Y	Y	Y	Y	Y
12 ***Devine***	Y	Y	Y	Y	Y	Y	Y	N
13 Pease	Y	Y	Y	Y	N	N	Y	Y
14 Seiberling	Y	Y	Y	N	Y	N	N	Y
15 ***Wylie***	Y	Y	Y	Y	Y	Y	Y	N
16 ***Regula***	Y	Y	Y	Y	Y	Y	Y	N
17 ***Ashbrook***	Y	Y	Y	Y	Y	N	Y	N
18 Applegate	N	Y	Y	Y	N	N	N	Y
19 Carney	Y	Y	Y	Y	N	N	N	Y
20 Oakar	?	?	?	?	?	?	?	?
21 Stokes	Y	Y	Y	Y	N	N	N	Y
22 Vanik	Y	N	Y	Y	Y	N	N	N
23 Mottl	N	N	Y	N	Y	Y	Y	N
OKLAHOMA								
1 Jones	Y	Y	Y	Y	N	Y	N	Y
2 Risenhoover	Y	Y	Y	Y	N	N	N	Y
3 Watkins	Y	Y	Y	Y	Y	#	N	N
4 Steed	Y	Y	Y	Y	N	N	N	Y
5 ***Edwards***	Y	Y	?	?	?	?	?	?
6 English	Y	Y	Y	Y	Y	Y	N	N
OREGON								
1 AuCoin	✓	#	#	✓	▮	X	X	✓
2 Ullman	Y	Y	Y	Y	Y	N	N	Y
3 Duncan	?	?	?	?	?	?	?	?
4 Weaver	Y	Y	Y	Y	N	N	N	Y
PENNSYLVANIA								
1 Myers, M.	Y	Y	Y	Y	N	N	N	Y
2 Nix	?	?	?	?	?	?	?	?
3 Lederer	Y	Y	Y	Y	N	N	N	Y
4 Eilberg	Y	Y	Y	Y	N	N	N	Y
5 ***Schulze***	Y	Y	Y	Y	Y	Y	Y	Y
6 Yatron	Y	Y	Y	Y	Y	N	Y	Y
7 Edgar	Y	Y	Y	Y	Y	N	N	Y
8 Kostmayer	N	N	Y	Y	Y	N	N	Y
9 ***Shuster***	Y	Y	Y	Y	Y	Y	Y	N
10 ***McDade***	Y	Y	Y	Y	N	Y	Y	Y
11 Flood	Y	Y	Y	Y	N	N	N	Y
12 Murtha	Y	Y	Y	Y	N	N	N	Y
13 ***Coughlin***	Y	Y	Y	Y	Y	N	Y	Y
14 Moorhead	Y	Y	Y	Y	N	N	N	Y
15 Rooney	Y	Y	Y	Y	N	N	N	Y
16 ***Walker***	Y	Y	Y	Y	Y	Y	Y	N
17 Ertel	Y	Y	Y	Y	Y	N	N	Y
18 Walgren	Y	Y	Y	Y	Y	N	Y	Y
19 ***Goodling, W.***	Y	Y	Y	Y	N	Y	Y	N
20 Gaydos	N	Y	Y	Y	N	N	N	Y
21 Dent	N	Y	Y	Y	N	N	X	Y
22 Murphy	N	Y	Y	Y	Y	N	N	Y
23 Ammerman	Y	Y	Y	N	?	?	?	✓
24 ***Marks***	Y	Y	Y	Y	N	N	N	Y
25 ***Myers, G.***	N	Y	Y	Y	Y	N	N	N
RHODE ISLAND								
1 St Germain	Y	Y	Y	Y	Y	N	N	Y
2 Beard	Y	Y	Y	Y	Y	N	N	Y
SOUTH CAROLINA								
1 Davis	Y	Y	Y	N	N	N	N	Y
2 ***Spence***	Y	Y	Y	Y	N	Y	N	Y
3 Derrick	Y	Y	Y	N	N	N	N	Y
4 Mann	Y	N	Y	Y	Y	N	?	Y
5 Holland	Y	Y	Y	N	N	?	N	Y
6 Jenrette	Y	Y	Y	Y	N	N	N	Y
SOUTH DAKOTA								
1 ***Pressler***	Y	Y	Y	Y	Y	N	Y	Y
2 ***Abdnor***	Y	Y	Y	Y	Y	N	Y	Y
TENNESSEE								
1 ***Quillen***	Y	Y	Y	Y	N	Y	Y	Y
2 ***Duncan***	Y	Y	Y	Y	Y	Y	Y	Y
3 Lloyd	Y	Y	Y	Y	Y	N	N	Y
4 Gore	Y	N	Y	Y	Y	N	N	Y
5 Allen	N	Y	Y	Y	N	N	N	Y
6 ***Beard***	Y	Y	Y	Y	Y	Y	Y	N
7 Jones	Y	Y	Y	Y	Y	N	N	Y
8 Ford	Y	Y	Y	Y	N	N	N	Y
TEXAS								
1 Hall	Y	Y	Y	Y	Y	Y	N	Y
2 Wilson, C.	Y	Y	Y	Y	N	N	▮	#
3 ***Collins***	Y	Y	Y	N	Y	Y	Y	N
4 Roberts	Y	Y	Y	Y	Y	Y	Y	N
5 Mattox	Y	Y	Y	Y	N	N	N	Y
6 Teague	?	?	?	?	?	✓	✓	X
7 ***Archer***	Y	Y	Y	Y	Y	Y	Y	Y
8 Eckhardt	Y	Y	Y	Y	N	N	N	Y
9 Brooks	Y	Y	Y	Y	N	N	N	Y
10 Pickle	Y	Y	Y	Y	N	Y	Y	Y
11 Poage	Y	Y	Y	Y	Y	Y	Y	N
12 Wright	Y	Y	Y	✓	N	N	N	Y
13 Hightower	Y	Y	Y	Y	N	N	N	Y
14 Young	?	?	?	?	?	?	?	?
15 de la Garza	Y	Y	Y	Y	N	N	Y	Y
16 White	Y	Y	Y	Y	N	N	Y	Y
17 Burleson	Y	Y	Y	Y	Y	Y	Y	N
18 Jordan	Y	Y	Y	Y	N	N	N	Y
19 Mahon	Y	Y	Y	Y	N	N	N	Y
20 Gonzalez	Y	N	Y	Y	N	N	Y	Y
21 Krueger	Y	Y	Y	Y	N	N	Y	Y
22 Gammage	Y	Y	Y	Y	N	N	Y	Y
23 Kazen	Y	Y	Y	Y	N	N	Y	Y
24 Milford	Y	Y	Y	?	?	Y	Y	Y
UTAH								
1 McKay	Y	Y	Y	Y	N	Y	Y	Y
2 ***Marriott***	Y	Y	Y	Y	Y	Y	Y	N
VERMONT								
AL ***Jeffords***	Y	Y	Y	Y	Y	Y	Y	N
VIRGINIA								
1 ***Trible***	Y	Y	Y	Y	N	N	N	Y
2 ***Whitehurst***	Y	Y	Y	Y	N	N	N	Y
3 Satterfield	Y	N	Y	Y	Y	Y	Y	Y
4 ***Daniel***	Y	Y	Y	Y	N	N	N	Y
5 Daniel	Y	Y	Y	Y	Y	N	Y	Y
6 ***Butler***	Y	Y	Y	Y	Y	Y	Y	N
7 ***Robinson***	Y	Y	Y	Y	Y	Y	Y	N
8 Harris	Y	Y	Y	Y	N	?	Y	N
9 ***Wampler***	Y	Y	Y	Y	N	N	N	Y
10 Fisher	Y	Y	Y	Y	N	N	Y	N
WASHINGTON								
1 ***Pritchard***	Y	Y	Y	#	N	N	N	Y
2 Meeds	Y	Y	Y	Y	N	N	N	Y
3 Bonker	Y	Y	Y	Y	N	N	N	Y
4 McCormack	Y	Y	Y	Y	N	N	N	Y
5 Foley	Y	Y	Y	Y	N	N	N	Y
6 Dicks	Y	Y	Y	Y	N	N	N	Y
7 ***Cunningham***	Y	Y	Y	Y	N	N	N	Y
WEST VIRGINIA								
1 Mollohan	N	Y	Y	N	N	N	N	Y
2 Staggers	Y	Y	Y	Y	N	N	N	Y
3 Slack	Y	Y	Y	Y	N	N	N	Y
4 Rahall	N	Y	Y	Y	N	N	N	Y
WISCONSIN								
1 Aspin	Y	Y	Y	Y	N	N	N	Y
2 Kastenmeier	Y	Y	Y	Y	Y	Y	Y	N
3 Baldus	Y	Y	Y	Y	N	N	N	Y
4 Zablocki	Y	Y	Y	Y	N	N	N	Y
5 Reuss	Y	Y	Y	Y	N	N	N	Y
6 ***Steiger***	Y	Y	Y	Y	Y	Y	Y	N
7 Obey	Y	Y	Y	Y	Y	N	N	Y
8 Cornell	Y	Y	Y	Y	N	N	N	Y
9 ***Kasten***	#	#	#	#	#	#	#	▮
WYOMING								
AL Roncalio	Y	Y	Y	Y	N	Y	Y	Y

Democrats ***Republicans***

311. HR 10929. Defense Procurement Authorization. Adoption of the rule (H Res 1188) providing for House floor consideration of the bill to authorize funds for weapons procurement and research. Adopted 330-71: R 74-62; D 256-9 (ND 178-4; SD 78-5), May 23, 1978.

312. HR 10929. Defense Procurement Authorization. Schroeder, D-Colo., amendment, to the Carr, D-Mich., substitute amendment to the bill *(see vote 313, below)*, to reinstate the Armed Services Committee recommended authorization levels for weapons research and development. Rejected 107-297: R 11-130; D 96-167 (ND 90-93; SD 6-74), May 24, 1978.

313. HR 10929. Defense Procurement Authorization. Carr, D-Mich., substitute amendment to replace the Armed Services Committee recommended authorization levels with those originally requested by the Carter administration. Rejected 115-287: R 11-131; D 104-156 (ND 99-81; SD 5-75), May 24, 1978.

314. HR 10929. Defense Procurement Authorization. Schroeder, D-Colo., amendment to delete $8.1 million for one Gulfstream executive jet for the Marine Corps. Adopted 266-136: R 75-62; D 191-74 (ND 141-42; SD 50-32), May 24, 1978.

315. HR 10929. Defense Procurement Authorization. Aspin, D-Wis., amendment to delete $2.1 billion for a nuclear-powered aircraft carrier and add $1.5 billion for a conventionally powered carrier. Rejected 139-264: R 11-129; D 128-135 (ND 113-69; SD 15-66), May 24, 1978. A "yea" was a vote supporting the president's position.

316. HR 10929. Defense Procurement Authorization. Carr, D-Mich., amendment to delete $2.1 billion for a nuclear-powered aircraft carrier. Rejected 106-293: R 17-122; D 89-171 (ND 83-96; SD 6-75), May 24, 1978.

317. HR 10929. Defense Procurement Authorization. Downey, D-N.Y., amendment to add $29.2 million for development of a wide-body cruise missile carrying aircraft. Rejected 145-246: R 21-117; D 124-129 (ND 102-72; SD 22-57), May 24, 1978. A "yea" was a vote supporting the president's position.

318. HR 10929. Defense Procurement Authorization. Stratton, D-N.Y., amendment to prohibit the use of any funds in the bill to reduce U.S. troop strength in South Korea below 26,000. Rejected 142-247: R 91-46; D 51-201 (ND 17-156; SD 34-45), May 24, 1978. A "nay" was a vote supporting the president's position.

KEY

- Y Voted for (yea).
- ✓ Paired for.
- † Announced for.
- # CQ Poll for.
- N Voted against (nay).
- X Paired against.
- \- Announced against.
- ▮ CQ Poll against.
- P Voted "present."
- ● Voted "present" to avoid possible conflict of interest.
- ? Did not vote or otherwise make a position known.

	311	312	313	314	315	316	317	318
ALABAMA								
1 Edwards	Y	N	N	N	Y	N	Y	N
2 Dickinson	N	N	N	N	N	N	N	Y
3 Nichols	Y	N	N	N	N	N	N	Y
4 Bevill	Y	N	N	N	N	N	N	N
5 Flippo	Y	N	N	N	N	N	N	N
6 Buchanan	Y	N	N	N	N	N	N	N
7 Flowers	Y	N	N	Y	N	N	N	N
ALASKA								
AL Young	?	?	?	#	▮	▮	▮	#
ARIZONA								
1 Rhodes	?	N	N	?	N	N	N	Y
2 Udall	Y	Y	Y	Y	Y	N	Y	N
3 Stump	N	N	N	N	N	N	N	Y
4 Rudd	N	N	N	N	N	N	N	Y
ARKANSAS								
1 Alexander	Y	?	?	?	?	?	?	?
2 Tucker	#	▮	▮	#	▮	▮	#	▮
3 Hammerschmidt	N	N	N	N	N	N	N	Y
4 Thornton	?	?	?	?	?	?	?	?
CALIFORNIA								
1 Johnson	Y	N	N	N	N	N	N	N
2 Clausen	N	N	N	Y	N	N	Y	Y
3 Moss	Y	N	N	Y	Y	Y	N	N
4 Leggett	Y	Y	Y	Y	Y	Y	?	Y
5 Burton, J.	Y	N	Y	Y	Y	Y	?	N
6 Burton, P.	Y	N	Y	Y	Y	Y	?	?
7 Miller	Y	?	?	✓	✓	✓	?	X
8 Dellums	Y	Y	Y	Y	Y	Y	N	N
9 Stark	Y	Y	Y	Y	Y	Y	Y	N
10 Edwards	Y	Y	Y	Y	Y	Y	Y	N
11 Ryan	Y	Y	N	Y	Y	Y	N	N
12 McCloskey	N	Y	Y	Y	N	Y	Y	N
13 Mineta	Y	Y	Y	Y	Y	Y	Y	N
14 McFall	Y	N	N	N	Y	N	N	Y
15 Sisk	?	N	N	N	N	N	N	Y
16 Panetta	Y	N	N	Y	Y	N	Y	N
17 Krebs	Y	N	N	Y	Y	N	Y	N
18 Ketchum	Y	N	N	Y	N	N	N	Y
19 Lagomarsino	N	N	N	N	N	N	N	Y
20 Goldwater	N	N	N	N	N	N	N	Y
21 Corman	Y	N	N	N	N	N	N	N
22 Moorhead	N	N	N	Y	N	N	N	Y
23 Beilenson	Y	Y	Y	Y	Y	Y	N	N
24 Waxman	Y	N	N	Y	Y	N	Y	N
25 Roybal	Y	N	Y	Y	Y	Y	N	N
26 Rousselot	N	N	N	Y	N	N	N	Y
27 Dornan	N	N	N	N	N	N	N	Y
28 Burke	#	#	▮	#	✓	✓	▮	X
29 Hawkins	Y	N	Y	Y	Y	Y	N	N
30 Danielson	Y	N	N	Y	N	N	N	N
31 Wilson, C.H.	Y	N	N	Y	▮	N	N	Y
32 Anderson	Y	N	N	Y	N	N	N	N
33 Clawson	N	N	N	N	N	N	?	?
34 Hannaford	Y	N	N	Y	N	N	Y	N
35 Lloyd	Y	N	N	N	N	N	N	N
36 Brown	Y	Y	Y	Y	Y	Y	Y	N
37 Pettis	N	N	N	N	N	N	N	Y
38 Patterson	Y	N	Y	Y	N	N	Y	N
39 Wiggins	Y	▮	N	N	N	N	N	Y
40 Badham	N	N	N	N	N	N	N	Y
41 Wilson, B.	N	N	N	N	N	N	N	Y
42 Van Deerlin	Y	N	N	Y	N	N	Y	N
43 Burgener	N	N	N	N	N	N	N	Y
COLORADO								
1 Schroeder	Y	Y	Y	Y	Y	Y	Y	N
2 Wirth	Y	Y	Y	Y	Y	Y	Y	N
3 Evans	Y	Y	Y	N	Y	Y	N	N
4 Johnson	Y	N	N	N	N	N	N	N
5 Armstrong	Y	Y	N	Y	N	N	N	Y
CONNECTICUT								
1 Cotter	Y	N	Y	Y	Y	N	Y	N
2 Dodd	Y	Y	Y	Y	Y	N	Y	?
3 Giaimo	Y	N	Y	Y	Y	Y	Y	N
4 McKinney	N	Y	Y	Y	Y	Y	Y	N
5 Sarasin	Y	▮	▮	#	#	▮	#	▮
6 Moffett	Y	Y	Y	Y	N	Y	Y	N
DELAWARE								
AL Evans	Y	N	N	Y	N	N	N	Y
FLORIDA								
1 Sikes	N	N	N	N	N	N	N	Y
2 Fuqua	Y	N	N	Y	N	N	N	N
3 Bennett	Y	N	N	Y	N	N	N	Y
4 Chappell	Y	N	N	N	N	N	N	Y
5 Kelly	N	N	N	N	N	N	N	Y
6 Young	N	N	N	N	N	N	N	Y
7 Gibbons	Y	N	Y	Y	Y	Y	Y	N
8 Ireland	Y	N	N	Y	N	N	Y	Y
9 Frey	?	N	N	N	N	N	N	Y
10 Bafalis	N	N	N	Y	N	N	N	Y
11 Rogers	Y	N	N	Y	Y	N	N	N
12 Burke	Y	N	N	Y	N	N	N	Y
13 Lehman	Y	Y	Y	Y	N	Y	Y	N
14 Pepper	Y	N	N	N	N	N	N	N
15 Fascell	Y	Y	Y	Y	N	N	Y	N
GEORGIA								
1 Ginn	Y	N	N	N	N	N	N	N
2 Mathis	Y	N	N	N	N	N	N	Y
3 Brinkley	Y	N	N	N	N	N	N	N
4 Levitas	Y	Y	N	Y	N	N	N	Y
5 Fowler	Y	N	N	Y	Y	N	Y	N
6 Flynt	Y	N	N	N	N	N	N	Y
7 McDonald	N	N	N	N	N	N	N	Y
8 Evans	Y	▮	#	N	▮	N	Y	#
9 Jenkins	Y	N	N	Y	N	N	Y	N
10 Barnard	Y	N	N	N	N	N	N	N
HAWAII								
1 Heftel	Y	N	N	N	N	N	N	N
2 Akaka	Y	N	N	X	N	N	N	N
IDAHO								
1 Symms	N	N	N	N	N	N	N	Y
2 Hansen, G.	N	N	N	Y	N	N	N	Y
ILLINOIS								
1 Metcalfe	Y	?	?	?	Y	Y	N	N
2 Murphy	Y	N	N	Y	N	N	N	N
3 Russo	Y	N	N	Y	Y	N	Y	N
4 Derwinski	Y	N	N	Y	N	N	N	Y
5 Fary	Y	N	N	N	N	N	N	N
6 Hyde	N	N	N	Y	N	N	N	N
7 Collins	Y	?	?	Y	Y	Y	N	N
8 Rostenkowski	Y	N	N	N	N	N	N	N
9 Yates	Y	N	Y	Y	Y	Y	Y	N
10 Mikva	Y	Y	Y	Y	Y	Y	Y	N
11 Annunzio	Y	N	N	Y	N	N	N	N
12 Crane	N	N	N	Y	N	N	N	Y
13 McClory	N	N	N	N	N	N	N	Y
14 Erlenborn	Y	N	N	Y	N	N	N	Y
15 Corcoran	Y	N	N	N	N	N	N	N
16 Anderson	Y	N	Y	Y	Y	?	?	?
17 O'Brien	N	N	N	Y	N	N	Y	Y
18 Michel	N	N	N	Y	N	N	N	Y
19 Railsback	N	N	N	Y	N	N	Y	N
20 Findley	N	N	N	Y	N	N	N	Y
21 Madigan	Y	N	N	N	N	N	N	Y
22 Shipley	Y	?	?	N	N	N	?	?
23 Price	Y	N	N	N	N	N	N	Y
24 Simon	†	?	†	†	†	†	†	†
INDIANA								
1 Benjamin	Y	Y	Y	Y	N	N	N	N
2 Fithian	Y	Y	N	Y	N	N	Y	N
3 Brademas	Y	Y	Y	Y	Y	Y	Y	N
4 Quayle	N	N	N	Y	N	N	Y	N
5 Hillis	N	N	N	N	N	N	N	N
6 Evans	Y	N	N	Y	N	N	Y	Y
7 Myers, J.	Y	N	N	Y	N	N	N	Y
8 Cornwell	Y	Y	N	Y	N	N	Y	Y
9 Hamilton	Y	Y	Y	Y	Y	N	Y	N
10 Sharp	Y	Y	Y	Y	Y	N	Y	N
11 Jacobs	Y	Y	Y	Y	Y	N	Y	N
IOWA								
1 Leach	N	N	N	Y	N	N	N	N
2 Blouin	Y	Y	Y	Y	Y	Y	Y	N
3 Grassley	N	N	N	Y	N	N	N	Y
4 Smith	Y	N	N	Y	N	Y	N	N
5 Harkin	Y	Y	Y	Y	N	#	Y	N
6 Bedell	Y	Y	Y	Y	Y	Y	Y	N

Democrats ***Republicans***

Corresponding to Congressional Record Votes 363, 365, 366, 367, 368, 369, 370, 371

	311	312	313	314	315	316	317	318
KANSAS								
1 Sebelius	Y	N	N	N	N	N	N	Y
2 Keys	Y	Y	Y	Y	Y	Y	Y	N
3 Winn	Y	N	N	N	N	N	N	Y
4 Glickman	Y	N	N	Y	Y	N	Y	N
5 Skubitz	Y	N	N	N	N	N	N	?
KENTUCKY								
1 Hubbard	Y	N	N	Y	N	N	N	Y
2 Natcher	Y	N	N	Y	Y	N	N	N
3 Mazzoli	#	N	N	Y	Y	N	Y	N
4 Snyder	Y	N	N	N	N	N	N	Y
5 Carter	?	N	N	N	N	N	N	Y
6 Breckinridge	†	-	-	-	-	-	-	†
7 Perkins	Y	N	N	Y	N	N	N	N
LOUISIANA								
1 Livingston	Y	N	N	N	N	N	N	Y
2 Boggs	Y	N	N	N	N	N	N	Y
3 Treen	N	N	N	N	N	N	N	Y
4 Waggonner	Y	N	N	N	N	N	N	Y
5 Huckaby	Y	N	N	N	N	N	Y	Y
6 Moore	Y	N	N	Y	N	N	N	Y
7 Breaux	Y	N	N	N	N	N	N	N
8 Long	Y	N	N	Y	N	N	N	N
MAINE								
1 Emery	N	N	N	Y	N	N	Y	N
2 Cohen	Y	N	N	Y	?	?	Y	Y
MARYLAND								
1 Bauman	N	N	N	Y	N	N	N	Y
2 Long	Y	N	N	Y	N	Y	N	Y
3 Mikulski	Y	Y	Y	Y	Y	N	Y	N
4 Holt	N	N	N	Y	N	N	N	Y
5 Spellman	Y	N	N	Y	N	N	▮	N
6 Byron	Y	N	N	N	N	N	N	Y
7 Mitchell	N	Y	Y	Y	P	Y	N	N
8 Steers	Y	N	Y	Y	Y	Y	N	N
MASSACHUSETTS								
1 Conte	Y	N	N	Y	Y	N	Y	N
2 Boland	Y	N	N	Y	Y	N	Y	N
3 Early	Y	Y	Y	Y	Y	Y	Y	N
4 Drinan	Y	N	Y	Y	Y	Y	N	N
5 Tsongas	#	N	Y	Y	Y	Y	Y	N
6 Harrington	N	Y	Y	Y	P	Y	N	N
7 Markey	Y	Y	Y	Y	Y	Y	Y	N
8 O'Neill								
9 Moakley	Y	Y	Y	Y	Y	N	Y	N
10 Heckler	Y	Y	N	Y	Y	N	Y	N
11 Burke	Y	N	N	N	N	N	N	N
12 Studds	Y	Y	Y	Y	Y	Y	Y	N
MICHIGAN								
1 Conyers	▮	N	Y	#	▮	Y	N	N
2 Pursell	Y	N	N	Y	N	Y	N	N
3 Brown	Y	N	N	Y	N	N	N	Y
4 Stockman	#	N	N	Y	N	Y	N	Y
5 Sawyer	Y	N	N	#	N	N	N	N
6 Carr	Y	Y	Y	Y	N	Y	Y	N
7 Kildee	Y	Y	Y	Y	Y	Y	Y	N
8 Traxler	Y	Y	N	Y	Y	N	Y	N
9 Vander Jagt	Y	N	N	?	N	N	N	Y
10 Cederberg	?	N	N	N	N	N	N	Y
11 Ruppe	Y	N	N	#	N	Y	N	N
12 Bonior	Y	Y	Y	Y	Y	Y	Y	N
13 Diggs	Y	Y	Y	Y	Y	#	Y	▮
14 Nedzi	Y	N	Y	N	Y	Y	Y	N
15 Ford	Y	Y	Y	N	Y	N	Y	?
16 Dingell	Y	N	Y	Y	Y	Y	Y	N
17 Brodhead	Y	Y	Y	Y	Y	Y	Y	N
18 Blanchard	Y	Y	Y	N	Y	N	Y	N
19 Broomfield	Y	N	N	Y	N	N	N	N
MINNESOTA								
1 Quie	Y	N	N	Y	N	Y	N	N
2 Hagedorn	N	N	N	N	N	N	N	Y
3 Frenzel	Y	N	N	Y	N	Y	N	N
4 Vento	Y	Y	Y	Y	Y	N	Y	N
5 Fraser	Y	Y	Y	Y	Y	Y	Y	N
6 Nolan	Y	Y	?	Y	Y	Y	N	N
7 Stangeland	N	N	N	N	N	N	N	Y
8 Oberstar	Y	Y	Y	Y	Y	Y	Y	N
MISSISSIPPI								
1 Whitten	Y	N	N	N	N	N	N	N
2 Bowen	Y	N	N	N	N	N	N	Y
3 Montgomery	Y	N	N	N	N	N	N	Y
4 Cochran	?	?	?	?	?	?	?	?
5 Lott	Y	N	N	N	N	N	N	Y
MISSOURI								
1 Clay	Y	Y	Y	Y	Y	Y	Y	N
2 Young	Y	N	N	N	N	Y	N	N
3 Gephardt	Y	#	#	Y	Y	Y	Y	N

	311	312	313	314	315	316	317	318
4 Skelton	Y	N	N	N	N	N	N	N
5 Bolling	Y	N	N	N	Y	N	#	▮
6 Coleman	Y	N	N	Y	N	N	N	Y
7 Taylor	N	N	N	N	N	N	N	Y
8 Ichord	Y	N	N	Y	N	N	N	Y
9 Volkmer	Y	Y	Y	Y	N	Y	N	N
10 Burlison	Y	N	N	Y	Y	Y	Y	N
MONTANA								
1 Baucus	Y	N	N	Y	Y	#	#	▮
2 Marlenee	N	N	N	Y	N	N	N	N
NEBRASKA								
1 Thone	Y	N	N	Y	N	N	N	N
2 Cavanaugh	Y	Y	Y	Y	Y	Y	Y	N
3 Smith	Y	N	N	Y	N	N	N	N
NEVADA								
AL Santini	Y	N	N	Y	N	N	Y	Y
NEW HAMPSHIRE								
1 D'Amours	Y	N	N	Y	N	N	Y	N
2 Cleveland	Y	N	N	Y	N	N	N	Y
NEW JERSEY								
1 Florio	Y	N	N	Y	Y	N	Y	N
2 Hughes	Y	N	N	Y	Y	N	Y	N
3 Howard	Y	▮	▮	#	#	#	▮	▮
4 Thompson	Y	Y	Y	Y	Y	Y	Y	N
5 Fenwick	Y	Y	Y	Y	N	Y	N	N
6 Forsythe	Y	N	Y	Y	Y	Y	N	N
7 Maguire	Y	Y	Y	Y	Y	Y	Y	N
8 Roe	Y	N	N	Y	N	N	N	N
9 Hollenbeck	Y	N	N	Y	N	N	N	N
10 Rodino	#	#	#	#	#	#	#	▮
11 Minish	Y	N	N	Y	Y	N	N	N
12 Rinaldo	Y	N	N	Y	N	N	N	N
13 Meyner	#	Y	Y	Y	N	Y	Y	N
14 LeFante	Y	N	N	N	N	N	N	N
15 Patten	Y	N	N	Y	N	N	Y	N
NEW MEXICO								
1 Lujan	Y	Y	N	Y	N	N	Y	Y
2 Runnels	?	?	?	✓	X	?	?	✓
NEW YORK								
1 Pike	Y	Y	Y	N	Y	Y	N	N
2 Downey	Y	N	N	Y	N	Y	Y	N
3 Ambro	Y	N	N	N	N	N	Y	N
4 Lent	Y	N	N	N	N	N	N	#
5 Wydler	Y	N	N	N	N	N	N	Y
6 Wolff	Y	N	N	N	Y	N	N	N
7 Addabbo	Y	Y	Y	Y	Y	Y	Y	N
8 Rosenthal	Y	Y	Y	Y	Y	Y	Y	N
9 Delaney	Y	N	?	?	Y	?	?	?
10 Biaggi	Y	N	N	Y	N	N	N	N
11 Scheuer	Y	Y	N	Y	Y	Y	Y	N
12 Chisholm	#	Y	Y	Y	Y	✓	Y	N
13 Solarz	Y	Y	Y	Y	Y	Y	Y	N
14 Richmond	Y	Y	Y	Y	Y	Y	Y	N
15 Zeferetti	Y	N	N	Y	N	N	N	Y
16 Holtzman	Y	Y	Y	Y	Y	Y	N	N
17 Murphy	Y	N	▮	N	N	N	N	Y
18 Green	Y	Y	Y	Y	N	Y	Y	N
19 Rangel	Y	Y	Y	Y	Y	Y	Y	N
20 Weiss	Y	Y	Y	Y	Y	Y	N	N
21 Garcia	Y	Y	Y	Y	Y	Y	Y	?
22 Bingham	Y	Y	Y	Y	Y	Y	Y	N
23 Caputo	N	Y	N	N	Y	Y	Y	N
24 Ottinger	Y	Y	Y	Y	Y	Y	Y	N
25 Fish	Y	N	N	N	N	N	N	Y
26 Gilman	Y	N	N	N	N	N	N	Y
27 McHugh	Y	Y	Y	Y	Y	Y	Y	N
28 Stratton	N	N	N	N	N	N	N	Y
29 Pattison	Y	Y	Y	Y	Y	Y	Y	N
30 McEwen	Y	N	N	N	N	N	N	N
31 Mitchell	N	N	N	N	N	N	N	Y
32 Hanley	Y	N	N	Y	N	N	N	N
33 Walsh	Y	N	N	N	N	N	N	N
34 Horton	Y	N	N	Y	N	N	N	N
35 Conable	N	N	N	Y	N	Y	N	N
36 LaFalce	Y	N	N	N	N	N	Y	N
37 Nowak	Y	Y	Y	Y	Y	Y	Y	N
38 Kemp	N	N	N	Y	N	N	N	Y
39 Lundine	Y	Y	Y	Y	Y	#	Y	N
NORTH CAROLINA								
1 Jones	Y	N	N	N	N	N	N	N
2 Fountain	Y	N	N	Y	N	N	N	Y
3 Whitley	Y	N	N	N	N	N	Y	N
4 Andrews	Y	N	N	N	N	N	?	?
5 Neal	Y	N	N	Y	N	N	N	N
6 Preyer	Y	N	N	N	Y	N	Y	N
7 Rose	Y	N	Y	Y	Y	N	▮	▮
8 Hefner	Y	N	N	Y	N	N	Y	N

	311	312	313	314	315	316	317	318
9 Martin	N	N	N	N	N	N	N	Y
10 Broyhill	Y	N	N	Y	N	N	Y	Y
11 Gudger	Y	N	N	N	N	N	N	Y
NORTH DAKOTA								
AL Andrews	Y	N	N	N	N	N	N	N
OHIO								
1 Gradison	Y	N	N	Y	N	N	N	Y
2 Luken	Y	N	N	Y	N	N	?	#
3 Whalen	#	Y	Y	Y	Y	Y	Y	N
4 Guyer	Y	N	N	Y	N	N	N	Y
5 Latta	Y	N	N	Y	N	N	N	Y
6 Harsha	Y	N	N	N	N	N	N	Y
7 Brown	N	N	N	N	N	N	N	Y
8 Kindness	Y	N	N	N	N	N	N	Y
9 Ashley	Y	N	Y	Y	Y	N	?	N
10 Miller	Y	N	N	Y	N	N	N	Y
11 Stanton	Y	N	N	Y	N	N	N	Y
12 Devine	Y	N	N	Y	N	N	N	Y
13 Pease	Y	Y	Y	Y	Y	Y	Y	N
14 Seiberling	Y	Y	Y	Y	Y	Y	Y	N
15 Wylie	Y	N	N	Y	N	N	N	N
16 Regula	Y	N	N	Y	N	N	N	N
17 Ashbrook	N	N	N	Y	N	N	N	Y
18 Applegate	Y	?	?	?	?	?	?	?
19 Carney	Y	N	N	N	N	N	N	N
20 Oakar	?	?	?	?	?	N	N	N
21 Stokes	Y	Y	Y	Y	Y	Y	N	N
22 Vanik	Y	Y	Y	Y	Y	Y	N	N
23 Mottl	Y	Y	N	Y	N	N	N	N
OKLAHOMA								
1 Jones	Y	N	N	Y	N	N	N	Y
2 Risenhoover	Y	N	N	Y	N	N	N	N
3 Watkins	Y	N	N	Y	N	N	N	Y
4 Steed	Y	N	N	Y	N	N	N	N
5 Edwards	?	N	N	Y	N	N	N	Y
6 English	Y	N	N	Y	N	N	N	Y
OREGON								
1 AuCoin	#	?	?	#	#	#	?	?
2 Ullman	Y	N	Y	N	N	N	▮	▮
3 Duncan	?	N	N	Y	Y	N	N	Y
4 Weaver	Y	Y	Y	Y	Y	Y	Y	N
PENNSYLVANIA								
1 Myers, M.	Y	N	Y	N	N	N	N	N
2 Nix	?	Y	Y	N	X	X	?	?
3 Lederer	Y	N	N	N	Y	N	Y	N
4 Eilberg	Y	Y	Y	Y	Y	N	Y	N
5 Schulze	N	N	N	N	N	N	N	Y
6 Yatron	Y	N	N	Y	N	N	Y	N
7 Edgar	Y	Y	Y	Y	Y	N	N	N
8 Kostmayer	Y	Y	Y	Y	Y	Y	Y	N
9 Shuster	N	N	N	Y	N	N	N	Y
10 McDade	Y	N	N	Y	N	N	Y	N
11 Flood	Y	N	N	N	N	N	Y	N
12 Murtha	Y	N	N	N	N	N	N	N
13 Coughlin	?	N	N	N	N	Y	N	N
14 Moorhead	Y	Y	Y	N	Y	Y	N	N
15 Rooney	Y	N	N	N	Y	N	N	N
16 Walker	N	N	N	?	N	N	N	Y
17 Ertel	Y	Y	Y	Y	Y	N	N	N
18 Walgren	Y	Y	Y	Y	Y	N	N	N
19 Goodling, W.	N	N	N	Y	N	N	N	N
20 Gaydos	Y	N	N	Y	N	N	Y	N
21 Dent	#	N	N	N	N	N	▮	▮
22 Murphy	Y	Y	Y	Y	N	N	N	N
23 Ammerman	?	?	?	?	?	?	?	?
24 Marks	Y	N	N	Y	N	N	?	N
25 Myers, G.	Y	N	N	Y	N	N	N	Y
RHODE ISLAND								
1 St Germain	Y	N	N	N	N	N	N	N
2 Beard	Y	N	N	Y	N	?	N	N
SOUTH CAROLINA								
1 Davis	Y	N	N	Y	Y	N	N	N
2 Spence	N	N	N	N	N	N	N	Y
3 Derrick	Y	N	N	Y	N	N	Y	N
4 Mann	Y	N	N	Y	N	N	N	Y
5 Holland	Y	?	?	Y	Y	N	N	N
6 Jenrette	Y	N	N	Y	N	N	N	N
SOUTH DAKOTA								
1 Pressler	Y	Y	N	Y	N	N	Y	N
2 Abdnor	Y	N	N	Y	N	N	N	Y
TENNESSEE								
1 Quillen	Y	N	N	N	N	N	N	Y
2 Duncan	Y	N	N	Y	N	N	N	Y
3 Lloyd	N	N	N	Y	N	N	N	Y
4 Gore	Y	N	N	Y	N	N	Y	N
5 Allen	Y	Y	N	Y	N	N	Y	N
6 Beard	Y	N	N	N	N	N	N	Y

	311	312	313	314	315	316	317	318
7 Jones	Y	N	N	Y	N	N	N	Y
8 Ford	Y	N	N	Y	N	N	N	N
TEXAS								
1 Hall	Y	N	N	Y	N	N	Y	Y
2 Wilson, C.	#	N	N	N	N	N	Y	Y
3 Collins	N	N	N	Y	N	N	N	N
4 Roberts	Y	N	N	N	N	N	N	N
5 Mattox	Y	Y	N	Y	Y	Y	Y	N
6 Teague	?	?	?	X	X	X	?	✓
7 Archer	N	?	?	?	✓	?	?	?
8 Eckhardt	Y	?	?	?	Y	Y	Y	N
9 Brooks	Y	N	N	Y	N	N	N	N
10 Pickle	Y	N	N	N	Y	N	N	Y
11 Poage	Y	N	N	Y	N	N	N	Y
12 Wright	Y	N	N	N	N	N	N	N
13 Hightower	Y	N	N	N	N	N	Y	N
14 Young	?	?	?	?	?	?	?	?
15 de la Garza	Y	N	N	Y	N	N	N	Y
16 White	Y	N	N	Y	N	N	N	Y
17 Burleson	Y	N	N	N	N	N	N	Y
18 Jordan	Y	Y	N	Y	Y	Y	N	N
19 Mahon	Y	N	N	Y	Y	N	Y	N
20 Gonzalez	Y	N	N	N	N	N	N	Y
21 Krueger	Y	N	N	Y	▮	▮	▮	#
22 Gammage	N	N	N	Y	N	N	N	Y
23 Kazen	Y	?	?	?	?	?	?	?
24 Milford	Y	N	N	Y	N	?	?	N
UTAH								
1 McKay	Y	N	N	Y	Y	#	▮	▮
2 Marriott	N	N	N	N	N	N	N	Y
VERMONT								
AL Jeffords	Y	Y	N	N	▮	X	▮	▮
VIRGINIA								
1 Trible	N	N	N	N	N	N	N	Y
2 Whitehurst	N	N	N	N	N	N	N	Y
3 Satterfield	Y	N	N	Y	N	N	N	Y
4 Daniel	N	N	N	N	N	N	N	Y
5 Daniel	N	N	N	Y	N	N	N	Y
6 Butler	N	N	N	Y	N	N	N	Y
7 Robinson	N	N	N	N	N	N	N	Y
8 Harris	Y	N	N	Y	N	N	Y	N
9 Wampler	Y	N	N	N	N	N	N	Y
10 Fisher	Y	N	Y	Y	Y	Y	Y	N
WASHINGTON								
1 Pritchard	Y	N	Y	Y	Y	Y	Y	N
2 Meeds	Y	N	N	N	Y	N	Y	N
3 Bonker	Y	N	N	Y	Y	N	Y	▮
4 McCormack	Y	N	N	Y	N	N	Y	N
5 Foley	Y	N	N	Y	N	N	Y	N
6 Dicks	Y	Y	N	Y	N	N	Y	N
7 Cunningham	N	N	N	Y	N	N	Y	Y
WEST VIRGINIA								
1 Mollohan	Y	N	N	N	N	N	N	N
2 Staggers	Y	N	N	Y	N	N	Y	N
3 Slack	Y	N	N	N	N	N	N	N
4 Rahall	Y	N	Y	Y	Y	N	N	N
WISCONSIN								
1 Aspin	Y	Y	Y	Y	Y	Y	Y	N
2 Kastenmeier	Y	Y	Y	Y	Y	Y	Y	N
3 Baldus	Y	Y	Y	Y	Y	Y	Y	N
4 Zablocki	Y	N	N	N	N	N	N	N
5 Reuss	Y	Y	Y	Y	Y	Y	Y	N
6 Steiger	N	N	N	Y	N	Y	N	N
7 Obey	Y	Y	Y	Y	Y	Y	Y	N
8 Cornell	Y	Y	Y	Y	Y	Y	Y	N
9 Kasten	#	▮	▮	#	▮	▮	▮	#
WYOMING								
AL Roncalio	Y	Y	Y	Y	N	N	N	Y

Democrats ***Republicans***

319. HR 10929. Defense Procurement Authorization. Passage of the bill to authorize $37,899,020,000 for Defense Department weapons procurement and military research programs in fiscal 1979. Passed 319-67: R 133-3; D 186-64 (ND 107-63; SD 79-1), May 24, 1978.

320. S J Res 137. North Atlantic Alliance Reaffirmation. Passage of the joint resolution to reaffirm the United States' commitment and the unity of the North Atlantic Alliance on the occasion of the summit meeting in Washington, D.C., May 30-31. Passed 370-0: R 125-0; D 245-0 (ND 167-0; SD 78-0), May 25, 1978.

321. HR 7814. Federal Employees' Flexible Schedules. Adoption of the rule (H Res 1165) providing for House floor consideration of the bill to authorize federal agencies to conduct a three-year experiment in compressed and flexible work schedules for federal employees and to suspend certain overtime and holiday pay provisions for purposes of the experiment. Adopted 360-0: R 123-0; D 237-0 (ND 161-0; SD 76-0), May 25, 1978.

322. HR 7814. Federal Employees' Flexible Schedules. Schroeder, D-Colo., motion that the House resolve itself into the Committee of the Whole to consider the bill. Motion agreed to 338-2: R 116-1; D 222-1 (ND 149-1; SD 73-0), May 25, 1978.

323. HR 7814. Federal Employees' Flexible Schedules. Passage of the bill to authorize federal agencies to conduct a three-year experiment in flexible and compressed work schedules for federal employees and to suspend certain overtime and holiday pay provisions for purposes of the experiment. Passed 288-57: R 95-21; D 193-36 (ND 147-8; SD 46-28), May 25, 1978.

324. HR 9400. Civil Rights of Institutionalized Persons. Railsback, R-Ill., amendment to reinstate coverage under the bill for persons confined to jails, prisons or correctional institutions, thereby allowing the attorney general to initiate lawsuits against a state correctional facility if there was a pattern or practice of abuse of constitutional rights and if a federal judge had asked for review by the attorney general. Adopted 178-109: R 41-56; D 137-53 (ND 110-17; SD 27-36), May 25, 1978.

KEY

Y Voted for (yea).
✓ Paired for.
† Announced for.
# CQ Poll for.
N Voted against (nay).
X Paired against.
- Announced against.
▮ CQ Poll against.
P Voted "present."
● Voted "present" to avoid possible conflict of interest.
? Did not vote or otherwise make a position known.

	319	320	321	322	323	324
ALABAMA						
1 Edwards	Y	Y	Y	Y	Y	N
2 Dickinson	Y	?	?	?	?	?
3 Nichols	Y	#	#	#	▮	#
4 Bevill	Y	Y	Y	Y	?	?
5 Flippo	✓	Y	Y	Y	Y	Y
6 Buchanan	Y	Y	?	Y	Y	Y
7 Flowers	Y	Y	Y	Y	?	?
ALASKA						
AL Young	#	#	#	?	?	?
ARIZONA						
1 Rhodes	Y	?	?	?	?	?
2 Udall	Y	Y	Y	Y	Y	Y
3 Stump	Y	Y	Y	Y	▮	▮
4 Rudd	Y	Y	Y	Y	?	?
ARKANSAS						
1 Alexander	?	Y	Y	Y	Y	?
2 Tucker	#	#	#	#	#	#
3 Hammerschmidt	Y	Y	Y	N	?	?
4 Thornton	?	?	?	?	?	?
CALIFORNIA						
1 Johnson	Y	Y	Y	Y	Y	Y
2 Clausen	Y	Y	Y	Y	Y	?
3 Moss	Y	Y	Y	Y	Y	Y
4 Leggett	Y	Y	Y	Y	N	Y
5 Burton, J.	N	?	?	?	?	?
6 Burton, P.	X	?	?	?	?	?
7 Miller	X	?	?	?	?	?
8 Dellums	N	#	#	#	#	#
9 Stark	N	Y	Y	Y	Y	Y
10 Edwards	N	Y	Y	Y	Y	Y
11 Ryan	Y	Y	Y	Y	Y	#
12 McCloskey	Y	?	?	?	?	?
13 Mineta	Y	Y	Y	Y	Y	Y
14 McFall	Y	Y	Y	Y	Y	?
15 Sisk	?	Y	Y	Y	Y	Y
16 Panetta	N	Y	Y	Y	Y	Y
17 Krebs	Y	Y	Y	Y	Y	Y
18 Ketchum	Y	Y	Y	Y	N	?
19 Lagomarsino	Y	Y	Y	Y	Y	N
20 Goldwater	Y	Y	Y	Y	Y	?
21 Corman	Y	Y	Y	Y	Y	?
22 Moorhead	Y	Y	Y	Y	Y	N
23 Beilenson	N	Y	Y	Y	#	#
24 Waxman	Y	Y	Y	#	Y	#
25 Roybal	N	Y	Y	Y	Y	?
26 Rousselot	Y	?	?	?	?	?
27 Dornan	Y	#	#	#	#	#
28 Burke	X	#	#	#	#	#
29 Hawkins	Y	Y	Y	Y	Y	Y
30 Danielson	Y	Y	Y	Y	Y	#
31 Wilson, C.H.	Y	#	#	#	#	#
32 Anderson	Y	Y	Y	Y	Y	Y
33 Clawson	?	?	?	?	?	?
34 Hannaford	Y	Y	Y	Y	#	Y
35 Lloyd	Y	Y	Y	N	Y	Y
36 Brown	N	Y	?	?	Y	?
37 Pettis	Y	Y	Y	Y	Y	Y
38 Patterson	Y	Y	Y	Y	Y	Y
39 Wiggins	Y	Y	#	Y	Y	N
40 Badham	Y	#	#	#	#	#
41 Wilson, B.	Y	Y	Y	?	Y	Y
42 Van Deerlin	Y	Y	Y	Y	Y	Y
43 Burgener	Y	Y	Y	Y	Y	Y
COLORADO						
1 Schroeder	N	Y	Y	Y	Y	Y
2 Wirth	Y	Y	Y	Y	Y	Y
3 Evans	Y	Y	Y	Y	Y	Y
4 Johnson	Y	Y	Y	Y	Y	Y
5 Armstrong	Y	Y	Y	Y	Y	?
CONNECTICUT						
1 Cotter	N	Y	Y	#	#	#
2 Dodd	?	?	?	?	?	?
3 Giaimo	N	Y	Y	Y	Y	Y
4 McKinney	Y	Y	Y	Y	Y	Y
5 Sarasin	#	#	#	#	#	#
6 Moffett	N	?	?	?	?	?
DELAWARE						
AL Evans	Y	Y	Y	Y	Y	N
FLORIDA						
1 Sikes	Y	Y	Y	Y	Y	N
2 Fuqua	Y	Y	Y	Y	Y	N
3 Bennett	Y	Y	Y	Y	N	Y
4 Chappell	Y	Y	Y	Y	N	N
5 Kelly	Y	Y	Y	Y	N	N
6 Young	Y	Y	Y	Y	N	N
7 Gibbons	Y	Y	Y	Y	N	Y
8 Ireland	Y	Y	?	Y	Y	N
9 Frey	Y	Y	Y	Y	Y	N
10 Bafalis	Y	Y	Y	Y	Y	?
11 Rogers	Y	Y	Y	Y	N	N
12 Burke	Y	Y	Y	Y	N	▮
13 Lehman	Y	Y	Y	Y	Y	#
14 Pepper	Y	Y	Y	Y	Y	Y
15 Fascell	Y	Y	Y	Y	Y	Y
GEORGIA						
1 Ginn	Y	Y	Y	Y	N	N
2 Mathis	Y	Y	?	Y	Y	N
3 Brinkley	Y	Y	Y	Y	N	N
4 Levitas	Y	Y	Y	Y	N	Y
5 Fowler	Y	Y	Y	Y	N	Y
6 Flynt	Y	Y	Y	Y	N	?
7 McDonald	Y	Y	Y	Y	N	N
8 Evans	Y	Y	Y	Y	Y	N
9 Jenkins	Y	Y	Y	Y	N	#
10 Barnard	Y	Y	Y	Y	N	N
HAWAII						
1 Heftel	Y	Y	Y	Y	Y	?
2 Akaka	Y	Y	Y	Y	Y	#
IDAHO						
1 Symms	Y	Y	Y	Y	?	?
2 Hansen, G.	Y	Y	Y	?	N	N
ILLINOIS						
1 Metcalfe	N	Y	?	?	?	?
2 Murphy	Y	Y	Y	#	#	?
3 Russo	N	Y	#	#	▮	▮
4 Derwinski	Y	Y	Y	Y	Y	Y
5 Fary	Y	?	?	?	?	?
6 Hyde	Y	Y	Y	Y	Y	Y
7 Collins	N	?	?	?	?	?
8 Rostenkowski	Y	Y	Y	#	#	?
9 Yates	N	Y	Y	Y	Y	Y
10 Mikva	N	Y	#	#	#	#
11 Annunzio	Y	Y	#	#	#	#
12 Crane	Y	Y	Y	Y	Y	N
13 McClory	Y	Y	Y	Y	Y	Y
14 Erlenborn	Y	Y	Y	Y	Y	Y
15 Corcoran	Y	Y	Y	Y	Y	Y
16 Anderson	?	?	?	?	?	?
17 O'Brien	Y	Y	Y	Y	Y	Y
18 Michel	Y	Y	#	#	#	#
19 Railsback	Y	Y	Y	Y	Y	Y
20 Findley	Y	Y	Y	Y	Y	Y
21 Madigan	Y	Y	Y	Y	Y	Y
22 Shipley	✓	?	?	?	?	?
23 Price	Y	Y	Y	Y	Y	Y
24 Simon	†	†	†	†	†	†
INDIANA						
1 Benjamin	Y	Y	Y	Y	N	Y
2 Fithian	Y	Y	Y	Y	Y	Y
3 Brademas	Y	Y	Y	Y	Y	Y
4 Quayle	Y	Y	Y	?	Y	N
5 Hillis	Y	Y	Y	Y	Y	?
6 Evans	Y	Y	Y	Y	Y	Y
7 Myers, J.	Y	Y	Y	Y	Y	N
8 Cornwell	Y	Y	Y	Y	N	N
9 Hamilton	Y	Y	Y	Y	Y	Y
10 Sharp	Y	Y	Y	Y	Y	Y
11 Jacobs	Y	Y	Y	Y	Y	Y
IOWA						
1 Leach	Y	Y	Y	Y	Y	Y
2 Blouin	N	Y	Y	Y	Y	?
3 Grassley	Y	Y	Y	Y	Y	N
4 Smith	Y	Y	Y	Y	Y	?
5 Harkin	N	Y	Y	#	Y	Y
6 Bedell	N	Y	Y	Y	Y	Y

Democrats ***Republicans***

Corresponding to Congressional Record Votes 372, 374, 375, 376, 377, 379

	319	320	321	322	323	324
KANSAS						
1 Sebelius	Y	Y	Y	Y	■	#
2 Keys	Y	Y	Y	Y	Y	Y
3 Winn	Y	Y	Y	Y	N	Y
4 Glickman	Y	Y	Y	Y	Y	Y
5 Skubitz	Y	Y	Y	Y	N	N
KENTUCKY						
1 Hubbard	Y	Y	Y	Y	N	N
2 Natcher	Y	Y	Y	Y	Y	Y
3 Mazzoli	Y	Y	Y	Y	Y	Y
4 Snyder	Y	Y	Y	Y	N	N
5 Carter	Y	Y	Y	Y	Y	Y
6 Breckinridge	†	†	†	†	†	†
7 Perkins	Y	Y	Y	Y	Y	Y
LOUISIANA						
1 Livingston	Y	Y	Y	Y	Y	N
2 Boggs	Y	Y	Y	Y	Y	N
3 Treen	Y	?	?	?	?	?
4 Waggonner	Y	Y	Y	Y	■	■
5 Huckaby	Y	Y	Y	Y	Y	N
6 Moore	Y	Y	Y	Y	Y	N
7 Breaux	Y	Y	Y	?	Y	N
8 Long	Y	Y	Y	Y	Y	N
MAINE						
1 Emery	Y	Y	Y	Y	Y	N
2 Cohen	Y	Y	Y	Y	Y	N
MARYLAND						
1 Bauman	Y	Y	Y	Y	N	N
2 Long	Y	?	Y	?	Y	Y
3 Mikulski	Y	#	Y	Y	Y	Y
4 Holt	Y	Y	Y	Y	Y	N
5 Spellman	Y	Y	Y	Y	Y	Y
6 Byron	?	Y	Y	Y	Y	Y
7 Mitchell	N	#	Y	#	Y	Y
8 Steers	Y	Y	Y	Y	Y	Y
MASSACHUSETTS						
1 Conte	Y	Y	Y	Y	Y	Y
2 Boland	Y	Y	Y	Y	Y	#
3 Early	N	Y	Y	Y	Y	?
4 Drinan	N	Y	Y	Y	Y	Y
5 Tsongas	Y	#	#	#	#	#
6 Harrington	N	#	#	#	#	#
7 Markey	N	Y	Y	Y	Y	Y
8 O'Neill						
9 Moakley	X	Y	Y	Y	Y	Y
10 Heckler	Y	Y	Y	Y	Y	Y
11 Burke	Y	Y	Y	Y	Y	Y
12 Studds	N	Y	Y	Y	Y	Y
MICHIGAN						
1 Conyers	N	#	#	#	#	#
2 Pursell	N	Y	Y	Y	Y	Y
3 Brown	Y	#	Y	Y	Y	N
4 Stockman	Y	Y	Y	Y	Y	N
5 Sawyer	Y	Y	Y	Y	Y	Y
6 Carr	N	Y	Y	Y	Y	Y
7 Kildee	N	Y	Y	Y	Y	Y
8 Traxler	Y	Y	Y	Y	Y	Y
9 Vander Jagt	?	Y	Y	Y	Y	N
10 Cederberg	Y	Y	Y	Y	Y	N
11 Ruppe	Y	Y	Y	Y	N	N
12 Bonior	N	Y	Y	Y	Y	?
13 Diggs	N	Y	#	#	Y	Y
14 Nedzi	N	Y	Y	Y	Y	Y
15 Ford	Y	Y	Y	Y	Y	Y
16 Dingell	Y	Y	Y	Y	N	Y
17 Brodhead	N	Y	Y	Y	Y	Y
18 Blanchard	N	Y	Y	Y	Y	Y
19 Broomfield	Y	Y	Y	#	Y	#
MINNESOTA						
1 Quie	Y	Y	Y	Y	#	#
2 Hagedorn	Y	Y	Y	Y	Y	?
3 Frenzel	Y	Y	Y	?	Y	N
4 Vento	N	Y	Y	Y	Y	Y
5 Fraser	N	Y	#	#	#	#
6 Nolan	N	Y	?	Y	Y	Y
7 Stangeland	Y	Y	Y	Y	#	■
8 Oberstar	N	Y	Y	Y	Y	Y
MISSISSIPPI						
1 Whitten	Y	Y	Y	#	N	#
2 Bowen	Y	Y	Y	Y	Y	N
3 Montgomery	Y	Y	Y	Y	N	N
4 Cochran	?	?	?	?	?	?
5 Lott	Y	Y	Y	Y	Y	N
MISSOURI						
1 Clay	N	Y	Y	Y	Y	?
2 Young	Y	Y	Y	Y	Y	N
3 Gephardt	Y	Y	Y	Y	Y	■

	319	320	321	322	323	324
4 Skelton	Y	Y	Y	Y	Y	N
5 Bolling	Y	Y	Y	#	#	#
6 Coleman	Y	Y	Y	Y	Y	N
7 Taylor	Y	Y	Y	Y	Y	N
8 Ichord	Y	Y	Y	Y	Y	N
9 Volkmer	N	Y	Y	Y	Y	?
10 Burlison	Y	?	Y	Y	Y	?
MONTANA						
1 Baucus	#	#	#	#	#	#
2 Marlenee	Y	Y	Y	Y	N	N
NEBRASKA						
1 Thone	Y	Y	Y	Y	Y	Y
2 Cavanaugh	Y	Y	Y	?	?	?
3 Smith	Y	Y	Y	#	Y	?
NEVADA						
AL Santini	Y	Y	Y	Y	Y	■
NEW HAMPSHIRE						
1 D'Amours	Y	Y	Y	Y	Y	N
2 Cleveland	Y	Y	Y	Y	Y	N
NEW JERSEY						
1 Florio	#	Y	Y	Y	Y	#
2 Hughes	N	Y	Y	Y	Y	#
3 Howard	Y	Y	#	#	#	#
4 Thompson	N	Y	Y	Y	Y	Y
5 Fenwick	N	Y	Y	#	Y	Y
6 Forsythe	N	Y	Y	Y	Y	N
7 Maguire	N	Y	Y	Y	Y	Y
8 Roe	Y	Y	Y	Y	Y	Y
9 Hollenbeck	Y	Y	Y	Y	Y	Y
10 Rodino	#	#	#	#	#	#
11 Minish	Y	Y	Y	Y	Y	Y
12 Rinaldo	Y	Y	Y	Y	Y	Y
13 Meyner	N	Y	#	#	Y	Y
14 LeFante	Y	Y	Y	Y	Y	Y
15 Patten	Y	Y	Y	Y	Y	Y
NEW MEXICO						
1 Lujan	Y	Y	Y	Y	Y	?
2 Runnels	#	#	#	#	?	?
NEW YORK						
1 Pike	Y	Y	Y	Y	Y	N
2 Downey	†	Y	Y	Y	Y	Y
3 Ambro	Y	?	Y	Y	Y	N
4 Lent	#	Y	Y	Y	Y	N
5 Wydler	Y	Y	Y	Y	Y	N
6 Wolff	Y	Y	Y	Y	Y	N
7 Addabbo	N	Y	Y	Y	Y	Y
8 Rosenthal	N	Y	Y	Y	Y	Y
9 Delaney	Y	Y	Y	?	?	?
10 Biaggi	Y	Y	Y	Y	Y	Y
11 Scheuer	N	Y	Y	Y	Y	Y
12 Chisholm	X	Y	Y	Y	Y	Y
13 Solarz	Y	Y	Y	Y	Y	Y
14 Richmond	N	Y	Y	Y	Y	Y
15 Zeferetti	Y	Y	Y	Y	#	■
16 Holtzman	N	Y	Y	Y	Y	Y
17 Murphy	Y	Y	Y	Y	Y	Y
18 Green	Y	Y	Y	Y	Y	Y
19 Rangel	N	Y	Y	Y	Y	Y
20 Weiss	N	Y	Y	Y	Y	?
21 Garcia	?	?	?	?	?	?
22 Bingham	N	Y	Y	Y	Y	Y
23 Caputo	Y	Y	Y	Y	Y	N
24 Ottinger	N	Y	Y	Y	Y	Y
25 Fish	Y	Y	Y	Y	Y	Y
26 Gilman	Y	Y	Y	Y	Y	†
27 McHugh	Y	Y	Y	Y	Y	Y
28 Stratton	Y	Y	Y	Y	Y	N
29 Pattison	N	Y	Y	Y	Y	Y
30 McEwen	Y	Y	Y	Y	?	?
31 Mitchell	Y	Y	Y	Y	Y	#
32 Hanley	Y	Y	Y	Y	Y	Y
33 Walsh	Y	Y	Y	Y	Y	Y
34 Horton	Y	#	Y	Y	Y	Y
35 Conable	Y	Y	Y	Y	Y	N
36 LaFalce	Y	Y	Y	Y	Y	Y
37 Nowak	Y	Y	Y	Y	Y	Y
38 Kemp	Y	?	?	?	?	?
39 Lundine	Y	Y	Y	Y	Y	#
NORTH CAROLINA						
1 Jones	Y	Y	Y	Y	Y	N
2 Fountain	Y	Y	Y	Y	N	N
3 Whitley	Y	Y	Y	Y	Y	N
4 Andrews	Y	Y	Y	Y	N	N
5 Neal	Y	Y	Y	Y	Y	N
6 Preyer	Y	Y	Y	Y	Y	Y
7 Rose	#	#	#	#	#	■
8 Hefner	Y	Y	Y	#	Y	N

	319	320	321	322	323	324
9 Martin	Y	Y	Y	#	N	N
10 Broyhill	Y	Y	Y	Y	N	N
11 Gudger	Y	Y	Y	Y	Y	N
NORTH DAKOTA						
AL Andrews	Y	#	#	#	#	#
OHIO						
1 Gradison	Y	Y	Y	Y	Y	#
2 Luken	#	Y	Y	Y	Y	Y
3 Whalen	Y	Y	Y	Y	#	#
4 Guyer	Y	Y	Y	Y	Y	Y
5 Latta	Y	Y	Y	Y	N	Y
6 Harsha	Y	Y	Y	Y	Y	N
7 Brown	Y	Y	Y	Y	?	?
8 Kindness	Y	Y	Y	Y	Y	N
9 Ashley	Y	Y	Y	Y	Y	Y
10 Miller	Y	Y	Y	Y	Y	N
11 Stanton	Y	Y	Y	Y	Y	N
12 Devine	Y	Y	Y	Y	Y	N
13 Pease	Y	Y	Y	Y	Y	Y
14 Seiberling	N	Y	Y	Y	Y	Y
15 Wylie	Y	Y	Y	Y	Y	Y
16 Regula	Y	Y	Y	Y	Y	Y
17 Ashbrook	Y	Y	Y	Y	N	■
18 Applegate	?	?	?	?	?	?
19 Carney	Y	Y	Y	?	Y	Y
20 Oakar	Y	Y	Y	Y	Y	Y
21 Stokes	N	Y	Y	Y	Y	Y
22 Vanik	■	Y	Y	Y	Y	Y
23 Mottl	Y	Y	Y	Y	N	N
OKLAHOMA						
1 Jones	Y	Y	Y	Y	Y	Y
2 Risenhoover	Y	Y	Y	Y	Y	?
3 Watkins	Y	#	Y	Y	N	N
4 Steed	Y	Y	Y	Y	Y	Y
5 Edwards	Y	Y	?	?	?	?
6 English	Y	Y	Y	Y	N	N
OREGON						
1 AuCoin	?	#	#	#	#	?
2 Ullman	#	Y	Y	Y	Y	#
3 Duncan	Y	Y	Y	Y	Y	Y
4 Weaver	N	Y	Y	Y	#	?
PENNSYLVANIA						
1 Myers, M.	Y	Y	Y	Y	Y	Y
2 Nix	?	?	?	?	?	?
3 Lederer	Y	Y	Y	Y	Y	Y
4 Eilberg	Y	Y	Y	Y	Y	#
5 Schulze	Y	Y	Y	Y	Y	Y
6 Yatron	Y	Y	Y	Y	Y	#
7 Edgar	Y	Y	Y	Y	Y	Y
8 Kostmayer	N	Y	Y	Y	Y	Y
9 Shuster	Y	Y	Y	Y	N	N
10 McDade	Y	Y	Y	Y	Y	?
11 Flood	Y	Y	Y	Y	Y	Y
12 Murtha	Y	Y	Y	Y	Y	N
13 Coughlin	Y	Y	Y	?	Y	N
14 Moorhead	Y	Y	Y	Y	Y	#
15 Rooney	?	Y	Y	Y	Y	Y
16 Walker	Y	Y	Y	Y	N	N
17 Ertel	Y	Y	Y	Y	Y	Y
18 Walgren	Y	Y	Y	?	Y	Y
19 Goodling, W.	?	?	?	?	?	?
20 Gaydos	Y	Y	Y	Y	Y	N
21 Dent	Y	Y	#	#	#	■
22 Murphy	Y	Y	Y	Y	Y	N
23 Ammerman	✓	Y	Y	Y	Y	Y
24 Marks	Y	Y	Y	Y	Y	Y
25 Myers, G.	Y	Y	Y	Y	Y	Y
RHODE ISLAND						
1 St Germain	Y	?	?	?	?	?
2 Beard	Y	?	?	Y	Y	?
SOUTH CAROLINA						
1 Davis	Y	Y	Y	Y	Y	N
2 Spence	Y	Y	Y	Y	Y	N
3 Derrick	Y	Y	Y	Y	Y	Y
4 Mann	Y	Y	Y	Y	Y	N
5 Holland	Y	#	#	#	#	?
6 Jenrette	Y	Y	#	#	Y	N
SOUTH DAKOTA						
1 Pressler	Y	Y	Y	Y	Y	Y
2 Abdnor	Y	Y	Y	Y	N	N
TENNESSEE						
1 Quillen	Y	Y	Y	Y	Y	■
2 Duncan	Y	Y	Y	Y	Y	N
3 Lloyd	Y	Y	Y	Y	N	N
4 Gore	Y	Y	Y	Y	Y	Y
5 Allen	Y	Y	Y	Y	Y	Y
6 Beard	Y	?	?	?	?	?

	319	320	321	322	323	324
7 Jones	Y	Y	Y	Y	N	Y
8 Ford	Y	?	?	?	?	?
TEXAS						
1 Hall	Y	Y	#	Y	■	■
2 Wilson, C.	Y	Y	Y	Y	Y	Y
3 Collins	Y	Y	Y	Y	N	N
4 Roberts	Y	Y	Y	Y	?	?
5 Mattox	N	Y	Y	Y	Y	Y
6 Teague	✓	?	?	?	?	?
7 Archer	?	?	?	?	?	?
8 Eckhardt	Y	Y	Y	Y	Y	?
9 Brooks	Y	Y	Y	Y	Y	Y
10 Pickle	Y	Y	Y	Y	N	■
11 Poage	Y	Y	Y	Y	N	N
12 Wright	Y	Y	Y	Y	Y	?
13 Hightower	Y	Y	Y	Y	?	?
14 Young	?	?	?	?	?	?
15 de la Garza	Y	Y	Y	Y	Y	Y
16 White	Y	Y	Y	Y	N	Y
17 Burleson	Y	Y	Y	Y	N	N
18 Jordan	Y	Y	Y	Y	Y	#
19 Mahon	Y	Y	Y	Y	N	N
20 Gonzalez	Y	P	Y	Y	Y	Y
21 Krueger	#	Y	Y	#	Y	Y
22 Gammage	Y	Y	Y	Y	Y	Y
23 Kazen	?	?	?	?	?	?
24 Milford	Y	Y	Y	?	N	?
UTAH						
1 McKay	#	#	#	#	#	■
2 Marriott	Y	Y	Y	Y	Y	N
VERMONT						
AL Jeffords	#	Y	Y	Y	Y	#
VIRGINIA						
1 Trible	Y	Y	Y	Y	Y	N
2 Whitehurst	Y	Y	Y	Y	#	■
3 Satterfield	Y	Y	Y	Y	N	N
4 Daniel	Y	Y	Y	Y	Y	N
5 Daniel	Y	Y	Y	?	Y	N
6 Butler	Y	?	?	Y	Y	Y
7 Robinson	Y	Y	Y	Y	Y	N
8 Harris	Y	Y	Y	Y	Y	Y
9 Wampler	Y	Y	Y	Y	N	?
10 Fisher	Y	Y	Y	Y	Y	Y
WASHINGTON						
1 Pritchard	Y	Y	Y	Y	Y	Y
2 Meeds	Y	Y	Y	Y	Y	Y
3 Bonker	#	Y	Y	Y	Y	Y
4 McCormack	Y	Y	Y	Y	Y	N
5 Foley	Y	Y	Y	Y	Y	N
6 Dicks	Y	Y	Y	Y	Y	Y
7 Cunningham	Y	Y	Y	Y	N	N
WEST VIRGINIA						
1 Mollohan	Y	Y	Y	Y	N	N
2 Staggers	✓	Y	Y	Y	Y	Y
3 Slack	Y	Y	Y	Y	N	N
4 Rahall	Y	Y	Y	Y	N	Y
WISCONSIN						
1 Aspin	N	Y	Y	Y	Y	Y
2 Kastenmeier	N	Y	Y	Y	Y	Y
3 Baldus	N	Y	Y	Y	Y	Y
4 Zablocki	Y	Y	Y	Y	Y	Y
5 Reuss	Y	Y	Y	Y	Y	Y
6 Steiger	Y	#	#	#	#	#
7 Obey	N	Y	Y	?	Y	Y
8 Cornell	N	Y	Y	Y	Y	Y
9 Kasten	#	#	#	#	#	#
WYOMING						
AL Roncalio	Y	Y	Y	Y	Y	?

Democrats ***Republicans***

325. Procedural Motion. Symms, R-Idaho, motion to approve the House *Journal* of Tuesday, May 30, 1978. Motion agreed to 318-14: R 101-7; D 217-7 (ND 151-6; SD 66-1), May 31, 1978.

326. H Res 1194. Korean Investigation. Zablocki, D-Wis., motion to suspend the rules and adopt the resolution expressing the sense of the House that the government of South Korea should cooperate in the House investigation of alleged bribery attempts by former Korean Ambassador to the United States Kim Dong Jo and stating that the House is prepared to deny or reduce economic aid to South Korea if such cooperation is not forthcoming. Motion agreed to 321-46: R 96-23; D 225-23 (ND 158-13; SD 67-10), May 31, 1978. A two-thirds majority vote (245 in this case) is required for adoption under suspension of the rules.

327. HR 7041. Glenn Cunningham and Standing Bear Lakes. Roberts, D-Texas, motion to suspend the rules and pass the bill to rename two lakes in the Papillion Creek project in Nebraska: Irvington Lake to Glenn Cunningham Lake, for former Rep. Glenn C. Cunningham, R-Neb. (1957-71), and Military Lake to Standing Bear Lake, for the Ponca Indian who in 1879 was declared a person, thus establishing constitutional rights for American Indians. Motion agreed to 369-0: R 120-0; D 249-0 (ND 172-0; SD 77-0), May 31, 1978. A two-thirds majority vote (246 in this case) is required for passage under suspension of the rules.

328. HR 212. R. Shaefer Heard Park. Roberts, D-Texas, motion to suspend the rules and pass the bill to rename the East Lake Park located in the West Point Lake Project in Georgia the R. Shaefer Heard Park, for the president of the Middle Chattahoochee River Development Association. Motion agreed to 359-4: R 117-0; D 242-4 (ND 167-4; SD 75-0), May 31, 1978. A two-thirds majority vote (242 in this case) is required for passage under suspension of the rules.

329. HR 12598. State Department Authorization. Adoption of the rule (H Res 1204) providing for House floor consideration of the bill to authorize $1.9 billion for State Department operations and related programs in fiscal 1979 and fiscal 1978 supplemental authorizations of $47 million. Adopted 363-10: R 120-5; D 243-5 (ND 171-1; SD 72-4), May 31, 1978.

330. HR 12598. State Department Authorization. Ashbrook, R-Ohio, amendment to delete language authorizing the establishment of a "commission on proposals for a center for conflict resolution." Adopted 237-135: R 109-15; D 128-120 (ND 66-105; SD 62-15), May 31, 1978.

331. HR 12598. State Department Authorization. Bauman, R-Md., amendment to delete language authorizing the establishment of an Institute for International Human Rights. Adopted 202-164: R 96-27; D 106-137 (ND 47-121; SD 59-16), May 31, 1978.

332. HR 12598. State Department Authorization. Hansen, R-Idaho, amendment to prohibit use of any funds in the bill to implement the Panama Canal treaties without specific congressional approval. Adopted 203-163: R 95-29; D 108-134 (ND 49-117; SD 59-17), May 31, 1978.

KEY

- Y Voted for (yea).
- ✓ Paired for.
- † Announced for.
- # CQ Poll for.
- N Voted against (nay).
- X Paired against.
- - Announced against.
- ▮ CQ Poll against.
- P Voted "present."
- ● Voted "present" to avoid possible conflict of interest.
- ? Did not vote or otherwise make a position known.

	325	326	327	328	329	330	331	332
ALABAMA								
1 ***Edwards***	Y	Y	Y	Y	Y	Y	Y	Y
2 ***Dickinson***	?	?	?	?	Y	Y	Y	N
3 Nichols	Y	Y	Y	Y	Y	Y	Y	Y
4 Bevill	Y	Y	Y	Y	Y	Y	Y	Y
5 Flippo	?	Y	Y	Y	Y	Y	Y	Y
6 ***Buchanan***	Y	†	Y	Y	Y	N	N	N
7 Flowers	?	?	?	?	?	?	?	?
ALASKA								
AL ***Young***	?	?	?	?	?	?	?	?
ARIZONA								
1 ***Rhodes***	?	?	?	?	?	?	?	?
2 Udall	Y	Y	Y	Y	Y	Y	N	N
3 Stump	#	▮	#	#	?	Y	Y	Y
4 ***Rudd***	?	?	?	?	?	✓	✓	✓
ARKANSAS								
1 Alexander	Y	Y	Y	Y	Y	?	?	?
2 Tucker	#	#	#	#	#	#	#	#
3 ***Hammerschmidt***	Y	N	Y	Y	Y	Y	Y	Y
4 Thornton	?	?	?	?	?	?	?	?
CALIFORNIA								
1 Johnson	Y	Y	Y	Y	Y	N	Y	Y
2 ***Clausen***	Y	Y	Y	Y	Y	Y	Y	Y
3 Moss	Y	N	Y	Y	Y	Y	N	N
4 Leggett	?	Y	Y	Y	?	N	Y	Y
5 Burton, J.	?	?	?	?	?	?	?	?
6 Burton, P.	Y	Y	Y	Y	Y	?	?	?
7 Miller	N	Y	Y	Y	Y	N	N	N
8 Dellums	Y	Y	Y	Y	Y	N	N	N
9 Stark	Y	#	#	#	Y	N	N	N
10 Edwards	Y	Y	Y	Y	Y	N	N	N
11 Ryan	#	#	#	#	#	#	#	▮
12 ***McCloskey***	Y	Y	Y	Y	Y	N	Y	N
13 Mineta	#	Y	Y	Y	Y	N	N	N
14 McFall	Y	Y	Y	Y	Y	N	N	N
15 Sisk	Y	N	Y	Y	Y	N	Y	?
16 Panetta	Y	Y	Y	Y	Y	Y	Y	N
17 Krebs	Y	Y	Y	Y	Y	Y	Y	N
18 ***Ketchum***	Y	N	Y	Y	Y	Y	Y	Y
19 ***Lagomarsino***	Y	Y	Y	Y	Y	Y	Y	Y
20 ***Goldwater***	?	?	?	?	?	?	✓	?
21 Corman	#	#	#	#	#	?	▮	▮
22 ***Moorhead***	Y	Y	Y	Y	Y	Y	Y	Y
23 Beilenson	N	Y	Y	N	Y	N	N	N
24 Waxman	Y	Y	Y	Y	Y	N	N	N
25 Roybal	Y	Y	Y	Y	Y	N	N	N
26 ***Rousselot***	?	?	?	?	?	✓	✓	✓
27 ***Dornan***	Y	Y	Y	Y	Y	Y	Y	Y
28 Burke	#	#	#	#	#	X	X	X
29 Hawkins	Y	Y	Y	Y	Y	X	X	X
30 Danielson	Y	Y	Y	Y	Y	N	N	N
31 Wilson, C.H.	#	▮	#	#	#	N	#	Y
32 Anderson	Y	?	Y	Y	Y	N	N	Y
33 ***Clawson***	?	N	Y	Y	Y	Y	Y	Y
34 Hannaford	Y	Y	Y	Y	Y	Y	N	Y
35 Lloyd	N	Y	Y	Y	Y	Y	Y	Y
36 Brown	Y	Y	Y	Y	Y	N	N	N
37 ***Pettis***	Y	Y	Y	Y	Y	?	?	?
38 Patterson	Y	Y	Y	Y	Y	N	N	Y
39 ***Wiggins***	#	#	#	#	#	#	#	▮
40 ***Badham***	#	#	#	#	Y	Y	Y	Y
41 ***Wilson, B.***	N	Y	Y	Y	Y	Y	Y	Y
42 Van Deerlin	Y	Y	Y	Y	Y	Y	N	N
43 ***Burgener***	?	?	?	?	?	✓	✓	?
COLORADO								
1 Schroeder	Y	Y	Y	Y	Y	N	N	N
2 Wirth	Y	Y	Y	Y	Y	N	N	N
3 Evans	Y	N	Y	Y	Y	Y	N	#
4 ***Johnson***	Y	Y	Y	Y	Y	N	Y	N
5 ***Armstrong***	Y	Y	Y	Y	Y	Y	Y	Y
CONNECTICUT								
1 Cotter	#	Y	Y	Y	Y	N	N	N
2 Dodd	Y	N	Y	Y	Y	N	N	N
3 Giaimo	?	?	?	?	?	?	?	?
4 ***McKinney***	Y	Y	Y	Y	Y	N	N	N
5 ***Sarasin***	-	Y	Y	Y	Y	Y	X	N
6 Moffett	Y	Y	Y	Y	Y	N	N	N
DELAWARE								
AL ***Evans***	Y	Y	Y	Y	Y	Y	Y	Y
FLORIDA								
1 Sikes	Y	N	Y	Y	Y	Y	Y	Y
2 Fuqua	Y	Y	Y	Y	Y	Y	Y	Y
3 Bennett	Y	Y	Y	Y	Y	N	Y	Y
4 Chappell	Y	N	Y	Y	Y	Y	Y	Y
5 ***Kelly***	Y	Y	Y	Y	Y	Y	Y	Y
6 ***Young***	?	Y	Y	Y	Y	Y	Y	Y
7 Gibbons	?	?	?	?	?	?	?	?
8 Ireland	Y	Y	Y	Y	Y	Y	Y	Y
9 ***Frey***	?	?	?	?	?	?	?	✓
10 ***Bafalis***	Y	Y	Y	Y	Y	Y	Y	Y
11 Rogers	Y	Y	Y	Y	Y	Y	Y	Y
12 ***Burke***	Y	Y	Y	Y	Y	Y	Y	Y
13 Lehman	Y	Y	Y	Y	Y	N	N	N
14 Pepper	Y	Y	Y	Y	Y	N	N	N
15 Fascell	#	Y	Y	Y	Y	N	▮	▮
GEORGIA								
1 Ginn	Y	Y	Y	Y	Y	Y	Y	Y
2 Mathis	?	N	Y	Y	Y	Y	Y	Y
3 Brinkley	Y	Y	Y	Y	Y	Y	Y	Y
4 Levitas	Y	Y	Y	Y	Y	Y	Y	Y
5 Fowler	Y	Y	Y	Y	Y	Y	Y	Y
6 Flynt	Y	Y	Y	?	Y	Y	Y	Y
7 McDonald	Y	N	Y	Y	N	Y	Y	Y
8 Evans	Y	N	Y	Y	Y	Y	Y	Y
9 Jenkins	Y	Y	Y	Y	Y	Y	Y	Y
10 Barnard	Y	Y	Y	Y	Y	Y	Y	Y
HAWAII								
1 Heftel	Y	Y	Y	Y	Y	Y	Y	N
2 Akaka	Y	Y	Y	Y	Y	N	N	N
IDAHO								
1 ***Symms***	Y	N	Y	Y	N	Y	Y	Y
2 ***Hansen, G.***	Y	N	Y	Y	Y	Y	Y	Y
ILLINOIS								
1 Metcalfe	Y	Y	Y	Y	Y	N	N	N
2 Murphy	#	Y	Y	Y	Y	Y	Y	Y
3 Russo	#	#	#	#	#	#	#	▮
4 ***Derwinski***	Y	Y	Y	Y	Y	N	N	N
5 Fary	Y	Y	Y	Y	Y	N	N	N
6 ***Hyde***	Y	Y	Y	Y	Y	#	#	#
7 Collins	Y	Y	Y	Y	Y	N	N	N
8 Rostenkowski	#	?	#	#	#	?	?	?
9 Yates	Y	Y	Y	Y	Y	Y	N	N
10 Mikva	Y	Y	Y	Y	Y	N	N	N
11 Annunzio	Y	Y	Y	Y	Y	Y	Y	Y
12 ***Crane***	Y	N	Y	Y	N	Y	Y	Y
13 ***McClory***	Y	Y	Y	Y	Y	Y	N	N
14 ***Erlenborn***	Y	Y	Y	#	Y	Y	N	N
15 ***Corcoran***	Y	Y	Y	Y	Y	Y	Y	Y
16 ***Anderson***	?	N	Y	Y	Y	N	N	N
17 ***O'Brien***	#	#	#	#	#	#	#	#
18 ***Michel***	#	#	#	#	#	#	?	#
19 ***Railsback***	#	#	#	#	#	#	▮	▮
20 ***Findley***	Y	N	Y	Y	Y	N	N	N
21 ***Madigan***	Y	Y	Y	Y	Y	Y	Y	Y
22 Shipley	?	?	?	?	?	X	X	X
23 Price	Y	Y	Y	Y	Y	N	N	N
24 Simon	†	?	†	†	†	-	-	-
INDIANA								
1 Benjamin	Y	Y	Y	Y	Y	Y	Y	Y
2 Fithian	Y	†	Y	Y	Y	Y	Y	Y
3 Brademas	Y	Y	Y	Y	Y	N	N	N
4 ***Quayle***	?	?	?	?	?	?	?	?
5 ***Hillis***	Y	Y	Y	Y	Y	Y	Y	Y
6 Evans	Y	Y	Y	Y	Y	Y	Y	Y
7 ***Myers, J.***	Y	Y	Y	Y	Y	Y	Y	Y
8 Cornwell	Y	Y	Y	Y	Y	Y	N	N
9 Hamilton	Y	Y	Y	Y	Y	Y	N	N
10 Sharp	Y	Y	Y	Y	Y	Y	N	N
11 Jacobs	N	Y	Y	Y	Y	N	Y	Y
IOWA								
1 ***Leach***	Y	Y	Y	Y	Y	Y	Y	Y
2 Blouin	Y	Y	Y	Y	Y	N	N	N
3 ***Grassley***	Y	Y	Y	Y	Y	Y	Y	Y
4 Smith	Y	Y	Y	Y	Y	Y	N	N
5 Harkin	Y	Y	Y	Y	Y	N	N	N
6 Bedell	Y	Y	Y	Y	Y	N	N	N

Democrats ***Republicans***

Corresponding to Congressional Record Votes 380, 382, 383, 384, 385, 387, 388, 389

	325	326	327	328	329	330	331	332
KANSAS								
1 Sebelius	#	#	#	#	#	?	✓	#
2 Keys	Y	Y	Y	Y	Y	N	N	N
3 Winn	Y	Y	Y	Y	Y	Y	N	Y
4 Glickman	Y	Y	Y	Y	Y	N	Y	Y
5 Skubitz	?	Y	Y	Y	Y	Y	Y	N
KENTUCKY								
1 Hubbard	Y	Y	Y	Y	Y	Y	Y	Y
2 Natcher	Y	Y	Y	Y	Y	Y	N	Y
3 Mazzoli	Y	Y	Y	Y	Y	Y	N	N
4 Snyder	Y	Y	Y	Y	Y	Y	Y	Y
5 Carter	Y	Y	Y	Y	Y	Y	Y	Y
6 Breckinridge	†	†	†	†	Y	Y	N	Y
7 Perkins	Y	Y	Y	Y	Y	N	N	Y
LOUISIANA								
1 Livingston	?	?	?	?	?	Y	Y	Y
2 Boggs	Y	Y	Y	Y	Y	N	N	Y
3 Treen	?	?	?	?	Y	Y	Y	Y
4 Waggonner	Y	Y	Y	Y	Y	Y	Y	Y
5 Huckaby	Y	Y	Y	Y	Y	Y	Y	Y
6 Moore	Y	N	Y	Y	Y	Y	Y	Y
7 Breaux	Y	Y	Y	Y	Y	Y	Y	Y
8 Long	Y	Y	Y	Y	Y	N	N	N
MAINE								
1 Emery	Y	Y	Y	Y	Y	Y	Y	Y
2 Cohen	Y	Y	Y	Y	Y	Y	N	Y
MARYLAND								
1 Bauman	Y	Y	Y	Y	N	Y	Y	Y
2 Long	Y	Y	Y	Y	Y	Y	Y	N
3 Mikulski	Y	Y	Y	Y	Y	N	N	N
4 Holt	Y	N	Y	Y	Y	Y	Y	Y
5 Spellman	Y	Y	Y	Y	Y	N	N	#
6 Byron	Y	Y	Y	Y	Y	Y	Y	Y
7 Mitchell	N	Y	Y	Y	Y	N	N	N
8 Steers	Y	Y	Y	Y	Y	N	N	N
MASSACHUSETTS								
1 Conte	Y	Y	Y	Y	Y	N	N	N
2 Boland	Y	Y	Y	Y	Y	Y	N	N
3 Early	Y	Y	Y	Y	Y	Y	N	N
4 Drinan	Y	Y	Y	Y	Y	N	N	N
5 Tsongas	Y	Y	Y	Y	Y	N	N	N
6 Harrington	#	Y	Y	Y	Y	N	N	N
7 Markey	Y	Y	Y	Y	Y	N	N	N
8 O'Neill								
9 Moakley	Y	Y	Y	Y	Y	N	N	N
10 Heckler	?	Y	Y	Y	Y	Y	N	Y
11 Burke	Y	Y	Y	Y	Y	N	N	Y
12 Studds	Y	Y	Y	Y	Y	N	N	N
MICHIGAN								
1 Conyers	#	#	#	#	#	▮	X	X
2 Pursell	Y	Y	Y	Y	Y	Y	Y	N
3 Brown	N	Y	Y	Y	Y	Y	N	Y
4 Stockman	Y	N	Y	Y	Y	Y	Y	Y
5 Sawyer	Y	Y	Y	Y	Y	Y	Y	Y
6 Carr	Y	Y	Y	Y	Y	N	N	N
7 Kildee	Y	Y	Y	Y	Y	N	N	N
8 Traxler	Y	Y	Y	Y	Y	Y	N	N
9 Vander Jagt	?	Y	Y	Y	Y	Y	Y	Y
10 Cederberg	?	Y	Y	Y	Y	Y	Y	N
11 Ruppe	Y	N	Y	Y	Y	Y	Y	N
12 Bonior	?	Y	Y	Y	Y	N	N	N
13 Diggs	#	Y	Y	Y	Y	N	N	N
14 Nedzi	Y	Y	Y	Y	Y	Y	Y	N
15 Ford	Y	Y	Y	Y	Y	N	N	N
16 Dingell	Y	N	Y	Y	?	Y	N	N
17 Brodhead	N	Y	Y	Y	Y	N	N	N
18 Blanchard	Y	Y	Y	Y	Y	N	?	▮
19 Broomfield	Y	Y	Y	Y	Y	Y	N	N
MINNESOTA								
1 Quie	#	#	#	#	Y	Y	Y	Y
2 Hagedorn	Y	Y	Y	Y	Y	Y	Y	Y
3 Frenzel	Y	Y	Y	Y	Y	Y	Y	Y
4 Vento	Y	Y	Y	Y	Y	N	N	N
5 Fraser	Y	Y	Y	Y	Y	N	N	N
6 Nolan	Y	Y	Y	Y	Y	N	N	N
7 Stangeland	Y	Y	Y	Y	Y	Y	Y	Y
8 Oberstar	Y	Y	Y	Y	Y	N	N	N
MISSISSIPPI								
1 Whitten	Y	Y	Y	#	Y	Y	✓	Y
2 Bowen	Y	Y	Y	Y	Y	Y	Y	Y
3 Montgomery	Y	Y	Y	Y	Y	Y	Y	Y
4 Cochran	?	?	?	?	?	?	?	?
5 Lott	Y	Y	Y	Y	Y	Y	Y	Y
MISSOURI								
1 Clay	Y	Y	Y	Y	Y	N	N	N
2 Young	#	#	#	#	#	▮	▮	#
3 Gephardt	Y	Y	Y	Y	Y	Y	Y	Y
4 Skelton	Y	Y	Y	Y	Y	Y	Y	Y
5 Bolling	Y	N	Y	Y	Y	N	N	N
6 Coleman	Y	Y	Y	Y	Y	Y	Y	Y
7 Taylor	Y	N	Y	Y	Y	Y	Y	Y
8 Ichord	Y	Y	Y	Y	Y	Y	Y	Y
9 Volkmer	Y	Y	Y	Y	Y	Y	Y	Y
10 Burlison	Y	Y	Y	Y	Y	N	N	N
MONTANA								
1 Baucus	#	#	#	#	#	#	#	#
2 Marlenee	Y	Y	Y	Y	Y	Y	Y	Y
NEBRASKA								
1 Thone	Y	Y	Y	Y	Y	Y	Y	Y
2 Cavanaugh	Y	Y	Y	Y	Y	N	N	N
3 Smith	Y	Y	Y	Y	Y	Y	Y	Y
NEVADA								
AL Santini	#	Y	Y	Y	Y	#	Y	Y
NEW HAMPSHIRE								
1 D'Amours	Y	Y	Y	Y	Y	Y	N	Y
2 Cleveland	Y	Y	Y	Y	Y	Y	Y	Y
NEW JERSEY								
1 Florio	Y	Y	Y	Y	Y	N	N	Y
2 Hughes	Y	Y	Y	Y	Y	N	N	Y
3 Howard	#	#	#	#	#	▮	▮	▮
4 Thompson	Y	Y	Y	Y	Y	N	N	N
5 Fenwick	Y	Y	Y	Y	Y	Y	N	N
6 Forsythe	N	Y	Y	Y	Y	Y	N	Y
7 Maguire	Y	Y	Y	Y	Y	N	N	N
8 Roe	P	Y	Y	Y	Y	N	N	Y
9 Hollenbeck	Y	Y	Y	Y	Y	N	N	N
10 Rodino	#	#	#	#	#	▮	▮	▮
11 Minish	Y	Y	Y	Y	Y	N	N	Y
12 Rinaldo	Y	Y	Y	Y	Y	Y	N	Y
13 Meyner	Y	Y	Y	Y	Y	N	N	N
14 LeFante	Y	Y	Y	Y	Y	N	X	✓
15 Patten	Y	Y	Y	Y	Y	N	N	N
NEW MEXICO								
1 Lujan	?	?	?	?	?	?	?	?
2 Runnels	#	?	#	#	#	?	?	?
NEW YORK								
1 Pike	Y	Y	Y	Y	Y	Y	Y	N
2 Downey	Y	Y	Y	Y	Y	N	N	N
3 Ambro	?	Y	?	?	Y	Y	N	N
4 Lent	Y	Y	Y	Y	Y	Y	Y	Y
5 Wydler	Y	Y	Y	Y	Y	Y	Y	Y
6 Wolff	Y	Y	Y	Y	Y	N	N	N
7 Addabbo	Y	Y	Y	Y	Y	N	N	N
8 Rosenthal	Y	Y	Y	Y	Y	N	N	N
9 Delaney	Y	Y	Y	Y	Y	Y	Y	Y
10 Biaggi	Y	Y	Y	Y	Y	N	N	Y
11 Scheuer	?	Y	Y	Y	Y	N	N	N
12 Chisholm	#	Y	Y	Y	Y	Y	N	N
13 Solarz	Y	Y	Y	Y	Y	N	N	N
14 Richmond	Y	Y	Y	Y	Y	X	X	X
15 Zeferetti	Y	Y	Y	Y	Y	Y	Y	Y
16 Holtzman	?	Y	Y	Y	Y	N	N	N
17 Murphy	Y	N	Y	Y	Y	N	Y	N
18 Green	Y	Y	Y	Y	Y	N	N	N
19 Rangel	?	?	?	?	?	X	X	X
20 Weiss	Y	Y	Y	N	Y	N	N	N
21 Garcia	Y	Y	Y	Y	Y	N	N	N
22 Bingham	Y	N	Y	Y	Y	N	N	N
23 Caputo	Y	Y	Y	Y	Y	Y	?	?
24 Ottinger	Y	Y	Y	Y	Y	N	N	N
25 Fish	?	Y	Y	Y	Y	Y	N	N
26 Gilman	Y	Y	Y	Y	Y	†	-	✓
27 McHugh	Y	Y	Y	Y	Y	Y	N	N
28 Stratton	Y	N	Y	Y	Y	Y	Y	Y
29 Pattison	Y	Y	Y	Y	Y	N	N	N
30 McEwen	Y	Y	Y	?	Y	Y	Y	Y
31 Mitchell	Y	Y	Y	Y	Y	Y	Y	Y
32 Hanley	Y	Y	Y	Y	Y	Y	Y	N
33 Walsh	Y	Y	Y	Y	Y	Y	Y	Y
34 Horton	Y	Y	Y	Y	Y	N	N	Y
35 Conable	Y	Y	Y	Y	Y	Y	Y	Y
36 LaFalce	Y	Y	Y	Y	Y	Y	N	N
37 Nowak	Y	Y	Y	Y	Y	N	N	N
38 Kemp	Y	Y	Y	Y	Y	Y	Y	Y
39 Lundine	Y	Y	Y	Y	Y	N	N	N
NORTH CAROLINA								
1 Jones	Y	Y	Y	Y	Y	N	Y	Y
2 Fountain	Y	Y	Y	Y	#	Y	Y	Y
3 Whitley	Y	Y	Y	Y	Y	Y	Y	Y
4 Andrews	Y	Y	Y	Y	Y	Y	Y	N
5 Neal	#	#	#	#	#	?	?	✓
6 Preyer	Y	Y	Y	Y	Y	Y	N	N
7 Rose	Y	Y	Y	Y	Y	N	N	Y
8 Hefner	Y	Y	Y	Y	Y	Y	Y	Y
9 Martin	#	#	#	#	#	#	#	#
10 Broyhill	Y	Y	Y	Y	Y	Y	Y	Y
11 Gudger	Y	Y	Y	Y	Y	Y	Y	Y
NORTH DAKOTA								
AL Andrews	Y	Y	Y	Y	Y	Y	Y	Y
OHIO								
1 Gradison	Y	N	Y	Y	Y	Y	Y	Y
2 Luken	Y	Y	Y	Y	Y	Y	Y	Y
3 Whalen	Y	Y	Y	#	Y	N	N	N
4 Guyer	Y	Y	Y	Y	Y	Y	Y	Y
5 Latta	Y	Y	Y	Y	Y	Y	Y	Y
6 Harsha	?	Y	Y	Y	Y	Y	Y	Y
7 Brown	Y	N	Y	Y	Y	Y	Y	Y
8 Kindness	Y	Y	Y	Y	Y	Y	Y	Y
9 Ashley	?	Y	Y	?	Y	Y	Y	N
10 Miller	Y	Y	Y	Y	Y	Y	Y	Y
11 Stanton	Y	Y	Y	Y	Y	Y	Y	N
12 Devine	Y	N	Y	Y	Y	Y	Y	Y
13 Pease	#	Y	Y	Y	Y	N	N	N
14 Seiberling	Y	Y	Y	Y	Y	N	N	N
15 Wylie	Y	Y	Y	Y	Y	Y	Y	Y
16 Regula	Y	Y	Y	Y	Y	Y	Y	Y
17 Ashbrook	Y	N	Y	Y	N	Y	Y	Y
18 Applegate	?	Y	Y	Y	Y	Y	Y	Y
19 Carney	?	?	?	?	?	X	X	X
20 Oakar	Y	Y	Y	Y	Y	?	?	?
21 Stokes	Y	Y	Y	Y	Y	X	X	X
22 Vanik	Y	Y	Y	Y	Y	N	N	N
23 Mottl	Y	Y	Y	Y	Y	Y	Y	Y
OKLAHOMA								
1 Jones	Y	N	Y	Y	Y	Y	Y	Y
2 Risenhoover	Y	Y	Y	Y	Y	Y	Y	Y
3 Watkins	#	Y	Y	Y	Y	Y	Y	Y
4 Steed	Y	Y	Y	Y	Y	Y	Y	Y
5 Edwards	Y	Y	Y	Y	Y	Y	Y	Y
6 English	Y	Y	Y	Y	Y	Y	Y	Y
OREGON								
1 AuCoin	Y	Y	Y	Y	#	Y	N	N
2 Ullman	Y	N	Y	Y	Y	N	▮	▮
3 Duncan	Y	N	Y	Y	Y	Y	Y	N
4 Weaver	Y	Y	Y	Y	Y	Y	N	N
PENNSYLVANIA								
1 Myers, M.	Y	Y	Y	Y	Y	Y	N	Y
2 Nix	Y	Y	Y	Y	Y	N	N	N
3 Lederer	Y	Y	Y	Y	Y	Y	N	Y
4 Eilberg	Y	Y	Y	Y	Y	Y	N	Y
5 Schulze	Y	Y	Y	Y	Y	Y	Y	Y
6 Yatron	Y	Y	Y	Y	Y	Y	Y	Y
7 Edgar	Y	Y	Y	Y	Y	N	N	N
8 Kostmayer	Y	Y	Y	N	Y	N	N	N
9 Shuster	Y	Y	Y	Y	Y	Y	Y	Y
10 McDade	Y	Y	Y	Y	Y	Y	N	Y
11 Flood	Y	Y	Y	Y	Y	N	N	Y
12 Murtha	Y	N	Y	Y	Y	Y	Y	Y
13 Coughlin	N	Y	Y	Y	Y	Y	Y	N
14 Moorhead	Y	Y	Y	Y	Y	N	N	N
15 Rooney	?	Y	Y	Y	Y	N	N	N
16 Walker	N	Y	Y	Y	Y	Y	Y	Y
17 Ertel	Y	Y	Y	Y	Y	Y	Y	Y
18 Walgren	Y	Y	Y	Y	Y	Y	Y	N
19 Goodling, W.	Y	Y	Y	Y	Y	N	Y	N
20 Gaydos	Y	Y	Y	Y	Y	Y	Y	Y
21 Dent	#	#	#	#	#	#	✓	#
22 Murphy	Y	Y	Y	Y	N	Y	Y	Y
23 Ammerman	Y	Y	Y	N	Y	Y	N	Y
24 Marks	Y	Y	Y	Y	Y	Y	N	Y
25 Myers, G.	Y	N	Y	Y	Y	Y	Y	N
RHODE ISLAND								
1 St Germain	Y	Y	Y	Y	Y	Y	N	Y
2 Beard	Y	Y	Y	Y	Y	Y	N	Y
SOUTH CAROLINA								
1 Davis	Y	Y	Y	Y	Y	Y	Y	Y
2 Spence	Y	Y	Y	Y	Y	Y	Y	Y
3 Derrick	Y	Y	Y	Y	#	Y	Y	Y
4 Mann	?	?	?	?	?	?	?	?
5 Holland	#	Y	Y	Y	Y	Y	Y	Y
6 Jenrette	Y	N	Y	Y	Y	N	Y	N
SOUTH DAKOTA								
1 Pressler	?	?	?	?	?	?	?	?
2 Abdnor	Y	Y	Y	Y	Y	Y	Y	Y
TENNESSEE								
1 Quillen	Y	Y	Y	Y	Y	Y	Y	Y
2 Duncan	Y	Y	Y	Y	Y	Y	Y	Y
3 Lloyd	?	Y	Y	Y	Y	Y	Y	Y
4 Gore	Y	Y	Y	Y	Y	Y	Y	N
5 Allen	?	?	?	?	?	?	?	?
6 Beard	?	?	?	?	Y	Y	Y	Y
7 Jones	Y	Y	Y	Y	Y	Y	Y	Y
8 Ford	?	Y	Y	Y	Y	Y	N	N
TEXAS								
1 Hall	Y	Y	Y	Y	Y	Y	Y	Y
2 Wilson, C.	Y	Y	Y	Y	Y	N	Y	N
3 Collins	N	Y	Y	Y	N	Y	Y	Y
4 Roberts	Y	Y	Y	Y	N	✓	✓	✓
5 Mattox	N	Y	Y	Y	Y	N	Y	Y
6 Teague	?	?	?	?	?	✓	✓	✓
7 Archer	?	?	?	?	?	✓	✓	?
8 Eckhardt	?	?	?	?	?	N	N	N
9 Brooks	Y	N	Y	Y	Y	Y	Y	N
10 Pickle	#	Y	Y	Y	Y	Y	Y	Y
11 Poage	Y	Y	Y	Y	N	Y	Y	Y
12 Wright	Y	Y	Y	Y	Y	N	N	N
13 Hightower	Y	Y	Y	Y	Y	Y	Y	Y
14 Young	?	?	?	?	?	?	?	?
15 de la Garza	Y	Y	Y	Y	Y	Y	Y	Y
16 White	Y	Y	Y	Y	Y	Y	Y	Y
17 Burleson	Y	Y	Y	Y	Y	Y	Y	Y
18 Jordan	#	Y	Y	Y	Y	Y	N	N
19 Mahon	Y	Y	Y	Y	Y	Y	Y	Y
20 Gonzalez	Y	N	Y	Y	Y	Y	Y	N
21 Krueger	#	#	#	#	#	#	▮	#
22 Gammage	?	Y	Y	Y	Y	Y	Y	Y
23 Kazen	Y	Y	Y	Y	Y	Y	Y	Y
24 Milford	?	?	?	?	?	?	?	?
UTAH								
1 McKay	Y	Y	Y	Y	Y	Y	Y	N
2 Marriott	Y	Y	Y	Y	Y	Y	Y	Y
VERMONT								
AL Jeffords	#	N	Y	Y	Y	N	N	Y
VIRGINIA								
1 Trible	?	?	?	?	?	Y	Y	Y
2 Whitehurst	Y	Y	Y	Y	Y	Y	Y	Y
3 Satterfield	Y	Y	Y	Y	N	Y	Y	Y
4 Daniel	Y	N	Y	Y	Y	Y	Y	Y
5 Daniel	Y	N	Y	Y	Y	Y	Y	Y
6 Butler	Y	N	Y	Y	Y	Y	Y	Y
7 Robinson	Y	N	Y	Y	Y	Y	Y	Y
8 Harris	Y	Y	Y	Y	Y	Y	N	N
9 Wampler	Y	Y	Y	Y	Y	Y	Y	Y
10 Fisher	Y	Y	Y	Y	Y	N	N	N
WASHINGTON								
1 Pritchard	#	#	#	#	#	#	N	N
2 Meeds	#	#	#	#	#	▮	▮	▮
3 Bonker	Y	Y	Y	Y	Y	N	N	N
4 McCormack	?	?	?	?	?	?	?	?
5 Foley	Y	Y	Y	Y	Y	Y	Y	N
6 Dicks	Y	Y	Y	Y	Y	N	Y	N
7 Cunningham	#	Y	Y	Y	Y	Y	Y	Y
WEST VIRGINIA								
1 Mollohan	Y	Y	Y	Y	Y	N	Y	N
2 Staggers	Y	Y	Y	Y	Y	N	Y	Y
3 Slack	Y	Y	Y	Y	Y	Y	Y	Y
4 Rahall	Y	Y	Y	Y	Y	Y	N	Y
WISCONSIN								
1 Aspin	Y	Y	Y	Y	Y	N	N	N
2 Kastenmeier	Y	Y	Y	Y	Y	N	Y	N
3 Baldus	Y	Y	Y	Y	Y	N	N	N
4 Zablocki	Y	Y	Y	Y	Y	N	N	N
5 Reuss	Y	Y	Y	Y	Y	N	N	N
6 Steiger	N	N	Y	Y	Y	Y	N	N
7 Obey	Y	Y	Y	Y	Y	Y	N	N
8 Cornell	Y	N	Y	Y	Y	Y	N	N
9 Kasten	#	#	#	#	#	✓	#	#
WYOMING								
AL Roncalio	?	?	?	?	Y	N	N	N

Democrats **Republicans**

333. HR 12598. State Department Authorization. Passage of the bill to authorize $1.9 billion for State Department operations and related activities in fiscal 1979 and a supplemental authorization for fiscal 1978 of $47 million. Passed 240-124: R 59-64; D 181-60 (ND 144-22; SD 37-38), May 31, 1978.

334. HR 12050. Tuition Tax Credits. Adoption of the rule (H Res 1178) providing for House floor consideration of the bill to provide federal income tax credits for school tuitions. Adopted 294-97: R 107-27; D 187-70 (ND 132-45; SD 55-25), June 1, 1978.

335. HR 12050. Tuition Tax Credits. Vanik, D-Ohio, amendment to provide a tax credit for private elementary and secondary school tuitions, up to a maximum of $50 in calendar year 1978 and $100 in each of 1979 and 1980. Adopted 209-194: R 102-35; D 107-159 (ND 88-97; SD 19-62), June 1, 1978.

336. HR 12050. Tuition Tax Credits. Vanik, D-Ohio, amendment to increase to 50 percent from 25 percent the amount of tuition eligible for a tax credit. Rejected 142-261: R 75-62; D 67-199 (ND 55-131; SD 12-68), June 1, 1978.

337. HR 12050. Tuition Tax Credits. Mikva, D-Ill., substitute amendment to the bill, to provide for deferral of income taxes equal to college tuition expenses, up to $2,000, to be repaid by the taxpayer within 10 years. Rejected 155-239: R 25-110; D 130-129 (ND 86-95; SD 44-34), June 1, 1978.

338. HR 12050. Tuition Tax Credits. Passage of the bill to provide an income tax credit for a three-year period (calendar 1978-80) equal to 25 percent of tuitions for private elementary and secondary schools and public and private colleges and universities, up to a limit by 1980 of $100 for elementary and secondary tuitions and $250 for college tuitions. Passed 237-158: R 115-20; D 122-138 (ND 99-83; SD 23-55), June 1, 1978. A "nay" was a vote supporting the president's position.

339. HR 12157. Export-Import Bank. Adoption of the rule (H Res 1168) providing for House floor consideration of the bill to extend the U.S. Export-Import Bank for five years, through 1983, and to increase its financing commitment to $40 billion from $25 billion. Adopted 364-4: R 128-2; D 236-2 (ND 167-2; SD 69-0), June 1, 1978.

340. HR 15. Elementary and Secondary Education Act Amendments. Adoption of the rule (H Res 1208) providing for House floor consideration of the bill to extend the 1965 Elementary and Secondary Education Act through fiscal year 1983. Adopted 339-13: R 116-11; D 223-2 (ND 159-0; SD 64-2), June 1, 1978.

KEY

- Y Voted for (yea).
- ✓ Paired for.
- † Announced for.
- # CQ Poll for.
- N Voted against (nay).
- X Paired against.
- \- Announced against.
- ▮ CQ Poll against.
- P Voted "present."
- ● Voted "present" to avoid possible conflict of interest.
- ? Did not vote or otherwise make a position known.

	333	334	335	336	337	338	339	340
ALABAMA								
1 Edwards	Y	Y	Y	N	N	Y	Y	Y
2 Dickinson	Y	Y	N	N	N	N	Y	Y
3 Nichols	Y	Y	N	N	N	N	Y	Y
4 Bevill	Y	Y	N	N	N	Y	?	?
5 Flippo	Y	Y	N	N	Y	N	Y	Y
6 Buchanan	Y	N	N	N	Y	N	Y	Y
7 Flowers	?	Y	N	N	Y	N	?	?
ALASKA								
AL Young	X	#	?	X	▮	✓	#	#
ARIZONA								
1 Rhodes	?	Y	N	N	Y	N	Y	Y
2 Udall	Y	Y	N	N	Y	N	Y	#
3 Stump	N	N	N	N	Y	N	Y	Y
4 Rudd	X	?	✓	✓	?	✓	?	?
ARKANSAS								
1 Alexander	?	✓	✓	✓	X	✓	?	?
2 Tucker	#	#	N	N	✓	N	#	#
3 Hammerschmidt	N	Y	N	N	N	Y	Y	Y
4 Thornton	?	?	?	?	?	?	?	?
CALIFORNIA								
1 Johnson	Y	Y	Y	N	N	Y	Y	Y
2 Clausen	N	Y	Y	Y	N	Y	?	Y
3 Moss	Y	?	N	N	Y	N	?	?
4 Leggett	Y	N	N	N	Y	N	N	?
5 Burton, J.	?	X	X	N	Y	N	Y	?
6 Burton, P.	?	N	N	N	Y	N	Y	Y
7 Miller	Y	N	N	N	Y	N	Y	Y
8 Dellums	Y	N	N	N	Y	N	Y	Y
9 Stark	Y	N	N	N	Y	N	Y	Y
10 Edwards	Y	N	N	N	Y	N	Y	Y
11 Ryan	#	✓	✓	✓	X	✓	#	#
12 McCloskey	Y	Y	N	N	Y	N	Y	Y
13 Mineta	Y	Y	N	N	Y	N	Y	Y
14 McFall	Y	Y	N	N	N	N	Y	Y
15 Sisk	?	N	N	N	Y	N	?	?
16 Panetta	N	Y	N	N	Y	Y	Y	Y
17 Krebs	Y	Y	N	N	Y	N	Y	Y
18 Ketchum	N	Y	N	N	Y	N	Y	Y
19 Lagomarsino	N	Y	Y	Y	N	Y	Y	Y
20 Goldwater	X	Y	Y	Y	Y	Y	Y	Y
21 Corman	#	N	N	N	Y	N	Y	Y
22 Moorhead	N	Y	Y	N	N	Y	Y	Y
23 Beilenson	Y	N	N	N	Y	N	Y	Y
24 Waxman	Y	N	N	N	Y	N	N	Y
25 Roybal	Y	Y	N	N	Y	N	Y	Y
26 Rousselot	X	N	Y	Y	N	Y	Y	?
27 Dornan	N	N	Y	Y	N	Y	Y	Y
28 Burke	✓	Y	N	N	✓	X	#	#
29 Hawkins	✓	Y	N	N	Y	N	Y	Y
30 Danielson	Y	Y	N	N	Y	N	Y	Y
31 Wilson, C.H.	Y	N	N	N	Y	N	?	?
32 Anderson	N	Y	N	N	Y	Y	Y	Y
33 Clawson	N	Y	Y	N	N	Y	Y	N
34 Hannaford	Y	Y	N	N	Y	N	Y	Y
35 Lloyd	Y	Y	N	N	Y	Y	Y	Y
36 Brown	Y	Y	Y	N	N	Y	?	?
37 Pettis	?	Y	Y	Y	N	Y	Y	Y
38 Patterson	Y	Y	N	N	Y	N	Y	Y
39 Wiggins	#	Y	N	N	Y	N	Y	Y
40 Badham	N	Y	N	N	Y	Y	Y	Y
41 Wilson, B.	Y	Y	Y	N	N	Y	Y	Y
42 Van Deerlin	Y	Y	Y	N	N	Y	Y	Y
43 Burgener	X	Y	Y	N	N	Y	Y	?
COLORADO								
1 Schroeder	Y	N	N	N	Y	N	Y	Y
2 Wirth	Y	Y	N	N	Y	N	Y	Y
3 Evans	▮	N	N	N	Y	N	?	?
4 Johnson	N	Y	N	Y	N	N	Y	Y
5 Armstrong	N	?	Y	N	N	Y	Y	Y
CONNECTICUT								
1 Cotter	Y	Y	Y	Y	N	Y	?	?
2 Dodd	Y	Y	N	N	Y	N	Y	?
3 Giaimo	?	Y	Y	N	N	Y	Y	?
4 McKinney	Y	Y	N	N	Y	Y	#	Y
5 Sarasin	Y	Y	Y	N	▮	#	#	#
6 Moffett	Y	N	N	N	Y	N	Y	Y
DELAWARE								
AL Evans	Y	Y	Y	Y	N	Y	Y	Y
FLORIDA								
1 Sikes	Y	Y	N	N	N	N	Y	Y
2 Fuqua	N	Y	N	N	Y	N	Y	Y
3 Bennett	Y	Y	N	N	Y	N	Y	Y
4 Chappell	Y	Y	Y	N	N	Y	Y	Y
5 Kelly	N	N	Y	Y	N	Y	Y	Y
6 Young	N	N	Y	N	N	Y	Y	Y
7 Gibbons	?	✓	✓	✓	?	✓	?	?
8 Ireland	Y	Y	N	N	N	N	Y	Y
9 Frey	X	Y	Y	N	N	Y	Y	?
10 Bafalis	N	N	Y	Y	N	Y	Y	Y
11 Rogers	Y	Y	Y	N	N	Y	Y	Y
12 Burke	N	Y	Y	Y	N	Y	Y	Y
13 Lehman	Y	Y	N	N	Y	N	Y	#
14 Pepper	Y	Y	N	N	N	N	Y	Y
15 Fascell	#	N	N	N	Y	N	#	#
GEORGIA								
1 Ginn	N	N	N	N	Y	N	Y	Y
2 Mathis	?	Y	Y	Y	N	Y	?	Y
3 Brinkley	N	N	N	N	N	Y	Y	Y
4 Levitas	N	N	Y	N	N	Y	Y	Y
5 Fowler	N	Y	Y	N	N	Y	Y	Y
6 Flynt	N	N	Y	N	N	Y	Y	Y
7 McDonald	N	N	Y	Y	N	Y	Y	▮
8 Evans	N	#	Y	Y	N	Y	Y	Y
9 Jenkins	N	N	N	N	Y	N	Y	Y
10 Barnard	N	N	Y	Y	N	Y	Y	Y
HAWAII								
1 Heftel	Y	Y	Y	N	Y	Y	Y	Y
2 Akaka	Y	Y	N	N	N	Y	Y	Y
IDAHO								
1 Symms	N	N	Y	Y	N	Y	Y	N
2 Hansen, G.	N	N	Y	Y	N	Y	Y	N
ILLINOIS								
1 Metcalfe	Y	Y	N	N	Y	N	Y	Y
2 Murphy	Y	Y	Y	Y	N	Y	Y	Y
3 Russo	▮	Y	Y	N	N	Y	Y	Y
4 Derwinski	Y	Y	Y	Y	N	Y	Y	Y
5 Fary	Y	Y	Y	Y	N	Y	Y	Y
6 Hyde	#	Y	Y	Y	N	Y	Y	Y
7 Collins	Y	Y	N	N	Y	N	Y	Y
8 Rostenkowski	✓	#	Y	N	N	Y	Y	Y
9 Yates	Y	Y	N	N	Y	N	Y	Y
. 10 Mikva	Y	Y	N	N	Y	N	Y	Y
11 Annunzio	Y	Y	Y	Y	N	Y	Y	Y
12 Crane	N	#	✓	?	▮	✓	#	#
13 McClory	Y	Y	N	N	Y	Y	Y	Y
14 Erlenborn	Y	Y	Y	N	N	Y	Y	Y
15 Corcoran	Y	Y	Y	Y	N	Y	Y	Y
16 Anderson	Y	Y	N	N	Y	N	Y	Y
17 O'Brien	✓	Y	Y	Y	N	Y	Y	Y
18 Michel	▮	Y	Y	N	N	Y	Y	Y
19 Railsback	✓	Y	Y	Y	N	Y	Y	#
20 Findley	Y	Y	N	N	Y	N	Y	Y
21 Madigan	Y	Y	N	N	N	Y	Y	Y
22 Shipley	?	?	?	?	?	✓	?	?
23 Price	Y	Y	Y	Y	N	Y	Y	Y
24 Simon	†	N	N	N	Y	N	Y	Y
INDIANA								
1 Benjamin	N	Y	Y	N	N	Y	Y	Y
2 Fithian	N	Y	N	N	Y	N	Y	Y
3 Brademas	Y	Y	N	N	Y	N	Y	Y
4 Quayle	X	N	Y	Y	N	Y	Y	N
5 Hillis	Y	Y	Y	N	N	Y	Y	Y
6 Evans	N	Y	N	N	Y	N	Y	Y
7 Myers, J.	N	N	Y	N	N	Y	Y	Y
8 Cornwell	Y	N	N	N	N	N	Y	Y
9 Hamilton	Y	Y	N	N	Y	N	Y	Y
10 Sharp	Y	N	N	N	Y	N	Y	Y
11 Jacobs	N	N	N	N	Y	N	Y	Y
IOWA								
1 Leach	N	Y	Y	Y	N	Y	Y	Y
2 Blouin	Y	Y	Y	Y	N	Y	Y	Y
3 Grassley	N	N	Y	Y	N	Y	Y	Y
4 Smith	Y	Y	Y	N	N	Y	Y	Y
5 Harkin	N	N	Y	N	N	Y	Y	Y
6 Bedell	Y	Y	N	N	Y	N	Y	Y

Democrats ***Republicans***

	333	334	335	336	337	338	339	340
KANSAS								
1 Sebelius	✓	#	?	#	▮	#	#	#
2 Keys	N	N	N	N	Y	N	Y	Y
3 Winn	Y	Y	Y	Y	N	Y	Y	Y
4 Glickman	N	Y	N	N	Y	Y	Y	Y
5 Skubitz	Y	Y	N	N	Y	N	Y	Y
KENTUCKY								
1 Hubbard	N	Y	?	?	?	?	?	?
2 Natcher	Y	Y	Y	Y	N	Y	Y	Y
3 Mazzoli	Y	Y	Y	N	Y	Y	Y	Y
4 Snyder	N	Y	Y	Y	N	Y	Y	Y
5 Carter	N	Y	Y	Y	N	Y	Y	Y
6 Breckinridge	Y	N	N	N	N	N	Y	Y
7 Perkins	Y	Y	N	N	N	N	Y	Y
LOUISIANA								
1 Livingston	N	N	Y	Y	N	Y	Y	Y
2 Boggs	Y	Y	Y	N	N	Y	Y	Y
3 Treen	N	N	Y	Y	N	Y	Y	Y
4 Waggonner	Y	Y	?	▮	#	▮	#	#
5 Huckaby	N	Y	N	N	Y	N	Y	Y
6 Moore	N	N	Y	Y	N	Y	Y	Y
7 Breaux	N	Y	Y	Y	N	Y	Y	Y
8 Long	Y	Y	Y	Y	N	Y	Y	Y
MAINE								
1 Emery	Y	Y	Y	N	N	Y	Y	Y
2 Cohen	Y	Y	Y	N	N	Y	Y	Y
MARYLAND								
1 Bauman	N	N	Y	Y	N	Y	Y	N
2 Long	Y	Y	N	N	Y	Y	Y	Y
3 Mikulski	Y	Y	Y	Y	N	Y	Y	Y
4 Holt	N	Y	Y	Y	N	Y	Y	Y
5 Spellman	✓	Y	N	N	N	Y	Y	Y
6 Byron	N	Y	N	Y	N	Y	Y	Y
7 Mitchell	Y	N	N	N	Y	N	Y	Y
8 Steers	Y	Y	Y	N	N	Y	Y	Y
MASSACHUSETTS								
1 Conte	Y	Y	Y	Y	N	Y	Y	Y
2 Boland	Y	Y	Y	Y	N	Y	Y	Y
3 Early	Y	Y	Y	Y	N	Y	Y	Y
4 Drinan	Y	N	N	N	Y	N	Y	Y
5 Tsongas	Y	Y	N	N	N	Y	Y	Y
6 Harrington	Y	Y	Y	Y	N	Y	Y	Y
7 Markey	Y	N	Y	N	N	Y	#	#
8 O'Neill								
9 Moakley	Y	Y	Y	Y	N	Y	Y	Y
10 Heckler	Y	Y	Y	Y	N	Y	Y	Y
11 Burke	Y	Y	Y	Y	N	Y	Y	Y
12 Studds	Y	N	N	N	Y	N	Y	Y
MICHIGAN								
1 Conyers	▮	X	X	X	✓	X	#	#
2 Pursell	Y	Y	N	Y	N	Y	?	?
3 Brown	Y	Y	Y	N	N	Y	Y	#
4 Stockman	N	Y	Y	N	N	Y	Y	Y
5 Sawyer	Y	Y	Y	Y	N	Y	Y	N
6 Carr	Y	N	N	N	Y	N	Y	Y
7 Kildee	Y	Y	Y	Y	N	Y	Y	Y
8 Traxler	Y	Y	Y	Y	#	Y	#	Y
9 Vander Jagt	Y	?	Y	Y	N	Y	Y	Y
10 Cederberg	Y	Y	N	N	N	Y	Y	Y
11 Ruppe	Y	Y	Y	Y	N	#	Y	Y
12 Bonior	Y	N	N	N	Y	N	Y	Y
13 Diggs	Y	X	X	X	✓	X	?	?
14 Nedzi	Y	Y	Y	N	N	Y	Y	Y
15 Ford	Y	N	N	N	Y	N	Y	Y
16 Dingell	Y	Y	N	N	N	Y	Y	Y
17 Brodhead	Y	Y	N	N	Y	N	Y	Y
18 Blanchard	#	Y	N	N	Y	Y	Y	Y
19 Broomfield	Y	Y	Y	Y	N	Y	Y	Y
MINNESOTA								
1 Quie	Y	Y	Y	N	N	Y	Y	Y
2 Hagedorn	N	Y	†	✓	▮	#	#	#
3 Frenzel	N	Y	Y	Y	N	Y	Y	Y
4 Vento	Y	Y	Y	N	N	N	Y	Y
5 Fraser	Y	Y	N	N	X	X	#	#
6 Nolan	Y	?	N	N	Y	N	Y	?
7 Stangeland	N	Y	Y	Y	N	Y	Y	Y
8 Oberstar	Y	Y	N	N	N	Y	Y	Y
MISSISSIPPI								
1 Whitten	N	Y	Y	Y	N	Y	Y	Y
2 Bowen	Y	Y	N	N	Y	N	Y	Y
3 Montgomery	N	Y	Y	N	N	Y	Y	Y
4 Cochran	X	?	?	?	?	?	?	?
5 Lott	N	Y	N	Y	Y	Y	Y	Y
MISSOURI								
1 Clay	Y	N	N	N	Y	N	Y	Y
2 Young	#	Y	Y	Y	N	Y	Y	Y
3 Gephardt	N	Y	N	Y	N	Y	Y	Y
4 Skelton	N	N	N	N	Y	N	Y	Y
5 Bolling	Y	#	N	N	N	N	#	#
6 Coleman	N	Y	Y	N	N	Y	Y	Y
7 Taylor	N	Y	N	N	Y	N	Y	Y
8 Ichord	N	Y	N	N	Y	N	Y	Y
9 Volkmer	N	N	Y	N	N	Y	Y	Y
10 Burlison	Y	Y	N	N	?	N	Y	Y
MONTANA								
1 Baucus	#	X	X	X	✓	X	#	#
2 Marlenee	N	Y	N	Y	N	Y	Y	Y
NEBRASKA								
1 Thone	N	Y	Y	Y	N	Y	Y	Y
2 Cavanaugh	Y	Y	Y	Y	N	Y	Y	Y
3 Smith	N	Y	Y	Y	N	Y	Y	Y
NEVADA								
AL Santini	Y	Y	Y	N	N	Y	Y	Y
NEW HAMPSHIRE								
1 D'Amours	N	N	Y	Y	N	Y	Y	Y
2 Cleveland	Y	Y	Y	Y	N	Y	Y	Y
NEW JERSEY								
1 Florio	Y	Y	Y	Y	N	Y	Y	Y
2 Hughes	N	N	Y	N	N	Y	Y	Y
3 Howard	#	✓	✓	✓	#	✓	#	#
4 Thompson	Y	Y	N	N	Y	N	Y	Y
5 Fenwick	Y	Y	N	N	N	N	Y	Y
6 Forsythe	Y	#	Y	Y	N	Y	#	#
7 Maguire	Y	Y	Y	N	Y	N	Y	Y
8 Roe	Y	Y	Y	Y	N	Y	Y	Y
9 Hollenbeck	Y	Y	Y	Y	N	Y	Y	#
10 Rodino	#	#	?	▮	▮	?	#	#
11 Minish	Y	Y	Y	Y	N	Y	Y	Y
12 Rinaldo	Y	Y	Y	Y	N	Y	Y	Y
13 Meyner	Y	Y	N	N	Y	Y	Y	#
14 LeFante	✓	Y	Y	Y	N	Y	Y	Y
15 Patten	Y	Y	Y	N	X	✓	#	#
NEW MEXICO								
1 Lujan	✓	?	?	?	?	?	?	?
2 Runnels	#	?	?	?	?	?	#	#
NEW YORK								
1 Pike	Y	Y	N	N	N	N	Y	Y
2 Downey	Y	Y	N	N	N	Y	Y	Y
3 Ambro	Y	Y	Y	Y	N	Y	Y	Y
4 Lent	Y	Y	Y	Y	N	Y	Y	Y
5 Wydler	Y	Y	Y	Y	N	Y	Y	Y
6 Wolff	Y	Y	Y	N	N	Y	Y	Y
7 Addabbo	Y	Y	Y	N	N	Y	Y	#
8 Rosenthal	Y	Y	N	N	Y	N	Y	Y
9 Delaney	Y	Y	Y	Y	N	Y	Y	?
10 Biaggi	Y	Y	Y	Y	N	Y	Y	Y
11 Scheuer	Y	Y	Y	Y	N	Y	#	Y
12 Chisholm	Y	N	N	N	Y	N	Y	Y
13 Solarz	Y	Y	Y	Y	N	Y	Y	Y
14 Richmond	✓	✓	N	N	Y	N	Y	Y
15 Zeferetti	Y	Y	Y	Y	N	Y	Y	Y
16 Holtzman	Y	N	N	N	Y	N	Y	Y
17 Murphy	Y	#	Y	N	N	Y	Y	Y
18 Green	Y	Y	Y	N	N	Y	Y	Y
19 Rangel	✓	N	N	N	Y	N	Y	Y
20 Weiss	Y	N	N	N	Y	X	†	†
21 Garcia	Y	Y	Y	Y	N	Y	Y	Y
22 Bingham	Y	N	Y	N	Y	Y	Y	Y
23 Caputo	?	Y	Y	Y	N	Y	Y	Y
24 Ottinger	Y	Y	Y	Y	N	Y	Y	Y
25 Fish	Y	Y	Y	Y	N	Y	Y	Y
26 Gilman	†	Y	Y	N	N	Y	Y	Y
27 McHugh	Y	Y	N	N	Y	N	Y	Y
28 Stratton	Y	Y	Y	Y	N	Y	Y	Y
29 Pattison	Y	Y	Y	N	Y	N	Y	Y
30 McEwen	Y	Y	Y	Y	N	Y	Y	Y
31 Mitchell	Y	Y	N	N	Y	Y	Y	Y
32 Hanley	Y	Y	Y	Y	N	Y	Y	Y
33 Walsh	Y	Y	Y	Y	N	Y	Y	Y
34 Horton	Y	Y	Y	N	N	Y	Y	Y
35 Conable	Y	Y	Y	N	Y	Y	Y	N
36 LaFalce	Y	N	Y	N	Y	Y	Y	Y
37 Nowak	Y	Y	Y	Y	N	Y	Y	Y
38 Kemp	N	Y	Y	Y	N	Y	Y	Y
39 Lundine	Y	N	N	N	Y	Y	Y	#
NORTH CAROLINA								
1 Jones	Y	Y	N	N	Y	N	Y	Y
2 Fountain	Y	Y	N	N	Y	N	Y	Y
3 Whitley	N	N	N	N	Y	N	Y	Y
4 Andrews	Y	Y	N	N	Y	N	Y	Y
5 Neal	X	Y	N	N	Y	N	Y	Y
6 Preyer	Y	N	N	N	Y	N	Y	Y
7 Rose	Y	N	N	N	Y	N	Y	#
8 Hefner	N	N	N	N	Y	N	Y	Y
9 Martin	X	Y	N	N	Y	N	#	#
10 Broyhill	N	Y	N	N	N	N	Y	Y
11 Gudger	Y	Y	N	N	Y	N	Y	Y
NORTH DAKOTA								
AL Andrews	N	Y	Y	Y	N	Y	Y	Y
OHIO								
1 Gradison	Y	Y	Y	Y	N	Y	Y	Y
2 Luken	Y	Y	Y	Y	N	Y	Y	Y
3 Whalen	Y	Y	N	N	N	N	Y	Y
4 Guyer	Y	Y	Y	Y	N	Y	Y	Y
5 Latta	N	Y	Y	Y	N	Y	Y	Y
6 Harsha	N	Y	Y	Y	N	Y	Y	Y
7 Brown	N	N	Y	N	N	Y	Y	Y
8 Kindness	N	N	Y	Y	N	Y	Y	Y
9 Ashley	Y	Y	Y	N	N	Y	?	?
10 Miller	N	Y	Y	Y	N	Y	Y	Y
11 Stanton	Y	Y	Y	Y	N	Y	Y	Y
12 Devine	N	Y	Y	Y	N	Y	Y	Y
13 Pease	Y	Y	Y	N	N	Y	Y	Y
14 Seiberling	Y	Y	Y	N	N	Y	Y	Y
15 Wylie	Y	Y	Y	Y	N	Y	Y	Y
16 Regula	Y	Y	Y	Y	N	Y	Y	Y
17 Ashbrook	N	N	Y	Y	N	Y	Y	Y
18 Applegate	Y	Y	Y	Y	N	Y	Y	Y
19 Carney	✓	Y	Y	Y	N	Y	Y	Y
20 Oakar	?	?	Y	Y	N	Y	Y	?
21 Stokes	✓	N	N	N	Y	N	Y	Y
22 Vanik	Y	Y	Y	Y	N	Y	Y	Y
23 Mottl	N	Y	Y	Y	N	Y	Y	Y
OKLAHOMA								
1 Jones	N	Y	N	N	N	N	Y	Y
2 Risenhoover	N	N	N	N	Y	N	Y	Y
3 Watkins	N	N	N	N	Y	N	Y	Y
4 Steed	N	Y	N	N	N	N	Y	Y
5 Edwards	N	N	Y	Y	N	Y	Y	N
6 English	N	Y	N	N	Y	N	Y	Y
OREGON								
1 AuCoin	Y	Y	N	N	Y	N	Y	Y
2 Ullman	#	Y	N	N	N	Y	#	#
3 Duncan	Y	Y	N	N	Y	N	Y	Y
4 Weaver	Y	N	N	N	Y	N	Y	Y
PENNSYLVANIA								
1 Myers, M.	Y	Y	Y	Y	N	Y	Y	Y
2 Nix	Y	N	Y	Y	N	Y	Y	Y
3 Lederer	Y	Y	Y	Y	N	Y	Y	Y
4 Eilberg	Y	Y	Y	Y	N	Y	Y	Y
5 Schulze	N	Y	Y	N	N	Y	Y	Y
6 Yatron	Y	Y	Y	Y	N	Y	Y	Y
7 Edgar	Y	Y	Y	Y	N	Y	Y	Y
8 Kostmayer	N	Y	Y	N	N	Y	Y	Y
9 Shuster	N	N	Y	Y	N	Y	Y	Y
10 McDade	Y	Y	Y	Y	N	Y	Y	Y
11 Flood	Y	Y	Y	Y	N	Y	Y	Y
12 Murtha	Y	Y	Y	Y	N	Y	Y	Y
13 Coughlin	Y	Y	Y	Y	N	Y	?	Y
14 Moorhead	Y	Y	N	N	Y	N	Y	Y
15 Rooney	Y	Y	Y	Y	N	Y	Y	Y
16 Walker	N	N	Y	N	N	Y	Y	N
17 Ertel	Y	Y	Y	Y	N	Y	Y	Y
18 Walgren	Y	Y	Y	Y	N	Y	Y	Y
19 Goodling, W.	Y	N	N	N	Y	Y	Y	Y
20 Gaydos	N	Y	Y	Y	N	Y	Y	Y
21 Dent	#	#	?	▮	▮	✓	#	#
22 Murphy	N	Y	Y	N	N	Y	Y	Y
23 Ammerman	Y	Y	Y	N	N	Y	Y	Y
24 Marks	Y	N	Y	N	N	Y	Y	Y
25 Myers, G.	N	N	N	N	N	N	Y	Y
RHODE ISLAND								
1 St Germain	Y	Y	Y	Y	N	Y	Y	Y
2 Beard	Y	Y	Y	Y	N	Y	Y	Y
SOUTH CAROLINA								
1 Davis	N	Y	N	N	Y	N	?	Y
2 Spence	N	Y	N	N	Y	N	Y	Y
3 Derrick	N	Y	N	?	#	X	#	#
4 Mann	?	Y	N	N	Y	N	Y	?
5 Holland	N	Y	N	N	Y	N	Y	#
6 Jenrette	N	Y	N	N	Y	X	#	#
SOUTH DAKOTA								
1 Pressler	?	?	?	?	?	?	?	?
2 Abdnor	N	Y	N	N	Y	N	Y	Y
TENNESSEE								
1 Quillen	N	Y	N	N	Y	N	N	Y
2 Duncan	N	Y	N	N	Y	N	N	Y
3 Lloyd	N	N	N	N	Y	N	Y	Y
4 Gore	N	N	N	N	#	X	#	#
5 Allen	?	?	?	?	?	?	?	?
6 Beard	N	Y	Y	N	N	Y	Y	Y
7 Jones	N	N	N	N	N	N	Y	Y
8 Ford	Y	N	N	N	Y	N	Y	Y
TEXAS								
1 Hall	N	Y	N	N	Y	N	Y	Y
2 Wilson, C.	Y	N	N	N	Y	N	#	#
3 Collins	N	Y	Y	Y	N	Y	Y	N
4 Roberts	X	Y	N	N	Y	N	Y	Y
5 Mattox	N	N	N	N	Y	N	Y	Y
6 Teague	X	X	N	N	N	N	?	?
7 Archer	X	Y	Y	Y	N	Y	Y	N
8 Eckhardt	Y	Y	N	N	Y	N	Y	Y
9 Brooks	N	Y	N	N	N	Y	Y	Y
10 Pickle	Y	Y	N	N	Y	N	Y	Y
11 Poage	N	Y	N	N	Y	N	Y	Y
12 Wright	Y	Y	N	N	Y	N	Y	Y
13 Hightower	N	N	N	N	Y	N	Y	Y
14 Young	?	?	?	?	?	?	?	?
15 de la Garza	Y	Y	Y	Y	N	Y	?	?
16 White	Y	Y	N	N	Y	N	Y	Y
17 Burleson	N	N	N	N	Y	N	Y	N
18 Jordan	Y	N	N	N	N	N	Y	Y
19 Mahon	Y	Y	N	N	N	N	Y	Y
20 Gonzalez	Y	N	N	Y	Y	N	Y	Y
21 Krueger	#	?	X	X	X	?	?	?
22 Gammage	N	Y	N	N	Y	N	Y	Y
23 Kazen	Y	Y	N	N	N	Y	Y	Y
24 Milford	?	?	?	?	?	?	?	?
UTAH								
1 McKay	Y	#	?	▮	▮	▮	#	#
2 Marriott	N	Y	Y	N	N	Y	Y	Y
VERMONT								
AL Jeffords	Y	N	Y	Y	N	Y	Y	Y
VIRGINIA								
1 Trible	N	N	N	N	N	Y	Y	Y
2 Whitehurst	Y	Y	N	N	Y	Y	Y	Y
3 Satterfield	N	Y	N	N	N	Y	Y	N
4 Daniel	N	Y	Y	Y	N	Y	Y	Y
5 Daniel	N	Y	Y	Y	N	Y	Y	Y
6 Butler	?	?	?	?	?	?	?	?
7 Robinson	N	Y	N	N	▮	Y	Y	Y
8 Harris	Y	Y	N	N	Y	N	Y	Y
9 Wampler	N	Y	N	N	Y	Y	Y	Y
10 Fisher	Y	Y	N	N	Y	N	Y	Y
WASHINGTON								
1 Pritchard	Y	#	Y	Y	N	Y	Y	Y
2 Meeds	#	#	N	N	Y	N	Y	#
3 Bonker	Y	Y	N	N	N	Y	Y	Y
4 McCormack	?	?	X	X	?	X	?	?
5 Foley	Y	Y	Y	Y	N	Y	?	?
6 Dicks	Y	Y	N	N	Y	N	Y	Y
7 Cunningham	N	N	Y	Y	N	Y	Y	Y
WEST VIRGINIA								
1 Mollohan	Y	Y	N	N	N	N	Y	Y
2 Staggers	Y	Y	N	N	N	N	Y	Y
3 Slack	Y	Y	Y	N	N	Y	Y	Y
4 Rahall	N	Y	N	N	Y	N	Y	Y
WISCONSIN								
1 Aspin	Y	N	N	N	Y	N	Y	Y
2 Kastenmeier	Y	N	N	N	Y	N	Y	Y
3 Baldus	Y	Y	N	N	Y	N	Y	Y
4 Zablocki	Y	Y	Y	Y	N	Y	Y	Y
5 Reuss	Y	Y	N	N	N	N	Y	Y
6 Steiger	Y	Y	Y	N	Y	Y	Y	Y
7 Obey	Y	Y	N	N	N	Y	Y	Y
8 Cornell	Y	Y	Y	Y	N	Y	Y	Y
9 Kasten	▮	#	?	#	▮	#	#	#
WYOMING								
AL Roncalio	Y	Y	Y	N	N	Y	Y	Y

Democrats ***Republicans***

341. HR 12157. Export-Import Bank. Neal, D-N.C., motion that the House resolve itself into the Committee of the Whole for the consideration of the bill to further extend the 1945 Export-Import Bank Act. Motion agreed to 314-13: R 114-7; D 200-6 (ND 138-5; SD 62-1), June 1, 1978.

342. HR 12157. Export-Import Bank. Kelly, R-Fla., amendment to permit the Export-Import Bank to guarantee, insure or extend credit to South Africa as long as it also extended credit or was authorized to extend credit to Communist countries. Rejected 157-190: R 91-32; D 66-158 (ND 24-136; SD 42-22), June 1, 1978.

343. HR 12157. Export-Import Bank. Neal, D-N.C., motion that the House resolve itself into the Committee of the Whole for further consideration of the bill to extend the 1945 Export-Import Bank Act. Motion agreed to 318-3: R 111-1; D 207-2 (ND 144-2; SD 63-0), June 2, 1978.

344. HR 12157. Export-Import Bank. Ashbrook, R-Ohio, amendment to eliminate language prohibiting the Export-Import Bank's participation in loan transactions with South Africa. Rejected 116-219: R 79-40; D 37-179 (ND 8-145; SD 29-34), June 2, 1978.

345. HR 12157. Export-Import Bank. Vanik, D-Ohio, amendment to exempt the People's Republic of China from the provision requiring a presidential determination before the Export-Import Bank could do business in a Communist country. Adopted 179-138: R 79-29; D 100-109 (ND 57-91; SD 43-18), June 2, 1978.

346. HR 185. Coast Guard Employee Transportation. Murphy, D-N.Y., motion to suspend the rules and pass the bill to authorize the secretary of transportation to provide transportation from their homes for Coast Guard employees to remote Loran-C (long range aids to navigation) sites. Motion agreed to 336-0: R 123-0; D 213-0 (ND 146-0; SD 67-0), June 5, 1978. A two-thirds majority vote (224 in this case) is required for passage under suspension of the rules.

347. HR 188. International Marine Pollution. Murphy, D-N.Y., motion to suspend the rules and pass the bill to amend the 1969 international convention dealing with oil pollution on the high seas by implementing the 1973 protocol to authorize the U.S. Coast Guard to take any necessary action, including destruction of ships, to prevent or remove damage to the U.S. coastline by spills of hazardous cargoes in addition to oil. Motion agreed to 344-1: R 124-0; D 220-1 (ND 151-0; SD 69-1), June 5, 1978. A two-thirds majority vote (230 in this case) is required for passage under suspension of the rules.

348. HR 12140. Water Pollution Control. Roberts, D-Texas, motion to suspend the rules and pass the bill to extend for fiscal 1979 and 1980 authorizations in the 1977 Federal Water Pollution Control Act for water quality monitoring, Great Lakes water quality monitoring and manpower planning and training. Motion agreed to 338-9: R 121-5; D 217-4 (ND 152-0; SD 65-4), June 5, 1978. A two-thirds majority vote (232 in this case) is required for passage under suspension of the rules.

KEY

- Y Voted for (yea).
- ✓ Paired for.
- † Announced for.
- # CQ Poll for.
- N Voted against (nay).
- X Paired against.
- - Announced against.
- ▮ CQ Poll against.
- P Voted "present."
- ● Voted "present" to avoid possible conflict of interest.
- ? Did not vote or otherwise make a position known.

	341	342	343	344	345	346	347	348
ALABAMA								
1 Edwards	Y	?	?	?	✓	Y	Y	Y
2 Dickinson	Y	Y	Y	Y	✓	Y	Y	Y
3 Nichols	Y	#	Y	N	Y	Y	Y	Y
4 Bevill	?	?	?	?	✓	?	?	?
5 Flippo	?	Y	Y	N	Y	Y	Y	Y
6 Buchanan	Y	N	Y	N	Y	Y	Y	Y
7 Flowers	?	?	?	?	?	?	?	?
ALASKA								
AL Young	#	#	#	#	#	#	#	#
ARIZONA								
1 Rhodes	Y	Y	Y	Y	Y	Y	Y	Y
2 Udall	#	N	Y	N	N	Y	Y	Y
3 Stump	Y	Y	#	#	#	#	#	#
4 Rudd	?	?	?	?	?	Y	Y	Y
ARKANSAS								
1 Alexander	?	?	?	?	?	?	?	?
2 Tucker	#	▮	#	▮	#	#	#	#
3 Hammerschmidt	Y	Y	Y	Y	Y	Y	Y	Y
4 Thornton	?	?	?	?	?	?	?	?
CALIFORNIA								
1 Johnson	Y	Y	Y	Y	N	Y	Y	Y
2 Clausen	Y	Y	?	?	?	Y	Y	Y
3 Moss	?	?	Y	?	N	Y	Y	Y
4 Leggett	?	N	Y	N	Y	Y	Y	Y
5 Burton, J.	N	?	?	?	X	Y	Y	Y
6 Burton, P.	Y	N	Y	N	N	Y	Y	Y
7 Miller	?	N	Y	N	N	Y	Y	Y
8 Dellums	Y	N	Y	N	N	#	#	#
9 Stark	N	N	Y	N	Y	Y	Y	Y
10 Edwards	Y	N	Y	N	N	Y	Y	Y
11 Ryan	#	▮	#	▮	#	#	#	#
12 McCloskey	Y	N	Y	N	N	?	?	?
13 Mineta	Y	N	Y	N	N	Y	Y	Y
14 McFall	Y	N	Y	N	N	Y	Y	Y
15 Sisk	?	?	?	?	?	Y	Y	Y
16 Panetta	Y	N	Y	N	Y	Y	Y	Y
17 Krebs	Y	N	Y	N	N	Y	Y	Y
18 Ketchum	Y	Y	Y	Y	Y	Y	Y	Y
19 Lagomarsino	Y	Y	Y	Y	Y	Y	Y	Y
20 Goldwater	Y	Y	?	Y	Y	Y	Y	Y
21 Corman	Y	N	Y	N	N	Y	Y	Y
22 Moorhead	Y	Y	Y	Y	Y	Y	Y	Y
23 Beilenson	Y	N	#	N	N	#	#	#
24 Waxman	Y	N	Y	▮	N	#	Y	Y
25 Roybal	Y	N	Y	N	N	?	?	?
26 Rousselot	?	?	?	?	✓	Y	Y	Y
27 Dornan	Y	Y	Y	Y	Y	?	?	?
28 Burke	#	▮	#	▮	X	#	#	#
29 Hawkins	Y	N	Y	N	N	Y	Y	Y
30 Danielson	Y	N	Y	N	N	#	#	#
31 Wilson, C.H.	?	?	?	?	?	?	?	?
32 Anderson	Y	N	Y	N	N	?	?	?
33 Clawson	N	?	Y	Y	Y	Y	Y	Y
34 Hannaford	Y	N	#	▮	X	#	#	#
35 Lloyd	Y	N	N	N	N	Y	Y	Y
36 Brown	?	?	?	?	?	?	?	?
37 Pettis	?	Y	Y	Y	N	Y	Y	Y
38 Patterson	Y	N	Y	Y	N	Y	Y	Y
39 Wiggins	#	Y	#	Y	Y	Y	Y	Y
40 Badham	Y	Y	Y	Y	Y	Y	Y	Y
41 Wilson, B.	N	Y	N	Y	N	?	?	?
42 Van Deerlin	Y	N	Y	N	N	?	?	?
43 Burgener	?	?	?	?	?	Y	Y	Y
COLORADO								
1 Schroeder	Y	N	Y	N	N	Y	Y	Y
2 Wirth	Y	N	Y	N	N	Y	Y	Y
3 Evans	?	?	?	N	N	Y	Y	Y
4 Johnson	Y	N	Y	N	N	Y	Y	Y
5 Armstrong	Y	Y	Y	Y	Y	?	?	?
CONNECTICUT								
1 Cotter	?	?	?	?	?	?	?	?
2 Dodd	?	N	Y	N	Y	Y	Y	Y
3 Giaimo	Y	N	Y	N	Y	?	?	?
4 McKinney	#	N	Y	N	Y	Y	Y	Y
5 Sarasin	†	-	Y	N	†	†	†	†
6 Moffett	N	N	Y	N	Y	Y	Y	Y
DELAWARE								
AL Evans	Y	Y	Y	N	N	#	Y	Y
FLORIDA								
1 Sikes	Y	Y	Y	?	?	Y	Y	Y
2 Fuqua	Y	Y	Y	N	▮	Y	Y	Y
3 Bennett	Y	Y	Y	N	Y	Y	Y	Y
4 Chappell	Y	Y	Y	Y	Y	Y	Y	Y
5 Kelly	Y	Y	Y	Y	Y	Y	Y	Y
6 Young	Y	Y	Y	Y	#	Y	Y	Y
7 Gibbons	?	?	?	?	?	?	?	?
8 Ireland	Y	Y	Y	Y	Y	Y	Y	Y
9 Frey	?	?	?	?	✓	?	?	?
10 Bafalis	Y	Y	Y	Y	Y	Y	Y	Y
11 Rogers	Y	N	Y	N	X	Y	Y	Y
12 Burke	Y	Y	Y	Y	#	Y	Y	Y
13 Lehman	Y	N	Y	N	N	Y	Y	Y
14 Pepper	Y	N	Y	N	Y	Y	Y	Y
15 Fascell	#	▮	Y	N	N	Y	Y	Y
GEORGIA								
1 Ginn	Y	Y	#	#	X	Y	Y	Y
2 Mathis	N	Y	?	?	?	Y	Y	Y
3 Brinkley	Y	Y	Y	N	Y	Y	Y	Y
4 Levitas	Y	Y	Y	N	Y	Y	Y	Y
5 Fowler	Y	N	Y	N	Y	Y	Y	Y
6 Flynt	Y	Y	Y	Y	Y	Y	Y	Y
7 McDonald	#	†	#	Y	†	Y	N	N
8 Evans	Y	Y	Y	#	#	Y	Y	Y
9 Jenkins	Y	Y	Y	N	Y	#	#	#
10 Barnard	Y	Y	Y	N	N	Y	Y	Y
HAWAII								
1 Heftel	Y	N	Y	N	N	Y	Y	Y
2 Akaka	Y	N	#	▮	X	Y	Y	Y
IDAHO								
1 Symms	Y	Y	Y	Y	Y	Y	Y	N
2 Hansen, G.	N	Y	Y	Y	Y	Y	Y	N
ILLINOIS								
1 Metcalfe	?	?	?	?	X	Y	Y	Y
2 Murphy	Y	N	Y	N	?	#	#	#
3 Russo	Y	N	Y	N	✓	Y	Y	Y
4 Derwinski	Y	N	Y	Y	Y	Y	Y	Y
5 Fary	Y	N	Y	N	✓	Y	Y	Y
6 Hyde	Y	Y	#	#	✓	Y	Y	Y
7 Collins	Y	N	Y	N	N	Y	Y	Y
8 Rostenkowski	Y	N	Y	N	Y	Y	Y	Y
9 Yates	Y	N	Y	N	N	Y	Y	Y
10 Mikva	Y	N	Y	Y	N	†	†	†
11 Annunzio	Y	N	Y	N	Y	Y	Y	Y
12 Crane	#	#	#	Y	Y	Y	Y	N
13 McClory	Y	Y	Y	Y	Y	Y	Y	Y
14 Erlenborn	Y	Y	Y	Y	N	Y	Y	Y
15 Corcoran	Y	Y	Y	Y	N	Y	Y	Y
16 Anderson	#	N	Y	N	#	#	#	#
17 O'Brien	Y	Y	Y	N	N	Y	Y	Y
18 Michel	Y	Y	Y	Y	Y	Y	Y	Y
19 Railsback	Y	N	Y	N	#	Y	Y	Y
20 Findley	Y	N	Y	Y	N	Y	Y	Y
21 Madigan	Y	Y	Y	Y	N	Y	Y	Y
22 Shipley	?	?	?	?	X	Y	Y	Y
23 Price	Y	N	Y	N	N	Y	Y	Y
24 Simon	Y	N	Y	N	N	?	?	?
INDIANA								
1 Benjamin	Y	N	Y	N	Y	Y	Y	Y
2 Fithian	Y	N	Y	N	N	Y	Y	Y
3 Brademas	Y	N	Y	N	N	Y	Y	Y
4 Quayle	N	Y	?	?	?	Y	Y	Y
5 Hillis	Y	Y	Y	N	N	Y	Y	Y
6 Evans	Y	N	Y	N	Y	Y	Y	Y
7 Myers, J.	Y	Y	Y	Y	Y	Y	Y	Y
8 Cornwell	Y	N	?	N	N	?	?	?
9 Hamilton	Y	N	Y	Y	N	Y	Y	Y
10 Sharp	Y	N	Y	N	N	Y	Y	Y
11 Jacobs	Y	Y	#	#	▮	Y	Y	Y
IOWA								
1 Leach	Y	N	Y	N	N	Y	Y	Y
2 Blouin	Y	N	Y	N	Y	Y	Y	Y
3 Grassley	Y	Y	Y	N	Y	Y	Y	Y
4 Smith	Y	N	Y	N	N	Y	Y	Y
5 Harkin	Y	N	Y	N	Y	Y	Y	Y
6 Bedell	Y	N	Y	N	N	?	#	#

Democrats ***Republicans***

	341	342	343	344	345	346	347	348
KANSAS								
1 Sebelius	#	#	#	#	▮	Y	Y	Y
2 Keys	Y	N	#	-	-	Y	Y	Y
3 Winn	#	Y	Y	Y	N	Y	Y	Y
4 Glickman	Y	N	Y	N	N	Y	Y	Y
5 Skubitz	Y	N	Y	Y	N	Y	Y	Y
KENTUCKY								
1 Hubbard	?	?	?	?	?	Y	Y	Y
2 Natcher	Y	N	Y	N	N	Y	Y	Y
3 Mazzoli	Y	N	Y	N	Y	Y	Y	Y
4 Snyder	Y	?	Y	Y	Y	Y	Y	Y
5 Carter	Y	Y	Y	N	N	Y	Y	Y
6 Breckinridge	Y	?	Y	N	Y	Y	Y	Y
7 Perkins	Y	N	Y	N	Y	Y	Y	Y
LOUISIANA								
1 Livingston	Y	Y	Y	Y	Y	?	?	?
2 Boggs	Y	N	Y	N	Y	Y	Y	Y
3 Treen	Y	Y	Y	Y	Y	Y	Y	Y
4 Waggonner	#	#	#	#	▮	Y	Y	Y
5 Huckaby	Y	Y	Y	Y	Y	Y	Y	Y
6 Moore	Y	Y	Y	Y	Y	Y	Y	Y
7 Breaux	Y	Y	?	?	✓	Y	Y	Y
8 Long	Y	Y	Y	N	Y	Y	Y	Y
MAINE								
1 Emery	Y	Y	#	▮	▮	#	#	#
2 Cohen	Y	Y	?	?	?	Y	Y	Y
MARYLAND								
1 Bauman	Y	Y	Y	Y	Y	Y	Y	Y
2 Long	?	Y	Y	N	Y	Y	Y	Y
3 Mikulski	Y	N	Y	N	N	Y	Y	Y
4 Holt	Y	Y	Y	Y	Y	Y	Y	Y
5 Spellman	Y	N	Y	N	N	Y	Y	Y
6 Byron	Y	Y	Y	N	Y	Y	Y	Y
7 Mitchell	Y	N	N	N	N	Y	Y	Y
8 Steers	Y	N	Y	N	Y	Y	Y	Y
MASSACHUSETTS								
1 Conte	Y	N	Y	N	Y	?	?	?
2 Boland	Y	N	Y	N	✓	Y	Y	Y
3 Early	Y	N	Y	N	Y	Y	Y	Y
4 Drinan	Y	N	Y	N	N	Y	Y	Y
5 Tsongas	Y	N	Y	N	N	#	#	#
6 Harrington	Y	▮	#	N	N	Y	Y	Y
7 Markey	#	▮	Y	N	N	Y	Y	Y
8 O'Neill								
9 Moakley	Y	N	Y	N	Y	Y	Y	Y
10 Heckler	Y	Y	#	N	Y	Y	Y	Y
11 Burke	Y	N	Y	N	Y	Y	Y	Y
12 Studds	Y	N	Y	N	Y	Y	Y	Y
MICHIGAN								
1 Conyers	#	▮	#	▮	X	#	#	#
2 Pursell	?	?	?	?	?	Y	Y	Y
3 Brown	Y	Y	Y	Y	Y	#	#	#
4 Stockman	Y	Y	Y	Y	N	Y	Y	Y
5 Sawyer	Y	Y	?	?	?	Y	Y	Y
6 Carr	Y	N	Y	-	-	Y	Y	Y
7 Kildee	Y	N	Y	N	N	Y	Y	Y
8 Traxler	Y	N	Y	N	Y	Y	Y	Y
9 Vander Jagt	Y	Y	?	Y	Y	Y	Y	Y
10 Cederberg	Y	Y	Y	Y	Y	?	?	Y
11 Ruppe	Y	Y	#	?	#	#	#	#
12 Bonior	?	N	Y	N	N	Y	Y	Y
13 Diggs	?	?	?	?	X	?	?	?
14 Nedzi	Y	N	Y	N	N	Y	Y	Y
15 Ford	Y	N	?	N	Y	?	Y	Y
16 Dingell	Y	Y	?	?	X	?	?	?
17 Brodhead	?	N	Y	N	N	Y	Y	Y
18 Blanchard	Y	N	Y	N	Y	Y	Y	Y
19 Broomfield	Y	N	Y	Y	Y	Y	Y	Y
MINNESOTA								
1 Quie	Y	Y	Y	N	▮	Y	Y	Y
2 Hagedorn	#	#	#	Y	N	Y	Y	Y
3 Frenzel	Y	N	?	?	?	Y	Y	Y
4 Vento	Y	N	Y	N	Y	Y	Y	Y
5 Fraser	#	▮	#	▮	▮	Y	Y	Y
6 Nolan	?	N	?	N	N	Y	Y	Y
7 Stangeland	Y	Y	Y	Y	N	Y	Y	Y
8 Oberstar	Y	N	Y	N	N	Y	Y	Y
MISSISSIPPI								
1 Whitten	#	#	Y	#	▮	#	#	#
2 Bowen	Y	Y	Y	Y	N	?	?	?
3 Montgomery	Y	?	Y	Y	Y	Y	Y	Y
4 Cochran	?	?	?	?	?	?	?	?
5 Lott	Y	Y	Y	Y	Y	Y	Y	Y
MISSOURI								
1 Clay	Y	?	Y	N	N	Y	Y	Y
2 Young	#	Y	Y	N	Y	Y	Y	Y
3 Gephardt	?	N	?	N	Y	Y	Y	Y

	341	342	343	344	345	346	347	348
4 Skelton	N	Y	#	▮	#	Y	Y	Y
5 Bolling	#	▮	Y	#	#	Y	Y	Y
6 Coleman	?	Y	Y	Y	Y	Y	Y	Y
7 Taylor	Y	Y	Y	Y	Y	Y	Y	Y
8 Ichord	Y	Y	Y	Y	Y	Y	Y	Y
9 Volkmer	?	Y	Y	N	Y	Y	Y	Y
10 Burlison	Y	N	Y	N	N	Y	Y	Y
MONTANA								
1 Baucus	#	▮	#	▮	✓	#	#	#
2 Marlenee	Y	N	?	?	?	Y	Y	Y
NEBRASKA								
1 Thone	#	▮	#	?	?	#	#	#
2 Cavanaugh	Y	N	Y	N	Y	Y	Y	Y
3 Smith	Y	Y	Y	Y	Y	Y	Y	Y
NEVADA								
AL Santini	Y	Y	#	?	?	#	#	#
NEW HAMPSHIRE								
1 D'Amours	#	N	Y	N	Y	Y	Y	Y
2 Cleveland	Y	Y	Y	N	N	Y	Y	Y
NEW JERSEY								
1 Florio	Y	Y	Y	N	Y	Y	Y	Y
2 Hughes	Y	N	Y	N	Y	Y	Y	Y
3 Howard	#	▮	#	▮	#	#	#	#
4 Thompson	Y	▮	Y	N	N	Y	Y	Y
5 Fenwick	Y	N	Y	N	Y	Y	Y	Y
6 Forsythe	†	-	†	-	✓	Y	Y	Y
7 Maguire	?	N	?	N	N	Y	Y	Y
8 Roe	Y	N	#	▮	#	#	#	#
9 Hollenbeck	Y	N	Y	N	Y	Y	Y	Y
10 Rodino	#	▮	#	▮	#	#	#	#
11 Minish	Y	N	?	?	?	?	?	?
12 Rinaldo	Y	N	Y	N	Y	Y	Y	Y
13 Meyner	#	▮	Y	N	N	Y	Y	Y
14 LeFante	Y	Y	Y	N	Y	Y	Y	Y
15 Patten	#	▮	#	▮	#	#	#	#
NEW MEXICO								
1 Lujan	?	?	?	?	?	Y	Y	Y
2 Runnels	#	?	#	?	?	#	#	#
NEW YORK								
1 Pike	Y	N	Y	N	Y	#	#	#
2 Downey	#	N	Y	N	N	Y	Y	Y
3 Ambro	?	Y	?	Y	Y	Y	Y	Y
4 Lent	Y	Y	Y	Y	Y	Y	Y	Y
5 Wydler	Y	Y	Y	N	Y	Y	Y	Y
6 Wolff	Y	N	Y	N	#	Y	Y	Y
7 Addabbo	#	N	Y	N	Y	Y	Y	Y
8 Rosenthal	#	N	Y	N	N	Y	Y	Y
9 Delaney	?	?	Y	N	Y	?	Y	Y
10 Biaggi	Y	N	Y	N	N	#	#	#
11 Scheuer	Y	N	Y	N	Y	Y	Y	Y
12 Chisholm	Y	N	#	N	N	Y	Y	Y
13 Solarz	Y	N	Y	N	N	Y	Y	Y
14 Richmond	Y	N	?	?	X	Y	Y	Y
15 Zeferetti	Y	N	Y	N	Y	?	?	?
16 Holtzman	Y	N	Y	N	N	Y	Y	Y
17 Murphy	Y	N	Y	N	Y	Y	Y	Y
18 Green	Y	N	Y	N	Y	Y	Y	Y
19 Rangel	Y	N	Y	N	N	Y	Y	Y
20 Weiss	†	-	†	-	X	Y	Y	Y
21 Garcia	Y	N	Y	N	N	Y	Y	Y
22 Bingham	#	▮	#	N	N	Y	Y	Y
23 Caputo	Y	Y	Y	N	Y	Y	Y	Y
24 Ottinger	Y	N	?	N	N	Y	Y	Y
25 Fish	Y	N	Y	N	Y	Y	Y	Y
26 Gilman	Y	N	Y	N	Y	Y	Y	Y
27 McHugh	Y	N	Y	N	Y	#	Y	Y
28 Stratton	Y	Y	Y	Y	✓	Y	Y	Y
29 Pattison	#	N	Y	N	N	Y	Y	Y
30 McEwen	Y	Y	Y	Y	Y	Y	Y	Y
31 Mitchell	#	Y	Y	Y	Y	Y	Y	Y
32 Hanley	Y	N	Y	N	N	Y	Y	Y
33 Walsh	Y	N	Y	N	Y	Y	Y	Y
34 Horton	Y	N	Y	N	✓	Y	Y	Y
35 Conable	Y	?	Y	Y	Y	Y	Y	Y
36 LaFalce	Y	N	Y	N	N	Y	Y	Y
37 Nowak	#	N	Y	N	N	Y	Y	Y
38 Kemp	Y	Y	Y	Y	?	Y	Y	Y
39 Lundine	#	N	Y	▮	N	Y	Y	Y
NORTH CAROLINA								
1 Jones	Y	N	Y	Y	Y	Y	Y	Y
2 Fountain	Y	Y	P	Y	Y	Y	Y	Y
3 Whitley	Y	Y	Y	Y	Y	Y	Y	Y
4 Andrews	Y	?	Y	Y	N	Y	Y	Y
5 Neal	Y	N	Y	N	N	Y	Y	Y
6 Preyer	#	N	Y	N	N	Y	Y	Y
7 Rose	Y	▮	#	▮	▮	#	#	#
8 Hefner	Y	N	#	Y	Y	Y	Y	Y

	341	342	343	344	345	346	347	348
9 Martin	#	Y	Y	Y	Y	#	#	#
10 Broyhill	Y	Y	Y	Y	Y	Y	Y	Y
11 Gudger	Y	N	Y	Y	Y	Y	Y	Y
NORTH DAKOTA								
AL Andrews	Y	Y	Y	Y	N	Y	Y	Y
OHIO								
1 Gradison	Y	Y	Y	N	Y	Y	Y	Y
2 Luken	Y	N	Y	N	Y	Y	Y	Y
3 Whalen	Y	N	#	▮	#	?	#	#
4 Guyer	Y	▮	Y	Y	Y	Y	Y	Y
5 Latta	Y	Y	Y	?	?	Y	Y	Y
6 Harsha	Y	Y	Y	Y	N	Y	Y	Y
7 Brown	Y	Y	Y	N	Y	Y	Y	Y
8 Kindness	N	?	Y	Y	Y	?	?	?
9 Ashley	?	?	?	?	X	Y	Y	Y
10 Miller	Y	Y	Y	Y	Y	Y	Y	Y
11 Stanton	Y	N	Y	N	N	Y	Y	Y
12 Devine	Y	Y	Y	Y	Y	Y	Y	Y
13 Pease	Y	N	Y	N	Y	Y	Y	Y
14 Seiberling	Y	N	#	N	N	Y	Y	Y
15 Wylie	Y	N	?	?	?	Y	Y	Y
16 Regula	Y	Y	Y	N	Y	Y	Y	Y
17 Ashbrook	Y	#	#	Y	Y	Y	Y	N
18 Applegate	Y	Y	Y	N	Y	?	?	?
19 Carney	#	N	Y	?	X	#	#	#
20 Oakar	?	N	?	?	?	?	?	?
21 Stokes	Y	N	Y	N	N	#	#	#
22 Vanik	Y	N	Y	N	Y	Y	Y	Y
23 Mottl	Y	Y	Y	#	X	Y	Y	Y
OKLAHOMA								
1 Jones	Y	N	Y	Y	Y	Y	Y	Y
2 Risenhoover	Y	Y	Y	N	Y	Y	Y	?
3 Watkins	Y	Y	#	#	#	Y	Y	Y
4 Steed	Y	N	Y	N	N	Y	Y	Y
5 Edwards	Y	Y	?	?	?	Y	Y	Y
6 English	Y	Y	Y	Y	Y	Y	Y	Y
OREGON								
1 AuCoin	Y	N	Y	Y	N	P	Y	Y
2 Ullman	#	▮	Y	▮	#	#	#	#
3 Duncan	Y	Y	?	N	N	?	?	?
4 Weaver	N	N	Y	N	N	Y	Y	Y
PENNSYLVANIA								
1 Myers, M.	Y	Y	Y	N	Y	Y	Y	Y
2 Nix	?	?	Y	N	N	?	?	?
3 Lederer	Y	Y	Y	N	Y	Y	Y	Y
4 Eilberg	Y	N	Y	N	Y	#	#	#
5 Schulze	Y	Y	Y	Y	Y	Y	Y	Y
6 Yatron	Y	N	Y	N	Y	Y	Y	Y
7 Edgar	Y	N	Y	N	N	Y	Y	Y
8 Kostmayer	Y	N	Y	N	Y	Y	Y	Y
9 Shuster	Y	Y	Y	Y	Y	Y	Y	Y
10 McDade	Y	N	Y	N	N	Y	Y	Y
11 Flood	Y	N	Y	N	Y	Y	Y	Y
12 Murtha	Y	Y	Y	N	Y	Y	Y	Y
13 Coughlin	Y	Y	Y	N	Y	?	?	Y
14 Moorhead	Y	N	Y	N	N	Y	Y	Y
15 Rooney	Y	N	Y	N	Y	Y	Y	Y
16 Walker	Y	N	Y	N	Y	Y	Y	Y
17 Ertel	Y	N	Y	N	Y	?	Y	Y
18 Walgren	?	N	Y	N	N	Y	Y	Y
19 Goodling, W.	Y	Y	Y	N	Y	Y	Y	Y
20 Gaydos	Y	Y	Y	N	Y	Y	Y	Y
21 Dent	#	#	#	▮	#	Y	#	Y
22 Murphy	Y	Y	Y	Y	Y	Y	Y	Y
23 Ammerman	Y	N	Y	N	Y	Y	Y	Y
24 Marks	Y	N	Y	N	Y	Y	Y	Y
25 Myers, G.	Y	N	Y	N	N	Y	Y	Y
RHODE ISLAND								
1 St Germain	Y	?	Y	?	X	Y	Y	Y
2 Beard	Y	N	Y	N	N	Y	Y	Y
SOUTH CAROLINA								
1 Davis	Y	Y	Y	N	Y	Y	Y	Y
2 Spence	Y	Y	Y	Y	Y	Y	Y	Y
3 Derrick	#	▮	#	▮	▮	Y	Y	Y
4 Mann	Y	Y	Y	Y	Y	?	?	?
5 Holland	#	#	?	?	?	#	#	#
6 Jenrette	?	▮	#	▮	✓	#	#	#
SOUTH DAKOTA								
1 Pressler	?	?	?	?	?	?	?	?
2 Abdnor	Y	Y	Y	Y	N	Y	Y	Y
TENNESSEE								
1 Quillen	Y	Y	Y	Y	#	Y	Y	Y
2 Duncan	Y	Y	Y	Y	Y	Y	Y	Y
3 Lloyd	Y	Y	Y	Y	Y	Y	Y	Y
4 Gore	#	▮	#	▮	✓	Y	Y	Y
5 Allen	?	?	?	?	?	?	?	?
6 Beard	Y	Y	Y	Y	Y	Y	Y	Y

	341	342	343	344	345	346	347	348
7 Jones	Y	Y	Y	N	N	#	#	#
8 Ford	Y	N	Y	?	?	?	?	?
TEXAS								
1 Hall	Y	Y	Y	Y	Y	Y	Y	N
2 Wilson, C.	#	Y	#	Y	N	Y	Y	Y
3 Collins	N	Y	#	#	▮	Y	Y	N
4 Roberts	Y	Y	Y	Y	Y	Y	Y	Y
5 Mattox	Y	N	Y	N	Y	Y	Y	Y
6 Teague	?	?	?	?	✓	?	?	?
7 Archer	Y	Y	Y	Y	Y	Y	Y	Y
8 Eckhardt	?	N	Y	N	N	Y	Y	Y
9 Brooks	?	Y	Y	N	N	?	Y	Y
10 Pickle	Y	Y	Y	Y	Y	Y	Y	Y
11 Poage	Y	Y	Y	Y	Y	?	Y	Y
12 Wright	Y	N	Y	N	Y	Y	Y	Y
13 Hightower	Y	Y	Y	Y	Y	Y	Y	Y
14 Young	?	?	?	?	?	?	?	?
15 de la Garza	?	?	Y	?	N	?	?	?
16 White	Y	Y	Y	N	Y	Y	Y	Y
17 Burleson	Y	Y	Y	Y	Y	Y	Y	Y
18 Jordan	Y	N	Y	N	N	Y	Y	Y
19 Mahon	Y	Y	Y	Y	N	Y	Y	Y
20 Gonzalez	Y	Y	Y	Y	Y	?	Y	Y
21 Krueger	?	?	?	?	✓	Y	Y	Y
22 Gammage	Y	Y	Y	N	Y	Y	Y	Y
23 Kazen	Y	Y	Y	Y	N	Y	Y	Y
24 Milford	?	?	?	?	?	?	?	?
UTAH								
1 McKay	#	▮	#	#	▮	Y	Y	Y
2 Marriott	Y	Y	Y	Y	Y	Y	Y	Y
VERMONT								
AL Jeffords	N	N	#	Y	Y	Y	Y	Y
VIRGINIA								
1 Trible	Y	Y	Y	N	?	Y	Y	Y
2 Whitehurst	Y	Y	Y	Y	N	Y	Y	Y
3 Satterfield	Y	Y	Y	Y	Y	Y	Y	N
4 Daniel	Y	Y	Y	Y	Y	Y	Y	Y
5 Daniel	?	Y	?	Y	Y	Y	Y	N
6 Butler	?	?	Y	Y	Y	Y	Y	Y
7 Robinson	Y	Y	Y	Y	Y	Y	Y	Y
8 Harris	Y	N	Y	N	N	Y	Y	Y
9 Wampler	Y	Y	Y	Y	Y	Y	Y	Y
10 Fisher	Y	N	Y	N	Y	Y	Y	Y
WASHINGTON								
1 Pritchard	Y	Y	Y	N	N	#	#	#
2 Meeds	#	N	#	N	N	Y	Y	Y
3 Bonker	Y	N	Y	Y	N	#	#	#
4 McCormack	?	?	?	?	?	Y	Y	Y
5 Foley	Y	N	?	?	?	Y	Y	Y
6 Dicks	Y	N	Y	N	N	Y	Y	Y
7 Cunningham	Y	Y	Y	Y	N	Y	Y	Y
WEST VIRGINIA								
1 Mollohan	Y	Y	Y	N	Y	#	#	#
2 Staggers	Y	N	Y	N	N	Y	Y	Y
3 Slack	Y	?	Y	N	N	Y	Y	Y
4 Rahall	Y	N	Y	N	X	Y	Y	Y
WISCONSIN								
1 Aspin	Y	N	Y	N	N	?	?	?
2 Kastenmeier	Y	N	Y	N	N	Y	Y	Y
3 Baldus	Y	N	Y	N	N	Y	Y	Y
4 Zablocki	Y	N	Y	N	Y	Y	Y	Y
5 Reuss	Y	N	Y	N	N	Y	Y	Y
6 Steiger	#	N	Y	Y	Y	Y	Y	Y
7 Obey	Y	N	Y	Y	N	Y	Y	Y
8 Cornell	Y	N	Y	N	Y	Y	Y	Y
9 Kasten	#	▮	#	#	#	#	?	#
WYOMING								
AL Roncalio	Y	?	?	N	N	Y	Y	Y

Democrats ***Republicans***

349. HR 12250. Boundary Waters Canoe Area. Adoption of the rule (H Res 1213) providing for House floor consideration of the bill to designate uses of the northern Minnesota Boundary Waters Canoe Area Wilderness. Adopted 339-1: R 125-0; D 214-1 (ND 148-0; SD 66-1), June 5, 1978.

350. HR 12250. Boundary Waters Canoe Area. Vento, D-Minn., substitute amendment, to the Oberstar, D-Minn., substitute amendment to the bill, to ban logging and mining in the wilderness and to end motorized use except on six peripheral lakes where boats up to 25 horsepower could be used and except on certain large lakes where motorized use would be phased out through 2010. Adopted 213-141: R 52-76; D 161-65 (ND 123-31; SD 38-34), June 5, 1978. (The amended Oberstar substitute amendment was adopted subsequently by voice vote.)

351. HR 12250. Boundary Waters Canoe Area. Passage of the bill to prohibit mining, logging, snowmobiling and most use of motor boats in the Boundary Waters Canoe Area Wilderness of the Superior National Forest in Minnesota. Passed 324-29: R 119-10; D 205-19 (ND 149-5; SD 56-14), June 5, 1978.

352. HR 12481. U.S. Territories Authorization. Adoption of the rule (H Res 1191) providing for House floor consideration of the bill to authorize funds for programs in the insular territories of the United States. Adopted 344-2: R 124-1; D 220-1 (ND 153-0; SD 67-1), June 5, 1978.

353. HR 12481. U.S. Territories Authorization. Passage of the bill to authorize $162.5 million for programs in Guam, the Virgin Islands, the Trust Territory of the Pacific Islands and the Northern Mariana Islands. Passed 292-54: R 87-37; D 205-17 (ND 143-10; SD 62-7), June 5, 1978.

354. HR 8394. Wildlife Refuge Revenue Sharing. Leggett, D-Calif., motion to suspend the rules and pass the bill to amend the 1935 Refuge Revenue Sharing Act to update and expand the payments compensating local governments for loss of tax revenue for lands included in the National Wildlife Refuge System. Motion agreed to 340-28: R 123-13; D 217-15 (ND 147-12; SD 70-3), June 6, 1978. A two-thirds majority vote (246 in this case) is required for passage under suspension of the rules.

355. HR 12367. U.S.-Japan Fisheries Convention. Leggett, D-Calif., motion to suspend the rules and pass the bill to authorize $3 million for fiscal 1979-81 to implement the protocol to the 1952 International Convention for the High Seas Fisheries of the North Pacific to limit Japanese fishing to 175°E longitude to conserve 265,000 salmon annually and to organize joint Japanese-U.S.-Canadian research on Pacific salmon and mammals. Motion agreed to 368-0: R 135-0; D 233-0 (ND 160-0; SD 73-0), June 6, 1978. A two-thirds majority vote (246 in this case) is required for passage under suspension of the rules.

356. HR 12668. Polar Marine Research. Leggett, D-Calif., motion to suspend the rules and pass the bill to authorize $44 million for fiscal 1979-82 for Commerce Department research on the living marine resources in both the north and south polar regions. Motion agreed to 268-103: R 78-58; D 190-45 (ND 137-27; SD 53-18), June 6, 1978. A two-thirds majority vote (248 in this case) is required for passage under suspension of the rules.

KEY

- Y Voted for (yea).
- ✓ Paired for.
- † Announced for.
- # CQ Poll for.
- N Voted against (nay).
- X Paired against.
- \- Announced against.
- ▮ CQ Poll against.
- P Voted "present."
- ● Voted "present" to avoid possible conflict of interest.
- ? Did not vote or otherwise make a position known.

	349	350	351	352	353	354	355	356
ALABAMA								
1 Edwards	Y	N	Y	Y	Y	?	?	?
2 Dickinson	Y	N	Y	Y	Y	?	?	?
3 Nichols	Y	N	Y	Y	Y	#	#	#
4 Bevill	?	X	?	?	?	?	?	?
5 Flippo	Y	N	Y	Y	Y	?	?	?
6 Buchanan	Y	Y	Y	Y	Y	?	?	?
7 Flowers	?	?	?	?	?	?	?	?
ALASKA								
AL Young	#	▮	▮	#	#	#	#	#
ARIZONA								
1 Rhodes	Y	N	Y	Y	Y	Y	Y	Y
2 Udall	Y	Y	Y	Y	Y	Y	Y	Y
3 Stump	#	▮	▮	#	▮	#	#	▮
4 Rudd	Y	N	N	Y	Y	N	Y	N
ARKANSAS								
1 Alexander	?	✓	?	?	?	?	?	?
2 Tucker	#	#	#	#	#	#	#	#
3 Hammerschmidt	Y	N	Y	Y	N	Y	Y	Y
4 Thornton	?	?	?	?	?	Y	Y	Y
CALIFORNIA								
1 Johnson	Y	N	Y	Y	Y	Y	Y	Y
2 Clausen	Y	N	Y	Y	Y	Y	Y	Y
3 Moss	Y	Y	Y	Y	Y	N	Y	Y
4 Leggett	Y	N	Y	Y	Y	Y	Y	Y
5 Burton, J.	Y	Y	Y	Y	Y	Y	Y	Y
6 Burton, P.	Y	Y	Y	Y	Y	Y	Y	Y
7 Miller	Y	Y	Y	Y	Y	Y	Y	Y
8 Dellums	#	#	#	#	#	#	#	#
9 Stark	Y	Y	Y	Y	Y	Y	Y	Y
10 Edwards	Y	Y	Y	Y	Y	Y	Y	Y
11 Ryan	#	#	#	#	#	#	#	#
12 McCloskey	?	✓	?	?	?	?	?	?
13 Mineta	Y	Y	Y	Y	Y	#	Y	Y
14 McFall	Y	N	Y	Y	Y	Y	Y	Y
15 Sisk	Y	N	N	Y	Y	Y	Y	Y
16 Panetta	Y	Y	Y	Y	Y	Y	Y	Y
17 Krebs	Y	Y	Y	Y	Y	N	Y	Y
18 Ketchum	Y	N	Y	Y	Y	Y	Y	N
19 Lagomarsino	Y	N	Y	Y	Y	Y	Y	Y
20 Goldwater	Y	N	Y	Y	Y	Y	Y	N
21 Corman	Y	Y	Y	Y	Y	Y	Y	Y
22 Moorhead	Y	N	Y	Y	Y	Y	Y	N
23 Beilenson	#	#	#	#	#	?	#	#
24 Waxman	Y	Y	Y	#	#	#	#	#
25 Roybal	?	?	?	?	?	?	?	?
26 Rousselot	Y	N	N	?	?	N	Y	N
27 Dornan	?	X	?	?	?	?	?	?
28 Burke	#	#	#	#	#	#	#	#
29 Hawkins	Y	✓	?	Y	Y	Y	Y	Y
30 Danielson	#	#	#	#	#	#	#	#
31 Wilson, C.H.	?	?	?	?	?	?	?	?
32 Anderson	?	?	?	?	?	Y	Y	Y
33 Clawson	Y	N	N	Y	N	N	Y	N
34 Hannaford	#	#	#	#	#	#	#	#
35 Lloyd	Y	Y	Y	Y	Y	Y	Y	Y
36 Brown	?	?	?	?	?	Y	Y	Y
37 Pettis	Y	Y	Y	Y	Y	Y	Y	Y
38 Patterson	Y	Y	Y	Y	Y	Y	Y	Y
39 Wiggins	Y	▮	#	Y	Y	N	Y	Y
40 Badham	Y	N	Y	Y	Y	N	Y	N
41 Wilson, B.	?	?	?	?	?	?	?	?
42 Van Deerlin	?	?	?	?	?	Y	Y	Y
43 Burgener	Y	N	Y	Y	Y	Y	Y	Y
COLORADO								
1 Schroeder	Y	Y	Y	Y	Y	Y	Y	Y
2 Wirth	Y	Y	#	Y	Y	N	Y	Y
3 Evans	Y	Y	Y	Y	Y	Y	Y	Y
4 Johnson	Y	Y	Y	Y	Y	Y	Y	Y
5 Armstrong	?	N	Y	Y	Y	Y	Y	N
CONNECTICUT								
1 Cotter	?	?	?	?	?	?	?	?
2 Dodd	Y	?	Y	Y	Y	Y	Y	N
3 Giaimo	?	?	?	?	?	?	Y	Y
4 McKinney	Y	Y	Y	Y	Y	Y	Y	Y
5 Sarasin	#	#	#	#	#	Y	Y	Y
6 Moffett	Y	Y	Y	Y	Y	Y	Y	Y
DELAWARE								
AL Evans	Y	Y	Y	Y	Y	Y	Y	Y
FLORIDA								
1 Sikes	Y	N	Y	Y	Y	Y	Y	Y
2 Fuqua	Y	Y	Y	Y	Y	Y	Y	Y
3 Bennett	Y	Y	Y	Y	Y	N	Y	Y
4 Chappell	Y	N	Y	Y	Y	Y	Y	Y
5 Kelly	Y	N	Y	Y	N	Y	Y	N
6 Young	Y	N	Y	Y	N	Y	Y	N
7 Gibbons	?	?	?	?	?	?	?	?
8 Ireland	?	Y	Y	Y	Y	Y	Y	Y
9 Frey	?	?	?	?	?	Y	Y	Y
10 Bafalis	Y	Y	Y	Y	Y	Y	Y	N
11 Rogers	Y	Y	Y	Y	Y	Y	Y	Y
12 Burke	Y	N	Y	Y	Y	Y	Y	N
13 Lehman	Y	Y	Y	Y	Y	Y	Y	Y
14 Pepper	Y	Y	Y	Y	Y	Y	Y	Y
15 Fascell	Y	Y	Y	Y	Y	Y	Y	Y
GEORGIA								
1 Ginn	Y	N	Y	Y	Y	Y	Y	Y
2 Mathis	?	Y	Y	Y	Y	Y	Y	Y
3 Brinkley	Y	Y	Y	Y	Y	Y	Y	Y
4 Levitas	Y	Y	Y	Y	Y	Y	Y	Y
5 Fowler	Y	Y	Y	Y	Y	Y	Y	Y
6 Flynt	Y	N	N	Y	Y	?	?	?
7 McDonald	N	N	N	N	N	N	Y	N
8 Evans	#	Y	Y	Y	Y	Y	Y	N
9 Jenkins	#	?	#	#	#	Y	Y	N
10 Barnard	Y	Y	Y	Y	Y	Y	Y	Y
HAWAII								
1 Heftel	Y	Y	Y	Y	Y	Y	Y	Y
2 Akaka	Y	Y	Y	Y	Y	Y	Y	Y
IDAHO								
1 Symms	Y	N	N	Y	N	Y	Y	N
2 Hansen, G.	Y	N	N	Y	N	Y	Y	N
ILLINOIS								
1 Metcalfe	Y	Y	Y	?	Y	Y	Y	Y
2 Murphy	#	Y	Y	Y	Y	Y	Y	N
3 Russo	Y	Y	Y	Y	N	Y	Y	Y
4 Derwinski	Y	Y	Y	Y	Y	Y	Y	Y
5 Fary	Y	N	Y	Y	Y	Y	Y	Y
6 Hyde	Y	N	Y	Y	Y	Y	Y	Y
7 Collins	?	Y	Y	Y	Y	Y	Y	Y
8 Rostenkowski	Y	N	Y	Y	Y	Y	Y	N
9 Yates	Y	Y	Y	Y	Y	N	Y	N
10 Mikva	#	Y	Y	Y	Y	N	Y	N
11 Annunzio	Y	Y	Y	Y	Y	Y	Y	N
12 Crane	Y	N	N	Y	N	Y	Y	N
13 McClory	Y	Y	Y	Y	Y	Y	Y	Y
14 Erlenborn	Y	N	Y	Y	N	Y	Y	Y
15 Corcoran	Y	Y	Y	Y	Y	Y	Y	N
16 Anderson	#	Y	Y	#	#	Y	Y	Y
17 O'Brien	Y	Y	Y	Y	Y	Y	Y	Y
18 Michel	Y	N	Y	Y	Y	Y	Y	Y
19 Railsback	Y	Y	Y	Y	Y	Y	Y	Y
20 Findley	Y	Y	Y	Y	Y	Y	Y	N
21 Madigan	Y	N	Y	Y	Y	Y	Y	N
22 Shipley	Y	N	N	Y	Y	Y	Y	Y
23 Price	Y	N	Y	Y	Y	Y	Y	Y
24 Simon	Y	Y	Y	Y	Y	?	†	-
INDIANA								
1 Benjamin	Y	N	N	Y	Y	N	Y	N
2 Fithian	Y	Y	Y	Y	Y	Y	Y	N
3 Brademas	Y	Y	Y	Y	Y	Y	Y	Y
4 Quayle	Y	Y	Y	Y	N	N	Y	N
5 Hillis	Y	Y	Y	Y	N	Y	Y	Y
6 Evans	Y	N	Y	Y	N	N	Y	N
7 Myers, J.	Y	N	Y	Y	Y	Y	Y	N
8 Cornwell	?	✓	?	?	?	Y	Y	Y
9 Hamilton	Y	Y	Y	Y	N	Y	Y	N
10 Sharp	Y	Y	Y	Y	Y	Y	Y	N
11 Jacobs	Y	Y	Y	Y	N	N	Y	N
IOWA								
1 Leach	Y	Y	Y	Y	Y	Y	Y	Y
2 Blouin	Y	Y	Y	Y	Y	Y	Y	Y
3 Grassley	Y	Y	Y	Y	N	Y	Y	N
4 Smith	Y	Y	Y	Y	Y	Y	Y	Y
5 Harkin	Y	Y	Y	Y	Y	Y	Y	Y
6 Bedell	Y	Y	Y	Y	Y	Y	Y	Y

Democrats ***Republicans***

Corresponding to Congressional Record Votes 408, 409, 410, 411, 412, 414, 415, 416

	349	350	351	352	353	354	355	356
KANSAS								
1 Sebelius	Y	Y	Y	Y	Y	Y	Y	N
2 Keys	Y	Y	Y	Y	N	Y	Y	N
3 Winn	Y	Y	Y	Y	Y	Y	Y	N
4 Glickman	Y	Y	Y	Y	Y	Y	Y	N
5 Skubitz	Y	?	Y	Y	Y	Y	Y	N
KENTUCKY								
1 Hubbard	Y	N	Y	Y	Y	Y	Y	Y
2 Natcher	Y	Y	Y	Y	Y	Y	Y	Y
3 Mazzoli	Y	Y	Y	Y	Y	Y	Y	N
4 Snyder	Y	N	Y	Y	Y	Y	Y	N
5 Carter	Y	N	Y	Y	Y	Y	Y	Y
6 Breckinridge	Y	Y	Y	Y	Y	Y	Y	Y
7 Perkins	Y	Y	Y	Y	Y	Y	Y	Y
LOUISIANA								
1 Livingston	?	X	?	?	?	Y	Y	N
2 Boggs	Y	N	Y	Y	Y	Y	Y	#
3 Treen	Y	N	Y	Y	N	Y	Y	Y
4 Waggonner	Y	N	N	Y	N	Y	Y	N
5 Huckaby	Y	N	N	Y	Y	Y	Y	N
6 Moore	Y	N	Y	Y	Y	Y	Y	Y
7 Breaux	Y	N	Y	Y	Y	Y	Y	Y
8 Long	Y	N	Y	Y	Y	Y	Y	?
MAINE								
1 Emery	#	Y	Y	Y	Y	Y	Y	Y
2 Cohen	Y	Y	Y	Y	Y	Y	Y	Y
MARYLAND								
1 Bauman	Y	N	Y	Y	N	Y	Y	N
2 Long	Y	Y	Y	Y	Y	Y	Y	Y
3 Mikulski	Y	Y	Y	Y	Y	Y	Y	Y
4 Holt	Y	N	Y	Y	Y	Y	?	N
5 Spellman	Y	Y	Y	Y	Y	Y	Y	Y
6 Byron	Y	Y	Y	Y	Y	Y	Y	Y
7 Mitchell	Y	Y	Y	Y	Y	Y	Y	Y
8 Steers	Y	Y	Y	Y	Y	Y	Y	Y
MASSACHUSETTS								
1 Conte	?	Y	Y	Y	Y	N	Y	Y
2 Boland	Y	Y	Y	Y	Y	Y	Y	Y
3 Early	Y	Y	Y	Y	Y	Y	Y	Y
4 Drinan	#	#	#	#	#	Y	Y	N
5 Tsongas	#	#	#	#	#	#	#	?
6 Harrington	Y	Y	Y	Y	Y	Y	Y	Y
7 Markey	Y	Y	Y	Y	Y	Y	Y	Y
8 O'Neill								
9 Moakley	Y	Y	Y	Y	Y	Y	Y	Y
10 Heckler	Y	Y	Y	Y	N	Y	Y	Y
11 Burke	Y	N	Y	Y	Y	Y	Y	Y
12 Studds	Y	Y	Y	Y	Y	Y	Y	Y
MICHIGAN								
1 Conyers	#	#	#	#	#	#	#	#
2 Pursell	Y	Y	Y	Y	N	Y	Y	N
3 Brown	#	#	#	#	#	Y	Y	Y
4 Stockman	Y	■	#	#	#	Y	Y	Y
5 Sawyer	Y	Y	Y	Y	Y	Y	Y	Y
6 Carr	Y	Y	Y	Y	Y	Y	Y	N
7 Kildee	Y	Y	Y	Y	Y	Y	Y	Y
8 Traxler	Y	Y	Y	Y	#	Y	Y	Y
9 Vander Jagt	Y	Y	Y	Y	Y	Y	Y	Y
10 Cederberg	Y	Y	Y	Y	Y	Y	Y	Y
11 Ruppe	#	?	?	#	#	Y	Y	Y
12 Bonior	Y	Y	Y	Y	Y	Y	Y	Y
13 Diggs	?	Y	Y	Y	Y	?	?	?
14 Nedzi	Y	Y	Y	Y	Y	Y	Y	Y
15 Ford	Y	Y	Y	Y	Y	?	?	Y
16 Dingell	?	X	?	?	?	Y	Y	Y
17 Brodhead	Y	Y	Y	Y	Y	Y	Y	Y
18 Blanchard	Y	Y	Y	Y	Y	N	Y	N
19 Broomfield	Y	N	Y	Y	Y	Y	Y	Y
MINNESOTA								
1 Quie	Y	N	Y	Y	Y	#	#	#
2 Hagedorn	Y	N	Y	Y	N	Y	Y	Y
3 Frenzel	Y	N	Y	Y	N	N	Y	Y
4 Vento	Y	Y	Y	Y	Y	Y	Y	Y
5 Fraser	Y	Y	Y	Y	Y	Y	Y	Y
6 Nolan	Y	Y	Y	Y	Y	Y	Y	Y
7 Stangeland	Y	N	Y	Y	N	Y	Y	Y
8 Oberstar	Y	N	N	Y	Y	Y	Y	Y
MISSISSIPPI								
1 Whitten	#	#	#	#	#	?	?	■
2 Bowen	?	?	?	?	?	?	?	?
3 Montgomery	Y	?	?	?	?	?	?	?
4 Cochran	?	?	?	?	?	?	?	?
5 Lott	Y	N	Y	Y	Y	Y	Y	N
MISSOURI								
1 Clay	Y	Y	Y	Y	Y	Y	Y	Y
2 Young	Y	N	Y	Y	Y	Y	Y	Y
3 Gephardt	Y	Y	Y	Y	Y	Y	Y	N

	349	350	351	352	353	354	355	356
4 Skelton	Y	N	Y	Y	Y	Y	Y	N
5 Bolling	Y	N	Y	Y	Y	Y	Y	Y
6 Coleman	Y	N	Y	Y	Y	Y	Y	Y
7 Taylor	Y	N	N	Y	Y	Y	Y	N
8 Ichord	Y	N	N	Y	Y	Y	Y	N
9 Volkmer	Y	N	Y	Y	Y	Y	Y	N
10 Burlison	Y	Y	Y	Y	Y	Y	Y	Y
MONTANA								
1 Baucus	#	#	#	#	#	#	#	#
2 Marlenee	Y	N	Y	Y	Y	Y	Y	N
NEBRASKA								
1 Thone	#	?	#	#	#	Y	Y	N
2 Cavanaugh	Y	Y	Y	Y	Y	Y	Y	Y
3 Smith	Y	N	Y	Y	Y	Y	Y	N
NEVADA								
AL Santini	#	#	#	#	#	#	#	#
NEW HAMPSHIRE								
1 D'Amours	Y	N	Y	Y	N	Y	#	Y
2 Cleveland	Y	N	Y	Y	N	Y	Y	Y
NEW JERSEY								
1 Florio	Y	Y	Y	Y	Y	#	#	#
2 Hughes	Y	N	Y	Y	N	Y	Y	Y
3 Howard	#	#	#	#	#	#	#	#
4 Thompson	#	Y	Y	Y	Y	Y	Y	Y
5 Fenwick	Y	Y	Y	Y	N	Y	Y	Y
6 Forsythe	Y	N	Y	Y	Y	Y	Y	Y
7 Maguire	Y	Y	Y	Y	Y	N	Y	Y
8 Roe	#	N	Y	Y	Y	Y	Y	Y
9 Hollenbeck	Y	Y	Y	Y	Y	Y	Y	Y
10 Rodino	#	#	#	#	#	#	#	#
11 Minish	?	?	?	?	?	?	?	?
12 Rinaldo	Y	Y	Y	Y	Y	Y	Y	Y
13 Meyner	Y	Y	Y	Y	Y	Y	Y	Y
14 LeFante	Y	Y	Y	Y	Y	Y	Y	Y
15 Patten	#	#	#	#	#	#	#	#
NEW MEXICO								
1 Lujan	Y	N	Y	Y	Y	N	Y	Y
2 Runnels	#	X	#	#	#	#	#	?
NEW YORK								
1 Pike	#	#	#	#	#	#	#	#
2 Downey	Y	Y	Y	Y	Y	Y	Y	Y
3 Ambro	Y	Y	Y	Y	Y	Y	Y	Y
4 Lent	Y	Y	Y	Y	Y	Y	Y	Y
5 Wydler	Y	Y	Y	Y	Y	Y	Y	N
6 Wolff	Y	Y	Y	#	#	Y	Y	Y
7 Addabbo	Y	Y	Y	#	Y	Y	Y	Y
8 Rosenthal	Y	#	#	#	#	Y	Y	Y
9 Delaney	Y	N	Y	Y	Y	Y	Y	Y
10 Biaggi	#	Y	Y	Y	Y	Y	Y	Y
11 Scheuer	Y	Y	Y	Y	Y	Y	Y	Y
12 Chisholm	Y	Y	#	Y	Y	Y	Y	Y
13 Solarz	Y	Y	Y	Y	Y	Y	Y	Y
14 Richmond	Y	Y	Y	Y	Y	Y	Y	Y
15 Zeferetti	?	✓	?	?	?	Y	Y	Y
16 Holtzman	Y	Y	Y	Y	Y	Y	Y	Y
17 Murphy	#	■	#	#	#	#	#	#
18 Green	Y	Y	Y	Y	Y	Y	Y	Y
19 Rangel	Y	Y	Y	Y	Y	Y	Y	Y
20 Weiss	Y	Y	Y	Y	Y	Y	Y	Y
21 Garcia	Y	Y	Y	Y	Y	Y	Y	Y
22 Bingham	Y	Y	Y	Y	Y	N	Y	Y
23 Caputo	Y	Y	Y	?	?	Y	Y	N
24 Ottinger	Y	Y	Y	Y	Y	Y	Y	N
25 Fish	Y	Y	Y	Y	N	Y	Y	Y
26 Gilman	Y	Y	Y	†	†	Y	Y	Y
27 McHugh	Y	Y	Y	Y	Y	Y	Y	Y
28 Stratton	Y	Y	Y	Y	Y	Y	Y	Y
29 Pattison	Y	✓	Y	Y	Y	Y	Y	Y
30 McEwen	Y	N	N	Y	N	Y	Y	N
31 Mitchell	Y	N	Y	Y	Y	Y	Y	Y
32 Hanley	Y	Y	Y	Y	Y	Y	Y	Y
33 Walsh	Y	N	N	Y	Y	Y	Y	Y
34 Horton	Y	N	Y	Y	Y	Y	Y	Y
35 Conable	Y	N	Y	Y	N	Y	Y	N
36 LaFalce	Y	N	Y	Y	Y	Y	Y	Y
37 Nowak	Y	N	Y	Y	Y	Y	Y	Y
38 Kemp	Y	N	Y	Y	N	Y	Y	N
39 Lundine	Y	Y	Y	Y	Y	Y	Y	N
NORTH CAROLINA								
1 Jones	Y	Y	Y	Y	Y	Y	Y	Y
2 Fountain	Y	N	Y	Y	Y	Y	Y	Y
3 Whitley	Y	Y	Y	Y	Y	Y	Y	Y
4 Andrews	Y	N	Y	Y	Y	Y	Y	Y
5 Neal	Y	?	#	#	#	Y	Y	Y
6 Preyer	Y	Y	Y	Y	Y	Y	Y	Y
7 Rose	#	#	#	#	#	Y	Y	Y
8 Hefner	Y	N	Y	Y	Y	Y	Y	Y

	349	350	351	352	353	354	355	356
9 Martin	#	N	Y	#	Y	Y	Y	Y
10 Broyhill	Y	N	Y	Y	Y	?	?	?
11 Gudger	Y	N	Y	Y	Y	Y	Y	Y
NORTH DAKOTA								
AL Andrews	Y	N	Y	Y	Y	Y	Y	Y
OHIO								
1 Gradison	Y	Y	Y	Y	Y	Y	Y	Y
2 Luken	Y	Y	Y	Y	N	Y	Y	N
3 Whalen	#	#	#	#	N	Y	Y	Y
4 Guyer	Y	N	Y	Y	Y	Y	Y	Y
5 Latta	Y	N	Y	Y	N	Y	Y	N
6 Harsha	Y	N	Y	Y	Y	Y	Y	Y
7 Brown	Y	N	Y	Y	N	Y	Y	N
8 Kindness	?	?	?	?	?	Y	Y	Y
9 Ashley	Y	Y	Y	Y	Y	Y	Y	Y
10 Miller	Y	N	Y	Y	N	Y	Y	N
11 Stanton	Y	Y	Y	Y	Y	Y	Y	Y
12 Devine	Y	N	Y	Y	N	Y	Y	N
13 Pease	Y	Y	Y	Y	Y	Y	Y	N
14 Seiberling	Y	Y	Y	Y	Y	Y	Y	N
15 Wylie	Y	Y	Y	Y	Y	Y	Y	Y
16 Regula	Y	Y	Y	Y	Y	Y	Y	Y
17 Ashbrook	Y	N	Y	Y	N	Y	Y	N
18 Applegate	?	?	?	?	?	?	?	?
19 Carney	#	✓	#	#	#	#	#	?
20 Oakar	?	?	?	?	?	?	?	?
21 Stokes	#	#	#	#	#	#	#	#
22 Vanik	#	Y	Y	Y	Y	Y	Y	Y
23 Mottl	Y	Y	Y	Y	Y	N	Y	N
OKLAHOMA								
1 Jones	Y	N	N	Y	Y	N	Y	N
2 Risenhoover	Y	N	N	Y	Y	Y	Y	Y
3 Watkins	Y	N	N	Y	N	Y	Y	N
4 Steed	Y	N	Y	Y	Y	Y	Y	Y
5 Edwards	Y	N	Y	Y	N	N	Y	N
6 English	Y	Y	Y	Y	Y	Y	Y	Y
OREGON								
1 AuCoin	Y	Y	Y	Y	Y	Y	Y	Y
2 Ullman	#	#	#	#	#	Y	Y	Y
3 Duncan	?	?	?	?	?	?	?	?
4 Weaver	Y	Y	Y	Y	Y	#	#	Y
PENNSYLVANIA								
1 Myers, M.	Y	N	Y	Y	Y	Y	Y	Y
2 Nix	?	?	?	?	?	?	?	?
3 Lederer	Y	N	Y	Y	Y	Y	Y	Y
4 Eilberg	#	#	#	#	#	Y	Y	Y
5 Schulze	Y	N	Y	Y	Y	Y	Y	Y
6 Yatron	Y	Y	Y	Y	Y	Y	Y	Y
7 Edgar	#	Y	Y	Y	Y	Y	Y	Y
8 Kostmayer	Y	Y	Y	Y	Y	Y	Y	Y
9 Shuster	Y	N	N	Y	N	Y	Y	N
10 McDade	Y	Y	Y	Y	#	N	Y	N
11 Flood	Y	Y	Y	Y	Y	Y	#	Y
12 Murtha	Y	Y	Y	Y	Y	Y	Y	Y
13 Coughlin	Y	Y	Y	Y	Y	Y	Y	Y
14 Moorhead	Y	Y	Y	Y	#	Y	Y	Y
15 Rooney	Y	N	Y	Y	Y	Y	Y	Y
16 Walker	Y	N	Y	Y	N	Y	Y	N
17 Ertel	Y	N	Y	Y	Y	Y	Y	Y
18 Walgren	Y	Y	Y	Y	Y	Y	Y	Y
19 Goodling, W.	Y	Y	Y	Y	N	Y	Y	N
20 Gaydos	Y	Y	Y	Y	N	Y	Y	Y
21 Dent	Y	N	Y	Y	N	#	#	#
22 Murphy	Y	Y	Y	Y	Y	Y	Y	Y
23 Ammerman	Y	Y	Y	Y	Y	Y	Y	Y
24 Marks	Y	Y	Y	Y	Y	Y	Y	N
25 Myers, G.	Y	N	Y	Y	#	Y	Y	Y
RHODE ISLAND								
1 St Germain	Y	Y	Y	Y	Y	Y	Y	Y
2 Beard	Y	Y	Y	Y	Y	Y	Y	Y
SOUTH CAROLINA								
1 Davis	?	Y	Y	Y	Y	Y	Y	Y
2 Spence	Y	Y	Y	Y	Y	Y	Y	Y
3 Derrick	Y	Y	Y	Y	Y	Y	Y	N
4 Mann	?	?	?	?	?	Y	Y	Y
5 Holland	#	?	#	#	#	#	#	#
6 Jenrette	#	X	#	#	#	#	#	#
SOUTH DAKOTA								
1 Pressler	†	†	†	?	?	?	?	?
2 Abdnor	Y	N	Y	Y	N	Y	Y	N
TENNESSEE								
1 Quillen	Y	Y	Y	Y	Y	Y	Y	Y
2 Duncan	Y	Y	Y	Y	Y	Y	Y	Y
3 Lloyd	Y	N	N	Y	Y	Y	Y	Y
4 Gore	Y	N	Y	Y	Y	Y	Y	N
5 Allen	?	?	?	?	?	?	?	?
6 Beard	Y	N	Y	Y	Y	Y	Y	N

	349	350	351	352	353	354	355	356
7 Jones	Y	N	N	Y	Y	Y	Y	Y
8 Ford	?	Y	Y	Y	Y	Y	Y	Y
TEXAS								
1 Hall	Y	N	N	Y	N	Y	Y	N
2 Wilson, C.	#	N	Y	Y	Y	Y	Y	Y
3 Collins	Y	N	Y	N	N	N	Y	N
4 Roberts	Y	N	Y	Y	Y	Y	Y	N
5 Mattox	Y	Y	Y	Y	Y	Y	Y	Y
6 Teague	?	X	?	?	?	?	?	?
7 Archer	Y	Y	Y	Y	Y	N	Y	N
8 Eckhardt	Y	Y	Y	Y	Y	Y	Y	Y
9 Brooks	Y	N	Y	Y	Y	Y	Y	Y
10 Pickle	Y	Y	Y	Y	Y	Y	Y	Y
11 Poage	Y	N	N	Y	N	Y	Y	N
12 Wright	Y	N	Y	?	?	Y	Y	Y
13 Hightower	Y	Y	Y	Y	Y	Y	Y	Y
14 Young	?	?	?	?	?	?	?	?
15 de la Garza	?	Y	?	?	?	Y	Y	Y
16 White	Y	Y	Y	Y	Y	Y	Y	Y
17 Burleson	Y	N	N	Y	Y	Y	Y	N
18 Jordan	Y	Y	Y	Y	Y	Y	Y	Y
19 Mahon	Y	Y	Y	Y	Y	Y	Y	Y
20 Gonzalez	Y	Y	Y	Y	Y	Y	Y	Y
21 Krueger	Y	Y	Y	Y	Y	?	?	?
22 Gammage	Y	Y	Y	Y	Y	Y	Y	N
23 Kazen	Y	Y	?	?	?	Y	Y	N
24 Milford	Y	N	N	?	Y	Y	Y	Y
UTAH								
1 McKay	Y	N	Y	Y	Y	Y	Y	Y
2 Marriott	Y	N	Y	Y	Y	Y	Y	Y
VERMONT								
AL Jeffords	#	Y	Y	Y	N	Y	Y	Y
VIRGINIA								
1 Trible	Y	Y	Y	Y	Y	Y	Y	Y
2 Whitehurst	Y	Y	Y	Y	Y	Y	Y	Y
3 Satterfield	Y	N	N	Y	N	Y	Y	N
4 Daniel	Y	N	Y	Y	Y	Y	Y	N
5 Daniel	Y	N	Y	Y	N	Y	Y	Y
6 Butler	Y	N	Y	Y	Y	Y	Y	N
7 Robinson	Y	N	Y	Y	Y	Y	Y	N
8 Harris	Y	Y	Y	Y	Y	Y	Y	Y
9 Wampler	Y	N	Y	Y	Y	Y	Y	Y
10 Fisher	Y	Y	Y	Y	Y	Y	Y	Y
WASHINGTON								
1 Pritchard	#	#	#	#	#	Y	Y	Y
2 Meeds	Y	Y	Y	Y	Y	Y	Y	Y
3 Bonker	#	#	#	#	#	Y	Y	Y
4 McCormack	Y	Y	Y	Y	Y	Y	Y	Y
5 Foley	Y	Y	Y	Y	Y	Y	Y	Y
6 Dicks	Y	Y	Y	Y	Y	Y	Y	Y
7 Cunningham	Y	N	Y	Y	N	Y	Y	N
WEST VIRGINIA								
1 Mollohan	#	#	#	#	#	#	#	■
2 Staggers	Y	Y	Y	Y	Y	Y	Y	Y
3 Slack	Y	Y	Y	Y	Y	Y	Y	Y
4 Rahall	Y	Y	Y	Y	Y	Y	Y	Y
WISCONSIN								
1 Aspin	?	Y	Y	Y	Y	Y	Y	Y
2 Kastenmeier	Y	Y	Y	Y	Y	Y	Y	Y
3 Baldus	Y	N	Y	Y	Y	Y	Y	Y
4 Zablocki	Y	N	Y	Y	Y	Y	Y	Y
5 Reuss	Y	Y	Y	Y	Y	Y	Y	Y
6 Steiger	Y	N	Y	Y	Y	Y	Y	Y
7 Obey	Y	Y	Y	Y	Y	?	Y	Y
8 Cornell	Y	Y	Y	Y	Y	Y	Y	Y
9 Kasten	#	#	#	#	#	Y	Y	Y
WYOMING								
AL Roncalio	Y	Y	Y	Y	Y	Y	Y	Y

Democrats ***Republicans***

357. HR 12240. Intelligence Authorization. Adoption of the rule (H Res 1205) providing for House floor consideration of the bill to authorize fiscal 1979 funds for the activities of various federal intelligence-gathering agencies. Adopted 322-48: R 129-9; D 193-39 (ND 124-37; SD 69-2), June 6, 1978.

358. HR 12240. Intelligence Authorization. Weiss, D-N.Y., amendment to delete the requirement in the bill specifying that the Attorney General notify the House and Senate Intelligence Committees when an alien was admitted to the country who he believed could be excluded by law. Rejected 60-312: R 0-134; D 60-178 (ND 56-108; SD 4-70), June 6, 1978.

359. HR 12240. Intelligence Authorization. Passage of the bill to authorize appropriations of an undisclosed amount for federal government intelligence operations and activities, including the Central Intelligence Agency and various Defense Department agencies, for fiscal 1979. Passed 323-43: R 131-2; D 192-41 (ND 119-40; SD 73-1), June 6, 1978.

360. HR 12426. New York City Aid. Adoption of the rule (H Res 1206) providing for House floor consideration of the bill to authorize up to $2 billion in federal loan guarantees for long-term New York City bonds. Adopted 339-21: R 117-16; D 222-5 (ND 154-0; SD 68-5), June 6, 1978.

KEY

- Y Voted for (yea).
- ✓ Paired for.
- † Announced for.
- # CQ Poll for.
- N Voted against (nay).
- X Paired against.
- \- Announced against.
- ▮ CQ Poll against.
- P Voted "present."
- ● Voted "present" to avoid possible conflict of interest.
- ? Did not vote or otherwise make a position known.

	357	358	359	360
ALABAMA				
1 Edwards	?	N	Y	Y
2 Dickinson	?	N	Y	Y
3 Nichols	#	N	Y	Y
4 Bevill	?	N	Y	Y
5 Flippo	?	N	Y	Y
6 Buchanan	?	N	Y	Y
7 Flowers	?	?	?	?
ALASKA				
AL Young	#	▮	#	#
ARIZONA				
1 Rhodes	Y	N	Y	Y
2 Udall	Y	N	Y	Y
3 Stump	#	▮	#	▮
4 Rudd	Y	N	Y	N
ARKANSAS				
1 Alexander	?	?	?	?
2 Tucker	#	▮	#	#
3 Hammerschmidt	Y	N	Y	Y
4 Thornton	?	Y	Y	Y
CALIFORNIA				
1 Johnson	Y	N	Y	Y
2 Clausen	Y	N	Y	Y
3 Moss	N	Y	N	Y
4 Leggett	?	Y	Y	Y
5 Burton, J.	N	Y	N	Y
6 Burton, P.	N	Y	N	Y
7 Miller	N	Y	N	Y
8 Dellums	#	✓	X	#
9 Stark	N	Y	N	Y
10 Edwards	Y	Y	Y	Y
11 Ryan	#	▮	#	#
12 McCloskey	?	?	?	?
13 Mineta	Y	N	Y	Y
14 McFall	Y	N	Y	Y
15 Sisk	Y	N	Y	Y
16 Panetta	N	N	Y	Y
17 Krebs	N	N	Y	Y
18 Ketchum	Y	N	Y	Y
19 Lagomarsino	Y	N	Y	Y
20 Goldwater	Y	N	Y	Y
21 Corman	Y	Y	Y	Y
22 Moorhead	Y	N	Y	Y
23 Beilenson	▮	#	▮	#
24 Waxman	?	?	#	#
25 Roybal	?	?	?	?
26 Rousselot	Y	N	Y	Y
27 Dornan	?	X	?	?
28 Burke	#	✓	X	#
29 Hawkins	Y	N	Y	Y
30 Danielson	#	▮	#	#
31 Wilson, C.H.	?	?	?	?
32 Anderson	Y	N	Y	Y
33 Clawson	Y	N	Y	N
34 Hannaford	#	▮	#	#
35 Lloyd	Y	N	Y	Y
36 Brown	Y	Y	N	?
37 Pettis	Y	N	Y	Y
38 Patterson	Y	N	Y	Y
39 Wiggins	Y	N	Y	Y
40 Badham	Y	N	Y	Y
41 Wilson, B.	?	?	?	?
42 Van Deerlin	Y	N	Y	Y
43 Burgener	Y	N	Y	Y
COLORADO				
1 Schroeder	N	Y	P	Y
2 Wirth	Y	Y	Y	Y
3 Evans	Y	N	N	?
4 Johnson	N	N	N	?
5 Armstrong	Y	N	Y	Y
CONNECTICUT				
1 Cotter	?	?	✓	?
2 Dodd	Y	Y	Y	Y
3 Giaimo	N	Y	N	Y
4 McKinney	Y	▮	#	#
5 Sarasin	Y	N	Y	Y
6 Moffett	N	Y	N	Y
DELAWARE				
AL Evans	Y	N	Y	Y
FLORIDA				
1 Sikes	Y	N	Y	Y
2 Fuqua	Y	N	Y	Y
3 Bennett	Y	N	Y	Y
4 Chappell	Y	#	#	#
5 Kelly	Y	N	Y	Y
6 Young	Y	N	Y	Y
7 Gibbons	?	?	?	?
8 Ireland	Y	N	Y	Y
9 Frey	Y	N	Y	N
10 Bafalis	Y	N	Y	Y
11 Rogers	Y	N	Y	Y
12 Burke	Y	N	Y	Y
13 Lehman	Y	N	Y	Y
14 Pepper	Y	N	Y	Y
15 Fascell	Y	N	Y	Y
GEORGIA				
1 Ginn	Y	N	Y	Y
2 Mathis	Y	N	Y	Y
3 Brinkley	Y	N	Y	Y
4 Levitas	Y	N	Y	Y
5 Fowler	Y	N	[illegible]	Y
6 Flynt	?	?	?	?
7 McDonald	Y	N	Y	N
8 Evans	Y	N	Y	Y
9 Jenkins	Y	N	Y	Y
10 Barnard	Y	N	Y	Y
HAWAII				
1 Heftel	Y	N	Y	?
2 Akaka	Y	N	Y	Y
IDAHO				
1 Symms	Y	N	Y	N
2 Hansen, G.	Y	N	Y	N
ILLINOIS				
1 Metcalfe	Y	N	N	Y
2 Murphy	Y	N	Y	Y
3 Russo	Y	N	Y	Y
4 Derwinski	Y	N	Y	Y
5 Fary	Y	N	Y	Y
6 Hyde	Y	▮	#	#
7 Collins	Y	Y	?	Y
8 Rostenkowski	Y	N	Y	Y
9 Yates	Y	Y	N	Y
10 Mikva	Y	Y	N	Y
11 Annunzio	Y	N	Y	Y
12 Crane	Y	N	Y	N
13 McClory	Y	N	Y	Y
14 Erlenborn	Y	N	Y	Y
15 Corcoran	Y	N	Y	Y
16 Anderson	Y	N	Y	Y
17 O'Brien	Y	N	Y	Y
18 Michel	Y	N	Y	Y
19 Railsback	Y	N	Y	Y
20 Findley	Y	N	Y	?
21 Madigan	Y	?	Y	Y
22 Shipley	Y	N	Y	Y
23 Price	Y	N	Y	Y
24 Simon	†	?	†	†
INDIANA				
1 Benjamin	Y	N	Y	Y
2 Fithian	Y	N	Y	Y
3 Brademas	Y	N	Y	Y
4 Quayle	N	N	Y	Y
5 Hillis	Y	N	Y	Y
6 Evans	Y	N	Y	Y
7 Myers, J.	Y	N	Y	Y
8 Cornwell	Y	N	Y	Y
9 Hamilton	Y	N	Y	Y
10 Sharp	Y	N	Y	Y
11 Jacobs	Y	N	Y	Y
IOWA				
1 Leach	Y	N	Y	Y
2 Blouin	Y	Y	Y	Y
3 Grassley	Y	N	Y	Y
4 Smith	Y	N	Y	Y
5 Harkin	Y	N	Y	Y
6 Bedell	#	Y	N	Y

Democrats ***Republicans***

	357	358	359	360
KANSAS				
1 Sebelius	Y	N	Y	Y
2 Keys	Y	N	Y	Y
3 Winn	Y	N	Y	Y
4 Glickman	N	N	N	Y
5 Skubitz	Y	N	P	Y
KENTUCKY				
1 Hubbard	?	?	?	?
2 Natcher	Y	N	Y	Y
3 Mazzoli	Y	N	Y	Y
4 Snyder	Y	N	Y	N
5 Carter	Y	N	Y	Y
6 Breckinridge	Y	N	Y	Y
7 Perkins	Y	N	Y	Y
LOUISIANA				
1 Livingston	Y	N	Y	Y
2 Boggs	Y	N	Y	Y
3 Treen	Y	N	Y	Y
4 Waggonner	Y	N	Y	Y
5 Huckaby	Y	N	Y	Y
6 Moore	Y	N	Y	Y
7 Breaux	Y	N	Y	Y
8 Long	Y	N	Y	Y
MAINE				
1 Emery	Y	N	Y	Y
2 Cohen	Y	N	Y	Y
MARYLAND				
1 Bauman	Y	N	Y	N
2 Long	Y	N	Y	Y
3 Mikulski	Y	Y	Y	Y
4 Holt	Y	N	Y	Y
5 Spellman	Y	N	Y	#
6 Byron	Y	N	Y	Y
7 Mitchell	N	Y	N	Y
8 Steers	Y	N	Y	Y
MASSACHUSETTS				
1 Conte	Y	N	Y	Y
2 Boland	Y	N	Y	Y
3 Early	Y	N	Y	Y
4 Drinan	N	Y	N	Y
5 Tsongas	#	?	?	#
6 Harrington	N	Y	N	Y
7 Markey	Y	Y	N	Y
8 O'Neill				
9 Moakley	Y	N	Y	Y
10 Heckler	Y	N	Y	Y
11 Burke	Y	N	Y	Y
12 Studds	N	Y	P	Y
MICHIGAN				
1 Conyers	#	✓	X	#
2 Pursell	N	N	Y	Y
3 Brown	Y	N	Y	Y
4 Stockman	Y	▮	#	#
5 Sawyer	Y	N	Y	Y
6 Carr	N	N	Y	Y
7 Kildee	N	Y	Y	Y
8 Traxler	Y	N	Y	Y
9 Vander Jagt	Y	X	?	?
10 Cederberg	Y	N	Y	Y
11 Ruppe	Y	N	P	Y
12 Bonior	N	Y	N	Y
13 Diggs	?	N	Y	Y
14 Nedzi	Y	N	Y	Y
15 Ford	Y	N	Y	Y
16 Dingell	Y	N	Y	Y
17 Brodhead	N	Y	N	Y
18 Blanchard	Y	N	Y	Y
19 Broomfield	Y	N	Y	Y
MINNESOTA				
1 Quie	#	▮	#	#
2 Hagedorn	Y	N	Y	Y
3 Frenzel	Y	N	Y	Y
4 Vento	Y	N	Y	Y
5 Fraser	Y	Y	Y	#
6 Nolan	N	Y	N	Y
7 Stangeland	Y	N	Y	Y
8 Oberstar	Y	N	Y	Y
MISSISSIPPI				
1 Whitten	#	▮	#	#
2 Bowen	Y	N	Y	Y
3 Montgomery	?	?	?	?
4 Cochran	?	?	?	?
5 Lott	Y	N	Y	Y
MISSOURI				
1 Clay	N	Y	N	Y
2 Young	Y	N	Y	Y
3 Gephardt	Y	N	Y	Y
4 Skelton	Y	N	Y	Y
5 Bolling	Y	N	Y	Y
6 Coleman	Y	N	Y	Y
7 Taylor	Y	N	Y	Y
8 Ichord	Y	N	Y	Y
9 Volkmer	Y	N	Y	Y
10 Burlison	Y	N	Y	Y
MONTANA				
1 Baucus	#	▮	#	#
2 Marlenee	N	N	Y	N
NEBRASKA				
1 Thone	Y	N	Y	Y
2 Cavanaugh	N	Y	N	Y
3 Smith	Y	N	Y	Y
NEVADA				
AL Santini	#	▮	#	#
NEW HAMPSHIRE				
1 D'Amours	Y	N	Y	Y
2 Cleveland	Y	N	Y	Y
NEW JERSEY				
1 Florio	#	#	#	#
2 Hughes	Y	N	Y	Y
3 Howard	#	▮	#	#
4 Thompson	Y	Y	N	Y
5 Fenwick	Y	N	Y	Y
6 Forsythe	Y	N	Y	Y
7 Maguire	N	Y	N	Y
8 Roe	Y	N	Y	Y
9 Hollenbeck	Y	N	Y	Y
10 Rodino	#	▮	#	#
11 Minish	?	?	?	?
12 Rinaldo	Y	N	Y	Y
13 Meyner	Y	N	Y	Y
14 LeFante	Y	N	Y	Y
15 Patten	#	?	#	#
NEW MEXICO				
1 Lujan	Y	N	Y	Y
2 Runnels	#	?	#	#
NEW YORK				
1 Pike	#	▮	#	#
2 Downey	N	Y	N	Y
3 Ambro	Y	N	Y	Y
4 Lent	Y	N	Y	Y
5 Wydler	Y	?	?	?
6 Wolff	Y	N	Y	Y
7 Addabbo	Y	N	Y	Y
8 Rosenthal	N	#	#	#
9 Delaney	Y	N	Y	Y
10 Biaggi	Y	Y	Y	Y
11 Scheuer	N	Y	Y	Y
12 Chisholm	N	Y	N	Y
13 Solarz	Y	N	Y	Y
14 Richmond	N	Y	N	Y
15 Zeferetti	Y	N	Y	Y
16 Holtzman	N	Y	N	Y
17 Murphy	#	▮	#	#
18 Green	Y	N	Y	Y
19 Rangel	N	Y	N	Y
20 Weiss	N	Y	N	Y
21 Garcia	N	Y	N	Y
22 Bingham	Y	N	Y	Y
23 Caputo	Y	N	Y	Y
24 Ottinger	N	Y	N	Y
25 Fish	Y	N	Y	Y
26 Gilman	Y	N	Y	Y
27 McHugh	N	Y	Y	Y
28 Stratton	?	N	Y	Y
29 Pattison	Y	N	N	Y
30 McEwen	Y	N	Y	Y
31 Mitchell	Y	N	Y	Y
32 Hanley	Y	N	Y	Y
33 Walsh	Y	N	Y	Y
34 Horton	Y	N	Y	Y
35 Conable	Y	N	Y	Y
36 LaFalce	Y	N	Y	Y
37 Nowak	Y	N	Y	Y
38 Kemp	Y	N	Y	Y
39 Lundine	Y	Y	N	Y
NORTH CAROLINA				
1 Jones	Y	N	Y	Y
2 Fountain	Y	N	Y	Y
3 Whitley	Y	N	Y	Y
4 Andrews	Y	N	Y	Y
5 Neal	Y	N	Y	Y
6 Preyer	Y	N	Y	Y
7 Rose	Y	N	Y	Y
8 Hefner	Y	N	Y	Y
9 Martin	Y	N	Y	Y
10 Broyhill	Y	N	Y	Y
11 Gudger	Y	N	Y	Y
NORTH DAKOTA				
AL Andrews	Y	N	Y	Y
OHIO				
1 Gradison	Y	N	Y	Y
2 Luken	Y	N	Y	Y
3 Whalen	Y	N	Y	Y
4 Guyer	Y	N	Y	Y
5 Latta	Y	N	Y	Y
6 Harsha	Y	N	Y	Y
7 Brown	Y	N	Y	Y
8 Kindness	Y	N	Y	Y
9 Ashley	Y	N	Y	Y
10 Miller	Y	N	Y	Y
11 Stanton	Y	N	Y	Y
12 Devine	Y	N	Y	N
13 Pease	Y	N	Y	Y
14 Seiberling	Y	Y	P	Y
15 Wylie	Y	N	Y	Y
16 Regula	Y	N	Y	N
17 Ashbrook	Y	N	Y	N
18 Applegate	?	?	?	?
19 Carney	?	X	✓	?
20 Oakar	?	?	?	?
21 Stokes	#	✓	X	#
22 Vanik	Y	Y	#	#
23 Mottl	Y	N	Y	Y
OKLAHOMA				
1 Jones	Y	N	Y	Y
2 Risenhoover	Y	N	Y	Y
3 Watkins	Y	N	Y	Y
4 Steed	Y	N	Y	Y
5 Edwards	N	N	Y	N
6 English	Y	N	Y	Y
OREGON				
1 AuCoin	Y	N	Y	Y
2 Ullman	Y	N	Y	#
3 Duncan	?	?	?	?
4 Weaver	N	Y	N	Y
PENNSYLVANIA				
1 Myers, M.	Y	N	Y	Y
2 Nix	Y	N	Y	?
3 Lederer	Y	N	Y	Y
4 Eilberg	Y	X	✓	#
5 Schulze	Y	N	Y	Y
6 Yatron	Y	N	Y	Y
7 Edgar	N	Y	N	Y
8 Kostmayer	N	Y	N	Y
9 Shuster	Y	N	Y	Y
10 McDade	Y	N	Y	Y
11 Flood	Y	N	Y	Y
12 Murtha	Y	N	Y	Y
13 Coughlin	N	N	Y	Y
14 Moorhead	Y	N	Y	Y
15 Rooney	Y	N	Y	Y
16 Walker	N	N	Y	Y
17 Ertel	Y	N	Y	Y
18 Walgren	Y	Y	Y	?
19 Goodling, W.	Y	N	Y	Y
20 Gaydos	Y	N	Y	Y
21 Dent	#	▮	#	#
22 Murphy	Y	N	Y	Y
23 Ammerman	Y	N	Y	Y
24 Marks	Y	N	Y	Y
25 Myers, G.	Y	N	Y	Y
RHODE ISLAND				
1 St Germain	Y	N	Y	Y
2 Beard	Y	N	Y	Y
SOUTH CAROLINA				
1 Davis	Y	N	Y	Y
2 Spence	Y	N	Y	Y
3 Derrick	Y	N	Y	Y
4 Mann	Y	N	Y	Y
5 Holland	#	▮	#	#
6 Jenrette	#	▮	✓	#
SOUTH DAKOTA				
1 Pressler	?	?	?	?
2 Abdnor	Y	N	Y	Y
TENNESSEE				
1 Quillen	Y	N	Y	Y
2 Duncan	Y	N	Y	Y
3 Lloyd	Y	N	Y	Y
4 Gore	Y	N	Y	Y
5 Allen	?	?	?	?
6 Beard	Y	N	Y	Y
7 Jones	Y	N	Y	Y
8 Ford	N	N	Y	Y
TEXAS				
1 Hall	Y	N	Y	Y
2 Wilson, C.	Y	▮	#	Y
3 Collins	Y	N	Y	N
4 Roberts	Y	N	Y	N
5 Mattox	Y	N	Y	Y
6 Teague	?	?	?	?
7 Archer	Y	N	Y	N
8 Eckhardt	Y	Y	Y	Y
9 Brooks	Y	N	Y	Y
10 Pickle	Y	N	Y	Y
11 Poage	Y	N	Y	N
12 Wright	Y	N	Y	Y
13 Hightower	Y	N	Y	Y
14 Young	?	?	?	?
15 de la Garza	Y	N	Y	Y
16 White	Y	N	Y	Y
17 Burleson	Y	N	Y	N
18 Jordan	Y	N	Y	Y
19 Mahon	Y	N	Y	Y
20 Gonzalez	N	Y	N	Y
21 Krueger	?	?	?	?
22 Gammage	Y	N	Y	N
23 Kazen	Y	N	Y	Y
24 Milford	Y	N	Y	?
UTAH				
1 McKay	Y	N	Y	Y
2 Marriott	Y	N	Y	Y
VERMONT				
AL Jeffords	N	N	N	Y
VIRGINIA				
1 Trible	Y	N	Y	Y
2 Whitehurst	Y	N	Y	Y
3 Satterfield	Y	N	Y	Y
4 Daniel	Y	N	Y	Y
5 Daniel	?	N	Y	Y
6 Butler	Y	N	Y	Y
7 Robinson	Y	N	Y	Y
8 Harris	Y	Y	Y	?
9 Wampler	Y	N	Y	Y
10 Fisher	Y	N	Y	Y
WASHINGTON				
1 Pritchard	Y	N	Y	Y
2 Meeds	Y	N	Y	Y
3 Bonker	Y	N	Y	Y
4 McCormack	Y	N	Y	Y
5 Foley	Y	N	Y	Y
6 Dicks	Y	N	Y	Y
7 Cunningham	Y	N	Y	N
WEST VIRGINIA				
1 Mollohan	#	▮	#	#
2 Staggers	Y	N	Y	Y
3 Slack	Y	N	Y	Y
4 Rahall	Y	N	Y	Y
WISCONSIN				
1 Aspin	Y	N	Y	Y
2 Kastenmeier	Y	Y	N	Y
3 Baldus	Y	N	Y	Y
4 Zablocki	Y	N	Y	Y
5 Reuss	Y	Y	Y	Y
6 Steiger	Y	N	Y	Y
7 Obey	N	Y	N	Y
8 Cornell	Y	Y	Y	Y
9 Kasten	Y	N	Y	Y
WYOMING				
AL Roncalio	Y	N	Y	?

Democrats ***Republicans***

361. Procedural Motion. Wydler, R-N.Y., motion to approve the House *Journal* of Tuesday, June 6, 1978. Motion agreed to 331-15: R 117-10; D 214-5 (ND 145-3; SD 69-2), June 7, 1978.

362. H Con Res 561. Printing of Capitol Brochure. Adoption of the concurrent resolution to authorize the printing of two million copies of a visitors' information brochure, "The United States Capitol." Adopted 349-24: R 124-11; D 225-13 (ND 158-7; SD 67-6), June 7, 1978.

363. S Con Res 89. Printing of "Korean Influence Inquiry." Adoption of the concurrent resolution to authorize the printing of 2,000 copies of Vol. II of *Korean Influence Inquiry*. Adopted 329-50: R 105-31; D 224-19 (ND 155-13; SD 69-6), June 7, 1978.

364. HR 12930. Treasury, Postal Service and General Government Appropriations, Fiscal 1979. Adoption of the rule (H Res 1218) providing for House floor consideration of the bill to appropriate $8,634,300,000 for fiscal 1979 operations of the Treasury Department, Postal Service, Executive Office of the President and certain independent agencies. Adopted 376-1: R 135-0; D 241-1 (ND 168-1; SD 73-0), June 7, 1978.

365. HR 12930. Treasury, Postal Service and General Government Appropriations, Fiscal 1979. McClory, R-Ill., amendment to restore $4.2 million requested for the operation of the Bureau of Alcohol, Tobacco and Firearms and to delete language barring use of funds in the bill to carry out proposed firearms regulations. Rejected 80-314: R 10-128; D 70-186 (ND 64-112; SD 6-74), June 7, 1978.

366. HR 12930. Treasury, Postal Service and General Government Appropriations, Fiscal 1979. Passage of the bill to appropriate $8,634,300,000 for fiscal 1979 operations of the Treasury Department, Postal Service, Executive Office of the President and certain independent agencies. Passed 297-98: R 95-44; D 202-54 (ND 134-42; SD 68-12), June 7, 1978. The president had requested $8,663,161,000.

367. HR 12929. Labor-HEW Appropriations, Fiscal 1979. Symms, D-Idaho, amendment to reduce the fiscal 1979 funding for the Occupational Safety and Health Administration by $28.4 million, from $167,474,000 to $139,070,000 — the fiscal 1978 spending level. Adopted 201-179: R 102-34; D 99-145 (ND 39-130; SD 60-15), June 7, 1978.

KEY

- Y Voted for (yea).
- ✓ Paired for.
- † Announced for.
- # CQ Poll for.
- N Voted against (nay).
- X Paired against.
- \- Announced against.
- ▮ CQ Poll against.
- P Voted "present."
- ● Voted "present" to avoid possible conflict of interest.
- ? Did not vote or otherwise make a position known.

	361	362	363	364	365	366	367
ALABAMA							
1 Edwards	Y	Y	Y	Y	N	Y	Y
2 Dickinson	Y	Y	Y	Y	N	N	Y
3 Nichols	Y	Y	Y	Y	N	Y	Y
4 Bevill	Y	Y	Y	Y	N	Y	Y
5 Flippo	Y	Y	Y	Y	N	Y	Y
6 Buchanan	Y	Y	Y	Y	N	Y	N
7 Flowers	?	?	?	?	?	?	?
ALASKA							
AL Young	#	Y	Y	Y	▮	Y	Y
ARIZONA							
1 Rhodes	Y	Y	Y	Y	N	Y	Y
2 Udall	Y	Y	Y	Y	N	Y	N
3 Stump	#	▮	▮	#	▮	X	#
4 Rudd	Y	Y	N	Y	N	N	Y
ARKANSAS							
1 Alexander	Y	Y	Y	Y	N	N	?
2 Tucker	#	#	#	#	▮	#	▮
3 Hammerschmidt	Y	Y	Y	Y	N	Y	Y
4 Thornton	Y	?	?	Y	N	Y	Y
CALIFORNIA							
1 Johnson	Y	Y	Y	Y	N	Y	N
2 Clausen	Y	Y	Y	Y	N	Y	Y
3 Moss	Y	Y	Y	Y	Y	Y	?
4 Leggett	Y	Y	?	?	Y	Y	?
5 Burton, J.	?	Y	Y	Y	N	N	N
6 Burton, P.	Y	Y	Y	Y	Y	N	N
7 Miller	Y	Y	Y	Y	Y	N	N
8 Dellums	#	#	#	#	✓	X	N
9 Stark	#	#	#	#	Y	N	N
10 Edwards	Y	Y	Y	Y	Y	N	N
11 Ryan	#	Y	Y	Y	Y	Y	Y
12 McCloskey	?	?	?	?	?	?	Y
13 Mineta	Y	Y	Y	Y	Y	Y	N
14 McFall	Y	Y	Y	Y	N	Y	N
15 Sisk	Y	Y	Y	Y	N	Y	?
16 Panetta	Y	Y	Y	Y	N	N	Y
17 Krebs	Y	Y	Y	Y	N	Y	Y
18 Ketchum	Y	Y	Y	Y	N	Y	Y
19 Lagomarsino	Y	Y	Y	Y	N	Y	Y
20 Goldwater	Y	Y	Y	Y	N	N	Y
21 Corman	Y	Y	Y	Y	Y	Y	N
22 Moorhead	Y	Y	Y	Y	N	Y	Y
23 Beilenson	#	#	#	#	#	▮	▮
24 Waxman	#	#	#	#	✓	#	▮
25 Roybal	Y	Y	Y	Y	N	Y	N
26 Rousselot	Y	Y	Y	Y	N	N	?
27 Dornan	?	?	?	?	N	Y	Y
28 Burke	#	#	#	#	✓	X	X
29 Hawkins	Y	Y	Y	Y	Y	Y	N
30 Danielson	#	#	#	#	#	#	N
31 Wilson, C.H.	?	?	?	?	?	?	?
32 Anderson	Y	Y	Y	Y	N	Y	N
33 Clawson	Y	Y	N	Y	N	Y	Y
34 Hannaford	#	Y	Y	Y	N	Y	N
35 Lloyd	N	Y	N	Y	N	Y	Y
36 Brown	Y	Y	Y	Y	N	Y	?
37 Pettis	Y	Y	N	Y	N	Y	Y
38 Patterson	Y	Y	Y	Y	N	Y	N
39 Wiggins	#	Y	Y	Y	Y	Y	#
40 Badham	Y	Y	Y	Y	N	N	Y
41 Wilson, B.	N	Y	N	Y	N	Y	Y
42 Van Deerlin	Y	Y	Y	Y	Y	Y	N
43 Burgener	Y	Y	Y	Y	N	Y	Y
COLORADO							
1 Schroeder	Y	N	Y	Y	Y	N	N
2 Wirth	Y	Y	N	Y	N	Y	N
3 Evans	Y	Y	Y	Y	Y	Y	?
4 Johnson	Y	Y	Y	?	N	Y	Y
5 Armstrong	Y	Y	Y	Y	N	Y	Y
CONNECTICUT							
1 Cotter	Y	Y	Y	Y	N	Y	Y
2 Dodd	?	Y	Y	Y	Y	N	N
3 Giaimo	?	?	Y	Y	N	Y	Y
4 McKinney	#	#	#	#	▮	#	▮
5 Sarasin	N	Y	Y	Y	N	Y	N
6 Moffett	Y	Y	Y	Y	Y	N	N
DELAWARE							
AL Evans	Y	Y	Y	Y	N	Y	Y
FLORIDA							
1 Sikes	Y	Y	Y	Y	N	Y	Y
2 Fuqua	Y	Y	Y	Y	N	Y	Y
3 Bennett	Y	N	Y	Y	N	N	Y
4 Chappell	#	Y	Y	Y	N	Y	✓
5 Kelly	Y	N	N	Y	N	N	Y
6 Young	Y	Y	N	Y	N	Y	Y
7 Gibbons	?	?	?	?	?	?	?
8 Ireland	Y	Y	?	Y	N	Y	Y
9 Frey	Y	Y	Y	Y	N	Y	Y
10 Bafalis	Y	Y	Y	Y	N	Y	Y
11 Rogers	Y	Y	Y	Y	N	Y	Y
12 Burke	Y	Y	Y	Y	N	Y	Y
13 Lehman	Y	Y	Y	Y	Y	N	N
14 Pepper	#	Y	Y	Y	N	Y	N
15 Fascell	Y	Y	Y	Y	Y	N	#
GEORGIA							
1 Ginn	Y	Y	Y	Y	N	Y	Y
2 Mathis	?	Y	Y	?	N	Y	Y
3 Brinkley	Y	Y	Y	Y	N	Y	Y
4 Levitas	Y	Y	Y	Y	N	Y	Y
5 Fowler	Y	Y	Y	Y	N	Y	Y
6 Flynt	Y	Y	Y	Y	N	Y	?
7 McDonald	#	N	N	Y	N	N	Y
8 Evans	Y	Y	N	Y	N	Y	Y
9 Jenkins	Y	Y	Y	Y	N	Y	Y
10 Barnard	Y	Y	Y	Y	N	Y	Y
HAWAII							
1 Heftel	Y	Y	Y	Y	Y	Y	Y
2 Akaka	Y	Y	Y	Y	N	Y	N
IDAHO							
1 Symms	Y	Y	N	Y	N	N	Y
2 Hansen, G.	Y	N	N	Y	N	N	Y
ILLINOIS							
1 Metcalfe	Y	Y	Y	Y	Y	N	N
2 Murphy	#	Y	Y	Y	Y	Y	Y
3 Russo	Y	Y	Y	Y	Y	N	Y
4 Derwinski	Y	Y	Y	Y	Y	Y	Y
5 Fary	Y	Y	Y	Y	N	Y	Y
6 Hyde	#	#	#	#	N	Y	Y
7 Collins	?	?	Y	Y	Y	Y	N
8 Rostenkowski	Y	Y	Y	Y	Y	Y	Y
9 Yates	Y	Y	Y	Y	Y	Y	N
. 10 Mikva	Y	Y	Y	Y	Y	N	N
11 Annunzio	Y	Y	Y	Y	N	Y	N
12 Crane	Y	Y	N	Y	N	N	Y
13 McClory	Y	Y	Y	Y	Y	N	Y
14 Erlenborn	Y	Y	Y	Y	Y	Y	N
15 Corcoran	Y	Y	Y	Y	N	Y	Y
16 Anderson	#	Y	Y	Y	Y	Y	N
17 O'Brien	Y	Y	Y	Y	N	Y	Y
18 Michel	Y	Y	Y	Y	N	Y	Y
19 Railsback	Y	Y	Y	Y	N	Y	N
20 Findley	Y	Y	Y	Y	N	Y	Y
21 Madigan	Y	Y	N	Y	N	Y	Y
22 Shipley	Y	Y	Y	Y	N	Y	N
23 Price	Y	Y	Y	Y	N	Y	▮
24 Simon	†	†	†	†	?	✓	?
INDIANA							
1 Benjamin	Y	Y	Y	Y	N	Y	N
2 Fithian	Y	Y	Y	Y	N	Y	Y
3 Brademas	Y	Y	Y	Y	Y	Y	N
4 Quayle	N	Y	N	Y	N	N	Y
5 Hillis	Y	N	N	Y	N	N	N
6 Evans	Y	N	N	Y	N	N	Y
7 Myers, J.	Y	Y	N	Y	N	N	Y
8 Cornwell	Y	Y	N	Y	N	Y	Y
9 Hamilton	?	?	?	?	X	Y	N
10 Sharp	Y	Y	N	Y	N	Y	N
11 Jacobs	N	Y	Y	#	N	N	Y
IOWA							
1 Leach	Y	Y	Y	Y	N	N	Y
2 Blouin	Y	Y	Y	?	N	N	Y
3 Grassley	Y	Y	N	Y	N	N	Y
4 Smith	Y	Y	Y	Y	N	Y	N
5 Harkin	#	Y	Y	Y	N	N	Y
6 Bedell	#	Y	Y	Y	N	Y	Y

Democrats ***Republicans***

	361	362	363	364	365	366	367
KANSAS							
1 Sebelius	Y	Y	N	Y	N	N	Y
2 Keys	Y	Y	Y	Y	N	N	N
3 Winn	Y	Y	N	Y	N	Y	Y
4 Glickman	Y	N	N	?	N	N	Y
5 Skubitz	P	Y	N	Y	N	Y	Y
KENTUCKY							
1 Hubbard	?	?	?	?	?	?	?
2 Natcher	Y	Y	Y	Y	N	Y	N
3 Mazzoli	Y	Y	Y	Y	Y	Y	N
4 Snyder	Y	Y	N	Y	N	Y	Y
5 Carter	Y	Y	Y	Y	N	Y	N
6 Breckinridge	Y	Y	Y	Y	N	Y	N
7 Perkins	Y	Y	Y	Y	N	Y	N
LOUISIANA							
1 Livingston	?	?	Y	Y	N	N	Y
2 Boggs	Y	Y	Y	Y	N	Y	N
3 Treen	Y	N	Y	Y	N	N	Y
4 Waggonner	Y	Y	Y	Y	N	Y	Y
5 Huckaby	Y	Y	Y	Y	N	Y	Y
6 Moore	Y	Y	Y	Y	N	N	Y
7 Breaux	Y	Y	Y	Y	N	Y	Y
8 Long	Y	Y	Y	Y	N	Y	Y
MAINE							
1 Emery	Y	Y	Y	Y	N	Y	Y
2 Cohen	Y	Y	Y	Y	N	Y	Y
MARYLAND							
1 Bauman	Y	Y	N	Y	N	N	Y
2 Long	Y	Y	Y	Y	N	Y	N
3 Mikulski	Y	Y	Y	Y	N	Y	N
4 Holt	?	?	?	?	N	Y	Y
5 Spellman	Y	Y	Y	Y	N	Y	N
6 Byron	?	Y	Y	Y	N	Y	Y
7 Mitchell	N	Y	Y	Y	Y	Y	N
8 Steers	Y	Y	Y	Y	Y	Y	N
MASSACHUSETTS							
1 Conte	Y	Y	Y	Y	N	Y	N
2 Boland	Y	Y	Y	Y	N	Y	N
3 Early	Y	Y	Y	Y	N	Y	N
4 Drinan	Y	Y	Y	Y	Y	Y	N
5 Tsongas	Y	Y	Y	Y	Y	Y	▮
6 Harrington	P	Y	Y	Y	Y	#	▮
7 Markey	Y	Y	Y	Y	Y	Y	N
8 O'Neill							
9 Moakley	Y	Y	Y	Y	Y	Y	N
10 Heckler	#	#	#	#	?	?	N
11 Burke	Y	Y	Y	Y	N	Y	N
12 Studds	Y	Y	Y	Y	Y	Y	N
MICHIGAN							
1 Conyers	#	Y	Y	Y	Y	N	N
2 Pursell	Y	Y	Y	Y	N	N	N
3 Brown	N	Y	Y	Y	N	Y	N
4 Stockman	Y	Y	Y	Y	N	N	#
5 Sawyer	Y	Y	Y	Y	N	N	Y
6 Carr	Y	N	N	Y	N	N	N
7 Kildee	Y	Y	Y	Y	N	Y	N
8 Traxler	Y	Y	Y	Y	N	N	N
9 Vander Jagt	?	?	?	?	N	Y	Y
10 Cederberg	Y	Y	Y	Y	N	Y	N
11 Ruppe	Y	Y	Y	Y	N	Y	?
12 Bonior	Y	Y	Y	Y	Y	N	N
13 Diggs	?	?	Y	Y	Y	X	X
14 Nedzi	Y	Y	Y	Y	?	?	?
15 Ford	Y	Y	Y	Y	N	Y	N
16 Dingell	?	Y	N	Y	N	Y	N
17 Brodhead	Y	Y	Y	Y	Y	N	N
18 Blanchard	Y	Y	Y	Y	N	N	N
19 Broomfield	Y	Y	N	Y	N	Y	Y
MINNESOTA							
1 Quie	#	#	#	#	▮	#	#
2 Hagedorn	Y	Y	N	Y	N	N	Y
3 Frenzel	Y	Y	Y	Y	N	N	N
4 Vento	Y	Y	Y	Y	N	Y	N
5 Fraser	#	#	#	#	Y	Y	N
6 Nolan	Y	Y	Y	Y	Y	N	N
7 Stangeland	Y	Y	N	Y	N	N	Y
8 Oberstar	Y	Y	Y	Y	N	Y	N
MISSISSIPPI							
1 Whitten	#	#	#	#	▮	#	Y
2 Bowen	Y	Y	Y	Y	N	Y	Y
3 Montgomery	?	?	?	?	N	Y	Y
4 Cochran	?	?	?	?	?	?	?
5 Lott	Y	Y	Y	Y	N	N	Y
MISSOURI							
1 Clay	Y	Y	Y	Y	Y	N	N
2 Young	Y	Y	#	Y	N	Y	N
3 Gephardt	?	Y	N	Y	N	N	Y
4 Skelton	Y	Y	Y	Y	N	Y	N
5 Bolling	#	#	#	Y	Y	Y	N
6 Coleman	Y	Y	Y	Y	N	Y	Y
7 Taylor	Y	Y	N	Y	N	Y	Y
8 Ichord	Y	Y	Y	Y	N	Y	Y
9 Volkmer	Y	Y	N	Y	N	Y	Y
10 Burlison	Y	Y	Y	Y	N	Y	N
MONTANA							
1 Baucus	#	#	#	#	▮	#	Y
2 Marlenee	Y	Y	Y	Y	N	Y	Y
NEBRASKA							
1 Thone	Y	Y	Y	Y	N	Y	Y
2 Cavanaugh	Y	Y	Y	Y	N	N	Y
3 Smith	Y	Y	Y	Y	N	Y	Y
NEVADA							
AL Santini	#	Y	Y	Y	N	Y	✓
NEW HAMPSHIRE							
1 D'Amours	Y	N	Y	Y	N	Y	Y
2 Cleveland	Y	Y	Y	Y	N	Y	Y
NEW JERSEY							
1 Florio	Y	Y	Y	Y	N	Y	N
2 Hughes	Y	Y	Y	Y	N	N	Y
3 Howard	#	#	#	#	▮	✓	▮
4 Thompson	Y	Y	Y	Y	Y	Y	N
5 Fenwick	Y	Y	Y	Y	Y	N	N
6 Forsythe	N	Y	Y	Y	N	N	Y
7 Maguire	Y	Y	Y	Y	Y	N	N
8 Roe	Y	Y	Y	Y	N	Y	N
9 Hollenbeck	Y	Y	Y	Y	N	Y	N
10 Rodino	#	#	#	#	#	#	▮
11 Minish	?	?	?	?	?	?	?
12 Rinaldo	Y	Y	Y	Y	N	N	N
13 Meyner	Y	Y	Y	Y	N	Y	N
14 LeFante	Y	Y	Y	Y	N	Y	N
15 Patten	#	Y	Y	Y	N	Y	N
NEW MEXICO							
1 Lujan	Y	Y	N	Y	N	Y	Y
2 Runnels	#	#	?	#	?	?	✓
NEW YORK							
1 Pike	#	#	#	#	▮	#	#
2 Downey	Y	Y	Y	Y	Y	Y	N
3 Ambro	?	?	Y	Y	N	Y	N
4 Lent	Y	Y	Y	Y	N	Y	Y
5 Wydler	Y	N	N	Y	N	Y	N
6 Wolff	Y	Y	Y	Y	Y	Y	Y
7 Addabbo	Y	Y	Y	Y	Y	Y	N
8 Rosenthal	Y	Y	Y	Y	Y	N	N
9 Delaney	Y	Y	Y	Y	Y	Y	N
10 Biaggi	#	#	#	#	N	Y	N
11 Scheuer	Y	Y	Y	Y	Y	Y	N
12 Chisholm	Y	Y	Y	Y	Y	Y	N
13 Solarz	Y	Y	Y	Y	Y	Y	N
14 Richmond	Y	Y	Y	Y	Y	N	N
15 Zeferetti	Y	Y	Y	Y	N	Y	N
16 Holtzman	Y	Y	Y	Y	Y	N	N
17 Murphy	#	#	#	#	▮	✓	X
18 Green	Y	Y	Y	Y	Y	Y	N
19 Rangel	Y	Y	Y	Y	Y	Y	N
20 Weiss	Y	Y	Y	Y	Y	N	N
21 Garcia	Y	Y	Y	Y	Y	N	N
22 Bingham	Y	Y	Y	Y	Y	Y	N
23 Caputo	Y	Y	Y	Y	N	Y	N
24 Ottinger	Y	Y	Y	N	Y	Y	N
25 Fish	Y	Y	Y	Y	N	Y	N
26 Gilman	†	†	†	†	-	†	N
27 McHugh	Y	Y	Y	Y	N	Y	N
28 Stratton	Y	Y	Y	Y	N	Y	Y
29 Pattison	Y	Y	Y	Y	N	Y	N
30 McEwen	P	Y	Y	Y	N	Y	Y
31 Mitchell	Y	Y	Y	Y	N	Y	Y
32 Hanley	Y	Y	Y	Y	N	Y	Y
33 Walsh	Y	Y	Y	Y	N	Y	Y
34 Horton	Y	Y	Y	Y	N	Y	N
35 Conable	Y	Y	Y	Y	?	?	?
36 LaFalce	Y	Y	Y	Y	N	Y	Y
37 Nowak	Y	Y	Y	Y	N	Y	N
38 Kemp	Y	Y	Y	Y	N	N	Y
39 Lundine	#	Y	Y	Y	N	Y	N
NORTH CAROLINA							
1 Jones	Y	Y	Y	Y	N	Y	Y
2 Fountain	#	#	#	#	N	N	Y
3 Whitley	Y	Y	Y	Y	N	Y	Y
4 Andrews	#	?	#	#	N	Y	Y
5 Neal	Y	N	Y	Y	N	N	Y
6 Preyer	Y	Y	Y	Y	N	Y	Y
7 Rose	Y	Y	Y	Y	N	Y	Y
8 Hefner	#	Y	Y	Y	N	Y	Y
9 Martin	Y	Y	N	Y	N	N	Y
10 Broyhill	Y	N	Y	Y	N	N	Y
11 Gudger	Y	Y	Y	Y	N	N	Y
NORTH DAKOTA							
AL Andrews	Y	Y	Y	Y	N	Y	Y
OHIO							
1 Gradison	Y	Y	Y	Y	N	Y	N
2 Luken	Y	Y	Y	Y	N	N	Y
3 Whalen	Y	Y	Y	Y	Y	Y	N
4 Guyer	Y	Y	Y	Y	N	Y	Y
5 Latta	Y	Y	Y	Y	N	Y	Y
6 Harsha	Y	Y	Y	Y	N	Y	Y
7 Brown	Y	Y	Y	Y	N	Y	Y
8 Kindness	Y	Y	Y	Y	N	Y	Y
9 Ashley	Y	Y	Y	Y	Y	Y	N
10 Miller	Y	Y	Y	Y	N	N	Y
11 Stanton	Y	Y	Y	Y	N	Y	N
12 Devine	Y	Y	Y	Y	N	Y	Y
13 Pease	Y	Y	N	Y	N	N	N
14 Seiberling	Y	Y	Y	Y	Y	Y	N
15 Wylie	Y	Y	Y	Y	N	Y	N
16 Regula	Y	Y	Y	Y	N	Y	N
17 Ashbrook	Y	Y	Y	Y	N	Y	Y
18 Applegate	?	?	?	?	?	?	?
19 Carney	?	?	?	?	X	✓	X
20 Oakar	?	?	?	?	?	Y	N
21 Stokes	Y	Y	Y	Y	Y	N	N
22 Vanik	#	#	#	#	Y	Y	N
23 Mottl	Y	N	N	Y	N	N	N
OKLAHOMA							
1 Jones	Y	Y	N	Y	N	Y	Y
2 Risenhoover	Y	Y	Y	Y	N	Y	Y
3 Watkins	Y	#	Y	Y	N	Y	Y
4 Steed	Y	Y	Y	Y	N	Y	N
5 Edwards	?	N	Y	Y	N	Y	Y
6 English	Y	Y	Y	Y	N	Y	Y
OREGON							
1 AuCoin	Y	Y	Y	Y	N	N	N
2 Ullman	Y	Y	Y	Y	N	Y	N
3 Duncan	?	?	Y	Y	N	Y	Y
4 Weaver	Y	Y	Y	Y	N	Y	Y
PENNSYLVANIA							
1 Myers, M.	Y	Y	Y	Y	N	Y	N
2 Nix	?	Y	Y	Y	N	Y	?
3 Lederer	Y	Y	Y	Y	N	Y	N
4 Eilberg	Y	Y	Y	Y	N	Y	N
5 Schulze	Y	Y	Y	Y	N	Y	Y
6 Yatron	Y	Y	Y	Y	N	Y	Y
7 Edgar	Y	Y	Y	Y	Y	Y	N
8 Kostmayer	Y	N	N	Y	N	N	N
9 Shuster	Y	Y	N	Y	N	N	Y
10 McDade	Y	Y	Y	Y	N	Y	N
11 Flood	Y	Y	Y	Y	N	Y	N
12 Murtha	Y	Y	Y	Y	N	Y	N
13 Coughlin	N	Y	Y	Y	N	N	N
14 Moorhead	Y	Y	Y	Y	N	Y	N
15 Rooney	Y	Y	Y	Y	N	Y	N
16 Walker	N	Y	Y	Y	N	N	Y
17 Ertel	Y	Y	Y	Y	N	Y	Y
18 Walgren	Y	Y	Y	Y	N	Y	Y
19 Goodling, W.	N	N	N	Y	N	N	Y
20 Gaydos	?	Y	Y	Y	N	Y	N
21 Dent	#	#	#	#	▮	#	▮
22 Murphy	Y	?	Y	Y	N	Y	N
23 Ammerman	Y	Y	Y	Y	N	Y	N
24 Marks	Y	Y	Y	Y	N	Y	N
25 Myers, G.	Y	N	Y	Y	N	N	▮
RHODE ISLAND							
1 St Germain	Y	Y	Y	Y	Y	Y	N
2 Beard	Y	Y	Y	Y	Y	Y	N
SOUTH CAROLINA							
1 Davis	Y	Y	Y	?	N	Y	N
2 Spence	Y	Y	Y	Y	N	Y	Y
3 Derrick	Y	N	N	Y	N	Y	Y
4 Mann	Y	Y	Y	Y	N	Y	Y
5 Holland	N	Y	Y	Y	N	Y	Y
6 Jenrette	Y	Y	Y	Y	N	Y	Y
SOUTH DAKOTA							
1 Pressler	?	?	?	?	?	?	?
2 Abdnor	N	Y	Y	Y	N	Y	Y
TENNESSEE							
1 Quillen	Y	Y	Y	Y	N	Y	Y
2 Duncan	Y	Y	Y	Y	N	Y	Y
3 Lloyd	Y	Y	N	Y	N	N	Y
4 Gore	Y	N	Y	Y	N	Y	N
5 Allen	?	?	?	?	?	?	?
6 Beard	?	Y	N	Y	N	N	Y
7 Jones	Y	Y	Y	Y	N	Y	Y
8 Ford	Y	Y	Y	Y	N	Y	N
TEXAS							
1 Hall	Y	Y	Y	Y	N	N	Y
2 Wilson, C.	Y	N	Y	Y	▮	#	#
3 Collins	Y	N	N	Y	N	N	Y
4 Roberts	Y	Y	Y	Y	N	Y	?
5 Mattox	N	Y	Y	?	N	N	N
6 Teague	?	?	?	?	?	?	✓
7 Archer	?	Y	Y	Y	N	N	Y
8 Eckhardt	Y	Y	Y	Y	N	Y	?
9 Brooks	Y	Y	Y	Y	N	Y	Y
10 Pickle	Y	Y	Y	Y	N	Y	Y
11 Poage	Y	Y	Y	Y	N	Y	Y
12 Wright	Y	?	Y	Y	N	Y	Y
13 Hightower	Y	Y	N	Y	N	Y	Y
14 Young	?	?	?	?	?	?	?
15 de la Garza	Y	?	Y	Y	N	Y	Y
16 White	Y	Y	Y	Y	N	Y	Y
17 Burleson	Y	Y	Y	Y	N	Y	Y
18 Jordan	Y	Y	Y	Y	Y	Y	N
19 Mahon	Y	Y	Y	Y	N	Y	Y
20 Gonzalez	Y	Y	Y	Y	Y	Y	N
21 Krueger	?	?	#	#	X	#	#
22 Gammage	Y	Y	Y	Y	N	N	Y
23 Kazen	Y	Y	Y	Y	N	Y	Y
24 Milford	?	?	?	Y	N	Y	Y
UTAH							
1 McKay	Y	Y	Y	Y	N	Y	Y
2 Marriott	Y	Y	Y	Y	N	Y	Y
VERMONT							
AL Jeffords	Y	Y	N	Y	N	Y	N
VIRGINIA							
1 Trible	Y	Y	Y	Y	N	Y	?
2 Whitehurst	Y	Y	Y	Y	N	Y	Y
3 Satterfield	Y	Y	Y	Y	N	Y	Y
4 Daniel	Y	Y	Y	Y	N	Y	Y
5 Daniel	Y	Y	Y	?	N	Y	Y
6 Butler	Y	Y	Y	Y	N	Y	Y
7 Robinson	Y	Y	Y	Y	N	Y	Y
8 Harris	#	Y	Y	Y	Y	Y	N
9 Wampler	Y	Y	Y	Y	N	Y	Y
10 Fisher	Y	Y	Y	Y	N	Y	Y
WASHINGTON							
1 Pritchard	Y	N	Y	Y	Y	Y	N
2 Meeds	Y	Y	Y	Y	N	Y	N
3 Bonker	Y	Y	Y	Y	N	Y	N
4 McCormack	Y	Y	Y	Y	N	Y	N
5 Foley	Y	Y	Y	Y	N	Y	N
6 Dicks	Y	Y	Y	Y	N	Y	N
7 Cunningham	Y	Y	Y	Y	N	Y	Y
WEST VIRGINIA							
1 Mollohan	#	#	#	#	N	Y	N
2 Staggers	Y	Y	Y	Y	N	Y	N
3 Slack	Y	Y	Y	Y	N	Y	Y
4 Rahall	Y	Y	Y	Y	N	Y	▮
WISCONSIN							
1 Aspin	Y	Y	Y	Y	N	Y	N
2 Kastenmeier	Y	Y	Y	Y	Y	N	N
3 Baldus	Y	Y	Y	Y	N	Y	N
4 Zablocki	Y	Y	Y	Y	N	Y	N
5 Reuss	Y	Y	Y	Y	N	Y	N
6 Steiger	N	Y	Y	Y	N	N	N
7 Obey	Y	Y	?	Y	N	Y	N
8 Cornell	Y	Y	Y	Y	N	Y	N
9 Kasten	Y	Y	Y	Y	N	N	Y
WYOMING							
AL Roncalio	?	Y	Y	Y	N	Y	N

Democrats ***Republicans***

368. HR 12426. New York City Aid. Moorhead, D-Pa., motion that the House resolve itself into the Committee of the Whole to consider the bill to provide federal loan guarantees to New York City. Motion agreed to 382-3: R 133-2; D 249-1 (ND 174-0; SD 75-1), June 8, 1978.

369. HR 12426. New York City Aid. Moorhead, D-Pa., technical amendment conforming the bill to the budget act. Adopted 401-0: R 140-0; D 261-0 (ND 181-0; SD 80-0), June 8, 1978.

370. HR 12426. New York City Aid. Stanton, R-Ohio, motion to recommit the bill to the Banking Committee with instructions to report it back with amendments extending seasonal loans rather than loan guarantees for New York City, and instructing that the loans be phased out in three years. Rejected 109-291: R 84-55; D 25-236 (ND 12-170; SD 13-66), June 8, 1978.

371. HR 12426. New York City Aid. Passage of the bill to authorize the secretary of the treasury to issue federal loan guarantees totaling $2 billion for up to 15 years for New York City bonds. Passed 247-155: R 44-96; D 203-59 (ND 166-17; SD 37-42), June 8, 1978. A "yea" was a vote supporting the president's position.

372. HR 12929. Labor-HEW Appropriations, Fiscal 1979. Michel, R-Ill., amendment to reduce the appropriations for the Department of Health, Education and Welfare by $1 billion, to $57 billion from the $58 billion in the bill, to be accomplished by a reduction in waste, fraud and abuse. Adopted 290-87: R 129-6; D 161-81 (ND 96-72; SD 65-9), June 8, 1978.

KEY

- Y Voted for (yea).
- ✓ Paired for.
- † Announced for.
- # CQ Poll for.
- N Voted against (nay).
- X Paired against.
- \- Announced against.
- ▮ CQ Poll against.
- P Voted "present."
- ● Voted "present" to avoid possible conflict of interest.
- ? Did not vote or otherwise make a position known.

	368	369	370	371	372
ALABAMA					
1 Edwards	Y	Y	N	N	Y
2 Dickinson	Y	Y	Y	N	Y
3 Nichols	Y	Y	N	N	Y
4 Bevill	Y	Y	N	N	Y
5 Flippo	Y	Y	N	N	Y
6 Buchanan	Y	Y	N	Y	N
7 Flowers	?	?	?	?	?
ALASKA					
AL Young	#	Y	N	N	Y
ARIZONA					
1 Rhodes	Y	Y	Y	N	Y
2 Udall	Y	Y	N	Y	#
3 Stump	#	#	✓	X	#
4 Rudd	Y	Y	Y	N	Y
ARKANSAS					
1 Alexander	Y	Y	N	Y	N
2 Tucker	#	#	▮	#	#
3 Hammerschmidt	Y	Y	N	N	Y
4 Thornton	Y	?	?	?	?
CALIFORNIA					
1 Johnson	Y	Y	N	Y	Y
2 Clausen	Y	Y	Y	N	Y
3 Moss	Y	Y	N	Y	?
4 Leggett	?	?	?	Y	N
5 Burton, J.	Y	Y	N	Y	N
6 Burton, P.	Y	Y	N	Y	?
7 Miller	Y	Y	N	Y	Y
8 Dellums	#	Y	N	Y	N
9 Stark	#	Y	N	Y	N
10 Edwards	Y	Y	N	Y	N
11 Ryan	Y	Y	N	Y	Y
12 McCloskey	Y	Y	N	Y	Y
13 Mineta	Y	Y	N	Y	N
14 McFall	Y	Y	N	Y	N
15 Sisk	Y	Y	N	Y	Y
16 Panetta	Y	Y	Y	Y	Y
17 Krebs	Y	Y	Y	Y	Y
18 Ketchum	Y	Y	Y	N	?
19 Lagomarsino	Y	Y	Y	N	Y
20 Goldwater	Y	Y	Y	N	Y
21 Corman	Y	Y	N	Y	N
22 Moorhead	Y	Y	Y	N	Y
23 Beilenson	#	Y	N	Y	N
24 Waxman	Y	Y	N	Y	N
25 Roybal	Y	Y	N	Y	N
26 Rousselot	Y	Y	Y	N	Y
27 Dornan	Y	Y	Y	Y	Y
28 Burke	#	#	▮	✓	▮
29 Hawkins	Y	Y	N	Y	N
30 Danielson	Y	Y	N	Y	N
31 Wilson, C.H.	?	?	?	?	?
32 Anderson	Y	Y	N	Y	Y
33 Clawson	Y	Y	Y	N	Y
34 Hannaford	Y	Y	N	Y	Y
35 Lloyd	Y	Y	Y	Y	Y
36 Brown	Y	Y	N	Y	N
37 Pettis	Y	Y	Y	N	Y
38 Patterson	Y	Y	N	Y	?
39 Wiggins	#	#	✓	X	#
40 Badham	Y	Y	Y	N	#
41 Wilson, B.	N	Y	Y	Y	Y
42 Van Deerlin	Y	Y	N	Y	Y
43 Burgener	Y	Y	Y	N	Y
COLORADO					
1 Schroeder	Y	Y	N	N	Y
2 Wirth	Y	Y	N	✓	#
3 Evans	Y	Y	N	Y	N
4 Johnson	Y	Y	Y	N	Y
5 Armstrong	Y	Y	Y	N	Y
CONNECTICUT					
1 Cotter	Y	Y	N	Y	Y
2 Dodd	Y	Y	N	Y	Y
3 Giaimo	Y	Y	N	Y	Y
4 McKinney	#	Y	N	Y	Y
5 Sarasin	Y	Y	N	Y	#
6 Moffett	Y	Y	N	Y	Y
DELAWARE					
AL Evans	Y	Y	Y	N	Y
FLORIDA					
1 Sikes	Y	Y	N	Y	Y
2 Fuqua	Y	Y	N	Y	Y
3 Bennett	Y	Y	N	N	Y
4 Chappell	Y	Y	N	N	Y
5 Kelly	Y	Y	N	N	Y
6 Young	#	Y	N	N	Y
7 Gibbons	?	?	?	?	?
8 Ireland	Y	Y	N	N	Y
9 Frey	?	?	✓	X	?
10 Bafalis	Y	Y	N	N	Y
11 Rogers	Y	Y	N	Y	?
12 Burke	Y	Y	Y	Y	Y
13 Lehman	#	#	▮	#	#
14 Pepper	Y	Y	N	Y	N
15 Fascell	Y	Y	N	Y	Y
GEORGIA					
1 Ginn	Y	Y	N	N	Y
2 Mathis	Y	Y	N	Y	Y
3 Brinkley	Y	Y	N	N	Y
4 Levitas	Y	Y	N	N	Y
5 Fowler	Y	Y	N	Y	Y
6 Flynt	Y	Y	N	N	Y
7 McDonald	N	Y	N	N	Y
8 Evans	Y	Y	N	Y	Y
9 Jenkins	Y	Y	N	N	Y
10 Barnard	Y	Y	N	Y	Y
HAWAII					
1 Heftel	Y	Y	N	Y	N
2 Akaka	Y	Y	N	Y	Y
IDAHO					
1 Symms	Y	Y	N	N	Y
2 Hansen, G.	Y	Y	Y	N	Y
ILLINOIS					
1 Metcalfe	Y	Y	N	Y	N
2 Murphy	Y	Y	N	Y	Y
3 Russo	Y	Y	N	Y	Y
4 Derwinski	Y	Y	Y	N	Y
5 Fary	Y	Y	N	Y	Y
6 Hyde	Y	Y	Y	Y	Y
7 Collins	?	Y	N	Y	N
8 Rostenkowski	Y	Y	N	Y	Y
9 Yates	Y	Y	N	Y	N
10 Mikva	Y	Y	N	Y	▮
11 Annunzio	Y	Y	N	Y	Y
12 Crane	Y	Y	N	N	Y
13 McClory	Y	Y	Y	N	Y
14 Erlenborn	Y	Y	Y	N	Y
15 Corcoran	Y	Y	N	N	Y
16 Anderson	Y	Y	N	Y	Y
17 O'Brien	Y	Y	Y	Y	Y
18 Michel	Y	Y	Y	Y	Y
19 Railsback	Y	Y	Y	N	Y
20 Findley	Y	Y	Y	Y	Y
21 Madigan	Y	Y	N	Y	Y
22 Shipley	Y	Y	N	Y	Y
23 Price	Y	Y	N	Y	Y
24 Simon	†	†	▮	✓	▮
INDIANA					
1 Benjamin	Y	Y	N	Y	Y
2 Fithian	Y	Y	N	Y	Y
3 Brademas	Y	Y	N	Y	N
4 Quayle	N	Y	Y	N	Y
5 Hillis	Y	Y	N	Y	Y
6 Evans	Y	Y	Y	N	Y
7 Myers, J.	Y	Y	Y	Y	Y
8 Cornwell	Y	Y	N	Y	Y
9 Hamilton	Y	Y	N	Y	Y
10 Sharp	Y	Y	N	Y	Y
11 Jacobs	Y	Y	N	Y	Y
IOWA					
1 Leach	Y	Y	Y	N	Y
2 Blouin	Y	Y	N	Y	Y
3 Grassley	Y	Y	Y	N	Y
4 Smith	Y	Y	N	Y	Y
5 Harkin	Y	Y	N	Y	Y
6 Bedell	Y	Y	N	Y	Y

Democrats ***Republicans***

	368	369	370	371	372
KANSAS					
1 ***Sebelius***	Y	Y	Y	N	Y
2 Keys	Y	Y	N	Y	Y
3 ***Winn***	Y	Y	Y	N	Y
4 Glickman	Y	Y	Y	Y	Y
5 ***Skubitz***	Y	Y	?	N	Y
KENTUCKY					
1 Hubbard	Y	Y	N	Y	Y
2 Natcher	Y	Y	N	Y	N
3 Mazzoli	Y	Y	N	N	Y
4 ***Snyder***	Y	Y	Y	N	Y
5 ***Carter***	Y	Y	Y	N	N
6 Breckinridge	?	Y	Y	N	Y
7 Perkins	Y	Y	N	Y	N
LOUISIANA					
1 ***Livingston***	Y	Y	Y	N	Y
2 Boggs	Y	Y	N	Y	Y
3 ***Treen***	Y	Y	Y	N	Y
4 Waggonner	Y	Y	N	N	Y
5 Huckaby	Y	Y	N	N	Y
6 ***Moore***	Y	Y	Y	N	Y
7 Breaux	P	Y	Y	N	Y
8 Long	Y	Y	N	Y	Y
MAINE					
1 ***Emery***	Y	Y	Y	N	Y
2 ***Cohen***	Y	Y	Y	N	Y
MARYLAND					
1 ***Bauman***	Y	Y	N	N	Y
2 Long	Y	Y	N	Y	Y
3 Mikulski	Y	Y	N	Y	Y
4 ***Holt***	Y	Y	N	Y	Y
5 Spellman	Y	Y	N	Y	N
6 Byron	Y	Y	N	N	Y
7 Mitchell	Y	Y	N	Y	N
8 ***Steers***	Y	Y	N	Y	Y
MASSACHUSETTS					
1 ***Conte***	Y	Y	N	Y	Y
2 Boland	Y	Y	N	Y	Y
3 Early	Y	Y	N	Y	N
4 Drinan	Y	Y	N	Y	N
5 Tsongas	#	#	▮	✓	?
6 Harrington	Y	Y	N	Y	▮
7 Markey	Y	Y	N	Y	Y
8 O'Neill					
9 Moakley	Y	Y	N	Y	N
10 ***Heckler***	Y	Y	Y	Y	Y
11 Burke	Y	Y	N	Y	N
12 Studds	Y	Y	N	Y	Y
MICHIGAN					
1 Conyers	Y	Y	N	Y	N
2 ***Pursell***	Y	Y	Y	N	Y
3 ***Brown***	Y	Y	Y	N	Y
4 ***Stockman***	#	#	#	▮	Y
5 ***Sawyer***	Y	Y	N	N	Y
6 Carr	Y	Y	N	Y	Y
7 Kildee	Y	Y	N	Y	Y
8 Traxler	Y	Y	N	N	Y
9 ***Vander Jagt***	Y	?	X	✓	?
10 ***Cederberg***	Y	Y	Y	N	Y
11 ***Ruppe***	Y	#	✓	X	Y
12 Bonior	?	Y	N	Y	N
13 Diggs	?	Y	N	Y	Y
14 Nedzi	?	?	X	✓	?
15 Ford	Y	Y	N	Y	N
16 Dingell	Y	Y	N	Y	N
17 Brodhead	Y	Y	N	Y	N
18 Blanchard	Y	Y	N	Y	Y
19 ***Broomfield***	Y	Y	Y	N	Y
MINNESOTA					
1 ***Quie***	#	#	#	#	#
2 ***Hagedorn***	Y	Y	Y	N	Y
3 ***Frenzel***	Y	Y	Y	N	Y
4 Vento	Y	Y	N	Y	N
5 Fraser	Y	Y	N	Y	N
6 Nolan	Y	Y	N	Y	Y
7 ***Stangeland***	Y	Y	Y	N	Y
8 Oberstar	Y	Y	N	Y	N
MISSISSIPPI					
1 Whitten	Y	Y	N	Y	N
2 Bowen	Y	Y	N	N	Y
3 Montgomery	Y	Y	N	N	Y
4 ***Cochran***	?	Y	Y	N	Y
5 ***Lott***	Y	Y	N	N	Y
MISSOURI					
1 Clay	Y	Y	N	Y	N
2 Young	Y	Y	N	Y	Y
3 Gephardt	Y	Y	Y	Y	Y

	368	369	370	371	372
4 Skelton	Y	Y	N	N	Y
5 Bolling	#	Y	N	Y	N
6 ***Coleman***	Y	Y	Y	N	Y
7 ***Taylor***	Y	Y	Y	N	Y
8 Ichord	Y	Y	N	N	Y
9 Volkmer	Y	Y	N	N	Y
10 Burlison	Y	Y	N	Y	N
MONTANA					
1 Baucus	Y	Y	N	Y	Y
2 ***Marlenee***	Y	Y	Y	N	Y
NEBRASKA					
1 ***Thone***	Y	Y	Y	N	Y
2 Cavanaugh	Y	Y	N	Y	Y
3 ***Smith***	Y	Y	Y	N	?
NEVADA					
AL Santini	Y	Y	N	Y	Y
NEW HAMPSHIRE					
1 D'Amours	Y	Y	Y	N	Y
2 ***Cleveland***	Y	Y	N	N	Y
NEW JERSEY					
1 Florio	Y	Y	N	Y	Y
2 Hughes	Y	Y	N	Y	Y
3 Howard	#	#	X	✓	#
4 Thompson	Y	Y	N	Y	N
5 ***Fenwick***	Y	Y	N	Y	Y
6 ***Forsythe***	Y	Y	N	Y	Y
7 Maguire	Y	Y	N	Y	Y
8 Roe	Y	Y	N	Y	#
9 ***Hollenbeck***	Y	Y	N	Y	Y
10 Rodino	#	#	▮	#	▮
11 Minish	Y	Y	N	Y	N
12 ***Rinaldo***	Y	Y	N	Y	Y
13 Meyner	#	Y	N	Y	Y
14 LeFante	Y	Y	N	Y	N
15 Patten	Y	Y	N	Y	N
NEW MEXICO					
1 ***Lujan***	?	?	?	X	?
2 Runnels	#	#	?	X	?
NEW YORK					
1 Pike	#	#	▮	#	#
2 Downey	Y	Y	N	Y	Y
3 Ambro	?	Y	N	Y	Y
4 ***Lent***	Y	Y	N	Y	Y
5 ***Wydler***	Y	Y	N	Y	Y
6 Wolff	Y	Y	N	Y	▮
7 Addabbo	Y	Y	N	Y	▮
8 Rosenthal	Y	Y	N	Y	N
9 Delaney	Y	Y	N	Y	Y
10 Biaggi	Y	Y	N	Y	N
11 Scheuer	Y	Y	N	Y	N
12 Chisholm	Y	Y	N	Y	N
13 Solarz	Y	Y	N	Y	N
14 Richmond	Y	Y	N	Y	?
15 Zeferetti	Y	Y	N	Y	#
16 Holtzman	Y	Y	N	Y	N
17 Murphy	#	#	X	✓	#
18 ***Green***	Y	Y	N	Y	N
19 Rangel	Y	Y	N	Y	N
20 Weiss	Y	Y	N	Y	?
21 Garcia	Y	Y	N	Y	N
22 Bingham	Y	Y	N	Y	N
23 ***Caputo***	Y	Y	N	Y	Y
24 Ottinger	Y	Y	N	Y	N
25 ***Fish***	Y	Y	N	Y	Y
26 ***Gilman***	Y	Y	N	Y	N
27 McHugh	Y	Y	N	Y	N
28 Stratton	Y	Y	N	Y	Y
29 Pattison	Y	Y	N	Y	Y
30 ***McEwen***	Y	Y	N	Y	Y
31 ***Mitchell***	Y	Y	N	Y	Y
32 Hanley	Y	Y	N	Y	Y
33 ***Walsh***	Y	Y	N	Y	Y
34 ***Horton***	Y	Y	N	Y	Y
35 ***Conable***	Y	Y	N	Y	Y
36 LaFalce	Y	Y	N	Y	N
37 Nowak	Y	Y	N	Y	N
38 ***Kemp***	Y	Y	N	Y	Y
39 Lundine	Y	Y	N	Y	N
NORTH CAROLINA					
1 Jones	Y	Y	N	Y	Y
2 Fountain	Y	Y	N	N	Y
3 Whitley	Y	Y	N	N	Y
4 Andrews	Y	Y	Y	Y	Y
5 Neal	Y	Y	Y	Y	Y
6 Preyer	Y	Y	N	Y	Y
7 Rose	Y	#	X	Y	#
8 Hefner	Y	Y	N	Y	Y

	368	369	370	371	372
9 ***Martin***	Y	Y	Y	Y	Y
10 ***Broyhill***	Y	Y	Y	N	Y
11 Gudger	Y	Y	Y	?	Y
NORTH DAKOTA					
AL ***Andrews***	Y	Y	Y	N	Y
OHIO					
1 ***Gradison***	Y	Y	Y	N	Y
2 Luken	Y	Y	Y	N	Y
3 ***Whalen***	Y	Y	N	Y	N
4 ***Guyer***	Y	Y	N	Y	Y
5 ***Latta***	Y	Y	Y	N	Y
6 ***Harsha***	Y	Y	Y	N	Y
7 ***Brown***	Y	Y	Y	Y	Y
8 ***Kindness***	Y	Y	Y	N	Y
9 Ashley	Y	Y	N	Y	Y
10 ***Miller***	Y	Y	Y	N	Y
11 ***Stanton***	Y	Y	Y	N	Y
12 ***Devine***	Y	Y	N	N	Y
13 Pease	Y	Y	N	Y	Y
14 Seiberling	Y	Y	N	Y	N
15 ***Wylie***	Y	Y	Y	N	Y
16 ***Regula***	Y	Y	Y	N	Y
17 ***Ashbrook***	Y	Y	N	N	#
18 Applegate	Y	?	N	Y	Y
19 Carney	?	?	X	✓	?
20 Oakar	Y	Y	N	Y	Y
21 Stokes	Y	Y	N	Y	N
22 Vanik	Y	Y	N	Y	N
23 Mottl	Y	Y	N	N	Y
OKLAHOMA					
1 Jones	Y	Y	Y	X	Y
2 Risenhoover	Y	Y	N	N	Y
3 Watkins	P	Y	Y	N	Y
4 Steed	Y	Y	N	Y	Y
5 ***Edwards***	Y	Y	N	N	Y
6 English	Y	Y	N	N	Y
OREGON					
1 AuCoin	Y	Y	Y	N	Y
2 Ullman	Y	Y	N	Y	#
3 Duncan	Y	Y	Y	Y	Y
4 Weaver	Y	Y	N	Y	Y
PENNSYLVANIA					
1 Myers, M.	Y	Y	N	Y	N
2 Nix	Y	Y	N	Y	?
3 Lederer	Y	Y	N	Y	N
4 Eilberg	Y	Y	N	Y	N
5 ***Schulze***	Y	Y	Y	N	Y
6 Yatron	Y	Y	Y	N	Y
7 Edgar	Y	Y	N	Y	Y
8 Kostmayer	Y	Y	N	Y	Y
9 ***Shuster***	Y	Y	N	N	Y
10 ***McDade***	Y	Y	N	N	Y
11 Flood	Y	Y	N	Y	N
12 Murtha	Y	Y	N	Y	N
13 ***Coughlin***	?	Y	Y	Y	Y
14 Moorhead	Y	Y	N	Y	#
15 Rooney	Y	Y	N	Y	Y
16 ***Walker***	Y	Y	N	N	Y
17 Ertel	Y	Y	Y	Y	Y
18 Walgren	Y	Y	N	Y	Y
19 ***Goodling, W.***	Y	Y	Y	N	Y
20 Gaydos	Y	Y	N	Y	N
21 Dent	#	#	▮	#	#
22 Murphy	Y	Y	N	N	Y
23 Ammerman	Y	Y	N	N	Y
24 ***Marks***	Y	Y	N	Y	Y
25 ***Myers, G.***	Y	Y	Y	N	Y
RHODE ISLAND					
1 St Germain	Y	Y	N	Y	N
2 Beard	Y	Y	N	Y	Y
SOUTH CAROLINA					
1 Davis	Y	Y	N	Y	Y
2 ***Spence***	Y	Y	Y	N	Y
3 Derrick	Y	Y	Y	N	Y
4 Mann	Y	Y	N	Y	Y
5 Holland	Y	Y	▮	Y	#
6 Jenrette	Y	Y	N	Y	Y
SOUTH DAKOTA					
1 ***Pressler***	Y	Y	Y	N	Y
2 ***Abdnor***	Y	Y	Y	N	Y
TENNESSEE					
1 ***Quillen***	Y	Y	N	N	Y
2 ***Duncan***	Y	Y	N	N	Y
3 Lloyd	Y	Y	N	N	#
4 Gore	Y	Y	N	Y	Y
5 Allen	?	?	?	?	?
6 ***Beard***	Y	Y	N	N	Y

	368	369	370	371	372
7 Jones	Y	Y	N	Y	Y
8 Ford	Y	Y	N	Y	Y
TEXAS					
1 Hall	Y	Y	N	N	Y
2 Wilson, C.	#	Y	N	Y	Y
3 ***Collins***	Y	Y	Y	N	Y
4 Roberts	?	?	✓	X	?
5 Mattox	Y	Y	N	N	Y
6 Teague	?	?	✓	X	?
7 ***Archer***	Y	Y	Y	N	Y
8 Eckhardt	Y	Y	N	Y	?
9 Brooks	Y	Y	Y	N	N
10 Pickle	Y	Y	N	N	Y
11 Poage	Y	Y	Y	N	Y
12 Wright	Y	Y	N	Y	?
13 Hightower	Y	Y	N	N	Y
14 Young	?	?	?	?	?
15 de la Garza	Y	Y	N	N	?
16 White	Y	Y	N	N	Y
17 Burleson	Y	Y	Y	N	Y
18 Jordan	Y	Y	N	Y	N
19 Mahon	Y	Y	N	N	Y
20 Gonzalez	Y	Y	N	Y	N
21 Krueger	Y	Y	Y	N	Y
22 Gammage	Y	Y	Y	N	Y
23 Kazen	Y	Y	N	N	N
24 Milford	?	Y	N	N	Y
UTAH					
1 McKay	Y	Y	N	Y	Y
2 ***Marriott***	Y	Y	Y	N	#
VERMONT					
AL ***Jeffords***	Y	Y	N	Y	Y
VIRGINIA					
1 ***Trible***	Y	Y	Y	N	Y
2 ***Whitehurst***	Y	Y	Y	N	#
3 Satterfield	Y	Y	N	N	Y
4 ***Daniel***	Y	Y	N	N	Y
5 Daniel	Y	Y	N	N	Y
6 ***Butler***	?	Y	Y	N	Y
7 ***Robinson***	Y	Y	Y	N	Y
8 Harris	?	Y	N	Y	Y
9 ***Wampler***	Y	Y	Y	N	Y
10 Fisher	Y	Y	N	Y	Y
WASHINGTON					
1 ***Pritchard***	Y	Y	N	Y	N
2 Meeds	Y	#	N	Y	Y
3 Bonker	Y	Y	N	Y	Y
4 McCormack	Y	Y	N	N	Y
5 Foley	Y	Y	N	Y	Y
6 Dicks	Y	Y	N	Y	Y
7 ***Cunningham***	Y	Y	N	N	Y
WEST VIRGINIA					
1 Mollohan	Y	Y	N	Y	Y
2 Staggers	Y	Y	N	Y	Y
3 Slack	Y	Y	N	N	Y
4 Rahall	Y	Y	N	N	Y
WISCONSIN					
1 Aspin	Y	Y	N	Y	Y
2 Kastenmeier	Y	Y	N	Y	N
3 Baldus	Y	Y	N	Y	N
4 Zablocki	Y	Y	N	Y	N
5 Reuss	Y	Y	N	Y	N
6 ***Steiger***	#	Y	Y	Y	Y
7 Obey	Y	Y	N	Y	N
8 Cornell	Y	Y	N	Y	Y
9 ***Kasten***	Y	Y	Y	N	Y
WYOMING					
AL Roncalio	Y	Y	?	Y	N

Democrats ***Republicans***

373. H J Res 945. Black Lung Supplemental Appropriation, Fiscal 1978. Passage of the joint resolution to appropriate $181,689,000 from the Black Lung Disability Trust Fund for benefit payments and administration costs resulting from 1978 legislation (PL 95-239) liberalizing miner eligibility for black lung claims. Passed 237-72: R 52-59; D 185-13 (ND 140-4; SD 45-9), June 9, 1978. The president had requested $183,870,000.

374. HR 12933. Transportation Appropriations, Fiscal 1979. Adoption of the rule (H Res 1219) providing for House floor consideration of the bill to appropriate $8.9 billion for the Transportation Department and related agencies for fiscal 1979. Adopted 309-16: R 108-10; D 201-6 (ND 145-3; SD 56-3), June 9, 1978.

375. H Con Res 612. Ugandan Human Rights. Bonker, D-Wash., motion to suspend the rules and pass the resolution condemning the government of Uganda headed by President Idi Amin for gross violations of human rights and urging President Carter to discourage U.S. trade with the country. Motion agreed to 377-0: R 132-0; D 245-0 (ND 169-0; SD 76-0), June 12, 1978. A two-thirds majority vote (252 in this case) is required for passage under suspension of the rules.

376. HR 12441. Toxic Substances Control. Eckhardt, D-Texas, motion to suspend the rules and pass the bill to increase to $50 million, from $16 million, the fiscal 1979 authorization for the implementation of the 1976 Toxic Substances Control Act to regulate marketing of hazardous chemicals. Motion rejected 190-188: R 33-99; D 157-89 (ND 130-40; SD 27-49), June 12, 1978. A two-thirds majority vote (252 in this case) is required for passage under suspension of the rules.

377. HR 12933. Transportation Appropriations, Fiscal 1979. Shuster, R-Pa., amendment to prevent the National Highway Traffic Safety Administration from using any funds appropriated by the bill to implement or enforce any regulation requiring motor vehicles to be equipped with a system of passive restraints other than seat belts. Adopted 237-143: R 118-16; D 119-127 (ND 61-110; SD 58-17), June 12, 1978. A "nay" was a vote supporting the president's position.

378. HR 12933. Transportation Appropriations, Fiscal 1979. Eckhardt, D-Texas, amendment to permit the use of funds appropriated by the bill for research and development relating to passive restraint systems or for any court action concerning any regulation requiring motor vehicles to be equipped with passive restraint systems other than seat belts. Rejected 180-194: R 16-116; D 164-78 (ND 132-36; SD 32-42), June 12, 1978.

379. HR 12933. Transportation Appropriations, Fiscal 1979. Passage of the bill to appropriate $8,847,296,096 in new budget authority for the Transportation Department and related agencies for fiscal year 1979. Passed 347-25: R 122-9; D 225-16 (ND 153-13; SD 72-3), June 12, 1978. The president had requested $9,068,623,096.

380. HR 12929. Labor-HEW Appropriations, Fiscal 1979. Flood, D-Pa., motion that the House resolve itself into the Committee of the Whole to consider the bill to appropriate fiscal 1979 funds for the Departments of Labor and Health, Education and Welfare and related agencies. Motion agreed to 383-5: R 131-3; D 252-2 (ND 177-1; SD 75-1), June 13, 1978.

KEY

- Y Voted for (yea).
- ✓ Paired for.
- † Announced for.
- # CQ Poll for.
- N Voted against (nay).
- X Paired against.
- - Announced against.
- ▮ CQ Poll against.
- P Voted "present."
- ● Voted "present" to avoid possible conflict of interest.
- ? Did not vote or otherwise make a position known.

	373	374	375	376	377	378	379	380
ALABAMA								
1 Edwards	Y	Y	Y	N	Y	N	Y	Y
2 Dickinson	N	Y	Y	N	Y	N	Y	Y
3 Nichols	#	#	Y	N	Y	N	Y	Y
4 Bevill	Y	Y	Y	N	N	Y	Y	Y
5 Flippo	Y	Y	Y	N	Y	Y	Y	Y
6 Buchanan	Y	Y	Y	Y	Y	N	Y	Y
7 Flowers	?	?	?	?	?	?	?	Y
ALASKA								
AL Young	X	#	Y	N	Y	N	Y	Y
ARIZONA								
1 Rhodes	?	?	?	?	?	?	?	Y
2 Udall	#	#	Y	Y	N	Y	Y	Y
3 Stump	X	#	#	▮	#	▮	▮	Y
4 Rudd	N	Y	Y	N	Y	N	Y	Y
ARKANSAS								
1 Alexander	Y	Y	Y	Y	Y	N	Y	?
2 Tucker	#	#	#	#	#	#	#	#
3 Hammerschmidt	Y	N	Y	N	Y	N	Y	Y
4 Thornton	?	?	Y	Y	Y	N	Y	?
CALIFORNIA								
1 Johnson	Y	Y	Y	N	N	Y	Y	Y
2 Clausen	✓	?	Y	Y	Y	N	Y	Y
3 Moss	Y	Y	Y	Y	N	Y	Y	Y
4 Leggett	?	?	Y	Y	Y	N	Y	Y
5 Burton, J.	?	Y	Y	Y	N	Y	N	Y
6 Burton, P.	✓	?	Y	Y	N	Y	Y	Y
7 Miller	Y	Y	Y	Y	N	Y	Y	Y
8 Dellums	Y	Y	Y	Y	N	Y	Y	Y
9 Stark	Y	N	Y	Y	N	Y	Y	Y
10 Edwards	Y	Y	Y	Y	N	?	?	?
11 Ryan	#	Y	Y	Y	N	N	Y	Y
12 McCloskey	Y	Y	Y	N	Y	N	Y	Y
13 Mineta	Y	Y	Y	Y	N	Y	Y	Y
14 McFall	Y	Y	Y	Y	N	Y	Y	Y
15 Sisk	Y	Y	Y	N	Y	N	Y	Y
16 Panetta	Y	Y	?	?	X	?	X	Y
17 Krebs	Y	Y	Y	N	Y	N	Y	Y
18 Ketchum	?	?	Y	N	Y	N	Y	Y
19 Lagomarsino	N	Y	Y	N	Y	N	Y	Y
20 Goldwater	X	?	Y	N	Y	N	Y	Y
21 Corman	#	#	Y	Y	N	Y	Y	Y
22 Moorhead	N	Y	Y	N	Y	N	Y	Y
23 Beilenson	Y	Y	#	#	▮	#	#	#
24 Waxman	#	#	#	✓	X	#	#	Y
25 Roybal	Y	Y	Y	Y	N	Y	Y	Y
26 Rousselot	N	N	Y	N	Y	N	Y	Y
27 Dornan	N	Y	Y	N	Y	N	Y	Y
28 Burke	#	#	#	✓	X	#	#	#
29 Hawkins	Y	Y	Y	Y	N	Y	Y	Y
30 Danielson	#	#	Y	Y	N	Y	Y	Y
31 Wilson, C.H.	?	?	Y	N	Y	N	Y	?
32 Anderson	Y	Y	Y	N	N	Y	Y	Y
33 Clawson	N	Y	?	X	✓	X	?	?
34 Hannaford	Y	Y	Y	Y	Y	Y	Y	Y
35 Lloyd	Y	Y	Y	Y	Y	N	Y	Y
36 Brown	Y	?	Y	Y	N	Y	Y	Y
37 Pettis	N	Y	Y	N	Y	Y	Y	Y
38 Patterson	?	?	Y	Y	N	N	Y	Y
39 Wiggins	X	#	Y	N	Y	N	Y	#
40 Badham	X	#	Y	N	Y	N	Y	Y
41 Wilson, B.	X	Y	Y	N	Y	N	Y	N
42 Van Deerlin	Y	Y	?	✓	X	?	?	Y
43 Burgener	Y	Y	Y	N	Y	N	Y	Y
COLORADO								
1 Schroeder	Y	Y	Y	Y	N	Y	Y	Y
2 Wirth	Y	Y	Y	Y	N	Y	N	Y
3 Evans	Y	Y	?	?	N	Y	Y	Y
4 Johnson	Y	Y	Y	N	Y	N	Y	Y
5 Armstrong	?	?	?	?	?	?	?	Y
CONNECTICUT								
1 Cotter	N	Y	Y	N	Y	N	Y	Y
2 Dodd	Y	Y	Y	Y	N	Y	Y	Y
3 Giaimo	?	?	Y	N	Y	Y	Y	Y
4 McKinney	Y	Y	Y	N	N	Y	Y	Y
5 Sarasin	▮	#	#	X	#	✓	#	Y
6 Moffett	Y	N	Y	Y	N	Y	N	Y
DELAWARE								
AL Evans	Y	Y	Y	N	Y	N	Y	Y
FLORIDA								
1 Sikes	Y	Y	Y	N	Y	N	Y	Y
2 Fuqua	Y	Y	Y	Y	Y	Y	Y	Y
3 Bennett	N	Y	Y	N	Y	Y	Y	Y
4 Chappell	#	Y	Y	N	Y	N	Y	Y
5 Kelly	N	N	#	X	✓	X	X	Y
6 Young	Y	Y	Y	N	Y	N	Y	Y
7 Gibbons	?	?	Y	Y	N	Y	Y	Y
8 Ireland	?	?	Y	N	Y	Y	Y	Y
9 Frey	X	?	?	X	✓	X	?	Y
10 Bafalis	●	Y	Y	N	Y	N	Y	Y
11 Rogers	X	?	Y	Y	N	Y	Y	Y
12 Burke	X	#	Y	N	Y	N	Y	Y
13 Lehman	#	#	Y	Y	P	Y	Y	Y
14 Pepper	#	#	#	✓	X	#	#	Y
15 Fascell	Y	Y	Y	Y	N	Y	Y	Y
GEORGIA								
1 Ginn	Y	Y	Y	Y	Y	N	Y	Y
2 Mathis	?	Y	Y	N	Y	N	Y	?
3 Brinkley	Y	Y	Y	N	Y	Y	Y	Y
4 Levitas	Y	Y	Y	Y	Y	Y	Y	Y
5 Fowler	Y	Y	Y	Y	N	Y	Y	Y
6 Flynt	?	?	Y	N	Y	N	Y	Y
7 McDonald	N	N	Y	N	Y	N	N	N
8 Evans	Y	Y	Y	N	Y	N	Y	Y
9 Jenkins	#	#	Y	N	Y	Y	Y	Y
10 Barnard	?	?	Y	N	Y	N	Y	Y
HAWAII								
1 Heftel	Y	Y	Y	Y	N	Y	Y	Y
2 Akaka	Y	Y	Y	Y	Y	Y	Y	Y
IDAHO								
1 Symms	N	N	Y	N	Y	N	N	Y
2 Hansen, G.	N	Y	Y	N	Y	N	Y	Y
ILLINOIS								
1 Metcalfe	?	?	?	✓	X	?	?	Y
2 Murphy	Y	Y	#	✓	✓	?	#	Y
3 Russo	Y	Y	Y	Y	Y	N	Y	Y
4 Derwinski	Y	Y	Y	N	Y	N	N	Y
5 Fary	Y	Y	Y	Y	N	Y	Y	Y
6 Hyde	N	Y	Y	N	Y	N	Y	Y
7 Collins	?	Y	Y	Y	N	Y	Y	Y
8 Rostenkowski	Y	Y	Y	Y	Y	N	Y	Y
9 Yates	Y	Y	Y	Y	N	Y	Y	Y
10 Mikva	Y	Y	Y	Y	N	Y	N	Y
11 Annunzio	Y	Y	#	✓	Y	N	Y	Y
12 Crane	N	Y	Y	N	Y	N	N	Y
13 McClory	N	Y	Y	N	Y	N	Y	Y
14 Erlenborn	N	Y	Y	N	Y	N	Y	Y
15 Corcoran	N	Y	Y	Y	Y	N	Y	Y
16 Anderson	Y	Y	#	▮	Y	N	Y	#
17 O'Brien	Y	Y	Y	N	Y	N	Y	Y
18 Michel	Y	Y	Y	N	Y	N	Y	Y
19 Railsback	Y	Y	Y	N	Y	N	Y	Y
20 Findley	Y	Y	Y	N	Y	N	Y	Y
21 Madigan	Y	Y	Y	N	N	Y	Y	Y
22 Shipley	✓	?	Y	Y	X	?	?	Y
23 Price	Y	Y	Y	Y	N	Y	Y	Y
24 Simon	†	†	Y	Y	N	Y	Y	?
INDIANA								
1 Benjamin	Y	Y	Y	N	N	Y	Y	Y
2 Fithian	Y	Y	Y	N	Y	N	Y	Y
3 Brademas	Y	Y	Y	Y	N	Y	Y	Y
4 Quayle	N	N	Y	N	Y	N	Y	N
5 Hillis	N	Y	Y	N	Y	N	?	?
6 Evans	Y	Y	Y	N	Y	Y	N	Y
7 Myers, J.	Y	Y	Y	N	Y	N	Y	Y
8 Cornwell	?	Y	Y	Y	N	Y	Y	?
9 Hamilton	Y	Y	Y	Y	N	Y	Y	Y
10 Sharp	Y	Y	Y	Y	N	Y	Y	Y
11 Jacobs	Y	Y	Y	N	Y	N	N	Y
IOWA								
1 Leach	Y	Y	Y	N	Y	N	Y	Y
2 Blouin	Y	Y	Y	Y	N	Y	?	Y
3 Grassley	N	Y	Y	N	Y	N	Y	Y
4 Smith	Y	Y	Y	Y	N	Y	Y	Y
5 Harkin	Y	Y	Y	Y	N	Y	Y	Y
6 Bedell	Y	Y	Y	Y	N	Y	N	Y

Democrats ***Republicans***

	373	374	375	376	377	378	379	380
KANSAS								
1 Sebelius	N	Y	Y	N	Y	N	Y	Y
2 Keys	Y	Y	Y	Y	Y	Y	Y	Y
3 Winn	N	Y	Y	N	Y	N	Y	Y
4 Glickman	Y	Y	Y	N	Y	Y	Y	Y
5 Skubitz	?	Y	Y	Y	Y	N	Y	Y
KENTUCKY								
1 Hubbard	?	?	Y	N	Y	N	Y	Y
2 Natcher	Y	Y	Y	N	Y	N	Y	Y
3 Mazzoli	Y	Y	Y	N	N	Y	Y	Y
4 Snyder	Y	Y	Y	N	Y	N	Y	Y
5 Carter	Y	Y	Y	Y	Y	P	Y	Y
6 Breckinridge	?	Y	Y	N	Y	N	Y	Y
7 Perkins	Y	Y	Y	Y	N	Y	Y	Y
LOUISIANA								
1 Livingston	N	Y	Y	N	Y	N	Y	Y
2 Boggs	Y	Y	Y	Y	N	■	Y	Y
3 Treen	Y	N	Y	Y	Y	N	Y	?
4 Waggonner	N	Y	Y	N	Y	N	Y	Y
5 Huckaby	?	?	?	?	?	?	?	Y
6 Moore	Y	Y	Y	N	Y	N	Y	Y
7 Breaux	Y	Y	Y	N	Y	N	Y	Y
8 Long	Y	Y	Y	Y	Y	Y	Y	Y
MAINE								
1 Emery	Y	Y	Y	■	Y	N	Y	Y
2 Cohen	Y	Y	Y	Y	Y	N	Y	Y
MARYLAND								
1 Bauman	N	N	Y	N	Y	N	Y	Y
2 Long	Y	Y	Y	Y	Y	Y	Y	Y
3 Mikulski	✓	#	Y	Y	N	Y	Y	Y
4 Holt	N	Y	Y	N	Y	N	Y	Y
5 Spellman	#	Y	Y	Y	Y	Y	#	Y
6 Byron	Y	Y	Y	N	Y	N	Y	Y
7 Mitchell	Y	Y	Y	Y	N	Y	Y	N
8 Steers	Y	Y	Y	Y	N	Y	Y	Y
MASSACHUSETTS								
1 Conte	Y	Y	Y	Y	N	Y	Y	Y
2 Boland	Y	Y	Y	Y	Y	Y	Y	Y
3 Early	Y	?	Y	Y	Y	Y	Y	Y
4 Drinan	Y	Y	Y	Y	N	Y	Y	Y
5 Tsongas	#	#	#	?	?	?	#	#
6 Harrington	Y	Y	Y	Y	N	Y	Y	Y
7 Markey	Y	Y	Y	Y	N	Y	Y	Y
8 O'Neill								
9 Moakley	Y	Y	Y	Y	N	Y	Y	Y
10 Heckler	✓	Y	Y	Y	Y	N	#	Y
11 Burke	Y	Y	Y	Y	Y	Y	Y	Y
12 Studds	Y	Y	Y	Y	N	Y	Y	Y
MICHIGAN								
1 Conyers	#	#	#	✓	N	Y	Y	#
2 Pursell	✓	Y	Y	Y	Y	N	Y	Y
3 Brown	X	#	Y	N	Y	N	N	Y
4 Stockman	N	Y	Y	N	Y	■	#	Y
5 Sawyer	Y	Y	Y	N	Y	N	Y	Y
6 Carr	Y	Y	Y	Y	Y	Y	Y	Y
7 Kildee	Y	Y	Y	Y	Y	Y	Y	Y
8 Traxler	Y	Y	Y	Y	Y	N	Y	Y
9 Vander Jagt	Y	Y	Y	N	Y	N	Y	Y
10 Cederberg	Y	Y	Y	Y	Y	N	Y	?
11 Ruppe	N	Y	Y	N	Y	N	Y	#
12 Bonior	Y	Y	?	✓	N	Y	Y	Y
13 Diggs	Y	Y	Y	Y	Y	N	Y	?
14 Nedzi	?	?	?	✓	✓	X	?	?
15 Ford	?	?	Y	Y	Y	N	Y	Y
16 Dingell	Y	Y	Y	Y	N	Y	Y	Y
17 Brodhead	Y	?	Y	Y	N	Y	N	Y
18 Blanchard	Y	Y	Y	Y	Y	Y	Y	Y
19 Broomfield	Y	Y	Y	N	Y	N	Y	Y
MINNESOTA								
1 Quie	#	#	#	#	#	■	#	#
2 Hagedorn	Y	Y	Y	N	Y	N	Y	Y
3 Frenzel	N	Y	Y	N	Y	N	Y	?
4 Vento	✓	?	Y	Y	N	Y	Y	Y
5 Fraser	#	#	Y	Y	■	#	#	#
6 Nolan	Y	Y	?	?	?	?	?	?
7 Stangeland	N	Y	Y	N	Y	N	Y	Y
8 Oberstar	Y	Y	Y	Y	N	Y	Y	Y
MISSISSIPPI								
1 Whitten	Y	Y	Y	N	Y	N	Y	Y
2 Bowen	Y	Y	Y	N	Y	N	Y	?
3 Montgomery	N	Y	Y	N	N	Y	Y	Y
4 Cochran	?	?	Y	N	N	Y	Y	Y
5 Lott	N	Y	Y	N	Y	N	Y	Y
MISSOURI								
1 Clay	?	?	Y	Y	N	Y	Y	Y
2 Young	Y	Y	Y	N	N	Y	Y	Y
3 Gephardt	Y	Y	Y	N	N	Y	N	Y

	373	374	375	376	377	378	379	380
4 Skelton	Y	Y	Y	N	Y	N	Y	Y
5 Bolling	#	#	Y	Y	N	Y	Y	Y
6 Coleman	Y	Y	Y	N	Y	N	Y	Y
7 Taylor	N	Y	Y	N	Y	N	Y	Y
8 Ichord	N	Y	Y	N	Y	N	Y	Y
9 Volkmer	Y	Y	Y	N	Y	Y	Y	Y
10 Burlison	?	?	Y	Y	Y	N	Y	Y
MONTANA								
1 Baucus	Y	Y	Y	N	N	Y	Y	Y
2 Marlenee	Y	Y	Y	N	Y	N	Y	Y
NEBRASKA								
1 Thone	N	Y	Y	N	Y	N	Y	Y
2 Cavanaugh	Y	N	?	?	Y	Y	Y	Y
3 Smith	X	?	Y	N	Y	N	Y	Y
NEVADA								
AL Santini	N	Y	Y	N	■	#	#	Y
NEW HAMPSHIRE								
1 D'Amours	Y	Y	Y	N	Y	N	Y	Y
2 Cleveland	?	?	Y	N	Y	N	Y	Y
NEW JERSEY								
1 Florio	Y	Y	Y	Y	N	Y	Y	Y
2 Hughes	N	Y	Y	Y	Y	Y	Y	Y
3 Howard	✓	#	Y	Y	N	Y	Y	Y
4 Thompson	Y	Y	Y	Y	N	Y	Y	Y
5 Fenwick	✓	#	Y	Y	Y	N	Y	Y
6 Forsythe	N	Y	Y	N	Y	N	Y	Y
7 Maguire	?	?	Y	Y	N	Y	N	Y
8 Roe	Y	Y	Y	Y	N	Y	Y	Y
9 Hollenbeck	Y	Y	Y	Y	Y	N	Y	Y
10 Rodino	#	#	#	#	■	#	#	Y
11 Minish	Y	Y	Y	Y	N	Y	Y	Y
12 Rinaldo	✓	#	Y	Y	Y	N	Y	Y
13 Meyner	Y	Y	#	✓	X	#	#	Y
14 LeFante	Y	Y	#	✓	X	✓	#	#
15 Patten	Y	Y	Y	Y	N	Y	Y	Y
NEW MEXICO								
1 Lujan	Y	Y	Y	N	Y	N	Y	Y
2 Runnels	?	#	#	X	✓	?	#	#
NEW YORK								
1 Pike	#	#	Y	N	Y	Y	Y	Y
2 Downey	Y	Y	Y	Y	N	Y	N	Y
3 Ambro	?	Y	Y	Y	Y	Y	Y	?
4 Lent	N	Y	Y	Y	N	N	Y	Y
5 Wydler	X	?	Y	Y	N	Y	Y	Y
6 Wolff	✓	#	#	✓	X	✓	#	Y
7 Addabbo	Y	Y	Y	Y	N	✓	✓	Y
8 Rosenthal	Y	Y	Y	Y	N	Y	Y	Y
9 Delaney	Y	Y	Y	Y	Y	N	Y	Y
10 Biaggi	✓	Y	Y	Y	N	Y	Y	Y
11 Scheuer	#	#	Y	Y	N	Y	Y	Y
12 Chisholm	Y	Y	Y	Y	N	Y	Y	Y
13 Solarz	Y	Y	#	✓	X	#	#	Y
14 Richmond	✓	?	Y	Y	N	Y	Y	Y
15 Zeferetti	✓	?	Y	N	Y	N	Y	Y
16 Holtzman	Y	Y	Y	Y	N	Y	Y	Y
17 Murphy	#	#	Y	Y	N	Y	Y	Y
18 Green	Y	Y	Y	Y	N	Y	Y	Y
19 Rangel	Y	Y	?	Y	N	Y	Y	Y
20 Weiss	†	†	Y	Y	N	Y	Y	Y
21 Garcia	Y	Y	Y	Y	N	Y	Y	Y
22 Bingham	Y	Y	Y	Y	N	Y	Y	Y
23 Caputo	Y	Y	?	✓	?	?	?	Y
24 Ottinger	†	†	Y	Y	N	Y	Y	Y
25 Fish	N	Y	Y	Y	Y	N	Y	Y
26 Gilman	✓	†	Y	Y	N	Y	Y	Y
27 McHugh	Y	Y	Y	Y	N	Y	Y	Y
28 Stratton	Y	Y	Y	N	N	Y	Y	Y
29 Pattison	#	#	Y	Y	N	Y	#	Y
30 McEwen	N	Y	Y	N	Y	N	Y	?
31 Mitchell	Y	Y	Y	Y	Y	N	Y	Y
32 Hanley	Y	Y	Y	Y	Y	Y	Y	Y
33 Walsh	?	?	Y	N	Y	N	Y	Y
34 Horton	X	#	Y	Y	Y	N	Y	Y
35 Conable	N	Y	Y	N	Y	N	Y	Y
36 LaFalce	Y	Y	Y	Y	N	Y	Y	Y
37 Nowak	Y	Y	Y	N	Y	Y	Y	Y
38 Kemp	N	Y	Y	N	Y	N	Y	?
39 Lundine	Y	Y	Y	Y	N	Y	Y	Y
NORTH CAROLINA								
1 Jones	Y	Y	Y	N	Y	N	Y	Y
2 Fountain	Y	Y	Y	N	Y	N	Y	Y
3 Whitley	Y	Y	Y	N	Y	N	Y	Y
4 Andrews	Y	Y	Y	N	Y	N	Y	Y
5 Neal	#	Y	Y	Y	Y	Y	Y	Y
6 Preyer	Y	Y	Y	Y	N	Y	Y	Y
7 Rose	✓	#	Y	N	N	Y	Y	Y
8 Hefner	Y	Y	Y	Y	Y	N	Y	Y

	373	374	375	376	377	378	379	380
9 Martin	N	Y	Y	N	Y	N	Y	Y
10 Broyhill	Y	Y	Y	Y	Y	N	N	Y
11 Gudger	Y	Y	Y	N	Y	N	Y	Y
NORTH DAKOTA								
AL Andrews	N	Y	Y	N	Y	N	Y	Y
OHIO								
1 Gradison	N	Y	Y	Y	Y	N	Y	Y
2 Luken	Y	Y	Y	Y	Y	N	Y	Y
3 Whalen	#	#	#	✓	X	✓	#	Y
4 Guyer	N	Y	Y	N	Y	N	Y	Y
5 Latta	N	Y	Y	N	Y	N	N	Y
6 Harsha	Y	Y	Y	N	Y	N	Y	?
7 Brown	?	?	Y	N	Y	N	Y	Y
8 Kindness	Y	Y	Y	N	Y	N	Y	Y
9 Ashley	?	Y	Y	N	N	Y	Y	Y
10 Miller	Y	Y	†	X	✓	X	?	Y
11 Stanton	Y	Y	Y	N	Y	N	Y	Y
12 Devine	N	Y	Y	N	Y	N	N	Y
13 Pease	Y	Y	Y	N	N	Y	Y	Y
14 Seiberling	Y	Y	Y	Y	N	Y	Y	Y
15 Wylie	X	?	Y	Y	N	Y	Y	Y
16 Regula	Y	Y	Y	N	Y	N	Y	Y
17 Ashbrook	X	Y	Y	N	Y	N	Y	Y
18 Applegate	Y	Y	Y	N	Y	Y	Y	Y
19 Carney	?	?	Y	Y	Y	N	Y	Y
20 Oakar	Y	Y	Y	Y	N	Y	Y	Y
21 Stokes	✓	#	Y	Y	N	Y	Y	Y
22 Vanik	Y	Y	Y	Y	N	Y	Y	Y
23 Mottl	Y	Y	Y	N	N	Y	N	Y
OKLAHOMA								
1 Jones	N	Y	Y	N	Y	N	N	Y
2 Risenhoover	Y	Y	Y	N	Y	N	Y	Y
3 Watkins	Y	Y	Y	N	Y	N	Y	Y
4 Steed	Y	Y	Y	N	Y	N	Y	Y
5 Edwards	N	N	Y	N	Y	N	Y	Y
6 English	N	Y	Y	N	Y	N	Y	Y
OREGON								
1 AuCoin	?	#	#	?	?	?	■	Y
2 Ullman	Y	Y	Y	N	N	N	Y	Y
3 Duncan	Y	Y	Y	Y	Y	N	Y	Y
4 Weaver	Y	Y	Y	Y	Y	N	N	Y
PENNSYLVANIA								
1 Myers, M.	Y	Y	Y	Y	Y	Y	Y	Y
2 Nix	?	?	?	?	✓	?	?	?
3 Lederer	Y	Y	Y	Y	Y	Y	Y	Y
4 Eilberg	Y	Y	Y	Y	N	N	Y	Y
5 Schulze	N	Y	Y	N	Y	N	?	?
6 Yatron	Y	Y	Y	N	Y	N	Y	Y
7 Edgar	Y	Y	Y	Y	N	Y	Y	Y
8 Kostmayer	Y	?	Y	Y	N	Y	Y	Y
9 Shuster	Y	Y	Y	N	Y	N	Y	Y
10 McDade	Y	Y	Y	Y	N	Y	Y	Y
11 Flood	Y	Y	Y	Y	N	Y	Y	Y
12 Murtha	Y	Y	Y	N	Y	N	Y	Y
13 Coughlin	✓	Y	Y	Y	Y	N	Y	Y
14 Moorhead	#	#	Y	Y	N	Y	Y	Y
15 Rooney	Y	Y	Y	Y	Y	N	Y	Y
16 Walker	N	Y	Y	N	Y	N	Y	Y
17 Ertel	Y	Y	Y	N	Y	Y	Y	Y
18 Walgren	Y	Y	Y	N	N	Y	Y	?
19 Goodling, W.	N	Y	?	?	?	?	?	Y
20 Gaydos	Y	Y	Y	N	Y	?	Y	Y
21 Dent	#	#	#	■	✓	■	#	#
22 Murphy	Y	Y	Y	Y	Y	Y	Y	Y
23 Ammerman	Y	Y	Y	N	N	Y	Y	Y
24 Marks	Y	Y	Y	Y	N	Y	Y	Y
25 Myers, G.	Y	Y	Y	Y	Y	N	Y	Y
RHODE ISLAND								
1 St Germain	Y	Y	?	X	✓	✓	?	Y
2 Beard	Y	Y	Y	N	Y	Y	Y	Y
SOUTH CAROLINA								
1 Davis	Y	Y	?	?	?	?	?	?
2 Spence	N	Y	Y	N	Y	N	Y	Y
3 Derrick	Y	Y	Y	Y	Y	Y	N	#
4 Mann	Y	Y	?	?	?	?	?	?
5 Holland	#	#	?	?	#	#	#	#
6 Jenrette	✓	#	#	✓	✓	■	#	#
SOUTH DAKOTA								
1 Pressler	?	?	Y	N	Y	N	Y	Y
2 Abdnor	N	Y	Y	N	Y	N	Y	Y
TENNESSEE								
1 Quillen	Y	Y	#	■	✓	X	✓	Y
2 Duncan	Y	Y	Y	N	Y	N	Y	Y
3 Lloyd	#	#	Y	N	Y	N	Y	Y
4 Gore	Y	Y	#	#	■	■	#	Y
5 Allen	?	?	?	?	?	?	?	?
6 Beard	N	Y	?	X	Y	N	Y	Y

	373	374	375	376	377	378	379	380
7 Jones	Y	Y	Y	N	Y	N	Y	Y
8 Ford	Y	Y	?	✓	X	?	?	?
TEXAS								
1 Hall	#	Y	Y	N	Y	N	Y	Y
2 Wilson, C.	#	Y	Y	N	Y	■	#	Y
3 Collins	N	N	Y	N	Y	N	N	N
4 Roberts	X	?	Y	N	Y	N	Y	Y
5 Mattox	Y	?	Y	Y	Y	Y	Y	Y
6 Teague	X	?	?	X	✓	X	?	?
7 Archer	N	Y	Y	N	Y	N	N	Y
8 Eckhardt	?	?	Y	Y	N	Y	Y	Y
9 Brooks	?	?	Y	Y	Y	N	Y	Y
10 Pickle	Y	Y	Y	Y	Y	Y	Y	Y
11 Poage	N	Y	Y	N	Y	N	Y	Y
12 Wright	?	?	Y	Y	N	Y	Y	Y
13 Hightower	Y	Y	Y	Y	Y	Y	Y	Y
14 Young	?	?	Y	N	?	?	?	Y
15 de la Garza	?	?	?	?	?	?	?	?
16 White	?	?	Y	Y	Y	Y	Y	Y
17 Burleson	N	Y	Y	N	Y	N	Y	Y
18 Jordan	Y	Y	Y	N	N	Y	Y	Y
19 Mahon	Y	Y	Y	N	Y	Y	Y	Y
20 Gonzalez	Y	N	Y	N	N	Y	Y	Y
21 Krueger	■	#	Y	Y	Y	N	Y	Y
22 Gammage	Y	Y	Y	N	Y	N	Y	Y
23 Kazen	?	?	Y	N	Y	Y	Y	Y
24 Milford	?	?	?	?	Y	N	Y	Y
UTAH								
1 McKay	#	#	Y	N	N	Y	Y	Y
2 Marriott	X	#	Y	N	Y	N	Y	Y
VERMONT								
AL Jeffords	■	#	Y	Y	N	Y	Y	Y
VIRGINIA								
1 Trible	N	Y	Y	N	N	Y	Y	Y
2 Whitehurst	N	Y	Y	N	Y	N	Y	Y
3 Satterfield	N	N	Y	N	Y	N	N	Y
4 Daniel	N	Y	Y	N	Y	N	Y	Y
5 Daniel	Y	Y	Y	N	Y	N	Y	Y
6 Butler	N	Y	Y	N	Y	N	Y	Y
7 Robinson	N	Y	Y	N	Y	N	Y	Y
8 Harris	Y	Y	Y	Y	N	Y	Y	Y
9 Wampler	Y	Y	Y	N	Y	N	Y	Y
10 Fisher	Y	Y	Y	Y	N	Y	Y	Y
WASHINGTON								
1 Pritchard	Y	Y	#	Y	N	Y	Y	Y
2 Meeds	Y	Y	Y	Y	N	Y	Y	Y
3 Bonker	Y	Y	Y	Y	N	Y	Y	Y
4 McCormack	Y	Y	Y	Y	N	Y	Y	Y
5 Foley	Y	Y	Y	Y	X	?	?	Y
6 Dicks	Y	Y	Y	Y	N	Y	Y	Y
7 Cunningham	N	Y	Y	N	Y	N	Y	Y
WEST VIRGINIA								
1 Mollohan	Y	Y	Y	N	Y	N	Y	Y
2 Staggers	Y	Y	Y	Y	N	Y	Y	Y
3 Slack	Y	Y	Y	N	Y	N	Y	Y
4 Rahall	Y	Y	Y	Y	N	Y	Y	Y
WISCONSIN								
1 Aspin	Y	Y	Y	Y	N	Y	Y	Y
2 Kastenmeier	Y	Y	Y	Y	N	Y	Y	Y
3 Baldus	Y	Y	Y	Y	N	Y	Y	Y
4 Zablocki	Y	Y	Y	Y	Y	N	Y	Y
5 Reuss	Y	Y	Y	Y	Y	Y	Y	Y
6 Steiger	N	N	Y	Y	✓	✓	Y	Y
7 Obey	Y	Y	Y	Y	N	Y	Y	Y
8 Cornell	Y	Y	Y	Y	N	Y	Y	Y
9 Kasten	X	#	Y	Y	Y	N	Y	Y
WYOMING								
AL Roncalio	?	?	?	?	?	?	?	?

Democrats ***Republicans***

381. **HR 12929. Labor-HEW Appropriations, Fiscal 1979.** Stokes, D-Ohio, amendment to delete from the bill language prohibiting use of funds for abortions unless the life of the mother was in danger. Rejected 122-287: R 19-124; D 103-163 (ND 87-97; SD 16-66), June 13, 1978.

382. **HR 12929. Labor-HEW Appropriations, Fiscal 1979.** Wright, D-Texas, amendment to substitute the provisions relating to abortion contained in the fiscal 1978 Labor-HEW appropriation bill for the language in HR 12929 as reported by committee. Rejected 198-212: R 31-110; D 167-102 (ND 118-68; SD 49-34), June 13, 1978.

383. **HR 12929. Labor-HEW Appropriations, Fiscal 1979.** Walker, R-Pa., amendment to prohibit the use of appropriated funds to implement quotas or other numerical requirements relating to race, creed or sex with respect to hiring, promotion or admissions policies. Adopted 232-177: R 112-31; D 120-146 (ND 61-123; SD 59-23), June 13, 1978.

384. **HR 12929. Labor-HEW Appropriations, Fiscal 1979.** Miller, R-Ohio, amendment to reduce controllable spending in the bill by 2 percent. Adopted 220-181: R 122-18; D 98-163 (ND 47-133; SD 51-30), June 13, 1978.

385. **HR 12929. Labor-HEW Appropriations, Fiscal 1979.** Symms, R-Idaho, amendment to reduce the appropriation for the Occupational Safety and Health Administration by $28.4 million. Rejected 184-216: R 103-35; D 81-181 (ND 27-154; SD 54-27), June 13, 1978.

386. **HR 12929. Labor-HEW Appropriations, Fiscal 1979.** Passage of the bill to appropriate $56.6 billion for the Departments of Labor and Health, Education and Welfare and related agencies for fiscal 1979. Passed 338-61: R 107-33; D 231-28 (ND 165-13; SD 66-15), June 13, 1978. The president had requested $57,338,938,000.

387. **HR 12935. Legislative Branch Appropriations, Fiscal 1979.** Shipley, D-Ill., motion that the House resolve itself into the Committee of the Whole for consideration of the bill to appropriate fiscal 1979 funds for the legislative branch. Motion agreed to 344-2: R 118-1; D 226-1 (ND 152-1; SD 74-0), June 14, 1978.

388. **HR 12934. State, Justice, Commerce, Judiciary Appropriations, Fiscal 1979.** Slack, D-W.Va., motion that the House resolve itself into the Committee of the Whole for further consideration of the bill to appropriate fiscal 1979 funds for the Departments of State, Justice and Commerce, the Judiciary and related agencies. Motion agreed to 368-6: R 130-3; D 238-3 (ND 165-3; SD 73-0), June 14, 1978.

KEY

- Y Voted for (yea).
- ✓ Paired for.
- † Announced for.
- # CQ Poll for.
- N Voted against (nay).
- X Paired against.
- \- Announced against.
- ▮ CQ Poll against.
- P Voted "present."
- ● Voted "present" to avoid possible conflict of interest.
- ? Did not vote or otherwise make a position known.

	381	382	383	384	385	386	387	388
ALABAMA								
1 Edwards	N	N	Y	Y	Y	Y	Y	Y
2 Dickinson	N	N	Y	Y	Y	Y	Y	Y
3 Nichols	N	N	Y	Y	Y	Y	Y	#
4 Bevill	N	N	Y	Y	Y	Y	Y	Y
5 Flippo	N	Y	Y	Y	?	?	Y	Y
6 Buchanan	Y	Y	N	Y	N	Y	?	Y
7 Flowers	N	N	Y	Y	N	Y	?	?
ALASKA								
AL Young	N	N	Y	Y	Y	Y	#	N
ARIZONA								
1 Rhodes	N	N	Y	Y	Y	Y	?	Y
2 Udall	N	Y	Y	N	N	Y	Y	Y
3 Stump	N	N	Y	Y	Y	N	#	#
4 Rudd	N	N	Y	Y	Y	N	Y	Y
ARKANSAS								
1 Alexander	N	Y	Y	N	N	Y	Y	Y
2 Tucker	▮	#	▮	#	▮	#	#	#
3 Hammerschmidt	N	N	Y	Y	Y	Y	Y	Y
4 Thornton	N	Y	N	?	Y	Y	?	Y
CALIFORNIA								
1 Johnson	N	Y	N	N	N	Y	Y	Y
2 Clausen	N	N	Y	Y	Y	Y	Y	Y
3 Moss	Y	Y	N	?	?	?	?	?
4 Leggett	Y	?	N	N	N	Y	?	Y
5 Burton, J.	Y	Y	N	N	N	N	Y	Y
6 Burton, P.	Y	Y	N	N	N	Y	Y	Y
7 Miller	Y	Y	N	N	N	N	Y	Y
8 Dellums	Y	Y	N	N	N	N	Y	Y
9 Stark	Y	Y	N	N	N	N	#	#
10 Edwards	✓	✓	X	?	?	?	Y	Y
11 Ryan	Y	Y	N	Y	N	Y	Y	Y
12 McCloskey	Y	Y	N	N	N	Y	?	Y
13 Mineta	Y	Y	N	N	N	Y	Y	Y
14 McFall	Y	Y	N	N	N	Y	Y	Y
15 Sisk	Y	Y	Y	Y	Y	Y	Y	Y
16 Panetta	N	Y	N	Y	N	Y	Y	Y
17 Krebs	Y	Y	Y	Y	N	Y	Y	Y
18 Ketchum	N	Y	Y	Y	Y	Y	Y	Y
19 Lagomarsino	N	N	Y	Y	Y	Y	Y	Y
20 Goldwater	N	N	Y	Y	Y	Y	?	Y
21 Corman	Y	Y	N	N	N	#	Y	Y
22 Moorhead	N	N	Y	Y	Y	Y	Y	Y
23 Beilenson	Y	Y	N	N	N	Y	#	Y
24 Waxman	Y	Y	Y	N	N	Y	Y	Y
25 Roybal	Y	Y	N	N	N	Y	Y	Y
26 Rousselot	N	N	Y	Y	Y	N	Y	Y
27 Dornan	N	N	Y	Y	Y	N	Y	Y
28 Burke	✓	✓	X	▮	X	#	Y	Y
29 Hawkins	Y	Y	N	N	N	Y	Y	Y
30 Danielson	Y	Y	N	N	N	Y	Y	Y
31 Wilson, C.H.	Y	Y	N	N	N	Y	Y	?
32 Anderson	Y	Y	N	N	N	Y	Y	Y
33 Clawson	X	?	?	?	?	X	?	?
34 Hannaford	Y	Y	Y	N	N	Y	Y	Y
35 Lloyd	Y	Y	Y	N	N	Y	N	N
36 Brown	Y	Y	N	N	N	Y	?	Y
37 Pettis	Y	?	Y	Y	Y	Y	Y	Y
38 Patterson	Y	Y	Y	N	N	Y	Y	Y
39 Wiggins	N	Y	Y	#	#	▮	Y	Y
40 Badham	N	N	Y	Y	Y	N	Y	Y
41 Wilson, B.	N	N	Y	Y	Y	Y	N	N
42 Van Deerlin	Y	Y	N	N	N	Y	Y	Y
43 Burgener	N	N	Y	Y	Y	Y	Y	Y
COLORADO								
1 Schroeder	Y	Y	N	Y	N	N	Y	Y
2 Wirth	Y	Y	N	Y	N	Y	Y	Y
3 Evans	Y	Y	N	Y	N	Y	Y	Y
4 Johnson	Y	Y	N	Y	Y	Y	Y	Y
5 Armstrong	N	N	Y	Y	?	N	Y	Y
CONNECTICUT								
1 Cotter	N	N	N	Y	Y	Y	Y	Y
2 Dodd	N	Y	N	N	N	Y	?	Y
3 Giaimo	Y	Y	N	Y	Y	Y	?	Y
4 McKinney	Y	Y	N	N	N	Y	Y	Y
5 Sarasin	N	Y	Y	Y	N	Y	Y	Y
6 Moffett	Y	Y	N	N	N	Y	Y	Y
DELAWARE								
AL Evans	Y	Y	Y	Y	Y	Y	Y	Y
FLORIDA								
1 Sikes	N	N	Y	Y	Y	Y	Y	Y
2 Fuqua	N	N	Y	Y	Y	Y	#	#
3 Bennett	N	N	Y	Y	Y	N	Y	Y
4 Chappell	N	N	Y	Y	Y	Y	Y	Y
5 Kelly	N	N	Y	Y	Y	N	Y	Y
6 Young	N	N	Y	Y	Y	Y	Y	Y
7 Gibbons	N	N	?	Y	N	Y	Y	Y
8 Ireland	N	N	Y	Y	Y	Y	Y	Y
9 Frey	N	N	Y	Y	Y	Y	Y	Y
10 Bafalis	N	N	Y	Y	Y	N	Y	Y
11 Rogers	N	Y	Y	N	N	Y	Y	Y
12 Burke	N	N	Y	Y	Y	Y	Y	Y
13 Lehman	Y	Y	Y	N	N	Y	Y	Y
14 Pepper	N	Y	N	N	N	Y	#	Y
15 Fascell	Y	Y	N	N	N	Y	Y	Y
GEORGIA								
1 Ginn	N	Y	Y	Y	Y	Y	Y	Y
2 Mathis	N	Y	Y	Y	Y	N	?	?
3 Brinkley	N	Y	Y	Y	Y	Y	Y	Y
4 Levitas	N	Y	Y	Y	N	Y	Y	Y
5 Fowler	N	Y	N	Y	N	Y	Y	Y
6 Flynt	N	N	Y	Y	Y	N	Y	Y
7 McDonald	N	N	Y	Y	Y	N	Y	Y
8 Evans	N	N	Y	Y	Y	N	Y	#
9 Jenkins	N	Y	Y	Y	Y	N	Y	Y
10 Barnard	N	Y	Y	Y	Y	Y	Y	Y
HAWAII								
1 Heftel	N	Y	N	Y	Y	Y	Y	Y
2 Akaka	N	Y	N	N	N	Y	Y	Y
IDAHO								
1 Symms	N	N	Y	Y	Y	N	Y	Y
2 Hansen, G.	N	N	Y	Y	Y	N	Y	Y
ILLINOIS								
1 Metcalfe	Y	Y	N	N	N	Y	Y	Y
2 Murphy	N	N	N	N	Y	Y	Y	Y
3 Russo	N	N	Y	Y	N	Y	#	Y
4 Derwinski	N	N	Y	Y	Y	N	Y	Y
5 Fary	N	N	N	N	N	Y	Y	Y
6 Hyde	N	N	Y	Y	Y	Y	Y	Y
7 Collins	Y	Y	N	N	N	Y	Y	?
8 Rostenkowski	N	N	N	N	Y	Y	#	Y
9 Yates	Y	Y	N	N	N	Y	Y	Y
. 10 Mikva	Y	Y	▮	▮	▮	#	#	#
11 Annunzio	N	N	Y	N	N	Y	Y	Y
12 Crane	N	N	Y	Y	Y	N	Y	Y
13 McClory	N	N	N	Y	Y	Y	Y	Y
14 Erlenborn	N	N	Y	Y	N	Y	#	Y
15 Corcoran	N	N	Y	Y	Y	Y	Y	Y
16 Anderson	Y	Y	N	N	N	Y	#	Y
17 O'Brien	N	N	N	N	Y	Y	#	#
18 Michel	N	N	Y	Y	Y	Y	Y	Y
19 Railsback	N	Y	N	Y	N	Y	#	Y
20 Findley	N	Y	N	Y	Y	Y	Y	Y
21 Madigan	N	N	Y	?	Y	Y	?	Y
22 Shipley	N	Y	Y	Y	?	Y	Y	Y
23 Price	N	N	N	N	N	Y	Y	Y
24 Simon	?	?	?	?	?	?	?	?
INDIANA								
1 Benjamin	N	N	Y	N	N	Y	Y	Y
2 Fithian	N	N	Y	Y	Y	Y	Y	Y
3 Brademas	Y	Y	N	N	N	Y	Y	Y
4 Quayle	N	N	Y	Y	Y	Y	?	N
5 Hillis	N	N	N	Y	N	Y	?	Y
6 Evans	N	N	Y	Y	Y	N	Y	Y
7 Myers, J.	N	N	Y	Y	Y	Y	Y	Y
8 Cornwell	N	Y	N	Y	Y	Y	?	Y
9 Hamilton	N	N	N	Y	N	Y	Y	Y
10 Sharp	N	N	N	Y	N	Y	Y	Y
11 Jacobs	N	Y	Y	Y	Y	Y	Y	Y
IOWA								
1 Leach	N	Y	Y	Y	Y	Y	Y	Y
2 Blouin	N	N	N	N	N	Y	Y	Y
3 Grassley	N	N	Y	Y	Y	Y	Y	Y
4 Smith	N	Y	N	N	N	Y	Y	Y
5 Harkin	N	Y	N	Y	N	Y	Y	Y
6 Bedell	N	Y	N	N	Y	Y	Y	Y

Democrats ***Republicans***

	381	382	383	384	385	386	387	388
KANSAS								
1 ***Sebelius***	N	N	Y	Y	Y	Y	Y	Y
2 Keys	Y	Y	N	N	N	Y	Y	Y
3 ***Winn***	N	N	Y	Y	Y	Y	Y	Y
4 Glickman	Y	Y	Y	N	Y	Y	Y	Y
5 ***Skubitz***	N	N	Y	Y	Y	Y	Y	?
KENTUCKY								
1 Hubbard	N	N	Y	Y	Y	Y	Y	Y
2 Natcher	N	N	N	N	N	Y	Y	Y
3 Mazzoli	N	N	Y	Y	N	Y	Y	Y
4 ***Snyder***	N	N	Y	Y	Y	N	Y	Y
5 ***Carter***	N	N	Y	N	Y	Y	Y	Y
6 Breckinridge	Y	Y	N	Y	N	Y	Y	Y
7 Perkins	N	N	N	N	N	Y	Y	Y
LOUISIANA								
1 ***Livingston***	N	N	Y	Y	Y	Y	Y	Y
2 Boggs	N	N	N	N	N	Y	Y	Y
3 ***Treen***	N	N	N	Y	✓	Y	Y	Y
4 Waggonner	N	N	Y	Y	Y	Y	Y	Y
5 Huckaby	N	N	Y	Y	Y	Y	Y	Y
6 ***Moore***	N	N	Y	Y	Y	Y	Y	Y
7 Breaux	N	N	Y	Y	Y	Y	Y	Y
8 Long	N	N	N	N	Y	Y	Y	Y
MAINE								
1 ***Emery***	N	N	Y	Y	Y	Y	Y	Y
2 ***Cohen***	Y	Y	Y	Y	Y	Y	Y	?
MARYLAND								
1 ***Bauman***	N	N	Y	Y	Y	N	Y	Y
2 Long	Y	Y	Y	Y	N	Y	?	Y
3 Mikulski	Y	Y	N	N	N	Y	#	Y
4 ***Holt***	N	N	Y	Y	Y	N	Y	Y
5 Spellman	Y	Y	N	#	N	Y	Y	#
6 Byron	N	N	Y	Y	N	Y	Y	Y
7 Mitchell	Y	Y	N	N	N	Y	#	N
8 ***Steers***	Y	Y	N	N	N	Y	Y	Y
MASSACHUSETTS								
1 ***Conte***	N	N	N	N	N	Y	Y	Y
2 Boland	N	N	N	N	N	Y	Y	Y
3 Early	N	N	N	N	N	Y	Y	Y
4 Drinan	Y	Y	N	N	N	Y	Y	Y
5 Tsongas	#	Y	N	N	N	Y	Y	Y
6 Harrington	Y	Y	N	N	N	Y	#	Y
7 Markey	N	N	N	N	N	#	Y	Y
8 O'Neill								
9 Moakley	N	N	N	N	N	Y	Y	Y
10 ***Heckler***	N	N	N	Y	N	Y	#	Y
11 Burke	N	N	N	N	N	Y	Y	Y
12 Studds	Y	Y	N	N	N	Y	Y	Y
MICHIGAN								
1 Conyers	✓	X	X	▮	X	#	#	Y
2 ***Pursell***	Y	Y	Y	N	N	Y	Y	Y
3 ***Brown***	N	Y	N	Y	N	Y	Y	Y
4 ***Stockman***	N	Y	Y	Y	Y	N	Y	Y
5 ***Sawyer***	N	N	Y	Y	Y	Y	Y	Y
6 Carr	Y	Y	N	N	N	Y	Y	Y
7 Kildee	N	N	N	N	N	Y	Y	Y
8 Traxler	N	N	Y	N	N	Y	Y	Y
9 ***Vander Jagt***	N	N	Y	Y	Y	Y	?	Y
10 ***Cederberg***	N	N	Y	N	Y	Y	Y	Y
11 ***Ruppe***	▮	N	N	Y	N	Y	Y	#
12 Bonior	N	N	N	N	N	Y	Y	Y
13 Diggs	Y	Y	N	N	N	Y	?	?
14 Nedzi	X	✓	✓	?	?	?	?	?
15 Ford	Y	Y	Y	N	N	Y	?	?
16 Dingell	Y	Y	Y	N	N	Y	?	N
17 Brodhead	Y	Y	N	N	N	N	?	?
18 Blanchard	N	Y	Y	N	N	Y	Y	Y
19 ***Broomfield***	N	N	Y	Y	Y	Y	Y	Y
MINNESOTA								
1 ***Quie***	X	▮	#	#	#	✓	#	#
2 ***Hagedorn***	N	N	Y	Y	Y	N	Y	Y
3 ***Frenzel***	✓	✓	?	?	X	X	?	?
4 Vento	N	N	N	N	N	Y	Y	Y
5 Fraser	Y	Y	N	N	N	Y	#	Y
6 Nolan	?	?	?	?	?	?	Y	Y
7 ***Stangeland***	N	N	Y	Y	Y	N	Y	Y
8 Oberstar	N	N	N	N	N	Y	Y	Y
MISSISSIPPI								
1 Whitten	N	Y	Y	N	Y	Y	Y	Y
2 Bowen	N	N	Y	Y	Y	Y	Y	Y
3 Montgomery	N	N	Y	Y	Y	Y	Y	Y
4 ***Cochran***	N	N	Y	Y	Y	Y	Y	Y
5 ***Lott***	N	N	Y	Y	Y	Y	Y	Y
MISSOURI								
1 Clay	Y	Y	N	N	N	Y	Y	Y
2 Young	N	N	N	Y	N	Y	Y	Y
3 Gephardt	N	N	Y	Y	Y	N	Y	Y
4 Skelton	N	N	#	?	▮	#	#	Y
5 Bolling	Y	Y	N	N	N	Y	#	Y
6 ***Coleman***	N	N	Y	Y	Y	Y	Y	Y
7 ***Taylor***	N	N	Y	Y	Y	Y	Y	Y
8 Ichord	N	N	Y	Y	Y	Y	Y	Y
9 Volkmer	N	N	N	Y	Y	Y	Y	Y
10 Burlison	N	N	N	N	N	Y	Y	Y
MONTANA								
1 Baucus	Y	Y	Y	Y	N	Y	Y	Y
2 ***Marlenee***	N	N	Y	Y	Y	Y	Y	Y
NEBRASKA								
1 ***Thone***	N	N	Y	Y	Y	Y	Y	Y
2 Cavanaugh	N	N	N	Y	Y	Y	Y	Y
3 ***Smith***	N	X	Y	Y	Y	Y	Y	Y
NEVADA								
AL Santini	N	Y	Y	Y	Y	Y	#	Y
NEW HAMPSHIRE								
1 D'Amours	N	N	Y	N	N	Y	#	Y
2 ***Cleveland***	Y	Y	Y	Y	Y	Y	Y	Y
NEW JERSEY								
1 Florio	N	Y	Y	N	N	#	Y	Y
2 Hughes	N	Y	✓	#	✓	X	Y	Y
3 Howard	Y	Y	Y	N	N	Y	Y	Y
4 Thompson	Y	Y	N	N	N	Y	#	Y
5 ***Fenwick***	Y	Y	N	Y	Y	Y	Y	Y
6 ***Forsythe***	Y	Y	Y	Y	Y	N	Y	Y
7 Maguire	Y	Y	N	N	N	Y	Y	Y
8 Roe	N	N	N	N	N	Y	Y	Y
9 ***Hollenbeck***	N	Y	N	N	N	Y	Y	Y
10 Rodino	▮	▮	▮	▮	▮	#	#	#
11 Minish	N	N	Y	N	N	Y	Y	Y
12 ***Rinaldo***	N	N	Y	N	N	Y	Y	Y
13 Meyner	Y	Y	N	N	N	Y	Y	#
14 LeFante	X	X	✓	▮	X	#	#	Y
15 Patten	N	N	N	N	N	Y	#	#
NEW MEXICO								
1 ***Lujan***	N	N	Y	Y	Y	Y	?	Y
2 Runnels	?	X	?	?	✓	?	#	#
NEW YORK								
1 Pike	N	Y	N	Y	Y	Y	Y	Y
2 Downey	Y	Y	N	Y	N	Y	Y	Y
3 Ambro	N	N	Y	Y	N	Y	?	Y
4 ***Lent***	N	N	Y	#	Y	Y	Y	Y
5 ***Wydler***	N	N	Y	Y	N	Y	Y	Y
6 Wolff	Y	Y	Y	N	N	Y	Y	#
7 Addabbo	N	Y	N	N	N	Y	Y	Y
8 Rosenthal	Y	Y	N	N	N	Y	Y	Y
9 Delaney	N	N	Y	Y	Y	Y	Y	Y
10 Biaggi	N	N	Y	▮	N	Y	#	#
11 Scheuer	Y	Y	Y	N	N	Y	Y	Y
12 Chisholm	Y	Y	N	N	N	Y	#	#
13 Solarz	Y	Y	Y	N	N	Y	Y	Y
14 Richmond	Y	Y	N	N	N	Y	?	Y
15 Zeferetti	N	N	Y	N	N	Y	Y	Y
16 Holtzman	Y	Y	N	N	N	Y	?	Y
17 Murphy	N	N	N	N	N	Y	Y	Y
18 ***Green***	Y	Y	N	N	N	Y	Y	Y
19 Rangel	Y	Y	N	N	N	✓	?	?
20 Weiss	Y	Y	N	N	N	N	Y	Y
21 Garcia	Y	Y	N	N	N	Y	Y	?
22 Bingham	Y	Y	N	N	N	Y	Y	Y
23 ***Caputo***	N	?	?	?	X	✓	?	?
24 Ottinger	Y	Y	N	N	N	Y	Y	Y
25 ***Fish***	N	N	N	Y	N	Y	Y	Y
26 ***Gilman***	Y	Y	N	N	N	Y	Y	Y
27 McHugh	N	N	N	N	N	Y	Y	Y
28 Stratton	N	N	N	Y	Y	Y	Y	?
29 Pattison	N	Y	N	N	N	Y	Y	Y
30 ***McEwen***	N	N	Y	Y	Y	Y	?	Y
31 ***Mitchell***	N	N	Y	N	Y	Y	?	Y
32 Hanley	N	N	Y	N	Y	Y	Y	Y
33 ***Walsh***	N	N	Y	N	Y	Y	Y	Y
34 ***Horton***	Y	Y	Y	N	N	Y	#	#
35 ***Conable***	N	Y	Y	Y	N	Y	Y	Y
36 LaFalce	N	N	N	N	N	Y	Y	Y
37 Nowak	N	N	Y	N	N	Y	Y	Y
38 ***Kemp***	N	N	Y	Y	Y	Y	?	Y
39 Lundine	Y	Y	N	N	N	Y	Y	Y
NORTH CAROLINA								
1 Jones	N	Y	Y	N	Y	Y	Y	Y
2 Fountain	N	Y	Y	Y	Y	Y	#	Y
3 Whitley	Y	Y	Y	Y	Y	Y	Y	Y
4 Andrews	?	Y	Y	Y	N	Y	#	Y
5 Neal	N	Y	Y	Y	Y	Y	Y	Y
6 Preyer	N	Y	N	N	N	Y	Y	Y
7 Rose	Y	Y	N	N	N	Y	Y	#
8 Hefner	N	Y	Y	Y	Y	Y	Y	Y
9 ***Martin***	N	Y	Y	Y	Y	Y	Y	Y
10 ***Broyhill***	N	Y	Y	Y	Y	N	Y	Y
11 Gudger	N	Y	Y	Y	Y	Y	?	Y
NORTH DAKOTA								
AL ***Andrews***	N	N	Y	Y	Y	Y	Y	Y
OHIO								
1 ***Gradison***	N	N	Y	Y	N	N	Y	Y
2 Luken	N	N	Y	Y	N	Y	Y	Y
3 ***Whalen***	N	N	N	N	N	Y	#	#
4 ***Guyer***	N	N	Y	Y	Y	Y	Y	Y
5 ***Latta***	N	N	Y	Y	Y	N	Y	Y
6 ***Harsha***	N	N	Y	Y	Y	Y	?	?
7 ***Brown***	N	N	N	Y	Y	Y	Y	Y
8 ***Kindness***	N	N	Y	Y	Y	Y	Y	Y
9 Ashley	Y	Y	N	N	N	Y	?	?
10 ***Miller***	N	N	Y	Y	Y	N	Y	Y
11 ***Stanton***	N	N	N	Y	N	Y	Y	Y
12 ***Devine***	N	N	Y	Y	Y	N	Y	Y
13 Pease	N	Y	N	N	N	Y	Y	Y
14 Seiberling	Y	Y	N	N	N	Y	#	Y
15 ***Wylie***	N	N	N	Y	N	Y	Y	Y
16 ***Regula***	N	N	N	Y	N	Y	Y	Y
17 ***Ashbrook***	N	N	Y	Y	✓	X	#	#
18 Applegate	N	N	Y	Y	N	Y	Y	Y
19 Carney	N	N	N	N	N	Y	Y	Y
20 Oakar	N	N	N	N	N	Y	Y	Y
21 Stokes	Y	Y	N	N	N	Y	Y	#
22 Vanik	N	Y	N	N	▮	#	Y	Y
23 Mottl	N	N	Y	Y	Y	N	Y	Y
OKLAHOMA								
1 Jones	N	Y	Y	Y	Y	N	Y	Y
2 Risenhoover	N	N	Y	Y	Y	Y	Y	?
3 Watkins	N	N	Y	Y	Y	Y	#	Y
4 Steed	Y	Y	N	N	Y	Y	Y	Y
5 ***Edwards***	N	N	Y	Y	Y	N	Y	Y
6 English	N	N	Y	Y	Y	N	Y	Y
OREGON								
1 AuCoin	Y	Y	Y	Y	N	N	Y	Y
2 Ullman	N	Y	Y	▮	▮	#	Y	#
3 Duncan	?	Y	Y	N	N	Y	Y	?
4 Weaver	Y	Y	N	Y	N	N	Y	Y
PENNSYLVANIA								
1 Myers, M.	N	N	Y	N	N	Y	Y	Y
2 Nix	?	Y	N	N	N	Y	Y	Y
3 Lederer	N	N	N	N	N	Y	Y	Y
4 Eilberg	N	N	N	N	N	Y	Y	Y
5 ***Schulze***	N	N	Y	Y	Y	N	Y	Y
6 Yatron	N	N	Y	Y	Y	Y	Y	Y
7 Edgar	Y	Y	N	N	N	Y	Y	Y
8 Kostmayer	Y	Y	Y	Y	N	Y	Y	Y
9 ***Shuster***	N	N	Y	Y	Y	N	Y	Y
10 ***McDade***	N	N	Y	N	N	Y	#	#
11 Flood	N	N	N	N	N	Y	Y	Y
12 Murtha	N	N	Y	Y	N	Y	Y	Y
13 ***Coughlin***	N	Y	Y	Y	N	✓	Y	Y
14 Moorhead	Y	Y	N	N	N	Y	Y	Y
15 Rooney	N	N	N	N	N	Y	Y	Y
16 ***Walker***	N	N	Y	Y	Y	N	Y	Y
17 Ertel	N	N	Y	Y	Y	Y	Y	Y
18 Walgren	#	Y	Y	N	Y	Y	?	?
19 ***Goodling, W.***	N	N	Y	Y	✓	Y	Y	?
20 Gaydos	N	N	Y	N	N	Y	Y	Y
21 Dent	N	Y	✓	▮	N	Y	#	Y
22 Murphy	N	N	Y	N	N	Y	Y	Y
23 Ammerman	N	N	N	N	N	Y	Y	Y
24 ***Marks***	N	N	N	Y	N	Y	Y	Y
25 ***Myers, G.***	N	N	Y	Y	N	Y	Y	Y
RHODE ISLAND								
1 St Germain	N	N	N	N	N	Y	Y	Y
2 Beard	N	X	N	N	N	Y	Y	Y
SOUTH CAROLINA								
1 Davis	Y	Y	Y	Y	N	Y	Y	Y
2 ***Spence***	N	N	Y	Y	Y	Y	Y	Y
3 Derrick	N	Y	Y	Y	Y	Y	Y	Y
4 Mann	?	?	?	?	?	?	Y	Y
5 Holland	▮	▮	?	?	?	#	#	#
6 Jenrette	✓	✓	X	#	X	✓	#	Y
SOUTH DAKOTA								
1 ***Pressler***	N	N	N	Y	Y	Y	Y	Y
2 ***Abdnor***	N	N	Y	Y	Y	Y	Y	Y
TENNESSEE								
1 ***Quillen***	N	N	Y	Y	Y	Y	Y	Y
2 ***Duncan***	N	N	Y	Y	Y	Y	Y	Y
3 Lloyd	N	N	Y	Y	Y	Y	Y	Y
4 Gore	N	N	N	N	N	Y	Y	Y
5 Allen	?	?	?	?	?	?	?	?
6 ***Beard***	N	N	Y	Y	Y	Y	Y	Y
7 Jones	N	Y	Y	N	Y	Y	#	#
8 Ford	Y	Y	N	N	N	Y	Y	Y
TEXAS								
1 Hall	N	N	Y	Y	Y	N	Y	Y
2 Wilson, C.	Y	Y	Y	N	N	Y	Y	#
3 ***Collins***	N	N	Y	Y	Y	N	Y	Y
4 Roberts	N	Y	Y	Y	Y	N	Y	Y
5 Mattox	N	Y	N	Y	N	Y	Y	Y
6 Teague	X	Y	N	?	✓	X	?	?
7 ***Archer***	N	N	Y	Y	Y	N	?	Y
8 Eckhardt	Y	Y	N	N	N	Y	Y	Y
9 Brooks	N	Y	Y	N	Y	Y	Y	Y
10 Pickle	Y	Y	Y	N	Y	Y	Y	Y
11 Poage	N	Y	Y	Y	N	Y	Y	Y
12 Wright	N	Y	Y	N	N	Y	Y	Y
13 Hightower	N	Y	Y	N	Y	Y	Y	Y
14 Young	N	?	?	?	?	?	Y	Y
15 de la Garza	?	?	?	?	?	?	Y	Y
16 White	N	Y	Y	N	Y	Y	Y	Y
17 Burleson	N	N	Y	Y	Y	N	Y	Y
18 Jordan	Y	Y	N	N	N	Y	Y	Y
19 Mahon	N	Y	Y	N	Y	Y	Y	Y
20 Gonzalez	Y	Y	N	N	N	Y	Y	Y
21 Krueger	Y	Y	N	Y	Y	Y	Y	#
22 Gammage	N	N	Y	Y	Y	Y	Y	Y
23 Kazen	N	N	N	N	Y	Y	Y	Y
24 Milford	N	Y	Y	Y	Y	N	?	?
UTAH								
1 McKay	N	N	Y	Y	Y	Y	Y	Y
2 ***Marriott***	N	N	Y	Y	Y	N	Y	Y
VERMONT								
AL ***Jeffords***	Y	Y	N	N	N	Y	Y	Y
VIRGINIA								
1 ***Trible***	N	N	Y	Y	Y	Y	Y	Y
2 ***Whitehurst***	N	N	Y	Y	Y	Y	Y	Y
3 Satterfield	N	N	Y	Y	Y	N	Y	Y
4 ***Daniel***	N	N	Y	Y	Y	N	Y	Y
5 Daniel	N	N	Y	Y	Y	N	Y	?
6 ***Butler***	Y	Y	Y	Y	Y	N	Y	Y
7 ***Robinson***	N	N	Y	Y	Y	N	Y	Y
8 Harris	Y	Y	N	N	N	Y	Y	Y
9 ***Wampler***	N	N	Y	Y	Y	Y	Y	Y
10 Fisher	Y	Y	N	Y	Y	Y	Y	#
WASHINGTON								
1 ***Pritchard***	Y	Y	N	Y	N	Y	Y	Y
2 Meeds	Y	Y	N	N	N	Y	Y	Y
3 Bonker	N	Y	Y	N	N	Y	Y	Y
4 McCormack	Y	Y	Y	Y	N	Y	Y	Y
5 Foley	Y	Y	Y	Y	N	Y	Y	Y
6 Dicks	Y	Y	Y	N	N	Y	Y	Y
7 ***Cunningham***	N	N	Y	Y	Y	Y	Y	Y
WEST VIRGINIA								
1 Mollohan	Y	Y	Y	N	N	Y	Y	Y
2 Staggers	N	Y	N	N	N	Y	Y	Y
3 Slack	Y	Y	Y	N	Y	Y	Y	Y
4 Rahall	N	Y	N	N	N	Y	Y	Y
WISCONSIN								
1 Aspin	N	N	N	Y	N	Y	Y	Y
2 Kastenmeier	Y	Y	N	N	N	Y	Y	Y
3 Baldus	N	N	N	N	N	Y	Y	Y
4 Zablocki	N	N	Y	N	N	Y	Y	Y
5 Reuss	N	Y	N	N	N	Y	Y	Y
6 ***Steiger***	N	N	N	Y	N	Y	Y	Y
7 Obey	N	Y	N	N	N	Y	Y	Y
8 Cornell	N	N	N	N	N	Y	Y	Y
9 ***Kasten***	N	N	N	Y	Y	Y	Y	Y
WYOMING								
AL Roncalio	Y	Y	N	N	N	Y	?	?

Democrats ***Republicans***

389. HR 12934. State, Justice, Commerce, Judiciary Appropriations, Fiscal 1979. Beard, R-Tenn., amendment to prohibit the use of Commerce Department funds for conducting trade with Cuba. Adopted 241-158: R 127-10; D 114-148 (ND 52-128; SD 62-20), June 14, 1978.

390. HR 12934. State, Justice, Commerce, Judiciary Appropriations, Fiscal 1979. Rousselot, R-Calif., amendment to reduce the appropriation for the Legal Services Corporation by $30 million. Rejected 200-203: R 112-24; D 88-179 (ND 35-148; SD 53-31), June 14, 1978.

391. HR 12934. State, Justice, Commerce, Judiciary Appropriations, Fiscal 1979. Moorhead, R-Calif., amendment to prohibit the use of appropriated funds for the Legal Services Corporation for publicity or propaganda purposes designed to support or defeat legislation pending before Congress or any state legislature. Adopted 264-131: R 128-7; D 136-124 (ND 71-108; SD 65-16), June 14, 1978.

392. HR 12934. State, Justice, Commerce, Judiciary Appropriations, Fiscal 1979. Passage of the bill to appropriate $4.6 billion for the Departments of State, Justice and Commerce, the Judiciary and 18 independent agencies. Passed 359-34: R 117-19; D 242-15 (ND 171-9; SD 71-6), June 14, 1978. The president had requested $8.6 billion.

KEY

- Y Voted for (yea).
- ✓ Paired for.
- † Announced for.
- # CQ Poll for.
- N Voted against (nay).
- X Paired against.
- \- Announced against.
- ▮ CQ Poll against.
- P Voted "present."
- ● Voted "present" to avoid possible conflict of interest.
- ? Did not vote or otherwise make a position known.

	389	390	391	392
ALABAMA				
1 Edwards	Y	Y	Y	Y
2 Dickinson	Y	Y	Y	Y
3 Nichols	Y	Y	Y	Y
4 Bevill	Y	Y	Y	Y
5 Flippo	Y	Y	Y	?
6 Buchanan	Y	Y	Y	Y
7 Flowers	Y	Y	?	?
ALASKA				
AL Young	Y	Y	Y	N
ARIZONA				
1 Rhodes	Y	Y	Y	Y
2 Udall	N	N	N	Y
3 Stump	#	#	#	▮
4 Rudd	Y	Y	Y	N
ARKANSAS				
1 Alexander	N	N	N	Y
2 Tucker	#	▮	#	#
3 Hammerschmidt	Y	Y	Y	Y
4 Thornton	N	N	?	?
CALIFORNIA				
1 Johnson	N	N	Y	Y
2 Clausen	Y	Y	Y	Y
3 Moss	X	N	N	Y
4 Leggett	N	Y	Y	Y
5 Burton, J.	N	N	N	Y
6 Burton, P.	N	N	N	Y
7 Miller	N	N	N	Y
8 Dellums	N	N	N	Y
9 Stark	N	N	N	Y
10 Edwards	N	N	N	Y
11 Ryan	N	N	N	Y
12 McCloskey	N	N	Y	Y
13 Mineta	N	N	N	Y
14 McFall	N	N	N	Y
15 Sisk	N	N	Y	Y
16 Panetta	Y	N	Y	Y
17 Krebs	Y	N	Y	Y
18 Ketchum	Y	Y	Y	Y
19 Lagomarsino	Y	Y	Y	Y
20 Goldwater	Y	Y	Y	Y
21 Corman	N	N	N	Y
22 Moorhead	Y	Y	Y	Y
23 Beilenson	N	N	N	Y
24 Waxman	N	N	N	Y
25 Roybal	N	N	N	Y
26 Rousselot	Y	Y	Y	Y
27 Dornan	Y	Y	Y	N
28 Burke	N	N	N	Y
29 Hawkins	N	N	N	Y
30 Danielson	N	N	N	Y
31 Wilson, C.H.	?	N	N	Y
32 Anderson	N	N	Y	Y
33 Clawson	?	✓	?	?
34 Hannaford	N	N	Y	Y
35 Lloyd	N	Y	Y	Y
36 Brown	N	N	N	Y
37 Pettis	Y	Y	Y	Y
38 Patterson	N	N	N	Y
39 Wiggins	Y	Y	Y	Y
40 Badham	Y	✓	#	#
41 Wilson, B.	Y	Y	Y	Y
42 Van Deerlin	N	N	N	Y
43 Burgener	Y	Y	Y	Y
COLORADO				
1 Schroeder	N	N	N	N
2 Wirth	▮	N	N	Y
3 Evans	N	N	N	Y
4 Johnson	N	Y	Y	Y
5 Armstrong	Y	Y	Y	Y
CONNECTICUT				
1 Cotter	N	Y	N	Y
2 Dodd	N	N	N	Y
3 Giaimo	N	N	N	Y
4 McKinney	N	N	Y	Y
5 Sarasin	Y	Y	Y	Y
6 Moffett	N	N	N	Y
DELAWARE				
AL Evans	Y	Y	Y	Y
FLORIDA				
1 Sikes	Y	Y	Y	Y
2 Fuqua	#	#	#	#
3 Bennett	Y	Y	Y	Y
4 Chappell	Y	Y	Y	Y
5 Kelly	Y	Y	Y	N
6 Young	Y	Y	Y	Y
7 Gibbons	Y	N	Y	Y
8 Ireland	Y	Y	Y	Y
9 Frey	Y	Y	Y	Y
10 Bafalis	Y	Y	Y	Y
11 Rogers	Y	Y	Y	Y
12 Burke	Y	Y	Y	Y
13 Lehman	N	N	N	Y
14 Pepper	Y	N	N	Y
15 Fascell	N	N	N	Y
GEORGIA				
1 Ginn	Y	Y	Y	Y
2 Mathis	Y	Y	Y	N
3 Brinkley	Y	Y	Y	Y
4 Levitas	Y	N	Y	Y
5 Fowler	N	N	Y	Y
6 Flynt	Y	N	Y	Y
7 McDonald	Y	Y	Y	N
8 Evans	Y	Y	Y	N
9 Jenkins	Y	Y	Y	Y
10 Barnard	Y	Y	Y	?
HAWAII				
1 Heftel	Y	Y	Y	Y
2 Akaka	N	N	N	Y
IDAHO				
1 Symms	Y	Y	Y	N
2 Hansen, G.	Y	✓	✓	?
ILLINOIS				
1 Metcalfe	N	N	N	Y
2 Murphy	Y	Y	N	Y
3 Russo	Y	Y	Y	Y
4 Derwinski	Y	Y	Y	Y
5 Fary	Y	Y	Y	Y
6 Hyde	Y	Y	Y	Y
7 Collins	N	N	?	Y
8 Rostenkowski	N	Y	Y	Y
9 Yates	N	N	N	Y
10 Mikva	▮	X	#	#
11 Annunzio	Y	Y	Y	Y
12 Crane	Y	Y	Y	N
13 McClory	N	N	Y	Y
14 Erlenborn	N	N	Y	Y
15 Corcoran	Y	Y	Y	Y
16 Anderson	Y	N	Y	Y
17 O'Brien	#	✓	#	#
18 Michel	Y	Y	Y	Y
19 Railsback	N	N	N	Y
20 Findley	N	N	Y	Y
21 Madigan	Y	Y	Y	Y
22 Shipley	N	Y	Y	Y
23 Price	N	N	N	#
24 Simon	?	?	?	?
INDIANA				
1 Benjamin	N	N	Y	Y
2 Fithian	Y	Y	Y	Y
3 Brademas	N	N	N	Y
4 Quayle	Y	Y	Y	Y
5 Hillis	Y	Y	Y	Y
6 Evans	Y	N	Y	N
7 Myers, J.	Y	Y	Y	Y
8 Cornwell	N	N	Y	N
9 Hamilton	Y	N	N	Y
10 Sharp	Y	N	N	Y
11 Jacobs	Y	N	Y	N
IOWA				
1 Leach	N	N	N	Y
2 Blouin	N	N	N	Y
3 Grassley	Y	Y	Y	Y
4 Smith	N	N	N	Y
5 Harkin	N	N	N	Y
6 Bedell	N	N	N	Y

Democrats ***Republicans***

	389	390	391	392
KANSAS				
1 ***Sebelius***	Y	Y	Y	Y
2 Keys	N	N	Y	Y
3 ***Winn***	Y	Y	Y	Y
4 Glickman	Y	Y	Y	Y
5 ***Skubitz***	N	Y	Y	Y
KENTUCKY				
1 Hubbard	Y	Y	Y	Y
2 Natcher	Y	N	Y	Y
3 Mazzoli	Y	N	N	Y
4 ***Snyder***	Y	Y	Y	Y
5 ***Carter***	Y	Y	Y	Y
6 Breckinridge	N	Y	N	Y
7 Perkins	Y	N	Y	Y
LOUISIANA				
1 ***Livingston***	Y	Y	Y	Y
2 Boggs	N	N	Y	Y
3 ***Treen***	Y	Y	Y	Y
4 Waggonner	Y	Y	Y	Y
5 Huckaby	Y	Y	Y	Y
6 ***Moore***	Y	Y	Y	Y
7 Breaux	Y	Y	Y	Y
8 Long	N	N	Y	Y
MAINE				
1 ***Emery***	Y	Y	Y	Y
2 ***Cohen***	?	?	?	?
MARYLAND				
1 ***Bauman***	Y	Y	Y	N
2 Long	N	N	N	Y
3 Mikulski	N	N	N	Y
4 ***Holt***	Y	Y	Y	Y
5 Spellman	N	N	N	Y
6 Byron	Y	Y	Y	Y
7 Mitchell	Y	N	N	Y
8 ***Steers***	Y	N	N	Y
MASSACHUSETTS				
1 ***Conte***	Y	N	Y	Y
2 Boland	N	N	Y	Y
3 Early	N	N	N	Y
4 Drinan	N	N	N	Y
5 Tsongas	N	▮	?	#
6 Harrington	N	N	N	Y
7 Markey	N	N	N	Y
8 O'Neill				
9 Moakley	Y	N	Y	Y
10 ***Heckler***	?	N	Y	Y
11 Burke	Y	Y	N	Y
12 Studds	N	N	Y	Y
MICHIGAN				
1 Conyers	X	N	N	N
2 ***Pursell***	Y	N	Y	Y
3 ***Brown***	Y	Y	Y	Y
4 ***Stockman***	Y	Y	#	Y
5 ***Sawyer***	Y	Y	Y	Y
6 Carr	N	N	N	Y
7 Kildee	N	N	Y	Y
8 Traxler	Y	N	Y	Y
9 ***Vander Jagt***	Y	Y	Y	Y
10 ***Cederberg***	Y	N	Y	Y
11 ***Ruppe***	Y	Y	Y	Y
12 Bonior	N	N	N	Y
13 Diggs	N	N	N	Y
14 Nedzi	X	X	X	?
15 Ford	N	N	N	Y
16 Dingell	N	N	?	Y
17 Brodhead	N	N	N	Y
18 Blanchard	N	N	Y	Y
19 ***Broomfield***	Y	Y	Y	N
MINNESOTA				
1 ***Quie***	#	#	#	#
2 ***Hagedorn***	Y	Y	Y	Y
3 ***Frenzel***	✔	?	?	?
4 Vento	N	N	N	Y
5 Fraser	N	N	N	Y
6 Nolan	N	N	N	Y
7 ***Stangeland***	Y	Y	Y	Y
8 Oberstar	N	N	N	Y
MISSISSIPPI				
1 Whitten	Y	Y	Y	Y
2 Bowen	Y	Y	Y	Y
3 Montgomery	Y	Y	Y	Y
4 ***Cochran***	Y	Y	Y	Y
5 ***Lott***	Y	Y	Y	Y
MISSOURI				
1 Clay	N	N	N	Y
2 Young	Y	Y	N	Y
3 Gephardt	Y	Y	N	Y
4 Skelton	Y	Y	Y	Y
5 Bolling	N	N	N	Y
6 ***Coleman***	Y	Y	Y	Y
7 ***Taylor***	Y	Y	Y	Y
8 Ichord	Y	Y	Y	Y
9 Volkmer	Y	Y	N	Y
10 Burlison	N	N	N	Y
MONTANA				
1 Baucus	Y	N	N	Y
2 ***Marlenee***	Y	Y	Y	N
NEBRASKA				
1 ***Thone***	Y	Y	Y	Y
2 Cavanaugh	N	N	Y	Y
3 ***Smith***	Y	Y	Y	Y
NEVADA				
AL Santini	Y	N	Y	Y
NEW HAMPSHIRE				
1 D'Amours	Y	N	Y	Y
2 ***Cleveland***	Y	Y	Y	Y
NEW JERSEY				
1 Florio	Y	N	N	Y
2 Hughes	Y	N	Y	Y
3 Howard	Y	N	N	Y
4 Thompson	N	N	N	Y
5 ***Fenwick***	Y	Y	Y	Y
6 ***Forsythe***	Y	Y	Y	N
7 Maguire	N	N	N	Y
8 Roe	Y	N	Y	Y
9 ***Hollenbeck***	Y	N	N	Y
10 Rodino	▮	▮	▮	#
11 Minish	Y	N	Y	Y
12 ***Rinaldo***	Y	Y	Y	Y
13 Meyner	N	N	▮	Y
14 LeFante	N	N	Y	Y
15 Patten	X	N	N	Y
NEW MEXICO				
1 ***Lujan***	Y	Y	Y	Y
2 Runnels	?	✔	?	#
NEW YORK				
1 Pike	Y	N	Y	Y
2 Downey	N	N	N	Y
3 Ambro	Y	Y	Y	Y
4 ***Lent***	Y	Y	Y	Y
5 ***Wydler***	Y	Y	Y	Y
6 Wolff	Y	N	Y	Y
7 Addabbo	N	N	Y	Y
8 Rosenthal	N	N	N	Y
9 Delaney	Y	Y	?	Y
10 Biaggi	✔	X	#	#
11 Scheuer	N	N	N	Y
12 Chisholm	X	X	X	#
13 Solarz	N	N	N	Y
14 Richmond	N	N	N	Y
15 Zeferetti	Y	Y	Y	Y
16 Holtzman	N	N	N	Y
17 Murphy	Y	X	#	#
18 ***Green***	Y	N	Y	Y
19 Rangel	X	X	X	?
20 Weiss	N	N	N	Y
21 Garcia	X	X	X	?
22 Bingham	N	N	N	Y
23 ***Caputo***	?	?	?	?
24 Ottinger	N	N	N	†
25 ***Fish***	Y	N	Y	Y
26 ***Gilman***	Y	Y	Y	†
27 McHugh	N	N	Y	Y
28 Stratton	✔	?	?	?
29 Pattison	N	N	N	Y
30 ***McEwen***	Y	Y	Y	Y
31 ***Mitchell***	Y	Y	Y	Y
32 Hanley	N	Y	Y	Y
33 ***Walsh***	Y	Y	Y	Y
34 ***Horton***	Y	Y	Y	Y
35 ***Conable***	Y	Y	Y	Y
36 LaFalce	N	N	N	Y
37 Nowak	N	N	Y	Y
38 ***Kemp***	Y	Y	Y	Y
39 Lundine	N	N	N	Y
NORTH CAROLINA				
1 Jones	Y	Y	Y	Y
2 Fountain	Y	Y	Y	Y
3 Whitley	Y	Y	Y	Y
4 Andrews	Y	Y	Y	Y
5 Neal	Y	Y	Y	#
6 Preyer	Y	N	N	Y
7 Rose	Y	N	N	Y
8 Hefner	Y	Y	Y	Y
9 ***Martin***	Y	Y	Y	Y
10 ***Broyhill***	Y	Y	Y	Y
11 Gudger	Y	Y	Y	Y
NORTH DAKOTA				
AL Andrews	Y	N	Y	Y
OHIO				
1 ***Gradison***	Y	Y	Y	Y
2 Luken	Y	Y	Y	Y
3 ***Whalen***	▮	X	X	#
4 ***Guyer***	Y	Y	Y	Y
5 ***Latta***	Y	Y	Y	N
6 ***Harsha***	Y	Y	Y	N
7 ***Brown***	Y	Y	Y	Y
8 ***Kindness***	Y	Y	Y	Y
9 Ashley	N	Y	Y	Y
10 ***Miller***	Y	Y	Y	N
11 ***Stanton***	Y	Y	Y	Y
12 ***Devine***	Y	Y	Y	Y
13 Pease	N	Y	N	Y
14 Seiberling	N	N	N	Y
15 ***Wylie***	Y	Y	Y	Y
16 ***Regula***	Y	Y	Y	Y
17 ***Ashbrook***	✔	✔	✔	N
18 Applegate	Y	Y	Y	Y
19 Carney	Y	N	Y	Y
20 Oakar	Y	N	N	N
21 Stokes	N	N	N	#
22 Vanik	N	N	N	Y
23 Mottl	Y	Y	Y	N
OKLAHOMA				
1 Jones	Y	Y	Y	N
2 Risenhoover	Y	Y	Y	Y
3 Watkins	Y	Y	Y	Y
4 Steed	N	N	N	Y
5 ***Edwards***	Y	Y	Y	Y
6 English	Y	Y	Y	Y
OREGON				
1 AuCoin	Y	N	Y	N
2 Ullman	N	N	Y	Y
3 Duncan	N	N	Y	Y
4 Weaver	N	N	N	Y
PENNSYLVANIA				
1 Myers, M.	N	N	Y	Y
2 Nix	N	N	N	Y
3 Lederer	N	N	Y	Y
4 Eilberg	N	N	Y	N
5 ***Schulze***	Y	Y	Y	Y
6 Yatron	N	Y	Y	Y
7 Edgar	N	N	N	Y
8 Kostmayer	N	N	Y	Y
9 ***Shuster***	Y	Y	Y	N
10 ***McDade***	✔	?	✔	#
11 Flood	N	N	N	Y
12 Murtha	N	Y	N	Y
13 ***Coughlin***	Y	Y	Y	Y
14 Moorhead	N	N	N	Y
15 Rooney	N	Y	Y	Y
16 ***Walker***	Y	Y	Y	N
17 Ertel	N	N	Y	Y
18 Walgren	Y	Y	N	Y
19 ***Goodling, W.***	Y	Y	Y	N
20 Gaydos	Y	N	Y	Y
21 Dent	Y	Y	Y	Y
22 Murphy	Y	Y	Y	Y
23 Ammerman	N	N	Y	Y
24 ***Marks***	Y	N	Y	Y
25 ***Myers, G.***	N	Y	Y	Y
RHODE ISLAND				
1 St Germain	N	N	Y	Y
2 Beard	N	N	N	Y
SOUTH CAROLINA				
1 Davis	Y	N	N	N
2 ***Spence***	Y	Y	Y	Y
3 Derrick	Y	N	Y	Y
4 Mann	Y	Y	Y	?
5 Holland	?	?	?	?
6 Jenrette	Y	N	Y	Y
SOUTH DAKOTA				
1 ***Pressler***	Y	N	Y	Y
2 ***Abdnor***	Y	Y	Y	Y
TENNESSEE				
1 ***Quillen***	Y	Y	Y	Y
2 ***Duncan***	Y	Y	Y	Y
3 Lloyd	Y	Y	Y	Y
4 Gore	Y	N	Y	Y
5 Allen	?	?	?	?
6 ***Beard***	Y	Y	Y	Y
7 Jones	✔	✔	✔	#
8 Ford	N	N	N	Y
TEXAS				
1 Hall	Y	Y	Y	Y
2 Wilson, C.	N	Y	Y	Y
3 ***Collins***	Y	Y	Y	N
4 Roberts	Y	Y	Y	Y
5 Mattox	Y	Y	N	Y
6 Teague	✔	✔	✔	?
7 ***Archer***	Y	Y	Y	N
8 Eckhardt	N	N	N	Y
9 Brooks	Y	Y	Y	Y
10 Pickle	Y	N	Y	Y
11 Poage	?	Y	Y	Y
12 Wright	N	N	Y	Y
13 Hightower	N	Y	Y	Y
14 Young	N	N	Y	Y
15 de la Garza	Y	Y	Y	Y
16 White	Y	Y	Y	Y
17 Burleson	Y	Y	Y	Y
18 Jordan	N	N	N	Y
19 Mahon	Y	N	Y	Y
20 Gonzalez	P	Y	Y	Y
21 Krueger	N	N	Y	Y
22 Gammage	Y	Y	Y	Y
23 Kazen	Y	Y	Y	Y
24 Milford	N	Y	?	?
UTAH				
1 McKay	Y	N	Y	Y
2 ***Marriott***	Y	Y	Y	Y
VERMONT				
AL Jeffords	Y	Y	N	Y
VIRGINIA				
1 ***Trible***	Y	N	Y	Y
2 ***Whitehurst***	Y	Y	Y	Y
3 Satterfield	Y	Y	Y	N
4 ***Daniel***	Y	Y	Y	Y
5 Daniel	Y	Y	Y	Y
6 ***Butler***	Y	N	Y	Y
7 ***Robinson***	Y	Y	Y	Y
8 Harris	N	N	N	Y
9 ***Wampler***	Y	N	Y	Y
10 Fisher	N	N	N	Y
WASHINGTON				
1 ***Pritchard***	Y	N	N	Y
2 Meeds	N	N	N	Y
3 Bonker	▮	▮	#	#
4 McCormack	Y	N	Y	Y
5 Foley	Y	N	Y	Y
6 Dicks	Y	N	N	Y
7 ***Cunningham***	Y	Y	Y	Y
WEST VIRGINIA				
1 Mollohan	N	N	N	Y
2 Staggers	Y	N	N	Y
3 Slack	N	N	N	Y
4 Rahall	N	N	N	Y
WISCONSIN				
1 Aspin	N	N	N	Y
2 Kastenmeier	N	N	N	Y
3 Baldus	N	N	Y	Y
4 Zablocki	N	Y	N	Y
5 Reuss	N	N	N	Y
6 ***Steiger***	Y	N	N	Y
7 Obey	N	N	N	Y
8 Cornell	N	N	Y	Y
9 ***Kasten***	Y	Y	Y	Y
WYOMING				
AL Roncalio	N	N	N	Y

Democrats ***Republicans***

393. HR 12935. Legislative Branch Appropriations, Fiscal 1979. Conte, R-Mass., amendment to reduce fiscal 1979 appropriations, for payments not required by law, for Congress and related agencies by 5 percent. Adopted 220-168: R 130-4; D 90-164 (ND 51-128; SD 39-36), June 14, 1978.

394. HR 12935. Legislative Branch Appropriations, Fiscal 1979. Anderson, R-Ill., amendment to prohibit use of funds in the bill to purchase new color television cameras and related equipment to broadcast House floor proceedings without prior approval of the House. Rejected 133-249: R 111-22; D 22-227 (ND 19-156; SD 3-71), June 14, 1978.

395. HR 12935. Legislative Branch Appropriations, Fiscal 1979. Benjamin, D-Ind., amendment to require that any system set up to televise House proceedings be operated by House employees. Adopted 235-150: R 25-108; D 210-42 (ND 138-35; SD 72-7), June 14, 1978.

396. HR 12935. Legislative Branch Appropriations, Fiscal 1979. Armstrong, R-Colo., amendment to require members to pay for calendars, Agriculture Yearbooks, Botanic Garden plants and shipment of trunks out of their official office allowances. Adopted 214-159: R 116-13; D 98-146 (ND 69-99; SD 29-47), June 14, 1978.

397. HR 12935. Legislative Branch Appropriations, Fiscal 1979. Passage of the bill to appropriate $922.5 million (less a 5 percent reduction in payments not required by law) for the House and related congressional agencies in fiscal 1979. Passed 279-90: R 72-54; D 207-36 (ND 140-28; SD 67-8), June 14, 1978. The president had requested $948,149,500.

398. HR 12928. Public Works, Energy Appropriations, Fiscal 1979. Adoption of the rule (H Res 1236) providing for House floor consideration of the bill to appropriate $10,315,174,900 for fiscal 1979 energy research and water development. Adopted 317-82: R 110-29; D 207-53 (ND 134-45; SD 73-8), June 15, 1978.

399. HR 12928. Public Works, Energy Appropriations, Fiscal 1979. Jacobs, D-Ind., amendments, to the Bevill, D-Ala., amendment, to delete $90.8 million earmarked for three water projects. Rejected 108-284: R 31-105; D 77-179 (ND 69-108; SD 8-71), June 15, 1978. (The Bevill amendment to appropriate $25.6 million for 11 new projects requested by President Carter was adopted subsequently by voice vote.)

400. HR 12928. Public Works, Energy Appropriations, Fiscal 1979. Edgar, D-Pa., amendments to prohibit use of fiscal 1979 appropriated funds for eight projects deleted from the fiscal 1978 appropriations bill at President Carter's request. Rejected 142-234: R 44-90; D 98-144 (ND 82-87; SD 16-57), June 15, 1978. A "yea" was a vote supporting the president's position.

KEY

Y Voted for (yea).
✓ Paired for.
† Announced for.
\# CQ Poll for.
N Voted against (nay).
X Paired against.
\- Announced against.
▮ CQ Poll against.
P Voted "present."
● Voted "present" to avoid possible conflict of interest.
? Did not vote or otherwise make a position known.

	393	394	395	396	397	398	399	400
ALABAMA								
1 ***Edwards***	Y	N	N	Y	Y	Y	N	N
2 ***Dickinson***	Y	N	N	Y	Y	Y	N	N
3 Nichols	Y	N	Y	N	Y	Y	N	X
4 Bevill	N	N	Y	N	Y	Y	N	N
5 Flippo	N	N	Y	N	Y	Y	N	N
6 ***Buchanan***	Y	Y	N	Y	Y	Y	N	N
7 Flowers	?	?	?	?	?	?	?	?
ALASKA								
AL Young	Y	N	Y	▮	#	Y	N	N
ARIZONA								
1 ***Rhodes***	Y	Y	N	Y	Y	Y	N	N
2 Udall	N	N	Y	#	#	Y	N	N
3 Stump	#	#	▮	#	▮	#	▮	▮
4 ***Rudd***	Y	Y	Y	Y	Y	Y	N	N
ARKANSAS								
1 Alexander	N	N	Y	?	?	?	N	N
2 Tucker	#	▮	#	#	#	#	N	N
3 ***Hammerschmidt***	Y	N	Y	Y	N	Y	N	N
4 Thornton	?	?	?	?	?	?	?	?
CALIFORNIA								
1 Johnson	N	N	Y	N	Y	Y	N	N
2 ***Clausen***	Y	Y	N	Y	N	Y	N	N
3 Moss	N	N	✓	?	?	N	N	N
4 Leggett	N	N	Y	N	Y	Y	N	N
5 Burton, J.	N	?	Y	N	N	Y	N	✓
6 Burton, P.	N	N	Y	N	Y	Y	Y	Y
7 Miller	N	N	Y	N	N	N	Y	Y
8 Dellums	N	N	Y	N	N	Y	Y	Y
9 Stark	N	Y	N	N	N	N	Y	✓
10 Edwards	N	N	Y	N	Y	Y	Y	✓
11 Ryan	N	Y	Y	N	Y	Y	Y	Y
12 ***McCloskey***	Y	Y	N	Y	Y	Y	Y	Y
13 Mineta	N	N	Y	N	Y	Y	N	N
14 McFall	N	N	Y	N	Y	Y	N	N
15 Sisk	N	?	✓	?	?	Y	N	X
16 Panetta	Y	N	Y	Y	Y	N	N	N
17 Krebs	Y	N	N	N	Y	N	N	N
18 ***Ketchum***	Y	Y	N	Y	Y	Y	N	N
19 ***Lagomarsino***	Y	Y	N	Y	N	Y	N	N
20 ***Goldwater***	Y	Y	N	Y	N	Y	N	N
21 Corman	N	N	Y	N	Y	Y	N	N
22 ***Moorhead***	Y	Y	N	Y	N	N	N	▮
23 Beilenson	N	N	Y	N	Y	▮	Y	Y
24 Waxman	N	N	N	N	Y	N	Y	Y
25 Roybal	N	N	Y	N	Y	Y	N	N
26 ***Rousselot***	Y	Y	N	N	N	N	N	N
27 ***Dornan***	Y	Y	N	Y	N	Y	N	N
28 Burke	N	N	Y	N	Y	Y	N	N
29 Hawkins	N	N	Y	N	Y	Y	N	N
30 Danielson	N	N	Y	N	Y	Y	N	N
31 Wilson, C.H.	N	N	?	?	?	Y	?	N
32 Anderson	Y	Y	N	Y	Y	Y	N	N
33 ***Clawson***	?	?	X	?	?	Y	?	N
34 Hannaford	Y	N	N	Y	Y	Y	N	N
35 Lloyd	N	N	Y	N	Y	Y	N	N
36 Brown	?	?	?	?	?	N	?	Y
37 ***Pettis***	Y	Y	N	Y	Y	Y	N	N
38 Patterson	N	N	Y	Y	N	Y	N	?
39 ***Wiggins***	Y	N	Y	Y	Y	Y	N	N
40 ***Badham***	#	#	X	#	#	#	▮	▮
41 ***Wilson, B.***	Y	Y	N	Y	Y	Y	N	N
42 Van Deerlin	N	Y	N	N	Y	Y	N	N
43 ***Burgener***	Y	Y	N	Y	Y	Y	N	N
COLORADO								
1 Schroeder	Y	Y	N	Y	Y	N	Y	Y
2 Wirth	Y	N	Y	Y	Y	N	N	N
3 Evans	N	N	N	Y	Y	Y	N	N
4 ***Johnson***	Y	Y	N	Y	Y	Y	N	N
5 ***Armstrong***	Y	Y	N	Y	N	Y	N	N
CONNECTICUT								
1 Cotter	Y	N	Y	Y	Y	Y	N	N
2 Dodd	N	N	Y	Y	Y	Y	Y	Y
3 Giaimo	N	N	Y	Y	Y	Y	N	Y
4 ***McKinney***	N	Y	N	N	Y	N	N	N
5 ***Sarasin***	Y	Y	N	Y	Y	N	▮	▮
6 Moffett	Y	N	Y	Y	N	N	Y	Y
DELAWARE								
AL Evans	Y	Y	N	Y	Y	Y	N	N
FLORIDA								
1 Sikes	N	N	Y	?	?	Y	N	X
2 Fuqua	N	N	Y	N	N	N	▮	▮
3 Bennett	Y	N	Y	Y	N	Y	N	N
4 Chappell	N	N	Y	N	Y	Y	N	N
5 ***Kelly***	Y	N	N	Y	N	N	N	N
6 ***Young***	Y	Y	N	Y	N	Y	N	N
7 Gibbons	Y	N	Y	Y	Y	Y	N	?
8 Ireland	Y	N	Y	Y	Y	Y	N	N
9 ***Frey***	Y	Y	X	?	?	?	?	X
10 ***Bafalis***	Y	Y	N	Y	N	Y	N	N
11 Rogers	N	?	Y	Y	Y	N	N	N
12 ***Burke***	Y	N	N	Y	N	Y	N	N
13 Lehman	N	N	Y	N	Y	Y	N	Y
14 Pepper	#	N	Y	N	Y	Y	N	N
15 Fascell	N	N	Y	Y	Y	Y	N	N
GEORGIA								
1 Ginn	N	N	Y	N	Y	Y	N	N
2 Mathis	N	?	Y	?	Y	Y	N	N
3 Brinkley	Y	N	N	Y	Y	Y	N	N
4 Levitas	Y	N	N	Y	N	N	N	Y
5 Fowler	Y	N	Y	Y	Y	N	N	Y
6 Flynt	N	N	Y	N	Y	Y	N	N
7 McDonald	Y	Y	Y	Y	N	N	Y	Y
8 Evans	N	▮	Y	N	Y	Y	N	N
9 Jenkins	#	#	#	#	#	#	?	▮
10 Barnard	?	?	?	?	?	Y	N	N
HAWAII								
1 Heftel	N	N	Y	Y	Y	Y	N	N
2 Akaka	N	N	Y	N	Y	Y	N	N
IDAHO								
1 ***Symms***	Y	Y	N	Y	?	Y	N	N
2 ***Hansen, G.***	?	?	X	?	?	?	?	X
ILLINOIS								
1 Metcalfe	N	N	Y	N	Y	Y	Y	Y
2 Murphy	N	N	Y	N	Y	Y	N	N
3 Russo	Y	N	Y	Y	Y	N	N	N
4 ***Derwinski***	Y	N	Y	Y	Y	N	N	Y
5 Fary	N	N	Y	N	Y	Y	N	N
6 ***Hyde***	Y	N	N	N	Y	Y	N	N
7 Collins	N	N	Y	N	Y	?	?	?
8 Rostenkowski	N	N	Y	N	Y	Y	N	N
9 Yates	N	N	✓	#	#	Y	Y	Y
10 Mikva	#	#	✓	#	#	Y	Y	Y
11 Annunzio	N	N	Y	N	Y	Y	N	N
12 ***Crane***	Y	Y	N	Y	▮	N	N	N
13 ***McClory***	Y	Y	N	Y	Y	Y	N	Y
14 ***Erlenborn***	Y	Y	N	Y	Y	Y	N	N
15 ***Corcoran***	Y	Y	N	Y	Y	Y	N	Y
16 ***Anderson***	Y	Y	N	Y	N	Y	Y	Y
17 ***O'Brien***	#	▮	X	#	#	Y	Y	Y
18 ***Michel***	Y	Y	N	Y	Y	Y	N	Y
19 ***Railsback***	Y	Y	N	Y	Y	Y	N	N
20 ***Findley***	Y	Y	Y	Y	Y	Y	N	N
21 ***Madigan***	N	Y	N	Y	N	Y	N	N
22 Shipley	N	N	Y	N	Y	?	?	?
23 Price	▮	▮	✓	#	#	Y	N	N
24 Simon	?	?	?	?	?	?	?	?
INDIANA								
1 Benjamin	N	N	Y	N	Y	Y	N	N
2 Fithian	Y	N	Y	Y	N	Y	N	N
3 Brademas	N	N	Y	N	Y	Y	N	Y
4 ***Quayle***	Y	Y	N	Y	N	N	Y	Y
5 ***Hillis***	Y	Y	N	Y	Y	Y	N	N
6 Evans	Y	N	Y	Y	N	Y	N	Y
7 ***Myers, J.***	Y	Y	N	N	N	Y	N	N
8 Cornwell	N	N	Y	N	N	Y	N	Y
9 Hamilton	Y	N	N	N	Y	Y	Y	Y
10 Sharp	Y	Y	N	Y	Y	N	Y	Y
11 Jacobs	Y	Y	N	Y	N	Y	Y	Y
IOWA								
1 ***Leach***	Y	Y	N	Y	N	Y	N	Y
2 Blouin	N	N	Y	Y	Y	Y	N	Y
3 ***Grassley***	Y	Y	Y	Y	N	Y	N	N
4 Smith	N	N	Y	N	Y	Y	N	N
5 Harkin	Y	Y	Y	Y	Y	N	Y	Y
6 Bedell	N	N	Y	Y	N	N	Y	Y

Democrats ***Republicans***

	393	394	395	396	397	398	399	400
KANSAS								
1 Sebelius	Y	Y	N	Y	Y	Y	N	N
2 Keys	Y	N	N	Y	Y	Y	Y	Y
3 Winn	Y	Y	N	Y	Y	Y	N	N
4 Glickman	Y	N	Y	Y	Y	Y	N	Y
5 Skubitz	?	?	N	?	?	Y	N	N
KENTUCKY								
1 Hubbard	Y	N	Y	N	Y	Y	N	N
2 Natcher	Y	N	Y	Y	Y	Y	N	N
3 Mazzoli	Y	N	N	Y	Y	Y	Y	Y
4 Snyder	Y	N	Y	Y	Y	Y	N	N
5 Carter	Y	N	Y	Y	Y	Y	N	N
6 Breckinridge	N	N	N	Y	Y	Y	N	N
7 Perkins	N	N	Y	N	Y	Y	N	N
LOUISIANA								
1 Livingston	Y	Y	N	Y	Y	Y	N	N
2 Boggs	N	N	Y	N	Y	Y	N	N
3 Treen	Y	Y	N	Y	Y	Y	N	N
4 Waggonner	N	N	Y	N	Y	Y	N	N
5 Huckaby	Y	?	N	Y	Y	Y	?	X
6 Moore	Y	Y	N	Y	Y	N	N	N
7 Breaux	Y	N	Y	Y	Y	Y	N	N
8 Long	N	N	Y	N	Y	Y	N	N
MAINE								
1 Emery	Y	Y	N	Y	N	Y	Y	Y
2 Cohen	?	?	X	?	?	Y	?	?
MARYLAND								
1 Bauman	Y	Y	N	Y	N	N	N	N
2 Long	N	N	Y	Y	Y	Y	N	N
3 Mikulski	N	N	Y	N	N	N	N	Y
4 Holt	Y	Y	Y	Y	N	Y	N	N
5 Spellman	Y	▮	Y	Y	Y	Y	N	Y
6 Byron	Y	N	Y	N	Y	Y	Y	Y
7 Mitchell	N	N	✓	#	#	Y	N	Y
8 Steers	Y	Y	N	Y	Y	Y	Y	Y
MASSACHUSETTS								
1 Conte	Y	N	Y	Y	Y	Y	Y	Y
2 Boland	Y	N	Y	Y	Y	Y	N	N
3 Early	N	N	Y	Y	Y	N	Y	Y
4 Drinan	Y	N	N	Y	N	N	Y	Y
5 Tsongas	?	?	?	?	?	?	?	?
6 Harrington	N	N	Y	Y	N	Y	Y	✓
7 Markey	N	▮	N	Y	Y	N	Y	Y
8 O'Neill								
9 Moakley	N	N	Y	N	Y	Y	Y	Y
10 Heckler	Y	?	X	?	?	Y	Y	Y
11 Burke	N	N	Y	N	Y	Y	Y	N
12 Studds	N	N	Y	Y	Y	N	Y	Y
MICHIGAN								
1 Conyers	N	N	✓	▮	#	#	#	✓
2 Pursell	Y	Y	N	Y	Y	N	Y	Y
3 Brown	Y	Y	N	Y	N	N	N	Y
4 Stockman	Y	Y	N	Y	Y	N	Y	Y
5 Sawyer	Y	Y	Y	Y	Y	Y	Y	✓
6 Carr	N	N	Y	Y	Y	N	Y	Y
7 Kildee	Y	Y	N	Y	Y	N	Y	Y
8 Traxler	N	N	Y	N	Y	#	N	N
9 Vander Jagt	Y	Y	N	N	Y	Y	N	Y
10 Cederberg	Y	Y	N	Y	Y	Y	N	N
11 Ruppe	Y	Y	N	Y	Y	Y	N	N
12 Bonior	N	N	Y	N	Y	N	Y	Y
13 Diggs	N	N	N	?	?	?	N	N
14 Nedzi	?	?	✓	?	?	?	?	✓
15 Ford	N	N	✓	?	?	Y	Y	Y
16 Dingell	?	N	Y	N	Y	N	Y	Y
17 Brodhead	N	Y	N	N	N	N	?	?
18 Blanchard	N	N	Y	Y	N	Y	Y	Y
19 Broomfield	Y	Y	N	Y	Y	N	N	Y
MINNESOTA								
1 Quie	#	▮	X	#	#	#	▮	▮
2 Hagedorn	Y	Y	N	Y	Y	Y	N	N
3 Frenzel	?	?	X	?	?	?	?	✓
4 Vento	N	N	Y	?	?	N	Y	✓
5 Fraser	N	Y	N	Y	Y	Y	#	✓
6 Nolan	N	Y	N	Y	Y	Y	Y	Y
7 Stangeland	Y	Y	N	Y	Y	Y	N	N
8 Oberstar	N	Y	N	N	Y	N	N	N
MISSISSIPPI								
1 Whitten	N	N	Y	N	Y	Y	N	N
2 Bowen	Y	N	Y	Y	Y	Y	N	N
3 Montgomery	Y	N	Y	N	?	Y	N	N
4 Cochran	Y	Y	N	?	?	Y	N	N
5 Lott	Y	Y	N	N	Y	Y	▮	▮
MISSOURI								
1 Clay	N	N	Y	N	Y	Y	?	N
2 Young	Y	N	Y	N	Y	Y	N	N
3 Gephardt	Y	N	Y	Y	Y	Y	Y	Y
4 Skelton	Y	N	Y	Y	Y	Y	N	N
5 Bolling	#	#	#	#	#	Y	Y	Y
6 Coleman	Y	Y	N	Y	N	Y	N	Y
7 Taylor	Y	N	Y	Y	Y	Y	N	N
8 Ichord	Y	N	Y	Y	Y	Y	N	N
9 Volkmer	Y	N	Y	Y	Y	N	N	Y
10 Burlison	N	N	Y	N	Y	Y	N	N
MONTANA								
1 Baucus	Y	N	Y	Y	N	Y	N	N
2 Marlenee	Y	Y	N	Y	N	Y	N	N
NEBRASKA								
1 Thone	Y	Y	N	Y	N	Y	N	N
2 Cavanaugh	N	N	Y	Y	Y	Y	Y	Y
3 Smith	Y	Y	N	Y	Y	Y	N	N
NEVADA								
AL Santini	#	▮	▮	#	#	N	N	N
NEW HAMPSHIRE								
1 D'Amours	Y	N	Y	Y	Y	Y	N	Y
2 Cleveland	Y	N	Y	Y	N	N	Y	#
NEW JERSEY								
1 Florio	N	N	Y	N	N	N	N	Y
2 Hughes	Y	N	Y	Y	Y	Y	N	Y
3 Howard	N	N	Y	N	Y	Y	N	N
4 Thompson	N	N	Y	N	Y	Y	N	N
5 Fenwick	Y	Y	N	Y	Y	Y	Y	Y
6 Forsythe	Y	Y	N	N	N	Y	N	Y
7 Maguire	Y	Y	N	Y	N	N	Y	Y
8 Roe	Y	N	Y	N	Y	Y	N	N
9 Hollenbeck	Y	Y	N	Y	Y	#	Y	Y
10 Rodino	▮	▮	#	▮	#	#	#	#
11 Minish	N	N	Y	Y	Y	Y	Y	?
12 Rinaldo	Y	Y	N	Y	Y	Y	Y	Y
13 Meyner	N	N	Y	Y	Y	Y	Y	Y
14 LeFante	N	N	Y	N	Y	#	#	X
15 Patten	N	N	Y	N	Y	Y	N	N
NEW MEXICO								
1 Lujan	Y	Y	Y	Y	N	Y	N	N
2 Runnels	?	?	?	?	#	?	?	?
NEW YORK								
1 Pike	Y	N	N	N	Y	#	#	#
2 Downey	Y	N	Y	Y	Y	Y	Y	Y
3 Ambro	Y	N	N	N	Y	N	N	Y
4 Lent	Y	Y	N	Y	Y	Y	N	Y
5 Wydler	Y	Y	N	Y	Y	Y	Y	Y
6 Wolff	N	N	Y	N	Y	Y	N	N
7 Addabbo	N	N	Y	N	Y	Y	N	N
8 Rosenthal	N	N	Y	N	Y	N	N	N
9 Delaney	Y	?	Y	N	Y	Y	N	N
10 Biaggi	#	#	✓	#	#	Y	N	N
11 Scheuer	N	N	Y	N	Y	N	N	N
12 Chisholm	?	?	✓	?	?	Y	N	Y
13 Solarz	N	N	Y	N	Y	N	Y	Y
14 Richmond	N	N	Y	N	Y	Y	Y	Y
15 Zeferetti	N	N	Y	N	Y	Y	N	N
16 Holtzman	N	N	Y	Y	Y	N	Y	Y
17 Murphy	N	N	Y	N	Y	Y	N	Y
18 Green	Y	Y	N	Y	Y	N	Y	Y
19 Rangel	?	?	✓	?	?	Y	N	N
20 Weiss	N	N	Y	Y	Y	N	Y	Y
21 Garcia	?	?	✓	?	?	Y	Y	✓
22 Bingham	N	N	Y	N	#	N	Y	Y
23 Caputo	?	?	X	?	?	?	?	?
24 Ottinger	N	Y	N	Y	N	N	Y	Y
25 Fish	Y	Y	N	Y	Y	Y	Y	Y
26 Gilman	†	†	X	†	†	Y	N	N
27 McHugh	N	N	N	Y	Y	Y	N	Y
28 Stratton	N	N	N	N	Y	Y	N	X
29 Pattison	N	N	Y	Y	Y	Y	Y	Y
30 McEwen	Y	Y	N	Y	N	Y	N	N
31 Mitchell	Y	Y	N	Y	Y	Y	N	Y
32 Hanley	N	N	N	N	Y	Y	N	N
33 Walsh	Y	N	N	Y	Y	Y	N	N
34 Horton	N	N	Y	N	Y	Y	N	N
35 Conable	Y	Y	N	N	N	Y	N	✓
36 LaFalce	Y	N	N	Y	Y	Y	N	N
37 Nowak	N	N	Y	N	Y	Y	N	N
38 Kemp	Y	Y	N	Y	Y	Y	N	N
39 Lundine	N	N	N	Y	Y	Y	N	N
NORTH CAROLINA								
1 Jones	N	N	Y	N	Y	Y	N	N
2 Fountain	Y	N	Y	Y	Y	Y	N	N
3 Whitley	Y	N	Y	N	Y	Y	N	N
4 Andrews	Y	N	Y	N	Y	Y	N	?
5 Neal	#	N	Y	Y	Y	Y	N	N
6 Preyer	N	N	Y	N	Y	Y	N	Y
7 Rose	N	N	Y	N	Y	Y	#	#
8 Hefner	Y	N	Y	N	Y	Y	N	N
9 Martin	Y	Y	Y	Y	Y	N	Y	N
10 Broyhill	Y	N	N	Y	N	N	N	Y
11 Gudger	Y	N	Y	N	Y	Y	Y	Y
NORTH DAKOTA								
AL Andrews	Y	Y	N	N	Y	Y	N	N
OHIO								
1 Gradison	Y	Y	N	Y	N	Y	Y	Y
2 Luken	Y	N	N	Y	Y	Y	N	N
3 Whalen	▮	▮	X	▮	#	#	Y	Y
4 Guyer	Y	Y	N	Y	Y	Y	N	N
5 Latta	Y	N	Y	Y	N	Y	Y	N
6 Harsha	Y	N	Y	Y	Y	Y	N	N
7 Brown	Y	Y	N	Y	Y	Y	N	N
8 Kindness	Y	Y	Y	N	?	N	?	N
9 Ashley	N	N	Y	N	Y	Y	N	Y
10 Miller	Y	Y	N	Y	N	Y	Y	Y
11 Stanton	Y	Y	N	Y	Y	Y	N	N
12 Devine	Y	Y	N	Y	N	N	N	N
13 Pease	Y	N	Y	Y	N	#	Y	Y
14 Seiberling	N	N	Y	N	Y	N	Y	Y
15 Wylie	Y	Y	N	Y	N	N	N	Y
16 Regula	Y	Y	N	Y	N	Y	N	N
17 Ashbrook	Y	N	Y	#	#	N	Y	N
18 Applegate	N	N	Y	N	N	N	Y	Y
19 Carney	N	N	Y	N	Y	Y	N	N
20 Oakar	N	Y	N	N	N	Y	N	N
21 Stokes	N	N	Y	N	Y	Y	N	N
22 Vanik	N	N	Y	N	Y	Y	#	#
23 Mottl	Y	Y	N	Y	N	Y	Y	Y
OKLAHOMA								
1 Jones	Y	N	Y	Y	Y	N	N	N
2 Risenhoover	Y	N	Y	Y	Y	Y	N	N
3 Watkins	Y	N	Y	Y	N	Y	N	N
4 Steed	N	N	Y	N	Y	Y	N	X
5 Edwards	Y	N	Y	Y	N	Y	N	N
6 English	Y	N	Y	Y	Y	Y	N	N
OREGON								
1 AuCoin	Y	N	N	Y	N	Y	N	N
2 Ullman	N	N	Y	N	Y	#	▮	▮
3 Duncan	N	N	Y	N	Y	Y	N	N
4 Weaver	Y	N	Y	N	Y	N	Y	Y
PENNSYLVANIA								
1 Myers, M.	N	N	Y	N	Y	?	Y	Y
2 Nix	N	N	Y	N	Y	Y	N	N
3 Lederer	N	N	Y	N	Y	Y	Y	Y
4 Eilberg	N	N	Y	N	Y	Y	N	N
5 Schulze	Y	Y	N	Y	N	N	Y	Y
6 Yatron	Y	N	Y	Y	Y	Y	Y	Y
7 Edgar	Y	N	Y	Y	N	N	Y	Y
8 Kostmayer	Y	N	Y	Y	Y	N	Y	Y
9 Shuster	Y	Y	Y	Y	N	Y	N	N
10 McDade	#	?	X	#	#	Y	N	N
11 Flood	N	N	Y	Y	Y	Y	N	N
12 Murtha	N	N	Y	N	Y	Y	N	N
13 Coughlin	Y	Y	N	Y	Y	Y	Y	Y
14 Moorhead	N	N	Y	N	Y	Y	Y	#
15 Rooney	N	N	Y	N	Y	Y	Y	Y
16 Walker	Y	Y	N	Y	N	N	Y	Y
17 Ertel	Y	N	Y	Y	Y	Y	N	N
18 Walgren	Y	N	Y	N	Y	Y	Y	Y
19 Goodling, W.	Y	Y	N	Y	N	Y	N	Y
20 Gaydos	N	N	Y	N	Y	Y	N	N
21 Dent	N	N	Y	N	Y	Y	▮	▮
22 Murphy	N	N	Y	N	Y	Y	Y	Y
23 Ammerman	N	N	Y	N	N	Y	N	Y
24 Marks	Y	Y	N	Y	N	Y	N	Y
25 Myers, G.	Y	Y	N	Y	Y	Y	Y	Y
RHODE ISLAND								
1 St Germain	N	N	Y	N	Y	Y	N	N
2 Beard	N	N	Y	N	Y	Y	N	N
SOUTH CAROLINA								
1 Davis	Y	N	Y	Y	Y	Y	N	N
2 Spence	Y	Y	N	Y	Y	Y	N	N
3 Derrick	Y	N	Y	N	Y	Y	Y	Y
4 Mann	?	N	Y	N	Y	Y	Y	Y
5 Holland	?	?	?	?	?	#	?	?
6 Jenrette	Y	N	Y	N	Y	Y	N	Y
SOUTH DAKOTA								
1 Pressler	Y	Y	N	Y	N	Y	N	N
2 Abdnor	Y	Y	N	Y	Y	Y	N	N
TENNESSEE								
1 Quillen	Y	Y	N	N	N	Y	N	N
2 Duncan	Y	Y	N	Y	N	Y	N	N
3 Lloyd	Y	N	Y	N	Y	Y	N	N
4 Gore	Y	N	Y	Y	Y	N	N	N
5 Allen	?	?	?	?	?	?	?	?
6 Beard	Y	Y	Y	Y	Y	Y	N	N
7 Jones	#	▮	✓	#	#	Y	N	N
8 Ford	N	N	Y	N	Y	Y	N	Y
TEXAS								
1 Hall	Y	N	Y	N	Y	Y	N	N
2 Wilson, C.	N	N	Y	N	Y	Y	N	N
3 Collins	Y	N	N	Y	N	N	Y	Y
4 Roberts	N	N	Y	N	?	Y	N	X
5 Mattox	Y	N	N	Y	N	Y	Y	Y
6 Teague	?	?	?	?	?	?	?	X
7 Archer	Y	Y	N	Y	N	N	N	Y
8 Eckhardt	N	?	Y	Y	Y	N	Y	Y
9 Brooks	N	N	Y	N	Y	Y	N	N
10 Pickle	#	N	Y	N	Y	Y	N	N
11 Poage	Y	Y	Y	N	Y	Y	N	N
12 Wright	N	N	Y	N	Y	Y	N	N
13 Hightower	Y	N	Y	N	Y	Y	N	N
14 Young	N	N	Y	N	Y	Y	N	N
15 de la Garza	Y	N	Y	N	Y	Y	N	N
16 White	N	N	Y	Y	Y	Y	N	N
17 Burleson	N	Y	Y	N	Y	Y	N	N
18 Jordan	N	N	Y	N	Y	Y	N	N
19 Mahon	N	N	Y	N	Y	Y	N	N
20 Gonzalez	N	N	Y	N	Y	Y	N	N
21 Krueger	#	▮	▮	#	#	#	▮	X
22 Gammage	Y	N	N	N	N	Y	N	N
23 Kazen	Y	N	Y	N	Y	Y	N	N
24 Milford	?	?	?	?	?	Y	?	✓
UTAH								
1 McKay	N	N	Y	N	Y	Y	N	N
2 Marriott	Y	Y	Y	Y	N	Y	N	N
VERMONT								
AL Jeffords	N	Y	N	Y	N	N	N	Y
VIRGINIA								
1 Trible	Y	Y	N	Y	N	Y	N	N
2 Whitehurst	#	#	X	#	#	Y	N	N
3 Satterfield	Y	N	Y	Y	Y	N	N	N
4 Daniel	Y	Y	N	Y	Y	Y	N	N
5 Daniel	Y	N	Y	Y	Y	Y	N	N
6 Butler	Y	Y	N	Y	Y	Y	N	N
7 Robinson	Y	Y	N	Y	Y	Y	N	N
8 Harris	N	N	Y	Y	Y	Y	Y	Y
9 Wampler	Y	Y	N	Y	Y	Y	N	N
10 Fisher	Y	N	Y	Y	Y	Y	N	Y
WASHINGTON								
1 Pritchard	Y	Y	N	Y	Y	Y	N	N
2 Meeds	N	N	Y	N	Y	N	N	N
3 Bonker	#	▮	#	#	#	#	▮	▮
4 McCormack	Y	N	Y	N	Y	Y	N	N
5 Foley	Y	N	Y	Y	Y	Y	N	N
6 Dicks	Y	N	Y	Y	Y	Y	N	N
7 Cunningham	Y	Y	N	Y	N	Y	N	N
WEST VIRGINIA								
1 Mollohan	N	N	Y	N	Y	Y	N	N
2 Staggers	N	N	Y	N	N	N	N	N
3 Slack	N	N	Y	?	?	Y	N	N
4 Rahall	N	N	Y	N	Y	Y	N	N
WISCONSIN								
1 Aspin	N	N	Y	Y	Y	Y	Y	Y
2 Kastenmeier	N	N	Y	N	Y	Y	Y	Y
3 Baldus	N	N	Y	N	Y	Y	N	N
4 Zablocki	N	N	Y	N	Y	Y	N	N
5 Reuss	N	N	Y	N	Y	N	Y	Y
6 Steiger	Y	Y	N	N	N	N	Y	Y
7 Obey	N	N	Y	?	Y	Y	Y	Y
8 Cornell	N	N	Y	Y	Y	Y	Y	Y
9 Kasten	Y	Y	N	Y	N	Y	Y	Y
WYOMING								
AL Roncalio	?	?	?	?	?	Y	N	N

Democrats ***Republicans***

401. HR 12928. Public Works, Energy Appropriations, Fiscal 1979. Bevill, D-Ala., motion that the House resolve itself into the Committee of the Whole for consideration of the bill to appropriate $10,315,174,900 for fiscal 1979 energy research and water development programs. Motion agreed to 300-4: R 106-2; D 194-2 (ND 134-2; SD 60-0), June 16, 1978.

402. HR 12928. Public Works, Energy Appropriations, Fiscal 1979. Weiss, D-N.Y., amendment to prohibit the use of fiscal 1979 appropriations in the bill for production of enhanced radiation weapons (neutron bombs). Rejected 67-259: R 5-109; D 62-150 (ND 60-84; SD 2-66), June 16, 1978.

403. HR 12928. Public Works, Energy Appropriations, Fiscal 1979. Conte, D-Mass., motion to recommit the bill to the Committee on Appropriations with instructions to report back the bill with an amendment to reduce the appropriations in the bill by 3 percent (except payments for programs required by law). Rejected 93-228: R 43-67; D 50-161 (ND 40-105; SD 10-56), June 16, 1978.

404. HR 12928. Public Works, Energy Appropriations, Fiscal 1979. Passage of the bill to appropriate $10,341,633,900 (less a 2 percent reduction in payments not required by law) for fiscal 1979 for energy research and water development. Passed 263-59: R 90-22; D 173-37 (ND 115-29; SD 58-8), June 16, 1978. The president had requested $10,368,899,000.

405. HR 12927. Military Construction Appropriations, Fiscal 1979. Passage of the bill to appropriate $3,844,887,000 for military construction programs of the Defense Department for fiscal 1979. Passed 278-13: R 95-3; D 183-10 (ND 122-10; SD 61-0), June 16, 1978. The president had requested $4,253,000,000.

406. HR 12936. HUD-Independent Agencies Appropriations, Fiscal 1979. Boland, D-Mass., motion that the House resolve itself into the Committee of the Whole for consideration of the bill to appropriate fiscal 1979 funds for the Department of Housing and Urban Development and 17 independent agencies. Motion agreed to 347-4: R 127-2; D 220-2 (ND 154-2; SD 66-0), June 19, 1978.

407. HR 12936. HUD-Independent Agencies Appropriations, Fiscal 1979. Brown, R-Mich., amendment to reduce the fiscal 1979 appropriation recommended in the bill for the Environmental Protection Agency by $133 million. Rejected 173-211: R 104-30; D 69-181 (ND 29-148; SD 40-33), June 19, 1978.

408. HR 12936. HUD-Independent Agency Appropriations, Fiscal 1979. Miller, R-Ohio, motion to recommit the bill to the Committee on Appropriations with instructions to reduce the appropriations in the bill by 2 percent (except payments for programs required by law). Rejected 156-222: R 101-33; D 55-189 (ND 32-138; SD 23-51), June 19, 1978.

KEY

- Y Voted for (yea).
- ✓ Paired for.
- † Announced for.
- # CQ Poll for.
- N Voted against (nay).
- X Paired against.
- \- Announced against.
- ▮ CQ Poll against.
- P Voted "present."
- ● Voted "present" to avoid possible conflict of interest.
- ? Did not vote or otherwise make a position known.

	401	402	403	404	405	406	407	408
ALABAMA								
1 Edwards	Y	N	N	Y	Y	Y	Y	Y
2 Dickinson	Y	N	Y	Y	Y	Y	Y	Y
3 Nichols	#	X	▮	#	?	Y	Y	N
4 Bevill	Y	N	N	Y	Y	Y	Y	N
5 Flippo	Y	N	N	Y	Y	Y	Y	N
6 Buchanan	?	?	?	?	Y	Y	Y	Y
7 Flowers	?	?	?	?	?	?	?	?
ALASKA								
AL Young	#	N	N	Y	Y	Y	Y	Y
ARIZONA								
1 Rhodes	Y	N	N	Y	Y	?	Y	Y
2 Udall	#	#	▮	#	?	Y	Y	N
3 Stump	#	▮	▮	#	?	Y	Y	Y
4 Rudd	Y	N	N	Y	Y	Y	Y	Y
ARKANSAS								
1 Alexander	Y	N	N	Y	Y	Y	N	N
2 Tucker	#	N	Y	Y	Y	#	▮	?
3 Hammerschmidt	?	?	?	?	?	Y	Y	N
4 Thornton	?	?	?	?	?	Y	Y	N
CALIFORNIA								
1 Johnson	Y	N	N	Y	Y	Y	N	N
2 Clausen	Y	N	N	Y	?	Y	N	Y
3 Moss	Y	N	N	Y	Y	?	N	N
4 Leggett	Y	N	▮	#	#	#	▮	?
5 Burton, J.	?	✓	?	?	?	?	N	N
6 Burton, P.	Y	Y	N	Y	Y	Y	N	N
7 Miller	Y	Y	N	N	Y	Y	N	N
8 Dellums	#	Y	Y	N	N	Y	N	N
9 Stark	#	✓	?	?	?	Y	N	?
10 Edwards	Y	Y	N	N	N	Y	N	N
11 Ryan	Y	N	N	Y	Y	Y	N	N
12 McCloskey	?	N	N	Y	Y	?	N	Y
13 Mineta	Y	N	N	Y	Y	Y	N	N
14 McFall	Y	N	N	Y	Y	Y	N	N
15 Sisk	?	?	?	?	?	Y	Y	N
16 Panetta	Y	Y	N	Y	Y	Y	Y	Y
17 Krebs	Y	N	N	Y	Y	Y	Y	Y
18 Ketchum	?	?	?	?	Y	Y	Y	Y
19 Lagomarsino	Y	N	N	Y	Y	Y	Y	Y
20 Goldwater	Y	N	N	Y	Y	Y	Y	Y
21 Corman	Y	N	N	Y	Y	#	▮	?
22 Moorhead	#	▮	▮	#	?	Y	Y	Y
23 Beilenson	#	Y	#	?	Y	Y	N	N
24 Waxman	Y	N	N	Y	Y	Y	N	N
25 Roybal	?	?	?	?	?	Y	N	N
26 Rousselot	?	?	?	?	?	Y	Y	Y
27 Dornan	#	▮	#	#	?	Y	Y	Y
28 Burke	Y	Y	N	Y	Y	Y	N	N
29 Hawkins	Y	Y	N	Y	?	Y	N	?
30 Danielson	Y	N	N	Y	Y	#	▮	▮
31 Wilson, C.H.	Y	N	▮	#	Y	Y	▮	N
32 Anderson	Y	N	N	Y	Y	Y	N	Y
33 Clawson	Y	N	Y	Y	Y	Y	Y	Y
34 Hannaford	Y	Y	Y	Y	Y	Y	Y	N
35 Lloyd	N	N	N	Y	Y	N	N	N
36 Brown	Y	Y	Y	Y	Y	Y	N	N
37 Pettis	?	N	N	Y	Y	Y	Y	Y
38 Patterson	#	▮	▮	#	?	Y	Y	N
39 Wiggins	#	N	Y	Y	Y	Y	Y	Y
40 Badham	#	▮	▮	#	?	Y	Y	Y
41 Wilson, B.	N	N	Y	Y	Y	N	Y	N
42 Van Deerlin	Y	N	N	Y	Y	?	?	?
43 Burgener	Y	N	N	Y	Y	Y	Y	Y
COLORADO								
1 Schroeder	Y	Y	Y	N	Y	Y	N	N
2 Wirth	Y	Y	N	Y	Y	Y	N	N
3 Evans	Y	N	N	Y	Y	Y	N	N
4 Johnson	Y	N	N	Y	Y	Y	Y	Y

	401	402	403	404	405	406	407	408
5 Armstrong	?	?	?	?	?	Y	Y	Y
CONNECTICUT								
1 Cotter	#	▮	▮	#	#	#	N	N
2 Dodd	Y	N	N	Y	Y	Y	N	N
3 Giaimo	?	?	?	?	?	?	?	?
4 McKinney	Y	N	N	Y	#	#	X	X
5 Sarasin	†	-	-	†	†	-	X	-
6 Moffett	Y	Y	Y	N	?	?	N	N
DELAWARE								
AL Evans	Y	N	?	?	?	Y	Y	X
FLORIDA								
1 Sikes	?	X	?	?	?	Y	Y	N
2 Fuqua	Y	N	N	Y	?	Y	Y	N
3 Bennett	Y	N	N	Y	Y	Y	Y	Y
4 Chappell	?	N	N	Y	Y	Y	Y	N
5 Kelly	Y	N	N	Y	Y	Y	Y	Y
6 Young	Y	N	N	Y	Y	Y	Y	N
7 Gibbons	?	?	?	?	?	Y	?	Y
8 Ireland	Y	N	N	Y	Y	Y	Y	N
9 Frey	?	?	?	?	?	?	✓	?
10 Bafalis	Y	N	N	Y	Y	Y	Y	Y
11 Rogers	?	X	?	?	?	Y	N	N
12 Burke	Y	N	N	Y	Y	Y	Y	Y
13 Lehman	Y	Y	N	Y	Y	Y	N	N
14 Pepper	#	N	N	Y	Y	Y	N	N
15 Fascell	Y	N	N	Y	Y	Y	N	N
GEORGIA								
1 Ginn	Y	N	N	Y	Y	Y	N	N
2 Mathis	Y	N	N	Y	?	?	?	?
3 Brinkley	Y	N	N	Y	Y	Y	N	Y
4 Levitas	Y	N	N	N	Y	Y	N	Y
5 Fowler	Y	N	N	Y	Y	Y	N	N
6 Flynt	Y	N	N	Y	Y	?	?	✓
7 McDonald	#	N	Y	N	Y	Y	Y	Y
8 Evans	Y	N	N	Y	Y	Y	Y	N
9 Jenkins	?	X	▮	#	#	#	#	✓
10 Barnard	Y	N	N	Y	Y	Y	Y	Y
HAWAII								
1 Heftel	Y	N	N	Y	Y	Y	Y	N
2 Akaka	Y	N	N	Y	Y	Y	N	N
IDAHO								
1 Symms	Y	N	N	Y	Y	Y	Y	Y
2 Hansen, G.	?	?	?	?	?	?	✓	✓
ILLINOIS								
1 Metcalfe	?	✓	?	?	?	Y	N	N
2 Murphy	#	X	▮	#	?	Y	N	N
3 Russo	#	▮	#	#	?	Y	Y	Y
4 Derwinski	Y	N	Y	N	?	Y	Y	Y
5 Fary	?	?	?	?	?	?	N	N
6 Hyde	Y	N	N	Y	Y	Y	Y	N
7 Collins	#	✓	▮	#	?	Y	N	N
8 Rostenkowski	#	?	?	?	?	Y	N	N
9 Yates	Y	Y	N	Y	Y	Y	N	N
10 Mikva	Y	Y	Y	N	Y	Y	N	N
11 Annunzio	Y	N	N	Y	Y	Y	N	N
12 Crane	#	▮	▮	?	?	Y	Y	Y
13 McClory	Y	N	N	Y	Y	Y	N	Y
14 Erlenborn	Y	▮	▮	#	?	Y	Y	Y
15 Corcoran	Y	N	N	Y	Y	Y	Y	Y
16 Anderson	Y	N	Y	N	Y	Y	Y	Y
17 O'Brien	#	▮	▮	#	?	Y	Y	Y
18 Michel	Y	▮	N	Y	Y	Y	Y	Y
19 Railsback	Y	N	▮	#	?	Y	Y	Y
20 Findley	Y	N	Y	Y	Y	Y	Y	Y
21 Madigan	Y	N	N	Y	Y	Y	Y	Y
22 Shipley	?	X	?	?	?	?	X	?
23 Price	Y	N	N	Y	Y	Y	N	N
24 Simon	Y	Y	Y	Y	?	Y	N	N
INDIANA								
1 Benjamin	Y	N	N	Y	Y	Y	Y	N
2 Fithian	?	?	?	?	?	Y	Y	Y
3 Brademas	Y	N	N	Y	Y	Y	N	N
4 Quayle	?	?	?	?	?	N	Y	Y
5 Hillis	Y	N	N	Y	?	Y	Y	N
6 Evans	Y	N	Y	N	Y	Y	Y	Y
7 Myers, J.	Y	N	N	Y	Y	Y	Y	Y
8 Cornwell	Y	N	N	Y	Y	Y	N	N
9 Hamilton	Y	N	Y	Y	Y	Y	N	Y
10 Sharp	Y	Y	Y	N	Y	Y	N	Y
11 Jacobs	#	#	#	▮	?	Y	Y	Y
IOWA								
1 Leach	Y	N	N	Y	Y	Y	Y	Y
2 Blouin	?	?	?	?	?	?	N	N
3 Grassley	Y	N	N	Y	Y	Y	Y	Y
4 Smith	Y	N	N	Y	Y	Y	N	N
5 Harkin	Y	Y	Y	N	N	Y	N	Y
6 Bedell	Y	Y	Y	N	Y	Y	N	N

Democrats ***Republicans***

Corresponding to Congressional Record Votes 464, 465, 466, 467, 468, 469, 471, 472

	401	402	403	404	405	406	407	408
KANSAS								
1 Sebelius	Y	N	N	Y	?	Y	Y	Y
2 Keys	#	#	#	#	†	Y	Y	Y
3 Winn	Y	N	N	Y	Y	Y	Y	Y
4 Glickman	#	✓	▮	#	?	Y	Y	Y
5 Skubitz	Y	N	N	Y	Y	Y	Y	Y
KENTUCKY								
1 Hubbard	Y	N	N	Y	Y	Y	Y	N
2 Natcher	Y	N	N	Y	Y	Y	N	N
3 Mazzoli	Y	Y	Y	N	Y	Y	N	Y
4 Snyder	Y	N	N	Y	Y	Y	N	Y
5 Carter	Y	N	N	Y	Y	Y	N	N
6 Breckinridge	Y	N	N	Y	Y	Y	N	N
7 Perkins	Y	N	N	Y	Y	Y	N	N
LOUISIANA								
1 Livingston	Y	N	N	Y	Y	?	?	?
2 Boggs	Y	N	N	Y	Y	Y	N	N
3 Treen	Y	N	N	Y	Y	Y	Y	Y
4 Waggonner	Y	N	N	Y	Y	Y	Y	N
5 Huckaby	?	X	?	?	?	?	Y	Y
6 Moore	Y	N	Y	Y	Y	Y	Y	Y
7 Breaux	?	X	?	?	?	Y	Y	Y
8 Long	Y	N	N	Y	Y	Y	N	N
MAINE								
1 Emery	Y	N	Y	Y	Y	Y	N	✓
2 Cohen	?	?	?	?	?	Y	N	N
MARYLAND								
1 Bauman	Y	N	N	Y	Y	Y	Y	Y
2 Long	Y	N	N	Y	Y	Y	N	N
3 Mikulski	Y	Y	N	Y	Y	Y	N	N
4 Holt	?	N	N	Y	Y	Y	Y	Y
5 Spellman	Y	?	Y	Y	Y	Y	N	N
6 Byron	Y	N	N	Y	Y	Y	Y	N
7 Mitchell	N	Y	N	Y	Y	N	N	N
8 Steers	Y	Y	Y	Y	Y	Y	N	N
MASSACHUSETTS								
1 Conte	Y	N	Y	N	Y	Y	N	N
2 Boland	Y	N	N	Y	Y	Y	N	N
3 Early	Y	Y	Y	N	Y	?	N	N
4 Drinan	Y	Y	Y	Y	Y	Y	N	N
5 Tsongas	?	?	?	?	?	?	?	?
6 Harrington	#	#	#	▮	?	Y	▮	?
7 Markey	Y	Y	Y	N	Y	Y	N	N
8 O'Neill								
9 Moakley	Y	Y	N	Y	?	Y	N	N
10 Heckler	#	N	Y	Y	Y	Y	N	N
11 Burke	Y	N	N	Y	Y	Y	N	N
12 Studds	Y	Y	N	N	Y	Y	N	N
MICHIGAN								
1 Conyers	#	✓	▮	▮	▮	#	X	▮
2 Pursell	Y	Y	N	N	Y	Y	Y	Y
3 Brown	Y	N	#	#	?	Y	Y	N
4 Stockman	N	N	Y	N	Y	Y	Y	Y
5 Sawyer	#	?	?	?	#	#	Y	Y
6 Carr	Y	N	Y	N	Y	Y	N	Y
7 Kildee	Y	Y	Y	N	Y	Y	N	N
8 Traxler	Y	N	N	Y	?	Y	N	N
9 Vander Jagt	Y	N	Y	Y	?	?	✓	Y
10 Cederberg	Y	N	N	Y	Y	Y	Y	N
11 Ruppe	Y	N	?	Y	Y	?	✓	?
12 Bonior	Y	Y	Y	N	Y	Y	N	N
13 Diggs	#	Y	N	Y	#	#	N	N
14 Nedzi	?	?	?	?	?	Y	N	N
15 Ford	?	?	N	Y	Y	Y	N	N
16 Dingell	?	N	N	Y	Y	?	N	N
17 Brodhead	Y	Y	Y	N	Y	Y	N	N
18 Blanchard	Y	N	Y	Y	Y	Y	N	N
19 Broomfield	Y	N	Y	N	Y	Y	Y	N
MINNESOTA								
1 Quie	?	?	?	?	?	?	?	?
2 Hagedorn	?	?	?	?	?	Y	Y	Y
3 Frenzel	?	?	?	?	?	Y	Y	Y
4 Vento	#	✓	#	▮	?	Y	N	N
5 Fraser	#	#	▮	▮	?	Y	▮	?
6 Nolan	Y	Y	N	N	?	Y	N	N
7 Stangeland	Y	N	N	Y	?	Y	Y	Y
8 Oberstar	Y	Y	N	Y	Y	Y	N	N
MISSISSIPPI								
1 Whitten	Y	N	N	Y	?	Y	Y	N
2 Bowen	Y	N	N	Y	Y	?	?	?
3 Montgomery	Y	N	N	Y	?	Y	Y	N
4 Cochran	Y	N	N	Y	?	Y	Y	Y
5 Lott	#	▮	▮	#	?	Y	Y	Y
MISSOURI								
1 Clay	?	Y	N	Y	?	Y	N	N
2 Young	Y	N	N	Y	†	Y	Y	N
3 Gephardt	Y	N	Y	N	Y	Y	Y	Y

	401	402	403	404	405	406	407	408
4 Skelton	Y	N	N	Y	Y	Y	Y	Y
5 Bolling	#	▮	N	Y	?	Y	N	N
6 Coleman	Y	N	Y	Y	Y	Y	Y	Y
7 Taylor	?	?	?	?	?	Y	Y	Y
8 Ichord	Y	N	N	Y	Y	Y	Y	Y
9 Volkmer	Y	N	N	Y	N	Y	Y	Y
10 Burlison	Y	N	Y	Y	Y	Y	N	N
MONTANA								
1 Baucus	Y	N	N	Y	Y	Y	N	Y
2 Marlenee	?	?	?	?	?	Y	Y	Y
NEBRASKA								
1 Thone	Y	N	Y	Y	Y	Y	Y	Y
2 Cavanaugh	Y	Y	N	Y	Y	Y	N	Y
3 Smith	Y	N	N	Y	?	Y	Y	Y
NEVADA								
AL Santini	#	N	Y	Y	Y	#	#	▮
NEW HAMPSHIRE								
1 D'Amours	Y	N	Y	Y	Y	Y	Y	Y
2 Cleveland	?	?	?	?	?	Y	Y	Y
NEW JERSEY								
1 Florio	Y	N	N	Y	Y	Y	N	N
2 Hughes	Y	N	N	Y	Y	Y	N	Y
3 Howard	Y	N	N	Y	Y	Y	N	N
4 Thompson	Y	Y	Y	N	Y	Y	N	X
5 Fenwick	Y	Y	Y	N	N	Y	N	Y
6 Forsythe	Y	Y	Y	N	N	Y	N	Y
7 Maguire	Y	Y	Y	N	N	Y	N	N
8 Roe	Y	N	N	Y	Y	Y	N	N
9 Hollenbeck	Y	N	Y	Y	Y	Y	N	N
10 Rodino	?	?	?	?	?	?	?	?
11 Minish	Y	N	Y	Y	Y	Y	X	?
12 Rinaldo	Y	N	Y	Y	Y	Y	N	N
13 Meyner	Y	Y	N	Y	?	Y	N	N
14 LeFante	†	-	-	†	†	Y	N	N
15 Patten	Y	N	N	Y	Y	#	X	▮
NEW MEXICO								
1 Lujan	Y	N	N	Y	Y	Y	Y	Y
2 Runnels	#	?	?	?	#	#	✓	?
NEW YORK								
1 Pike	#	?	?	?	?	?	?	?
2 Downey	Y	N	N	Y	Y	Y	N	N
3 Ambro	?	X	N	Y	?	Y	N	N
4 Lent	Y	N	Y	N	Y	Y	Y	Y
5 Wydler	?	?	?	?	?	Y	Y	Y
6 Wolff	Y	N	Y	Y	Y	Y	N	N
7 Addabbo	#	✓	▮	#	#	#	N	N
8 Rosenthal	Y	Y	N	Y	Y	#	N	N
9 Delaney	Y	N	N	Y	Y	Y	N	N
10 Biaggi	#	✓	▮	#	#	#	N	Y
11 Scheuer	Y	N	N	Y	Y	▮	?	?
12 Chisholm	#	Y	N	Y	Y	?	N	N
13 Solarz	#	X	▮	#	#	#	N	▮
14 Richmond	?	✓	?	?	?	#	N	X
15 Zeferetti	#	✓	▮	#	#	#	N	N
16 Holtzman	Y	Y	N	N	N	Y	N	N
17 Murphy	Y	N	N	Y	Y	Y	N	?
18 Green	Y	N	Y	N	Y	Y	X	N
19 Rangel	Y	Y	N	Y	Y	Y	N	X
20 Weiss	Y	Y	Y	N	Y	Y	N	N
21 Garcia	#	✓	#	▮	#	#	N	N
22 Bingham	Y	Y	Y	Y	Y	Y	N	N
23 Caputo	?	?	?	?	?	?	X	?
24 Ottinger	Y	Y	N	†	-	†	N	N
25 Fish	Y	N	N	Y	?	Y	N	N
26 Gilman	Y	N	†	Y	Y	Y	N	N
27 McHugh	Y	Y	N	Y	Y	Y	N	N
28 Stratton	Y	N	Y	Y	Y	Y	N	N
29 Pattison	#	▮	▮	?	?	Y	N	N
30 McEwen	Y	N	N	Y	?	Y	Y	N
31 Mitchell	Y	N	Y	Y	Y	Y	Y	Y
32 Hanley	Y	N	Y	Y	Y	Y	Y	N
33 Walsh	?	?	?	?	?	Y	Y	N
34 Horton	#	▮	▮	#	?	Y	Y	N
35 Conable	Y	N	N	N	Y	Y	Y	Y
36 LaFalce	Y	N	N	Y	Y	Y	N	N
37 Nowak	Y	N	N	Y	Y	#	N	N
38 Kemp	Y	N	N	Y	Y	?	Y	Y
39 Lundine	Y	Y	N	Y	Y	Y	N	N
NORTH CAROLINA								
1 Jones	Y	N	N	Y	Y	Y	N	N
2 Fountain	Y	N	Y	Y	Y	Y	Y	Y
3 Whitley	Y	N	Y	Y	Y	Y	Y	Y
4 Andrews	?	N	N	Y	Y	?	?	?
5 Neal	Y	N	N	N	Y	Y	Y	Y
6 Preyer	Y	N	N	Y	Y	Y	N	N
7 Rose	Y	N	N	Y	Y	?	?	?
8 Hefner	Y	N	N	Y	Y	Y	N	N

	401	402	403	404	405	406	407	408
9 Martin	Y	N	Y	N	Y	Y	Y	Y
10 Broyhill	Y	N	Y	N	Y	Y	N	Y
11 Gudger	Y	N	Y	N	Y	#	▮	▮
NORTH DAKOTA								
AL Andrews	Y	N	N	Y	Y	Y	Y	N
OHIO								
1 Gradison	Y	N	Y	N	Y	#	N	N
2 Luken	Y	N	Y	N	Y	Y	N	N
3 Whalen	Y	N	Y	N	Y	Y	N	N
4 Guyer	Y	N	N	Y	?	Y	Y	Y
5 Latta	Y	N	Y	N	?	Y	Y	Y
6 Harsha	?	N	N	Y	Y	Y	N	Y
7 Brown	Y	N	Y	Y	Y	Y	Y	Y
8 Kindness	Y	N	N	Y	Y	Y	Y	Y
9 Ashley	?	X	?	?	?	Y	N	N
10 Miller	Y	N	Y	N	N	Y	Y	✓
11 Stanton	Y	N	N	Y	Y	Y	Y	N
12 Devine	Y	N	Y	N	Y	Y	Y	Y
13 Pease	Y	Y	N	Y	Y	Y	N	N
14 Seiberling	Y	Y	N	Y	Y	Y	N	N
15 Wylie	Y	N	Y	Y	Y	Y	N	Y
16 Regula	Y	N	N	Y	Y	Y	N	N
17 Ashbrook	Y	N	Y	Y	?	Y	Y	Y
18 Applegate	Y	N	N	Y	Y	Y	Y	Y
19 Carney	Y	N	N	Y	Y	Y	Y	N
20 Oakar	?	?	?	?	?	?	N	N
21 Stokes	Y	Y	N	Y	Y	Y	N	#
22 Vanik	#	Y	Y	N	Y	Y	N	N
23 Mottl	#	✓	#	▮	?	Y	N	Y
OKLAHOMA								
1 Jones	#	N	N	Y	Y	#	#	#
2 Risenhoover	Y	N	N	Y	Y	Y	Y	N
3 Watkins	Y	N	N	Y	Y	#	Y	N
4 Steed	#	X	▮	#	?	Y	Y	N
5 Edwards	?	N	N	Y	Y	Y	Y	Y
6 English	Y	N	N	Y	Y	Y	Y	Y
OREGON								
1 AuCoin	Y	Y	N	Y	N	Y	N	N
2 Ullman	#	▮	▮	#	?	Y	N	N
3 Duncan	Y	N	N	Y	Y	Y	N	N
4 Weaver	Y	Y	Y	N	Y	Y	N	N
PENNSYLVANIA								
1 Myers, M.	Y	N	N	Y	Y	Y	N	N
2 Nix	Y	N	N	Y	?	?	?	?
3 Lederer	Y	N	N	Y	Y	Y	N	N
4 Eilberg	Y	Y	N	Y	Y	Y	N	N
5 Schulze	Y	N	N	Y	Y	Y	Y	Y
6 Yatron	Y	N	Y	Y	Y	Y	Y	Y
7 Edgar	Y	Y	Y	N	Y	Y	N	N
8 Kostmayer	Y	Y	Y	N	Y	Y	N	Y
9 Shuster	Y	N	N	Y	?	Y	N	Y
10 McDade	Y	N	Y	Y	Y	Y	N	N
11 Flood	Y	N	N	Y	Y	Y	N	N
12 Murtha	Y	N	N	Y	Y	Y	Y	N
13 Coughlin	Y	N	Y	Y	Y	Y	N	N
14 Moorhead	#	▮	▮	#	?	Y	N	N
15 Rooney	Y	N	N	Y	Y	Y	N	N
16 Walker	Y	N	N	Y	Y	Y	Y	Y
17 Ertel	Y	N	N	Y	Y	Y	N	Y
18 Walgren	Y	Y	Y	Y	Y	Y	N	N
19 Goodling, W.	Y	?	?	?	?	?	Y	Y
20 Gaydos	?	N	N	Y	Y	Y	N	N
21 Dent	?	?	?	?	?	?	✓	?
22 Murphy	Y	N	Y	Y	N	N	N	N
23 Ammerman	Y	N	N	Y	Y	Y	N	Y
24 Marks	Y	N	Y	N	Y	Y	N	Y
25 Myers, G.	Y	N	Y	Y	Y	Y	N	Y
RHODE ISLAND								
1 St Germain	?	✓	?	?	?	Y	N	N
2 Beard	?	✓	?	?	?	Y	N	N
SOUTH CAROLINA								
1 Davis	Y	N	?	?	?	Y	Y	N
2 Spence	Y	N	N	Y	Y	Y	Y	Y
3 Derrick	Y	N	Y	N	Y	?	Y	N
4 Mann	?	?	?	?	?	?	Y	Y
5 Holland	?	?	?	?	?	Y	Y	N
6 Jenrette	Y	N	N	Y	Y	Y	Y	Y
SOUTH DAKOTA								
1 Pressler	?	Y	N	Y	Y	?	?	?
2 Abdnor	Y	N	N	Y	Y	Y	Y	Y
TENNESSEE								
1 Quillen	Y	N	N	Y	Y	Y	Y	N
2 Duncan	Y	N	N	Y	Y	Y	Y	N
3 Lloyd	Y	N	N	Y	Y	Y	Y	N
4 Gore	Y	N	N	Y	Y	Y	N	N
5 Allen †	?	?	?	?	?			
6 Beard	Y	N	N	Y	Y	#	✓	X

	401	402	403	404	405	406	407	408
7 Jones	Y	N	N	Y	Y	Y	Y	N
8 Ford	?	?	?	?	?	?	N	N
TEXAS								
1 Hall	Y	N	N	Y	Y	Y	Y	N
2 Wilson, C.	#	N	▮	#	#	#	▮	▮
3 Collins	Y	N	Y	N	Y	Y	Y	Y
4 Roberts	?	X	?	?	?	Y	N	N
5 Mattox	Y	N	Y	N	Y	Y	N	Y
6 Teague	?	?	?	?	?	?	?	?
7 Archer	?	?	?	?	?	?	Y	Y
8 Eckhardt	?	?	?	?	?	?	N	N
9 Brooks	Y	N	N	Y	Y	Y	?	N
10 Pickle	#	X	▮	#	?	Y	N	Y
11 Poage	Y	N	N	Y	Y	?	Y	Y
12 Wright	?	?	?	?	?	Y	N	N
13 Hightower	Y	N	N	Y	Y	Y	N	Y
14 Young	Y	N	N	Y	?	Y	Y	?
15 de la Garza	Y	N	N	Y	Y	Y	N	N
16 White	Y	N	N	Y	Y	Y	Y	N
17 Burleson	Y	N	N	Y	Y	Y	Y	Y
18 Jordan	Y	N	N	Y	Y	Y	N	N
19 Mahon	Y	N	N	Y	Y	Y	N	N
20 Gonzalez	Y	N	N	Y	Y	#	N	N
21 Krueger	#	▮	▮	#	?	Y	N	Y
22 Gammage	Y	N	N	Y	Y	#	✓	✓
23 Kazen	Y	N	N	Y	Y	Y	Y	N
24 Milford	?	X	?	?	?	?	?	?
UTAH								
1 McKay	Y	N	N	Y	Y	Y	N	N
2 Marriott	Y	N	N	Y	Y	Y	Y	Y
VERMONT								
AL Jeffords	Y	N	Y	Y	Y	Y	N	N
VIRGINIA								
1 Trible	Y	N	N	Y	Y	Y	Y	N
2 Whitehurst	#	▮	▮	#	?	Y	Y	N
3 Satterfield	?	X	?	?	?	Y	Y	Y
4 Daniel	Y	N	N	Y	Y	Y	Y	Y
5 Daniel	Y	N	N	Y	Y	Y	Y	Y
6 Butler	Y	N	N	Y	Y	Y	Y	Y
7 Robinson	Y	N	N	Y	Y	Y	Y	Y
8 Harris	#	N	N	Y	Y	#	N	N
9 Wampler	Y	N	Y	Y	?	?	Y	Y
10 Fisher	Y	N	Y	N	Y	Y	N	N
WASHINGTON								
1 Pritchard	Y	N	N	Y	Y	Y	▮	Y
2 Meeds	Y	N	N	Y	?	Y	N	N
3 Bonker	#	#	▮	#	#	#	N	N
4 McCormack	Y	N	N	Y	Y	#	Y	N
5 Foley	?	?	?	?	?	Y	Y	Y
6 Dicks	Y	N	N	Y	Y	Y	N	N
7 Cunningham	Y	N	N	Y	Y	#	Y	Y
WEST VIRGINIA								
1 Mollohan	Y	N	N	Y	Y	Y	N	Y
2 Staggers	Y	N	N	Y	Y	?	N	N
3 Slack	Y	N	N	Y	Y	Y	N	Y
4 Rahall	Y	Y	N	Y	Y	#	N	N
WISCONSIN								
1 Aspin	?	?	?	?	?	Y	N	N
2 Kastenmeier	Y	Y	N	Y	N	Y	N	N
3 Baldus	Y	Y	N	Y	Y	Y	N	N
4 Zablocki	Y	N	N	Y	Y	Y	N	N
5 Reuss	Y	N	N	Y	Y	Y	N	N
6 Steiger	Y	N	Y	N	Y	Y	N	Y
7 Obey	Y	N	N	N	N	Y	N	N
8 Cornell	Y	Y	N	Y	Y	#	N	N
9 Kasten	#	▮	#	▮	?	Y	N	Y
WYOMING								
AL Roncalio	Y	N	N	Y	Y	Y	N	N

†Rep. Clifford Allen, D-Tenn., died June 18, 1978.

Democrats ***Republicans***

409. HR 12936. HUD-Independent Agencies Appropriations, Fiscal 1979. Passage of bill to appropriate $68,208,848,000 for the Department of Housing and Urban Development and 17 other agencies, including the Environmental Protection Agency, National Aeronautics and Space Administration and the Veterans Administration, for fiscal 1979. Passed 332-47: R 101-34; D 231-13 (ND 160-10; SD 71-3), June 19, 1978. The president had requested $69,517,534,000.

410. HR 12932. Interior, Energy Appropriations, Fiscal 1979. Adoption of the rule (H Res 1230) providing for House floor consideration of the bill to appropriate $12,700,544,000 for fiscal 1979 for the Interior Department, the Energy Department, the Forest Service and other agencies. Adopted 353-27: R 115-16; D 238-11 (ND 164-8; SD 74-3), June 21, 1978.

411. HR 12932. Interior, Energy Appropriations, Fiscal 1979. Yates, D-Ill., amendment, to the Moffett, D-Conn., amendment *(see vote 412, below)*, to limit to $100,000 the use of appropriated funds to pay for expenses of citizens intervening in regulatory proceedings before the Economic Regulatory Administration. Rejected 190-221: R 21-120; D 169-101 (ND 142-48; SD 27-53), June 21, 1978.

412. HR 12932. Interior, Energy Appropriations, Fiscal 1979. Moffett, D-Conn., amendment to delete language from the bill prohibiting use of appropriated funds to pay for expenses of citizens intervening in regulatory proceedings before the Economic Regulatory Administration. Rejected 126-282: R 5-138; D 121-144 (ND 109-77; SD 12-67), June 21, 1978.

413. HR 12932. Interior, Energy Appropriations, Fiscal 1979. Miller, R-Ohio, amendment to reduce fiscal 1979 appropriations for payments not required by law for the Interior Department, the Energy Department and other agencies in the bill by 2 percent. Rejected 198-211: R 108-35; D 90-176 (ND 44-142; SD 46-34), June 21, 1978.

414. HR 12932. Interior, Energy Appropriations, Fiscal 1979. Passage of the bill to appropriate $12,690,544,000 for fiscal 1979 for the Interior Department, the Energy Department, the Forest Service and other agencies. Passed 356-50: R 105-34; D 251-16 (ND 180-7; SD 71-9), June 21, 1978. The president had requested $12,874,757,000.

415. HR 11493. Amtrak Improvements. Adoption of the rule (H Res 1212) providing for House floor consideration of the bill to authorize $768 million for the National Railroad Passenger Corp. (Amtrak) for fiscal 1979. Adopted 375-25: R 121-18; D 254-7 (ND 179-3; SD 75-4), June 21, 1978.

KEY

- Y Voted for (yea).
- ✓ Paired for.
- † Announced for.
- # CQ Poll for.
- N Voted against (nay).
- X Paired against.
- \- Announced against.
- ▮ CQ Poll against.
- P Voted "present."
- ● Voted "present" to avoid possible conflict of interest.
- ? Did not vote or otherwise make a position known.

	409	410	411	412	413	414	415
ALABAMA							
1 Edwards	Y	Y	N	N	Y	Y	Y
2 Dickinson	Y	Y	N	N	Y	Y	Y
3 Nichols	Y	Y	N	N	Y	Y	Y
4 Bevill	Y	Y	N	N	Y	Y	Y
5 Flippo	Y	Y	N	N	Y	Y	Y
6 Buchanan	Y	N	N	N	Y	Y	Y
7 Flowers	?	Y	Y	?	?	?	?
ALASKA							
AL Young	Y	#	N	N	N	Y	N
ARIZONA							
1 Rhodes	Y	Y	N	N	N	Y	Y
2 Udall	Y	Y	Y	Y	N	Y	Y
3 Stump	N	Y	N	N	Y	N	N
4 Rudd	N	Y	N	N	Y	Y	N
ARKANSAS							
1 Alexander	Y	Y	Y	N	N	Y	Y
2 Tucker	#	#	#	▮	#	?	?
3 Hammerschmidt	Y	Y	N	N	Y	Y	Y
4 Thornton	Y	Y	?	?	N	Y	?
CALIFORNIA							
1 Johnson	Y	Y	N	N	N	Y	Y
2 Clausen	Y	Y	N	N	Y	Y	Y
3 Moss	Y	?	?	?	?	?	?
4 Leggett	#	#	Y	N	N	Y	Y
5 Burton, J.	Y	?	Y	Y	N	Y	Y
6 Burton, P.	Y	Y	Y	Y	N	Y	?
7 Miller	Y	Y	Y	Y	N	Y	Y
8 Dellums	Y	Y	Y	Y	N	Y	Y
9 Stark	Y	Y	Y	Y	N	Y	Y
10 Edwards	Y	Y	Y	Y	N	Y	Y
11 Ryan	Y	Y	Y	N	N	Y	Y
12 McCloskey	Y	?	Y	Y	N	Y	Y
13 Mineta	Y	Y	Y	Y	N	Y	Y
14 McFall	Y	Y	N	N	N	Y	Y
15 Sisk	?	Y	N	N	N	Y	Y
16 Panetta	Y	Y	Y	Y	Y	Y	Y
17 Krebs	Y	N	Y	N	N	Y	Y
18 Ketchum	Y	Y	N	N	Y	Y	Y
19 Lagomarsino	Y	Y	N	N	N	Y	Y
20 Goldwater	Y	Y	N	N	Y	Y	Y
21 Corman	#	Y	Y	Y	N	Y	Y
22 Moorhead	N	Y	N	N	Y	Y	N
23 Beilenson	Y	#	Y	Y	N	Y	Y
24 Waxman	Y	#	#	✓	#	#	#
25 Roybal	Y	Y	Y	Y	N	Y	Y
26 Rousselot	N	Y	N	N	Y	Y	N
27 Dornan	N	Y	N	N	Y	Y	Y
28 Burke	Y	Y	Y	Y	N	Y	Y
29 Hawkins	?	P	Y	Y	N	Y	Y
30 Danielson	#	Y	Y	Y	N	Y	#
31 Wilson, C.H.	Y	Y	N	▮	N	Y	#
32 Anderson	Y	Y	Y	Y	Y	Y	Y
33 Clawson	N	Y	N	N	Y	Y	N
34 Hannaford	Y	Y	Y	Y	Y	Y	Y
35 Lloyd	Y	Y	Y	N	N	Y	Y
36 Brown	Y	Y	Y	Y	N	Y	Y
37 Pettis	Y	Y	N	N	N	Y	Y
38 Patterson	Y	Y	Y	Y	N	Y	Y
39 Wiggins	Y	#	▮	Y	Y	Y	Y
40 Badham	N	Y	N	N	Y	N	Y
41 Wilson, B.	Y	N	N	N	Y	Y	Y
42 Van Deerlin	?	Y	Y	N	N	Y	Y
43 Burgener	Y	Y	N	N	Y	Y	Y
COLORADO							
1 Schroeder	N	Y	Y	Y	N	N	Y
2 Wirth	Y	Y	Y	Y	N	Y	Y
3 Evans	Y	Y	N	N	N	Y	Y
4 Johnson	Y	Y	N	N	N	Y	Y
5 Armstrong	N	Y	N	N	Y	Y	Y
CONNECTICUT							
1 Cotter	Y	Y	Y	N	Y	Y	Y
2 Dodd	Y	Y	Y	Y	N	Y	Y
3 Giaimo	?	Y	N	N	Y	Y	Y
4 McKinney	#	#	N	N	N	Y	Y
5 Sarasin	#	Y	N	N	Y	#	#
6 Moffett	Y	Y	Y	Y	Y	Y	Y
DELAWARE							
AL Evans	✓	Y	N	N	Y	Y	Y
FLORIDA							
1 Sikes	Y	Y	N	N	N	Y	Y
2 Fuqua	Y	Y	N	N	N	Y	Y
3 Bennett	N	Y	Y	N	Y	Y	Y
4 Chappell	Y	?	N	N	N	Y	Y
5 Kelly	N	N	N	N	Y	N	Y
6 Young	Y	Y	N	N	Y	Y	Y
7 Gibbons	Y	Y	Y	N	Y	Y	?
8 Ireland	Y	Y	N	N	Y	Y	Y
9 Frey	?	Y	N	N	Y	Y	Y
10 Bafalis	Y	Y	N	N	Y	Y	Y
11 Rogers	Y	Y	Y	N	Y	Y	Y
12 Burke	Y	Y	N	N	Y	Y	Y
13 Lehman	Y	Y	Y	N	N	Y	Y
14 Pepper	Y	Y	Y	Y	N	Y	Y
15 Fascell	N	Y	Y	Y	N	Y	N
GEORGIA							
1 Ginn	Y	Y	N	N	Y	Y	Y
2 Mathis	?	Y	N	N	Y	N	Y
3 Brinkley	Y	Y	Y	N	Y	Y	Y
4 Levitas	Y	N	Y	Y	Y	Y	Y
5 Fowler	Y	Y	Y	?	?	?	Y
6 Flynt	X	Y	Y	N	N	Y	Y
7 McDonald	N	N	N	N	Y	N	N
8 Evans	Y	Y	N	N	Y	N	Y
9 Jenkins	X	Y	N	N	Y	Y	Y
10 Barnard	Y	Y	N	N	Y	Y	Y
HAWAII							
1 Heftel	Y	Y	N	N	N	Y	Y
2 Akaka	Y	Y	N	N	N	Y	Y
IDAHO							
1 Symms	N	Y	N	N	Y	N	N
2 Hansen, G.	X	Y	N	N	Y	Y	N
ILLINOIS							
1 Metcalfe	Y	Y	Y	N	N	Y	Y
2 Murphy	Y	Y	N	N	Y	Y	Y
3 Russo	N	Y	N	N	Y	Y	Y
4 Derwinski	N	Y	N	N	Y	N	Y
5 Fary	Y	Y	Y	N	N	Y	Y
6 Hyde	Y	Y	N	N	Y	Y	Y
7 Collins	Y	Y	Y	Y	N	Y	Y
8 Rostenkowski	Y	Y	Y	N	N	Y	Y
9 Yates	Y	Y	Y	Y	N	Y	Y
10 Mikva	Y	Y	Y	Y	N	Y	Y
11 Annunzio	Y	Y	N	N	N	Y	Y
12 Crane	N	N	N	N	Y	N	N
13 McClory	Y	#	N	N	N	Y	Y
14 Erlenborn	Y	Y	N	N	Y	N	Y
15 Corcoran	Y	Y	N	N	Y	Y	Y
16 Anderson	Y	Y	Y	N	N	Y	Y
17 O'Brien	Y	Y	N	N	Y	Y	Y
18 Michel	Y	Y	N	N	N	Y	Y
19 Railsback	Y	Y	Y	N	N	Y	Y
20 Findley	Y	Y	N	N	N	Y	Y
21 Madigan	Y	Y	N	N	Y	Y	Y
22 Shipley	?	?	?	X	?	?	?
23 Price	Y	Y	Y	Y	N	Y	Y
24 Simon	Y	?	?	?	?	?	?
INDIANA							
1 Benjamin	Y	Y	Y	N	Y	Y	Y
2 Fithian	Y	Y	N	N	Y	Y	Y
3 Brademas	Y	Y	Y	Y	N	Y	Y
4 Quayle	N	N	N	N	Y	N	Y
5 Hillis	Y	Y	N	N	Y	Y	Y
6 Evans	N	Y	N	N	Y	N	Y
7 Myers, J.	Y	Y	N	N	Y	Y	Y
8 Cornwell	Y	Y	Y	Y	N	Y	?
9 Hamilton	Y	Y	Y	Y	Y	Y	Y
10 Sharp	Y	Y	Y	Y	Y	Y	Y
11 Jacobs	N	Y	N	N	Y	N	Y
IOWA							
1 Leach	Y	#	Y	N	Y	Y	Y
2 Blouin	Y	Y	Y	N	Y	Y	Y
3 Grassley	Y	Y	N	N	Y	N	Y
4 Smith	Y	Y	Y	N	N	Y	Y
5 Harkin	Y	Y	Y	Y	Y	Y	Y
6 Bedell	Y	Y	Y	Y	N	Y	Y

Democrats ***Republicans***

	409	410	411	412	413	414	415
KANSAS							
1 ***Sebelius***	Y	Y	N	N	N	Y	Y
2 Keys	Y	Y	N	Y	Y	Y	Y
3 ***Winn***	Y	Y	N	N	Y	Y	Y
4 Glickman	Y	Y	N	Y	Y	Y	Y
5 ***Skubitz***	Y	Y	N	N	N	Y	Y
KENTUCKY							
1 Hubbard	Y	Y	Y	N	N	Y	Y
2 Natcher	Y	Y	N	N	N	Y	Y
3 Mazzoli	Y	Y	Y	N	Y	Y	Y
4 ***Snyder***	Y	Y	N	N	Y	Y	Y
5 ***Carter***	Y	Y	N	N	N	Y	Y
6 Breckinridge	Y	Y	N	Y	N	Y	Y
7 Perkins	Y	Y	N	N	N	Y	Y
LOUISIANA							
1 ***Livingston***	✓	Y	N	N	Y	Y	Y
2 Boggs	Y	Y	N	N	N	Y	Y
3 ***Treen***	N	Y	N	N	Y	Y	Y
4 Waggonner	Y	Y	N	N	Y	Y	Y
5 Huckaby	Y	Y	N	N	Y	Y	Y
6 ***Moore***	Y	N	N	N	Y	N	Y
7 Breaux	Y	?	N	N	Y	Y	Y
8 Long	Y	Y	N	N	N	Y	Y
MAINE							
1 ***Emery***	X	Y	N	N	Y	Y	Y
2 ***Cohen***	Y	Y	N	N	Y	Y	Y
MARYLAND							
1 ***Bauman***	N	N	N	N	Y	N	N
2 Long	Y	Y	Y	N	N	Y	Y
3 Mikulski	Y	N	Y	Y	N	Y	Y
4 ***Holt***	N	N	N	N	Y	N	N
5 Spellman	Y	Y	Y	Y	N	Y	Y
6 Byron	Y	Y	Y	N	Y	Y	Y
7 Mitchell	Y	Y	Y	Y	N	Y	Y
8 ***Steers***	Y	Y	Y	Y	Y	Y	Y
MASSACHUSETTS							
1 ***Conte***	Y	Y	Y	N	N	Y	Y
2 Boland	Y	Y	Y	Y	N	Y	Y
3 Early	Y	Y	Y	Y	N	Y	Y
4 Drinan	Y	Y	Y	Y	N	Y	Y
5 Tsongas	?	Y	Y	Y	?	Y	Y
6 Harrington	#	#	Y	Y	N	Y	Y
7 Markey	Y	Y	Y	Y	N	Y	Y
8 O'Neill							
9 Moakley	Y	Y	Y	Y	N	Y	Y
10 ***Heckler***	Y	#	Y	N	Y	Y	Y
11 Burke	Y	Y	N	N	N	Y	Y
12 Studds	Y	Y	Y	Y	N	Y	Y
MICHIGAN							
1 Conyers	#	Y	▮	✓	▮	#	#
2 ***Pursell***	N	Y	Y	N	Y	N	Y
3 ***Brown***	Y	Y	N	N	Y	N	Y
4 ***Stockman***	N	N	N	N	Y	N	N
5 ***Sawyer***	Y	Y	N	N	Y	N	Y
6 Carr	Y	Y	Y	Y	N	Y	Y
7 Kildee	Y	Y	Y	Y	N	Y	Y
8 Traxler	Y	Y	Y	▮	#	#	#
9 ***Vander Jagt***	Y	?	N	N	Y	Y	Y
10 ***Cederberg***	Y	Y	N	N	Y	Y	Y
11 ***Ruppe***	?	P	N	N	Y	Y	Y
12 Bonior	Y	?	Y	Y	N	Y	Y
13 Diggs	Y	#	Y	Y	N	Y	Y
14 Nedzi	Y	Y	N	N	N	Y	Y
15 Ford	Y	Y	Y	?	N	Y	Y
16 Dingell	Y	N	Y	Y	N	Y	Y
17 Brodhead	N	Y	Y	Y	N	N	Y
18 Blanchard	Y	Y	Y	Y	Y	Y	Y
19 ***Broomfield***	Y	Y	N	N	Y	Y	N
MINNESOTA							
1 ***Quie***	?	?	?	?	?	?	?
2 ***Hagedorn***	N	Y	N	N	Y	Y	Y
3 ***Frenzel***	N	Y	N	N	Y	N	Y
4 Vento	Y	Y	Y	Y	N	Y	Y
5 Fraser	Y	Y	Y	Y	N	Y	Y
6 Nolan	Y	Y	Y	Y	N	Y	Y
7 ***Stangeland***	N	N	N	N	Y	N	Y
8 Oberstar	Y	Y	Y	Y	N	Y	Y
MISSISSIPPI							
1 Whitten	Y	Y	N	N	N	Y	Y
2 Bowen	?	Y	N	N	N	Y	Y
3 Montgomery	Y	Y	N	N	Y	N	Y
4 ***Cochran***	Y	Y	N	N	N	Y	Y
5 ***Lott***	Y	Y	Y	N	Y	N	Y
MISSOURI							
1 Clay	Y	Y	Y	Y	N	Y	Y
2 Young	Y	Y	Y	N	N	Y	Y
3 Gephardt	N	Y	Y	N	Y	Y	Y
4 Skelton	Y	Y	Y	N	Y	Y	Y
5 Bolling	Y	Y	Y	N	N	Y	Y
6 ***Coleman***	N	N	N	N	Y	Y	Y
7 ***Taylor***	Y	Y	N	N	Y	Y	N
8 Ichord	Y	Y	N	N	Y	Y	Y
9 Volkmer	Y	N	Y	Y	Y	N	N
10 Burlison	Y	Y	Y	N	N	Y	Y
MONTANA							
1 Baucus	Y	Y	Y	Y	N	Y	Y
2 ***Marlenee***	Y	Y	N	N	Y	Y	Y
NEBRASKA							
1 ***Thone***	Y	Y	N	N	Y	Y	Y
2 Cavanaugh	Y	Y	Y	Y	Y	Y	N
3 ***Smith***	Y	Y	N	N	Y	Y	Y
NEVADA							
AL Santini	#	Y	N	N	Y	Y	Y
NEW HAMPSHIRE							
1 D'Amours	Y	Y	Y	Y	Y	Y	Y
2 ***Cleveland***	Y	Y	Y	N	Y	Y	Y
NEW JERSEY							
1 Florio	Y	Y	Y	N	N	Y	Y
2 Hughes	Y	Y	N	N	Y	Y	Y
3 Howard	Y	Y	Y	Y	N	Y	Y
4 Thompson	#	Y	Y	N	N	Y	Y
5 ***Fenwick***	N	Y	N	N	Y	N	Y
6 ***Forsythe***	Y	Y	N	N	Y	Y	Y
7 Maguire	Y	Y	Y	Y	N	Y	Y
8 Roe	Y	Y	N	N	Y	Y	Y
9 ***Hollenbeck***	Y	Y	N	N	N	Y	Y
10 Rodino	?	?	Y	?	?	?	?
11 Minish	?	Y	Y	Y	Y	Y	Y
12 ***Rinaldo***	Y	Y	N	N	Y	Y	Y
13 Meyner	Y	Y	Y	Y	N	Y	Y
14 LeFante	Y	Y	N	N	N	Y	Y
15 Patten	#	Y	Y	N	N	Y	Y
NEW MEXICO							
1 ***Lujan***	Y	Y	N	N	N	Y	Y
2 Runnels	?	#	?	?	?	#	?
NEW YORK							
1 Pike	?	Y	N	N	Y	Y	Y
2 Downey	Y	Y	Y	Y	N	Y	Y
3 Ambro	Y	?	N	Y	Y	Y	Y
4 ***Lent***	Y	Y	N	N	Y	Y	Y
5 ***Wydler***	Y	Y	N	N	Y	Y	Y
6 Wolff	Y	Y	Y	N	N	Y	Y
7 Addabbo	Y	Y	Y	N	N	Y	Y
8 Rosenthal	Y	#	Y	Y	N	Y	Y
9 Delaney	Y	Y	N	N	Y	Y	Y
10 Biaggi	Y	Y	N	N	N	Y	Y
11 Scheuer	?	Y	Y	Y	N	Y	Y
12 Chisholm	Y	Y	Y	Y	N	Y	Y
13 Solarz	#	Y	N	Y	N	Y	Y
14 Richmond	✓	?	Y	Y	N	Y	Y
15 Zeferetti	Y	Y	N	N	N	Y	Y
16 Holtzman	Y	?	Y	Y	N	Y	Y
17 Murphy	?	Y	Y	N	N	Y	Y
18 ***Green***	Y	Y	Y	Y	N	Y	Y
19 Rangel	?	Y	Y	Y	N	Y	Y
20 Weiss	N	N	Y	Y	N	Y	Y
21 Garcia	Y	#	Y	Y	N	Y	Y
22 Bingham	Y	Y	Y	Y	N	Y	Y
23 ***Caputo***	?	Y	N	N	Y	N	Y
24 Ottinger	Y	N	Y	Y	N	Y	Y
25 ***Fish***	Y	Y	N	N	N	Y	Y
26 ***Gilman***	Y	Y	Y	N	Y	Y	Y
27 McHugh	Y	Y	Y	Y	N	Y	Y
28 Stratton	Y	Y	Y	N	N	Y	Y
29 Pattison	Y	#	Y	Y	N	Y	Y
30 ***McEwen***	Y	Y	N	N	N	Y	Y
31 ***Mitchell***	Y	Y	N	N	N	#	#
32 Hanley	Y	Y	N	N	Y	Y	Y
33 ***Walsh***	Y	Y	N	N	N	Y	Y
34 ***Horton***	Y	Y	N	N	N	Y	Y
35 ***Conable***	N	Y	N	N	N	N	N
36 LaFalce	Y	#	Y	Y	Y	Y	Y
37 Nowak	Y	#	Y	Y	Y	Y	Y
38 ***Kemp***	Y	Y	N	N	Y	N	Y
39 Lundine	Y	Y	Y	Y	N	Y	Y
NORTH CAROLINA							
1 Jones	Y	Y	N	N	N	Y	N
2 Fountain	Y	Y	N	N	Y	Y	Y
3 Whitley	Y	Y	N	N	Y	Y	N
4 Andrews	?	?	Y	Y	Y	Y	Y
5 Neal	Y	Y	Y	N	Y	Y	Y
6 Preyer	Y	Y	N	N	Y	Y	Y
7 Rose	?	Y	Y	N	N	Y	Y
8 Hefner	Y	Y	N	N	Y	Y	Y
9 ***Martin***	N	Y	#	N	Y	N	Y
10 ***Broyhill***	Y	Y	N	N	Y	Y	Y
11 Gudger	#	Y	N	N	N	Y	Y
NORTH DAKOTA							
AL ***Andrews***	Y	Y	Y	N	N	Y	Y
OHIO							
1 ***Gradison***	Y	Y	N	N	Y	Y	Y
2 Luken	Y	Y	N	N	Y	Y	Y
3 ***Whalen***	Y	#	#	#	▮	#	#
4 ***Guyer***	Y	Y	N	N	Y	Y	Y
5 ***Latta***	N	Y	N	N	Y	N	Y
6 ***Harsha***	Y	Y	N	N	Y	Y	N
7 ***Brown***	Y	N	N	N	Y	Y	Y
8 ***Kindness***	Y	Y	N	N	Y	Y	Y
9 Ashley	Y	Y	Y	Y	N	Y	Y
10 ***Miller***	N	Y	N	N	Y	N	Y
11 ***Stanton***	Y	Y	N	N	Y	Y	Y
12 ***Devine***	N	Y	N	N	Y	N	Y
13 Pease	Y	#	Y	N	Y	Y	Y
14 Seiberling	Y	#	Y	Y	N	Y	Y
15 ***Wylie***	Y	?	N	N	Y	Y	Y
16 ***Regula***	Y	Y	N	N	Y	Y	Y
17 ***Ashbrook***	N	#	▮	X	#	▮	#
18 Applegate	Y	Y	Y	N	N	Y	Y
19 Carney	Y	Y	Y	Y	N	Y	#
20 Oakar	Y	Y	Y	Y	N	Y	Y
21 Stokes	?	Y	Y	Y	N	Y	Y
22 Vanik	Y	Y	Y	Y	N	Y	Y
23 Mottl	N	Y	Y	Y	Y	N	Y
OKLAHOMA							
1 Jones	▮	Y	N	N	Y	N	Y
2 Risenhoover	Y	Y	Y	N	?	Y	Y
3 Watkins	Y	Y	N	N	N	Y	Y
4 Steed	Y	Y	N	N	N	Y	Y
5 ***Edwards***	N	Y	N	N	Y	N	Y
6 English	Y	Y	#	N	Y	Y	Y
OREGON							
1 AuCoin	Y	Y	Y	Y	N	Y	Y
2 Ullman	Y	Y	N	N	N	Y	Y
3 Duncan	Y	Y	N	N	N	Y	Y
4 Weaver	Y	Y	Y	Y	N	Y	Y
PENNSYLVANIA							
1 Myers, M.	Y	Y	N	Y	N	Y	Y
2 Nix	?	Y	Y	?	?	?	?
3 Lederer	Y	Y	N	Y	N	Y	Y
4 Eilberg	Y	Y	Y	N	N	Y	Y
5 ***Schulze***	N	Y	N	Y	Y	Y	Y
6 Yatron	Y	Y	N	N	Y	Y	Y
7 Edgar	Y	Y	Y	Y	N	Y	Y
8 Kostmayer	Y	?	Y	Y	N	Y	Y
9 ***Shuster***	N	Y	N	N	Y	N	Y
10 ***McDade***	Y	Y	Y	N	N	Y	Y
11 Flood	Y	Y	Y	N	N	Y	Y
12 Murtha	Y	Y	Y	N	N	Y	Y
13 ***Coughlin***	Y	Y	N	N	N	Y	Y
14 Moorhead	Y	Y	Y	N	N	Y	Y
15 Rooney	Y	Y	Y	N	N	Y	Y
16 ***Walker***	N	Y	N	N	Y	N	Y
17 Ertel	Y	Y	N	N	Y	Y	Y
18 Walgren	Y	Y	Y	Y	N	Y	Y
19 ***Goodling, W.***	Y	Y	N	N	Y	Y	Y
20 Gaydos	Y	Y	N	N	Y	Y	Y
21 Dent	?	?	?	N	N	Y	Y
22 Murphy	Y	Y	N	N	N	Y	Y
23 Ammerman	Y	Y	N	Y	Y	Y	Y
24 ***Marks***	Y	N	N	N	Y	Y	Y
25 ***Myers, G.***	Y	Y	N	N	Y	N	Y
RHODE ISLAND							
1 St Germain	Y	Y	Y	Y	N	Y	Y
2 Beard	Y	Y	Y	Y	N	Y	Y
SOUTH CAROLINA							
1 Davis	Y	Y	N	Y	Y	Y	?
2 ***Spence***	Y	Y	N	N	Y	Y	Y
3 Derrick	Y	Y	Y	Y	Y	Y	Y
4 Mann	Y	Y	Y	N	Y	Y	Y
5 Holland	Y	Y	Y	Y	Y	Y	Y
6 Jenrette	Y	?	?	✓	?	?	?
SOUTH DAKOTA							
1 ***Pressler***	?	Y	Y	Y	N	Y	Y
2 ***Abdnor***	Y	Y	N	N	Y	Y	Y
TENNESSEE							
1 ***Quillen***	Y	Y	N	N	Y	Y	Y
2 ***Duncan***	Y	Y	N	N	N	?	N
3 Lloyd	Y	Y	N	N	Y	Y	Y
4 Gore	Y	Y	Y	Y	N	Y	Y
5 Vacancy							
6 ***Beard***	#	Y	N	N	Y	Y	Y
7 Jones	Y	Y	N	N	Y	Y	Y
8 Ford	Y	?	?	?	?	?	?
TEXAS							
1 Hall	Y	#	N	N	Y	Y	Y
2 Wilson, C.	#	#	N	N	N	Y	Y
3 ***Collins***	N	N	N	N	Y	N	N
4 Roberts	Y	Y	N	N	Y	N	Y
5 Mattox	Y	Y	Y	Y	Y	N	Y
6 Teague	?	?	?	?	?	?	?
7 ***Archer***	N	Y	N	N	Y	N	Y
8 Eckhardt	Y	Y	Y	Y	N	?	Y
9 Brooks	Y	Y	N	N	N	Y	Y
10 Pickle	Y	Y	▮	N	N	Y	Y
11 Poage	Y	Y	N	N	Y	Y	Y
12 Wright	Y	Y	N	N	N	Y	Y
13 Hightower	Y	Y	N	N	Y	Y	Y
14 Young	?	?	?	?	?	?	?
15 de la Garza	Y	Y	N	N	N	Y	Y
16 White	Y	Y	N	N	N	Y	Y
17 Burleson	Y	Y	N	N	Y	Y	Y
18 Jordan	Y	#	Y	Y	N	Y	Y
19 Mahon	Y	Y	N	N	N	Y	Y
20 Gonzalez	Y	Y	N	N	N	Y	Y
21 Krueger	Y	N	N	N	Y	Y	Y
22 Gammage	✓	Y	N	N	Y	Y	Y
23 Kazen	Y	Y	N	N	N	Y	Y
24 Milford	?	?	?	?	?	?	?
UTAH							
1 McKay	Y	Y	N	N	N	Y	Y
2 ***Marriott***	Y	Y	N	N	Y	N	Y
VERMONT							
AL ***Jeffords***	Y	#	Y	Y	N	Y	Y
VIRGINIA							
1 ***Trible***	Y	Y	N	N	Y	Y	Y
2 ***Whitehurst***	Y	Y	N	N	Y	Y	Y
3 Satterfield	Y	Y	N	N	Y	N	Y
4 ***Daniel***	Y	Y	N	N	Y	Y	Y
5 Daniel	Y	Y	N	N	Y	Y	Y
6 ***Butler***	Y	?	?	X	?	?	?
7 ***Robinson***	Y	Y	N	N	Y	Y	Y
8 Harris	Y	Y	Y	?	N	Y	Y
9 ***Wampler***	Y	Y	N	N	Y	Y	Y
10 Fisher	Y	Y	Y	Y	N	Y	Y
WASHINGTON							
1 ***Pritchard***	Y	Y	Y	N	Y	#	#
2 Meeds	Y	N	N	N	N	Y	Y
3 Bonker	Y	Y	Y	N	N	Y	Y
4 McCormack	N	Y	N	N	N	Y	Y
5 Foley	Y	Y	Y	N	N	Y	Y
6 Dicks	Y	Y	Y	Y	N	Y	Y
7 ***Cunningham***	Y	N	N	N	N	Y	N
WEST VIRGINIA							
1 Mollohan	Y	Y	N	N	N	Y	Y
2 Staggers	Y	N	Y	Y	N	Y	Y
3 Slack	Y	Y	N	N	N	Y	Y
4 Rahall	Y	Y	N	N	#	#	#
WISCONSIN							
1 Aspin	Y	Y	Y	Y	N	Y	Y
2 Kastenmeier	Y	Y	Y	Y	N	Y	Y
3 Baldus	Y	Y	Y	Y	N	Y	Y
4 Zablocki	Y	Y	Y	N	N	Y	Y
5 Reuss	Y	Y	Y	Y	N	Y	Y
6 ***Steiger***	Y	N	Y	N	Y	N	Y
7 Obey	?	Y	Y	Y	N	Y	Y
8 Cornell	Y	Y	Y	Y	N	Y	Y
9 ***Kasten***	Y	#	Y	N	N	Y	#
WYOMING							
AL Roncalio	Y	Y	N	N	N	Y	Y

Democrats ***Republicans***

416. HR 13125. Agriculture Appropriations, Fiscal 1979. Whitten, D-Miss., motion that the House resolve itself into the Committee of the Whole to consider the bill to appropriate $18,014,000,000 for fiscal 1979 operations and programs of the Department of Agriculture and related agencies. Motion agreed to 369-5: R 127-3; D 242-2 (ND 165-1; SD 77-1), June 22, 1978.

417. HR 13125. Agriculture Appropriations, Fiscal 1979. Symms, R-Idaho, amendment to reduce by $290,200,000 the appropriation for the food stamp program. Rejected 194-201: R 120-14; D 74-187 (ND 22-162; SD 52-25), June 22, 1978.

418. HR 13125. Agriculture Appropriations, Fiscal 1979. Wright, D-Texas, amendment to prohibit the use of appropriated funds to finance economic assistance to South Korea under the Food for Peace program. Adopted 273-125: R 68-67; D 205-58 (ND 144-39; SD 61-19), June 22, 1978.

419. HR 13125. Agriculture Appropriations, Fiscal 1979. Miller, R-Ohio, amendment to reduce by 2 percent appropriated funds for all operations and programs of the Agriculture Department and related agencies, except the Agriculture Research Service, the Cooperative State Research Service and the Extension Service. Rejected 189-201: R 100-33; D 89-168 (ND 59-119; SD 30-49), June 22, 1978.

420. HR 13125. Agriculture Appropriations, Fiscal 1979. Passage of the bill to appropriate $18,014,000,000 for fiscal 1979 operations and programs of the Department of Agriculture and related agencies. Passed 326-59: R 93-38; D 233-21 (ND 159-16; SD 74-5), June 22, 1978. The president had requested $18,090,000,000 in new budget authority.

421. HR 12505. Solar Satellite Program. Passage of the bill to authorize $25 million for a feasibility study by the Energy Department and NASA of a research, development and demonstration program for collecting solar energy by satellite and transmitting the energy to earth to generate electricity. Passed 267-96: R 92-29; D 175-67 (ND 111-56; SD 64-11), June 22, 1978.

KEY

Y Voted for (yea).
✓ Paired for.
† Announced for.
# CQ Poll for.
N Voted against (nay).
X Paired against.
\- Announced against.
▮ CQ Poll against.
P Voted "present."
● Voted "present" to avoid possible conflict of interest.
? Did not vote or otherwise make a position known.

	416	417	418	419	420	421
ALABAMA						
1 Edwards	Y	Y	N	N	Y	Y
2 Dickinson	Y	Y	Y	Y	Y	Y
3 Nichols	#	✓	X	#	#	#
4 Bevill	Y	Y	Y	Y	Y	Y
5 Flippo	Y	Y	Y	Y	Y	Y
6 Buchanan	Y	N	Y	Y	Y	Y
7 Flowers	?	?	?	?	?	?
ALASKA						
AL Young	#	#	#	▮	#	#
ARIZONA						
1 Rhodes	Y	Y	Y	Y	Y	Y
2 Udall	Y	N	Y	N	Y	N
3 Stump	Y	Y	N	Y	N	Y
4 Rudd	Y	Y	N	Y	N	?
ARKANSAS						
1 Alexander	Y	N	Y	N	Y	Y
2 Tucker	#	▮	#	▮	#	#
3 Hammerschmidt	Y	Y	N	Y	Y	Y
4 Thornton	Y	?	Y	N	Y	Y
CALIFORNIA						
1 Johnson	Y	N	N	N	Y	Y
2 Clausen	Y	Y	Y	Y	Y	Y
3 Moss	Y	N	X	?	?	N
4 Leggett	Y	N	N	N	Y	Y
5 Burton, J.	?	X	✓	?	?	?
6 Burton, P.	Y	N	Y	N	Y	N
7 Miller	Y	N	Y	Y	Y	N
8 Dellums	Y	N	Y	N	#	▮
9 Stark	#	N	Y	N	Y	N
10 Edwards	Y	N	N	N	Y	N
11 Ryan	Y	N	Y	Y	Y	X
12 McCloskey	Y	Y	Y	N	Y	Y
13 Mineta	Y	N	Y	N	Y	N
14 McFall	Y	N	Y	N	Y	Y
15 Sisk	Y	N	N	N	Y	Y
16 Panetta	Y	Y	Y	Y	Y	Y
17 Krebs	Y	N	Y	N	Y	Y
18 Ketchum	Y	Y	N	Y	N	?
19 Lagomarsino	Y	Y	Y	Y	N	Y
20 Goldwater	?	Y	N	Y	Y	Y
21 Corman	Y	N	Y	N	Y	Y
22 Moorhead	Y	Y	N	Y	N	Y
23 Beilenson	#	N	N	N	Y	N
24 Waxman	#	X	✓	▮	#	#
25 Roybal	Y	N	N	N	Y	Y
26 Rousselot	?	Y	?	?	N	Y
27 Dornan	Y	Y	Y	Y	N	Y
28 Burke	Y	N	N	N	Y	Y
29 Hawkins	Y	X	Y	N	Y	Y
30 Danielson	#	N	Y	N	Y	Y
31 Wilson, C.H.	Y	▮	N	▮	#	#
32 Anderson	Y	N	Y	Y	N	Y
33 Clawson	Y	Y	N	Y	N	N
34 Hannaford	Y	Y	Y	Y	Y	Y
35 Lloyd	N	N	Y	N	Y	✓
36 Brown	Y	N	Y	?	Y	N
37 Pettis	Y	Y	N	Y	Y	Y
38 Patterson	Y	Y	Y	N	Y	Y
39 Wiggins	Y	Y	N	Y	N	Y
40 Badham	Y	Y	N	Y	N	Y
41 Wilson, B.	N	Y	N	Y	N	Y
42 Van Deerlin	Y	N	Y	N	Y	N
43 Burgener	Y	Y	N	Y	N	Y
COLORADO						
1 Schroeder	Y	N	Y	Y	N	Y
2 Wirth	Y	N	Y	Y	Y	Y
3 Evans	Y	N	N	N	Y	Y
4 Johnson	Y	Y	Y	N	Y	Y
5 Armstrong	Y	Y	N	Y	N	N
CONNECTICUT						
1 Cotter	Y	N	Y	Y	Y	Y
2 Dodd	?	N	N	N	Y	?
3 Giaimo	Y	N	Y	Y	Y	Y
4 McKinney	Y	N	Y	Y	Y	N
5 Sarasin	Y	Y	Y	Y	Y	#
6 Moffett	Y	N	Y	Y	Y	?
DELAWARE						
AL Evans	Y	Y	Y	Y	Y	Y
FLORIDA						
1 Sikes	Y	Y	N	N	Y	Y
2 Fuqua	Y	Y	Y	N	Y	Y
3 Bennett	Y	Y	Y	Y	N	Y
4 Chappell	Y	Y	Y	N	Y	Y
5 Kelly	Y	Y	Y	Y	N	N
6 Young	Y	Y	Y	Y	N	Y
7 Gibbons	?	Y	Y	Y	Y	Y
8 Ireland	Y	Y	Y	Y	Y	Y
9 Frey	Y	Y	Y	Y	Y	?
10 Bafalis	Y	Y	Y	Y	Y	Y
11 Rogers	Y	?	Y	Y	Y	Y
12 Burke	Y	Y	N	Y	Y	Y
13 Lehman	Y	N	Y	N	Y	N
14 Pepper	Y	N	Y	N	Y	Y
15 Fascell	Y	N	Y	N	Y	Y
GEORGIA						
1 Ginn	Y	Y	Y	N	Y	Y
2 Mathis	Y	Y	N	?	Y	Y
3 Brinkley	Y	Y	Y	N	Y	Y
4 Levitas	Y	Y	Y	Y	Y	Y
5 Fowler	Y	N	?	?	?	?
6 Flynt	Y	Y	Y	Y	Y	Y
7 McDonald	N	Y	N	Y	N	N
8 Evans	Y	Y	N	Y	Y	N
9 Jenkins	Y	Y	Y	Y	Y	Y
10 Barnard	Y	Y	Y	Y	Y	?
HAWAII						
1 Heftel	Y	N	Y	N	Y	Y
2 Akaka	Y	N	Y	N	Y	Y
IDAHO						
1 Symms	Y	Y	N	Y	N	?
2 Hansen, G.	Y	Y	N	Y	N	N
ILLINOIS						
1 Metcalfe	Y	N	Y	N	Y	?
2 Murphy	Y	N	Y	N	Y	N
3 Russo	Y	N	Y	Y	N	N
4 Derwinski	Y	Y	N	Y	N	Y
5 Fary	Y	N	Y	N	Y	Y
6 Hyde	Y	Y	Y	Y	Y	N
7 Collins	#	N	Y	N	Y	Y
8 Rostenkowski	Y	N	Y	N	Y	Y
9 Yates	Y	N	Y	N	Y	N
10 Mikva	Y	N	Y	Y	N	N
11 Annunzio	Y	N	N	Y	Y	Y
12 Crane	Y	Y	N	Y	N	N
13 McClory	Y	Y	N	Y	Y	Y
14 Erlenborn	Y	Y	N	Y	N	N
15 Corcoran	Y	Y	Y	Y	Y	Y
16 Anderson	Y	Y	N	N	Y	N
17 O'Brien	Y	Y	Y	N	Y	N
18 Michel	Y	Y	N	Y	Y	Y
19 Railsback	Y	Y	Y	Y	Y	Y
20 Findley	Y	Y	N	Y	Y	?
21 Madigan	Y	Y	Y	Y	Y	Y
22 Shipley	?	X	X	?	?	?
23 Price	Y	N	Y	N	Y	Y
24 Simon	?	?	?	?	?	?
INDIANA						
1 Benjamin	Y	N	Y	Y	Y	Y
2 Fithian	Y	N	Y	N	Y	Y
3 Brademas	Y	N	Y	N	Y	Y
4 Quayle	N	Y	Y	Y	N	Y
5 Hillis	Y	Y	N	Y	Y	N
6 Evans	Y	Y	Y	N	Y	Y
7 Myers, J.	Y	Y	N	Y	?	?
8 Cornwell	Y	N	Y	N	Y	Y
9 Hamilton	Y	N	Y	Y	Y	Y
10 Sharp	Y	N	Y	Y	Y	Y
11 Jacobs	#	Y	Y	Y	N	N
IOWA						
1 Leach	Y	Y	Y	Y	Y	Y
2 Blouin	Y	N	Y	N	Y	N
3 Grassley	Y	Y	Y	Y	Y	N
4 Smith	Y	N	N	N	Y	Y
5 Harkin	Y	N	Y	Y	Y	Y
6 Bedell	Y	N	Y	N	Y	N

Democrats ***Republicans***

	416	417	418	419	420	421
KANSAS						
1 Sebelius	Y	Y	N	N	Y	N
2 Keys	Y	N	Y	Y	Y	N
3 Winn	Y	Y	N	N	Y	Y
4 Glickman	Y	Y	Y	N	Y	Y
5 Skubitz	Y	?	N	?	?	Y
KENTUCKY						
1 Hubbard	Y	Y	Y	N	Y	Y
2 Natcher	Y	N	Y	N	Y	Y
3 Mazzoli	Y	N	Y	Y	Y	Y
4 Snyder	Y	Y	Y	Y	N	Y
5 Carter	Y	N	N	N	Y	Y
6 Breckinridge	Y	Y	N	N	Y	Y
7 Perkins	Y	N	Y	N	Y	Y
LOUISIANA						
1 Livingston	Y	N	N	Y	Y	Y
2 Boggs	Y	N	N	N	Y	Y
3 Treen	Y	Y	N	Y	Y	Y
4 Waggonner	#	✔	Y	N	Y	Y
5 Huckaby	Y	N	Y	N	Y	?
6 Moore	Y	Y	N	N	Y	Y
7 Breaux	Y	Y	Y	Y	Y	Y
8 Long	Y	N	Y	N	Y	Y
MAINE						
1 Emery	Y	Y	Y	Y	Y	Y
2 Cohen	Y	Y	Y	Y	Y	?
MARYLAND						
1 Bauman	Y	Y	N	Y	Y	N
2 Long	Y	N	Y	N	Y	N
3 Mikulski	Y	N	N	Y	Y	Y
4 Holt	Y	Y	N	Y	Y	Y
5 Spellman	Y	N	Y	N	?	Y
6 Byron	?	Y	Y	Y	Y	Y
7 Mitchell	#	N	Y	N	Y	Y
8 Steers	Y	N	Y	Y	Y	Y
MASSACHUSETTS						
1 Conte	Y	Y	N	N	Y	Y
2 Boland	Y	N	Y	N	Y	Y
3 Early	Y	N	Y	N	Y	N
4 Drinan	Y	N	Y	N	Y	N
5 Tsongas	?	?	?	?	?	?
6 Harrington	#	N	Y	N	Y	▮
7 Markey	Y	N	Y	?	?	?
8 O'Neill						
9 Moakley	Y	N	Y	N	Y	N
10 Heckler	Y	N	Y	Y	?	#
11 Burke	Y	N	N	N	Y	Y
12 Studds	Y	N	Y	N	Y	N
MICHIGAN						
1 Conyers	#	X	#	▮	#	▮
2 Pursell	Y	Y	N	Y	Y	Y
3 Brown	Y	Y	Y	Y	N	N
4 Stockman	Y	Y	N	Y	N	Y
5 Sawyer	#	✔	#	?	#	#
6 Carr	Y	N	Y	Y	Y	Y
7 Kildee	Y	N	Y	N	Y	Y
8 Traxler	#	▮	#	▮	#	#
9 Vander Jagt	?	?	?	?	?	?
10 Cederberg	#	Y	Y	Y	Y	Y
11 Ruppe	Y	Y	Y	N	Y	Y
12 Bonior	Y	N	N	N	Y	N
13 Diggs	#	N	Y	N	Y	Y
14 Nedzi	Y	N	Y	N	Y	Y
15 Ford	Y	N	Y	N	Y	Y
16 Dingell	?	N	N	N	?	Y
17 Brodhead	Y	N	Y	N	N	N
18 Blanchard	Y	N	Y	N	N	Y
19 Broomfield	Y	Y	Y	Y	N	Y
MINNESOTA						
1 Quie	?	?	?	?	?	?
2 Hagedorn	Y	Y	N	N	Y	Y
3 Frenzel	Y	Y	?	?	?	?
4 Vento	Y	N	Y	N	Y	N
5 Fraser	Y	N	Y	▮	#	▮
6 Nolan	Y	N	Y	N	Y	N
7 Stangeland	Y	Y	Y	Y	Y	Y
8 Oberstar	Y	N	Y	N	Y	Y
MISSISSIPPI						
1 Whitten	Y	N	Y	N	Y	#
2 Bowen	Y	?	?	?	?	?
3 Montgomery	Y	Y	Y	N	Y	N
4 Cochran	Y	Y	Y	N	Y	N
5 Lott	Y	Y	Y	N	Y	N
MISSOURI						
1 Clay	Y	N	N	N	Y	Y
2 Young	Y	N	Y	Y	Y	Y
3 Gephardt	Y	Y	Y	Y	N	Y

	416	417	418	419	420	421
4 Skelton	Y	Y	Y	Y	Y	Y
5 Bolling	Y	N	N	N	Y	Y
6 Coleman	Y	Y	Y	N	Y	Y
7 Taylor	Y	Y	N	Y	Y	Y
8 Ichord	Y	Y	Y	Y	Y	Y
9 Volkmer	Y	Y	Y	Y	Y	Y
10 Burlison	Y	N	Y	N	Y	Y
MONTANA						
1 Baucus	Y	N	Y	N	Y	Y
2 Marlenee	Y	Y	Y	N	Y	N
NEBRASKA						
1 Thone	Y	Y	N	Y	Y	#
2 Cavanaugh	Y	N	Y	N	Y	Y
3 Smith	Y	Y	N	N	Y	Y
NEVADA						
AL Santini	Y	Y	Y	Y	Y	#
NEW HAMPSHIRE						
1 D'Amours	Y	N	Y	Y	Y	Y
2 Cleveland	Y	Y	Y	Y	N	?
NEW JERSEY						
1 Florio	Y	N	Y	N	Y	N
2 Hughes	Y	Y	Y	Y	Y	Y
3 Howard	Y	N	Y	N	Y	Y
4 Thompson	Y	N	Y	N	#	Y
5 Fenwick	Y	Y	Y	Y	N	N
6 Forsythe	Y	Y	Y	Y	N	Y
7 Maguire	Y	N	Y	Y	Y	N
8 Roe	Y	N	Y	Y	Y	Y
9 Hollenbeck	Y	N	Y	Y	Y	Y
10 Rodino	?	?	?	?	?	?
11 Minish	Y	N	Y	Y	Y	Y
12 Rinaldo	Y	N	Y	Y	Y	Y
13 Meyner	#	N	Y	N	Y	Y
14 LeFante	#	X	✔	▮	#	#
15 Patten	Y	N	Y	N	Y	Y
NEW MEXICO						
1 Lujan	Y	Y	N	Y	Y	Y
2 Runnels	#	✔	X	?	?	#
NEW YORK						
1 Pike	Y	Y	Y	Y	N	Y
2 Downey	Y	N	Y	Y	Y	N
3 Ambro	?	Y	Y	Y	Y	Y
4 Lent	Y	Y	Y	Y	Y	Y
5 Wydler	Y	Y	Y	Y	N	Y
6 Wolff	Y	N	N	Y	N	Y
7 Addabbo	Y	N	Y	N	Y	Y
8 Rosenthal	#	N	Y	Y	Y	N
9 Delaney	Y	N	Y	Y	Y	N
10 Biaggi	Y	N	N	Y	Y	N
11 Scheuer	Y	N	Y	N	Y	Y
12 Chisholm	Y	N	Y	N	Y	N
13 Solarz	Y	N	Y	N	Y	N
14 Richmond	Y	N	Y	N	Y	N
15 Zeferetti	Y	N	Y	Y	Y	#
16 Holtzman	Y	N	Y	N	Y	N
17 Murphy	Y	N	N	N	Y	Y
18 Green	Y	N	N	N	Y	N
19 Rangel	?	N	Y	N	Y	N
20 Weiss	Y	N	N	N	Y	X
21 Garcia	#	X	✔	N	Y	N
22 Bingham	Y	N	N	N	Y	N
23 Caputo	Y	N	Y	?	?	?
24 Ottinger	Y	N	Y	N	Y	N
25 Fish	Y	Y	Y	Y	Y	Y
26 Gilman	Y	N	Y	N	Y	Y
27 McHugh	Y	N	Y	N	Y	Y
28 Stratton	Y	N	N	Y	N	Y
29 Pattison	Y	N	Y	N	Y	Y
30 McEwen	?	Y	Y	Y	Y	Y
31 Mitchell	Y	Y	N	Y	Y	Y
32 Hanley	Y	N	Y	#	#	#
33 Walsh	Y	Y	N	Y	Y	Y
34 Horton	Y	N	N	Y	Y	Y
35 Conable	Y	Y	Y	Y	N	N
36 LaFalce	Y	N	Y	Y	Y	N
37 Nowak	Y	N	Y	N	Y	Y
38 Kemp	Y	Y	N	Y	N	Y
39 Lundine	Y	N	Y	Y	Y	N
NORTH CAROLINA						
1 Jones	Y	Y	N	N	Y	Y
2 Fountain	Y	Y	Y	N	Y	Y
3 Whitley	Y	Y	Y	Y	Y	Y
4 Andrews	Y	Y	Y	N	Y	Y
5 Neal	Y	Y	Y	Y	Y	Y
6 Preyer	Y	Y	Y	N	Y	N
7 Rose	Y	N	Y	N	Y	Y
8 Hefner	Y	Y	Y	N	Y	Y

	416	417	418	419	420	421
9 Martin	Y	Y	N	Y	Y	Y
10 Broyhill	Y	Y	Y	Y	N	Y
11 Gudger	Y	Y	Y	Y	Y	Y
NORTH DAKOTA						
AL Andrews	Y	Y	N	N	Y	Y
OHIO						
1 Gradison	Y	Y	N	Y	N	N
2 Luken	Y	N	Y	N	Y	?
3 Whalen	#	▮	▮	▮	#	#
4 Guyer	?	✔	?	?	?	?
5 Latta	Y	Y	Y	Y	Y	N
6 Harsha	?	Y	Y	Y	Y	Y
7 Brown	Y	Y	N	Y	Y	?
8 Kindness	?	Y	Y	Y	Y	Y
9 Ashley	?	N	N	N	Y	N
10 Miller	Y	Y	N	Y	N	Y
11 Stanton	Y	Y	Y	Y	Y	Y
12 Devine	Y	Y	N	Y	N	Y
13 Pease	Y	N	N	Y	Y	N
14 Seiberling	Y	N	Y	Y	Y	N
15 Wylie	Y	Y	Y	Y	Y	N
16 Regula	Y	Y	N	Y	Y	Y
17 Ashbrook	#	✔	▮	#	#	#
18 Applegate	Y	N	Y	N	Y	Y
19 Carney	Y	N	Y	N	Y	Y
20 Oakar	Y	N	Y	N	Y	Y
21 Stokes	Y	N	N	N	Y	N
22 Vanik	Y	N	Y	Y	N	#
23 Mottl	Y	Y	Y	Y	N	Y
OKLAHOMA						
1 Jones	Y	Y	N	N	Y	Y
2 Risenhoover	Y	Y	Y	N	Y	Y
3 Watkins	Y	Y	Y	N	Y	Y
4 Steed	Y	N	N	N	Y	Y
5 Edwards	Y	Y	Y	N	Y	N
6 English	Y	Y	Y	N	Y	Y
OREGON						
1 AuCoin	Y	Y	Y	Y	N	N
2 Ullman	Y	N	N	N	Y	Y
3 Duncan	Y	N	N	N	Y	Y
4 Weaver	Y	Y	N	Y	Y	N
PENNSYLVANIA						
1 Myers, M.	Y	N	N	Y	Y	Y
2 Nix	?	N	X	?	?	?
3 Lederer	Y	N	Y	N	Y	Y
4 Eilberg	Y	N	Y	Y	Y	Y
5 Schulze	Y	Y	Y	Y	Y	Y
6 Yatron	Y	N	Y	Y	Y	Y
7 Edgar	Y	N	Y	Y	N	N
8 Kostmayer	Y	N	Y	Y	Y	N
9 Shuster	Y	Y	Y	Y	N	Y
10 McDade	Y	▮	Y	N	Y	Y
11 Flood	Y	N	Y	N	Y	Y
12 Murtha	Y	N	N	N	Y	Y
13 Coughlin	Y	Y	Y	Y	N	Y
14 Moorhead	Y	N	Y	N	Y	Y
15 Rooney	Y	N	Y	N	Y	Y
16 Walker	Y	?	Y	Y	N	Y
17 Ertel	Y	Y	Y	N	Y	Y
18 Walgren	Y	N	N	Y	Y	Y
19 Goodling, W.	?	Y	N	Y	Y	N
20 Gaydos	Y	N	Y	Y	Y	Y
21 Dent	?	N	X	?	?	?
22 Murphy	Y	N	Y	N	Y	Y
23 Ammerman	Y	N	Y	N	Y	N
24 Marks	Y	Y	N	N	Y	Y
25 Myers, G.	Y	Y	N	Y	Y	Y
RHODE ISLAND						
1 St Germain	Y	N	Y	N	Y	?
2 Beard	Y	N	Y	N	Y	Y
SOUTH CAROLINA						
1 Davis	Y	Y	Y	Y	Y	Y
2 Spence	Y	Y	Y	Y	Y	Y
3 Derrick	Y	Y	Y	Y	Y	N
4 Mann	Y	N	N	Y	Y	Y
5 Holland	Y	Y	Y	Y	?	?
6 Jenrette	?	X	✔	?	?	✔
SOUTH DAKOTA						
1 Pressler	Y	N	N	N	Y	Y
2 Abdnor	Y	Y	N	N	Y	Y
TENNESSEE						
1 Quillen	Y	Y	Y	N	Y	Y
2 Duncan	Y	Y	N	Y	Y	Y
3 Lloyd	Y	Y	N	N	Y	Y
4 Gore	Y	N	Y	N	Y	Y
5 Vacancy						
6 Beard	Y	Y	N	N	Y	Y

	416	417	418	419	420	421
7 Jones	Y	Y	Y	N	Y	Y
8 Ford	?	?	Y	N	Y	Y
TEXAS						
1 Hall	Y	Y	Y	Y	Y	N
2 Wilson, C.	Y	Y	N	Y	Y	Y
3 Collins	N	Y	Y	Y	N	N
4 Roberts	Y	Y	Y	N	Y	Y
5 Mattox	Y	Y	Y	Y	N	N
6 Teague	?	✔	Y	?	?	?
7 Archer	Y	Y	Y	Y	N	Y
8 Eckhardt	Y	N	N	N	Y	Y
9 Brooks	Y	Y	N	N	Y	Y
10 Pickle	Y	Y	Y	N	Y	#
11 Poage	Y	Y	N	N	Y	Y
12 Wright	Y	N	Y	N	Y	Y
13 Hightower	Y	Y	Y	Y	Y	Y
14 Young	Y	N	Y	N	Y	Y
15 de la Garza	Y	N	P	N	Y	Y
16 White	Y	Y	Y	N	Y	Y
17 Burleson	Y	Y	Y	Y	Y	N
18 Jordan	Y	N	Y	N	Y	N
19 Mahon	Y	N	Y	N	Y	Y
20 Gonzalez	Y	N	N	N	Y	Y
21 Krueger	#	▮	✔	▮	#	#
22 Gammage	Y	Y	Y	Y	Y	Y
23 Kazen	Y	N	Y	N	Y	Y
24 Milford	?	?	?	?	?	?
UTAH						
1 McKay	Y	Y	N	N	Y	Y
2 Marriott	Y	Y	N	Y	#	#
VERMONT						
AL Jeffords	Y	N	Y	N	Y	N
VIRGINIA						
1 Trible	Y	Y	Y	N	Y	Y
2 Whitehurst	Y	Y	N	Y	Y	Y
3 Satterfield	Y	Y	N	Y	Y	N
4 Daniel	Y	Y	N	N	Y	Y
5 Daniel	?	Y	N	N	Y	Y
6 Butler	?	✔	?	?	?	?
7 Robinson	Y	Y	N	N	Y	Y
8 Harris	Y	N	N	Y	N	Y
9 Wampler	Y	Y	N	N	Y	Y
10 Fisher	Y	Y	Y	Y	N	Y
WASHINGTON						
1 Pritchard	#	▮	▮	#	#	#
2 Meeds	Y	N	Y	N	Y	Y
3 Bonker	Y	N	N	N	Y	Y
4 McCormack	Y	N	Y	N	Y	Y
5 Foley	?	N	Y	N	Y	Y
6 Dicks	Y	N	Y	N	Y	Y
7 Cunningham	Y	Y	Y	Y	Y	#
WEST VIRGINIA						
1 Mollohan	Y	N	Y	N	Y	Y
2 Staggers	Y	N	Y	N	Y	Y
3 Slack	Y	Y	Y	?	?	Y
4 Rahall	Y	N	Y	N	Y	Y
WISCONSIN						
1 Aspin	Y	N	N	Y	Y	Y
2 Kastenmeier	Y	N	Y	N	Y	N
3 Baldus	Y	N	Y	N	Y	Y
4 Zablocki	Y	N	N	N	Y	Y
5 Reuss	Y	N	Y	N	Y	N
6 Steiger	Y	Y	N	Y	Y	N
7 Obey	Y	N	Y	N	Y	N
8 Cornell	Y	N	N	N	Y	N
9 Kasten	#	#	#	#	#	▮
WYOMING						
AL Roncalio	?	N	Y	N	Y	?

Democrats ***Republicans***

422. HR 11493. Amtrak Improvements. Steiger, R-Wis., amendment to delete from the bill a provision requiring the National Railroad Passenger Corp. (Amtrak) to buy American goods and materials for purchases of more than $100,000, unless waived by the transportation secretary. Rejected 93-207: R 44-62; D 49-145 (ND 36-102; SD 13-43), June 23, 1978.

423. HR 11493. Amtrak Improvements. Madigan, R-Ill., amendment to require Amtrak to drop service on a rail passenger route if the federal subsidy for that route rose above $100 per passenger per ride. Rejected 119-186: R 82-20; D 37-166 (ND 13-129; SD 24-37), June 23, 1978.

424. HR 11493. Amtrak Improvements. Neal, D-N.C., amendment to give the president's special trade representative, rather than the transportation secretary, the authority to waive the requirement that Amtrak buy American goods and materials for purchases of more than $100,000. Rejected 121-178: R 44-57; D 77-121 (ND 54-86; SD 23-35), June 23, 1978.

425. HR 11493. Amtrak Improvements. Passage of the bill to authorize a federal subsidy of $755,250,000 for the National Railroad Passenger Corp. (Amtrak) for fiscal 1979, to require approval by both houses of Congress of a new basic route system to be recommended by the transportation secretary, and to prohibit changes in the existing route structure before Oct. 1, 1979. Passed 204-89: R 53-47; D 151-42 (ND 124-12; SD 27-30), June 23, 1978.

426. HR 12433. Housing and Community Development. Adoption of the rule (H Res 1214) providing for House floor consideration of the bill to extend and amend the federal laws related to housing, community and neighborhood development and preservation. Adopted 282-5: R 94-3; D 188-2 (ND 132-1; SD 56-1), June 23, 1978.

427. HR 10341. Reserve Enlisted Members' Retirement. Nichols, D-Ala., motion to suspend the rules and pass the bill to allow reserve enlisted members of the Army and Air Force to retire after 20 years of active duty. Passed 283-35: R 104-5; D 179-30 (ND 119-26; SD 60-4), June 26, 1978. A two-thirds majority vote (212 in this case) is required for passage under suspension of the rules.

428. HR 10342. Military Retired Pay Calculation. Nichols, D-Ala., motion to suspend the rules and pass the bill to revise the rules for calculating the pay of military retirees who were recalled to active duty between 1963 and 1973. Passed 292-30: R 106-3; D 186-27 (ND 121-27; SD 65-0), June 26, 1978. A two-thirds majority vote (215 in this case) is required for passage under suspension of the rules.

429. S 666. Indian Bureau Employee Retirement. Spellman, D-Md., motion to suspend the rules and pass the bill to provide special retirement preference to non-Indian employees of the Bureau of Indian Affairs and Indian Health Service who had been adversely affected by BIA policies that gave preference to Indians for BIA positions and promotions. Motion rejected 118-204: R 28-81; D 90-123 (ND 67-81; SD 23-42), June 26, 1978. A two-thirds majority vote (215 in this case) is required for passage under suspension of the rules.

KEY

- Y Voted for (yea).
- ✓ Paired for.
- † Announced for.
- # CQ Poll for.
- N Voted against (nay).
- X Paired against.
- \- Announced against.
- ▮ CQ Poll against.
- P Voted "present."
- ● Voted "present" to avoid possible conflict of interest.
- ? Did not vote or otherwise make a position known.

	422	423	424	425	426	427	428	429
ALABAMA								
1 Edwards	N	Y	N	N	Y	Y	Y	N
2 Dickinson	N	Y	N	N	Y	Y	Y	Y
3 Nichols	▮	✓	▮	▮	#	Y	Y	N
4 Bevill	N	N	N	N	Y	Y	Y	N
5 Flippo	N	N	N	N	Y	?	?	?
6 Buchanan	N	N	N	Y	Y	Y	Y	N
7 Flowers	?	?	?	?	?	?	?	?
ALASKA								
AL Young	▮	✓	▮	#	#	Y	Y	Y
ARIZONA								
1 Rhodes	Y	Y	N	Y	Y	Y	Y	Y
2 Udall	Y	N	Y	Y	Y	#	#	?
3 Stump	Y	Y	Y	N	Y	#	#	#
4 Rudd	?	?	?	?	?	Y	Y	Y
ARKANSAS								
1 Alexander	N	N	?	?	?	Y	Y	Y
2 Tucker	▮	▮	▮	#	#	N	Y	N
3 Hammerschmidt	?	?	?	?	?	Y	Y	Y
4 Thornton	?	?	?	?	?	Y	Y	Y
CALIFORNIA								
1 Johnson	N	N	N	Y	Y	Y	Y	Y
2 Clausen	N	Y	N	Y	Y	Y	Y	Y
3 Moss	Y	N	Y	Y	Y	Y	Y	N
4 Leggett	N	N	N	#	#	#	#	#
5 Burton, J.	?	?	?	?	?	Y	Y	Y
6 Burton, P.	Y	N	Y	Y	Y	Y	Y	Y
7 Miller	?	?	?	?	?	N	Y	N
8 Dellums	#	▮	#	#	#	N	N	Y
9 Stark	?	?	?	?	?	N	N	N
10 Edwards	N	N	Y	Y	Y	Y	Y	Y
11 Ryan	▮	#	#	#	#	#	†	▮
12 McCloskey	Y	Y	Y	Y	Y	?	?	?
13 Mineta	Y	N	Y	Y	Y	Y	Y	Y
14 McFall	N	N	N	Y	Y	?	Y	Y
15 Sisk	Y	N	Y	?	?	Y	Y	N
16 Panetta	▮	✓	▮	#	#	Y	Y	N
17 Krebs	Y	N	Y	Y	Y	N	N	N
18 Ketchum[1]	?	?	?	?	?			
19 Lagomarsino	Y	Y	Y	N	Y	Y	Y	N
20 Goldwater	?	✓	?	?	?	Y	Y	N
21 Corman	?	?	#	#	?	Y	Y	Y
22 Moorhead	N	Y	N	N	Y	Y	Y	N
23 Beilenson	?	N	Y	Y	Y	N	Y	Y
24 Waxman	▮	N	Y	Y	Y	#	#	▮
25 Roybal	N	N	N	Y	Y	N	Y	Y
26 Rousselot	✓	✓	?	X	?	Y	Y	N
27 Dornan	Y	Y	N	N	Y	Y	Y	N
28 Burke	N	N	N	Y	Y	#	#	#
29 Hawkins	N	N	N	?	?	Y	Y	?
30 Danielson	N	N	N	Y	Y	Y	Y	N
31 Wilson, C.H.	▮	▮	▮	#	#	#	#	#
32 Anderson	N	Y	Y	Y	Y	?	#	#
33 Clawson	Y	Y	Y	N	Y	Y	Y	N
34 Hannaford	Y	N	Y	Y	Y	Y	Y	N
35 Lloyd	N	N	N	Y	Y	Y	Y	Y
36 Brown	?	?	?	?	?	?	?	?
37 Pettis	Y	Y	Y	Y	Y	Y	Y	N
38 Patterson	N	N	N	Y	Y	Y	Y	N
39 Wiggins	▮	#	Y	N	Y	#	#	▮
40 Badham	Y	Y	Y	N	Y	Y	Y	N
41 Wilson, B.	N	N	Y	Y	Y	Y	Y	Y
42 Van Deerlin	Y	Y	?	Y	?	Y	Y	Y
43 Burgener	?	✓	?	?	?	?	?	?
COLORADO								
1 Schroeder	N	N	N	N	Y	Y	Y	Y
2 Wirth	Y	N	Y	Y	Y	#	#	#
3 Evans	N	N	Y	Y	Y	Y	Y	N
4 Johnson	Y	Y	N	Y	Y	?	?	?
5 Armstrong	?	?	?	?	?	?	?	?
CONNECTICUT								
1 Cotter	▮	▮	▮	#	#	#	#	#
2 Dodd	N	N	N	Y	Y	N	Y	N
3 Giaimo	?	?	?	?	?	?	?	?
4 McKinney	N	N	N	Y	Y	Y	Y	N
5 Sarasin	▮	X	▮	#	#	#	#	▮
6 Moffett	Y	N	Y	Y	Y	?	?	?
DELAWARE								
AL Evans	N	Y	N	Y	Y	Y	Y	N
FLORIDA								
1 Sikes	N	N	N	N	Y	Y	Y	N
2 Fuqua	N	N	N	Y	#	Y	Y	N
3 Bennett	N	N	N	Y	Y	Y	Y	N
4 Chappell	N	N	N	Y	Y	Y	Y	N
5 Kelly	Y	Y	N	N	Y	Y	N	N
6 Young	N	N	Y	Y	Y	Y	Y	N
7 Gibbons	?	?	?	?	?	?	?	?
8 Ireland	?	?	?	?	?	Y	Y	N
9 Frey	?	?	?	?	?	?	?	?
10 Bafalis	?	?	?	?	?	Y	Y	N
11 Rogers	?	?	?	Y	Y	?	?	?
12 Burke	Y	Y	N	Y	Y	Y	Y	N
13 Lehman	Y	N	Y	Y	Y	Y	Y	N
14 Pepper	▮	N	N	Y	Y	#	#	#
15 Fascell	N	N	N	N	Y	Y	Y	Y
GEORGIA								
1 Ginn	N	N	N	Y	Y	Y	Y	Y
2 Mathis	?	?	?	?	?	Y	Y	N
3 Brinkley	N	Y	Y	Y	Y	Y	Y	N
4 Levitas	N	N	Y	N	Y	Y	Y	N
5 Fowler	?	?	?	?	?	?	?	?
6 Flynt	N	Y	N	N	Y	?	?	?
7 McDonald	#	Y	Y	N	N	#	#	▮
8 Evans	N	N	▮	#	#	#	#	▮
9 Jenkins	N	N	N	N	Y	Y	Y	N
10 Barnard	?	?	?	?	?	Y	Y	N
HAWAII								
1 Heftel	N	Y	N	Y	Y	Y	Y	N
2 Akaka	N	N	Y	Y	Y	Y	Y	Y
IDAHO								
1 Symms	?	X	?	X	?	Y	Y	N
2 Hansen, G.	N	N	N	N	N	Y	Y	N
ILLINOIS								
1 Metcalfe	?	?	?	?	?	Y	Y	Y
2 Murphy	▮	X	?	#	#	Y	Y	N
3 Russo	N	N	N	N	Y	#	#	▮
4 Derwinski	N	Y	N	Y	Y	N	Y	N
5 Fary	N	N	N	Y	Y	Y	Y	N
6 Hyde	Y	Y	Y	Y	Y	Y	Y	N
7 Collins	N	▮	N	Y	Y	Y	Y	Y
8 Rostenkowski	?	?	?	?	#	#	#	?
9 Yates	Y	N	Y	Y	Y	N	N	N
10 Mikva	Y	Y	Y	N	Y	N	N	N
11 Annunzio	N	N	N	Y	Y	Y	Y	N
12 Crane	?	✓	#	▮	#	#	#	▮
13 McClory	✓	✓	#	#	#	Y	Y	N
14 Erlenborn	Y	Y	Y	N	Y	Y	Y	Y
15 Corcoran	Y	Y	Y	Y	Y	Y	Y	N
16 Anderson	Y	Y	Y	Y	#	#	#	▮
17 O'Brien	Y	Y	Y	Y	Y	N	Y	N
18 Michel	Y	Y	#	#	#	#	#	?
19 Railsback	Y	Y	Y	Y	Y	#	#	▮
20 Findley	Y	Y	Y	N	Y	Y	Y	N
21 Madigan	Y	Y	Y	Y	?	Y	Y	N
22 Shipley	?	?	?	?	?	?	?	?
23 Price	N	N	N	Y	Y	Y	Y	Y
24 Simon	?	?	?	?	?	?	?	?
INDIANA								
1 Benjamin	N	N	N	Y	Y	N	N	N
2 Fithian	?	?	?	?	?	?	?	?
3 Brademas	N	N	N	Y	Y	Y	Y	N
4 Quayle	Y	Y	Y	N	Y	?	?	?
5 Hillis	N	Y	N	Y	Y	Y	Y	N
6 Evans	N	N	N	Y	?	Y	Y	N
7 Myers, J.	N	Y	N	Y	Y	Y	Y	Y
8 Cornwell	?	?	?	?	?	?	?	?
9 Hamilton	N	N	N	Y	Y	Y	Y	N
10 Sharp	N	N	N	Y	Y	Y	Y	N
11 Jacobs	Y	Y	Y	N	Y	N	Y	N
IOWA								
1 Leach	Y	N	Y	Y	Y	Y	Y	Y
2 Blouin	Y	N	Y	Y	Y	Y	Y	Y
3 Grassley	N	N	N	N	Y	Y	Y	N
4 Smith	Y	N	Y	Y	Y	Y	Y	N
5 Harkin	N	N	Y	Y	Y	Y	N	N
6 Bedell	N	N	N	N	Y	N	N	N

Democrats ***Republicans***

[1] *Rep. William M. Ketchum, R-Calif., died June 24, 1978.*

	422	423	424	425	426	427	428	429
KANSAS								
1 Sebelius	Y	Y	N	N	Y	Y	Y	Y
2 Keys	Y	N	Y	Y	Y	N	N	N
3 Winn	▮	▮	▮	#	#	Y	Y	N
4 Glickman	N	Y	N	Y	Y	Y	Y	N
5 Skubitz	N	Y	N	Y	?	Y	Y	N
KENTUCKY								
1 Hubbard	N	N	N	Y	Y	Y	Y	N
2 Natcher	N	N	N	Y	Y	Y	Y	N
3 Mazzoli	Y	N	Y	Y	Y	Y	Y	N
4 Snyder	N	N	N	N	Y	Y	Y	N
5 Carter	N	N	N	Y	Y	Y	Y	Y
6 Breckinridge	Y	N	N	†	Y	Y	Y	N
7 Perkins	▮	▮	▮	#	#	Y	Y	N
LOUISIANA								
1 Livingston	N	Y	N	N	Y	Y	Y	N
2 Boggs	Y	N	?	?	?	Y	Y	N
3 Treen	N	Y	?	?	?	Y	Y	N
4 Waggonner	Y	Y	Y	N	Y	Y	Y	N
5 Huckaby	?	?	?	?	?	Y	Y	N
6 Moore	N	Y	N	N	Y	Y	Y	N
7 Breaux	N	Y	?	?	?	Y	Y	N
8 Long	?	?	?	?	?	Y	Y	N
MAINE								
1 Emery	N	Y	N	Y	Y	#	#	▮
2 Cohen	?	?	?	?	?	?	?	?
MARYLAND								
1 Bauman	N	Y	N	Y	N	Y	Y	N
2 Long	Y	Y	N	Y	Y	Y	Y	N
3 Mikulski	N	N	N	Y	Y	Y	Y	Y
4 Holt	N	Y	N	N	Y	Y	Y	N
5 Spellman	N	N	Y	Y	Y	Y	Y	Y
6 Byron	N	N	N	Y	Y	Y	Y	N
7 Mitchell	N	N	N	Y	Y	Y	Y	Y
8 Steers	Y	Y	Y	Y	Y	Y	Y	Y
MASSACHUSETTS								
1 Conte	N	Y	N	Y	Y	?	?	?
2 Boland	N	Y	N	Y	Y	Y	Y	Y
3 Early	?	?	?	?	?	N	N	N
4 Drinan	N	N	N	Y	Y	Y	Y	N
5 Tsongas	?	?	?	?	?	?	?	?
6 Harrington	▮	X	#	#	#	Y	N	Y
7 Markey	N	N	N	Y	Y	Y	Y	Y
8 O'Neill								
9 Moakley	X	X	▮	#	#	#	#	?
10 Heckler	N	?	?	✓	#	Y	Y	N
11 Burke	N	N	N	Y	Y	Y	Y	Y
12 Studds	N	N	N	Y	Y	Y	Y	N
MICHIGAN								
1 Conyers	▮	▮	▮	#	#	▮	▮	#
2 Pursell	N	Y	Y	Y	Y	?	?	?
3 Brown	Y	Y	Y	Y	Y	#	#	▮
4 Stockman	Y	Y	Y	▮	#	Y	Y	N
5 Sawyer	?	?	?	✓	#	#	#	?
6 Carr	Y	N	Y	Y	Y	N	N	Y
7 Kildee	N	N	Y	Y	Y	Y	Y	N
8 Traxler	#	▮	▮	#	#	#	#	#
9 Vander Jagt	?	?	?	?	?	?	?	?
10 Cederberg	Y	Y	Y	N	Y	Y	Y	N
11 Ruppe	Y	✓	?	?	?	?	?	?
12 Bonior	N	N	Y	Y	?	Y	Y	Y
13 Diggs	N	N	Y	Y	#	Y	Y	Y
14 Nedzi	N	N	Y	?	?	Y	Y	N
15 Ford	N	N	N	Y	Y	?	?	?
16 Dingell	N	N	N	?	Y	Y	Y	N
17 Brodhead	N	N	Y	Y	Y	N	Y	N
18 Blanchard	N	N	Y	Y	Y	N	Y	Y
19 Broomfield	Y	Y	Y	N	Y	Y	Y	N
MINNESOTA								
1 Quie	?	?	?	?	?	?	?	?
2 Hagedorn	Y	Y	Y	N	Y	?	?	?
3 Frenzel	✓	?	?	X	?	Y	Y	Y
4 Vento	N	N	N	Y	Y	N	N	N
5 Fraser	#	▮	#	?	#	#	#	#
6 Nolan	N	N	N	Y	Y	Y	Y	Y
7 Stangeland	#	#	#	✓	#	Y	Y	Y
8 Oberstar	N	N	N	Y	Y	Y	Y	Y
MISSISSIPPI								
1 Whitten	▮	✓	▮	#	#	#	#	#
2 Bowen	?	?	Y	N	Y	?	?	?
3 Montgomery	N	Y	N	N	Y	Y	Y	Y
4 Cochran	Y	N	Y	Y	Y	?	?	?
5 Lott	N	Y	N	N	Y	Y	Y	Y
MISSOURI								
1 Clay	N	N	N	Y	Y	?	Y	Y
2 Young	N	N	N	Y	Y	Y	Y	N
3 Gephardt	N	Y	N	N	Y	#	#	▮
4 Skelton	N	N	N	N	Y	Y	Y	N
5 Bolling	Y	N	Y	Y	Y	Y	Y	Y
6 Coleman	N	N	N	N	Y	Y	Y	N
7 Taylor	N	Y	N	N	Y	Y	Y	N
8 Ichord	?	?	?	?	?	?	?	N
9 Volkmer	N	Y	N	N	Y	N	Y	N
10 Burlison	N	N	N	Y	Y	Y	Y	N
MONTANA								
1 Baucus	▮	X	▮	#	#	Y	Y	Y
2 Marlenee	N	N	Y	Y	Y	Y	Y	Y
NEBRASKA								
1 Thone	?	X	?	X	#	Y	Y	Y
2 Cavanaugh	Y	N	N	Y	Y	Y	Y	Y
3 Smith	Y	N	N	Y	Y	Y	Y	Y
NEVADA								
AL Santini	▮	▮	▮	#	#	Y	Y	N
NEW HAMPSHIRE								
1 D'Amours	?	?	?	#	#	Y	Y	N
2 Cleveland	?	?	?	?	?	Y	Y	N
NEW JERSEY								
1 Florio	N	N	N	Y	Y	Y	Y	N
2 Hughes	N	N	N	Y	Y	Y	Y	N
3 Howard	N	N	N	Y	Y	#	#	#
4 Thompson	N	N	N	Y	Y	#	#	▮
5 Fenwick	Y	Y	Y	N	Y	Y	Y	N
6 Forsythe	Y	Y	Y	N	Y	Y	Y	N
7 Maguire	Y	N	Y	Y	Y	N	N	N
8 Roe	N	N	N	Y	Y	Y	Y	N
9 Hollenbeck	N	N	N	Y	Y	Y	Y	N
10 Rodino	?	?	?	?	?	?	?	?
11 Minish	N	N	N	Y	Y	Y	Y	N
12 Rinaldo	N	N	N	Y	Y	Y	Y	N
13 Meyner	Y	N	Y	Y	Y	Y	Y	Y
14 LeFante	▮	▮	▮	#	#	#	#	▮
15 Patten	N	N	N	Y	Y	Y	Y	Y
NEW MEXICO								
1 Lujan	N	Y	Y	Y	Y	N	Y	Y
2 Runnels	?	✓	?	?	#	#	Y	Y
NEW YORK								
1 Pike	?	?	?	?	?	Y	N	N
2 Downey	Y	N	Y	Y	Y	Y	Y	N
3 Ambro	?	?	?	?	Y	Y	Y	Y
4 Lent	?	?	?	?	?	Y	Y	N
5 Wydler	?	?	?	?	?	Y	N	N
6 Wolff	✓	X	▮	#	#	#	#	▮
7 Addabbo	X	X	▮	#	#	#	#	▮
8 Rosenthal	N	N	N	Y	Y	N	Y	Y
9 Delaney	N	N	N	Y	Y	Y	Y	N
10 Biaggi	▮	▮	?	#	#	Y	Y	N
11 Scheuer	Y	N	Y	Y	Y	?	?	?
12 Chisholm	N	N	N	Y	Y	Y	Y	Y
13 Solarz	N	N	#	Y	Y	#	#	#
14 Richmond	?	X	?	?	?	Y	Y	Y
15 Zeferetti	▮	▮	▮	#	#	#	#	▮
16 Holtzman	Y	N	Y	Y	Y	?	?	?
17 Murphy	?	?	?	?	?	?	?	?
18 Green	Y	Y	Y	Y	Y	N	N	N
19 Rangel	?	X	?	?	?	N	N	Y
20 Weiss	-	-	-	†	†	Y	Y	N
21 Garcia	▮	▮	▮	#	#	?	?	▮
22 Bingham	Y	N	Y	Y	Y	Y	Y	Y
23 Caputo	?	?	?	?	?	?	?	?
24 Ottinger	†	-	†	†	†	Y	Y	N
25 Fish	Y	Y	Y	Y	Y	Y	Y	N
26 Gilman	N	N	N	Y	Y	Y	Y	N
27 McHugh	Y	N	Y	Y	Y	Y	Y	Y
28 Stratton	N	N	N	Y	Y	Y	Y	N
29 Pattison	Y	N	Y	Y	Y	#	#	▮
30 McEwen	?	?	?	?	?	Y	Y	N
31 Mitchell	N	N	N	Y	Y	Y	Y	N
32 Hanley	▮	X	▮	#	#	Y	Y	Y
33 Walsh	?	?	?	?	?	Y	Y	N
34 Horton	N	N	N	Y	Y	Y	Y	Y
35 Conable	Y	Y	Y	N	Y	Y	Y	N
36 LaFalce	Y	N	Y	Y	Y	Y	Y	N
37 Nowak	N	N	N	Y	Y	#	#	▮
38 Kemp	Y	N	Y	N	Y	Y	Y	N
39 Lundine	N	N	N	Y	Y	#	#	▮
NORTH CAROLINA								
1 Jones	N	N	N	N	Y	Y	Y	Y
2 Fountain	N	Y	Y	N	Y	Y	Y	N
3 Whitley	N	Y	N	N	Y	?	?	?
4 Andrews	?	Y	Y	N	Y	Y	Y	N
5 Neal	Y	Y	Y	N	Y	#	Y	N
6 Preyer	N	N	N	Y	Y	Y	Y	Y
7 Rose	?	N	Y	Y	Y	Y	Y	Y
8 Hefner	N	Y	N	N	Y	?	?	?
9 Martin	N	Y	Y	N	Y	Y	Y	N
10 Broyhill	N	Y	Y	N	Y	#	#	▮
11 Gudger	N	Y	N	N	Y	Y	Y	Y
NORTH DAKOTA								
AL Andrews	Y	N	Y	Y	Y	?	?	?
OHIO								
1 Gradison	Y	Y	Y	N	Y	Y	Y	N
2 Luken	?	?	?	?	?	Y	Y	N
3 Whalen	#	#	?	#	#	#	#	▮
4 Guyer	N	Y	N	Y	Y	Y	Y	N
5 Latta	N	Y	N	N	Y	Y	Y	N
6 Harsha	?	?	?	?	?	?	?	?
7 Brown	?	?	?	?	?	?	?	?
8 Kindness	N	Y	N	Y	Y	N	Y	N
9 Ashley	?	N	Y	Y	Y	Y	Y	N
10 Miller	N	Y	N	N	Y	Y	Y	N
11 Stanton	N	Y	Y	Y	Y	Y	Y	N
12 Devine	N	Y	N	N	Y	Y	Y	N
13 Pease	Y	N	N	Y	Y	?	?	?
14 Seiberling	N	N	N	Y	Y	Y	N	N
15 Wylie	Y	Y	Y	Y	Y	?	?	?
16 Regula	N	Y	N	Y	Y	Y	Y	N
17 Ashbrook	▮	✓	▮	X	#	Y	Y	N
18 Applegate	N	N	N	Y	Y	Y	Y	Y
19 Carney	N	N	N	Y	Y	Y	Y	Y
20 Oakar	N	N	N	Y	Y	Y	Y	Y
21 Stokes	?	X	?	?	?	Y	Y	Y
22 Vanik	Y	N	Y	Y	Y	Y	Y	N
23 Mottl	▮	✓	▮	▮	#	Y	N	N
OKLAHOMA								
1 Jones	Y	Y	Y	N	Y	Y	Y	Y
2 Risenhoover	N	Y	N	N	Y	Y	Y	Y
3 Watkins	N	Y	N	N	Y	Y	Y	Y
4 Steed	N	Y	N	Y	Y	Y	Y	Y
5 Edwards	N	Y	N	N	Y	Y	Y	Y
6 English	N	N	N	N	Y	Y	Y	Y
OREGON								
1 AuCoin	▮	N	Y	Y	Y	Y	Y	N
2 Ullman	▮	▮	#	#	#	Y	Y	Y
3 Duncan	N	N	Y	N	Y	N	Y	Y
4 Weaver	N	N	N	?	?	Y	Y	N
PENNSYLVANIA								
1 Myers, M.	N	N	N	Y	Y	Y	N	N
2 Nix	?	?	?	?	?	?	?	?
3 Lederer	N	N	N	Y	Y	Y	N	N
4 Eilberg	N	N	N	Y	Y	Y	Y	Y
5 Schulze	N	Y	N	Y	Y	?	?	?
6 Yatron	N	N	N	Y	Y	Y	N	N
7 Edgar	N	N	N	Y	Y	N	N	Y
8 Kostmayer	Y	N	N	Y	Y	Y	Y	Y
9 Shuster	N	Y	N	N	Y	Y	Y	N
10 McDade	N	▮	▮	#	#	#	#	▮
11 Flood	N	N	N	Y	Y	Y	Y	Y
12 Murtha	N	N	N	Y	Y	Y	Y	Y
13 Coughlin	N	Y	N	Y	Y	Y	Y	N
14 Moorhead	N	N	Y	Y	Y	#	#	?
15 Rooney	N	N	N	Y	Y	Y	Y	Y
16 Walker	✓	?	?	X	?	?	?	?
17 Ertel	N	Y	N	Y	Y	Y	Y	N
18 Walgren	N	Y	N	Y	Y	Y	N	N
19 Goodling, W.	N	Y	N	Y	Y	Y	Y	Y
20 Gaydos	N	N	N	Y	Y	N	N	N
21 Dent	?	?	?	?	?	?	?	?
22 Murphy	N	N	N	Y	N	Y	N	N
23 Ammerman	N	N	N	Y	Y	Y	Y	N
24 Marks	N	Y	N	Y	Y	Y	Y	N
25 Myers, G.	N	Y	N	N	Y	Y	Y	Y
RHODE ISLAND								
1 St Germain	?	X	?	?	?	Y	Y	N
2 Beard	N	N	N	Y	Y	Y	Y	N
SOUTH CAROLINA								
1 Davis	N	Y	N	Y	Y	?	?	?
2 Spence	N	Y	N	Y	Y	Y	Y	N
3 Derrick	N	N	N	N	Y	N	Y	N
4 Mann	?	?	?	?	?	?	?	?
5 Holland	?	?	?	?	?	?	?	?
6 Jenrette	?	X	?	?	?	?	?	?
SOUTH DAKOTA								
1 Pressler	N	?	?	?	?	?	?	?
2 Abdnor	▮	#	▮	▮	#	Y	Y	Y
TENNESSEE								
1 Quillen	N	Y	N	N	Y	Y	Y	Y
2 Duncan	N	Y	N	N	Y	Y	Y	N
3 Lloyd	N	N	N	Y	Y	Y	Y	N
4 Gore	Y	N	Y	Y	Y	N	Y	Y
5 Vacancy								
6 Beard	N	Y	Y	Y	Y	#	#	▮
7 Jones	N	N	N	Y	Y	Y	Y	N
8 Ford	Y	N	N	Y	Y	?	?	?
TEXAS								
1 Hall	▮	Y	Y	▮	Y	Y	Y	N
2 Wilson, C.	▮	#	#	#	#	#	#	?
3 Collins	Y	Y	Y	N	N	Y	Y	N
4 Roberts	N	Y	N	N	Y	Y	Y	N
5 Mattox	Y	N	Y	Y	?	N	Y	N
6 Teague	?	✓	?	?	?	?	?	?
7 Archer	Y	Y	Y	N	Y	Y	Y	N
8 Eckhardt	?	?	?	?	?	?	?	?
9 Brooks	?	?	?	?	?	Y	Y	N
10 Pickle	▮	?	#	#	#	#	#	▮
11 Poage	N	N	N	N	Y	Y	Y	N
12 Wright	?	?	?	?	?	Y	Y	N
13 Hightower	N	N	Y	Y	Y	Y	Y	Y
14 Young	N	N	Y	Y	Y	Y	Y	Y
15 de la Garza	N	Y	Y	N	Y	Y	Y	Y
16 White	N	N	N	Y	Y	Y	Y	Y
17 Burleson	Y	Y	Y	N	Y	Y	Y	N
18 Jordan	▮	▮	▮	#	#	Y	Y	N
19 Mahon	N	Y	N	N	Y	Y	Y	N
20 Gonzalez	N	N	N	Y	Y	Y	Y	Y
21 Krueger	▮	X	▮	#	#	Y	Y	N
22 Gammage	X	X	▮	#	#	Y	Y	N
23 Kazen	N	N	Y	Y	Y	Y	Y	Y
24 Milford	?	?	?	?	?	?	?	?
UTAH								
1 McKay	N	N	N	Y	Y	#	#	#
2 Marriott	X	✓	▮	✓	#	Y	Y	N
VERMONT								
AL Jeffords	?	?	?	#	#	Y	Y	N
VIRGINIA								
1 Trible	N	Y	N	N	Y	Y	Y	N
2 Whitehurst	Y	Y	N	N	Y	Y	Y	N
3 Satterfield	N	Y	Y	N	Y	Y	Y	N
4 Daniel	N	Y	N	N	Y	Y	Y	N
5 Daniel	N	Y	N	N	Y	?	?	?
6 Butler	?	✓	?	?	?	Y	Y	N
7 Robinson	N	Y	N	N	Y	Y	Y	N
8 Harris	Y	N	Y	Y	Y	Y	Y	Y
9 Wampler	N	Y	N	Y	Y	Y	Y	Y
10 Fisher	Y	N	Y	Y	Y	Y	Y	Y
WASHINGTON								
1 Pritchard	▮	?	#	✓	#	#	#	#
2 Meeds	?	N	?	?	?	?	?	?
3 Bonker	N	N	Y	Y	Y	Y	Y	Y
4 McCormack	N	N	Y	Y	Y	Y	Y	Y
5 Foley	N	N	Y	Y	Y	Y	Y	N
6 Dicks	N	N	Y	Y	Y	?	?	?
7 Cunningham	X	▮	▮	✓	#	Y	Y	N
WEST VIRGINIA								
1 Mollohan	N	N	N	Y	Y	Y	Y	N
2 Staggers	N	N	N	Y	Y	Y	Y	N
3 Slack	N	N	N	Y	Y	Y	Y	N
4 Rahall	N	N	N	Y	#	Y	Y	Y
WISCONSIN								
1 Aspin	N	N	Y	Y	Y	Y	Y	Y
2 Kastenmeier	Y	N	Y	Y	Y	N	N	N
3 Baldus	#	#	#	#	#	Y	Y	Y
4 Zablocki	N	N	N	Y	Y	Y	Y	Y
5 Reuss	#	#	#	#	#	Y	Y	N
6 Steiger	Y	Y	Y	N	Y	Y	Y	Y
7 Obey	Y	N	Y	N	Y	Y	N	Y
8 Cornell	Y	N	Y	N	Y	Y	Y	Y
9 Kasten	▮	?	#	▮	#	#	#	#
WYOMING								
AL Roncalio	N	N	N	Y	Y	Y	Y	Y

Democrats ***Republicans***

430. HR 12536. National Parks and Recreation. Adoption of the rule (H Res 1243) providing for House floor consideration of the bill, the National Park and Recreation Act of 1978, to authorize $1.4 billion for new parks and improvement of existing parks, trails and other recreation areas. Adopted 311-2: R 108-0; D 203-2 (ND 143-1; SD 60-1), June 26, 1978.

431. HR 12432. Civil Rights Commission. Adoption of the rule (H Res 1235) providing for House floor consideration of the bill to extend the Commission on Civil Rights for five years. Adopted 303-16: R 95-13; D 208-3 (ND 147-0; SD 61-3), June 26, 1978.

432. Procedural Motion. Bauman, R-Md., motion to approve the House *Journal* of Tuesday, June 27, 1978. Motion agreed to 326-11: R 111-8; D 215-3 (ND 144-2; SD 71-1), June 28, 1978.

433. HR 3161. Federal Firefighters. Schroeder, D-Colo., motion to refer to the Post Office and Civil Service Committee President Carter's message on his veto of the bill, along with the accompanying bill, to reduce the basic workweek of firefighting personnel of federal agencies from 72 hours to 56 hours. Motion agreed to 279-109: R 62-71; D 217-38 (ND 153-21; SD 64-17), June 28, 1978.

434. HR 11886. Veterans Disability Compensation. Hammerschmidt, R-Ark., demand for a second on the Roberts, D-Texas, motion to suspend the rules and pass the bill *(see vote 439, p. 126-H).* Second ordered 378-1: R 132-1; D 246-0 (ND 169-0; SD 77-0), June 28, 1978.

435. HR 11888. Dependents Allowance for Disabled Veterans. Hammerschmidt, R-Ark., demand for a second on the Roberts, D-Texas, motion to suspend the rules and pass the bill *(see vote 440, p. 126-H).* Second ordered 379-2: R 132-1; D 247-1 (ND 165-1; SD 82-0), June 28, 1978.

436. HR 12841. Taxation of Fringe Benefits. Conable, R-N.Y., demand for a second on the Ullman, D-Ore., motion *(see vote 442, p. 126-H)* to suspend the rules and pass the bill to prohibit the issuance of regulations on the taxation of fringe benefits between May 1, 1978, and Dec. 31, 1979. Second ordered 379-3: R 132-3; D 247-0 (ND 164-0; SD 83-0), June 28, 1978.

437. HR 12589. International Investment Survey Act. Broomfield, R-Mich., demand for a second on the Bingham, D-N.Y., motion *(see vote 443, p. 126-H)* to suspend the rules and pass the bill to authorize $4 million for fiscal 1979 to carry out the International Investment Survey Act of 1976. Second ordered 384-3: R 127-2; D 257-1 (ND 176-0; SD 81-1), June 28, 1978.

KEY

- Y Voted for (yea).
- ✓ Paired for.
- † Announced for.
- # CQ Poll for.
- N Voted against (nay).
- X Paired against.
- \- Announced against.
- ▮ CQ Poll against.
- P Voted "present."
- ● Voted "present" to avoid possible conflict of interest.
- ? Did not vote or otherwise make a position known.

	430	431	432	433	434	435	436	437
ALABAMA								
1 Edwards	Y	Y	Y	Y	Y	Y	Y	Y
2 Dickinson	Y	Y	Y	Y	Y	Y	Y	?
3 Nichols	Y	Y	?	Y	Y	Y	Y	Y
4 Bevill	Y	Y	Y	Y	Y	Y	Y	Y
5 Flippo	?	?	Y	Y	Y	Y	Y	Y
6 Buchanan	Y	Y	Y	Y	Y	Y	Y	Y
7 Flowers	?	?	?	?	?	?	?	?
ALASKA								
AL Young	Y	Y	?	▮	Y	#	Y	Y
ARIZONA								
1 Rhodes	Y	Y	?	Y	Y	Y	Y	Y
2 Udall	?	?	?	Y	Y	Y	Y	Y
3 Stump	?	?	Y	N	Y	Y	Y	Y
4 Rudd	Y	N	Y	N	Y	Y	Y	Y
ARKANSAS								
1 Alexander	Y	Y	?	?	?	?	?	?
2 Tucker	Y	Y	?	#	#	#	Y	Y
3 Hammerschmidt	Y	Y	Y	N	Y	Y	Y	Y
4 Thornton	Y	Y	Y	N	?	Y	Y	Y
CALIFORNIA								
1 Johnson	Y	Y	Y	Y	Y	Y	Y	Y
2 Clausen	Y	Y	Y	Y	Y	Y	?	?
3 Moss	Y	?	Y	Y	Y	Y	Y	Y
4 Leggett	?	?	Y	Y	#	Y	#	#
5 Burton, J.	Y	Y	?	?	?	?	?	?
6 Burton, P.	Y	Y	Y	Y	Y	Y	Y	Y
7 Miller	Y	Y	Y	Y	Y	Y	Y	Y
8 Dellums	Y	Y	?	Y	Y	#	#	Y
9 Stark	Y	Y	?	#	Y	Y	?	Y
10 Edwards	Y	Y	Y	Y	?	?	Y	Y
11 Ryan	†	†	?	N	Y	Y	Y	Y
12 McCloskey	?	?	?	?	?	?	?	?
13 Mineta	Y	Y	Y	Y	Y	Y	Y	Y
14 McFall	Y	Y	Y	Y	Y	Y	Y	Y
15 Sisk	Y	?	Y	N	Y	Y	Y	Y
16 Panetta	Y	Y	Y	Y	Y	Y	Y	Y
17 Krebs	Y	Y	Y	Y	Y	Y	Y	Y
18 Vacancy								
19 Lagomarsino	Y	Y	Y	N	Y	Y	Y	Y
20 Goldwater	Y	Y	Y	N	Y	Y	Y	Y
21 Corman	Y	Y	Y	Y	Y	Y	Y	Y
22 Moorhead	Y	Y	Y	N	Y	Y	Y	Y
23 Beilenson	Y	Y	?	Y	#	Y	Y	#
24 Waxman	Y	Y	Y	Y	Y	Y	Y	#
25 Roybal	Y	Y	Y	Y	Y	Y	Y	Y
26 Rousselot	Y	N	Y	N	Y	Y	Y	Y
27 Dornan	Y	Y	Y	N	Y	Y	Y	Y
28 Burke	?	?	?	Y	Y	Y	Y	Y
29 Hawkins	?	?	Y	Y	Y	Y	Y	Y
30 Danielson	Y	Y	Y	Y	#	Y	Y	Y
31 Wilson, C.H.	?	?	Y	N	#	#	#	#
32 Anderson	?	?	Y	Y	Y	Y	Y	Y
33 Clawson	Y	N	Y	N	Y	Y	Y	Y
34 Hannaford	Y	Y	Y	Y	Y	Y	Y	Y
35 Lloyd	Y	Y	N	Y	Y	Y	?	Y
36 Brown	?	?	Y	Y	Y	?	Y	Y
37 Pettis	Y	Y	?	?	?	?	?	?
38 Patterson	Y	Y	Y	Y	Y	Y	Y	Y
39 Wiggins	?	?	?	Y	Y	Y	Y	Y
40 Badham	Y	Y	Y	N	Y	Y	Y	Y
41 Wilson, B.	Y	Y	N	Y	Y	Y	Y	Y
42 Van Deerlin	Y	Y	Y	N	Y	Y	Y	Y
43 Burgener	?	?	Y	N	Y	Y	Y	Y
COLORADO								
1 Schroeder	Y	Y	Y	Y	Y	Y	#	Y
2 Wirth	?	?	Y	Y	Y	Y	Y	Y
3 Evans	Y	Y	?	?	?	Y	Y	Y
4 Johnson	?	?	?	?	?	?	?	?
5 Armstrong	?	?	?	?	?	?	?	?
CONNECTICUT								
1 Cotter	?	?	?	#	#	#	Y	Y
2 Dodd	Y	Y	Y	?	Y	Y	Y	Y
3 Giaimo	?	?	?	Y	Y	Y	Y	Y
4 McKinney	Y	Y	Y	Y	Y	Y	Y	Y
5 Sarasin	†	†	N	N	Y	Y	Y	Y
6 Moffett	?	?	?	Y	Y	Y	Y	Y
DELAWARE								
AL Evans	Y	Y	Y	N	Y	Y	Y	Y
FLORIDA								
1 Sikes	Y	Y	Y	Y	Y	?	Y	Y
2 Fuqua	Y	Y	Y	Y	Y	Y	Y	Y
3 Bennett	Y	Y	Y	Y	Y	Y	Y	Y
4 Chappell	Y	Y	Y	Y	Y	Y	Y	Y
5 Kelly	Y	N	Y	N	Y	Y	Y	Y
6 Young	Y	Y	Y	N	Y	Y	Y	Y
7 Gibbons	?	?	Y	Y	Y	Y	Y	Y
8 Ireland	Y	Y	P	N	?	Y	Y	Y
9 Frey	?	?	Y	N	Y	Y	Y	Y
10 Bafalis	Y	Y	Y	N	Y	Y	Y	Y
11 Rogers	?	?	Y	Y	Y	Y	Y	Y
12 Burke	Y	Y	Y	Y	Y	Y	Y	Y
13 Lehman	?	Y	Y	Y	Y	Y	Y	Y
14 Pepper	?	?	?	Y	Y	Y	Y	Y
15 Fascell	Y	Y	Y	Y	Y	Y	Y	Y
GEORGIA								
1 Ginn	Y	Y	Y	Y	Y	Y	Y	Y
2 Mathis	?	?	Y	N	?	Y	Y	Y
3 Brinkley	Y	Y	Y	N	Y	Y	Y	Y
4 Levitas	Y	Y	Y	Y	Y	Y	Y	Y
5 Fowler	?	?	Y	N	Y	Y	Y	Y
6 Flynt	?	?	?	N	Y	Y	Y	Y
7 McDonald	N	N	?	N	Y	Y	Y	N
8 Evans	?	?	Y	Y	Y	Y	Y	Y
9 Jenkins	Y	Y	Y	N	Y	Y	Y	Y
10 Barnard	Y	Y	Y	N	Y	Y	Y	Y
HAWAII								
1 Heftel	Y	Y	Y	Y	Y	Y	Y	Y
2 Akaka	Y	Y	Y	Y	Y	Y	Y	Y
IDAHO								
1 Symms	Y	N	?	?	?	Y	Y	Y
2 Hansen, G.	Y	N	Y	N	Y	Y	Y	Y
ILLINOIS								
1 Metcalfe	Y	Y	Y	Y	Y	Y	?	Y
2 Murphy	Y	Y	Y	Y	Y	Y	Y	Y
3 Russo	?	?	Y	Y	Y	Y	Y	Y
4 Derwinski	Y	Y	Y	Y	Y	Y	Y	Y
5 Fary	Y	Y	?	?	?	?	Y	Y
6 Hyde	Y	Y	Y	N	Y	Y	Y	Y
7 Collins	Y	Y	Y	Y	Y	Y	Y	Y
8 Rostenkowski	?	?	?	?	#	#	#	#
9 Yates	Y	Y	?	Y	Y	Y	Y	Y
10 Mikva	Y	Y	Y	Y	#	#	Y	Y
11 Annunzio	Y	Y	Y	Y	Y	Y	Y	Y
12 Crane	?	?	Y	N	Y	Y	Y	Y
13 McClory	Y	Y	Y	Y	Y	Y	Y	Y
14 Erlenborn	Y	Y	Y	Y	Y	Y	Y	#
15 Corcoran	Y	Y	?	#	#	#	#	#
16 Anderson	Y	Y	Y	Y	Y	Y	Y	Y
17 O'Brien	Y	Y	?	Y	Y	Y	Y	Y
18 Michel	?	?	?	#	#	#	#	#
19 Railsback	?	?	Y	Y	Y	Y	Y	Y
20 Findley	Y	Y	Y	Y	Y	Y	Y	Y
21 Madigan	Y	?	Y	Y	Y	Y	Y	Y
22 Shipley	?	?	?	?	?	?	?	?
23 Price	Y	Y	Y	Y	Y	Y	Y	Y
24 Simon	?	?	?	?	?	?	?	?
INDIANA								
1 Benjamin	Y	Y	Y	Y	Y	Y	Y	Y
2 Fithian	?	?	Y	Y	Y	Y	Y	Y
3 Brademas	Y	Y	Y	Y	Y	Y	Y	Y
4 Quayle	?	?	N	Y	Y	Y	N	N
5 Hillis	Y	Y	Y	N	Y	Y	Y	Y
6 Evans	Y	Y	Y	N	Y	Y	Y	Y
7 Myers, J.	Y	Y	Y	N	Y	Y	Y	Y
8 Cornwell	?	?	Y	Y	Y	Y	Y	Y
9 Hamilton	Y	Y	Y	Y	Y	Y	Y	Y
10 Sharp	Y	Y	Y	Y	Y	Y	Y	Y
11 Jacobs	Y	Y	?	Y	Y	Y	Y	Y
IOWA								
1 Leach	Y	Y	Y	Y	Y	Y	Y	Y
2 Blouin	Y	Y	Y	Y	Y	Y	Y	Y
3 Grassley	Y	Y	Y	Y	Y	Y	Y	Y
4 Smith	Y	Y	Y	Y	Y	Y	Y	Y
5 Harkin	Y	Y	Y	Y	Y	Y	Y	Y
6 Bedell	Y	Y	Y	Y	Y	Y	Y	Y

Democrats ***Republicans***

	430	431	432	433	434	435	436	437
KANSAS								
1 ***Sebelius***	Y	Y	Y	N	Y	Y	Y	Y
2 Keys	Y	Y	?	Y	Y	Y	Y	Y
3 ***Winn***	Y	Y	Y	Y	Y	Y	Y	Y
4 Glickman	Y	Y	Y	Y	Y	Y	Y	Y
5 ***Skubitz***	Y	Y	P	Y	Y	Y	Y	Y
KENTUCKY								
1 Hubbard	Y	Y	Y	Y	Y	Y	Y	Y
2 Natcher	Y	Y	Y	Y	Y	Y	Y	Y
3 Mazzoli	Y	Y	Y	Y	Y	Y	Y	Y
4 ***Snyder***	Y	Y	Y	N	Y	Y	Y	Y
5 ***Carter***	Y	Y	Y	N	Y	Y	Y	Y
6 Breckinridge	Y	Y	N	N	Y	Y	Y	Y
7 Perkins	Y	Y	Y	Y	Y	Y	Y	Y
LOUISIANA								
1 ***Livingston***	Y	Y	Y	Y	Y	Y	Y	Y
2 Boggs	Y	Y	Y	Y	?	Y	Y	Y
3 ***Treen***	Y	Y	?	N	Y	Y	Y	Y
4 Waggonner	Y	Y	Y	Y	Y	Y	Y	Y
5 Huckaby	Y	Y	Y	N	Y	Y	Y	Y
6 ***Moore***	Y	Y	Y	Y	Y	Y	Y	Y
7 Breaux	?	Y	Y	Y	Y	Y	Y	Y
8 Long	Y	Y	Y	Y	Y	Y	Y	Y
MAINE								
1 ***Emery***	Y	Y	Y	N	Y	Y	Y	Y
2 ***Cohen***	?	?	Y	Y	Y	Y	Y	Y
MARYLAND								
1 ***Bauman***	Y	N	Y	N	Y	Y	Y	Y
2 Long	Y	Y	Y	?	Y	Y	Y	Y
3 Mikulski	Y	Y	?	Y	Y	Y	Y	Y
4 ***Holt***	Y	Y	N	N	Y	Y	Y	Y
5 Spellman	Y	Y	Y	Y	Y	Y	Y	Y
6 Byron	Y	Y	Y	Y	Y	Y	Y	Y
7 Mitchell	Y	Y	N	Y	Y	#	#	Y
8 ***Steers***	Y	Y	Y	Y	Y	Y	Y	Y
MASSACHUSETTS								
1 ***Conte***	?	?	Y	Y	Y	Y	N	Y
2 Boland	Y	Y	?	#	#	#	Y	Y
3 Early	Y	Y	Y	N	Y	Y	Y	Y
4 Drinan	Y	Y	Y	Y	Y	Y	Y	Y
5 Tsongas	?	?	?	?	?	?	?	?
6 Harrington	?	?	#	#	#	#	#	#
7 Markey	Y	Y	Y	Y	Y	Y	Y	Y
8 O'Neill								
9 Moakley	†	?	Y	Y	Y	Y	Y	Y
10 ***Heckler***	Y	Y	Y	Y	Y	Y	Y	Y
11 Burke	Y	Y	Y	N	Y	Y	Y	Y
12 Studds	Y	Y	Y	Y	Y	Y	Y	Y
MICHIGAN								
1 Conyers	?	?	#	#	#	#	Y	#
2 ***Pursell***	?	?	Y	Y	Y	Y	Y	Y
3 ***Brown***	?	?	N	N	Y	Y	Y	Y
4 ***Stockman***	Y	Y	Y	■	Y	Y	Y	Y
5 ***Sawyer***	?	?	Y	Y	Y	Y	Y	Y
6 Carr	Y	Y	Y	Y	Y	Y	?	Y
7 Kildee	Y	Y	Y	Y	Y	Y	Y	Y
8 Traxler	?	?	Y	Y	Y	Y	Y	Y
9 ***Vander Jagt***	?	?	Y	Y	Y	Y	Y	Y
10 ***Cederberg***	?	?	Y	N	Y	Y	Y	Y
11 ***Ruppe***	?	?	?	?	?	?	?	?
12 Bonior	Y	Y	?	Y	Y	Y	Y	Y
13 Diggs	?	?	#	Y	Y	#	#	#
14 Nedzi	Y	Y	Y	Y	Y	Y	Y	Y
15 Ford	?	?	?	Y	Y	?	Y	Y
16 Dingell	?	Y	?	Y	Y	Y	Y	Y
17 Brodhead	Y	Y	Y	Y	Y	Y	Y	Y
18 Blanchard	Y	Y	Y	Y	Y	Y	Y	Y
19 ***Broomfield***	Y	Y	Y	N	Y	Y	Y	Y
MINNESOTA								
1 ***Quie***	?	?	?	?	?	?	?	?
2 ***Hagedorn***	?	?	Y	N	Y	Y	Y	Y
3 ***Frenzel***	Y	Y	Y	Y	Y	Y	Y	Y
4 Vento	Y	Y	Y	Y	Y	Y	Y	Y
5 Fraser	?	?	Y	Y	#	#	#	Y
6 Nolan	?	Y	?	Y	Y	Y	Y	Y
7 ***Stangeland***	Y	Y	Y	N	Y	Y	Y	Y
8 Oberstar	N	Y	Y	Y	Y	Y	Y	Y
MISSISSIPPI								
1 Whitten	?	?	Y	Y	Y	Y	#	Y
2 Bowen	?	?	Y	Y	Y	Y	Y	Y
3 Montgomery	?	?	Y	Y	Y	Y	Y	Y
4 ***Cochran***	?	?	?	Y	Y	?	Y	?
5 ***Lott***	Y	Y	Y	Y	Y	Y	Y	#
MISSOURI								
1 Clay	Y	Y	?	?	Y	Y	?	?
2 Young	Y	Y	Y	Y	Y	Y	Y	Y
3 Gephardt	?	?	#	Y	Y	Y	Y	Y

	430	431	432	433	434	435	436	437
4 Skelton	Y	Y	Y	Y	Y	Y	Y	Y
5 Bolling	Y	Y	?	Y	Y	Y	Y	Y
6 ***Coleman***	Y	N	Y	N	Y	Y	Y	Y
7 ***Taylor***	Y	Y	Y	N	Y	Y	Y	Y
8 Ichord	Y	Y	Y	N	Y	Y	Y	Y
9 Volkmer	Y	Y	Y	Y	Y	Y	Y	Y
10 Burlison	Y	Y	Y	Y	Y	Y	Y	Y
MONTANA								
1 Baucus	Y	Y	Y	Y	Y	Y	Y	Y
2 ***Marlenee***	Y	Y	Y	Y	Y	Y	Y	Y
NEBRASKA								
1 ***Thone***	Y	Y	?	N	Y	Y	Y	Y
2 Cavanaugh	Y	Y	Y	N	Y	Y	Y	Y
3 ***Smith***	Y	Y	Y	N	Y	Y	Y	Y
NEVADA								
AL Santini	Y	Y	Y	Y	Y	Y	Y	Y
NEW HAMPSHIRE								
1 D'Amours	Y	Y	Y	Y	Y	Y	Y	Y
2 ***Cleveland***	Y	Y	Y	N	Y	Y	Y	Y
NEW JERSEY								
1 Florio	Y	Y	?	#	#	#	Y	Y
2 Hughes	Y	Y	Y	Y	Y	Y	Y	Y
3 Howard	?	?	#	Y	Y	Y	#	Y
4 Thompson	?	?	Y	Y	Y	Y	Y	Y
5 ***Fenwick***	Y	Y	Y	N	Y	Y	Y	Y
6 ***Forsythe***	Y	N	N	N	#	Y	Y	Y
7 Maguire	Y	Y	Y	Y	Y	Y	Y	Y
8 Roe	Y	Y	Y	Y	Y	Y	Y	Y
9 ***Hollenbeck***	Y	Y	Y	Y	Y	Y	Y	Y
10 Rodino	?	?	?	?	#	#	#	#
11 Minish	Y	Y	Y	Y	Y	Y	Y	Y
12 ***Rinaldo***	Y	Y	Y	Y	Y	Y	Y	Y
13 Meyner	Y	Y	†	#	#	#	#	#
14 LeFante	?	?	#	#	#	#	#	#
15 Patten	Y	Y	Y	Y	Y	Y	Y	Y
NEW MEXICO								
1 ***Lujan***	Y	Y	Y	Y	Y	Y	Y	Y
2 Runnels	Y	Y	?	#	?	#	#	#
NEW YORK								
1 Pike	Y	Y	Y	Y	Y	Y	Y	Y
2 Downey	Y	Y	Y	Y	Y	Y	Y	Y
3 Ambro	Y	Y	?	Y	Y	Y	Y	Y
4 ***Lent***	Y	Y	Y	N	Y	Y	Y	Y
5 ***Wydler***	Y	Y	?	Y	Y	Y	Y	Y
6 Wolff	?	Y	Y	Y	Y	Y	Y	Y
7 Addabbo	?	?	Y	Y	#	#	Y	Y
8 Rosenthal	Y	Y	Y	Y	#	#	Y	Y
9 Delaney	Y	Y	Y	N	Y	Y	Y	Y
10 Biaggi	Y	Y	Y	Y	Y	Y	Y	Y
11 Scheuer	?	?	Y	Y	Y	Y	Y	Y
12 Chisholm	?	?	#	Y	Y	Y	#	Y
13 Solarz	?	?	Y	Y	Y	Y	Y	Y
14 Richmond	Y	Y	Y	Y	Y	Y	Y	Y
15 Zeferetti	?	?	Y	Y	Y	Y	Y	Y
16 Holtzman	?	?	Y	Y	Y	Y	Y	Y
17 Murphy	?	?	Y	Y	Y	Y	?	Y
18 ***Green***	Y	Y	Y	N	Y	Y	Y	Y
19 Rangel	?	Y	Y	Y	Y	Y	Y	Y
20 Weiss	Y	Y	Y	Y	Y	Y	Y	Y
21 Garcia	?	?	#	#	#	#	#	?
22 Bingham	Y	Y	Y	Y	Y	Y	Y	Y
23 ***Caputo***	?	?	Y	Y	Y	Y	Y	Y
24 Ottinger	Y	Y	Y	Y	Y	Y	Y	Y
25 ***Fish***	Y	Y	Y	N	Y	Y	Y	Y
26 ***Gilman***	Y	Y	Y	Y	Y	Y	Y	Y
27 McHugh	Y	Y	Y	N	Y	Y	Y	Y
28 Stratton	Y	Y	Y	Y	Y	Y	Y	Y
29 Pattison	?	?	Y	Y	Y	Y	Y	Y
30 ***McEwen***	Y	Y	P	Y	Y	Y	Y	Y
31 ***Mitchell***	Y	Y	Y	N	Y	Y	Y	Y
32 Hanley	Y	Y	Y	Y	Y	Y	Y	Y
33 ***Walsh***	Y	Y	Y	N	Y	Y	Y	Y
34 ***Horton***	?	Y	?	Y	Y	Y	Y	#
35 ***Conable***	Y	Y	Y	N	Y	Y	Y	Y
36 LaFalce	Y	Y	Y	N	Y	Y	Y	Y
37 Nowak	Y	Y	Y	N	Y	Y	Y	Y
38 ***Kemp***	Y	Y	Y	N	Y	Y	Y	Y
39 Lundine	?	?	Y	N	Y	Y	Y	Y
NORTH CAROLINA								
1 Jones	Y	Y	Y	Y	Y	Y	Y	Y
2 Fountain	Y	Y	?	Y	Y	Y	Y	Y
3 Whitley	?	?	Y	Y	Y	Y	Y	Y
4 Andrews	?	?	Y	Y	?	Y	Y	Y
5 Neal	Y	Y	?	Y	Y	Y	Y	Y
6 Preyer	Y	Y	Y	Y	Y	Y	Y	Y
7 Rose	Y	Y	Y	?	?	Y	Y	Y
8 Hefner	?	?	Y	Y	Y	Y	Y	Y

	430	431	432	433	434	435	436	437
9 ***Martin***	Y	Y	Y	Y	Y	Y	Y	Y
10 ***Broyhill***	?	?	Y	N	Y	Y	Y	Y
11 Gudger	Y	Y	Y	Y	Y	Y	Y	Y
NORTH DAKOTA								
AL ***Andrews***	?	?	Y	Y	Y	Y	Y	Y
OHIO								
1 ***Gradison***	Y	Y	Y	Y	Y	Y	Y	Y
2 Luken	Y	Y	Y	Y	Y	Y	Y	Y
3 ***Whalen***	?	?	#	#	#	#	#	#
4 ***Guyer***	Y	Y	Y	N	Y	Y	Y	Y
5 ***Latta***	Y	Y	Y	N	Y	Y	Y	Y
6 ***Harsha***	?	?	Y	Y	Y	Y	Y	Y
7 ***Brown***	?	?	?	?	?	?	?	?
8 ***Kindness***	Y	Y	Y	N	?	Y	Y	Y
9 Ashley	Y	Y	Y	Y	Y	N	Y	Y
10 ***Miller***	Y	Y	Y	Y	Y	Y	Y	Y
11 ***Stanton***	Y	Y	Y	N	Y	Y	Y	Y
12 ***Devine***	Y	N	Y	N	Y	Y	Y	Y
13 Pease	?	?	Y	N	Y	Y	#	Y
14 Seiberling	Y	Y	Y	Y	#	#	#	Y
15 ***Wylie***	?	?	?	Y	Y	Y	Y	Y
16 ***Regula***	Y	Y	Y	Y	Y	Y	Y	Y
17 ***Ashbrook***	Y	N	Y	N	Y	Y	Y	Y
18 Applegate	Y	Y	Y	N	Y	Y	Y	Y
19 Carney	Y	Y	Y	Y	Y	Y	Y	Y
20 Oakar	Y	Y	Y	N	Y	Y	Y	Y
21 Stokes	Y	Y	Y	Y	Y	Y	?	Y
22 Vanik	Y	Y	Y	Y	Y	Y	Y	Y
23 Mottl	Y	Y	Y	N	Y	Y	Y	Y
OKLAHOMA								
1 Jones	Y	Y	Y	Y	Y	Y	Y	Y
2 Risenhoover	Y	Y	Y	Y	Y	Y	Y	Y
3 Watkins	Y	Y	Y	Y	Y	Y	Y	Y
4 Steed	Y	Y	Y	Y	Y	Y	Y	Y
5 ***Edwards***	Y	Y	Y	Y	Y	Y	Y	Y
6 English	Y	Y	Y	Y	Y	Y	Y	Y
OREGON								
1 AuCoin	Y	Y	Y	Y	Y	#	#	Y
2 Ullman	Y	Y	?	Y	Y	Y	Y	Y
3 Duncan	Y	Y	?	Y	Y	?	Y	Y
4 Weaver	Y	Y	?	Y	Y	Y	Y	Y
PENNSYLVANIA								
1 Myers, M.	Y	Y	?	Y	Y	Y	Y	Y
2 Nix	Y	Y	?	Y	Y	Y	Y	?
3 Lederer	Y	Y	?	Y	Y	Y	Y	Y
4 Eilberg	Y	Y	Y	Y	Y	Y	Y	Y
5 ***Schulze***	?	?	Y	N	Y	Y	Y	Y
6 Yatron	Y	Y	Y	Y	Y	Y	Y	Y
7 Edgar	Y	Y	Y	N	Y	Y	Y	#
8 Kostmayer	Y	Y	Y	Y	Y	Y	Y	Y
9 ***Shuster***	Y	Y	Y	N	Y	Y	Y	Y
10 ***McDade***	?	?	#	Y	Y	Y	Y	Y
11 Flood	Y	Y	Y	Y	Y	Y	Y	Y
12 Murtha	Y	Y	Y	Y	Y	Y	Y	Y
13 ***Coughlin***	Y	Y	?	Y	Y	Y	Y	Y
14 Moorhead	?	?	Y	Y	Y	Y	Y	Y
15 Rooney	Y	Y	Y	Y	Y	Y	Y	Y
16 ***Walker***	?	?	N	N	Y	Y	Y	Y
17 Ertel	Y	Y	Y	Y	Y	Y	Y	Y
18 Walgren	Y	Y	Y	Y	Y	Y	Y	Y
19 ***Goodling, W.***	?	?	Y	N	Y	Y	Y	Y
20 Gaydos	Y	Y	Y	Y	Y	Y	?	Y
21 Dent	?	?	?	?	?	?	?	?
22 Murphy	Y	Y	?	Y	Y	Y	Y	Y
23 Ammerman	Y	Y	Y	Y	Y	Y	Y	Y
24 ***Marks***	Y	Y	Y	Y	Y	Y	Y	Y
25 ***Myers, G.***	Y	Y	Y	Y	N	Y	Y	Y
RHODE ISLAND								
1 St Germain	Y	Y	Y	Y	Y	Y	Y	Y
2 Beard	Y	Y	Y	Y	Y	Y	Y	Y
SOUTH CAROLINA								
1 Davis	?	?	Y	Y	Y	Y	Y	Y
2 ***Spence***	Y	Y	Y	Y	Y	Y	Y	Y
3 Derrick	Y	Y	Y	Y	Y	Y	Y	Y
4 Mann	?	?	Y	Y	Y	Y	Y	Y
5 Holland	?	Y	?	?	?	?	?	?
6 Jenrette	?	?	?	?	Y	Y	Y	Y
SOUTH DAKOTA								
1 ***Pressler***	?	?	Y	Y	Y	Y	Y	?
2 ***Abdnor***	Y	Y	Y	N	Y	Y	Y	Y
TENNESSEE								
1 ***Quillen***	Y	Y	Y	N	Y	Y	Y	Y
2 ***Duncan***	Y	Y	Y	Y	Y	Y	Y	Y
3 Lloyd	Y	Y	Y	Y	Y	Y	Y	Y
4 Gore	Y	Y	Y	Y	Y	Y	Y	Y
5 Vacancy								
6 ***Beard***	?	?	Y	Y	Y	Y	Y	Y

	430	431	432	433	434	435	436	437
7 Jones	Y	Y	Y	Y	Y	Y	Y	Y
8 Ford	?	?	Y	Y	Y	Y	Y	Y
TEXAS								
1 Hall	Y	Y	Y	Y	Y	Y	Y	Y
2 Wilson, C.	?	?	?	#	#	#	#	#
3 ***Collins***	Y	N	?	N	Y	N	N	N
4 Roberts	Y	Y	Y	Y	Y	Y	Y	Y
5 Mattox	Y	Y	Y	Y	Y	Y	Y	Y
6 Teague	?	?	Y	Y	Y	Y	Y	Y
7 ***Archer***	Y	Y	Y	N	Y	Y	Y	Y
8 Eckhardt	?	?	Y	Y	Y	Y	Y	Y
9 Brooks	Y	Y	Y	Y	Y	Y	Y	Y
10 Pickle	?	?	Y	Y	Y	Y	Y	Y
11 Poage	Y	N	Y	N	Y	Y	Y	Y
12 Wright	Y	Y	Y	Y	Y	Y	Y	Y
13 Hightower	Y	Y	Y	Y	Y	Y	Y	Y
14 Young	Y	Y	?	N	Y	Y	Y	?
15 de la Garza	Y	Y	Y	Y	Y	Y	Y	Y
16 White	Y	Y	?	Y	Y	Y	Y	Y
17 Burleson	Y	Y	Y	N	Y	Y	Y	Y
18 Jordan	Y	Y	Y	Y	Y	Y	Y	Y
19 Mahon	Y	Y	Y	N	Y	Y	Y	Y
20 Gonzalez	Y	Y	Y	Y	Y	Y	Y	Y
21 Krueger	Y	Y	Y	Y	Y	Y	Y	#
22 Gammage	Y	Y	Y	Y	Y	Y	Y	Y
23 Kazen	Y	Y	Y	Y	Y	Y	Y	Y
24 Milford	?	?	?	?	?	?	?	?
UTAH								
1 McKay	?	Y	Y	Y	Y	Y	Y	Y
2 ***Marriott***	Y	Y	Y	N	Y	Y	Y	Y
VERMONT								
AL ***Jeffords***	Y	Y	Y	Y	Y	Y	Y	Y
VIRGINIA								
1 ***Trible***	Y	Y	Y	N	Y	Y	Y	Y
2 ***Whitehurst***	Y	Y	Y	N	Y	Y	Y	Y
3 Satterfield	Y	N	Y	N	Y	Y	Y	Y
4 ***Daniel***	Y	Y	Y	N	Y	Y	Y	Y
5 Daniel	?	?	?	N	Y	Y	Y	Y
6 ***Butler***	Y	Y	Y	N	Y	Y	Y	Y
7 ***Robinson***	Y	Y	Y	N	Y	Y	Y	Y
8 Harris	Y	Y	Y	Y	Y	Y	Y	Y
9 ***Wampler***	Y	Y	Y	N	Y	Y	Y	Y
10 Fisher	Y	Y	Y	Y	Y	Y	Y	Y
WASHINGTON								
1 ***Pritchard***	?	?	N	N	Y	Y	Y	Y
2 Meeds	?	?	Y	Y	Y	Y	Y	Y
3 Bonker	Y	Y	Y	Y	Y	Y	Y	Y
4 McCormack	Y	Y	Y	Y	Y	Y	Y	Y
5 Foley	Y	Y	Y	Y	Y	Y	Y	Y
6 Dicks	?	?	Y	Y	Y	Y	Y	Y
7 ***Cunningham***	Y	Y	Y	N	Y	Y	Y	Y
WEST VIRGINIA								
1 Mollohan	Y	Y	?	Y	Y	Y	Y	Y
2 Staggers	Y	Y	Y	Y	Y	Y	Y	Y
3 Slack	Y	Y	Y	Y	Y	Y	Y	Y
4 Rahall	Y	Y	Y	Y	Y	Y	Y	Y
WISCONSIN								
1 Aspin	Y	Y	Y	N	Y	Y	Y	Y
2 Kastenmeier	Y	Y	Y	Y	Y	Y	Y	Y
3 Baldus	Y	Y	Y	Y	Y	Y	Y	Y
4 Zablocki	Y	Y	Y	Y	Y	Y	Y	Y
5 Reuss	Y	Y	?	#	Y	Y	Y	Y
6 ***Steiger***	Y	N	?	Y	Y	#	Y	Y
7 Obey	?	?	Y	Y	Y	Y	Y	Y
8 Cornell	Y	Y	Y	Y	Y	Y	Y	Y
9 ***Kasten***	?	?	Y	Y	Y	Y	Y	Y
WYOMING								
AL Roncalio	Y	Y	?	Y	Y	Y	?	Y

Democrats ***Republicans***

438. HR 12874. Solar Power Research. Goldwater, R-Calif., demand for a second on the McCormack, D-Wash., motion *(see vote 444, below)* to suspend the rules and pass the bill to provide for accelerated federal research on developing energy cells to convert sunlight to electricity. Second ordered 376-5: R 126-2; D 250-3 (ND 170-1; SD 80-2), June 28, 1978.

439. HR 11886. Veterans' Disability Compensation. Roberts, D-Texas, motion to suspend the rules and pass the bill to increase by 6.5 percent the compensation paid to veterans disabled in the course of their military service. Motion agreed to 400-1: R 135-1; D 265-0 (ND 183-0; SD 82-0), June 28, 1978. A two-thirds majority vote (268 in this case) is required for passage under suspension of the rules.

440. HR 11888. Dependents Allowance for Disabled Veterans. Roberts, D-Texas, motion to suspend the rules and pass the bill to lower to 40 percent, from 50 percent, the level of disability at which veterans become eligible for additional payments for each dependent. Motion agreed to 385-16: R 136-0; D 249-16 (ND 168-15; SD 81-1), June 28, 1978. A two-thirds majority vote (268 in this case) is required for passage under suspension of the rules.

441. HR 10173. Veterans' and Survivors' Pension Improvements. Roberts, D-Texas, motion to suspend the rules and pass the bill to pay non-disabled war veterans a pension sufficient to bring their total income to a specified minimum level. Motion agreed to 398-5: R 136-1; D 262-4 (ND 180-3; SD 82-1), June 28, 1978. A two-thirds majority vote (269 in this case) is required for passage under suspension of the rules.

442. HR 12841. Taxation of Fringe Benefits. Ullman, D-Ore., motion to suspend the rules and pass the bill to prohibit the issuance of regulations on the taxation of fringe benefits between May 1, 1978, and Dec. 31, 1979. Motion agreed to 386-12: R 132-0; D 254-12 (ND 175-9; SD 79-3), June 28, 1978. A two-thirds majority vote (266 in this case) is required for passage under suspension of the rules.

443. HR 12589. International Investment Survey Act. Bingham, D-N.Y., motion to suspend the rules and pass the bill to authorize $4 million for fiscal 1979 for the collection of regular and periodic information on foreign investment in the United States and U.S. investments abroad. Motion agreed to 344-54: R 109-27; D 235-27 (ND 173-9; SD 62-18), June 28, 1978. A two-thirds majority vote (266 in this case) is required for passage under suspension of the rules.

444. HR 12874. Solar Power Research. McCormack, D-Wash., motion to suspend the rules and pass the bill to provide accelerated federal research on developing energy cells to convert sunlight to electricity. Motion agreed to 385-14: R 127-7; D 258-7 (ND 179-4; SD 79-3), June 28, 1978. A two-thirds majority vote (266 in this case) is required for passage under suspension of the rules.

445. HR 12433. Housing and Community Development. Hagedorn, R-Minn., amendment to waive Davis-Bacon Act prevailing wage requirements for housing rehabilitation projects performed by neighborhood-based, non-profit organizations. Rejected 173-218: R 106-26; D 67-192 (ND 16-165; SD 51-27), June 28, 1978.

KEY

- Y Voted for (yea).
- ✓ Paired for.
- † Announced for.
- # CQ Poll for.
- N Voted against (nay).
- X Paired against.
- \- Announced against.
- ▮ CQ Poll against.
- P Voted "present."
- ● Voted "present" to avoid possible conflict of interest.
- ? Did not vote or otherwise make a position known.

	438	439	440	441	442	443	444	445
ALABAMA								
1 Edwards	Y	Y	Y	Y	Y	Y	Y	Y
2 Dickinson	Y	Y	Y	Y	Y	Y	Y	Y
3 Nichols	Y	Y	Y	Y	Y	Y	Y	Y
4 Bevill	Y	Y	Y	Y	Y	Y	Y	N
5 Flippo	Y	Y	Y	Y	?	Y	Y	N
6 Buchanan	Y	Y	Y	Y	Y	Y	Y	N
7 Flowers	?	?	?	?	?	?	?	?
ALASKA								
AL Young	Y	Y	Y	Y	Y	N	Y	N
ARIZONA								
1 Rhodes	Y	Y	Y	Y	Y	Y	Y	Y
2 Udall	Y	Y	Y	Y	Y	Y	Y	N
3 Stump	Y	Y	Y	Y	Y	N	N	Y
4 Rudd	Y	Y	Y	Y	Y	N	Y	Y
ARKANSAS								
1 Alexander	?	?	?	?	?	?	?	?
2 Tucker	Y	Y	Y	Y	Y	Y	Y	Y
3 Hammerschmidt	Y	Y	Y	Y	Y	Y	Y	Y
4 Thornton	Y	Y	Y	Y	Y	Y	Y	Y
CALIFORNIA								
1 Johnson	Y	Y	Y	Y	Y	Y	Y	N
2 Clausen	?	Y	Y	Y	Y	Y	Y	N
3 Moss	Y	Y	Y	Y	Y	Y	Y	N
4 Leggett	#	#	#	#	#	#	#	N
5 Burton, J.	Y	Y	Y	Y	Y	Y	Y	N
6 Burton, P.	Y	Y	Y	Y	Y	Y	Y	N
7 Miller	Y	Y	Y	Y	Y	Y	Y	N
8 Dellums	Y	Y	Y	Y	Y	Y	Y	N
9 Stark	Y	Y	Y	Y	N	Y	Y	N
10 Edwards	Y	Y	Y	Y	Y	Y	Y	N
11 Ryan	Y	Y	Y	Y	Y	Y	Y	N
12 McCloskey	?	?	?	?	?	?	?	?
13 Mineta	Y	Y	Y	Y	Y	Y	Y	N
14 McFall	Y	Y	Y	Y	Y	Y	Y	N
15 Sisk	Y	Y	Y	N	Y	Y	Y	N
16 Panetta	Y	Y	Y	Y	Y	Y	Y	N
17 Krebs	Y	Y	N	Y	Y	Y	Y	N
18 Vacancy								
19 Lagomarsino	Y	Y	Y	Y	Y	Y	Y	Y
20 Goldwater	Y	Y	Y	Y	Y	Y	Y	Y
21 Corman	Y	Y	Y	Y	Y	Y	Y	N
22 Moorhead	Y	Y	Y	Y	Y	N	Y	Y
23 Beilenson	Y	Y	N	N	N	Y	Y	N
24 Waxman	Y	Y	Y	Y	Y	Y	Y	N
25 Roybal	Y	Y	Y	Y	Y	Y	Y	N
26 Rousselot	Y	Y	Y	Y	?	N	Y	Y
27 Dornan	Y	Y	Y	Y	Y	Y	Y	Y
28 Burke	Y	Y	Y	Y	Y	Y	Y	N
29 Hawkins	Y	Y	Y	Y	Y	Y	Y	N
30 Danielson	Y	#	#	#	#	#	#	N
31 Wilson, C.H.	#	Y	Y	Y	Y	Y	Y	N
32 Anderson	Y	Y	Y	N	Y	Y	Y	N
33 Clawson	Y	Y	Y	Y	Y	Y	Y	Y
34 Hannaford	Y	Y	Y	Y	Y	Y	Y	N
35 Lloyd	Y	Y	Y	Y	Y	?	Y	N
36 Brown	?	Y	Y	Y	Y	Y	Y	N
37 Pettis	?	?	?	?	?	?	?	?
38 Patterson	Y	Y	Y	Y	Y	Y	Y	N
39 Wiggins	#	Y	Y	Y	Y	N	Y	✓
40 Badham	Y	Y	Y	Y	Y	N	Y	Y
41 Wilson, B.	Y	Y	Y	Y	Y	Y	Y	Y
42 Van Deerlin	Y	Y	N	Y	Y	Y	Y	Y
43 Burgener	Y	Y	Y	Y	Y	Y	Y	Y
COLORADO								
1 Schroeder	Y	Y	Y	Y	Y	Y	Y	N
2 Wirth	Y	Y	Y	Y	Y	Y	Y	Y
3 Evans	Y	Y	Y	Y	Y	Y	Y	Y
4 Johnson	?	?	?	?	?	?	?	?
5 Armstrong	?	?	?	?	?	?	?	?
CONNECTICUT								
1 Cotter	Y	Y	Y	Y	Y	Y	Y	N
2 Dodd	Y	Y	Y	Y	Y	N	Y	N
3 Giaimo	Y	Y	Y	Y	Y	Y	Y	N
4 McKinney	Y	Y	Y	Y	Y	Y	Y	Y
5 Sarasin	Y	Y	Y	Y	Y	Y	Y	N
6 Moffett	Y	Y	Y	Y	N	Y	Y	N
DELAWARE								
AL Evans	Y	Y	Y	Y	Y	Y	Y	Y
FLORIDA								
1 Sikes	Y	Y	Y	Y	Y	Y	Y	Y
2 Fuqua	Y	Y	Y	Y	Y	Y	Y	Y
3 Bennett	Y	Y	Y	Y	N	N	Y	Y
4 Chappell	Y	Y	Y	Y	Y	Y	Y	Y
5 Kelly	Y	Y	Y	Y	Y	N	Y	Y
6 Young	Y	Y	Y	Y	Y	Y	Y	Y
7 Gibbons	Y	Y	Y	Y	N	N	Y	Y
8 Ireland	Y	Y	Y	Y	Y	Y	Y	?
9 Frey	Y	Y	Y	Y	Y	Y	Y	Y
10 Bafalis	Y	Y	Y	Y	Y	Y	Y	Y
11 Rogers	Y	Y	Y	Y	Y	Y	Y	Y
12 Burke	Y	Y	Y	Y	Y	Y	Y	Y
13 Lehman	Y	Y	Y	Y	Y	Y	Y	N
14 Pepper	Y	Y	Y	Y	Y	Y	Y	N
15 Fascell	Y	Y	Y	N	Y	Y	#	N
GEORGIA								
1 Ginn	Y	Y	Y	Y	Y	Y	Y	N
2 Mathis	Y	Y	Y	Y	Y	Y	Y	Y
3 Brinkley	Y	Y	Y	Y	Y	Y	Y	N
4 Levitas	Y	Y	Y	Y	Y	Y	Y	N
5 Fowler	Y	Y	Y	Y	Y	Y	Y	N
6 Flynt	Y	Y	Y	Y	Y	N	Y	Y
7 McDonald	N	Y	Y	Y	Y	N	N	Y
8 Evans	Y	Y	Y	Y	Y	Y	Y	Y
9 Jenkins	Y	Y	Y	Y	Y	Y	Y	#
10 Barnard	Y	Y	Y	Y	Y	Y	N	Y
HAWAII								
1 Heftel	Y	Y	Y	?	Y	Y	Y	Y
2 Akaka	Y	Y	Y	Y	Y	Y	Y	N
IDAHO								
1 Symms	Y	Y	Y	Y	Y	N	N	Y
2 Hansen, G.	Y	Y	Y	Y	Y	N	Y	Y
ILLINOIS								
1 Metcalfe	Y	Y	Y	Y	Y	Y	Y	N
2 Murphy	Y	Y	Y	Y	Y	Y	Y	N
3 Russo	Y	Y	Y	Y	Y	Y	Y	N
4 Derwinski	Y	Y	Y	Y	Y	Y	Y	N
5 Fary	Y	Y	Y	Y	Y	Y	Y	N
6 Hyde	Y	Y	Y	Y	Y	N	N	Y
7 Collins	Y	Y	Y	Y	Y	Y	Y	N
8 Rostenkowski	#	#	#	#	#	?	#	X
9 Yates	Y	Y	N	Y	Y	Y	Y	N
10 Mikva	Y	Y	N	Y	N	Y	Y	N
11 Annunzio	Y	Y	Y	Y	Y	Y	Y	N
12 Crane	Y	Y	Y	Y	Y	N	N	✓
13 McClory	Y	Y	Y	Y	Y	Y	Y	Y
14 Erlenborn	Y	Y	Y	Y	Y	Y	Y	Y
15 Corcoran	#	#	#	#	#	#	#	✓
16 Anderson	Y	Y	Y	Y	Y	Y	Y	Y
17 O'Brien	Y	Y	Y	Y	Y	Y	Y	Y
18 Michel	#	Y	Y	Y	Y	Y	Y	Y
19 Railsback	Y	Y	#	Y	#	Y	Y	Y
20 Findley	Y	Y	Y	Y	Y	Y	Y	Y
21 Madigan	?	Y	Y	Y	Y	Y	Y	Y
22 Shipley	?	?	?	?	?	?	?	X
23 Price	Y	Y	Y	Y	Y	Y	Y	N
24 Simon	?	?	?	?	?	?	?	?
INDIANA								
1 Benjamin	Y	Y	N	Y	Y	N	N	N
2 Fithian	Y	Y	Y	Y	Y	Y	Y	Y
3 Brademas	Y	Y	Y	Y	Y	Y	Y	N
4 Quayle	N	Y	Y	Y	Y	Y	Y	Y
5 Hillis	Y	Y	Y	Y	Y	Y	Y	N
6 Evans	Y	Y	Y	Y	Y	Y	Y	N
7 Myers, J.	Y	Y	Y	Y	Y	Y	Y	Y
8 Cornwell	?	Y	Y	Y	Y	Y	Y	N
9 Hamilton	Y	Y	Y	Y	N	Y	Y	N
10 Sharp	Y	Y	Y	Y	Y	Y	Y	N
11 Jacobs	Y	Y	N	Y	Y	N	N	Y
IOWA								
1 Leach	#	Y	Y	Y	Y	Y	Y	Y
2 Blouin	Y	Y	Y	Y	Y	Y	Y	N
3 Grassley	Y	Y	Y	Y	Y	Y	Y	Y
4 Smith	Y	Y	Y	Y	Y	Y	Y	N
5 Harkin	Y	Y	Y	Y	Y	Y	Y	N
6 Bedell	Y	Y	N	Y	Y	Y	Y	Y

Democrats ***Republicans***

	438	439	440	441	442	443	444	445
KANSAS								
1 Sebelius	Y	Y	Y	Y	Y	Y	Y	Y
2 Keys	Y	Y	N	Y	Y	Y	Y	Y
3 Winn	Y	Y	Y	Y	#	Y	Y	Y
4 Glickman	Y	Y	N	Y	Y	Y	Y	N
5 Skubitz	Y	Y	Y	Y	Y	N	Y	Y
KENTUCKY								
1 Hubbard	Y	Y	Y	Y	Y	Y	Y	N
2 Natcher	Y	Y	Y	Y	Y	Y	Y	N
3 Mazzoli	Y	Y	Y	Y	Y	Y	Y	N
4 Snyder	Y	Y	Y	Y	Y	Y	Y	Y
5 Carter	Y	Y	Y	Y	Y	Y	Y	Y
6 Breckinridge	Y	Y	Y	Y	Y	Y	Y	Y
7 Perkins	Y	Y	Y	Y	Y	Y	Y	N
LOUISIANA								
1 Livingston	Y	Y	Y	Y	Y	Y	N	Y
2 Boggs	Y	Y	Y	Y	Y	Y	Y	Y
3 Treen	Y	Y	Y	Y	Y	Y	Y	Y
4 Waggonner	Y	Y	Y	Y	Y	N	Y	Y
5 Huckaby	Y	Y	Y	Y	Y	Y	Y	Y
6 Moore	Y	Y	Y	Y	Y	Y	Y	Y
7 Breaux	Y	Y	Y	Y	Y	?	Y	Y
8 Long	Y	?	?	Y	Y	Y	Y	Y
MAINE								
1 Emery	Y	Y	Y	Y	Y	Y	Y	Y
2 Cohen	Y	Y	Y	Y	Y	Y	Y	Y
MARYLAND								
1 Bauman	Y	Y	Y	Y	Y	Y	N	Y
2 Long	Y	Y	Y	Y	Y	Y	Y	Y
3 Mikulski	N	Y	Y	Y	Y	Y	Y	N
4 Holt	Y	Y	Y	Y	Y	N	Y	Y
5 Spellman	Y	Y	Y	Y	Y	Y	Y	N
6 Byron	Y	Y	Y	Y	Y	Y	Y	Y
7 Mitchell	Y	Y	Y	Y	Y	Y	Y	N
8 Steers	Y	Y	Y	Y	Y	Y	Y	N
MASSACHUSETTS								
1 Conte	Y	Y	Y	Y	Y	Y	Y	N
2 Boland	Y	Y	Y	Y	Y	Y	Y	N
3 Early	Y	Y	Y	Y	Y	Y	Y	N
4 Drinan	Y	Y	Y	Y	N	Y	Y	N
5 Tsongas	?	?	?	?	?	?	?	X
6 Harrington	#	#	#	#	#	#	#	X
7 Markey	Y	Y	Y	Y	Y	Y	Y	N
8 O'Neill								
9 Moakley	Y	Y	Y	Y	Y	Y	Y	N
10 Heckler	Y	Y	Y	Y	Y	Y	Y	N
11 Burke	Y	Y	Y	Y	Y	Y	Y	N
12 Studds	Y	Y	Y	Y	Y	Y	Y	N
MICHIGAN								
1 Conyers	#	Y	Y	Y	Y	#	Y	N
2 Pursell	Y	Y	Y	Y	Y	Y	Y	N
3 Brown	#	Y	Y	Y	Y	N	Y	Y
4 Stockman	Y	Y	Y	Y	Y	Y	N	Y
5 Sawyer	Y	Y	Y	Y	Y	Y	Y	Y
6 Carr	Y	Y	Y	Y	Y	Y	Y	N
7 Kildee	Y	Y	Y	Y	Y	Y	Y	N
8 Traxler	Y	Y	Y	Y	Y	Y	Y	N
9 Vander Jagt	Y	Y	Y	Y	Y	Y	Y	Y
10 Cederberg	Y	Y	Y	Y	Y	Y	Y	Y
11 Ruppe	?	?	?	?	?	?	?	✓
12 Bonior	Y	Y	Y	Y	Y	Y	Y	N
13 Diggs	#	#	#	Y	Y	Y	Y	N
14 Nedzi	Y	Y	Y	Y	Y	Y	Y	N
15 Ford	?	Y	Y	Y	Y	Y	Y	N
16 Dingell	Y	Y	Y	Y	Y	Y	Y	N
17 Brodhead	Y	Y	Y	Y	Y	Y	Y	N
18 Blanchard	Y	Y	Y	Y	Y	Y	Y	N
19 Broomfield	Y	Y	Y	Y	Y	Y	Y	Y
MINNESOTA								
1 Quie	?	?	?	?	?	?	?	?
2 Hagedorn	Y	Y	Y	Y	Y	Y	Y	Y
3 Frenzel	Y	Y	Y	Y	Y	Y	Y	Y
4 Vento	Y	Y	Y	Y	Y	Y	Y	N
5 Fraser	#	Y	Y	Y	Y	Y	Y	N
6 Nolan	Y	Y	Y	Y	Y	Y	Y	N
7 Stangeland	Y	Y	Y	Y	Y	Y	Y	Y
8 Oberstar	Y	Y	Y	Y	Y	Y	Y	N
MISSISSIPPI								
1 Whitten	Y	Y	Y	Y	Y	Y	Y	Y
2 Bowen	Y	Y	Y	Y	Y	Y	Y	Y
3 Montgomery	Y	Y	Y	Y	Y	N	Y	Y
4 Cochran	Y	Y	Y	Y	Y	Y	Y	Y
5 Lott	Y	Y	Y	Y	Y	Y	Y	Y
MISSOURI								
1 Clay	?	Y	Y	Y	Y	Y	Y	N
2 Young	Y	Y	Y	Y	Y	Y	Y	N
3 Gephardt	Y	Y	Y	Y	Y	Y	Y	N
4 Skelton	Y	Y	Y	Y	Y	Y	#	▮
5 Bolling	Y	Y	Y	Y	Y	Y	Y	▮
6 Coleman	Y	Y	Y	Y	Y	Y	Y	Y
7 Taylor	Y	Y	Y	Y	Y	Y	Y	Y
8 Ichord	Y	Y	Y	Y	Y	Y	Y	Y
9 Volkmer	Y	Y	N	Y	Y	Y	Y	N
10 Burlison	Y	Y	Y	Y	Y	Y	Y	N
MONTANA								
1 Baucus	Y	Y	Y	Y	Y	Y	Y	N
2 Marlenee	Y	Y	Y	Y	Y	Y	Y	N
NEBRASKA								
1 Thone	Y	Y	Y	Y	Y	Y	#	Y
2 Cavanaugh	Y	Y	Y	Y	Y	Y	Y	N
3 Smith	Y	Y	Y	Y	Y	Y	Y	Y
NEVADA								
AL Santini	Y	Y	Y	Y	Y	Y	Y	?
NEW HAMPSHIRE								
1 D'Amours	Y	Y	Y	Y	Y	Y	Y	N
2 Cleveland	Y	Y	Y	Y	Y	Y	Y	Y
NEW JERSEY								
1 Florio	Y	Y	Y	Y	Y	Y	Y	N
2 Hughes	Y	Y	Y	Y	Y	Y	Y	N
3 Howard	#	Y	Y	Y	Y	Y	Y	N
4 Thompson	Y	Y	Y	Y	Y	Y	Y	N
5 Fenwick	#	Y	Y	Y	Y	Y	Y	Y
6 Forsythe	#	Y	Y	Y	Y	Y	Y	#
7 Maguire	Y	Y	Y	Y	Y	Y	Y	N
8 Roe	Y	Y	Y	Y	Y	Y	Y	N
9 Hollenbeck	Y	Y	Y	Y	Y	Y	Y	N
10 Rodino	#	#	#	#	#	#	#	▮
11 Minish	Y	Y	Y	Y	Y	Y	Y	N
12 Rinaldo	Y	Y	Y	Y	Y	Y	Y	N
13 Meyner	#	#	#	#	#	#	#	▮
14 LeFante	#	#	#	#	#	#	#	X
15 Patten	Y	Y	Y	Y	Y	Y	Y	N
NEW MEXICO								
1 Lujan	Y	Y	Y	Y	Y	N	Y	Y
2 Runnels	#	Y	Y	Y	Y	N	Y	✓
NEW YORK								
1 Pike	Y	Y	N	Y	Y	N	Y	N
2 Downey	Y	Y	Y	Y	Y	Y	Y	N
3 Ambro	Y	Y	Y	Y	Y	Y	Y	N
4 Lent	Y	Y	Y	Y	Y	Y	Y	Y
5 Wydler	Y	Y	Y	Y	Y	N	Y	N
6 Wolff	Y	Y	Y	Y	Y	Y	Y	N
7 Addabbo	Y	Y	Y	Y	Y	Y	Y	N
8 Rosenthal	Y	Y	Y	Y	N	Y	Y	N
9 Delaney	Y	Y	Y	Y	Y	Y	Y	?
10 Biaggi	Y	Y	Y	Y	Y	Y	Y	N
11 Scheuer	Y	Y	Y	Y	Y	Y	N	N
12 Chisholm	Y	Y	#	#	Y	#	Y	N
13 Solarz	Y	Y	Y	Y	Y	Y	Y	N
14 Richmond	Y	Y	Y	Y	Y	Y	Y	N
15 Zeferetti	Y	Y	Y	Y	Y	Y	Y	N
16 Holtzman	Y	Y	Y	Y	Y	Y	Y	N
17 Murphy	Y	Y	Y	Y	Y	Y	Y	N
18 Green	Y	Y	Y	Y	Y	Y	Y	Y
19 Rangel	?	Y	Y	Y	Y	Y	Y	N
20 Weiss	Y	Y	Y	Y	Y	Y	Y	N
21 Garcia	#	Y	Y	Y	Y	Y	Y	N
22 Bingham	Y	Y	Y	Y	Y	Y	Y	N
23 Caputo	Y	Y	Y	Y	Y	Y	Y	?
24 Ottinger	Y	Y	Y	Y	Y	Y	Y	N
25 Fish	Y	Y	Y	Y	Y	Y	Y	N
26 Gilman	Y	Y	Y	Y	Y	Y	Y	N
27 McHugh	Y	Y	N	Y	Y	Y	Y	N
28 Stratton	Y	Y	Y	Y	Y	N	Y	N
29 Pattison	Y	Y	Y	Y	Y	Y	Y	Y
30 McEwen	Y	Y	Y	Y	Y	Y	Y	Y
31 Mitchell	Y	Y	Y	Y	Y	Y	Y	Y
32 Hanley	Y	Y	Y	Y	Y	Y	Y	N
33 Walsh	Y	Y	Y	Y	Y	Y	Y	N
34 Horton	Y	Y	Y	Y	Y	Y	Y	N
35 Conable	Y	Y	Y	Y	Y	N	Y	Y
36 LaFalce	Y	Y	Y	Y	Y	Y	Y	N
37 Nowak	Y	Y	Y	Y	Y	Y	Y	N
38 Kemp	Y	Y	Y	Y	Y	N	Y	Y
39 Lundine	Y	Y	Y	Y	Y	Y	Y	N
NORTH CAROLINA								
1 Jones	Y	Y	Y	Y	Y	Y	Y	Y
2 Fountain	Y	Y	Y	Y	Y	#	Y	Y
3 Whitley	Y	Y	Y	Y	Y	Y	Y	Y
4 Andrews	Y	Y	Y	Y	Y	Y	Y	Y
5 Neal	Y	Y	Y	Y	Y	Y	Y	Y
6 Preyer	Y	Y	Y	Y	Y	Y	Y	Y
7 Rose	Y	Y	Y	Y	Y	Y	Y	Y
8 Hefner	Y	Y	Y	Y	Y	Y	Y	Y
9 Martin	Y	Y	Y	Y	Y	Y	Y	Y
10 Broyhill	Y	Y	Y	Y	Y	Y	Y	Y
11 Gudger	Y	Y	Y	Y	Y	Y	Y	Y
NORTH DAKOTA								
AL Andrews	Y	Y	Y	Y	Y	Y	Y	Y
OHIO								
1 Gradison	Y	Y	Y	Y	Y	Y	Y	Y
2 Luken	Y	Y	Y	Y	Y	Y	Y	N
3 Whalen	#	#	#	#	#	#	#	X
4 Guyer	Y	Y	Y	Y	Y	Y	Y	Y
5 Latta	Y	Y	Y	Y	Y	Y	Y	Y
6 Harsha	Y	Y	Y	Y	Y	Y	Y	N
7 Brown	?	?	?	?	?	?	?	✓
8 Kindness	Y	Y	Y	Y	Y	Y	Y	Y
9 Ashley	?	Y	Y	Y	Y	Y	Y	N
10 Miller	Y	Y	Y	Y	Y	Y	Y	Y
11 Stanton	Y	Y	Y	Y	Y	Y	Y	Y
12 Devine	Y	Y	Y	Y	Y	Y	Y	Y
13 Pease	Y	Y	Y	Y	Y	N	Y	N
14 Seiberling	Y	Y	N	Y	Y	Y	Y	N
15 Wylie	Y	Y	Y	Y	Y	Y	Y	N
16 Regula	Y	Y	Y	Y	Y	Y	Y	Y
17 Ashbrook	Y	Y	Y	Y	Y	N	Y	Y
18 Applegate	Y	Y	Y	Y	Y	Y	Y	N
19 Carney	Y	Y	Y	Y	Y	Y	Y	N
20 Oakar	Y	Y	Y	Y	Y	N	Y	N
21 Stokes	Y	Y	Y	Y	Y	Y	Y	N
22 Vanik	Y	Y	Y	Y	Y	Y	Y	N
23 Mottl	Y	Y	Y	Y	Y	Y	Y	N
OKLAHOMA								
1 Jones	Y	Y	N	Y	Y	N	Y	Y
2 Risenhoover	Y	Y	Y	Y	Y	Y	Y	Y
3 Watkins	Y	Y	Y	Y	Y	N	Y	Y
4 Steed	Y	Y	Y	Y	Y	Y	Y	Y
5 Edwards	Y	Y	Y	Y	Y	N	Y	Y
6 English	Y	Y	Y	Y	Y	Y	Y	Y
OREGON								
1 AuCoin	#	Y	Y	Y	Y	Y	Y	N
2 Ullman	Y	Y	Y	Y	Y	Y	Y	Y
3 Duncan	Y	Y	Y	Y	Y	Y	Y	Y
4 Weaver	Y	Y	Y	Y	Y	Y	Y	?
PENNSYLVANIA								
1 Myers, M.	Y	Y	Y	Y	Y	Y	?	N
2 Nix	?	?	?	?	?	?	?	?
3 Lederer	Y	Y	Y	Y	Y	Y	Y	N
4 Eilberg	Y	Y	Y	Y	Y	Y	Y	N
5 Schulze	Y	Y	Y	Y	Y	Y	Y	Y
6 Yatron	Y	Y	Y	Y	Y	Y	Y	N
7 Edgar	Y	Y	Y	Y	Y	Y	Y	N
8 Kostmayer	Y	Y	Y	Y	Y	Y	Y	N
9 Shuster	Y	Y	Y	Y	Y	N	Y	Y
10 McDade	Y	Y	Y	Y	Y	Y	Y	N
11 Flood	Y	Y	Y	Y	Y	Y	Y	N
12 Murtha	Y	Y	Y	Y	Y	Y	Y	N
13 Coughlin	?	Y	Y	Y	Y	Y	Y	Y
14 Moorhead	Y	Y	Y	Y	Y	Y	Y	N
15 Rooney	Y	Y	Y	Y	Y	Y	Y	N
16 Walker	Y	Y	Y	Y	Y	Y	Y	Y
17 Ertel	Y	Y	Y	Y	Y	Y	Y	N
18 Walgren	Y	Y	Y	Y	Y	Y	Y	N
19 Goodling, W.	Y	Y	Y	Y	Y	N	Y	Y
20 Gaydos	Y	?	Y	Y	Y	Y	Y	N
21 Dent	?	?	?	?	?	?	?	X
22 Murphy	Y	Y	Y	Y	Y	Y	Y	N
23 Ammerman	Y	Y	Y	Y	Y	Y	Y	N
24 Marks	Y	Y	Y	Y	?	Y	Y	N
25 Myers, G.	Y	N	Y	N	Y	Y	Y	Y
RHODE ISLAND								
1 St Germain	Y	Y	Y	Y	Y	Y	Y	N
2 Beard	Y	Y	Y	Y	Y	Y	Y	N
SOUTH CAROLINA								
1 Davis	Y	Y	Y	Y	Y	Y	Y	N
2 Spence	Y	Y	Y	Y	Y	Y	Y	Y
3 Derrick	Y	Y	Y	Y	Y	Y	Y	?
4 Mann	Y	Y	Y	Y	Y	Y	Y	Y
5 Holland	?	?	?	?	?	?	?	N
6 Jenrette	Y	Y	Y	Y	Y	Y	Y	N
SOUTH DAKOTA								
1 Pressler	Y	?	Y	Y	Y	Y	Y	N
2 Abdnor	Y	Y	Y	Y	Y	Y	Y	Y
TENNESSEE								
1 Quillen	Y	Y	Y	Y	Y	N	Y	N
2 Duncan	Y	Y	Y	Y	Y	N	?	Y
3 Lloyd	Y	Y	Y	Y	Y	N	Y	Y
4 Gore	Y	Y	Y	Y	N	Y	Y	Y
5 Vacancy								
6 Beard	Y	Y	Y	Y	Y	Y	Y	Y
7 Jones	Y	Y	Y	Y	Y	N	Y	Y
8 Ford	Y	Y	Y	Y	Y	Y	Y	N
TEXAS								
1 Hall	Y	Y	Y	Y	Y	N	Y	Y
2 Wilson, C.	#	#	#	#	#	#	#	#
3 Collins	N	Y	Y	Y	Y	N	N	Y
4 Roberts	Y	Y	Y	Y	Y	Y	Y	Y
5 Mattox	Y	Y	Y	Y	Y	Y	Y	N
6 Teague	?	Y	Y	Y	Y	N	Y	✓
7 Archer	Y	Y	Y	Y	Y	N	Y	Y
8 Eckhardt	Y	Y	Y	Y	Y	Y	Y	N
9 Brooks	Y	Y	Y	Y	Y	N	Y	N
10 Pickle	Y	Y	Y	Y	Y	N	Y	N
11 Poage	Y	Y	Y	Y	Y	Y	Y	?
12 Wright	?	Y	Y	Y	Y	Y	Y	N
13 Hightower	Y	Y	Y	Y	Y	Y	Y	Y
14 Young	Y	Y	Y	Y	Y	Y	Y	?
15 de la Garza	Y	Y	Y	Y	Y	Y	Y	Y
16 White	Y	Y	Y	Y	Y	Y	Y	Y
17 Burleson	Y	Y	Y	Y	Y	N	Y	Y
18 Jordan	Y	Y	Y	Y	Y	Y	Y	N
19 Mahon	Y	Y	Y	Y	Y	Y	Y	Y
20 Gonzalez	Y	Y	Y	Y	Y	P	Y	N
21 Krueger	N	#	#	#	#	#	#	▮
22 Gammage	Y	Y	Y	Y	Y	N	Y	N
23 Kazen	Y	Y	Y	Y	Y	Y	Y	Y
24 Milford	?	?	?	?	?	?	?	?
UTAH								
1 McKay	Y	Y	Y	Y	Y	Y	Y	Y
2 Marriott	Y	Y	Y	Y	Y	Y	Y	Y
VERMONT								
AL Jeffords	Y	Y	Y	Y	Y	Y	Y	N
VIRGINIA								
1 Trible	Y	Y	Y	Y	Y	Y	Y	Y
2 Whitehurst	Y	Y	Y	Y	Y	Y	Y	Y
3 Satterfield	Y	Y	Y	Y	Y	N	N	Y
4 Daniel	Y	Y	Y	Y	Y	Y	Y	Y
5 Daniel	Y	Y	Y	Y	Y	N	Y	Y
6 Butler	Y	Y	Y	Y	Y	Y	Y	Y
7 Robinson	Y	Y	Y	Y	Y	Y	Y	Y
8 Harris	Y	Y	Y	Y	Y	Y	Y	N
9 Wampler	Y	Y	Y	Y	Y	Y	Y	Y
10 Fisher	Y	Y	Y	Y	Y	Y	Y	N
WASHINGTON								
1 Pritchard	Y	Y	Y	Y	Y	Y	Y	Y
2 Meeds	Y	Y	Y	Y	Y	Y	Y	N
3 Bonker	#	Y	Y	Y	Y	Y	Y	N
4 McCormack	Y	Y	Y	Y	Y	Y	Y	N
5 Foley	Y	Y	Y	Y	Y	Y	Y	N
6 Dicks	Y	Y	Y	Y	Y	Y	Y	N
7 Cunningham	Y	Y	Y	Y	Y	N	Y	N
WEST VIRGINIA								
1 Mollohan	Y	Y	Y	Y	Y	Y	Y	N
2 Staggers	Y	Y	Y	Y	Y	Y	Y	N
3 Slack	Y	Y	Y	Y	Y	Y	Y	N
4 Rahall	Y	Y	Y	Y	Y	Y	Y	N
WISCONSIN								
1 Aspin	Y	Y	N	Y	Y	Y	Y	N
2 Kastenmeier	Y	Y	Y	Y	N	Y	Y	N
3 Baldus	Y	Y	Y	Y	Y	Y	Y	N
4 Zablocki	Y	Y	Y	Y	Y	Y	Y	N
5 Reuss	Y	Y	Y	Y	N	Y	Y	N
6 Steiger	Y	Y	Y	Y	#	#	#	#
7 Obey	Y	Y	Y	Y	Y	Y	Y	N
8 Cornell	Y	Y	Y	Y	Y	Y	Y	N
9 Kasten	Y	Y	Y	Y	Y	Y	Y	Y
WYOMING								
AL Roncalio	Y	Y	Y	Y	?	Y	Y	N

Democrats ***Republicans***

446. Procedural Motion. Broomfield, R-Mich., motion to approve the House *Journal* of Wednesday, June 28, 1978. Motion agreed to 338-11: R 113-8; D 225-3 (ND 156-1; SD 69-2), June 29, 1978.

447. HR 12433. Housing and Community Development. Ashley, D-Ohio, motion that the House resolve itself into the Committee of the Whole for consideration of the bill to revise and extend certain federal housing and community development laws. Motion agreed to 362-3: R 129-1; D 233-2 (ND 160-1; SD 73-1), June 29, 1978.

448. HR 12433. Housing and Community Development. Brown, R-Mich., amendment to permit either the House or Senate to veto rules or regulations prescribed by the Department of Housing and Urban Development. Adopted 244-140: R 126-3; D 118-137 (ND 64-113; SD 54-24), June 29, 1978. A "nay" was a vote supporting the president's position.

449. HR 12433. Housing and Community Development. Russo, D-Ill., amendment to require the Department of Housing and Urban Development to provide pre-purchase counseling to first-time purchasers of single family dwellings who apply for Federal Housing Administration mortgages. Rejected 93-285: R 16-113; D 77-172 (ND 63-111; SD 14-61), June 29, 1978.

450. HR 8099. Ak-Chin Indian Claims. Passage of the bill to authorize $43 million for fiscal 1979-83 for the construction of water wells and pumping and delivery facilities for the Ak-Chin Indian community in Arizona to fulfill a 1912 federal trust responsibility. Passed 292-80: R 74-53; D 218-27 (ND 154-15; SD 64-12), June 29, 1978.

KEY

- Y Voted for (yea).
- ✓ Paired for.
- † Announced for.
- # CQ Poll for.
- N Voted against (nay).
- X Paired against.
- \- Announced against.
- ▮ CQ Poll against.
- P Voted "present."
- ● Voted "present" to avoid possible conflict of interest.
- ? Did not vote or otherwise make a position known.

	446	447	448	449	450
ALABAMA					
1 Edwards	Y	Y	Y	N	Y
2 Dickinson	Y	Y	Y	N	?
3 Nichols	Y	Y	Y	N	Y
4 Bevill	Y	Y	✓	X	?
5 Flippo	Y	Y	N	Y	Y
6 Buchanan	Y	Y	Y	Y	Y
7 Flowers	?	?	?	?	?
ALASKA					
AL Young	#	Y	Y	N	Y
ARIZONA					
1 Rhodes	Y	Y	?	?	Y
2 Udall	Y	Y	N	N	Y
3 Stump	Y	Y	Y	N	▮
4 Rudd	Y	Y	Y	N	Y
ARKANSAS					
1 Alexander	Y	Y	Y	Y	Y
2 Tucker	Y	Y	Y	Y	Y
3 Hammerschmidt	Y	Y	Y	N	N
4 Thornton	Y	Y	Y	N	Y
CALIFORNIA					
1 Johnson	Y	Y	N	N	Y
2 Clausen	Y	Y	Y	N	Y
3 Moss	P	Y	N	N	Y
4 Leggett	#	#	#	Y	#
5 Burton, J.	?	Y	N	N	Y
6 Burton, P.	Y	Y	N	Y	Y
7 Miller	Y	Y	N	N	Y
8 Dellums	Y	Y	N	N	Y
9 Stark	Y	Y	N	N	Y
10 Edwards	Y	Y	N	N	Y
11 Ryan	Y	#	Y	N	N
12 McCloskey	?	?	?	?	?
13 Mineta	Y	Y	N	N	Y
14 McFall	Y	Y	N	N	Y
15 Sisk	Y	?	Y	Y	Y
16 Panetta	Y	Y	Y	N	Y
17 Krebs	Y	Y	Y	N	Y
18 Vacancy					
19 Lagomarsino	Y	Y	Y	N	N
20 Goldwater	Y	Y	Y	N	Y
21 Corman	Y	Y	N	N	Y
22 Moorhead	Y	Y	Y	N	N
23 Beilenson	#	#	N	Y	Y
24 Waxman	Y	Y	N	Y	Y
25 Roybal	Y	Y	N	N	Y
26 Rousselot	Y	Y	Y	N	N
27 Dornan	Y	Y	Y	N	N
28 Burke	#	Y	N	Y	Y
29 Hawkins	Y	?	N	Y	Y
30 Danielson	P	P	N	N	Y
31 Wilson, C.H.	Y	Y	N	▮	▮
32 Anderson	Y	Y	N	Y	Y
33 Clawson	Y	Y	Y	N	Y
34 Hannaford	Y	Y	N	N	Y
35 Lloyd	N	N	N	Y	Y
36 Brown	Y	Y	N	N	?
37 Pettis	?	?	?	?	?
38 Patterson	Y	Y	N	N	Y
39 Wiggins	#	#	Y	N	N
40 Badham	Y	Y	Y	N	N
41 Wilson, B.	N	N	✓	?	Y
42 Van Deerlin	Y	Y	N	Y	Y
43 Burgener	Y	Y	Y	N	Y
COLORADO					
1 Schroeder	#	#	Y	N	Y
2 Wirth	Y	Y	N	N	Y
3 Evans	Y	Y	N	N	Y
4 Johnson	?	?	?	?	?
5 Armstrong	?	?	?	?	?
CONNECTICUT					
1 Cotter	Y	Y	N	Y	Y
2 Dodd	Y	Y	Y	Y	Y
3 Giaimo	Y	Y	N	?	Y
4 McKinney	Y	Y	Y	N	Y
5 Sarasin	N	Y	Y	N	Y
6 Moffett	Y	Y	N	Y	Y
DELAWARE					
AL Evans	Y	Y	Y	N	N
FLORIDA					
1 Sikes	Y	Y	Y	N	Y
2 Fuqua	Y	Y	Y	N	Y
3 Bennett	Y	Y	Y	N	Y
4 Chappell	Y	Y	Y	N	Y
5 Kelly	Y	Y	Y	N	N
6 Young	Y	Y	Y	N	N
7 Gibbons	Y	Y	N	N	Y
8 Ireland	Y	Y	Y	N	N
9 Frey	Y	Y	Y	N	Y
10 Bafalis	Y	Y	Y	N	Y
11 Rogers	Y	Y	Y	N	Y
12 Burke	Y	Y	Y	N	N
13 Lehman	Y	Y	N	N	Y
14 Pepper	#	Y	N	N	Y
15 Fascell	Y	Y	N	N	Y
GEORGIA					
1 Ginn	Y	Y	Y	Y	Y
2 Mathis	?	?	?	?	?
3 Brinkley	?	?	?	?	?
4 Levitas	Y	Y	Y	Y	Y
5 Fowler	Y	Y	N	Y	Y
6 Flynt	Y	Y	Y	N	N
7 McDonald	#	N	Y	N	N
8 Evans	#	#	Y	N	N
9 Jenkins	#	#	#	▮	#
10 Barnard	Y	Y	Y	N	Y
HAWAII					
1 Heftel	Y	Y	Y	Y	Y
2 Akaka	Y	Y	N	N	Y
IDAHO					
1 Symms	Y	Y	Y	N	N
2 Hansen, G.	Y	Y	Y	N	N
ILLINOIS					
1 Metcalfe	Y	Y	N	Y	Y
2 Murphy	Y	Y	N	Y	Y
3 Russo	Y	Y	Y	Y	Y
4 Derwinski	Y	Y	Y	N	Y
5 Fary	Y	Y	N	Y	Y
6 Hyde	Y	Y	Y	Y	Y
7 Collins	Y	Y	N	Y	Y
8 Rostenkowski	Y	Y	N	Y	Y
9 Yates	Y	Y	N	N	#
10 Mikva	Y	Y	N	Y	Y
11 Annunzio	Y	Y	N	Y	Y
12 Crane	#	Y	Y	N	N
13 McClory	Y	Y	Y	N	Y
14 Erlenborn	Y	Y	Y	N	Y
15 Corcoran	#	#	✓	#	▮
16 Anderson	#	#	#	▮	#
17 O'Brien	#	Y	Y	Y	Y
18 Michel	Y	Y	Y	Y	N
19 Railsback	Y	Y	Y	Y	?
20 Findley	Y	Y	?	?	?
21 Madigan	Y	Y	Y	N	Y
22 Shipley	?	?	X	X	?
23 Price	Y	Y	N	Y	Y
24 Simon	Y	Y	N	Y	Y
INDIANA					
1 Benjamin	Y	Y	Y	Y	Y
2 Fithian	Y	Y	Y	Y	Y
3 Brademas	#	#	X	X	#
4 Quayle	N	Y	Y	N	Y
5 Hillis	Y	Y	Y	Y	Y
6 Evans	Y	Y	Y	N	N
7 Myers, J.	Y	Y	Y	N	Y
8 Cornwell	?	?	?	?	?
9 Hamilton	Y	Y	Y	N	Y
10 Sharp	Y	Y	Y	N	Y
11 Jacobs	Y	Y	Y	N	N
IOWA					
1 Leach	Y	Y	Y	N	Y
2 Blouin	Y	Y	Y	Y	Y
3 Grassley	Y	Y	Y	N	N
4 Smith	Y	Y	Y	▮	#
5 Harkin	Y	Y	Y	Y	Y
6 Bedell	#	#	N	N	Y

Democrats ***Republicans***

	446	447	448	449	450
KANSAS					
1 ***Sebelius***	Y	Y	Y	N	Y
2 Keys	Y	Y	Y	N	Y
3 ***Winn***	Y	Y	✓	N	#
4 Glickman	Y	Y	Y	N	Y
5 ***Skubitz***	?	Y	Y	?	?
KENTUCKY					
1 Hubbard	Y	Y	Y	N	Y
2 Natcher	Y	Y	N	N	Y
3 Mazzoli	Y	Y	Y	N	Y
4 ***Snyder***	Y	Y	Y	N	N
5 ***Carter***	Y	Y	Y	N	Y
6 Breckinridge	P	Y	Y	N	Y
7 Perkins	Y	Y	N	N	Y
LOUISIANA					
1 ***Livingston***	Y	Y	Y	N	Y
2 Boggs	?	Y	N	N	Y
3 ***Treen***	Y	Y	Y	N	N
4 Waggonner	Y	Y	Y	▮	▮
5 Huckaby	Y	Y	Y	N	Y
6 ***Moore***	Y	Y	Y	N	N
7 Breaux	Y	Y	Y	N	N
8 Long	Y	Y	N	Y	Y
MAINE					
1 ***Emery***	Y	Y	Y	Y	Y
2 ***Cohen***	Y	Y	Y	Y	Y
MARYLAND					
1 ***Bauman***	Y	Y	Y	N	N
2 Long	Y	Y	Y	Y	Y
3 Mikulski	Y	Y	N	Y	Y
4 ***Holt***	Y	Y	Y	N	N
5 Spellman	Y	Y	Y	Y	Y
6 Byron	Y	Y	Y	N	Y
7 Mitchell	#	#	N	N	Y
8 ***Steers***	Y	Y	Y	N	Y
MASSACHUSETTS					
1 ***Conte***	Y	Y	N	Y	Y
2 Boland	Y	Y	N	N	Y
3 Early	Y	Y	N	Y	Y
4 Drinan	Y	Y	N	N	Y
5 Tsongas	?	?	X	?	?
6 Harrington	#	#	X	?	#
7 Markey	Y	Y	N	Y	Y
8 O'Neill					
9 Moakley	Y	Y	N	N	Y
10 ***Heckler***	#	Y	N	Y	N
11 Burke	Y	Y	N	N	Y
12 Studds	Y	Y	N	N	Y
MICHIGAN					
1 Conyers	#	#	X	#	#
2 ***Pursell***	Y	Y	Y	N	Y
3 ***Brown***	N	Y	Y	N	Y
4 ***Stockman***	#	#	#	N	N
5 ***Sawyer***	Y	Y	Y	N	Y
6 Carr	Y	Y	Y	Y	Y
7 Kildee	Y	Y	Y	N	Y
8 Traxler	Y	Y	N	N	#
9 ***Vander Jagt***	Y	Y	Y	Y	Y
10 ***Cederberg***	Y	Y	Y	Y	Y
11 ***Ruppe***	?	?	?	?	?
12 Bonior	Y	Y	N	N	Y
13 Diggs	#	#	N	#	#
14 Nedzi	Y	Y	Y	N	Y
15 Ford	?	?	Y	N	Y
16 Dingell	?	Y	Y	N	N
17 Brodhead	?	Y	N	Y	Y
18 Blanchard	Y	Y	Y	N	Y
19 ***Broomfield***	Y	Y	Y	N	Y
MINNESOTA					
1 ***Quie***	?	?	?	?	?
2 ***Hagedorn***	P	Y	Y	N	Y
3 ***Frenzel***	Y	Y	Y	N	Y
4 Vento	Y	Y	N	N	Y
5 Fraser	#	#	N	Y	#
6 Nolan	?	Y	?	Y	?
7 ***Stangeland***	Y	Y	Y	N	Y
8 Oberstar	Y	Y	N	Y	Y
MISSISSIPPI					
1 Whitten	Y	#	Y	N	Y
2 Bowen	Y	Y	Y	N	Y
3 Montgomery	Y	Y	Y	N	N
4 ***Cochran***	?	Y	Y	N	Y
5 ***Lott***	Y	Y	Y	N	Y
MISSOURI					
1 Clay	?	?	N	N	?
2 Young	Y	Y	Y	N	Y
3 Gephardt	Y	Y	Y	N	Y

	446	447	448	449	450
4 Skelton	#	#	Y	N	Y
5 Bolling	#	#	N	▮	Y
6 ***Coleman***	Y	Y	Y	N	Y
7 ***Taylor***	Y	Y	Y	N	N
8 Ichord	?	Y	Y	N	N
9 Volkmer	Y	Y	Y	N	Y
10 Burlison	Y	Y	N	N	Y
MONTANA					
1 Baucus	Y	Y	Y	N	Y
2 ***Marlenee***	Y	Y	Y	N	Y
NEBRASKA					
1 ***Thone***	Y	Y	Y	N	N
2 Cavanaugh	Y	Y	Y	N	Y
3 ***Smith***	?	Y	Y	N	N
NEVADA					
AL Santini	Y	Y	Y	N	#
NEW HAMPSHIRE					
1 D'Amours	Y	Y	Y	N	Y
2 ***Cleveland***	Y	Y	Y	N	N
NEW JERSEY					
1 Florio	#	#	X	✓	#
2 Hughes	Y	Y	Y	N	N
3 Howard	Y	Y	N	Y	Y
4 Thompson	Y	Y	Y	N	Y
5 ***Fenwick***	Y	Y	Y	N	N
6 ***Forsythe***	N	#	Y	N	N
7 Maguire	Y	Y	N	Y	Y
8 Roe	Y	Y	Y	N	Y
9 ***Hollenbeck***	Y	Y	Y	Y	Y
10 Rodino	#	#	▮	▮	#
11 Minish	Y	Y	N	N	Y
12 ***Rinaldo***	Y	Y	Y	N	Y
13 Meyner	#	#	✓	✓	#
14 LeFante	#	#	X	X	#
15 Patten	Y	Y	N	Y	N
NEW MEXICO					
1 ***Lujan***	Y	Y	Y	N	N
2 Runnels	#	#	✓	?	?
NEW YORK					
1 Pike	Y	Y	Y	N	Y
2 Downey	Y	Y	N	Y	Y
3 Ambro	?	?	Y	Y	Y
4 ***Lent***	Y	Y	Y	N	N
5 ***Wydler***	Y	Y	Y	N	N
6 Wolff	Y	#	Y	N	Y
7 Addabbo	Y	Y	N	Y	Y
8 Rosenthal	Y	Y	N	Y	Y
9 Delaney	Y	Y	Y	N	Y
10 Biaggi	Y	Y	N	Y	Y
11 Scheuer	Y	Y	N	Y	Y
12 Chisholm	#	Y	N	Y	Y
13 Solarz	Y	Y	N	Y	Y
14 Richmond	Y	Y	N	N	Y
15 Zeferetti	Y	Y	Y	Y	Y
16 Holtzman	Y	Y	N	N	Y
17 Murphy	Y	Y	N	?	Y
18 ***Green***	Y	Y	Y	N	Y
19 Rangel	Y	Y	N	Y	Y
20 Weiss	Y	Y	N	Y	Y
21 Garcia	#	#	X	#	Y
22 Bingham	#	#	X	✓	#
23 ***Caputo***	Y	Y	Y	N	Y
24 Ottinger	Y	Y	N	N	Y
25 ***Fish***	Y	Y	Y	N	N
26 ***Gilman***	Y	Y	Y	N	Y
27 McHugh	?	Y	N	N	Y
28 Stratton	Y	Y	N	N	N
29 Pattison	Y	Y	N	N	Y
30 ***McEwen***	?	?	Y	N	Y
31 ***Mitchell***	Y	Y	Y	N	Y
32 Hanley	Y	Y	N	N	Y
33 ***Walsh***	Y	Y	Y	N	Y
34 ***Horton***	Y	Y	Y	N	#
35 ***Conable***	Y	Y	Y	N	Y
36 LaFalce	Y	Y	N	N	Y
37 Nowak	Y	Y	Y	N	Y
38 ***Kemp***	Y	Y	Y	?	Y
39 Lundine	Y	Y	▮	N	Y
NORTH CAROLINA					
1 Jones	Y	Y	Y	N	Y
2 Fountain	Y	Y	Y	N	Y
3 Whitley	Y	Y	Y	N	Y
4 Andrews	Y	Y	Y	N	Y
5 Neal	Y	Y	Y	N	Y
6 Preyer	?	Y	Y	N	Y
7 Rose	Y	Y	N	N	Y
8 Hefner	Y	Y	Y	N	Y

	446	447	448	449	450
9 ***Martin***	Y	Y	Y	N	N
10 ***Broyhill***	#	Y	Y	N	Y
11 Gudger	#	#	#	▮	Y
NORTH DAKOTA					
AL ***Andrews***	Y	Y	Y	N	Y
OHIO					
1 ***Gradison***	Y	Y	Y	Y	N
2 Luken	Y	Y	Y	N	N
3 ***Whalen***	#	#	▮	#	#
4 ***Guyer***	Y	Y	Y	N	Y
5 ***Latta***	Y	Y	Y	N	#
6 ***Harsha***	Y	Y	Y	N	Y
7 ***Brown***	?	?	✓	?	?
8 ***Kindness***	Y	Y	Y	N	N
9 Ashley	Y	Y	N	N	N
10 ***Miller***	Y	Y	Y	N	N
11 ***Stanton***	Y	Y	Y	N	Y
12 ***Devine***	Y	Y	Y	N	Y
13 Pease	Y	Y	N	N	Y
14 Seiberling	#	Y	N	N	Y
15 ***Wylie***	Y	Y	Y	N	N
16 ***Regula***	Y	Y	Y	N	Y
17 ***Ashbrook***	Y	Y	Y	N	N
18 Applegate	Y	?	Y	N	Y
19 Carney	Y	Y	N	N	Y
20 Oakar	Y	Y	N	Y	Y
21 Stokes	Y	Y	N	Y	Y
22 Vanik	Y	Y	N	N	Y
23 Mottl	Y	Y	Y	Y	▮
OKLAHOMA					
1 Jones	Y	Y	N	N	N
2 Risenhoover	Y	Y	Y	N	Y
3 Watkins	Y	Y	Y	▮	?
4 Steed	Y	Y	N	N	Y
5 ***Edwards***	Y	Y	Y	N	N
6 English	Y	Y	Y	N	N
OREGON					
1 AuCoin	Y	Y	Y	N	N
2 Ullman	Y	Y	Y	N	Y
3 Duncan	Y	Y	Y	?	Y
4 Weaver	?	?	?	?	?
PENNSYLVANIA					
1 Myers, M.	Y	Y	N	Y	Y
2 Nix	?	?	X	?	?
3 Lederer	Y	Y	N	Y	Y
4 Eilberg	Y	Y	Y	Y	Y
5 ***Schulze***	Y	Y	Y	N	N
6 Yatron	Y	Y	Y	Y	N
7 Edgar	Y	Y	N	N	Y
8 Kostmayer	Y	Y	N	N	Y
9 ***Shuster***	Y	Y	Y	N	Y
10 ***McDade***	Y	Y	Y	N	Y
11 Flood	Y	Y	N	N	Y
12 Murtha	Y	Y	Y	N	N
13 ***Coughlin***	?	Y	Y	N	N
14 Moorhead	Y	Y	N	N	Y
15 Rooney	Y	Y	N	N	Y
16 ***Walker***	N	Y	Y	N	N
17 Ertel	Y	Y	Y	Y	Y
18 Walgren	Y	Y	N	Y	Y
19 ***Goodling, W.***	N	Y	Y	N	N
20 Gaydos	Y	Y	Y	N	N
21 Dent	?	?	?	X	?
22 Murphy	Y	Y	Y	N	Y
23 Ammerman	Y	Y	Y	N	Y
24 ***Marks***	Y	Y	Y	N	Y
25 ***Myers, G.***	Y	Y	N	Y	N
RHODE ISLAND					
1 St Germain	Y	Y	N	N	Y
2 Beard	Y	Y	N	N	Y
SOUTH CAROLINA					
1 Davis	Y	Y	Y	Y	Y
2 ***Spence***	Y	Y	Y	N	Y
3 Derrick	Y	Y	N	Y	Y
4 Mann	Y	Y	Y	N	Y
5 Holland	Y	Y	N	N	?
6 Jenrette	N	Y	N	✓	Y
SOUTH DAKOTA					
1 ***Pressler***	Y	Y	Y	N	Y
2 ***Abdnor***	Y	Y	Y	N	Y
TENNESSEE					
1 ***Quillen***	Y	Y	Y	N	Y
2 ***Duncan***	Y	Y	Y	N	Y
3 Lloyd	Y	Y	Y	N	Y
4 Gore	Y	Y	Y	N	Y
5 Vacancy					
6 ***Beard***	Y	Y	Y	N	N

	446	447	448	449	450
7 Jones	Y	Y	Y	N	Y
8 Ford	Y	Y	N	Y	Y
TEXAS					
1 Hall	Y	Y	Y	N	Y
2 Wilson, C.	#	#	Y	N	#
3 ***Collins***	N	Y	Y	N	N
4 Roberts	Y	?	Y	Y	Y
5 Mattox	N	Y	Y	N	N
6 Teague	?	?	✓	?	?
7 ***Archer***	Y	Y	Y	N	N
8 Eckhardt	?	?	X	?	?
9 Brooks	Y	Y	N	N	Y
10 Pickle	Y	Y	Y	N	Y
11 Poage	Y	?	Y	N	Y
12 Wright	Y	Y	N	?	Y
13 Hightower	Y	Y	N	Y	Y
14 Young	?	?	?	N	Y
15 de la Garza	Y	Y	Y	N	N
16 White	#	Y	Y	N	Y
17 Burleson	Y	Y	Y	Y	Y
18 Jordan	Y	Y	N	N	Y
19 Mahon	Y	Y	N	N	Y
20 Gonzalez	Y	Y	N	N	Y
21 Krueger	?	#	✓	✓	#
22 Gammage	Y	Y	Y	N	Y
23 Kazen	Y	Y	Y	N	Y
24 Milford	?	?	?	?	?
UTAH					
1 McKay	Y	Y	Y	N	Y
2 ***Marriott***	Y	Y	Y	N	Y
VERMONT					
AL ***Jeffords***	Y	Y	Y	Y	Y
VIRGINIA					
1 ***Trible***	Y	Y	Y	N	N
2 ***Whitehurst***	Y	Y	Y	N	N
3 Satterfield	Y	Y	Y	N	N
4 ***Daniel***	Y	Y	Y	N	N
5 Daniel	Y	Y	Y	N	N
6 ***Butler***	?	?	✓	?	?
7 ***Robinson***	Y	Y	Y	N	N
8 Harris	Y	Y	Y	Y	Y
9 ***Wampler***	Y	Y	Y	N	Y
10 Fisher	Y	Y	N	N	Y
WASHINGTON					
1 ***Pritchard***	Y	Y	Y	N	Y
2 Meeds	Y	Y	N	Y	Y
3 Bonker	Y	Y	N	N	Y
4 McCormack	Y	Y	N	N	Y
5 Foley	Y	Y	N	N	N
6 Dicks	Y	Y	?	N	Y
7 ***Cunningham***	Y	Y	Y	N	N
WEST VIRGINIA					
1 Mollohan	Y	Y	Y	N	Y
2 Staggers	Y	Y	N	N	Y
3 Slack	Y	?	Y	N	Y
4 Rahall	Y	Y	Y	N	Y
WISCONSIN					
1 Aspin	Y	Y	N	N	Y
2 Kastenmeier	Y	Y	N	Y	Y
3 Baldus	Y	Y	N	N	Y
4 Zablocki	Y	Y	N	N	Y
5 Reuss	#	#	N	N	Y
6 ***Steiger***	▮	#	✓	▮	#
7 Obey	Y	Y	N	N	Y
8 Cornell	Y	Y	N	N	Y
9 ***Kasten***	Y	Y	Y	N	Y
WYOMING					
AL Roncalio	Y	Y	N	N	Y

Democrats ***Republicans***

451. H J Res 13. National Grandparents Day. Lehman, D-Fla., motion to suspend the rules and pass the joint resolution to request the president to designate the first Sunday in September after Labor Day in 1978 as National Grandparents Day. Motion agreed to 362-8: R 130-1; D 232-7 (ND 165-7; SD 67-0), July 10, 1978. A two-thirds majority vote (247 in this case) is required for passage under suspension of the rules.

452. H J Res 1007. Asian/Pacific American Heritage Week. Lehman, D-Fla., motion to suspend the rules and pass the joint resolution to request the president to designate a week in the first 10 days of May 1979 to be designated Asian/Pacific American Heritage Week to commemorate the contributions and accomplishments of the two million Americans of Asian and Pacific descent. Motion agreed to 360-6: R 129-1; D 231-5 (ND 164-5; SD 67-0), July 10, 1978. A two-thirds majority vote (244 in this case) is required for passage under suspension of the rules.

453. H J Res 773. National Port Week. Lehman, D-Fla., motion to suspend the rules and pass the joint resolution to request the president to designate the week of Sept. 17, 1978, as National Port Week to recognize the economic and national security importance of the nation's ports. Motion agreed to 363-11: R 129-3; D 234-8 (ND 167-7; SD 67-1), July 10, 1978. A two-thirds majority vote (250 in this case) is required for passage under suspension of the rules.

454. HR 13087. Substitute Treasury Checks. Mitchell, D-Md., motion to suspend the rules and pass the bill to authorize the Treasury secretary, at his discretion, to issue substitute checks for stolen or lost Social Security checks without indemnification by the recipient. Motion agreed to 375-0: R 132-0; D 243-0 (ND 175-0; SD 68-0), July 10, 1978. A two-thirds majority vote (250 in this case) is required for passage under suspension of the rules.

455. HR 12106. Transportation Safety Board. Anderson, D-Calif., motion to suspend the rules and pass the bill to extend the National Transportation Safety Board for one year with an authorization of $16.4 million for the board's operations in fiscal 1979. Motion agreed to 340-32: R 120-11; D 220-21 (ND 165-9; SD 55-12), July 10, 1978. A two-thirds majority vote (248 in this case) is required for passage under suspension of the rules.

456. HR 12536. National Parks Additions. Thompson, D-N.J., amendments, en bloc, to delete a provision in the bill to authorize the Interior Department secretary to acquire all lands within the present boundary of the Delaware Water Gap National Recreation Area in Pennsylvania and New York for the wild and scenic rivers system and for recreational purposes (thus giving the Interior Department priority over U.S. Corps of Engineers projects). Rejected 110-275: R 25-110; D 85-165 (ND 52-127; SD 33-38), July 10, 1978.

457. H J Res 1024. Agriculture Supplemental Appropriations, Fiscal 1978. Passage of the joint resolution to appropriate $57,145,000 for staff salaries for the Agricultural Stabilization and Conservation Service (ASCS) and to increase transfer authority from the Commodity Credit Corporation fund to ASCS by $23,391,000, for fiscal 1978. Passed 340-48: R 110-26; D 230-22 (ND 160-19; SD 70-3), July 11, 1978.

458. HR 11827. Strip Mining. Roncalio, D-Wyo., motion to suspend the rules and pass the bill to amend the 1977 Surface Mining Control and Reclamation Act (PL 95-87) to authorize an additional $25 million each in fiscal 1979-80 for Interior Department inspections of mines and assistance to small operators. Motion agreed to 323-74: R 91-44; D 232-30 (ND 174-10; SD 58-20), July 11, 1978. A two-thirds majority vote (265 in this case) is required for passage under suspension of the rules.

KEY

- Y Voted for (yea).
- ✓ Paired for.
- † Announced for.
- # CQ Poll for.
- N Voted against (nay).
- X Paired against.
- - Announced against.
- ▮ CQ Poll against.
- P Voted "present."
- ● Voted "present" to avoid possible conflict of interest.
- ? Did not vote or otherwise make a position known.

	451	452	453	454	455	456	457	458
ALABAMA								
1 Edwards	Y	Y	Y	Y	Y	N	Y	Y
2 Dickinson	Y	Y	Y	Y	Y	Y	Y	Y
3 Nichols	Y	Y	Y	Y	Y	Y	Y	Y
4 Bevill	Y	Y	Y	Y	Y	Y	Y	Y
5 Flippo	Y	Y	Y	Y	N	Y	Y	Y
6 Buchanan	Y	Y	Y	Y	Y	N	Y	Y
7 Flowers	?	?	?	?	?	?	Y	Y
ALASKA								
AL Young	Y	Y	N	Y	Y	Y	Y	Y
ARIZONA								
1 Rhodes	Y	Y	Y	Y	Y	Y	Y	Y
2 Udall	Y	Y	Y	Y	Y	Y	#	Y
3 Stump	Y	Y	Y	Y	N	Y	Y	N
4 Rudd	Y	Y	Y	Y	N	Y	Y	N
ARKANSAS								
1 Alexander	Y	Y	Y	Y	Y	Y	Y	Y
2 Tucker	Y	Y	Y	Y	Y	N	Y	Y
3 Hammerschmidt	Y	Y	Y	Y	N	N	Y	N
4 Thornton	?	Y	Y	Y	Y	N	?	Y
CALIFORNIA								
1 Johnson	Y	Y	Y	Y	Y	Y	Y	Y
2 Clausen	Y	Y	Y	Y	Y	Y	Y	Y
3 Moss	Y	P	P	Y	Y	Y	Y	Y
4 Leggett	#	#	#	#	#	▮	#	#
5 Burton, J.	Y	Y	Y	Y	Y	N	Y	Y
6 Burton, P.	Y	Y	Y	Y	Y	N	Y	Y
7 Miller	Y	Y	Y	Y	Y	N	?	Y
8 Dellums	Y	Y	Y	Y	Y	N	Y	Y
9 Stark	Y	Y	Y	Y	Y	N	Y	Y
10 Edwards	Y	Y	Y	Y	Y	N	Y	Y
11 Ryan	Y	Y	Y	Y	Y	N	Y	Y
12 McCloskey	Y	Y	Y	Y	Y	N	Y	Y
13 Mineta	Y	Y	Y	Y	Y	N	Y	Y
14 McFall	Y	?	Y	Y	Y	Y	Y	Y
15 Sisk	Y	Y	Y	Y	Y	Y	Y	Y
16 Panetta	Y	Y	Y	Y	Y	N	Y	Y
17 Krebs	Y	Y	Y	Y	Y	N	Y	Y
18 Vacancy								
19 Lagomarsino	Y	Y	Y	Y	Y	N	Y	Y
20 Goldwater	Y	Y	Y	Y	Y	N	Y	Y
21 Corman	Y	Y	Y	Y	Y	N	Y	Y
22 Moorhead	Y	Y	Y	Y	Y	N	N	N
23 Beilenson	N	Y	N	Y	Y	N	Y	Y
24 Waxman	Y	Y	Y	Y	Y	N	Y	Y
25 Roybal	Y	?	Y	Y	Y	N	Y	Y
26 Rousselot	Y	Y	Y	Y	N	N	N	Y
27 Dornan	Y	Y	Y	Y	Y	N	Y	#
28 Burke	Y	Y	Y	Y	Y	N	Y	Y
29 Hawkins	Y	Y	Y	Y	Y	Y	Y	Y
30 Danielson	Y	Y	Y	Y	Y	N	Y	Y
31 Wilson, C.H.	Y	Y	Y	Y	Y	Y	Y	#
32 Anderson	Y	Y	Y	Y	Y	Y	N	Y
33 Clawson	Y	Y	Y	Y	Y	N	N	N
34 Hannaford	Y	Y	Y	Y	Y	N	Y	Y
35 Lloyd	Y	Y	Y	Y	Y	N	Y	Y
36 Brown	Y	Y	Y	Y	Y	N	Y	Y
37 Pettis	?	?	?	?	?	?	Y	Y
38 Patterson	Y	Y	Y	Y	Y	N	Y	Y
39 Wiggins	Y	Y	Y	Y	Y	N	N	Y
40 Badham	Y	Y	Y	Y	Y	Y	Y	N
41 Wilson, B.	Y	Y	Y	Y	Y	N	Y	N
42 Van Deerlin	Y	Y	Y	Y	Y	Y	Y	Y
43 Burgener	Y	Y	Y	Y	Y	Y	Y	Y
COLORADO								
1 Schroeder	N	N	N	Y	Y	N	N	Y
2 Wirth	#	#	#	#	#	✓	Y	Y
3 Evans	N	N	N	Y	Y	Y	Y	Y
4 Johnson	?	?	?	?	?	?	?	?
5 Armstrong	?	?	?	?	?	?	?	Y
CONNECTICUT								
1 Cotter	Y	Y	Y	Y	Y	Y	Y	Y
2 Dodd	Y	Y	Y	Y	Y	N	?	Y
3 Giaimo	Y	Y	Y	Y	Y	N	Y	Y
4 McKinney	Y	Y	Y	Y	Y	N	Y	Y
5 Sarasin	†	†	†	†	†	-	N	Y
6 Moffett	Y	Y	Y	Y	?	N	N	Y
DELAWARE								
AL Evans	Y	Y	Y	Y	Y	N	Y	Y
FLORIDA								
1 Sikes	Y	Y	Y	Y	Y	N	Y	Y
2 Fuqua	#	#	#	#	#	▮	Y	Y
3 Bennett	Y	Y	Y	Y	Y	N	Y	Y
4 Chappell	?	?	?	?	?	X	?	?
5 Kelly	Y	Y	Y	Y	N	N	N	N
6 Young	Y	Y	Y	Y	Y	N	N	Y
7 Gibbons	Y	Y	Y	Y	Y	N	N	N
8 Ireland	Y	Y	Y	Y	Y	N	Y	Y
9 Frey	?	?	?	?	?	?	?	?
10 Bafalis	Y	Y	Y	Y	Y	N	Y	●
11 Rogers	Y	Y	Y	Y	Y	Y	Y	?
12 Burke	?	?	?	?	?	?	?	?
13 Lehman	Y	Y	Y	Y	Y	N	Y	Y
14 Pepper	Y	Y	Y	Y	Y	N	Y	Y
15 Fascell	Y	Y	Y	Y	Y	N	#	Y
GEORGIA								
1 Ginn	Y	Y	Y	Y	Y	N	Y	Y
2 Mathis	Y	Y	Y	Y	Y	Y	?	?
3 Brinkley	Y	Y	Y	Y	Y	N	Y	N
4 Levitas	Y	Y	Y	Y	Y	N	Y	Y
5 Fowler	Y	Y	Y	Y	Y	N	Y	Y
6 Flynt	Y	Y	Y	Y	Y	Y	Y	N
7 McDonald	Y	Y	Y	Y	N	Y	N	N
8 Evans	#	#	#	#	#	▮	#	#
9 Jenkins	Y	Y	Y	Y	Y	N	Y	N
10 Barnard	?	?	?	?	?	?	Y	N
HAWAII								
1 Heftel	Y	Y	Y	Y	N	N	Y	Y
2 Akaka	Y	Y	Y	Y	Y	N	Y	Y
IDAHO								
1 Symms	?	?	?	?	?	N	N	N
2 Hansen, G.	Y	Y	Y	Y	N	N	N	N
ILLINOIS								
1 Metcalfe	Y	Y	Y	Y	Y	N	Y	Y
2 Murphy	Y	Y	Y	Y	Y	N	N	Y
3 Russo	Y	Y	Y	Y	Y	N	N	N
4 Derwinski	Y	Y	Y	Y	Y	N	N	Y
5 Fary	Y	Y	Y	Y	Y	Y	Y	Y
6 Hyde	Y	Y	Y	Y	Y	N	Y	Y
7 Collins	Y	Y	Y	Y	Y	N	Y	Y
8 Rostenkowski	Y	Y	Y	Y	Y	Y	Y	Y
9 Yates	Y	Y	Y	Y	Y	N	N	Y
10 Mikva	Y	Y	Y	Y	Y	N	N	Y
11 Annunzio	Y	Y	Y	Y	Y	Y	Y	Y
12 Crane	Y	Y	Y	Y	N	N	N	N
13 McClory	Y	Y	Y	Y	Y	N	Y	Y
14 Erlenborn	Y	Y	Y	Y	Y	N	Y	Y
15 Corcoran	Y	Y	Y	Y	Y	N	Y	Y
16 Anderson	#	#	#	#	#	▮	#	#
17 O'Brien	Y	Y	Y	Y	Y	N	Y	Y
18 Michel	Y	Y	Y	Y	Y	N	Y	Y
19 Railsback	Y	Y	Y	Y	Y	N	Y	Y
20 Findley	Y	Y	Y	Y	Y	N	Y	Y
21 Madigan	Y	Y	Y	Y	Y	Y	Y	Y
22 Shipley	Y	?	Y	Y	Y	Y	Y	Y
23 Price	Y	Y	Y	Y	Y	Y	Y	Y
24 Simon	Y	Y	Y	Y	Y	N	Y	Y
INDIANA								
1 Benjamin	Y	Y	Y	Y	Y	N	Y	Y
2 Fithian	Y	Y	Y	Y	Y	N	Y	Y
3 Brademas	Y	Y	Y	Y	Y	Y	Y	Y
4 Quayle	Y	Y	Y	Y	Y	N	N	Y
5 Hillis	Y	Y	Y	Y	Y	N	Y	Y
6 Evans	Y	?	Y	Y	N	Y	Y	N
7 Myers, J.	Y	Y	Y	Y	Y	Y	Y	Y
8 Cornwell	Y	Y	Y	Y	Y	N	Y	Y
9 Hamilton	Y	Y	Y	Y	Y	N	Y	Y
10 Sharp	Y	Y	Y	Y	Y	N	Y	Y
11 Jacobs	Y	Y	Y	Y	Y	N	Y	N
IOWA								
1 Leach	Y	Y	Y	Y	Y	N	Y	Y
2 Blouin	Y	Y	Y	Y	Y	N	Y	Y
3 Grassley	Y	Y	Y	Y	Y	N	Y	N
4 Smith	Y	Y	Y	Y	Y	N	Y	Y
5 Harkin	Y	Y	Y	Y	Y	N	Y	Y
6 Bedell	Y	Y	Y	Y	Y	N	Y	Y

Democrats ***Republicans***

Corresponding to Congressional Record Votes 519, 520, 521, 522, 523, 524, 525, 526

	451	452	453	454	455	456	457	458
KANSAS								
1 Sebelius	Y	Y	Y	Y	Y	N	Y	N
2 Keys	Y	Y	Y	Y	Y	N	Y	Y
3 Winn	#	#	#	#	#	▮	#	#
4 Glickman	Y	Y	Y	Y	Y	N	Y	Y
5 Skubitz	Y	Y	Y	Y	Y	N	Y	Y
KENTUCKY								
1 Hubbard	Y	Y	Y	Y	Y	Y	Y	Y
2 Natcher	Y	Y	Y	Y	Y	Y	Y	Y
3 Mazzoli	Y	Y	Y	Y	Y	N	Y	Y
4 Snyder	Y	Y	Y	Y	Y	Y	Y	N
5 Carter	Y	Y	Y	Y	Y	Y	Y	Y
6 Breckinridge	Y	Y	Y	Y	Y	Y	Y	Y
7 Perkins	Y	Y	Y	Y	Y	Y	Y	Y
LOUISIANA								
1 Livingston	Y	?	Y	Y	Y	Y	Y	N
2 Boggs	?	?	?	?	?	?	?	?
3 Treen	Y	Y	Y	Y	Y	N	Y	N
4 Waggonner	Y	Y	Y	Y	N	Y	Y	N
5 Huckaby	?	?	?	?	?	?	?	?
6 Moore	Y	Y	Y	Y	Y	N	Y	N
7 Breaux	Y	Y	Y	Y	Y	Y	Y	Y
8 Long	Y	Y	Y	Y	Y	Y	Y	Y
MAINE								
1 Emery	Y	Y	Y	Y	Y	N	Y	Y
2 Cohen	Y	Y	Y	Y	Y	N	Y	Y
MARYLAND								
1 Bauman	Y	Y	Y	Y	Y	N	Y	N
2 Long	Y	Y	Y	Y	Y	N	Y	Y
3 Mikulski	Y	Y	Y	Y	Y	N	Y	Y
4 Holt	Y	Y	Y	Y	Y	N	Y	N
5 Spellman	Y	Y	Y	Y	Y	N	Y	Y
6 Byron	?	?	?	?	?	N	Y	Y
7 Mitchell	Y	Y	Y	Y	Y	▮	Y	Y
8 Steers	Y	#	Y	Y	Y	N	Y	Y
MASSACHUSETTS								
1 Conte	Y	Y	Y	Y	Y	N	Y	Y
2 Boland	Y	Y	Y	Y	Y	N	Y	Y
3 Early	Y	Y	Y	Y	Y	N	Y	Y
4 Drinan	Y	Y	Y	Y	Y	N	Y	Y
5 Tsongas	?	?	?	?	?	?	Y	Y
6 Harrington	?	?	?	#	#	▮	#	Y
7 Markey	Y	Y	Y	Y	Y	N	Y	Y
8 O'Neill								
9 Moakley	Y	Y	Y	Y	Y	N	Y	Y
10 Heckler	Y	Y	Y	Y	Y	N	Y	Y
11 Burke	Y	Y	Y	Y	Y	Y	Y	Y
12 Studds	Y	Y	Y	Y	Y	N	Y	Y
MICHIGAN								
1 Conyers	#	#	#	#	#	▮	N	Y
2 Pursell	Y	Y	Y	Y	Y	N	Y	Y
3 Brown	Y	Y	Y	Y	Y	N	Y	Y
4 Stockman	Y	Y	Y	Y	Y	N	Y	N
5 Sawyer	Y	Y	Y	Y	Y	N	Y	Y
6 Carr	Y	Y	Y	Y	Y	N	Y	Y
7 Kildee	Y	Y	Y	Y	Y	N	Y	Y
8 Traxler	Y	Y	Y	Y	Y	N	Y	Y
9 Vander Jagt	Y	Y	Y	Y	Y	N	Y	Y
10 Cederberg	Y	Y	Y	Y	Y	Y	Y	Y
11 Ruppe	Y	Y	Y	Y	Y	N	Y	Y
12 Bonior	Y	Y	Y	Y	Y	N	Y	Y
13 Diggs	Y	Y	Y	Y	Y	Y	Y	Y
14 Nedzi	Y	Y	Y	Y	Y	Y	Y	Y
15 Ford	Y	Y	Y	Y	Y	Y	?	?
16 Dingell	N	N	Y	Y	Y	Y	Y	Y
17 Brodhead	Y	Y	Y	Y	Y	N	N	Y
18 Blanchard	Y	Y	Y	Y	Y	N	Y	Y
19 Broomfield	Y	Y	Y	Y	Y	N	N	Y
MINNESOTA								
1 Quie	Y	Y	Y	Y	Y	N	Y	Y
2 Hagedorn	Y	Y	Y	Y	Y	N	Y	N
3 Frenzel	Y	Y	Y	Y	Y	Y	N	Y
4 Vento	Y	Y	Y	Y	Y	N	Y	Y
5 Fraser	Y	Y	Y	Y	Y	N	Y	Y
6 Nolan	Y	Y	Y	Y	Y	N	?	Y
7 Stangeland	Y	Y	Y	Y	Y	Y	Y	N
8 Oberstar	Y	Y	Y	Y	Y	Y	Y	Y
MISSISSIPPI								
1 Whitten	Y	#	Y	Y	Y	Y	Y	N
2 Bowen	?	?	?	?	?	Y	Y	N
3 Montgomery	Y	Y	Y	Y	N	N	Y	N
4 Cochran	Y	Y	Y	Y	Y	N	Y	N
5 Lott	Y	Y	Y	Y	Y	N	Y	N
MISSOURI								
1 Clay	Y	Y	Y	Y	Y	Y	Y	Y
2 Young	Y	Y	Y	Y	Y	Y	Y	N
3 Gephardt	Y	Y	Y	Y	Y	N	N	N

	451	452	453	454	455	456	457	458
4 Skelton	Y	Y	Y	Y	N	N	Y	Y
5 Bolling	Y	Y	Y	Y	Y	Y	Y	Y
6 Coleman	Y	Y	Y	Y	Y	N	Y	Y
7 Taylor	Y	Y	Y	Y	N	Y	Y	N
8 Ichord	?	?	?	?	?	?	Y	N
9 Volkmer	Y	Y	Y	Y	N	N	Y	N
10 Burlison	Y	Y	Y	Y	Y	Y	Y	Y
MONTANA								
1 Baucus	Y	Y	Y	Y	Y	N	Y	Y
2 Marlenee	Y	Y	Y	Y	N	N	Y	Y
NEBRASKA								
1 Thone	Y	Y	Y	Y	Y	N	Y	Y
2 Cavanaugh	Y	Y	Y	Y	Y	N	Y	Y
3 Smith	Y	Y	Y	Y	Y	N	Y	Y
NEVADA								
AL Santini	#	#	#	Y	Y	▮	Y	Y
NEW HAMPSHIRE								
1 D'Amours	Y	Y	Y	Y	Y	N	Y	Y
2 Cleveland	Y	Y	Y	Y	Y	N	Y	N
NEW JERSEY								
1 Florio	#	Y	Y	Y	Y	N	Y	Y
2 Hughes	Y	Y	Y	Y	Y	N	N	Y
3 Howard	Y	Y	Y	Y	Y	Y	Y	Y
4 Thompson	Y	Y	Y	#	Y	Y	Y	Y
5 Fenwick	Y	Y	Y	Y	Y	N	N	Y
6 Forsythe	Y	Y	Y	Y	Y	Y	N	Y
7 Maguire	Y	Y	Y	Y	Y	N	Y	Y
8 Roe	Y	Y	Y	Y	Y	N	Y	Y
9 Hollenbeck	Y	Y	Y	Y	Y	N	N	Y
10 Rodino	Y	Y	Y	Y	Y	▮	#	#
11 Minish	Y	Y	Y	Y	Y	N	N	Y
12 Rinaldo	Y	Y	Y	Y	Y	N	N	Y
13 Meyner	Y	Y	Y	Y	Y	N	Y	Y
14 LeFante	#	#	#	#	#	▮	#	#
15 Patten	Y	Y	Y	Y	Y	Y	Y	Y
NEW MEXICO								
1 Lujan	Y	Y	Y	Y	Y	Y	Y	Y
2 Runnels	Y	Y	Y	Y	N	Y	Y	N
NEW YORK								
1 Pike	?	?	?	?	?	?	?	?
2 Downey	Y	Y	Y	Y	Y	N	Y	Y
3 Ambro	Y	Y	Y	Y	Y	N	Y	Y
4 Lent	Y	Y	Y	Y	Y	N	N	Y
5 Wydler	Y	Y	Y	Y	Y	N	N	Y
6 Wolff	#	#	#	#	#	X	▮	#
7 Addabbo	Y	Y	Y	Y	Y	Y	Y	Y
8 Rosenthal	Y	Y	Y	Y	Y	N	Y	Y
9 Delaney	?	?	?	?	?	?	Y	Y
10 Biaggi	Y	Y	Y	Y	Y	N	Y	Y
11 Scheuer	Y	Y	Y	Y	Y	N	Y	Y
12 Chisholm	Y	Y	Y	Y	Y	N	Y	Y
13 Solarz	#	#	#	#	#	N	Y	Y
14 Richmond	?	Y	Y	Y	Y	N	Y	Y
15 Zeferetti	#	Y	Y	Y	Y	N	Y	Y
16 Holtzman	Y	Y	Y	Y	Y	N	Y	Y
17 Murphy	?	?	?	?	?	?	?	Y
18 Green	Y	Y	Y	Y	Y	N	N	Y
19 Rangel	?	?	?	?	?	?	?	?
20 Weiss	Y	Y	Y	Y	Y	N	Y	Y
21 Garcia	Y	Y	Y	Y	Y	N	Y	Y
22 Bingham	#	#	#	#	#	N	Y	Y
23 Caputo	Y	Y	Y	Y	Y	N	Y	Y
24 Ottinger	N	Y	N	Y	Y	N	Y	Y
25 Fish	Y	Y	Y	Y	Y	N	Y	Y
26 Gilman	?	Y	Y	Y	Y	N	Y	Y
27 McHugh	Y	Y	Y	Y	Y	N	?	?
28 Stratton	Y	Y	Y	Y	Y	N	N	Y
29 Pattison	Y	Y	Y	Y	#	N	Y	Y
30 McEwen	Y	Y	Y	Y	Y	N	Y	Y
31 Mitchell	Y	Y	Y	Y	Y	N	Y	Y
32 Hanley	Y	Y	Y	Y	Y	N	Y	Y
33 Walsh	Y	Y	Y	Y	Y	N	Y	Y
34 Horton	Y	Y	Y	Y	Y	N	Y	Y
35 Conable	Y	Y	N	Y	Y	N	N	Y
36 LaFalce	Y	Y	Y	Y	Y	N	Y	Y
37 Nowak	#	#	#	#	#	▮	Y	Y
38 Kemp	Y	Y	Y	Y	Y	N	Y	?
39 Lundine	Y	Y	Y	Y	Y	N	Y	Y
NORTH CAROLINA								
1 Jones	Y	Y	Y	Y	Y	N	Y	Y
2 Fountain	#	#	#	#	#	▮	#	#
3 Whitley	Y	Y	Y	Y	N	N	Y	Y
4 Andrews	?	?	?	?	?	?	?	?
5 Neal	Y	Y	Y	Y	Y	N	Y	Y
6 Preyer	Y	Y	Y	Y	Y	N	Y	Y
7 Rose	?	?	?	?	?	Y	Y	Y
8 Hefner	Y	Y	Y	Y	Y	N	Y	Y

	451	452	453	454	455	456	457	458
9 Martin	Y	Y	Y	Y	Y	N	Y	Y
10 Broyhill	Y	Y	Y	Y	Y	N	Y	Y
11 Gudger	Y	Y	Y	Y	Y	N	Y	Y
NORTH DAKOTA								
AL Andrews	Y	Y	Y	Y	Y	N	Y	Y
OHIO								
1 Gradison	Y	Y	Y	Y	Y	N	N	Y
2 Luken	?	?	?	?	?	?	N	Y
3 Whalen	Y	Y	Y	Y	Y	N	Y	Y
4 Guyer	?	?	?	?	?	?	?	?
5 Latta	Y	Y	Y	Y	N	N	Y	N
6 Harsha	Y	Y	Y	Y	Y	Y	Y	N
7 Brown	Y	Y	Y	Y	?	N	Y	N
8 Kindness	Y	Y	Y	Y	Y	N	Y	N
9 Ashley	N	Y	Y	Y	Y	N	Y	Y
10 Miller	Y	Y	Y	Y	Y	N	Y	N
11 Stanton	Y	Y	Y	Y	Y	N	Y	Y
12 Devine	Y	Y	Y	Y	N	N	Y	N
13 Pease	Y	Y	Y	Y	Y	N	Y	Y
14 Seiberling	Y	N	N	Y	Y	N	N	Y
15 Wylie	Y	Y	Y	Y	Y	N	Y	Y
16 Regula	Y	Y	Y	Y	Y	N	Y	Y
17 Ashbrook	Y	Y	Y	Y	Y	Y	Y	N
18 Applegate	Y	Y	Y	Y	Y	N	Y	Y
19 Carney	Y	#	Y	Y	Y	Y	Y	Y
20 Oakar	Y	Y	Y	Y	Y	N	Y	Y
21 Stokes	Y	Y	Y	Y	Y	Y	Y	Y
22 Vanik	Y	Y	Y	Y	Y	N	Y	Y
23 Mottl	Y	Y	Y	Y	N	N	N	N
OKLAHOMA								
1 Jones	#	#	#	#	#	Y	Y	N
2 Risenhoover	Y	Y	Y	Y	N	?	?	Y
3 Watkins	?	?	?	#	#	?	Y	N
4 Steed	#	#	#	#	#	▮	Y	Y
5 Edwards	?	?	?	#	?	N	Y	N
6 English	#	#	#	?	#	▮	Y	N
OREGON								
1 AuCoin	Y	Y	Y	Y	Y	N	N	Y
2 Ullman	Y	Y	Y	Y	Y	Y	Y	Y
3 Duncan	?	?	?	?	?	?	?	?
4 Weaver	Y	Y	Y	Y	Y	N	N	Y
PENNSYLVANIA								
1 Myers, M.	Y	Y	Y	Y	Y	Y	Y	Y
2 Nix	?	?	?	?	?	Y	Y	?
3 Lederer	Y	Y	Y	Y	Y	Y	Y	Y
4 Eilberg	Y	Y	Y	Y	Y	Y	Y	Y
5 Schulze	Y	Y	Y	Y	Y	N	Y	N
6 Yatron	Y	Y	Y	Y	Y	N	Y	Y
7 Edgar	Y	Y	Y	Y	Y	N	Y	Y
8 Kostmayer	Y	Y	Y	Y	Y	N	N	Y
9 Shuster	Y	Y	Y	Y	Y	N	Y	N
10 McDade	Y	Y	Y	Y	Y	N	Y	Y
11 Flood	Y	Y	Y	Y	Y	N	Y	Y
12 Murtha	Y	Y	Y	Y	Y	Y	Y	Y
13 Coughlin	Y	Y	Y	Y	Y	N	Y	Y
14 Moorhead	Y	Y	Y	Y	Y	Y	Y	Y
15 Rooney	Y	Y	Y	Y	Y	N	Y	Y
16 Walker	Y	Y	Y	Y	Y	N	Y	Y
17 Ertel	Y	Y	Y	Y	Y	N	Y	Y
18 Walgren	Y	Y	Y	Y	N	N	Y	Y
19 Goodling, W.	Y	Y	Y	Y	Y	N	?	?
20 Gaydos	Y	Y	Y	Y	Y	Y	Y	Y
21 Dent	?	?	?	?	?	?	Y	Y
22 Murphy	Y	Y	Y	Y	Y	Y	Y	Y
23 Ammerman	Y	Y	N	Y	N	N	Y	Y
24 Marks	Y	Y	Y	Y	Y	Y	†	Y
25 Myers, G.	N	N	N	Y	Y	N	N	Y
RHODE ISLAND								
1 St Germain	Y	Y	Y	Y	Y	Y	Y	Y
2 Beard	Y	Y	Y	Y	Y	Y	Y	Y
SOUTH CAROLINA								
1 Davis	Y	Y	Y	Y	Y	Y	Y	Y
2 Spence	Y	Y	Y	Y	Y	Y	Y	Y
3 Derrick	Y	Y	Y	Y	Y	N	Y	Y
4 Mann	?	?	?	?	?	?	?	?
5 Holland	Y	Y	Y	Y	Y	Y	Y	Y
6 Jenrette	Y	Y	Y	Y	Y	Y	Y	N
SOUTH DAKOTA								
1 Pressler	Y	Y	Y	Y	Y	N	Y	Y
2 Abdnor	Y	Y	Y	Y	Y	N	Y	Y
TENNESSEE								
1 Quillen	Y	Y	Y	Y	Y	N	Y	N
2 Duncan	Y	Y	Y	Y	Y	Y	Y	Y
3 Lloyd	Y	Y	Y	Y	Y	N	Y	Y
4 Gore	Y	Y	Y	Y	Y	N	Y	Y
5 Vacancy								
6 Beard	Y	Y	Y	Y	Y	N	Y	N

	451	452	453	454	455	456	457	458
7 Jones	Y	Y	Y	Y	Y	Y	Y	Y
8 Ford	Y	Y	Y	Y	Y	Y	Y	Y
TEXAS								
1 Hall	Y	Y	Y	Y	N	Y	Y	N
2 Wilson, C.	#	#	#	#	#	N	#	Y
3 Collins	Y	Y	Y	Y	N	N	N	N
4 Roberts	?	?	?	?	?	✓	?	?
5 Mattox	Y	Y	Y	Y	N	N	Y	Y
6 Teague	?	?	?	?	?	?	?	?
7 Archer	Y	Y	Y	Y	Y	N	N	N
8 Eckhardt	Y	Y	Y	Y	Y	N	Y	Y
9 Brooks	Y	Y	Y	Y	Y	Y	Y	Y
10 Pickle	Y	Y	Y	Y	Y	N	Y	Y
11 Poage	Y	Y	N	Y	N	Y	Y	Y
12 Wright	Y	Y	Y	Y	Y	Y	Y	Y
13 Hightower	Y	Y	Y	Y	N	N	Y	Y
14 Young	Y	Y	Y	Y	Y	Y	Y	Y
15 de la Garza	?	?	?	?	?	?	?	?
16 White	Y	Y	Y	Y	Y	N	Y	Y
17 Burleson	Y	Y	Y	Y	N	Y	Y	N
18 Jordan	Y	Y	Y	Y	Y	Y	Y	Y
19 Mahon	Y	Y	Y	Y	Y	N	Y	Y
20 Gonzalez	Y	Y	Y	Y	Y	Y	Y	Y
21 Krueger	Y	Y	Y	Y	Y	N	Y	Y
22 Gammage	Y	Y	Y	Y	N	N	Y	N
23 Kazen	Y	Y	Y	Y	?	N	Y	Y
24 Milford	?	?	?	?	?	?	?	N
UTAH								
1 McKay	#	#	▮	#	#	Y	Y	Y
2 Marriott	Y	Y	Y	Y	Y	N	Y	Y
VERMONT								
AL Jeffords	#	#	#	#	#	N	Y	Y
VIRGINIA								
1 Trible	Y	Y	Y	Y	Y	N	Y	N
2 Whitehurst	Y	Y	Y	Y	Y	N	Y	Y
3 Satterfield	Y	Y	Y	Y	Y	Y	Y	N
4 Daniel	Y	Y	Y	Y	Y	N	Y	N
5 Daniel	Y	Y	Y	Y	Y	N	Y	N
6 Butler	Y	Y	Y	Y	Y	Y	Y	N
7 Robinson	Y	Y	Y	Y	Y	N	Y	N
8 Harris	Y	Y	Y	Y	Y	N	N	Y
9 Wampler	Y	Y	Y	Y	Y	Y	Y	N
10 Fisher	Y	Y	Y	Y	Y	N	Y	Y
WASHINGTON								
1 Pritchard	#	#	#	#	#	▮	Y	Y
2 Meeds	Y	Y	Y	Y	Y	N	Y	Y
3 Bonker	Y	Y	Y	Y	Y	N	Y	Y
4 McCormack	Y	Y	Y	Y	Y	N	#	Y
5 Foley	Y	Y	Y	Y	Y	N	Y	Y
6 Dicks	Y	Y	Y	Y	Y	N	Y	Y
7 Cunningham	Y	Y	Y	Y	Y	N	Y	Y
WEST VIRGINIA								
1 Mollohan	Y	Y	Y	Y	Y	N	Y	Y
2 Staggers	Y	Y	Y	Y	Y	N	Y	Y
3 Slack	Y	Y	Y	Y	Y	Y	?	?
4 Rahall	Y	Y	Y	Y	Y	N	Y	Y
WISCONSIN								
1 Aspin	Y	Y	Y	Y	Y	N	Y	Y
2 Kastenmeier	Y	Y	Y	Y	Y	N	Y	Y
3 Baldus	Y	Y	Y	Y	Y	N	#	Y
4 Zablocki	Y	Y	Y	Y	Y	Y	Y	Y
5 Reuss	Y	Y	Y	Y	Y	Y	Y	#
6 Steiger	Y	Y	Y	Y	Y	N	Y	Y
7 Obey	N	N	N	Y	Y	N	Y	Y
8 Cornell	Y	Y	Y	Y	Y	N	Y	Y
9 Kasten	#	#	#	#	#	▮	#	#
WYOMING								
AL Roncalio	Y	Y	Y	Y	Y	N	Y	Y

Democrats ***Republicans***

459. HR 12536. National Parks Additions. Baucus, D-Mont., amendment to delete a provision in the bill to designate 927,550 acres in Glacier National Park in Montana as wilderness. Adopted 216-181: R 62-74; D 154-107 (ND 92-91; SD 62-16), July 11, 1978.

460. HR 12536. National Parks Additions. Symms, R-Idaho, amendment to provide for the exclusion of 4,400 acres of the Blue Jacket Mine area in Idaho from the Hells Canyon Recreation Area. Rejected 147-249: R 95-41; D 52-208 (ND 16-166; SD 36-42), July 11, 1978.

461. HR 12536. National Parks Additions. Oberstar, D-Minn., amendment to provide for a master development plan, to be submitted to Congress one year after enactment of the bill, for inclusion of segments of the Upper Mississippi River in Minnesota in the Wild and Scenic Rivers system. Adopted 205-192: R 116-20; D 89-172 (ND 50-134; SD 39-38), July 11, 1978.

462. HR 12536. National Parks Additions. Oberstar, D-Minn., amendment to delete the provision in the bill to amend the Wild and Scenic Rivers Act deleting the limitation on acquisition authority of the St. Croix River in Minnesota and Wisconsin. Rejected 175-218: R 100-38; D 75-180 (ND 43-135; SD 32-45), July 11, 1978.

463. HR 12536. National Parks Additions. Passage of the bill to authorize $1.25 billion in fiscal 1979-83 for establishment of new areas and additions in the national park, national trails, wild and scenic rivers and wilderness systems. Passed 341-61: R 104-33; D 237-28 (ND 173-12; SD 64-16), July 12, 1978.

464. S Con Res 95. Soviet Dissident Trials. Zablocki, D-Wis., motion to table (kill) the Ashbrook, R-Ohio, motion to appeal the ruling of the chair sustaining a point of order against a motion to commit the resolution *(see vote 465, below)* to the International Relations Committee with instructions to report it back with an amendment stating that it was the sense of Congress that U.S. representatives to the strategic arm limitation talks with the Soviet Union be recalled to show U.S. commitment to human rights principles. Motion agreed to 277-120: R 45-90; D 232-30 (ND 176-9; SD 56-21), July 12, 1978.

465. S Con Res 95. Soviet Dissident Trials. Adoption of the concurrent resolution urging the Soviet Union and its leadership "to seek a humanitarian resolution" to the "deplorable" trials of Anatoly Shcharansky, Viktoras Petkus and Aleksandr Ilyich Ginzburg, who defended the principles of the Helsinki agreement in the Soviet Union. Adopted (thus completing congressional action) 380-10: R 127-1; D 253-9 (ND 179-5; SD 74-4), July 12, 1978.

466. H Con Res 599. Uranium Export to India. Adoption of the resolution to disapprove the president's approval of the export of low-enriched uranium to India. Rejected 181-227: R 81-56; D 100-171 (ND 79-110; SD 21-61), July 12, 1978. A "nay" was a vote supporting the president's position.

KEY

- Y Voted for (yea).
- ✓ Paired for.
- † Announced for.
- # CQ Poll for.
- N Voted against (nay).
- X Paired against.
- \- Announced against.
- ▮ CQ Poll against.
- P Voted "present."
- ● Voted "present" to avoid possible conflict of interest.
- ? Did not vote or otherwise make a position known.

	459	460	461	462	463	464	465	466
ALABAMA								
1 Edwards	Y	Y	Y	Y	Y	Y	Y	Y
2 Dickinson	Y	Y	Y	Y	Y	N	Y	Y
3 Nichols	Y	Y	Y	Y	Y	Y	Y	N
4 Bevill	Y	Y	Y	Y	Y	Y	Y	N
5 Flippo	Y	Y	Y	N	Y	Y	Y	N
6 Buchanan	N	N	Y	Y	Y	Y	Y	Y
7 Flowers	Y	N	Y	Y	Y	N	Y	N
ALASKA								
AL Young	Y	Y	Y	Y	N	N	#	Y
ARIZONA								
1 Rhodes	N	Y	Y	Y	Y	Y	Y	Y
2 Udall	N	N	N	N	Y	Y	Y	N
3 Stump	Y	Y	Y	Y	N	N	Y	N
4 Rudd	Y	Y	Y	Y	N	N	Y	Y
ARKANSAS								
1 Alexander	Y	N	Y	?	Y	Y	Y	Y
2 Tucker	N	N	N	N	Y	Y	Y	N
3 Hammerschmidt	N	Y	Y	Y	Y	N	Y	N
4 Thornton	N	N	N	N	Y	Y	Y	N
CALIFORNIA								
1 Johnson	N	N	N	N	?	Y	Y	N
2 Clausen	N	Y	Y	Y	Y	N	Y	Y
3 Moss	Y	N	N	?	Y	Y	Y	N
4 Leggett	?	▮	#	?	Y	#	#	N
5 Burton, J.	N	N	N	N	Y	Y	Y	Y
6 Burton, P.	N	N	N	N	Y	Y	Y	Y
7 Miller	N	N	N	N	Y	Y	Y	Y
8 Dellums	N	N	N	N	Y	Y	Y	Y
9 Stark	N	N	N	N	Y	Y	Y	Y
10 Edwards	N	N	N	N	Y	Y	Y	Y
11 Ryan	Y	N	N	N	Y	Y	Y	N
12 McCloskey	Y	Y	Y	N	Y	?	Y	N
13 Mineta	N	N	N	N	Y	Y	Y	Y
14 McFall	Y	N	Y	Y	Y	Y	Y	N
15 Sisk	Y	Y	Y	Y	Y	Y	Y	N
16 Panetta	Y	N	N	N	Y	Y	Y	Y
17 Krebs	N	N	N	N	Y	Y	Y	Y
18 Vacancy								
19 Lagomarsino	Y	N	Y	N	Y	N	Y	Y
20 Goldwater	N	Y	Y	Y	Y	N	Y	Y
21 Corman	N	N	N	N	Y	Y	Y	N
22 Moorhead	N	Y	Y	Y	Y	N	Y	Y
23 Beilenson	N	N	N	N	Y	Y	Y	Y
24 Waxman	N	N	N	N	Y	Y	Y	Y
25 Roybal	N	N	N	N	Y	Y	Y	Y
26 Rousselot	Y	Y	Y	Y	N	N	Y	Y
27 Dornan	Y	Y	Y	Y	N	N	Y	Y
28 Burke	N	N	N	N	Y	Y	Y	Y
29 Hawkins	N	N	X	X	Y	Y	Y	N
30 Danielson	N	N	N	N	Y	Y	Y	N
31 Wilson, C.H.	Y	#	Y	▮	Y	#	#	N
32 Anderson	Y	N	N	N	Y	Y	Y	Y
33 Clawson	Y	Y	Y	Y	Y	N	Y	Y
34 Hannaford	Y	N	N	N	Y	Y	Y	N
35 Lloyd	Y	N	N	N	Y	Y	Y	Y
36 Brown	N	N	N	N	Y	Y	Y	Y
37 Pettis	Y	Y	Y	Y	Y	Y	Y	N
38 Patterson	Y	N	N	N	Y	Y	Y	Y
39 Wiggins	Y	Y	?	Y	N	Y	Y	Y
40 Badham	Y	Y	Y	Y	N	N	P	N
41 Wilson, B.	N	Y	Y	Y	Y	N	Y	N
42 Van Deerlin	N	N	N	N	Y	Y	Y	N
43 Burgener	N	Y	Y	Y	Y	N	Y	Y
COLORADO								
1 Schroeder	N	N	Y	N	Y	Y	Y	Y
2 Wirth	Y	N	N	N	Y	Y	Y	Y
3 Evans	Y	N	Y	Y	Y	Y	Y	N
4 Johnson	?	Y	Y	Y	Y	Y	P	Y
5 Armstrong	Y	Y	Y	Y	Y	N	?	Y
CONNECTICUT								
1 Cotter	N	N	N	Y	Y	Y	Y	Y
2 Dodd	Y	N	N	N	Y	Y	Y	Y
3 Giaimo	N	N	N	N	Y	?	Y	Y
4 McKinney	Y	N	Y	Y	Y	Y	Y	Y
5 Sarasin	N	N	Y	Y	Y	Y	Y	Y
6 Moffett	N	?	N	N	Y	Y	Y	Y
DELAWARE								
AL Evans	N	Y	Y	Y	Y	Y	Y	N
FLORIDA								
1 Sikes	Y	N	Y	N	Y	N	Y	Y
2 Fuqua	Y	N	N	N	Y	Y	Y	Y
3 Bennett	Y	N	Y	N	Y	Y	Y	Y
4 Chappell	?	?	✓	?	✓	Y	N	Y
5 Kelly	Y	Y	Y	Y	N	N	Y	Y
6 Young	N	N	Y	Y	Y	N	Y	Y
7 Gibbons	N	N	N	N	Y	Y	Y	Y
8 Ireland	N	N	N	N	Y	N	Y	Y
9 Frey	?	?	?	?	?	?	?	?
10 Bafalis	N	N	Y	Y	Y	Y	Y	Y
11 Rogers	Y	N	N	N	Y	?	Y	N
12 Burke	?	?	?	?	?	?	?	?
13 Lehman	Y	N	N	N	Y	Y	Y	N
14 Pepper	N	N	N	N	Y	Y	#	N
15 Fascell	Y	N	N	N	Y	Y	Y	N
GEORGIA								
1 Ginn	Y	Y	Y	N	Y	Y	Y	N
2 Mathis	?	?	N	N	Y	?	Y	N
3 Brinkley	Y	Y	Y	Y	Y	Y	Y	N
4 Levitas	Y	N	Y	N	Y	P	Y	Y
5 Fowler	Y	N	N	N	Y	Y	Y	N
6 Flynt	Y	Y	?	?	?	?	?	?
7 McDonald	Y	Y	Y	Y	N	N	Y	Y
8 Evans	#	#	#	#	#	▮	#	#
9 Jenkins	Y	Y	Y	N	N	N	Y	N
10 Barnard	Y	Y	Y	Y	Y	N	Y	Y
HAWAII								
1 Heftel	Y	Y	N	N	Y	Y	Y	N
2 Akaka	Y	N	N	N	Y	Y	Y	N
IDAHO								
1 Symms	Y	Y	Y	Y	N	N	Y	Y
2 Hansen, G.	?	Y	Y	Y	N	N	Y	Y
ILLINOIS								
1 Metcalfe	N	N	N	N	Y	Y	Y	N
2 Murphy	N	N	Y	Y	Y	Y	Y	N
3 Russo	Y	N	Y	Y	Y	Y	Y	Y
4 Derwinski	N	Y	N	N	Y	N	Y	N
5 Fary	Y	N	Y	Y	Y	Y	Y	N
6 Hyde	N	Y	Y	Y	Y	N	Y	N
7 Collins	N	N	N	?	Y	Y	Y	N
8 Rostenkowski	Y	N	Y	Y	Y	Y	Y	N
9 Yates	Y	N	N	Y	Y	Y	Y	Y
10 Mikva	N	N	N	N	Y	Y	#	N
11 Annunzio	N	N	Y	Y	Y	Y	Y	N
12 Crane	Y	Y	Y	Y	N	N	Y	Y
13 McClory	N	Y	Y	Y	Y	N	Y	N
14 Erlenborn	Y	Y	Y	Y	Y	Y	P	N
15 Corcoran	N	N	N	N	Y	N	Y	Y
16 Anderson	▮	▮	#	▮	#	#	#	▮
17 O'Brien	N	Y	Y	Y	N	N	Y	N
18 Michel	N	Y	Y	Y	N	N	Y	N
19 Railsback	N	N	Y	Y	Y	Y	Y	N
20 Findley	N	Y	Y	Y	Y	Y	Y	N
21 Madigan	N	Y	Y	Y	Y	Y	Y	N
22 Shipley	Y	N	Y	N	Y	Y	Y	N
23 Price	Y	N	Y	Y	Y	Y	Y	N
24 Simon	Y	N	N	N	Y	Y	Y	N
INDIANA								
1 Benjamin	N	N	N	N	Y	Y	Y	N
2 Fithian	N	N	N	N	N	Y	Y	Y
3 Brademas	Y	N	N	N	Y	Y	Y	N
4 Quayle	Y	Y	Y	N	Y	N	Y	N
5 Hillis	N	N	Y	Y	Y	N	Y	Y
6 Evans	Y	N	N	Y	N	Y	Y	Y
7 Myers, J.	Y	Y	Y	Y	Y	Y	Y	N
8 Cornwell	N	N	N	N	Y	N	Y	Y
9 Hamilton	Y	N	N	N	Y	Y	Y	N
10 Sharp	Y	N	N	N	Y	Y	Y	N
11 Jacobs	Y	N	N	Y	Y	Y	Y	N
IOWA								
1 Leach	N	N	N	Y	Y	Y	Y	Y
2 Blouin	Y	N	N	N	Y	Y	Y	Y
3 Grassley	Y	Y	Y	Y	N	N	Y	Y
4 Smith	Y	N	N	N	Y	N	Y	N
5 Harkin	N	N	N	N	Y	Y	Y	Y
6 Bedell	Y	N	N	N	Y	Y	Y	Y

Democrats ***Republicans***

Corresponding to Congressional Record Votes 527, 528, 529, 530, 532, 533, 534, 535

	459	460	461	462	463	464	465	466
KANSAS								
1 Sebelius	N	Y	N	N	Y	N	Y	N
2 Keys	Y	N	N	N	Y	Y	Y	Y
3 Winn	▮	▮	▮	▮	#	▮	#	#
4 Glickman	Y	N	N	N	Y	Y	Y	N
5 Skubitz	N	N	N	N	Y	?	Y	?
KENTUCKY								
1 Hubbard	Y	Y	N	Y	Y	N	Y	N
2 Natcher	Y	N	N	N	Y	Y	Y	N
3 Mazzoli	N	N	N	N	Y	Y	Y	Y
4 Snyder	Y	Y	Y	Y	N	N	Y	Y
5 Carter	Y	Y	Y	N	Y	N	Y	Y
6 Breckinridge	N	?	N	N	Y	Y	Y	N
7 Perkins	N	N	N	N	Y	Y	Y	N
LOUISIANA								
1 Livingston	Y	Y	Y	Y	Y	N	Y	Y
2 Boggs	?	?	X	✓	Y	Y	Y	N
3 Treen	Y	Y	Y	Y	Y	N	P	N
4 Waggonner	Y	Y	Y	Y	X	N	N	N
5 Huckaby	?	?	?	?	Y	N	Y	Y
6 Moore	Y	N	Y	Y	Y	N	Y	Y
7 Breaux	Y	Y	Y	Y	Y	N	Y	N
8 Long	Y	N	N	Y	Y	Y	Y	N
MAINE								
1 Emery	N	Y	Y	Y	Y	N	Y	Y
2 Cohen	N	Y	Y	Y	Y	N	Y	Y
MARYLAND								
1 Bauman	N	Y	Y	Y	Y	N	Y	Y
2 Long	N	N	N	N	Y	Y	Y	Y
3 Mikulski	Y	N	Y	N	Y	Y	Y	Y
4 Holt	N	Y	Y	Y	N	N	Y	Y
5 Spellman	N	N	N	N	Y	Y	Y	Y
6 Byron	N	N	N	N	Y	N	Y	Y
7 Mitchell	Y	N	N	N	Y	Y	Y	Y
8 Steers	N	N	N	N	Y	Y	Y	N
MASSACHUSETTS								
1 Conte	N	N	N	N	Y	Y	Y	Y
2 Boland	Y	N	N	N	Y	Y	Y	N
3 Early	Y	N	N	N	Y	Y	Y	Y
4 Drinan	N	N	N	N	Y	Y	Y	Y
5 Tsongas	Y	N	N	?	?	?	?	?
6 Harrington	N	N	N	N	Y	Y	Y	N
7 Markey	N	N	N	N	Y	Y	Y	Y
8 O'Neill								
9 Moakley	N	N	N	N	Y	Y	Y	Y
10 Heckler	N	Y	Y	N	Y	N	Y	Y
11 Burke	N	N	N	N	Y	Y	Y	N
12 Studds	N	N	N	N	Y	Y	Y	N
MICHIGAN								
1 Conyers	N	N	N	N	Y	#	#	Y
2 Pursell	N	?	Y	N	Y	Y	Y	Y
3 Brown	N	N	Y	Y	Y	N	Y	N
4 Stockman	Y	Y	Y	Y	Y	N	#	N
5 Sawyer	N	N	Y	N	Y	N	Y	N
6 Carr	N	N	N	N	Y	Y	Y	Y
7 Kildee	N	N	N	N	Y	Y	Y	Y
8 Traxler	Y	N	Y	N	#	Y	Y	N
9 Vander Jagt	N	N	?	N	Y	Y	Y	Y
10 Cederberg	N	Y	Y	N	Y	#	Y	N
11 Ruppe	Y	N	Y	Y	Y	Y	Y	Y
12 Bonior	N	X	N	N	Y	Y	Y	Y
13 Diggs	Y	N	▮	▮	Y	Y	Y	▮
14 Nedzi	N	N	N	N	Y	Y	Y	N
15 Ford	N	N	N	N	Y	Y	Y	N
16 Dingell	N	N	Y	Y	Y	Y	Y	N
17 Brodhead	N	N	N	N	Y	Y	Y	Y
18 Blanchard	Y	N	Y	N	Y	Y	Y	N
19 Broomfield	N	N	Y	Y	Y	Y	Y	N
MINNESOTA								
1 Quie	Y	Y	Y	Y	Y	Y	Y	N
2 Hagedorn	N	Y	Y	Y	Y	N	Y	N
3 Frenzel	Y	Y	Y	Y	Y	Y	Y	N
4 Vento	N	N	N	Y	Y	Y	Y	N
5 Fraser	N	N	N	N	Y	Y	Y	#
6 Nolan	?	N	N	N	Y	Y	?	Y
7 Stangeland	Y	Y	Y	Y	N	N	#	Y
8 Oberstar	Y	Y	Y	Y	Y	Y	Y	Y
MISSISSIPPI								
1 Whitten	Y	Y	Y	Y	Y	Y	Y	N
2 Bowen	Y	Y	Y	Y	Y	Y	Y	N
3 Montgomery	Y	Y	Y	Y	N	N	Y	Y
4 Cochran	Y	Y	Y	Y	Y	N	Y	Y
5 Lott	Y	Y	Y	Y	Y	N	Y	Y
MISSOURI								
1 Clay	N	N	N	N	Y	Y	Y	Y
2 Young	Y	Y	N	Y	Y	Y	Y	N
3 Gephardt	Y	N	N	N	N	Y	Y	N
4 Skelton	Y	Y	Y	N	Y	Y	Y	N
5 Bolling	Y	▮	Y	Y	Y	Y	Y	N
6 Coleman	Y	Y	Y	Y	Y	N	Y	Y
7 Taylor	Y	Y	Y	Y	Y	N	Y	Y
8 Ichord	?	Y	Y	Y	Y	N	Y	N
9 Volkmer	Y	N	Y	Y	N	Y	Y	N
10 Burlison	Y	N	N	N	Y	Y	Y	N
MONTANA								
1 Baucus	Y	N	N	N	Y	Y	Y	Y
2 Marlenee	Y	Y	Y	N	Y	N	Y	Y
NEBRASKA								
1 Thone	N	Y	Y	Y	Y	N	#	?
2 Cavanaugh	Y	N	N	N	Y	Y	Y	N
3 Smith	N	Y	Y	Y	Y	N	Y	Y
NEVADA								
AL Santini	Y	Y	Y	Y	Y	Y	Y	N
NEW HAMPSHIRE								
1 D'Amours	Y	N	Y	N	Y	Y	Y	Y
2 Cleveland	Y	Y	Y	Y	N	N	Y	N
NEW JERSEY								
1 Florio	Y	N	N	N	Y	Y	Y	Y
2 Hughes	Y	N	N	Y	Y	Y	Y	Y
3 Howard	Y	N	N	N	Y	Y	Y	N
4 Thompson	N	N	Y	Y	✓	#	#	N
5 Fenwick	N	N	N	N	Y	Y	Y	N
6 Forsythe	Y	Y	Y	Y	Y	Y	Y	N
7 Maguire	N	N	N	N	Y	Y	Y	Y
8 Roe	N	N	N	Y	✓	Y	Y	N
9 Hollenbeck	Y	N	Y	N	Y	N	Y	Y
10 Rodino	▮	▮	#	▮	#	#	#	▮
11 Minish	Y	N	N	N	Y	Y	Y	Y
12 Rinaldo	N	N	N	N	Y	N	Y	Y
13 Meyner	Y	N	N	N	Y	Y	Y	N
14 LeFante	▮	▮	#	#	#	#	#	✓
15 Patten	Y	N	Y	Y	Y	Y	Y	N
NEW MEXICO								
1 Lujan	N	Y	Y	Y	Y	N	Y	N
2 Runnels	?	✓	✓	✓	Y	Y	Y	N
NEW YORK								
1 Pike	?	?	?	?	Y	Y	Y	Y
2 Downey	N	N	N	N	Y	Y	Y	Y
3 Ambro	N	N	N	N	Y	Y	Y	Y
4 Lent	N	Y	Y	N	Y	N	Y	Y
5 Wydler	N	Y	Y	N	Y	N	Y	N
6 Wolff	▮	X	#	▮	#	#	#	X
7 Addabbo	N	N	Y	X	Y	Y	Y	N
8 Rosenthal	▮	N	N	N	Y	Y	Y	N
9 Delaney	Y	N	N	N	Y	Y	Y	N
10 Biaggi	Y	N	Y	N	Y	Y	Y	N
11 Scheuer	N	N	N	N	Y	Y	Y	N
12 Chisholm	N	N	N	N	Y	Y	Y	N
13 Solarz	N	N	N	N	Y	Y	Y	N
14 Richmond	N	N	N	N	Y	Y	Y	Y
15 Zeferetti	Y	Y	Y	N	Y	N	Y	Y
16 Holtzman	N	N	N	N	Y	Y	Y	Y
17 Murphy	N	N	N	N	Y	N	Y	N
18 Green	N	N	N	N	Y	Y	Y	Y
19 Rangel	?	X	X	X	?	?	?	✓
20 Weiss	N	N	N	N	Y	Y	Y	Y
21 Garcia	N	N	N	N	Y	Y	Y	N
22 Bingham	N	N	N	N	Y	Y	Y	N
23 Caputo	N	N	N	Y	Y	N	Y	Y
24 Ottinger	N	N	N	N	Y	Y	Y	Y
25 Fish	N	N	N	N	Y	Y	Y	Y
26 Gilman	N	N	N	N	Y	N	Y	Y
27 McHugh	N	N	N	N	Y	Y	Y	N
28 Stratton	N	Y	Y	N	Y	Y	Y	N
29 Pattison	Y	N	N	▮	Y	Y	Y	Y
30 McEwen	N	Y	Y	Y	Y	?	Y	N
31 Mitchell	N	N	Y	N	Y	Y	Y	N
32 Hanley	Y	N	Y	Y	Y	N	Y	N
33 Walsh	N	N	Y	Y	Y	Y	Y	N
34 Horton	N	N	Y	N	Y	N	Y	N
35 Conable	N	Y	Y	Y	N	Y	Y	N
36 LaFalce	Y	N	Y	N	Y	Y	Y	Y
37 Nowak	N	N	N	Y	Y	Y	Y	Y
38 Kemp	N	?	Y	Y	Y	N	Y	Y
39 Lundine	Y	▮	N	Y	Y	Y	Y	N
NORTH CAROLINA								
1 Jones	Y	Y	Y	N	Y	Y	Y	N
2 Fountain	▮	#	#	#	▮	#	#	#
3 Whitley	Y	Y	Y	N	N	Y	Y	N
4 Andrews	Y	N	N	N	Y	Y	Y	N
5 Neal	Y	N	Y	Y	Y	Y	Y	N
6 Preyer	Y	N	N	N	Y	Y	Y	N
7 Rose	N	N	N	N	Y	Y	Y	N
8 Hefner	Y	Y	Y	Y	Y	Y	Y	Y
9 Martin	Y	Y	Y	Y	Y	Y	Y	Y
10 Broyhill	Y	Y	Y	Y	Y	Y	Y	Y
11 Gudger	Y	N	Y	N	Y	Y	Y	N
NORTH DAKOTA								
AL Andrews	N	N	N	N	Y	N	Y	Y
OHIO								
1 Gradison	Y	N	N	N	Y	Y	Y	N
2 Luken	Y	N	N	N	N	Y	Y	N
3 Whalen	Y	N	N	N	Y	Y	Y	N
4 Guyer	?	?	?	?	?	?	?	?
5 Latta	Y	Y	Y	Y	N	N	Y	Y
6 Harsha	N	N	N	N	N	N	Y	N
7 Brown	?	?	?	?	Y	N	Y	N
8 Kindness	Y	Y	Y	Y	N	N	P	N
9 Ashley	Y	N	X	X	Y	Y	Y	N
10 Miller	N	Y	Y	Y	N	N	Y	Y
11 Stanton	N	Y	Y	Y	Y	Y	Y	N
12 Devine	Y	Y	Y	Y	N	N	Y	Y
13 Pease	N	N	N	N	Y	Y	Y	N
14 Seiberling	N	N	N	N	Y	Y	Y	N
15 Wylie	N	N	Y	N	Y	Y	Y	Y
16 Regula	N	N	Y	Y	Y	Y	Y	N
17 Ashbrook	Y	Y	Y	Y	N	N	P	Y
18 Applegate	Y	N	Y	Y	Y	Y	Y	Y
19 Carney	Y	N	N	N	Y	Y	Y	N
20 Oakar	N	N	Y	N	Y	Y	Y	Y
21 Stokes	N	N	N	N	Y	Y	Y	Y
22 Vanik	N	N	N	N	Y	Y	Y	N
23 Mottl	N	Y	Y	Y	Y	Y	Y	Y
OKLAHOMA								
1 Jones	N	Y	Y	Y	N	N	Y	N
2 Risenhoover	Y	Y	Y	Y	N	N	Y	N
3 Watkins	Y	Y	Y	Y	N	N	Y	N
4 Steed	Y	N	N	Y	N	Y	Y	N
5 Edwards	N	Y	Y	Y	N	N	Y	Y
6 English	Y	Y	Y	Y	N	N	Y	Y
OREGON								
1 AuCoin	Y	N	N	N	Y	Y	Y	Y
2 Ullman	Y	N	N	N	Y	Y	Y	N
3 Duncan	?	?	?	?	N	Y	Y	N
4 Weaver	N	N	N	N	Y	Y	Y	Y
PENNSYLVANIA								
1 Myers, M.	N	N	Y	Y	Y	Y	Y	N
2 Nix	?	?	?	?	?	?	?	?
3 Lederer	N	N	Y	Y	Y	Y	Y	N
4 Eilberg	Y	N	Y	Y	Y	Y	Y	Y
5 Schulze	N	Y	Y	Y	N	N	Y	Y
6 Yatron	N	N	N	Y	Y	Y	Y	N
7 Edgar	Y	N	N	N	Y	Y	Y	Y
8 Kostmayer	N	N	N	N	Y	Y	Y	N
9 Shuster	Y	Y	Y	Y	N	N	Y	Y
10 McDade	N	Y	Y	Y	Y	Y	Y	Y
11 Flood	Y	N	Y	Y	Y	Y	Y	N
12 Murtha	Y	Y	Y	Y	N	Y	N	N
13 Coughlin	N	Y	Y	N	Y	N	Y	N
14 Moorhead	N	N	Y	N	Y	Y	Y	N
15 Rooney	?	N	N	N	Y	Y	Y	N
16 Walker	Y	Y	Y	Y	?	N	Y	Y
17 Ertel	Y	N	Y	Y	N	Y	Y	N
18 Walgren	Y	N	N	N	Y	Y	Y	Y
19 Goodling, W.	?	?	?	?	X	?	?	?
20 Gaydos	Y	N	N	N	Y	Y	Y	N
21 Dent	Y	Y	Y	Y	N	Y	N	N
22 Murphy	N	N	N	N	Y	Y	Y	N
23 Ammerman	N	N	N	N	Y	Y	Y	Y
24 Marks	N	N	Y	N	Y	Y	Y	N
25 Myers, G.	Y	Y	Y	Y	N	Y	N	N
RHODE ISLAND								
1 St Germain	N	N	Y	N	Y	Y	Y	N
2 Beard	Y	N	Y	N	Y	Y	Y	N
SOUTH CAROLINA								
1 Davis	Y	N	N	N	Y	?	Y	N
2 Spence	N	Y	Y	N	Y	N	Y	N
3 Derrick	Y	N	Y	N	Y	Y	Y	N
4 Mann	?	?	?	?	?	?	?	?
5 Holland	Y	N	N	N	Y	?	?	N
6 Jenrette	Y	N	N	N	Y	Y	Y	N
SOUTH DAKOTA								
1 Pressler	Y	Y	N	N	Y	N	Y	Y
2 Abdnor	N	Y	Y	Y	Y	N	Y	Y
TENNESSEE								
1 Quillen	N	N	Y	N	Y	N	Y	Y
2 Duncan	N	Y	Y	Y	Y	N	Y	N
3 Lloyd	Y	Y	Y	Y	Y	N	Y	N
4 Gore	Y	N	N	N	Y	Y	Y	N
5 Vacancy								
6 Beard	N	Y	Y	Y	Y	N	Y	N
7 Jones	Y	Y	Y	Y	Y	Y	Y	Y
8 Ford	N	N	N	N	Y	Y	Y	Y
TEXAS								
1 Hall	Y	Y	Y	Y	N	N	Y	N
2 Wilson, C.	Y	Y	?	Y	Y	Y	Y	N
3 Collins	Y	Y	Y	Y	N	N	Y	Y
4 Roberts	?	✓	✓	✓	N	Y	?	N
5 Mattox	N	N	N	N	Y	Y	Y	N
6 Teague	?	✓	✓	✓	X	?	?	X
7 Archer	N	Y	Y	Y	Y	N	Y	Y
8 Eckhardt	N	N	N	N	Y	Y	Y	Y
9 Brooks	Y	N	N	N	?	Y	Y	N
10 Pickle	Y	Y	N	N	N	Y	Y	N
11 Poage	Y	Y	Y	Y	Y	Y	N	N
12 Wright	Y	N	Y	N	Y	Y	Y	N
13 Hightower	Y	Y	N	N	Y	Y	Y	N
14 Young	Y	N	?	?	Y	Y	Y	N
15 de la Garza	?	?	?	?	?	?	?	?
16 White	Y	Y	Y	Y	Y	Y	Y	N
17 Burleson	Y	Y	Y	Y	N	N	N	N
18 Jordan	▮	N	N	N	Y	Y	Y	Y
19 Mahon	Y	N	N	N	Y	Y	Y	N
20 Gonzalez	Y	N	N	N	Y	Y	Y	N
21 Krueger	Y	N	N	Y	Y	Y	#	▮
22 Gammage	Y	Y	Y	Y	Y	N	Y	Y
23 Kazen	N	N	N	N	Y	Y	Y	N
24 Milford	Y	Y	Y	Y	N	P	?	N
UTAH								
1 McKay	Y	Y	Y	N	Y	Y	Y	N
2 Marriott	Y	Y	Y	Y	Y	N	Y	N
VERMONT								
AL Jeffords	N	N	N	Y	#	N	Y	Y
VIRGINIA								
1 Trible	Y	Y	Y	Y	Y	Y	Y	Y
2 Whitehurst	Y	Y	Y	Y	Y	Y	Y	Y
3 Satterfield	Y	Y	Y	Y	N	N	Y	N
4 Daniel	Y	Y	Y	Y	Y	N	Y	N
5 Daniel	Y	Y	Y	Y	N	N	Y	N
6 Butler	Y	Y	Y	Y	N	N	Y	N
7 Robinson	Y	Y	Y	Y	N	N	Y	N
8 Harris	N	N	N	N	Y	Y	Y	Y
9 Wampler	Y	Y	Y	Y	N	N	Y	Y
10 Fisher	N	N	N	N	Y	Y	Y	N
WASHINGTON								
1 Pritchard	Y	N	Y	N	Y	Y	Y	Y
2 Meeds	N	N	N	N	Y	Y	Y	N
3 Bonker	Y	N	Y	N	Y	Y	Y	N
4 McCormack	Y	N	Y	N	Y	Y	Y	N
5 Foley	Y	Y	N	N	Y	Y	Y	N
6 Dicks	Y	N	N	N	Y	Y	Y	N
7 Cunningham	Y	Y	Y	Y	N	N	Y	Y
WEST VIRGINIA								
1 Mollohan	Y	N	Y	Y	N	Y	Y	N
2 Staggers	N	N	Y	Y	?	Y	Y	N
3 Slack	?	?	?	?	N	Y	N	Y
4 Rahall	N	N	N	N	Y	Y	N	N
WISCONSIN								
1 Aspin	Y	N	N	N	Y	Y	Y	N
2 Kastenmeier	N	N	N	N	Y	Y	N	N
3 Baldus	Y	N	N	Y	Y	Y	Y	Y
4 Zablocki	Y	Y	N	Y	Y	Y	Y	N
5 Reuss	N	N	N	N	Y	Y	Y	N
6 Steiger	Y	N	N	N	Y	Y	Y	N
7 Obey	Y	N	N	N	?	?	?	N
8 Cornell	Y	N	N	N	Y	Y	Y	Y
9 Kasten	#	▮	▮	▮	#	#	#	▮
WYOMING								
AL Roncalio	Y	N	N	N	Y	Y	Y	N

Democrats ***Republicans***

467. HR 15. Elementary and Secondary Education. Quie, R-Minn., amendment to allow local education agencies, as well as states, to qualify for special matching federal grants if they had their own compensatory education programs. Rejected 150-240: R 93-41; D 57-199 (ND 33-144; SD 24-55), July 12, 1978.

468. HR 15. Elementary and Secondary Education. Edwards, R-Okla., amendment to count two-thirds instead of 100 percent of the children in each state from families receiving Aid to Families with Dependent Children payments in excess of the poverty level, for the purposes of determining state compensatory education allocations. Rejected 175-212: R 80-51; D 95-161 (ND 28-153; SD 67-8), July 12, 1978.

469. H Res 1267. Andrew Young Impeachment. Wright, D-Texas, motion to table (kill) the McDonald, D-Ga., resolution to impeach U.S. Ambassador to the United Nations Andrew Young. Motion agreed to 293-82: R 61-67; D 232-15 (ND 166-5; SD 66-10), July 13, 1978. A "yea" was a vote supporting the president's position.

470. HR 15. Elementary and Secondary Education. Kildee, D-Mich., substitute amendment, to the Holt, R-Md., amendment, to prohibit duplication by community education programs of services offered by other government agencies, unless the commissioner of education determined that collaboration existed between the education agency and the other government agencies. Adopted 197-195: R 6-128; D 191-67 (ND 165-18; SD 26-49), July 13, 1978. (The Holt amendment subsequently was adopted by voice vote.)

471. HR 15. Elementary and Secondary Education. Ashbrook, R-Ohio, substitute for the bill to distribute funds authorized by the bill in block grants to states. Rejected 79-290: R 61-61; D 18-229 (ND 7-170; SD 11-59), July 13, 1978.

472. HR 15. Elementary and Secondary Education. Passage of the bill to extend the Elementary and Secondary Education Act of 1965 for five years, through fiscal 1983. Passed 350-20: R 110-14; D 240-6 (ND 177-0; SD 63-6), July 13, 1978.

KEY

Y Voted for (yea).
✓ Paired for.
† Announced for.
# CQ Poll for.
N Voted against (nay).
X Paired against.
- Announced against.
▮ CQ Poll against.
P Voted "present."
● Voted "present" to avoid possible conflict of interest.
? Did not vote or otherwise make a position known.

	467	468	469	470	471	472
ALABAMA						
1 Edwards	Y	Y	Y	N	N	Y
2 Dickinson	Y	Y	N	N	Y	Y
3 Nichols	X	✓	Y	N	▮	#
4 Bevill	N	Y	Y	N	N	Y
5 Flippo	N	Y	Y	N	N	Y
6 Buchanan	Y	Y	Y	N	N	Y
7 Flowers	N	Y	Y	N	?	?
ALASKA						
AL Young	N	Y	#	N	N	Y
ARIZONA						
1 Rhodes	Y	Y	N	N	N	Y
2 Udall	Y	Y	Y	Y	N	Y
3 Stump	Y	Y	N	N	N	Y
4 Rudd	Y	Y	N	N	Y	N
ARKANSAS						
1 Alexander	N	N	Y	?	?	?
2 Tucker	N	Y	Y	Y	N	Y
3 Hammerschmidt	N	Y	N	N	Y	Y
4 Thornton	N	Y	Y	?	N	Y
CALIFORNIA						
1 Johnson	N	N	Y	Y	N	Y
2 Clausen	Y	N	?	N	Y	Y
3 Moss	?	?	Y	Y	?	?
4 Leggett	▮	N	#	▮	N	Y
5 Burton, J.	?	N	?	Y	N	Y
6 Burton, P.	N	N	Y	Y	N	Y
7 Miller	N	N	Y	Y	N	Y
8 Dellums	N	N	Y	Y	N	Y
9 Stark	N	N	Y	Y	N	Y
10 Edwards	N	N	Y	Y	N	Y
11 Ryan	N	N	Y	N	Y	Y
12 McCloskey	Y	N	Y	N	N	Y
13 Mineta	N	N	Y	Y	N	Y
14 McFall	N	N	Y	Y	N	Y
15 Sisk	?	?	?	Y	N	Y
16 Panetta	N	N	Y	Y	N	Y
17 Krebs	N	N	Y	Y	N	Y
18 Vacancy						
19 Lagomarsino	Y	N	N	N	Y	Y
20 Goldwater	Y	?	N	N	Y	Y
21 Corman	N	N	Y	Y	N	Y
22 Moorhead	Y	N	N	N	N	Y
23 Beilenson	N	N	#	Y	N	Y
24 Waxman	N	N	Y	Y	▮	#
25 Roybal	N	N	Y	Y	N	Y
26 Rousselot	Y	N	N	N	Y	N
27 Dornan	Y	N	N	N	N	Y
28 Burke	N	N	Y	Y	N	Y
29 Hawkins	N	N	Y	Y	N	Y
30 Danielson	N	N	Y	#	N	Y
31 Wilson, C.H.	▮	▮	Y	#	?	Y
32 Anderson	N	N	Y	Y	N	Y
33 Clawson	Y	N	N	N	?	?
34 Hannaford	N	N	Y	Y	N	Y
35 Lloyd	N	N	Y	Y	N	Y
36 Brown	?	?	?	Y	N	Y
37 Pettis	Y	N	Y	N	N	Y
38 Patterson	N	N	Y	Y	N	Y
39 Wiggins	Y	N	N	N	#	#
40 Badham	Y	N	N	N	Y	N
41 Wilson, B.	N	N	N	N	?	Y
42 Van Deerlin	N	N	Y	Y	N	Y
43 Burgener	N	N	N	N	N	Y
COLORADO						
1 Schroeder	Y	N	Y	Y	N	Y
2 Wirth	Y	N	Y	Y	N	Y
3 Evans	?	?	?	?	?	?
4 Johnson	Y	Y	Y	N	N	Y
5 Armstrong	Y	Y	N	N	Y	Y
CONNECTICUT						
1 Cotter	N	N	Y	N	N	Y
2 Dodd	N	N	Y	Y	N	Y
3 Giaimo	N	N	Y	N	N	Y
4 McKinney	Y	N	#	N	N	Y
5 Sarasin	N	N	Y	N	▮	#
6 Moffett	N	N	Y	Y	?	?
DELAWARE						
AL Evans	N	Y	Y	N	Y	Y
FLORIDA						
1 Sikes	N	?	Y	N	N	Y
2 Fuqua	N	Y	Y	Y	N	Y
3 Bennett	N	Y	Y	N	N	Y
4 Chappell	N	Y	N	N	N	Y
5 Kelly	N	Y	N	N	Y	N
6 Young	N	Y	N	N	N	Y
7 Gibbons	N	Y	N	N	?	?
8 Ireland	N	Y	N	?	N	Y
9 Frey	?	?	?	?	?	?
10 Bafalis	N	Y	N	N	Y	Y
11 Rogers	N	?	Y	Y	N	Y
12 Burke	?	?	?	?	?	?
13 Lehman	N	N	Y	Y	N	Y
14 Pepper	N	N	Y	Y	N	Y
15 Fascell	N	N	Y	Y	N	Y
GEORGIA						
1 Ginn	N	Y	Y	N	N	Y
2 Mathis	N	Y	Y	N	?	?
3 Brinkley	N	Y	Y	N	Y	Y
4 Levitas	N	Y	Y	Y	Y	Y
5 Fowler	N	N	Y	Y	N	Y
6 Flynt	?	?	?	?	?	?
7 McDonald	Y	Y	N	N	Y	N
8 Evans	▮	▮	#	#	?	?
9 Jenkins	N	#	#	#	▮	#
10 Barnard	N	Y	?	N	▮	#
HAWAII						
1 Heftel	N	N	Y	Y	N	Y
2 Akaka	N	N	Y	Y	N	Y
IDAHO						
1 Symms	Y	Y	N	N	Y	N
2 Hansen, G.	Y	Y	N	N	Y	N
ILLINOIS						
1 Metcalfe	N	N	Y	?	?	?
2 Murphy	N	N	Y	Y	N	Y
3 Russo	N	N	Y	Y	N	Y
4 Derwinski	Y	N	Y	N	Y	Y
5 Fary	N	N	Y	Y	N	Y
6 Hyde	Y	N	Y	N	Y	Y
7 Collins	N	N	Y	Y	N	Y
8 Rostenkowski	N	N	Y	Y	N	Y
9 Yates	N	N	Y	Y	N	Y
10 Mikva	N	N	Y	Y	N	Y
11 Annunzio	N	N	Y	Y	N	Y
12 Crane	Y	Y	N	N	#	▮
13 McClory	Y	N	Y	N	N	Y
14 Erlenborn	Y	Y	Y	N	Y	Y
15 Corcoran	Y	Y	N	N	Y	Y
16 Anderson	#	▮	#	▮	▮	#
17 O'Brien	Y	N	N	N	Y	Y
18 Michel	Y	Y	Y	N	Y	Y
19 Railsback	Y	Y	Y	N	?	?
20 Findley	Y	Y	Y	N	Y	Y
21 Madigan	N	Y	N	N	N	Y
22 Shipley	N	X	Y	Y	N	Y
23 Price	N	N	Y	Y	N	Y
24 Simon	N	N	Y	Y	N	Y
INDIANA						
1 Benjamin	Y	N	Y	Y	N	Y
2 Fithian	Y	Y	Y	Y	N	Y
3 Brademas	N	N	Y	Y	N	Y
4 Quayle	Y	?	Y	N	Y	Y
5 Hillis	Y	Y	N	N	N	Y
6 Evans	Y	Y	Y	Y	N	Y
7 Myers, J.	Y	Y	N	N	N	Y
8 Cornwell	Y	Y	Y	Y	N	Y
9 Hamilton	Y	Y	Y	Y	Y	Y
10 Sharp	Y	Y	Y	Y	Y	Y
11 Jacobs	Y	Y	Y	Y	N	Y
IOWA						
1 Leach	Y	Y	Y	N	N	Y
2 Blouin	N	N	Y	Y	▮	#
3 Grassley	Y	Y	Y	N	Y	Y
4 Smith	N	Y	Y	N	Y	Y
5 Harkin	N	N	Y	Y	N	Y
6 Bedell	N	N	Y	Y	N	Y

Democrats ***Republicans***

	467	468	469	470	471	472
KANSAS						
1 Sebelius	Y	Y	N	N	N	Y
2 Keys	Y	Y	Y	Y	N	Y
3 Winn	#	#	#	▮	▮	#
4 Glickman	Y	Y	Y	N	N	Y
5 Skubitz	?	?	N	N	N	Y
KENTUCKY						
1 Hubbard	N	Y	Y	N	N	Y
2 Natcher	N	Y	Y	Y	N	Y
3 Mazzoli	N	N	Y	Y	N	Y
4 Snyder	Y	Y	N	N	N	Y
5 Carter	Y	Y	Y	N	N	Y
6 Breckinridge	N	Y	Y	Y	?	?
7 Perkins	N	N	Y	Y	N	Y
LOUISIANA						
1 Livingston	Y	Y	N	N	Y	Y
2 Boggs	Y	Y	Y	Y	N	Y
3 Treen	Y	Y	Y	N	Y	N
4 Waggonner	Y	Y	N	N	Y	Y
5 Huckaby	Y	Y	N	N	Y	Y
6 Moore	Y	Y	N	N	Y	Y
7 Breaux	Y	Y	?	X	?	?
8 Long	Y	Y	?	Y	N	Y
MAINE						
1 Emery	N	Y	Y	N	N	Y
2 Cohen	Y	Y	Y	N	N	Y
MARYLAND						
1 Bauman	Y	Y	N	N	Y	N
2 Long	Y	N	Y	Y	N	Y
3 Mikulski	N	Y	Y	Y	N	Y
4 Holt	Y	Y	N	N	Y	N
5 Spellman	N	Y	Y	X	N	Y
6 Byron	?	?	?	Y	N	Y
7 Mitchell	N	N	Y	Y	N	Y
8 Steers	N	Y	Y	Y	N	Y
MASSACHUSETTS						
1 Conte	N	N	Y	N	N	Y
2 Boland	N	N	Y	N	N	Y
3 Early	N	N	Y	N	N	Y
4 Drinan	N	N	Y	Y	N	Y
5 Tsongas	?	?	?	?	?	?
6 Harrington	▮	N	#	Y	▮	#
7 Markey	N	N	Y	Y	N	Y
8 O'Neill						
9 Moakley	N	N	#	Y	N	Y
10 Heckler	N	N	?	N	N	Y
11 Burke	N	N	Y	Y	N	Y
12 Studds	Y	N	Y	Y	N	Y
MICHIGAN						
1 Conyers	N	N	#	Y	N	Y
2 Pursell	N	?	?	?	N	Y
3 Brown	N	N	Y	N	?	?
4 Stockman	N	N	Y	N	N	Y
5 Sawyer	Y	N	N	N	▮	#
6 Carr	N	N	Y	Y	N	Y
7 Kildee	N	N	Y	Y	N	Y
8 Traxler	N	N	Y	Y	N	Y
9 Vander Jagt	N	N	N	N	Y	Y
10 Cederberg	N	N	N	▮	?	?
11 Ruppe	Y	N	Y	N	?	?
12 Bonior	N	N	Y	Y	N	Y
13 Diggs	▮	#	#	Y	▮	Y
14 Nedzi	N	N	Y	Y	N	Y
15 Ford	N	N	Y	Y	N	Y
16 Dingell	N	N	?	Y	N	Y
17 Brodhead	N	N	Y	Y	N	Y
18 Blanchard	N	N	Y	Y	N	Y
19 Broomfield	Y	▮	Y	N	Y	Y
MINNESOTA						
1 Quie	Y	Y	Y	N	N	Y
2 Hagedorn	Y	Y	N	N	Y	Y
3 Frenzel	Y	Y	Y	N	N	Y
4 Vento	Y	N	Y	Y	N	Y
5 Fraser	#	▮	#	#	?	?
6 Nolan	Y	N	Y	Y	N	Y
7 Stangeland	Y	Y	N	N	Y	Y
8 Oberstar	Y	N	Y	Y	N	Y
MISSISSIPPI						
1 Whitten	N	Y	Y	N	N	Y
2 Bowen	Y	Y	Y	N	N	Y
3 Montgomery	N	Y	N	N	N	Y
4 Cochran	N	Y	Y	N	?	?
5 Lott	N	Y	N	N	N	Y
MISSOURI						
1 Clay	N	N	Y	Y	N	Y
2 Young	Y	Y	Y	N	N	Y
3 Gephardt	Y	Y	Y	Y	Y	Y
4 Skelton	Y	Y	Y	Y	N	Y
5 Bolling	▮	▮	Y	Y	N	Y
6 Coleman	Y	Y	N	N	Y	Y
7 Taylor	Y	Y	N	N	Y	Y
8 Ichord	Y	Y	N	N	Y	Y
9 Volkmer	Y	Y	Y	Y	N	Y
10 Burlison	N	N	Y	Y	N	Y
MONTANA						
1 Baucus	Y	Y	Y	Y	▮	#
2 Marlenee	Y	Y	Y	N	N	Y
NEBRASKA						
1 Thone	✓	?	?	?	?	?
2 Cavanaugh	Y	Y	Y	Y	N	Y
3 Smith	Y	Y	N	N	#	?
NEVADA						
AL Santini	N	Y	#	N	N	Y
NEW HAMPSHIRE						
1 D'Amours	N	N	Y	N	N	Y
2 Cleveland	Y	Y	Y	N	Y	Y
NEW JERSEY						
1 Florio	N	N	Y	Y	N	Y
2 Hughes	N	N	Y	Y	N	Y
3 Howard	N	N	Y	Y	N	Y
4 Thompson	N	N	Y	Y	N	Y
5 Fenwick	N	N	#	Y	N	Y
6 Forsythe	▮	N	Y	N	Y	N
7 Maguire	N	N	Y	N	N	Y
8 Roe	N	N	Y	Y	N	Y
9 Hollenbeck	N	N	Y	Y	N	Y
10 Rodino	▮	▮	#	#	▮	#
11 Minish	N	N	Y	Y	N	Y
12 Rinaldo	N	N	Y	Y	N	Y
13 Meyner	N	N	Y	Y	N	Y
14 LeFante	▮	X	#	✓	▮	#
15 Patten	N	N	Y	Y	N	Y
NEW MEXICO						
1 Lujan	N	Y	N	N	Y	Y
2 Runnels	N	Y	N	N	Y	Y
NEW YORK						
1 Pike	N	N	Y	N	N	Y
2 Downey	N	N	Y	Y	N	Y
3 Ambro	N	N	Y	Y	N	Y
4 Lent	N	N	N	N	N	Y
5 Wydler	Y	N	N	N	N	Y
6 Wolff	#	▮	#	#	?	?
7 Addabbo	N	N	Y	Y	N	Y
8 Rosenthal	▮	N	Y	Y	N	Y
9 Delaney	▮	N	Y	Y	N	Y
10 Biaggi	N	N	Y	Y	N	Y
11 Scheuer	N	N	#	Y	N	Y
12 Chisholm	N	N	Y	Y	N	Y
13 Solarz	N	N	Y	Y	N	Y
14 Richmond	N	N	Y	Y	N	Y
15 Zeferetti	N	N	Y	Y	N	Y
16 Holtzman	N	N	Y	Y	N	Y
17 Murphy	N	N	?	Y	N	Y
18 Green	N	N	Y	N	N	Y
19 Rangel	?	X	?	✓	?	?
20 Weiss	N	N	Y	Y	N	Y
21 Garcia	N	N	#	Y	N	Y
22 Bingham	N	N	Y	Y	N	Y
23 Caputo	?	?	?	?	?	?
24 Ottinger	N	N	Y	Y	N	Y
25 Fish	N	N	Y	N	N	Y
26 Gilman	N	N	Y	N	N	Y
27 McHugh	N	N	Y	?	N	Y
28 Stratton	N	N	Y	Y	N	Y
29 Pattison	N	N	Y	Y	N	Y
30 McEwen	N	N	N	N	Y	Y
31 Mitchell	#	▮	N	N	▮	#
32 Hanley	N	N	Y	Y	N	Y
33 Walsh	N	N	N	N	N	Y
34 Horton	N	N	N	N	N	Y
35 Conable	Y	N	Y	N	Y	Y
36 LaFalce	N	N	Y	Y	N	Y
37 Nowak	N	N	Y	Y	N	Y
38 Kemp	N	N	Y	N	Y	Y
39 Lundine	N	N	Y	N	▮	#
NORTH CAROLINA						
1 Jones	Y	Y	Y	N	Y	Y
2 Fountain	#	#	#	▮	▮	#
3 Whitley	Y	Y	Y	N	N	Y
4 Andrews	N	Y	?	?	?	?
5 Neal	Y	Y	Y	N	N	Y
6 Preyer	Y	Y	Y	N	N	Y
7 Rose	N	Y	Y	N	N	Y
8 Hefner	Y	Y	Y	N	N	†
9 Martin	Y	Y	Y	N	Y	Y
10 Broyhill	Y	Y	Y	N	Y	Y
11 Gudger	N	Y	Y	N	N	Y
NORTH DAKOTA						
AL Andrews	Y	Y	N	N	Y	Y
OHIO						
1 Gradison	Y	Y	Y	N	N	Y
2 Luken	N	N	Y	N	N	Y
3 Whalen	N	N	Y	Y	N	Y
4 Guyer	?	?	?	?	▮	#
5 Latta	Y	Y	N	N	Y	Y
6 Harsha	N	Y	Y	N	N	Y
7 Brown	Y	Y	Y	N	Y	Y
8 Kindness	Y	Y	N	N	Y	Y
9 Ashley	N	N	?	N	N	Y
10 Miller	Y	Y	N	N	Y	N
11 Stanton	Y	Y	Y	N	N	Y
12 Devine	Y	Y	N	N	Y	Y
13 Pease	N	N	Y	Y	N	Y
14 Seiberling	N	N	Y	Y	N	Y
15 Wylie	Y	Y	Y	?	N	Y
16 Regula	Y	Y	Y	N	N	Y
17 Ashbrook	Y	Y	N	N	Y	N
18 Applegate	N	Y	Y	Y	N	Y
19 Carney	N	N	Y	Y	N	?
20 Oakar	N	N	Y	Y	N	Y
21 Stokes	N	N	Y	Y	N	Y
22 Vanik	N	N	Y	Y	N	Y
23 Mottl	N	Y	N	Y	▮	#
OKLAHOMA						
1 Jones	Y	Y	Y	N	N	Y
2 Risenhoover	Y	Y	Y	N	N	Y
3 Watkins	Y	Y	Y	N	N	Y
4 Steed	#	▮	Y	Y	N	Y
5 Edwards	Y	Y	?	N	Y	Y
6 English	Y	Y	Y	N	N	Y
OREGON						
1 AuCoin	Y	N	Y	Y	▮	#
2 Ullman	N	N	Y	Y	N	Y
3 Duncan	Y	N	Y	Y	N	Y
4 Weaver	Y	N	Y	Y	N	Y
PENNSYLVANIA						
1 Myers, M.	N	N	Y	Y	N	Y
2 Nix	?	?	?	Y	N	Y
3 Lederer	N	N	Y	Y	N	Y
4 Eilberg	N	N	Y	Y	N	Y
5 Schulze	Y	N	N	N	Y	Y
6 Yatron	N	N	Y	Y	N	Y
7 Edgar	N	N	Y	Y	N	Y
8 Kostmayer	N	N	Y	Y	N	Y
9 Shuster	Y	N	N	N	Y	Y
10 McDade	N	N	#	N	N	Y
11 Flood	N	N	Y	Y	N	Y
12 Murtha	N	N	Y	Y	N	Y
13 Coughlin	Y	N	Y	N	▮	Y
14 Moorhead	N	N	Y	Y	N	Y
15 Rooney	N	N	Y	Y	N	Y
16 Walker	N	N	N	N	Y	Y
17 Ertel	N	N	Y	Y	N	Y
18 Walgren	N	N	Y	Y	N	Y
19 Goodling, W.	?	?	?	?	?	?
20 Gaydos	N	N	Y	Y	N	Y
21 Dent	?	N	Y	Y	▮	#
22 Murphy	N	N	Y	Y	N	Y
23 Ammerman	N	N	Y	Y	N	Y
24 Marks	N	N	Y	N	N	Y
25 Myers, G.	N	N	Y	Y	N	Y
RHODE ISLAND						
1 St Germain	N	N	Y	Y	N	Y
2 Beard	N	N	Y	Y	N	Y
SOUTH CAROLINA						
1 Davis	N	Y	Y	N	N	Y
2 Spence	Y	Y	Y	N	N	Y
3 Derrick	N	Y	Y	N	N	Y
4 Mann	?	?	?	?	?	?
5 Holland	N	Y	Y	Y	N	Y
6 Jenrette	N	Y	Y	N	N	Y
SOUTH DAKOTA						
1 Pressler	Y	Y	N	N	N	Y
2 Abdnor	Y	Y	N	N	N	Y
TENNESSEE						
1 Quillen	N	N	Y	N	▮	#
2 Duncan	Y	Y	Y	N	N	Y
3 Lloyd	Y	Y	Y	N	N	Y
4 Gore	N	Y	Y	Y	N	Y
5 Vacancy						
6 Beard	Y	Y	#	N	N	Y
7 Jones	Y	Y	Y	Y	N	Y
8 Ford	N	Y	Y	Y	N	Y
TEXAS						
1 Hall	Y	Y	Y	N	Y	Y
2 Wilson, C.	N	Y	Y	?	N	Y
3 Collins	Y	Y	N	N	Y	N
4 Roberts	N	✓	Y	N	?	?
5 Mattox	N	Y	Y	N	N	Y
6 Teague	?	✓	?	X	?	?
7 Archer	Y	Y	N	N	Y	N
8 Eckhardt	N	Y	Y	Y	N	Y
9 Brooks	N	Y	Y	Y	N	Y
10 Pickle	Y	Y	Y	N	N	Y
11 Poage	N	Y	Y	N	N	N
12 Wright	N	Y	Y	Y	N	Y
13 Hightower	N	Y	Y	N	N	Y
14 Young	?	?	?	Y	N	Y
15 de la Garza	?	?	?	?	?	?
16 White	N	Y	Y	N	N	Y
17 Burleson	N	Y	N	N	Y	N
18 Jordan	N	Y	Y	Y	N	Y
19 Mahon	N	Y	Y	N	N	Y
20 Gonzalez	N	Y	Y	N	N	Y
21 Krueger	▮	#	#	#	▮	#
22 Gammage	Y	Y	Y	N	▮	#
23 Kazen	N	Y	Y	N	N	Y
24 Milford	N	Y	Y	N	Y	N
UTAH						
1 McKay	N	Y	Y	Y	N	Y
2 Marriott	Y	Y	N	N	Y	Y
VERMONT						
AL Jeffords	Y	N	Y	N	N	Y
VIRGINIA						
1 Trible	Y	Y	Y	N	N	Y
2 Whitehurst	Y	Y	N	N	Y	Y
3 Satterfield	Y	Y	N	N	Y	N
4 Daniel	Y	Y	N	N	Y	Y
5 Daniel	Y	Y	N	N	Y	N
6 Butler	Y	Y	N	N	Y	Y
7 Robinson	Y	Y	N	N	Y	Y
8 Harris	N	N	Y	Y	N	Y
9 Wampler	Y	Y	Y	N	N	Y
10 Fisher	Y	Y	Y	Y	N	Y
WASHINGTON						
1 Pritchard	N	N	Y	N	N	Y
2 Meeds	Y	N	Y	Y	N	#
3 Bonker	N	N	Y	Y	N	Y
4 McCormack	N	N	Y	Y	N	Y
5 Foley	Y	N	?	Y	N	Y
6 Dicks	N	N	Y	Y	N	Y
7 Cunningham	Y	Y	N	N	Y	Y
WEST VIRGINIA						
1 Mollohan	N	Y	Y	Y	N	Y
2 Staggers	N	Y	Y	Y	N	Y
3 Slack	N	Y	Y	Y	N	Y
4 Rahall	N	N	#	✓	N	Y
WISCONSIN						
1 Aspin	Y	N	Y	Y	N	Y
2 Kastenmeier	N	N	Y	Y	N	Y
3 Baldus	Y	N	Y	Y	N	Y
4 Zablocki	N	N	Y	Y	N	Y
5 Reuss	N	N	Y	Y	N	Y
6 Steiger	Y	Y	Y	N	N	Y
7 Obey	Y	N	Y	Y	N	Y
8 Cornell	N	N	Y	Y	N	Y
9 Kasten	#	#	#	▮	?	?
WYOMING						
AL Roncalio	N	N	Y	Y	N	Y

Democrats ***Republicans***

473. H 10929. Defense Procurement Authorization. Price, D-Ill., motion to close to the public the conference committee meetings on the bill to authorize fiscal 1979 funds for Defense Department weapons procurement and military research and development when classified national security items were being discussed, as authorized under House rules, but to allow the attendance of members of Congress at all meetings. Motion agreed to 312-5: R 104-0; D 208-5 (ND 144-5; SD 64-0), July 14, 1978.

474. HR 12163. Energy Department Authorization. Flowers, D-Ala., amendment to reduce funding for the Clinch River nuclear breeder reactor project by $159 million, to limit work on that project to completion of studies and tests and to require a study of advanced breeder reactor technologies to be prepared by March 1, 1981. Rejected 142-187: R 20-91; D 122-96 (ND 96-56; SD 26-40), July 14, 1978. A "yea" was a vote supporting the president's position.

475. HR 12163. Energy Department Authorization. Flowers, D-Ala., amendment to add $75 million for initial construction costs for a facility to demonstrate the SRC-II (solvent refined coal) process of producing liquid boiler fuels from coal. Adopted 165-132: R 33-62; D 132-70 (ND 78-60; SD 54-10), July 14, 1978.

476. HR 12028. Veterans' Home Loan Program. Roberts, D-Texas, motion to suspend the rules and pass the bill to amend the U.S. Code to increase to $30,000 grants for specially adapted housing for certain disabled veterans, to $25,000 for VA loan guarantees, and to permit Vietnam-era veterans with 90 days of service to qualify for VA home loan programs. Motion agreed to 373-0: R 120-0; D 253-0 (ND 175-0; SD 78-0), July 17, 1978. A two-thirds majority vote (249 in this case) is required for passage under suspension of the rules.

477. HR 12232. Unemployment Compensation Amendments. Corman, D-Calif., motion to suspend the rules and pass the bill to amend the 1976 Unemployment Compensation Amendments to: 1) pay members of the National Commission on Unemployment Compensation who were not full-time federal employees; 2) extend for one year, to May 31, 1981, the effective date of the provision that unemployment compensation benefits be reduced by the amount of retirement benefits received; and 3) extend for two years the exemption for farm employers of the payment of employment taxes for seasonal alien agricultural workers. Motion agreed to 300-81: R 82-41; D 218-40 (ND 158-22; SD 60-18), July 17, 1978. A two-thirds majority vote (254 in this case) is required for passage under suspension of the rules.

478. HR 12380. Extended Unemployment Benefits. Corman, D-Calif, motion to suspend the rules and pass the bill to limit to two years beyond the regular unemployment period the time within which an individual may receive extended unemployment benefits under the 1970 Federal-State Extended Unemployment Compensation Act. Motion agreed to 381-4: R 124-0; D 257-4 (ND 181-1; SD 76-3) July 17, 1978. A two-thirds majority vote (257 in this case) is required for passage under suspension of the rules.

479. HR 10848. Supplemental Security Income (SSI) Benefits. Corman, D-Calif., motion to suspend the rules and pass the bill to allow persons whose SSI payments were discontinued because they became employed to be considered disabled and immediately receive SSI benefits for three months, pending a review by the Social Security Administration, if they had received SSI benefits within the previous five years. Motion agreed to 351-32: R 114-10; D 237-22 (ND 171-9; SD 66-13), July 17, 1978. A two-thirds majority vote (256 in this case) is required for passage under suspension of the rules.

480. HR 12163. Energy Department Authorization. Fish, R-N.Y., motion to recommit the bill to the Science and Technology Committee with instructions to report the bill back to the House with an amendment containing language called for in the rejected Flowers, D-Ala., amendment *(see vote 474, above)*. Motion rejected 157-238: R 23-107; D 134-131 (ND 113-70; SD 21-61), July 17, 1978. A "yea" was a vote supporting the president's position.

KEY

- Y Voted for (yea).
- ✓ Paired for.
- † Announced for.
- # CQ Poll for.
- N Voted against (nay).
- X Paired against.
- \- Announced against.
- ▮ CQ Poll against.
- P Voted "present."
- ● Voted "present" to avoid possible conflict of interest.
- ? Did not vote or otherwise make a position known.

	473	474	475	476	477	478	479	480
ALABAMA								
1 Edwards	Y	N	N	Y	Y	Y	Y	N
2 Dickinson	Y	N	Y	Y	Y	Y	Y	N
3 Nichols	#	X	#	Y	Y	Y	Y	N
4 Bevill	Y	N	Y	Y	Y	Y	Y	N
5 Flippo	Y	Y	Y	Y	Y	Y	Y	N
6 Buchanan	Y	N	Y	Y	Y	Y	Y	N
7 Flowers	Y	Y	Y	?	?	?	?	✓
ALASKA								
AL Young	Y	N	#	Y	N	Y	Y	N
ARIZONA								
1 Rhodes	Y	N	N	Y	Y	Y	Y	N
2 Udall	Y	Y	▮	Y	Y	Y	Y	Y
3 Stump	?	▮	#	Y	Y	Y	N	N
4 Rudd	Y	N	N	Y	Y	Y	N	N
ARKANSAS								
1 Alexander	?	?	?	?	?	?	?	?
2 Tucker	#	#	#	Y	Y	Y	Y	Y
3 Hammerschmidt	Y	N	Y	Y	N	Y	Y	N
4 Thornton	?	N	Y	Y	Y	Y	N	N
CALIFORNIA								
1 Johnson	Y	N	Y	Y	Y	Y	Y	N
2 Clausen	?	N	N	Y	Y	Y	Y	N
3 Moss	Y	Y	N	Y	Y	Y	Y	Y
4 Leggett	Y	?	Y	?	?	?	?	X
5 Burton, J.	?	Y	N	Y	Y	Y	Y	Y
6 Burton, P.	Y	Y	N	Y	Y	Y	Y	Y
7 Miller	Y	Y	N	Y	Y	Y	Y	Y
8 Dellums	N	Y	N	Y	Y	Y	Y	Y
9 Stark	▮	Y	N	Y	Y	Y	Y	Y
10 Edwards	Y	Y	Y	Y	Y	Y	Y	Y
11 Ryan	Y	Y	N	Y	Y	Y	Y	Y
12 McCloskey	?	N	N	Y	Y	Y	Y	N
13 Mineta	Y	N	Y	Y	Y	Y	Y	N
14 McFall	Y	N	Y	Y	Y	Y	Y	N
15 Sisk	Y	N	?	Y	Y	Y	Y	N
16 Panetta	Y	Y	Y	Y	Y	Y	Y	Y
17 Krebs	N	Y	Y	Y	Y	Y	Y	Y
18 Vacancy								
19 Lagomarsino	Y	N	N	Y	N	Y	Y	N
20 Goldwater	Y	N	Y	Y	Y	Y	Y	N
21 Corman	Y	Y	Y	Y	Y	Y	Y	Y
22 Moorhead	Y	N	N	Y	N	Y	Y	N
23 Beilenson	#	Y	N	Y	Y	Y	Y	Y
24 Waxman	#	#	N	Y	Y	Y	Y	Y
25 Roybal	Y	Y	N	Y	Y	Y	Y	Y
26 Rousselot	Y	N	?	Y	N	Y	N	N
27 Dornan	Y	N	N	Y	N	Y	Y	N
28 Burke	#	#	#	#	#	#	#	✓
29 Hawkins	?	✓	?	Y	Y	Y	Y	Y
30 Danielson	Y	Y	Y	Y	Y	Y	Y	N
31 Wilson, C.H.	Y	?	?	Y	Y	Y	Y	N
32 Anderson	Y	N	Y	Y	Y	Y	Y	N
33 Clawson	?	?	?	?	?	?	?	?
34 Hannaford	Y	N	Y	Y	Y	Y	Y	N
35 Lloyd	Y	Y	Y	Y	Y	Y	Y	Y
36 Brown	Y	Y	N	Y	Y	Y	Y	Y
37 Pettis	Y	N	Y	Y	Y	Y	Y	N
38 Patterson	Y	Y	Y	#	#	#	#	▮
39 Wiggins	#	▮	#	#	#	#	#	▮
40 Badham	Y	N	N	Y	N	Y	Y	N
41 Wilson, B.	Y	N	Y	Y	Y	Y	Y	N
42 Van Deerlin	?	?	?	Y	Y	Y	Y	Y
43 Burgener	Y	N	N	Y	Y	Y	Y	N
COLORADO								
1 Schroeder	N	Y	Y	Y	Y	Y	Y	Y
2 Wirth	Y	Y	N	Y	N	Y	N	Y
3 Evans	?	?	?	Y	Y	Y	Y	Y
4 Johnson	Y	N	?	?	?	?	?	?
5 Armstrong	Y	N	N	?	?	?	?	?
CONNECTICUT								
1 Cotter	#	▮	▮	Y	Y	Y	Y	Y
2 Dodd	Y	Y	Y	Y	Y	Y	Y	Y
3 Giaimo	Y	Y	N	Y	Y	Y	Y	Y
4 McKinney	Y	Y	Y	#	Y	Y	Y	Y
5 Sarasin	#	X	#	#	#	#	#	▮
6 Moffett	Y	✓	?	?	?	Y	Y	Y
DELAWARE								
AL Evans	Y	N	N	?	?	Y	Y	N
FLORIDA								
1 Sikes	?	X	?	Y	N	Y	N	N
2 Fuqua	Y	Y	Y	#	#	Y	Y	Y
3 Bennett	Y	N	Y	Y	Y	Y	Y	N
4 Chappell	Y	N	Y	Y	N	Y	N	N
5 Kelly	Y	N	N	Y	Y	Y	Y	N
6 Young	Y	N	?	Y	Y	Y	Y	N
7 Gibbons	?	?	?	?	?	?	?	?
8 Ireland	Y	Y	Y	Y	Y	Y	Y	Y
9 Frey	?	?	?	?	?	?	?	?
10 Bafalis	Y	N	?	Y	Y	Y	Y	N
11 Rogers	Y	Y	Y	Y	Y	Y	Y	Y
12 Burke	?	?	?	Y	?	?	?	N
13 Lehman	Y	Y	N	Y	N	Y	Y	Y
14 Pepper	Y	Y	Y	Y	Y	Y	Y	Y
15 Fascell	Y	Y	Y	Y	N	Y	Y	Y
GEORGIA								
1 Ginn	Y	N	Y	#	#	#	#	N
2 Mathis	?	?	?	Y	Y	Y	Y	N
3 Brinkley	Y	?	?	Y	Y	Y	N	N
4 Levitas	Y	Y	Y	Y	Y	Y	N	Y
5 Fowler	Y	Y	Y	Y	Y	Y	Y	Y
6 Flynt	?	?	?	?	?	?	?	?
7 McDonald	Y	N	N	Y	N	Y	N	N
8 Evans	?	?	?	?	?	?	?	N
9 Jenkins	#	#	#	Y	Y	Y	N	Y
10 Barnard	#	▮	#	Y	Y	Y	N	N
HAWAII								
1 Heftel	Y	Y	Y	Y	Y	Y	Y	Y
2 Akaka	Y	N	Y	Y	Y	Y	Y	N
IDAHO								
1 Symms	?	?	?	Y	N	Y	N	N
2 Hansen, G.	?	N	N	Y	N	Y	N	N
ILLINOIS								
1 Metcalfe	?	?	?	Y	Y	Y	Y	N
2 Murphy	Y	N	Y	Y	Y	Y	Y	N
3 Russo	Y	N	▮	Y	Y	Y	Y	N
4 Derwinski	Y	N	N	Y	Y	Y	Y	N
5 Fary	Y	N	Y	Y	Y	Y	Y	N
6 Hyde	Y	N	N	Y	Y	Y	Y	N
7 Collins	?	?	?	Y	Y	Y	Y	N
8 Rostenkowski	Y	N	?	Y	Y	Y	Y	N
9 Yates	Y	Y	Y	Y	Y	Y	Y	Y
10 Mikva	Y	Y	N	Y	Y	Y	Y	Y
11 Annunzio	Y	N	Y	Y	Y	Y	Y	N
12 Crane	Y	N	N	Y	N	Y	N	N
13 McClory	Y	▮	▮	Y	Y	Y	Y	N
14 Erlenborn	Y	N	N	#	#	#	#	▮
15 Corcoran	Y	N	N	Y	Y	Y	Y	N
16 Anderson	#	▮	#	Y	Y	Y	Y	N
17 O'Brien	Y	N	N	Y	Y	Y	Y	N
18 Michel	Y	N	N	Y	Y	Y	Y	N
19 Railsback	?	?	?	Y	Y	Y	?	N
20 Findley	Y	Y	Y	Y	N	Y	Y	Y
21 Madigan	Y	?	?	Y	Y	Y	Y	N
22 Shipley	?	X	?	?	?	?	?	X
23 Price	Y	N	Y	Y	Y	Y	Y	N
24 Simon	?	?	?	Y	Y	Y	Y	Y
INDIANA								
1 Benjamin	Y	N	Y	Y	Y	Y	Y	N
2 Fithian	Y	Y	N	Y	Y	Y	Y	Y
3 Brademas	Y	Y	Y	Y	Y	Y	Y	Y
4 Quayle	?	?	?	Y	N	Y	Y	Y
5 Hillis	Y	N	Y	Y	N	Y	Y	N
6 Evans	Y	N	N	Y	N	Y	Y	N
7 Myers, J.	Y	N	N	Y	N	Y	Y	N
8 Cornwell	Y	N	#	Y	Y	Y	N	N
9 Hamilton	Y	Y	N	Y	Y	Y	Y	Y
10 Sharp	Y	Y	N	Y	N	Y	Y	Y
11 Jacobs	Y	Y	N	Y	N	Y	Y	Y
IOWA								
1 Leach	Y	Y	N	Y	Y	Y	Y	Y
2 Blouin	▮	#	▮	#	#	#	#	✓
3 Grassley	Y	N	N	Y	N	Y	Y	N
4 Smith	Y	N	Y	Y	Y	Y	Y	N
5 Harkin	Y	Y	Y	Y	Y	Y	Y	Y
6 Bedell	Y	#	▮	Y	N	Y	Y	Y

Democrats ***Republicans***

	473	474	475	476	477	478	479	480
KANSAS								
1 Sebelius	Y	N	?	?	?	?	?	?
2 Keys	Y	Y	N	Y	Y	Y	Y	Y
3 Winn	#	▮	▮	Y	Y	Y	Y	N
4 Glickman	Y	Y	Y	Y	N	Y	Y	Y
5 Skubitz	Y	N	N	?	?	?	?	N
KENTUCKY								
1 Hubbard	Y	N	Y	Y	Y	Y	Y	N
2 Natcher	Y	Y	Y	Y	Y	Y	Y	Y
3 Mazzoli	Y	N	Y	Y	Y	Y	Y	N
4 Snyder	Y	N	N	Y	Y	Y	Y	N
5 Carter	Y	N	Y	Y	Y	Y	Y	N
6 Breckinridge	?	?	?	Y	Y	Y	Y	N
7 Perkins	Y	N	Y	Y	Y	Y	Y	N
LOUISIANA								
1 Livingston	?	X	?	Y	N	Y	Y	N
2 Boggs	Y	N	Y	Y	Y	Y	Y	N
3 Treen	?	?	?	Y	N	Y	Y	N
4 Waggonner	#	N	Y	Y	N	N	N	N
5 Huckaby	Y	N	N	Y	Y	Y	Y	N
6 Moore	Y	N	N	Y	Y	Y	Y	N
7 Breaux	?	X	?	?	?	?	?	X
8 Long	Y	Y	N	Y	Y	Y	Y	Y
MAINE								
1 Emery	Y	Y	N	Y	Y	Y	Y	Y
2 Cohen	#	#	#	Y	Y	Y	Y	Y
MARYLAND								
1 Bauman	Y	N	N	Y	N	Y	Y	N
2 Long	Y	Y	Y	Y	Y	Y	Y	Y
3 Mikulski	Y	N	N	Y	Y	Y	Y	Y
4 Holt	Y	N	N	Y	N	Y	Y	N
5 Spellman	#	#	Y	Y	Y	Y	Y	Y
6 Byron	?	?	?	?	N	Y	Y	N
7 Mitchell	N	Y	N	Y	Y	Y	Y	Y
8 Steers	Y	Y	N	Y	Y	Y	Y	Y
MASSACHUSETTS								
1 Conte	Y	Y	Y	Y	Y	Y	Y	Y
2 Boland	Y	Y	▮	Y	Y	Y	Y	Y
3 Early	Y	Y	N	Y	Y	Y	Y	Y
4 Drinan	Y	Y	N	Y	Y	Y	Y	Y
5 Tsongas	?	✓	?	?	?	?	?	?
6 Harrington	▮	✓	▮	#	#	#	#	✓
7 Markey	?	Y	?	Y	Y	Y	Y	Y
8 O'Neill								
9 Moakley	Y	#	?	Y	Y	Y	Y	Y
10 Heckler	Y	Y	N	Y	Y	Y	Y	Y
11 Burke	Y	N	Y	Y	Y	Y	Y	N
12 Studds	Y	Y	N	Y	Y	Y	Y	Y
MICHIGAN								
1 Conyers	▮	Y	Y	Y	Y	Y	Y	N
2 Pursell	Y	Y	Y	Y	Y	Y	Y	Y
3 Brown	?	?	?	Y	Y	Y	Y	N
4 Stockman	#	Y	N	Y	N	Y	Y	Y
5 Sawyer	#	?	?	#	#	#	#	N
6 Carr	N	Y	N	Y	Y	Y	Y	Y
7 Kildee	Y	Y	N	Y	Y	Y	Y	Y
8 Traxler	Y	Y	▮	#	#	#	Y	Y
9 Vander Jagt	Y	N	?	?	?	?	Y	N
10 Cederberg	?	?	?	Y	Y	Y	Y	N
11 Ruppe	?	?	?	?	?	?	?	?
12 Bonior	Y	Y	N	Y	Y	Y	Y	Y
13 Diggs	Y	Y	N	Y	Y	Y	Y	N
14 Nedzi	Y	Y	N	?	Y	Y	Y	Y
15 Ford	?	?	?	Y	Y	Y	?	Y
16 Dingell	Y	Y	N	Y	Y	Y	Y	Y
17 Brodhead	Y	Y	N	Y	Y	Y	Y	Y
18 Blanchard	Y	Y	Y	Y	Y	Y	Y	Y
19 Broomfield	Y	N	N	Y	Y	Y	Y	N
MINNESOTA								
1 Quie	?	?	?	?	?	?	?	?
2 Hagedorn	Y	N	?	Y	N	Y	Y	N
3 Frenzel	Y	N	N	Y	N	Y	Y	N
4 Vento	Y	Y	?	Y	N	Y	Y	Y
5 Fraser	?	✓	?	Y	Y	Y	Y	Y
6 Nolan	Y	Y	▮	Y	Y	Y	Y	Y
7 Stangeland	Y	N	▮	Y	N	Y	Y	N
8 Oberstar	Y	Y	Y	Y	Y	Y	Y	Y
MISSISSIPPI								
1 Whitten	Y	N	Y	Y	Y	Y	Y	N
2 Bowen	Y	N	Y	Y	Y	Y	Y	N
3 Montgomery	Y	N	Y	Y	Y	Y	Y	N
4 Cochran	?	?	?	Y	Y	Y	Y	N
5 Lott	#	N	#	Y	Y	Y	Y	N
MISSOURI								
1 Clay	?	?	?	Y	Y	Y	Y	Y
2 Young	Y	N	Y	Y	Y	Y	Y	N
3 Gephardt	Y	Y	Y	Y	Y	Y	Y	Y

	473	474	475	476	477	478	479	480
4 Skelton	Y	Y	Y	Y	Y	Y	Y	N
5 Bolling	Y	Y	Y	Y	Y	Y	Y	Y
6 Coleman	Y	N	Y	Y	N	Y	Y	N
7 Taylor	Y	N	N	Y	Y	Y	Y	N
8 Ichord	Y	N	Y	Y	N	Y	N	N
9 Volkmer	Y	N	Y	Y	N	Y	N	N
10 Burlison	Y	N	Y	Y	Y	Y	?	N
MONTANA								
1 Baucus	#	?	?	Y	Y	Y	Y	Y
2 Marlenee	Y	Y	N	Y	Y	Y	Y	Y
NEBRASKA								
1 Thone	?	?	?	?	?	?	?	N
2 Cavanaugh	?	Y	?	Y	N	Y	Y	Y
3 Smith	?	?	?	Y	N	Y	Y	N
NEVADA								
AL Santini	Y	N	N	#	#	#	#	X
NEW HAMPSHIRE								
1 D'Amours	Y	Y	N	Y	N	Y	Y	Y
2 Cleveland	?	?	?	Y	Y	Y	Y	N
NEW JERSEY								
1 Florio	Y	N	N	Y	Y	Y	Y	N
2 Hughes	Y	N	N	Y	Y	Y	Y	X
3 Howard	Y	Y	Y	Y	Y	Y	Y	Y
4 Thompson	Y	Y	Y	Y	Y	Y	Y	Y
5 Fenwick	Y	Y	N	Y	N	Y	Y	Y
6 Forsythe	Y	N	N	Y	Y	Y	Y	N
7 Maguire	Y	Y	N	Y	Y	Y	Y	Y
8 Roe	Y	N	Y	Y	Y	Y	Y	N
9 Hollenbeck	Y	N	▮	Y	Y	Y	Y	N
10 Rodino	#	#	▮	#	#	#	#	▮
11 Minish	Y	N	N	Y	Y	Y	Y	N
12 Rinaldo	Y	N	N	Y	Y	Y	Y	N
13 Meyner	Y	N	Y	Y	Y	Y	Y	N
14 LeFante	#	X	#	#	#	#	#	X
15 Patten	Y	N	N	#	#	#	#	N
NEW MEXICO								
1 Lujan	Y	N	Y	Y	N	Y	Y	N
2 Runnels	Y	N	Y	Y	N	Y	Y	N
NEW YORK								
1 Pike	Y	Y	N	Y	Y	Y	Y	Y
2 Downey	Y	Y	Y	Y	Y	Y	#	Y
3 Ambro	?	Y	Y	Y	Y	Y	Y	Y
4 Lent	?	N	Y	Y	Y	Y	Y	N
5 Wydler	Y	N	Y	Y	Y	Y	Y	N
6 Wolff	?	?	?	Y	Y	Y	Y	Y
7 Addabbo	?	✓	?	Y	Y	Y	Y	Y
8 Rosenthal	#	#	▮	Y	Y	Y	Y	Y
9 Delaney	Y	Y	Y	Y	Y	Y	Y	Y
10 Biaggi	Y	N	Y	?	Y	Y	Y	N
11 Scheuer	Y	N	Y	Y	Y	Y	Y	N
12 Chisholm	#	Y	N	Y	Y	Y	Y	Y
13 Solarz	Y	Y	Y	Y	Y	Y	Y	Y
14 Richmond	#	✓	▮	#	#	#	#	✓
15 Zeferetti	#	✓	#	#	Y	Y	Y	N
16 Holtzman	Y	Y	N	Y	Y	Y	Y	Y
17 Murphy	#	▮	?	Y	Y	Y	Y	N
18 Green	Y	N	N	Y	Y	Y	Y	N
19 Rangel	?	✓	?	Y	Y	Y	Y	Y
20 Weiss	†	✓	-	Y	Y	N	Y	Y
21 Garcia	Y	Y	▮	#	Y	Y	Y	Y
22 Bingham	Y	Y	Y	Y	Y	Y	Y	Y
23 Caputo	?	?	?	?	?	?	?	?
24 Ottinger	Y	Y	N	†	†	†	†	✓
25 Fish	Y	Y	Y	?	Y	Y	Y	Y
26 Gilman	Y	Y	Y	Y	Y	Y	Y	Y
27 McHugh	Y	Y	N	Y	Y	Y	Y	Y
28 Stratton	Y	N	Y	Y	Y	Y	Y	N
29 Pattison	Y	Y	N	Y	Y	Y	Y	Y
30 McEwen	Y	N	N	Y	Y	Y	Y	N
31 Mitchell	Y	Y	Y	Y	Y	Y	Y	Y
32 Hanley	Y	Y	N	Y	Y	Y	Y	Y
33 Walsh	?	?	?	Y	Y	Y	Y	N
34 Horton	Y	N	Y	Y	Y	Y	Y	N
35 Conable	Y	N	N	Y	N	Y	Y	N
36 LaFalce	Y	Y	?	Y	Y	Y	Y	Y
37 Nowak	Y	Y	Y	Y	Y	Y	Y	Y
38 Kemp	?	N	N	Y	Y	Y	Y	N
39 Lundine	#	✓	▮	Y	Y	Y	Y	Y
NORTH CAROLINA								
1 Jones	Y	N	Y	Y	Y	Y	Y	N
2 Fountain	#	▮	▮	Y	Y	Y	Y	N
3 Whitley	Y	N	?	Y	Y	Y	Y	N
4 Andrews	?	?	?	Y	Y	Y	Y	N
5 Neal	Y	Y	Y	Y	Y	Y	Y	Y
6 Preyer	Y	N	Y	Y	Y	Y	Y	N
7 Rose	Y	N	Y	Y	Y	Y	Y	N
8 Hefner	Y	N	Y	Y	Y	Y	Y	N

	473	474	475	476	477	478	479	480
9 Martin	Y	N	Y	Y	N	Y	Y	N
10 Broyhill	Y	N	N	Y	Y	Y	Y	N
11 Gudger	Y	N	Y	Y	Y	Y	Y	N
NORTH DAKOTA								
AL Andrews	Y	N	#	Y	Y	Y	Y	N
OHIO								
1 Gradison	Y	N	N	Y	Y	Y	Y	N
2 Luken	Y	N	N	Y	N	Y	Y	N
3 Whalen	Y	Y	N	Y	Y	Y	Y	Y
4 Guyer	#	▮	#	Y	Y	Y	Y	N
5 Latta	Y	N	▮	Y	N	Y	N	N
6 Harsha	Y	N	Y	Y	Y	Y	Y	N
7 Brown	?	?	?	?	?	?	?	?
8 Kindness	Y	N	N	Y	N	Y	Y	N
9 Ashley	?	Y	Y	Y	Y	Y	Y	Y
10 Miller	Y	N	Y	Y	N	Y	N	N
11 Stanton	Y	N	N	Y	Y	Y	Y	N
12 Devine	Y	N	Y	Y	Y	Y	N	N
13 Pease	Y	N	N	Y	N	Y	N	N
14 Seiberling	Y	Y	N	Y	Y	Y	Y	Y
15 Wylie	?	?	?	Y	Y	Y	Y	N
16 Regula	Y	N	N	Y	Y	Y	Y	N
17 Ashbrook	#	▮	#	#	▮	#	▮	#
18 Applegate	Y	N	Y	Y	Y	Y	Y	N
19 Carney	?	?	?	Y	Y	Y	Y	N
20 Oakar	Y	Y	?	Y	Y	Y	Y	Y
21 Stokes	#	#	▮	Y	Y	Y	Y	Y
22 Vanik	Y	Y	N	Y	Y	Y	Y	Y
23 Mottl	#	X	▮	Y	N	Y	N	N
OKLAHOMA								
1 Jones	Y	N	Y	Y	Y	Y	N	N
2 Risenhoover	Y	N	Y	Y	N	Y	Y	N
3 Watkins	Y	N	Y	Y	Y	Y	Y	N
4 Steed	Y	Y	Y	Y	Y	Y	Y	N
5 Edwards	Y	N	N	?	?	?	?	?
6 English	Y	N	N	Y	N	Y	Y	N
OREGON								
1 AuCoin	?	#	?	Y	Y	Y	N	Y
2 Ullman	#	N	Y	Y	Y	Y	Y	N
3 Duncan	Y	N	Y	Y	Y	Y	Y	N
4 Weaver	Y	Y	N	Y	Y	Y	Y	Y
PENNSYLVANIA								
1 Myers, M.	Y	N	Y	Y	Y	Y	Y	N
2 Nix	Y	N	?	Y	Y	Y	Y	N
3 Lederer	Y	N	Y	Y	Y	Y	Y	N
4 Eilberg	Y	N	?	Y	Y	Y	Y	N
5 Schulze	Y	N	N	Y	Y	Y	Y	N
6 Yatron	Y	N	Y	Y	Y	Y	Y	N
7 Edgar	Y	Y	Y	Y	Y	Y	Y	Y
8 Kostmayer	Y	Y	N	Y	N	Y	Y	Y
9 Shuster	Y	N	N	Y	Y	Y	Y	N
10 McDade	#	Y	Y	Y	Y	Y	Y	Y
11 Flood	?	X	?	Y	Y	Y	Y	N
12 Murtha	Y	N	Y	Y	Y	Y	Y	N
13 Coughlin	Y	Y	Y	Y	Y	Y	Y	Y
14 Moorhead	Y	Y	Y	Y	Y	Y	Y	Y
15 Rooney	Y	N	Y	Y	Y	Y	Y	N
16 Walker	Y	N	N	Y	N	Y	Y	N
17 Ertel	Y	N	Y	Y	Y	Y	Y	N
18 Walgren	Y	✓	?	Y	Y	Y	Y	Y
19 Goodling, W.	?	?	?	Y	Y	Y	Y	N
20 Gaydos	Y	N	Y	Y	Y	Y	Y	N
21 Dent	#	X	▮	#	#	Y	Y	N
22 Murphy	Y	N	Y	Y	N	Y	N	N
23 Ammerman	Y	Y	Y	Y	Y	Y	Y	Y
24 Marks	Y	N	?	Y	Y	Y	Y	N
25 Myers, G.	Y	N	Y	Y	Y	Y	Y	N
RHODE ISLAND								
1 St Germain	Y	?	?	Y	Y	Y	Y	Y
2 Beard	Y	Y	Y	Y	Y	Y	Y	N
SOUTH CAROLINA								
1 Davis	Y	Y	Y	Y	Y	Y	Y	N
2 Spence	Y	N	Y	Y	Y	Y	Y	N
3 Derrick	Y	Y	Y	Y	Y	Y	Y	N
4 Mann	?	?	?	?	?	?	?	?
5 Holland	Y	?	?	Y	Y	Y	Y	N
6 Jenrette	Y	N	Y	#	#	#	#	N
SOUTH DAKOTA								
1 Pressler	?	Y	?	?	?	?	?	?
2 Abdnor	Y	N	Y	Y	N	Y	Y	N
TENNESSEE								
1 Quillen	#	#	#	#	Y	Y	Y	N
2 Duncan	Y	N	Y	Y	Y	Y	Y	N
3 Lloyd	Y	N	Y	Y	N	Y	Y	N
4 Gore	Y	N	N	Y	N	Y	Y	N
5 Vacancy								
6 Beard	Y	N	N	Y	N	Y	Y	N

	473	474	475	476	477	478	479	480
7 Jones	Y	N	N	Y	N	Y	Y	N
8 Ford	?	?	?	Y	Y	Y	Y	N
TEXAS								
1 Hall	Y	N	Y	Y	N	Y	Y	N
2 Wilson, C.	#	N	Y	Y	Y	Y	Y	N
3 Collins	Y	N	N	Y	N	Y	N	N
4 Roberts	?	X	?	Y	N	Y	Y	N
5 Mattox	Y	Y	Y	Y	Y	Y	Y	Y
6 Teague	Y	Y	Y	Y	Y	Y	Y	Y
7 Archer	Y	N	Y	Y	N	Y	Y	N
8 Eckhardt	Y	Y	N	Y	Y	Y	Y	Y
9 Brooks	?	?	?	Y	Y	Y	Y	N
10 Pickle	Y	Y	Y	Y	Y	Y	N	Y
11 Poage	Y	N	Y	Y	N	N	Y	N
12 Wright	Y	Y	Y	Y	Y	Y	Y	Y
13 Hightower	Y	Y	?	Y	Y	Y	Y	Y
14 Young	?	?	Y	Y	Y	Y	Y	N
15 de la Garza	?	?	?	Y	Y	Y	Y	N
16 White	Y	N	Y	Y	Y	Y	Y	N
17 Burleson	Y	N	Y	Y	N	N	N	N
18 Jordan	Y	Y	Y	Y	Y	Y	Y	Y
19 Mahon	Y	N	Y	Y	Y	Y	Y	N
20 Gonzalez	Y	N	Y	Y	Y	Y	Y	N
21 Krueger	#	X	#	Y	Y	Y	Y	N
22 Gammage	Y	N	Y	Y	N	Y	Y	N
23 Kazen	Y	N	Y	Y	N	Y	Y	N
24 Milford	?	Y	?	?	?	?	?	?
UTAH								
1 McKay	Y	N	Y	Y	N	Y	Y	N
2 Marriott	Y	N	Y	Y	Y	Y	Y	N
VERMONT								
AL Jeffords	Y	Y	#	Y	N	Y	N	Y
VIRGINIA								
1 Trible	Y	N	N	Y	Y	Y	Y	N
2 Whitehurst	Y	N	N	Y	Y	Y	Y	N
3 Satterfield	Y	N	N	Y	N	Y	N	N
4 Daniel	Y	N	N	Y	N	Y	Y	N
5 Daniel	Y	N	Y	Y	Y	Y	Y	N
6 Butler	Y	N	N	?	N	Y	Y	N
7 Robinson	Y	N	N	Y	Y	Y	Y	N
8 Harris	Y	Y	N	Y	Y	Y	Y	Y
9 Wampler	?	?	?	?	?	?	?	N
10 Fisher	Y	Y	Y	Y	Y	Y	Y	N
WASHINGTON								
1 Pritchard	Y	Y	Y	Y	Y	Y	Y	Y
2 Meeds	Y	#	#	Y	Y	Y	Y	Y
3 Bonker	P	Y	N	Y	Y	Y	Y	Y
4 McCormack	Y	N	Y	Y	Y	Y	Y	N
5 Foley	Y	N	Y	Y	Y	Y	Y	N
6 Dicks	Y	N	?	Y	N	Y	Y	N
7 Cunningham	Y	N	N	Y	N	Y	Y	N
WEST VIRGINIA								
1 Mollohan	Y	N	Y	Y	N	Y	Y	N
2 Staggers	Y	Y	N	Y	Y	Y	Y	N
3 Slack	Y	N	Y	Y	Y	Y	Y	N
4 Rahall	Y	Y	Y	Y	Y	Y	Y	Y
WISCONSIN								
1 Aspin	Y	Y	N	Y	Y	Y	Y	Y
2 Kastenmeier	Y	Y	N	Y	Y	Y	Y	Y
3 Baldus	Y	Y	N	Y	Y	Y	Y	Y
4 Zablocki	Y	N	Y	Y	Y	Y	Y	N
5 Reuss	Y	Y	N	Y	Y	Y	Y	Y
6 Steiger	#	✓	▮	Y	Y	Y	Y	Y
7 Obey	Y	Y	N	Y	N	Y	Y	Y
8 Cornell	Y	Y	N	Y	Y	Y	Y	Y
9 Kasten	?	X	?	?	?	?	?	?
WYOMING								
AL Roncalio	Y	Y	Y	#	#	#	#	▮

Democrats ***Republicans***

481. HR 12163. Energy Department Authorization. Passage of the bill to authorize $4.5 billion in fiscal 1979 for research and development programs and activities of the Energy Department. Passed 325-67: R 119-11; D 206-56 (ND 126-54; SD 80-2), July 17, 1978.

482. HR 1609. Coal Slurry Pipelines. Adoption of the rule (H Res 1252) providing for House floor consideration of the bill to encourage construction of coal slurry pipelines. Adopted 376-7: R 124-4; D 252-3 (ND 173-2; SD 79-1), July 17, 1978.

483. HR 1609. Coal Slurry Pipelines. Udall, D-Ariz., motion that the House resolve itself into the Committee of the Whole for consideration of the bill to promote development of coal slurry pipelines. Motion agreed to 344-23: R 111-13; D 233-10 (ND 157-7; SD 76-3), July 17, 1978.

484. H J Res 738. Native American Religious Freedom. Johnson, R-Colo., demand for a second on the Udall, D-Ariz., motion *(see vote 491, p. 140-H)* to suspend the rules and pass the joint resolution to express the sense of Congress that the president direct the federal agencies to re-evaluate existing laws and regulations that prevented native Americans from practicing their traditional religions. Second ordered 396-2: R 136-2; D 260-0 (ND 181-0; SD 79-0), July 18, 1978.

485. HR 12443. Immigration Policy Revision. Eilberg, D-Pa., motion to suspend the rules and pass the bill to amend the Immigration and Nationality Act to provide a single worldwide ceiling on immigration into the United States and to establish a Select Commission on Immigration and Refugee Policy to study U.S. immigration policies. Motion agreed to 396-20: R 133-8; D 263-12 (ND 187-5; SD 76-7), July 18, 1978. A two-thirds majority vote (278 in this case) is required for passage under suspension of the rules.

486. HR 12508. Immigration of Adopted Children. Eilberg, D-Pa., motion to suspend the rules and pass the bill to amend the Immigration and Nationality Act to raise the limit for immigration preference on the number of children that could be adopted by a single family, and to liberalize immigration and naturalization requirements for children of parents applying for U.S. citizenship. Motion agreed to 413-0: R 139-0; D 274-0 (ND 191-0; SD 83-0), July 18, 1978. A two-thirds majority vote (276 in this case) is required for passage under suspension of the rules.

487. HR 12252. Payment to States' Veterans Cemeteries. Roberts, D-Texas, motion to suspend the rules and pass the bill to pay state and local governments $150 to cover the expenses of burying any veteran in a veterans' cemetery operated by a state or local government. Motion agreed to 407-9: R 136-4; D 271-5 (ND 186-5; SD 85-0), July 18, 1978. A two-third majority vote (278 in this case) is required for passage under suspension of the rules.

488. HR 12011. Hospital Care for Veterans in U.S. Territories. Roberts, D-Texas, motion to suspend the rules and pass the bill to extend indefinitely the authority of the Veterans Administration to contract with private hospitals for medical care of veterans in Alaska, Hawaii and U.S.-controlled territories. Motion agreed to 415-0: R 138-0; D 277-0 (ND 192-0; SD 85-0), July 18, 1978. A two-thirds majority vote (277 in this case) is required for passage under suspension of the rules.

KEY

Y	Voted for (yea).
✓	Paired for.
†	Announced for.
#	CQ Poll for.
N	Voted against (nay).
X	Paired against.
-	Announced against.
▮	CQ Poll against.
P	Voted "present."
●	Voted "present" to avoid possible conflict of interest.
?	Did not vote or otherwise make a position known.

	481	482	483	484	485	486	487	488
ALABAMA								
1 Edwards	Y	Y	Y	Y	Y	Y	Y	Y
2 Dickinson	Y	Y	Y	Y	Y	Y	Y	Y
3 Nichols	Y	Y	Y	Y	Y	Y	Y	Y
4 Bevill	Y	Y	Y	Y	Y	Y	Y	Y
5 Flippo	Y	Y	Y	Y	N	Y	Y	Y
6 Buchanan	Y	Y	Y	Y	Y	Y	Y	Y
7 Flowers	?	?	?	?	?	?	Y	Y
ALASKA								
AL Young	Y	Y	▮	Y	Y	Y	Y	Y
ARIZONA								
1 Rhodes	Y	Y	Y	Y	Y	Y	Y	Y
2 Udall	Y	Y	Y	Y	Y	Y	Y	Y
3 Stump	Y	Y	Y	Y	N	Y	Y	Y
4 Rudd	Y	Y	N	Y	N	Y	Y	Y
ARKANSAS								
1 Alexander	?	?	?	?	?	?	?	?
2 Tucker	Y	Y	Y	#	Y	Y	Y	Y
3 Hammerschmidt	Y	Y	Y	Y	Y	Y	Y	Y
4 Thornton	Y	Y	Y	Y	Y	Y	Y	Y
CALIFORNIA								
1 Johnson	Y	Y	Y	Y	Y	Y	Y	Y
2 Clausen	Y	Y	?	Y	Y	Y	Y	Y
3 Moss	Y	Y	Y	?	Y	Y	Y	Y
4 Leggett	?	Y	Y	Y	Y	Y	?	Y
5 Burton, J.	N	Y	Y	?	Y	Y	Y	Y
6 Burton, P.	N	Y	Y	Y	Y	Y	Y	Y
7 Miller	N	Y	Y	Y	Y	Y	Y	Y
8 Dellums	N	Y	Y	Y	Y	Y	Y	Y
9 Stark	N	Y	Y	Y	Y	Y	Y	Y
10 Edwards	Y	Y	Y	Y	Y	Y	Y	Y
11 Ryan	Y	Y	Y	Y	Y	Y	Y	Y
12 McCloskey	Y	Y	?	Y	Y	Y	Y	Y
13 Mineta	Y	Y	Y	Y	Y	Y	Y	Y
14 McFall	Y	Y	Y	Y	Y	Y	Y	Y
15 Sisk	Y	Y	Y	Y	Y	Y	Y	Y
16 Panetta	N	Y	Y	Y	Y	Y	Y	Y
17 Krebs	N	Y	Y	Y	Y	Y	Y	Y
18 Vacancy								
19 Lagomarsino	Y	Y	Y	Y	Y	Y	Y	Y
20 Goldwater	Y	Y	N	Y	Y	Y	Y	Y
21 Corman	Y	Y	Y	Y	Y	Y	Y	Y
22 Moorhead	Y	Y	Y	Y	Y	Y	Y	Y
23 Beilenson	N	Y	Y	Y	Y	Y	N	Y
24 Waxman	N	Y	Y	Y	Y	Y	Y	Y
25 Roybal	N	Y	Y	Y	Y	Y	Y	Y
26 Rousselot	Y	Y	Y	Y	Y	Y	Y	Y
27 Dornan	Y	Y	N	Y	Y	Y	Y	Y
28 Burke	#	#	#	Y	Y	Y	Y	Y
29 Hawkins	Y	Y	Y	Y	Y	Y	Y	Y
30 Danielson	Y	#	Y	Y	Y	Y	Y	Y
31 Wilson, C.H.	Y	Y	?	Y	Y	Y	Y	Y
32 Anderson	Y	Y	Y	Y	Y	Y	Y	Y
33 Clawson	?	?	?	?	?	?	?	?
34 Hannaford	Y	Y	Y	Y	Y	Y	Y	Y
35 Lloyd	Y	Y	N	Y	Y	Y	Y	Y
36 Brown	N	Y	Y	?	Y	Y	Y	Y
37 Pettis	Y	Y	Y	Y	Y	Y	Y	Y
38 Patterson	#	#	#	Y	Y	Y	Y	Y
39 Wiggins	#	#	#	Y	Y	Y	N	Y
40 Badham	Y	Y	#	Y	Y	Y	Y	Y
41 Wilson, B.	Y	Y	N	N	Y	Y	Y	Y
42 Van Deerlin	Y	Y	Y	Y	Y	Y	Y	Y
43 Burgener	Y	Y	Y	Y	Y	Y	Y	Y
COLORADO								
1 Schroeder	N	Y	#	Y	Y	Y	Y	Y
2 Wirth	?	Y	Y	Y	Y	Y	N	Y
3 Evans	Y	Y	Y	Y	Y	Y	Y	Y
4 Johnson	Y	Y	Y	Y	Y	Y	N	Y
5 Armstrong	N	Y	Y	Y	Y	Y	N	Y
CONNECTICUT								
1 Cotter	Y	Y	Y	Y	Y	Y	Y	Y
2 Dodd	N	Y	P	Y	Y	Y	Y	Y
3 Giaimo	Y	Y	Y	Y	Y	Y	Y	Y
4 McKinney	Y	Y	Y	Y	Y	Y	Y	Y
5 Sarasin	#	#	#	Y	Y	Y	Y	Y
6 Moffett	N	Y	Y	Y	Y	Y	Y	Y
DELAWARE								
AL Evans	Y	Y	Y	Y	Y	Y	Y	Y
FLORIDA								
1 Sikes	Y	Y	Y	Y	Y	Y	Y	Y
2 Fuqua	Y	Y	Y	Y	Y	Y	Y	Y
3 Bennett	Y	Y	Y	Y	Y	Y	Y	Y
4 Chappell	Y	Y	Y	Y	Y	Y	Y	Y
5 Kelly	Y	Y	Y	Y	N	Y	Y	Y
6 Young	Y	Y	Y	Y	Y	Y	Y	Y
7 Gibbons	?	?	?	?	?	?	?	?
8 Ireland	Y	?	?	Y	Y	Y	Y	Y
9 Frey	?	?	?	?	?	?	?	?
10 Bafalis	Y	●	●	Y	Y	Y	Y	Y
11 Rogers	Y	Y	Y	Y	Y	Y	Y	Y
12 Burke	Y	Y	Y	Y	Y	Y	Y	Y
13 Lehman	Y	Y	Y	Y	Y	Y	Y	Y
14 Pepper	Y	Y	Y	Y	Y	Y	Y	Y
15 Fascell	Y	Y	Y	Y	Y	Y	Y	Y
GEORGIA								
1 Ginn	Y	Y	Y	Y	Y	Y	Y	Y
2 Mathis	Y	Y	Y	?	Y	Y	Y	Y
3 Brinkley	Y	Y	Y	Y	Y	Y	Y	Y
4 Levitas	Y	Y	Y	Y	Y	Y	Y	Y
5 Fowler	Y	Y	Y	Y	Y	Y	Y	Y
6 Flynt	?	?	?	?	?	?	?	?
7 McDonald	N	Y	N	Y	N	Y	Y	Y
8 Evans	N	N	N	Y	Y	Y	Y	Y
9 Jenkins	Y	Y	Y	Y	Y	Y	Y	Y
10 Barnard	Y	Y	Y	Y	Y	Y	Y	Y
HAWAII								
1 Heftel	Y	Y	Y	Y	Y	Y	Y	Y
2 Akaka	Y	Y	Y	Y	Y	Y	Y	Y
IDAHO								
1 Symms	N	N	N	Y	Y	Y	Y	Y
2 Hansen, G.	N	N	?	Y	Y	Y	Y	Y
ILLINOIS								
1 Metcalfe	Y	Y	Y	Y	Y	Y	Y	Y
2 Murphy	Y	#	Y	Y	Y	Y	Y	Y
3 Russo	Y	Y	Y	Y	Y	Y	Y	Y
4 Derwinski	Y	Y	Y	Y	Y	Y	Y	Y
5 Fary	Y	Y	Y	Y	Y	Y	Y	Y
6 Hyde	Y	Y	Y	Y	Y	Y	Y	Y
7 Collins	Y	Y	Y	Y	Y	Y	Y	Y
8 Rostenkowski	Y	Y	Y	Y	Y	Y	Y	Y
9 Yates	Y	Y	Y	Y	Y	Y	Y	Y
10 Mikva	N	Y	Y	Y	Y	Y	Y	Y
11 Annunzio	Y	Y	Y	Y	Y	Y	Y	Y
12 Crane	N	Y	N	Y	Y	Y	Y	Y
13 McClory	Y	Y	Y	Y	Y	Y	Y	Y
14 Erlenborn	#	#	#	Y	Y	Y	Y	Y
15 Corcoran	Y	Y	Y	Y	Y	Y	Y	Y
16 Anderson	Y	Y	Y	Y	Y	#	Y	Y
17 O'Brien	Y	Y	Y	Y	Y	Y	Y	Y
18 Michel	Y	Y	Y	Y	Y	Y	Y	Y
19 Railsback	?	Y	Y	Y	Y	?	Y	Y
20 Findley	Y	Y	Y	Y	Y	Y	Y	?
21 Madigan	Y	?	Y	Y	Y	Y	Y	Y
22 Shipley	?	?	?	?	?	?	?	?
23 Price	Y	Y	Y	Y	Y	Y	Y	Y
24 Simon	Y	Y	Y	Y	Y	Y	Y	Y
INDIANA								
1 Benjamin	N	Y	Y	Y	Y	Y	N	Y
2 Fithian	Y	Y	Y	Y	Y	Y	Y	Y
3 Brademas	Y	Y	Y	Y	Y	Y	Y	Y
4 Quayle	Y	Y	N	Y	Y	Y	Y	Y
5 Hillis	Y	Y	Y	Y	Y	Y	Y	Y
6 Evans	Y	Y	Y	Y	Y	Y	Y	Y
7 Myers, J.	Y	Y	Y	Y	Y	Y	Y	Y
8 Cornwell	Y	Y	#	Y	Y	Y	Y	Y
9 Hamilton	Y	Y	Y	Y	Y	Y	Y	Y
10 Sharp	Y	Y	Y	Y	Y	Y	Y	Y
11 Jacobs	N	Y	Y	#	Y	Y	Y	Y
IOWA								
1 Leach	Y	Y	Y	Y	Y	Y	Y	Y
2 Blouin	X	#	#	Y	Y	Y	Y	Y
3 Grassley	Y	Y	Y	Y	Y	Y	Y	Y
4 Smith	Y	Y	Y	Y	Y	Y	Y	Y
5 Harkin	Y	Y	Y	Y	Y	Y	Y	Y
6 Bedell	N	Y	Y	Y	Y	Y	N	Y

Democrats ***Republicans***

	481	482	483	484	485	486	487	488
KANSAS								
1 Sebelius	?	?	?	Y	Y	Y	Y	Y
2 Keys	N	Y	Y	#	Y	Y	Y	Y
3 Winn	Y	Y	Y	Y	Y	Y	Y	Y
4 Glickman	Y	Y	Y	Y	N	Y	Y	Y
5 Skubitz	Y	Y	N	Y	Y	Y	Y	Y
KENTUCKY								
1 Hubbard	Y	Y	Y	Y	Y	Y	Y	Y
2 Natcher	Y	Y	Y	Y	Y	Y	Y	Y
3 Mazzoli	Y	Y	Y	Y	Y	Y	Y	Y
4 Snyder	Y	Y	Y	Y	Y	Y	Y	Y
5 Carter	Y	Y	Y	Y	Y	Y	Y	Y
6 Breckinridge	Y	Y	Y	Y	Y	Y	Y	Y
7 Perkins	Y	Y	Y	Y	Y	Y	Y	Y
LOUISIANA								
1 Livingston	Y	Y	Y	Y	N	Y	Y	Y
2 Boggs	Y	Y	Y	Y	Y	Y	Y	Y
3 Treen	Y	Y	Y	Y	N	Y	Y	Y
4 Waggonner	Y	Y	Y	Y	N	Y	Y	Y
5 Huckaby	Y	Y	Y	Y	Y	Y	Y	Y
6 Moore	Y	Y	Y	Y	Y	Y	Y	Y
7 Breaux	✓	?	?	Y	Y	Y	Y	Y
8 Long	Y	Y	Y	Y	Y	Y	Y	Y
MAINE								
1 Emery	Y	Y	Y	Y	Y	Y	Y	Y
2 Cohen	Y	Y	Y	Y	Y	Y	Y	Y
MARYLAND								
1 Bauman	Y	Y	N	Y	Y	Y	Y	Y
2 Long	N	N	N	Y	Y	Y	Y	Y
3 Mikulski	N	Y	?	Y	Y	Y	Y	Y
4 Holt	Y	Y	Y	Y	Y	Y	Y	Y
5 Spellman	Y	Y	Y	Y	Y	Y	Y	Y
6 Byron	Y	Y	Y	Y	Y	Y	Y	Y
7 Mitchell	N	Y	N	Y	Y	Y	Y	Y
8 Steers	N	Y	Y	Y	Y	Y	Y	▮
MASSACHUSETTS								
1 Conte	Y	Y	Y	Y	Y	Y	Y	Y
2 Boland	Y	Y	Y	Y	Y	Y	Y	Y
3 Early	N	Y	Y	?	Y	Y	Y	Y
4 Drinan	Y	Y	Y	Y	Y	Y	Y	Y
5 Tsongas	?	?	?	?	?	?	?	?
6 Harrington	X	#	#	Y	Y	Y	Y	Y
7 Markey	N	Y	Y	Y	Y	Y	Y	Y
8 O'Neill								
9 Moakley	Y	Y	Y	Y	Y	Y	Y	Y
10 Heckler	Y	Y	Y	Y	Y	Y	Y	Y
11 Burke	Y	Y	?	Y	Y	Y	Y	Y
12 Studds	N	Y	N	Y	Y	Y	Y	Y
MICHIGAN								
1 Conyers	N	Y	Y	#	Y	Y	Y	Y
2 Pursell	Y	Y	Y	Y	Y	Y	Y	Y
3 Brown	Y	Y	Y	Y	Y	Y	N	Y
4 Stockman	N	#	Y	Y	Y	Y	Y	Y
5 Sawyer	Y	Y	Y	Y	Y	Y	Y	Y
6 Carr	N	Y	Y	Y	Y	Y	Y	Y
7 Kildee	Y	Y	Y	Y	Y	Y	Y	Y
8 Traxler	Y	Y	Y	Y	Y	Y	Y	Y
9 Vander Jagt	Y	Y	Y	Y	Y	Y	Y	Y
10 Cederberg	Y	Y	Y	Y	Y	Y	Y	Y
11 Ruppe	?	?	?	?	?	?	?	?
12 Bonior	N	Y	#	Y	Y	Y	Y	Y
13 Diggs	Y	#	#	Y	Y	Y	Y	Y
14 Nedzi	Y	Y	Y	Y	Y	Y	Y	Y
15 Ford	Y	Y	Y	Y	Y	Y	Y	Y
16 Dingell	Y	Y	Y	Y	Y	Y	Y	Y
17 Brodhead	N	?	Y	Y	Y	Y	Y	Y
18 Blanchard	Y	Y	Y	Y	Y	Y	Y	Y
19 Broomfield	Y	Y	#	Y	Y	Y	Y	Y
MINNESOTA								
1 Quie	?	?	?	Y	Y	Y	Y	Y
2 Hagedorn	Y	Y	Y	Y	Y	Y	Y	Y
3 Frenzel	Y	Y	Y	Y	Y	Y	Y	Y
4 Vento	Y	Y	Y	Y	Y	Y	N	Y
5 Fraser	Y	Y	?	Y	Y	Y	Y	Y
6 Nolan	N	Y	Y	Y	Y	Y	Y	Y
7 Stangeland	Y	Y	N	Y	Y	Y	Y	Y
8 Oberstar	Y	Y	Y	Y	Y	Y	Y	Y
MISSISSIPPI								
1 Whitten	Y	Y	#	Y	Y	Y	Y	Y
2 Bowen	Y	Y	Y	Y	Y	Y	Y	Y
3 Montgomery	Y	Y	Y	Y	N	Y	Y	Y
4 Cochran	Y	Y	Y	Y	Y	Y	Y	Y
5 Lott	Y	Y	Y	Y	N	Y	Y	Y
MISSOURI								
1 Clay	N	Y	?	Y	Y	Y	Y	Y
2 Young	Y	Y	Y	Y	Y	Y	Y	Y
3 Gephardt	Y	Y	Y	Y	Y	Y	Y	Y

	481	482	483	484	485	486	487	488
4 Skelton	Y	Y	?	Y	N	Y	Y	Y
5 Bolling	Y	#	#	Y	Y	Y	Y	Y
6 Coleman	Y	Y	Y	Y	Y	Y	Y	Y
7 Taylor	Y	Y	Y	Y	Y	Y	Y	Y
8 Ichord	Y	Y	Y	Y	Y	Y	Y	Y
9 Volkmer	Y	Y	N	Y	Y	Y	Y	Y
10 Burlison	Y	Y	Y	Y	Y	Y	Y	Y
MONTANA								
1 Baucus	Y	Y	N	Y	Y	Y	Y	Y
2 Marlenee	Y	Y	Y	Y	Y	Y	Y	Y
NEBRASKA								
1 Thone	Y	Y	Y	Y	Y	Y	Y	Y
2 Cavanaugh	Y	Y	Y	Y	Y	Y	Y	Y
3 Smith	Y	Y	Y	Y	Y	Y	Y	Y
NEVADA								
AL Santini	✓	#	#	Y	Y	Y	Y	Y
NEW HAMPSHIRE								
1 D'Amours	Y	Y	Y	Y	Y	Y	Y	Y
2 Cleveland	Y	Y	Y	Y	Y	Y	Y	Y
NEW JERSEY								
1 Florio	Y	Y	Y	Y	Y	Y	Y	Y
2 Hughes	✓	?	?	Y	Y	Y	Y	Y
3 Howard	Y	Y	Y	Y	Y	Y	Y	Y
4 Thompson	Y	Y	Y	Y	Y	Y	Y	Y
5 Fenwick	N	Y	Y	Y	Y	Y	Y	Y
6 Forsythe	Y	N	Y	Y	Y	Y	Y	Y
7 Maguire	N	Y	Y	Y	Y	Y	Y	Y
8 Roe	Y	Y	Y	Y	Y	Y	Y	Y
9 Hollenbeck	Y	Y	Y	Y	Y	Y	Y	Y
10 Rodino	#	?	#	Y	Y	Y	Y	Y
11 Minish	Y	Y	Y	Y	Y	Y	Y	Y
12 Rinaldo	Y	Y	Y	Y	Y	Y	Y	Y
13 Meyner	Y	Y	Y	Y	Y	Y	Y	Y
14 LeFante	#	#	#	#	#	#	#	#
15 Patten	Y	Y	Y	Y	Y	Y	Y	Y
NEW MEXICO								
1 Lujan	Y	Y	Y	Y	Y	Y	Y	Y
2 Runnels	Y	Y	Y	Y	Y	Y	Y	Y
NEW YORK								
1 Pike	Y	Y	#	Y	Y	Y	Y	Y
2 Downey	N	Y	Y	Y	Y	Y	Y	Y
3 Ambro	Y	Y	Y	?	?	?	?	?
4 Lent	Y	Y	Y	Y	Y	Y	Y	Y
5 Wydler	Y	Y	Y	Y	Y	Y	Y	Y
6 Wolff	Y	Y	Y	Y	Y	Y	Y	Y
7 Addabbo	Y	Y	Y	?	?	?	?	?
8 Rosenthal	Y	Y	Y	Y	Y	Y	Y	Y
9 Delaney	Y	Y	Y	Y	Y	Y	Y	Y
10 Biaggi	Y	Y	Y	Y	Y	Y	Y	Y
11 Scheuer	Y	Y	Y	Y	Y	Y	Y	Y
12 Chisholm	Y	Y	Y	Y	Y	Y	Y	Y
13 Solarz	N	Y	Y	Y	Y	Y	Y	Y
14 Richmond	X	#	#	Y	Y	Y	Y	Y
15 Zeferetti	Y	Y	Y	Y	Y	Y	Y	Y
16 Holtzman	N	Y	Y	Y	Y	Y	Y	Y
17 Murphy	Y	Y	Y	Y	Y	Y	Y	Y
18 Green	Y	Y	Y	Y	Y	Y	Y	Y
19 Rangel	Y	Y	Y	Y	Y	Y	Y	Y
20 Weiss	N	Y	Y	Y	Y	Y	Y	Y
21 Garcia	N	Y	#	Y	Y	Y	Y	Y
22 Bingham	N	Y	Y	Y	Y	Y	Y	Y
23 Caputo	?	?	?	Y	Y	Y	Y	Y
24 Ottinger	-	-	†	Y	Y	Y	Y	Y
25 Fish	N	Y	Y	Y	Y	Y	Y	Y
26 Gilman	Y	Y	Y	Y	Y	Y	Y	Y
27 McHugh	N	Y	Y	Y	Y	Y	Y	Y
28 Stratton	Y	Y	Y	Y	Y	Y	Y	Y
29 Pattison	N	Y	#	Y	Y	#	Y	Y
30 McEwen	Y	?	Y	Y	Y	Y	Y	Y
31 Mitchell	Y	Y	Y	#	Y	Y	Y	Y
32 Hanley	Y	Y	Y	Y	Y	Y	Y	Y
33 Walsh	Y	Y	Y	Y	Y	Y	?	Y
34 Horton	Y	Y	Y	#	Y	Y	Y	Y
35 Conable	Y	Y	Y	Y	Y	Y	Y	Y
36 LaFalce	N	Y	Y	Y	Y	Y	Y	Y
37 Nowak	N	Y	Y	Y	Y	Y	Y	Y
38 Kemp	N	Y	Y	Y	Y	Y	Y	Y
39 Lundine	N	Y	Y	#	Y	Y	Y	Y
NORTH CAROLINA								
1 Jones	Y	Y	Y	Y	Y	Y	Y	Y
2 Fountain	Y	Y	Y	Y	Y	Y	Y	Y
3 Whitley	Y	Y	Y	Y	Y	Y	Y	Y
4 Andrews	Y	Y	Y	Y	Y	Y	Y	Y
5 Neal	Y	Y	Y	#	Y	Y	Y	Y
6 Preyer	Y	Y	Y	Y	Y	Y	Y	Y
7 Rose	Y	Y	Y	Y	Y	Y	Y	Y
8 Hefner	Y	Y	?	Y	Y	Y	Y	Y

	481	482	483	484	485	486	487	488
9 Martin	Y	Y	Y	Y	Y	Y	Y	Y
10 Broyhill	Y	Y	Y	Y	Y	Y	Y	Y
11 Gudger	Y	Y	Y	Y	Y	Y	Y	Y
NORTH DAKOTA								
AL Andrews	Y	Y	Y	Y	Y	Y	Y	Y
OHIO								
1 Gradison	Y	Y	Y	Y	Y	Y	Y	Y
2 Luken	Y	Y	Y	Y	Y	Y	Y	Y
3 Whalen	N	Y	Y	Y	Y	Y	Y	#
4 Guyer	Y	Y	Y	Y	Y	Y	Y	Y
5 Latta	Y	Y	Y	Y	Y	Y	Y	Y
6 Harsha	Y	N	N	?	Y	Y	Y	Y
7 Brown	?	?	?	Y	Y	Y	Y	Y
8 Kindness	Y	Y	N	Y	Y	Y	Y	Y
9 Ashley	Y	Y	Y	Y	Y	Y	Y	Y
10 Miller	Y	Y	#	Y	N	Y	Y	Y
11 Stanton	Y	Y	Y	Y	Y	Y	Y	Y
12 Devine	Y	Y	Y	Y	Y	Y	Y	Y
13 Pease	Y	Y	Y	Y	Y	Y	Y	Y
14 Seiberling	N	Y	Y	Y	Y	Y	Y	Y
15 Wylie	Y	Y	Y	Y	Y	Y	Y	Y
16 Regula	Y	Y	Y	Y	Y	Y	Y	Y
17 Ashbrook	▮	▮	#	#	▮	#	#	#
18 Applegate	Y	Y	Y	Y	Y	Y	Y	Y
19 Carney	Y	Y	?	Y	Y	Y	Y	Y
20 Oakar	N	?	Y	Y	Y	Y	Y	Y
21 Stokes	N	Y	Y	#	Y	Y	Y	Y
22 Vanik	Y	Y	Y	Y	Y	Y	Y	Y
23 Mottl	N	Y	Y	Y	N	Y	Y	Y
OKLAHOMA								
1 Jones	Y	Y	Y	Y	Y	Y	Y	Y
2 Risenhoover	Y	?	Y	Y	Y	Y	Y	Y
3 Watkins	Y	Y	Y	Y	Y	Y	Y	Y
4 Steed	Y	Y	Y	Y	Y	Y	Y	Y
5 Edwards	?	?	?	Y	Y	Y	Y	Y
6 English	Y	Y	Y	Y	Y	Y	Y	Y
OREGON								
1 AuCoin	N	Y	Y	Y	Y	Y	Y	Y
2 Ullman	Y	Y	Y	Y	Y	Y	Y	Y
3 Duncan	Y	#	#	Y	Y	Y	Y	Y
4 Weaver	N	Y	Y	Y	Y	Y	Y	Y
PENNSYLVANIA								
1 Myers, M.	Y	Y	Y	Y	Y	Y	Y	Y
2 Nix	Y	Y	?	Y	Y	Y	Y	Y
3 Lederer	Y	Y	Y	Y	Y	Y	Y	Y
4 Eilberg	Y	Y	Y	Y	Y	Y	Y	Y
5 Schulze	Y	Y	Y	Y	Y	Y	Y	Y
6 Yatron	Y	Y	Y	Y	Y	Y	Y	Y
7 Edgar	N	Y	N	Y	Y	Y	Y	Y
8 Kostmayer	N	Y	Y	Y	N	Y	Y	Y
9 Shuster	Y	Y	Y	Y	Y	Y	Y	Y
10 McDade	Y	Y	Y	Y	Y	Y	Y	Y
11 Flood	Y	Y	Y	Y	Y	Y	Y	Y
12 Murtha	Y	Y	Y	Y	Y	Y	Y	Y
13 Coughlin	Y	Y	Y	Y	Y	Y	Y	Y
14 Moorhead	Y	Y	Y	Y	Y	Y	Y	Y
15 Rooney	Y	Y	Y	Y	Y	Y	Y	Y
16 Walker	Y	Y	Y	Y	Y	Y	Y	Y
17 Ertel	?	Y	Y	Y	Y	Y	Y	Y
18 Walgren	Y	Y	Y	Y	Y	Y	Y	Y
19 Goodling, W.	Y	Y	Y	Y	Y	Y	Y	Y
20 Gaydos	Y	Y	Y	Y	Y	Y	Y	Y
21 Dent	Y	Y	Y	#	Y	Y	Y	Y
22 Murphy	N	N	?	Y	Y	Y	Y	Y
23 Ammerman	Y	Y	Y	Y	Y	Y	Y	Y
24 Marks	Y	Y	Y	Y	Y	Y	Y	Y
25 Myers, G.	Y	Y	Y	N	Y	Y	Y	Y
RHODE ISLAND								
1 St Germain	Y	Y	Y	Y	Y	Y	Y	Y
2 Beard	Y	Y	#	Y	Y	Y	Y	Y
SOUTH CAROLINA								
1 Davis	Y	Y	N	Y	Y	Y	Y	Y
2 Spence	Y	Y	Y	Y	N	Y	Y	Y
3 Derrick	Y	Y	Y	Y	Y	Y	Y	Y
4 Mann	?	?	?	Y	Y	Y	Y	Y
5 Holland	Y	Y	Y	Y	Y	Y	Y	Y
6 Jenrette	Y	Y	Y	Y	Y	Y	Y	Y
SOUTH DAKOTA								
1 Pressler	?	?	?	Y	Y	Y	Y	Y
2 Abdnor	Y	Y	N	Y	Y	Y	Y	Y
TENNESSEE								
1 Quillen	Y	Y	Y	Y	Y	Y	Y	Y
2 Duncan	Y	Y	Y	Y	Y	Y	Y	Y
3 Lloyd	Y	Y	Y	Y	Y	Y	Y	Y
4 Gore	Y	Y	Y	Y	N	Y	Y	Y
5 Vacancy								
6 Beard	Y	Y	Y	Y	Y	Y	Y	Y

	481	482	483	484	485	486	487	488
7 Jones	Y	Y	Y	Y	Y	Y	Y	Y
8 Ford	Y	Y	Y	Y	Y	Y	Y	Y
TEXAS								
1 Hall	Y	Y	Y	Y	Y	Y	Y	Y
2 Wilson, C.	Y	Y	Y	Y	Y	Y	Y	Y
3 Collins	N	Y	Y	Y	Y	Y	Y	Y
4 Roberts	Y	Y	Y	Y	Y	Y	Y	Y
5 Mattox	Y	Y	Y	Y	Y	Y	Y	Y
6 Teague	Y	Y	Y	Y	Y	Y	Y	Y
7 Archer	Y	Y	Y	Y	N	Y	Y	Y
8 Eckhardt	Y	Y	Y	Y	Y	Y	Y	Y
9 Brooks	Y	Y	Y	Y	Y	Y	Y	Y
10 Pickle	Y	Y	Y	Y	Y	#	Y	Y
11 Poage	Y	Y	Y	Y	Y	Y	Y	Y
12 Wright	Y	Y	Y	Y	Y	Y	Y	Y
13 Hightower	Y	Y	Y	?	?	?	?	?
14 Young	Y	Y	Y	?	Y	Y	Y	Y
15 de la Garza	Y	Y	Y	?	N	Y	Y	Y
16 White	Y	Y	Y	Y	Y	Y	Y	Y
17 Burleson	Y	Y	Y	Y	Y	Y	Y	Y
18 Jordan	Y	Y	Y	Y	Y	Y	Y	Y
19 Mahon	Y	Y	Y	Y	Y	Y	Y	Y
20 Gonzalez	Y	Y	Y	Y	Y	Y	Y	Y
21 Krueger	Y	Y	Y	Y	Y	Y	Y	Y
22 Gammage	Y	Y	Y	Y	Y	Y	Y	Y
23 Kazen	Y	Y	Y	Y	Y	Y	Y	Y
24 Milford	?	?	?	Y	?	Y	Y	Y
UTAH								
1 McKay	Y	Y	Y	Y	Y	Y	Y	Y
2 Marriott	Y	Y	Y	Y	Y	Y	Y	Y
VERMONT								
AL Jeffords	Y	Y	Y	Y	Y	Y	Y	Y
VIRGINIA								
1 Trible	Y	Y	Y	Y	Y	Y	Y	Y
2 Whitehurst	Y	Y	Y	Y	Y	Y	Y	Y
3 Satterfield	Y	Y	Y	Y	N	Y	Y	Y
4 Daniel	Y	Y	Y	Y	Y	Y	Y	Y
5 Daniel	Y	Y	Y	Y	Y	Y	Y	Y
6 Butler	?	Y	Y	Y	Y	Y	Y	Y
7 Robinson	Y	Y	Y	Y	Y	Y	Y	Y
8 Harris	Y	Y	Y	Y	Y	Y	Y	Y
9 Wampler	Y	Y	Y	Y	Y	Y	Y	Y
10 Fisher	Y	Y	Y	Y	Y	Y	Y	Y
WASHINGTON								
1 Pritchard	Y	Y	Y	Y	Y	Y	Y	Y
2 Meeds	Y	Y	Y	Y	Y	Y	Y	Y
3 Bonker	Y	Y	Y	Y	Y	Y	Y	Y
4 McCormack	Y	Y	Y	Y	Y	Y	Y	Y
5 Foley	Y	Y	Y	Y	Y	Y	Y	Y
6 Dicks	Y	Y	Y	Y	Y	Y	Y	Y
7 Cunningham	Y	Y	Y	Y	Y	Y	Y	Y
WEST VIRGINIA								
1 Mollohan	Y	Y	Y	#	Y	Y	Y	Y
2 Staggers	Y	Y	Y	Y	Y	Y	Y	Y
3 Slack	Y	Y	Y	Y	Y	Y	Y	Y
4 Rahall	Y	Y	Y	Y	Y	Y	Y	Y
WISCONSIN								
1 Aspin	Y	?	Y	Y	Y	Y	Y	Y
2 Kastenmeier	▮	Y	Y	Y	Y	Y	Y	Y
3 Baldus	Y	Y	Y	Y	Y	Y	Y	Y
4 Zablocki	Y	#	Y	Y	Y	Y	Y	Y
5 Reuss	Y	Y	Y	Y	Y	Y	Y	Y
6 Steiger	Y	Y	Y	Y	Y	Y	Y	Y
7 Obey	N	Y	Y	Y	Y	Y	Y	Y
8 Cornell	N	Y	Y	Y	Y	Y	Y	Y
9 Kasten	?	?	?	?	?	?	?	?
WYOMING								
AL Roncalio	#	▮	#	Y	Y	Y	Y	Y

Democrats ***Republicans***

489. HR 11891. Disabled Veterans' Medical Aid. Roberts, D-Texas, motion to suspend the rules and pass the bill to establish higher benefits payments for home health care for disabled veterans requiring constant medical attention. Motion agreed to 418-0: R 140-0; D 278-0 (ND 192-0; SD 86-0), July 18, 1978. A two-thirds majority vote (279 in this case) is required for passage under suspension of the rules.

490. HR 6075. Pregnancy Disability. Hawkins, D-Calif., motion to suspend the rules and pass the bill to prohibit employment discrimination based on pregnancy. Motion agreed to 376-43: R 116-25; D 260-18 (ND 183-9; SD 77-9), July 18, 1978. A two-thirds majority vote (280 in this case) is required for passage under suspension of the rules.

491. H J Res 738. Native American Religious Freedom. Udall, D-Ariz., motion to suspend the rules and pass the joint resolution to express the sense of Congress that the president direct the federal agencies concerned to re-evaluate existing laws and regulations that prevented native Americans from practicing their traditional religions by denying them access to sacred lands, instruments or ceremonial practices. Passed 337-81: R 94-46; D 243-35 (ND 173-19; SD 70-16), July 18, 1978. A two-thirds majority vote (279 in this case) is required for passage under suspension of the rules.

492. HR 1609. Coal Slurry Pipelines. Passage of the bill to promote development of coal slurry pipelines. Rejected 161-246: R 45-90; D 116-156 (ND 73-115; SD 43-41), July 19, 1978.

493. HR 11983. Federal Election Commission-Public Financing. Sisk, D-Calif., motion to order the previous question (thus ending debate) on the adoption of the rule (H Res 1172) providing for House floor consideration of the fiscal 1979 authorization bill for the Federal Election Commission. (Opponents of the rule sought to defeat the previous question in order to permit drafting an alternative rule that would allow a House vote on public financing of House general elections.) Motion agreed to 213-196: R 106-30; D 107-166 (ND 45-144; SD 62-22), July 19, 1978. The rule subsequently was adopted by voice vote.

494. HR 11983. Federal Election Commission. Passage of the bill to authorize $8.6 million for the Federal Election Commission for fiscal year 1979, with the stipulation that none of the money could be used to fund random audits of candidates for the House and Senate. Passed 366-37: R 112-22; D 254-15 (ND 179-7; SD 75-8), July 19, 1978.

495. HR 13385. Debt Limit Increase. Adoption of the rule (H Res 1277) providing for House floor consideration of the bill to provide for a temporary increase in the public debt ceiling. Adopted 303-98: R 61-76; D 242-22 (ND 174-9; SD 68-13), July 19, 1978.

496. HR 13385. Debt Limit Increase. Vanik, D-Ohio, amendment to reduce the temporary increase in the public debt ceiling by $16 billion, to $798 billion from $814 billion. Adopted 363-37: R 124-12; D 239-25 (ND 164-19; SD 75-6), July 19, 1978.

KEY

- Y Voted for (yea).
- ✓ Paired for.
- † Announced for.
- # CQ Poll for.
- N Voted against (nay).
- X Paired against.
- \- Announced against.
- ▮ CQ Poll against.
- P Voted "present."
- ● Voted "present" to avoid possible conflict of interest.
- ? Did not vote or otherwise make a position known.

	489	490	491	492	493	494	495	496
ALABAMA								
1 Edwards	Y	Y	Y	N	Y	Y	Y	Y
2 Dickinson	Y	Y	N	N	Y	Y	Y	Y
3 Nichols	Y	Y	Y	N	Y	Y	Y	Y
4 Bevill	Y	Y	Y	N	Y	Y	Y	Y
5 Flippo	Y	N	Y	N	Y	Y	Y	Y
6 Buchanan	Y	Y	Y	N	Y	Y	N	Y
7 Flowers	Y	Y	Y	N	?	?	?	?
ALASKA								
AL Young	Y	Y	Y	Y	Y	N	N	Y
ARIZONA								
1 Rhodes	Y	Y	Y	N	Y	Y	Y	Y
2 Udall	Y	Y	Y	Y	N	Y	Y	Y
3 Stump	Y	N	N	Y	Y	N	N	Y
4 Rudd	Y	N	Y	N	Y	Y	N	Y
ARKANSAS								
1 Alexander	Y	Y	Y	Y	Y	Y	Y	Y
2 Tucker	Y	Y	Y	Y	Y	Y	Y	Y
3 Hammerschmidt	Y	Y	N	Y	Y	N	N	N
4 Thornton	Y	Y	Y	Y	Y	Y	Y	?
CALIFORNIA								
1 Johnson	Y	Y	Y	Y	N	Y	Y	Y
2 Clausen	Y	Y	Y	Y	Y	Y	N	Y
3 Moss	Y	Y	Y	N	N	Y	Y	N
4 Leggett	Y	Y	Y	Y	Y	Y	Y	?
5 Burton, J.	Y	Y	Y	Y	N	Y	Y	Y
6 Burton, P.	Y	Y	Y	Y	N	Y	Y	?
7 Miller	Y	N	Y	Y	N	Y	Y	Y
8 Dellums	Y	Y	Y	Y	N	Y	Y	Y
9 Stark	Y	Y	Y	Y	N	Y	Y	Y
10 Edwards	Y	Y	Y	?	N	Y	Y	Y
11 Ryan	Y	N	N	Y	N	N	Y	Y
12 McCloskey	Y	Y	Y	Y	N	Y	Y	Y
13 Mineta	Y	Y	Y	Y	N	Y	Y	N
14 McFall	Y	Y	Y	Y	Y	Y	Y	Y
15 Sisk	Y	Y	Y	Y	Y	Y	Y	N
16 Panetta	Y	Y	Y	Y	N	Y	Y	Y
17 Krebs	Y	Y	N	Y	N	Y	Y	Y
18 Vacancy								
19 Lagomarsino	Y	Y	Y	Y	Y	Y	N	Y
20 Goldwater	Y	N	Y	Y	Y	Y	N	Y
21 Corman	Y	Y	Y	Y	N	Y	Y	N
22 Moorhead	Y	Y	N	Y	Y	N	N	Y
23 Beilenson	Y	N	Y	Y	N	Y	Y	N
24 Waxman	Y	Y	Y	Y	N	Y	Y	N
25 Roybal	Y	Y	Y	Y	N	Y	Y	?
26 Rousselot	Y	Y	N	Y	Y	N	N	Y
27 Dornan	Y	Y	Y	?	Y	Y	N	Y
28 Burke	Y	Y	Y	Y	N	Y	Y	Y
29 Hawkins	Y	Y	Y	N	Y	Y	Y	N
30 Danielson	Y	Y	Y	Y	N	Y	Y	N
31 Wilson, C.H.	Y	Y	N	Y	Y	Y	?	?
32 Anderson	Y	Y	Y	Y	N	Y	Y	Y
33 Clawson	?	?	?	?	?	?	?	?
34 Hannaford	Y	Y	Y	Y	N	Y	Y	Y
35 Lloyd	Y	Y	N	Y	N	Y	Y	Y
36 Brown	Y	Y	Y	Y	N	Y	Y	Y
37 Pettis	Y	Y	N	Y	Y	Y	Y	Y
38 Patterson	Y	Y	Y	Y	N	Y	Y	Y
39 Wiggins	Y	N	N	Y	Y	Y	Y	#
40 Badham	Y	N	N	Y	Y	N	N	Y
41 Wilson, B.	Y	Y	Y	Y	Y	N	Y	Y
42 Van Deerlin	Y	Y	Y	N	N	Y	Y	Y
43 Burgener	Y	Y	Y	N	Y	Y	Y	Y
COLORADO								
1 Schroeder	Y	Y	Y	N	N	Y	N	Y
2 Wirth	Y	Y	Y	N	N	Y	Y	Y
3 Evans	Y	Y	Y	N	N	Y	Y	N
4 Johnson	Y	N	Y	N	N	Y	Y	Y

	489	490	491	492	493	494	495	496
5 Armstrong	Y	N	Y	N	Y	N	N	Y
CONNECTICUT								
1 Cotter	Y	Y	Y	Y	Y	Y	Y	Y
2 Dodd	Y	Y	Y	Y	N	Y	Y	Y
3 Giaimo	Y	Y	Y	N	N	Y	Y	Y
4 McKinney	Y	N	Y	N	N	Y	Y	Y
5 Sarasin	Y	Y	Y	Y	Y	Y	Y	Y
6 Moffett	Y	Y	Y	N	N	Y	Y	Y
DELAWARE								
AL Evans	Y	N	Y	N	N	Y	N	Y
FLORIDA								
1 Sikes	Y	Y	Y	N	Y	Y	Y	Y
2 Fuqua	Y	Y	Y	Y	Y	Y	Y	Y
3 Bennett	Y	Y	Y	Y	Y	Y	Y	Y
4 Chappell	Y	Y	Y	Y	Y	Y	Y	Y
5 Kelly	Y	Y	N	✓	✓	?	?	?
6 Young	Y	Y	N	N	Y	Y	N	Y
7 Gibbons	?	?	?	?	?	?	?	?
8 Ireland	Y	N	N	N	N	Y	Y	Y
9 Frey	?	?	?	?	?	?	?	?
10 Bafalis	Y	Y	Y	●	Y	Y	N	Y
11 Rogers	Y	Y	Y	N	N	Y	Y	Y
12 Burke	Y	Y	Y	N	Y	Y	N	Y
13 Lehman	Y	Y	Y	Y	N	Y	Y	Y
14 Pepper	Y	Y	Y	N	Y	Y	Y	Y
15 Fascell	Y	Y	Y	Y	N	Y	Y	Y
GEORGIA								
1 Ginn	Y	Y	N	N	Y	Y	Y	Y
2 Mathis	Y	Y	Y	N	Y	Y	Y	Y
3 Brinkley	Y	Y	Y	N	N	Y	N	Y
4 Levitas	Y	Y	Y	N	N	Y	N	Y
5 Fowler	Y	Y	Y	N	N	Y	Y	Y
6 Flynt	?	?	?	?	?	?	?	?
7 McDonald	Y	N	N	N	Y	N	N	Y
8 Evans	Y	Y	N	N	Y	?	Y	Y
9 Jenkins	Y	Y	Y	N	Y	Y	Y	Y
10 Barnard	Y	Y	N	N	Y	Y	N	Y
HAWAII								
1 Heftel	Y	Y	Y	N	-	Y	Y	Y
2 Akaka	Y	Y	Y	Y	N	Y	Y	Y
IDAHO								
1 Symms	Y	Y	N	N	Y	N	N	Y
2 Hansen, G.	Y	Y	N	N	Y	N	N	Y
ILLINOIS								
1 Metcalfe	Y	Y	Y	N	N	Y	Y	Y
2 Murphy	Y	Y	Y	N	Y	Y	Y	Y
3 Russo	Y	Y	Y	N	N	Y	Y	Y
4 Derwinski	Y	Y	Y	N	Y	N	Y	Y
5 Fary	Y	Y	Y	Y	Y	Y	Y	Y
6 Hyde	Y	Y	Y	N	Y	Y	Y	Y
7 Collins	Y	Y	Y	N	Y	Y	Y	Y
8 Rostenkowski	Y	Y	Y	X	X	?	?	?
9 Yates	Y	Y	Y	N	N	Y	Y	Y
10 Mikva	Y	Y	Y	N	N	#	Y	Y
11 Annunzio	Y	Y	Y	N	Y	Y	Y	Y
12 Crane	Y	N	N	▮	#	N	N	Y
13 McClory	Y	Y	N	Y	Y	Y	Y	N
14 Erlenborn	Y	Y	Y	N	Y	Y	Y	Y
15 Corcoran	Y	N	Y	▮	✓	#	▮	Y
16 Anderson	Y	Y	Y	Y	N	Y	Y	N
17 O'Brien	Y	Y	Y	N	Y	Y	N	Y
18 Michel	Y	Y	N	Y	Y	Y	Y	Y
19 Railsback	Y	Y	Y	N	N	Y	Y	Y
20 Findley	?	Y	N	N	Y	Y	Y	Y
21 Madigan	Y	Y	N	N	Y	Y	Y	Y
22 Shipley	?	?	?	✓	✓	?	?	?
23 Price	Y	Y	Y	N	N	Y	Y	Y
24 Simon	Y	Y	Y	N	N	Y	Y	Y
INDIANA								
1 Benjamin	Y	Y	Y	N	Y	Y	Y	Y
2 Fithian	Y	Y	Y	N	N	Y	Y	Y
3 Brademas	Y	Y	Y	N	N	Y	Y	Y
4 Quayle	Y	Y	Y	Y	Y	Y	N	Y
5 Hillis	Y	Y	Y	N	N	Y	N	Y
6 Evans	Y	Y	Y	N	N	N	Y	Y
7 Myers, J.	Y	Y	Y	Y	Y	Y	N	Y
8 Cornwell	Y	Y	Y	Y	N	Y	#	Y
9 Hamilton	Y	Y	Y	N	N	Y	Y	Y
10 Sharp	Y	Y	Y	Y	N	Y	Y	Y
11 Jacobs	Y	Y	Y	N	N	#	Y	Y
IOWA								
1 Leach	Y	Y	Y	N	N	Y	N	Y
2 Blouin	Y	Y	Y	N	N	Y	Y	Y
3 Grassley	Y	Y	Y	N	Y	Y	N	Y
4 Smith	Y	Y	Y	Y	N	Y	Y	Y
5 Harkin	Y	Y	Y	N	N	Y	Y	Y
6 Bedell	Y	Y	Y	N	N	Y	Y	Y

Democrats ***Republicans***

	489	490	491	492	493	494	495	496
KANSAS								
1 Sebelius	Y	Y	Y	Y	Y	Y	N	Y
2 Keys	Y	Y	Y	N	N	Y	Y	Y
3 Winn	Y	Y	Y	Y	Y	Y	N	Y
4 Glickman	Y	Y	Y	Y	N	Y	Y	Y
5 Skubitz	Y	N	Y	N	Y	?	Y	Y
KENTUCKY								
1 Hubbard	Y	Y	Y	▮	N	Y	Y	Y
2 Natcher	Y	Y	Y	N	Y	Y	Y	Y
3 Mazzoli	Y	Y	N	N	N	Y	Y	Y
4 Snyder	Y	Y	Y	N	Y	Y	N	Y
5 Carter	Y	Y	Y	N	Y	Y	Y	Y
6 Breckinridge	Y	Y	Y	Y	N	Y	Y	N
7 Perkins	Y	Y	Y	N	Y	Y	Y	Y
LOUISIANA								
1 Livingston	Y	Y	N	Y	Y	Y	N	Y
2 Boggs	Y	Y	Y	Y	Y	Y	Y	N
3 Treen	Y	N	N	Y	Y	Y	Y	Y
4 Waggonner	Y	N	N	Y	Y	N	Y	N
5 Huckaby	Y	Y	Y	Y	Y	Y	N	Y
6 Moore	Y	Y	Y	Y	Y	Y	N	Y
7 Breaux	Y	Y	N	Y	Y	Y	Y	Y
8 Long	Y	Y	Y	Y	Y	Y	Y	N
MAINE								
1 Emery	Y	Y	Y	N	N	Y	Y	Y
2 Cohen	Y	Y	N	N	N	Y	Y	Y
MARYLAND								
1 Bauman	Y	Y	N	N	Y	N	N	Y
2 Long	Y	Y	Y	N	N	Y	Y	Y
3 Mikulski	Y	Y	Y	N	N	Y	Y	Y
4 Holt	Y	Y	N	N	Y	N	N	Y
5 Spellman	Y	Y	Y	N	N	Y	Y	Y
6 Byron	Y	Y	Y	N	Y	Y	Y	Y
7 Mitchell	Y	Y	Y	N	N	Y	Y	N
8 Steers	Y	Y	Y	Y	N	Y	Y	Y
MASSACHUSETTS								
1 Conte	Y	Y	Y	N	N	Y	Y	N
2 Boland	Y	Y	Y	N	N	Y	Y	Y
3 Early	Y	Y	Y	N	Y	Y	N	Y
4 Drinan	Y	Y	Y	N	N	Y	Y	Y
5 Tsongas	?	?	?	?	?	?	?	?
6 Harrington	Y	Y	Y	Y	N	Y	#	N
7 Markey	Y	Y	Y	N	N	Y	Y	Y
8 O'Neill								
9 Moakley	Y	Y	Y	N	N	Y	Y	Y
10 Heckler	Y	Y	Y	N	N	Y	Y	Y
11 Burke	Y	Y	Y	Y	Y	Y	Y	N
12 Studds	Y	Y	Y	N	N	Y	Y	Y
MICHIGAN								
1 Conyers	Y	Y	Y	N	N	Y	#	N
2 Pursell	Y	Y	Y	N	N	Y	N	Y
3 Brown	Y	Y	Y	N	Y	Y	Y	Y
4 Stockman	Y	Y	N	N	N	#	Y	#
5 Sawyer	Y	Y	Y	Y	Y	Y	N	Y
6 Carr	Y	Y	Y	N	N	Y	Y	Y
7 Kildee	Y	Y	Y	N	N	Y	Y	Y
8 Traxler	Y	Y	Y	N	N	Y	Y	Y
9 Vander Jagt	Y	Y	Y	N	Y	Y	Y	Y
10 Cederberg	Y	Y	Y	N	Y	Y	Y	Y
11 Ruppe	?	?	?	Y	N	Y	Y	Y
12 Bonior	Y	Y	Y	N	N	Y	Y	Y
13 Diggs	Y	Y	Y	N	Y	Y	Y	#
14 Nedzi	Y	Y	N	N	Y	Y	Y	Y
15 Ford	Y	Y	N	N	N	Y	Y	Y
16 Dingell	Y	Y	N	N	Y	Y	Y	Y
17 Brodhead	Y	Y	Y	N	N	Y	Y	Y
18 Blanchard	Y	Y	N	N	N	Y	Y	Y
19 Broomfield	Y	Y	Y	N	Y	Y	N	Y
MINNESOTA								
1 Quie	Y	Y	Y	?	?	?	?	?
2 Hagedorn	Y	N	N	N	Y	Y	Y	Y
3 Frenzel	Y	Y	Y	N	Y	N	Y	N
4 Vento	Y	Y	Y	N	N	Y	Y	Y
5 Fraser	Y	Y	Y	N	N	Y	Y	Y
6 Nolan	Y	Y	Y	N	N	Y	Y	Y
7 Stangeland	Y	N	N	N	Y	N	N	Y
8 Oberstar	Y	Y	Y	N	N	Y	Y	Y
MISSISSIPPI								
1 Whitten	Y	Y	Y	Y	Y	Y	Y	Y
2 Bowen	Y	N	Y	Y	Y	Y	Y	Y
3 Montgomery	Y	Y	N	Y	Y	Y	#	#
4 Cochran	Y	Y	Y	Y	N	Y	N	Y
5 Lott	Y	Y	N	Y	Y	Y	N	Y
MISSOURI								
1 Clay	Y	Y	Y	N	Y	Y	Y	Y
2 Young	Y	Y	Y	Y	Y	Y	Y	Y
3 Gephardt	Y	Y	Y	Y	N	Y	Y	N
4 Skelton	Y	Y	N	N	Y	Y	Y	Y
5 Bolling	Y	Y	Y	Y	N	Y	Y	N
6 Coleman	Y	Y	Y	N	Y	Y	N	Y
7 Taylor	Y	Y	N	N	Y	Y	N	Y
8 Ichord	Y	N	N	N	Y	Y	Y	Y
9 Volkmer	Y	Y	Y	N	N	Y	Y	Y
10 Burlison	Y	Y	Y	?	N	Y	?	Y
MONTANA								
1 Baucus	Y	Y	N	N	N	Y	Y	Y
2 Marlenee	Y	N	N	N	Y	Y	N	Y
NEBRASKA								
1 Thone	Y	Y	Y	N	Y	Y	N	Y
2 Cavanaugh	Y	Y	Y	N	N	Y	Y	Y
3 Smith	Y	Y	Y	N	Y	Y	N	Y
NEVADA								
AL Santini	Y	Y	Y	N	N	Y	Y	Y
NEW HAMPSHIRE								
1 D'Amours	Y	Y	Y	N	N	Y	Y	Y
2 Cleveland	Y	Y	Y	N	N	Y	Y	Y
NEW JERSEY								
1 Florio	Y	Y	Y	N	N	Y	Y	Y
2 Hughes	Y	Y	Y	N	N	Y	Y	Y
3 Howard	Y	Y	Y	Y	N	Y	Y	Y
4 Thompson	Y	Y	Y	Y	N	Y	Y	Y
5 Fenwick	Y	Y	Y	N	N	Y	N	Y
6 Forsythe	Y	Y	Y	N	Y	Y	N	Y
7 Maguire	Y	Y	Y	N	N	Y	Y	Y
8 Roe	Y	Y	Y	Y	N	Y	Y	Y
9 Hollenbeck	Y	Y	Y	Y	N	Y	Y	Y
10 Rodino	Y	Y	Y	#	#	#	#	#
11 Minish	Y	Y	Y	N	N	Y	Y	Y
12 Rinaldo	Y	Y	Y	N	N	Y	N	Y
13 Meyner	Y	Y	Y	Y	N	Y	Y	Y
14 LeFante	#	#	?	X	X	#	#	#
15 Patten	Y	Y	Y	▮	X	#	#	#
NEW MEXICO								
1 Lujan	Y	Y	Y	Y	Y	Y	N	Y
2 Runnels	Y	N	Y	Y	Y	Y	?	Y
NEW YORK								
1 Pike	Y	Y	Y	Y	N	Y	Y	Y
2 Downey	Y	Y	Y	N	N	Y	Y	Y
3 Ambro	?	?	?	Y	N	Y	Y	Y
4 Lent	Y	N	N	N	Y	Y	N	Y
5 Wydler	Y	N	N	Y	Y	Y	N	Y
6 Wolff	Y	Y	Y	N	N	Y	Y	Y
7 Addabbo	?	?	?	Y	N	Y	Y	Y
8 Rosenthal	Y	Y	Y	Y	N	Y	Y	Y
9 Delaney	Y	Y	Y	Y	Y	N	Y	N
10 Biaggi	Y	Y	Y	Y	Y	Y	Y	Y
11 Scheuer	Y	Y	Y	Y	N	Y	Y	Y
12 Chisholm	Y	Y	Y	Y	N	Y	Y	Y
13 Solarz	Y	Y	Y	Y	N	Y	Y	Y
14 Richmond	Y	Y	Y	N	N	Y	Y	Y
15 Zeferetti	Y	Y	Y	Y	Y	Y	Y	Y
16 Holtzman	Y	Y	Y	N	N	Y	Y	Y
17 Murphy	Y	Y	Y	N	Y	Y	Y	Y
18 Green	Y	Y	Y	N	N	Y	Y	Y
19 Rangel	Y	Y	Y	N	N	Y	Y	Y
20 Weiss	Y	N	Y	Y	N	Y	Y	Y
21 Garcia	Y	Y	Y	Y	N	Y	Y	Y
22 Bingham	Y	Y	Y	Y	N	Y	Y	Y
23 Caputo	Y	Y	Y	?	?	?	?	?
24 Ottinger	Y	N	Y	N	N	Y	N	N
25 Fish	Y	Y	Y	N	Y	Y	Y	Y
26 Gilman	Y	Y	Y	N	N	Y	Y	Y
27 McHugh	Y	Y	Y	N	N	Y	Y	Y
28 Stratton	Y	Y	Y	Y	Y	Y	Y	Y
29 Pattison	Y	Y	Y	Y	N	Y	Y	Y
30 McEwen	Y	Y	N	N	Y	Y	Y	N
31 Mitchell	Y	Y	Y	Y	N	Y	Y	Y
32 Hanley	Y	Y	Y	Y	N	Y	Y	Y
33 Walsh	Y	Y	Y	N	Y	N	Y	Y
34 Horton	Y	Y	Y	Y	Y	#	Y	Y
35 Conable	Y	Y	N	Y	N	Y	Y	N
36 LaFalce	Y	Y	Y	N	N	Y	Y	Y
37 Nowak	Y	Y	Y	N	N	Y	Y	Y
38 Kemp	Y	Y	Y	Y	Y	Y	N	Y
39 Lundine	Y	Y	Y	Y	N	Y	Y	Y
NORTH CAROLINA								
1 Jones	Y	Y	Y	N	Y	Y	Y	Y
2 Fountain	Y	Y	Y	Y	Y	Y	Y	Y
3 Whitley	Y	Y	Y	N	Y	Y	Y	Y
4 Andrews	Y	Y	Y	Y	Y	Y	Y	Y
5 Neal	Y	Y	Y	Y	Y	Y	Y	Y
6 Preyer	Y	Y	Y	N	N	Y	?	?
7 Rose	Y	Y	Y	?	?	?	?	?
8 Hefner	Y	Y	Y	N	Y	Y	Y	Y
9 Martin	Y	Y	N	Y	Y	N	Y	Y
10 Broyhill	Y	Y	Y	Y	Y	Y	Y	Y
11 Gudger	Y	Y	Y	Y	N	Y	Y	Y
NORTH DAKOTA								
AL Andrews	Y	Y	Y	N	Y	Y	Y	Y
OHIO								
1 Gradison	Y	Y	Y	N	Y	Y	Y	N
2 Luken	Y	Y	Y	N	N	Y	Y	Y
3 Whalen	Y	Y	Y	N	N	Y	Y	Y
4 Guyer	Y	Y	Y	N	Y	Y	N	Y
5 Latta	Y	Y	Y	N	Y	Y	N	Y
6 Harsha	Y	Y	Y	N	Y	Y	N	Y
7 Brown	Y	N	N	N	Y	Y	N	Y
8 Kindness	Y	Y	Y	N	Y	N	N	Y
9 Ashley	Y	Y	Y	Y	N	Y	Y	Y
10 Miller	Y	Y	Y	N	Y	Y	N	Y
11 Stanton	Y	Y	Y	N	Y	Y	Y	N
12 Devine	Y	Y	N	N	Y	Y	N	Y
13 Pease	Y	Y	Y	N	N	Y	Y	Y
14 Seiberling	Y	Y	Y	Y	N	Y	Y	Y
15 Wylie	Y	Y	Y	N	Y	Y	N	Y
16 Regula	Y	Y	Y	N	Y	Y	N	Y
17 Ashbrook	#	▮	▮	▮	▮	▮	▮	▮
18 Applegate	Y	Y	Y	N	Y	Y	Y	Y
19 Carney	Y	Y	Y	N	Y	Y	?	Y
20 Oakar	Y	Y	Y	N	N	Y	Y	Y
21 Stokes	Y	Y	Y	N	N	Y	Y	Y
22 Vanik	Y	Y	Y	Y	N	Y	Y	Y
23 Mottl	Y	N	Y	N	N	N	Y	Y
OKLAHOMA								
1 Jones	Y	Y	Y	Y	Y	N	Y	Y
2 Risenhoover	Y	Y	Y	Y	Y	Y	Y	Y
3 Watkins	Y	Y	Y	Y	Y	Y	Y	Y
4 Steed	Y	Y	Y	Y	Y	Y	Y	Y
5 Edwards	Y	Y	Y	Y	Y	Y	N	Y
6 English	Y	Y	Y	Y	Y	Y	N	Y
OREGON								
1 AuCoin	Y	Y	N	N	N	#	Y	Y
2 Ullman	Y	Y	Y	N	Y	#	Y	N
3 Duncan	Y	Y	Y	N	Y	Y	Y	Y
4 Weaver	Y	Y	Y	N	N	N	N	Y
PENNSYLVANIA								
1 Myers, M.	Y	Y	Y	Y	Y	Y	Y	Y
2 Nix	Y	Y	Y	Y	X	?	?	?
3 Lederer	Y	Y	Y	N	N	Y	Y	N
4 Eilberg	Y	Y	Y	N	N	Y	Y	Y
5 Schulze	Y	N	Y	Y	Y	Y	Y	Y
6 Yatron	Y	Y	Y	N	Y	Y	N	Y
7 Edgar	Y	Y	Y	N	N	Y	N	Y
8 Kostmayer	Y	Y	Y	Y	N	Y	Y	Y
9 Shuster	Y	Y	N	N	Y	N	N	Y
10 McDade	Y	Y	Y	N	Y	Y	Y	Y
11 Flood	Y	Y	Y	N	Y	Y	Y	Y
12 Murtha	Y	Y	N	N	Y	Y	Y	Y
13 Coughlin	Y	Y	Y	N	Y	Y	Y	Y
14 Moorhead	Y	Y	Y	N	N	Y	Y	Y
15 Rooney	Y	Y	Y	N	N	Y	Y	Y
16 Walker	Y	Y	N	N	Y	Y	N	Y
17 Ertel	Y	Y	Y	Y	Y	Y	Y	Y
18 Walgren	Y	Y	Y	Y	N	Y	Y	Y
19 Goodling, W.	Y	Y	N	N	Y	Y	N	Y
20 Gaydos	Y	Y	N	Y	Y	Y	N	Y
21 Dent	Y	Y	Y	▮	Y	N	N	#
22 Murphy	Y	Y	Y	N	N	Y	Y	Y
23 Ammerman	Y	Y	Y	N	N	Y	Y	Y
24 Marks	Y	Y	Y	N	N	Y	Y	Y
25 Myers, G.	Y	N	N	Y	N	N	Y	N
RHODE ISLAND								
1 St Germain	Y	Y	Y	N	N	Y	Y	Y
2 Beard	Y	Y	Y	N	N	Y	Y	Y
SOUTH CAROLINA								
1 Davis	Y	Y	Y	N	Y	Y	N	Y
2 Spence	Y	Y	N	N	Y	Y	N	Y
3 Derrick	Y	Y	Y	N	N	Y	Y	Y
4 Mann	Y	Y	Y	N	Y	Y	Y	Y
5 Holland	Y	Y	Y	N	Y	N	Y	Y
6 Jenrette	Y	Y	Y	N	N	N	Y	Y
SOUTH DAKOTA								
1 Pressler	Y	Y	Y	N	Y	Y	Y	Y
2 Abdnor	Y	N	Y	N	Y	Y	Y	Y
TENNESSEE								
1 Quillen	Y	Y	Y	N	Y	Y	N	Y
2 Duncan	Y	Y	Y	N	Y	Y	N	Y
3 Lloyd	Y	Y	Y	N	Y	Y	Y	Y
4 Gore	Y	Y	Y	N	N	Y	Y	Y
5 Vacancy								
6 Beard	Y	Y	N	N	Y	Y	N	Y
7 Jones	Y	Y	Y	N	Y	Y	Y	Y
8 Ford	Y	Y	Y	N	N	Y	Y	Y
TEXAS								
1 Hall	Y	Y	N	N	Y	Y	N	Y
2 Wilson, C.	Y	Y	Y	Y	Y	Y	#	Y
3 Collins	Y	N	N	Y	Y	N	N	Y
4 Roberts	Y	Y	N	Y	Y	Y	Y	Y
5 Mattox	Y	Y	N	N	N	Y	Y	Y
6 Teague	Y	Y	Y	N	Y	N	?	?
7 Archer	Y	Y	N	Y	Y	Y	N	Y
8 Eckhardt	Y	Y	Y	Y	N	Y	Y	Y
9 Brooks	Y	Y	Y	Y	Y	Y	Y	Y
10 Pickle	Y	Y	Y	Y	Y	Y	Y	Y
11 Poage	Y	N	Y	N	Y	N	N	Y
12 Wright	Y	Y	Y	Y	N	Y	Y	Y
13 Hightower	?	?	?	N	Y	Y	Y	Y
14 Young	Y	Y	Y	?	?	?	Y	Y
15 de la Garza	Y	Y	N	Y	Y	Y	N	Y
16 White	Y	Y	Y	N	Y	Y	Y	Y
17 Burleson	Y	N	Y	Y	Y	Y	Y	N
18 Jordan	Y	Y	Y	Y	N	Y	Y	N
19 Mahon	Y	Y	Y	Y	Y	Y	Y	Y
20 Gonzalez	Y	Y	Y	Y	Y	Y	Y	Y
21 Krueger	Y	Y	Y	Y	Y	Y	N	Y
22 Gammage	Y	Y	Y	Y	Y	N	N	Y
23 Kazen	Y	Y	Y	Y	Y	Y	Y	Y
24 Milford	Y	Y	N	Y	Y	Y	Y	Y
UTAH								
1 McKay	Y	Y	Y	N	Y	Y	Y	Y
2 Marriott	Y	Y	Y	Y	Y	Y	Y	Y
VERMONT								
AL Jeffords	Y	Y	Y	N	N	Y	Y	N
VIRGINIA								
1 Trible	Y	Y	Y	N	Y	Y	N	Y
2 Whitehurst	Y	Y	Y	N	Y	Y	Y	Y
3 Satterfield	Y	N	N	N	Y	Y	N	Y
4 Daniel	Y	N	N	N	Y	Y	N	Y
5 Daniel	Y	N	N	N	Y	Y	Y	Y
6 Butler	Y	N	N	N	Y	Y	N	Y
7 Robinson	Y	N	N	N	Y	Y	N	Y
8 Harris	Y	Y	Y	Y	N	Y	Y	Y
9 Wampler	Y	Y	Y	N	Y	Y	N	Y
10 Fisher	Y	Y	Y	Y	N	Y	Y	Y
WASHINGTON								
1 Pritchard	Y	Y	#	Y	N	Y	N	Y
2 Meeds	Y	Y	Y	Y	N	Y	Y	Y
3 Bonker	Y	Y	N	N	N	Y	Y	Y
4 McCormack	Y	Y	N	Y	N	Y	Y	Y
5 Foley	Y	Y	N	N	N	Y	Y	Y
6 Dicks	Y	Y	N	N	N	Y	Y	Y
7 Cunningham	Y	Y	N	N	Y	Y	N	Y
WEST VIRGINIA								
1 Mollohan	Y	Y	Y	N	Y	Y	Y	Y
2 Staggers	Y	Y	Y	N	Y	Y	Y	Y
3 Slack	Y	Y	Y	N	Y	Y	Y	Y
4 Rahall	Y	Y	Y	N	Y	Y	Y	Y
WISCONSIN								
1 Aspin	Y	Y	Y	N	N	Y	Y	Y
2 Kastenmeier	Y	Y	Y	N	N	Y	Y	Y
3 Baldus	Y	Y	Y	N	N	Y	Y	Y
4 Zablocki	Y	Y	Y	N	Y	Y	Y	Y
5 Reuss	Y	Y	Y	N	N	Y	Y	Y
6 Steiger	Y	Y	Y	Y	Y	N	Y	N
7 Obey	Y	Y	Y	N	N	Y	Y	Y
8 Cornell	Y	Y	Y	N	N	Y	Y	Y
9 Kasten	?	?	?	?	✓	?	?	?
WYOMING								
AL Roncalio	Y	Y	Y	N	N	Y	Y	#

Democrats ***Republicans***

497. HR 13385. Temporary Debt Limit. Passage of the bill to increase the temporary public debt limit to $798 billion through March 31, 1979. Passed 205-202: R 9-128; D 196-74 (ND 140-46; SD 56-28), July 19, 1978.

498. HR 11504. Agricultural Credit. Richmond, D-N.Y., motion to order the previous question (thus ending debate) on the Symms, R-Idaho, motion to recommit to a House-Senate conference committee the conference report on the bill to revise existing farm credit programs, to create an economic emergency loan program for farmers and ranchers and to extend the Emergency Livestock Credit Act through Sept. 13, 1979. Motion agreed to 282-105: R 121-14; D 161-91 (ND 90-86; SD 71-5), July 19, 1978. (The Symms motion to recommit the conference report was rejected subsequently by voice vote.)

499. HR 11504. Agricultural Credit. Adoption of the conference report on the bill to revise existing farm credit programs, to create an economic emergency loan program for farmers and ranchers and to extend the Emergency Livestock Credit Act through Sept. 30, 1979. Adopted 362-28: R 119-18; D 243-10 (ND 167-8; SD 76-2), July 19, 1978.

KEY

- Y Voted for (yea).
- ✓ Paired for.
- † Announced for.
- # CQ Poll for.
- N Voted against (nay).
- X Paired against.
- \- Announced against.
- ▮ CQ Poll against.
- P Voted "present."
- ● Voted "present" to avoid possible conflict of interest.
- ? Did not vote or otherwise make a position known.

	497	498	499
ALABAMA			
1 Edwards	N	Y	Y
2 Dickinson	N	Y	Y
3 Nichols	N	#	#
4 Bevill	Y	Y	Y
5 Flippo	N	Y	Y
6 Buchanan	N	Y	Y
7 Flowers	?	?	?
ALASKA			
AL Young	N	Y	N
ARIZONA			
1 Rhodes	N	Y	Y
2 Udall	Y	#	Y
3 Stump	N	Y	Y
4 Rudd	N	Y	Y
ARKANSAS			
1 Alexander	Y	Y	Y
2 Tucker	Y	Y	Y
3 Hammerschmidt	N	Y	Y
4 Thornton	Y	Y	Y
CALIFORNIA			
1 Johnson	Y	Y	Y
2 Clausen	N	Y	Y
3 Moss	Y	?	?
4 Leggett	Y	?	?
5 Burton, J.	N	N	Y
6 Burton, P.	Y	N	?
7 Miller	N	N	Y
8 Dellums	N	N	Y
9 Stark	N	N	Y
10 Edwards .	Y	N	Y
11 Ryan	Y	Y	Y
12 McCloskey	Y	Y	Y
13 Mineta	Y	Y	Y
14 McFall	Y	Y	Y
15 Sisk	Y	?	?
16 Panetta	Y	Y	Y
17 Krebs	Y	Y	Y
18 Vacancy			
19 Lagomarsino	N	Y	Y
20 Goldwater	N	?	?
21 Corman	Y	Y	Y
22 Moorhead	N	Y	Y
23 Beilenson	Y	N	Y
24 Waxman	Y	N	Y
25 Roybal	Y	N	Y
26 Rousselot	N	?	?
27 Dornan	N	Y	Y
28 Burke	Y	N	Y
29 Hawkins	Y	Y	Y
30 Danielson	Y	Y	Y
31 Wilson, C.H.	Y	?	?
32 Anderson	N	N	N
33 Clawson	?	?	?
34 Hannaford	Y	N	Y
35 Lloyd	N	Y	Y
36 Brown	Y	?	?
37 Pettis	?	Y	Y
38 Patterson	Y	N	Y
39 Wiggins	Y	Y	Y
40 Badham	N	Y	N
41 Wilson, B.	N	Y	Y
42 Van Deerlin	Y	N	Y
43 Burgener	N	Y	Y
COLORADO			
1 Schroeder	N	Y	Y
2 Wirth	Y	Y	Y
3 Evans	Y	?	?
4 Johnson	N	Y	Y
5 Armstrong	N	Y	Y
CONNECTICUT			
1 Cotter	Y	Y	Y
2 Dodd	Y	N	Y
3 Giaimo	Y	?	?
4 McKinney	Y	Y	Y
5 Sarasin	N	Y	Y
6 Moffett	N	N	Y
DELAWARE			
AL Evans	N	Y	Y
FLORIDA			
1 Sikes	Y	Y	Y
2 Fuqua	Y	Y	Y
3 Bennett	Y	N	Y
4 Chappell	N	Y	Y
5 Kelly	X	Y	N
6 Young	N	Y	Y
7 Gibbons	?	?	?
8 Ireland	N	Y	Y
9 Frey	?	?	?
10 Bafalis	N	Y	Y
11 Rogers	Y	Y	Y
12 Burke	N	Y	Y
13 Lehman	Y	Y	Y
14 Pepper	Y	Y	Y
15 Fascell	Y	N	Y
GEORGIA			
1 Ginn	Y	Y	Y
2 Mathis	Y	Y	Y
3 Brinkley	N	Y	Y
4 Levitas	N	Y	Y
5 Fowler	Y	Y	Y
6 Flynt	?	?	?
7 McDonald	N	N	N
8 Evans	N	Y	Y
9 Jenkins	Y	#	#
10 Barnard	N	?	Y
HAWAII			
1 Heftel	Y	Y	Y
2 Akaka	Y	Y	Y
IDAHO			
1 Symms	N	Y	N
2 Hansen, G.	N	Y	N
ILLINOIS			
1 Metcalfe	Y	N	Y
2 Murphy	Y	Y	Y
3 Russo	N	N	Y
4 Derwinski	Y	Y	N
5 Fary	Y	Y	Y
6 Hyde	N	Y	Y
7 Collins	Y	N	Y
8 Rostenkowski	?	?	?
9 Yates	Y	N	N
10 Mikva	Y	N	Y
11 Annunzio	Y	Y	Y
12 Crane	N	N	N
13 McClory	N	Y	Y
14 Erlenborn	N	Y	Y
15 Corcoran	N	Y	Y
16 Anderson	N	Y	Y
17 O'Brien	N	Y	Y
18 Michel	N	Y	Y
19 Railsback	N	Y	Y
20 Findley	Y	Y	Y
21 Madigan	N	Y	Y
22 Shipley	✓	?	?
23 Price	Y	Y	Y
24 Simon	Y	N	Y
INDIANA			
1 Benjamin	Y	N	Y
2 Fithian	N	Y	Y
3 Brademas	Y	N	Y
4 Quayle	N	Y	Y
5 Hillis	N	Y	Y
6 Evans	N	Y	Y
7 Myers, J.	N	Y	Y
8 Cornwell	Y	Y	Y
9 Hamilton	Y	Y	Y
10 Sharp	Y	Y	Y
11 Jacobs	N	Y	Y
IOWA			
1 Leach	N	Y	Y
2 Blouin	Y	Y	Y
3 Grassley	N	Y	Y
4 Smith	Y	Y	Y
5 Harkin	N	Y	Y
6 Bedell	Y	Y	Y

Democrats ***Republicans***

	497	498	499
KANSAS			
1 Sebelius	N	Y	Y
2 Keys	Y	Y	Y
3 Winn	N	Y	Y
4 Glickman	N	Y	Y
5 Skubitz	N	Y	Y
KENTUCKY			
1 Hubbard	Y	Y	Y
2 Natcher	Y	Y	Y
3 Mazzoli	Y	Y	Y
4 Snyder	N	Y	Y
5 Carter	N	Y	Y
6 Breckinridge	Y	Y	Y
7 Perkins	Y	Y	Y
LOUISIANA			
1 Livingston	N	Y	Y
2 Boggs	Y	Y	Y
3 Treen	N	Y	Y
4 Waggonner	Y	Y	Y
5 Huckaby	N	Y	Y
6 Moore	N	Y	Y
7 Breaux	N	Y	Y
8 Long	Y	Y	Y
MAINE			
1 Emery	N	N	Y
2 Cohen	N	Y	Y
MARYLAND			
1 Bauman	N	Y	Y
2 Long	Y	N	N
3 Mikulski	N	Y	Y
4 Holt	N	Y	Y
5 Spellman	Y	N	Y
6 Byron	N	Y	Y
7 Mitchell	Y	Y	Y
8 Steers	Y	Y	Y
MASSACHUSETTS			
1 Conte	Y	N	N
2 Boland	Y	N	Y
3 Early	N	N	Y
4 Drinan	Y	N	Y
5 Tsongas	?	?	?
6 Harrington	Y	#	#
7 Markey	Y	N	Y
8 O'Neill			
9 Moakley	Y	Y	Y
10 Heckler	N	N	Y
11 Burke	N	N	Y
12 Studds	Y	N	Y
MICHIGAN			
1 Conyers	X	▮	#
2 Pursell	N	Y	Y
3 Brown	N	Y	Y
4 Stockman	N	Y	Y
5 Sawyer	N	Y	Y
6 Carr	N	N	Y
7 Kildee	Y	Y	Y
8 Traxler	Y	Y	Y
9 Vander Jagt	N	Y	Y
10 Cederberg	N	Y	Y
11 Ruppe	N	Y	Y
12 Bonior	Y	N	Y
13 Diggs	X	▮	#
14 Nedzi	Y	Y	Y
15 Ford	Y	?	?
16 Dingell	Y	Y	Y
17 Brodhead	Y	N	Y
18 Blanchard	Y	N	Y
19 Broomfield	N	Y	N
MINNESOTA			
1 Quie	X	?	?
2 Hagedorn	N	Y	Y
3 Frenzel	N	N	Y
4 Vento	Y	Y	Y
5 Fraser	Y	N	Y
6 Nolan	N	N	Y
7 Stangeland	N	Y	Y
8 Oberstar	Y	N	Y
MISSISSIPPI			
1 Whitten	Y	Y	Y
2 Bowen	N	Y	Y
3 Montgomery	N	Y	Y
4 Cochran	N	Y	Y
5 Lott	N	Y	Y
MISSOURI			
1 Clay	Y	N	?
2 Young	Y	Y	Y
3 Gephardt	Y	Y	Y
4 Skelton	N	Y	Y
5 Bolling	Y	#	#
6 Coleman	N	Y	Y
7 Taylor	N	Y	Y
8 Ichord	N	Y	Y
9 Volkmer	Y	Y	Y
10 Burlison	Y	Y	Y
MONTANA			
1 Baucus	N	Y	Y
2 Marlenee	N	Y	Y
NEBRASKA			
1 Thone	N	Y	Y
2 Cavanaugh	N	Y	Y
3 Smith	N	Y	Y
NEVADA			
AL Santini	N	Y	Y
NEW HAMPSHIRE			
1 D'Amours	N	N	Y
2 Cleveland	N	N	Y
NEW JERSEY			
1 Florio	N	N	Y
2 Hughes	N	N	Y
3 Howard	Y	N	Y
4 Thompson	Y	N	Y
5 Fenwick	N	Y	N
6 Forsythe	N	#	N
7 Maguire	N	N	Y
8 Roe	Y	Y	Y
9 Hollenbeck	N	Y	N
10 Rodino	#	#	?
11 Minish	Y	N	Y
12 Rinaldo	N	N	Y
13 Meyner	Y	Y	Y
14 LeFante	✓	▮	#
15 Patten	✓	Y	Y
NEW MEXICO			
1 Lujan	N	Y	Y
2 Runnels	N	Y	Y
NEW YORK			
1 Pike	Y	N	Y
2 Downey	N	Y	Y
3 Ambro	N	Y	Y
4 Lent	N	Y	Y
5 Wydler	N	N	N
6 Wolff	N	N	N
7 Addabbo	Y	N	Y
8 Rosenthal	Y	N	Y
9 Delaney	Y	N	Y
10 Biaggi	N	N	Y
11 Scheuer	Y	N	Y
12 Chisholm	Y	N	Y
13 Solarz	Y	N	Y
14 Richmond	Y	N	Y
15 Zeferetti	N	N	Y
16 Holtzman	Y	N	Y
17 Murphy	Y	Y	Y
18 Green	N	N	Y
19 Rangel	Y	N	Y
20 Weiss	N	N	Y
21 Garcia	Y	N	Y
22 Bingham	Y	N	Y
23 Caputo	?	?	?
24 Ottinger	Y	N	Y
25 Fish	N	Y	Y
26 Gilman	N	N	Y
27 McHugh	Y	N	Y
28 Stratton	Y	N	Y
29 Pattison	Y	Y	Y
30 McEwen	N	Y	Y
31 Mitchell	N	Y	Y
32 Hanley	N	Y	Y
33 Walsh	N	N	Y
34 Horton	N	Y	Y
35 Conable	N	Y	N
36 LaFalce	Y	N	Y
37 Nowak	Y	N	Y
38 Kemp	N	Y	Y
39 Lundine	Y	Y	Y
NORTH CAROLINA			
1 Jones	Y	Y	Y
2 Fountain	N	Y	Y
3 Whitley	N	Y	Y
4 Andrews	Y	Y	Y
5 Neal	N	Y	Y
6 Preyer	Y	Y	Y
7 Rose	✓	?	?
8 Hefner	Y	Y	Y
9 Martin	N	Y	Y
10 Broyhill	N	Y	Y
11 Gudger	N	Y	Y
NORTH DAKOTA			
AL Andrews	N	Y	Y
OHIO			
1 Gradison	N	Y	N
2 Luken	N	Y	Y
3 Whalen	Y	N	N
4 Guyer	N	Y	Y
5 Latta	N	Y	Y
6 Harsha	N	Y	Y
7 Brown	N	Y	Y
8 Kindness	N	?	Y
9 Ashley	Y	Y	Y
10 Miller	N	N	Y
11 Stanton	N	Y	Y
12 Devine	N	Y	Y
13 Pease	Y	N	Y
14 Seiberling	Y	N	Y
15 Wylie	N	Y	Y
16 Regula	N	Y	Y
17 Ashbrook	▮	▮	#
18 Applegate	Y	Y	Y
19 Carney	Y	Y	Y
20 Oakar	Y	N	Y
21 Stokes	Y	N	Y
22 Vanik	Y	N	Y
23 Mottl	N	N	N
OKLAHOMA			
1 Jones	Y	Y	Y
2 Risenhoover	N	Y	Y
3 Watkins	Y	Y	Y
4 Steed	Y	Y	Y
5 Edwards	N	Y	Y
6 English	N	Y	Y
OREGON			
1 AuCoin	N	Y	Y
2 Ullman	Y	Y	Y
3 Duncan	Y	Y	Y
4 Weaver	N	N	N
PENNSYLVANIA			
1 Myers, M.	Y	Y	Y
2 Nix	?	?	?
3 Lederer	Y	Y	Y
4 Eilberg	Y	N	Y
5 Schulze	N	Y	Y
6 Yatron	N	Y	Y
7 Edgar	Y	N	Y
8 Kostmayer	N	N	N
9 Shuster	N	Y	Y
10 McDade	N	Y	Y
11 Flood	Y	Y	Y
12 Murtha	Y	Y	Y
13 Coughlin	N	Y	Y
14 Moorhead	Y	Y	Y
15 Rooney	Y	Y	Y
16 Walker	N	Y	Y
17 Ertel	N	Y	Y
18 Walgren	Y	N	Y
19 Goodling, W.	N	Y	Y
20 Gaydos	N	Y	Y
21 Dent	#	#	#
22 Murphy	Y	Y	Y
23 Ammerman	Y	N	Y
24 Marks	N	Y	Y
25 Myers, G.	N	N	N
RHODE ISLAND			
1 St Germain	Y	Y	Y
2 Beard	Y	Y	Y
SOUTH CAROLINA			
1 Davis	N	Y	Y
2 Spence	N	Y	Y
3 Derrick	Y	Y	Y
4 Mann	Y	?	?
5 Holland	Y	Y	Y
6 Jenrette	Y	Y	Y
SOUTH DAKOTA			
1 Pressler	?	?	?
2 Abdnor	N	Y	Y
TENNESSEE			
1 Quillen	N	Y	Y
2 Duncan	N	Y	Y
3 Lloyd	N	Y	Y
4 Gore	Y	Y	Y
5 Vacancy			
6 Beard	N	Y	Y
7 Jones	N	Y	Y
8 Ford	Y	Y	Y
TEXAS			
1 Hall	N	Y	Y
2 Wilson, C.	Y	Y	Y
3 Collins	N	Y	N
4 Roberts	Y	?	?
5 Mattox	Y	Y	Y
6 Teague	?	?	?
7 Archer	N	Y	Y
8 Eckhardt	Y	Y	Y
9 Brooks	Y	Y	Y
10 Pickle	Y	N	Y
11 Poage	N	Y	Y
12 Wright	Y	Y	Y
13 Hightower	Y	Y	Y
14 Young	Y	?	?
15 de la Garza	Y	Y	Y
16 White	N	Y	Y
17 Burleson	Y	Y	Y
18 Jordan	Y	Y	Y
19 Mahon	Y	Y	Y
20 Gonzalez	Y	Y	Y
21 Krueger	N	#	#
22 Gammage	N	Y	Y
23 Kazen	Y	Y	Y
24 Milford	Y	?	N
UTAH			
1 McKay	Y	Y	Y
2 Marriott	N	Y	Y
VERMONT			
AL Jeffords	N	Y	Y
VIRGINIA			
1 Trible	N	Y	Y
2 Whitehurst	Y	Y	Y
3 Satterfield	N	Y	Y
4 Daniel	N	Y	Y
5 Daniel	Y	Y	Y
6 Butler	N	Y	Y
7 Robinson	N	Y	Y
8 Harris	Y	N	Y
9 Wampler	N	Y	Y
10 Fisher	Y	Y	Y
WASHINGTON			
1 Pritchard	N	Y	Y
2 Meeds	Y	Y	Y
3 Bonker	Y	Y	Y
4 McCormack	Y	Y	Y
5 Foley	Y	Y	Y
6 Dicks	Y	Y	N
7 Cunningham	N	Y	Y
WEST VIRGINIA			
1 Mollohan	Y	Y	Y
2 Staggers	Y	Y	Y
3 Slack	Y	Y	Y
4 Rahall	Y	Y	Y
WISCONSIN			
1 Aspin	Y	N	Y
2 Kastenmeier	Y	N	Y
3 Baldus	Y	N	Y
4 Zablocki	Y	Y	Y
5 Reuss	Y	N	Y
6 Steiger	N	Y	Y
7 Obey	Y	N	Y
8 Cornell	Y	N	Y
9 Kasten	?	?	?
WYOMING			
AL Roncalio	✓	#	#

Democrats ***Republicans***

KEY

- Y Voted for (yea).
- ✓ Paired for.
- † Announced for.
- # CQ Poll for.
- N Voted against (nay).
- X Paired against.
- \- Announced against.
- ▮ CQ Poll against.
- P Voted "present."
- ● Voted "present" to avoid possible conflict of interest.
- ? Did not vote or otherwise make a position known.

500. HR 13467. Second Supplemental Appropriations, Fiscal 1978. Mahon, D-Texas, motion that the House resolve itself into the Committee of the Whole to consider the bill. Motion agreed to 357-3: R 126-2; D 231-1 (ND 159-1; SD 72-0), July 20, 1978.

501. HR 13467. Second Supplemental Appropriations, Fiscal 1978. Moss, D-Calif., amendment to delete $15 million in the bill for a Center for Disease Control influenza immunization program and add $3 million for influenza vaccine research programs of the National Institute for Allergy and Infectious Diseases. Adopted 268-127: R 86-47; D 182-80 (ND 127-57; SD 55-23), July 20, 1978.

502. HR 13467. Second Supplemental Appropriations, Fiscal 1978. Gore, D-Tenn., amendment to add $26 million to the $5 million in the bill for "pinpoint" assistance to schools in federally declared disaster areas. Rejected 166-233: R 38-98; D 128-135 (ND 89-96; SD 39-39), July 20, 1978.

503. HR 13467. Second Supplemental Appropriations, Fiscal 1978. McHugh, D-N.Y., amendment to add $9.9 million to the $5 million in the bill for "pinpoint" assistance to schools in federally declared disaster areas. Rejected 156-237: R 37-97; D 119-140 (ND 87-96; SD 32-44), July 20, 1978.

504. HR 13467. Second Supplemental Appropriations, Fiscal 1978. Crane, R-Ill., amendment to delete the $275,000 appropriation for the U.S. Metric Board. Rejected 75-302: R 46-85; D 29-217 (ND 11-161; SD 18-56), July 20, 1978.

505. HR 13467. Second Supplemental Appropriations, Fiscal 1978. Miller, R-Ohio, amendment to reduce all spending in the bill, except for payments required by law, by 2 percent, provided that no one program be cut by more than 5 percent. Adopted 256-114: R 115-11; D 141-103 (ND 81-89; SD 60-14), July 20, 1978.

506. HR 13467. Second Supplemental Appropriations, Fiscal 1978. Passage of the bill to appropriate $6.3 billion in supplemental funds for fiscal 1978 operations of the government, including $3.2 billion for federal employee pay raises. Passed 311-60: R 94-32; D 217-28 (ND 153-18; SD 64-10), July 20, 1978. The president had requested $6,675,886,486 in supplemental new budget authority for fiscal 1978.

	500	501	502	503	504	505	506
ALABAMA							
1 Edwards	Y	N	N	N	N	Y	Y
2 Dickinson	Y	Y	N	N	N	Y	Y
3 Nichols	#	✓	X	X	▮	#	#
4 Bevill	Y	N	Y	N	N	Y	Y
5 Flippo	Y	N	Y	N	N	Y	Y
6 Buchanan	Y	N	Y	Y	N	Y	Y
7 Flowers	?	?	?	?	?	?	?
ALASKA							
AL Young	#	Y	Y	N	N	Y	Y
ARIZONA							
1 Rhodes	Y	Y	N	N	N	N	Y
2 Udall	Y	Y	N	N	N	Y	Y
3 Stump	Y	Y	N	N	Y	Y	N
4 Rudd	Y	Y	N	N	Y	?	?
ARKANSAS							
1 Alexander	Y	Y	N	N	N	N	Y
2 Tucker	Y	Y	Y	Y	N	Y	Y
3 Hammerschmidt	Y	N	Y	Y	Y	Y	Y
4 Thornton	Y	Y	Y	Y	N	Y	Y
CALIFORNIA							
1 Johnson	Y	Y	N	N	N	N	Y
2 Clausen	Y	Y	Y	Y	Y	Y	Y
3 Moss	Y	Y	N	N	N	N	Y
4 Leggett	Y	Y	Y	Y	N	N	Y
5 Burton, J.	Y	Y	Y	Y	N	N	N
6 Burton, P.	Y	Y	Y	Y	?	?	?
7 Miller	Y	Y	Y	Y	N	N	Y
8 Dellums	Y	Y	Y	✓	N	N	Y
9 Stark	Y	?	Y	Y	N	N	Y
10 Edwards	Y	Y	Y	Y	?	?	?
11 Ryan	Y	Y	Y	N	N	Y	Y
12 McCloskey	Y	N	Y	Y	N	Y	Y
13 Mineta	Y	Y	N	N	N	N	Y
14 McFall	Y	N	N	N	N	N	Y
15 Sisk	Y	Y	Y	N	N	Y	Y
16 Panetta	Y	Y	N	N	Y	Y	Y
17 Krebs	Y	Y	N	N	N	Y	Y
18 Vacancy							
19 Lagomarsino	Y	Y	N	N	Y	Y	Y
20 Goldwater	Y	Y	Y	Y	N	Y	Y
21 Corman	Y	Y	Y	Y	N	N	Y
22 Moorhead	Y	Y	N	N	Y	Y	N
23 Beilenson	Y	N	N	N	N	N	Y
24 Waxman	#	Y	✓	Y	▮	▮	#
25 Roybal	?	?	?	?	?	?	?
26 Rousselot	?	?	?	?	?	?	?
27 Dornan	?	Y	N	N	N	Y	N
28 Burke	Y	Y	Y	Y	N	N	Y
29 Hawkins	Y	Y	Y	Y	N	N	Y
30 Danielson	Y	Y	N	N	N	N	Y
31 Wilson, C.H.	Y	N	N	N	N	?	Y
32 Anderson	Y	Y	Y	Y	N	Y	Y
33 Clawson	?	?	?	?	?	?	?
34 Hannaford	Y	Y	N	N	N	N	Y
35 Lloyd	N	Y	N	N	N	N	Y
36 Brown	Y	Y	Y	Y	N	N	?
37 Pettis	Y	N	N	N	Y	Y	Y
38 Patterson	Y	Y	Y	Y	N	Y	Y
39 Wiggins	#	?	N	N	N	Y	Y
40 Badham	Y	Y	N	N	Y	#	▮
41 Wilson, B.	N	N	N	N	N	Y	Y
42 Van Deerlin	?	Y	Y	Y	N	N	Y
43 Burgener	Y	N	N	N	Y	Y	Y
COLORADO							
1 Schroeder	Y	Y	N	N	N	Y	Y
2 Wirth	Y	Y	N	N	N	Y	N
3 Evans	?	N	N	N	N	N	Y
4 Johnson	Y	N	N	?	?	?	?
5 Armstrong	Y	Y	N	N	N	Y	N
CONNECTICUT							
1 Cotter	Y	Y	N	N	N	Y	Y
2 Dodd	Y	Y	N	N	N	N	Y
3 Giaimo	Y	N	N	?	N	Y	Y
4 McKinney	Y	N	Y	Y	N	Y	Y
5 Sarasin	#	N	N	N	N	#	#
6 Moffett	Y	Y	N	Y	N	Y	Y
DELAWARE							
AL Evans	Y	Y	N	N	Y	Y	Y
FLORIDA							
1 Sikes	Y	Y	N	N	N	Y	Y
2 Fuqua	Y	Y	Y	Y	N	#	#
3 Bennett	Y	Y	N	N	N	Y	Y
4 Chappell	Y	Y	N	N	N	Y	Y
5 Kelly	Y	Y	N	N	N	Y	N
6 Young	Y	N	Y	Y	Y	Y	Y
7 Gibbons	?	?	?	?	?	?	?
8 Ireland	?	Y	N	N	Y	Y	Y
9 Frey	?	?	?	?	?	?	?
10 Bafalis	Y	N	N	N	Y	Y	Y
11 Rogers	Y	N	Y	Y	N	Y	Y
12 Burke	Y	Y	N	Y	N	Y	Y
13 Lehman	Y	Y	N	N	N	N	Y
14 Pepper	Y	N	Y	Y	N	N	Y
15 Fascell	Y	Y	N	N	N	N	Y
GEORGIA							
1 Ginn	Y	N	N	N	N	Y	Y
2 Mathis	?	Y	N	N	Y	Y	Y
3 Brinkley	Y	N	N	N	N	Y	Y
4 Levitas	Y	Y	N	N	N	Y	N
5 Fowler	Y	N	Y	N	?	?	?
6 Flynt	?	?	?	?	?	?	?
7 McDonald	Y	Y	N	N	Y	Y	N
8 Evans	Y	Y	N	N	Y	Y	N
9 Jenkins	#	#	#	#	#	#	#
10 Barnard	Y	Y	N	?	?	#	?
HAWAII							
1 Heftel	Y	N	Y	Y	N	Y	Y
2 Akaka	Y	N	Y	Y	N	N	Y
IDAHO							
1 Symms	Y	Y	N	N	Y	Y	N
2 Hansen, G.	Y	Y	N	N	Y	Y	N
ILLINOIS							
1 Metcalfe	Y	Y	N	Y	N	N	Y
2 Murphy	Y	Y	N	N	N	Y	Y
3 Russo	Y	Y	N	N	N	Y	N
4 Derwinski	Y	N	N	N	Y	Y	N
5 Fary	Y	Y	N	N	N	Y	Y
6 Hyde	Y	Y	N	N	N	Y	Y
7 Collins	Y	Y	Y	N	?	?	?
8 Rostenkowski	?	?	?	?	?	?	?
9 Yates	Y	N	N	N	N	N	Y
10 Mikva	Y	Y	N	N	N	Y	Y
11 Annunzio	Y	Y	N	N	N	Y	Y
12 Crane	#	Y	N	N	Y	#	▮
13 McClory	Y	N	N	N	N	Y	Y
14 Erlenborn	Y	Y	N	N	N	Y	Y
15 Corcoran	Y	Y	N	N	Y	Y	N
16 Anderson	Y	Y	N	N	N	#	#
17 O'Brien	Y	N	N	N	Y	Y	Y
18 Michel	Y	Y	N	N	N	Y	Y
19 Railsback	Y	?	N	N	N	Y	Y
20 Findley	Y	Y	N	N	N	Y	N
21 Madigan	Y	N	N	Y	N	Y	Y
22 Shipley	?	X	X	X	?	?	?
23 Price	Y	Y	N	N	N	N	Y
24 Simon	Y	N	N	N	N	N	Y
INDIANA							
1 Benjamin	Y	N	N	N	N	N	Y
2 Fithian	Y	Y	Y	Y	Y	Y	Y
3 Brademas	Y	N	N	N	N	N	Y
4 Quayle	N	Y	Y	N	Y	Y	Y
5 Hillis	Y	Y	?	?	?	?	?
6 Evans	Y	Y	Y	Y	Y	Y	N
7 Myers, J.	Y	Y	N	N	Y	Y	N
8 Cornwell	#	Y	Y	Y	N	Y	N
9 Hamilton	Y	Y	Y	Y	N	Y	Y
10 Sharp	Y	Y	Y	Y	N	Y	N
11 Jacobs	#	Y	Y	Y	N	Y	N
IOWA							
1 Leach	Y	N	N	N	N	Y	Y
2 Blouin	Y	Y	N	N	N	Y	Y
3 Grassley	Y	Y	N	N	N	Y	N
4 Smith	Y	N	Y	?	?	?	?
5 Harkin	Y	Y	N	N	N	Y	N
6 Bedell	Y	Y	N	N	N	Y	Y

Democrats ***Republicans***

	500	501	502	503	504	505	506
KANSAS							
1 ***Sebelius***	Y	Y	N	N	N	?	?
2 Keys	#	N	Y	Y	N	Y	Y
3 ***Winn***	Y	Y	N	N	N	Y	Y
4 Glickman	Y	Y	N	N	N	Y	N
5 ***Skubitz***	Y	?	Y	Y	?	Y	Y
KENTUCKY							
1 Hubbard	Y	Y	Y	Y	Y	Y	N
2 Natcher	Y	N	N	N	N	Y	Y
3 Mazzoli	Y	Y	Y	N	N	Y	Y
4 ***Snyder***	Y	N	Y	N	Y	Y	N
5 ***Carter***	Y	N	Y	Y	N	N	Y
6 Breckinridge	Y	N	N	N	N	N	Y
7 Perkins	Y	N	Y	Y	N	N	Y
LOUISIANA							
1 ***Livingston***	Y	Y	Y	Y	Y	Y	Y
2 Boggs	Y	N	Y	N	N	Y	Y
3 ***Treen***	Y	Y	N	N	N	Y	Y
4 Waggonner	Y	Y	N	N	Y	Y	N
5 Huckaby	Y	Y	Y	Y	?	?	?
6 ***Moore***	Y	Y	N	N	N	Y	Y
7 Breaux	?	Y	Y	Y	Y	Y	N
8 Long	Y	Y	N	N	N	Y	Y
MAINE							
1 ***Emery***	Y	Y	N	N	N	Y	Y
2 ***Cohen***	Y	Y	N	N	N	Y	Y
MARYLAND							
1 ***Bauman***	Y	Y	N	N	Y	Y	N
2 Long	Y	Y	N	N	N	N	Y
3 Mikulski	Y	Y	N	N	N	N	Y
4 ***Holt***	Y	Y	N	N	Y	Y	N
5 Spellman	Y	Y	N	N	N	Y	Y
6 Byron	?	Y	N	N	N	Y	Y
7 Mitchell	P	Y	Y	Y	N	N	Y
8 ***Steers***	Y	N	Y	Y	N	Y	Y
MASSACHUSETTS							
1 ***Conte***	Y	N	N	N	N	N	Y
2 Boland	Y	Y	N	N	N	N	Y
3 Early	Y	N	N	N	N	N	Y
4 Drinan	Y	Y	N	N	N	Y	Y
5 Tsongas	?	?	?	?	?	?	?
6 Harrington	#	#	N	Y	▮	▮	#
7 Markey	Y	Y	Y	Y	N	N	Y
8 O'Neill							
9 Moakley	Y	N	N	N	▮	#	#
10 ***Heckler***	?	Y	N	N	Y	Y	Y
11 Burke	Y	N	Y	Y	N	N	Y
12 Studds	Y	N	Y	Y	N	N	Y
MICHIGAN							
1 Conyers	#	Y	N	#	▮	▮	#
2 ***Pursell***	Y	?	?	?	?	?	?
3 ***Brown***	Y	Y	Y	Y	N	Y	Y
4 ***Stockman***	Y	Y	Y	Y	N	Y	N
5 ***Sawyer***	Y	?	N	N	N	Y	Y
6 Carr	Y	N	Y	Y	N	N	Y
7 Kildee	Y	N	Y	Y	N	N	Y
8 Traxler	Y	N	N	N	N	Y	Y
9 ***Vander Jagt***	Y	N	N	N	N	Y	Y
10 ***Cederberg***	Y	N	N	N	N	Y	Y
11 ***Ruppe***	Y	Y	N	N	N	Y	Y
12 Bonior	#	Y	Y	#	▮	N	Y
13 Diggs	#	N	Y	Y	▮	?	#
14 Nedzi	Y	Y	Y	Y	N	N	Y
15 Ford	?	Y	N	N	N	N	Y
16 Dingell	?	Y	✓	N	?	?	?
17 Brodhead	Y	Y	Y	Y	N	Y	N
18 Blanchard	Y	Y	Y	Y	N	N	Y
19 ***Broomfield***	Y	Y	N	N	N	Y	Y
MINNESOTA							
1 ***Quie***	?	?	?	?	?	?	?
2 ***Hagedorn***	Y	N	N	N	N	Y	N
3 ***Frenzel***	Y	N	N	N	N	Y	N
4 Vento	Y	Y	Y	Y	N	Y	Y
5 Fraser	?	N	Y	Y	N	N	Y
6 Nolan	Y	Y	Y	Y	N	N	Y
7 ***Stangeland***	Y	N	N	N	Y	Y	Y
8 Oberstar	Y	Y	Y	Y	N	N	Y
MISSISSIPPI							
1 Whitten	Y	N	N	Y	N	N	Y
2 Bowen	Y	Y	Y	Y	N	Y	Y
3 Montgomery	Y	Y	N	N	N	Y	N
4 ***Cochran***	Y	Y	N	?	?	?	?
5 ***Lott***	Y	Y	Y	Y	Y	Y	Y
MISSOURI							
1 Clay	Y	Y	Y	Y	N	N	Y
2 Young	Y	Y	N	Y	N	Y	Y
3 Gephardt	Y	Y	Y	Y	N	Y	Y

	500	501	502	503	504	505	506
4 Skelton	Y	Y	N	N	?	?	?
5 Bolling	#	#	#	#	▮	▮	#
6 ***Coleman***	Y	Y	N	Y	N	Y	N
7 ***Taylor***	Y	Y	N	N	Y	Y	N
8 Ichord	Y	Y	N	N	N	Y	N
9 Volkmer	Y	Y	N	N	N	Y	Y
10 Burlison	Y	N	N	N	N	N	Y
MONTANA							
1 Baucus	Y	Y	N	Y	N	Y	Y
2 ***Marlenee***	Y	Y	Y	Y	Y	Y	Y
NEBRASKA							
1 ***Thone***	Y	Y	N	N	?	?	?
2 Cavanaugh	?	N	N	N	N	Y	N
3 ***Smith***	Y	Y	N	N	Y	Y	N
NEVADA							
AL Santini	#	Y	N	N	N	Y	Y
NEW HAMPSHIRE							
1 D'Amours	Y	Y	Y	Y	Y	Y	N
2 ***Cleveland***	Y	N	Y	Y	Y	Y	Y
NEW JERSEY							
1 Florio	Y	Y	Y	Y	Y	Y	Y
2 Hughes	Y	Y	Y	Y	N	Y	N
3 Howard	Y	N	Y	Y	N	N	Y
4 Thompson	Y	N	N	N	N	N	Y
5 ***Fenwick***	Y	Y	N	N	N	Y	Y
6 ***Forsythe***	Y	Y	N	N	N	Y	Y
7 Maguire	Y	N	Y	Y	N	?	?
8 Roe	Y	Y	Y	Y	N	Y	Y
9 ***Hollenbeck***	Y	Y	Y	Y	N	Y	Y
10 Rodino	#	#	▮	▮	▮	▮	#
11 Minish	Y	N	Y	Y	N	Y	Y
12 ***Rinaldo***	Y	Y	Y	Y	N	Y	Y
13 Meyner	Y	N	Y	Y	N	N	Y
14 LeFante	#	X	✓	✓	▮	#	#
15 Patten	Y	N	Y	Y	N	N	Y
NEW MEXICO							
1 ***Lujan***	Y	Y	N	N	?	?	?
2 Runnels	Y	Y	N	N	Y	Y	Y
NEW YORK							
1 Pike	Y	Y	N	N	N	Y	Y
2 Downey	Y	Y	Y	Y	N	Y	Y
3 Ambro	?	Y	N	Y	N	Y	Y
4 ***Lent***	Y	N	N	N	N	Y	Y
5 ***Wydler***	Y	Y	N	N	Y	Y	Y
6 Wolff	Y	N	Y	Y	N	Y	Y
7 Addabbo	Y	N	Y	Y	?	?	?
8 Rosenthal	Y	Y	Y	Y	N	Y	Y
9 Delaney	Y	Y	N	N	N	Y	Y
10 Biaggi	Y	Y	Y	Y	N	?	Y
11 Scheuer	Y	Y	Y	Y	N	N	Y
12 Chisholm	#	Y	Y	Y	N	N	Y
13 Solarz	#	Y	Y	Y	N	N	Y
14 Richmond	Y	Y	Y	Y	N	N	Y
15 Zeferetti	Y	Y	Y	Y	N	Y	Y
16 Holtzman	Y	Y	Y	Y	N	N	Y
17 Murphy	Y	Y	Y	Y	N	N	Y
18 ***Green***	Y	N	Y	Y	N	N	Y
19 Rangel	Y	Y	Y	Y	N	N	Y
20 Weiss	Y	Y	Y	Y	N	N	Y
21 Garcia	#	Y	Y	Y	N	N	Y
22 Bingham	Y	Y	Y	Y	N	N	Y
23 ***Caputo***	?	N	Y	Y	Y	N	Y
24 Ottinger	Y	Y	Y	Y	N	N	Y
25 ***Fish***	Y	Y	N	N	N	Y	Y
26 ***Gilman***	Y	N	Y	Y	N	Y	Y
27 McHugh	#	N	Y	Y	N	N	Y
28 Stratton	Y	Y	N	N	N	Y	Y
29 Pattison	#	#	N	N	N	N	Y
30 ***McEwen***	Y	N	N	N	N	N	Y
31 ***Mitchell***	Y	Y	Y	Y	N	Y	Y
32 Hanley	Y	Y	N	Y	N	Y	Y
33 ***Walsh***	Y	N	Y	Y	N	Y	Y
34 ***Horton***	Y	Y	N	N	N	N	Y
35 ***Conable***	Y	Y	N	N	N	Y	N
36 LaFalce	?	N	N	Y	N	Y	Y
37 Nowak	Y	N	N	N	N	Y	Y
38 ***Kemp***	?	Y	N	N	N	Y	Y
39 Lundine	#	N	Y	Y	N	N	Y
NORTH CAROLINA							
1 Jones	Y	Y	Y	Y	N	Y	Y
2 Fountain	Y	Y	N	N	N	Y	Y
3 Whitley	Y	Y	Y	N	N	Y	Y
4 Andrews	Y	N	N	N	N	Y	Y
5 Neal	Y	Y	N	N	N	Y	Y
6 Preyer	Y	N	Y	N	N	Y	Y
7 Rose	Y	Y	Y	Y	N	Y	Y
8 Hefner	Y	N	Y	N	N	Y	Y

	500	501	502	503	504	505	506
9 ***Martin***	Y	Y	N	N	N	Y	Y
10 ***Broyhill***	Y	Y	N	N	N	Y	Y
11 Gudger	Y	N	N	N	N	Y	Y
NORTH DAKOTA							
AL ***Andrews***	Y	Y	N	N	N	N	Y
OHIO							
1 ***Gradison***	Y	Y	N	N	N	Y	Y
2 Luken	?	?	?	?	?	?	?
3 ***Whalen***	Y	Y	Y	Y	N	N	Y
4 ***Guyer***	Y	N	N	N	N	Y	N
5 ***Latta***	Y	Y	N	N	N	Y	N
6 ***Harsha***	Y	N	Y	Y	Y	Y	Y
7 ***Brown***	Y	N	Y	Y	N	Y	Y
8 ***Kindness***	Y	N	N	N	Y	Y	Y
9 Ashley	Y	N	Y	Y	Y	N	Y
10 ***Miller***	Y	Y	N	N	N	Y	N
11 ***Stanton***	Y	N	N	N	N	Y	Y
12 ***Devine***	Y	Y	N	N	Y	Y	N
13 Pease	Y	Y	Y	N	▮	Y	Y
14 Seiberling	Y	Y	N	N	N	N	Y
15 ***Wylie***	Y	Y	N	N	N	Y	Y
16 ***Regula***	Y	Y	N	N	N	Y	Y
17 ***Ashbrook***	#	?	?	?	?	?	?
18 Applegate	Y	N	N	N	N	Y	Y
19 Carney	Y	Y	N	N	N	?	Y
20 Oakar	Y	N	N	N	Y	N	Y
21 Stokes	Y	Y	Y	Y	N	N	Y
22 Vanik	Y	Y	N	N	N	Y	Y
23 Mottl	Y	Y	N	N	Y	Y	N
OKLAHOMA							
1 Jones	Y	Y	Y	Y	Y	Y	Y
2 Risenhoover	Y	Y	Y	Y	Y	Y	Y
3 Watkins	Y	Y	Y	Y	Y	Y	Y
4 Steed	Y	Y	N	N	N	N	Y
5 ***Edwards***	?	Y	Y	N	Y	Y	N
6 English	Y	Y	Y	Y	Y	Y	Y
OREGON							
1 AuCoin	Y	Y	N	N	N	Y	N
2 Ullman	Y	Y	N	N	N	N	Y
3 Duncan	Y	N	N	N	N	N	Y
4 Weaver	Y	Y	N	N	N	Y	?
PENNSYLVANIA							
1 Myers, M.	Y	N	Y	Y	N	N	Y
2 Nix	Y	N	Y	N	N	N	Y
3 Lederer	Y	N	Y	Y	N	N	Y
4 Eilberg	Y	N	Y	Y	N	N	Y
5 ***Schulze***	Y	N	N	N	N	Y	N
6 Yatron	Y	Y	N	N	N	Y	Y
7 Edgar	Y	Y	N	N	N	Y	Y
8 Kostmayer	?	Y	N	N	N	Y	N
9 ***Shuster***	Y	Y	N	N	Y	Y	N
10 ***McDade***	Y	N	Y	Y	N	Y	Y
11 Flood	Y	N	N	N	N	N	Y
12 Murtha	Y	Y	N	N	N	Y	Y
13 ***Coughlin***	Y	N	N	N	N	Y	Y
14 Moorhead	Y	N	N	N	N	N	Y
15 Rooney	Y	N	N	N	N	N	Y
16 ***Walker***	Y	Y	N	N	Y	Y	N
17 Ertel	Y	Y	Y	Y	N	Y	Y
18 Walgren	Y	N	Y	Y	N	Y	Y
19 ***Goodling, W.***	Y	N	N	N	Y	Y	N
20 Gaydos	Y	Y	Y	Y	N	Y	Y
21 Dent	#	✓	X	▮	▮	#	#
22 Murphy	Y	Y	Y	Y	N	Y	Y
23 Ammerman	Y	Y	N	N	N	Y	Y
24 ***Marks***	Y	N	Y	Y	N	Y	Y
25 ***Myers, G.***	Y	N	N	N	N	Y	Y
RHODE ISLAND							
1 St Germain	Y	Y	N	N	N	?	?
2 Beard	Y	N	Y	N	N	N	Y
SOUTH CAROLINA							
1 Davis	?	Y	Y	Y	N	Y	Y
2 ***Spence***	Y	Y	Y	Y	Y	Y	Y
3 Derrick	#	?	▮	#	▮	#	#
4 Mann	?	?	?	?	?	?	?
5 Holland	Y	Y	Y	N	Y	Y	Y
6 Jenrette	#	N	N	Y	▮	Y	Y
SOUTH DAKOTA							
1 ***Pressler***	?	?	?	?	?	?	?
2 ***Abdnor***	Y	Y	N	N	Y	Y	Y
TENNESSEE							
1 ***Quillen***	Y	N	Y	Y	N	N	Y
2 ***Duncan***	Y	N	Y	Y	N	Y	Y
3 Lloyd	Y	Y	Y	Y	N	Y	Y
4 Gore	Y	Y	Y	Y	N	Y	Y
5 Vacancy							
6 ***Beard***	Y	Y	Y	Y	N	Y	Y

	500	501	502	503	504	505	506
7 Jones	Y	Y	Y	N	N	Y	Y
8 Ford	Y	Y	Y	Y	N	?	?
TEXAS							
1 Hall	Y	Y	N	▮	Y	Y	Y
2 Wilson, C.	#	Y	▮	#	N	Y	Y
3 ***Collins***	#	#	▮	▮	#	#	▮
4 Roberts	Y	Y	N	N	Y	Y	Y
5 Mattox	Y	N	Y	Y	Y	Y	N
6 Teague	?	?	X	?	?	?	?
7 ***Archer***	Y	Y	N	N	Y	Y	N
8 Eckhardt	Y	Y	Y	Y	N	N	Y
9 Brooks	Y	Y	Y	Y	N	Y	Y
10 Pickle	Y	N	Y	Y	N	Y	Y
11 Poage	Y	Y	N	N	N	Y	Y
12 Wright	Y	?	Y	Y	N	N	Y
13 Hightower	Y	Y	Y	Y	Y	Y	Y
14 Young	?	?	?	?	?	?	?
15 de la Garza	Y	N	Y	Y	N	Y	Y
16 White	Y	Y	N	N	N	Y	Y
17 Burleson	Y	Y	N	N	Y	Y	Y
18 Jordan	Y	Y	Y	Y	N	N	Y
19 Mahon	Y	N	N	N	N	N	Y
20 Gonzalez	Y	Y	Y	Y	N	N	Y
21 Krueger	#	#	#	#	▮	#	#
22 Gammage	Y	Y	N	N	Y	Y	N
23 Kazen	Y	Y	Y	Y	Y	Y	Y
24 Milford	Y	N	N	N	?	Y	Y
UTAH							
1 McKay	#	Y	N	N	Y	N	Y
2 ***Marriott***	Y	Y	N	N	N	Y	N
VERMONT							
AL ***Jeffords***	Y	Y	N	N	N	N	Y
VIRGINIA							
1 ***Trible***	Y	Y	N	N	Y	Y	Y
2 ***Whitehurst***	Y	Y	N	N	N	Y	Y
3 Satterfield	Y	Y	N	N	N	Y	N
4 ***Daniel***	Y	Y	N	N	Y	Y	Y
5 Daniel	Y	Y	N	N	N	Y	Y
6 ***Butler***	?	Y	N	N	N	Y	Y
7 ***Robinson***	Y	Y	N	N	Y	Y	Y
8 Harris	#	Y	N	N	N	N	Y
9 ***Wampler***	Y	Y	Y	Y	N	Y	Y
10 Fisher	Y	N	N	N	N	Y	Y
WASHINGTON							
1 ***Pritchard***	Y	N	N	N	N	Y	Y
2 Meeds	Y	Y	N	N	N	N	Y
3 Bonker	Y	Y	Y	N	N	Y	Y
4 McCormack	Y	N	Y	Y	N	Y	Y
5 Foley	Y	Y	N	N	N	Y	Y
6 Dicks	Y	Y	Y	N	N	Y	Y
7 ***Cunningham***	Y	Y	N	N	Y	Y	Y
WEST VIRGINIA							
1 Mollohan	Y	Y	N	N	▮	▮	#
2 Staggers	Y	N	Y	N	N	Y	Y
3 Slack	Y	Y	N	N	N	N	Y
4 Rahall	Y	Y	Y	Y	N	N	Y
WISCONSIN							
1 Aspin	Y	N	N	N	N	Y	Y
2 Kastenmeier	Y	N	Y	Y	N	N	Y
3 Baldus	Y	N	N	N	N	N	Y
4 Zablocki	Y	N	N	N	N	N	Y
5 Reuss	Y	N	N	N	N	N	Y
6 ***Steiger***	Y	Y	Y	Y	N	Y	Y
7 Obey	Y	N	N	N	?	N	Y
8 Cornell	Y	N	N	N	N	N	Y
9 ***Kasten***	?	?	?	?	?	?	?
WYOMING							
AL Roncalio	#	#	✓	Y	N	N	Y

Democrats ***Republicans***

507. HR 12433. Housing and Community Development. Ashley, D-Ohio, motion that the House resolve itself into the Committee of the Whole for consideration of the bill to revise and extend certain federal housing and community development laws. Motion agreed to 268-6: R 90-2; D 178-4 (ND 127-3; SD 51-1), July 21, 1978.

508. HR 12433. Housing and Community Development. Abdnor, R-S.D., amendment to prohibit the Department of Housing and Urban Development from carrying out a reorganization of its field offices. Rejected 133-160: R 82-13; D 51-147 (ND 35-105; SD 16-42), July 21, 1978.

509. HR 12433. Housing and Community Development. Brown, R-Mich., amendment to delete a provision in the bill to limit property insurance rates under state-operated FAIR (Fair Access to Insurance Requirements) plans. Rejected 119-185: R 84-16; D 35-169 (ND 15-131; SD 20-38), July 21, 1978.

510. HR 12433. Housing and Community Development. Duncan, R-Tenn., amendment to prohibit Social Security cost-of-living increases from being counted as income when calculating rents in assisted housing. Adopted 256-38: R 91-5; D 165-33 (ND 116-29; SD 49-4), July 21, 1978.

511. HR 12433. Housing and Community Development. Passage of the bill to revise, extend and authorize $29.3 billion for various housing and community development programs. Passed 270-26: R 85-14; D 185-12 (ND 139-5; SD 46-7), July 21, 1978.

512. HR 13468. District of Columbia Appropriations, Fiscal 1979. Passage of the bill to appropriate $274,300,000 in federal funds and establish a fiscal 1979 budget for the District of Columbia of $1,348,185,100. Passed 215-32: R 59-21; D 156-11 (ND 115-3; SD 41-8), July 21, 1978. The president had requested $457,090,000 in federal funds and a budget of $1,428,442,000.

513. H J Res 946. National Guard Day. Lehman, D-Fla., motion to suspend the rules and pass the joint resolution to designate Oct. 7, 1978, as National Guard Day to commemorate the contributions to the national defense of the national guard since 1636. Passed 264-10: R 76-1; D 188-9 (ND 124-8; SD 64-1), July 24, 1978. A two-thirds majority vote (183 in this case) is required for passage under suspension of the rule.

KEY

- Y Voted for (yea).
- ✓ Paired for.
- † Announced for.
- # CQ Poll for.
- N Voted against (nay).
- X Paired against.
- \- Announced against.
- ▮ CQ Poll against.
- P Voted "present."
- ● Voted "present" to avoid possible conflict of interest.
- ? Did not vote or otherwise make a position known.

	507	508	509	510	511	512	513
ALABAMA							
1 Edwards	Y	Y	Y	Y	Y	Y	Y
2 Dickinson	Y	Y	Y	Y	Y	Y	Y
3 Nichols	#	✓	✓	#	#	#	Y
4 Bevill	?	?	?	?	?	?	Y
5 Flippo	Y	N	Y	Y	Y	Y	Y
6 Buchanan	Y	Y	Y	Y	Y	Y	Y
7 Flowers	?	?	?	?	?	?	Y
ALASKA							
AL Young	#	#	▮	#	#	#	#
ARIZONA							
1 Rhodes	?	?	?	?	?	?	?
2 Udall	Y	N	N	Y	Y	Y	#
3 Stump	Y	Y	Y	Y	N	N	Y
4 Rudd	?	?	?	?	?	?	?
ARKANSAS							
1 Alexander	Y	Y	N	Y	Y	Y	Y
2 Tucker	Y	Y	N	N	Y	Y	#
3 Hammerschmidt	Y	Y	N	Y	Y	N	Y
4 Thornton	?	Y	N	Y	Y	Y	Y
CALIFORNIA							
1 Johnson	Y	Y	N	Y	Y	Y	Y
2 Clausen	?	?	?	?	?	?	?
3 Moss	Y	Y	N	N	Y	Y	Y
4 Leggett	?	?	?	?	Y	Y	?
5 Burton, J.	?	?	?	?	?	?	?
6 Burton, P.	?	X	X	?	?	?	Y
7 Miller	Y	N	N	N	Y	Y	N
8 Dellums	▮	▮	▮	#	#	#	▮
9 Stark	#	▮	N	Y	Y	Y	N
10 Edwards	?	?	?	?	?	?	Y
11 Ryan	Y	N	N	Y	Y	Y	Y
12 McCloskey	Y	N	Y	Y	?	?	?
13 Mineta	Y	N	Y	Y	Y	Y	Y
14 McFall	Y	N	N	N	Y	Y	Y
15 Sisk	Y	Y	Y	Y	Y	Y	Y
16 Panetta	Y	N	N	Y	Y	N	Y
17 Krebs	Y	N	N	Y	Y	Y	Y
18 Vacancy							
19 Lagomarsino	Y	Y	Y	Y	Y	Y	Y
20 Goldwater	?	?	Y	Y	Y	Y	?
21 Corman	Y	N	N	N	#	#	Y
22 Moorhead	Y	Y	Y	Y	Y	N	Y
23 Beilenson	Y	N	N	N	Y	Y	N
24 Waxman	#	▮	▮	#	#	#	#
25 Roybal	?	?	?	?	?	?	Y
26 Rousselot	?	?	?	?	?	?	?
27 Dornan	Y	Y	Y	Y	Y	N	Y
28 Burke	Y	N	N	Y	Y	Y	?
29 Hawkins	?	?	?	?	?	?	Y
30 Danielson	Y	N	N	N	Y	Y	#
31 Wilson, C.H.	Y	N	N	Y	Y	?	?
32 Anderson	Y	N	N	Y	Y	Y	#
33 Clawson	?	?	?	?	?	?	?
34 Hannaford	Y	N	N	Y	Y	Y	Y
35 Lloyd	N	N	N	N	Y	Y	Y
36 Brown	?	?	?	?	?	?	Y
37 Pettis	?	?	?	?	?	?	?
38 Patterson	Y	N	N	Y	Y	Y	Y
39 Wiggins	Y	Y	Y	N	Y	Y	#
40 Badham	#	#	#	#	▮	▮	#
41 Wilson, B.	N	Y	Y	Y	Y	Y	?
42 Van Deerlin	Y	Y	N	Y	Y	Y	Y
43 Burgener	Y	Y	Y	Y	Y	Y	?
COLORADO							
1 Schroeder	Y	N	N	Y	Y	#	N
2 Wirth	Y	N	N	Y	Y	Y	Y
3 Evans	?	N	N	N	Y	Y	N
4 Johnson	?	?	?	?	?	?	?
5 Armstrong	?	?	?	?	?	?	?
CONNECTICUT							
1 Cotter	#	▮	▮	#	#	#	#
2 Dodd	Y	N	N	Y	Y	?	?
3 Giaimo	Y	?	N	N	Y	Y	?
4 McKinney	Y	Y	Y	Y	Y	Y	#
5 Sarasin	#	#	▮	#	#	#	#
6 Moffett	?	?	?	?	?	?	Y
DELAWARE							
AL Evans	Y	Y	Y	Y	Y	Y	?
FLORIDA							
1 Sikes	Y	N	N	Y	Y	?	Y
2 Fuqua	#	▮	▮	#	#	#	Y
3 Bennett	Y	N	N	Y	Y	Y	Y
4 Chappell	Y	N	Y	Y	Y	Y	Y
5 Kelly	Y	Y	Y	Y	N	N	Y
6 Young	Y	Y	Y	Y	Y	?	Y
7 Gibbons	?	?	?	?	?	?	Y
8 Ireland	Y	N	Y	Y	Y	Y	?
9 Frey	?	?	?	?	?	?	?
10 Bafalis	Y	Y	Y	Y	Y	N	Y
11 Rogers	Y	N	N	Y	Y	Y	N
12 Burke	Y	Y	Y	Y	Y	Y	Y
13 Lehman	Y	N	N	Y	Y	Y	Y
14 Pepper	#	#	#	#	#	#	#
15 Fascell	Y	N	N	Y	Y	Y	#
GEORGIA							
1 Ginn	Y	N	N	Y	Y	Y	Y
2 Mathis	?	?	?	?	?	?	?
3 Brinkley	Y	N	Y	?	?	?	?
4 Levitas	Y	N	N	Y	Y	Y	?
5 Fowler	?	?	?	?	?	?	Y
6 Flynt	?	?	?	?	?	?	Y
7 McDonald	Y	Y	Y	Y	N	▮	Y
8 Evans	Y	N	Y	?	?	?	?
9 Jenkins	#	▮	▮	#	#	#	#
10 Barnard	?	?	?	?	?	?	#
HAWAII							
1 Heftel	Y	N	N	Y	Y	Y	Y
2 Akaka	Y	N	N	Y	Y	Y	Y
IDAHO							
1 Symms	Y	Y	Y	Y	N	N	?
2 Hansen, G.	Y	Y	Y	Y	N	N	Y
ILLINOIS							
1 Metcalfe	?	?	?	?	?	?	?
2 Murphy	#	▮	?	#	#	#	Y
3 Russo	Y	Y	N	Y	N	#	#
4 Derwinski	Y	Y	Y	Y	N	?	Y
5 Fary	Y	N	N	Y	Y	Y	Y
6 Hyde	Y	Y	N	Y	Y	Y	Y
7 Collins	?	?	?	?	?	?	?
8 Rostenkowski	?	?	?	?	?	?	?
9 Yates	Y	N	N	Y	Y	Y	#
10 Mikva	Y	N	N	N	Y	Y	#
11 Annunzio	Y	N	N	Y	Y	Y	Y
12 Crane	#	#	#	#	?	▮	Y
13 McClory	Y	Y	Y	Y	Y	Y	Y
14 Erlenborn	#	Y	Y	Y	Y	Y	Y
15 Corcoran	Y	Y	Y	Y	Y	Y	Y
16 Anderson	Y	Y	Y	#	Y	Y	#
17 O'Brien	Y	Y	Y	Y	Y	Y	#
18 Michel	?	?	?	?	?	?	?
19 Railsback	Y	Y	N	Y	Y	?	?
20 Findley	Y	Y	Y	Y	N	Y	Y
21 Madigan	?	?	Y	Y	Y	Y	Y
22 Shipley	?	?	?	?	?	?	?
23 Price	Y	N	N	Y	Y	Y	Y
24 Simon	Y	N	N	N	Y	Y	Y
INDIANA							
1 Benjamin	Y	Y	N	Y	Y	Y	Y
2 Fithian	Y	N	Y	Y	Y	?	Y
3 Brademas	Y	N	N	N	Y	Y	Y
4 Quayle	?	?	?	?	?	?	?
5 Hillis	?	?	?	?	?	?	?
6 Evans	Y	N	Y	Y	Y	N	Y
7 Myers, J.	Y	Y	Y	Y	Y	N	Y
8 Cornwell	?	N	Y	Y	Y	?	Y
9 Hamilton	Y	N	Y	Y	Y	Y	Y
10 Sharp	Y	N	N	N	Y	Y	Y
11 Jacobs	Y	Y	Y	Y	Y	Y	Y
IOWA							
1 Leach	Y	Y	Y	Y	Y	N	Y
2 Blouin	Y	Y	N	Y	Y	Y	#
3 Grassley	Y	Y	Y	Y	Y	N	Y
4 Smith	?	?	?	?	?	?	Y
5 Harkin	Y	Y	N	Y	Y	?	Y
6 Bedell	#	#	▮	#	#	#	Y

Democrats ***Republicans***

	507	508	509	510	511	512	513
KANSAS							
1 ***Sebelius***	?	?	?	?	?	?	?
2 Keys	Y	Y	Y	Y	Y	Y	Y
3 ***Winn***	#	#	▮	#	#	#	#
4 Glickman	Y	Y	N	Y	Y	Y	Y
5 ***Skubitz***	?	Y	Y	Y	Y	Y	Y
KENTUCKY							
1 Hubbard	Y	Y	N	Y	Y	Y	Y
2 Natcher	Y	N	N	Y	Y	Y	Y
3 Mazzoli	#	▮	▮	#	#	#	Y
4 ***Snyder***	Y	Y	Y	Y	Y	Y	Y
5 ***Carter***	Y	Y	Y	Y	Y	Y	Y
6 Breckinridge	Y	Y	N	?	?	Y	Y
7 Perkins	Y	N	N	Y	Y	Y	Y
LOUISIANA							
1 ***Livingston***	Y	Y	Y	Y	Y	Y	Y
2 Boggs	N	N	N	Y	Y	Y	Y
3 ***Treen***	Y	Y	Y	N	Y	?	?
4 Waggonner	#	#	▮	#	#	▮	Y
5 Huckaby	?	?	?	?	?	?	Y
6 ***Moore***	Y	Y	Y	Y	Y	Y	Y
7 Breaux	?	?	?	?	?	?	Y
8 Long	?	?	?	Y	Y	?	Y
MAINE							
1 ***Emery***	Y	Y	N	Y	Y	N	Y
2 ***Cohen***	#	?	?	?	?	#	#
MARYLAND							
1 ***Bauman***	Y	Y	Y	Y	N	N	Y
2 Long	Y	N	N	Y	Y	Y	Y
3 Mikulski	N	N	N	Y	Y	Y	?
4 ***Holt***	Y	Y	Y	Y	N	?	Y
5 Spellman	?	?	N	Y	Y	Y	?
6 Byron	?	?	Y	Y	Y	Y	Y
7 Mitchell	N	N	N	Y	Y	Y	Y
8 ***Steers***	Y	N	Y	Y	Y	Y	Y
MASSACHUSETTS							
1 ***Conte***	Y	N	N	Y	Y	Y	Y
2 Boland	Y	N	N	Y	Y	#	#
3 Early	?	?	?	?	?	?	?
4 Drinan	Y	N	N	Y	Y	Y	Y
5 Tsongas	?	?	?	?	?	?	?
6 Harrington	#	▮	▮	#	#	#	▮
7 Markey	Y	?	N	Y	Y	Y	Y
8 O'Neill							
9 Moakley	#	▮	▮	#	#	#	#
10 ***Heckler***	?	?	N	?	Y	Y	?
11 Burke	Y	N	N	N	Y	Y	Y
12 Studds	Y	N	N	Y	Y	Y	Y
MICHIGAN							
1 Conyers	#	▮	▮	#	#	#	#
2 ***Pursell***	?	?	?	?	?	?	?
3 ***Brown***	Y	Y	Y	Y	Y	Y	Y
4 ***Stockman***	Y	#	Y	Y	Y	#	Y
5 ***Sawyer***	#	#	?	#	#	#	Y
6 Carr	Y	Y	N	N	Y	Y	Y
7 Kildee	Y	N	N	Y	Y	Y	Y
8 Traxler	Y	N	N	Y	Y	#	#
9 ***Vander Jagt***	?	?	?	?	?	?	?
10 ***Cederberg***	Y	Y	Y	Y	Y	N	?
11 ***Ruppe***	Y	Y	Y	N	Y	?	?
12 Bonior	Y	N	N	Y	Y	Y	#
13 Diggs	#	▮	?	#	#	#	#
14 Nedzi	Y	N	N	N	Y	Y	Y
15 Ford	?	?	N	Y	Y	Y	?
16 Dingell	Y	N	N	Y	Y	Y	Y
17 Brodhead	Y	N	N	Y	N	Y	Y
18 Blanchard	Y	N	N	Y	Y	Y	Y
19 ***Broomfield***	Y	Y	N	Y	Y	Y	Y
MINNESOTA							
1 ***Quie***	?	?	?	?	?	?	?
2 ***Hagedorn***	Y	Y	Y	Y	Y	Y	?
3 ***Frenzel***	Y	N	Y	Y	Y	?	Y
4 Vento	Y	N	N	Y	Y	?	Y
5 Fraser	?	N	N	Y	Y	Y	?
6 Nolan	Y	?	?	?	?	?	Y
7 ***Stangeland***	Y	Y	Y	Y	Y	#	Y
8 Oberstar	Y	N	N	Y	Y	Y	Y
MISSISSIPPI							
1 Whitten	Y	▮	▮	#	#	#	#
2 Bowen	Y	N	N	Y	Y	Y	Y
3 Montgomery	Y	Y	Y	Y	N	Y	Y
4 ***Cochran***	?	?	?	?	?	?	?
5 ***Lott***	#	#	#	#	#	▮	#
MISSOURI							
1 Clay	?	?	?	?	?	?	Y
2 Young	Y	Y	N	Y	Y	#	Y
3 Gephardt	Y	Y	N	N	Y	▮	Y
4 Skelton	?	?	?	?	?	?	Y
5 Bolling	#	N	N	N	Y	Y	Y
6 ***Coleman***	Y	N	Y	Y	Y	Y	?
7 ***Taylor***	?	?	?	?	?	?	Y
8 Ichord	Y	Y	Y	Y	N	Y	Y
9 Volkmer	Y	Y	Y	Y	Y	Y	Y
10 Burlison	Y	N	N	N	Y	Y	?
MONTANA							
1 Baucus	#	#	▮	#	#	#	Y
2 ***Marlenee***	?	?	?	?	?	?	Y
NEBRASKA							
1 ***Thone***	?	?	?	?	?	?	?
2 Cavanaugh	?	N	N	Y	?	Y	?
3 ***Smith***	Y	Y	Y	Y	Y	Y	Y
NEVADA							
AL Santini	#	Y	N	Y	Y	Y	#
NEW HAMPSHIRE							
1 D'Amours	Y	Y	N	Y	Y	?	Y
2 ***Cleveland***	Y	Y	Y	Y	Y	?	?
NEW JERSEY							
1 Florio	Y	N	N	Y	Y	Y	Y
2 Hughes	Y	Y	N	Y	N	Y	Y
3 Howard	Y	Y	N	Y	Y	Y	#
4 Thompson	Y	N	N	N	Y	Y	Y
5 ***Fenwick***	Y	Y	N	Y	Y	Y	?
6 ***Forsythe***	Y	Y	Y	Y	Y	Y	Y
7 Maguire	?	?	?	?	?	?	?
8 Roe	Y	Y	N	Y	Y	Y	Y
9 ***Hollenbeck***	Y	Y	N	Y	Y	?	#
10 Rodino	#	▮	▮	#	#	#	#
11 Minish	Y	N	N	Y	Y	?	Y
12 ***Rinaldo***	Y	Y	N	Y	Y	#	Y
13 Meyner	#	N	N	#	#	#	#
14 LeFante	#	▮	▮	#	#	#	#
15 Patten	Y	Y	N	Y	Y	Y	#
NEW MEXICO							
1 ***Lujan***	?	?	?	?	?	?	Y
2 Runnels	?	?	?	?	?	?	Y
NEW YORK							
1 Pike	Y	N	N	Y	Y	Y	N
2 Downey	Y	N	N	Y	Y	Y	Y
3 Ambro	?	?	N	Y	Y	Y	Y
4 ***Lent***	?	?	✓	?	?	?	?
5 ***Wydler***	?	?	?	?	?	?	?
6 Wolff	Y	N	N	Y	Y	Y	?
7 Addabbo	?	X	X	?	?	?	?
8 Rosenthal	#	N	N	Y	Y	#	#
9 Delaney	Y	N	N	Y	Y	Y	Y
10 Biaggi	?	?	?	?	?	?	?
11 Scheuer	Y	N	N	Y	Y	Y	?
12 Chisholm	#	?	?	#	#	#	#
13 Solarz	Y	N	N	Y	Y	Y	Y
14 Richmond	?	?	X	?	?	?	?
15 Zeferetti	#	▮	▮	#	#	#	#
16 Holtzman	Y	N	N	Y	Y	Y	?
17 Murphy	?	?	?	?	?	?	Y
18 ***Green***	#	▮	▮	#	#	#	?
19 Rangel	Y	N	N	Y	Y	Y	Y
20 Weiss	?	?	?	?	?	?	?
21 Garcia	Y	N	N	Y	Y	Y	#
22 Bingham	Y	N	N	Y	Y	Y	Y
23 ***Caputo***	?	?	?	?	?	?	?
24 Ottinger	Y	N	N	Y	Y	Y	N
25 ***Fish***	Y	Y	Y	Y	Y	Y	?
26 ***Gilman***	?	Y	N	Y	Y	Y	Y
27 McHugh	Y	Y	N	Y	Y	Y	Y
28 Stratton	Y	Y	N	Y	Y	Y	Y
29 Pattison	#	#	N	#	#	#	Y
30 ***McEwen***	?	?	?	?	?	?	?
31 ***Mitchell***	#	▮	▮	#	#	#	Y
32 Hanley	Y	N	N	Y	#	#	#
33 ***Walsh***	?	?	?	?	?	?	Y
34 ***Horton***	?	?	?	?	?	?	Y
35 ***Conable***	Y	Y	Y	Y	Y	Y	Y
36 LaFalce	Y	N	N	N	Y	#	Y
37 Nowak	Y	N	N	Y	Y	Y	Y
38 ***Kemp***	?	?	Y	Y	Y	Y	Y
39 Lundine	#	N	N	N	Y	Y	#
NORTH CAROLINA							
1 Jones	#	▮	#	#	#	#	Y
2 Fountain	#	N	Y	Y	Y	Y	#
3 Whitley	?	?	?	?	?	?	?
4 Andrews	Y	N	Y	Y	Y	Y	Y
5 Neal	Y	N	N	Y	Y	N	Y
6 Preyer	Y	N	N	Y	Y	Y	#
7 Rose	Y	N	N	Y	Y	Y	?
8 Hefner	Y	N	Y	Y	Y	Y	?
9 ***Martin***	Y	Y	Y	Y	Y	Y	Y
10 ***Broyhill***	Y	Y	Y	Y	Y	Y	?
11 Gudger	Y	N	N	Y	Y	Y	Y
NORTH DAKOTA							
AL ***Andrews***	#	#	▮	#	#	#	#
OHIO							
1 ***Gradison***	Y	Y	Y	Y	Y	Y	Y
2 Luken	Y	Y	Y	Y	Y	Y	Y
3 ***Whalen***	Y	N	N	Y	Y	#	#
4 ***Guyer***	Y	Y	Y	Y	Y	Y	Y
5 ***Latta***	Y	Y	Y	Y	N	▮	Y
6 ***Harsha***	?	?	?	?	?	?	Y
7 ***Brown***	?	?	?	?	?	?	Y
8 ***Kindness***	Y	Y	Y	?	N	Y	Y
9 Ashley	Y	N	N	N	Y	Y	?
10 ***Miller***	Y	Y	Y	Y	N	N	Y
11 ***Stanton***	Y	Y	Y	N	Y	Y	Y
12 ***Devine***	#	#	#	#	▮	▮	#
13 Pease	Y	N	Y	N	Y	Y	Y
14 Seiberling	Y	N	N	Y	Y	Y	Y
15 ***Wylie***	Y	Y	Y	Y	Y	Y	Y
16 ***Regula***	Y	Y	Y	Y	Y	Y	Y
17 ***Ashbrook***	?	?	?	?	?	?	?
18 Applegate	Y	N	Y	Y	Y	Y	Y
19 Carney	?	?	?	?	?	?	Y
20 Oakar	?	N	N	Y	Y	?	?
21 Stokes	?	?	?	?	?	?	?
22 Vanik	?	?	?	?	?	?	Y
23 Mottl	#	✓	✓	#	▮	▮	#
OKLAHOMA							
1 Jones	Y	Y	N	Y	Y	Y	Y
2 Risenhoover	?	N	N	?	?	?	Y
3 Watkins	?	?	?	?	?	?	Y
4 Steed	Y	Y	N	Y	Y	Y	Y
5 ***Edwards***	?	N	Y	Y	Y	N	Y
6 English	?	N	N	Y	Y	N	Y
OREGON							
1 AuCoin	Y	N	N	N	Y	Y	Y
2 Ullman	Y	Y	N	N	Y	Y	Y
3 Duncan	Y	N	N	N	Y	#	Y
4 Weaver	?	?	?	?	?	?	Y
PENNSYLVANIA							
1 Myers, M.	Y	N	N	Y	Y	Y	Y
2 Nix	Y	N	N	Y	Y	?	?
3 Lederer	Y	N	N	Y	Y	Y	Y
4 Eilberg	Y	N	N	Y	Y	Y	Y
5 ***Schulze***	Y	Y	Y	Y	Y	Y	?
6 Yatron	Y	Y	N	Y	Y	Y	Y
7 Edgar	#	▮	▮	#	#	#	Y
8 Kostmayer	Y	N	N	Y	Y	Y	Y
9 ***Shuster***	Y	Y	Y	Y	N	N	Y
10 ***McDade***	Y	N	Y	Y	Y	Y	#
11 Flood	Y	N	N	Y	Y	Y	Y
12 Murtha	Y	N	N	Y	Y	?	Y
13 ***Coughlin***	Y	N	Y	Y	Y	Y	Y
14 Moorhead	#	▮	▮	#	#	#	Y
15 Rooney	Y	N	N	N	Y	Y	Y
16 ***Walker***	Y	Y	Y	Y	N	N	?
17 Ertel	Y	Y	N	Y	Y	Y	Y
18 Walgren	Y	N	N	Y	Y	Y	Y
19 ***Goodling, W.***	Y	Y	Y	Y	Y	?	?
20 Gaydos	Y	N	N	Y	Y	?	Y
21 Dent	#	▮	▮	#	#	#	#
22 Murphy	Y	N	N	Y	Y	Y	Y
23 Ammerman	Y	N	N	Y	Y	Y	Y
24 ***Marks***	Y	N	N	Y	Y	Y	Y
25 ***Myers, G.***	Y	N	Y	N	Y	Y	N
RHODE ISLAND							
1 St Germain	?	?	?	?	?	?	Y
2 Beard	Y	N	▮	#	Y	#	Y
SOUTH CAROLINA							
1 Davis	?	?	?	?	?	?	?
2 ***Spence***	Y	Y	Y	Y	Y	Y	Y
3 Derrick	#	▮	▮	#	#	#	Y
4 Mann	?	?	?	?	?	?	?
5 Holland	?	?	?	?	?	?	Y
6 Jenrette	#	X	X	#	#	#	Y
SOUTH DAKOTA							
1 ***Pressler***	?	✓	?	?	?	?	?
2 ***Abdnor***	Y	Y	Y	Y	Y	Y	#
TENNESSEE							
1 ***Quillen***	Y	N	Y	Y	Y	▮	#
2 ***Duncan***	Y	Y	Y	Y	Y	Y	Y
3 Lloyd	Y	Y	N	#	#	#	Y
4 Gore	Y	N	N	Y	Y	Y	Y
5 Vacancy							
6 ***Beard***	Y	Y	Y	#	Y	Y	Y
7 Jones	Y	N	Y	Y	Y	#	Y
8 Ford	?	?	?	?	?	?	?
TEXAS							
1 Hall	Y	Y	Y	Y	Y	N	Y
2 Wilson, C.	Y	N	N	Y	Y	Y	#
3 ***Collins***	N	Y	Y	Y	N	N	Y
4 Roberts	Y	N	Y	Y	Y	N	Y
5 Mattox	Y	N	Y	Y	Y	N	Y
6 Teague	?	?	✓	?	?	?	?
7 ***Archer***	Y	Y	Y	Y	N	N	?
8 Eckhardt	?	N	N	?	?	?	Y
9 Brooks	Y	N	Y	Y	Y	Y	Y
10 Pickle	Y	N	N	Y	Y	Y	Y
11 Poage	Y	Y	Y	N	N	Y	Y
12 Wright	?	?	?	?	?	?	Y
13 Hightower	Y	N	N	Y	Y	?	Y
14 Young	?	?	?	?	?	?	Y
15 de la Garza	Y	N	N	Y	Y	Y	Y
16 White	Y	Y	N	Y	Y	Y	Y
17 Burleson	Y	N	Y	N	N	N	Y
18 Jordan	Y	N	N	Y	Y	Y	Y
19 Mahon	Y	N	N	Y	N	Y	Y
20 Gonzalez	Y	N	N	Y	Y	Y	?
21 Krueger	#	▮	▮	#	#	#	Y
22 Gammage	?	N	Y	Y	Y	N	Y
23 Kazen	Y	N	N	Y	Y	Y	Y
24 Milford	?	?	?	?	?	?	?
UTAH							
1 McKay	Y	Y	N	Y	Y	Y	#
2 ***Marriott***	Y	Y	Y	Y	Y	#	#
VERMONT							
AL ***Jeffords***	Y	Y	N	Y	Y	Y	?
VIRGINIA							
1 ***Trible***	Y	Y	Y	Y	Y	Y	Y
2 ***Whitehurst***	#	▮	#	#	#	▮	Y
3 Satterfield	?	Y	Y	Y	N	?	Y
4 ***Daniel***	Y	Y	Y	Y	Y	N	Y
5 Daniel	Y	Y	Y	Y	N	N	?
6 ***Butler***	Y	Y	Y	Y	Y	?	?
7 ***Robinson***	Y	Y	Y	Y	Y	N	Y
8 Harris	Y	Y	N	Y	Y	Y	Y
9 ***Wampler***	?	?	?	?	?	?	?
10 Fisher	Y	N	N	N	Y	Y	Y
WASHINGTON							
1 ***Pritchard***	Y	N	N	Y	Y	#	#
2 Meeds	Y	Y	N	Y	Y	#	#
3 Bonker	Y	N	N	Y	Y	Y	Y
4 McCormack	Y	Y	N	Y	Y	Y	Y
5 Foley	Y	Y	N	Y	Y	Y	Y
6 Dicks	Y	Y	N	Y	Y	?	?
7 ***Cunningham***	Y	Y	Y	Y	Y	Y	Y
WEST VIRGINIA							
1 Mollohan	Y	N	N	Y	Y	Y	Y
2 Staggers	Y	N	N	Y	Y	Y	Y
3 Slack	?	?	?	?	?	?	Y
4 Rahall	#	N	N	Y	Y	#	Y
WISCONSIN							
1 Aspin	Y	N	N	Y	Y	Y	Y
2 Kastenmeier	Y	N	N	Y	Y	?	Y
3 Baldus	Y	N	N	Y	Y	Y	Y
4 Zablocki	Y	N	N	Y	Y	Y	Y
5 Reuss	Y	N	N	N	Y	Y	Y
6 ***Steiger***	Y	Y	Y	Y	Y	Y	Y
7 Obey	?	N	N	Y	Y	?	N
8 Cornell	Y	N	N	Y	Y	Y	Y
9 ***Kasten***	?	?	?	?	?	▮	#
WYOMING							
AL Roncalio	#	Y	N	Y	Y	Y	#

Democrats ***Republicans***

514. HR 11823. Reservists' Retirement Eligibility. Nichols, D-Ala., motion to suspend the rules and pass the bill to liberalize eligibility for retired pay of members of reserve branches of the military. Motion agreed to 390-8: R 129-5; D 261-3 (ND 177-3; SD 84-0), July 25, 1978. A two-thirds majority vote (266 in this case) is required for passage under suspension of the rules.

515. HR 12349. DuNoir Basin Wilderness. Roncalio, D-Wyo., motion to suspend the rules and pass the bill to add a 34,500-acre area known as DuNoir Basin to the Washakie Wilderness in Wyoming. Motion agreed to 372-22: R 120-12; D 252-10 (ND 176-2; SD 76-8), July 25, 1978. A two-thirds majority vote (263 in this case) is required for passage under suspension of the rules.

516. HR 12973. Social Services Amendments. Corman, D-Calif., motion to suspend the rules and pass the bill to increase spending ceilings to $2.7 billion for fiscal 1979, $3.15 billion for 1980 and $3.45 billion for 1981 for child day care, home assistance for aged and disabled, employment training and other social services programs under Title XX of the Social Security Act. Motion agreed to 346-54: R 106-30; D 240-24 (ND 171-8; SD 69-16), July 25, 1978. A two-thirds majority vote (267 in this case) is required for passage under suspension of the rules.

517. HR 11889. Pension for Medal of Honor Recipients. Roberts, D-Texas, motion to suspend the rules and pass the bill to increase to $200 the additional monthly pension paid by the Veterans Administration to eligible persons who held the Congressional Medal of Honor. Motion agreed to 394-4: R 135-0; D 259-4 (ND 175-4; SD 84-0), July 25, 1978. A two-thirds majority vote (266 in this case) is required for passage under suspension of the rules.

518. HR 11890. Benefits for Survivors of Disabled Veterans. Roberts, D-Texas, motion to suspend the rules and pass the bill to liberalize eligibility for the benefits paid to survivors of permanently disabled veterans. Motion agreed to 393-9: R 136-0; D 257-9 (ND 172-9; SD 85-0), July 25, 1978. A two-thirds majority vote (269 in this case) is required for passage under suspension of the rules.

519. HR 12426. New York City Aid. Adoption of the conference report on the bill to provide up to $1.65 billion in long-term federal loan guarantees to New York City. Adopted 244-157: R 41-95; D 203-62 (ND 163-19; SD 40-43), July 25, 1978. A "yea" was a vote supporting the president's position.

520. HR 11877. Peace Corps. Adoption of the conference report on the bill to authorize $112,424,000 for fiscal 1979 plus supplemental funds of $3.7 million for fiscal 1978 programs of the Peace Corps, and to amend the Peace Corps Act to emphasize assistance to the poorest countries, the need to integrate women into the economies of third world nations and to make various administrative changes. Adopted (thus cleared for the president) 276-120: R 70-65; D 206-55 (ND 165-14; SD 41-41), July 25, 1978.

KEY

- Y Voted for (yea).
- ✓ Paired for.
- † Announced for.
- # CQ Poll for.
- N Voted against (nay).
- X Paired against.
- - Announced against.
- ▮ CQ Poll against.
- P Voted "present."
- ● Voted "present" to avoid possible conflict of interest.
- ? Did not vote or otherwise make a position known.

	514	515	516	517	518	519	520
ALABAMA							
1 Edwards	Y	Y	Y	Y	Y	N	Y
2 Dickinson	Y	Y	Y	Y	Y	N	N
3 Nichols	Y	Y	Y	Y	Y	N	N
4 Bevill	Y	Y	Y	Y	Y	N	N
5 Flippo	Y	Y	Y	Y	Y	N	N
6 Buchanan	Y	Y	Y	Y	Y	Y	Y
7 Flowers	Y	Y	Y	Y	Y	?	?
ALASKA							
AL Young	Y	N	Y	Y	Y	N	N
ARIZONA							
1 Rhodes	Y	Y	N	Y	Y	Y	Y
2 Udall	#	#	#	#	#	#	#
3 Stump	Y	N	N	Y	Y	N	N
4 Rudd	N	N	N	Y	Y	N	N
ARKANSAS							
1 Alexander	Y	Y	Y	Y	Y	Y	Y
2 Tucker	Y	Y	Y	Y	Y	Y	Y
3 Hammerschmidt	Y	N	Y	Y	Y	N	N
4 Thornton	Y	Y	Y	Y	Y	Y	Y
CALIFORNIA							
1 Johnson	Y	Y	Y	Y	Y	Y	Y
2 Clausen	Y	Y	Y	Y	Y	N	Y
3 Moss	Y	Y	Y	Y	Y	Y	Y
4 Leggett	Y	Y	Y	Y	Y	Y	Y
5 Burton, J.	Y	Y	Y	Y	Y	Y	Y
6 Burton, P.	Y	Y	Y	Y	Y	Y	?
7 Miller	Y	Y	Y	N	Y	Y	Y
8 Dellums	Y	Y	Y	Y	Y	Y	Y
9 Stark	N	Y	Y	Y	Y	Y	Y
10 Edwards	Y	Y	Y	Y	Y	Y	Y
11 Ryan	?	?	?	?	?	Y	Y
12 McCloskey	Y	Y	Y	Y	Y	Y	Y
13 Mineta	Y	Y	Y	Y	N	Y	Y
14 McFall	Y	Y	Y	Y	Y	Y	Y
15 Sisk	Y	Y	Y	Y	Y	Y	Y
16 Panetta	Y	Y	Y	Y	Y	Y	Y
17 Krebs	Y	Y	Y	Y	Y	Y	Y
18 Vacancy							
19 Lagomarsino	Y	Y	Y	Y	Y	N	N
20 Goldwater	Y	Y	Y	Y	Y	N	N
21 Corman	Y	Y	Y	Y	Y	Y	Y
22 Moorhead	Y	Y	N	Y	Y	N	N
23 Beilenson	Y	Y	Y	Y	N	Y	Y
24 Waxman	Y	Y	Y	Y	Y	Y	Y
25 Roybal	Y	Y	Y	Y	Y	Y	Y
26 Rousselot	Y	N	N	Y	Y	N	N
27 Dornan	Y	Y	Y	Y	Y	N	N
28 Burke	Y	Y	Y	Y	Y	Y	Y
29 Hawkins	Y	Y	Y	Y	Y	Y	Y
30 Danielson	#	#	#	#	#	#	#
31 Wilson, C.H.	Y	Y	Y	Y	Y	N	?
32 Anderson	Y	Y	Y	Y	Y	Y	Y
33 Clawson	?	?	?	?	?	?	?
34 Hannaford	Y	Y	Y	Y	Y	Y	Y
35 Lloyd	Y	Y	Y	Y	Y	Y	Y
36 Brown	Y	Y	Y	Y	Y	Y	Y
37 Pettis	Y	Y	Y	Y	Y	N	Y
38 Patterson	Y	Y	#	Y	Y	Y	Y
39 Wiggins	#	#	#	#	#	▮	▮
40 Badham	Y	N	N	Y	Y	N	N
41 Wilson, B.	Y	?	Y	Y	Y	N	N
42 Van Deerlin	Y	?	Y	Y	Y	Y	Y
43 Burgener	Y	Y	Y	Y	Y	N	Y
COLORADO							
1 Schroeder	Y	Y	Y	Y	Y	N	Y
2 Wirth	Y	Y	Y	Y	Y	Y	Y
3 Evans	Y	Y	Y	Y	Y	Y	Y
4 Johnson	Y	Y	Y	Y	Y	N	Y
5 Armstrong	?	?	?	?	?	?	?
CONNECTICUT							
1 Cotter	?	#	#	#	#	✓	#
2 Dodd	?	?	?	Y	Y	Y	Y
3 Giaimo	Y	Y	Y	Y	Y	Y	?
4 McKinney	Y	Y	Y	Y	Y	Y	Y
5 Sarasin	#	#	#	#	#	#	#
6 Moffett	?	?	?	?	?	✓	Y
DELAWARE							
AL Evans	Y	Y	Y	Y	Y	N	Y
FLORIDA							
1 Sikes	Y	Y	Y	Y	Y	Y	N
2 Fuqua	Y	Y	N	Y	Y	Y	N
3 Bennett	Y	Y	N	Y	Y	N	N
4 Chappell	Y	Y	N	Y	Y	N	N
5 Kelly	Y	Y	Y	Y	Y	N	N
6 Young	Y	Y	Y	Y	Y	N	N
7 Gibbons	Y	Y	Y	Y	Y	N	Y
8 Ireland	Y	Y	Y	Y	Y	N	N
9 Frey	?	?	?	?	?	?	?
10 Bafalis	Y	Y	Y	Y	Y	N	N
11 Rogers	Y	Y	Y	Y	Y	Y	Y
12 Burke	Y	Y	Y	Y	Y	N	N
13 Lehman	Y	Y	Y	Y	Y	Y	Y
14 Pepper	Y	Y	Y	Y	Y	Y	Y
15 Fascell	Y	Y	Y	Y	Y	Y	Y
GEORGIA							
1 Ginn	Y	Y	Y	Y	Y	N	Y
2 Mathis	Y	Y	Y	Y	Y	Y	N
3 Brinkley	Y	Y	N	Y	Y	N	N
4 Levitas	Y	Y	Y	Y	Y	N	Y
5 Fowler	Y	Y	Y	Y	Y	Y	Y
6 Flynt	Y	Y	N	Y	Y	N	N
7 McDonald	Y	N	N	Y	Y	N	N
8 Evans	?	?	?	?	?	Y	N
9 Jenkins	Y	Y	N	Y	Y	N	N
10 Barnard	Y	Y	N	Y	Y	Y	N
HAWAII							
1 Heftel	Y	Y	Y	Y	Y	Y	Y
2 Akaka	Y	Y	Y	Y	Y	Y	Y
IDAHO							
1 Symms	Y	N	N	Y	Y	N	N
2 Hansen, G.	Y	N	N	Y	Y	N	N
ILLINOIS							
1 Metcalfe	Y	Y	Y	?	Y	Y	Y
2 Murphy	Y	Y	Y	Y	Y	Y	Y
3 Russo	Y	Y	Y	Y	Y	Y	Y
4 Derwinski	Y	Y	Y	Y	Y	N	Y
5 Fary	Y	Y	Y	Y	Y	Y	Y
6 Hyde	Y	Y	Y	Y	Y	Y	N
7 Collins	?	?	?	?	?	?	?
8 Rostenkowski	Y	Y	Y	Y	Y	Y	Y
9 Yates	Y	Y	Y	Y	Y	Y	Y
10 Mikva	Y	Y	Y	Y	Y	Y	Y
11 Annunzio	Y	Y	Y	Y	Y	Y	Y
12 Crane	Y	N	N	Y	Y	N	N
13 McClory	Y	Y	Y	Y	Y	N	Y
14 Erlenborn	Y	Y	Y	Y	Y	Y	Y
15 Corcoran	Y	Y	Y	Y	Y	N	Y
16 Anderson	Y	Y	Y	Y	Y	Y	Y
17 O'Brien	Y	Y	Y	Y	Y	Y	N
18 Michel	Y	Y	N	Y	Y	Y	Y
19 Railsback	Y	Y	Y	Y	Y	N	Y
20 Findley	Y	?	Y	Y	Y	Y	Y
21 Madigan	Y	Y	Y	Y	Y	Y	Y
22 Shipley	?	?	?	?	?	?	?
23 Price	Y	Y	Y	Y	Y	Y	Y
24 Simon	Y	Y	N	Y	Y	Y	Y
INDIANA							
1 Benjamin	N	Y	Y	Y	N	Y	N
2 Fithian	Y	Y	Y	Y	Y	Y	Y
3 Brademas	Y	Y	Y	Y	Y	Y	Y
4 Quayle	Y	Y	N	Y	Y	N	Y
5 Hillis	Y	Y	Y	Y	Y	Y	N
6 Evans	Y	Y	Y	Y	Y	N	Y
7 Myers, J.	Y	Y	Y	Y	Y	Y	N
8 Cornwell	Y	Y	N	Y	Y	Y	Y
9 Hamilton	Y	Y	Y	Y	Y	Y	Y
10 Sharp	Y	Y	Y	Y	Y	Y	Y
11 Jacobs	Y	N	N	Y	Y	Y	Y
IOWA							
1 Leach	Y	Y	Y	Y	Y	N	Y
2 Blouin	Y	Y	Y	Y	Y	Y	Y
3 Grassley	Y	Y	Y	Y	Y	N	N
4 Smith	?	?	?	?	?	Y	Y
5 Harkin	Y	Y	Y	N	Y	Y	Y
6 Bedell	Y	Y	Y	N	N	Y	Y

Democrats ***Republicans***

	514	515	516	517	518	519	520
KANSAS							
1 Sebelius	Y	Y	Y	Y	Y	N	N
2 Keys	Y	Y	Y	Y	Y	Y	Y
3 Winn	Y	Y	Y	Y	Y	N	Y
4 Glickman	Y	Y	Y	Y	Y	Y	N
5 Skubitz	Y	Y	Y	Y	Y	N	Y
KENTUCKY							
1 Hubbard	Y	Y	Y	Y	Y	Y	N
2 Natcher	Y	Y	Y	Y	Y	Y	Y
3 Mazzoli	Y	Y	Y	Y	Y	Y	Y
4 Snyder	Y	Y	N	Y	Y	N	N
5 Carter	Y	Y	Y	Y	Y	N	Y
6 Breckinridge	Y	Y	Y	Y	Y	N	Y
7 Perkins	Y	Y	Y	Y	Y	Y	Y
LOUISIANA							
1 Livingston	Y	Y	N	Y	Y	N	N
2 Boggs	Y	Y	Y	Y	Y	Y	Y
3 Treen	Y	Y	N	Y	Y	N	N
4 Waggonner	Y	N	N	Y	Y	N	N
5 Huckaby	Y	Y	Y	Y	Y	N	N
6 Moore	Y	Y	Y	Y	Y	N	N
7 Breaux	Y	Y	Y	Y	Y	N	Y
8 Long	Y	Y	Y	Y	Y	Y	Y
MAINE							
1 Emery	Y	Y	Y	Y	Y	N	Y
2 Cohen	Y	Y	Y	Y	Y	N	Y
MARYLAND							
1 Bauman	Y	Y	N	Y	Y	N	N
2 Long	Y	Y	N	Y	Y	Y	Y
3 Mikulski	Y	Y	Y	N	N	Y	Y
4 Holt	Y	Y	N	Y	Y	N	N
5 Spellman	Y	Y	Y	Y	Y	Y	Y
6 Byron	Y	Y	Y	Y	Y	N	N
7 Mitchell	Y	Y	Y	Y	Y	Y	Y
8 Steers	Y	Y	Y	#	Y	Y	Y
MASSACHUSETTS							
1 Conte	Y	Y	Y	Y	Y	Y	Y
2 Boland	Y	Y	Y	Y	Y	Y	Y
3 Early	Y	Y	Y	Y	Y	Y	Y
4 Drinan	Y	Y	Y	Y	Y	Y	Y
5 Tsongas	?	?	?	?	?	✓	?
6 Harrington	#	#	#	#	#	Y	Y
7 Markey	Y	Y	Y	Y	Y	Y	Y
8 O'Neill							
9 Moakley	Y	Y	Y	Y	Y	Y	Y
10 Heckler	Y	Y	Y	Y	Y	Y	Y
11 Burke	Y	Y	Y	Y	Y	Y	Y
12 Studds	Y	Y	Y	Y	Y	Y	Y
MICHIGAN							
1 Conyers	Y	Y	Y	Y	Y	Y	Y
2 Pursell	?	Y	Y	Y	Y	Y	Y
3 Brown	Y	Y	Y	Y	Y	N	Y
4 Stockman	Y	Y	N	Y	Y	N	N
5 Sawyer	Y	#	Y	Y	Y	N	Y
6 Carr	Y	Y	Y	Y	Y	Y	Y
7 Kildee	Y	Y	Y	Y	Y	Y	Y
8 Traxler	Y	Y	Y	Y	Y	N	Y
9 Vander Jagt	Y	Y	Y	Y	Y	Y	N
10 Cederberg	Y	Y	Y	Y	Y	N	N
11 Ruppe	Y	Y	Y	Y	Y	N	Y
12 Bonior	Y	Y	Y	Y	Y	Y	Y
13 Diggs	#	#	#	#	#	#	Y
14 Nedzi	Y	Y	Y	Y	Y	Y	Y
15 Ford	Y	Y	Y	Y	Y	Y	Y
16 Dingell	Y	Y	Y	Y	Y	Y	Y
17 Brodhead	Y	Y	Y	Y	Y	Y	Y
18 Blanchard	Y	Y	Y	Y	Y	Y	Y
19 Broomfield	Y	Y	Y	Y	Y	N	Y
MINNESOTA							
1 Quie	?	?	?	?	?	?	?
2 Hagedorn	Y	Y	Y	Y	Y	N	Y
3 Frenzel	Y	Y	Y	Y	Y	N	Y
4 Vento	Y	Y	Y	Y	Y	Y	Y
5 Fraser	?	?	?	?	?	?	?
6 Nolan	Y	Y	Y	Y	Y	Y	Y
7 Stangeland	Y	Y	Y	Y	Y	N	Y
8 Oberstar	Y	Y	Y	Y	Y	Y	Y
MISSISSIPPI							
1 Whitten	?	#	#	#	#	#	#
2 Bowen	Y	Y	Y	Y	Y	N	Y
3 Montgomery	Y	Y	N	Y	Y	N	N
4 Cochran	?	?	?	?	?	?	?
5 Lott	Y	Y	N	Y	Y	N	N
MISSOURI							
1 Clay	Y	Y	Y	Y	Y	Y	Y
2 Young	Y	Y	Y	Y	Y	Y	Y
3 Gephardt	Y	Y	Y	Y	Y	Y	N

	514	515	516	517	518	519	520
4 Skelton	Y	Y	N	Y	Y	N	?
5 Bolling	Y	Y	Y	Y	Y	Y	Y
6 Coleman	Y	Y	Y	Y	Y	N	Y
7 Taylor	Y	Y	N	Y	Y	N	N
8 Ichord	Y	Y	N	Y	Y	N	N
9 Volkmer	N	Y	N	Y	N	Y	N
10 Burlison	Y	Y	Y	Y	Y	Y	Y
MONTANA							
1 Baucus	Y	#	Y	Y	Y	Y	Y
2 Marlenee	Y	Y	Y	Y	Y	N	N
NEBRASKA							
1 Thone	Y	Y	Y	Y	Y	N	Y
2 Cavanaugh	Y	Y	Y	Y	Y	Y	Y
3 Smith	Y	Y	Y	Y	Y	N	N
NEVADA							
AL Santini	Y	Y	Y	Y	Y	Y	Y
NEW HAMPSHIRE							
1 D'Amours	Y	Y	Y	Y	Y	N	Y
2 Cleveland	Y	Y	Y	Y	Y	N	Y
NEW JERSEY							
1 Florio	Y	Y	Y	Y	Y	Y	Y
2 Hughes	Y	Y	Y	Y	Y	Y	Y
3 Howard	Y	Y	Y	Y	Y	Y	Y
4 Thompson	Y	Y	Y	Y	Y	Y	Y
5 Fenwick	Y	Y	Y	Y	Y	Y	Y
6 Forsythe	Y	Y	Y	Y	Y	Y	Y
7 Maguire	?	?	?	?	?	?	?
8 Roe	Y	Y	Y	Y	Y	Y	Y
9 Hollenbeck	Y	Y	Y	Y	Y	Y	Y
10 Rodino	Y	Y	Y	Y	Y	#	#
11 Minish	Y	Y	Y	Y	Y	Y	Y
12 Rinaldo	Y	Y	Y	Y	Y	Y	Y
13 Meyner	Y	Y	Y	Y	Y	Y	Y
14 LeFante	#	#	#	#	#	✓	#
15 Patten	Y	Y	Y	Y	Y	Y	Y
NEW MEXICO							
1 Lujan	Y	Y	Y	Y	Y	N	N
2 Runnels	Y	Y	Y	Y	Y	N	N
NEW YORK							
1 Pike	Y	Y	Y	Y	Y	Y	Y
2 Downey	Y	Y	Y	Y	Y	Y	Y
3 Ambro	Y	Y	Y	Y	Y	Y	Y
4 Lent	Y	Y	Y	Y	Y	Y	Y
5 Wydler	Y	Y	Y	Y	Y	Y	N
6 Wolff	Y	Y	Y	Y	Y	Y	Y
7 Addabbo	Y	Y	Y	Y	Y	Y	Y
8 Rosenthal	Y	Y	Y	Y	Y	Y	Y
9 Delaney	Y	Y	Y	Y	Y	Y	Y
10 Biaggi	Y	Y	Y	Y	Y	Y	?
11 Scheuer	Y	Y	Y	Y	Y	Y	Y
12 Chisholm	Y	Y	Y	Y	Y	Y	Y
13 Solarz	Y	Y	Y	Y	Y	Y	Y
14 Richmond	Y	Y	Y	Y	Y	Y	Y
15 Zeferetti	Y	Y	Y	Y	Y	Y	Y
16 Holtzman	Y	Y	Y	Y	Y	Y	Y
17 Murphy	Y	Y	Y	Y	Y	Y	Y
18 Green	Y	Y	Y	Y	Y	Y	Y
19 Rangel	Y	Y	Y	Y	Y	Y	Y
20 Weiss	Y	Y	Y	Y	N	Y	Y
21 Garcia	Y	Y	Y	Y	Y	Y	Y
22 Bingham	Y	Y	Y	Y	Y	Y	Y
23 Caputo	Y	Y	Y	Y	Y	Y	Y
24 Ottinger	Y	Y	Y	Y	Y	Y	Y
25 Fish	Y	Y	Y	Y	Y	Y	Y
26 Gilman	?	Y	Y	Y	Y	Y	Y
27 McHugh	Y	Y	Y	Y	Y	Y	Y
28 Stratton	Y	Y	Y	Y	Y	Y	Y
29 Pattison	Y	Y	Y	Y	Y	Y	Y
30 McEwen	Y	Y	Y	Y	Y	Y	N
31 Mitchell	Y	Y	Y	Y	Y	Y	Y
32 Hanley	Y	Y	Y	Y	Y	Y	Y
33 Walsh	Y	Y	Y	Y	Y	Y	Y
34 Horton	Y	Y	Y	Y	Y	Y	Y
35 Conable	Y	Y	Y	Y	Y	Y	Y
36 LaFalce	Y	Y	Y	Y	Y	Y	Y
37 Nowak	Y	Y	Y	Y	Y	Y	Y
38 Kemp	Y	Y	Y	Y	Y	Y	Y
39 Lundine	Y	Y	Y	Y	Y	Y	Y
NORTH CAROLINA							
1 Jones	Y	Y	Y	Y	Y	Y	N
2 Fountain	Y	Y	Y	Y	Y	N	N
3 Whitley	Y	Y	Y	Y	Y	N	N
4 Andrews	Y	Y	Y	Y	Y	Y	Y
5 Neal	Y	Y	Y	Y	Y	Y	Y
6 Preyer	Y	Y	Y	Y	Y	Y	Y
7 Rose	Y	Y	Y	Y	Y	Y	Y
8 Hefner	Y	Y	Y	Y	Y	Y	N

	514	515	516	517	518	519	520
9 Martin	Y	Y	Y	Y	Y	Y	Y
10 Broyhill	Y	Y	Y	Y	Y	N	Y
11 Gudger	Y	Y	Y	Y	Y	N	Y
NORTH DAKOTA							
AL Andrews	Y	Y	Y	Y	Y	N	N
OHIO							
1 Gradison	Y	Y	Y	Y	Y	N	Y
2 Luken	Y	Y	Y	Y	Y	N	N
3 Whalen	#	#	#	#	#	#	#
4 Guyer	Y	Y	Y	Y	Y	Y	N
5 Latta	Y	N	N	Y	Y	N	N
6 Harsha	Y	Y	Y	Y	Y	N	N
7 Brown	Y	?	N	Y	Y	Y	Y
8 Kindness	Y	Y	Y	Y	Y	N	N
9 Ashley	Y	Y	Y	Y	N	Y	?
10 Miller	Y	Y	N	Y	Y	N	N
11 Stanton	Y	Y	Y	Y	Y	Y	N
12 Devine	N	N	N	Y	Y	N	N
13 Pease	Y	Y	Y	Y	Y	Y	Y
14 Seiberling	Y	Y	Y	Y	N	Y	Y
15 Wylie	Y	Y	Y	Y	Y	N	Y
16 Regula	Y	Y	Y	Y	Y	N	N
17 Ashbrook	Y	Y	N	Y	Y	N	N
18 Applegate	Y	Y	Y	Y	Y	Y	Y
19 Carney	Y	Y	Y	Y	Y	Y	Y
20 Oakar	Y	Y	Y	Y	Y	Y	Y
21 Stokes	?	?	?	?	?	?	?
22 Vanik	Y	Y	Y	Y	Y	Y	Y
23 Mottl	Y	Y	Y	Y	Y	N	N
OKLAHOMA							
1 Jones	Y	Y	Y	Y	Y	N	N
2 Risenhoover	Y	N	Y	Y	Y	X	?
3 Watkins	Y	N	Y	Y	Y	N	N
4 Steed	Y	Y	Y	#	Y	Y	N
5 Edwards	Y	Y	N	Y	Y	N	N
6 English	Y	Y	Y	Y	Y	N	Y
OREGON							
1 AuCoin	Y	Y	Y	Y	Y	N	Y
2 Ullman	Y	Y	Y	Y	Y	Y	Y
3 Duncan	Y	Y	Y	Y	Y	Y	Y
4 Weaver	Y	Y	Y	Y	Y	Y	Y
PENNSYLVANIA							
1 Myers, M.	Y	Y	Y	Y	Y	Y	Y
2 Nix	Y	Y	Y	Y	Y	Y	Y
3 Lederer	Y	Y	Y	Y	Y	Y	Y
4 Eilberg	Y	Y	Y	Y	Y	Y	Y
5 Schulze	Y	Y	Y	Y	Y	N	Y
6 Yatron	Y	Y	Y	Y	Y	N	Y
7 Edgar	Y	Y	Y	Y	Y	Y	Y
8 Kostmayer	Y	Y	Y	Y	Y	Y	Y
9 Shuster	Y	Y	N	Y	Y	N	N
10 McDade	Y	Y	Y	Y	Y	N	Y
11 Flood	Y	Y	Y	Y	Y	Y	Y
12 Murtha	Y	Y	Y	Y	Y	Y	Y
13 Coughlin	Y	Y	Y	Y	Y	Y	Y
14 Moorhead	Y	Y	Y	Y	Y	Y	Y
15 Rooney	Y	Y	Y	Y	Y	Y	Y
16 Walker	Y	Y	Y	Y	Y	N	N
17 Ertel	Y	Y	Y	Y	Y	Y	Y
18 Walgren	Y	Y	Y	Y	Y	Y	Y
19 Goodling, W.	N	N	Y	Y	Y	N	Y
20 Gaydos	Y	Y	Y	Y	Y	Y	N
21 Dent	Y	Y	Y	#	Y	#	Y
22 Murphy	Y	Y	Y	Y	Y	N	Y
23 Ammerman	Y	Y	Y	Y	Y	N	Y
24 Marks	Y	Y	Y	Y	Y	Y	Y
25 Myers, G.	N	Y	Y	Y	Y	N	N
RHODE ISLAND							
1 St Germain	Y	Y	Y	Y	Y	Y	Y
2 Beard	Y	Y	Y	Y	Y	Y	Y
SOUTH CAROLINA							
1 Davis	Y	Y	Y	Y	Y	Y	N
2 Spence	Y	Y	Y	Y	Y	N	N
3 Derrick	Y	Y	Y	Y	Y	N	Y
4 Mann	?	?	?	?	?	?	?
5 Holland	?	?	Y	Y	Y	Y	Y
6 Jenrette	Y	Y	Y	Y	Y	Y	#
SOUTH DAKOTA							
1 Pressler	Y	Y	Y	Y	Y	N	Y
2 Abdnor	Y	Y	Y	Y	Y	N	#
TENNESSEE							
1 Quillen	Y	Y	Y	Y	Y	N	N
2 Duncan	Y	Y	Y	Y	Y	N	N
3 Lloyd	Y	Y	Y	Y	Y	N	N
4 Gore	Y	Y	Y	Y	Y	Y	Y
5 Vacancy							
6 Beard	Y	Y	N	Y	Y	N	N

	514	515	516	517	518	519	520
7 Jones	Y	Y	Y	Y	Y	Y	N
8 Ford	Y	Y	Y	Y	Y	Y	Y
TEXAS							
1 Hall	Y	N	N	Y	Y	N	N
2 Wilson, C.	Y	Y	Y	Y	Y	Y	Y
3 Collins	N	N	N	Y	Y	N	N
4 Roberts	Y	Y	Y	Y	Y	N	N
5 Mattox	Y	Y	Y	Y	Y	N	Y
6 Teague	?	?	?	?	?	X	?
7 Archer	Y	Y	N	Y	Y	N	N
8 Eckhardt	Y	Y	Y	Y	Y	Y	Y
9 Brooks	Y	Y	Y	Y	Y	N	Y
10 Pickle	Y	Y	Y	Y	Y	N	Y
11 Poage	Y	Y	N	Y	Y	N	N
12 Wright	Y	Y	Y	Y	Y	Y	Y
13 Hightower	Y	Y	Y	Y	Y	N	Y
14 Young	Y	Y	Y	Y	Y	Y	?
15 de la Garza	Y	Y	Y	Y	Y	N	N
16 White	Y	Y	Y	Y	Y	N	N
17 Burleson	Y	N	N	Y	Y	N	N
18 Jordan	Y	Y	Y	Y	Y	Y	Y
19 Mahon	Y	Y	Y	Y	Y	N	N
20 Gonzalez	Y	Y	Y	Y	Y	Y	Y
21 Krueger	Y	Y	Y	Y	Y	N	Y
22 Gammage	Y	Y	Y	Y	Y	N	N
23 Kazen	Y	Y	Y	Y	Y	N	N
24 Milford	Y	Y	N	Y	Y	X	N
UTAH							
1 McKay	Y	Y	Y	Y	Y	Y	Y
2 Marriott	Y	Y	Y	Y	Y	N	N
VERMONT							
AL Jeffords	Y	Y	Y	Y	Y	Y	Y
VIRGINIA							
1 Trible	Y	Y	Y	Y	Y	N	Y
2 Whitehurst	Y	Y	Y	Y	Y	N	Y
3 Satterfield	Y	N	N	Y	Y	N	N
4 Daniel	Y	Y	N	Y	Y	N	N
5 Daniel	Y	N	N	Y	Y	N	N
6 Butler	Y	Y	Y	Y	Y	N	N
7 Robinson	Y	Y	N	Y	Y	N	N
8 Harris	Y	Y	Y	Y	Y	Y	Y
9 Wampler	Y	Y	Y	Y	Y	N	Y
10 Fisher	Y	Y	Y	Y	Y	Y	Y
WASHINGTON							
1 Pritchard	#	#	#	#	#	#	#
2 Meeds	#	#	#	#	#	#	#
3 Bonker	Y	Y	Y	Y	Y	Y	Y
4 McCormack	Y	Y	Y	Y	Y	N	Y
5 Foley	Y	Y	Y	Y	Y	Y	Y
6 Dicks	Y	Y	Y	Y	Y	Y	Y
7 Cunningham	Y	Y	Y	Y	Y	N	N
WEST VIRGINIA							
1 Mollohan	Y	Y	Y	Y	Y	N	N
2 Staggers	Y	Y	Y	Y	Y	Y	N
3 Slack	Y	Y	Y	Y	Y	N	N
4 Rahall	Y	Y	Y	Y	Y	Y	Y
WISCONSIN							
1 Aspin	Y	Y	Y	Y	Y	Y	Y
2 Kastenmeier	Y	Y	Y	Y	Y	Y	Y
3 Baldus	Y	Y	Y	Y	Y	Y	Y
4 Zablocki	Y	Y	Y	Y	Y	Y	Y
5 Reuss	Y	Y	Y	Y	Y	Y	Y
6 Steiger	Y	Y	Y	Y	Y	N	Y
7 Obey	Y	Y	Y	Y	Y	Y	Y
8 Cornell	Y	Y	Y	Y	Y	Y	Y
9 Kasten	#	#	#	#	#	X	#
WYOMING							
AL Roncalio	Y	Y	Y	Y	Y	Y	Y

Democrats ***Republicans***

521. HR 10285. Commodity Exchange Act. Foley, D-Wash., motion that the House resolve itself into the Committee of the Whole for consideration of the bill to extend the Commodity Exchange Act and authorize appropriations as needed for the operations of the Commodity Futures Trading Commission (CFTC) through fiscal year 1981. Motion agreed to 362-2: R 127-1; D 235-1 (ND 161-1; SD 74-0), July 26, 1978.

522. HR 10285. Commodity Exchange Act. Baldus, D-Wis., amendment to permit states to enact and enforce their own commodity futures trading laws that were identical to certain sections of the Commodity Exchange Act. Rejected 141-260: R 27-109; D 114-151 (ND 96-85; SD 18-66), July 26, 1978.

523. HR 10285. Commodity Exchange Act. Smith, D-Iowa amendment to require reporting within 48 hours of export commodity sales and certain related information to the Commodity Futures Trading Commission, and to require the commission to publish this information. Adopted 273-125: R 82-55; D 191-70 (ND 139-39; SD 52-31), July 26, 1978.

524. HR 10285. Commodity Exchange Act. Passage of the bill to extend the Commodity Exchange Act and to authorize appropriations as needed for the operations of the Commodity Futures Trading Commission through fiscal year 1981. Passed 401-6: R 133-5; D 268-1 (ND 185-0; SD 83-1), July 26, 1978.

525. HR 3350. Ocean Mining. Breaux, D-La., substitute amendment, to the Udall, D-Ariz., amendment, to place responsibility for the Deep Seabed Mineral Resources program in the Department of Commerce. Adopted 214-184: R 97-38; D 117-146 (ND 69-112; SD 48-34), July 26, 1978. (The Udall amendment, as amended, was adopted subsequently by voice vote. The Udall amendment had specified the Interior Department; the bill did not specify the responsible agency.)

526. HR 3350. Ocean Mining. McCloskey, R-Calif., amendment to reword language in the bill to state more clearly that in granting mining permits the United States was not claiming jurisdiction over any areas beyond the 200-mile limit. Rejected 199-202: R 73-64; D 126-138 (ND 109-75; SD 17-63), July 26, 1978.

527. HR 3350. Ocean Mining. Passage of the bill to provide for interim federal regulation and taxation of ocean mining of hard minerals by U.S. citizens until an international agreement was reached by the Law of the Sea Conference. Passed 312-80: R 118-19; D 194-61 (ND 124-56; SD 70-5), July 26, 1978.

528. HR 7577. Economic Opportunity Amendments. Goodling, R-Pa., amendment to alter the proposed funding formula for community action agencies to require 60 percent federal contributions and 40 percent local contributions. Rejected 158-224: R 95-41; D 63-183 (ND 35-136; SD 28-47), July 26, 1978.

KEY

- Y Voted for (yea).
- ✓ Paired for.
- † Announced for.
- # CQ Poll for.
- N Voted against (nay).
- X Paired against.
- \- Announced against.
- ▮ CQ Poll against.
- P Voted "present."
- ● Voted "present" to avoid possible conflict of interest.
- ? Did not vote or otherwise make a position known.

	521	522	523	524	525	526	527	528
ALABAMA								
1 Edwards	Y	N	Y	Y	Y	N	Y	N
2 Dickinson	Y	N	Y	Y	Y	N	Y	Y
3 Nichols	Y	N	Y	Y	Y	N	Y	Y
4 Bevill	Y	N	Y	Y	Y	N	Y	N
5 Flippo	Y	N	Y	Y	Y	N	Y	N
6 Buchanan	?	?	?	?	?	?	?	?
7 Flowers	?	?	?	?	?	?	?	?
ALASKA								
AL Young	#	Y	Y	Y	Y	N	Y	N
ARIZONA								
1 Rhodes	Y	N	N	Y	Y	Y	Y	Y
2 Udall	Y	Y	Y	Y	N	Y	Y	N
3 Stump	Y	Y	N	Y	Y	N	Y	Y
4 Rudd	Y	N	N	Y	Y	N	Y	Y
ARKANSAS								
1 Alexander	Y	N	?	Y	Y	N	Y	N
2 Tucker	Y	Y	Y	Y	Y	Y	Y	N
3 Hammerschmidt	Y	N	N	Y	Y	Y	N	Y
4 Thornton	Y	N	N	Y	Y	N	Y	N
CALIFORNIA								
1 Johnson	Y	N	N	Y	N	N	Y	N
2 Clausen	Y	Y	Y	Y	N	N	Y	N
3 Moss	Y	N	Y	Y	Y	N	?	?
4 Leggett	?	Y	?	Y	Y	N	Y	N
5 Burton, J.	Y	Y	N	Y	N	Y	Y	N
6 Burton, P.	Y	Y	Y	Y	N	Y	Y	N
7 Miller	Y	Y	Y	Y	N	Y	N	N
8 Dellums	#	Y	Y	Y	N	Y	N	N
9 Stark	Y	▮	#	Y	N	Y	X	▮
10 Edwards	Y	N	Y	Y	N	Y	N	N
11 Ryan	Y	N	N	Y	N	Y	N	N
12 McCloskey	Y	N	Y	Y	Y	Y	N	N
13 Mineta	Y	Y	N	Y	N	Y	N	N
14 McFall	Y	N	Y	Y	Y	N	Y	N
15 Sisk	Y	N	N	Y	Y	N	?	?
16 Panetta	Y	Y	Y	Y	N	Y	N	Y
17 Krebs	Y	N	N	Y	N	Y	Y	Y
18 Vacancy								
19 Lagomarsino	Y	Y	Y	Y	N	N	Y	N
20 Goldwater	Y	N	N	Y	Y	N	Y	?
21 Corman	Y	N	N	Y	Y	N	Y	N
22 Moorhead	Y	N	Y	Y	Y	N	Y	Y
23 Beilenson	#	Y	Y	Y	N	Y	N	N
24 Waxman	Y	Y	Y	Y	N	Y	N	N
25 Roybal	Y	N	N	Y	N	Y	Y	N
26 Rousselot	Y	N	N	N	Y	N	Y	Y
27 Dornan	?	Y	Y	Y	Y	N	Y	Y
28 Burke	?	Y	Y	Y	Y	Y	Y	N
29 Hawkins	Y	Y	Y	Y	N	N	Y	N
30 Danielson	#	#	▮	#	▮	#	#	▮
31 Wilson, C.H.	Y	N	Y	Y	N	N	Y	?
32 Anderson	Y	Y	N	Y	Y	N	Y	N
33 Clawson	?	?	?	?	?	?	?	?
34 Hannaford	Y	N	N	Y	N	Y	Y	N
35 Lloyd	N	N	N	Y	N	Y	Y	N
36 Brown	Y	N	Y	Y	N	Y	N	?
37 Pettis	Y	N	N	Y	N	Y	Y	Y
38 Patterson	Y	Y	Y	Y	Y	Y	Y	N
39 Wiggins	#	N	N	Y	#	Y	Y	Y
40 Badham	Y	Y	N	Y	Y	N	Y	Y
41 Wilson, B.	N	N	Y	Y	N	Y	Y	Y
42 Van Deerlin	Y	Y	Y	Y	N	Y	Y	N
43 Burgener	Y	N	Y	Y	Y	Y	Y	N
COLORADO								
1 Schroeder	Y	N	Y	Y	N	Y	N	N
2 Wirth	Y	Y	N	Y	Y	Y	Y	Y
3 Evans	Y	N	Y	Y	N	Y	?	?
4 Johnson	Y	N	N	Y	N	Y	Y	Y

	521	522	523	524	525	526	527	528
5 Armstrong	?	?	?	?	?	?	N	Y
CONNECTICUT								
1 Cotter	#	▮	?	?	?	?	?	▮
2 Dodd	Y	Y	N	Y	N	Y	N	N
3 Giaimo	?	N	?	Y	?	N	Y	N
4 McKinney	Y	N	Y	Y	N	Y	N	N
5 Sarasin	#	▮	#	#			#	▮
6 Moffett	Y	Y	Y	Y	N	Y	N	?
DELAWARE								
AL Evans	Y	N	N	Y	Y	Y	Y	Y
FLORIDA								
1 Sikes	Y	N	Y	Y	N	N	Y	?
2 Fuqua	Y	N	Y	Y	N	N	Y	Y
3 Bennett	Y	Y	Y	Y	N	Y	N	Y
4 Chappell	Y	N	Y	Y	Y	N	Y	Y
5 Kelly	Y	N	Y	Y	Y	N	Y	Y
6 Young	Y	N	Y	Y	Y	N	Y	Y
7 Gibbons	Y	N	Y	Y	N	Y	Y	N
8 Ireland	Y	N	Y	Y	Y	N	Y	?
9 Frey	?	?	?	?	?	?	?	?
10 Bafalis	Y	N	N	Y	Y	N	Y	Y
11 Rogers	Y	N	Y	Y	Y	N	#	Y
12 Burke	Y	N	Y	Y	Y	N	Y	Y
13 Lehman	Y	N	Y	Y	N	Y	N	N
14 Pepper	#	N	Y	Y	Y	N	#	N
15 Fascell	#	N	Y	Y	N	Y	Y	N
GEORGIA								
1 Ginn	Y	N	Y	Y	Y	N	Y	N
2 Mathis	Y	Y	Y	Y	?	N	Y	Y
3 Brinkley	Y	Y	Y	Y	N	Y	Y	N
4 Levitas	Y	Y	Y	Y	N	Y	Y	Y
5 Fowler	Y	N	Y	Y	Y	Y	Y	N
6 Flynt	Y	N	Y	Y	Y	N	?	?
7 McDonald	#	N	N	N	Y	N	Y	Y
8 Evans	Y	Y	Y	Y	N	Y	?	Y
9 Jenkins	Y	Y	Y	Y	#	#	#	#
10 Barnard	Y	Y	N	Y	Y	N	Y	Y
HAWAII								
1 Heftel	Y	Y	Y	Y	Y	N	Y	N
2 Akaka	Y	N	N	Y	Y	N	Y	N
IDAHO								
1 Symms	Y	N	N	N	Y	N	Y	Y
2 Hansen, G.	Y	N	N	N	Y	N	Y	Y
ILLINOIS								
1 Metcalfe	Y	N	N	Y	Y	N	N	N
2 Murphy	Y	N	N	Y	Y	N	Y	N
3 Russo	Y	N	Y	Y	Y	N	Y	Y
4 Derwinski	Y	N	Y	Y	Y	N	Y	Y
5 Fary	Y	N	Y	Y	Y	N	Y	N
6 Hyde	Y	N	Y	Y	Y	Y	Y	Y
7 Collins	?	X	?	?	✓	✓	X	?
8 Rostenkowski	Y	N	Y	Y	Y	N	Y	N
9 Yates	Y	N	Y	Y	N	Y	N	N
10 Mikva	Y	N	Y	Y	N	Y	N	N
11 Annunzio	Y	N	N	Y	Y	N	Y	N
12 Crane	Y	N	N	N	Y	N	Y	Y
13 McClory	Y	N	N	Y	Y	Y	Y	Y
14 Erlenborn	Y	N	N	Y	Y	Y	Y	Y
15 Corcoran	Y	N	N	Y	N	Y	Y	Y
16 Anderson	Y	N	N	Y	N	Y	N	Y
17 O'Brien	Y	N	N	Y	Y	Y	Y	N
18 Michel	Y	N	N	Y	Y	Y	Y	Y
19 Railsback	Y	N	Y	Y	Y	Y	Y	?
20 Findley	Y	N	N	Y	N	Y	N	Y
21 Madigan	Y	N	N	Y	Y	Y	N	N
22 Shipley	?	X	X	?	✓	X	?	?
23 Price	Y	N	Y	Y	N	Y	Y	N
24 Simon	Y	N	Y	Y	N	Y	N	Y
INDIANA								
1 Benjamin	Y	Y	Y	Y	Y	Y	Y	N
2 Fithian	Y	N	Y	Y	N	Y	N	N
3 Brademas	Y	N	N	Y	N	Y	Y	N
4 Quayle	Y	N	N	Y	Y	Y	Y	Y
5 Hillis	Y	N	N	Y	Y	Y	Y	Y
6 Evans	Y	N	Y	Y	Y	Y	Y	N
7 Myers, J.	Y	N	N	Y	Y	Y	Y	N
8 Cornwell	Y	Y	Y	Y	N	Y	N	?
9 Hamilton	Y	N	Y	Y	Y	Y	Y	N
10 Sharp	Y	N	Y	Y	N	Y	N	N
11 Jacobs	Y	N	Y	Y	P	Y	Y	N
IOWA								
1 Leach	Y	N	Y	Y	Y	Y	N	Y
2 Blouin	Y	Y	Y	Y	N	Y	Y	N
3 Grassley	Y	N	Y	Y	Y	N	Y	Y
4 Smith	Y	N	Y	Y	N	Y	Y	N
5 Harkin	Y	Y	Y	Y	N	Y	N	Y
6 Bedell	Y	Y	Y	Y	N	Y	N	Y

Democrats ***Republicans***

Corresponding to Congressional Record Votes 597, 598, 599, 600, 601, 602, 603, 604

	521	522	523	524	525	526	527	528
KANSAS								
1 Sebelius	Y	N	Y	Y	N	N	Y	Y
2 Keys	Y	Y	Y	Y	N	Y	N	N
3 Winn	Y	N	N	Y	Y	N	Y	N
4 Glickman	Y	Y	Y	Y	N	Y	Y	Y
5 Skubitz	?	N	Y	Y	N	Y	Y	Y
KENTUCKY								
1 Hubbard	Y	N	N	Y	Y	N	Y	N
2 Natcher	Y	N	N	Y	N	N	Y	N
3 Mazzoli	Y	Y	Y	Y	N	Y	Y	N
4 Snyder	Y	N	Y	Y	Y	N	Y	Y
5 Carter	Y	Y	Y	Y	N	N	Y	N
6 Breckinridge	Y	N	Y	Y	Y	Y	Y	N
7 Perkins	Y	N	Y	Y	N	N	Y	N
LOUISIANA								
1 Livingston	Y	N	Y	Y	Y	N	Y	Y
2 Boggs	Y	N	N	Y	Y	N	Y	N
3 Treen	Y	N	N	Y	Y	N	Y	Y
4 Waggonner	P	N	N	Y	N	N	Y	Y
5 Huckaby	Y	N	Y	Y	N	N	Y	N
6 Moore	Y	N	N	Y	Y	N	Y	Y
7 Breaux	Y	N	Y	Y	Y	N	Y	?
8 Long	Y	N	Y	Y	Y	N	Y	N
MAINE								
1 Emery	Y	Y	Y	Y	Y	Y	Y	Y
2 Cohen	Y	Y	Y	Y	N	Y	Y	Y
MARYLAND								
1 Bauman	Y	Y	Y	Y	Y	N	Y	Y
2 Long	Y	Y	Y	Y	N	Y	Y	Y
3 Mikulski	Y	Y	Y	Y	Y	Y	Y	N
4 Holt	Y	N	Y	Y	Y	N	Y	N
5 Spellman	?	N	Y	Y	N	Y	N	N
6 Byron	?	N	Y	Y	Y	N	Y	Y
7 Mitchell	#	Y	#	Y	N	Y	N	▮
8 Steers	Y	N	Y	Y	N	Y	N	N
MASSACHUSETTS								
1 Conte	Y	Y	Y	Y	N	Y	N	N
2 Boland	Y	N	Y	Y	N	#	N	Y
3 Early	?	?	?	?	?	?	?	?
4 Drinan	Y	Y	Y	Y	N	Y	N	N
5 Tsongas	?	?	?	?	?	?	N	N
6 Harrington	#	Y	Y	Y	N	Y	N	▮
7 Markey	Y	Y	Y	Y	N	Y	Y	N
8 O'Neill								
9 Moakley	Y	Y	Y	Y	▮	N	Y	▮
10 Heckler	?	Y	Y	Y	Y	Y	N	N
11 Burke	Y	N	Y	Y	Y	X	✓	?
12 Studds	Y	Y	Y	Y	Y	Y	N	N
MICHIGAN								
1 Conyers	#	Y	#	Y	N	Y	▮	▮
2 Pursell	Y	N	Y	Y	Y	?	N	Y
3 Brown	Y	N	Y	Y	Y	N	Y	Y
4 Stockman	Y	N	N	Y	Y	N	Y	Y
5 Sawyer	Y	N	N	Y	Y	Y	Y	?
6 Carr	Y	Y	Y	Y	N	Y	N	Y
7 Kildee	Y	Y	Y	Y	N	Y	Y	N
8 Traxler	Y	Y	Y	Y	Y	Y	Y	N
9 Vander Jagt	Y	N	Y	Y	Y	Y	Y	Y
10 Cederberg	Y	N	Y	Y	N	Y	Y	Y
11 Ruppe	Y	N	N	Y	Y	Y	Y	Y
12 Bonior	#	Y	Y	Y	Y	Y	N	N
13 Diggs	#	Y	Y	Y	N	Y	N	N
14 Nedzi	Y	N	Y	Y	N	Y	Y	N
15 Ford	?	Y	Y	Y	N	N	Y	N
16 Dingell	?	Y	Y	Y	Y	N	Y	N
17 Brodhead	Y	Y	Y	Y	N	Y	N	N
18 Blanchard	Y	Y	Y	Y	Y	Y	Y	N
19 Broomfield	Y	Y	Y	Y	Y	N	Y	Y
MINNESOTA								
1 Quie	?	?	?	?	?	?	?	?
2 Hagedorn	Y	N	N	Y	Y	N	Y	Y
3 Frenzel	Y	N	Y	Y	Y	Y	Y	Y
4 Vento	Y	Y	Y	Y	N	Y	Y	N
5 Fraser	?	✓	?	?	X	✓	?	?
6 Nolan	Y	Y	Y	Y	N	Y	N	N
7 Stangeland	Y	N	Y	Y	Y	N	Y	Y
8 Oberstar	Y	Y	Y	Y	Y	N	Y	N
MISSISSIPPI								
1 Whitten	Y	N	N	Y	Y	N	Y	▮
2 Bowen	Y	N	N	Y	Y	N	Y	Y
3 Montgomery	Y	N	N	Y	Y	N	Y	Y
4 Cochran	Y	N	N	Y	Y	N	Y	Y
5 Lott	Y	N	N	Y	Y	N	Y	Y
MISSOURI								
1 Clay	Y	Y	?	Y	N	N	N	N
2 Young	Y	N	Y	Y	Y	N	Y	N
3 Gephardt	Y	Y	Y	Y	N	Y	N	N

	521	522	523	524	525	526	527	528
4 Skelton	Y	Y	N	Y	N	N	Y	N
5 Bolling	#	▮	N	Y	N	Y	#	▮
6 Coleman	Y	N	Y	Y	Y	N	Y	Y
7 Taylor	Y	N	Y	Y	Y	N	Y	Y
8 Ichord	Y	N	Y	Y	Y	N	Y	Y
9 Volkmer	Y	N	Y	Y	N	Y	N	N
10 Burlison	Y	N	Y	Y	N	Y	Y	N
MONTANA								
1 Baucus	Y	Y	Y	Y	N	Y	Y	N
2 Marlenee	Y	Y	Y	Y	N	Y	Y	Y
NEBRASKA								
1 Thone	Y	N	Y	Y	N	Y	Y	Y
2 Cavanaugh	Y	Y	Y	Y	?	Y	Y	Y
3 Smith	Y	N	Y	Y	N	Y	Y	Y
NEVADA								
AL Santini	#	Y	Y	Y	N	N	Y	Y
NEW HAMPSHIRE								
1 D'Amours	Y	Y	Y	Y	Y	Y	Y	Y
2 Cleveland	Y	Y	Y	Y	Y	Y	Y	Y
NEW JERSEY								
1 Florio	Y	Y	Y	Y	Y	N	Y	N
2 Hughes	Y	Y	N	Y	Y	N	Y	Y
3 Howard	Y	Y	#	#	N	Y	Y	N
4 Thompson	Y	N	N	Y	Y	N	Y	N
5 Fenwick	Y	Y	Y	Y	N	Y	N	Y
6 Forsythe	Y	Y	N	Y	Y	N	N	Y
7 Maguire	?	?	?	?	?	?	?	?
8 Roe	#	#	Y	Y	Y	N	Y	N
9 Hollenbeck	?	Y	N	Y	Y	N	Y	N
10 Rodino	#	▮	#	#	▮	#	#	▮
11 Minish	Y	Y	Y	Y	Y	N	Y	N
12 Rinaldo	Y	Y	Y	Y	Y	Y	Y	N
13 Meyner	Y	✓	✓	Y	N	Y	N	N
14 LeFante	#	#	#	#	✓	X	#	▮
15 Patten	Y	N	Y	Y	Y	N	Y	N
NEW MEXICO								
1 Lujan	Y	N	Y	Y	N	N	N	Y
2 Runnels	Y	N	Y	Y	N	N	Y	Y
NEW YORK								
1 Pike	Y	N	Y	Y	N	N	Y	Y
2 Downey	Y	Y	N	Y	N	Y	N	N
3 Ambro	?	Y	Y	Y	N	Y	Y	Y
4 Lent	Y	Y	N	Y	Y	Y	Y	Y
5 Wydler	Y	Y	Y	Y	Y	Y	?	N
6 Wolff	Y	Y	Y	Y	N	N	Y	N
7 Addabbo	Y	Y	Y	Y	Y	N	Y	N
8 Rosenthal	Y	Y	Y	Y	N	N	Y	N
9 Delaney	Y	N	Y	Y	N	N	Y	Y
10 Biaggi	Y	Y	Y	Y	Y	N	Y	N
11 Scheuer	Y	N	Y	Y	N	N	Y	N
12 Chisholm	#	Y	Y	Y	N	N	Y	N
13 Solarz	Y	Y	Y	Y	N	Y	N	N
14 Richmond	Y	Y	Y	Y	N	Y	Y	Y
15 Zeferetti	Y	Y	Y	Y	Y	N	Y	N
16 Holtzman	Y	Y	Y	Y	N	Y	N	N
17 Murphy	Y	N	N	Y	Y	N	Y	N
18 Green	Y	Y	Y	Y	N	Y	Y	N
19 Rangel	Y	Y	Y	Y	N	Y	Y	N
20 Weiss	Y	Y	Y	Y	N	Y	N	N
21 Garcia	#	Y	Y	Y	N	Y	Y	N
22 Bingham	Y	Y	N	Y	N	Y	Y	N
23 Caputo	Y	N	?	Y	Y	N	Y	N
24 Ottinger	Y	Y	Y	Y	N	Y	N	N
25 Fish	Y	Y	Y	Y	Y	Y	Y	Y
26 Gilman	Y	Y	Y	Y	Y	Y	Y	N
27 McHugh	Y	Y	Y	Y	N	Y	Y	Y
28 Stratton	Y	N	Y	Y	Y	N	Y	N
29 Pattison	Y	Y	Y	Y	N	Y	N	Y
30 McEwen	Y	N	Y	Y	Y	N	Y	N
31 Mitchell	#	N	Y	Y	N	Y	Y	N
32 Hanley	Y	N	Y	Y	N	N	Y	N
33 Walsh	Y	N	N	Y	Y	Y	Y	N
34 Horton	Y	N	Y	Y	?	Y	Y	N
35 Conable	Y	N	N	Y	Y	Y	Y	N
36 LaFalce	#	N	N	Y	Y	Y	Y	Y
37 Nowak	Y	N	Y	Y	Y	N	Y	N
38 Kemp	Y	N	N	Y	Y	Y	Y	Y
39 Lundine	Y	Y	Y	Y	Y	Y	Y	N
NORTH CAROLINA								
1 Jones	Y	N	Y	Y	Y	N	Y	N
2 Fountain	Y	Y	Y	Y	Y	N	Y	Y
3 Whitley	Y	N	Y	Y	Y	N	Y	N
4 Andrews	Y	Y	N	Y	Y	N	Y	N
5 Neal	Y	N	Y	#	Y	N	Y	N
6 Preyer	Y	N	Y	Y	Y	Y	Y	N
7 Rose	?	?	?	Y	N	Y	Y	N
8 Hefner	Y	N	Y	Y	Y	N	Y	N

	521	522	523	524	525	526	527	528
9 Martin	Y	N	Y	Y	Y	N	Y	Y
10 Broyhill	Y	N	Y	Y	Y	N	Y	Y
11 Gudger	Y	N	Y	Y	N	N	Y	N
NORTH DAKOTA								
AL Andrews	Y	N	Y	Y	N	Y	Y	Y
OHIO								
1 Gradison	Y	N	Y	Y	Y	Y	Y	Y
2 Luken	Y	N	Y	Y	Y	Y	Y	Y
3 Whalen	#	▮	#	#	▮	#	#	▮
4 Guyer	Y	N	N	Y	Y	N	Y	Y
5 Latta	Y	N	N	Y	Y	N	Y	Y
6 Harsha	Y	N	N	Y	Y	N	Y	Y
7 Brown	Y	N	N	Y	Y	N	Y	Y
8 Kindness	Y	N	Y	Y	Y	N	Y	Y
9 Ashley	?	Y	N	Y	Y	Y	Y	N
10 Miller	Y	N	Y	Y	Y	Y	Y	Y
11 Stanton	Y	N	N	Y	Y	Y	N	Y
12 Devine	Y	N	N	Y	Y	N	Y	Y
13 Pease	Y	Y	Y	Y	N	Y	N	N
14 Seiberling	Y	N	Y	Y	N	Y	N	N
15 Wylie	Y	N	N	Y	N	Y	Y	N
16 Regula	Y	N	Y	Y	N	Y	Y	Y
17 Ashbrook	Y	N	N	Y	Y	N	Y	Y
18 Applegate	Y	Y	Y	Y	Y	Y	Y	N
19 Carney	Y	N	Y	Y	Y	N	Y	N
20 Oakar	Y	Y	Y	Y	N	N	Y	N
21 Stokes	Y	?	N	Y	N	Y	N	N
22 Vanik	Y	N	Y	Y	N	Y	N	N
23 Mottl	Y	Y	Y	Y	N	Y	Y	N
OKLAHOMA								
1 Jones	Y	N	Y	Y	N	N	Y	Y
2 Risenhoover	?	N	N	Y	N	N	Y	N
3 Watkins	Y	N	Y	Y	N	N	Y	N
4 Steed	#	N	Y	Y	N	N	Y	Y
5 Edwards	?	N	Y	Y	N	N	Y	Y
6 English	Y	N	Y	Y	N	N	Y	Y
OREGON								
1 AuCoin	Y	N	N	Y	Y	N	Y	N
2 Ullman	Y	N	N	Y	Y	N	Y	N
3 Duncan	#	N	N	Y	N	N	Y	Y
4 Weaver	Y	Y	Y	Y	N	Y	N	N
PENNSYLVANIA								
1 Myers, M.	?	N	Y	Y	Y	N	Y	N
2 Nix	Y	N	Y	Y	N	Y	Y	N
3 Lederer	Y	N	Y	Y	Y	N	Y	N
4 Eilberg	Y	N	Y	Y	Y	N	Y	N
5 Schulze	Y	N	Y	Y	Y	N	Y	Y
6 Yatron	Y	Y	Y	Y	Y	N	Y	Y
7 Edgar	Y	Y	Y	Y	N	Y	N	N
8 Kostmayer	Y	Y	Y	Y	N	Y	N	N
9 Shuster	Y	N	N	Y	N	Y	Y	Y
10 McDade	#	▮	Y	Y	N	Y	Y	N
11 Flood	Y	N	Y	Y	Y	N	Y	N
12 Murtha	Y	N	Y	Y	Y	N	Y	N
13 Coughlin	Y	N	Y	Y	N	Y	N	N
14 Moorhead	Y	N	Y	Y	Y	N	Y	N
15 Rooney	Y	N	N	Y	N	N	Y	N
16 Walker	Y	N	Y	Y	Y	Y	Y	Y
17 Ertel	Y	N	Y	Y	Y	N	Y	Y
18 Walgren	Y	N	Y	Y	N	Y	N	?
19 Goodling, W.	Y	N	Y	Y	N	Y	Y	Y
20 Gaydos	Y	N	Y	Y	Y	N	Y	N
21 Dent	Y	N	Y	Y	Y	N	Y	▮
22 Murphy	Y	Y	Y	Y	N	N	Y	Y
23 Ammerman	Y	N	Y	Y	Y	N	Y	N
24 Marks	Y	Y	Y	Y	N	Y	Y	N
25 Myers, G.	Y	N	Y	Y	N	Y	N	Y
RHODE ISLAND								
1 St Germain	Y	N	Y	Y	Y	Y	Y	N
2 Beard	Y	N	Y	Y	N	Y	Y	N
SOUTH CAROLINA								
1 Davis	?	?	?	?	?	?	?	N
2 Spence	Y	N	Y	Y	?	N	Y	N
3 Derrick	Y	N	Y	Y	N	Y	Y	N
4 Mann	?	Y	Y	Y	Y	N	Y	Y
5 Holland	Y	N	Y	Y	Y	N	Y	N
6 Jenrette	#	✓	✓	#	X	✓	✓	▮
SOUTH DAKOTA								
1 Pressler	Y	Y	Y	Y	N	Y	Y	N
2 Abdnor	Y	N	Y	Y	N	Y	Y	N
TENNESSEE								
1 Quillen	Y	N	N	Y	Y	Y	Y	N
2 Duncan	Y	Y	Y	Y	Y	N	Y	N
3 Lloyd	Y	Y	Y	Y	Y	N	Y	N
4 Gore	Y	Y	N	Y	Y	N	Y	N
5 Vacancy								
6 Beard	Y	N	Y	Y	Y	N	Y	Y

	521	522	523	524	525	526	527	528
7 Jones	Y	Y	N	Y	Y	N	Y	N
8 Ford	Y	Y	N	Y	Y	?	?	?
TEXAS								
1 Hall	Y	N	N	Y	Y	N	Y	Y
2 Wilson, C.	#	N	N	Y	Y	N	Y	N
3 Collins	Y	N	Y	N	Y	N	Y	Y
4 Roberts	Y	N	N	Y	Y	?	?	?
5 Mattox	Y	N	Y	Y	Y	N	Y	N
6 Teague	?	X	X	?	?	?	?	?
7 Archer	Y	N	Y	Y	Y	N	Y	Y
8 Eckhardt	Y	N	Y	Y	N	Y	N	N
9 Brooks	Y	N	N	Y	Y	N	Y	Y
10 Pickle	Y	N	Y	Y	N	N	Y	Y
11 Poage	Y	N	N	Y	N	N	Y	Y
12 Wright	Y	N	N	Y	N	N	Y	N
13 Hightower	Y	N	N	Y	N	N	Y	Y
14 Young	?	N	N	Y	N	N	?	?
15 de la Garza	Y	Y	Y	Y	N	N	Y	N
16 White	Y	N	N	Y	Y	N	Y	Y
17 Burleson	Y	N	N	Y	N	N	Y	Y
18 Jordan	Y	N	N	Y	Y	N	Y	N
19 Mahon	Y	N	N	Y	N	N	Y	Y
20 Gonzalez	Y	N	N	Y	N	N	Y	N
21 Krueger	Y	N	N	Y	Y	N	#	▮
22 Gammage	Y	N	Y	Y	Y	N	Y	Y
23 Kazen	Y	N	N	Y	N	N	Y	N
24 Milford	?	N	N	Y	?	?	?	?
UTAH								
1 McKay	Y	N	N	Y	N	N	Y	Y
2 Marriott	Y	N	Y	Y	N	Y	Y	Y
VERMONT								
AL Jeffords	Y	Y	Y	Y	N	Y	N	N
VIRGINIA								
1 Trible	?	?	Y	Y	Y	N	Y	N
2 Whitehurst	Y	N	Y	Y	Y	N	#	Y
3 Satterfield	Y	Y	Y	Y	Y	?	Y	Y
4 Daniel	Y	N	Y	Y	Y	N	Y	Y
5 Daniel	Y	N	Y	Y	Y	N	Y	N
6 Butler	Y	N	N	Y	Y	Y	Y	N
7 Robinson	Y	N	Y	Y	Y	N	Y	Y
8 Harris	Y	N	Y	Y	N	Y	N	N
9 Wampler	Y	N	N	Y	Y	N	Y	N
10 Fisher	Y	N	Y	Y	N	Y	N	N
WASHINGTON								
1 Pritchard	Y	N	N	Y	Y	Y	Y	Y
2 Meeds	#	▮	#	#	▮	#	#	▮
3 Bonker	Y	N	N	Y	Y	N	Y	N
4 McCormack	Y	N	N	Y	Y	N	Y	N
5 Foley	Y	N	N	Y	Y	N	Y	N
6 Dicks	Y	N	N	Y	Y	N	Y	Y
7 Cunningham	Y	N	N	Y	Y	N	Y	Y
WEST VIRGINIA								
1 Mollohan	Y	N	Y	Y	N	Y	Y	Y
2 Staggers	Y	N	Y	Y	X	N	Y	N
3 Slack	Y	N	Y	Y	Y	N	Y	N
4 Rahall	Y	N	Y	Y	N	Y	Y	N
WISCONSIN								
1 Aspin	Y	Y	Y	Y	N	Y	Y	N
2 Kastenmeier	Y	Y	Y	Y	N	Y	N	N
3 Baldus	Y	Y	Y	Y	N	Y	N	N
4 Zablocki	Y	Y	Y	Y	N	N	Y	N
5 Reuss	Y	Y	Y	Y	N	Y	Y	N
6 Steiger	Y	N	N	Y	Y	Y	Y	N
7 Obey	Y	Y	Y	Y	N	Y	Y	N
8 Cornell	Y	Y	Y	Y	Y	N	N	Y
9 Kasten	#	?	?	?	?	?	?	?
WYOMING								
AL Roncalio	Y	Y	Y	Y	N	Y	N	N

Democrats ***Republicans***

529. HR 7577. Economic Opportunity Act Amendments. Passage of the bill to extend the Economic Opportunity Act of 1964 for three years, through fiscal 1981, and to make changes in various anti-poverty programs covered under the act. Passed 346-38: R 113-24; D 233-14 (ND 165-5; SD 68-9), July 26, 1978.

530. S Con Res 98. Congressional Adjournment. Adoption of the concurrent resolution to allow Congress to continue meeting beyond the mandatory adjournment date of July 31 provided for in the 1946 Legislative Reorganization Act, as amended. Adopted 302-44: R 100-32; D 202-12 (ND 136-7; SD 66-5), July 27, 1978.

531. HR 12157. Export-Import Bank. Long, D-Md., amendment to prohibit the Export-Import Bank from providing loans to produce any commodity unless the president certified that the commodity was not in surplus in the United States and its importation would not injure U.S. firms and employees producing the same or competing commodity. Rejected 197-199: R 67-71; D 130-128 (ND 79-101; SD 51-27), July 27, 1978.

532. HR 12157. Export-Import Bank. Harkin, D-Iowa, amendment to prohibit the Export-Import Bank from participating in transactions with countries that the secretary of state has determined grossly violate internationally recognized human rights. Rejected 103-286: R 28-109; D 75-177 (ND 64-111; SD 11-66), July 27, 1978. A "nay" was a vote supporting the president's position.

533. HR 12157. Export-Import Bank. Brown, R-Mich., amendment to prohibit the Export-Import Bank from extending credit to purchasers of exports whom the secretary of state certifies do not endorse fair and equal employment principles. Rejected 90-288: R 51-82; D 39-206 (ND 30-142; SD 9-64), July 27, 1978.

534. HR 12157. Export-Import Bank. Cavanaugh, D-Neb., amendment to require the Export-Import Bank to submit to Congress an evaluation, based on analyses by the Nuclear Regulatory Commission, of the nuclear safety standards in effect in nations with which the bank conducts a transaction for the sale of nuclear reactors. Rejected 106-266: R 12-118; D 94-148 (ND 90-78; SD 4-70), July 27, 1978.

535. HR 12157. Export-Import Bank. Passage of the bill to extend the authority of the Export-Import Bank through September 1983 and increase its loan ceiling to $40 million from $25 million. Passed 314-47: R 102-26; D 212-21 (ND 150-11; SD 62-10), July 27, 1978.

KEY

Y Voted for (yea).
✓ Paired for.
† Announced for.
# CQ Poll for.
N Voted against (nay).
X Paired against.
- Announced against.
▮ CQ Poll against.
P Voted "present."
● Voted "present" to avoid possible conflict of interest.
? Did not vote or otherwise make a position known.

	529	530	531	532	533	534	535
ALABAMA							
1 Edwards	Y	Y	Y	N	N	N	Y
2 Dickinson	Y	Y	Y	N	N	N	Y
3 Nichols	Y	Y	Y	N	N	N	Y
4 Bevill	Y	Y	Y	N	N	N	Y
5 Flippo	Y	Y	Y	N	N	N	Y
6 Buchanan	Y	?	Y	Y	Y	N	Y
7 Flowers	?	?	?	?	?	?	?
ALASKA							
AL Young	Y	#	#	N	Y	N	N
ARIZONA							
1 Rhodes	Y	Y	N	N	N	N	Y
2 Udall	Y	Y	N	N	N	Y	Y
3 Stump	N	N	Y	N	Y	N	Y
4 Rudd	N	Y	N	N	Y	N	Y
ARKANSAS							
1 Alexander	Y	Y	N	N	N	N	Y
2 Tucker	Y	Y	N	N	▮	▮	#
3 Hammerschmidt	Y	Y	Y	N	Y	N	N
4 Thornton	Y	Y	N	N	N	N	Y
CALIFORNIA							
1 Johnson	Y	Y	N	N	N	N	Y
2 Clausen	Y	?	Y	N	N	?	?
3 Moss	?	Y	N	N	N	N	Y
4 Leggett	Y	?	Y	N	N	N	Y
5 Burton, J.	Y	Y	Y	Y	Y	Y	Y
6 Burton, P.	Y	Y	N	Y	?	?	?
7 Miller	Y	Y	Y	Y	Y	Y	Y
8 Dellums	Y	#	N	Y	Y	Y	Y
9 Stark	#	Y	N	Y	Y	#	#
10 Edwards	Y	Y	N	N	N	Y	?
11 Ryan	Y	Y	Y	Y	?	Y	Y
12 McCloskey	Y	Y	N	N	N	Y	Y
13 Mineta	Y	Y	N	N	N	N	Y
14 McFall	Y	Y	N	N	N	N	Y
15 Sisk	?	Y	N	?	N	N	Y
16 Panetta	Y	Y	Y	Y	N	Y	Y
17 Krebs	Y	Y	N	Y	N	Y	Y
18 Vacancy							
19 Lagomarsino	Y	N	N	N	N	N	Y
20 Goldwater	?	Y	N	N	N	N	Y
21 Corman	Y	Y	N	N	N	N	Y
22 Moorhead	N	Y	N	N	Y	N	#
23 Beilenson	Y	#	N	Y	N	Y	Y
24 Waxman	Y	#	N	Y	N	Y	Y
25 Roybal	Y	Y	?	Y	N	Y	Y
26 Rousselot	N	?	?	N	Y	N	N
27 Dornan	Y	Y	Y	N	Y	N	Y
28 Burke	Y	Y	N	Y	Y	Y	Y
29 Hawkins	Y	Y	Y	Y	Y	N	Y
30 Danielson	#	#	▮	▮	▮	▮	#
31 Wilson, C.H.	Y	Y	Y	?	N	N	N
32 Anderson	Y	Y	Y	Y	N	Y	Y
33 Clawson	?	Y	N	N	N	N	Y
34 Hannaford	Y	Y	N	N	N	N	Y
35 Lloyd	Y	?	Y	N	N	N	Y
36 Brown	?	?	Y	N	N	N	Y
37 Pettis	Y	Y	N	N	N	N	Y
38 Patterson	Y	Y	N	N	N	N	Y
39 Wiggins	Y	Y	N	N	Y	N	Y
40 Badham	N	Y	N	N	#	▮	#
41 Wilson, B.	Y	Y	N	N	Y	N	Y
42 Van Deerlin	Y	Y	N	N	N	Y	Y
43 Burgener	Y	Y	N	N	N	N	Y
COLORADO							
1 Schroeder	Y	N	N	Y	N	Y	Y
2 Wirth	Y	?	N	N	N	N	?
3 Evans	?	?	N	N	N	N	Y
4 Johnson	Y	Y	N	N	N	N	Y
5 Armstrong	N	N	Y	N	N	N	N
CONNECTICUT							
1 Cotter	#	Y	Y	Y	N	N	Y
2 Dodd	Y	?	N	Y	N	Y	?
3 Giaimo	Y	Y	N	N	N	?	Y
4 McKinney	Y	Y	N	N	N	N	Y
5 Sarasin	#	#	▮	▮	▮	▮	#
6 Moffett	?	?	N	Y	N	?	Y
DELAWARE							
AL Evans	Y	?	N	N	N	N	Y
FLORIDA							
1 Sikes	Y	Y	Y	N	N	N	Y
2 Fuqua	Y	Y	Y	N	N	N	N
3 Bennett	Y	Y	Y	Y	N	N	Y
4 Chappell	Y	Y	Y	N	Y	N	Y
5 Kelly	N	N	N	N	Y	N	N
6 Young	Y	N	Y	Y	N	Y	N
7 Gibbons	Y	N	N	N	N	N	Y
8 Ireland	?	Y	Y	N	N	N	Y
9 Frey	?	?	?	?	?	?	?
10 Bafalis	Y	N	Y	Y	N	N	N
11 Rogers	Y	Y	Y	N	▮	N	Y
12 Burke	Y	Y	Y	N	Y	Y	Y
13 Lehman	Y	Y	N	Y	Y	N	Y
14 Pepper	Y	Y	N	Y	N	N	Y
15 Fascell	Y	N	N	N	N	N	Y
GEORGIA							
1 Ginn	Y	Y	Y	N	N	N	N
2 Mathis	N	Y	Y	?	?	N	N
3 Brinkley	Y	Y	N	N	N	N	Y
4 Levitas	Y	Y	Y	N	N	N	Y
5 Fowler	Y	Y	Y	N	N	N	Y
6 Flynt	?	N	Y	N	N	N	Y
7 McDonald	N	#	N	Y	Y	N	N
8 Evans	Y	Y	Y	N	N	N	N
9 Jenkins	#	#	▮	▮	▮	▮	#
10 Barnard	Y	Y	N	?	?	?	?
HAWAII							
1 Heftel	Y	Y	Y	N	N	Y	?
2 Akaka	Y	Y	Y	N	N	Y	Y
IDAHO							
1 Symms	N	N	N	Y	Y	N	N
2 Hansen, G.	N	N	N	N	Y	N	N
ILLINOIS							
1 Metcalfe	Y	Y	Y	N	Y	Y	?
2 Murphy	Y	Y	Y	N	N	N	Y
3 Russo	Y	#	N	N	N	N	Y
4 Derwinski	Y	Y	N	N	Y	N	Y
5 Fary	Y	Y	N	N	N	N	Y
6 Hyde	Y	Y	N	N	N	N	Y
7 Collins	?	?	?	?	?	?	?
8 Rostenkowski	Y	Y	N	N	N	N	?
9 Yates	Y	Y	N	Y	N	Y	Y
10 Mikva	Y	#	N	Y	N	Y	Y
11 Annunzio	Y	Y	N	N	N	N	Y
12 Crane	N	N	N	Y	Y	N	N
13 McClory	Y	Y	N	N	N	N	Y
14 Erlenborn	Y	Y	N	N	N	N	Y
15 Corcoran	Y	Y	N	Y	N	N	Y
16 Anderson	Y	Y	N	Y	N	N	Y
17 O'Brien	Y	Y	N	N	N	N	Y
18 Michel	Y	Y	N	N	N	N	Y
19 Railsback	?	Y	N	N	N	N	Y
20 Findley	Y	Y	N	N	N	N	Y
21 Madigan	Y	Y	Y	N	N	N	Y
22 Shipley	?	?	X	?	?	?	?
23 Price	Y	Y	N	N	N	N	Y
24 Simon	Y	?	N	N	N	Y	Y
INDIANA							
1 Benjamin	Y	Y	Y	Y	N	Y	Y
2 Fithian	Y	?	N	N	N	N	Y
3 Brademas	Y	Y	N	Y	N	Y	Y
4 Quayle	Y	N	N	N	N	N	Y
5 Hillis	Y	Y	Y	N	N	N	Y
6 Evans	?	?	?	?	?	?	?
7 Myers, J.	Y	Y	Y	N	N	N	Y
8 Cornwell	Y	Y	Y	Y	?	?	?
9 Hamilton	Y	Y	?	N	N	N	Y
10 Sharp	Y	?	N	N	N	N	Y
11 Jacobs	Y	N	N	?	Y	N	Y
IOWA							
1 Leach	Y	N	N	N	N	N	Y
2 Blouin	Y	#	N	N	N	N	Y
3 Grassley	Y	Y	Y	N	N	N	Y
4 Smith	Y	Y	N	Y	N	N	Y
5 Harkin	Y	Y	Y	Y	Y	Y	N
6 Bedell	Y	#	N	Y	N	Y	Y

Democrats ***Republicans***

	529	530	531	532	533	534	535
KANSAS							
1 Sebelius	Y	Y	N	N	N	N	Y
2 Keys	Y	Y	N	Y	N	Y	Y
3 Winn	Y	Y	N	N	N	N	Y
4 Glickman	Y	Y	N	N	N	Y	Y
5 Skubitz	Y	Y	N	N	N	?	Y
KENTUCKY							
1 Hubbard	Y	Y	N	N	N	N	Y
2 Natcher	Y	Y	Y	N	N	N	Y
3 Mazzoli	Y	Y	N	N	N	N	Y
4 Snyder	N	N	Y	Y	Y	N	N
5 Carter	Y	Y	Y	N	N	N	Y
6 Breckinridge	Y	Y	N	N	N	N	Y
7 Perkins	Y	Y	Y	N	N	N	Y
LOUISIANA							
1 Livingston	Y	?	?	?	?	?	?
2 Boggs	Y	Y	N	N	N	N	Y
3 Treen	Y	N	Y	N	Y	N	Y
4 Waggonner	N	Y	Y	N	N	N	Y
5 Huckaby	Y	Y	Y	N	N	N	?
6 Moore	Y	Y	Y	N	N	N	Y
7 Breaux	?	Y	Y	N	N	N	Y
8 Long	Y	Y	Y	N	N	N	Y
MAINE							
1 Emery	Y	Y	Y	N	N	Y	Y
2 Cohen	Y	Y	Y	?	?	?	?
MARYLAND							
1 Bauman	N	N	Y	Y	Y	N	N
2 Long	Y	Y	Y	Y	Y	Y	Y
3 Mikulski	Y	?	Y	Y	Y	Y	N
4 Holt	Y	N	Y	N	Y	N	N
5 Spellman	Y	Y	Y	Y	N	Y	Y
6 Byron	Y	Y	Y	N	Y	N	N
7 Mitchell	#	N	Y	P	Y	Y	N
8 Steers	Y	Y	Y	Y	N	Y	Y
MASSACHUSETTS							
1 Conte	Y	Y	N	N	N	N	Y
2 Boland	Y	Y	N	N	N	N	Y
3 Early	?	Y	N	Y	N	Y	Y
4 Drinan	Y	Y	Y	Y	N	Y	Y
5 Tsongas	?	?	N	N	N	N	?
6 Harrington	#	#	X	?	?	#	#
7 Markey	Y	Y	N	Y	N	Y	Y
8 O'Neill							
9 Moakley	Y	Y	N	Y	N	Y	Y
10 Heckler	Y	Y	Y	Y	N	Y	Y
11 Burke	?	?	X	?	?	?	✓
12 Studds	Y	Y	N	N	N	Y	Y
MICHIGAN							
1 Conyers	#	Y	N	?	#	#	#
2 Pursell	Y	Y	N	Y	N	N	Y
3 Brown	Y	Y	N	N	Y	N	Y
4 Stockman	N	Y	N	N	Y	N	N
5 Sawyer	Y	Y	N	N	Y	N	Y
6 Carr	Y	?	N	Y	?	Y	Y
7 Kildee	Y	Y	N	Y	N	Y	Y
8 Traxler	Y	Y	Y	N	N	N	Y
9 Vander Jagt	Y	Y	N	N	Y	?	?
10 Cederberg	Y	Y	N	N	N	N	Y
11 Ruppe	Y	Y	N	Y	N	N	Y
12 Bonior	Y	#	N	Y	Y	Y	#
13 Diggs	Y	Y	?	N	N	Y	Y
14 Nedzi	Y	Y	N	N	N	N	Y
15 Ford	Y	Y	Y	N	N	N	Y
16 Dingell	Y	Y	Y	N	N	N	Y
17 Brodhead	Y	Y	?	N	N	Y	Y
18 Blanchard	Y	#	N	N	N	N	Y
19 Broomfield	Y	N	N	N	Y	N	Y
MINNESOTA							
1 Quie	?	?	?	?	?	?	?
2 Hagedorn	Y	N	Y	N	N	Y	Y
3 Frenzel	Y	Y	N	N	N	N	Y
4 Vento	Y	Y	N	✓	?	?	?
5 Fraser	?	?	?	?	?	?	?
6 Nolan	Y	?	Y	Y	N	Y	Y
7 Stangeland	Y	Y	Y	N	N	N	Y
8 Oberstar	Y	Y	Y	N	N	Y	Y
MISSISSIPPI							
1 Whitten	Y	#	Y	N	N	N	Y
2 Bowen	Y	Y	Y	N	N	N	Y
3 Montgomery	N	Y	Y	N	N	N	Y
4 Cochran	Y	Y	Y	N	N	N	Y
5 Lott	N	Y	Y	N	N	N	Y
MISSOURI							
1 Clay	Y	Y	N	?	Y	?	Y
2 Young	Y	Y	Y	N	N	N	Y
3 Gephardt	N	Y	Y	N	N	Y	Y
4 Skelton	Y	Y	Y	N	Y	N	Y
5 Bolling	#	Y	N	N	N	N	Y
6 Coleman	Y	Y	Y	N	?	N	Y
7 Taylor	N	N	N	N	Y	N	N
8 Ichord	N	N	Y	N	Y	N	N
9 Volkmer	Y	Y	Y	Y	Y	Y	N
10 Burlison	Y	Y	Y	N	N	N	Y
MONTANA							
1 Baucus	Y	#	N	N	N	N	Y
2 Marlenee	Y	N	Y	Y	N	N	?
NEBRASKA							
1 Thone	Y	Y	N	N	Y	?	?
2 Cavanaugh	Y	Y	N	Y	N	Y	Y
3 Smith	Y	Y	N	N	N	Y	Y
NEVADA							
AL Santini	Y	#	Y	N	N	N	N
NEW HAMPSHIRE							
1 D'Amours	Y	Y	Y	N	N	N	Y
2 Cleveland	Y	Y	Y	N	Y	N	Y
NEW JERSEY							
1 Florio	Y	Y	Y	Y	N	Y	Y
2 Hughes	Y	?	Y	N	N	N	Y
3 Howard	Y	Y	Y	N	N	N	Y
4 Thompson	Y	Y	N	N	N	N	Y
5 Fenwick	Y	Y	N	N	N	N	Y
6 Forsythe	N	Y	N	N	N	N	Y
7 Maguire	?	?	?	?	?	?	?
8 Roe	Y	Y	Y	N	N	Y	Y
9 Hollenbeck	Y	Y	Y	Y	N	N	Y
10 Rodino	#	#	▮	▮	▮	▮	#
11 Minish	Y	Y	Y	N	N	N	Y
12 Rinaldo	Y	Y	Y	Y	N	N	Y
13 Meyner	Y	Y	N	N	N	Y	Y
14 LeFante	#	#	✓	▮	▮	▮	#
15 Patten	Y	Y	N	N	N	Y	Y
NEW MEXICO							
1 Lujan	Y	N	Y	Y	Y	N	?
2 Runnels	Y	N	Y	N	?	?	?
NEW YORK							
1 Pike	N	Y	Y	Y	N	Y	Y
2 Downey	Y	#	N	N	N	Y	Y
3 Ambro	Y	?	Y	Y	Y	Y	Y
4 Lent	Y	Y	Y	Y	Y	N	Y
5 Wydler	Y	Y	Y	N	Y	N	Y
6 Wolff	Y	Y	Y	Y	N	Y	Y
7 Addabbo	Y	Y	Y	Y	?	?	✓
8 Rosenthal	Y	#	N	Y	N	Y	Y
9 Delaney	Y	N	N	N	N	N	Y
10 Biaggi	Y	Y	N	Y	N	N	Y
11 Scheuer	Y	?	N	Y	N	Y	Y
12 Chisholm	#	#	N	Y	Y	Y	Y
13 Solarz	Y	Y	N	Y	N	Y	Y
14 Richmond	Y	?	N	Y	Y	Y	?
15 Zeferetti	Y	#	Y	N	Y	N	Y
16 Holtzman	Y	?	N	Y	Y	Y	N
17 Murphy	Y	Y	N	N	N	N	Y
18 Green	Y	Y	N	Y	N	Y	Y
19 Rangel	Y	Y	Y	N	Y	Y	Y
20 Weiss	Y	Y	N	Y	N	Y	Y
21 Garcia	Y	Y	Y	Y	Y	Y	Y
22 Bingham	Y	Y	N	N	N	Y	Y
23 Caputo	Y	Y	Y	Y	?	?	?
24 Ottinger	Y	?	Y	Y	N	Y	Y
25 Fish	?	Y	N	N	N	Y	Y
26 Gilman	Y	Y	Y	Y	N	N	N
27 McHugh	Y	Y	N	N	N	N	Y
28 Stratton	Y	Y	Y	N	N	N	Y
29 Pattison	Y	#	N	N	N	Y	Y
30 McEwen	Y	Y	Y	N	N	N	Y
31 Mitchell	Y	Y	Y	N	Y	N	Y
32 Hanley	Y	Y	N	N	N	N	Y
33 Walsh	Y	Y	Y	N	N	N	Y
34 Horton	Y	Y	N	N	N	N	Y
35 Conable	Y	Y	N	N	N	N	Y
36 LaFalce	#	#	N	N	N	Y	Y
37 Nowak	Y	Y	Y	Y	N	Y	Y
38 Kemp	Y	Y	N	N	Y	N	N
39 Lundine	Y	Y	N	N	N	N	Y
NORTH CAROLINA							
1 Jones	Y	Y	Y	N	N	N	Y
2 Fountain	Y	Y	Y	N	N	N	Y
3 Whitley	Y	Y	Y	N	N	N	Y
4 Andrews	Y	Y	N	N	N	N	Y
5 Neal	Y	Y	N	N	N	N	Y
6 Preyer	Y	#	✓	▮	▮	▮	#
7 Rose	Y	Y	Y	N	N	N	Y
8 Hefner	Y	?	Y	N	N	?	?
9 Martin	Y	#	Y	Y	Y	N	Y
10 Broyhill	Y	Y	Y	N	N	N	Y
11 Gudger	Y	Y	Y	N	N	N	Y
NORTH DAKOTA							
AL Andrews	Y	Y	Y	N	Y	N	Y
OHIO							
1 Gradison	Y	Y	N	N	N	N	Y
2 Luken	Y	Y	Y	N	N	N	Y
3 Whalen	#	#	▮	▮	▮	#	#
4 Guyer	Y	Y	N	N	N	N	Y
5 Latta	N	Y	Y	N	N	N	Y
6 Harsha	Y	Y	Y	N	Y	N	N
7 Brown	Y	N	N	?	?	?	?
8 Kindness	N	N	Y	N	N	N	N
9 Ashley	Y	Y	X	?	?	?	?
10 Miller	Y	N	Y	N	Y	Y	Y
11 Stanton	Y	Y	N	N	N	N	Y
12 Devine	N	Y	N	N	Y	N	Y
13 Pease	Y	Y	N	N	N	Y	Y
14 Seiberling	Y	Y	Y	Y	N	Y	Y
15 Wylie	Y	Y	N	N	N	N	Y
16 Regula	Y	Y	Y	N	N	N	Y
17 Ashbrook	N	N	Y	?	?	?	?
18 Applegate	Y	Y	Y	N	Y	N	Y
19 Carney	Y	Y	Y	N	?	N	Y
20 Oakar	Y	Y	N	Y	Y	Y	Y
21 Stokes	Y	Y	N	N	Y	Y	Y
22 Vanik	Y	Y	N	N	N	Y	Y
23 Mottl	Y	Y	Y	Y	Y	Y	Y
OKLAHOMA							
1 Jones	Y	Y	N	N	N	N	Y
2 Risenhoover	Y	?	Y	N	N	N	N
3 Watkins	Y	Y	Y	N	?	N	Y
4 Steed	Y	N	N	N	N	N	#
5 Edwards	Y	?	N	Y	?	N	Y
6 English	Y	Y	N	Y	N	N	Y
OREGON							
1 AuCoin	Y	Y	N	N	N	?	#
2 Ullman	Y	Y	N	N	N	N	Y
3 Duncan	Y	Y	N	N	N	▮	#
4 Weaver	Y	Y	Y	Y	Y	Y	N
PENNSYLVANIA							
1 Myers, M.	Y	Y	Y	N	N	Y	Y
2 Nix	?	Y	Y	?	?	?	?
3 Lederer	Y	Y	Y	N	N	Y	Y
4 Eilberg	Y	Y	Y	Y	N	Y	Y
5 Schulze	Y	N	Y	N	Y	N	Y
6 Yatron	Y	Y	Y	N	N	N	Y
7 Edgar	Y	#	N	N	N	Y	Y
8 Kostmayer	Y	Y	N	Y	N	Y	Y
9 Shuster	N	N	Y	N	Y	N	N
10 McDade	Y	Y	Y	N	N	N	Y
11 Flood	Y	Y	Y	N	N	N	Y
12 Murtha	Y	Y	Y	N	N	N	Y
13 Coughlin	Y	Y	Y	N	Y	N	Y
14 Moorhead	Y	Y	N	N	N	N	Y
15 Rooney	Y	Y	Y	N	N	N	Y
16 Walker	Y	Y	N	Y	Y	N	Y
17 Ertel	Y	Y	Y	N	N	N	Y
18 Walgren	Y	Y	N	Y	N	N	Y
19 Goodling, W.	Y	N	Y	N	Y	N	Y
20 Gaydos	Y	Y	Y	N	N	N	Y
21 Dent	#	#	✓	▮	▮	▮	#
22 Murphy	Y	Y	Y	N	N	Y	Y
23 Ammerman	Y	Y	Y	N	N	Y	Y
24 Marks	Y	Y	Y	Y	N	N	Y
25 Myers, G.	N	Y	N	Y	N	N	Y
RHODE ISLAND							
1 St Germain	Y	Y	Y	N	N	?	?
2 Beard	Y	#	Y	N	N	N	Y
SOUTH CAROLINA							
1 Davis	Y	Y	Y	Y	Y	N	N
2 Spence	Y	Y	Y	Y	Y	N	N
3 Derrick	Y	#	Y	N	N	N	Y
4 Mann	Y	Y	Y	N	N	N	Y
5 Holland	Y	?	Y	Y	Y	N	Y
6 Jenrette	#	#	X	X	▮	▮	X
SOUTH DAKOTA							
1 Pressler	Y	?	Y	Y	Y	Y	N
2 Abdnor	Y	N	N	N	N	▮	#
TENNESSEE							
1 Quillen	Y	N	Y	N	Y	N	N
2 Duncan	Y	N	Y	Y	Y	N	N
3 Lloyd	Y	Y	#	▮	▮	▮	▮
4 Gore	Y	Y	N	Y	N	Y	Y
5 Vacancy							
6 Beard	Y	Y	N	N	N	N	Y
7 Jones	Y	Y	Y	N	N	N	Y
8 Ford	?	?	?	Y	N	N	Y
TEXAS							
1 Hall	N	Y	Y	N	N	N	N
2 Wilson, C.	Y	Y	N	N	N	▮	#
3 Collins	N	N	N	N	Y	N	N
4 Roberts	?	?	✓	?	?	?	X
5 Mattox	Y	Y	N	N	N	N	Y
6 Teague	?	?	✓	?	?	?	?
7 Archer	N	Y	N	N	N	N	Y
8 Eckhardt	Y	Y	N	N	N	Y	Y
9 Brooks	Y	Y	Y	N	N	N	Y
10 Pickle	Y	Y	Y	N	N	N	Y
11 Poage	N	Y	Y	N	Y	N	Y
12 Wright	Y	Y	N	N	N	N	Y
13 Hightower	Y	?	Y	N	N	N	Y
14 Young	?	?	?	?	?	?	?
15 de la Garza	Y	Y	Y	N	N	N	Y
16 White	Y	Y	Y	N	N	N	Y
17 Burleson	N	Y	Y	N	Y	N	Y
18 Jordan	Y	Y	Y	N	N	N	Y
19 Mahon	Y	Y	Y	N	N	N	Y
20 Gonzalez	Y	Y	Y	Y	N	N	Y
21 Krueger	#	#	▮	▮	▮	▮	#
22 Gammage	Y	Y	N	N	N	N	N
23 Kazen	Y	Y	Y	N	?	?	?
24 Milford	?	?	?	?	?	?	?
UTAH							
1 McKay	N	Y	Y	N	N	N	Y
2 Marriott	Y	Y	N	N	N	N	Y
VERMONT							
AL Jeffords	Y	Y	Y	N	N	Y	Y
VIRGINIA							
1 Trible	Y	Y	Y	N	N	N	Y
2 Whitehurst	Y	Y	Y	N	N	N	Y
3 Satterfield	N	?	Y	N	Y	N	N
4 Daniel	Y	Y	Y	N	Y	N	Y
5 Daniel	N	N	Y	N	Y	N	Y
6 Butler	Y	Y	N	N	N	N	Y
7 Robinson	N	N	Y	N	Y	N	N
8 Harris	Y	Y	N	N	N	Y	Y
9 Wampler	Y	Y	Y	N	Y	N	Y
10 Fisher	Y	Y	N	Y	N	Y	Y
WASHINGTON							
1 Pritchard	Y	Y	N	N	N	N	Y
2 Meeds	#	#	▮	▮	▮	▮	#
3 Bonker	Y	#	N	N	▮	Y	Y
4 McCormack	Y	Y	N	N	N	N	Y
5 Foley	Y	Y	N	N	N	N	Y
6 Dicks	Y	Y	N	N	N	?	?
7 Cunningham	Y	N	N	N	N	N	Y
WEST VIRGINIA							
1 Mollohan	Y	Y	Y	N	N	N	Y
2 Staggers	Y	Y	Y	N	N	N	Y
3 Slack	Y	Y	Y	N	N	N	N
4 Rahall	Y	Y	Y	N	N	Y	Y
WISCONSIN							
1 Aspin	Y	Y	N	N	N	Y	?
2 Kastenmeier	Y	Y	N	N	N	Y	Y
3 Baldus	Y	#	N	N	N	Y	Y
4 Zablocki	Y	Y	N	N	N	N	Y
5 Reuss	Y	Y	N	N	N	N	Y
6 Steiger	Y	Y	N	N	N	N	Y
7 Obey	Y	Y	N	N	N	Y	Y
8 Cornell	Y	#	N	N	N	Y	Y
9 Kasten	?	?	?	?	?	?	?
WYOMING							
AL Roncalio	Y	Y	N	▮	#	#	#

Democrats ***Republicans***

536. HR 9400. Civil Rights of Institutionalized Persons. Kastenmeier, D-Wis., motion to resolve into the Committee of the Whole to consider the bill to allow the attorney general to sue or intervene in suits to protect the constitutional rights of persons living in state-run nursing homes, prisons, juvenile facilities and institutions for the chronically ill. Motion agreed to 304-4: R 113-2; D 191-2 (ND 127-2; SD 64-0), July 28, 1978.

537. HR 9400. Civil Rights of Institutionalized Persons. Passage of the bill to allow the attorney general to sue or intervene in suits to protect the constitutional rights of persons living in state-run nursing homes, prisons, juvenile facilities and institutions for the chronically ill. Passed 254-69: R 77-37; D 177-32 (ND 130-10; SD 47-22), July 28, 1978.

538. HR 12432. Civil Rights Commission. Edwards, D-Calif., motion to resolve into the Committee of the Whole to consider the bill to extend the Commission on Civil Rights for five years and to authorize funds for the commission. Motion agreed to 303-5: R 108-3; D 195-2 (ND 130-1; SD 65-1), July 28, 1978.

539. HR 12432. Civil Rights Commission. Butler, R-Va., amendments, en bloc, to delete provisions to give the commission authority to study discrimination based on age or handicap, including $2 million allocated for such studies. Rejected 87-224: R 63-50; D 24-174 (ND 8-124; SD 16-50), July 28, 1978.

540. HR 12432. Civil Rights Commission. Butler, R-Va., amendment to prohibit the commission from engaging in lobbying on legislation before Congress or state legislatures. Adopted 159-125: R 85-14; D 74-111 (ND 33-90; SD 41-21), July 28, 1978.

541. HR 9998. Ocean Shipping Predatory Pricing. Murphy, D-N.Y., motion to suspend the rules and pass the bill to authorize the Federal Maritime Commission to prevent ocean shipping fleets controlled by certain foreign governments from setting predatory prices for transporting goods between the United States and other nations, subject to presidential disapproval for national defense. Motion agreed to 329-6: R 114-6; D 215-0 (ND 150-0; SD 65-0), July 31, 1978. A two-thirds majority vote (224 in this case) is required for passage under suspension of the rules.

542. HR 12514. Foreign Military Aid. Adoption of the rule (H Res 1286) providing for House floor consideration of the bill to authorize $999.3 million for foreign military assistance programs for fiscal 1979. Adopted 323-21: R 107-15; D 216-6 (ND 152-2; SD 64-4), July 31, 1978.

543. HR 12931. Foreign Aid Appropriations, Fiscal 1979. Adoption of the rule (H Res 1247) providing for House floor consideration of the bill to appropriate $7.4 billion for foreign aid programs for fiscal 1979. Adopted 265-84: R 65-57; D 200-27 (ND 147-12; SD 53-15), July 31, 1978.

KEY

Y Voted for (yea).
✓ Paired for.
+ Announced for.
# CQ Poll for.
N Voted against (nay).
X Paired against.
- Announced against.
▮ CQ Poll against.
P Voted "present."
● Voted "present" to avoid possible conflict of interest.
? Did not vote or otherwise make a position known.

	536	537	538	539	540	541	542	543
ALABAMA								
1 Edwards	Y	Y	Y	Y	?	Y	Y	Y
2 Dickinson	?	?	?	?	?	Y	Y	Y
3 Nichols	#	X	#	#	#	Y	Y	Y
4 Bevill	Y	Y	Y	Y	Y	Y	Y	Y
5 Flippo	Y	Y	Y	?	Y	Y	Y	Y
6 Buchanan	?	Y	Y	N	N	Y	Y	?
7 Flowers	?	?	?	?	?	?	?	?
ALASKA								
AL Young	▮	Y	Y	N	#	Y	Y	N
ARIZONA								
1 Rhodes	Y	Y	Y	Y	Y	Y	Y	Y
2 Udall	Y	Y	#	▮	Y	Y	Y	Y
3 Stump	Y	N	Y	N	Y	Y	Y	N
4 Rudd	Y	N	Y	Y	Y	Y	N	Y
ARKANSAS								
1 Alexander	Y	Y	Y	N	?	Y	Y	Y
2 Tucker	#	#	#	▮	▮	#	?	#
3 Hammerschmidt	Y	N	Y	Y	Y	Y	Y	N
4 Thornton	?	Y	Y	Y	N	Y	Y	Y
CALIFORNIA								
1 Johnson	Y	Y	Y	N	N	Y	Y	Y
2 Clausen	?	?	?	?	?	Y	Y	Y
3 Moss	Y	Y	?	N	N	Y	Y	Y
4 Leggett	Y	Y	?	?	?	Y	?	?
5 Burton, J.	?	Y	?	N	N	Y	Y	Y
6 Burton, P.	Y	Y	Y	N	N	Y	Y	Y
7 Miller	Y	#	Y	N	N	Y	Y	N
8 Dellums	#	Y	Y	N	N	Y	Y	#
9 Stark	#	#	#	▮	▮	Y	Y	Y
10 Edwards	Y	Y	Y	N	N	Y	Y	Y
11 Ryan	Y	Y	Y	N	N	Y	Y	Y
12 McCloskey	Y	Y	Y	Y	Y	Y	Y	Y
13 Mineta	Y	Y	Y	N	N	Y	Y	Y
14 McFall	Y	Y	Y	N	N	Y	?	Y
15 Sisk	?	Y	Y	N	N	Y	Y	Y
16 Panetta	Y	Y	Y	N	N	Y	Y	Y
17 Krebs	Y	Y	Y	N	N	Y	Y	Y
18 Vacancy								
19 Lagomarsino	Y	N	Y	Y	Y	Y	Y	Y
20 Goldwater	?	N	Y	?	Y	?	?	?
21 Corman	Y	Y	Y	N	N	Y	Y	Y
22 Moorhead	#	#	#	▮	#	Y	Y	N
23 Beilenson	#	Y	Y	N	N	Y	Y	Y
24 Waxman	#	#	#	▮	▮	?	#	#
25 Roybal	Y	Y	Y	N	N	Y	Y	Y
26 Rousselot	Y	N	Y	Y	Y	Y	N	N
27 Dornan	Y	N	Y	N	Y	Y	Y	Y
28 Burke	Y	Y	Y	N	N	?	?	?
29 Hawkins	Y	Y	?	?	?	Y	Y	Y
30 Danielson	#	#	#	▮	▮	Y	Y	Y
31 Wilson, C.H.	Y	Y	?	?	?	?	Y	Y
32 Anderson	Y	Y	Y	N	N	Y	Y	Y
33 Clawson	Y	N	Y	Y	Y	Y	N	N
34 Hannaford	Y	Y	Y	N	N	Y	Y	Y
35 Lloyd	N	Y	N	N	N	Y	Y	Y
36 Brown	Y	Y	Y	?	?	Y	Y	Y
37 Pettis	Y	Y	Y	Y	Y	?	?	?
38 Patterson	Y	Y	Y	N	N	Y	Y	Y
39 Wiggins	Y	N	Y	Y	Y	Y	#	#
40 Badham	#	▮	#	#	#	Y	Y	N
41 Wilson, B.	N	Y	N	N	N	Y	Y	Y
42 Van Deerlin	Y	Y	?	N	N	Y	Y	N
43 Burgener	Y	Y	Y	N	Y	Y	Y	N
COLORADO								
1 Schroeder	Y	Y	Y	N	N	Y	Y	N
2 Wirth	?	?	?	?	?	?	?	?
3 Evans	Y	Y	Y	N	N	Y	Y	?
4 Johnson	Y	Y	?	Y	?	?	?	?
5 Armstrong	Y	Y	Y	Y	Y	Y	Y	N
CONNECTICUT								
1 Cotter	Y	Y	Y	N	?	Y	Y	Y
2 Dodd	Y	Y	Y	N	?	Y	Y	Y
3 Giaimo	?	Y	Y	N	N	Y	Y	Y
4 McKinney	Y	Y	#	▮	▮	Y	Y	Y
5 Sarasin	#	#	#	▮	#	#	#	#
6 Moffett	Y	Y	Y	N	N	Y	Y	Y
DELAWARE								
AL Evans	Y	Y	Y	N	Y	Y	Y	Y
FLORIDA								
1 Sikes	Y	Y	Y	Y	Y	Y	Y	Y
2 Fuqua	Y	Y	Y	N	Y	Y	Y	Y
3 Bennett	Y	Y	Y	N	Y	Y	Y	Y
4 Chappell	Y	Y	Y	Y	Y	Y	Y	Y
5 Kelly	Y	N	Y	Y	Y	Y	N	N
6 Young	Y	Y	Y	N	Y	Y	Y	Y
7 Gibbons	Y	Y	Y	N	Y	Y	Y	Y
8 Ireland	Y	?	?	Y	?	Y	Y	?
9 Frey	?	?	?	?	?	?	?	?
10 Bafalis	Y	?	?	?	?	Y	Y	N
11 Rogers	Y	Y	?	N	Y	Y	Y	Y
12 Burke	Y	Y	Y	N	Y	Y	Y	Y
13 Lehman	Y	Y	Y	N	N	Y	Y	Y
14 Pepper	Y	Y	Y	N	N	#	#	#
15 Fascell	Y	Y	Y	N	N	Y	Y	Y
GEORGIA								
1 Ginn	Y	Y	Y	N	Y	Y	Y	Y
2 Mathis	?	N	?	N	?	?	?	?
3 Brinkley	Y	Y	Y	N	Y	?	?	?
4 Levitas	Y	Y	Y	N	Y	?	?	?
5 Fowler	?	?	?	?	?	?	?	?
6 Flynt	Y	N	Y	Y	Y	Y	Y	N
7 McDonald	#	N	N	Y	Y	▮	▮	▮
8 Evans	Y	Y	Y	N	N	Y	Y	Y
9 Jenkins	#	#	#	#	#	#	#	#
10 Barnard	?	?	?	?	?	Y	Y	Y
HAWAII								
1 Heftel	?	?	?	?	?	Y	Y	Y
2 Akaka	Y	Y	Y	▮	N	#	#	#
IDAHO								
1 Symms	Y	N	Y	Y	Y	Y	N	N
2 Hansen, G.	Y	N	Y	Y	Y	Y	N	N
ILLINOIS								
1 Metcalfe	?	?	?	?	?	?	?	?
2 Murphy	#	#	#	?	?	Y	Y	Y
3 Russo	Y	Y	Y	#	#	Y	Y	Y
4 Derwinski	Y	Y	Y	N	Y	Y	Y	Y
5 Fary	Y	Y	Y	N	N	Y	Y	Y
6 Hyde	Y	Y	Y	N	Y	Y	Y	Y
7 Collins	?	?	?	?	?	?	?	?
8 Rostenkowski	Y	Y	Y	N	N	Y	Y	Y
9 Yates	Y	Y	Y	N	N	Y	Y	Y
10 Mikva	Y	Y	Y	N	▮	Y	Y	Y
11 Annunzio	Y	Y	Y	N	N	Y	Y	Y
12 Crane	#	▮	#	#	#	Y	N	▮
13 McClory	Y	Y	Y	N	Y	Y	Y	N
14 Erlenborn	Y	N	Y	N	Y	Y	Y	Y
15 Corcoran	Y	Y	Y	N	Y	Y	Y	N
16 Anderson	Y	Y	#	N	#	Y	Y	Y
17 O'Brien	Y	Y	Y	N	Y	Y	Y	N
18 Michel	Y	Y	Y	Y	Y	Y	Y	N
19 Railsback	Y	Y	?	?	?	N	Y	Y
20 Findley	Y	Y	Y	N	Y	Y	Y	Y
21 Madigan	Y	Y	Y	N	Y	?	?	Y
22 Shipley	?	?	?	?	?	?	?	?
23 Price	Y	Y	Y	N	N	Y	Y	Y
24 Simon	Y	Y	Y	N	N	Y	Y	Y
INDIANA								
1 Benjamin	Y	Y	Y	Y	Y	Y	Y	Y
2 Fithian	Y	Y	?	N	N	Y	Y	Y
3 Brademas	Y	Y	Y	N	N	Y	Y	Y
4 Quayle	N	N	N	N	Y	Y	Y	N
5 Hillis	Y	Y	Y	?	?	Y	Y	Y
6 Evans	?	Y	Y	N	Y	Y	Y	Y
7 Myers, J.	Y	Y	Y	Y	Y	Y	Y	N
8 Cornwell	?	?	?	?	?	Y	Y	Y
9 Hamilton	Y	Y	Y	N	Y	Y	Y	Y
10 Sharp	Y	Y	Y	N	Y	Y	Y	Y
11 Jacobs	#	#	#	▮	#	Y	Y	Y
IOWA								
1 Leach	Y	Y	Y	N	Y	N	Y	N
2 Blouin	Y	Y	Y	N	N	Y	Y	Y
3 Grassley	Y	N	Y	N	Y	Y	Y	N
4 Smith	Y	Y	Y	N	Y	Y	Y	Y
5 Harkin	?	?	?	?	?	?	?	?
6 Bedell	#	?	#	▮	▮	Y	Y	Y

Democrats ***Republicans***

	536	537	538	539	540	541	542	543
KANSAS								
1 Sebelius	Y	Y	Y	Y	?	Y	Y	Y
2 Keys	#	#	#	▮	▮	Y	Y	Y
3 Winn	Y	Y	Y	Y	Y	Y	Y	Y
4 Glickman	Y	Y	Y	N	Y	Y	Y	Y
5 Skubitz	P	Y	Y	Y	?	Y	Y	Y
KENTUCKY								
1 Hubbard	Y	Y	Y	N	Y	#	#	#
2 Natcher	Y	Y	Y	N	N	Y	Y	Y
3 Mazzoli	Y	Y	Y	N	N	Y	Y	Y
4 Snyder	Y	Y	Y	Y	Y	Y	N	N
5 Carter	Y	Y	Y	N	Y	Y	Y	Y
6 Breckinridge	Y	Y	Y	N	N	Y	Y	Y
7 Perkins	Y	Y	Y	N	N	Y	Y	Y
LOUISIANA								
1 Livingston	?	?	?	?	?	Y	Y	Y
2 Boggs	Y	Y	Y	N	N	Y	Y	Y
3 Treen	Y	N	Y	Y	Y	Y	Y	Y
4 Waggonner	Y	N	Y	Y	Y	Y	Y	N
5 Huckaby	?	?	?	?	?	Y	Y	N
6 Moore	Y	N	Y	Y	Y	Y	Y	Y
7 Breaux	?	X	?	?	?	?	?	?
8 Long	?	Y	Y	N	N	Y	Y	Y
MAINE								
1 Emery	Y	Y	Y	N	Y	Y	Y	Y
2 Cohen	#	#	?	?	?	#	#	#
MARYLAND								
1 Bauman	Y	N	Y	Y	Y	Y	N	N
2 Long	Y	Y	Y	N	N	Y	Y	Y
3 Mikulski	Y	Y	Y	N	N	Y	Y	Y
4 Holt	Y	N	Y	Y	Y	Y	Y	N
5 Spellman	?	Y	Y	N	N	Y	Y	Y
6 Byron	Y	Y	Y	N	Y	Y	Y	N
7 Mitchell	N	Y	#	N	N	Y	Y	Y
8 Steers	Y	Y	Y	N	N	Y	Y	Y
MASSACHUSETTS								
1 Conte	Y	Y	Y	N	N	Y	Y	Y
2 Boland	Y	Y	Y	▮	▮	Y	Y	Y
3 Early	Y	Y	Y	N	?	Y	Y	N
4 Drinan	Y	Y	Y	N	N	Y	Y	Y
5 Tsongas	?	?	?	?	?	?	?	?
6 Harrington	#	#	#	▮	▮	#	#	#
7 Markey	Y	Y	Y	N	N	?	Y	Y
8 O'Neill								
9 Moakley	Y	Y	Y	N	?	Y	Y	Y
10 Heckler	Y	Y	Y	N	N	Y	Y	Y
11 Burke	?	✓	?	?	?	?	?	?
12 Studds	Y	Y	Y	N	N	Y	Y	Y
MICHIGAN								
1 Conyers	#	#	#	▮	▮	#	▮	#
2 Pursell	Y	Y	Y	N	Y	?	?	?
3 Brown	Y	Y	Y	N	Y	Y	Y	Y
4 Stockman	Y	Y	Y	Y	Y	▮	Y	N
5 Sawyer	Y	Y	Y	Y	?	#	#	#
6 Carr	Y	Y	Y	N	N	Y	Y	Y
7 Kildee	Y	Y	Y	N	N	Y	Y	Y
8 Traxler	Y	N	Y	N	#	#	#	Y
9 Vander Jagt	Y	Y	Y	Y	?	?	?	N
10 Cederberg	Y	?	Y	N	Y	?	?	?
11 Ruppe	?	?	?	?	?	?	?	?
12 Bonior	#	Y	Y	N	N	Y	Y	Y
13 Diggs	#	#	#	▮	▮	#	#	Y
14 Nedzi	Y	Y	Y	N	Y	Y	Y	Y
15 Ford	?	?	Y	N	N	?	?	?
16 Dingell	?	N	Y	N	Y	Y	?	Y
17 Brodhead	Y	Y	Y	N	N	Y	Y	Y
18 Blanchard	Y	Y	Y	N	?	Y	Y	Y
19 Broomfield	Y	Y	Y	Y	#	Y	Y	Y
MINNESOTA								
1 Quie	?	?	?	?	?	?	?	?
2 Hagedorn	Y	Y	Y	Y	?	Y	Y	Y
3 Frenzel	Y	Y	Y	N	?	Y	Y	Y
4 Vento	?	✓	?	?	?	?	Y	Y
5 Fraser	?	?	?	?	?	?	?	?
6 Nolan	?	?	?	?	?	?	?	?
7 Stangeland	Y	Y	Y	Y	#	Y	Y	Y
8 Oberstar	Y	Y	Y	N	N	Y	Y	Y
MISSISSIPPI								
1 Whitten	#	#	#	▮	#	Y	Y	Y
2 Bowen	Y	?	Y	Y	Y	Y	Y	Y
3 Montgomery	Y	N	Y	#	#	Y	Y	N
4 Cochran	?	?	?	?	?	Y	Y	N
5 Lott	Y	N	Y	Y	#	Y	Y	N
MISSOURI								
1 Clay	?	?	?	?	?	Y	Y	Y
2 Young	Y	Y	Y	▮	#	Y	Y	Y
3 Gephardt	▮	N	Y	N	Y	Y	Y	Y
4 Skelton	Y	N	Y	N	Y	Y	Y	Y
5 Bolling	#	#	Y	N	N	Y	Y	Y
6 Coleman	Y	?	Y	N	Y	Y	Y	N
7 Taylor	Y	N	Y	Y	?	Y	N	N
8 Ichord	Y	N	Y	Y	Y	Y	N	N
9 Volkmer	Y	Y	Y	N	?	Y	Y	Y
10 Burlison	Y	Y	Y	N	N	Y	Y	Y
MONTANA								
1 Baucus	#	#	#	▮	▮	Y	Y	Y
2 Marlenee	Y	?	Y	N	Y	Y	Y	Y
NEBRASKA								
1 Thone	?	?	?	?	?	?	?	?
2 Cavanaugh	Y	Y	?	?	N	Y	Y	Y
3 Smith	Y	Y	Y	?	?	Y	Y	N
NEVADA								
AL Santini	Y	Y	Y	N	Y	Y	Y	Y
NEW HAMPSHIRE								
1 D'Amours	Y	Y	#	N	Y	Y	Y	Y
2 Cleveland	?	X	?	?	?	?	?	?
NEW JERSEY								
1 Florio	Y	Y	Y	N	Y	Y	Y	Y
2 Hughes	Y	Y	Y	N	Y	Y	Y	Y
3 Howard	Y	Y	Y	N	Y	Y	Y	Y
4 Thompson	Y	Y	Y	N	N	Y	Y	Y
5 Fenwick	Y	Y	Y	Y	N	Y	Y	Y
6 Forsythe	Y	#	#	Y	N	Y	Y	Y
7 Maguire	?	?	?	?	?	?	?	?
8 Roe	Y	Y	Y	N	N	#	#	Y
9 Hollenbeck	Y	Y	Y	N	?	Y	Y	Y
10 Rodino	#	#	#	▮	▮	#	#	#
11 Minish	Y	Y	Y	N	N	Y	Y	Y
12 Rinaldo	Y	Y	Y	N	N	Y	Y	Y
13 Meyner	#	Y	Y	▮	▮	Y	Y	Y
14 LeFante	#	#	#	▮	▮	#	#	#
15 Patten	Y	Y	Y	Y	N	#	Y	Y
NEW MEXICO								
1 Lujan	Y	Y	Y	N	Y	Y	N	N
2 Runnels	?	?	?	?	?	Y	N	N
NEW YORK								
1 Pike	Y	Y	Y	Y	Y	Y	Y	Y
2 Downey	Y	Y	Y	N	N	Y	Y	Y
3 Ambro	?	Y	Y	N	N	Y	Y	Y
4 Lent	?	?	?	?	?	?	Y	Y
5 Wydler	?	?	?	?	?	Y	Y	Y
6 Wolff	Y	Y	Y	N	Y	Y	Y	Y
7 Addabbo	?	✓	?	?	?	?	?	?
8 Rosenthal	#	#	#	▮	▮	Y	Y	Y
9 Delaney	Y	Y	Y	N	N	Y	Y	Y
10 Biaggi	?	✓	?	?	?	?	Y	?
11 Scheuer	Y	Y	Y	N	N	Y	Y	Y
12 Chisholm	#	Y	Y	N	N	Y	Y	Y
13 Solarz	Y	Y	Y	N	N	Y	Y	Y
14 Richmond	?	?	?	?	?	?	?	?
15 Zeferetti	#	X	#	▮	#	#	#	#
16 Holtzman	Y	Y	Y	N	N	?	Y	Y
17 Murphy	?	?	?	?	?	Y	Y	Y
18 Green	Y	Y	Y	N	N	#	Y	Y
19 Rangel	Y	Y	Y	N	N	?	?	?
20 Weiss	Y	Y	Y	N	N	?	?	?
21 Garcia	#	#	#	▮	▮	#	#	#
22 Bingham	#	#	#	▮	▮	Y	Y	N
23 Caputo	?	?	?	?	?	?	?	?
24 Ottinger	Y	Y	Y	N	N	Y	Y	N
25 Fish	Y	Y	Y	N	Y	Y	Y	Y
26 Gilman	Y	Y	?	N	Y	Y	Y	Y
27 McHugh	Y	Y	Y	▮	N	Y	Y	Y
28 Stratton	Y	Y	Y	N	N	Y	Y	Y
29 Pattison	#	Y	Y	N	N	Y	Y	Y
30 McEwen	?	?	?	?	?	Y	Y	Y
31 Mitchell	Y	Y	Y	N	Y	#	#	#
32 Hanley	Y	Y	Y	N	N	#	Y	Y
33 Walsh	?	?	?	?	?	Y	Y	Y
34 Horton	?	?	?	?	?	Y	Y	Y
35 Conable	Y	N	Y	Y	Y	N	Y	Y
36 LaFalce	Y	Y	Y	N	Y	Y	Y	Y
37 Nowak	Y	Y	Y	N	N	#	#	Y
38 Kemp	?	?	?	?	?	?	?	?
39 Lundine	Y	Y	#	N	N	#	#	#
NORTH CAROLINA								
1 Jones	Y	N	Y	Y	Y	Y	Y	Y
2 Fountain	Y	N	Y	N	Y	Y	Y	Y
3 Whitley	Y	N	Y	N	Y	Y	Y	N
4 Andrews	Y	N	Y	Y	Y	Y	Y	Y
5 Neal	Y	Y	Y	N	Y	Y	Y	N
6 Preyer	Y	Y	Y	N	Y	Y	Y	Y
7 Rose	Y	Y	Y	?	?	Y	N	Y
8 Hefner	?	?	?	?	?	Y	Y	Y
9 Martin	Y	Y	Y	Y	Y	Y	Y	N
10 Broyhill	Y	N	Y	Y	Y	Y	Y	N
11 Gudger	Y	N	Y	Y	Y	#	#	Y
NORTH DAKOTA								
AL Andrews	Y	Y	Y	N	Y	Y	Y	Y
OHIO								
1 Gradison	Y	Y	Y	N	Y	Y	Y	Y
2 Luken	Y	Y	Y	N	Y	?	?	?
3 Whalen	#	#	#	▮	▮	#	#	#
4 Guyer	Y	Y	Y	Y	Y	Y	Y	N
5 Latta	Y	N	Y	Y	Y	Y	N	N
6 Harsha	Y	Y	Y	Y	Y	Y	N	N
7 Brown	?	?	?	?	?	Y	Y	N
8 Kindness	Y	N	Y	Y	Y	Y	Y	N
9 Ashley	?	N	Y	N	N	?	?	Y
10 Miller	Y	N	Y	Y	Y	Y	Y	Y
11 Stanton	Y	Y	Y	Y	Y	Y	Y	Y
12 Devine	Y	N	Y	Y	Y	Y	Y	N
13 Pease	Y	Y	Y	N	?	Y	Y	Y
14 Seiberling	Y	Y	Y	N	N	Y	Y	N
15 Wylie	Y	Y	Y	Y	N	Y	Y	Y
16 Regula	Y	Y	Y	N	Y	Y	Y	Y
17 Ashbrook	Y	N	Y	Y	Y	Y	Y	N
18 Applegate	Y	Y	Y	N	Y	Y	Y	Y
19 Carney	?	?	?	?	?	Y	Y	Y
20 Oakar	Y	Y	Y	N	?	Y	Y	Y
21 Stokes	Y	Y	Y	N	N	Y	Y	Y
22 Vanik	Y	Y	Y	N	N	Y	Y	Y
23 Mottl	Y	Y	Y	N	#	Y	Y	Y
OKLAHOMA								
1 Jones	Y	Y	Y	N	Y	?	Y	N
2 Risenhoover	Y	N	Y	N	Y	?	?	?
3 Watkins	Y	N	?	?	?	Y	Y	N
4 Steed	#	#	#	▮	#	Y	Y	Y
5 Edwards	Y	N	Y	Y	Y	Y	Y	N
6 English	Y	N	Y	N	?	Y	Y	N
OREGON								
1 AuCoin	#	#	#	?	?	Y	Y	Y
2 Ullman	Y	Y	Y	N	N	Y	Y	Y
3 Duncan	#	#	#	▮	?	#	#	#
4 Weaver	Y	N	Y	N	N	Y	Y	N
PENNSYLVANIA								
1 Myers, M.	Y	?	?	?	?	Y	Y	Y
2 Nix	?	?	?	?	?	?	?	?
3 Lederer	Y	✓	?	?	?	Y	Y	Y
4 Eilberg	Y	Y	Y	N	N	Y	Y	Y
5 Schulze	Y	Y	Y	Y	Y	Y	Y	N
6 Yatron	Y	Y	Y	N	Y	Y	Y	Y
7 Edgar	Y	Y	Y	N	N	Y	Y	Y
8 Kostmayer	Y	Y	Y	N	N	Y	Y	Y
9 Shuster	Y	N	Y	Y	Y	Y	Y	N
10 McDade	Y	Y	Y	N	N	#	#	#
11 Flood	Y	Y	Y	N	N	Y	Y	Y
12 Murtha	Y	Y	Y	Y	Y	Y	Y	Y
13 Coughlin	Y	Y	Y	N	Y	Y	Y	Y
14 Moorhead	Y	Y	Y	N	N	Y	Y	Y
15 Rooney	Y	Y	?	N	?	?	?	?
16 Walker	Y	N	Y	Y	Y	Y	N	N
17 Ertel	Y	Y	Y	N	Y	?	?	Y
18 Walgren	Y	Y	Y	N	N	Y	Y	Y
19 Goodling, W.	Y	N	Y	Y	Y	?	?	?
20 Gaydos	?	?	?	?	?	Y	Y	Y
21 Dent	#	#	#	▮	#	Y	Y	Y
22 Murphy	Y	#	#	▮	?	Y	Y	Y
23 Ammerman	Y	✓	?	?	?	?	?	?
24 Marks	Y	Y	Y	N	N	Y	Y	Y
25 Myers, G.	Y	Y	Y	Y	Y	Y	Y	Y
RHODE ISLAND								
1 St Germain	?	?	?	?	?	Y	Y	Y
2 Beard	#	Y	Y	N	N	Y	Y	Y
SOUTH CAROLINA								
1 Davis	Y	N	?	N	Y	Y	N	N
2 Spence	Y	N	Y	N	Y	Y	Y	N
3 Derrick	Y	Y	Y	N	N	Y	Y	Y
4 Mann	Y	N	Y	?	Y	?	?	?
5 Holland	Y	Y	Y	N	Y	Y	Y	Y
6 Jenrette	Y	N	Y	N	Y	Y	Y	N
SOUTH DAKOTA								
1 Pressler	Y	Y	Y	N	Y	Y	Y	Y
2 Abdnor	#	#	#	#	#	Y	Y	Y
TENNESSEE								
1 Quillen	Y	Y	Y	Y	Y	N	Y	N
2 Duncan	Y	Y	Y	Y	Y	Y	Y	N
3 Lloyd	#	#	#	▮	#	#	#	#
4 Gore	Y	Y	Y	N	N	Y	Y	?
5 Vacancy								
6 Beard	#	#	#	▮	#	Y	Y	N
7 Jones	Y	Y	Y	N	Y	#	#	#
8 Ford	Y	Y	Y	N	N	?	?	?
TEXAS								
1 Hall	Y	N	Y	Y	Y	Y	Y	Y
2 Wilson, C.	Y	Y	Y	N	?	Y	Y	Y
3 Collins	Y	N	N	Y	Y	N	N	N
4 Roberts	?	X	?	?	?	Y	N	N
5 Mattox	Y	Y	Y	N	N	Y	Y	Y
6 Teague	?	X	?	?	?	?	?	?
7 Archer	Y	N	?	Y	Y	Y	Y	N
8 Eckhardt	Y	Y	Y	N	N	?	?	?
9 Brooks	Y	Y	Y	N	Y	Y	Y	Y
10 Pickle	#	#	#	▮	#	#	Y	Y
11 Poage	Y	N	Y	Y	Y	Y	N	N
12 Wright	Y	Y	Y	N	N	Y	Y	Y
13 Hightower	Y	Y	Y	N	?	Y	Y	Y
14 Young	?	Y	Y	N	Y	Y	?	Y
15 de la Garza	Y	Y	Y	N	Y	Y	Y	Y
16 White	Y	Y	Y	N	Y	Y	Y	Y
17 Burleson	Y	N	Y	N	Y	Y	Y	N
18 Jordan	Y	Y	Y	N	N	Y	Y	Y
19 Mahon	Y	N	Y	N	Y	Y	Y	Y
20 Gonzalez	?	Y	Y	N	N	?	Y	Y
21 Krueger	#	#	#	▮	#	#	Y	Y
22 Gammage	Y	Y	Y	N	Y	Y	Y	Y
23 Kazen	?	?	?	?	?	Y	Y	Y
24 Milford	?	?	?	?	?	?	?	?
UTAH								
1 McKay	Y	Y	Y	Y	Y	#	#	#
2 Marriott	Y	N	Y	Y	Y	Y	Y	Y
VERMONT								
AL Jeffords	Y	Y	Y	N	N	?	?	?
VIRGINIA								
1 Trible	Y	Y	Y	Y	Y	Y	Y	N
2 Whitehurst	Y	Y	Y	Y	Y	Y	Y	Y
3 Satterfield	Y	N	Y	Y	Y	Y	Y	N
4 Daniel	Y	N	Y	Y	Y	Y	Y	N
5 Daniel	Y	N	Y	Y	Y	Y	Y	Y
6 Butler	Y	Y	Y	Y	Y	?	?	?
7 Robinson	Y	Y	Y	Y	Y	Y	Y	N
8 Harris	#	Y	Y	N	N	Y	Y	Y
9 Wampler	?	?	?	?	?	Y	Y	N
10 Fisher	Y	Y	Y	N	N	Y	Y	Y
WASHINGTON								
1 Pritchard	Y	Y	Y	N	N	Y	Y	Y
2 Meeds	#	#	#	▮	▮	Y	Y	Y
3 Bonker	#	#	#	▮	#	#	#	#
4 McCormack	?	N	Y	N	Y	?	?	?
5 Foley	Y	N	Y	N	Y	Y	Y	Y
6 Dicks	?	?	?	?	?	Y	Y	Y
7 Cunningham	Y	N	Y	N	Y	Y	Y	N
WEST VIRGINIA								
1 Mollohan	Y	Y	Y	Y	Y	Y	Y	Y
2 Staggers	Y	Y	Y	N	N	Y	Y	Y
3 Slack	Y	Y	Y	Y	Y	Y	Y	Y
4 Rahall	Y	†	Y	N	N	Y	Y	Y
WISCONSIN								
1 Aspin	?	?	?	?	?	Y	Y	Y
2 Kastenmeier	Y	Y	Y	N	?	Y	Y	Y
3 Baldus	Y	Y	Y	N	N	Y	Y	Y
4 Zablocki	Y	Y	Y	N	Y	Y	Y	Y
5 Reuss	Y	Y	Y	N	N	Y	Y	Y
6 Steiger	Y	Y	Y	N	Y	N	Y	N
7 Obey	?	?	?	?	?	Y	Y	Y
8 Cornell	Y	Y	Y	N	N	Y	Y	Y
9 Kasten	?	?	?	?	?	Y	Y	N
WYOMING								
AL Roncalio	#	#	#	▮	▮	#	#	#

Democrats ***Republicans***

544. HR 12514. Foreign Military Aid. Zablocki, D-Wis., motion to resolve into the Committee of the Whole to consider the bill to authorize fiscal 1979 funds. Motion agreed to 317-11: R 111-8; D 206-3 (ND 144-2; SD 62-1), July 31, 1978.

545. HR 12972. Social Security Work Disincentives. Corman, D-Calif., motion to suspend the rules and pass the bill to remove certain work disincentives for the disabled under the Supplemental Security Income benefits program. Motion agreed to 399-4: R 136-1; D 263-3 (ND 186-1; SD 77-2), Aug. 1, 1978. A two-thirds majority vote (269 in this case) is required for passage under suspension of the rules.

546. H J Res 963. National POW-MIA Recognition Day. Lehman, D-Fla., motion to suspend the rules and pass the joint resolution to declare July 18, 1979, to be National POW-MIA Recognition Day. Motion agreed to 401-2: R 136-1; D 265-1 (ND 187-1; SD 78-0), Aug. 1, 1978. A two-thirds majority vote (269 in this case) is required for passage under suspension of the rules.

547. HR 4030. Private Foundations' Stock Holdings. Passage of the bill to amend the Internal Revenue Code to allow certain private foundations to retain for 10 years the excess over the legal existing amount of the stock of certain public utilities without being subject to the excise tax on excess business holdings. Passed 317-86: R 136-2; D 181-84 (ND 111-74; SD 70-10), Aug. 1, 1978.

548. HR 12514. Foreign Military Aid. Wright, D-Texas, amendment, to the Fascell, D-Fla., amendment, to lift the U.S. arms embargo against Turkey when the president certified to Congress that the action was in the national interest of the United States and NATO and that Turkey was acting in good faith to achieve a settlement of the Cyprus problem. Adopted 208-205: R 78-64; D 130-141 (ND 64-123; SD 66-18), Aug. 1, 1978. A "yea" was a vote supporting the president's position. (The Fascell amendment, as amended, was adopted subsequently by voice vote.)

549. HR 12514. Foreign Military Aid. Derwinski, R-Ill., substitute amendment, to the Stratton, D-N.Y., amendment *(see vote 550, below)*, to express the sense of Congress that further withdrawal of U.S. ground forces from South Korea "may risk upsetting" the military balance in that region, and to require "full advance consultation with Congress" before any withdrawal occurs. Adopted 212-189: R 43-97; D 169-92 (ND 145-33; SD 24-59), Aug. 1, 1978. A "yea" was a vote supporting the president's position. (This language replaced Stratton's proposal that would have cut to $90 million from $800 million — the amount President Carter requested — the authorization for the transfer to South Korea of U.S. military equipment pursuant to the troop withdrawal; Stratton's purpose was to undercut Carter's withdrawal plan.)

550. HR 12514. Foreign Military Aid. Stratton, D-N.Y., amendment, as amended by the Derwinski, R-Ill., substitute amendment *(see vote 549, above)*. Adopted 279-117: R 129-10; D 150-107 (ND 73-101; SD 77-6), Aug. 1, 1978. A "yea" was a vote supporting the president's position.

KEY

- Y Voted for (yea).
- ✓ Paired for.
- † Announced for.
- # CQ Poll for.
- N Voted against (nay).
- X Paired against.
- \- Announced against.
- ▮ CQ Poll against.
- P Voted "present."
- ● Voted "present" to avoid possible conflict of interest.
- ? Did not vote or otherwise make a position known.

	544	545	546	547	548	549	550
ALABAMA							
1 Edwards	Y	Y	Y	Y	Y	N	Y
2 Dickinson	Y	Y	Y	Y	Y	N	N
3 Nichols	Y	Y	Y	Y	Y	N	Y
4 Bevill	Y	Y	Y	Y	Y	N	Y
5 Flippo	Y	Y	Y	N	Y	N	Y
6 Buchanan	Y	Y	Y	Y	N	Y	Y
7 Flowers	?	Y	Y	Y	N	N	Y
ALASKA							
AL Young	Y	Y	Y	Y	N	N	Y
ARIZONA							
1 Rhodes	Y	Y	Y	Y	Y	Y	Y
2 Udall	Y	Y	Y	Y	Y	Y	N
3 Stump	N	Y	Y	Y	Y	N	Y
4 Rudd	Y	Y	Y	Y	Y	N	Y
ARKANSAS							
1 Alexander	Y	Y	Y	Y	Y	N	Y
2 Tucker	#	Y	Y	#	Y	Y	Y
3 Hammerschmidt	Y	Y	Y	Y	Y	N	Y
4 Thornton	Y	Y	Y	Y	Y	Y	Y
CALIFORNIA							
1 Johnson	Y	Y	Y	Y	N	Y	N
2 Clausen	Y	Y	Y	Y	N	Y	Y
3 Moss	Y	Y	Y	Y	Y	?	?
4 Leggett	Y	Y	Y	Y	Y	Y	Y
5 Burton, J.	?	Y	Y	N	N	Y	N
6 Burton, P.	Y	Y	Y	N	N	Y	N
7 Miller	Y	Y	Y	N	N	Y	?
8 Dellums	Y	Y	Y	N	N	N	N
9 Stark	Y	Y	Y	Y	N	Y	▮
10 Edwards	Y	Y	Y	Y	N	Y	N
11 Ryan	Y	Y	Y	N	Y	?	Y
12 McCloskey	?	Y	?	Y	Y	Y	Y
13 Mineta	Y	Y	Y	Y	N	Y	N
14 McFall	Y	Y	Y	Y	Y	Y	N
15 Sisk	?	Y	Y	Y	Y	?	?
16 Panetta	Y	Y	Y	N	N	Y	Y
17 Krebs	Y	Y	Y	N	N	Y	N
18 Vacancy							
19 Lagomarsino	Y	Y	Y	Y	Y	N	Y
20 Goldwater	?	Y	Y	Y	Y	N	Y
21 Corman	Y	Y	Y	N	Y	Y	N
22 Moorhead	Y	Y	Y	Y	N	N	Y
23 Beilenson	Y	Y	Y	Y	N	Y	N
24 Waxman	#	Y	Y	N	N	Y	N
25 Roybal	Y	Y	Y	N	N	Y	N
26 Rousselot	N	?	?	?	N	N	Y
27 Dornan	Y	Y	Y	Y	N	N	Y
28 Burke	?	Y	Y	#	N	Y	N
29 Hawkins	Y	Y	Y	N	Y	✓	?
30 Danielson	Y	Y	Y	Y	Y	Y	N
31 Wilson, C.H.	Y	Y	Y	?	Y	?	?
32 Anderson	Y	Y	Y	N	N	Y	N
33 Clawson	Y	Y	Y	Y	N	N	Y
34 Hannaford	Y	Y	Y	Y	N	Y	N
35 Lloyd	?	Y	Y	Y	Y	N	Y
36 Brown	?	Y	Y	N	Y	Y	Y
37 Pettis	?	Y	Y	Y	Y	N	Y
38 Patterson	Y	Y	Y	N	N	Y	N
39 Wiggins	Y	Y	Y	Y	Y	N	Y
40 Badham	Y	Y	Y	Y	Y	N	Y
41 Wilson, B.	N	Y	Y	Y	Y	N	Y
42 Van Deerlin	Y	Y	Y	N	Y	?	?
43 Burgener	Y	Y	Y	Y	Y	N	Y
COLORADO							
1 Schroeder	Y	Y	N	N	N	Y	N
2 Wirth	?	Y	Y	Y	Y	Y	N
3 Evans	?	Y	Y	N	Y	Y	N
4 Johnson	?	Y	Y	Y	N	N	N
5 Armstrong	Y	Y	Y	Y	N	N	Y
CONNECTICUT							
1 Cotter	Y	Y	Y	Y	N	Y	Y
2 Dodd	Y	Y	Y	Y	N	Y	Y
3 Giaimo	Y	Y	Y	Y	N	?	?
4 McKinney	Y	Y	Y	Y	N	Y	Y
5 Sarasin	#	#	#	#	▮	#	#
6 Moffett	Y	Y	Y	Y	N	Y	N
DELAWARE							
AL Evans	Y	Y	Y	Y	N	N	Y
FLORIDA							
1 Sikes	Y	Y	Y	Y	Y	N	Y
2 Fuqua	Y	Y	Y	Y	N	Y	Y
3 Bennett	Y	N	Y	N	Y	N	Y
4 Chappell	Y	Y	Y	Y	Y	N	N
5 Kelly	Y	Y	Y	Y	N	Y	Y
6 Young	Y	Y	Y	Y	Y	N	Y
7 Gibbons	Y	Y	Y	N	Y	Y	Y
8 Ireland	Y	Y	Y	N	N	N	Y
9 Frey	?	Y	Y	Y	N	N	Y
10 Bafalis	Y	Y	Y	Y	Y	N	Y
11 Rogers	Y	Y	#	Y	Y	Y	Y
12 Burke	Y	Y	Y	Y	N	N	Y
13 Lehman	Y	Y	Y	N	Y	Y	Y
14 Pepper	#	Y	Y	Y	Y	Y	Y
15 Fascell	Y	Y	Y	N	N	Y	N
GEORGIA							
1 Ginn	Y	Y	Y	Y	Y	N	Y
2 Mathis	?	?	?	?	?	?	?
3 Brinkley	?	Y	Y	Y	Y	N	N
4 Levitas	?	Y	Y	Y	N	N	Y
5 Fowler	?	?	?	Y	N	N	Y
6 Flynt	Y	Y	Y	Y	Y	N	Y
7 McDonald	▮	Y	Y	Y	Y	N	Y
8 Evans	?	Y	Y	Y	Y	N	Y
9 Jenkins	#	#	?	#	#	#	#
10 Barnard	Y	Y	Y	Y	N	N	Y
HAWAII							
1 Heftel	Y	Y	Y	Y	Y	Y	Y
2 Akaka	#	Y	Y	Y	Y	N	Y
IDAHO							
1 Symms	N	Y	Y	Y	Y	N	Y
2 Hansen, G.	N	Y	Y	Y	N	N	Y
ILLINOIS							
1 Metcalfe	?	Y	Y	N	N	Y	N
2 Murphy	Y	Y	Y	Y	N	Y	Y
3 Russo	#	Y	Y	Y	N	Y	Y
4 Derwinski	Y	Y	Y	Y	N	Y	Y
5 Fary	Y	Y	Y	Y	N	Y	N
6 Hyde	Y	Y	Y	Y	Y	N	Y
7 Collins	?	?	?	?	?	?	?
8 Rostenkowski	Y	Y	Y	Y	Y	Y	Y
9 Yates	Y	Y	Y	N	N	Y	N
10 Mikva	Y	Y	Y	Y	N	Y	N
11 Annunzio	Y	Y	Y	Y	N	Y	N
12 Crane	Y	Y	Y	Y	N	N	Y
13 McClory	#	Y	Y	Y	Y	N	Y
14 Erlenborn	#	Y	Y	Y	Y	Y	Y
15 Corcoran	Y	Y	Y	Y	N	N	Y
16 Anderson	Y	Y	Y	Y	Y	Y	Y
17 O'Brien	Y	Y	Y	Y	N	Y	Y
18 Michel	Y	Y	Y	Y	Y	Y	Y
19 Railsback	?	Y	Y	Y	Y	Y	Y
20 Findley	Y	Y	Y	Y	Y	N	Y
21 Madigan	Y	Y	Y	Y	Y	?	?
22 Shipley	?	Y	Y	Y	Y	Y	Y
23 Price	Y	Y	Y	Y	Y	N	N
24 Simon	Y	Y	Y	Y	Y	Y	Y
INDIANA							
1 Benjamin	Y	Y	Y	N	N	Y	Y
2 Fithian	Y	Y	Y	Y	N	Y	Y
3 Brademas	Y	Y	Y	Y	N	Y	Y
4 Quayle	N	Y	Y	Y	Y	Y	Y
5 Hillis	Y	Y	Y	Y	Y	N	Y
6 Evans	Y	Y	Y	N	N	N	Y
7 Myers, J.	Y	Y	Y	Y	N	N	Y
8 Cornwell	?	Y	Y	Y	Y	Y	Y
9 Hamilton	Y	Y	Y	Y	Y	Y	Y
10 Sharp	Y	Y	Y	Y	Y	Y	N
11 Jacobs	Y	Y	Y	N	N	N	N
IOWA							
1 Leach	Y	Y	Y	Y	Y	Y	N
2 Blouin	Y	Y	Y	Y	N	Y	N
3 Grassley	Y	Y	Y	Y	N	N	Y
4 Smith	Y	Y	Y	Y	Y	Y	Y
5 Harkin	?	Y	Y	N	N	Y	N
6 Bedell	Y	N	Y	N	Y	Y	N

Democrats ***Republicans***

	544	545	546	547	548	549	550
KANSAS							
1 Sebelius	Y	Y	Y	Y	Y	N	Y
2 Keys	Y	Y	Y	N	Y	N	N
3 Winn	Y	Y	Y	Y	Y	N	Y
4 Glickman	Y	Y	Y	Y	Y	Y	Y
5 Skubitz	?	Y	Y	Y	Y	N	Y
KENTUCKY							
1 Hubbard	#	Y	Y	Y	Y	N	Y
2 Natcher	Y	Y	Y	Y	Y	N	Y
3 Mazzoli	Y	Y	Y	Y	Y	Y	Y
4 Snyder	Y	Y	Y	Y	Y	N	Y
5 Carter	Y	Y	Y	Y	Y	N	Y
6 Breckinridge	Y	Y	Y	Y	Y	N	Y
7 Perkins	Y	Y	Y	Y	Y	N	Y
LOUISIANA							
1 Livingston	Y	Y	Y	Y	Y	N	Y
2 Boggs	Y	Y	Y	Y	N	N	Y
3 Treen	Y	Y	Y	Y	Y	N	Y
4 Waggonner	Y	Y	Y	Y	Y	N	Y
5 Huckaby	Y	Y	Y	Y	Y	N	Y
6 Moore	Y	Y	Y	Y	Y	N	Y
7 Breaux	?	?	?	?	✓	X	?
8 Long	Y	Y	Y	Y	Y	Y	Y
MAINE							
1 Emery	Y	Y	Y	Y	N	N	Y
2 Cohen	#	Y	Y	Y	N	N	Y
MARYLAND							
1 Bauman	Y	Y	Y	Y	N	N	Y
2 Long	Y	Y	Y	Y	N	N	Y
3 Mikulski	?	Y	Y	Y	N	Y	N
4 Holt	Y	Y	Y	Y	N	N	Y
5 Spellman	Y	Y	Y	Y	N	Y	Y
6 Byron	Y	Y	Y	N	N	N	Y
7 Mitchell	N	Y	Y	N	N	Y	N
8 Steers	Y	Y	Y	Y	N	Y	Y
MASSACHUSETTS							
1 Conte	Y	Y	Y	Y	N	Y	Y
2 Boland	Y	Y	Y	Y	N	Y	Y
3 Early	Y	Y	Y	Y	Y	Y	N
4 Drinan	Y	Y	Y	N	N	Y	N
5 Tsongas	?	Y	Y	N	N	Y	?
6 Harrington	#	#	?	▮	N	Y	N
7 Markey	Y	Y	Y	N	N	?	?
8 O'Neill							
9 Moakley	Y	Y	Y	Y	N	Y	Y
10 Heckler	Y	Y	Y	?	N	Y	N
11 Burke	?	?	?	?	X	✓	?
12 Studds	Y	Y	Y	N	N	Y	N
MICHIGAN							
1 Conyers	▮	#	#	▮	▮	✓	▮
2 Pursell	?	?	Y	Y	N	Y	Y
3 Brown	Y	Y	Y	Y	Y	N	Y
4 Stockman	Y	Y	Y	Y	Y	N	#
5 Sawyer	#	Y	Y	Y	Y	N	Y
6 Carr	Y	Y	Y	N	N	Y	N
7 Kildee	Y	Y	Y	N	N	Y	N
8 Traxler	Y	Y	Y	Y	N	Y	N
9 Vander Jagt	Y	Y	Y	Y	Y	N	Y
10 Cederberg	?	Y	Y	Y	Y	Y	Y
11 Ruppe	?	Y	Y	Y	Y	Y	Y
12 Bonior	#	Y	Y	N	N	Y	N
13 Diggs	Y	Y	Y	Y	N	Y	?
14 Nedzi	Y	Y	Y	Y	N	Y	N
15 Ford	?	Y	Y	Y	N	Y	N
16 Dingell	Y	Y	Y	N	N	Y	N
17 Brodhead	Y	Y	Y	N	N	Y	N
18 Blanchard	Y	Y	Y	Y	N	Y	N
19 Broomfield	Y	Y	Y	Y	Y	Y	Y
MINNESOTA							
1 Quie	?	Y	Y	Y	N	Y	Y
2 Hagedorn	Y	Y	Y	Y	Y	N	Y
3 Frenzel	Y	Y	Y	Y	Y	Y	Y
4 Vento	Y	Y	Y	N	N	Y	N
5 Fraser	?	?	?	?	?	?	?
6 Nolan	?	Y	Y	Y	N	Y	N
7 Stangeland	Y	Y	Y	Y	N	N	Y
8 Oberstar	Y	Y	Y	Y	N	Y	N
MISSISSIPPI							
1 Whitten	Y	Y	#	Y	Y	N	Y
2 Bowen	Y	Y	Y	Y	Y	N	Y
3 Montgomery	Y	Y	Y	Y	Y	N	Y
4 Cochran	Y	Y	Y	Y	N	?	?
5 Lott	Y	Y	Y	Y	Y	N	Y
MISSOURI							
1 Clay	?	Y	Y	?	N	Y	N
2 Young	Y	Y	Y	N	Y	N	Y
3 Gephardt	Y	Y	Y	Y	Y	Y	Y
4 Skelton	Y	Y	Y	Y	Y	N	Y
5 Bolling	Y	Y	Y	Y	Y	N	N
6 Coleman	?	Y	Y	Y	Y	N	N
7 Taylor	Y	Y	Y	Y	Y	N	Y
8 Ichord	Y	Y	Y	Y	Y	N	Y
9 Volkmer	Y	Y	Y	N	Y	Y	Y
10 Burlison	Y	Y	Y	N	?	?	?
MONTANA							
1 Baucus	Y	Y	Y	Y	N	Y	?
2 Marlenee	Y	Y	Y	Y	N	Y	Y
NEBRASKA							
1 Thone	?	Y	Y	Y	Y	N	Y
2 Cavanaugh	Y	Y	Y	N	N	Y	N
3 Smith	Y	Y	Y	Y	Y	N	Y
NEVADA							
AL Santini	#	Y	Y	Y	N	N	Y
NEW HAMPSHIRE							
1 D'Amours	Y	Y	Y	Y	N	Y	Y
2 Cleveland	?	Y	Y	Y	Y	N	Y
NEW JERSEY							
1 Florio	Y	Y	Y	Y	N	Y	Y
2 Hughes	Y	Y	Y	Y	N	Y	Y
3 Howard	Y	Y	Y	Y	N	Y	Y
4 Thompson	Y	Y	Y	N	N	Y	N
5 Fenwick	Y	Y	Y	Y	Y	Y	N
6 Forsythe	#	Y	Y	Y	N	Y	Y
7 Maguire	?	#	#	?	▮	▮	?
8 Roe	Y	Y	Y	Y	N	Y	Y
9 Hollenbeck	Y	Y	Y	Y	N	N	Y
10 Rodino	#	#	#	#	▮	#	#
11 Minish	Y	Y	Y	N	N	Y	Y
12 Rinaldo	Y	Y	Y	Y	N	Y	Y
13 Meyner	Y	Y	Y	Y	N	Y	N
14 LeFante	#	#	#	#	X	#	#
15 Patten	Y	Y	Y	Y	Y	Y	N
NEW MEXICO							
1 Lujan	N	Y	Y	Y	N	N	Y
2 Runnels	?	Y	Y	Y	Y	N	Y
NEW YORK							
1 Pike	Y	Y	Y	Y	N	Y	N
2 Downey	#	Y	Y	Y	N	Y	N
3 Ambro	Y	Y	Y	Y	N	Y	Y
4 Lent	Y	Y	Y	Y	N	N	Y
5 Wydler	Y	Y	Y	N	N	N	Y
6 Wolff	Y	Y	Y	Y	N	Y	N
7 Addabbo	?	Y	Y	Y	N	Y	N
8 Rosenthal	Y	Y	Y	N	N	Y	N
9 Delaney	Y	Y	Y	N	N	N	N
10 Biaggi	?	Y	Y	Y	N	Y	N
11 Scheuer	Y	Y	Y	N	N	Y	N
12 Chisholm	Y	Y	Y	N	N	Y	N
13 Solarz	Y	Y	Y	Y	Y	Y	N
14 Richmond	?	Y	Y	N	N	Y	N
15 Zeferetti	#	Y	Y	Y	N	N	Y
16 Holtzman	Y	Y	Y	N	N	Y	N
17 Murphy	Y	Y	Y	Y	N	Y	Y
18 Green	Y	Y	Y	Y	N	Y	N
19 Rangel	?	Y	Y	N	N	Y	Y
20 Weiss	?	Y	Y	N	N	Y	N
21 Garcia	#	#	Y	N	Y	Y	Y
22 Bingham	Y	Y	Y	Y	Y	Y	N
23 Caputo	?	Y	Y	Y	N	?	?
24 Ottinger	Y	Y	Y	N	N	Y	N
25 Fish	Y	Y	Y	Y	N	N	Y
26 Gilman	Y	Y	Y	Y	N	N	Y
27 McHugh	Y	Y	Y	Y	Y	Y	N
28 Stratton	Y	Y	Y	Y	Y	N	Y
29 Pattison	Y	Y	Y	N	Y	Y	N
30 McEwen	Y	Y	Y	Y	Y	Y	N
31 Mitchell	?	Y	Y	Y	Y	N	Y
32 Hanley	Y	Y	Y	Y	N	Y	N
33 Walsh	Y	Y	Y	Y	Y	Y	Y
34 Horton	Y	Y	Y	Y	N	Y	Y
35 Conable	Y	Y	Y	Y	Y	Y	Y
36 LaFalce	#	Y	Y	Y	Y	Y	N
37 Nowak	Y	?	?	Y	Y	N	Y
38 Kemp	Y	Y	Y	Y	Y	Y	Y
39 Lundine	Y	Y	Y	Y	Y	Y	N
NORTH CAROLINA							
1 Jones	Y	Y	Y	Y	Y	N	Y
2 Fountain	Y	Y	Y	Y	Y	N	Y
3 Whitley	Y	Y	Y	Y	N	N	Y
4 Andrews	Y	Y	Y	Y	Y	Y	Y
5 Neal	Y	Y	Y	Y	Y	Y	Y
6 Preyer	Y	Y	Y	Y	Y	Y	Y
7 Rose	?	Y	Y	Y	N	N	Y
8 Hefner	Y	Y	Y	Y	Y	N	Y
9 Martin	Y	Y	Y	Y	N	N	Y
10 Broyhill	Y	Y	Y	Y	Y	N	Y
11 Gudger	Y	Y	Y	Y	N	Y	Y
NORTH DAKOTA							
AL Andrews	Y	Y	Y	Y	N	N	Y
OHIO							
1 Gradison	Y	Y	Y	Y	Y	Y	Y
2 Luken	?	Y	Y	Y	N	N	N
3 Whalen	#	#	#	#	✓	▮	?
4 Guyer	Y	Y	Y	Y	N	Y	Y
5 Latta	Y	Y	Y	Y	Y	N	Y
6 Harsha	Y	Y	Y	Y	N	N	N
7 Brown	Y	?	?	?	Y	N	Y
8 Kindness	Y	Y	Y	Y	Y	N	Y
9 Ashley	Y	Y	Y	Y	N	Y	Y
10 Miller	Y	Y	Y	Y	N	N	Y
11 Stanton	Y	Y	Y	Y	Y	Y	Y
12 Devine	Y	Y	Y	Y	N	N	Y
13 Pease	Y	Y	Y	N	Y	Y	N
14 Seiberling	Y	Y	Y	N	N	Y	N
15 Wylie	Y	Y	Y	Y	N	N	Y
16 Regula	Y	Y	Y	Y	Y	Y	Y
17 Ashbrook	Y	Y	Y	Y	N	N	Y
18 Applegate	Y	Y	Y	Y	N	N	Y
19 Carney	Y	Y	Y	N	N	Y	Y
20 Oakar	Y	Y	Y	N	N	N	Y
21 Stokes	Y	Y	Y	N	N	Y	N
22 Vanik	Y	Y	Y	N	N	Y	Y
23 Mottl	Y	Y	Y	N	N	N	Y
OKLAHOMA							
1 Jones	Y	Y	Y	Y	Y	N	Y
2 Risenhoover	?	Y	Y	Y	✓	X	?
3 Watkins	Y	Y	Y	Y	Y	N	Y
4 Steed	Y	Y	Y	Y	Y	N	Y
5 Edwards	N	Y	Y	Y	N	N	Y
6 English	?	Y	Y	Y	Y	N	Y
OREGON							
1 AuCoin	#	Y	Y	N	N	Y	N
2 Ullman	Y	Y	Y	Y	Y	▮	#
3 Duncan	#	Y	Y	Y	Y	N	Y
4 Weaver	Y	Y	Y	N	Y	Y	N
PENNSYLVANIA							
1 Myers, M.	?	Y	Y	Y	N	Y	Y
2 Nix	?	Y	Y	Y	Y	Y	Y
3 Lederer	Y	Y	Y	Y	N	Y	Y
4 Eilberg	Y	Y	Y	Y	X	✓	?
5 Schulze	Y	Y	Y	Y	Y	N	Y
6 Yatron	Y	Y	Y	N	N	Y	N
7 Edgar	#	Y	Y	N	N	Y	N
8 Kostmayer	Y	Y	Y	N	N	Y	Y
9 Shuster	Y	Y	Y	Y	Y	N	Y
10 McDade	#	?	?	?	?	?	?
11 Flood	Y	Y	Y	Y	N	Y	Y
12 Murtha	Y	Y	Y	Y	Y	N	Y
13 Coughlin	Y	Y	Y	Y	Y	Y	Y
14 Moorhead	Y	Y	Y	Y	Y	Y	N
15 Rooney	?	Y	Y	N	N	Y	N
16 Walker	Y	Y	Y	Y	N	N	Y
17 Ertel	Y	Y	Y	Y	N	N	Y
18 Walgren	Y	Y	Y	Y	N	Y	Y
19 Goodling, W.	?	?	?	?	?	?	Y
20 Gaydos	Y	Y	Y	Y	N	N	Y
21 Dent	Y	?	#	#	X	X	#
22 Murphy	#	Y	Y	N	N	N	Y
23 Ammerman	?	Y	Y	Y	Y	Y	Y
24 Marks	Y	Y	Y	Y	N	Y	Y
25 Myers, G.	Y	N	N	N	N	N	N
RHODE ISLAND							
1 St Germain	Y	Y	Y	N	N	Y	N
2 Beard	Y	Y	Y	Y	N	N	N
SOUTH CAROLINA							
1 Davis	N	Y	Y	Y	N	N	Y
2 Spence	Y	Y	Y	Y	N	N	Y
3 Derrick	Y	Y	Y	Y	Y	Y	N
4 Mann	?	Y	Y	Y	Y	N	Y
5 Holland	Y	Y	Y	?	Y	Y	Y
6 Jenrette	Y	Y	Y	Y	Y	N	Y
SOUTH DAKOTA							
1 Pressler	Y	Y	Y	Y	N	Y	Y
2 Abdnor	Y	Y	Y	Y	Y	N	Y
TENNESSEE							
1 Quillen	Y	Y	Y	Y	Y	N	Y
2 Duncan	Y	Y	Y	Y	N	N	Y
3 Lloyd	#	Y	Y	Y	Y	N	Y
4 Gore	#	Y	Y	N	Y	Y	Y
5 Vacancy							
6 Beard	#	#	#	Y	Y	N	Y
7 Jones	#	#	#	?	Y	N	Y
8 Ford	?	?	?	?	N	Y	Y
TEXAS							
1 Hall	Y	Y	Y	Y	Y	N	Y
2 Wilson, C.	Y	Y	Y	Y	Y	N	Y
3 Collins	N	Y	Y	Y	Y	N	Y
4 Roberts	Y	Y	Y	Y	Y	N	Y
5 Mattox	Y	Y	Y	N	N	Y	N
6 Teague	?	?	?	?	✓	X	?
7 Archer	Y	Y	Y	Y	Y	N	Y
8 Eckhardt	?	?	Y	Y	N	Y	N
9 Brooks	Y	Y	Y	Y	Y	N	Y
10 Pickle	Y	N	Y	Y	Y	Y	Y
11 Poage	Y	Y	Y	Y	Y	N	Y
12 Wright	Y	Y	Y	Y	Y	N	Y
13 Hightower	Y	Y	Y	Y	Y	N	Y
14 Young	?	?	?	Y	Y	?	?
15 de la Garza	Y	Y	Y	Y	Y	N	Y
16 White	Y	Y	Y	Y	Y	N	Y
17 Burleson	Y	Y	Y	Y	Y	N	Y
18 Jordan	Y	Y	Y	Y	Y	Y	Y
19 Mahon	Y	Y	Y	Y	Y	N	Y
20 Gonzalez	Y	Y	Y	Y	Y	N	Y
21 Krueger	Y	Y	Y	Y	Y	N	Y
22 Gammage	Y	Y	Y	Y	N	N	Y
23 Kazen	Y	Y	Y	Y	Y	N	Y
24 Milford	?	?	?	?	Y	N	Y
UTAH							
1 McKay	#	Y	Y	Y	Y	Y	Y
2 Marriott	Y	Y	Y	Y	N	N	Y
VERMONT							
AL Jeffords	?	Y	Y	Y	Y	Y	Y
VIRGINIA							
1 Trible	Y	Y	Y	Y	N	N	Y
2 Whitehurst	Y	Y	Y	Y	N	N	Y
3 Satterfield	?	Y	Y	N	Y	N	Y
4 Daniel	Y	Y	Y	Y	Y	N	Y
5 Daniel	?	Y	Y	Y	Y	N	Y
6 Butler	Y	Y	Y	Y	Y	N	Y
7 Robinson	Y	Y	Y	Y	Y	N	Y
8 Harris	Y	Y	Y	N	N	Y	Y
9 Wampler	Y	Y	Y	Y	Y	N	Y
10 Fisher	Y	Y	Y	Y	N	Y	Y
WASHINGTON							
1 Pritchard	Y	Y	Y	Y	Y	Y	Y
2 Meeds	Y	Y	Y	Y	Y	Y	N
3 Bonker	#	Y	Y	Y	Y	Y	N
4 McCormack	Y	Y	Y	Y	Y	Y	N
5 Foley	Y	Y	Y	Y	N	Y	Y
6 Dicks	Y	Y	Y	Y	Y	Y	Y
7 Cunningham	Y	Y	Y	Y	N	N	Y
WEST VIRGINIA							
1 Mollohan	Y	Y	Y	Y	N	N	Y
2 Staggers	Y	Y	Y	Y	Y	N	N
3 Slack	Y	Y	Y	Y	N	N	Y
4 Rahall	Y	Y	Y	N	Y	Y	N
WISCONSIN							
1 Aspin	Y	Y	Y	N	Y	Y	N
2 Kastenmeier	Y	Y	Y	N	N	Y	N
3 Baldus	Y	Y	Y	Y	Y	Y	N
4 Zablocki	Y	Y	Y	Y	Y	Y	N
5 Reuss	Y	Y	Y	N	N	Y	N
6 Steiger	Y	Y	Y	▮	Y	Y	Y
7 Obey	Y	Y	Y	Y	Y	Y	N
8 Cornell	Y	Y	Y	Y	Y	N	N
9 Kasten	Y	Y	Y	Y	N	N	Y
WYOMING							
AL Roncalio	#	Y	Y	Y	N	N	Y

Democrats ***Republicans***

551. HR 12514. Foreign Military Aid. Zablocki, D-Wis., motion to resolve into the Committee of the Whole to consider the bill to authorize $999.3 million for foreign military assistance programs for fiscal 1979. Motion agreed to 372-7: R 129-3; D 243-4 (ND 169-2; SD 74-2), Aug. 2, 1978.

552. HR 12514. Foreign Military Aid. Stark, D-Calif., amendment to prohibit delivery of weapons to Chile sold before enactment of the bill. Rejected 146-260: R 19-120; D 127-140 (ND 119-67; SD 8-73), Aug. 2, 1978.

553. HR 12514. Foreign Military Aid. Zablocki, D-Wis., motion to end all debate on the Harkin, D-Iowa, amendment *(see vote 557, below)* to prohibit delivery of weapons sold to Chile before enactment of the bill until the Chilean government turned over to the United States those Chileans indicted for the murders of Orlando Letelier and Ronni Moffitt. Motion rejected 171-228: R 59-78; D 112-150 (ND 65-115; SD 47-35), Aug. 2, 1978.

554. HR 12514. Foreign Military Aid. Jacobs, D-Ind., amendment to prohibit the use of funds in the bill for South Korea until former Korean Ambassador to the United States Kim Dong Jo had given testimony to the Standards of Official Conduct Committee on congressional influence-buying by the Korean government. Rejected 147-257: R 34-103; D 113-154 (ND 103-80; SD 10-74), Aug. 2, 1978.

555. HR 12514. Foreign Military Aid. Findley, R-Ill., amendment, to the Zablocki, D-Wis., substitute amendment to the Bauman, R-Md., amendment *(see vote 556, below)*, to prohibit the enforcement of economic sanctions against Rhodesia before Oct. 1, 1978, but to allow the president to reimpose sanctions if he determined the government of Rhodesia had "refused to participate in good faith" in an all-parties conference and had failed "to schedule for an early date free elections." Rejected 176-229: R 113-25; D 63-204 (ND 15-170; SD 48-34), Aug. 2, 1978. A "nay" was a vote supporting the president's position.

556. HR 12514. Foreign Military Aid. Ichord, D-Mo., amendment, to the Zablocki, D-Wis., substitute amendment to the Bauman, R-Md., amendment, to prohibit the enforcement of sanctions against Rhodesia after Dec. 31, 1978, unless the president determined that a government had not been installed, which was chosen by free elections in which all political groups were allowed to participate freely. Adopted 229-180: R 127-13; D 102-167 (ND 36-151; SD 66-16), Aug. 2, 1978. A "nay" was a vote supporting the president's position. (Both the Zablocki and Bauman amendments, as amended by Ichord, were adopted subsequently by voice votes.) (The Harkin amendment had previously been adopted by voice vote in Committee of the Whole.)

557. HR 12514. Foreign Military Aid. Harkin, D-Iowa, amendment to prohibit delivery of weapons sold to Chile before enactment of the bill until the Chilean government turned over to the United States those Chileans indicted on Aug. 1, 1978, in Washington, D. C., for the murders of Orlando Letelier and Ronni Moffitt in September 1976. Rejected 166-243: R 23-116; D 143-127 (ND 128-60; SD 15-67), Aug. 2, 1978.

558. HR 12514. Foreign Military Aid. Passage of the bill to authorize $999.3 million for foreign military assistance programs of the State Department in fiscal 1979. Passed 255-156: R 73-66; D 182-90 (ND 144-45; SD 38-45), Aug. 2, 1978.

KEY

- Y Voted for (yea).
- ✓ Paired for.
- † Announced for.
- # CQ Poll for.
- N Voted against (nay).
- X Paired against.
- \- Announced against.
- ▮ CQ Poll against.
- P Voted "present."
- ● Voted "present" to avoid possible conflict of interest.
- ? Did not vote or otherwise make a position known.

	551	552	553	554	555	556	557	558
ALABAMA								
1 Edwards	Y	N	Y	N	Y	Y	N	N
2 Dickinson	Y	N	Y	N	Y	Y	N	N
3 Nichols	Y	N	Y	N	Y	Y	N	N
4 Bevill	Y	N	N	N	Y	Y	N	N
5 Flippo	Y	N	Y	Y	Y	Y	N	N
6 Buchanan	?	N	N	N	N	Y	N	Y
7 Flowers	?	?	?	?	?	?	?	?
ALASKA								
AL Young	#	N	Y	N	Y	Y	N	N
ARIZONA								
1 Rhodes	Y	N	Y	Y	Y	Y	N	Y
2 Udall	Y	Y	▮	Y	N	N	Y	Y
3 Stump	Y	N	Y	N	Y	Y	N	N
4 Rudd	Y	N	Y	N	Y	Y	N	N
ARKANSAS								
1 Alexander	Y	N	N	N	N	Y	N	Y
2 Tucker	Y	Y	▮	Y	N	N	Y	Y
3 Hammerschmidt	Y	N	N	N	?	Y	N	N
4 Thornton	Y	N	N	N	N	Y	N	Y
CALIFORNIA								
1 Johnson	Y	N	N	N	N	N	N	Y
2 Clausen	?	N	?	N	Y	Y	Y	N
3 Moss	Y	Y	Y	N	N	N	N	Y
4 Leggett	Y	Y	?	N	Y	Y	Y	Y
5 Burton, J.	?	Y	N	Y	N	N	Y	N
6 Burton, P.	Y	Y	N	Y	N	N	Y	Y
7 Miller	Y	Y	N	Y	N	N	Y	N
8 Dellums	Y	Y	N	#	N	N	Y	N
9 Stark	Y	Y	N	▮	N	N	Y	N
10 Edwards	Y	Y	N	Y	N	N	Y	Y
11 Ryan	Y	Y	Y	Y	N	N	Y	N
12 McCloskey	?	Y	?	Y	N	N	N	Y
13 Mineta	Y	Y	N	Y	N	N	Y	Y
14 McFall	Y	N	Y	N	N	N	N	Y
15 Sisk	Y	N	?	N	N	Y	N	Y
16 Panetta	Y	Y	N	Y	N	N	Y	N
17 Krebs	Y	Y	N	Y	N	N	Y	N
18 Vacancy								
19 Lagomarsino	Y	N	Y	N	Y	Y	N	Y
20 Goldwater	Y	N	N	N	Y	Y	N	Y
21 Corman	Y	Y	N	N	N	N	Y	Y
22 Moorhead	Y	N	N	N	Y	Y	N	N
23 Beilenson	#	Y	N	Y	N	N	Y	Y
24 Waxman	Y	Y	N	Y	N	N	Y	Y
25 Roybal	Y	Y	Y	Y	N	N	Y	N
26 Rousselot	Y	N	N	N	Y	Y	N	N
27 Dornan	Y	Y	N	N	Y	Y	Y	Y
28 Burke	#	Y	N	Y	N	N	Y	Y
29 Hawkins	Y	Y	N	Y	N	N	Y	Y
30 Danielson	Y	N	N	N	N	N	N	Y
31 Wilson, C.H.	Y	N	Y	N	?	Y	N	Y
32 Anderson	Y	Y	N	Y	N	N	Y	N
33 Clawson	Y	N	N	N	Y	Y	N	N
34 Hannaford	Y	Y	Y	Y	N	N	Y	Y
35 Lloyd	N	N	Y	N	N	Y	Y	Y
36 Brown	Y	Y	N	Y	N	N	Y	Y
37 Pettis	Y	N	Y	N	Y	Y	N	Y
38 Patterson	Y	Y	Y	Y	N	N	Y	Y
39 Wiggins	#	▮	Y	N	Y	Y	N	Y
40 Badham	Y	N	N	N	Y	Y	N	N
41 Wilson, B.	N	N	Y	N	Y	Y	N	Y
42 Van Deerlin	Y	Y	Y	N	N	N	Y	Y
43 Burgener	Y	N	N	N	Y	Y	N	Y
COLORADO								
1 Schroeder	Y	Y	N	Y	N	N	Y	N
2 Wirth	Y	Y	Y	N	N	N	Y	Y
3 Evans	#	N	Y	N	N	Y	N	Y
4 Johnson	Y	Y	N	Y	Y	Y	Y	N
5 Armstrong	Y	N	N	Y	Y	Y	N	N
CONNECTICUT								
1 Cotter	Y	N	Y	N	N	N	N	Y
2 Dodd	?	Y	N	N	N	N	Y	Y
3 Giaimo	Y	N	N	N	N	N	N	Y
4 McKinney	Y	Y	N	N	N	Y	Y	Y
5 Sarasin	Y	N	N	N	Y	Y	N	Y
6 Moffett	Y	Y	N	Y	N	N	Y	N
DELAWARE								
AL Evans	Y	N	N	N	Y	Y	N	Y
FLORIDA								
1 Sikes	Y	?	Y	N	Y	Y	N	Y
2 Fuqua	Y	N	Y	N	N	Y	N	Y
3 Bennett	Y	N	N	N	N	Y	N	N
4 Chappell	Y	N	Y	N	Y	Y	N	N
5 Kelly	Y	N	N	N	Y	Y	N	N
6 Young	Y	N	N	N	Y	Y	N	Y
7 Gibbons	Y	N	Y	N	Y	Y	Y	Y
8 Ireland	?	N	Y	N	Y	Y	N	Y
9 Frey	Y	N	Y	N	Y	Y	N	Y
10 Bafalis	Y	N	N	Y	Y	Y	N	Y
11 Rogers	Y	N	N	Y	Y	Y	N	Y
12 Burke	Y	Y	N	N	Y	Y	N	Y
13 Lehman	Y	Y	N	Y	N	N	Y	Y
14 Pepper	Y	N	Y	N	N	N	N	Y
15 Fascell	Y	N	Y	N	N	N	N	Y
GEORGIA								
1 Ginn	Y	N	Y	N	Y	Y	N	N
2 Mathis	?	?	?	?	?	?	?	?
3 Brinkley	Y	N	Y	N	Y	Y	N	N
4 Levitas	Y	N	N	N	N	Y	N	Y
5 Fowler	Y	N	N	N	N	N	N	Y
6 Flynt	Y	N	Y	N	Y	Y	N	N
7 McDonald	N	N	N	N	Y	Y	N	N
8 Evans	Y	N	Y	N	Y	Y	N	Y
9 Jenkins	#	▮	▮	#	#	#	▮	X
10 Barnard	Y	?	N	N	Y	Y	N	N
HAWAII								
1 Heftel	Y	N	Y	Y	N	N	N	Y
2 Akaka	Y	Y	Y	N	N	N	N	Y
IDAHO								
1 Symms	Y	?	?	?	✓	?	?	?
2 Hansen, G.	Y	N	N	N	Y	Y	N	N
ILLINOIS								
1 Metcalfe	Y	Y	N	Y	N	N	Y	Y
2 Murphy	Y	N	Y	N	N	N	N	Y
3 Russo	Y	N	N	Y	Y	Y	N	N
4 Derwinski	Y	N	N	N	Y	Y	N	Y
5 Fary	Y	N	Y	N	N	N	N	Y
6 Hyde	Y	N	Y	N	Y	Y	N	Y
7 Collins	?	✓	?	?	?	?	✓	✓
8 Rostenkowski	Y	N	Y	N	N	N	N	Y
9 Yates	Y	Y	N	N	N	N	Y	Y
10 Mikva	Y	Y	N	Y	N	N	Y	Y
11 Annunzio	Y	N	Y	N	N	N	N	Y
12 Crane	#	N	N	N	Y	Y	N	N
13 McClory	Y	N	N	N	Y	Y	N	Y
14 Erlenborn	Y	N	Y	N	Y	Y	N	Y
15 Corcoran	Y	N	N	N	Y	Y	N	Y
16 Anderson	Y	Y	N	N	N	N	Y	Y
17 O'Brien	Y	N	N	N	Y	Y	N	Y
18 Michel	Y	N	Y	N	Y	Y	N	Y
19 Railsback	Y	N	Y	Y	Y	Y	N	Y
20 Findley	Y	N	Y	N	Y	Y	N	Y
21 Madigan	Y	N	Y	N	Y	Y	N	Y
22 Shipley	Y	N	Y	N	N	N	N	Y
23 Price	Y	N	N	N	N	N	N	Y
24 Simon	Y	N	N	N	N	N	N	Y
INDIANA								
1 Benjamin	Y	Y	N	Y	N	N	Y	Y
2 Fithian	Y	N	N	N	N	Y	Y	N
3 Brademas	Y	Y	N	Y	N	N	Y	Y
4 Quayle	N	N	N	Y	Y	Y	N	N
5 Hillis	Y	N	Y	N	Y	Y	N	N
6 Evans	Y	Y	N	Y	Y	Y	Y	N
7 Myers, J.	Y	N	Y	N	Y	Y	N	N
8 Cornwell	Y	N	N	Y	N	N	Y	Y
9 Hamilton	Y	N	N	N	N	N	N	Y
10 Sharp	Y	N	N	Y	N	N	Y	Y
11 Jacobs	Y	Y	N	Y	N	N	Y	N
IOWA								
1 Leach	Y	N	N	Y	N	N	Y	N
2 Blouin	Y	Y	N	Y	N	N	N	N
3 Grassley	Y	N	N	N	Y	Y	N	N
4 Smith	Y	N	?	N	N	N	N	Y
5 Harkin	Y	Y	N	Y	N	N	Y	N
6 Bedell	Y	Y	N	Y	N	N	Y	N

Democrats ***Republicans***

Corresponding to Congressional Record Votes 630, 631, 632, 633, 634, 635, 636, 637

	551	552	553	554	555	556	557	558
KANSAS								
1 Sebelius	Y	N	Y	N	Y	Y	N	N
2 Keys	Y	Y	N	Y	N	N	Y	N
3 Winn	Y	N	Y	N	Y	Y	N	Y
4 Glickman	Y	Y	N	Y	N	N	Y	Y
5 Skubitz	Y	N	Y	N	Y	Y	N	Y
KENTUCKY								
1 Hubbard	Y	N	N	N	Y	Y	N	N
2 Natcher	Y	N	Y	N	Y	Y	N	N
3 Mazzoli	Y	Y	N	Y	N	Y	Y	Y
4 Snyder	Y	N	Y	N	Y	Y	N	N
5 Carter	Y	N	Y	N	Y	Y	N	N
6 Breckinridge	Y	N	N	N	Y	Y	?	Y
7 Perkins	Y	N	Y	N	N	Y	N	Y
LOUISIANA								
1 Livingston	Y	N	N	N	Y	Y	N	Y
2 Boggs	#	N	Y	N	N	N	N	Y
3 Treen	Y	N	N	N	Y	Y	N	Y
4 Waggonner	Y	N	Y	N	Y	Y	N	Y
5 Huckaby	Y	N	N	N	Y	Y	N	Y
6 Moore	Y	N	N	N	Y	Y	N	Y
7 Breaux	?	X	?	N	Y	Y	N	Y
8 Long	Y	N	Y	N	N	N	N	Y
MAINE								
1 Emery	Y	Y	N	Y	Y	Y	Y	N
2 Cohen	Y	N	N	Y	Y	Y	N	Y
MARYLAND								
1 Bauman	Y	N	N	N	Y	Y	N	N
2 Long	Y	Y	N	N	N	Y	Y	Y
3 Mikulski	Y	Y	N	Y	N	N	Y	Y
4 Holt	Y	N	N	N	Y	Y	N	N
5 Spellman	#	N	N	#	N	N	N	Y
6 Byron	Y	N	Y	N	Y	Y	N	N
7 Mitchell	▮	Y	N	Y	N	N	Y	N
8 Steers	Y	N	Y	Y	N	N	Y	Y
MASSACHUSETTS								
1 Conte	Y	N	N	N	N	N	Y	Y
2 Boland	Y	Y	Y	Y	N	N	Y	Y
3 Early	Y	Y	N	Y	N	N	Y	Y
4 Drinan	Y	Y	N	N	N	N	Y	Y
5 Tsongas	?	✓	?	?	X	?	?	✓
6 Harrington	#	Y	N	#	▮	▮	#	▮
7 Markey	?	Y	N	Y	N	N	Y	N
8 O'Neill								
9 Moakley	Y	Y	N	Y	N	N	Y	Y
10 Heckler	?	Y	N	Y	N	Y	Y	Y
11 Burke	?	X	?	?	X	X	X	✓
12 Studds	Y	Y	N	Y	N	N	Y	N
MICHIGAN								
1 Conyers	#	✓	▮	#	▮	X	✓	X
2 Pursell	Y	N	N	Y	N	Y	Y	N
3 Brown	Y	N	N	N	N	Y	N	Y
4 Stockman	Y	N	N	N	Y	Y	N	Y
5 Sawyer	Y	N	Y	N	Y	Y	N	Y
6 Carr	Y	Y	N	Y	N	N	Y	Y
7 Kildee	Y	Y	N	Y	N	N	Y	Y
8 Traxler	Y	Y	Y	N	N	N	N	Y
9 Vander Jagt	?	N	N	N	Y	Y	N	Y
10 Cederberg	Y	N	Y	N	Y	Y	N	Y
11 Ruppe	Y	N	Y	Y	N	N	N	Y
12 Bonior	Y	Y	N	#	N	N	Y	N
13 Diggs	Y	Y	N	Y	N	N	Y	Y
14 Nedzi	Y	N	Y	N	N	N	N	Y
15 Ford	?	?	?	N	N	N	Y	Y
16 Dingell	?	N	?	N	N	Y	N	Y
17 Brodhead	Y	Y	N	Y	N	N	Y	Y
18 Blanchard	Y	Y	Y	Y	N	N	Y	Y
19 Broomfield	Y	N	Y	N	Y	Y	N	Y
MINNESOTA								
1 Quie	?	?	?	?	?	?	?	?
2 Hagedorn	Y	N	N	N	Y	Y	N	Y
3 Frenzel	Y	N	Y	Y	Y	Y	N	Y
4 Vento	Y	Y	N	Y	N	N	Y	Y
5 Fraser	?	Y	?	Y	N	N	Y	Y
6 Nolan	Y	Y	N	Y	?	?	Y	N
7 Stangeland	Y	N	Y	N	Y	Y	N	N
8 Oberstar	Y	Y	N	Y	N	N	Y	Y
MISSISSIPPI								
1 Whitten	#	N	Y	N	Y	Y	N	N
2 Bowen	Y	N	Y	N	Y	Y	N	N
3 Montgomery	Y	N	Y	N	Y	Y	N	N
4 Cochran	?	?	?	?	?	?	?	?
5 Lott	Y	N	Y	N	Y	Y	N	N
MISSOURI								
1 Clay	Y	Y	N	?	N	N	Y	N
2 Young	Y	Y	Y	Y	Y	Y	N	Y
3 Gephardt	Y	N	N	Y	N	Y	Y	N

	551	552	553	554	555	556	557	558
4 Skelton	Y	N	N	Y	N	Y	N	Y
5 Bolling	Y	N	N	N	N	N	N	Y
6 Coleman	Y	N	N	Y	Y	Y	N	Y
7 Taylor	Y	N	Y	N	Y	Y	N	N
8 Ichord	Y	N	Y	Y	Y	Y	N	Y
9 Volkmer	Y	-	N	Y	N	Y	Y	N
10 Burlison	?	N	Y	Y	N	Y	N	Y
MONTANA								
1 Baucus	Y	Y	N	Y	N	N	Y	Y
2 Marlenee	Y	N	Y	Y	N	Y	Y	N
NEBRASKA								
1 Thone	Y	N	N	N	Y	Y	N	N
2 Cavanaugh	Y	Y	N	N	N	N	Y	Y
3 Smith	Y	N	Y	N	Y	Y	N	N
NEVADA								
AL Santini	Y	N	Y	Y	Y	Y	N	Y
NEW HAMPSHIRE								
1 D'Amours	Y	Y	N	Y	N	Y	Y	Y
2 Cleveland	Y	N	Y	Y	Y	Y	N	N
NEW JERSEY								
1 Florio	Y	Y	Y	Y	N	N	Y	N
2 Hughes	Y	Y	N	Y	N	N	Y	N
3 Howard	Y	Y	N	Y	N	N	Y	Y
4 Thompson	Y	Y	N	N	N	N	Y	Y
5 Fenwick	Y	Y	Y	?	N	N	Y	Y
6 Forsythe	Y	Y	Y	Y	Y	Y	N	N
7 Maguire	#	#	▮	#	X	N	Y	N
8 Roe	Y	Y	Y	Y	N	Y	Y	Y
9 Hollenbeck	Y	Y	Y	Y	N	N	Y	Y
10 Rodino	Y	Y	▮	N	▮	▮	#	#
11 Minish	Y	N	Y	Y	N	N	Y	Y
12 Rinaldo	Y	N	N	Y	N	N	Y	Y
13 Meyner	Y	N	N	N	N	N	Y	Y
14 LeFante	#	X	▮	▮	▮	▮	✓	✓
15 Patten	Y	N	Y	N	N	N	N	Y
NEW MEXICO								
1 Lujan	Y	N	N	Y	Y	Y	N	N
2 Runnels	Y	N	Y	N	Y	Y	N	N
NEW YORK								
1 Pike	Y	N	Y	Y	N	N	N	N
2 Downey	Y	Y	N	Y	N	N	Y	Y
3 Ambro	Y	N	N	N	Y	N	Y	Y
4 Lent	Y	N	Y	N	Y	Y	N	Y
5 Wydler	Y	N	N	N	Y	Y	N	Y
6 Wolff	Y	Y	Y	N	N	N	Y	Y
7 Addabbo	Y	Y	Y	N	N	N	Y	Y
8 Rosenthal	Y	Y	N	Y	N	N	Y	Y
9 Delaney	Y	N	Y	N	N	N	Y	Y
10 Biaggi	Y	N	Y	N	N	N	Y	Y
11 Scheuer	Y	Y	N	Y	N	Y	Y	Y
12 Chisholm	#	Y	N	Y	N	N	Y	Y
13 Solarz	Y	Y	Y	N	N	N	Y	Y
14 Richmond	Y	Y	N	Y	N	N	Y	Y
15 Zeferetti	Y	N	Y	N	Y	Y	Y	Y
16 Holtzman	Y	Y	N	Y	N	N	Y	Y
17 Murphy	Y	N	Y	N	?	?	?	Y
18 Green	Y	Y	N	Y	N	Y	Y	Y
19 Rangel	Y	Y	N	Y	N	N	Y	Y
20 Weiss	Y	Y	N	Y	N	N	Y	Y
21 Garcia	#	Y	N	Y	N	N	Y	Y
22 Bingham	Y	Y	N	N	N	N	N	Y
23 Caputo	Y	Y	N	N	N	Y	Y	?
24 Ottinger	Y	Y	N	Y	N	N	Y	Y
25 Fish	Y	N	N	Y	N	Y	N	Y
26 Gilman	Y	Y	N	Y	N	N	Y	Y
27 McHugh	Y	Y	N	N	N	N	Y	Y
28 Stratton	Y	N	Y	N	Y	Y	N	Y
29 Pattison	N	Y	N	N	N	N	Y	Y
30 McEwen	Y	N	N	N	Y	Y	N	Y
31 Mitchell	Y	N	N	N	Y	Y	N	Y
32 Hanley	Y	Y	N	N	N	N	Y	Y
33 Walsh	Y	N	Y	N	Y	Y	N	Y
34 Horton	Y	N	N	N	Y	Y	N	Y
35 Conable	Y	N	Y	N	?	Y	N	Y
36 LaFalce	Y	N	N	N	N	N	N	Y
37 Nowak	Y	Y	Y	N	N	N	Y	Y
38 Kemp	Y	N	N	?	Y	Y	N	Y
39 Lundine	#	Y	N	Y	N	N	Y	Y
NORTH CAROLINA								
1 Jones	Y	N	Y	N	N	N	N	N
2 Fountain	Y	N	Y	N	Y	Y	N	N
3 Whitley	Y	N	Y	N	N	Y	N	N
4 Andrews	?	N	N	Y	Y	Y	N	N
5 Neal	#	N	N	N	N	Y	N	N
6 Preyer	Y	N	N	N	N	N	N	Y
7 Rose	Y	Y	N	N	N	N	Y	N
8 Hefner	Y	N	Y	N	Y	Y	Y	N

	551	552	553	554	555	556	557	558
9 Martin	Y	N	N	N	Y	Y	N	N
10 Broyhill	Y	N	Y	N	Y	Y	N	N
11 Gudger	Y	N	N	N	N	Y	N	Y
NORTH DAKOTA								
AL Andrews	Y	N	Y	Y	Y	Y	N	N
OHIO								
1 Gradison	Y	N	Y	N	Y	Y	N	Y
2 Luken	Y	N	N	Y	Y	N	Y	Y
3 Whalen	#	▮	▮	▮	▮	#	▮	#
4 Guyer	Y	Y	N	N	Y	Y	N	N
5 Latta	Y	N	Y	N	Y	Y	N	N
6 Harsha	Y	N	Y	N	Y	Y	N	N
7 Brown	Y	N	Y	N	Y	Y	N	N
8 Kindness	Y	N	N	N	Y	Y	N	N
9 Ashley	Y	?	?	N	Y	N	N	Y
10 Miller	Y	N	N	Y	Y	Y	N	N
11 Stanton	Y	N	Y	N	N	Y	N	Y
12 Devine	Y	N	Y	N	Y	Y	N	N
13 Pease	Y	Y	N	N	N	N	Y	Y
14 Seiberling	#	Y	N	Y	N	N	N	Y
15 Wylie	Y	N	Y	N	Y	Y	N	N
16 Regula	Y	N	N	N	Y	Y	N	Y
17 Ashbrook	Y	N	N	N	Y	Y	N	N
18 Applegate	Y	Y	Y	Y	N	Y	Y	N
19 Carney	Y	N	Y	N	N	N	N	Y
20 Oakar	Y	Y	N	Y	N	N	Y	N
21 Stokes	Y	Y	N	Y	N	N	Y	N
22 Vanik	Y	Y	N	Y	N	N	Y	Y
23 Mottl	Y	Y	Y	Y	Y	Y	Y	N
OKLAHOMA								
1 Jones	Y	N	Y	N	N	Y	Y	N
2 Risenhoover	Y	N	Y	N	Y	Y	N	N
3 Watkins	Y	N	Y	N	Y	Y	N	N
4 Steed	Y	N	Y	N	Y	Y	N	N
5 Edwards	Y	N	N	N	Y	Y	Y	N
6 English	Y	Y	N	Y	Y	Y	Y	N
OREGON								
1 AuCoin	Y	Y	N	Y	N	N	Y	Y
2 Ullman	Y	▮	Y	N	N	N	N	Y
3 Duncan	Y	N	#	▮	N	Y	N	Y
4 Weaver	Y	Y	N	Y	N	N	Y	N
PENNSYLVANIA								
1 Myers, M.	Y	Y	N	N	N	N	Y	Y
2 Nix	Y	N	Y	N	N	N	N	Y
3 Lederer	Y	Y	N	N	N	N	Y	Y
4 Eilberg	Y	Y	N	Y	N	N	Y	Y
5 Schulze	Y	N	N	Y	Y	Y	?	N
6 Yatron	Y	N	N	N	N	N	N	Y
7 Edgar	Y	Y	N	Y	N	N	Y	Y
8 Kostmayer	Y	Y	N	Y	N	N	Y	Y
9 Shuster	Y	N	Y	Y	Y	Y	N	N
10 McDade	?	?	?	?	?	?	?	?
11 Flood	Y	N	Y	N	N	N	N	Y
12 Murtha	Y	N	Y	N	N	Y	N	Y
13 Coughlin	Y	N	N	N	Y	Y	N	Y
14 Moorhead	Y	N	N	N	N	N	N	Y
15 Rooney	Y	N	Y	N	N	N	N	Y
16 Walker	Y	N	N	Y	Y	Y	N	N
17 Ertel	Y	Y	N	Y	N	N	N	Y
18 Walgren	Y	Y	N	Y	N	N	Y	Y
19 Goodling, W.	Y	N	?	N	Y	Y	N	N
20 Gaydos	Y	Y	Y	N	N	N	Y	Y
21 Dent	#	▮	#	▮	✓	✓	X	X
22 Murphy	Y	Y	N	Y	N	Y	Y	Y
23 Ammerman	Y	Y	N	Y	N	N	Y	Y
24 Marks	Y	Y	N	N	N	N	Y	Y
25 Myers, G.	Y	Y	N	N	N	N	Y	N
RHODE ISLAND								
1 St Germain	?	Y	N	N	N	N	Y	N
2 Beard	Y	N	Y	Y	N	N	Y	N
SOUTH CAROLINA								
1 Davis	Y	N	Y	N	N	Y	N	N
2 Spence	Y	N	N	N	Y	Y	N	Y
3 Derrick	Y	N	N	N	N	Y	Y	N
4 Mann	Y	N	N	N	Y	Y	N	N
5 Holland	Y	N	N	N	N	Y	N	N
6 Jenrette	N	N	N	N	N	Y	N	N
SOUTH DAKOTA								
1 Pressler	Y	Y	N	Y	Y	Y	Y	N
2 Abdnor	Y	N	N	Y	Y	Y	N	N
TENNESSEE								
1 Quillen	Y	N	Y	N	Y	Y	N	N
2 Duncan	Y	N	Y	?	Y	Y	N	N
3 Lloyd	Y	N	Y	N	Y	Y	N	N
4 Gore	Y	Y	N	Y	N	N	Y	Y
5 Vacancy								
6 Beard	Y	N	Y	N	Y	Y	N	Y

	551	552	553	554	555	556	557	558
7 Jones	Y	N	Y	N	Y	Y	N	N
8 Ford	Y	Y	N	?	?	?	?	?
TEXAS								
1 Hall	Y	N	Y	Y	Y	Y	Y	N
2 Wilson, C.	#	N	N	N	Y	Y	N	Y
3 Collins	N	N	Y	Y	Y	Y	N	N
4 Roberts	Y	N	Y	N	Y	Y	N	N
5 Mattox	Y	N	N	Y	N	Y	Y	N
6 Teague	?	?	?	?	✓	✓	X	X
7 Archer	Y	N	N	N	Y	Y	N	N
8 Eckhardt	Y	Y	N	N	N	N	Y	Y
9 Brooks	Y	N	Y	N	N	Y	N	Y
10 Pickle	Y	N	N	N	Y	Y	Y	Y
11 Poage	Y	N	Y	N	Y	Y	N	N
12 Wright	Y	N	Y	N	N	N	N	Y
13 Hightower	Y	N	Y	N	Y	Y	N	Y
14 Young	?	?	?	N	?	?	?	?
15 de la Garza	Y	N	N	N	Y	Y	N	N
16 White	Y	N	Y	N	Y	Y	N	Y
17 Burleson	Y	N	Y	N	Y	Y	N	N
18 Jordan	Y	N	Y	N	N	N	N	Y
19 Mahon	Y	N	Y	N	Y	Y	N	N
20 Gonzalez	Y	N	Y	N	N	N	Y	Y
21 Krueger	#	N	Y	Y	N	N	Y	Y
22 Gammage	Y	N	N	N	Y	Y	N	N
23 Kazen	Y	N	N	N	Y	Y	N	Y
24 Milford	Y	N	Y	N	?	?	N	Y
UTAH								
1 McKay	Y	N	Y	N	Y	Y	N	Y
2 Marriott	Y	N	N	N	Y	Y	N	N
VERMONT								
AL Jeffords	Y	Y	N	N	Y	Y	Y	Y
VIRGINIA								
1 Trible	Y	N	N	N	Y	Y	N	N
2 Whitehurst	Y	N	Y	N	Y	Y	N	Y
3 Satterfield	Y	N	N	N	Y	Y	N	N
4 Daniel	Y	N	Y	N	Y	Y	N	N
5 Daniel	Y	N	Y	N	Y	Y	N	N
6 Butler	Y	N	Y	N	Y	Y	N	N
7 Robinson	Y	N	Y	N	Y	Y	N	N
8 Harris	Y	N	N	N	Y	Y	N	N
9 Wampler	Y	N	N	N	Y	Y	N	N
10 Fisher	Y	N	N	N	N	N	N	Y
WASHINGTON								
1 Pritchard	Y	N	N	N	N	Y	N	Y
2 Meeds	Y	N	Y	Y	N	N	Y	Y
3 Bonker	#	Y	N	N	N	N	Y	Y
4 McCormack	Y	Y	N	N	N	N	N	Y
5 Foley	Y	N	N	Y	N	Y	Y	Y
6 Dicks	Y	N	N	N	N	Y	Y	Y
7 Cunningham	Y	N	N	N	Y	Y	N	Y
WEST VIRGINIA								
1 Mollohan	Y	N	Y	N	N	Y	N	Y
2 Staggers	Y	N	Y	N	N	N	N	N
3 Slack	Y	N	Y	N	N	Y	N	N
4 Rahall	Y	Y	Y	Y	N	N	Y	Y
WISCONSIN								
1 Aspin	Y	Y	N	N	N	N	N	Y
2 Kastenmeier	Y	Y	Y	Y	N	N	Y	N
3 Baldus	Y	N	Y	N	N	N	Y	Y
4 Zablocki	Y	N	Y	N	N	N	N	Y
5 Reuss	Y	Y	Y	Y	N	N	Y	Y
6 Steiger	#	N	N	N	Y	Y	N	Y
7 Obey	Y	N	Y	Y	N	N	N	Y
8 Cornell	Y	Y	N	N	N	N	Y	Y
9 Kasten	?	?	?	?	?	?	?	?
WYOMING								
AL Roncalio	Y	N	Y	N	N	N	Y	N

Democrats ***Republicans***

559. HR 12931. Foreign Aid Appropriations, Fiscal 1979. Young, R-Fla., amendment to delete $49 million from the bill for the purchase of rupees from India. Rejected 194-200: R 106-31; D 88-169 (ND 35-143; SD 53-26), Aug. 2, 1978. A "nay" was a vote supporting the president's position.

560. HR 12931. Foreign Aid Appropriations, Fiscal 1979. Young, R-Fla., amendment to reduce the appropriations for the United Nations Development Program by $6.8 million. Rejected 189-202: R 104-33; D 85-169 (ND 30-145; SD 55-24), Aug. 2, 1978. A "nay" was a vote supporting the president's position.

561. HR 12931. Foreign Aid Appropriations, Fiscal 1979. Derwinski, R-Ill., amendment to delete $90 million from the bill that was earmarked for Syria. Adopted 280-103: R 123-13; D 157-90 (ND 98-72; SD 59-18), Aug. 2, 1978. A "nay" was a vote supporting the president's position.

562. Procedural Motion. Ashbrook, R-Ohio, motion to approve the House *Journal* of Wednesday, Aug. 2, 1978. Motion agreed to 362-14: R 121-10; D 241-4 (ND 170-3; SD 71-1), Aug. 3, 1978.

563. HR 12931. Foreign Aid Appropriations, Fiscal 1979. Ryan, D-Calif., amendment to reduce the $13.1 million appropriation for the Philippines by $5 million. Rejected 142-264: R 25-112; D 117-152 (ND 104-84; SD 13-68), Aug. 3, 1978. A "nay" was a vote supporting the president's position.

564. HR 12931. Foreign Aid Appropriations, Fiscal 1979. Ashbrook, R-Ohio, amendment to delete the $600,000 appropriation for military education and training assistance to Afghanistan. Rejected 152-236: R 83-49; D 69-187 (ND 37-143; SD 32-44), Aug. 3, 1978. A "nay" was a vote supporting the president's position.

565. HR 12931. Foreign Aid Appropriations, Fiscal 1979. Harkin, D-Iowa, amendment to the Young, R-Fla., amendment *(see vote 566, below)*, to prohibit indirect U.S. aid to Chile, Argentina, Uruguay, South Korea, Nicaragua, Indonesia and the Philippines. Rejected 41-360: R 3-133; D 38-227 (ND 33-152; SD 5-75), Aug. 3, 1978. A "nay" was a vote supporting the president's position.

566. HR 12931. Foreign Aid Appropriations, Fiscal 1979. Young, R-Fla., amendment to prohibit indirect U.S. aid to Uganda, Cambodia, Laos and Vietnam. Rejected 198-203: R 101-35; D 97-168 (ND 52-134; SD 45-34), Aug. 3, 1978. A "nay" was a vote supporting the president's position.

KEY

- Y Voted for (yea).
- ✓ Paired for.
- † Announced for.
- # CQ Poll for.
- N Voted against (nay).
- X Paired against.
- \- Announced against.
- ▮ CQ Poll against.
- P Voted "present."
- ● Voted "present" to avoid possible conflict of interest.
- ? Did not vote or otherwise make a position known.

	559	560	561	562	563	564	565	566
ALABAMA								
1 Edwards	Y	Y	Y	Y	N	Y	N	Y
2 Dickinson	Y	Y	Y	Y	N	Y	N	Y
3 Nichols	Y	Y	Y	#	N	Y	N	Y
4 Bevill	Y	Y	Y	Y	Y	Y	N	Y
5 Flippo	Y	Y	Y	Y	N	Y	N	Y
6 Buchanan	N	Y	Y	Y	Y	Y	N	Y
7 Flowers	?	?	?	?	?	?	?	?
ALASKA								
AL Young	Y	#	#	#	▮	#	▮	#
ARIZONA								
1 Rhodes	Y	Y	Y	Y	N	Y	N	N
2 Udall	N	N	N	Y	Y	N	N	N
3 Stump	Y	Y	Y	Y	N	Y	N	Y
4 Rudd	Y	Y	Y	Y	N	Y	N	Y
ARKANSAS								
1 Alexander	N	N	N	Y	N	?	N	Y
2 Tucker	N	N	Y	#	Y	Y	N	N
3 Hammerschmidt	Y	Y	Y	Y	N	N	N	Y
4 Thornton	?	N	N	Y	N	?	N	N
CALIFORNIA								
1 Johnson	N	N	?	Y	N	N	N	N
2 Clausen	Y	Y	Y	Y	N	Y	N	Y
3 Moss	N	?	?	Y	N	N	N	N
4 Leggett	N	?	N	Y	N	N	N	N
5 Burton, J.	N	N	Y	N	Y	N	Y	N
6 Burton, P.	X	?	Y	Y	Y	N	Y	N
7 Miller	N	N	N	Y	Y	N	Y	N
8 Dellums	N	N	N	#	Y	N	N	N
9 Stark	N	N	N	Y	Y	N	Y	N
10 Edwards	N	N	Y	Y	Y	N	Y	N
11 Ryan	N	N	Y	Y	Y	Y	Y	N
12 McCloskey	N	N	Y	Y	Y	N	N	N
13 Mineta	N	N	Y	Y	Y	N	Y	N
14 McFall	N	N	N	Y	N	N	N	N
15 Sisk	?	?	?	Y	N	N	?	Y
16 Panetta	N	Y	Y	Y	N	N	Y	Y
17 Krebs	N	N	Y	Y	Y	N	Y	N
18 Vacancy								
19 Lagomarsino	Y	Y	Y	Y	N	N	N	Y
20 Goldwater	Y	?	?	Y	N	N	N	Y
21 Corman	N	N	Y	Y	Y	N	N	N
22 Moorhead	Y	Y	Y	Y	N	Y	N	Y
23 Beilenson	N	N	N	▮	Y	N	N	N
24 Waxman	N	N	Y	#	Y	N	N	N
25 Roybal	N	N	N	Y	Y	N	N	N
26 Rousselot	Y	Y	Y	N	N	Y	N	Y
27 Dornan	Y	Y	Y	Y	Y	Y	N	Y
28 Burke	N	N	Y	Y	Y	N	Y	N
29 Hawkins	N	X	Y	Y	Y	N	Y	N
30 Danielson	N	N	N	Y	N	N	N	N
31 Wilson, C.H.	Y	?	?	Y	N	?	N	Y
32 Anderson	Y	N	Y	Y	Y	Y	Y	Y
33 Clawson	Y	Y	Y	Y	N	Y	N	Y
34 Hannaford	N	N	Y	Y	Y	N	N	N
35 Lloyd	N	N	Y	N	N	N	N	Y
36 Brown	?	?	?	Y	Y	N	Y	N
37 Pettis	N	N	N	Y	N	?	N	N
38 Patterson	N	N	N	Y	N	N	N	N
39 Wiggins	Y	Y	Y	#	N	N	N	Y
40 Badham	Y	Y	Y	Y	N	Y	N	Y
41 Wilson, B.	Y	Y	N	Y	N	?	N	Y
42 Van Deerlin	N	N	Y	Y	N	N	N	N
43 Burgener	Y	Y	Y	Y	N	N	N	Y
COLORADO								
1 Schroeder	N	N	Y	Y	Y	N	N	N
2 Wirth	N	N	N	Y	Y	N	N	N
3 Evans	▮	▮	#	#	Y	N	N	N
4 Johnson	Y	Y	Y	Y	Y	Y	Y	Y
5 Armstrong	Y	Y	Y	Y	N	Y	N	Y
CONNECTICUT								
1 Cotter	N	N	N	Y	N	N	N	N
2 Dodd	N	N	Y	Y	Y	Y	N	N
3 Giaimo	N	N	N	Y	N	N	N	N
4 McKinney	N	N	N	Y	N	Y	N	N
5 Sarasin	N	N	N	N	N	N	N	N
6 Moffett	N	N	N	Y	Y	N	Y	N
DELAWARE								
AL Evans	N	Y	Y	Y	N	N	N	Y
FLORIDA								
1 Sikes	Y	Y	Y	Y	N	N	N	Y
2 Fuqua	Y	Y	Y	Y	N	N	N	Y
3 Bennett	Y	Y	Y	Y	N	N	N	Y
4 Chappell	✓	✓	✓	?	?	Y	N	Y
5 Kelly	Y	Y	Y	Y	N	Y	N	Y
6 Young	Y	Y	Y	Y	N	Y	N	Y
7 Gibbons	Y	Y	Y	Y	N	N	N	Y
8 Ireland	Y	Y	Y	?	N	Y	N	Y
9 Frey	Y	Y	Y	?	?	?	?	?
10 Bafalis	Y	Y	Y	Y	N	Y	N	Y
11 Rogers	N	N	Y	Y	Y	✓	N	Y
12 Burke	Y	Y	Y	Y	N	Y	Y	Y
13 Lehman	N	N	Y	Y	Y	N	N	N
14 Pepper	N	N	Y	Y	N	N	N	N
15 Fascell	N	N	N	Y	N	N	N	N
GEORGIA								
1 Ginn	Y	Y	Y	Y	N	N	N	Y
2 Mathis	?	?	?	?	?	?	?	?
3 Brinkley	Y	Y	Y	Y	N	Y	N	Y
4 Levitas	Y	Y	Y	Y	N	N	N	Y
5 Fowler	N	Y	Y	Y	N	N	N	N
6 Flynt	?	?	?	?	N	N	N	Y
7 McDonald	Y	Y	Y	Y	N	Y	N	Y
8 Evans	Y	Y	Y	Y	N	N	N	Y
9 Jenkins	#	#	#	#	#	#	▮	#
10 Barnard	Y	Y	?	?	?	?	?	?
HAWAII								
1 Heftel	N	N	Y	Y	N	N	N	N
2 Akaka	N	N	N	Y	N	N	N	N
IDAHO								
1 Symms	?	Y	Y	Y	N	Y	N	Y
2 Hansen, G.	Y	Y	Y	Y	N	Y	N	Y
ILLINOIS								
1 Metcalfe	N	N	Y	Y	Y	N	N	N
2 Murphy	N	N	N	Y	N	Y	N	N
3 Russo	Y	Y	Y	Y	Y	Y	Y	Y
4 Derwinski	Y	N	Y	Y	N	N	N	N
5 Fary	N	N	Y	Y	N	N	N	N
6 Hyde	N	Y	Y	Y	N	N	N	N
7 Collins	?	?	?	?	?	?	?	X
8 Rostenkowski	N	N	N	Y	N	N	N	N
9 Yates	N	N	Y	Y	Y	N	N	N
10 Mikva	N	N	Y	Y	Y	N	N	N
11 Annunzio	N	N	Y	Y	N	N	N	N
12 Crane	#	Y	Y	Y	N	Y	N	Y
13 McClory	Y	N	Y	Y	Y	Y	N	N
14 Erlenborn	N	N	Y	Y	N	N	N	N
15 Corcoran	Y	Y	Y	Y	N	Y	N	Y
16 Anderson	N	N	Y	Y	N	N	N	N
17 O'Brien	Y	Y	Y	Y	N	Y	N	N
18 Michel	Y	Y	Y	Y	N	N	N	N
19 Railsback	N	N	Y	Y	N	N	N	N
20 Findley	N	N	N	Y	N	N	N	N
21 Madigan	Y	Y	Y	Y	N	?	N	N
22 Shipley	Y	X	X	Y	N	?	N	Y
23 Price	N	N	N	Y	N	N	N	N
24 Simon	N	N	N	Y	N	N	N	N
INDIANA								
1 Benjamin	N	Y	Y	Y	Y	N	Y	Y
2 Fithian	N	Y	Y	Y	Y	N	N	N
3 Brademas	N	N	Y	Y	N	N	N	N
4 Quayle	Y	Y	Y	N	Y	Y	N	Y
5 Hillis	Y	Y	Y	Y	N	Y	N	Y
6 Evans	Y	Y	Y	Y	Y	Y	N	Y
7 Myers, J.	Y	Y	N	Y	N	Y	N	Y
8 Cornwell	N	N	Y	Y	Y	N	N	N
9 Hamilton	N	N	N	Y	Y	N	N	N
10 Sharp	N	N	N	Y	Y	N	N	N
11 Jacobs	Y	Y	N	Y	Y	Y	N	N
IOWA								
1 Leach	N	N	Y	Y	Y	Y	N	N
2 Blouin	N	N	N	Y	Y	N	N	N
3 Grassley	Y	N	Y	Y	Y	Y	N	Y
4 Smith	N	N	N	Y	N	N	N	N
5 Harkin	N	N	N	Y	Y	Y	Y	N
6 Bedell	N	N	N	Y	Y	Y	Y	N

Democrats ***Republicans***

Corresponding to Congressional Record Votes 638, 639, 640, 641, 642, 643, 644, 645

	559	560	561	562	563	564	565	566
KANSAS								
1 Sebelius	Y	Y	Y	Y	N	N	N	Y
2 Keys	N	N	N	Y	Y	Y	N	N
3 Winn	Y	Y	Y	Y	N	N	N	Y
4 Glickman	N	Y	N	Y	N	N	N	Y
5 Skubitz	Y	Y	Y	?	N	N	N	Y
KENTUCKY								
1 Hubbard	Y	Y	Y	Y	N	N	N	Y
2 Natcher	N	Y	Y	Y	N	N	N	N
3 Mazzoli	Y	N	N	Y	N	N	N	N
4 Snyder	Y	Y	Y	Y	N	Y	N	Y
5 Carter	Y	Y	Y	Y	N	N	N	Y
6 Breckinridge	N	N	Y	Y	N	N	N	N
7 Perkins	N	N	Y	Y	N	N	N	N
LOUISIANA								
1 Livingston	Y	Y	Y	Y	N	Y	N	Y
2 Boggs	N	N	Y	Y	N	N	N	N
3 Treen	Y	Y	Y	Y	N	N	N	Y
4 Waggonner	Y	Y	Y	Y	N	Y	N	Y
5 Huckaby	Y	Y	Y	Y	N	Y	N	Y
6 Moore	Y	Y	Y	Y	N	Y	N	Y
7 Breaux	Y	Y	Y	Y	N	Y	N	Y
8 Long	Y	N	Y	Y	Y	Y	Y	N
MAINE								
1 Emery	N	Y	Y	Y	Y	Y	N	Y
2 Cohen	Y	Y	Y	Y	N	Y	N	Y
MARYLAND								
1 Bauman	Y	Y	Y	Y	N	Y	N	Y
2 Long	N	N	N	Y	N	N	N	N
3 Mikulski	N	N	Y	Y	Y	N	N	N
4 Holt	Y	Y	Y	Y	N	Y	N	Y
5 Spellman	N	N	Y	Y	N	N	N	N
6 Byron	Y	Y	Y	?	N	Y	N	Y
7 Mitchell	N	N	N	N	Y	N	N	N
8 Steers	N	N	Y	Y	N	N	N	N
MASSACHUSETTS								
1 Conte	N	N	N	Y	N	N	N	N
2 Boland	N	N	N	Y	N	N	N	N
3 Early	N	Y	Y	Y	Y	Y	N	Y
4 Drinan	N	N	Y	Y	Y	Y	N	N
5 Tsongas	?	X	✓	?	?	?	?	X
6 Harrington	▮	▮	#	#	#	▮	#	▮
7 Markey	N	N	Y	Y	Y	N	N	N
8 O'Neill								
9 Moakley	N	N	Y	Y	Y	Y	N	N
10 Heckler	N	N	Y	Y	N	N	N	N
11 Burke	X	X	X	?	X	X	?	X
12 Studds	N	N	N	Y	Y	N	N	N
MICHIGAN								
1 Conyers	X	X	X	#	✓	✓	#	X
2 Pursell	Y	N	Y	Y	N	N	N	N
3 Brown	Y	N	N	N	N	Y	N	N
4 Stockman	Y	Y	Y	Y	N	Y	N	Y
5 Sawyer	Y	Y	Y	Y	Y	Y	N	N
6 Carr	?	N	Y	Y	Y	N	Y	N
7 Kildee	N	N	Y	Y	Y	N	N	N
8 Traxler	N	N	Y	Y	Y	N	N	Y
9 Vander Jagt	Y	Y	Y	Y	N	Y	N	Y
10 Cederberg	Y	N	Y	Y	N	Y	N	Y
11 Ruppe	Y	N	N	Y	N	Y	N	N
12 Bonior	N	N	Y	Y	Y	N	N	N
13 Diggs	?	?	?	#	N	▮	▮	X
14 Nedzi	N	N	N	Y	N	N	N	N
15 Ford	N	N	?	?	N	N	N	N
16 Dingell	Y	N	N	Y	N	N	N	N
17 Brodhead	N	N	Y	Y	Y	N	N	N
18 Blanchard	N	N	Y	Y	N	N	N	N
19 Broomfield	Y	Y	Y	Y	N	Y	N	Y
MINNESOTA								
1 Quie	?	?	?	?	?	?	?	?
2 Hagedorn	Y	N	Y	Y	N	N	N	Y
3 Frenzel	Y	Y	Y	Y	N	N	N	N
4 Vento	N	N	N	Y	Y	N	N	N
5 Fraser	N	N	N	?	?	?	?	?
6 Nolan	?	N	N	Y	Y	?	Y	N
7 Stangeland	Y	Y	#	Y	Y	N	N	Y
8 Oberstar	N	N	Y	Y	Y	N	N	N
MISSISSIPPI								
1 Whitten	Y	✓	#	#	N	N	N	N
2 Bowen	Y	Y	N	Y	N	Y	N	N
3 Montgomery	Y	Y	Y	Y	N	Y	Y	N
4 Cochran	?	?	?	?	?	?	?	?
5 Lott	Y	Y	Y	Y	N	Y	N	Y
MISSOURI								
1 Clay	N	N	?	Y	Y	N	N	N
2 Young	Y	Y	Y	Y	N	N	N	N
3 Gephardt	N	N	N	Y	N	N	N	N

	559	560	561	562	563	564	565	566
4 Skelton	Y	Y	Y	Y	N	Y	?	?
5 Bolling	▮	▮	▮	Y	N	N	N	N
6 Coleman	Y	Y	Y	Y	N	Y	N	Y
7 Taylor	Y	Y	Y	Y	N	Y	N	Y
8 Ichord	Y	Y	Y	Y	N	Y	N	Y
9 Volkmer	Y	Y	N	Y	Y	N	N	Y
10 Burlison	N	N	N	Y	N	N	N	N
MONTANA								
1 Baucus	N	N	Y	Y	Y	N	N	N
2 Marlenee	Y	Y	Y	?	Y	Y	N	Y
NEBRASKA								
1 Thone	Y	Y	Y	?	?	?	?	?
2 Cavanaugh	N	N	N	Y	N	N	N	N
3 Smith	Y	Y	Y	Y	N	Y	N	Y
NEVADA								
AL Santini	Y	Y	Y	#	N	Y	Y	Y
NEW HAMPSHIRE								
1 D'Amours	N	N	Y	Y	Y	Y	N	N
2 Cleveland	Y	Y	Y	Y	N	N	N	Y
NEW JERSEY								
1 Florio	N	N	Y	Y	Y	N	N	Y
2 Hughes	N	N	Y	Y	N	N	N	N
3 Howard	N	N	#	Y	N	N	N	N
4 Thompson	N	N	N	Y	N	X	N	N
5 Fenwick	N	N	Y	Y	Y	N	N	N
6 Forsythe	N	Y	Y	N	N	N	N	Y
7 Maguire	N	N	N	Y	Y	N	Y	N
8 Roe	Y	N	#	#	N	N	N	Y
9 Hollenbeck	N	N	Y	Y	Y	N	N	N
10 Rodino	▮	▮	▮	#	▮	▮	▮	▮
11 Minish	N	Y	Y	Y	Y	N	N	Y
12 Rinaldo	Y	N	Y	Y	Y	N	N	Y
13 Meyner	N	N	N	Y	Y	N	N	N
14 LeFante	▮	✓	▮	#	✓	X	▮	✓
15 Patten	N	N	N	Y	N	N	N	N
NEW MEXICO								
1 Lujan	Y	Y	Y	Y	Y	Y	?	?
2 Runnels	Y	Y	Y	Y	N	Y	N	Y
NEW YORK								
1 Pike	N	N	Y	Y	Y	Y	Y	Y
2 Downey	N	N	Y	Y	Y	N	N	N
3 Ambro	Y	N	Y	Y	Y	N	N	Y
4 Lent	Y	Y	Y	Y	N	Y	N	Y
5 Wydler	Y	Y	Y	Y	N	Y	N	Y
6 Wolff	N	Y	Y	Y	N	Y	N	Y
7 Addabbo	N	N	Y	Y	N	N	N	Y
8 Rosenthal	N	N	Y	Y	Y	N	N	N
9 Delaney	N	N	?	Y	N	N	N	Y
10 Biaggi	Y	N	Y	Y	N	N	N	Y
11 Scheuer	N	N	Y	Y	Y	N	N	N
12 Chisholm	N	N	N	Y	Y	N	N	N
13 Solarz	N	N	N	Y	Y	N	N	N
14 Richmond	N	N	Y	Y	Y	N	Y	N
15 Zeferetti	N	Y	Y	Y	N	Y	N	Y
16 Holtzman	N	N	Y	Y	Y	N	N	N
17 Murphy	N	N	N	Y	N	N	N	Y
18 Green	N	N	Y	Y	Y	N	N	N
19 Rangel	N	N	Y	Y	Y	N	N	N
20 Weiss	N	N	Y	Y	Y	N	N	N
21 Garcia	N	N	✓	#	Y	N	N	N
22 Bingham	N	N	Y	Y	Y	N	N	N
23 Caputo	?	?	?	?	Y	Y	Y	Y
24 Ottinger	N	N	Y	Y	Y	N	N	N
25 Fish	N	N	Y	Y	N	N	N	Y
26 Gilman	Y	Y	Y	Y	N	Y	N	Y
27 McHugh	N	N	N	Y	Y	N	N	N
28 Stratton	Y	Y	N	Y	N	Y	N	Y
29 Pattison	N	N	N	Y	Y	Y	N	N
30 McEwen	Y	Y	Y	P	N	N	N	Y
31 Mitchell	N	Y	Y	Y	N	N	N	Y
32 Hanley	N	N	N	Y	Y	N	N	Y
33 Walsh	Y	Y	Y	Y	N	N	N	Y
34 Horton	Y	Y	Y	Y	N	N	N	N
35 Conable	Y	N	Y	Y	N	N	N	N
36 LaFalce	N	N	N	Y	Y	N	N	N
37 Nowak	N	N	Y	Y	N	N	N	N
38 Kemp	Y	Y	Y	Y	N	?	N	Y
39 Lundine	N	N	#	Y	Y	N	N	N
NORTH CAROLINA								
1 Jones	Y	Y	Y	Y	N	Y	N	Y
2 Fountain	Y	Y	Y	Y	N	N	N	Y
3 Whitley	Y	Y	Y	Y	N	Y	N	Y
4 Andrews	Y	Y	?	?	N	N	N	Y
5 Neal	Y	Y	Y	Y	N	N	N	N
6 Preyer	Y	Y	N	Y	N	N	N	N
7 Rose	Y	Y	Y	Y	N	Y	N	N
8 Hefner	Y	Y	Y	Y	N	N	Y	Y

	559	560	561	562	563	564	565	566
9 Martin	Y	Y	Y	Y	N	N	N	Y
10 Broyhill	Y	Y	Y	Y	N	Y	N	Y
11 Gudger	Y	Y	Y	Y	N	Y	N	Y
NORTH DAKOTA								
AL Andrews	N	Y	Y	Y	N	N	N	Y
OHIO								
1 Gradison	Y	Y	Y	Y	N	Y	N	Y
2 Luken	N	N	Y	Y	Y	Y	N	Y
3 Whalen	▮	▮	▮	#	▮	▮	▮	▮
4 Guyer	Y	Y	Y	Y	N	N	N	Y
5 Latta	Y	Y	Y	Y	N	?	N	Y
6 Harsha	Y	Y	Y	Y	N	Y	N	Y
7 Brown	Y	Y	Y	Y	N	N	N	Y
8 Kindness	Y	Y	?	Y	Y	Y	N	Y
9 Ashley	N	N	N	Y	N	N	N	N
10 Miller	Y	Y	Y	Y	Y	Y	N	Y
11 Stanton	N	N	N	Y	N	N	N	N
12 Devine	Y	Y	Y	Y	N	Y	N	Y
13 Pease	N	N	N	Y	N	Y	N	N
14 Seiberling	N	N	N	#	Y	N	N	N
15 Wylie	Y	Y	Y	Y	N	Y	N	Y
16 Regula	N	Y	Y	Y	N	N	N	Y
17 Ashbrook	Y	Y	Y	Y	Y	Y	N	Y
18 Applegate	Y	Y	Y	Y	Y	Y	N	Y
19 Carney	?	?	Y	Y	N	N	N	N
20 Oakar	N	N	N	Y	N	Y	N	Y
21 Stokes	N	N	N	Y	Y	N	Y	N
22 Vanik	Y	N	Y	Y	Y	N	N	N
23 Mottl	Y	Y	Y	Y	Y	Y	Y	Y
OKLAHOMA								
1 Jones	Y	Y	Y	Y	N	N	N	Y
2 Risenhoover	Y	Y	Y	Y	Y	Y	N	Y
3 Watkins	Y	Y	Y	Y	Y	Y	N	Y
4 Steed	Y	Y	Y	Y	N	Y	N	Y
5 Edwards	Y	Y	Y	?	N	Y	N	Y
6 English	Y	Y	Y	Y	Y	Y	N	Y
OREGON								
1 AuCoin	Y	N	Y	Y	Y	N	N	Y
2 Ullman	N	N	N	Y	N	N	N	N
3 Duncan	N	N	N	#	N	N	N	N
4 Weaver	Y	N	Y	Y	Y	Y	Y	Y
PENNSYLVANIA								
1 Myers, M.	N	N	Y	Y	N	N	N	Y
2 Nix	?	?	X	Y	N	N	N	N
3 Lederer	N	N	N	Y	N	N	N	Y
4 Eilberg	N	Y	Y	Y	N	N	N	Y
5 Schulze	Y	Y	Y	Y	N	Y	N	Y
6 Yatron	Y	Y	Y	Y	N	N	N	Y
7 Edgar	N	N	N	Y	Y	N	N	N
8 Kostmayer	N	N	N	Y	Y	N	N	N
9 Shuster	Y	Y	Y	Y	Y	Y	N	Y
10 McDade	?	?	?	?	?	?	?	?
11 Flood	N	N	Y	Y	N	N	N	Y
12 Murtha	Y	Y	Y	Y	N	N	N	Y
13 Coughlin	N	N	Y	N	N	Y	N	Y
14 Moorhead	N	N	N	Y	N	N	N	N
15 Rooney	N	N	Y	Y	N	?	N	N
16 Walker	Y	Y	Y	N	Y	Y	N	Y
17 Ertel	Y	Y	Y	Y	Y	Y	N	Y
18 Walgren	N	N	Y	Y	Y	N	N	Y
19 Goodling, W.	Y	Y	Y	N	N	N	N	Y
20 Gaydos	Y	Y	Y	Y	Y	Y	Y	Y
21 Dent	✓	✓	✓	#	✓	✓	▮	✓
22 Murphy	Y	Y	Y	Y	Y	Y	Y	Y
23 Ammerman	N	N	Y	Y	Y	Y	Y	Y
24 Marks	N	N	Y	Y	N	Y	N	N
25 Myers, G.	N	N	Y	Y	N	Y	N	N
RHODE ISLAND								
1 St Germain	Y	N	Y	Y	N	Y	Y	Y
2 Beard	Y	Y	Y	Y	Y	✓	N	Y
SOUTH CAROLINA								
1 Davis	Y	Y	N	Y	Y	Y	N	Y
2 Spence	Y	Y	N	Y	N	Y	N	Y
3 Derrick	Y	N	N	Y	N	N	N	N
4 Mann	N	Y	N	Y	N	N	N	N
5 Holland	N	N	N	Y	N	N	Y	Y
6 Jenrette	N	Y	N	N	N	N	N	N
SOUTH DAKOTA								
1 Pressler	Y	Y	Y	?	?	?	?	?
2 Abdnor	Y	Y	Y	Y	N	Y	N	Y
TENNESSEE								
1 Quillen	Y	Y	Y	Y	N	Y	N	Y
2 Duncan	Y	Y	Y	Y	N	Y	N	Y
3 Lloyd	Y	Y	Y	Y	N	Y	N	✓
4 Gore	N	N	Y	Y	N	N	N	N
5 Vacancy								
6 Beard	Y	Y	Y	Y	N	Y	N	Y

	559	560	561	562	563	564	565	566
7 Jones	Y	Y	Y	Y	Y	✓	?	✓
8 Ford	?	?	?	?	?	?	?	X
TEXAS								
1 Hall	Y	Y	Y	Y	N	Y	N	Y
2 Wilson, C.	N	N	N	Y	N	N	N	N
3 Collins	Y	Y	Y	N	Y	Y	N	Y
4 Roberts	Y	Y	Y	Y	N	Y	N	Y
5 Mattox	Y	N	N	Y	Y	Y	Y	Y
6 Teague	✓	✓	?	?	X	X	?	✓
7 Archer	Y	Y	Y	Y	N	Y	N	Y
8 Eckhardt	N	N	N	?	Y	N	N	N
9 Brooks	N	Y	Y	Y	N	N	N	N
10 Pickle	N	Y	Y	Y	N	?	N	N
11 Poage	Y	Y	Y	Y	Y	N	N	Y
12 Wright	N	N	Y	Y	N	N	N	N
13 Hightower	Y	Y	Y	Y	N	N	N	N
14 Young	?	?	?	?	N	?	?	?
15 de la Garza	Y	Y	Y	Y	N	N	N	Y
16 White	Y	Y	Y	Y	N	Y	N	Y
17 Burleson	Y	Y	?	Y	N	N	N	Y
18 Jordan	N	N	N	Y	N	N	N	N
19 Mahon	N	Y	N	Y	N	N	N	N
20 Gonzalez	N	N	Y	Y	N	N	N	N
21 Krueger	N	N	Y	#	X	X	▮	✓
22 Gammage	Y	Y	Y	Y	N	Y	N	Y
23 Kazen	Y	Y	Y	Y	N	Y	N	Y
24 Milford	?	?	Y	?	N	N	N	N
UTAH								
1 McKay	Y	N	Y	#	Y	N	N	N
2 Marriott	Y	Y	Y	Y	N	Y	N	Y
VERMONT								
AL Jeffords	N	N	Y	Y	Y	N	N	N
VIRGINIA								
1 Trible	Y	Y	Y	Y	N	Y	N	Y
2 Whitehurst	Y	Y	Y	Y	N	Y	N	Y
3 Satterfield	Y	Y	Y	Y	N	Y	N	Y
4 Daniel	Y	Y	Y	Y	N	Y	N	Y
5 Daniel	Y	Y	Y	Y	N	Y	N	Y
6 Butler	Y	Y	Y	Y	N	Y	N	Y
7 Robinson	Y	Y	Y	Y	N	Y	N	Y
8 Harris	N	N	N	Y	N	N	N	N
9 Wampler	?	?	Y	Y	N	Y	N	Y
10 Fisher	N	N	N	Y	N	N	N	N
WASHINGTON								
1 Pritchard	N	N	N	Y	N	N	N	N
2 Meeds	▮	N	?	#	N	N	N	N
3 Bonker	N	N	Y	Y	N	N	N	N
4 McCormack	N	N	Y	Y	N	N	N	N
5 Foley	N	N	N	Y	N	N	N	N
6 Dicks	N	N	Y	Y	N	N	N	N
7 Cunningham	Y	Y	Y	Y	N	Y	N	Y
WEST VIRGINIA								
1 Mollohan	Y	Y	Y	Y	N	N	N	N
2 Staggers	N	N	Y	Y	N	N	N	Y
3 Slack	Y	?	?	Y	Y	N	N	Y
4 Rahall	Y	N	Y	Y	N	N	N	N
WISCONSIN								
1 Aspin	N	N	Y	Y	Y	N	N	N
2 Kastenmeier	N	N	N	Y	Y	N	N	N
3 Baldus	N	N	N	Y	N	N	N	N
4 Zablocki	N	N	N	Y	N	N	N	N
5 Reuss	N	N	N	Y	Y	N	N	N
6 Steiger	N	N	N	N	N	N	N	N
7 Obey	N	N	N	Y	N	N	N	N
8 Cornell	N	N	N	Y	Y	Y	Y	N
9 Kasten	?	?	?	?	?	?	?	?
WYOMING								
AL Roncalio	N	N	N	#	Y	#	Y	N

Democrats ***Republicans***

567. HR 12931. Foreign Aid Appropriations, Fiscal 1979. Harkin, D-Iowa, amendment to reduce spending for Title I programs by 2 percent, or $44 million, except for the $1.628 billion of the Economic Support Fund allocated to Israel, Egypt and Jordan. Adopted 293-52: R 116-5; D 177-47 (ND 113-46; SD 64-1), Aug. 3, 1978. A "nay" was a vote supporting the president's position.

568. HR 12931. Foreign Aid Appropriations, Fiscal 1979. Long, D-Md., motion that the House resolve itself into the Committee of the Whole for further consideration of the bill to appropriate fiscal 1979 funds for foreign assistance programs of the State Department. Motion agreed to 272-7: R 99-4; D 173-3 (ND 124-1; SD 49-2), Aug. 4, 1978.

569. HR 12931. Foreign Aid Appropriations, Fiscal 1979. Harkin, D-Iowa, amendment, as amended by Obey, D-Wis., amendment, to reduce the appropriation for foreign military credit sales by $12,600,000 and to specify that of the total appropriation for this category, $2.5 million would be available for Lebanon and $8.5 million would be available for Jordan. Adopted 300-29: R 101-14; D 199-15 (ND 139-15; SD 60-0), Aug. 4, 1978. A "nay" was a vote supporting the president's position.

570. HR 13635. Defense Appropriations, Fiscal 1979. Adoption of the rule (H Res 1291) providing for House floor consideration of the bill to appropriate fiscal 1979 funds for Defense Department operations and programs. Adopted 330-7: R 115-1; D 215-6 (ND 153-5; SD 62-1), Aug. 4, 1978.

571. HR 13635. Defense Appropriations, Fiscal 1979. Mahon, D-Texas, motion that the House resolve itself into the Committee of the Whole for further consideration of the bill. Motion agreed to 320-6: R 115-3; D 205-3 (ND 144-3; SD 61-0), Aug. 7, 1978.

572. HR 13635. Defense Appropriations, Fiscal 1979. Montgomery, D-Miss., amendment to add $15.5 million for reserve recruiting incentives. Adopted 257-121: R 102-27; D 155-94 (ND 85-86; SD 70-8), Aug. 7, 1978.

573. HR 13635. Defense Appropriations, Fiscal 1979. Volkmer, D-Mo., amendment to reduce by 2 percent appropriations for Title I of the bill. Rejected 53-327: R 11-121; D 42-206 (ND 42-130; SD 0-76), Aug. 7, 1978.

574. HR 13635. Defense Appropriations, Fiscal 1979. Dickinson, R-Ala., amendment to consolidate helicopter basic training by transferring Navy helicopter pilot training to Army control. Adopted 252-128: R 113-18; D 139-110 (ND 114-58; SD 25-52), Aug. 7, 1978.

KEY

- Y Voted for (yea).
- ✓ Paired for.
- † Announced for.
- # CQ Poll for.
- N Voted against (nay).
- X Paired against.
- - Announced against.
- ▮ CQ Poll against.
- P Voted "present."
- ● Voted "present" to avoid possible conflict of interest.
- ? Did not vote or otherwise make a position known.

	567	568	569	570	571	572	573	574
ALABAMA								
1 Edwards	Y	Y	Y	Y	Y	N	N	Y
2 Dickinson	Y	Y	Y	Y	Y	Y	N	Y
3 Nichols	Y	Y	Y	Y	Y	Y	N	Y
4 Bevill	Y	Y	Y	Y	Y	Y	N	Y
5 Flippo	Y	Y	Y	Y	Y	Y	N	Y
6 Buchanan	Y	Y	Y	Y	Y	Y	N	Y
7 Flowers	?	?	?	?	?	?	?	?
ALASKA								
AL Young	▮	#	#	#	#	Y	N	Y
ARIZONA								
1 Rhodes	Y	Y	Y	Y	?	?	?	?
2 Udall	Y	#	Y	Y	#	#	N	Y
3 Stump	Y	Y	Y	Y	Y	Y	N	N
4 Rudd	Y	?	?	?	Y	Y	N	N
ARKANSAS								
1 Alexander	P	Y	?	Y	?	Y	N	N
2 Tucker	Y	#	#	#	#	Y	N	N
3 Hammerschmidt	Y	Y	Y	Y	Y	Y	N	Y
4 Thornton	Y	?	Y	Y	Y	Y	?	?
CALIFORNIA								
1 Johnson	N	Y	Y	Y	Y	Y	N	N
2 Clausen	Y	Y	Y	Y	Y	Y	N	Y
3 Moss	?	Y	?	?	?	N	N	N
4 Leggett	Y	?	?	Y	Y	Y	N	Y
5 Burton, J.	Y	?	Y	Y	Y	N	Y	Y
6 Burton, P.	N	Y	Y	?	Y	N	Y	Y
7 Miller	Y	Y	Y	Y	Y	N	N	Y
8 Dellums	N	#	Y	Y	Y	N	Y	Y
9 Stark	Y	#	Y	Y	Y	N	Y	Y
10 Edwards	N	Y	Y	Y	Y	N	Y	Y
11 Ryan	Y	Y	Y	Y	Y	N	N	Y
12 McCloskey	Y	Y	Y	Y	Y	N	N	Y
13 Mineta	Y	Y	Y	Y	Y	N	N	Y
14 McFall	N	Y	Y	Y	Y	N	N	N
15 Sisk	?	?	?	Y	?	?	?	?
16 Panetta	Y	Y	Y	Y	Y	Y	N	N
17 Krebs	Y	Y	Y	Y	Y	N	N	N
18 Vacancy								
19 Lagomarsino	Y	Y	N	Y	Y	Y	N	Y
20 Goldwater	Y	?	N	Y	?	Y	N	Y
21 Corman	N	?	Y	Y	Y	N	N	Y
22 Moorhead	Y	Y	Y	Y	Y	Y	N	Y
23 Beilenson	N	Y	N	Y	#	▮	▮	#
24 Waxman	Y	Y	#	Y	Y	N	Y	Y
25 Roybal	Y	Y	Y	Y	Y	N	N	Y
26 Rousselot	Y	?	?	?	?	Y	N	Y
27 Dornan	Y	Y	Y	N	Y	Y	N	Y
28 Burke	#	#	#	#	#	X	▮	X
29 Hawkins	?	?	?	?	Y	N	N	Y
30 Danielson	Y	?	?	?	Y	N	N	N
31 Wilson, C.H.	?	Y	N	Y	?	?	?	?
32 Anderson	Y	Y	Y	Y	Y	N	N	Y
33 Clawson	Y	Y	Y	Y	Y	Y	N	Y
34 Hannaford	Y	Y	Y	Y	Y	Y	N	Y
35 Lloyd	Y	N	Y	Y	N	Y	N	Y
36 Brown	?	?	Y	Y	?	?	?	?
37 Pettis	Y	Y	Y	Y	Y	Y	N	Y
38 Patterson	Y	Y	Y	Y	Y	Y	N	Y
39 Wiggins	#	#	#	#	#	Y	N	Y
40 Badham	Y	Y	Y	Y	Y	Y	N	Y
41 Wilson, B.	Y	N	N	Y	N	Y	N	Y
42 Van Deerlin	Y	Y	Y	Y	Y	N	N	Y
43 Burgener	Y	Y	Y	Y	Y	Y	N	Y
COLORADO								
1 Schroeder	Y	Y	#	Y	Y	N	N	Y
2 Wirth	Y	Y	Y	?	?	✓	?	✓
3 Evans	▮	#	Y	Y	Y	N	N	Y
4 Johnson	Y	Y	Y	Y	?	?	Y	Y
5 Armstrong	N	N	Y	Y	?	?	N	Y
CONNECTICUT								
1 Cotter	Y	Y	Y	Y	#	N	N	N
2 Dodd	Y	?	?	Y	?	N	N	Y
3 Giaimo	Y	?	Y	N	Y	N	N	N
4 McKinney	Y	Y	Y	Y	#	Y	N	Y
5 Sarasin	#	#	#	#	#	#	▮	#
6 Moffett	?	?	Y	Y	Y	N	Y	Y
DELAWARE								
AL Evans	Y	Y	Y	Y	Y	Y	N	Y
FLORIDA								
1 Sikes	Y	Y	Y	Y	Y	Y	N	N
2 Fuqua	Y	Y	Y	Y	Y	Y	N	N
3 Bennett	Y	Y	Y	Y	Y	Y	N	N
4 Chappell	Y	?	Y	Y	Y	Y	N	N
5 Kelly	Y	Y	N	Y	Y	Y	N	N
6 Young	Y	Y	Y	Y	Y	Y	N	N
7 Gibbons	Y	Y	Y	Y	Y	Y	N	N
8 Ireland	Y	?	?	?	Y	Y	N	N
9 Frey	?	?	?	?	?	?	?	?
10 Bafalis	Y	Y	Y	Y	Y	Y	N	N
11 Rogers	Y	Y	Y	Y	Y	Y	N	N
12 Burke	Y	Y	Y	Y	Y	N	N	Y
13 Lehman	Y	Y	Y	Y	Y	N	N	▮
14 Pepper	Y	#	Y	Y	#	#	N	N
15 Fascell	Y	Y	Y	N	Y	Y	N	N
GEORGIA								
1 Ginn	Y	#	#	#	Y	Y	N	N
2 Mathis	?	?	?	?	?	?	?	?
3 Brinkley	Y	Y	Y	Y	Y	Y	N	N
4 Levitas	Y	Y	Y	Y	Y	Y	N	Y
5 Fowler	?	?	?	?	?	?	?	?
6 Flynt	?	Y	Y	Y	Y	Y	N	N
7 McDonald	Y	N	Y	Y	#	Y	N	N
8 Evans	Y	Y	Y	Y	?	Y	N	Y
9 Jenkins	#	#	#	#	#	#	▮	#
10 Barnard	?	?	?	?	?	?	?	?
HAWAII								
1 Heftel	?	?	?	?	Y	Y	N	Y
2 Akaka	Y	Y	Y	Y	Y	Y	N	Y
IDAHO								
1 Symms	Y	Y	Y	Y	Y	Y	N	N
2 Hansen, G.	Y	Y	Y	Y	?	?	?	?
ILLINOIS								
1 Metcalfe	?	?	?	?	Y	N	N	Y
2 Murphy	Y	Y	Y	Y	Y	N	N	Y
3 Russo	Y	Y	Y	Y	Y	?	Y	Y
4 Derwinski	Y	Y	?	Y	Y	N	N	Y
5 Fary	N	Y	Y	Y	Y	N	N	N
6 Hyde	Y	Y	Y	Y	Y	N	N	N
7 Collins	?	Y	Y	Y	Y	Y	Y	Y
8 Rostenkowski	N	Y	Y	Y	Y	N	N	N
9 Yates	N	Y	Y	Y	Y	N	N	Y
10 Mikva	#	#	#	#	Y	Y	Y	Y
11 Annunzio	N	Y	Y	Y	Y	Y	N	Y
12 Crane	Y	Y	Y	Y	Y	Y	N	Y
13 McClory	Y	Y	Y	Y	Y	Y	N	Y
14 Erlenborn	Y	Y	Y	Y	Y	N	N	Y
15 Corcoran	Y	Y	Y	Y	Y	N	N	Y
16 Anderson	Y	Y	N	Y	Y	N	N	Y
17 O'Brien	#	#	#	#	Y	Y	N	Y
18 Michel	Y	Y	Y	Y	Y	N	N	Y
19 Railsback	?	Y	?	Y	Y	N	?	Y
20 Findley	N	Y	N	Y	Y	N	N	Y
21 Madigan	Y	Y	Y	Y	Y	Y	N	N
22 Shipley	?	?	?	?	?	X	?	X
23 Price	N	Y	Y	Y	Y	Y	N	N
24 Simon	N	Y	N	Y	Y	Y	N	Y
INDIANA								
1 Benjamin	Y	Y	Y	Y	Y	N	N	Y
2 Fithian	Y	Y	Y	Y	Y	Y	N	Y
3 Brademas	Y	Y	Y	Y	Y	N	N	N
4 Quayle	?	N	Y	Y	N	N	N	Y
5 Hillis	Y	Y	Y	Y	?	Y	N	Y
6 Evans	Y	Y	Y	Y	Y	Y	N	Y
7 Myers, J.	?	?	Y	Y	Y	Y	N	Y
8 Cornwell	Y	?	?	?	Y	Y	N	?
9 Hamilton	Y	Y	Y	Y	Y	Y	N	Y
10 Sharp	Y	Y	Y	Y	Y	Y	Y	Y
11 Jacobs	Y	#	Y	Y	#	N	Y	Y
IOWA								
1 Leach	Y	Y	Y	Y	Y	Y	N	Y
2 Blouin	Y	?	?	?	Y	N	Y	Y
3 Grassley	Y	Y	Y	Y	Y	Y	N	Y
4 Smith	Y	?	Y	Y	Y	Y	N	Y
5 Harkin	Y	Y	Y	Y	Y	N	Y	N
6 Bedell	N	Y	Y	Y	Y	N	N	Y

Democrats ***Republicans***

	567	568	569	570	571	572	573	574
KANSAS								
1 Sebelius	Y	?	?	?	Y	Y	N	Y
2 Keys	Y	#	Y	Y	Y	N	Y	Y
3 Winn	Y	Y	Y	Y	Y	Y	N	Y
4 Glickman	Y	Y	Y	Y	Y	Y	N	N
5 Skubitz	Y	Y	Y	?	Y	?	N	N
KENTUCKY								
1 Hubbard	#	#	#	#	Y	Y	N	N
2 Natcher	Y	Y	Y	Y	Y	Y	N	N
3 Mazzoli	Y	Y	Y	Y	Y	Y	N	Y
4 Snyder	Y	Y	Y	Y	Y	Y	N	Y
5 Carter	Y	Y	Y	Y	Y	Y	N	Y
6 Breckinridge	Y	Y	Y	Y	Y	Y	N	N
7 Perkins	Y	Y	Y	Y	Y	Y	N	Y
LOUISIANA								
1 Livingston	Y	Y	Y	Y	Y	Y	N	N
2 Boggs	Y	Y	Y	Y	Y	Y	N	N
3 Treen	Y	Y	N	Y	Y	Y	N	Y
4 Waggonner	Y	#	Y	Y	Y	Y	N	N
5 Huckaby	?	?	?	?	Y	Y	N	N
6 Moore	Y	Y	Y	Y	Y	Y	N	Y
7 Breaux	?	?	?	?	Y	Y	N	N
8 Long	Y	Y	Y	?	Y	Y	N	N
MAINE								
1 Emery	Y	#	#	#	Y	Y	N	Y
2 Cohen	?	#	?	#	Y	Y	N	Y
MARYLAND								
1 Bauman	Y	Y	Y	Y	Y	Y	N	Y
2 Long	N	Y	Y	Y	Y	Y	N	N
3 Mikulski	N	Y	Y	Y	?	Y	N	Y
4 Holt	Y	Y	Y	Y	Y	Y	N	Y
5 Spellman	Y	#	Y	Y	#	✓	N	Y
6 Byron	Y	?	Y	Y	Y	Y	N	N
7 Mitchell	N	#	Y	Y	N	N	✓	✓
8 Steers	Y	Y	Y	Y	Y	N	Y	Y
MASSACHUSETTS								
1 Conte	Y	Y	N	Y	?	N	N	Y
2 Boland	Y	#	Y	Y	#	N	N	Y
3 Early	N	Y	Y	Y	Y	N	N	Y
4 Drinan	Y	Y	Y	Y	Y	N	Y	Y
5 Tsongas	?	?	?	?	Y	N	?	Y
6 Harrington	#	#	#	#	#	●	#	#
7 Markey	?	Y	Y	Y	Y	N	Y	Y
8 O'Neill								
9 Moakley	Y	#	#	#	#	Y	N	Y
10 Heckler	?	?	?	?	Y	Y	N	Y
11 Burke	?	?	?	?	?	X	X	X
12 Studds	N	Y	Y	Y	Y	N	N	Y
MICHIGAN								
1 Conyers	●	#	#	#	#	X	✓	✓
2 Pursell	Y	?	Y	Y	Y	Y	Y	Y
3 Brown	Y	Y	Y	Y	Y	Y	N	Y
4 Stockman	#	#	Y	Y	Y	N	N	Y
5 Sawyer	Y	#	Y	Y	#	#	●	?
6 Carr	Y	Y	Y	Y	?	N	Y	Y
7 Kildee	Y	Y	Y	Y	Y	Y	N	Y
8 Traxler	Y	Y	Y	Y	#	Y	N	Y
9 Vander Jagt	Y	?	Y	Y	Y	Y	N	Y
10 Cederberg	Y	Y	Y	Y	?	Y	N	Y
11 Ruppe	Y	?	Y	Y	?	?	?	?
12 Bonior	N	#	N	Y	Y	N	Y	Y
13 Diggs	#	#	#	#	#	?	●	?
14 Nedzi	N	Y	N	Y	Y	Y	N	Y
15 Ford	Y	?	Y	Y	?	Y	N	N
16 Dingell	Y	Y	Y	N	Y	Y	N	N
17 Brodhead	Y	?	Y	Y	Y	N	N	Y
18 Blanchard	Y	Y	Y	Y	Y	Y	N	Y
19 Broomfield	Y	Y	Y	Y	Y	Y	N	N
MINNESOTA								
1 Quie	?	?	?	?	?	?	?	?
2 Hagedorn	Y	?	Y	Y	Y	Y	N	Y
3 Frenzel	Y	Y	Y	?	Y	Y	N	Y
4 Vento	N	Y	Y	Y	Y	N	N	Y
5 Fraser	?	?	?	?	?	?	?	?
6 Nolan	Y	?	Y	Y	Y	Y	Y	Y
7 Stangeland	Y	Y	Y	Y	Y	Y	N	Y
8 Oberstar	N	Y	Y	Y	Y	Y	N	N
MISSISSIPPI								
1 Whitten	Y	Y	Y	Y	Y	Y	N	N
2 Bowen	Y	?	Y	Y	?	Y	N	N
3 Montgomery	Y	Y	Y	Y	Y	Y	N	N
4 Cochran	?	?	?	?	?	?	?	?
5 Lott	Y	N	Y	Y	?	Y	N	N
MISSOURI								
1 Clay	?	?	?	?	?	?	?	?
2 Young	Y	Y	Y	Y	Y	Y	N	Y
3 Gephardt	Y	●	Y	Y	Y	N	Y	Y

	567	568	569	570	571	572	573	574
4 Skelton	?	?	?	?	?	?	?	?
5 Bolling	Y	#	#	#	#	#	●	●
6 Coleman	Y	Y	Y	Y	Y	Y	N	Y
7 Taylor	Y	Y	Y	Y	Y	Y	N	N
8 Ichord	Y	Y	Y	Y	Y	Y	N	Y
9 Volkmer	Y	Y	Y	Y	Y	N	Y	Y
10 Burlison	Y	Y	Y	Y	Y	N	N	N
MONTANA								
1 Baucus	Y	?	?	?	?	?	?	?
2 Marlenee	Y	Y	Y	Y	Y	Y	N	Y
NEBRASKA								
1 Thone	?	?	?	?	?	?	N	Y
2 Cavanaugh	N	?	Y	Y	Y	Y	N	Y
3 Smith	Y	Y	Y	Y	Y	Y	N	Y
NEVADA								
AL Santini	Y	Y	Y	Y	#	✓	✓	✓
NEW HAMPSHIRE								
1 D'Amours	Y	#	Y	Y	Y	Y	N	Y
2 Cleveland	Y	?	?	?	Y	Y	N	Y
NEW JERSEY								
1 Florio	Y	Y	[illegible]	Y	Y	Y	N	N
2 Hughes	?	Y	Y	Y	Y	Y	N	N
3 Howard	N	Y	Y	Y	Y	Y	N	N
4 Thompson	?	Y	Y	Y	Y	N	N	N
5 Fenwick	Y	Y	Y	Y	Y	N	Y	Y
6 Forsythe	Y	#	Y	Y	Y	Y	Y	Y
7 Maguire	#	Y	Y	Y	Y	?	Y	Y
8 Roe	Y	Y	Y	Y	Y	Y	N	N
9 Hollenbeck	#	Y	Y	Y	Y	N	Y	Y
10 Rodino	●	#	?	#	#	●	●	Y
11 Minish	Y	Y	Y	Y	Y	N	N	Y
12 Rinaldo	Y	Y	N	Y	Y	Y	N	Y
13 Meyner	Y	#	#	#	Y	N	N	Y
14 LeFante	#	#	#	#	#	X	●	#
15 Patten	N	#	Y	Y	#	Y	N	N
NEW MEXICO								
1 Lujan	?	?	?	?	Y	Y	Y	Y
2 Runnels	Y	Y	Y	Y	Y	Y	N	Y
NEW YORK								
1 Pike	Y	Y	Y	Y	Y	N	Y	Y
2 Downey	Y	Y	Y	Y	Y	N	Y	N
3 Ambro	Y	?	Y	Y	?	N	N	Y
4 Lent	Y	?	Y	Y	Y	Y	N	Y
5 Wydler	Y	?	?	?	Y	Y	N	Y
6 Wolff	Y	Y	Y	Y	Y	Y	N	N
7 Addabbo	Y	P	Y	Y	Y	N	N	N
8 Rosenthal	N	Y	N	Y	#	N	Y	N
9 Delaney	Y	Y	Y	Y	Y	N	N	N
10 Biaggi	Y	?	?	?	Y	Y	N	N
11 Scheuer	Y	Y	Y	Y	Y	N	Y	N
12 Chisholm	#	#	#	#	#	N	N	N
13 Solarz	N	Y	N	Y	Y	N	N	Y
14 Richmond	?	?	?	?	?	N	Y	Y
15 Zeferetti	#	#	#	#	#	Y	N	N
16 Holtzman	N	Y	Y	Y	Y	N	Y	Y
17 Murphy	N	?	?	?	Y	Y	?	N
18 Green	N	Y	N	Y	Y	N	N	Y
19 Rangel	N	?	?	?	Y	Y	N	N
20 Weiss	N	Y	Y	Y	Y	N	Y	Y
21 Garcia	●	#	#	#	#	Y	Y	Y
22 Bingham	Y	Y	Y	N	Y	N	Y	Y
23 Caputo	?	?	?	?	?	?	?	?
24 Ottinger	Y	Y	Y	N	Y	N	Y	X
25 Fish	Y	Y	Y	Y	Y	Y	N	Y
26 Gilman	Y	Y	N	Y	Y	Y	N	Y
27 McHugh	N	Y	Y	Y	Y	N	N	Y
28 Stratton	Y	Y	N	Y	Y	Y	N	N
29 Pattison	Y	#	Y	Y	Y	N	N	Y
30 McEwen	?	?	?	?	Y	N	N	Y
31 Mitchell	#	#	#	#	Y	Y	N	N
32 Hanley	Y	Y	Y	Y	#	Y	N	Y
33 Walsh	Y	?	?	?	Y	Y	N	Y
34 Horton	Y	Y	Y	Y	Y	Y	N	#
35 Conable	Y	Y	N	Y	Y	Y	N	Y
36 LaFalce	Y	#	N	Y	#	●	●	#
37 Nowak	Y	Y	Y	Y	Y	Y	N	Y
38 Kemp	?	?	?	?	Y	N	N	N
39 Lundine	Y	#	#	Y	N	N	N	Y
NORTH CAROLINA								
1 Jones	#	#	#	?	Y	Y	N	N
2 Fountain	Y	Y	Y	Y	#	Y	N	Y
3 Whitley	?	?	?	?	Y	Y	N	N
4 Andrews	Y	?	Y	Y	Y	Y	N	N
5 Neal	Y	Y	Y	Y	#	Y	N	Y
6 Preyer	Y	Y	Y	Y	Y	Y	N	Y
7 Rose	Y	Y	Y	Y	Y	Y	N	N
8 Hefner	Y	Y	Y	Y	Y	Y	N	Y

	567	568	569	570	571	572	573	574
9 Martin	Y	#	Y	Y	Y	Y	N	Y
10 Broyhill	Y	Y	Y	Y	Y	Y	N	Y
11 Gudger	Y	#	Y	Y	Y	Y	N	Y
NORTH DAKOTA								
AL Andrews	Y	Y	Y	Y	Y	Y	N	Y
OHIO								
1 Gradison	Y	?	?	?	Y	N	N	Y
2 Luken	?	?	Y	Y	Y	Y	N	Y
3 Whalen	#	#	Y	Y	Y	N	N	Y
4 Guyer	Y	Y	Y	Y	Y	Y	N	Y
5 Latta	Y	?	Y	Y	Y	Y	N	N
6 Harsha	Y	Y	Y	Y	Y	Y	N	N
7 Brown	?	?	?	?	?	?	?	?
8 Kindness	Y	Y	Y	Y	Y	Y	N	?
9 Ashley	N	?	?	?	Y	N	N	Y
10 Miller	Y	Y	Y	Y	Y	N	Y	N
11 Stanton	Y	Y	Y	Y	Y	Y	N	Y
12 Devine	Y	Y	Y	Y	Y	Y	N	Y
13 Pease	N	Y	Y	Y	Y	N	N	Y
14 Seiberling	N	#	Y	Y	Y	Y	Y	Y
15 Wylie	Y	Y	Y	Y	Y	Y	N	Y
16 Regula	Y	Y	Y	Y	Y	Y	N	Y
17 Ashbrook	Y	Y	Y	Y	Y	Y	N	Y
18 Applegate	Y	?	Y	Y	?	Y	N	N
19 Carney	Y	Y	Y	Y	Y	Y	N	N
20 Oakar	?	Y	N	Y	?	Y	N	Y
21 Stokes	N	Y	N	Y	?	N	Y	Y
22 Vanik	Y	Y	Y	Y	Y	N	N	Y
23 Mottl	#	#	#	#	Y	Y	N	N
OKLAHOMA								
1 Jones	Y	Y	Y	Y	Y	Y	N	N
2 Risenhoover	Y	?	?	Y	Y	Y	N	Y
3 Watkins	Y	Y	Y	Y	Y	Y	N	N
4 Steed	Y	Y	Y	Y	#	#	●	#
5 Edwards	Y	Y	Y	Y	Y	Y	N	Y
6 English	Y	?	?	Y	?	Y	N	N
OREGON								
1 AuCoin	Y	Y	Y	Y	Y	N	Y	Y
2 Ullman	Y	Y	Y	Y	Y	Y	N	N
3 Duncan	N	Y	N	Y	Y	Y	N	Y
4 Weaver	Y	Y	Y	N	Y	N	Y	Y
PENNSYLVANIA								
1 Myers, M.	N	Y	Y	Y	Y	Y	N	N
2 Nix	?	Y	N	Y	Y	N	N	N
3 Lederer	N	Y	Y	Y	Y	Y	N	N
4 Eilberg	Y	Y	Y	Y	Y	Y	N	Y
5 Schulze	Y	Y	Y	Y	Y	Y	N	Y
6 Yatron	Y	Y	Y	Y	Y	Y	N	Y
7 Edgar	#	Y	Y	Y	Y	N	N	Y
8 Kostmayer	N	Y	Y	Y	Y	N	Y	Y
9 Shuster	Y	Y	Y	Y	Y	Y	N	Y
10 McDade	?	Y	Y	Y	Y	Y	N	Y
11 Flood	Y	Y	Y	Y	Y	Y	N	N
12 Murtha	Y	Y	Y	Y	Y	Y	N	N
13 Coughlin	Y	Y	Y	Y	Y	Y	N	Y
14 Moorhead	Y	Y	Y	Y	#	N	N	Y
15 Rooney	Y	Y	Y	Y	Y	Y	N	Y
16 Walker	Y	Y	Y	Y	Y	Y	Y	Y
17 Ertel	Y	Y	Y	Y	Y	Y	N	N
18 Walgren	Y	Y	Y	Y	Y	Y	Y	N
19 Goodling, W.	N	Y	N	Y	Y	Y	N	Y
20 Gaydos	Y	?	?	?	Y	Y	N	N
21 Dent	#	#	#	#	Y	Y	N	X
22 Murphy	Y	Y	Y	Y	Y	Y	N	N
23 Ammerman	Y	Y	Y	Y	?	Y	Y	Y
24 Marks	Y	Y	Y	Y	Y	Y	N	Y
25 Myers, G.	N	Y	N	Y	Y	N	Y	Y
RHODE ISLAND								
1 St Germain	Y	Y	Y	Y	Y	N	N	Y
2 Beard	Y	Y	Y	Y	#	Y	N	N
SOUTH CAROLINA								
1 Davis	Y	N	Y	Y	?	Y	N	Y
2 Spence	Y	Y	Y	Y	Y	Y	N	Y
3 Derrick	Y	Y	Y	Y	Y	Y	N	Y
4 Mann	Y	Y	Y	Y	?	?	?	?
5 Holland	Y	?	?	?	Y	Y	N	N
6 Jenrette	#	#	#	#	Y	Y	N	N
SOUTH DAKOTA								
1 Pressler	?	?	?	?	?	?	?	?
2 Abdnor	Y	#	#	#	Y	Y	N	Y
TENNESSEE								
1 Quillen	Y	Y	Y	Y	Y	Y	N	Y
2 Duncan	Y	Y	Y	Y	Y	Y	N	Y
3 Lloyd	#	#	#	#	Y	Y	N	N
4 Gore	#	#	#	#	Y	N	N	Y
5 Vacancy								
6 Beard	Y	Y	Y	Y	Y	Y	N	N

	567	568	569	570	571	572	573	574
7 Jones	#	#	#	#	#	Y	N	N
8 Ford	?	?	?	?	?	N	N	Y
TEXAS								
1 Hall	Y	Y	Y	Y	Y	Y	N	Y
2 Wilson, C.	Y	#	#	#	#	?	●	●
3 Collins	Y	?	Y	Y	N	N	N	Y
4 Roberts	Y	Y	Y	Y	Y	Y	N	N
5 Mattox	Y	?	Y	Y	Y	N	N	Y
6 Teague	?	?	?	?	?	✓	?	X
7 Archer	Y	Y	Y	Y	Y	Y	N	Y
8 Eckhardt	Y	?	Y	Y	?	N	N	Y
9 Brooks	Y	Y	Y	Y	Y	Y	N	N
10 Pickle	?	?	?	?	Y	Y	N	N
11 Poage	Y	Y	Y	Y	Y	Y	N	N
12 Wright	Y	Y	Y	Y	?	Y	N	N
13 Hightower	Y	Y	Y	Y	?	Y	N	N
14 Young	?	?	?	Y	Y	Y	?	N
15 de la Garza	Y	Y	Y	Y	?	Y	N	N
16 White	#	#	#	#	Y	Y	N	N
17 Burleson	Y	Y	Y	Y	Y	Y	N	N
18 Jordan	N	Y	Y	Y	Y	N	N	Y
19 Mahon	Y	Y	Y	Y	Y	N	N	N
20 Gonzalez	Y	Y	Y	Y	#	Y	N	N
21 Krueger	#	#	#	#	Y	Y	N	N
22 Gammage	Y	#	Y	Y	#	✓	X	✓
23 Kazen	Y	Y	Y	Y	Y	Y	N	N
24 Milford	?	?	?	?	?	Y	?	Y
UTAH								
1 McKay	Y	Y	Y	Y	Y	N	N	N
2 Marriott	Y	Y	Y	Y	Y	Y	N	Y
VERMONT								
AL Jeffords	Y	#	#	Y	#	Y	N	Y
VIRGINIA								
1 Trible	Y	?	?	?	Y	Y	N	Y
2 Whitehurst	Y	Y	Y	Y	Y	Y	N	Y
3 Satterfield	Y	Y	Y	Y	Y	Y	N	N
4 Daniel	Y	Y	Y	Y	Y	Y	N	Y
5 Daniel	Y	Y	Y	Y	Y	Y	N	N
6 Butler	Y	Y	Y	Y	?	?	?	?
7 Robinson	Y	Y	Y	Y	Y	N	N	Y
8 Harris	Y	Y	Y	Y	Y	Y	N	Y
9 Wampler	Y	Y	Y	Y	?	Y	N	Y
10 Fisher	?	Y	Y	Y	Y	N	N	Y
WASHINGTON								
1 Pritchard	Y	Y	Y	Y	Y	N	Y	Y
2 Meeds	N	#	#	#	Y	Y	N	N
3 Bonker	N	Y	Y	Y	Y	N	N	Y
4 McCormack	Y	?	Y	Y	Y	Y	N	Y
5 Foley	Y	Y	Y	Y	Y	Y	N	Y
6 Dicks	Y	Y	Y	Y	Y	Y	N	Y
7 Cunningham	Y	Y	Y	Y	#	Y	N	Y
WEST VIRGINIA								
1 Mollohan	Y	Y	Y	Y	N	Y	N	N
2 Staggers	N	Y	Y	Y	Y	Y	N	N
3 Slack	Y	Y	Y	Y	Y	Y	N	Y
4 Rahall	Y	Y	Y	Y	Y	Y	Y	Y
WISCONSIN								
1 Aspin	Y	Y	Y	Y	Y	N	N	Y
2 Kastenmeier	N	Y	Y	Y	Y	Y	Y	Y
3 Baldus	Y	Y	Y	Y	#	X	X	✓
4 Zablocki	N	Y	N	Y	Y	Y	N	N
5 Reuss	Y	Y	Y	Y	Y	N	N	Y
6 Steiger	Y	Y	Y	Y	Y	Y	N	Y
7 Obey	Y	Y	Y	Y	?	N	N	Y
8 Cornell	Y	Y	Y	Y	#	Y	N	Y
9 Kasten	?	?	?	?	?	✓	?	?
WYOMING								
AL Roncalio	#	#	#	#	#	#	●	#

Democrats ***Republicans***

575. HR 13635. Defense Appropriations, Fiscal 1979. Yates, D-Ill., amendment to delete $2.1 billion for a nuclear-powered aircraft carrier. Rejected 156-218: R 23-104; D 133-114 (ND 117-53; SD 16-61), Aug. 7, 1978. A "yea" was a vote supporting the president's position.

576. HR 13635. Defense Appropriations, Fiscal 1979. Giaimo, D-Conn., amendment to delete $3 million for development of a diesel engine for future combat vehicles. Rejected 107-269: R 10-128; D 97-141 (ND 91-70; SD 6-71), Aug. 8, 1978.

577. HR 13635. Defense Appropriations, Fiscal 1979. Heckler, R-Mass., amendment to add $1 million for Army food research. Rejected 103-277: R 69-68; D 34-209 (ND 29-136; SD 5-73), Aug. 8, 1978.

578. HR 13635. Defense Appropriations, Fiscal 1979. Howard, D-N.J., amendment to allow up to 10 percent of Defense Department procurement contracts to be targeted to areas of high unemployment. Rejected 165-213: R 45-93; D 120-120 (ND 111-51; SD 9-69), Aug. 8, 1978.

579. HR 13635. Defense Appropriations, Fiscal 1979. Brown, R-Mich., amendment to prohibit purchase of foreign manufactured trucks to haul cargo in combat areas. Rejected 72-302: R 28-107; D 44-195 (ND 41-121; SD 3-74), Aug. 8, 1978.

580. HR 13635. Defense Appropriations, Fiscal 1979. Conte, R-Mass., to delete limitations on the use of competitive bidding to award contracts for moving household goods. Adopted 269-96: R 115-17; D 154-79 (ND 114-47; SD 40-32), Aug. 8, 1978.

581. HR 13635. Defense Appropriations, Fiscal 1979. Mitchell, D-Md., substitute amendment, to the Harkin, D-Iowa, amendment *(see vote 582, below)*, to reduce by 1 percent the funds appropriated by the bill. Rejected 136-222: R 34-98; D 102-124 (ND 93-57; SD 9-67), Aug. 8, 1978.

582. HR 13635. Defense Appropriations, Fiscal 1979. Harkin, D-Iowa, amendment to reduce by 2 percent the funds appropriated by the bill. Rejected 102-252: R 23-108; D 79-144 (ND 77-70; SD 2-74), Aug. 8, 1978.

KEY

- Y Voted for (yea).
- ✓ Paired for.
- † Announced for.
- # CQ Poll for.
- N Voted against (nay).
- X Paired against.
- \- Announced against.
- ▮ CQ Poll against.
- P Voted "present."
- ● Voted "present" to avoid possible conflict of interest.
- ? Did not vote or otherwise make a position known.

	575	576	577	578	579	580	581	582
ALABAMA								
1 Edwards	Y	N	Y	N	N	Y	N	N
2 Dickinson	?	N	Y	N	N	Y	N	N
3 Nichols	N	N	N	N	N	Y	N	N
4 Bevill	N	N	N	N	N	Y	N	N
5 Flippo	N	N	N	N	N	Y	N	N
6 Buchanan	N	N	Y	N	N	Y	N	N
7 Flowers	?	?	?	?	?	?	?	?
ALASKA								
AL Young	N	N	Y	N	N	N	N	N
ARIZONA								
1 Rhodes	?	?	?	?	?	?	?	?
2 Udall	Y	Y	N	N	N	Y	?	?
3 Stump	N	N	N	N	N	Y	N	N
4 Rudd	N	N	N	N	N	Y	N	N
ARKANSAS								
1 Alexander	N	N	N	N	N	N	N	N
2 Tucker	N	▮	#	▮	▮	#	N	Y
3 Hammerschmic	N	N	Y	N	N	Y	N	N
4 Thornton	N	N	N	N	N	?	N	N
CALIFORNIA								
1 Johnson	N	N	N	Y	N	N	N	N
2 Clausen	N	N	Y	Y	N	Y	N	N
3 Moss	?	N	N	N	N	?	?	?
4 Leggett	Y	N	Y	N	N	Y	Y	Y
5 Burton, J.	Y	Y	N	Y	Y	Y	Y	Y
6 Burton, P.	?	Y	?	Y	N	Y	Y	?
7 Miller	Y	Y	N	Y	N	Y	Y	Y
8 Dellums	Y	Y	N	Y	N	Y	Y	Y
9 Stark	Y	Y	N	Y	N	Y	Y	?
10 Edwards	Y	Y	N	Y	N	Y	Y	Y
11 Ryan	Y	N	N	N	Y	Y	Y	Y
12 McCloskey	Y	N	Y	N	N	Y	N	N
13 Mineta	Y	Y	Y	Y	N	Y	Y	Y
14 McFall	N	N	N	N	N	N	N	N
15 Sisk	X	?	?	?	?	X	?	X
16 Panetta	Y	N	N	N	N	Y	Y	Y
17 Krebs	Y	N	N	Y	N	Y	Y	N
18 Vacancy								
19 Lagomarsino	N	N	N	N	N	N	N	N
20 Goldwater	N	N	N	N	N	Y	N	N
21 Corman	N	N	N	N	N	N	Y	N
22 Moorhead	N	N	N	N	N	Y	N	N
23 Beilenson	✓	#	▮	#	▮	#	#	#
24 Waxman	Y	Y	N	N	N	N	#	#
25 Roybal	Y	Y	N	Y	N	Y	Y	Y
26 Rousselot	N	N	N	N	N	Y	N	Y
27 Dornan	N	N	N	N	N	Y	N	?
28 Burke	✓	▮	▮	▮	▮	?	#	#
29 Hawkins	?	Y	N	Y	N	Y	Y	N
30 Danielson	N	Y	N	N	N	N	?	?
31 Wilson, C.H.	?	?	?	?	?	?	?	?
32 Anderson	N	N	N	Y	Y	N	Y	Y
33 Clawson	N	N	N	N	N	Y	N	N
34 Hannaford	N	N	N	Y	N	N	N	N
35 Lloyd	N	N	N	N	N	N	N	N
36 Brown	?	Y	N	Y	N	Y	Y	Y
37 Pettis	N	N	Y	N	N	Y	N	N
38 Patterson	N	N	N	N	N	Y	Y	N
39 Wiggins	N	N	N	N	▮	Y	N	N
40 Badham	N	N	N	N	N	Y	N	N
41 Wilson, B.	N	N	Y	Y	N	Y	N	N
42 Van Deerlin	N	Y	N	N	N	Y	N	N
43 Burgener	N	N	Y	N	N	Y	N	N
COLORADO								
1 Schroeder	Y	Y	N	Y	N	Y	Y	Y
2 Wirth	✓	Y	N	N	N	Y	Y	Y
3 Evans	Y	N	N	Y	N	N	▮	▮
4 Johnson	N	Y	N	N	N	Y	Y	Y

	575	576	577	578	579	580	581	582
5 Armstrong	N	N	N	N	N	Y	N	N
CONNECTICUT								
1 Cotter	Y	Y	N	Y	N	N	Y	Y
2 Dodd	Y	Y	N	Y	N	Y	N	N
3 Giaimo	Y	Y	N	?	N	N	Y	N
4 McKinney	Y	Y	N	Y	N	Y	Y	Y
5 Sarasin	#	Y	N	Y	N	Y	Y	N
6 Moffett	Y	Y	N	Y	N	Y	?	Y
DELAWARE								
AL Evans	N	N	Y	Y	N	Y	N	N
FLORIDA								
1 Sikes	N	N	N	N	N	N	N	N
2 Fuqua	N	N	N	N	N	N	N	N
3 Bennett	N	N	N	N	N	Y	N	N
4 Chappell	N	N	N	N	N	N	N	N
5 Kelly	N	N	N	N	N	Y	N	N
6 Young	N	N	Y	N	Y	N	N	N
7 Gibbons	Y	Y	N	N	N	Y	N	N
8 Ireland	N	N	N	N	?	?	?	?
9 Frey	?	?	?	?	?	?	?	?
10 Bafalis	N	N	N	N	N	Y	N	N
11 Rogers	Y	N	N	N	N	Y	N	N
12 Burke	N	N	N	N	N	Y	Y	N
13 Lehman	Y	Y	N	Y	N	Y	Y	N
14 Pepper	N	N	Y	Y	N	Y	Y	N
15 Fascell	N	N	N	Y	N	N	N	N
GEORGIA								
1 Ginn	N	N	N	N	N	N	N	N
2 Mathis	?	?	?	?	?	?	?	?
3 Brinkley	N	N	N	N	N	N	N	N
4 Levitas	Y	X	?	?	?	?	?	?
5 Fowler	?	?	?	?	?	?	?	?
6 Flynt	N	X	?	X	?	X	?	X
7 McDonald	N	N	N	N	N	Y	N	N
8 Evans	?	N	N	Y	N	Y	N	N
9 Jenkins	#	▮	▮	▮	▮	#	▮	▮
10 Barnard	?	?	?	?	?	?	?	?
HAWAII								
1 Heftel	Y	N	N	N	N	N	N	N
2 Akaka	N	N	N	N	N	N	Y	N
IDAHO								
1 Symms	N	N	Y	N	N	Y	N	N
2 Hansen, G.	?	?	?	?	?	?	?	?
ILLINOIS								
1 Metcalfe	Y	Y	N	Y	N	Y	Y	Y
2 Murphy	Y	Y	N	Y	Y	N	Y	Y
3 Russo	Y	N	N	Y	N	Y	Y	Y
4 Derwinski	N	N	N	N	N	Y	N	N
5 Fary	Y	N	Y	N	N	N	N	N
6 Hyde	N	N	N	Y	N	Y	N	N
7 Collins	Y	Y	N	Y	Y	N	Y	Y
8 Rostenkowski	Y	Y	N	Y	N	N	N	N
9 Yates	Y	Y	N	Y	N	Y	N	N
10 Mikva	Y	N	N	Y	N	Y	#	#
11 Annunzio	N	N	Y	N	N	N	Y	N
12 Crane	▮	N	N	N	N	Y	N	N
13 McClory	N	N	N	N	N	#	N	N
14 Erlenborn	Y	N	N	N	N	Y	N	N
15 Corcoran	N	N	N	N	N	Y	Y	Y
16 Anderson	Y	N	Y	N	N	Y	N	N
17 O'Brien	N	N	N	N	N	Y	N	N
18 Michel	N	N	Y	N	N	Y	N	N
19 Railsback	N	N	Y	N	N	Y	Y	N
20 Findley	Y	N	Y	N	N	Y	N	N
21 Madigan	Y	N	Y	Y	N	Y	N	N
22 Shipley	X	N	N	X	N	N	N	N
23 Price	N	N	Y	N	N	Y	N	N
24 Simon	Y	Y	N	N	N	Y	Y	Y
INDIANA								
1 Benjamin	Y	N	N	Y	Y	Y	Y	N
2 Fithian	N	N	N	Y	Y	Y	Y	N
3 Brademas	Y	Y	N	Y	Y	Y	Y	Y
4 Quayle	N	N	Y	N	N	Y	N	Y
5 Hillis	N	N	Y	Y	N	Y	N	N
6 Evans	N	N	?	?	?	?	?	?
7 Myers, J.	N	N	Y	N	N	N	N	Y
8 Cornwell	Y	Y	N	Y	Y	?	Y	Y
9 Hamilton	Y	Y	N	Y	N	Y	Y	Y
10 Sharp	Y	Y	N	Y	N	Y	Y	Y
11 Jacobs	Y	N	N	N	N	Y	N	Y
IOWA								
1 Leach	N	N	Y	N	N	Y	N	Y
2 Blouin	Y	Y	N	N	N	N	Y	Y
3 Grassley	N	N	N	N	N	Y	N	N
4 Smith	Y	N	Y	N	N	Y	N	Y
5 Harkin	Y	Y	N	N	N	N	Y	Y
6 Bedell	Y	Y	N	N	N	Y	Y	Y

Democrats ***Republicans***

	575	576	577	578	579	580	581	582
KANSAS								
1 Sebelius	N	N	Y	N	N	N	Y	N
2 Keys	Y	Y	N	N	N	Y	N	Y
3 Winn	N	N	Y	N	N	N	N	N
4 Glickman	Y	Y	N	N	N	Y	Y	N
5 Skubitz	?	N	?	N	N	Y	?	?
KENTUCKY								
1 Hubbard	N	N	N	N	N	N	N	N
2 Natcher	Y	N	N	N	N	N	N	N
3 Mazzoli	N	N	N	N	N	Y	Y	N
4 Snyder	N	N	N	N	Y	N	N	N
5 Carter	N	N	N	Y	Y	Y	N	N
6 Breckinridge	N	N	N	N	N	N	N	N
7 Perkins	N	N	N	Y	N	N	N	N
LOUISIANA								
1 Livingston	N	N	N	N	N	Y	N	N
2 Boggs	N	N	N	N	N	N	N	N
3 Treen	N	N	Y	N	N	Y	N	N
4 Waggonner	N	N	N	N	N	N	N	N
5 Huckaby	N	N	N	N	N	Y	N	N
6 Moore	N	N	N	N	N	Y	N	N
7 Breaux	N	N	N	N	N	N	N	N
8 Long	N	N	N	N	N	N	N	N
MAINE								
1 Emery	N	N	Y	Y	Y	Y	N	N
2 Cohen	Y	N	Y	Y	Y	Y	N	N
MARYLAND								
1 Bauman	N	N	N	N	N	N	N	N
2 Long	N	N	N	N	N	Y	N	N
3 Mikulski	Y	Y	Y	Y	Y	N	Y	Y
4 Holt	N	N	N	N	N	N	N	N
5 Spellman	Y	Y	Y	Y	N	Y	N	N
6 Byron	N	N	N	N	N	N	N	N
7 Mitchell	✔	Y	N	Y	N	Y	Y	Y
8 Steers	Y	N	Y	Y	Y	Y	Y	Y
MASSACHUSETTS								
1 Conte	Y	N	Y	Y	Y	Y	N	N
2 Boland	Y	Y	Y	Y	N	Y	N	N
3 Early	Y	Y	Y	Y	N	Y	N	N
4 Drinan	Y	Y	Y	Y	N	Y	†	†
5 Tsongas	?	?	?	?	?	?	?	?
6 Harrington	#	Y	Y	Y	▮	Y	P	P
7 Markey	Y	Y	Y	Y	N	Y	Y	Y
8 O'Neill								
9 Moakley	Y	Y	Y	Y	N	Y	Y	N
10 Heckler	Y	Y	Y	Y	?	?	?	?
11 Burke	X	N	Y	Y	N	Y	N	N
12 Studds	Y	Y	Y	Y	N	Y	N	N
MICHIGAN								
1 Conyers	✔	✔	▮	#	▮	✔	#	✔
2 Pursell	?	N	Y	Y	Y	Y	Y	Y
3 Brown	N	N	N	N	Y	?	?	?
4 Stockman	Y	N	N	N	N	Y	N	N
5 Sawyer	?	N	Y	N	N	Y	N	N
6 Carr	Y	Y	N	Y	Y	Y	Y	Y
7 Kildee	Y	Y	N	Y	Y	Y	Y	Y
8 Traxler	Y	Y	N	Y	Y	Y	N	N
9 Vander Jagt	N	N	Y	Y	Y	Y	Y	Y
10 Cederberg	N	N	Y	Y	Y	Y	N	Y
11 Ruppe	?	N	N	Y	N	Y	Y	Y
12 Bonior	Y	Y	N	#	?	✔	#	✔
13 Diggs	#	▮	▮	?	▮	#	#	?
14 Nedzi	Y	Y	N	N	N	Y	N	N
15 Ford	Y	Y	N	Y	Y	Y	Y	Y
16 Dingell	Y	?	N	Y	Y	Y	?	?
17 Brodhead	Y	Y	N	Y	Y	Y	Y	Y
18 Blanchard	Y	Y	N	Y	Y	Y	Y	Y
19 Broomfield	N	N	Y	N	Y	Y	Y	N
MINNESOTA								
1 Quie	?	N	Y	N	N	Y	Y	N
2 Hagedorn	N	N	Y	N	N	Y	N	N
3 Frenzel	Y	N	Y	N	N	Y	N	N
4 Vento	Y	Y	N	Y	N	Y	Y	N
5 Fraser	?	?	N	Y	N	Y	Y	Y
6 Nolan	Y	Y	N	Y	N	Y	Y	Y
7 Stangeland	N	N	N	N	Y	Y	N	N
8 Oberstar	Y	N	N	Y	N	N	Y	N
MISSISSIPPI								
1 Whitten	N	N	N	N	N	N	N	N
2 Bowen	N	N	N	N	N	N	N	N
3 Montgomery	N	N	Y	N	N	Y	N	N
4 Cochran	?	N	N	?	N	Y	N	N
5 Lott	N	N	N	N	▮	N	N	N
MISSOURI								
1 Clay	✔	?	?	?	?	?	?	?
2 Young	Y	X	▮	X	▮	#	▮	X
3 Gephardt	Y	Y	N	▮	▮	#	▮	#

	575	576	577	578	579	580	581	582
4 Skelton	X	?	?	?	?	?	?	?
5 Bolling	#	▮	▮	▮	▮	#	▮	▮
6 Coleman	N	N	N	N	Y	Y	N	N
7 Taylor	N	N	N	N	Y	Y	N	N
8 Ichord	N	N	N	N	N	Y	N	N
9 Volkmer	Y	Y	N	N	N	N	Y	Y
10 Burlison	Y	?	?	?	?	?	?	?
MONTANA								
1 Baucus	?	N	N	N	N	Y	Y	N
2 Marlenee	N	N	N	N	N	Y	Y	N
NEBRASKA								
1 Thone	N	N	N	N	N	Y	Y	N
2 Cavanaugh	Y	Y	N	N	N	N	Y	Y
3 Smith	N	N	Y	N	N	Y	Y	N
NEVADA								
AL Santini	X	N	N	N	N	Y	Y	Y
NEW HAMPSHIRE								
1 D'Amours	Y	N	N	Y	N	Y	Y	Y
2 Cleveland	N	N	Y	Y	N	Y	N	N
NEW JERSEY								
1 Florio	Y	Y	N	Y	Y	Y	Y	Y
2 Hughes	Y	N	N	Y	N	Y	Y	Y
3 Howard	Y	Y	Y	Y	N	Y	N	N
4 Thompson	Y	Y	N	Y	Y	Y	Y	Y
5 Fenwick	Y	Y	Y	Y	N	Y	Y	Y
6 Forsythe	Y	Y	Y	Y	N	N	Y	Y
7 Maguire	Y	Y	N	Y	N	Y	Y	Y
8 Roe	N	▮	N	Y	Y	Y	#	Y
9 Hollenbeck	?	Y	Y	Y	N	Y	Y	Y
10 Rodino	Y	Y	N	#	▮	#	#	#
11 Minish	N	Y	N	Y	Y	Y	Y	Y
12 Rinaldo	N	Y	Y	Y	Y	Y	Y	N
13 Meyner	Y	Y	N	Y	N	Y	Y	Y
14 LeFante	#	✔	▮	✔	▮	#	#	#
15 Patten	N	N	Y	Y	N	#	▮	N
NEW MEXICO								
1 Lujan	N	N	N	Y	Y	Y	Y	Y
2 Runnels	N	N	N	N	N	N	N	N
NEW YORK								
1 Pike	Y	Y	N	Y	N	Y	Y	Y
2 Downey	N	Y	N	Y	N	Y	Y	Y
3 Ambro	N	N	N	Y	N	Y	N	N
4 Lent	N	N	N	Y	N	Y	N	N
5 Wydler	N	N	Y	Y	N	Y	N	Y
6 Wolff	N	?	?	?	?	✔	?	?
7 Addabbo	Y	X	?	✔	?	X	?	✔
8 Rosenthal	Y	#	#	#	▮	#	#	#
9 Delaney	Y	?	?	?	?	?	?	?
10 Biaggi	Y	?	?	?	?	?	?	?
11 Scheuer	Y	?	?	?	?	?	?	?
12 Chisholm	Y	✔	?	✔	?	✔	?	✔
13 Solarz	Y	?	?	?	?	?	?	?
14 Richmond	Y	✔	?	✔	?	✔	?	✔
15 Zeferetti	N	X	▮	✔	▮	X	▮	X
16 Holtzman	Y	?	?	?	?	?	?	?
17 Murphy	N	?	?	?	?	?	?	?
18 Green	#	#	▮	#	▮	#	#	#
19 Rangel	Y	✔	?	?	?	✔	?	✔
20 Weiss	Y	✔	?	?	?	✔	?	✔
21 Garcia	Y	✔	▮	#	▮	✔	#	✔
22 Bingham	Y	Y	N	Y	N	Y	Y	#
23 Caputo	?	?	?	?	?	?	?	?
24 Ottinger	✔	Y	N	Y	N	Y	†	†
25 Fish	N	N	Y	Y	N	Y	N	N
26 Gilman	N	Y	Y	Y	N	Y	Y	N
27 McHugh	Y	Y	N	Y	N	Y	N	N
28 Stratton	N	N	N	Y	Y	N	N	N
29 Pattison	Y	N	N	Y	N	Y	N	▮
30 McEwen	Y	N	Y	Y	Y	Y	N	N
31 Mitchell	N	N	Y	Y	Y	Y	N	N
32 Hanley	Y	N	Y	Y	N	Y	Y	Y
33 Walsh	N	N	Y	Y	Y	Y	N	N
34 Horton	N	N	Y	Y	N	Y	Y	N
35 Conable	Y	N	Y	Y	N	Y	?	?
36 LaFalce	#	N	N	Y	N	Y	N	N
37 Nowak	Y	Y	N	Y	Y	Y	Y	Y
38 Kemp	N	N	Y	N	N	Y	N	N
39 Lundine	Y	N	N	Y	N	Y	N	N
NORTH CAROLINA								
1 Jones	N	N	N	N	N	N	N	N
2 Fountain	N	N	N	N	N	Y	N	N
3 Whitley	N	N	N	N	N	N	N	N
4 Andrews	Y	N	N	N	N	N	N	N
5 Neal	N	N	N	N	N	Y	N	N
6 Preyer	Y	N	N	N	N	Y	N	N
7 Rose	N	N	N	N	N	N	N	N
8 Hefner	Y	N	N	N	N	Y	N	N

	575	576	577	578	579	580	581	582
9 Martin	N	N	▮	N	N	Y	N	N
10 Broyhill	N	N	N	N	N	Y	Y	N
11 Gudger	▮	▮	▮	▮	▮	#	▮	▮
NORTH DAKOTA								
AL Andrews	N	N	N	N	N	Y	N	N
OHIO								
1 Gradison	N	N	N	N	N	Y	Y	N
2 Luken	N	N	N	Y	Y	Y	N	N
3 Whalen	Y	N	N	N	N	Y	Y	Y
4 Guyer	N	N	Y	N	N	Y	N	N
5 Latta	N	N	N	N	N	Y	N	Y
6 Harsha	N	N	N	N	N	Y	N	N
7 Brown	?	N	Y	N	N	Y	N	N
8 Kindness	N	N	N	Y	Y	Y	N	N
9 Ashley	Y	✔	?	?	?	X	?	X
10 Miller	Y	Y	N	Y	N	N	Y	Y
11 Stanton	N	N	Y	Y	N	Y	Y	N
12 Devine	N	N	N	N	N	Y	N	Y
13 Pease	Y	Y	N	Y	N	Y	Y	Y
14 Seiberling	Y	Y	N	Y	N	Y	Y	Y
15 Wylie	N	N	N	N	N	Y	Y	Y
16 Regula	N	N	N	N	N	N	N	N
17 Ashbrook	N	N	N	N	N	N	N	N
18 Applegate	N	N	N	Y	Y	N	N	N
19 Carney	N	N	N	Y	N	N	Y	Y
20 Oakar	N	N	Y	Y	Y	N	Y	N
21 Stokes	Y	Y	N	Y	N	Y	Y	Y
22 Vanik	Y	Y	N	Y	N	N	Y	Y
23 Mottl	N	N	N	Y	Y	Y	N	N
OKLAHOMA								
1 Jones	N	N	N	N	N	Y	N	N
2 Risenhoover	N	N	Y	Y	Y	Y	N	N
3 Watkins	N	N	N	Y	N	Y	N	N
4 Steed	N	N	N	N	N	N	N	N
5 Edwards	N	N	N	N	N	Y	N	N
6 English	N	N	N	N	N	Y	N	N
OREGON								
1 AuCoin	Y	?	N	N	N	N	Y	Y
2 Ullman	N	▮	N	N	N	N	N	N
3 Duncan	Y	▮	Y	N	N	Y	N	N
4 Weaver	Y	Y	N	Y	Y	Y	Y	?
PENNSYLVANIA								
1 Myers, M.	N	N	N	Y	Y	N	N	N
2 Nix	N	N	N	N	N	N	?	X
3 Lederer	N	N	N	Y	Y	Y	N	N
4 Eilberg	N	Y	N	Y	Y	N	N	N
5 Schulze	N	N	Y	Y	N	Y	N	N
6 Yatron	N	Y	N	Y	Y	Y	Y	Y
7 Edgar	N	N	N	Y	N	Y	Y	Y
8 Kostmayer	Y	Y	N	Y	N	Y	Y	Y
9 Shuster	N	N	Y	Y	Y	Y	N	N
10 McDade	Y	N	N	Y	N	Y	N	N
11 Flood	N	N	N	Y	N	N	N	N
12 Murtha	N	N	N	Y	Y	N	N	N
13 Coughlin	Y	N	Y	Y	N	Y	Y	N
14 Moorhead	Y	Y	N	Y	N	Y	Y	Y
15 Rooney	Y	Y	Y	Y	N	Y	Y	Y
16 Walker	N	N	N	Y	Y	Y	N	N
17 Ertel	Y	N	N	Y	N	Y	N	N
18 Walgren	Y	Y	Y	Y	Y	Y	Y	Y
19 Goodling, W.	N	N	N	Y	Y	Y	N	N
20 Gaydos	N	N	N	Y	Y	Y	Y	Y
21 Dent	N	X	▮	Y	Y	N	Y	Y
22 Murphy	N	Y	N	Y	Y	N	Y	Y
23 Ammerman	Y	N	N	Y	Y	Y	Y	Y
24 Marks	N	N	Y	Y	N	Y	N	N
25 Myers, G.	N	N	N	Y	N	Y	Y	N
RHODE ISLAND								
1 St Germain	Y	Y	Y	Y	Y	Y	Y	Y
2 Beard	N	Y	Y	Y	N	Y	N	N
SOUTH CAROLINA								
1 Davis	N	N	N	N	N	X	?	X
2 Spence	N	N	Y	N	N	Y	N	N
3 Derrick	N	N	N	N	N	Y	Y	N
4 Mann	?	N	N	N	N	Y	?	?
5 Holland	?	N	N	N	N	N	N	N
6 Jenrette	N	N	N	N	N	#	N	N
SOUTH DAKOTA								
1 Pressler	?	?	?	?	?	?	?	?
2 Abdnor	N	N	Y	N	▮	#	#	▮
TENNESSEE								
1 Quillen	N	N	N	N	Y	#	▮	▮
2 Duncan	N	▮	N	N	Y	Y	N	N
3 Lloyd	N	X	#	X	#	X	▮	X
4 Gore	N	N	N	N	N	N	N	N
5 Vacancy								
6 Beard	N	N	N	N	N	#	N	N

	575	576	577	578	579	580	581	582
7 Jones	N	N	N	N	N	N	N	N
8 Ford	Y	N	N	N	Y	N	Y	N
TEXAS								
1 Hall	N	N	N	N	N	Y	Y	N
2 Wilson, C.	▮	N	N	N	N	#	N	N
3 Collins	N	N	N	N	N	Y	N	N
4 Roberts	N	N	N	N	N	N	N	N
5 Mattox	Y	Y	N	N	N	Y	Y	N
6 Teague	X	X	?	X	?	X	?	X
7 Archer	N	N	N	N	N	Y	N	N
8 Eckhardt	Y	Y	N	N	N	Y	Y	Y
9 Brooks	N	N	N	N	N	Y	N	N
10 Pickle	Y	N	Y	N	N	Y	N	N
11 Poage	N	N	N	N	N	N	N	N
12 Wright	N	?	N	N	N	N	N	N
13 Hightower	N	N	N	N	N	N	N	N
14 Young	N	Y	N	N	N	Y	N	N
15 de la Garza	N	N	N	N	N	Y	N	N
16 White	N	N	N	Y	N	Y	N	N
17 Burleson	N	N	N	N	N	N	N	N
18 Jordan	Y	N	N	N	N	Y	Y	N
19 Mahon	Y	N	Y	N	N	N	N	N
20 Gonzalez	N	N	N	N	N	Y	N	N
21 Krueger	N	N	N	N	N	Y	N	N
22 Gammage	X	N	N	N	N	Y	N	N
23 Kazen	N	N	N	Y	N	Y	N	N
24 Milford	Y	N	N	N	N	?	N	N
UTAH								
1 McKay	Y	N	N	N	N	Y	N	N
2 Marriott	N	N	N	N	N	Y	N	N
VERMONT								
AL Jeffords	N	N	Y	Y	Y	Y	N	N
VIRGINIA								
1 Trible	N	N	N	N	N	?	?	?
2 Whitehurst	N	N	Y	N	N	Y	N	N
3 Satterfield	N	N	N	N	N	Y	N	N
4 Daniel	N	N	N	N	N	Y	N	N
5 Daniel	N	N	N	N	N	Y	N	N
6 Butler	?	N	Y	N	N	Y	N	N
7 Robinson	N	N	Y	N	N	N	N	N
8 Harris	N	N	N	N	N	Y	N	N
9 Wampler	N	N	Y	N	N	Y	N	N
10 Fisher	Y	Y	N	N	N	Y	Y	N
WASHINGTON								
1 Pritchard	Y	N	Y	N	N	N	Y	Y
2 Meeds	Y	N	N	N	N	N	N	N
3 Bonker	Y	N	N	N	N	N	N	N
4 McCormack	N	N	N	N	N	N	Y	Y
5 Foley	N	N	N	N	N	N	Y	Y
6 Dicks	N	N	N	N	N	N	N	N
7 Cunningham	N	N	N	N	N	N	Y	N
WEST VIRGINIA								
1 Mollohan	N	N	N	N	N	Y	N	N
2 Staggers	N	N	N	Y	N	Y	N	N
3 Slack	N	N	Y	N	N	N	N	N
4 Rahall	Y	Y	Y	Y	N	Y	Y	Y
WISCONSIN								
1 Aspin	Y	Y	N	N	Y	Y	Y	Y
2 Kastenmeier	Y	Y	Y	Y	N	Y	Y	Y
3 Baldus	✔	N	N	Y	▮	Y	N	N
4 Zablocki	N	N	N	N	Y	Y	N	N
5 Reuss	Y	Y	N	Y	N	Y	Y	N
6 Steiger	Y	N	Y	N	N	Y	N	N
7 Obey	Y	Y	N	Y	N	Y	N	N
8 Cornell	Y	Y	N	Y	N	Y	N	N
9 Kasten	?	?	?	?	?	?	?	?
WYOMING								
AL Roncalio	X	N	Y	N	N	Y	N	#

Democrats ***Republicans***

583. HR 13635. Defense Appropriations, Fiscal 1979. Mahon, D-Texas, motion that the House resolve itself into the Committee of the Whole for further consideration of the bill. Motion agreed to 367-4: R 133-2; D 234-2 (ND 163-2; SD 71-0), Aug. 9, 1978.

584. HR 13635. Defense Appropriations, Fiscal 1979. Dornan, R-Calif., amendment to prohibit use of funds appropriated in the bill for any abortion not required to save the life of the mother. Adopted 226-163: R 107-27; D 119-136 (ND 79-100; SD 40-36), Aug. 9, 1978.

585. HR 13635. Defense Appropriations, Fiscal 1979. Passage of the bill to appropriate $119,017,218,000 for programs of the Defense Department in fiscal 1979. Passed 339-60: R 131-4; D 208-56 (ND 131-56; SD 77-0), Aug. 9, 1978. The president had requested $119,300,283,000.

586. HR 2777. National Consumer Cooperative Bank. Adoption of the conference report on the bill to establish a national consumer cooperative bank; to establish within the bank an office to provide technical assistance to cooperatives; and to authorize a total of $300 million over fiscal 1979-83 for the bank's initial capitalization, $75 million for fiscal 1979-81 for technical assistance and $4 million for fiscal 1979 and additional sums as necessary for fiscal 1980-81 for the administrative costs of the bank and technical assistance programs. Adopted 236-164: R 35-96; D 201-68 (ND 170-20; SD 31-48), Aug. 9, 1978.

587. H Res 11280. Civil Service Reorganization. Adoption of the resolution to disapprove President Carter's Reorganization Plan No. 2 to reorganize the Civil Service System. Rejected 19-381: R 17-119; D 2-262 (ND 1-184; SD 1-78), Aug. 9, 1978. A "nay" was a vote supporting the president's position.

KEY

Y Voted for (yea).
✓ Paired for.
† Announced for.
# CQ Poll for.
N Voted against (nay).
X Paired against.
\- Announced against.
▮ CQ Poll against.
P Voted "present."
● Voted "present" to avoid possible conflict of interest.
? Did not vote or otherwise make a position known.

	583	584	585	586	587
ALABAMA					
1 ***Edwards***	Y	Y	Y	N	N
2 ***Dickinson***	Y	?	?	N	N
3 Nichols	Y	Y	Y	N	N
4 Bevill	Y	Y	Y	N	N
5 Flippo	Y	N	Y	N	N
6 ***Buchanan***	Y	Y	Y	N	N
7 Flowers	?	?	?	?	?
ALASKA					
AL ***Young***	?	?	?	?	?
ARIZONA					
1 ***Rhodes***	?	?	?	?	?
2 Udall	Y	N	Y	Y	N
3 Stump	Y	Y	Y	N	N
4 ***Rudd***	Y	Y	Y	N	Y
ARKANSAS					
1 Alexander	Y	N	Y	Y	N
2 Tucker	Y	N	Y	Y	N
3 ***Hammerschmidt***	Y	Y	Y	N	Y
4 Thornton	Y	N	Y	Y	N
CALIFORNIA					
1 Johnson	Y	N	Y	Y	N
2 ***Clausen***	Y	Y	Y	N	N
3 Moss	Y	N	Y	Y	N
4 Leggett	?	N	Y	Y	N
5 Burton, J.	Y	N	N	Y	N
6 Burton, P.	Y	N	N	Y	N
7 Miller	?	X	X	✓	?
8 Dellums	Y	N	N	Y	N
9 Stark	Y	N	N	Y	N
10 Edwards	Y	N	N	Y	N
11 Ryan	Y	N	Y	Y	N
12 ***McCloskey***	Y	N	Y	Y	N
13 Mineta	Y	N	Y	Y	N
14 McFall	Y	N	Y	Y	N
15 Sisk	?	?	?	?	?
16 Panetta	Y	N	Y	Y	N
17 Krebs	Y	N	Y	Y	N
18 Vacancy					
19 ***Lagomarsino***	Y	Y	Y	N	N
20 ***Goldwater***	?	Y	Y	N	N
21 Corman	Y	N	Y	Y	N
22 ***Moorhead***	Y	Y	Y	N	N
23 Beilenson	#	▮	N	Y	N
24 Waxman	Y	N	Y	Y	▮
25 Roybal	Y	N	N	Y	N
26 ***Rousselot***	Y	Y	Y	N	N
27 ***Dornan***	Y	Y	Y	N	N
28 Burke	Y	N	Y	Y	N
29 Hawkins	Y	N	Y	Y	N
30 Danielson	Y	N	Y	Y	N
31 Wilson, C.H.	Y	N	Y	Y	?
32 Anderson	Y	N	Y	Y	N
33 ***Clawson***	Y	Y	Y	N	N
34 Hannaford	Y	N	Y	N	N
35 Lloyd	N	N	Y	Y	N
36 Brown	?	N	N	Y	N
37 ***Pettis***	Y	N	Y	N	N
38 Patterson	Y	N	Y	Y	N
39 ***Wiggins***	Y	N	Y	▮	N
40 ***Badham***	Y	Y	Y	N	N
41 ***Wilson, B.***	N	Y	Y	N	N
42 Van Deerlin	Y	N	Y	Y	N
43 ***Burgener***	Y	Y	Y	N	N
COLORADO					
1 Schroeder	Y	N	N	Y	N
2 Wirth	Y	N	N	Y	N
3 Evans	#	N	Y	Y	N
4 ***Johnson***	Y	N	Y	N	N
5 ***Armstrong***	Y	Y	Y	N	Y
CONNECTICUT					
1 Cotter	Y	Y	Y	Y	N
2 Dodd	Y	N	Y	Y	N
3 Giaimo	?	N	Y	N	N
4 ***McKinney***	Y	N	Y	Y	N
5 ***Sarasin***	Y	N	Y	Y	N
6 Moffett	Y	N	N	Y	N
DELAWARE					
AL ***Evans***	?	?	?	?	?
FLORIDA					
1 Sikes	Y	N	Y	N	N
2 Fuqua	Y	Y	Y	N	N
3 Bennett	Y	Y	Y	N	N
4 Chappell	Y	Y	Y	N	N
5 ***Kelly***	Y	Y	Y	N	N
6 ***Young***	Y	Y	Y	N	N
7 Gibbons	Y	Y	Y	Y	N
8 Ireland	Y	Y	Y	N	N
9 ***Frey***	?	?	?	?	?
10 ***Bafalis***	Y	Y	Y	N	N
11 Rogers	Y	N	Y	Y	N
12 ***Burke***	Y	Y	Y	N	N
13 Lehman	Y	N	Y	Y	N
14 Pepper	Y	N	Y	Y	N
15 Fascell	Y	N	Y	Y	N
GEORGIA					
1 Ginn	Y	Y	Y	N	N
2 Mathis	?	?	?	?	?
3 Brinkley	Y	N	Y	N	N
4 Levitas	Y	N	Y	N	N
5 Fowler	?	?	?	Y	N
6 Flynt	Y	Y	Y	N	N
7 McDonald	#	✓	#	X	✓
8 Evans	Y	Y	Y	Y	N
9 Jenkins	#	#	#	▮	▮
10 Barnard	?	?	?	N	N
HAWAII					
1 Heftel	Y	N	Y	Y	N
2 Akaka	Y	N	Y	Y	N
IDAHO					
1 ***Symms***	Y	?	Y	N	Y
2 ***Hansen, G.***	?	?	?	?	?
ILLINOIS					
1 Metcalfe	Y	N	N	Y	N
2 Murphy	Y	Y	Y	Y	N
3 Russo	Y	Y	Y	Y	N
4 ***Derwinski***	Y	Y	Y	N	N
5 Fary	Y	Y	Y	Y	N
6 ***Hyde***	Y	Y	Y	N	N
7 Collins	Y	N	N	Y	N
8 Rostenkowski	Y	Y	Y	Y	N
9 Yates	Y	N	N	Y	N
10 Mikva	Y	N	N	Y	N
11 Annunzio	Y	Y	Y	Y	N
12 ***Crane***	Y	Y	Y	N	N
13 ***McClory***	Y	Y	Y	N	N
14 ***Erlenborn***	Y	Y	Y	N	N
15 ***Corcoran***	Y	Y	Y	N	N
16 ***Anderson***	Y	N	Y	Y	N
17 ***O'Brien***	Y	Y	Y	P	N
18 ***Michel***	Y	Y	Y	N	N
19 ***Railsback***	Y	Y	Y	Y	N
20 ***Findley***	Y	N	Y	Y	N
21 ***Madigan***	Y	Y	Y	Y	N
22 Shipley	Y	Y	Y	Y	N
23 Price	Y	N	Y	Y	N
24 Simon	Y	N	Y	Y	N
INDIANA					
1 Benjamin	Y	Y	Y	Y	N
2 Fithian	Y	Y	Y	N	N
3 Brademas	Y	N	Y	Y	N
4 ***Quayle***	N	Y	Y	N	N
5 ***Hillis***	Y	Y	Y	N	N
6 Evans	Y	Y	Y	Y	N
7 ***Myers, J.***	Y	Y	Y	N	N
8 Cornwell	Y	Y	N	N	N
9 Hamilton	Y	Y	Y	N	N
10 Sharp	Y	Y	Y	N	N
11 Jacobs	Y	Y	Y	N	N
IOWA					
1 ***Leach***	Y	Y	Y	N	N
2 Blouin	Y	Y	Y	Y	N
3 ***Grassley***	Y	Y	Y	N	N
4 Smith	Y	Y	Y	Y	N
5 Harkin	Y	Y	N	Y	N
6 Bedell	Y	Y	N	Y	N

Democrats ***Republicans***

	583	584	585	586	587
KANSAS					
1 Sebelius	Y	Y	Y	N	N
2 Keys	Y	N	Y	Y	N
3 Winn	Y	Y	Y	P	N
4 Glickman	Y	-	Y	Y	N
5 Skubitz	Y	Y	Y	N	N
KENTUCKY					
1 Hubbard	Y	Y	Y	Y	N
2 Natcher	Y	Y	Y	N	N
3 Mazzoli	Y	Y	Y	Y	N
4 Snyder	Y	Y	Y	N	N
5 Carter	Y	Y	Y	N	N
6 Breckinridge	Y	N	Y	Y	N
7 Perkins	Y	Y	Y	N	N
LOUISIANA					
1 Livingston	Y	Y	Y	N	N
2 Boggs	Y	Y	Y	Y	N
3 Treen	Y	Y	Y	N	N
4 Waggonner	Y	Y	Y	N	N
5 Huckaby	Y	Y	Y	N	N
6 Moore	Y	Y	Y	N	N
7 Breaux	Y	Y	Y	Y	N
8 Long	?	Y	Y	Y	N
MAINE					
1 Emery	Y	Y	Y	Y	N
2 Cohen	Y	Y	Y	Y	?
MARYLAND					
1 Bauman	Y	Y	Y	N	Y
2 Long	Y	N	Y	Y	N
3 Mikulski	Y	N	Y	Y	N
4 Holt	Y	Y	Y	N	Y
5 Spellman	Y	N	Y	Y	N
6 Byron	Y	Y	Y	N	N
7 Mitchell	N	N	N	Y	N
8 Steers	Y	▮	N	Y	Y
MASSACHUSETTS					
1 Conte	Y	Y	Y	Y	N
2 Boland	Y	Y	Y	Y	N
3 Early	Y	Y	N	Y	N
4 Drinan	Y	N	N	Y	N
5 Tsongas	?	?	?	?	?
6 Harrington	#	N	N	Y	▮
7 Markey	Y	Y	N	Y	N
8 O'Neill					
9 Moakley	Y	Y	Y	Y	N
10 Heckler	Y	Y	Y	Y	Y
11 Burke	Y	Y	Y	Y	N
12 Studds	Y	N	N	Y	N
MICHIGAN					
1 Conyers	#	N	N	Y	N
2 Pursell	Y	N	N	Y	N
3 Brown	?	?	?	N	N
4 Stockman	Y	N	Y	N	N
5 Sawyer	Y	Y	Y	N	N
6 Carr	Y	-	N	Y	N
7 Kildee	Y	Y	Y	Y	N
8 Traxler	Y	Y	Y	Y	N
9 Vander Jagt	Y	?	?	N	N
10 Cederberg	Y	Y	Y	N	N
11 Ruppe	Y	Y	Y	?	?
12 Bonior	#	X	▮	Y	N
13 Diggs	#	X	N	✓	▮
14 Nedzi	Y	Y	Y	Y	N
15 Ford	?	N	Y	Y	?
16 Dingell	Y	N	Y	Y	N
17 Brodhead	Y	N	Y	Y	N
18 Blanchard	Y	N	Y	Y	N
19 Broomfield	Y	Y	Y	N	N
MINNESOTA					
1 Quie	Y	Y	Y	Y	N
2 Hagedorn	Y	Y	Y	N	N
3 Frenzel	Y	N	Y	N	N
4 Vento	Y	Y	N	Y	N
5 Fraser	Y	N	N	Y	N
6 Nolan	Y	Y	N	Y	N
7 Stangeland	Y	Y	Y	N	N
8 Oberstar	Y	Y	N	Y	N
MISSISSIPPI					
1 Whitten	Y	Y	Y	N	N
2 Bowen	Y	Y	Y	N	N
3 Montgomery	Y	Y	Y	N	N
4 Cochran	Y	Y	Y	N	N
5 Lott	Y	Y	Y	N	N
MISSOURI					
1 Clay	?	X	N	Y	N
2 Young	#	✓	Y	Y	N
3 Gephardt	#	#	N	Y	N

	583	584	585	586	587
4 Skelton	?	?	Y	N	N
5 Bolling	Y	N	Y	Y	N
6 Coleman	Y	Y	Y	N	N
7 Taylor	Y	Y	Y	N	N
8 Ichord	Y	Y	Y	N	N
9 Volkmer	Y	Y	Y	Y	N
10 Burlison	?	Y	Y	N	N
MONTANA					
1 Baucus	Y	N	Y	Y	N
2 Marlenee	Y	N	Y	N	N
NEBRASKA					
1 Thone	Y	Y	Y	N	N
2 Cavanaugh	Y	Y	Y	N	N
3 Smith	Y	Y	Y	N	N
NEVADA					
AL Santini	Y	Y	Y	Y	N
NEW HAMPSHIRE					
1 D'Amours	Y	Y	Y	Y	N
2 Cleveland	Y	N	Y	Y	N
NEW JERSEY					
1 Florio	Y	N	Y	Y	N
2 Hughes	Y	N	Y	Y	N
3 Howard	Y	N	Y	Y	N
4 Thompson	Y	N	N	Y	N
5 Fenwick	Y	N	N	Y	N
6 Forsythe	Y	N	N	N	N
7 Maguire	Y	N	N	Y	N
8 Roe	#	#	#	Y	N
9 Hollenbeck	Y	N	Y	Y	N
10 Rodino	#	#	#	#	X
11 Minish	Y	Y	Y	Y	N
12 Rinaldo	Y	Y	Y	Y	N
13 Meyner	Y	N	Y	Y	N
14 LeFante	#	✓	#	✓	▮
15 Patten	Y	Y	Y	Y	N
NEW MEXICO					
1 Lujan	Y	Y	Y	Y	N
2 Runnels	Y	Y	Y	N	N
NEW YORK					
1 Pike	Y	N	Y	Y	N
2 Downey	Y	-	Y	Y	N
3 Ambro	?	?	Y	Y	N
4 Lent	Y	Y	?	Y	N
5 Wydler	Y	Y	Y	N	N
6 Wolff	Y	N	Y	Y	N
7 Addabbo	Y	N	Y	Y	N
8 Rosenthal	Y	N	N	Y	N
9 Delaney	Y	Y	Y	Y	N
10 Biaggi	Y	Y	Y	Y	N
11 Scheuer	Y	N	?	Y	N
12 Chisholm	#	N	N	Y	N
13 Solarz	Y	N	Y	Y	N
14 Richmond	?	X	X	Y	N
15 Zeferetti	Y	Y	Y	Y	N
16 Holtzman	Y	N	N	Y	N
17 Murphy	Y	Y	?	Y	N
18 Green	Y	N	Y	Y	N
19 Rangel	Y	N	N	Y	N
20 Weiss	Y	N	N	Y	N
21 Garcia	#	N	N	Y	N
22 Bingham	Y	N	N	Y	N
23 Caputo	P	Y	Y	Y	Y
24 Ottinger	Y	N	N	Y	N
25 Fish	Y	Y	Y	?	?
26 Gilman	Y	N	Y	Y	Y
27 McHugh	Y	Y	N	Y	N
28 Stratton	Y	Y	Y	Y	N
29 Pattison	#	N	N	Y	N
30 McEwen	Y	Y	Y	N	N
31 Mitchell	Y	Y	Y	N	N
32 Hanley	Y	Y	Y	N	N
33 Walsh	Y	Y	Y	P	Y
34 Horton	Y	N	Y	Y	N
35 Conable	Y	N	Y	N	N
36 LaFalce	#	Y	Y	N	▮
37 Nowak	Y	Y	Y	Y	N
38 Kemp	Y	Y	Y	?	N
39 Lundine	Y	N	N	Y	N
NORTH CAROLINA					
1 Jones	Y	N	Y	N	N
2 Fountain	Y	Y	Y	N	N
3 Whitley	Y	N	Y	N	N
4 Andrews	?	?	?	N	N
5 Neal	#	N	Y	N	N
6 Preyer	Y	N	Y	N	N
7 Rose	?	N	?	Y	N
8 Hefner	Y	N	Y	N	N

	583	584	585	586	587
9 Martin	Y	N	Y	N	N
10 Broyhill	Y	N	Y	N	N
11 Gudger	Y	N	Y	N	N
NORTH DAKOTA					
AL Andrews	Y	Y	Y	Y	N
OHIO					
1 Gradison	Y	Y	Y	N	N
2 Luken	Y	Y	Y	N	N
3 Whalen	Y	Y	Y	Y	N
4 Guyer	Y	Y	Y	Y	N
5 Latta	Y	Y	Y	N	N
6 Harsha	Y	Y	Y	Y	N
7 Brown	Y	N	Y	Y	N
8 Kindness	Y	Y	Y	N	N
9 Ashley	Y	N	Y	N	N
10 Miller	Y	Y	Y	N	N
11 Stanton	Y	Y	Y	N	N
12 Devine	Y	Y	Y	N	N
13 Pease	Y	N	Y	Y	N
14 Seiberling	Y	N	N	Y	N
15 Wylie	Y	Y	Y	Y	N
16 Regula	Y	Y	Y	N	N
17 Ashbrook	Y	Y	Y	N	Y
18 Applegate	Y	Y	Y	N	N
19 Carney	Y	Y	Y	Y	N
20 Oakar	Y	Y	Y	Y	N
21 Stokes	Y	N	N	Y	N
22 Vanik	Y	Y	N	Y	N
23 Mottl	Y	Y	Y	Y	N
OKLAHOMA					
1 Jones	Y	N	Y	N	N
2 Risenhoover	?	Y	Y	N	N
3 Watkins	Y	Y	Y	N	N
4 Steed	Y	N	Y	N	N
5 Edwards	?	Y	Y	N	Y
6 English	Y	Y	Y	N	N
OREGON					
1 AuCoin	Y	N	N	Y	N
2 Ullman	Y	N	Y	Y	N
3 Duncan	Y	N	Y	Y	N
4 Weaver	Y	N	N	Y	N
PENNSYLVANIA					
1 Myers, M.	Y	Y	Y	Y	N
2 Nix	?	N	Y	Y	N
3 Lederer	Y	Y	Y	Y	N
4 Eilberg	Y	Y	Y	Y	Y
5 Schulze	Y	Y	Y	N	N
6 Yatron	Y	Y	Y	Y	N
7 Edgar	Y	N	Y	Y	N
8 Kostmayer	Y	N	Y	Y	N
9 Shuster	Y	Y	Y	N	N
10 McDade	Y	Y	Y	Y	N
11 Flood	Y	Y	Y	Y	N
12 Murtha	Y	Y	Y	Y	N
13 Coughlin	Y	N	Y	N	N
14 Moorhead	Y	Y	Y	Y	N
15 Rooney	Y	Y	Y	Y	N
16 Walker	Y	Y	Y	N	N
17 Ertel	Y	Y	Y	Y	N
18 Walgren	Y	N	Y	Y	N
19 Goodling, W.	Y	Y	Y	N	N
20 Gaydos	Y	Y	Y	Y	N
21 Dent	#	Y	Y	#	N
22 Murphy	Y	Y	Y	Y	N
23 Ammerman	Y	Y	Y	Y	N
24 Marks	Y	Y	Y	?	N
25 Myers, G.	Y	Y	Y	N	Y
RHODE ISLAND					
1 St Germain	?	Y	Y	Y	N
2 Beard	Y	Y	Y	Y	N
SOUTH CAROLINA					
1 Davis	?	?	✓	?	N
2 Spence	Y	Y	Y	N	N
3 Derrick	Y	N	Y	Y	N
4 Mann	Y	N	Y	N	?
5 Holland	?	?	Y	Y	N
6 Jenrette	Y	N	Y	Y	N
SOUTH DAKOTA					
1 Pressler	Y	Y	Y	Y	N
2 Abdnor	#	#	#	▮	▮
TENNESSEE					
1 Quillen	Y	Y	Y	N	Y
2 Duncan	Y	Y	Y	N	Y
3 Lloyd	#	✓	✓	X	▮
4 Gore	Y	Y	Y	N	N
5 Vacancy					
6 Beard	Y	Y	Y	N	N

	583	584	585	586	587
7 Jones	Y	N	Y	N	N
8 Ford	Y	N	Y	Y	N
TEXAS					
1 Hall	Y	Y	Y	N	N
2 Wilson, C.	Y	N	Y	Y	N
3 Collins	Y	Y	Y	N	Y
4 Roberts	Y	Y	Y	N	N
5 Mattox	?	?	?	?	N
6 Teague	?	?	?	X	?
7 Archer	Y	Y	Y	N	N
8 Eckhardt	Y	N	Y	Y	N
9 Brooks	Y	N	Y	Y	N
10 Pickle	Y	N	Y	N	N
11 Poage	Y	Y	Y	N	N
12 Wright	Y	Y	Y	Y	N
13 Hightower	Y	Y	Y	Y	N
14 Young	?	?	Y	Y	N
15 de la Garza	Y	Y	Y	N	?
16 White	Y	Y	Y	Y	N
17 Burleson	Y	Y	Y	N	N
18 Jordan	Y	N	Y	Y	N
19 Mahon	Y	N	Y	N	N
20 Gonzalez	Y	N	Y	N	N
21 Krueger	Y	N	Y	▮	▮
22 Gammage	Y	Y	Y	N	N
23 Kazen	Y	Y	Y	N	N
24 Milford	?	Y	Y	?	?
UTAH					
1 McKay	Y	Y	Y	Y	N
2 Marriott	Y	Y	Y	N	N
VERMONT					
AL Jeffords	Y	N	Y	Y	N
VIRGINIA					
1 Trible	Y	Y	Y	N	N
2 Whitehurst	Y	Y	Y	N	N
3 Satterfield	Y	Y	Y	N	N
4 Daniel	Y	Y	Y	N	N
5 Daniel	Y	Y	Y	N	N
6 Butler	Y	N	Y	N	N
7 Robinson	Y	Y	Y	N	N
8 Harris	Y	N	Y	Y	Y
9 Wampler	Y	Y	Y	N	N
10 Fisher	Y	N	Y	Y	N
WASHINGTON					
1 Pritchard	Y	N	Y	Y	N
2 Meeds	#	N	Y	Y	N
3 Bonker	Y	Y	Y	Y	N
4 McCormack	Y	N	Y	Y	N
5 Foley	Y	N	Y	Y	N
6 Dicks	Y	N	Y	Y	N
7 Cunningham	Y	Y	Y	N	N
WEST VIRGINIA					
1 Mollohan	Y	N	Y	N	N
2 Staggers	Y	Y	Y	Y	N
3 Slack	Y	N	Y	Y	N
4 Rahall	Y	Y	Y	Y	N
WISCONSIN					
1 Aspin	Y	Y	Y	Y	N
2 Kastenmeier	Y	N	N	Y	N
3 Baldus	Y	Y	N	Y	N
4 Zablocki	Y	Y	Y	Y	N
5 Reuss	Y	N	N	Y	N
6 Steiger	Y	Y	Y	Y	N
7 Obey	Y	Y	N	Y	N
8 Cornell	Y	Y	N	Y	N
9 Kasten	?	✓	?	?	?
WYOMING					
AL Roncalio	#	N	Y	Y	▮

Democrats ***Republicans***

588. HR 12452. CETA Amendments. Adoption of the rule (H Res 1294) providing for House floor consideration of the bill to extend and amend the Comprehensive Employment and Training Act (CETA). Adopted 376-20: R 114-20; D 262-0 (ND 186-0; SD 76-0), Aug. 9, 1978.

589. HR 12452. CETA Amendments. Cornell, D-Wis., amendment to require the secretary of labor to withhold funds, or to seek repayment of funds already distributed, from local government prime sponsors found to have used federal funds to substitute CETA workers for regular employees. Adopted 407-1: R 139-1; D 268-0 (ND 188-0; SD 80-0), Aug. 9, 1978.

590. HR 12452. CETA Amendments. Goodling, R-Pa., amendment, to the Erlenborn, R-Ill., amendment *(see vote 592, below)*, to allow local governments the option of not paying unemployment insurance for CETA workers. Rejected 197-211: R 122-18; D 75-193 (ND 22-168; SD 53-25), Aug. 9, 1978.

591. HR 12452. CETA Amendments. Ashbrook, R-Ohio, amendment, to the Krebs, D-Calif., substitute to the Erlenborn, R-Ill., amendment *(see vote 592, below)*, to delete the provision allowing use of CETA funds to make contributions to retirement plans if the CETA worker had a reasonable chance of benefiting in the future from the plan. Adopted 209-194: R 127-13; D 82-181 (ND 34-149; SD 48-32), Aug. 9, 1978. (The Krebs amendment, as amended, was subsequently rejected by voice vote, thus nullifying the Ashbrook amendment.)

592. HR 12452. CETA Amendments. Erlenborn, D-Ill., amendment to prohibit use of CETA funds for retirement plan payments after Jan. 1, 1980. Adopted 254-148: R 132-8; D 122-140 (ND 59-124; SD 63-16), Aug. 9, 1978.

593. HR 12452. CETA Amendments. Obey, D-Wis., amendments, considered en bloc, to limit maximum CETA wages to $10,000 annually ($12,000 in high-wage areas) and to set the average CETA worker's wage at $7,000, to be adjusted according to the consumer price index. Adopted 230-175: R 116-23; D 114-152 (ND 54-132; SD 60-20), Aug. 9, 1978.

594. HR 12452. CETA Amendments. Jeffords, R-Vt., amendment to set a $3.2 billion ceiling on spending for Title VI public service employment, and to increase by $500 million the authorizations for youth employment and private sector jobs programs. Adopted 221-181: R 120-19; D 101-162 (ND 44-141; SD 57-21), Aug. 9, 1978.

595. HR 12452. CETA Amendments. Maguire, D-N.J., amendment to permit use of CETA funds to pay outside legal consultants, provided neither the local government nor the Labor Department could perform the task and the consultant charged reasonable fees. Adopted 200-198: R 17-123; D 183-75 (ND 145-36; SD 38-39), Aug. 9, 1978.

KEY

- Y Voted for (yea).
- ✓ Paired for.
- † Announced for.
- # CQ Poll for.
- N Voted against (nay).
- X Paired against.
- - Announced against.
- ■ CQ Poll against.
- P Voted "present."
- ● Voted "present" to avoid possible conflict of interest.
- ? Did not vote or otherwise make a position known.

	588	589	590	591	592	593	594	595
ALABAMA								
1 Edwards	Y	Y	Y	Y	Y	Y	Y	N
2 Dickinson	Y	Y	Y	Y	Y	Y	Y	N
3 Nichols	Y	Y	Y	Y	Y	Y	Y	N
4 Bevill	Y	Y	Y	Y	Y	Y	Y	N
5 Flippo	Y	Y	Y	Y	?	Y	Y	Y
6 Buchanan	Y	Y	N	Y	Y	Y	N	N
7 Flowers	?	?	?	?	?	?	?	?
ALASKA								
AL Young	?	Y	N	Y	Y	N	N	Y
ARIZONA								
1 Rhodes	?	?	?	?	?	?	?	?
2 Udall	Y	Y	N	N	Y	Y	N	Y
3 Stump	Y	Y	Y	Y	Y	Y	Y	N
4 Rudd	N	Y	Y	Y	Y	Y	Y	N
ARKANSAS								
1 Alexander	Y	Y	N	N	Y	Y	N	Y
2 Tucker	Y	Y	N	N	N	N	Y	N
3 Hammerschmidt	Y	Y	Y	Y	Y	Y	Y	N
4 Thornton	Y	Y	N	N	Y	?	N	N
CALIFORNIA								
1 Johnson	Y	Y	N	N	N	N	N	Y
2 Clausen	?	Y	Y	N	Y	Y	Y	N
3 Moss	Y	Y	N	?	?	?	?	?
4 Leggett	?	Y	N	?	?	?	N	?
5 Burton, J.	Y	Y	N	N	N	N	N	Y
6 Burton, P.	Y	Y	N	N	N	N	N	N
7 Miller	?	?	X	X	?	?	X	?
8 Dellums	Y	Y	N	N	N	N	N	N
9 Stark	Y	Y	N	N	N	N	N	Y
10 Edwards	Y	Y	N	N	N	N	N	Y
11 Ryan	Y	Y	Y	N	Y	N	Y	N
12 McCloskey	?	Y	N	Y	Y	Y	Y	N
13 Mineta	Y	Y	N	N	N	N	N	N
14 McFall	Y	Y	N	N	N	N	N	Y
15 Sisk	?	?	?	?	?	?	?	?
16 Panetta	Y	Y	N	N	N	Y	Y	Y
17 Krebs	Y	Y	N	N	N	Y	N	Y
18 Vacancy								
19 Lagomarsino	Y	Y	Y	N	N	Y	Y	N
20 Goldwater	?	Y	Y	Y	Y	?	?	?
21 Corman	Y	Y	N	N	N	N	N	Y
22 Moorhead	Y	Y	Y	Y	Y	Y	Y	N
23 Beilenson	Y	Y	N	N	N	N	■	Y
24 Waxman	Y	Y	N	N	N	N	N	Y
25 Roybal	Y	Y	N	N	N	Y	N	Y
26 Rousselot	N	Y	Y	Y	Y	Y	Y	N
27 Dornan	Y	Y	Y	?	Y	Y	Y	N
28 Burke	Y	Y	N	N	N	N	N	Y
29 Hawkins	Y	Y	N	N	N	N	N	Y
30 Danielson	Y	Y	N	Y	N	N	N	Y
31 Wilson, C.H.	Y	Y	N	N	N	N	?	?
32 Anderson	Y	Y	N	N	N	N	N	Y
33 Clawson	N	Y	Y	Y	Y	?	Y	N
34 Hannaford	Y	Y	N	N	N	N	N	Y
35 Lloyd	Y	Y	N	N	N	N	N	N
36 Brown	?	?	N	N	N	N	N	Y
37 Pettis	Y	Y	Y	Y	Y	Y	Y	N
38 Patterson	Y	Y	N	N	N	N	N	N
39 Wiggins	Y	Y	Y	Y	#	Y	Y	N
40 Badham	N	Y	Y	Y	Y	Y	Y	N
41 Wilson, B.	Y	Y	Y	Y	Y	Y	Y	N
42 Van Deerlin	Y	Y	N	N	Y	N	N	Y
43 Burgener	Y	Y	Y	Y	Y	Y	Y	N
COLORADO								
1 Schroeder	Y	Y	N	N	N	N	N	Y
2 Wirth	Y	Y	N	Y	Y	Y	Y	Y
3 Evans	Y	Y	Y	Y	Y	Y	Y	#
4 Johnson	Y	Y	N	Y	Y	Y	Y	N
5 Armstrong	N	Y	Y	Y	Y	Y	Y	N
CONNECTICUT								
1 Cotter	Y	Y	N	Y	Y	Y	N	N
2 Dodd	Y	Y	N	N	N	N	N	N
3 Giaimo	?	Y	N	?	?	Y	N	N
4 McKinney	Y	Y	Y	Y	Y	N	N	N
5 Sarasin	Y	Y	Y	Y	Y	Y	Y	N
6 Moffett	Y	Y	N	N	Y	Y	N	Y
DELAWARE								
AL Evans	?	Y	Y	Y	Y	Y	Y	N
FLORIDA								
1 Sikes	Y	Y	Y	Y	Y	Y	✓	?
2 Fuqua	Y	Y	Y	Y	Y	Y	Y	Y
3 Bennett	Y	Y	Y	Y	Y	Y	Y	Y
4 Chappell	Y	Y	Y	Y	Y	Y	Y	N
5 Kelly	Y	Y	Y	Y	Y	Y	Y	N
6 Young	Y	Y	Y	Y	Y	Y	Y	N
7 Gibbons	Y	Y	N	Y	Y	Y	Y	Y
8 Ireland	?	Y	Y	Y	Y	Y	Y	N
9 Frey	?	?	?	?	?	?	?	?
10 Bafalis	Y	Y	Y	Y	Y	Y	Y	Y
11 Rogers	Y	Y	Y	N	Y	Y	Y	Y
12 Burke	Y	Y	Y	Y	Y	Y	Y	N
13 Lehman	Y	Y	Y	N	N	Y	Y	Y
14 Pepper	Y	Y	N	N	N	N	N	Y
15 Fascell	Y	Y	N	N	N	Y	N	Y
GEORGIA								
1 Ginn	Y	Y	Y	Y	Y	Y	Y	N
2 Mathis	?	?	?	?	?	?	?	?
3 Brinkley	Y	Y	Y	Y	Y	Y	Y	N
4 Levitas	Y	Y	Y	N	Y	N	Y	Y
5 Fowler	Y	Y	Y	N	Y	Y	Y	N
6 Flynt	Y	Y	✓	✓	✓	Y	✓	N
7 McDonald	■	#	✓	✓	✓	✓	✓	■
8 Evans	Y	Y	Y	N	Y	Y	N	N
9 Jenkins	#	#	#	#	#	#	#	#
10 Barnard	Y	Y	Y	Y	Y	Y	Y	Y
HAWAII								
1 Heftel	Y	Y	N	N	N	N	Y	N
2 Akaka	Y	Y	N	N	N	N	N	N
IDAHO								
1 Symms	N	Y	Y	Y	Y	Y	Y	N
2 Hansen, G.	?	?	?	?	?	?	?	?
ILLINOIS								
1 Metcalfe	Y	Y	N	N	N	N	N	Y
2 Murphy	Y	Y	N	N	Y	Y	N	N
3 Russo	Y	Y	Y	Y	Y	Y	N	Y
4 Derwinski	Y	Y	Y	Y	Y	Y	Y	Y
5 Fary	Y	Y	N	N	Y	N	N	N
6 Hyde	Y	Y	Y	Y	Y	Y	Y	N
7 Collins	Y	Y	N	N	N	N	N	Y
8 Rostenkowski	Y	Y	N	N	Y	Y	N	Y
9 Yates	Y	Y	N	N	N	N	N	Y
10 Mikva	Y	Y	N	N	N	N	N	Y
11 Annunzio	Y	Y	N	N	Y	N	N	N
12 Crane	N	Y	Y	Y	Y	Y	Y	N
13 McClory	Y	Y	Y	Y	Y	Y	Y	N
14 Erlenborn	Y	Y	Y	Y	Y	Y	Y	N
15 Corcoran	Y	Y	Y	Y	Y	Y	Y	N
16 Anderson	Y	Y	Y	Y	Y	Y	Y	Y
17 O'Brien	Y	Y	Y	Y	Y	N	Y	Y
18 Michel	Y	Y	Y	Y	Y	Y	Y	N
19 Railsback	Y	Y	Y	Y	Y	Y	Y	N
20 Findley	Y	Y	Y	Y	Y	Y	Y	N
21 Madigan	Y	Y	Y	Y	Y	Y	Y	N
22 Shipley	Y	Y	N	N	Y	?	N	?
23 Price	Y	Y	N	N	Y	N	N	Y
24 Simon	Y	Y	N	N	N	N	Y	Y
INDIANA								
1 Benjamin	Y	Y	N	N	N	N	N	Y
2 Fithian	Y	Y	N	N	Y	Y	Y	Y
3 Brademas	Y	Y	N	N	N	N	N	Y
4 Quayle	N	Y	Y	Y	Y	Y	Y	N
5 Hillis	Y	Y	Y	Y	Y	Y	Y	N
6 Evans	Y	Y	N	N	N	N	N	N
7 Myers, J.	Y	Y	Y	Y	Y	Y	Y	N
8 Cornwell	Y	Y	Y	N	Y	Y	Y	Y
9 Hamilton	Y	Y	N	N	N	Y	Y	N
10 Sharp	Y	Y	N	N	Y	N	Y	N
11 Jacobs	Y	Y	N	N	N	Y	Y	Y
IOWA								
1 Leach	Y	Y	Y	Y	Y	Y	Y	N
2 Blouin	Y	Y	N	N	N	N	N	Y
3 Grassley	Y	Y	Y	Y	Y	Y	Y	N
4 Smith	Y	Y	N	Y	Y	Y	Y	Y
5 Harkin	Y	Y	N	N	N	Y	Y	Y
6 Bedell	Y	Y	N	N	N	Y	Y	Y

Democrats ***Republicans***

	588	589	590	591	592	593	594	595
KANSAS								
1 Sebelius	Y	Y	Y	Y	Y	Y	Y	N
2 Keys	Y	Y	N	N	Y	Y	Y	Y
3 Winn	Y	Y	Y	Y	Y	Y	Y	N
4 Glickman	Y	Y	N	Y	Y	Y	Y	Y
5 Skubitz	Y	Y	Y	Y	Y	Y	Y	N
KENTUCKY								
1 Hubbard	Y	Y	Y	Y	Y	N	Y	N
2 Natcher	Y	Y	N	N	Y	Y	N	Y
3 Mazzoli	Y	Y	N	N	N	Y	Y	N
4 Snyder	Y	Y	Y	N	Y	Y	N	Y
5 Carter	Y	Y	N	Y	Y	Y	N	N
6 Breckinridge	Y	Y	N	N	N	N	Y	Y
7 Perkins	Y	Y	N	N	N	N	N	N
LOUISIANA								
1 Livingston	Y	Y	Y	Y	Y	Y	N	N
2 Boggs	Y	Y	N	N	N	N	N	N
3 Treen	Y	Y	Y	Y	Y	Y	Y	N
4 Waggonner	Y	Y	Y	Y	Y	Y	Y	N
5 Huckaby	Y	Y	N	N	N	N	N	Y
6 Moore	Y	Y	Y	Y	Y	Y	Y	N
7 Breaux	Y	Y	Y	Y	Y	Y	Y	N
8 Long	Y	Y	N	N	N	N	N	N
MAINE								
1 Emery	Y	Y	Y	Y	Y	Y	Y	N
2 Cohen	Y	Y	Y	Y	Y	Y	Y	N
MARYLAND								
1 Bauman	N	Y	Y	Y	Y	Y	Y	N
2 Long	Y	Y	Y	Y	Y	Y	Y	Y
3 Mikulski	Y	Y	N	N	N	N	Y	Y
4 Holt	N	Y	Y	Y	Y	Y	Y	N
5 Spellman	Y	Y	N	N	N	N	X	Y
6 Byron	Y	Y	Y	Y	Y	Y	Y	N
7 Mitchell	Y	Y	N	N	N	N	N	Y
8 Steers	Y	Y	N	N	N	N	N	N
MASSACHUSETTS								
1 Conte	Y	Y	N	Y	Y	Y	Y	N
2 Boland	Y	Y	N	N	Y	N	N	Y
3 Early	Y	Y	N	N	Y	N	N	Y
4 Drinan	Y	Y	N	N	Y	N	N	Y
5 Tsongas	?	?	?	?	?	?	?	?
6 Harrington	Y	Y	N	Y	Y	N	N	N
7 Markey	Y	Y	N	N	N	N	N	Y
8 O'Neill								
9 Moakley	Y	Y	N	▮	▮	N	N	#
10 Heckler	Y	Y	N	Y	Y	N	N	Y
11 Burke	Y	Y	N	X	X	X	X	?
12 Studds	Y	Y	N	N	N	N	N	Y
MICHIGAN								
1 Conyers	Y	Y	N	N	N	N	N	Y
2 Pursell	Y	Y	Y	Y	N	N	Y	Y
3 Brown	Y	Y	N	N	Y	N	Y	N
4 Stockman	#	Y	Y	Y	Y	Y	Y	N
5 Sawyer	Y	Y	Y	Y	Y	Y	Y	N
6 Carr	Y	Y	N	N	N	N	N	Y
7 Kildee	Y	Y	N	N	N	N	N	Y
8 Traxler	Y	Y	N	N	N	N	N	N
9 Vander Jagt	Y	Y	Y	Y	Y	N	Y	N
10 Cederberg	Y	Y	Y	Y	Y	N	Y	N
11 Ruppe	Y	Y	Y	Y	Y	Y	Y	N
12 Bonior	Y	Y	N	N	N	N	N	Y
13 Diggs	Y	Y	N	N	N	N	▮	?
14 Nedzi	Y	Y	N	N	N	N	N	Y
15 Ford	Y	Y	N	N	N	N	N	Y
16 Dingell	Y	Y	N	N	N	N	N	Y
17 Brodhead	Y	Y	N	N	N	N	N	Y
18 Blanchard	Y	Y	N	N	N	N	N	Y
19 Broomfield	Y	Y	Y	Y	Y	Y	Y	N
MINNESOTA								
1 Quie	Y	Y	Y	Y	Y	Y	Y	N
2 Hagedorn	Y	Y	Y	Y	Y	Y	Y	N
3 Frenzel	Y	Y	Y	Y	Y	Y	Y	N
4 Vento	Y	Y	N	N	N	N	N	Y
5 Fraser	Y	Y	N	N	N	N	N	Y
6 Nolan	Y	Y	N	N	?	N	N	Y
7 Stangeland	Y	Y	Y	Y	Y	Y	Y	Y
8 Oberstar	Y	Y	N	N	N	N	N	Y
MISSISSIPPI								
1 Whitten	Y	Y	Y	Y	Y	Y	✓	▮
2 Bowen	Y	Y	Y	Y	Y	Y	Y	N
3 Montgomery	Y	Y	Y	Y	Y	Y	Y	N
4 Cochran	Y	Y	Y	Y	Y	Y	Y	N
5 Lott	Y	Y	Y	Y	Y	Y	Y	N
MISSOURI								
1 Clay	Y	Y	N	N	N	N	N	Y
2 Young	Y	Y	N	N	N	N	Y	Y
3 Gephardt	Y	Y	N	N	N	N	Y	Y

	588	589	590	591	592	593	594	595
4 Skelton	Y	Y	N	N	N	N	Y	N
5 Bolling	Y	Y	N	N	N	#	N	Y
6 Coleman	Y	Y	Y	Y	Y	Y	Y	N
7 Taylor	N	Y	Y	Y	Y	Y	Y	N
8 Ichord	Y	Y	Y	Y	Y	Y	N	Y
9 Volkmer	Y	Y	N	N	Y	N	Y	Y
10 Burlison	Y	Y	N	N	N	Y	N	N
MONTANA								
1 Baucus	Y	Y	N	N	Y	Y	Y	Y
2 Marlenee	Y	Y	Y	Y	Y	Y	Y	N
NEBRASKA								
1 Thone	Y	Y	Y	Y	Y	Y	Y	N
2 Cavanaugh	Y	Y	N	Y	Y	N	N	Y
3 Smith	Y	Y	Y	Y	Y	Y	Y	N
NEVADA								
AL Santini	Y	Y	N	N	N	Y	Y	Y
NEW HAMPSHIRE								
1 D'Amours	Y	Y	Y	N	Y	N	N	Y
2 Cleveland	Y	Y	Y	Y	Y	Y	Y	N
NEW JERSEY								
1 Florio	Y	Y	N	Y	Y	Y	Y	Y
2 Hughes	Y	Y	Y	Y	Y	N	N	Y
3 Howard	Y	Y	N	N	N	N	N	Y
4 Thompson	Y	Y	N	N	N	N	N	Y
5 Fenwick	Y	Y	Y	Y	Y	Y	Y	N
6 Forsythe	Y	Y	Y	Y	Y	Y	Y	N
7 Maguire	Y	Y	N	N	N	N	N	Y
8 Roe	Y	Y	N	N	N	N	N	N
9 Hollenbeck	Y	Y	N	Y	Y	N	N	Y
10 Rodino	#	#	X	X	X	X	X	#
11 Minish	Y	Y	N	Y	Y	Y	Y	Y
12 Rinaldo	Y	Y	N	N	Y	N	N	Y
13 Meyner	Y	Y	N	N	N	N	N	Y
14 LeFante	#	#	X	X	X	#	▮	#
15 Patten	Y	Y	N	Y	Y	N	N	Y
NEW MEXICO								
1 Lujan	Y	Y	Y	Y	Y	Y	Y	Y
2 Runnels	Y	Y	Y	Y	Y	Y	Y	N
NEW YORK								
1 Pike	Y	Y	Y	Y	Y	Y	Y	N
2 Downey	Y	Y	N	N	N	N	N	Y
3 Ambro	Y	Y	Y	N	N	Y	Y	Y
4 Lent	Y	Y	Y	Y	Y	Y	Y	N
5 Wydler	Y	Y	Y	Y	Y	Y	Y	N
6 Wolff	Y	Y	N	Y	N	Y	N	Y
7 Addabbo	Y	Y	N	N	N	N	N	Y
8 Rosenthal	Y	Y	N	N	N	N	N	Y
9 Delaney	Y	Y	Y	?	Y	Y	N	N
10 Biaggi	Y	Y	Y	Y	Y	Y	N	Y
11 Scheuer	Y	Y	N	N	N	N	N	Y
12 Chisholm	Y	Y	N	N	N	N	N	Y
13 Solarz	Y	Y	N	N	N	N	N	Y
14 Richmond	Y	Y	N	N	N	N	N	Y
15 Zeferetti	Y	Y	N	Y	Y	N	N	N
16 Holtzman	Y	Y	N	N	N	N	N	Y
17 Murphy	Y	Y	N	N	N	Y	N	N
18 Green	Y	Y	N	N	N	N	N	N
19 Rangel	Y	Y	N	N	N	N	N	Y
20 Weiss	Y	Y	N	N	N	N	N	N
21 Garcia	Y	Y	N	N	N	N	N	Y
22 Bingham	Y	Y	N	N	N	N	N	Y
23 Caputo	Y	Y	N	N	N	N	N	Y
24 Ottinger	Y	Y	N	N	N	N	N	Y
25 Fish	?	Y	Y	Y	Y	Y	Y	N
26 Gilman	Y	Y	N	Y	Y	N	N	N
27 McHugh	Y	Y	N	N	N	N	N	Y
28 Stratton	Y	Y	N	N	N	N	N	Y
29 Pattison	Y	Y	N	N	N	N	Y	Y
30 McEwen	Y	Y	Y	Y	Y	Y	Y	N
31 Mitchell	Y	Y	Y	Y	Y	N	Y	N
32 Hanley	Y	Y	Y	Y	Y	Y	N	Y
33 Walsh	Y	Y	Y	Y	Y	Y	Y	N
34 Horton	Y	Y	Y	Y	Y	N	N	N
35 Conable	Y	Y	Y	Y	Y	Y	Y	N
36 LaFalce	#	#	#	#	N	N	Y	Y
37 Nowak	Y	Y	N	N	N	N	N	Y
38 Kemp	Y	Y	Y	Y	Y	Y	Y	N
39 Lundine	Y	Y	N	N	N	N	N	Y
NORTH CAROLINA								
1 Jones	Y	Y	Y	Y	Y	Y	Y	N
2 Fountain	Y	Y	Y	Y	Y	Y	Y	N
3 Whitley	Y	Y	Y	Y	Y	Y	Y	N
4 Andrews	Y	Y	Y	Y	Y	N	Y	Y
5 Neal	Y	Y	Y	Y	Y	Y	Y	Y
6 Preyer	Y	Y	Y	Y	Y	Y	Y	Y
7 Rose	Y	?	?	N	Y	Y	Y	Y
8 Hefner	Y	Y	Y	Y	Y	Y	Y	N

	588	589	590	591	592	593	594	595
9 Martin	Y	Y	Y	Y	Y	Y	Y	N
10 Broyhill	Y	Y	Y	Y	Y	Y	Y	N
11 Gudger	Y	Y	▮	Y	Y	Y	Y	Y
NORTH DAKOTA								
AL Andrews	Y	Y	Y	Y	Y	N	Y	N
OHIO								
1 Gradison	Y	Y	Y	Y	Y	Y	Y	N
2 Luken	Y	Y	Y	N	N	N	Y	Y
3 Whalen	Y	Y	N	N	N	N	▮	N
4 Guyer	Y	Y	Y	Y	Y	Y	Y	N
5 Latta	Y	Y	Y	Y	Y	Y	Y	N
6 Harsha	Y	Y	Y	N	N	N	N	Y
7 Brown	N	Y	Y	Y	Y	Y	Y	N
8 Kindness	N	N	Y	N	Y	Y	Y	N
9 Ashley	Y	Y	N	Y	Y	Y	N	N
10 Miller	Y	Y	Y	Y	Y	Y	N	Y
11 Stanton	Y	Y	Y	Y	Y	Y	Y	N
12 Devine	Y	Y	Y	Y	Y	Y	Y	N
13 Pease	Y	Y	N	N	N	N	N	Y
14 Seiberling	Y	Y	N	N	N	N	N	Y
15 Wylie	Y	Y	?	N	Y	N	Y	N
16 Regula	Y	Y	Y	Y	Y	Y	Y	N
17 Ashbrook	N	Y	Y	Y	Y	Y	Y	N
18 Applegate	Y	Y	N	N	P	Y	Y	Y
19 Carney	Y	Y	N	N	N	N	N	Y
20 Oakar	Y	Y	N	N	N	N	N	N
21 Stokes	Y	Y	N	N	N	N	N	Y
22 Vanik	Y	Y	N	N	?	?	N	Y
23 Mottl	Y	Y	N	Y	Y	Y	N	N
OKLAHOMA								
1 Jones	Y	Y	Y	Y	Y	Y	Y	Y
2 Risenhoover	Y	Y	N	N	Y	Y	N	N
3 Watkins	Y	Y	Y	Y	Y	Y	N	N
4 Steed	Y	Y	Y	Y	Y	Y	Y	Y
5 Edwards	Y	Y	Y	Y	Y	Y	Y	N
6 English	Y	Y	Y	Y	Y	Y	Y	N
OREGON								
1 AuCoin	Y	Y	N	Y	Y	N	Y	Y
2 Ullman	Y	Y	N	▮	N	Y	Y	Y
3 Duncan	Y	Y	Y	N	Y	N	Y	Y
4 Weaver	Y	Y	N	N	N	N	N	Y
PENNSYLVANIA								
1 Myers, M.	Y	Y	N	N	N	N	N	Y
2 Nix	Y	Y	N	✓	N	N	N	N
3 Lederer	Y	Y	N	N	N	N	N	Y
4 Eilberg	Y	Y	N	N	N	N	N	Y
5 Schulze	Y	Y	Y	Y	Y	Y	Y	N
6 Yatron	Y	Y	N	Y	Y	N	N	Y
7 Edgar	Y	Y	N	N	N	N	N	Y
8 Kostmayer	Y	Y	Y	Y	Y	N	Y	Y
9 Shuster	N	Y	Y	Y	Y	Y	Y	N
10 McDade	Y	Y	N	Y	Y	Y	Y	N
11 Flood	Y	Y	N	N	Y	N	N	Y
12 Murtha	Y	Y	N	Y	Y	N	N	Y
13 Coughlin	Y	Y	Y	Y	Y	Y	Y	N
14 Moorhead	Y	Y	N	N	N	Y	N	Y
15 Rooney	Y	Y	N	N	N	N	X	?
16 Walker	Y	Y	Y	Y	Y	Y	Y	N
17 Ertel	Y	Y	Y	Y	Y	Y	Y	Y
18 Walgren	Y	Y	N	N	Y	N	N	Y
19 Goodling, W.	Y	Y	Y	Y	Y	Y	Y	N
20 Gaydos	Y	Y	N	N	N	N	N	Y
21 Dent	Y	Y	▮	N	Y	Y	N	Y
22 Murphy	Y	Y	N	N	N	N	N	Y
23 Ammerman	Y	Y	N	Y	Y	Y	N	Y
24 Marks	Y	Y	N	Y	Y	Y	N	N
25 Myers, G.	N	Y	Y	Y	Y	Y	Y	Y
RHODE ISLAND								
1 St Germain	Y	Y	N	N	N	Y	N	Y
2 Beard	Y	Y	N	N	N	N	N	Y
SOUTH CAROLINA								
1 Davis	Y	Y	N	N	Y	N	Y	N
2 Spence	Y	Y	Y	Y	Y	Y	Y	N
3 Derrick	Y	Y	N	N	N	N	N	▮
4 Mann	Y	Y	Y	Y	Y	Y	Y	Y
5 Holland	Y	Y	N	N	Y	N	N	N
6 Jenrette	Y	Y	N	N	Y	Y	Y	N
SOUTH DAKOTA								
1 Pressler	Y	Y	N	N	N	N	Y	N
2 Abdnor	#	#	#	#	#	#	#	▮
TENNESSEE								
1 Quillen	Y	Y	Y	Y	Y	Y	Y	N
2 Duncan	Y	Y	Y	Y	Y	Y	Y	N
3 Lloyd	#	#	✓	✓	✓	▮	✓	▮
4 Gore	Y	Y	N	N	Y	N	Y	Y
5 Vacancy								
6 Beard	Y	Y	Y	Y	Y	Y	Y	Y

	588	589	590	591	592	593	594	595
7 Jones	Y	Y	Y	Y	Y	N	Y	N
8 Ford	Y	Y	N	N	Y	N	N	Y
TEXAS								
1 Hall	Y	Y	Y	Y	Y	Y	Y	N
2 Wilson, C.	Y	Y	Y	Y	Y	Y	Y	Y
3 Collins	N	Y	Y	Y	Y	Y	Y	N
4 Roberts	?	Y	Y	Y	Y	Y	Y	N
5 Mattox	?	Y	Y	Y	Y	Y	Y	Y
6 Teague	?	?	✓	✓	✓	✓	✓	?
7 Archer	N	Y	Y	Y	Y	Y	Y	N
8 Eckhardt	Y	Y	N	N	N	N	N	Y
9 Brooks	Y	Y	N	N	Y	Y	Y	Y
10 Pickle	Y	Y	Y	Y	Y	Y	Y	Y
11 Poage	Y	Y	Y	Y	Y	Y	N	N
12 Wright	Y	Y	N	N	N	Y	N	Y
13 Hightower	Y	Y	Y	Y	Y	Y	Y	Y
14 Young	Y	Y	?	?	?	?	?	?
15 de la Garza	Y	Y	Y	Y	Y	Y	Y	Y
16 White	#	Y	Y	Y	Y	Y	Y	N
17 Burleson	Y	Y	Y	Y	Y	Y	Y	N
18 Jordan	Y	Y	Y	N	N	Y	N	Y
19 Mahon	Y	Y	Y	Y	Y	Y	Y	Y
20 Gonzalez	Y	Y	Y	N	N	N	N	Y
21 Krueger	#	#	X	X	X	#	X	▮
22 Gammage	Y	Y	Y	Y	Y	Y	Y	Y
23 Kazen	Y	Y	Y	Y	Y	Y	Y	Y
24 Milford	?	?	Y	Y	Y	Y	Y	?
UTAH								
1 McKay	Y	#	N	Y	Y	Y	Y	Y
2 Marriott	Y	#	Y	Y	Y	Y	Y	N
VERMONT								
AL Jeffords	Y	Y	Y	Y	Y	Y	Y	N
VIRGINIA								
1 Trible	Y	Y	Y	Y	Y	Y	Y	N
2 Whitehurst	Y	Y	Y	Y	Y	Y	Y	N
3 Satterfield	?	Y	Y	Y	Y	Y	Y	N
4 Daniel	Y	Y	Y	Y	Y	Y	Y	N
5 Daniel	Y	Y	Y	Y	Y	Y	Y	N
6 Butler	Y	Y	Y	Y	Y	Y	Y	N
7 Robinson	N	Y	Y	Y	Y	Y	Y	N
8 Harris	Y	Y	N	N	N	N	N	Y
9 Wampler	Y	Y	Y	Y	Y	Y	Y	N
10 Fisher	Y	Y	N	N	N	N	Y	N
WASHINGTON								
1 Pritchard	Y	Y	Y	Y	Y	Y	Y	N
2 Meeds	Y	Y	N	N	▮	N	N	Y
3 Bonker	Y	#	N	N	N	N	N	#
4 McCormack	Y	Y	Y	N	N	N	Y	Y
5 Foley	?	Y	Y	N	N	N	Y	Y
6 Dicks	Y	Y	N	N	N	N	Y	Y
7 Cunningham	N	Y	Y	Y	Y	Y	Y	N
WEST VIRGINIA								
1 Mollohan	#	Y	N	Y	Y	Y	Y	Y
2 Staggers	Y	Y	N	N	Y	N	Y	Y
3 Slack	Y	Y	N	Y	Y	Y	N	N
4 Rahall	Y	Y	N	N	N	N	N	Y
WISCONSIN								
1 Aspin	Y	Y	N	N	N	Y	N	Y
2 Kastenmeier	Y	Y	N	N	N	N	N	Y
3 Baldus	Y	Y	N	N	N	N	N	Y
4 Zablocki	Y	Y	N	N	Y	Y	N	N
5 Reuss	Y	Y	N	N	Y	N	N	Y
6 Steiger	Y	Y	Y	Y	Y	Y	N	N
7 Obey	Y	Y	N	N	N	Y	N	Y
8 Cornell	Y	Y	N	N	N	N	N	Y
9 Kasten	?	?	?	?	?	?	?	?
WYOMING								
AL Roncalio	Y	Y	N	N	N	N	N	#

Democrats ***Republicans***

596. HR 13511. Revenue Act of 1978. Murphy, D-Ill., motion to order the previous question (thus ending debate) on the adoption of the rule (H Res 1306) providing for House floor consideration of the bill. Motion agreed to 284-130: R 136-8; D 148-122 (ND 80-106; SD 68-16), Aug. 10, 1978.

597. HR 13511. Revenue Act of 1978. Adoption of the Ways and Means Committee amendments to modify the earned income tax credit, extend investment tax credits to rehabilitation of structures, revise the jobs credit, establish an alternative minimum tax on capital gains, exempt up to $100,000 in profits from the sale of residences from capital gains taxes once in a taxpayer's lifetime and other measures. Adopted 409-1: R 142-0; D 267-1 (ND 184-0; SD 83-1), Aug. 10, 1978.

598. HR 13511. Revenue Act of 1978. Adoption of Ways and Means Committee amendment to provide for indexation of capital gains taxes for inflation beginning in 1980. Adopted 249-167: R 142-1; D 107-166 (ND 48-140; SD 59-26), Aug. 10, 1978.

599. HR 13511. Revenue Act of 1978. Vanik, D-Ohio, substitute amendment for the bill to extend tax cuts due to expire at the end of 1978 and enact no new tax cut. Rejected 57-356: R 2-140; D 55-216 (ND 47-141; SD 8-75), Aug. 10, 1978.

600. HR 13511. Revenue Act of 1978. Corman, D-Calif., amendment to provide an $18.1 billion tax cut including more benefits to taxpayers earning less than $50,000, and less to those earning more. Rejected 193-225: R 8-134; D 185-91 (ND 164-27; SD 21-64), Aug. 10, 1978. A "yea" was a vote supporting the president's position.

601. HR 13511. Revenue Act of 1978. Kemp, R-N.Y., motion to recommit the bill to the Ways and Means Committee with instructions to report it back with an amendment to reduce individual income tax rates by one-third over the next three years. Rejected 177-240: R 140-3; D 37-237 (ND 17-173; SD 20-64), Aug. 10, 1978. A "nay" was a vote supporting the president's position.

602. HR 13511. Revenue Act of 1978. Passage of the bill to provide $16.3 billion in individual, corporate and capital gains tax cuts. Passed 362-49: R 138-2; D 224-47 (ND 143-44; SD 81-3), Aug. 10, 1978.

KEY

- Y Voted for (yea).
- ✓ Paired for.
- † Announced for.
- # CQ Poll for.
- N Voted against (nay).
- X Paired against.
- \- Announced against.
- ▮ CQ Poll against.
- P Voted "present."
- ● Voted "present" to avoid possible conflict of interest.
- ? Did not vote or otherwise make a position known.

	596	597	598	599	600	601	602
ALABAMA							
1 Edwards	Y	Y	Y	N	N	Y	Y
2 Dickinson	Y	Y	Y	N	N	Y	Y
3 Nichols	Y	Y	Y	N	N	N	Y
4 Bevill	Y	Y	Y	N	N	N	Y
5 Flippo	Y	Y	Y	N	N	N	Y
6 Buchanan	Y	Y	Y	N	N	Y	Y
7 Flowers	?	Y	Y	N	N	N	Y
ALASKA							
AL Young	#	Y	Y	N	N	Y	Y
ARIZONA							
1 Rhodes	Y	Y	Y	N	N	Y	Y
2 Udall	N	Y	N	N	Y	N	Y
3 Stump	Y	Y	Y	N	N	Y	Y
4 Rudd	Y	Y	Y	?	X	✓	?
ARKANSAS							
1 Alexander	Y	Y	N	N	N	N	Y
2 Tucker	N	Y	Y	N	Y	N	Y
3 Hammerschmidt	Y	Y	Y	N	N	Y	Y
4 Thornton	Y	Y	Y	N	N	N	Y
CALIFORNIA							
1 Johnson	Y	Y	N	N	Y	N	Y
2 Clausen	Y	Y	Y	N	N	Y	Y
3 Moss	N	P	N	N	Y	N	N
4 Leggett	N	?	?	N	Y	N	Y
5 Burton, J.	N	Y	N	Y	Y	Y	N
6 Burton, P.	N	Y	N	Y	Y	N	N
7 Miller	X	?	X	?	✓	X	?
8 Dellums	X	#	N	Y	Y	N	N
9 Stark	X	#	X	Y	Y	N	N
10 Edwards	N	Y	N	Y	Y	N	N
11 Ryan	Y	Y	Y	Y	Y	N	Y
12 McCloskey	Y	Y	Y	N	N	Y	Y
13 Mineta	Y	Y	N	N	Y	N	Y
14 McFall	Y	Y	N	N	Y	N	Y
15 Sisk	✓	?	?	?	?	?	?
16 Panetta	N	Y	N	N	Y	N	Y
17 Krebs	N	Y	N	N	Y	N	Y
18 Vacancy							
19 Lagomarsino	Y	Y	Y	N	N	Y	Y
20 Goldwater	Y	Y	Y	N	N	Y	Y
21 Corman	Y	Y	N	N	Y	N	Y
22 Moorhead	Y	Y	Y	N	N	Y	Y
23 Beilenson	N	Y	N	N	Y	N	N
24 Waxman	N	Y	N	Y	Y	N	Y
25 Roybal	Y	Y	N	N	Y	N	N
26 Rousselot	Y	Y	Y	N	N	Y	Y
27 Dornan	Y	Y	Y	N	N	Y	Y
28 Burke	P	Y	N	N	✓	X	#
29 Hawkins	Y	Y	N	N	Y	N	Y
30 Danielson	Y	Y	N	N	Y	N	Y
31 Wilson, C.H.	Y	?	N	N	Y	Y	Y
32 Anderson	N	Y	N	N	Y	N	Y
33 Clawson	Y	Y	Y	N	N	Y	Y
34 Hannaford	N	Y	Y	N	Y	Y	Y
35 Lloyd	N	Y	N	N	Y	Y	Y
36 Brown	Y	Y	N	N	Y	N	Y
37 Pettis	Y	Y	Y	N	N	Y	Y
38 Patterson	N	Y	N	N	Y	N	Y
39 Wiggins	Y	Y	Y	N	N	Y	Y
40 Badham	Y	Y	Y	N	N	Y	Y
41 Wilson, B.	Y	Y	Y	N	N	Y	Y
42 Van Deerlin	Y	Y	N	N	Y	N	Y
43 Burgener	Y	Y	Y	N	N	Y	Y
COLORADO							
1 Schroeder	N	Y	N	Y	Y	N	Y
2 Wirth	N	Y	N	Y	Y	N	Y
3 Evans	Y	Y	Y	N	N	N	Y
4 Johnson	Y	Y	Y	N	N	Y	Y
5 Armstrong	Y	Y	Y	N	N	Y	?
CONNECTICUT							
1 Cotter	Y	Y	N	N	N	N	Y
2 Dodd	N	Y	N	Y	Y	N	N
3 Giaimo	Y	Y	N	N	N	N	Y
4 McKinney	Y	Y	Y	N	N	Y	Y
5 Sarasin	Y	Y	Y	N	N	Y	Y
6 Moffett	N	Y	N	Y	Y	N	N
DELAWARE							
AL Evans	Y	Y	Y	N	N	Y	Y
FLORIDA							
1 Sikes	Y	Y	Y	N	N	Y	Y
2 Fuqua	Y	Y	Y	N	N	N	Y
3 Bennett	Y	Y	Y	Y	N	N	N
4 Chappell	Y	Y	Y	N	N	Y	Y
5 Kelly	Y	Y	Y	N	N	Y	Y
6 Young	Y	Y	Y	N	N	Y	Y
7 Gibbons	Y	Y	Y	N	N	N	Y
8 Ireland	Y	Y	Y	N	N	Y	Y
9 Frey	?	?	Y	N	N	Y	Y
10 Bafalis	Y	Y	Y	N	N	Y	Y
11 Rogers	Y	Y	N	N	Y	N	Y
12 Burke	Y	Y	Y	N	N	Y	Y
13 Lehman	N	Y	N	N	Y	N	Y
14 Pepper	N	Y	N	N	Y	N	Y
15 Fascell	Y	Y	N	Y	Y	N	Y
GEORGIA							
1 Ginn	Y	Y	Y	N	N	N	Y
2 Mathis	Y	Y	?	?	N	Y	Y
3 Brinkley	Y	Y	Y	N	N	Y	Y
4 Levitas	N	Y	Y	N	Y	Y	Y
5 Fowler	N	Y	N	N	N	N	Y
6 Flynt	Y	Y	Y	N	N	Y	Y
7 McDonald	✓	#	✓	?	X	✓	#
8 Evans	Y	Y	Y	N	N	N	Y
9 Jenkins	Y	Y	N	N	N	N	Y
10 Barnard	Y	?	Y	N	N	Y	Y
HAWAII							
1 Heftel	Y	Y	Y	N	N	N	Y
2 Akaka	Y	Y	N	N	N	N	?
IDAHO							
1 Symms	Y	Y	Y	N	N	Y	Y
2 Hansen, G.	Y	Y	✓	N	N	Y	Y
ILLINOIS							
1 Metcalfe	N	Y	N	N	Y	?	?
2 Murphy	Y	Y	N	N	Y	N	Y
3 Russo	Y	Y	Y	N	N	Y	Y
4 Derwinski	Y	Y	Y	N	N	Y	Y
5 Fary	Y	Y	N	N	Y	N	Y
6 Hyde	Y	Y	Y	N	N	Y	Y
7 Collins	Y	Y	N	N	Y	N	Y
8 Rostenkowski	Y	Y	N	N	Y	N	Y
9 Yates	Y	Y	N	Y	Y	N	N
10 Mikva	N	Y	N	Y	Y	N	Y
11 Annunzio	Y	Y	N	N	Y	N	Y
12 Crane	Y	Y	Y	N	N	Y	Y
13 McClory	Y	Y	Y	N	N	Y	Y
14 Erlenborn	Y	Y	Y	N	N	Y	Y
15 Corcoran	Y	Y	Y	N	N	Y	Y
16 Anderson	Y	Y	Y	N	N	Y	Y
17 O'Brien	Y	Y	Y	N	N	Y	Y
18 Michel	Y	Y	Y	N	N	Y	Y
19 Railsback	Y	Y	Y	N	N	Y	Y
20 Findley	Y	Y	N	Y	N	N	N
21 Madigan	Y	Y	Y	N	N	Y	Y
22 Shipley	Y	Y	N	N	N	N	Y
23 Price	Y	Y	N	N	Y	N	Y
24 Simon	N	Y	N	Y	Y	N	N
INDIANA							
1 Benjamin	N	Y	N	N	Y	N	Y
2 Fithian	Y	Y	N	N	Y	N	Y
3 Brademas	Y	Y	N	N	Y	N	Y
4 Quayle	Y	Y	Y	N	N	Y	Y
5 Hillis	Y	Y	Y	N	N	Y	Y
6 Evans	Y	Y	N	N	Y	Y	Y
7 Myers, J.	Y	Y	Y	N	N	Y	Y
8 Cornwell	Y	Y	N	N	N	N	Y
9 Hamilton	Y	Y	N	N	Y	N	Y
10 Sharp	Y	Y	N	N	Y	N	Y
11 Jacobs	N	#	N	Y	Y	N	N
IOWA							
1 Leach	Y	Y	Y	N	N	Y	Y
2 Blouin	Y	Y	Y	N	Y	N	Y
3 Grassley	Y	Y	Y	N	N	Y	Y
4 Smith	Y	Y	Y	N	N	N	Y
5 Harkin	N	Y	Y	Y	Y	N	Y
6 Bedell	N	Y	N	Y	Y	N	N

Democrats ***Republicans***

	596	597	598	599	600	601	602
KANSAS							
1 Sebelius	Y	Y	Y	N	N	Y	Y
2 Keys	N	Y	N	Y	Y	N	Y
3 Winn	Y	Y	Y	N	N	Y	Y
4 Glickman	N	Y	Y	N	Y	N	Y
5 Skubitz	Y	Y	Y	Y	N	Y	Y
KENTUCKY							
1 Hubbard	Y	Y	Y	N	Y	N	Y
2 Natcher	Y	Y	Y	N	N	N	Y
3 Mazzoli	Y	Y	Y	N	N	N	Y
4 Snyder	Y	Y	Y	N	N	Y	Y
5 Carter	Y	Y	Y	N	N	Y	Y
6 Breckinridge	Y	Y	Y	N	Y	N	Y
7 Perkins	Y	Y	Y	N	N	N	Y
LOUISIANA							
1 Livingston	Y	Y	Y	N	N	Y	Y
2 Boggs	Y	Y	Y	N	N	N	Y
3 Treen	Y	Y	Y	N	N	Y	Y
4 Waggonner	Y	Y	Y	N	N	N	Y
5 Huckaby	Y	Y	Y	N	N	Y	Y
6 Moore	Y	Y	Y	N	N	Y	Y
7 Breaux	Y	Y	Y	N	N	Y	Y
8 Long	Y	Y	Y	N	N	N	Y
MAINE							
1 Emery	Y	Y	Y	N	N	Y	Y
2 Cohen	Y	Y	Y	N	N	Y	Y
MARYLAND							
1 Bauman	Y	Y	Y	N	N	Y	Y
2 Long	Y	Y	Y	N	N	N	Y
3 Mikulski	N	Y	N	Y	Y	N	N
4 Holt	Y	Y	Y	N	N	Y	Y
5 Spellman	N	Y	N	?	Y	N	Y
6 Byron	Y	Y	Y	N	N	N	Y
7 Mitchell	N	Y	N	N	Y	N	N
8 Steers	N	Y	Y	N	Y	Y	Y
MASSACHUSETTS							
1 Conte	Y	Y	Y	N	N	Y	Y
2 Boland	Y	Y	N	N	Y	N	Y
3 Early	N	Y	N	N	Y	Y	Y
4 Drinan	N	Y	N	N	Y	N	N
5 Tsongas	?	Y	N	N	Y	N	Y
6 Harrington	N	Y	N	N	Y	N	N
7 Markey	N	Y	N	N	Y	N	N
8 O'Neill							
9 Moakley	Y	Y	N	N	Y	N	Y
10 Heckler	N	Y	N	Y	Y	Y	Y
11 Burke	N	Y	Y	N	Y	Y	Y
12 Studds	N	Y	N	N	Y	N	N
MICHIGAN							
1 Conyers	X	Y	N	Y	Y	N	N
2 Pursell	Y	Y	Y	N	N	Y	Y
3 Brown	Y	Y	Y	N	N	Y	Y
4 Stockman	Y	Y	Y	N	N	Y	Y
5 Sawyer	Y	#	✓	?	?	✓	#
6 Carr	N	Y	N	N	Y	Y	Y
7 Kildee	N	Y	N	N	Y	N	Y
8 Traxler	N	Y	N	N	Y	Y	Y
9 Vander Jagt	Y	Y	Y	N	N	Y	Y
10 Cederberg	Y	Y	Y	N	N	Y	Y
11 Ruppe	Y	Y	Y	N	N	Y	Y
12 Bonior	N	Y	N	Y	Y	N	N
13 Diggs	#	#	X	N	Y	N	N
14 Nedzi	N	Y	N	Y	Y	N	Y
15 Ford	N	Y	N	N	Y	N	Y
16 Dingell	N	Y	N	N	Y	N	Y
17 Brodhead	N	Y	N	Y	Y	N	N
18 Blanchard	N	Y	N	N	Y	N	Y
19 Broomfield	Y	Y	Y	N	N	Y	Y
MINNESOTA							
1 Quie	Y	Y	Y	N	N	Y	?
2 Hagedorn	Y	Y	Y	N	N	Y	Y
3 Frenzel	Y	Y	Y	N	N	Y	Y
4 Vento	N	Y	N	N	Y	N	Y
5 Fraser	N	Y	Y	?	?	?	?
6 Nolan	N	Y	N	Y	Y	N	N
7 Stangeland	Y	Y	Y	N	N	Y	Y
8 Oberstar	N	Y	N	N	Y	N	N
MISSISSIPPI							
1 Whitten	Y	Y	Y	N	Y	N	Y
2 Bowen	Y	Y	Y	N	N	Y	Y
3 Montgomery	Y	Y	Y	N	N	N	Y
4 Cochran	Y	?	Y	N	N	Y	Y
5 Lott	Y	Y	Y	N	N	Y	Y
MISSOURI							
1 Clay	N	Y	N	N	Y	N	N
2 Young	N	Y	Y	N	Y	N	Y
3 Gephardt	N	Y	N	N	Y	N	Y

	596	597	598	599	600	601	602
4 Skelton	N	Y	Y	N	Y	N	Y
5 Bolling	N	Y	N	N	Y	N	Y
6 Coleman	Y	Y	Y	N	N	Y	Y
7 Taylor	Y	Y	Y	N	N	Y	Y
8 Ichord	Y	Y	Y	Y	N	N	Y
9 Volkmer	N	Y	N	Y	Y	N	Y
10 Burlison	Y	Y	N	Y	Y	N	Y
MONTANA							
1 Baucus	N	Y	Y	N	Y	N	Y
2 Marlenee	N	Y	Y	N	N	Y	Y
NEBRASKA							
1 Thone	Y	Y	Y	N	N	Y	?
2 Cavanaugh	N	Y	Y	N	Y	N	Y
3 Smith	Y	Y	Y	N	N	Y	Y
NEVADA							
AL Santini	N	Y	Y	N	Y	N	#
NEW HAMPSHIRE							
1 D'Amours	N	Y	N	N	Y	N	Y
2 Cleveland	Y	Y	Y	N	N	Y	Y
NEW JERSEY							
1 Florio	Y	Y	Y	N	Y	N	Y
2 Hughes	N	Y	N	N	Y	N	Y
3 Howard	Y	Y	N	N	Y	N	Y
4 Thompson	N	Y	N	N	Y	N	Y
5 Fenwick	Y	Y	Y	N	N	N	Y
6 Forsythe	Y	Y	Y	N	N	Y	Y
7 Maguire	N	Y	N	?	Y	N	N
8 Roe	N	Y	Y	N	Y	N	Y
9 Hollenbeck	N	Y	Y	N	Y	Y	Y
10 Rodino	X	#	X	?	✓	X	#
11 Minish	N	Y	Y	N	Y	N	Y
12 Rinaldo	N	Y	Y	N	Y	Y	Y
13 Meyner	N	Y	N	N	Y	N	Y
14 LeFante	▮	#	#	?	✓	X	#
15 Patten	Y	Y	N	N	Y	N	Y
NEW MEXICO							
1 Lujan	Y	Y	Y	N	N	Y	Y
2 Runnels	Y	Y	Y	N	N	Y	Y
NEW YORK							
1 Pike	Y	Y	Y	Y	N	N	N
2 Downey	N	Y	N	Y	Y	N	Y
3 Ambro	Y	Y	Y	N	Y	Y	Y
4 Lent	Y	Y	Y	N	N	Y	Y
5 Wydler	Y	Y	Y	N	N	Y	Y
6 Wolff	Y	Y	Y	?	Y	N	Y
7 Addabbo	N	Y	N	N	Y	N	Y
8 Rosenthal	N	Y	N	N	Y	N	Y
9 Delaney	Y	Y	Y	N	Y	N	Y
10 Biaggi	Y	Y	Y	N	Y	N	Y
11 Scheuer	N	Y	N	N	Y	N	N
12 Chisholm	N	Y	N	?	Y	N	N
13 Solarz	N	Y	N	Y	Y	N	N
14 Richmond	N	Y	N	Y	Y	N	N
15 Zeferetti	Y	Y	Y	N	Y	N	Y
16 Holtzman	N	Y	N	N	Y	N	N
17 Murphy	Y	Y	N	N	Y	N	Y
18 Green	Y	Y	Y	N	N	Y	Y
19 Rangel	Y	Y	N	N	Y	N	Y
20 Weiss	N	Y	N	Y	Y	N	N
21 Garcia	N	Y	N	Y	Y	N	N
22 Bingham	N	Y	N	Y	Y	N	N
23 Caputo	Y	Y	Y	N	Y	Y	Y
24 Ottinger	N	Y	N	Y	Y	N	Y
25 Fish	Y	Y	Y	N	N	Y	Y
26 Gilman	N	Y	Y	N	Y	Y	Y
27 McHugh	N	Y	N	N	Y	N	Y
28 Stratton	Y	Y	Y	N	N	N	Y
29 Pattison	N	Y	Y	Y	Y	N	Y
30 McEwen	Y	Y	Y	N	N	Y	Y
31 Mitchell	Y	Y	Y	N	N	Y	Y
32 Hanley	Y	Y	Y	N	Y	N	Y
33 Walsh	Y	Y	Y	N	N	Y	Y
34 Horton	Y	Y	Y	N	N	Y	Y
35 Conable	Y	Y	Y	N	N	Y	Y
36 LaFalce	N	Y	Y	N	Y	N	Y
37 Nowak	N	Y	Y	N	Y	N	Y
38 Kemp	Y	Y	Y	N	N	Y	N
39 Lundine	N	Y	Y	N	Y	N	Y
NORTH CAROLINA							
1 Jones	Y	Y	N	N	N	N	Y
2 Fountain	Y	Y	Y	N	N	N	Y
3 Whitley	Y	Y	N	N	N	N	Y
4 Andrews	Y	Y	N	N	N	N	Y
5 Neal	N	Y	Y	N	N	N	Y
6 Preyer	N	Y	N	N	Y	N	Y
7 Rose	N	Y	N	N	Y	N	Y
8 Hefner	Y	Y	Y	N	N	N	Y

	596	597	598	599	600	601	602
9 Martin	Y	Y	Y	N	N	Y	Y
10 Broyhill	Y	Y	Y	N	N	Y	Y
11 Gudger	N	Y	N	N	N	N	Y
NORTH DAKOTA							
AL Andrews	Y	Y	Y	N	N	Y	Y
OHIO							
1 Gradison	Y	Y	Y	N	N	Y	Y
2 Luken	N	Y	Y	N	N	Y	Y
3 Whalen	N	Y	Y	N	Y	N	Y
4 Guyer	Y	Y	Y	N	N	Y	Y
5 Latta	Y	Y	Y	N	N	Y	Y
6 Harsha	Y	Y	Y	N	N	Y	Y
7 Brown	Y	Y	Y	N	N	Y	Y
8 Kindness	Y	Y	Y	N	N	Y	Y
9 Ashley	Y	Y	X	N	Y	N	Y
10 Miller	Y	Y	Y	N	N	Y	Y
11 Stanton	Y	Y	Y	N	N	Y	Y
12 Devine	Y	Y	Y	?	X	✓	#
13 Pease	N	Y	N	Y	Y	N	Y
14 Seiberling	N	Y	N	Y	Y	N	N
15 Wylie	Y	Y	Y	N	N	Y	Y
16 Regula	Y	Y	Y	N	N	Y	Y
17 Ashbrook	Y	Y	Y	N	N	Y	Y
18 Applegate	Y	Y	Y	N	Y	Y	Y
19 Carney	N	Y	N	N	Y	N	Y
20 Oakar	N	Y	N	N	Y	N	Y
21 Stokes	N	Y	N	N	Y	N	N
22 Vanik	N	Y	N	Y	Y	N	Y
23 Mottl	Y	Y	Y	N	Y	Y	Y
OKLAHOMA							
1 Jones	Y	Y	N	N	N	N	Y
2 Risenhoover	Y	Y	Y	N	N	Y	Y
3 Watkins	Y	Y	Y	N	N	Y	Y
4 Steed	Y	Y	N	N	N	N	Y
5 Edwards	Y	Y	Y	N	N	Y	Y
6 English	Y	Y	Y	N	N	Y	Y
OREGON							
1 AuCoin	Y	Y	N	N	N	N	Y
2 Ullman	Y	Y	N	N	N	N	Y
3 Duncan	Y	Y	N	Y	N	N	Y
4 Weaver	N	Y	N	N	Y	N	N
PENNSYLVANIA							
1 Myers, M.	Y	Y	N	N	Y	N	Y
2 Nix	Y	Y	N	N	Y	N	Y
3 Lederer	Y	Y	N	N	N	N	Y
4 Eilberg	N	Y	N	N	Y	N	Y
5 Schulze	Y	?	✓	?	?	Y	Y
6 Yatron	Y	Y	Y	N	Y	Y	Y
7 Edgar	N	Y	N	N	Y	N	Y
8 Kostmayer	N	Y	N	Y	Y	N	Y
9 Shuster	Y	Y	Y	N	N	Y	Y
10 McDade	Y	Y	Y	N	N	Y	Y
11 Flood	Y	Y	N	N	Y	N	Y
12 Murtha	Y	Y	N	N	N	N	Y
13 Coughlin	Y	Y	Y	N	N	Y	Y
14 Moorhead	Y	Y	Y	N	Y	N	Y
15 Rooney	N	Y	Y	N	Y	N	Y
16 Walker	Y	Y	Y	N	N	Y	Y
17 Ertel	?	Y	Y	N	Y	N	Y
18 Walgren	N	Y	Y	N	Y	N	Y
19 Goodling, W.	Y	Y	Y	N	N	Y	Y
20 Gaydos	Y	Y	Y	N	Y	N	Y
21 Dent	Y	Y	Y	N	Y	N	Y
22 Murphy	Y	Y	Y	Y	Y	N	Y
23 Ammerman	N	Y	N	Y	Y	N	Y
24 Marks	Y	Y	Y	N	Y	Y	Y
25 Myers, G.	Y	Y	Y	N	N	Y	Y
RHODE ISLAND							
1 St Germain	N	Y	N	N	Y	N	Y
2 Beard	N	Y	N	N	Y	N	Y
SOUTH CAROLINA							
1 Davis	Y	Y	Y	N	N	Y	Y
2 Spence	Y	Y	Y	N	N	Y	Y
3 Derrick	Y	Y	Y	N	Y	N	Y
4 Mann	Y	Y	Y	N	N	N	Y
5 Holland	Y	Y	Y	N	N	N	Y
6 Jenrette	Y	Y	N	?	✓	X	#
SOUTH DAKOTA							
1 Pressler	Y	Y	Y	N	N	Y	Y
2 Abdnor	Y	Y	Y	N	N	Y	Y
TENNESSEE							
1 Quillen	Y	Y	Y	N	N	Y	Y
2 Duncan	Y	Y	Y	N	N	Y	Y
3 Lloyd	✓	#	✓	?	X	✓	#
4 Gore	N	N	N	Y	Y	N	N
5 Vacancy							
6 Beard	Y	Y	Y	N	N	Y	Y

	596	597	598	599	600	601	602
7 Jones	Y	Y	N	N	N	Y	Y
8 Ford	N	Y	N	Y	Y	N	Y
TEXAS							
1 Hall	Y	Y	Y	N	N	N	Y
2 Wilson, C.	Y	Y	Y	N	N	N	Y
3 Collins	Y	Y	Y	N	N	Y	Y
4 Roberts	Y	Y	Y	N	N	N	Y
5 Mattox	N	Y	Y	N	Y	N	Y
6 Teague	✓	?	✓	?	X	?	?
7 Archer	Y	Y	Y	N	N	Y	Y
8 Eckhardt	N	Y	N	N	Y	N	Y
9 Brooks	Y	Y	Y	N	N	N	Y
10 Pickle	Y	Y	Y	Y	N	N	Y
11 Poage	Y	Y	Y	N	N	N	Y
12 Wright	Y	Y	N	N	Y	N	Y
13 Hightower	Y	Y	Y	N	N	N	Y
14 Young	Y	Y	Y	N	N	N	Y
15 de la Garza	N	Y	Y	Y	N	Y	Y
16 White	Y	Y	Y	N	N	N	Y
17 Burleson	Y	Y	Y	N	N	N	Y
18 Jordan	Y	Y	N	N	Y	N	Y
19 Mahon	Y	Y	Y	Y	N	N	Y
20 Gonzalez	N	Y	N	Y	Y	N	N
21 Krueger	✓	Y	Y	N	N	N	Y
22 Gammage	Y	Y	Y	N	N	Y	Y
23 Kazen	Y	Y	Y	N	N	N	Y
24 Milford	Y	?	Y	?	N	?	?
UTAH							
1 McKay	Y	Y	N	N	N	N	Y
2 Marriott	Y	Y	Y	N	N	Y	Y
VERMONT							
AL Jeffords	N	Y	Y	N	N	Y	Y
VIRGINIA							
1 Trible	Y	Y	Y	N	N	Y	Y
2 Whitehurst	Y	Y	Y	N	N	Y	Y
3 Satterfield	Y	Y	N	N	N	Y	Y
4 Daniel	Y	Y	Y	N	N	Y	Y
5 Daniel	Y	Y	Y	N	N	Y	Y
6 Butler	Y	Y	Y	N	N	Y	Y
7 Robinson	Y	Y	Y	N	N	Y	Y
8 Harris	N	Y	N	N	Y	N	Y
9 Wampler	Y	Y	Y	N	N	Y	Y
10 Fisher	Y	Y	N	N	Y	N	Y
WASHINGTON							
1 Pritchard	Y	Y	Y	N	N	Y	Y
2 Meeds	N	Y	N	Y	Y	N	N
3 Bonker	N	Y	N	N	Y	N	Y
4 McCormack	Y	Y	N	N	N	N	Y
5 Foley	Y	Y	N	N	Y	N	Y
6 Dicks	N	Y	Y	N	Y	N	Y
7 Cunningham	Y	Y	Y	N	N	Y	Y
WEST VIRGINIA							
1 Mollohan	Y	Y	N	N	N	N	Y
2 Staggers	Y	Y	X	N	Y	N	?
3 Slack	Y	Y	N	N	N	N	Y
4 Rahall	Y	Y	N	N	N	N	Y
WISCONSIN							
1 Aspin	N	Y	N	N	Y	N	Y
2 Kastenmeier	N	Y	N	Y	Y	N	N
3 Baldus	Y	Y	N	N	Y	N	Y
4 Zablocki	Y	Y	N	N	Y	N	Y
5 Reuss	N	#	N	Y	Y	N	N
6 Steiger	Y	Y	Y	N	N	Y	Y
7 Obey	N	Y	N	N	Y	N	Y
8 Cornell	N	Y	N	Y	Y	N	N
9 Kasten	Y	Y	Y	N	N	Y	Y
WYOMING							
AL Roncalio	Y	#	N	N	Y	N	Y

Democrats ***Republicans***

603. Procedural Motion. Symms, R-Idaho, motion to approve the House *Journal* of Thursday, Aug. 10, 1978. Motion agreed to 325-13: R 111-9; D 214-4 (ND 145-4; SD 69-0), Aug. 11, 1978.

604. HR 11280. Civil Service Reform. Adoption of the rule (H Res 1307) providing for House floor consideration of the bill to revise the Civil Service System. Adopted 357-18: R 116-10; D 241-8 (ND 171-5; SD 70-3), Aug. 11, 1978.

605. HR 11280. Civil Service Reform. Udall, D-Ariz., motion that the House resolve itself into the Committee of the Whole to consider the bill. Motion agreed to 340-13: R 118-4; D 222-9 (ND 159-6; SD 63-3), Aug. 11, 1978.

606. HR 11280. Civil Service Reform. Udall, D-Ariz., motion to table (kill) the Clay, D-Mo., motion to reconsider the vote *(vote 605, above)* by which the motion that the House resolve itself into the Committee of the Whole was agreed to. Motion agreed to 327-8: R 108-4; D 219-4 (ND 153-4; SD 66-0), Aug. 11, 1978.

607. HR 13007. Electronic Funds Transfers. Passage of the bill to establish the rights and liabilities of financial institutions offering electronic fund transfer services and of consumers using such services and to provide for the federal regulation of electronic fund transfer systems. Passed 314-2: R 103-0; D 211-2 (ND 146-2; SD 65-0), Aug. 11, 1978.

608. Procedural Motion. Stangeland, R-Minn., motion to approve the House *Journal* of Friday, Aug. 11, 1978. Motion agreed to 321-14: R 108-9; D 213-5 (ND 142-5; SD 71-0), Aug. 14, 1978.

609. HR 12931. Foreign Aid Appropriations, Fiscal 1979. Obey, D-Wis., amendment, to the Long, D-Md., amendment, to reduce by $24,880,100 the appropriation for the Inter-American Development Bank and the International Development Association (thus superseding the Long amendment *(see vote 610, below)* that would have reduced the appropriation by $548 million). Adopted 241-153: R 67-68; D 174-85 (ND 140-40; SD 34-45), Aug. 14, 1978. A "yea" was a vote supporting the president's position.

610. HR 12931. Foreign Aid Appropriations, Fiscal 1979. Long, D-Md., amendment, as amended by the Obey, D-Wis., amendment *(vote 609, above)*. Adopted 359-27: R 127-6; D 232-21 (ND 155-20; SD 77-1), Aug. 14, 1978.

KEY

Y Voted for (yea).
✓ Paired for.
† Announced for.
# CQ Poll for.
N Voted against (nay).
X Paired against.
\- Announced against.
▮ CQ Poll against.
P Voted "present."
● Voted "present" to avoid possible conflict of interest.
? Did not vote or otherwise make a position known.

	603	604	605	606	607	608	609	610
ALABAMA								
1 Edwards	?	Y	Y	Y	Y	Y	N	Y
2 Dickinson	Y	Y	Y	N	Y	Y	N	Y
3 Nichols	Y	Y	Y	#	Y	Y	N	Y
4 Bevill	Y	Y	Y	?	Y	Y	N	Y
5 Flippo	Y	Y	Y	Y	Y	Y	N	Y
6 Buchanan	Y	Y	Y	Y	Y	Y	Y	Y
7 Flowers	Y	Y	Y	Y	?	?	?	?
ALASKA								
AL Young	?	Y	Y	Y	Y	#	#	#
ARIZONA								
1 Rhodes	Y	Y	Y	Y	Y	Y	Y	Y
2 Udall	#	Y	Y	Y	Y	Y	Y	Y
3 Stump	Y	Y	Y	Y	Y	Y	N	Y
4 Rudd	†	†	†	†	†	Y	N	Y
ARKANSAS								
1 Alexander	Y	Y	Y	Y	Y	Y	Y	Y
2 Tucker	#	Y	#	Y	#	#	Y	Y
3 Hammerschmidt	Y	Y	Y	Y	Y	Y	N	Y
4 Thornton	Y	Y	Y	Y	Y	Y	Y	Y
CALIFORNIA								
1 Johnson	Y	Y	Y	Y	Y	Y	Y	Y
2 Clausen	Y	Y	Y	Y	Y	Y	N	Y
3 Moss	P	Y	?	?	N	?	Y	Y
4 Leggett	?	Y	?	?	Y	?	Y	Y
5 Burton, J.	?	Y	Y	?	?	Y	Y	Y
6 Burton, P.	Y	Y	?	?	Y	?	Y	Y
7 Miller	?	?	?	?	?	?	?	?
8 Dellums	Y	Y	Y	#	Y	Y	Y	N
9 Stark	#	#	#	#	Y	Y	Y	Y
10 Edwards	Y	Y	Y	Y	Y	Y	Y	Y
11 Ryan	Y	Y	Y	Y	Y	Y	Y	Y
12 McCloskey	Y	Y	Y	Y	Y	?	Y	Y
13 Mineta	?	Y	Y	Y	Y	Y	Y	Y
14 McFall	Y	Y	Y	Y	Y	Y	Y	Y
15 Sisk	?	?	?	?	?	?	?	?
16 Panetta	Y	Y	Y	Y	Y	Y	Y	Y
17 Krebs	Y	Y	Y	Y	Y	Y	Y	Y
18 Vacancy								
19 Lagomarsino	Y	Y	Y	Y	Y	Y	N	Y
20 Goldwater	?	Y	Y	Y	Y	?	N	Y
21 Corman	Y	Y	Y	Y	?	Y	Y	Y
22 Moorhead	Y	Y	Y	Y	Y	Y	N	Y
23 Beilenson	▮	Y	Y	Y	Y	Y	Y	N
24 Waxman	#	Y	Y	Y	Y	Y	N	Y
25 Roybal	Y	Y	Y	Y	Y	Y	N	Y
26 Rousselot	Y	Y	Y	Y	Y	N	N	Y
27 Dornan	Y	Y	Y	Y	?	Y	N	Y
28 Burke	#	#	#	#	#	Y	Y	Y
29 Hawkins	Y	Y	N	Y	?	Y	Y	Y
30 Danielson	Y	Y	Y	Y	Y	Y	Y	Y
31 Wilson, C.H.	Y	N	N	?	?	Y	N	Y
32 Anderson	Y	Y	Y	Y	Y	Y	N	Y
33 Clawson	Y	Y	Y	Y	Y	Y	N	Y
34 Hannaford	Y	Y	Y	Y	Y	Y	Y	Y
35 Lloyd	N	Y	N	Y	Y	N	N	Y
36 Brown	Y	Y	Y	?	Y	Y	Y	Y
37 Pettis	Y	Y	Y	Y	Y	Y	Y	Y
38 Patterson	Y	Y	Y	Y	Y	#	▮	#
39 Wiggins	Y	Y	#	#	Y	Y	Y	Y
40 Badham	Y	Y	Y	Y	Y	Y	Y	Y
41 Wilson, B.	N	Y	N	N	Y	N	Y	Y
42 Van Deerlin	Y	Y	Y	Y	Y	Y	Y	Y
43 Burgener	Y	Y	Y	Y	Y	Y	N	Y
COLORADO								
1 Schroeder	Y	Y	Y	Y	Y	Y	Y	Y
2 Wirth	Y	Y	P	Y	Y	Y	Y	Y
3 Evans	#	Y	#	#	Y	Y	Y	Y
4 Johnson	Y	Y	?	?	?	?	Y	Y
5 Armstrong	?	?	?	?	?	?	Y	Y
CONNECTICUT								
1 Cotter	Y	Y	Y	Y	#	#	N	Y
2 Dodd	Y	Y	Y	Y	Y	Y	Y	Y
3 Giaimo	?	?	?	?	?	?	Y	Y
4 McKinney	Y	Y	Y	Y	Y	Y	Y	N
5 Sarasin	▮	#	#	#	#	N	Y	Y
6 Moffett	Y	Y	Y	Y	Y	Y	Y	Y
DELAWARE								
AL Evans	Y	Y	Y	Y	Y	Y	Y	Y
FLORIDA								
1 Sikes	Y	Y	Y	?	Y	?	X	?
2 Fuqua	Y	Y	Y	Y	Y	Y	N	Y
3 Bennett	Y	Y	Y	Y	Y	Y	N	Y
4 Chappell	?	Y	Y	Y	Y	Y	N	Y
5 Kelly	Y	Y	Y	Y	Y	Y	N	Y
6 Young	Y	Y	Y	Y	Y	Y	N	Y
7 Gibbons	?	?	?	?	?	Y	Y	Y
8 Ireland	?	?	?	Y	Y	Y	N	Y
9 Frey	?	?	?	?	?	Y	N	Y
10 Bafalis	Y	Y	Y	Y	Y	Y	N	Y
11 Rogers	Y	Y	Y	Y	Y	Y	N	Y
12 Burke	Y	Y	Y	Y	Y	Y	N	Y
13 Lehman	Y	Y	Y	#	Y	Y	Y	Y
14 Pepper	Y	Y	Y	Y	Y	#	Y	Y
15 Fascell	Y	Y	Y	Y	#	Y	Y	Y
GEORGIA								
1 Ginn	Y	Y	Y	Y	Y	Y	N	Y
2 Mathis	?	Y	Y	Y	Y	Y	N	Y
3 Brinkley	Y	Y	Y	Y	Y	Y	N	Y
4 Levitas	Y	Y	Y	Y	Y	Y	Y	Y
5 Fowler	Y	Y	?	?	Y	Y	Y	Y
6 Flynt	Y	Y	Y	Y	Y	Y	N	Y
7 McDonald	#	X	#	#	#	#	X	#
8 Evans	Y	Y	Y	Y	Y	Y	N	Y
9 Jenkins	Y	Y	Y	Y	Y	Y	N	Y
10 Barnard	Y	Y	Y	Y	Y	Y	N	Y
HAWAII								
1 Heftel	?	Y	Y	Y	Y	Y	Y	Y
2 Akaka	Y	Y	Y	Y	Y	Y	Y	Y
IDAHO								
1 Symms	Y	?	?	?	?	?	?	?
2 Hansen, G.	Y	N	Y	Y	Y	Y	N	Y
ILLINOIS								
1 Metcalfe	?	?	?	?	?	?	?	?
2 Murphy	Y	Y	Y	Y	#	Y	Y	Y
3 Russo	Y	Y	Y	Y	#	#	#	?
4 Derwinski	Y	Y	Y	Y	Y	Y	Y	Y
5 Fary	Y	Y	Y	Y	Y	Y	Y	Y
6 Hyde	Y	Y	Y	Y	Y	Y	Y	Y
7 Collins	Y	Y	Y	?	Y	?	Y	Y
8 Rostenkowski	Y	Y	Y	Y	?	Y	Y	Y
9 Yates	Y	Y	Y	Y	Y	Y	Y	Y
10 Mikva	Y	Y	Y	Y	Y	Y	Y	Y
11 Annunzio	Y	Y	Y	Y	Y	Y	Y	Y
12 Crane	Y	N	Y	Y	Y	Y	N	Y
13 McClory	Y	Y	Y	Y	Y	Y	Y	Y
14 Erlenborn	Y	Y	Y	#	Y	Y	Y	Y
15 Corcoran	Y	Y	Y	Y	Y	Y	N	Y
16 Anderson	Y	Y	Y	#	Y	Y	Y	Y
17 O'Brien	Y	Y	Y	Y	Y	Y	Y	Y
18 Michel	Y	Y	Y	Y	#	Y	Y	Y
19 Railsback	Y	Y	Y	Y	Y	Y	Y	Y
20 Findley	Y	Y	Y	Y	Y	Y	Y	Y
21 Madigan	Y	Y	Y	Y	Y	Y	Y	?
22 Shipley	?	?	?	?	?	?	?	?
23 Price	Y	Y	Y	Y	Y	Y	Y	Y
24 Simon	Y	Y	Y	Y	Y	Y	Y	N
INDIANA								
1 Benjamin	Y	Y	Y	Y	Y	Y	Y	Y
2 Fithian	Y	Y	Y	Y	Y	Y	Y	Y
3 Brademas	Y	Y	Y	Y	Y	Y	Y	Y
4 Quayle	N	Y	N	?	?	N	Y	Y
5 Hillis	Y	Y	Y	Y	?	?	Y	Y
6 Evans	Y	Y	Y	Y	?	Y	Y	Y
7 Myers, J.	Y	Y	Y	Y	Y	Y	N	Y
8 Cornwell	Y	Y	?	?	?	Y	N	Y
9 Hamilton	Y	Y	Y	Y	Y	Y	Y	Y
10 Sharp	Y	Y	Y	Y	Y	Y	Y	Y
11 Jacobs	▮	Y	Y	Y	Y	N	Y	Y
IOWA								
1 Leach	Y	Y	Y	Y	Y	Y	Y	Y
2 Blouin	?	Y	Y	Y	Y	?	?	?
3 Grassley	Y	Y	Y	Y	Y	Y	N	Y
4 Smith	Y	Y	Y	Y	Y	Y	Y	Y
5 Harkin	Y	Y	Y	Y	Y	Y	Y	Y
6 Bedell	Y	Y	Y	Y	Y	Y	Y	N

Democrats ***Republicans***

	603	604	605	606	607	608	609	610
KANSAS								
1 ***Sebelius***	Y	Y	Y	Y	?	Y	N	Y
2 Keys	#	Y	Y	Y	Y	Y	Y	Y
3 ***Winn***	Y	Y	Y	Y	Y	Y	Y	Y
4 Glickman	Y	Y	Y	Y	Y	Y	Y	Y
5 ***Skubitz***	P	?	Y	?	Y	?	Y	Y
KENTUCKY								
1 Hubbard	#	#	#	#	#	Y	Y	Y
2 Natcher	Y	Y	Y	Y	Y	Y	N	Y
3 Mazzoli	Y	Y	Y	Y	Y	Y	Y	Y
4 ***Snyder***	Y	Y	Y	Y	Y	Y	N	Y
5 ***Carter***	Y	Y	Y	Y	Y	Y	Y	Y
6 Breckinridge	?	?	?	?	?	Y	Y	Y
7 Perkins	Y	Y	Y	Y	Y	Y	N	Y
LOUISIANA								
1 ***Livingston***	Y	N	Y	Y	Y	Y	N	Y
2 Boggs	Y	#	#	#	Y	Y	Y	Y
3 ***Treen***	Y	Y	Y	Y	Y	Y	N	Y
4 Waggonner	Y	Y	Y	Y	#	Y	N	Y
5 Huckaby	?	?	?	?	?	Y	N	Y
6 ***Moore***	Y	Y	Y	Y	Y	Y	N	Y
7 Breaux	?	?	?	?	?	?	X	?
8 Long	?	?	?	?	?	Y	Y	Y
MAINE								
1 ***Emery***	Y	Y	Y	Y	Y	Y	Y	Y
2 ***Cohen***	#	#	#	#	#	#	?	?
MARYLAND								
1 ***Bauman***	Y	N	Y	Y	Y	Y	N	Y
2 Long	Y	Y	Y	Y	Y	Y	N	Y
3 Mikulski	Y	N	N	N	Y	Y	N	Y
4 ***Holt***	Y	N	Y	Y	Y	Y	N	Y
5 Spellman	Y	N	N	Y	Y	Y	N	Y
6 Byron	Y	Y	Y	Y	Y	Y	N	Y
7 Mitchell	▮	N	N	▮	Y	N	Y	Y
8 ***Steers***	Y	N	N	N	Y	Y	Y	N
MASSACHUSETTS								
1 ***Conte***	Y	Y	Y	Y	Y	Y	Y	N
2 Boland	Y	Y	Y	Y	#	#	Y	Y
3 Early	Y	Y	Y	Y	Y	?	N	N
4 Drinan	Y	Y	Y	Y	Y	Y	Y	Y
5 Tsongas	?	?	?	?	?	?	✓	?
6 Harrington	#	#	#	#	#	#	▮	▮
7 Markey	Y	Y	Y	Y	Y	Y	Y	Y
8 O'Neill								
9 Moakley	Y	Y	Y	Y	Y	Y	Y	Y
10 ***Heckler***	Y	Y	Y	Y	Y	Y	Y	Y
11 Burke	?	Y	Y	Y	Y	Y	N	Y
12 Studds	Y	Y	Y	Y	Y	Y	Y	N
MICHIGAN								
1 Conyers	#	Y	Y	N	Y	#	Y	N
2 ***Pursell***	?	N	Y	N	Y	?	Y	Y
3 ***Brown***	N	Y	Y	?	Y	N	Y	Y
4 ***Stockman***	N	Y	Y	#	Y	Y	Y	Y
5 ***Sawyer***	#	#	#	#	#	Y	N	Y
6 Carr	Y	Y	?	Y	Y	Y	Y	Y
7 Kildee	Y	Y	Y	Y	Y	Y	Y	Y
8 Traxler	Y	Y	Y	Y	#	#	Y	Y
9 ***Vander Jagt***	Y	Y	Y	Y	Y	?	N	Y
10 ***Cederberg***	Y	Y	Y	Y	Y	Y	Y	Y
11 ***Ruppe***	?	?	?	?	?	?	?	?
12 Bonior	Y	Y	Y	Y	Y	#	Y	N
13 Diggs	#	X	#	#	#	#	Y	#
14 Nedzi	Y	Y	Y	Y	Y	Y	Y	Y
15 Ford	?	Y	Y	Y	Y	Y	Y	Y
16 Dingell	Y	Y	Y	Y	Y	?	✓	?
17 Brodhead	N	Y	Y	?	Y	Y	Y	Y
18 Blanchard	Y	Y	Y	Y	Y	Y	Y	Y
19 ***Broomfield***	Y	Y	Y	Y	#	Y	Y	Y
MINNESOTA								
1 ***Quie***	?	?	?	?	?	?	?	?
2 ***Hagedorn***	Y	Y	Y	Y	?	Y	N	Y
3 ***Frenzel***	Y	Y	Y	Y	?	?	Y	Y
4 Vento	Y	Y	Y	?	Y	Y	Y	Y
5 Fraser	?	?	?	?	?	?	?	?
6 Nolan	?	?	?	?	?	Y	Y	Y
7 ***Stangeland***	Y	Y	Y	Y	#	Y	N	Y
8 Oberstar	Y	Y	Y	Y	Y	Y	N	N
MISSISSIPPI								
1 Whitten	Y	Y	Y	Y	Y	Y	N	Y
2 Bowen	Y	?	?	Y	Y	Y	N	Y
3 Montgomery	Y	Y	#	Y	Y	Y	N	Y
4 ***Cochran***	?	?	?	?	?	?	?	?
5 ***Lott***	Y	Y	#	Y	#	Y	N	Y
MISSOURI								
1 Clay	Y	N	Y	N	Y	?	?	?
2 Young	Y	Y	Y	Y	#	Y	N	Y
3 Gephardt	Y	Y	Y	Y	N	#	Y	Y

	603	604	605	606	607	608	609	610
4 Skelton	Y	Y	Y	Y	?	?	Y	Y
5 Bolling	Y	Y	Y	Y	Y	Y	Y	Y
6 ***Coleman***	Y	Y	Y	Y	Y	#	N	Y
7 ***Taylor***	Y	Y	Y	?	Y	?	N	Y
8 Ichord	Y	Y	Y	Y	?	?	N	Y
9 Volkmer	Y	Y	Y	Y	Y	Y	Y	Y
10 Burlison	Y	Y	Y	Y	Y	?	N	Y
MONTANA								
1 Baucus	Y	Y	Y	Y	Y	?	Y	Y
2 ***Marlenee***	Y	Y	Y	Y	Y	Y	N	Y
NEBRASKA								
1 ***Thone***	?	?	?	?	?	?	Y	Y
2 Cavanaugh	?	Y	Y	Y	Y	Y	Y	Y
3 ***Smith***	Y	Y	Y	Y	?	Y	Y	Y
NEVADA								
AL Santini	#	Y	#	Y	Y	Y	N	Y
NEW HAMPSHIRE								
1 D'Amours	N	Y	Y	Y	Y	Y	Y	Y
2 ***Cleveland***	Y	Y	Y	Y	?	Y	N	Y
NEW JERSEY								
1 Florio	Y	Y	Y	Y	Y	Y	N	Y
2 Hughes	Y	Y	Y	Y	Y	Y	N	Y
3 Howard	Y	Y	Y	Y	Y	Y	Y	Y
4 Thompson	Y	Y	Y	Y	Y	Y	Y	Y
5 ***Fenwick***	Y	Y	Y	Y	Y	Y	Y	Y
6 ***Forsythe***	N	Y	Y	#	Y	▮	Y	N
7 Maguire	Y	Y	#	#	Y	Y	Y	Y
8 Roe	Y	Y	Y	Y	Y	#	Y	Y
9 ***Hollenbeck***	#	Y	Y	Y	Y	#	N	Y
10 Rodino	#	✓	#	#	#	#	#	#
11 Minish	Y	Y	Y	Y	Y	Y	Y	Y
12 ***Rinaldo***	Y	Y	Y	Y	Y	Y	Y	Y
13 Meyner	Y	Y	#	#	#	#	Y	Y
14 LeFante	#	#	#	#	#	#	✓	#
15 Patten	Y	Y	Y	Y	Y	Y	Y	Y
NEW MEXICO								
1 ***Lujan***	Y	Y	?	Y	Y	?	?	?
2 Runnels	Y	Y	Y	Y	?	Y	N	Y
NEW YORK								
1 Pike	N	Y	Y	Y	Y	Y	N	Y
2 Downey	Y	Y	Y	#	#	Y	Y	Y
3 Ambro	?	?	?	Y	Y	?	Y	Y
4 ***Lent***	Y	Y	Y	Y	Y	Y	Y	Y
5 ***Wydler***	?	?	?	?	?	Y	N	Y
6 Wolff	Y	Y	Y	Y	Y	Y	N	Y
7 Addabbo	Y	Y	Y	Y	Y	Y	Y	Y
8 Rosenthal	#	Y	Y	Y	Y	Y	Y	Y
9 Delaney	Y	Y	Y	Y	Y	Y	Y	Y
10 Biaggi	Y	Y	Y	Y	Y	?	Y	Y
11 Scheuer	Y	Y	Y	Y	Y	Y	Y	Y
12 Chisholm	#	Y	Y	Y	Y	#	Y	Y
13 Solarz	Y	Y	Y	Y	Y	Y	Y	N
14 Richmond	?	✓	?	?	?	?	?	Y
15 Zeferetti	Y	Y	Y	Y	Y	Y	N	Y
16 Holtzman	Y	Y	Y	Y	Y	Y	Y	N
17 Murphy	?	?	?	?	?	?	?	?
18 ***Green***	Y	Y	Y	Y	Y	#	Y	N
19 Rangel	Y	Y	Y	Y	Y	Y	Y	N
20 Weiss	Y	Y	Y	Y	Y	Y	Y	N
21 Garcia	Y	Y	Y	Y	Y	Y	Y	N
22 Bingham	Y	Y	Y	Y	Y	Y	Y	N
23 ***Caputo***	?	?	?	?	?	?	?	?
24 Ottinger	Y	Y	Y	Y	#	Y	Y	Y
25 ***Fish***	Y	Y	Y	Y	?	Y	Y	?
26 ***Gilman***	Y	N	Y	Y	Y	Y	Y	Y
27 McHugh	Y	Y	Y	Y	Y	Y	Y	N
28 Stratton	Y	Y	Y	Y	Y	Y	N	Y
29 Pattison	#	#	#	#	#	Y	Y	Y
30 ***McEwen***	P	Y	Y	?	Y	P	N	Y
31 ***Mitchell***	Y	Y	Y	Y	Y	Y	Y	Y
32 Hanley	Y	Y	Y	Y	Y	#	✓	#
33 ***Walsh***	?	?	?	?	?	Y	Y	Y
34 ***Horton***	Y	Y	#	#	#	Y	Y	Y
35 ***Conable***	Y	Y	Y	Y	Y	Y	Y	Y
36 LaFalce	Y	Y	Y	Y	Y	Y	Y	Y
37 Nowak	Y	Y	Y	Y	Y	#	Y	Y
38 ***Kemp***	Y	Y	Y	Y	?	Y	Y	Y
39 Lundine	Y	Y	Y	Y	Y	#	Y	Y
NORTH CAROLINA								
1 Jones	Y	Y	Y	Y	Y	Y	N	Y
2 Fountain	Y	Y	Y	#	Y	Y	N	Y
3 Whitley	Y	Y	Y	Y	Y	Y	N	Y
4 Andrews	Y	Y	Y	Y	Y	?	Y	?
5 Neal	Y	Y	Y	Y	Y	Y	Y	Y
6 Preyer	Y	Y	Y	Y	Y	Y	Y	Y
7 Rose	Y	Y	Y	Y	Y	Y	Y	Y
8 Hefner	Y	Y	Y	Y	Y	Y	N	Y

	603	604	605	606	607	608	609	610
9 ***Martin***	Y	Y	Y	Y	Y	Y	N	Y
10 ***Broyhill***	Y	Y	Y	Y	Y	Y	N	Y
11 Gudger	Y	Y	Y	Y	#	Y	N	Y
NORTH DAKOTA								
AL ***Andrews***	Y	Y	Y	Y	Y	Y	N	Y
OHIO								
1 ***Gradison***	Y	Y	Y	Y	Y	Y	Y	Y
2 Luken	?	?	?	?	?	?	Y	Y
3 ***Whalen***	Y	Y	Y	Y	Y	Y	Y	Y
4 ***Guyer***	Y	Y	Y	Y	Y	Y	Y	Y
5 ***Latta***	?	?	?	?	?	N	N	Y
6 ***Harsha***	?	?	?	?	?	Y	N	Y
7 ***Brown***	Y	Y	Y	Y	Y	Y	N	Y
8 ***Kindness***	Y	Y	Y	?	Y	Y	N	Y
9 Ashley	?	Y	Y	Y	Y	Y	Y	?
10 ***Miller***	Y	Y	Y	Y	Y	Y	N	Y
11 ***Stanton***	Y	Y	Y	Y	#	Y	Y	Y
12 ***Devine***	#	Y	Y	Y	Y	Y	N	Y
13 Pease	Y	Y	Y	Y	#	Y	Y	Y
14 Seiberling	#	Y	Y	Y	Y	Y	Y	Y
15 ***Wylie***	Y	Y	Y	Y	Y	Y	Y	Y
16 ***Regula***	Y	Y	Y	Y	Y	Y	Y	Y
17 ***Ashbrook***	Y	N	Y	Y	Y	Y	N	Y
18 Applegate	Y	Y	Y	Y	?	N	N	Y
19 Carney	Y	Y	Y	Y	Y	Y	N	Y
20 Oakar	?	Y	Y	Y	?	Y	Y	?
21 Stokes	Y	Y	Y	Y	Y	?	Y	N
22 Vanik	Y	Y	Y	Y	?	Y	Y	Y
23 Mottl	Y	Y	Y	Y	▮	Y	Y	Y
OKLAHOMA								
1 Jones	Y	Y	Y	Y	Y	Y	N	Y
2 Risenhoover	?	Y	Y	Y	?	?	?	?
3 Watkins	Y	Y	Y	Y	?	Y	N	Y
4 Steed	Y	Y	Y	Y	Y	Y	Y	Y
5 ***Edwards***	Y	Y	Y	Y	Y	Y	N	Y
6 English	Y	Y	?	Y	Y	?	N	Y
OREGON								
1 AuCoin	Y	Y	Y	Y	Y	N	Y	Y
2 Ullman	Y	Y	Y	Y	Y	Y	Y	Y
3 Duncan	Y	Y	Y	Y	Y	#	Y	Y
4 Weaver	Y	Y	Y	Y	Y	Y	N	Y
PENNSYLVANIA								
1 Myers, M.	Y	Y	Y	Y	Y	Y	N	Y
2 Nix	?	Y	Y	Y	?	Y	N	Y
3 Lederer	Y	Y	Y	N	Y	Y	N	Y
4 Eilberg	Y	Y	Y	Y	Y	Y	Y	Y
5 ***Schulze***	Y	Y	Y	Y	Y	Y	N	Y
6 Yatron	Y	Y	Y	Y	Y	Y	Y	Y
7 Edgar	#	Y	Y	#	Y	Y	Y	Y
8 Kostmayer	Y	Y	Y	Y	Y	Y	Y	N
9 ***Shuster***	Y	Y	Y	Y	?	?	?	?
10 ***McDade***	Y	Y	Y	Y	Y	Y	Y	Y
11 Flood	Y	Y	Y	Y	Y	Y	Y	Y
12 Murtha	Y	Y	Y	Y	Y	Y	N	Y
13 ***Coughlin***	Y	Y	Y	Y	Y	▮	Y	Y
14 Moorhead	#	Y	Y	Y	#	Y	Y	Y
15 Rooney	Y	Y	Y	Y	Y	Y	Y	Y
16 ***Walker***	N	Y	Y	Y	Y	N	N	Y
17 Ertel	Y	Y	Y	Y	Y	Y	Y	Y
18 Walgren	Y	Y	Y	Y	Y	Y	Y	Y
19 ***Goodling, W.***	N	Y	Y	?	Y	?	?	?
20 Gaydos	Y	Y	Y	?	Y	Y	N	Y
21 Dent	#	#	#	#	#	#	N	Y
22 Murphy	Y	Y	Y	Y	Y	Y	N	Y
23 Ammerman	Y	Y	Y	Y	?	Y	N	Y
24 ***Marks***	Y	Y	Y	Y	Y	Y	Y	Y
25 ***Myers, G.***	Y	Y	Y	Y	Y	Y	Y	N
RHODE ISLAND								
1 St Germain	Y	Y	Y	Y	?	Y	Y	?
2 Beard	Y	Y	Y	Y	Y	Y	Y	Y
SOUTH CAROLINA								
1 Davis	?	N	?	Y	Y	Y	N	Y
2 ***Spence***	Y	Y	Y	Y	Y	Y	N	Y
3 Derrick	Y	Y	Y	Y	Y	Y	N	Y
4 Mann	Y	Y	?	Y	Y	Y	Y	Y
5 Holland	Y	Y	Y	Y	Y	?	N	Y
6 Jenrette	#	#	#	#	#	Y	N	Y
SOUTH DAKOTA								
1 ***Pressler***	Y	?	?	?	?	Y	Y	Y
2 ***Abdnor***	Y	Y	Y	Y	#	Y	N	Y
TENNESSEE								
1 ***Quillen***	Y	Y	Y	Y	Y	Y	Y	Y
2 ***Duncan***	#	Y	Y	Y	Y	Y	N	Y
3 Lloyd	#	#	#	#	#	#	✓	#
4 Gore	Y	Y	Y	Y	Y	Y	Y	Y
5 Vacancy								
6 ***Beard***	Y	Y	Y	#	Y	Y	N	Y

	603	604	605	606	607	608	609	610
7 Jones	Y	Y	Y	Y	Y	#	Y	Y
8 Ford	Y	Y	Y	Y	?	Y	Y	Y
TEXAS								
1 Hall	Y	Y	Y	Y	Y	Y	N	Y
2 Wilson, C.	Y	Y	Y	Y	Y	#	Y	Y
3 ***Collins***	N	Y	N	Y	Y	N	N	Y
4 Roberts	Y	N	N	Y	Y	Y	N	N
5 Mattox	Y	Y	Y	Y	P	Y	N	Y
6 Teague	?	?	?	?	?	?	X	?
7 ***Archer***	Y	Y	Y	Y	Y	Y	N	Y
8 Eckhardt	Y	Y	Y	Y	Y	Y	Y	Y
9 Brooks	?	?	?	?	?	Y	Y	Y
10 Pickle	Y	Y	Y	Y	Y	Y	Y	Y
11 Poage	P	?	?	?	Y	Y	N	Y
12 Wright	Y	Y	Y	?	Y	Y	Y	Y
13 Hightower	Y	Y	Y	Y	Y	Y	N	Y
14 Young	?	Y	N	?	?	?	?	?
15 de la Garza	Y	Y	Y	Y	Y	Y	Y	Y
16 White	Y	Y	Y	Y	Y	Y	N	Y
17 Burleson	Y	Y	Y	Y	Y	Y	N	Y
18 Jordan	Y	Y	Y	Y	Y	Y	Y	Y
19 Mahon	Y	Y	Y	Y	Y	Y	N	Y
20 Gonzalez	Y	Y	Y	Y	Y	#	Y	Y
21 Krueger	Y	Y	Y	Y	?	#	X	#
22 Gammage	Y	Y	Y	Y	Y	Y	N	Y
23 Kazen	Y	Y	Y	Y	Y	Y	Y	Y
24 Milford	?	?	?	?	?	?	?	?
UTAH								
1 McKay	Y	Y	Y	#	Y	Y	N	Y
2 ***Marriott***	#	#	#	#	#	Y	Y	Y
VERMONT								
AL ***Jeffords***	Y	Y	Y	Y	#	Y	N	Y
VIRGINIA								
1 ***Trible***	Y	Y	Y	Y	Y	Y	N	Y
2 ***Whitehurst***	Y	Y	Y	Y	#	Y	N	Y
3 Satterfield	Y	Y	Y	?	Y	Y	N	Y
4 ***Daniel***	Y	Y	Y	Y	Y	Y	N	Y
5 Daniel	Y	Y	?	Y	Y	Y	N	Y
6 ***Butler***	Y	Y	Y	Y	?	Y	N	Y
7 ***Robinson***	Y	Y	Y	Y	Y	Y	N	Y
8 Harris	Y	N	N	Y	Y	Y	Y	Y
9 ***Wampler***	?	?	?	?	?	Y	N	Y
10 Fisher	Y	Y	Y	Y	Y	Y	Y	Y
WASHINGTON								
1 ***Pritchard***	Y	Y	Y	Y	Y	Y	Y	Y
2 Meeds	Y	Y	Y	Y	Y	Y	Y	N
3 Bonker	#	Y	Y	#	Y	Y	Y	Y
4 McCormack	Y	Y	Y	Y	Y	Y	Y	?
5 Foley	Y	Y	Y	Y	Y	Y	Y	Y
6 Dicks	Y	Y	Y	Y	?	Y	Y	Y
7 ***Cunningham***	Y	Y	Y	Y	#	#	N	Y
WEST VIRGINIA								
1 Mollohan	Y	Y	Y	Y	Y	Y	N	Y
2 Staggers	Y	Y	Y	Y	Y	Y	Y	Y
3 Slack	Y	Y	Y	Y	Y	Y	N	Y
4 Rahall	Y	Y	Y	Y	Y	Y	Y	Y
WISCONSIN								
1 Aspin	Y	Y	Y	Y	Y	?	Y	Y
2 Kastenmeier	Y	Y	Y	Y	Y	Y	Y	N
3 Baldus	Y	Y	Y	Y	Y	#	Y	Y
4 Zablocki	Y	Y	Y	Y	Y	Y	Y	Y
5 Reuss	Y	Y	#	Y	Y	Y	Y	Y
6 ***Steiger***	N	N	Y	Y	Y	N	Y	Y
7 Obey	Y	Y	Y	Y	Y	Y	Y	Y
8 Cornell	Y	Y	Y	Y	Y	#	Y	Y
9 ***Kasten***	Y	Y	Y	Y	Y	?	?	?
WYOMING								
AL Roncalio	#	#	#	#	#	#	#	#

Democrats ***Republicans***

611. HR 12931. Foreign Aid Appropriations, Fiscal 1979. Young, R-Fla., amendment to prohibit use of U.S. funds by the International Development Association for aid or reparation to Vietnam. Adopted 234-152: R 111-21; D 123-131 (ND 66-112; SD 57-19), Aug. 14, 1978. A "nay" was a vote supporting the president's position.

612. HR 12931. Foreign Aid Appropriations, Fiscal 1979. Mathis, D-Ga., amendment to prohibit funds appropriated for international financial institutions to be used to establish or expand production for export of steel, grains, sugar, palm oil, citrus crops, tobacco or tires. Rejected 143-239: R 64-68; D 79-171 (ND 34-138; SD 45-33), Aug. 14, 1978. A "nay" was a vote supporting the president's position.

613. HR 12931. Foreign Aid Appropriations, Fiscal 1979. Hansen, R-Idaho, amendment to prohibit use of funds appropriated in the bill for aid to Panama. Rejected 172-202: R 87-39; D 85-163 (ND 36-135; SD 49-28), Aug. 14, 1978. A "nay" was a vote supporting the president's position.

614. HR 12931. Foreign Aid Appropriations, Fiscal 1979. Miller, R-Ohio, amendment, to the Young, R-Fla., amendment *(see vote 616, below)*, to reduce all appropriations in the bill by 8 percent except funds for Israel and Egypt. Rejected 184-199: R 88-43; D 96-156 (ND 42-133; SD 54-23), Aug. 14, 1978. A "nay" was a vote supporting the president's position.

615. HR 12931. Foreign Aid Appropriations, Fiscal 1979. Harkin, D-Iowa, substitute amendment, to the Young, R-Fla., amendment *(see vote 616, below)*, to provide a 2 percent reduction in items in the bill not previously reduced by 2 percent by floor amendments or otherwise exempted from cuts, including funds for Israel and Egypt (Harkin's amendment replaced Young's which provided a 2 percent cut in *all* items, except funds for Israel and Egypt, regardless of whether they had been previously cut by floor amendments). Adopted 289-95: R 88-43; D 201-52 (ND 148-27; SD 53-25), Aug. 14, 1978. A "yea" was a vote supporting the president's position.

616. HR 12931, Foreign Aid Appropriations, Fiscal 1979. Young, R-Fla., amendment as amended *(see vote 615, above)*. Adopted 341-44: R 124-5; D 217-39 (ND 141-37; SD 76-2), Aug. 14, 1978.

617. HR 12931. Foreign Aid Appropriations, Fiscal 1979. Passage of the bill to appropriate $7,174,634,653 for foreign aid programs in fiscal 1979. Passed 223-167: R 57-74; D 166-93 (ND 140-40; SD 26-53), Aug. 14, 1978. The president had requested $8,444,320,919.

KEY

- Y Voted for (yea).
- ✓ Paired for.
- † Announced for.
- # CQ Poll for.
- N Voted against (nay).
- X Paired against.
- \- Announced against.
- ▮ CQ Poll against.
- P Voted "present."
- ● Voted "present" to avoid possible conflict of interest.
- ? Did not vote or otherwise make a position known.

	611	612	613	614	615	616	617
ALABAMA							
1 Edwards	?	N	Y	Y	Y	Y	N
2 Dickinson	Y	Y	Y	Y	Y	Y	N
3 Nichols	Y	Y	Y	Y	N	Y	N
4 Bevill	Y	Y	Y	Y	Y	Y	N
5 Flippo	Y	Y	Y	Y	Y	Y	N
6 Buchanan	Y	Y	Y	N	Y	Y	Y
7 Flowers	?	?	?	?	?	?	?
ALASKA							
AL Young	#	▮	#	#	#	#	▮
ARIZONA							
1 Rhodes	Y	N	?	N	Y	Y	Y
2 Udall	▮	N	▮	▮	Y	Y	Y
3 Stump	Y	Y	Y	Y	Y	Y	N
4 Rudd	Y	Y	Y	Y	Y	Y	N
ARKANSAS							
1 Alexander	Y	N	N	N	Y	N	Y
2 Tucker	N	N	N	N	Y	Y	Y
3 Hammerschmidt	Y	Y	Y	Y	N	Y	N
4 Thornton	N	N	N	Y	N	Y	N
CALIFORNIA							
1 Johnson	N	N	Y	N	Y	Y	Y
2 Clausen	Y	N	Y	Y	Y	Y	N
3 Moss	N	?	?	?	?	?	?
4 Leggett	N	?	Y	N	Y	Y	Y
5 Burton, J.	N	N	N	N	Y	Y	Y
6 Burton, P.	N	N	N	N	N	N	Y
7 Miller	X	X	?	X	?	?	✓
8 Dellums	N	N	N	N	N	N	N
9 Stark	N	N	N	N	Y	N	N
10 Edwards	N	N	N	N	Y	Y	Y
11 Ryan	Y	N	N	N	Y	Y	Y
12 McCloskey	N	N	N	N	Y	Y	Y
13 Mineta	N	N	N	N	Y	Y	Y
14 McFall	N	N	N	N	N	Y	Y
15 Sisk	?	?	?	?	?	?	?
16 Panetta	Y	N	N	N	Y	Y	N
17 Krebs	Y	N	N	N	Y	Y	Y
18 Vacancy							
19 Lagomarsino	Y	N	Y	Y	N	Y	N
20 Goldwater	Y	N	Y	Y	N	Y	N
21 Corman	N	N	N	N	Y	Y	Y
22 Moorhead	Y	Y	Y	Y	Y	Y	N
23 Beilenson	N	N	N	N	Y	N	Y
24 Waxman	N	N	N	N	Y	Y	Y
25 Roybal	N	N	N	N	Y	Y	N
26 Rousselot	Y	Y	Y	Y	Y	Y	N
27 Dornan	Y	N	Y	N	Y	Y	Y
28 Burke	N	N	N	N	Y	Y	Y
29 Hawkins	N	N	X	X	?	?	✓
30 Danielson	N	N	N	N	Y	Y	Y
31 Wilson, C.H.	Y	▮	#	Y	N	N	Y
32 Anderson	Y	N	Y	Y	Y	Y	N
33 Clawson	Y	Y	Y	?	?	?	?
34 Hannaford	Y	N	N	Y	Y	Y	Y
35 Lloyd	N	N	Y	N	N	N	Y
36 Brown	N	N	N	N	Y	Y	Y
37 Pettis	?	N	N	N	Y	Y	Y
38 Patterson	#	▮	▮	▮	#	#	#
39 Wiggins	Y	▮	N	N	Y	Y	Y
40 Badham	Y	Y	Y	Y	Y	Y	N
41 Wilson, B.	Y	N	Y	Y	Y	Y	Y
42 Van Deerlin	N	N	N	N	Y	Y	Y
43 Burgener	Y	Y	Y	Y	Y	Y	N
COLORADO							
1 Schroeder	N	N	N	N	Y	Y	N
2 Wirth	N	N	N	N	Y	Y	Y
3 Evans	N	N	?	▮	▮	▮	#
4 Johnson	Y	Y	N	Y	Y	Y	N
5 Armstrong	Y	Y	Y	Y	Y	Y	N
CONNECTICUT							
1 Cotter	Y	Y	N	Y	Y	Y	Y
2 Dodd	N	N	N	N	Y	Y	Y
3 Giaimo	N	N	N	N	Y	Y	Y
4 McKinney	N	N	N	N	Y	Y	Y
5 Sarasin	Y	N	?	▮	#	#	Y
6 Moffett	N	N	N	N	Y	Y	N
DELAWARE							
AL Evans	Y	N	Y	N	Y	Y	Y
FLORIDA							
1 Sikes	✓	✓	✓	✓	N	Y	N
2 Fuqua	Y	Y	Y	Y	N	Y	Y
3 Bennett	Y	Y	Y	Y	N	Y	N
4 Chappell	Y	Y	Y	Y	N	Y	N
5 Kelly	Y	Y	Y	Y	N	Y	N
6 Young	Y	Y	Y	Y	N	Y	N
7 Gibbons	Y	N	N	N	N	Y	N
8 Ireland	Y	Y	Y	Y	N	Y	Y
9 Frey	Y	Y	Y	Y	Y	Y	N
10 Bafalis	Y	Y	Y	Y	Y	Y	N
11 Rogers	Y	N	N	N	Y	Y	Y
12 Burke	Y	Y	Y	Y	Y	Y	Y
13 Lehman	N	N	N	N	Y	Y	Y
14 Pepper	Y	N	N	N	Y	Y	Y
15 Fascell	N	N	N	N	Y	Y	Y
GEORGIA							
1 Ginn	Y	Y	Y	Y	N	Y	N
2 Mathis	Y	Y	Y	Y	N	Y	N
3 Brinkley	Y	Y	Y	Y	N	Y	N
4 Levitas	Y	N	?	?	?	?	Y
5 Fowler	Y	Y	Y	Y	Y	Y	Y
6 Flynt	Y	Y	Y	Y	N	Y	N
7 McDonald	✓	✓	✓	✓	#	#	X
8 Evans	Y	Y	Y	N	Y	Y	Y
9 Jenkins	Y	Y	Y	Y	N	Y	N
10 Barnard	Y	Y	Y	Y	N	Y	N
HAWAII							
1 Heftel	Y	Y	N	N	Y	Y	Y
2 Akaka	Y	N	N	N	Y	Y	Y
IDAHO							
1 Symms	?	?	?	?	?	?	?
2 Hansen, G.	Y	Y	Y	Y	N	Y	N
ILLINOIS							
1 Metcalfe	X	?	?	?	?	?	?
2 Murphy	Y	N	N	Y	Y	Y	Y
3 Russo	#	▮	▮	#	#	#	X
4 Derwinski	Y	N	N	N	Y	Y	Y
5 Fary	N	N	N	N	Y	Y	Y
6 Hyde	N	N	N	N	Y	Y	Y
7 Collins	Y	N	N	N	Y	N	Y
8 Rostenkowski	N	N	N	N	N	N	Y
9 Yates	N	N	N	N	Y	Y	Y
10 Mikva	N	N	N	N	Y	Y	Y
11 Annunzio	Y	N	N	N	Y	Y	Y
12 Crane	Y	Y	Y	Y	N	Y	N
13 McClory	Y	N	N	N	Y	Y	Y
14 Erlenborn	N	N	N	N	Y	Y	Y
15 Corcoran	Y	Y	Y	Y	N	Y	N
16 Anderson	N	N	N	N	Y	#	Y
17 O'Brien	Y	N	Y	Y	Y	Y	Y
18 Michel	Y	N	N	N	N	Y	Y
19 Railsback	Y	N	N	N	Y	Y	Y
20 Findley	?	?	?	?	?	?	?
21 Madigan	Y	N	?	?	?	?	?
22 Shipley	X	X	?	X	?	?	?
23 Price	N	N	N	N	Y	Y	Y
24 Simon	N	N	N	N	Y	N	Y
INDIANA							
1 Benjamin	Y	Y	N	Y	Y	Y	Y
2 Fithian	N	Y	Y	Y	Y	Y	N
3 Brademas	N	N	N	N	Y	Y	Y
4 Quayle	Y	N	N	Y	Y	Y	N
5 Hillis	Y	Y	Y	Y	Y	Y	N
6 Evans	Y	Y	Y	Y	Y	Y	N
7 Myers, J.	Y	Y	Y	Y	N	Y	N
8 Cornwell	Y	N	Y	Y	Y	Y	N
9 Hamilton	N	N	N	N	Y	Y	Y
10 Sharp	N	N	N	N	Y	Y	Y
11 Jacobs	N	N	N	Y	Y	Y	N
IOWA							
1 Leach	N	N	N	Y	Y	Y	Y
2 Blouin	N	N	N	N	Y	Y	Y
3 Grassley	Y	Y	Y	Y	N	Y	N
4 Smith	Y	N	N	Y	Y	Y	Y
5 Harkin	N	N	N	N	Y	Y	N
6 Bedell	N	N	N	N	Y	N	Y

Democrats ***Republicans***

	611	612	613	614	615	616	617
KANSAS							
1 Sebelius	Y	N	?	Y	N	Y	Y
2 Keys	N	N	N	N	Y	Y	Y
3 Winn	Y	N	Y	N	Y	Y	Y
4 Glickman	Y	N	N	N	Y	Y	Y
5 Skubitz	Y	N	N	N	N	Y	Y
KENTUCKY							
1 Hubbard	Y	Y	Y	Y	Y	Y	N
2 Natcher	Y	N	Y	Y	Y	Y	N
3 Mazzoli	▮	N	N	Y	Y	Y	Y
4 Snyder	Y	Y	Y	Y	Y	Y	N
5 Carter	Y	Y	Y	Y	N	Y	N
6 Breckinridge	N	N	N	N	Y	Y	Y
7 Perkins	N	N	Y	Y	Y	Y	N
LOUISIANA							
1 Livingston	Y	Y	Y	Y	N	Y	N
2 Boggs	N	N	Y	N	Y	Y	Y
3 Treen	Y	Y	Y	Y	N	Y	N
4 Waggonner	Y	Y	N	Y	N	Y	N
5 Huckaby	Y	Y	Y	Y	Y	Y	N
6 Moore	Y	Y	Y	Y	N	Y	N
7 Breaux	✓	✓	?	✓	?	?	X
8 Long	?	N	Y	N	Y	Y	Y
MAINE							
1 Emery	Y	Y	Y	Y	Y	Y	N
2 Cohen	?	?	?	?	?	?	#
MARYLAND							
1 Bauman	Y	Y	Y	Y	Y	Y	N
2 Long	N	N	N	N	Y	N	Y
3 Mikulski	N	Y	N	N	Y	Y	Y
4 Holt	Y	Y	Y	Y	N	Y	N
5 Spellman	N	N	N	N	Y	Y	Y
6 Byron	Y	Y	Y	Y	Y	Y	N
7 Mitchell	X	X	X	X	▮	▮	✓
8 Steers	N	N	N	N	Y	N	Y
MASSACHUSETTS							
1 Conte	N	N	N	N	Y	N	Y
2 Boland	Y	N	N	N	Y	Y	Y
3 Early	Y	N	N	N	N	N	N
4 Drinan	N	N	N	N	N	Y	N
5 Tsongas	?	?	?	X	?	?	✓
6 Harrington	▮	▮	▮	▮	▮	▮	#
7 Markey	N	N	N	N	Y	N	Y
8 O'Neill							
9 Moakley	Y	▮	N	N	Y	Y	Y
10 Heckler	Y	N	?	Y	Y	Y	Y
11 Burke	Y	N	Y	N	N	N	Y
12 Studds	N	N	N	N	N	N	Y
MICHIGAN							
1 Conyers	N	N	N	N	N	N	Y
2 Pursell	N	N	N	N	Y	Y	Y
3 Brown	N	N	N	N	Y	Y	Y
4 Stockman	Y	N	N	Y	Y	Y	Y
5 Sawyer	Y	N	N	N	Y	Y	Y
6 Carr	N	N	N	N	Y	Y	Y
7 Kildee	N	N	N	N	Y	Y	Y
8 Traxler	Y	N	N	N	Y	Y	Y
9 Vander Jagt	Y	Y	Y	Y	N	Y	Y
10 Cederberg	Y	N	Y	N	N	Y	N
11 Ruppe	?	?	?	?	?	?	?
12 Bonior	N	N	N	N	N	N	Y
13 Diggs	N	N	N	?	?	?	Y
14 Nedzi	N	N	N	N	Y	Y	Y
15 Ford	N	?	N	N	Y	Y	Y
16 Dingell	X	X	X	N	Y	Y	Y
17 Brodhead	N	N	N	N	Y	Y	Y
18 Blanchard	N	N	N	N	Y	Y	Y
19 Broomfield	Y	N	Y	N	Y	Y	Y
MINNESOTA							
1 Quie	?	?	?	?	?	?	?
2 Hagedorn	Y	Y	?	Y	Y	Y	N
3 Frenzel	N	N	N	N	Y	Y	Y
4 Vento	N	N	N	N	Y	Y	Y
5 Fraser	?	?	?	?	?	?	Y
6 Nolan	N	?	N	Y	Y	Y	N
7 Stangeland	Y	Y	#	Y	N	Y	N
8 Oberstar	N	Y	N	N	Y	Y	Y
MISSISSIPPI							
1 Whitten	Y	Y	Y	Y	Y	Y	N
2 Bowen	Y	N	Y	Y	Y	Y	N
3 Montgomery	N	Y	Y	Y	N	Y	N
4 Cochran	?	Y	Y	Y	N	Y	N
5 Lott	Y	Y	Y	Y	N	Y	N
MISSOURI							
1 Clay	X	?	?	?	?	N	Y
2 Young	Y	Y	Y	Y	Y	Y	N
3 Gephardt	Y	N	Y	Y	Y	Y	N

	611	612	613	614	615	616	617
4 Skelton	Y	Y	Y	N	Y	Y	Y
5 Bolling	N	N	N	N	N	N	Y
6 Coleman	Y	Y	Y	Y	Y	Y	N
7 Taylor	Y	Y	Y	Y	Y	Y	N
8 Ichord	Y	Y	Y	Y	Y	Y	N
9 Volkmer	Y	Y	Y	N	Y	Y	N
10 Burlison	N	N	N	N	Y	Y	Y
MONTANA							
1 Baucus	Y	N	N	Y	Y	Y	N
2 Marlenee	Y	Y	Y	Y	N	Y	N
NEBRASKA							
1 Thone	Y	N	Y	Y	Y	Y	N
2 Cavanaugh	N	N	N	N	Y	Y	Y
3 Smith	Y	N	Y	Y	Y	Y	N
NEVADA							
AL Santini	Y	N	Y	N	Y	Y	Y
NEW HAMPSHIRE							
1 D'Amours	N	N	Y	Y	Y	Y	Y
2 Cleveland	Y	N	N	Y	Y	Y	N
NEW JERSEY							
1 Florio	Y	Y	N	Y	Y	Y	Y
2 Hughes	N	N	N	Y	Y	Y	Y
3 Howard	N	N	N	N	Y	Y	Y
4 Thompson	N	N	N	N	N	N	Y
5 Fenwick	N	N	N	N	Y	Y	Y
6 Forsythe	N	N	N	N	Y	Y	Y
7 Maguire	N	N	N	N	Y	Y	Y
8 Roe	Y	N	N	N	Y	Y	Y
9 Hollenbeck	N	N	N	N	Y	Y	Y
10 Rodino	N	N	N	N	Y	Y	Y
11 Minish	Y	N	N	Y	Y	Y	Y
12 Rinaldo	Y	N	Y	Y	Y	Y	Y
13 Meyner	N	N	N	N	Y	Y	Y
14 LeFante	✓	X	▮	▮	#	#	#
15 Patten	N	N	N	N	Y	Y	Y
NEW MEXICO							
1 Lujan	?	?	?	Y	Y	Y	N
2 Runnels	Y	Y	Y	Y	Y	Y	N
NEW YORK							
1 Pike	Y	N	N	Y	N	Y	N
2 Downey	N	N	N	N	N	Y	Y
3 Ambro	Y	N	N	N	Y	Y	Y
4 Lent	Y	?	Y	Y	Y	Y	Y
5 Wydler	Y	N	Y	Y	Y	Y	Y
6 Wolff	Y	N	Y	N	Y	Y	Y
7 Addabbo	Y	Y	N	N	Y	Y	Y
8 Rosenthal	N	N	▮	N	Y	N	Y
9 Delaney	N	N	N	N	Y	Y	Y
10 Biaggi	Y	Y	Y	N	Y	Y	Y
11 Scheuer	N	N	N	N	Y	N	Y
12 Chisholm	N	N	N	N	Y	Y	Y
13 Solarz	N	N	N	N	N	N	Y
14 Richmond	X	X	X	X	?	?	✓
15 Zeferetti	Y	Y	Y	Y	Y	Y	Y
16 Holtzman	N	N	N	N	Y	N	Y
17 Murphy	?	?	?	?	?	?	?
18 Green	N	N	N	N	Y	N	Y
19 Rangel	N	N	N	N	Y	N	Y
20 Weiss	N	N	N	N	Y	N	Y
21 Garcia	N	N	N	N	#	N	Y
22 Bingham	N	N	N	N	N	N	Y
23 Caputo	?	?	?	?	?	?	?
24 Ottinger	N	N	N	N	Y	Y	Y
25 Fish	Y	N	N	N	Y	Y	Y
26 Gilman	Y	N	Y	N	Y	Y	Y
27 McHugh	N	N	N	N	N	N	Y
28 Stratton	Y	Y	Y	Y	Y	Y	Y
29 Pattison	N	N	N	N	Y	Y	Y
30 McEwen	Y	N	Y	Y	N	Y	N
31 Mitchell	Y	N	Y	N	Y	Y	Y
32 Hanley	#	▮	▮	▮	#	Y	Y
33 Walsh	Y	Y	Y	Y	Y	Y	Y
34 Horton	Y	N	Y	N	Y	Y	Y
35 Conable	N	N	N	N	Y	Y	Y
36 LaFalce	N	N	N	N	Y	Y	Y
37 Nowak	N	N	N	N	Y	Y	Y
38 Kemp	Y	N	?	?	?	?	?
39 Lundine	N	N	N	N	Y	Y	Y
NORTH CAROLINA							
1 Jones	Y	Y	Y	Y	Y	Y	N
2 Fountain	Y	Y	Y	Y	Y	Y	N
3 Whitley	Y	Y	Y	Y	Y	Y	N
4 Andrews	Y	N	N	Y	Y	Y	N
5 Neal	Y	N	N	Y	Y	Y	N
6 Preyer	N	N	N	N	Y	Y	Y
7 Rose	Y	Y	Y	Y	Y	Y	N
8 Hefner	Y	Y	Y	Y	Y	Y	N

	611	612	613	614	615	616	617
9 Martin	Y	Y	Y	Y	N	Y	N
10 Broyhill	Y	Y	N	Y	Y	?	?
11 Gudger	Y	Y	Y	Y	Y	Y	N
NORTH DAKOTA							
AL Andrews	Y	N	Y	Y	Y	Y	N
OHIO							
1 Gradison	Y	N	N	N	Y	Y	Y
2 Luken	Y	N	Y	N	Y	Y	Y
3 Whalen	N	N	N	N	Y	N	Y
4 Guyer	Y	Y	Y	Y	Y	Y	N
5 Latta	Y	Y	Y	Y	N	Y	N
6 Harsha	Y	Y	Y	Y	Y	Y	N
7 Brown	Y	N	Y	Y	Y	Y	N
8 Kindness	Y	Y	Y	Y	N	Y	N
9 Ashley	N	N	N	N	Y	Y	Y
10 Miller	Y	Y	Y	Y	N	Y	N
11 Stanton	Y	N	N	N	Y	Y	Y
12 Devine	Y	Y	Y	Y	Y	Y	N
13 Pease	N	N	N	N	Y	Y	Y
14 Seiberling	N	N	N	N	Y	Y	Y
15 Wylie	Y	N	Y	Y	N	Y	N
16 Regula	Y	N	Y	Y	Y	Y	Y
17 Ashbrook	Y	Y	Y	Y	N	Y	N
18 Applegate	Y	Y	Y	Y	Y	Y	N
19 Carney	Y	Y	N	N	Y	Y	Y
20 Oakar	Y	N	Y	N	N	N	N
21 Stokes	N	N	?	?	?	?	?
22 Vanik	N	N	N	N	Y	Y	Y
23 Mottl	Y	Y	Y	Y	Y	Y	N
OKLAHOMA							
1 Jones	Y	N	Y	Y	Y	Y	N
2 Risenhoover	✓	✓	✓	?	?	?	?
3 Watkins	Y	Y	Y	Y	Y	Y	N
4 Steed	Y	N	N	Y	Y	Y	N
5 Edwards	Y	Y	Y	Y	N	Y	N
6 English	Y	Y	Y	Y	N	Y	N
OREGON							
1 AuCoin	Y	N	N	Y	Y	Y	N
2 Ullman	N	N	N	N	Y	Y	Y
3 Duncan	N	N	N	N	Y	Y	Y
4 Weaver	Y	N	Y	Y	Y	Y	N
PENNSYLVANIA							
1 Myers, M.	Y	Y	N	N	Y	Y	Y
2 Nix	N	N	N	N	N	N	Y
3 Lederer	N	Y	N	N	Y	Y	Y
4 Eilberg	✓	X	X	N	Y	Y	Y
5 Schulze	Y	Y	Y	Y	N	Y	N
6 Yatron	Y	Y	Y	Y	Y	Y	Y
7 Edgar	N	N	N	N	Y	Y	Y
8 Kostmayer	N	N	N	N	Y	Y	Y
9 Shuster	?	?	?	?	?	?	?
10 McDade	Y	Y	N	Y	Y	Y	Y
11 Flood	N	N	Y	N	N	N	Y
12 Murtha	Y	Y	N	Y	Y	Y	N
13 Coughlin	Y	N	N	N	Y	Y	Y
14 Moorhead	N	N	N	N	Y	Y	Y
15 Rooney	Y	Y	N	N	Y	Y	Y
16 Walker	Y	Y	Y	Y	N	Y	N
17 Ertel	Y	Y	N	Y	Y	Y	N
18 Walgren	Y	N	N	N	Y	Y	Y
19 Goodling, W.	?	?	?	?	?	?	?
20 Gaydos	Y	Y	Y	Y	Y	Y	N
21 Dent	Y	Y	Y	Y	Y	Y	N
22 Murphy	Y	Y	Y	Y	Y	Y	N
23 Ammerman	Y	Y	Y	Y	Y	Y	N
24 Marks	N	N	N	N	Y	Y	Y
25 Myers, G.	N	N	N	N	N	N	Y
RHODE ISLAND							
1 St Germain	Y	N	N	Y	Y	Y	Y
2 Beard	Y	N	N	N	Y	Y	N
SOUTH CAROLINA							
1 Davis	Y	Y	Y	Y	N	Y	N
2 Spence	Y	Y	Y	Y	N	Y	N
3 Derrick	N	Y	Y	Y	Y	Y	N
4 Mann	Y	N	N	Y	Y	Y	Y
5 Holland	Y	Y	Y	Y	Y	Y	N
6 Jenrette	Y	Y	Y	Y	Y	Y	N
SOUTH DAKOTA							
1 Pressler	Y	Y	Y	Y	Y	Y	N
2 Abdnor	Y	▮	#	#	#	#	▮
TENNESSEE							
1 Quillen	Y	Y	Y	Y	Y	Y	N
2 Duncan	Y	Y	Y	Y	Y	Y	N
3 Lloyd	✓	✓	#	✓	#	#	X
4 Gore	Y	N	N	N	Y	Y	Y
5 Vacancy							
6 Beard	Y	Y	Y	Y	Y	Y	N

	611	612	613	614	615	616	617
7 Jones	Y	Y	Y	Y	Y	Y	N
8 Ford	N	N	N	N	Y	Y	Y
TEXAS							
1 Hall	Y	Y	Y	Y	Y	Y	N
2 Wilson, C.	N	N	N	N	Y	Y	Y
3 Collins	Y	Y	Y	Y	Y	Y	N
4 Roberts	Y	Y	Y	Y	N	Y	N
5 Mattox	N	N	N	N	Y	Y	N
6 Teague	?	✓	✓	✓	?	?	X
7 Archer	Y	Y	Y	Y	Y	Y	N
8 Eckhardt	N	N	N	N	Y	N	Y
9 Brooks	Y	Y	N	Y	N	Y	N
10 Pickle	Y	Y	Y	Y	Y	Y	N
11 Poage	Y	Y	Y	Y	N	Y	N
12 Wright	?	N	N	N	Y	Y	Y
13 Hightower	Y	N	Y	Y	Y	Y	N
14 Young	?	?	?	?	?	?	?
15 de la Garza	Y	Y	Y	Y	Y	Y	N
16 White	Y	Y	Y	Y	Y	Y	N
17 Burleson	Y	Y	Y	Y	N	Y	N
18 Jordan	N	N	N	N	Y	Y	Y
19 Mahon	N	Y	N	N	Y	Y	N
20 Gonzalez	N	N	N	N	Y	Y	Y
21 Krueger	#	▮	▮	▮	#	#	✓
22 Gammage	Y	✓	✓	✓	#	#	X
23 Kazen	Y	Y	Y	Y	Y	Y	N
24 Milford	?	?	?	?	?	?	?
UTAH							
1 McKay	Y	Y	Y	Y	Y	Y	N
2 Marriott	Y	Y	Y	Y	Y	Y	N
VERMONT							
AL Jeffords	Y	N	N	N	Y	Y	Y
VIRGINIA							
1 Trible	Y	N	Y	Y	N	Y	N
2 Whitehurst	Y	N	Y	Y	N	Y	N
3 Satterfield	Y	Y	Y	Y	N	Y	N
4 Daniel	Y	Y	Y	Y	N	Y	N
5 Daniel	Y	Y	Y	Y	N	Y	N
6 Butler	Y	N	Y	Y	N	Y	N
7 Robinson	Y	Y	Y	Y	N	Y	N
8 Harris	N	N	N	N	Y	Y	Y
9 Wampler	Y	Y	Y	Y	N	Y	N
10 Fisher	N	N	N	N	Y	Y	Y
WASHINGTON							
1 Pritchard	N	N	N	N	Y	Y	Y
2 Meeds	N	▮	N	N	Y	Y	Y
3 Bonker	N	N	N	N	Y	Y	Y
4 McCormack	N	N	N	N	Y	Y	Y
5 Foley	N	N	N	N	Y	Y	Y
6 Dicks	N	N	N	N	Y	Y	Y
7 Cunningham	Y	Y	Y	Y	N	Y	N
WEST VIRGINIA							
1 Mollohan	Y	N	N	Y	N	Y	Y
2 Staggers	Y	N	Y	Y	N	N	N
3 Slack	Y	Y	Y	Y	N	Y	N
4 Rahall	Y	N	N	N	Y	Y	N
WISCONSIN							
1 Aspin	N	N	N	N	Y	Y	Y
2 Kastenmeier	N	N	N	N	N	N	Y
3 Baldus	N	N	N	N	Y	Y	Y
4 Zablocki	N	N	N	N	N	N	Y
5 Reuss	N	N	N	N	Y	Y	Y
6 Steiger	N	N	N	N	Y	Y	Y
7 Obey	N	N	N	N	Y	Y	Y
8 Cornell	N	N	N	N	N	N	N
9 Kasten	?	?	?	?	?	?	?
WYOMING							
AL Roncalio	▮	▮	▮	#	#	#	#

Democrats ***Republicans***

618. H J Res 638. ERA Deadline Extension. Chisholm, D-N.Y., motion to order the previous question (thus ending debate) on the adoption of the rule (H Res 1295) providing for floor consideration of the resolution to extend by 39 months the deadline for states to ratify the Equal Rights Amendment (ERA) to the Constitution and allowing for passage of the extension by a simple majority vote. Motion agreed to 243-171: R 43-100; D 200-71 (ND 164-24; SD 36-47), Aug. 15, 1978.

619. H J Res 638. ERA Deadline Extension. Edwards, D-Calif., motion to table (kill) the resolution (H Res 1315) to require a two-thirds vote of members present and voting for passage of H J Res 638 to extend the deadline for ratification of the Equal Rights Amendment to the Constitution. Motion agreed to 230-183: R 44-98; D 186-85 (ND 156-32; SD 30-53), Aug. 15, 1978.

620. H J Res 638. ERA Deadline Extension. Railsback, R-Ill., amendment to allow states to rescind their ratification of the ERA during the proposed 39-month extension period. Rejected 196-227: R 108-36; D 88-191 (ND 34-160; SD 54-31), Aug. 15, 1978. A "nay" was a vote supporting the president's position.

621. H J Res 638. ERA Deadline Extension. Passage of the joint resolution to provide an additional 39 months, until June 30, 1982, for states to ratify the Equal Rights Amendment to the Constitution under which discrimination on the basis of sex would be prohibited. Passed 233-189: R 41-103; D 192-86 (ND 162-31; SD 30-55), Aug. 15, 1978. A "yea" was a vote supporting the president's position.

622. H Con Res 683. Fiscal 1979 Binding Budget Levels. Holt, R-Md., amendment to the Giaimo, D-Conn., substitute amendment, to provide for the following budget aggregates: budget authority, $539 billion; outlays, $480 billion; revenues, $445 billion; deficit, $35 billion. Rejected 201-206: R 140-1; D 61-205 (ND 22-163; SD 39-42), Aug. 16, 1978.

623. H Con Res 683. Fiscal 1979 Binding Budget Levels. Mattox, D-Texas, amendment, to the Giaimo, D-Conn., substitute amendment, to reduce budget authority by $223 billion and outlays by $673 billion to reflect Senate committee cuts in anti-recession aid to states and cities and House cuts in the Comprehensive Employment and Training Act. Adopted 271-134: R 126-15; D 145-119 (ND 78-106; SD 67-13), Aug. 16, 1978.

624. H Con Res 683. Fiscal 1979 Binding Budget Levels. Latta, R-Ohio, amendment, to the Giaimo, D-Conn., substitute amendment, to provide for the following budget aggregates: budget authority, $539 billion; outlays, $480 billion; revenues, $450 billion; deficit, $30 billion. Rejected 198-204: R 135-5; D 63-199 (ND 32-152; SD 31-47), Aug. 16, 1978.

625. H Con Res 683. Fiscal 1979 Binding Budget Levels. Fisher, D-Va., amendment, to the Giaimo, D-Conn., substitute amendment, to reduce budget authority and outlays by $5 billion. Rejected 155-241: R 88-50; D 67-191 (ND 51-128; SD 16-63), Aug. 16, 1978. (The Giaimo substitute amendment, as amended by the Mattox, D-Texas, amendment *(see vote 623, above)*, subsequently was adopted by voice vote.)

KEY

Y Voted for (yea).
✓ Paired for.
† Announced for.
# CQ Poll for.
N Voted against (nay).
X Paired against.
\- Announced against.
▮ CQ Poll against.
P Voted "present."
● Voted "present" to avoid possible conflict of interest.
? Did not vote or otherwise make a position known.

	618	619	620	621	622	623	624	625
ALABAMA								
1 Edwards	N	N	Y	N	Y	Y	Y	Y
2 Dickinson	N	N	Y	N	Y	Y	Y	Y
3 Nichols	N	N	Y	N	Y	Y	Y	N
4 Bevill	N	N	Y	N	N	Y	N	N
5 Flippo	N	N	Y	N	N	Y	N	N
6 Buchanan	Y	Y	Y	Y	Y	?	Y	N
7 Flowers	N	N	Y	N	?	?	?	?
ALASKA								
AL Young	#	▮	#	▮	✓	#	#	▮
ARIZONA								
1 Rhodes	N	N	Y	N	Y	Y	Y	N
2 Udall	Y	Y	N	Y	N	Y	N	N
3 Stump	N	N	Y	N	Y	Y	Y	Y
4 Rudd	N	N	Y	N	Y	Y	Y	N
ARKANSAS								
1 Alexander	Y	Y	N	N	N	N	N	N
2 Tucker	Y	Y	N	N	N	N	N	N
3 Hammerschmidt	N	N	Y	N	Y	Y	Y	Y
4 Thornton	Y	N	Y	Y	N	N	N	N
CALIFORNIA								
1 Johnson	Y	N	N	N	N	N	N	N
2 Clausen	Y	Y	N	Y	Y	Y	Y	Y
3 Moss	Y	Y	N	Y	N	N	N	?
4 Leggett	Y	Y	N	Y	N	Y	N	Y
5 Burton, J.	Y	Y	N	Y	N	N	N	N
6 Burton, P.	Y	Y	N	Y	N	N	N	N
7 Miller	Y	Y	N	Y	X	?	?	?
8 Dellums	Y	Y	N	Y	X	X	▮	▮
9 Stark	Y	Y	N	Y	N	N	N	Y
10 Edwards	Y	Y	N	Y	N	?	N	N
11 Ryan	Y	Y	N	Y	N	Y	N	N
12 McCloskey	Y	Y	N	Y	Y	N	Y	Y
13 Mineta	Y	Y	N	Y	N	N	N	N
14 McFall	Y	Y	N	Y	N	Y	N	N
15 Sisk	?	?	?	?	?	?	?	?
16 Panetta	Y	Y	N	Y	Y	N	Y	Y
17 Krebs	Y	Y	N	Y	Y	Y	N	Y
18 Vacancy								
19 Lagomarsino	N	N	Y	N	Y	Y	Y	N
20 Goldwater	N	N	Y	N	Y	Y	Y	Y
21 Corman	Y	Y	N	Y	N	N	N	N
22 Moorhead	N	N	Y	N	Y	Y	Y	Y
23 Beilenson	Y	Y	N	Y	N	N	N	N
24 Waxman	Y	Y	N	Y	N	N	N	N
25 Roybal	Y	Y	N	Y	N	N	N	N
26 Rousselot	N	N	Y	N	Y	Y	Y	Y
27 Dornan	N	N	Y	N	Y	Y	Y	Y
28 Burke	Y	Y	N	Y	X	X	▮	▮
29 Hawkins	Y	Y	N	Y	N	N	N	N
30 Danielson	Y	Y	N	Y	N	Y	N	N
31 Wilson, C.H.	Y	N	Y	Y	▮	▮	▮	▮
32 Anderson	Y	Y	N	Y	N	N	N	Y
33 Clawson	N	N	Y	N	Y	Y	Y	Y
34 Hannaford	Y	Y	N	Y	N	Y	N	Y
35 Lloyd	Y	Y	N	Y	N	N	N	N
36 Brown	Y	Y	N	Y	N	N	N	Y
37 Pettis	Y	Y	Y	Y	Y	Y	Y	Y
38 Patterson	Y	Y	N	Y	N	N	N	N
39 Wiggins	N	N	Y	N	Y	Y	#	N
40 Badham	N	N	N	N	Y	Y	Y	Y
41 Wilson, B.	Y	Y	N	Y	Y	Y	Y	N
42 Van Deerlin	Y	Y	N	N	N	N	N	N
43 Burgener	Y	Y	N	N	Y	Y	Y	Y
COLORADO								
1 Schroeder	Y	Y	N	Y	N	N	Y	Y
2 Wirth	Y	Y	N	Y	N	Y	Y	Y
3 Evans	Y	Y	N	Y	N	Y	N	N
4 Johnson	Y	Y	Y	Y	Y	Y	Y	Y
5 Armstrong	N	N	Y	N	Y	Y	Y	Y
CONNECTICUT								
1 Cotter	Y	Y	N	Y	N	N	N	N
2 Dodd	Y	Y	N	Y	N	Y	N	N
3 Giaimo	Y	Y	N	Y	N	Y	N	N
4 McKinney	Y	Y	N	Y	Y	Y	Y	N
5 Sarasin	Y	Y	N	Y	Y	Y	Y	N
6 Moffett	✓	?	N	Y	N	Y	N	Y
DELAWARE								
AL Evans	Y	Y	Y	N	Y	Y	Y	Y
FLORIDA								
1 Sikes	N	N	Y	N	N	Y	?	?
2 Fuqua	N	N	Y	N	Y	Y	Y	N
3 Bennett	N	N	Y	N	Y	Y	Y	N
4 Chappell	N	N	Y	N	N	Y	N	N
5 Kelly	N	N	Y	N	Y	Y	Y	N
6 Young	N	N	Y	N	Y	Y	Y	N
7 Gibbons	N	N	Y	N	Y	Y	Y	Y
8 Ireland	N	N	Y	N	Y	Y	N	Y
9 Frey	N	N	Y	N	✓	?	?	?
10 Bafalis	N	N	Y	N	Y	Y	Y	Y
11 Rogers	Y	Y	N	Y	N	Y	N	N
12 Burke	N	N	Y	N	Y	Y	Y	N
13 Lehman	Y	Y	N	Y	N	Y	N	N
14 Pepper	Y	Y	N	Y	N	Y	N	N
15 Fascell	Y	Y	N	Y	N	Y	N	N
GEORGIA								
1 Ginn	N	N	N	N	N	Y	N	N
2 Mathis	N	N	Y	N	Y	Y	Y	Y
3 Brinkley	N	N	Y	N	Y	Y	Y	N
4 Levitas	Y	N	Y	Y	Y	Y	N	N
5 Fowler	Y	N	N	Y	N	Y	Y	N
6 Flynt	N	N	Y	N	✓	?	?	?
7 McDonald	N	N	Y	N	✓	✓	#	✓
8 Evans	N	N	Y	N	Y	Y	Y	Y
9 Jenkins	N	N	Y	N	Y	Y	Y	N
10 Barnard	N	N	Y	N	Y	Y	N	N
HAWAII								
1 Heftel	Y	Y	N	Y	N	Y	N	Y
2 Akaka	Y	Y	N	Y	N	Y	N	N
IDAHO								
1 Symms	N	N	Y	N	Y	Y	Y	N
2 Hansen, G.	N	N	Y	N	Y	Y	Y	Y
ILLINOIS								
1 Metcalfe	Y	Y	N	Y	N	N	N	N
2 Murphy	Y	Y	Y	Y	N	N	N	N
3 Russo	X	X	N	Y	N	Y	N	N
4 Derwinski	N	N	Y	N	Y	Y	Y	?
5 Fary	Y	Y	Y	Y	N	N	N	N
6 Hyde	N	N	Y	N	Y	Y	Y	N
7 Collins	Y	Y	N	Y	N	N	N	N
8 Rostenkowski	Y	N	Y	Y	N	N	N	N
9 Yates	Y	Y	N	Y	N	N	N	N
10 Mikva	Y	Y	N	Y	N	N	N	N
11 Annunzio	Y	Y	Y	Y	N	Y	N	N
12 Crane	N	N	Y	N	✓	Y	Y	N
13 McClory	N	N	N	N	Y	Y	Y	Y
14 Erlenborn	N	N	Y	N	Y	Y	Y	Y
15 Corcoran	N	N	Y	N	Y	Y	Y	Y
16 Anderson	Y	Y	N	Y	Y	Y	Y	N
17 O'Brien	N	N	Y	N	Y	Y	Y	#
18 Michel	N	N	Y	N	Y	Y	Y	Y
19 Railsback	N	Y	Y	N	Y	Y	Y	N
20 Findley	N	N	Y	Y	Y	Y	Y	Y
21 Madigan	N	N	Y	N	Y	Y	Y	N
22 Shipley	X	?	X	✓	X	?	?	?
23 Price	Y	Y	N	Y	N	Y	N	N
24 Simon	Y	Y	N	Y	N	N	N	N
INDIANA								
1 Benjamin	Y	Y	N	Y	N	N	N	N
2 Fithian	Y	N	N	N	N	Y	N	N
3 Brademas	Y	Y	N	Y	N	Y	N	N
4 Quayle	N	N	Y	N	Y	Y	Y	Y
5 Hillis	N	N	Y	N	Y	Y	Y	Y
6 Evans	Y	Y	Y	Y	Y	Y	Y	N
7 Myers, J.	N	N	Y	N	Y	Y	Y	Y
8 Cornwell	Y	Y	N	Y	Y	N	N	N
9 Hamilton	N	N	Y	N	N	Y	N	Y
10 Sharp	Y	Y	N	Y	N	Y	Y	Y
11 Jacobs	N	N	N	Y	Y	Y	Y	#
IOWA								
1 Leach	Y	Y	N	Y	Y	Y	Y	Y
2 Blouin	Y	Y	N	Y	N	Y	N	Y
3 Grassley	N	N	Y	N	Y	Y	Y	Y
4 Smith	Y	Y	N	Y	N	Y	N	N
5 Harkin	Y	Y	N	Y	N	Y	N	Y
6 Bedell	Y	Y	Y	Y	N	Y	N	N

Democrats ***Republicans***

	618	619	620	621	622	623	624	625
KANSAS								
1 Sebelius	N	N	Y	N	Y	Y	Y	Y
2 Keys	Y	Y	N	Y	N	Y	N	Y
3 Winn	N	N	Y	N	Y	Y	Y	Y
4 Glickman	Y	Y	N	Y	Y	Y	Y	Y
5 Skubitz	N	N	Y	N	✓	Y	N	Y
KENTUCKY								
1 Hubbard	N	N	Y	N	N	Y	N	Y
2 Natcher	Y	Y	Y	Y	N	Y	N	N
3 Mazzoli	N	Y	N	N	Y	Y	N	N
4 Snyder	N	N	Y	N	Y	Y	Y	Y
5 Carter	Y	N	Y	Y	Y	N	Y	N
6 Breckinridge	Y	N	Y	N	Y	Y	N	N
7 Perkins	Y	Y	Y	Y	N	N	N	N
LOUISIANA								
1 Livingston	N	N	Y	N	Y	Y	Y	N
2 Boggs	Y	Y	N	Y	N	N	N	N
3 Treen	N	N	Y	N	Y	Y	Y	Y
4 Waggonner	N	N	Y	N	Y	Y	#	N
5 Huckaby	N	N	N	N	✓	?	?	?
6 Moore	N	N	Y	N	Y	Y	Y	Y
7 Breaux	X	Y	Y	N	Y	Y	Y	Y
8 Long	Y	Y	N	Y	N	Y	N	N
MAINE								
1 Emery	Y	Y	N	Y	Y	Y	Y	Y
2 Cohen	Y	Y	N	Y	Y	Y	Y	Y
MARYLAND								
1 Bauman	N	N	Y	N	Y	Y	Y	Y
2 Long	Y	Y	N	?	N	Y	N	N
3 Mikulski	Y	Y	N	Y	N	N	N	N
4 Holt	Y	Y	Y	Y	Y	Y	Y	N
5 Spellman	Y	Y	N	Y	N	N	Y	Y
6 Byron	Y	Y	Y	Y	Y	Y	Y	N
7 Mitchell	✓	✓	N	Y	N	N	N	N
8 Steers	Y	Y	N	Y	Y	N	Y	Y
MASSACHUSETTS								
1 Conte	Y	Y	N	Y	Y	Y	N	N
2 Boland	Y	Y	Y	Y	N	N	N	N
3 Early	Y	Y	N	Y	Y	N	Y	N
4 Drinan	Y	Y	N	Y	N	Y	N	N
5 Tsongas	?	?	N	Y	N	N	N	?
6 Harrington	#	#	N	Y	N	N	N	#
7 Markey	Y	Y	N	Y	N	N	N	N
8 O'Neill								
9 Moakley	Y	Y	N	Y	N	N	N	N
10 Heckler	Y	Y	N	Y	Y	N	Y	N
11 Burke	Y	N	N	Y	N	N	N	N
12 Studds	Y	Y	N	Y	N	N	N	N
MICHIGAN								
1 Conyers	Y	Y	N	Y	▮	N	N	N
2 Pursell	Y	?	N	Y	Y	Y	Y	Y
3 Brown	N	N	Y	N	Y	Y	Y	N
4 Stockman	Y	Y	Y	Y	Y	Y	Y	Y
5 Sawyer	N	Y	N	Y	Y	Y	Y	Y
6 Carr	Y	Y	N	Y	Y	N	Y	Y
7 Kildee	Y	Y	N	Y	N	N	N	N
8 Traxler	Y	Y	N	Y	Y	N	▮	Y
9 Vander Jagt	Y	Y	Y	Y	Y	Y	Y	?
10 Cederberg	N	N	Y	N	Y	N	Y	Y
11 Ruppe	?	?	N	Y	Y	Y	Y	Y
12 Bonior	Y	Y	N	Y	N	N	N	N
13 Diggs	Y	Y	N	Y	N	N	N	▮
14 Nedzi	N	N	Y	N	N	Y	N	N
15 Ford	Y	Y	N	Y	N	N	N	N
16 Dingell	N	N	Y	N	N	N	N	N
17 Brodhead	Y	Y	N	Y	N	N	N	N
18 Blanchard	Y	Y	N	Y	N	N	N	N
19 Broomfield	Y	N	Y	Y	Y	Y	Y	Y
MINNESOTA								
1 Quie	N	N	Y	N	Y	Y	Y	Y
2 Hagedorn	N	N	Y	N	Y	Y	?	?
3 Frenzel	Y	Y	N	Y	Y	Y	Y	Y
4 Vento	Y	Y	N	Y	N	N	N	N
5 Fraser	Y	Y	N	Y	N	N	N	?
6 Nolan	Y	Y	N	Y	N	N	N	N
7 Stangeland	N	N	Y	N	Y	Y	Y	Y
8 Oberstar	Y	Y	Y	Y	N	N	N	N
MISSISSIPPI								
1 Whitten	Y	Y	N	N	N	Y	N	N
2 Bowen	Y	N	Y	N	Y	Y	Y	Y
3 Montgomery	N	N	Y	N	Y	Y	Y	N
4 Cochran	N	N	Y	N	Y	Y	Y	Y
5 Lott	N	N	Y	N	Y	Y	Y	Y
MISSOURI								
1 Clay	Y	Y	N	Y	N	N	N	N
2 Young	N	N	N	N	N	Y	N	N
3 Gephardt	N	N	N	N	N	Y	N	Y
4 Skelton	N	N	N	N	N	Y	Y	N
5 Bolling	Y	Y	N	Y	N	N	N	N
6 Coleman	N	N	Y	N	Y	Y	Y	N
7 Taylor	N	N	Y	N	Y	Y	Y	N
8 Ichord	N	N	Y	N	Y	Y	Y	N
9 Volkmer	N	N	N	N	N	Y	N	Y
10 Burlison	Y	Y	N	N	N	Y	N	N
MONTANA								
1 Baucus	Y	Y	N	Y	N	Y	Y	Y
2 Marlenee	N	N	Y	N	Y	Y	Y	N
NEBRASKA								
1 Thone	N	N	Y	N	Y	Y	Y	Y
2 Cavanaugh	N	Y	N	Y	Y	Y	Y	Y
3 Smith	Y	Y	Y	Y	Y	Y	Y	Y
NEVADA								
AL Santini	N	N	Y	N	Y	Y	Y	Y
NEW HAMPSHIRE								
1 D'Amours	Y	Y	Y	Y	N	Y	Y	Y
2 Cleveland	Y	Y	Y	N	Y	Y	Y	N
NEW JERSEY								
1 Florio	Y	Y	N	Y	N	N	N	N
2 Hughes	Y	Y	N	Y	N	Y	Y	Y
3 Howard	Y	Y	N	Y	N	N	N	N
4 Thompson	Y	Y	N	Y	X	✓	?	X
5 Fenwick	Y	Y	N	Y	Y	Y	Y	Y
6 Forsythe	Y	Y	N	Y	Y	Y	Y	Y
7 Maguire	Y	Y	N	Y	N	N	N	N
8 Roe	Y	Y	N	Y	N	N	N	N
9 Hollenbeck	Y	Y	N	Y	Y	N	Y	N
10 Rodino	Y	Y	N	Y	N	N	▮	▮
11 Minish	Y	Y	N	Y	N	N	N	Y
12 Rinaldo	Y	Y	N	Y	Y	N	Y	N
13 Meyner	Y	Y	N	Y	N	N	▮	▮
14 LeFante	✓	#	X	✓	X	X	▮	▮
15 Patten	Y	Y	N	Y	N	N	N	N
NEW MEXICO								
1 Lujan	N	N	Y	N	Y	Y	Y	Y
2 Runnels	N	N	Y	N	Y	✓	Y	N
NEW YORK								
1 Pike	N	N	Y	N	Y	Y	Y	Y
2 Downey	Y	Y	N	Y	N	N	N	N
3 Ambro	N	N	Y	Y	Y	N	N	N
4 Lent	N	N	Y	N	Y	N	Y	Y
5 Wydler	N	N	Y	N	Y	N	Y	Y
6 Wolff	Y	Y	N	Y	N	N	N	Y
7 Addabbo	Y	Y	N	Y	N	N	N	N
8 Rosenthal	Y	Y	N	Y	N	N	N	N
9 Delaney	N	N	Y	N	N	N	N	N
10 Biaggi	Y	Y	N	Y	N	N	N	N
11 Scheuer	Y	Y	N	Y	N	N	N	N
12 Chisholm	Y	Y	N	Y	N	N	N	N
13 Solarz	Y	Y	N	Y	N	N	N	N
14 Richmond	Y	Y	N	Y	N	N	N	N
15 Zeferetti	Y	N	N	N	N	N	N	N
16 Holtzman	Y	Y	N	Y	N	N	N	N
17 Murphy	Y	Y	N	Y	N	N	N	N
18 Green	Y	Y	N	Y	Y	N	Y	N
19 Rangel	Y	Y	N	Y	N	N	N	N
20 Weiss	Y	Y	N	Y	N	N	N	N
21 Garcia	Y	Y	N	Y	X	N	N	N
22 Bingham	Y	Y	N	Y	N	N	N	N
23 Caputo	?	?	?	?	Y	Y	Y	Y
24 Ottinger	Y	Y	N	Y	N	N	N	N
25 Fish	Y	Y	N	Y	Y	?	Y	Y
26 Gilman	Y	Y	N	Y	Y	N	Y	N
27 McHugh	Y	Y	N	N	N	Y	N	N
28 Stratton	N	N	N	Y	N	N	N	N
29 Pattison	Y	Y	N	Y	N	Y	N	N
30 McEwen	N	N	Y	N	Y	Y	Y	N
31 Mitchell	N	Y	Y	N	Y	N	Y	N
32 Hanley	Y	Y	N	Y	N	Y	N	N
33 Walsh	N	N	Y	N	Y	Y	N	N
34 Horton	Y	Y	N	N	Y	N	Y	N
35 Conable	Y	Y	N	Y	Y	Y	Y	Y
36 LaFalce	N	Y	N	N	N	N	Y	Y
37 Nowak	Y	Y	N	Y	N	N	Y	Y
38 Kemp	N	Y	Y	N	Y	Y	Y	Y
39 Lundine	Y	Y	N	Y	N	N	N	Y
NORTH CAROLINA								
1 Jones	N	N	Y	N	Y	Y	N	N
2 Fountain	N	N	Y	N	Y	Y	Y	N
3 Whitley	N	N	Y	N	Y	Y	N	N
4 Andrews	Y	Y	Y	N	Y	Y	Y	N
5 Neal	Y	N	Y	Y	Y	Y	Y	N
6 Preyer	Y	Y	Y	Y	N	Y	N	Y
7 Rose	N	Y	N	Y	N	Y	Y	N
8 Hefner	N	N	Y	N	Y	Y	N	N
9 Martin	N	N	Y	N	Y	Y	Y	Y
10 Broyhill	N	N	Y	N	Y	Y	Y	Y
11 Gudger	N	N	Y	Y	Y	Y	Y	N
NORTH DAKOTA								
AL Andrews	N	N	Y	N	Y	Y	Y	Y
OHIO								
1 Gradison	N	N	Y	N	Y	Y	Y	Y
2 Luken	Y	Y	Y	N	Y	Y	Y	Y
3 Whalen	Y	Y	N	Y	N	N	N	N
4 Guyer	N	N	Y	N	Y	Y	Y	N
5 Latta	N	N	Y	N	Y	Y	Y	Y
6 Harsha	N	N	Y	N	Y	Y	Y	N
7 Brown	Y	N	N	N	Y	Y	Y	Y
8 Kindness	N	N	Y	N	Y	Y	Y	Y
9 Ashley	Y	Y	N	Y	N	Y	N	N
10 Miller	N	N	Y	N	Y	Y	Y	Y
11 Stanton	N	N	Y	N	Y	Y	Y	Y
12 Devine	N	N	Y	N	Y	Y	Y	Y
13 Pease	Y	Y	N	Y	N	Y	N	N
14 Seiberling	Y	Y	N	Y	N	N	N	Y
15 Wylie	N	N	Y	N	Y	Y	Y	Y
16 Regula	N	N	N	N	Y	Y	Y	Y
17 Ashbrook	N	N	Y	N	Y	Y	Y	Y
18 Applegate	Y	N	Y	N	Y	Y	Y	Y
19 Carney	Y	Y	N	Y	N	N	N	N
20 Oakar	Y	Y	N	Y	N	Y	N	N
21 Stokes	Y	Y	N	Y	X	N	?	?
22 Vanik	Y	Y	N	Y	N	N	Y	Y
23 Mottl	N	N	Y	N	Y	Y	Y	Y
OKLAHOMA								
1 Jones	N	N	N	N	N	Y	N	N
2 Risenhoover	?	?	?	?	?	X	?	?
3 Watkins	N	N	N	N	N	Y	N	N
4 Steed	Y	N	Y	N	N	N	N	N
5 Edwards	N	N	Y	N	Y	Y	Y	Y
6 English	N	N	Y	N	Y	Y	Y	Y
OREGON								
1 AuCoin	Y	Y	N	Y	N	Y	Y	Y
2 Ullman	Y	Y	Y	Y	N	Y	N	N
3 Duncan	N	N	Y	N	N	Y	N	N
4 Weaver	Y	Y	N	Y	N	Y	Y	Y
PENNSYLVANIA								
1 Myers, M.	Y	Y	N	Y	N	N	N	N
2 Nix	Y	Y	N	Y	N	N	N	N
3 Lederer	Y	Y	N	Y	N	N	N	N
4 Eilberg	Y	Y	N	Y	N	N	N	N
5 Schulze	N	N	Y	N	Y	Y	?	?
6 Yatron	Y	Y	N	Y	Y	Y	Y	Y
7 Edgar	Y	Y	N	Y	N	N	N	N
8 Kostmayer	Y	Y	N	Y	N	Y	Y	Y
9 Shuster	N	N	Y	N	Y	Y	Y	Y
10 McDade	N	Y	N	N	Y	N	N	N
11 Flood	Y	Y	N	Y	N	Y	N	N
12 Murtha	Y	N	N	N	N	N	N	N
13 Coughlin	Y	Y	Y	Y	Y	Y	Y	Y
14 Moorhead	Y	Y	N	Y	N	N	N	N
15 Rooney	Y	Y	N	Y	N	N	N	N
16 Walker	N	Y	Y	N	Y	Y	Y	Y
17 Ertel	Y	Y	Y	Y	N	Y	N	Y
18 Walgren	Y	Y	N	Y	N	Y	N	Y
19 Goodling, W.	N	N	Y	Y	Y	Y	Y	Y
20 Gaydos	Y	Y	Y	Y	N	N	N	Y
21 Dent	#	#	Y	Y	X	X	▮	▮
22 Murphy	Y	Y	N	Y	Y	Y	Y	Y
23 Ammerman	Y	Y	N	Y	N	Y	N	Y
24 Marks	Y	Y	N	Y	Y	Y	Y	Y
25 Myers, G.	N	N	Y	N	Y	Y	Y	Y
RHODE ISLAND								
1 St Germain	N	Y	Y	N	N	N	N	N
2 Beard	Y	Y	N	Y	N	Y	N	N
SOUTH CAROLINA								
1 Davis	N	N	Y	N	Y	N	N	N
2 Spence	N	N	Y	N	Y	Y	Y	N
3 Derrick	Y	Y	N	Y	N	Y	N	N
4 Mann	N	N	Y	N	N	Y	Y	N
5 Holland	Y	Y	N	N	N	Y	N	N
6 Jenrette	Y	Y	Y	Y	#	X	▮	#
SOUTH DAKOTA								
1 Pressler	Y	Y	N	Y	Y	Y	Y	N
2 Abdnor	N	N	N	N	Y	Y	Y	Y
TENNESSEE								
1 Quillen	N	N	Y	N	Y	Y	Y	N
2 Duncan	N	N	Y	N	Y	Y	Y	N
3 Lloyd	X	X	✓	X	✓	✓	#	#
4 Gore	N	N	N	N	N	N	N	N
5 Vacancy								
6 Beard	N	N	Y	N	Y	Y	Y	Y
7 Jones	N	N	Y	N	Y	Y	N	N
8 Ford	Y	Y	N	Y	Y	N	N	N
TEXAS								
1 Hall	N	N	Y	N	Y	Y	N	Y
2 Wilson, C.	Y	▮	N	Y	N	Y	N	N
3 Collins	N	N	Y	N	Y	Y	Y	Y
4 Roberts	N	N	Y	N	Y	Y	N	N
5 Mattox	Y	Y	N	Y	N	Y	Y	Y
6 Teague	✓	✓	✓	X	?	✓	?	?
7 Archer	N	N	Y	N	Y	Y	Y	Y
8 Eckhardt	Y	Y	Y	N	N	N	N	N
9 Brooks	N	N	Y	N	N	Y	N	N
10 Pickle	Y	Y	N	N	N	Y	Y	Y
11 Poage	N	N	Y	N	N	Y	Y	N
12 Wright	Y	Y	Y	Y	N	Y	N	N
13 Hightower	N	N	N	N	Y	Y	N	N
14 Young	?	?	N	Y	N	?	?	?
15 de la Garza	N	N	Y	N	Y	Y	Y	Y
16 White	N	N	Y	Y	Y	Y	Y	N
17 Burleson	N	N	Y	N	Y	Y	Y	N
18 Jordan	Y	Y	N	Y	N	N	N	N
19 Mahon	Y	N	Y	N	N	Y	N	N
20 Gonzalez	Y	Y	N	Y	N	N	N	N
21 Krueger	Y	Y	N	Y	N	Y	Y	N
22 Gammage	Y	Y	N	Y	Y	Y	Y	Y
23 Kazen	N	N	Y	N	Y	Y	N	N
24 Milford	?	?	Y	Y	Y	Y	Y	N
UTAH								
1 McKay	N	N	Y	N	N	Y	N	N
2 Marriott	N	N	Y	N	Y	Y	Y	Y
VERMONT								
AL Jeffords	Y	Y	Y	Y	Y	Y	Y	N
VIRGINIA								
1 Trible	N	N	Y	N	Y	Y	Y	N
2 Whitehurst	N	N	Y	N	Y	Y	Y	N
3 Satterfield	N	N	Y	N	Y	Y	Y	N
4 Daniel	N	N	Y	N	Y	Y	Y	N
5 Daniel	N	N	?	?	Y	Y	Y	N
6 Butler	N	N	Y	N	Y	Y	Y	Y
7 Robinson	N	N	Y	N	Y	Y	Y	N
8 Harris	Y	Y	N	Y	N	N	Y	Y
9 Wampler	N	N	Y	N	Y	Y	Y	N
10 Fisher	Y	Y	N	Y	N	Y	N	Y
WASHINGTON								
1 Pritchard	Y	Y	N	Y	Y	Y	Y	Y
2 Meeds	Y	Y	N	Y	N	N	N	N
3 Bonker	Y	Y	N	Y	N	#	N	Y
4 McCormack	Y	Y	N	Y	N	Y	N	Y
5 Foley	Y	Y	N	Y	N	Y	N	N
6 Dicks	Y	Y	N	Y	N	Y	N	N
7 Cunningham	N	N	Y	N	Y	Y	Y	N
WEST VIRGINIA								
1 Mollohan	Y	N	Y	Y	N	Y	N	N
2 Staggers	Y	Y	N	N	N	Y	N	N
3 Slack	N	N	Y	N	N	Y	N	N
4 Rahall	Y	N	N	Y	N	Y	N	N
WISCONSIN								
1 Aspin	Y	Y	N	Y	N	N	N	N
2 Kastenmeier	Y	Y	N	Y	N	N	N	N
3 Baldus	Y	Y	N	Y	N	Y	N	N
4 Zablocki	Y	N	Y	N	N	Y	N	N
5 Reuss	Y	Y	N	Y	N	N	N	N
6 Steiger	Y	N	Y	N	Y	Y	Y	Y
7 Obey	Y	Y	N	N	N	Y	N	N
8 Cornell	N	N	N	Y	N	N	N	N
9 Kasten	N	N	Y	N	✓	✓	?	?
WYOMING								
AL Roncalio	Y	Y	N	Y	N	#	N	Y

Democrats ***Republicans***

626. H Con Res 683. Fiscal 1979 Binding Budget Levels. Levitas, D-Ga., amendment, to the Giaimo, D-Conn., substitute amendment, to reduce budget authority and outlays by $753 million to reflect elimination of all money for anti-recession aid to states and cities. Rejected 187-208: R 97-42; D 90-166 (ND 33-147; SD 57-19), Aug. 16, 1978.

627. H Con Res 683. Fiscal 1979 Binding Budget Levels. Rousselot, R-Calif., substitute, to the Giaimo, D-Conn., substitute amendment, to balance the budget at the following levels: budget authority, $519 billion; outlays, $464.1 billion; revenues, $464.1 billion. Rejected 153-235: R 100-37; D 53-198 (ND 20-156; SD 33-42), Aug. 16, 1978. (The Giaimo substitute amendment, as amended by the Mattox, D-Texas, amendment *(see vote 623, p. 176-H),* subsequently was adopted by voice vote.)

628. H Con Res 683. Fiscal 1979 Binding Budget Levels. Adoption of the second budget resolution setting the following budget levels: budget authority, $561 billion; outlays, $489.8 billion; revenues, $450 billion; deficit, $39.8 billion. Adopted 217-178: R 2-136; D 215-42 (ND 154-25; SD 61-17), Aug. 16, 1978.

629. HR 13467. Second Supplemental Appropriations, Fiscal 1978. Adoption of the conference report on the bill to appropriate $6,808,778,686 in supplemental funds for fiscal 1978 operations of the government, including $3.2 billion for federal employee pay raises. Adopted 198-191: R 24-113; D 174-78 (ND 127-54; SD 47-24), Aug. 17, 1978. The president had requested $7,168,446,986 in supplemental funds for fiscal 1978.

630. HR 13467. Second Supplemental Appropriations, Fiscal 1978. Mahon, D-Texas, motion that the House recede from its disagreement to the Senate amendment appropriating $54,853,000 for the new Hart Senate office building. Rejected 133-245: R 16-119; D 117-126 (ND 84-85; SD 33-41), Aug. 17, 1978.

KEY

Y Voted for (yea).
✓ Paired for.
† Announced for.
# CQ Poll for.
N Voted against (nay).
X Paired against.
- Announced against.
▮ CQ Poll against.
P Voted "present."
● Voted "present" to avoid possible conflict of interest.
? Did not vote or otherwise make a position known.

	626	627	628	629	630
ALABAMA					
1 Edwards	Y	Y	N	N	N
2 Dickinson	Y	Y	N	N	N
3 Nichols	Y	N	Y	N	N
4 Bevill	Y	N	Y	Y	N
5 Flippo	Y	N	Y	Y	N
6 Buchanan	N	Y	N	N	N
7 Flowers	?	?	?	?	?
ALASKA					
AL Young	#	#	#	#	▮
ARIZONA					
1 Rhodes	Y	N	N	N	Y
2 Udall	N	N	Y	Y	N
3 Stump	Y	Y	N	N	N
4 Rudd	Y	Y	N	N	N
ARKANSAS					
1 Alexander	?	N	Y	Y	Y
2 Tucker	N	N	Y	Y	N
3 Hammerschmidt	Y	Y	N	N	N
4 Thornton	N	N	Y	Y	Y
CALIFORNIA					
1 Johnson	N	N	Y	Y	Y
2 Clausen	N	Y	N	N	N
3 Moss	?	?	?	Y	Y
4 Leggett	N	N	Y	Y	Y
5 Burton, J.	N	Y	N	N	P
6 Burton, P.	N	N	Y	Y	Y
7 Miller	?	?	?	?	?
8 Dellums	▮	▮	#	Y	▮
9 Stark	N	N	Y	N	Y
10 Edwards	N	N	Y	Y	?
11 Ryan	N	N	Y	Y	Y
12 McCloskey	Y	Y	N	N	Y
13 Mineta	N	N	Y	Y	Y
14 McFall	N	N	Y	Y	Y
15 Sisk	?	?	?	?	?
16 Panetta	N	Y	Y	N	N
17 Krebs	N	N	Y	N	Y
18 Vacancy					
19 Lagomarsino	Y	Y	N	N	N
20 Goldwater	Y	Y	N	N	Y
21 Corman	N	N	Y	Y	Y
22 Moorhead	Y	Y	N	N	N
23 Beilenson	N	N	Y	N	N
24 Waxman	N	N	Y	Y	Y
25 Roybal	N	N	Y	Y	Y
26 Rousselot	Y	Y	N	N	N
27 Dornan	Y	Y	N	N	N
28 Burke	X	X	✓	#	#
29 Hawkins	X	N	Y	Y	Y
30 Danielson	N	N	Y	Y	Y
31 Wilson, C.H.	▮	▮	#	#	#
32 Anderson	N	N	Y	N	N
33 Clawson	Y	Y	N	N	N
34 Hannaford	Y	Y	Y	Y	N
35 Lloyd	Y	Y	Y	N	Y
36 Brown	N	N	Y	Y	Y
37 Pettis	Y	Y	N	Y	Y
38 Patterson	N	N	Y	Y	N
39 Wiggins	Y	Y	N	N	P
40 Badham	Y	Y	N	N	N
41 Wilson, B.	Y	Y	N	Y	Y
42 Van Deerlin	N	N	Y	Y	N
43 Burgener	Y	Y	N	Y	N
COLORADO					
1 Schroeder	N	Y	Y	N	N
2 Wirth	N	N	Y	N	N
3 Evans	Y	▮	#	?	▮
4 Johnson	Y	Y	N	N	N
5 Armstrong	Y	Y	N	N	N
CONNECTICUT					
1 Cotter	N	N	Y	Y	Y
2 Dodd	N	N	Y	Y	P
3 Giaimo	N	N	Y	Y	Y
4 McKinney	N	Y	N	N	Y
5 Sarasin	N	?	▮	▮	▮
6 Moffett	N	N	Y	N	N
DELAWARE					
AL Evans	N	N	N	N	N
FLORIDA					
1 Sikes	✓	✓	X	?	?
2 Fuqua	Y	N	Y	Y	N
3 Bennett	Y	N	N	N	N
4 Chappell	Y	Y	N	Y	Y
5 Kelly	Y	Y	N	N	N
6 Young	Y	Y	N	N	N
7 Gibbons	Y	N	N	N	N
8 Ireland	Y	?	N	N	N
9 Frey	?	?	X	?	?
10 Bafalis	Y	Y	N	N	N
11 Rogers	Y	▮	Y	Y	Y
12 Burke	Y	Y	N	N	N
13 Lehman	Y	N	Y	#	N
14 Pepper	N	N	Y	Y	Y
15 Fascell	Y	N	Y	#	#
GEORGIA					
1 Ginn	Y	Y	Y	Y	Y
2 Mathis	Y	Y	N	N	N
3 Brinkley	Y	Y	Y	Y	N
4 Levitas	Y	Y	Y	N	Y
5 Fowler	N	Y	Y	?	?
6 Flynt	?	?	?	?	?
7 McDonald	✓	✓	X	X	▮
8 Evans	Y	Y	N	N	N
9 Jenkins	Y	N	Y	Y	#
10 Barnard	Y	Y	Y	N	Y
HAWAII					
1 Heftel	N	N	Y	Y	N
2 Akaka	N	N	Y	Y	Y
IDAHO					
1 Symms	Y	Y	N	N	N
2 Hansen, G.	Y	Y	N	N	N
ILLINOIS					
1 Metcalfe	N	N	Y	Y	Y
2 Murphy	N	N	Y	Y	Y
3 Russo	N	N	Y	N	N
4 Derwinski	N	Y	N	N	Y
5 Fary	N	N	Y	Y	Y
6 Hyde	N	Y	N	N	N
7 Collins	N	N	Y	Y	Y
8 Rostenkowski	N	N	Y	Y	Y
9 Yates	N	N	Y	Y	Y
10 Mikva	N	N	Y	#	▮
11 Annunzio	N	N	Y	Y	Y
12 Crane	Y	Y	N	N	N
13 McClory	Y	Y	N	N	N
14 Erlenborn	Y	N	N	N	N
15 Corcoran	Y	Y	N	N	N
16 Anderson	N	N	N	N	Y
17 O'Brien	Y	Y	N	N	N
18 Michel	Y	#	N	Y	Y
19 Railsback	N	N	N	N	N
20 Findley	Y	Y	N	N	N
21 Madigan	N	Y	N	N	N
22 Shipley	?	?	?	?	?
23 Price	N	N	Y	Y	Y
24 Simon	N	N	Y	Y	Y
INDIANA					
1 Benjamin	N	N	Y	Y	Y
2 Fithian	Y	Y	N	N	N
3 Brademas	N	N	Y	Y	Y
4 Quayle	Y	Y	N	N	N
5 Hillis	Y	Y	N	N	N
6 Evans	Y	Y	N	N	N
7 Myers, J.	Y	Y	N	N	N
8 Cornwell	Y	N	Y	Y	N
9 Hamilton	Y	N	Y	Y	N
10 Sharp	Y	N	Y	N	N
11 Jacobs	Y	N	N	N	N
IOWA					
1 Leach	Y	Y	N	N	N
2 Blouin	N	N	Y	N	N
3 Grassley	Y	Y	N	N	N
4 Smith	Y	N	Y	Y	Y
5 Harkin	Y	N	N	N	N
6 Bedell	N	N	Y	Y	N

Democrats ***Republicans***

	626	627	628	629	630
KANSAS					
1 Sebelius	Y	Y	N	N	N
2 Keys	N	N	Y	N	N
3 Winn	Y	Y	N	N	N
4 Glickman	Y	N	Y	N	N
5 Skubitz	N	N	N	N	Y
KENTUCKY					
1 Hubbard	Y	Y	Y	Y	N
2 Natcher	N	N	Y	Y	Y
3 Mazzoli	N	N	Y	Y	Y
4 Snyder	Y	Y	N	N	N
5 Carter	N	Y	N	Y	Y
6 Breckinridge	Y	N	Y	Y	Y
7 Perkins	N	N	Y	Y	N
LOUISIANA					
1 Livingston	N	Y	N	Y	N
2 Boggs	N	N	Y	Y	Y
3 Treen	Y	Y	N	Y	N
4 Waggonner	Y	N	Y	N	Y
5 Huckaby	?	?	X	?	?
6 Moore	Y	Y	N	N	N
7 Breaux	Y	Y	N	N	N
8 Long	N	N	Y	Y	N
MAINE					
1 Emery	N	N	Y	N	N
2 Cohen	N	N	N	N	N
MARYLAND					
1 Bauman	Y	Y	N	N	N
2 Long	Y	N	Y	Y	Y
3 Mikulski	N	N	Y	Y	N
4 Holt	Y	Y	N	N	N
5 Spellman	N	N	Y	Y	N
6 Byron	Y	Y	N	N	N
7 Mitchell	N	N	Y	Y	Y
8 Steers	Y	N	Y	Y	N
MASSACHUSETTS					
1 Conte	N	N	N	N	N
2 Boland	N	N	Y	Y	N
3 Early	N	N	N	Y	N
4 Drinan	N	N	Y	N	N
5 Tsongas	N	?	?	?	?
6 Harrington	▮	▮	#	#	▮
7 Markey	N	N	Y	Y	N
8 O'Neill					
9 Moakley	N	N	Y	Y	N
10 Heckler	N	N	N	N	Y
11 Burke	N	N	Y	Y	Y
12 Studds	N	N	Y	Y	N
MICHIGAN					
1 Conyers	N	N	N	N	#
2 Pursell	N	N	N	N	?
3 Brown	Y	Y	N	N	N
4 Stockman	Y	Y	N	N	N
5 Sawyer	Y	Y	N	N	N
6 Carr	N	Y	N	N	Y
7 Kildee	N	N	Y	N	N
8 Traxler	N	Y	Y	Y	Y
9 Vander Jagt	N	Y	N	N	N
10 Cederberg	N	Y	N	?	?
11 Ruppe	N	N	N	N	N
12 Bonior	N	N	Y	N	N
13 Diggs	N	N	Y	N	Y
14 Nedzi	N	N	Y	Y	Y
15 Ford	N	?	Y	Y	Y
16 Dingell	N	N	Y	Y	N
17 Brodhead	N	Y	Y	Y	N
18 Blanchard	N	N	Y	N	Y
19 Broomfield	Y	Y	N	N	N
MINNESOTA					
1 Quie	Y	N	N	Y	N
2 Hagedorn	?	?	?	?	?
3 Frenzel	Y	N	N	N	N
4 Vento	?	N	Y	Y	N
5 Fraser	?	?	?	?	?
6 Nolan	N	N	Y	Y	Y
7 Stangeland	#	#	X	▮	▮
8 Oberstar	N	N	Y	Y	N
MISSISSIPPI					
1 Whitten	N	N	Y	Y	N
2 Bowen	Y	Y	Y	N	N
3 Montgomery	Y	Y	Y	N	N
4 Cochran	Y	Y	N	N	N
5 Lott	Y	Y	N	N	P
MISSOURI					
1 Clay	N	?	Y	N	Y
2 Young	N	N	Y	Y	N
3 Gephardt	N	N	Y	N	N

	626	627	628	629	630
4 Skelton	Y	Y	Y	Y	N
5 Bolling	N	N	Y	#	#
6 Coleman	Y	Y	N	N	N
7 Taylor	Y	Y	N	N	N
8 Ichord	Y	Y	N	N	N
9 Volkmer	Y	N	Y	N	Y
10 Burlison	Y	N	Y	Y	Y
MONTANA					
1 Baucus	N	N	N	N	?
2 Marlenee	Y	Y	N	Y	N
NEBRASKA					
1 Thone	Y	Y	N	N	N
2 Cavanaugh	Y	N	N	N	N
3 Smith	Y	Y	N	N	N
NEVADA					
AL Santini	N	N	N	Y	N
NEW HAMPSHIRE					
1 D'Amours	N	N	Y	N	N
2 Cleveland	Y	Y	N	Y	N
NEW JERSEY					
1 Florio	N	N	Y	Y	N
2 Hughes	N	N	N	N	N
3 Howard	N	N	Y	Y	Y
4 Thompson	X	X	✓	✓	?
5 Fenwick	Y	N	N	N	N
6 Forsythe	Y	N	N	N	N
7 Maguire	N	N	Y	N	Y
8 Roe	N	N	Y	Y	N
9 Hollenbeck	N	N	N	N	N
10 Rodino	X	X	✓	#	▮
11 Minish	N	N	Y	Y	N
12 Rinaldo	N	N	N	N	N
13 Meyner	X	▮	✓	Y	Y
14 LeFante	▮	X	✓	#	▮
15 Patten	N	N	Y	Y	Y
NEW MEXICO					
1 Lujan	Y	Y	N	N	N
2 Runnels	Y	Y	N	N	N
NEW YORK					
1 Pike	Y	N	N	N	N
2 Downey	N	N	Y	Y	Y
3 Ambro	N	N	Y	Y	N
4 Lent	N	N	N	Y	N
5 Wydler	N	N	N	N	N
6 Wolff	N	N	Y	Y	N
7 Addabbo	N	N	Y	Y	Y
8 Rosenthal	N	N	Y	Y	▮
9 Delaney	N	N	Y	Y	Y
10 Biaggi	N	N	Y	Y	Y
11 Scheuer	N	N	Y	Y	P
12 Chisholm	N	N	Y	Y	Y
13 Solarz	N	N	Y	N	N
14 Richmond	N	N	Y	Y	N
15 Zeferetti	N	N	Y	Y	Y
16 Holtzman	N	N	Y	N	Y
17 Murphy	N	N	Y	Y	Y
18 Green	N	N	N	Y	N
19 Rangel	N	N	Y	Y	N
20 Weiss	N	N	Y	N	N
21 Garcia	N	N	Y	Y	Y
22 Bingham	N	N	Y	Y	Y
23 Caputo	N	Y	N	N	N
24 Ottinger	N	N	N	Y	Y
25 Fish	N	N	N	N	N
26 Gilman	N	N	N	N	N
27 McHugh	N	N	Y	Y	N
28 Stratton	N	N	Y	Y	Y
29 Pattison	N	N	Y	N	Y
30 McEwen	N	N	N	N	Y
31 Mitchell	N	Y	N	N	N
32 Hanley	N	N	Y	Y	Y
33 Walsh	N	Y	N	N	N
34 Horton	N	N	N	N	N
35 Conable	Y	N	N	N	N
36 LaFalce	N	N	Y	N	N
37 Nowak	N	N	Y	Y	Y
38 Kemp	Y	Y	N	N	N
39 Lundine	N	N	Y	Y	Y
NORTH CAROLINA					
1 Jones	Y	Y	Y	Y	N
2 Fountain	✓	#	▮	▮	▮
3 Whitley	Y	Y	Y	N	N
4 Andrews	Y	Y	Y	Y	Y
5 Neal	Y	Y	N	N	N
6 Preyer	Y	N	Y	#	Y
7 Rose	Y	Y	Y	?	Y
8 Hefner	Y	Y	Y	Y	N

	626	627	628	629	630
9 Martin	Y	Y	N	N	N
10 Broyhill	Y	Y	N	N	N
11 Gudger	Y	Y	N	N	N
NORTH DAKOTA					
AL Andrews	N	Y	N	Y	N
OHIO					
1 Gradison	Y	N	N	Y	N
2 Luken	Y	N	N	N	N
3 Whalen	N	N	Y	N	Y
4 Guyer	#	#	▮	N	N
5 Latta	Y	Y	N	N	N
6 Harsha	Y	Y	N	N	N
7 Brown	Y	Y	N	N	N
8 Kindness	Y	Y	N	N	N
9 Ashley	N	?	Y	Y	N
10 Miller	Y	Y	N	N	N
11 Stanton	N	N	N	Y	N
12 Devine	Y	Y	N	N	N
13 Pease	Y	N	Y	N	N
14 Seiberling	N	N	Y	Y	P
15 Wylie	Y	Y	N	N	N
16 Regula	N	N	N	Y	N
17 Ashbrook	Y	Y	N	N	N
18 Applegate	N	N	Y	Y	N
19 Carney	N	N	Y	Y	Y
20 Oakar	N	Y	Y	Y	N
21 Stokes	X	?	✓	?	?
22 Vanik	N	N	Y	N	N
23 Mottl	Y	Y	N	N	N
OKLAHOMA					
1 Jones	Y	Y	Y	N	N
2 Risenhoover	✓	✓	?	?	?
3 Watkins	Y	Y	Y	Y	N
4 Steed	Y	N	Y	Y	Y
5 Edwards	Y	Y	N	N	N
6 English	Y	Y	Y	N	N
OREGON					
1 AuCoin	N	N	N	N	N
2 Ullman	N	N	Y	Y	Y
3 Duncan	Y	N	Y	Y	N
4 Weaver	N	N	N	N	N
PENNSYLVANIA					
1 Myers, M.	N	N	Y	Y	Y
2 Nix	N	N	Y	Y	Y
3 Lederer	N	N	Y	Y	Y
4 Eilberg	N	N	Y	Y	Y
5 Schulze	?	?	?	?	?
6 Yatron	Y	Y	Y	Y	N
7 Edgar	N	N	Y	N	N
8 Kostmayer	N	Y	N	N	N
9 Shuster	Y	Y	N	N	N
10 McDade	N	N	N	Y	N
11 Flood	N	N	Y	Y	Y
12 Murtha	N	N	Y	Y	Y
13 Coughlin	Y	N	N	Y	Y
14 Moorhead	N	N	Y	Y	Y
15 Rooney	N	N	Y	Y	Y
16 Walker	Y	Y	N	N	N
17 Ertel	Y	N	N	N	N
18 Walgren	N	N	Y	Y	?
19 Goodling, W.	N	Y	N	N	N
20 Gaydos	N	N	Y	Y	Y
21 Dent	▮	▮	#	#	▮
22 Murphy	N	Y	N	Y	N
23 Ammerman	Y	N	Y	Y	N
24 Marks	N	Y	N	Y	Y
25 Myers, G.	Y	N	N	N	N
RHODE ISLAND					
1 St Germain	N	N	Y	Y	N
2 Beard	N	N	Y	Y	Y
SOUTH CAROLINA					
1 Davis	Y	Y	Y	N	N
2 Spence	Y	Y	N	N	N
3 Derrick	N	N	Y	Y	N
4 Mann	Y	N	Y	Y	Y
5 Holland	N	N	Y	?	?
6 Jenrette	#	▮	#	Y	N
SOUTH DAKOTA					
1 Pressler	N	N	N	Y	N
2 Abdnor	Y	Y	N	N	N
TENNESSEE					
1 Quillen	Y	Y	N	Y	N
2 Duncan	Y	Y	N	?	N
3 Lloyd	✓	✓	X	#	▮
4 Gore	N	N	Y	Y	Y
5 Vacancy					
6 Beard	Y	Y	N	N	N

	626	627	628	629	630
7 Jones	Y	Y	N	Y	Y
8 Ford	Y	N	Y	Y	N
TEXAS					
1 Hall	Y	Y	N	N	N
2 Wilson, C.	Y	N	Y	Y	Y
3 Collins	Y	Y	N	N	N
4 Roberts	Y	N	Y	Y	Y
5 Mattox	Y	Y	Y	N	Y
6 Teague	✓	?	?	?	?
7 Archer	Y	Y	N	N	N
8 Eckhardt	N	N	Y	?	Y
9 Brooks	Y	N	Y	Y	Y
10 Pickle	Y	N	Y	N	Y
11 Poage	Y	N	Y	Y	Y
12 Wright	N	N	Y	Y	Y
13 Hightower	N	N	Y	Y	N
14 Young	?	?	?	?	?
15 de la Garza	N	Y	Y	Y	N
16 White	Y	Y	N	Y	Y
17 Burleson	Y	Y	Y	Y	Y
18 Jordan	Y	N	Y	Y	Y
19 Mahon	Y	N	Y	Y	Y
20 Gonzalez	Y	N	Y	Y	Y
21 Krueger	Y	Y	N	Y	N
22 Gammage	Y	Y	N	N	N
23 Kazen	Y	N	Y	Y	N
24 Milford	?	?	Y	?	?
UTAH					
1 McKay	Y	N	Y	Y	Y
2 Marriott	Y	Y	N	N	N
VERMONT					
AL Jeffords	N	N	N	Y	N
VIRGINIA					
1 Trible	Y	Y	N	N	N
2 Whitehurst	Y	Y	N	N	N
3 Satterfield	Y	Y	N	N	N
4 Daniel	Y	Y	N	N	N
5 Daniel	Y	Y	N	N	N
6 Butler	Y	Y	N	N	N
7 Robinson	Y	Y	N	N	N
8 Harris	N	N	N	Y	N
9 Wampler	Y	Y	N	Y	N
10 Fisher	N	N	Y	Y	N
WASHINGTON					
1 Pritchard	Y	N	N	N	N
2 Meeds	N	N	Y	Y	Y
3 Bonker	N	▮	#	Y	N
4 McCormack	Y	N	Y	N	N
5 Foley	Y	N	Y	Y	Y
6 Dicks	Y	N	Y	Y	Y
7 Cunningham	Y	Y	N	N	N
WEST VIRGINIA					
1 Mollohan	N	N	Y	Y	Y
2 Staggers	N	N	Y	Y	Y
3 Slack	N	N	Y	Y	Y
4 Rahall	N	N	Y	Y	Y
WISCONSIN					
1 Aspin	N	N	Y	Y	N
2 Kastenmeier	N	N	Y	Y	▮
3 Baldus	N	N	Y	Y	N
4 Zablocki	N	N	Y	Y	N
5 Reuss	N	N	Y	Y	N
6 Steiger	Y	N	N	N	N
7 Obey	N	N	Y	Y	?
8 Cornell	N	N	Y	Y	N
9 Kasten	?	?	?	?	?
WYOMING					
AL Roncalio	N	N	Y	Y	Y

Democrats ***Republicans***

631. HR 12935. Legislative Branch Appropriations, Fiscal 1979. Adoption of the conference report on the bill to appropriate $1.118 billion (less a 5 percent reduction in payments not required by law) for operations of Congress and related agencies for fiscal 1979. Adopted 255-123: R 54-81; D 201-42 (ND 144-30; SD 57-12), Aug. 17, 1978. The president had requested $1,143,824,100 in new budget authority.

632. HR 12927. Military Construction Appropriations, Fiscal 1979. Adoption of the conference report on the bill to appropriate $3,880,863,000 for construction projects of the Department of Defense for fiscal 1979. Adopted 355-24: R 128-6; D 227-18 (ND 155-18; SD 72-0), Aug. 17, 1978. The president had requested $4,253,-000,000.

633. HR 13468. District of Columbia Appropriations, Fiscal 1979. Adoption of the conference report on the bill to appropriate $1,597,317,700 for fiscal 1979 (the appropriation was composed of $235 million in federal funds and $1,362,317,700 in revenues raised by the city). Adopted 339-31: R 110-20; D 229-11 (ND 163-7; SD 66-4), Aug. 17, 1978. The president had requested $1,745,442,000 in new budget authority.

634. S 9. Outer Continental Shelf Lands. Adoption of the conference report on the bill to revise federal leasing procedures, upgrading environmental standards and to increase state participation in federal decisions regarding the development of oil and gas on the Outer Continental Shelf. Adopted 338-18: R 113-10; D 225-8 (ND 164-0; SD 61-8), Aug. 17, 1978. A "yea" was a vote supporting the president's position.

635. HR 12230. Intelligence Authorizations. Adoption of the conference report on the bill to authorize a secret amount for intelligence operations for fiscal 1979. Adopted 323-30: R 119-0; D 204-30 (ND 135-30; SD 69-0), Aug. 17, 1978.

636. HR 10898. United States Railway Association. Adoption of the rule (H Res 1321) providing for House floor consideration of the bill to authorize appropriations for the United States Railway Association for fiscal 1979. Adopted 323-6: R 106-4; D 217-2 (ND 155-1; SD 62-1), Aug. 17, 1978.

637. HR 10898. United States Railway Association. Passage of the bill to authorize $27.2 million for the United States Railway Association for fiscal 1979; to permit the association to modify loan guarantees to permit the continuation of rail service found by the association to be desirable; and to extend by 195 days the 900-day period during which the Consolidated Rail Corp. was permitted to sell surplus trackage, stations and rights of way to states at the net liquidation price. Passed 253-67: R 67-40; D 186-27 (ND 150-5; SD 36-22), Aug. 17, 1978.

KEY

Y Voted for (yea).
✓ Paired for.
† Announced for.
# CQ Poll for.
N Voted against (nay).
X Paired against.
\- Announced against.
▮ CQ Poll against.
P Voted "present."
● Voted "present" to avoid possible conflict of interest.
? Did not vote or otherwise make a position known.

	631	632	633	634	635	636	637
ALABAMA							
1 Edwards	Y	Y	Y	Y	Y	?	?
2 Dickinson	Y	Y	Y	Y	Y	Y	N
3 Nichols	Y	Y	Y	Y	Y	Y	N
4 Bevill	Y	Y	Y	Y	Y	Y	N
5 Flippo	Y	Y	?	?	?	?	?
6 Buchanan	N	Y	Y	Y	Y	Y	Y
7 Flowers	?	?	?	?	?	?	?
ALASKA							
AL Young	#	#	▮	#	#	#	#
ARIZONA							
1 Rhodes	N	Y	Y	Y	Y	Y	Y
2 Udall	Y	Y	Y	Y	Y	Y	Y
3 Stump	N	Y	N	▮	#	#	▮
4 Rudd	N	Y	N	Y	Y	Y	N
ARKANSAS							
1 Alexander	Y	Y	Y	?	?	Y	?
2 Tucker	#	Y	Y	Y	Y	Y	Y
3 Hammerschmidt	N	Y	Y	N	Y	Y	N
4 Thornton	Y	Y	Y	Y	Y	Y	Y
CALIFORNIA							
1 Johnson	Y	Y	Y	Y	Y	Y	Y
2 Clausen	?	Y	Y	Y	Y	Y	?
3 Moss	Y	Y	Y	Y	Y	Y	Y
4 Leggett	Y	?	Y	?	Y	?	Y
5 Burton, J.	N	N	Y	Y	N	Y	Y
6 Burton, P.	Y	Y	Y	Y	N	?	?
7 Miller	?	?	?	?	?	?	?
8 Dellums	Y	N	Y	Y	N	Y	Y
9 Stark	#	▮	Y	Y	N	Y	Y
10 Edwards	Y	N	Y	Y	Y	Y	Y
11 Ryan	Y	Y	Y	Y	Y	Y	?
12 McCloskey	Y	Y	Y	Y	Y	Y	N
13 Mineta	Y	Y	Y	Y	Y	Y	Y
14 McFall	Y	Y	Y	Y	Y	Y	Y
15 Sisk	?	?	?	?	?	?	?
16 Panetta	Y	Y	Y	Y	Y	Y	Y
17 Krebs	Y	Y	Y	Y	Y	Y	Y
18 Vacancy							
19 Lagomarsino	N	Y	Y	Y	Y	Y	N
20 Goldwater	N	Y	Y	?	Y	Y	N
21 Corman	Y	Y	Y	Y	Y	Y	Y
22 Moorhead	N	Y	N	Y	Y	Y	N
23 Beilenson	Y	Y	Y	Y	N	Y	Y
24 Waxman	Y	Y	#	Y	Y	#	Y
25 Roybal	Y	Y	Y	Y	N	Y	Y
26 Rousselot	N	Y	N	Y	Y	Y	N
27 Dornan	N	Y	N	Y	Y	Y	N
28 Burke	#	#	#	#	#	#	#
29 Hawkins	?	Y	Y	Y	N	Y	Y
30 Danielson	?	Y	Y	Y	Y	Y	Y
31 Wilson, C.H.	#	#	#	#	#	#	#
32 Anderson	N	N	Y	Y	N	Y	N
33 Clawson	N	Y	Y	Y	?	?	?
34 Hannaford	Y	Y	Y	Y	Y	#	#
35 Lloyd	Y	Y	Y	Y	Y	Y	Y
36 Brown	Y	Y	Y	?	Y	Y	Y
37 Pettis	Y	Y	Y	?	Y	Y	Y
38 Patterson	Y	Y	Y	Y	Y	Y	Y
39 Wiggins	Y	Y	N	#	Y	#	Y
40 Badham	N	Y	Y	Y	Y	Y	N
41 Wilson, B.	Y	Y	Y	Y	Y	Y	N
42 Van Deerlin	Y	Y	Y	Y	Y	Y	?
43 Burgener	N	Y	Y	Y	Y	?	?
COLORADO							
1 Schroeder	N	Y	Y	Y	P	Y	Y
2 Wirth	N	Y	Y	Y	Y	Y	Y
3 Evans	#	#	#	#	#	#	#
4 Johnson	Y	Y	Y	?	?	?	?
5 Armstrong	N	Y	?	?	?	?	?
CONNECTICUT							
1 Cotter	Y	Y	Y	Y	Y	Y	Y
2 Dodd	Y	Y	Y	Y	Y	Y	Y
3 Giaimo	Y	Y	Y	Y	Y	Y	Y
4 McKinney	Y	Y	Y	Y	Y	Y	Y
5 Sarasin	#	#	#	#	#	#	#
6 Moffett	Y	Y	Y	Y	N	Y	Y
DELAWARE							
AL Evans	N	Y	Y	Y	Y	Y	Y
FLORIDA							
1 Sikes	?	?	?	?	?	?	?
2 Fuqua	N	Y	Y	Y	Y	Y	#
3 Bennett	N	Y	Y	Y	Y	Y	N
4 Chappell	Y	Y	Y	Y	Y	Y	Y
5 Kelly	N	Y	N	Y	Y	Y	N
6 Young	N	Y	Y	Y	Y	Y	N
7 Gibbons	N	Y	Y	Y	Y	Y	Y
8 Ireland	?	?	Y	Y	Y	?	?
9 Frey	?	?	?	?	?	?	?
10 Bafalis	N	Y	Y	Y	?	Y	N
11 Rogers	Y	Y	Y	Y	Y	Y	Y
12 Burke	N	Y	Y	Y	Y	Y	Y
13 Lehman	Y	Y	Y	Y	Y	Y	Y
14 Pepper	Y	Y	Y	Y	Y	Y	Y
15 Fascell	#	#	#	#	#	#	#
GEORGIA							
1 Ginn	Y	Y	Y	Y	Y	Y	Y
2 Mathis	Y	Y	Y	Y	Y	?	N
3 Brinkley	Y	Y	Y	Y	Y	?	?
4 Levitas	N	Y	Y	Y	Y	Y	N
5 Fowler	?	?	?	?	?	?	?
6 Flynt	?	?	?	?	?	?	?
7 McDonald	X	#	▮	▮	#	▮	▮
8 Evans	Y	Y	Y	N	Y	N	N
9 Jenkins	#	#	#	#	#	#	#
10 Barnard	?	?	?	?	?	?	?
HAWAII							
1 Heftel	N	Y	Y	Y	Y	Y	Y
2 Akaka	Y	Y	Y	Y	Y	Y	Y
IDAHO							
1 Symms	N	Y	N	N	Y	N	?
2 Hansen, G.	N	Y	N	N	Y	Y	N
ILLINOIS							
1 Metcalfe	Y	Y	Y	Y	N	Y	Y
2 Murphy	Y	Y	Y	Y	Y	Y	Y
3 Russo	N	Y	Y	Y	Y	Y	Y
4 Derwinski	N	Y	Y	Y	Y	Y	Y
5 Fary	Y	Y	Y	Y	Y	Y	Y
6 Hyde	Y	Y	Y	Y	Y	Y	Y
7 Collins	Y	Y	Y	Y	Y	?	?
8 Rostenkowski	Y	Y	Y	Y	Y	Y	Y
9 Yates	Y	Y	#	#	#	#	#
10 Mikva	#	#	#	#	▮	#	#
11 Annunzio	Y	Y	Y	Y	Y	Y	Y
12 Crane	N	Y	N	#	#	#	▮
13 McClory	Y	Y	Y	Y	Y	Y	Y
14 Erlenborn	Y	Y	Y	Y	Y	Y	Y
15 Corcoran	Y	Y	Y	Y	Y	Y	N
16 Anderson	Y	Y	Y	Y	Y	Y	Y
17 O'Brien	Y	Y	Y	Y	Y	Y	Y
18 Michel	Y	Y	Y	Y	Y	Y	#
19 Railsback	Y	Y	Y	Y	Y	Y	Y
20 Findley	Y	Y	Y	Y	Y	Y	N
21 Madigan	N	Y	Y	Y	Y	Y	Y
22 Shipley	?	?	?	?	?	?	?
23 Price	Y	Y	Y	Y	Y	Y	Y
24 Simon	Y	Y	Y	Y	Y	Y	Y
INDIANA							
1 Benjamin	Y	Y	Y	Y	Y	Y	Y
2 Fithian	N	Y	N	?	?	?	Y
3 Brademas	Y	Y	Y	Y	Y	Y	Y
4 Quayle	N	Y	Y	Y	Y	Y	N
5 Hillis	Y	Y	Y	Y	Y	?	?
6 Evans	N	Y	N	Y	Y	Y	Y
7 Myers, J.	N	Y	Y	Y	Y	Y	Y
8 Cornwell	?	?	?	?	?	?	?
9 Hamilton	Y	Y	Y	Y	Y	Y	Y
10 Sharp	Y	Y	Y	Y	Y	Y	Y
11 Jacobs	N	Y	Y	Y	Y	Y	N
IOWA							
1 Leach	N	Y	Y	Y	Y	Y	N
2 Blouin	N	Y	Y	Y	Y	Y	Y
3 Grassley	N	Y	Y	Y	Y	Y	Y
4 Smith	Y	Y	Y	Y	Y	Y	Y
5 Harkin	Y	N	Y	Y	Y	Y	Y
6 Bedell	Y	N	Y	Y	N	Y	Y

Democrats ***Republicans***

	631	632	633	634	635	636	637
KANSAS							
1 Sebelius	Y	Y	Y	Y	#	#	▮
2 Keys	N	Y	Y	Y	Y	Y	Y
3 Winn	Y	Y	#	Y	Y	Y	Y
4 Glickman	Y	Y	Y	Y	Y	Y	N
5 Skubitz	Y	Y	Y	Y	Y	?	Y
KENTUCKY							
1 Hubbard	N	Y	Y	Y	Y	Y	Y
2 Natcher	Y	Y	Y	Y	Y	Y	Y
3 Mazzoli	Y	Y	Y	Y	Y	Y	Y
4 Snyder	N	Y	Y	N	Y	Y	N
5 Carter	Y	Y	Y	Y	Y	Y	Y
6 Breckinridge	Y	Y	Y	Y	Y	Y	Y
7 Perkins	Y	Y	Y	Y	Y	Y	Y
LOUISIANA							
1 Livingston	Y	Y	Y	Y	?	?	?
2 Boggs	Y	Y	#	Y	Y	Y	Y
3 Treen	Y	Y	Y	Y	Y	Y	Y
4 Waggonner	Y	Y	Y	Y	Y	Y	#
5 Huckaby	?	?	?	?	?	?	?
6 Moore	Y	Y	Y	N	Y	Y	Y
7 Breaux	Y	Y	Y	Y	Y	Y	Y
8 Long	Y	Y	Y	Y	Y	Y	Y
MAINE							
1 Emery	N	Y	Y	Y	Y	Y	Y
2 Cohen	N	Y	Y	Y	Y	Y	Y
MARYLAND							
1 Bauman	N	Y	N	Y	Y	N	N
2 Long	Y	Y	Y	Y	Y	Y	Y
3 Mikulski	N	Y	Y	Y	Y	Y	Y
4 Holt	N	Y	Y	Y	Y	Y	N
5 Spellman	Y	Y	Y	Y	Y	Y	Y
6 Byron	N	Y	Y	Y	Y	Y	Y
7 Mitchell	Y	Y	Y	Y	N	Y	Y
8 Steers	N	Y	Y	Y	Y	Y	Y
MASSACHUSETTS							
1 Conte	Y	Y	Y	Y	Y	Y	Y
2 Boland	Y	Y	Y	Y	Y	#	#
3 Early	Y	Y	Y	Y	Y	Y	Y
4 Drinan	Y	Y	Y	Y	N	Y	Y
5 Tsongas	?	?	?	?	?	?	?
6 Harrington	#	▮	#	#	▮	#	#
7 Markey	Y	Y	Y	Y	N	Y	Y
8 O'Neill							
9 Moakley	Y	Y	Y	Y	Y	Y	Y
10 Heckler	Y	N	Y	Y	Y	Y	Y
11 Burke	Y	Y	Y	Y	Y	Y	Y
12 Studds	Y	Y	Y	Y	P	Y	Y
MICHIGAN							
1 Conyers	Y	N	Y	Y	▮	#	Y
2 Pursell	Y	Y	Y	Y	?	?	?
3 Brown	N	Y	Y	?	Y	Y	Y
4 Stockman	Y	Y	Y	Y	Y	Y	N
5 Sawyer	Y	Y	Y	Y	Y	Y	Y
6 Carr	Y	N	Y	Y	Y	Y	Y
7 Kildee	Y	Y	Y	Y	Y	Y	Y
8 Traxler	Y	Y	#	#	#	#	#
9 Vander Jagt	Y	Y	Y	Y	Y	Y	Y
10 Cederberg	?	?	?	?	?	?	?
11 Ruppe	N	Y	Y	Y	?	Y	N
12 Bonior	Y	Y	Y	Y	N	Y	Y
13 Diggs	#	Y	#	#	#	#	#
14 Nedzi	Y	Y	Y	Y	Y	Y	Y
15 Ford	Y	Y	Y	Y	Y	Y	Y
16 Dingell	Y	Y	Y	Y	Y	Y	Y
17 Brodhead	Y	Y	Y	Y	Y	Y	Y
18 Blanchard	Y	Y	Y	Y	Y	Y	Y
19 Broomfield	N	Y	Y	Y	Y	#	#
MINNESOTA							
1 Quie	Y	Y	?	?	?	?	?
2 Hagedorn	?	?	?	?	?	?	?
3 Frenzel	N	N	Y	Y	Y	Y	Y
4 Vento	Y	N	?	?	?	?	?
5 Fraser	?	?	?	?	?	?	?
6 Nolan	Y	N	?	?	?	?	?
7 Stangeland	#	#	#	▮	#	#	▮
8 Oberstar	Y	Y	Y	Y	Y	Y	Y
MISSISSIPPI							
1 Whitten	Y	Y	Y	Y	Y	Y	Y
2 Bowen	N	Y	Y	Y	Y	Y	Y
3 Montgomery	N	Y	Y	Y	Y	Y	N
4 Cochran	N	Y	Y	Y	Y	Y	Y
5 Lott	N	Y	N	Y	Y	Y	Y
MISSOURI							
1 Clay	?	?	?	Y	N	Y	Y
2 Young	Y	Y	Y	Y	Y	Y	Y
3 Gephardt	Y	Y	N	Y	Y	Y	Y

	631	632	633	634	635	636	637
4 Skelton	Y	Y	Y	Y	Y	Y	Y
5 Bolling	#	#	#	#	#	#	#
6 Coleman	N	Y	N	Y	Y	Y	Y
7 Taylor	N	Y	Y	Y	Y	?	?
8 Ichord	N	Y	Y	Y	Y	?	?
9 Volkmer	Y	Y	N	Y	Y	Y	Y
10 Burlison	Y	Y	Y	Y	Y	Y	Y
MONTANA							
1 Baucus	N	Y	Y	Y	Y	?	?
2 Marlenee	N	Y	Y	Y	Y	Y	Y
NEBRASKA							
1 Thone	N	Y	Y	Y	?	?	?
2 Cavanaugh	N	Y	Y	Y	Y	Y	Y
3 Smith	?	?	?	?	?	?	?
NEVADA							
AL Santini	N	Y	Y	Y	Y	Y	#
NEW HAMPSHIRE							
1 D'Amours	Y	Y	Y	Y	Y	Y	Y
2 Cleveland	N	Y	Y	Y	Y	Y	Y
NEW JERSEY							
1 Florio	Y	Y	Y	Y	Y	Y	Y
2 Hughes	N	N	Y	Y	Y	Y	Y
3 Howard	Y	Y	Y	Y	Y	Y	Y
4 Thompson	✓	?	?	?	?	?	?
5 Fenwick	N	N	Y	Y	Y	Y	Y
6 Forsythe	N	N	Y	N	Y	Y	Y
7 Maguire	Y	N	Y	Y	N	Y	Y
8 Roe	Y	Y	Y	Y	Y	Y	Y
9 Hollenbeck	Y	Y	Y	Y	Y	Y	Y
10 Rodino	✓	#	#	#	#	#	#
11 Minish	Y	Y	Y	Y	Y	Y	Y
12 Rinaldo	Y	Y	Y	Y	Y	Y	Y
13 Meyner	Y	Y	Y	Y	Y	Y	Y
14 LeFante	#	#	#	#	#	#	#
15 Patten	Y	Y	Y	Y	Y	Y	Y
NEW MEXICO							
1 Lujan	N	Y	Y	?	?	?	?
2 Runnels	Y	Y	Y	Y	Y	Y	N
NEW YORK							
1 Pike	Y	Y	Y	Y	Y	N	Y
2 Downey	Y	Y	Y	Y	Y	Y	Y
3 Ambro	Y	Y	Y	Y	Y	Y	Y
4 Lent	Y	Y	Y	Y	?	Y	Y
5 Wydler	Y	Y	Y	Y	Y	Y	Y
6 Wolff	Y	Y	Y	Y	Y	Y	Y
7 Addabbo	Y	Y	Y	Y	Y	Y	?
8 Rosenthal	Y	Y	Y	Y	N	Y	Y
9 Delaney	?	?	?	?	?	?	?
10 Biaggi	Y	Y	Y	Y	Y	Y	Y
11 Scheuer	Y	N	Y	Y	N	Y	Y
12 Chisholm	Y	N	Y	#	N	Y	Y
13 Solarz	Y	Y	Y	Y	Y	Y	Y
14 Richmond	Y	Y	Y	Y	N	Y	Y
15 Zeferetti	Y	Y	Y	#	#	#	#
16 Holtzman	Y	N	Y	Y	N	Y	Y
17 Murphy	Y	Y	Y	Y	Y	Y	Y
18 Green	Y	Y	Y	Y	Y	Y	Y
19 Rangel	Y	N	Y	Y	Y	Y	Y
20 Weiss	Y	Y	Y	Y	N	Y	Y
21 Garcia	Y	Y	Y	Y	N	Y	Y
22 Bingham	Y	Y	Y	Y	Y	Y	Y
23 Caputo	Y	Y	Y	N	Y	Y	Y
24 Ottinger	Y	Y	Y	Y	N	Y	Y
25 Fish	Y	Y	Y	Y	?	?	?
26 Gilman	N	Y	Y	Y	Y	Y	Y
27 McHugh	Y	Y	Y	Y	Y	#	Y
28 Stratton	Y	Y	Y	Y	Y	Y	Y
29 Pattison	Y	#	Y	Y	Y	Y	Y
30 McEwen	N	Y	Y	Y	Y	Y	Y
31 Mitchell	Y	Y	Y	Y	Y	Y	Y
32 Hanley	Y	Y	Y	Y	Y	Y	Y
33 Walsh	Y	Y	Y	Y	Y	Y	Y
34 Horton	Y	Y	Y	Y	Y	Y	Y
35 Conable	N	Y	Y	Y	Y	Y	Y
36 LaFalce	N	Y	Y	Y	Y	#	Y
37 Nowak	Y	Y	Y	Y	Y	Y	#
38 Kemp	N	Y	Y	Y	Y	Y	Y
39 Lundine	Y	Y	Y	Y	N	Y	Y
NORTH CAROLINA							
1 Jones	Y	Y	Y	Y	Y	#	#
2 Fountain	#	#	#	#	#	#	#
3 Whitley	Y	Y	Y	Y	Y	Y	N
4 Andrews	Y	Y	Y	Y	Y	Y	Y
5 Neal	N	Y	N	Y	Y	Y	N
6 Preyer	Y	Y	#	#	#	?	Y
7 Rose	Y	Y	?	Y	Y	Y	Y
8 Hefner	Y	Y	Y	Y	Y	Y	Y

	631	632	633	634	635	636	637
9 Martin	N	Y	Y	Y	Y	Y	N
10 Broyhill	N	Y	Y	Y	Y	Y	N
11 Gudger	Y	Y	Y	Y	Y	Y	Y
NORTH DAKOTA							
AL Andrews	Y	Y	Y	Y	Y	Y	?
OHIO							
1 Gradison	N	Y	Y	Y	Y	Y	N
2 Luken	N	Y	Y	Y	Y	Y	Y
3 Whalen	Y	Y	Y	Y	Y	Y	Y
4 Guyer	N	Y	Y	Y	Y	Y	Y
5 Latta	N	Y	N	Y	Y	Y	N
6 Harsha	N	Y	Y	Y	Y	Y	Y
7 Brown	Y	Y	Y	Y	Y	Y	N
8 Kindness	N	Y	Y	Y	Y	Y	Y
9 Ashley	Y	Y	Y	Y	Y	Y	Y
10 Miller	N	N	N	Y	Y	Y	N
11 Stanton	Y	Y	Y	#	#	#	#
12 Devine	N	Y	Y	Y	Y	Y	N
13 Pease	N	Y	Y	Y	Y	Y	Y
14 Seiberling	Y	Y	Y	Y	Y	Y	Y
15 Wylie	N	Y	Y	Y	Y	Y	Y
16 Regula	N	Y	Y	Y	Y	Y	Y
17 Ashbrook	N	Y	N	Y	Y	#	#
18 Applegate	Y	Y	Y	Y	Y	Y	Y
19 Carney	Y	Y	Y	Y	Y	Y	Y
20 Oakar	Y	Y	Y	Y	Y	Y	Y
21 Stokes	?	?	?	?	N	Y	Y
22 Vanik	Y	Y	Y	Y	Y	Y	Y
23 Mottl	N	Y	N	Y	Y	Y	N
OKLAHOMA							
1 Jones	N	Y	Y	Y	Y	Y	N
2 Risenhoover	?	?	?	?	?	?	?
3 Watkins	N	Y	N	Y	Y	Y	N
4 Steed	Y	Y	Y	Y	Y	#	Y
5 Edwards	N	Y	N	Y	Y	N	N
6 English	?	Y	N	Y	Y	Y	N
OREGON							
1 AuCoin	N	N	Y	#	#	#	#
2 Ullman	Y	Y	Y	Y	Y	Y	Y
3 Duncan	Y	Y	Y	Y	Y	Y	Y
4 Weaver	N	Y	N	Y	N	Y	?
PENNSYLVANIA							
1 Myers, M.	Y	Y	Y	Y	Y	Y	Y
2 Nix	Y	?	?	?	?	?	?
3 Lederer	Y	Y	Y	Y	Y	Y	Y
4 Eilberg	Y	Y	Y	Y	Y	Y	Y
5 Schulze	?	?	?	?	?	?	?
6 Yatron	Y	Y	Y	Y	Y	Y	#
7 Edgar	Y	Y	Y	#	Y	Y	Y
8 Kostmayer	N	Y	Y	Y	N	Y	Y
9 Shuster	N	Y	N	Y	Y	Y	Y
10 McDade	Y	Y	?	?	Y	Y	Y
11 Flood	Y	Y	Y	Y	Y	Y	Y
12 Murtha	Y	Y	Y	Y	Y	Y	Y
13 Coughlin	Y	Y	Y	Y	Y	Y	Y
14 Moorhead	Y	Y	Y	Y	Y	Y	Y
15 Rooney	Y	Y	Y	Y	Y	Y	Y
16 Walker	N	Y	Y	Y	Y	Y	N
17 Ertel	N	Y	Y	Y	Y	Y	Y
18 Walgren	N	Y	Y	Y	Y	Y	Y
19 Goodling, W.	N	Y	Y	Y	Y	Y	Y
20 Gaydos	Y	Y	Y	Y	Y	Y	Y
21 Dent	#	#	#	#	#	#	#
22 Murphy	N	Y	Y	Y	Y	Y	Y
23 Ammerman	N	Y	Y	Y	Y	Y	Y
24 Marks	N	Y	Y	Y	Y	Y	Y
25 Myers, G.	N	Y	Y	N	Y	Y	N
RHODE ISLAND							
1 St Germain	Y	Y	Y	Y	Y	?	?
2 Beard	Y	Y	Y	Y	Y	Y	Y
SOUTH CAROLINA							
1 Davis	Y	Y	Y	Y	Y	?	?
2 Spence	N	Y	Y	Y	Y	Y	Y
3 Derrick	Y	Y	Y	#	Y	Y	Y
4 Mann	Y	Y	Y	Y	Y	Y	Y
5 Holland	?	?	?	?	?	?	?
6 Jenrette	Y	Y	Y	Y	Y	Y	Y
SOUTH DAKOTA							
1 Pressler	N	Y	Y	Y	Y	Y	Y
2 Abdnor	N	Y	Y	Y	Y	#	N
TENNESSEE							
1 Quillen	N	Y	N	Y	Y	#	▮
2 Duncan	N	Y	Y	Y	Y	Y	N
3 Lloyd	#	#	#	#	#	#	#
4 Gore	Y	Y	Y	Y	Y	Y	Y
5 Vacancy							
6 Beard	N	Y	Y	Y	Y	Y	#

	631	632	633	634	635	636	637
7 Jones	Y	Y	Y	Y	Y	Y	Y
8 Ford	Y	Y	Y	Y	Y	Y	Y
TEXAS							
1 Hall	Y	Y	Y	N	Y	Y	N
2 Wilson, C.	Y	Y	Y	Y	Y	Y	#
3 Collins	N	N	N	N	Y	N	N
4 Roberts	Y	Y	Y	N	Y	?	?
5 Mattox	N	Y	Y	Y	Y	Y	N
6 Teague	?	?	?	?	?	?	?
7 Archer	N	Y	N	N	Y	Y	N
8 Eckhardt	?	?	Y	?	Y	Y	Y
9 Brooks	Y	Y	Y	Y	Y	Y	Y
10 Pickle	Y	Y	Y	Y	Y	Y	?
11 Poage	Y	Y	Y	N	Y	Y	N
12 Wright	Y	Y	Y	Y	Y	Y	Y
13 Hightower	Y	Y	Y	N	?	?	?
14 Young	?	Y	Y	N	?	?	?
15 de la Garza	Y	Y	Y	Y	Y	Y	N
16 White	Y	Y	Y	Y	Y	Y	#
17 Burleson	Y	Y	Y	Y	Y	Y	N
18 Jordan	Y	Y	Y	Y	Y	Y	Y
19 Mahon	Y	Y	Y	Y	Y	Y	N
20 Gonzalez	Y	Y	Y	Y	Y	Y	N
21 Krueger	Y	Y	Y	N	Y	Y	#
22 Gammage	N	Y	N	N	Y	Y	N
23 Kazen	Y	Y	Y	Y	Y	Y	N
24 Milford	?	?	?	?	?	?	?
UTAH							
1 McKay	Y	Y	Y	Y	Y	Y	Y
2 Marriott	N	Y	Y	Y	Y	#	#
VERMONT							
AL Jeffords	N	Y	Y	Y	Y	Y	Y
VIRGINIA							
1 Trible	N	Y	Y	Y	Y	Y	N
2 Whitehurst	Y	Y	Y	Y	Y	Y	▮
3 Satterfield	Y	Y	Y	Y	Y	Y	N
4 Daniel	Y	Y	Y	Y	Y	Y	Y
5 Daniel	Y	Y	Y	Y	Y	Y	?
6 Butler	Y	Y	Y	Y	Y	Y	Y
7 Robinson	Y	Y	Y	Y	Y	Y	N
8 Harris	Y	Y	Y	Y	Y	Y	Y
9 Wampler	Y	Y	Y	Y	Y	?	?
10 Fisher	Y	Y	Y	Y	Y	Y	Y
WASHINGTON							
1 Pritchard	Y	#	#	#	#	#	#
2 Meeds	Y	Y	Y	Y	Y	Y	Y
3 Bonker	Y	Y	Y	Y	Y	Y	Y
4 McCormack	Y	Y	Y	Y	Y	Y	Y
5 Foley	Y	Y	Y	Y	Y	Y	Y
6 Dicks	Y	?	?	?	?	?	?
7 Cunningham	N	#	▮	#	#	#	▮
WEST VIRGINIA							
1 Mollohan	Y	Y	Y	Y	Y	Y	Y
2 Staggers	Y	Y	Y	Y	Y	Y	Y
3 Slack	Y	Y	Y	Y	Y	Y	Y
4 Rahall	Y	Y	Y	Y	Y	Y	Y
WISCONSIN							
1 Aspin	Y	Y	Y	Y	Y	Y	Y
2 Kastenmeier	Y	N	Y	Y	N	Y	Y
3 Baldus	Y	Y	Y	Y	#	#	#
4 Zablocki	Y	Y	Y	Y	Y	Y	Y
5 Reuss	Y	Y	Y	Y	Y	Y	Y
6 Steiger	▮	#	#	#	#	#	#
7 Obey	Y	Y	Y	Y	Y	Y	Y
8 Cornell	Y	Y	Y	Y	Y	Y	Y
9 Kasten	X	?	?	?	?	?	?
WYOMING							
AL Roncalio	Y	Y	Y	Y	Y	Y	Y

Democrats ***Republicans***

KEY

- Y Voted for (yea).
- ✓ Paired for.
- † Announced for.
- # CQ Poll for.
- N Voted against (nay).
- X Paired against.
- \- Announced against.
- ▮ CQ Poll against.
- P Voted "present."
- ● Voted "present" to avoid possible conflict of interest.
- ? Did not vote or otherwise make a position known.

638. HR 12432. Civil Rights Commission. Treen, R-La., amendment to prohibit the Commission on Civil Rights from appraising or studying and collecting information about laws and policies of the federal government, or any other governmental authority, with respect to the issue of abortion. Adopted 234-131: R 106-14, D 128-117 (ND 81-92; SD 47-25), Sept. 6, 1978.

639. H J Res 1088. New York City Loan Guarantees. Adoption of joint resolution to permit the secretary of the Treasury to guarantee up to $1.65 billion in New York City bonds, as authorized under the New York City Loan Guarantee Act of 1978 (PL 95-339), and to appropriate funds necessary to pay guaranteed loans if the city defaulted on them. Passed 233-132: R 40-80; D 193-52 (ND 156-15; SD 37-37), Sept. 6, 1978. A "yea" was a vote supporting the president's position.

640. HR 7308. Foreign Intelligence Surveillance. McClory, R-Ill., amendment to allow wiretapping of non-U.S. persons without a warrant, provided that a certificate was issued by the attorney general and a designated executive branch official in the area of national security who had been confirmed by the Senate. Adopted 178-176: R 107-11; D 71-165 (ND 30-132; SD 41-33), Sept. 6, 1978. A "nay" was a vote supporting the president's position.

641. HR 7308. Foreign Intelligence Surveillance. Ertel, D-Pa., amendment to eliminate a provision in the bill to establish a special court to hear government applications for warrants to conduct electronic surveillance in the foreign intelligence area. Adopted 224-103: R 96-9; D 128-94 (ND 77-76; SD 51-18), Sept. 6, 1978.

642. HR 10929. Defense Procurement Authorization. Passage, over the president's Aug. 17 veto, of the bill to authorize $36,956,969,000 for Defense Department weapons procurement and military research programs in fiscal 1979. Rejected 191-206: R 107-23; D 84-183 (ND 34-150; SD 50-33), Sept. 7, 1978. A two thirds majority vote (265 in this case) is required for passage over a veto. A "nay" was a vote supporting the president's position.

643. HR 12930. Treasury, Postal Service Appropriations, Fiscal 1979. Brown, R-Ohio, motion to instruct House conferees to the House-Senate conference committee on the bill to appropriate fiscal 1979 funds for the Treasury, Postal Service, Executive Office of the President and other independent agencies to agree to the Senate amendment to prohibit the president from imposing fees or quotas on oil imports. Rejected 194-201: R 124-6; D 70-195 (ND 40-143; SD 30-52), Sept. 7, 1978. A "nay" was a vote supporting the president's position.

	638	639	640	641	642	643
ALABAMA						
1 Edwards	Y	N	Y	Y	N	Y
2 Dickinson	?	?	?	?	Y	Y
3 Nichols	Y	N	#	#	Y	Y
4 Bevill	?	?	?	Y	Y	N
5 Flippo	?	?	?	Y	N	N
6 Buchanan	?	?	Y	Y	Y	Y
7 Flowers	?	?	?	?	N	Y
ALASKA						
AL Young	#	#	#	#	✓	#
ARIZONA						
1 Rhodes	Y	Y	Y	?	Y	Y
2 Udall	N	Y	N	Y	N	N
3 Stump	#	▮	#	#	Y	Y
4 Rudd	Y	N	Y	Y	Y	Y
ARKANSAS						
1 Alexander	?	?	Y	N	Y	N
2 Tucker	N	N	N	N	N	N
3 Hammerschmidt	Y	N	Y	Y	Y	Y
4 Thornton	N	Y	Y	Y	N	N
CALIFORNIA						
1 Johnson	N	Y	N	Y	Y	N
2 Clausen	Y	N	Y	Y	Y	Y
3 Moss	N	Y	?	?	N	Y
4 Leggett	N	Y	?	N	N	N
5 Burton, J.	N	Y	N	N	N	N
6 Burton, P.	N	Y	N	?	N	N
7 Miller	?	?	?	?	?	?
8 Dellums	N	Y	N	N	N	N
9 Stark	N	Y	N	?	N	N
10 Edwards	N	Y	N	N	N	N
11 Ryan	N	Y	N	?	N	N
12 McCloskey	N	Y	N	?	N	N
13 Mineta	N	Y	N	N	N	N
14 McFall	N	Y	N	Y	N	N
15 Sisk	?	?	?	?	?	?
16 Panetta	N	Y	N	Y	N	N
17 Krebs	N	Y	N	Y	N	N
18 Vacancy						
19 Lagomarsino	Y	N	Y	Y	Y	Y
20 Goldwater	Y	N	Y	Y	Y	Y
21 Corman	N	Y	N	N	N	N
22 Moorhead	Y	N	Y	Y	Y	Y
23 Beilenson	▮	#	▮	▮	X	?
24 Waxman	N	Y	N	N	N	▮
25 Roybal	N	Y	N	Y	N	N
26 Rousselot	Y	N	Y	Y	Y	Y
27 Dornan	?	?	?	?	Y	Y
28 Burke	X	#	▮	#	X	▮
29 Hawkins	N	Y	?	?	X	?
30 Danielson	N	Y	N	N	N	N
31 Wilson, C.H.	N	N	#	#	Y	N
32 Anderson	N	Y	N	Y	N	N
33 Clawson	?	?	?	?	✓	?
34 Hannaford	N	Y	N	Y	Y	N
35 Lloyd	N	Y	Y	N	Y	N
36 Brown	N	Y	N	N	N	N
37 Pettis	?	?	?	?	✓	?
38 Patterson	N	Y	N	N	N	N
39 Wiggins	▮	▮	#	#	#	▮
40 Badham	Y	N	Y	Y	Y	Y
41 Wilson, B.	Y	N	Y	Y	Y	Y
42 Van Deerlin	N	Y	N	?	N	N
43 Burgener	Y	N	Y	Y	Y	Y
COLORADO						
1 Schroeder	N	N	N	Y	N	N
2 Wirth	▮	#	▮	▮	N	N
3 Evans	N	Y	#	#	N	N
4 Johnson	?	?	?	?	Y	Y
5 Armstrong	?	?	?	?	Y	Y
CONNECTICUT						
1 Cotter	Y	Y	N	N	N	Y
2 Dodd	N	Y	N	N	N	N
3 Giaimo	N	Y	N	N	N	N
4 McKinney	N	Y	Y	Y	N	Y
5 Sarasin	N	Y	Y	Y	Y	Y
6 Moffett	N	Y	N	?	N	N
DELAWARE						
AL Evans	Y	N	Y	Y	Y	Y
FLORIDA						
1 Sikes	Y	Y	Y	?	Y	N
2 Fuqua	#	#	Y	Y	Y	Y
3 Bennett	Y	N	Y	Y	Y	N
4 Chappell	?	?	?	Y	Y	Y
5 Kelly	Y	N	Y	Y	Y	Y
6 Young	Y	N	Y	Y	Y	Y
7 Gibbons	?	?	?	?	?	?
8 Ireland	Y	N	?	?	Y	N
9 Frey	?	?	?	?	✓	?
10 Bafalis	Y	N	Y	Y	Y	Y
11 Rogers	N	Y	N	#	N	N
12 Burke	?	?	?	?	✓	?
13 Lehman	▮	#	▮	▮	X	▮
14 Pepper	N	Y	#	#	Y	N
15 Fascell	N	Y	▮	N	N	N
GEORGIA						
1 Ginn	Y	N	N	N	Y	N
2 Mathis	Y	Y	Y	Y	Y	N
3 Brinkley	N	N	Y	N	N	N
4 Levitas	N	N	N	N	N	N
5 Fowler	N	?	N	N	N	N
6 Flynt	?	N	Y	Y	Y	Y
7 McDonald	Y	N	Y	Y	Y	Y
8 Evans	Y	Y	Y	Y	N	▮
9 Jenkins	Y	N	Y	N	N	N
10 Barnard	Y	Y	N	?	Y	N
HAWAII						
1 Heftel	Y	Y	Y	Y	N	N
2 Akaka	Y	Y	N	Y	N	N
IDAHO						
1 Symms	?	?	?	?	✓	?
2 Hansen, G.	?	?	?	?	✓	?
ILLINOIS						
1 Metcalfe	N	Y	N	N	N	N
2 Murphy	Y	Y	N	N	N	N
3 Russo	Y	Y	N	N	N	N
4 Derwinski	Y	N	Y	N	Y	Y
5 Fary	Y	Y	N	?	✓	?
6 Hyde	Y	Y	#	#	Y	Y
7 Collins	N	Y	N	Y	N	N
8 Rostenkowski	?	?	?	?	N	N
9 Yates	N	Y	N	N	N	N
10 Mikva	▮	#	▮	▮	X	▮
11 Annunzio	Y	Y	N	N	N	N
12 Crane	Y	N	Y	Y	Y	Y
13 McClory	Y	N	Y	Y	Y	Y
14 Erlenborn	Y	N	#	#	X	#
15 Corcoran	Y	N	Y	Y	Y	Y
16 Anderson	N	#	Y	#	N	Y
17 O'Brien	Y	Y	Y	#	Y	Y
18 Michel	Y	Y	Y	Y	Y	Y
19 Railsback	Y	N	N	?	Y	Y
20 Findley	N	N	N	Y	Y	Y
21 Madigan	?	Y	Y	Y	N	Y
22 Shipley	?	?	?	?	✓	?
23 Price	Y	#	N	N	Y	N
24 Simon	N	Y	N	Y	N	N
INDIANA						
1 Benjamin	Y	Y	N	Y	N	Y
2 Fithian	Y	Y	N	N	N	N
3 Brademas	N	Y	N	N	N	N
4 Quayle	Y	N	Y	?	Y	Y
5 Hillis	Y	Y	Y	Y	Y	Y
6 Evans	Y	N	Y	Y	Y	Y
7 Myers, J.	Y	N	Y	Y	Y	Y
8 Cornwell	✓	?	?	?	N	N
9 Hamilton	N	Y	N	N	N	N
10 Sharp	N	Y	N	N	N	N
11 Jacobs	Y	N	N	Y	N	Y
IOWA						
1 Leach	Y	N	Y	Y	N	Y
2 Blouin	Y	Y	N	N	N	N
3 Grassley	Y	N	Y	Y	Y	Y
4 Smith	N	Y	?	?	Y	N
5 Harkin	N	Y	N	N	N	N
6 Bedell	N	Y	N	Y	N	N

Democrats ***Republicans***

	638	639	640	641	642	643
KANSAS						
1 Sebelius	Y	N	Y	Y	Y	Y
2 Keys	N	Y	N	N	N	Y
3 Winn	Y	N	Y	Y	Y	Y
4 Glickman	Y	Y	Y	N	Y	N
5 Skubitz	Y	Y	?	?	N	Y
KENTUCKY						
1 Hubbard	Y	Y	Y	Y	N	N
2 Natcher	Y	Y	N	Y	N	N
3 Mazzoli	Y	Y	N	N	N	N
4 Snyder	Y	N	Y	Y	Y	Y
5 Carter	Y	N	Y	Y	Y	Y
6 Breckinridge	N	N	N	N	Y	N
7 Perkins	Y	Y	N	Y	N	N
LOUISIANA						
1 Livingston	Y	N	Y	Y	Y	Y
2 Boggs	Y	Y	N	#	Y	N
3 Treen	Y	N	Y	Y	Y	Y
4 Waggonner	Y	N	Y	Y	Y	N
5 Huckaby	?	?	?	?	✓	?
6 Moore	Y	N	Y	Y	Y	Y
7 Breaux	Y	N	Y	Y	Y	Y
8 Long	Y	Y	N	N	Y	N
MAINE						
1 Emery	Y	N	Y	Y	Y	Y
2 Cohen	Y	N	Y	Y	N	Y
MARYLAND						
1 Bauman	Y	N	Y	Y	Y	Y
2 Long	N	Y	N	N	Y	N
3 Mikulski	N	Y	N	Y	N	N
4 Holt	Y	N	Y	Y	Y	Y
5 Spellman	▮	Y	N	N	N	N
6 Byron	?	?	?	?	Y	N
7 Mitchell	N	Y	N	▮	N	N
8 Steers	N	Y	N	N	N	N
MASSACHUSETTS						
1 Conte	Y	Y	Y	N	N	Y
2 Boland	Y	Y	N	N	N	N
3 Early	Y	Y	N	N	N	Y
4 Drinan	N	Y	N	Y	N	Y
5 Tsongas	?	?	?	?	X	Y
6 Harrington	▮	#	▮	▮	N	N
7 Markey	Y	Y	N	N	N	Y
8 O'Neill						
9 Moakley	Y	Y	N	▮	N	N
10 Heckler	Y	Y	Y	N	?	Y
11 Burke	Y	Y	?	?	N	Y
12 Studds	N	Y	N	N	N	Y
MICHIGAN						
1 Conyers	N	Y	N	Y	N	N
2 Pursell	Y	Y	N	Y	Y	Y
3 Brown	Y	Y	Y	Y	Y	Y
4 Stockman	Y	N	Y	#	N	Y
5 Sawyer	Y	N	Y	Y	Y	Y
6 Carr	N	Y	N	N	N	N
7 Kildee	Y	Y	N	Y	N	N
8 Traxler	Y	N	N	#	N	N
9 Vander Jagt	Y	Y	Y	Y	Y	Y
10 Cederberg	Y	N	Y	Y	Y	Y
11 Ruppe	?	?	Y	Y	N	Y
12 Bonior	Y	Y	N	N	N	N
13 Diggs	N	Y	?	?	N	N
14 Nedzi	N	Y	Y	Y	N	N
15 Ford	N	Y	?	N	N	N
16 Dingell	Y	Y	Y	Y	N	N
17 Brodhead	N	Y	N	N	N	N
18 Blanchard	N	Y	Y	N	N	N
19 Broomfield	Y	N	Y	#	Y	Y
MINNESOTA						
1 Quie	?	?	?	?	?	?
2 Hagedorn	Y	N	Y	Y	Y	Y
3 Frenzel	N	N	Y	Y	Y	Y
4 Vento	Y	Y	N	N	N	N
5 Fraser	?	?	?	?	?	?
6 Nolan	Y	Y	N	N	N	N
7 Stangeland	Y	N	Y	Y	Y	Y
8 Oberstar	Y	Y	N	Y	N	N
MISSISSIPPI						
1 Whitten	Y	Y	Y	Y	Y	N
2 Bowen	Y	N	Y	?	Y	Y
3 Montgomery	Y	N	Y	Y	Y	Y
4 Cochran	?	?	?	?	Y	?
5 Lott	Y	N	Y	Y	Y	Y
MISSOURI						
1 Clay	N	Y	?	N	N	N
2 Young	Y	Y	Y	Y	N	N
3 Gephardt	Y	Y	Y	N	N	N
4 Skelton	Y	N	Y	Y	Y	N
5 Bolling	N	Y	N	N	N	N
6 Coleman	Y	N	Y	Y	Y	Y
7 Taylor	Y	N	Y	Y	Y	Y
8 Ichord	Y	N	Y	Y	Y	Y
9 Volkmer	Y	Y	Y	N	N	N
10 Burlison	Y	Y	N	N	N	N
MONTANA						
1 Baucus	N	?	N	Y	N	N
2 Marlenee	Y	N	Y	Y	Y	Y
NEBRASKA						
1 Thone	?	?	?	?	✓	?
2 Cavanaugh	N	Y	N	Y	N	N
3 Smith	Y	N	Y	Y	Y	Y
NEVADA						
AL Santini	Y	Y	N	N	Y	Y
NEW HAMPSHIRE						
1 D'Amours	Y	N	Y	Y	N	Y
2 Cleveland	N	N	Y	Y	Y	Y
NEW JERSEY						
1 Florio	Y	Y	N	N	N	▮
2 Hughes	Y	Y	N	N	N	N
3 Howard	Y	Y	N	N	N	N
4 Thompson	N	Y	N	N	N	N
5 Fenwick	N	Y	N	N	N	Y
6 Forsythe	#	#	#	#	N	Y
7 Maguire	N	Y	N	Y	N	Y
8 Roe	Y	Y	N	Y	N	Y
9 Hollenbeck	Y	Y	N	Y	N	Y
10 Rodino	#	#	N	N	N	N
11 Minish	Y	Y	N	Y	N	Y
12 Rinaldo	Y	Y	N	Y	Y	Y
13 Meyner	N	Y	N	▮	N	N
14 LeFante	Y	Y	N	Y	N	N
15 Patten	Y	Y	N	N	N	N
NEW MEXICO						
1 Lujan	Y	N	Y	Y	Y	Y
2 Runnels	Y	N	Y	Y	Y	Y
NEW YORK						
1 Pike	Y	Y	N	N	Y	N
2 Downey	N	Y	N	N	Y	N
3 Ambro	Y	Y	Y	Y	Y	Y
4 Lent	Y	Y	Y	Y	Y	Y
5 Wydler	?	?	?	?	Y	Y
6 Wolff	Y	Y	Y	Y	Y	Y
7 Addabbo	N	Y	N	N	N	Y
8 Rosenthal	N	Y	N	N	N	N
9 Delaney	Y	Y	N	Y	N	N
10 Biaggi	Y	Y	N	N	N	Y
11 Scheuer	N	Y	N	N	N	N
12 Chisholm	N	Y	?	?	N	Y
13 Solarz	N	Y	N	N	N	N
14 Richmond	?	✓	?	?	N	N
15 Zeferetti	Y	Y	N	Y	Y	Y
16 Holtzman	N	Y	N	Y	N	Y
17 Murphy	Y	Y	?	?	?	N
18 Green	N	Y	N	N	N	Y
19 Rangel	N	Y	N	N	N	N
20 Weiss	N	Y	N	Y	N	N
21 Garcia	▮	#	▮	▮	N	N
22 Bingham	N	Y	N	N	N	N
23 Caputo	Y	Y	?	?	Y	Y
24 Ottinger	N	Y	N	Y	N	N
25 Fish	Y	Y	Y	?	Y	Y
26 Gilman	N	Y	Y	Y	Y	Y
27 McHugh	Y	Y	N	Y	N	Y
28 Stratton	Y	Y	Y	Y	Y	N
29 Pattison	▮	✓	▮	▮	N	N
30 McEwen	Y	Y	Y	Y	N	Y
31 Mitchell	Y	Y	Y	Y	Y	Y
32 Hanley	Y	Y	N	Y	Y	Y
33 Walsh	Y	Y	Y	Y	Y	Y
34 Horton	N	Y	Y	Y	Y	Y
35 Conable	Y	Y	Y	Y	N	N
36 LaFalce	#	Y	N	N	N	Y
37 Nowak	Y	Y	N	Y	N	N
38 Kemp	Y	Y	Y	?	Y	Y
39 Lundine	N	Y	N	N	N	N
NORTH CAROLINA						
1 Jones	Y	Y	Y	Y	Y	N
2 Fountain	Y	N	Y	Y	Y	N
3 Whitley	Y	N	Y	Y	Y	N
4 Andrews	Y	Y	Y	?	N	N
5 Neal	Y	Y	N	Y	N	Y
6 Preyer	N	Y	N	Y	N	N
7 Rose	N	Y	N	N	N	Y
8 Hefner	Y	Y	N	?	N	N
9 Martin	Y	Y	Y	Y	Y	Y
10 Broyhill	?	N	Y	Y	Y	Y
11 Gudger	Y	N	Y	Y	Y	N
NORTH DAKOTA						
AL Andrews	Y	N	Y	Y	Y	Y
OHIO						
1 Gradison	Y	N	Y	Y	Y	N
2 Luken	Y	N	Y	Y	Y	N
3 Whalen	Y	Y	N	N	N	N
4 Guyer	Y	Y	Y	Y	Y	Y
5 Latta	Y	N	Y	Y	Y	Y
6 Harsha	?	?	?	?	Y	Y
7 Brown	Y	Y	Y	Y	Y	Y
8 Kindness	Y	N	Y	?	Y	Y
9 Ashley	N	Y	?	?	N	N
10 Miller	Y	N	Y	Y	Y	Y
11 Stanton	Y	Y	Y	#	Y	Y
12 Devine	Y	N	Y	Y	Y	Y
13 Pease	N	Y	N	Y	N	N
14 Seiberling	N	#	N	Y	N	N
15 Wylie	Y	N	Y	Y	N	Y
16 Regula	Y	N	Y	Y	Y	Y
17 Ashbrook	Y	N	Y	Y	Y	Y
18 Applegate	Y	Y	Y	Y	N	Y
19 Carney	Y	Y	N	Y	N	N
20 Oakar	Y	Y	N	Y	Y	N
21 Stokes	N	Y	N	N	N	N
22 Vanik	N	Y	N	Y	N	N
23 Mottl	Y	N	Y	Y	Y	Y
OKLAHOMA						
1 Jones	Y	N	N	Y	Y	N
2 Risenhoover	Y	Y	Y	Y	Y	Y
3 Watkins	?	N	Y	Y	Y	Y
4 Steed	Y	Y	Y	Y	Y	N
5 Edwards	Y	N	Y	Y	Y	Y
6 English	Y	N	Y	Y	Y	Y
OREGON						
1 AuCoin	N	N	N	Y	N	?
2 Ullman	Y	Y	▮	#	N	N
3 Duncan	#	#	#	#	#	▮
4 Weaver	N	Y	N	Y	N	N
PENNSYLVANIA						
1 Myers, M.	Y	Y	N	N	N	Y
2 Nix	N	Y	N	?	N	N
3 Lederer	Y	Y	N	Y	N	N
4 Eilberg	Y	#	N	N	N	Y
5 Schulze	Y	N	Y	Y	Y	Y
6 Yatron	Y	N	Y	Y	Y	Y
7 Edgar	N	Y	N	Y	N	N
8 Kostmayer	N	Y	N	Y	N	Y
9 Shuster	Y	N	Y	Y	Y	Y
10 McDade	Y	Y	Y	N	Y	Y
11 Flood	?	?	?	Y	N	N
12 Murtha	Y	Y	N	Y	Y	N
13 Coughlin	Y	Y	Y	Y	Y	Y
14 Moorhead	N	Y	N	N	N	N
15 Rooney	Y	Y	?	?	N	N
16 Walker	Y	N	Y	Y	Y	Y
17 Ertel	Y	Y	Y	Y	N	Y
18 Walgren	N	Y	Y	Y	N	N
19 Goodling, W.	Y	N	Y	Y	Y	Y
20 Gaydos	Y	Y	N	Y	N	N
21 Dent	Y	Y	N	Y	Y	N
22 Murphy	Y	N	Y	Y	N	N
23 Ammerman	?	X	?	?	X	?
24 Marks	Y	Y	N	N	N	Y
25 Myers, G.	Y	N	Y	Y	Y	Y
RHODE ISLAND						
1 St Germain	Y	Y	N	Y	N	N
2 Beard	Y	Y	N	Y	N	Y
SOUTH CAROLINA						
1 Davis	Y	N	Y	Y	Y	N
2 Spence	Y	N	Y	Y	Y	Y
3 Derrick	N	N	N	N	Y	N
4 Mann	N	Y	Y	N	Y	N
5 Holland	Y	Y	N	Y	N	N
6 Jenrette	N	Y	Y	Y	N	N
SOUTH DAKOTA						
1 Pressler	?	?	?	?	?	?
2 Abdnor	#	▮	#	#	✓	#
TENNESSEE						
1 Quillen	#	▮	▮	#	✓	#
2 Duncan	Y	N	Y	Y	Y	Y
3 Lloyd	#	N	Y	Y	Y	Y
, Gore	N	Y	N	Y	Y	N
5 Vacancy						
6 Beard	Y	N	Y	#	Y	Y
7 Jones	Y	Y	Y	Y	Y	Y
8 Ford	N	Y	N	Y	N	N
TEXAS						
1 Hall	Y	N	N	Y	Y	Y
2 Wilson, C.	N	Y	Y	Y	Y	N
3 Collins	Y	N	Y	Y	Y	Y
4 Roberts	Y	N	?	Y	Y	Y
5 Mattox	N	N	N	N	N	N
6 Teague	?	?	?	?	✓	?
7 Archer	Y	N	Y	Y	Y	Y
8 Eckhardt	N	Y	N	Y	N	Y
9 Brooks	N	N	N	?	N	N
10 Pickle	N	N	N	Y	N	N
11 Poage	?	?	Y	Y	Y	Y
12 Wright	Y	Y	N	N	N	N
13 Hightower	Y	N	Y	?	Y	Y
14 Young	?	?	?	?	?	?
15 de la Garza	Y	N	Y	Y	Y	Y
16 White	Y	N	Y	Y	Y	Y
17 Burleson	Y	N	Y	?	Y	Y
18 Jordan	N	Y	N	Y	N	N
19 Mahon	Y	Y	N	Y	N	N
20 Gonzalez	N	Y	N	Y	Y	Y
21 Krueger	X	X	▮	#	✓	#
22 Gammage	Y	N	N	Y	Y	Y
23 Kazen	Y	N	Y	Y	Y	Y
24 Milford	?	?	Y	Y	N	N
UTAH						
1 McKay	Y	Y	Y	Y	N	N
2 Marriott	Y	N	Y	Y	Y	Y
VERMONT						
AL Jeffords	N	Y	▮	#	Y	Y
VIRGINIA						
1 Trible	Y	N	Y	Y	Y	Y
2 Whitehurst	Y	N	Y	Y	Y	Y
3 Satterfield	Y	N	Y	Y	Y	Y
4 Daniel	Y	N	Y	Y	Y	Y
5 Daniel	Y	N	Y	Y	Y	Y
6 Butler	Y	N	Y	Y	Y	Y
7 Robinson	Y	N	Y	Y	Y	Y
8 Harris	N	Y	N	N	N	Y
9 Wampler	Y	N	Y	Y	Y	Y
10 Fisher	N	Y	N	N	N	N
WASHINGTON						
1 Pritchard	N	Y	Y	Y	N	Y
2 Meeds	N	Y	N	?	N	N
3 Bonker	#	#	N	Y	N	N
4 McCormack	N	N	Y	Y	Y	Y
5 Foley	N	Y	N	Y	N	N
6 Dicks	N	Y	N	Y	Y	N
7 Cunningham	Y	N	Y	Y	Y	Y
WEST VIRGINIA						
1 Mollohan	Y	Y	Y	Y	Y	N
2 Staggers	Y	Y	Y	Y	Y	Y
3 Slack	Y	Y	Y	?	Y	N
4 Rahall	Y	Y	Y	Y	N	N
WISCONSIN						
1 Aspin	Y	Y	N	N	N	N
2 Kastenmeier	N	Y	N	N	N	N
3 Baldus	Y	Y	N	N	N	N
4 Zablocki	Y	Y	N	N	Y	N
5 Reuss	N	Y	N	N	N	N
6 Steiger	Y	#	#	#	N	N
7 Obey	Y	Y	N	N	N	N
8 Cornell	Y	Y	N	N	N	N
9 Kasten	✓	?	?	?	✓	?
WYOMING						
AL Roncalio	N	Y	N	N	N	N

Democrats ***Republicans***

644. HR 7308. Foreign Intelligence Surveillance. Kemp, R-N.Y., amendment to require the president to inform the House and Senate Intelligence committees when he had reason to believe an individual with diplomatic immunity was engaged in electronic surveillance in the United States, to inform the target of the surveillance and to demand the foreign power cease such surveillance if he determined that to do so would not cause serious damage to national security. Rejected 154-230: R 117-6; D 37-224 (ND 22-156; SD 15-68), Sept. 7, 1978.

645. HR 7308. Foreign Intelligence Surveillance. McClory, R-Ill., substitute amendment to delete from the bill the requirement for a warrant to conduct electronic surveillance in the foreign intelligence area, delete the criminal standard for surveillance of U.S. persons, and allow surveillance of a U.S. person if certified by the president, the attorney general and an executive branch official confirmed by the Senate. Rejected 128-249: R 93-27; D 35-222 (ND 7-170; SD 28-52), Sept. 7, 1978.

646. HR 7308. Foreign Intelligence Surveillance. McClory, R-Ill, amendment to allow wiretapping of non-U.S. persons without a warrant, provided that a certificate was issued by the attorney general and a designated executive branch official in the area of national security who had been confirmed by the Senate. Rejected 176-200: R 112-9; D 64-191 (ND 23-153; SD 41-38), Sept. 7, 1978. A "nay" was a vote supporting the president's position. (This amendment had previously been adopted *(see vote 640, p. 182-H)* in the Committee of the Whole.)

647. HR 7308. Foreign Intelligence Surveillance. McClory, R-Ill., motion to recommit the bill to the Select Committee on Intelligence with instructions to report it back containing an amendment that would allow warrantless surveillance of official foreign powers. Rejected 164-207: R 111-10; D 53-197 (ND 13-160; SD 40-37), Sept. 7, 1978. A "nay" was a vote supporting the president's position.

648. HR 7308. Foreign Intelligence Surveillance. Passage of the bill to require the U.S. government to obtain judicial warrants for most electronic surveillance operations conducted within the United States for purposes of gathering foreign intelligence information. Passed 246-128: R 32-90; D 214-38 (ND 162-13; SD 52-25), Sept. 7, 1978. A "yea" was a vote supporting the president's position.

KEY

- Y Voted for (yea).
- ✓ Paired for.
- † Announced for.
- # CQ Poll for.
- N Voted against (nay).
- X Paired against.
- \- Announced against.
- ▮ CQ Poll against.
- P Voted "present."
- ● Voted "present" to avoid possible conflict of interest.
- ? Did not vote or otherwise make a position known.

	644	645	646	647	648
ALABAMA					
1 Edwards	Y	Y	Y	Y	N
2 Dickinson	Y	Y	Y	Y	N
3 Nichols	Y	Y	Y	Y	N
4 Bevill	N	Y	Y	Y	N
5 Flippo	N	Y	Y	Y	N
6 Buchanan	Y	Y	Y	Y	N
7 Flowers	Y	Y	Y	Y	N
ALASKA					
AL Young	#	#	#	#	?
ARIZONA					
1 Rhodes	Y	?	✓	✓	X
2 Udall	N	N	N	N	Y
3 Stump	Y	Y	Y	Y	N
4 Rudd	Y	Y	Y	Y	N
ARKANSAS					
1 Alexander	N	N	Y	N	Y
2 Tucker	N	N	N	N	Y
3 Hammerschmidt	Y	Y	Y	Y	N
4 Thornton	N	N	?	?	?
CALIFORNIA					
1 Johnson	N	N	N	N	Y
2 Clausen	Y	Y	Y	Y	N
3 Moss	N	N	N	N	?
4 Leggett	Y	N	N	N	Y
5 Burton, J.	N	N	N	N	Y
6 Burton, P.	N	N	N	N	Y
7 Miller	?	?	X	?	✓
8 Dellums	N	N	N	N	Y
9 Stark	N	N	N	N	Y
10 Edwards	N	N	N	N	Y
11 Ryan	N	N	N	N	Y
12 McCloskey	N	N	N	N	Y
13 Mineta	N	N	N	N	Y
14 McFall	N	N	N	N	Y
15 Sisk	?	?	?	?	?
16 Panetta	N	N	N	N	Y
17 Krebs	N	N	N	N	Y
18 Vacancy					
19 Lagomarsino	Y	Y	Y	Y	N
20 Goldwater	Y	Y	Y	Y	N
21 Corman	N	N	N	N	Y
22 Moorhead	Y	Y	Y	Y	N
23 Beilenson	▮	▮	▮	▮	?
24 Waxman	N	N	N	N	Y
25 Roybal	N	N	N	N	Y
26 Rousselot	Y	Y	Y	Y	N
27 Dornan	Y	Y	Y	Y	N
28 Burke	▮	▮	X	X	✓
29 Hawkins	?	?	X	X	✓
30 Danielson	N	N	N	N	Y
31 Wilson, C.H.	N	N	Y	Y	N
32 Anderson	N	N	N	N	Y
33 Clawson	?	?	?	?	X
34 Hannaford	N	N	N	N	Y
35 Lloyd	N	N	N	N	Y
36 Brown	N	N	N	N	Y
37 Pettis	?	?	?	?	?
38 Patterson	N	N	N	N	Y
39 Wiggins	▮	#	#	#	X
40 Badham	#	#	✓	✓	X
41 Wilson, B.	Y	Y	Y	Y	N
42 Van Deerlin	N	N	N	N	Y
43 Burgener	Y	Y	Y	Y	N
COLORADO					
1 Schroeder	N	N	N	N	Y
2 Wirth	N	N	N	N	Y
3 Evans	N	N	N	N	Y
4 Johnson	Y	?	?	?	?
5 Armstrong	?	?	?	?	?
CONNECTICUT					
1 Cotter	N	N	N	N	Y
2 Dodd	N	N	N	N	Y
3 Giaimo	N	N	N	N	Y
4 McKinney	Y	N	Y	Y	Y
5 Sarasin	Y	N	Y	Y	Y
6 Moffett	N	N	N	N	Y
DELAWARE					
AL Evans	Y	Y	Y	Y	N
FLORIDA					
1 Sikes	N	Y	Y	Y	N
2 Fuqua	N	#	✓	▮	✓
3 Bennett	Y	N	Y	Y	N
4 Chappell	N	Y	Y	Y	N
5 Kelly	N	Y	Y	Y	N
6 Young	Y	Y	Y	Y	N
7 Gibbons	?	?	?	?	?
8 Ireland	N	N	N	N	Y
9 Frey	?	?	?	?	?
10 Bafalis	Y	Y	Y	Y	N
11 Rogers	N	N	N	N	Y
12 Burke	?	?	?	?	?
13 Lehman	▮	▮	▮	▮	✓
14 Pepper	N	N	N	N	Y
15 Fascell	N	N	N	N	Y
GEORGIA					
1 Ginn	N	N	N	N	Y
2 Mathis	Y	Y	Y	Y	Y
3 Brinkley	Y	Y	Y	Y	Y
4 Levitas	Y	N	N	N	Y
5 Fowler	N	N	N	N	Y
6 Flynt	N	Y	Y	Y	N
7 McDonald	Y	Y	Y	Y	N
8 Evans	N	N	N	N	Y
9 Jenkins	N	Y	Y	Y	Y
10 Barnard	N	N	N	N	Y
HAWAII					
1 Heftel	N	N	N	N	Y
2 Akaka	N	N	N	N	Y
IDAHO					
1 Symms	?	?	✓	✓	X
2 Hansen, G.	?	?	✓	✓	X
ILLINOIS					
1 Metcalfe	N	N	N	N	Y
2 Murphy	N	N	N	N	Y
3 Russo	N	N	N	N	Y
4 Derwinski	Y	N	Y	Y	Y
5 Fary	?	?	X	X	✓
6 Hyde	Y	Y	Y	Y	N
7 Collins	N	N	N	N	Y
8 Rostenkowski	N	N	N	N	Y
9 Yates	N	N	N	N	Y
10 Mikva	▮	▮	X	X	✓
11 Annunzio	N	N	N	N	Y
12 Crane	#	#	#	#	X
13 McClory	Y	Y	Y	Y	N
14 Erlenborn	#	Y	Y	Y	N
15 Corcoran	Y	Y	Y	Y	N
16 Anderson	Y	N	Y	Y	Y
17 O'Brien	Y	Y	Y	Y	N
18 Michel	Y	Y	Y	Y	N
19 Railsback	Y	N	N	N	Y
20 Findley	Y	N	N	N	Y
21 Madigan	Y	Y	Y	Y	Y
22 Shipley	?	?	?	?	✓
23 Price	N	N	N	N	Y
24 Simon	N	N	N	N	Y
INDIANA					
1 Benjamin	N	N	N	N	Y
2 Fithian	N	N	N	N	Y
3 Brademas	N	N	N	N	Y
4 Quayle	Y	Y	Y	Y	Y
5 Hillis	Y	Y	Y	Y	N
6 Evans	Y	N	Y	Y	Y
7 Myers, J.	Y	Y	Y	Y	N
8 Cornwell	N	N	N	N	Y
9 Hamilton	N	N	N	N	Y
10 Sharp	N	N	N	N	Y
11 Jacobs	N	N	N	N	Y
IOWA					
1 Leach	Y	N	Y	Y	Y
2 Blouin	N	N	N	N	Y
3 Grassley	Y	Y	Y	Y	N
4 Smith	N	N	N	N	Y
5 Harkin	N	N	N	N	Y
6 Bedell	N	N	N	N	Y

Democrats ***Republicans***

Corresponding to Congressional Record Votes 733, 734, 735, 736, 737

	644	645	646	647	648
KANSAS					
1 Sebelius	Y	Y	Y	Y	N
2 Keys	N	N	N	N	Y
3 Winn	Y	#	Y	Y	N
4 Glickman	N	N	N	N	Y
5 Skubitz	?	Y	?	Y	N
KENTUCKY					
1 Hubbard	N	N	Y	N	Y
2 Natcher	N	N	N	N	Y
3 Mazzoli	N	N	N	N	Y
4 Snyder	Y	Y	Y	Y	N
5 Carter	Y	Y	Y	Y	N
6 Breckinridge	N	N	N	N	?
7 Perkins	N	N	N	N	Y
LOUISIANA					
1 Livingston	Y	Y	Y	Y	N
2 Boggs	N	N	N	N	Y
3 Treen	Y	Y	Y	Y	N
4 Waggonner	#	#	✓	✓	X
5 Huckaby	?	?	?	?	?
6 Moore	Y	Y	Y	Y	N
7 Breaux	Y	Y	Y	Y	N
8 Long	N	N	N	N	Y
MAINE					
1 Emery	Y	N	Y	Y	N
2 Cohen	Y	N	Y	Y	Y
MARYLAND					
1 Bauman	Y	Y	Y	Y	N
2 Long	N	N	N	N	Y
3 Mikulski	Y	N	N	N	Y
4 Holt	Y	Y	Y	Y	N
5 Spellman	N	N	N	N	Y
6 Byron	N	N	?	?	?
7 Mitchell	N	N	N	N	Y
8 Steers	N	N	N	N	Y
MASSACHUSETTS					
1 Conte	Y	N	Y	Y	Y
2 Boland	N	N	N	N	Y
3 Early	N	N	N	N	Y
4 Drinan	Y	▮	X	X	X
5 Tsongas	?	?	?	?	?
6 Harrington	N	N	N	N	Y
7 Markey	Y	N	N	N	Y
8 O'Neill					
9 Moakley	N	N	N	X	Y
10 Heckler	Y	N	Y	Y	Y
11 Burke	N	N	N	N	Y
12 Studds	N	N	N	N	Y
MICHIGAN					
1 Conyers	N	N	N	N	Y
2 Pursell	Y	Y	Y	N	Y
3 Brown	Y	Y	Y	Y	N
4 Stockman	Y	Y	Y	Y	N
5 Sawyer	Y	?	Y	Y	Y
6 Carr	N	N	N	N	Y
7 Kildee	Y	N	N	N	Y
8 Traxler	N	N	N	N	Y
9 Vander Jagt	Y	Y	Y	Y	N
10 Cederberg	Y	Y	Y	Y	N
11 Ruppe	Y	Y	Y	Y	N
12 Bonior	N	N	N	N	Y
13 Diggs	?	N	X	N	Y
14 Nedzi	N	Y	Y	Y	N
15 Ford	N	N	N	N	Y
16 Dingell	N	N	Y	Y	Y
17 Brodhead	N	N	N	N	N
18 Blanchard	N	N	Y	N	Y
19 Broomfield	Y	Y	Y	Y	Y
MINNESOTA					
1 Quie	?	?	?	?	?
2 Hagedorn	?	?	✓	✓	X
3 Frenzel	Y	N	Y	Y	N
4 Vento	N	N	N	N	Y
5 Fraser	?	?	?	?	?
6 Nolan	N	N	N	N	Y
7 Stangeland	Y	Y	Y	Y	N
8 Oberstar	Y	N	N	N	Y
MISSISSIPPI					
1 Whitten	N	N	Y	▮	Y
2 Bowen	Y	Y	Y	Y	N
3 Montgomery	N	N	Y	Y	Y
4 Cochran	?	?	?	?	?
5 Lott	Y	Y	Y	Y	N
MISSOURI					
1 Clay	N	N	N	N	Y
2 Young	N	N	N	N	Y
3 Gephardt	N	N	N	N	Y

	644	645	646	647	648
4 Skelton	N	N	N	N	Y
5 Bolling	N	N	N	N	Y
6 Coleman	Y	Y	Y	Y	N
7 Taylor	Y	Y	Y	Y	N
8 Ichord	Y	Y	Y	Y	N
9 Volkmer	N	N	N	N	Y
10 Burlison	N	N	N	N	Y
MONTANA					
1 Baucus	N	N	N	N	Y
2 Marlenee	Y	N	Y	?	Y
NEBRASKA					
1 Thone	?	?	?	?	?
2 Cavanaugh	N	N	N	N	Y
3 Smith	Y	Y	Y	Y	N
NEVADA					
AL Santini	Y	N	N	N	Y
NEW HAMPSHIRE					
1 D'Amours	N	N	Y	N	Y
2 Cleveland	Y	N	Y	Y	Y
NEW JERSEY					
1 Florio	N	N	N	N	Y
2 Hughes	N	N	N	N	Y
3 Howard	N	N	N	N	Y
4 Thompson	N	N	N	N	Y
5 Fenwick	Y	N	N	N	Y
6 Forsythe	Y	Y	Y	Y	N
7 Maguire	Y	N	N	N	Y
8 Roe	N	N	N	N	Y
9 Hollenbeck	N	N	N	N	Y
10 Rodino	N	N	N	▮	✓
11 Minish	N	N	N	N	Y
12 Rinaldo	Y	Y	Y	Y	Y
13 Meyner	N	▮	N	N	Y
14 LeFante	N	N	N	N	Y
15 Patten	N	N	N	N	Y
NEW MEXICO					
1 Lujan	Y	Y	Y	Y	N
2 Runnels	Y	Y	Y	Y	N
NEW YORK					
1 Pike	N	N	N	N	Y
2 Downey	N	N	N	N	Y
3 Ambro	N	N	Y	Y	Y
4 Lent	Y	Y	Y	Y	N
5 Wydler	N	Y	Y	Y	Y
6 Wolff	N	N	Y	Y	Y
7 Addabbo	N	N	N	N	Y
8 Rosenthal	N	N	N	N	Y
9 Delaney	N	N	N	N	Y
10 Biaggi	Y	N	N	N	Y
11 Scheuer	N	N	N	N	Y
12 Chisholm	N	N	N	N	Y
13 Solarz	N	N	N	N	Y
14 Richmond	N	X	X	X	✓
15 Zeferetti	?	X	X	X	✓
16 Holtzman	Y	N	N	N	N
17 Murphy	N	Y	Y	N	Y
18 Green	Y	N	N	N	Y
19 Rangel	N	N	?	X	✓
20 Weiss	Y	N	N	N	Y
21 Garcia	N	N	N	N	Y
22 Bingham	N	N	N	N	Y
23 Caputo	Y	?	?	?	?
24 Ottinger	N	N	N	N	Y
25 Fish	?	Y	Y	Y	N
26 Gilman	Y	N	Y	Y	Y
27 McHugh	N	N	N	N	Y
28 Stratton	Y	Y	Y	Y	N
29 Pattison	N	N	N	N	Y
30 McEwen	Y	Y	Y	Y	N
31 Mitchell	Y	Y	Y	Y	N
32 Hanley	N	N	N	N	Y
33 Walsh	Y	Y	Y	Y	N
34 Horton	Y	N	Y	Y	Y
35 Conable	Y	Y	Y	Y	N
36 LaFalce	Y	N	N	N	Y
37 Nowak	Y	N	N	N	Y
38 Kemp	Y	?	✓	✓	X
39 Lundine	N	N	N	N	Y
NORTH CAROLINA					
1 Jones	N	Y	Y	N	Y
2 Fountain	N	Y	Y	Y	N
3 Whitley	N	Y	Y	Y	N
4 Andrews	N	N	N	Y	N
5 Neal	N	N	N	N	Y
6 Preyer	N	N	N	N	Y
7 Rose	N	N	N	N	Y
8 Hefner	N	N	N	Y	Y

	644	645	646	647	648
9 Martin	Y	Y	Y	Y	N
10 Broyhill	Y	Y	Y	Y	N
11 Gudger	N	N	Y	Y	Y
NORTH DAKOTA					
AL Andrews	Y	Y	Y	Y	N
OHIO					
1 Gradison	N	Y	Y	Y	N
2 Luken	N	N	Y	?	Y
3 Whalen	Y	N	N	N	Y
4 Guyer	#	▮	✓	✓	X
5 Latta	Y	Y	Y	Y	N
6 Harsha	Y	Y	Y	Y	N
7 Brown	Y	Y	Y	Y	N
8 Kindness	Y	Y	Y	Y	N
9 Ashley	N	N	N	N	Y
10 Miller	Y	Y	Y	Y	N
11 Stanton	Y	Y	Y	Y	Y
12 Devine	Y	Y	Y	Y	N
13 Pease	N	N	N	N	Y
14 Seiberling	N	N	N	N	Y
15 Wylie	Y	Y	Y	Y	N
16 Regula	Y	Y	Y	Y	N
17 Ashbrook	Y	Y	Y	Y	N
18 Applegate	Y	Y	Y	N	Y
19 Carney	N	N	N	N	Y
20 Oakar	N	N	N	N	N
21 Stokes	N	N	N	N	Y
22 Vanik	N	N	N	N	Y
23 Mottl	Y	N	Y	N	Y
OKLAHOMA					
1 Jones	N	N	N	N	Y
2 Risenhoover	N	N	Y	Y	Y
3 Watkins	Y	Y	Y	Y	N
4 Steed	N	N	N	N	Y
5 Edwards	Y	N	Y	Y	N
6 English	N	Y	Y	Y	N
OREGON					
1 AuCoin	Y	N	N	N	Y
2 Ullman	N	N	N	N	Y
3 Duncan	#	#	#	#	?
4 Weaver	N	N	N	N	Y
PENNSYLVANIA					
1 Myers, M.	N	N	N	N	Y
2 Nix	N	N	N	N	Y
3 Lederer	N	N	N	N	Y
4 Eilberg	N	N	N	N	Y
5 Schulze	Y	Y	Y	Y	N
6 Yatron	#	#	X	X	✓
7 Edgar	N	N	N	N	Y
8 Kostmayer	N	N	N	N	Y
9 Shuster	Y	Y	Y	Y	N
10 McDade	Y	N	Y	Y	Y
11 Flood	N	N	N	N	Y
12 Murtha	N	N	N	N	Y
13 Coughlin	Y	Y	Y	Y	N
14 Moorhead	N	N	N	N	Y
15 Rooney	?	?	?	?	✓
16 Walker	Y	Y	Y	Y	N
17 Ertel	N	N	Y	Y	N
18 Walgren	N	N	Y	N	Y
19 Goodling, W.	Y	Y	Y	Y	N
20 Gaydos	Y	N	N	N	Y
21 Dent	▮	▮	X	X	✓
22 Murphy	▮	N	N	N	Y
23 Ammerman	?	?	?	?	?
24 Marks	Y	N	N	N	Y
25 Myers, G.	Y	Y	Y	Y	N
RHODE ISLAND					
1 St Germain	N	N	N	N	Y
2 Beard	N	N	N	N	Y
SOUTH CAROLINA					
1 Davis	Y	N	Y	Y	N
2 Spence	Y	Y	Y	Y	N
3 Derrick	N	N	N	N	Y
4 Mann	N	N	N	N	Y
5 Holland	N	N	N	N	Y
6 Jenrette	N	N	N	Y	N
SOUTH DAKOTA					
1 Pressler	?	?	?	?	?
2 Abdnor	#	#	#	✓	X
TENNESSEE					
1 Quillen	#	▮	▮	#	?
2 Duncan	Y	Y	Y	Y	N
3 Lloyd	N	N	Y	Y	N
4 Gore	Y	N	N	N	Y
5 Vacancy					
6 Beard	Y	Y	Y	Y	N

	644	645	646	647	648
7 Jones	N	N	Y	N	Y
8 Ford	N	N	N	N	Y
TEXAS					
1 Hall	N	Y	Y	Y	Y
2 Wilson, C.	N	N	N	Y	Y
3 Collins	Y	Y	Y	Y	N
4 Roberts	N	Y	Y	Y	Y
5 Mattox	N	N	N	N	Y
6 Teague	?	✓	✓	✓	X
7 Archer	Y	Y	Y	Y	N
8 Eckhardt	N	N	N	N	Y
9 Brooks	N	N	Y	?	Y
10 Pickle	N	N	N	N	Y
11 Poage	N	Y	Y	Y	N
12 Wright	N	N	N	N	Y
13 Hightower	N	Y	Y	Y	N
14 Young	N	?	?	?	?
15 de la Garza	N	N	Y	Y	Y
16 White	N	N	Y	Y	Y
17 Burleson	N	Y	Y	Y	N
18 Jordan	N	▮	▮	▮	?
19 Mahon	N	Y	N	N	Y
20 Gonzalez	N	N	N	Y	N
21 Krueger	▮	▮	▮	▮	?
22 Gammage	Y	Y	Y	Y	Y
23 Kazen	N	N	Y	Y	Y
24 Milford	N	Y	Y	Y	?
UTAH					
1 McKay	N	N	Y	N	Y
2 Marriott	Y	Y	Y	Y	N
VERMONT					
AL Jeffords	Y	N	Y	Y	Y
VIRGINIA					
1 Trible	Y	Y	Y	Y	N
2 Whitehurst	Y	Y	Y	Y	N
3 Satterfield	Y	Y	Y	Y	N
4 Daniel	Y	Y	Y	Y	N
5 Daniel	Y	Y	Y	Y	N
6 Butler	Y	Y	Y	Y	N
7 Robinson	Y	Y	Y	Y	N
8 Harris	N	N	N	N	Y
9 Wampler	Y	Y	Y	Y	N
10 Fisher	N	N	N	N	Y
WASHINGTON					
1 Pritchard	Y	N	Y	Y	Y
2 Meeds	N	N	N	N	Y
3 Bonker	N	N	N	N	Y
4 McCormack	N	N	Y	Y	N
5 Foley	N	?	N	?	Y
6 Dicks	N	N	N	N	Y
7 Cunningham	Y	Y	Y	Y	N
WEST VIRGINIA					
1 Mollohan	N	N	Y	Y	N
2 Staggers	?	N	Y	N	Y
3 Slack	N	N	Y	N	N
4 Rahall	N	N	N	N	Y
WISCONSIN					
1 Aspin	N	N	N	N	Y
2 Kastenmeier	N	N	N	N	Y
3 Baldus	N	N	N	N	Y
4 Zablocki	N	N	N	N	Y
5 Reuss	N	N	N	N	Y
6 Steiger	Y	Y	Y	Y	N
7 Obey	N	N	N	N	Y
8 Cornell	N	N	N	N	Y
9 Kasten	?	✓	✓	✓	X
WYOMING					
AL Roncalio	N	N	N	N	Y

Democrats ***Republicans***

649. HR 11280. Civil Service Reform. Udall, D-Ariz., motion that the House resolve itself into the Committee of the Whole to consider the bill to reorganize the U.S. Civil Service. Motion agreed to 307-10: R 103-5; D 204-5 (ND 142-4; SD 62-1), Sept. 7, 1978.

650. HR 11280. Civil Service Reform. Udall, D-Ariz., motion to table (kill) the Clay, D-Mo., motion to reconsider the vote *(vote 649, above)* by which the House resolved itself into the Committee of the Whole. Motion agreed to 296-18: R 100-7: D 196-11 (ND 141-9; SD 55-2) Sept. 7, 1978.

651 HR 11711. Trade Adjustment Assistance. Adoption of the rule (H Res 1288) providing for House floor consideration of the bill to broaden coverage and liberalize certain benefits to workers and firms under the adjustment assistance programs of the Trade Act of 1974. Adopted 333-2: R 110-1; D 223-1 (ND 155-1; SD 68-0), Sept. 8, 1978.

652. S J Res 4. Hawaiian Native Claims. Bauman, R-Md., motion to recommit to the Interior and Insular Affairs Committee, and thus kill, the joint resolution to establish a commission to study the claims of aboriginal Hawaiians resulting from the 1893 overthrow of the Hawaiian government. Motion agreed to 190-148: R 95-14; D 95-134 (ND 54-106: SD 41-28), Sept. 8, 1978.

653. HR 11711. Trade Adjustment Assistance. Ways and Means Committee amendment to extend adjustment assistance coverage to workers in firms adversely affected by foreign imports who were employed at least 26 of the preceding 52 weeks, as under current law, or 40 of the preceding 104 weeks. Adopted 206-110: R 34-70; D 172-40 (ND 141-4; SD 31-36), Sept. 8, 1978. A "nay" was a vote supporting the president's position.

654. HR 11711. Trade Adjustment Assistance. Passage of the bill to broaden coverage and liberalize certain benefits to workers and firms that were adversely affected by foreign imports under the adjustment assistance programs of the Trade Act of 1974. Passed 261-24: R 86-7; D 175-17 (ND 131-3; SD 44-14), Sept. 8, 1978. A "yea" was a vote supporting the president's position.

KEY

- Y Voted for (yea).
- ✓ Paired for.
- † Announced for.
- # CQ Poll for.
- N Voted against (nay).
- X Paired against.
- \- Announced against.
- ▮ CQ Poll against.
- P Voted "present."
- ● Voted "present" to avoid possible conflict of interest.
- ? Did not vote or otherwise make a position known.

	649	650	651	652	653	654
ALABAMA						
1 Edwards	Y	Y	Y	Y	Y	Y
2 Dickinson	N	Y	Y	Y	N	Y
3 Nichols	Y	Y	Y	Y	Y	Y
4 Bevill	Y	Y	Y	Y	Y	Y
5 Flippo	Y	?	Y	Y	Y	Y
6 Buchanan	Y	?	Y	Y	Y	?
7 Flowers	?	?	?	Y	Y	Y
ALASKA						
AL Young	#	?	?	▮	▮	#
ARIZONA						
1 Rhodes	?	?	?	?	?	?
2 Udall	Y	Y	Y	N	Y	Y
3 Stump	#	?	Y	Y	N	▮
4 Rudd	Y	Y	Y	Y	N	?
ARKANSAS						
1 Alexander	Y	Y	Y	N	Y	Y
2 Tucker	Y	Y	Y	N	Y	▮
3 Hammerschmidt	Y	Y	Y	?	?	?
4 Thornton	?	?	?	?	?	?
CALIFORNIA						
1 Johnson	Y	Y	Y	N	Y	Y
2 Clausen	Y	Y	Y	N	Y	Y
3 Moss	?	?	Y	N	Y	Y
4 Leggett	?	N	Y	Y	?	Y
5 Burton, J.	?	?	Y	N	Y	Y
6 Burton, P.	?	?	Y	N	Y	?
7 Miller	?	?	?	?	?	?
8 Dellums	Y	Y	Y	N	Y	?
9 Stark	Y	Y	Y	N	Y	Y
10 Edwards	Y	Y	Y	N	Y	Y
11 Ryan	Y	Y	Y	N	Y	Y
12 McCloskey	Y	Y	Y	N	N	Y
13 Mineta	Y	Y	Y	N	Y	Y
14 McFall	Y	Y	Y	N	Y	Y
15 Sisk	?	?	?	?	?	?
16 Panetta	Y	Y	Y	Y	Y	Y
17 Krebs	Y	Y	Y	N	Y	Y
18 Vacancy						
19 Lagomarsino	Y	Y	Y	Y	N	Y
20 Goldwater	Y	Y	Y	N	N	Y
21 Corman	Y	Y	?	?	?	?
22 Moorhead	Y	Y	Y	Y	N	Y
23 Beilenson	#	?	?	▮	?	?
24 Waxman	#	?	?	▮	#	?
25 Roybal	Y	Y	Y	N	Y	Y
26 Rousselot	Y	Y	Y	Y	N	Y
27 Dornan	Y	Y	Y	Y	N	Y
28 Burke	#	?	?	#	#	#
29 Hawkins	?	?	?	?	?	?
30 Danielson	Y	Y	Y	Y	Y	Y
31 Wilson, C.H.	N	N	Y	Y	#	#
32 Anderson	Y	Y	Y	N	Y	Y
33 Clawson	?	?	?	?	?	?
34 Hannaford	Y	Y	Y	N	Y	Y
35 Lloyd	N	?	Y	Y	Y	Y
36 Brown	?	?	Y	N	Y	Y
37 Pettis	?	?	?	?	?	?
38 Patterson	Y	Y	Y	N	Y	Y
39 Wiggins	#	?	?	#	▮	▮
40 Badham	#	?	?	#	▮	?
41 Wilson, B.	N	N	Y	Y	N	Y
42 Van Deerlin	Y	Y	?	N	Y	Y
43 Burgener	Y	Y	Y	N	N	Y
COLORADO						
1 Schroeder	Y	Y	Y	N	Y	Y
2 Wirth	Y	Y	Y	N	Y	Y
3 Evans	#	?	Y	N	Y	Y
4 Johnson	?	?	Y	N	N	Y
5 Armstrong	?	?	?	?	?	?
CONNECTICUT						
1 Cotter	#	?	?	#	#	?
2 Dodd	Y	Y	Y	?	?	?
3 Giaimo	Y	Y	Y	Y	Y	Y
4 McKinney	Y	?	†	-	†	†
5 Sarasin	?	?	?	?	?	?
6 Moffett	Y	Y	Y	?	?	?
DELAWARE						
AL Evans	Y	Y	Y	Y	N	Y
FLORIDA						
1 Sikes	?	?	Y	Y	N	?
2 Fuqua	#	?	?	#	#	#
3 Bennett	Y	Y	Y	Y	N	N
4 Chappell	Y	Y	Y	Y	N	?
5 Kelly	Y	Y	Y	Y	N	N
6 Young	?	N	Y	Y	N	N
7 Gibbons	?	?	?	?	?	?
8 Ireland	Y	Y	?	?	?	?
9 Frey	?	?	?	?	?	?
10 Bafalis	Y	Y	Y	Y	N	Y
11 Rogers	#	#	Y	Y	?	Y
12 Burke	?	?	?	?	?	?
13 Lehman	#	#	?	▮	?	#
14 Pepper	Y	Y	?	N	Y	?
15 Fascell	Y	Y	Y	N	Y	Y
GEORGIA						
1 Ginn	Y	Y	Y	Y	N	Y
2 Mathis	?	?	?	?	?	?
3 Brinkley	Y	Y	?	?	?	?
4 Levitas	Y	Y	Y	N	N	Y
5 Fowler	Y	?	Y	N	N	Y
6 Flynt	Y	Y	?	?	?	?
7 McDonald	Y	Y	Y	Y	N	N
8 Evans	Y	Y	Y	N	N	Y
9 Jenkins	Y	?	Y	Y	N	Y
10 Barnard	Y	Y	Y	Y	N	Y
HAWAII						
1 Heftel	Y	Y	Y	N	Y	Y
2 Akaka	Y	Y	Y	N	Y	Y
IDAHO						
1 Symms	?	?	?	?	?	?
2 Hansen, G.	?	?	?	?	?	?
ILLINOIS						
1 Metcalfe	?	N	?	N	Y	?
2 Murphy	Y	Y	?	?	#	#
3 Russo	Y	Y	Y	Y	Y	Y
4 Derwinski	Y	Y	Y	Y	Y	Y
5 Fary	?	?	?	?	?	?
6 Hyde	Y	Y	Y	Y	Y	?
7 Collins	Y	N	?	▮	#	?
8 Rostenkowski	Y	Y	?	?	?	?
9 Yates	Y	Y	Y	N	Y	Y
10 Mikva	?	?	?	?	?	?
11 Annunzio	Y	Y	Y	Y	Y	Y
12 Crane	?	?	Y	Y	N	N
13 McClory	Y	Y	Y	Y	N	Y
14 Erlenborn	Y	?	Y	Y	N	Y
15 Corcoran	Y	Y	Y	Y	N	Y
16 Anderson	#	Y	Y	Y	Y	Y
17 O'Brien	Y	Y	Y	Y	Y	Y
18 Michel	Y	Y	Y	Y	N	Y
19 Railsback	Y	Y	Y	Y	N	Y
20 Findley	Y	Y	Y	Y	Y	?
21 Madigan	Y	Y	Y	Y	?	?
22 Shipley	?	?	?	?	?	?
23 Price	Y	Y	Y	Y	Y	Y
24 Simon	Y	Y	P	N	Y	Y
INDIANA						
1 Benjamin	Y	Y	Y	Y	Y	Y
2 Fithian	Y	Y	Y	N	Y	Y
3 Brademas	Y	Y	Y	N	Y	?
4 Quayle	?	N	Y	Y	Y	Y
5 Hillis	Y	Y	?	?	?	?
6 Evans	Y	Y	Y	Y	?	?
7 Myers, J.	Y	Y	Y	Y	N	Y
8 Cornwell	#	Y	Y	N	Y	?
9 Hamilton	Y	Y	Y	N	Y	Y
10 Sharp	Y	Y	Y	N	Y	Y
11 Jacobs	Y	?	Y	#	#	?
IOWA						
1 Leach	Y	Y	Y	Y	N	Y
2 Blouin	Y	Y	Y	N	?	?
3 Grassley	Y	Y	Y	Y	N	Y
4 Smith	Y	Y	Y	N	Y	Y
5 Harkin	Y	Y	Y	N	?	?
6 Bedell	Y	Y	Y	Y	Y	Y

Democrats ***Republicans***

	649	650	651	652	653	654
KANSAS						
1 Sebelius	Y	Y	Y	N	N	Y
2 Keys	Y	?	Y	-	†	†
3 Winn	Y	Y	?	#	#	?
4 Glickman	Y	Y	Y	Y	Y	Y
5 Skubitz	Y	Y	?	N	?	Y
KENTUCKY						
1 Hubbard	Y	Y	Y	N	Y	Y
2 Natcher	Y	Y	Y	N	Y	Y
3 Mazzoli	Y	Y	Y	Y	Y	Y
4 Snyder	?	?	?	?	?	?
5 Carter	Y	Y	Y	Y	Y	Y
6 Breckinridge	Y	?	Y	N	N	Y
7 Perkins	Y	Y	Y	N	Y	Y
LOUISIANA						
1 Livingston	?	Y	Y	Y	N	Y
2 Boggs	Y	Y	Y	N	N	Y
3 Treen	?	Y	Y	Y	N	Y
4 Waggonner	#	?	?	#	#	?
5 Huckaby	?	?	?	?	?	?
6 Moore	Y	Y	N	Y	N	Y
7 Breaux	Y	?	?	?	?	?
8 Long	Y	Y	Y	Y	N	?
MAINE						
1 Emery	Y	Y	Y	Y	N	Y
2 Cohen	Y	Y	?	?	#	#
MARYLAND						
1 Bauman	Y	Y	Y	Y	N	N
2 Long	Y	Y	Y	Y	N	Y
3 Mikulski	Y	N	Y	N	Y	Y
4 Holt	Y	N	Y	Y	N	Y
5 Spellman	N	N	Y	N	Y	Y
6 Byron	?	?	?	?	?	?
7 Mitchell	N	Y	Y	N	Y	Y
8 Steers	N	N	Y	Y	Y	Y
MASSACHUSETTS						
1 Conte	Y	Y	Y	Y	Y	Y
2 Boland	#	Y	Y	▮	#	?
3 Early	?	Y	Y	N	Y	Y
4 Drinan	?	?	Y	N	Y	Y
5 Tsongas	?	?	?	?	?	?
6 Harrington	#	?	?	▮	#	?
7 Markey	Y	Y	Y	N	Y	Y
8 O'Neill						
9 Moakley	#	?	Y	N	Y	Y
10 Heckler	N	Y	?	?	?	?
11 Burke	Y	Y	Y	Y	Y	Y
12 Studds	Y	Y	Y	N	Y	Y
MICHIGAN						
1 Conyers	Y	Y	?	N	Y	Y
2 Pursell	Y	?	Y	N	N	Y
3 Brown	Y	Y	Y	Y	N	Y
4 Stockman	Y	Y	Y	Y	N	?
5 Sawyer	Y	Y	Y	Y	N	▮
6 Carr	Y	Y	Y	N	Y	Y
7 Kildee	Y	Y	Y	N	Y	Y
8 Traxler	Y	Y	Y	N	Y	#
9 Vander Jagt	Y	Y	Y	Y	N	Y
10 Cederberg	Y	Y	Y	Y	N	Y
11 Ruppe	?	?	Y	N	N	Y
12 Bonior	Y	Y	Y	N	Y	Y
13 Diggs	#	?	Y	N	#	?
14 Nedzi	Y	Y	Y	Y	Y	Y
15 Ford	Y	?	?	Y	Y	Y
16 Dingell	?	?	Y	Y	Y	Y
17 Brodhead	Y	Y	Y	Y	Y	Y
18 Blanchard	Y	Y	Y	Y	Y	Y
19 Broomfield	Y	N	Y	Y	N	Y
MINNESOTA						
1 Quie	?	?	?	?	?	?
2 Hagedorn	?	?	?	?	?	?
3 Frenzel	Y	Y	Y	Y	N	Y
4 Vento	Y	Y	Y	N	Y	?
5 Fraser	?	?	?	?	?	?
6 Nolan	Y	Y	?	N	Y	?
7 Stangeland	Y	Y	Y	Y	N	Y
8 Oberstar	Y	Y	Y	N	Y	Y
MISSISSIPPI						
1 Whitten	#	?	Y	N	N	Y
2 Bowen	?	?	Y	Y	N	Y
3 Montgomery	Y	?	Y	Y	N	N
4 Cochran	?	?	?	?	?	?
5 Lott	Y	Y	Y	Y	N	Y
MISSOURI						
1 Clay	Y	N	Y	N	?	?
2 Young	Y	Y	Y	N	Y	Y
3 Gephardt	Y	Y	Y	N	Y	Y
4 Skelton	Y	Y	Y	N	?	?
5 Bolling	Y	Y	Y	Y	Y	Y
6 Coleman	Y	Y	Y	Y	N	Y
7 Taylor	Y	Y	Y	Y	N	N
8 Ichord	?	Y	Y	Y	Y	Y
9 Volkmer	?	Y	N	N	Y	Y
10 Burlison	?	Y	Y	N	Y	Y
MONTANA						
1 Baucus	Y	Y	Y	Y	?	?
2 Marlenee	?	Y	Y	N	Y	Y
NEBRASKA						
1 Thone	?	?	?	?	?	?
2 Cavanaugh	Y	Y	Y	Y	Y	Y
3 Smith	Y	Y	Y	Y	?	?
NEVADA						
AL Santini	Y	Y	?	N	Y	Y
NEW HAMPSHIRE						
1 D'Amours	Y	Y	Y	N	Y	Y
2 Cleveland	Y	Y	Y	Y	N	Y
NEW JERSEY						
1 Florio	Y	Y	Y	Y	Y	?
2 Hughes	Y	Y	Y	N	Y	Y
3 Howard	Y	?	Y	#	#	#
4 Thompson	Y	?	Y	N	Y	Y
5 Fenwick	Y	Y	Y	Y	N	Y
6 Forsythe	#	?	Y	N	N	?
7 Maguire	Y	Y	?	?	?	?
8 Roe	Y	?	Y	N	Y	Y
9 Hollenbeck	#	?	Y	Y	Y	?
10 Rodino	#	?	?	▮	#	#
11 Minish	Y	Y	Y	Y	Y	?
12 Rinaldo	Y	Y	Y	#	#	#
13 Meyner	Y	?	Y	Y	Y	Y
14 LeFante	Y	Y	Y	N	Y	Y
15 Patten	Y	Y	Y	N	Y	Y
NEW MEXICO						
1 Lujan	Y	Y	?	?	?	?
2 Runnels	Y	Y	Y	Y	N	N
NEW YORK						
1 Pike	#	?	Y	N	N	N
2 Downey	#	Y	Y	N	Y	Y
3 Ambro	?	Y	Y	N	Y	Y
4 Lent	?	?	Y	Y	Y	Y
5 Wydler	N	Y	Y	Y	Y	N
6 Wolff	Y	Y	Y	Y	Y	Y
7 Addabbo	?	?	Y	N	Y	?
8 Rosenthal	Y	Y	Y	N	Y	Y
9 Delaney	Y	Y	Y	Y	?	Y
10 Biaggi	Y	Y	Y	Y	Y	?
11 Scheuer	Y	?	Y	?	Y	Y
12 Chisholm	Y	Y	?	N	Y	Y
13 Solarz	Y	Y	Y	N	Y	Y
14 Richmond	?	?	?	N	?	?
15 Zeferetti	#	?	?	#	#	#
16 Holtzman	Y	Y	Y	N	Y	Y
17 Murphy	Y	Y	Y	N	?	Y
18 Green	Y	Y	Y	Y	Y	Y
19 Rangel	?	?	?	?	?	?
20 Weiss	Y	Y	Y	N	Y	Y
21 Garcia	Y	Y	Y	N	Y	Y
22 Bingham	Y	Y	Y	N	Y	Y
23 Caputo	?	?	?	?	?	?
24 Ottinger	Y	Y	Y	N	Y	Y
25 Fish	Y	Y	?	?	?	?
26 Gilman	Y	N	Y	Y	Y	Y
27 McHugh	Y	Y	Y	N	Y	Y
28 Stratton	Y	Y	Y	Y	Y	Y
29 Pattison	Y	Y	Y	N	Y	Y
30 McEwen	Y	Y	Y	Y	Y	Y
31 Mitchell	Y	Y	Y	Y	Y	Y
32 Hanley	Y	Y	Y	N	Y	Y
33 Walsh	Y	Y	Y	Y	Y	Y
34 Horton	Y	Y	Y	#	#	#
35 Conable	Y	Y	Y	Y	N	Y
36 LaFalce	Y	Y	Y	Y	Y	Y
37 Nowak	Y	Y	Y	Y	Y	Y
38 Kemp	?	?	Y	Y	Y	Y
39 Lundine	Y	Y	Y	N	Y	Y
NORTH CAROLINA						
1 Jones	Y	?	Y	Y	N	N
2 Fountain	Y	Y	Y	Y	N	N
3 Whitley	Y	Y	Y	N	N	N
4 Andrews	Y	Y	Y	N	N	N
5 Neal	Y	Y	Y	Y	Y	Y
6 Preyer	Y	Y	Y	N	Y	Y
7 Rose	Y	Y	Y	N	N	N
8 Hefner	Y	Y	Y	Y	N	Y
9 Martin	Y	Y	Y	Y	N	Y
10 Broyhill	Y	Y	Y	Y	N	Y
11 Gudger	Y	Y	Y	N	Y	Y
NORTH DAKOTA						
AL Andrews	Y	Y	Y	Y	N	Y
OHIO						
1 Gradison	Y	Y	Y	Y	N	Y
2 Luken	Y	Y	Y	Y	Y	Y
3 Whalen	Y	Y	Y	Y	Y	?
4 Guyer	#	?	?	#	#	#
5 Latta	Y	Y	Y	Y	N	?
6 Harsha	Y	?	Y	Y	N	Y
7 Brown	Y	Y	Y	Y	Y	Y
8 Kindness	?	?	Y	Y	N	Y
9 Ashley	?	?	Y	Y	Y	Y
10 Miller	Y	Y	Y	Y	N	Y
11 Stanton	Y	Y	Y	Y	Y	Y
12 Devine	Y	Y	Y	Y	N	Y
13 Pease	Y	Y	Y	N	Y	?
14 Seiberling	Y	Y	Y	N	Y	Y
15 Wylie	Y	Y	Y	Y	N	Y
16 Regula	Y	Y	Y	Y	Y	Y
17 Ashbrook	Y	Y	?	#	▮	▮
18 Applegate	Y	Y	?	N	Y	Y
19 Carney	?	Y	Y	Y	Y	Y
20 Oakar	Y	Y	?	?	?	?
21 Stokes	Y	N	Y	N	Y	Y
22 Vanik	Y	Y	Y	Y	Y	Y
23 Mottl	Y	Y	Y	N	Y	?
OKLAHOMA						
1 Jones	Y	Y	Y	?	N	Y
2 Risenhoover	Y	Y	Y	Y	Y	Y
3 Watkins	Y	?	Y	Y	N	Y
4 Steed	Y	Y	Y	N	Y	N
5 Edwards	Y	Y	Y	Y	N	?
6 English	Y	Y	Y	?	N	Y
OREGON						
1 AuCoin	#	?	Y	?	?	Y
2 Ullman	Y	Y	Y	Y	Y	Y
3 Duncan	#	?	?	#	#	#
4 Weaver	Y	Y	Y	N	Y	Y
PENNSYLVANIA						
1 Myers, M.	Y	Y	Y	N	Y	Y
2 Nix	Y	Y	Y	?	?	?
3 Lederer	Y	Y	Y	N	Y	Y
4 Eilberg	Y	Y	P	Y	Y	Y
5 Schulze	Y	Y	Y	Y	Y	Y
6 Yatron	#	?	Y	Y	Y	Y
7 Edgar	Y	Y	Y	N	Y	Y
8 Kostmayer	Y	Y	Y	N	Y	Y
9 Shuster	Y	Y	Y	Y	Y	Y
10 McDade	Y	Y	Y	Y	Y	?
11 Flood	Y	Y	Y	Y	Y	Y
12 Murtha	Y	Y	Y	Y	Y	Y
13 Coughlin	Y	?	Y	Y	#	?
14 Moorhead	Y	Y	Y	N	Y	Y
15 Rooney	#	?	P	N	Y	Y
16 Walker	Y	Y	Y	Y	Y	Y
17 Ertel	Y	Y	Y	Y	Y	Y
18 Walgren	Y	Y	Y	N	Y	Y
19 Goodling, W.	Y	Y	Y	Y	N	Y
20 Gaydos	P	Y	?	N	Y	Y
21 Dent	#	?	?	▮	#	#
22 Murphy	Y	Y	Y	N	Y	Y
23 Ammerman	?	?	?	?	?	?
24 Marks	Y	Y	Y	N	Y	Y
25 Myers, G.	Y	Y	?	▮	#	#
RHODE ISLAND						
1 St Germain	Y	Y	?	?	?	?
2 Beard	Y	Y	Y	N	#	Y
SOUTH CAROLINA						
1 Davis	Y	N	Y	Y	N	Y
2 Spence	Y	Y	Y	Y	N	Y
3 Derrick	Y	Y	Y	#	#	#
4 Mann	Y	?	Y	Y	Y	Y
5 Holland	?	?	Y	Y	Y	Y
6 Jenrette	Y	?	Y	Y	#	?
SOUTH DAKOTA						
1 Pressler	?	?	?	?	?	?
2 Abdnor	#	#	?	?	#	#
TENNESSEE						
1 Quillen	#	?	?	#	#	#
2 Duncan	Y	Y	Y	Y	N	Y
3 Lloyd	Y	Y	Y	Y	Y	Y
4 Gore	Y	Y	Y	N	Y	Y
5 Vacancy						
6 Beard	Y	Y	Y	Y	N	Y
7 Jones	Y	Y	Y	N	Y	?
8 Ford	Y	Y	Y	N	Y	?
TEXAS						
1 Hall	#	Y	Y	Y	N	N
2 Wilson, C.	#	?	Y	N	Y	?
3 Collins	Y	Y	?	#	▮	▮
4 Roberts	?	?	?	Y	N	N
5 Mattox	Y	Y	Y	Y	Y	Y
6 Teague	?	?	?	?	?	?
7 Archer	?	Y	Y	Y	N	N
8 Eckhardt	?	Y	Y	N	Y	Y
9 Brooks	Y	Y	?	?	?	?
10 Pickle	#	?	Y	Y	?	?
11 Poage	Y	Y	Y	Y	N	N
12 Wright	?	Y	Y	N	Y	?
13 Hightower	Y	Y	Y	Y	N	?
14 Young	?	?	?	?	?	Y
15 de la Garza	Y	Y	Y	Y	N	Y
16 White	Y	Y	Y	Y	Y	Y
17 Burleson	Y	Y	Y	Y	N	N
18 Jordan	?	?	?	?	?	?
19 Mahon	Y	Y	?	Y	N	N
20 Gonzalez	Y	Y	Y	N	Y	Y
21 Krueger	#	?	?	#	#	#
22 Gammage	Y	Y	Y	Y	▮	?
23 Kazen	Y	?	Y	Y	N	?
24 Milford	?	?	?	?	?	?
UTAH						
1 McKay	Y	Y	Y	N	Y	N
2 Marriott	Y	Y	Y	Y	N	Y
VERMONT						
AL Jeffords	Y	Y	Y	N	Y	Y
VIRGINIA						
1 Trible	Y	Y	Y	Y	Y	Y
2 Whitehurst	Y	Y	Y	Y	N	Y
3 Satterfield	?	Y	Y	Y	N	Y
4 Daniel	Y	Y	Y	Y	N	Y
5 Daniel	?	Y	Y	Y	N	Y
6 Butler	Y	Y	Y	Y	N	Y
7 Robinson	Y	Y	Y	Y	N	Y
8 Harris	N	N	Y	N	Y	Y
9 Wampler	Y	Y	?	?	?	?
10 Fisher	Y	Y	Y	N	Y	Y
WASHINGTON						
1 Pritchard	Y	?	Y	Y	Y	Y
2 Meeds	Y	Y	Y	N	?	Y
3 Bonker	#	?	?	?	#	#
4 McCormack	Y	Y	Y	Y	Y	Y
5 Foley	Y	Y	Y	Y	Y	Y
6 Dicks	Y	Y	Y	Y	?	?
7 Cunningham	Y	Y	Y	Y	?	?
WEST VIRGINIA						
1 Mollohan	Y	Y	Y	Y	Y	Y
2 Staggers	Y	N	Y	N	Y	Y
3 Slack	Y	Y	Y	Y	Y	?
4 Rahall	Y	Y	Y	N	Y	Y
WISCONSIN						
1 Aspin	Y	Y	Y	Y	Y	?
2 Kastenmeier	Y	Y	Y	N	Y	Y
3 Baldus	Y	Y	Y	N	Y	Y
4 Zablocki	Y	Y	Y	Y	Y	Y
5 Reuss	Y	Y	Y	Y	Y	Y
6 Steiger	Y	?	Y	N	N	Y
7 Obey	Y	Y	Y	Y	Y	Y
8 Cornell	Y	Y	Y	N	Y	Y
9 Kasten	?	?	?	?	?	?
WYOMING						
AL Roncalio	#	Y	Y	N	#	#

Democrats ***Republicans***

655. HR 11280. Civil Service Reform. Udall, D-Ariz., motion that the House resolve itself into the Committee of the Whole for further consideration of the bill to reorganize the U.S Civil Service. Motion agreed to 318-4: R 108-2; D 210-2 (ND 145-2; SD 65-0), Sept. 11, 1978.

656. HR 11280. Civil Service Reform. Harris, D-Va., amendment to require each federal agency to establish a personnel office to be headed by a career civil servant. Rejected 16-336: R 5-108; D 11-228 (ND 6-161; SD 5-67), Sept. 11, 1978.

657. HR 11280. Civil Service Reform. Bonior, D-Mich., amendment to extend the use of veterans preference to Vietnam War combat veterans for 15 years after leaving the service or until 1986, whichever came later. Rejected 149-222: R 26-91; D 123-131 (ND 105-72; SD 18-59), Sept. 11, 1978. A "yea" was a vote supporting the president's position.

658. HR 11280. Civil Service Reform. Hanley, D-N.Y., amendments, en bloc, to delete provisions changing the veterans preference program. Adopted 281-88: R 107-9; D 174-79 (ND 104-72; SD 70-7), Sept. 11, 1978. A "nay" was a vote supporting the president's position.

659. HR 11280. Civil Service Reform. Leach, R-Iowa, amendment to limit the number of federal employees one year after enactment of the bill to the employment level on Jan. 1, 1977, and to impose the ceiling until Jan. 20, 1981. Adopted 251-96: R 110-2; D 141-94 (ND 86-78; SD 55-16), Sept. 11, 1978.

660. HR 11280. Civil Service Reform. Collins, R-Texas, amendment to guarantee the FBI at least 140 positions at the senior executive service levels equivalent to GS-16, GS-17, GS-18. Rejected 124-217: R 71-40; D 53-177 (ND 26-134; SD 27-43), Sept. 11, 1978.

661. HR 11280. Civil Service Reform. Erlenborn, R-Ill., amendment to delete the labor-management relations provisions from the bill. Rejected 125-217: R 78-30; D 47-187 (ND 5-156; SD 42-31), Sept. 11, 1978.

662. HR 11280. Civil Service Reform. Wilson, D-Calif., motion that the Committee of the Whole rise and report the bill back to the House with the recommendation that the enacting clause be stricken. Rejected 46-286: R 32-76; D 14-210 (ND 6-151; SD 8-59), Sept. 11, 1978. A "nay" was a vote supporting the president's position.

KEY

- Y Voted for (yea).
- ✓ Paired for.
- † Announced for.
- # CQ Poll for.
- N Voted against (nay).
- X Paired against.
- \- Announced against.
- ▮ CQ Poll against.
- P Voted "present."
- ● Voted "present" to avoid possible conflict of interest.
- ? Did not vote or otherwise make a position known.

	655	656	657	658	659	660	661	662
ALABAMA								
1 Edwards	Y	N	N	Y	Y	N	Y	N
2 Dickinson	Y	N	N	?	?	?	?	?
3 Nichols	Y	N	N	Y	Y	N	Y	N
4 Bevill	Y	N	N	Y	Y	N	N	N
5 Flippo	Y	N	N	Y	Y	N	Y	N
6 Buchanan	Y	N	N	Y	Y	Y	?	?
7 Flowers	?	?	?	?	?	?	?	?
ALASKA								
AL Young	?	▮	▮	#	#	#	#	▮
ARIZONA								
1 Rhodes	Y	N	N	Y	Y	N	N	Y
2 Udall	Y	N	Y	N	N	N	N	N
3 Stump	?	▮	▮	#	#	#	#	▮
4 Rudd	?	?	?	?	?	?	?	?
ARKANSAS								
1 Alexander	Y	N	Y	Y	N	Y	N	N
2 Tucker	Y	N	Y	Y	N	Y	N	N
3 Hammerschmidt	Y	N	N	Y	Y	Y	N	Y
4 Thornton	?	?	?	?	?	N	N	N
CALIFORNIA								
1 Johnson	Y	N	N	Y	N	Y	N	N
2 Clausen	Y	N	N	Y	Y	Y	Y	N
3 Moss	Y	N	Y	N	?	?	?	?
4 Leggett	Y	N	Y	N	N	N	N	Y
5 Burton, J.	Y	N	Y	N	N	N	N	?
6 Burton, P.	Y	N	Y	N	?	?	?	?
7 Miller	?	?	✓	X	?	?	?	?
8 Dellums	Y	N	Y	N	N	N	N	N
9 Stark	Y	N	Y	N	N	N	N	N
10 Edwards	Y	N	Y	N	N	N	N	N
11 Ryan	Y	N	Y	N	?	?	N	?
12 McCloskey	?	N	Y	N	Y	N	N	N
13 Mineta	Y	N	Y	N	N	N	N	N
14 McFall	Y	N	N	Y	N	N	N	N
15 Sisk	Y	N	N	Y	?	?	?	?
16 Panetta	?	N	N	Y	Y	N	N	N
17 Krebs	Y	N	Y	Y	Y	N	N	N
18 Vacancy								
19 Lagomarsino	Y	N	N	Y	Y	Y	Y	N
20 Goldwater	?	N	N	Y	Y	Y	Y	N
21 Corman	Y	N	Y	N	N	N	N	N
22 Moorhead	?	?	#	#	#	#	#	?
23 Beilenson	?	N	Y	N	N	N	N	N
24 Waxman	Y	N	Y	N	N	N	N	N
25 Roybal	Y	N	Y	Y	N	N	N	N
26 Rousselot	?	?	?	?	?	?	?	?
27 Dornan	Y	N	N	Y	Y	Y	Y	Y
28 Burke	?	▮	✓	X	#	▮	▮	▮
29 Hawkins	Y	N	Y	N	N	N	?	?
30 Danielson	Y	N	Y	Y	N	N	N	N
31 Wilson, C.H.	Y	▮	N	Y	#	N	Y	Y
32 Anderson	Y	N	N	Y	N	N	N	N
33 Clawson	?	?	?	?	?	?	?	?
34 Hannaford	Y	Y	N	Y	N	N	N	N
35 Lloyd	N	Y	N	Y	Y	Y	N	N
36 Brown	Y	N	Y	N	?	N	N	?
37 Pettis	?	?	?	?	?	?	?	?
38 Patterson	Y	N	Y	N	N	N	N	N
39 Wiggins	?	▮	▮	▮	#	▮	#	▮
40 Badham	Y	N	N	Y	Y	Y	Y	N
41 Wilson, B.	?	?	?	?	?	?	?	?
42 Van Deerlin	Y	N	Y	N	N	N	N	N
43 Burgener	?	?	?	?	?	?	?	?
COLORADO								
1 Schroeder	Y	N	Y	N	Y	N	N	N
2 Wirth	Y	N	Y	Y	Y	N	N	N
3 Evans	Y	?	Y	N	N	#	#	#
4 Johnson	?	?	?	?	?	?	?	?
5 Armstrong	?	?	?	?	?	?	?	?
CONNECTICUT								
1 Cotter	?	N	Y	Y	Y	N	N	N
2 Dodd	?	N	Y	Y	Y	N	N	N
3 Giaimo	Y	N	Y	Y	N	N	?	N
4 McKinney	Y	N	Y	Y	Y	N	?	?
5 Sarasin	?	?	?	?	?	?	▮	▮
6 Moffett	?	N	Y	N	Y	?	N	?
DELAWARE								
AL Evans	Y	N	N	Y	?	?	?	?
FLORIDA								
1 Sikes	Y	N	N	Y	Y	Y	N	N
2 Fuqua	?	?	▮	#	#	▮	▮	▮
3 Bennett	Y	Y	N	Y	Y	N	Y	N
4 Chappell	?	?	X	✓	?	?	?	?
5 Kelly	?	?	N	Y	Y	Y	Y	N
6 Young	Y	N	N	Y	Y	Y	N	N
7 Gibbons	?	?	?	?	?	?	?	?
8 Ireland	?	N	N	Y	Y	?	Y	N
9 Frey	?	?	?	?	?	?	?	?
10 Bafalis	Y	N	N	Y	Y	Y	Y	N
11 Rogers	Y	N	N	Y	Y	N	N	N
12 Burke	?	?	?	?	?	?	?	?
13 Lehman	?	▮	#	▮	▮	▮	▮	▮
14 Pepper	?	N	N	Y	Y	N	N	N
15 Fascell	Y	N	Y	N	Y	N	N	N
GEORGIA								
1 Ginn	Y	N	N	Y	Y	Y	Y	N
2 Mathis	Y	N	N	Y	?	Y	Y	?
3 Brinkley	Y	N	Y	Y	Y	Y	Y	N
4 Levitas	Y	N	N	Y	Y	Y	Y	N
5 Fowler	Y	N	Y	Y	Y	Y	N	N
6 Flynt	Y	N	N	Y	Y	?	Y	Y
7 McDonald	Y	N	N	Y	Y	Y	Y	Y
8 Evans	Y	N	N	Y	#	N	Y	#
9 Jenkins	?	?	#	#	#	#	▮	▮
10 Barnard	Y	N	Y	Y	Y	Y	Y	Y
HAWAII								
1 Heftel	Y	N	N	Y	Y	N	N	N
2 Akaka	Y	N	N	Y	N	N	N	N
IDAHO								
1 Symms	Y	N	N	Y	Y	Y	Y	Y
2 Hansen, G.	?	?	?	?	?	?	?	?
ILLINOIS								
1 Metcalfe	Y	N	Y	N	N	N	N	N
2 Murphy	?	▮	N	Y	N	N	N	N
3 Russo	Y	N	N	Y	Y	N	N	N
4 Derwinski	Y	N	N	Y	Y	N	N	N
5 Fary	?	?	X	✓	?	?	?	?
6 Hyde	Y	N	N	Y	Y	Y	Y	N
7 Collins	Y	N	#	Y	N	N	N	N
8 Rostenkowski	Y	N	Y	Y	N	N	N	N
9 Yates	Y	N	Y	N	N	N	N	N
10 Mikva	Y	N	Y	N	#	?	?	?
11 Annunzio	Y	N	N	Y	Y	Y	▮	▮
12 Crane	Y	N	N	Y	Y	Y	Y	Y
13 McClory	Y	N	N	Y	Y	Y	Y	N
14 Erlenborn	Y	N	N	N	Y	N	Y	N
15 Corcoran	Y	N	✓	X	#	?	?	?
16 Anderson	Y	?	Y	N	Y	N	N	N
17 O'Brien	Y	N	N	Y	Y	Y	N	N
18 Michel	Y	N	Y	Y	Y	N	Y	N
19 Railsback	Y	N	Y	Y	Y	N	N	N
20 Findley	Y	N	Y	Y	Y	N	Y	N
21 Madigan	Y	N	Y	Y	Y	Y	Y	N
22 Shipley	?	N	N	?	?	?	?	?
23 Price	Y	N	N	Y	N	N	N	N
24 Simon	Y	N	Y	N	N	N	N	N
INDIANA								
1 Benjamin	Y	N	Y	Y	Y	N	N	N
2 Fithian	Y	N	Y	Y	Y	N	N	N
3 Brademas	Y	N	Y	Y	Y	N	N	N
4 Quayle	N	N	Y	Y	Y	N	Y	Y
5 Hillis	Y	N	N	Y	Y	Y	N	N
6 Evans	Y	N	N	Y	Y	N	N	N
7 Myers, J.	Y	N	N	Y	Y	Y	Y	Y
8 Cornwell	Y	N	Y	Y	Y	N	N	N
9 Hamilton	Y	N	Y	Y	Y	N	N	N
10 Sharp	Y	N	Y	Y	Y	N	N	N
11 Jacobs	Y	N	Y	N	Y	N	N	N
IOWA								
1 Leach	Y	N	Y	N	Y	Y	Y	N
2 Blouin	Y	N	Y	N	Y	N	N	N
3 Grassley	Y	N	N	Y	Y	N	Y	N
4 Smith	Y	N	Y	N	Y	Y	N	N
5 Harkin	Y	N	Y	N	Y	N	N	N
6 Bedell	Y	Y	Y	N	Y	N	N	N

Democrats ***Republicans***

	655	656	657	658	659	660	661	662
KANSAS								
1 Sebelius	Y	N	N	Y	Y	N	Y	Y
2 Keys	Y	N	Y	N	Y	N	N	N
3 Winn	Y	N	N	Y	Y	N	Y	N
4 Glickman	Y	N	Y	Y	Y	N	N	N
5 Skubitz	?	N	N	Y	?	N	N	N
KENTUCKY								
1 Hubbard	Y	N	N	Y	Y	Y	Y	N
2 Natcher	Y	N	N	Y	Y	N	N	N
3 Mazzoli	Y	N	Y	N	Y	N	N	Y
4 Snyder	Y	N	N	Y	Y	Y	Y	Y
5 Carter	Y	N	N	Y	Y	Y	Y	Y
6 Breckinridge	Y	Y	Y	Y	Y	N	Y	Y
7 Perkins	Y	N	N	Y	Y	N	N	N
LOUISIANA								
1 Livingston	Y	N	N	Y	Y	Y	Y	N
2 Boggs	Y	N	N	Y	N	N	N	N
3 Treen	Y	N	N	Y	Y	Y	Y	N
4 Waggonner	Y	N	N	Y	Y	Y	Y	Y
5 Huckaby	?	?	?	?	?	?	?	?
6 Moore	Y	N	N	Y	Y	Y	Y	N
7 Breaux	?	?	X	✓	?	?	✓	?
8 Long	Y	N	N	Y	Y	N	N	N
MAINE								
1 Emery	Y	N	X	?	?	?	?	?
2 Cohen	?	▮	?	#	?	?	?	▮
MARYLAND								
1 Bauman	Y	N	N	Y	Y	Y	Y	Y
2 Long	Y	N	N	Y	N	N	N	N
3 Mikulski	Y	N	Y	N	Y	N	N	N
4 Holt	Y	Y	N	Y	Y	?	Y	Y
5 Spellman	Y	Y	Y	Y	Y	Y	N	Y
6 Byron	?	?	?	?	?	?	?	?
7 Mitchell	N	N	Y	N	▮	▮	X	▮
8 Steers	Y	Y	Y	N	N	Y	N	Y
MASSACHUSETTS								
1 Conte	Y	N	Y	Y	Y	N	N	N
2 Boland	?	N	N	Y	#	▮	N	N
3 Early	Y	N	N	Y	Y	N	N	N
4 Drinan	Y	N	Y	N	Y	N	N	N
5 Tsongas	?	?	?	?	?	?	?	?
6 Harrington	Y	N	Y	N	Y	▮	▮	▮
7 Markey	Y	N	Y	N	Y	N	N	N
8 O'Neill								
9 Moakley	Y	N	N	Y	Y	N	N	N
10 Heckler	Y	N	N	Y	Y	N	N	N
11 Burke	Y	N	N	Y	Y	Y	?	?
12 Studds	Y	N	Y	N	Y	N	N	N
MICHIGAN								
1 Conyers	?	N	Y	N	▮	▮	▮	▮
2 Pursell	?	?	Y	Y	Y	N	?	?
3 Brown	?	?	?	?	?	?	?	?
4 Stockman	Y	N	Y	Y	Y	N	Y	N
5 Sawyer	Y	N	N	Y	Y	N	N	Y
6 Carr	Y	N	Y	N	N	N	N	N
7 Kildee	Y	N	N	Y	Y	N	N	N
8 Traxler	?	▮	▮	#	#	▮	▮	▮
9 Vander Jagt	?	?	?	?	?	?	?	?
10 Cederberg	Y	N	N	Y	Y	Y	Y	N
11 Ruppe	Y	N	Y	Y	Y	Y	Y	N
12 Bonior	Y	N	Y	N	N	N	N	N
13 Diggs	?	N	Y	X	N	▮	N	N
14 Nedzi	Y	N	Y	N	N	N	N	N
15 Ford	Y	N	Y	N	N	N	N	N
16 Dingell	Y	N	N	Y	?	N	N	?
17 Brodhead	Y	N	Y	N	Y	N	N	N
18 Blanchard	Y	N	Y	N	Y	N	N	N
19 Broomfield	Y	N	N	Y	Y	Y	Y	Y
MINNESOTA								
1 Quie	?	?	?	?	?	?	?	?
2 Hagedorn	?	?	?	?	?	?	?	?
3 Frenzel	Y	N	N	Y	Y	Y	Y	N
4 Vento	Y	N	Y	Y	Y	N	N	N
5 Fraser	?	?	?	?	?	?	?	?
6 Nolan	Y	N	Y	N	N	N	N	N
7 Stangeland	Y	N	N	Y	Y	Y	Y	Y
8 Oberstar	Y	N	N	Y	N	N	N	N
MISSISSIPPI								
1 Whitten	Y	N	N	Y	Y	▮	▮	▮
2 Bowen	Y	N	N	Y	Y	Y	Y	N
3 Montgomery	Y	N	N	Y	Y	Y	Y	▮
4 Cochran	?	?	?	?	?	?	?	?
5 Lott	Y	N	N	Y	Y	Y	Y	N
MISSOURI								
1 Clay	Y	N	Y	N	N	N	N	N
2 Young	Y	N	N	Y	Y	Y	N	N
3 Gephardt	?	N	N	Y	Y	Y	N	N

	655	656	657	658	659	660	661	662
4 Skelton	Y	N	N	Y	Y	Y	N	N
5 Bolling	Y	N	Y	N	N	N	N	N
6 Coleman	Y	N	N	Y	Y	Y	N	Y
7 Taylor	Y	N	N	Y	Y	Y	Y	Y
8 Ichord	Y	N	N	Y	Y	Y	Y	?
9 Volkmer	Y	N	N	Y	Y	Y	N	N
10 Burlison	Y	N	N	Y	Y	N	N	N
MONTANA								
1 Baucus	Y	N	N	Y	Y	N	N	N
2 Marlenee	N	N	N	Y	Y	N	Y	Y
NEBRASKA								
1 Thone	Y	N	N	Y	Y	N	Y	N
2 Cavanaugh	Y	N	Y	Y	Y	?	N	?
3 Smith	Y	N	N	Y	Y	?	?	?
NEVADA								
AL Santini	Y	N	N	Y	Y	N	N	N
NEW HAMPSHIRE								
1 D'Amours	Y	N	N	Y	Y	N	N	N
2 Cleveland	Y	N	N	Y	Y	Y	N	N
NEW JERSEY								
1 Florio	Y	N	N	Y	Y	N	N	N
2 Hughes	Y	N	Y	Y	Y	N	N	N
3 Howard	?	N	Y	Y	N	N	N	N
4 Thompson	Y	N	Y	Y	N	N	N	N
5 Fenwick	Y	N	Y	N	Y	N	N	N
6 Forsythe	Y	N	Y	Y	Y	▮	#	▮
7 Maguire	Y	N	Y	N	Y	N	N	N
8 Roe	Y	N	N	Y	Y	N	N	N
9 Hollenbeck	Y	N	Y	Y	#	N	?	▮
10 Rodino	?	?	#	#	#	▮	▮	▮
11 Minish	Y	N	N	Y	N	Y	N	N
12 Rinaldo	Y	N	N	Y	#	▮	▮	▮
13 Meyner	Y	N	N	Y	N	N	N	N
14 LeFante	Y	N	N	Y	N	N	N	N
15 Patten	P	N	N	Y	N	N	N	N
NEW MEXICO								
1 Lujan	?	?	?	?	?	?	✓	?
2 Runnels	Y	N	N	Y	Y	Y	Y	Y
NEW YORK								
1 Pike	Y	N	Y	N	Y	N	N	N
2 Downey	Y	N	Y	N	N	N	N	N
3 Ambro	Y	N	N	Y	Y	N	N	N
4 Lent	Y	N	N	Y	Y	Y	N	N
5 Wydler	Y	N	N	Y	Y	Y	Y	N
6 Wolff	Y	N	N	Y	Y	Y	N	N
7 Addabbo	Y	N	N	Y	N	?	X	N
8 Rosenthal	Y	N	Y	Y	N	N	N	N
9 Delaney	?	?	?	?	?	?	?	?
10 Biaggi	?	N	N	Y	?	?	?	?
11 Scheuer	Y	N	Y	N	N	N	N	N
12 Chisholm	?	?	✓	X	?	▮	?	▮
13 Solarz	Y	N	Y	N	N	N	N	N
14 Richmond	?	?	✓	X	?	?	X	?
15 Zeferetti	?	?	X	✓	#	?	X	▮
16 Holtzman	?	?	Y	N	N	N	N	N
17 Murphy	Y	N	N	Y	N	N	N	N
18 Green	Y	N	Y	N	Y	N	N	N
19 Rangel	Y	N	Y	N	?	?	?	?
20 Weiss	Y	N	Y	N	N	N	N	N
21 Garcia	?	N	Y	N	N	N	N	N
22 Bingham	Y	N	Y	N	N	?	N	N
23 Caputo	?	?	N	Y	Y	N	N	N
24 Ottinger	Y	N	Y	N	N	N	N	N
25 Fish	?	Y	N	Y	Y	?	?	?
26 Gilman	Y	Y	N	Y	Y	Y	N	N
27 McHugh	Y	N	Y	N	N	N	N	N
28 Stratton	?	?	X	✓	#	#	▮	▮
29 Pattison	Y	N	Y	N	N	N	▮	N
30 McEwen	Y	N	N	Y	Y	Y	Y	Y
31 Mitchell	Y	N	N	Y	Y	Y	N	N
32 Hanley	Y	N	N	Y	▮	▮	N	N
33 Walsh	Y	N	N	Y	Y	Y	N	Y
34 Horton	Y	?	N	Y	Y	N	Y	N
35 Conable	Y	N	Y	Y	Y	N	Y	N
36 LaFalce	?	N	Y	N	N	N	N	▮
37 Nowak	?	?	Y	Y	Y	N	N	N
38 Kemp	?	?	?	?	?	?	?	?
39 Lundine	Y	N	Y	Y	Y	N	N	N
NORTH CAROLINA								
1 Jones	Y	N	N	Y	Y	Y	Y	N
2 Fountain	Y	N	N	Y	Y	Y	Y	N
3 Whitley	Y	N	N	Y	Y	N	Y	N
4 Andrews	Y	N	N	Y	N	N	Y	N
5 Neal	?	?	N	Y	Y	Y	Y	N
6 Preyer	Y	N	N	Y	N	N	Y	N
7 Rose	Y	N	N	Y	Y	Y	Y	N
8 Hefner	Y	N	N	Y	Y	N	Y	N

	655	656	657	658	659	660	661	662
9 Martin	Y	N	N	Y	Y	Y	Y	N
10 Broyhill	Y	N	N	Y	Y	Y	Y	Y
11 Gudger	Y	N	N	Y	Y	Y	Y	N
NORTH DAKOTA								
AL Andrews	Y	N	N	Y	Y	Y	N	N
OHIO								
1 Gradison	Y	N	Y	Y	Y	Y	Y	N
2 Luken	Y	N	N	Y	Y	N	N	N
3 Whalen	Y	N	Y	N	Y	N	N	N
4 Guyer	Y	N	N	Y	Y	Y	Y	N
5 Latta	?	?	?	?	?	?	?	?
6 Harsha	Y	N	N	Y	Y	Y	Y	N
7 Brown	?	?	?	#	?	?	#	?
8 Kindness	Y	N	N	Y	Y	Y	Y	Y
9 Ashley	Y	N	Y	N	N	N	N	N
10 Miller	Y	N	N	Y	Y	Y	Y	N
11 Stanton	Y	N	N	Y	Y	Y	Y	N
12 Devine	Y	N	N	Y	Y	Y	Y	N
13 Pease	?	N	Y	N	N	N	N	N
14 Seiberling	Y	N	Y	N	N	N	N	N
15 Wylie	Y	N	N	Y	Y	Y	Y	N
16 Regula	Y	N	N	Y	Y	Y	Y	N
17 Ashbrook	Y	N	N	Y	Y	Y	Y	Y
18 Applegate	?	?	N	Y	Y	Y	N	Y
19 Carney	Y	Y	N	Y	Y	N	N	N
20 Oakar	?	?	Y	N	Y	N	N	N
21 Stokes	Y	N	Y	N	N	N	?	N
22 Vanik	?	N	Y	Y	Y	Y	N	N
23 Mottl	Y	N	Y	Y	Y	Y	N	N
OKLAHOMA								
1 Jones	Y	N	Y	N	Y	N	Y	N
2 Risenhoover	Y	N	N	Y	?	?	?	?
3 Watkins	Y	N	N	Y	Y	Y	Y	N
4 Steed	Y	N	N	Y	Y	N	N	N
5 Edwards	Y	N	N	Y	Y	Y	Y	Y
6 English	Y	N	N	Y	Y	Y	Y	N
OREGON								
1 AuCoin	Y	N	Y	Y	Y	N	N	N
2 Ullman	Y	N	Y	Y	N	N	N	N
3 Duncan	Y	N	N	Y	N	N	Y	N
4 Weaver	Y	N	Y	Y	Y	N	N	N
PENNSYLVANIA								
1 Myers, M.	Y	N	N	Y	N	N	N	N
2 Nix	Y	N	Y	N	N	N	N	N
3 Lederer	Y	N	N	Y	Y	Y	N	N
4 Eilberg	?	?	N	Y	Y	N	N	N
5 Schulze	Y	N	N	Y	Y	Y	Y	Y
6 Yatron	Y	N	N	Y	Y	Y	N	N
7 Edgar	Y	N	Y	N	Y	N	N	N
8 Kostmayer	Y	N	N	Y	Y	N	N	N
9 Shuster	Y	N	N	Y	Y	Y	Y	Y
10 McDade	Y	N	N	Y	N	N	N	N
11 Flood	?	?	✓	X	?	?	?	?
12 Murtha	Y	N	N	Y	N	Y	N	Y
13 Coughlin	Y	N	Y	Y	Y	N	Y	N
14 Moorhead	?	?	N	Y	N	N	N	N
15 Rooney	Y	N	N	Y	N	Y	N	N
16 Walker	Y	N	N	Y	Y	N	Y	N
17 Ertel	Y	N	N	Y	Y	N	Y	N
18 Walgren	Y	N	Y	Y	Y	N	N	N
19 Goodling, W.	P	N	N	Y	Y	N	Y	N
20 Gaydos	Y	N	N	Y	Y	Y	N	N
21 Dent	?	N	N	Y	Y	Y	N	N
22 Murphy	Y	Y	N	Y	Y	N	N	N
23 Ammerman	?	?	?	✓	?	?	?	?
24 Marks	Y	N	N	Y	Y	N	N	N
25 Myers, G.	Y	Y	N	Y	N	Y	Y	Y
RHODE ISLAND								
1 St Germain	?	?	?	✓	?	?	?	?
2 Beard	?	N	N	Y	Y	N	N	N
SOUTH CAROLINA								
1 Davis	Y	N	N	Y	N	N	N	Y
2 Spence	Y	N	N	Y	Y	Y	Y	N
3 Derrick	Y	?	N	Y	Y	N	N	N
4 Mann	?	?	N	Y	Y	N	N	N
5 Holland	Y	N	N	Y	Y	N	N	N
6 Jenrette	?	N	N	Y	Y	N	N	N
SOUTH DAKOTA								
1 Pressler	Y	N	N	Y	Y	N	N	N
2 Abdnor	Y	?	N	Y	Y	N	Y	N
TENNESSEE								
1 Quillen	Y	N	N	Y	Y	Y	Y	Y
2 Duncan	Y	N	N	Y	Y	Y	Y	Y
3 Lloyd	Y	N	N	Y	N	Y	Y	N
4 Gore	Y	N	Y	Y	N	N	N	N
5 Vacancy								
6 Beard	Y	N	N	Y	Y	Y	Y	N

	655	656	657	658	659	660	661	662
7 Jones	?	N	N	Y	N	N	Y	N
8 Ford	?	N	Y	N	N	N	N	N
TEXAS								
1 Hall	Y	N	N	Y	Y	Y	Y	N
2 Wilson, C.	Y	N	Y	N	#	N	N	▮
3 Collins	Y	N	N	Y	Y	Y	Y	Y
4 Roberts	Y	N	N	Y	Y	Y	Y	N
5 Mattox	Y	N	Y	Y	Y	N	N	N
6 Teague	?	?	X	?	?	?	✓	?
7 Archer	Y	N	N	Y	Y	Y	Y	N
8 Eckhardt	?	?	✓	X	?	?	?	?
9 Brooks	Y	?	N	Y	N	N	N	N
10 Pickle	?	N	N	Y	Y	N	N	N
11 Poage	Y	N	Y	N	Y	N	Y	N
12 Wright	Y	N	N	Y	?	?	?	?
13 Hightower	Y	N	Y	Y	Y	N	Y	N
14 Young	?	?	N	Y	?	?	?	?
15 de la Garza	Y	N	N	Y	Y	N	Y	N
16 White	Y	N	N	Y	Y	N	Y	N
17 Burleson	Y	N	N	Y	Y	#	✓	#
18 Jordan	?	N	Y	N	N	N	N	N
19 Mahon	Y	N	N	Y	Y	N	Y	N
20 Gonzalez	?	Y	N	Y	N	P	N	#
21 Krueger	?	?	▮	✓	#	▮	▮	▮
22 Gammage	Y	N	N	Y	Y	N	N	N
23 Kazen	Y	N	N	Y	Y	N	Y	N
24 Milford	?	N	N	Y	Y	N	Y	?
UTAH								
1 McKay	?	?	N	Y	Y	N	N	N
2 Marriott	Y	N	N	Y	Y	Y	Y	N
VERMONT								
AL Jeffords	Y	N	Y	Y	Y	N	N	N
VIRGINIA								
1 Trible	Y	N	N	Y	Y	N	Y	N
2 Whitehurst	Y	N	Y	Y	Y	Y	Y	N
3 Satterfield	Y	N	N	Y	Y	Y	Y	N
4 Daniel	Y	N	N	Y	Y	Y	Y	N
5 Daniel	Y	N	N	Y	Y	Y	Y	N
6 Butler	?	N	Y	Y	Y	Y	Y	N
7 Robinson	Y	N	N	Y	Y	Y	Y	N
8 Harris	Y	Y	Y	Y	N	Y	N	Y
9 Wampler	Y	N	N	Y	Y	Y	Y	N
10 Fisher	Y	Y	Y	Y	N	N	N	N
WASHINGTON								
1 Pritchard	Y	N	Y	N	Y	N	Y	N
2 Meeds	Y	N	Y	N	N	N	?	N
3 Bonker	?	#	?	#	#	▮	N	N
4 McCormack	Y	N	Y	Y	Y	N	N	N
5 Foley	Y	N	Y	Y	Y	N	N	N
6 Dicks	Y	N	N	Y	N	N	N	N
7 Cunningham	Y	N	N	Y	Y	Y	Y	N
WEST VIRGINIA								
1 Mollohan	Y	N	N	Y	Y	Y	N	N
2 Staggers	?	N	N	Y	Y	N	N	N
3 Slack	Y	N	N	Y	N	Y	N	N
4 Rahall	?	N	N	Y	N	N	N	N
WISCONSIN								
1 Aspin	?	?	Y	N	Y	N	N	N
2 Kastenmeier	Y	N	Y	N	N	N	N	N
3 Baldus	Y	N	Y	Y	Y	N	N	N
4 Zablocki	Y	N	N	Y	Y	Y	N	N
5 Reuss	Y	N	Y	N	N	N	N	N
6 Steiger	?	?	▮	#	#	Y	N	N
7 Obey	Y	N	Y	N	N	N	N	N
8 Cornell	Y	N	N	Y	Y	N	N	N
9 Kasten	?	?	?	?	?	?	?	?
WYOMING								
AL Roncalio	?	▮	#	?	N	N	▮	▮

Democrats ***Republicans***

663. HR 12860. Rhode Island Indian Claims. Roncalio, D-Wyo., motion to suspend the rules and pass the bill to authorize $3.5 million to purchase land in Charlestown, R.I., and to establish a Rhode Island-chartered Narragansett Indian corporation to oversee the federally purchased private land and the 900 acres of state land ceded by Rhode Island in settlement of violations of the 1790 Indian Trade and Intercourse Act. Motion agreed to 249-122: R 33-95; D 216-27 (ND 155-11; SD 61-16), Sept. 12, 1978. A two-thirds majority vote (248 in this case) is required for passage under suspension of the rules.

664. HR 13311. Ports and Waterways Safety. Biaggi, D-N.Y., motion to suspend the rules and pass the bill to mandate higher standards for ship construction and safety equipment. Motion agreed to 366-6: R 124-4; D 242-2 (ND 168-0; SD 74-2), Sept. 12, 1978. A two-thirds majority vote (248 in this case) is required for passage under suspension of the rules.

665. HR 12026. Indian Peaks Wilderness Area. Roncalio, D-Wyo., motion to suspend the rules and pass the bill to create the Indian Peaks Wilderness Area and the Arapaho National Recreation Area and to authorize the secretary of the interior to study the feasibility of revising the boundaries of the Rocky Mountain National Park. Motion agreed to 360-9: R 124-4; D 236-5 (ND 162-2; SD 74-3), Sept. 12, 1978. A two-thirds majority vote (246 in this case) is required for passage under suspension of the rules.

666. HR 5265. Fluorspar Duty Suspension. Vanik, D-Ohio, motion to suspend the rules and pass the bill to provide for suspension of the duty on importation of fluorspar through June 30, 1980. Motion rejected 205-166: R 100-28; D 105-138 (ND 76-92; SD 29-46), Sept. 12, 1978. A two-thirds majority vote (248 in this case) is required for passage under suspension of the rules.

667. HR 1337. Tax Law Changes. Corman, D-Calif., motion to suspend the rules and adopt the resolution (H Res 1342) providing that the House concur, with amendments, in Senate amendments to the bill making certain changes in tax laws and in the Supplemental Security Income program. Motion agreed to 304-69: R 88-41; D 216-28 (ND 161-6; SD 55-22), Sept. 12, 1978. A two-thirds majority vote (249 in this case) is required for adoption under suspension of the rules.

668. HR 13331. Federal District Court Amendments. Kastenmeier, D-Wis., motion to suspend the rules and pass the bill to make certain changes in the location of federal district courts, in the divisions within judicial districts, and in judicial district dividing lines. Motion agreed to 362-9: R 124-5; D 238-4 (ND 162-3; SD 76-1), Sept. 12, 1978. A two-thirds majority vote (248 in this case) is required for passage under suspension of the rules.

669. S 3119. District of Columbia Land Transfer. Passage of the bill to transfer title of a parcel of federal land adjacent to the Southwest Urban Renewal Project area in the District of Columbia to the D.C. Redevelopment Land Agency. Passed 354-1: R 124-1; D 230-0 (ND 158-0; SD 72-0), Sept. 12, 1978.

670. S 3075. Foreign Military Aid. Adoption of the conference report on the bill to authorize $2,817,500,000 for foreign military assistance, arms sales and economic support programs of the State Department for fiscal 1979. Adopted (thus clearing for the president) 225-126: R 70-54; D 155-72 (ND 119-34; SD 36-38), Sept. 12, 1978.

KEY

- Y Voted for (yea).
- ✓ Paired for.
- † Announced for.
- # CQ Poll for.
- N Voted against (nay).
- X Paired against.
- - Announced against.
- ▮ CQ Poll against.
- P Voted "present."
- ● Voted "present" to avoid possible conflict of interest.
- ? Did not vote or otherwise make a position known.

	663	664	665	666	667	668	669	670
ALABAMA								
1 ***Edwards***	Y	Y	Y	Y	N	Y	Y	N
2 ***Dickinson***	?	?	?	?	?	?	?	?
3 Nichols	Y	Y	Y	N	Y	Y	Y	N
4 Bevill	Y	Y	Y	N	Y	Y	Y	N
5 Flippo	Y	Y	Y	N	Y	Y	Y	N
6 ***Buchanan***	Y	Y	Y	Y	Y	Y	Y	Y
7 Flowers	?	?	?	?	?	?	?	?
ALASKA								
AL ***Young***	#	#	?	#	#	▮	#	#
ARIZONA								
1 ***Rhodes***	N	Y	Y	Y	N	Y	Y	Y
2 Udall	Y	Y	Y	N	Y	Y	Y	Y
3 Stump	▮	#	?	#	#	#	#	X
4 ***Rudd***	?	?	?	?	?	?	?	?
ARKANSAS								
1 Alexander	Y	Y	Y	Y	Y	Y	Y	Y
2 Tucker	Y	Y	Y	Y	Y	Y	Y	Y
3 ***Hammerschmidt***	N	Y	Y	Y	N	Y	Y	N
4 Thornton	Y	Y	Y	Y	Y	Y	?	Y
CALIFORNIA								
1 Johnson	Y	Y	Y	N	Y	Y	Y	Y
2 ***Clausen***	Y	Y	Y	Y	Y	Y	Y	N
3 Moss	Y	Y	Y	N	Y	Y	Y	?
4 Leggett	Y	Y	?	Y	Y	Y	?	?
5 Burton, J.	Y	Y	Y	N	Y	Y	Y	N
6 Burton, P.	Y	Y	Y	N	Y	Y	?	Y
7 Miller	?	?	?	?	?	?	?	X
8 Dellums	Y	Y	Y	N	Y	Y	Y	N
9 Stark	Y	Y	Y	N	Y	Y	Y	N
10 Edwards	Y	Y	Y	N	Y	Y	Y	Y
11 Ryan	Y	Y	Y	N	Y	Y	Y	Y
12 ***McCloskey***	Y	Y	Y	Y	Y	Y	Y	Y
13 Mineta	Y	Y	Y	N	Y	Y	Y	Y
14 McFall	Y	Y	Y	Y	Y	Y	Y	Y
15 Sisk	Y	Y	Y	Y	Y	Y	Y	Y
16 Panetta	Y	Y	Y	N	Y	Y	Y	N
17 Krebs	Y	Y	Y	N	Y	Y	Y	N
18 Vacancy								
19 ***Lagomarsino***	Y	Y	Y	Y	Y	Y	Y	Y
20 ***Goldwater***	Y	Y	Y	Y	Y	Y	Y	?
21 Corman	Y	Y	Y	Y	Y	Y	Y	Y
22 ***Moorhead***	N	Y	Y	Y	Y	Y	Y	N
23 Beilenson	Y	Y	Y	Y	Y	Y	Y	Y
24 Waxman	Y	Y	Y	N	Y	Y	Y	Y
25 Roybal	Y	Y	?	N	Y	Y	Y	N
26 ***Rousselot***	N	Y	Y	N	Y	Y	Y	N
27 ***Dornan***	N	Y	Y	Y	Y	Y	Y	Y
28 Burke	#	#	?	▮	#	#	#	#
29 Hawkins	Y	Y	Y	N	Y	Y	Y	✓
30 Danielson	Y	Y	Y	Y	Y	Y	Y	Y
31 Wilson, C.H.	Y	Y	Y	Y	Y	Y	#	#
32 Anderson	Y	Y	Y	N	Y	Y	Y	N
33 ***Clawson***	?	?	?	?	?	?	?	?
34 Hannaford	Y	Y	Y	N	Y	Y	Y	Y
35 Lloyd	Y	Y	Y	N	Y	Y	Y	Y
36 Brown	Y	Y	Y	N	Y	Y	?	Y
37 ***Pettis***	N	Y	Y	Y	Y	Y	Y	Y
38 Patterson	Y	Y	Y	N	Y	Y	Y	Y
39 ***Wiggins***	▮	#	?	#	#	#	#	#
40 ***Badham***	N	Y	Y	Y	N	Y	Y	N
41 ***Wilson, B.***	Y	Y	Y	Y	Y	Y	Y	Y
42 Van Deerlin	Y	Y	Y	Y	Y	Y	Y	Y
43 ***Burgener***	N	Y	Y	Y	Y	Y	Y	Y
COLORADO								
1 Schroeder	Y	Y	Y	N	Y	Y	#	N
2 Wirth	Y	Y	Y	Y	Y	Y	Y	Y
3 Evans	Y	Y	Y	N	Y	Y	Y	Y
4 ***Johnson***	?	?	?	?	?	?	?	?
5 ***Armstrong***	?	?	?	?	?	?	?	?
CONNECTICUT								
1 Cotter	Y	Y	Y	Y	Y	Y	Y	Y
2 Dodd	Y	Y	Y	N	Y	Y	Y	Y
3 Giaimo	Y	Y	Y	N	Y	Y	Y	Y
4 ***McKinney***	Y	Y	Y	Y	Y	Y	Y	Y
5 ***Sarasin***	?	?	?	?	?	?	?	?
6 Moffett	Y	Y	Y	N	Y	?	Y	N
DELAWARE								
AL ***Evans***	N	Y	Y	Y	Y	Y	Y	Y
FLORIDA								
1 Sikes	Y	Y	Y	Y	Y	Y	Y	Y
2 Fuqua	#	#	?	#	#	#	#	✓
3 Bennett	N	Y	Y	Y	N	Y	Y	N
4 Chappell	Y	Y	Y	Y	Y	Y	Y	N
5 ***Kelly***	N	N	Y	Y	N	Y	N	N
6 ***Young***	N	Y	Y	Y	N	Y	Y	N
7 Gibbons	?	?	?	?	?	?	?	?
8 Ireland	?	?	?	?	?	?	?	?
9 ***Frey***	?	?	?	?	?	?	?	?
10 ***Bafalis***	Y	Y	Y	Y	N	Y	Y	N
11 Rogers	Y	Y	Y	N	Y	Y	Y	Y
12 ***Burke***	?	?	?	?	?	?	?	?
13 Lehman	#	#	?	▮	#	#	#	#
14 Pepper	Y	Y	Y	Y	Y	Y	Y	Y
15 Fascell	Y	Y	Y	N	Y	Y	Y	Y
GEORGIA								
1 Ginn	Y	Y	Y	Y	N	Y	Y	N
2 Mathis	N	Y	Y	?	Y	Y	Y	N
3 Brinkley	Y	Y	Y	Y	N	Y	Y	N
4 Levitas	Y	Y	Y	N	N	Y	Y	Y
5 Fowler	Y	Y	Y	N	N	Y	Y	Y
6 Flynt	N	Y	Y	Y	N	Y	Y	N
7 McDonald	N	N	N	Y	N	N	Y	N
8 Evans	N	Y	Y	Y	Y	Y	Y	N
9 Jenkins	Y	Y	Y	Y	N	Y	Y	N
10 Barnard	?	?	?	?	?	?	?	?
HAWAII								
1 Heftel	N	Y	Y	N	Y	Y	Y	Y
2 Akaka	Y	Y	Y	N	Y	Y	Y	Y
IDAHO								
1 ***Symms***	N	N	N	Y	N	N	Y	?
2 ***Hansen, G.***	?	?	?	?	?	?	?	X
ILLINOIS								
1 Metcalfe	Y	Y	Y	N	Y	Y	Y	Y
2 Murphy	Y	Y	Y	N	Y	Y	Y	Y
3 Russo	Y	Y	Y	N	Y	Y	Y	N
4 ***Derwinski***	Y	Y	Y	Y	Y	Y	Y	Y
5 Fary	?	?	?	?	?	?	?	✓
6 ***Hyde***	N	Y	Y	Y	N	Y	Y	Y
7 Collins	Y	Y	Y	N	Y	Y	Y	Y
8 Rostenkowski	Y	Y	Y	Y	?	?	?	?
9 Yates	Y	Y	Y	N	Y	Y	Y	Y
10 Mikva	Y	Y	Y	N	N	Y	Y	Y
11 Annunzio	Y	Y	Y	Y	Y	Y	Y	Y
12 ***Crane***	N	N	N	Y	N	N	Y	N
13 ***McClory***	N	Y	Y	Y	N	Y	Y	Y
14 ***Erlenborn***	N	Y	Y	N	Y	Y	Y	Y
15 ***Corcoran***	N	Y	Y	N	Y	Y	Y	Y
16 ***Anderson***	N	Y	Y	N	Y	Y	Y	Y
17 ***O'Brien***	N	Y	Y	#	Y	N	Y	Y
18 ***Michel***	N	Y	Y	N	Y	Y	Y	Y
19 ***Railsback***	N	Y	Y	N	Y	Y	Y	Y
20 ***Findley***	N	Y	Y	Y	Y	Y	Y	Y
21 ***Madigan***	N	Y	Y	Y	Y	Y	Y	Y
22 Shipley	Y	Y	Y	N	Y	Y	Y	Y
23 Price	Y	Y	Y	Y	Y	Y	Y	Y
24 Simon	Y	Y	Y	N	Y	Y	Y	Y
INDIANA								
1 Benjamin	Y	Y	Y	Y	Y	Y	Y	Y
2 Fithian	N	Y	Y	Y	Y	Y	Y	N
3 Brademas	Y	Y	Y	N	Y	Y	Y	Y
4 ***Quayle***	N	Y	Y	Y	Y	Y	Y	Y
5 ***Hillis***	N	Y	Y	Y	Y	Y	Y	Y
6 Evans	?	Y	N	Y	N	Y	Y	N
7 ***Myers, J.***	N	Y	Y	Y	Y	Y	Y	N
8 Cornwell	Y	Y	Y	N	Y	Y	Y	#
9 Hamilton	Y	Y	Y	Y	Y	Y	Y	Y
10 Sharp	Y	Y	Y	Y	Y	Y	Y	Y
11 Jacobs	Y	Y	N	N	Y	N	Y	N
IOWA								
1 ***Leach***	Y	Y	Y	Y	Y	Y	Y	Y
2 Blouin	Y	Y	Y	N	Y	Y	Y	N
3 ***Grassley***	N	Y	Y	Y	N	Y	Y	N
4 Smith	Y	Y	Y	Y	Y	Y	Y	Y
5 Harkin	Y	Y	Y	N	Y	Y	Y	N
6 Bedell	Y	Y	Y	N	N	Y	Y	N

Democrats ***Republicans***

	663	664	665	666	667	668	669	670
KANSAS								
1 ***Sebelius***	Y	Y	Y	N	Y	Y	Y	N
2 Keys	Y	Y	?	Y	Y	Y	Y	Y
3 ***Winn***	Y	Y	Y	Y	Y	Y	Y	Y
4 Glickman	Y	Y	Y	Y	Y	Y	Y	Y
5 ***Skubitz***	?	?	?	?	Y	Y	Y	Y
KENTUCKY								
1 Hubbard	#	?	?	▮	#	#	#	▮
2 Natcher	Y	Y	Y	N	Y	Y	Y	Y
3 Mazzoli	N	Y	Y	N	N	Y	Y	Y
4 ***Snyder***	N	Y	Y	Y	N	Y	Y	Y
5 ***Carter***	N	Y	Y	N	Y	Y	Y	N
6 Breckinridge	Y	Y	Y	N	Y	Y	Y	Y
7 Perkins	Y	Y	Y	N	Y	Y	Y	Y
LOUISIANA								
1 ***Livingston***	N	Y	Y	Y	N	Y	?	Y
2 Boggs	Y	Y	Y	N	Y	Y	Y	Y
3 ***Treen***	N	Y	Y	Y	N	Y	Y	Y
4 Waggonner	N	N	N	Y	Y	Y	#	N
5 Huckaby	?	?	?	?	?	?	?	?
6 ***Moore***	Y	Y	Y	Y	N	Y	Y	Y
7 Breaux	?	?	?	?	?	?	?	X
8 Long	Y	Y	Y	N	Y	Y	Y	Y
MAINE								
1 ***Emery***	N	Y	Y	N	Y	Y	Y	N
2 ***Cohen***	N	Y	Y	N	Y	Y	Y	Y
MARYLAND								
1 ***Bauman***	N	Y	N	Y	N	N	Y	N
2 Long	?	?	?	?	?	?	?	?
3 Mikulski	?	?	?	?	?	?	?	?
4 ***Holt***	N	Y	Y	Y	N	N	Y	N
5 Spellman	Y	Y	Y	Y	Y	Y	Y	#
6 Byron	?	?	?	?	?	?	?	X
7 Mitchell	#	#	?	#	#	#	#	X
8 ***Steers***	Y	Y	Y	Y	Y	Y	Y	Y
MASSACHUSETTS								
1 ***Conte***	Y	Y	Y	Y	Y	Y	Y	Y
2 Boland	Y	Y	Y	Y	Y	Y	Y	Y
3 Early	Y	Y	Y	Y	Y	Y	Y	Y
4 Drinan	Y	Y	?	N	Y	Y	Y	Y
5 Tsongas	?	?	?	?	?	?	?	?
6 Harrington	#	#	?	▮	?	#	#	▮
7 Markey	Y	Y	Y	N	Y	Y	Y	Y
8 O'Neill								
9 Moakley	Y	Y	Y	Y	Y	Y	Y	Y
10 ***Heckler***	Y	Y	Y	Y	Y	Y	Y	Y
11 Burke	Y	Y	Y	N	Y	Y	Y	N
12 Studds	Y	Y	Y	N	Y	Y	Y	Y
MICHIGAN								
1 Conyers	#	#	#	▮	#	#	#	X
2 ***Pursell***	Y	Y	Y	Y	Y	Y	Y	N
3 ***Brown***	N	Y	Y	N	Y	Y	Y	Y
4 ***Stockman***	N	Y	?	Y	Y	Y	Y	Y
5 ***Sawyer***	Y	Y	Y	Y	Y	Y	Y	Y
6 Carr	Y	Y	Y	N	Y	Y	Y	Y
7 Kildee	Y	Y	Y	N	Y	Y	Y	Y
8 Traxler	Y	Y	Y	Y	Y	Y	Y	Y
9 ***Vander Jagt***	?	?	?	?	?	?	?	?
10 ***Cederberg***	N	Y	Y	Y	Y	Y	Y	Y
11 ***Ruppe***	?	?	Y	Y	Y	Y	?	Y
12 Bonior	Y	Y	Y	N	Y	Y	Y	N
13 Diggs	#	#	?	#	#	#	#	?
14 Nedzi	Y	Y	Y	Y	Y	Y	Y	Y
15 Ford	?	Y	Y	Y	Y	Y	Y	Y
16 Dingell	N	Y	Y	Y	Y	Y	Y	Y
17 Brodhead	Y	Y	Y	N	Y	Y	Y	Y
18 Blanchard	Y	Y	Y	Y	Y	Y	Y	Y
19 ***Broomfield***	N	Y	Y	N	Y	Y	Y	Y
MINNESOTA								
1 ***Quie***	?	?	?	?	?	?	?	?
2 ***Hagedorn***	N	Y	Y	Y	Y	Y	Y	Y
3 ***Frenzel***	N	Y	Y	Y	Y	Y	Y	#
4 Vento	Y	Y	Y	Y	Y	Y	Y	Y
5 Fraser	?	?	?	?	?	?	?	?
6 Nolan	Y	Y	Y	N	Y	Y	?	Y
7 ***Stangeland***	N	Y	Y	Y	Y	Y	Y	N
8 Oberstar	Y	Y	Y	N	Y	Y	Y	Y
MISSISSIPPI								
1 Whitten	Y	Y	Y	N	Y	Y	#	X
2 Bowen	Y	Y	Y	Y	Y	Y	Y	N
3 Montgomery	Y	Y	Y	N	Y	Y	Y	N
4 ***Cochran***	?	?	?	?	?	?	?	?
5 ***Lott***	N	Y	Y	Y	N	Y	Y	N
MISSOURI								
1 Clay	Y	Y	Y	N	Y	Y	Y	Y
2 Young	Y	Y	Y	N	Y	Y	Y	✓
3 Gephardt	Y	Y	Y	Y	Y	Y	Y	N
4 Skelton	N	Y	Y	Y	Y	Y	Y	Y
5 Bolling	Y	Y	Y	Y	Y	Y	Y	#
6 ***Coleman***	N	Y	Y	Y	Y	Y	Y	Y
7 ***Taylor***	N	Y	Y	Y	N	Y	Y	N
8 Ichord	N	Y	Y	Y	N	Y	Y	N
9 Volkmer	Y	Y	Y	N	Y	Y	Y	N
10 Burlison	Y	Y	Y	N	Y	Y	Y	Y
MONTANA								
1 Baucus	Y	Y	Y	N	Y	Y	Y	Y
2 ***Marlenee***	Y	Y	Y	Y	N	Y	Y	N
NEBRASKA								
1 ***Thone***	N	Y	Y	N	Y	Y	Y	N
2 Cavanaugh	?	Y	Y	Y	Y	Y	Y	Y
3 ***Smith***	N	Y	Y	N	Y	Y	Y	N
NEVADA								
AL Santini	Y	Y	Y	N	Y	Y	Y	Y
NEW HAMPSHIRE								
1 D'Amours	?	#	?	?	?	#	#	?
2 ***Cleveland***	N	Y	Y	N	N	Y	Y	N
NEW JERSEY								
1 Florio	Y	Y	Y	N	Y	Y	Y	#
2 Hughes	Y	Y	Y	N	Y	Y	Y	N
3 Howard	Y	Y	Y	N	Y	Y	Y	Y
4 Thompson	Y	Y	Y	N	Y	Y	Y	Y
5 ***Fenwick***	Y	Y	Y	Y	Y	Y	Y	Y
6 ***Forsythe***	N	Y	Y	N	Y	Y	Y	N
7 Maguire	Y	Y	Y	N	N	Y	Y	Y
8 Roe	Y	Y	Y	N	Y	Y	Y	Y
9 ***Hollenbeck***	N	Y	Y	Y	Y	Y	Y	Y
10 Rodino	#	#	?	#	?	#	#	#
11 Minish	Y	Y	Y	N	Y	Y	Y	Y
12 ***Rinaldo***	Y	Y	Y	Y	Y	Y	Y	Y
13 Meyner	Y	Y	Y	Y	Y	Y	Y	Y
14 LeFante	Y	Y	Y	Y	Y	Y	Y	Y
15 Patten	Y	Y	Y	N	Y	Y	Y	Y
NEW MEXICO								
1 ***Lujan***	Y	Y	Y	Y	Y	Y	Y	N
2 Runnels	N	Y	Y	Y	Y	Y	Y	N
NEW YORK								
1 Pike	Y	Y	Y	Y	Y	Y	Y	N
2 Downey	Y	Y	Y	N	Y	Y	Y	Y
3 Ambro	Y	Y	Y	Y	Y	Y	Y	Y
4 ***Lent***	N	Y	Y	Y	Y	Y	Y	Y
5 ***Wydler***	N	Y	Y	N	Y	Y	Y	Y
6 Wolff	N	Y	Y	Y	Y	Y	Y	Y
7 Addabbo	?	?	?	?	?	?	?	✓
8 Rosenthal	Y	Y	Y	N	Y	Y	Y	Y
9 Delaney	?	?	?	?	?	?	?	?
10 Biaggi	Y	Y	Y	N	Y	Y	Y	Y
11 Scheuer	?	?	?	?	?	?	?	?
12 Chisholm	#	#	?	▮	#	#	#	✓
13 Solarz	Y	Y	Y	Y	Y	Y	Y	Y
14 Richmond	?	?	?	?	?	?	?	✓
15 Zeferetti	#	#	?	#	#	#	#	✓
16 Holtzman	?	?	?	?	?	?	?	✓
17 Murphy	?	?	?	?	?	?	?	?
18 ***Green***	N	Y	Y	Y	Y	Y	Y	Y
19 Rangel	Y	Y	Y	N	Y	Y	Y	Y
20 Weiss	Y	Y	Y	N	Y	Y	Y	✓
21 Garcia	#	#	?	#	#	#	#	✓
22 Bingham	Y	Y	Y	Y	Y	Y	Y	Y
23 ***Caputo***	N	Y	Y	Y	Y	Y	?	?
24 Ottinger	Y	Y	Y	N	Y	Y	Y	Y
25 ***Fish***	Y	Y	Y	Y	Y	Y	?	?
26 ***Gilman***	N	Y	Y	Y	Y	Y	Y	Y
27 McHugh	Y	Y	Y	Y	Y	Y	Y	Y
28 Stratton	▮	#	?	▮	#	#	#	#
29 Pattison	Y	Y	Y	Y	Y	Y	Y	Y
30 ***McEwen***	N	Y	Y	N	N	Y	Y	Y
31 ***Mitchell***	N	Y	Y	N	Y	Y	Y	Y
32 Hanley	Y	Y	Y	Y	Y	Y	Y	Y
33 ***Walsh***	Y	Y	Y	Y	Y	Y	Y	Y
34 ***Horton***	Y	Y	Y	Y	Y	Y	Y	Y
35 ***Conable***	N	Y	Y	Y	Y	Y	Y	Y
36 LaFalce	Y	Y	Y	Y	Y	Y	#	Y
37 Nowak	Y	Y	Y	Y	Y	Y	Y	Y
38 ***Kemp***	N	Y	Y	Y	Y	Y	Y	Y
39 Lundine	Y	Y	Y	Y	Y	Y	#	Y
NORTH CAROLINA								
1 Jones	Y	Y	Y	N	Y	Y	Y	N
2 Fountain	Y	Y	Y	N	N	Y	Y	N
3 Whitley	Y	Y	Y	Y	Y	Y	Y	N
4 Andrews	Y	Y	Y	N	N	Y	Y	N
5 Neal	Y	Y	Y	N	N	Y	Y	N
6 Preyer	Y	Y	Y	N	Y	Y	Y	Y
7 Rose	Y	Y	Y	Y	Y	Y	Y	N
8 Hefner	Y	Y	Y	N	N	Y	Y	N
9 ***Martin***	N	Y	Y	Y	Y	Y	Y	N
10 ***Broyhill***	N	Y	Y	N	Y	Y	Y	N
11 Gudger	Y	Y	Y	N	Y	Y	Y	N
NORTH DAKOTA								
AL ***Andrews***	Y	Y	Y	Y	Y	Y	Y	Y
OHIO								
1 ***Gradison***	N	Y	Y	Y	Y	Y	Y	Y
2 Luken	Y	Y	Y	N	Y	Y	Y	Y
3 ***Whalen***	Y	Y	Y	N	Y	Y	Y	Y
4 ***Guyer***	N	Y	Y	Y	Y	Y	Y	N
5 ***Latta***	N	Y	Y	Y	N	Y	Y	N
6 ***Harsha***	N	Y	Y	Y	Y	Y	Y	N
7 ***Brown***	?	?	?	?	?	?	?	?
8 ***Kindness***	N	Y	Y	Y	N	Y	Y	N
9 Ashley	?	?	?	?	?	?	?	✓
10 ***Miller***	N	Y	Y	Y	N	Y	Y	N
11 ***Stanton***	N	Y	Y	Y	Y	Y	Y	Y
12 ***Devine***	N	Y	Y	Y	N	Y	Y	N
13 Pease	Y	Y	Y	N	Y	Y	Y	Y
14 Seiberling	Y	Y	Y	Y	Y	Y	Y	Y
15 ***Wylie***	N	Y	Y	Y	Y	Y	Y	N
16 ***Regula***	N	Y	Y	Y	Y	Y	Y	Y
17 ***Ashbrook***	N	Y	Y	N	N	Y	Y	N
18 Applegate	Y	Y	Y	N	Y	Y	Y	N
19 Carney	Y	Y	Y	Y	Y	Y	Y	Y
20 Oakar	Y	Y	Y	N	Y	N	Y	N
21 Stokes	Y	Y	Y	N	Y	Y	?	N
22 Vanik	Y	Y	Y	Y	Y	Y	Y	Y
23 Mottl	Y	Y	Y	N	N	N	Y	N
OKLAHOMA								
1 Jones	N	Y	Y	N	Y	Y	Y	N
2 Risenhoover	?	?	?	?	?	?	?	X
3 Watkins	Y	Y	Y	N	Y	Y	Y	N
4 Steed	Y	Y	Y	Y	Y	Y	Y	N
5 ***Edwards***	N	Y	Y	Y	N	Y	Y	?
6 English	N	Y	Y	N	Y	Y	Y	N
OREGON								
1 AuCoin	Y	Y	Y	Y	Y	Y	Y	Y
2 Ullman	Y	Y	Y	Y	Y	Y	Y	Y
3 Duncan	Y	Y	Y	Y	Y	Y	Y	Y
4 Weaver	Y	Y	Y	Y	Y	Y	Y	N
PENNSYLVANIA								
1 Myers, M.	Y	Y	Y	N	Y	Y	Y	Y
2 Nix	Y	Y	Y	Y	Y	Y	Y	Y
3 Lederer	Y	Y	Y	N	Y	Y	Y	Y
4 Eilberg	Y	Y	Y	Y	Y	Y	Y	Y
5 ***Schulze***	N	Y	Y	Y	?	Y	Y	Y
6 Yatron	Y	Y	Y	Y	Y	Y	Y	Y
7 Edgar	Y	Y	Y	N	Y	Y	Y	Y
8 Kostmayer	Y	Y	Y	N	Y	Y	Y	Y
9 ***Shuster***	N	Y	Y	N	N	Y	Y	N
10 ***McDade***	N	Y	Y	Y	Y	Y	Y	Y
11 Flood	Y	Y	Y	N	Y	Y	Y	Y
12 Murtha	Y	Y	Y	N	Y	Y	Y	Y
13 ***Coughlin***	N	Y	Y	N	Y	Y	Y	Y
14 Moorhead	Y	Y	Y	Y	Y	Y	Y	Y
15 Rooney	Y	Y	Y	Y	Y	Y	Y	Y
16 ***Walker***	N	Y	Y	N	Y	Y	Y	N
17 Ertel	Y	Y	Y	Y	Y	Y	Y	?
18 Walgren	Y	Y	Y	Y	Y	Y	Y	Y
19 ***Goodling, W.***	N	Y	Y	N	Y	Y	Y	N
20 Gaydos	Y	Y	Y	N	Y	Y	Y	Y
21 Dent	Y	Y	Y	N	Y	Y	Y	Y
22 Murphy	Y	Y	Y	Y	Y	Y	Y	N
23 Ammerman	?	?	?	?	?	?	?	?
24 ***Marks***	Y	Y	Y	Y	Y	Y	Y	Y
25 ***Myers, G.***	N	Y	Y	Y	N	Y	Y	N
RHODE ISLAND								
1 St Germain	?	?	?	?	?	?	?	X
2 Beard	Y	#	?	#	#	#	#	X
SOUTH CAROLINA								
1 Davis	Y	Y	Y	N	Y	Y	Y	N
2 ***Spence***	N	Y	Y	Y	Y	Y	Y	Y
3 Derrick	Y	Y	Y	Y	Y	Y	Y	Y
4 Mann	Y	Y	Y	N	Y	Y	Y	Y
5 Holland	Y	Y	Y	N	Y	Y	Y	Y
6 Jenrette	Y	Y	Y	N	Y	Y	Y	N
SOUTH DAKOTA								
1 ***Pressler***	Y	Y	Y	Y	Y	Y	Y	N
2 ***Abdnor***	Y	Y	Y	Y	Y	Y	Y	N
TENNESSEE								
1 ***Quillen***	Y	Y	Y	Y	N	Y	Y	N
2 ***Duncan***	N	Y	Y	Y	Y	Y	Y	N
3 Lloyd	Y	Y	Y	N	Y	Y	Y	N
4 Gore	Y	Y	Y	N	Y	Y	Y	Y
5 Vacancy								
6 ***Beard***	N	Y	Y	N	N	#	Y	Y
7 Jones	Y	Y	Y	N	Y	Y	Y	N
8 Ford	Y	Y	Y	N	Y	Y	Y	Y
TEXAS								
1 Hall	Y	Y	N	N	N	Y	Y	N
2 Wilson, C.	Y	Y	Y	Y	Y	Y	Y	Y
3 ***Collins***	N	N	N	Y	N	Y	Y	N
4 Roberts	N	Y	Y	N	N	Y	Y	Y
5 Mattox	Y	Y	Y	?	Y	Y	Y	?
6 Teague	?	?	?	?	?	?	?	X
7 ***Archer***	N	Y	Y	Y	N	Y	Y	N
8 Eckhardt	Y	Y	Y	Y	Y	Y	Y	Y
9 Brooks	Y	?	Y	N	Y	Y	Y	Y
10 Pickle	Y	Y	Y	N	Y	Y	Y	Y
11 Poage	N	Y	Y	N	N	Y	Y	N
12 Wright	Y	Y	Y	Y	Y	Y	Y	Y
13 Hightower	Y	Y	Y	N	Y	Y	Y	Y
14 Young	Y	Y	Y	N	N	Y	?	?
15 de la Garza	N	Y	Y	Y	Y	Y	Y	N
16 White	Y	Y	Y	N	Y	Y	Y	Y
17 Burleson	N	Y	Y	N	N	Y	Y	N
18 Jordan	Y	Y	Y	N	Y	Y	Y	Y
19 Mahon	Y	Y	Y	N	N	Y	Y	Y
20 Gonzalez	Y	Y	Y	Y	Y	Y	Y	Y
21 Krueger	#	#	?	#	#	#	#	✓
22 Gammage	N	Y	Y	Y	N	Y	Y	N
23 Kazen	Y	Y	Y	N	Y	Y	Y	Y
24 Milford	Y	Y	Y	N	Y	Y	?	Y
UTAH								
1 McKay	Y	Y	Y	N	Y	Y	Y	Y
2 ***Marriott***	N	Y	Y	Y	Y	Y	Y	N
VERMONT								
AL ***Jeffords***	Y	Y	Y	N	Y	Y	Y	Y
VIRGINIA								
1 ***Trible***	N	Y	Y	Y	N	Y	Y	N
2 ***Whitehurst***	N	Y	Y	Y	N	Y	Y	Y
3 Satterfield	N	Y	Y	Y	N	Y	Y	N
4 ***Daniel***	N	Y	Y	Y	N	Y	Y	N
5 Daniel	N	Y	Y	Y	N	Y	Y	N
6 ***Butler***	N	Y	Y	Y	N	Y	Y	N
7 ***Robinson***	N	Y	Y	Y	N	Y	Y	N
8 Harris	Y	Y	Y	Y	Y	Y	Y	Y
9 ***Wampler***	N	Y	Y	Y	Y	Y	Y	N
10 Fisher	Y	Y	Y	Y	Y	Y	Y	Y
WASHINGTON								
1 ***Pritchard***	N	Y	Y	Y	Y	Y	#	Y
2 Meeds	Y	Y	Y	Y	Y	Y	?	?
3 Bonker	N	Y	Y	Y	Y	Y	Y	Y
4 McCormack	N	Y	Y	Y	Y	Y	Y	Y
5 Foley	N	Y	Y	Y	Y	Y	Y	Y
6 Dicks	N	Y	Y	Y	Y	Y	Y	Y
7 ***Cunningham***	N	Y	Y	Y	N	Y	Y	N
WEST VIRGINIA								
1 Mollohan	Y	Y	Y	N	Y	Y	Y	Y
2 Staggers	Y	Y	Y	N	Y	Y	Y	Y
3 Slack	Y	Y	Y	N	Y	Y	Y	N
4 Rahall	Y	Y	Y	N	Y	Y	Y	Y
WISCONSIN								
1 Aspin	Y	Y	Y	N	Y	Y	Y	Y
2 Kastenmeier	Y	Y	Y	Y	Y	Y	Y	N
3 Baldus	Y	Y	Y	N	Y	Y	Y	Y
4 Zablocki	Y	Y	Y	Y	Y	#	Y	Y
5 Reuss	Y	Y	Y	Y	Y	Y	Y	Y
6 ***Steiger***	N	Y	Y	Y	Y	Y	Y	Y
7 Obey	Y	Y	Y	Y	Y	Y	Y	Y
8 Cornell	Y	Y	Y	Y	Y	Y	Y	N
9 ***Kasten***	?	?	?	?	?	#	#	#
WYOMING								
AL Roncalio	Y	Y	Y	Y	Y	Y	Y	X

Democrats ***Republicans***

671. HR 11280. Civil Service Reform. Udall, D-Ariz., motion that the House resolve itself into the Committee of the Whole for further consideration of the bill to reorganize the U.S. Civil Service. Motion agreed to 328-5: R 115-3; D 213-2 (ND 147-2; SD 66-0), Sept. 13, 1978.

672. HR 11280. Civil Service Reform. Erlenborn, R-Ill., amendment, to the Udall, D-Ariz., substitute amendment to the Collins, R-Texas, amendment *(see vote 673, below),* to prohibit Federal Election Commission employees from being represented by a union that maintained a political action committee or advocated the election or defeat of any candidate for federal office. Rejected 166-217: R 113-12; D 53-205 (ND 20-158; SD 33-47), Sept. 13, 1978.

673. HR 11280. Civil Service Reform. Collins, R-Texas, amendment, as amended by the Udall, D-Ariz., substitute amendment (adopted by voice vote), to establish the right of federal employees to union representation, and to define other federal employee rights. Adopted 381-0: R 122-0; D 259-0 (ND 182-0; SD 77-0), Sept. 13, 1978.

674. HR 11280. Civil Service Reform. Ashbrook, R-Ohio, amendment to limit the outside income of federal employees at levels GS-13 and above to 15 percent of their federal salaries. Rejected 134-254: R 46-81; D 88-173 (ND 55-128; SD 33-45), Sept. 13, 1978.

675. HR 11280. Civil Service Reform. Hanley, D-N.Y., amendments, en bloc, to delete from the bill changes in the veterans preference program (this amendment had previously been adopted in the Committee of the Whole *(see vote 658, p. 188-H).* Adopted 327-70: R 120-9; D 207-61 (ND 131-57; SD 76-4), Sept. 13, 1978. A "nay" was a vote supporting the president's position.

676. HR 11280. Civil Service Reform. Passage of the bill to revise the federal civil service system. Passed 385-10: R 124-4; D 261-6 (ND 183-4; SD 78-2), Sept. 13, 1978. A "yea" was a vote supporting the president's position.

677. HR 8729. Aviation Noise Reduction. Bolling, D-Mo., motion to order the previous question (thus ending debate) on the adoption of the rule *(see vote 678, below)* providing for House floor consideration of the bill to provide federal grants for airport operators for airport noise control programs and to provide federal assistance to aircraft operators to comply with federal noise standards. Motion agreed to 199-193: R 67-61; D 132-132 (ND 93-90; SD 39-42), Sept. 13, 1978.

678. HR 8729. Aviation Noise Reduction. Adoption of the rule (H Res 1292) providing for House floor consideration of the bill to provide federal grants for airport operators for airport noise control programs and to provide federal assistance to aircraft operators to comply with federal noise standards. Adopted 236-155: R 80-48; D 156-107 (ND 105-78; SD 51-29), Sept. 13, 1978.

KEY

- Y Voted for (yea).
- ✓ Paired for.
- † Announced for.
- # CQ Poll for.
- N Voted against (nay).
- X Paired against.
- \- Announced against.
- ▮ CQ Poll against.
- P Voted "present."
- ● Voted "present" to avoid possible conflict of interest.
- ? Did not vote or otherwise make a position known.

	671	672	673	674	675	676	677	678
ALABAMA								
1 Edwards	Y	Y	Y	N	Y	Y	Y	Y
2 Dickinson	?	Y	Y	Y	Y	Y	Y	N
3 Nichols	Y	N	Y	N	Y	Y	Y	N
4 Bevill	Y	N	Y	N	Y	Y	Y	Y
5 Flippo	Y	N	Y	Y	Y	Y	N	N
6 Buchanan	?	Y	Y	N	Y	Y	Y	Y
7 Flowers	?	?	?	?	?	?	?	?
ALASKA								
AL Young	?	?	#	▮	#	#	?	?
ARIZONA								
1 Rhodes	Y	Y	Y	Y	Y	Y	N	Y
2 Udall	Y	N	Y	N	Y	Y	Y	Y
3 Stump	?	?	#	#	#	#	N	N
4 Rudd	Y	Y	Y	Y	Y	Y	N	N
ARKANSAS								
1 Alexander	Y	N	Y	N	Y	Y	Y	Y
2 Tucker	Y	N	Y	Y	Y	Y	N	Y
3 Hammerschmidt	Y	Y	Y	N	Y	Y	Y	Y
4 Thornton	Y	N	Y	N	Y	Y	Y	Y
CALIFORNIA								
1 Johnson	Y	N	Y	Y	Y	Y	Y	Y
2 Clausen	Y	Y	Y	Y	Y	Y	Y	Y
3 Moss	?	N	Y	N	Y	N	N	N
4 Leggett	?	N	?	N	N	Y	Y	Y
5 Burton, J.	Y	N	Y	N	Y	Y	N	N
6 Burton, P.	Y	N	Y	N	N	Y	N	Y
7 Miller	?	X	?	?	X	?	?	?
8 Dellums	?	N	Y	N	N	Y	N	N
9 Stark	Y	N	Y	N	N	Y	N	N
10 Edwards	Y	N	Y	N	N	Y	Y	Y
11 Ryan	Y	Y	Y	N	Y	Y	N	N
12 McCloskey	?	Y	Y	N	Y	?	N	Y
13 Mineta	Y	N	Y	N	N	Y	Y	Y
14 McFall	Y	N	Y	N	Y	Y	Y	Y
15 Sisk	Y	N	Y	?	Y	Y	Y	Y
16 Panetta	Y	N	Y	Y	Y	Y	N	N
17 Krebs	Y	N	Y	N	Y	Y	Y	Y
18 Vacancy								
19 Lagomarsino	Y	Y	Y	N	Y	Y	Y	Y
20 Goldwater	Y	Y	Y	N	Y	Y	Y	Y
21 Corman	Y	N	Y	N	N	Y	Y	Y
22 Moorhead	Y	Y	Y	N	Y	Y	Y	Y
23 Beilenson	?	N	Y	N	N	Y	N	N
24 Waxman	?	N	Y	N	N	Y	N	N
25 Roybal	Y	N	Y	N	Y	Y	Y	Y
26 Rousselot	Y	Y	Y	Y	Y	Y	Y	Y
27 Dornan	?	Y	Y	N	Y	Y	N	Y
28 Burke	?	X	#	▮	X	#	?	?
29 Hawkins	?	X	Y	?	N	Y	Y	Y
30 Danielson	Y	N	Y	N	Y	Y	Y	Y
31 Wilson, C.H.	N	N	Y	Y	Y	N	Y	Y
32 Anderson	Y	N	Y	N	Y	Y	Y	Y
33 Clawson	?	✓	?	?	?	?	?	?
34 Hannaford	Y	N	Y	N	Y	Y	Y	Y
35 Lloyd	N	N	Y	N	Y	Y	Y	Y
36 Brown	?	N	Y	N	Y	Y	?	?
37 Pettis	Y	Y	Y	N	Y	Y	Y	Y
38 Patterson	Y	N	Y	N	Y	Y	Y	Y
39 Wiggins	?	✓	#	▮	▮	#	?	?
40 Badham	Y	Y	Y	N	Y	Y	Y	Y
41 Wilson, B.	N	Y	Y	Y	Y	Y	Y	Y
42 Van Deerlin	?	N	Y	N	Y	Y	Y	Y
43 Burgener	Y	Y	Y	N	Y	Y	Y	Y
COLORADO								
1 Schroeder	Y	N	Y	Y	N	Y	Y	Y
2 Wirth	Y	N	Y	▮	Y	Y	Y	Y
3 Evans	Y	N	Y	N	N	Y	N	N
4 Johnson	?	?	?	?	?	?	?	?
5 Armstrong	?	?	?	?	?	?	?	?
CONNECTICUT								
1 Cotter	Y	N	Y	Y	Y	Y	N	N
2 Dodd	Y	N	Y	N	Y	Y	Y	Y
3 Giaimo	?	N	Y	N	Y	Y	N	Y
4 McKinney	?	?	#	▮	#	#	?	?
5 Sarasin	?	?	?	?	?	?	?	?
6 Moffett	Y	N	Y	Y	N	Y	N	N
DELAWARE								
AL Evans	Y	Y	Y	N	Y	Y	Y	Y
FLORIDA								
1 Sikes	Y	N	Y	N	Y	Y	Y	Y
2 Fuqua	?	N	Y	N	Y	Y	Y	Y
3 Bennett	Y	N	Y	N	Y	Y	N	N
4 Chappell	Y	N	Y	N	Y	Y	N	Y
5 Kelly	Y	Y	Y	Y	Y	Y	N	N
6 Young	Y	Y	Y	Y	Y	Y	N	Y
7 Gibbons	?	?	?	?	?	?	?	?
8 Ireland	Y	Y	Y	Y	Y	Y	Y	Y
9 Frey	?	Y	Y	Y	Y	Y	Y	Y
10 Bafalis	Y	Y	Y	Y	Y	Y	Y	Y
11 Rogers	Y	Y	Y	Y	Y	Y	Y	Y
12 Burke	?	✓	?	?	?	?	?	?
13 Lehman	?	?	#	▮	#	#	?	?
14 Pepper	?	N	Y	Y	Y	Y	Y	Y
15 Fascell	?	N	Y	Y	N	Y	Y	Y
GEORGIA								
1 Ginn	Y	N	Y	Y	Y	Y	Y	Y
2 Mathis	?	N	Y	N	Y	Y	Y	Y
3 Brinkley	Y	N	Y	Y	Y	Y	Y	Y
4 Levitas	?	N	Y	Y	Y	Y	Y	Y
5 Fowler	Y	N	Y	Y	Y	Y	N	Y
6 Flynt	Y	N	Y	Y	Y	Y	Y	Y
7 McDonald	?	Y	Y	N	Y	Y	N	N
8 Evans	Y	N	Y	Y	Y	Y	Y	Y
9 Jenkins	Y	Y	Y	Y	Y	Y	Y	Y
10 Barnard	Y	Y	Y	Y	Y	Y	N	Y
HAWAII								
1 Heftel	?	N	Y	N	Y	Y	Y	Y
2 Akaka	Y	N	Y	N	Y	Y	Y	Y
IDAHO								
1 Symms	Y	Y	Y	N	Y	Y	N	N
2 Hansen, G.	Y	Y	Y	N	Y	Y	N	N
ILLINOIS								
1 Metcalfe	Y	N	Y	?	?	?	?	?
2 Murphy	Y	N	Y	N	Y	Y	Y	Y
3 Russo	Y	N	Y	N	Y	Y	N	N
4 Derwinski	Y	Y	Y	N	Y	Y	Y	Y
5 Fary	?	X	?	?	✓	?	✓	✓
6 Hyde	Y	Y	Y	N	Y	Y	Y	Y
7 Collins	?	N	Y	▮	Y	Y	Y	Y
8 Rostenkowski	Y	N	Y	N	Y	Y	Y	Y
9 Yates	Y	N	Y	N	N	Y	N	N
10 Mikva	Y	N	Y	N	N	Y	?	?
11 Annunzio	Y	N	Y	N	Y	Y	Y	Y
12 Crane	Y	Y	?	Y	Y	Y	Y	Y
13 McClory	Y	Y	Y	N	Y	Y	Y	Y
14 Erlenborn	Y	Y	Y	N	N	Y	Y	Y
15 Corcoran	Y	Y	Y	Y	N	Y	Y	Y
16 Anderson	?	?	Y	N	N	Y	N	N
17 O'Brien	?	Y	Y	N	Y	Y	Y	?
18 Michel	Y	Y	Y	N	Y	Y	N	Y
19 Railsback	Y	Y	Y	N	Y	Y	N	Y
20 Findley	Y	Y	Y	N	Y	Y	N	Y
21 Madigan	Y	Y	Y	N	Y	Y	Y	Y
22 Shipley	Y	N	?	N	Y	Y	Y	Y
23 Price	Y	N	Y	N	Y	Y	Y	Y
24 Simon	Y	N	Y	N	N	Y	N	N
INDIANA								
1 Benjamin	Y	N	Y	N	Y	Y	N	N
2 Fithian	Y	N	Y	Y	Y	Y	Y	Y
3 Brademas	Y	N	Y	N	Y	Y	Y	Y
4 Quayle	N	Y	Y	N	Y	Y	N	N
5 Hillis	Y	Y	Y	Y	Y	Y	Y	Y
6 Evans	Y	N	Y	Y	Y	Y	Y	Y
7 Myers, J.	Y	Y	Y	N	Y	Y	N	N
8 Cornwell	Y	N	Y	Y	Y	Y	Y	Y
9 Hamilton	Y	N	Y	Y	Y	Y	N	N
10 Sharp	Y	Y	Y	Y	Y	Y	N	N
11 Jacobs	?	N	Y	Y	N	Y	N	N
IOWA								
1 Leach	Y	Y	Y	Y	N	Y	N	N
2 Blouin	?	Y	Y	Y	N	Y	N	N
3 Grassley	Y	Y	Y	N	Y	Y	Y	N
4 Smith	Y	N	Y	N	N	Y	N	Y
5 Harkin	Y	N	Y	Y	N	Y	N	N
6 Bedell	Y	N	Y	Y	N	Y	N	N

Democrats ***Republicans***

Corresponding to Congressional Record Votes 762, 763, 764, 765, 766, 767, 768, 769

	671	672	673	674	675	676	677	678
KANSAS								
1 Sebelius	Y	Y	Y	N	Y	Y	Y	Y
2 Keys	?	N	Y	N	N	Y	Y	?
3 Winn	Y	Y	Y	N	Y	Y	Y	Y
4 Glickman	Y	Y	Y	N	Y	Y	Y	Y
5 Skubitz	Y	Y	Y	N	Y	Y	Y	Y
KENTUCKY								
1 Hubbard	Y	N	Y	N	Y	Y	N	N
2 Natcher	Y	N	Y	N	Y	Y	N	N
3 Mazzoli	Y	Y	Y	N	N	Y	N	N
4 Snyder	Y	N	Y	N	Y	Y	N	N
5 Carter	Y	Y	Y	N	Y	Y	N	Y
6 Breckinridge	Y	Y	?	N	Y	Y	N	N
7 Perkins	Y	N	Y	N	Y	Y	N	N
LOUISIANA								
1 Livingston	Y	Y	Y	N	Y	Y	Y	Y
2 Boggs	Y	N	Y	N	Y	Y	Y	?
3 Treen	Y	Y	?	?	?	?	?	?
4 Waggonner	?	Y	Y	N	Y	Y	Y	Y
5 Huckaby	?	?	?	?	?	?	?	?
6 Moore	Y	Y	Y	Y	Y	Y	N	N
7 Breaux	?	✓	?	?	?	?	?	?
8 Long	Y	N	Y	N	Y	Y	Y	Y
MAINE								
1 Emery	Y	Y	Y	Y	Y	Y	N	N
2 Cohen	Y	Y	Y	Y	Y	Y	N	N
MARYLAND								
1 Bauman	Y	Y	Y	N	Y	Y	N	N
2 Long	Y	N	Y	N	Y	?	N	N
3 Mikulski	?	N	Y	N	N	Y	Y	Y
4 Holt	Y	Y	Y	N	Y	N	Y	Y
5 Spellman	?	N	Y	N	Y	N	N	N
6 Byron	?	?	Y	Y	Y	Y	N	N
7 Mitchell	?	N	Y	N	N	N	N	N
8 Steers	Y	N	Y	N	N	N	N	N
MASSACHUSETTS								
1 Conte	Y	N	Y	N	Y	Y	Y	Y
2 Boland	Y	N	Y	N	Y	Y	N	Y
3 Early	Y	N	Y	N	Y	Y	N	N
4 Drinan	Y	N	Y	N	N	Y	N	N
5 Tsongas	?	?	?	?	?	?	?	?
6 Harrington	?	N	Y	N	N	Y	N	N
7 Markey	Y	N	Y	N	N	Y	Y	Y
8 O'Neill								
9 Moakley	Y	N	Y	N	Y	Y	Y	Y
10 Heckler	Y	N	Y	N	Y	Y	Y	N
11 Burke	Y	N	Y	N	Y	Y	Y	Y
12 Studds	Y	N	Y	Y	N	Y	N	N
MICHIGAN								
1 Conyers	?	X	Y	N	N	Y	N	N
2 Pursell	Y	Y	Y	?	Y	Y	Y	N
3 Brown	Y	Y	Y	N	Y	Y	Y	Y
4 Stockman	Y	Y	Y	N	Y	Y	N	N
5 Sawyer	Y	Y	#	Y	Y	Y	N	Y
6 Carr	Y	N	Y	Y	N	Y	N	N
7 Kildee	Y	N	Y	Y	Y	Y	N	N
8 Traxler	Y	N	Y	Y	Y	Y	N	N
9 Vander Jagt	?	✓	?	?	?	?	Y	Y
10 Cederberg	Y	Y	Y	Y	Y	Y	Y	Y
11 Ruppe	?	✓	Y	N	Y	Y	N	Y
12 Bonior	Y	N	Y	Y	N	Y	N	N
13 Diggs	?	N	Y	N	Y	Y	?	Y
14 Nedzi	Y	N	Y	N	Y	Y	N	N
15 Ford	Y	N	Y	N	Y	Y	Y	Y
16 Dingell	?	N	Y	N	Y	Y	Y	Y
17 Brodhead	?	N	Y	N	Y	Y	N	N
18 Blanchard	Y	N	Y	N	Y	Y	N	N
19 Broomfield	?	✓	#	#	#	#	?	?
MINNESOTA								
1 Quie	?	?	?	?	?	?	?	?
2 Hagedorn	Y	Y	Y	Y	Y	Y	Y	Y
3 Frenzel	?	✓	#	#	#	#	?	?
4 Vento	Y	N	Y	Y	Y	Y	N	N
5 Fraser	?	?	?	?	?	?	Y	Y
6 Nolan	?	?	Y	Y	N	Y	N	N
7 Stangeland	Y	Y	Y	Y	Y	Y	Y	Y
8 Oberstar	Y	N	Y	Y	Y	Y	N	Y
MISSISSIPPI								
1 Whitten	?	N	#	▮	Y	Y	N	Y
2 Bowen	Y	Y	Y	N	Y	Y	Y	Y
3 Montgomery	Y	Y	Y	N	Y	Y	Y	Y
4 Cochran	?	?	?	?	?	?	?	?
5 Lott	Y	Y	Y	N	Y	Y	Y	Y
MISSOURI								
1 Clay	Y	N	Y	N	N	Y	Y	Y
2 Young	Y	N	Y	Y	Y	Y	Y	Y
3 Gephardt	Y	Y	Y	Y	Y	Y	N	N

	671	672	673	674	675	676	677	678
4 Skelton	Y	N	Y	N	Y	Y	Y	Y
5 Bolling	?	N	Y	N	N	Y	Y	Y
6 Coleman	Y	Y	Y	N	Y	Y	Y	Y
7 Taylor	Y	Y	Y	N	Y	Y	Y	Y
8 Ichord	Y	Y	Y	Y	Y	Y	N	N
9 Volkmer	Y	N	?	Y	Y	Y	N	N
10 Burlison	Y	N	Y	N	Y	Y	Y	Y
MONTANA								
1 Baucus	Y	Y	Y	N	Y	Y	N	Y
2 Marlenee	Y	?	Y	Y	Y	Y	N	Y
NEBRASKA								
1 Thone	Y	Y	Y	Y	Y	Y	N	Y
2 Cavanaugh	?	Y	Y	Y	Y	Y	N	N
3 Smith	Y	Y	Y	Y	Y	Y	N	Y
NEVADA								
AL Santini	Y	Y	#	Y	Y	Y	N	N
NEW HAMPSHIRE								
1 D'Amours	Y	Y	Y	Y	Y	Y	N	N
2 Cleveland	Y	Y	Y	N	Y	Y	N	N
NEW JERSEY								
1 Florio	Y	N	Y	N	Y	Y	Y	Y
2 Hughes	Y	Y	Y	N	Y	Y	N	N
3 Howard	Y	N	Y	N	Y	Y	Y	Y
4 Thompson	?	N	Y	N	Y	Y	Y	Y
5 Fenwick	Y	N	Y	Y	N	Y	N	N
6 Forsythe	Y	Y	Y	N	Y	Y	N	N
7 Maguire	Y	N	Y	Y	N	Y	N	N
8 Roe	?	?	Y	N	Y	Y	Y	Y
9 Hollenbeck	?	?	Y	Y	Y	Y	Y	Y
10 Rodino	Y	N	Y	N	Y	Y	Y	Y
11 Minish	Y	N	Y	Y	Y	Y	N	N
12 Rinaldo	Y	Y	Y	N	Y	Y	Y	Y
13 Meyner	Y	N	Y	N	Y	Y	N	N
14 LeFante	Y	N	Y	N	Y	Y	Y	Y
15 Patten	Y	N	Y	N	Y	Y	Y	Y
NEW MEXICO								
1 Lujan	Y	Y	Y	N	Y	Y	N	N
2 Runnels	Y	Y	Y	N	Y	Y	N	N
NEW YORK								
1 Pike	Y	N	Y	N	N	Y	N	N
2 Downey	Y	N	Y	N	N	Y	N	N
3 Ambro	?	?	Y	Y	Y	Y	Y	?
4 Lent	?	Y	Y	N	Y	Y	Y	Y
5 Wydler	Y	Y	Y	N	Y	Y	Y	Y
6 Wolff	Y	N	Y	N	Y	Y	Y	Y
7 Addabbo	Y	N	Y	N	Y	Y	Y	Y
8 Rosenthal	Y	N	Y	N	Y	Y	N	N
9 Delaney	Y	N	Y	Y	Y	Y	N	N
10 Biaggi	Y	N	Y	N	Y	Y	N	N
11 Scheuer	Y	N	Y	N	N	Y	Y	Y
12 Chisholm	?	N	Y	N	N	Y	N	Y
13 Solarz	Y	N	Y	N	Y	Y	N	N
14 Richmond	?	X	?	?	X	?	X	X
15 Zeferetti	Y	N	Y	N	Y	Y	Y	Y
16 Holtzman	Y	N	Y	N	N	Y	N	N
17 Murphy	?	N	Y	N	Y	Y	Y	Y
18 Green	Y	N	Y	Y	N	Y	Y	Y
19 Rangel	Y	N	Y	?	N	Y	N	N
20 Weiss	Y	N	Y	Y	N	Y	N	N
21 Garcia	?	X	Y	N	N	Y	N	N
22 Bingham	Y	N	Y	N	N	Y	N	N
23 Caputo	?	?	?	?	?	?	?	?
24 Ottinger	Y	N	Y	N	N	Y	N	N
25 Fish	Y	N	Y	N	Y	Y	N	N
26 Gilman	Y	N	Y	N	Y	Y	N	Y
27 McHugh	Y	N	Y	Y	N	Y	?	?
28 Stratton	Y	N	Y	Y	Y	Y	Y	Y
29 Pattison	Y	N	Y	N	N	Y	N	Y
30 McEwen	Y	Y	?	N	Y	Y	Y	Y
31 Mitchell	Y	Y	Y	N	Y	Y	N	Y
32 Hanley	Y	N	Y	N	Y	Y	Y	N
33 Walsh	Y	Y	Y	N	Y	Y	Y	Y
34 Horton	Y	Y	Y	N	Y	Y	Y	Y
35 Conable	?	?	?	?	N	Y	Y	Y
36 LaFalce	?	?	#	N	Y	Y	N	Y
37 Nowak	Y	N	Y	N	Y	Y	Y	Y
38 Kemp	Y	Y	Y	N	Y	Y	N	N
39 Lundine	Y	Y	Y	Y	Y	Y	Y	Y
NORTH CAROLINA								
1 Jones	Y	Y	Y	Y	Y	Y	N	N
2 Fountain	Y	Y	Y	Y	Y	Y	N	N
3 Whitley	Y	Y	Y	Y	Y	Y	N	N
4 Andrews	Y	Y	Y	Y	Y	Y	N	Y
5 Neal	Y	Y	Y	Y	Y	Y	N	N
6 Preyer	?	Y	Y	N	Y	Y	N	N
7 Rose	?	Y	Y	Y	Y	Y	N	Y
8 Hefner	Y	Y	Y	Y	Y	Y	N	N

	671	672	673	674	675	676	677	678
9 Martin	Y	Y	Y	Y	Y	Y	N	N
10 Broyhill	Y	Y	Y	N	Y	Y	N	N
11 Gudger	Y	Y	#	Y	Y	Y	N	N
NORTH DAKOTA								
AL Andrews	Y	Y	Y	Y	Y	Y	Y	Y
OHIO								
1 Gradison	Y	Y	Y	N	Y	Y	N	N
2 Luken	Y	N	Y	N	Y	Y	Y	Y
3 Whalen	?	?	#	N	N	Y	N	N
4 Guyer	Y	Y	Y	N	Y	Y	N	N
5 Latta	Y	Y	Y	Y	Y	Y	N	N
6 Harsha	Y	N	Y	N	Y	Y	Y	Y
7 Brown	Y	Y	?	?	Y	Y	N	Y
8 Kindness	Y	Y	Y	N	Y	Y	N	N
9 Ashley	?	N	Y	N	N	Y	Y	Y
10 Miller	Y	Y	Y	Y	Y	Y	N	N
11 Stanton	Y	N	Y	N	Y	Y	Y	Y
12 Devine	Y	Y	Y	Y	Y	Y	N	N
13 Pease	Y	Y	Y	N	Y	Y	N	N
14 Seiberling	Y	N	Y	N	N	Y	N	N
15 Wylie	Y	Y	Y	Y	Y	Y	N	N
16 Regula	Y	Y	Y	Y	Y	Y	N	N
17 Ashbrook	Y	Y	Y	Y	Y	N	N	N
18 Applegate	Y	N	Y	Y	Y	Y	?	Y
19 Carney	Y	N	Y	N	Y	Y	Y	Y
20 Oakar	Y	N	Y	N	N	Y	N	N
21 Stokes	Y	N	Y	N	N	Y	N	N
22 Vanik	Y	N	Y	Y	Y	Y	N	N
23 Mottl	Y	N	Y	Y	Y	Y	N	N
OKLAHOMA								
1 Jones	Y	Y	Y	Y	Y	Y	Y	Y
2 Risenhoover	?	✓	?	?	?	?	Y	Y
3 Watkins	Y	Y	Y	Y	Y	Y	N	Y
4 Steed	Y	N	Y	N	Y	Y	N	N
5 Edwards	Y	Y	P	Y	Y	Y	N	N
6 English	Y	Y	Y	?	Y	Y	N	N
OREGON								
1 AuCoin	Y	Y	Y	Y	Y	Y	Y	Y
2 Ullman	?	N	Y	N	Y	Y	Y	Y
3 Duncan	Y	Y	Y	N	Y	Y	Y	?
4 Weaver	Y	N	Y	Y	Y	Y	N	N
PENNSYLVANIA								
1 Myers, M.	Y	N	Y	N	Y	Y	Y	Y
2 Nix	Y	N	Y	N	Y	Y	Y	Y
3 Lederer	Y	N	Y	N	Y	Y	Y	Y
4 Eilberg	Y	N	Y	N	Y	Y	Y	Y
5 Schulze	Y	Y	Y	Y	Y	Y	N	N
6 Yatron	Y	N	Y	Y	Y	Y	Y	Y
7 Edgar	Y	N	Y	Y	N	Y	N	N
8 Kostmayer	Y	Y	Y	Y	Y	Y	N	N
9 Shuster	Y	Y	Y	N	Y	Y	Y	Y
10 McDade	Y	Y	Y	N	Y	Y	N	Y
11 Flood	Y	N	Y	N	Y	Y	N	Y
12 Murtha	Y	N	Y	N	Y	Y	Y	Y
13 Coughlin	Y	Y	Y	N	Y	Y	N	N
14 Moorhead	Y	N	Y	N	Y	Y	Y	Y
15 Rooney	Y	N	Y	N	Y	Y	Y	Y
16 Walker	Y	Y	Y	Y	Y	Y	Y	Y
17 Ertel	Y	Y	Y	N	Y	Y	Y	Y
18 Walgren	Y	Y	Y	N	Y	Y	Y	Y
19 Goodling, W.	Y	Y	Y	N	Y	Y	N	N
20 Gaydos	Y	N	Y	N	Y	Y	Y	Y
21 Dent	Y	N	Y	N	Y	Y	Y	Y
22 Murphy	Y	N	Y	Y	Y	Y	Y	Y
23 Ammerman	?	X	?	?	✓	?	✓	?
24 Marks	Y	Y	Y	N	Y	Y	Y	Y
25 Myers, G.	N	Y	Y	Y	Y	N	Y	Y
RHODE ISLAND								
1 St Germain	?	X	Y	N	Y	Y	Y	Y
2 Beard	?	X	Y	N	Y	Y	Y	Y
SOUTH CAROLINA								
1 Davis	Y	N	Y	N	Y	N	Y	Y
2 Spence	Y	Y	Y	Y	Y	Y	Y	Y
3 Derrick	?	N	Y	?	Y	Y	N	N
4 Mann	Y	Y	Y	N	Y	Y	N	Y
5 Holland	Y	N	Y	N	Y	Y	Y	Y
6 Jenrette	Y	N	Y	N	Y	Y	Y	Y
SOUTH DAKOTA								
1 Pressler	?	Y	Y	Y	Y	Y	?	Y
2 Abdnor	Y	Y	Y	Y	Y	Y	Y	Y
TENNESSEE								
1 Quillen	Y	Y	Y	N	Y	Y	Y	Y
2 Duncan	Y	Y	Y	Y	Y	Y	Y	Y
3 Lloyd	Y	N	Y	N	Y	Y	Y	Y
4 Gore	Y	N	Y	N	Y	Y	N	N
5 Vacancy								
6 Beard	Y	Y	#	▮	#	#	?	?

	671	672	673	674	675	676	677	678
7 Jones	Y	N	Y	N	Y	Y	Y	Y
8 Ford	Y	N	Y	N	Y	Y	N	N
TEXAS								
1 Hall	Y	Y	Y	Y	Y	Y	Y	Y
2 Wilson, C.	Y	N	Y	N	Y	Y	Y	Y
3 Collins	Y	Y	Y	N	Y	Y	N	N
4 Roberts	Y	N	Y	Y	Y	Y	Y	Y
5 Mattox	?	N	Y	N	Y	Y	N	Y
6 Teague	?	✓	?	?	✓	?	?	?
7 Archer	Y	Y	Y	Y	Y	Y	Y	Y
8 Eckhardt	?	N	Y	N	Y	Y	N	Y
9 Brooks	Y	N	Y	N	Y	Y	N	Y
10 Pickle	Y	N	Y	Y	Y	Y	N	N
11 Poage	Y	Y	Y	Y	N	Y	N	N
12 Wright	Y	N	Y	N	Y	Y	Y	Y
13 Hightower	Y	Y	Y	N	Y	Y	Y	Y
14 Young	?	Y	?	?	?	?	?	?
15 de la Garza	Y	Y	Y	Y	Y	Y	N	N
16 White	Y	Y	Y	N	Y	Y	Y	Y
17 Burleson	Y	✓	Y	Y	Y	Y	Y	Y
18 Jordan	Y	N	Y	N	N	Y	N	N
19 Mahon	Y	Y	Y	Y	Y	Y	N	Y
20 Gonzalez	Y	N	Y	N	Y	Y	N	N
21 Krueger	?	X	#	▮	#	#	?	?
22 Gammage	Y	N	Y	Y	Y	Y	Y	Y
23 Kazen	Y	Y	Y	N	Y	Y	N	N
24 Milford	?	Y	Y	N	Y	Y	Y	Y
UTAH								
1 McKay	Y	Y	#	N	Y	Y	Y	Y
2 Marriott	Y	Y	Y	Y	Y	Y	Y	Y
VERMONT								
AL Jeffords	Y	Y	Y	N	Y	Y	N	N
VIRGINIA								
1 Trible	Y	Y	Y	N	Y	Y	N	N
2 Whitehurst	Y	Y	Y	N	Y	Y	N	N
3 Satterfield	Y	Y	Y	N	Y	Y	N	N
4 Daniel	Y	Y	Y	N	Y	Y	N	N
5 Daniel	Y	N	Y	N	Y	Y	N	N
6 Butler	Y	Y	Y	N	Y	Y	N	Y
7 Robinson	Y	Y	Y	Y	Y	Y	Y	N
8 Harris	Y	N	Y	N	Y	N	N	Y
9 Wampler	Y	N	Y	N	Y	Y	Y	Y
10 Fisher	Y	N	Y	N	Y	Y	Y	Y
WASHINGTON								
1 Pritchard	Y	N	Y	N	N	Y	Y	Y
2 Meeds	?	N	Y	N	N	Y	Y	Y
3 Bonker	Y	N	Y	N	Y	Y	Y	Y
4 McCormack	Y	N	Y	N	Y	Y	?	✓
5 Foley	Y	N	Y	N	Y	Y	?	Y
6 Dicks	Y	N	Y	N	Y	Y	Y	Y
7 Cunningham	Y	Y	Y	N	Y	Y	Y	N
WEST VIRGINIA								
1 Mollohan	Y	N	Y	N	Y	Y	N	N
2 Staggers	Y	N	Y	N	Y	Y	Y	Y
3 Slack	?	?	?	N	Y	Y	N	Y
4 Rahall	Y	N	Y	N	Y	Y	Y	Y
WISCONSIN								
1 Aspin	Y	N	Y	Y	N	Y	Y	Y
2 Kastenmeier	Y	N	Y	N	N	Y	N	N
3 Baldus	Y	N	Y	Y	Y	Y	N	N
4 Zablocki	Y	N	Y	Y	Y	Y	N	Y
5 Reuss	Y	N	Y	Y	N	Y	N	Y
6 Steiger	Y	Y	Y	N	Y	Y	X	X
7 Obey	Y	N	Y	Y	Y	Y	N	N
8 Cornell	Y	N	Y	Y	Y	Y	N	N
9 Kasten	?	?	#	▮	#	#	?	?
WYOMING								
AL Roncalio	?	N	Y	N	N	Y	Y	Y

Democrats ***Republicans***

679. HR 8729. Aviation Noise Reduction. Florio, D-N.J., amendment to require airports, whose noise in the opinion of the transportation secretary affected communities in adjacent states, to prepare airport noise compatibility programs. Rejected 127-246: R 23-101; D 104-145 (ND 96-78; SD 8-67), Sept. 13, 1978.

680. HR 8729. Aviation Noise Reduction. Skubitz, R-Kan., amendment to authorize the expenditure from the Airport and Airway Trust Fund of $25 million annually for fiscal years 1979 and 1980 for the development of general aviation airports, and to divide the funds equally among the 50 states. Adopted 213-147: R 104-16; D 109-131 (ND 71-99; SD 38-32), Sept. 13, 1978.

681. Procedural Motion. Mottl, D-Ohio, motion to approve the House *Journal* of Wednesday, Sept. 13, 1978. Motion agreed to 336-12: R 111-7; D 225-5 (ND 152-5; SD 73-0), Sept. 14, 1978.

682. HR 8729. Aviation Noise Reduction. Ullman, D-Ore., amendment to substitute provisions of the bill as drafted by the Ways and Means Committee (HR 11986) for the Public Works Committee's provisions on changes in air transportation taxes and tax credits and refunds for retrofitting and replacing noisy aircraft. Adopted 266-133: R 98-37; D 168-96 (ND 115-70; SD 53-26), Sept. 14, 1978.

683. HR 8729. Aviation Noise Reduction. Snyder, R-Ky., motion to recommit the bill to the Public Works Committee with instructions to delete the provisions of the bill imposing a 2 percent tax on commercial airline passenger tickets and freight charges for the purpose of providing federal assistance for aircraft operators to comply with federal noise standards. Rejected 170-227: R 57-75; D 113-152 (ND 78-106; SD 35-46), Sept. 14, 1978.

684. HR 8729. Aviation Noise Reduction. Passage of the bill to provide federal grants to airport operators for airport noise control programs and to provide federal assistance to aircraft operators to comply with federal noise control standards. Passed 272-123: R 93-39; D 179-84 (ND 132-51; SD 47-33), Sept. 14, 1978.

685. HR 12928. Public Works, Energy Appropriations, Fiscal 1979. Adoption of the conference report on the bill to appropriate $10,160,483,000 in fiscal 1979 for energy and water development programs of the Interior and Energy Departments. Adopted 319-71: R 111-23; D 208-48 (ND 139-43; SD 69-5), Sept. 14, 1978. The president had requested $11,039,449,000 in new budget authority.

686. HR 9214. IMF-Witteveen Facility. Grassley, R-Iowa, motion to instruct House conferees on the bill to authorize U.S. participation in the Supplementary Financing (Witteveen) Facility of the International Monetary Fund to accept Senate language to require a balanced federal budget beginning in fiscal 1981 and direct the U.S. executive director to the IMF to oppose aid to countries that aided or abetted international terrorists. Motion agreed to 286-91: R 122-6; D 164-85 (ND 98-78; SD 66-7), Sept. 14, 1978.

KEY

- Y Voted for (yea).
- ✓ Paired for.
- † Announced for.
- # CQ Poll for.
- N Voted against (nay).
- X Paired against.
- - Announced against.
- ▮ CQ Poll against.
- P Voted "present."
- ● Voted "present" to avoid possible conflict of interest.
- ? Did not vote or otherwise make a position known.

	679	680	681	682	683	684	685	686
ALABAMA								
1 Edwards	N	Y	Y	Y	N	Y	Y	Y
2 Dickinson	N	Y	Y	Y	Y	N	Y	Y
3 Nichols	N	Y	Y	Y	Y	N	Y	Y
4 Bevill	N	Y	Y	Y	Y	N	Y	Y
5 Flippo	N	N	Y	Y	Y	N	Y	Y
6 Buchanan	N	Y	Y	Y	N	Y	Y	Y
7 Flowers	?	?	?	?	?	?	?	?
ALASKA								
AL Young	▮	#	?	Y	N	Y	Y	Y
ARIZONA								
1 Rhodes	N	N	Y	Y	N	Y	Y	Y
2 Udall	▮	Y	Y	Y	▮	#	Y	Y
3 Stump	N	Y	Y	N	Y	N	Y	Y
4 Rudd	N	Y	Y	N	Y	N	Y	Y
ARKANSAS								
1 Alexander	Y	?	Y	N	N	Y	Y	Y
2 Tucker	Y	Y	Y	N	Y	Y	Y	Y
3 Hammerschmidt	N	Y	Y	Y	N	Y	Y	Y
4 Thornton	N	Y	Y	Y	N	Y	Y	Y
CALIFORNIA								
1 Johnson	N	N	Y	Y	N	Y	Y	N
2 Clausen	N	Y	Y	Y	N	Y	Y	Y
3 Moss	?	?	P	N	Y	?	?	N
4 Leggett	?	?	?	Y	N	Y	Y	Y
5 Burton, J.	Y	Y	Y	N	Y	N	✓	Y
6 Burton, P.	Y	Y	Y	N	Y	N	N	N
7 Miller	?	?	?	?	?	?	X	?
8 Dellums	Y	Y	?	N	Y	N	▮	N
9 Stark	Y	Y	?	N	Y	N	Y	#
10 Edwards	N	N	Y	Y	N	Y	N	N
11 Ryan	?	Y	Y	N	Y	Y	Y	N
12 McCloskey	Y	Y	?	N	N	Y	Y	Y
13 Mineta	N	N	Y	Y	N	Y	Y	N
14 McFall	N	Y	Y	Y	N	Y	Y	N
15 Sisk	?	?	Y	Y	N	Y	Y	N
16 Panetta	N	Y	Y	Y	N	Y	Y	Y
17 Krebs	Y	N	Y	Y	N	Y	Y	Y
18 Vacancy								
19 Lagomarsino	N	Y	Y	Y	N	Y	Y	Y
20 Goldwater	N	Y	?	Y	N	Y	Y	Y
21 Corman	N	N	Y	Y	N	Y	Y	N
22 Moorhead	N	Y	Y	Y	N	Y	Y	Y
23 Beilenson	N	N	?	N	Y	N	N	N
24 Waxman	Y	N	?	N	Y	N	N	N
25 Roybal	N	N	?	Y	Y	Y	Y	N
26 Rousselot	N	Y	Y	Y	N	Y	Y	Y
27 Dornan	N	Y	Y	Y	N	Y	Y	Y
28 Burke	X	#	?	#	✓	#	#	▮
29 Hawkins	N	N	Y	Y	N	Y	Y	N
30 Danielson	N	N	P	Y	N	Y	Y	N
31 Wilson, C.H.	▮	#	?	Y	N	Y	Y	N
32 Anderson	N	N	?	Y	N	Y	Y	Y
33 Clawson	?	?	?	?	?	?	?	?
34 Hannaford	N	N	Y	Y	N	Y	Y	?
35 Lloyd	N	Y	N	Y	N	Y	Y	Y
36 Brown	N	Y	Y	Y	N	Y	Y	N
37 Pettis	N	Y	?	Y	N	Y	Y	Y
38 Patterson	Y	N	Y	Y	N	Y	Y	Y
39 Wiggins	▮	#	?	#	▮	#	#	▮
40 Badham	N	Y	Y	Y	N	Y	Y	Y
41 Wilson, B.	N	Y	N	Y	N	Y	Y	Y
42 Van Deerlin	N	N	?	Y	N	Y	Y	N
43 Burgener	N	Y	Y	Y	N	Y	Y	Y
COLORADO								
1 Schroeder	N	N	Y	Y	N	Y	N	Y
2 Wirth	Y	N	Y	Y	N	Y	Y	▮
3 Evans	▮	#	Y	Y	N	Y	Y	N
4 Johnson	?	?	Y	Y	Y	Y	Y	Y
5 Armstrong	?	?	?	?	?	?	?	?
CONNECTICUT								
1 Cotter	N	N	?	▮	✓	X	#	#
2 Dodd	Y	N	Y	N	Y	Y	N	N
3 Giaimo	N	N	?	Y	N	Y	Y	N
4 McKinney	▮	#	?	✓	▮	#	#	#
5 Sarasin	?	?	?	✓	▮	#	#	?
6 Moffett	Y	N	Y	Y	N	Y	N	Y
DELAWARE								
AL Evans	Y	Y	Y	N	Y	N	Y	Y
FLORIDA								
1 Sikes	N	Y	Y	Y	N	Y	Y	Y
2 Fuqua	N	Y	Y	Y	N	Y	Y	Y
3 Bennett	N	N	P	Y	Y	N	Y	Y
4 Chappell	N	Y	Y	Y	N	Y	Y	Y
5 Kelly	N	N	Y	N	Y	N	Y	Y
6 Young	Y	Y	Y	Y	Y	N	Y	Y
7 Gibbons	?	?	?	?	?	?	?	?
8 Ireland	?	N	Y	Y	N	Y	?	Y
9 Frey	N	Y	Y	Y	?	?	Y	Y
10 Bafalis	N	Y	Y	Y	N	Y	Y	Y
11 Rogers	N	Y	?	Y	N	#	Y	Y
12 Burke	?	?	?	?	?	?	?	?
13 Lehman	▮	▮	?	#	▮	#	▮	▮
14 Pepper	N	N	Y	Y	N	Y	Y	Y
15 Fascell	N	N	Y	Y	N	Y	Y	#
GEORGIA								
1 Ginn	N	N	Y	Y	N	Y	Y	Y
2 Mathis	N	Y	Y	Y	N	N	?	?
3 Brinkley	Y	Y	Y	N	Y	N	Y	Y
4 Levitas	N	N	Y	Y	N	Y	Y	Y
5 Fowler	N	?	Y	Y	N	Y	Y	Y
6 Flynt	N	N	Y	Y	N	Y	Y	Y
7 McDonald	N	Y	?	Y	Y	N	N	Y
8 Evans	N	Y	Y	Y	N	Y	Y	Y
9 Jenkins	N	N	Y	Y	Y	N	Y	Y
10 Barnard	N	N	Y	Y	N	Y	Y	Y
HAWAII								
1 Heftel	N	Y	?	Y	N	Y	Y	Y
2 Akaka	N	Y	Y	Y	N	Y	Y	Y
IDAHO								
1 Symms	N	Y	Y	Y	Y	N	Y	Y
2 Hansen, G.	N	Y	Y	Y	Y	N	Y	Y
ILLINOIS								
1 Metcalfe	✓	?	Y	Y	N	Y	Y	N
2 Murphy	Y	N	Y	Y	N	Y	Y	Y
3 Russo	Y	N	Y	Y	Y	Y	Y	Y
4 Derwinski	N	N	Y	Y	N	Y	N	Y
5 Fary	✓	?	?	?	X	Y	Y	N
6 Hyde	Y	Y	Y	Y	N	Y	Y	Y
7 Collins	Y	▮	Y	Y	N	Y	Y	N
8 Rostenkowski	N	N	Y	Y	N	Y	Y	N
9 Yates	Y	N	Y	N	Y	N	Y	Y
10 Mikva	Y	N	Y	Y	N	Y	N	Y
11 Annunzio	Y	N	Y	Y	N	Y	Y	N
12 Crane	N	Y	?	Y	▮	#	N	Y
13 McClory	▮	N	Y	Y	N	Y	Y	Y
14 Erlenborn	N	N	Y	Y	N	Y	Y	Y
15 Corcoran	N	Y	Y	Y	N	Y	Y	Y
16 Anderson	Y	N	?	N	Y	N	Y	#
17 O'Brien	N	Y	Y	Y	N	Y	Y	Y
18 Michel	N	Y	?	Y	N	Y	Y	Y
19 Railsback	N	Y	Y	Y	N	Y	Y	Y
20 Findley	N	Y	Y	Y	Y	N	Y	N
21 Madigan	N	Y	Y	Y	N	Y	Y	Y
22 Shipley	Y	?	N	N	N	Y	Y	?
23 Price	N	N	Y	Y	N	Y	Y	N
24 Simon	Y	Y	Y	N	Y	N	Y	N
INDIANA								
1 Benjamin	Y	Y	Y	Y	Y	Y	Y	Y
2 Fithian	N	Y	Y	Y	N	Y	Y	Y
3 Brademas	N	N	Y	N	Y	Y	Y	N
4 Quayle	N	Y	N	N	Y	Y	N	Y
5 Hillis	N	Y	Y	Y	N	Y	Y	Y
6 Evans	?	?	Y	Y	N	Y	Y	Y
7 Myers, J.	N	Y	Y	N	Y	N	Y	Y
8 Cornwell	N	Y	?	Y	N	Y	Y	Y
9 Hamilton	N	Y	Y	N	Y	Y	Y	N
10 Sharp	N	N	Y	N	Y	Y	N	Y
11 Jacobs	N	Y	N	Y	N	Y	N	Y
IOWA								
1 Leach	▮	#	?	X	#	▮	▮	#
2 Blouin	N	Y	Y	N	Y	N	Y	Y
3 Grassley	N	Y	Y	Y	Y	Y	Y	Y
4 Smith	N	N	Y	Y	N	Y	Y	Y
5 Harkin	Y	Y	Y	N	N	Y	N	Y
6 Bedell	Y	Y	Y	N	Y	N	N	Y

Democrats ***Republicans***

	679	680	681	682	683	684	685	686
KANSAS								
1 Sebelius	N	Y	Y	Y	N	Y	#	#
2 Keys	N	Y	Y	Y	N	Y	Y	Y
3 Winn	Y	#	Y	Y	N	Y	Y	Y
4 Glickman	N	Y	Y	Y	N	Y	Y	Y
5 Skubitz	Y	Y	?	Y	N	Y	Y	?
KENTUCKY								
1 Hubbard	N	Y	Y	Y	Y	N	Y	Y
2 Natcher	N	Y	Y	N	Y	N	Y	Y
3 Mazzoli	N	N	Y	N	Y	N	Y	N
4 Snyder	N	Y	Y	N	Y	N	Y	Y
5 Carter	N	Y	Y	N	Y	Y	Y	Y
6 Breckinridge	N	Y	Y	N	Y	N	?	N
7 Perkins	N	N	Y	Y	Y	N	Y	Y
LOUISIANA								
1 Livingston	N	Y	Y	Y	N	Y	Y	Y
2 Boggs	N	N	Y	Y	N	Y	Y	#
3 Treen	?	?	?	Y	N	Y	Y	Y
4 Waggonner	N	N	Y	Y	N	Y	Y	Y
5 Huckaby	?	?	?	?	?	?	?	?
6 Moore	N	Y	Y	Y	Y	N	Y	Y
7 Breaux	X	?	?	?	X	✓	?	?
8 Long	N	N	Y	Y	N	Y	Y	Y
MAINE								
1 Emery	N	Y	Y	Y	Y	N	N	Y
2 Cohen	?	?	Y	N	Y	N	N	Y
MARYLAND								
1 Bauman	N	Y	Y	N	Y	N	Y	Y
2 Long	N	N	Y	Y	N	Y	Y	Y
3 Mikulski	Y	N	Y	N	Y	N	Y	Y
4 Holt	Y	Y	Y	Y	N	Y	Y	Y
5 Spellman	N	Y	?	#	▮	#	#	▮
6 Byron	Y	Y	?	N	Y	Y	Y	Y
7 Mitchell	Y	N	N	Y	Y	N	Y	N
8 Steers	Y	N	Y	N	Y	N	Y	N
MASSACHUSETTS								
1 Conte	Y	Y	Y	Y	Y	Y	N	N
2 Boland	N	N	Y	Y	N	N	Y	N
3 Early	Y	N	Y	N	Y	N	N	Y
4 Drinan	Y	N	Y	N	Y	N	Y	Y
5 Tsongas	?	?	?	?	?	?	?	?
6 Harrington	#	▮	?	N	Y	Y	N	N
7 Markey	Y	N	Y	Y	N	Y	N	N
8 O'Neill								
9 Moakley	Y	N	Y	Y	N	#	N	N
10 Heckler	?	Y	?	Y	N	Y	N	Y
11 Burke	Y	N	Y	Y	N	Y	Y	N
12 Studds	Y	N	Y	N	Y	N	N	N
MICHIGAN								
1 Conyers	Y	Y	#	N	Y	?	N	▮
2 Pursell	N	Y	Y	N	Y	N	Y	Y
3 Brown	N	Y	N	N	Y	Y	N	Y
4 Stockman	N	N	Y	N	Y	N	N	Y
5 Sawyer	N	#	Y	Y	Y	Y	Y	Y
6 Carr	Y	Y	Y	Y	Y	N	?	?
7 Kildee	Y	Y	Y	N	Y	N	N	Y
8 Traxler	Y	N	Y	N	Y	N	Y	Y
9 Vander Jagt	N	Y	Y	Y	Y	Y	Y	Y
10 Cederberg	N	Y	Y	Y	N	Y	Y	Y
11 Ruppe	N	Y	?	N	Y	Y	Y	Y
12 Bonior	Y	Y	Y	N	Y	N	N	Y
13 Diggs	▮	?	?	?	N	Y	Y	N
14 Nedzi	Y	N	Y	N	Y	N	N	N
15 Ford	✓	?	?	Y	N	Y	Y	N
16 Dingell	N	Y	?	Y	N	Y	Y	N
17 Brodhead	Y	N	Y	N	Y	N	N	N
18 Blanchard	Y	N	Y	N	Y	N	N	Y
19 Broomfield	▮	#	?	X	#	#	#	▮
MINNESOTA								
1 Quie	?	?	?	?	?	?	?	?
2 Hagedorn	N	Y	Y	Y	N	Y	Y	Y
3 Frenzel	?	?	?	N	Y	N	Y	?
4 Vento	Y	N	Y	N	Y	N	N	N
5 Fraser	Y	Y	Y	Y	Y	Y	N	N
6 Nolan	?	Y	?	N	Y	Y	N	N
7 Stangeland	N	Y	Y	Y	N	Y	Y	Y
8 Oberstar	N	N	Y	Y	N	Y	Y	Y
MISSISSIPPI								
1 Whitten	N	Y	Y	N	Y	N	Y	Y
2 Bowen	N	Y	?	Y	N	Y	Y	Y
3 Montgomery	N	Y	?	#	X	✓	#	#
4 Cochran	?	?	?	?	?	?	?	?
5 Lott	N	Y	Y	Y	N	Y	Y	Y
MISSOURI								
1 Clay	Y	N	Y	Y	N	Y	Y	N
2 Young	N	Y	Y	Y	N	Y	Y	Y
3 Gephardt	N	Y	Y	N	Y	N	N	Y
4 Skelton	N	Y	Y	Y	N	Y	Y	Y
5 Bolling	N	N	Y	Y	N	Y	Y	N
6 Coleman	N	Y	Y	Y	N	Y	Y	Y
7 Taylor	N	Y	Y	Y	N	Y	Y	Y
8 Ichord	N	Y	Y	N	Y	N	Y	Y
9 Volkmer	N	Y	Y	Y	N	Y	Y	Y
10 Burlison	N	N	?	Y	N	Y	Y	N
MONTANA								
1 Baucus	N	Y	Y	N	Y	Y	Y	Y
2 Marlenee	Y	Y	?	N	Y	Y	Y	Y
NEBRASKA								
1 Thone	N	Y	Y	Y	Y	Y	?	?
2 Cavanaugh	N	Y	Y	N	Y	N	Y	Y
3 Smith	?	?	Y	Y	Y	Y	Y	Y
NEVADA								
AL Santini	N	#	Y	N	Y	Y	Y	Y
NEW HAMPSHIRE								
1 D'Amours	N	Y	Y	N	Y	Y	Y	Y
2 Cleveland	N	Y	Y	N	Y	N	N	Y
NEW JERSEY								
1 Florio	Y	Y	Y	Y	N	Y	Y	Y
2 Hughes	Y	Y	Y	Y	Y	N	Y	Y
3 Howard	Y	N	Y	Y	N	Y	Y	N
4 Thompson	Y	N	Y	Y	N	Y	Y	N
5 Fenwick	Y	N	Y	N	Y	N	Y	Y
6 Forsythe	Y	N	N	Y	N	Y	Y	Y
7 Maguire	Y	Y	Y	N	Y	N	N	Y
8 Roe	Y	Y	Y	Y	N	Y	Y	Y
9 Hollenbeck	?	?	Y	Y	N	Y	Y	Y
10 Rodino	Y	N	Y	Y	N	Y	Y	▮
11 Minish	Y	N	Y	N	Y	Y	Y	Y
12 Rinaldo	Y	N	Y	Y	N	Y	Y	Y
13 Meyner	Y	N	Y	Y	N	Y	Y	Y
14 LeFante	Y	Y	Y	Y	N	Y	Y	N
15 Patten	Y	Y	Y	Y	N	Y	Y	N
NEW MEXICO								
1 Lujan	N	Y	Y	Y	N	Y	Y	Y
2 Runnels	?	?	?	Y	N	Y	Y	Y
NEW YORK								
1 Pike	Y	N	N	N	Y	N	N	Y
2 Downey	Y	Y	?	Y	N	Y	N	Y
3 Ambro	Y	N	?	Y	N	Y	Y	Y
4 Lent	Y	Y	Y	Y	N	Y	N	Y
5 Wydler	Y	Y	Y	N	N	Y	Y	Y
6 Wolff	Y	Y	Y	Y	N	Y	Y	Y
7 Addabbo	Y	Y	Y	Y	N	Y	Y	?
8 Rosenthal	Y	N	Y	N	Y	N	Y	N
9 Delaney	Y	Y	Y	N	Y	N	Y	Y
10 Biaggi	Y	Y	Y	Y	Y	Y	Y	Y
11 Scheuer	Y	N	Y	Y	N	Y	Y	Y
12 Chisholm	Y	▮	?	Y	N	Y	Y	N
13 Solarz	Y	N	?	X	✓	X	Y	N
14 Richmond	✓	?	Y	N	Y	Y	N	N
15 Zeferetti	Y	N	Y	Y	N	Y	Y	Y
16 Holtzman	Y	N	Y	N	Y	N	N	N
17 Murphy	N	N	Y	?	N	Y	Y	Y
18 Green	Y	N	Y	Y	N	Y	N	Y
19 Rangel	Y	N	Y	N	Y	N	Y	N
20 Weiss	Y	N	Y	N	Y	N	N	Y
21 Garcia	Y	Y	?	N	N	Y	Y	N
22 Bingham	Y	N	Y	N	Y	N	Y	N
23 Caputo	?	?	?	Y	N	Y	Y	Y
24 Ottinger	Y	Y	Y	N	Y	N	Y	Y
25 Fish	Y	Y	Y	N	Y	?	N	Y
26 Gilman	Y	Y	Y	Y	N	Y	Y	Y
27 McHugh	Y	Y	Y	Y	N	Y	Y	Y
28 Stratton	N	N	Y	Y	N	Y	Y	Y
29 Pattison	Y	Y	Y	Y	N	Y	Y	Y
30 McEwen	N	?	P	Y	N	Y	Y	Y
31 Mitchell	N	Y	Y	Y	N	Y	Y	Y
32 Hanley	N	N	Y	Y	N	Y	Y	Y
33 Walsh	N	?	Y	Y	N	Y	Y	Y
34 Horton	N	Y	Y	Y	N	Y	Y	Y
35 Conable	N	Y	Y	Y	N	Y	Y	Y
36 LaFalce	Y	Y	Y	N	Y	N	Y	N
37 Nowak	N	N	Y	Y	N	Y	Y	Y
38 Kemp	N	Y	Y	Y	Y	Y	Y	Y
39 Lundine	N	Y	Y	Y	N	Y	Y	N
NORTH CAROLINA								
1 Jones	N	Y	Y	N	Y	N	#	▮
2 Fountain	N	Y	?	N	Y	N	Y	Y
3 Whitley	N	Y	Y	N	Y	N	Y	Y
4 Andrews	N	Y	Y	N	Y	N	Y	Y
5 Neal	N	?	Y	Y	N	Y	N	Y
6 Preyer	N	?	Y	N	Y	Y	Y	Y
7 Rose	N	Y	Y	Y	N	Y	?	?
8 Hefner	?	?	Y	N	Y	N	Y	Y
9 Martin	N	Y	Y	N	Y	Y	N	Y
10 Broyhill	N	Y	Y	N	Y	N	N	Y
11 Gudger	N	Y	Y	N	Y	N	N	Y
NORTH DAKOTA								
AL Andrews	N	Y	Y	Y	N	Y	Y	Y
OHIO								
1 Gradison	Y	N	Y	N	Y	N	N	Y
2 Luken	Y	N	Y	Y	N	Y	N	Y
3 Whalen	N	Y	Y	N	Y	N	Y	N
4 Guyer	N	Y	Y	Y	Y	N	Y	Y
5 Latta	N	Y	Y	Y	Y	N	N	Y
6 Harsha	N	N	Y	Y	N	Y	Y	Y
7 Brown	N	Y	Y	?	?	?	Y	Y
8 Kindness	N	Y	Y	Y	Y	Y	Y	Y
9 Ashley	Y	N	Y	Y	N	Y	Y	N
10 Miller	N	Y	Y	Y	Y	N	N	Y
11 Stanton	N	#	Y	N	Y	N	Y	Y
12 Devine	N	Y	Y	N	Y	N	Y	Y
13 Pease	Y	Y	Y	N	Y	N	N	Y
14 Seiberling	Y	N	Y	N	Y	N	N	Y
15 Wylie	N	Y	Y	N	?	N	N	Y
16 Regula	N	Y	Y	N	Y	N	Y	Y
17 Ashbrook	N	Y	Y	N	Y	N	Y	Y
18 Applegate	N	N	Y	Y	N	Y	Y	Y
19 Carney	N	Y	Y	Y	N	Y	Y	?
20 Oakar	Y	N	Y	N	N	Y	Y	Y
21 Stokes	Y	Y	?	N	Y	Y	Y	?
22 Vanik	N	N	Y	N	Y	N	N	Y
23 Mottl	Y	N	Y	N	Y	Y	N	Y
OKLAHOMA								
1 Jones	N	N	Y	Y	N	Y	Y	Y
2 Risenhoover	?	?	Y	Y	N	Y	Y	Y
3 Watkins	N	Y	Y	Y	Y	Y	Y	Y
4 Steed	Y	N	Y	N	Y	N	Y	Y
5 Edwards	N	Y	Y	Y	N	Y	Y	Y
6 English	N	Y	Y	Y	N	Y	Y	Y
OREGON								
1 AuCoin	N	N	Y	Y	N	Y	Y	Y
2 Ullman	N	N	Y	Y	▮	Y	Y	N
3 Duncan	N	N	Y	N	Y	N	#	N
4 Weaver	N	N	Y	N	Y	N	N	Y
PENNSYLVANIA								
1 Myers, M.	Y	N	Y	?	?	?	?	?
2 Nix	✓	?	Y	Y	?	?	?	?
3 Lederer	Y	Y	Y	Y	N	Y	Y	N
4 Eilberg	Y	N	Y	Y	N	Y	Y	N
5 Schulze	N	Y	Y	Y	Y	N	Y	Y
6 Yatron	N	N	Y	Y	N	Y	Y	Y
7 Edgar	Y	N	Y	N	Y	N	N	N
8 Kostmayer	Y	N	Y	N	Y	N	N	Y
9 Shuster	N	Y	Y	Y	N	Y	Y	Y
10 McDade	N	Y	?	Y	N	Y	Y	Y
11 Flood	N	N	Y	Y	N	Y	Y	N
12 Murtha	N	N	Y	Y	N	Y	Y	Y
13 Coughlin	Y	Y	N	Y	N	Y	Y	Y
14 Moorhead	Y	N	Y	Y	N	Y	#	▮
15 Rooney	Y	Y	Y	Y	N	Y	Y	Y
16 Walker	N	▮	N	Y	N	Y	Y	Y
17 Ertel	N	Y	Y	Y	N	Y	Y	Y
18 Walgren	Y	N	Y	Y	N	Y	Y	Y
19 Goodling, W.	N	Y	Y	Y	N	N	Y	Y
20 Gaydos	N	N	Y	Y	N	Y	Y	Y
21 Dent	X	#	Y	Y	Y	Y	Y	▮
22 Murphy	Y	Y	Y	Y	N	Y	Y	Y
23 Ammerman	?	?	?	?	?	?	?	?
24 Marks	N	Y	Y	Y	N	Y	Y	Y
25 Myers, G.	Y	N	Y	Y	N	Y	Y	N
RHODE ISLAND								
1 St Germain	N	N	Y	Y	Y	Y	Y	N
2 Beard	N	N	Y	Y	Y	Y	Y	Y
SOUTH CAROLINA								
1 Davis	N	Y	Y	Y	N	Y	Y	Y
2 Spence	N	Y	Y	Y	N	Y	Y	Y
3 Derrick	N	N	Y	N	Y	Y	N	Y
4 Mann	N	?	Y	Y	Y	N	Y	Y
5 Holland	?	?	?	Y	N	Y	Y	Y
6 Jenrette	N	#	Y	N	Y	N	#	▮
SOUTH DAKOTA								
1 Pressler	N	Y	?	Y	N	Y	Y	?
2 Abdnor	N	Y	Y	Y	N	Y	Y	Y
TENNESSEE								
1 Quillen	N	Y	Y	Y	N	Y	Y	Y
2 Duncan	N	Y	Y	Y	N	Y	Y	Y
3 Lloyd	N	Y	Y	Y	N	Y	Y	Y
4 Gore	N	Y	Y	N	Y	N	Y	Y
5 Vacancy								
6 Beard	▮	#	Y	N	Y	Y	Y	Y
7 Jones	N	#	Y	Y	N	Y	Y	Y
8 Ford	N	Y	Y	Y	N	Y	Y	Y
TEXAS								
1 Hall	N	N	Y	Y	N	N	Y	Y
2 Wilson, C.	▮	Y	Y	Y	N	Y	Y	Y
3 Collins	N	N	Y	Y	Y	N	N	Y
4 Roberts	N	N	Y	Y	N	Y	Y	Y
5 Mattox	Y	N	Y	?	N	Y	Y	Y
6 Teague	X	?	?	?	?	?	?	?
7 Archer	N	Y	Y	Y	N	Y	Y	Y
8 Eckhardt	Y	N	Y	?	N	Y	?	N
9 Brooks	?	?	Y	N	Y	Y	Y	N
10 Pickle	N	N	Y	Y	N	Y	Y	Y
11 Poage	N	N	Y	N	Y	N	Y	?
12 Wright	N	N	Y	Y	N	Y	Y	Y
13 Hightower	N	N	Y	Y	N	Y	Y	Y
14 Young	?	?	?	Y	N	Y	Y	?
15 de la Garza	N	Y	Y	N	Y	N	Y	Y
16 White	N	Y	Y	Y	N	Y	Y	Y
17 Burleson	N	N	Y	Y	N	Y	Y	Y
18 Jordan	N	N	Y	N	N	N	Y	N
19 Mahon	N	N	Y	Y	N	N	Y	N
20 Gonzalez	N	N	Y	N	Y	N	Y	N
21 Krueger	▮	#	?	#	✓	X	#	▮
22 Gammage	N	Y	Y	Y	N	Y	Y	Y
23 Kazen	N	Y	Y	N	Y	N	Y	Y
24 Milford	N	N	?	Y	N	Y	Y	Y
UTAH								
1 McKay	N	N	?	Y	N	Y	Y	Y
2 Marriott	N	Y	Y	Y	N	Y	Y	#
VERMONT								
AL Jeffords	Y	Y	Y	N	Y	Y	N	Y
VIRGINIA								
1 Trible	N	Y	Y	Y	Y	Y	Y	Y
2 Whitehurst	N	Y	Y	Y	Y	Y	Y	Y
3 Satterfield	N	Y	Y	N	Y	N	Y	Y
4 Daniel	N	Y	Y	N	Y	N	Y	Y
5 Daniel	N	Y	Y	Y	Y	N	Y	Y
6 Butler	N	Y	Y	Y	N	Y	Y	Y
7 Robinson	N	Y	Y	N	Y	N	Y	Y
8 Harris	Y	Y	Y	N	Y	Y	Y	Y
9 Wampler	N	Y	Y	Y	Y	N	Y	Y
10 Fisher	Y	N	Y	Y	N	Y	N	Y
WASHINGTON								
1 Pritchard	N	Y	Y	Y	N	Y	Y	▮
2 Meeds	N	N	?	Y	N	Y	Y	N
3 Bonker	Y	?	Y	Y	N	Y	Y	Y
4 McCormack	X	?	?	✓	X	✓	?	?
5 Foley	N	Y	Y	N	Y	Y	Y	Y
6 Dicks	N	Y	Y	Y	N	Y	Y	Y
7 Cunningham	N	Y	Y	Y	N	Y	Y	Y
WEST VIRGINIA								
1 Mollohan	N	N	Y	N	Y	N	Y	N
2 Staggers	Y	N	Y	Y	N	Y	Y	Y
3 Slack	N	?	Y	Y	N	Y	Y	Y
4 Rahall	N	N	Y	Y	N	Y	Y	N
WISCONSIN								
1 Aspin	N	N	Y	Y	Y	Y	Y	N
2 Kastenmeier	N	Y	Y	N	Y	N	Y	N
3 Baldus	Y	Y	Y	N	Y	N	Y	Y
4 Zablocki	Y	Y	Y	Y	N	Y	Y	N
5 Reuss	Y	N	Y	N	Y	Y	N	Y
6 Steiger	N	Y	N	N	Y	N	N	N
7 Obey	Y	N	Y	N	Y	N	N	N
8 Cornell	Y	Y	Y	N	Y	N	Y	Y
9 Kasten	▮	#	?	N	N	Y	N	Y
WYOMING								
AL Roncalio	N	#	?	Y	N	Y	Y	N

Democrats ***Republicans***

687. H Res 1242. Emergency Preparedness Reorganization. Adoption of the resolution to disapprove the president's Reorganization Plan No. 3 of 1978 for the reorganization of federal emergency preparedness and disaster relief programs. Disapproval resolution rejected 40-327: R 37-89; D 3-238 (ND 0-171; SD 3-67), Sept. 14, 1978. A "nay" was a vote supporting the president's position.

688. HR 12611. Airline Deregulation. Adoption of the rule (H Res 1324) providing for House floor consideration of the bill to increase competition in the commercial passenger airline industry, to facilitate the granting of new route authority by the Civil Aeronautics Board (CAB), to expedite CAB proceedings, to grant airlines flexibility to alter their fares within certain limits and to terminate the CAB on Dec. 31, 1982, unless Congress acted to renew it. Adopted 344-1: R 122-0; D 222-1 (ND 155-0; SD 67-1), Sept. 14, 1978.

689. HR 12611. Airline Deregulation. Anderson, D-Calif., motion that the House resolve itself into the Committee of the Whole for consideration of the bill to partially deregulate the commercial passenger airline industry. Motion agreed to 300-8: R 106-6; D 194-2 (ND 134-2; SD 60-0), Sept. 14, 1978.

690. Procedural Motion. Mottl, D-Ohio, motion to approve the House *Journal* of Thursday, Sept. 14, 1978. Motion agreed to 293-10: R 88-7; D 205-3 (ND 143-3; SD 62-0), Sept. 15, 1978.

691. S 2701. Water Resources Planning. Adoption of the conference report on the bill to authorize $11,733,900 for the Water Resources Council for fiscal 1979. Adopted 304-22: R 90-10; D 214-12 (ND 153-5; SD 61-7), Sept. 15, 1978.

692. H Res 1350. Hancho C. Kim Contempt Citation. Adoption of the resolution to cite Hancho C. Kim for criminal contempt of Congress and to recommend prosecution of Kim for contempt for refusing to respond to questions by the Committee on Standards of Official Conduct in connection with its investigation of South Korean influence-buying on Capitol Hill. Adopted 319-2: R 100-0; D 219-2 (ND 152-1; SD 67-1), Sept. 15, 1978.

693. HR 11733. Surface Transportation Assistance Act. Adoption of the rule (H Res 1326) providing for House floor consideration of the bill to authorize $66.5 billion for fiscal years 1979-82 for federal assistance programs for highway construction and safety and urban mass transportation. Adopted 318-4: R 99-2; D 219-2 (ND 153-0; SD 66-2), Sept. 15, 1978.

694. HR 11733. Surface Transportation Assistance Act. Howard, D-N.J., motion that the House resolve itself into the Committee of the Whole for consideration of the bill to authorize $66.5 billion for fiscal years 1979-82 for federal assistance programs for highway construction and safety and urban mass transportation. Motion agreed to 303-6: R 91-4; D 212-2 (ND 145-1; SD 67-1), Sept. 15, 1978.

KEY

- Y Voted for (yea).
- ✓ Paired for.
- † Announced for.
- # CQ Poll for.
- N Voted against (nay).
- X Paired against.
- \- Announced against.
- ▮ CQ Poll against.
- P Voted "present."
- ● Voted "present" to avoid possible conflict of interest.
- ? Did not vote or otherwise make a position known.

	687	688	689	690	691	692	693	694
ALABAMA								
1 ***Edwards***	N	Y	Y	?	?	?	?	?
2 ***Dickinson***	N	Y	N	Y	Y	Y	Y	Y
3 Nichols	N	Y	Y	Y	Y	Y	Y	Y
4 Bevill	N	Y	Y	Y	Y	Y	Y	Y
5 Flippo	N	Y	Y	Y	N	Y	Y	Y
6 ***Buchanan***	N	Y	Y	?	Y	Y	Y	Y
7 Flowers	?	?	?	?	?	?	?	?
ALASKA								
AL Young	N	Y	Y	?	#	#	?	?
ARIZONA								
1 ***Rhodes***	N	Y	N	Y	Y	Y	Y	Y
2 Udall	N	Y	Y	Y	Y	Y	Y	Y
3 Stump	N	Y	Y	Y	N	Y	Y	Y
4 ***Rudd***	N	Y	Y	Y	Y	Y	Y	Y
ARKANSAS								
1 Alexander	N	Y	Y	Y	Y	Y	Y	Y
2 Tucker	N	Y	Y	Y	Y	Y	Y	Y
3 ***Hammerschmidt***	Y	Y	Y	Y	Y	Y	Y	Y
4 Thornton	N	Y	Y	Y	Y	?	Y	Y
CALIFORNIA								
1 Johnson	N	Y	Y	Y	Y	Y	Y	Y
2 ***Clausen***	N	Y	Y	?	?	?	?	?
3 Moss	N	?	?	P	Y	Y	Y	Y
4 Leggett	N	?	?	Y	Y	?	Y	?
5 Burton, J.	N	Y	Y	?	?	?	?	?
6 Burton, P.	N	Y	Y	Y	Y	P	Y	Y
7 Miller	?	?	?	?	?	?	?	?
8 Dellums	▮	?	?	?	#	#	?	?
9 Stark	▮	?	?	?	#	#	?	?
10 Edwards	N	Y	Y	Y	Y	Y	Y	Y
11 Ryan	N	Y	Y	Y	?	?	?	Y
12 ***McCloskey***	N	Y	Y	?	?	?	?	?
13 Mineta	N	Y	Y	Y	Y	Y	Y	Y
14 McFall	N	Y	?	Y	Y	Y	Y	Y
15 Sisk	?	Y	Y	?	?	?	?	?
16 Panetta	N	?	Y	Y	Y	Y	Y	Y
17 Krebs	N	Y	Y	Y	Y	Y	Y	Y
18 Vacancy								
19 ***Lagomarsino***	Y	Y	Y	Y	Y	Y	Y	Y
20 ***Goldwater***	N	Y	Y	?	?	?	?	?
21 Corman	N	Y	Y	?	?	?	?	?
22 ***Moorhead***	Y	Y	Y	Y	Y	Y	Y	Y
23 Beilenson	N	Y	Y	Y	Y	Y	Y	Y
24 Waxman	N	?	?	?	#	#	?	?
25 Roybal	N	Y	Y	Y	Y	Y	Y	Y
26 ***Rousselot***	Y	Y	Y	?	?	?	?	?
27 ***Dornan***	Y	Y	Y	Y	Y	Y	Y	Y
28 Burke	▮	?	?	?	#	#	?	?
29 Hawkins	N	Y	?	Y	Y	Y	Y	?
30 Danielson	N	Y	Y	Y	Y	Y	Y	Y
31 Wilson, C.H.	?	Y	Y	Y	Y	P	Y	Y
32 Anderson	N	Y	Y	Y	Y	Y	Y	Y
33 ***Clawson***	?	?	?	Y	N	Y	Y	Y
34 Hannaford	?	?	?	?	?	?	?	?
35 Lloyd	N	Y	N	N	Y	Y	Y	N
36 Brown	N	?	?	Y	Y	Y	Y	Y
37 ***Pettis***	N	Y	Y	Y	Y	Y	Y	Y
38 Patterson	N	Y	Y	?	#	Y	Y	Y
39 ***Wiggins***	▮	?	?	?	Y	Y	Y	Y
40 ***Badham***	Y	Y	Y	?	#	#	?	?
41 ***Wilson, B.***	N	Y	Y	N	Y	Y	Y	N
42 Van Deerlin	N	Y	Y	Y	Y	Y	Y	?
43 ***Burgener***	N	Y	Y	?	?	?	?	?
COLORADO								
1 Schroeder	N	Y	?	Y	Y	Y	Y	Y
2 Wirth	▮	?	?	Y	Y	Y	Y	Y
3 Evans	N	?	?	Y	Y	Y	Y	Y
4 ***Johnson***	N	?	?	Y	Y	Y	Y	Y
5 ***Armstrong***	?	?	?	?	?	?	?	?
CONNECTICUT								
1 Cotter	▮	?	?	?	#	#	?	?
2 Dodd	N	Y	Y	Y	Y	Y	Y	Y
3 Giaimo	N	?	?	Y	Y	Y	Y	Y
4 ***McKinney***	▮	?	?	?	#	#	?	?
5 ***Sarasin***	-	†	†	-	†	†	†	†
6 Moffett	N	?	?	Y	Y	Y	Y	Y
DELAWARE								
AL Evans	N	Y	Y	?	?	Y	Y	Y
FLORIDA								
1 Sikes	N	Y	Y	Y	Y	Y	Y	Y
2 Fuqua	N	Y	Y	Y	Y	Y	Y	Y
3 Bennett	N	Y	Y	Y	Y	Y	Y	Y
4 Chappell	N	Y	Y	Y	N	Y	Y	Y
5 ***Kelly***	Y	Y	Y	Y	?	?	?	?
6 ***Young***	N	Y	Y	Y	Y	Y	Y	Y
7 Gibbons	?	?	?	?	?	?	?	?
8 Ireland	?	?	?	?	?	Y	Y	Y
9 ***Frey***	N	Y	Y	?	?	?	?	?
10 ***Bafalis***	?	Y	Y	Y	Y	Y	Y	Y
11 Rogers	N	Y	?	Y	Y	Y	Y	?
12 ***Burke***	?	?	?	?	?	?	?	?
13 Lehman	▮	?	?	Y	Y	Y	Y	Y
14 Pepper	?	?	?	?	#	#	?	?
15 Fascell	▮	?	?	?	Y	Y	Y	Y
GEORGIA								
1 Ginn	N	Y	Y	Y	Y	Y	Y	Y
2 Mathis	?	?	?	?	?	?	?	?
3 Brinkley	N	Y	Y	Y	Y	Y	Y	Y
4 Levitas	N	Y	Y	Y	Y	Y	Y	Y
5 Fowler	N	Y	Y	Y	Y	Y	Y	Y
6 Flynt	N	Y	?	Y	Y	Y	Y	Y
7 McDonald	Y	Y	Y	?	X	Y	N	N
8 Evans	N	N	Y	?	Y	Y	Y	Y
9 Jenkins	N	Y	Y	Y	Y	Y	Y	Y
10 Barnard	N	Y	?	Y	Y	Y	Y	Y
HAWAII								
1 Heftel	N	Y	Y	?	Y	Y	Y	Y
2 Akaka	N	Y	Y	Y	Y	Y	Y	Y
IDAHO								
1 ***Symms***	Y	Y	Y	Y	Y	Y	Y	?
2 ***Hansen, G.***	Y	Y	N	Y	Y	Y	Y	Y
ILLINOIS								
1 Metcalfe	N	Y	Y	?	?	?	?	?
2 Murphy	N	Y	Y	?	#	#	?	?
3 Russo	N	Y	Y	Y	Y	Y	Y	Y
4 ***Derwinski***	N	Y	Y	Y	Y	Y	Y	?
5 Fary	N	Y	Y	Y	Y	Y	Y	Y
6 ***Hyde***	Y	Y	Y	Y	Y	Y	Y	Y
7 Collins	N	Y	Y	Y	Y	Y	Y	Y
8 Rostenkowski	N	Y	Y	?	?	?	?	?
9 Yates	N	Y	Y	Y	Y	Y	Y	Y
10 Mikva	N	Y	Y	Y	Y	Y	Y	Y
11 Annunzio	N	?	?	Y	Y	Y	Y	Y
12 ***Crane***	Y	Y	Y	?	#	#	?	?
13 ***McClory***	N	Y	Y	Y	Y	Y	Y	Y
14 ***Erlenborn***	N	Y	?	Y	Y	Y	Y	Y
15 ***Corcoran***	N	Y	Y	Y	Y	Y	Y	Y
16 ***Anderson***	▮	?	?	?	#	#	?	?
17 ***O'Brien***	Y	Y	Y	?	Y	Y	Y	Y
18 ***Michel***	N	Y	Y	Y	Y	Y	Y	Y
19 ***Railsback***	N	Y	Y	Y	Y	Y	Y	Y
20 ***Findley***	N	Y	Y	Y	Y	Y	Y	Y
21 ***Madigan***	N	Y	Y	Y	Y	Y	Y	Y
22 Shipley	?	?	?	?	?	?	?	?
23 Price	N	Y	Y	Y	Y	Y	Y	Y
24 Simon	N	Y	Y	Y	Y	Y	Y	Y
INDIANA								
1 Benjamin	N	Y	Y	Y	Y	Y	Y	Y
2 Fithian	N	Y	Y	Y	Y	Y	Y	Y
3 Brademas	N	Y	Y	Y	Y	Y	Y	Y
4 ***Quayle***	N	Y	N	N	?	Y	Y	N
5 ***Hillis***	Y	Y	Y	Y	Y	Y	Y	Y
6 Evans	N	Y	Y	Y	Y	Y	Y	?
7 ***Myers, J.***	N	Y	Y	?	?	?	?	?
8 Cornwell	?	?	?	Y	Y	#	?	?
9 Hamilton	N	Y	Y	Y	Y	Y	Y	Y
10 Sharp	N	Y	Y	Y	Y	Y	Y	Y
11 Jacobs	N	Y	Y	N	Y	Y	?	?
IOWA								
1 ***Leach***	▮	?	?	Y	Y	Y	Y	Y
2 Blouin	N	Y	?	Y	Y	Y	Y	Y
3 ***Grassley***	N	Y	Y	Y	N	Y	Y	Y
4 Smith	N	Y	Y	?	?	?	?	?
5 Harkin	N	?	Y	Y	Y	Y	Y	Y
6 Bedell	N	Y	Y	Y	Y	Y	Y	Y

Democrats ***Republicans***

	687	688	689	690	691	692	693	694
KANSAS								
1 Sebelius	▌	?	?	?	#	#	?	?
2 Keys	N	Y	?	Y	Y	Y	?	?
3 Winn	N	Y	Y	Y	Y	Y	Y	Y
4 Glickman	N	Y	Y	Y	Y	Y	Y	?
5 Skubitz	?	?	?	?	?	?	?	?
KENTUCKY								
1 Hubbard	N	Y	Y	Y	Y	Y	Y	Y
2 Natcher	N	Y	Y	Y	Y	Y	Y	Y
3 Mazzoli	N	Y	Y	Y	Y	Y	Y	Y
4 Snyder	N	Y	Y	?	Y	Y	Y	Y
5 Carter	N	Y	Y	Y	Y	Y	Y	Y
6 Breckinridge	?	Y	Y	Y	Y	Y	Y	Y
7 Perkins	N	Y	Y	Y	Y	Y	Y	Y
LOUISIANA								
1 Livingston	N	Y	Y	Y	Y	Y	Y	Y
2 Boggs	▌	?	?	?	✓	#	?	?
3 Treen	N	Y	Y	Y	Y	Y	Y	Y
4 Waggonner	N	Y	Y	Y	Y	Y	Y	Y
5 Huckaby	?	?	?	?	?	?	?	?
6 Moore	N	Y	Y	Y	Y	Y	N	Y
7 Breaux	?	?	?	?	?	?	?	?
8 Long	N	Y	Y	Y	Y	Y	Y	Y
MAINE								
1 Emery	Y	Y	Y	Y	Y	Y	Y	?
2 Cohen	Y	?	?	?	#	#	?	?
MARYLAND								
1 Bauman	Y	Y	Y	Y	N	Y	N	Y
2 Long	N	Y	Y	Y	Y	Y	Y	Y
3 Mikulski	N	Y	Y	Y	Y	Y	Y	Y
4 Holt	Y	Y	?	Y	N	Y	Y	Y
5 Spellman	▌	?	?	?	#	?	?	?
6 Byron	N	Y	Y	?	Y	Y	Y	Y
7 Mitchell	N	Y	N	?	Y	Y	Y	Y
8 Steers	N	Y	Y	Y	Y	Y	Y	Y
MASSACHUSETTS								
1 Conte	N	Y	Y	Y	Y	Y	Y	Y
2 Boland	N	Y	?	Y	Y	Y	Y	Y
3 Early	N	Y	Y	Y	Y	Y	Y	Y
4 Drinan	N	Y	Y	Y	Y	Y	Y	Y
5 Tsongas	?	?	?	?	?	?	?	?
6 Harrington	N	?	?	?	#	#	?	?
7 Markey	N	Y	?	Y	Y	Y	Y	?
8 O'Neill								
9 Moakley	N	Y	?	Y	Y	Y	Y	Y
10 Heckler	N	Y	?	?	?	?	?	?
11 Burke	N	Y	Y	Y	Y	Y	?	Y
12 Studds	N	Y	Y	Y	Y	Y	Y	Y
MICHIGAN								
1 Conyers	▌	?	?	?	#	#	?	?
2 Pursell	Y	Y	Y	Y	Y	Y	Y	Y
3 Brown	N	Y	Y	N	N	Y	Y	Y
4 Stockman	N	Y	Y	Y	Y	Y	Y	Y
5 Sawyer	N	Y	Y	Y	Y	Y	Y	Y
6 Carr	-	†	†	Y	Y	Y	Y	Y
7 Kildee	N	Y	Y	Y	Y	Y	Y	Y
8 Traxler	N	Y	Y	Y	Y	Y	Y	Y
9 Vander Jagt	N	Y	Y	Y	N	Y	Y	Y
10 Cederberg	N	Y	Y	Y	Y	Y	Y	Y
11 Ruppe	N	Y	Y	Y	N	Y	Y	?
12 Bonior	N	Y	?	Y	Y	Y	Y	Y
13 Diggs	N	Y	Y	?	#	#	?	?
14 Nedzi	N	Y	Y	Y	Y	Y	Y	Y
15 Ford	N	Y	Y	Y	Y	Y	?	?
16 Dingell	N	Y	?	?	Y	Y	Y	?
17 Brodhead	N	Y	Y	Y	N	Y	Y	Y
18 Blanchard	N	Y	Y	Y	Y	Y	Y	Y
19 Broomfield	▌	?	?	?	#	#	?	?
MINNESOTA								
1 Quie	?	?	?	?	?	?	?	?
2 Hagedorn	N	Y	Y	Y	Y	Y	Y	Y
3 Frenzel	N	Y	Y	Y	Y	Y	Y	Y
4 Vento	N	Y	Y	Y	Y	Y	Y	Y
5 Fraser	N	Y	Y	?	Y	Y	Y	?
6 Nolan	N	?	Y	?	?	?	Y	Y
7 Stangeland	N	Y	Y	Y	Y	Y	Y	Y
8 Oberstar	N	Y	Y	Y	Y	Y	Y	Y
MISSISSIPPI								
1 Whitten	N	?	?	Y	Y	Y	Y	Y
2 Bowen	N	Y	Y	Y	Y	Y	Y	Y
3 Montgomery	▌	?	?	Y	N	Y	Y	Y
4 Cochran	?	?	?	?	?	?	?	?
5 Lott	?	?	?	?	#	#	?	?
MISSOURI								
1 Clay	N	Y	?	?	?	Y	Y	?
2 Young	N	Y	Y	Y	Y	Y	Y	Y
3 Gephardt	N	Y	Y	Y	Y	Y	Y	Y
4 Skelton	N	Y	Y	Y	Y	Y	Y	Y
5 Bolling	N	Y	?	Y	Y	Y	Y	Y
6 Coleman	?	Y	Y	Y	Y	Y	Y	Y
7 Taylor	Y	Y	Y	Y	?	?	?	?
8 Ichord	N	Y	Y	N	N	Y	Y	Y
9 Volkmer	N	Y	Y	Y	Y	Y	Y	Y
10 Burlison	N	Y	Y	Y	Y	Y	Y	Y
MONTANA								
1 Baucus	N	Y	Y	Y	Y	Y	Y	Y
2 Marlenee	N	Y	Y	?	?	?	?	?
NEBRASKA								
1 Thone	?	?	?	?	?	?	?	?
2 Cavanaugh	N	Y	Y	?	Y	Y	Y	Y
3 Smith	N	Y	Y	Y	Y	?	?	?
NEVADA								
AL Santini	N	Y	Y	?	#	#	?	?
NEW HAMPSHIRE								
1 D'Amours	N	Y	Y	Y	Y	Y	Y	Y
2 Cleveland	N	?	?	?	?	?	?	?
NEW JERSEY								
1 Florio	N	Y	?	Y	Y	Y	Y	Y
2 Hughes	N	Y	?	Y	Y	Y	Y	Y
3 Howard	N	Y	Y	Y	Y	Y	Y	Y
4 Thompson	N	Y	Y	Y	Y	Y	Y	Y
5 Fenwick	N	Y	?	Y	Y	Y	Y	Y
6 Forsythe	Y	Y	?	N	Y	Y	Y	Y
7 Maguire	N	?	Y	Y	Y	Y	Y	Y
8 Roe	N	Y	Y	Y	Y	Y	Y	Y
9 Hollenbeck	N	Y	Y	Y	Y	Y	Y	Y
10 Rodino	▌	?	?	?	#	#	?	?
11 Minish	N	Y	Y	Y	Y	Y	Y	Y
12 Rinaldo	N	Y	Y	Y	Y	Y	Y	Y
13 Meyner	N	?	Y	Y	Y	Y	Y	Y
14 LeFante	N	Y	Y	Y	Y	Y	Y	Y
15 Patten	N	Y	Y	Y	Y	Y	Y	Y
NEW MEXICO								
1 Lujan	N	Y	N	?	?	?	?	?
2 Runnels	N	Y	Y	?	?	?	?	?
NEW YORK								
1 Pike	N	Y	Y	?	#	#	?	?
2 Downey	N	?	?	Y	Y	Y	Y	Y
3 Ambro	N	Y	Y	?	?	Y	Y	Y
4 Lent	Y	Y	Y	Y	Y	Y	Y	?
5 Wydler	Y	Y	N	?	?	?	?	?
6 Wolff	N	Y	Y	Y	Y	Y	Y	Y
7 Addabbo	?	?	?	?	Y	Y	Y	?
8 Rosenthal	N	Y	Y	Y	Y	Y	Y	Y
9 Delaney	N	Y	?	Y	Y	Y	Y	Y
10 Biaggi	N	Y	Y	Y	Y	Y	Y	Y
11 Scheuer	N	Y	Y	Y	Y	Y	Y	Y
12 Chisholm	N	Y	?	?	Y	Y	Y	?
13 Solarz	N	Y	Y	Y	Y	Y	Y	Y
14 Richmond	N	Y	Y	Y	Y	Y	Y	Y
15 Zeferetti	N	?	?	Y	Y	Y	Y	Y
16 Holtzman	N	Y	Y	Y	Y	N	Y	Y
17 Murphy	N	Y	Y	Y	Y	Y	?	Y
18 Green	N	Y	Y	Y	Y	Y	Y	Y
19 Rangel	N	Y	?	?	Y	Y	Y	Y
20 Weiss	N	Y	Y	Y	Y	Y	Y	Y
21 Garcia	N	Y	Y	?	Y	Y	Y	Y
22 Bingham	N	Y	Y	Y	Y	Y	Y	Y
23 Caputo	N	Y	?	?	?	?	?	?
24 Ottinger	N	Y	Y	Y	Y	Y	Y	Y
25 Fish	N	Y	Y	Y	Y	Y	Y	Y
26 Gilman	N	Y	Y	Y	Y	Y	Y	Y
27 McHugh	N	Y	Y	Y	Y	#	Y	Y
28 Stratton	N	Y	Y	Y	Y	Y	Y	Y
29 Pattison	N	?	?	Y	Y	Y	Y	Y
30 McEwen	N	Y	?	P	Y	Y	Y	Y
31 Mitchell	N	Y	Y	Y	Y	Y	Y	Y
32 Hanley	N	Y	Y	Y	Y	Y	Y	Y
33 Walsh	N	Y	Y	?	?	?	?	?
34 Horton	N	Y	?	Y	Y	Y	Y	?
35 Conable	N	Y	Y	Y	Y	Y	Y	N
36 LaFalce	N	?	?	Y	Y	Y	Y	Y
37 Nowak	N	Y	Y	Y	Y	Y	Y	Y
38 Kemp	N	Y	Y	?	Y	Y	Y	Y
39 Lundine	?	?	?	Y	Y	Y	Y	Y
NORTH CAROLINA								
1 Jones	▌	?	?	?	#	#	?	?
2 Fountain	N	Y	Y	Y	N	Y	Y	Y
3 Whitley	N	Y	Y	Y	Y	Y	Y	Y
4 Andrews	N	Y	Y	Y	Y	Y	Y	Y
5 Neal	N	Y	Y	?	Y	Y	Y	Y
6 Preyer	N	Y	Y	?	Y	Y	Y	Y
7 Rose	?	?	?	Y	Y	Y	Y	Y
8 Hefner	N	Y	Y	Y	Y	Y	Y	Y
9 Martin	N	Y	Y	Y	Y	Y	Y	Y
10 Broyhill	N	Y	Y	Y	Y	Y	Y	Y
11 Gudger	N	Y	Y	Y	Y	Y	Y	Y
NORTH DAKOTA								
AL Andrews	N	Y	Y	Y	Y	Y	Y	Y
OHIO								
1 Gradison	N	Y	Y	Y	Y	Y	Y	Y
2 Luken	N	Y	Y	?	?	?	?	?
3 Whalen	N	Y	Y	Y	Y	Y	Y	Y
4 Guyer	N	Y	Y	Y	Y	P	Y	Y
5 Latta	Y	Y	Y	Y	Y	Y	Y	Y
6 Harsha	N	Y	Y	?	?	?	?	?
7 Brown	N	Y	Y	?	?	?	?	?
8 Kindness	Y	Y	Y	Y	Y	Y	Y	Y
9 Ashley	N	Y	Y	Y	Y	Y	Y	Y
10 Miller	N	Y	Y	Y	Y	Y	Y	Y
11 Stanton	N	Y	Y	P	Y	Y	Y	Y
12 Devine	Y	?	?	Y	N	Y	Y	Y
13 Pease	N	Y	Y	Y	Y	Y	Y	Y
14 Seiberling	N	Y	Y	?	Y	Y	?	Y
15 Wylie	N	Y	Y	Y	Y	Y	Y	Y
16 Regula	N	Y	Y	Y	Y	Y	Y	Y
17 Ashbrook	Y	Y	Y	?	#	#	?	?
18 Applegate	N	Y	Y	Y	Y	Y	Y	Y
19 Carney	N	Y	Y	?	?	?	?	?
20 Oakar	N	Y	Y	?	?	?	?	?
21 Stokes	N	Y	?	Y	Y	Y	Y	Y
22 Vanik	N	Y	Y	Y	Y	Y	Y	Y
23 Mottl	?	?	?	Y	Y	Y	Y	Y
OKLAHOMA								
1 Jones	N	Y	?	Y	Y	Y	Y	Y
2 Risenhoover	N	Y	?	?	?	?	?	?
3 Watkins	N	Y	Y	Y	Y	Y	Y	Y
4 Steed	N	Y	Y	Y	Y	Y	Y	Y
5 Edwards	N	Y	Y	?	Y	Y	Y	Y
6 English	N	Y	Y	Y	Y	Y	Y	Y
OREGON								
1 AuCoin	N	Y	Y	Y	Y	Y	Y	Y
2 Ullman	N	Y	?	Y	Y	Y	Y	Y
3 Duncan	N	Y	?	Y	Y	Y	Y	Y
4 Weaver	N	Y	?	Y	Y	Y	Y	Y
PENNSYLVANIA								
1 Myers, M.	?	Y	Y	Y	Y	Y	Y	?
2 Nix	?	?	?	?	?	?	?	?
3 Lederer	N	Y	Y	Y	Y	Y	Y	Y
4 Eilberg	N	Y	Y	Y	Y	Y	Y	Y
5 Schulze	Y	Y	Y	Y	Y	Y	Y	Y
6 Yatron	N	Y	Y	Y	Y	Y	Y	Y
7 Edgar	N	Y	Y	Y	Y	Y	Y	Y
8 Kostmayer	N	Y	Y	Y	Y	Y	Y	Y
9 Shuster	Y	Y	Y	Y	Y	Y	Y	Y
10 McDade	N	?	?	Y	Y	Y	Y	Y
11 Flood	N	Y	Y	Y	Y	Y	Y	Y
12 Murtha	N	Y	Y	Y	Y	Y	Y	Y
13 Coughlin	N	Y	Y	N	Y	Y	Y	Y
14 Moorhead	▌	?	?	?	#	#	?	?
15 Rooney	▌	?	?	?	#	#	?	?
16 Walker	Y	Y	Y	N	Y	Y	Y	Y
17 Ertel	N	Y	Y	Y	Y	Y	Y	Y
18 Walgren	N	Y	Y	Y	Y	?	Y	Y
19 Goodling, W.	N	Y	Y	Y	Y	Y	Y	Y
20 Gaydos	N	Y	Y	?	?	?	?	?
21 Dent	▌	?	?	?	#	#	?	?
22 Murphy	N	Y	Y	Y	Y	Y	Y	Y
23 Ammerman	?	?	?	?	?	?	?	?
24 Marks	N	Y	Y	Y	Y	Y	Y	Y
25 Myers, G.	N	Y	Y	?	#	▌	?	?
RHODE ISLAND								
1 St Germain	N	Y	Y	Y	Y	Y	Y	Y
2 Beard	N	Y	?	Y	Y	#	?	?
SOUTH CAROLINA								
1 Davis	N	Y	?	Y	Y	Y	Y	Y
2 Spence	Y	Y	Y	Y	Y	Y	Y	Y
3 Derrick	N	Y	Y	Y	Y	Y	Y	Y
4 Mann	N	Y	Y	?	?	?	?	?
5 Holland	N	Y	Y	?	Y	Y	Y	Y
6 Jenrette	▌	?	?	?	#	#	?	?
SOUTH DAKOTA								
1 Pressler	N	?	?	?	?	?	?	?
2 Abdnor	N	Y	Y	Y	Y	Y	Y	Y
TENNESSEE								
1 Quillen	N	Y	Y	Y	Y	Y	Y	Y
2 Duncan	N	Y	Y	Y	Y	Y	Y	Y
3 Lloyd	N	Y	Y	Y	Y	Y	Y	Y
4 Gore	N	Y	Y	Y	Y	Y	Y	Y
5 Vacancy								
6 Beard	Y	Y	Y	?	#	#	?	?
7 Jones	N	Y	Y	Y	Y	Y	Y	Y
8 Ford	N	Y	Y	Y	Y	Y	Y	Y
TEXAS								
1 Hall	N	Y	Y	Y	Y	Y	Y	Y
2 Wilson, C.	N	Y	Y	?	#	#	?	?
3 Collins	Y	Y	Y	N	N	Y	Y	N
4 Roberts	N	Y	Y	Y	N	Y	Y	Y
5 Mattox	N	Y	Y	Y	Y	Y	Y	Y
6 Teague	?	?	?	?	?	?	?	?
7 Archer	Y	Y	Y	Y	N	Y	Y	Y
8 Eckhardt	N	Y	Y	Y	Y	?	?	Y
9 Brooks	N	Y	Y	Y	Y	Y	Y	Y
10 Pickle	N	Y	Y	?	#	#	?	?
11 Poage	?	?	?	?	?	?	?	?
12 Wright	N	Y	Y	?	?	?	?	?
13 Hightower	N	Y	Y	Y	Y	Y	Y	Y
14 Young	N	?	?	?	Y	Y	?	?
15 de la Garza	N	Y	Y	Y	Y	Y	Y	Y
16 White	▌	?	?	?	#	#	?	?
17 Burleson	N	Y	Y	Y	N	Y	Y	Y
18 Jordan	N	Y	?	Y	Y	Y	Y	Y
19 Mahon	N	Y	?	Y	Y	Y	Y	Y
20 Gonzalez	N	Y	Y	Y	Y	N	N	Y
21 Krueger	▌	?	?	?	#	#	?	?
22 Gammage	N	Y	Y	Y	Y	Y	Y	Y
23 Kazen	N	Y	Y	Y	Y	Y	Y	Y
24 Milford	N	?	?	?	?	?	?	?
UTAH								
1 McKay	N	Y	Y	?	Y	Y	Y	Y
2 Marriott	▌	?	?	?	#	#	?	?
VERMONT								
AL Jeffords	N	Y	Y	?	#	#	?	?
VIRGINIA								
1 Trible	N	Y	Y	Y	Y	Y	Y	Y
2 Whitehurst	Y	Y	?	Y	Y	Y	Y	Y
3 Satterfield	Y	Y	Y	Y	Y	Y	Y	Y
4 Daniel	Y	Y	Y	Y	Y	Y	Y	Y
5 Daniel	Y	Y	Y	Y	N	Y	Y	Y
6 Butler	N	Y	Y	Y	Y	Y	Y	Y
7 Robinson	Y	Y	Y	Y	Y	Y	Y	Y
8 Harris	N	Y	Y	Y	Y	Y	Y	Y
9 Wampler	N	Y	Y	Y	Y	Y	Y	Y
10 Fisher	N	Y	Y	Y	Y	Y	Y	Y
WASHINGTON								
1 Pritchard	▌	?	?	?	#	#	?	?
2 Meeds	N	Y	?	Y	Y	Y	Y	Y
3 Bonker	N	Y	Y	Y	Y	Y	?	Y
4 McCormack	?	?	?	?	?	?	?	?
5 Foley	N	Y	Y	Y	Y	Y	Y	Y
6 Dicks	N	?	Y	Y	N	Y	Y	Y
7 Cunningham	Y	Y	Y	Y	Y	Y	Y	Y
WEST VIRGINIA								
1 Mollohan	N	Y	Y	Y	Y	Y	Y	Y
2 Staggers	N	Y	Y	Y	Y	Y	Y	Y
3 Slack	N	Y	Y	Y	Y	Y	Y	Y
4 Rahall	N	Y	?	Y	N	Y	Y	Y
WISCONSIN								
1 Aspin	N	Y	Y	Y	Y	Y	Y	Y
2 Kastenmeier	N	Y	Y	Y	Y	Y	Y	Y
3 Baldus	N	Y	Y	Y	Y	Y	Y	Y
4 Zablocki	N	Y	Y	Y	Y	Y	Y	Y
5 Reuss	N	Y	Y	Y	Y	Y	Y	Y
6 Steiger	N	Y	?	?	?	#	?	?
7 Obey	N	Y	Y	Y	Y	Y	Y	Y
8 Cornell	N	Y	Y	Y	Y	Y	Y	Y
9 Kasten	▌	?	?	?	#	#	?	?
WYOMING								
AL Roncalio	N	Y	?	Y	Y	#	Y	Y

Democrats ***Republicans***

695. HR 13097. Medicare Amendments. Rostenkowski, D-Ill., motion to suspend the rules and pass the bill to liberalize home health benefits and provide certain other benefits for Medicare beneficiaries, through fiscal 1983. Motion agreed to 398-2: R 137-0; D 261-2 (ND 182-0; SD 79-2), Sept. 18, 1978. A two-thirds majority vote (267 in this case) is required for passage under suspension of the rules.

696. HR 13817. Health Program Amendments. Rostenkowski, D-Ill., motion to suspend the rules and pass the bill to increase nonphysician health professionals' participation in federal professional standards review organizations, authorize Medicare and Medicaid reimbursement for certain long-term nursing care and require coordinated Medicare and Medicaid audits. Motion agreed to 359-40: R 108-27; D 251-13 (ND 178-3; SD 73-10), Sept. 18, 1978. A two-thirds majority vote (266 in this case) is required for passage under suspension of the rules.

697. HR 10792. Smithsonian African Art Museum. Nedzi, D-Mich., motion to suspend the rules and pass the bill to allow the Smithsonian Institution to acquire the Museum of African Art, in Washington, D.C., and to authorize $1 million in fiscal 1979. Motion agreed to 350-54: R 104-33; D 246-21 (ND 172-12; SD 74-9), Sept. 18, 1978. A two-thirds majority vote (270 in this case) is required for passage under suspension of the rules.

698. HR 7819. Diplomatic Immunity. Fascell, D-Fla., motion to suspend the rules and pass the bill to repeal a 1790 statute granting full criminal and civil immunity to the staffs and servants of diplomats posted in the United States. Motion agreed to 397-7: R 130-7; D 267-0 (ND 184-0; SD 83-0), Sept. 18, 1978. A two-thirds majority vote (270 in this case) is required for passage under suspension of the rules.

699. HR 11488. Health Planning. Rogers, D-Fla., motion to suspend the rules and pass the bill to authorize $1.49 billion through fiscal 1981 for health resources planning and development programs. Motion rejected 261-141: R 55-83; D 206-58 (ND 167-16; SD 39-42), Sept. 18, 1978. A two-thirds majority vote (268 in this case) is required for passage under suspension of the rules.

700. HR 12326. Developmental Disabilities. Rogers, D-Fla., motion to suspend the rules and pass the bill to extend through fiscal 1981 the Developmental Disabilities Act and to authorize up to $399 million for fiscal 1979-81 for programs operated under the act. Motion agreed to 397-3: R 136-2; D 261-1 (ND 183-0; SD 78-1), Sept. 19, 1978. A two-thirds majority vote (267 in this case) is required for passage under suspension of the rules.

701. HR 12303. Nurse Training. Rogers, D-Fla., motion to suspend the rules and pass the bill to authorize $553.5 million in fiscal 1979-81 for construction or renovation of nursing schools and grants to support nurse training. Motion agreed to 393-12: R 134-5; D 259-7 (ND 183-2; SD 76-5), Sept. 19, 1978. A two-thirds majority vote (270 in this case) is required for passage under suspension of the rules.

702. HR 12460. Health Centers Amendments. Rogers, D-Fla., motion to suspend the rules and pass the bill to authorize $1.98 billion in fiscal 1979-81 for community mental health centers, migrant and community health centers and other health programs. Motion agreed to 302-102: R 70-68; D 232-34 (ND 171-15; SD 61-19), Sept. 19, 1978. A two-thirds majority vote (270 in this case) is required for passage under suspension of the rules.

KEY

- Y Voted for (yea).
- ✓ Paired for.
- † Announced for.
- # CQ Poll for.
- N Voted against (nay).
- X Paired against.
- \- Announced against.
- ▮ CQ Poll against.
- P Voted "present."
- ● Voted "present" to avoid possible conflict of interest.
- ? Did not vote or otherwise make a position known.

	695	696	697	698	699	700	701	702
ALABAMA								
1 Edwards	Y	Y	Y	Y	Y	Y	Y	N
2 Dickinson	?	?	?	?	?	?	?	?
3 Nichols	Y	Y	Y	Y	Y	Y	Y	Y
4 Bevill	Y	Y	N	Y	N	Y	Y	Y
5 Flippo	Y	Y	Y	Y	Y	Y	Y	Y
6 Buchanan	Y	Y	Y	Y	N	Y	Y	Y
7 Flowers	?	Y	Y	Y	Y	?	?	?
ALASKA								
AL Young	Y	Y	Y	Y	N	Y	Y	Y
ARIZONA								
1 Rhodes	Y	Y	Y	Y	N	Y	Y	Y
2 Udall	Y	Y	Y	Y	Y	Y	Y	Y
3 Stump	Y	N	N	Y	N	Y	N	N
4 Rudd	Y	N	N	Y	N	Y	Y	N
ARKANSAS								
1 Alexander	Y	Y	Y	Y	Y	Y	Y	Y
2 Tucker	Y	Y	Y	Y	Y	Y	Y	Y
3 Hammerschmidt	Y	Y	N	Y	Y	Y	Y	Y
4 Thornton	Y	Y	Y	Y	Y	Y	Y	Y
CALIFORNIA								
1 Johnson	Y	Y	Y	Y	Y	Y	Y	Y
2 Clausen	Y	Y	N	Y	Y	Y	Y	Y
3 Moss	Y	Y	Y	Y	Y	Y	Y	Y
4 Leggett	Y	Y	Y	Y	Y	Y	Y	Y
5 Burton, J.	Y	Y	Y	Y	Y	Y	Y	Y
6 Burton, P.	Y	Y	Y	Y	Y	Y	Y	Y
7 Miller	?	?	?	?	?	?	?	?
8 Dellums	Y	Y	Y	Y	Y	Y	Y	Y
9 Stark	Y	Y	Y	Y	Y	Y	Y	Y
10 Edwards	Y	Y	Y	Y	Y	Y	Y	Y
11 Ryan	Y	Y	Y	Y	Y	Y	Y	N
12 McCloskey	Y	Y	Y	Y	Y	Y	Y	Y
13 Mineta	Y	Y	Y	Y	Y	Y	Y	Y
14 McFall	Y	Y	Y	Y	Y	Y	Y	Y
15 Sisk	Y	Y	Y	Y	Y	Y	Y	Y
16 Panetta	Y	Y	Y	Y	N	Y	Y	Y
17 Krebs	Y	Y	Y	Y	Y	Y	Y	Y
18 Vacancy								
19 Lagomarsino	Y	Y	N	Y	N	Y	Y	N
20 Goldwater	Y	N	Y	?	N	?	Y	N
21 Corman	?	?	?	?	?	Y	Y	Y
22 Moorhead	Y	N	N	N	N	Y	Y	N
23 Beilenson	#	#	#	#	#	Y	Y	Y
24 Waxman	Y	Y	Y	Y	Y	Y	Y	Y
25 Roybal	Y	Y	Y	Y	Y	Y	Y	Y
26 Rousselot	Y	N	N	Y	N	Y	Y	N
27 Dornan	Y	Y	Y	Y	N	Y	Y	N
28 Burke	#	#	#	#	#	#	#	#
29 Hawkins	Y	Y	Y	Y	Y	Y	Y	Y
30 Danielson	Y	Y	Y	Y	Y	Y	Y	Y
31 Wilson, C.H.	Y	Y	N	Y	Y	Y	Y	Y
32 Anderson	Y	Y	Y	Y	Y	Y	Y	Y
33 Clawson	Y	N	N	Y	N	Y	Y	N
34 Hannaford	Y	Y	Y	Y	Y	Y	Y	Y
35 Lloyd	Y	Y	Y	Y	Y	Y	Y	Y
36 Brown	Y	Y	Y	Y	Y	Y	Y	Y
37 Pettis	Y	N	Y	Y	N	Y	Y	N
38 Patterson	Y	Y	Y	Y	Y	Y	Y	Y
39 Wiggins	Y	N	Y	N	N	Y	Y	N
40 Badham	Y	N	N	Y	N	Y	N	N
41 Wilson, B.	Y	Y	Y	Y	Y	Y	Y	N
42 Van Deerlin	?	?	Y	Y	Y	Y	Y	Y
43 Burgener	Y	Y	Y	Y	N	Y	Y	Y
COLORADO								
1 Schroeder	Y	Y	Y	Y	Y	Y	Y	Y
2 Wirth	#	#	#	#	#	Y	Y	Y
3 Evans	Y	#	Y	Y	Y	Y	Y	Y
4 Johnson	Y	Y	Y	Y	Y	Y	Y	Y
5 Armstrong	?	?	?	?	?	?	?	?
CONNECTICUT								
1 Cotter	Y	Y	Y	Y	Y	#	#	✓
2 Dodd	Y	Y	Y	Y	Y	Y	Y	Y
3 Giaimo	Y	Y	Y	Y	Y	Y	Y	Y
4 McKinney	Y	Y	Y	Y	Y	Y	Y	Y
5 Sarasin	†	†	†	†	†	Y	Y	Y
6 Moffett	Y	Y	Y	Y	Y	Y	Y	Y
DELAWARE								
AL Evans	Y	Y	Y	Y	Y	Y	Y	Y
FLORIDA								
1 Sikes	Y	Y	Y	Y	N	Y	Y	Y
2 Fuqua	Y	Y	Y	Y	Y	Y	Y	Y
3 Bennett	N	Y	Y	Y	N	Y	N	N
4 Chappell	Y	N	Y	Y	N	Y	Y	Y
5 Kelly	Y	Y	N	Y	N	Y	N	N
6 Young	Y	Y	Y	Y	N	Y	Y	Y
7 Gibbons	Y	Y	N	Y	Y	Y	Y	N
8 Ireland	Y	Y	Y	Y	N	Y	Y	Y
9 Frey	?	?	?	?	?	?	?	?
10 Bafalis	Y	Y	Y	Y	N	Y	Y	Y
11 Rogers	Y	Y	Y	Y	Y	Y	Y	Y
12 Burke	Y	Y	Y	Y	N	Y	Y	Y
13 Lehman	Y	Y	Y	Y	Y	Y	Y	Y
14 Pepper	Y	Y	Y	Y	Y	#	#	✓
15 Fascell	Y	Y	Y	Y	Y	Y	Y	Y
GEORGIA								
1 Ginn	Y	Y	Y	Y	Y	Y	Y	Y
2 Mathis	Y	Y	Y	Y	N	Y	Y	Y
3 Brinkley	Y	Y	Y	Y	N	Y	Y	Y
4 Levitas	Y	Y	Y	Y	N	Y	Y	Y
5 Fowler	Y	Y	Y	Y	Y	Y	Y	Y
6 Flynt	Y	N	N	Y	N	Y	Y	N
7 McDonald	N	N	N	Y	N	N	N	N
8 Evans	Y	Y	Y	Y	Y	Y	Y	N
9 Jenkins	Y	Y	Y	Y	N	Y	Y	Y
10 Barnard	Y	Y	Y	Y	N	Y	Y	Y
HAWAII								
1 Heftel	Y	Y	Y	Y	Y	Y	Y	Y
2 Akaka	Y	Y	Y	Y	Y	Y	Y	Y
IDAHO								
1 Symms	Y	N	N	Y	N	N	N	N
2 Hansen, G.	Y	N	N	Y	N	Y	N	N
ILLINOIS								
1 Metcalfe	Y	Y	Y	Y	Y	Y	Y	Y
2 Murphy	Y	Y	Y	Y	Y	Y	Y	Y
3 Russo	Y	Y	Y	Y	N	Y	Y	N
4 Derwinski	Y	Y	Y	Y	N	Y	Y	Y
5 Fary	Y	Y	Y	Y	Y	Y	Y	Y
6 Hyde	#	#	#	#	▮	Y	Y	N
7 Collins	Y	Y	Y	Y	Y	Y	Y	Y
8 Rostenkowski	Y	Y	Y	Y	Y	Y	Y	Y
9 Yates	Y	Y	Y	Y	Y	Y	Y	Y
10 Mikva	Y	Y	Y	Y	Y	#	Y	Y
11 Annunzio	Y	Y	Y	Y	Y	Y	Y	Y
12 Crane	Y	N	N	Y	N	#	▮	▮
13 McClory	Y	Y	N	N	Y	Y	Y	N
14 Erlenborn	Y	Y	Y	Y	Y	Y	Y	N
15 Corcoran	Y	Y	Y	Y	Y	Y	Y	N
16 Anderson	Y	Y	Y	Y	Y	Y	Y	Y
17 O'Brien	Y	Y	Y	Y	Y	Y	Y	N
18 Michel	Y	Y	N	Y	N	Y	Y	N
19 Railsback	Y	Y	Y	Y	Y	Y	Y	Y
20 Findley	Y	Y	N	Y	Y	Y	Y	Y
21 Madigan	Y	Y	Y	Y	Y	Y	Y	N
22 Shipley	?	?	?	?	?	?	?	?
23 Price	Y	Y	Y	Y	Y	Y	Y	Y
24 Simon	Y	Y	Y	Y	Y	Y	Y	Y
INDIANA								
1 Benjamin	Y	Y	Y	Y	Y	Y	Y	Y
2 Fithian	Y	Y	Y	Y	N	Y	Y	Y
3 Brademas	Y	Y	Y	Y	Y	Y	Y	Y
4 Quayle	Y	Y	Y	Y	N	Y	Y	N
5 Hillis	Y	Y	Y	Y	N	Y	Y	Y
6 Evans	Y	Y	N	Y	N	Y	Y	Y
7 Myers, J.	Y	Y	Y	Y	N	Y	Y	Y
8 Cornwell	#	#	#	#	#	Y	Y	Y
9 Hamilton	Y	Y	Y	Y	Y	Y	Y	Y
10 Sharp	Y	Y	Y	Y	Y	Y	Y	Y
11 Jacobs	Y	Y	Y	Y	Y	Y	Y	N
IOWA								
1 Leach	Y	Y	Y	Y	Y	#	#	#
2 Blouin	Y	Y	Y	Y	Y	Y	Y	N
3 Grassley	Y	Y	N	Y	N	Y	Y	N
4 Smith	Y	Y	Y	Y	Y	Y	Y	Y
5 Harkin	Y	Y	Y	Y	Y	Y	Y	Y
6 Bedell	Y	Y	Y	Y	Y	Y	Y	Y

Democrats ***Republicans***

	695	696	697	698	699	700	701	702
KANSAS								
1 ***Sebelius***	Y	Y	Y	Y	N	Y	Y	Y
2 Keys	Y	Y	Y	Y	Y	Y	Y	Y
3 ***Winn***	Y	Y	Y	Y	Y	Y	Y	Y
4 Glickman	Y	Y	Y	Y	Y	Y	Y	Y
5 ***Skubitz***	Y	Y	Y	Y	Y	Y	Y	?
KENTUCKY								
1 Hubbard	Y	Y	N	Y	N	Y	Y	N
2 Natcher	Y	Y	Y	Y	Y	Y	Y	Y
3 Mazzoli	Y	Y	Y	Y	Y	Y	Y	Y
4 ***Snyder***	Y	N	Y	Y	Y	Y	Y	Y
5 ***Carter***	Y	Y	Y	Y	Y	Y	Y	Y
6 Breckinridge	Y	Y	Y	Y	Y	Y	Y	Y
7 Perkins	Y	Y	Y	Y	Y	Y	Y	Y
LOUISIANA								
1 ***Livingston***	Y	Y	Y	Y	N	Y	Y	N
2 Boggs	Y	Y	Y	Y	Y	Y	Y	Y
3 ***Treen***	Y	Y	Y	Y	N	Y	Y	N
4 Waggonner	Y	Y	Y	Y	N	Y	N	N
5 Huckaby	Y	Y	Y	Y	Y	Y	Y	Y
6 ***Moore***	Y	Y	Y	Y	Y	Y	Y	N
7 Breaux	Y	Y	Y	Y	Y	Y	Y	X
8 Long	Y	Y	Y	Y	Y	Y	Y	Y
MAINE								
1 ***Emery***	Y	Y	Y	Y	Y	Y	Y	Y
2 ***Cohen***	Y	Y	Y	Y	N	Y	Y	Y
MARYLAND								
1 ***Bauman***	Y	N	N	Y	N	Y	Y	N
2 Long	Y	Y	Y	Y	Y	Y	Y	Y
3 Mikulski	Y	Y	Y	Y	Y	Y	Y	Y
4 ***Holt***	Y	Y	N	Y	N	Y	Y	N
5 Spellman	Y	Y	Y	Y	Y	Y	Y	Y
6 Byron	Y	Y	Y	Y	Y	Y	Y	Y
7 Mitchell	Y	Y	Y	Y	Y	Y	Y	Y
8 ***Steers***	Y	Y	Y	Y	Y	Y	Y	Y
MASSACHUSETTS								
1 ***Conte***	Y	Y	Y	Y	Y	Y	Y	Y
2 Boland	Y	Y	Y	Y	Y	Y	Y	Y
3 Early	Y	Y	Y	Y	Y	?	?	?
4 Drinan	Y	Y	Y	Y	Y	Y	Y	Y
5 Tsongas	?	?	?	?	?	?	?	?
6 Harrington	Y	Y	Y	Y	Y	#	#	#
7 Markey	Y	Y	Y	Y	Y	Y	Y	Y
8 O'Neill								
9 Moakley	Y	Y	Y	Y	Y	Y	Y	Y
10 ***Heckler***	Y	Y	Y	Y	Y	Y	Y	Y
11 Burke	Y	Y	Y	Y	Y	Y	Y	Y
12 Studds	Y	Y	Y	Y	Y	Y	Y	Y
MICHIGAN								
1 Conyers	#	#	#	#	#	Y	Y	Y
2 ***Pursell***	Y	Y	Y	Y	Y	Y	Y	Y
3 ***Brown***	Y	Y	Y	Y	N	Y	Y	N
4 ***Stockman***	Y	#	Y	Y	N	Y	Y	N
5 ***Sawyer***	Y	Y	Y	Y	N	Y	Y	Y
6 Carr	Y	Y	Y	Y	Y	Y	Y	Y
7 Kildee	Y	Y	Y	Y	Y	Y	Y	Y
8 Traxler	#	#	#	#	#	Y	Y	Y
9 ***Vander Jagt***	Y	Y	Y	Y	Y	Y	Y	Y
10 ***Cederberg***	Y	Y	Y	Y	Y	Y	Y	Y
11 ***Ruppe***	Y	Y	Y	Y	N	Y	Y	N
12 Bonior	Y	Y	Y	Y	Y	Y	Y	Y
13 Diggs	Y	Y	Y	Y	Y	#	#	#
14 Nedzi	Y	Y	Y	Y	Y	Y	Y	Y
15 Ford	Y	Y	Y	Y	Y	Y	Y	Y
16 Dingell	Y	Y	Y	Y	Y	Y	Y	Y
17 Brodhead	Y	Y	Y	Y	Y	Y	Y	Y
18 Blanchard	Y	Y	Y	Y	Y	Y	Y	Y
19 ***Broomfield***	Y	Y	Y	Y	N	Y	Y	N
MINNESOTA								
1 ***Quie***	?	?	?	?	?	?	?	?
2 ***Hagedorn***	Y	Y	N	Y	N	Y	Y	N
3 ***Frenzel***	Y	Y	Y	Y	Y	Y	Y	N
4 Vento	Y	Y	Y	Y	Y	Y	Y	Y
5 Fraser	Y	Y	Y	Y	Y	Y	Y	Y
6 Nolan	Y	Y	Y	Y	Y	Y	Y	Y
7 ***Stangeland***	Y	Y	N	Y	N	Y	Y	Y
8 Oberstar	Y	Y	Y	Y	Y	Y	Y	Y
MISSISSIPPI								
1 Whitten	Y	Y	Y	Y	Y	Y	Y	Y
2 Bowen	Y	Y	Y	Y	Y	Y	Y	Y
3 Montgomery	Y	N	N	Y	N	Y	Y	N
4 ***Cochran***	Y	N	Y	Y	Y	Y	Y	Y
5 ***Lott***	Y	N	N	Y	N	Y	Y	N
MISSOURI								
1 Clay	Y	Y	Y	Y	Y	?	?	Y
2 Young	Y	Y	Y	Y	Y	Y	Y	Y
3 Gephardt	Y	Y	N	Y	Y	Y	Y	N

	695	696	697	698	699	700	701	702
4 Skelton	Y	Y	N	Y	N	Y	Y	N
5 Bolling	Y	Y	Y	Y	Y	Y	Y	Y
6 ***Coleman***	#	#	#	Y	N	Y	Y	Y
7 ***Taylor***	Y	N	N	Y	N	Y	Y	N
8 Ichord	Y	Y	N	Y	N	Y	Y	N
9 Volkmer	Y	N	Y	Y	N	Y	Y	Y
10 Burlison	Y	Y	Y	Y	N	Y	Y	N
MONTANA								
1 Baucus	Y	Y	Y	Y	Y	Y	Y	Y
2 ***Marlenee***	Y	Y	Y	Y	Y	Y	Y	Y
NEBRASKA								
1 ***Thone***	Y	Y	Y	Y	N	Y	Y	Y
2 Cavanaugh	Y	Y	Y	Y	N	Y	Y	Y
3 ***Smith***	Y	Y	Y	Y	N	Y	Y	Y
NEVADA								
AL Santini	Y	Y	Y	Y	Y	Y	Y	Y
NEW HAMPSHIRE								
1 D'Amours	Y	Y	Y	Y	Y	Y	Y	N
2 ***Cleveland***	Y	Y	Y	Y	Y	Y	Y	N
NEW JERSEY								
1 Florio	Y	Y	Y	Y	Y	Y	Y	Y
2 Hughes	Y	Y	Y	Y	N	Y	Y	Y
3 Howard	Y	Y	Y	Y	Y	Y	Y	Y
4 Thompson	Y	Y	Y	Y	Y	Y	Y	Y
5 ***Fenwick***	Y	Y	Y	Y	N	Y	Y	N
6 ***Forsythe***	Y	Y	Y	Y	N	Y	Y	Y
7 Maguire	Y	Y	Y	Y	Y	Y	Y	Y
8 Roe	Y	Y	Y	Y	Y	Y	Y	Y
9 ***Hollenbeck***	Y	Y	Y	Y	Y	Y	Y	Y
10 Rodino	#	#	#	#	#	Y	Y	Y
11 Minish	Y	Y	Y	Y	Y	Y	Y	Y
12 ***Rinaldo***	Y	Y	Y	Y	Y	Y	Y	Y
13 Meyner	Y	Y	Y	Y	Y	Y	Y	Y
14 LeFante	Y	Y	Y	Y	Y	Y	Y	Y
15 Patten	Y	Y	Y	Y	Y	Y	Y	Y
NEW MEXICO								
1 ***Lujan***	Y	Y	Y	Y	N	Y	Y	Y
2 Runnels	Y	Y	Y	Y	N	Y	Y	N
NEW YORK								
1 Pike	Y	Y	Y	Y	Y	Y	N	N
2 Downey	Y	Y	Y	Y	Y	Y	Y	Y
3 Ambro	Y	Y	Y	Y	Y	Y	Y	Y
4 ***Lent***	Y	Y	Y	Y	Y	Y	Y	Y
5 ***Wydler***	Y	Y	Y	Y	N	Y	Y	N
6 Wolff	Y	Y	Y	Y	Y	Y	Y	Y
7 Addabbo	Y	Y	Y	Y	Y	Y	Y	Y
8 Rosenthal	Y	Y	Y	Y	Y	Y	Y	Y
9 Delaney	Y	Y	Y	Y	Y	Y	Y	Y
10 Biaggi	Y	Y	Y	Y	Y	Y	Y	Y
11 Scheuer	Y	Y	Y	Y	Y	Y	Y	Y
12 Chisholm	Y	Y	Y	Y	Y	Y	Y	Y
13 Solarz	Y	Y	Y	Y	Y	Y	Y	Y
14 Richmond	Y	Y	Y	Y	Y	Y	Y	Y
15 Zeferetti	Y	Y	Y	Y	Y	Y	Y	Y
16 Holtzman	Y	Y	Y	Y	Y	Y	Y	Y
17 Murphy	Y	Y	Y	Y	Y	Y	Y	Y
18 ***Green***	Y	Y	Y	Y	Y	Y	Y	Y
19 Rangel	Y	Y	Y	Y	Y	Y	Y	Y
20 Weiss	Y	Y	Y	Y	Y	Y	Y	Y
21 Garcia	Y	Y	Y	Y	Y	Y	Y	Y
22 Bingham	Y	Y	Y	Y	Y	Y	Y	Y
23 ***Caputo***	?	?	?	?	?	Y	Y	Y
24 Ottinger	Y	Y	Y	Y	Y	Y	Y	Y
25 ***Fish***	Y	Y	Y	Y	N	Y	Y	Y
26 ***Gilman***	Y	Y	Y	Y	Y	Y	Y	Y
27 McHugh	Y	Y	Y	Y	Y	Y	Y	Y
28 Stratton	Y	N	Y	Y	Y	Y	Y	Y
29 Pattison	Y	Y	Y	Y	Y	Y	Y	Y
30 ***McEwen***	Y	Y	N	Y	N	Y	Y	N
31 ***Mitchell***	Y	Y	Y	Y	Y	Y	Y	Y
32 Hanley	Y	Y	Y	Y	Y	Y	Y	Y
33 ***Walsh***	Y	Y	Y	Y	Y	Y	Y	Y
34 ***Horton***	Y	Y	Y	Y	Y	Y	Y	Y
35 ***Conable***	Y	Y	Y	Y	N	Y	Y	N
36 LaFalce	Y	Y	Y	Y	#	Y	Y	Y
37 Nowak	Y	Y	Y	Y	Y	Y	Y	Y
38 ***Kemp***	Y	Y	Y	Y	N	Y	Y	N
39 Lundine	Y	Y	Y	Y	Y	Y	Y	Y
NORTH CAROLINA								
1 Jones	Y	Y	Y	Y	N	Y	Y	Y
2 Fountain	Y	Y	Y	Y	N	Y	Y	Y
3 Whitley	Y	Y	Y	Y	N	Y	Y	Y
4 Andrews	Y	Y	Y	Y	N	Y	Y	Y
5 Neal	Y	Y	Y	Y	Y	#	Y	Y
6 Preyer	Y	Y	Y	Y	Y	Y	Y	Y
7 Rose	Y	Y	Y	Y	?	Y	Y	Y
8 Hefner	?	?	?	?	?	Y	Y	Y

	695	696	697	698	699	700	701	702
9 ***Martin***	Y	Y	Y	Y	N	Y	Y	N
10 ***Broyhill***	Y	Y	Y	Y	Y	Y	Y	N
11 Gudger	Y	Y	Y	Y	N	Y	Y	Y
NORTH DAKOTA								
AL ***Andrews***	Y	Y	N	Y	N	Y	Y	Y
OHIO								
1 ***Gradison***	Y	Y	Y	N	Y	Y	Y	N
2 Luken	Y	Y	N	Y	Y	?	?	?
3 ***Whalen***	Y	Y	Y	Y	Y	Y	Y	Y
4 ***Guyer***	Y	Y	Y	Y	N	Y	Y	N
5 ***Latta***	Y	?	Y	Y	N	Y	Y	N
6 ***Harsha***	Y	Y	Y	Y	N	Y	Y	Y
7 ***Brown***	Y	Y	Y	Y	N	Y	Y	N
8 ***Kindness***	Y	N	Y	N	N	Y	Y	Y
9 Ashley	Y	Y	Y	Y	Y	Y	Y	Y
10 ***Miller***	Y	N	N	Y	N	Y	Y	N
11 ***Stanton***	Y	Y	Y	Y	N	Y	Y	N
12 ***Devine***	Y	N	N	Y	N	Y	Y	N
13 Pease	Y	Y	Y	Y	N	Y	Y	N
14 Seiberling	Y	Y	Y	Y	Y	Y	Y	Y
15 ***Wylie***	Y	Y	Y	Y	N	Y	Y	Y
16 ***Regula***	Y	Y	Y	Y	N	Y	Y	Y
17 ***Ashbrook***	Y	N	N	Y	N	Y	Y	N
18 Applegate	Y	Y	Y	Y	Y	Y	Y	Y
19 Carney	Y	Y	Y	Y	Y	Y	Y	Y
20 Oakar	Y	Y	Y	Y	Y	Y	Y	Y
21 Stokes	Y	Y	Y	Y	Y	Y	Y	Y
22 Vanik	Y	Y	Y	Y	Y	Y	Y	Y
23 Mottl	Y	Y	Y	Y	Y	Y	Y	Y
OKLAHOMA								
1 Jones	Y	N	Y	Y	N	Y	Y	Y
2 Risenhoover	Y	Y	Y	Y	N	?	?	?
3 Watkins	Y	N	Y	Y	N	Y	Y	Y
4 Steed	#	#	#	#	▮	#	#	#
5 ***Edwards***	Y	N	Y	Y	Y	Y	Y	Y
6 English	Y	N	Y	Y	N	Y	Y	N
OREGON								
1 AuCoin	Y	Y	N	Y	Y	Y	Y	Y
2 Ullman	Y	Y	Y	Y	Y	Y	Y	Y
3 Duncan	Y	Y	N	Y	Y	Y	Y	Y
4 Weaver	Y	Y	Y	Y	Y	Y	Y	Y
PENNSYLVANIA								
1 Myers, M.	Y	Y	Y	Y	Y	Y	Y	Y
2 Nix	Y	Y	Y	Y	Y	Y	Y	Y
3 Lederer	Y	Y	Y	Y	Y	Y	Y	Y
4 Eilberg	Y	Y	Y	Y	Y	Y	Y	Y
5 ***Schulze***	Y	Y	Y	Y	N	Y	Y	N
6 Yatron	Y	Y	Y	Y	Y	Y	Y	Y
7 Edgar	Y	Y	Y	Y	Y	Y	Y	Y
8 Kostmayer	Y	Y	N	Y	N	Y	Y	Y
9 ***Shuster***	Y	Y	Y	Y	N	Y	Y	N
10 ***McDade***	Y	Y	Y	Y	Y	Y	Y	N
11 Flood	Y	Y	Y	Y	Y	Y	Y	Y
12 Murtha	Y	Y	Y	Y	Y	Y	Y	Y
13 ***Coughlin***	Y	Y	Y	Y	N	Y	Y	Y
14 Moorhead	Y	Y	Y	Y	Y	Y	Y	Y
15 Rooney	Y	Y	Y	Y	Y	Y	Y	Y
16 ***Walker***	Y	N	N	Y	N	Y	Y	N
17 Ertel	Y	Y	Y	Y	Y	Y	Y	Y
18 Walgren	?	?	Y	Y	Y	Y	Y	Y
19 ***Goodling, W.***	Y	Y	Y	Y	N	Y	Y	Y
20 Gaydos	Y	Y	Y	Y	Y	Y	Y	Y
21 Dent	Y	Y	Y	Y	Y	#	Y	Y
22 Murphy	Y	Y	Y	Y	Y	Y	Y	Y
23 Ammerman	?	?	?	?	?	?	?	✓
24 ***Marks***	Y	Y	Y	Y	Y	Y	Y	Y
25 ***Myers, G.***	Y	Y	Y	Y	Y	Y	Y	N
RHODE ISLAND								
1 St Germain	Y	Y	Y	Y	Y	Y	Y	Y
2 Beard	Y	Y	Y	Y	Y	Y	Y	Y
SOUTH CAROLINA								
1 Davis	Y	N	Y	Y	Y	Y	Y	Y
2 ***Spence***	Y	N	Y	Y	Y	Y	Y	Y
3 Derrick	#	Y	Y	Y	Y	Y	Y	Y
4 Mann	Y	Y	Y	Y	Y	Y	Y	Y
5 Holland	Y	Y	Y	Y	Y	Y	Y	Y
6 Jenrette	Y	Y	Y	Y	Y	Y	Y	Y
SOUTH DAKOTA								
1 ***Pressler***	Y	Y	Y	Y	Y	Y	Y	Y
2 ***Abdnor***	Y	Y	Y	Y	N	Y	Y	Y
TENNESSEE								
1 ***Quillen***	Y	Y	N	Y	Y	Y	Y	Y
2 ***Duncan***	Y	Y	Y	Y	N	Y	Y	Y
3 Lloyd	Y	Y	Y	Y	N	Y	Y	Y
4 Gore	Y	Y	Y	Y	Y	Y	Y	Y
5 Vacancy								
6 ***Beard***	Y	Y	Y	Y	N	Y	Y	Y

	695	696	697	698	699	700	701	702
7 Jones	Y	Y	Y	Y	N	Y	Y	Y
8 Ford	Y	Y	Y	Y	Y	Y	Y	Y
TEXAS								
1 Hall	Y	Y	Y	Y	N	Y	Y	N
2 Wilson, C.	Y	Y	Y	Y	Y	Y	Y	Y
3 ***Collins***	Y	N	N	N	N	N	N	N
4 Roberts	Y	Y	Y	Y	N	Y	Y	N
5 Mattox	Y	Y	Y	Y	N	Y	Y	Y
6 Teague	?	?	?	?	?	?	?	X
7 ***Archer***	Y	Y	N	Y	N	Y	Y	N
8 Eckhardt	?	?	?	?	?	?	Y	Y
9 Brooks	Y	Y	Y	Y	N	Y	Y	N
10 Pickle	Y	Y	Y	Y	N	Y	Y	Y
11 Poage	Y	Y	N	Y	N	Y	N	N
12 Wright	?	?	?	?	?	Y	Y	Y
13 Hightower	Y	Y	Y	Y	N	Y	Y	N
14 Young	Y	Y	Y	Y	N	Y	Y	N
15 de la Garza	Y	Y	Y	Y	N	Y	Y	Y
16 White	Y	Y	Y	Y	N	Y	Y	N
17 Burleson	Y	Y	N	Y	N	Y	N	N
18 Jordan	Y	Y	Y	Y	Y	Y	Y	Y
19 Mahon	Y	Y	Y	Y	N	Y	Y	N
20 Gonzalez	Y	Y	Y	Y	P	Y	Y	Y
21 Krueger	Y	Y	Y	Y	N	#	#	#
22 Gammage	Y	Y	Y	Y	N	#	#	✓
23 Kazen	Y	Y	Y	Y	N	Y	Y	Y
24 Milford	?	?	?	?	?	?	?	?
UTAH								
1 McKay	Y	Y	N	Y	N	Y	Y	N
2 ***Marriott***	Y	Y	Y	Y	N	Y	Y	N
VERMONT								
AL ***Jeffords***	Y	Y	Y	Y	Y	Y	Y	N
VIRGINIA								
1 ***Trible***	Y	Y	Y	Y	N	Y	Y	Y
2 ***Whitehurst***	Y	N	Y	Y	Y	Y	Y	Y
3 Satterfield	Y	N	N	Y	N	Y	Y	N
4 ***Daniel***	Y	Y	N	Y	N	Y	Y	N
5 Daniel	Y	N	Y	Y	Y	Y	Y	Y
6 ***Butler***	Y	N	Y	N	N	Y	Y	N
7 ***Robinson***	Y	Y	Y	Y	N	Y	Y	N
8 Harris	Y	Y	Y	Y	Y	Y	Y	Y
9 ***Wampler***	Y	Y	Y	Y	Y	Y	Y	Y
10 Fisher	Y	Y	Y	Y	Y	Y	Y	Y
WASHINGTON								
1 ***Pritchard***	Y	Y	Y	Y	Y	#	#	#
2 Meeds	?	?	?	?	?	?	?	?
3 Bonker	Y	Y	Y	Y	Y	Y	Y	Y
4 McCormack	Y	Y	Y	Y	Y	Y	Y	Y
5 Foley	Y	Y	Y	Y	N	Y	Y	N
6 Dicks	Y	Y	Y	Y	Y	Y	Y	Y
7 ***Cunningham***	Y	N	N	Y	N	Y	Y	N
WEST VIRGINIA								
1 Mollohan	Y	Y	N	Y	Y	Y	Y	Y
2 Staggers	Y	Y	Y	Y	Y	Y	Y	Y
3 Slack	Y	Y	Y	Y	Y	Y	Y	Y
4 Rahall	Y	Y	Y	Y	Y	Y	Y	Y
WISCONSIN								
1 Aspin	Y	Y	Y	Y	Y	Y	Y	Y
2 Kastenmeier	Y	Y	Y	Y	Y	Y	Y	Y
3 Baldus	Y	Y	Y	Y	Y	Y	Y	Y
4 Zablocki	Y	Y	Y	Y	Y	Y	Y	Y
5 Reuss	Y	Y	Y	Y	Y	Y	Y	Y
6 ***Steiger***	Y	Y	Y	Y	N	Y	Y	N
7 Obey	Y	Y	Y	Y	Y	Y	Y	Y
8 Cornell	Y	Y	Y	Y	Y	Y	Y	Y
9 ***Kasten***	#	#	#	?	▮	Y	Y	N
WYOMING								
AL Roncalio	Y	Y	Y	Y	Y	Y	Y	Y

Democrats ***Republicans***

703. S 703. Overseas Citizens' Voting Rights. Thompson, D-N.J., motion to suspend the rules and pass the bill to allow U.S. citizens living overseas to vote in federal elections in the state of their last domicile without becoming subject to the taxes of that state. Motion agreed to 327-78: R 103-36; D 224-42 (ND 172-13; SD 52-29), Sept. 19, 1978. A two-thirds majority vote (270 in this case) is required for passage under suspension of the rules.

704. HR 12101. Farmer-to-Consumer Direct Marketing. Foley, D-Wash., motion to suspend the rules and pass the bill to authorize $1.5 million in fiscal 1979 for farmer-to-consumer direct marketing demonstration projects. Motion rejected 237-163: R 23-113; D 214-50 (ND 162-21; SD 52-29), Sept. 19, 1978. A two-thirds majority vote (267 in this case) is required for passage under suspension of the rules.

705. S 3040. Amtrak Improvements. Adoption of the conference report on the bill to authorize a subsidy for fiscal 1979 of $755 million for the National Railroad Passenger Corp. (Amtrak). Adopted 267-127: R 60-73; D 207-54 (ND 162-17; SD 45-37), Sept. 19, 1978.

706. HR 12598. State Department Authorization. Adoption of the conference report on the bill to authorize $1,969,710,000 for the State Department and related programs in fiscal 1979. Adopted 240-153: R 51-82; D 189-71 (ND 151-27; SD 38-44), Sept. 19, 1978.

707. HR 12222. Foreign Economic Aid. Adoption of the conference report on the bill to authorize $1,795,000,000 for bilateral economic aid programs in fiscal 1979. Adopted 232-159: R 57-77; D 175-82 (ND 153-26; SD 22-56), Sept. 19, 1978.

708. HR 11401. NASA Authorization. Adoption of the conference report on the bill to authorize $4,401,600,000 for fiscal 1979 research and development and construction programs of the National Aeronautics and Space Administration. Adopted (thus cleared for the president) 321-54: R 113-16; D 208-38 (ND 133-35; SD 75-3), Sept. 19, 1978.

709. HR 8149. Customs Procedures Reform. Adoption of the conference report on the bill to modernize and simplify numerous procedures of U.S. customs law and to raise the personal duty exemption to $300, from $100. Adopted (thus cleared for the president) 360-1: R 124-0; D 236-1 (ND 161-1; SD 75-0), Sept. 19, 1978.

KEY

- Y Voted for (yea).
- ✓ Paired for.
- † Announced for.
- # CQ Poll for.
- N Voted against (nay).
- X Paired against.
- \- Announced against.
- ▮ CQ Poll against.
- P Voted "present."
- ● Voted "present" to avoid possible conflict of interest.
- ? Did not vote or otherwise make a position known.

	703	704	705	706	707	708	709
ALABAMA							
1 Edwards	Y	N	N	Y	N	Y	Y
2 Dickinson	?	?	?	?	?	?	?
3 Nichols	N	N	N	N	N	Y	Y
4 Bevill	N	N	N	N	N	Y	Y
5 Flippo	N	N	N	N	N	Y	Y
6 Buchanan	Y	N	Y	Y	Y	Y	Y
7 Flowers	?	?	?	?	?	?	?
ALASKA							
AL Young	N	N	N	N	N	Y	#
ARIZONA							
1 Rhodes	Y	N	Y	N	Y	Y	Y
2 Udall	Y	Y	Y	Y	Y	Y	Y
3 Stump	N	N	N	N	N	Y	Y
4 Rudd	N	N	?	?	?	?	?
ARKANSAS							
1 Alexander	Y	Y	Y	Y	Y	Y	Y
2 Tucker	Y	Y	Y	Y	Y	Y	Y
3 Hammerschmidt	Y	N	N	N	N	Y	Y
4 Thornton	Y	Y	N	Y	Y	Y	Y
CALIFORNIA							
1 Johnson	Y	Y	Y	Y	Y	Y	Y
2 Clausen	Y	N	Y	N	N	Y	Y
3 Moss	Y	Y	Y	Y	Y	?	?
4 Leggett	Y	Y	Y	?	Y	?	Y
5 Burton, J.	Y	Y	Y	Y	Y	?	?
6 Burton, P.	Y	Y	?	Y	Y	Y	?
7 Miller	?	?	?	?	?	?	?
8 Dellums	Y	Y	Y	Y	Y	N	Y
9 Stark	Y	Y	Y	Y	Y	N	Y
10 Edwards	Y	Y	Y	Y	Y	Y	Y
11 Ryan	Y	Y	N	Y	Y	Y	Y
12 McCloskey	Y	N	Y	Y	Y	Y	Y
13 Mineta	Y	Y	Y	Y	Y	Y	Y
14 McFall	Y	?	?	Y	Y	Y	Y
15 Sisk	Y	Y	Y	Y	Y	?	?
16 Panetta	Y	Y	N	Y	N	Y	Y
17 Krebs	Y	Y	N	Y	Y	N	Y
18 Vacancy							
19 Lagomarsino	N	N	N	N	N	Y	Y
20 Goldwater	N	N	N	N	N	Y	Y
21 Corman	Y	Y	Y	Y	Y	Y	Y
22 Moorhead	N	N	N	N	N	Y	Y
23 Beilenson	Y	Y	Y	Y	Y	Y	Y
24 Waxman	Y	Y	Y	Y	Y	#	#
25 Roybal	Y	Y	Y	Y	N	N	Y
26 Rousselot	N	N	N	N	N	Y	Y
27 Dornan	Y	N	N	Y	Y	Y	Y
28 Burke	#	✓	#	#	#	#	#
29 Hawkins	Y	Y	Y	Y	Y	Y	Y
30 Danielson	Y	Y	Y	Y	Y	Y	Y
31 Wilson, C.H.	Y	Y	▮	#	N	#	#
32 Anderson	Y	Y	N	N	Y	Y	Y
33 Clawson	Y	N	N	N	N	Y	Y
34 Hannaford	Y	Y	Y	Y	Y	Y	Y
35 Lloyd	Y	Y	Y	Y	Y	Y	Y
36 Brown	Y	Y	Y	Y	Y	Y	Y
37 Pettis	N	N	Y	Y	Y	Y	Y
38 Patterson	Y	Y	Y	Y	Y	Y	Y
39 Wiggins	N	N	N	#	Y	Y	Y
40 Badham	Y	N	N	N	N	Y	Y
41 Wilson, B.	Y	N	N	Y	N	Y	Y
42 Van Deerlin	Y	Y	Y	Y	Y	Y	Y
43 Burgener	Y	N	N	N	N	Y	Y
COLORADO							
1 Schroeder	Y	Y	Y	Y	Y	Y	Y
2 Wirth	Y	Y	Y	Y	Y	Y	#
3 Evans	Y	Y	Y	Y	Y	Y	Y
4 Johnson	Y	N	Y	N	Y	Y	Y
5 Armstrong	?	?	?	?	?	?	?
CONNECTICUT							
1 Cotter	#	✓	#	✓	✓	#	#
2 Dodd	Y	Y	?	Y	Y	Y	Y
3 Giaimo	Y	Y	Y	Y	?	Y	Y
4 McKinney	Y	N	Y	Y	Y	Y	Y
5 Sarasin	Y	Y	?	?	?	?	?
6 Moffett	Y	Y	Y	Y	Y	Y	Y
DELAWARE							
AL Evans	Y	N	Y	N	?	?	?
FLORIDA							
1 Sikes	N	Y	N	N	N	Y	Y
2 Fuqua	N	N	Y	N	N	Y	Y
3 Bennett	N	N	Y	N	N	Y	Y
4 Chappell	N	N	Y	N	N	Y	Y
5 Kelly	N	N	N	N	N	Y	Y
6 Young	Y	N	Y	N	N	Y	Y
7 Gibbons	Y	N	N	Y	N	N	Y
8 Ireland	N	N	Y	Y	N	?	?
9 Frey	?	?	?	?	N	Y	Y
10 Bafalis	Y	N	N	N	N	Y	Y
11 Rogers	Y	Y	Y	Y	N	Y	Y
12 Burke	Y	N	N	Y	N	Y	Y
13 Lehman	Y	N	Y	Y	Y	#	Y
14 Pepper	#	✓	#	#	#	#	#
15 Fascell	Y	Y	Y	Y	Y	Y	Y
GEORGIA							
1 Ginn	Y	Y	Y	N	N	Y	Y
2 Mathis	Y	Y	N	N	N	Y	Y
3 Brinkley	Y	Y	Y	N	N	Y	Y
4 Levitas	Y	Y	N	N	N	Y	Y
5 Fowler	N	Y	Y	Y	Y	Y	Y
6 Flynt	N	N	N	N	N	Y	Y
7 McDonald	N	N	N	N	N	N	Y
8 Evans	N	N	Y	N	N	Y	Y
9 Jenkins	N	Y	N	N	N	Y	Y
10 Barnard	N	Y	N	N	N	Y	Y
HAWAII							
1 Heftel	Y	N	N	Y	Y	Y	Y
2 Akaka	Y	Y	Y	Y	Y	Y	Y
IDAHO							
1 Symms	N	N	N	N	N	Y	Y
2 Hansen, G.	N	N	N	N	N	Y	Y
ILLINOIS							
1 Metcalfe	Y	Y	Y	Y	Y	Y	Y
2 Murphy	Y	N	Y	Y	Y	Y	Y
3 Russo	Y	N	N	N	N	N	Y
4 Derwinski	Y	N	Y	Y	N	Y	Y
5 Fary	Y	Y	Y	Y	Y	Y	Y
6 Hyde	Y	N	Y	Y	Y	N	Y
7 Collins	Y	Y	Y	Y	Y	Y	Y
8 Rostenkowski	Y	N	Y	Y	Y	Y	Y
9 Yates	Y	Y	Y	Y	Y	N	Y
10 Mikva	Y	Y	Y	Y	Y	N	Y
11 Annunzio	Y	Y	Y	Y	Y	Y	Y
12 Crane	▮	▮	N	N	N	Y	Y
13 McClory	Y	N	Y	N	N	Y	Y
14 Erlenborn	N	N	N	Y	Y	Y	Y
15 Corcoran	Y	N	Y	Y	N	Y	Y
16 Anderson	Y	N	Y	Y	Y	Y	#
17 O'Brien	N	N	#	#	#	#	#
18 Michel	Y	N	N	N	N	N	Y
19 Railsback	Y	N	Y	N	Y	Y	?
20 Findley	Y	N	?	Y	Y	N	Y
21 Madigan	Y	N	Y	Y	Y	Y	Y
22 Shipley	?	?	?	?	?	?	?
23 Price	Y	Y	Y	Y	Y	Y	Y
24 Simon	Y	Y	Y	Y	Y	N	Y
INDIANA							
1 Benjamin	Y	Y	Y	N	Y	Y	Y
2 Fithian	Y	Y	Y	N	N	Y	Y
3 Brademas	Y	Y	Y	Y	Y	Y	#
4 Quayle	Y	Y	N	N	N	N	?
5 Hillis	Y	N	Y	Y	Y	Y	Y
6 Evans	Y	Y	Y	N	N	N	Y
7 Myers, J.	Y	N	N	N	N	Y	Y
8 Cornwell	N	Y	Y	Y	Y	Y	#
9 Hamilton	Y	Y	Y	Y	Y	Y	Y
10 Sharp	Y	Y	Y	Y	Y	Y	Y
11 Jacobs	Y	N	N	N	N	N	Y
IOWA							
1 Leach	▮	X	▮	▮	#	#	#
2 Blouin	Y	Y	Y	Y	Y	Y	Y
3 Grassley	N	N	N	N	N	Y	Y
4 Smith	Y	Y	Y	Y	Y	Y	Y
5 Harkin	Y	Y	Y	N	Y	Y	Y
6 Bedell	Y	Y	Y	Y	Y	N	N

Democrats ***Republicans***

	703	704	705	706	707	708	709
KANSAS							
1 Sebelius	Y	Y	N	N	N	Y	Y
2 Keys	Y	Y	Y	N	Y	N	Y
3 Winn	Y	N	Y	Y	Y	Y	Y
4 Glickman	Y	Y	Y	N	Y	Y	Y
5 Skubitz	Y	Y	Y	Y	Y	N	Y
KENTUCKY							
1 Hubbard	N	N	Y	N	N	Y	Y
2 Natcher	Y	Y	Y	Y	Y	Y	Y
3 Mazzoli	Y	N	Y	Y	Y	Y	Y
4 Snyder	Y	N	N	N	N	Y	Y
5 Carter	Y	N	Y	Y	Y	Y	Y
6 Breckinridge	Y	Y	Y	Y	?	Y	?
7 Perkins	Y	Y	Y	Y	Y	Y	Y
LOUISIANA							
1 Livingston	N	N	N	N	N	Y	Y
2 Boggs	Y	Y	Y	Y	Y	Y	Y
3 Treen	N	N	N	N	Y	Y	Y
4 Waggonner	N	N	N	N	N	Y	Y
5 Huckaby	N	Y	N	N	N	Y	Y
6 Moore	Y	Y	N	N	N	Y	Y
7 Breaux	Y	Y	N	N	N	Y	Y
8 Long	N	Y	Y	Y	Y	Y	Y
MAINE							
1 Emery	Y	Y	Y	N	N	Y	Y
2 Cohen	Y	Y	Y	N	Y	Y	Y
MARYLAND							
1 Bauman	N	N	Y	N	N	Y	Y
2 Long	Y	Y	Y	Y	Y	Y	Y
3 Mikulski	Y	Y	Y	Y	Y	Y	Y
4 Holt	Y	N	N	N	N	Y	Y
5 Spellman	Y	Y	Y	Y	Y	Y	Y
6 Byron	Y	Y	Y	N	N	Y	Y
7 Mitchell	Y	Y	Y	Y	Y	Y	Y
8 Steers	Y	#	Y	Y	Y	Y	Y
MASSACHUSETTS							
1 Conte	Y	N	Y	Y	Y	Y	Y
2 Boland	Y	Y	Y	Y	Y	Y	Y
3 Early	?	✓	Y	Y	Y	Y	Y
4 Drinan	Y	Y	Y	Y	✓	?	?
5 Tsongas	?	?	?	?	?	?	?
6 Harrington	#	#	#	#	#	▮	#
7 Markey	Y	Y	?	?	?	?	?
8 O'Neill							
9 Moakley	Y	Y	Y	Y	Y	Y	Y
10 Heckler	Y	Y	Y	Y	Y	?	?
11 Burke	Y	Y	Y	Y	Y	?	?
12 Studds	Y	Y	Y	Y	Y	N	Y
MICHIGAN							
1 Conyers	Y	Y	Y	N	Y	▮	#
2 Pursell	Y	Y	Y	Y	Y	Y	Y
3 Brown	Y	N	Y	Y	Y	Y	Y
4 Stockman	Y	N	N	N	Y	Y	Y
5 Sawyer	Y	N	Y	Y	N	Y	Y
6 Carr	Y	Y	Y	Y	Y	Y	Y
7 Kildee	Y	Y	Y	Y	Y	Y	Y
8 Traxler	Y	Y	Y	Y	Y	Y	Y
9 Vander Jagt	Y	N	N	Y	Y	Y	Y
10 Cederberg	Y	?	N	Y	Y	Y	Y
11 Ruppe	Y	N	N	Y	Y	Y	Y
12 Bonior	Y	Y	Y	Y	Y	Y	Y
13 Diggs	#	?	#	#	#	#	#
14 Nedzi	?	✓	Y	Y	Y	Y	Y
15 Ford	Y	Y	Y	Y	Y	Y	Y
16 Dingell	Y	Y	Y	?	?	?	Y
17 Brodhead	Y	Y	Y	Y	Y	N	Y
18 Blanchard	Y	Y	Y	Y	Y	Y	Y
19 Broomfield	Y	N	Y	Y	Y	Y	Y
MINNESOTA							
1 Quie	?	?	?	?	?	?	?
2 Hagedorn	Y	N	N	N	N	Y	Y
3 Frenzel	Y	N	Y	N	Y	N	Y
4 Vento	Y	Y	Y	Y	Y	N	Y
5 Fraser	Y	Y	Y	Y	Y	Y	Y
6 Nolan	Y	Y	Y	Y	Y	N	Y
7 Stangeland	Y	N	Y	N	N	Y	Y
8 Oberstar	Y	Y	Y	Y	Y	Y	Y
MISSISSIPPI							
1 Whitten	Y	Y	N	Y	N	Y	?
2 Bowen	Y	Y	N	Y	N	Y	Y
3 Montgomery	N	Y	N	Y	N	Y	Y
4 Cochran	N	Y	Y	N	N	Y	Y
5 Lott	N	N	N	N	N	Y	Y
MISSOURI							
1 Clay	Y	Y	Y	Y	Y	Y	?
2 Young	Y	Y	Y	Y	Y	Y	Y
3 Gephardt	N	Y	N	N	Y	N	Y
4 Skelton	N	Y	N	N	N	N	Y
5 Bolling	Y	Y	Y	Y	Y	#	#
6 Coleman	Y	Y	N	N	N	#	Y
7 Taylor	N	N	N	N	N	Y	Y
8 Ichord	N	N	Y	N	N	Y	Y
9 Volkmer	N	N	N	N	Y	N	Y
10 Burlison	N	Y	Y	Y	Y	Y	Y
MONTANA							
1 Baucus	Y	Y	Y	N	Y	Y	Y
2 Marlenee	Y	Y	Y	N	N	Y	Y
NEBRASKA							
1 Thone	Y	N	Y	N	N	Y	Y
2 Cavanaugh	Y	Y	Y	Y	Y	Y	Y
3 Smith	Y	N	Y	N	N	?	?
NEVADA							
AL Santini	Y	N	Y	Y	N	Y	Y
NEW HAMPSHIRE							
1 D'Amours	Y	Y	Y	Y	Y	Y	Y
2 Cleveland	Y	N	Y	Y	N	Y	Y
NEW JERSEY							
1 Florio	Y	Y	Y	Y	N	Y	#
2 Hughes	Y	Y	Y	N	Y	N	Y
3 Howard	Y	Y	Y	Y	Y	Y	Y
4 Thompson	Y	Y	Y	Y	Y	Y	Y
5 Fenwick	Y	N	N	Y	Y	N	Y
6 Forsythe	Y	N	N	Y	Y	Y	Y
7 Maguire	Y	Y	Y	Y	Y	N	Y
8 Roe	Y	Y	Y	Y	Y	Y	Y
9 Hollenbeck	Y	N	Y	Y	Y	Y	Y
10 Rodino	Y	Y	Y	✓	Y	Y	Y
11 Minish	Y	Y	Y	Y	Y	N	Y
12 Rinaldo	Y	Y	Y	Y	Y	Y	Y
13 Meyner	Y	Y	Y	Y	Y	#	Y
14 LeFante	Y	Y	Y	Y	Y	Y	Y
15 Patten	Y	N	Y	Y	Y	Y	Y
NEW MEXICO							
1 Lujan	Y	N	N	N	N	Y	Y
2 Runnels	N	N	N	N	N	Y	Y
NEW YORK							
1 Pike	N	N	Y	Y	N	Y	Y
2 Downey	Y	Y	Y	Y	Y	Y	Y
3 Ambro	Y	Y	Y	Y	Y	Y	Y
4 Lent	Y	N	Y	Y	Y	Y	?
5 Wydler	Y	N	N	Y	Y	Y	Y
6 Wolff	Y	N	Y	Y	Y	Y	Y
7 Addabbo	Y	Y	Y	Y	Y	Y	Y
8 Rosenthal	Y	Y	Y	Y	Y	N	Y
9 Delaney	Y	N	Y	Y	Y	Y	Y
10 Biaggi	Y	Y	Y	Y	Y	Y	?
11 Scheuer	Y	Y	Y	Y	Y	Y	Y
12 Chisholm	Y	Y	Y	Y	Y	Y	Y
13 Solarz	Y	Y	Y	Y	Y	Y	Y
14 Richmond	Y	Y	Y	Y	Y	N	Y
15 Zeferetti	Y	Y	Y	Y	Y	Y	Y
16 Holtzman	Y	Y	Y	Y	Y	N	Y
17 Murphy	Y	Y	?	?	?	?	?
18 Green	Y	Y	Y	Y	Y	Y	Y
19 Rangel	Y	Y	Y	Y	Y	Y	Y
20 Weiss	Y	Y	Y	Y	Y	N	Y
21 Garcia	Y	Y	Y	Y	Y	Y	Y
22 Bingham	Y	Y	Y	Y	Y	Y	Y
23 Caputo	Y	Y	?	?	?	?	?
24 Ottinger	Y	Y	Y	Y	Y	N	Y
25 Fish	Y	N	Y	Y	Y	N	Y
26 Gilman	Y	Y	Y	Y	Y	Y	Y
27 McHugh	Y	Y	Y	Y	Y	Y	Y
28 Stratton	Y	N	Y	Y	Y	Y	Y
29 Pattison	Y	Y	Y	Y	Y	Y	Y
30 McEwen	Y	N	?	?	Y	Y	Y
31 Mitchell	Y	Y	Y	Y	Y	Y	Y
32 Hanley	Y	Y	Y	Y	Y	Y	Y
33 Walsh	Y	N	Y	Y	N	Y	Y
34 Horton	Y	N	Y	Y	Y	Y	#
35 Conable	Y	N	N	N	Y	Y	Y
36 LaFalce	Y	Y	Y	Y	Y	Y	Y
37 Nowak	Y	Y	Y	Y	Y	Y	Y
38 Kemp	Y	N	N	N	?	?	?
39 Lundine	Y	Y	Y	Y	Y	Y	Y
NORTH CAROLINA							
1 Jones	Y	Y	N	N	N	Y	Y
2 Fountain	Y	N	N	N	▮	Y	Y
3 Whitley	Y	N	N	N	N	Y	Y
4 Andrews	Y	N	N	N	N	Y	Y
5 Neal	Y	Y	N	Y	N	Y	Y
6 Preyer	Y	N	Y	Y	Y	Y	Y
7 Rose	Y	Y	Y	N	N	Y	Y
8 Hefner	Y	N	Y	N	N	Y	Y
9 Martin	N	N	N	N	Y	N	Y
10 Broyhill	N	N	N	Y	N	N	Y
11 Gudger	Y	Y	N	N	N	Y	Y
NORTH DAKOTA							
AL Andrews	Y	N	Y	N	N	Y	Y
OHIO							
1 Gradison	Y	N	N	Y	Y	Y	Y
2 Luken	?	?	?	?	?	?	?
3 Whalen	Y	Y	Y	Y	Y	Y	Y
4 Guyer	Y	N	Y	N	N	Y	Y
5 Latta	N	N	N	N	N	N	Y
6 Harsha	Y	N	N	N	N	Y	Y
7 Brown	N	N	N	N	N	Y	Y
8 Kindness	N	N	Y	N	N	Y	Y
9 Ashley	Y	Y	Y	Y	Y	Y	Y
10 Miller	N	N	N	N	N	N	Y
11 Stanton	Y	N	Y	Y	Y	Y	Y
12 Devine	N	N	N	N	N	N	Y
13 Pease	Y	N	Y	Y	Y	Y	Y
14 Seiberling	Y	Y	Y	Y	Y	N	#
15 Wylie	Y	N	Y	N	Y	Y	Y
16 Regula	Y	N	Y	N	N	Y	Y
17 Ashbrook	N	N	Y	N	N	Y	Y
18 Applegate	Y	Y	Y	Y	N	Y	Y
19 Carney	Y	Y	Y	?	✓	Y	Y
20 Oakar	Y	Y	Y	N	N	Y	Y
21 Stokes	Y	Y	Y	Y	Y	Y	?
22 Vanik	Y	Y	Y	Y	Y	Y	Y
23 Mottl	N	N	N	N	N	N	Y
OKLAHOMA							
1 Jones	N	N	N	N	N	Y	Y
2 Risenhoover	?	?	?	X	X	?	?
3 Watkins	N	N	N	N	N	Y	Y
4 Steed	#	#	N	N	N	Y	Y
5 Edwards	N	N	N	N	N	Y	Y
6 English	N	N	N	N	N	Y	Y
OREGON							
1 AuCoin	Y	Y	Y	Y	Y	Y	Y
2 Ullman	Y	Y	Y	Y	Y	#	#
3 Duncan	Y	#	N	Y	Y	Y	Y
4 Weaver	Y	Y	Y	N	N	N	Y
PENNSYLVANIA							
1 Myers, M.	Y	Y	Y	Y	Y	Y	Y
2 Nix	Y	Y	Y	Y	Y	Y	Y
3 Lederer	Y	Y	Y	Y	Y	Y	Y
4 Eilberg	Y	Y	?	✓	?	?	?
5 Schulze	Y	N	Y	N	Y	Y	Y
6 Yatron	Y	Y	Y	Y	Y	Y	Y
7 Edgar	Y	Y	Y	Y	Y	Y	Y
8 Kostmayer	Y	Y	Y	N	Y	N	Y
9 Shuster	Y	N	N	N	N	Y	Y
10 McDade	Y	N	Y	Y	Y	Y	Y
11 Flood	Y	Y	Y	Y	Y	Y	Y
12 Murtha	Y	N	Y	Y	Y	Y	Y
13 Coughlin	Y	N	Y	Y	Y	Y	Y
14 Moorhead	Y	Y	Y	Y	Y	Y	Y
15 Rooney	Y	Y	Y	Y	Y	Y	Y
16 Walker	Y	N	N	N	N	Y	Y
17 Ertel	Y	Y	Y	Y	N	Y	Y
18 Walgren	Y	N	Y	Y	Y	Y	Y
19 Goodling, W.	Y	N	N	N	Y	N	Y
20 Gaydos	Y	Y	Y	N	N	Y	Y
21 Dent	Y	Y	Y	Y	N	#	#
22 Murphy	Y	Y	Y	N	N	Y	Y
23 Ammerman	?	✓	?	?	?	?	?
24 Marks	Y	N	Y	Y	Y	Y	Y
25 Myers, G.	N	N	N	N	Y	Y	Y
RHODE ISLAND							
1 St Germain	Y	Y	Y	Y	Y	Y	Y
2 Beard	Y	Y	Y	Y	Y	#	Y
SOUTH CAROLINA							
1 Davis	Y	Y	Y	Y	N	Y	Y
2 Spence	Y	Y	Y	N	N	?	?
3 Derrick	Y	Y	Y	N	N	Y	Y
4 Mann	N	N	Y	Y	Y	Y	Y
5 Holland	Y	Y	Y	Y	?	Y	Y
6 Jenrette	N	Y	Y	N	N	Y	#
SOUTH DAKOTA							
1 Pressler	Y	Y	N	N	N	Y	Y
2 Abdnor	Y	Y	N	N	N	Y	Y
TENNESSEE							
1 Quillen	Y	#	N	N	N	Y	Y
2 Duncan	Y	N	N	N	N	Y	Y
3 Lloyd	Y	Y	Y	N	N	Y	Y
4 Gore	Y	Y	Y	Y	Y	Y	Y
5 Vacancy							
6 Beard	Y	N	N	N	N	#	#
7 Jones	Y	Y	Y	N	N	Y	Y
8 Ford	Y	Y	Y	Y	Y	Y	Y
TEXAS							
1 Hall	N	N	N	N	N	Y	Y
2 Wilson, C.	Y	Y	Y	Y	Y	Y	Y
3 Collins	N	N	N	N	N	N	Y
4 Roberts	N	N	N	Y	N	Y	Y
5 Mattox	Y	Y	Y	N	N	N	Y
6 Teague	?	X	?	X	X	?	?
7 Archer	N	N	N	N	N	Y	Y
8 Eckhardt	Y	Y	Y	Y	Y	?	?
9 Brooks	Y	Y	N	N	N	Y	Y
10 Pickle	Y	Y	Y	Y	N	Y	Y
11 Poage	N	N	N	Y	N	Y	Y
12 Wright	Y	Y	Y	Y	Y	Y	Y
13 Hightower	Y	Y	Y	N	N	Y	Y
14 Young	Y	Y	Y	?	?	?	?
15 de la Garza	Y	Y	N	Y	N	Y	Y
16 White	Y	Y	Y	N	N	#	Y
17 Burleson	N	N	N	N	N	Y	?
18 Jordan	Y	Y	Y	Y	Y	Y	Y
19 Mahon	Y	Y	N	Y	N	Y	Y
20 Gonzalez	Y	Y	Y	Y	Y	Y	Y
21 Krueger	#	#	#	#	#	#	#
22 Gammage	#	X	▮	X	X	#	#
23 Kazen	Y	Y	Y	N	N	Y	Y
24 Milford	?	?	N	Y	?	Y	?
UTAH							
1 McKay	Y	Y	Y	Y	Y	Y	Y
2 Marriott	Y	N	N	N	N	Y	Y
VERMONT							
AL Jeffords	Y	Y	#	#	?	?	#
VIRGINIA							
1 Trible	Y	N	N	N	N	Y	Y
2 Whitehurst	Y	N	N	Y	▮	#	#
3 Satterfield	N	N	?	N	N	Y	Y
4 Daniel	Y	N	N	N	N	Y	Y
5 Daniel	Y	Y	N	N	N	Y	Y
6 Butler	N	N	N	N	N	Y	Y
7 Robinson	N	N	N	N	N	Y	Y
8 Harris	Y	Y	Y	Y	Y	Y	Y
9 Wampler	N	Y	Y	N	N	Y	Y
10 Fisher	Y	Y	Y	Y	Y	Y	Y
WASHINGTON							
1 Pritchard	#	#	#	#	Y	Y	Y
2 Meeds	?	?	?	?	?	?	?
3 Bonker	Y	Y	Y	Y	Y	Y	Y
4 McCormack	Y	Y	Y	Y	Y	Y	Y
5 Foley	Y	Y	?	?	?	?	?
6 Dicks	Y	Y	Y	Y	Y	Y	Y
7 Cunningham	N	N	N	N	N	Y	Y
WEST VIRGINIA							
1 Mollohan	Y	N	Y	Y	Y	Y	Y
2 Staggers	Y	Y	Y	N	N	Y	Y
3 Slack	N	N	Y	Y	N	Y	Y
4 Rahall	N	Y	Y	N	N	N	Y
WISCONSIN							
1 Aspin	Y	Y	Y	Y	Y	Y	Y
2 Kastenmeier	Y	Y	Y	Y	Y	Y	Y
3 Baldus	Y	Y	Y	Y	Y	N	Y
4 Zablocki	Y	Y	Y	Y	Y	Y	#
5 Reuss	Y	Y	Y	Y	Y	Y	Y
6 Steiger	Y	N	N	Y	Y	N	Y
7 Obey	Y	Y	N	Y	Y	N	Y
8 Cornell	Y	Y	N	Y	Y	N	Y
9 Kasten	Y	N	N	N	N	Y	Y
WYOMING							
AL Roncalio	N	Y	N	Y	Y	Y	Y

Democrats ***Republicans***

710. HR 1. Ethics in Government. Adoption of the rule (H Res 1323) providing for House floor consideration of the bill to require financial disclosure by high-level federal officials, including members of Congress and federal judges. Adopted 331-50: R 95-34; D 236-16 (ND 168-7; SD 68-9), Sept. 20, 1978.

711. HR 1. Ethics in Government. Danielson, D-Calif., motion that the House resolve itself into the Committtee of the Whole for consideration of the bill to require financial disclosure by high-level federal officials, including members of Congress and federal judges. Motion agreed to 361-4: R 122-3; D 239-1 (ND 164-1; SD 75-0), Sept. 20, 1978.

712. HR 1. Ethics in Government. Wiggins, R-Calif., amendment to exempt candidates for congressional office from the bill's financial disclosure requirements. Rejected 34-365: R 22-108; D 12-257 (ND 8-181; SD 4-76), Sept. 20, 1978.

713. HR l. Ethics in Government. Myers, R-Pa., amendments, en bloc, to require candidates for federal office to report the source but not the amount of income that must be reported under the bill. Rejected 39-353: R 29-102; D 10-251 (ND 6-179; SD 4-72), Sept. 20, 1978.

714. HR 1. Ethics in Government. Quillen, R-Tenn., amendment to repeal House Rule 47 limiting members' outside earned income to 15 percent of their congressional salaries. Rejected 97-290: R 47-82; D 50-208 (ND 30-150; SD 20-58), Sept. 20, 1978.

715. HR 1. Ethics in Government. Moorhead, R-Calif., amendment to delete provisions in the bill that prohibit a former government employee from making business contacts with his or her former agency for one year after leaving the agency. Rejected 112-259: R 65-59; D 47-200 (ND 16-155; SD 31-45), Sept. 20, 1978.

KEY

Y Voted for (yea).
✓ Paired for.
† Announced for.
# CQ Poll for.
N Voted against (nay).
X Paired against.
\- Announced against.
▮ CQ Poll against.
P Voted "present."
● Voted "present" to avoid possible conflict of interest.
? Did not vote or otherwise make a position known.

	710	711	712	713	714	715
ALABAMA						
1 Edwards	Y	Y	N	N	N	N
2 Dickinson	?	?	?	?	?	?
3 Nichols	?	?	▮	▮	▮	X
4 Bevill	Y	Y	N	N	N	N
5 Flippo	Y	Y	N	N	N	N
6 Buchanan	Y	Y	N	N	N	N
7 Flowers	?	?	?	?	?	?
ALASKA						
AL Young	N	Y	N	N	Y	N
ARIZONA						
1 Rhodes	?	?	?	?	?	?
2 Udall	Y	Y	N	N	N	▮
3 Stump	Y	Y	N	N	Y	Y
4 Rudd	?	?	?	?	?	?
ARKANSAS						
1 Alexander	Y	Y	N	N	N	Y
2 Tucker	Y	Y	N	▮	▮	▮
3 Hammerschmidt	N	N	Y	Y	Y	Y
4 Thornton	Y	Y	N	N	N	N
CALIFORNIA						
1 Johnson	Y	Y	N	N	N	N
2 Clausen	Y	Y	N	N	N	N
3 Moss	N	Y	N	N	?	?
4 Leggett	?	?	N	N	Y	?
5 Burton, J.	Y	?	N	N	N	N
6 Burton, P.	?	Y	Y	N	N	N
7 Miller	?	?	?	?	?	?
8 Dellums	Y	Y	N	N	Y	N
9 Stark	Y	Y	N	N	N	N
10 Edwards	Y	?	N	N	N	N
11 Ryan	Y	Y	N	N	N	N
12 McCloskey	Y	?	N	N	N	N
13 Mineta	Y	Y	N	N	N	N
14 McFall	Y	Y	N	N	N	Y
15 Sisk	N	Y	N	N	Y	?
16 Panetta	Y	Y	N	N	N	N
17 Krebs	Y	Y	N	Y	N	N
18 Vacancy						
19 Lagomarsino	Y	Y	N	N	N	Y
20 Goldwater	?	?	?	Y	Y	Y
21 Corman	Y	Y	N	N	Y	N
22 Moorhead	Y	Y	Y	N	Y	Y
23 Beilenson	Y	Y	N	N	N	N
24 Waxman	Y	Y	Y	N	N	N
25 Roybal	Y	Y	N	N	#	X
26 Rousselot	N	Y	N	N	Y	Y
27 Dornan	N	Y	Y	N	Y	Y
28 Burke	?	?	▮	▮	▮	#
29 Hawkins	Y	Y	N	N	N	N
30 Danielson	Y	Y	N	N	N	N
31 Wilson, C.H.	Y	Y	N	▮	Y	N
32 Anderson	Y	Y	Y	N	N	N
33 Clawson	N	Y	N	N	Y	Y
34 Hannaford	Y	Y	N	N	N	N
35 Lloyd	Y	N	N	N	N	N
36 Brown	Y	Y	N	N	Y	?
37 Pettis	Y	Y	N	N	Y	Y
38 Patterson	Y	Y	N	N	N	N
39 Wiggins	N	Y	Y	▮	#	#
40 Badham	N	Y	N	N	Y	Y
41 Wilson, B.	Y	Y	N	N	N	N
42 Van Deerlin	Y	Y	N	Y	N	Y
43 Burgener	Y	Y	Y	Y	N	Y
COLORADO						
1 Schroeder	Y	Y	N	N	N	N
2 Wirth	Y	Y	N	N	N	Y
3 Evans	Y	Y	N	N	▮	▮
4 Johnson	Y	Y	N	N	N	✓
5 Armstrong	?	?	?	?	?	?
CONNECTICUT						
1 Cotter	Y	Y	N	N	Y	N
2 Dodd	Y	?	N	N	N	N
3 Giaimo	Y	Y	N	N	N	N
4 McKinney	Y	Y	N	N	N	N
5 Sarasin	Y	Y	?	?	?	?
6 Moffett	Y	Y	N	N	N	N
DELAWARE						
AL Evans	N	Y	N	N	Y	Y
FLORIDA						
1 Sikes	Y	Y	N	N	Y	Y
2 Fuqua	Y	Y	N	N	N	N
3 Bennett	Y	Y	N	N	N	N
4 Chappell	Y	Y	N	N	Y	Y
5 Kelly	N	Y	Y	N	N	N
6 Young	Y	Y	N	N	N	Y
7 Gibbons	Y	Y	N	N	Y	N
8 Ireland	?	Y	?	N	N	N
9 Frey	Y	Y	N	N	N	Y
10 Bafalis	Y	Y	N	N	N	N
11 Rogers	Y	Y	N	N	N	N
12 Burke	Y	Y	N	N	N	N
13 Lehman	Y	Y	N	N	N	N
14 Pepper	?	?	▮	▮	#	X
15 Fascell	Y	Y	N	N	N	N
GEORGIA						
1 Ginn	Y	Y	N	N	N	N
2 Mathis	Y	Y	N	N	Y	Y
3 Brinkley	Y	Y	N	N	N	N
4 Levitas	Y	Y	N	N	N	N
5 Fowler	Y	Y	N	N	N	N
6 Flynt	Y	Y	N	N	Y	Y
7 McDonald	N	Y	Y	Y	Y	Y
8 Evans	Y	Y	N	N	N	N
9 Jenkins	Y	Y	N	N	N	N
10 Barnard	Y	Y	N	N	N	N
HAWAII						
1 Heftel	Y	Y	N	N	N	N
2 Akaka	Y	Y	N	N	N	N
IDAHO						
1 Symms	N	Y	Y	Y	Y	✓
2 Hansen, G.	N	Y	N	Y	Y	Y
ILLINOIS						
1 Metcalfe	Y	Y	N	N	N	N
2 Murphy	Y	Y	N	N	Y	N
3 Russo	Y	Y	N	N	Y	N
4 Derwinski	Y	Y	N	N	N	N
5 Fary	Y	Y	N	N	Y	N
6 Hyde	Y	Y	N	Y	Y	Y
7 Collins	Y	Y	N	N	Y	N
8 Rostenkowski	Y	Y	Y	Y	Y	N
9 Yates	Y	Y	N	N	N	N
10 Mikva	Y	Y	N	N	N	N
11 Annunzio	Y	Y	N	N	Y	▮
12 Crane	N	Y	N	Y	Y	N
13 McClory	Y	Y	Y	Y	Y	Y
14 Erlenborn	Y	Y	N	N	Y	Y
15 Corcoran	Y	Y	N	N	N	N
16 Anderson	?	?	▮	▮	▮	#
17 O'Brien	?	?	Y	N	Y	Y
18 Michel	N	Y	?	?	?	?
19 Railsback	?	?	?	?	Y	N
20 Findley	?	?	N	N	N	Y
21 Madigan	Y	Y	N	N	N	N
22 Shipley	?	?	?	?	?	✓
23 Price	Y	Y	N	N	N	N
24 Simon	Y	Y	N	N	N	N
INDIANA						
1 Benjamin	Y	Y	N	N	N	N
2 Fithian	?	Y	N	N	N	N
3 Brademas	Y	Y	N	N	N	N
4 Quayle	N	N	N	Y	Y	?
5 Hillis	Y	Y	N	N	N	Y
6 Evans	Y	Y	N	N	N	Y
7 Myers, J.	Y	Y	N	?	?	?
8 Cornwell	Y	Y	N	N	N	N
9 Hamilton	Y	Y	N	N	N	N
10 Sharp	Y	Y	N	N	N	N
11 Jacobs	N	Y	N	N	N	N
IOWA						
1 Leach	Y	Y	N	N	N	N
2 Blouin	Y	Y	N	N	N	N
3 Grassley	Y	Y	N	N	N	N
4 Smith	Y	Y	N	N	N	N
5 Harkin	Y	Y	N	N	N	N
6 Bedell	Y	Y	N	N	N	N

Democrats ***Republicans***

Corresponding to Congressional Record Votes 804, 805, 806, 807, 808, 809

	710	711	712	713	714	715
KANSAS						
1 Sebelius	Y	Y	N	N	N	Y
2 Keys	Y	Y	N	N	N	N
3 Winn	Y	Y	N	N	N	Y
4 Glickman	Y	Y	N	N	N	Y
5 Skubitz	Y	Y	?	N	?	?
KENTUCKY						
1 Hubbard	Y	Y	N	N	N	N
2 Natcher	Y	Y	N	N	N	N
3 Mazzoli	Y	Y	N	N	N	N
4 Snyder	Y	Y	N	N	Y	Y
5 Carter	Y	Y	N	N	Y	Y
6 Breckinridge	Y	Y	N	N	N	Y
7 Perkins	Y	Y	N	N	N	N
LOUISIANA						
1 Livingston	Y	Y	N	N	Y	Y
2 Boggs	Y	Y	N	N	Y	▮
3 Treen	Y	Y	Y	Y	N	Y
4 Waggonner	N	Y	N	N	Y	Y
5 Huckaby	Y	Y	N	N	N	N
6 Moore	N	Y	N	N	N	Y
7 Breaux	?	?	?	?	?	✓
8 Long	Y	Y	N	N	N	N
MAINE						
1 Emery	Y	Y	N	N	N	N
2 Cohen	Y	Y	N	N	N	▮
MARYLAND						
1 Bauman	N	Y	N	N	Y	Y
2 Long	Y	Y	N	N	N	N
3 Mikulski	Y	Y	N	N	N	N
4 Holt	N	Y	N	Y	Y	?
5 Spellman	Y	Y	N	N	N	N
6 Byron	?	Y	N	N	N	?
7 Mitchell	Y	?	N	▮	N	N
8 Steers	Y	Y	N	N	N	N
MASSACHUSETTS						
1 Conte	Y	Y	N	N	N	N
2 Boland	Y	Y	N	N	N	Y
3 Early	Y	Y	Y	N	N	N
4 Drinan	Y	Y	N	N	N	N
5 Tsongas	?	?	?	?	?	?
6 Harrington	Y	Y	N	N	Y	▮
7 Markey	?	?	N	N	N	N
8 O'Neill						
9 Moakley	Y	Y	N	N	N	N
10 Heckler	Y	Y	N	N	N	N
11 Burke	Y	Y	N	N	Y	N
12 Studds	Y	Y	N	N	N	N
MICHIGAN						
1 Conyers	?	?	N	N	N	N
2 Pursell	Y	Y	Y	N	N	N
3 Brown	N	Y	N	N	N	N
4 Stockman	?	?	▮	▮	▮	?
5 Sawyer	Y	Y	N	N	N	N
6 Carr	Y	Y	N	N	N	N
7 Kildee	Y	Y	N	N	N	N
8 Traxler	Y	Y	N	N	N	N
9 Vander Jagt	Y	Y	Y	Y	Y	N
10 Cederberg	Y	Y	N	N	N	Y
11 Ruppe	Y	Y	N	N	N	N
12 Bonior	Y	Y	N	N	N	N
13 Diggs	Y	Y	▮	▮	N	N
14 Nedzi	Y	Y	N	N	N	N
15 Ford	Y	Y	N	N	Y	N
16 Dingell	Y	?	N	N	N	N
17 Brodhead	Y	Y	N	N	N	N
18 Blanchard	Y	Y	N	N	N	N
19 Broomfield	Y	Y	N	N	N	N
MINNESOTA						
1 Quie	Y	Y	N	N	N	N
2 Hagedorn	Y	Y	N	N	N	?
3 Frenzel	Y	Y	Y	Y	Y	Y
4 Vento	Y	Y	N	N	N	N
5 Fraser	Y	Y	N	N	N	?
6 Nolan	Y	Y	N	N	N	N
7 Stangeland	Y	?	N	N	N	Y
8 Oberstar	Y	Y	N	N	N	N
MISSISSIPPI						
1 Whitten	Y	Y	N	N	N	Y
2 Bowen	Y	Y	N	N	Y	Y
3 Montgomery	Y	Y	N	N	N	Y
4 Cochran	Y	Y	N	N	N	Y
5 Lott	Y	Y	N	N	Y	Y
MISSOURI						
1 Clay	Y	?	N	?	Y	N
2 Young	Y	Y	N	N	N	N
3 Gephardt	Y	Y	N	N	N	N

	710	711	712	713	714	715
4 Skelton	Y	Y	N	N	N	N
5 Bolling	Y	Y	N	N	N	N
6 Coleman	Y	Y	N	N	N	N
7 Taylor	Y	Y	N	Y	Y	Y
8 Ichord	Y	Y	N	N	N	N
9 Volkmer	N	Y	N	N	N	N
10 Burlison	Y	Y	N	N	N	N
MONTANA						
1 Baucus	Y	Y	N	N	N	N
2 Marlenee	Y	Y	N	N	N	N
NEBRASKA						
1 Thone	Y	Y	N	N	N	N
2 Cavanaugh	Y	Y	N	N	N	N
3 Smith	Y	Y	N	N	?	?
NEVADA						
AL Santini	Y	Y	N	N	N	N
NEW HAMPSHIRE						
1 D'Amours	Y	Y	N	N	N	N
2 Cleveland	Y	Y	Y	Y	Y	N
NEW JERSEY						
1 Florio	?	?	N	N	N	N
2 Hughes	?	?	▮	N	P	N
3 Howard	?	?	N	N	N	N
4 Thompson	?	?	N	N	N	N
5 Fenwick	Y	Y	N	N	N	N
6 Forsythe	N	?	N	N	Y	Y
7 Maguire	Y	Y	N	N	N	N
8 Roe	?	?	N	N	N	N
9 Hollenbeck	Y	Y	N	N	N	N
10 Rodino	?	?	N	N	N	N
11 Minish	?	?	N	N	N	N
12 Rinaldo	Y	Y	N	N	N	N
13 Meyner	?	?	N	N	N	N
14 LeFante	Y	Y	N	N	N	N
15 Patten	Y	Y	N	N	N	N
NEW MEXICO						
1 Lujan	?	?	?	N	N	N
2 Runnels	Y	Y	N	N	N	N
NEW YORK						
1 Pike	N	Y	N	N	#	▮
2 Downey	Y	Y	N	N	N	N
3 Ambro	?	?	N	N	N	N
4 Lent	N	Y	N	N	N	Y
5 Wydler	N	Y	Y	Y	Y	N
6 Wolff	Y	Y	N	N	N	N
7 Addabbo	Y	Y	N	N	?	X
8 Rosenthal	Y	?	N	N	N	N
9 Delaney	Y	Y	N	N	Y	?
10 Biaggi	Y	Y	N	N	Y	N
11 Scheuer	Y	Y	N	Y	N	N
12 Chisholm	Y	Y	N	N	Y	N
13 Solarz	Y	Y	N	N	N	N
14 Richmond	Y	Y	N	N	N	N
15 Zeferetti	Y	Y	N	N	Y	N
16 Holtzman	Y	Y	N	N	N	N
17 Murphy	Y	Y	N	N	Y	N
18 Green	Y	Y	N	N	N	N
19 Rangel	Y	Y	N	N	N	N
20 Weiss	Y	Y	N	N	N	?
21 Garcia	Y	Y	N	N	▮	▮
22 Bingham	Y	Y	N	N	N	N
23 Caputo	?	?	?	?	?	?
24 Ottinger	Y	Y	N	N	Y	N
25 Fish	Y	Y	N	N	Y	Y
26 Gilman	Y	Y	N	N	N	N
27 McHugh	Y	Y	N	N	N	N
28 Stratton	Y	Y	N	N	N	Y
29 Pattison	Y	Y	Y	Y	N	N
30 McEwen	Y	Y	N	N	Y	Y
31 Mitchell	Y	Y	N	N	N	Y
32 Hanley	Y	Y	N	N	N	N
33 Walsh	N	Y	N	N	?	?
34 Horton	Y	Y	N	N	N	N
35 Conable	Y	Y	Y	Y	?	?
36 LaFalce	Y	Y	N	N	Y	N
37 Nowak	Y	Y	N	N	N	N
38 Kemp	?	?	?	?	?	?
39 Lundine	Y	Y	N	N	N	N
NORTH CAROLINA						
1 Jones	N	Y	N	N	Y	N
2 Fountain	Y	Y	N	N	N	N
3 Whitley	Y	Y	N	N	N	N
4 Andrews	?	?	N	N	?	N
5 Neal	Y	Y	N	▮	▮	X
6 Preyer	Y	Y	N	N	N	N
7 Rose	Y	Y	N	N	N	Y
8 Hefner	Y	Y	N	N	N	N

	710	711	712	713	714	715
9 Martin	Y	Y	N	N	N	Y
10 Broyhill	Y	Y	N	Y	N	Y
11 Gudger	Y	Y	N	N	N	N
NORTH DAKOTA						
AL Andrews	Y	Y	N	N	N	N
OHIO						
1 Gradison	Y	Y	N	N	Y	Y
2 Luken	Y	Y	N	N	N	N
3 Whalen	Y	Y	N	N	N	N
4 Guyer	?	?	▮	▮	▮	Y
5 Latta	Y	Y	N	N	N	Y
6 Harsha	Y	Y	N	N	Y	N
7 Brown	?	?	N	Y	Y	N
8 Kindness	Y	Y	N	Y	Y	Y
9 Ashley	Y	Y	N	N	N	Y
10 Miller	Y	Y	N	Y	N	Y
11 Stanton	Y	Y	N	N	Y	Y
12 Devine	Y	?	N	N	N	Y
13 Pease	Y	Y	N	N	N	N
14 Seiberling	Y	?	N	N	N	N
15 Wylie	Y	Y	?	?	N	N
16 Regula	Y	Y	N	N	N	Y
17 Ashbrook	N	Y	N	Y	N	Y
18 Applegate	Y	Y	N	N	N	N
19 Carney	Y	?	N	N	N	N
20 Oakar	Y	?	N	N	N	?
21 Stokes	Y	?	N	?	Y	N
22 Vanik	Y	Y	N	N	N	N
23 Mottl	Y	Y	N	N	Y	N
OKLAHOMA						
1 Jones	N	Y	N	N	N	Y
2 Risenhoover	?	?	?	?	N	N
3 Watkins	Y	Y	N	N	N	N
4 Steed	Y	Y	N	Y	N	Y
5 Edwards	N	Y	N	N	N	N
6 English	Y	Y	N	N	N	N
OREGON						
1 AuCoin	Y	Y	N	N	N	N
2 Ullman	Y	Y	N	N	N	N
3 Duncan	Y	Y	N	N	Y	Y
4 Weaver	Y	Y	N	N	N	N
PENNSYLVANIA						
1 Myers, M.	Y	Y	N	N	N	N
2 Nix	N	Y	N	N	?	?
3 Lederer	Y	Y	N	N	N	N
4 Eilberg	Y	Y	N	N	N	N
5 Schulze	N	Y	N	N	N	N
6 Yatron	Y	Y	N	N	N	Y
7 Edgar	Y	?	N	N	N	N
8 Kostmayer	Y	Y	N	N	N	N
9 Shuster	N	Y	N	Y	Y	Y
10 McDade	Y	Y	N	N	N	N
11 Flood	Y	Y	N	N	?	N
12 Murtha	Y	Y	Y	N	Y	Y
13 Coughlin	Y	Y	Y	N	N	N
14 Moorhead	Y	Y	N	N	Y	N
15 Rooney	Y	Y	N	N	N	N
16 Walker	N	Y	N	N	N	N
17 Ertel	Y	Y	N	N	N	N
18 Walgren	Y	Y	N	Y	N	N
19 Goodling, W.	N	Y	N	N	Y	N
20 Gaydos	?	Y	N	N	?	?
21 Dent	Y	?	N	▮	▮	N
22 Murphy	Y	Y	N	N	N	N
23 Ammerman	?	?	?	?	?	?
24 Marks	Y	Y	N	N	N	N
25 Myers, G.	N	Y	N	Y	N	N
RHODE ISLAND						
1 St Germain	Y	Y	N	N	N	N
2 Beard	Y	Y	N	N	N	N
SOUTH CAROLINA						
1 Davis	N	Y	N	N	Y	Y
2 Spence	Y	Y	N	N	N	Y
3 Derrick	Y	?	N	N	N	N
4 Mann	Y	Y	N	N	Y	N
5 Holland	N	Y	N	N	Y	Y
6 Jenrette	N	Y	N	N	▮	X
SOUTH DAKOTA						
1 Pressler	Y	Y	N	N	N	N
2 Abdnor	Y	Y	N	N	N	N
TENNESSEE						
1 Quillen	Y	Y	Y	N	Y	Y
2 Duncan	Y	Y	N	N	N	Y
3 Lloyd	Y	Y	N	N	N	Y
4 Gore	Y	Y	N	N	N	N
5 Vacancy						
6 Beard	?	?	N	N	N	Y

	710	711	712	713	714	715
7 Jones	Y	Y	N	N	N	Y
8 Ford	Y	Y	N	N	N	N
TEXAS						
1 Hall	Y	Y	Y	N	N	Y
2 Wilson, C.	Y	Y	N	N	Y	N
3 Collins	N	N	Y	Y	Y	Y
4 Roberts	Y	?	N	N	N	Y
5 Mattox	Y	Y	N	N	N	N
6 Teague	?	?	?	?	?	?
7 Archer	Y	Y	N	N	N	Y
8 Eckhardt	Y	?	N	N	N	Y
9 Brooks	N	Y	N	N	Y	Y
10 Pickle	Y	Y	N	N	N	Y
11 Poage	Y	Y	Y	N	N	N
12 Wright	Y	Y	N	?	N	N
13 Hightower	Y	Y	N	N	Y	N
14 Young	Y	Y	N	?	?	?
15 de la Garza	Y	Y	N	N	N	?
16 White	Y	Y	N	▮	N	Y
17 Burleson	Y	Y	Y	Y	Y	?
18 Jordan	Y	Y	N	N	N	Y
19 Mahon	Y	Y	N	N	N	N
20 Gonzalez	N	Y	N	N	Y	Y
21 Krueger	?	?	▮	▮	#	▮
22 Gammage	?	?	N	N	N	Y
23 Kazen	Y	Y	N	N	N	Y
24 Milford	?	?	?	?	Y	Y
UTAH						
1 McKay	Y	Y	N	N	N	Y
2 Marriott	Y	Y	N	N	N	N
VERMONT						
AL Jeffords	Y	Y	N	N	Y	Y
VIRGINIA						
1 Trible	Y	Y	N	N	N	N
2 Whitehurst	?	?	N	N	N	Y
3 Satterfield	?	?	N	Y	N	Y
4 Daniel	Y	Y	N	N	Y	Y
5 Daniel	Y	Y	N	N	Y	Y
6 Butler	Y	Y	Y	Y	N	N
7 Robinson	N	Y	N	Y	Y	Y
8 Harris	Y	Y	N	N	N	N
9 Wampler	N	Y	N	Y	N	Y
10 Fisher	Y	Y	N	N	N	N
WASHINGTON						
1 Pritchard	Y	Y	N	N	N	Y
2 Meeds	?	?	?	?	?	?
3 Bonker	Y	Y	N	N	N	N
4 McCormack	Y	Y	N	N	N	Y
5 Foley	Y	Y	N	N	N	Y
6 Dicks	Y	Y	N	N	N	N
7 Cunningham	N	Y	N	N	N	N
WEST VIRGINIA						
1 Mollohan	Y	Y	N	N	N	N
2 Staggers	Y	Y	N	N	N	N
3 Slack	N	Y	N	N	N	?
4 Rahall	Y	Y	N	N	N	N
WISCONSIN						
1 Aspin	Y	Y	N	N	N	N
2 Kastenmeier	Y	Y	N	N	N	N
3 Baldus	Y	Y	N	N	N	N
4 Zablocki	Y	Y	N	N	N	N
5 Reuss	Y	Y	N	N	N	N
6 Steiger	N	Y	Y	Y	Y	Y
7 Obey	Y	Y	N	N	N	N
8 Cornell	Y	Y	N	N	N	N
9 Kasten	Y	Y	N	Y	N	Y
WYOMING						
AL Roncalio	Y	?	Y	N	N	Y

Democrats ***Republicans***

716. H Con Res 683. Fiscal 1979 Binding Budget Levels. Giaimo, D-Conn., motion to approve the conference committee's version of the resolution setting the following binding budget levels for fiscal 1979: budget authority, $555.65 billion; outlays, $487.5 billion; revenues, $448.7 billion; deficit, $38.8 billion. Motion agreed to 225-162: R 7-123; D 218-39 (ND 158-22; SD 60-17), Sept. 21, 1978.

717. HR 12611. Airline Deregulation. Ertel, D-Pa., amendment to direct the Civil Aeronautics Board (CAB) to authorize a proposed air transportation service unless it determined that the proposed service was inconsistent with public convenience and necessity. Adopted 300-86: R 100-31; D 200-55 (ND 145-34; SD 55-21), Sept. 21, 1978.

718. HR 12611. Airline Deregulation. Oberstar, D-Minn., amendment to declare unlawful the pooling of revenues by air carriers in order to provide financial aid to carriers shut down by strikes. Adopted 299-78: R 72-52; D 227-26 (ND 174-3; SD 53-23), Sept. 21, 1978.

719. HR 12611. Airline Deregulation. Passage of the bill to encourage airline industry competition by increasing airlines' flexibility to set fares and enter additional routes. Passed 363-8: R 118-3; D 245-5 (ND 175-3; SD 70-2), Sept. 21, 1978. A "yea" was a vote supporting the president's position.

KEY

- Y Voted for (yea).
- ✓ Paired for.
- † Announced for.
- # CQ Poll for.
- N Voted against (nay).
- X Paired against.
- \- Announced against.
- ▮ CQ Poll against.
- P Voted "present."
- ● Voted "present" to avoid possible conflict of interest.
- ? Did not vote or otherwise make a position known.

	716	717	718	719
ALABAMA				
1 Edwards	N	N	Y	Y
2 Dickinson	X	?	?	?
3 Nichols	✓	✓	X	#
4 Bevill	Y	Y	Y	Y
5 Flippo	Y	Y	Y	Y
6 Buchanan	N	Y	Y	Y
7 Flowers	?	?	?	?
ALASKA				
AL Young	N	N	Y	Y
ARIZONA				
1 Rhodes	?	?	?	?
2 Udall	Y	Y	Y	Y
3 Stump	N	N	N	N
4 Rudd	X	?	?	?
ARKANSAS				
1 Alexander	Y	Y	Y	Y
2 Tucker	✓	✓	#	#
3 Hammerschmidt	N	N	Y	Y
4 Thornton	Y	N	Y	Y
CALIFORNIA				
1 Johnson	Y	N	Y	Y
2 Clausen	N	Y	Y	Y
3 Moss	Y	Y	Y	Y
4 Leggett	Y	Y	Y	Y
5 Burton, J.	N	Y	Y	Y
6 Burton, P.	Y	Y	Y	Y
7 Miller	?	?	?	?
8 Dellums	Y	Y	Y	Y
9 Stark	Y	Y	Y	Y
10 Edwards	Y	Y	Y	Y
11 Ryan	Y	Y	Y	Y
12 McCloskey	Y	Y	Y	Y
13 Mineta	Y	Y	Y	Y
14 McFall	Y	Y	Y	Y
15 Sisk	Y	N	Y	Y
16 Panetta	Y	Y	Y	Y
17 Krebs	Y	Y	Y	Y
18 Vacancy				
19 Lagomarsino	N	Y	Y	Y
20 Goldwater	N	N	Y	Y
21 Corman	✓	N	Y	Y
22 Moorhead	N	Y	N	Y
23 Beilenson	Y	Y	Y	Y
24 Waxman	Y	?	Y	Y
25 Roybal	Y	N	Y	Y
26 Rousselot	N	Y	N	Y
27 Dornan	N	Y	N	Y
28 Burke	#	#	#	?
29 Hawkins	Y	N	Y	Y
30 Danielson	Y	?	Y	Y
31 Wilson, C.H.	Y	?	Y	?
32 Anderson	Y	N	Y	Y
33 Clawson	N	Y	N	Y
34 Hannaford	Y	Y	Y	Y
35 Lloyd	Y	N	Y	Y
36 Brown	Y	Y	Y	Y
37 Pettis	N	?	N	Y
38 Patterson	#	#	#	▮
39 Wiggins	X	#	▮	#
40 Badham	N	N	N	Y
41 Wilson, B.	N	N	N	Y
42 Van Deerlin	Y	Y	Y	Y
43 Burgener	N	N	N	Y
COLORADO				
1 Schroeder	Y	Y	Y	Y
2 Wirth	Y	Y	Y	Y
3 Evans	Y	Y	Y	Y
4 Johnson	N	N	Y	Y

	716	717	718	719
5 Armstrong	?	?	?	?
CONNECTICUT				
1 Cotter	Y	N	Y	Y
2 Dodd	Y	Y	Y	Y
3 Giaimo	Y	Y	?	Y
4 McKinney	N	Y	Y	#
5 Sarasin	▮	#	#	#
6 Moffett	Y	Y	Y	Y
DELAWARE				
AL Evans	N	Y	N	Y
FLORIDA				
1 Sikes	X	X	X	?
2 Fuqua	Y	Y	Y	Y
3 Bennett	Y	Y	N	Y
4 Chappell	N	N	N	Y
5 Kelly	N	Y	N	Y
6 Young	N	Y	Y	Y
7 Gibbons	?	N	N	?
8 Ireland	N	Y	Y	Y
9 Frey	N	Y	Y	Y
10 Bafalis	N	N	N	Y
11 Rogers	Y	Y	Y	Y
12 Burke	N	N	Y	Y
13 Lehman	Y	Y	Y	Y
14 Pepper	✓	#	#	▮
15 Fascell	Y	▮	#	#
GEORGIA				
1 Ginn	Y	Y	Y	Y
2 Mathis	N	Y	N	?
3 Brinkley	Y	Y	Y	Y
4 Levitas	Y	N	Y	Y
5 Fowler	Y	Y	Y	Y
6 Flynt	N	N	N	Y
7 McDonald	N	Y	N	Y
8 Evans	N	Y	Y	Y
9 Jenkins	Y	N	Y	Y
10 Barnard	Y	Y	Y	Y
HAWAII				
1 Heftel	Y	N	Y	Y
2 Akaka	Y	N	Y	Y
IDAHO				
1 Symms	N	Y	N	Y
2 Hansen, G.	X	?	?	?
ILLINOIS				
1 Metcalfe	Y	Y	Y	Y
2 Murphy	Y	Y	Y	Y
3 Russo	Y	Y	Y	Y
4 Derwinski	N	Y	Y	Y
5 Fary	Y	N	Y	Y
6 Hyde	N	Y	Y	Y
7 Collins	Y	Y	Y	Y
8 Rostenkowski	Y	Y	Y	Y
9 Yates	Y	Y	Y	Y
10 Mikva	Y	Y	Y	Y
11 Annunzio	Y	Y	Y	Y
12 Crane	X	Y	?	#
13 McClory	N	Y	N	Y
14 Erlenborn	N	Y	N	Y
15 Corcoran	N	Y	N	Y
16 Anderson	X	#	#	#
17 O'Brien	N	Y	Y	Y
18 Michel	X	Y	Y	Y
19 Railsback	N	Y	?	?
20 Findley	N	Y	Y	Y
21 Madigan	N	Y	Y	Y
22 Shipley	✓	?	?	?
23 Price	Y	Y	Y	Y
24 Simon	Y	Y	Y	Y
INDIANA				
1 Benjamin	Y	Y	Y	Y
2 Fithian	N	Y	Y	Y
3 Brademas	Y	Y	Y	Y
4 Quayle	N	?	?	?
5 Hillis	N	Y	Y	Y
6 Evans	N	Y	Y	Y
7 Myers, J.	N	Y	Y	Y
8 Cornwell	Y	#	✓	#
9 Hamilton	Y	Y	Y	Y
10 Sharp	Y	Y	Y	Y
11 Jacobs	N	Y	Y	Y
IOWA				
1 Leach	N	Y	Y	Y
2 Blouin	Y	Y	Y	Y
3 Grassley	N	Y	Y	Y
4 Smith	Y	Y	Y	Y
5 Harkin	Y	Y	Y	Y
6 Bedell	Y	Y	Y	Y

Democrats ***Republicans***

	716	717	718	719
KANSAS				
1 Sebelius	N	Y	N	Y
2 Keys	Y	Y	Y	Y
3 Winn	Y	Y	N	Y
4 Glickman	Y	Y	Y	Y
5 Skubitz	Y	N	N	Y
KENTUCKY				
1 Hubbard	Y	Y	Y	Y
2 Natcher	Y	Y	Y	Y
3 Mazzoli	Y	Y	Y	Y
4 Snyder	N	N	Y	Y
5 Carter	N	N	Y	Y
6 Breckinridge	Y	Y	N	Y
7 Perkins	Y	N	Y	Y
LOUISIANA				
1 Livingston	N	N	Y	Y
2 Boggs	Y	Y	Y	Y
3 Treen	N	Y	N	Y
4 Waggonner	Y	Y	N	Y
5 Huckaby	N	Y	N	Y
6 Moore	N	Y	N	Y
7 Breaux	N	N	N	Y
8 Long	Y	Y	Y	Y
MAINE				
1 Emery	N	Y	Y	Y
2 Cohen	X	?	?	#
MARYLAND				
1 Bauman	N	Y	N	Y
2 Long	Y	Y	Y	Y
3 Mikulski	Y	Y	Y	Y
4 Holt	Y	Y	N	Y
5 Spellman	Y	Y	Y	Y
6 Byron	Y	Y	Y	Y
7 Mitchell	✓	Y	Y	Y
8 Steers	Y	Y	Y	Y
MASSACHUSETTS				
1 Conte	Y	Y	Y	Y
2 Boland	Y	Y	Y	Y
3 Early	N	Y	Y	Y
4 Drinan	Y	Y	Y	Y
5 Tsongas	?	?	?	?
6 Harrington	#	Y	Y	Y
7 Markey	Y	Y	Y	Y
8 O'Neill				
9 Moakley	Y	Y	Y	Y
10 Heckler	N	Y	Y	Y
11 Burke	Y	N	Y	Y
12 Studds	Y	Y	Y	Y
MICHIGAN				
1 Conyers	▮	#	Y	Y
2 Pursell	N	Y	Y	Y
3 Brown	N	Y	N	Y
4 Stockman	▮	Y	Y	Y
5 Sawyer	N	Y	Y	Y
6 Carr	N	Y	Y	Y
7 Kildee	Y	Y	Y	Y
8 Traxler	Y	Y	Y	Y
9 Vander Jagt	N	N	Y	Y
10 Cederberg	N	Y	Y	Y
11 Ruppe	N	N	N	?
12 Bonior	Y	Y	Y	Y
13 Diggs	Y	#	#	Y
14 Nedzi	Y	Y	Y	Y
15 Ford	Y	N	Y	Y
16 Dingell	Y	N	Y	N
17 Brodhead	Y	Y	Y	Y
18 Blanchard	Y	Y	Y	Y
19 Broomfield	N	Y	Y	Y
MINNESOTA				
1 Quie	X	?	?	?
2 Hagedorn	N	Y	Y	Y
3 Frenzel	N	Y	N	Y
4 Vento	Y	N	Y	Y
5 Fraser	Y	Y	?	Y
6 Nolan	Y	Y	Y	Y
7 Stangeland	N	N	N	Y
8 Oberstar	Y	Y	Y	Y
MISSISSIPPI				
1 Whitten	Y	Y	Y	Y
2 Bowen	Y	Y	Y	Y
3 Montgomery	Y	Y	N	Y
4 Cochran	X	?	?	?
5 Lott	N	Y	Y	Y
MISSOURI				
1 Clay	Y	Y	Y	Y
2 Young	Y	N	Y	Y
3 Gephardt	Y	Y	N	Y
4 Skelton	Y	N	Y	Y
5 Bolling	Y	N	Y	Y
6 Coleman	N	N	Y	Y
7 Taylor	N	N	Y	Y
8 Ichord	N	Y	Y	Y
9 Volkmer	Y	N	Y	Y
10 Burlison	Y	Y	Y	Y
MONTANA				
1 Baucus	N	Y	Y	N
2 Marlenee	N	Y	Y	N
NEBRASKA				
1 Thone	N	Y	?	?
2 Cavanaugh	N	Y	Y	Y
3 Smith	N	Y	N	Y
NEVADA				
AL Santini	N	Y	?	Y
NEW HAMPSHIRE				
1 D'Amours	N	Y	Y	Y
2 Cleveland	N	Y	Y	Y
NEW JERSEY				
1 Florio	Y	Y	Y	Y
2 Hughes	N	Y	Y	Y
3 Howard	Y	N	Y	Y
4 Thompson	Y	Y	Y	Y
5 Fenwick	N	Y	N	Y
6 Forsythe	N	Y	▮	#
7 Maguire	Y	Y	Y	Y
8 Roe	Y	Y	Y	Y
9 Hollenbeck	N	N	Y	Y
10 Rodino	Y	#	#	#
11 Minish	Y	Y	Y	Y
12 Rinaldo	N	Y	Y	Y
13 Meyner	✓	Y	Y	Y
14 LeFante	Y	Y	Y	Y
15 Patten	Y	N	Y	Y
NEW MEXICO				
1 Lujan	N	Y	Y	Y
2 Runnels	?	Y	Y	Y
NEW YORK				
1 Pike	N	Y	Y	Y
2 Downey	Y	Y	Y	Y
3 Ambro	Y	N	Y	Y
4 Lent	N	Y	Y	Y
5 Wydler	N	Y	Y	Y
6 Wolff	Y	Y	Y	Y
7 Addabbo	Y	N	Y	?
8 Rosenthal	Y	Y	Y	Y
9 Delaney	Y	Y	Y	Y
10 Biaggi	Y	Y	Y	Y
11 Scheuer	Y	Y	Y	Y
12 Chisholm	✓	N	Y	Y
13 Solarz	Y	Y	Y	Y
14 Richmond	Y	Y	Y	Y
15 Zeferetti	Y	Y	Y	#
16 Holtzman	Y	Y	Y	Y
17 Murphy	Y	Y	Y	Y
18 Green	N	Y	Y	Y
19 Rangel	Y	Y	Y	Y
20 Weiss	Y	Y	Y	Y
21 Garcia	Y	Y	Y	Y
22 Bingham	Y	Y	Y	Y
23 Caputo	?	?	?	?
24 Ottinger	N	Y	Y	Y
25 Fish	N	Y	Y	Y
26 Gilman	N	Y	Y	Y
27 McHugh	Y	Y	Y	Y
28 Stratton	Y	Y	N	Y
29 Pattison	Y	Y	Y	Y
30 McEwen	N	Y	N	Y
31 Mitchell	N	Y	#	#
32 Hanley	Y	Y	Y	Y
33 Walsh	N	N	Y	Y
34 Horton	N	Y	Y	Y
35 Conable	X	?	?	?
36 LaFalce	Y	Y	Y	Y
37 Nowak	Y	N	Y	Y
38 Kemp	N	Y	?	?
39 Lundine	Y	Y	Y	Y
NORTH CAROLINA				
1 Jones	Y	Y	Y	Y
2 Fountain	N	Y	N	Y
3 Whitley	Y	Y	N	Y
4 Andrews	N	Y	Y	Y
5 Neal	N	N	Y	Y
6 Preyer	Y	Y	Y	Y
7 Rose	Y	N	Y	Y
8 Hefner	Y	Y	Y	Y
9 Martin	N	Y	N	Y
10 Broyhill	N	Y	N	Y
11 Gudger	N	Y	Y	Y
NORTH DAKOTA				
AL Andrews	N	N	Y	Y
OHIO				
1 Gradison	N	Y	N	#
2 Luken	N	Y	Y	Y
3 Whalen	Y	Y	Y	Y
4 Guyer	N	N	Y	Y
5 Latta	N	Y	N	Y
6 Harsha	N	N	Y	Y
7 Brown	N	N	?	?
8 Kindness	N	Y	N	Y
9 Ashley	Y	N	Y	Y
10 Miller	N	N	Y	Y
11 Stanton	N	N	Y	Y
12 Devine	N	Y	N	Y
13 Pease	Y	Y	Y	Y
14 Seiberling	Y	Y	Y	Y
15 Wylie	N	Y	Y	Y
16 Regula	N	Y	N	Y
17 Ashbrook	N	Y	N	Y
18 Applegate	Y	Y	Y	Y
19 Carney	Y	N	Y	Y
20 Oakar	Y	Y	?	?
21 Stokes	Y	Y	Y	?
22 Vanik	Y	Y	Y	#
23 Mottl	N	Y	Y	Y
OKLAHOMA				
1 Jones	Y	N	N	Y
2 Risenhoover	N	X	Y	Y
3 Watkins	Y	Y	N	Y
4 Steed	Y	N	Y	Y
5 Edwards	N	Y	N	Y
6 English	Y	Y	N	Y
OREGON				
1 AuCoin	N	N	Y	Y
2 Ullman	Y	Y	Y	Y
3 Duncan	Y	Y	Y	Y
4 Weaver	N	Y	?	?
PENNSYLVANIA				
1 Myers, M.	Y	Y	Y	Y
2 Nix	Y	X	?	?
3 Lederer	Y	Y	Y	Y
4 Eilberg	Y	N	✓	?
5 Schulze	N	N	Y	N
6 Yatron	Y	Y	Y	Y
7 Edgar	Y	Y	Y	Y
8 Kostmayer	N	Y	Y	Y
9 Shuster	N	N	Y	Y
10 McDade	N	Y	Y	Y
11 Flood	Y	Y	Y	Y
12 Murtha	Y	Y	Y	Y
13 Coughlin	N	Y	Y	Y
14 Moorhead	Y	Y	Y	Y
15 Rooney	Y	Y	Y	Y
16 Walker	N	Y	N	Y
17 Ertel	N	Y	Y	Y
18 Walgren	Y	Y	Y	Y
19 Goodling, W.	N	Y	N	Y
20 Gaydos	?	?	?	Y
21 Dent	✓	#	#	#
22 Murphy	N	Y	Y	Y
23 Ammerman	✓	✓	✓	?
24 Marks	N	Y	Y	Y
25 Myers, G.	N	N	N	Y
RHODE ISLAND				
1 St Germain	Y	Y	Y	Y
2 Beard	Y	Y	Y	Y
SOUTH CAROLINA				
1 Davis	Y	Y	Y	Y
2 Spence	N	Y	N	Y
3 Derrick	Y	Y	#	#
4 Mann	Y	Y	Y	Y
5 Holland	Y	?	Y	Y
6 Jenrette	#	Y	Y	Y
SOUTH DAKOTA				
1 Pressler	N	N	Y	N
2 Abdnor	N	N	N	N
TENNESSEE				
1 Quillen	N	Y	#	#
2 Duncan	N	Y	Y	Y
3 Lloyd	Y	N	Y	Y
4 Gore	Y	Y	Y	Y
5 Vacancy				
6 Beard	N	Y	N	Y
7 Jones	Y	Y	Y	Y
8 Ford	Y	Y	Y	Y
TEXAS				
1 Hall	Y	Y	N	Y
2 Wilson, C.	#	Y	Y	#
3 Collins	N	Y	N	Y
4 Roberts	Y	N	Y	Y
5 Mattox	Y	Y	Y	Y
6 Teague	?	X	X	?
7 Archer	N	Y	N	Y
8 Eckhardt	Y	Y	?	?
9 Brooks	Y	Y	Y	Y
10 Pickle	Y	Y	N	Y
11 Poage	Y	N	N	N
12 Wright	Y	N	Y	Y
13 Hightower	?	?	?	?
14 Young	Y	N	?	?
15 de la Garza	?	?	?	?
16 White	Y	Y	Y	Y
17 Burleson	Y	N	N	Y
18 Jordan	Y	Y	Y	Y
19 Mahon	Y	N	Y	Y
20 Gonzalez	Y	Y	Y	#
21 Krueger	#	✓	#	#
22 Gammage	N	#	Y	Y
23 Kazen	Y	N	Y	Y
24 Milford	Y	N	N	N
UTAH				
1 McKay	Y	Y	Y	Y
2 Marriott	N	Y	Y	Y
VERMONT				
AL Jeffords	N	Y	Y	Y
VIRGINIA				
1 Trible	N	Y	N	Y
2 Whitehurst	N	Y	N	Y
3 Satterfield	N	Y	N	Y
4 Daniel	N	Y	N	Y
5 Daniel	N	Y	N	Y
6 Butler	N	Y	N	Y
7 Robinson	N	Y	N	Y
8 Harris	N	Y	Y	Y
9 Wampler	N	Y	Y	Y
10 Fisher	Y	Y	Y	Y
WASHINGTON				
1 Pritchard	N	Y	Y	Y
2 Meeds	✓	?	?	?
3 Bonker	Y	Y	Y	Y
4 McCormack	Y	N	Y	Y
5 Foley	Y	Y	Y	Y
6 Dicks	Y	Y	Y	Y
7 Cunningham	N	Y	Y	Y
WEST VIRGINIA				
1 Mollohan	Y	N	Y	Y
2 Staggers	Y	N	Y	Y
3 Slack	Y	Y	Y	Y
4 Rahall	✓	#	#	Y
WISCONSIN				
1 Aspin	Y	Y	Y	Y
2 Kastenmeier	Y	Y	Y	Y
3 Baldus	Y	Y	Y	Y
4 Zablocki	Y	Y	Y	Y
5 Reuss	Y	Y	Y	Y
6 Steiger	N	Y	Y	Y
7 Obey	Y	Y	Y	Y
8 Cornell	Y	Y	Y	Y
9 Kasten	N	Y	Y	Y
WYOMING				
AL Roncalio	Y	N	Y	Y

Democrats ***Republicans***

720. HR 11733. Surface Transportation Assistance Act. Giaimo, D-Conn., amendment to declare it to be national policy that expenditures from the Highway Trust Fund be "closely related" to the fund's anticipated annual revenues. Rejected 111-238: R 18-95; D 93-143 (ND 75-92; SD 18-51), Sept. 21, 1978. A "yea" was a vote supporting the president's position.

721. HR 12452. CETA Amendments. Flippo, D-Ala., amendment, to the Jeffords, R-Vt., substitute to the bill, to add approximately 100,000 countercyclical public service jobs by increasing the target for jobs to be provided under CETA Title VI to 25 percent, from 20 percent, of the total number of unemployed in excess of 4 percent of the work force. Rejected 1-335: R 0-110; D 1-225 (ND 0-158; SD 1-67), Sept. 22, 1978. (The Jeffords substitute amendment, which reduced the number of public service jobs and public service wages contained in the Education and Labor Committee-reported bill, was subsequently adopted by voice vote.)

722. HR 12452. CETA Amendments. Ashbrook, R-Ohio, motion to recommit the bill to the Education and Labor Committee with instructions to report it back with an amendment limiting spending on public service jobs programs to no more than 30 percent of the amount appropriated for CETA. Motion rejected 81-252: R 58-52; D 23-200 (ND 6-150; SD 17-50), Sept. 22, 1978.

723. HR 12452. CETA Amendments. Passage of the bill to extend major jobs programs under the Comprehensive Employment and Training Act through fiscal 1982. Passed 284-50: R 78-32; D 206-18 (ND 151-5; SD 55-13), Sept. 22, 1978. A "yea" was a vote supporting the president's position.

724. HR 11733. Surface Transportation Assistance Act. Kostmayer, D-Pa., amendments, en bloc, to delete from the bill provisions making changes in the 1965 Highway Beautification Act (PL 89-285). Rejected 76-199: R 14-74; D 62-125 (ND 52-74; SD 10-51), Sept. 22, 1978.

725. HR 10584. Agricultural Exports. Foley, D-Wash., motion to suspend the rules and pass the bill to promote the sale of U.S. agricultural commodities by providing intermediate term (three to 10 years) credit under the Commodity Credit Corporation, to make certain non-market economy countries eligible for short-term (up to three years) credit, and to establish six to 16 agricultural trade offices overseas. Motion agreed to 325-62: R 110-24; D 215-38 (ND 145-28; SD 70-10), Sept. 25, 1978. A two-thirds majority vote (258 in this case) is required for passage under suspension of the rules.

726. HR 11870. U.S. Tourism. Rooney, D-Pa., motion to suspend the rules and pass the bill to authorize $1,008,000 for fiscal 1979 to carry out the domestic tourism programs administered by the Commerce Department's U.S. Travel Service. Motion agreed to 289-96: R 78-56; D 211-40 (ND 150-22; SD 61-18), Sept. 25, 1978. A two-thirds majority vote (257 in this case) is required for passage under suspension of the rules.

727. HR 12162. Rail Public Counsel. Rooney, D-Pa., motion to suspend the rules and pass the bill to authorize $2.2 million for fiscal 1979 for the Interstate Commerce Commission's Office of Rail Public Counsel. Motion rejected 188-196: R 34-99; D 154-97 (ND 133-40; SD 21-57), Sept. 25, 1978. A two-thirds majority vote (256 in this case) is required for passage under suspension of the rules.

KEY

- Y Voted for (yea).
- ✓ Paired for.
- † Announced for.
- # CQ Poll for.
- N Voted against (nay).
- X Paired against.
- - Announced against.
- ▮ CQ Poll against.
- P Voted "present."
- ● Voted "present" to avoid possible conflict of interest.
- ? Did not vote or otherwise make a position known.

	720	721	722	723	724	725	726	727
ALABAMA								
1 Edwards	N	N	N	Y	?	Y	Y	N
2 Dickinson	?	?	?	?	?	Y	Y	N
3 Nichols	▮	N	Y	Y	N	Y	N	N
4 Bevill	N	N	N	Y	N	Y	N	N
5 Flippo	N	Y	N	Y	N	Y	N	N
6 Buchanan	N	N	N	Y	N	N	Y	N
7 Flowers	?	?	?	?	?	?	?	?
ALASKA								
AL Young	N	N	N	Y	N	Y	N	Y
ARIZONA								
1 Rhodes	?	?	?	?	?	Y	Y	Y
2 Udall	Y	N	N	Y	Y	Y	Y	Y
3 Stump	N	N	Y	N	N	Y	N	N
4 Rudd	?	?	?	?	?	?	?	?
ARKANSAS								
1 Alexander	N	?	?	?	?	Y	Y	Y
2 Tucker	?	▮	▮	?	?	Y	Y	Y
3 Hammerschmidt	N	N	Y	Y	N	Y	Y	N
4 Thornton	?	?	?	?	?	Y	Y	Y
CALIFORNIA								
1 Johnson	N	N	N	Y	N	Y	Y	Y
2 Clausen	N	N	Y	Y	N	Y	Y	N
3 Moss	?	?	N	Y	N	?	?	?
4 Leggett	Y	?	N	Y	N	Y	Y	Y
5 Burton, J.	N	?	?	?	?	?	?	?
6 Burton, P.	N	N	N	Y	Y	Y	Y	Y
7 Miller	?	?	?	?	?	?	?	?
8 Dellums	Y	▮	N	Y	Y	Y	Y	Y
9 Stark	Y	N	N	Y	Y	Y	Y	Y
10 Edwards	Y	N	N	Y	Y	Y	Y	Y
11 Ryan	N	N	N	Y	Y	Y	Y	Y
12 McCloskey	Y	N	N	Y	Y	Y	Y	N
13 Mineta	N	N	N	Y	N	Y	Y	Y
14 McFall	Y	N	N	Y	N	Y	Y	Y
15 Sisk	?	N	?	?	?	Y	Y	Y
16 Panetta	Y	N	N	Y	Y	Y	N	N
17 Krebs	Y	N	N	Y	N	Y	Y	N
18 Vacancy								
19 Lagomarsino	N	N	Y	Y	N	Y	N	N
20 Goldwater	N	N	Y	N	N	Y	N	N
21 Corman	N	?	?	?	X	Y	Y	Y
22 Moorhead	N	N	?	?	?	N	N	N
23 Beilenson	Y	N	N	Y	Y	Y	Y	Y
24 Waxman	Y	N	N	Y	Y	N	Y	Y
25 Roybal	N	N	N	Y	Y	Y	Y	Y
26 Rousselot	N	N	Y	N	N	N	N	N
27 Dornan	N	N	Y	N	N	Y	N	N
28 Burke	▮	▮	?	?	?	#	#	✓
29 Hawkins	?	N	N	Y	N	Y	Y	Y
30 Danielson	Y	N	N	Y	N	Y	Y	Y
31 Wilson, C.H.	?	N	N	Y	?	N	Y	N
32 Anderson	N	N	N	Y	N	?	?	?
33 Clawson	N	N	Y	N	N	N	N	N
34 Hannaford	N	N	N	Y	Y	Y	Y	N
35 Lloyd	N	N	N	Y	N	Y	Y	Y
36 Brown	?	?	?	?	?	Y	Y	Y
37 Pettis	N	?	N	Y	N	Y	Y	N
38 Patterson	▮	▮	?	?	?	Y	Y	Y
39 Wiggins	#	▮	?	?	?	Y	N	N
40 Badham	N	N	Y	N	N	N	N	N
41 Wilson, B.	N	N	N	Y	N	Y	Y	Y
42 Van Deerlin	N	N	N	Y	N	Y	Y	Y
43 Burgener	N	N	Y	Y	N	Y	Y	N
COLORADO								
1 Schroeder	Y	N	N	Y	?	Y	N	Y
2 Wirth	Y	▮	?	?	?	✓	#	✓
3 Evans	▮	N	N	Y	?	Y	Y	Y
4 Johnson	N	N	N	Y	?	Y	Y	N
5 Armstrong	?	?	?	?	?	?	?	?
CONNECTICUT								
1 Cotter	N	▮	?	?	?	Y	Y	N
2 Dodd	N	N	N	Y	?	Y	Y	Y
3 Giaimo	Y	N	N	Y	Y	Y	Y	Y
4 McKinney	#	▮	?	?	?	Y	Y	Y
5 Sarasin	▮	▮	?	?	?	#	#	#
6 Moffett	Y	N	N	Y	✓	Y	Y	Y
DELAWARE								
AL Evans	N	▮	?	?	?	Y	Y	Y
FLORIDA								
1 Sikes	?	?	?	?	?	Y	Y	N
2 Fuqua	N	?	?	?	?	Y	Y	N
3 Bennett	Y	N	Y	N	N	Y	N	N
4 Chappell	N	N	N	N	N	Y	Y	N
5 Kelly	N	N	Y	N	N	Y	N	N
6 Young	N	N	N	Y	N	Y	Y	N
7 Gibbons	?	?	?	?	?	Y	Y	N
8 Ireland	?	N	N	N	N	Y	Y	?
9 Frey	N	N	N	Y	N	Y	N	N
10 Bafalis	N	N	Y	N	N	Y	Y	N
11 Rogers	Y	N	N	Y	N	Y	Y	N
12 Burke	N	N	N	Y	N	Y	Y	Y
13 Lehman	Y	N	N	Y	Y	Y	Y	Y
14 Pepper	▮	?	?	?	#	?	#	✓
15 Fascell	▮	?	?	?	?	Y	Y	Y
GEORGIA								
1 Ginn	N	N	Y	Y	N	Y	Y	N
2 Mathis	N	N	N	Y	N	Y	Y	N
3 Brinkley	Y	N	Y	Y	Y	Y	Y	N
4 Levitas	N	N	Y	Y	Y	N	Y	Y
5 Fowler	N	N	N	Y	N	Y	N	N
6 Flynt	?	?	?	?	?	Y	Y	N
7 McDonald	N	N	Y	N	N	N	N	N
8 Evans	N	N	N	Y	N	N	N	N
9 Jenkins	Y	N	Y	Y	N	N	Y	N
10 Barnard	N	?	?	?	?	Y	Y	N
HAWAII								
1 Heftel	N	N	N	Y	N	Y	Y	N
2 Akaka	N	N	N	Y	N	Y	Y	Y
IDAHO								
1 Symms	N	N	Y	N	?	Y	N	N
2 Hansen, G.	?	?	?	?	?	N	N	N
ILLINOIS								
1 Metcalfe	?	?	?	?	?	Y	Y	Y
2 Murphy	Y	?	?	?	X	Y	Y	Y
3 Russo	Y	N	N	Y	?	Y	Y	Y
4 Derwinski	N	N	Y	Y	N	N	Y	N
5 Fary	N	N	N	Y	N	Y	Y	Y
6 Hyde	Y	N	Y	Y	N	Y	Y	N
7 Collins	N	?	?	?	?	Y	Y	Y
8 Rostenkowski	Y	N	N	Y	X	Y	Y	Y
9 Yates	Y	N	N	Y	Y	N	N	Y
10 Mikva	Y	N	N	Y	Y	Y	Y	Y
11 Annunzio	N	N	N	Y	N	Y	Y	Y
12 Crane	?	?	?	?	?	N	N	N
13 McClory	N	N	Y	Y	Y	#	#	X
14 Erlenborn	#	?	?	?	?	Y	Y	N
15 Corcoran	N	N	Y	Y	N	Y	Y	N
16 Anderson	▮	N	N	Y	N	#	#	▮
17 O'Brien	N	N	Y	Y	N	Y	Y	Y
18 Michel	N	N	Y	Y	N	Y	N	N
19 Railsback	?	?	?	?	?	Y	Y	Y
20 Findley	N	N	Y	Y	?	Y	Y	N
21 Madigan	N	?	?	?	?	Y	Y	Y
22 Shipley	?	?	?	?	?	?	?	✓
23 Price	▮	N	N	Y	N	Y	Y	Y
24 Simon	Y	N	N	Y	Y	Y	Y	Y
INDIANA								
1 Benjamin	N	N	N	Y	N	N	N	Y
2 Fithian	N	N	N	Y	N	Y	Y	Y
3 Brademas	Y	N	N	Y	N	Y	Y	Y
4 Quayle	?	N	Y	N	N	Y	N	N
5 Hillis	N	N	N	Y	?	Y	N	N
6 Evans	N	N	N	Y	N	Y	N	Y
7 Myers, J.	N	N	Y	Y	N	Y	N	N
8 Cornwell	#	?	?	?	X	Y	Y	Y
9 Hamilton	Y	N	N	Y	N	Y	Y	Y
10 Sharp	Y	N	N	Y	N	Y	N	Y
11 Jacobs	Y	N	?	?	?	Y	Y	Y
IOWA								
1 Leach	N	N	Y	Y	Y	Y	N	N
2 Blouin	N	N	N	Y	?	Y	Y	N
3 Grassley	N	N	Y	N	N	Y	N	N
4 Smith	N	N	N	Y	N	Y	Y	N
5 Harkin	N	N	N	Y	?	Y	Y	Y
6 Bedell	Y	N	N	Y	?	Y	Y	N

Democrats *Republicans*

Corresponding to Congressional Record Votes 815, 816, 817, 818, 819, 820, 822, 823

	720	721	722	723	724	725	726	727
KANSAS								
1 Sebelius	N	N	Y	Y	N	Y	Y	N
2 Keys	N	N	?	?	?	Y	Y	Y
3 Winn	▮	?	?	?	?	Y	N	N
4 Glickman	N	N	Y	Y	?	Y	N	N
5 Skubitz	?	N	N	Y	?	Y	Y	Y
KENTUCKY								
1 Hubbard	N	N	N	Y	N	Y	N	Y
2 Natcher	N	N	N	Y	N	Y	Y	Y
3 Mazzoli	Y	N	N	Y	N	Y	Y	N
4 Snyder	N	N	N	Y	N	Y	Y	N
5 Carter	N	N	N	Y	N	Y	Y	Y
6 Breckinridge	N	N	N	Y	N	Y	Y	Y
7 Perkins	N	N	N	Y	N	Y	Y	N
LOUISIANA								
1 Livingston	N	N	N	Y	N	Y	Y	N
2 Boggs	N	N	N	Y	N	Y	#	Y
3 Treen	N	N	Y	Y	N	Y	N	N
4 Waggonner	N	N	Y	N	N	Y	Y	N
5 Huckaby	N	N	N	Y	N	Y	Y	N
6 Moore	N	N	N	Y	N	Y	Y	N
7 Breaux	N	N	N	Y	N	Y	Y	N
8 Long	Y	N	N	Y	N	Y	Y	N
MAINE								
1 Emery	N	N	N	Y	N	N	N	N
2 Cohen	?	?	?	?	?	#	?	?
MARYLAND								
1 Bauman	?	N	Y	N	N	Y	N	N
2 Long	Y	N	N	Y	N	N	Y	Y
3 Mikulski	Y	N	N	Y	N	N	Y	Y
4 Holt	N	N	Y	N	N	Y	N	N
5 Spellman	Y	N	N	Y	Y	Y	N	N
6 Byron	?	N	N	Y	N	Y	Y	N
7 Mitchell	N	N	N	Y	N	Y	Y	Y
8 Steers	Y	N	N	Y	Y	Y	Y	Y
MASSACHUSETTS								
1 Conte	N	N	N	Y	?	Y	Y	Y
2 Boland	▮	?	?	?	?	Y	Y	Y
3 Early	Y	N	N	Y	Y	Y	N	Y
4 Drinan	Y	N	N	Y	Y	N	Y	Y
5 Tsongas	?	N	N	Y	Y	Y	Y	Y
6 Harrington	#	?	?	?	?	#	#	#
7 Markey	Y	N	N	Y	Y	Y	Y	Y
8 O'Neill								
9 Moakley	N	N	N	Y	N	Y	Y	Y
10 Heckler	N	N	N	Y	N	Y	Y	Y
11 Burke	N	N	N	?	N	Y	Y	Y
12 Studds	Y	N	N	Y	Y	Y	Y	Y
MICHIGAN								
1 Conyers	N	?	?	?	✓	Y	Y	Y
2 Pursell	N	N	N	Y	Y	Y	Y	Y
3 Brown	N	N	N	Y	N	Y	Y	Y
4 Stockman	Y	N	Y	N	Y	Y	N	N
5 Sawyer	N	N	N	Y	Y	Y	Y	N
6 Carr	Y	?	N	Y	Y	Y	Y	Y
7 Kildee	N	N	N	Y	Y	Y	Y	Y
8 Traxler	N	N	N	Y	?	Y	Y	Y
9 Vander Jagt	N	N	N	Y	N	Y	Y	N
10 Cederberg	N	N	N	Y	N	Y	Y	N
11 Ruppe	?	?	?	?	?	?	?	X
12 Bonior	?	N	N	Y	Y	Y	Y	Y
13 Diggs	Y	N	N	Y	?	#	#	?
14 Nedzi	Y	N	N	Y	N	Y	Y	Y
15 Ford	Y	?	N	Y	N	Y	Y	Y
16 Dingell	N	N	N	Y	Y	Y	Y	Y
17 Brodhead	Y	N	N	Y	Y	?	?	Y
18 Blanchard	Y	N	N	Y	?	Y	Y	Y
19 Broomfield	N	N	?	?	?	Y	Y	N
MINNESOTA								
1 Quie	?	?	?	?	?	?	?	X
2 Hagedorn	N	N	Y	N	?	Y	Y	N
3 Frenzel	Y	N	Y	Y	Y	Y	Y	N
4 Vento	N	N	N	Y	?	Y	N	Y
5 Fraser	Y	?	?	?	?	Y	Y	Y
6 Nolan	Y	N	N	Y	N	Y	Y	Y
7 Stangeland	N	N	Y	Y	N	Y	Y	N
8 Oberstar	N	N	N	Y	?	Y	Y	Y
MISSISSIPPI								
1 Whitten	N	N	N	Y	N	Y	Y	N
2 Bowen	N	N	N	Y	N	Y	Y	N
3 Montgomery	N	N	?	?	?	Y	Y	N
4 Cochran	?	?	?	?	?	?	?	X
5 Lott	N	N	N	Y	N	N	Y	N
MISSOURI								
1 Clay	N	N	N	Y	?	Y	Y	Y
2 Young	N	N	N	Y	N	Y	Y	N
3 Gephardt	Y	N	N	Y	Y	Y	N	N

	720	721	722	723	724	725	726	727
4 Skelton	N	N	N	Y	N	Y	N	N
5 Bolling	N	N	N	Y	N	#	#	#
6 Coleman	N	N	Y	Y	N	Y	Y	N
7 Taylor	N	N	Y	N	N	Y	Y	N
8 Ichord	Y	?	?	?	?	N	N	N
9 Volkmer	Y	N	N	Y	N	Y	Y	N
10 Burlison	Y	N	N	Y	N	Y	Y	N
MONTANA								
1 Baucus	N	N	?	?	?	?	?	✓
2 Marlenee	N	?	?	?	?	Y	N	Y
NEBRASKA								
1 Thone	?	?	?	?	?	?	?	X
2 Cavanaugh	Y	?	?	?	?	Y	N	N
3 Smith	?	N	Y	Y	?	Y	Y	N
NEVADA								
AL Santini	N	N	N	Y	N	Y	Y	N
NEW HAMPSHIRE								
1 D'Amours	N	N	Y	Y	Y	N	N	Y
2 Cleveland	N	N	Y	N	N	N	N	N
NEW JERSEY								
1 Florio	N	N	N	Y	?	Y	Y	Y
2 Hughes	N	N	N	Y	N	Y	Y	Y
3 Howard	N	N	N	Y	N	Y	Y	Y
4 Thompson	N	N	N	Y	Y	✓	?	✓
5 Fenwick	Y	N	N	Y	Y	N	Y	N
6 Forsythe	▮	N	N	Y	N	N	N	N
7 Maguire	Y	N	N	Y	?	Y	Y	Y
8 Roe	N	N	N	Y	N	N	Y	Y
9 Hollenbeck	N	N	N	Y	?	N	N	Y
10 Rodino	▮	?	?	?	?	#	#	✓
11 Minish	N	N	N	Y	N	N	Y	Y
12 Rinaldo	N	N	N	Y	?	Y	Y	Y
13 Meyner	N	N	N	Y	N	Y	Y	Y
14 LeFante	N	N	?	?	?	Y	Y	Y
15 Patten	N	N	N	Y	N	Y	Y	Y
NEW MEXICO								
1 Lujan	N	N	Y	Y	N	Y	Y	N
2 Runnels	N	N	Y	N	N	Y	N	N
NEW YORK								
1 Pike	Y	N	Y	N	Y	Y	Y	N
2 Downey	N	N	N	Y	Y	N	Y	Y
3 Ambro	N	N	N	Y	N	Y	Y	N
4 Lent	Y	N	N	Y	?	N	N	Y
5 Wydler	N	N	N	Y	?	N	N	N
6 Wolff	N	N	N	Y	Y	N	Y	Y
7 Addabbo	X	N	N	Y	?	Y	Y	Y
8 Rosenthal	N	N	N	Y	N	Y	Y	Y
9 Delaney	Y	N	N	N	N	N	Y	N
10 Biaggi	N	N	N	Y	?	Y	Y	Y
11 Scheuer	Y	N	N	Y	Y	N	?	Y
12 Chisholm	N	N	N	Y	Y	✓	#	✓
13 Solarz	N	N	N	Y	N	Y	Y	Y
14 Richmond	Y	?	?	?	✓	N	Y	Y
15 Zeferetti	X	?	?	?	?	N	Y	Y
16 Holtzman	Y	N	N	Y	Y	N	N	Y
17 Murphy	N	N	?	?	?	Y	Y	✓
18 Green	N	?	N	Y	Y	Y	Y	Y
19 Rangel	Y	N	N	Y	N	Y	Y	Y
20 Weiss	Y	N	N	Y	Y	Y	Y	Y
21 Garcia	Y	?	?	?	?	N	Y	Y
22 Bingham	N	N	N	Y	Y	Y	Y	Y
23 Caputo	?	?	?	?	?	?	?	?
24 Ottinger	N	N	N	Y	Y	Y	Y	Y
25 Fish	N	N	N	Y	?	Y	Y	?
26 Gilman	N	N	N	Y	?	N	N	N
27 McHugh	Y	N	N	Y	N	Y	Y	Y
28 Stratton	N	N	N	Y	N	Y	Y	N
29 Pattison	Y	?	?	?	?	Y	Y	Y
30 McEwen	N	N	N	Y	?	Y	Y	N
31 Mitchell	▮	?	?	?	?	Y	Y	Y
32 Hanley	Y	N	N	Y	N	Y	Y	N
33 Walsh	N	N	N	Y	N	Y	Y	Y
34 Horton	N	N	?	?	?	Y	Y	N
35 Conable	?	?	?	?	?	Y	N	N
36 LaFalce	Y	N	N	Y	N	Y	Y	Y
37 Nowak	N	N	N	Y	N	Y	Y	Y
38 Kemp	?	?	?	?	?	Y	Y	N
39 Lundine	N	N	N	Y	?	Y	Y	Y
NORTH CAROLINA								
1 Jones	N	N	N	Y	N	Y	Y	N
2 Fountain	N	N	N	Y	N	Y	Y	N
3 Whitley	Y	N	N	Y	N	Y	Y	N
4 Andrews	Y	?	N	Y	N	Y	Y	N
5 Neal	Y	?	?	?	?	N	Y	N
6 Preyer	Y	N	N	Y	N	Y	Y	Y
7 Rose	N	N	N	Y	?	Y	Y	N
8 Hefner	N	N	N	Y	?	Y	Y	N

	720	721	722	723	724	725	726	727
9 Martin	Y	?	Y	N	N	Y	N	N
10 Broyhill	Y	N	Y	N	N	N	Y	N
11 Gudger	Y	N	N	Y	?	Y	Y	N
NORTH DAKOTA								
AL Andrews	N	?	?	?	?	Y	Y	Y
OHIO								
1 Gradison	#	N	N	Y	Y	Y	Y	N
2 Luken	N	N	N	Y	N	Y	Y	N
3 Whalen	Y	N	N	Y	Y	Y	Y	Y
4 Guyer	N	N	Y	Y	N	Y	Y	N
5 Latta	Y	N	Y	Y	?	Y	N	N
6 Harsha	N	N	N	Y	N	Y	Y	N
7 Brown	?	?	?	?	?	Y	N	Y
8 Kindness	N	N	Y	N	?	Y	Y	N
9 Ashley	Y	N	N	Y	?	Y	Y	N
10 Miller	N	N	Y	Y	N	Y	N	N
11 Stanton	N	N	N	Y	?	Y	Y	Y
12 Devine	N	N	Y	N	N	Y	N	N
13 Pease	Y	N	N	Y	?	Y	Y	Y
14 Seiberling	Y	N	N	Y	Y	N	Y	Y
15 Wylie	Y	N	Y	Y	N	Y	N	N
16 Regula	Y	N	N	Y	N	Y	Y	N
17 Ashbrook	N	N	Y	N	N	N	N	N
18 Applegate	N	N	N	Y	?	?	?	✓
19 Carney	?	?	?	?	?	Y	Y	Y
20 Oakar	?	?	?	?	?	?	?	?
21 Stokes	N	N	N	Y	Y	Y	Y	Y
22 Vanik	#	N	N	Y	Y	N	Y	Y
23 Mottl	Y	?	?	?	✓	N	N	N
OKLAHOMA								
1 Jones	N	N	Y	N	N	#	#	#
2 Risenhoover	N	N	N	Y	N	X	?	?
3 Watkins	N	N	?	?	?	Y	Y	N
4 Steed	N	N	N	Y	N	Y	Y	N
5 Edwards	N	N	Y	N	N	Y	N	N
6 English	N	N	Y	N	N	Y	Y	N
OREGON								
1 AuCoin	Y	?	N	Y	Y	#	#	?
2 Ullman	N	?	?	?	?	Y	Y	Y
3 Duncan	Y	N	?	Y	N	Y	Y	N
4 Weaver	?	?	?	?	?	Y	N	N
PENNSYLVANIA								
1 Myers, M.	N	N	N	Y	N	Y	Y	Y
2 Nix	?	?	?	?	?	N	Y	Y
3 Lederer	N	N	N	Y	N	Y	Y	Y
4 Eilberg	X	N	N	Y	✓	X	?	✓
5 Schulze	N	N	Y	Y	N	Y	Y	N
6 Yatron	N	N	N	Y	?	Y	Y	Y
7 Edgar	N	N	N	Y	Y	Y	Y	Y
8 Kostmayer	Y	N	N	Y	Y	N	Y	Y
9 Shuster	N	N	N	N	N	Y	N	N
10 McDade	N	?	?	?	?	Y	Y	Y
11 Flood	N	N	N	Y	?	?	?	✓
12 Murtha	N	N	N	Y	N	Y	Y	Y
13 Coughlin	▮	N	N	Y	Y	Y	N	N
14 Moorhead	N	N	N	Y	N	Y	Y	Y
15 Rooney	N	N	N	Y	N	Y	Y	Y
16 Walker	N	N	Y	N	N	Y	N	N
17 Ertel	N	N	N	Y	Y	Y	Y	N
18 Walgren	N	N	N	Y	Y	Y	N	N
19 Goodling, W.	N	N	Y	Y	N	Y	N	N
20 Gaydos	N	N	N	Y	N	N	Y	N
21 Dent	▮	?	?	?	?	N	Y	N
22 Murphy	N	N	N	Y	N	Y	Y	Y
23 Ammerman	?	?	?	?	?	?	?	✓
24 Marks	Y	N	N	Y	?	Y	Y	Y
25 Myers, G.	Y	N	Y	N	N	N	N	Y
RHODE ISLAND								
1 St Germain	N	N	?	?	?	Y	Y	Y
2 Beard	N	N	N	Y	?	Y	Y	Y
SOUTH CAROLINA								
1 Davis	N	N	N	Y	?	N	Y	Y
2 Spence	N	N	N	Y	N	N	Y	N
3 Derrick	✓	N	N	Y	?	N	Y	Y
4 Mann	Y	N	?	Y	?	N	Y	N
5 Holland	?	?	?	?	?	N	Y	N
6 Jenrette	N	N	N	Y	?	Y	Y	N
SOUTH DAKOTA								
1 Pressler	?	?	?	?	?	?	?	?
2 Abdnor	N	N	Y	N	N	Y	Y	N
TENNESSEE								
1 Quillen	▮	?	?	?	?	Y	Y	Y
2 Duncan	Y	N	N	Y	N	Y	Y	Y
3 Lloyd	N	N	N	Y	N	N	N	N
4 Gore	N	N	N	Y	Y	Y	N	Y
5 Vacancy								
6 Beard	N	?	?	?	?	Y	N	N

	720	721	722	723	724	725	726	727
7 Jones	N	N	N	Y	N	Y	N	Y
8 Ford	N	N	N	Y	Y	Y	Y	Y
TEXAS								
1 Hall	N	N	Y	N	N	Y	N	N
2 Wilson, C.	N	N	N	Y	N	Y	Y	▮
3 Collins	N	N	Y	N	N	N	N	N
4 Roberts	N	N	Y	N	N	Y	N	N
5 Mattox	Y	N	N	Y	Y	Y	Y	N
6 Teague	✓	?	?	?	?	?	?	X
7 Archer	N	N	Y	N	N	N	N	N
8 Eckhardt	?	?	N	Y	Y	?	?	?
9 Brooks	N	N	N	Y	N	Y	Y	N
10 Pickle	N	N	Y	Y	Y	Y	Y	Y
11 Poage	Y	N	N	Y	N	Y	Y	N
12 Wright	N	N	N	Y	N	?	?	?
13 Hightower	?	N	N	Y	N	Y	Y	N
14 Young	?	?	?	?	?	Y	Y	N
15 de la Garza	?	?	?	?	?	Y	Y	N
16 White	N	N	N	Y	N	Y	Y	N
17 Burleson	Y	N	Y	N	N	Y	N	N
18 Jordan	N	N	N	Y	N	Y	Y	Y
19 Mahon	N	N	N	Y	N	Y	N	N
20 Gonzalez	N	N	N	Y	N	Y	Y	Y
21 Krueger	▮	?	?	?	?	#	#	✓
22 Gammage	✓	?	?	?	X	✓	#	X
23 Kazen	N	N	N	Y	N	Y	N	N
24 Milford	?	?	?	?	?	Y	Y	N
UTAH								
1 McKay	N	N	Y	N	Y	Y	Y	N
2 Marriott	N	N	Y	N	N	Y	N	N
VERMONT								
AL Jeffords	Y	N	N	Y	?	Y	Y	Y
VIRGINIA								
1 Trible	N	?	?	?	?	Y	Y	N
2 Whitehurst	N	N	N	Y	Y	Y	N	N
3 Satterfield	N	N	Y	N	N	Y	N	N
4 Daniel	N	N	Y	N	N	Y	N	N
5 Daniel	N	N	Y	N	N	Y	N	N
6 Butler	N	N	Y	N	?	Y	Y	N
7 Robinson	N	N	Y	N	N	Y	Y	N
8 Harris	Y	N	N	Y	Y	Y	N	Y
9 Wampler	N	N	N	Y	N	Y	Y	Y
10 Fisher	Y	N	N	Y	Y	Y	Y	Y
WASHINGTON								
1 Pritchard	Y	N	N	Y	N	Y	Y	N
2 Meeds	?	?	?	?	?	?	?	?
3 Bonker	Y	N	N	Y	N	#	#	?
4 McCormack	N	N	N	Y	N	Y	Y	Y
5 Foley	Y	N	N	Y	N	Y	Y	N
6 Dicks	N	N	N	Y	N	Y	Y	Y
7 Cunningham	N	?	?	?	?	N	N	N
WEST VIRGINIA								
1 Mollohan	Y	N	N	Y	N	Y	Y	Y
2 Staggers	Y	N	N	Y	N	Y	Y	Y
3 Slack	N	N	N	Y	N	Y	Y	N
4 Rahall	N	N	N	Y	N	Y	N	Y
WISCONSIN								
1 Aspin	Y	N	N	Y	?	Y	Y	Y
2 Kastenmeier	Y	N	N	Y	Y	Y	Y	Y
3 Baldus	N	N	N	Y	N	Y	Y	Y
4 Zablocki	N	N	N	Y	N	Y	Y	Y
5 Reuss	Y	N	N	Y	Y	Y	Y	Y
6 Steiger	#	?	?	?	?	Y	N	N
7 Obey	Y	N	N	Y	?	Y	Y	Y
8 Cornell	Y	N	N	Y	N	Y	Y	Y
9 Kasten	N	N	Y	Y	N	Y	N	N
WYOMING								
AL Roncalio	N	N	N	Y	Y	#	#	#

Democrats ***Republicans***

728. HR 13655. Health Maintenance Organizations. Rogers, D-Fla., motion to suspend the rules and pass the bill to authorize $126 million for fiscal 1980-81 for federal assistance to prepaid group medical practices (HMOs) and to make certain revisions in the program. Motion agreed to 327-60: R 96-38; D 231-22 (ND 170-4; SD 61-18), Sept. 25, 1978. A two-thirds majority vote (258 in this case) is required for passage under suspension of the rules.

729. HR 12584. Health Services Research. Rogers, D-Fla., motion to suspend the rules and pass the bill to authorize $429 million in fiscal 1979-81 for the National Center for Health Services Research and the National Center for Health Statistics and to authorize a Center for Health Care Technology. Motion agreed to 306-77: R 98-34; D 208-43 (ND 153-20; SD 55-23), Sept. 25, 1978. A two-thirds majority vote (256 in this case) is required for passage under suspension of the rules.

730. HR 12370. Health Services Programs. Rogers, D-Fla., motion to suspend the rules and pass the bill to authorize $2.7 billion for family planning services and other public health programs through fiscal 1981 (except for hypertension and comprehensive health programs, which were authorized through fiscal 1982). Motion rejected 193-193: R 38-96; D 155-97 (ND 114-59; SD 41-38), Sept. 25, 1978. A two-thirds majority vote (258 in this case) is required for passage under suspension of the rules.

731. HR 9486. International Tin Buffer Stock. Bingham, D-N.Y., motion to suspend the rules and pass the bill to authorize the president to contribute 5,000 long tons of tin to the tin buffer stock in accordance with the 1976 5th International Tin Agreement to stabilize the world tin market. Motion agreed to 308-75: R 83-48; D 225-27 (ND 166-7; SD 59-20), Sept. 25, 1978. A two-thirds majority vote (256 in this case) is required for passage under suspension of the rules.

732. HR 13597. Rayburn Building Solar Collectors. Mineta, D-Calif., motion to suspend the rules and pass the bill to authorize $3 million to install solar collectors to provide a portion of the energy needs of the Rayburn House office building. Motion agreed to 332-48: R 104-27; D 228-21 (ND 163-7; SD 65-14), Sept. 25, 1978. A two-thirds majority vote (254 in this case) is required for passage under suspension of the rules.

733. HR 13488. Foreign Earned Income. Ullman, D-Ore., motion to suspend the rules and pass the bill to ease the income tax burden on Americans working aboad. Motion agreed to 282-94: R 126-3; D 156-91 (ND 89-81; SD 67-10), Sept. 25, 1978. A two-thirds majority vote (251 in this case) is required for passage under suspension of the rules.

734. S 274. Military Unionization. Stratton, D-N.Y., motion to suspend the rules and pass the bill to prohibit union activity in the U.S. armed forces. Motion agreed to 395-12: R 137-0; D 258-12 (ND 174-12; SD 84-0), Sept. 26, 1978. A two-thirds majority vote (272 in this case) is required for passage under suspension of the rules.

735. HR 9333. Hydroelectric Powerplants. Meeds, D-Wash., motion to suspend the rules and pass the bill to authorize feasibility studies of eight hydroelectric improvement projects and $151,700,000 for additional construction at three existing projects. Motion rejected 263-143: R 106-31; D 157-112 (ND 101-85; SD 56-27), Sept. 26, 1978. A two-thirds majority vote (271 in this case) is required for passage under suspension of the rules.

KEY

- Y Voted for (yea).
- ✓ Paired for.
- † Announced for.
- # CQ Poll for.
- N Voted against (nay).
- X Paired against.
- \- Announced against.
- ▮ CQ Poll against.
- P Voted "present."
- ● Voted "present" to avoid possible conflict of interest.
- ? Did not vote or otherwise make a position known.

	728	729	730	731	732	733	734	735
ALABAMA								
1 Edwards	Y	Y	Y	Y	Y	Y	Y	Y
2 Dickinson	Y	Y	N	Y	N	Y	Y	Y
3 Nichols	Y	Y	Y	Y	Y	Y	Y	N
4 Bevill	Y	Y	Y	Y	Y	?	Y	Y
5 Flippo	Y	Y	Y	Y	N	Y	Y	Y
6 Buchanan	Y	Y	Y	Y	Y	Y	Y	Y
7 Flowers	?	?	?	?	?	?	?	?
ALASKA								
AL Young	Y	Y	Y	N	N	Y	Y	Y
ARIZONA								
1 Rhodes	Y	Y	N	Y	Y	Y	Y	Y
2 Udall	Y	Y	Y	Y	Y	Y	Y	Y
3 Stump	N	N	N	Y	N	Y	Y	Y
4 Rudd	?	?	X	?	?	?	Y	Y
ARKANSAS								
1 Alexander	Y	?	?	?	?	?	Y	Y
2 Tucker	Y	Y	Y	N	Y	Y	Y	N
3 Hammerschmidt	N	Y	Y	N	Y	Y	Y	N
4 Thornton	Y	Y	Y	N	Y	Y	Y	Y
CALIFORNIA								
1 Johnson	Y	Y	N	Y	Y	Y	Y	Y
2 Clausen	Y	Y	Y	N	Y	Y	Y	Y
3 Moss	?	?	?	?	?	?	N	Y
4 Leggett	Y	Y	Y	Y	Y	Y	Y	Y
5 Burton, J.	?	?	?	?	?	?	?	?
6 Burton, P.	Y	Y	Y	Y	Y	N	Y	Y
7 Miller	?	?	✓	?	?	?	?	?
8 Dellums	Y	Y	Y	Y	Y	N	N	N
9 Stark	Y	Y	Y	Y	Y	N	N	Y
10 Edwards	Y	Y	Y	Y	Y	N	Y	Y
11 Ryan	Y	Y	Y	Y	Y	Y	Y	N
12 McCloskey	Y	?	Y	Y	Y	Y	Y	Y
13 Mineta	Y	Y	Y	Y	Y	Y	Y	Y
14 McFall	Y	Y	Y	Y	Y	Y	Y	Y
15 Sisk	Y	Y	Y	N	?	?	Y	Y
16 Panetta	Y	N	Y	Y	Y	N	Y	Y
17 Krebs	Y	N	Y	Y	Y	N	Y	Y
18 Vacancy								
19 Lagomarsino	Y	Y	N	N	Y	Y	Y	Y
20 Goldwater	N	N	N	N	Y	Y	Y	Y
21 Corman	Y	Y	Y	Y	Y	?	Y	Y
22 Moorhead	Y	Y	N	N	Y	Y	Y	Y
23 Beilenson	Y	Y	Y	Y	Y	N	N	Y
24 Waxman	Y	Y	Y	Y	Y	N	Y	Y
25 Roybal	Y	Y	Y	Y	Y	N	Y	Y
26 Rousselot	N	N	N	N	Y	Y	Y	Y
27 Dornan	N	Y	N	N	Y	Y	Y	Y
28 Burke	#	#	✓	#	#	✓	#	▮
29 Hawkins	Y	Y	Y	Y	Y	N	Y	Y
30 Danielson	Y	Y	Y	Y	Y	Y	Y	Y
31 Wilson, C.H.	Y	Y	Y	Y	Y	Y	N	Y
32 Anderson	?	?	?	?	?	?	Y	Y
33 Clawson	N	N	N	N	N	Y	Y	Y
34 Hannaford	Y	Y	Y	Y	Y	Y	Y	Y
35 Lloyd	Y	Y	Y	Y	Y	Y	Y	Y
36 Brown	Y	Y	Y	Y	Y	Y	Y	Y
37 Pettis	Y	Y	N	Y	Y	Y	Y	Y
38 Patterson	Y	Y	Y	Y	Y	N	Y	Y
39 Wiggins	Y	Y	N	Y	Y	Y	Y	Y
40 Badham	N	Y	N	N	Y	Y	Y	Y
41 Wilson, B.	Y	Y	Y	Y	Y	Y	Y	Y
42 Van Deerlin	Y	Y	Y	Y	Y	N	Y	Y
43 Burgener	Y	Y	Y	Y	Y	Y	Y	Y
COLORADO								
1 Schroeder	Y	Y	Y	Y	Y	N	Y	Y
2 Wirth	#	#	✓	#	#	✓	Y	Y
3 Evans	Y	▮	▮	▮	▮	#	Y	Y
4 Johnson	N	Y	N	Y	Y	Y	Y	Y
5 Armstrong	?	?	?	?	?	?	?	?
CONNECTICUT								
1 Cotter	Y	Y	N	Y	Y	Y	Y	N
2 Dodd	Y	Y	Y	Y	Y	Y	Y	N
3 Giaimo	Y	Y	Y	Y	Y	Y	Y	N
4 McKinney	Y	Y	N	Y	Y	Y	Y	Y
5 Sarasin	#	#	▮	#	#	#	#	#
6 Moffett	Y	Y	Y	Y	Y	N	Y	N
DELAWARE								
AL Evans	Y	N	Y	Y	Y	Y	Y	Y
FLORIDA								
1 Sikes	N	Y	N	Y	Y	Y	Y	Y
2 Fuqua	Y	Y	Y	Y	Y	Y	Y	N
3 Bennett	N	N	N	Y	Y	N	Y	N
4 Chappell	Y	Y	N	Y	Y	N	Y	Y
5 Kelly	N	N	N	N	N	Y	Y	Y
6 Young	Y	Y	N	N	Y	Y	Y	N
7 Gibbons	Y	Y	Y	Y	Y	Y	Y	N
8 Ireland	?	?	?	?	?	?	Y	Y
9 Frey	Y	Y	N	N	Y	Y	Y	N
10 Bafalis	Y	Y	N	?	Y	Y	Y	Y
11 Rogers	Y	Y	Y	Y	Y	#	Y	Y
12 Burke	Y	Y	Y	Y	Y	Y	Y	N
13 Lehman	Y	Y	Y	Y	Y	Y	Y	Y
14 Pepper	#	#	✓	#	#	✓	#	#
15 Fascell	Y	Y	Y	Y	Y	Y	Y	Y
GEORGIA								
1 Ginn	Y	Y	Y	N	Y	Y	Y	Y
2 Mathis	Y	N	Y	Y	Y	Y	Y	Y
3 Brinkley	Y	Y	Y	Y	N	N	Y	N
4 Levitas	Y	Y	Y	N	Y	Y	Y	Y
5 Fowler	Y	Y	Y	Y	Y	Y	Y	N
6 Flynt	N	N	N	Y	Y	Y	Y	Y
7 McDonald	N	N	N	N	N	Y	#	X
8 Evans	N	N	N	N	N	Y	Y	Y
9 Jenkins	Y	N	N	Y	N	Y	Y	Y
10 Barnard	N	N	Y	Y	N	Y	Y	Y
HAWAII								
1 Heftel	Y	Y	N	Y	Y	Y	Y	N
2 Akaka	Y	Y	Y	Y	Y	Y	Y	Y
IDAHO								
1 Symms	N	N	N	N	N	Y	Y	Y
2 Hansen, G.	N	N	N	N	N	Y	?	?
ILLINOIS								
1 Metcalfe	Y	Y	Y	Y	Y	Y	Y	Y
2 Murphy	Y	Y	Y	Y	Y	Y	Y	N
3 Russo	Y	Y	N	Y	Y	Y	Y	N
4 Derwinski	Y	N	N	N	N	Y	Y	Y
5 Fary	Y	Y	N	Y	Y	Y	Y	N
6 Hyde	N	Y	N	Y	Y	Y	Y	Y
7 Collins	Y	Y	Y	Y	Y	Y	Y	N
8 Rostenkowski	Y	Y	N	Y	Y	Y	Y	Y
9 Yates	Y	Y	Y	Y	Y	N	Y	N
10 Mikva	Y	Y	Y	Y	Y	N	Y	N
11 Annunzio	Y	Y	N	Y	Y	Y	Y	N
12 Crane	N	N	N	N	N	Y	Y	N
13 McClory	#	#	X	#	#	#	Y	Y
14 Erlenborn	N	Y	Y	Y	N	Y	Y	Y
15 Corcoran	Y	Y	N	Y	Y	Y	Y	Y
16 Anderson	?	?	#	#	#	#	#	#
17 O'Brien	Y	N	N	Y	Y	Y	Y	N
18 Michel	Y	Y	N	N	Y	Y	Y	N
19 Railsback	Y	Y	N	Y	Y	Y	Y	N
20 Findley	Y	Y	N	Y	Y	Y	Y	N
21 Madigan	Y	Y	Y	N	Y	Y	Y	Y
22 Shipley	?	?	✓	?	?	?	?	?
23 Price	Y	Y	N	Y	Y	Y	Y	N
24 Simon	Y	Y	Y	Y	Y	N	Y	Y
INDIANA								
1 Benjamin	Y	N	N	Y	Y	N	Y	Y
2 Fithian	Y	N	N	Y	Y	N	Y	N
3 Brademas	Y	Y	Y	Y	Y	Y	Y	Y
4 Quayle	Y	N	N	N	N	Y	Y	N
5 Hillis	Y	Y	Y	Y	Y	Y	Y	Y
6 Evans	Y	N	N	Y	N	N	Y	N
7 Myers, J.	N	Y	N	N	Y	Y	Y	Y
8 Cornwell	Y	Y	Y	Y	Y	N	Y	N
9 Hamilton	Y	Y	Y	Y	Y	Y	Y	Y
10 Sharp	Y	Y	Y	Y	Y	N	Y	N
11 Jacobs	Y	Y	Y	Y	N	N	Y	N
IOWA								
1 Leach	Y	Y	N	N	N	Y	Y	Y
2 Blouin	Y	N	N	Y	Y	Y	Y	Y
3 Grassley	Y	N	N	N	Y	Y	Y	Y
4 Smith	Y	Y	Y	Y	Y	Y	Y	Y
5 Harkin	Y	Y	Y	Y	Y	N	Y	Y
6 Bedell	Y	Y	Y	Y	Y	N	Y	Y

Democrats ***Republicans***

	728	729	730	731	732	733	734	735
KANSAS								
1 Sebelius	N	Y	N	Y	Y	Y	Y	Y
2 Keys	Y	Y	Y	Y	Y	N	Y	Y
3 Winn	Y	Y	N	Y	Y	#	Y	Y
4 Glickman	Y	N	Y	Y	Y	Y	Y	Y
5 Skubitz	Y	Y	Y	Y	N	Y	Y	Y
KENTUCKY								
1 Hubbard	Y	Y	N	Y	Y	Y	Y	Y
2 Natcher	Y	Y	N	Y	Y	N	Y	Y
3 Mazzoli	Y	Y	N	Y	Y	Y	Y	Y
4 Snyder	Y	Y	N	N	Y	N	Y	Y
5 Carter	Y	Y	Y	N	Y	Y	Y	Y
6 Breckinridge	Y	Y	Y	Y	Y	Y	Y	Y
7 Perkins	Y	Y	N	Y	Y	Y	Y	Y
LOUISIANA								
1 Livingston	N	Y	N	Y	Y	Y	Y	Y
2 Boggs	Y	Y	Y	Y	Y	Y	Y	Y
3 Treen	N	N	N	Y	N	Y	Y	Y
4 Waggonner	N	N	N	Y	Y	Y	Y	N
5 Huckaby	Y	Y	N	Y	Y	Y	Y	Y
6 Moore	Y	Y	N	Y	Y	Y	Y	Y
7 Breaux	Y	Y	N	Y	Y	Y	Y	Y
8 Long	Y	Y	Y	Y	Y	Y	Y	Y
MAINE								
1 Emery	Y	Y	N	Y	Y	N	Y	Y
2 Cohen	?	?	?	#	#	#	?	?
MARYLAND								
1 Bauman	N	N	N	N	N	Y	Y	N
2 Long	Y	Y	Y	Y	Y	Y	Y	N
3 Mikulski	Y	Y	Y	Y	Y	N	Y	N
4 Holt	N	N	N	Y	Y	Y	Y	N
5 Spellman	Y	Y	Y	Y	Y	N	Y	Y
6 Byron	Y	Y	N	Y	Y	Y	Y	Y
7 Mitchell	Y	Y	Y	Y	Y	N	N	N
8 Steers	Y	Y	Y	Y	Y	Y	Y	Y
MASSACHUSETTS								
1 Conte	Y	Y	N	Y	Y	Y	Y	N
2 Boland	Y	Y	N	Y	Y	N	Y	N
3 Early	Y	Y	Y	Y	Y	N	Y	N
4 Drinan	Y	Y	Y	Y	Y	N	N	N
5 Tsongas	Y	Y	Y	Y	Y	N	Y	Y
6 Harrington	#	#	#	#	#	▮	?	▮
7 Markey	Y	Y	Y	Y	Y	N	Y	N
8 O'Neill								
9 Moakley	Y	Y	Y	Y	Y	Y	Y	Y
10 Heckler	Y	Y	N	Y	Y	Y	Y	Y
11 Burke	Y	Y	N	Y	Y	Y	Y	Y
12 Studds	Y	Y	Y	Y	Y	N	Y	N
MICHIGAN								
1 Conyers	Y	Y	Y	Y	Y	N	N	N
2 Pursell	Y	Y	Y	N	Y	Y	Y	N
3 Brown	Y	Y	N	N	Y	Y	Y	N
4 Stockman	Y	N	N	N	N	Y	Y	N
5 Sawyer	Y	Y	N	N	Y	Y	Y	Y
6 Carr	Y	Y	Y	Y	Y	N	Y	N
7 Kildee	Y	Y	N	Y	Y	N	Y	N
8 Traxler	Y	Y	N	Y	Y	Y	Y	Y
9 Vander Jagt	Y	Y	N	Y	Y	Y	Y	Y
10 Cederberg	Y	Y	N	Y	Y	Y	Y	Y
11 Ruppe	?	?	?	?	?	?	Y	Y
12 Bonior	Y	Y	N	Y	Y	N	N	N
13 Diggs	#	#	✓	#	#	#	#	#
14 Nedzi	Y	Y	Y	Y	Y	N	Y	N
15 Ford	Y	Y	Y	Y	Y	Y	Y	Y
16 Dingell	Y	Y	Y	N	Y	N	Y	Y
17 Brodhead	Y	Y	Y	Y	Y	N	Y	N
18 Blanchard	Y	Y	Y	Y	Y	Y	Y	N
19 Broomfield	Y	Y	N	Y	Y	Y	Y	N
MINNESOTA								
1 Quie	?	?	?	?	?	?	Y	Y
2 Hagedorn	N	Y	N	Y	Y	Y	Y	Y
3 Frenzel	Y	Y	N	Y	Y	Y	Y	Y
4 Vento	Y	Y	N	Y	Y	N	Y	Y
5 Fraser	Y	Y	Y	Y	Y	N	Y	N
6 Nolan	Y	Y	Y	Y	Y	N	Y	Y
7 Stangeland	Y	N	N	N	Y	Y	Y	Y
8 Oberstar	Y	Y	N	Y	Y	N	Y	Y
MISSISSIPPI								
1 Whitten	N	Y	N	Y	N	Y	Y	Y
2 Bowen	N	Y	Y	Y	Y	Y	Y	Y
3 Montgomery	N	N	N	Y	Y	Y	Y	Y
4 Cochran	?	?	?	?	?	?	?	?
5 Lott	N	N	N	Y	Y	Y	Y	Y
MISSOURI								
1 Clay	Y	Y	Y	Y	Y	N	Y	N
2 Young	Y	Y	N	Y	Y	Y	Y	Y
3 Gephardt	Y	Y	N	Y	N	Y	Y	N
4 Skelton	Y	Y	N	Y	Y	Y	Y	Y
5 Bolling	#	#	#	#	#	#	Y	Y
6 Coleman	N	Y	Y	Y	Y	Y	Y	Y
7 Taylor	N	Y	N	N	Y	Y	Y	Y
8 Ichord	N	N	N	Y	Y	N	Y	Y
9 Volkmer	N	N	N	Y	Y	N	Y	N
10 Burlison	Y	N	N	Y	Y	N	Y	Y
MONTANA								
1 Baucus	?	?	✓	?	?	?	Y	Y
2 Marlenee	N	Y	Y	Y	Y	Y	Y	Y
NEBRASKA								
1 Thone	?	?	X	?	?	?	?	?
2 Cavanaugh	Y	Y	N	Y	Y	Y	Y	N
3 Smith	Y	Y	N	Y	Y	Y	Y	Y
NEVADA								
AL Santini	Y	Y	N	Y	Y	Y	Y	Y
NEW HAMPSHIRE								
1 D'Amours	Y	N	Y	Y	N	N	Y	Y
2 Cleveland	Y	Y	Y	Y	Y	Y	Y	Y
NEW JERSEY								
1 Florio	Y	Y	Y	Y	Y	Y	Y	N
2 Hughes	Y	N	N	Y	Y	N	Y	N
3 Howard	Y	Y	Y	Y	Y	Y	Y	Y
4 Thompson	?	?	✓	?	?	✓	Y	Y
5 Fenwick	Y	N	Y	Y	Y	Y	Y	Y
6 Forsythe	N	Y	N	Y	Y	Y	Y	N
7 Maguire	Y	Y	Y	N	Y	N	Y	N
8 Roe	Y	Y	N	Y	Y	Y	Y	N
9 Hollenbeck	Y	Y	Y	Y	Y	Y	Y	N
10 Rodino	#	✓	✓	#	#	✓	Y	N
11 Minish	Y	Y	Y	Y	Y	Y	Y	N
12 Rinaldo	Y	Y	N	Y	Y	Y	Y	Y
13 Meyner	Y	Y	Y	Y	#	#	Y	N
14 LeFante	Y	Y	Y	Y	Y	Y	Y	N
15 Patten	Y	Y	Y	Y	Y	Y	Y	N
NEW MEXICO								
1 Lujan	Y	Y	Y	Y	Y	N	Y	Y
2 Runnels	Y	N	N	N	Y	Y	Y	N
NEW YORK								
1 Pike	Y	N	N	Y	Y	N	Y	N
2 Downey	Y	Y	Y	Y	Y	Y	#	▮
3 Ambro	Y	Y	N	Y	Y	Y	Y	N
4 Lent	Y	Y	N	Y	Y	Y	Y	N
5 Wydler	Y	Y	N	Y	Y	Y	Y	N
6 Wolff	Y	Y	Y	Y	Y	Y	Y	N
7 Addabbo	Y	Y	Y	Y	Y	Y	Y	N
8 Rosenthal	Y	Y	Y	Y	Y	N	Y	Y
9 Delaney	Y	Y	N	Y	Y	Y	Y	Y
10 Biaggi	Y	Y	N	Y	Y	Y	Y	Y
11 Scheuer	Y	Y	Y	Y	Y	Y	Y	Y
12 Chisholm	#	✓	✓	#	#	X	Y	Y
13 Solarz	Y	Y	Y	Y	Y	N	Y	Y
14 Richmond	Y	Y	Y	Y	Y	N	N	N
15 Zeferetti	Y	Y	N	Y	Y	Y	Y	N
16 Holtzman	Y	Y	Y	Y	Y	N	Y	N
17 Murphy	Y	Y	Y	Y	Y	Y	?	?
18 Green	Y	Y	Y	Y	Y	Y	Y	Y
19 Rangel	Y	Y	Y	Y	Y	N	Y	N
20 Weiss	Y	Y	Y	Y	Y	N	N	Y
21 Garcia	Y	Y	Y	Y	Y	N	N	Y
22 Bingham	Y	Y	Y	Y	Y	Y	Y	Y
23 Caputo	?	?	?	?	?	?	?	?
24 Ottinger	Y	Y	Y	Y	Y	N	#	✓
25 Fish	Y	?	N	Y	Y	Y	Y	Y
26 Gilman	Y	Y	Y	Y	Y	Y	Y	Y
27 McHugh	Y	Y	Y	Y	Y	Y	Y	N
28 Stratton	Y	Y	N	N	Y	Y	Y	Y
29 Pattison	Y	Y	Y	Y	Y	Y	Y	Y
30 McEwen	Y	N	N	Y	N	Y	Y	Y
31 Mitchell	Y	Y	Y	Y	Y	Y	Y	Y
32 Hanley	Y	Y	N	Y	Y	N	Y	Y
33 Walsh	Y	Y	N	Y	Y	Y	?	?
34 Horton	Y	Y	Y	Y	Y	Y	Y	Y
35 Conable	Y	N	N	Y	N	Y	Y	Y
36 LaFalce	Y	Y	Y	Y	Y	N	Y	Y
37 Nowak	Y	Y	N	Y	Y	Y	Y	Y
38 Kemp	Y	Y	N	N	?	?	Y	Y
39 Lundine	Y	Y	Y	Y	Y	Y	Y	Y
NORTH CAROLINA								
1 Jones	Y	Y	N	Y	Y	Y	Y	N
2 Fountain	Y	N	N	N	Y	Y	Y	N
3 Whitley	Y	Y	N	Y	Y	Y	Y	N
4 Andrews	Y	Y	N	N	Y	Y	Y	N
5 Neal	Y	Y	N	N	Y	Y	Y	N
6 Preyer	Y	Y	Y	Y	Y	Y	Y	Y
7 Rose	Y	Y	N	Y	Y	Y	Y	Y
8 Hefner	Y	Y	N	N	Y	Y	Y	Y
9 Martin	Y	Y	N	N	Y	Y	Y	N
10 Broyhill	Y	Y	N	N	Y	Y	Y	Y
11 Gudger	Y	Y	N	N	Y	Y	Y	N
NORTH DAKOTA								
AL Andrews	Y	Y	Y	Y	Y	Y	Y	Y
OHIO								
1 Gradison	Y	Y	Y	Y	Y	Y	Y	Y
2 Luken	Y	Y	N	Y	Y	Y	Y	N
3 Whalen	Y	Y	Y	Y	Y	Y	Y	N
4 Guyer	Y	Y	N	Y	Y	Y	Y	Y
5 Latta	N	Y	N	N	N	Y	Y	Y
6 Harsha	Y	N	N	Y	Y	Y	Y	Y
7 Brown	Y	Y	Y	N	Y	Y	Y	Y
8 Kindness	Y	Y	N	Y	Y	Y	Y	Y
9 Ashley	Y	Y	Y	Y	Y	Y	Y	N
10 Miller	N	Y	N	▮	Y	Y	Y	Y
11 Stanton	N	Y	N	Y	N	#	Y	N
12 Devine	N	N	N	N	Y	Y	Y	Y
13 Pease	Y	N	N	Y	Y	Y	Y	N
14 Seiberling	Y	Y	Y	Y	Y	Y	Y	N
15 Wylie	Y	Y	N	Y	Y	Y	Y	Y
16 Regula	Y	Y	N	Y	N	Y	Y	Y
17 Ashbrook	N	N	N	N	N	Y	Y	N
18 Applegate	?	?	?	?	?	?	Y	N
19 Carney	Y	Y	Y	Y	Y	N	Y	Y
20 Oakar	?	?	?	?	?	?	Y	Y
21 Stokes	Y	Y	Y	Y	Y	N	Y	N
22 Vanik	Y	Y	Y	Y	Y	Y	Y	N
23 Mottl	N	N	N	N	Y	N	Y	N
OKLAHOMA								
1 Jones	#	#	#	#	#	#	Y	N
2 Risenhoover	?	?	N	N	N	Y	Y	Y
3 Watkins	Y	N	N	N	N	Y	Y	Y
4 Steed	Y	Y	N	Y	N	Y	Y	Y
5 Edwards	N	N	N	N	N	Y	Y	N
6 English	Y	N	N	N	N	Y	Y	N
OREGON								
1 AuCoin	#	#	#	?	#	#	Y	Y
2 Ullman	Y	Y	Y	Y	Y	Y	Y	Y
3 Duncan	Y	N	Y	Y	Y	Y	Y	Y
4 Weaver	Y	Y	Y	Y	Y	N	Y	Y
PENNSYLVANIA								
1 Myers, M.	Y	Y	N	Y	Y	Y	Y	N
2 Nix	Y	Y	Y	Y	Y	N	Y	Y
3 Lederer	Y	Y	N	Y	Y	Y	Y	N
4 Eilberg	?	✓	X	?	?	X	Y	N
5 Schulze	Y	Y	N	N	Y	Y	Y	Y
6 Yatron	Y	Y	N	Y	Y	Y	Y	N
7 Edgar	Y	Y	N	Y	Y	N	Y	N
8 Kostmayer	Y	Y	Y	Y	Y	N	Y	N
9 Shuster	N	Y	N	N	Y	Y	Y	Y
10 McDade	Y	Y	N	N	Y	Y	Y	N
11 Flood	?	?	X	?	?	X	Y	Y
12 Murtha	Y	Y	N	Y	Y	Y	Y	N
13 Coughlin	Y	Y	Y	Y	Y	Y	Y	N
14 Moorhead	Y	Y	Y	Y	Y	N	Y	N
15 Rooney	Y	Y	N	Y	Y	Y	Y	Y
16 Walker	Y	Y	N	N	#	#	Y	Y
17 Ertel	Y	N	N	Y	Y	Y	Y	N
18 Walgren	Y	Y	Y	Y	Y	Y	Y	N
19 Goodling, W.	Y	N	N	Y	N	Y	Y	N
20 Gaydos	Y	Y	N	Y	Y	Y	Y	N
21 Dent	Y	Y	N	Y	Y	Y	Y	N
22 Murphy	Y	Y	N	Y	Y	Y	Y	N
23 Ammerman	?	?	?	?	?	?	?	?
24 Marks	Y	Y	N	Y	Y	Y	Y	Y
25 Myers, G.	N	N	N	Y	Y	Y	Y	N
RHODE ISLAND								
1 St Germain	Y	Y	N	Y	Y	N	Y	Y
2 Beard	Y	Y	N	Y	Y	Y	Y	Y
SOUTH CAROLINA								
1 Davis	Y	N	Y	Y	Y	N	Y	N
2 Spence	Y	Y	Y	Y	Y	Y	Y	Y
3 Derrick	Y	N	Y	Y	Y	N	Y	N
4 Mann	Y	N	N	Y	Y	Y	Y	N
5 Holland	Y	Y	Y	Y	Y	Y	Y	Y
6 Jenrette	Y	N	Y	Y	Y	N	Y	N
SOUTH DAKOTA								
1 Pressler	?	?	?	?	?	?	Y	Y
2 Abdnor	N	N	N	Y	Y	Y	Y	Y
TENNESSEE								
1 Quillen	Y	Y	Y	Y	Y	Y	Y	Y
2 Duncan	Y	Y	Y	Y	Y	Y	Y	Y
3 Lloyd	Y	Y	Y	N	Y	Y	Y	Y
4 Gore	Y	Y	Y	N	Y	N	Y	Y
5 Vacancy								
6 Beard	Y	N	N	N	Y	Y	Y	Y
7 Jones	Y	Y	Y	Y	Y	Y	Y	Y
8 Ford	Y	Y	Y	Y	Y	N	Y	Y
TEXAS								
1 Hall	N	N	N	Y	Y	Y	Y	N
2 Wilson, C.	Y	Y	Y	Y	Y	Y	Y	Y
3 Collins	N	N	N	N	N	Y	Y	N
4 Roberts	N	N	N	N	Y	Y	Y	Y
5 Mattox	Y	Y	Y	Y	Y	Y	Y	N
6 Teague	?	X	X	?	?	✓	?	?
7 Archer	N	N	N	N	Y	Y	Y	Y
8 Eckhardt	?	?	?	?	?	?	Y	Y
9 Brooks	Y	Y	Y	Y	Y	Y	Y	N
10 Pickle	Y	Y	Y	N	Y	Y	Y	Y
11 Poage	N	N	N	Y	Y	Y	Y	Y
12 Wright	?	?	?	?	?	?	Y	Y
13 Hightower	Y	Y	Y	Y	N	Y	Y	Y
14 Young	Y	Y	N	Y	Y	Y	Y	Y
15 de la Garza	Y	Y	Y	Y	Y	Y	Y	Y
16 White	Y	Y	N	Y	Y	Y	Y	Y
17 Burleson	N	N	N	Y	Y	Y	Y	Y
18 Jordan	Y	Y	Y	Y	Y	Y	Y	N
19 Mahon	N	N	N	Y	Y	Y	Y	Y
20 Gonzalez	Y	Y	Y	N	Y	Y	Y	P
21 Krueger	#	✓	✓	#	#	✓	#	#
22 Gammage	▮	X	✓	#	#	✓	Y	N
23 Kazen	Y	Y	Y	Y	Y	Y	Y	Y
24 Milford	N	N	N	Y	N	Y	Y	Y
UTAH								
1 McKay	Y	N	N	N	N	N	Y	Y
2 Marriott	Y	N	N	Y	Y	Y	Y	Y
VERMONT								
AL Jeffords	Y	Y	Y	Y	Y	Y	Y	Y
VIRGINIA								
1 Trible	Y	Y	N	?	?	?	Y	Y
2 Whitehurst	Y	Y	N	Y	Y	Y	Y	Y
3 Satterfield	N	Y	N	N	N	Y	Y	Y
4 Daniel	N	Y	N	N	N	Y	Y	Y
5 Daniel	N	N	Y	Y	Y	Y	Y	Y
6 Butler	Y	Y	N	Y	N	Y	Y	Y
7 Robinson	N	Y	N	Y	Y	Y	Y	Y
8 Harris	Y	Y	Y	Y	Y	Y	Y	N
9 Wampler	Y	Y	Y	Y	Y	Y	Y	Y
10 Fisher	Y	Y	Y	Y	Y	N	Y	N
WASHINGTON								
1 Pritchard	Y	Y	Y	Y	Y	Y	Y	Y
2 Meeds	?	?	?	?	?	?	Y	Y
3 Bonker	#	#	#	#	#	#	Y	Y
4 McCormack	Y	Y	Y	Y	P	Y	Y	Y
5 Foley	Y	Y	Y	Y	Y	Y	Y	Y
6 Dicks	Y	Y	Y	Y	Y	Y	Y	Y
7 Cunningham	Y	N	N	Y	N	Y	Y	Y
WEST VIRGINIA								
1 Mollohan	Y	Y	Y	Y	Y	Y	Y	✓
2 Staggers	Y	Y	Y	Y	Y	N	Y	Y
3 Slack	Y	Y	Y	Y	Y	Y	?	Y
4 Rahall	Y	Y	Y	Y	Y	N	Y	N
WISCONSIN								
1 Aspin	Y	Y	Y	Y	Y	N	Y	N
2 Kastenmeier	Y	Y	Y	Y	Y	N	Y	Y
3 Baldus	Y	Y	N	Y	Y	Y	Y	Y
4 Zablocki	Y	Y	N	Y	Y	Y	Y	Y
5 Reuss	Y	Y	Y	Y	Y	N	Y	N
6 Steiger	Y	Y	N	Y	Y	Y	Y	Y
7 Obey	Y	Y	Y	Y	Y	N	Y	N
8 Cornell	Y	Y	N	Y	N	N	Y	N
9 Kasten	Y	N	N	Y	Y	Y	Y	Y
WYOMING								
AL Roncalio	#	#	#	#	#	?	Y	Y

Democrats ***Republicans***

KEY

- Y Voted for (yea).
- ✓ Paired for.
- † Announced for.
- # CQ Poll for.
- N Voted against (nay).
- X Paired against.
- \- Announced against.
- ▮ CQ Poll against.
- P Voted "present."
- ● Voted "present" to avoid possible conflict of interest.
- ? Did not vote or otherwise make a position known.

736. HR 12728. Susan B. Anthony Dollar Coin. Oakar, D-Ohio, motion to suspend the rules and pass the bill to authorize the minting of a new dollar coin bearing the likeness of women's suffrage leader Susan B. Anthony. Motion agreed to 368-38: R 110-26; D 258-12 (ND 180-6; SD 78-6), Sept. 26, 1978. A two-thirds majority vote (271 in this case) is required for passage under suspension of the rules.

737. S 2727. Amateur Sports. Danielson, D-Calif., motion to suspend the rules and pass the bill to authorize $30 million for fiscal 1980 for athletic training, medicine and administration, and to amend the federal charter of the United States Olympic Committee. Motion rejected 244-158: R 87-47; D 157-111 (ND 119-65; SD 38-46), Sept. 26, 1978. A two-thirds majority vote (268 in this case) is required for passage under suspension of the rules.

738. HR 12005. Justice Department Authorization. Adoption of the Collins, R-Texas, amendment to prohibit use of funds to bring action to require, directly or indirectly, the busing of students to a school other than the one nearest the student's home, except for mentally or physically handicapped students requiring special education. Adopted 235-158: R 106-26; D 129-132 (ND 72-109; SD 57-23), Sept. 26, 1978.

739. H J Res 1139. Continuing Appropriations. Passage of the joint resolution to continue appropriations for existing programs funded in the Labor-HEW-related agencies and defense appropriations bills, which were not expected to be enacted before fiscal 1979 began Oct. 1. Passed 349-30: R 108-20; D 241-10 (ND 167-6; SD 74-4), Sept. 26, 1978.

740. HR 13125. Agriculture Appropriations, Fiscal 1979. Passage of the bill to appropriate $19,699,776,000 for fiscal 1979 operations and programs of the Department of Agriculture and related agencies. Passed 328-31: R 98-22; D 230-9 (ND 156-9; SD 74-0), Sept. 26, 1978. The president had requested $19,501,727,000.

741. HR 1. Ethics in Government. Danielson, D-Calif., motion that the House resolve itself into the Committee of the Whole for consideration of the bill to require financial disclosure by high-level federal officials, including members of Congress and federal judges. Motion agreed to 365-6: R 121-4; D 244-2 (ND 169-2; SD 75-0), Sept. 27, 1978.

742. HR 1. Ethics in Government. Mazzoli, D-Ky., amendment to allow undercover intelligence agents to falsify the name of their employer and their salary in their financial disclosure reports if the president found it was necessary for national interest, and to provide for review of their reports by the director of the Office of Government Ethics under Central Intelligence Agency procedures. Rejected 53-347: R 1-133; D 52-214 (ND 47-136; SD 5-78), Sept. 27, 1978.

743. HR 1. Ethics in Government. Ryan, D-Calif., amendment to require repeal after five years of the bill's provisions requiring financial disclosure by executive branch employees and establishing an Office of Government Ethics. Rejected 138-266: R 73-63; D 65-203 (ND 31-154; SD 34-49), Sept. 27, 1978.

	736	737	738	739	740	741	742	743
ALABAMA								
1 Edwards	Y	N	Y	Y	Y	Y	N	Y
2 Dickinson	N	Y	Y	Y	?	?	N	Y
3 Nichols	Y	N	Y	Y	Y	Y	N	Y
4 Bevill	Y	N	Y	Y	Y	Y	N	Y
5 Flippo	Y	N	Y	Y	Y	Y	N	Y
6 Buchanan	Y	Y	Y	Y	Y	?	N	N
7 Flowers	?	?	?	?	?	?	?	Y
ALASKA								
AL Young	Y	Y	✓	#	?	?	▮	▮
ARIZONA								
1 Rhodes	N	Y	Y	Y	Y	Y	N	Y
2 Udall	Y	N	N	Y	Y	Y	N	N
3 Stump	N	N	Y	Y	▮	Y	N	Y
4 Rudd	Y	N	Y	Y	N	Y	N	Y
ARKANSAS								
1 Alexander	Y	Y	Y	Y	Y	Y	N	N
2 Tucker	Y	Y	N	Y	Y	Y	N	N
3 Hammerschmidt	Y	Y	Y	N	Y	N	N	N
4 Thornton	Y	Y	?	Y	Y	Y	N	?
CALIFORNIA								
1 Johnson	Y	Y	N	Y	Y	Y	N	N
2 Clausen	Y	Y	Y	Y	?	Y	N	N
3 Moss	Y	Y	?	?	?	Y	?	N
4 Leggett	N	Y	N	Y	Y	?	N	N
5 Burton, J.	?	?	?	?	?	Y	Y	N
6 Burton, P.	Y	Y	N	Y	Y	Y	Y	N
7 Miller	?	?	X	?	?	?	?	?
8 Dellums	Y	Y	N	Y	Y	Y	Y	N
9 Stark	Y	N	N	Y	#	Y	Y	N
10 Edwards	Y	?	N	Y	Y	Y	Y	N
11 Ryan	Y	Y	Y	N	Y	Y	N	Y
12 McCloskey	Y	Y	N	Y	Y	Y	N	N
13 Mineta	Y	Y	N	Y	Y	Y	N	Y
14 McFall	Y	Y	N	Y	Y	Y	N	N
15 Sisk	Y	Y	Y	Y	Y	Y	N	Y
16 Panetta	Y	N	N	Y	Y	Y	N	Y
17 Krebs	Y	N	Y	Y	Y	Y	N	Y
18 Vacancy								
19 Lagomarsino	Y	N	Y	N	N	Y	N	Y
20 Goldwater	Y	Y	Y	Y	Y	?	?	Y
21 Corman	Y	Y	N	Y	Y	Y	N	N
22 Moorhead	Y	Y	Y	Y	N	Y	N	Y
23 Beilenson	Y	N	N	Y	Y	Y	Y	N
24 Waxman	Y	Y	N	?	?	Y	N	N
25 Roybal	Y	Y	N	Y	Y	Y	Y	N
26 Rousselot	Y	Y	Y	N	N	Y	N	Y
27 Dornan	Y	Y	Y	N	Y	Y	N	Y
28 Burke	#	✓	X	#	?	?	▮	#
29 Hawkins	Y	Y	N	Y	?	Y	?	N
30 Danielson	Y	N	N	?	?	Y	N	N
31 Wilson, C.H.	N	N	?	Y	?	Y	N	?
32 Anderson	Y	Y	Y	Y	Y	Y	N	N
33 Clawson	N	N	Y	N	N	Y	N	Y
34 Hannaford	Y	Y	Y	Y	Y	Y	N	Y
35 Lloyd	Y	Y	Y	Y	Y	N	N	Y
36 Brown	Y	Y	N	Y	Y	Y	N	N
37 Pettis	Y	Y	Y	Y	Y	?	N	Y
38 Patterson	Y	Y	N	Y	Y	Y	N	N
39 Wiggins	Y	Y	N	#	?	?	N	Y
40 Badham	N	N	Y	Y	Y	Y	N	N
41 Wilson, B.	N	Y	Y	Y	?	P	N	N
42 Van Deerlin	Y	Y	N	Y	N	Y	N	N
43 Burgener	N	Y	Y	Y	Y	Y	N	N
COLORADO								
1 Schroeder	Y	N	N	#	?	Y	Y	N
2 Wirth	Y	N	N	Y	Y	Y	N	N
3 Evans	Y	Y	N	▮	?	?	N	Y
4 Johnson	Y	N	N	Y	Y	Y	N	Y
5 Armstrong	?	?	?	?	?	?	?	?
CONNECTICUT								
1 Cotter	Y	Y	Y	Y	Y	Y	N	N
2 Dodd	Y	Y	N	Y	Y	Y	N	Y
3 Giaimo	Y	Y	?	Y	Y	?	Y	N
4 McKinney	Y	Y	▮	#	?	?	▮	▮
5 Sarasin	?	#	#	#	?	?	▮	▮
6 Moffett	Y	Y	N	Y	Y	Y	Y	N
DELAWARE								
AL Evans	N	Y	Y	Y	Y	P	N	Y
FLORIDA								
1 Sikes	Y	N	✓	?	Y	Y	N	Y
2 Fuqua	Y	N	Y	Y	Y	Y	N	Y
3 Bennett	Y	N	Y	Y	Y	Y	N	N
4 Chappell	Y	N	Y	Y	Y	?	N	N
5 Kelly	Y	N	Y	Y	N	Y	N	Y
6 Young	N	N	Y	Y	N	Y	N	Y
7 Gibbons	Y	N	Y	Y	Y	Y	N	Y
8 Ireland	Y	N	?	Y	?	?	N	N
9 Frey	Y	Y	Y	Y	Y	Y	N	N
10 Bafalis	Y	Y	Y	Y	Y	Y	N	N
11 Rogers	Y	Y	N	Y	Y	Y	N	N
12 Burke	Y	N	Y	Y	Y	Y	N	Y
13 Lehman	Y	N	N	Y	Y	?	#	N
14 Pepper	#	✓	X	#	?	?	▮	▮
15 Fascell	Y	Y	N	Y	Y	Y	Y	N
GEORGIA								
1 Ginn	Y	Y	Y	Y	Y	Y	N	N
2 Mathis	Y	N	Y	Y	?	?	N	N
3 Brinkley	Y	N	Y	Y	Y	Y	N	N
4 Levitas	Y	Y	Y	Y	Y	Y	N	Y
5 Fowler	Y	N	N	Y	Y	Y	N	N
6 Flynt	N	N	Y	Y	Y	Y	N	N
7 McDonald	X	X	✓	X	?	Y	N	Y
8 Evans	Y	Y	Y	Y	#	Y	N	N
9 Jenkins	Y	N	Y	Y	#	Y	N	N
10 Barnard	Y	Y	Y	Y	Y	Y	N	Y
HAWAII								
1 Heftel	Y	Y	Y	Y	Y	?	N	Y
2 Akaka	Y	Y	N	Y	Y	Y	N	Y
IDAHO								
1 Symms	N	N	Y	N	N	Y	N	Y
2 Hansen, G.	?	?	✓	?	?	?	?	?
ILLINOIS								
1 Metcalfe	Y	Y	N	Y	Y	Y	N	N
2 Murphy	Y	Y	N	Y	Y	Y	N	N
3 Russo	Y	Y	Y	N	N	Y	N	N
4 Derwinski	Y	Y	Y	Y	N	Y	N	N
5 Fary	Y	Y	Y	Y	Y	Y	N	N
6 Hyde	Y	N	Y	N	Y	Y	N	N
7 Collins	Y	Y	N	Y	Y	?	N	N
8 Rostenkowski	Y	Y	N	Y	Y	Y	N	N
9 Yates	Y	N	N	Y	Y	Y	Y	N
10 Mikva	Y	Y	N	Y	N	Y	Y	N
11 Annunzio	Y	Y	Y	Y	Y	Y	N	N
12 Crane	N	N	✓	▮	?	?	N	Y
13 McClory	Y	Y	N	Y	Y	Y	N	Y
14 Erlenborn	Y	N	N	Y	#	Y	N	Y
15 Corcoran	Y	Y	Y	Y	Y	Y	N	Y
16 Anderson	#	#	▮	#	?	?	▮	▮
17 O'Brien	Y	Y	Y	Y	Y	Y	N	N
18 Michel	N	Y	Y	Y	Y	Y	N	N
19 Railsback	Y	Y	N	Y	?	Y	N	N
20 Findley	Y	N	N	Y	Y	Y	N	Y
21 Madigan	Y	Y	Y	Y	Y	Y	N	N
22 Shipley	?	✓	?	?	?	?	?	?
23 Price	Y	Y	Y	Y	Y	Y	N	N
24 Simon	Y	Y	N	Y	Y	?	Y	N
INDIANA								
1 Benjamin	Y	Y	N	Y	Y	Y	N	N
2 Fithian	Y	N	Y	Y	Y	Y	N	N
3 Brademas	Y	Y	N	Y	Y	Y	N	N
4 Quayle	N	Y	Y	?	?	N	N	Y
5 Hillis	Y	Y	Y	Y	Y	Y	N	N
6 Evans	Y	N	Y	Y	Y	Y	N	N
7 Myers, J.	Y	Y	Y	Y	Y	Y	N	Y
8 Cornwell	N	Y	Y	Y	Y	Y	N	N
9 Hamilton	Y	Y	Y	Y	Y	Y	N	N
10 Sharp	Y	Y	Y	Y	Y	Y	N	N
11 Jacobs	N	N	Y	Y	N	Y	N	Y
IOWA								
1 Leach	Y	Y	Y	Y	Y	Y	N	N
2 Blouin	Y	N	N	Y	Y	Y	N	N
3 Grassley	N	N	Y	Y	Y	Y	N	N
4 Smith	Y	N	N	Y	Y	Y	N	Y
5 Harkin	Y	N	?	?	?	Y	N	N
6 Bedell	Y	N	N	Y	Y	Y	N	Y

Democrats ***Republicans***

	736	737	738	739	740	741	742	743
KANSAS								
1 Sebelius	Y	Y	Y	Y	Y	?	N	Y
2 Keys	Y	N	Y	Y	Y	Y	N	N
3 Winn	N	Y	Y	Y	Y	Y	N	Y
4 Glickman	Y	Y	Y	Y	Y	Y	N	N
5 Skubitz	N	Y	Y	Y	?	Y	N	N
KENTUCKY								
1 Hubbard	Y	Y	Y	#	?	?	N	Y
2 Natcher	Y	Y	Y	Y	Y	Y	N	N
3 Mazzoli	Y	N	N	Y	Y	Y	Y	N
4 Snyder	Y	N	Y	N	Y	Y	N	N
5 Carter	Y	Y	Y	Y	Y	Y	N	Y
6 Breckinridge	Y	N	N	Y	?	Y	N	N
7 Perkins	Y	Y	N	Y	Y	Y	N	N
LOUISIANA								
1 Livingston	Y	Y	Y	Y	Y	Y	N	N
2 Boggs	Y	Y	Y	Y	Y	?	Y	N
3 Treen	Y	N	Y	Y	Y	Y	N	N
4 Waggonner	Y	Y	Y	Y	Y	Y	N	Y
5 Huckaby	Y	Y	Y	Y	Y	Y	N	N
6 Moore	Y	Y	Y	Y	Y	Y	N	N
7 Breaux	Y	Y	Y	Y	Y	Y	N	Y
8 Long	Y	N	Y	Y	Y	?	N	N
MAINE								
1 Emery	Y	Y	N	Y	Y	Y	N	N
2 Cohen	#	?	?	#	?	Y	N	?
MARYLAND								
1 Bauman	Y	N	Y	N	Y	Y	N	N
2 Long	Y	N	N	Y	Y	Y	N	N
3 Mikulski	Y	Y	Y	Y	Y	P	Y	N
4 Holt	Y	Y	Y	N	Y	Y	N	N
5 Spellman	Y	N	Y	Y	Y	Y	N	N
6 Byron	Y	Y	Y	?	?	Y	N	N
7 Mitchell	Y	Y	N	Y	Y	?	N	N
8 Steers	Y	N	N	Y	Y	Y	N	N
MASSACHUSETTS								
1 Conte	Y	Y	N	Y	Y	Y	Y	N
2 Boland	Y	N	Y	Y	Y	Y	Y	N
3 Early	Y	Y	N	Y	?	Y	N	Y
4 Drinan	Y	N	N	Y	?	Y	Y	N
5 Tsongas	Y	Y	N	Y	Y	?	N	N
6 Harrington	#	#	▮	#	?	?	Y	N
7 Markey	Y	Y	N	Y	Y	Y	N	N
8 O'Neill								
9 Moakley	Y	N	Y	Y	Y	Y	N	N
10 Heckler	Y	Y	Y	Y	N	Y	N	N
11 Burke	Y	Y	Y	Y	Y	Y	N	N
12 Studds	Y	Y	N	Y	Y	Y	N	N
MICHIGAN								
1 Conyers	Y	N	N	N	?	?	▮	N
2 Pursell	Y	Y	Y	?	?	Y	N	N
3 Brown	Y	Y	N	Y	Y	Y	N	Y
4 Stockman	Y	N	Y	Y	Y	Y	N	Y
5 Sawyer	Y	Y	Y	Y	Y	Y	N	N
6 Carr	Y	N	N	Y	Y	Y	Y	N
7 Kildee	Y	N	N	Y	Y	Y	N	N
8 Traxler	Y	N	Y	Y	Y	Y	N	N
9 Vander Jagt	Y	Y	Y	Y	Y	Y	N	Y
10 Cederberg	Y	Y	Y	Y	Y	Y	N	Y
11 Ruppe	Y	Y	Y	Y	?	?	N	Y
12 Bonior	Y	N	Y	Y	Y	Y	Y	N
13 Diggs	#	#	?	#	?	?	▮	?
14 Nedzi	Y	N	Y	Y	Y	Y	N	N
15 Ford	Y	Y	Y	Y	Y	Y	N	N
16 Dingell	Y	N	Y	Y	Y	N	N	N
17 Brodhead	Y	Y	N	Y	Y	Y	Y	N
18 Blanchard	Y	Y	Y	Y	Y	Y	N	N
19 Broomfield	Y	Y	Y	Y	Y	Y	N	Y
MINNESOTA								
1 Quie	Y	Y	N	Y	Y	Y	N	N
2 Hagedorn	Y	Y	Y	Y	Y	Y	N	?
3 Frenzel	Y	Y	N	Y	N	Y	N	Y
4 Vento	Y	N	N	Y	Y	Y	Y	N
5 Fraser	Y	Y	N	?	Y	Y	Y	N
6 Nolan	Y	Y	N	Y	Y	Y	Y	N
7 Stangeland	Y	Y	Y	Y	Y	Y	N	Y
8 Oberstar	Y	Y	N	Y	Y	Y	Y	N
MISSISSIPPI								
1 Whitten	Y	Y	Y	Y	Y	Y	N	N
2 Bowen	Y	Y	Y	Y	Y	Y	N	Y
3 Montgomery	Y	Y	Y	Y	Y	Y	N	Y
4 Cochran	?	?	?	?	?	?	?	N
5 Lott	Y	Y	Y	Y	Y	Y	N	Y
MISSOURI								
1 Clay	Y	Y	N	Y	Y	Y	N	N
2 Young	Y	Y	Y	Y	Y	Y	N	N
3 Gephardt	Y	N	Y	Y	N	Y	N	N
4 Skelton	Y	Y	Y	Y	Y	Y	N	N
5 Bolling	Y	Y	N	Y	Y	?	N	N
6 Coleman	Y	Y	Y	Y	Y	Y	N	N
7 Taylor	N	N	Y	Y	Y	Y	N	N
8 Ichord	Y	N	Y	Y	Y	Y	N	N
9 Volkmer	Y	N	N	N	Y	Y	Y	N
10 Burlison	Y	Y	Y	Y	Y	Y	Y	N
MONTANA								
1 Baucus	Y	N	N	Y	Y	Y	N	Y
2 Marlenee	Y	N	Y	Y	Y	Y	N	Y
NEBRASKA								
1 Thone	?	?	?	?	?	?	?	?
2 Cavanaugh	Y	N	N	Y	Y	Y	N	Y
3 Smith	Y	Y	?	?	Y	Y	N	N
NEVADA								
AL Santini	Y	Y	Y	Y	Y	Y	N	N
NEW HAMPSHIRE								
1 D'Amours	Y	Y	Y	Y	Y	Y	N	N
2 Cleveland	Y	N	Y	Y	N	Y	N	N
NEW JERSEY								
1 Florio	Y	N	Y	Y	Y	Y	N	Y
2 Hughes	Y	N	N	Y	Y	Y	N	Y
3 Howard	Y	Y	N	Y	Y	Y	N	N
4 Thompson	Y	Y	N	Y	Y	Y	N	N
5 Fenwick	Y	N	N	?	N	Y	N	N
6 Forsythe	N	Y	N	Y	Y	Y	N	Y
7 Maguire	Y	Y	N	Y	Y	Y	Y	N
8 Roe	Y	N	Y	Y	Y	Y	N	N
9 Hollenbeck	Y	N	Y	Y	?	Y	N	N
10 Rodino	Y	Y	N	Y	Y	Y	Y	N
11 Minish	Y	Y	N	Y	Y	Y	Y	N
12 Rinaldo	Y	N	Y	Y	Y	Y	N	N
13 Meyner	Y	Y	N	Y	Y	Y	N	Y
14 LeFante	Y	Y	Y	Y	Y	Y	N	N
15 Patten	Y	Y	N	#	Y	Y	N	N
NEW MEXICO								
1 Lujan	Y	N	Y	Y	Y	Y	N	Y
2 Runnels	Y	N	Y	Y	Y	Y	?	?
NEW YORK								
1 Pike	Y	N	N	Y	Y	Y	N	#
2 Downey	#	#	Y	Y	Y	Y	Y	N
3 Ambro	Y	Y	Y	Y	Y	Y	N	N
4 Lent	Y	Y	Y	Y	Y	Y	N	Y
5 Wydler	?	?	?	?	?	Y	N	N
6 Wolff	Y	Y	Y	?	N	Y	N	Y
7 Addabbo	Y	Y	N	Y	Y	Y	N	N
8 Rosenthal	Y	N	N	Y	?	Y	Y	N
9 Delaney	Y	N	Y	Y	Y	Y	N	N
10 Biaggi	Y	Y	Y	Y	Y	Y	N	N
11 Scheuer	Y	N	N	Y	Y	Y	Y	N
12 Chisholm	Y	Y	N	Y	Y	Y	N	N
13 Solarz	Y	Y	N	Y	Y	Y	Y	N
14 Richmond	Y	Y	N	Y	Y	Y	Y	N
15 Zeferetti	Y	Y	Y	Y	Y	Y	N	N
16 Holtzman	Y	Y	N	Y	Y	Y	Y	N
17 Murphy	?	?	?	✓	?	?	?	?
18 Green	Y	Y	N	Y	Y	Y	N	N
19 Rangel	Y	Y	N	Y	Y	Y	N	N
20 Weiss	Y	Y	N	Y	Y	Y	Y	N
21 Garcia	Y	Y	X	#	?	Y	Y	N
22 Bingham	Y	N	N	Y	?	Y	Y	N
23 Caputo	?	?	?	?	?	Y	N	Y
24 Ottinger	✓	X	X	#	?	Y	N	N
25 Fish	Y	Y	N	Y	Y	?	?	?
26 Gilman	Y	Y	N	Y	Y	Y	N	Y
27 McHugh	Y	Y	N	Y	Y	Y	N	N
28 Stratton	Y	Y	Y	Y	Y	Y	N	N
29 Pattison	Y	Y	N	Y	Y	?	N	N
30 McEwen	Y	Y	Y	Y	Y	Y	N	Y
31 Mitchell	Y	Y	Y	Y	Y	Y	N	Y
32 Hanley	Y	N	Y	Y	Y	Y	N	Y
33 Walsh	?	?	Y	Y	Y	Y	N	Y
34 Horton	Y	Y	N	Y	Y	Y	N	Y
35 Conable	Y	Y	N	Y	Y	Y	N	Y
36 LaFalce	Y	Y	N	Y	Y	?	N	Y
37 Nowak	Y	Y	N	Y	Y	Y	N	N
38 Kemp	Y	Y	?	?	?	?	?	N
39 Lundine	Y	Y	N	Y	Y	Y	N	N
NORTH CAROLINA								
1 Jones	Y	N	Y	Y	Y	Y	N	Y
2 Fountain	Y	N	Y	Y	Y	Y	N	Y
3 Whitley	Y	N	N	Y	Y	Y	Y	N
4 Andrews	Y	Y	Y	Y	Y	Y	N	N
5 Neal	N	N	Y	Y	Y	Y	N	N
6 Preyer	Y	Y	N	Y	Y	?	N	N
7 Rose	Y	Y	N	Y	Y	Y	N	N
8 Hefner	Y	N	Y	Y	Y	Y	N	N
9 Martin	Y	N	Y	Y	N	Y	N	Y
10 Broyhill	N	N	Y	Y	N	Y	N	Y
11 Gudger	Y	Y	Y	Y	Y	Y	N	N
NORTH DAKOTA								
AL Andrews	Y	N	Y	Y	Y	Y	N	N
OHIO								
1 Gradison	Y	N	Y	Y	N	Y	N	Y
2 Luken	Y	N	Y	Y	Y	Y	N	N
3 Whalen	Y	Y	N	Y	Y	Y	N	N
4 Guyer	Y	Y	Y	Y	Y	Y	N	Y
5 Latta	Y	N	Y	N	Y	?	N	N
6 Harsha	Y	N	Y	Y	Y	Y	N	N
7 Brown	Y	P	N	Y	Y	Y	N	Y
8 Kindness	Y	N	Y	N	Y	Y	N	N
9 Ashley	Y	?	N	Y	Y	Y	N	N
10 Miller	Y	N	Y	N	N	Y	N	Y
11 Stanton	N	Y	Y	Y	Y	Y	N	Y
12 Devine	N	Y	Y	Y	N	Y	N	Y
13 Pease	Y	N	Y	Y	Y	Y	Y	N
14 Seiberling	Y	N	N	Y	Y	?	Y	N
15 Wylie	Y	Y	Y	Y	Y	Y	N	N
16 Regula	Y	N	Y	Y	Y	Y	N	N
17 Ashbrook	N	N	Y	N	N	Y	N	Y
18 Applegate	Y	N	Y	Y	Y	Y	N	N
19 Carney	Y	N	N	Y	Y	Y	N	N
20 Oakar	Y	Y	Y	Y	Y	Y	N	N
21 Stokes	Y	Y	N	Y	?	?	Y	N
22 Vanik	Y	Y	Y	Y	Y	Y	N	N
23 Mottl	Y	N	Y	N	N	Y	N	N
OKLAHOMA								
1 Jones	Y	N	Y	Y	Y	Y	N	Y
2 Risenhoover	Y	N	Y	Y	Y	?	N	N
3 Watkins	Y	N	Y	Y	Y	Y	N	N
4 Steed	N	N	Y	Y	Y	Y	N	N
5 Edwards	Y	N	Y	N	Y	Y	N	N
6 English	Y	N	Y	Y	Y	Y	N	Y
OREGON								
1 AuCoin	Y	Y	N	Y	Y	Y	N	N
2 Ullman	Y	Y	N	Y	Y	Y	N	N
3 Duncan	Y	N	N	Y	Y	Y	Y	N
4 Weaver	Y	N	N	N	N	Y	N	Y
PENNSYLVANIA								
1 Myers, M.	Y	Y	Y	Y	Y	Y	N	N
2 Nix	Y	Y	N	?	?	?	N	?
3 Lederer	Y	Y	Y	Y	Y	Y	N	N
4 Eilberg	Y	Y	Y	Y	Y	Y	N	N
5 Schulze	N	Y	Y	Y	Y	Y	N	Y
6 Yatron	Y	Y	Y	Y	Y	Y	N	Y
7 Edgar	Y	N	N	Y	N	Y	N	N
8 Kostmayer	Y	N	N	Y	Y	Y	N	Y
9 Shuster	Y	N	Y	Y	Y	Y	N	Y
10 McDade	Y	N	Y	Y	Y	Y	N	Y
11 Flood	Y	Y	Y	Y	?	Y	N	Y
12 Murtha	Y	N	Y	Y	Y	Y	N	N
13 Coughlin	N	Y	Y	Y	Y	Y	N	Y
14 Moorhead	Y	Y	N	Y	Y	Y	N	N
15 Rooney	Y	Y	Y	Y	Y	Y	N	N
16 Walker	N	Y	Y	Y	?	Y	N	N
17 Ertel	Y	N	N	Y	Y	Y	N	Y
18 Walgren	Y	N	Y	Y	Y	Y	Y	N
19 Goodling, W.	Y	Y	Y	Y	Y	N	N	N
20 Gaydos	Y	N	Y	Y	Y	Y	N	N
21 Dent	Y	N	N	Y	Y	Y	N	▮
22 Murphy	N	Y	Y	Y	Y	Y	N	Y
23 Ammerman	✓	✓	?	?	?	?	?	?
24 Marks	Y	Y	N	Y	Y	Y	N	N
25 Myers, G.	Y	Y	Y	N	N	Y	N	N
RHODE ISLAND								
1 St Germain	Y	Y	N	Y	Y	Y	?	N
2 Beard	Y	Y	N	Y	Y	Y	N	N
SOUTH CAROLINA								
1 Davis	Y	Y	N	Y	?	Y	N	Y
2 Spence	Y	Y	Y	Y	Y	Y	N	N
3 Derrick	Y	Y	N	Y	Y	Y	N	N
4 Mann	Y	Y	N	?	?	Y	N	N
5 Holland	Y	Y	Y	?	Y	Y	N	Y
6 Jenrette	Y	Y	N	Y	Y	Y	Y	N
SOUTH DAKOTA								
1 Pressler	Y	Y	N	Y	Y	Y	N	Y
2 Abdnor	Y	Y	Y	Y	Y	Y	N	N
TENNESSEE								
1 Quillen	Y	Y	Y	Y	Y	Y	N	Y
2 Duncan	Y	N	Y	Y	Y	Y	N	N
3 Lloyd	Y	N	Y	Y	Y	Y	N	N
4 Gore	Y	N	N	Y	Y	Y	N	Y
5 Vacancy								
6 Beard	N	N	Y	Y	Y	Y	?	Y
7 Jones	Y	N	Y	Y	Y	Y	N	Y
8 Ford	Y	Y	N	Y	Y	Y	N	N
TEXAS								
1 Hall	Y	N	Y	Y	Y	Y	N	Y
2 Wilson, C.	Y	Y	Y	Y	Y	Y	N	N
3 Collins	N	N	Y	N	N	N	N	Y
4 Roberts	Y	N	Y	Y	Y	Y	N	Y
5 Mattox	Y	N	Y	N	Y	Y	N	Y
6 Teague	X	X	✓	?	?	?	?	?
7 Archer	Y	Y	Y	N	N	Y	N	N
8 Eckhardt	Y	Y	N	Y	Y	Y	N	N
9 Brooks	Y	Y	N	Y	Y	Y	N	N
10 Pickle	Y	Y	Y	Y	Y	Y	N	N
11 Poage	N	N	Y	?	Y	Y	N	Y
12 Wright	Y	Y	Y	Y	Y	Y	N	?
13 Hightower	Y	N	Y	Y	Y	Y	N	Y
14 Young	Y	Y	?	Y	Y	?	?	N
15 de la Garza	Y	N	Y	Y	Y	Y	N	Y
16 White	Y	N	Y	Y	Y	Y	N	Y
17 Burleson	N	N	Y	Y	Y	Y	N	Y
18 Jordan	Y	Y	N	Y	Y	Y	N	N
19 Mahon	Y	N	Y	Y	Y	Y	N	N
20 Gonzalez	Y	Y	N	Y	Y	Y	N	Y
21 Krueger	✓	✓	#	#	?	?	▮	▮
22 Gammage	Y	N	Y	X	?	Y	N	N
23 Kazen	Y	N	Y	Y	Y	Y	N	N
24 Milford	N	N	Y	N	?	Y	N	?
UTAH								
1 McKay	Y	N	Y	Y	Y	?	N	N
2 Marriott	Y	Y	Y	Y	Y	Y	N	N
VERMONT								
AL Jeffords	Y	N	N	N	Y	Y	N	Y
VIRGINIA								
1 Trible	Y	N	Y	Y	Y	Y	N	N
2 Whitehurst	Y	Y	Y	Y	Y	Y	N	Y
3 Satterfield	Y	N	Y	N	Y	Y	N	Y
4 Daniel	Y	N	Y	Y	Y	Y	N	Y
5 Daniel	Y	N	Y	N	Y	Y	N	Y
6 Butler	Y	?	Y	Y	Y	Y	N	Y
7 Robinson	Y	Y	Y	Y	Y	Y	N	Y
8 Harris	Y	N	N	Y	Y	Y	N	N
9 Wampler	Y	Y	Y	Y	Y	Y	N	Y
10 Fisher	Y	Y	N	Y	Y	Y	N	N
WASHINGTON								
1 Pritchard	Y	Y	Y	Y	Y	Y	N	N
2 Meeds	Y	Y	N	Y	Y	Y	?	N
3 Bonker	Y	Y	N	Y	Y	?	N	N
4 McCormack	Y	Y	N	Y	Y	Y	N	N
5 Foley	Y	Y	N	Y	Y	Y	N	N
6 Dicks	Y	Y	N	Y	Y	Y	N	N
7 Cunningham	Y	N	Y	N	Y	Y	N	N
WEST VIRGINIA								
1 Mollohan	✓	✓	X	✓	?	Y	N	N
2 Staggers	Y	Y	N	Y	Y	Y	N	N
3 Slack	Y	Y	?	?	?	?	?	?
4 Rahall	Y	Y	Y	Y	Y	Y	Y	Y
WISCONSIN								
1 Aspin	Y	Y	N	Y	Y	Y	?	N
2 Kastenmeier	Y	Y	N	Y	Y	Y	Y	N
3 Baldus	Y	Y	N	Y	Y	Y	N	N
4 Zablocki	Y	Y	Y	Y	Y	Y	N	N
5 Reuss	Y	Y	N	Y	Y	Y	N	N
6 Steiger	Y	Y	N	Y	Y	Y	N	Y
7 Obey	Y	N	N	Y	Y	Y	Y	N
8 Cornell	Y	N	N	Y	Y	Y	N	N
9 Kasten	Y	Y	Y	Y	?	Y	N	Y
WYOMING								
AL Roncalio	Y	Y	N	#	?	Y	N	N

Democrats ***Republicans***

744. HR 1. Ethics in Government. Gonzalez, D-Texas, amendment to remove criminal sanctions from the bill's executive branch conflict-of-interest provisions. Rejected 129-269: R 67-65; D 62-204 (ND 21-164; SD 41-40), Sept. 27, 1978.

745. HR 1. Ethics in Government. Wiggins, R-Calif., amendment to delete the provisions in the bill to require public financial disclosure by federal judges and top judicial branch employees. Rejected 75-316: R 37-94; D 38-222 (ND 24-154; SD 14-68), Sept. 27, 1978.

746. HR 1. Ethics in Government. Passage of the bill to require financial disclosure by high-level federal officials, including members of Congress and federal judges. Passed 368-30: R 120-13; D 248-17 (ND 174-10; SD 74-7), Sept. 27, 1978. A "yea" was a vote supporting the president's position.

747. HR 11733. Surface Transportation Assistance Act. Howard, D-N.J., motion that the House resolve itself into the Committee of the Whole for further consideration of the bill to authorize $66.5 billion for fiscal 1979-82 for federal assistance programs for highway construction and safety and urban mass transportation. Motion agreed to 355-6: R 124-3; D 231-3 (ND 160-2; SD 71-1), Sept. 28, 1978.

748. HR 11733. Surface Transportation Assistance Act. Goldwater, R-Calif., amendment to delete from the bill language to authorize the Federal Aviation Administration to have access to information in the National Driver Registry. Rejected 12-380: R 8-125; D 4-255 (ND 2-178; SD 2-77), Sept. 28, 1978.

749. HR 11733. Surface Transportation Assistance Act. Passage of the bill to authorize $60.9 billion for fiscal 1979-82 for federal assistance programs for highway construction and safety and urban mass transportation. Passed 367-28: R 123-9; D 244-19 (ND 169-14; SD 75-5), Sept. 28, 1978.

750. HR 3816. FTC Act Amendments. Adoption of the conference report on the bill to strengthen and expedit the Federal Trade Commission's powers for enforcing its rules and subpoenas and to authorize funds for the FTC for fiscal 1978-81. Rejected 175-214: R 15-116; D 160-98 (ND 133-46; SD 27-52), Sept. 28, 1978.

751. HR 9214. IMF-Witteveen Facility. Adoption of the conference report on the bill to authorize $1.8 billion for United States participation in the International Monetary Fund's new Witteveen Facility to assist developing nations meet balance of payments deficits. Adopted 238-138: R 68-57; D 170-81 (ND 125-47; SD 45-34), Sept. 28, 1978. A "yea" was a vote supporting the president's position.

KEY

- Y Voted for (yea).
- ✓ Paired for.
- † Announced for.
- # CQ Poll for.
- N Voted against (nay).
- X Paired against.
- \- Announced against.
- ▮ CQ Poll against.
- P Voted "present."
- ● Voted "present" to avoid possible conflict of interest.
- ? Did not vote or otherwise make a position known.

	744	745	746	747	748	749	750	751
ALABAMA								
1 Edwards	N	N	Y	Y	N	Y	N	Y
2 Dickinson	Y	N	Y	Y	N	Y	N	N
3 Nichols	Y	N	Y	Y	N	Y	X	N
4 Bevill	Y	N	Y	Y	N	Y	N	N
5 Flippo	Y	N	Y	Y	N	Y	N	Y
6 Buchanan	N	N	Y	Y	N	Y	N	N
7 Flowers	Y	N	Y	Y	N	Y	N	N
ALASKA								
AL Young	▮	#	#	?	▮	#	▮	X
ARIZONA								
1 Rhodes	Y	N	Y	Y	N	Y	N	Y
2 Udall	N	N	Y	Y	N	Y	Y	Y
3 Stump	Y	N	Y	Y	N	Y	N	N
4 Rudd	N	N	Y	Y	N	Y	N	N
ARKANSAS								
1 Alexander	Y	?	?	Y	N	Y	N	Y
2 Tucker	N	▮	Y	Y	N	Y	Y	Y
3 Hammerschmidt	Y	Y	Y	Y	N	Y	N	N
4 Thornton	?	N	Y	Y	?	?	Y	Y
CALIFORNIA								
1 Johnson	N	N	Y	Y	N	Y	N	Y
2 Clausen	N	N	Y	Y	N	Y	N	N
3 Moss	N	?	?	?	N	?	Y	?
4 Leggett	N	N	Y	?	?	?	N	Y
5 Burton, J.	N	?	Y	?	N	Y	Y	?
6 Burton, P.	?	Y	Y	Y	?	Y	Y	N
7 Miller	?	?	?	?	?	?	✓	?
8 Dellums	N	N	Y	?	N	Y	Y	N
9 Stark	N	N	Y	Y	N	Y	Y	N
10 Edwards	N	N	Y	Y	N	Y	Y	N
11 Ryan	Y	Y	N	Y	N	Y	N	Y
12 McCloskey	N	Y	Y	?	N	Y	Y	Y
13 Mineta	N	N	Y	Y	N	Y	Y	Y
14 McFall	N	N	Y	Y	N	Y	Y	Y
15 Sisk	Y	Y	N	?	N	Y	N	Y
16 Panetta	N	N	Y	Y	N	N	Y	N
17 Krebs	N	N	Y	Y	N	Y	Y	N
18 Vacancy								
19 Lagomarsino	Y	Y	Y	Y	N	Y	N	N
20 Goldwater	Y	Y	Y	?	Y	Y	N	N
21 Corman	N	Y	Y	Y	N	Y	Y	Y
22 Moorhead	Y	Y	Y	Y	N	Y	N	N
23 Beilenson	N	N	Y	Y	N	N	Y	Y
24 Waxman	N	N	Y	Y	N	Y	Y	?
25 Roybal	▮	Y	#	Y	N	Y	Y	N
26 Rousselot	Y	N	N	Y	Y	Y	N	N
27 Dornan	Y	N	Y	Y	N	Y	N	N
28 Burke	X	▮	#	?	▮	#	✓	X
29 Hawkins	N	N	Y	N	N	Y	Y	Y
30 Danielson	N	N	Y	Y	N	Y	Y	Y
31 Wilson, C.H.	?	?	N	Y	N	Y	N	Y
32 Anderson	N	N	Y	Y	N	Y	N	Y
33 Clawson	Y	Y	N	Y	N	Y	N	N
34 Hannaford	N	N	Y	Y	N	Y	Y	Y
35 Lloyd	N	N	Y	N	N	Y	N	Y
36 Brown	N	N	Y	Y	Y	Y	Y	Y
37 Pettis	Y	N	Y	?	?	?	?	?
38 Patterson	N	N	Y	Y	N	Y	Y	Y
39 Wiggins	Y	Y	N	?	N	Y	N	Y
40 Badham	Y	N	N	Y	N	Y	N	X
41 Wilson, B.	Y	N	Y	N	N	Y	N	N
42 Van Deerlin	N	N	Y	Y	N	Y	Y	Y
43 Burgener	N	Y	Y	Y	N	Y	N	N
COLORADO								
1 Schroeder	N	N	Y	Y	N	Y	N	N
2 Wirth	N	N	Y	Y	N	Y	Y	Y
3 Evans	Y	Y	N	?	N	Y	Y	Y
4 Johnson	N	N	Y	Y	N	Y	N	Y
5 Armstrong	?	?	?	?	?	?	?	?
CONNECTICUT								
1 Cotter	N	N	Y	Y	N	Y	N	Y
2 Dodd	N	N	Y	?	N	Y	N	N
3 Giaimo	N	N	Y	Y	N	N	N	Y
4 McKinney	▮	▮	#	Y	N	Y	N	Y
5 Sarasin	▮	#	#	?	▮	#	X	#
6 Moffett	N	N	Y	Y	N	N	Y	N
DELAWARE								
AL Evans	Y	N	Y	?	?	#	X	Y
FLORIDA								
1 Sikes	Y	N	N	Y	N	Y	N	Y
2 Fuqua	N	N	Y	Y	N	Y	N	N
3 Bennett	N	N	Y	Y	N	N	N	N
4 Chappell	Y	N	N	Y	N	Y	N	Y
5 Kelly	N	N	Y	Y	N	Y	N	N
6 Young	N	N	Y	Y	N	Y	N	Y
7 Gibbons	Y	Y	Y	Y	N	Y	Y	Y
8 Ireland	Y	N	Y	Y	?	?	N	N
9 Frey	N	N	Y	Y	N	Y	N	N
10 Bafalis	N	N	Y	Y	N	Y	N	N
11 Rogers	N	N	Y	Y	N	Y	Y	N
12 Burke	N	▮	Y	Y	N	Y	N	Y
13 Lehman	N	N	Y	Y	N	N	Y	Y
14 Pepper	X	▮	#	?	▮	#	✓	✓
15 Fascell	N	N	Y	Y	N	Y	Y	Y
GEORGIA								
1 Ginn	N	N	Y	Y	N	Y	N	Y
2 Mathis	N	N	Y	?	N	Y	N	N
3 Brinkley	N	N	Y	Y	N	Y	N	N
4 Levitas	N	N	Y	Y	N	Y	N	Y
5 Fowler	N	N	Y	Y	N	Y	Y	Y
6 Flynt	Y	N	Y	Y	N	Y	N	N
7 McDonald	Y	Y	N	N	N	N	N	N
8 Evans	N	N	Y	Y	N	Y	N	N
9 Jenkins	Y	Y	Y	Y	N	Y	N	N
10 Barnard	Y	N	Y	Y	N	Y	N	Y
HAWAII								
1 Heftel	N	N	Y	Y	N	Y	Y	Y
2 Akaka	N	N	Y	Y	N	Y	Y	Y
IDAHO								
1 Symms	Y	Y	N	Y	Y	Y	N	N
2 Hansen, G.	?	?	?	Y	N	Y	N	N
ILLINOIS								
1 Metcalfe	Y	N	Y	Y	N	Y	Y	?
2 Murphy	N	N	Y	Y	N	Y	N	Y
3 Russo	N	N	Y	Y	N	N	N	N
4 Derwinski	Y	N	Y	Y	N	Y	N	Y
5 Fary	Y	Y	Y	Y	N	Y	Y	Y
6 Hyde	Y	N	Y	Y	N	N	N	Y
7 Collins	N	N	Y	Y	▮	#	✓	Y
8 Rostenkowski	N	Y	N	Y	N	Y	Y	Y
9 Yates	N	N	Y	Y	N	N	Y	Y
10 Mikva	N	N	Y	Y	N	N	Y	▮
11 Annunzio	Y	Y	N	Y	N	Y	Y	Y
12 Crane	Y	Y	N	Y	N	Y	N	N
13 McClory	Y	Y	Y	Y	N	Y	N	Y
14 Erlenborn	Y	N	N	Y	N	Y	N	✓
15 Corcoran	N	N	Y	?	▮	#	X	X
16 Anderson	▮	▮	#	Y	N	Y	Y	✓
17 O'Brien	Y	Y	N	Y	N	Y	N	Y
18 Michel	N	Y	Y	Y	N	Y	N	Y
19 Railsback	N	N	Y	Y	N	Y	Y	Y
20 Findley	N	N	Y	Y	N	Y	N	Y
21 Madigan	N	N	Y	Y	?	?	X	✓
22 Shipley	?	?	?	?	?	?	✓	X
23 Price	N	N	Y	Y	N	Y	Y	Y
24 Simon	N	N	Y	Y	N	Y	Y	Y
INDIANA								
1 Benjamin	N	N	Y	Y	N	Y	N	N
2 Fithian	N	N	Y	Y	N	Y	N	?
3 Brademas	N	N	Y	Y	N	Y	Y	Y
4 Quayle	N	N	Y	N	N	Y	N	Y
5 Hillis	N	Y	Y	Y	N	Y	N	Y
6 Evans	N	N	Y	Y	N	Y	N	N
7 Myers, J.	N	N	Y	Y	N	Y	N	N
8 Cornwell	N	N	Y	?	N	Y	Y	N
9 Hamilton	N	N	Y	Y	N	Y	N	Y
10 Sharp	N	N	Y	Y	N	Y	N	Y
11 Jacobs	N	N	Y	Y	N	Y	N	Y
IOWA								
1 Leach	N	N	Y	Y	N	Y	N	Y
2 Blouin	N	N	Y	?	N	Y	N	Y
3 Grassley	N	N	Y	Y	N	Y	N	Y
4 Smith	N	N	Y	Y	N	Y	Y	Y
5 Harkin	N	N	Y	Y	N	Y	Y	N
6 Bedell	N	N	Y	Y	N	Y	Y	N

Democrats ***Republicans***

Corresponding to Congressional Record Votes 844, 845, 846, 847, 848, 849, 850, 851

	744	745	746	747	748	749	750	751
KANSAS								
1 Sebelius	Y	Y	Y	Y	N	Y	N	Y
2 Keys	N	N	Y	?	N	Y	N	Y
3 Winn	Y	Y	Y	Y	N	Y	N	Y
4 Glickman	N	N	Y	Y	Y	Y	Y	Y
5 Skubitz	?	?	?	Y	N	Y	N	Y
KENTUCKY								
1 Hubbard	N	N	Y	Y	N	Y	N	Y
2 Natcher	N	N	Y	Y	N	Y	Y	Y
3 Mazzoli	N	N	Y	Y	N	Y	N	Y
4 Snyder	Y	Y	Y	Y	N	Y	N	Y
5 Carter	Y	N	Y	Y	N	Y	N	Y
6 Breckinridge	N	Y	Y	?	N	Y	N	Y
7 Perkins	N	N	Y	Y	N	Y	Y	Y
LOUISIANA								
1 Livingston	Y	N	Y	Y	N	?	N	N
2 Boggs	Y	N	Y	Y	Y	Y	N	Y
3 Treen	Y	Y	N	Y	N	Y	N	Y
4 Waggonner	Y	Y	N	Y	N	Y	N	Y
5 Huckaby	Y	N	Y	Y	N	Y	N	N
6 Moore	Y	N	Y	Y	N	Y	N	Y
7 Breaux	Y	Y	Y	?	N	Y	N	Y
8 Long	Y	N	Y	Y	N	Y	Y	Y
MAINE								
1 Emery	N	N	Y	Y	N	Y	N	N
2 Cohen	?	■	#	Y	N	Y	N	Y
MARYLAND								
1 Bauman	Y	N	Y	Y	N	Y	N	N
2 Long	N	N	Y	Y	N	Y	Y	Y
3 Mikulski	N	N	Y	Y	N	Y	Y	N
4 Holt	Y	N	Y	Y	N	Y	N	N
5 Spellman	N	N	Y	Y	N	Y	N	Y
6 Byron	N	N	Y	Y	N	Y	N	N
7 Mitchell	N	N	Y	Y	N	Y	Y	Y
8 Steers	N	N	Y	Y	N	Y	Y	N
MASSACHUSETTS								
1 Conte	N	N	Y	Y	N	Y	Y	Y
2 Boland	N	Y	Y	Y	N	Y	Y	Y
3 Early	N	N	Y	Y	N	N	Y	?
4 Drinan	N	N	Y	Y	N	Y	Y	N
5 Tsongas	N	?	?	?	?	?	?	?
6 Harrington	N	N	Y	?	N	Y	Y	Y
7 Markey	N	N	Y	Y	N	Y	Y	N
8 O'Neill								
9 Moakley	N	N	Y	Y	N	Y	Y	Y
10 Heckler	Y	N	Y	?	N	Y	Y	Y
11 Burke	Y	N	Y	Y	N	Y	Y	Y
12 Studds	N	N	Y	Y	N	Y	Y	Y
MICHIGAN								
1 Conyers	N	■	Y	?	■	#	Y	N
2 Pursell	Y	N	Y	Y	N	Y	N	?
3 Brown	Y	N	Y	Y	N	Y	N	Y
4 Stockman	Y	N	Y	Y	■	N	N	Y
5 Sawyer	N	N	Y	Y	N	Y	X	✓
6 Carr	N	N	Y	Y	Y	Y	N	N
7 Kildee	N	N	Y	Y	N	Y	N	Y
8 Traxler	N	N	Y	Y	N	Y	N	Y
9 Vander Jagt	Y	N	Y	Y	N	Y	N	Y
10 Cederberg	N	N	Y	Y	N	Y	N	Y
11 Ruppe	N	N	Y	Y	N	Y	N	Y
12 Bonior	N	N	Y	Y	N	Y	Y	N
13 Diggs	?	■	#	?	■	#	✓	✓
14 Nedzi	N	N	Y	Y	N	Y	Y	Y
15 Ford	N	N	?	?	?	Y	✓	✓
16 Dingell	Y	N	Y	Y	N	Y	Y	Y
17 Brodhead	N	N	Y	Y	N	N	Y	Y
18 Blanchard	N	N	Y	Y	N	Y	N	Y
19 Broomfield	Y	Y	Y	Y	N	Y	N	Y
MINNESOTA								
1 Quie	N	N	Y	?	?	?	?	?
2 Hagedorn	Y	N	Y	Y	N	Y	N	Y
3 Frenzel	N	N	Y	Y	N	Y	N	Y
4 Vento	N	N	Y	Y	N	Y	Y	Y
5 Fraser	N	Y	Y	Y	N	Y	Y	Y
6 Nolan	N	N	Y	Y	N	Y	Y	N
7 Stangeland	N	N	Y	Y	N	Y	N	Y
8 Oberstar	N	N	Y	Y	N	Y	N	Y
MISSISSIPPI								
1 Whitten	Y	N	Y	Y	N	Y	N	N
2 Bowen	Y	N	Y	Y	N	Y	N	N
3 Montgomery	Y	N	Y	?	?	?	N	N
4 Cochran	N	N	Y	?	?	?	X	X
5 Lott	Y	N	Y	Y	N	Y	N	N
MISSOURI								
1 Clay	?	?	Y	?	?	Y	Y	N
2 Young	N	N	Y	Y	N	Y	N	Y
3 Gephardt	N	N	Y	Y	N	Y	Y	Y
4 Skelton	N	Y	Y	?	N	Y	N	Y
5 Bolling	N	N	Y	Y	N	Y	Y	Y
6 Coleman	N	N	Y	Y	N	Y	N	N
7 Taylor	N	Y	Y	Y	N	Y	N	N
8 Ichord	N	N	Y	Y	N	Y	N	N
9 Volkmer	N	N	Y	Y	N	Y	Y	N
10 Burlison	N	N	Y	Y	N	Y	Y	Y
MONTANA								
1 Baucus	N	N	Y	Y	N	Y	N	Y
2 Marlenee	?	N	Y	Y	Y	Y	N	N
NEBRASKA								
1 Thone	?	?	?	?	?	?	X	?
2 Cavanaugh	N	N	Y	Y	N	Y	Y	Y
3 Smith	Y	N	Y	Y	N	Y	N	Y
NEVADA								
AL Santini	N	■	Y	?	N	Y	N	N
NEW HAMPSHIRE								
1 D'Amours	N	N	Y	Y	N	Y	?	?
2 Cleveland	Y	N	Y	Y	N	Y	N	N
NEW JERSEY								
1 Florio	N	N	Y	Y	N	Y	Y	N
2 Hughes	N	Y	Y	Y	N	Y	N	Y
3 Howard	N	Y	Y	Y	N	Y	Y	Y
4 Thompson	N	N	Y	Y	N	Y	Y	Y
5 Fenwick	N	N	Y	Y	N	N	N	Y
6 Forsythe	Y	Y	N	Y	N	Y	N	Y
7 Maguire	N	N	Y	Y	N	N	Y	N
8 Roe	N	N	Y	Y	N	Y	N	Y
9 Hollenbeck	N	Y	Y	?	N	Y	Y	Y
10 Rodino	N	N	Y	Y	N	Y	Y	#
11 Minish	N	Y	Y	Y	N	Y	Y	Y
12 Rinaldo	N	N	Y	Y	N	Y	Y	Y
13 Meyner	N	■	Y	Y	N	Y	✓	Y
14 LeFante	N	■	Y	Y	N	Y	Y	Y
15 Patten	Y	N	Y	Y	N	Y	Y	Y
NEW MEXICO								
1 Lujan	Y	N	Y	Y	N	Y	N	N
2 Runnels	Y	N	Y	?	?	?	?	X
NEW YORK								
1 Pike	■	■	■	?	■	#	#	#
2 Downey	N	N	Y	Y	N	Y	Y	Y
3 Ambro	N	N	Y	?	N	Y	Y	Y
4 Lent	N	N	Y	Y	N	Y	N	Y
5 Wydler	N	N	Y	Y	N	Y	N	Y
6 Wolff	N	N	Y	Y	N	Y	N	Y
7 Addabbo	Y	N	Y	Y	N	Y	Y	Y
8 Rosenthal	N	N	Y	Y	N	Y	Y	Y
9 Delaney	N	N	N	?	N	Y	N	Y
10 Biaggi	N	N	Y	Y	N	Y	Y	Y
11 Scheuer	N	N	Y	Y	N	Y	Y	Y
12 Chisholm	N	N	Y	?	N	Y	Y	Y
13 Solarz	N	N	Y	Y	N	Y	Y	Y
14 Richmond	N	N	Y	Y	N	Y	Y	N
15 Zeferetti	Y	N	Y	Y	N	Y	N	Y
16 Holtzman	N	N	Y	Y	N	Y	Y	N
17 Murphy	?	?	?	Y	N	Y	?	Y
18 Green	N	N	Y	Y	N	Y	Y	Y
19 Rangel	N	N	Y	Y	N	Y	Y	Y
20 Weiss	N	N	Y	Y	N	Y	Y	N
21 Garcia	N	■	#	?	N	Y	Y	N
22 Bingham	N	N	Y	Y	N	Y	Y	Y
23 Caputo	?	?	?	?	?	?	?	?
24 Ottinger	N	N	Y	Y	N	Y	Y	Y
25 Fish	Y	N	Y	Y	Y	Y	N	Y
26 Gilman	N	N	Y	Y	N	Y	Y	N
27 McHugh	N	N	Y	Y	N	Y	Y	Y
28 Stratton	N	N	Y	Y	N	Y	Y	Y
29 Pattison	N	N	Y	Y	N	Y	Y	Y
30 McEwen	Y	?	Y	?	N	Y	N	Y
31 Mitchell	N	N	Y	Y	N	Y	N	Y
32 Hanley	N	N	Y	Y	N	Y	Y	Y
33 Walsh	N	N	Y	Y	N	Y	N	Y
34 Horton	Y	N	Y	Y	N	Y	N	Y
35 Conable	Y	Y	Y	Y	N	Y	N	✓
36 LaFalce	Y	N	Y	?	N	Y	Y	Y
37 Nowak	N	N	Y	Y	N	Y	Y	N
38 Kemp	N	N	Y	Y	N	Y	N	N
39 Lundine	N	N	Y	Y	N	Y	Y	Y
NORTH CAROLINA								
1 Jones	N	N	#	Y	N	Y	N	Y
2 Fountain	N	N	Y	Y	N	Y	N	N
3 Whitley	N	N	Y	Y	N	Y	N	N
4 Andrews	N	N	Y	?	N	Y	N	Y
5 Neal	N	N	Y	Y	N	N	N	Y
6 Preyer	N	N	Y	?	Y	Y	Y	Y
7 Rose	N	N	Y	Y	N	Y	N	Y
8 Hefner	N	N	Y	Y	N	Y	N	Y
9 Martin	Y	N	Y	Y	N	Y	N	N
10 Broyhill	Y	N	Y	Y	N	Y	N	Y
11 Gudger	N	N	Y	Y	■	#	■	■
NORTH DAKOTA								
AL Andrews	N	N	Y	Y	N	Y	N	Y
OHIO								
1 Gradison	Y	N	Y	Y	N	N	N	Y
2 Luken	N	N	Y	Y	N	Y	Y	Y
3 Whalen	N	N	Y	Y	N	Y	#	Y
4 Guyer	Y	Y	Y	Y	N	Y	N	Y
5 Latta	N	N	Y	Y	N	N	N	N
6 Harsha	Y	Y	Y	Y	N	Y	N	N
7 Brown	?	?	?	Y	N	Y	N	Y
8 Kindness	N	N	Y	Y	N	N	N	Y
9 Ashley	N	N	Y	Y	N	Y	Y	Y
10 Miller	N	N	Y	Y	Y	Y	N	N
11 Stanton	Y	Y	Y	Y	N	Y	N	Y
12 Devine	N	N	Y	Y	N	N	N	N
13 Pease	N	N	Y	Y	N	Y	Y	Y
14 Seiberling	N	N	Y	Y	N	Y	Y	N
15 Wylie	N	N	Y	Y	?	?	N	Y
16 Regula	N	N	Y	Y	N	Y	N	Y
17 Ashbrook	#	#	■	?	■	#	X	X
18 Applegate	N	N	Y	Y	N	Y	N	Y
19 Carney	N	?	Y	Y	N	Y	Y	Y
20 Oakar	N	N	Y	Y	N	Y	Y	N
21 Stokes	N	N	Y	?	N	Y	✓	Y
22 Vanik	N	N	Y	Y	N	N	Y	Y
23 Mottl	N	N	Y	Y	N	N	N	N
OKLAHOMA								
1 Jones	Y	N	Y	Y	N	Y	N	■
2 Risenhoover	?	N	Y	?	?	Y	?	X
3 Watkins	N	N	Y	Y	N	Y	N	N
4 Steed	Y	Y	Y	Y	N	Y	N	Y
5 Edwards	N	N	Y	Y	N	Y	?	?
6 English	N	N	Y	Y	N	Y	N	N
OREGON								
1 AuCoin	N	N	Y	Y	N	Y	N	Y
2 Ullman	Y	N	Y	Y	N	Y	N	Y
3 Duncan	Y	Y	N	Y	N	N	N	Y
4 Weaver	N	N	Y	Y	N	N	Y	N
PENNSYLVANIA								
1 Myers, M.	N	N	Y	Y	N	Y	Y	Y
2 Nix	Y	Y	Y	?	N	Y	✓	?
3 Lederer	N	N	Y	Y	N	Y	Y	✓
4 Eilberg	N	N	Y	Y	N	Y	Y	X
5 Schulze	Y	N	Y	Y	N	Y	N	N
6 Yatron	N	Y	Y	Y	N	Y	Y	Y
7 Edgar	N	N	Y	Y	N	Y	Y	N
8 Kostmayer	N	N	Y	Y	N	Y	Y	Y
9 Shuster	Y	Y	Y	Y	N	Y	N	N
10 McDade	N	N	Y	Y	N	Y	N	Y
11 Flood	N	N	Y	Y	N	Y	Y	Y
12 Murtha	Y	Y	N	Y	N	Y	Y	Y
13 Coughlin	N	N	Y	Y	N	Y	N	N
14 Moorhead	N	N	Y	Y	N	Y	✓	✓
15 Rooney	N	N	Y	Y	N	Y	Y	Y
16 Walker	N	N	Y	Y	N	Y	N	N
17 Ertel	N	N	Y	Y	N	Y	Y	Y
18 Walgren	N	N	Y	Y	N	Y	Y	N
19 Goodling, W.	Y	Y	Y	Y	N	Y	N	N
20 Gaydos	N	Y	Y	Y	N	Y	Y	N
21 Dent	Y	Y	Y	Y	N	Y	Y	N
22 Murphy	N	N	Y	Y	N	Y	Y	N
23 Ammerman	?	?	?	?	?	?	?	?
24 Marks	Y	N	Y	Y	N	Y	Y	Y
25 Myers, G.	N	N	Y	Y	N	N	Y	Y
RHODE ISLAND								
1 St Germain	N	N	Y	Y	N	Y	Y	Y
2 Beard	N	N	Y	Y	N	Y	Y	Y
SOUTH CAROLINA								
1 Davis	N	N	Y	Y	N	Y	Y	N
2 Spence	N	N	Y	Y	N	Y	N	?
3 Derrick	N	N	Y	Y	N	N	Y	Y
4 Mann	Y	Y	Y	?	N	Y	Y	Y
5 Holland	N	Y	P	?	?	?	?	?
6 Jenrette	N	Y	Y	Y	N	Y	Y	N
SOUTH DAKOTA								
1 Pressler	N	N	Y	?	N	Y	N	?
2 Abdnor	N	N	Y	Y	N	Y	N	N
TENNESSEE								
1 Quillen	Y	Y	Y	Y	Y	Y	N	N
2 Duncan	N	N	Y	Y	N	Y	N	N
3 Lloyd	Y	N	Y	Y	N	Y	N	N
4 Gore	N	N	Y	Y	N	Y	Y	N
5 Vacancy								
6 Beard	Y	N	Y	Y	N	Y	N	N
7 Jones	Y	N	Y	Y	N	Y	N	N
8 Ford	N	N	Y	Y	N	Y	Y	N
TEXAS								
1 Hall	Y	N	Y	?	N	Y	N	N
2 Wilson, C.	N	N	■	?	N	Y	Y	Y
3 Collins	Y	Y	N	N	N	N	N	N
4 Roberts	Y	N	Y	Y	N	Y	N	N
5 Mattox	Y	N	Y	Y	N	Y	Y	Y
6 Teague	✓	?	?	?	?	?	X	X
7 Archer	N	N	Y	Y	N	Y	N	N
8 Eckhardt	N	Y	Y	Y	N	Y	Y	Y
9 Brooks	Y	Y	N	Y	N	Y	Y	Y
10 Pickle	Y	N	Y	Y	N	Y	N	Y
11 Poage	Y	N	Y	Y	N	Y	?	?
12 Wright	Y	N	Y	Y	N	Y	N	Y
13 Hightower	Y	N	Y	Y	N	Y	Y	Y
14 Young	?	?	Y	?	N	Y	?	?
15 de la Garza	Y	N	Y	Y	N	Y	N	N
16 White	N	N	Y	Y	N	Y	N	Y
17 Burleson	✓	#	#	?	?	#	X	X
18 Jordan	Y	N	Y	Y	N	Y	Y	Y
19 Mahon	Y	N	Y	Y	N	Y	Y	Y
20 Gonzalez	Y	Y	N	Y	N	Y	Y	N
21 Krueger	■	■	#	?	■	#	X	✓
22 Gammage	N	N	Y	Y	N	Y	N	N
23 Kazen	Y	N	Y	Y	N	Y	N	Y
24 Milford	?	N	Y	?	N	Y	N	Y
UTAH								
1 McKay	Y	Y	Y	?	N	Y	N	Y
2 Marriott	Y	N	Y	Y	N	Y	N	■
VERMONT								
AL Jeffords	N	Y	Y	Y	N	Y	Y	Y
VIRGINIA								
1 Trible	N	N	Y	Y	N	Y	N	N
2 Whitehurst	Y	Y	Y	Y	N	Y	N	N
3 Satterfield	Y	N	Y	Y	N	Y	N	N
4 Daniel	Y	Y	Y	Y	N	Y	N	N
5 Daniel	Y	Y	N	Y	N	Y	N	N
6 Butler	Y	Y	N	?	N	Y	N	N
7 Robinson	Y	Y	Y	Y	N	Y	N	N
8 Harris	N	N	Y	Y	N	Y	Y	Y
9 Wampler	Y	Y	Y	Y	N	Y	N	N
10 Fisher	N	N	Y	Y	N	Y	Y	Y
WASHINGTON								
1 Pritchard	Y	N	Y	Y	N	Y	Y	Y
2 Meeds	N	N	Y	Y	N	Y	Y	Y
3 Bonker	N	N	Y	Y	N	Y	Y	Y
4 McCormack	N	N	Y	?	?	?	✓	?
5 Foley	N	N	Y	Y	N	Y	Y	Y
6 Dicks	N	N	Y	Y	N	Y	Y	Y
7 Cunningham	N	N	Y	Y	N	Y	N	N
WEST VIRGINIA								
1 Mollohan	N	N	Y	Y	N	Y	Y	Y
2 Staggers	N	N	Y	Y	N	Y	Y	N
3 Slack	?	?	?	?	?	?	Y	✓
4 Rahall	N	N	Y	Y	N	Y	Y	Y
WISCONSIN								
1 Aspin	N	N	Y	Y	N	Y	Y	Y
2 Kastenmeier	N	N	Y	Y	N	Y	Y	Y
3 Baldus	N	N	Y	Y	N	Y	Y	Y
4 Zablocki	N	Y	Y	Y	N	Y	Y	Y
5 Reuss	N	N	Y	Y	N	Y	Y	Y
6 Steiger	Y	Y	N	Y	N	Y	Y	Y
7 Obey	N	N	Y	Y	N	Y	Y	Y
8 Cornell	N	N	Y	Y	N	Y	Y	Y
9 Kasten	■	■	#	Y	N	Y	N	N
WYOMING								
AL Roncalio	Y	Y	N	?	N	Y	?	?

Democrats ***Republicans***

752. HR 12005. Justice Department Authorization. Seiberling, D-Ohio, amendment to require the attorney general to promulgate advisory procedures to assist the president in selecting federal district court judges on the basis of merit. Adopted 206-151: R 112-9; D 94-142 (ND 80-82; SD 14-60), Sept. 28, 1978.

753. HR 12005. Justice Department Authorization. Passage of the bill to authorize $1,657,224,000 for Justice Department operations for fiscal 1979. Passed 322-21: R 116-4; D 206-17 (ND 138-14; SD 68-3), Sept. 28, 1978.

754. HR 12934. State-Justice-Commerce-Judiciary Appropriations, Fiscal 1979. Adoption of the conference report on the bill to appropriate $8,515,354,000 for fiscal 1979 programs and operations of the Departments of State, Justice, Commerce, the federal judiciary and related agencies. Adopted 276-61: R 80-33; D 196-28 (ND 136-16; SD 60-12), Sept. 28, 1978. The president had requested $8,660,076,000.

755. HR 12934. State-Justice-Commerce-Judiciary Appropriations, Fiscal 1979. Smith, D-Iowa, motion to recede and concur in the Senate amendment to the conference report to provide $355,392,000 for obligations to international organizations such as the United Nations rather than the $327,676,000 recommended by the House Appropriations Committee. Motion rejected 143-191: R 22-95; D 121-96 (ND 100-51; SD 21-45), Sept. 29, 1978. A "yea" was a vote supporting the president's position.

756. HR 12934. State-Justice-Commerce-Judiciary Appropriations, Fiscal 1979. Smith, D-Iowa, motion that the House recede from its position and agree to the Senate amendment to the conference report to state that it is the sense of Congress that the attorney general admit into the United States 7,500 Cambodian refugees in fiscal 1979 and 7,500 in fiscal 1980 "in view of the magnitude and severity of the violations of human rights" committed by the government of Cambodia. Motion agreed to 231-105: R 68-48; D 163-57 (ND 130-21; SD 33-36), Sept. 29, 1978.

757. HR 10909. Clinical Laboratory Improvements. Adoption of the rule (H Res 1348) providing for House floor consideration of the bill to revise national standards and licensing for clinical laboratories and to revise Medicare and Medicaid reimbursement for clinical laboratory services. Adopted 328-0: R 113-0; D 215-0 (ND 149-0; SD 66-0), Sept. 29, 1978.

758. HR 14042. Defense Procurement Authorization. Downey, D-N.Y., amendment to eliminate from the authorization $209 million earmarked for the payment of naval shipbuilding contract claims. Rejected 97-187: R 28-69; D 69-118 (ND 58-71; SD 11-47), Sept. 29, 1978.

KEY

- Y Voted for (yea).
- ✓ Paired for.
- † Announced for.
- # CQ Poll for.
- N Voted against (nay).
- X Paired against.
- - Announced against.
- ▮ CQ Poll against.
- P Voted "present."
- ● Voted "present" to avoid possible conflict of interest.
- ? Did not vote or otherwise make a position known.

	752	753	754	755	756	757	758
ALABAMA							
1 Edwards	Y	Y	Y	N	Y	Y	?
2 Dickinson	N	Y	?	X	?	?	?
3 Nichols	Y	Y	Y	X	X	?	X
4 Bevill	N	Y	Y	N	N	Y	N
5 Flippo	Y	Y	Y	N	N	Y	N
6 Buchanan	Y	Y	Y	Y	Y	Y	N
7 Flowers	N	Y	Y	N	N	Y	N
ALASKA							
AL Young	✓	#	#	X	#	?	#
ARIZONA							
1 Rhodes	Y	Y	Y	?	?	?	?
2 Udall	Y	Y	#	N	Y	Y	▮
3 Stump	N	Y	N	N	N	Y	N
4 Rudd	Y	Y	N	N	N	Y	N
ARKANSAS							
1 Alexander	N	?	Y	Y	Y	Y	N
2 Tucker	N	Y	Y	▮	Y	?	#
3 Hammerschmidt	Y	Y	Y	N	N	?	?
4 Thornton	?	?	?	Y	Y	Y	N
CALIFORNIA							
1 Johnson	N	Y	Y	N	Y	Y	N
2 Clausen	Y	Y	Y	N	Y	Y	?
3 Moss	?	?	?	Y	N	Y	N
4 Leggett	N	Y	Y	Y	Y	?	N
5 Burton, J.	Y	N	?	?	?	?	?
6 Burton, P.	N	Y	Y	Y	Y	Y	Y
7 Miller	X	?	?	?	?	?	?
8 Dellums	N	N	Y	Y	Y	Y	Y
9 Stark	N	N	Y	Y	Y	Y	Y
10 Edwards	N	Y	Y	Y	Y	?	N
11 Ryan	N	Y	Y	Y	N	Y	Y
12 McCloskey	Y	Y	Y	?	?	?	?
13 Mineta	N	Y	Y	Y	Y	Y	N
14 McFall	N	Y	Y	Y	Y	Y	N
15 Sisk	?	?	?	N	Y	?	?
16 Panetta	Y	Y	N	N	Y	Y	▮
17 Krebs	N	Y	Y	N	N	Y	N
18 Vacancy							
19 Lagomarsino	Y	Y	N	N	Y	Y	N
20 Goldwater	Y	Y	N	X	?	?	?
21 Corman	N	Y	Y	Y	Y	Y	N
22 Moorhead	Y	Y	N	N	N	Y	N
23 Beilenson	N	Y	Y	Y	Y	Y	N
24 Waxman	N	Y	Y	Y	Y	Y	Y
25 Roybal	Y	N	Y	✓	Y	Y	N
26 Rousselot	Y	Y	N	N	N	Y	N
27 Dornan	Y	Y	N	N	Y	Y	N
28 Burke	X	#	#	Y	Y	Y	N
29 Hawkins	N	Y	?	Y	Y	Y	?
30 Danielson	N	Y	Y	Y	Y	Y	N
31 Wilson, C.H.	?	Y	?	N	?	Y	N
32 Anderson	N	N	Y	Y	Y	Y	N
33 Clawson	Y	Y	N	N	N	Y	N
34 Hannaford	Y	Y	Y	N	N	Y	N
35 Lloyd	N	Y	Y	Y	Y	Y	N
36 Brown	N	Y	Y	Y	Y	Y	N
37 Pettis	?	?	?	?	?	?	?
38 Patterson	N	Y	Y	N	Y	Y	N
39 Wiggins	N	Y	#	Y	N	Y	N
40 Badham	✓	#	#	X	▮	?	▮
41 Wilson, B.	Y	Y	Y	N	Y	Y	N
42 Van Deerlin	N	Y	Y	✓	?	?	?
43 Burgener	Y	Y	Y	N	N	Y	N
COLORADO							
1 Schroeder	Y	Y	N	Y	N	Y	#
2 Wirth	Y	Y	Y	#	#	?	#
3 Evans	N	▮	▮	Y	Y	Y	Y
4 Johnson	N	Y	Y	N	Y	Y	P
5 Armstrong	?	?	?	?	?	?	?
CONNECTICUT							
1 Cotter	N	Y	#	✓	#	?	X
2 Dodd	N	?	Y	Y	Y	Y	N
3 Giaimo	N	Y	?	Y	Y	Y	N
4 McKinney	N	Y	Y	Y	Y	Y	N
5 Sarasin	▮	#	#	Y	Y	Y	N
6 Moffett	Y	Y	Y	?	Y	Y	N
DELAWARE							
AL Evans	Y	Y	Y	N	Y	Y	N
FLORIDA							
1 Sikes	N	Y	Y	X	?	?	X
2 Fuqua	N	Y	Y	N	N	Y	▮
3 Bennett	Y	Y	N	N	Y	Y	N
4 Chappell	N	Y	Y	N	Y	Y	X
5 Kelly	Y	Y	N	N	N	Y	Y
6 Young	Y	Y	Y	N	Y	Y	Y
7 Gibbons	Y	Y	Y	Y	Y	?	?
8 Ireland	?	Y	?	?	?	?	?
9 Frey	Y	?	?	X	?	?	?
10 Bafalis	Y	Y	N	N	Y	Y	Y
11 Rogers	N	#	Y	Y	Y	Y	N
12 Burke	Y	Y	#	N	Y	Y	N
13 Lehman	N	Y	N	Y	Y	Y	▮
14 Pepper	X	?	#	✓	#	?	▮
15 Fascell	N	Y	Y	Y	Y	Y	N
GEORGIA							
1 Ginn	N	Y	Y	N	N	Y	N
2 Mathis	?	?	?	?	?	?	?
3 Brinkley	Y	Y	Y	N	N	Y	N
4 Levitas	N	Y	Y	N	Y	Y	N
5 Fowler	N	Y	N	N	N	Y	N
6 Flynt	N	Y	Y	Y	Y	Y	N
7 McDonald	Y	N	N	N	Y	Y	N
8 Evans	N	Y	Y	N	N	Y	▮
9 Jenkins	N	Y	N	N	N	Y	Y
10 Barnard	N	Y	N	N	N	Y	?
HAWAII							
1 Heftel	Y	N	N	N	N	Y	N
2 Akaka	N	Y	Y	Y	Y	Y	N
IDAHO							
1 Symms	Y	N	N	N	Y	Y	Y
2 Hansen, G.	Y	Y	N	N	N	Y	N
ILLINOIS							
1 Metcalfe	X	?	?	Y	Y	Y	?
2 Murphy	N	Y	Y	✓	?	?	X
3 Russo	Y	Y	Y	▮	#	?	#
4 Derwinski	Y	Y	N	Y	Y	Y	N
5 Fary	N	Y	Y	Y	Y	Y	N
6 Hyde	Y	Y	Y	N	Y	Y	N
7 Collins	N	Y	Y	✓	P	Y	✓
8 Rostenkowski	N	Y	Y	Y	Y	Y	N
9 Yates	Y	Y	Y	Y	Y	Y	#
10 Mikva	#	#	#	✓	#	?	#
11 Annunzio	N	Y	Y	Y	Y	Y	N
12 Crane	Y	#	▮	N	Y	Y	Y
13 McClory	Y	Y	Y	N	N	Y	▮
14 Erlenborn	✓	#	#	▮	#	▮	?
15 Corcoran	✓	#	#	N	Y	Y	Y
16 Anderson	✓	#	#	#	#	?	▮
17 O'Brien	Y	Y	Y	Y	N	Y	N
18 Michel	Y	Y	Y	N	N	Y	N
19 Railsback	✓	?	?	Y	Y	Y	?
20 Findley	Y	Y	Y	Y	Y	Y	N
21 Madigan	✓	?	?	?	?	Y	N
22 Shipley	X	?	?	✓	?	?	?
23 Price	N	#	#	Y	Y	Y	N
24 Simon	?	Y	Y	Y	Y	Y	N
INDIANA							
1 Benjamin	Y	Y	Y	N	Y	Y	N
2 Fithian	Y	Y	Y	N	N	Y	N
3 Brademas	N	Y	Y	Y	Y	Y	N
4 Quayle	Y	Y	?	N	Y	Y	Y
5 Hillis	Y	Y	Y	N	Y	Y	N
6 Evans	Y	N	N	N	Y	Y	Y
7 Myers, J.	Y	Y	Y	N	N	Y	N
8 Cornwell	Y	Y	Y	N	Y	?	Y
9 Hamilton	Y	Y	Y	Y	Y	Y	Y
10 Sharp	Y	Y	Y	N	Y	Y	Y
11 Jacobs	Y	Y	N	N	Y	Y	Y
IOWA							
1 Leach	Y	Y	Y	N	Y	Y	Y
2 Blouin	Y	Y	?	?	?	?	?
3 Grassley	Y	Y	Y	N	Y	Y	N
4 Smith	N	Y	Y	Y	Y	Y	?
5 Harkin	Y	?	?	?	?	?	?
6 Bedell	Y	Y	Y	Y	Y	Y	Y

Democrats ***Republicans***

	752	753	754	755	756	757	758
KANSAS							
1 Sebelius	Y	Y	Y	N	N	Y	N
2 Keys	Y	Y	Y	Y	#	#	?
3 Winn	Y	Y	Y	Y	Y	Y	N
4 Glickman	Y	Y	N	N	Y	Y	Y
5 Skubitz	Y	Y	Y	N	N	Y	N
KENTUCKY							
1 Hubbard	N	Y	Y	Y	N	Y	N
2 Natcher	N	Y	Y	Y	N	Y	N
3 Mazzoli	N	Y	Y	▮	#	?	#
4 Snyder	Y	Y	N	N	N	Y	Y
5 Carter	Y	Y	Y	N	Y	Y	N
6 Breckinridge	Y	Y	?	?	N	Y	Y
7 Perkins	N	Y	Y	Y	Y	Y	N
LOUISIANA							
1 Livingston	Y	Y	Y	N	N	Y	N
2 Boggs	N	Y	Y	Y	Y	Y	N
3 Treen	Y	Y	Y	?	N	Y	N
4 Waggonner	N	Y	Y	N	N	Y	N
5 Huckaby	Y	Y	Y	N	N	Y	?
6 Moore	Y	Y	Y	N	N	Y	N
7 Breaux	N	Y	Y	N	N	?	X
8 Long	N	Y	Y	?	N	Y	N
MAINE							
1 Emery	Y	Y	Y	N	Y	Y	N
2 Cohen	Y	Y	Y	?	?	?	?
MARYLAND							
1 Bauman	Y	N	N	N	Y	Y	Y
2 Long	Y	Y	Y	N	N	Y	Y
3 Mikulski	N	Y	Y	Y	Y	Y	Y
4 Holt	Y	Y	N	N	Y	Y	N
5 Spellman	Y	Y	Y	Y	?	Y	N
6 Byron	N	?	Y	N	Y	Y	N
7 Mitchell	N	Y	Y	✓	✓	?	✓
8 Steers	Y	Y	Y	Y	Y	Y	Y
MASSACHUSETTS							
1 Conte	Y	Y	Y	Y	Y	Y	Y
2 Boland	Y	Y	Y	Y	Y	Y	X
3 Early	?	?	?	Y	Y	Y	Y
4 Drinan	N	N	Y	Y	Y	Y	Y
5 Tsongas	?	?	?	?	?	?	?
6 Harrington	#	#	#	#	#	?	#
7 Markey	N	Y	Y	Y	Y	Y	Y
8 O'Neill							
9 Moakley	N	Y	Y	Y	Y	Y	N
10 Heckler	Y	Y	Y	?	?	?	?
11 Burke	N	Y	Y	Y	Y	Y	N
12 Studds	Y	Y	Y	Y	Y	Y	N
MICHIGAN							
1 Conyers	N	N	#	#	#	?	✓
2 Pursell	Y	Y	Y	Y	Y	Y	N
3 Brown	Y	Y	Y	N	Y	Y	N
4 Stockman	Y	Y	Y	N	Y	Y	N
5 Sawyer	✓	#	#	#	?	?	?
6 Carr	Y	Y	Y	Y	Y	Y	N
7 Kildee	Y	Y	Y	Y	Y	Y	Y
8 Traxler	N	Y	N	▮	Y	Y	▮
9 Vander Jagt	Y	Y	Y	Y	Y	Y	N
10 Cederberg	Y	Y	Y	Y	Y	Y	?
11 Ruppe	Y	Y	Y	N	N	Y	N
12 Bonior	N	Y	Y	?	Y	Y	Y
13 Diggs	X	#	#	✓	?	?	✓
14 Nedzi	?	?	?	Y	Y	Y	N
15 Ford	X	?	?	✓	?	Y	N
16 Dingell	N	?	Y	✓	?	?	?
17 Brodhead	N	Y	Y	Y	Y	Y	Y
18 Blanchard	N	Y	Y	Y	Y	Y	N
19 Broomfield	Y	Y	#	N	Y	Y	Y
MINNESOTA							
1 Quie	?	?	?	?	?	?	?
2 Hagedorn	Y	Y	Y	N	?	?	?
3 Frenzel	Y	Y	N	?	?	?	N
4 Vento	N	Y	Y	Y	Y	Y	X
5 Fraser	?	Y	?	Y	?	Y	Y
6 Nolan	N	?	Y	?	Y	Y	Y
7 Stangeland	Y	Y	Y	N	N	Y	N
8 Oberstar	Y	Y	Y	Y	Y	Y	Y
MISSISSIPPI							
1 Whitten	N	#	Y	N	N	Y	N
2 Bowen	N	Y	Y	N	N	Y	N
3 Montgomery	N	Y	Y	N	N	Y	N
4 Cochran	✓	?	?	X	?	?	?
5 Lott	Y	Y	N	N	N	Y	N
MISSOURI							
1 Clay	N	?	?	Y	Y	Y	Y
2 Young	N	Y	Y	N	Y	Y	N
3 Gephardt	Y	Y	Y	N	Y	Y	N
4 Skelton	N	?	?	N	Y	Y	?
5 Bolling	N	Y	#	Y	Y	Y	N
6 Coleman	Y	Y	N	N	N	Y	N
7 Taylor	Y	Y	N	N	N	Y	N
8 Ichord	Y	Y	N	N	N	Y	N
9 Volkmer	N	Y	Y	N	N	Y	X
10 Burlison	N	Y	Y	Y	Y	Y	N
MONTANA							
1 Baucus	Y	Y	N	N	Y	Y	?
2 Marlenee	Y	Y	Y	N	N	Y	Y
NEBRASKA							
1 Thone	✓	?	?	X	?	?	?
2 Cavanaugh	N	Y	Y	N	Y	Y	N
3 Smith	✓	?	?	N	N	Y	?
NEVADA							
AL Santini	Y	Y	Y	N	Y	Y	#
NEW HAMPSHIRE							
1 D'Amours	#	#	?	?	✓	?	?
2 Cleveland	Y	Y	N	?	?	?	?
NEW JERSEY							
1 Florio	Y	Y	Y	Y	Y	?	▮
2 Hughes	Y	Y	N	N	N	Y	Y
3 Howard	N	Y	Y	✓	#	?	▮
4 Thompson	N	Y	Y	Y	Y	Y	N
5 Fenwick	Y	Y	Y	Y	Y	Y	N
6 Forsythe	Y	Y	Y	N	N	?	▮
7 Maguire	Y	Y	Y	Y	Y	Y	Y
8 Roe	Y	Y	Y	N	Y	Y	N
9 Hollenbeck	Y	Y	Y	Y	Y	?	?
10 Rodino	X	#	#	✓	X	▮	?
11 Minish	?	?	?	N	Y	Y	Y
12 Rinaldo	Y	Y	Y	N	Y	Y	Y
13 Meyner	Y	Y	Y	Y	Y	?	N
14 LeFante	Y	Y	Y	Y	Y	Y	N
15 Patten	Y	Y	Y	Y	Y	Y	Y
NEW MEXICO							
1 Lujan	Y	Y	Y	N	N	Y	Y
2 Runnels	✓	?	?	X	X	?	✓
NEW YORK							
1 Pike	#	#	#	#	#	?	#
2 Downey	N	Y	Y	Y	Y	Y	Y
3 Ambro	Y	Y	Y	N	Y	Y	Y
4 Lent	Y	Y	Y	N	Y	Y	?
5 Wydler	Y	Y	Y	X	?	?	?
6 Wolff	N	Y	Y	N	Y	Y	Y
7 Addabbo	N	Y	Y	N	Y	Y	X
8 Rosenthal	X	Y	Y	Y	Y	?	#
9 Delaney	N	?	?	X	?	?	?
10 Biaggi	X	?	?	X	✓	?	X
11 Scheuer	Y	Y	Y	Y	Y	Y	Y
12 Chisholm	N	Y	Y	✓	✓	?	✓
13 Solarz	Y	Y	Y	Y	Y	Y	Y
14 Richmond	Y	Y	Y	✓	?	?	✓
15 Zeferetti	N	Y	Y	N	Y	Y	X
16 Holtzman	Y	N	Y	Y	N	Y	Y
17 Murphy	N	?	Y	N	Y	Y	N
18 Green	Y	Y	Y	Y	Y	Y	N
19 Rangel	N	Y	Y	Y	Y	Y	Y
20 Weiss	Y	N	Y	Y	Y	Y	Y
21 Garcia	N	Y	Y	✓	?	?	✓
22 Bingham	Y	Y	Y	Y	Y	Y	Y
23 Caputo	?	?	?	?	?	?	?
24 Ottinger	Y	Y	Y	Y	Y	?	Y
25 Fish	Y	Y	Y	N	N	?	?
26 Gilman	Y	Y	Y	N	Y	Y	Y
27 McHugh	Y	Y	Y	Y	Y	Y	Y
28 Stratton	Y	Y	Y	N	Y	Y	Y
29 Pattison	Y	Y	Y	Y	Y	Y	Y
30 McEwen	Y	Y	?	N	Y	Y	?
31 Mitchell	Y	Y	Y	N	Y	Y	N
32 Hanley	Y	Y	Y	▮	✓	Y	N
33 Walsh	Y	Y	Y	X	?	?	?
34 Horton	Y	Y	Y	N	?	?	▮
35 Conable	✓	?	?	N	Y	Y	N
36 LaFalce	N	Y	Y	Y	Y	Y	N
37 Nowak	Y	Y	Y	Y	Y	Y	Y
38 Kemp	?	?	?	N	Y	Y	N
39 Lundine	N	Y	Y	Y	Y	Y	#
NORTH CAROLINA							
1 Jones	N	Y	Y	N	N	Y	✓
2 Fountain	N	Y	N	N	N	Y	N
3 Whitley	N	Y	Y	N	N	Y	Y
4 Andrews	N	Y	Y	N	N	Y	N
5 Neal	N	Y	Y	N	Y	Y	Y
6 Preyer	N	Y	Y	Y	Y	Y	N
7 Rose	N	Y	Y	N	N	?	N
8 Hefner	N	Y	Y	N	N	Y	Y
9 Martin	Y	Y	N	N	Y	Y	N
10 Broyhill	Y	Y	Y	N	N	Y	N
11 Gudger	#	#	#	▮	#	?	▮
NORTH DAKOTA							
AL Andrews	Y	Y	Y	N	Y	Y	N
OHIO							
1 Gradison	Y	Y	Y	N	Y	Y	N
2 Luken	Y	Y	Y	N	Y	Y	N
3 Whalen	Y	Y	Y	Y	Y	Y	Y
4 Guyer	Y	Y	Y	N	Y	Y	N
5 Latta	Y	Y	N	N	N	Y	?
6 Harsha	Y	Y	N	N	N	Y	N
7 Brown	Y	Y	N	N	Y	Y	?
8 Kindness	Y	Y	Y	N	N	Y	?
9 Ashley	Y	?	Y	Y	Y	Y	N
10 Miller	Y	Y	N	N	N	Y	Y
11 Stanton	Y	Y	Y	Y	Y	Y	N
12 Devine	Y	Y	N	N	N	Y	Y
13 Pease	Y	Y	Y	Y	Y	Y	Y
14 Seiberling	Y	Y	Y	#	#	?	#
15 Wylie	Y	Y	Y	X	?	?	?
16 Regula	Y	Y	Y	N	Y	Y	N
17 Ashbrook	✓	▮	▮	N	Y	Y	Y
18 Applegate	N	Y	Y	N	N	Y	Y
19 Carney	X	?	?	✓	?	?	X
20 Oakar	Y	N	N	?	?	?	?
21 Stokes	X	?	?	✓	?	?	✓
22 Vanik	Y	Y	Y	Y	Y	Y	Y
23 Mottl	Y	N	N	N	N	Y	✓
OKLAHOMA							
1 Jones	N	N	N	N	Y	Y	N
2 Risenhoover	?	?	?	X	?	?	✓
3 Watkins	N	Y	N	N	N	Y	N
4 Steed	N	Y	Y	N	Y	Y	Y
5 Edwards	?	?	?	?	?	?	Y
6 English	N	Y	N	N	N	Y	Y
OREGON							
1 AuCoin	Y	Y	N	Y	Y	Y	Y
2 Ullman	N	#	Y	Y	Y	Y	N
3 Duncan	N	Y	Y	Y	Y	Y	N
4 Weaver	Y	N	N	Y	Y	?	Y
PENNSYLVANIA							
1 Myers, M.	N	Y	Y	Y	Y	Y	N
2 Nix	X	?	?	?	?	?	✓
3 Lederer	?	#	?	N	N	Y	N
4 Eilberg	X	?	?	?	X	?	?
5 Schulze	Y	Y	Y	N	N	Y	N
6 Yatron	Y	Y	Y	N	N	Y	▮
7 Edgar	Y	Y	Y	Y	Y	Y	Y
8 Kostmayer	Y	Y	N	N	Y	Y	Y
9 Shuster	N	Y	N	N	N	Y	Y
10 McDade	Y	Y	Y	Y	Y	Y	?
11 Flood	N	Y	Y	Y	Y	Y	X
12 Murtha	N	Y	Y	?	✓	Y	N
13 Coughlin	Y	Y	Y	N	N	Y	▮
14 Moorhead	X	#	#	✓	#	?	▮
15 Rooney	Y	#	Y	Y	Y	Y	N
16 Walker	✓	Y	N	N	Y	Y	Y
17 Ertel	Y	Y	Y	N	Y	Y	Y
18 Walgren	Y	Y	Y	Y	Y	Y	?
19 Goodling, W.	✓	Y	Y	✓	?	?	?
20 Gaydos	Y	Y	Y	N	N	Y	?
21 Dent	Y	Y	Y	X	?	?	▮
22 Murphy	N	Y	Y	N	N	Y	Y
23 Ammerman	?	?	?	?	?	?	?
24 Marks	Y	Y	Y	Y	Y	Y	Y
25 Myers, G.	Y	Y	Y	N	N	Y	Y
RHODE ISLAND							
1 St Germain	Y	Y	Y	N	Y	Y	N
2 Beard	#	#	Y	N	Y	Y	N
SOUTH CAROLINA							
1 Davis	?	Y	Y	N	N	Y	N
2 Spence	✓	?	?	N	N	Y	N
3 Derrick	N	Y	Y	Y	Y	Y	N
4 Mann	Y	Y	Y	?	?	?	?
5 Holland	?	?	?	N	Y	Y	N
6 Jenrette	N	Y	Y	N	N	Y	N
SOUTH DAKOTA							
1 Pressler	Y	Y	Y	?	?	?	?
2 Abdnor	Y	Y	Y	N	N	Y	N
TENNESSEE							
1 Quillen	Y	Y	N	N	N	Y	N
2 Duncan	Y	Y	Y	N	Y	Y	N
3 Lloyd	N	Y	Y	N	Y	Y	N
4 Gore	N	Y	Y	Y	Y	Y	Y
5 Vacancy							
6 Beard	✓	?	?	N	N	Y	N
7 Jones	N	Y	Y	N	Y	Y	N
8 Ford	N	Y	Y	?	Y	Y	N
TEXAS							
1 Hall	N	Y	Y	N	N	Y	Y
2 Wilson, C.	N	Y	Y	Y	Y	Y	N
3 Collins	Y	N	N	N	N	Y	Y
4 Roberts	N	Y	Y	N	N	Y	?
5 Mattox	N	Y	N	N	N	Y	?
6 Teague	X	?	?	X	X	?	✓
7 Archer	Y	N	N	N	N	Y	N
8 Eckhardt	N	?	Y	Y	?	Y	N
9 Brooks	N	Y	?	?	?	?	?
10 Pickle	N	Y	Y	N	Y	Y	N
11 Poage	?	?	?	?	?	?	?
12 Wright	?	?	?	?	?	?	?
13 Hightower	N	Y	Y	N	Y	Y	?
14 Young	?	?	?	?	?	?	N
15 de la Garza	N	Y	Y	N	Y	Y	N
16 White	Y	Y	Y	N	N	Y	N
17 Burleson	X	#	?	X	X	?	✓
18 Jordan	N	Y	Y	Y	Y	Y	Y
19 Mahon	N	Y	Y	?	?	?	?
20 Gonzalez	N	▮	Y	Y	Y	Y	N
21 Krueger	X	#	#	?	X	?	X
22 Gammage	Y	N	▮	▮	▮	?	✓
23 Kazen	N	Y	Y	Y	Y	Y	N
24 Milford	?	?	?	?	?	?	?
UTAH							
1 McKay	N	Y	Y	Y	N	Y	N
2 Marriott	✓	#	▮	X	#	?	▮
VERMONT							
AL Jeffords	Y	Y	Y	Y	Y	Y	▮
VIRGINIA							
1 Trible	Y	Y	?	N	Y	Y	N
2 Whitehurst	Y	Y	Y	N	Y	Y	▮
3 Satterfield	N	Y	N	N	N	Y	N
4 Daniel	Y	Y	N	N	N	Y	N
5 Daniel	Y	Y	Y	N	N	Y	N
6 Butler	N	Y	Y	N	N	Y	N
7 Robinson	N	Y	Y	N	N	Y	N
8 Harris	Y	Y	Y	Y	Y	Y	N
9 Wampler	N	Y	Y	N	Y	Y	N
10 Fisher	Y	Y	Y	Y	Y	Y	Y
WASHINGTON							
1 Pritchard	Y	#	Y	N	Y	Y	▮
2 Meeds	?	?	?	Y	Y	Y	N
3 Bonker	Y	Y	Y	Y	N	Y	Y
4 McCormack	?	?	?	Y	Y	Y	N
5 Foley	Y	Y	Y	Y	Y	Y	Y
6 Dicks	Y	Y	Y	Y	Y	Y	N
7 Cunningham	Y	Y	Y	N	Y	Y	Y
WEST VIRGINIA							
1 Mollohan	N	Y	Y	N	Y	Y	N
2 Staggers	N	?	Y	N	Y	Y	X
3 Slack	X	?	?	✓	✓	?	X
4 Rahall	Y	Y	Y	N	Y	Y	✓
WISCONSIN							
1 Aspin	N	Y	Y	Y	Y	Y	?
2 Kastenmeier	N	Y	Y	Y	Y	?	Y
3 Baldus	▮	Y	Y	Y	Y	Y	Y
4 Zablocki	Y	Y	Y	Y	Y	Y	N
5 Reuss	Y	Y	Y	Y	Y	Y	▮
6 Steiger	N	Y	N	N	Y	Y	N
7 Obey	N	Y	Y	Y	Y	Y	Y
8 Cornell	Y	Y	Y	N	Y	Y	Y
9 Kasten	Y	Y	#	N	Y	Y	Y
WYOMING							
AL Roncalio	Y	Y	Y	Y	?	Y	N

Democrats ***Republicans***

759. HR 12930. Treasury, Postal Service Appropriations, Fiscal 1979. Adoption of the conference report on the bill to appropriate $8,983,261,000 for fiscal 1979 for the Treasury, Postal Service, Executive Office of the President and various independent agencies. Adopted 247-137: R 61-71; D 186-66 (ND 134-40; SD 52-26), Oct. 4, 1978. The president had requested $9,203,261,000 in new budget authority.

760. HR 12930. Treasury, Postal Service Appropriations, Fiscal 1979. Steed, D-Okla., motion that the House recede from its disagreement and concur in the Senate amendment to provide a 5.5 percent ceiling on salary increases for federal blue-collar workers. Motion agreed to 284-111: R 109-28; D 175-83 (ND 117-62; SD 58-21), Oct. 4, 1978. A "yea" was a vote supporting the president's position.

761. HR 12930. Treasury, Postal Service Appropriations, Fiscal 1979. Steed, D-Okla., motion to table (kill) the Walker, R-Pa., motion to reconsider the votes by which action was taken on the conference report and on amendments reported in disagreement. Motion agreed to 392-4: R 136-4; D 256-0 (ND 178-0; SD 78-0), Oct. 4, 1978.

762. HR 12255. Older Americans Act. Adoption of the conference report on the bill to extend for three years the 1965 Older Americans Act and authorize $4.042 billion for various programs for elderly Americans for fiscal 1979-81. Adopted 399-3: R 134-2; D 265-1 (ND 182-0; SD 83-1), Oct. 4, 1978.

763. HR 11302. EPA Research Authorization. Adoption of the conference report on the bill to authorize $400,564,000 for research, development and demonstration programs of the Environmental Protection Agency for fiscal 1979. Adopted (thus cleared for the president) 387-15: R 130-7; D 257-8 (ND 178-3; SD 79-5), Oct. 4, 1978.

764. HR 11445. Small Business Administration. Adoption of the conference report on the bill to authorize $1.635 billion for the Small Business Administration (SBA) for fiscal 1979, $1.616 billion for 1980, $1.607 billion for 1981 and $1.943 billion for 1982; to subsidize the interest rate on SBA natural disaster relief loans; to strengthen and expand federal small business aid programs; to authorize a new type of SBA small business investment company, and to authorize $5 million for a White House conference on small business. Adopted 396-10: R 134-6; D 262-4 (ND 178-3; SD 84-1), Oct. 4, 1978.

765. HR 7843. Omnibus Judgeships Bill. Rodino, D-N.J., motion to order the previous question (thus ending debate) on the Rodino motion that the House recede and concur in the Senate amendment to the bill, *(see vote 766, below)*. Motion agreed to 285-114: R 63-74; D 222-40 (ND 151-28; SD 71-12), Oct. 4, 1978.

766. HR 7843. Omnibus Judgeships Bill. Rodino, D-N.J., motion that the House recede and concur in the Senate amendment to the bill, with an amendment stipulating the areas of agreement between the House and Senate conferees on the bill to provide for creation of 117 new federal district court judgeships (the motion was equivalent to a vote on adoption of a conference report). Motion agreed to 292-112: R 55-81; D 237-31 (ND 160-22; SD 77-9), Oct. 4, 1978. A "yea" was a vote supporting the president's position.

KEY

- Y Voted for (yea).
- ✓ Paired for.
- † Announced for.
- # CQ Poll for.
- N Voted against (nay).
- X Paired against.
- \- Announced against.
- ▮ CQ Poll against.
- P Voted "present."
- ● Voted "present" to avoid possible conflict of interest.
- ? Did not vote or otherwise make a position known.

	759	760	761	762	763	764	765	766
ALABAMA								
1 Edwards	N	N	Y	Y	Y	Y	N	N
2 Dickinson	?	?	?	?	?	?	?	?
3 Nichols	Y	Y	Y	Y	Y	Y	Y	Y
4 Bevill	Y	Y	Y	Y	Y	Y	N	Y
5 Flippo	Y	N	Y	Y	Y	Y	Y	Y
6 Buchanan	N	N	Y	Y	Y	Y	Y	Y
7 Flowers	Y	Y	Y	Y	Y	Y	Y	Y
ALASKA								
AL Young	#	N	Y	Y	Y	Y	Y	Y
ARIZONA								
1 Rhodes	Y	Y	Y	Y	Y	Y	Y	?
2 Udall	Y	Y	Y	Y	Y	Y	Y	Y
3 Stump	Y	Y	Y	Y	N	Y	N	N
4 Rudd	N	Y	Y	Y	N	Y	N	N
ARKANSAS								
1 Alexander	Y	Y	Y	Y	Y	Y	Y	Y
2 Tucker	#	Y	Y	Y	Y	Y	Y	Y
3 Hammerschmidt	N	Y	Y	Y	Y	Y	Y	Y
4 Thornton	Y	Y	Y	Y	Y	Y	Y	Y
CALIFORNIA								
1 Johnson	Y	Y	Y	Y	Y	Y	Y	Y
2 Clausen	N	N	Y	Y	Y	Y	Y	N
3 Moss	Y	?	Y	Y	?	Y	Y	Y
4 Leggett	Y	Y	Y	Y	Y	?	Y	Y
5 Burton, J.	N	?	?	Y	Y	Y	Y	Y
6 Burton, P.	Y	N	Y	Y	Y	Y	Y	Y
7 Miller	?	?	?	?	?	?	?	?
8 Dellums	Y	N	Y	#	Y	Y	Y	Y
9 Stark	Y	N	Y	Y	Y	Y	Y	Y
10 Edwards	Y	N	Y	Y	Y	Y	Y	Y
11 Ryan	Y	Y	Y	Y	Y	Y	Y	Y
12 McCloskey	Y	Y	Y	Y	Y	Y	N	Y
13 Mineta	Y	Y	Y	Y	Y	Y	Y	Y
14 McFall	Y	Y	Y	Y	Y	Y	Y	Y
15 Sisk	Y	N	Y	Y	Y	?	?	Y
16 Panetta	N	Y	Y	Y	Y	Y	N	N
17 Krebs	N	N	Y	Y	Y	Y	Y	Y
18 Vacancy								
19 Lagomarsino	N	Y	Y	Y	Y	Y	Y	N
20 Goldwater	?	Y	Y	Y	Y	Y	N	N
21 Corman	Y	Y	Y	Y	Y	N	N	Y
22 Moorhead	N	Y	Y	Y	Y	Y	Y	N
23 Beilenson	Y	Y	Y	Y	Y	N	Y	N
24 Waxman	Y	N	Y	Y	Y	Y	Y	Y
25 Roybal	Y	Y	Y	Y	Y	#	Y	Y
26 Rousselot	N	Y	Y	Y	Y	Y	N	N
27 Dornan	N	Y	Y	Y	Y	Y	N	N
28 Burke	#	#	#	#	#	#	?	#
29 Hawkins	Y	N	Y	Y	Y	?	Y	Y
30 Danielson	Y	Y	Y	Y	Y	Y	Y	Y
31 Wilson, C.H.	Y	N	Y	Y	?	Y	Y	N
32 Anderson	Y	N	Y	Y	Y	Y	N	N
33 Clawson	N	Y	Y	Y	Y	Y	N	N
34 Hannaford	Y	N	Y	Y	Y	Y	Y	Y
35 Lloyd	Y	Y	Y	Y	Y	Y	Y	Y
36 Brown	Y	Y	Y	Y	Y	Y	Y	Y
37 Pettis	?	?	?	?	?	?	?	?
38 Patterson	Y	Y	Y	Y	Y	Y	?	Y
39 Wiggins	#	Y	Y	#	#	Y	Y	Y
40 Badham	N	Y	Y	Y	Y	Y	Y	N
41 Wilson, B.	Y	N	Y	Y	Y	Y	Y	Y
42 Van Deerlin	Y	?	?	Y	Y	Y	N	Y
43 Burgener	Y	Y	Y	Y	Y	Y	Y	Y
COLORADO								
1 Schroeder	N	N	Y	Y	Y	Y	Y	Y
2 Wirth	N	N	Y	Y	Y	Y	Y	Y
3 Evans	Y	Y	Y	Y	Y	Y	Y	Y
4 Johnson	Y	Y	Y	Y	Y	Y	Y	Y
5 Armstrong	N	Y	Y	Y	Y	Y	N	N
CONNECTICUT								
1 Cotter	Y	Y	Y	Y	Y	Y	Y	Y
2 Dodd	N	Y	Y	Y	Y	Y	Y	Y
3 Giaimo	N	Y	Y	Y	Y	Y	?	?
4 McKinney	Y	Y	Y	Y	Y	Y	Y	Y
5 Sarasin	▮	#	#	#	#	#	?	#
6 Moffett	N	N	Y	Y	Y	Y	Y	Y
DELAWARE								
AL Evans	N	Y	Y	Y	Y	Y	N	N
FLORIDA								
1 Sikes	Y	N	Y	Y	Y	Y	Y	Y
2 Fuqua	Y	Y	Y	Y	Y	Y	Y	Y
3 Bennett	Y	Y	Y	Y	Y	Y	N	Y
4 Chappell	?	?	?	Y	Y	Y	Y	Y
5 Kelly	N	Y	Y	Y	N	N	N	N
6 Young	N	Y	Y	Y	Y	Y	Y	Y
7 Gibbons	N	Y	Y	Y	Y	Y	Y	Y
8 Ireland	Y	Y	?	?	Y	Y	Y	Y
9 Frey	Y	Y	Y	Y	Y	Y	Y	Y
10 Bafalis	N	Y	Y	Y	Y	Y	Y	Y
11 Rogers	Y	Y	Y	Y	Y	Y	Y	Y
12 Burke	Y	Y	Y	Y	Y	Y	Y	Y
13 Lehman	N	#	Y	Y	Y	Y	Y	Y
14 Pepper	Y	Y	Y	Y	Y	Y	Y	Y
15 Fascell	Y	Y	Y	Y	Y	Y	Y	Y
GEORGIA								
1 Ginn	Y	Y	Y	Y	Y	Y	Y	Y
2 Mathis	N	N	Y	Y	Y	Y	Y	Y
3 Brinkley	N	N	Y	Y	Y	Y	N	Y
4 Levitas	N	N	Y	Y	Y	Y	N	Y
5 Fowler	Y	Y	Y	Y	Y	Y	Y	Y
6 Flynt	Y	Y	Y	Y	Y	Y	Y	Y
7 McDonald	N	Y	Y	N	N	N	N	N
8 Evans	N	N	Y	Y	Y	Y	Y	Y
9 Jenkins	N	Y	Y	Y	Y	Y	N	Y
10 Barnard	N	Y	Y	Y	Y	Y	Y	Y
HAWAII								
1 Heftel	Y	Y	Y	Y	Y	Y	Y	Y
2 Akaka	Y	N	Y	Y	Y	Y	Y	Y
IDAHO								
1 Symms	N	Y	Y	Y	N	N	N	N
2 Hansen, G.	N	Y	Y	Y	N	Y	N	N
ILLINOIS								
1 Metcalfe	Y	N	Y	Y	Y	Y	Y	Y
2 Murphy	?	Y	Y	Y	Y	Y	Y	Y
3 Russo	N	Y	Y	Y	Y	Y	Y	Y
4 Derwinski	Y	Y	Y	Y	Y	Y	N	N
5 Fary	Y	Y	Y	Y	Y	Y	Y	Y
6 Hyde	Y	Y	Y	Y	Y	Y	N	N
7 Collins	Y	N	Y	Y	Y	Y	Y	Y
8 Rostenkowski	Y	Y	Y	Y	Y	Y	Y	Y
9 Yates	Y	Y	Y	Y	Y	Y	Y	Y
10 Mikva	N	Y	Y	#	Y	Y	?	?
11 Annunzio	Y	Y	Y	Y	Y	Y	Y	Y
12 Crane	N	Y	Y	N	N	N	N	N
13 McClory	N	Y	Y	Y	Y	Y	N	N
14 Erlenborn	Y	Y	Y	Y	Y	Y	Y	N
15 Corcoran	Y	Y	Y	Y	Y	Y	N	N
16 Anderson	Y	Y	Y	Y	Y	Y	Y	Y
17 O'Brien	Y	Y	Y	Y	Y	Y	N	Y
18 Michel	Y	Y	Y	Y	Y	Y	N	N
19 Railsback	N	N	Y	?	Y	Y	Y	Y
20 Findley	Y	Y	Y	Y	Y	Y	N	N
21 Madigan	Y	Y	Y	Y	Y	Y	N	Y
22 Shipley	?	?	?	?	?	?	?	?
23 Price	Y	Y	Y	Y	Y	Y	Y	Y
24 Simon	N	Y	Y	Y	Y	?	Y	Y
INDIANA								
1 Benjamin	Y	Y	Y	Y	Y	Y	Y	Y
2 Fithian	Y	Y	Y	Y	Y	Y	Y	Y
3 Brademas	Y	Y	Y	Y	Y	Y	Y	Y
4 Quayle	N	Y	Y	Y	Y	Y	N	Y
5 Hillis	?	?	Y	Y	Y	Y	N	N
6 Evans	N	Y	Y	Y	N	Y	Y	Y
7 Myers, J.	N	Y	Y	Y	Y	Y	N	N
8 Cornwell	#	#	#	#	#	#	?	#
9 Hamilton	Y	Y	Y	Y	Y	Y	N	Y
10 Sharp	N	Y	Y	Y	Y	Y	N	Y
11 Jacobs	N	Y	Y	Y	Y	N	N	N
IOWA								
1 Leach	N	N	Y	Y	Y	Y	Y	Y
2 Blouin	?	?	?	?	?	?	?	✓
3 Grassley	N	Y	Y	Y	Y	Y	N	N
4 Smith	Y	N	Y	Y	Y	Y	Y	Y
5 Harkin	?	?	?	Y	Y	Y	N	Y
6 Bedell	Y	Y	Y	Y	Y	Y	Y	Y

Democrats ***Republicans***

Corresponding to Congressional Record Votes 860, 861, 862, 863, 864, 865, 866, 867

	759	760	761	762	763	764	765	766
KANSAS								
1 Sebelius	N	Y	Y	Y	Y	Y	N	N
2 Keys	N	N	Y	Y	Y	Y	N	N
3 Winn	N	Y	Y	#	Y	Y	Y	N
4 Glickman	N	Y	Y	Y	Y	Y	N	N
5 Skubitz	Y	Y	Y	Y	Y	Y	N	N
KENTUCKY								
1 Hubbard	Y	N	Y	Y	Y	Y	Y	Y
2 Natcher	Y	Y	Y	Y	Y	Y	Y	Y
3 Mazzoli	Y	Y	Y	Y	Y	Y	Y	Y
4 Snyder	N	Y	Y	Y	Y	Y	Y	Y
5 Carter	Y	Y	Y	Y	Y	Y	N	Y
6 Breckinridge	Y	Y	Y	Y	Y	Y	Y	Y
7 Perkins	Y	Y	Y	Y	Y	Y	Y	Y
LOUISIANA								
1 Livingston	N	Y	Y	Y	Y	Y	N	N
2 Boggs	Y	N	Y	Y	Y	Y	Y	Y
3 Treen	N	Y	Y	Y	Y	Y	N	N
4 Waggonner	Y	Y	Y	Y	N	Y	Y	Y
5 Huckaby	Y	Y	Y	Y	Y	Y	Y	Y
6 Moore	N	Y	Y	Y	Y	Y	Y	Y
7 Breaux	Y	Y	Y	Y	Y	Y	Y	Y
8 Long	Y	Y	Y	Y	Y	Y	Y	Y
MAINE								
1 Emery	Y	Y	Y	Y	Y	Y	Y	Y
2 Cohen	Y	Y	Y	Y	Y	Y	Y	Y
MARYLAND								
1 Bauman	N	Y	N	Y	Y	Y	N	N
2 Long	Y	Y	Y	Y	Y	Y	Y	Y
3 Mikulski	Y	N	Y	Y	Y	Y	Y	?
4 Holt	N	N	Y	Y	Y	Y	N	N
5 Spellman	Y	N	#	Y	Y	Y	Y	Y
6 Byron	?	N	Y	Y	Y	Y	N	N
7 Mitchell	Y	N	Y	Y	Y	Y	Y	Y
8 Steers	Y	N	N	Y	#	Y	Y	Y
MASSACHUSETTS								
1 Conte	Y	Y	Y	Y	Y	Y	Y	Y
2 Boland	Y	Y	Y	Y	Y	Y	Y	Y
3 Early	Y	Y	Y	Y	Y	Y	Y	Y
4 Drinan	Y	Y	Y	Y	Y	Y	Y	Y
5 Tsongas	?	?	?	?	?	?	?	?
6 Harrington	#	Y	Y	Y	#	Y	Y	Y
7 Markey	Y	Y	Y	Y	Y	Y	Y	Y
8 O'Neill								
9 Moakley	Y	N	Y	Y	Y	Y	?	Y
10 Heckler	Y	?	Y	Y	Y	Y	Y	?
11 Burke	Y	N	Y	Y	Y	Y	Y	Y
12 Studds	N	Y	Y	Y	Y	Y	Y	Y
MICHIGAN								
1 Conyers	Y	N	#	Y	Y	#	?	#
2 Pursell	N	Y	Y	#	Y	Y	N	Y
3 Brown	Y	Y	Y	Y	Y	Y	Y	Y
4 Stockman	N	Y	Y	Y	Y	Y	N	N
5 Sawyer	N	Y	Y	Y	Y	Y	Y	Y
6 Carr	Y	Y	Y	Y	Y	Y	Y	Y
7 Kildee	Y	N	Y	Y	Y	Y	Y	Y
8 Traxler	Y	Y	Y	Y	Y	Y	Y	Y
9 Vander Jagt	Y	Y	Y	Y	Y	Y	Y	Y
10 Cederberg	Y	Y	Y	Y	Y	Y	N	N
11 Ruppe	Y	N	Y	Y	Y	Y	N	N
12 Bonior	Y	Y	Y	Y	Y	Y	Y	Y
13 Diggs	#	#	#	#	#	#	?	#
14 Nedzi	Y	Y	Y	Y	Y	Y	Y	Y
15 Ford	?	?	Y	Y	Y	Y	Y	Y
16 Dingell	?	?	?	?	?	?	?	X
17 Brodhead	Y	Y	Y	Y	Y	Y	Y	Y
18 Blanchard	Y	Y	Y	Y	Y	Y	Y	Y
19 Broomfield	N	Y	Y	Y	Y	Y	Y	N
MINNESOTA								
1 Quie	?	?	Y	Y	Y	Y	Y	Y
2 Hagedorn	N	Y	Y	Y	Y	Y	N	N
3 Frenzel	N	Y	Y	Y	Y	Y	Y	Y
4 Vento	Y	N	Y	Y	Y	Y	Y	Y
5 Fraser	Y	N	Y	Y	Y	Y	?	Y
6 Nolan	N	N	Y	Y	Y	Y	Y	Y
7 Stangeland	N	Y	Y	Y	Y	Y	N	N
8 Oberstar	Y	N	Y	Y	Y	Y	Y	Y
MISSISSIPPI								
1 Whitten	#	Y	Y	Y	Y	Y	Y	Y
2 Bowen	N	Y	Y	Y	Y	Y	Y	N
3 Montgomery	N	Y	Y	Y	Y	Y	N	N
4 Cochran	?	?	?	?	?	?	?	?
5 Lott	N	Y	Y	Y	Y	Y	N	N
MISSOURI								
1 Clay	Y	N	Y	Y	Y	Y	Y	Y
2 Young	N	N	Y	Y	Y	Y	Y	Y
3 Gephardt	N	Y	Y	Y	Y	Y	N	Y

	759	760	761	762	763	764	765	766
4 Skelton	N	Y	Y	Y	Y	Y	Y	Y
5 Bolling	Y	Y	Y	Y	Y	Y	Y	Y
6 Coleman	N	N	Y	Y	Y	Y	Y	Y
7 Taylor	N	Y	Y	Y	Y	Y	Y	N
8 Ichord	N	Y	Y	Y	Y	Y	N	Y
9 Volkmer	N	Y	Y	Y	Y	Y	Y	Y
10 Burlison	Y	Y	Y	Y	Y	Y	Y	Y
MONTANA								
1 Baucus	N	Y	Y	Y	Y	Y	Y	Y
2 Marlenee	Y	Y	Y	Y	Y	Y	N	N
NEBRASKA								
1 Thone	?	?	?	?	?	?	?	?
2 Cavanaugh	N	Y	Y	Y	Y	Y	Y	Y
3 Smith	Y	Y	Y	Y	Y	Y	N	N
NEVADA								
AL Santini	Y	#	Y	Y	Y	Y	Y	Y
NEW HAMPSHIRE								
1 D'Amours	N	N	Y	Y	#	Y	N	Y
2 Cleveland	N	Y	Y	Y	Y	Y	N	N
NEW JERSEY								
1 Florio	Y	Y	Y	Y	Y	Y	Y	Y
2 Hughes	N	Y	Y	Y	Y	Y	Y	Y
3 Howard	Y	Y	Y	Y	Y	Y	Y	Y
4 Thompson	Y	Y	Y	Y	Y	Y	Y	Y
5 Fenwick	N	Y	Y	Y	Y	Y	N	N
6 Forsythe	N	Y	Y	Y	Y	Y	N	N
7 Maguire	N	Y	Y	Y	Y	Y	Y	Y
8 Roe	#	?	?	Y	Y	Y	Y	Y
9 Hollenbeck	N	Y	Y	Y	Y	Y	Y	Y
10 Rodino	Y	N	Y	Y	Y	Y	Y	Y
11 Minish	Y	Y	Y	Y	Y	Y	Y	Y
12 Rinaldo	Y	Y	Y	Y	Y	Y	Y	Y
13 Meyner	Y	Y	Y	Y	Y	Y	Y	Y
14 LeFante	Y	Y	Y	Y	Y	Y	Y	Y
15 Patten	Y	N	Y	Y	Y	Y	Y	Y
NEW MEXICO								
1 Lujan	?	?	?	?	?	?	?	?
2 Runnels	N	Y	?	?	?	Y	Y	Y
NEW YORK								
1 Pike	#	#	Y	Y	Y	Y	Y	Y
2 Downey	Y	N	Y	Y	Y	Y	Y	Y
3 Ambro	?	Y	Y	Y	Y	Y	Y	Y
4 Lent	Y	Y	Y	Y	Y	Y	Y	Y
5 Wydler	Y	N	Y	Y	Y	Y	Y	N
6 Wolff	Y	N	Y	Y	Y	Y	Y	Y
7 Addabbo	Y	N	Y	Y	Y	Y	Y	Y
8 Rosenthal	Y	N	Y	Y	Y	Y	Y	Y
9 Delaney	Y	Y	Y	Y	?	Y	Y	Y
10 Biaggi	Y	N	Y	Y	Y	Y	Y	?
11 Scheuer	Y	Y	Y	Y	Y	Y	Y	Y
12 Chisholm	Y	N	Y	Y	Y	Y	Y	Y
13 Solarz	Y	N	Y	Y	Y	Y	Y	Y
14 Richmond	Y	N	Y	Y	Y	Y	Y	Y
15 Zeferetti	Y	N	Y	Y	Y	Y	Y	Y
16 Holtzman	?	N	Y	Y	Y	Y	Y	Y
17 Murphy	Y	Y	Y	Y	Y	Y	Y	Y
18 Green	Y	Y	Y	Y	Y	Y	Y	Y
19 Rangel	Y	N	Y	Y	Y	Y	Y	Y
20 Weiss	Y	N	Y	Y	Y	Y	Y	Y
21 Garcia	Y	N	Y	Y	Y	Y	Y	Y
22 Bingham	Y	N	Y	Y	Y	Y	Y	Y
23 Caputo	Y	Y	Y	Y	Y	Y	?	?
24 Ottinger	Y	N	Y	Y	Y	Y	Y	Y
25 Fish	Y	Y	Y	Y	Y	Y	Y	Y
26 Gilman	N	N	Y	Y	Y	Y	Y	Y
27 McHugh	#	Y	Y	Y	Y	Y	Y	Y
28 Stratton	N	Y	Y	Y	Y	Y	Y	Y
29 Pattison	Y	Y	#	Y	Y	Y	Y	Y
30 McEwen	?	Y	Y	Y	Y	Y	Y	Y
31 Mitchell	#	N	Y	Y	Y	Y	N	N
32 Hanley	Y	N	Y	Y	Y	Y	Y	Y
33 Walsh	Y	N	Y	Y	Y	Y	Y	Y
34 Horton	Y	Y	Y	Y	Y	Y	Y	Y
35 Conable	N	Y	Y	Y	Y	N	N	N
36 LaFalce	N	Y	Y	Y	Y	▮	Y	Y
37 Nowak	Y	Y	Y	Y	Y	Y	Y	Y
38 Kemp	N	Y	Y	Y	Y	Y	?	?
39 Lundine	N	Y	Y	Y	Y	Y	Y	Y
NORTH CAROLINA								
1 Jones	Y	Y	Y	Y	Y	Y	Y	Y
2 Fountain	N	Y	Y	Y	Y	Y	Y	Y
3 Whitley	N	N	Y	Y	Y	Y	Y	Y
4 Andrews	Y	Y	Y	Y	Y	Y	Y	Y
5 Neal	N	Y	Y	Y	Y	Y	Y	Y
6 Preyer	Y	Y	Y	Y	Y	Y	Y	Y
7 Rose	Y	Y	Y	Y	Y	Y	Y	Y
8 Hefner	Y	N	Y	Y	Y	Y	Y	Y

	759	760	761	762	763	764	765	766
9 Martin	N	Y	Y	Y	Y	Y	Y	N
10 Broyhill	N	Y	Y	Y	Y	Y	Y	N
11 Gudger	N	Y	Y	Y	Y	Y	Y	Y
NORTH DAKOTA								
AL Andrews	Y	N	Y	Y	Y	Y	N	N
OHIO								
1 Gradison	Y	Y	Y	Y	Y	Y	N	N
2 Luken	N	Y	Y	Y	Y	Y	Y	Y
3 Whalen	Y	N	Y	Y	Y	Y	Y	Y
4 Guyer	Y	Y	Y	Y	Y	Y	N	N
5 Latta	N	Y	Y	Y	Y	Y	N	N
6 Harsha	N	N	Y	Y	Y	Y	Y	Y
7 Brown	N	N	Y	Y	Y	Y	N	N
8 Kindness	Y	Y	Y	Y	Y	Y	N	N
9 Ashley	?	N	Y	Y	Y	Y	Y	Y
10 Miller	N	Y	Y	Y	Y	Y	N	N
11 Stanton	Y	Y	Y	Y	Y	Y	N	N
12 Devine	N	Y	Y	Y	Y	Y	N	N
13 Pease	Y	Y	Y	Y	Y	Y	Y	Y
14 Seiberling	Y	Y	Y	Y	Y	Y	Y	Y
15 Wylie	N	Y	Y	Y	Y	Y	N	N
16 Regula	N	Y	Y	Y	Y	Y	N	N
17 Ashbrook	▮	Y	N	Y	Y	Y	N	N
18 Applegate	Y	Y	?	Y	Y	Y	N	N
19 Carney	Y	N	Y	Y	Y	Y	N	N
20 Oakar	Y	Y	Y	Y	Y	Y	N	N
21 Stokes	Y	N	Y	Y	Y	Y	Y	Y
22 Vanik	Y	Y	Y	Y	Y	Y	Y	Y
23 Mottl	N	Y	Y	Y	N	Y	N	N
OKLAHOMA								
1 Jones	Y	Y	Y	Y	Y	Y	Y	Y
2 Risenhoover	Y	Y	Y	Y	?	Y	?	Y
3 Watkins	Y	Y	Y	Y	Y	Y	Y	Y
4 Steed	Y	Y	Y	Y	Y	Y	Y	Y
5 Edwards	Y	Y	Y	Y	Y	Y	N	N
6 English	Y	Y	Y	Y	Y	Y	Y	Y
OREGON								
1 AuCoin	N	Y	Y	Y	Y	Y	Y	Y
2 Ullman	Y	Y	Y	Y	Y	Y	N	Y
3 Duncan	Y	Y	Y	#	Y	Y	Y	Y
4 Weaver	N	Y	Y	Y	Y	Y	N	Y
PENNSYLVANIA								
1 Myers, M.	Y	Y	Y	Y	Y	Y	N	N
2 Nix	Y	Y	Y	Y	Y	Y	Y	Y
3 Lederer	Y	Y	Y	Y	Y	Y	N	N
4 Eilberg	Y	Y	Y	Y	Y	Y	Y	Y
5 Schulze	Y	Y	Y	Y	Y	Y	N	N
6 Yatron	Y	Y	Y	Y	Y	Y	N	N
7 Edgar	N	Y	Y	Y	Y	Y	Y	Y
8 Kostmayer	Y	Y	Y	Y	Y	Y	Y	N
9 Shuster	N	Y	Y	Y	Y	Y	N	Y
10 McDade	Y	N	Y	Y	Y	Y	N	Y
11 Flood	Y	Y	Y	Y	Y	Y	Y	Y
12 Murtha	Y	Y	Y	Y	Y	Y	Y	N
13 Coughlin	N	Y	Y	Y	Y	Y	?	N
14 Moorhead	Y	Y	Y	Y	Y	Y	Y	Y
15 Rooney	Y	Y	Y	Y	Y	Y	Y	Y
16 Walker	N	Y	Y	Y	Y	Y	N	N
17 Ertel	N	Y	Y	Y	Y	Y	Y	Y
18 Walgren	?	?	Y	Y	Y	Y	Y	Y
19 Goodling, W.	N	N	N	Y	Y	Y	Y	Y
20 Gaydos	Y	Y	Y	Y	Y	Y	Y	N
21 Dent	Y	Y	Y	Y	Y	Y	Y	Y
22 Murphy	Y	Y	Y	Y	Y	Y	N	N
23 Ammerman	?	?	?	?	?	?	?	X
24 Marks	Y	Y	Y	Y	Y	Y	Y	Y
25 Myers, G.	N	Y	Y	Y	Y	N	N	N
RHODE ISLAND								
1 St Germain	Y	N	Y	Y	Y	Y	Y	Y
2 Beard	Y	N	Y	Y	Y	Y	Y	Y
SOUTH CAROLINA								
1 Davis	Y	N	Y	Y	Y	Y	Y	Y
2 Spence	Y	N	Y	Y	Y	Y	Y	Y
3 Derrick	Y	Y	Y	Y	Y	Y	Y	Y
4 Mann	Y	Y	Y	Y	Y	Y	Y	Y
5 Holland	?	?	?	Y	Y	Y	Y	Y
6 Jenrette	N	N	Y	Y	Y	Y	Y	Y
SOUTH DAKOTA								
1 Pressler	Y	N	Y	Y	Y	Y	Y	Y
2 Abdnor	Y	Y	Y	Y	Y	Y	Y	Y
TENNESSEE								
1 Quillen	Y	N	Y	Y	N	Y	Y	N
2 Duncan	Y	Y	Y	Y	?	Y	N	N
3 Lloyd	N	Y	Y	Y	Y	Y	Y	Y
4 Gore	Y	Y	Y	Y	Y	Y	Y	Y
5 Vacancy								
6 Beard	N	Y	Y	Y	Y	Y	N	N

	759	760	761	762	763	764	765	766
7 Jones	#	#	#	Y	Y	Y	Y	Y
8 Ford	Y	N	Y	Y	Y	Y	Y	Y
TEXAS								
1 Hall	Y	Y	Y	Y	N	Y	Y	Y
2 Wilson, C.	#	#	#	Y	Y	Y	?	Y
3 Collins	N	Y	Y	N	N	N	N	N
4 Roberts	N	Y	Y	Y	N	Y	Y	Y
5 Mattox	N	Y	Y	Y	Y	Y	N	N
6 Teague	?	?	?	?	?	?	?	?
7 Archer	N	Y	Y	Y	Y	Y	Y	Y
8 Eckhardt	Y	N	Y	Y	Y	Y	Y	Y
9 Brooks	Y	Y	Y	Y	Y	Y	Y	Y
10 Pickle	N	N	Y	Y	Y	Y	N	N
11 Poage	N	Y	Y	Y	Y	Y	N	N
12 Wright	Y	Y	Y	Y	Y	Y	Y	Y
13 Hightower	?	?	?	?	?	?	Y	Y
14 Young	?	?	?	?	?	?	?	?
15 de la Garza	N	N	Y	Y	Y	Y	Y	Y
16 White	Y	N	Y	Y	Y	Y	Y	Y
17 Burleson	N	Y	Y	Y	Y	Y	Y	N
18 Jordan	Y	Y	Y	Y	Y	Y	Y	Y
19 Mahon	Y	Y	Y	Y	Y	Y	Y	Y
20 Gonzalez	Y	N	Y	Y	Y	Y	Y	Y
21 Krueger	#	?	#	#	#	#	?	✓
22 Gammage	N	Y	Y	Y	Y	Y	Y	Y
23 Kazen	Y	N	Y	Y	Y	Y	Y	Y
24 Milford	?	?	?	Y	Y	Y	?	Y
UTAH								
1 McKay	?	N	Y	Y	Y	Y	N	Y
2 Marriott	Y	Y	Y	Y	Y	Y	Y	Y
VERMONT								
AL Jeffords	N	Y	Y	Y	Y	Y	N	N
VIRGINIA								
1 Trible	Y	N	Y	Y	Y	Y	Y	Y
2 Whitehurst	Y	N	Y	Y	Y	Y	Y	N
3 Satterfield	N	Y	Y	Y	N	Y	N	N
4 Daniel	Y	N	Y	Y	Y	Y	N	N
5 Daniel	N	Y	?	Y	Y	Y	N	N
6 Butler	Y	Y	Y	Y	Y	Y	Y	N
7 Robinson	Y	Y	Y	Y	Y	Y	N	N
8 Harris	Y	N	Y	Y	Y	Y	Y	Y
9 Wampler	Y	Y	Y	Y	Y	Y	N	N
10 Fisher	Y	N	Y	Y	Y	Y	Y	Y
WASHINGTON								
1 Pritchard	Y	Y	Y	Y	Y	Y	Y	Y
2 Meeds	Y	Y	Y	Y	Y	Y	?	?
3 Bonker	#	Y	Y	Y	Y	Y	Y	Y
4 McCormack	Y	Y	Y	Y	Y	Y	Y	Y
5 Foley	N	Y	Y	Y	Y	Y	Y	Y
6 Dicks	Y	N	Y	Y	Y	Y	Y	Y
7 Cunningham	N	N	Y	Y	Y	Y	N	N
WEST VIRGINIA								
1 Mollohan	Y	Y	Y	#	Y	Y	N	N
2 Staggers	Y	Y	Y	Y	Y	Y	Y	Y
3 Slack	Y	Y	Y	Y	Y	Y	N	N
4 Rahall	Y	N	Y	Y	Y	Y	Y	Y
WISCONSIN								
1 Aspin	Y	Y	Y	Y	Y	Y	Y	Y
2 Kastenmeier	Y	N	Y	Y	Y	Y	Y	Y
3 Baldus	Y	N	Y	Y	Y	Y	Y	Y
4 Zablocki	Y	Y	Y	Y	Y	Y	Y	Y
5 Reuss	Y	Y	Y	Y	Y	Y	Y	Y
6 Steiger	N	Y	Y	Y	Y	Y	N	N
7 Obey	Y	Y	Y	Y	Y	Y	?	Y
8 Cornell	N	Y	Y	Y	Y	Y	Y	Y
9 Kasten	N	Y	Y	Y	Y	Y	N	N
WYOMING								
AL Roncalio	Y	Y	#	#	#	Y	Y	Y

Democrats ***Republicans***

767. HR 13845. Perishable Agricultural Commodities. Richmond, D-N.Y., motion to suspend the rules and pass the bill to raise license fees and make certain other revisions in the Perishable Agricultural Commodities Act. Motion agreed to 399-7: R 133-3; D 266-4 (ND 184-2; SD 82-2), Oct. 4, 1978. A two-thirds majority vote (271 in this case) is required for passage under suspension of the rules.

768. HR 12917. Rural Transportation. Fithian, D-Ind., motion to suspend the rules and pass the bill to establish an interagency task force to study rural transportation problems and recommend improvements in railroad transportation for the agriculture industry. Motion agreed to 352-49: R 103-32; D 249-17 (ND 173-8; SD 76-9), Oct. 4, 1978. A two-thirds majority vote (268 in this case) is required for passage under suspension of the rules.

769. HR 14042. Defense Procurement Authorization. Downey, D-N.Y., amendment to require approval by both houses of Congress of any future contract claims settlement negotiated under PL 85-804 that cost more than $25 million. Rejected 111-275: R 19-113; D 92-162 (ND 81-90; SD 11-72), Oct. 4, 1978.

770. HR 14042. Defense Procurement Authorization. Passage of the bill to authorize $35,235,969,000 for weapons procurement and military research projects of the Defense Department for fiscal 1979. Passed 367-22: R 131-2; D 236-20 (ND 152-20; SD 84-0), Oct. 4, 1978.

KEY

Y Voted for (yea).
✓ Paired for.
† Announced for.
# CQ Poll for.
N Voted against (nay).
X Paired against.
\- Announced against.
▮ CQ Poll against.
P Voted "present."
● Voted "present" to avoid possible conflict of interest.
? Did not vote or otherwise make a position known.

	767	768	769	770
ALABAMA				
1 Edwards	Y	Y	N	Y
2 Dickinson	?	?	?	?
3 Nichols	Y	Y	N	Y
4 Bevill	Y	Y	N	Y
5 Flippo	Y	Y	N	Y
6 Buchanan	Y	Y	N	Y
7 Flowers	?	Y	N	Y
ALASKA				
AL Young	Y	Y	N	#
ARIZONA				
1 Rhodes	Y	Y	N	Y
2 Udall	Y	Y	N	Y
3 Stump	Y	N	N	Y
4 Rudd	Y	N	N	Y
ARKANSAS				
1 Alexander	Y	Y	N	Y
2 Tucker	Y	Y	N	Y
3 Hammerschmidt	Y	Y	N	Y
4 Thornton	Y	Y	N	Y
CALIFORNIA				
1 Johnson	Y	Y	N	Y
2 Clausen	Y	Y	N	Y
3 Moss	?	?	?	?
4 Leggett	Y	Y	N	Y
5 Burton, J.	Y	Y	Y	?
6 Burton, P.	Y	Y	Y	?
7 Miller	?	?	?	?
8 Dellums	Y	Y	Y	N
9 Stark	Y	Y	Y	▮
10 Edwards	Y	Y	Y	N
11 Ryan	Y	?	Y	Y
12 McCloskey	Y	N	N	Y
13 Mineta	Y	Y	N	Y
14 McFall	?	Y	N	Y
15 Sisk	Y	Y	?	?
16 Panetta	Y	Y	Y	Y
17 Krebs	Y	Y	N	Y
18 Vacancy				
19 Lagomarsino	Y	N	N	Y
20 Goldwater	Y	N	N	Y
21 Corman	Y	Y	N	Y
22 Moorhead	Y	N	N	Y
23 Beilenson	Y	Y	N	Y
24 Waxman	Y	Y	Y	Y
25 Roybal	Y	Y	Y	N
26 Rousselot	Y	N	N	Y
27 Dornan	Y	N	N	Y
28 Burke	#	#	▮	#
29 Hawkins	Y	Y	Y	Y
30 Danielson	Y	Y	N	Y
31 Wilson, C.H.	Y	Y	?	Y
32 Anderson	Y	Y	N	Y
33 Clawson	Y	N	N	Y
34 Hannaford	Y	Y	N	Y
35 Lloyd	Y	Y	N	Y
36 Brown	Y	Y	N	Y
37 Pettis	?	?	?	?
38 Patterson	Y	#	N	Y
39 Wiggins	Y	N	N	Y
40 Badham	Y	N	N	Y
41 Wilson, B.	Y	N	N	Y
42 Van Deerlin	Y	Y	N	Y
43 Burgener	Y	Y	N	Y
COLORADO				
1 Schroeder	Y	Y	Y	Y
2 Wirth	Y	Y	Y	Y
3 Evans	Y	Y	▮	#
4 Johnson	Y	Y	N	Y
5 Armstrong	Y	Y	?	?
CONNECTICUT				
1 Cotter	Y	Y	N	Y
2 Dodd	Y	Y	N	Y
3 Giaimo	Y	Y	N	Y
4 McKinney	Y	N	N	Y
5 Sarasin	#	▮	▮	#
6 Moffett	Y	Y	Y	Y
DELAWARE				
AL Evans	Y	Y	N	Y
FLORIDA				
1 Sikes	Y	Y	N	Y
2 Fuqua	Y	Y	N	Y
3 Bennett	Y	Y	N	Y
4 Chappell	Y	Y	Y	Y
5 Kelly	Y	Y	N	Y
6 Young	Y	Y	N	Y
7 Gibbons	Y	N	N	Y
8 Ireland	Y	Y	?	Y
9 Frey	Y	Y	N	Y
10 Bafalis	Y	Y	N	Y
11 Rogers	Y	Y	N	Y
12 Burke	Y	Y	N	Y
13 Lehman	Y	Y	N	Y
14 Pepper	Y	Y	▮	#
15 Fascell	Y	Y	N	Y
GEORGIA				
1 Ginn	Y	Y	N	Y
2 Mathis	Y	Y	N	Y
3 Brinkley	Y	Y	Y	Y
4 Levitas	Y	Y	N	Y
5 Fowler	Y	Y	N	Y
6 Flynt	Y	N	N	Y
7 McDonald	N	N	N	Y
8 Evans	Y	Y	N	Y
9 Jenkins	Y	Y	N	Y
10 Barnard	Y	Y	N	Y
HAWAII				
1 Heftel	Y	Y	N	Y
2 Akaka	Y	Y	N	Y
IDAHO				
1 Symms	Y	N	N	Y
2 Hansen, G.	Y	N	N	Y
ILLINOIS				
1 Metcalfe	Y	Y	N	N
2 Murphy	Y	Y	N	Y
3 Russo	Y	N	Y	Y
4 Derwinski	Y	N	Y	Y
5 Fary	Y	Y	N	Y
6 Hyde	Y	Y	N	Y
7 Collins	Y	Y	Y	N
8 Rostenkowski	Y	Y	N	Y
9 Yates	Y	Y	Y	Y
10 Mikva	Y	Y	#	#
11 Annunzio	Y	Y	N	Y
12 Crane	Y	N	N	Y
13 McClory	Y	Y	N	Y
14 Erlenborn	Y	Y	N	Y
15 Corcoran	Y	Y	N	Y
16 Anderson	Y	Y	▮	#
17 O'Brien	Y	Y	N	Y
18 Michel	Y	Y	N	Y
19 Railsback	Y	Y	N	Y
20 Findley	Y	Y	N	Y
21 Madigan	Y	Y	N	Y
22 Shipley	?	?	?	?
23 Price	Y	Y	N	Y
24 Simon	Y	Y	N	Y
INDIANA				
1 Benjamin	Y	Y	N	Y
2 Fithian	Y	Y	Y	Y
3 Brademas	Y	Y	N	Y
4 Quayle	Y	Y	Y	Y
5 Hillis	Y	Y	N	Y
6 Evans	Y	Y	Y	Y
7 Myers, J.	Y	Y	N	Y
8 Cornwell	Y	Y	Y	Y
9 Hamilton	Y	Y	N	Y
10 Sharp	Y	Y	Y	Y
11 Jacobs	Y	#	Y	Y
IOWA				
1 Leach	Y	Y	Y	Y
2 Blouin	X	?	?	?
3 Grassley	N	Y	N	Y
4 Smith	Y	Y	Y	Y
5 Harkin	Y	Y	Y	Y
6 Bedell	Y	Y	Y	N

Democrats ***Republicans***

	767	768	769	770
KANSAS				
1 Sebelius	Y	Y	N	Y
2 Keys	Y	Y	Y	Y
3 Winn	Y	Y	N	Y
4 Glickman	Y	Y	Y	Y
5 Skubitz	?	?	?	Y
KENTUCKY				
1 Hubbard	Y	Y	N	Y
2 Natcher	Y	Y	N	Y
3 Mazzoli	Y	Y	N	Y
4 Snyder	Y	Y	N	Y
5 Carter	Y	Y	N	Y
6 Breckinridge	Y	Y	Y	?
7 Perkins	Y	Y	N	Y
LOUISIANA				
1 Livingston	Y	Y	N	Y
2 Boggs	N	Y	N	Y
3 Treen	Y	N	N	Y
4 Waggonner	Y	Y	N	Y
5 Huckaby	Y	Y	N	Y
6 Moore	Y	Y	N	Y
7 Breaux	Y	Y	N	Y
8 Long	Y	Y	N	Y
MAINE				
1 Emery	Y	Y	N	Y
2 Cohen	Y	Y	N	Y
MARYLAND				
1 Bauman	Y	Y	N	Y
2 Long	Y	Y	N	Y
3 Mikulski	Y	Y	Y	Y
4 Holt	Y	Y	N	Y
5 Spellman	Y	Y	Y	Y
6 Byron	Y	Y	N	Y
7 Mitchell	Y	Y	Y	N
8 Steers	Y	Y	Y	Y
MASSACHUSETTS				
1 Conte	Y	Y	Y	Y
2 Boland	Y	Y	N	Y
3 Early	Y	Y	Y	Y
4 Drinan	Y	N	Y	Y
5 Tsongas	?	?	?	?
6 Harrington	Y	Y	#	■
7 Markey	Y	Y	Y	Y
8 O'Neill				
9 Moakley	Y	Y	N	Y
10 Heckler	?	?	?	?
11 Burke	Y	Y	N	Y
12 Studds	Y	Y	Y	Y
MICHIGAN				
1 Conyers	#	#	#	■
2 Pursell	Y	Y	Y	Y
3 Brown	Y	Y	N	Y
4 Stockman	Y	N	N	Y
5 Sawyer	Y	Y	N	Y
6 Carr	Y	Y	Y	Y
7 Kildee	Y	Y	Y	Y
8 Traxler	Y	Y	■	Y
9 Vander Jagt	Y	Y	N	Y
10 Cederberg	Y	Y	N	Y
11 Ruppe	Y	?	N	Y
12 Bonior	Y	Y	Y	Y
13 Diggs	#	#	?	#
14 Nedzi	Y	Y	N	Y
15 Ford	Y	Y	?	Y
16 Dingell	✓	?	X	?
17 Brodhead	Y	Y	Y	Y
18 Blanchard	Y	Y	N	Y
19 Broomfield	Y	N	N	Y
MINNESOTA				
1 Quie	Y	Y	N	Y
2 Hagedorn	Y	Y	N	Y
3 Frenzel	Y	Y	N	Y
4 Vento	Y	Y	Y	Y
5 Fraser	Y	Y	N	Y
6 Nolan	Y	#	Y	N
7 Stangeland	Y	Y	N	Y
8 Oberstar	Y	Y	Y	Y
MISSISSIPPI				
1 Whitten	Y	Y	N	Y
2 Bowen	Y	Y	N	Y
3 Montgomery	Y	Y	N	Y
4 Cochran	?	?	?	?
5 Lott	Y	Y	N	Y
MISSOURI				
1 Clay	Y	Y	?	N
2 Young	Y	Y	N	Y
3 Gephardt	Y	Y	N	Y

	767	768	769	770
4 Skelton	Y	Y	N	Y
5 Bolling	Y	Y	N	#
6 Coleman	Y	Y	N	Y
7 Taylor	Y	N	N	Y
8 Ichord	Y	Y	N	Y
9 Volkmer	Y	Y	Y	Y
10 Burlison	Y	Y	N	Y
MONTANA				
1 Baucus	Y	Y	N	Y
2 Marlenee	Y	Y	N	Y
NEBRASKA				
1 Thone	?	?	?	?
2 Cavanaugh	Y	Y	Y	Y
3 Smith	Y	Y	?	Y
NEVADA				
AL Santini	Y	Y	N	Y
NEW HAMPSHIRE				
1 D'Amours	Y	Y	N	Y
2 Cleveland	Y	N	N	Y
NEW JERSEY				
1 Florio	Y	Y	Y	Y
2 Hughes	Y	#	Y	Y
3 Howard	Y	Y	Y	Y
4 Thompson	Y	Y	N	Y
5 Fenwick	Y	Y	N	Y
6 Forsythe	Y	Y	N	N
7 Maguire	Y	Y	Y	N
8 Roe	Y	Y	Y	Y
9 Hollenbeck	Y	Y	N	Y
10 Rodino	Y	Y	Y	Y
11 Minish	Y	Y	Y	Y
12 Rinaldo	Y	Y	Y	Y
13 Meyner	Y	Y	Y	Y
14 LeFante	Y	Y	N	Y
15 Patten	Y	N	N	Y
NEW MEXICO				
1 Lujan	?	?	?	?
2 Runnels	Y	Y	N	Y
NEW YORK				
1 Pike	Y	Y	Y	Y
2 Downey	Y	Y	Y	Y
3 Ambro	Y	Y	N	Y
4 Lent	Y	Y	Y	Y
5 Wydler	N	N	Y	Y
6 Wolff	Y	Y	N	Y
7 Addabbo	Y	Y	N	Y
8 Rosenthal	Y	Y	Y	Y
9 Delaney	Y	Y	?	?
10 Biaggi	Y	Y	N	Y
11 Scheuer	Y	Y	Y	Y
12 Chisholm	Y	Y	Y	N
13 Solarz	Y	Y	Y	Y
14 Richmond	Y	Y	✓	X
15 Zeferetti	Y	Y	N	Y
16 Holtzman	Y	Y	Y	N
17 Murphy	Y	Y	N	Y
18 Green	Y	Y	N	Y
19 Rangel	Y	Y	Y	N
20 Weiss	Y	Y	Y	N
21 Garcia	Y	Y	Y	■
22 Bingham	Y	Y	Y	N
23 Caputo	?	?	?	?
24 Ottinger	Y	Y	Y	N
25 Fish	Y	Y	N	Y
26 Gilman	Y	Y	N	Y
27 McHugh	Y	Y	Y	Y
28 Stratton	Y	N	Y	Y
29 Pattison	Y	Y	Y	Y
30 McEwen	Y	Y	N	Y
31 Mitchell	Y	Y	N	Y
32 Hanley	Y	Y	N	Y
33 Walsh	Y	Y	N	Y
34 Horton	Y	Y	N	Y
35 Conable	Y	N	N	Y
36 LaFalce	Y	Y	N	Y
37 Nowak	Y	Y	Y	Y
38 Kemp	?	?	?	?
39 Lundine	Y	Y	Y	Y
NORTH CAROLINA				
1 Jones	Y	N	Y	Y
2 Fountain	Y	Y	N	#
3 Whitley	Y	N	N	Y
4 Andrews	Y	Y	N	Y
5 Neal	Y	Y	Y	Y
6 Preyer	Y	Y	N	Y
7 Rose	Y	Y	N	Y
8 Hefner	Y	Y	Y	Y

	767	768	769	770
9 Martin	Y	Y	N	Y
10 Broyhill	Y	Y	N	Y
11 Gudger	Y	Y	N	Y
NORTH DAKOTA				
AL Andrews	Y	Y	Y	Y
OHIO				
1 Gradison	Y	Y	N	Y
2 Luken	Y	N	N	Y
3 Whalen	Y	Y	Y	Y
4 Guyer	Y	Y	N	Y
5 Latta	Y	Y	N	Y
6 Harsha	Y	Y	N	Y
7 Brown	Y	Y	N	Y
8 Kindness	Y	Y	N	Y
9 Ashley	Y	Y	N	Y
10 Miller	Y	Y	N	Y
11 Stanton	Y	Y	N	Y
12 Devine	Y	N	N	Y
13 Pease	Y	Y	N	Y
14 Seiberling	Y	Y	Y	N
15 Wylie	Y	Y	N	Y
16 Regula	Y	Y	N	Y
17 Ashbrook	Y	Y	Y	Y
18 Applegate	Y	Y	?	Y
19 Carney	Y	Y	?	Y
20 Oakar	Y	Y	N	Y
21 Stokes	Y	Y	Y	N
22 Vanik	Y	Y	Y	Y
23 Mottl	Y	N	Y	Y
OKLAHOMA				
1 Jones	Y	Y	N	Y
2 Risenhoover	Y	Y	N	Y
3 Watkins	Y	Y	N	Y
4 Steed	Y	Y	N	Y
5 Edwards	Y	N	Y	Y
6 English	Y	Y	N	Y
OREGON				
1 AuCoin	Y	Y	Y	Y
2 Ullman	Y	Y	N	Y
3 Duncan	Y	Y	N	Y
4 Weaver	Y	Y	Y	Y
PENNSYLVANIA				
1 Myers, M.	Y	Y	N	Y
2 Nix	Y	Y	N	Y
3 Lederer	Y	Y	N	Y
4 Eilberg	Y	Y	✓	✓
5 Schulze	Y	Y	N	Y
6 Yatron	Y	Y	N	Y
7 Edgar	Y	Y	Y	Y
8 Kostmayer	N	N	Y	Y
9 Shuster	Y	Y	N	Y
10 McDade	Y	Y	N	Y
11 Flood	Y	Y	N	Y
12 Murtha	Y	Y	N	Y
13 Coughlin	Y	N	N	Y
14 Moorhead	Y	Y	N	Y
15 Rooney	Y	Y	N	Y
16 Walker	Y	N	N	Y
17 Ertel	Y	Y	N	Y
18 Walgren	Y	Y	Y	Y
19 Goodling, W.	Y	Y	N	?
20 Gaydos	Y	Y	N	Y
21 Dent	Y	Y	N	Y
22 Murphy	N	N	Y	Y
23 Ammerman	?	?	✓	?
24 Marks	Y	Y	Y	Y
25 Myers, G.	Y	N	N	N
RHODE ISLAND				
1 St Germain	Y	Y	N	Y
2 Beard	Y	Y	N	Y
SOUTH CAROLINA				
1 Davis	Y	Y	N	Y
2 Spence	Y	Y	N	Y
3 Derrick	Y	Y	N	Y
4 Mann	Y	Y	N	Y
5 Holland	Y	Y	N	Y
6 Jenrette	Y	Y	Y	Y
SOUTH DAKOTA				
1 Pressler	Y	Y	Y	Y
2 Abdnor	Y	Y	Y	Y
TENNESSEE				
1 Quillen	Y	Y	N	Y
2 Duncan	Y	Y	N	Y
3 Lloyd	Y	Y	N	Y
4 Gore	Y	Y	Y	Y
5 Vacancy				
6 Beard	Y	N	N	Y

	767	768	769	770
7 Jones	Y	Y	N	Y
8 Ford	Y	Y	N	Y
TEXAS				
1 Hall	Y	Y	N	Y
2 Wilson, C.	Y	Y	N	Y
3 Collins	N	N	Y	Y
4 Roberts	Y	Y	N	Y
5 Mattox	Y	N	Y	Y
6 Teague	?	?	X	?
7 Archer	Y	N	N	Y
8 Eckhardt	?	?	?	Y
9 Brooks	Y	Y	N	Y
10 Pickle	Y	Y	N	Y
11 Poage	Y	?	N	Y
12 Wright	Y	Y	N	Y
13 Hightower	Y	Y	N	Y
14 Young	?	?	N	Y
15 de la Garza	Y	Y	N	Y
16 White	Y	Y	N	Y
17 Burleson	Y	Y	N	Y
18 Jordan	Y	Y	Y	Y
19 Mahon	Y	Y	N	Y
20 Gonzalez	Y	Y	N	Y
21 Krueger	✓	#	X	#
22 Gammage	Y	N	N	Y
23 Kazen	Y	Y	N	Y
24 Milford	Y	N	?	Y
UTAH				
1 McKay	Y	Y	N	Y
2 Marriott	Y	Y	N	Y
VERMONT				
AL Jeffords	Y	Y	#	Y
VIRGINIA				
1 Trible	Y	Y	N	Y
2 Whitehurst	Y	Y	N	Y
3 Satterfield	Y	Y	N	Y
4 Daniel	Y	Y	N	Y
5 Daniel	Y	Y	N	Y
6 Butler	Y	Y	N	Y
7 Robinson	Y	Y	N	Y
8 Harris	Y	Y	N	Y
9 Wampler	Y	Y	N	Y
10 Fisher	Y	Y	Y	Y
WASHINGTON				
1 Pritchard	Y	Y	Y	Y
2 Meeds	Y	Y	?	?
3 Bonker	Y	Y	■	Y
4 McCormack	Y	Y	N	Y
5 Foley	Y	Y	N	Y
6 Dicks	Y	Y	N	Y
7 Cunningham	Y	N	N	Y
WEST VIRGINIA				
1 Mollohan	Y	Y	N	Y
2 Staggers	Y	Y	N	Y
3 Slack	Y	Y	?	?
4 Rahall	Y	Y	Y	Y
WISCONSIN				
1 Aspin	Y	Y	N	Y
2 Kastenmeier	Y	Y	Y	N
3 Baldus	Y	Y	N	■
4 Zablocki	Y	Y	N	Y
5 Reuss	Y	Y	N	Y
6 Steiger	Y	Y	N	Y
7 Obey	Y	Y	N	N
8 Cornell	Y	Y	Y	Y
9 Kasten	Y	Y	Y	Y
WYOMING				
AL Roncalio	Y	Y	Y	Y

Democrats ***Republicans***

771. S 1613. Magistrate Act of 1978/U.S. District Court Jurisdiction. Passage of the bill to enlarge the civil and criminal jurisdiction of U.S. magistrates, and to abolish "diversity of citizenship" as a ground for requesting federal district court jurisdiction in most cases involving disputes between residents of different states. Passed 323-49: R 109-16; D 214-33 (ND 141-24; SD 73-9), Oct. 4, 1978. A "yea" was a vote supporting the president's position.

772. HR 13059. Water Projects Authorization. Passage of the bill to authorize $1.29 billion for certain water projects of the Army Corps of Engineers. Passed 303-73: R 99-25; D 204-48 (ND 127-41; SD 77-7), Oct. 4, 1978.

773. HR 12932. Interior Appropriations, Fiscal 1979. Adoption of the conference report on the bill to appropriate $11,578,692,000 for fiscal 1979 for the programs of the Interior Department and various programs of the Energy Department and related agencies. Adopted 382-12: R 129-7; D 253-5 (ND 171-3; SD 82-2), Oct. 5, 1978. The president had requested $12,878,467,000.

774. HR 12928. Public Works — Energy Appropriations, Fiscal 1979. Passage, over the president's Oct. 5 veto, of the bill to appropriate $10,160,483,000 for energy and water development programs of the Corps of Engineers and the Interior and Energy Departments. Rejected 223-190: R 73-62; D 150-128 (ND 92-99; SD 58-29), Oct. 5, 1978. A two-thirds majority vote (276 in this case) is required to override a veto. The president had requested $11,039,449,000. A "nay" was a vote supporting the president's position.

775. HR 13635. Defense Department Appropriations, Fiscal 1979. Sikes, D-Fla., motion to table (kill) the Dickinson, R-Ala., motion to instruct House conferees to maintain the House position in support of consolidating Army and Navy basic helicopter pilot training. Rejected 165-225: R 14-118; D 151-107 (ND 97-83; SD 54-24), Oct. 5, 1978. (The Dickinson motion subsequently was agreed to by voice vote.)

776. HR 13635. Defense Department Appropriations, Fiscal 1979. Mahon, D-Texas, motion to close to the public the conference committee meetings on the bill to appropriate fiscal 1979 funds for the Defense Department when classified national security information was being discussed, as authorized under House rules, but to allow the attendance of members of Congress at all meetings. Motion agreed to 387-0: R 128-0; D 259-0 (ND 179-0; SD 80-0), Oct. 5, 1978.

777. HR 12932. Interior Appropriations, Fiscal 1979. Yates, D-Ill. motion that the House recede from its disagreement and concur in the Senate amendment stating that a basin-wide environmental impact statement would not be required for water projects in the Colorado River basin for which individual environmental impact statements had been filed. Motion agreed to 206-186: R 87-40; D 119-146 (ND 59-123; SD 60-23), Oct. 5, 1978.

KEY

- Y Voted for (yea).
- ✓ Paired for.
- † Announced for.
- # CQ Poll for.
- N Voted against (nay).
- X Paired against.
- \- Announced against.
- ▮ CQ Poll against.
- P Voted "present."
- ● Voted "present" to avoid possible conflict of interest.
- ? Did not vote or otherwise make a position known.

	771	772	773	774	775	776	777
ALABAMA							
1 Edwards	Y	Y	Y	Y	N	Y	Y
2 Dickinson	?	?	Y	Y	N	Y	Y
3 Nichols	Y	Y	Y	Y	▮	#	#
4 Bevill	Y	Y	Y	Y	N	Y	Y
5 Flippo	Y	Y	Y	Y	N	Y	Y
6 Buchanan	Y	Y	Y	Y	N	Y	N
7 Flowers	Y	Y	Y	N	N	Y	Y
ALASKA							
AL Young	#	#	Y	Y	N	Y	Y
ARIZONA							
1 Rhodes	Y	Y	Y	Y	N	Y	Y
2 Udall	#	Y	Y	Y	N	Y	Y
3 Stump	N	Y	Y	Y	Y	Y	Y
4 Rudd	N	Y	Y	Y	N	Y	Y
ARKANSAS							
1 Alexander	Y	Y	Y	Y	Y	Y	Y
2 Tucker	Y	Y	Y	N	Y	Y	Y
3 Hammerschmidt	Y	Y	Y	Y	N	Y	Y
4 Thornton	Y	Y	N	Y	Y	Y	Y
CALIFORNIA							
1 Johnson	Y	Y	Y	Y	Y	Y	Y
2 Clausen	Y	Y	Y	Y	N	Y	Y
3 Moss	?	?	?	Y	?	?	?
4 Leggett	?	Y	Y	Y	Y	Y	Y
5 Burton, J.	?	Y	Y	N	Y	Y	N
6 Burton, P.	Y	Y	Y	N	N	Y	N
7 Miller	?	?	?	N	?	?	?
8 Dellums	N	N	#	N	#	Y	N
9 Stark	Y	N	Y	N	Y	Y	N
10 Edwards	Y	Y	?	N	N	Y	N
11 Ryan	Y	Y	Y	Y	N	Y	Y
12 McCloskey	Y	N	Y	N	N	Y	N
13 Mineta	Y	Y	Y	Y	N	Y	N
14 McFall	Y	Y	Y	Y	Y	Y	Y
15 Sisk	?	?	Y	Y	Y	Y	Y
16 Panetta	Y	Y	Y	N	Y	Y	#
17 Krebs	Y	Y	Y	Y	Y	Y	N
18 Vacancy							
19 Lagomarsino	Y	Y	Y	Y	N	Y	Y
20 Goldwater	Y	Y	Y	Y	N	Y	Y
21 Corman	Y	Y	Y	Y	Y	Y	N
22 Moorhead	Y	Y	Y	N	N	Y	Y
23 Beilenson	N	N	#	N	N	Y	N
24 Waxman	Y	N	Y	N	N	#	N
25 Roybal	N	Y	Y	N	N	Y	N
26 Rousselot	Y	Y	Y	Y	N	Y	Y
27 Dornan	N	Y	Y	N	N	Y	Y
28 Burke	#	#	#	▮	▮	#	#
29 Hawkins	?	Y	Y	Y	Y	Y	N
30 Danielson	Y	Y	Y	Y	N	Y	Y
31 Wilson, C.H.	?	?	Y	N	?	?	Y
32 Anderson	Y	Y	Y	Y	Y	Y	Y
33 Clawson	Y	Y	Y	Y	N	Y	Y
34 Hannaford	Y	Y	Y	N	N	Y	N
35 Lloyd	Y	Y	Y	Y	N	Y	Y
36 Brown	Y	Y	Y	N	Y	Y	N
37 Pettis	?	?	?	?	?	?	?
38 Patterson	Y	Y	Y	N	N	Y	N
39 Wiggins	Y	#	#	#	▮	#	#
40 Badham	#	Y	Y	Y	N	Y	Y
41 Wilson, B.	?	Y	Y	Y	N	Y	Y
42 Van Deerlin	?	?	N	Y	N	Y	N
43 Burgener	?	Y	Y	Y	N	Y	Y
COLORADO							
1 Schroeder	Y	Y	Y	N	N	Y	Y
2 Wirth	Y	Y	Y	Y	▮	Y	Y
3 Evans	#	#	Y	Y	N	Y	Y
4 Johnson	Y	Y	Y	Y	N	Y	Y

	771	772	773	774	775	776	777
5 Armstrong	?	Y	Y	Y	N	?	✓
CONNECTICUT							
1 Cotter	Y	Y	Y	Y	Y	Y	N
2 Dodd	N	N	Y	Y	Y	Y	N
3 Giaimo	?	?	?	Y	Y	Y	N
4 McKinney	Y	Y	Y	Y	N	Y	N
5 Sarasin	#	#	#	✓	#	#	X
6 Moffett	N	N	Y	N	N	Y	N
DELAWARE							
AL Evans	Y	Y	Y	Y	N	Y	N
FLORIDA							
1 Sikes	Y	Y	Y	Y	Y	Y	Y
2 Fuqua	Y	Y	Y	Y	Y	Y	N
3 Bennett	N	Y	Y	N	Y	Y	N
4 Chappell	Y	Y	Y	Y	Y	Y	Y
5 Kelly	N	N	Y	Y	Y	Y	Y
6 Young	N	N	Y	Y	Y	Y	Y
7 Gibbons	Y	Y	Y	N	Y	Y	N
8 Ireland	Y	Y	Y	Y	Y	Y	N
9 Frey	Y	?	Y	N	Y	Y	Y
10 Bafalis	N	Y	Y	Y	Y	Y	N
11 Rogers	Y	Y	Y	N	Y	Y	N
12 Burke	Y	Y	Y	Y	Y	Y	N
13 Lehman	N	N	Y	N	Y	Y	N
14 Pepper	#	Y	Y	N	Y	Y	Y
15 Fascell	Y	N	Y	Y	Y	Y	N
GEORGIA							
1 Ginn	Y	Y	Y	Y	Y	Y	Y
2 Mathis	Y	Y	Y	Y	Y	Y	Y
3 Brinkley	Y	Y	Y	Y	Y	Y	Y
4 Levitas	Y	Y	Y	N	Y	Y	Y
5 Fowler	Y	Y	Y	N	Y	Y	Y
6 Flynt	Y	Y	Y	Y	Y	Y	Y
7 McDonald	N	N	N	▮	▮	#	Y
8 Evans	Y	Y	Y	Y	Y	Y	Y
9 Jenkins	Y	Y	Y	Y	Y	Y	Y
10 Barnard	Y	Y	Y	Y	Y	Y	?
HAWAII							
1 Heftel	Y	Y	Y	Y	N	Y	Y
2 Akaka	Y	Y	Y	Y	N	Y	Y
IDAHO							
1 Symms	N	Y	Y	Y	Y	Y	Y
2 Hansen, G.	N	Y	Y	Y	N	Y	Y
ILLINOIS							
1 Metcalfe	Y	Y	Y	N	Y	Y	N
2 Murphy	Y	Y	Y	Y	Y	Y	Y
3 Russo	Y	Y	Y	N	N	Y	N
4 Derwinski	Y	Y	Y	N	N	Y	Y
5 Fary	Y	Y	Y	Y	Y	Y	N
6 Hyde	Y	N	Y	N	N	Y	Y
7 Collins	Y	Y	Y	Y	Y	Y	N
8 Rostenkowski	Y	Y	Y	Y	Y	Y	N
9 Yates	Y	N	Y	Y	Y	Y	N
10 Mikva	▮	▮	Y	N	Y	Y	▮
11 Annunzio	Y	Y	Y	Y	Y	Y	N
12 Crane	N	N	N	▮	N	Y	#
13 McClory	Y	Y	Y	Y	N	Y	Y
14 Erlenborn	Y	Y	Y	N	▮	Y	Y
15 Corcoran	Y	Y	Y	Y	N	Y	N
16 Anderson	#	#	Y	N	N	Y	N
17 O'Brien	Y	Y	Y	N	N	Y	N
18 Michel	Y	Y	Y	N	?	?	?
19 Railsback	Y	Y	Y	N	N	Y	N
20 Findley	Y	Y	Y	Y	N	Y	N
21 Madigan	Y	N	Y	N	N	?	?
22 Shipley	?	?	?	✓	?	?	?
23 Price	Y	Y	Y	Y	Y	Y	Y
24 Simon	Y	Y	Y	N	N	Y	N
INDIANA							
1 Benjamin	Y	Y	Y	Y	Y	Y	N
2 Fithian	Y	N	Y	N	Y	Y	N
3 Brademas	Y	Y	Y	Y	Y	Y	N
4 Quayle	Y	?	Y	N	N	Y	Y
5 Hillis	?	?	Y	Y	N	Y	N
6 Evans	Y	N	N	N	N	Y	Y
7 Myers, J.	Y	Y	Y	Y	Y	Y	Y
8 Cornwell	Y	Y	Y	N	Y	Y	Y
9 Hamilton	Y	Y	Y	N	N	Y	N
10 Sharp	Y	N	Y	N	N	Y	N
11 Jacobs	Y	N	Y	N	N	Y	N
IOWA							
1 Leach	Y	Y	Y	N	N	Y	Y
2 Blouin	?	?	?	?	?	?	?
3 Grassley	Y	N	Y	Y	N	Y	N
4 Smith	Y	Y	Y	Y	N	Y	Y
5 Harkin	Y	N	Y	N	N	Y	N
6 Bedell	Y	N	#	N	N	Y	N

Democrats ***Republicans***

	771	772	773	774	775	776	777
KANSAS							
1 Sebelius	Y	Y	Y	Y	N	Y	Y
2 Keys	Y	Y	Y	N	N	Y	Y
3 Winn	Y	Y	Y	Y	N	Y	Y
4 Glickman	N	Y	Y	N	Y	Y	Y
5 Skubitz	?	?	Y	Y	N	?	?
KENTUCKY							
1 Hubbard	Y	Y	Y	Y	Y	Y	Y
2 Natcher	Y	Y	Y	Y	Y	Y	N
3 Mazzoli	Y	N	Y	Y	N	Y	N
4 Snyder	Y	Y	Y	Y	N	Y	Y
5 Carter	Y	Y	Y	Y	N	Y	Y
6 Breckinridge	?	?	?	Y	?	?	?
7 Perkins	Y	Y	Y	Y	N	Y	N
LOUISIANA							
1 Livingston	Y	Y	Y	Y	Y	Y	?
2 Boggs	Y	Y	Y	Y	Y	Y	N
3 Treen	Y	Y	Y	Y	N	Y	Y
4 Waggonner	Y	Y	Y	Y	Y	Y	Y
5 Huckaby	Y	Y	Y	Y	Y	Y	Y
6 Moore	Y	Y	Y	Y	N	Y	Y
7 Breaux	Y	Y	Y	Y	Y	Y	Y
8 Long	Y	Y	Y	Y	Y	Y	Y
MAINE							
1 Emery	Y	N	Y	N	N	Y	Y
2 Cohen	Y	N	Y	N	N	Y	N
MARYLAND							
1 Bauman	N	Y	Y	N	N	Y	Y
2 Long	N	Y	Y	Y	Y	Y	N
3 Mikulski	Y	Y	Y	Y	Y	Y	N
4 Holt	Y	Y	Y	N	N	Y	Y
5 Spellman	Y	Y	#	Y	Y	Y	N
6 Byron	Y	Y	Y	N	N	?	Y
7 Mitchell	N	Y	Y	Y	Y	Y	#
8 Steers	Y	N	Y	N	N	Y	N
MASSACHUSETTS							
1 Conte	Y	N	Y	N	N	Y	N
2 Boland	Y	Y	Y	Y	Y	Y	N
3 Early	Y	N	Y	N	N	Y	N
4 Drinan	N	N	Y	N	N	Y	N
5 Tsongas	?	?	Y	N	?	?	?
6 Harrington	#	▮	#	N	▮	#	▮
7 Markey	N	N	Y	N	N	Y	N
8 O'Neill							
9 Moakley	Y	Y	Y	Y	N	Y	N
10 Heckler	?	?	Y	N	N	Y	N
11 Burke	Y	Y	Y	Y	N	Y	Y
12 Studds	Y	N	Y	N	N	Y	N
MICHIGAN							
1 Conyers	#	N	#	N	▮	#	▮
2 Pursell	Y	Y	Y	Y	N	Y	Y
3 Brown	Y	N	Y	N	N	Y	N
4 Stockman	#	N	Y	N	N	Y	N
5 Sawyer	Y	Y	Y	N	N	Y	N
6 Carr	N	N	Y	N	N	Y	N
7 Kildee	Y	N	Y	N	N	Y	N
8 Traxler	Y	Y	Y	Y	Y	Y	N
9 Vander Jagt	Y	Y	Y	?	N	Y	Y
10 Cederberg	Y	Y	Y	N	N	Y	Y
11 Ruppe	Y	Y	Y	N	?	?	Y
12 Bonior	N	N	Y	N	N	Y	N
13 Diggs	#	#	#	X	?	#	#
14 Nedzi	Y	N	?	N	N	Y	N
15 Ford	?	?	?	Y	Y	Y	N
16 Dingell	?	?	Y	N	Y	Y	N
17 Brodhead	Y	N	Y	N	N	Y	N
18 Blanchard	?	N	Y	N	N	Y	N
19 Broomfield	#	▮	Y	N	N	Y	N
MINNESOTA							
1 Quie	Y	Y	Y	Y	N	?	?
2 Hagedorn	Y	Y	Y	Y	N	Y	?
3 Frenzel	Y	Y	N	N	N	Y	Y
4 Vento	Y	N	Y	N	N	Y	N
5 Fraser	Y	Y	Y	N	N	Y	N
6 Nolan	Y	?	Y	N	?	#	N
7 Stangeland	Y	Y	Y	Y	N	Y	Y
8 Oberstar	Y	Y	Y	Y	Y	Y	N
MISSISSIPPI							
1 Whitten	Y	Y	Y	Y	?	Y	Y
2 Bowen	Y	Y	Y	Y	Y	Y	Y
3 Montgomery	Y	Y	Y	Y	Y	Y	Y
4 Cochran	?	?	?	✓	?	?	?
5 Lott	Y	Y	Y	Y	Y	Y	Y
MISSOURI							
1 Clay	?	?	Y	Y	Y	?	N
2 Young	Y	Y	Y	N	Y	Y	Y
3 Gephardt	Y	N	Y	N	N	Y	Y

	771	772	773	774	775	776	777
4 Skelton	Y	Y	Y	N	Y	Y	Y
5 Bolling	#	#	Y	N	▮	Y	Y
6 Coleman	Y	Y	Y	N	N	Y	Y
7 Taylor	Y	Y	Y	Y	N	Y	Y
8 Ichord	Y	Y	Y	Y	N	Y	Y
9 Volkmer	Y	N	Y	N	N	Y	N
10 Burlison	Y	Y	Y	Y	Y	Y	Y
MONTANA							
1 Baucus	Y	Y	Y	Y	N	Y	Y
2 Marlenee	Y	Y	Y	Y	N	Y	Y
NEBRASKA							
1 Thone	?	?	?	✓	?	?	?
2 Cavanaugh	Y	Y	Y	Y	N	Y	N
3 Smith	?	?	Y	Y	N	Y	Y
NEVADA							
AL Santini	Y	Y	Y	N	Y	Y	Y
NEW HAMPSHIRE							
1 D'Amours	Y	N	Y	N	N	Y	N
2 Cleveland	Y	Y	Y	N	N	Y	Y
NEW JERSEY							
1 Florio	Y	Y	Y	N	Y	Y	N
2 Hughes	Y	N	Y	N	Y	Y	N
3 Howard	Y	Y	Y	Y	Y	Y	N
4 Thompson	Y	Y	Y	Y	Y	Y	N
5 Fenwick	Y	N	N	N	N	Y	N
6 Forsythe	Y	N	Y	N	N	Y	N
7 Maguire	N	N	Y	N	N	Y	N
8 Roe	Y	Y	Y	Y	Y	Y	N
9 Hollenbeck	Y	Y	#	N	N	Y	N
10 Rodino	Y	Y	Y	N	Y	Y	N
11 Minish	Y	Y	Y	N	N	Y	N
12 Rinaldo	Y	Y	Y	Y	N	Y	N
13 Meyner	Y	Y	Y	N	N	Y	N
14 LeFante	Y	Y	Y	N	Y	Y	Y
15 Patten	Y	Y	Y	N	Y	Y	N
NEW MEXICO							
1 Lujan	?	?	?	?	?	?	?
2 Runnels	Y	Y	Y	N	Y	Y	Y
NEW YORK							
1 Pike	Y	Y	Y	N	N	Y	N
2 Downey	Y	N	#	N	Y	Y	N
3 Ambro	Y	Y	?	N	Y	Y	N
4 Lent	Y	Y	Y	N	N	Y	Y
5 Wydler	N	Y	Y	N	N	Y	N
6 Wolff	Y	Y	Y	N	Y	Y	Y
7 Addabbo	Y	Y	Y	Y	Y	Y	N
8 Rosenthal	Y	N	Y	N	Y	Y	N
9 Delaney	?	?	Y	N	Y	Y	Y
10 Biaggi	Y	Y	Y	N	Y	Y	N
11 Scheuer	Y	Y	Y	Y	Y	Y	N
12 Chisholm	Y	Y	#	Y	Y	Y	N
13 Solarz	Y	Y	Y	N	N	Y	N
14 Richmond	?	?	Y	Y	Y	Y	N
15 Zeferetti	Y	Y	Y	Y	Y	Y	Y
16 Holtzman	N	Y	Y	N	N	Y	N
17 Murphy	Y	Y	Y	Y	Y	Y	N
18 Green	Y	Y	Y	N	N	Y	N
19 Rangel	Y	Y	Y	Y	Y	Y	N
20 Weiss	N	Y	Y	N	N	Y	N
21 Garcia	▮	▮	#	N	Y	Y	N
22 Bingham	Y	Y	Y	N	Y	Y	N
23 Caputo	?	?	?	?	?	?	?
24 Ottinger	Y	Y	Y	N	N	Y	N
25 Fish	Y	?	Y	N	N	Y	Y
26 Gilman	Y	Y	Y	Y	?	?	N
27 McHugh	Y	Y	Y	N	Y	Y	N
28 Stratton	Y	Y	Y	N	Y	Y	Y
29 Pattison	Y	N	Y	N	N	Y	N
30 McEwen	N	Y	Y	Y	N	Y	Y
31 Mitchell	Y	Y	Y	N	▮	Y	N
32 Hanley	Y	Y	Y	N	N	Y	Y
33 Walsh	Y	Y	Y	Y	N	Y	Y
34 Horton	Y	Y	Y	Y	N	#	N
35 Conable	Y	N	Y	N	N	Y	Y
36 LaFalce	Y	Y	Y	N	Y	Y	N
37 Nowak	Y	Y	Y	Y	N	Y	N
38 Kemp	?	?	Y	Y	Y	Y	Y
39 Lundine	Y	Y	Y	Y	N	Y	N
NORTH CAROLINA							
1 Jones	Y	Y	Y	Y	Y	Y	Y
2 Fountain	Y	Y	Y	N	N	Y	Y
3 Whitley	Y	Y	Y	Y	Y	Y	Y
4 Andrews	Y	Y	Y	Y	N	Y	N
5 Neal	Y	Y	Y	N	N	Y	N
6 Preyer	Y	Y	Y	N	N	Y	N
7 Rose	Y	Y	Y	N	?	?	N
8 Hefner	Y	Y	Y	N	N	Y	Y

	771	772	773	774	775	776	777
9 Martin	Y	N	N	N	N	#	?
10 Broyhill	Y	N	Y	N	N	Y	Y
11 Gudger	Y	Y	Y	N	N	Y	Y
NORTH DAKOTA							
AL Andrews	Y	Y	Y	Y	✓	Y	Y
OHIO							
1 Gradison	Y	N	Y	N	N	Y	N
2 Luken	Y	?	?	N	N	Y	N
3 Whalen	Y	N	#	X	▮	#	#
4 Guyer	Y	Y	Y	N	N	Y	Y
5 Latta	N	Y	Y	N	N	Y	Y
6 Harsha	Y	Y	Y	Y	Y	Y	Y
7 Brown	Y	Y	Y	N	N	Y	Y
8 Kindness	N	Y	Y	N	N	Y	Y
9 Ashley	Y	Y	Y	?	N	Y	N
10 Miller	N	Y	N	N	Y	Y	Y
11 Stanton	Y	Y	Y	Y	N	Y	Y
12 Devine	Y	N	Y	N	N	Y	Y
13 Pease	N	N	Y	N	N	Y	N
14 Seiberling	N	N	Y	N	N	Y	N
15 Wylie	Y	N	Y	N	N	Y	N
16 Regula	Y	Y	Y	N	N	Y	Y
17 Ashbrook	N	Y	Y	N	N	Y	Y
18 Applegate	N	Y	Y	Y	Y	Y	Y
19 Carney	Y	Y	Y	Y	Y	Y	N
20 Oakar	N	Y	Y	Y	Y	Y	Y
21 Stokes	Y	Y	Y	Y	Y	Y	N
22 Vanik	Y	Y	Y	N	Y	Y	N
23 Mottl	N	N	Y	N	Y	Y	N
OKLAHOMA							
1 Jones	Y	Y	Y	Y	Y	?	Y
2 Risenhoover	Y	Y	Y	N	Y	Y	Y
3 Watkins	Y	Y	Y	Y	Y	Y	Y
4 Steed	Y	Y	Y	Y	Y	Y	Y
5 Edwards	Y	Y	Y	Y	N	Y	Y
6 English	Y	Y	Y	N	?	Y	Y
OREGON							
1 AuCoin	Y	Y	Y	Y	N	Y	N
2 Ullman	Y	#	Y	Y	Y	Y	Y
3 Duncan	?	Y	Y	Y	N	Y	Y
4 Weaver	N	Y	Y	N	N	Y	N
PENNSYLVANIA							
1 Myers, M.	Y	Y	Y	Y	Y	?	N
2 Nix	Y	Y	Y	N	Y	Y	Y
3 Lederer	Y	Y	Y	Y	Y	Y	Y
4 Eilberg	?	?	?	Y	Y	Y	Y
5 Schulze	Y	?	?	✓	Y	N	N
6 Yatron	Y	Y	Y	Y	N	Y	N
7 Edgar	Y	N	Y	N	N	Y	N
8 Kostmayer	N	N	Y	N	N	Y	N
9 Shuster	Y	Y	Y	Y	N	Y	Y
10 McDade	Y	Y	Y	Y	N	Y	Y
11 Flood	Y	Y	Y	Y	?	Y	Y
12 Murtha	Y	Y	Y	Y	Y	Y	Y
13 Coughlin	Y	Y	Y	N	N	Y	Y
14 Moorhead	Y	Y	Y	N	Y	Y	N
15 Rooney	Y	Y	Y	Y	N	Y	N
16 Walker	Y	N	Y	N	N	Y	Y
17 Ertel	Y	Y	Y	Y	N	Y	Y
18 Walgren	Y	Y	Y	N	Y	Y	N
19 Goodling, W.	Y	Y	Y	N	N	Y	?
20 Gaydos	Y	Y	Y	Y	Y	Y	N
21 Dent	Y	Y	Y	Y	Y	#	#
22 Murphy	N	Y	Y	N	Y	Y	Y
23 Ammerman	?	?	?	X	?	?	?
24 Marks	Y	Y	Y	N	N	Y	N
25 Myers, G.	N	Y	N	Y	N	Y	N
RHODE ISLAND							
1 St Germain	Y	Y	Y	N	Y	Y	N
2 Beard	Y	Y	Y	Y	Y	Y	N
SOUTH CAROLINA							
1 Davis	Y	Y	Y	N	N	Y	Y
2 Spence	Y	Y	Y	Y	N	Y	N
3 Derrick	Y	N	Y	N	Y	Y	N
4 Mann	Y	Y	Y	N	N	Y	Y
5 Holland	Y	Y	Y	N	N	Y	Y
6 Jenrette	Y	Y	Y	Y	N	Y	Y
SOUTH DAKOTA							
1 Pressler	Y	Y	Y	Y	N	Y	?
2 Abdnor	Y	Y	Y	Y	N	Y	Y
TENNESSEE							
1 Quillen	Y	Y	Y	Y	N	Y	Y
2 Duncan	Y	Y	Y	Y	N	Y	Y
3 Lloyd	Y	Y	Y	Y	Y	Y	Y
4 Gore	N	Y	Y	Y	N	Y	Y
5 Vacancy							
6 Beard	#	Y	Y	Y	Y	Y	Y

	771	772	773	774	775	776	777
7 Jones	Y	Y	Y	Y	Y	Y	Y
8 Ford	Y	Y	Y	N	N	Y	N
TEXAS							
1 Hall	Y	Y	Y	Y	Y	Y	Y
2 Wilson, C.	Y	Y	#	Y	Y	Y	Y
3 Collins	Y	N	N	N	N	Y	Y
4 Roberts	N	Y	Y	Y	Y	Y	Y
5 Mattox	N	N	Y	N	N	Y	N
6 Teague	?	?	?	Y	?	?	?
7 Archer	Y	Y	Y	N	N	Y	Y
8 Eckhardt	Y	Y	Y	N	Y	Y	N
9 Brooks	?	?	Y	Y	Y	Y	Y
10 Pickle	#	#	Y	Y	Y	Y	N
11 Poage	N	Y	Y	Y	Y	Y	Y
12 Wright	Y	Y	Y	Y	?	Y	Y
13 Hightower	Y	Y	Y	Y	N	Y	Y
14 Young	?	Y	?	Y	N	?	?
15 de la Garza	Y	Y	Y	Y	N	Y	Y
16 White	N	Y	Y	Y	Y	Y	Y
17 Burleson	Y	Y	Y	N	Y	Y	Y
18 Jordan	Y	Y	Y	Y	Y	Y	N
19 Mahon	Y	Y	Y	Y	Y	Y	Y
20 Gonzalez	Y	Y	Y	Y	P	Y	Y
21 Krueger	#	#	#	✓	?	#	?
22 Gammage	Y	Y	Y	N	N	Y	Y
23 Kazen	Y	Y	Y	Y	N	Y	Y
24 Milford	Y	Y	Y	N	?	?	Y
UTAH							
1 McKay	Y	Y	Y	Y	Y	Y	Y
2 Marriott	Y	Y	Y	Y	▮	Y	Y
VERMONT							
AL Jeffords	Y	N	Y	N	N	Y	N
VIRGINIA							
1 Trible	Y	Y	Y	Y	N	Y	Y
2 Whitehurst	Y	Y	Y	Y	N	Y	Y
3 Satterfield	N	Y	Y	Y	Y	Y	Y
4 Daniel	Y	Y	Y	Y	N	Y	Y
5 Daniel	Y	Y	Y	Y	Y	Y	Y
6 Butler	Y	Y	Y	Y	N	Y	Y
7 Robinson	Y	Y	Y	Y	N	Y	Y
8 Harris	Y	Y	Y	N	Y	Y	N
9 Wampler	Y	Y	Y	Y	N	Y	Y
10 Fisher	Y	N	Y	N	N	Y	N
WASHINGTON							
1 Pritchard	Y	Y	Y	N	N	Y	N
2 Meeds	?	?	Y	Y	N	Y	Y
3 Bonker	Y	Y	Y	Y	N	Y	N
4 McCormack	Y	Y	N	Y	N	Y	Y
5 Foley	Y	Y	Y	Y	Y	Y	Y
6 Dicks	Y	Y	Y	Y	N	Y	Y
7 Cunningham	Y	Y	Y	N	N	Y	N
WEST VIRGINIA							
1 Mollohan	Y	Y	Y	Y	Y	Y	N
2 Staggers	Y	Y	Y	N	Y	?	?
3 Slack	?	?	Y	Y	Y	Y	N
4 Rahall	Y	Y	Y	Y	Y	Y	N
WISCONSIN							
1 Aspin	Y	?	Y	N	?	Y	N
2 Kastenmeier	Y	Y	Y	Y	N	Y	N
3 Baldus	Y	Y	Y	Y	N	Y	N
4 Zablocki	Y	Y	Y	Y	Y	Y	Y
5 Reuss	Y	N	Y	N	N	Y	N
6 Steiger	Y	▮	Y	N	N	#	Y
7 Obey	Y	N	Y	Y	Y	Y	N
8 Cornell	Y	N	Y	N	N	Y	N
9 Kasten	Y	▮	Y	N	N	Y	N
WYOMING							
AL Roncalio	Y	Y	Y	Y	Y	Y	Y

Democrats ***Republicans***

778. HR 13471. Financial Institutions Regulatory Act. Kindness, R-Ohio, amendment to authorize payment of attorneys' fees and court costs to persons who win appeals against federal agencies covered under the act. Rejected 153-222: R 93-26; D 60-196 (ND 18-157; SD 42-39), Oct. 5, 1978.

779. HR 13471. Financial Institutions Regulatory Act. Stark, D-Calif., amendment to delete the exemption from privacy provisions for the Securities and Exchange Commission. Adopted 328-26: R 111-1; D 217-25 (ND 143-22; SD 74-3), Oct. 5, 1978.

780. HR 13471. Financial Institutions Regulatory Act. Hanley, D-N.Y. amendments, en bloc, to delete the "grandfather" clause for bank holding company insurance affiliates that had applied for authority to engage in insurance activities before June 6, 1978. Adopted 252-72: R 67-32; D 185-40 (ND 128-22; SD 57-18), Oct. 5, 1978.

781. H Res 1404. Consideration of Conference Reports. Adoption of the resolution to waive House rules to allow the House, through Oct. 15, 1978, to consider on the same day as filed conference committee reports and amendments reported in disagreement by conference committees, and to authorize the Speaker at any time to declare recesses and to allow motions to suspend the rules. Adopted 300-56: R 62-55; D 238-1 (ND 163-0; SD 75-1), Oct. 6, 1978.

782. HR 12442. Consumer Product Safety Commission. Adoption of the rule (H Res 1410) providing for House floor consideration of the bill to authorize appropriations for the Consumer Product Safety Commission of $55 million for fiscal 1979, $60 million for 1980 and $65 million for 1981 and to grant the agency increased flexibility in the development of mandatory safety standards. Adopted 360-6: R 116-1; D 244-5 (ND 169-1; SD 75-4), Oct. 6, 1978.

783. S 2640. Civil Service Reform. Adoption of the conference report on the bill to revise the federal civil service system. Adopted (thus cleared for the president) 365-8: R 119-3; D 246-5 (ND 168-2; SD 78-3) Oct. 6, 1978. A "yea" was a vote supporting the president's position.

784. HR 13750. Sugar Stabilization Act. Steiger, R-Wis., amendment, to the Ways and Means amendment, to add an automatic inflation adjustment for the support price for domestic sugar producers. Adopted 194-164: R 73-45; D 121-119 (ND 66-98; SD 55-21), Oct. 6, 1978. A "nay" was a vote supporting the president's position.

785. HR 13750. Sugar Stabilization Act. Passage of the bill to authorize U.S. participation in the International Sugar Agreement, to set a support price for domestic sugar producers and authorize import quotas and fees to maintain that price, and to establish minimum wages and other benefits for sugar industry workers. Passed 186-159: R 54-61; D 132-98 (ND 75-79; SD 57-19), Oct. 6, 1978. A "nay" was a vote supporting the president's position.

KEY

- Y Voted for (yea).
- ✓ Paired for.
- † Announced for.
- # CQ Poll for.
- N Voted against (nay).
- X Paired against.
- \- Announced against.
- ▮ CQ Poll against.
- P Voted "present."
- ● Voted "present" to avoid possible conflict of interest.
- ? Did not vote or otherwise make a position known.

	778	779	780	781	782	783	784	785
ALABAMA								
1 Edwards	N	Y	N	Y	Y	Y	Y	Y
2 Dickinson	N	Y	?	Y	Y	Y	Y	Y
3 Nichols	▮	#	▮	Y	Y	Y	Y	Y
4 Bevill	N	Y	N	Y	Y	Y	Y	Y
5 Flippo	N	Y	Y	Y	Y	Y	Y	?
6 Buchanan	N	Y	N	N	Y	Y	Y	N
7 Flowers	Y	Y	Y	Y	?	?	Y	?
ALASKA								
AL Young	Y	Y	#	N	Y	Y	Y	Y
ARIZONA								
1 Rhodes	Y	Y	N	?	?	?	?	?
2 Udall	N	#	#	Y	Y	Y	N	N
3 Stump	N	Y	Y	Y	Y	Y	Y	Y
4 Rudd	?	?	?	?	?	?	?	?
ARKANSAS								
1 Alexander	N	Y	Y	?	?	?	?	?
2 Tucker	Y	Y	Y	?	Y	Y	Y	Y
3 Hammerschmidt	Y	Y	Y	N	N	Y	Y	N
4 Thornton	N	Y	Y	Y	Y	Y	Y	Y
CALIFORNIA								
1 Johnson	N	Y	N	Y	Y	Y	Y	Y
2 Clausen	Y	Y	Y	N	Y	Y	Y	Y
3 Moss	?	?	?	?	?	?	?	?
4 Leggett	N	Y	?	Y	Y	?	Y	Y
5 Burton, J.	Y	Y	Y	?	?	Y	Y	Y
6 Burton, P.	N	?	?	Y	Y	Y	Y	Y
7 Miller	N	?	?	Y	Y	Y	Y	N
8 Dellums	N	Y	Y	Y	Y	Y	Y	Y
9 Stark	N	Y	#	?	Y	Y	N	▮
10 Edwards	N	Y	?	Y	Y	Y	N	Y
11 Ryan	N	Y	Y	Y	Y	Y	Y	Y
12 McCloskey	Y	Y	Y	?	Y	Y	Y	Y
13 Mineta	N	Y	P	Y	Y	Y	Y	Y
14 McFall	N	Y	Y	Y	Y	Y	Y	Y
15 Sisk	Y	Y	?	Y	Y	?	?	Y
16 Panetta	N	Y	Y	Y	?	#	#	✓
17 Krebs	N	Y	Y	Y	Y	Y	Y	Y
18 Vacancy								
19 Lagomarsino	Y	Y	Y	N	Y	Y	Y	Y
20 Goldwater	Y	Y	?	?	Y	Y	Y	Y
21 Corman	N	Y	Y	Y	?	Y	N	Y
22 Moorhead	Y	Y	Y	N	Y	Y	Y	N
23 Beilenson	N	N	#	Y	Y	Y	N	N
24 Waxman	N	Y	Y	?	Y	Y	Y	Y
25 Roybal	N	Y	Y	Y	Y	Y	Y	Y
26 Rousselot	Y	Y	Y	N	Y	Y	Y	N
27 Dornan	Y	Y	N	N	Y	Y	Y	N
28 Burke	▮	#	#	?	?	#	#	#
29 Hawkins	N	Y	N	Y	Y	Y	Y	Y
30 Danielson	N	N	Y	Y	Y	Y	N	N
31 Wilson, C.H.	N	Y	?	Y	Y	N	N	Y
32 Anderson	N	N	Y	Y	?	Y	N	N
33 Clawson	Y	Y	Y	N	Y	Y	Y	N
34 Hannaford	N	Y	Y	Y	Y	Y	N	Y
35 Lloyd	N	N	Y	Y	Y	Y	N	Y
36 Brown	N	Y	Y	Y	Y	Y	Y	Y
37 Pettis	?	?	?	?	?	?	?	?
38 Patterson	N	Y	N	Y	Y	Y	N	Y
39 Wiggins	▮	#	#	?	?	#	#	#
40 Badham	Y	Y	Y	N	Y	Y	Y	Y
41 Wilson, B.	N	Y	Y	Y	Y	Y	Y	Y
42 Van Deerlin	N	Y	?	Y	Y	Y	N	N
43 Burgener	Y	Y	Y	N	Y	Y	Y	Y
COLORADO								
1 Schroeder	N	Y	Y	?	Y	Y	Y	Y
2 Wirth	N	Y	Y	Y	Y	Y	Y	Y
3 Evans	N	#	#	Y	Y	Y	Y	Y
4 Johnson	Y	?	Y	Y	Y	Y	Y	Y
5 Armstrong	?	?	?	?	?	?	✓	✓
CONNECTICUT								
1 Cotter	N	Y	Y	?	?	#	▮	?
2 Dodd	?	?	?	Y	Y	Y	Y	N
3 Giaimo	N	Y	?	?	?	?	?	?
4 McKinney	N	Y	Y	Y	Y	Y	N	N
5 Sarasin	▮	#	#	?	?	#	X	X
6 Moffett	N	?	?	Y	Y	Y	N	N
DELAWARE								
AL Evans	Y	Y	?	Y	Y	Y	N	N
FLORIDA								
1 Sikes	N	?	Y	Y	Y	Y	Y	Y
2 Fuqua	N	Y	Y	Y	Y	Y	#	#
3 Bennett	N	Y	Y	Y	Y	Y	N	N
4 Chappell	Y	N	Y	Y	Y	?	?	✓
5 Kelly	Y	Y	N	N	Y	Y	Y	N
6 Young	P	Y	Y	Y	Y	Y	Y	N
7 Gibbons	?	?	?	Y	N	Y	N	N
8 Ireland	Y	Y	Y	?	Y	Y	Y	Y
9 Frey	Y	Y	Y	N	?	Y	Y	Y
10 Bafalis	Y	Y	Y	Y	Y	Y	Y	Y
11 Rogers	P	?	?	Y	Y	Y	✓	Y
12 Burke	Y	Y	?	Y	Y	Y	Y	Y
13 Lehman	N	Y	Y	Y	Y	Y	N	Y
14 Pepper	N	Y	Y	Y	Y	Y	N	Y
15 Fascell	N	Y	Y	Y	Y	Y	N	N
GEORGIA								
1 Ginn	N	Y	N	Y	Y	Y	N	N
2 Mathis	Y	Y	?	?	N	Y	Y	Y
3 Brinkley	Y	Y	Y	Y	N	Y	Y	Y
4 Levitas	N	Y	N	Y	Y	Y	N	N
5 Fowler	N	Y	N	Y	Y	Y	N	N
6 Flynt	Y	Y	N	Y	Y	Y	Y	Y
7 McDonald	Y	Y	Y	N	N	Y	Y	N
8 Evans	Y	Y	Y	Y	Y	Y	Y	Y
9 Jenkins	N	Y	N	Y	Y	Y	N	N
10 Barnard	N	Y	N	Y	Y	Y	Y	N
HAWAII								
1 Heftel	N	Y	Y	Y	Y	Y	Y	Y
2 Akaka	N	Y	Y	Y	Y	Y	Y	Y
IDAHO								
1 Symms	Y	Y	Y	N	Y	Y	Y	Y
2 Hansen, G.	Y	Y	Y	N	Y	Y	Y	Y
ILLINOIS								
1 Metcalfe	N	Y	Y	Y	Y	Y	Y	Y
2 Murphy	N	Y	Y	?	?	#	?	?
3 Russo	N	Y	Y	Y	Y	Y	N	N
4 Derwinski	N	Y	Y	Y	Y	Y	Y	Y
5 Fary	N	Y	Y	Y	Y	Y	Y	Y
6 Hyde	Y	Y	N	N	Y	Y	N	N
7 Collins	N	Y	Y	?	?	#	▮	✓
8 Rostenkowski	N	Y	Y	Y	Y	Y	N	Y
9 Yates	N	Y	Y	Y	Y	Y	N	N
10 Mikva	▮	#	#	?	?	#	▮	X
11 Annunzio	N	Y	Y	Y	Y	Y	Y	Y
12 Crane	#	#	▮	?	?	#	?	?
13 McClory	Y	N	Y	N	Y	Y	N	N
14 Erlenborn	N	Y	N	Y	Y	Y	N	N
15 Corcoran	Y	Y	N	Y	Y	Y	X	X
16 Anderson	Y	#	#	Y	Y	Y	N	N
17 O'Brien	Y	P	P	Y	Y	Y	Y	Y
18 Michel	?	?	?	?	Y	Y	Y	Y
19 Railsback	N	?	?	?	?	?	?	?
20 Findley	Y	Y	?	Y	Y	Y	N	N
21 Madigan	?	?	?	?	?	Y	Y	Y
22 Shipley	?	?	?	?	?	?	?	?
23 Price	N	Y	Y	Y	Y	Y	Y	N
24 Simon	N	Y	?	Y	Y	Y	N	N
INDIANA								
1 Benjamin	N	N	Y	Y	Y	Y	Y	Y
2 Fithian	N	Y	Y	Y	Y	Y	Y	Y
3 Brademas	N	Y	Y	Y	Y	Y	N	N
4 Quayle	Y	Y	?	Y	Y	Y	N	N
5 Hillis	N	Y	?	?	?	?	?	?
6 Evans	N	?	Y	Y	Y	Y	Y	Y
7 Myers, J.	P	Y	Y	N	Y	Y	Y	Y
8 Cornwell	N	#	#	Y	Y	Y	N	N
9 Hamilton	N	Y	Y	Y	Y	Y	N	N
10 Sharp	N	Y	Y	Y	Y	Y	N	N
11 Jacobs	N	Y	Y	Y	Y	Y	N	N
IOWA								
1 Leach	Y	Y	Y	Y	Y	Y	Y	Y
2 Blouin	?	?	?	Y	Y	Y	Y	?
3 Grassley	Y	Y	Y	N	Y	Y	Y	Y
4 Smith	N	Y	N	Y	Y	Y	Y	Y
5 Harkin	N	Y	Y	Y	Y	Y	Y	Y
6 Bedell	Y	Y	N	Y	Y	#	Y	Y

Democrats ***Republicans***

	778	779	780	781	782	783	784	785
KANSAS								
1 Sebelius	Y	Y	Y	Y	Y	Y	✔	✔
2 Keys	N	N	Y	Y	Y	Y	N	Y
3 Winn	P	Y	P	N	Y	Y	Y	Y
4 Glickman	N	N	Y	Y	Y	Y	Y	Y
5 Skubitz	Y	?	Y	Y	Y	Y	?	✔
KENTUCKY								
1 Hubbard	Y	Y	Y	Y	Y	Y	Y	Y
2 Natcher	Y	Y	Y	Y	Y	Y	Y	Y
3 Mazzoli	N	Y	N	Y	Y	Y	N	N
4 Snyder	Y	Y	N	N	Y	Y	N	Y
5 Carter	Y	Y	N	Y	Y	Y	N	Y
6 Breckinridge	?	?	?	?	?	?	?	?
7 Perkins	N	Y	Y	Y	Y	Y	N	Y
LOUISIANA								
1 Livingston	?	#	?	N	Y	Y	Y	Y
2 Boggs	Y	?	Y	Y	Y	Y	Y	Y
3 Treen	Y	Y	N	N	Y	Y	Y	Y
4 Waggonner	Y	Y	N	Y	Y	Y	Y	Y
5 Huckaby	Y	Y	N	Y	Y	Y	Y	Y
6 Moore	Y	Y	N	N	Y	Y	Y	Y
7 Breaux	Y	Y	Y	Y	Y	Y	Y	Y
8 Long	Y	Y	N	Y	Y	Y	Y	Y
MAINE								
1 Emery	Y	Y	Y	Y	Y	Y	N	N
2 Cohen	Y	?	?	?	?	#	?	X
MARYLAND								
1 Bauman	N	Y	Y	N	Y	Y	Y	N
2 Long	N	Y	Y	Y	Y	Y	N	N
3 Mikulski	N	Y	Y	?	Y	Y	N	N
4 Holt	Y	Y	Y	N	Y	N	Y	N
5 Spellman	N	Y	Y	Y	Y	N	N	N
6 Byron	N	Y	N	Y	?	Y	Y	N
7 Mitchell	N	Y	N	Y	Y	Y	Y	Y
8 Steers	P	P	P	Y	Y	N	N	N
MASSACHUSETTS								
1 Conte	N	Y	Y	Y	Y	Y	N	N
2 Boland	N	Y	Y	?	Y	Y	▮	▮
3 Early	N	Y	Y	Y	Y	Y	N	N
4 Drinan	N	Y	Y	Y	Y	Y	N	N
5 Tsongas	?	?	?	?	?	?	?	?
6 Harrington	▮	#	#	?	?	#	▮	?
7 Markey	N	Y	Y	Y	Y	Y	N	N
8 O'Neill								
9 Moakley	N	Y	Y	Y	Y	Y	N	N
10 Heckler	N	Y	Y	?	Y	Y	N	N
11 Burke	N	N	Y	Y	Y	Y	N	N
12 Studds	N	Y	Y	Y	Y	Y	N	N
MICHIGAN								
1 Conyers	✔	#	#	?	?	#	▮	N
2 Pursell	N	Y	Y	Y	Y	Y	Y	N
3 Brown	N	Y	Y	N	Y	Y	N	N
4 Stockman	Y	Y	?	N	?	Y	N	N
5 Sawyer	Y	Y	Y	N	Y	Y	N	N
6 Carr	N	Y	Y	Y	Y	Y	Y	Y
7 Kildee	N	Y	Y	Y	Y	Y	Y	Y
8 Traxler	N	Y	Y	Y	Y	Y	Y	Y
9 Vander Jagt	Y	Y	N	?	Y	Y	Y	Y
10 Cederberg	Y	Y	Y	Y	Y	Y	Y	Y
11 Ruppe	?	?	?	Y	Y	?	N	N
12 Bonior	N	Y	Y	Y	Y	Y	Y	Y
13 Diggs	X	#	#	?	?	#	?	?
14 Nedzi	N	Y	Y	Y	Y	Y	Y	N
15 Ford	N	Y	Y	?	Y	Y	N	N
16 Dingell	?	Y	Y	Y	Y	Y	N	Y
17 Brodhead	N	Y	?	Y	Y	Y	N	N
18 Blanchard	N	Y	Y	?	Y	Y	N	?
19 Broomfield	Y	#	#	N	Y	Y	N	N
MINNESOTA								
1 Quie	?	?	?	?	?	?	✔	✔
2 Hagedorn	?	?	?	?	?	?	?	✔
3 Frenzel	Y	Y	N	Y	Y	Y	Y	Y
4 Vento	N	Y	N	Y	Y	Y	✔	✔
5 Fraser	N	?	Y	Y	Y	Y	Y	?
6 Nolan	N	Y	N	Y	Y	Y	Y	Y
7 Stangeland	Y	Y	N	N	Y	Y	Y	Y
8 Oberstar	N	Y	N	Y	Y	Y	Y	Y
MISSISSIPPI								
1 Whitten	Y	Y	Y	?	Y	Y	Y	Y
2 Bowen	Y	Y	Y	Y	Y	Y	Y	Y
3 Montgomery	Y	Y	Y	Y	Y	Y	Y	Y
4 Cochran	?	?	?	?	?	?	?	✔
5 Lott	Y	Y	Y	N	Y	Y	Y	Y
MISSOURI								
1 Clay	N	Y	Y	Y	Y	Y	Y	Y
2 Young	N	Y	N	Y	Y	Y	N	N
3 Gephardt	N	Y	Y	Y	Y	Y	Y	Y

	778	779	780	781	782	783	784	785
4 Skelton	P	P	P	?	?	?	?	?
5 Bolling	N	Y	N	Y	Y	Y	#	#
6 Coleman	Y	Y	Y	Y	Y	Y	Y	Y
7 Taylor	Y	Y	Y	N	Y	Y	Y	Y
8 Ichord	Y	Y	Y	?	Y	Y	Y	Y
9 Volkmer	N	Y	Y	Y	Y	Y	Y	Y
10 Burlison	N	Y	Y	Y	Y	Y	Y	Y
MONTANA								
1 Baucus	N	Y	Y	Y	Y	Y	Y	Y
2 Marlenee	Y	Y	Y	N	Y	Y	Y	Y
NEBRASKA								
1 Thone	?	?	?	?	?	?	?	✔
2 Cavanaugh	N	N	Y	Y	Y	Y	Y	Y
3 Smith	Y	?	?	Y	Y	Y	Y	Y
NEVADA								
AL Santini	Y	Y	Y	Y	Y	Y	N	N
NEW HAMPSHIRE								
1 D'Amours	N	Y	#	Y	Y	Y	N	N
2 Cleveland	P	P	?	?	?	?	X	X
NEW JERSEY								
1 Florio	N	Y	Y	Y	Y	Y	N	N
2 Hughes	N	Y	Y	Y	Y	Y	N	N
3 Howard	N	Y	Y	?	Y	Y	N	Y
4 Thompson	N	Y	Y	Y	Y	?	?	?
5 Fenwick	N	Y	N	Y	Y	Y	N	N
6 Forsythe	Y	Y	N	Y	Y	Y	N	N
7 Maguire	▮	#	#	Y	Y	Y	N	N
8 Roe	N	Y	Y	Y	Y	Y	?	?
9 Hollenbeck	Y	Y	Y	?	?	#	X	X
10 Rodino	N	▮	#	?	?	#	▮	▮
11 Minish	N	Y	Y	Y	Y	Y	N	N
12 Rinaldo	Y	Y	Y	Y	Y	Y	N	N
13 Meyner	N	Y	Y	Y	Y	?	N	N
14 LeFante	Y	Y	Y	Y	Y	Y	N	N
15 Patten	Y	Y	Y	Y	Y	Y	N	N
NEW MEXICO								
1 Lujan	?	?	?	?	?	?	✔	X
2 Runnels	Y	Y	Y	Y	Y	Y	Y	N
NEW YORK								
1 Pike	P	#	Y	Y	Y	Y	N	N
2 Downey	N	N	Y	Y	Y	Y	N	N
3 Ambro	N	Y	Y	?	Y	Y	N	N
4 Lent	Y	Y	Y	N	Y	Y	N	N
5 Wydler	N	Y	N	Y	Y	Y	N	N
6 Wolff	N	Y	?	Y	Y	Y	N	N
7 Addabbo	N	Y	Y	Y	Y	Y	N	N
8 Rosenthal	N	Y	Y	Y	Y	#	N	N
9 Delaney	N	Y	?	Y	Y	Y	N	Y
10 Biaggi	?	Y	Y	Y	Y	Y	N	N
11 Scheuer	N	Y	N	Y	Y	Y	N	N
12 Chisholm	N	Y	Y	Y	Y	Y	Y	Y
13 Solarz	N	Y	Y	Y	Y	Y	N	N
14 Richmond	N	Y	?	Y	Y	Y	N	N
15 Zeferetti	N	Y	Y	Y	Y	Y	X	#
16 Holtzman	N	Y	Y	?	Y	Y	N	N
17 Murphy	N	Y	Y	Y	Y	Y	N	N
18 Green	N	Y	N	Y	Y	Y	N	N
19 Rangel	N	Y	Y	Y	Y	Y	N	Y
20 Weiss	N	Y	Y	Y	Y	Y	N	N
21 Garcia	N	Y	Y	Y	Y	Y	X	▮
22 Bingham	N	Y	Y	Y	Y	Y	N	Y
23 Caputo	?	?	?	?	?	?	?	?
24 Ottinger	N	Y	Y	Y	Y	Y	N	?
25 Fish	Y	Y	Y	Y	Y	Y	N	X
26 Gilman	N	Y	Y	Y	Y	Y	N	N
27 McHugh	N	Y	Y	Y	Y	Y	N	N
28 Stratton	N	N	Y	Y	Y	Y	N	N
29 Pattison	N	N	N	?	Y	Y	N	N
30 McEwen	P	?	Y	N	Y	?	Y	?
31 Mitchell	Y	Y	Y	Y	Y	Y	Y	X
32 Hanley	N	Y	Y	Y	Y	Y	N	Y
33 Walsh	P	Y	P	?	?	?	X	X
34 Horton	Y	Y	Y	Y	Y	Y	X	X
35 Conable	N	N	Y	Y	Y	Y	?	X
36 LaFalce	N	N	N	Y	Y	Y	N	N
37 Nowak	N	Y	N	Y	Y	Y	N	N
38 Kemp	Y	?	?	N	Y	Y	N	N
39 Lundine	N	N	Y	Y	Y	Y	N	N
NORTH CAROLINA								
1 Jones	N	Y	Y	Y	Y	Y	Y	Y
2 Fountain	Y	#	Y	Y	Y	Y	Y	Y
3 Whitley	N	Y	Y	Y	Y	Y	Y	Y
4 Andrews	Y	Y	Y	Y	Y	Y	Y	Y
5 Neal	N	Y	Y	Y	Y	Y	Y	Y
6 Preyer	N	Y	Y	Y	Y	Y	Y	Y
7 Rose	N	Y	N	Y	Y	Y	Y	Y
8 Hefner	N	Y	Y	Y	Y	Y	Y	Y

	778	779	780	781	782	783	784	785
9 Martin	#	#	#	?	?	#	✔	#
10 Broyhill	Y	?	?	?	?	?	✔	?
11 Gudger	Y	Y	Y	Y	Y	Y	Y	Y
NORTH DAKOTA								
AL Andrews	Y	Y	Y	Y	Y	Y	Y	Y
OHIO								
1 Gradison	N	Y	Y	Y	Y	Y	N	N
2 Luken	Y	Y	Y	Y	Y	Y	N	N
3 Whalen	▮	Y	N	Y	Y	Y	N	N
4 Guyer	Y	Y	Y	Y	Y	Y	Y	Y
5 Latta	Y	Y	Y	Y	Y	Y	Y	Y
6 Harsha	Y	Y	Y	N	Y	Y	N	?
7 Brown	Y	Y	?	N	Y	Y	N	N
8 Kindness	Y	Y	Y	?	?	Y	Y	Y
9 Ashley	N	Y	N	Y	Y	Y	?	?
10 Miller	Y	Y	N	Y	Y	Y	Y	Y
11 Stanton	Y	Y	N	Y	Y	Y	N	N
12 Devine	Y	Y	Y	Y	Y	Y	Y	N
13 Pease	N	Y	Y	Y	Y	Y	X	✔
14 Seiberling	N	Y	Y	Y	Y	Y	N	N
15 Wylie	Y	Y	Y	Y	Y	Y	N	N
16 Regula	N	Y	N	N	Y	Y	N	N
17 Ashbrook	Y	Y	Y	N	Y	Y	Y	N
18 Applegate	Y	Y	Y	Y	Y	Y	N	N
19 Carney	N	Y	?	?	?	?	?	?
20 Oakar	N	Y	Y	Y	Y	Y	Y	Y
21 Stokes	N	Y	Y	Y	Y	Y	Y	Y
22 Vanik	N	Y	Y	Y	Y	Y	N	N
23 Mottl	Y	N	Y	Y	Y	Y	N	X
OKLAHOMA								
1 Jones	Y	Y	?	Y	Y	Y	N	Y
2 Risenhoover	Y	Y	Y	Y	Y	?	?	?
3 Watkins	Y	Y	N	Y	?	Y	Y	Y
4 Steed	N	#	N	Y	Y	Y	Y	Y
5 Edwards	N	Y	Y	N	Y	Y	Y	N
6 English	Y	Y	Y	Y	Y	Y	Y	Y
OREGON								
1 AuCoin	Y	Y	Y	Y	Y	Y	N	N
2 Ullman	N	#	#	Y	Y	Y	N	N
3 Duncan	N	N	N	Y	Y	Y	N	Y
4 Weaver	?	?	?	?	?	?	?	?
PENNSYLVANIA								
1 Myers, M.	N	Y	Y	Y	Y	Y	N	N
2 Nix	N	Y	?	Y	Y	Y	N	Y
3 Lederer	N	Y	Y	Y	Y	Y	N	N
4 Eilberg	N	?	?	Y	Y	Y	N	X
5 Schulze	Y	?	?	N	Y	Y	N	N
6 Yatron	Y	Y	Y	Y	?	Y	Y	Y
7 Edgar	Y	Y	N	Y	Y	Y	N	N
8 Kostmayer	N	Y	N	Y	Y	Y	N	N
9 Shuster	Y	Y	Y	N	Y	Y	Y	Y
10 McDade	Y	Y	Y	Y	Y	Y	N	N
11 Flood	N	Y	Y	Y	Y	Y	Y	Y
12 Murtha	N	N	Y	Y	Y	Y	N	Y
13 Coughlin	Y	Y	#	N	Y	Y	N	N
14 Moorhead	N	Y	Y	Y	Y	Y	N	N
15 Rooney	Y	#	▮	Y	Y	Y	Y	?
16 Walker	Y	#	#	N	Y	Y	N	N
17 Ertel	Y	Y	Y	Y	Y	Y	N	N
18 Walgren	N	Y	Y	Y	Y	Y	N	?
19 Goodling, W.	?	?	?	N	Y	Y	N	N
20 Gaydos	Y	?	Y	Y	Y	Y	N	N
21 Dent	N	Y	Y	?	Y	Y	N	#
22 Murphy	Y	Y	Y	Y	Y	Y	N	N
23 Ammerman	?	?	?	?	?	?	?	X
24 Marks	N	Y	?	Y	Y	Y	N	N
25 Myers, G.	N	Y	Y	Y	Y	N	N	N
RHODE ISLAND								
1 St Germain	N	N	Y	Y	Y	Y	N	N
2 Beard	N	Y	Y	Y	Y	Y	N	N
SOUTH CAROLINA								
1 Davis	Y	Y	?	Y	Y	N	?	?
2 Spence	Y	Y	Y	Y	Y	Y	Y	Y
3 Derrick	N	Y	Y	Y	Y	Y	Y	Y
4 Mann	Y	Y	Y	Y	Y	Y	?	N
5 Holland	N	Y	Y	Y	Y	Y	Y	Y
6 Jenrette	Y	Y	Y	Y	Y	Y	Y	Y
SOUTH DAKOTA								
1 Pressler	N	Y	Y	N	Y	Y	Y	Y
2 Abdnor	Y	Y	N	Y	Y	Y	Y	Y
TENNESSEE								
1 Quillen	P	P	P	Y	?	Y	N	N
2 Duncan	Y	Y	Y	Y	?	Y	N	N
3 Lloyd	N	Y	Y	Y	Y	Y	N	?
4 Gore	N	Y	Y	Y	Y	Y	Y	Y
5 Vacancy								
6 Beard	Y	Y	#	Y	?	Y	Y	Y

	778	779	780	781	782	783	784	785
7 Jones	N	Y	Y	Y	Y	Y	Y	Y
8 Ford	N	Y	N	Y	Y	Y	Y	Y
TEXAS								
1 Hall	Y	Y	Y	Y	Y	Y	Y	N
2 Wilson, C.	Y	Y	Y	Y	Y	Y	#	Y
3 Collins	Y	Y	Y	N	Y	Y	Y	N
4 Roberts	N	N	Y	Y	Y	Y	?	?
5 Mattox	N	Y	Y	Y	Y	Y	N	N
6 Teague	?	?	?	?	?	?	?	?
7 Archer	Y	Y	Y	N	Y	Y	Y	N
8 Eckhardt	N	N	N	?	Y	Y	N	N
9 Brooks	N	Y	Y	Y	Y	Y	N	Y
10 Pickle	N	Y	Y	Y	Y	Y	N	N
11 Poage	Y	Y	Y	Y	Y	Y	Y	Y
12 Wright	?	Y	?	Y	Y	Y	Y	Y
13 Hightower	Y	Y	Y	Y	Y	Y	Y	Y
14 Young	?	?	?	?	?	?	Y	Y
15 de la Garza	Y	Y	Y	Y	Y	Y	Y	Y
16 White	Y	Y	Y	Y	Y	Y	Y	Y
17 Burleson	Y	Y	Y	Y	Y	Y	Y	Y
18 Jordan	Y	Y	N	Y	Y	Y	Y	Y
19 Mahon	N	Y	Y	Y	Y	Y	Y	Y
20 Gonzalez	N	Y	Y	Y	Y	Y	Y	Y
21 Krueger	#	#	?	?	?	#	#	✔
22 Gammage	Y	Y	#	?	?	?	#	#
23 Kazen	Y	Y	Y	Y	Y	Y	Y	Y
24 Milford	Y	?	?	?	?	Y	N	N
UTAH								
1 McKay	N	N	N	Y	N	#	#	✔
2 Marriott	Y	Y	Y	N	Y	Y	Y	Y
VERMONT								
AL Jeffords	N	Y	Y	N	Y	Y	N	Y
VIRGINIA								
1 Trible	Y	Y	N	Y	Y	Y	Y	N
2 Whitehurst	Y	Y	N	?	?	?	#	▮
3 Satterfield	Y	Y	N	?	Y	Y	Y	Y
4 Daniel	Y	Y	N	N	Y	Y	Y	N
5 Daniel	Y	Y	P	Y	Y	Y	Y	Y
6 Butler	Y	Y	N	Y	Y	Y	Y	N
7 Robinson	Y	Y	P	Y	Y	Y	Y	Y
8 Harris	N	Y	Y	Y	Y	N	N	N
9 Wampler	Y	Y	Y	Y	Y	Y	Y	Y
10 Fisher	N	Y	Y	Y	Y	Y	N	N
WASHINGTON								
1 Pritchard	Y	Y	N	Y	Y	Y	Y	N
2 Meeds	N	?	?	Y	Y	Y	?	?
3 Bonker	?	Y	Y	Y	Y	Y	Y	Y
4 McCormack	N	Y	Y	?	Y	Y	Y	Y
5 Foley	N	N	N	Y	Y	Y	Y	Y
6 Dicks	?	?	?	?	?	?	?	?
7 Cunningham	Y	Y	N	N	Y	Y	Y	N
WEST VIRGINIA								
1 Mollohan	N	Y	Y	Y	Y	Y	N	N
2 Staggers	?	?	?	?	?	?	?	?
3 Slack	?	Y	Y	Y	Y	Y	Y	Y
4 Rahall	N	Y	Y	Y	Y	#	✔	✔
WISCONSIN								
1 Aspin	N	?	?	Y	Y	Y	N	?
2 Kastenmeier	N	N	Y	Y	Y	Y	N	N
3 Baldus	N	Y	Y	Y	Y	Y	Y	Y
4 Zablocki	N	Y	Y	Y	Y	Y	Y	Y
5 Reuss	N	N	Y	Y	Y	Y	N	N
6 Steiger	Y	Y	N	Y	Y	Y	Y	Y
7 Obey	N	Y	?	Y	Y	Y	Y	Y
8 Cornell	N	Y	Y	Y	Y	Y	Y	Y
9 Kasten	Y	Y	Y	N	Y	Y	#	Y
WYOMING								
AL Roncalio	▮	Y	Y	Y	?	Y	Y	#

Democrats ***Republicans***

786. HR 11545. Meat Import Act. Burleson, D-Texas, amendment to set the minimum annual level of meat imports at 739 million pounds, instead of 1.2 billion as provided by the bill. Rejected 131-139: R 59-32; D 72-107 (ND 22-92; SD 50-15), Oct. 6, 1978. A "nay" was a vote supporting the president's position.

787. HR 12929. Labor-HEW Appropriations, Fiscal 1979. Walker, R-Pa., motion to recommit the conference report to the conference committee with instructions to the House conferees to agree to the Senate amendment to prohibit use of appropriated funds to implement admission quota policies at higher education institutions. Motion rejected 187-200: R 102-32; D 85-168 (ND 38-136; SD 47-32), Oct. 12, 1978.

788. HR 12929. Labor-HEW Appropriations, Fiscal 1979. Flood, D-Pa., motion that the House concur in the Senate amendment to the conference report to provide 788 full-time permanent positions at the National Heart, Lung and Blood Institute. Motion agreed to 385-11: R 125-8; D 260-3 (ND 181-0; SD 79-3), Oct. 12, 1978.

789. HR 12929. Labor-HEW Apprmedian. Fiscal 1979. Flood, D-Pa., motion that the House concur in the Senate amendment to the conference report to earmark $7.5 million for special projects for Indochinese refugees under the Indochina Migration and Refugee Assistance Act. Motion agreed to 391-0: R 130-0; D 261-0 (ND 179-0; SD 82-0), Oct. 12, 1978.

KEY

- Y Voted for (yea).
- ✓ Paired for.
- † Announced for.
- # CQ Poll for.
- N Voted against (nay).
- X Paired against.
- \- Announced against.
- ▮ CQ Poll against.
- P Voted "present."
- ● Voted "present" to avoid possible conflict of interest.
- ? Did not vote or otherwise make a position known.

	786	787	788	789
ALABAMA				
1 Edwards	Y	Y	Y	Y
2 Dickinson	Y	Y	Y	Y
3 Nichols	Y	Y	Y	Y
4 Bevill	Y	Y	Y	Y
5 Flippo	?	Y	Y	Y
6 Buchanan	Y	Y	Y	Y
7 Flowers	?	Y	Y	?
ALASKA				
AL Young	Y	N	Y	Y
ARIZONA				
1 Rhodes	?	?	?	Y
2 Udall	N	N	Y	Y
3 Stump	#	Y	Y	Y
4 Rudd	?	Y	Y	Y
ARKANSAS				
1 Alexander	?	N	Y	Y
2 Tucker	Y	N	Y	Y
3 Hammerschmidt	Y	Y	Y	Y
4 Thornton	Y	N	Y	Y
CALIFORNIA				
1 Johnson	Y	N	Y	Y
2 Clausen	Y	Y	Y	Y
3 Moss	?	?	?	?
4 Leggett	Y	N	Y	?
5 Burton, J.	?	N	?	Y
6 Burton, P.	?	N	Y	Y
7 Miller	?	N	Y	Y
8 Dellums	▮	N	Y	Y
9 Stark	▮	N	Y	Y
10 Edwards	?	N	Y	Y
11 Ryan	N	N	Y	Y
12 McCloskey	N	N	Y	Y
13 Mineta	N	N	Y	Y
14 McFall	N	N	Y	Y
15 Sisk	N	?	?	?
16 Panetta	#	N	Y	Y
17 Krebs	N	N	Y	Y
18 Vacancy				
19 Lagomarsino	Y	Y	Y	Y
20 Goldwater	?	Y	Y	Y
21 Corman	N	N	Y	Y
22 Moorhead	N	Y	Y	Y
23 Beilenson	N	N	Y	Y
24 Waxman	N	N	Y	Y
25 Roybal	N	N	Y	Y
26 Rousselot	?	Y	N	Y
27 Dornan	?	Y	Y	Y
28 Burke	▮	▮	#	#
29 Hawkins	N	N	?	Y
30 Danielson	N	N	Y	Y
31 Wilson, C.H.	?	N	Y	Y
32 Anderson	N	N	Y	Y
33 Clawson	Y	Y	Y	Y
34 Hannaford	?	N	Y	Y
35 Lloyd	?	N	Y	Y
36 Brown	N	N	Y	Y
37 Pettis	?	?	?	?
38 Patterson	N	N	Y	Y
39 Wiggins	▮	Y	#	Y
40 Badham	#	Y	Y	Y
41 Wilson, B.	Y	N	Y	Y
42 Van Deerlin	N	N	Y	Y
43 Burgener	Y	Y	Y	Y
COLORADO				
1 Schroeder	Y	N	Y	Y
2 Wirth	Y	N	Y	Y
3 Evans	Y	N	Y	Y
4 Johnson	Y	Y	Y	Y
5 Armstrong	X	Y	Y	Y
CONNECTICUT				
1 Cotter	▮	N	Y	Y
2 Dodd	?	N	Y	Y
3 Giaimo	?	N	?	?
4 McKinney	N	Y	Y	Y
5 Sarasin	X	X	#	#
6 Moffett	N	N	Y	Y
DELAWARE				
AL Evans	?	Y	Y	Y
FLORIDA				
1 Sikes	Y	Y	Y	Y
2 Fuqua	#	Y	Y	Y
3 Bennett	N	Y	N	Y
4 Chappell	✓	Y	Y	Y
5 Kelly	Y	Y	N	Y
6 Young	N	Y	Y	Y
7 Gibbons	N	Y	Y	Y
8 Ireland	Y	?	?	?
9 Frey	?	Y	Y	?
10 Bafalis	Y	Y	Y	Y
11 Rogers	N	N	Y	Y
12 Burke	N	Y	Y	Y
13 Lehman	N	N	Y	Y
14 Pepper	▮	N	Y	Y
15 Fascell	N	N	Y	Y
GEORGIA				
1 Ginn	Y	Y	Y	Y
2 Mathis	Y	?	Y	Y
3 Brinkley	Y	Y	Y	Y
4 Levitas	N	Y	Y	Y
5 Fowler	Y	N	Y	Y
6 Flynt	Y	Y	Y	Y
7 McDonald	X	Y	N	Y
8 Evans	Y	#	Y	Y
9 Jenkins	Y	Y	Y	Y
10 Barnard	Y	Y	Y	Y
HAWAII				
1 Heftel	?	?	Y	Y
2 Akaka	#	N	Y	Y
IDAHO				
1 Symms	Y	Y	N	Y
2 Hansen, G.	Y	Y	Y	Y
ILLINOIS				
1 Metcalfe[†]	N			
2 Murphy	?	N	Y	Y
3 Russo	N	Y	Y	Y
4 Derwinski	N	Y	Y	Y
5 Fary	N	N	Y	Y
6 Hyde	?	✓	Y	Y
7 Collins	▮	N	Y	Y
8 Rostenkowski	N	N	Y	Y
9 Yates	N	N	Y	Y
10 Mikva	▮	N	Y	Y
11 Annunzio	N	N	Y	#
12 Crane	#	✓	▮	?
13 McClory	▮	N	Y	Y
14 Erlenborn	N	Y	Y	Y
15 Corcoran	✓	Y	Y	Y
16 Anderson	N	N	Y	Y
17 O'Brien	✓	N	Y	Y
18 Michel	N	Y	N	Y
19 Railsback	?	N	Y	Y
20 Findley	N	N	Y	Y
21 Madigan	Y	N	Y	Y
22 Shipley	✓	?	?	?
23 Price	N	N	Y	Y
24 Simon	N	N	Y	Y
INDIANA				
1 Benjamin	N	N	Y	Y
2 Fithian	N	?	Y	Y
3 Brademas	N	N	Y	Y
4 Quayle	N	Y	Y	Y
5 Hillis	?	N	Y	Y
6 Evans	?	Y	Y	Y
7 Myers, J.	?	Y	Y	Y
8 Cornwell	N	?	Y	Y
9 Hamilton	Y	N	Y	Y
10 Sharp	Y	N	Y	Y
11 Jacobs	Y	#	Y	Y
IOWA				
1 Leach	Y	Y	Y	Y
2 Blouin	Y	?	Y	Y
3 Grassley	Y	N	Y	Y
4 Smith	?	N	Y	Y
5 Harkin	Y	N	Y	Y
6 Bedell	Y	N	Y	Y

Democrats ***Republicans***

	786	787	788	789
KANSAS				
1 Sebelius	✓	Y	Y	Y
2 Keys	Y	▮	Y	Y
3 Winn	Y	Y	Y	Y
4 Glickman	#	Y	Y	Y
5 Skubitz	Y	Y	Y	Y
KENTUCKY				
1 Hubbard	▮	Y	Y	Y
2 Natcher	N	N	Y	Y
3 Mazzoli	N	N	Y	Y
4 Snyder	?	Y	Y	Y
5 Carter	Y	Y	Y	Y
6 Breckinridge	?	N	Y	Y
7 Perkins	?	N	Y	Y
LOUISIANA				
1 Livingston	N	Y	Y	Y
2 Boggs	N	N	Y	Y
3 Treen	Y	Y	Y	Y
4 Waggonner	Y	Y	Y	Y
5 Huckaby	Y	Y	Y	Y
6 Moore	Y	Y	Y	Y
7 Breaux	Y	Y	Y	Y
8 Long	Y	Y	Y	Y
MAINE				
1 Emery	N	Y	Y	Y
2 Cohen	?	Y	Y	Y
MARYLAND				
1 Bauman	Y	Y	N	Y
2 Long	N	N	Y	Y
3 Mikulski	N	N	Y	Y
4 Holt	Y	Y	?	Y
5 Spellman	N	N	Y	Y
6 Byron*	N			
7 Mitchell	N	N	Y	Y
8 Steers	N	N	Y	Y
MASSACHUSETTS				
1 Conte	N	N	Y	Y
2 Boland	?	N	Y	Y
3 Early	N	Y	Y	Y
4 Drinan	N	N	Y	Y
5 Tsongas	?	?	Y	Y
6 Harrington	▮	▮	#	#
7 Markey	N	N	Y	Y
8 O'Neill				
9 Moakley	N	Y	Y	Y
10 Heckler	N	Y	Y	Y
11 Burke	N	N	Y	Y
12 Studds	N	N	Y	Y
MICHIGAN				
1 Conyers	#	▮	#	#
2 Pursell	N	N	Y	Y
3 Brown	Y	X	?	?
4 Stockman	N	#	#	#
5 Sawyer	Y	✓	Y	Y
6 Carr	Y	N	Y	Y
7 Kildee	N	N	Y	Y
8 Traxler	?	Y	Y	Y
9 Vander Jagt	?	Y	Y	Y
10 Cederberg	Y	Y	Y	Y
11 Ruppe	Y	Y	Y	Y
12 Bonior	?	N	Y	Y
13 Diggs	X	?	?	?
14 Nedzi	N	N	Y	Y
15 Ford	?	N	Y	Y
16 Dingell	N	N	Y	Y
17 Brodhead	N	N	Y	Y
18 Blanchard	?	N	Y	Y
19 Broomfield	?	N	Y	Y
MINNESOTA				
1 Quie	?	?	?	?
2 Hagedorn	?	Y	Y	Y
3 Frenzel	N	Y	Y	Y
4 Vento	?	N	Y	?
5 Fraser	Y	N	?	Y
6 Nolan	Y	N	Y	Y
7 Stangeland	Y	Y	Y	Y
8 Oberstar	N	N	Y	Y
MISSISSIPPI				
1 Whitten	Y	Y	Y	Y
2 Bowen	Y	Y	Y	Y
3 Montgomery	Y	Y	Y	#
4 Cochran	✓	✓	?	?
5 Lott	Y	Y	Y	Y
MISSOURI				
1 Clay	N	N	Y	Y
2 Young	?	N	Y	Y
3 Gephardt	Y	Y	Y	Y
4 Skelton	?	Y	Y	Y
5 Bolling	▮	N	Y	Y
6 Coleman	Y	Y	Y	Y
7 Taylor	Y	Y	Y	Y
8 Ichord	?	Y	Y	Y
9 Volkmer	Y	N	Y	Y
10 Burlison	Y	N	Y	Y
MONTANA				
1 Baucus	Y	Y	Y	Y
2 Marlenee	Y	Y	Y	Y
NEBRASKA				
1 Thone	?	Y	Y	Y
2 Cavanaugh	?	?	Y	Y
3 Smith	Y	Y	Y	Y
NEVADA				
AL Santini	X	Y	Y	Y
NEW HAMPSHIRE				
1 D'Amours	N	Y	Y	Y
2 Cleveland	X	Y	Y	?
NEW JERSEY				
1 Florio	▮	Y	Y	Y
2 Hughes	N	Y	Y	Y
3 Howard	#	N	Y	Y
4 Thompson	?	N	Y	Y
5 Fenwick	N	N	Y	Y
6 Forsythe	▮	Y	Y	Y
7 Maguire	N	N	Y	Y
8 Roe	N	Y	Y	Y
9 Hollenbeck	X	N	Y	Y
10 Rodino	▮	N	Y	Y
11 Minish	?	Y	Y	?
12 Rinaldo	X	Y	Y	#
13 Meyner	N	N	Y	Y
14 LeFante	▮	▮	Y	Y
15 Patten	N	N	Y	Y
NEW MEXICO				
1 Lujan	✓	N	Y	Y
2 Runnels	Y	Y	Y	Y
NEW YORK				
1 Pike	N	N	Y	Y
2 Downey	N	N	Y	Y
3 Ambro	?	Y	Y	Y
4 Lent	N	Y	Y	Y
5 Wydler	?	Y	Y	Y
6 Wolff	?	Y	Y	Y
7 Addabbo	N	N	Y	Y
8 Rosenthal	N	N	Y	Y
9 Delaney	?	N	Y	Y
10 Biaggi	N	Y	Y	Y
11 Scheuer	N	N	Y	Y
12 Chisholm	N	N	Y	Y
13 Solarz	N	N	Y	Y
14 Richmond	N	N	Y	Y
15 Zeferetti	#	Y	Y	Y
16 Holtzman	N	N	Y	Y
17 Murphy	N	Y	Y	Y
18 Green	N	N	Y	Y
19 Rangel	N	N	Y	Y
20 Weiss	N	N	Y	Y
21 Garcia	X	N	Y	Y
22 Bingham	N	N	Y	Y
23 Caputo	?	?	?	?
24 Ottinger	N	N	Y	Y
25 Fish	?	N	Y	Y
26 Gilman	N	N	Y	Y
27 McHugh	N	N	Y	Y
28 Stratton	N	N	Y	Y
29 Pattison	N	N	Y	Y
30 McEwen	?	Y	Y	Y
31 Mitchell	▮	Y	Y	Y
32 Hanley	#	Y	Y	Y
33 Walsh	X	Y	Y	Y
34 Horton	?	N	Y	Y
35 Conable	?	N	Y	Y
36 LaFalce	N	N	#	Y
37 Nowak	N	N	Y	Y
38 Kemp	N	Y	Y	Y
39 Lundine	#	▮	Y	Y
NORTH CAROLINA				
1 Jones	Y	Y	Y	Y
2 Fountain	N	Y	Y	Y
3 Whitley	Y	?	Y	Y
4 Andrews	Y	Y	Y	Y
5 Neal	?	Y	#	Y
6 Preyer	Y	Y	Y	Y
7 Rose	Y	N	Y	Y
8 Hefner	Y	?	Y	Y
9 Martin	#	Y	Y	Y
10 Broyhill	?	✓	?	?
11 Gudger	Y	Y	Y	Y
NORTH DAKOTA				
AL Andrews	Y	N	Y	Y
OHIO				
1 Gradison	N	Y	Y	Y
2 Luken	?	Y	Y	Y
3 Whalen	N	N	Y	Y
4 Guyer	Y	Y	Y	Y
5 Latta	Y	Y	Y	Y
6 Harsha	?	Y	Y	?
7 Brown	Y	Y	Y	Y
8 Kindness	Y	Y	Y	Y
9 Ashley	?	N	Y	Y
10 Miller	Y	Y	N	Y
11 Stanton	Y	N	Y	Y
12 Devine	Y	Y	Y	Y
13 Pease	?	?	Y	Y
14 Seiberling	N	N	Y	Y
15 Wylie	?	N	Y	Y
16 Regula	Y	Y	Y	Y
17 Ashbrook	Y	Y	Y	Y
18 Applegate	N	Y	Y	Y
19 Carney	?	N	Y	Y
20 Oakar	N	?	Y	Y
21 Stokes	N	N	Y	Y
22 Vanik	N	N	Y	Y
23 Mottl	?	Y	Y	Y
OKLAHOMA				
1 Jones	Y	Y	Y	Y
2 Risenhoover	?	N	Y	Y
3 Watkins	Y	Y	Y	Y
4 Steed	Y	N	Y	Y
5 Edwards	Y	Y	Y	Y
6 English	Y	Y	Y	Y
OREGON				
1 AuCoin	?	Y	Y	Y
2 Ullman	N	N	Y	Y
3 Duncan	N	N	Y	Y
4 Weaver	?	N	Y	?
PENNSYLVANIA				
1 Myers, M.	N	N	Y	Y
2 Nix	?	N	Y	Y
3 Lederer	N	N	Y	Y
4 Eilberg	X	N	Y	Y
5 Schulze	X	Y	Y	Y
6 Yatron	#	Y	Y	Y
7 Edgar	▮	N	Y	Y
8 Kostmayer	N	Y	Y	Y
9 Shuster	?	Y	Y	Y
10 McDade	N	Y	Y	Y
11 Flood	N	N	Y	Y
12 Murtha	N	N	Y	Y
13 Coughlin	N	Y	Y	Y
14 Moorhead	▮	Y	Y	Y
15 Rooney	▮	N	Y	Y
16 Walker	Y	Y	Y	Y
17 Ertel	Y	N	Y	Y
18 Walgren	?	Y	Y	Y
19 Goodling, W.	Y	Y	Y	?
20 Gaydos	?	Y	Y	Y
21 Dent	▮	N	Y	Y
22 Murphy	N	Y	Y	Y
23 Ammerman	?	X	?	?
24 Marks	N	N	Y	Y
25 Myers, G.	N	Y	Y	Y
RHODE ISLAND				
1 St Germain	?	N	Y	Y
2 Beard	?	N	Y	Y
SOUTH CAROLINA				
1 Davis	?	N	N	Y
2 Spence	Y	Y	Y	Y
3 Derrick	#	N	Y	Y
4 Mann	Y	Y	Y	Y
5 Holland	Y	N	Y	Y
6 Jenrette	N	N	Y	Y
SOUTH DAKOTA				
1 Pressler	Y	N	Y	Y
2 Abdnor	Y	Y	#	Y
TENNESSEE				
1 Quillen	#	Y	Y	Y
2 Duncan	?	Y	Y	Y
3 Lloyd	?	Y	Y	Y
4 Gore	Y	N	Y	Y
5 Vacancy				
6 Beard	▮	Y	Y	#
7 Jones	#	N	Y	Y
8 Ford	?	?	?	Y
TEXAS				
1 Hall	Y	Y	Y	Y
2 Wilson, C.	Y	N	Y	Y
3 Collins	Y	Y	N	Y
4 Roberts	?	Y	Y	Y
5 Mattox	?	N	Y	Y
6 Teague	?	?	?	?
7 Archer	Y	Y	N	Y
8 Eckhardt	N	N	Y	Y
9 Brooks	Y	Y	Y	Y
10 Pickle	Y	N	Y	Y
11 Poage	?	Y	Y	Y
12 Wright	Y	N	Y	Y
13 Hightower	Y	Y	Y	Y
14 Young	Y	Y	Y	Y
15 de la Garza	Y	Y	Y	Y
16 White	Y	X	#	#
17 Burleson	Y	Y	Y	Y
18 Jordan	N	N	Y	Y
19 Mahon	Y	N	Y	Y
20 Gonzalez	Y	▮	#	#
21 Krueger	✓	▮	#	#
22 Gammage	#	Y	Y	Y
23 Kazen	Y	Y	Y	Y
24 Milford	?	N	Y	Y
UTAH				
1 McKay	✓	N	Y	Y
2 Marriott	✓	Y	Y	Y
VERMONT				
AL Jeffords	Y	N	Y	Y
VIRGINIA				
1 Trible	Y	Y	Y	Y
2 Whitehurst	#	Y	Y	#
3 Satterfield	Y	Y	Y	Y
4 Daniel	Y	Y	Y	Y
5 Daniel	Y	Y	Y	Y
6 Butler	Y	Y	Y	Y
7 Robinson	Y	Y	Y	Y
8 Harris	N	N	Y	Y
9 Wampler	Y	Y	Y	Y
10 Fisher	N	N	Y	Y
WASHINGTON				
1 Pritchard	▮	N	Y	Y
2 Meeds	?	N	Y	Y
3 Bonker	#	N	Y	#
4 McCormack	✓	N	Y	Y
5 Foley	Y	Y	Y	Y
6 Dicks	?	N	Y	Y
7 Cunningham	▮	Y	Y	Y
WEST VIRGINIA				
1 Mollohan	N	Y	Y	Y
2 Staggers	X	N	Y	Y
3 Slack	N	Y	Y	Y
4 Rahall	▮	X	#	#
WISCONSIN				
1 Aspin	?	N	Y	Y
2 Kastenmeier	N	N	Y	Y
3 Baldus	N	N	Y	Y
4 Zablocki	N	Y	Y	Y
5 Reuss	N	N	Y	Y
6 Steiger	N	N	Y	Y
7 Obey	N	N	Y	Y
8 Cornell	▮	N	Y	Y
9 Kasten	N	Y	Y	Y
WYOMING				
AL Roncalio	#	N	Y	Y

† *Rep. Ralph H. Metcalfe, D-Ill., died Oct. 10, 1978.*

* *Rep. Goodloe E. Byron, D-Md., died Oct. 11, 1978.*

Democrats ***Republicans***

790. HR 12929. Labor-HEW Appropriations, Fiscal 1979. Mahon, D-Texas, motion to recede from the House position and concur in the Senate amendment with an amendment to prohibit the use of appropriated funds for abortions except when the life of the mother was in danger or in cases of rape or incest that had been promptly reported to health or law enforcement agencies or if the pregnancy would cause long-lasting physical health damage to the mother as determined by two physicians. Motion rejected 188-216: R 30-108; D 158-108 (ND 112-72; SD 46-36), Oct. 12, 1978.

791. HR 13511. Revenue Act of 1978. Conable, R-N.Y., motion that the House conferees be instructed to concur in the Senate amendment to reduce individual income taxes by about 5 percent annually in 1980-83, provided that federal outlays increase by no more than 1 percent annually in real terms, that the federal share of gross national product decline each year by specified amounts and that the federal budget be balanced by 1982. Motion agreed to 268-135: R 136-1; D 132-134 (ND 78-105; SD 54-29), Oct. 12, 1978. A "nay" was a vote supporting the president's position.

792. S 1566. Foreign Intelligence Surveillance. Adoption of the conference report on the bill to require a judicial warrant for most national security electronic surveillance conducted within the United States for foreign intelligence purposes and to require evidence of criminal intent before such a warrant was issued against a U.S. citizen. Adopted (thus cleared for the president) 226-176: R 18-118; D 208-58 (ND 161-23; SD 47-35), Oct. 12, 1978. A "yea" was a vote supporting the president's position.

793. S 555. Ethics in Government. Wiggins, R-Calif., motion to reject Title VI, to establish a mechanism for appointing a temporary special prosecutor to investigate alleged criminal wrongdoing by high-level executive branch officials. Rejected 49-344: R 29-104; D 20-240 (ND 10-172; SD 10-68), Oct. 12, 1978.

794. S 555. Ethics in Government. Adoption of the conference report on the bill requiring public financial disclosure by top officials in all three branches of the federal government, and putting new restrictions on revolving door relationships between government and private employment. Adopted (thus cleared for the president) 370-23: R 119-14; D 251-9 (ND 178-4; SD 73-5), Oct. 12, 1978. A "yea" was a vote supporting the president's position.

795. HR 9893. Tax Credit for the Elderly. Ullman, D-Ore., motion to suspend the rules and pass the bill to amend the 1954 Internal Revenue Code to liberalize the income tax credit for persons aged 65 and older. Motion agreed to 388-5: R 134-0; D 254-5 (ND 178-1; SD 76-4), Oct. 12, 1978. A two-thirds majority vote (262 in this case) is required for passage under suspension of the rules.

796. S 957. Small Claims Disputes. Eckhardt, D-Texas, motion to suspend the rules and pass the bill to authorize $3 million in fiscal 1979 and $23 million in each of fiscal 1980-83 to establish a grant program through the Justice Department to encourage state and local governments to improve small claims courts procedures and to facilitate resolution of minor civil disputes quickly and inexpensively. Motion rejected 224-166: R 30-101; D 194-65 (ND 146-32; SD 48-33), Oct. 12, 1978. A two-thirds majority vote (260 in this case) is required for passage under suspension of the rules.

797. S 1503. Tris Claims. Vanik, D-Ohio, motion to suspend the rules and pass the bill as amended to allow the U.S. Court of Claims to hear claims for losses sustained by manufacturers and distributors of children's sleepwear as a result of the ban on garments treated with the flame retardant chemical, Tris. Motion agreed to 304-90: R 115-19; D 189-71 (ND 124-55; SD 65-16), Oct. 12, 1978. A two-thirds majority vote (263 in this case) is required for passage under suspension of the rules.

KEY

- Y Voted for (yea).
- ✓ Paired for.
- † Announced for.
- # CQ Poll for.
- N Voted against (nay).
- X Paired against.
- \- Announced against.
- ▮ CQ Poll against.
- P Voted "present."
- ● Voted "present" to avoid possible conflict of interest.
- ? Did not vote or otherwise make a position known.

	790	791	792	793	794	795	796	797
ALABAMA								
1 Edwards	N	Y	N	Y	Y	Y	N	Y
2 Dickinson	N	Y	N	Y	Y	Y	N	Y
3 Nichols	N	Y	N	N	Y	Y	N	Y
4 Bevill	N	Y	N	N	Y	Y	N	Y
5 Flippo	Y	Y	N	N	Y	Y	N	Y
6 Buchanan	Y	Y	N	N	Y	Y	N	Y
7 Flowers	Y	Y	N	N	Y	Y	N	Y
ALASKA								
AL Young	N	Y	N	Y	Y	Y	N	Y
ARIZONA								
1 Rhodes	N	Y	N	Y	Y	Y	N	Y
2 Udall	Y	Y	Y	N	Y	Y	Y	N
3 Stump	N	Y	N	Y	Y	Y	N	Y
4 Rudd	N	Y	X	?	?	?	?	?
ARKANSAS								
1 Alexander	Y	N	?	?	Y	Y	Y	Y
2 Tucker	Y	Y	Y	N	Y	Y	Y	Y
3 Hammerschmidt	N	Y	N	Y	N	Y	N	Y
4 Thornton	?	N	Y	N	Y	Y	Y	Y
CALIFORNIA								
1 Johnson	Y	-N	Y	N	Y	Y	Y	Y
2 Clausen	N	Y	N	N	Y	Y	N	Y
3 Moss	?	?	?	?	?	?	?	?
4 Leggett	?	N	Y	?	?	?	?	?
5 Burton, J.	Y	Y	Y	N	Y	Y	Y	N
6 Burton, P.	Y	N	Y	?	Y	Y	Y	Y
7 Miller	Y	N	?	N	Y	?	?	?
8 Dellums	Y	N	Y	N	Y	Y	Y	N
9 Stark	Y	N	N	N	Y	#	#	▮
10 Edwards	Y	N	Y	N	Y	Y	?	?
11 Ryan	Y	N	N	Y	Y	Y	Y	Y
12 McCloskey	Y	Y	Y	N	Y	Y	N	Y
13 Mineta	Y	N	Y	N	Y	Y	Y	Y
14 McFall	Y	N	Y	N	Y	?	?	Y
15 Sisk	?	?	Y	N	?	Y	Y	Y
16 Panetta	Y	Y	Y	N	Y	Y	Y	N
17 Krebs	Y	Y	Y	N	Y	Y	Y	N
18 Vacancy								
19 Lagomarsino	N	Y	N	N	Y	Y	Y	Y
20 Goldwater	X	✓	N	N	Y	Y	N	Y
21 Corman	Y	N	Y	N	Y	Y	Y	Y
22 Moorhead	N	Y	N	N	Y	Y	N	Y
23 Beilenson	Y	N	Y	N	Y	N	Y	N
24 Waxman	Y	N	Y	N	Y	Y	Y	N
25 Roybal	Y	N	Y	N	Y	Y	Y	Y
26 Rousselot	N	Y	N	N	N	Y	N	Y
27 Dornan	N	Y	N	N	Y	Y	Y	Y
28 Burke	✓	#	✓	?	#	#	✓	#
29 Hawkins	Y	N	Y	N	Y	?	?	?
30 Danielson	Y	N	Y	N	Y	Y	Y	Y
31 Wilson, C.H.	Y	?	?	?	?	Y	Y	Y
32 Anderson	Y	N	Y	N	Y	Y	Y	Y
33 Clawson	N	Y	N	Y	N	Y	N	Y
34 Hannaford	Y	Y	Y	N	Y	Y	Y	Y
35 Lloyd	Y	Y	N	N	Y	Y	Y	Y
36 Brown	Y	N	Y	N	Y	Y	Y	N
37 Pettis	?	?	?	?	?	?	?	?
38 Patterson	Y	Y	Y	N	Y	Y	Y	Y
39 Wiggins	Y	Y	N	Y	N	Y	N	Y
40 Badham	N	Y	▮	▮	▮	#	▮	#
41 Wilson, B.	Y	Y	N	Y	Y	Y	N	Y
42 Van Deerlin	Y	N	Y	N	Y	Y	Y	Y
43 Burgener	N	Y	N	N	Y	Y	Y	Y
COLORADO								
1 Schroeder	Y	Y	N	N	Y	Y	Y	Y
2 Wirth	Y	Y	Y	N	Y	Y	Y	Y
3 Evans	Y	Y	Y	N	N	#	#	#
4 Johnson	Y	Y	Y	N	Y	Y	N	Y
5 Armstrong	N	Y	N	N	N	Y	N	Y
CONNECTICUT								
1 Cotter	X	N	Y	N	Y	Y	Y	N
2 Dodd	Y	Y	Y	N	Y	Y	Y	Y
3 Giaimo	?	N	Y	N	Y	Y	Y	Y
4 McKinney	Y	Y	Y	N	Y	Y	Y	Y
5 Sarasin	?	#	#	?	#	#	#	#
6 Moffett	Y	Y	Y	N	Y	Y	Y	Y
DELAWARE								
AL Evans	Y	Y	N	N	Y	Y	Y	N
FLORIDA								
1 Sikes	Y	N	N	?	Y	Y	N	Y
2 Fuqua	Y	Y	N	N	Y	Y	Y	N
3 Bennett	Y	Y	N	N	Y	N	N	N
4 Chappell	Y	X	X	?	?	?	?	?
5 Kelly	N	Y	N	Y	Y	Y	N	Y
6 Young	N	Y	N	N	Y	Y	N	Y
7 Gibbons	N	N	Y	Y	Y	Y	Y	N
8 Ireland	N	Y	Y	?	?	?	?	?
9 Frey	N	Y	N	?	?	?	?	?
10 Bafalis	N	Y	N	N	Y	Y	N	N
11 Rogers	Y	N	Y	N	Y	Y	Y	N
12 Burke	N	Y	N	N	?	Y	N	Y
13 Lehman	Y	N	Y	N	#	Y	Y	N
14 Pepper	Y	N	Y	N	Y	Y	Y	Y
15 Fascell	Y	N	Y	N	Y	Y	Y	Y
GEORGIA								
1 Ginn	Y	Y	Y	N	Y	Y	Y	Y
2 Mathis	N	Y	Y	N	Y	Y	Y	Y
3 Brinkley	Y	Y	Y	N	Y	Y	N	Y
4 Levitas	Y	Y	N	N	Y	Y	Y	N
5 Fowler	Y	Y	Y	N	Y	Y	Y	Y
6 Flynt	Y	Y	Y	?	Y	Y	N	Y
7 McDonald	N	Y	N	Y	N	N	N	Y
8 Evans	N	Y	Y	N	Y	Y	N	Y
9 Jenkins	N	Y	N	N	Y	Y	Y	Y
10 Barnard	N	Y	Y	N	Y	Y	Y	N
HAWAII								
1 Heftel	Y	Y	Y	N	Y	Y	Y	N
2 Akaka	Y	N	Y	N	Y	Y	Y	Y
IDAHO								
1 Symms	N	Y	N	N	N	Y	N	Y
2 Hansen, G.	N	Y	N	N	N	Y	N	N
ILLINOIS								
1 Vacancy								
2 Murphy	N	N	Y	N	Y	Y	Y	Y
3 Russo	N	Y	Y	N	Y	Y	N	Y
4 Derwinski	N	Y	N	N	Y	Y	N	Y
5 Fary	N	N	Y	N	Y	Y	Y	Y
6 Hyde	N	Y	N	N	Y	Y	N	Y
7 Collins	Y	N	Y	N	Y	Y	Y	N
8 Rostenkowski	N	N	Y	Y	N	Y	Y	Y
9 Yates	Y	N	Y	N	Y	Y	Y	N
10 Mikva	Y	N	Y	N	Y	Y	Y	Y
11 Annunzio	N	N	Y	N	Y	Y	Y	Y
12 Crane	X	✓	X	?	?	#	X	#
13 McClory	N	Y	N	Y	Y	Y	Y	Y
14 Erlenborn	N	Y	N	Y	N	Y	N	Y
15 Corcoran	N	Y	N	N	Y	Y	N	Y
16 Anderson	Y	Y	Y	N	Y	Y	N	Y
17 O'Brien	N	Y	N	N	N	Y	Y	Y
18 Michel	N	Y	N	N	Y	Y	N	Y
19 Railsback	Y	Y	Y	N	Y	Y	Y	Y
20 Findley	Y	Y	Y	Y	Y	Y	Y	N
21 Madigan	N	Y	N	?	Y	Y	N	Y
22 Shipley	✓	?	?	?	?	?	?	?
23 Price	N	N	Y	N	Y	Y	Y	Y
24 Simon	Y	N	Y	N	Y	Y	N	N
INDIANA								
1 Benjamin	N	Y	Y	N	Y	Y	Y	N
2 Fithian	N	Y	Y	N	Y	Y	Y	Y
3 Brademas	Y	N	Y	N	Y	Y	Y	N
4 Quayle	N	Y	Y	Y	Y	Y	N	Y
5 Hillis	N	Y	?	?	?	?	?	?
6 Evans	N	Y	Y	N	Y	Y	Y	Y
7 Myers, J.	N	Y	N	Y	Y	Y	N	Y
8 Cornwell	Y	Y	Y	N	Y	Y	Y	Y
9 Hamilton	Y	N	Y	N	Y	Y	Y	Y
10 Sharp	Y	Y	Y	N	Y	Y	Y	Y
11 Jacobs	Y	Y	Y	N	Y	Y	N	N
IOWA								
1 Leach	Y	Y	N	N	Y	Y	#	Y
2 Blouin	N	N	Y	N	Y	Y	Y	Y
3 Grassley	N	Y	N	N	Y	Y	N	N
4 Smith	Y	N	Y	N	Y	Y	Y	Y
5 Harkin	Y	Y	Y	N	Y	Y	Y	N
6 Bedell	N	N	Y	N	Y	Y	Y	N

Democrats ***Republicans***

	790	791	792	793	794	795	796	797
KANSAS								
1 Sebelius	N	Y	N	N	Y	Y	N	Y
2 Keys	Y	Y	Y	N	Y	Y	N	N
3 Winn	N	Y	N	Y	Y	Y	N	Y
4 Glickman	Y	Y	Y	N	Y	Y	N	N
5 Skubitz	N	Y	X	N	Y	Y	N	Y
KENTUCKY								
1 Hubbard	N	Y	Y	N	Y	Y	Y	N
2 Natcher	N	N	Y	N	Y	Y	N	N
3 Mazzoli	N	N	Y	N	Y	Y	Y	Y
4 Snyder	N	Y	N	N	Y	Y	N	N
5 Carter	N	Y	N	N	Y	Y	Y	Y
6 Breckinridge	Y	Y	N	N	Y	Y	N	Y
7 Perkins	N	N	Y	N	Y	Y	N	N
LOUISIANA								
1 Livingston	N	Y	N	Y	Y	Y	N	N
2 Boggs	N	N	N	?	Y	Y	Y	Y
3 Treen	N	Y	N	N	N	Y	N	N
4 Waggonner	N	N	N	Y	N	Y	N	Y
5 Huckaby	N	Y	N	N	Y	Y	Y	Y
6 Moore	N	Y	N	N	Y	Y	N	Y
7 Breaux	N	Y	N	N	Y	Y	Y	Y
8 Long	N	N	Y	N	?	Y	Y	Y
MAINE								
1 Emery	N	Y	N	N	Y	Y	N	Y
2 Cohen	Y	Y	N	N	Y	Y	N	Y
MARYLAND								
1 Bauman	N	Y	N	N	Y	Y	N	Y
2 Long	Y	N	Y	N	Y	Y	Y	N
3 Mikulski	Y	N	Y	N	Y	Y	Y	Y
4 Holt	N	Y	N	N	Y	Y	N	Y
5 Spellman	Y	Y	Y	N	Y	Y	Y	Y
6 Vacancy								
7 Mitchell	Y	N	Y	N	Y	Y	Y	N
8 Steers	Y	Y	Y	N	Y	Y	Y	Y
MASSACHUSETTS								
1 Conte	N	Y	Y	N	Y	Y	N	Y
2 Boland	N	N	Y	N	Y	Y	Y	Y
3 Early	N	Y	Y	N	Y	Y	Y	N
4 Drinan	Y	N	N	N	Y	Y	Y	N
5 Tsongas	Y	N	Y	?	?	?	?	?
6 Harrington	✓	▮	▮	?	#	#	#	#
7 Markey	N	N	Y	N	Y	Y	Y	N
8 O'Neill								
9 Moakley	N	N	Y	N	Y	Y	Y	Y
10 Heckler	N	Y	Y	N	Y	Y	Y	Y
11 Burke	N	Y	Y	N	Y	Y	Y	Y
12 Studds	Y	N	Y	N	Y	Y	Y	Y
MICHIGAN								
1 Conyers	Y	N	#	?	Y	#	#	▮
2 Pursell	Y	Y	Y	N	Y	Y	Y	Y
3 Brown	?	?	N	N	Y	Y	Y	N
4 Stockman	Y	Y	N	N	Y	Y	✓	Y
5 Sawyer	N	Y	N	N	Y	Y	N	Y
6 Carr	Y	Y	Y	N	Y	Y	Y	Y
7 Kildee	N	N	Y	N	Y	Y	Y	N
8 Traxler	N	Y	Y	N	Y	Y	Y	Y
9 Vander Jagt	N	Y	N	N	Y	Y	?	Y
10 Cederberg	N	Y	N	N	Y	Y	N	Y
11 Ruppe	N	Y	N	Y	Y	Y	Y	Y
12 Bonior	N	N	Y	N	Y	Y	Y	Y
13 Diggs	✓	?	?	?	?	?	?	?
14 Nedzi	Y	N	N	Y	Y	Y	Y	Y
15 Ford	Y	N	Y	N	Y	Y	Y	Y
16 Dingell	Y	N	Y	Y	Y	Y	Y	Y
17 Brodhead	Y	N	Y	N	Y	Y	Y	Y
18 Blanchard	Y	N	Y	N	Y	Y	Y	Y
19 Broomfield	N	Y	N	N	Y	Y	N	Y
MINNESOTA								
1 Quie	X	?	?	?	?	?	?	?
2 Hagedorn	N	Y	N	N	Y	Y	N	Y
3 Frenzel	Y	Y	N	Y	Y	Y	Y	Y
4 Vento	N	Y	Y	N	Y	Y	Y	Y
5 Fraser	Y	N	Y	N	Y	Y	Y	Y
6 Nolan	N	Y	Y	N	Y	Y	Y	Y
7 Stangeland	N	Y	N	N	Y	Y	N	Y
8 Oberstar	N	N	Y	N	Y	Y	Y	Y
MISSISSIPPI								
1 Whitten	N	Y	Y	N	Y	Y	N	Y
2 Bowen	N	Y	Y	N	Y	Y	N	Y
3 Montgomery	N	Y	Y	N	#	#	▮	#
4 Cochran	?	?	?	?	?	?	?	?
5 Lott	N	Y	N	?	#	#	X	#
MISSOURI								
1 Clay	Y	N	Y	N	Y	Y	Y	Y
2 Young	N	Y	N	N	Y	Y	N	Y
3 Gephardt	N	Y	N	N	Y	Y	Y	N

	790	791	792	793	794	795	796	797
4 Skelton	N	Y	Y	N	Y	Y	N	Y
5 Bolling	Y	N	Y	N	Y	Y	Y	Y
6 Coleman	N	Y	N	N	Y	Y	N	N
7 Taylor	N	Y	N	N	Y	Y	N	N
8 Ichord	N	Y	N	N	Y	Y	N	N
9 Volkmer	N	Y	N	N	Y	Y	N	N
10 Burlison	N	N	Y	N	Y	Y	N	Y
MONTANA								
1 Baucus	Y	Y	Y	N	Y	Y	Y	N
2 Marlenee	N	Y	Y	N	Y	Y	N	N
NEBRASKA								
1 Thone	N	Y	N	N	Y	Y	N	Y
2 Cavanaugh	N	Y	Y	N	Y	Y	Y	N
3 Smith	N	Y	N	?	?	Y	N	Y
NEVADA								
AL Santini	Y	Y	Y	N	Y	Y	Y	Y
NEW HAMPSHIRE								
1 D'Amours	N	Y	Y	N	Y	Y	Y	Y
2 Cleveland	Y	Y	N	N	Y	Y	N	Y
NEW JERSEY								
1 Florio	N	Y	Y	N	Y	Y	Y	N
2 Hughes	Y	Y	Y	N	Y	Y	N	N
3 Howard	Y	N	Y	N	Y	Y	Y	Y
4 Thompson	Y	N	Y	N	Y	Y	Y	Y
5 Fenwick	Y	Y	Y	N	Y	Y	N	Y
6 Forsythe	Y	Y	N	N	N	Y	N	Y
7 Maguire	Y	Y	Y	N	Y	Y	Y	N
8 Roe	N	Y	Y	N	Y	Y	Y	Y
9 Hollenbeck	Y	✓	#	?	#	#	✓	#
10 Rodino	N	N	Y	N	Y	Y	Y	Y
11 Minish	N	Y	Y	N	Y	Y	Y	N
12 Rinaldo	N	Y	N	N	Y	Y	Y	N
13 Meyner	Y	Y	Y	N	Y	Y	Y	Y
14 LeFante	N	N	Y	N	Y	Y	Y	Y
15 Patten	N	N	N	N	Y	Y	Y	Y
NEW MEXICO								
1 Lujan	N	Y	N	N	Y	Y	N	Y
2 Runnels	N	Y	N	N	Y	Y	N	Y
NEW YORK								
1 Pike	Y	N	Y	N	Y	Y	Y	Y
2 Downey	Y	Y	Y	N	Y	Y	N	Y
3 Ambro	N	Y	Y	N	Y	Y	Y	N
4 Lent	N	Y	N	Y	Y	Y	N	Y
5 Wydler	N	Y	N	N	Y	Y	N	Y
6 Wolff	Y	Y	N	Y	Y	Y	Y	Y
7 Addabbo	Y	N	Y	N	Y	Y	Y	Y
8 Rosenthal	Y	N	Y	N	#	Y	Y	N
9 Delaney	N	Y	Y	Y	N	Y	N	Y
10 Biaggi	N	Y	Y	N	Y	Y	Y	Y
11 Scheuer	Y	?	Y	N	Y	Y	Y	Y
12 Chisholm	Y	N	Y	N	Y	Y	Y	Y
13 Solarz	Y	N	Y	N	Y	Y	Y	Y
14 Richmond	Y	N	Y	N	Y	Y	Y	N
15 Zeferetti	N	Y	Y	N	Y	Y	Y	Y
16 Holtzman	Y	N	N	N	Y	Y	Y	N
17 Murphy	N	N	Y	N	Y	Y	Y	Y
18 Green	Y	Y	Y	N	Y	Y	Y	Y
19 Rangel	Y	N	Y	N	Y	Y	Y	N
20 Weiss	Y	N	Y	N	Y	Y	Y	Y
21 Garcia	Y	N	Y	N	Y	Y	Y	Y
22 Bingham	Y	N	Y	?	Y	Y	Y	N
23 Caputo	?	Y	Y	N	Y	Y	Y	Y
24 Ottinger	Y	N	Y	N	Y	Y	Y	Y
25 Fish	N	Y	N	N	Y	Y	Y	Y
26 Gilman	Y	Y	N	N	Y	Y	Y	Y
27 McHugh	Y	▮	Y	N	Y	Y	N	N
28 Stratton	N	Y	X	N	Y	Y	N	Y
29 Pattison	Y	Y	Y	N	Y	Y	Y	Y
30 McEwen	N	Y	N	N	Y	Y	N	Y
31 Mitchell	N	Y	N	N	Y	Y	Y	Y
32 Hanley	N	Y	Y	N	Y	Y	N	Y
33 Walsh	N	Y	N	N	Y	Y	N	Y
34 Horton	Y	Y	N	N	Y	Y	Y	Y
35 Conable	Y	Y	N	Y	Y	Y	N	Y
36 LaFalce	N	N	Y	N	Y	Y	Y	N
37 Nowak	N	Y	Y	N	Y	Y	Y	Y
38 Kemp	N	Y	N	N	Y	Y	N	Y
39 Lundine	Y	N	Y	N	Y	Y	Y	Y
NORTH CAROLINA								
1 Jones	Y	Y	Y	Y	N	Y	Y	Y
2 Fountain	Y	Y	N	N	Y	Y	Y	Y
3 Whitley	Y	Y	Y	N	Y	Y	Y	Y
4 Andrews	Y	Y	N	N	Y	Y	Y	Y
5 Neal	Y	Y	Y	N	Y	Y	Y	Y
6 Preyer	?	N	Y	N	Y	Y	Y	Y
7 Rose	Y	Y	Y	N	Y	Y	Y	Y
8 Hefner	Y	Y	Y	N	Y	Y	Y	Y

	790	791	792	793	794	795	796	797
9 Martin	Y	Y	N	N	Y	Y	N	Y
10 Broyhill	Y	Y	N	N	Y	Y	Y	Y
11 Gudger	Y	Y	N	N	Y	Y	Y	Y
NORTH DAKOTA								
AL Andrews	N	Y	N	N	Y	Y	N	Y
OHIO								
1 Gradison	N	Y	N	N	Y	Y	N	N
2 Luken	N	Y	N	N	Y	Y	N	Y
3 Whalen	N	N	Y	N	Y	Y	N	N
4 Guyer	N	Y	N	N	Y	Y	N	Y
5 Latta	N	Y	N	N	Y	Y	N	Y
6 Harsha	N	Y	N	N	Y	Y	N	Y
7 Brown	N	Y	N	Y	Y	Y	N	Y
8 Kindness	N	Y	N	Y	Y	Y	N	Y
9 Ashley	Y	N	Y	N	Y	Y	N	Y
10 Miller	N	Y	N	Y	Y	Y	N	N
11 Stanton	N	Y	N	N	Y	Y	N	Y
12 Devine	N	Y	N	N	Y	Y	N	Y
13 Pease	Y	Y	Y	N	Y	Y	N	N
14 Seiberling	Y	N	Y	N	Y	Y	N	Y
15 Wylie	N	Y	N	N	Y	Y	N	Y
16 Regula	N	Y	N	N	Y	Y	N	Y
17 Ashbrook	N	Y	N	N	Y	Y	N	N
18 Applegate	N	Y	Y	N	Y	Y	Y	Y
19 Carney	N	Y	Y	N	Y	Y	Y	Y
20 Oakar	N	Y	N	N	Y	Y	Y	N
21 Stokes	Y	N	Y	N	Y	Y	Y	Y
22 Vanik	N	N	Y	N	Y	Y	Y	N
23 Mottl	N	Y	Y	N	Y	Y	N	N
OKLAHOMA								
1 Jones	N	Y	Y	Y	Y	Y	Y	Y
2 Risenhoover	Y	Y	?	N	Y	Y	N	Y
3 Watkins	N	Y	N	N	Y	Y	N	Y
4 Steed	Y	N	Y	Y	Y	Y	Y	N
5 Edwards	N	Y	N	N	Y	Y	N	Y
6 English	N	Y	N	N	Y	Y	N	Y
OREGON								
1 AuCoin	Y	Y	Y	N	Y	Y	Y	Y
2 Ullman	Y	N	Y	N	Y	Y	Y	Y
3 Duncan	Y	N	Y	N	Y	Y	Y	Y
4 Weaver	Y	N	Y	N	Y	Y	Y	Y
PENNSYLVANIA								
1 Myers, M.	N	N	Y	N	Y	Y	Y	Y
2 Nix	Y	N	Y	N	Y	Y	Y	Y
3 Lederer	N	N	Y	N	Y	Y	Y	Y
4 Eilberg	N	Y	Y	N	Y	Y	Y	Y
5 Schulze	N	Y	N	N	Y	?	?	?
6 Yatron	N	Y	Y	N	Y	Y	Y	Y
7 Edgar	Y	N	Y	N	Y	Y	Y	N
8 Kostmayer	Y	Y	Y	N	Y	Y	N	N
9 Shuster	N	Y	N	N	Y	Y	N	Y
10 McDade	N	Y	N	N	Y	Y	N	Y
11 Flood	N	N	Y	N	Y	Y	Y	Y
12 Murtha	N	N	Y	N	Y	Y	N	Y
13 Coughlin	Y	Y	N	N	Y	Y	Y	Y
14 Moorhead	Y	N	Y	N	Y	Y	Y	Y
15 Rooney	N	N	Y	N	Y	Y	Y	Y
16 Walker	N	Y	N	N	Y	Y	Y	Y
17 Ertel	N	Y	N	N	Y	Y	Y	Y
18 Walgren	Y	Y	Y	N	Y	Y	Y	Y
19 Goodling, W.	N	Y	N	N	Y	Y	Y	Y
20 Gaydos	N	N	Y	N	Y	Y	N	Y
21 Dent	N	N	Y	N	Y	Y	N	Y
22 Murphy	N	Y	Y	N	Y	Y	Y	Y
23 Ammerman	?	X	✓	?	?	?	?	?
24 Marks	N	Y	Y	N	Y	Y	N	Y
25 Myers, G.	N	Y	N	N	Y	Y	N	N
RHODE ISLAND								
1 St Germain	N	Y	Y	N	Y	Y	Y	Y
2 Beard	N	Y	Y	N	Y	Y	Y	Y
SOUTH CAROLINA								
1 Davis	Y	Y	N	N	Y	Y	Y	Y
2 Spence	N	Y	N	N	Y	Y	N	Y
3 Derrick	Y	N	Y	N	#	#	#	#
4 Mann	Y	Y	Y	N	Y	Y	Y	Y
5 Holland	Y	N	Y	N	Y	Y	Y	Y
6 Jenrette	N	N	N	N	Y	Y	Y	Y
SOUTH DAKOTA								
1 Pressler	N	Y	N	N	Y	Y	Y	Y
2 Abdnor	N	Y	N	N	Y	Y	N	Y
TENNESSEE								
1 Quillen	N	Y	N	Y	Y	Y	N	Y
2 Duncan	N	Y	N	Y	Y	Y	N	Y
3 Lloyd	N	Y	N	N	Y	Y	N	Y
4 Gore	N	N	Y	N	Y	Y	Y	Y
5 Vacancy								
6 Beard	N	Y	N	N	Y	Y	N	Y

	790	791	792	793	794	795	796	797
7 Jones	Y	N	Y	N	Y	Y	Y	Y
8 Ford	Y	N	Y	N	Y	Y	Y	Y
TEXAS								
1 Hall	N	Y	N	N	Y	Y	N	N
2 Wilson, C.	Y	Y	Y	N	Y	Y	Y	Y
3 Collins	N	Y	N	Y	N	Y	N	Y
4 Roberts	N	Y	N	N	Y	Y	N	Y
5 Mattox	Y	Y	Y	N	Y	Y	Y	Y
6 Teague	?	?	?	?	?	?	?	?
7 Archer	N	Y	N	N	Y	Y	N	Y
8 Eckhardt	Y	N	N	N	Y	Y	Y	Y
9 Brooks	Y	N	Y	Y	N	Y	N	N
10 Pickle	Y	Y	Y	N	Y	N	N	Y
11 Poage	Y	Y	N	N	Y	N	N	N
12 Wright	Y	N	Y	N	Y	Y	Y	Y
13 Hightower	N	Y	N	N	Y	Y	N	Y
14 Young	?	?	Y	?	?	?	?	?
15 de la Garza	N	Y	N	N	Y	Y	N	Y
16 White	?	✓	✓	?	#	#	▮	X
17 Burleson	N	N	N	N	Y	Y	N	Y
18 Jordan	Y	N	Y	N	Y	Y	Y	N
19 Mahon	Y	N	Y	N	Y	Y	N	N
20 Gonzalez	?	▮	▮	Y	N	Y	Y	Y
21 Krueger	#	#	✓	?	#	#	✓	✓
22 Gammage	N	Y	N	N	Y	Y	N	Y
23 Kazen	N	N	N	N	Y	Y	Y	Y
24 Milford	Y	Y	N	?	?	?	N	Y
UTAH								
1 McKay	N	Y	Y	Y	#	#	#	✓
2 Marriott	N	Y	N	N	Y	Y	N	Y
VERMONT								
AL Jeffords	Y	Y	N	N	Y	Y	N	Y
VIRGINIA								
1 Trible	N	Y	N	N	Y	Y	N	Y
2 Whitehurst	N	Y	N	N	Y	Y	N	Y
3 Satterfield	N	Y	N	Y	Y	Y	N	Y
4 Daniel	N	Y	N	Y	Y	Y	N	Y
5 Daniel	N	Y	N	Y	Y	Y	N	Y
6 Butler	Y	Y	N	Y	N	Y	N	N
7 Robinson	N	Y	N	N	Y	Y	N	Y
8 Harris	Y	Y	Y	N	Y	Y	Y	Y
9 Wampler	N	Y	N	N	Y	Y	N	Y
10 Fisher	Y	Y	Y	N	Y	Y	Y	Y
WASHINGTON								
1 Pritchard	Y	Y	Y	N	Y	Y	Y	Y
2 Meeds	Y	N	Y	?	?	?	?	?
3 Bonker	Y	Y	Y	Y	Y	Y	Y	Y
4 McCormack	Y	Y	N	N	Y	Y	Y	Y
5 Foley	Y	Y	N	N	Y	Y	Y	Y
6 Dicks	Y	Y	Y	N	Y	Y	Y	Y
7 Cunningham	N	Y	N	N	Y	Y	N	Y
WEST VIRGINIA								
1 Mollohan	Y	N	N	N	Y	Y	N	N
2 Staggers	N	N	N	Y	Y	Y	Y	N
3 Slack	Y	N	N	N	Y	Y	N	Y
4 Rahall	?	X	✓	N	Y	Y	Y	Y
WISCONSIN								
1 Aspin	N	Y	N	Y	Y	Y	Y	Y
2 Kastenmeier	Y	N	Y	N	Y	Y	Y	N
3 Baldus	N	N	Y	N	Y	Y	Y	Y
4 Zablocki	N	N	Y	N	Y	Y	N	Y
5 Reuss	Y	N	Y	N	Y	Y	N	N
6 Steiger	N	X	N	Y	N	Y	Y	Y
7 Obey	Y	N	Y	Y	Y	Y	Y	N
8 Cornell	N	N	Y	N	Y	Y	N	N
9 Kasten	N	Y	N	N	Y	Y	N	Y
WYOMING								
AL Roncalio	Y	#	Y	N	N	Y	Y	Y

Democrats ***Republicans***

798. HR 12050. Tuition Tax Credits. Gradison, R-Ohio, motion to recommit the conference report on the bill to provide income tax credits for college and vocational school tuitions to the conference committee, with instructions that House conferees insist on a provision making tuitions paid to private elementary and secondary schools eligible for a credit. Motion agreed to 207-185: R 100-33; D 107-152 (ND 91-86; SD 16-66), Oct. 12, 1978. A "nay" was a vote supporting the president's position.

799. HR 12931. Foreign Aid Appropriations, Fiscal 1979. Cederberg, R-Mich., motion to recommit, and thus kill, the conference report on the bill to appropriate $9,135,031,948 for U.S. foreign assistance programs in fiscal 1979. Motion rejected 191-201: R 91-38; D 100-163 (ND 44-138; SD 56-25), Oct. 12, 1978. A "nay" was a vote supporting the president's position.

800. HR 12931. Foreign Aid Appropriations, Fiscal 1979. Adoption of the conference report on the bill to appropriate $9,-135,031,948 for U.S. foreign assistance programs for fiscal 1979. Adopted 203-188: R 45-85; D 158-103 (ND 137-42; SD 21-61), Oct. 12, 1978. The president had requested $10,387,760,919.

801. HR 12931. Foreign Aid Appropriations, Fiscal 1979. Long, D-Md., motion to recede and concur in the Senate amendment to provide that the president could waive a prohibition on direct U.S. aid to Angola or Mozambique if he determined the aid would further U.S. policy interests. Motion rejected 161-204: R 17-107; D 144-97 (ND 122-41; SD 22-56), Oct. 12, 1978. A "yea" was a vote supporting the president's position.

802. HR 11545. Meat Import Act. Passage of the bill to revise the import quota formula in the 1964 Meat Import Act, to authorize suspension of the quota only in cases of national emergency or natural disaster, and to include processed meats in the quota system. Passed 289-66: R 100-21; D 189-45 (ND 115-40; SD 74-5), Oct. 12, 1978. A "nay" was a vote supporting the president's position.

803. H Res 1426. Consideration of Rules Committee Reports. Adoption of the resolution to waive the provision in House rule XI, 4(b), that requires a two-thirds vote to consider reports from the Rules Committee on the same day they were reported. Adopted 260-134: R 1-128; D 259-6 (ND 176-4; SD 83-2), Oct. 13, 1978.

804. H Res 1432. Waterway User Tax/Lock and Dam 26. Frenzel, R-Minn., demand for a second on the Ullman, D-Ore., motion to suspend the rules and adopt the resolution agreeing to the bill (HR 8533) together with the Senate amendment to establish a waterway user tax and to authorize a new lock and dam on the Mississippi River. Second ordered 374-4: R 124-3; D 250-1 (ND 169-0; SD 81-1), Oct. 13, 1978.

805. H Res 1432. Waterway User Tax/Lock and Dam 26. Ullman, D-Ore. motion to suspend the rules and adopt the resolution agreeing to the bill (HR 8533) together with the Senate amendment to impose a tax on barge fuel, beginning at four cents a gallon on Oct. 1, 1980, and rising to a maximum of 10 cents after Sept. 30, 1985, and to authorize $421 million for the construction of a new lock and dam on the Mississippi River at Alton, Ill. Motion agreed to (thus cleared for the president) 287-123: R 109-26; D 178-97 (ND 105-85; SD 73-12), Oct. 13, 1978. A two-thirds majority vote (274 in this case) is required for adoption under suspension of the rules. A "yea" was a vote supporting the president's position.

KEY

Y Voted for (yea).
✓ Paired for.
† Announced for.
# CQ Poll for.
N Voted against (nay).
X Paired against.
- Announced against.
▮ CQ Poll against.
P Voted "present."
● Voted "present" to avoid possible conflict of interest.
? Did not vote or otherwise make a position known.

	798	799	800	801	802	803	804	805
ALABAMA								
1 Edwards	Y	Y	N	N	Y	N	Y	Y
2 Dickinson	N	Y	N	N	Y	?	?	?
3 Nichols	N	Y	N	N	Y	Y	Y	Y
4 Bevill	N	Y	N	N	Y	Y	Y	Y
5 Flippo	N	Y	N	N	Y	Y	Y	Y
6 Buchanan	N	N	Y	Y	Y	N	Y	Y
7 Flowers	N	Y	N	N	Y	Y	?	Y
ALASKA								
AL Young	N	Y	N	?	#	N	Y	Y
ARIZONA								
1 Rhodes	N	Y	N	N	Y	N	Y	Y
2 Udall	N	N	Y	Y	#	Y	Y	Y
3 Stump	N	Y	N	N	Y	Y	Y	Y
4 Rudd	✓	✓	?	?	?	?	?	?
ARKANSAS								
1 Alexander	N	N	Y	Y	Y	Y	Y	Y
2 Tucker	N	X	Y	Y	#	Y	Y	N
3 Hammerschmidt	N	Y	N	N	Y	N	Y	Y
4 Thornton	N	N	N	Y	Y	Y	Y	N
CALIFORNIA								
1 Johnson	Y	Y	Y	Y	Y	Y	Y	Y
2 Clausen	Y	Y	N	N	Y	N	?	Y
3 Moss	?	?	?	?	?	?	?	N
4 Leggett	?	N	Y	?	?	Y	Y	?
5 Burton, J.	N	N	Y	?	N	Y	?	N
6 Burton, P.	N	N	Y	?	?	Y	Y	N
7 Miller	?	N	N	?	?	Y	Y	N
8 Dellums	N	N	N	Y	N	Y	Y	N
9 Stark	N	N	N	?	▮	Y	?	N
10 Edwards	?	N	Y	?	?	Y	?	N
11 Ryan	Y	N	Y	Y	Y	Y	Y	Y
12 McCloskey	N	N	Y	Y	Y	N	Y	Y
13 Mineta	N	N	Y	Y	Y	Y	Y	Y
14 McFall	N	N	Y	Y	?	Y	Y	Y
15 Sisk	N	?	?	?	?	Y	Y	Y
16 Panetta	N	Y	N	Y	Y	Y	Y	Y
17 Krebs	N	N	Y	Y	Y	Y	Y	N
18 Vacancy								
19 Lagomarsino	Y	Y	N	N	Y	N	Y	Y
20 Goldwater	Y	Y	N	N	?	?	Y	Y
21 Corman	N	N	Y	Y	Y	Y	Y	Y
22 Moorhead	Y	Y	N	N	Y	N	Y	Y
23 Beilenson	N	N	Y	Y	N	Y	Y	N
24 Waxman	N	N	Y	Y	N	Y	#	N
25 Roybal	N	N	N	Y	N	#	Y	Y
26 Rousselot	Y	Y	N	N	Y	N	Y	Y
27 Dornan	Y	N	Y	N	Y	N	Y	Y
28 Burke	X	X	✓	?	#	#	?	#
29 Hawkins	N	N	?	Y	Y	Y	Y	Y
30 Danielson	N	N	Y	Y	Y	Y	Y	Y
31 Wilson, C.H.	N	?	?	?	?	N	Y	Y
32 Anderson	N	Y	Y	N	N	Y	Y	Y
33 Clawson	Y	Y	N	N	Y	N	Y	Y
34 Hannaford	N	N	Y	Y	?	Y	Y	N
35 Lloyd	N	N	Y	N	Y	Y	Y	Y
36 Brown	N	N	Y	?	Y	Y	Y	Y
37 Pettis	?	?	?	?	?	?	?	?
38 Patterson	N	N	Y	Y	Y	Y	Y	Y
39 Wiggins	N	✓	▮	?	#	▮	?	Y
40 Badham	▮	✓	X	?	#	▮	?	#
41 Wilson, B.	Y	Y	N	N	Y	N	N	Y
42 Van Deerlin	Y	N	Y	Y	Y	Y	Y	Y
43 Burgener	Y	Y	N	N	Y	N	Y	Y
COLORADO								
1 Schroeder	N	Y	N	Y	Y	N	Y	N
2 Wirth	N	N	Y	Y	Y	Y	Y	N
3 Evans	#	?	#	?	#	Y	Y	Y
4 Johnson	N	Y	N	N	Y	N	Y	N
5 Armstrong	Y	✓	?	?	?	N	Y	N
CONNECTICUT								
1 Cotter	Y	N	Y	Y	N	Y	Y	Y
2 Dodd	N	N	Y	Y	Y	Y	Y	N
3 Giaimo	Y	N	Y	?	?	?	?	Y
4 McKinney	N	N	Y	Y	Y	N	Y	Y
5 Sarasin	#	X	✓	?	#	▮	?	#
6 Moffett	N	N	Y	Y	?	Y	Y	N
DELAWARE								
AL Evans	Y	Y	Y	N	Y	N	Y	Y
FLORIDA								
1 Sikes	N	?	?	?	?	?	Y	Y
2 Fuqua	N	Y	N	N	Y	Y	?	N
3 Bennett	N	Y	N	N	Y	Y	Y	Y
4 Chappell	X	?	X	?	✓	Y	Y	Y
5 Kelly	Y	Y	N	N	Y	N	Y	Y
6 Young	N	Y	N	N	N	N	Y	Y
7 Gibbons	Y	N	N	N	N	Y	Y	Y
8 Ireland	?	?	?	?	Y	?	Y	?
9 Frey	?	✓	?	?	?	?	?	?
10 Bafalis	Y	Y	N	N	Y	N	Y	Y
11 Rogers	N	N	Y	Y	Y	Y	Y	Y
12 Burke	Y	Y	N	N	Y	N	Y	Y
13 Lehman	N	N	Y	Y	Y	Y	Y	Y
14 Pepper	N	N	Y	Y	Y	Y	Y	Y
15 Fascell	N	N	Y	Y	Y	Y	Y	Y
GEORGIA								
1 Ginn	N	Y	N	N	Y	Y	Y	Y
2 Mathis	Y	Y	N	N	Y	Y	Y	?
3 Brinkley	Y	Y	N	N	Y	Y	Y	Y
4 Levitas	Y	Y	N	Y	Y	Y	Y	Y
5 Fowler	N	N	Y	N	Y	Y	Y	Y
6 Flynt	Y	Y	N	N	Y	Y	Y	Y
7 McDonald	Y	Y	N	N	Y	N	N	N
8 Evans	Y	N	Y	N	Y	Y	Y	N
9 Jenkins	N	Y	N	N	Y	Y	Y	Y
10 Barnard	Y	Y	N	N	Y	Y	Y	Y
HAWAII								
1 Heftel	Y	Y	N	N	Y	Y	Y	Y
2 Akaka	N	N	Y	N	Y	Y	Y	Y
IDAHO								
1 Symms	Y	Y	N	N	Y	N	Y	N
2 Hansen, G.	Y	Y	N	N	Y	N	Y	N
ILLINOIS								
1 Vacancy								
2 Murphy	Y	N	Y	N	Y	Y	Y	N
3 Russo	Y	Y	N	N	N	Y	Y	N
4 Derwinski	Y	N	Y	N	N	N	Y	N
5 Fary	Y	Y	Y	Y	Y	Y	Y	Y
6 Hyde	Y	N	Y	N	N	N	Y	Y
7 Collins	N	N	Y	Y	Y	Y	Y	Y
8 Rostenkowski	Y	N	Y	Y	Y	Y	Y	N
9 Yates	N	N	Y	?	▮	Y	Y	N
10 Mikva	N	N	Y	Y	Y	Y	?	N
11 Annunzio	Y	N	Y	?	#	Y	Y	Y
12 Crane	✓	✓	X	?	#	▮	?	?
13 McClory	N	N	N	N	Y	N	Y	Y
14 Erlenborn	Y	N	Y	N	N	N	Y	Y
15 Corcoran	Y	Y	N	N	Y	N	Y	Y
16 Anderson	N	N	Y	Y	#	N	Y	Y
17 O'Brien	Y	Y	Y	N	Y	N	Y	Y
18 Michel	Y	Y	N	N	Y	N	Y	Y
19 Railsback	Y	N	Y	N	Y	N	Y	Y
20 Findley	N	N	Y	Y	Y	N	Y	Y
21 Madigan	?	Y	Y	N	Y	N	Y	Y
22 Shipley	?	X	?	?	?	?	?	?
23 Price	Y	N	Y	Y	Y	Y	Y	Y
24 Simon	N	N	Y	Y	Y	Y	Y	Y
INDIANA								
1 Benjamin	Y	Y	N	Y	N	Y	Y	N
2 Fithian	N	Y	N	N	Y	Y	Y	Y
3 Brademas	N	N	Y	Y	N	Y	Y	Y
4 Quayle	Y	?	?	?	?	N	Y	Y
5 Hillis	?	?	?	?	?	N	Y	Y
6 Evans	N	Y	N	N	Y	Y	Y	Y
7 Myers, J.	Y	Y	N	N	Y	N	Y	Y
8 Cornwell	N	N	Y	Y	Y	Y	Y	Y
9 Hamilton	N	N	Y	Y	Y	Y	Y	Y
10 Sharp	N	N	N	Y	Y	Y	Y	Y
11 Jacobs	▮	N	N	Y	Y	N	Y	N
IOWA								
1 Leach	Y	Y	Y	Y	Y	N	Y	Y
2 Blouin	Y	N	Y	Y	Y	Y	Y	Y
3 Grassley	Y	Y	N	N	Y	N	Y	Y
4 Smith	N	Y	Y	Y	Y	Y	Y	Y
5 Harkin	Y	Y	N	Y	Y	Y	Y	Y
6 Bedell	N	N	Y	Y	Y	Y	Y	N

Democrats ***Republicans***

	798	799	800	801	802	803	804	805
KANSAS								
1 Sebelius	Y	Y	N	N	Y	▮	Y	Y
2 Keys	N	N	Y	Y	Y	Y	Y	Y
3 Winn	Y	Y	Y	N	Y	N	Y	Y
4 Glickman	N	N	Y	N	Y	Y	Y	Y
5 Skubitz	N	✓	?	?	?	N	Y	N
KENTUCKY								
1 Hubbard	N	N	N	N	Y	Y	Y	Y
2 Natcher	Y	Y	N	Y	Y	Y	Y	Y
3 Mazzoli	Y	N	Y	N	N	Y	Y	Y
4 Snyder	Y	Y	N	N	Y	N	Y	Y
5 Carter	N	Y	N	N	Y	N	Y	Y
6 Breckinridge	N	N	Y	N	Y	Y	Y	Y
7 Perkins	N	Y	N	Y	Y	Y	Y	Y
LOUISIANA								
1 Livingston	Y	Y	N	N	N	N	Y	Y
2 Boggs	Y	N	Y	Y	N	Y	Y	Y
3 Treen	Y	Y	N	N	Y	N	Y	Y
4 Waggonner	N	Y	N	N	Y	Y	Y	Y
5 Huckaby	N	Y	N	N	Y	Y	Y	Y
6 Moore	Y	Y	N	N	Y	N	Y	N
7 Breaux	Y	Y	N	N	Y	Y	Y	Y
8 Long	Y	Y	N	Y	Y	Y	Y	N
MAINE								
1 Emery	Y	Y	N	N	?	N	Y	Y
2 Cohen	Y	Y	N	N	?	N	Y	N
MARYLAND								
1 Bauman	Y	Y	N	N	Y	N	Y	Y
2 Long	N	N	Y	Y	Y	Y	Y	N
3 Mikulski	Y	N	Y	Y	N	Y	Y	Y
4 Holt	Y	Y	N	N	Y	N	Y	N
5 Spellman	N	N	Y	Y	Y	Y	Y	Y
6 Vacancy								
7 Mitchell	#	N	#	Y	#	Y	?	Y
8 Steers	Y	N	Y	Y	Y	Y	Y	N
MASSACHUSETTS								
1 Conte	Y	N	Y	Y	N	N	Y	N
2 Boland	Y	N	Y	Y	Y	Y	Y	Y
3 Early	Y	Y	N	N	N	Y	Y	N
4 Drinan	N	N	Y	Y	N	Y	Y	N
5 Tsongas	N	N	Y	?	?	Y	Y	N
6 Harrington	✓	?	#	?	▮	#	?	N
7 Markey	Y	N	Y	Y	N	Y	Y	N
8 O'Neill								
9 Moakley	Y	N	Y	N	Y	Y	Y	N
10 Heckler	Y	N	Y	Y	N	N	Y	N
11 Burke	Y	Y	Y	N	Y	Y	Y	Y
12 Studds	N	N	Y	Y	N	Y	Y	N
MICHIGAN								
1 Conyers	Y	?	▮	?	X	Y	?	N
2 Pursell	N	N	Y	Y	Y	N	Y	N
3 Brown	Y	N	Y	N	Y	N	?	N
4 Stockman	Y	?	Y	N	N	N	▮	N
5 Sawyer	Y	Y	N	?	Y	N	Y	Y
6 Carr	N	N	Y	Y	Y	Y	Y	N
7 Kildee	Y	N	Y	Y	Y	Y	Y	N
8 Traxler	Y	N	Y	?	#	Y	Y	Y
9 Vander Jagt	Y	Y	N	N	Y	N	Y	Y
10 Cederberg	Y	Y	N	N	Y	N	?	Y
11 Ruppe	Y	N	Y	N	Y	N	Y	Y
12 Bonior	N	N	Y	Y	#	Y	Y	N
13 Diggs	?	X	✓	?	?	?	?	?
14 Nedzi	Y	N	Y	Y	N	Y	Y	N
15 Ford	N	N	Y	Y	Y	Y	Y	N
16 Dingell	N	N	Y	?	N	Y	?	N
17 Brodhead	N	N	Y	Y	N	Y	Y	N
18 Blanchard	N	N	Y	Y	N	Y	Y	N
19 Broomfield	Y	?	#	?	#	N	Y	Y
MINNESOTA								
1 Quie	?	?	?	?	?	?	?	?
2 Hagedorn	Y	Y	N	N	Y	N	Y	Y
3 Frenzel	Y	N	Y	N	Y	N	Y	Y
4 Vento	Y	N	Y	Y	Y	Y	Y	Y
5 Fraser	N	N	Y	Y	Y	?	Y	Y
6 Nolan	N	N	Y	Y	Y	Y	Y	Y
7 Stangeland	Y	Y	N	N	Y	N	Y	Y
8 Oberstar	N	N	Y	Y	Y	Y	Y	Y
MISSISSIPPI								
1 Whitten	Y	Y	N	N	Y	Y	Y	Y
2 Bowen	N	Y	N	N	Y	Y	Y	Y
3 Montgomery	#	Y	N	N	Y	Y	Y	Y
4 Cochran	?	?	?	?	?	?	?	?
5 Lott	▮	Y	N	N	Y	N	Y	Y
MISSOURI								
1 Clay	N	N	Y	?	?	Y	?	Y
2 Young	Y	N	Y	N	Y	Y	Y	Y
3 Gephardt	Y	Y	N	N	Y	Y	Y	Y
4 Skelton	N	N	Y	N	Y	Y	Y	Y
5 Bolling	N	N	#	?	#	Y	Y	Y
6 Coleman	Y	Y	N	N	Y	N	Y	Y
7 Taylor	N	Y	N	N	Y	N	Y	Y
8 Ichord	N	Y	N	N	Y	Y	Y	Y
9 Volkmer	Y	N	N	N	Y	Y	Y	Y
10 Burlison	N	N	Y	Y	Y	Y	Y	Y
MONTANA								
1 Baucus	N	Y	N	?	Y	Y	Y	Y
2 Marlenee	N	Y	N	N	Y	N	Y	N
NEBRASKA								
1 Thone	Y	Y	N	N	Y	N	Y	Y
2 Cavanaugh	Y	N	Y	Y	Y	Y	Y	N
3 Smith	Y	Y	N	N	Y	N	Y	Y
NEVADA								
AL Santini	Y	N	Y	N	Y	Y	?	Y
NEW HAMPSHIRE								
1 D'Amours	Y	Y	N	N	N	Y	Y	N
2 Cleveland	Y	Y	N	N	N	N	Y	N
NEW JERSEY								
1 Florio	Y	N	Y	Y	N	Y	Y	N
2 Hughes	Y	Y	N	Y	N	Y	Y	N
3 Howard	Y	N	Y	Y	#	Y	Y	Y
4 Thompson	N	N	Y	Y	N	Y	Y	N
5 Fenwick	N	N	Y	Y	N	N	Y	N
6 Forsythe	Y	N	Y	N	Y	N	Y	Y
7 Maguire	Y	N	Y	Y	N	Y	Y	N
8 Roe	Y	N	Y	Y	?	Y	Y	Y
9 Hollenbeck	✓	?	Y	?	Y	#	?	Y
10 Rodino	Y	N	Y	Y	N	Y	Y	N
11 Minish	Y	N	Y	Y	N	Y	?	N
12 Rinaldo	Y	N	Y	N	N	N	Y	N
13 Meyner	Y	N	Y	?	▮	Y	Y	N
14 LeFante	Y	Y	Y	Y	N	Y	Y	N
15 Patten	Y	N	Y	Y	N	Y	Y	Y
NEW MEXICO								
1 Lujan	Y	Y	?	N	?	?	?	?
2 Runnels	Y	Y	N	N	?	Y	Y	Y
NEW YORK								
1 Pike	N	Y	N	N	Y	Y	Y	Y
2 Downey	N	N	Y	Y	Y	Y	Y	N
3 Ambro	Y	N	Y	N	Y	?	?	N
4 Lent	Y	N	Y	N	Y	N	Y	Y
5 Wydler	Y	Y	Y	N	N	N	Y	N
6 Wolff	Y	N	Y	N	N	Y	Y	Y
7 Addabbo	Y	N	Y	Y	Y	Y	Y	N
8 Rosenthal	N	X	Y	?	#	Y	?	N
9 Delaney	Y	Y	N	N	Y	Y	Y	Y
10 Biaggi	Y	N	Y	N	Y	Y	Y	N
11 Scheuer	Y	N	Y	Y	N	Y	Y	N
12 Chisholm	N	N	Y	Y	Y	Y	Y	Y
13 Solarz	Y	N	Y	Y	N	Y	Y	N
14 Richmond	N	N	Y	Y	N	Y	Y	N
15 Zeferetti	Y	N	Y	N	#	Y	Y	Y
16 Holtzman	N	N	Y	Y	N	Y	Y	N
17 Murphy	Y	N	Y	N	Y	Y	Y	Y
18 Green	Y	N	Y	Y	N	N	Y	Y
19 Rangel	N	N	Y	Y	Y	Y	Y	N
20 Weiss	N	N	Y	Y	N	Y	Y	N
21 Garcia	Y	#	?	?	▮	Y	Y	N
22 Bingham	Y	N	Y	Y	N	Y	Y	Y
23 Caputo	Y	N	Y	N	N	?	?	Y
24 Ottinger	Y	N	Y	Y	?	Y	Y	N
25 Fish	Y	N	Y	?	?	N	Y	Y
26 Gilman	Y	N	Y	N	N	N	Y	Y
27 McHugh	N	N	Y	Y	Y	#	?	N
28 Stratton	Y	N	Y	N	Y	Y	Y	Y
29 Pattison	Y	N	Y	Y	Y	#	Y	N
30 McEwen	Y	Y	N	N	Y	N	Y	Y
31 Mitchell	N	N	Y	N	Y	N	Y	Y
32 Hanley	Y	N	Y	Y	Y	#	?	N
33 Walsh	Y	Y	N	N	Y	N	Y	Y
34 Horton	Y	N	Y	N	Y	N	Y	Y
35 Conable	Y	N	Y	N	N	N	Y	Y
36 LaFalce	N	N	Y	Y	Y	Y	?	Y
37 Nowak	Y	N	Y	Y	Y	Y	Y	Y
38 Kemp	Y	Y	N	N	N	N	Y	Y
39 Lundine	▮	N	Y	Y	Y	Y	Y	N
NORTH CAROLINA								
1 Jones	N	Y	N	N	Y	Y	Y	Y
2 Fountain	N	Y	N	N	Y	N	Y	Y
3 Whitley	N	Y	N	N	Y	Y	Y	Y
4 Andrews	N	Y	N	N	Y	Y	Y	Y
5 Neal	N	Y	N	?	Y	Y	Y	Y
6 Preyer	N	N	Y	N	Y	Y	Y	Y
7 Rose	N	Y	N	N	Y	Y	Y	Y
8 Hefner	N	Y	N	N	Y	Y	Y	Y
9 Martin	N	Y	N	N	Y	N	Y	Y
10 Broyhill	N	Y	N	N	Y	N	Y	Y
11 Gudger	N	Y	N	N	Y	Y	?	Y
NORTH DAKOTA								
AL Andrews	Y	Y	N	Y	Y	N	Y	Y
OHIO								
1 Gradison	Y	N	Y	N	N	N	Y	Y
2 Luken	Y	N	Y	N	Y	Y	Y	Y
3 Whalen	N	N	Y	Y	N	N	Y	Y
4 Guyer	Y	Y	N	N	Y	N	Y	Y
5 Latta	Y	Y	N	N	Y	N	Y	Y
6 Harsha	Y	Y	N	N	Y	N	Y	Y
7 Brown	Y	Y	N	N	Y	N	Y	Y
8 Kindness	Y	Y	N	?	?	N	Y	Y
9 Ashley	Y	N	?	Y	Y	Y	Y	Y
10 Miller	Y	Y	N	N	Y	N	Y	Y
11 Stanton	Y	N	Y	N	#	N	Y	Y
12 Devine	Y	Y	N	N	Y	N	Y	Y
13 Pease	Y	N	Y	Y	Y	Y	Y	Y
14 Seiberling	Y	N	Y	Y	Y	Y	?	N
15 Wylie	Y	Y	N	N	Y	N	Y	Y
16 Regula	Y	Y	N	N	Y	N	Y	N
17 Ashbrook	Y	Y	N	N	Y	N	N	Y
18 Applegate	Y	Y	N	N	Y	Y	Y	N
19 Carney	Y	Y	N	Y	Y	Y	Y	Y
20 Oakar	Y	Y	N	Y	Y	Y	Y	N
21 Stokes	N	N	Y	Y	Y	Y	Y	Y
22 Vanik	Y	N	Y	Y	Y	Y	Y	N
23 Mottl	Y	Y	N	N	?	Y	Y	N
OKLAHOMA								
1 Jones	N	Y	N	N	Y	Y	Y	Y
2 Risenhoover	N	Y	N	N	Y	Y	Y	?
3 Watkins	N	Y	N	N	Y	Y	Y	Y
4 Steed	N	Y	N	N	#	Y	Y	Y
5 Edwards	Y	Y	N	N	Y	N	Y	Y
6 English	N	Y	N	N	Y	Y	?	Y
OREGON								
1 AuCoin	?	N	N	N	Y	Y	Y	Y
2 Ullman	N	N	Y	N	Y	Y	Y	Y
3 Duncan	N	N	Y	Y	Y	Y	Y	Y
4 Weaver	N	Y	N	Y	Y	Y	Y	N
PENNSYLVANIA								
1 Myers, M.	Y	Y	Y	N	N	Y	Y	Y
2 Nix	Y	N	Y	Y	Y	?	Y	N
3 Lederer	Y	Y	Y	Y	N	Y	Y	Y
4 Eilberg	Y	N	Y	Y	?	Y	Y	Y
5 Schulze	?	?	?	?	?	?	?	?
6 Yatron	Y	N	Y	Y	Y	Y	Y	N
7 Edgar	Y	N	Y	Y	Y	N	Y	N
8 Kostmayer	Y	N	Y	Y	N	Y	Y	N
9 Shuster	Y	Y	N	N	Y	N	Y	Y
10 McDade	Y	Y	Y	N	N	N	Y	N
11 Flood	Y	N	Y	Y	Y	Y	Y	N
12 Murtha	Y	Y	N	Y	Y	Y	Y	N
13 Coughlin	Y	N	Y	N	Y	N	Y	Y
14 Moorhead	N	N	Y	Y	Y	Y	Y	Y
15 Rooney	Y	N	Y	Y	Y	Y	Y	N
16 Walker	Y	Y	N	N	Y	N	Y	Y
17 Ertel	Y	Y	N	N	Y	Y	Y	Y
18 Walgren	Y	N	Y	Y	Y	Y	Y	N
19 Goodling, W.	Y	Y	N	N	Y	N	Y	Y
20 Gaydos	Y	Y	N	Y	Y	Y	Y	N
21 Dent	Y	Y	N	Y	Y	Y	Y	N
22 Murphy	Y	Y	N	N	Y	Y	Y	N
23 Ammerman	?	?	X	?	?	?	?	?
24 Marks	Y	N	N	Y	Y	N	Y	Y
25 Myers, G.	N	N	Y	N	N	N	N	N
RHODE ISLAND								
1 St Germain	Y	N	Y	Y	N	Y	Y	Y
2 Beard	Y	Y	N	N	Y	Y	Y	Y
SOUTH CAROLINA								
1 Davis	N	Y	N	N	Y	Y	?	Y
2 Spence	N	Y	N	N	Y	N	Y	Y
3 Derrick	N	Y	N	N	Y	Y	Y	N
4 Mann	N	N	Y	Y	Y	Y	Y	Y
5 Holland	N	Y	N	N	Y	Y	Y	Y
6 Jenrette	N	Y	N	N	Y	Y	Y	Y
SOUTH DAKOTA								
1 Pressler	Y	Y	N	N	Y	?	?	Y
2 Abdnor	N	Y	N	N	Y	N	Y	Y
TENNESSEE								
1 Quillen	N	Y	N	N	Y	N	Y	N
2 Duncan	N	Y	N	N	Y	N	Y	Y
3 Lloyd	N	Y	N	N	Y	Y	Y	Y
4 Gore	N	N	Y	Y	Y	Y	Y	Y
5 Vacancy								
6 Beard	Y	Y	N	?	#	N	Y	Y
7 Jones	N	Y	N	N	Y	Y	Y	Y
8 Ford	N	N	Y	Y	Y	Y	Y	Y
TEXAS								
1 Hall	N	Y	N	N	Y	Y	Y	Y
2 Wilson, C.	N	N	Y	?	Y	Y	Y	Y
3 Collins	Y	Y	N	N	Y	N	Y	N
4 Roberts	N	Y	N	N	Y	Y	Y	Y
5 Mattox	N	N	N	Y	Y	Y	Y	N
6 Teague	?	?	?	?	?	?	?	?
7 Archer	Y	Y	N	N	Y	N	Y	Y
8 Eckhardt	N	N	Y	Y	N	Y	Y	Y
9 Brooks	Y	Y	N	N	Y	Y	Y	Y
10 Pickle	N	Y	N	Y	Y	Y	Y	N
11 Poage	N	Y	N	N	Y	Y	Y	Y
12 Wright	N	N	Y	Y	Y	Y	?	Y
13 Hightower	N	Y	N	N	Y	Y	Y	Y
14 Young	?	?	?	?	?	?	Y	Y
15 de la Garza	Y	Y	N	N	Y	Y	Y	Y
16 White	X	?	▮	?	#	Y	Y	Y
17 Burleson	N	Y	N	N	Y	Y	Y	N
18 Jordan	N	N	Y	?	?	Y	Y	Y
19 Mahon	N	N	N	Y	Y	Y	Y	N
20 Gonzalez	N	N	Y	N	Y	Y	Y	Y
21 Krueger	X	X	✓	?	#	Y	Y	Y
22 Gammage	N	Y	N	N	Y	Y	Y	Y
23 Kazen	N	Y	N	N	Y	Y	Y	Y
24 Milford	N	Y	N	?	?	Y	Y	Y
UTAH								
1 McKay	#	Y	N	N	Y	Y	Y	Y
2 Marriott	Y	Y	N	N	Y	N	Y	Y
VERMONT								
AL Jeffords	Y	N	Y	Y	Y	N	Y	Y
VIRGINIA								
1 Trible	N	Y	N	N	Y	N	Y	Y
2 Whitehurst	N	Y	N	N	Y	N	Y	Y
3 Satterfield	N	Y	N	N	Y	Y	Y	Y
4 Daniel	Y	Y	N	N	Y	N	Y	Y
5 Daniel	N	Y	N	N	Y	Y	Y	Y
6 Butler	N	Y	N	N	Y	N	Y	Y
7 Robinson	N	Y	N	N	Y	N	Y	Y
8 Harris	N	Y	N	Y	N	Y	Y	N
9 Wampler	N	Y	N	N	Y	N	Y	Y
10 Fisher	N	N	Y	Y	Y	Y	Y	Y
WASHINGTON								
1 Pritchard	Y	N	Y	Y	Y	N	Y	N
2 Meeds	?	?	?	?	?	Y	Y	Y
3 Bonker	▮	N	Y	Y	Y	Y	Y	Y
4 McCormack	N	Y	Y	N	Y	Y	Y	Y
5 Foley	Y	Y	Y	Y	Y	Y	Y	Y
6 Dicks	N	N	Y	Y	Y	Y	Y	Y
7 Cunningham	Y	Y	N	N	Y	N	Y	Y
WEST VIRGINIA								
1 Mollohan	N	N	Y	Y	Y	Y	Y	Y
2 Staggers	Y	Y	N	N	Y	Y	Y	N
3 Slack	Y	Y	N	?	?	Y	Y	Y
4 Rahall	N	Y	N	Y	Y	Y	Y	Y
WISCONSIN								
1 Aspin	N	N	Y	?	Y	Y	Y	Y
2 Kastenmeier	N	N	Y	Y	Y	Y	?	Y
3 Baldus	N	N	Y	Y	Y	Y	Y	Y
4 Zablocki	Y	N	Y	Y	Y	Y	Y	Y
5 Reuss	▮	N	Y	Y	N	Y	Y	Y
6 Steiger	Y	N	Y	N	Y	N	Y	Y
7 Obey	N	N	Y	Y	Y	Y	?	Y
8 Cornell	Y	Y	N	Y	Y	Y	Y	Y
9 Kasten	Y	Y	N	?	Y	N	Y	Y
WYOMING								
AL Roncalio	Y	N	Y	Y	Y	#	Y	Y

Democrats ***Republicans***

806. H Res 1434. National Energy Act. Bolling, D-Mo., motion to order the previous question (thus ending debate) on adoption of the resolution to waive all points of order so that the House could consider en bloc the conference reports on the five pieces of the National Energy Act — HR 5263, HR 5037, HR 5289, HR 5146, HR 4018. (The vote prevented a separate vote on the natural gas pricing section of the bill, which had been sought by its opponents). Motion agreed to 207-206: R 8-127; D 199-79 (ND 136-55; SD 63-24), Oct. 13, 1978. A "yea" was a vote supporting the president's position.

807. H Res 1414. Reprimand of Charles H. Wilson. Adoption of the resolution that the House agree to the report by the Committee on Standards of Official Conduct recommending a "reprimand" of Charles H. Wilson, D-Calif., for false statement made by Wilson in response to a committee questionnaire concerning a gift of $1,000 he received from Tongsun Park, an alleged Korean government agent. Adopted 329-41: R 115-11; D 214-30 (ND 140-20; SD 74-10), Oct. 13, 1978.

808. H Res 1416. Censure of Edward R. Roybal. Bob Wilson, R-Calif., motion to recommit to the Committee on Standards of Official Conduct the resolution recommending that the House censure Edward R. Roybal, D-Calif., and report back the resolution with a recommendation that the House reprimand Roybal for false statements made on four occasions to the committee concerning receipt of a $1,000 campaign contribution from Tongsun Park, an alleged agent of South Korea, for converting the campaign contribution to his own use, and for failure to report the campaign contribution as required by law. Motion agreed to 219-170: R 41-83; D 178-87 (ND 127-53; SD 51-34), Oct. 13, 1978.

809. HR 12370. Health Services Amendments. Rogers, D-Fla., motion that the House resolve itself into the Committee of the Whole to consider the bill to extend through fiscal 1982 the authorization for hypertension screening and control programs, and, through fiscal 1981, other categorical health programs, for a total authorization in the bill of $2,704,861,000. Motion agreed to 327-6: R 110-1; D 217-5 (ND 149-3; SD 68-2), Oct. 13, 1978.

810. HR 12370. Health Services Amendments. Dornan, R-Calif., motion to recommit the bill to committee with instructions to report it back with an amendment to prohibit use of any appropriated funds to support family programs that provided directly or indirectly for abortions, abortion counseling or referral services. Motion rejected 137-232: R 72-48; D 65-184 (ND 42-127; SD 23-57), Oct. 13, 1978.

811. HR 12370. Health Services Amendments. Passage of the bill to authorize $2,316,861,000 for fiscal 1979-81 for hypertension screening and control and other categorical federal health programs. Passed 343-27: R 107-13; D 236-14 (ND 158-10; SD 78-4), Oct. 13, 1978.

812. HR 2534. Health Maintenance Organizations. Adoption of the conference report on the bill to authorize $164 million for federal programs supporting prepaid group medical practices (HMOs) for fiscal 1979-81. Adopted 309-33: R 88-26; D 221-7 (ND 149-3; SD 72-4), Oct. 13, 1978.

813. HR 14104. Endangered Species Act Amendments. Duncan, R-Tenn., amendment to exempt the Tellico Dam in Tennessee from provisions of the act. Adopted 231-157: R 99-30; D 132-127 (ND 61-116; SD 71-11), Oct. 14, 1978.

KEY

- Y Voted for (yea).
- ✓ Paired for.
- † Announced for.
- # CQ Poll for.
- N Voted against (nay).
- X Paired against.
- - Announced against.
- ▮ CQ Poll against.
- P Voted "present."
- ● Voted "present" to avoid possible conflict of interest.
- ? Did not vote or otherwise make a position known.

	806	807	808	809	810	811	812	813
ALABAMA								
1 Edwards	N	Y	N	Y	N	Y	Y	Y
2 Dickinson	?	?	?	?	?	?	?	✓
3 Nichols	Y	Y	Y	?	Y	Y	Y	?
4 Bevill	Y	N	Y	Y	Y	Y	Y	Y
5 Flippo	Y	Y	Y	Y	N	Y	Y	Y
6 Buchanan	Y	Y	?	Y	N	Y	Y	Y
7 Flowers	Y	Y	N	?	N	Y	Y	Y
ALASKA								
AL Young	Y	N	N	Y	Y	Y	Y	Y
ARIZONA								
1 Rhodes	N	Y	Y	Y	Y	Y	Y	Y
2 Udall	Y	Y	Y	Y	N	Y	Y	N
3 Stump	Y	Y	N	Y	Y	N	N	Y
4 Rudd	X	?	?	?	✓	?	?	✓
ARKANSAS								
1 Alexander	Y	P	Y	?	X	?	Y	Y
2 Tucker	Y	Y	?	?	?	Y	?	Y
3 Hammerschmidt	N	?	?	Y	Y	Y	N	Y
4 Thornton	Y	Y	N	Y	N	Y	Y	Y
CALIFORNIA								
1 Johnson	Y	P	Y	Y	N	N	Y	Y
2 Clausen	N	Y	Y	Y	Y	Y	Y	Y
3 Moss	N	?	?	?	?	?	?	?
4 Leggett	Y	P	Y	?	N	Y	?	N
5 Burton, J.	N	P	Y	?	N	Y	?	N
6 Burton, P.	N	P	Y	?	?	?	?	N
7 Miller	N	P	Y	?	?	?	?	N
8 Dellums	N	P	Y	Y	N	Y	Y	N
9 Stark	N	P	Y	Y	N	Y	Y	N
10 Edwards	Y	P	Y	?	N	Y	Y	N
11 Ryan	Y	P	Y	Y	N	Y	?	N
12 McCloskey	N	Y	Y	Y	N	Y	Y	N
13 Mineta	Y	Y	Y	Y	N	Y	Y	N
14 McFall	Y	?	?	?	?	?	?	?
15 Sisk	Y	N	Y	Y	N	?	Y	Y
16 Panetta	Y	Y	Y	Y	N	Y	Y	N
17 Krebs	Y	Y	Y	Y	N	Y	Y	N
18 Vacancy								
19 Lagomarsino	N	Y	Y	Y	Y	Y	Y	Y
20 Goldwater	N	Y	Y	Y	Y	Y	N	Y
21 Corman	Y	N	Y	Y	N	Y	Y	N
22 Moorhead	N	Y	Y	Y	Y	N	Y	Y
23 Beilenson	Y	P	Y	Y	N	Y	Y	N
24 Waxman	N	?	Y	Y	N	Y	?	N
25 Roybal	Y	N	?	Y	N	Y	Y	N
26 Rousselot	N	N	Y	Y	Y	N	N	Y
27 Dornan	N	Y	Y	Y	Y	P	Y	Y
28 Burke	✓	#	?	?	X	?	?	X
29 Hawkins	Y	N	Y	?	N	?	Y	N
30 Danielson	Y	P	Y	Y	N	Y	Y	N
31 Wilson, C.H.	Y	●	Y	?	?	?	?	Y
32 Anderson	Y	P	Y	Y	N	Y	Y	Y
33 Clawson	N	N	Y	?	?	?	N	Y
34 Hannaford	Y	Y	Y	Y	N	Y	Y	N
35 Lloyd	Y	Y	Y	N	N	Y	Y	Y
36 Brown	Y	P	Y	?	N	Y	Y	N
37 Pettis	?	?	?	?	?	?	?	?
38 Patterson	Y	Y	Y	Y	N	Y	?	N
39 Wiggins	N	Y	N	?	N	Y	Y	Y
40 Badham	✓	#	?	?	?	?	?	?
41 Wilson, B.	N	N	Y	N	Y	?	Y	Y
42 Van Deerlin	Y	P	Y	Y	N	Y	Y	N
43 Burgener	N	Y	Y	Y	N	Y	Y	Y
COLORADO								
1 Schroeder	N	Y	Y	Y	N	Y	Y	Y
2 Wirth	Y	Y	N	Y	N	Y	Y	N
3 Evans	Y	Y	Y	Y	?	?	?	Y
4 Johnson	N	Y	N	?	N	Y	Y	Y
5 Armstrong	N	?	?	?	?	?	?	?
CONNECTICUT								
1 Cotter	Y	Y	Y	Y	N	Y	Y	Y
2 Dodd	Y	Y	N	Y	N	Y	Y	N
3 Giaimo	Y	Y	Y	?	?	?	?	Y
4 McKinney	N	Y	Y	?	N	Y	Y	N
5 Sarasin	?	#	?	?	X	?	?	?
6 Moffett	N	Y	Y	?	N	Y	Y	N
DELAWARE								
AL Evans	Y	?	N	?	N	Y	Y	Y
FLORIDA								
1 Sikes	Y	P	Y	Y	N	Y	?	Y
2 Fuqua	Y	Y	Y	Y	N	Y	Y	Y
3 Bennett	Y	Y	N	Y	N	Y	N	Y
4 Chappell	N	Y	Y	Y	N	Y	Y	Y
5 Kelly	N	Y	N	Y	Y	N	N	Y
6 Young	N	Y	?	?	✓	?	?	Y
7 Gibbons	Y	Y	N	Y	N	?	?	Y
8 Ireland	Y	Y	?	?	?	Y	?	?
9 Frey	?	?	?	?	?	?	?	✓
10 Bafalis	N	Y	N	Y	Y	Y	Y	N
11 Rogers	Y	Y	N	Y	N	Y	Y	N
12 Burke	N	Y	Y	Y	?	?	?	?
13 Lehman	Y	Y	N	?	N	Y	Y	?
14 Pepper	Y	Y	Y	?	N	Y	?	N
15 Fascell	Y	Y	N	Y	N	Y	Y	N
GEORGIA								
1 Ginn	Y	Y	N	Y	N	Y	Y	Y
2 Mathis	Y	Y	N	?	?	Y	?	Y
3 Brinkley	Y	Y	N	Y	Y	Y	Y	Y
4 Levitas	Y	Y	N	Y	N	Y	Y	Y
5 Fowler	Y	Y	N	?	N	Y	Y	N
6 Flynt	Y	Y	N	Y	?	?	Y	?
7 McDonald	N	Y	N	N	Y	N	N	Y
8 Evans	Y	Y	Y	Y	Y	Y	Y	Y
9 Jenkins	Y	Y	N	Y	N	Y	Y	Y
10 Barnard	Y	Y	N	Y	N	Y	Y	Y
HAWAII								
1 Heftel	Y	Y	Y	?	N	Y	Y	Y
2 Akaka	Y	P	Y	Y	N	Y	Y	N
IDAHO								
1 Symms	N	Y	Y	Y	Y	N	N	Y
2 Hansen, G.	N	Y	?	Y	Y	N	N	Y
ILLINOIS								
1 Vacancy								
2 Murphy	Y	Y	Y	Y	N	Y	Y	Y
3 Russo	Y	Y	Y	?	Y	Y	?	N
4 Derwinski	N	N	N	Y	Y	Y	Y	Y
5 Fary	Y	Y	Y	Y	X	?	?	Y
6 Hyde	N	?	?	?	✓	?	?	Y
7 Collins	N	N	Y	Y	N	Y	Y	Y
8 Rostenkowski	Y	Y	Y	Y	N	Y	Y	Y
9 Yates	N	Y	Y	Y	N	Y	Y	N
10 Mikva	N	Y	N	?	N	Y	Y	X
11 Annunzio	Y	Y	Y	Y	N	Y	?	Y
12 Crane	X	#	?	?	✓	?	?	✓
13 McClory	N	N	N	Y	N	Y	Y	N
14 Erlenborn	N	Y	N	Y	Y	Y	Y	Y
15 Corcoran	N	Y	N	Y	Y	Y	Y	N
16 Anderson	N	Y	N	Y	N	Y	Y	Y
17 O'Brien	N	Y	Y	Y	Y	Y	Y	Y
18 Michel	N	Y	N	Y	N	Y	Y	Y
19 Railsback	N	Y	Y	?	N	Y	Y	Y
20 Findley	N	Y	Y	Y	N	Y	Y	Y
21 Madigan	N	Y	N	Y	N	Y	?	N
22 Shipley	?	?	?	?	?	?	?	?
23 Price	Y	P	Y	Y	N	Y	?	Y
24 Simon	Y	Y	Y	Y	N	Y	Y	Y
INDIANA								
1 Benjamin	N	Y	Y	Y	Y	Y	Y	Y
2 Fithian	Y	Y	N	Y	N	Y	Y	N
3 Brademas	Y	Y	N	Y	N	Y	Y	N
4 Quayle	N	Y	N	Y	N	Y	?	Y
5 Hillis	N	N	N	Y	N	Y	?	Y
6 Evans	Y	Y	N	Y	Y	Y	Y	Y
7 Myers, J.	N	Y	Y	Y	?	?	?	Y
8 Cornwell	Y	Y	?	Y	N	Y	Y	Y
9 Hamilton	Y	Y	N	Y	N	Y	Y	N
10 Sharp	Y	Y	N	Y	N	Y	Y	N
11 Jacobs	Y	Y	N	Y	N	Y	Y	Y
IOWA								
1 Leach	N	Y	N	Y	Y	Y	Y	Y
2 Blouin	Y	Y	N	Y	Y	Y	Y	N
3 Grassley	N	Y	N	Y	Y	Y	Y	Y
4 Smith	Y	Y	Y	Y	N	Y	Y	N
5 Harkin	N	Y	N	Y	N	Y	Y	N
6 Bedell	N	Y	N	Y	N	Y	Y	N

Democrats ***Republicans***

Corresponding to Congressional Record Votes 912, 914, 915, 916, 917, 918, 919, 920

	806	807	808	809	810	811	812	813
KANSAS								
1 Sebelius	N	Y	N	Y	?	?	?	Y
2 Keys	Y	Y	N	Y	N	Y	Y	N
3 Winn	N	Y	N	?	Y	Y	Y	N
4 Glickman	Y	Y	N	Y	N	Y	Y	N
5 Skubitz	Y	?	Y	?	?	?	?	?
KENTUCKY								
1 Hubbard	Y	Y	Y	Y	Y	Y	Y	Y
2 Natcher	Y	Y	Y	Y	Y	Y	Y	Y
3 Mazzoli	Y	Y	N	?	Y	Y	Y	Y
4 Snyder	N	Y	N	Y	Y	Y	Y	Y
5 Carter	N	Y	Y	Y	N	Y	Y	Y
6 Breckinridge	Y	Y	Y	Y	N	Y	Y	Y
7 Perkins	N	Y	Y	Y	N	Y	Y	Y
LOUISIANA								
1 Livingston	N	Y	N	Y	Y	Y	N	Y
2 Boggs	N	P	Y	Y	Y	Y	Y	Y
3 Treen	N	Y	N	?	Y	N	N	?
4 Waggonner	N	N	Y	Y	Y	N	N	Y
5 Huckaby	N	Y	Y	?	Y	Y	Y	Y
6 Moore	N	Y	N	Y	Y	Y	Y	Y
7 Breaux	N	Y	Y	Y	Y	Y	Y	Y
8 Long	N	Y	N	Y	Y	Y	Y	Y
MAINE								
1 Emery	N	Y	N	Y	Y	Y	Y	N
2 Cohen	N	Y	?	?	?	?	?	?
MARYLAND								
1 Bauman	N	Y	N	Y	Y	N	N	Y
2 Long	Y	Y	Y	Y	N	Y	Y	N
3 Mikulski	N	Y	Y	Y	N	Y	Y	N
4 Holt	N	N	Y	Y	Y	Y	N	Y
5 Spellman	N	P	Y	?	N	Y	Y	N
6 Vacancy								
7 Mitchell	N	N	Y	N	N	Y	?	?
8 Steers	N	Y	N	Y	N	Y	Y	N
MASSACHUSETTS								
1 Conte	Y	Y	Y	Y	Y	Y	Y	N
2 Boland	N	Y	Y	Y	N	Y	Y	N
3 Early	Y	Y	Y	?	N	Y	Y	N
4 Drinan	N	Y	Y	Y	N	Y	Y	N
5 Tsongas	Y	Y	N	Y	X	?	?	N
6 Harrington	Y	P	Y	?	X	?	?	Y
7 Markey	N	Y	Y	Y	N	Y	Y	N
8 O'Neill								
9 Moakley	Y	Y	Y	Y	Y	Y	Y	N
10 Heckler	N	Y	N	?	Y	Y	Y	X
11 Burke	N	N	Y	Y	Y	Y	Y	N
12 Studds	N	Y	N	Y	N	Y	Y	N
MICHIGAN								
1 Conyers	N	Y	?	?	?	?	?	N
2 Pursell	N	Y	Y	Y	N	Y	Y	?
3 Brown	N	Y	N	?	Y	Y	Y	N
4 Stockman	N	Y	N	Y	N	Y	?	Y
5 Sawyer	N	Y	N	Y	N	Y	Y	N
6 Carr	Y	Y	N	Y	N	Y	Y	N
7 Kildee	N	Y	N	Y	Y	Y	Y	N
8 Traxler	Y	Y	Y	Y	Y	Y	Y	N
9 Vander Jagt	N	Y	Y	Y	Y	Y	Y	Y
10 Cederberg	N	Y	Y	Y	Y	Y	?	Y
11 Ruppe	N	Y	N	Y	Y	Y	Y	Y
12 Bonior	N	Y	N	?	Y	Y	Y	N
13 Diggs	?	?	?	?	?	?	?	?
14 Nedzi	Y	Y	Y	Y	N	Y	Y	N
15 Ford	Y	N	Y	Y	N	Y	Y	N
16 Dingell	Y	N	Y	Y	N	Y	Y	N
17 Brodhead	Y	Y	N	Y	N	Y	Y	N
18 Blanchard	Y	Y	N	Y	N	Y	Y	N
19 Broomfield	N	P	Y	Y	Y	Y	?	Y
MINNESOTA								
1 Quie	?	?	?	?	✓	?	?	?
2 Hagedorn	N	Y	N	Y	Y	Y	?	Y
3 Frenzel	N	Y	N	Y	N	Y	Y	N
4 Vento	N	Y	Y	Y	N	Y	Y	N
5 Fraser	N	Y	Y	Y	N	Y	Y	N
6 Nolan	Y	Y	Y	Y	N	Y	Y	N
7 Stangeland	N	Y	N	Y	Y	Y	Y	Y
8 Oberstar	Y	Y	Y	Y	Y	Y	Y	Y
MISSISSIPPI								
1 Whitten	Y	Y	Y	Y	N	Y	Y	Y
2 Bowen	Y	Y	Y	Y	N	Y	Y	Y
3 Montgomery	Y	Y	N	Y	Y	Y	Y	Y
4 Cochran	X	?	?	?	?	?	?	Y
5 Lott	N	Y	N	?	Y	Y	N	Y
MISSOURI								
1 Clay	N	N	Y	?	?	Y	?	N
2 Young	N	Y	Y	Y	Y	N	Y	Y
3 Gephardt	Y	Y	N	Y	Y	N	Y	Y

	806	807	808	809	810	811	812	813
4 Skelton	Y	Y	N	Y	Y	Y	Y	Y
5 Bolling	Y	Y	N	?	?	?	?	Y
6 Coleman	N	Y	N	Y	Y	Y	N	Y
7 Taylor	N	Y	N	Y	Y	N	N	Y
8 Ichord	Y	Y	Y	Y	Y	N	N	?
9 Volkmer	N	Y	N	Y	Y	N	N	Y
10 Burlison	Y	Y	N	Y	N	Y	Y	Y
MONTANA								
1 Baucus	Y	Y	N	Y	N	Y	Y	N
2 Marlenee	N	?	?	?	?	?	?	?
NEBRASKA								
1 Thone	N	Y	N	Y	Y	Y	Y	Y
2 Cavanaugh	Y	Y	N	Y	Y	Y	Y	N
3 Smith	N	?	?	?	✓	?	?	Y
NEVADA								
AL Santini	N	Y	Y	Y	Y	Y	?	Y
NEW HAMPSHIRE								
1 D'Amours	Y	Y	N	Y	Y	Y	Y	Y
2 Cleveland	N	Y	N	Y	N	Y	Y	Y
NEW JERSEY								
1 Florio	N	Y	Y	Y	N	Y	?	N
2 Hughes	Y	Y	N	Y	N	Y	Y	N
3 Howard	Y	Y	?	?	N	Y	Y	N
4 Thompson	Y	Y	Y	Y	N	Y	Y	Y
5 Fenwick	✓	Y	N	Y	N	Y	Y	N
6 Forsythe	N	Y	N	Y	N	Y	N	N
7 Maguire	N	Y	N	Y	N	Y	Y	N
8 Roe	Y	Y	Y	Y	Y	Y	Y	N
9 Hollenbeck	Y	Y	Y	Y	N	Y	Y	N
10 Rodino	Y	Y	Y	?	N	Y	Y	N
11 Minish	Y	Y	N	Y	Y	Y	Y	N
12 Rinaldo	N	Y	N	Y	Y	Y	Y	N
13 Meyner	N	Y	Y	Y	N	Y	Y	N
14 LeFante	Y	Y	Y	Y	?	?	?	?
15 Patten	Y	?	?	?	?	?	?	N
NEW MEXICO								
1 Lujan	?	?	?	?	✓	?	?	?
2 Runnels	N	P	Y	Y	Y	Y	?	Y
NEW YORK								
1 Pike	Y	Y	N	Y	N	N	Y	N
2 Downey	Y	Y	N	Y	N	Y	Y	N
3 Ambro	Y	Y	N	Y	Y	Y	Y	N
4 Lent	N	N	N	Y	Y	Y	Y	N
5 Wydler	N	Y	N	Y	?	?	?	N
6 Wolff	Y	Y	Y	Y	N	Y	Y	N
7 Addabbo	Y	Y	Y	?	N	Y	Y	Y
8 Rosenthal	N	Y	Y	Y	N	Y	Y	N
9 Delaney	Y	N	Y	?	Y	Y	?	Y
10 Biaggi	Y	P	Y	Y	Y	Y	?	N
11 Scheuer	Y	Y	Y	Y	N	Y	Y	N
12 Chisholm	N	P	Y	Y	N	Y	Y	?
13 Solarz	Y	Y	Y	Y	N	Y	Y	N
14 Richmond	Y	Y	Y	Y	N	Y	Y	N
15 Zeferetti	Y	Y	Y	?	Y	Y	Y	Y
16 Holtzman	N	Y	Y	Y	N	Y	Y	N
17 Murphy	Y	N	Y	Y	N	Y	Y	?
18 Green	Y	Y	Y	Y	N	Y	Y	N
19 Rangel	Y	N	Y	Y	N	Y	Y	N
20 Weiss	N	Y	Y	Y	N	Y	Y	N
21 Garcia	Y	N	Y	Y	N	Y	Y	X
22 Bingham	Y	Y	Y	?	N	Y	Y	N
23 Caputo	N	Y	N	Y	?	Y	Y	Y
24 Ottinger	N	P	Y	Y	N	Y	Y	N
25 Fish	Y	Y	Y	Y	N	Y	Y	N
26 Gilman	N	Y	Y	Y	N	Y	Y	Y
27 McHugh	Y	Y	Y	Y	N	Y	Y	N
28 Stratton	Y	Y	N	?	X	Y	Y	N
29 Pattison	N	Y	N	Y	N	Y	Y	N
30 McEwen	N	Y	N	Y	Y	Y	Y	Y
31 Mitchell	N	Y	Y	Y	Y	Y	Y	N
32 Hanley	Y	Y	Y	Y	N	Y	Y	Y
33 Walsh	N	Y	Y	?	Y	Y	Y	Y
34 Horton	N	Y	Y	Y	N	Y	Y	Y
35 Conable	N	Y	N	Y	N	Y	Y	Y
36 LaFalce	Y	Y	Y	Y	N	Y	?	Y
37 Nowak	Y	Y	Y	Y	N	Y	Y	N
38 Kemp	N	Y	Y	Y	Y	Y	Y	Y
39 Lundine	Y	Y	N	Y	N	Y	Y	Y
NORTH CAROLINA								
1 Jones	Y	Y	Y	Y	N	Y	Y	Y
2 Fountain	Y	Y	Y	Y	N	Y	Y	Y
3 Whitley	Y	Y	Y	Y	N	Y	Y	Y
4 Andrews	Y	Y	Y	Y	N	Y	Y	Y
5 Neal	Y	Y	N	Y	N	Y	?	?
6 Preyer	Y	Y	N	Y	N	Y	Y	Y
7 Rose	Y	Y	Y	Y	N	Y	Y	Y
8 Hefner	Y	Y	N	Y	N	Y	Y	Y

	806	807	808	809	810	811	812	813
9 Martin	N	Y	N	Y	N	Y	Y	Y
10 Broyhill	N	Y	N	Y	N	Y	Y	Y
11 Gudger	Y	Y	Y	Y	N	Y	Y	Y
NORTH DAKOTA								
AL Andrews	N	Y	N	Y	Y	Y	Y	✓
OHIO								
1 Gradison	N	Y	Y	Y	N	Y	Y	N
2 Luken	N	Y	Y	N	Y	N	Y	Y
3 Whalen	N	Y	N	Y	N	Y	Y	N
4 Guyer	N	Y	N	Y	Y	Y	Y	Y
5 Latta	N	Y	N	Y	?	N	N	Y
6 Harsha	N	Y	N	Y	Y	Y	Y	Y
7 Brown	N	Y	N	Y	Y	Y	Y	Y
8 Kindness	N	Y	N	?	Y	Y	Y	Y
9 Ashley	Y	Y	Y	Y	N	Y	?	N
10 Miller	N	Y	N	Y	Y	Y	N	Y
11 Stanton	N	Y	Y	Y	Y	Y	?	Y
12 Devine	N	Y	N	Y	Y	Y	N	Y
13 Pease	Y	Y	Y	Y	Y	N	Y	N
14 Seiberling	N	Y	Y	Y	N	Y	Y	N
15 Wylie	N	Y	N	Y	N	Y	Y	Y
16 Regula	N	Y	N	Y	Y	Y	Y	Y
17 Ashbrook	N	N	Y	Y	Y	N	N	Y
18 Applegate	N	Y	?	?	?	?	?	?
19 Carney	Y	P	Y	?	?	?	?	?
20 Oakar	N	Y	Y	Y	Y	Y	Y	?
21 Stokes	N	N	Y	Y	N	Y	Y	N
22 Vanik	N	Y	Y	Y	N	Y	Y	N
23 Mottl	Y	Y	N	Y	Y	Y	Y	N
OKLAHOMA								
1 Jones	N	N	N	Y	N	Y	Y	Y
2 Risenhoover	Y	N	Y	?	N	Y	Y	Y
3 Watkins	N	Y	N	Y	Y	Y	Y	Y
4 Steed	Y	Y	Y	Y	N	Y	Y	Y
5 Edwards	N	Y	N	Y	Y	Y	N	Y
6 English	Y	Y	N	Y	Y	Y	Y	Y
OREGON								
1 AuCoin	Y	Y	N	Y	N	Y	Y	N
2 Ullman	Y	Y	Y	Y	?	?	?	Y
3 Duncan	Y	P	Y	?	N	Y	Y	Y
4 Weaver	Y	Y	Y	?	N	Y	Y	N
PENNSYLVANIA								
1 Myers, M.	Y	N	Y	Y	N	Y	Y	?
2 Nix	Y	N	Y	Y	N	Y	Y	Y
3 Lederer	Y	N	Y	Y	Y	Y	Y	Y
4 Eilberg	N	?	P	?	Y	Y	?	N
5 Schulze	N	Y	N	Y	Y	Y	Y	Y
6 Yatron	Y	Y	N	Y	Y	Y	Y	Y
7 Edgar	N	Y	N	Y	N	Y	Y	N
8 Kostmayer	N	Y	N	Y	N	Y	Y	N
9 Shuster	N	Y	?	?	?	?	?	Y
10 McDade	N	Y	N	Y	Y	Y	Y	N
11 Flood	Y	?	?	Y	Y	N	Y	Y
12 Murtha	Y	N	Y	Y	Y	Y	Y	Y
13 Coughlin	N	Y	N	Y	Y	Y	Y	Y
14 Moorhead	Y	Y	Y	Y	N	Y	Y	Y
15 Rooney	Y	Y	Y	?	Y	Y	Y	N
16 Walker	N	Y	N	Y	Y	Y	Y	Y
17 Ertel	Y	Y	Y	Y	N	Y	Y	Y
18 Walgren	Y	Y	?	?	?	?	?	N
19 Goodling, W.	N	Y	N	P	N	Y	Y	Y
20 Gaydos	Y	Y	Y	Y	Y	Y	Y	Y
21 Dent	Y	#	Y	Y	Y	Y	Y	Y
22 Murphy	Y	Y	Y	Y	Y	Y	Y	N
23 Ammerman	X	?	?	?	?	?	?	?
24 Marks	N	N	Y	Y	N	Y	Y	N
25 Myers, G.	Y	Y	N	Y	Y	N	N	N
RHODE ISLAND								
1 St Germain	N	Y	Y	Y	N	Y	Y	N
2 Beard	Y	Y	Y	Y	N	Y	Y	N
SOUTH CAROLINA								
1 Davis	N	N	N	?	N	Y	Y	N
2 Spence	N	Y	N	Y	Y	Y	Y	Y
3 Derrick	Y	Y	Y	Y	N	Y	Y	N
4 Mann	Y	Y	N	?	N	Y	Y	N
5 Holland	Y	N	Y	Y	N	Y	Y	Y
6 Jenrette	Y	N	N	Y	N	Y	Y	Y
SOUTH DAKOTA								
1 Pressler	N	Y	N	Y	Y	Y	?	Y
2 Abdnor	N	Y	N	Y	Y	Y	N	Y
TENNESSEE								
1 Quillen	N	Y	N	Y	N	Y	Y	Y
2 Duncan	N	Y	N	Y	N	Y	Y	Y
3 Lloyd	Y	Y	N	Y	Y	Y	Y	Y
4 Gore	N	Y	N	Y	N	Y	Y	Y
5 Vacancy								
6 Beard	N	Y	N	?	N	Y	Y	Y

	806	807	808	809	810	811	812	813
7 Jones	Y	Y	N	Y	N	Y	Y	Y
8 Ford	Y	Y	Y	Y	N	Y	Y	Y
TEXAS								
1 Hall	N	Y	Y	Y	Y	Y	Y	Y
2 Wilson, C.	Y	N	Y	Y	N	Y	?	Y
3 Collins	N	Y	Y	Y	Y	N	N	Y
4 Roberts	N	Y	Y	Y	N	?	?	Y
5 Mattox	Y	Y	Y	N	N	Y	Y	Y
6 Teague	?	?	?	?	?	?	?	?
7 Archer	N	Y	N	Y	Y	Y	N	Y
8 Eckhardt	Y	Y	Y	?	N	Y	Y	N
9 Brooks	Y	Y	Y	Y	N	Y	Y	Y
10 Pickle	Y	Y	Y	?	N	Y	Y	Y
11 Poage	Y	Y	Y	Y	N	Y	Y	Y
12 Wright	Y	Y	Y	Y	N	Y	Y	Y
13 Hightower	N	Y	Y	Y	N	Y	Y	Y
14 Young	Y	?	?	?	?	?	?	Y
15 de la Garza	N	Y	Y	Y	Y	Y	Y	Y
16 White	N	Y	Y	Y	N	Y	Y	Y
17 Burleson	N	Y	Y	Y	?	?	?	Y
18 Jordan	N	Y	Y	Y	N	Y	?	N
19 Mahon	N	Y	Y	Y	N	N	Y	Y
20 Gonzalez	✓	N	Y	Y	N	Y	Y	Y
21 Krueger	N	Y	Y	Y	N	Y	Y	Y
22 Gammage	N	Y	Y	Y	Y	Y	Y	Y
23 Kazen	Y	Y	Y	Y	Y	Y	Y	Y
24 Milford	Y	Y	N	?	?	N	Y	?
UTAH								
1 McKay	Y	Y	Y	Y	Y	Y	Y	Y
2 Marriott	N	Y	N	Y	Y	Y	Y	Y
VERMONT								
AL Jeffords	N	Y	N	Y	N	Y	Y	N
VIRGINIA								
1 Trible	N	Y	N	Y	N	Y	Y	Y
2 Whitehurst	N	#	?	?	?	?	?	Y
3 Satterfield	N	Y	Y	Y	Y	Y	Y	Y
4 Daniel	N	Y	Y	Y	Y	N	N	Y
5 Daniel	Y	N	Y	Y	Y	Y	N	Y
6 Butler	N	Y	N	Y	N	Y	Y	Y
7 Robinson	N	Y	?	?	Y	Y	N	Y
8 Harris	N	Y	Y	Y	N	Y	Y	N
9 Wampler	N	Y	Y	Y	N	Y	Y	Y
10 Fisher	Y	Y	N	Y	N	Y	Y	N
WASHINGTON								
1 Pritchard	N	Y	N	Y	N	Y	Y	N
2 Meeds	Y	Y	N	?	?	?	?	?
3 Bonker	Y	Y	N	Y	N	?	Y	N
4 McCormack	Y	Y	N	Y	N	Y	Y	Y
5 Foley	Y	Y	N	Y	N	Y	Y	Y
6 Dicks	Y	Y	N	Y	N	Y	Y	Y
7 Cunningham	N	Y	N	Y	Y	Y	Y	Y
WEST VIRGINIA								
1 Mollohan	Y	Y	Y	Y	N	Y	Y	Y
2 Staggers	Y	Y	Y	Y	N	Y	Y	N
3 Slack	Y	Y	Y	?	?	?	?	Y
4 Rahall	Y	Y	N	Y	N	Y	Y	Y
WISCONSIN								
1 Aspin	Y	Y	N	Y	N	Y	?	N
2 Kastenmeier	N	Y	Y	Y	N	Y	Y	N
3 Baldus	Y	Y	N	Y	N	Y	Y	N
4 Zablocki	Y	Y	Y	Y	Y	Y	Y	Y
5 Reuss	N	Y	Y	Y	N	Y	Y	N
6 Steiger	N	Y	Y	Y	N	Y	Y	N
7 Obey	Y	Y	Y	Y	N	Y	Y	N
8 Cornell	N	Y	N	Y	Y	Y	Y	N
9 Kasten	N	Y	N	Y	N	Y	Y	Y
WYOMING								
AL Roncalio	Y	N	Y	Y	N	Y	Y	Y

Democrats ***Republicans***

814. HR 14104. Endangered Species Act Amendments. Passage of the bill to authorize $40.5 million in fiscal 1979 and the first half of fiscal 1980 and to establish a two-step review for federal public works projects seeking exemption from the Endangered Species Act. Passed 384-12: R 133-1; D 251-11 (ND 168-11; SD 83-0), Oct. 14, 1978.

815. HR 12929. Labor-HEW Appropriations, Fiscal 1979. Mahon, D-Texas, motion to recede from the House position and concur in the Senate amendment with an amendment to prohibit the use of appropriated funds for abortions except when the life of the mother was in danger or in cases of rape or incest that had been promptly reported to health or law enforcement agencies or if the pregnancy would cause long-lasting physical health damage to the mother as determined by two physicians. Motion agreed to (thus cleared for the president) 198-195: R 32-101; D 166-94 (ND 112-63; SD 54-31), Oct. 14, 1978.

816. HR 11274. Middle Income Student Assistance. Adoption of the rule (H Res 1425) providing for House floor consideration of the bill to increase existing federal programs of assistance to college students. Adopted 342-38: R 105-28; D 237-10 (ND 165-5; SD 72-5), Oct. 14, 1978.

817. HR 11274. Middle Income Student Assistance. Erlenborn, R-Ill., amendment, to the Ford, D-Mich., substitute for the bill, to limit eligibility for federal interest subsidies on guaranteed student loans to students from families with adjusted gross annual incomes of less than $40,000. Rejected 86-301: R 72-58; D 14-243 (ND 6-170; SD 8-73), Oct. 14, 1978. (The bill to increase existing federal programs of assistance to college students, as modified by the Ford amendment, was adopted subsequently by voice vote.) A "yea" was a vote supporting the president's position.

818. HR 10173. Veterans' and Survivors' Pension Improvements. Adoption of the conference report on the bill to establish a new pension program for indigent war veterans who were either fully disabled or 65 years of age or older, and for their survivors. Adopted (thus cleared for the president) 387-1: R 133-0; D 254-1 (ND 175-0; SD 79-1), Oct. 14, 1978.

819. S 3151. Justice Department Authorization. Adoption of the conference report on the bill to authorize appropriations of $1.69 billion for fiscal 1979 operations of the Department of Justice. Adopted 271-93: R 64-61; D 207-32 (ND 147-15; SD 60-17), Oct. 14, 1978. A "yea" was a vote supporting the president's position.

820. HR 7010. Victims of Crime. Adoption of the conference report on the bill to provide federal funds to states to compensate victims of violent crimes. Rejected 184-199: R 30-100; D 154-99 (ND 122-52; SD 32-47), Oct. 14, 1978.

KEY

- Y Voted for (yea).
- ✓ Paired for.
- † Announced for.
- # CQ Poll for.
- N Voted against (nay).
- X Paired against.
- \- Announced against.
- ▮ CQ Poll against.
- P Voted "present."
- ● Voted "present" to avoid possible conflict of interest.
- ? Did not vote or otherwise make a position known.

	814	815	816	817	818	819	820
ALABAMA							
1 Edwards	Y	N	N	N	Y	Y	N
2 Dickinson	?	?	?	?	?	?	X
3 Nichols	Y	N	Y	N	N	Y	?
4 Bevill	Y	N	Y	N	Y	Y	N
5 Flippo	Y	Y	Y	N	Y	Y	N
6 Buchanan	Y	Y	Y	N	Y	Y	N
7 Flowers	Y	Y	Y	N	Y	?	?
ALASKA							
AL Young	Y	N	Y	N	Y	N	N
ARIZONA							
1 Rhodes	Y	N	Y	Y	Y	Y	N
2 Udall	Y	Y	Y	N	Y	Y	Y
3 Stump	Y	N	Y	N	Y	N	N
4 Rudd	?	?	?	?	?	?	?
ARKANSAS							
1 Alexander	Y	Y	Y	N	Y	Y	Y
2 Tucker	Y	Y	Y	N	Y	Y	N
3 Hammerschmidt	Y	N	Y	Y	Y	Y	Y
4 Thornton	Y	Y	?	N	Y	?	Y
CALIFORNIA							
1 Johnson	Y	Y	Y	N	Y	Y	N
2 Clausen	Y	N	Y	?	Y	N	N
3 Moss	?	?	?	?	?	?	?
4 Leggett	Y	?	Y	N	Y	?	N
5 Burton, J.	N	Y	?	N	Y	?	Y
6 Burton, P.	N	Y	Y	N	Y	Y	Y
7 Miller	N	Y	?	N	Y	Y	?
8 Dellums	N	Y	Y	N	?	Y	Y
9 Stark	N	Y	?	?	Y	N	?
10 Edwards	Y	Y	Y	N	Y	Y	Y
11 Ryan	Y	Y	Y	N	?	Y	Y
12 McCloskey	Y	Y	Y	N	Y	Y	Y
13 Mineta	Y	Y	Y	N	Y	Y	Y
14 McFall	?	?	?	?	?	?	?
15 Sisk	Y	Y	Y	N	Y	?	N
16 Panetta	Y	Y	Y	N	Y	Y	Y
17 Krebs	Y	Y	Y	N	Y	Y	N
18 Vacancy							
19 Lagomarsino	Y	N	Y	Y	Y	N	N
20 Goldwater	Y	N	Y	Y	Y	N	N
21 Corman	Y	Y	Y	N	Y	Y	N
22 Moorhead	Y	N	Y	Y	Y	N	N
23 Beilenson	N	Y	Y	N	Y	Y	Y
24 Waxman	Y	Y	?	N	Y	Y	Y
25 Roybal	Y	Y	Y	N	Y	Y	Y
26 Rousselot	Y	N	N	N	Y	N	N
27 Dornan	Y	N	Y	N	Y	N	N
28 Burke	?	?	?	?	?	?	?
29 Hawkins	Y	Y	Y	N	Y	Y	Y
30 Danielson	Y	Y	Y	N	Y	Y	Y
31 Wilson, C.H.	?	?	?	N	?	?	?
32 Anderson	Y	Y	Y	N	Y	N	Y
33 Clawson	Y	N	N	Y	Y	N	N
34 Hannaford	Y	Y	Y	N	Y	Y	N
35 Lloyd	Y	Y	Y	N	Y	Y	Y
36 Brown	Y	Y	?	N	Y	?	Y
37 Pettis	?	?	?	?	?	?	?
38 Patterson	Y	Y	Y	N	Y	Y	Y
39 Wiggins	Y	Y	Y	Y	Y	Y	N
40 Badham	?	?	?	?	?	?	?
41 Wilson, B.	Y	Y	Y	Y	Y	Y	N
42 Van Deerlin	Y	Y	Y	N	Y	Y	N
43 Burgener	Y	N	Y	Y	Y	N	N
COLORADO							
1 Schroeder	Y	Y	Y	N	Y	Y	Y
2 Wirth	Y	Y	Y	N	Y	Y	Y
3 Evans	Y	?	?	?	?	?	?
4 Johnson	Y	Y	Y	N	Y	Y	N
5 Armstrong	?	?	?	?	?	?	?
CONNECTICUT							
1 Cotter	Y	N	Y	N	Y	Y	N
2 Dodd	Y	Y	Y	N	Y	Y	Y
3 Giaimo	Y	Y	?	N	Y	Y	N
4 McKinney	Y	Y	Y	N	Y	Y	Y
5 Sarasin	Y	Y	Y	N	Y	Y	N
6 Moffett	Y	Y	Y	N	Y	?	N
DELAWARE							
AL Evans	Y	Y	Y	Y	Y	N	Y
FLORIDA							
1 Sikes	Y	Y	Y	?	?	Y	Y
2 Fuqua	Y	Y	Y	N	Y	Y	N
3 Bennett	Y	Y	Y	Y	Y	Y	N
4 Chappell	†	Y	Y	N	Y	N	N
5 Kelly	Y	N	Y	N	Y	Y	N
6 Young	Y	N	Y	N	Y	N	N
7 Gibbons	Y	N	Y	N	Y	?	?
8 Ireland	Y	Y	?	?	Y	Y	N
9 Frey	?	?	?	?	?	?	?
10 Bafalis	Y	N	Y	N	Y	Y	N
11 Rogers	Y	Y	?	N	Y	Y	N
12 Burke	?	?	?	?	?	?	X
13 Lehman	?	?	?	?	?	?	?
14 Pepper	Y	Y	Y	Y	Y	Y	Y
15 Fascell	Y	Y	Y	N	Y	Y	Y
GEORGIA							
1 Ginn	Y	Y	Y	N	Y	Y	N
2 Mathis	Y	Y	?	N	Y	?	Y
3 Brinkley	Y	Y	Y	N	Y	N	Y
4 Levitas	Y	Y	Y	N	Y	Y	N
5 Fowler	Y	Y	Y	?	Y	Y	N
6 Flynt	?	?	?	?	?	?	?
7 McDonald	Y	N	N	N	Y	N	N
8 Evans	Y	N	?	N	Y	?	Y
9 Jenkins	Y	N	?	Y	Y	Y	N
10 Barnard	Y	N	Y	Y	Y	Y	N
HAWAII							
1 Heftel	Y	Y	Y	N	Y	Y	Y
2 Akaka	Y	Y	Y	N	Y	Y	Y
IDAHO							
1 Symms	Y	N	N	N	Y	N	N
2 Hansen, G.	Y	N	Y	N	Y	N	N
ILLINOIS							
1 Vacancy							
2 Murphy	Y	N	Y	N	Y	Y	Y
3 Russo	Y	N	?	N	Y	N	Y
4 Derwinski	Y	N	N	Y	Y	N	Y
5 Fary	Y	N	Y	N	Y	Y	Y
6 Hyde	Y	N	Y	Y	Y	N	Y
7 Collins	Y	Y	Y	N	Y	Y	Y
8 Rostenkowski	Y	N	?	N	Y	Y	N
9 Yates	Y	Y	Y	N	Y	Y	Y
10 Mikva	?	?	?	?	?	?	✓
11 Annunzio	Y	N	Y	N	Y	Y	Y
12 Crane	Y	N	Y	N	Y	N	N
13 McClory	Y	N	Y	Y	Y	N	N
14 Erlenborn	Y	?	N	Y	Y	Y	N
15 Corcoran	Y	N	N	Y	Y	Y	N
16 Anderson	Y	Y	Y	Y	Y	Y	Y
17 O'Brien	Y	N	Y	N	Y	Y	N
18 Michel	Y	N	Y	Y	Y	Y	N
19 Railsback	Y	Y	Y	P	Y	Y	N
20 Findley	Y	Y	Y	Y	Y	Y	Y
21 Madigan	Y	N	Y	Y	Y	Y	N
22 Shipley	?	?	?	?	?	?	?
23 Price	Y	N	Y	N	Y	Y	Y
24 Simon	N	Y	Y	N	Y	Y	Y
INDIANA							
1 Benjamin	Y	N	Y	N	Y	Y	Y
2 Fithian	Y	N	Y	N	Y	Y	N
3 Brademas	Y	Y	Y	N	Y	Y	Y
4 Quayle	Y	N	N	Y	Y	Y	N
5 Hillis	Y	N	Y	Y	Y	Y	N
6 Evans	Y	N	Y	N	Y	N	N
7 Myers, J.	Y	N	Y	Y	Y	N	N
8 Cornwell	Y	Y	Y	N	Y	Y	N
9 Hamilton	Y	Y	Y	N	Y	Y	N
10 Sharp	Y	Y	Y	N	Y	Y	N
11 Jacobs	P	Y	Y	N	Y	N	Y
IOWA							
1 Leach	Y	Y	Y	Y	Y	Y	N
2 Blouin	Y	N	Y	N	Y	Y	N
3 Grassley	Y	N	Y	Y	Y	N	N
4 Smith	Y	Y	Y	N	Y	Y	Y
5 Harkin	Y	Y	Y	N	Y	Y	Y
6 Bedell	Y	Y	Y	N	Y	Y	Y

Democrats ***Republicans***

	814	815	816	817	818	819	820
KANSAS							
1 ***Sebelius***	Y	N	Y	Y	Y	N	N
2 Keys	Y	Y	Y	N	Y	N	Y
3 ***Winn***	Y	N	N	Y	Y	N	N
4 Glickman	Y	Y	Y	N	Y	N	N
5 ***Skubitz***	?	?	Y	?	Y	?	?
KENTUCKY							
1 Hubbard	Y	N	Y	N	Y	N	N
2 Natcher	Y	N	Y	N	Y	Y	Y
3 Mazzoli	Y	N	Y	N	Y	Y	Y
4 ***Snyder***	Y	N	Y	N	Y	N	N
5 ***Carter***	Y	Y	Y	N	Y	Y	N
6 Breckinridge	Y	Y	Y	N	Y	Y	N
7 Perkins	Y	Y	Y	N	Y	Y	Y
LOUISIANA							
1 ***Livingston***	Y	N	N	Y	Y	Y	N
2 Boggs	Y	N	Y	N	?	Y	Y
3 ***Treen***	Y	N	Y	N	Y	N	N
4 Waggonner	Y	N	Y	N	Y	N	N
5 Huckaby	Y	N	?	N	Y	Y	N
6 ***Moore***	Y	N	Y	N	Y	Y	N
7 Breaux	Y	N	Y	N	Y	Y	Y
8 Long	Y	N	Y	N	Y	Y	Y
MAINE							
1 ***Emery***	Y	N	Y	Y	Y	Y	N
2 ***Cohen***	?	?	Y	Y	Y	Y	N
MARYLAND							
1 ***Bauman***	Y	N	Y	N	Y	N	N
2 Long	Y	Y	Y	N	?	Y	Y
3 Mikulski	Y	Y	Y	N	Y	Y	Y
4 ***Holt***	Y	N	Y	N	Y	N	N
5 Spellman	Y	Y	Y	N	Y	Y	Y
6 Vacancy							
7 Mitchell	Y	Y	Y	N	Y	Y	Y
8 ***Steers***	Y	Y	Y	N	Y	?	Y
MASSACHUSETTS							
1 ***Conte***	Y	N	Y	Y	Y	Y	N
2 Boland	Y	N	Y	N	Y	Y	N
3 Early	Y	N	Y	N	Y	Y	N
4 Drinan	Y	Y	Y	N	Y	N	Y
5 Tsongas	Y	Y	Y	N	Y	Y	Y
6 Harrington	Y	?	?	?	?	?	?
7 Markey	Y	N	Y	N	Y	Y	Y
8 O'Neill							
9 Moakley	Y	N	Y	N	Y	Y	Y
10 ***Heckler***	Y	N	Y	N	Y	?	Y
11 Burke	Y	N	Y	N	Y	Y	Y
12 Studds	Y	Y	Y	N	Y	Y	Y
MICHIGAN							
1 Conyers	N	?	?	?	Y	Y	?
2 ***Pursell***	Y	Y	Y	N	Y	?	N
3 ***Brown***	Y	N	?	Y	Y	N	N
4 ***Stockman***	Y	Y	N	?	Y	N	N
5 ***Sawyer***	Y	N	Y	N	Y	Y	Y
6 Carr	Y	Y	Y	N	Y	Y	Y
7 Kildee	Y	N	Y	N	Y	Y	Y
8 Traxler	Y	?	Y	N	Y	Y	Y
9 ***Vander Jagt***	Y	N	N	N	Y	N	N
10 ***Cederberg***	Y	N	Y	Y	Y	Y	N
11 ***Ruppe***	Y	N	Y	Y	Y	?	N
12 Bonior	N	N	Y	N	Y	?	Y
13 Diggs	?	?	?	?	?	?	?
14 Nedzi	Y	Y	Y	N	Y	Y	Y
15 Ford	Y	Y	Y	N	Y	?	?
16 Dingell	Y	Y	Y	N	Y	?	?
17 Brodhead	Y	Y	Y	N	Y	Y	Y
18 Blanchard	Y	Y	Y	N	Y	Y	Y
19 ***Broomfield***	Y	N	Y	Y	Y	Y	N
MINNESOTA							
1 ***Quie***	?	?	?	?	?	?	?
2 ***Hagedorn***	Y	N	Y	N	Y	N	N
3 ***Frenzel***	Y	Y	Y	N	Y	Y	N
4 Vento	Y	N	Y	N	Y	Y	Y
5 Fraser	Y	Y	?	N	Y	Y	Y
6 Nolan	Y	N	Y	N	Y	?	Y
7 ***Stangeland***	Y	N	N	Y	Y	Y	N
8 Oberstar	Y	N	Y	N	Y	Y	Y
MISSISSIPPI							
1 Whitten	Y	N	Y	?	Y	N	N
2 Bowen	Y	N	Y	N	Y	?	N
3 Montgomery	Y	N	Y	N	Y	N	N
4 ***Cochran***	Y	N	Y	N	Y	N	N
5 ***Lott***	Y	N	Y	Y	Y	N	N
MISSOURI							
1 Clay	Y	Y	Y	N	Y	Y	Y
2 Young	Y	N	Y	N	Y	Y	N
3 Gephardt	Y	N	Y	N	Y	Y	N
4 Skelton	Y	N	Y	N	Y	Y	N
5 Bolling	Y	Y	Y	N	Y	Y	Y
6 ***Coleman***	Y	N	Y	Y	Y	Y	Y
7 ***Taylor***	Y	N	Y	N	Y	N	N
8 Ichord	?	?	?	?	?	?	?
9 Volkmer	Y	N	Y	Y	Y	Y	N
10 Burlison	Y	N	Y	N	Y	Y	N
MONTANA							
1 Baucus	Y	Y	Y	N	Y	Y	Y
2 ***Marlenee***	?	?	?	?	?	?	?
NEBRASKA							
1 ***Thone***	Y	N	Y	?	?	?	?
2 Cavanaugh	Y	N	Y	N	Y	Y	N
3 ***Smith***	Y	N	?	?	?	?	?
NEVADA							
AL Santini	Y	Y	Y	N	Y	Y	N
NEW HAMPSHIRE							
1 D'Amours	Y	N	Y	N	Y	Y	N
2 ***Cleveland***	Y	Y	Y	Y	Y	N	N
NEW JERSEY							
1 Florio	Y	Y	Y	N	Y	Y	Y
2 Hughes	Y	Y	Y	N	Y	Y	Y
3 Howard	Y	Y	Y	N	Y	Y	Y
4 Thompson	Y	Y	Y	N	Y	Y	Y
5 ***Fenwick***	Y	Y	Y	Y	Y	N	Y
6 ***Forsythe***	Y	Y	N	N	Y	?	?
7 Maguire	Y	Y	Y	N	Y	?	Y
8 Roe	Y	N	Y	N	Y	Y	Y
9 ***Hollenbeck***	Y	Y	Y	N	Y	Y	Y
10 Rodino	Y	N	Y	N	Y	Y	Y
11 Minish	Y	N	Y	N	Y	Y	Y
12 ***Rinaldo***	Y	N	Y	N	Y	Y	Y
13 Meyner	Y	?	Y	N	Y	Y	Y
14 LeFante	?	N	Y	N	Y	Y	Y
15 Patten	Y	N	Y	N	Y	Y	Y
NEW MEXICO							
1 ***Lujan***	?	?	?	?	?	?	?
2 Runnels	Y	N	Y	N	?	N	N
NEW YORK							
1 Pike	Y	Y	Y	Y	Y	Y	N
2 Downey	Y	Y	Y	N	Y	?	N
3 Ambro	Y	N	Y	N	Y	Y	Y
4 ***Lent***	Y	N	Y	N	Y	N	Y
5 ***Wydler***	Y	N	Y	N	Y	N	N
6 Wolff	Y	Y	Y	N	Y	Y	Y
7 Addabbo	Y	Y	Y	N	Y	Y	Y
8 Rosenthal	Y	Y	Y	N	Y	Y	Y
9 Delaney	Y	N	N	N	Y	Y	Y
10 Biaggi	?	?	?	?	?	?	?
11 Scheuer	Y	Y	Y	N	Y	Y	Y
12 Chisholm	Y	Y	Y	N	Y	Y	Y
13 Solarz	Y	Y	Y	N	Y	Y	Y
14 Richmond	Y	Y	Y	N	Y	Y	Y
15 Zeferetti	Y	N	Y	N	Y	Y	Y
16 Holtzman	N	Y	Y	N	Y	N	Y
17 Murphy	Y	N	Y	N	?	?	Y
18 ***Green***	Y	Y	Y	N	Y	N	Y
19 Rangel	Y	Y	Y	Y	Y	Y	Y
20 Weiss	N	Y	Y	N	Y	N	Y
21 Garcia	?	?	Y	N	Y	Y	Y
22 Bingham	Y	Y	Y	?	Y	Y	Y
23 ***Caputo***	Y	N	Y	N	Y	N	Y
24 Ottinger	Y	Y	Y	N	Y	Y	Y
25 ***Fish***	Y	Y	Y	N	Y	Y	Y
26 ***Gilman***	Y	Y	Y	N	Y	Y	†
27 McHugh	Y	Y	Y	N	Y	Y	Y
28 Stratton	Y	?	?	?	?	?	N
29 Pattison	Y	Y	Y	N	Y	?	N
30 ***McEwen***	Y	N	N	Y	Y	Y	N
31 ***Mitchell***	Y	N	Y	Y	Y	Y	Y
32 Hanley	Y	N	Y	N	Y	Y	Y
33 ***Walsh***	Y	N	Y	N	Y	Y	?
34 ***Horton***	Y	Y	Y	N	Y	Y	N
35 ***Conable***	Y	Y	N	Y	Y	N	N
36 LaFalce	Y	N	Y	N	Y	?	Y
37 Nowak	Y	N	Y	N	Y	Y	Y
38 ***Kemp***	Y	N	Y	Y	Y	N	N
39 Lundine	Y	Y	Y	N	Y	Y	Y
NORTH CAROLINA							
1 Jones	Y	Y	Y	N	Y	Y	N
2 Fountain	Y	Y	Y	Y	Y	Y	N
3 Whitley	Y	Y	Y	N	Y	Y	N
4 Andrews	Y	Y	Y	N	Y	Y	N
5 Neal	Y	Y	Y	N	Y	Y	Y
6 Preyer	Y	Y	Y	N	Y	Y	Y
7 Rose	Y	Y	Y	N	Y	Y	Y
8 Hefner	Y	Y	Y	N	Y	Y	Y
9 ***Martin***	Y	Y	Y	Y	Y	N	N
10 ***Broyhill***	Y	Y	Y	N	Y	Y	N
11 Gudger	Y	Y	Y	N	Y	Y	Y
NORTH DAKOTA							
AL ***Andrews***	Y	N	Y	N	Y	Y	Y
OHIO							
1 ***Gradison***	Y	N	Y	N	Y	Y	N
2 Luken	Y	N	N	N	Y	Y	N
3 ***Whalen***	Y	N	Y	N	Y	Y	Y
4 ***Guyer***	Y	N	Y	Y	Y	N	N
5 ***Latta***	Y	N	N	N	Y	N	N
6 ***Harsha***	Y	N	?	N	Y	Y	N
7 ***Brown***	Y	N	Y	Y	Y	N	N
8 ***Kindness***	Y	N	N	Y	Y	N	N
9 Ashley	Y	Y	Y	N	Y	Y	N
10 ***Miller***	Y	N	N	Y	Y	N	N
11 ***Stanton***	Y	N	Y	N	Y	Y	N
12 ***Devine***	Y	N	N	Y	Y	N	N
13 Pease	Y	Y	Y	N	Y	Y	N
14 Seiberling	Y	Y	Y	?	Y	Y	Y
15 ***Wylie***	Y	N	Y	Y	Y	N	N
16 ***Regula***	Y	N	Y	Y	Y	N	Y
17 ***Ashbrook***	N	N	Y	N	?	?	N
18 Applegate	?	?	?	?	?	?	✓
19 Carney	?	?	?	?	?	?	?
20 Oakar	Y	N	Y	N	Y	N	Y
21 Stokes	Y	Y	Y	N	Y	Y	Y
22 Vanik	Y	N	Y	N	Y	Y	Y
23 Mottl	Y	N	Y	N	Y	N	Y
OKLAHOMA							
1 Jones	Y	N	Y	N	Y	N	N
2 Risenhoover	?	Y	?	N	?	?	?
3 Watkins	Y	N	Y	N	Y	Y	N
4 Steed	Y	Y	Y	N	?	Y	N
5 ***Edwards***	Y	N	Y	Y	Y	N	N
6 English	Y	N	Y	Y	Y	Y	N
OREGON							
1 AuCoin	Y	Y	Y	N	Y	?	N
2 Ullman	Y	Y	Y	N	Y	Y	N
3 Duncan	Y	Y	Y	Y	Y	Y	N
4 Weaver	Y	Y	Y	N	Y	N	N
PENNSYLVANIA							
1 Myers, M.	?	N	Y	?	Y	Y	Y
2 Nix	Y	Y	Y	N	Y	Y	Y
3 Lederer	Y	N	Y	N	Y	Y	Y
4 Eilberg	Y	N	Y	N	Y	Y	Y
5 ***Schulze***	Y	N	Y	Y	Y	N	N
6 Yatron	Y	N	Y	N	Y	Y	Y
7 Edgar	Y	Y	Y	N	Y	Y	Y
8 Kostmayer	Y	Y	Y	N	Y	Y	Y
9 ***Shuster***	Y	N	N	Y	Y	N	N
10 ***McDade***	Y	N	Y	Y	Y	Y	N
11 Flood	Y	N	Y	N	Y	Y	Y
12 Murtha	Y	N	N	N	Y	Y	N
13 ***Coughlin***	Y	Y	Y	N	Y	Y	Y
14 Moorhead	Y	Y	Y	N	Y	Y	Y
15 Rooney	Y	N	Y	N	Y	Y	N
16 ***Walker***	Y	N	N	Y	Y	N	Y
17 Ertel	Y	N	Y	N	Y	Y	Y
18 Walgren	Y	Y	Y	N	Y	Y	Y
19 ***Goodling, W.***	Y	N	Y	Y	Y	N	N
20 Gaydos	Y	N	Y	N	Y	Y	Y
21 Dent	Y	N	Y	N	Y	Y	Y
22 Murphy	Y	N	Y	N	Y	Y	Y
23 Ammerman	?	?	?	?	?	?	?
24 ***Marks***	Y	N	Y	N	Y	Y	Y
25 ***Myers, G.***	Y	N	Y	N	Y	N	Y
RHODE ISLAND							
1 St Germain	Y	Y	N	Y	Y	Y	Y
2 Beard	Y	N	N	Y	Y	Y	Y
SOUTH CAROLINA							
1 Davis	Y	Y	Y	N	Y	Y	?
2 ***Spence***	Y	N	Y	Y	Y	Y	Y
3 Derrick	Y	Y	Y	N	Y	Y	N
4 Mann	Y	Y	Y	N	Y	Y	Y
5 Holland	Y	Y	Y	N	Y	Y	Y
6 Jenrette	?	Y	N	Y	Y	Y	Y
SOUTH DAKOTA							
1 ***Pressler***	Y	N	Y	Y	Y	Y	N
2 ***Abdnor***	Y	N	Y	Y	Y	Y	N
TENNESSEE							
1 ***Quillen***	Y	N	N	Y	Y	Y	N
2 ***Duncan***	Y	N	Y	Y	Y	Y	N
3 Lloyd	Y	N	Y	N	Y	N	N
4 Gore	Y	N	Y	N	Y	Y	Y
5 Vacancy							
6 ***Beard***	Y	N	Y	N	Y	?	N
7 Jones	Y	Y	Y	N	Y	Y	N
8 Ford	Y	Y	Y	N	Y	?	Y
TEXAS							
1 Hall	Y	N	Y	N	Y	N	N
2 Wilson, C.	Y	Y	Y	N	?	Y	N
3 ***Collins***	Y	N	N	N	Y	N	N
4 Roberts	Y	Y	Y	N	Y	N	N
5 Mattox	Y	Y	Y	N	Y	N	Y
6 Teague	?	?	?	?	?	?	?
7 ***Archer***	Y	N	N	Y	Y	N	N
8 Eckhardt	Y	Y	Y	N	Y	Y	Y
9 Brooks	Y	Y	Y	N	Y	Y	N
10 Pickle	Y	Y	Y	N	Y	Y	N
11 Poage	Y	Y	N	N	Y	N	N
12 Wright	Y	Y	Y	N	Y	Y	?
13 Hightower	Y	Y	Y	N	Y	Y	N
14 Young	Y	?	Y	N	Y	Y	Y
15 de la Garza	Y	N	Y	N	Y	Y	N
16 White	Y	N	Y	N	Y	Y	N
17 Burleson	Y	N	N	N	Y	?	N
18 Jordan	Y	Y	Y	N	Y	Y	Y
19 Mahon	Y	Y	Y	N	Y	Y	N
20 Gonzalez	Y	Y	Y	N	Y	Y	Y
21 Krueger	Y	Y	Y	N	Y	Y	?
22 Gammage	Y	N	Y	N	Y	N	N
23 Kazen	Y	N	Y	N	Y	Y	Y
24 Milford	Y	Y	?	?	?	N	N
UTAH							
1 McKay	Y	N	Y	N	Y	Y	N
2 ***Marriott***	Y	N	Y	Y	Y	Y	N
VERMONT							
AL ***Jeffords***	Y	Y	N	Y	Y	N	Y
VIRGINIA							
1 ***Trible***	Y	N	Y	N	Y	Y	N
2 ***Whitehurst***	Y	N	Y	N	Y	Y	N
3 Satterfield	Y	N	N	Y	Y	N	N
4 ***Daniel***	Y	N	Y	Y	Y	Y	N
5 Daniel	Y	N	Y	N	Y	N	N
6 ***Butler***	Y	Y	Y	Y	Y	Y	N
7 ***Robinson***	Y	N	Y	Y	Y	N	N
8 Harris	Y	Y	Y	N	Y	Y	Y
9 ***Wampler***	Y	N	Y	Y	Y	Y	N
10 Fisher	Y	Y	Y	N	Y	Y	Y
WASHINGTON							
1 ***Pritchard***	Y	Y	Y	N	Y	?	Y
2 Meeds	Y	Y	Y	N	Y	Y	?
3 Bonker	Y	Y	Y	N	Y	Y	Y
4 McCormack	Y	Y	Y	N	Y	Y	N
5 Foley	Y	Y	Y	N	Y	Y	N
6 Dicks	Y	Y	Y	N	Y	?	Y
7 ***Cunningham***	Y	N	Y	N	Y	N	N
WEST VIRGINIA							
1 Mollohan	Y	Y	Y	N	Y	Y	N
2 Staggers	Y	N	Y	N	Y	Y	Y
3 Slack	Y	Y	Y	N	Y	Y	N
4 Rahall	Y	Y	Y	N	Y	Y	N
WISCONSIN							
1 Aspin	Y	N	Y	N	Y	Y	Y
2 Kastenmeier	Y	Y	Y	N	Y	Y	N
3 Baldus	Y	Y	Y	N	Y	Y	Y
4 Zablocki	Y	N	Y	N	Y	Y	Y
5 Reuss	Y	Y	Y	N	Y	Y	N
6 ***Steiger***	Y	N	Y	Y	Y	Y	N
7 Obey	Y	Y	Y	N	Y	?	?
8 Cornell	Y	N	Y	N	Y	Y	N
9 ***Kasten***	Y	N	N	Y	Y	N	N
WYOMING							
AL Roncalio	Y	Y	Y	N	Y	?	Y

Democrats ***Republicans***

821. S 1487. Illegal Cigarette Sales. Adoption of the conference report on the bill to expand federal anti-racketeering laws to assist states in controlling illegal interstate traffic in cigarettes. Adopted 366-0: R 127-0; D 239-0 (ND 164-0; SD 75-0), Oct. 15, 1978.

822. HR 14279. Banking Regulation. Rousselot, R-Calif., demand for a second on the St Germain, D-R.I., motion to suspend the rules and adopt the resolution (H Res 1439) providing that the House concur, with amendments, in the Senate amendments to the bill to strengthen federal regulation of financial institutions and make certain other changes in banking laws. Second ordered 331-14: R 112-9; D 219-5 (ND 146-4; SD 73-1), Oct. 15, 1978.

823. HR 14279. Banking Regulation. St Germain, D-R.I., motion to suspend the rules and adopt the resolution (H Res 1439) providing that the House concur, with amendments, in the Senate amendments to the bill to strengthen federal regulation of financial institutions and make certain other changes in banking laws. Motion agreed to 341-32: R 110-16; D 231-16 (ND 164-3; SD 67-13), Oct. 15, 1978. A two-thirds majority vote (249 in this case) is required for adoption under suspension of the rules.

824. HR 5289, HR 5037, HR 5146, HR 4018, HR 5263. National Energy Act. Adoption of the five energy conference reports, considered en bloc, on the bills on natural gas pricing, conservation, coal conversion, utility rate reform and energy taxes. Adopted (thus cleared for the president) 231-168: R 46-87; D 185-81 (ND 130-50; SD 55-31), Oct. 15, 1978. A "yea" was a vote supporting the president's position.

825. HR 12250. Boundary Waters Canoe Area. Adoption of the conference report on the bill to restrict use of motorboats and to prohibit logging and mining in the Boundary Waters Canoe Area in northern Minnesota. Adopted 248-111: R 73-47; D 175-64 (ND 130-31; SD 45-33), Oct. 15, 1978.

826. S 2493. Airline Deregulation. Adoption of the conference report on the bill to increase competition in the commercial passenger airline industry by phasing out federal regulation of fares and air routes and mandating the abolition of the Civil Aeronautics Board (CAB) unless Congress acted to retain it. Adopted (thus cleared for the president) 356-6: R 121-3; D 235-3 (ND 161-2; SD 74-1), Oct. 15, 1978. A "yea" was a vote supporting the president's position.

827. S 3447. Agricultural Trade. Adoption of the conference report on the bill to promote the sale of U.S. agricultural commodities by providing intermediate term (three to 10 years) credit under the Commodity Credit Corporation, to make the People's Republic of China eligible for short-term (up to three years) credit, and to establish from six to 25 agricultural trade offices abroad. Adopted (thus cleared for the president) 356-4: R 123-1; D 233-3 (ND 160-2; SD 73-1), Oct. 15, 1978. A "yea" was a vote supporting the president's position.

KEY

- Y Voted for (yea).
- ✓ Paired for.
- † Announced for.
- # CQ Poll for.
- N Voted against (nay).
- X Paired against.
- - Announced against.
- ▮ CQ Poll against.
- P Voted "present."
- ● Voted "present" to avoid possible conflict of interest.
- ? Did not vote or otherwise make a position known.

	821	822	823	824	825	826	827
ALABAMA							
1 Edwards	Y	Y	Y	N	Y	Y	Y
2 Dickinson	?	?	?	?	?	?	?
3 Nichols	Y	Y	N	N	N	Y	Y
4 Bevill	Y	Y	Y	Y	N	Y	Y
5 Flippo	Y	Y	N	Y	N	Y	Y
6 Buchanan	Y	Y	Y	Y	Y	Y	Y
7 Flowers	?	Y	Y	Y	Y	Y	Y
ALASKA							
AL Young	Y	Y	Y	Y	N	Y	Y
ARIZONA							
1 Rhodes	Y	Y	Y	N	?	Y	Y
2 Udall	?	?	?	Y	Y	?	?
3 Stump	Y	Y	N	N	N	N	Y
4 Rudd	?	?	?	X	?	?	?
ARKANSAS							
1 Alexander	Y	Y	Y	Y	N	Y	Y
2 Tucker	Y	Y	Y	Y	Y	Y	Y
3 Hammerschmidt	Y	Y	N	N	N	Y	Y
4 Thornton	Y	Y	N	Y	Y	Y	Y
CALIFORNIA							
1 Johnson	Y	Y	Y	Y	Y	Y	Y
2 Clausen	Y	Y	Y	Y	N	Y	Y
3 Moss	?	?	?	?	?	?	?
4 Leggett	?	?	?	N	N	Y	Y
5 Burton, J.	?	?	?	N	?	?	?
6 Burton, P.	Y	Y	Y	N	Y	?	Y
7 Miller	Y	Y	Y	N	Y	Y	Y
8 Dellums	Y	Y	Y	N	Y	Y	Y
9 Stark	Y	Y	Y	N	?	?	?
10 Edwards	Y	P	Y	Y	Y	Y	Y
11 Ryan	?	Y	Y	?	Y	Y	?
12 McCloskey	Y	Y	Y	Y	Y	Y	Y
13 Mineta	Y	Y	Y	Y	Y	Y	Y
14 McFall	?	?	?	?	?	?	?
15 Sisk	Y	Y	Y	?	?	?	?
16 Panetta	Y	Y	Y	Y	Y	Y	Y
17 Krebs	Y	Y	Y	Y	Y	Y	Y
18 Vacancy							
19 Lagomarsino	Y	Y	Y	N	Y	Y	Y
20 Goldwater	Y	Y	Y	N	Y	Y	?
21 Corman	Y	?	Y	Y	Y	Y	Y
22 Moorhead	Y	Y	Y	N	Y	Y	Y
23 Beilenson	Y	?	Y	Y	Y	Y	Y
24 Waxman	Y	?	?	N	Y	Y	Y
25 Roybal	Y	Y	Y	Y	Y	Y	Y
26 Rousselot	Y	Y	N	N	N	Y	Y
27 Dornan	Y	N	Y	Y	N	Y	Y
28 Burke	?	?	?	?	?	?	?
29 Hawkins	Y	Y	Y	Y	Y	Y	Y
30 Danielson	Y	Y	Y	Y	Y	Y	Y
31 Wilson, C.H.	?	?	?	?	?	?	?
32 Anderson	Y	Y	Y	Y	Y	Y	Y
33 Clawson	Y	N	N	N	N	Y	?
34 Hannaford	Y	Y	Y	Y	Y	Y	Y
35 Lloyd	Y	N	Y	Y	Y	Y	Y
36 Brown	Y	?	Y	Y	Y	Y	Y
37 Pettis	?	?	?	?	?	?	?
38 Patterson	Y	Y	Y	Y	Y	Y	Y
39 Wiggins	Y	Y	Y	Y	?	Y	?
40 Badham	?	?	?	X	?	?	?
41 Wilson, B.	Y	N	N	Y	Y	Y	Y
42 Van Deerlin	Y	Y	Y	Y	N	Y	Y
43 Burgener	Y	Y	Y	Y	Y	Y	Y
COLORADO							
1 Schroeder	Y	Y	Y	N	Y	Y	Y
2 Wirth	Y	Y	Y	Y	Y	Y	Y
3 Evans	?	?	?	?	?	?	?
4 Johnson	Y	Y	Y	N	Y	Y	Y

	821	822	823	824	825	826	827
5 Armstrong	?	?	?	?	?	?	?
CONNECTICUT							
1 Cotter	Y	Y	Y	Y	N	Y	Y
2 Dodd	Y	Y	Y	Y	Y	Y	Y
3 Giaimo	Y	Y	Y	Y	N	Y	Y
4 McKinney	Y	Y	Y	Y	Y	Y	Y
5 Sarasin	Y	Y	Y	N	N	Y	Y
6 Moffett	Y	Y	Y	N	?	?	?
DELAWARE							
AL Evans	Y	Y	Y	Y	Y	Y	Y
FLORIDA							
1 Sikes	Y	Y	Y	Y	?	?	?
2 Fuqua	Y	Y	Y	Y	Y	Y	Y
3 Bennett	Y	Y	Y	Y	Y	Y	Y
4 Chappell	Y	Y	N	Y	N	Y	Y
5 Kelly	Y	N	N	N	N	Y	Y
6 Young	Y	Y	Y	N	Y	Y	Y
7 Gibbons	Y	?	?	Y	Y	Y	Y
8 Ireland	Y	Y	Y	Y	Y	Y	?
9 Frey	?	?	?	✓	?	?	?
10 Bafalis	Y	Y	Y	Y	Y	Y	Y
11 Rogers	Y	Y	P	Y	N	Y	Y
12 Burke	?	?	?	X	?	?	?
13 Lehman	?	?	?	?	?	?	?
14 Pepper	Y	Y	Y	Y	Y	Y	Y
15 Fascell	Y	Y	Y	Y	Y	Y	Y
GEORGIA							
1 Ginn	Y	Y	N	Y	N	Y	Y
2 Mathis	?	?	Y	Y	?	Y	Y
3 Brinkley	Y	Y	Y	Y	Y	Y	Y
4 Levitas	?	Y	Y	Y	Y	Y	Y
5 Fowler	Y	Y	Y	Y	Y	Y	Y
6 Flynt	?	?	?	?	?	?	?
7 McDonald	Y	N	N	N	N	Y	N
8 Evans	?	?	Y	Y	?	?	?
9 Jenkins	Y	Y	N	Y	N	Y	Y
10 Barnard	Y	Y	Y	Y	N	Y	Y
HAWAII							
1 Heftel	Y	Y	Y	Y	N	Y	Y
2 Akaka	Y	Y	Y	Y	Y	Y	Y
IDAHO							
1 Symms	Y	Y	N	N	N	Y	Y
2 Hansen, G.	Y	Y	Y	N	N	Y	Y
ILLINOIS							
1 Vacancy							
2 Murphy	Y	?	Y	Y	Y	Y	Y
3 Russo	Y	Y	Y	Y	Y	Y	Y
4 Derwinski	Y	N	Y	N	Y	Y	Y
5 Fary	Y	Y	Y	Y	N	Y	Y
6 Hyde	Y	Y	Y	N	Y	Y	Y
7 Collins	Y	Y	Y	Y	Y	Y	Y
8 Rostenkowski	Y	?	Y	Y	Y	Y	Y
9 Yates	Y	Y	Y	Y	Y	Y	Y
10 Mikva	?	?	?	✓	?	?	?
11 Annunzio	Y	Y	Y	Y	Y	Y	Y
12 Crane	Y	Y	N	N	?	?	?
13 McClory	Y	Y	Y	N	Y	Y	Y
14 Erlenborn	Y	Y	Y	N	N	Y	Y
15 Corcoran	Y	Y	Y	N	Y	Y	Y
16 Anderson	Y	Y	Y	N	Y	Y	Y
17 O'Brien	Y	P	P	N	N	Y	Y
18 Michel	Y	Y	Y	N	N	Y	Y
19 Railsback	Y	Y	Y	N	Y	Y	Y
20 Findley	Y	Y	Y	N	Y	Y	Y
21 Madigan	Y	Y	Y	N	N	Y	Y
22 Shipley	?	?	?	?	?	?	?
23 Price	Y	Y	Y	Y	N	Y	Y
24 Simon	Y	N	Y	Y	Y	Y	Y
INDIANA							
1 Benjamin	Y	Y	N	N	N	Y	Y
2 Fithian	Y	Y	Y	Y	Y	Y	Y
3 Brademas	Y	Y	Y	Y	Y	Y	Y
4 Quayle	Y	?	?	N	Y	Y	Y
5 Hillis	Y	Y	Y	Y	Y	Y	Y
6 Evans	Y	Y	Y	Y	Y	Y	Y
7 Myers, J.	Y	Y	Y	N	N	Y	Y
8 Cornwell	Y	?	Y	Y	Y	Y	Y
9 Hamilton	Y	Y	Y	Y	Y	Y	Y
10 Sharp	Y	Y	Y	Y	Y	Y	Y
11 Jacobs	Y	Y	Y	N	?	?	Y
IOWA							
1 Leach	Y	Y	Y	Y	Y	Y	Y
2 Blouin	?	Y	Y	Y	?	Y	Y
3 Grassley	Y	Y	N	N	Y	Y	Y
4 Smith	Y	Y	Y	Y	Y	Y	Y
5 Harkin	?	Y	Y	N	Y	Y	Y
6 Bedell	Y	Y	Y	Y	Y	Y	Y

Democrats ***Republicans***

Corresponding to Congressional Record Votes 928, 929, 930, 932, 933, 934, 935

	821	822	823	824	825	826	827
KANSAS							
1 Sebelius	Y	Y	N	N	Y	Y	Y
2 Keys	Y	Y	Y	Y	Y	?	?
3 Winn	Y	Y	P	N	Y	Y	Y
4 Glickman	Y	Y	Y	Y	Y	Y	Y
5 Skubitz	Y	Y	Y	Y	?	Y	Y
KENTUCKY							
1 Hubbard	Y	Y	Y	N	N	Y	Y
2 Natcher	Y	Y	Y	Y	Y	Y	Y
3 Mazzoli	Y	?	Y	Y	Y	?	?
4 Snyder	Y	Y	Y	Y	N	Y	Y
5 Carter	Y	Y	Y	N	N	Y	Y
6 Breckinridge	Y	Y	Y	N	Y	Y	Y
7 Perkins	Y	Y	Y	Y	Y	Y	Y
LOUISIANA							
1 Livingston	Y	Y	N	N	N	Y	Y
2 Boggs	Y	Y	Y	N	N	?	?
3 Treen	?	?	Y	N	Y	Y	Y
4 Waggonner	Y	Y	Y	N	N	Y	Y
5 Huckaby	Y	Y	Y	N	Y	Y	Y
6 Moore	Y	Y	Y	N	Y	Y	Y
7 Breaux	Y	Y	Y	N	N	Y	Y
8 Long	Y	Y	Y	N	Y	Y	Y
MAINE							
1 Emery	Y	Y	Y	Y	?	Y	Y
2 Cohen	Y	Y	Y	Y	Y	Y	Y
MARYLAND							
1 Bauman	Y	N	Y	N	Y	Y	Y
2 Long	Y	Y	Y	Y	Y	Y	Y
3 Mikulski	Y	Y	Y	N	Y	Y	Y
4 Holt	Y	Y	Y	N	Y	Y	Y
5 Spellman	Y	Y	Y	N	Y	Y	Y
6 Vacancy							
7 Mitchell	?	?	?	N	Y	Y	Y
8 Steers	Y	P	P	N	Y	Y	Y
MASSACHUSETTS							
1 Conte	Y	Y	Y	Y	Y	Y	Y
2 Boland	Y	Y	Y	Y	Y	Y	Y
3 Early	Y	?	Y	Y	Y	Y	Y
4 Drinan	Y	Y	Y	N	Y	Y	Y
5 Tsongas	Y	Y	Y	Y	Y	Y	Y
6 Harrington	?	Y	Y	Y	?	?	?
7 Markey	Y	Y	Y	N	Y	Y	Y
8 O'Neill							
9 Moakley	Y	Y	Y	Y	?	Y	Y
10 Heckler	Y	Y	Y	Y	?	?	Y
11 Burke	Y	Y	Y	N	N	Y	Y
12 Studds	Y	Y	Y	Y	Y	Y	Y
MICHIGAN							
1 Conyers	?	?	?	N	Y	?	?
2 Pursell	Y	Y	Y	Y	Y	Y	Y
3 Brown	Y	?	N	Y	Y	Y	Y
4 Stockman	?	?	Y	N	?	?	?
5 Sawyer	Y	Y	Y	Y	?	?	Y
6 Carr	Y	Y	Y	Y	Y	Y	Y
7 Kildee	Y	Y	Y	N	Y	Y	Y
8 Traxler	Y	Y	Y	Y	Y	Y	Y
9 Vander Jagt	Y	Y	Y	?	?	Y	Y
10 Cederberg	Y	?	Y	N	Y	Y	Y
11 Ruppe	Y	Y	Y	Y	?	?	?
12 Bonior	?	?	Y	N	Y	Y	Y
13 Diggs	?	?	?	?	?	?	?
14 Nedzi	Y	Y	Y	Y	Y	?	?
15 Ford	?	?	?	Y	?	?	?
16 Dingell	?	?	Y	Y	N	?	Y
17 Brodhead	Y	Y	Y	Y	Y	Y	Y
18 Blanchard	Y	Y	Y	Y	Y	Y	Y
19 Broomfield	Y	Y	Y	Y	N	Y	Y
MINNESOTA							
1 Quie	?	?	?	✓	?	?	?
2 Hagedorn	Y	Y	Y	N	Y	Y	Y
3 Frenzel	Y	Y	Y	Y	Y	Y	Y
4 Vento	Y	Y	Y	N	Y	Y	Y
5 Fraser	Y	Y	Y	N	Y	Y	Y
6 Nolan	Y	Y	Y	N	Y	Y	Y
7 Stangeland	Y	Y	Y	Y	Y	Y	Y
8 Oberstar	Y	Y	Y	N	N	Y	Y
MISSISSIPPI							
1 Whitten	Y	Y	Y	Y	N	Y	Y
2 Bowen	Y	?	Y	Y	N	Y	Y
3 Montgomery	Y	Y	Y	Y	N	Y	Y
4 Cochran	Y	Y	Y	N	N	Y	Y
5 Lott	Y	Y	Y	N	N	Y	Y
MISSOURI							
1 Clay	Y	?	Y	N	?	Y	Y
2 Young	Y	Y	Y	N	N	Y	Y
3 Gephardt	Y	Y	Y	Y	Y	Y	Y

	821	822	823	824	825	826	827
4 Skelton	Y	Y	P	Y	Y	Y	Y
5 Bolling	Y	Y	Y	Y	?	Y	Y
6 Coleman	Y	Y	Y	Y	N	Y	Y
7 Taylor	Y	Y	Y	N	N	Y	Y
8 Ichord	?	?	?	X	?	?	?
9 Volkmer	Y	Y	Y	Y	N	Y	Y
10 Burlison	Y	Y	Y	Y	Y	Y	Y
MONTANA							
1 Baucus	Y	Y	Y	Y	Y	N	Y
2 Marlenee	?	?	?	✓	?	?	?
NEBRASKA							
1 Thone	?	?	?	Y	?	?	?
2 Cavanaugh	Y	Y	Y	Y	Y	Y	Y
3 Smith	?	Y	?	Y	?	?	?
NEVADA							
AL Santini	Y	Y	Y	Y	?	Y	?
NEW HAMPSHIRE							
1 D'Amours	Y	Y	Y	Y	Y	Y	Y
2 Cleveland	Y	P	P	N	Y	Y	Y
NEW JERSEY							
1 Florio	Y	Y	Y	N	Y	Y	Y
2 Hughes	Y	Y	Y	Y	N	Y	Y
3 Howard	Y	Y	Y	Y	Y	Y	Y
4 Thompson	Y	Y	Y	Y	Y	Y	Y
5 Fenwick	Y	Y	Y	Y	Y	Y	Y
6 Forsythe	?	?	Y	N	N	?	Y
7 Maguire	Y	Y	Y	N	Y	Y	Y
8 Roe	Y	Y	Y	Y	Y	Y	Y
9 Hollenbeck	Y	Y	Y	Y	?	?	Y
10 Rodino	Y	Y	Y	N	Y	Y	Y
11 Minish	Y	Y	Y	Y	Y	Y	Y
12 Rinaldo	Y	Y	Y	Y	Y	Y	Y
13 Meyner	Y	Y	Y	Y	?	Y	Y
14 LeFante	Y	Y	Y	Y	Y	Y	Y
15 Patten	Y	Y	Y	Y	Y	Y	Y
NEW MEXICO							
1 Lujan	?	?	?	?	?	?	?
2 Runnels	?	?	Y	N	Y	Y	Y
NEW YORK							
1 Pike	Y	Y	Y	Y	Y	Y	Y
2 Downey	Y	Y	Y	Y	?	?	?
3 Ambro	Y	?	Y	Y	?	Y	Y
4 Lent	Y	Y	Y	N	Y	Y	Y
5 Wydler	Y	Y	Y	N	Y	Y	Y
6 Wolff	Y	Y	Y	Y	Y	Y	Y
7 Addabbo	Y	Y	Y	Y	Y	Y	Y
8 Rosenthal	Y	Y	Y	Y	Y	Y	Y
9 Delaney	Y	?	?	Y	N	?	Y
10 Biaggi	?	?	?	✓	?	?	?
11 Scheuer	Y	Y	Y	Y	Y	Y	Y
12 Chisholm	Y	Y	Y	N	Y	Y	Y
13 Solarz	Y	Y	Y	Y	Y	Y	Y
14 Richmond	Y	Y	Y	Y	Y	Y	Y
15 Zeferetti	Y	Y	?	Y	N	Y	Y
16 Holtzman	Y	Y	Y	N	Y	Y	Y
17 Murphy	Y	?	Y	Y	N	Y	Y
18 Green	Y	Y	Y	Y	Y	Y	Y
19 Rangel	Y	?	?	Y	Y	Y	Y
20 Weiss	Y	Y	Y	N	Y	Y	Y
21 Garcia	Y	Y	Y	Y	Y	Y	Y
22 Bingham	Y	Y	Y	Y	Y	Y	Y
23 Caputo	?	Y	Y	✓	?	?	?
24 Ottinger	Y	Y	Y	N	Y	Y	Y
25 Fish	Y	Y	Y	N	Y	Y	Y
26 Gilman	Y	Y	Y	N	Y	Y	Y
27 McHugh	Y	Y	Y	Y	Y	Y	Y
28 Stratton	Y	Y	Y	Y	Y	Y	Y
29 Pattison	Y	Y	Y	Y	Y	Y	Y
30 McEwen	Y	Y	P	N	N	Y	Y
31 Mitchell	Y	Y	Y	Y	Y	Y	Y
32 Hanley	Y	Y	Y	Y	N	Y	Y
33 Walsh	Y	P	P	N	N	Y	Y
34 Horton	Y	Y	Y	N	Y	Y	Y
35 Conable	Y	Y	Y	N	Y	Y	Y
36 LaFalce	Y	Y	Y	Y	Y	Y	?
37 Nowak	Y	Y	Y	Y	N	Y	?
38 Kemp	Y	Y	Y	N	N	Y	Y
39 Lundine	Y	Y	Y	Y	Y	Y	Y
NORTH CAROLINA							
1 Jones	Y	Y	Y	Y	N	Y	Y
2 Fountain	Y	Y	Y	Y	N	Y	Y
3 Whitley	Y	Y	Y	Y	Y	Y	Y
4 Andrews	Y	Y	Y	Y	Y	Y	Y
5 Neal	Y	Y	Y	Y	Y	Y	Y
6 Preyer	Y	Y	Y	Y	Y	Y	?
7 Rose	Y	?	Y	Y	Y	Y	Y
8 Hefner	Y	Y	Y	Y	N	Y	Y

	821	822	823	824	825	826	827
9 Martin	Y	Y	Y	Y	N	Y	?
10 Broyhill	Y	Y	Y	Y	Y	Y	Y
11 Gudger	Y	Y	Y	Y	N	Y	Y
NORTH DAKOTA							
AL Andrews	Y	Y	Y	Y	N	Y	Y
OHIO							
1 Gradison	Y	Y	Y	Y	Y	Y	Y
2 Luken	Y	Y	Y	N	Y	Y	Y
3 Whalen	Y	Y	Y	N	Y	Y	Y
4 Guyer	Y	Y	Y	N	Y	Y	Y
5 Latta	Y	Y	Y	N	N	Y	Y
6 Harsha	Y	?	Y	N	N	Y	Y
7 Brown	Y	Y	Y	N	N	Y	Y
8 Kindness	Y	Y	N	N	N	?	Y
9 Ashley	Y	Y	Y	Y	Y	Y	Y
10 Miller	Y	Y	Y	N	N	Y	Y
11 Stanton	Y	Y	Y	N	?	Y	?
12 Devine	Y	Y	Y	N	N	Y	Y
13 Pease	Y	?	Y	Y	Y	Y	Y
14 Seiberling	Y	Y	Y	Y	Y	Y	Y
15 Wylie	Y	Y	Y	N	Y	Y	Y
16 Regula	Y	Y	Y	N	Y	Y	Y
17 Ashbrook	Y	Y	N	N	N	Y	Y
18 Applegate	?	?	?	X	?	?	?
19 Carney	?	?	?	X	?	?	?
20 Oakar	?	Y	Y	N	N	Y	Y
21 Stokes	Y	?	?	Y	N	Y	Y
22 Vanik	Y	Y	Y	N	Y	Y	Y
23 Mottl	Y	Y	N	N	?	?	?
OKLAHOMA							
1 Jones	Y	Y	N	N	N	Y	Y
2 Risenhoover	?	?	?	Y	?	?	?
3 Watkins	Y	Y	N	N	N	Y	Y
4 Steed	?	?	Y	N	?	?	?
5 Edwards	Y	Y	N	N	N	Y	Y
6 English	Y	Y	?	N	Y	Y	Y
OREGON							
1 AuCoin	Y	Y	Y	Y	Y	Y	Y
2 Ullman	Y	?	?	Y	N	Y	Y
3 Duncan	?	?	?	Y	N	Y	Y
4 Weaver	Y	?	Y	Y	?	?	?
PENNSYLVANIA							
1 Myers, M.	Y	N	Y	Y	N	Y	N
2 Nix	Y	Y	Y	Y	Y	Y	Y
3 Lederer	Y	Y	Y	Y	N	Y	Y
4 Eilberg	Y	Y	Y	N	Y	Y	Y
5 Schulze	Y	Y	Y	N	N	Y	Y
6 Yatron	Y	Y	Y	Y	Y	Y	Y
7 Edgar	Y	Y	Y	Y	Y	Y	Y
8 Kostmayer	Y	Y	Y	N	Y	Y	Y
9 Shuster	Y	N	Y	N	N	Y	Y
10 McDade	Y	Y	Y	N	Y	Y	Y
11 Flood	Y	Y	Y	Y	Y	Y	Y
12 Murtha	Y	N	Y	Y	N	Y	Y
13 Coughlin	?	Y	Y	N	Y	?	Y
14 Moorhead	Y	Y	Y	Y	Y	Y	Y
15 Rooney	Y	Y	Y	Y	Y	Y	Y
16 Walker	Y	Y	Y	N	N	Y	Y
17 Ertel	Y	Y	Y	Y	N	Y	Y
18 Walgren	Y	Y	?	Y	?	?	?
19 Goodling, W.	Y	N	Y	N	N	Y	?
20 Gaydos	Y	Y	Y	N	Y	Y	Y
21 Dent	Y	Y	Y	N	Y	Y	Y
22 Murphy	Y	Y	Y	Y	Y	Y	N
23 Ammerman	?	?	?	?	?	?	?
24 Marks	Y	Y	Y	Y	Y	Y	Y
25 Myers, G.	Y	N	N	Y	Y	N	N
RHODE ISLAND							
1 St Germain	Y	Y	Y	Y	Y	Y	Y
2 Beard	Y	Y	Y	N	Y	Y	Y
SOUTH CAROLINA							
1 Davis	?	Y	Y	N	Y	Y	Y
2 Spence	Y	Y	Y	Y	Y	Y	Y
3 Derrick	Y	Y	Y	Y	Y	Y	Y
4 Mann	Y	Y	Y	Y	Y	Y	Y
5 Holland	Y	Y	Y	Y	Y	Y	Y
6 Jenrette	Y	Y	Y	Y	Y	Y	?
SOUTH DAKOTA							
1 Pressler	Y	Y	Y	N	Y	N	Y
2 Abdnor	Y	Y	Y	N	N	N	Y
TENNESSEE							
1 Quillen	Y	P	P	Y	Y	Y	Y
2 Duncan	Y	Y	Y	N	Y	Y	Y
3 Lloyd	Y	Y	Y	Y	N	Y	Y
4 Gore	Y	Y	Y	N	Y	Y	Y
5 Vacancy							
6 Beard	?	?	Y	Y	?	Y	Y

	821	822	823	824	825	826	827
7 Jones	Y	Y	Y	Y	N	Y	Y
8 Ford	Y	Y	Y	Y	Y	Y	Y
TEXAS							
1 Hall	Y	Y	N	N	N	Y	Y
2 Wilson, C.	?	Y	Y	Y	?	Y	Y
3 Collins	Y	Y	N	N	N	Y	Y
4 Roberts	Y	Y	Y	N	N	Y	Y
5 Mattox	Y	Y	Y	N	Y	?	?
6 Teague	?	?	?	?	?	?	?
7 Archer	Y	Y	Y	N	Y	Y	Y
8 Eckhardt	Y	Y	Y	Y	Y	?	Y
9 Brooks	Y	Y	Y	Y	Y	Y	Y
10 Pickle	Y	Y	Y	N	Y	Y	Y
11 Poage	Y	Y	N	Y	N	N	Y
12 Wright	Y	Y	Y	Y	N	Y	Y
13 Hightower	Y	Y	Y	N	Y	Y	Y
14 Young	?	?	?	Y	Y	?	Y
15 de la Garza	Y	Y	Y	N	Y	Y	Y
16 White	Y	Y	Y	N	Y	Y	Y
17 Burleson	Y	?	N	N	N	Y	Y
18 Jordan	Y	Y	Y	Y	?	?	?
19 Mahon	Y	Y	Y	N	?	Y	Y
20 Gonzalez	Y	Y	Y	N	Y	Y	Y
21 Krueger	?	?	Y	N	Y	Y	Y
22 Gammage	Y	Y	N	N	Y	Y	Y
23 Kazen	Y	Y	Y	N	Y	Y	Y
24 Milford	?	?	?	N	N	?	?
UTAH							
1 McKay	Y	Y	Y	N	N	Y	Y
2 Marriott	Y	Y	Y	N	Y	Y	Y
VERMONT							
AL Jeffords	Y	Y	Y	Y	Y	Y	Y
VIRGINIA							
1 Trible	Y	Y	Y	N	Y	Y	Y
2 Whitehurst	Y	Y	Y	N	Y	Y	Y
3 Satterfield	Y	Y	Y	N	N	Y	Y
4 Daniel	Y	Y	Y	N	Y	Y	Y
5 Daniel	Y	Y	Y	Y	N	Y	Y
6 Butler	Y	Y	Y	Y	N	Y	Y
7 Robinson	Y	Y	Y	N	N	Y	Y
8 Harris	Y	Y	Y	N	Y	Y	Y
9 Wampler	Y	Y	Y	Y	N	Y	Y
10 Fisher	Y	Y	Y	Y	Y	Y	Y
WASHINGTON							
1 Pritchard	Y	Y	Y	Y	Y	Y	Y
2 Meeds	?	?	Y	Y	?	?	?
3 Bonker	Y	?	Y	Y	?	Y	?
4 McCormack	Y	Y	Y	Y	N	Y	Y
5 Foley	Y	Y	Y	Y	Y	Y	Y
6 Dicks	Y	Y	Y	Y	Y	Y	Y
7 Cunningham	Y	Y	Y	N	N	Y	Y
WEST VIRGINIA							
1 Mollohan	Y	Y	Y	Y	N	Y	Y
2 Staggers	Y	Y	Y	Y	Y	Y	Y
3 Slack	Y	Y	Y	Y	Y	Y	Y
4 Rahall	Y	Y	Y	Y	Y	Y	Y
WISCONSIN							
1 Aspin	Y	Y	Y	Y	Y	Y	Y
2 Kastenmeier	Y	Y	Y	N	Y	Y	Y
3 Baldus	Y	Y	?	Y	Y	Y	Y
4 Zablocki	Y	Y	Y	Y	N	Y	Y
5 Reuss	Y	Y	Y	Y	Y	Y	Y
6 Steiger	Y	Y	Y	N	Y	Y	Y
7 Obey	?	?	Y	N	?	Y	Y
8 Cornell	Y	Y	Y	N	Y	Y	Y
9 Kasten	?	?	Y	N	Y	Y	Y
WYOMING							
AL Roncalio	?	?	Y	Y	Y	Y	Y

Democrats ***Republicans***

828. HR 15. Elementary and Secondary Education. Adoption of the conference report on the bill to extend the Elementary and Secondary Education Act of 1965 for five years, through fiscal 1983. Adopted 349-18: R 113-13; D 236-5 (ND 165-0; SD 71-5), Oct. 15, 1978.

829. HR 12467. Rehabilitation Act Amendments. Adoption of the conference report on the bill to extend the Rehabilitation Act of 1973 for four years, through fiscal 1982, and to authorize up to $4.9 billion for fiscal 1979-82 for rehabilitation and service programs. Adopted 365-2: R 126-1; D 239-1 (ND 165-0; SD 74-1), Oct. 15, 1978.

830. HR 13750. Sugar Stabilization Act. Adoption of the rule (H Res 1448) providing for House floor consideration of the conference report on the bill *(see vote 831, below)*. Adopted 261-107: R 76-50; D 185-57 (ND 117-47; SD 68-10), Oct. 15, 1978.

831. HR 13750. Sugar Stabilization Act. Adoption of the conference report on the bill to authorize, through fiscal 1983, U.S. participation in the International Sugar Agreement, to maintain a minimum per-pound price for U.S. sugar producers through import quotas and fees and (for fiscal 1979 only) direct payments, to establish minimum wages and other benefits for sugar industry workers, to extend through Feb. 15, 1979, the president's authority to waive countervailing duties, and to authorize sales and contributions to an international stockpile of stockpiled U.S. tin. Rejected 177-194: R 23-104; D 154-90 (ND 93-75; SD 61-15), Oct. 15, 1978. A "yea" was a vote supporting the president's position.

832. HR 13511. Revenue Act of 1978. Adoption of the conference report on the bill to reduce taxes by $18.7 billion in 1979. Adopted (thus cleared for the president) 337-38: R 125-1; D 212-37 (ND 138-34; SD 74-3), Oct. 15, 1978.

833. HR 9937. Carson City Silver Dollars/Textile Negotiations. Adoption of the conference report on the bill to authorize the General Services Administration to dispose of $24 million worth of Carson City silver dollars and to prohibit a reduction or elimination in trade negotiations of duties or import restrictions on certain imported textiles and textile products. Adopted (thus cleared for the president) 198-29: R 48-15; D 150-14 (ND 97-10; SD 53-4), Oct. 15, 1978. A "nay" was a vote supporting the president's position.

834. HR 10979. Water Projects/Emergency Highway and Transportation Repair Act. Ertel, D-Pa., motion to suspend the rules and agree to the Senate amendments to the bill to authorize $1.4 billion for 158 water projects (road repair provisions previously had been dropped). Motion failed due to lack of a quorum 129-31: R 40-8; D 89-12 (ND 51-20; SD 38-3), Oct. 15, 1978. A two-thirds majority vote is required for passage under suspension of the rules; a quorum was 216.

KEY

- Y Voted for (yea).
- ✓ Paired for.
- † Announced for.
- # CQ Poll for.
- N Voted against (nay).
- X Paired against.
- - Announced against.
- ▮ CQ Poll against.
- P Voted "present."
- ● Voted "present" to avoid possible conflict of interest.
- ? Did not vote or otherwise make a position known.

	828	829	830	831	832	833	834
ALABAMA							
1 Edwards	Y	Y	Y	N	Y	?	Y
2 Dickinson	?	?	?	X	?	?	?
3 Nichols	Y	Y	Y	Y	Y	?	?
4 Bevill	Y	Y	Y	Y	Y	Y	?
5 Flippo	Y	Y	Y	Y	Y	Y	?
6 Buchanan	Y	Y	Y	N	Y	Y	Y
7 Flowers	Y	?	Y	Y	Y	Y	?
ALASKA							
AL Young	Y	Y	Y	N	Y	?	?
ARIZONA							
1 Rhodes	Y	Y	?	N	?	?	?
2 Udall	?	?	?	?	?	?	?
3 Stump	Y	Y	Y	Y	Y	Y	Y
4 Rudd	?	?	?	?	?	?	?
ARKANSAS							
1 Alexander	Y	?	Y	Y	Y	Y	Y
2 Tucker	Y	Y	Y	Y	Y	Y	Y
3 Hammerschmidt	Y	Y	N	N	Y	?	?
4 Thornton	Y	Y	Y	Y	Y	Y	Y
CALIFORNIA							
1 Johnson	Y	Y	Y	Y	Y	Y	Y
2 Clausen	Y	Y	Y	Y	Y	Y	Y
3 Moss	?	?	?	?	?	?	?
4 Leggett	?	?	?	?	Y	?	?
5 Burton, J.	?	?	?	?	X	?	?
6 Burton, P.	Y	Y	?	?	?	?	?
7 Miller	Y	Y	Y	Y	Y	?	?
8 Dellums	Y	Y	Y	Y	N	Y	N
9 Stark	?	?	?	N	N	?	?
10 Edwards	Y	Y	Y	Y	N	?	?
11 Ryan	?	Y	?	Y	Y	?	?
12 McCloskey	Y	Y	Y	N	Y	N	Y
13 Mineta	Y	Y	Y	Y	Y	Y	Y
14 McFall	?	?	?	?	?	?	?
15 Sisk	?	?	?	?	?	?	?
16 Panetta	Y	Y	Y	Y	Y	Y	?
17 Krebs	Y	Y	Y	Y	Y	Y	?
18 Vacancy							
19 Lagomarsino	Y	Y	Y	N	Y	N	Y
20 Goldwater	?	Y	Y	N	Y	N	Y
21 Corman	Y	Y	Y	Y	Y	Y	?
22 Moorhead	Y	Y	Y	N	Y	?	?
23 Beilenson	Y	Y	Y	Y	Y	N	N
24 Waxman	?	Y	Y	Y	N	?	?
25 Roybal	Y	Y	N	Y	N	Y	Y
26 Rousselot	N	Y	Y	N	Y	N	Y
27 Dornan	N	Y	Y	Y	Y	?	?
28 Burke	?	?	?	?	?	?	?
29 Hawkins	Y	Y	Y	Y	N	Y	?
30 Danielson	Y	Y	Y	Y	Y	Y	P
31 Wilson, C.H.	?	?	?	?	?	?	?
32 Anderson	Y	Y	N	N	Y	Y	Y
33 Clawson	?	Y	N	N	Y	N	Y
34 Hannaford	Y	?	Y	N	Y	?	?
35 Lloyd	Y	Y	Y	N	Y	?	?
36 Brown	Y	Y	Y	Y	Y	Y	?
37 Pettis	?	?	?	?	?	?	?
38 Patterson	Y	Y	N	Y	Y	Y	P
39 Wiggins	?	?	?	?	?	?	?
40 Badham	?	?	?	?	?	?	?
41 Wilson, B.	Y	Y	?	N	Y	Y	Y
42 Van Deerlin	Y	?	N	N	Y	N	N
43 Burgener	Y	Y	Y	Y	Y	?	?
COLORADO							
1 Schroeder	Y	Y	Y	Y	Y	?	?
2 Wirth	Y	Y	Y	N	Y	?	?
3 Evans	?	?	?	?	?	?	?
4 Johnson	Y	Y	Y	N	Y	?	?
5 Armstrong	?	?	?	?	?	?	?
CONNECTICUT							
1 Cotter	Y	Y	?	?	Y	Y	?
2 Dodd	Y	Y	Y	N	N	Y	N
3 Giaimo	Y	Y	Y	N	Y	?	?
4 McKinney	Y	Y	N	N	Y	Y	Y
5 Sarasin	Y	Y	N	N	Y	?	?
6 Moffett	Y	Y	Y	N	Y	Y	N
DELAWARE							
AL Evans	Y	Y	N	N	Y	Y	Y
FLORIDA							
1 Sikes	?	?	Y	Y	Y	?	?
2 Fuqua	Y	Y	Y	✓	?	?	?
3 Bennett	Y	Y	Y	Y	N	N	Y
4 Chappell	Y	Y	Y	Y	Y	Y	?
5 Kelly	N	Y	Y	N	Y	Y	N
6 Young	Y	Y	N	N	Y	?	?
7 Gibbons	Y	Y	N	Y	Y	?	?
8 Ireland	?	?	?	Y	Y	?	?
9 Frey	?	?	?	?	?	?	?
10 Bafalis	Y	Y	Y	Y	Y	N	Y
11 Rogers	Y	Y	Y	Y	Y	?	?
12 Burke	?	?	?	?	?	?	?
13 Lehman	?	?	?	?	?	?	?
14 Pepper	Y	Y	Y	Y	Y	?	?
15 Fascell	Y	Y	Y	Y	Y	?	?
GEORGIA							
1 Ginn	Y	Y	N	N	Y	Y	Y
2 Mathis	Y	Y	Y	?	Y	Y	Y
3 Brinkley	Y	Y	Y	Y	Y	Y	?
4 Levitas	Y	Y	Y	N	Y	Y	Y
5 Fowler	Y	Y	N	N	Y	Y	Y
6 Flynt	?	?	?	?	?	?	?
7 McDonald	N	N	N	N	Y	Y	N
8 Evans	?	?	Y	Y	Y	Y	Y
9 Jenkins	Y	Y	N	Y	Y	Y	?
10 Barnard	Y	Y	Y	N	Y	Y	Y
HAWAII							
1 Heftel	Y	Y	Y	Y	Y	Y	Y
2 Akaka	Y	Y	Y	Y	Y	Y	Y
IDAHO							
1 Symms	N	Y	Y	N	Y	Y	?
2 Hansen, G.	N	Y	Y	N	Y	Y	Y
ILLINOIS							
1 Vacancy							
2 Murphy	Y	Y	Y	Y	Y	Y	Y
3 Russo	Y	Y	N	N	Y	?	?
4 Derwinski	Y	Y	N	N	Y	Y	Y
5 Fary	Y	Y	Y	Y	Y	Y	Y
6 Hyde	Y	Y	Y	N	Y	?	?
7 Collins	Y	Y	Y	Y	Y	Y	?
8 Rostenkowski	Y	Y	Y	Y	Y	Y	Y
9 Yates	Y	Y	N	N	N	Y	?
10 Mikva	?	?	?	?	✓	?	?
11 Annunzio	Y	Y	Y	Y	Y	?	?
12 Crane	?	?	?	X	?	?	?
13 McClory	Y	Y	N	N	Y	?	?
14 Erlenborn	Y	Y	N	N	Y	?	?
15 Corcoran	Y	Y	N	N	Y	?	?
16 Anderson	Y	Y	N	N	Y	?	?
17 O'Brien	Y	Y	N	N	Y	?	?
18 Michel	Y	Y	N	N	Y	Y	Y
19 Railsback	Y	Y	N	?	?	?	?
20 Findley	Y	Y	N	N	N	?	?
21 Madigan	Y	Y	N	N	Y	?	?
22 Shipley	?	?	?	?	?	?	?
23 Price	Y	?	Y	Y	Y	Y	Y
24 Simon	Y	Y	N	Y	N	Y	?
INDIANA							
1 Benjamin	Y	Y	N	N	Y	Y	Y
2 Fithian	Y	Y	N	N	Y	?	?
3 Brademas	Y	Y	Y	N	Y	N	Y
4 Quayle	Y	?	N	N	Y	?	?
5 Hillis	Y	Y	Y	N	Y	?	?
6 Evans	Y	Y	Y	N	Y	Y	?
7 Myers, J.	Y	Y	N	N	Y	?	?
8 Cornwell	?	?	N	N	Y	Y	Y
9 Hamilton	Y	Y	N	N	Y	N	Y
10 Sharp	Y	Y	N	N	Y	Y	N
11 Jacobs	Y	Y	N	Y	N	?	?
IOWA							
1 Leach	Y	Y	N	N	Y	N	Y
2 Blouin	Y	Y	Y	N	Y	Y	Y
3 Grassley	Y	Y	N	N	Y	N	Y
4 Smith	Y	Y	N	N	Y	N	Y
5 Harkin	Y	Y	Y	N	Y	Y	N
6 Bedell	Y	Y	Y	Y	N	N	N

Democrats ***Republicans***

	828	829	830	831	832	833	834
KANSAS							
1 Sebelius	?	?	Y	N	Y	Y	?
2 Keys	Y	Y	N	Y	Y	?	?
3 Winn	Y	Y	Y	N	Y	?	?
4 Glickman	Y	Y	Y	N	Y	Y	?
5 Skubitz	Y	Y	Y	N	Y	Y	?
KENTUCKY							
1 Hubbard	Y	Y	Y	Y	Y	Y	Y
2 Natcher	Y	Y	Y	N	Y	Y	Y
3 Mazzoli	Y	Y	Y	N	Y	?	?
4 Snyder	Y	Y	Y	Y	Y	?	?
5 Carter	Y	Y	Y	N	Y	Y	Y
6 Breckinridge	Y	Y	Y	N	Y	N	Y
7 Perkins	Y	Y	Y	N	Y	?	?
LOUISIANA							
1 Livingston	Y	Y	Y	Y	Y	Y	Y
2 Boggs	Y	Y	Y	Y	Y	Y	Y
3 Treen	N	Y	Y	Y	Y	Y	Y
4 Waggonner	N	Y	Y	Y	Y	Y	Y
5 Huckaby	Y	Y	Y	Y	Y	Y	Y
6 Moore	Y	Y	Y	Y	Y	Y	Y
7 Breaux	Y	Y	Y	Y	Y	Y	Y
8 Long	Y	Y	Y	Y	Y	Y	?
MAINE							
1 Emery	Y	Y	N	N	Y	?	?
2 Cohen	Y	Y	N	N	Y	?	?
MARYLAND							
1 Bauman	N	Y	Y	N	Y	Y	Y
2 Long	Y	Y	N	N	Y	Y	Y
3 Mikulski	Y	Y	Y	N	Y	Y	?
4 Holt	N	Y	Y	N	Y	?	?
5 Spellman	Y	Y	Y	N	Y	Y	Y
6 Vacancy							
7 Mitchell	Y	Y	Y	Y	N	Y	?
8 Steers	Y	Y	N	N	Y	N	N
MASSACHUSETTS							
1 Conte	Y	Y	Y	N	Y	Y	N
2 Boland	Y	Y	Y	N	Y	?	?
3 Early	Y	Y	N	N	Y	?	?
4 Drinan	Y	Y	N	N	Y	?	?
5 Tsongas	Y	Y	Y	N	Y	Y	N
6 Harrington	?	?	?	?	X	?	?
7 Markey	Y	Y	Y	N	N	Y	?
8 O'Neill							
9 Moakley	Y	Y	Y	N	Y	Y	Y
10 Heckler	Y	Y	N	N	Y	Y	?
11 Burke	Y	Y	Y	N	N	Y	Y
12 Studds	Y	Y	N	N	N	Y	N
MICHIGAN							
1 Conyers	Y	Y	?	N	N	?	Y
2 Pursell	Y	Y	Y	N	Y	?	?
3 Brown	Y	Y	N	N	Y	?	?
4 Stockman	?	?	N	N	Y	?	?
5 Sawyer	Y	Y	Y	N	Y	Y	N
6 Carr	Y	Y	Y	Y	Y	Y	N
7 Kildee	Y	Y	Y	Y	Y	Y	P
8 Traxler	?	Y	Y	Y	Y	?	?
9 Vander Jagt	Y	Y	Y	N	Y	Y	Y
10 Cederberg	Y	Y	Y	Y	Y	?	?
11 Ruppe	?	?	?	?	?	?	?
12 Bonior	Y	Y	Y	Y	N	Y	N
13 Diggs	?	?	?	?	?	?	?
14 Nedzi	?	Y	Y	N	Y	?	?
15 Ford	Y	Y	Y	?	Y	Y	?
16 Dingell	Y	Y	Y	Y	Y	Y	?
17 Brodhead	Y	Y	Y	Y	N	?	?
18 Blanchard	Y	Y	Y	Y	Y	Y	N
19 Broomfield	Y	Y	N	N	Y	?	?
MINNESOTA							
1 Quie	?	?	?	?	?	?	?
2 Hagedorn	Y	Y	Y	N	Y	?	?
3 Frenzel	Y	Y	N	N	?	?	?
4 Vento	Y	Y	Y	Y	Y	?	?
5 Fraser	Y	Y	Y	Y	N	N	?
6 Nolan	Y	Y	Y	Y	N	?	?
7 Stangeland	Y	Y	Y	Y	Y	?	?
8 Oberstar	Y	Y	Y	Y	Y	Y	Y
MISSISSIPPI							
1 Whitten	Y	Y	Y	Y	Y	Y	Y
2 Bowen	Y	Y	Y	Y	Y	Y	Y
3 Montgomery	Y	Y	Y	Y	Y	Y	Y
4 Cochran	Y	Y	Y	N	Y	Y	Y
5 Lott	Y	Y	Y	Y	Y	?	?
MISSOURI							
1 Clay	Y	Y	Y	Y	N	?	?
2 Young	Y	Y	N	N	Y	?	?
3 Gephardt	Y	Y	Y	N	Y	Y	?

	828	829	830	831	832	833	834
4 Skelton	Y	Y	Y	Y	Y	Y	?
5 Bolling	Y	Y	Y	Y	Y	?	?
6 Coleman	Y	Y	Y	N	Y	?	?
7 Taylor	Y	Y	Y	N	Y	Y	Y
8 Ichord	?	?	?	?	✓	?	?
9 Volkmer	Y	Y	Y	Y	Y	Y	P
10 Burlison	Y	Y	Y	Y	Y	Y	Y
MONTANA							
1 Baucus	Y	Y	Y	Y	Y	?	?
2 Marlenee	?	?	?	?	?	?	?
NEBRASKA							
1 Thone	?	?	?	?	?	?	?
2 Cavanaugh	Y	Y	Y	Y	Y	Y	?
3 Smith	?	?	?	?	?	?	?
NEVADA							
AL Santini	Y	Y	N	N	?	?	?
NEW HAMPSHIRE							
1 D'Amours	Y	Y	N	N	Y	?	?
2 Cleveland	Y	Y	N	N	Y	?	?
NEW JERSEY							
1 Florio	Y	Y	N	N	Y	Y	Y
2 Hughes	Y	Y	N	N	Y	Y	N
3 Howard	Y	Y	Y	Y	Y	Y	Y
4 Thompson	Y	Y	Y	Y	Y	?	?
5 Fenwick	Y	Y	N	N	Y	?	?
6 Forsythe	Y	Y	Y	N	Y	?	?
7 Maguire	Y	Y	N	N	Y	Y	?
8 Roe	Y	Y	Y	N	Y	Y	Y
9 Hollenbeck	Y	Y	Y	Y	Y	?	?
10 Rodino	Y	Y	?	N	Y	?	?
11 Minish	Y	Y	N	N	Y	?	?
12 Rinaldo	Y	Y	N	N	Y	?	?
13 Meyner	Y	Y	N	N	Y	Y	?
14 LeFante	Y	Y	N	N	Y	?	?
15 Patten	Y	Y	N	Y	Y	Y	?
NEW MEXICO							
1 Lujan	?	?	?	✓	?	?	?
2 Runnels	Y	Y	Y	Y	Y	Y	?
NEW YORK							
1 Pike	Y	Y	Y	?	N	?	?
2 Downey	?	?	?	N	Y	?	?
3 Ambro	Y	Y	Y	N	Y	?	?
4 Lent	Y	Y	N	N	Y	Y	?
5 Wydler	Y	Y	N	N	Y	?	?
6 Wolff	Y	Y	N	N	Y	Y	?
7 Addabbo	Y	Y	Y	N	Y	?	?
8 Rosenthal	Y	Y	?	?	?	?	?
9 Delaney	?	?	Y	?	Y	?	?
10 Biaggi	?	Y	N	N	Y	Y	Y
11 Scheuer	Y	Y	N	N	?	?	?
12 Chisholm	Y	Y	Y	N	N	Y	?
13 Solarz	Y	Y	?	✓	N	?	?
14 Richmond	Y	Y	Y	N	N	?	?
15 Zeferetti	Y	Y	Y	Y	Y	?	?
16 Holtzman	Y	Y	N	N	N	Y	Y
17 Murphy	Y	?	Y	N	Y	Y	Y
18 Green	Y	Y	N	N	Y	N	Y
19 Rangel	Y	Y	Y	Y	Y	?	?
20 Weiss	Y	Y	N	Y	N	Y	Y
21 Garcia	Y	Y	Y	N	N	Y	Y
22 Bingham	Y	Y	Y	Y	N	Y	?
23 Caputo	?	?	?	?	Y	Y	Y
24 Ottinger	Y	Y	N	N	Y	Y	?
25 Fish	Y	Y	N	N	Y	Y	?
26 Gilman	Y	Y	Y	N	Y	Y	?
27 McHugh	Y	Y	Y	N	Y	Y	N
28 Stratton	Y	Y	N	N	Y	?	?
29 Pattison	Y	Y	Y	N	Y	?	?
30 McEwen	Y	Y	?	?	?	?	?
31 Mitchell	Y	Y	Y	N	Y	Y	?
32 Hanley	Y	?	Y	Y	Y	?	?
33 Walsh	Y	Y	Y	N	Y	?	?
34 Horton	Y	Y	?	?	?	?	?
35 Conable	Y	Y	N	N	Y	N	?
36 LaFalce	Y	Y	Y	N	Y	?	?
37 Nowak	Y	Y	Y	N	Y	Y	Y
38 Kemp	Y	Y	Y	N	Y	?	?
39 Lundine	Y	Y	Y	N	?	?	?
NORTH CAROLINA							
1 Jones	Y	?	Y	Y	Y	Y	?
2 Fountain	?	Y	Y	Y	Y	Y	Y
3 Whitley	Y	Y	Y	Y	Y	Y	?
4 Andrews	Y	Y	Y	Y	?	?	Y
5 Neal	Y	Y	Y	Y	Y	Y	P
6 Preyer	Y	Y	Y	Y	Y	Y	?
7 Rose	Y	Y	?	Y	Y	Y	?
8 Hefner	Y	Y	Y	Y	Y	Y	?

	828	829	830	831	832	833	834
9 Martin	Y	Y	Y	N	Y	Y	?
10 Broyhill	Y	Y	Y	N	Y	Y	N
11 Gudger	Y	Y	Y	Y	Y	Y	Y
NORTH DAKOTA							
AL Andrews	Y	Y	Y	Y	Y	?	?
OHIO							
1 Gradison	Y	Y	N	N	Y	?	?
2 Luken	Y	Y	N	N	N	?	?
3 Whalen	Y	Y	N	N	Y	?	?
4 Guyer	Y	Y	Y	Y	Y	?	?
5 Latta	Y	Y	Y	Y	Y	?	?
6 Harsha	Y	Y	Y	N	Y	Y	Y
7 Brown	N	Y	Y	N	Y	N	Y
8 Kindness	Y	Y	Y	N	Y	Y	?
9 Ashley	Y	Y	?	Y	Y	?	?
10 Miller	N	Y	Y	Y	Y	Y	Y
11 Stanton	Y	Y	Y	N	Y	?	?
12 Devine	Y	Y	N	N	Y	?	?
13 Pease	Y	Y	N	Y	Y	N	N
14 Seiberling	Y	Y	Y	Y	N	?	?
15 Wylie	Y	Y	N	N	Y	?	?
16 Regula	Y	Y	Y	N	Y	N	Y
17 Ashbrook	N	Y	Y	N	Y	Y	?
18 Applegate	?	?	?	?	?	?	?
19 Carney	?	?	?	?	?	?	?
20 Oakar	Y	Y	Y	?	Y	?	?
21 Stokes	Y	Y	Y	Y	N	Y	?
22 Vanik	Y	Y	Y	Y	Y	Y	Y
23 Mottl	?	?	?	?	?	?	?
OKLAHOMA							
1 Jones	Y	Y	Y	Y	Y	?	?
2 Risenhoover	?	?	?	?	Y	?	?
3 Watkins	Y	Y	Y	Y	Y	Y	?
4 Steed	?	?	?	?	?	?	?
5 Edwards	Y	Y	Y	N	Y	Y	Y
6 English	Y	Y	Y	Y	Y	?	?
OREGON							
1 AuCoin	Y	Y	?	N	Y	?	?
2 Ullman	Y	?	Y	Y	Y	?	?
3 Duncan	Y	Y	Y	Y	N	?	Y
4 Weaver	?	?	?	?	?	?	?
PENNSYLVANIA							
1 Myers, M.	Y	Y	N	Y	Y	Y	Y
2 Nix	Y	Y	Y	Y	Y	?	?
3 Lederer	Y	Y	N	Y	Y	Y	Y
4 Eilberg	Y	Y	N	Y	Y	?	?
5 Schulze	Y	Y	Y	N	Y	?	?
6 Yatron	Y	Y	Y	Y	Y	?	?
7 Edgar	Y	Y	N	N	Y	Y	N
8 Kostmayer	Y	Y	N	N	Y	N	N
9 Shuster	Y	Y	Y	Y	Y	?	Y
10 McDade	Y	Y	N	N	Y	Y	?
11 Flood	Y	Y	Y	Y	Y	Y	Y
12 Murtha	Y	Y	Y	Y	Y	Y	Y
13 Coughlin	Y	Y	N	N	Y	Y	N
14 Moorhead	Y	Y	Y	Y	Y	?	?
15 Rooney	Y	Y	Y	Y	Y	Y	Y
16 Walker	Y	Y	N	N	Y	Y	N
17 Ertel	Y	Y	Y	Y	Y	Y	Y
18 Walgren	?	?	Y	Y	Y	?	?
19 Goodling, W.	Y	Y	Y	N	Y	Y	?
20 Gaydos	Y	Y	N	N	Y	Y	Y
21 Dent	Y	Y	Y	Y	Y	Y	Y
22 Murphy	Y	Y	N	Y	Y	Y	Y
23 Ammerman	?	?	?	X	?	?	?
24 Marks	Y	Y	Y	N	Y	Y	?
25 Myers, G.	Y	Y	N	N	Y	N	Y
RHODE ISLAND							
1 St Germain	Y	Y	N	N	Y	Y	?
2 Beard	Y	Y	Y	N	Y	Y	?
SOUTH CAROLINA							
1 Davis	Y	Y	N	Y	Y	Y	Y
2 Spence	Y	Y	Y	Y	Y	?	?
3 Derrick	?	Y	Y	Y	Y	Y	?
4 Mann	Y	Y	Y	Y	Y	Y	N
5 Holland	Y	Y	N	Y	Y	Y	Y
6 Jenrette	?	?	?	?	?	?	?
SOUTH DAKOTA							
1 Pressler	Y	Y	Y	N	Y	?	?
2 Abdnor	Y	Y	Y	N	Y	Y	Y
TENNESSEE							
1 Quillen	Y	Y	Y	Y	Y	?	?
2 Duncan	Y	Y	Y	N	Y	Y	Y
3 Lloyd	Y	Y	Y	Y	Y	Y	Y
4 Gore	Y	Y	Y	Y	N	Y	Y
5 Vacancy							
6 Beard	Y	Y	Y	Y	Y	?	?

	828	829	830	831	832	833	834
7 Jones	Y	Y	Y	Y	Y	Y	Y
8 Ford	Y	Y	Y	Y	Y	?	?
TEXAS							
1 Hall	Y	Y	Y	Y	Y	?	?
2 Wilson, C.	Y	Y	Y	N	Y	Y	?
3 Collins	N	N	Y	?	?	?	?
4 Roberts	Y	Y	?	?	?	?	?
5 Mattox	?	?	?	?	?	?	?
6 Teague	?	?	?	N	Y	?	?
7 Archer	N	Y	N	Y	Y	N	Y
8 Eckhardt	Y	Y	Y	Y	Y	Y	Y
9 Brooks	Y	Y	Y	Y	Y	Y	Y
10 Pickle	Y	Y	Y	?	?	?	?
11 Poage	N	Y	Y	Y	Y	?	?
12 Wright	Y	Y	Y	Y	Y	?	?
13 Hightower	Y	Y	Y	Y	Y	Y	Y
14 Young	?	?	Y	Y	Y	Y	Y
15 de la Garza	Y	Y	Y	Y	Y	Y	Y
16 White	Y	Y	Y	Y	Y	?	?
17 Burleson	N	Y	Y	Y	Y	Y	N
18 Jordan	Y	Y	Y	Y	Y	?	?
19 Mahon	Y	Y	Y	Y	Y	Y	Y
20 Gonzalez	Y	Y	N	N	N	Y	Y
21 Krueger	Y	Y	Y	?	?	?	?
22 Gammage	Y	Y	N	N	Y	?	?
23 Kazen	Y	Y	Y	Y	Y	Y	Y
24 Milford	Y	Y	?	?	?	?	?
UTAH							
1 McKay	Y	Y	Y	Y	Y	Y	Y
2 Marriott	Y	Y	Y	Y	Y	?	?
VERMONT							
AL Jeffords	Y	Y	Y	Y	Y	?	?
VIRGINIA							
1 Trible	Y	Y	N	N	Y	Y	Y
2 Whitehurst	Y	Y	Y	N	Y	?	?
3 Satterfield	N	Y	Y	N	Y	Y	?
4 Daniel	Y	Y	N	N	Y	Y	Y
5 Daniel	Y	Y	Y	N	Y	Y	Y
6 Butler	Y	Y	N	N	Y	?	?
7 Robinson	Y	Y	Y	N	Y	Y	Y
8 Harris	Y	Y	N	N	Y	Y	N
9 Wampler	Y	Y	Y	Y	Y	Y	Y
10 Fisher	Y	Y	Y	N	Y	N	?
WASHINGTON							
1 Pritchard	Y	Y	N	N	Y	Y	Y
2 Meeds	Y	Y	Y	Y	Y	?	?
3 Bonker	?	Y	Y	Y	Y	Y	?
4 McCormack	Y	Y	Y	Y	Y	Y	Y
5 Foley	Y	Y	Y	Y	Y	N	Y
6 Dicks	Y	Y	Y	Y	Y	Y	Y
7 Cunningham	Y	Y	Y	N	Y	?	?
WEST VIRGINIA							
1 Mollohan	Y	Y	Y	Y	Y	?	?
2 Staggers	Y	Y	Y	Y	Y	Y	?
3 Slack	Y	Y	Y	Y	Y	Y	Y
4 Rahall	Y	Y	Y	Y	Y	Y	Y
WISCONSIN							
1 Aspin	Y	Y	?	N	Y	?	?
2 Kastenmeier	Y	Y	N	N	Y	Y	?
3 Baldus	Y	Y	Y	Y	Y	?	?
4 Zablocki	Y	Y	Y	Y	Y	Y	Y
5 Reuss	Y	Y	Y	Y	N	?	?
6 Steiger	Y	Y	N	N	Y	N	N
7 Obey	Y	Y	Y	Y	Y	Y	N
8 Cornell	Y	Y	N	N	Y	Y	N
9 Kasten	Y	Y	Y	N	Y	?	?
WYOMING							
AL Roncalio	Y	Y	Y	Y	Y	Y	?

Democrats ***Republicans***

INDEX

A

INDEX

B

C

D

E

F

H

K

L

M

N

X, Y, Z